FOREWORD - FINAL EDITION

I share your sadness that this is our last edition. It will, unfortunately, no longer be viable to have *Rail Times* printed. However, as Network Rail still have the timetables and index to stations online, those who wish to do so can download these and print their chosen tables. If you are **devoid of a computer**, please show this page to a friend, local library or printing shop that offer a download and print service.

We plan to continue with our biannual update of route diagrams, if necessary, in a *Guide to Rail Times*, to keep Rail Times users well-informed. We will update the table numbers on the route diagrams, which span 13 pages, as these have been discontinued by Network Rail. Additionally, the large (A1) *National Rail Passenger Network Diagram* will again be available from us (please see page 3).

TO COPY & PRINT TABLES:

For those who wish to download and print particular tables, the NR website link is: *https://www.networkrail.co.uk/running-the-railway/the-timetable/electronic-national-rail-timetable/* From this webpage, the folder of NR timetables for the latest validity period is available to save. They are downloadable as PDF files (A4 size), with each table as a separate file. Single tables can therefore be printed easily. The entire volume could be stored in a computer or on disc. To do so on paper would involve a large box for storage of the pages.

European Rail Timetable Ltd (01832 270198) continues to print their European product, which includes abbreviated timetables for the principal routes in Britain.

The fortnightly journal *RAIL* contains the most detailed study of timetable issues and Barry Doe is its specialist contributor. We are, as ever, grateful to him for his efforts over the years.

Network Rail has stated that minor amendments are in progress for some tables and updated files will be uploaded in January 2020. Owing to this and the number of emergency cancellations and diversions, we always recommend confirming train times by visiting *www.nationalrail.co.uk* or telephoning **03457 48 49 50**.

As a final note, I wish to say thank you to all our faithful *Rail Times* customers, and wish you continued happy train travelling.

(Foreword updates continue on page 2)

Vic Bradshaw-Mitchell

GW00580238

CONTENTS

Cover picture: Rebuilt Royal Scot no. 46115 Scots Guardsman *heads north over the Forth Bridge on 28th April 2012 towards North Queensferry station. This image also appears on the cover of Middleton Press's recent publication,* Edinburgh to Inverkeithing, *which includes Port Edgar, North Queensferry, South Queensferry and Rosyth Dockyard branches. (R.McDermaid)*

Published by

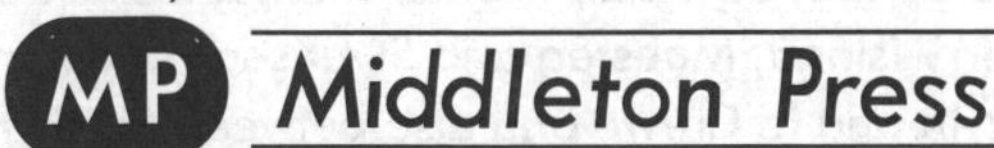

Easebourne Lane
Midhurst, West Sussex, GU29 9AZ
Tel: 01730 813169
info@middletonpress.co.uk www.middletonpress.co.uk

ISBN 978 1 910356-37-1

Data and monochrome diagrams
Copyright © 2019 Network Rail

Printed and bound by CPI Group (UK) Ltd, Croydon, CR0 4YY

(FOREWORD continued from page 1)

UPDATES:

A new station is scheduled to open at Worcestershire Parkway (southeast of Worcester). This serves both lines in the area – that from Birmingham to Cheltenham Spa and that from Oxford to Worcester. Most CrossCountry Nottingham to Cardiff trains and GWR Worcester to London Paddington services will call at the station. A new station will also open at Warrington West and will receive two trains per hour between Liverpool and Manchester.

Some CrossCountry services will be retimed to offer faster journey times. A small number, taking advantage of the recently completed improvements at Derby station, will see journey time improvements of up to 30 minutes. East Midlands Railway will run additional services between Kettering and Corby and will also provide additional winter trains to Skegness and Cleethorpes. On Great Northern, New Southgate and Oakleigh Park stations will see train services increased to six per hour. Due to extensive maintenance on the tunnels approaching Moorgate, weekday services will finish earlier in the evening and none will run at weekends.

GWR sees major changes to its timetable, with most services amended. Journey times will be improved, frequencies increased, and more capacity provided. London Paddington to both the North and South Cotswolds becomes hourly. From London Paddington to Bristol Temple Meads and South Wales, additional services will be provided, and journey times improved. Later in the timetable, two new trains per hour will operate from London Paddington to Bristol Temple Meads, via Bristol Parkway. The London Paddington to West of England service will run non-stop from Reading to Taunton and additional services will be provided for intermediate stations. In the far southwest, Exeter St David's to Paignton services become half-hourly, additional services will operate between Plymouth and Penzance and both the Barnstaple and Looe branches will become hourly.

Greater Anglia will introduce new hourly services between Stansted Airport and Norwich and between Cambridge North and London Liverpool Street. Sunday services between Cambridge and Ipswich will also be increased to an hourly frequency. London Northwestern Railway will cut back London Euston to Rugeley Trent Valley services to Walsall. A new Sunday service from London Euston to Liverpool Lime Street via Birmingham New Street will be introduced. On London North Eastern Railway, five direct services will be introduced between London King's Cross and Harrogate. Some services from London Kings Cross to Newcastle will be extended to Edinburgh Waverley.

Northern will introduce a range of new services. The hourly service from Leeds to Selby will be extended to run from Halifax to Hull; in line with this, the Huddersfield to Leeds service will operate to Bradford Interchange only. Services from Wigan to Alderley Edge and Stalybridge will start back from Southport; services from Southport to Blackburn and Leeds will start forward from Wigan. Sheffield to Bridlington services will be extended to Scarborough, while York to Hull and Hull to Bridlington services will be joined. Services between Manchester Piccadilly and New Mills Central will be doubled to half-hourly, while the Middlesbrough to Whitby branch sees two additional trains a day.

Southern is introducing additional calls at Cooksbridge. TfL Rail will commence operation of London Paddington to Reading services, in advance of the future opening of the Crossrail tunnels. Saturday Thameslink Peterborough to London King's Cross and London Bridge to Horsham services will be joined. Thameslink will no longer serve Cambridge North. TransPennine Express is introducing new trains, which will enable some changes to timetables. Some stations will see additional calls, while Liverpool Lime Street to Newcastle via Leeds services will be extended to Edinburgh Waverley. Transport for Wales is introducing enhanced Sunday services, with additional trains from Cardiff Central to Rhymney, Caerphilly, Treherbert, Barry Island, Maesteg and Swansea. Additional services will also operate from Shrewsbury to Aberystwyth and to Crewe and also between Machynlleth and Pwllheli; Chester and Crewe; Llandudno Junction and Llandudno Town; Llandudno Junction and Blaenau Ffestiniog; and Holyhead and Manchester. West Midlands Railway will operate an additional train each hour between Birmingham International and Birmingham New Street.

CONTACT TELEPHONE NUMBERS

Nationwide Rail Times TELEPHONE Traveline	03457 48 49 50 24 Hours Daily

Nationwide Bus Times TELEPHONE Traveline 0871 200 22 33

Timetable and fares available at:
www.nationalrail.co.uk

National Rail Enquiries provides up-to-the-minute advice on all aspects of journey planning, fares and buying tickets, live train running updates and other useful information.

Feedback or complaint about National Rail Enquiries?

Email: customer.relations@nationalrail.co.uk
Phone: 0800 022 3720 (Open Monday to Friday 09:00 to 17:00 except Bank Holidays)
Customer Relations Team, Suite 410, 1 Northumberland Avenue,
Trafalgar Square, London WC2N 5BW

These contact details are only for those wishing to comment on National Rail Enquiries. Comments, complaints and feedback about delays, refunds and claims, train journeys, stations or ticket offices should be sent to the appropriate Train Operating Company or station operator.

TIMETABLES COMPILED BY NETWORK RAIL:
YOUR FEEDBACK IS VALUABLE

If you have any comments on these timetables or feedback on how you feel they could be improved, please contact the Network Rail Publications Manager by writing to:
Planning Publication, Network Rail, The Quadrant: MK, Elder Gate, Milton Keynes, MK9 1EN
Or e-mail: NRT-WTT@networkrail.co.uk

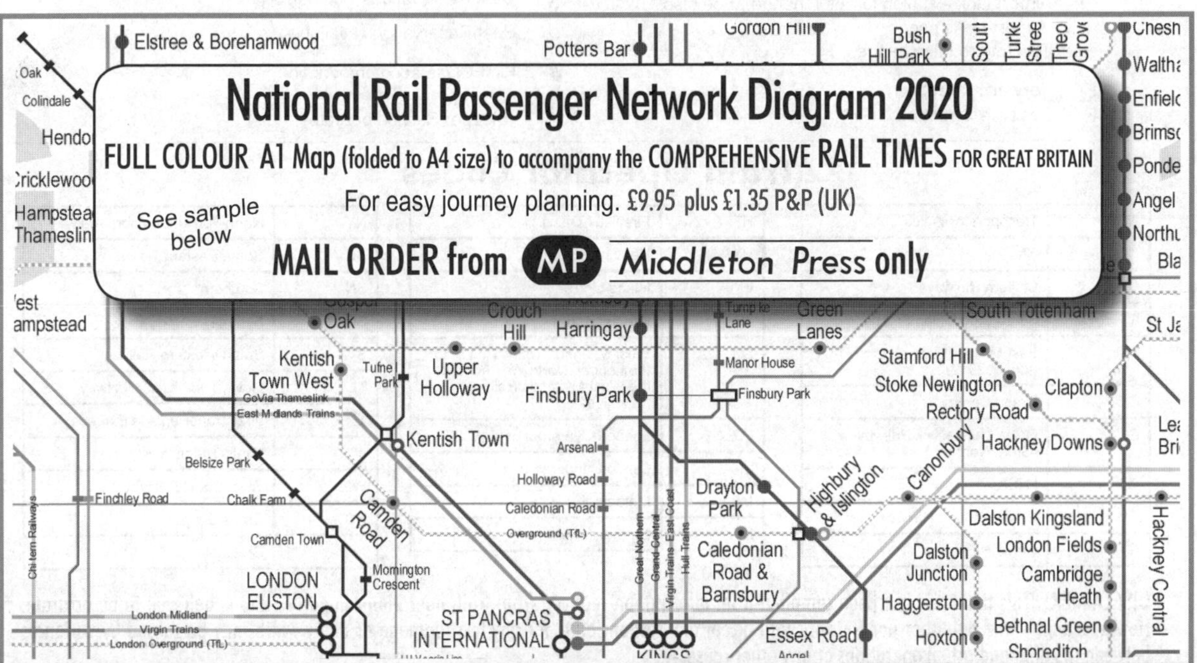

References and Symbols used in this Timetable

Date and Time Symbols

- **a** Arrival time
- **d** Departure time
- **p** Previous night
- **s** Stops to set down only
- **u** Stops to pick up only
- **x** Stops on request.

- **M** Monday
- **T** Tuesday
- **W** Wednesday
- **Th** Thursday
- **F** Friday
- **S** Saturday
- **Su** Sunday
- • Adding **'O'** to the abbreviation for the day or days (eg **WO**) means the train runs **only** on the day or days preceding the **'O'**
- • Adding **'X'** to the abbreviation for the day or days (eg **FX**) means the train runs on all the days in this section of the Timetable **except** the day or days preceding the **'X'**

Wavy Line between train times indicates that this train does **not** run during the full period of the Timetable on which the train is shown

BHX Does not run on designated Bank Holidays

Train continued in a later column

Train continued from an earlier column

Station Symbols

- Stations having interchange with London Underground services
- **10** Figure in box indicates the minimum Interchange Time in minutes to allow between trains at this station; example shows 10 minutes. For stations where no time is shown, the recommended minimum interchange time is 5 minutes
- Airport Link – station for interchange. See also Airport Links pages
- Tram/Metro Interchange
- **F** **Forward Direction**
- **R** **Reverse Direction**

Train Numbers

On certain tables, route codes are shown as part of the column heading information. These codes correspond with numbers that will be displayed on trains which are equipped to display such information.

Train Symbols

Catering Symbols

Services are available for First and Standard Class ticket holders, for all or part of the journey, unless otherwise shown.

Alterations may apply at Bank Holiday periods. See the directory of Train Operators for further information and availability of complimentary refreshments.

- Complimentary restaurant or full meal service where available, consisting of breakfast, light lunch or evening meal served at seat for First Class ticket holders only. Also a counter buffet service of hot and cold snacks, sandwiches, hot/cold drinks is available to all passengers for the sale of refreshments, for all or part of the journey, unless otherwise shown.
- A Restaurant (table) service (for First Class ticket holders, also Standard Class ticket holders if accommodation is available), and a buffet service of hot and cold snacks, sandwiches, hot/cold drinks is available for the sale of refreshments, for all or part of the journey, unless otherwise shown.
- A service of hot light meals to order and also a buffet service of snacks, sandwiches, hot/cold drinks is available for the sale of refreshments, for all or part of the journey, unless otherwise shown.
- A counter buffet service of hot and cold snacks, sandwiches, hot/cold drinks is available to all passengers for the sale of refreshments, for all or part of the journey, unless otherwise shown.
- An at-seat trolley service of cold snacks, sandwiches and hot and cold drinks is available for the sale of refreshments, for all or part of the journey, unless otherwise shown.

Other Symbols

- R Seat Reservations recommended.
- R Seat Reservations compulsory.
- ◇ Seat Reservations available.
- 1 First Class accommodation.
- Sleeper Service operates

Train Operator Codes

AW	Transport for Wales
CC	c2c
CH	Chiltern Railways
CS	Serco Caledonian Sleeper
EM	East Midland Railway (from 18 August 2019)
GC	Grand Central
GN	Govia Thameslink Railway (Great Northern)
GR	LNER
GW	Great Western Railway
GX	Gatwick Express
HT	First Hull Trains
HX	Heathrow Express
IL	Island Line
LE	Greater Anglia
LM	West Midlands Trains (run both the London North Western and the West Midlands Railway franchises)
LO	London Overground
LT	London Underground
ME	Merseyrail
NT	Northern Rail
NY	North Yorkshire Moors Railway
SE	South Eastern Trains
SN	Southern
SR	Scotrail
SW	South Western Railway
TL	Govia Thameslink Railway
TP	First TransPennine Express
VT	Virgin Trains West Coast
WR	West Coast Railway
XC	Cross Country
XR	Crossrail

DISCLAIMER: This timetable has been compiled from information received from train operation companies and is believed to be accurate. However, neither the publisher nor Network Rail accept any responsibility for any loss, damage or delay which may be caused by variances between the data and actual operations or any other cause.

Heritage Railways

Keith & Dufftown
Alford
Strathspey
Royal Deeside
Caledonian Rly (Brechin)
Kerrs
Almond
Prestongrange
PSPS
Bo'ness & Kinneil
Summerlee
EDINBURGH
Glasgow Museum
Heatherslaw
Leadhills
Scottish
North Tyneside/Stephenson
Bowes
Tanfield
Giant's Causeway
County Donegal
RPSI
Fintown
Ulster
BELFAST
Downpatrick
South Tynedale
Beamish
Monkwearmouth
Weardale
Locomotion
Head of Steam (Darlington)
Saltburn
North Bay
Haig
Eden
North Yorkshire Moors
Wensleydale
Ravenglass & Eskdale
Lightwater
Snaefell Mountain
Great Laxey
Groudle Glen
Manx Electric
I.O.M. Steam Railway
Lakeside & Haverthwaite
National Railway Museum
Embsay & Bolton Abbey
Keighley & Worth Valley
Abbey Light
Derwent
Cavan & Leitrim
VCT
Blackpool
Leeds Museum
Middleton
Appleby Frodingham (Scunthorpe)
West Lancashire
Ribble
Elsecar
Windmill Farm
Lakeside
National Coal
East Lancashire
Kirklees
Cleethorpes Coast
Museum (Manchester)
Astley Green
Penrhyn
Brookside
Lincolnshire Wolds
DUBLIN
Rheilffordd Eryri
Rhyl
Wirral
Peak Rail
Hills
Barrow Hill
North Ings
Great Orme
Moseley
Crich
North Norfolk
Churnet Valley
Midland/Golden Valley
Llanberis Lake
Snowdon Mountain
Conwy
Crewe
Rudyard
Ecclesbourne
Ashmanhaugh
Llangollen
Foxfield
Wells & Walsingham
Nottingham
Bure Valley
West Clare
Welsh Highland
Ffestiniog
Oswestry
Rudyard
Amerton
Whitewell
Great Central
Chasewater
Silk Mill
Mid Norfolk
Abbey
Bala Lake
Cambrian
Battlefield Line
Irish Steam
Ironbridge
Railworld
Fairbourne
Rutland
EATM
Corris
Telford
Nene Valley
Welshpool & Llanfair
Tyseley
Bressingham
Northampton & Lamport
Talyllyn
Kidderminster
Irchester
Vale of Rheidol
Irish Traction Group
Mid-Suffolk
Severn Valley
Northants Ironstone
Coventry
Waterford
Evesham
Great Whipsnade
Gloucestershire Warwickshire
Leighton Buzzard
Audley End
Teifi
Winchcombe
Brecon Mountain
Colne Valley
Gwili
Buckinghamshire
EARM
Perrygrove
National Waterways
Didcot
Waltham Abbey
Mangapps Farm
Llanelli
Dean Forest
Chinnor
Ruislip
Epping
Pontypool
Cholsey
LONDON
Swindon & Cricklade
Steam
Gawr
CARDIFF
Great Cockcrow
Sittingbourne & Kemsley
Bristol
Bredgar
East Kent
West Somerset
Avon Valley
Spa Valley
Midsomer Norton
Kent & East Sussex
Lynton
Longleat
S&DJRT
East Somerset
Mid-Hants
Old Kiln
Bluebell
Romney, Hythe & Dymchurch
Hollycombe
Rother Valley
Lavender
Yeovil
Gartell
Amberley
Volks
Hayling
Shillingstone
Moors
South Downs
Devon Railway Centre
Seaton
Royal Victoria
Launceston
Swanage
Burlesdon
Beer
Exbury
Dartmoor
Bicton
Isle of Wight
Eastleigh
Bickington
Bodmin & Wenford
South Devon
Paignton & Dartmouth
LONDON
Kew Bridge, LT Depot
Science Museum,
Southall, LT Museum
Lappa
Alderney
Plym Valley
Pallot (Jersey)
Helston

EUROSTAR

For further information, telephone Eurostar on 03432 186 186

LONDON - LILLE - PARIS and BRUSSELS *by Eurostar*

Minimum check-in time is 30 minutes, but passengers are advised to allow longer due to immigration procedures. Not available for London - Ebbsfleet - Ashford or v.v. Special fares payable that include three classes of service: business premier, standard premier and standard. All times shown are local times (France and Belgium are one hour ahead of Great Britain). All Eurostar services are 🅁, non-smoking and convey ✕ in Business Premier and Standard Premier, 🍸 in Standard.

Service Dec. 15 - Jan. 4. No service Dec. 25. See below service Jan. 5 - Feb. 1. See next page for service Feb. 2 - May 16.

km	km	*train number*	9080	9002	9110	9110	9004	9114	9008	9008	9010	9010	9116	9014	9018	9018	9020	9126	9022	9024	9132	9028
		notes	①–⑤	⑥	①–⑤	⑥	①–⑤	①–⑥	⑥	①–⑤	⑦	①⑤⑥				Ⓑ	⑥		⑤⑥⑦			
		notes	C		C		C	A		C	D				E	F		A	G			
0	0	**London** St Pancras d.	0540	0618	0647	0657	0701	0716	0752	0755	0819	0831	0855	0924	1014	1024	1101	1104	1131	1224	1258	1331
35	35	Ebbsfleet International d.	0558**t**	│	0704**b**	│	│	│	0812**k**	0812**t**	0838**g**	│	0912**b**	0941**b**	1034	1042**b**	│	│	│	1242**b**	1315**b**	│
90	90	Ashford International d.	0624**h**	0655**j**	0728**h**	0728**r**	│	│	│	│	│	│	│	│	│	│	│	│	│	│	│	│
166	166	Calais Fréthun a.	│	│	│	│	│	│	│	│	│	│	1056	│	│	│	│	│	│	│	1459	│
267	267	Lille Europe a.	│	│	0926	0926	│	│	│	│	│	│	1127	│	│	│	│	1326	│	│	1530	│
	373	**Brussels** Midi / Zuid a.	│	│	1007	1005	│	1012	│	│	│	│	1205	│	│	│	│	1405	│	│	1608	│
492		**Paris** Nord a.	0917	0947	...	...	1017	...	1117	1117	1147	1147	...	1247	1347	1347	1417	...	1447	1547	...	1647

train number	9032	9140	9036	9038	9040	9042	9148	9150	9152	9046	9152	9048	9050	9158	9054	9056						
notes				⑤⑦		Ⓑ	⑥	Ⓑ	⑦	①–⑥	①–⑤	⑤⑦				⑦						
notes				G				A	G	H	H	G	J	J	H	G						
London St Pancras d.	1422	1504	1531	1601	1631	1701	1704	1716**f**	1755	1801	1804	1831	1901	1934	2001	2031	...	...	...	...	...	...
Ebbsfleet International d.	│	│	│	│	│	│	│	│	│	│	│	│	│	│	│	│	...	...	...	...	...	...
Ashford International d.	1455**p**	│	│	│	│	│	│	│	1828**q**	│	│	│	│	│	│	│	...	...	...	...	...	...
Calais Fréthun a.	│	│	│	│	│	│	│	│	│	│	│	│	│	2129	│	│	...	...	...	...	...	...
Lille Europe a.	│	1726	│	│	│	│	1926	│	2026	│	2026	│	│	2200	│	│	...	...	...	...	...	...
Brussels Midi / Zuid a.	│	1805	│	│	│	│	2005	2012	2105	│	2105	│	│	2238	│	│	...	...	...	...	...	...
Paris Nord a.	1747	...	1847	1920	1947	2020	...	...	...	2117	...	2147	2217	...	2317	2347	...	...	...	...	...	...

train number	9109	9005	9007	9113	9009	9011	9117	9013	9015	9019	9019	9121	9023	9023	9129	9025	9027	9133	9031	9033	9035	9037
notes	①	①	①–⑥	①–⑥	①–⑤	⑥⑦		①–⑤		②–⑦	①	①–⑥	①	②–⑥	⑦	⑦	⑤⑥⑦	①–⑥		⑦	⑥	⑤⑦
notes			C	C	C	G		C				N	K	L		G	G	C		D		G
Paris Nord d.	...	0643	0713	...	0743	0813	...	0843	0913	1013	1013	...	1113	1113	...	1128	1213	...	1313	1328	1413	1443
Brussels Midi / Zuid d.	0656	│	│	0756	│	│	0852	│	│	│	│	1056	│	│	1156	│	│	1252	│	│	│	│
Lille Europe d.	0736	│	│	0835	│	│	0930	│	│	│	│	1135	│	│	1235	│	│	1330	│	│	│	│
Calais Fréthun d.	│	│	│	│	│	│	1001	│	│	│	│	│	│	│	│	│	│	│	│	│	│
Ashford International a.	│	│	│	│	│	│	│	│	│	│	1107	│	│	1207	│	1237**q**	│	│	│	│	│	│
Ebbsfleet International a.	│	│	│	│	│	│	│	│	1015	│	│	│	1226	1226	│	│	│	1345	1418	│	1518	│
London St Pancras a.	0759	0802	0832	0857	0900	0930	0957	1000	1039	1130	1143	1157	1247	1247	1257	1309	1330	1405	1439	1500	1539	1602

train number	9141	9039	9043	9045	9149	9047	9049	9153	9153	9051	9157	9055	9067	9059	9163	9061	9063					
notes				⑦		①–⑥	⑦	⑦	①–⑥	Ⓑ	Ⓑ		⑤⑦			⑤⑦	Ⓑ					
notes				G		C	G	P	Q	J	R	J	M	B	J	G	J					
Paris Nord d.	...	1513	1613	1643	...	1713	1743	...	...	1813	...	1913	1943	2013	...	2043	2113	...	...	...	...	...
Brussels Midi / Zuid d.	1452	│	│	│	1656	│	│	1756	1756	│	1856	│	│	│	2022	│	│	...	...	...	...	...
Lille Europe d.	1530	│	│	│	1735	│	│	1835	1835	│	1935	│	│	│	2100	│	│	...	...	...	...	...
Calais Fréthun d.	1601	│	│	│	│	│	│	│	│	│	│	│	│	│	2131	│	│	...	...	...	...	...
Ashford International a.	│	│	│	│	│	│	│	│	1835	│	│	2007**v**	2048	│	│	│	│	...	...	...	...	...
Ebbsfleet International a.	1545	1618	1718	│	1745	│	│	1845	1857	1918	│	2027	│	2118	2115	│	2218	...	...	...	...	...
London St Pancras a.	1605	1639	1739	1800	1806	1832	1900	1903	1915	1939	1957	2049	2113	2139	2133	2200	2239	...	...	...	...	...

- **A** – To Amsterdam, see Table **18**.
- **B** – ①②③④⑥ (not Dec. 24, 26, 31, Jan. 1).
- **C** – Not Dec. 26, Jan. 1.
- **D** – Also Jan. 1.
- **E** – Dec. 15, 24, 26, 27, 29.
- **F** – Not Dec. 15, 24–29.
- **G** – Also Dec. 26, Jan. 1.
- **H** – Not Dec. 24, 26, 31, Jan. 1.
- **J** – Not Dec. 24, 31.
- **K** – Also Dec. 24, 27, 28, Jan. 4.
- **L** – Not Dec. 24, 26, 27, 28, Jan. 1, 4.
- **M** – Also Dec. 26, Jan. 1; not Dec. 15.
- **N** – Not Jan. 4.
- **P** – Also Dec. 24, 26, 27, 28, Jan. 4.
- **Q** – Not Dec. 24, 26, 27, 28, Jan. 4.
- **R** – Not Dec. 24, 26, 27, 29, 31.
- **b** – Not Dec. 18–21, Jan. 1, 2.
- **f** – 1719 on ⑦.
- **g** – Not Jan. 1.
- **h** – Not Dec. 24, 27.
- **j** – Not Dec. 28.
- **k** – Not Dec. 21.
- **p** – Not Dec. 15, 24–29, Jan. 4.
- **q** – Not Dec. 15, 26, 29.
- **r** – Not Dec. 28, Jan. 4.
- **t** – Not Dec. 18–20, Jan. 2.
- **v** – Not Dec. 15, 26–29, Jan. 4.

Service Jan. 5 – Feb. 1. See above for service Dec. 15 - Jan. 4. See next page for Feb. 2 - May 16.

km	km	*train number*	9080	9002	9110	9110	9004	9112	9008	9008	9010	9010	9116	9014	9018	9018	9020	9126	9022	9024	9132	9028
		notes	①–⑤	⑥	①–⑤	⑥	①–⑤	①–⑥	⑥	①–⑤	⑦	①⑤⑥				Ⓑ	⑥		⑤⑥⑦			⑤
		notes						A							E	F		A				
0	0	**London** St Pancras d.	0540	0618	0647	0657	0701	0716	0752	0755	0819	0831	0855	0924	1014	1024	1101	1104	1131	1224	1258	1331
35	35	Ebbsfleet International d.	0558	│	0704	│	│	│	0812	0812	0842	│	0912	0941	1034	1042	│	│	│	1242**b**	1315	│
90	90	Ashford International d.	0624	0655	0728	0728	│	│	│	│	│	│	│	│	│	│	│	│	│	│	│	│
166	166	Calais Fréthun a.	│	│	0859	│	│	│	│	│	│	│	1056	│	│	│	│	│	│	│	1459	│
267	267	Lille Europe a.	│	│	0926	0926	│	│	│	│	│	│	1127	│	│	│	│	1326	│	│	1530	│
	373	**Brussels** Midi / Zuid a.	│	│	1008	1005	│	1012	│	│	│	│	1205	│	│	│	│	1405	│	│	1608	│
492		**Paris** Nord a.	0927	0957	...	...	1027	...	1127	1127	1157**y**	1157	...	1257**y**	1347	1357	1427	...	1457**y**	1557**y**	...	1657

train number	9032	9140	9036	9038	9040	9042	9148	9150	9150	9152	9046	9152	9048	9050	9158	9054	9054	9056				
notes				⑤⑦		Ⓑ	⑥	①–⑤	⑦	⑦	①–⑥	①–⑤	⑦			①–⑤	⑥⑦	⑦				
notes								A	A													
London St Pancras d.	1422	1504	1531	1601	1631	1701	1704	1716	1719	1755	1801	1804	1831	1901	1934	1925	2000	2031	...	...	...	...
Ebbsfleet International d.	│	│	│	│	│	│	│	│	│	│	│	│	│	│	│	│	│	│	...	...	...	...
Ashford International d.	1455**h**	│	│	│	│	│	│	│	│	1828**h**	│	│	│	│	│	│	│	│	...	...	...	...
Calais Fréthun a.	│	│	│	│	│	│	│	│	│	│	│	│	│	│	2129	│	│	│	...	...	...	...
Lille Europe a.	│	1726	│	│	│	│	1926	│	│	2026	│	2026	│	│	2200	│	│	│	...	...	...	...
Brussels Midi / Zuid a.	│	1805	│	│	│	│	2005	2012	2012	2105	│	2105	│	│	2238	│	│	│	...	...	...	...
Paris Nord a.	1757	...	1857**y**	1930**y**	1957**y**	2030**y**	...	...	...	...	2127	...	2157**y**	2227**y**	...	2327	2327**y**	2347**y**	...	...	...	...

train number	9109	9005	9007	9113	9009	9011	9117	9013	9015	9019	9125	9023	9129	9025	9027	9133	9031	9033	9035	9037	9141	9039
notes	①	①	①–⑥	①–⑥	①–⑤	⑥⑦		①–⑤		⑤	①–⑥	①–⑥	⑦	⑦	⑤⑥⑦	①–⑥		⑦	⑥	⑦		
notes																						
Paris Nord d.	...	0633	0703	...	0733	0803**g**	...	0833	0903**g**	1003	...	1103	...	1125	1203**g**	...	1303**g**	1325	1403	1433**g**	...	1503**g**
Brussels Midi / Zuid d.	0656	│	│	0756	│	│	0852	│	│	│	1052	│	1156	│	│	1252	│	│	│	│	1452	│
Lille Europe d.	0735	│	│	0835	│	│	0930	│	│	│	1135	│	1235	│	│	1330	│	│	│	│	1530	│
Calais Fréthun d.	│	│	│	│	│	│	1001	│	│	│	│	│	│	│	│	│	│	│	│	│	1601	│
Ashford International a.	│	│	│	│	│	│	│	│	│	│	│	1207	│	1237**h**	│	│	│	│	│	│	│	│
Ebbsfleet International a.	│	│	│	│	│	│	│	│	1015	│	│	1226	│	│	│	1345	1418	│	1518	│	1545	1618
London St Pancras a.	0759	0802	0832	0859	0900	0930	0957	1000	1039	1130	1157	1247	1257	1309	1330	1405	1439	1500	1539	1602	1605	1639

train number	9043	9045	9149	9149	9149	9149	9047	9049	9153	9153	9153	9051	9157	9055	9055	9067	9059	9163	9061	9063		
notes		⑦	②③④⑤	⑦	⑥	①	①–⑥	⑦	②–⑦	①		Ⓑ	Ⓑ			⑤⑦			⑤⑦	Ⓑ		
notes									F		E			F	E		B					
Paris Nord d.	1603	1633**g**	...	...	...	...	1703	1733**g**	...	...	...	1803**g**	...	1903	1913	1933**g**	2003	...	2033**g**	2103**g**	...	...
Brussels Midi / Zuid d.	│	│	1700	1700	1700	1700	│	│	1756	1756	1756	│	1856	│	│	│	│	2022	│	│	...	...
Lille Europe d.	│	│	│	1736	1739	│	│	│	1835	1835	1835	│	1935	│	│	│	│	2100	│	│	...	...
Calais Fréthun d.	│	│	│	│	│	│	│	│	│	│	│	│	│	│	│	│	│	2131	│	│	...	...
Ashford International a.	│	│	│	│	│	1734	│	│	1835	│	│	│	│	2007	│	│	│	│	│	│	...	...
Ebbsfleet International a.	1718	│	1745	1745	1748	1753	│	│	1856	1856	1856	1918	│	2027	2018	2048	2118	2115	│	2218	...	...
London St Pancras a.	1739	1800	1806	1806	1810	1814	1832	1900	1915	1915	1915	1939	1957	2049	2049	2113	2139	2133	2200	2239	...	...

- **A** – To Amsterdam, see Table **18**.
- **B** – ①②③④⑥.
- **E** – Jan. 5.
- **F** – Not Jan. 5.
- **g** – 10 minutes later on Jan. 5.
- **h** – Not Jan. 5.
- **y** – 10 minutes earlier on Jan. 5.

Provided by European Rail Timetable Ltd
(www.europeanrailtimetable.eu 01832 270198)

LONDON - LILLE - PARIS and BRUSSELS *by Eurostar*

Minimum check-in time is 30 minutes, but passengers are advised to allow longer due to immigration procedures. Not available for London - Ebbsfleet - Ashford or v.v. Special fares payable that include three classes of service: business premier, standard premier and standard. All times shown are local times (France and Belgium are one hour ahead of Great Britain). All Eurostar services are Ⓡ, non-smoking and convey ✕ in Business Premier and Standard Premier, 🍸 in Standard.

Service Feb. 2 - Mar. 28. See previous page for service Dec. 15 - Feb. 1. See below for service Mar. 29 - May 16.

km	*km*	*train number*	**9080**	**9002**	**9110**	**9110**	**9004**	**9114**	**9008**	**9008**	**9010**	**9010**	**9116**	**9014**	**9018**	**9018**	**9018**	**9020**	**9126**	**9022**	**9024**	**9132**	**9028**	**9032**
		notes	①–⑤	⑥	①–⑤	⑥	①–⑤	①–⑥	⑥	①–⑤	⑦	①⑤⑥				Ⓑ		⑥		⑤⑥⑦				
		notes						**A**							**C**	**D**	**E**		**A**					
0	*0*	**London** St Pancras .... d.	0540	0618	0647	0657	0701	0716	0752	0755S	0819	0831	0855	0924	1014	1024	1024	1101	1104	1131	1224	1258	1331	1422
35	*35*	Ebbsfleet International .... d.	0558**f**	│	0704**f**	│	│	│	0812**j**	│	0842	│	0912**p**	0941**p**	1034	1042	│	│	│	│	1242**p**	1315**p**	│	│
90	*90*	Ashford International .... d.	0624	0655**h**	0728	0728**h**	│	│	│	│	│	│	│	│	│	│	│	│	│	│	│	│	│	1455**k**
166	*166*	Calais Fréthun .... a.	│	│	│	│	│	│	│	│	│	│	1056	│	│	│	│	│	│	│	│	1459	│	│
267	*267*	Lille Europe .... a.	│	│	0926	0926	│	│	│	│	│	│	1127	│	│	│	│	│	1326	│	│	1530	│	│
	373	**Brussels** Midi / Zuid .... a.	│	│	1007	1005	│	1012	│	**1127**	│	│	1205	│	│	│	│	│	1405	│	│	1608	│	│
492		**Paris** Nord .... a.	0927	0957	...	...	1027	...	1127		1157	1157	...	1300	1357	1357	1357	1427	...	1457	1557	...	1657	1757

train number	**9140**	**9036**	**9038**	**9040**	**9042**	**9150**	**9150**	**9150**	**9152**	**9046**	**9152**	**9048**	**9050**	**9054**	**9158**	**9054**	**9158**	**9056**						
notes			⑤⑦		Ⓑ	⑥	①–⑤	⑦	⑦	①–⑥	①–⑤	⑤⑦		①–⑤		⑥⑦	Ⓑ	⑦						
notes							**A**	**A**							**G**									
London St Pancras .... d.	1504	1531	1601	1631	1701	1704	1716	1719	1755	1801	1804	1831	1901	1925	1934	2000	2004	2031	...	...	...	...	...	...
Ebbsfleet International .... d.	│	│	│	│	│	│	│	│	│	│	│	│	│	│	│	│	│	│	...	...	...	...	...	...
Ashford International .... d.	│	│	│	│	│	│	│	│	1828**q**	│	│	│	│	│	│	│	│	│	...	...	...	...	...	...
Calais Fréthun .... a.	│	│	│	│	│	│	│	│	│	│	│	│	│	│	2129	│	2159	│	...	...	...	...	...	...
Lille Europe .... a.	1726	│	│	│	│	1926	│	│	2026	│	2026	│	│	│	2200	│	2230	│	...	...	...	...	...	...
Brussels Midi / Zuid .... a.	1805	│	│	│	│	2005	2012	2012	2105	│	2105	│	│	│	2238	│	2308	│	...	...	...	...	...	...
Paris Nord .... a.	...	1857	1930	1957	2020	...	...	...	...	2127	...	2157	2227	2327	...	2327	...	2357	...	...	...	...	...	...

train number	**9109**	**9005**	**9007**	**9113**	**9009**	**9011**	**9117**	**9013**	**9015**	**9019**	**9019**	**9125**	**9023**	**9023**	**9129**	**9025**	**9027**	**9133**	**9031**	**9033**	**9035**	**9037**	**9141**	**9039**
notes	①	①	①–⑥	①–⑥	①–⑤	⑥⑦		①–⑤		②–⑦	①	①–⑥	①	②–⑥	⑦	⑦	⑤⑥⑦	①–⑥		⑦	⑥	⑤⑦		
notes																								
Paris Nord .... d.	...	0633	0703	...	0733	0803	...	0833	0903	1003	1003	...	1103	1103	...	1125	1203	...	1303	1325	1403	1433	...	1503
Brussels Midi / Zuid .... d.	0656	│	│	0756	│	│	0852	│	│	│	│	1052	│	│	1156	│	│	1252	│	│	│	│	1452	│
Lille Europe .... d.	0735	│	│	0835	│	│	0930	│	│	│	│	1135	│	│	1235	│	│	1330	│	│	│	│	1530	│
Calais Fréthun .... d.	│	│	│	│	│	│	1001	│	│	│	│	│	│	│	│	│	│	│	│	│	│	│	1601	│
Ashford International .... a.	│	│	│	│	│	│	│	│	│	│	1107	│	│	1207**h**	│	1237**q**	│	│	│	│	│	│	│	│
Ebbsfleet International .... a.	│	│	│	│	│	│	0944	│	1015	│	│	│	1226	1226	│	│	│	1345	1418	│	1518	│	1545	1618
London St Pancras .... a.	0759	0802	0832	0859	0900	0930	1002	1000	1039	1130	1143	1157	1247	1247	1257	1309	1330	1405	1439	1500	1539	1602	1605	1639

train number	**9043**	**9045**	**9149**	**9149**	**9149**	**9149**	**9047**	**9049**	**9153**	**9153**	**9153**	**9051**	**9157**	**9055**	**9067**	**9059**	**9163**	**9061**	**9063**					
notes		⑦	②③④⑤	⑦	⑥	①	①–⑥	⑦	②–⑦	①		Ⓑ	Ⓑ		⑤⑦			⑤⑦	Ⓑ					
notes									**k**		**H**					**B**								
Paris Nord .... d.	1603	1633	...	...	...	...	1703	1733	...	...	...	1803	...	1903	1933	2003	...	2033	2103	...	...	...	...	...
Brussels Midi / Zuid .... d.	│	│	1700	1700	1700	1700	│	│	1756	1756	1756	│	1856	│	│	│	2022	│	│	...	...	...	...	...
Lille Europe .... d.	│	│	│	1736	1739	│	│	│	1835	1835	1835	│	1935	│	│	│	2100	│	│	...	...	...	...	...
Calais Fréthun .... d.	│	│	│	│	│	│	│	│	│	│	│	│	│	│	│	│	2131	│	│	...	...	...	...	...
Ashford International .... a.	│	│	│	│	│	1734	│	│	1835	│	│	│	│	2007**k**	│	│	│	│	│	...	...	...	...	...
Ebbsfleet International .... a.	1718	│	1745	1745	1748	1753	│	│	1856	1856	1856	1918	│	2027	2048	2118	2115	│	2218	...	...	...	...	...
London St Pancras .... a.	1739	1800	1806	1806	1810	1814	1832	1900	1915	1915	1915	1939	1957	2049	2113	2139	2133	2200	2239	...	...	...	...	...

A – To Amsterdam, see Table **18**.
B – ①②③④⑥.
C – Feb. 23.
D – Ⓑ (not Feb. 14, 23).
E – Feb. 14.
G – ①②③④⑥⑦.
H – Feb. 22, 23.
f – Not Feb. 14.
h – Not Feb. 22.
j – Not Feb. 15.
k – Not Feb. 22, 23.
p – Not Feb. 14, 15.
q – Not Feb. 23.

Service Mar. 29 - May 16. See above for service Feb. 2 - Mar. 28. See previous page for service Dec. 15 - Feb. 1.

km	*km*	*train number*	**9080**	**9002**	**9110**	**9110**	**9004**	**9114**	**9008**	**9008**	**9010**	**9010**	**9116**	**9014**	**9018**	**9020**	**9126**	**9022**	**9024**	**9132**	**9028**	**9030**	**9136**	**9032**
		notes	①–⑤	⑥	①–⑤	⑥	①–⑤	①–⑥	⑥	①–⑤	⑦	①⑤⑥			Ⓑ	⑥								
		notes						**A**									**A**					⑤	⑤	
0	*0*	**London** St Pancras .... d.	0540	0618	0647	0657	0701	0716	0752	0755	0819	0831	0855	0924	1024	1101	1104	1131	1224	1258	1331	1401	1404	1422
35	*35*	Ebbsfleet International .... d.	0558**f**	│	0704**f**	│	│	│	0812	0812**f**	0842	│	0912**f**	0941**f**	1042**f**	│	│	│	1242**f**	1315**f**	│	│	│	│
90	*90*	Ashford International .... d.	0624	0655	0728	0728	│	│	│	│	│	│	│	│	│	│	│	│	│	│	│	│	│	1455
166	*166*	Calais Fréthun .... a.	│	│	│	│	│	│	│	│	│	│	1056	│	│	│	│	│	│	1459	│	│	│	│
267	*267*	Lille Europe .... a.	│	│	0926	0926	│	│	│	│	│	│	1127	│	│	│	1326	│	│	1530	│	│	1626	│
	373	**Brussels** Midi / Zuid .... a.	│	│	1007	1005	│	1012	│	│	│	│	1205	│	│	│	1405	│	│	1608	│	│	1705	│
492		**Paris** Nord .... a.	0927	0957	...	...	1027	...	1127	1127	1157	1157	...	1300	1357	1427	...	1457	1557	...	1657	1727	...	1757

train number	**9140**	**9036**	**9038**	**9040**	**9042**	**9150**	**9150**	**9150**	**9152**	**9046**	**9152**	**9048**	**9050**	**9054**	**9158**	**9054**	**9158**	**9056**						
notes			⑤⑦		Ⓑ	⑥	①–⑤	⑦	⑦	①–⑥	①–⑤	⑤⑦		①–⑤		⑥⑦		⑦						
notes							**A**	**A**							**h**		**C**							
London St Pancras .... d.	1504	1531	1601	1631	1701	1704	1716	1719	1755	1801	1804	1831	1901	1925	1934	2000	2004	2031	...	...	...	...	...	...
Ebbsfleet International .... d.	│	│	│	│	│	│	│	│	│	│	│	│	│	│	│	│	│	│	...	...	...	...	...	...
Ashford International .... d.	│	│	│	│	│	│	│	│	1828	│	│	│	│	│	│	│	│	│	...	...	...	...	...	...
Calais Fréthun .... a.	│	│	│	│	│	│	│	│	│	│	│	│	│	│	2129	│	2159	│	...	...	...	...	...	...
Lille Europe .... a.	1726	│	│	│	│	1926	│	│	2026	│	2026	│	│	│	2200	│	2230	│	...	...	...	...	...	...
Brussels Midi / Zuid .... a.	1805	│	│1930	│	│	2005	2012	2012	2105	│	2105	│	│	│	2238	│	2308	│	...	...	...	...	...	...
Paris Nord .... a.	...	1857		1957	2020	...	...	...	...	2127	...	2157	2227	2327	...	2327	...	2357	...	...	...	...	...	...

train number	**9109**	**9005**	**9007**	**9113**	**9009**	**9011**	**9117**	**9013**	**9015**	**9119**	**9019**	**9019**	**9125**	**9021**	**9023**	**9023**	**9129**	**9025**	**9027**	**9133**	**9031**	**9033**	**9035**	**9037**
notes	①	①	①–⑥	①–⑥	①–⑤	⑥⑦		①–⑤		①–⑥	②–⑦	①	①–⑥	⑤	①	②–⑥	⑦	⑦		①–⑥		⑦	⑥	⑤⑦
notes										**A E**														
Paris Nord .... d.	...	0633	0703	...	0733	0803	...	0833	0903	...	1003	1003	...	1033	1103	1103	...	1125	1203	...	1303	1325	1403	1433
Brussels Midi / Zuid .... d.	0656	│	│	0756	│	│	0852	│	│	1005	│	│	1052	│	│	│	1156	│	│	1252	│	│	│	│
Lille Europe .... d.	0735	│	│	0835	│	│	0930	│	│	│	│	│	1135	│	│	│	1235	│	│	1330	│	│	│	│
Calais Fréthun .... d.	│	│	│	│	│	│	1001	│	│	│	│	│	│	│	│	│	│	│	│	│	│	│	│	│
Ashford International .... a.	│	│	│	│	│	│	│	│	│	│	│	│	│	│	│	1207	│	1237	│	│	│	│	│	│
Ebbsfleet International .... a.	│	│	│	│	│	│	0944	│	1015	│	│	1107	│	1148	1226	1226	│	│	│	1345	1418	│	1518	│
London St Pancras .... a.	0759	0802	0832	0859	0900	0930	1002	1000	1039	1057	1130	1143	1157	1209	1247	1247	1257	1309	1330	1405	1439	1500	1539	1602

train number	**9141**	**9039**	**9145**	**9043**	**9045**	**9149**	**9149**	**9149**	**9149**	**9047**	**9049**	**9153**	**9051**	**9157**	**9055**	**9067**	**9059**	**9163**	**9167**	**9061**	**9063**			
notes					⑦	②③④⑤	⑦	⑥	①	①–⑥	⑦		Ⓑ	Ⓑ		⑤⑦			Ⓑ	⑤⑦	Ⓑ			
notes			**A E**														**B**		**A E**					
Paris Nord .... d.	...	1503	...	1603	1633	...	...	...	...	1703	1733	...	1803	...	1903	1933	2003	...	...	2033	2103	...	...	...
Brussels Midi / Zuid .... d.	1452	│	1556	│	│	1700	1700	1700	1700	│	│	1756	│	1856	│	│	│	2022	2105	│	│	...	...	...
Lille Europe .... d.	1530	│	1635	│	│	│	1736	1739	│	│	│	1835	│	1935	│	│	│	2100	│	│	│	...	...	...
Calais Fréthun .... d.	1601	│	│	│	│	│	│	│	│	│	│	│	│	│	│	│	│	2131	│	│	│	...	...	...
Ashford International .... a.	│	│	│	│	│	│	│	│	1734	│	│	1835	│	│	2007	│	│	│	│	│	│	...	...	...
Ebbsfleet International .... a.	1545	1618	│	1718	│	1745	1745	1748	1753	│	│	1856	1918	│	2027	2048	2118	2115	│	│	2218	...	...	...
London St Pancras .... a.	1605	1639	1657	1739	1800	1806	1806	1810	1814	1832	1900	1915	1939	1957	2049	2109	2139	2133	2157	2200	2239	...	...	...

A – To / from Amsterdam, see Table **18**.
B – ①②③④⑥.
C – Apr. 3.
E – From Mar. 31.
f – Not Apr. 9, 10, 13.
h – Not Apr. 3.

Newslines (Provided by European Rail Timetable Limited, 01832 270198)

Great Western Railway

This company has the biggest timetable change – everything has changed – below is a summary of these.

Paddington to Bristol

The headline here is the introduction of fast, non-stop services between Paddington and Bristol Parkway on Mondays to Fridays – 5 from Paddington and 4 from Bristol Parkway, then to and from Bristol Temple Meads, giving a journey time of around 1hr 20 mins. Additionally there are 3 services each way non-stop Paddington to Chippenham and v.v. (one is fast from Swindon to Paddington).

Paddington to South Wales

Journey times have been accelerated by up to 12 minutes in each direction.

On Mondays to Fridays 2 fast services have been introduced in both directions which are non-stop between Paddington and Bristol Parkway giving a journey time of between 1 hour 43 minutes and 1 hour 49 minutes to and from Cardiff.

On Saturdays Cardiff has 12 additional services from Paddington – 3 of which continue to Swansea; on Sundays 9 additional services, 2 of which continue to Swansea. In the other direction on Saturdays there are an additional 9 services from Cardiff and on Sundays, also an additional 9 services with 3 of those originating at Swansea.

Paddington to Plymouth and Penzance

There has been an overhaul of the services here. There is now an hourly fast service from Paddington to Exeter and beyond and every 2 hours a service stopping at the Berks and Hants stations and v.v. During most of the day on Mondays to Saturdays there is now a half hourly service between Plymouth and Penzance.

Paddington to Hereford via Worcester

The headline news here is the opening of Worcestershire Parkway Station. The timetable has been re-cast with most trains now starting from Paddington at xx50 on Mondays to Saturdays, instead of xx22, and speeded up by about 10 minutes.

On Sundays an additional train has been added from London while in the other direction 2 extra trains have been added giving 14 in each direction. This gives an even, hourly spread through the day in each direction through the core Oxford to Worcester route.

Paddington to Oxford

This service has been speeded up by between 5 and 10 minutes depending on service. In the evening peak from Paddington 4 trains now run fast to Oxford.

Bristol to Westbury, Brighton, Portsmouth and Weymouth

On Mondays to Fridays the 0549 Westbury to Portsmouth starts back at Bristol at 0500. Also the 1645 Bristol to Weymouth has been accelerated by 14 minutes – arrival is now 1900 instead of 1916 – the 2046 is similarly accelerated.

On Mondays to Saturdays the 1730 from Weymouth (1723 on Mondays to Fridays) now has an arrival time into Bristol of 1949 instead of 2009. The wait of around 15 minutes at Westbury has now been eliminated.

Swindon to Westbury

Completely re-cast – There is one less train from Swindon to Westbury on Mondays to Fridays but an additional one on Sundays at 2110. The early morning service from Gloucester is now truncated to start from Swindon, as is the Saturday evening service.

In the other direction there is a new early morning service on Mondays to Fridays at 0517 from Westbury and the Sunday evening service to Cheltenham Spa now terminates at Swindon.

The Sunday service to and from Weymouth is retained.

Northern Trains

Leeds to Morecambe

On Sundays all trains (except the first one) have been retimed to leave at xx32 and go through to Morecambe instead of terminating at Lancaster. The 1032 now goes through to Heysham Port, returning at 1305. The service from Morecambe to Leeds has been re-cast with all trains starting from Morecambe instead of Lancaster.

The local trains from Lancaster to Morecambe and v.v. have been recast and are now irregular.

Leeds to Carlisle

On Sundays the 1250 and 1502 from Carlisle have been retimed to 1225 and 1520. The 1520 timing gives a much better connection with the DalesRail service at Hellifield (8 minutes instead of 21).

Scarborough to Hull

This service has been recast now leaving during most of the day at xx00 every day instead of xx20 Mondays to Saturdays and xx02 on Sundays. On the return from Hull timings are now xx21 instead of xx30 Mondays to Saturdays and xx 01 instead of xx02 on Sundays. The timings have also been tweaked to achieve a 5 to 7 minute time saving. Most trains now also come from/go to Sheffield.

Hull to Sheffield

On Mondays to Saturdays this service has been re-cast to give an hourly service – mostly coming through from Scarborough instead of Bridlington.

Leeds to Manchester Victoria via Halifax

To give a better spread of departures the xx18 and xx38 services from Leeds are now at xx12 and xx42. The xx12 trains have also been speeded up by about 7 minutes.

Blackpool North to Leeds and York

On Sundays this service has been extended to/from York.

Middlesbrough to Whitby

The headline here is the addition of 2 extra services each way on Mondays to Saturdays.

The new services start from Middlesbrough at 0458 and 2043 returning at 0633 and 2221. To accommodate the early trains several station calls are missed out between Glaisdale and Whitby (including Grosmont).

Southwestern Railway

London Waterloo to Exeter St Davids

On Mondays to Fridays the 2120 Waterloo to Yeovil Junction has been extended to Exeter St Davids and the 2220 Waterloo to Gillingham has been extended to Yeovil Junction.

On Monday to Saturday the 0619 from Honiton to Waterloo now starts back at Exeter St Davids at 0530 but has a 20 minute wait at Honiton to take up the same path (departs at 0620).

On Mondays to Fridays the 2300 from Exeter to Salisbury has been replaced by a 2225 Exeter to Salisbury and a 2327 Exeter to Yeovil Junction.

The Summer Saturday train from Waterloo to Weymouth and v.v. and the short workings to/from Yeovil Junction continue throughout the year.

On Sundays the 0706 from Salisbury has been retimed to start at 0654 giving an earlier arrival in Exeter at 0843 instead of 0859.

The 1745, 1845 and 1945 fast services to Waterloo to Salisbury now have stops at Woking and Basingstoke with the 1745 being extended to Yeovil Pen Mill via Westbury.

The 2215 Waterloo to Salisbury has been retimed to 2220 and extended to Yeovil Junction.

The 0858 Honiton to Waterloo now starts back at Exeter at 0824.

The 1621 Gillingham to Waterloo starts back at Yeovil Junction at 1543.

West Midland Railway

Birmingham New Street to Hereford

On Saturdays the 1850 Birmingham to Great Malvern has been extended to Hereford arriving at 2014 with a return at 2035 taking up the path of the 2130 from Worcester.

London Northwestern Railway

London to Birmingham, Crewe and Liverpool via Northampton

On Sundays the service from Birmingham to Liverpool now starts back at/is extended to London Euston. Also the Birmingham to Crewe service via Stoke-on-Trent starts back at/is extended to Coventry and has been recast. Also on Sundays the xx34 trains from Euston to Birmingham are extended to/from Stafford or Crewe. On Mondays to Fridays the 1305 and 1405 departures from Liverpool now run non-stop between Northampton and London giving up to a 29 minute earlier arrival. Also the 1505, 1605 and 1805 are fast from Milton Keynes giving a similar acceleration. On Monday to Fridays the xx35 Liverpool to London and xx01 Crewe to London via Stoke on Trent services combine at Birmingham New Street.

Bedford to Bletchley

With the introduction of the "new" class 230 rolling stock the timetable has been re-cast.

Newslines (Provided by European Rail Timetable Limited, 01832 270198)

Chiltern Trains

Stratford upon Avon to Marylebone

On Sundays the 1219 from Stratford now departs at 1257 so avoiding the 35 minute wait at Banbury.

Greater Anglia

Norwich to Cambridge and Stansted Airport

This service has been recast to allow trains to continue from Cambridge to Stansted Airport through much of the day – every day of the week; 7 services on Mondays to Fridays; 15 on Saturdays and 13 on Sundays. This gives the sparse service from Cambridge to Stansted and v.v. a much needed boost on Mondays to Fridays.

Ipswich to Lowestoft

On Sundays the service in both directions doubles to become hourly.

Ipswich to Cambridge

On Sundays this has also become hourly in each direction and has been recast.

London North Eastern Railway

The headline news here are the 6 through trains from Kings Cross to Lincoln (5 on Sundays) and Harrogate each day.

The Lincoln trains are extensions of the Kings Cross to Newark Northgate services with one new departure at 0806 on Mondays to Saturdays returning at 2025. The Saturday service was introduced one week earlier than the timetable change to cater for the Lincoln Christmas Market. On Sundays these are new services at 0933, 1133, 1435, and 1533 from King Cross returning from Lincoln at 1121, 1249, 1446, 1723 and 1825

The Harrogate trains are extensions of Kings Cross to Leeds trains and are every 2 hours starting at 0903; on the return from Harrogate they start at 0815.

On Mondays to Fridays the 0830, 1230 and 1430 trains from Kings Cross to Newcastle have been extended to Edinburgh. In the other direction the 1225 and 1625 departures from Newcastle now start from Edinburgh at 1100 and 1500

Transport for Wales

Gloucester to Cardiff

On Sundays an early train has been introduced from Cardiff to Cheltenham Spa at 0823 returning at 1037 taking up the path of the 1048 from Gloucester.

Also on Sundays a much earlier first train has been introduced at 0845 from Gloucester to Cardiff.

Birmingham and Shrewsbury to Aberystwyth and Pwllheli

On Sundays there are additional services from Shrewsbury to Aberystwyth at 1027 and 1429; in the other direction additional services from Aberystwyth start at 0830, 1229, 1430 and 1630.

Also on Sundays the service to/from Pwllheli has increased from one to five services each way, 4 of which start from/return to Birmingham International.

On Mondays to Saturdays the 1029 and 1827 (1831 on Saturdays) from Shrewsbury start back from Birmingham International as a portion of a service to Chester.

Holyhead, Chester and Shrewsbury to Birmingham and Cardiff

Manchester to Cardiff

On Mondays to Fridays the 0721 Cardiff to Holyhead now starts at 0702 and is accelerated by 44 minutes giving an arrival time of 1120. Part of this acceleration is due to the fact that it is now non-stop between Shrewsbury and Wrexham.

Also on Sundays the 1232, 1630 and 1830 services from Manchester are accelerated by up to 15 minutes into Cardiff.

On Mondays to Fridays the 1232 from Manchester is retimed to depart at 1134 with an arrival into Cardiff at 1615 instead of 1716 – it also has full restaurant facilities. To compensate for the earlier departure above the 1128 Holyhead to Birmingham is retimed to depart at 1148 with an acceleration of 20 minutes. The 1735 from Cardiff to Manchester now starts at 1754 and also has a 20 minute earlier arrival.

Llandudno to Llandudno Junction and Blaenau Ffestiniog

On Sundays the line from Llandudno to Llandudno Junction now has 16 trains out and 15 on the return all year round. Also the line to Blaenau Ffestiniog enjoys 4 return services every Sunday.

CrossCountry Trains

Nottingham to Cardiff via Birmingham

The headline news here is the opening of Worcestershire Parkway station on the Worcester avoiding line. Nearly all trains now stop here with some slight adjustments to running times.

Reading to Newcastle

On Mondays to Fridays the 0745, 0850, 1345 and 1743 departures from Reading to Newcastle have been speeded up by up to 30 minutes by cutting out the lengthy waits in Derby and Sheffield. On Saturdays the same applies to the 0845, 0945, 1045, 1145 and 1645 departures from Reading.

Hull Trains

On Mondays to Fridays an additional train starts back at Beverley at 0753 returning as the 1548 from Kings Cross.

East Midlands Railway

Kettering to Corby

On Mondays to Fridays East Midland Railway have introduced additional shuttles between Kettering and Corby at 0940, 1206, 1124, 1526, 1626 and 1723 from Kettering and 0848, 1010, 1105, 1505, 1605 and 1705 from Corby.

Transpennine Express

Manchester Airport to Scotland via Preston

On Saturdays a late train has been introduced from Manchester Airport to Carlisle at 2310.

Liverpool and Manchester to Leeds, York, Newcastle and Edinburgh

The headline for this is the extension of services to Edinburgh and Redcar on a daily basis – along with the start of the 3 services per day between Liverpool and Glasgow via Carlisle.

During most of the day the xx24 (xx25 on Sundays) trains from Liverpool continue to Edinburgh via Newcastle but on the return they vary between xx11 and xx33 from Edinburgh.

Redcar is reached by an extension of services to Middlesbrough during most of the day.

Stalybridge calls have moved from the Manchester to Huddersfield service to the Liverpool to Scarborough service.

Dewsbury has been moved from the Manchester to Hull service and is now included in the Manchester to Newcastle service.

The services to Glasgow from Liverpool leave at 0812, 1211 and 1612 Mondays to Saturdays (with an additional short working to Oxenholme at 2012 on Mondays to Fridays) returning at 0745 (0805 on Saturdays), 1205 and 1629. On Sundays the service from Liverpool is at 1012, 1412 and 1812 returning from Glasgow at 1013, 1405 and 1847.

Thameslink

The only significant change this time around is the start of Saturday services from Peterborough through the core to Horsham. The same timings are used as Mondays to Fridays.

ScotRail

On the Aberdeen to Inverness line the number of services from Aberdeen to Dyce has risen to 78 per day and to Inverurie 76. Cross-Aberdeen services from Inverurie to Montrose have increased from 5 to 28 per day.

EUROPEAN RAIL TIMETABLE

Your Perfect Travel Companions

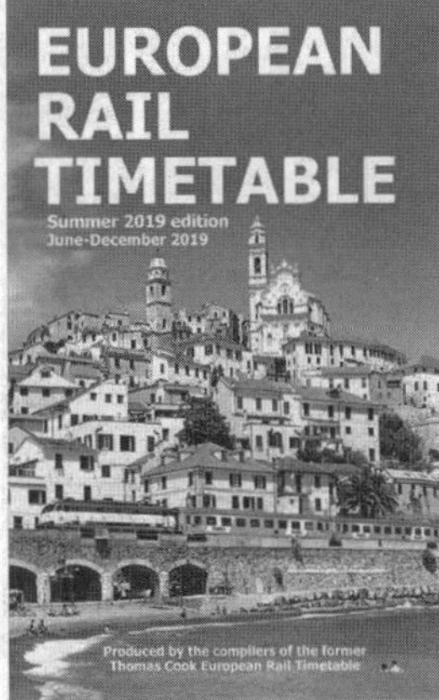

Published in June
£19.99

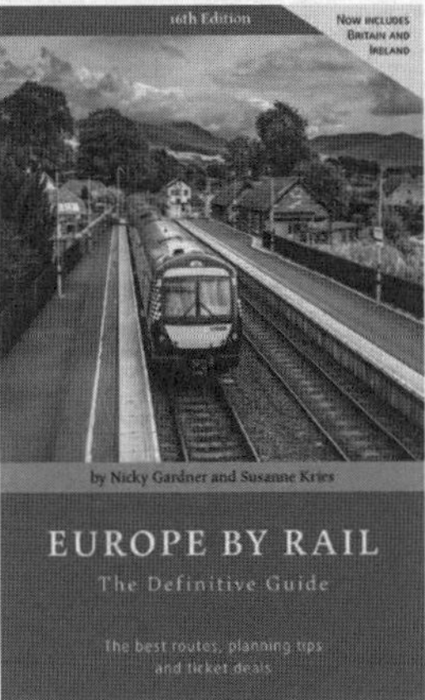

Available now
£16.99

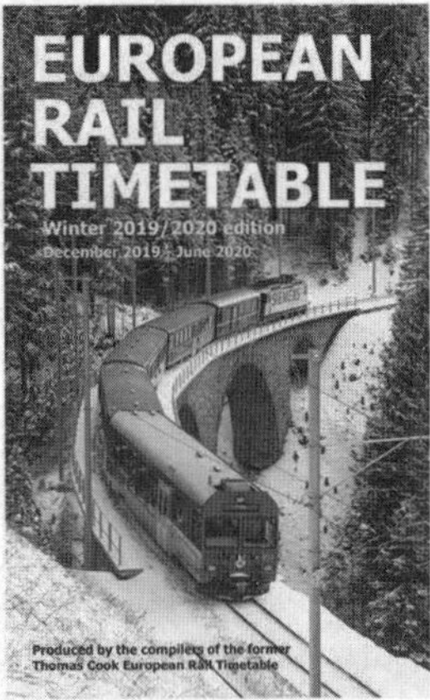

Published in December
£19.99

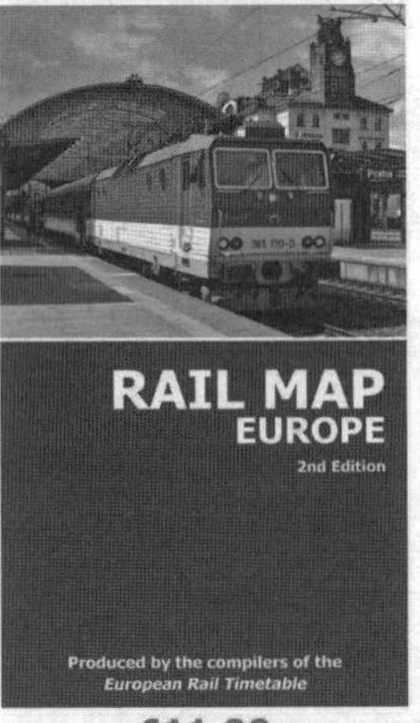

£11.99

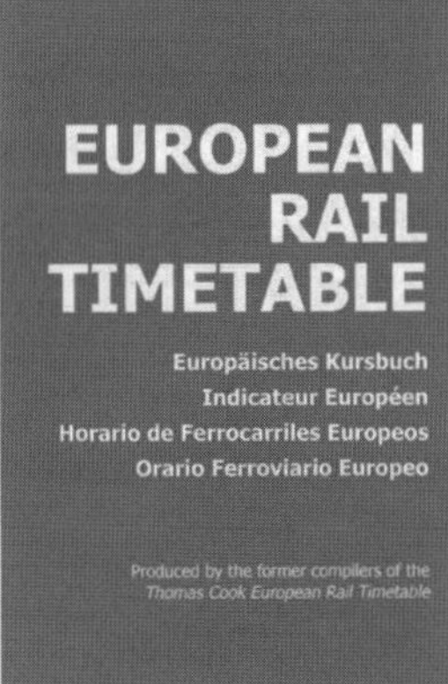

Printed every two months £17.99

ERT

Digital edition from
£11.99

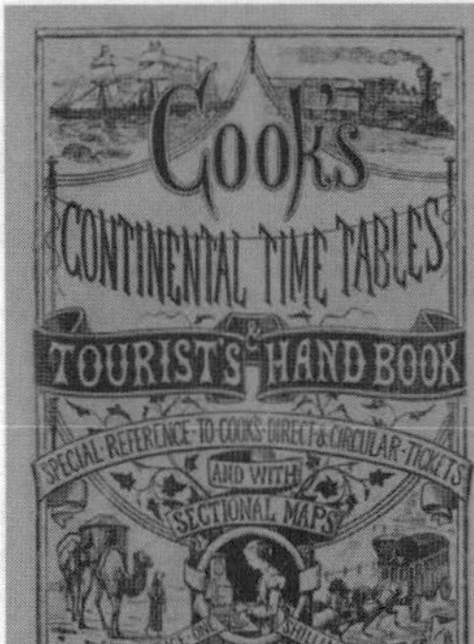

Reprint £13.99

Timetable available in printed format every two months. Digital edition every month to view on your Tablet, Smart phone or Computer

Why not have a yearly subscription? From £104

ORDER FROM

www.europeanrailtimetable.eu

01832 270198

28 Monson Way, Oundle, Northamptonshire PE8 4QG U.K.

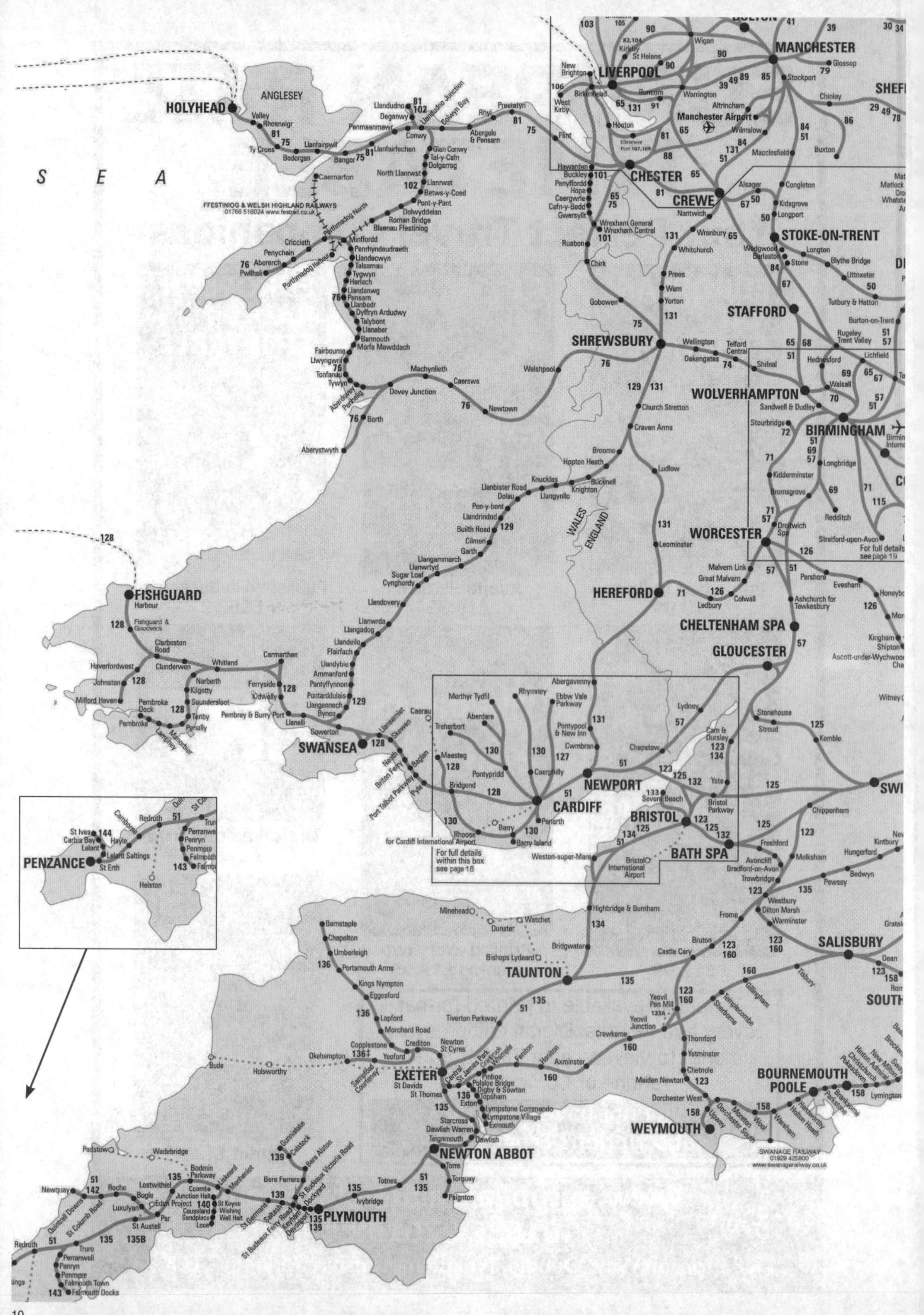
S E A
HOLYHEAD
ANGLESEY
Valley
Rhosneigr
Ty Croes
Bodorgan
Llanfairpwll
Bangor
Llanfairfechan
Penmaenmawr
Conwy
Llandudno
Deganwy
Llandudno Junction
Colwyn Bay
Abergele & Pensarn
Rhyl
Prestatyn
Flint
Glan Conwy
Tal-y-Cafn
Dolgarrog
North Llanrwst
Llanrwst
Betws-y-Coed
Pont-y-Pant
Dolwyddelan
Roman Bridge
Blaenau Ffestiniog
Caernarfon
FFESTINIOG & WELSH HIGHLAND RAILWAYS
01766 516024 www.festrail.co.uk
Porthmadog North
Porthmadog Harbour
Minffordd
Penrhyndeudraeth
Llandecwyn
Talsarnau
Tygwyn
Harlech
Llandanwg
Pensarn
Llanbedr
Dyffryn Ardudwy
Talybont
Llanaber
Barmouth
Morfa Mawddach
Fairbourne
Llwyngwril
Tonfanau
Tywyn
Aberdovey
Penhelig
Dovey Junction
Borth
Aberystwyth
Machynlleth
Caersws
Newtown
Welshpool
Criccieth
Penychain
Abererch
Pwllheli
LIVERPOOL
New Brighton
West Kirby
Birkenhead
Hooton
Ellesmere Port
Kirkby
St Helens
Wigan
Runcorn
Warrington
BOLTON
MANCHESTER
Glossop
Stockport
Chinley
Altrincham
Manchester Airport
Wilmslow
Macclesfield
Buxton
SHEFF
CHESTER
CREWE
Hawarden
Buckley
Penyffordd
Hope
Caergwrle
Cefn-y-Bedd
Gwersyllt
Wrexham General
Wrexham Central
Ruabon
Chirk
Gobowen
Nantwich
Wrenbury
Whitchurch
Prees
Wem
Yorton
Alsager
Congleton
Kidsgrove
Longport
STOKE-ON-TRENT
Wedgwood
Barlaston
Stone
Longton
Blythe Bridge
Uttoxeter
Tutbury & Hatton
Burton-on-Trent
STAFFORD
Rugeley Trent Valley
Lichfield
Hednesford
Walsall
SHREWSBURY
Wellington
Telford Central
Oakengates
Shifnal
WOLVERHAMPTON
Sandwell & Dudley
Stourbridge
BIRMINGHAM
Longbridge
Kidderminster
Bromsgrove
Redditch
Droitwich Spa
Stratford-upon-Avon
For full details see page 19
WORCESTER
Church Stretton
Craven Arms
Broome
Hopton Heath
Bucknell
Knighton
Knucklas
Llangynllo
Llanbister Road
Dolau
Pen-y-bont
Llandrindod
Builth Road
Cilmeri
Garth
Llangammarch
Llanwrtyd
Sugar Loaf
Cynghordy
Llandovery
Llanwrda
Llangadog
Llandeilo
Ffairfach
Llandybie
Ammanford
Pantyffynnon
Pontarddulais
Llangennech
Bynea
Ludlow
Leominster
WALES
ENGLAND
HEREFORD
Ledbury
Colwall
Great Malvern
Malvern Link
Pershore
Evesham
Honeybo
Ashchurch for Tewkesbury
CHELTENHAM SPA
GLOUCESTER
Kingham
Shipton
Ascott-under-Wychwood
FISHGUARD
Harbour
Fishguard & Goodwick
Clarbeston Road
Haverfordwest
Johnston
Milford Haven
Clunderwen
Whitland
Narberth
Kilgetty
Saundersfoot
Tenby
Penally
Manorbier
Lamphey
Pembroke
Pembroke Dock
Carmarthen
Ferryside
Kidwelly
Pembrey & Burry Port
Llanelli
Gowerton
SWANSEA
Llansamlet
Skewen
Neath
Briton Ferry
Baglan
Port Talbot Parkway
Pyle
Bridgend
Maesteg
Caerau
Treherbert
Aberdare
Merthyr Tydfil
Rhymney
Ebbw Vale Parkway
Pontypool & New Inn
Cwmbran
Abergavenny
Pontypridd
Caerphilly
CARDIFF
NEWPORT
Penarth
Barry
Barry Island
Rhoose
for Cardiff International Airport
For full details within this box see page 18
Lydney
Chepstow
Severn Beach
Bristol Parkway
Yate
Cam & Dursley
Stonehouse
Stroud
Kemble
BRISTOL
BATH SPA
Weston-super-Mare
Bristol International Airport
Chippenham
Freshford
Avoncliff
Bradford-on-Avon
Trowbridge
Melksham
Westbury
Dilton Marsh
Warminster
Frome
Pewsey
Bedwyn
Hungerford
Kintbury
SALISBURY
Dean
Tisbury
Gillingham
Templecombe
Sherborne
Highbridge & Burnham
Bridgwater
Minehead
Dunster
Watchet
Bishops Lydeard
TAUNTON
Bruton
Castle Cary
Yeovil Pen Mill
Yeovil Junction
Crewkerne
Thornford
Yetminster
Chetnole
Maiden Newton
Dorchester West
Dorchester South
Upwey
WEYMOUTH
Moreton
Wool
Wareham
Hamworthy
Holton Heath
Parkstone
Branksome
BOURNEMOUTH
POOLE
Pokesdown
Christchurch
Hinton Admiral
New Milton
Lymington
SWANAGE RAILWAY
01929 425800
www.swanagerailway.co.uk
Barnstaple
Chapelton
Umberleigh
Portsmouth Arms
Kings Nympton
Eggesford
Lapford
Morchard Road
Copplestone
Yeoford
Crediton
Newton St Cyres
Okehampton
Sampford Courtenay
Bude
Holsworthy
Tiverton Parkway
EXETER
Central
St James Park
Polsloe Bridge
Pinhoe
Whimple
Feniton
Honiton
Axminster
St Davids
St Thomas
Digby & Sowton
Topsham
Exton
Lympstone Commando
Lympstone Village
Exmouth
Starcross
Dawlish Warren
Dawlish
Teignmouth
NEWTON ABBOT
Torre
Torquay
Paignton
Totnes
Ivybridge
PLYMOUTH
Gunnislake
Calstock
Bere Alston
Bere Ferrers
St Budeaux Victoria Road
St Budeaux Ferry Road
Keyham
Devonport
Dockyard
Saltash
St Germans
Menheniot
Liskeard
Coombe Junction Halt
St Keyne Wishing Well Halt
Causeland
Sandplace
Looe
Bodmin Parkway
Lostwithiel
Wadebridge
Padstow
Newquay
Quintrell Downs
St Columb Road
Roche
Bugle
Luxulyan
Eden Project
Par
St Austell
Truro
Redruth
Perranwell
Penryn
Penmere
Falmouth Town
Falmouth Docks
PENZANCE
St Ives
Carbis Bay
Lelant
Lelant Saltings
St Erth
Hayle
Camborne
Helston

GRIMSBY
DONCASTER
Robin Hood Airport
Scunthorpe
Barnsley
Brigg
Kirton Lindsey
Gainsborough Central
Gainsborough Lea Road
Market Rasen
Healing
Great Coates
Docks
New Clee
Cleethorpes
SHEFFIELD
Rotherham
Worksop
RETFORD
Creswell
Whitwell
Shirebrook
Langwith-Whaley Thorns
Mansfield Woodhouse
Mansfield
Chesterfield
Saxilby
LINCOLN
Hykeham
Swinderby
Collingham
Metheringham
Ruskington
Sutton Parkway
Kirkby-in-Ashfield
Newstead
Hucknall
Bulwell
Matlock
Matlock Bath
Cromford
Whatstandwell
Ambergate
Alfreton
Langley Mill
Ilkeston
Belper
Duffield
NEWARK
North Gate
Newark Castle
Rolleston
Fiskerton
Bleasby
Thurgarton
Lowdham
Burton Joyce
Carlton
Rauceby
Sleaford
Ancaster
Heckington
Swineshead
Hubberts Bridge
Boston
Thorpe Culvert
Wainfleet
Havenhouse
Skegness
NOTTINGHAM
DERBY
Peartree
Spondon
Beeston
Attenborough
Netherfield
Radcliffe
Bingham
Aslockton
Elton & Orston
Bottesford
GRANTHAM
Long Eaton
East Midlands Parkway
Willington
Loughborough
Barrow-on-Soar
Sileby
Syston
Melton Mowbray
Oakham
Stamford
Spalding
Hunstanton
Sandringham
Sheringham
West Runton
Cromer
Roughton Road
Gunton
North Walsham
Worstead
Hoveton & Wroxham
Salhouse
KINGS LYNN
Watlington
Downham Market
Swaffham
Dereham
Wisbech
NORWICH
Brundall Gardens
Brundall
Lingwood
Acle
Great Yarmouth
Berney Arms
Haddiscoe
Somerleyton
Oulton Broad North
Lowestoft
Oulton Broad South
Beccles
Buckenham
Cantley
Reedham
Wymondham
Spooner Row
Attleborough
Eccles Road
Harling Road
Thetford
Brandon
Lakenheath
Shippea Hill
Littleport
Diss
Brampton
Halesworth
Darsham
Saxmundham
LEICESTER
South Wigston
Narborough
Hinckley
Nuneaton
Tamworth
Lichfield
Birmingham International
COVENTRY
Leamington Spa
For full details within this box see page 19
PETERBOROUGH
Whittlesea
March
Manea
Ely
Waterbeach
Corby
Oundle
Market Harborough
KETTERING
Wellingborough
RUGBY
Long Buckby
NORTHAMPTON
Huntingdon
Cambridge North
Newmarket
Bury St Edmunds
Stowmarket
CAMBRIDGE
St Neots
Bedford
Westerfield
IPSWICH
Felixstowe
Sudbury
Royston
Letchworth
Hitchin
STANSTED Airport
MILTON KEYNES
Bletchley
Banbury
Honeybourne
Moreton-in-Marsh
Kingham
Chipping Norton
Shipton
Charlbury
Finstock
Combe
Hanborough
Buckingham
Bicester
Luton
Stevenage
COLCHESTER
Manningtree
HARWICH
Walton-on-the-Naze
Clacton-on-Sea
Marks Tey
Braintree
Witham
Bishops Stortford
Aylesbury Parkway
Aylesbury
Dunstable
Welwyn Garden City
Hertford
Harlow
Witney
Abingdon
OXFORD
Hemel Hempstead
St Albans
Chelmsford
Southminster
Princes Risborough
Chinnor
Amersham
Watford
Chingford
Shenfield
Wickford
Southend Airport
Romford
Basildon
SOUTHEND
Shoeburyness
Upminster
Didcot Parkway
Henley-on-Thames
High Wycombe
Marlow
Maidenhead
Slough
SWINDON
LONDON
Barking
Tilbury
Heathrow Airport
Twyford
READING
Windsor
Richmond
Staines
Ascot
Surbiton
Dartford
Ebbsfleet International
Sheerness-on-Sea
MARGATE
Herne Bay
Sittingbourne
Chatham
Gillingham
Faversham
RAMSGATE
Newbury
Thatcham
Kintbury
Newbury Racecourse
Midgham
Theale
Aldermaston
Woking
East Croydon
Oxted
Maidstone
CANTERBURY
Deal
Basingstoke
Aldershot
Guildford
Dorking
Redhill
Sevenoaks
Tonbridge
Tunbridge Wells
Overton
Whitchurch
Andover
Grateley
GATWICK Airport
ASHFORD
DOVER
FOLKESTONE
CHANNEL TUNNEL
Micheldever
Winchester
Shawford
Eastleigh
Alton
Haslemere
Crawley
East Grinstead
Dean
Mottisfont & Dunbridge
Romsey
Chandlers Ford
Horsham
Haywards Heath
Uckfield
Rye
SOUTHAMPTON
Totton
Southampton Airport Parkway
For full details within this box see pages 14-15
LEWES
HASTINGS
Bexhill
Fareham
Havant
CHICHESTER
WORTHING
Hove
BRIGHTON
Newhaven
Seaford
Littlehampton
Bognor Regis
EASTBOURNE
For full details within this box see pages 14-17
PORTSMOUTH
Lymington Town
Lymington Pier
See 167A
Pier Head
Ryde
Esplanade
St Johns Road
Brading
Sandown
Lake
Shanklin
Ventnor
ISLE OF WIGHT
ENGLISH CHANNEL
Fréthun-Calais
BOULOGNE
Etaples

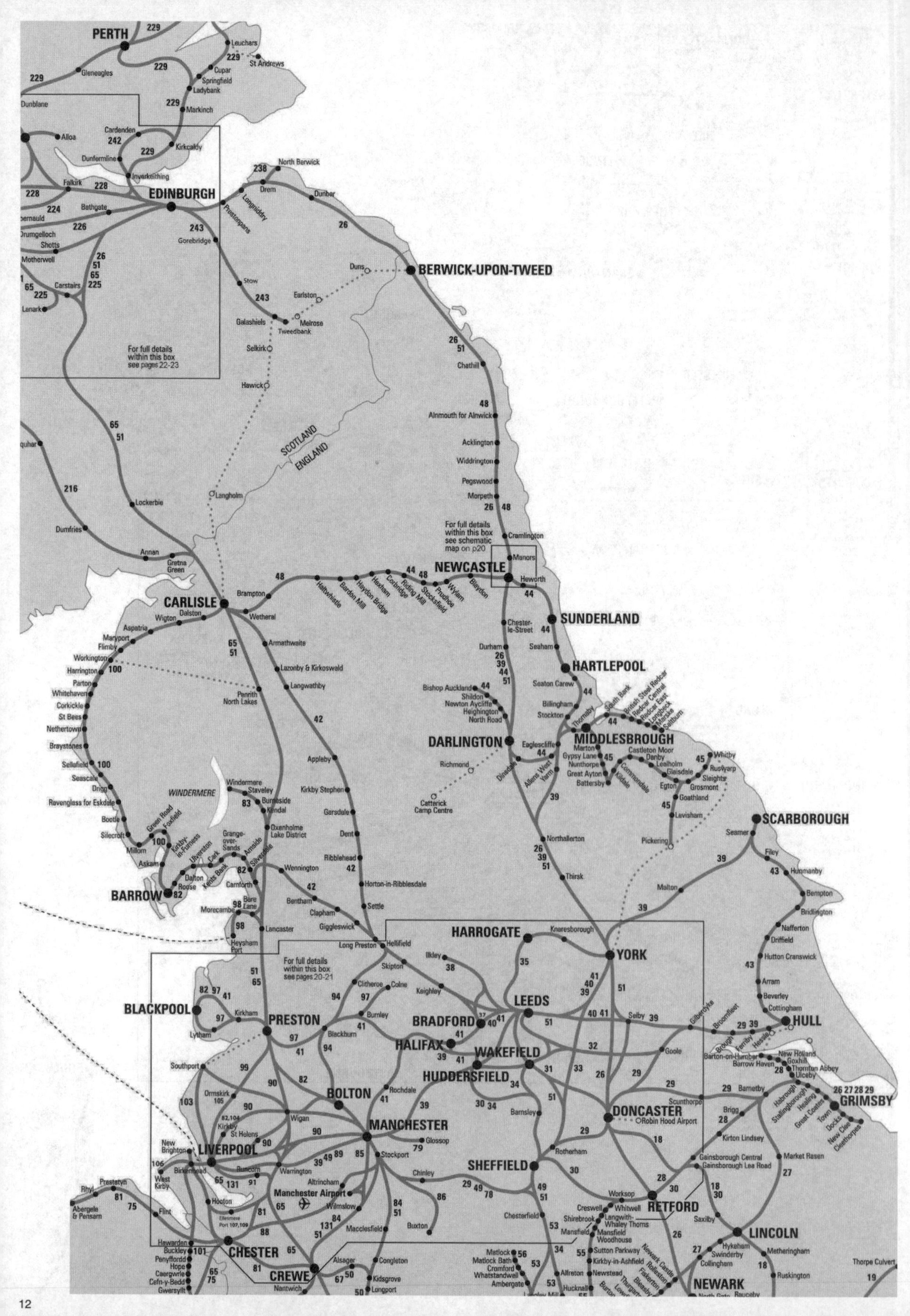

PERTH
Leuchars
St Andrews
Gleneagles
Cupar
Springfield
Ladybank
Markinch
Dunblane
Alloa
Cardenden
Kirkcaldy
Dunfermline
Inverkeithing
North Berwick
Drem
Dunbar
Falkirk
EDINBURGH
Longniddry
Prestonpans
Bathgate
Drumgelloch
Shotts
Motherwell
Gorebridge
Carstairs
Lanark
Stow
Galashiels
Tweedbank
Melrose
Earlston
Duns
BERWICK-UPON-TWEED
Selkirk
Hawick
For full details within this box see pages 22-23
Chathill
Alnmouth for Alnwick
Acklington
Widdrington
Pegswood
Morpeth
SCOTLAND
ENGLAND
Langholm
Lockerbie
Dumfries
Annan
Gretna Green
Cramlington
For full details within this box see schematic map on p20
Manors
NEWCASTLE
Heworth
Brampton
Haltwhistle
Bardon Mill
Haydon Bridge
Hexham
Corbridge
Riding Mill
Stocksfield
Prudhoe
Wylam
Blaydon
CARLISLE
Wetheral
Dalston
Wigton
Aspatria
Maryport
Flimby
Workington
Harrington
Parton
Whitehaven
Corkickle
St Bees
Nethertown
Braystones
Sellafield
Seascale
Drigg
Ravenglass for Eskdale
Bootle
Silecroft
Millom
Green Road
Foxfield
Kirkby-in-Furness
Askam
BARROW
Roose
Dalton
Ulverston
Cark
Kents Bank
Grange-over-Sands
Arnside
Silverdale
Carnforth
Armathwaite
Lazonby & Kirkoswald
Langwathby
Penrith North Lakes
Appleby
Kirkby Stephen
Garsdale
Dent
Ribblehead
Horton-in-Ribblesdale
Settle
Windermere
Staveley
Burneside
Kendal
Oxenholme Lake District
WINDERMERE
Wennington
Bentham
Clapham
Giggleswick
Morecambe
Bare Lane
Lancaster
Heysham Port
Long Preston
Hellifield
Chester-le-Street
SUNDERLAND
Seaham
Durham
HARTLEPOOL
Seaton Carew
Billingham
Stockton
Thornaby
Bishop Auckland
Shildon
Newton Aycliffe
Heighington
North Road
DARLINGTON
Eaglescliffe
MIDDLESBROUGH
South Bank
British Steel Redcar
Redcar Central
Redcar East
Longbeck
Marske
Saltburn
Marton
Gypsy Lane
Nunthorpe
Great Ayton
Battersby
Kildale
Castleton Moor
Commondale
Danby
Lealholm
Glaisdale
Egton
Grosmont
Sleights
Ruswarp
Whitby
Goathland
Levisham
Pickering
Richmond
Catterick Camp Centre
Dinsdale
Allens West
Yarm
Northallerton
Thirsk
SCARBOROUGH
Seamer
Filey
Hunmanby
Malton
Bempton
Bridlington
Nafferton
Driffield
Hutton Cranswick
Arram
Beverley
Cottingham
HULL
HARROGATE
Knaresborough
YORK
For full details within this box see pages 20-21
Ilkley
Skipton
Clitheroe
Colne
Keighley
BLACKPOOL
Kirkham
Lytham
PRESTON
Burnley
Blackburn
LEEDS
BRADFORD
HALIFAX
WAKEFIELD
HUDDERSFIELD
Selby
Gilberdyke
Broomfleet
Brough
Ferriby
Hessle
Goole
Barton-on-Humber
Barrow Haven
New Holland
Goxhill
Thornton Abbey
Ulceby
Southport
Ormskirk
BOLTON
Rochdale
Barnsley
Scunthorpe
Barnetby
Habrough
Stallingborough
Healing
Great Coates
GRIMSBY
Town
Docks
New Clee
Cleethorpes
Brigg
Kirton Lindsey
Kirkby
St Helens
Wigan
MANCHESTER
Glossop
DONCASTER
Robin Hood Airport
New Brighton
LIVERPOOL
Birkenhead
West Kirby
Runcorn
Warrington
Stockport
Rotherham
SHEFFIELD
Gainsborough Central
Gainsborough Lea Road
Market Rasen
Chinley
Altrincham
Manchester Airport
Wilmslow
Rhyl
Prestatyn
Abergele & Pensarn
Hooton
Flint
Ellesmere Port
Macclesfield
Buxton
Chesterfield
Worksop
Whitwell
Creswell
Shirebrook
Langwith-Whaley Thorns
Mansfield
Mansfield Woodhouse
RETFORD
Saxilby
LINCOLN
Hawarden
Buckley
Penyffordd
Hope
Caergwrle
Cefn-y-Bedd
Gwersyllt
CHESTER
CREWE
Nantwich
Alsager
Congleton
Kidsgrove
Longport
Matlock
Matlock Bath
Cromford
Whatstandwell
Ambergate
Sutton Parkway
Kirkby-in-Ashfield
Newstead
Alfreton
Hucknall
Newark Castle
Rolleston
Fiskerton
Bleasby
Thurgarton
Hykeham
Swinderby
Collingham
Metheringham
Ruskington
NEWARK
Thorpe Culvert

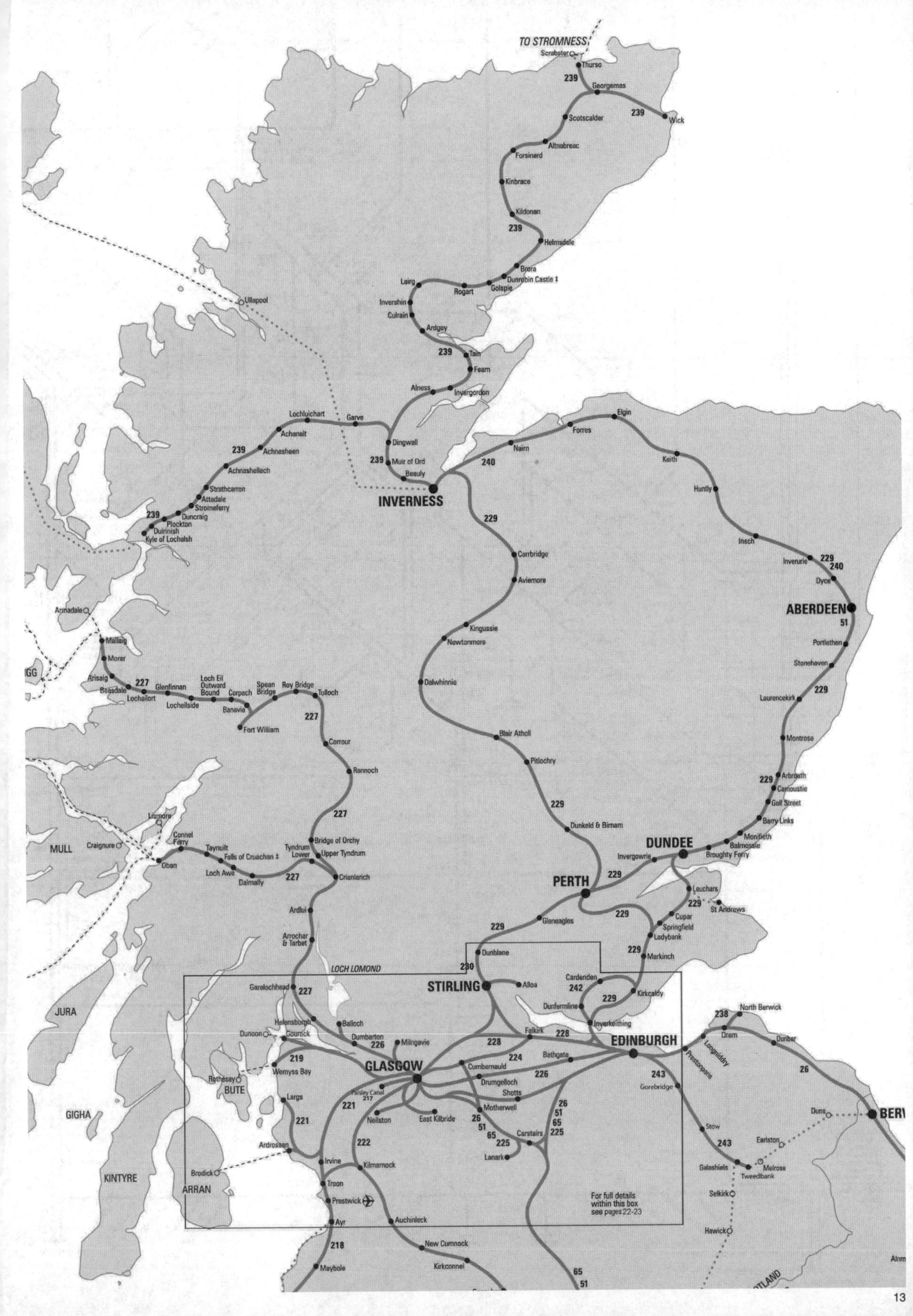

TO STROMNESS
Scrabster
Thurso
Georgemas
Wick
Scotscalder
Altnabreac
Forsinard
Kinbrace
Kildonan
Helmsdale
Brora
Dunrobin Castle ‡
Golspie
Rogart
Lairg
Invershin
Culrain
Ardgay
Tain
Fearn
Invergordon
Alness
Ullapool
Lochluichart
Garve
Achanalt
Achnasheen
Achnashellach
Strathcarron
Attadale
Stromeferry
Duncraig
Plockton
Duirinish
Kyle of Lochalsh
Dingwall
Muir of Ord
Beauly
INVERNESS
Nairn
Forres
Elgin
Keith
Huntly
Insch
Inverurie
Dyce
ABERDEEN
Portlethen
Stonehaven
Laurencekirk
Montrose
Arbroath
Carnoustie
Golf Street
Barry Links
Monifieth
Balmossie
Broughty Ferry
DUNDEE
Invergowrie
Carrbridge
Aviemore
Kingussie
Newtonmore
Dalwhinnie
Blair Atholl
Pitlochry
Dunkeld & Birnam
PERTH
Leuchars
St Andrews
Cupar
Springfield
Ladybank
Markinch
Kirkcaldy
Gleneagles
Dunblane
Armadale
Mallaig
Morar
Arisaig
Beasdale
Lochailort
Glenfinnan
Locheilside
Loch Eil Outward Bound
Corpach
Banavie
Fort William
Spean Bridge
Roy Bridge
Tulloch
Corrour
Rannoch
Bridge of Orchy
Tyndrum Lower
Upper Tyndrum
Crianlarich
Lismore
MULL
Craignure
Connel Ferry
Oban
Taynuilt
Falls of Cruachan ‡
Loch Awe
Dalmally
Ardlui
Arrochar & Tarbet
LOCH LOMOND
Garelochhead
STIRLING
Alloa
Cardenden
Dunfermline
Inverkeithing
JURA
Helensburgh
Balloch
Dunoon
Gourock
Dumbarton
Milngavie
Falkirk
EDINBURGH
North Berwick
Drem
Longniddry
Prestonpans
Dunbar
Wemyss Bay
Rothesay
BUTE
GLASGOW
Cumbernauld
Bathgate
Drumgelloch
Shotts
Paisley Canal
Largs
Neilston
East Kilbride
Motherwell
Gorebridge
GIGHA
Carstairs
Lanark
Stow
Duns
BERW
Earlston
Ardrossan
Irvine
Kilmarnock
Galashiels
Melrose
Tweedbank
Brodick
KINTYRE
ARRAN
Troon
Prestwick
Selkirk
Ayr
Auchinleck
For full details within this box see pages 22-23
Hawick
New Cumnock
Maybole
Kirkconnel
Alnm
239
240
229
51
227
230
242
228
224
226
219
217
221
222
225
26
65
243
238
218

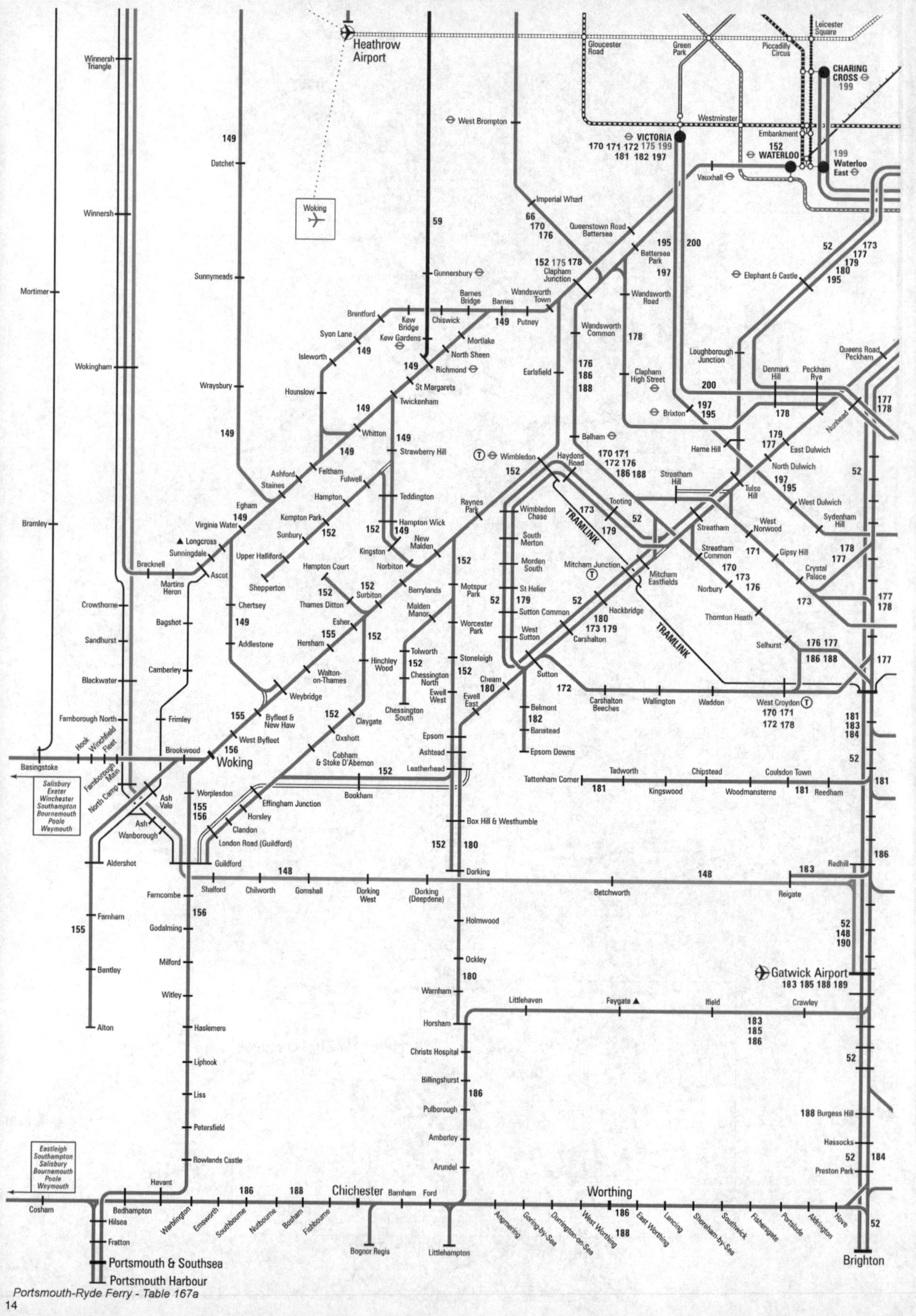

Portsmouth-Ryde Ferry - Table 167a

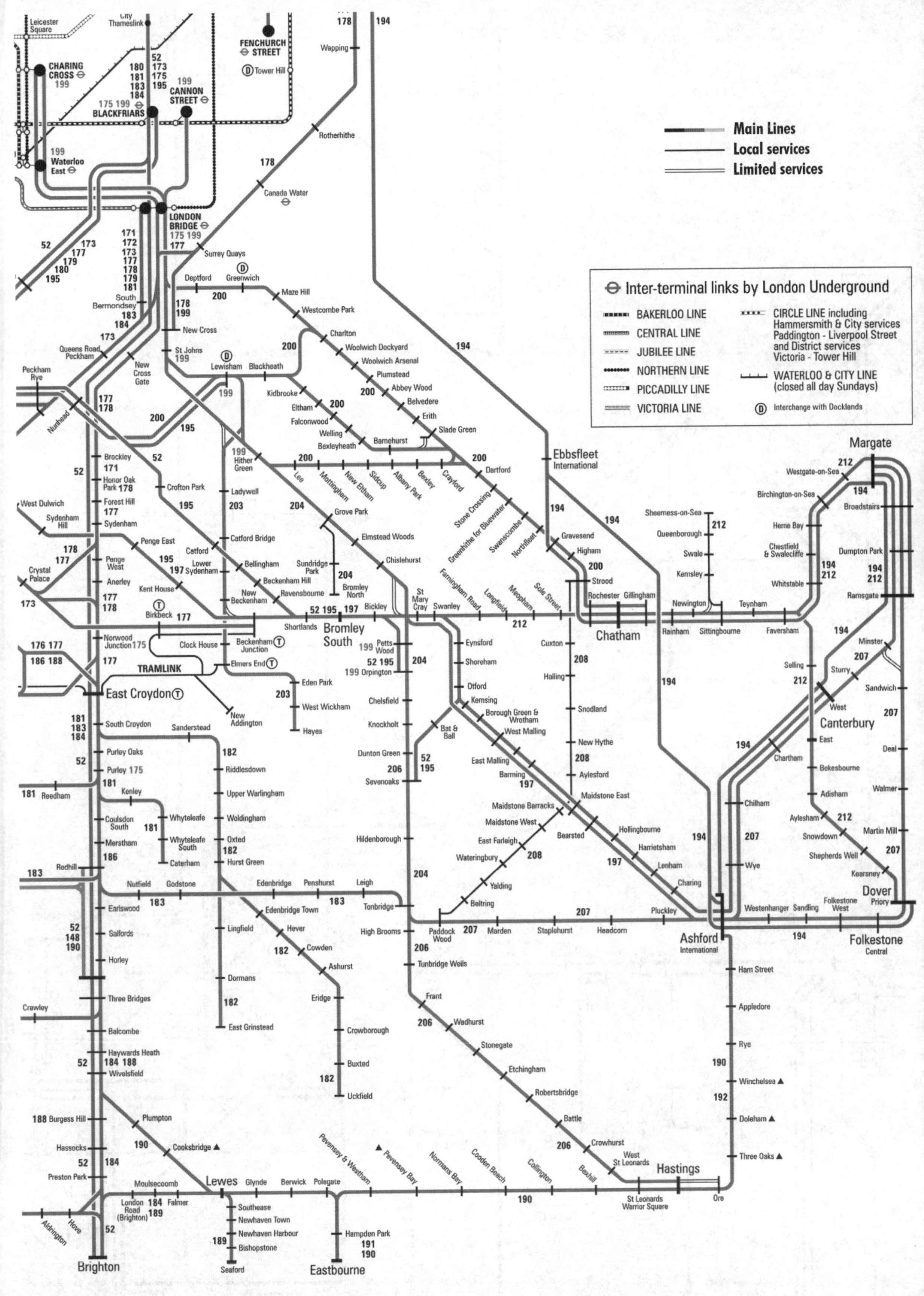
Main Lines
Local services
Limited services
Inter-terminal links by London Underground
BAKERLOO LINE
CENTRAL LINE
JUBILEE LINE
NORTHERN LINE
PICCADILLY LINE
VICTORIA LINE
CIRCLE LINE including Hammersmith & City services Paddington - Liverpool Street and District services Victoria - Tower Hill
WATERLOO & CITY LINE (closed all day Sundays)
Interchange with Docklands
Leicester Square
City Thameslink
CHARING CROSS
FENCHURCH STREET
Tower Hill
BLACKFRIARS
CANNON STREET
Wapping
Rotherhithe
Waterloo East
Canada Water
LONDON BRIDGE
Surrey Quays
Deptford
Greenwich
Maze Hill
Westcombe Park
Charlton
Woolwich Dockyard
Woolwich Arsenal
Plumstead
Abbey Wood
Belvedere
Erith
Slade Green
South Bermondsey
New Cross
Queens Road Peckham
New Cross Gate
St Johns
Lewisham
Blackheath
Kidbrooke
Eltham
Falconwood
Welling
Bexleyheath
Barnehurst
Peckham Rye
Nunhead
Hither Green
Lee
Mottingham
New Eltham
Sidcup
Albany Park
Bexley
Crayford
Dartford
Stone Crossing
Greenhithe for Bluewater
Swanscombe
Northfleet
Ebbsfleet International
Gravesend
Higham
Strood
Rochester
Gillingham
Chatham
Rainham
Newington
Sittingbourne
Teynham
Faversham
Sheerness-on-Sea
Queenborough
Swale
Kemsley
Margate
Westgate-on-Sea
Birchington-on-Sea
Broadstairs
Herne Bay
Chestfield & Swalecliffe
Dumpton Park
Whitstable
Ramsgate
Minster
Sturry
Sandwich
Selling
Canterbury West
Canterbury East
Chartham
Bekesbourne
Deal
Adisham
Walmer
Aylesham
Snowdown
Martin Mill
Shepherds Well
Kearsney
Dover Priory
Folkestone West
Folkestone Central
Sandling
Westenhanger
Brockley
Honor Oak Park
Crofton Park
West Dulwich
Forest Hill
Sydenham Hill
Sydenham
Ladywell
Grove Park
Elmstead Woods
Chislehurst
Catford Bridge
Catford
Penge East
Penge West
Crystal Palace
Anerley
Kent House
Lower Sydenham
Bellingham
Beckenham Hill
Sundridge Park
Bromley North
Ravensbourne
New Beckenham
Birkbeck
Shortlands
Bromley South
Bickley
St Mary Cray
Swanley
Farningham Road
Longfield
Meopham
Sole Street
Cuxton
Halling
Snodland
New Hythe
Aylesford
Norwood Junction
Clock House
Beckenham Junction
Elmers End
TRAMLINK
East Croydon
New Addington
Eden Park
West Wickham
Hayes
Petts Wood
Orpington
Chelsfield
Knockholt
Dunton Green
Sevenoaks
Bat & Ball
Eynsford
Shoreham
Otford
Kemsing
Borough Green & Wrotham
West Malling
East Malling
Barming
Maidstone Barracks
Maidstone East
Maidstone West
Bearsted
Hollingbourne
Harrietsham
Lenham
Charing
East Farleigh
Wateringbury
Yalding
Beltring
Paddock Wood
Marden
Staplehurst
Headcorn
Pluckley
Ashford International
South Croydon
Sanderstead
Purley Oaks
Purley
Riddlesdown
Upper Warlingham
Reedham
Kenley
Coulsdon South
Whyteleafe
Woldingham
Whyteleafe South
Oxted
Caterham
Hurst Green
Merstham
Redhill
Nutfield
Godstone
Edenbridge
Penshurst
Leigh
Tonbridge
Hildenborough
Earlswood
Edenbridge Town
Hever
Cowden
Ashurst
Lingfield
Salfords
Horley
Dormans
High Brooms
Tunbridge Wells
Frant
Wadhurst
Stonegate
Etchingham
Robertsbridge
Battle
Crowhurst
West St Leonards
Hastings
Ore
St Leonards Warrior Square
Bexhill
Collington
Cooden Beach
Normans Bay
Pevensey Bay
Pevensey & Westham
Crawley
Three Bridges
East Grinstead
Eridge
Crowborough
Buxted
Uckfield
Balcombe
Haywards Heath
Wivelsfield
Burgess Hill
Plumpton
Cooksbridge
Hassocks
Preston Park
Moulsecoomb
London Road (Brighton)
Falmer
Lewes
Glynde
Berwick
Polegate
Southease
Newhaven Town
Newhaven Harbour
Bishopstone
Seaford
Hampden Park
Eastbourne
Aldrington
Hove
Brighton
Ham Street
Appledore
Rye
Winchelsea
Doleham
Three Oaks

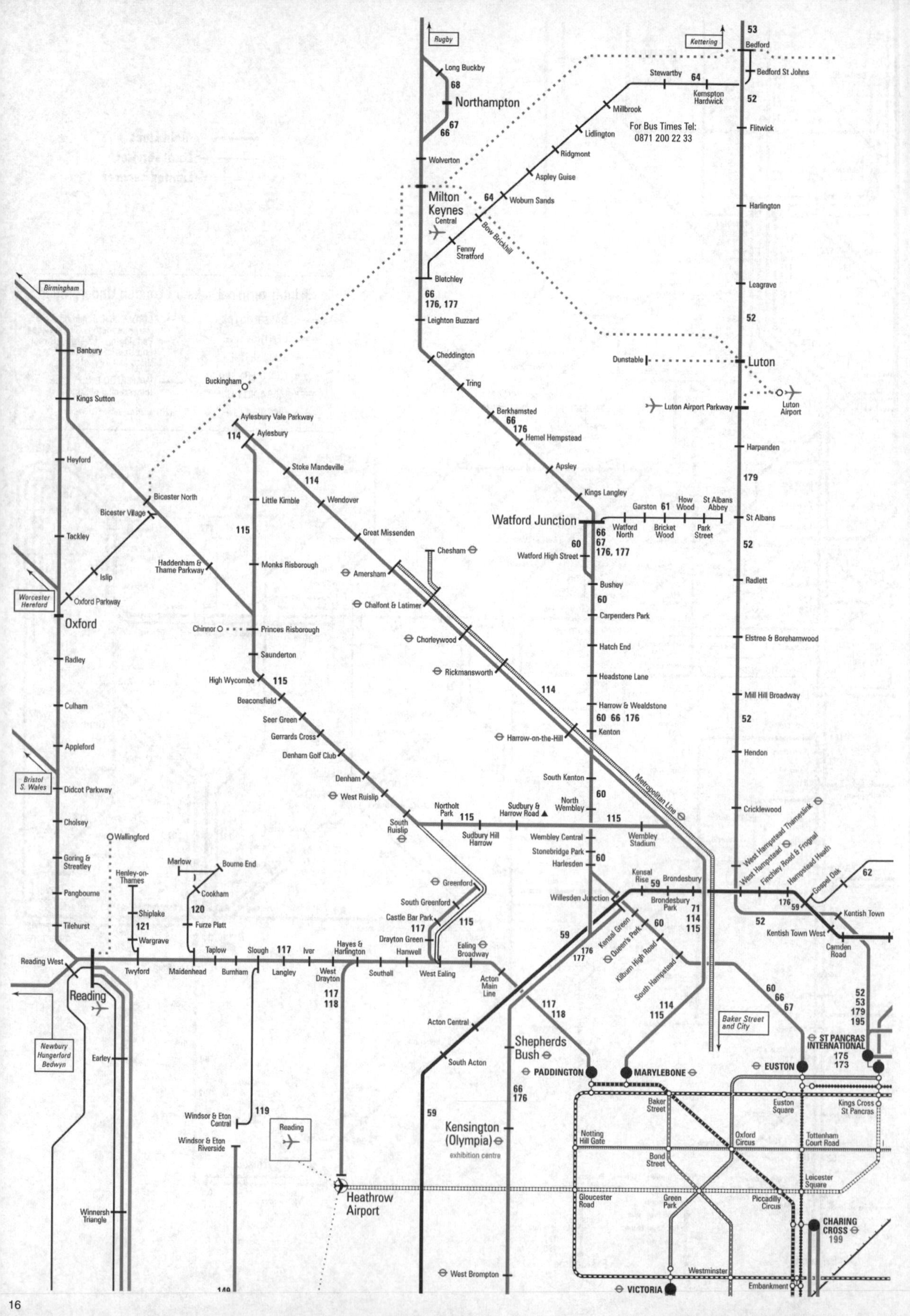
Rugby
Kettering
Birmingham
Worcester Hereford
Bristol S. Wales
Newbury Hungerford Bedwyn
Long Buckby
Northampton
Wolverton
Milton Keynes Central
Fenny Stratford
Bow Brickhill
Woburn Sands
Aspley Guise
Ridgmont
Lidlington
Millbrook
Stewartby
Kempston Hardwick
Bedford
Bedford St Johns
Flitwick
Harlington
Leagrave
Luton
Dunstable
Luton Airport Parkway
Luton Airport
Harpenden
St Albans
Radlett
Elstree & Borehamwood
Mill Hill Broadway
Hendon
Cricklewood
For Bus Times Tel:
0871 200 22 33
Bletchley
Leighton Buzzard
Cheddington
Tring
Berkhamsted
Hemel Hempstead
Apsley
Kings Langley
Watford Junction
Watford North
Garston
Bricket Wood
How Wood
Park Street
St Albans Abbey
Watford High Street
Bushey
Carpenders Park
Hatch End
Headstone Lane
Harrow & Wealdstone
Kenton
South Kenton
North Wembley
Wembley Central
Stonebridge Park
Harlesden
Willesden Junction
Kensal Rise
Brondesbury
Brondesbury Park
Kensal Green
Queen's Park
Kilburn High Road
South Hampstead
West Hampstead Thameslink
West Hampstead
Finchley Road & Frognal
Hampstead Heath
Gospel Oak
Kentish Town
Kentish Town West
Camden Road
Banbury
Kings Sutton
Heyford
Bicester North
Bicester Village
Buckingham
Tackley
Islip
Oxford Parkway
Oxford
Radley
Culham
Appleford
Didcot Parkway
Cholsey
Goring & Streatley
Pangbourne
Tilehurst
Reading West
Reading
Earley
Winnersh Triangle
Wallingford
Henley-on-Thames
Shiplake
Wargrave
Twyford
Marlow
Bourne End
Cookham
Furze Platt
Maidenhead
Taplow
Burnham
Slough
Langley
Iver
West Drayton
Hayes & Harlington
Southall
Hanwell
West Ealing
Ealing Broadway
Acton Main Line
Acton Central
South Acton
Windsor & Eton Central
Windsor & Eton Riverside
Heathrow Airport
Aylesbury Vale Parkway
Aylesbury
Stoke Mandeville
Wendover
Great Missenden
Little Kimble
Monks Risborough
Haddenham & Thame Parkway
Chinnor
Princes Risborough
Saunderton
High Wycombe
Beaconsfield
Seer Green
Gerrards Cross
Denham Golf Club
Denham
West Ruislip
South Ruislip
Northolt Park
Sudbury Hill Harrow
Sudbury & Harrow Road
Wembley Stadium
Greenford
South Greenford
Castle Bar Park
Drayton Green
Chesham
Amersham
Chalfont & Latimer
Chorleywood
Rickmansworth
Harrow-on-the-Hill
Metropolitan Line
Baker Street and City
Shepherds Bush
Kensington (Olympia)
exhibition centre
West Brompton
PADDINGTON
MARYLEBONE
EUSTON
ST PANCRAS INTERNATIONAL
Baker Street
Euston Square
Kings Cross St Pancras
Notting Hill Gate
Oxford Circus
Tottenham Court Road
Bond Street
Leicester Square
Gloucester Road
Green Park
Piccadilly Circus
CHARING CROSS
Westminster
Embankment
VICTORIA
52 53 59 60 61 62 64 66 67 68 71 114 115 117 118 119 120 121 149 173 175 176 177 179 195 199

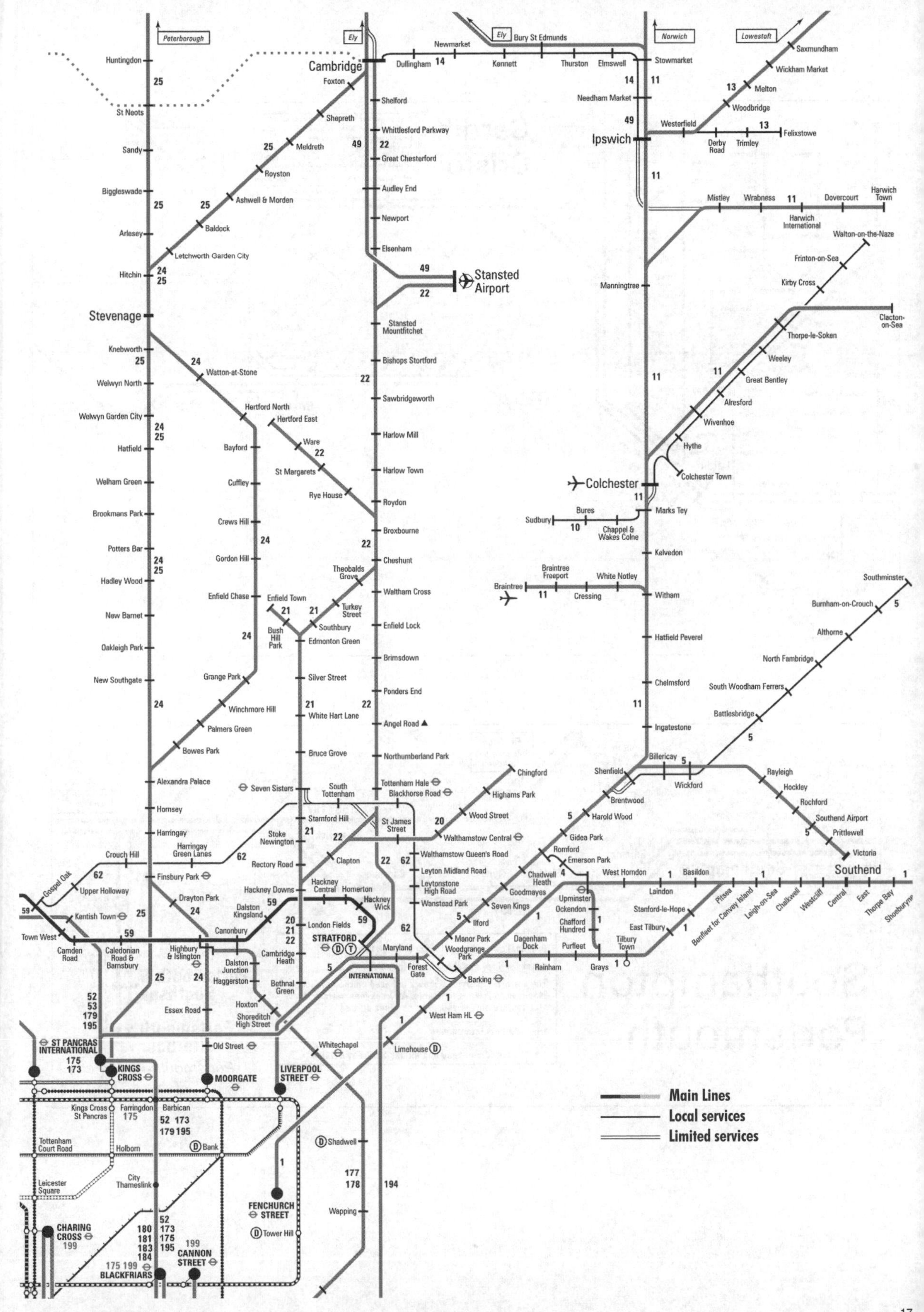

Peterborough
Ely
Ely
Bury St Edmunds
Norwich
Lowestoft
Huntingdon
Cambridge
Newmarket
Dullingham
Kennett
Thurston
Elmswell
Stowmarket
Saxmundham
Wickham Market
Melton
Woodbridge
Foxton
Shelford
St Neots
Shepreth
Whittlesford Parkway
Needham Market
Westerfield
Felixstowe
Derby Road
Trimley
Ipswich
Sandy
Meldreth
Great Chesterford
Royston
Audley End
Biggleswade
Ashwell & Morden
Newport
Mistley
Wrabness
Dovercourt
Harwich Town
Harwich International
Arlesey
Baldock
Elsenham
Walton-on-the-Naze
Frinton-on-Sea
Letchworth Garden City
Kirby Cross
Hitchin
Stansted Airport
Manningtree
Stevenage
Clacton-on-Sea
Stansted Mountfitchet
Thorpe-le-Soken
Knebworth
Bishops Stortford
Weeley
Watton-at-Stone
Great Bentley
Welwyn North
Sawbridgeworth
Alresford
Hertford North
Welwyn Garden City
Hertford East
Wivenhoe
Ware
Harlow Mill
Hythe
Hatfield
Bayford
St Margarets
Harlow Town
Colchester Town
Welham Green
Cuffley
Colchester
Rye House
Roydon
Brookmans Park
Marks Tey
Bures
Crews Hill
Sudbury
Broxbourne
Chappel & Wakes Colne
Potters Bar
Gordon Hill
Kelvedon
Cheshunt
Theobalds Grove
Hadley Wood
Braintree Freeport
White Notley
Waltham Cross
Braintree
Witham
Cressing
Southminster
Enfield Chase
Enfield Town
Turkey Street
New Barnet
Burnham-on-Crouch
Southbury
Enfield Lock
Bush Hill Park
Althorne
Oakleigh Park
Edmonton Green
Hatfield Peverel
Brimsdown
North Fambridge
Grange Park
New Southgate
Silver Street
Chelmsford
Ponders End
South Woodham Ferrers
Winchmore Hill
White Hart Lane
Battlesbridge
Angel Road
Palmers Green
Ingatestone
Bruce Grove
Bowes Park
Northumberland Park
Billericay
Chingford
Shenfield
Rayleigh
Alexandra Palace
Tottenham Hale
Seven Sisters
South Tottenham
Wickford
Blackhorse Road
Hockley
Highams Park
Hornsey
Brentwood
Stamford Hill
Rochford
Wood Street
Harold Wood
St James Street
Southend Airport
Harringay
Stoke Newington
Walthamstow Central
Gidea Park
Prittlewell
Crouch Hill
Harringay Green Lanes
Romford
Walthamstow Queen's Road
Victoria
Rectory Road
Clapton
Emerson Park
Southend
Leyton Midland Road
Gospel Oak
Finsbury Park
Chadwell Heath
West Horndon
Basildon
Leytonstone High Road
Upper Holloway
Hackney Downs
Hackney Central
Homerton
Goodmayes
Laindon
Pitsea
Leigh-on-Sea
Chalkwell
Westcliff
Central
East
Thorpe Bay
Shoeburyness
Drayton Park
Hackney Wick
Upminster
Dalston Kingsland
Wanstead Park
Seven Kings
Ockendon
Stanford-le-Hope
Benfleet for Canvey Island
Kentish Town
Ilford
Chafford Hundred
East Tilbury
Town West
London Fields
Canonbury
Manor Park
Camden Road
Caledonian Road & Barnsbury
Highbury & Islington
Stratford
Maryland
Dagenham Dock
Purfleet
Tilbury Town
Woodgrange Park
Cambridge Heath
Dalston Junction
International
Forest Gate
Rainham
Grays
Haggerston
Barking
Bethnal Green
Hoxton
Essex Road
Shoreditch High Street
West Ham HL
Old Street
Whitechapel
Limehouse
St Pancras International
Kings Cross
Moorgate
Liverpool Street
Kings Cross St Pancras
Farringdon
Barbican
Shadwell
Tottenham Court Road
Holborn
Bank
City Thameslink
Leicester Square
Fenchurch Street
Wapping
Charing Cross
Tower Hill
Cannon Street
Blackfriars
Main Lines
Local services
Limited services

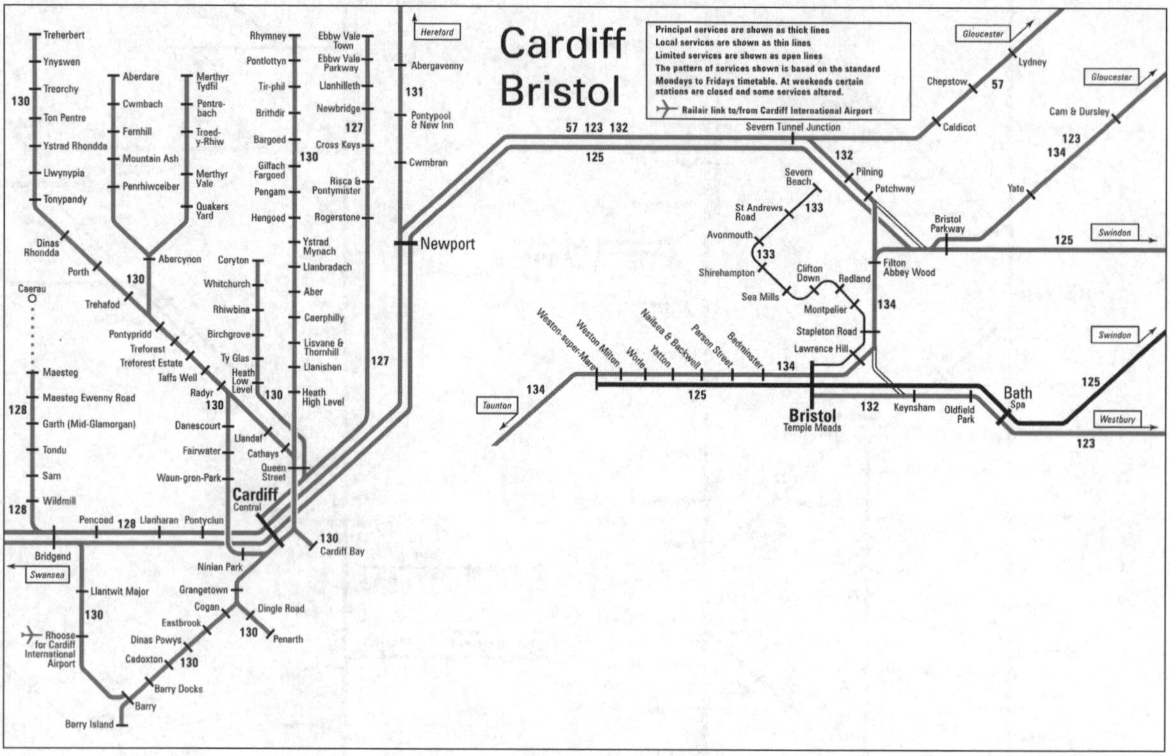

Cardiff Bristol

Principal services are shown as thick lines
Local services are shown as thin lines
Limited services are shown as open lines
The pattern of services shown is based on the standard Mondays to Fridays timetable. At weekends certain stations are closed and some services altered.
Railair link to/from Cardiff International Airport

Treherbert
Ynyswen
Treorchy
130
Ton Pentre
Ystrad Rhondda
Llwynypia
Tonypandy
Dinas Rhondda
Porth
Trehafod
Aberdare
Cwmbach
Fernhill
Mountain Ash
Penrhiwceiber
Merthyr Tydfil
Pentre-bach
Troed-y-Rhiw
Merthyr Vale
Quakers Yard
Abercynon
130
Pontypridd
Treforest
Treforest Estate
Taffs Well
Radyr
130
Caerau
Maesteg
Maesteg Ewenny Road
128
Garth (Mid-Glamorgan)
Tondu
Sarn
Wildmill
128
Pencoed
128
Llanharan
Pontyclun
Bridgend
Swansea
Llantwit Major
130
Rhoose for Cardiff International Airport
Cadoxton
130
Barry Docks
Barry
Barry Island
Dinas Powys
Eastbrook
Cogan
Grangetown
Dingle Road
130
Penarth
Ninian Park
Danescourt
Fairwater
Waun-gron-Park
Coryton
Whitchurch
Rhiwbina
Birchgrove
Ty Glas
Heath Low Level
130
Llandaf
Cathays
Queen Street
Cardiff Central
130
Cardiff Bay
Rhymney
Pontlottyn
Tir-phil
Brithdir
Bargoed
Gilfach Fargoed
Pengam
Hengoed
130
Ystrad Mynach
Llanbradach
Aber
Caerphilly
Lisvane & Thornhill
Llanishen
Heath High Level
Ebbw Vale Town
Ebbw Vale Parkway
Llanhilleth
Newbridge
127
Cross Keys
Risca & Pontymister
Rogerstone
127
Hereford
Abergavenny
131
Pontypool & New Inn
Cwmbran
Newport
57 123 132
125
Severn Tunnel Junction
Gloucester
Lydney
Chepstow
57
Caldicot
Gloucester
Cam & Dursley
123
134
Yate
132
Pilning
Patchway
Severn Beach
St Andrews Road
133
Avonmouth
133
Shirehampton
Sea Mills
Clifton Down
Redland
Montpelier
Filton Abbey Wood
134
Bristol Parkway
125
Swindon
Stapleton Road
Lawrence Hill
Swindon
Weston-super-Mare
Weston Milton
Worle
Yatton
Nailsea & Backwell
Parson Street
Bedminster
134
134
Taunton
125
Bristol Temple Meads
132
Keynsham
Oldfield Park
Bath Spa
125
Westbury
123

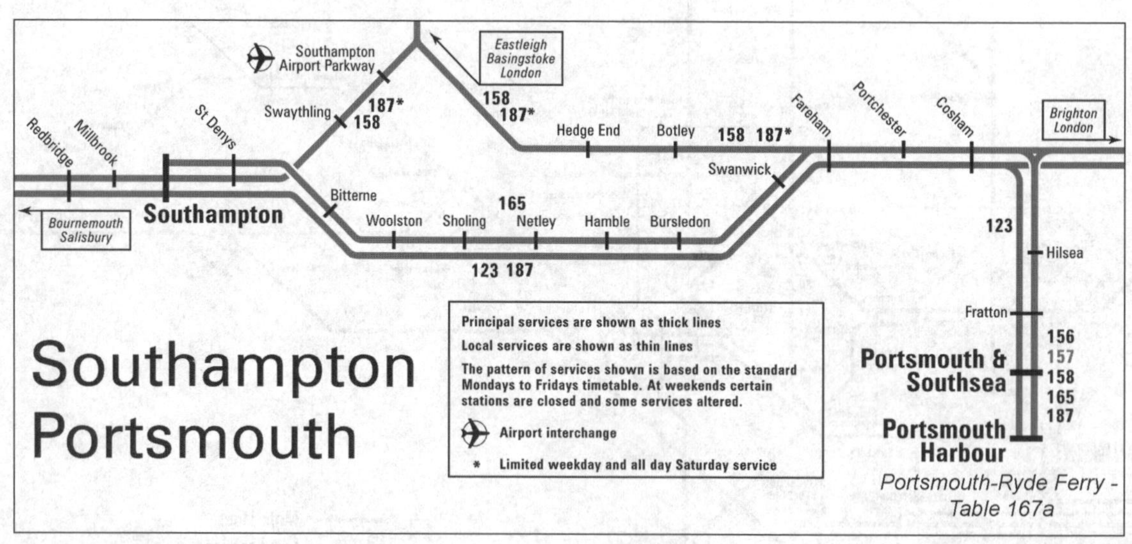

CENTRAL LONDON UNDERGROUND

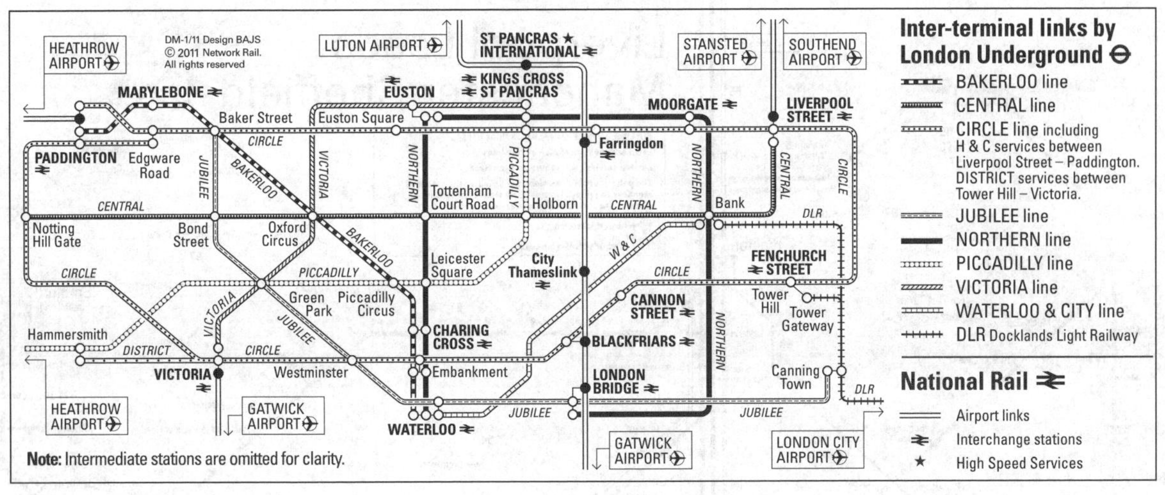

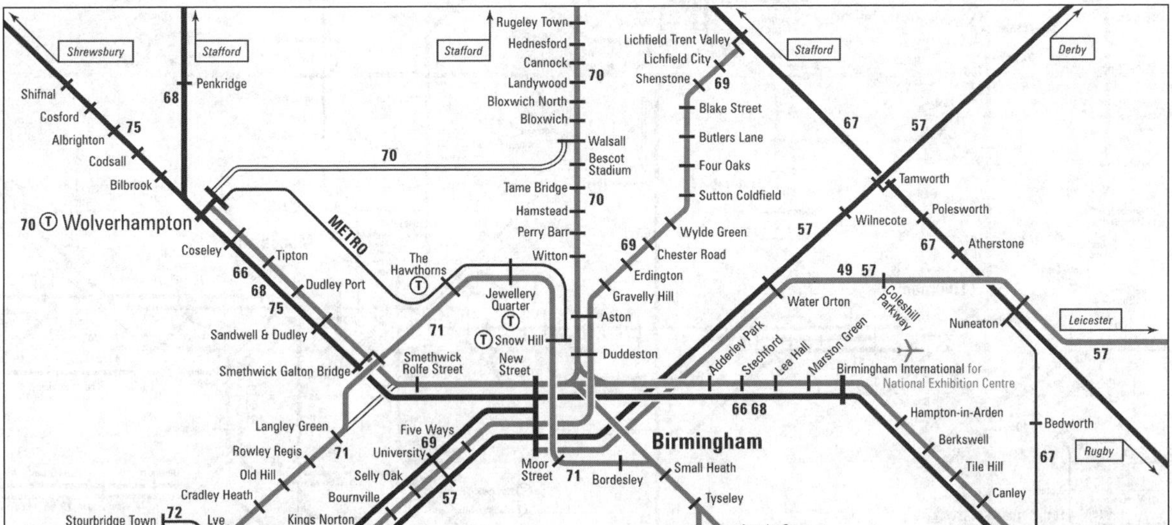

Shrewsbury
Stafford
Penkridge
Shifnal
Cosford
Albrighton
Codsall
Bilbrook
70 Ⓣ Wolverhampton
Coseley
Tipton
Dudley Port
Sandwell & Dudley
Smethwick Galton Bridge
METRO
The Hawthorns Ⓣ
Jewellery Quarter Ⓣ
Ⓣ Snow Hill
Smethwick Rolfe Street
New Street
Rugeley Town
Hednesford
Cannock
Landywood
Bloxwich North
Bloxwich
Walsall
Bescot Stadium
Tame Bridge
Hamstead
Perry Barr
Witton
Aston
Duddeston
Lichfield Trent Valley
Lichfield City
Shenstone
Blake Street
Butlers Lane
Four Oaks
Sutton Coldfield
Wylde Green
Chester Road
Erdington
Gravelly Hill
Derby
Tamworth
Wilnecote
Polesworth
Atherstone
Water Orton
Coleshill Parkway
Nuneaton
Leicester
Adderley Park
Stechford
Lea Hall
Marston Green
Birmingham International for National Exhibition Centre
Birmingham
Hampton-in-Arden
Berkswell
Tile Hill
Canley
Coventry
Bedworth
Rugby
Langley Green
Rowley Regis
Old Hill
Cradley Heath
Lye
Stourbridge Town
Stourbridge Junction
Hagley
Blakedown
Kidderminster
Hartlebury
Bromsgrove
Droitwich Spa
Hereford
Shrub Hill
Worc. Parkway
Foregate Street
Worcester
Great Malvern
Cheltenham Spa
Evesham
Five Ways
University
Selly Oak
Bournville
Kings Norton
Northfield
Longbridge
Barnt Green
Alvechurch
Redditch
Moor Street
Bordesley
Small Heath
Tyseley
Acocks Green
Olton
Solihull
Widney Manor
Dorridge
Lapworth
Spring Road
Hall Green
Yardley Wood
Shirley
Whitlocks End
Wythall
Earlswood
The Lakes
Wood End
Danzey
Henley-in-Arden
Wootton Wawen
Wilmcote
Stratford-upon-Avon
Hatton
Claverdon
Bearley
Warwick Parkway
Warwick
Leamington Spa
Kenilworth
Banbury

Birmingham West Midlands

Principal services are shown as thick lines
Local services are shown as thin lines
Limited services are shown as open lines
The pattern of services shown is based on the standard Mondays to Fridays timetable. At weekends certain stations are closed and some services altered.
Railair link to/from Birmingham Airport
Ⓣ Tram/Metro Interchange

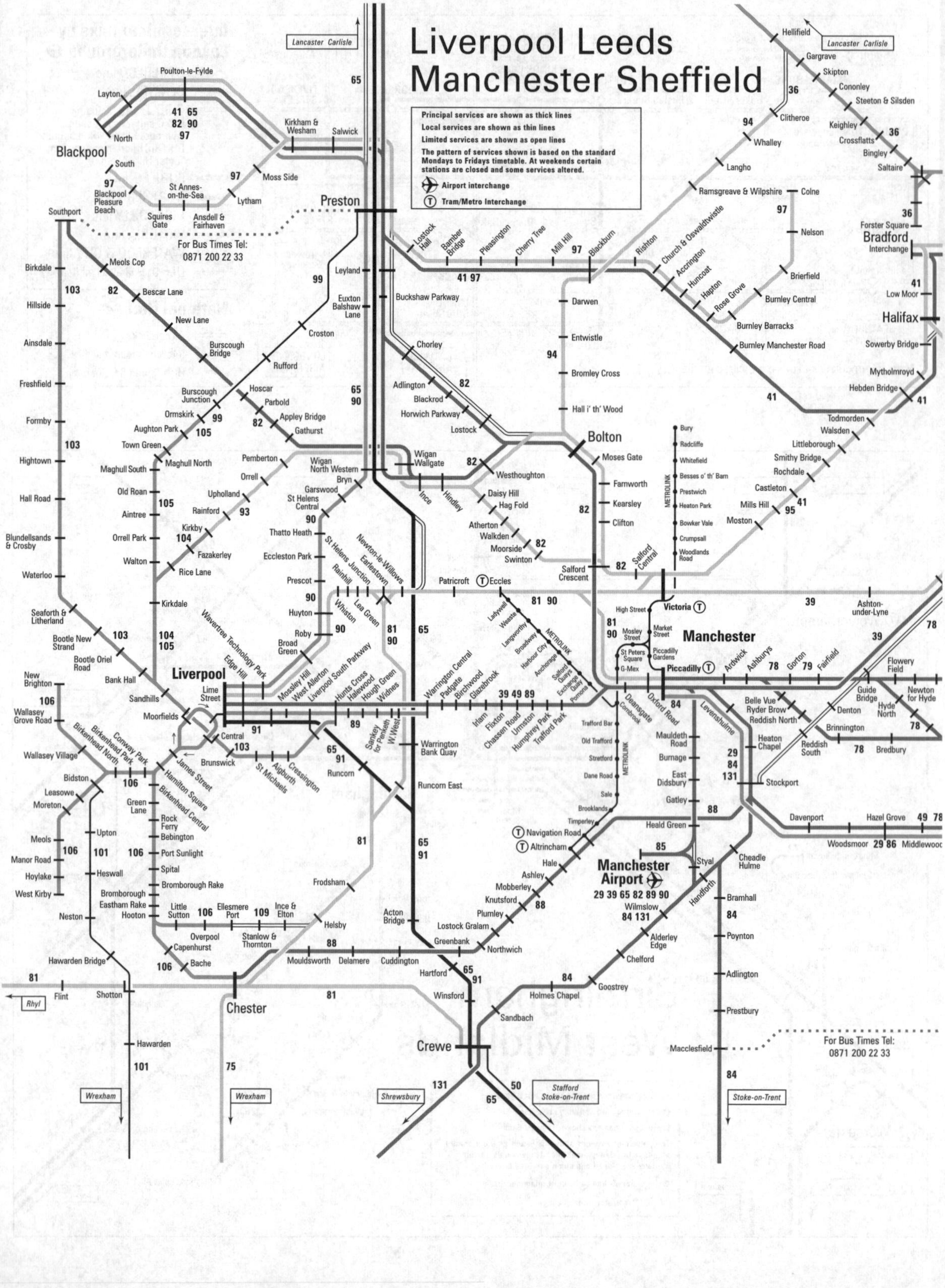

Liverpool Leeds
Manchester Sheffield
Principal services are shown as thick lines
Local services are shown as thin lines
Limited services are shown as open lines
The pattern of services shown is based on the standard Mondays to Fridays timetable. At weekends certain stations are closed and some services altered.
Airport interchange
Tram/Metro Interchange
For Bus Times Tel:
0871 200 22 33
Lancaster Carlisle
Lancaster Carlisle
Poulton-le-Fylde
Layton
North
Blackpool
South
Blackpool Pleasure Beach
St Annes-on-the-Sea
Squires Gate
Ansdell & Fairhaven
Lytham
Moss Side
Kirkham & Wesham
Salwick
Preston
Southport
Birkdale
Hillside
Ainsdale
Freshfield
Formby
Hightown
Hall Road
Blundellsands & Crosby
Waterloo
Seaforth & Litherland
Bootle New Strand
Bootle Oriel Road
Bank Hall
Sandhills
Moorfields
Lime Street
Liverpool
Central
Brunswick
St Michaels
Aigburth
Cressington
James Street
Hamilton Square
Birkenhead Central
Conway Park
Birkenhead Park
Birkenhead North
Wallasey Village
Wallasey Grove Road
New Brighton
Bidston
Leasowe
Moreton
Meols
Manor Road
Hoylake
West Kirby
Upton
Heswall
Neston
Hawarden Bridge
Shotton
Flint
Rhyl
Hawarden
Wrexham
Wrexham
Green Lane
Rock Ferry
Bebington
Port Sunlight
Spital
Bromborough Rake
Bromborough
Eastham Rake
Hooton
Little Sutton
Overpool
Capenhurst
Bache
Ellesmere Port
Stanlow & Thornton
Ince & Elton
Helsby
Chester
Mouldsworth
Delamere
Cuddington
Greenbank
Hartford
Winsford
Northwich
Lostock Gralam
Plumley
Knutsford
Mobberley
Ashley
Hale
Altrincham
Navigation Road
Timperley
Brooklands
Sale
Dane Road
Stretford
Old Trafford
Trafford Bar
Cornbrook
Deansgate
Oxford Road
Meols Cop
Bescar Lane
New Lane
Burscough Bridge
Hoscar
Parbold
Appley Bridge
Gathurst
Burscough Junction
Ormskirk
Aughton Park
Town Green
Maghull North
Maghull South
Old Roan
Aintree
Orrell Park
Walton
Kirkdale
Rice Lane
Fazakerley
Kirkby
Rainford
Upholland
Orrell
Pemberton
Rufford
Croston
Leyland
Euxton Balshaw Lane
Buckshaw Parkway
Chorley
Adlington
Blackrod
Horwich Parkway
Lostock
Lostock Hall
Bamber Bridge
Pleasington
Cherry Tree
Mill Hill
Blackburn
Rishton
Church & Oswaldtwistle
Accrington
Huncoat
Hapton
Rose Grove
Burnley Barracks
Burnley Manchester Road
Burnley Central
Brierfield
Nelson
Colne
Ramsgreave & Wilpshire
Langho
Whalley
Clitheroe
Hellifield
Gargrave
Skipton
Cononley
Steeton & Silsden
Keighley
Crossflatts
Bingley
Saltaire
Forster Square
Bradford
Interchange
Low Moor
Halifax
Sowerby Bridge
Mytholmroyd
Hebden Bridge
Todmorden
Walsden
Littleborough
Smithy Bridge
Rochdale
Castleton
Mills Hill
Moston
Darwen
Entwistle
Bromley Cross
Hall i' th' Wood
Bolton
Moses Gate
Farnworth
Kearsley
Clifton
Salford Crescent
Salford Central
Wigan Wallgate
Wigan North Western
Ince
Hindley
Westhoughton
Daisy Hill
Hag Fold
Atherton
Walkden
Moorside
Swinton
Bryn
Garswood
St Helens Central
Thatto Heath
Eccleston Park
Prescot
Huyton
Roby
Broad Green
St Helens Junction
Rainhill
Whiston
Lea Green
Newton-le-Willows
Earlestown
Patricroft
Eccles
Wavertree Technology Park
Edge Hill
Mossley Hill
West Allerton
Liverpool South Parkway
Hunts Cross
Halewood
Hough Green
Widnes
Sankey for Penketh
W. West
Warrington Central
Padgate
Birchwood
Glazebrook
Irlam
Flixton
Chassen Road
Urmston
Humphrey Park
Trafford Park
Warrington Bank Quay
Runcorn
Runcorn East
Frodsham
Acton Bridge
Crewe
Shrewsbury
Stafford Stoke-on-Trent
Stoke-on-Trent
Sandbach
Holmes Chapel
Goostrey
Chelford
Alderley Edge
Wilmslow
Handforth
Styal
Manchester Airport
29 39 65 82 89 90
84 131
Heald Green
Gatley
East Didsbury
Burnage
Mauldeth Road
Levenshulme
Heaton Chapel
Stockport
Davenport
Hazel Grove
Woodsmoor
Middlewood
Cheadle Hulme
Bramhall
Poynton
Adlington
Prestbury
Macclesfield
Manchester
Piccadilly
Victoria
High Street
Market Street
Mosley Street
St Peters Square
Piccadilly Gardens
G-Mex
Ardwick
Ashburys
Gorton
Fairfield
Belle Vue
Ryder Brow
Reddish North
Reddish South
Denton
Guide Bridge
Flowery Field
Newton for Hyde
Hyde North
Brinnington
Bredbury
Ashton-under-Lyne
Ladywell
Weaste
Langworthy
Broadway
Harbour City
Anchorage
Salford Quays
Exchange Quay
Pomona
METROLINK
Bury
Radcliffe
Whitefield
Besses o' th' Barn
Prestwich
Heaton Park
Bowker Vale
Crumpsall
Woodlands Road

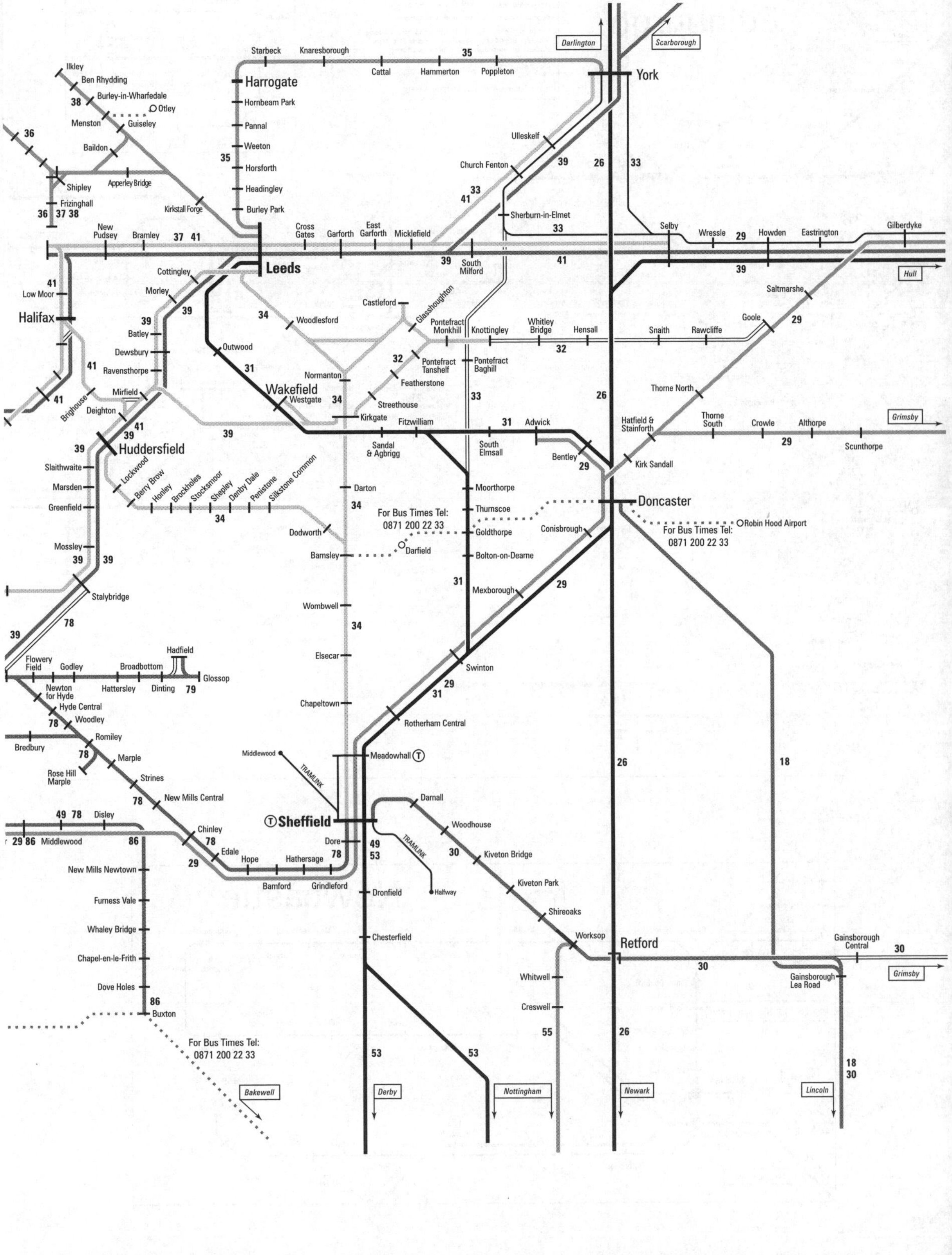

Darlington
Scarborough
York
Starbeck
Knaresborough
35
Cattal
Hammerton
Poppleton
Harrogate
Hornbeam Park
Pannal
Weeton
35
Horsforth
Headingley
Burley Park
Ilkley
Ben Rhydding
38
Burley-in-Wharfedale
Otley
Menston
Guiseley
36
Baildon
Shipley
Apperley Bridge
Frizinghall
36 37 38
Kirkstall Forge
Ulleskelf
Church Fenton
39
26
33
33
41
Sherburn-in-Elmet
33
Selby
Wressle
29
Howden
Eastrington
Gilberdyke
New Pudsey
Bramley
37 41
Cross Gates
Garforth
East Garforth
Micklefield
39
South Milford
41
39
Hull
Leeds
Cottingley
41
Low Moor
Halifax
Morley
39
39
Batley
Dewsbury
Ravensthorpe
41
41
Brighouse
Mirfield
Deighton
41
39
Huddersfield
39
34
Woodlesford
Castleford
Glasshoughton
Pontefract Monkhill
Knottingley
Whitley Bridge
Hensall
Snaith
Rawcliffe
Goole
Saltmarshe
29
32
Outwood
31
Normanton
32
Pontefract Tanshelf
Featherstone
Pontefract Baghill
Wakefield Westgate
34
Streethouse
33
26
Thorne North
Kirkgate
Fitzwilliam
31
Adwick
Sandal & Agbrigg
South Elmsall
Hatfield & Stainforth
Thorne South
Crowle
Althorpe
29
Grimsby
Scunthorpe
Bentley
29
Kirk Sandall
Slaithwaite
Marsden
Greenfield
Lockwood
Berry Brow
Honley
Brockholes
Stocksmoor
Shepley
Denby Dale
Penistone
Silkstone Common
34
Darton
34
Moorthorpe
Thurnscoe
Goldthorpe
Bolton-on-Dearne
Doncaster
For Bus Times Tel:
0871 200 22 33
Conisbrough
For Bus Times Tel:
0871 200 22 33
Robin Hood Airport
Dodworth
Darfield
Barnsley
Mossley
39
39
Stalybridge
78
39
31
Mexborough
29
Wombwell
34
Elsecar
Hadfield
Flowery Field
Godley
Broadbottom
Glossop
Newton for Hyde
Hattersley
Dinting
79
Swinton
29
31
Chapeltown
Hyde Central
78
Woodley
Romiley
Rotherham Central
Bredbury
78
Marple
Rose Hill Marple
Strines
78
New Mills Central
Middlewood
Meadowhall
TRAMLINK
18
26
Darnall
49 78
Disley
Chinley
78
Sheffield
Woodhouse
29 86
Middlewood
86
Edale
Dore
78
49
53
30
Kiveton Bridge
TRAMLINK
29
Hope
Hathersage
New Mills Newtown
Bamford
Grindleford
Dronfield
Halfway
Kiveton Park
Furness Vale
Shireoaks
Whaley Bridge
Chesterfield
Worksop
Retford
Gainsborough Central
30
Chapel-en-le-Frith
30
Grimsby
Whitwell
Gainsborough Lea Road
Dove Holes
Creswell
86
Buxton
55
26
For Bus Times Tel:
0871 200 22 33
53
53
18
30
Bakewell
Derby
Nottingham
Newark
Lincoln

Glasgow Edinburgh

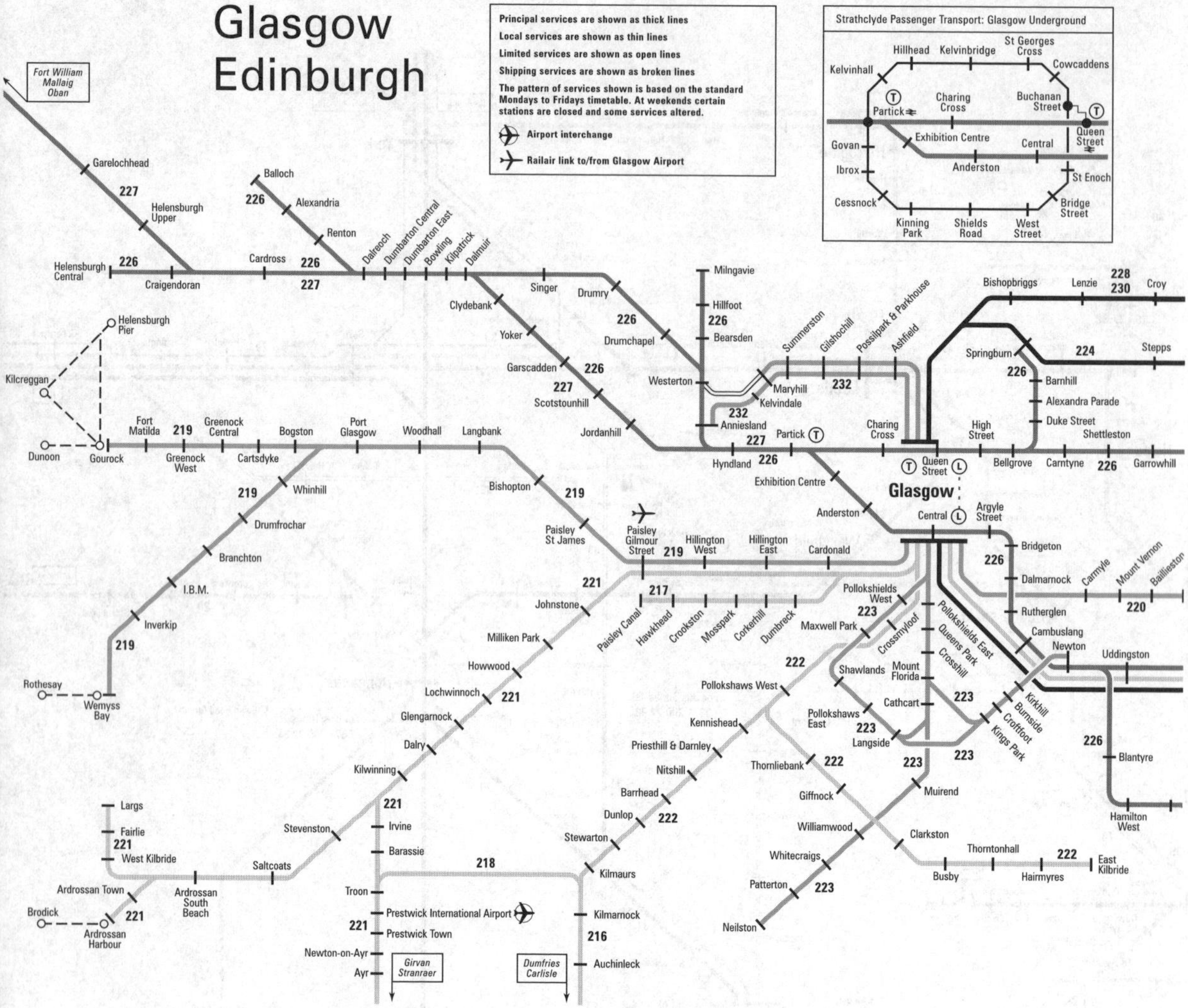

Principal services are shown as thick lines
Local services are shown as thin lines
Limited services are shown as open lines
Shipping services are shown as broken lines
The pattern of services shown is based on the standard Mondays to Fridays timetable. At weekends certain stations are closed and some services altered.
Airport interchange
Railair link to/from Glasgow Airport
Strathclyde Passenger Transport: Glasgow Underground
Hillhead
Kelvinbridge
St Georges Cross
Kelvinhall
Cowcaddens
Partick
Charing Cross
Buchanan Street
Queen Street
Exhibition Centre
Govan
Central
Ibrox
Anderston
St Enoch
Cessnock
Bridge Street
Kinning Park
Shields Road
West Street
Fort William Mallaig Oban
Garelochhead
227
Helensburgh Upper
Helensburgh Central
226
Craigendoran
Balloch
226
Alexandria
Renton
Cardross
226
227
Dalreoch
Dumbarton Central
Dumbarton East
Bowling
Kilpatrick
Dalmuir
Singer
Drumry
Clydebank
226
Yoker
Drumchapel
Garscadden
226
227
Scotstounhill
Westerton
Jordanhill
Milngavie
Hillfoot
226
Bearsden
Summerston
Gilshochill
Possilpark & Parkhouse
Ashfield
232
Maryhill
Kelvindale
232
Anniesland
227
Partick
Charing Cross
Hyndland
226
Exhibition Centre
Anderston
Queen Street
Glasgow
Central
Argyle Street
Bishopbriggs
Lenzie
228
230
Croy
Springburn
224
Stepps
226
Barnhill
Alexandra Parade
Duke Street
High Street
Shettleston
Bellgrove
Carntyne
226
Garrowhill
Helensburgh Pier
Kilcreggan
Dunoon
Gourock
Fort Matilda
219
Greenock Central
Greenock West
Bogston
Cartsdyke
Port Glasgow
Woodhall
Langbank
Bishopton
219
Whinhill
219
Drumfrochar
Branchton
I.B.M.
Inverkip
219
Rothesay
Wemyss Bay
Paisley St James
Paisley Gilmour Street
219
Hillington West
Hillington East
Cardonald
221
Johnstone
217
Paisley Canal
Hawkhead
Crookston
Mosspark
Corkerhill
Dumbreck
Milliken Park
Howwood
Lochwinnoch
221
Glengarnock
Dalry
Kilwinning
Pollokshields West
223
Maxwell Park
Crossmyloof
Pollokshields East
Queens Park
Crosshill
Bridgeton
226
Dalmarnock
Carmyle
Mount Vernon
Baillieston
220
Rutherglen
Cambuslang
Newton
Uddingston
222
Shawlands
Mount Florida
Pollokshaws West
Kennishead
Pollokshaws East
223
Cathcart
223
Kirkhill
Burnside
Croftfoot
Kings Park
Langside
Priesthill & Darnley
Thornliebank
222
223
223
226
Blantyre
Nitshill
Barrhead
Giffnock
Muirend
Hamilton West
Dunlop
222
Stewarton
Williamwood
Clarkston
Thorntonhall
222
East Kilbride
Whitecraigs
Busby
Hairmyres
Patterton
223
Neilston
Largs
Fairlie
221
West Kilbride
221
Irvine
Barassie
Stevenston
Saltcoats
218
Kilmaurs
Ardrossan Town
Ardrossan South Beach
Brodick
221
Ardrossan Harbour
Troon
Prestwick International Airport
221
Prestwick Town
Kilmarnock
216
Newton-on-Ayr
Ayr
Girvan Stranraer
Dumfries Carlisle
Auchinleck

Newcastle

Airport
Callerton Park
Kingston Park
Wansbeck Road
Bank Foot
Fawdon
Regent Centre
Berwick Edinburgh
26
48
Longbenton
Four Lane Ends
Benton
Northumberland Park
West Monkseaton
Whitley Bay
Palmersville
Shiremoor
Monkseaton
Cullercoats
South Gosforth
Tyne & Wear Transport: Metro
Ilford Road
West Jesmond
Jesmond
Haymarket
Tynemouth
Chillingham Road
Wallsend
Howdon
Meadow Well
Byker
Walkergate
Hadrian Road
Percy Main
North Shields
Manors
Hexham Carlisle
St James
Monument
South Shields
Metro Centre
Dunston
44
48
Newcastle
Central
Heworth
Chichester
Pelaw
Jarrow
Simonside
26
39
44
Darlington York
Gateshead
Gateshead Stadium
Felling
Hebburn
Bede
Tyne Dock
44
Sunderland

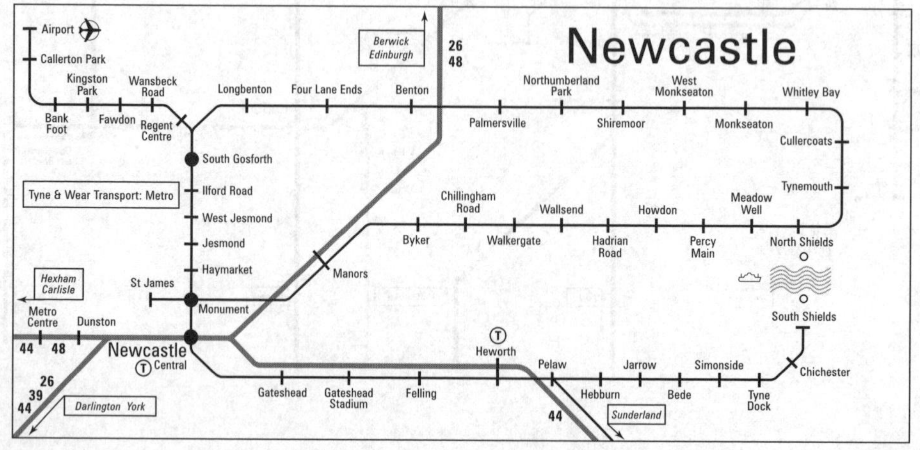

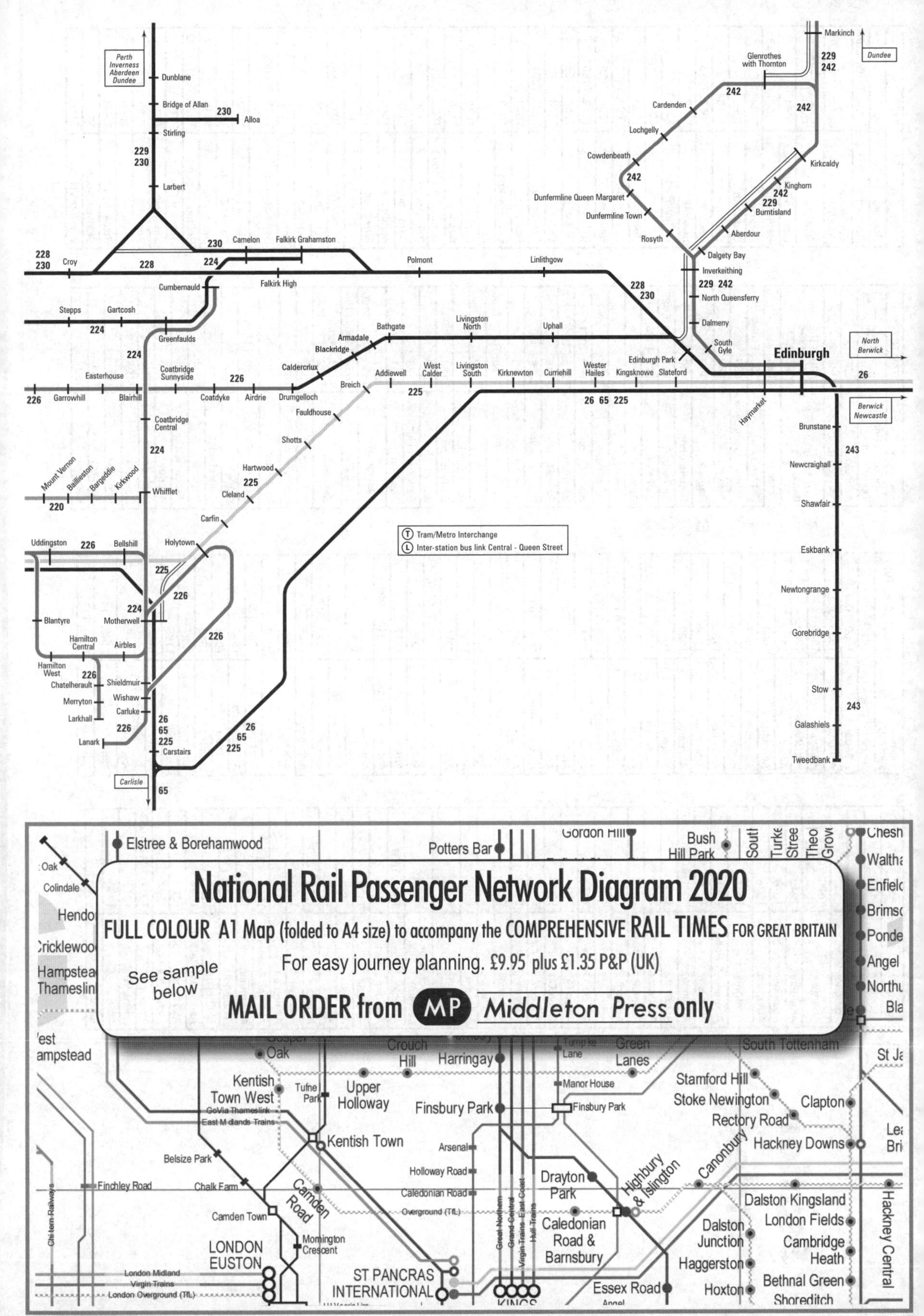

Perth
Inverness
Aberdeen
Dundee
Dunblane
Bridge of Allan
230
Alloa
Stirling
229
230
Larbert
Camelon
Falkirk Grahamston
228
230
Croy
228
224
Polmont
Linlithgow
Cumbernauld
Falkirk High
228
230
Stepps
Gartcosh
224
Greenfaulds
224
Bathgate
Livingston North
Uphall
Armadale
Blackridge
Caldercruix
Easterhouse
Coatbridge Sunnyside
226
Addiewell
West Calder
Livingston South
Kirknewton
Curriehill
Wester Hailes
Kingsknowe
Slateford
Breich
225
226
Garrowhill
Blairhill
Coatdyke
Airdrie
Drumgelloch
Fauldhouse
26 65 225
Coatbridge Central
224
Shotts
Mount Vernon
Baillieston
Bargeddie
Kirkwood
Whifflet
220
Hartwood
225
Cleland
Carfin
Holytown
Uddingston
226
Bellshill
225
226
224
Blantyre
Motherwell
Hamilton Central
Airbles
226
Hamilton West
226
Chatelherault
Shieldmuir
Merryton
Wishaw
Larkhall
Carluke
226
Lanark
26
65
225
Carstairs
26
65
225
Carlisle
65
Markinch
Dundee
Glenrothes with Thornton
229
242
242
Cardenden
242
Lochgelly
Cowdenbeath
Kirkcaldy
242
Kinghorn
Dunfermline Queen Margaret
242
229
Burntisland
Dunfermline Town
Aberdour
Rosyth
Dalgety Bay
Inverkeithing
229 242
North Queensferry
Dalmeny
South Gyle
Edinburgh Park
Edinburgh
North Berwick
26
Haymarket
Berwick Newcastle
Brunstane
243
Newcraighall
Shawfair
Eskbank
Newtongrange
Gorebridge
Stow
243
Galashiels
Tweedbank
T Tram/Metro Interchange
L Inter-station bus link Central - Queen Street
National Rail Passenger Network Diagram 2020
FULL COLOUR A1 Map (folded to A4 size) to accompany the COMPREHENSIVE RAIL TIMES FOR GREAT BRITAIN
For easy journey planning. £9.95 plus £1.35 P&P (UK)
See sample below
MAIL ORDER from MP Middleton Press only
Elstree & Borehamwood
Potters Bar
Colindale
Finchley Road
Belsize Park
Chalk Farm
Camden Town
Camden Road
Kentish Town West
Kentish Town
Tufnell Park
Upper Holloway
Harringay
Finsbury Park
Manor House
Arsenal
Holloway Road
Caledonian Road
Overground (TfL)
Drayton Park
Caledonian Road & Barnsbury
Highbury & Islington
Canonbury
Mornington Crescent
LONDON EUSTON
ST PANCRAS INTERNATIONAL
London Midland
Virgin Trains
London Overground (TfL)
GoVia Thameslink
East Midlands Trains
Chiltern Railways
Great Northern
Grand Central
Virgin Trains East Coast
Hull Trains
Green Lanes
South Tottenham
Stamford Hill
Stoke Newington
Clapton
Rectory Road
Hackney Downs
Dalston Kingsland
London Fields
Dalston Junction
Cambridge Heath
Haggerston
Bethnal Green
Hoxton
Shoreditch
Essex Road
Hackney Central
Crouch Hill

Station Index

A

B

Bickley	T052, T195, T196
Bidston	T101, T106
Biggleswade	T025
Bilbrook	T074
Billericay	T006
Billingham	T044
Billingshurst	T186
Bingham	T019
Bingley	T036, T042
Birchgrove	T130
Birchington-on-Sea	T194, T212
Birchwood	T039, T089
Birkbeck	T173
Birkdale	T103
Birkenhead 12 Quays	T098A
Birkenhead Central	T107
Birkenhead North	T106
Birkenhead Park	T106
Birmingham Int'l Bus Stn	T047A
Birmingham International	T051, T065, T066, T068, T071, T074, T075, T076, T116
Birmingham Moor Street	T071, T115
Birmingham New Street	"T047, T051, T057, T065, T066, T068, T069, T070, T071, T074, T075, T076, T081, T084, T091, T116, T135"
Birmingham Snow Hill	T071, T115
Bishop Auckland	T044
Bishopbriggs	T228, T230
Bishops Lydeard L Arms	T135E
Bishops Stortford	T022
Bishopstone	T189
Bishopton	T219
Bitterne	T165
Blackburn	T041, T042, T094, T095, T097
Blackheath	T200
Blackhorse Road	T062
Blackpool North	T041, T042, T065, T082, T090, T094, T097
Blackpool Pleasure Beach	T097
Blackpool South	T097

Blackridge	T226, T226
Blackrod	T082
Blackwater	T148
Blackwood	T130A
Blaenau Ffestiniog	T102
Blair Atholl	T229
Blairhill	T226, T226
Blake Street	T069
Blakedown	T071
Blantyre	T225
Blaydon	T048
Bleasby	T027
Bletchley	T064, T066, T176
Bloxwich	T070
Bloxwich North	T070
Blundellsands & Crosby	T103
Blythe Bridge	T050
Bodmin Mount Folly	T135C
Bodmin Parkway	T051, T135C, T135
Bodorgan	T081
Bognor Regis	T186, T188
Bogston	T219
Bolton	T065, T082, T094
Bolton-upon-Dearne	T031
Bookham	T152
Bootle	T100
Bootle New Strand	T103
Bootle Oriel Road	T103
Bordesley	T071
Borough Green & Wrotham	T196, T197
Borth	T076
Bosham	T186
Boston	T019
Botley	T158
Bottesford	T019
Bourne End	T120
Bournemouth	T051, T158
Bournville	T069
Bow Brickhill	T064
Bowes Park	T024
Bowling	T226, T226
Box Hill & West-humble	T152, T180
Bracknell	T149
Bradford Forster Square	T026, T036, T037, T038
Bradford Inter-change	T026, T032, T037, T040, T041

Bradford-on-Avon	T123, T160
Brading	T167
Braintree	T011
Braintree Freeport	T011
Bramhall	T084
Bramley	T037, T041
Bramley (Hants)	T122
Brampton (Cum-bria)	T048
Brampton (Suffolk)	T013
Branchton	T219
Brandon	T017
Branksome	T158
Braystones	T100
Bredbury	T078
Breich	T224
Brentford	T149
Brentwood	T005
Bricket Wood	T061
Bridge Of Allan	T229, T230
Bridge Of Orchy	T227
Bridgend	T125, T128, T130
Bridgeton	T225
Bridgwater	T134, T135
Bridlington	T043
Brierfield	T097
Brigg	T028
Brighouse	T026, T032, T041
Brighton	T025, T052, T123, T184, T186, T188, T189, T190, T192
Brimsdown	T022
Brinnington	T078
Bristol Internatl Airport	T125B
Bristol Parkway	T051, T057, T058, T123, T125, T128, T132, T134, T135
Bristol Temple Meads	T051, T057, T058, T123, T125B, T125, T132, T133, T134, T135, T160
Brithdir	T130
British Steel Redcar	T044
Briton Ferry	T128
Brixton	T195
Broad Green	T090
Broadbottom	T079
Broadstairs	T194, T207, T212
Brockenhurst	T051, T158, T159
Brockholes	T034

Brockley	T171, T177, T178
Brodick	T221A
Bromborough	T107
Bromborough Rake	T107
Bromley Cross	T094
Bromley North	T204
Bromley South	T052, T195, T196, T197, T212
Bromsgrove	T069, T071
Brondesbury	T059
Brondesbury Park	T059
Brookmans Park	T024
Brookwood	T155
Broome	T129
Broomfleet	T029
Brora	T239
Brough	T029, T039
Broughty Ferry	T229
Broxbourne	T022
Bruce Grove	T021
Brundall	T015
Brundall Gardens	T015
Brunstane	T243
Brunswick	T103
Bruton	T123, T160
Bryn	T090
Buckenham	T015
Buckley	T101
Bucknell	T129
Buckshaw Parkway	T082
Bude Strand	T135D
Bugle	T142
Builth Road	T129
Bulwell	T055
Bures	T010
Burgess Hill	T052, T184
Burley Park	T035
Burley-in-wharfedale	T038
Burnage	T085
Burneside	T083
Burnham	T117
Burnham-on-Crouch	T006
Burnley Barracks	T097
Burnley Central	T097
Burnley Manchester Road	T041, T095, T097
Burnside	T223
Burntisland	T242
Burscough Bridge	T082

Burscough Junction	T099
Bursledon	T165
Burton Joyce	T027
Burton-on-Trent	T051, T057
Bury St Edmunds	T014
Busby	T222
Bush Hill Park	T021
Bushey	T066
Bushey	T060
Butlers Lane	T069
Buxted	T182
Buxton	T086
Byfleet & New Haw	T155
Bynea	T129

C

Cadoxton	T130
Caergwrle	T101
Caerphilly	T130
Caersws	T076
Cairnryan (Loch Ryan Port)	T221B
Caldercruix	T226, T226
Caldicot	T057
Caledonian Rd & Barnsbury	T059
Calstock	T139
Cam & Dursley	T123, T134
Camberley	T149
Camborne	T051, T135
Cambridge	T014, T017, T022, T025, T047, T052, T196
Cambridge Heath	T021
Cambridge North	T017, T022, T025
Cambuslang	T224, T225
Camden Road	T059
Camelon	T226, T230, T231
Canada Water	T177, T178
Canley	T068
Canna	T227A
Cannock	T070
Canonbury	T059, T177, T178
Canonbury Ell	T177, T178
Canterbury East	T212
Canterbury West	T194, T197, T207
Cantley	T015
Capenhurst	T107
Carbis Bay	T144
Cardenden	T242
Cardiff Bay	T124

Cardiff Central	"T051, T057, T058, T075, T081, T123, T125, T127, T128, T130, T131, T132, T134, T135"
Cardiff Central Bus Stn	T125C
Cardiff Int'l Airport	T125C
Cardiff Queen Street	T124, T130
Cardonald	T219
Cardross	T226, T226
Carfin	T224
Cark	T082
Carlisle	T042, T048, T051, T065, T100, T216
Carlton	T027
Carluke	T224, T225
Carmarthen	T128
Carmyle	T225
Carnforth	T042, T082
Carnoustie	T229
Carntyne	T226, T226
Carpenders Park	T060
Carrbridge	T229
Carshalton	T052, T173, T179, T180
Carshalton Beeches	T172
Carstairs	T065, T224, T225
Cartsdyke	T219
Castle Bar Park	T117
Castle Cary	T123, T135, T160
Castlebay	T227C
Castleford	T032, T034, T039
Castleton	T041
Castleton Moor	T045
Caterham	T181
Catford	T052, T195, T196
Catford Bridge	T203
Cathays	T130
Cathcart	T223
Cattal	T035
Catterick Camp Centre	T026H
Catterick Garrison Kemmel	T026H
Catterick Garrison Tesco	T026H
Causeland	T140

Cefn-y-Bedd	T101
Chadwell Heath	T005
Chafford Hundred Lakeside	T001
Chalfont & Latimer	T114
Chalkwell	T001
Chandlers Ford	T158
Chapel-en-le-frith	T086
Chapelton	T136
Chapeltown	T034
Chappel & Wakes Colne	T010
Charing	T196, T197
Charing Cross	T226, T226
Charlbury	T126
Charlton	T200, T201
Chartham	T197, T207
Chassen Road	T089
Chatelherault	T225
Chatham	T194, T200, T201, T212
Chathill	T048
Cheadle Hulme	T084
Cheam	T180
Cheddington	T066
Chelford	T084
Chelmsford	T011
Chelsfield	T204, T206
Cheltenham Spa	T051, T057, T058, T123, T125
Chepstow	T057
Cherry Tree	T097
Chertsey	T149
Cheshunt	T021, T022
Chessington North	T152
Chessington South	T152
Chester	T065, T075, T081, T088, T091, T107, T131
Chester Road	T069
Chester-le-street	T026, T039, T044, T051
Chesterfield	T034, T049, T051, T053
Chestfield & Swalecliffe	T212
Chetnole	T123
Chichester	T123, T165, T186, T188
Chilham	T197, T207
Chilworth	T148
Chingford	T020

Chinley	T078
Chinnor	T115A
Chippenham	T123, T125
Chipping Norton West St	T126A
Chipstead	T181
Chirk	T075, T131
Chislehurst	T204
Chiswick	T149
Cholsey	T116
Chorley	T082
Chorleywood	T114
Christchurch	T158
Christs Hospital	T186
Church & Oswaldtwistle	T097
Church Fenton	T033, T040
Church Stretton	T129, T131
Cilmeri	T129
City Thameslink	"T024, T025, T052, T052MML, T173, T175, T179, T180, T181, T182, T183, T184, T185, T188, T195, T196, T197, T201"
Clacton-on-Sea	T011
Clandon	T152
Clapham (Nth Yorkshire)	T042
Clapham High Street	T178
Clapham Junction	T059, T066, T149, T152, T155, T156, T158, T160, T170, T171, T172, T175, T176, T178, T180, T181, T182, T183, T184, T185, T186, T188, T189, T190
Clapton	T020
Clarbeston Road	T128
Clarkston	T222
Claverdon	T115
Claygate	T152
Cleethorpes	T027, T028, T029
Cleland	T224
Clifton	T082
Clifton Down	T133
Clitheroe	T042, T094, T097
Clock House	T203

Clunderwen	T128
Clydebank	T226, T226
Coatbridge Central	T225, T231
Coatbridge Sunnyside	T226, T226
Coatdyke	T226, T226
Cobham & Stoke D'abernon	T152
Codsall	T074
Cogan	T130
Colchester	T010, T011, T014
Colchester Town	T011
Coleshill Parkway	T047A, T047
Coll	T227B
Collingham	T027
Collington	T190, T192
Colne	T097
Colonsay	T227B
Colwall	T071, T126
Colwyn Bay	T075, T081
Combe	T126
Commondale	T045
Congleton	T051, T084
Conisbrough	T029
Connel Ferry	T227
Conon Bridge	T239
Cononley	T036
Conway Park	T106
Conwy	T081
Cooden Beach	T190, T192
Cookham	T120
Cooksbridge	T190
Coombe Junction Halt	T140
Copplestone	T136
Corbridge	T048
Corby	T053
Corby George Street	T026B
Corkerhill	T217
Corkickle	T100
Corpach	T227
Corrour	T227
Coryton	T130
Coseley	T068
Cosford	T074
Cosham	T123, T158, T165, T186
Cottingham	T043
Cottingley	T039
Coulsdon South	T183

Coulsdon Town	T181
Coventry	T051, T063, T065, T066, T068, T071, T091, T116, T116A
Coventry Arena	T063
Cowden	T182
Cowdenbeath	T242
Cradley Heath	T071, T115
Craigendoran	T226, T226
Craignure	T227B
Cramlington	T048
Cranbrook	T160
Craven Arms	T129, T131
Crawley	T183, T185, T186
Crayford	T200
Crediton	T136
Cressing	T011
Cressington	T103
Creswell (Derbys)	T055
Crewe	T050, T051, T065, T067, T081, T084, T085, T091, T131
Crewkerne	T160
Crews Hill	T024
Crianlarich	T227
Criccieth	T076
Cricklewood	T052, T052MML
Croftfoot	T223
Crofton Park	T052, T195, T196
Cromer	T016
Cromford	T056
Crookston	T217
Cross Gates	T039, T040
Cross Keys	T127
Crossflatts	T036
Crosshill	T223
Crossmyloof	T222
Croston	T099
Crouch Hill	T062
Crowborough	T182
Crowhurst	T206
Crowle	T029
Crowthorne	T148
Croy	T228, T230
Crystal Palace	T171, T173, T177, T178
Cuddington	T088
Cuffley	T024
Culham	T116

D

Culrain	T239
Cumbernauld	T225, T226, T226
Cupar	T051, T229
Curriehill	T224
Cuxton	T208
Cwmbach	T130
Cwmbran	T131
Cynghordy	T129
Dagenham Dock	T001
Daisy Hill	T082
Dalgety Bay	T242
Dalmally	T227
Dalmarnock	T225
Dalmeny	T242
Dalmuir	T226, T226, T227
Dalreoch	T226, T226
Dalry	T221
Dalston	T100
Dalston Junction	T177, T178
Dalston Kingsland	T059
Dalton	T082
Dalwhinnie	T229
Danby	T045
Danescourt	T130
Danzey	T071
Darlington	T026, T026H, T039, T044, T051
Darnall	T030
Darsham	T013
Dartford	T052, T200, T201, T212
Darton	T034
Darwen	T094
Datchet	T149
Davenport	T086
Dawlish	T051, T135
Dawlish Warren	T135
Deal	T194, T207
Dean	T158
Deansgate	T082, T084, T085, T086, T089
Deganwy	T081, T102
Deighton	T039
Delamere	T088
Denby Dale	T034
Denham	T115
Denham Golf Club	T115
Denmark Hill	T052, T178, T195, T196, T200
Dent	T042

Denton	T078A
Deptford	T200, T201
Derby	T050, T051, T053A, T053, T056, T057
Derby Road	T013
Dereham Market Place	T026A
Devonport	T135, T139
Dewsbury	T039, T041
Didcot Parkway	T116, T125, T126
Digby & Sowton	T136
Dilton Marsh	T123
Dinas Powys	T130
Dinas Rhondda	T130
Dingle Road	T130
Dingwall	T239
Dinsdale	T044
Dinting	T079
Disley	T086
Diss	T011
Dockyard	T135, T139
Dodworth	T034
Dolau	T129
Doleham	T192
Dolgarrog	T102
Dolwyddelan	T102
Doncaster	T018, T026, T029, T031, T051, T053
Dorchester South	T158
Dorchester West	T123, T158
Dore & Totley	T078
Dorking	T152, T180
Dorking Deepdene	T148
Dorking West	T148
Dormans	T182
Dorridge	T071, T115
Douglas (Isle Of Man)	T098A
Dove Holes	T086
Dover Priory	T194, T207, T212
Dovercourt	T011
Dovey Junction	T076
Downham Market	T017, T025
Drayton Green	T117
Drayton Park	T024
Drem	T238
Driffield	T043
Drigg	T100
Droitwich Spa	T071

Dronfield	T034, T053
Drumchapel	T226, T226_
Drumfrochar	T219
Drumgelloch	T226, T226
Drumry	T226, T226
Dublin Ferryport	T081A
Dublin Port - Stena	T081A
Duddeston	T069, T070
Dudley Port	T068
Duffield	T056
Duirinish	T239
Duke Street	T226, T226
Dullingham	T014
Dumbarton Central	T226, T226, T227
Dumbarton East	T226, T226
Dumbreck	T217
Dumfries	T216
Dumpton Park	T212
Dunbar	T026, T051, T238
Dunblane	T229, T230
Duncraig	T239
Dundee	T026, T051, T065, T229
Dunfermline Queen Margaret	T242
Dunfermline Town	T242
Dunkeld & Birnam	T229
Dunlop	T222
Dunoon	T219A
Dunrobin Castle	T239
Duns	T026K
Dunstable Asda	T052A
Dunster Steep	T135E
Dunston	T048
Dunton Green	T204
Durham	T026, T039, T044, T051
Durrington-on-Sea	T186, T188
Dyce	T229, T240
Dyffryn Ardudwy	T076

E

Eaglescliffe	T026, T044
Ealing Broadway	T116, T117
Earlestown	T081, T090
Earley	T149
Earlsfield	T152, T155
Earlston	T026K
Earlswood (Surrey)	T183
Earlswood (West Midlands)	T071

East Croydon	"T025, T052, T066, T170, T173, T175, T176, T177, T181, T182, T183, T184, T185, T186, T188, T189, T190"
East Didsbury	T085
East Dulwich	T173
East Farleigh	T208
East Garforth	T040
East Grinstead	T182
East Kilbride	T222
East Malling	T196, T197
East Midlands Airport (Bus)	T053A
East Midlands Parkway	T049, T053
East Tilbury	T001
East Worthing	T188
Eastbourne	T190, T192
Eastbrook	T130
Easterhouse	T226, T226
Eastham Rake	T107
Eastleigh	T158, T165
Eastrington	T029
Ebbsfleet International	T192, T194, T200, T207, T212
Ebbw Vale Parkway	T127
Ebbw Vale Town	T127
Eccles	T090
Eccles Road	T017
Eccleston Park	T090
Edale	T078
Eden Camp	T026G
Eden Park	T203
Eden Project	T135B
Edenbridge	T183
Edenbridge Town	T182
Edge Hill	T089, T090, T091
Edinburgh	T026, T039, T042, T051, T065, T224, T225, T226, T227, T228, T229, T230, T231, T238, T239B, T242, T243
Edinburgh Gateway	T229, T242
Edinburgh Park	T226, T230, T231
Edmonton Green	T021

Effingham Junction	T152
Eggesford	T136
Egham	T149
Egton	T045
Eigg	T227A
Elephant & Castle	T052, T052MML, T173, T179, T180, T195, T196, T212
Elgin	T240
Ellesmere Port	T107, T109
Elmers End	T203
Elmstead Woods	T204
Elmswell	T014
Elsecar	T034
Elsenham	T022
Elstree & Borehamwood	T052, T052MML
Eltham	T200
Elton & Orston	T019
Ely	T014, T017, T025, T047, T049
Emerson Park	T004
Emsworth	T186
Energlyn & Churchill Park	T130
Enfield Chase	T024
Enfield Lock	T022
Enfield Town	T021
Entwistle	T094
Epsom	T152, T180
Epsom Downs	T172, T180
Erdington	T069
Eridge	T182
Erith	T200, T201
Esher	T155
Eskbank	T243
Essex Road	T024
Etchingham	T206
Euxton Balshaw Lane	T090
Evesham	T126
Ewell East	T180
Ewell West	T152
Exeter Airport	T135G
Exeter Central	T135, T136, T160
Exeter St Davids	T051, T135D, T135, T135G, T136, T160
Exeter St Thomas	T135
Exhibition Centre	T225, T226
Exmouth	T135, T136

F

Station	Tables
Exton	T136
Eynsford	T052, T195, T196
Fairbourne	T076
Fairfield	T078
Fairlie	T221
Fairwater	T130
Falconwood	T200
Falkirk Grahamston	T226, T228, T230, T231
Falkirk High	T228
Falls Of Cruachan	T227
Falmer	T189, T190
Falmouth Docks	T143
Falmouth Town	T143
Fareham	T123, T158, T165, T186, T188
Farnborough (Main)	T155, T158
Farnborough North	T148
Farncombe	T156
Farnham	T155
Farningham Road	T212
Farnworth	T082
Farringdon	"T024, T025, T052, T052MML, T173, T175, T179, T180, T181, T182, T183, T184, T185, T188, T195, T196, T197, T201"
Fauldhouse	T224
Faversham	T194, T212
Faygate	T183
Fazakerley	T104
Fearn	T239
Featherstone	T032
Felixstowe	T013
Feltham	T149
Feniton	T160
Fenny Stratford	T064
Fernhill	T130
Ferriby	T029
Ferryside	T128
Ffairfach	T129
Filey	T043
Filton Abbey Wood	T123, T132, T134, T135
Finchley Road & Frognal	T059
Finsbury Park	T024, T025, T052, T196
Finstock	T126
Fishbourne (Sussex)	T186
Fishersgate	T188
Fishguard & Goodwick	T128
Fishguard Harbour	T128
Fiskerton	T027
Fitzwilliam	T031
Five Ways	T069
Flamingo Land	T026G
Fleet	T155, T158
Flimby	T100
Flint	T075, T081
Flitwick	T052, T052MML
Flixton	T089
Flowery Field	T079
Folkestone Central	T194, T207
Folkestone West	T194, T207
Ford	T186,
Forest Gate	T005
Forest Hill	T171, T177, T178
Formby	T103
Forres	T240
Forsinard	T239
Fort Matilda	T219
Fort William	T065, T227A, T227
Four Oaks	T069
Foxfield	T100
Foxton	T025
Frant	T206
Fratton	T123, T156, T157, T158, T165, T186
Freshfield	T103
Freshford	T123
Frimley	T149
Frinton-on-Sea	T011
Frizinghall	T036, T037, T038
Frodsham	T081
Frome	T123, T135, T160
Fulwell	T149, T152
Furness Vale	T086
Furze Platt	T120

G

Station	Tables
Gainsborough Central	T028, T030
Gainsborough Lea Road	T018, T030
Galashiels	T243
Galashiels Bus Station	T026K
Garelochhead	T227
Garforth	T039, T040
Gargrave	T042
Garrowhill	T226, T226
Garscadden	T226, T226
Garsdale	T042
Garston (Hertfordshire)	T061
Garswood	T090
Gartcosh	T226, T231
Garth (Mid Glamorgan)	T128
Garth (Powys)	T129
Garve	T239
Gathurst	T082
Gatley	T039, T085
Gatwick Airport	"T025, T052, T052MML, T148, T183, T184, T185, T186, T188, T189, T190"
Georgemas Junction	T239
Gerrards Cross	T115
Gidea Park	T005
Giffnock	T222
Giggleswick	T042
Gilberdyke	T029
Gilfach Fargoed	T130
Gillingham (Dorset)	T160
Gillingham (Kent)	T194, T200, T201, T212
Gilshochill	T232
Gipsy Hill	T171, T173
Girvan	T218
Glaisdale	T045
Glan Conwy	T102
Glasgow Central	T026, T042, T051, T065, T216, T217, T218, T219, T221, T222, T223, T224
Glasgow Central L. Level	T225, T226
Glasgow Queen St high level	"T226, T227, T228, T229, T230, T231, T232, T239B"
Glasgow Queen St low level	T226, T226, T227
Glasshoughton	T032
Glazebrook	T089
Gleneagles	T229
Glenfinnan	T227
Glengarnock	T221
Glenrothes With Thornton	T242
Glossop	T079
Gloucester	T051, T057, T058, T123, T125, T128, T134
Glynde	T190
Goathland	T045
Gobowen	T075, T131
Godalming	T156
Godley	T079
Godstone	T183
Goldthorpe	T031
Golf Street	T229
Golspie	T239
Gomshall	T148
Goodmayes	T005
Goole	T029, T032
Goostrey	T084
Gordon Hill	T024
Gorebridge	T243
Goring & Streatley	T116
Goring-by-sea	T186, T188
Gorton	T078, T079
Gospel Oak	T059, T062, T176
Gourock	T219A, T219
Gowerton	T128, T129
Goxhill	T028
Grange Park	T024
Grange-over-sands	T082
Grangetown	T130
Grantham	T019, T026, T049
Grateley	T160
Gravelly Hill	T069
Gravesend	T194, T200, T201, T212
Grays	T001
Great Ayton	T045
Great Bentley	T011
Great Chesterford	T022
Great Coates	T028
Great Malvern	T071, T123, T126
Great Missenden	T114
Great Yarmouth	T015
Green Lane	T107
Green Road	T100
Greenbank	T088
Greenfaulds	T225, T226, T226, T231
Greenfield	T039
Greenford	T117
Greenhithe For Bluewater	T200, T201, T212
Greenock Central	T219
Greenock West	T219
Greenwich	T052, T200, T201
Gretna Green	T216
Grimsby Docks	T028
Grimsby Town	T027, T028, T029
Grindleford	T078
Grosmont	T045
Grosmont North Yorks Moors	T045
Grove Park	T204
Guide Bridge	T078A, T078, T079
Guildford	T051, T148, T149, T152, T155, T156, T180
Guiseley	T038
Gunnersbury	T059
Gunnislake	T139
Gunton	T016
Gwersyllt	T101
Gypsy Lane	T045

H

Station	Tables
Habrough	T027, T028, T029
Hackbridge	T052, T173, T179, T180
Hackney Central	T059
Hackney Downs	T020, T021, T022
Hackney Wick	T059
Haddenham & Thame Parkway	T115
Haddiscoe	T015
Hadfield	T079
Hadley Wood	T024
Hag Fold	T082
Haggerston	T177, T178
Hagley	T071
Hairmyres	T222
Hale	T088
Halesworth	T013
Halewood	T089
Halifax	T026, T032, T041
Hall Green	T071
Hall I' Th' Wood	T094
Hall Road	T103
Halling	T208
Haltwhistle	T048
Ham Street	T192

Hamble	T165
Hamilton Central	T225
Hamilton Square	T106, T107
Hamilton West	T225
Hammerton	T035
Hampden Park	T190, T192
Hampstead Heath	T059
Hampton	T152
Hampton Court	T152
Hampton Wick	T149, T152
Hampton-in-arden	T068
Hamstead	T070
Hamworthy	T158
Hanborough	T126
Handforth	T084
Hanley Bus Station	T067
Hanwell	T117
Hapton	T097
Harlech	T076
Harlesden	T060
Harling Road	T017
Harlington	T052, T052MML
Harlow Mill	T022
Harlow Town	T022
Harold Wood	T005
Harpenden	T052, T052MML
Harrietsham	T196, T197
Harringay	T024
Harringay Green Lanes	T062
Harrington	T100
Harrogate	T026, T035
Harrow & Weald-stone	T066, T176
Harrow & Weald-stone	T060
Harrow-on-the-Hill	T114
Hartford	T091
Hartlebury	T071
Hartlepool	T026, T044
Hartwood	T224
Harwich International	T011, T013, T014
Harwich Town	T011
Haslemere	T156
Hassocks	T052, T184
Hastings	T190, T192, T206
Hatch End	T060
Hatfield	T024, T025
Hatfield & Stainforth	T029
Hatfield Bus	T052C

Hatfield Peverel	T011
Hathersage	T078
Hattersley	T079
Hatton	T071, T115
Havant	T123, T156, T157, T165, T186, T188
Havenhouse	T019
Haverfordwest	T128
Hawarden	T101
Hawarden Bridge	T101
Hawkhead	T217
Haydon Bridge	T048
Haydons Road	T052, T173, T179
Hayes	T203
Hayes & Harlington	T117
Hayle	T051, T135
Haymarket	"T026, T051, T065, T224, T225, T226, T226, T228, T229, T230, T231, T238, T242"
Haywards Heath	T052, T184, T188, T189, T190
Hazel Grove	T078, T086
Headcorn	T207
Headingley	T035
Headstone Lane	T060
Heald Green	T082, T085
Healing	T028
Heath High Level	T130
Heath Low Level	T130
Heathrow Termi-nal 4	T117, T118
Heathrow Termi-nal 5	T117, T118
Heathrow Terminals 2 & 3	" T117, T118"
Heaton Chapel	T084, T086
Hebden Bridge	T041
Heckington	T019
Hedge End	T158
Hednesford	T070
Heighington	T044
Helensburgh Central	T226, T226
Helensburgh Upper	T226, T226, T227
Hellifield	T042
Helmsdale	T239
Helsby	T081, T109
Helston Coinagehall St	T135A

Hemel Hempstead	T066, T176
Hendon	T052, T052MML
Hengoed	T130
Henley-in-Arden	T071
Henley-on-Thames	T121
Hensall	T032
Hereford	T071, T075, T126, T131
Herne Bay	T194, T212
Herne Hill	T052, T173, T179, T180, T195
Hersham	T155
Hertford East	T022
Hertford North	T024, T025
Hessle	T029
Heswall	T101
Hever	T182
Heworth	T044
Hexham	T044, T048
Heyford	T116
Heysham Port	T042, T098A, T098
High Brooms	T206
High Street	T226, T226
High Wycombe	T115
Higham	T200, T201
Highams Park	T020
Highbridge & Burnham	T134
Highbury & Islington	T024, T059, T176, T177, T178
Hightown	T103
Hildenborough	T204, T206, T207
Hillfoot	T226
Hillington East	T219
Hillington West	T219
Hillside	T103
Hilsea	T156, T157, T158, T165, T186
Hinchley Wood	T152
Hinckley	T047
Hindley	T082
Hinton Admiral	T158
Hitchin	T024, T025, T052
Hither Green	T199, T200, T204
Hockley	T006
Hollingbourne	T196, T197
Holmes Chapel	T084
Holmwood	T180
Holsworthy Church	T135D
Holsworthy Library	T135D
Holton Heath	T158

Holyhead	T065, T075, T081A, T081, T131
Holytown	T224, T225
Homerton	T059
Honeybourne	T126
Honiton	T160
Honley	T034
Honor Oak Park	T171, T177, T178
Hook	T155
Hooton	T107
Hope (Derbyshire)	T078
Hope (Flintshire)	T101
Hopton Heath	T129
Horley	T183, T184
Hornbeam Park	T035
Hornsey	T024
Horsforth	T035
Horsham	T052, T180, T183, T185, T186
Horsley	T152
Horton-in-Ribbles-dale	T042
Horwich Parkway	T082
Hoscar	T082
Hough Green	T089
Hounslow	T149
Hove	T123, T184, T186, T188
Hoveton & Wrox-ham	T016
How Wood	T061
Howden	T029, T039
Howwood	T221
Hoxton	T177, T178
Hoylake	T106
Hubberts Bridge	T019
Hucknall	T055
Huddersfield	T031, T034, T039, T041
Hull	T026, T029, T033, T039, T043
Hull Paragon Interchange	T028
Humphrey Park	T089
Huncoat	T097
Hungerford	T116, T135
Hunmanby	T043
Huntingdon	T025, T052
Huntly	T240
Hunts Cross	T089, T103
Hurst Green	T182

Hutton Cranswick	T043
Huyton	T090
Hyde Central	T078
Hyde North	T078
Hykeham	T027
Hyndland	T225, T226, T226
Hythe	T011

I

I.B.M.	T219
Ifield	T183
Ilford	T005
Ilkeston	T034, T049
Ilkley	T038
Imperial Wharf	T059, T066, T170, T176
Ince	T082
Ince & Elton	T109
Ingatestone	T011
Insch	T240
Invergordon	T239
Invergowrie	T229
Inverkeithing	T026, T051, T229, T242
Inverkip	T219
Inverness	T026, T065, T229, T239A, T239B, T239, T240
Invershin	T239
Inverurie	T229, T240
Ipswich	T011, T013, T014, T017
Irlam	T089
Irvine	T221
Isleworth	T149
Islip	T115
Iver	T117
Ivybridge	T135

J

James Cook	T045
James Street	T106, T107
Jewellery Quarter	T071
Johnston	T128
Johnstone	T221
Jordanhill	T226, T226

K

Kearsley	T082
Kearsney	T212
Keighley	T026, T036, T042
Keith	T240
Kelvedon	T011
Kelvindale	T232

Kemble	T125
Kempston Hardwick	T064
Kempton Park	T152
Kemsing	T196, T197
Kemsley	T212
Kendal	T083
Kenilworth	T116A
Kenley	T181
Kennett	T014
Kennishead	T222
Kensal Green	T060
Kensal Rise	T059
Kensington (Olympia)	T059, T066, T170, T176
Kent House	T195
Kentish Town	T052, T052MML, T195, T196
Kentish Town West	T059
Kenton	T060
Kents Bank	T082
Kettering	T053
Kettering Library	T026B
Kew Bridge	T149
Kew Gardens	T059
Keyham	T135, T139
Keynsham	T123, T132
Kidbrooke	T200
Kidderminster	T071, T115
Kidsgrove	T050, T067, T084
Kidwelly	T128
Kilburn High Road	T060
Kilcreggan	T219A
Kildale	T045
Kildonan	T239
Kilgetty	T128
Kilmarnock	T216, T218, T222
Kilmaurs	T222
Kilpatrick	T226, T226
Kilwinning	T218, T221
Kinbrace	T239
Kingham	T126A, T126
Kinghorn	T242
Kings Langley	T066
Kings Lynn	T017, T025
Kings Lynn Bus Station	T026A
Kings Norton	T069
Kings Nympton	T136
Kings Park	T223
Kings Sutton	T115, T116

Kingsknowe	T224
Kingston	T149, T152
Kingswood	T181
Kingussie	T229
Kintbury	T116
Kirby Cross	T011
Kirk Sandall	T029
Kirkby	T082, T104
Kirkby In Ashfield	T055
Kirkby Stephen	T042
Kirkby-in-furness	T100
Kirkcaldy	T026, T051, T229, T242
Kirkconnel	T216
Kirkdale	T104, T105
Kirkham & Wesham	T082, T097
Kirkhill	T223
Kirknewton	T224
Kirkstall Forge	T036, T037, T038
Kirkwood	T225
Kirton Lindsey	T028
Kiveton Bridge	T030
Kiveton Park	T030
Knaresborough	T035
Knebworth	T024, T025
Knighton	T129
Knockholt	T204
Knottingley	T032
Knucklas	T129
Knutsford	T088
Kyle Of Lochalsh	T239B, T239

L

Ladybank	T051, T229
Ladywell	T203
Laindon	T001
Lairg	T239
Lake	T167
Lakenheath	T017
Lamphey	T128
Lanark	T225
Lancaster	T042, T051, T065, T082, T098, T100
Lancing	T186, T188
Landywood	T070
Langbank	T219
Langho	T094
Langley	T117
Langley Green	T071
Langley Mill	T034, T049, T053
Langside	T223
Langwathby	T042
Langwith - Whaley Thorns	T055
Lapford	T136
Lapworth	T071, T115
Larbert	T229, T230
Largs	T221
Larkhall	T225
Laurencekirk	T229
Lawrence Hill	T133, T134
Layton	T082, T097
Lazonby & Kirkoswald	T042
Lea Bridge	T022
Lea Green	T039, T090
Lea Hall	T068
Leagrave	T052, T052MML
Lealholm	T045
Leamington Spa	T051, T071, T115, T116, T116A
Leasowe	T106
Leatherhead	T152, T180
Ledbury	T071, T126
Lee	T200
Leeds	"T026, T031, T032, T034, T035, T036, T037, T038, T039, T040, T041, T042, T051, T053, T097"
Leicester	T047, T053
Leigh (Kent)	T183
Leigh-on-Sea	T001
Leighton Buzzard	T066, T176
Lelant	T144
Lelant Saltings	T144
Lenham	T196, T197
Lenzie	T228, T230
Leominster	T131
Letchworth Garden City	T024, T025, T052
Leuchars	T026, T051, T229A, T229
Levenshulme	T084, T086
Levisham	T045
Lewes	T184, T189, T190, T192
Lewisham	T195, T199, T200, T203, T204
Leyland	T082, T090

Leyton Midland Road	T062
Leytonstone High Road	T062
Lichfield City	T069
Lichfield Trent Valley	T065, T067, T069
Lidlington	T064
Limehouse	T001
Lincoln	T018, T026, T027, T030, T053
Lingfield	T182
Lingwood	T015
Linlithgow	T228, T230, T231
Liphook	T156
Liskeard	T051, T135, T140
Lismore	T227B
Liss	T156
Lisvane & Thornhill	T130
Little Kimble	T115
Little Sutton	T107
Littleborough	T041
Littlehampton	T186, T188
Littlehaven	T183
Littleport	T017, T025
Liverpool Central	T103, T104, T105, T106, T107
Liverpool Lime Street	T039, T049, T065, T081, T089, T090, T091, T106, T107
Liverpool South Parkway (Sth)	T049, T065, T081, T091, T103
Livingston North	T226, T226
Livingston South	T224
Llanaber	T076
Llanbedr	T076
Llanbister Road	T129
Llanbradach	T130
Llandaf	T130
Llandanwg	T076
Llandecwyn	T076
Llandeilo	T129
Llandovery	T129
Llandrindod	T129
Llandudno	T075, T081, T102, T131
Llandudno Junction	T065, T075, T081, T102, T131
Llandybie	T129
Llanelli	T128, T129
Llanfairfechan	T081
Llanfairpwll	T081

Llangadog	T129
Llangammarch	T129
Llangennech	T129
Llangynllo	T129
Llanharan	T128
Llanhilleth	T127
Llanishen	T130
Llanrwst	T102
Llansamlet	T128
Llantwit Major	T130
Llanwrda	T129
Llanwrtyd	T129
Llwyngwril	T076
Llwynypia	T130
Loch Awe	T227
Loch Eil Outward Bound	T227
Lochailort	T227
Lochboisdale	T227C
Locheilside	T227
Lochgelly	T242
Lochluichart	T239
Lochmaddy	T239B
Lochwinnoch	T221
Lockerbie	T051, T065
Lockwood	T034
London Blackfriars	"T024, T025, T052, T052MML, T173, T175, T179, T180, T181, T182, T183, T184, T185, T188, T195, T196, T197, T199, T201, T212"
London Bridge	"T024, T025, T052, T052MML, T170, T171, T172, T173, T175, T177, T179, T180, T181, T182, T183, T184, T185, T186, T188, T189, T190, T196, T197, T199, T200, T201, T203, T204, T206, T207, T212"
London Cannon Street	T199, T200, T201, T203, T204, T206, T207, T212

London Charing Cross	T199, T200, T201, T203, T204, T206, T207, T212
London Euston	T060, T065, T066, T067, T068, T081, T084, T091
London Fenchurch St	T001
London Fields	T021
London Kings Cross	T017, T024, T025, T026, T029, T032, T041, T044
London Liverpool St	T001, T005, T006, T011, T015, T017, T020, T021, T022
London Luton Airport	T052B
London Marylebone	T071, T114, T115
London Paddington	T116, T117, T118, T123, T125, T126, T128, T135
London Road (Brighton)	T189, T190
London Road (Guildford)	T152
London Victoria	T170, T171, T172, T175, T180, T181, T182, T183, T184, T185, T186, T188, T189, T190, T195, T197,T199, T200, T201, T212
London Waterloo	" T149, T152, T155, T156, T158, T160, T180"
London Waterloo (East)	T199, T200, T201, T203, T204, T206, T207, T212
Long Buckby	T066, T068
Long Eaton	T053, T056, T057
Long Preston	T042
Longbeck	T044
Longbridge	T069
Longcross	T149
Longfield	T212
Longniddry	T238
Longport	T050, T084
Longton	T050
Looe	T140
Lostock	T082

M

Lostock Gralam	T088
Lostock Hall	T097
Lostwithiel	T051, T135
Loughborough	T053
Loughborough Jn	T052, T173, T179, T180, T195
Low Moor	T041
Lowdham	T027
Lower Sydenham	T203
Lowestoft	T013, T015
Ludlow	T131
Luton	T052, T052MML, T053, T179, T201
Luton Airport Parkway	T052B, T052, T052MML, T053, T179, T201
Luton Station Interchange	T052A
Luxulyan	T142
Lydney	T057
Lye	T071
Lymington Pier	T159
Lymington Town	T159
Lympstone Commando	T136
Lympstone Village	T136
Lytham	T097
Macclesfield	T051, T065, T084
Machynlleth	T076
Maesteg	T128
Maesteg (Ewenny Road)	T128
Maghull	T105
Maghull North	T105
Maiden Newton	T123
Maidenhead	T116, T117, T120
Maidstone Barracks	T208
Maidstone East	T025, T052, T196, T197
Maidstone West	T207, T208
Malden Manor	T152
Mallaig	T227A, T227
Malton	T039
Malvern Link	T071, T123, T126
Manchester Airport	T029, T039, T065, T078, T081, T082, T084, T085, T089, T090
Manchester Oxford Road	T039, T049, T081, T082, T084, T085, T086, T089, T090

Manchester Piccadilly	"T029, T039, T049, T051, T053, T065, T078, T079, T081, T082, T084, T085, T086, T088, T089, T090, T094, T128, T131"
Manchester Victoria	T039, T041, T081, T082, T085, T090, T094, T095, T097
Manea	T014, T017
Manningtree	T011, T014
Manor Park	T005
Manor Road	T106
Manorbier	T128
Manors	T048
Mansfield	T055
Mansfield Woodhouse	T055
March	T014, T017, T047, T049
Marden	T207
Margate	T194, T207, T212
Market Harborough	T053
Market Rasen	T027
Markinch	T051, T229
Marks Tey	T010, T011
Marlborough High St Bus	T116A
Marlow	T120
Marple	T078
Marsden	T039
Marske	T044
Marston Green	T068
Martin Mill	T207
Martins Heron	T149
Marton	T045
Maryhill	T232
Maryland	T005
Maryport	T100
Matlock	T056
Matlock Bath	T056
Mauldeth Road	T085
Maxwell Park	T223
Maybole	T218
Maze Hill	T200, T201
Meadowhall	T029, T030, T031, T033, T034
Meldreth	T025
Melksham	T123

Melrose	T026K
Melton	T013
Melton Mowbray	T047, T053
Menheniot	T135
Menston	T038
Meols	T106
Meols Cop	T082
Meopham	T212
Meridian Water	T022
Merryton	T225
Merstham	T183
Merthyr Tydfil	T130
Merthyr Vale	T130
Metheringham	T018
Metrocentre	T044, T048
Mexborough	T029
Micheldever	T158
Micklefield	T040
Middlesbrough	T026, T039, T044, T045
Middlewood	T086
Midgham	T116
Milford (Surrey)	T156
Milford Haven	T128
Mill Hill (Lan-cashire)	T097
Mill Hill Broadway	T052, T052MML
Millbrook (Bedfordshire)	T064
Millbrook (Hants)	T158
Milliken Park	T221
Millom	T100
Mills Hill	T041
Milngavie	T226, T226
Milton Keynes Central	T065, T066, T067, T176
Minehead Bancks Street	T135E
Minehead Butlins	T135E
Minehead Parade	T135E
Minffordd	T076
Minster	T207
Mirfield	T026, T032, T039, T041
Mistley	T011
Mitcham Eastfields	T052, T173, T179, T180
Mitcham Junction	T052, T173, T179, T180
Mobberley	T088
Monifieth	T229
Monks Risborough	T115

Montpelier	T133
Montrose	T026, T051, T229
Moorfields	T103, T104, T105, T106, T107
Moorgate	T024
Moorside	T082
Moorthorpe	T031, T033
Morar	T227
Morchard Road	T136
Morden South	T052, T179
Morecambe	T042, T098
Moreton	T106
Moreton (Dorset)	T158
Moreton-in-marsh	T126
Morfa Mawddach	T076
Morley	T039
Morpeth	T026, T039, T048, T051
Mortimer	T122
Mortlake	T149
Moses Gate	T082
Moss Side	T097
Mossley (Grtr Manchester)	T039
Mossley Hill	T089, T091
Mosspark	T217
Moston	T041
Motherwell	T026, T051, T065, T224, T225, T231
Motspur Park	T152
Mottingham	T200
Mottisfont & Dunbridge	T158
Mouldsworth	T088
Moulsecoomb	T189, T190
Mount Florida	T223
Mount Vernon	T225
Mountain Ash	T130
Muck	T227A
Muir Of Ord	T239
Muirend	T223
Musselburgh	T238
Mytholmroyd	T041

N

Nafferton	T043
Nailsea & Backwell	T134
Nairn	T240
Nantwich	T131
Narberth	T128
Narborough	T047
Navigation Road	T088

Neath	T125, T128
Needham Market	T011, T014
Neilston	T223
Nelson	T097
Neston	T101
Netherfield	T019
Nethertown	T100
Netley	T165
New Barnet	T024
New Beckenham	T203
New Brighton	T106
New Clee	T028
New Cross	T178, T199, T200, T203, T204
New Cross Gate	T171, T175, T177, T178, T181, T183
New Cumnock	T216
New Eltham	T200
New Holland	T028
New Hythe	T208
New Lane	T082
New Malden	T152
New Mills Central	T078
New Mills Newtown	T086
New Milton	T158
New Pudsey	T037, T041
New Southgate	T024
Newark Castle	T027, T053
Newark North Gate	T026, T027
Newbridge (Ebbw Vale)	T127
Newbury	T116, T135
Newbury Racecourse	T116
Newcastle	T026, T039, T044, T045, T048, T051, T216
Newcourt	T136
Newcraighall	T243
Newhaven Harbour	T189
Newhaven Town	T189
Newington	T212
Newmarket	T014
Newport (Essex)	T022
Newport (South Wales)	T051, T057, T075, T123, T125, T128, T131, T132, T135
Newquay	T135, T142
Newstead	T055
Newton	T223, T225

Newton Abbot	T051, T135
Newton Aycliffe	T044
Newton For Hyde	T079
Newton St Cyres	T136
Newton-le-Willows	T039, T081, T090
Newton-on-Ayr	T221
Newtongrange	T243
Newtonmore	T229
Newtown (Powys)	T076
Ninian Park	T130
Nitshill	T222
Norbiton	T152
Norbury	T170, T173, T176
Normans Bay	T190, T192
Normanton	T034, T039
North Berwick	T238
North Camp	T148
North Dulwich	T173
North Fambridge	T006
North Llanrwst	T102
North Queensferry	T242
North Road	T044
North Sheen	T149
North Walsham	T016
North Wembley	T060
Northallerton	T026, T039
Northampton	T066, T067, T068
Northfield	T069
Northfleet	T200, T201
Northolt Park	T115
Northumberland Park	T022
Northwich	T088
Norton Bridge Station Drv	T067
Norwich	T011, T015, T016, T017, T026, T049
Norwood Junction	T171, T172, T175, T177, T178, T180, T181, T182, T183
Nottingham	T019, T027, T034, T049, T051, T053, T055, T056, T057
Nuneaton	T047, T063, T065, T066, T067
Nunhead	T052, T195, T196, T200
Nunthorpe	T045
Nutbourne	T186

Nutfield	T183

O

Oakengates	T074
Oakham	T047, T053
Oakleigh Park	T024
Oban	T227B, T227C, T227
Ockendon	T001
Ockley	T180
Okehampton	T136
Okehampton West Street	T135D
Old Hill	T071
Old Roan	T105
Old Street	T024
Oldfield Park	T123, T132
Olton	T071
Ore	T190, T192, T206
Ormskirk	T099, T105
Orpington	T052, T195, T196, T199, T204, T206, T207
Orrell	T082
Orrell Park	T105
Otford	T052, T195, T196, T197
Oulton Broad North	T015
Oulton Broad South	T013
Oundle Market Place	T026B
Outwood	T031
Overpool	T107
Overton	T160
Oxenholme Lake District	T051, T065, T082, T083
Oxford	T051, T115, T116, T117, T126
Oxford Parkway	T115
Oxshott	T152
Oxted	T182
Oxted Bay	T182

P

Paddock Wood	T207, T208
Padgate	T089
Padstow Old Rly Station	T135C
Paignton	T051, T135
Paisley Canal	T217
Paisley Gilmour St.	T218, T219A, T219B, T219, T221A, T221
Paisley St James	T219
Palmers Green	T024

Pangbourne	T116
Pannal	T035
Pantyffynnon	T129
Par	T051, T135, T142
Parbold	T082
Park Street	T061
Parkstone (Dorset)	T158
Parson Street	T134
Partick	T225, T226, T226
Parton	T100
Patchway	T132
Patricroft	T090
Patterton	T223
Peartree	T050
Peckham Rye	T052, T173, T178, T195, T196, T200
Pegswood	T048
Pemberton	T082
Pembrey & Burry Port	T128
Pembroke	T128
Pembroke Dock	T128
Pen-y-bont	T129
Penally	T128
Penarth	T130
Pencoed	T128
Pengam	T130
Penge East	T195
Penge West	T177, T178
Penhelig	T076
Penistone	T034
Penkridge	T065, T068
Penmaenmawr	T081
Penmere	T143
Penrhiwceiber	T130
Penrhyndeudraeth	T076
Penrith North Lakes	T051, T065
Penryn	T143
Pensarn	T076
Penshurst	T183
Pentre-bach	T130
Penychain	T076
Penyffordd	T101
Penzance	T051, T135, T144
Penzance Quay	T135F
Perranwell	T143
Perry Barr	T070
Pershore	T126
Perth	T026, T065, T229

Peterborough	T014, T017, T018, T025, T026A, T026, T047, T049, T052
Peterborough Queensgate	T026B
Petersfield	T156
Petts Wood	T195, T196, T199, T204
Pevensey & Westham	T190, T192
Pevensey Bay	T190, T192
Pewsey	T135
Pickering	T045
Pickering Eastgate	T026G
Pilning	T132
Pinhoe	T160
Pitlochry	T229
Pitsea	T001
Pleasington	T097
Plockton	T239
Pluckley	T207
Plumley	T088
Plumpton	T190
Plumstead	T200, T201
Plymouth	T051, T135, T139
Pokesdown	T158
Polegate	T190
Polesworth	T067
Pollokshaws East	T223
Pollokshaws West	T222
Pollokshields East	T223
Pollokshields West	T223
Polmont	T228, T230, T231
Polsloe Bridge	T136
Ponders End	T022
Pont-y-Pant	T102
Pontarddulais	T129
Pontefract Baghill	T033
Pontefract Monkhill	T026, T031, T032
Pontefract Tanshelf	T032
Pontlottyn	T130
Pontyclun	T128
Pontypool And New Inn	T131
Pontypridd	T130
Poole	T158
Poppleton	T035
Port Glasgow	T219
Port Sunlight	T107
Port Talbot Parkway	T125, T128

Station	Tables
Portchester	T158, T165, T186
Porth	T130
Porthmadog	T076
Portlethen	T229
Portslade	T186, T188
Portsmouth & Southsea	T123, T156, T157, T158, T165, T186, T188
Portsmouth Arms	T136
Portsmouth Harbour	T123, T156, T157, T158, T165, T167A, T186, T188
Possilpark & Parkhouse	T232
Potters Bar	T024, T025
Poulton-le-fylde	T041, T082, T097
Poynton	T084
Prees	T131
Prescot	T090
Prestatyn	T075, T081
Prestbury	T084
Preston	T041, T042, T051, T065, T082, T090, T094, T097, T099
Preston Park	T052, T184, T188
Prestonpans	T238
Prestwick Int. Airport	T218, T221
Prestwick Town	T218, T221
Priesthill & Darnley	T222
Princes Risborough	T115A, T115
Prittlewell	T006
Prudhoe	T048
Pulborough	T186
Purfleet	T001
Purley	T170, T177, T181, T183
Purley Oaks	T181
Putney	T149
Pwllheli	T076
Pye Corner	T127
Pyle	T128

Q

Station	Tables
Quakers Yard	T130
Queen's Park (London)	T060
Queenborough	T212
Queens Park	T223
Queens Rd Peckham	T173, T178
Queenstown Rd.(Battersea)	T149
Quintrell Downs	T142

R

Station	Tables
Radcliffe (Notts)	T019
Radlett	T052, T052MML
Radley	T116
Radyr	T130
Rainford	T082
Rainham	T001
Rainham (Kent)	T052, T194, T200, T201, T212
Rainhill	T090
Ramsgate	T194, T207, T212
Ramsgreave & Wilpshire	T094
Rannoch	T227
Rauceby	T019
Ravenglass For Eskdale	T100
Ravensbourne	T052, T195, T196
Ravensthorpe	T039
Rawcliffe	T032
Rayleigh	T006
Raynes Park	T152
Reading	"T051, T116, T117, T122, T125A, T125, T126, T128, T135, T148, T149, T158"
Reading Bus	T122
Reading West	T116, T122
Rectory Road	T021
Redbridge	T158
Redcar Central	T039, T044
Redcar East	T044
Reddish North	T078
Reddish South	T078A
Redditch	T069
Redhill	T052, T148, T183, T184
Redland	T133
Redruth	T051, T135A, T135
Reedham	T181
Reedham (Norfolk)	T015
Reigate	T148, T183
Renton	T226, T226
Retford	T026, T028, T030
Rhiwbina	T130
Rhoose Cardiff Int'l Airport	T125C, T130
Rhosneigr	T081
Rhyl	T075, T081
Rhymney	T130
Ribblehead	T042
Rice Lane	T104
Richmond	T059, T149
Richmond (Market)	T026H
Rickmansworth	T114
Riddlesdown	T182
Ridgmont	T064
Riding Mill	T048
Risca & Pontymister	T127
Rishton	T097
Robertsbridge	T206
Roby	T090
Rochdale	T041, T082, T095, T097
Roche	T142
Rochester	T194, T200, T201, T212
Rochford	T006
Rock Ferry	T107
Rogart	T239
Rogerstone	T127
Rolleston	T027
Roman Bridge	T102
Romford	T004, T005, T006, T011
Romiley	T078
Romsey	T123, T158
Roose	T082
Rose Grove	T097
Rose Hill Marple	T078
Rosslare Harbour	T128
Rosyth	T242
Rotherham Central	T029, T031, T033
Rotherhithe	T177, T178
Rothesay	T219B
Roughton Road	T016
Rowlands Castle	T156
Rowley Regis	T071, T115
Roy Bridge	T227
Roydon	T022
Royston	T025, T052
Ruabon	T075, T131
Rufford	T099
Rugby	T065, T066, T067, T068
Rugeley Town	T070
Rugeley Trent Valley	T067, T070
Rum	T227A
Runcorn	T065, T081, T091
Runcorn East	T081
Ruskington	T018
Ruswarp	T045
Rutherglen	T225
Ryde Esplanade	T167
Ryde Pier Head	T167A, T167
Ryde St Johns Road	T167
Ryder Brow	T078
Rye	T190, T192
Rye House	T022

S

Station	Tables
Salford Central	T082, T094
Salford Crescent	T082, T094
Salfords	T183
Salhouse	T016
Salisbury	T123, T158, T160
Saltaire	T036
Saltash	T135
Saltburn	T044
Saltcoats	T221
Saltmarshe	T029
Salwick	T097
Sampford Courtenay	T136
Sandal & Agbrigg	T031
Sandbach	T084
Sanderstead	T181, T182
Sandhills	T103, T104, T105
Sandhurst	T148
Sandling	T207
Sandown	T167
Sandplace	T140
Sandwell & Dudley	T066, T068, T074
Sandwich	T194, T207
Sandy	T025
Sankey For Penketh	T089
Sanquhar	T216
Sarn	T128
Saundersfoot	T128
Saunderton	T115
Sawbridgeworth	T022
Saxilby	T018, T030
Saxmundham	T013
Scarborough	T026, T039, T043, T090
Scotscalder	T239
Scotstounhill	T226, T226
Scrabster	T239A
Scunthorpe	T029
Sea Mills	T133
Seaford	T189
Seaforth & Litherland	T103
Seaham	T044
Seamer	T039, T043
Seascale	T100
Seaton Carew	T044
Seer Green	T115
Selby	T026, T029, T033, T039, T040, T041
Selhurst	T052, T170, T173, T176
Sellafield	T100
Selling	T212
Selly Oak	T069
Settle	T042
Seven Kings	T005
Seven Sisters	T021, T022
Sevenoaks	T052, T195, T196, T204, T206, T207
Severn Beach	T133
Severn Tunnel Jn	T057, T123, T132
Shadwell	T177, T178
Shalford	T148
Shanklin	T167
Shawfair	T243
Shawford	T158
Shawlands	T223
Sheerness-on-sea	T212
Sheffield	"T018, T026, T029, T030, T031, T033, T034, T049, T051, T053, T078, T089"
Shelford	T022
Shenfield	T005, T006, T011
Shenstone	T069
Shepherd's Bush	T059, T066, T170, T176
Shepherds Well	T212
Shepley	T034
Shepperton	T152
Shepreth	T025
Sherborne	T160
Sherburn-in-Elmet	T033
Sheringham	T016

Shettleston	T226, T226
Shieldmuir	T225
Shifnal	T074
Shildon	T044
Shiplake	T121
Shipley	T026, T036, T037, T038, T042
Shippea Hill	T017
Shipton	T126
Shirebrook	T055
Shirehampton	T133
Shireoaks	T030
Shirley	T071
Shoeburyness	T001
Sholing	T165
Shoreditch High Street	T177, T178
Shoreham (Kent)	T052, T195, T196
Shoreham-by-sea	T123, T186, T188
Shortlands	T052, T195, T196
Shotton	T081
Shotton High Level	T101
Shotts	T224
Shrewsbury	T074, T075, T076, T129, T131
Sidcup	T200
Sileby	T053
Silecroft	T100
Silkstone Common	T034
Silver Street	T021
Silverdale	T082
Singer	T226
Sittingbourne	T194, T212
Skegness	T019
Skewen	T128
Skipton	T026, T036, T042
Slade Green	T200, T201
Slaithwaite	T039
Slateford	T224
Sleaford	T018, T019
Sleights	T045
Slough	T116, T117, T119, T125, T126, T135
Small Heath	T071
Smallbrook Junc-tion	T167
Smethwick Galton Bridge	T071, T068, T074, T075, T076
Smethwick Rolfe Street	T068
Smithy Bridge	T041
Snaith	T032
Snodland	T208
Snowdown	T212
Sole Street	T212
Solihull	T071, T115
Somerleyton	T015
South Acton	T059
South Bank	T044
South Bermondsey	T173
South Croydon	T176, T181, T182
South Elmsall	T031
South Greenford	T117
South Gyle	T242
South Hampstead	T060
South Kenton	T060
South Merton	T052, T179
South Milford	T039, T040
South Ruislip	T115
South Tottenham	T062
South Wigston	T047
South Woodham Ferrers	T006
Southall	T117
Southampton Airport Pkway	T051, T158, T165
Southampton Central	T051, T123, T158, T165, T186, T188
Southbourne	T186
Southbury	T021
Southease	T189
Southend Airport	T006
Southend Central	T001
Southend East	T001
Southend Victoria	T006
Southminster	T006
Southport	T082, T103
Southwick	T186, T188
Sowerby Bridge	T041
Spalding	T018
Spean Bridge	T227
Spital	T107
Spondon	T056
Spooner Row	T017
Spring Road	T071
Springburn	T226, T231
Springfield	T229
Squires Gate	T097
St Albans Abbey	T061
St Albans Bus	T052C
St Albans City	T052, T052MML, T179, T201
St Andrews Bus Station	T229A, T229
St Andrews Road	T133
St Annes-on-the-sea	T097
St Austell	T051, T135B, T135
St Bees	T100
St Budeaux Ferry Road	T135, T139
St Budeaux Victoria Road	T139
St Columb Road	T142
St Denys	T158, T165
St Erth	T051, T135, T144
St Germans	T135
St Helens Central	T090
St Helens Junction	T090
St Helier	T052, T179
St Ives	T144
St James Street	T020
St James' Park	T136
St Johns	T199, T200, T203, T204
St Keyne Wishing Well Halt	T140
St Leonards Warrior Sq	T190, T192, T206
St Margarets	T149
St Margarets (Herts)	T022
St Mary Cray	T052, T195, T196, T197, T212
St Michaels	T103
St Neots	T025
St Pancras International	T024, T025, T052, T052MML, T053, T173, T175, T179, T180, T181, T182, T183, T184, T185, T188, T192, T194, T195, T196, T197, T200, T201, T207, T212
St. Marys Quay	T135F
Stafford	T051, T065, T067, T068, T084
Staines	T149
Stallingborough	T028
Stalybridge	T039, T078A
Stamford	T047
Stamford Hill	T021
Stanford-le-hope	T001
Stanlow & Thornton	T109
Stansted Airport	T017, T022, T047
Stansted Mountfitchet	T022
Staplehurst	T207
Stapleton Road	T133, T134
Starbeck	T035
Starcross	T135
Staveley	T083
Stechford	T068
Steeton & Silsden	T036
Stepps	T226, T231
Stevenage	T024, T025, T026, T052, T196
Stevenston	T221
Stewartby	T064
Stewarton	T222
Stirling	T026, T229, T230
Stockport	"T029, T049, T051, T065, T078A, T078, T082, T084, T086, T088, T089, T131"
Stocksfield	T048
Stocksmoor	T034
Stockton	T044
Stoke Mandeville	T114
Stoke Newington	T021
Stoke-on-trent	T050, T051, T065, T067, T084
Stone	T067
Stone Crossing	T200, T201
Stone Crown Street	T067
Stone Granville Square	T067
Stonebridge Park	T060
Stonegate	T206
Stonehaven	T026, T051, T229
Stonehouse	T125
Stoneleigh	T152
Stornoway	T239B
Stourbridge Junc-tion	T071, T072, T115
Stourbridge Town	T072
Stow	T243
Stowmarket	T011, T014
Stranraer	T218
Stratford	T001, T005, T006, T011, T022, T059, T176
Stratford International	T192, T194, T200, T207, T212, Table
Stratford-upon-avon	T071, T115
Stratford-upon-avon Parkway	T071, T115, T175, T181
Strathcarron	T239
Strawberry Hill	T149, T152
Streatham	T052, T173, T179, T180
Streatham Common	T170, T173, T176
Streatham Hill	T171
Streethouse	T032
Strines	T078
Stromeferry	T239
Stromness	T239A
Strood	T194, T200, T201, T208, T212
Stroud	T125
Sturry	T207
Styal	T084
Sudbury	T010
Sudbury & Harrow Road	T115
Sudbury Hill Harrow	T115
Sugar Loaf	T129
Summerston	T232
Sunbury	T152
Sunderland	T026, T044, T048
Sundridge Park	T204
Sunningdale	T149
Sunnymeads	T149
Surbiton	T152, T155
Surrey Quays	T177, T178
Sutton	T052, T170, T171, T172, T173, T179, T180
Sutton Coldfield	T069
Sutton Common	T052, T179
Sutton Parkway	T055
Swaffham Market Place	T026A
Swale	T212
Swanley	T052, T195, T196, T197, T212
Swanscombe	T200, T201
Swansea	T125, T128, T129, T131
Swanwick	T165, T186
Sway	T158

Swaythling	T158
Swinderby	T027
Swindon	T123, T125, T135
Swineshead	T019
Swinton	T082
Swinton (S.Yorks)	T029, T031, T033
Sydenham	T171, T177, T178
Sydenham Hill	T195
Syon Lane	T149
Syston	T053

T

Tackley	T116
Tadworth	T181
Taffs Well	T130
Tain	T239
Tal-y-cafn	T102
Talsarnau	T076
Talybont	T076
Tame Bridge Parkway	T070
Tamworth	T051, T057
Tamworth Low Level	T065, T067
Taplow	T117
Tarbert	T239B
Tattenham Corner	T181
Taunton	T051, T125, T134, T135E, T135
Taynuilt	T227
Teddington	T149, T152
Tees-side Airport	T044
Teignmouth	T051, T135
Telford Central	T074, T075, T076
Templecombe	T160
Tenby	T128
Teynham	T212
Thames Ditton	T152
Thatcham	T116, T135
Thatto Heath	T090
The Hawthorns	T071
The Lakes	T071
Theale	T116, T135
Theobalds Grove	T021
Thetford	T017, T049
Thirsk	T026, T039
Thornaby	T039, T044
Thorne North	T029
Thorne South	T029
Thornford	T123
Thornliebank	T222
Thornton Abbey	T028
Thornton Heath	T170, T173, T176
Thorntonhall	T222
Thorpe Bay	T001
Thorpe Culvert	T019
Thorpe-le-soken	T011
Three Bridges	T052, T183, T184, T185, T186
Three Oaks	T192
Thurgarton	T027
Thurnscoe	T031
Thurso	T239A, T239
Thurston	T014
Tilbury Town	T001
Tile Hill	T068
Tilehurst	T116
Tipton	T068
Tir-phil	T130
Tiree	T227B
Tisbury	T160
Tiverton Parkway	T051, T135
Todmorden	T041, T095, T097
Tolworth	T152
Ton Pentre	T130
Tonbridge	T183, T204, T206, T207, T208
Tondu	T128
Tonfanau	T076
Tonypandy	T130
Tooting	T052, T173, T179
Topsham	T136
Torquay	T051, T135
Torre	T135
Totnes	T051, T135
Tottenham Hale	T022
Totton	T158
Town Green	T105
Trafford Park	T089
Trefforest	T130
Trefforest Estate	T130
Trehafod	T130
Treherbert	T130
Treorchy	T130
Trimley	T013
Tring	T066, T176
Troed Y Rhiw	T130
Troon	T218, T221
Trowbridge	T123, T160
Truro	T051, T135, T143
Tulloch	T227
Tulse Hill	T052, T173, T179, T180
Tunbridge Wells	T206
Turkey Street	T021
Tutbury & Hatton	T050
Tweedbank	T243
Twickenham	T149
Twyford	T116, T117, T121
Ty Croes	T081
Ty Glas	T130
Tygwyn	T076
Tyndrum Lower	T227
Tyseley	T071
Tywyn	T076

U

Uckfield	T182
Uddingston	T224, T225
Uig	T239B
Ulceby	T028
Ullapool	T239B
Ulleskelf	T033, T040
Ulverston	T082
Umberleigh	T136
University	T057, T069, T071
Uphall	T226, T226
Upholland	T082
Upminster	T001, T004
Upper Halliford	T152
Upper Holloway	T062
Upper Tyndrum	T227
Upper Warlingham	T181, T182
Upton	T101
Upwey	T123, T158
Urmston	T089
Uttoxeter	T050

V

Valley	T081
Vauxhall	T149, T152, T155
Virginia Water	T149

W

Waddon	T172
Wadebridge Bus Station	T135C
Wadhurst	T206
Wainfleet	T019
Wakefield Kirkgate	T026, T031, T032, T034, T039, T053
Wakefield Westgate	T026, T031, T032, T039, T051, T053
Walkden	T082
Wallasey Grove Road	T106
Wallasey Village	T106
Wallington	T172
Wallyford	T238
Walmer	T207
Walsall	T070
Walsden	T041
Waltham Cross	T022
Walthamstow Central	T020
Walthamstow Queen's Road	T062
Walton	T105
Walton-on-thames	T155
Walton-on-the-naze	T011
Wanborough	T148, T149
Wandsworth Common	T170, T171, T176
Wandsworth Road	T178
Wandsworth Town	T149
Wanstead Park	T062
Wapping	T177, T178
Warblington	T186
Ware	T022
Wareham	T158
Wargrave	T121
Warminster	T123, T160
Warnham	T180
Warrington Bank Quay	T051, T065, T081, T090, T109
Warrington Central	T039, T049, T089
Warwick	T071, T115
Warwick Parkway	T071, T115
Watchet (West Somerset Rly)	T135E
Water Orton	T047, T057
Waterbeach	T017, T025
Wateringbury	T208
Waterloo	T103
Watford High Street	T060
Watford Junction	T060, T061, T065, T066, T067, T176
Watford North	T061
Watlington	T017, T025
Watton-at-stone	T024
Waun-gron Park	T130
Wavertree Technology Park	T090
Wedgwood Old Road Bridge	T067
Weeley	T011
Weeton	T035
Welham Green	T024
Welling	T200
Wellingborough	T053
Wellington (Shropshire)	T074, T075, T076
Welshpool	T076
Welwyn Garden City	T024, T025, T052, T196
Welwyn North	T024, T025
Wem	T131
Wembley Central	T060, T066, T176
Wembley Stadium	T115
Wemyss Bay	T219B, T219
Wendover	T114
Wennington	T042
West Allerton	T089, T091
West Brompton	T059, T066, T170, T176
West Byfleet	T155
West Calder	T224
West Croydon	T170, T171, T172, T177, T178, T180
West Drayton	T117
West Dulwich	T195
West Ealing	T115, T117
West Ham	T001
West Hampstead	T059, T176
West Hampstead Thameslink	T052, T052MML, T179, T201
West Horndon	T001
West Kilbride	T221
West Kirby	T106
West Malling	T196, T197
West Norwood	T171, T173
West Ruislip	T115
West Runton	T016
West St Leonards	T206
West Sutton	T052, T179
West Wickham	T203
West Worthing	T186, T188
Westbury	T123, T135, T160
Westcliff	T001
Westcombe Park	T200, T201
Westenhanger	T207
Wester Hailes	T224
Westerfield	T013
Westerton	T226
Westgate-on-sea	T212

RECENT PUBLICATIONS

Eastern Main Lines
SCUNTHORPE TO DONCASTER
Including the Axholme Joint Railway plus the Whitton and Elsham lines
Vic Mitchell and Keith Smith

Country Railway Routes
UTTOXETER TO BUXTON
via ASHBOURNE
Vic Mitchell and Keith Smith

Country Railway Routes
CROMFORD & HIGH PEAK by RAIL and TRAIL
Vic Mitchell and Keith Smith
MP Middleton Press

Eastern Main Lines
NEWCASTLE TO ALNMOUTH
and the Amble branch
Roger R Darsley and Dennis A Lovett
MP Middleton Press

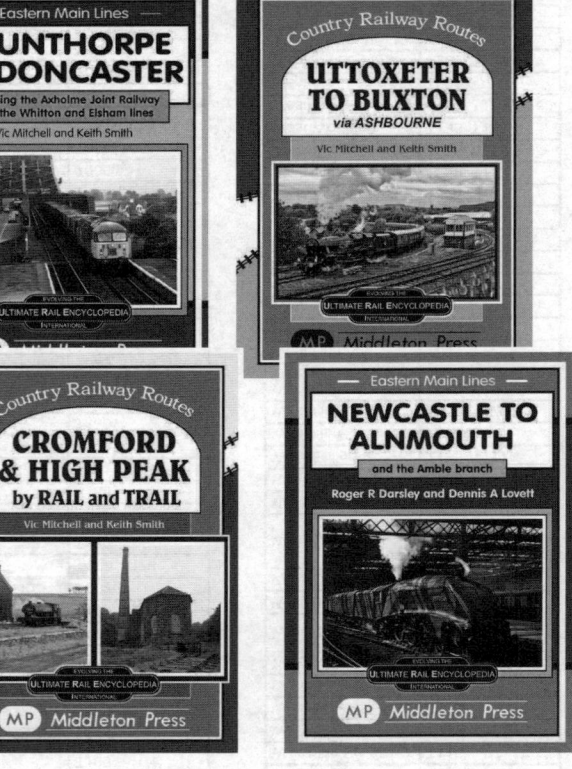

Leisurely armchair journeys back in time.
Each station is visited in geographical order.
Photographs give a visual history of each location.
Over 400 albums bound in attractive glossy hardback covers.

MP Middleton Press

Easebourne Lane, Midhurst, West Sussex, GU29 9AZ
Tel: 01730 813169 ● sales@middletonpress.co.uk
● www.middletonpress.co.uk

Table T001-F

Mondays to Fridays

16 December to 15 May

London - Southend Central and Shoeburyness

Miles	Miles	Miles	Miles	Station	CC MX A	CC MO B	CC MX A	CC MO A	CC MX A	CC MO A	CC MX A	CC MX A	CC MX A	CC MX C	CC MO	CC MX	CC MX A	CC MX	CC MX	CC	CC	CC
0	0	0	—	**London Fenchurch St** ⊖ d										00 11	00 11	00 19		00 25	00 34		05 00	
1¾	1¾	1¾	—	Limehouse d										00 15	00 15	00 23		00 29	00 38		05 04	
4	4	4	—	West Ham ⊖ d									00 04	00 20	00 20	00 28		00 34	00 43		05 09	
—	—	—	0	**London Liverpool St** ⊖ d																		
—	—	—	4	Stratford ⊖ d																		
7½	7½	7½	8	Barking ⊖ d							00 03		00 09	00 25	00 26	00 33		00 39	00 49	04 53	05 14	05 20
15¼	—	15¼	—	Upminster ⊖ d						00 05	00 11	00 04		00 33	00 34	00 41			00 57	05 01	05 22	
—	—	18½	—	Ockendon d								00 09		00 39						05 06		
—	—	21	—	Chafford Hundred Lakeside d								00 13		00 42						05 10		
—	10½	—	—	Dagenham Dock d									00 14					00 44				05 24
—	12¾	—	—	Rainham d									00 17					00 47				05 28
—	16	—	—	Purfleet d									00 22					00 52				05 33
—	19¾	23	—	Grays d								00 18	00a30	00 46				00a59		05 15		05a40
—	21½	24¾	—	Tilbury Town d								00 21		00 49						05 18		
—	25¼	28¼	—	East Tilbury d								00 27		00 55						05 24		
—	27¼	30½	—	Stanford-le-Hope d				00 01				00 30		00 59						05 27		
19¾	—	—	—	West Horndon d						00 10	00 16				00 39	00 46			01 02		05 27	
22¾	—	—	—	Laindon d			00 01			00 15	00 21				00 44	00 51			01 07		05 32	
24¼	—	—	—	Basildon d			00 04			00 18	00 24				00 47	00 54	←		01 10		05 35	
26½	32½	35¾	—	Pitsea d			00 08	00 09	00 12	00 22	00 28	00 39		01 07	00 51	00 58	01 07		01 14	05 35	05 39	
29¼	35¼	38½	—	Benfleet d		00 03	00 11	00 13	00 16	00 25	00 31	00 42		→	00 54	01 01	01 11		01 17	05 39	05 42	
32½	38½	41¾	—	Leigh-on-Sea d		00 07	00 16	00 17	00 20	00 30	00 36	00 47			00 59	01 06	01 15		01 22	05 43	05 47	
33¾	39¾	43	—	Chalkwell d		00 10	00 18	00 20	00 23	00 32	00 38	00 49			01 01	01 08	01 18		01 24	05 46	05 49	
34¾	40¾	44	—	Westcliff d		00 12	00 20	00 22	00 25	00 34	00 40	00 51			01 03	01 10	01 20		01 26	05 48	05 51	
35¾	41¾	45	—	Southend Central a		00 14	00 23	00 24	00 27	00 37	00 43	00 54			01 06	01 13	01 22		01 29	05 51	05 54	
—	—	—	—	d		00 15	00 23	00 25	00 27	00 37	00 43	00 54			01 06	01 13	01 22		01 29		05 55	
36½	42½	45¾	—	Southend East d		00 17	00 25	00 27	00 29	00 39	00 45	00 56			01 08	01 15	01 24		01 31		05 57	
38	44	47¼	—	Thorpe Bay d	00 03	00 19	00 28	00 29	00 32	00 42	00 48	00 58			01 11	01 18	01 27		01 34		05 59	
39½	45½	48¾	—	**Shoeburyness** a	00 07	00 25	00 32	00 35	00 36	00 48	00 52	01 02			01 17	01 22	01 31		01 38		06 03	

Station	CC	CC	CC	CC	CC	CC	CC	CC	CC	CC	CC	CC	CC	CC	CC	CC	CC	CC	CC	CC	CC	CC
London Fenchurch St ⊖ d	05 07	05 24	05 30	05 40		06 00	06 04	06 08	06 19	06 26	06 35	06 39	06 42	06 46	06 49	06 56	06 59	07 02	07 07	07 13	07 17	07 20
Limehouse d	05 11	05 28	05 34	05 44		06 05	06 08	06 13	06 23	06 31	06 40	06 44	06 46	06 50	06 53		07 03	07 06	07 12		07 21	07 25
West Ham ⊖ d	05 16	05 33	05 39	05 49		06 10	06 13	06 18	06 28	06 36	06 45	06 49	06 51	06 55	06 59		07 08	07 11	07 17		07 27	07 30
London Liverpool St ⊖ d																						
Stratford ⊖ d																						
Barking ⊖ d	05 22	05 39	05 44	05 54	06 01	06 16	06 18	06 24	06 34	06 43	06 50	06 54	06 57	07 01	07 04	07 09	07 14	07 17	07 23	07 27	07 34	07 36
Upminster ⊖ d	05 30		05 53	06 02			06 26	06 32	06 42		06 59	07 03		07 09	07 13		07 23		07 33			07 44
Ockendon d	05 36			06 08				06 40				07 10							07 40			
Chafford Hundred Lakeside d	05 39			06 11				06 43				07 14							07 44			
Dagenham Dock d		05 43			06 05	06 20				06 47			07 01					07 21			07 38	
Rainham d		05 47			06 09	06 24				06 51			07 05					07 25			07 42	
Purfleet d		05 52			06 14	06 29				06 56			07 10					07 30			07 47	
Grays d	05 44	05a59		06 16	06a21	06a36		06 48		07a04		07a21	07 16					07a37	07 48		07a54	
Tilbury Town d	05 47			06 19				06 51					07 19						07 51			
East Tilbury d	05 53			06 25				06 57					07 25						07 57			
Stanford-le-Hope d	05 56			06 28				07 00					07 29						08 01			
West Horndon d			05 58				06 31				07 04						07 28					
Laindon d			06 03				06 36		06 50		07 09			07 18	07 21	07a24	07 34					07 52
Basildon d			06 06				06 39		06 54		07 12			07 21	07 25		07 38			07 45		07 56
Pitsea d	06 04		06 10	06 39			06 43	07a08			07 16		07a38	07 25	07 29		07 42		08a09			07 59
Benfleet d	06 08		06 13	06 42			06 46		06 59		07 20			07 28	07 33		07 45					08 03
Leigh-on-Sea d	06 13		06 18	06 47			06 51		07 04		07 25			07 33	07 38		07 50			07a54		08 07
Chalkwell d	06 15		06 20	06 49			06 53		07 06		07 27			07 36	07 41		07 53					08 10
Westcliff d	06 17		06 22	06 51			06 55		07 08		07 29			07 38	07 43		07 55					08 12
Southend Central a	06 20		06 25	06 55			06 58		07 11		07 32			07 41	07 46		07 58					08 14
d			06 25				06 58		07 11		07 32			07 41	07 47		07 58					08 15
Southend East d			06 27				07 00		07 13		07 34			07 43	07 49		08 00					08 17
Thorpe Bay d			06 29				07 03		07 16		07 37			07 46	07 51		08 03					08 19
Shoeburyness a			06 33				07 08		07 23		07 43			07 50	07 55		08 07					08 23

Station	CC	CC	CC	CC	CC	CC	CC	CC	CC	CC	CC	CC	CC	CC	CC	CC	CC	CC	CC	CC	CC	CC D
London Fenchurch St ⊖ d	07 26	07 29	07 32	07 35	07 37	07 40	07 44	07 47	07 50	07 52	07 56	07 59	08 02	08 05	08 08	08 11	08 14	08 17	08 20	08 26	08 32	08 35
Limehouse d	07 30	07 33	07 36	07 39	07 42		07 48	07 51	07 54	07 57		08 03	08 06	08 09			08 18		08 24	08 30		08 40
West Ham ⊖ d	07 35	07 38	07 41	07 44	07 47	07 50	07 53	07 56	07 59	08 02	08 05	08 08	08 11	08 14		08 19	08 24	08 27	08 30	08 35	08 40	08 45
London Liverpool St ⊖ d																						
Stratford ⊖ d																						
Barking ⊖ d	07 40	07 43	07 47	07 49	07 53	07 55	07 58	08 02	08 05	08 07	08 10	08 13	08 17	08 19		08 24	08 30	08 32	08 35	08 42	08 46	08 52
Upminster ⊖ d				07 57	08 02							08 22		08 27		08 33			08 43		08 54	09 03
Ockendon d					08 10											08 40						09 10
Chafford Hundred Lakeside d					08 13											08 44						09 14
Dagenham Dock d			07 51						08 10				08 22				08 35			08 46		
Rainham d			07 55						08 13				08 26				08 39			08 50		
Purfleet d			08 00						08 18				08 31				08 45			08 57		
Grays d			08 06		08 19	08a11			08a25				08a37			08 48	08a52			09a05		09 18
Tilbury Town d			08 09		08 22											08 51						09 21
East Tilbury d			08 15		08 28											08 57						09 27
Stanford-le-Hope d			08 18		08 31											09 00						09 31
West Horndon d				08 02								08 27							08 48		08 59	
Laindon d	07a55	08 00		08 07				08 17		08a22	08 26	08 32		08 35	08 40				08 52		09 03	
Basildon d		08 03		08 10			08 14	08 20			08 29	08 35		08 39	08 43			08 48	08 56		09 07	
Pitsea d		08 06	08a26	08 14	08a39			08 23			08 33	08 39		08 42		09a08			08 59		09 10	09 41
Benfleet d		08 10		08 17				08 27			08 36	08 42		08 46	08 50			08 54	09 03		09 14	→
Leigh-on-Sea d		08 14		08 22			08a26	08 32			08 41	08 47		08 50	08 55			08 59	09 07		09 18	
Chalkwell d		08 17		08 24				08 34			08 43	08 49		08 53	08 58			09 02	09 10		09 21	
Westcliff d		08 19		08 26				08 36			08 45	08 51		08 55	09 00			09 04	09 12		09 23	
Southend Central a		08 22		08 29				08 39			08 48	08 54		08 58	09 02			09 06	09 15		09 25	
d				08 29							08 48				09 03			09 07	09 16		09 26	
Southend East d				08 31							08 50				09 05			09 09	09 18		09 28	
Thorpe Bay d				08 34							08 53				09 08			09 12	09 20		09 30	
Shoeburyness a				08 39							08 57				09 14			09 17	09 24		09 34	

A From London Fenchurch Street
B From London Liverpool Street
C To Shoeburyness
D To Southend Central

For services between London Liverpool Street and Southend Victoria refer to Table T006

Table T001-F

Mondays to Fridays

16 December to 15 May

London - Southend Central and Shoeburyness

Station	CC	CC	CC A	CC	CC	CC B	CC	CC A	CC	CC	CC C	CC	CC A	CC	CC	CC C	CC	CC A	CC	CC	CC C
London Fenchurch St ⊖ d	08 41	08 47		08 50	09 05	09 08	09 20		09 23	09 34	09 41	09 51		09 55	10 04	10 11	10 19		10 25	10 34	10 41
Limehouse d		08 51			09 09	09 13	09 24		09 28	09 39	09 45	09 55		09 59	10 08	10 15	10 23		10 29	10 38	10 45
West Ham ⊖ d	08 51	08 56		08 59	09 14	09 18	09 29		09 33	09 44	09 50	10 00		10 04	10 13	10 20	10 28		10 34	10 43	10 50
London Liverpool St ⊖ d																					
Stratford ⊖ d																					
Barking ⊖ d	08 57	09 01		09 09	09 20	09 24	09 34		09 39	09 49	09 55	10 05		10 09	10 18	10 25	10 33		10 39	10 48	10 55
Upminster ⊖ d		09 09			09 28	09 32	09 42			09 57	10 03	10 13			10 26	10 33	10 41			10 56	11 03
Ockendon d						09 39					10 09					10 39					11 09
Chafford Hundred Lakeside d						09 43					10 13					10 43					11 13
Dagenham Dock d				09 14					09 44					10 14					10 44		
Rainham d				09 17					09 47					10 17					10 47		
Purfleet d				09 22					09 52					10 22					10 52		
Grays d				09a29		09 47			09a59		10 17			10a29		10 47			10a59		11 17
Tilbury Town d						09 50					10 20					10 50					11 20
East Tilbury d						09 56					10 26					10 56					11 26
Stanford-le-Hope d						10 00					10 30					11 00					11 30
West Horndon d		09 14			09 33					10 02					10 31					11 01	
Laindon d	09 13	09 19			09 38		09 50			10 07		10 21			10 36		10 49			11 06	
Basildon d	09 17	09 22	←		09 41		09 54	←		10 10		10 25			10 39		10 53			11 09	
Pitsea d		09 26	09 41		09 45	10 09	09 57	10 09		10 14	10 38		←		10 43	11 09		←		11 13	11 38
Benfleet d	09 23	09 29	09 45		09 48	→	10 01	10 13		10 17	10 42	10 30	10 42		10 46	11 13	10 58	11 13		11 16	11 42
Leigh-on-Sea d	09 27	09 34	09 50		09 53		10 05	10 17		10 22	→	10 35	10 46		10 51	→	11 03	11 17		11 21	→
Chalkwell d	09 30	09 36	09 52		09 56		10 08	10 20		10 24		10 37	10 49		10 53		11 05	11 20		11 23	
Westcliff d	09 32	09 38	09 54		09 58		10 10	10 22		10 26		10 39	10 51		10 55		11 07	11 22		11 25	
Southend Central a	09 34	09 41	09 57		10 00		10 12	10 24		10 29		10 42	10 54		10 58		11 10	11 25		11 28	
d	09 35	09 41			10 00		10 13	10 25		10 29		10 42			10 58		11 10			11 28	
Southend East d	09 37	09 43			10 02		10 15	10 27		10 31		10 44			11 00		11 12			11 30	
Thorpe Bay d	09 39	09 46			10 05		10 17	10 29		10 34		10 47			11 03		11 15			11 33	
Shoeburyness a	09 44	09 50			10 09		10 21	10 33		10 38		10 51			11 07		11 19			11 37	

Station	CC	CC A	CC	CC	CC C	CC	CC A	CC	CC	CC C	CC	CC A	CC	CC	CC C	CC	CC A	CC	CC	CC C	CC	CC A
London Fenchurch St ⊖ d	10 49		10 55	11 04	11 12	11 19		11 25	11 34	11 39	11 49		11 55	12 04	12 11	12 19		12 25	12 34	12 41	12 49	
Limehouse d	10 53		10 59	11 08	11 16	11 23		11 29	11 38	11 43	11 53		11 59	12 08	12 15	12 23		12 29	12 38	12 45	12 53	
West Ham ⊖ d	10 58		11 04	11 13	11 21	11 28		11 34	11 43	11 48	11 58		12 04	12 13	12 20	12 28		12 34	12 43	12 50	12 58	
London Liverpool St ⊖ d																						
Stratford ⊖ d																						
Barking ⊖ d	11 03		11 09	11 18	11 26	11 33		11 39	11 48	11 53	12 03		12 09	12 18	12 25	12 33		12 39	12 48	12 55	13 03	
Upminster ⊖ d	11 11			11 26	11 34	11 41			11 56	12 02	12 11			12 26	12 33	12 41			12 56	13 03	13 11	
Ockendon d					11 40					12 07					12 39					13 09		
Chafford Hundred Lakeside d					11 44					12 11					12 43					13 13		
Dagenham Dock d			11 14					11 44					12 14					12 44				
Rainham d			11 17					11 47					12 17					12 47				
Purfleet d			11 22					11 52					12 22					12 52				
Grays d			11a29		11 48			11a59		12 17			12a29		12 47			12a59		13 17		
Tilbury Town d					11 51					12 20					12 50					13 20		
East Tilbury d					11 57					12 26					12 56					13 26		
Stanford-le-Hope d					12 01					12 30					13 00					13 30		
West Horndon d				11 31					12 01					12 31					13 01			
Laindon d	11 19			11 36		11 49			12 06		12 19			12 36		12 49			13 06		13 19	
Basildon d	11 23			11 39		11 53			12 09		12 23			12 39		12 53			13 09		13 23	
Pitsea d		←		11 43	12 09		←		12 13	12 38		←		12 43	13 08		←		13 13	13 38		←
Benfleet d	11 28	11 42		11 46	12 13	11 58	12 13		12 16	12 42	12 28	12 42		12 46	13 12	12 58	13 12		13 16	13 42	13 28	13 42
Leigh-on-Sea d	11 33	11 46		11 51	→	12 03	12 17		12 21	→	12 33	12 46		12 51	→	13 03	13 16		13 21	→	13 33	13 46
Chalkwell d	11 35	11 49		11 53		12 05	12 20		12 23		12 35	12 49		12 53		13 05	13 19		13 23		13 35	13 49
Westcliff d	11 37	11 51		11 55		12 07	12 22		12 25		12 37	12 51		12 55		13 07	13 21		13 25		13 37	13 51
Southend Central a	11 40	11 54		11 58		12 10	12 25		12 28		12 40	12 54		12 58		13 10	13 24		13 28		13 40	13 54
d	11 40			11 58		12 10			12 28		12 40			12 58		13 10			13 28		13 40	
Southend East d	11 42			12 00		12 12			12 30		12 42			13 00		13 12			13 30		13 42	
Thorpe Bay d	11 45			12 03		12 15			12 33		12 45			13 03		13 15			13 33		13 45	
Shoeburyness a	11 49			12 07		12 19			12 37		12 50			13 07		13 19			13 38		13 49	

Station	CC	CC	CC C	CC	CC A	CC	CC	CC C	CC	CC A	CC	CC	CC C	CC	CC A	CC	CC	CC C	CC	CC A	CC
London Fenchurch St ⊖ d	12 55	13 04	13 11	13 19		13 25	13 34	13 41	13 49		13 55	14 04	14 11	14 19		14 25	14 34	14 41	14 49		14 55
Limehouse d	12 59	13 08	13 16	13 23		13 29	13 38	13 45	13 53		13 59	14 08	14 15	14 23		14 29	14 38	14 45	14 53		14 59
West Ham ⊖ d	13 04	13 13	13 21	13 28		13 34	13 43	13 50	13 58		14 04	14 13	14 20	14 28		14 34	14 43	14 50	14 58		15 04
London Liverpool St ⊖ d																					
Stratford ⊖ d																					
Barking ⊖ d	13 09	13 18	13 26	13 33		13 39	13 48	13 55	14 03		14 09	14 18	14 25	14 33		14 39	14 48	14 55	15 03		15 09
Upminster ⊖ d		13 26	13 34	13 41			13 56	14 03	14 11			14 26	14 33	14 41			14 56	15 03	15 11		
Ockendon d			13 39					14 09					14 39					15 09			
Chafford Hundred Lakeside d			13 43					14 13					14 43					15 13			
Dagenham Dock d	13 14					13 44					14 14					14 44					15 14
Rainham d	13 17					13 47					14 17					14 47					15 17
Purfleet d	13 22					13 52					14 22					14 52					15 22
Grays d	13a29		13 47			13a59		14 17			14a29		14 47			14a59		15 17			15a29
Tilbury Town d			13 50					14 20					14 50					15 20			
East Tilbury d			13 56					14 26					14 56					15 26			
Stanford-le-Hope d			14 00					14 30					15 00					15 30			
West Horndon d		13 31					14 01					14 31					15 01				
Laindon d		13 36		13 49			14 06		14 19			14 36		14 49			15 06		15 19		
Basildon d		13 39		13 53			14 09		14 23			14 39		14 53			15 09		15 23		
Pitsea d		13 43	14 08		←		14 13	14 38		←		14 43	15 08		←		15 13	15 38		←	
Benfleet d		13 46	14 12	13 58	14 12		14 16	14 42	14 28	14 42		14 46	15 12	14 58	15 12		15 16	15 42	15 28	15 42	
Leigh-on-Sea d		13 51	→	14 03	14 16		14 21	→	14 33	14 46		14 51	→	15 03	15 16		15 21	→	15 33	15 46	
Chalkwell d		13 53		14 05	14 19		14 23		14 35	14 49		14 53		15 05	15 19		15 23		15 35	15 49	
Westcliff d		13 55		14 07	14 21		14 25		14 37	14 51		14 55		15 07	15 21		15 25		15 37	15 51	
Southend Central a		13 58		14 10	14 25		14 28		14 40	14 54		14 58		15 10	15 24		15 28		15 40	15 54	
d		13 58		14 10			14 28		14 40			14 58		15 10			15 28		15 40		
Southend East d		14 00		14 12			14 30		14 42			15 00		15 12			15 30		15 42		
Thorpe Bay d		14 03		14 15			14 33		14 45			15 03		15 15			15 33		15 45		
Shoeburyness a		14 07		14 19			14 37		14 49			15 07		15 19			15 37		15 50		

A From London Fenchurch Street
B To Shoeburyness
C To Southend Central

For services between London Liverpool Street and Southend Victoria refer to Table T006

London - Southend Central and Shoeburyness

		CC	CC A	CC	CC B	CC	CC	CC	CC	CC		CC	CC	CC	CC	CC	CC	CC	CC	CC		CC	CC	CC C	CC
London Fenchurch St 7 ⊖	d	15 04	15 11	15 19		15 25	15 34	15 41	15 49	15 55		16 00	16 04	16 07	16 10	16 16	16 19	16 22	16 25	16 28		16 31	16 34	16 37	16 40
Limehouse	d	15 08	15 15	15 23		15 29	15 38	15 45	15 53	15 59		16 05	16 09	16 12	16 15	16 21	16 24	16 27	16 30	16 33		16 36	16 39	16 42	16 45
West Ham ⊖	d	15 13	15 20	15 28		15 35	15 44	15 50	15 59	16 05		16 10	16 14	16 17	16 21	16 26	16 29	16 32	16 35	16 38		16 41	16 44	16 47	16 50
London Liverpool St 15 ⊖	d																								
Stratford 7 ⊖	d																								
Barking ⊖	d	15 18	15 25	15 33		15 40	15 49	15 56	16 04	16 11		16 16	16 20	16 23	16 26	16 32	16 35	16 38	16 41	16 44				16 53	16 56
Upminster ⊖	d	15 26	15 33	15 41			15 58	16 04	16 13			16 24	16 29		16 35	16 40	16 44		16 49	16 53			16 59		17 04
Ockendon	d		15 39					16 10							16 40				16 57						17 10
Chafford Hundred Lakeside	d		15 43					16 14							16 44				17 01						17 14
Dagenham Dock	d					15 45				16 16				16 28				16 42						16 57	
Rainham	d					15 49				16 20				16 31				16 46						17 01	
Purfleet	d					15 55				16 25				16 36				16 52						17 07	
Grays	d		15 47			16a01		16 19		16a31				16a44	16 49			16 58	17a08					17 13	17a22
Tilbury Town 3	d		15 50					16 22							16 52			17 01						17 16	
East Tilbury	d		15 56					16 28							16 58			17 07						17 22	
Stanford-le-Hope	d		16 00					16 32							17 01			17 11						17 26	
West Horndon	d	15 31					16 03						16 34				16 49						17 04		
Laindon	d	15 36		15 49			16 07		16 21				16 39			16 49	16 54					17 04	17 09		
Basildon	d	15 39		15 53			16 10		16 24			16 34	16 42				16 57			17 02			17 13		
Pitsea	d	15 43	16 08		←		16 14	16a40					16 46		17a11		17 01	17a21					17 16	17 41	
Benfleet	d	15 46	16 11	15 58	16 11		16 17		16 30			16 40	16 50				17 05			17 09			17 20	→	
Leigh-on-Sea	d	15 51	→	16 03	16 16		16 22		16 34			16 45	16 55				17 10			17a16			17 25		
Chalkwell	d	15 53		16 05	16 18		16 24		16 37			16 47	16 57			17 01	17 12					17 19	17 28		
Westcliff	d	15 55		16 09	16 20		16 27		16 39			16 49	16 59			17 03	17 14					17 21	17 30		
Southend Central	a	15 58		16 12	16 24		16 29		16 41			16 52	17 04			17 05	17 19					17 23	17 35		
	d	15 58		16 12			16 30		16 42			16 52				17 06						17 24			
Southend East	d	16 00		16 14			16 32		16 44			16 54				17 08						17 26			
Thorpe Bay	d	16 03		16 17			16 34		16 46			16 57				17 10						17 28			
Shoeburyness	a	16 07		16 21			16 38		16 52			17 03				17 16						17 34			

		CC	CC D	CC	CC	CC		CC	CC B	CC	CC	CC	CC	CC	CC	CC		CC	CC	CC	CC	CC	CC	CC	CC
London Fenchurch St 7 ⊖	d	16 45		16 51	16 54	16 57		17 01		17 04	17 07	17 10	17 13	17 16	17 19	17 22		17 25	17 28	17 31	17 34	17 37	17 40	17 43	17 46
Limehouse	d	16 50		16 56	16 59	17 02		17 06		17 09	17 12	17 15	17 18	17 21	17 24	17 27		17 30	17 33	17 36	17 39	17 42	17 45	17 48	17 51
West Ham ⊖	d	16 55		17 01	17 04	17 07				17 14	17 17		17 23	17 26	17 29	17 32		17 35		17 41	17 44	17 47	17 50	17 53	
London Liverpool St 15 ⊖	d																								
Stratford 7 ⊖	d																								
Barking ⊖	d	17 01		17 07	17 10	17 13		17 16		17 20	17 24	17 26				17 39		17 41	17 44		17 50	17 54			18 01
Upminster ⊖	d	17 09			17 18	17 22				17 29		17 34	17 38		17 44			17 49		17 55	17 59		18 04		18 11
Ockendon	d				17 26							17 40						17 57					18 10		
Chafford Hundred Lakeside	d				17 30							17 44						18 01					18 14		
Dagenham Dock	d			17 12							17 29					17 44						17 59			
Rainham	d			17 16							17 33					17 48						18 03			
Purfleet	d			17 21							17 38					17 53						18 08			
Grays	d			17 27	17a37						17 44	17a50				17 59		18a07				18 14	18a21		
Tilbury Town 3	d			17 30							17 47					18 02						18 17			
East Tilbury	d			17 36							17 53					18 08						18 23			
Stanford-le-Hope	d			17 40							17 57					18 12						18 27			
West Horndon	d	17 14								17 34					17 49						18 04				
Laindon	d	17 19				17 30				17 39			17 46	17 50	17 54				18 00		18 09			18 15	18 19
Basildon	d	17 23	←					17 35		17 43				17 54	17 58					18 06	18 12				18 23
Pitsea	d	17 26	17 41	17a50					←	17 46	18a07				18 01	18a22					18 16	18a37			
Benfleet	d	17 30	17 45			17 37		17 41	17 45	17 50			17 54		18 05				18 09	18 12	18 20			18 24	18 29
Leigh-on-Sea	d	17 35	→			17a44		17 46	17 50	17 55			18a01		18 10				18a16		18 25			18 29	18a35
Chalkwell	d	17 38						17 49	17 52	17 58				18 04	18 13					18 18	18 27			18 31	
Westcliff	d	17 40						17 51	17 54	18 00				18 07	18 15					18 20	18 29			18 33	
Southend Central	a	17 42						17 53	17 57	18 02				18 09	18 17					18 23	18 32			18 36	
	d	17 43						17 54	17 57	18 03				18 10	18 18					18 23	18 32			18 36	
Southend East	d	17 45						17 56	17 59	18 05				18 12	18 20					18 25	18 34			18 38	
Thorpe Bay	d	17 47						17 58	18 02	18 07				18 15	18 22					18 28	18 37			18 41	
Shoeburyness	a	17 54						18 03	18 07	18 14				18 19	18 28					18 33	18 43			18 46	

		CC		CC	CC	CC	CC	CC	CC	CC	CC	CC		CC	CC	CC A	CC	CC	CC	CC A	CC	CC B		CC	CC E
London Fenchurch St 7 ⊖	d	17 49		17 52	17 55	17 58	18 01	18 04	18 07	18 10	18 13	18 16		18 19	18 22	18 25	18 31	18 34	18 37	18 40	18 46			18 52	
Limehouse	d	17 54		17 57	18 00	18 03	18 06	18 09	18 12	18 15	18 18	18 21		18 24	18 27	18 30	18 36	18 39	18 42	18 45	18 51			18 57	
West Ham ⊖	d	17 59		18 02		18 08	18 11	18 14		18 20	18 23	18 26		18 29	18 32	18 35	18 41		18 47	18 50	18 56			19 02	
London Liverpool St 15 ⊖	d																								
Stratford 7 ⊖	d																								
Barking ⊖	d			18 09	18 11		18 17	18 20	18 23	18 26				18 35	18 38			18 50	18 53	18 56				19 08	
Upminster ⊖	d	18 14			18 19		18 26	18 29		18 34				18 44		18 48	18 54	18 59		19 04				19 16	
Ockendon	d				18 27					18 40						18 57				19 10					
Chafford Hundred Lakeside	d				18 31					18 44						19 01				19 14					
Dagenham Dock	d			18 13					18 27						18 43				18 57						
Rainham	d			18 17					18 31						18 47				19 01						
Purfleet	d			18 23					18 37						18 52				19 07						
Grays	d			18 29	18a38				18 43	18a50					18 58	19 05			19a15	19 18					
Tilbury Town 3	d			18 32					18 46						19 01	19 08				19 21					
East Tilbury	d			18 38					18 52						19 07	19 14				19 27					
Stanford-le-Hope	d			18 42					18 56						19 10	19 18				19 31					
West Horndon	d	18 19						18 34						18 49				19 04						19 21	
Laindon	d	18 24				18 31		18 39				18 48		18 54				19 09			19 15			19 26	
Basildon	d	18 28					18 36	18 43						18 58			19 04	19 13			19 19	←		19 30	←
Pitsea	d	18 31		18a52				18 46	19a06					19 01	19a20	19 28		19 16		19 42		19 28		19 33	19 42
Benfleet	d	18 35				18 39	18 43	18 50			18 54			19 05		→	19 10	19 20		→	19 25	19 31		19 37	19 46
Leigh-on-Sea	d	18 40				18 44	18 50	18 55			19a01			19 10			19 15	19 25			19 30	19 36		19 42	→
Chalkwell	d	18 43				18 47		18 58				19 04		19 13			19 17	19 27			19 32	19 38		19 45	
Westcliff	d	18 45				18 49		19 00				19 06		19 15			19 19	19 29			19 34	19 40		19 47	
Southend Central	a	18 48				18 52	18 58	19 02				19 08		19 17			19 22	19 34			19 37	19 44		19 49	
	d	18 48				18 52		19 03				19 09		19 18			19 22				19 37			19 50	
Southend East	d	18 50				18 54		19 05				19 11		19 20			19 24				19 39			19 52	
Thorpe Bay	d	18 53				18 57		19 07				19 13		19 22			19 27				19 42			19 54	
Shoeburyness	a	18 58				19 02		19 13				19 20		19 28			19 33				19 48			20 00	

A To Southend Central
B From London Fenchurch Street
C To Shoeburyness
D From London Fenchurch Street to Shoeburyness
E From London Fenchurch Street to Southend Central

For services between London Liverpool Street and Southend Victoria refer to Table T006

Table T001-F

Mondays to Fridays

16 December to 15 May

London - Southend Central and Shoeburyness

		CC	CC	CC A	CC	CC B	CC	CC A		CC	CC	CC C	CC	CC A	CC	CC	CC C	CC		CC A	CC	CC	CC C	CC	CC A
London Fenchurch St 7 ⊖	d	18 55	19 03		19 06	19 11	19 20			19 25	19 34	19 41	19 49		19 56	20 05	20 11	20 19			20 25	20 34	20 41	20 49	
Limehouse	d	19 00	19 08		19 11	19 15	19 25			19 29	19 38	19 45	19 53		20 00	20 09	20 15	20 23			20 29	20 38	20 45	20 53	
West Ham ⊖	d	19 05	19 13		19 16	19 20	19 30			19 34	19 43	19 50	19 58		20 05	20 14	20 20	20 28			20 34	20 43	20 50	20 58	
London Liverpool St 15 ⊖	d																								
Stratford 7 ⊖	d																								
Barking ⊖	d	19 11			19 22	19 25	19 36			19 40	19 49	19 55	20 04		20 11	20 19	20 25	20 33			20 40	20 48	20 55	21 03	
Upminster ⊖	d				19 30	19 33	19 44				19 57	20 03	20 12			20 27	20 33	20 41				20 56	21 03	21 11	
Ockendon	d					19 39						20 09					20 39						21 09		
Chafford Hundred Lakeside	d					19 43						20 13					20 43						21 13		
Dagenham Dock	d	19 15								19 44					20 15						20 44				
Rainham	d	19 19								19 48					20 19						20 48				
Purfleet	d	19 25								19 54					20 25						20 55				
Grays	d	19 31				19 47				20a01		20 17			20a32		20 48				21a01		21 17		
Tilbury Town 3	d	19 34				19 50						20 20					20 51						21 20		
East Tilbury	d	19 40				19 56						20 26					20 57						21 26		
Stanford-le-Hope	d	19 44				20 00						20 30					21 01						21 30		
West Horndon	d				19 35						20 02					20 32						21 01			
Laindon	d		19 32		19 40		19 53				20 06		20 20			20 37		20 49				21 06		21 19	
Basildon	d		19 36		19 44		19 56	←			20 10		20 23			20 40		20 53				21 09		21 23	
Pitsea	d	19a54		←	19 48	20 08	20 00	20 08			20 13	20 38		←		20 44	21 09			←		21 13	21 38		←
Benfleet	d		19 42	19 46	19 52	→	20 03	20 12			20 17	20 42	20 29	20 42		20 47	21 12	20 58		21 12		21 16	21 42	21 28	21 42
Leigh-on-Sea	d		19 47	19 51	19 57		20 08	20 16			20 22	→	20 33	20 46		20 52	→	21 03		21 17		21 21	→	21 33	21 46
Chalkwell	d		19 49	19 53	19 59		20 10	20 19			20 25		20 36	20 49		20 54		21 05		21 19		21 23		21 35	21 49
Westcliff	d		19 51	19 55	20 01		20 12	20 21			20 27		20 38	20 51		20 56		21 07		21 21		21 25		21 37	21 51
Southend Central	a		19 54	19 59	20 04		20 15	20 23			20 29		20 40	20 55		20 59		21 10		21 25		21 28		21 40	21 55
	d		19 54		20 04		20 15	20 24			20 30		20 41			20 59		21 10				21 28		21 40	
Southend East	d		19 56		20 06		20 17	20 26			20 32		20 43			21 01		21 12				21 30		21 42	
Thorpe Bay	d		19 59		20 09		20 20	20 28			20 34		20 45			21 04		21 15				21 33		21 45	
Shoeburyness	a		20 03		20 13		20 24	20 32			20 39		20 49			21 08		21 19				21 37		21 49	

		CC	CC	CC C		CC	CC A	CC	CC	CC C	CC	CC A	CC	CC		CC B	CC	CC	CC A	CC B	CC	CC A	CC	CC	
London Fenchurch St 7 ⊖	d	20 55	21 04	21 11		21 19		21 25	21 34	21 41	21 49		21 55	22 04		22 11	22 25	22 29		22 41	22 49		22 55	23 04	
Limehouse	d	20 59	21 08	21 15		21 23		21 29	21 38	21 45	21 53		21 59	22 08		22 15	22 29	22 33		22 45	22 53		22 59	23 08	
West Ham ⊖	d	21 04	21 13	21 20		21 28		21 34	21 43	21 50	21 58		22 04	22 13		22 20	22 34	22 38		22 50	22 58		23 04	23 13	
London Liverpool St 15 ⊖	d																								
Stratford 7 ⊖	d																								
Barking ⊖	d	21 09	21 18	21 25		21 33		21 39	21 49	21 55	22 03		22 09	22 18		22 25	22 39	22 43		22 55	23 03		23 09	23 18	
Upminster ⊖	d		21 26	21 33		21 41			21 57	22 03	22 11			22 26		22 33		22 51		23 03	23 11			23 26	
Ockendon	d			21 39						22 09						22 39				23 09					
Chafford Hundred Lakeside	d			21 43						22 13						22 43				23 13					
Dagenham Dock	d	21 14						21 44					22 14				22 44						23 14		
Rainham	d	21 17						21 47					22 17				22 47						23 17		
Purfleet	d	21 22						21 52					22 22				22 52						23 22		
Grays	d	21a29		21 47				21a59		22 17			22a29			22 47	22a59			23 17			23a29		
Tilbury Town 3	d			21 50						22 20						22 50				23 20					
East Tilbury	d			21 56						22 26						22 56				23 26					
Stanford-le-Hope	d			22 00						22 30						23 00				23 30					
West Horndon	d		21 31						22 02					22 31				22 56			23 16			23 31	
Laindon	d		21 36			21 49			22 07		22 19			22 36				23 01			23 21			23 36	
Basildon	d		21 39			21 53			22 10		22 23			22 39				23 04	←		23 24	←		23 39	
Pitsea	d		21 43	22 08			←		22 14	22 38		←		22 43		23 12		23 08	23 12	23 38	23 28	23 38		23 43	
Benfleet	d		21 46	22 12		21 58	22 12		22 18	22 42	22 28	22 42		22 46		→		23 11	23 16	→	23 31	23 42		23 46	
Leigh-on-Sea	d		21 51	→		22 03	22 16		22 23	→	22 33	22 46		22 51				23 16	23 20		23 36	23 46		23 51	
Chalkwell	d		21 53			22 05	22 19		22 25		22 35	22 49		22 53				23 18	23 23		23 38	23 49		23 53	
Westcliff	d		21 55			22 07	22 21		22 27		22 37	22 51		22 55				23 20	23 25		23 40	23 51		23 55	
Southend Central	a		21 58			22 10	22 25		22 30		22 40	22 55		22 58				23 23	23 27		23 43	23 54		23 58	
	d		21 58			22 10			22 30		22 40			22 58				23 23	23 28		23 43	23 54		23 58	
Southend East	d		22 00			22 12			22 32		22 42			23 00				23 25	23 30		23 45	23 56		23 59	
Thorpe Bay	d		22 03			22 15			22 35		22 45			23 03				23 28	23 32		23 48	23 58		00 03	
Shoeburyness	a		22 07			22 19			22 39		22 49			23 07				23 32	23 36		23 52	00 03		00 07	

		CC B	CC	CC	CC A	CC B	CC	CC A	CC
London Fenchurch St 7 ⊖	d	23 11	23 25	23 29		23 41	23 49		23 55
Limehouse	d	23 15	23 29	23 33		23 45	23 53		23 59
West Ham ⊖	d	23 20	23 34	23 38		23 50	23 58		00 04
London Liverpool St 15 ⊖	d								
Stratford 7 ⊖	d								
Barking ⊖	d	23 25	23 39	23 43		23 55	00 03		00 09
Upminster ⊖	d	23 33		23 51		00 04	00 11		
Ockendon	d	23 39				00 09			
Chafford Hundred Lakeside	d	23 43				00 13			
Dagenham Dock	d		23 44						00 14
Rainham	d		23 47						00 17
Purfleet	d		23 52						00 22
Grays	d	23 47	23a59			00 18			00a30
Tilbury Town 3	d	23 50				00 21			
East Tilbury	d	23 56				00 27			
Stanford-le-Hope	d	23 59				00 30			
West Horndon	d			23 56			00 16		
Laindon	d			00 01			00 21		
Basildon	d			00 04	←		00 24	←	
Pitsea	d	00 12		00 08	00 12	00 39	00 28	00 39	
Benfleet	d	→		00 11	00 16	→	00 31	00 42	
Leigh-on-Sea	d			00 16	00 20		00 36	00 47	
Chalkwell	d			00 18	00 23		00 38	00 49	
Westcliff	d			00 20	00 25		00 40	00 51	
Southend Central	a			00 23	00 27		00 43	00 54	
	d			00 23	00 27		00 43	00 54	
Southend East	d			00 25	00 29		00 45	00 56	
Thorpe Bay	d			00 28	00 32		00 48	00 58	
Shoeburyness	a			00 32	00 36		00 52	01 02	

A From London Fenchurch Street
B To Shoeburyness
C To Southend Central

For services between London Liverpool Street and Southend Victoria refer to Table T006

Table T001-F

Saturdays

21 December to 16 May

London - Southend Central and Shoeburyness

		CC A	CC A	CC A	CC A	CC A	CC A	CC B	CC	CC A		CC	CC	CC	CC	CC	CC B	CC	CC A	CC		CC B	CC	CC A	CC
London Fenchurch St 7 ⊖	d							00 11	00 19			00 25	00 34	05 00			05 23	05 28		05 35		05 53	05 58		06 08
Limehouse	d							00 15	00 23			00 29	00 38	05 04			05 27	05 32		05 40		05 57	06 02		06 12
West Ham ⊖	d						00 04	00 20	00 28			00 34	00 43	05 09			05 33	05 37		05 45		06 03	06 07		06 17
London Liverpool St 15 ⊖	d																								
Stratford 7 ⊖	d																								
Barking ⊖	d				00 03		00 09	00 25	00 33			00 39	00 49	05 14	05 08	05 23	05 38	05 42		05 53		06 08	06 12		06 23
Upminster ⊖	d				00 11	00 04		00 33	00 41				00 57	05 23	05 17		05 47	05 51				06 17	06 21		
Ockendon	d					00 09		00 39							05 22		05 52					06 22			
Chafford Hundred Lakeside	d					00 13		00 42							05 26		05 56					06 26			
Dagenham Dock	d						00 14					00 44				05 27				05 57					06 27
Rainham	d						00 17					00 47				05 31				06 01					06 31
Purfleet	d						00 22					00 52				05 36				06 06					06 36
Grays	d					00 18	00a30	00 46				00a59			05 30	05a43	06 00			06a13		06 30			06a43
Tilbury Town 3	d					00 21		00 49							05 33		06 03					06 33			
East Tilbury	d					00 27		00 55							05 39		06 09					06 39			
Stanford-le-Hope	d					00 30		00 59							05 43		06 13					06 43			
West Horndon	d				00 16				00 46				01 02	05 28				05 56					06 26		
Laindon	d		00 01		00 21				00 51				01 07	05 32				06 00					06 30		
Basildon	d		00 04		00 24				00 54	←			01 10	05 36				06 04	←				06 34	←	
Pitsea	d		00 08	00 12	00 28	00 39		01 07	00 58	01 07			01 14	05 39	05 51		06 21	06 07	06 21			06 51	06 37	06 51	
Benfleet	d		00 11	00 16	00 31	00 42		→	01 01	01 11			01 17	05 43	05 55		→	06 11	06 25			→	06 41	06 55	
Leigh-on-Sea	d		00 16	00 20	00 36	00 47			01 06	01 15			01 22	05 47	06 00			06 15	06 30				06 45	07 00	
Chalkwell	d		00 18	00 23	00 38	00 49			01 08	01 18			01 24	05 50	06 02			06 18	06 32				06 48	07 02	
Westcliff	d		00 20	00 25	00 40	00 51			01 10	01 20			01 26	05 52	06 04			06 20	06 34				06 50	07 04	
Southend Central	a		00 23	00 27	00 43	00 54			01 13	01 22			01 29	05 54	06 07			06 22	06 37				06 52	07 07	
	d		00 23	00 27	00 43	00 54			01 13	01 22			01 29	05 55	06 07			06 23	06 37				06 53	07 07	
Southend East	d		00 25	00 29	00 45	00 56			01 15	01 24			01 31	05 57	06 09			06 25	06 39				06 55	07 09	
Thorpe Bay	d	00 03	00 28	00 32	00 48	00 58			01 18	01 27			01 34	05 59	06 12			06 27	06 42				06 57	07 12	
Shoeburyness	a	00 07	00 32	00 36	00 52	01 02			01 22	01 31			01 38	06 05	06 19			06 33	06 49				07 03	07 19	

		CC B	CC	CC A	CC	CC B		CC	CC A	CC	CC B	CC	CC A	CC	CC B	CC		CC A	CC	CC B	CC	CC A	CC	CC	CC B
London Fenchurch St 7 ⊖	d	06 23	06 28		06 38	06 53		06 58		07 08	07 23	07 28		07 38	07 53	07 58			08 08	08 23	08 28		08 38		08 53
Limehouse	d	06 27	06 32		06 42	06 57		07 02		07 12	07 27	07 32		07 42	07 57	08 02			08 12	08 27	08 32		08 42		08 57
West Ham ⊖	d	06 33	06 37		06 47	07 03		07 07		07 17	07 33	07 37		07 47	08 03	08 07			08 17	08 33	08 37		08 47		09 03
London Liverpool St 15 ⊖	d																							08 45	
Stratford 7 ⊖	d																							08 52	
Barking ⊖	d	06 38	06 42		06 53	07 08		07 12		07 23	07 38	07 42		07 53	08 08	08 12			08 23	08 38	08 42		08 53	09 03	09 08
Upminster ⊖	d	06 47	06 51			07 17		07 21			07 47	07 51			08 17	08 21				08 47	08 51			09 13	09 17
Ockendon	d	06 52				07 22					07 52				08 22					08 52					09 22
Chafford Hundred Lakeside	d	06 56				07 26					07 56				08 26					08 56					09 26
Dagenham Dock	d				06 57					07 27				07 57					08 27				08 57		
Rainham	d				07 01					07 31				08 01					08 31				09 01		
Purfleet	d				07 06					07 36				08 06					08 36				09 06		
Grays	d	07 00			07a13	07 30				07a43	08 00			08a13	08 30				08a43	09 00			09a13		09 30
Tilbury Town 3	d	07 03				07 33					08 03				08 33					09 03					09 33
East Tilbury	d	07 09				07 39					08 09				08 39					09 09					09 39
Stanford-le-Hope	d	07 13				07 43					08 13				08 43					09 13					09 43
West Horndon	d		06 56					07 26				07 56				08 26					08 56				
Laindon	d		07 00					07 30				08 00				08 30					09 00			09 21	
Basildon	d		07 04	←				07 34	←			08 04	←			08 34		←			09 04	←		09 24	
Pitsea	d	07 21	07 07	07 21		07 51		07 37	07 51		08 21	08 07	08 21		08 51	08 37		08 51		09 21	09 07	09 21			09 51
Benfleet	d	→	07 11	07 25		→		07 41	07 55		→	08 11	08 25		→	08 41		08 55		→	09 11	09 25		09 30	→
Leigh-on-Sea	d		07 15	07 30				07 45	08 00			08 15	08 30			08 45		09 00			09 15	09 30		09 34	
Chalkwell	d		07 18	07 32				07 48	08 02			08 18	08 32			08 48		09 02			09 18	09 32		09 37	
Westcliff	d		07 20	07 34				07 50	08 04			08 20	08 34			08 50		09 04			09 20	09 34		09 39	
Southend Central	a		07 22	07 37				07 52	08 07			08 22	08 37			08 52		09 07			09 22	09 37		09 41	
	d		07 23	07 37				07 53	08 07			08 23	08 37			08 53		09 07			09 23	09 37		09 42	
Southend East	d		07 25	07 39				07 55	08 09			08 25	08 39			08 55		09 09			09 25	09 39		09 44	
Thorpe Bay	d		07 27	07 42				07 57	08 12			08 27	08 42			08 57		09 12			09 27	09 42		09 46	
Shoeburyness	a		07 33	07 49				08 03	08 19			08 33	08 49			09 03		09 19			09 33	09 49		09 52	

		CC	CC A	CC	CC		CC B	CC	CC A	CC	CC	CC B	CC	CC A	CC	CC		CC B	CC	CC A	CC	CC	CC B	CC
London Fenchurch St 7 ⊖	d	08 58		09 08			20 23	20 28		20 38		20 53	20 58		21 08			21 23	21 28		21 38		21 53	21 58
Limehouse	d	09 02		09 12			20 27	20 32		20 42		20 57	21 02		21 12			21 27	21 32		21 42		21 57	22 02
West Ham ⊖	d	09 07		09 17			20 33	20 37		20 47		21 03	21 07		21 17			21 33	21 37		21 47		22 03	22 07
London Liverpool St 15 ⊖	d				09 15						20 45					21 15						21 45		
Stratford 7 ⊖	d				09 22						20 52					21 22						21 52		
Barking ⊖	d	09 12		09 23	09 33		20 38	20 42		20 53	21 03	21 08	21 12		21 23	21 33		21 38	21 42		21 53	22 03	22 08	22 12
Upminster ⊖	d	09 21			09 43		20 47	20 51			21 13	21 17	21 21			21 43		21 47	21 51			22 13	22 17	22 21
Ockendon	d						20 52					21 22						21 52					22 22	
Chafford Hundred Lakeside	d						20 56					21 26						21 56					22 26	
Dagenham Dock	d			09 27						20 57					21 27						21 57			
Rainham	d			09 31						21 01					21 31						22 01			
Purfleet	d			09 36						21 06					21 36						22 06			
Grays	d			09a43		and at the same minutes past each hour until	21 00			21a13		21 30			21a43			22 00			22a13		22 30	
Tilbury Town 3	d						21 03					21 33						22 03					22 33	
East Tilbury	d						21 09					21 39						22 09					22 39	
Stanford-le-Hope	d						21 13					21 43						22 13					22 43	
West Horndon	d	09 26						20 56					21 26						21 56					22 26
Laindon	d	09 30			09 51			21 00			21 21		21 30			21 51			22 00			22 21		22 30
Basildon	d	09 34	←		09 54			21 04	←		21 24		21 34	←		21 54			22 04	←		22 24		22 34
Pitsea	d	09 37	09 51				21 21	21 07	21 21			21 51	21 37	21 51				22 21	22 07	22 21			22 51	22 37
Benfleet	d	09 41	09 55		10 00		→	21 11	21 25		21 30	→	21 41	21 55		22 00		→	22 11	22 25		22 30	→	22 41
Leigh-on-Sea	d	09 45	10 00		10 04			21 15	21 30		21 34		21 45	22 00		22 04			22 15	22 30		22 34		22 45
Chalkwell	d	09 48	10 02		10 07			21 18	21 32		21 37		21 48	22 02		22 07			22 18	22 32		22 37		22 48
Westcliff	d	09 50	10 04		10 09			21 20	21 34		21 39		21 50	22 04		22 09			22 20	22 34		22 39		22 50
Southend Central	a	09 52	10 07		10 11			21 22	21 37		21 41		21 52	22 07		22 11			22 22	22 37		22 41		22 52
	d	09 53	10 07		10 12			21 23	21 37		21 42		21 53	22 07		22 12			22 23	22 37		22 42		22 53
Southend East	d	09 55	10 09		10 14			21 25	21 39		21 44		21 55	22 09		22 14			22 25	22 39		22 44		22 55
Thorpe Bay	d	09 57	10 12		10 16			21 27	21 42		21 46		21 57	22 12		22 16			22 27	22 42		22 46		22 57
Shoeburyness	a	10 03	10 19		10 22			21 33	21 49		21 52		22 03	22 19		22 22			22 33	22 49		22 52		23 03

A From London Fenchurch Street
B To Shoeburyness

Table T001-F

Saturdays

21 December to 16 May

London - Southend Central and Shoeburyness

		CC A	CC		CC	CC B	CC	CC A	CC	CC	CC B	CC	CC A		CC	CC	CC B	CC	CC A	CC	CC	CC			
London Fenchurch St 7 ⊖	d		22 08			22 23	22 28		22 38		22 53	22 58				23 08	23 23	23 28			23 43	23 59			
Limehouse	d		22 12			22 27	22 32		22 42		22 57	23 02				23 12	23 27	23 32			23 47	00 03			
West Ham ⊖	d		22 17			22 33	22 37		22 47		23 03	23 07				23 17	23 33	23 37			23 53	00 08			
London Liverpool St 15 ⊖	d				22 15					22 45					23 15					23 45					
Stratford 7 ⊖	d				22 23					22 52					23 23					23 52					
Barking ⊖	d		22 23		22 33	22 38	22 42		22 53	23 03	23 08	23 12			23 33	23 23	23 38	23 42		00 05	23 58	00 15			
Upminster ⊖	d				22 43	22 47	22 51			23 13	23 17	23 21			23 43		23 47	23 51		00 14	00 07				
Ockendon	d					22 52					23 22						23 52				00 12				
Chafford Hundred Lakeside	d					22 56					23 26						23 56				00 16				
Dagenham Dock	d		22 27						22 57							23 27						00 19			
Rainham	d		22 31						23 01							23 31						00 23			
Purfleet	d		22 36						23 06							23 36						00 28			
Grays	d		22a43			23 00			23a13		23 30					23 42	00 02				00 20	00 34			
Tilbury Town 3	d					23 03					23 33					23 45	00 05				00 23	00 37			
East Tilbury	d					23 09					23 39					23 51	00 11				00 29	00 43			
Stanford-le-Hope	d					23 13					23 43					23 54	00 14				00 33	00 46			
West Horndon	d						22 56					23 26						23 56		00 19					
Laindon	d				22 51		23 00			23 21		23 30			23 51			23 59		00 24					
Basildon	d	←			22 54		23 04	←		23 24		23 34	←		23 54			00 04	←	00 27					
Pitsea	d	22 51				23 21	23 07	23 21			23 51	23 37	23 51			00 03	00 22	00 07	00 22	00 32	00 41	00 55			
Benfleet	d	22 55			23 00	→	23 11	23 25		23 30	→	23 41	23 55		23 59	00 06	→	00 11	00 26	00 36	00 45	00 58			
Leigh-on-Sea	d	23 00			23 04		23 15	23 30		23 34		23 45	23 59		00 04	00 11		00 15	00 30	00 40	00 49	01 03			
Chalkwell	d	23 02			23 07		23 18	23 32		23 37		23 48	00 02		00 07	00 13		00 18	00 33	00 43	00 52	01 05			
Westcliff	d	23 04			23 09		23 20	23 34		23 39		23 50	00 04		00 09	00 15		00 20	00 35	00 45	00 54	01 07			
Southend Central	a	23 07			23 11		23 22	23 37		23 41		23 52	00 06		00 11	00 18		00 22	00 37	00 47	00 56	01 10			
	d	23 07			23 12		23 23	23 37		23 42		23 53	00 07		00 12	00 18		00 23	00 37	00 48	00 56	01 10			
Southend East	d	23 09			23 14		23 25	23 39		23 44		23 55	00 09		00 14	00 20		00 25	00 39	00 50	00 58	01 12			
Thorpe Bay	d	23 12			23 16		23 27	23 42		23 46		23 57	00 11		00 16	00 22		00 27	00 42	00 52	01 01	01 14			
Shoeburyness	a	23 19			23 22		23 33	23 49		23 52		00 03	00 17		00 22	00 27		00 33	00 48	00 58	01 07	01 19			

Sundays

15 December to 10 May

		CC C	CC D	CC C	CC C	CC C	CC D	CC C	CC	CC C		CC	CC	CC	CC	CC	CC	CC	CC	CC		CC	CC	CC	CC
London Fenchurch St 7 ⊖	d								00 05			00 15	00 41	06 38		07 18	07 23	07 35	07 48	07 53		08 05	08 18	08 23	08 35
Limehouse	d								00 09	00 03		00 19	00 45	06 42		07 22	07 27	07 39	07 52	07 57		08 09	08 22	08 27	08 39
West Ham ⊖	d								00 14	00 08		00 25	00 50	06 47		07 27	07 32	07 44	07 57	08 02		08 14	08 27	08 32	08 44
London Liverpool St 15 ⊖	d																								
Stratford 7 ⊖	d																								
Barking ⊖	d						00 05		00 20	00 15		00 30	00 56	06 53	06 58	07 33	07 38	07 50	08 03	08 08		08 20	08 33	08 38	08 50
Upminster ⊖	d						00 14	00 07	00 28			00 39	01 04	07 02	07 07	07 42	07 46		08 12	08 16			08 42	08 46	
Ockendon	d							00 12				00 44			07 12		07 52			08 22				08 52	
Chafford Hundred Lakeside	d							00 16				00 48			07 16		07 56			08 26				08 56	
Dagenham Dock	d									00 19								07 54				08 24			08 54
Rainham	d									00 23								07 58				08 28			08 58
Purfleet	d									00 28								08 03				08 33			09 03
Grays	d					00 02		00 20		00 34		00 52			07 21		08 00	08a10		08 30		08a40		09 00	09a10
Tilbury Town 3	d					00 05		00 23		00 37		00 55			07 24		08 03			08 33				09 03	
East Tilbury	d					00 11		00 29		00 43		01 01			07 30		08 09			08 39				09 09	
Stanford-le-Hope	d					00 14		00 33		00 46		01 05			07 33		08 13			08 43				09 13	
West Horndon	d						00 19		00 33				01 09	07 07		07 47			08 17				08 47		
Laindon	d						00 24		00 38				01 14	07 12		07 52			08 22				08 52		
Basildon	d				00 04		00 27		00 41				01 17	07 15		07 55			08 25				08 55		
Pitsea	d			00 03	00 07	00 22	00 32	00 41	00 45	00 55		01 13	01 21	07 19	07 42	07 59	08 22		08 29	08 52			08 59	09 22	
Benfleet	d			00 06	00 11	00 26	00 36	00 45	00 48	00 58		01 17	01 24	07 22	07 45	08 02	08 25		08 32	08 55			09 02	09 25	
Leigh-on-Sea	d		00 04	00 11	00 15	00 30	00 40	00 49	00 53	01 03		01 21	01 29	07 27	07 50	08 07	08 30		08 37	09 00			09 07	09 30	
Chalkwell	d	00 02	00 07	00 13	00 18	00 33	00 43	00 52	00 55	01 05		01 24	01 31	07 29	07 52	08 09	08 32		08 39	09 02			09 09	09 32	
Westcliff	d	00 04	00 09	00 15	00 20	00 35	00 45	00 54	00 57	01 07		01 26	01 33	07 31	07 54	08 11	08 34		08 41	09 04			09 11	09 34	
Southend Central	a	00 06	00 11	00 18	00 22	00 37	00 47	00 56	01 00	01 10		01 28	01 36	07 34	07 57	08 14	08 37		08 44	09 07			09 14	09 37	
	d	00 07	00 12	00 18	00 23	00 37	00 48	00 56	01 00	01 10		01 28	01 36	07 34	07 57	08 14	08 37		08 44	09 07			09 14	09 37	
Southend East	d	00 09	00 14	00 20	00 25	00 39	00 50	00 58	01 02	01 12		01 30	01 38	07 36	07 59	08 16	08 39		08 46	09 09			09 16	09 39	
Thorpe Bay	d	00 11	00 16	00 22	00 27	00 42	00 52	01 01	01 05	01 14		01 33	01 41	07 39	08 02	08 19	08 42		08 49	09 12			09 19	09 42	
Shoeburyness	a	00 17	00 22	00 27	00 33	00 48	00 58	01 07	01 11	01 19		01 39	01 47	07 45	08 08	08 25	08 48		08 55	09 18			09 25	09 48	

A From London Fenchurch Street
B To Shoeburyness
C not 15 December. From London Fenchurch Street
D not 15 December. From London Liverpool Street

For services between London Liverpool Street and Southend Victoria refer to Table T006

Table T001-F

Sundays

15 December to 10 May

London - Southend Central and Shoeburyness

		CC	CC	CC	CC	CC	CC	CC	CC	CC	CC		CC	CC	CC	CC	CC	CC	CC	CC	CC	CC	CC
London Fenchurch St 7 ⊖	d	08 48	08 53	09 05	09 18	09 23	09 35		09 53	10 05			20 23	20 35		20 53	21 05		21 23	21 38		21 53	
Limehouse	d	08 52	08 57	09 09	09 22	09 27	09 39		09 57	10 09			20 27	20 39		20 57	21 09		21 27	21 42		21 57	
West Ham ⊖	d	08 57	09 02	09 14	09 27	09 32	09 44		10 02	10 14			20 32	20 44		21 02	21 14		21 32	21 47		22 02	
London Liverpool St 15 ⊖	d							09 45			10 15				20 45			21 15			21 45		22 15
Stratford 7 ⊖	d							09 52			10 22				20 52			21 22			21 52		22 22
Barking ⊖	d	09 03	09 08	09 20	09 33	09 38	09 50	10 03	10 08	10 20	10 33		20 38	20 50	21 03	21 08	21 20	21 33	21 38	21 53	22 03	22 08	22 33
Upminster ⊖	d	09 12	09 16		09 42	09 46		10 12	10 16		10 42		20 46		21 12	21 16		21 42	21 46		22 12	22 16	22 42
Ockendon	d		09 22			09 52			10 22				20 52			21 22			21 52			22 22	
Chafford Hundred Lakeside	d		09 26			09 56			10 26				20 56			21 26			21 56			22 26	
Dagenham Dock	d			09 24			09 54			10 24				20 54			21 24			21 57			
Rainham	d			09 28			09 58			10 28				20 58			21 28			22 01			
Purfleet	d			09 33			10 03			10 33		and at the same minutes past each hour until		21 03			21 33			22 06			
Grays	d		09 30	09a40		10 00	10a10		10 30	10a40			21 00	21a10		21 30	21a40		22 00	22a13		22 30	
Tilbury Town 3	d		09 33			10 03			10 33				21 03			21 33			22 03			22 33	
East Tilbury	d		09 39			10 09			10 39				21 09			21 39			22 09			22 39	
Stanford-le-Hope	d		09 43			10 13			10 43				21 13			21 43			22 13			22 43	
West Horndon	d	09 17			09 47			10 17			10 47				21 17			21 47			22 17		22 47
Laindon	d	09 22			09 52			10 22			10 52				21 22			21 52			22 22		22 52
Basildon	d	09 25			09 55			10 26			10 56				21 26			21 56			22 26		22 56
Pitsea	d	09 29	09 52		09 59	10 22		10 29	10 52		10 59		21 22		21 29	21 52		21 59	22 22		22 29	22 52	22 59
Benfleet	d	09 32	09 55		10 02	10 25		10 33	10 55		11 03		21 25		21 33	21 55		22 03	22 25		22 33	22 55	23 03
Leigh-on-Sea	d	09 37	10 00		10 07	10 30		10 37	11 00		11 07		21 30		21 37	22 00		22 07	22 30		22 37	23 00	23 07
Chalkwell	d	09 39	10 02		10 09	10 32		10 40	11 02		11 10		21 32		21 40	22 02		22 10	22 32		22 40	23 02	23 10
Westcliff	d	09 41	10 04		10 11	10 34		10 42	11 04		11 12		21 34		21 42	22 04		22 12	22 34		22 42	23 04	23 12
Southend Central	a	09 44	10 07		10 14	10 37		10 44	11 07		11 14		21 37		21 44	22 07		22 14	22 37		22 44	23 07	23 14
	d	09 44	10 07		10 14	10 37		10 45	11 07		11 15		21 37		21 45	22 07		22 15	22 37		22 45	23 07	23 15
Southend East	d	09 46	10 09		10 16	10 39		10 47	11 09		11 17		21 39		21 47	22 09		22 17	22 39		22 47	23 09	23 17
Thorpe Bay	d	09 49	10 12		10 19	10 42		10 49	11 12		11 19		21 42		21 49	22 12		22 19	22 42		22 49	23 12	23 19
Shoeburyness	a	09 55	10 18		10 25	10 48		10 55	11 18		11 25		21 48		21 55	22 18		22 25	22 48		22 55	23 18	23 25

		CC	CC	CC	CC	CC
London Fenchurch St 7 ⊖	d	22 23			23 11	23 41
Limehouse	d	22 27			23 15	23 45
West Ham ⊖	d	22 32			23 20	23 50
London Liverpool St 15 ⊖	d		22 45	23 15		
Stratford 7 ⊖	d		22 52	23 22		
Barking ⊖	d	22 38	23 03	23 33	23 26	23 56
Upminster ⊖	d	22 46	23 12	23 42	23 34	00 05
Ockendon	d	22 52			23 40	
Chafford Hundred Lakeside	d	22 56			23 44	
Dagenham Dock	d					
Rainham	d					
Purfleet	d					
Grays	d	23 00			23 48	
Tilbury Town 3	d	23 03			23 51	
East Tilbury	d	23 09			23 57	
Stanford-le-Hope	d	23 13			00 01	
West Horndon	d		23 17	23 47		00 10
Laindon	d		23 22	23 52		00 15
Basildon	d		23 26	23 56		00 18
Pitsea	d	23 22	23 29	23 59	00 09	00 22
Benfleet	d	23 25	23 33	00 03	00 13	00 25
Leigh-on-Sea	d	23 30	23 37	00 07	00 17	00 30
Chalkwell	d	23 32	23 40	00 10	00 20	00 32
Westcliff	d	23 34	23 42	00 12	00 22	00 34
Southend Central	a	23 37	23 44	00 14	00 24	00 37
	d	23 37	23 45	00 15	00 25	00 37
Southend East	d	23 39	23 47	00 17	00 27	00 39
Thorpe Bay	d	23 42	23 49	00 19	00 29	00 42
Shoeburyness	a	23 48	23 55	00 25	00 35	00 48

For services between London Liverpool Street and Southend Victoria refer to Table T006

Table T001-R

Mondays to Fridays

16 December to 15 May

Shoeburyness and Southend Central - London

Miles	Miles	Miles	Miles			CC MX A	CC MX B	CC MX C	CC D	CC	CC E	CC	CC	CC	CC	CC D	CC	CC E	CC	CC D	CC	CC D	CC D
0	0	0	—	**Shoeburyness**	d					04 15					04 59		05 13				05 28		05 34
1½	1½	1½	—	Thorpe Bay	d				04 06	04 18			04 35		05 03	05 08	05 17				05 32		05 38
3	3	3	—	Southend East	d				04 08	04 21			04 37		05 05	05 10	05 19				05 34		05 40
3¾	3¾	3¾	—	**Southend Central**	a				04 11	04 23			04 40		05 08	05 13	05 22				05 37		05 43
—	—	—	—		d				04 11	04 24			04 40		05 08	05 13	05 22				05 37		05 43
4¾	4¾	4¾	—	Westcliff	d				04 14	04 26			04 42		05 10	05 15	05 24				05 39		05 45
5¾	5¾	5¾	—	Chalkwell	d				04 16	04 28			04 44		05 13	05 17	05 27				05 42		05 48
7	7	7	—	Leigh-on-Sea	d				04 19	04 31			04 47		05 15	05 20	05 30				05 44		05 50
10¼	10¼	10¼	—	Benfleet	d				04 23	04 36			04 51		05 20	05 24	05 35				05 49		05 55
13	13	13	—	Pitsea	d				04 28	04 40			04 56		05 23	05 29	05 38			05 48	05 52		06 04
15¼	—	—	—	Basildon	d					04 43					05 27		05 42				05 56		
16¾	—	—	—	Laindon	d					04 46					05 31		05 46				06 00		
20¼	—	—	—	West Horndon	d			00 03		04 51					05 35		05 50				06 04		
—	18¼	18¼	—	Stanford-le-Hope	d				04 34				05 02			05 35				05 54			06 10
—	20½	20½	—	East Tilbury	d				04 37				05 06			05 38				05 58			06 14
—	24	24	—	**Tilbury Town** 3	d				04 43				05 12			05 44				06 04			06 20
—	25¾	25¾	—	Grays	d				04 46			04 53	05 15	05 25		05 47			05 53	06 07		06 15	06 23
—	29¼	—	—	Purfleet	d							04 59		05 31					05 59	06 13			06 29
—	32¾	—	—	Rainham	d							05 04		05 36					06 04	06 18			06 34
—	35	—	—	Dagenham Dock	d						←	05 07		05 39				←	06 08	06 22			06 38
—	—	27¾	—	Chafford Hundred Lakeside	d				04 50		04 50		05 19			05 51		05 51				06 19	
—	—	30¼	—	Ockendon	d				→		04 54		05 23			→		05 55				→	
24¼	—	33½	—	Upminster ⊖	d		00 01	00 08		04 56	05 00		05 30		05 41		05 56	06 02			06 10		
32	38	41¼	0	Barking ⊖	d		00 09	00 16		05 05	05 08	05 13	05 38	05 45	05 49		06 04	06 10	06 14	06 28	06 18		06 44
—	—	—	4	Stratford 7 ⊖	a															→			→
—	—	—	8	**London Liverpool St** 15 ⊖	a																		
34¾	40¾	44	—	West Ham ⊖	d	00 05	00 14	00 21		05 10	05 13	05 18	05 43	05 50	05 55		06 10	06 16	06 19		06 23		
35½	41½	44¾	—	Limehouse	d	00 10	00 19	00 26		05 15	05 18	05 23	05 48	05 55	06 00		06 15	06 21	06 24		06 28		
39½	45½	48¾	—	**London Fenchurch St** 7 ⊖	a	00 15	00 24	00 32		05 20	05 23	05 28	05 53	06 00	06 04		06 19	06 26	06 29		06 33		

		CC	CC F	CC	CC A	CC C	CC D	CC D	CC	CC D	CC	CC A	CC E	CC	CC	CC B	CC	CC D	CC D	CC	CC	CC	CC F
Shoeburyness	d	05 38		05 44					05 57		06 07			06 11						06 25			
Thorpe Bay	d	05 42		05 48				05 56	06 01		06 11			06 15						06 29	06 38		
Southend East	d	05 44		05 50				05 58	06 03		06 13			06 17						06 31	06 40		
Southend Central	a	05 47		05 53				06 01	06 06					06 20						06 34			
	d	05 47		05 53				06 01	06 06	06 11				06 20						06 34			
Westcliff	d	05 49		05 55				06 03	06 08	06 13				06 22						06 36			
Chalkwell	d	05 52		05 57				06 06	06 11	06 16				06 25						06 39			
Leigh-on-Sea	d	05 54		06 00				06 08	06 14	06 18	06 22			06 28	06 35					06 42	06 47		
Benfleet	d	05 59		06 05				06 13	06 19	06 23	06 27			06 33	06 40					06 47	06 53		
Pitsea	d			06 08				06 19	06 23	06 28	06 31			06 37					06 45	06 51			
Basildon	d			06 12					06 27		06 35			06 41	06 46					06 55	06 59		
Laindon	d	06 06		06 16					06 30		06 39			06 44	06 49					06 58		07 04	
West Horndon	d			06 20					06 35						06 54							07 09	
Stanford-le-Hope	d							06 25		06 34									06 51				
East Tilbury	d							06 29		06 37									06 54				
Tilbury Town 3	d							06 35		06 43									07 00				
Grays	d						06 31	06 38		06 47							06 52	07 01	07 04				
Purfleet	d							06 44									06 58		07 09				
Rainham	d							06 49									07 03		07 15				
Dagenham Dock	d				←			06 53				←				←	07 07		07 18				
Chafford Hundred Lakeside	d				06 19		06 35			06 51		06 35				06 51		07 06					
Ockendon	d				06 24		→			→		06 40				06 56		→					
Upminster ⊖	d	06 15	←	06 26	06 31	←			06 40			06 49	←	06 54	06 59	07 03				07 08		07 14	←
Barking ⊖	d		06 28		06 39	06 44		07 00			06 54		07 00	07 03	07 08	07 11	07 14		07 25			07 23	07 25
Stratford 7 ⊖	a							→											→				
London Liverpool St 15 ⊖	a																						
West Ham ⊖	d	06 27	06 33	06 39	06 44	06 49			06 53		06 59	07 02	07 05	07 09	07 13	07 17	07 20			07 23	07 26	07 29	07 32
Limehouse	d	06 33	06 39	06 44	06 49	06 55			06 59		07 05	07 08	07 11	07 14	07 19	07 22	07 25			07 28	07 31	07 34	07 37
London Fenchurch St 7 ⊖	a	06 37	06 44	06 49	06 54	07 00			07 06		07 11	07 14	07 17	07 21	07 25	07 29	07 32			07 35	07 38	07 41	07 44

A From Grays
B From Southend Central
C From Shoeburyness
D To London Fenchurch Street
E From Thorpe Bay
F From Pitsea

For services between Southend Victoria and London Liverpool Street refer to Table 6

Table T001-R

Mondays to Fridays

16 December to 15 May

Shoeburyness and Southend Central - London

		CC A		CC B	CC B	CC	CC	CC	CC A	CC C	CC	CC		CC	CC	CC	CC	CC	CC	CC	CC	CC		CC	CC
Shoeburyness	d					06 41	06 48								07 02			07 18						07 31	
Thorpe Bay	d					06 45	06 52								07 06		07 12	07 22				07 29		07 35	
Southend East	d					06 47	06 54								07 08		07 14	07 24				07 31		07 37	
Southend Central	a					06 50	06 57								07 11		07 17	07 27				07 34		07 40	
	d				06 46	06 50	06 57							07 04	07 11		07 17	07 27				07 34		07 40	
Westcliff	d				06 49	06 52	06 59							07 06	07 13		07 19	07 29				07 36		07 42	
Chalkwell	d				06 51	06 55	07 02							07 09	07 16		07 22	07 32				07 39		07 45	
Leigh-on-Sea	d				06 54	06 58	07 05	07 08						07 11		07 21	07 25		07 37			07 42		07 48	
Benfleet	d				06 58	07 03	07 10	07 13						07 17		07 26	07 30		07 42			07 47		07 53	
Pitsea	d				07 05	07 06		07 17						07 22		07 30	07 34				07 35	07 51			
Basildon	d					07 10		07 21								07 34	07 38	07 42	07 48					07 59	
Laindon	d					07 14	07 18				07 31						07 45		07 52						08 04
West Horndon	d					07 18					07 36						07 51								08 09
Stanford-le-Hope	d				07 12									07 28							07 42				
East Tilbury	d				07 15									07 31							07 45				
Tilbury Town	d				07 22									07 37							07 51				
Grays	d			07 17	07 25							07 31		07 41						07 47	07 56				
Purfleet	d				07 31									07 46							08 02				
Rainham	d				07 36									07 52							08 07				
Dagenham Dock	d	←			07 40									07 55							08 11				
Chafford Hundred Lakeside	d	07 06		07 21								07 35								07 51					
Ockendon	d	07 11		07 26								07 41								07 56					
Upminster ⊖	d	07 19		07 33					←	←	07 41	07 48					07 57			08 03		08 06			08 14
Barking ⊖	d	07 28		07 41	07 46	07 35			07 41	07 46	07 50	07 56		08 02						08 11	08 19				08 23
Stratford ⊖	a			→	→																				
London Liverpool St ⊖	a																								
West Ham ⊖	d	07 35				07 41		07 44	07 47	07 53	07 56	08 02		08 08	07 50	07 59	08 11	08 05	08 14	08 17	08 26	08 20		08 23	08 29
Limehouse	d	07 40				07 46		07 49	07 52	07 58	08 01	08 07		08 13	07 55	08 04	08 16		08 19	08 22	08 31	08 25		08 28	08 34
London Fenchurch St ⊖	a	07 47				07 53	07 48	07 56	07 59	08 05	08 08	08 14		08 20	08 02	08 11	08 23	08 16	08 26	08 29	08 38	08 32		08 35	08 41

		CC	CC	CC B	CC B	CC	CC	CC		CC A	CC C	CC	CC	CC	CC	CC B	CC B	CC		CC	CC A	CC D	CC B	CC B	CC
Shoeburyness	d					07 39	07 45					08 00						08 15							
Thorpe Bay	d					07 43	07 49					08 04						08 19							
Southend East	d					07 45	07 51					08 06						08 21							
Southend Central	a					07 48	07 54					08 09						08 24							
	d				07 44	07 48	07 54					08 09						08 24							08 34
Westcliff	d				07 46	07 50	07 56					08 11						08 26							08 36
Chalkwell	d				07 49	07 53	07 59					08 14						08 29							08 39
Leigh-on-Sea	d				07 52	07 56		08 04				08 17						08 32		08 36					08 42
Benfleet	d				07 56	08 01		08 09				08 22						08 37		08 41					08 47
Pitsea	d		07 52		08 03	08 04		08 13							08 19		08 34	08 40						08 49	08 50
Basildon	d					08 08	08 13	08 17				08 28						08 44							08 54
Laindon	d					08 12		08 22					08 34							08 50					08 58
West Horndon	d						08 21						08 39												09 02
Stanford-le-Hope	d		07 58		08 10										08 25		08 40							08 55	
East Tilbury	d		08 02		08 13										08 29		08 44							08 59	
Tilbury Town	d		08 08		08 19										08 35		08 50							09 05	
Grays	d	08 01	08 11	08 18	08 23									08 31	08 38	08 47	08 53						09 02	09 08	
Purfleet	d		08 17		08 28										08 44		08 59							09 14	
Rainham	d		08 22		08 34										08 49		09 04							09 19	
Dagenham Dock	d		08 26		08 37					←					08 53		09 08				←			09 23	
Chafford Hundred Lakeside	d	08 05		08 22						08 22				08 35		08 51					08 51		09 06		
Ockendon	d	08 10		→						08 26				08 41		→					08 56		→		
Upminster ⊖	d	08 18				08 21	08 26			08 33	←		08 44	08 48				08 54			09 03	←			09 08
Barking ⊖	d	08 26	08 32		08 44			08 38		08 41	08 44	08 47	08 53	08 56	08 59		09 14	09 03			09 11	09 14		09 29	09 17
Stratford ⊖	a				→												→							→	
London Liverpool St ⊖	a																								
West Ham ⊖	d	08 32	08 38			08 35	08 41	08 44		08 47	08 50	08 53	08 59	09 02	09 05			09 08		09 13	09 17	09 20			09 23
Limehouse	d	08 37	08 43			08 40	08 46	08 49		08 52	08 55	08 58	09 04	09 07	09 10			09 14		09 18	09 22	09 25			09 28
London Fenchurch St ⊖	a	08 44	08 50			08 47	08 53	08 56		08 59	09 02	09 05	09 11	09 14	09 17			09 20		09 25	09 28	09 32			09 35

		CC	CC A	CC D		CC	CC	CC	CC B	CC	CC D	CC B	CC B	CC B		CC	CC A	CC C	CC	CC B	CC B	CC	CC A	CC C	
Shoeburyness	d	08 34					08 49									09 10			09 27			09 41			
Thorpe Bay	d	08 38					08 53									09 14			09 31			09 45			
Southend East	d	08 40					08 55									09 16			09 33			09 47			
Southend Central	a	08 43					08 58									09 19			09 36			09 50			
	d	08 43				08 50	08 58			09 03			09 12			09 19			09 36	09 42		09 50			
Westcliff	d	08 45				08 52	09 00			09 06			09 15			09 21			09 38	09 45		09 52			
Chalkwell	d	08 48				08 55	09 03			09 08			09 17			09 24			09 41	09 47		09 55			
Leigh-on-Sea	d	08 51				08 58	09 05			09 11			09 20			09 27			09 43	09 50		09 57			
Benfleet	d	08 56				09 03	09 10			09 16			09 24			09 32			09 48	09 54		10 02			
Pitsea	d					09 06			09 15	09 20			09 29						09 51	09 59					
Basildon	d	09 02				09 10	09 16			09 24						09 38			09 55			10 08			
Laindon	d	09 05				09 14	09 20			09 27						09 41			09 58			10 11			
West Horndon	d					09 18				09 32									10 03						
Stanford-le-Hope	d								09 21				09 35							10 05					
East Tilbury	d								09 25				09 38							10 08					
Tilbury Town	d								09 31				09 44							10 14					
Grays	d							09 17	09 34			09 41	09 48	10 10						10 17	10 40				
Purfleet	d								09 40			09 47		10 16							10 46				
Rainham	d								09 45			09 52		10 21							10 52				
Dagenham Dock	d		←						09 48			09 55		10 24				←			10 56			←	
Chafford Hundred Lakeside	d		09 06					09 21					09 52					09 52		10 21				10 21	
Ockendon	d		09 11					09 25					→					09 56		→				10 25	
Upminster ⊖	d	09 14	09 18	←		09 24	09 28	09 32		09 37	←					09 49	←	10 03	10 08			10 19	←	10 31	
Barking ⊖	d	09 22	09 26	09 29		09 32	09 36	09 40	09 54	09 46	09 54	10 02		10 30		09 58	10 02	10 11	10 17		11 04	10 27	10 30	10 39	
Stratford ⊖	a								→			→		→							→				
London Liverpool St ⊖	a																								
West Ham ⊖	d	09 28	09 32	09 35		09 38	09 42	09 46		09 51	09 59					10 03	10 07	10 16	10 22			10 32	10 35	10 44	
Limehouse	d	09 33	09 37	09 40		09 43	09 47	09 51		09 57	10 05					10 08	10 12	10 21	10 28			10 37	10 40	10 49	
London Fenchurch St ⊖	a	09 40	09 44	09 47		09 50	09 54	09 58		10 01	10 10					10 13	10 17	10 26	10 32			10 41	10 45	10 55	

A From Grays
B To London Fenchurch Street
C From Southend Central
D From Pitsea

Table T001-R

Mondays to Fridays

16 December to 15 May

Shoeburyness and Southend Central - London

		CC	CC A	CC A	CC	CC B	CC C	CC	CC A	CC A		CC	CC B	CC C	CC	CC A	CC A	CC	CC B	CC C		CC	CC A	CC A	CC
Shoeburyness	d	09 57			10 11			10 27				10 41			10 57			11 11				11 27			11 41
Thorpe Bay	d	10 01			10 15			10 31				10 45			11 01			11 15				11 31			11 45
Southend East	d	10 03			10 17			10 33				10 47			11 03			11 17				11 33			11 47
Southend Central	a	10 06			10 20			10 36				10 50			11 06			11 20				11 36			11 50
	d	10 06	10 12		10 20			10 36	10 42			10 50			11 06	11 12		11 20				11 36	11 39		11 50
Westcliff	d	10 08	10 15		10 22			10 38	10 45			10 52			11 08	11 15		11 22				11 38	11 42		11 52
Chalkwell	d	10 11	10 17		10 25			10 41	10 47			10 55			11 11	11 17		11 25				11 41	11 44		11 55
Leigh-on-Sea	d	10 13	10 20		10 28			10 43	10 50			10 57			11 13	11 20		11 27				11 43	11 47		11 57
Benfleet	d	10 18	10 24		10 33			10 48	10 54			11 02			11 18	11 24		11 32				11 48	11 51		12 02
Pitsea	d	10 21	10 29					10 51	10 59						11 21	11 29						11 51	11 56		
Basildon	d	10 25			10 39			10 55				11 08			11 25			11 38				11 55			12 08
Laindon	d	10 28			10 42			10 58				11 11			11 28			11 41				11 58			12 11
West Horndon	d	10 33						11 03							11 33							12 03			
Stanford-le-Hope	d		10 35						11 05							11 35							12 02		
East Tilbury	d		10 38						11 08							11 38							12 05		
Tilbury Town	d		10 44						11 14							11 44							12 11		
Grays	d		10 47	11 10					11 17	11 40						11 47	12 10						12 14	12 40	
Purfleet	d			11 16						11 46							12 16							12 46	
Rainham	d			11 21						11 51							12 21							12 51	
Dagenham Dock	d			11 24			←			11 54				←			12 24			←				12 54	
Chafford Hundred Lakeside	d		10 51				10 51		11 21					11 21		11 51				11 51			12 18		
Ockendon	d		→				10 55		→					11 25		→				11 55			→		
Upminster ⊖	d	10 39			10 50	←	11 01	11 08				11 19	←	11 31	11 38			11 49	←	12 01		12 08			12 19
Barking ⊖	d	10 47		11 30	10 58	11 04	11 09	11 17		12 00		11 27	11 30	11 39	11 47		12 30	11 57	12 00	12 09		12 16		13 00	12 27
Stratford ⊖	a			→						→							→							→	
London Liverpool St ⊖	a																								
West Ham ⊖	d	10 53			11 03	11 09	11 14	11 22				11 32	11 35	11 44	11 52			12 02	12 05	12 14		12 21			12 32
Limehouse	d	10 58			11 08	11 14	11 19	11 27				11 37	11 40	11 49	11 57			12 07	12 10	12 19		12 26			12 37
London Fenchurch St ⊖	a	11 02			11 12	11 18	11 25	11 31				11 41	11 45	11 54	12 01			12 11	12 15	12 24		12 31			12 41

		CC B	CC C	CC	CC A	CC A		CC	CC B	CC C	CC	CC A	CC A	CC	CC B	CC C		CC	CC A	CC A	CC	CC B	CC C	CC	CC A
Shoeburyness	d			11 57				12 11			12 27			12 41				12 57			13 11			13 27	
Thorpe Bay	d			12 01				12 15			12 31			12 45				13 01			13 15			13 31	
Southend East	d			12 03				12 17			12 33			12 47				13 03			13 17			13 33	
Southend Central	a			12 06				12 20			12 36			12 50				13 06			13 20			13 36	
	d			12 06	12 12			12 20			12 36	12 42		12 50				13 06	13 11		13 20			13 36	13 42
Westcliff	d			12 08	12 15			12 22			12 38	12 45		12 52				13 08	13 14		13 22			13 38	13 45
Chalkwell	d			12 11	12 17			12 25			12 41	12 47		12 55				13 11	13 16		13 25			13 41	13 47
Leigh-on-Sea	d			12 13	12 20			12 27			12 43	12 50		12 57				13 13	13 19		13 27			13 43	13 50
Benfleet	d			12 18	12 24			12 32			12 48	12 54		13 02				13 18	13 23		13 32			13 48	13 54
Pitsea	d			12 21	12 29						12 51	12 59						13 21	13 28					13 51	13 59
Basildon	d			12 25				12 38			12 55			13 08				13 25			13 38			13 55	
Laindon	d			12 28				12 41			12 58			13 11				13 28			13 41			13 58	
West Horndon	d			12 33							13 03							13 33						14 03	
Stanford-le-Hope	d				12 35							13 05							13 34						14 05
East Tilbury	d				12 38							13 08							13 37						14 08
Tilbury Town	d				12 44							13 14							13 43						14 14
Grays	d				12 47	13 10						13 17	13 40						13 46	14 10					14 17
Purfleet	d					13 16							13 46							14 16					
Rainham	d					13 21							13 51							14 21					
Dagenham Dock	d		←			13 24				←			13 54			←				14 24			←		
Chafford Hundred Lakeside	d		12 18		12 51					12 51		13 21				13 21			13 50				13 50		14 21
Ockendon	d		12 22		→					12 55		→				13 25			→				13 54		→
Upminster ⊖	d	←	12 28	12 38				12 49	←	13 01	13 08			13 19	←	13 31		13 38			13 49	←	14 01	14 08	
Barking ⊖	d	12 30	12 36	12 46		13 30		12 57	13 00	13 09	13 16		14 00	13 27	13 30	13 39		13 46		14 30	13 57	14 00	14 09	14 16	
Stratford ⊖	a					→							→							→					
London Liverpool St ⊖	a																								
West Ham ⊖	d	12 35	12 42	12 52				13 02	13 05	13 14	13 21			13 32	13 35	13 44		13 51			14 02	14 05	14 14	14 21	
Limehouse	d	12 40	12 47	12 57				13 07	13 10	13 19	13 26			13 37	13 40	13 49		13 56			14 07	14 10	14 19	14 26	
London Fenchurch St ⊖	a	12 45	12 53	13 01				13 11	13 16	13 25	13 31			13 41	13 45	13 55		14 02			14 11	14 15	14 24	14 31	

		CC A		CC	CC B	CC C	CC	CC A	CC A	CC	CC B	CC C		CC	CC A	CC A	CC	CC B	CC C	CC	CC A	CC A		CC	CC B
Shoeburyness	d			13 41			13 57			14 11				14 27			14 41			14 57				15 10	
Thorpe Bay	d			13 45			14 01			14 15				14 31			14 45			15 01				15 14	
Southend East	d			13 47			14 03			14 17				14 33			14 47			15 03				15 16	
Southend Central	a			13 50			14 06			14 20				14 36			14 50			15 06				15 19	
	d			13 50			14 06	14 12		14 20				14 36	14 42		14 50			15 06	15 11			15 19	
Westcliff	d			13 52			14 08	14 15		14 22				14 38	14 45		14 52			15 08	15 14			15 21	
Chalkwell	d			13 55			14 11	14 17		14 25				14 41	14 47		14 55			15 11	15 16			15 24	
Leigh-on-Sea	d			13 57			14 13	14 20		14 27				14 43	14 50		14 57			15 13	15 19			15 26	
Benfleet	d			14 02			14 18	14 24		14 32				14 48	14 54		15 02			15 18	15 23			15 31	
Pitsea	d						14 21	14 29						14 51	14 59					15 21	15 28				
Basildon	d			14 08			14 25			14 38				14 55			15 08			15 25				15 37	
Laindon	d			14 11			14 28			14 41				14 58			15 11			15 28				15 40	
West Horndon	d						14 33							15 03						15 33					
Stanford-le-Hope	d							14 35							15 05						15 34				
East Tilbury	d							14 38							15 08						15 37				
Tilbury Town	d							14 44							15 14						15 43				
Grays	d	14 40						14 47	15 10						15 17	15 40					15 46	16 09			
Purfleet	d	14 46							15 16							15 46						16 15			
Rainham	d	14 51							15 21							15 51						16 20			
Dagenham Dock	d	14 54				←			15 24			←				15 54			←			16 24			
Chafford Hundred Lakeside	d					14 21		14 51				14 51			15 21				15 21		15 50				
Ockendon	d					14 25		→				14 55			→				15 25		→				
Upminster ⊖	d			14 19	←	14 31	14 38			14 49	←	15 01		15 08			15 19	←	15 31	15 38				15 48	←
Barking ⊖	d	15 00		14 27	14 30	14 39	14 46		15 30	14 57	15 00	15 09		15 16		16 00	15 27	15 30	15 39	15 46		16 31		15 57	16 00
Stratford ⊖	a	→							→							→						→			
London Liverpool St ⊖	a																								
West Ham ⊖	d			14 32	14 35	14 44	14 51			15 02	15 05	15 14		15 21			15 32	15 35	15 44	15 51				16 02	16 06
Limehouse	d			14 37	14 40	14 49	14 56			15 07	15 10	15 19		15 27			15 37	15 40	15 49	15 56				16 07	16 11
London Fenchurch St ⊖	a			14 41	14 45	14 54	15 00			15 11	15 15	15 25		15 31			15 42	15 45	15 54	16 00				16 12	16 16

A To London Fenchurch Street
B From Grays
C From Southend Central

Table T001-R

Shoeburyness and Southend Central - London

		CC A	CC	CC B	CC	CC C	CC A	CC	CC	CC	CC B	CC B	CC	CC	CC D	CC C	CC B	CC	CC	CC E	CC	CC	CC
Shoeburyness	d		15 27		15 39			15 55	16 00			16 03	16 12	16 18							16 40	16 49	
Thorpe Bay	d		15 31		15 43			15 59	16 04			16 07	16 16	16 22					16 38		16 44	16 53	
Southend East	d		15 33		15 45			16 01	16 06			16 09	16 18	16 24					16 40		16 46	16 55	
Southend Central	a		15 36		15 48			16 04	16 09			16 12	16 21	16 27					16 43		16 49	16 58	
	d		15 36	15 42	15 48			16 04	16 09			16 13	16 21	16 27				16 35	16 43		16 49	16 58	
Westcliff	d		15 38	15 44	15 50			16 06	16 11			16 15	16 23	16 29				16 37	16 45		16 51	17 00	
Chalkwell	d		15 41	15 47	15 53			16 09	16 14			16 17	16 26	16 32				16 40	16 48		16 54	17 03	
Leigh-on-Sea	d		15 43	15 50	15 55			16 12	16 16			16 20	16 29	16 34				16 42	16 51		16 57	17 05	
Benfleet	d		15 48	15 54	16 00			16 17	16 21			16 25	16 34	16 39				16 47	16 56		17 02	17 10	
Pitsea	d		15 51	15 59	16 03				16 25			16 29		16 43			16 49	16 51			17 06	17 15	
Basildon	d		15 55		16 07			16 23	16 29				16 40	16 47				16 55	17 02		17 10	17 19	
Laindon	d		15 59		16 11			16 26	16 33				16 43	16 51				16 58	17 05		17 13	17 22	
West Horndon	d		16 03		16 15			16 31					16 48					17 03			17 18		
Stanford-le-Hope	d			16 05								16 36					16 55						
East Tilbury	d			16 08								16 39					16 59						
Tilbury Town 3	d			16 15								16 45					17 05						
Grays	d			16 19						16 38	16 48	16 49					17 08						17 17
Purfleet	d									16 44		16 55					17 13						
Rainham	d									16 49		17 01					17 18						
Dagenham Dock	d	←					←			16 53		17 04				←	17 22						
Chafford Hundred Lakeside	d	15 50		16 22			16 22				16 52					16 52							17 21
Ockendon	d	15 54		→			16 26				→					16 57							17 27
Upminster ⊖	d	16 01	16 09		16 21	←	16 33		16 41				16 53	16 59	←	17 04		17 08	17 14	←	17 25		17 34
Barking ⊖	d	16 11	16 17		16 29	16 31	16 41		16 52	16 59		17 10	17 01	17 07	17 10	17 13	17 28	17 17	17 22	17 28	17 34	17 39	17 43
Stratford 7 ⊖	a											→					→						
London Liverpool St 15 ⊖	a																						
West Ham ⊖	d	16 16	16 22		16 34	16 37	16 46	16 50	16 57	17 04			17 07	17 13	17 16	17 18		17 22	17 29		17 40	17 46	17 49
Limehouse	d	16 21	16 27		16 39	16 42	16 51		17 02	17 09			17 12		17 21	17 24		17 27		17 39			17 54
London Fenchurch St 7 ⊖	a	16 26	16 32		16 44	16 48	16 56	16 59	17 07	17 14			17 17	17 23	17 26	17 29		17 32	17 38	17 44	17 50	17 55	17 59

		CC	CC	CC B	CC	CC	CC	CC E	CC	CC	CC	CC	CC	CC	CC B	CC	CC E	CC	CC	CC	CC	CC B
Shoeburyness	d	16 57			17 05		17 15				17 27					17 43				17 59		
Thorpe Bay	d	17 01			17 09		17 19				17 31					17 47				18 03		
Southend East	d	17 03			17 11		17 21				17 33					17 49				18 05		
Southend Central	a	17 06			17 14		17 24				17 36					17 52				18 08		
	d	17 06			17 14		17 24		17 28		17 36			17 46		17 52				18 08		
Westcliff	d	17 08			17 16		17 26		17 31		17 38			17 48		17 54				18 10		
Chalkwell	d	17 11			17 19		17 29		17 33		17 40			17 51		17 57				18 13		
Leigh-on-Sea	d	17 13			17 21	17 24	17 31		17 36		17 43		17 50	17 53		17 59		18 06		18 15		
Benfleet	d	17 18			17 26	17 30	17 36		17 41		17 47			17 58		18 04		18 12		18 20		
Pitsea	d	17 21		17 25	17 29				17 44		17 51				17 54	18 07				18 23		
Basildon	d	17 25			17 33	17 37	17 43		17 48		17 55		17 59	18 04		18 11		18 18		18 27		
Laindon	d	17 28			17 36		17 46		17 51		17 58			18 08		18 14		18 22		18 30		
West Horndon	d	17 33									18 03					18 19				18 35		
Stanford-le-Hope	d			17 31											18 00							
East Tilbury	d			17 35											18 04							
Tilbury Town 3	d			17 41											18 10							
Grays	d		17 28	17 44						17 47		17 55			18 13				18 17		18 31	18 44
Purfleet	d		17 34	17 49								18 01			18 19						18 37	18 50
Rainham	d		17 40	17 54								18 07			18 24						18 42	18 56
Dagenham Dock	d		17 43	17 58								18 10			18 28						18 46	19 00
Chafford Hundred Lakeside	d									17 51									18 21			
Ockendon	d									17 57									18 28			
Upminster ⊖	d	17 38			17 45			←	17 59	18 05	18 08		18 12	18 16		18 24	←	18 30	18 35	18 40		
Barking ⊖	d	17 47	17 50	18 05	17 53			18 05	18 07	18 13	18 16	18 18		18 25	18 35	18 32	18 35	18 39	18 43	18 48	18 52	19 07
Stratford 7 ⊖	a			→											→							→
London Liverpool St 15 ⊖	a																					
West Ham ⊖	d	17 52	17 55		17 58		18 06	18 10	18 13	18 19	18 22	18 24		18 30		18 37	18 40	18 44	18 48	18 54	18 58	
Limehouse	d	17 57			18 03				18 18	18 24	18 27	18 30		18 35		18 42	18 45	18 50	18 53	18 59	19 04	
London Fenchurch St 7 ⊖	a	18 02	18 05		18 08	18 10	18 15	18 19	18 23	18 29	18 31	18 34	18 37	18 40		18 47	18 50	18 54	18 58	19 04	19 08	

		CC B	CC	CC C	CC E	CC B	CC	CC E	CC	CC	CC	CC	CC B	CC B	CC B	CC	CC E	CC A	CC	CC B	CC	CC C	CC A
Shoeburyness	d		18 14				18 28		18 44			18 59				19 14			19 27		19 41		
Thorpe Bay	d		18 18				18 32		18 48			19 03				19 18			19 31		19 45		
Southend East	d		18 20				18 34		18 50			19 05				19 20			19 33		19 47		
Southend Central	a		18 23				18 37		18 53			19 08				19 23			19 36		19 50		
	d		18 23				18 37		18 53			19 08		19 12		19 23			19 36	19 42	19 50		
Westcliff	d		18 25				18 39		18 55			19 10		19 15		19 25			19 38	19 45	19 52		
Chalkwell	d		18 28				18 42		18 58			19 13		19 17		19 28			19 41	19 47	19 55		
Leigh-on-Sea	d		18 30				18 44		19 00			19 15		19 20		19 30			19 43	19 50	19 57		
Benfleet	d		18 35				18 49		19 05			19 20		19 24		19 35			19 48	19 54	20 02		
Pitsea	d	18 27	18 38			18 42	18 53			18 59		19 23	19 25	19 29					19 51	19 59			
Basildon	d		18 42				18 57		19 11			19 27				19 41			19 55		20 08		
Laindon	d		18 45				19 00		19 14			19 30				19 44			19 58		20 11		
West Horndon	d		18 50				19 04					19 35							20 03				
Stanford-le-Hope	d	18 34				18 49				19 05				19 35						20 05			
East Tilbury	d	18 37				18 52				19 09				19 38						20 08			
Tilbury Town 3	d	18 43				18 58				19 15				19 44						20 14			
Grays	d	18 47				19 02				19 19	19 23		19 42	19 47	20 10					20 17			
Purfleet	d					19 07					19 29		19 48		20 16								
Rainham	d					19 12					19 34		19 53		20 21								
Dagenham Dock	d				←	19 16					19 37		19 56		20 24			←					←
Chafford Hundred Lakeside	d	18 51			18 51					19 22				19 51				19 51		20 21			20 21
Ockendon	d	→			18 57					19 26				→				19 55		→			20 25
Upminster ⊖	d		18 55	←	19 04		19 09	←	19 22	19 33		19 40				19 52	←	20 01	20 08		20 19	←	20 31
Barking ⊖	d		19 03	19 07	19 12	19 22	19 17	19 22	19 30	19 41	19 43	19 48	20 03		20 30	20 00	20 03	20 10	20 16		20 27	20 30	20 39
Stratford 7 ⊖	a					→							→		→								
London Liverpool St 15 ⊖	a																						
West Ham ⊖	d		19 08	19 12	19 17		19 22	19 27	19 35	19 46	19 49	19 53				20 05	20 08	20 15	20 22		20 32	20 35	20 44
Limehouse	d		19 13	19 18	19 22		19 27	19 32		19 51	19 54	19 58				20 10	20 13	20 20	20 27		20 37	20 40	20 49
London Fenchurch St 7 ⊖	a		19 18	19 24	19 27		19 32	19 38	19 45	19 56	19 59	20 04				20 14	20 19	20 24	20 31		20 41	20 44	20 54

A From Southend Central
B To London Fenchurch Street
C From Grays
D From Shoeburyness
E From Pitsea

For services between Southend Victoria and London Liverpool Street refer to Table 6

Table T001-R

Shoeburyness and Southend Central - London

		CC	CC	CC	CC A	CC	CC A	CC	CC B	CC C	CC	CC	CC	CC A	CC	CC A	CC	CC B	CC C	CC	CC	CC	CC
Shoeburyness	d	19 57				20 27		20 41			20 57				21 27		21 41			21 57			22 27
Thorpe Bay	d	20 01				20 31		20 45			21 01				21 31		21 45			22 01			22 31
Southend East	d	20 03				20 33		20 47			21 03				21 33		21 47			22 03			22 33
Southend Central	a	20 06				20 36		20 50			21 06				21 36		21 50			22 06			22 36
	d	20 06		20 12		20 36	20 42	20 50			21 06		21 12		21 36	21 42	21 50			22 06		22 12	22 36
Westcliff	d	20 08		20 15		20 38	20 45	20 52			21 08		21 15		21 38	21 45	21 52			22 08		22 15	22 38
Chalkwell	d	20 11		20 17		20 41	20 47	20 55			21 11		21 17		21 41	21 47	21 55			22 11		22 17	22 41
Leigh-on-Sea	d	20 13		20 20		20 43	20 50	20 57			21 13		21 20		21 43	21 50	21 57			22 13		22 20	22 43
Benfleet	d	20 18		20 24		20 48	20 54	21 02			21 18		21 24		21 48	21 54	22 02			22 18		22 24	22 48
Pitsea	d	20 21		20 29		20 51	20 59				21 21		21 29		21 51	21 59				22 21		22 29	22 51
Basildon	d	20 25				20 55		21 08			21 25				21 55		22 08			22 25			22 55
Laindon	d	20 28				20 58		21 11			21 28				21 58		22 11			22 28			22 58
West Horndon	d	20 33				21 03					21 33				22 03					22 33			23 03
Stanford-le-Hope	d			20 35			21 05						21 35			22 05						22 35	
East Tilbury	d			20 38			21 08						21 38			22 08						22 38	
Tilbury Town 3	d			20 44			21 14						21 44			22 14						22 44	
Grays	d		20 40	20 47	21 10		21 17					21 43	21 47	22 10		22 17					22 40	22 47	
Purfleet	d		20 46		21 16							21 49		22 16							22 46		
Rainham	d		20 51		21 21							21 54		22 21							22 51		
Dagenham Dock	d		20 54		21 24					←		21 58		22 24					←		22 54		
Chafford Hundred Lakeside	d			20 51			21 21			21 21			21 51			22 21			22 21			22 51	
Ockendon	d			20 55			→			21 25			21 55			→			22 25			22 55	
Upminster ⊖	d	20 38		21 01		21 08		21 19	←	21 31	21 38		22 01		22 08		22 19	←	22 31	22 38		23 01	23 08
Barking ⊖	d	20 46	21 00	21 09	21 30	21 16		21 27	21 30	21 39	21 46	22 05	22 09	22 30	22 16		22 27	22 30	22 39	22 46	23 00	23 09	23 16
Stratford 7 ⊖	a				→									→									
London Liverpool St 15 ⊖	a																						
West Ham ⊖	d	20 51	21 05	21 14		21 21		21 32	21 35	21 44	21 51	22 10	22 14		22 21		22 32	22 35	22 44	22 51	23 05	23 14	23 21
Limehouse	d	20 56	21 10	21 19		21 26		21 37	21 40	21 49	21 56	22 15	22 19		22 26		22 37	22 40	22 49	22 56	23 10	23 19	23 26
London Fenchurch St 7 ⊖	a	21 00	21 14	21 24		21 30		21 41	21 45	21 54	22 00	22 19	22 24		22 31		22 41	22 45	22 54	23 00	23 14	23 24	23 30

		CC	CC	CC	CC	CC	CC
Shoeburyness	d			22 57			23 27
Thorpe Bay	d			23 01			23 31
Southend East	d			23 03			23 33
Southend Central	a			23 06			23 36
	d		22 42	23 06		23 12	23 36
Westcliff	d		22 45	23 08		23 15	23 38
Chalkwell	d		22 47	23 11		23 17	23 41
Leigh-on-Sea	d		22 50	23 13		23 20	23 43
Benfleet	d		22 54	23 18		23 24	23 48
Pitsea	d		22 59	23 21		23 29	23 51
Basildon	d			23 25			23 55
Laindon	d			23 28			23 58
West Horndon	d			23 33			00 03
Stanford-le-Hope	d		23 05			23 35	
East Tilbury	d		23 08			23 38	
Tilbury Town 3	d		23 14			23 44	
Grays	d	23 10	23 17		23 39	23 47	
Purfleet	d	23 16			23 45		
Rainham	d	23 21			23 50		
Dagenham Dock	d	23 24			23 54		
Chafford Hundred Lakeside	d		23 21			23 51	
Ockendon	d		23 25			23 55	
Upminster ⊖	d		23 31	23 38		00 01	00 08
Barking ⊖	d	23 30	23 39	23 46	23 59	00 09	00 16
Stratford 7 ⊖	a						
London Liverpool St 15 ⊖	a						
West Ham ⊖	d	23 35	23 44	23 51	00 05	00 14	00 21
Limehouse	d	23 40	23 49	23 56	00 10	00 19	00 26
London Fenchurch St 7 ⊖	a	23 45	23 54	00 01	00 15	00 24	00 32

A To London Fenchurch Street
B From Grays
C From Southend Central

For services between Southend Victoria and London Liverpool Street refer to Table 6

Table T001-R

Saturdays

21 December to 16 May

Shoeburyness and Southend Central - London

		CC A	CC B	CC C	CC	CC	CC	CC	CC	CC	CC	CC	CC	CC	CC	CC	CC	CC	CC	CC D	CC	CC D	CC D
Shoeburyness	d					04 25	04 43	05 09		05 13	05 39		05 43	06 09		06 13	06 39		06 43		07 09	07 13	
Thorpe Bay	d					04 29	04 47	05 13		05 17	05 43		05 47	06 13		06 17	06 43		06 47		07 13	07 17	
Southend East	d					04 31	04 49	05 15		05 19	05 45		05 49	06 15		06 19	06 45		06 49		07 15	07 19	
Southend Central	a					04 34	04 52	05 18		05 22	05 48		05 52	06 18		06 22	06 48		06 52		07 18	07 22	
	d				04 14	04 34	04 52	05 18		05 22	05 48		05 52	06 18		06 22	06 48		06 52		07 18	07 22	
Westcliff	d				04 16	04 36	04 54	05 20		05 24	05 50		05 54	06 20		06 24	06 50		06 54		07 20	07 24	
Chalkwell	d				04 18	04 39	04 57	05 23		05 27	05 53		05 57	06 23		06 27	06 53		06 57		07 23	07 27	
Leigh-on-Sea	d				04 21	04 41	05 00	05 26		05 30	05 56		06 00	06 26		06 30	06 56		07 00		07 26	07 30	
Benfleet	d				04 25	04 46	05 05	05 31		05 35	06 01		06 05	06 31		06 35	07 01		07 05		07 31	07 35	
Pitsea	d				04 30	04 49	05 10	05 34		05 40	06 04		06 10	06 34		06 40	07 04		07 10		07 34	07 40	
Basildon	d					04 53		05 38			06 08			06 38			07 08				07 38		
Laindon	d					04 56		05 42			06 12			06 42			07 12				07 42		
West Horndon	d			00 03		05 01		05 46			06 16			06 46			07 16				07 46		
Stanford-le-Hope	d				04 36		05 16			05 46			06 16			06 46			07 16			07 46	
East Tilbury	d				04 39		05 20			05 50			06 20			06 50			07 20			07 50	
Tilbury Town 3	d				04 45		05 26			05 56			06 26			06 56			07 26			07 56	
Grays	d				04 49		05 30		05 55	06 00		06 25	06 30		06 55	07 00		07 25	07 30	07 55		08 00	08 25
Purfleet	d								06 01			06 31			07 01			07 31		08 01			08 31
Rainham	d								06 06			06 36			07 06			07 36		08 06			08 36
Dagenham Dock	d								06 09			06 39			07 09			07 39		08 09			08 39
Chafford Hundred Lakeside	d				04 52		05 34			06 04			06 34			07 04			07 34			08 04	
Ockendon	d				04 56		05 38			06 08			06 38			07 08			07 38			→	
Upminster ⊖	d		00 01	00 08	05 03	05 06	05 44	05 52		06 14	06 22		06 44	06 52		07 14	07 22		07 44		07 52		
Barking ⊖	d		00 09	00 16	05 11	05 14	05 53	06 00	06 15	06 23	06 30	06 45	06 53	07 00	07 15	07 23	07 30	07 45	07 53	08 15	08 00		08 45
Stratford 7 ⊖	a																			→			→
London Liverpool St 15 ⊖	a																						
West Ham ⊖	d	00 05	00 14	00 21	05 16	05 19	05 58	06 06	06 20	06 28	06 36	06 50	06 58	07 06	07 20	07 28	07 36	07 50	07 58		08 06		
Limehouse	d	00 10	00 19	00 26	05 21	05 24	06 03	06 11	06 25	06 33	06 41	06 55	07 03	07 11	07 25	07 33	07 41	07 55	08 03		08 11		
London Fenchurch St 7 ⊖	a	00 15	00 24	00 32	05 28	05 30	06 09	06 16	06 30	06 39	06 46	07 01	07 09	07 16	07 31	07 39	07 46	08 01	08 09		08 16		

		CC	CC A	CC C	CC	CC D	CC D	CC	CC A	CC C	CC	CC D	CC D	CC	CC A	CC C	CC	CC D	CC D	CC	CC A	CC C
Shoeburyness	d	07 22			07 39	07 43		07 52			08 09	08 13		08 22			08 39	08 43		08 52		
Thorpe Bay	d	07 26			07 43	07 47		07 56			08 13	08 17		08 26			08 43	08 47		08 56		
Southend East	d	07 28			07 45	07 49		07 58			08 15	08 19		08 28			08 45	08 49		08 58		
Southend Central	a	07 31			07 48	07 52		08 01			08 18	08 22		08 31			08 48	08 52		09 01		
	d	07 31			07 48	07 52		08 01			08 18	08 22		08 31			08 48	08 52		09 01		
Westcliff	d	07 33			07 50	07 54		08 03			08 20	08 24		08 33			08 50	08 54		09 03		
Chalkwell	d	07 36			07 53	07 57		08 06			08 23	08 27		08 36			08 53	08 57		09 06		
Leigh-on-Sea	d	07 38			07 56	08 00		08 08			08 26	08 30		08 38			08 56	09 00		09 08		
Benfleet	d	07 43			08 01	08 05		08 13			08 31	08 35		08 43			09 01	09 05		09 13		
Pitsea	d				08 04	08 10					08 34	08 40					09 04	09 10				
Basildon	d	07 49			08 08			08 19			08 38			08 49			09 08			09 19		
Laindon	d	07 52			08 12			08 22			08 42			08 52			09 12			09 22		
West Horndon	d				08 16						08 46						09 16					
Stanford-le-Hope	d					08 16						08 46						09 16				
East Tilbury	d					08 20						08 50						09 20				
Tilbury Town 3	d					08 26						08 56						09 26				
Grays	d					08 30	08 55					09 00	09 25					09 30	09 55			
Purfleet	d						09 01						09 31						10 01			
Rainham	d						09 06						09 36						10 06			
Dagenham Dock	d			←			09 09			←			09 39			←			10 09			←
Chafford Hundred Lakeside	d			08 04		08 34				08 34		09 04				09 04		09 34				09 34
Ockendon	d			08 08		→				08 38		→				09 08		→				09 38
Upminster ⊖	d	08 00	←	08 14	08 22			08 30	←	08 44	08 52			09 00	←	09 14	09 22			09 30	←	09 44
Barking ⊖	d	08 10	08 15	08 23	08 30		09 15	08 40	08 45	08 53	09 00		09 45	09 10	09 15	09 23	09 30		10 15	09 40	09 45	09 53
Stratford 7 ⊖	a	08 21					→	08 51					→	09 21					→	09 51		
London Liverpool St 15 ⊖	a	08 31						09 01						09 31						10 01		
West Ham ⊖	d		08 20	08 28	08 36				08 50	08 58	09 06				09 20	09 28	09 36				09 50	09 58
Limehouse	d		08 25	08 33	08 41				08 55	09 03	09 11				09 25	09 33	09 41				09 55	10 03
London Fenchurch St 7 ⊖	a		08 31	08 39	08 46				09 01	09 09	09 16				09 31	09 39	09 46				10 01	10 09

		CC	CC D	CC D	CC	CC A	CC C	CC	CC D	CC D	CC	CC A	CC C	CC	CC D	CC D	CC	CC A	CC C	CC	CC D	CC D	CC
Shoeburyness	d	09 09	09 13		09 22			09 39	09 43		09 52			10 09	10 13		10 22			10 39	10 43		10 52
Thorpe Bay	d	09 13	09 17		09 26			09 43	09 47		09 56			10 13	10 17		10 26			10 43	10 47		10 56
Southend East	d	09 15	09 19		09 28			09 45	09 49		09 58			10 15	10 19		10 28			10 45	10 49		10 58
Southend Central	a	09 18	09 22		09 31			09 48	09 52		10 01			10 18	10 22		10 31			10 48	10 52		11 01
	d	09 18	09 22		09 31			09 48	09 52		10 01			10 18	10 22		10 31			10 48	10 52		11 01
Westcliff	d	09 20	09 24		09 33			09 50	09 54		10 03			10 20	10 24		10 33			10 50	10 54		11 03
Chalkwell	d	09 23	09 27		09 36			09 53	09 57		10 06			10 23	10 27		10 36			10 53	10 57		11 06
Leigh-on-Sea	d	09 26	09 30		09 38			09 56	10 00		10 08			10 26	10 30		10 38			10 56	11 00		11 08
Benfleet	d	09 31	09 35		09 43			10 01	10 05		10 13			10 31	10 35		10 43			11 01	11 05		11 13
Pitsea	d	09 34	09 40					10 04	10 10					10 34	10 40					11 04	11 10		
Basildon	d	09 38			09 49			10 08			10 19			10 38			10 49			11 08			11 19
Laindon	d	09 42			09 52			10 12			10 22			10 42			10 52			11 12			11 22
West Horndon	d	09 46						10 16						10 46						11 16			
Stanford-le-Hope	d		09 46						10 16						10 46						11 16		
East Tilbury	d		09 50						10 20						10 50						11 20		
Tilbury Town 3	d		09 56						10 26						10 56						11 26		
Grays	d		10 00	10 25					10 30	10 55					11 00	11 25					11 30	11 55	
Purfleet	d			10 31						11 01						11 31						12 01	
Rainham	d			10 36						11 06						11 36						12 06	
Dagenham Dock	d			10 39			←			11 09			←			11 39			←			12 09	
Chafford Hundred Lakeside	d		10 04				10 04		10 34				10 34		11 04				11 04		11 34		
Ockendon	d		→				10 08		→				10 38		→				11 08		→		
Upminster ⊖	d	09 52			10 00	←	10 14	10 22			10 30	←	10 44	10 52			11 00	←	11 14	11 22			11 30
Barking ⊖	d	10 00		10 45	10 10	10 15	10 23	10 30		11 15	10 41	10 45	10 53	11 00		11 45	11 10	11 15	11 23	11 30		12 15	11 40
Stratford 7 ⊖	a			→	10 21					→	10 51					→	11 21					→	11 51
London Liverpool St 15 ⊖	a				10 31						11 01						11 31						12 01
West Ham ⊖	d	10 06				10 20	10 28	10 36				10 50	10 58	11 06				11 20	11 28	11 36			
Limehouse	d	10 11				10 25	10 33	10 41				10 55	11 03	11 11				11 25	11 33	11 41			
London Fenchurch St 7 ⊖	a	10 16				10 31	10 39	10 46				11 01	11 09	11 16				11 31	11 39	11 46			

A From Grays
B From Southend Central
C From Shoeburyness
D To London Fenchurch Street

NRT DECEMBER 19 EDITION

Table T001-R

Saturdays

21 December to 16 May

Shoeburyness and Southend Central - London

		CC A	CC B	CC	CC C	CC C	CC	CC A	CC B	CC	CC C	CC C	CC	CC A	CC B	CC	CC C	CC C	CC	CC A	CC B	CC
Shoeburyness	d			11 09	11 13		11 22			11 39	11 43		11 52			12 09	12 13		12 22			12 39
Thorpe Bay	d			11 13	11 17		11 26			11 43	11 47		11 56			12 13	12 17		12 26			12 43
Southend East	d			11 15	11 19		11 28			11 45	11 49		11 58			12 15	12 19		12 28			12 45
Southend Central	a			11 18	11 22		11 31			11 48	11 52		12 01			12 18	12 22		12 31			12 48
	d			11 18	11 22		11 31			11 48	11 52		12 01			12 18	12 22		12 31			12 48
Westcliff	d			11 20	11 24		11 33			11 50	11 54		12 03			12 20	12 24		12 33			12 50
Chalkwell	d			11 23	11 27		11 36			11 53	11 57		12 06			12 23	12 27		12 36			12 53
Leigh-on-Sea	d			11 26	11 30		11 38			11 56	12 00		12 08			12 26	12 30		12 38			12 56
Benfleet	d			11 31	11 35		11 43			12 01	12 05		12 13			12 31	12 35		12 43			13 01
Pitsea	d			11 34	11 40					12 04	12 10					12 34	12 40					13 04
Basildon	d			11 38			11 49			12 08			12 19			12 38			12 49			13 08
Laindon	d			11 42			11 52			12 12			12 22			12 42			12 52			13 12
West Horndon	d			11 46						12 16						12 46						13 16
Stanford-le-Hope	d				11 46						12 16						12 46					
East Tilbury	d				11 50						12 20						12 50					
Tilbury Town 3	d				11 56						12 26						12 56					
Grays	d				12 00	12 25					12 30	12 55					13 00	13 25				
Purfleet	d					12 31						13 01						13 31				
Rainham	d					12 36						13 06						13 36				
Dagenham Dock	d		←			12 39			←			13 09			←			13 39			←	
Chafford Hundred Lakeside	d		11 34		12 04				12 04		12 34				12 34		13 04				13 04	
Ockendon	d		11 38		→				12 08		→				12 38		→				13 08	
Upminster ⊖	d	←	11 44	11 52			12 00	←	12 14	12 22			12 30	←	12 44	12 52			13 00	←	13 14	13 22
Barking ⊖	d	11 45	11 53	12 00		12 45	12 10	12 15	12 23	12 30		13 15	12 40	12 45	12 53	13 00		13 45	13 11	13 15	13 23	13 30
Stratford 7 ⊖	a					→	12 21					→	12 51					→	13 21			
London Liverpool St 15 ⊖	a						12 31						13 01						13 31			
West Ham ⊖	d	11 50	11 58	12 06				12 20	12 28	12 36				12 50	12 58	13 06				13 20	13 28	13 36
Limehouse	d	11 55	12 03	12 11				12 25	12 33	12 41				12 55	13 03	13 11				13 25	13 33	13 41
London Fenchurch St 7 ⊖	a	12 01	12 09	12 16				12 31	12 39	12 46				13 01	13 09	13 16				13 31	13 39	13 46

		CC C	CC C	CC	CC A	CC B	CC	CC C	CC C	CC	CC A	CC B	CC	CC C	CC C	CC	CC A	CC B	CC	CC C	CC C	CC	CC A
Shoeburyness	d	12 43		12 52			13 09	13 13		13 22			13 39	13 43		13 52			14 09	14 13		14 22	
Thorpe Bay	d	12 47		12 56			13 13	13 17		13 26			13 43	13 47		13 56			14 13	14 17		14 26	
Southend East	d	12 49		12 58			13 15	13 19		13 28			13 45	13 49		13 58			14 15	14 19		14 28	
Southend Central	a	12 52		13 01			13 18	13 22		13 31			13 48	13 52		14 01			14 18	14 22		14 31	
	d	12 52		13 01			13 18	13 22		13 31			13 48	13 52		14 01			14 18	14 22		14 31	
Westcliff	d	12 54		13 03			13 20	13 24		13 33			13 50	13 54		14 03			14 20	14 24		14 33	
Chalkwell	d	12 57		13 06			13 23	13 27		13 36			13 53	13 57		14 06			14 23	14 27		14 36	
Leigh-on-Sea	d	13 00		13 08			13 26	13 30		13 38			13 56	14 00		14 08			14 26	14 30		14 38	
Benfleet	d	13 05		13 13			13 31	13 35		13 43			14 01	14 05		14 13			14 31	14 35		14 43	
Pitsea	d	13 10					13 34	13 40					14 04	14 10					14 34	14 40			
Basildon	d			13 19			13 38			13 49			14 08			14 19			14 38			14 49	
Laindon	d			13 22			13 42			13 52			14 12			14 22			14 42			14 52	
West Horndon	d						13 46						14 16						14 46				
Stanford-le-Hope	d	13 16						13 46						14 16						14 46			
East Tilbury	d	13 20						13 50						14 20						14 50			
Tilbury Town 3	d	13 26						13 56						14 26						14 56			
Grays	d	13 30	13 55					14 00	14 25					14 30	14 55					15 00	15 25		
Purfleet	d		14 01						14 31						15 01						15 31		
Rainham	d		14 06						14 36						15 06						15 36		
Dagenham Dock	d		14 09			←			14 39			←			15 09			←			15 39		
Chafford Hundred Lakeside	d	13 34				13 34		14 04				14 04		14 34				14 34		15 04			
Ockendon	d	→				13 38		→				14 08		→				14 38		→			
Upminster ⊖	d			13 30	←	13 44	13 52			14 00	←	14 14	14 22			14 30	←	14 44	14 52			15 00	←
Barking ⊖	d		14 15	13 40	13 45	13 53	14 00		14 45	14 10	14 15	14 23	14 30		15 15	14 40	14 45	14 53	15 00		15 45	15 10	15 15
Stratford 7 ⊖	a		→	13 51					→	14 21					→	14 51					→	15 21	
London Liverpool St 15 ⊖	a			14 01						14 31						15 01						15 31	
West Ham ⊖	d				13 50	13 58	14 06				14 20	14 28	14 36				14 50	14 58	15 06				15 20
Limehouse	d				13 55	14 03	14 11				14 25	14 33	14 41				14 55	15 03	15 11				15 25
London Fenchurch St 7 ⊖	a				14 01	14 09	14 16				14 31	14 39	14 46				15 01	15 09	15 16				15 31

		CC B	CC	CC C	CC C	CC	CC A	CC B	CC	CC C	CC C	CC	CC A	CC B	CC	CC C	CC C	CC	CC A	CC B	CC	CC C	CC C
Shoeburyness	d		14 39	14 43		14 52			15 09	15 13		15 22			15 39	15 43		15 52			16 09	16 13	
Thorpe Bay	d		14 43	14 47		14 56			15 13	15 17		15 26			15 43	15 47		15 56			16 13	16 17	
Southend East	d		14 45	14 49		14 58			15 15	15 19		15 28			15 45	15 49		15 58			16 15	16 19	
Southend Central	a		14 48	14 52		15 01			15 18	15 22		15 31			15 48	15 52		16 01			16 18	16 22	
	d		14 48	14 52		15 01			15 18	15 22		15 31			15 48	15 52		16 01			16 18	16 22	
Westcliff	d		14 50	14 54		15 03			15 20	15 24		15 33			15 50	15 54		16 03			16 20	16 24	
Chalkwell	d		14 53	14 57		15 06			15 23	15 27		15 36			15 53	15 57		16 06			16 23	16 27	
Leigh-on-Sea	d		14 56	15 00		15 08			15 26	15 30		15 38			15 56	16 00		16 08			16 26	16 30	
Benfleet	d		15 01	15 05		15 13			15 31	15 35		15 43			16 01	16 05		16 13			16 31	16 35	
Pitsea	d		15 04	15 10					15 34	15 40					16 04	16 10					16 34	16 40	
Basildon	d		15 08			15 19			15 38			15 49			16 08			16 19			16 38		
Laindon	d		15 12			15 22			15 42			15 52			16 12			16 22			16 42		
West Horndon	d		15 16						15 46						16 16						16 46		
Stanford-le-Hope	d			15 16						15 46						16 16						16 46	
East Tilbury	d			15 20						15 50						16 20						16 50	
Tilbury Town 3	d			15 26						15 56						16 26						16 56	
Grays	d			15 30	15 55					16 00	16 25					16 30	16 55					17 00	17 25
Purfleet	d				16 01						16 31						17 01						17 31
Rainham	d				16 06						16 36						17 06						17 36
Dagenham Dock	d	←			16 09			←			16 39			←			17 09			←			17 39
Chafford Hundred Lakeside	d	15 04		15 34				15 34		16 04				16 04		16 34				16 34		17 04	
Ockendon	d	15 08		→				15 38		→				16 08		→				16 38		→	
Upminster ⊖	d	15 14	15 22			15 30	←	15 44	15 52			16 00	←	16 14	16 22			16 30	←	16 44	16 52		
Barking ⊖	d	15 23	15 30		16 15	15 41	15 45	15 53	16 00		16 45	16 10	16 15	16 23	16 30		17 15	16 40	16 45	16 53	17 00		17 45
Stratford 7 ⊖	a				→	15 51					→	16 21					→	16 51					→
London Liverpool St 15 ⊖	a					16 01						16 31						17 01					
West Ham ⊖	d	15 28	15 36				15 50	15 58	16 06				16 20	16 28	16 36				16 50	16 58	17 06		
Limehouse	d	15 33	15 41				15 55	16 03	16 11				16 25	16 33	16 41				16 55	17 03	17 11		
London Fenchurch St 7 ⊖	a	15 39	15 46				16 01	16 09	16 16				16 31	16 39	16 46				17 01	17 09	17 16		

A From Grays
B From Shoeburyness
C To London Fenchurch Street

Table T001-R

Saturdays

21 December to 16 May

Shoeburyness and Southend Central - London

		CC		CC A	CC B	CC	CC C	CC C	CC	CC A	CC B	CC		CC C	CC C	CC	CC A	CC B	CC	CC C	CC C	CC		CC A	CC B
Shoeburyness	d	16 22				16 39	16 43		16 52			17 09		17 13		17 22			17 39	17 43		17 52			
Thorpe Bay	d	16 26				16 43	16 47		16 56			17 13		17 17		17 26			17 43	17 47		17 56			
Southend East	d	16 28				16 45	16 49		16 58			17 15		17 19		17 28			17 45	17 49		17 58			
Southend Central	a	16 31				16 48	16 52		17 01			17 18		17 22		17 31			17 48	17 52		18 01			
	d	16 31				16 48	16 52		17 01			17 18		17 22		17 31			17 48	17 52		18 01			
Westcliff	d	16 33				16 50	16 54		17 03			17 20		17 24		17 33			17 50	17 54		18 03			
Chalkwell	d	16 36				16 53	16 57		17 06			17 23		17 27		17 36			17 53	17 57		18 06			
Leigh-on-Sea	d	16 38				16 56	17 00		17 08			17 26		17 30		17 38			17 56	18 00		18 08			
Benfleet	d	16 43				17 01	17 05		17 13			17 31		17 35		17 43			18 01	18 05		18 13			
Pitsea	d					17 04	17 10					17 34		17 40					18 04	18 10					
Basildon	d	16 49				17 08			17 19			17 38				17 49			18 08			18 19			
Laindon	d	16 52				17 12			17 22			17 42				17 52			18 12			18 22			
West Horndon	d					17 16						17 46							18 16						
Stanford-le-Hope	d						17 16							17 46						18 16					
East Tilbury	d						17 20							17 50						18 20					
Tilbury Town 3	d						17 26							17 56						18 26					
Grays	d						17 30	17 55						18 00	18 25					18 30	18 55				
Purfleet	d							18 01							18 31						19 01				
Rainham	d							18 06							18 36						19 06				
Dagenham Dock	d				←			18 09			←				18 39			←			19 09				←
Chafford Hundred Lakeside	d				17 04		17 34				17 34			18 04				18 04		18 34					18 34
Ockendon	d				17 08		→				17 38			→				18 08		→					18 38
Upminster ⊖	d	17 00		←	17 14	17 22			17 30	←	17 44	17 52				18 00	←	18 14	18 22			18 30		←	18 44
Barking ⊖	d	17 10		17 15	17 23	17 30		18 15	17 40	17 45	17 53	18 00			18 45	18 10	18 15	18 23	18 30		19 15	18 40		18 45	18 53
Stratford 7 ⊖	a	17 21						→	17 51						→	18 21					→	18 51			
London Liverpool St 15 ⊖	a	17 31							18 01							18 31						19 01			
West Ham ⊖	d			17 20	17 28	17 36				17 50	17 58	18 06					18 20	18 28	18 36					18 50	18 58
Limehouse	d			17 25	17 33	17 41				17 55	18 03	18 11					18 25	18 33	18 41					18 55	19 03
London Fenchurch St 7 ⊖	a			17 31	17 39	17 46				18 01	18 09	18 16					18 31	18 39	18 46					19 01	19 09

		CC	CC C	CC C	CC	CC A	CC B	CC		CC C	CC C	CC	CC A	CC B	CC	CC C	CC C	CC		CC A	CC B	CC	CC C	CC C	CC
Shoeburyness	d	18 09	18 13		18 22			18 39		18 43		18 52			19 09	19 13		19 22				19 39	19 43		19 52
Thorpe Bay	d	18 13	18 17		18 26			18 43		18 47		18 56			19 13	19 17		19 26				19 43	19 47		19 56
Southend East	d	18 15	18 19		18 28			18 45		18 49		18 58			19 15	19 19		19 28				19 45	19 49		19 58
Southend Central	a	18 18	18 22		18 31			18 48		18 52		19 01			19 18	19 22		19 31				19 48	19 52		20 01
	d	18 18	18 22		18 31			18 48		18 52		19 01			19 18	19 22		19 31				19 48	19 52		20 01
Westcliff	d	18 20	18 24		18 33			18 50		18 54		19 03			19 20	19 24		19 33				19 50	19 54		20 03
Chalkwell	d	18 23	18 27		18 36			18 53		18 57		19 06			19 23	19 27		19 36				19 53	19 57		20 06
Leigh-on-Sea	d	18 26	18 30		18 38			18 56		19 00		19 08			19 26	19 30		19 38				19 56	20 00		20 08
Benfleet	d	18 31	18 35		18 43			19 01		19 05		19 13			19 31	19 35		19 43				20 01	20 05		20 13
Pitsea	d	18 34	18 40					19 04		19 10					19 34	19 40						20 04	20 10		
Basildon	d	18 38			18 49			19 08				19 19			19 38			19 49				20 08			20 19
Laindon	d	18 42			18 52			19 12				19 22			19 42			19 52				20 12			20 22
West Horndon	d	18 46						19 16							19 46							20 16			
Stanford-le-Hope	d		18 46							19 16						19 46							20 16		
East Tilbury	d		18 50							19 20						19 50							20 20		
Tilbury Town 3	d		18 56							19 26						19 56							20 26		
Grays	d		19 00	19 25						19 30	19 55					20 00	20 25						20 30	20 55	
Purfleet	d			19 31							20 01						20 31							21 01	
Rainham	d			19 36							20 06						20 36							21 06	
Dagenham Dock	d			19 39			←				20 09			←			20 39				←			21 09	
Chafford Hundred Lakeside	d		19 04				19 04			19 34				19 34		20 04					20 04		20 34		
Ockendon	d		→				19 08			→				19 38		→					20 08		→		
Upminster ⊖	d	18 52			19 00	←	19 14	19 22				19 30	←	19 44	19 52			20 00		←	20 14	20 22			20 30
Barking ⊖	d	19 00		19 45	19 10	19 15	19 23	19 30			20 15	19 40	19 45	19 53	20 00		20 45	20 10		20 15	20 23	20 30		21 15	20 40
Stratford 7 ⊖	a			→	19 21						→	19 51					→	20 21						→	20 51
London Liverpool St 15 ⊖	a				19 31							20 01						20 31							21 01
West Ham ⊖	d	19 06				19 20	19 28	19 36					19 50	19 58	20 06					20 20	20 28	20 36			
Limehouse	d	19 11				19 25	19 33	19 41					19 55	20 03	20 11					20 25	20 33	20 41			
London Fenchurch St 7 ⊖	a	19 16				19 31	19 39	19 46					20 01	20 09	20 16					20 31	20 39	20 46			

		CC A	CC B	CC		CC C	CC C	CC	CC A	CC B	CC	CC C	CC C	CC		CC A	CC B	CC	CC C	CC C	CC	CC A	CC B	CC	
Shoeburyness	d			20 09		20 13		20 22			20 39	20 43		20 52				21 09	21 13		21 22			21 39	
Thorpe Bay	d			20 13		20 17		20 26			20 43	20 47		20 56				21 13	21 17		21 26			21 43	
Southend East	d			20 15		20 19		20 28			20 45	20 49		20 58				21 15	21 19		21 28			21 45	
Southend Central	a			20 18		20 22		20 31			20 48	20 52		21 01				21 18	21 22		21 31			21 48	
	d			20 18		20 22		20 31			20 48	20 52		21 01				21 18	21 22		21 31			21 48	
Westcliff	d			20 20		20 24		20 33			20 50	20 54		21 03				21 20	21 24		21 33			21 50	
Chalkwell	d			20 23		20 27		20 36			20 53	20 57		21 06				21 23	21 27		21 36			21 53	
Leigh-on-Sea	d			20 26		20 30		20 38			20 56	21 00		21 08				21 26	21 30		21 38			21 56	
Benfleet	d			20 31		20 35		20 43			21 01	21 05		21 13				21 31	21 35		21 43			22 01	
Pitsea	d			20 34		20 40					21 04	21 10						21 34	21 40					22 04	
Basildon	d			20 38				20 49			21 08			21 19				21 38			21 49			22 08	
Laindon	d			20 42				20 52			21 12			21 22				21 42			21 52			22 12	
West Horndon	d			20 46							21 16							21 46						22 16	
Stanford-le-Hope	d					20 46						21 16							21 46						
East Tilbury	d					20 50						21 20							21 50						
Tilbury Town 3	d					20 56						21 26							21 56						
Grays	d					21 00	21 25					21 30	21 55						22 00	22 25					
Purfleet	d						21 31						22 01							22 31					
Rainham	d						21 36						22 06							22 36					
Dagenham Dock	d		←				21 39			←			22 09				←			22 39			←		
Chafford Hundred Lakeside	d		20 34			21 04				21 04		21 34					21 34		22 04				22 04		
Ockendon	d		20 38			→				21 08		→					21 38		→				22 08		
Upminster ⊖	d	←	20 44	20 52				21 00	←	21 14	21 22			21 30		←	21 44	21 52			22 00	←	22 14	22 22	
Barking ⊖	d	20 45	20 53	21 00			21 45	21 10	21 15	21 23	21 30		22 15	21 40		21 45	21 53	22 00		22 45	22 10	22 15	22 23	22 30	
Stratford 7 ⊖	a						→	21 21					→	21 51						→	22 21				
London Liverpool St 15 ⊖	a							21 31						22 01							22 31				
West Ham ⊖	d	20 50	20 58	21 06					21 20	21 28	21 36					21 50	21 58	22 06				22 20	22 28	22 36	
Limehouse	d	20 55	21 03	21 11					21 25	21 33	21 41					21 55	22 03	22 11				22 25	22 33	22 41	
London Fenchurch St 7 ⊖	a	21 01	21 09	21 16					21 31	21 39	21 46					22 01	22 09	22 16				22 31	22 39	22 46	

A From Grays B From Shoeburyness C To London Fenchurch Street

For services between Southend Victoria and London Liverpool Street refer to Table 6

Table T001-R

Saturdays

21 December to 16 May

Shoeburyness and Southend Central - London

		CC A	CC A	CC	CC B	CC C	CC	CC A	CC	CC B		CC C	CC	CC	CC	CC	CC	CC
Shoeburyness	d	21 43		21 52			22 09	22 13	22 22				22 39		22 43	23 09	23 29	23 33
Thorpe Bay	d	21 47		21 56			22 13	22 17	22 26				22 43		22 47	23 13	23 33	23 37
Southend East	d	21 49		21 58			22 15	22 19	22 28				22 45		22 49	23 15	23 35	23 39
Southend Central	a	21 52		22 01			22 18	22 22	22 31				22 48		22 52	23 18	23 38	23 42
	d	21 52		22 01			22 18	22 22	22 31				22 48		22 52	23 18	23 38	23 42
Westcliff	d	21 54		22 03			22 20	22 24	22 33				22 50		22 54	23 20	23 40	23 44
Chalkwell	d	21 57		22 06			22 23	22 27	22 36				22 53		22 57	23 23	23 43	23 47
Leigh-on-Sea	d	22 00		22 08			22 26	22 30	22 38				22 56		23 00	23 26	23 46	23 50
Benfleet	d	22 05		22 13			22 31	22 35	22 43				23 01		23 05	23 31	23 51	23 54
Pitsea	d	22 10					22 34	22 40					23 04		23 10	23 34	23 54	23 59
Basildon	d			22 19			22 38		22 49				23 08			23 38	23 58	
Laindon	d			22 22			22 42		22 52				23 12			23 42	00 01	
West Horndon	d						22 46						23 16			23 46	00 06	
Stanford-le-Hope	d	22 16						22 46							23 16			00 05
East Tilbury	d	22 20						22 50							23 20			00 09
Tilbury Town 3	d	22 26						22 56							23 26			00 15
Grays	d	22 30	22 55					23 00						23 25	23 30			00 19
Purfleet	d		23 01											23 31				
Rainham	d		23 06											23 36				
Dagenham Dock	d		23 09			←						←		23 39				
Chafford Hundred Lakeside	d	22 34				22 34		23 04				23 04			23 34			00 24
Ockendon	d	→				22 38		→				23 08			23 38			00 28
Upminster ⊖	d			22 30	←	22 44	22 52		23 00	←		23 14	23 22		23 44	23 52	00 11	00 34
Barking ⊖	d		23 15	22 40	22 45	22 53	23 00		23 09	23 15		23 23	23 30	23 45	23 53	23 59	00 20	00a43
Stratford 7 ⊖	a		→	22 51					23 21									
London Liverpool St 15 ⊖	a			23 01					23 31									
West Ham ⊖	d				22 50	22 58	23 06			23 20		23 28	23 36	23 50	23 58	00 06	00 25	
Limehouse	d				22 55	23 03	23 11			23 25		23 33	23 41	23 55	00 03	00 11	00 30	
London Fenchurch St 7 ⊖	a				23 01	23 09	23 16			23 31		23 39	23 46	00 02	00 10	00 16	00 36	

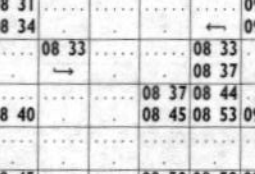
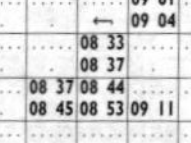

Sundays

15 December to 10 May

		CC D	CC D	CC D	CC D	CC	CC A	CC	CC C	CC		CC A	CC	CC C	CC	CC A	CC	CC C	CC	CC A		CC	CC C	CC
Shoeburyness	d					05 40	06 02	06 10		06 26		06 43	06 56			07 13	07 26			07 43		07 56		
Thorpe Bay	d					05 44	06 06	06 14		06 30		06 47	07 00			07 17	07 30			07 47		08 00		
Southend East	d					05 46	06 08	06 16		06 32		06 49	07 02			07 19	07 32			07 49		08 02		
Southend Central	a					05 49	06 11	06 19		06 35		06 52	07 05			07 22	07 35			07 52		08 05		
	d					05 49	06 11	06 19		06 35		06 52	07 05			07 22	07 35			07 52		08 05		
Westcliff	d					05 51	06 13	06 21		06 37		06 54	07 07			07 24	07 37			07 54		08 07		
Chalkwell	d					05 54	06 16	06 24		06 40		06 57	07 10			07 27	07 40			07 57		08 10		
Leigh-on-Sea	d					05 56	06 19	06 26		06 42		07 00	07 12			07 30	07 42			08 00		08 12		
Benfleet	d					06 01	06 24	06 31		06 47		07 05	07 17			07 35	07 47			08 05		08 17		
Pitsea	d					06 04	06 29	06 34		06 50		07 10	07 20			07 40	07 50			08 10		08 20		
Basildon	d					06 08		06 38		06 54			07 24				07 54					08 24		
Laindon	d			00 01		06 11		06 41		06 57			07 27				07 57					08 27		
West Horndon	d			00 06		06 16		06 46		07 02			07 32				08 02					08 32		
Stanford-le-Hope	d				00 05		06 35					07 16				07 46				08 16				
East Tilbury	d				00 09		06 38					07 19				07 49				08 19				
Tilbury Town 3	d				00 15		06 44					07 25				07 55				08 25				
Grays	d				00 19		06 48					07 30			07 40	08 00			08 20	08 30				08 50
Purfleet	d														07 46				08 26					08 56
Rainham	d														07 51				08 31					09 01
Dagenham Dock	d								←					←	07 54			←	08 34				←	09 04
Chafford Hundred Lakeside	d				00 24		06 51		06 51			07 33		07 33		08 03		08 03		08 33			08 33	
Ockendon	d				00 28		→		06 55			→		07 37		→		08 07		→			08 37	
Upminster ⊖	d			00 11	00 34	06 21		06 51	07 02	07 07			07 37	07 44			08 07	08 14				08 37	08 44	
Barking ⊖	d			00 20	00a43	06 29		06 59	07 11	07 15			07 45	07 53	08 00		08 15	08 23	08 40			08 45	08 53	09 11
Stratford 7 ⊖	a																							
London Liverpool St 15 ⊖	a																							
West Ham ⊖	d		00 06	00 25		06 34		07 04	07 16	07 20			07 50	07 58	08 05		08 20	08 28	08 45			08 50	08 58	09 16
Limehouse	d	00 03	00 11	00 30		06 39		07 09	07 21	07 25			07 55	08 03	08 10		08 25	08 33	08 50			08 55	09 03	09 21
London Fenchurch St 7 ⊖	a	00 10	00 16	00 36		06 45		07 16	07 28	07 32			08 02	08 09	08 15		08 32	08 39	08 55			09 02	09 09	09 25

A To London Fenchurch Street
B From Grays
C From Shoeburyness
D not 15 December. From Shoeburyness

For services between Southend Victoria and London Liverpool Street refer to Table 6

Table T001-R

Sundays

15 December to 10 May

Shoeburyness and Southend Central - London

		CC A	CC	CC B	CC	CC A	CC	CC B	CC		CC A	CC	CC B	CC	CC A	CC	CC B	CC		CC A	CC	CC B	CC A	CC
Shoeburyness	d	08 13	08 26			08 43	08 56				20 13	20 26			20 43	20 56				21 13	21 26		21 43	21 56
Thorpe Bay	d	08 17	08 30			08 47	09 00				20 17	20 30			20 47	21 00				21 17	21 30		21 47	22 00
Southend East	d	08 19	08 32			08 49	09 02				20 19	20 32			20 49	21 02				21 19	21 32		21 49	22 02
Southend Central	a	08 22	08 35			08 52	09 05				20 22	20 35			20 52	21 05				21 22	21 35		21 52	22 05
	d	08 22	08 35			08 52	09 05				20 22	20 35			20 52	21 05				21 22	21 35		21 52	22 05
Westcliff	d	08 24	08 37			08 54	09 07				20 24	20 37			20 54	21 07				21 24	21 37		21 54	22 07
Chalkwell	d	08 27	08 40			08 57	09 10				20 27	20 40			20 57	21 10				21 27	21 40		21 57	22 10
Leigh-on-Sea	d	08 30	08 42			09 00	09 12				20 30	20 42			21 00	21 12				21 30	21 42		22 00	22 12
Benfleet	d	08 35	08 47			09 05	09 17				20 35	20 47			21 05	21 17				21 35	21 47		22 05	22 17
Pitsea	d	08 40	08 50			09 10	09 20				20 40	20 50			21 10	21 20				21 40	21 50		22 10	22 20
Basildon	d		08 54				09 24			and at the same minutes past each hour until		20 54				21 24					21 54			22 24
Laindon	d		08 57				09 27					20 57				21 27					21 57			22 27
West Horndon	d		09 02				09 32					21 02				21 32					22 02			22 32
Stanford-le-Hope	d	08 46				09 16					20 46				21 16					21 46			22 16	
East Tilbury	d	08 49				09 19					20 49				21 19					21 49			22 19	
Tilbury Town	d	08 55				09 25					20 55				21 25					21 55			22 25	
Grays	d	09 00			09 20	09 30			09 50		21 00			21 20	21 30			21 50		22 00			22 30	
Purfleet	d				09 26				09 56					21 26				21 56						
Rainham	d				09 31				10 01					21 31				22 01						
Dagenham Dock	d			←	09 34			←	10 04				←	21 34			←	22 04				←		
Chafford Hundred Lakeside	d	09 03		09 03		09 33		09 33			21 03		21 03		21 33		21 33			22 03		22 03	22 33	
Ockendon	d	→		09 07		→		09 37			→		21 07		→		21 37			→		22 07	→	
Upminster	d		09 07	09 14			09 37	09 44				21 07	21 14			21 37	21 44				22 07	22 14		22 37
Barking	d		09 17	09 23	09 40		09 47	09 53	10 10			21 17	21 23	21 40		21 47	21 53	22 10			22 17	22 23		22 47
Stratford	a		09 25				09 55					21 25				21 55					22 25			22 55
London Liverpool St	a		09 35				10 05					21 35				22 05					22 35			23 05
West Ham	d			09 28	09 45			09 58	10 15				21 28	21 45			21 58	22 15				22 28		
Limehouse	d			09 33	09 50			10 03	10 20				21 33	21 50			22 03	22 20				22 33		
London Fenchurch St	a			09 39	09 55			10 09	10 25				21 39	21 55			22 09	22 25				22 39		

		CC B	CC	CC	CC A		CC	CC B
Shoeburyness	d			22 10	22 26		22 40	
Thorpe Bay	d			22 14	22 30		22 44	
Southend East	d			22 16	22 32		22 46	
Southend Central	a			22 19	22 35		22 49	
	d			22 19	22 35		22 49	
Westcliff	d			22 21	22 37		22 51	
Chalkwell	d			22 24	22 40		22 54	
Leigh-on-Sea	d			22 26	22 43		22 56	
Benfleet	d			22 31	22 48		23 01	
Pitsea	d			22 34	22 53		23 04	
Basildon	d			22 38			23 08	
Laindon	d			22 41			23 11	
West Horndon	d			22 46			23 16	
Stanford-le-Hope	d				22 59			
East Tilbury	d				23 02			
Tilbury Town	d				23 08			
Grays	d		22 35		23 12			
Purfleet	d		22 41					
Rainham	d		22 46					
Dagenham Dock	d	←	22 49					←
Chafford Hundred Lakeside	d	22 33			23 15			23 15
Ockendon	d	22 37			→			23 19
Upminster	d	22 44		22 51			23 21	23 26
Barking	d	22 53	22 56	22 59			23 29	23 35
Stratford	a							
London Liverpool St	a							
West Ham	d	22 58	23 01	23 04			23 34	23 40
Limehouse	d	23 03	23 06	23 09			23 39	23 45
London Fenchurch St	a	23 09	23 11	23 16			23 46	23 51

A To London Fenchurch Street **B** From Shoeburyness

For services between Southend Victoria and London Liverpool Street refer to Table 6

Table T004-F

Mondays to Saturdays

16 December to 16 May

Romford - Upminster

Miles			LO	LO	LO	LO	LO	LO	LO	LO	LO		LO	LO	LO	LO	LO	LO	LO	LO	LO		LO	LO	LO
0	**Romford**	d	06 11	06 41	07 11	07 41	08 11	08 41	09 11	09 41	10 11		10 41	11 11	11 41	12 11	12 41	13 11	13 41	14 11	14 41		15 11	15 41	16 11
2	Emerson Park	d	06 15	06 45	07 15	07 45	08 15	08 45	09 15	09 45	10 15		10 45	11 15	11 45	12 15	12 45	13 15	13 45	14 15	14 45		15 15	15 45	16 15
3½	**Upminster**	a	06 20	06 50	07 20	07 50	08 20	08 50	09 20	09 50	10 20		10 50	11 20	11 50	12 20	12 50	13 20	13 50	14 20	14 50		15 20	15 50	16 20

		LO	LO	LO	LO	LO	LO		LO	LO	LO	LO	LO
Romford	d	16 41	17 11	17 41	18 11	18 41	19 11		19 41	20 11	20 41	21 11	21 41
Emerson Park	d	16 45	17 15	17 45	18 15	18 45	19 15		19 45	20 15	20 45	21 15	21 45
Upminster	a	16 50	17 20	17 50	18 20	18 50	19 20		19 50	20 20	20 50	21 20	21 50

Sundays

15 December to 10 May

		LO	LO	LO	LO	LO	LO	LO	LO	LO		LO	LO	LO	LO	LO	LO	LO	LO	LO		LO	LO	LO	LO
Romford	d	08 41	09 11	09 41	10 11	10 41	11 11	11 41	12 11	12 41		13 11	13 41	14 11	14 41	15 11	15 41	16 11	16 41	17 11		17 41	18 11	18 41	19 11
Emerson Park	d	08 45	09 15	09 45	10 15	10 45	11 15	11 45	12 15	12 45		13 15	13 45	14 15	14 45	15 15	15 45	16 15	16 45	17 15		17 45	18 15	18 45	19 15
Upminster	a	08 50	09 20	09 50	10 20	10 50	11 20	11 50	12 20	12 50		13 20	13 50	14 20	14 50	15 20	15 50	16 20	16 50	17 20		17 50	18 20	18 50	19 20

		LO
Romford	d	19 41
Emerson Park	d	19 45
Upminster	a	19 50

Table T004-R

Mondays to Saturdays

16 December to 16 May

Upminster - Romford

Miles			LO	LO	LO	LO	LO	LO		LO	LO	LO	LO	LO	LO	LO	LO	LO		LO	LO	LO	LO	LO	LO
0	**Upminster**	d	06 24	06 54	07 24	07 54	08 24	08 54		09 24	09 54	10 24	10 54	11 24	11 54	12 24	12 54	13 24		13 54	14 24	14 54	15 24	15 54	16 24
1½	Emerson Park	d	06 28	06 58	07 28	07 58	08 28	08 58		09 28	09 58	10 28	10 58	11 28	11 58	12 28	12 58	13 28		13 58	14 28	14 58	15 28	15 58	16 28
3½	**Romford**	a	06 33	07 03	07 33	08 03	08 33	09 03		09 33	10 03	10 33	11 03	11 33	12 03	12 33	13 03	13 33		14 03	14 33	15 03	15 33	16 03	16 33

		LO	LO	LO		LO	LO	LO	LO	LO	LO	LO	LO
Upminster	d	16 54	17 24	17 54		18 24	18 54	19 24	19 54	20 24	20 54	21 24	21 54
Emerson Park	d	16 58	17 28	17 58		18 28	18 58	19 28	19 58	20 28	20 58	21 28	21 58
Romford	a	17 03	17 33	18 03		18 33	19 03	19 33	20 03	20 33	21 03	21 33	22 03

Sundays

15 December to 10 May

		LO	LO	LO	LO	LO	LO	LO	LO	LO		LO	LO	LO	LO	LO	LO	LO	LO	LO		LO	LO	LO	LO
Upminster	d	08 54	09 24	09 54	10 24	10 54	11 24	11 54	12 24	12 54		13 24	13 54	14 24	14 54	15 24	15 54	16 24	16 54	17 24		17 54	18 24	18 54	19 24
Emerson Park	d	08 58	09 28	09 58	10 28	10 58	11 28	11 58	12 28	12 58		13 28	13 58	14 28	14 58	15 28	15 58	16 28	16 58	17 28		17 58	18 28	18 58	19 28
Romford	a	09 03	09 33	10 03	10 33	11 03	11 33	12 03	12 33	13 03		13 33	14 03	14 33	15 03	15 33	16 03	16 33	17 03	17 33		18 03	18 33	19 03	19 33

		LO
Upminster	d	19 54
Emerson Park	d	19 58
Romford	a	20 03

Table T005-F

London Liverpool Street - Ilford - Shenfield

Mondays to Fridays
16 December to 15 May

Miles	Station		XR MO A	XR MX	XR MO	LE MO B	LE MX 1 B	XR	XR MX	XR MO	LE MO B	LE MX 1 C	LE MX 1 B	XR	LE ◇1 D	XR	XR	XR	XR	XR	XR	XR	XR
0	**London Liverpool Street** 15 ⊖	d		00 01	00 05	00 14	00 15	00 20	00 32	00 35	00 44	00 46	00 50	00 55	05 23	05 24	05 40	06 00	06 10	06 20	06 30	06 40	06 50
4	Stratford 7 ⊖	d		00 08	00 12	00 21	00 22	00 27	00 39	00 42	00 51	00 53	00 57	01 02	05 30	05 31	05 47	06 07	06 17	06 27	06 37	06 47	06 57
4½	Maryland	d		00 10	00 14			00 29	00 41	00 44				01 04		05 33	05 49	06 09	06 19	06 29	06 39	06 49	06 59
5¼	Forest Gate	d		00 12	00 16			00 31	00 43	00 46				01 06		05 35	05 51	06 11	06 21	06 31	06 41	06 51	07 01
6¼	Manor Park	d	00 02	00 14	00 18			00 33	00 45	00 48				01 08		05 37	05 53	06 13	06 23	06 33	06 43	06 53	07 03
7¼	Ilford 2	d	00 05	00 17	00 21			00 36	00 48	00 51				01 11		05 40	05 56	06 16	06 26	06 36	06 46	06 56	07 06
8½	Seven Kings	d	00 07	00 19	00 23			00 38	00 50	00 53				01 13		05 42	05 58	06 18	06 28	06 38	06 48	06 58	07 08
9¼	Goodmayes	d	00 09	00 21	00 25			00 40	00 52	00 55				01 15		05 44	06 00	06 20	06 30	06 40	06 50	07 00	07 10
10	Chadwell Heath	d	00 11	00 23	00 27			00 42	00 54	00 57				01 17		05 46	06 02	06 22	06 32	06 42	06 52	07 02	07 12
12½	Romford	d	00 15	00 27	00 31	00 36	00 32	00 46	00 58	01 01	01 05		01 08	01 21	05 38	05 50	06 06	06 26	06 36	06 46	06 56	07 06	07 16
13½	Gidea Park 2	a	00 18	00 33	00 37			00 50	01 04	01 07		01 06		01 25		05 54	06 10	06 30	06 40	06 50	07 00	07 10	07 20
—		d	00 18					00 50				01 06		01 25		05 54	06 10	06 30	06 40	06 50	07 00	07 10	07 20
15	Harold Wood	d	00 21					00 53						01 28		05 57	06 13	06 33	06 43	06 53	07 03	07 13	07 23
18¾	Brentwood	d	00 25					00 57						01 32		06 01	06 17	06 37	06 47	06 57	07 07	07 17	07 27
20¼	**Shenfield** 3	a	00 31			00 49	00 44	01 05			01 19	01 16	01 20	01 40	05 47	06 07	06 23	06 43	06 53	07 04	07 13	07 23	07 33

Station		XR	XR	XR	LE 1 E	XR	XR	XR	XR	XR	XR	XR	XR	XR	XR	XR	XR	XR	XR	XR	XR	XR	XR
London Liverpool Street 15 ⊖	d	06 57	07 00	07 07	07 08	07 10	07 17	07 20	07 27	07 30	07 37	07 40	07 47	07 50	07 57	08 00	08 07	08 10	08 17	08 20	08 27	08 30	08 37
Stratford 7 ⊖	d	07 04	07 07	07 14	07 15	07 17	07 24	07 27	07 34	07 37	07 44	07 47	07 54	07 57	08 04	08 07	08 14	08 17	08 24	08 27	08 34	08 37	08 44
Maryland	d		07 09			07 19		07 29		07 39		07 49		07 59		08 09		08 19		08 29		08 39	
Forest Gate	d		07 11			07 21		07 31		07 41		07 51		08 01		08 11		08 21		08 31		08 41	
Manor Park	d		07 13			07 23		07 33		07 43		07 53		08 03		08 13		08 23		08 33		08 43	
Ilford 2	d	07 11	07 16	07 21		07 26	07 31	07 36	07 41	07 46	07 51	07 56	08 01	08 06	08 11	08 16	08 21	08 26	08 31	08 36	08 41	08 46	08 51
Seven Kings	d	07 13	07 18	07 23		07 28	07 33	07 38	07 43	07 48	07 53	07 58	08 03	08 08		08 18	08 23	08 28		08 38	08 43	08 48	
Goodmayes	d	07 15	07 20	07 25		07 30	07 35	07 40	07 45	07 50	07 55	08 00	08 05	08 10		08 20	08 25	08 30		08 40	08 45	08 50	
Chadwell Heath	d	07 17	07 22	07 27		07 32	07 37	07 42	07 47	07 52	07 57	08 02	08 07	08 12		08 22	08 27	08 32		08 42	08 47	08 52	
Romford	d	07 21	07 26	07 31	07 23	07 36	07 41	07 46	07 51	07 56	08 01	08 06	08 11	08 16	08 20	08 26	08 31	08 36	08 40	08 46	08 51	08 56	09 00
Gidea Park 2	a	07 27	07 30	07 37		07 40	07 47	07 50	07 57	08 00	08 07	08 10	08 17	08 20	08 27	08 30	08 37	08 40	08 47	08 50	08 57	09 00	09 07
	d		07 30			07 40		07 50		08 00		08 10		08 20		08 30		08 40		08 50		09 00	
Harold Wood	d		07 33			07 43		07 53		08 03		08 13		08 23		08 33		08 43		08 53		09 03	
Brentwood	d		07 37			07 47		07 57		08 07		08 17		08 27		08 37		08 47		08 57		09 07	
Shenfield 3	a		07 43		07 32	07 53		08 05		08 13		08 25		08 33		08 45		08 53		09 05		09 13	

Station		XR	XR	XR	XR	XR	XR	LE 1 F	XR	XR	XR	XR	LE ◇1 B	XR	XR	LE 1 F	XR	XR	XR	XR	LE ◇1 B	XR	XR
London Liverpool Street 15 ⊖	d	08 40	08 50	09 00	09 10	09 20	09 30	09 38	09 40	09 50	10 00	10 10	10 13	10 20	10 30	10 34	10 40	10 50	11 00	11 10	11 13	11 20	11 30
Stratford 7 ⊖	d	08 47	08 57	09 07	09 17	09 27	09 37	09 45	09 47	09 57	10 07	10 17	10 20	10 27	10 37	10 41	10 47	10 57	11 07	11 17	11 20	11 27	11 37
Maryland	d	08 49	08 59	09 09	09 19	09 29	09 39		09 49	09 59	10 09	10 19		10 29	10 39		10 49	10 59	11 09	11 19		11 29	11 39
Forest Gate	d	08 51	09 01	09 11	09 21	09 31	09 41		09 51	10 01	10 11	10 21		10 31	10 41		10 51	11 01	11 11	11 21		11 31	11 41
Manor Park	d	08 53	09 03	09 13	09 23	09 33	09 43		09 53	10 03	10 13	10 23		10 33	10 43		10 53	11 03	11 13	11 23		11 33	11 43
Ilford 2	d	08 56	09 06	09 16	09 26	09 36	09 46		09 56	10 06	10 16	10 26		10 36	10 46		10 56	11 06	11 16	11 26		11 36	11 46
Seven Kings	d	08 58	09 08	09 18	09 28	09 38	09 48		09 58	10 08	10 18	10 28		10 38	10 48		10 58	11 08	11 18	11 28		11 38	11 48
Goodmayes	d	09 00	09 10	09 20	09 30	09 40	09 50		10 00	10 10	10 20	10 30		10 40	10 50		11 00	11 10	11 20	11 30		11 40	11 50
Chadwell Heath	d	09 02	09 12	09 22	09 32	09 42	09 52		10 02	10 12	10 22	10 32		10 42	10 52		11 02	11 12	11 22	11 32		11 42	11 52
Romford	d	09 06	09 16	09 26	09 36	09 46	09 56	09 53	10 06	10 16	10 26	10 36	10 28	10 46	10 56	10 49	11 06	11 16	11 26	11 36	11 28	11 46	11 56
Gidea Park 2	a	09 10	09 20	09 30	09 40	09 50	10 00		10 10	10 20	10 30	10 40		10 50	11 00		11 10	11 20	11 30	11 40		11 50	12 00
	d	09 10	09 20	09 30	09 40	09 50	10 00		10 10	10 20	10 30	10 40		10 50	11 00		11 10	11 20	11 30	11 40		11 50	12 00
Harold Wood	d	09 13	09 23	09 33	09 43	09 53	10 03		10 13	10 23	10 33	10 43		10 53	11 03		11 13	11 23	11 33	11 43		11 53	12 03
Brentwood	d	09 17	09 27	09 37	09 47	09 57	10 07		10 17	10 27	10 37	10 47		10 57	11 07		11 17	11 27	11 37	11 47		11 57	12 07
Shenfield 3	a	09 23	09 33	09 43	09 53	10 03	10 13	10 02	10 23	10 33	10 43	10 53	10 37	11 03	11 13	10 58	11 23	11 33	11 43	11 53	11 37	12 03	12 13

Station		LE 1 F		XR	XR	XR	XR	LE 1 B	XR	XR	LE 1 F	XR	XR	XR	XR	XR	XR	XR	XR	XR	XR	XR
London Liverpool Street 15 ⊖	d	11 38	and at the same minutes past each hour until	14 40	14 50	15 00	15 10	15 13	15 20	15 30	15 38	15 40	15 50	16 00	16 08	16 15	16 22	16 29	16 36	16 40	16 47	16 50
Stratford 7 ⊖	d	11 45		14 47	14 57	15 07	15 17	15 20	15 27	15 37	15 45	15 47	15 57	16 07	16 15	16 22	16 29	16 36	16 43	16 47	16 54	16 57
Maryland	d			14 49	14 59	15 09	15 19		15 29	15 39		15 49	15 59	16 09	16 17	16 24	16 31	16 38		16 49		16 59
Forest Gate	d			14 51	15 01	15 11	15 21		15 31	15 41		15 51	16 01	16 11	16 19	16 26	16 33	16 40		16 51		17 01
Manor Park	d			14 53	15 03	15 13	15 23		15 33	15 43		15 53	16 03	16 13	16 21	16 28	16 35	16 42		16 53		17 03
Ilford 2	d			14 56	15 06	15 16	15 26		15 36	15 46		15 56	16 06	16 16	16 24	16 31	16 38	16 45	16 50	16 56	17 00	17 06
Seven Kings	d			14 58	15 08	15 18	15 28		15 38	15 48		15 58	16 08	16 18	16 26	16 34	16 40	16 48	16 52		17 02	
Goodmayes	d			15 00	15 10	15 20	15 30		15 40	15 50		16 00	16 10	16 20	16 28	16 36	16 42	16 50	16 54		17 04	
Chadwell Heath	d			15 02	15 12	15 22	15 32		15 42	15 52		16 02	16 12	16 22	16 30	16 38	16 44	16 52	16 56	17 00	17 06	17 10
Romford	d	11 53		15 06	15 16	15 26	15 36	15 28	15 46	15 56	15 53	16 06	16 16	16 26	16 34	16 42	16 48	16 56	17 00	17 04	17 10	17 14
Gidea Park 2	a			15 10	15 20	15 30	15 40		15 50	16 00		16 10	16 20	16 30	16 38	16 47	16 53	17 01	17 04	17 10	17 14	17 20
	d			15 10	15 20	15 30	15 40		15 50	16 00		16 10	16 20	16 30	16 38		16 53		17 04		17 14	
Harold Wood	d			15 13	15 23	15 33	15 43		15 53	16 03		16 13	16 23	16 33	16 41		16 56		17 07		17 17	
Brentwood	d			15 17	15 27	15 37	15 47		15 57	16 07		16 17	16 27	16 37	16 45		17 00		17 11		17 21	
Shenfield 3	a	12 02		15 23	15 33	15 43	15 53	15 37	16 03	16 13	16 02	16 23	16 33	16 45	16 53		17 09		17 19		17 30	

Station		XR	XR	XR	XR	XR	XR	XR	XR	XR	XR	XR	XR	XR	XR	XR	XR	XR	XR	XR	XR	XR	XR
London Liverpool Street 15 ⊖	d	16 57	17 00	17 07	17 10	17 17	17 20	17 27	17 30	17 36	17 39	17 42	17 46	17 49	17 52	17 56	18 00	18 04	18 08	18 12	18 16	18 20	18 24
Stratford 7 ⊖	d	17 04	17 07	17 14	17 17	17 24	17 27	17 34	17 37	17 43	17 46	17 49	17 53	17 56	17 59	18 03	18 07	18 11	18 15	18 19	18 23	18 27	18 31
Maryland	d		17 09		17 19		17 29		17 39	17 45			17 55			18 05		18 13		18 21		18 29	
Forest Gate	d		17 11		17 21		17 31		17 41			17 52			18 02		18 10		18 18		18 26		18 34
Manor Park	d		17 13		17 23		17 33		17 43		17 50			18 00		18 08		18 16		18 24			
Ilford 2	d	17 10	17 16	17 20	17 26	17 30	17 36	17 40	17 46	17 50	17 53	17 56	18 00	18 03	18 06	18 11	18 14	18 19	18 22	18 27	18 30	18 35	18 38
Seven Kings	d	17 12		17 22		17 32		17 42		17 52	17 56	17 59	18 02	18 06	18 09	18 14	18 17	18 22	18 25	18 30	18 33	18 38	18 41
Goodmayes	d	17 14		17 24		17 34		17 44		17 54	17 58	18 01	18 04	18 08	18 11	18 16	18 19	18 24	18 27	18 32	18 35	18 40	18 43
Chadwell Heath	d	17 16	17 20	17 26	17 30	17 36	17 40	17 46	17 50	17 56	18 00	18 03	18 06	18 10	18 13	18 18	18 21	18 26	18 29	18 34	18 37	18 42	18 45
Romford	d	17 20	17 24	17 30	17 34	17 40	17 44	17 50	17 54	18 00	18 04	18 07	18 10	18 14	18 17	18 22	18 25	18 30	18 33	18 38	18 41	18 46	18 49
Gidea Park 2	a	17 24	17 30	17 34	17 40	17 44	17 50	17 54	17 58	18 04	18 08	18 11	18 14	18 18	18 21	18 25	18 29	18 33	18 36	18 41	18 44	18 49	18 54
	d	17 24		17 34		17 44		17 54		18 04	18 08		18 14	18 18		18 25		18 33		18 41		18 49	
Harold Wood	d	17 27		17 37		17 47		17 57		18 07	18 10		18 17	18 20		18 28		18 36		18 44		18 52	
Brentwood	d	17 31		17 41		17 51		18 01		18 11	18 14		18 21	18 25		18 33		18 41		18 49		18 57	
Shenfield 3	a	17 40		17 50		18 00		18 10		18 19	18 23		18 29	18 33		18 41		18 49		18 57		19 05	

A From London Liverpool Street
B To Southend Victoria
C To Colchester
D To Clacton-on-Sea
E To Ipswich
F To Colchester Town

Table T005-F

London Liverpool Street - Ilford - Shenfield

Mondays to Fridays
16 December to 15 May

Station		XR	XR	XR	XR	XR	XR	XR	XR	XR	XR	XR	XR	XR	XR	XR	XR	XR	LE ◇1 A	XR	XR	LE ◇1 A	XR
London Liverpool Street 15 ⊖	d	18 28	18 33	18 38	18 43	18 48	18 53	18 58	19 03	19 08	19 15	19 22	19 30	19 38	19 45	19 52	20 00	20 10	20 13	20 20	20 30	20 35	20 40
Stratford 7 ⊖	d	18 35	18 40	18 45	18 50	18 55	19 00	19 05	19 10	19 15	19 22	19 29	19 37	19 45	19 52	19 59	20 07	20 17	20 20	20 27	20 37	20 42	20 47
Maryland	d	18 37		18 47		18 57		19 07		19 17	19 24	19 31	19 39	19 47	19 54	20 01	20 09	20 19		20 29	20 39		20 49
Forest Gate	d		18 43		18 53		19 03		19 13	19 19	19 26	19 33	19 41	19 49	19 56	20 03	20 11	20 21		20 31	20 41		20 51
Manor Park	d	18 40		18 50		19 00		19 10		19 21	19 28	19 35	19 43	19 51	19 58	20 05	20 13	20 23		20 33	20 43		20 53
Ilford 2	d	18 43	18 47	18 53	18 57	19 03	19 07	19 13	19 17	19 24	19 31	19 38	19 46	19 54	20 01	20 08	20 16	20 26		20 36	20 46		20 56
Seven Kings	d	18 46	18 50	18 56	19 00	19 06	19 10	19 16	19 20	19 26	19 33	19 40	19 48	19 56	20 03	20 10	20 18	20 28		20 38	20 48		20 58
Goodmayes	d	18 48	18 52	18 58	19 02	19 08	19 12	19 18	19 22	19 28	19 35	19 42	19 50	19 58	20 05	20 12	20 20	20 30		20 40	20 50		21 00
Chadwell Heath	d	18 50	18 54	19 00	19 04	19 10	19 14	19 20	19 24	19 30	19 37	19 44	19 52	20 00	20 07	20 14	20 22	20 32		20 42	20 52		21 02
Romford	d	18 54	18 58	19 04	19 08	19 14	19 18	19 24	19 28	19 34	19 41	19 48	19 56	20 04	20 11	20 18	20 26	20 36	20 28	20 46	20 56	20 50	21 06
Gidea Park 2	a	18 57	19 03	19 07	19 13	19 17	19 23	19 27	19 31	19 38	19 45	19 52	20 00	20 08	20 15	20 22	20 30	20 40		20 50	21 00		21 10
	d	18 57		19 07		19 17		19 27	19 31	19 38	19 45	19 52	20 00	20 08		20 22	20 30	20 40		20 50	21 00		21 10
Harold Wood	d	19 00		19 10		19 20		19 30	19 34	19 41	19 48	19 55	20 03	20 11		20 25	20 33	20 43		20 53	21 03		21 13
Brentwood	d	19 05		19 15		19 25		19 35	19 39	19 45	19 52	19 59	20 07	20 15		20 29	20 37	20 47		20 57	21 07		21 17
Shenfield 3	a	19 13		19 23		19 33		19 43	19 47	19 51	19 58	20 07	20 13	20 21		20 35	20 43	20 53	20 37	21 03	21 13	20 59	21 23

Station		XR	XR	XR	LE ◇1 A	XR	XR	LE 1 B	XR	XR	XR	XR	LE ◇1 A	XR	XR		XR
London Liverpool Street 15 ⊖	d	20 50	21 00	21 10	21 13	21 20	21 30	21 38	21 40	21 50	22 00	22 10	22 13	22 20	22 35	and every 15 minutes until	23 50
Stratford 7 ⊖	d	20 57	21 07	21 17	21 20	21 27	21 37	21 45	21 47	21 57	22 07	22 17	22 20	22 27	22 42		23 57
Maryland	d	20 59	21 09	21 19		21 29	21 39		21 49	21 59	22 09	22 19		22 29	22 44		23 59
Forest Gate	d	21 01	21 11	21 21		21 31	21 41		21 51	22 01	22 11	22 21		22 31	22 46		00 01
Manor Park	d	21 03	21 13	21 23		21 33	21 43		21 53	22 03	22 13	22 23		22 33	22 48		00 03
Ilford 2	d	21 06	21 16	21 26		21 36	21 46		21 56	22 06	22 16	22 26		22 36	22 51		00 06
Seven Kings	d	21 08	21 18	21 28		21 38	21 48		21 58	22 08	22 18	22 28		22 38	22 53		00 08
Goodmayes	d	21 10	21 20	21 30		21 40	21 50		22 00	22 10	22 20	22 30		22 40	22 55		00 10
Chadwell Heath	d	21 12	21 22	21 32		21 42	21 52		22 02	22 12	22 22	22 32		22 42	22 57		00 12
Romford	d	21 16	21 26	21 36	21 28	21 46	21 56	21 53	22 06	22 16	22 26	22 36	22 28	22 46	23 01		00 16
Gidea Park 2	a	21 20	21 30	21 40		21 50	22 00		22 10	22 20	22 30	22 40		22 50	23 05		00 20
	d	21 20	21 30	21 40		21 50	22 00		22 10	22 20	22 30	22 40		22 50	23 05		00 20
Harold Wood	d	21 23	21 33	21 43		21 53	22 03		22 13	22 23	22 33	22 43		22 53	23 08		00 23
Brentwood	d	21 27	21 37	21 47		21 57	22 07		22 17	22 27	22 37	22 47		22 57	23 12		00 27
Shenfield 3	a	21 33	21 43	21 53	21 37	22 03	22 13	22 02	22 23	22 33	22 43	22 53	22 37	23 03	23 20		00 35

Saturdays
21 December to 16 May

Station		XR	LE 1 A	XR	XR	LE 1 C	LE 1 A	XR	XR	LE 1 D	XR	XR	XR	XR	LE 1 E	XR	XR	XR	LE 1 A	XR	XR	LE 1 B	XR
London Liverpool Street 15 ⊖	d	00 01	00 15	00 20	00 32	00 46	00 50	00 55	05 20	05 34		05 50	06 10	06 30	06 38	06 45	07 00	07 10	07 13	07 20	07 30	07 38	07 40
Stratford 7 ⊖	d	00 08	00 22	00 27	00 39	00 53	00 57	01 02	05 27	05 41		05 57	06 17	06 37	06 45	06 52	07 07	07 17	07 20	07 27	07 37	07 45	07 47
Maryland	d	00 10		00 29	00 41			01 04	05 29			05 59	06 19	06 39		06 54	07 09	07 19		07 29	07 39		07 49
Forest Gate	d	00 12		00 31	00 43			01 06	05 31			06 01	06 21	06 41		06 56	07 11	07 21		07 31	07 41		07 51
Manor Park	d	00 14		00 33	00 45			01 08	05 33			06 03	06 23	06 43		06 58	07 13	07 23		07 33	07 43		07 53
Ilford 2	d	00 17		00 36	00 48			01 11	05 36			06 06	06 26	06 46		07 01	07 16	07 26		07 36	07 46		07 56
Seven Kings	d	00 19		00 38	00 50			01 13	05 38		05 53	06 08	06 28	06 48		07 03	07 18	07 28		07 38	07 48		07 58
Goodmayes	d	00 21		00 40	00 52			01 15	05 40		05 55	06 10	06 30	06 50		07 05	07 20	07 30		07 40	07 50		08 00
Chadwell Heath	d	00 23		00 42	00 54			01 17	05 42		05 57	06 12	06 32	06 52		07 07	07 22	07 32		07 42	07 52		08 02
Romford	d	00 27	00 32	00 46	00 58		01 08	01 21	05 46	05 49	06 01	06 16	06 36	06 56	06 53	07 11	07 26	07 36	07 28	07 46	07 56	07 53	08 06
Gidea Park 2	a	00 33		00 50	01 04	01 06		01 25	05 50		06 05	06 20	06 40	07 00		07 15	07 30	07 40		07 50	08 00		08 10
	d			00 50		01 06		01 25	05 50		06 05	06 20	06 40	07 00		07 15	07 30	07 40		07 50	08 00		08 10
Harold Wood	d			00 53				01 28	05 53		06 08	06 23	06 43	07 03		07 18	07 33	07 43		07 53	08 03		08 13
Brentwood	d			00 57				01 32	05 57		06 12	06 27	06 47	07 07		07 22	07 37	07 47		07 57	08 07		08 17
Shenfield 3	a		00 45	01 05		01 16	01 20	01 40	06 03	05 58	06 18	06 33	06 53	07 13	07 02	07 28	07 43	07 53	07 37	08 03	08 13	08 02	08 23

Station		XR	XR	XR	LE 1 A	XR	XR	LE 1 B	XR	XR	XR	XR	LE ◇1 A	XR	XR	LE 1 B	XR	XR	XR	XR	LE ◇1 A	XR	XR
London Liverpool Street 15 ⊖	d	07 50	08 00	08 10	08 13	08 20	08 30	08 38	08 40	08 50	09 00	09 10	09 13	09 20	09 30	09 38	09 40	09 50	10 00	10 10	10 13	10 20	10 30
Stratford 7 ⊖	d	07 57	08 07	08 17	08 20	08 27	08 37	08 45	08 47	08 57	09 07	09 17	09 20	09 27	09 37	09 45	09 47	09 57	10 07	10 17	10 20	10 27	10 37
Maryland	d	07 59	08 09	08 19		08 29	08 39		08 49	08 59	09 09	09 19		09 29	09 39		09 49	09 59	10 09	10 19		10 29	10 39
Forest Gate	d	08 01	08 11	08 21		08 31	08 41		08 51	09 01	09 11	09 21		09 31	09 41		09 51	10 01	10 11	10 21		10 31	10 41
Manor Park	d	08 03	08 13	08 23		08 33	08 43		08 53	09 03	09 13	09 23		09 33	09 43		09 53	10 03	10 13	10 23		10 33	10 43
Ilford 2	d	08 06	08 16	08 26		08 36	08 46		08 56	09 06	09 16	09 26		09 36	09 46		09 56	10 06	10 16	10 26		10 36	10 46
Seven Kings	d	08 08	08 18	08 28		08 38	08 48		08 58	09 08	09 18	09 28		09 38	09 48		09 58	10 08	10 18	10 28		10 38	10 48
Goodmayes	d	08 10	08 20	08 30		08 40	08 50		09 00	09 10	09 20	09 30		09 40	09 50		10 00	10 10	10 20	10 30		10 40	10 50
Chadwell Heath	d	08 12	08 22	08 32		08 42	08 52		09 02	09 12	09 22	09 32		09 42	09 52		10 02	10 12	10 22	10 32		10 42	10 52
Romford	d	08 16	08 26	08 36	08 28	08 46	08 56	08 53	09 06	09 16	09 26	09 36	09 28	09 46	09 56	09 53	10 06	10 16	10 26	10 36	10 28	10 46	10 56
Gidea Park 2	a	08 20	08 30	08 40		08 50	09 00		09 10	09 20	09 30	09 40		09 50	10 00		10 10	10 20	10 30	10 40		10 50	11 00
	d	08 20	08 30	08 40		08 50	09 00		09 10	09 20	09 30	09 40		09 50	10 00		10 10	10 20	10 30	10 40		10 50	11 00
Harold Wood	d	08 23	08 33	08 43		08 53	09 03		09 13	09 23	09 33	09 43		09 53	10 03		10 13	10 23	10 33	10 43		10 53	11 03
Brentwood	d	08 27	08 37	08 47		08 57	09 07		09 17	09 27	09 37	09 47		09 57	10 07		10 17	10 27	10 37	10 47		10 57	11 07
Shenfield 3	a	08 33	08 43	08 53	08 38	09 03	09 13	09 02	09 23	09 33	09 43	09 53	09 37	10 03	10 13	10 02	10 23	10 33	10 43	10 53	10 37	11 03	11 13

A To Southend Victoria
B To Colchester Town
C To Colchester
D To Ipswich
E To Harwich International

Table T005-F

Saturdays

21 December to 16 May

London Liverpool Street - Ilford - Shenfield

Station		LE [1] A	XR	XR	XR	XR	LE ◇[1] B	XR	XR	LE [1] A		XR	XR	XR	XR	LE [1] B	XR	XR	LE [1] A	XR	XR	XR	XR
London Liverpool Street [15] ⊖	d	10 34	10 40	10 50	11 00	11 10	11 13	11 20	11 30	11 38	and at the same minutes past each hour until	15 40	15 50	16 00	16 10	16 13	16 20	16 30	16 38	16 40	16 50	17 00	17 10
Stratford [7] ⊖	d	10 41	10 47	10 57	11 07	11 17	11 20	11 27	11 37	11 45		15 47	15 57	16 07	16 17	16 20	16 27	16 37	16 45	16 47	16 57	17 07	17 17
Maryland	d		10 49	10 59	11 09	11 19		11 29	11 39			15 49	15 59	16 09	16 19		16 29	16 39		16 49	16 59	17 09	17 19
Forest Gate	d		10 51	11 01	11 11	11 21		11 31	11 41			15 51	16 01	16 11	16 21		16 31	16 41		16 51	17 01	17 11	17 21
Manor Park	d		10 53	11 03	11 13	11 23		11 33	11 43			15 53	16 03	16 13	16 23		16 33	16 43		16 53	17 03	17 13	17 23
Ilford [2]	d		10 56	11 06	11 16	11 26		11 36	11 46			15 56	16 06	16 16	16 26		16 36	16 46		16 56	17 06	17 16	17 26
Seven Kings	d		10 58	11 08	11 18	11 28		11 38	11 48			15 58	16 08	16 18	16 28		16 38	16 48		16 58	17 08	17 18	17 28
Goodmayes	d		11 00	11 10	11 20	11 30		11 40	11 50			16 00	16 10	16 20	16 30		16 40	16 50		17 00	17 10	17 20	17 30
Chadwell Heath	d		11 02	11 12	11 22	11 32		11 42	11 52			16 02	16 12	16 22	16 32		16 42	16 52		17 02	17 12	17 22	17 32
Romford	d	10 49	11 06	11 16	11 26	11 36	11 28	11 46	11 56	11 53		16 06	16 16	16 26	16 36	16 28	16 46	16 56	16 53	17 06	17 16	17 26	17 36
Gidea Park [2]	a		11 10	11 20	11 30	11 40		11 50	12 00			16 10	16 20	16 30	16 40		16 50	17 00		17 10	17 20	17 30	17 40
	d		11 10	11 20	11 30	11 40		11 50	12 00			16 10	16 20	16 30	16 40		16 50	17 00		17 10	17 20	17 30	17 40
Harold Wood	d		11 13	11 23	11 33	11 43		11 53	12 03			16 13	16 23	16 33	16 43		16 53	17 03		17 13	17 23	17 33	17 43
Brentwood	d		11 17	11 27	11 37	11 47		11 57	12 07			16 17	16 27	16 37	16 47		16 57	17 07		17 17	17 27	17 37	17 47
Shenfield [3]	a	10 58	11 23	11 33	11 43	11 53	11 37	12 03	12 13	12 02		16 23	16 33	16 43	16 53	16 37	17 03	17 13	17 02	17 23	17 33	17 43	17 53

Station		LE [1] B	XR	XR	LE [1] A	XR	XR	XR	XR	LE [1] B	XR	XR	LE [1] A	XR	XR	XR	XR	LE ◇[1] B	XR	XR	LE [1] A	XR	XR
London Liverpool Street [15] ⊖	d	17 13	17 20	17 30	17 38	17 40	17 50	18 00	18 10	18 13	18 20	18 30	18 34	18 40	18 50	19 00	19 10	19 13	19 20	19 30	19 38	19 40	19 50
Stratford [7] ⊖	d	17 21	17 27	17 37	17 45	17 47	17 57	18 07	18 17	18 21	18 27	18 37	18 41	18 47	18 57	19 07	19 17	19 20	19 27	19 37	19 46	19 47	19 57
Maryland	d		17 29	17 39		17 49	17 59	18 09	18 19		18 29	18 39		18 49	18 59	19 09	19 19		19 29	19 39		19 49	19 59
Forest Gate	d		17 31	17 41		17 51	18 01	18 11	18 21		18 31	18 41		18 51	19 01	19 11	19 21		19 31	19 41		19 51	20 01
Manor Park	d		17 33	17 43		17 53	18 03	18 13	18 23		18 33	18 43		18 53	19 03	19 13	19 23		19 33	19 43		19 53	20 03
Ilford [2]	d		17 36	17 46		17 56	18 06	18 16	18 26		18 36	18 46		18 56	19 06	19 16	19 26		19 36	19 46		19 56	20 06
Seven Kings	d		17 38	17 48		17 58	18 08	18 18	18 28		18 38	18 48		18 58	19 08	19 18	19 28		19 38	19 48		19 58	20 08
Goodmayes	d		17 40	17 50		18 00	18 10	18 20	18 30		18 40	18 50		19 00	19 10	19 20	19 30		19 40	19 50		20 00	20 10
Chadwell Heath	d		17 42	17 52		18 02	18 12	18 22	18 32		18 42	18 52		19 02	19 12	19 22	19 32		19 42	19 52		20 02	20 12
Romford	d	17 30	17 46	17 56	17 54	18 06	18 16	18 26	18 36	18 30	18 46	18 56	18 50	19 06	19 16	19 26	19 36	19 28	19 46	19 56	19 54	20 06	20 16
Gidea Park [2]	a		17 50	18 00		18 10	18 20	18 30	18 40		18 50	19 00		19 10	19 20	19 30	19 40		19 50	20 00		20 10	20 20
	d		17 50	18 00		18 10	18 20	18 30	18 40		18 50	19 00		19 10	19 20	19 30	19 40		19 50	20 00		20 10	20 20
Harold Wood	d		17 53	18 03		18 13	18 23	18 33	18 43		18 53	19 03		19 13	19 23	19 33	19 43		19 53	20 03		20 13	20 23
Brentwood	d		17 57	18 07		18 17	18 27	18 37	18 47		18 57	19 07		19 17	19 27	19 37	19 47		19 57	20 07		20 17	20 27
Shenfield [3]	a	17 39	18 03	18 13	18 03	18 23	18 33	18 43	18 53	18 39	19 03	19 13	18 59	19 23	19 33	19 43	19 53	19 37	20 03	20 13	20 03	20 23	20 33

Station		XR	XR	LE ◇[1] B	XR	XR	LE [1] A	XR	XR	XR	XR	LE ◇[1] B	XR	XR	LE [1] A	XR	XR	LE ◇[1] B	XR		XR
London Liverpool Street [15] ⊖	d	20 00	20 10	20 13	20 20	20 30	20 38	20 40	20 50	21 00	21 10	21 13	21 20	21 35	21 38	21 50	22 05	22 13	22 20	and every 15 minutes until	23 20
Stratford [7] ⊖	d	20 07	20 17	20 20	20 27	20 37	20 45	20 47	20 57	21 07	21 17	21 20	21 27	21 42	21 45	21 57	22 12	22 20	22 27		23 27
Maryland	d	20 09	20 19		20 29	20 39		20 49	20 59	21 09	21 19		21 29	21 44		21 59	22 14		22 29		23 29
Forest Gate	d	20 11	20 21		20 31	20 41		20 51	21 01	21 11	21 21		21 31	21 46		22 01	22 16		22 31		23 31
Manor Park	d	20 13	20 23		20 33	20 43		20 53	21 03	21 13	21 23		21 33	21 48		22 03	22 18		22 33		23 33
Ilford [2]	d	20 16	20 26		20 36	20 46		20 56	21 06	21 16	21 26		21 36	21 51		22 06	22 21		22 36		23 36
Seven Kings	d	20 18	20 28		20 38	20 48		20 58	21 08	21 18	21 28		21 38	21 53		22 08	22 23		22 38		23 38
Goodmayes	d	20 20	20 30		20 40	20 50		21 00	21 10	21 20	21 30		21 40	21 55		22 10	22 25		22 40		23 40
Chadwell Heath	d	20 22	20 32		20 42	20 52		21 02	21 12	21 22	21 32		21 42	21 57		22 12	22 27		22 42		23 42
Romford	d	20 26	20 36	20 28	20 46	20 56	20 53	21 06	21 16	21 26	21 36	21 28	21 46	22 01	21 53	22 16	22 31	22 28	22 46		23 46
Gidea Park [2]	a	20 30	20 40		20 50	21 00		21 10	21 20	21 30	21 40		21 50	22 05		22 20	22 35		22 50		23 50
	d	20 30	20 40		20 50	21 00		21 10	21 20	21 30	21 40		21 50	22 05		22 20	22 35		22 50		23 50
Harold Wood	d	20 33	20 43		20 53	21 03		21 13	21 23	21 33	21 43		21 53	22 08		22 23	22 38		22 53		23 53
Brentwood	d	20 37	20 47		20 57	21 07		21 17	21 27	21 37	21 47		21 57	22 12		22 27	22 42		22 57		23 57
Shenfield [3]	a	20 43	20 53	20 37	21 03	21 13	21 02	21 23	21 33	21 43	21 53	21 37	22 03	22 18	22 02	22 33	22 48	22 37	23 03		00 03

Station		XR	XR
London Liverpool Street [15] ⊖	d	23 35	23 50
Stratford [7] ⊖	d	23 42	23 57
Maryland	d	23 44	23 59
Forest Gate	d	23 46	00 01
Manor Park	d	23 48	00 03
Ilford [2]	d	23 51	00 06
Seven Kings	d	23 53	00 08
Goodmayes	d	23 55	00 10
Chadwell Heath	d	23 57	00 12
Romford	d	00 01	00 16
Gidea Park [2]	a	00 05	00 20
	d	00 05	00 20
Harold Wood	d	00 08	00 23
Brentwood	d	00 12	00 27
Shenfield [3]	a	00 20	00 35

A To Colchester Town **B** To Southend Victoria **C** To Ipswich

NRT DECEMBER 19 EDITION

Table T005-F

Sundays

15 December to 10 May

London Liverpool Street - Ilford - Shenfield

Station		XR	LE [1] B	XR	XR	LE [1] B	XR	XR	XR	XR	LE [1] B	XR	XR	LE [1] B	XR	LE [1] C	XR	LE [1] B	XR	XR	LE [1] B	XR
London Liverpool Street [15] ⊖	d	00 01	00 15	00 20	00 35	00 50	00 55	06 33	06 48	07 02	07 14	07 18	07 32	07 44	07 48	08 00	08 03	08 15	08 18	08 33	08 45	08 48
Stratford [7] ⊖	d	00 08	00 22	00 27	00 42	00 57	01 02	06 40	06 55	07 09	07 21	07 25	07 39	07 51	07 55	08 07	08 10	08 22	08 25	08 40	08 52	08 55
Maryland	d	00 10		00 29	00 44		01 04	06 42	06 57	07 11		07 27	07 41		07 57		08 12		08 27	08 42		08 57
Forest Gate	d	00 12		00 31	00 46		01 06	06 44	06 59	07 13		07 29	07 43		07 59		08 14		08 29	08 44		08 59
Manor Park	d	00 14		00 33	00 48		01 08	06 47	07 02	07 16		07 32	07 46		08 02		08 17		08 32	08 47		09 02
Ilford [2]	d	00 17		00 36	00 51		01 11	06 50	07 05	07 19		07 35	07 49		08 05		08 20		08 35	08 50		09 05
Seven Kings	d	00 19		00 38	00 53		01 13	06 52	07 07	07 21		07 37	07 51		08 07		08 22		08 37	08 52		09 07
Goodmayes	d	00 21		00 40	00 55		01 15	06 54	07 09	07 23		07 39	07 53		08 09		08 24		08 39	08 54		09 09
Chadwell Heath	d	00 23		00 42	00 57		01 17	06 56	07 11	07 25		07 41	07 55		08 11		08 26		08 41	08 56		09 11
Romford	d	00 27	00 32	00 46	01 01	01 08	01 21	07 00	07 15	07 29	07 32	07 45	07 59	08 02	08 15	08 20	08 30	08 33	08 45	09 00	09 03	09 15
Gidea Park [2]	a	00 33		00 50	01 07		01 25	07 03	07 18	07 32		07 48	08 02		08 18		08 33		08 48	09 03		09 18
	d			00 50			01 25	07 03	07 18	07 32		07 48	08 02		08 18		08 33		08 48	09 03		09 18
Harold Wood	d			00 53			01 28	07 06	07 21	07 35		07 51	08 05		08 21		08 36		08 51	09 06		09 21
Brentwood	d			00 57			01 32	07 10	07 25	07 39		07 55	08 09		08 25		08 40		08 55	09 10		09 25
Shenfield [3]	a		00 44	01 05		01 20	01 40	07 16	07 31	07 45	07 45	08 01	08 15	08 15	08 31	08 34	08 46	08 46	09 01	09 16	09 16	09 31

A To Colchester Town **B** To Southend Victoria **C** To Ipswich

Station		XR	XR	LE ◇[1] A	XR	XR	LE ◇[1] A		XR	XR	LE [1] A	XR	XR	LE ◇[1] A	XR	XR	LE [1] A	XR	LE [1] A	XR
London Liverpool Street [15] ⊖	d	09 03	09 18	09 23	09 33	09 48	09 53	and at the same minutes past each hour until	22 03	22 18	22 23	22 33	22 48	22 53	23 03	23 18	23 23	23 33	23 42	23 48
Stratford [7] ⊖	d	09 10	09 25	09 30	09 40	09 55	10 00		22 10	22 25	22 30	22 40	22 55	23 00	23 10	23 25	23 30	23 40	23 49	23 55
Maryland	d	09 12	09 27		09 42	09 57			22 12	22 27		22 42	22 57		23 12	23 27		23 42		23 57
Forest Gate	d	09 14	09 29		09 44	09 59			22 14	22 29		22 44	22 59		23 14	23 29		23 44		23 59
Manor Park	d	09 17	09 32		09 47	10 02			22 17	22 32		22 47	23 02		23 17	23 32		23 47		00 02
Ilford [2]	d	09 20	09 35		09 50	10 05			22 20	22 35		22 50	23 05		23 20	23 35		23 50		00 05
Seven Kings	d	09 22	09 37		09 52	10 07			22 22	22 37		22 52	23 07		23 22	23 37		23 52		00 07
Goodmayes	d	09 24	09 39		09 54	10 09			22 24	22 39		22 54	23 09		23 24	23 39		23 54		00 09
Chadwell Heath	d	09 26	09 41		09 56	10 11			22 26	22 41		22 56	23 11		23 26	23 41		23 56		00 11
Romford	d	09 30	09 45	09 39	10 00	10 15	10 09		22 30	22 45	22 39	23 00	23 15	23 09	23 30	23 45	23 39	23 59	00 01	00 15
Gidea Park [2]	a	09 33	09 48		10 03	10 18			22 33	22 48		23 03	23 18		23 33	23 48		00 03		00 18
	d	09 33	09 48		10 03	10 18			22 33	22 48		23 03	23 18		23 33	23 48		00 03		00 18
Harold Wood	d	09 36	09 51		10 06	10 21			22 36	22 51		23 06	23 21		23 36	23 51		00 06		00 21
Brentwood	d	09 40	09 55		10 10	10 25			22 40	22 55		23 10	23 25		23 40	23 55		00 10		00 25
Shenfield [3]	a	09 46	10 01	09 48	10 16	10 31	10 18		22 46	23 01	22 48	23 16	23 31	23 18	23 46	00 01	23 48	00 16	00 16	00 31

A To Southend Victoria

Shenfield - Ilford - London Liverpool Street

Mondays to Fridays
16 December to 15 May

Miles	Station		XR MO A	XR MX A	XR MO A	XR MX A	XR MO A	XR	XR	XR	LE 1 B	XR	XR	XR	XR	XR	XR	XR	XR	XR	XR	XR	XR
0	Shenfield 3	d						04 44		05 12	05 24	05 29		05 44		05 59		06 14	06 24		06 34		06 44
2	Brentwood	d					00 01	04 47		05 15		05 32		05 47		06 02		06 17	06 27		06 37		06 47
5¼	Harold Wood	d					00 04	04 52		05 20		05 37		05 52		06 07		06 22	06 32		06 42		06 52
6¾	Gidea Park 2	d					00 07	04 56	05 11	05 24		05 41	05 49	05 56	06 04	06 11	06 19	06 26	06 35	06 39	06 45	06 49	06 55
7½	Romford	d					00 10	04 58	05 13	05 26	05 32	05 43	05 51	05 58	06 06	06 13	06 21	06 28	06 38	06 41	06 48	06 51	06 58
10¼	Chadwell Heath	d				00 02	00 14	05 02	05 17	05 30		05 47	05 55	06 02	06 10	06 17	06 25	06 32	06 42	06 45	06 52	06 55	07 02
11	Goodmayes	d			00 01	00 04	00 16	05 04	05 19	05 32		05 49	05 57	06 04	06 12	06 19	06 27	06 34	06 44	06 47		06 57	
11¾	Seven Kings	d			00 03	00 06	00 18	05 06	05 21	05 34	05 37	05 51	05 59	06 06	06 14	06 21	06 29	06 36	06 46	06 49		06 59	
12¾	Ilford 2	d			00 06	00 09	00 21	05 09	05 24	05 37		05 54	06 03	06 09	06 17	06 26	06 32	06 39	06 49	06 52	06 57	07 02	07 07
14	Manor Park	d			00 09	00 12	00 24	05 12	05 27	05 40		05 57	06 05	06 12	06 20	06 30	06 35	06 42		06 55		07 05	
15	Forest Gate	d			00 11	00 14	00 26	05 14	05 29	05 42		05 59	06 08	06 14	06 22	06 32	06 37	06 44		06 57		07 07	
15¾	Maryland	d		00 01	00 13	00 16	00 28	05 16	05 31	05 44		06 01	06 10	06 16	06 24	06 34	06 39	06 46		06 59		07 09	
16¼	Stratford 7 ⊖	d	00 02	00 04	00 16	00 19	00 31	05 19	05 34	05 47	05 45	06 04	06 12	06 19	06 27	06 37	06 42	06 49	06 55	07 02	07 05	07 12	07 15
20¼	**London Liverpool Street 15 ⊖**	a	00 10	00 15	00 25	00 30	00 40	05 27	05 44	05 55	05 53	06 12	06 22	06 27	06 37	06 45	06 52	06 57	07 07	07 12	07 17	07 22	07 27

Station		XR	XR	XR	XR	XR	XR	XR	XR	XR	XR	XR	XR	XR	XR	XR	XR	XR	XR	XR	XR	XR
Shenfield 3	d		06 54		07 01		07 10		07 19		07 28		07 37	07 42		07 49		07 56		08 02		08 12
Brentwood	d		06 57		07 04		07 13		07 22		07 31		07 40	07 45		07 52		07 59		08 05		08 15
Harold Wood	d		07 02		07 09		07 18		07 27		07 36		07 45	07 50		07 57		08 04		08 10		08 20
Gidea Park 2	d	06 59	07 05	07 09	07 13	07 18	07 22	07 27	07 31	07 36	07 40	07 45	07 49	07 54	07 58	08 01	08 05	08 08	08 12	08 15	08 19	08 24
Romford	d	07 01	07 08	07 11	07 16	07 20	07 25	07 29	07 34	07 38	07 43	07 47	07 52	07 56	08 00	08 03	08 07	08 10	08 14	08 17	08 21	08 26
Chadwell Heath	d	07 05	07 12	07 15	07 20	07 24	07 29	07 33	07 38	07 42	07 47	07 51	07 56	08 00	08 04	08 07	08 11	08 14	08 18	08 21	08 25	08 30
Goodmayes	d	07 07		07 17	07 22	07 26	07 31	07 35	07 40	07 44	07 49	07 53	07 58	08 02	08 06	08 09	08 13	08 16	08 20	08 23	08 27	08 32
Seven Kings	d	07 09		07 19	07 24	07 28	07 33	07 37	07 42	07 46	07 51	07 55	08 00	08 04	08 08	08 11	08 15	08 18	08 22	08 25	08 29	08 34
Ilford 2	d	07 12	07 17	07 22	07 27	07 31	07 36	07 40	07 45	07 49	07 54	07 58	08 03	08 07	08 11	08 14	08 18	08 21	08 25	08 28	08 32	08 37
Manor Park	d	07 15		07 25		07 34		07 43		07 52		08 01		08 10		08 17			08 28			08 40
Forest Gate	d	07 17		07 27	07 31		07 40		07 49		07 58		08 07		08 15			08 25			08 36	
Maryland	d	07 19		07 29		07 37		07 46		07 55		08 04		08 13			08 23			08 33		
Stratford 7 ⊖	d	07 22	07 25	07 32	07 35	07 39	07 43	07 48	07 52	07 57	08 01	08 06	08 10	08 15	08 19	08 22	08 25	08 29	08 32	08 36	08 40	08 44
London Liverpool Street 15 ⊖	a	07 33	07 37	07 42	07 45	07 51	07 53	08 00	08 02	08 09	08 11	08 18	08 21	08 26	08 31	08 33	08 38	08 41	08 45	08 47	08 52	08 55

Station		XR	XR	XR	XR	XR	XR	LE 1 C	XR	XR	XR	XR	XR	XR	XR	XR	XR	LE 1 C	XR	XR	XR	XR	XR
Shenfield 3	d		08 22		08 32		08 42	08 46		08 52		09 02		09 14	09 24	09 34	09 44	09 46	09 54	10 04	10 14	10 24	10 34
Brentwood	d		08 25		08 35		08 45			08 55		09 05		09 17	09 27	09 37	09 47		09 57	10 07	10 17	10 27	10 37
Harold Wood	d		08 30		08 40		08 50			09 00		09 10		09 22	09 32	09 42	09 52		10 02	10 12	10 22	10 32	10 42
Gidea Park 2	d	08 29	08 33	08 37	08 44	08 49	08 53		08 57	09 04	09 09	09 13	09 17	09 26	09 36	09 46	09 56		10 06	10 16	10 26	10 36	10 46
Romford	d	08 31	08 36	08 39	08 46	08 51	08 56	08 55	08 59	09 06	09 11	09 16	09 19	09 28	09 38	09 48	09 58	09 55	10 08	10 18	10 28	10 38	10 48
Chadwell Heath	d	08 35	08 40	08 43	08 50	08 55	09 00		09 03	09 10	09 15	09 20	09 23	09 32	09 42	09 52	10 02		10 12	10 22	10 32	10 42	10 52
Goodmayes	d		08 42	08 45	08 52		09 02		09 05	09 12		09 22	09 25	09 34	09 44	09 54	10 04		10 14	10 24	10 34	10 44	10 54
Seven Kings	d		08 44	08 47	08 54		09 04		09 07	09 14		09 24	09 27	09 36	09 46	09 56	10 06		10 16	10 26	10 36	10 46	10 56
Ilford 2	d	08 40	08 47	08 50	08 57	09 00	09 07		09 10	09 17	09 20	09 27	09 30	09 39	09 49	09 59	10 09		10 19	10 29	10 39	10 49	10 59
Manor Park	d	08 43		08 53		09 03			09 13		09 23		09 33	09 42	09 52	10 02	10 12		10 22	10 32	10 42	10 52	11 02
Forest Gate	d	08 45		08 55		09 05			09 15		09 25		09 35	09 44	09 54	10 04	10 14		10 24	10 34	10 44	10 54	11 04
Maryland	d	08 47		08 57		09 07			09 17		09 27		09 37	09 46	09 56	10 06	10 16		10 26	10 36	10 46	10 56	11 06
Stratford 7 ⊖	d	08 50	08 53	09 00	09 03	09 10	09 13	09s06	09 20	09 23	09 30	09 33	09 40	09 49	09 59	10 09	10 19	10 04	10 29	10 39	10 49	10 59	11 09
London Liverpool Street 15 ⊖	a	09 02	09 05	09 11	09 15	09 22	09 25	09 16	09 31	09 35	09 42	09 45	09 51	09 59	10 07	10 17	10 27	10 12	10 37	10 47	10 59	11 09	11 19

Station		XR	LE 1 C	XR	XR	XR	LE 1 D	XR	XR	XR	LE 1 C	XR	XR	XR	LE 1 D	XR	XR	XR	LE ◇1 C	XR	XR	XR	LE 1 D
Shenfield 3	d	10 44	10 46	10 54	11 04	11 14	11 20	11 24	11 34	11 44	11 45	11 54	12 04	12 14	12 20	12 24	12 34	12 44	12 45	12 54	13 04	13 14	13 20
Brentwood	d	10 47		10 57	11 07	11 17		11 27	11 37	11 47		11 57	12 07	12 17		12 27	12 37	12 47		12 57	13 07	13 17	
Harold Wood	d	10 52		11 02	11 12	11 22		11 32	11 42	11 52		12 02	12 12	12 22		12 32	12 42	12 52		13 02	13 12	13 22	
Gidea Park 2	d	10 56		11 06	11 16	11 26		11 36	11 46	11 56		12 06	12 16	12 26		12 36	12 46	12 56		13 06	13 16	13 26	
Romford	d	10 58	10 55	11 08	11 18	11 28	11 28	11 38	11 48	11 58	11 53	12 08	12 18	12 28	12 28	12 38	12 48	12 58	12 53	13 08	13 18	13 28	13 28
Chadwell Heath	d	11 02		11 12	11 22	11 32		11 42	11 52	12 02		12 12	12 22	12 32		12 42	12 52	13 02		13 12	13 22	13 32	
Goodmayes	d	11 04		11 14	11 24	11 34		11 44	11 54	12 04		12 14	12 24	12 34		12 44	12 54	13 04		13 14	13 24	13 34	
Seven Kings	d	11 06		11 16	11 26	11 36		11 46	11 56	12 06		12 16	12 26	12 36		12 46	12 56	13 06		13 16	13 26	13 36	
Ilford 2	d	11 09		11 19	11 29	11 39		11 49	11 59	12 09		12 19	12 29	12 39		12 49	12 59	13 09		13 19	13 29	13 39	
Manor Park	d	11 12		11 22	11 32	11 42		11 52	12 02	12 12		12 22	12 32	12 42		12 52	13 02	13 12		13 22	13 32	13 42	
Forest Gate	d	11 14		11 24	11 34	11 44		11 54	12 04	12 14		12 24	12 34	12 44		12 54	13 04	13 14		13 24	13 34	13 44	
Maryland	d	11 16		11 26	11 36	11 46		11 56	12 06	12 16		12 26	12 36	12 46		12 56	13 06	13 16		13 26	13 36	13 46	
Stratford 7 ⊖	d	11 19	11 05	11 29	11 39	11 49	11 37	11 59	12 09	12 19	12 02	12 29	12 39	12 49	12 37	12 59	13 09	13 19	13 01	13 29	13 39	13 49	13 37
London Liverpool Street 15 ⊖	a	11 29	11 13	11 39	11 47	11 57	11 45	12 07	12 17	12 27	12 10	12 37	12 47	12 57	12 45	13 07	13 17	13 27	13 10	13 37	13 47	13 57	13 45

Station		XR	XR	XR	LE ◇1 C	XR	XR	XR	LE 1 D	XR	XR	XR	LE ◇1 C	XR	XR	XR	LE 1 D	XR	XR	XR	LE ◇1 C	XR
Shenfield 3	d	13 24	13 34	13 44	13 45	13 54	14 04	14 14	14 20	14 24	14 34	14 44	14 45	14 54	15 04	15 14	15 20	15 24	15 34	15 44	15 45	15 54
Brentwood	d	13 27	13 37	13 47		13 57	14 07	14 17		14 27	14 37	14 47		14 57	15 07	15 17		15 27	15 37	15 47		15 57
Harold Wood	d	13 32	13 42	13 52		14 02	14 12	14 22		14 32	14 42	14 52		15 02	15 12	15 22		15 32	15 42	15 52		16 02
Gidea Park 2	d	13 36	13 46	13 56		14 06	14 16	14 26		14 36	14 46	14 56		15 06	15 16	15 26		15 36	15 46	15 56		16 06
Romford	d	13 38	13 48	13 58	13 53	14 08	14 18	14 28	14 28	14 38	14 48	14 58	14 53	15 08	15 18	15 28	15 28	15 38	15 48	15 58	15 53	16 08
Chadwell Heath	d	13 42	13 52	14 02		14 12	14 22	14 32		14 42	14 52	15 02		15 12	15 22	15 32		15 42	15 52	16 02		16 12
Goodmayes	d	13 44	13 54	14 04		14 14	14 24	14 34		14 44	14 54	15 04		15 14	15 24	15 34		15 44	15 54	16 04		16 14
Seven Kings	d	13 46	13 56	14 06		14 16	14 26	14 36		14 46	14 56	15 06		15 16	15 26	15 36		15 46	15 56	16 06		16 16
Ilford 2	d	13 49	13 59	14 09		14 19	14 29	14 39		14 49	14 59	15 09		15 19	15 29	15 39		15 49	15 59	16 09		16 19
Manor Park	d	13 52	14 02	14 12		14 22	14 32	14 42		14 52	15 02	15 12		15 22	15 32	15 42		15 52	16 02	16 12		16 22
Forest Gate	d	13 54	14 04	14 14		14 24	14 34	14 44		14 54	15 04	15 14		15 24	15 34	15 44		15 54	16 04	16 14		16 24
Maryland	d	13 56	14 06	14 16		14 26	14 36	14 46		14 56	15 06	15 16		15 26	15 36	15 46		15 56	16 06	16 16		16 26
Stratford 7 ⊖	d	13 59	14 09	14 19	14 02	14 29	14 39	14 49	14 37	14 59	15 09	15 19	15 02	15 29	15 39	15 49	15 37	15 59	16 09	16 19	16 02	16 29
London Liverpool Street 15 ⊖	a	14 07	14 17	14 27	14 10	14 37	14 47	14 57	14 45	15 07	15 17	15 27	15 10	15 37	15 47	15 57	15 45	16 07	16 17	16 27	16 11	16 37

A From Shenfield
B From Colchester
C From Southend Victoria
D From Colchester Town

Shenfield - Ilford - London Liverpool Street

Mondays to Fridays
16 December to 15 May

Station		XR	XR	XR	XR	XR	XR	XR	XR	XR	XR	XR	XR	XR	XR	XR	XR	XR	XR	XR	XR	XR
Shenfield 3	d	16 04	16 14	16 24	16 34	16 44		16 54		17 04		17 14		17 24		17 34		17 44		17 54		18 04
Brentwood	d	16 07	16 17	16 27	16 37	16 47		16 57		17 07		17 17		17 27		17 37		17 47		17 57		18 07
Harold Wood	d	16 12	16 22	16 32	16 42	16 52		17 02		17 12		17 22		17 32		17 42		17 52		18 02		18 12
Gidea Park 2	d	16 16	16 26	16 36	16 46	16 56	17 02	17 06	17 12	17 16	17 22	17 26	17 32	17 37	17 42	17 46	17 52	17 56	18 02	18 06	18 12	18 16
Romford	d	16 18	16 28	16 38	16 48	16 58	17 04	17 08	17 14	17 18	17 24	17 28	17 34	17 39	17 44	17 48	17 54	17 58	18 04	18 08	18 14	18 18
Chadwell Heath	d	16 22	16 32	16 42	16 52	17 02		17 12		17 22		17 32		17 43		17 52		18 02		18 12		18 22
Goodmayes	d	16 24	16 34	16 44	16 54	17 04		17 14		17 24		17 34		17 45		17 54		18 04		18 14		18 24
Seven Kings	d	16 26	16 36	16 46	16 56	17 06		17 16		17 26		17 36		17 47		17 56		18 06		18 16		18 26
Ilford 2	d	16 29	16 39	16 49	16 59	17 09	17 12	17 19	17 22	17 29	17 32	17 39	17 42	17 50	17 53	17 59	18 02	18 09	18 12	18 19	18 22	18 29
Manor Park	d	16 32	16 42	16 52	17 02	17 12	17 15		17 25		17 35		17 45		17 56		18 06		18 15		18 25	
Forest Gate	d	16 34	16 44	16 54	17 04	17 14	17 17		17 27		17 37		17 47		17 58		18 08		18 17		18 27	
Maryland	d	16 36	16 46	16 56	17 06	17 16	17 19		17 29		17 39		17 49		18 00		18 10		18 19		18 29	
Stratford 7 ⊖	d	16 39	16 49	16 59	17 09	17 19	17 22	17 27	17 32	17 37	17 42	17 45	17 52	17 57	18 03	18 06	18 13	18 16	18 22	18 25	18 32	18 35
London Liverpool Street 15 ⊖	a	16 47	16 57	17 07	17 17	17 27	17 34	17 37	17 44	17 47	17 54	17 57	18 04	18 07	18 14	18 17	18 24	18 27	18 34	18 37	18 44	18 47

Station		XR	XR	XR	XR	LE 1 A	XR	XR	XR	XR	XR	XR	LE 1 B	XR	XR	XR	LE ◇1 C	XR	XR	XR	LE 1 A	XR	XR
Shenfield 3	d		18 14		18 24	18 28		18 34	18 44	18 54	19 04	19 14	19 20	19 24	19 34	19 44	19 45	19 54	20 04	20 14	20 20	20 24	20 34
Brentwood	d		18 17		18 27			18 37	18 47	18 57	19 07	19 17		19 27	19 37	19 47		19 57	20 07	20 17		20 27	20 37
Harold Wood	d		18 22		18 32			18 42	18 52	19 02	19 12	19 22		19 32	19 42	19 52		20 02	20 12	20 22		20 32	20 42
Gidea Park 2	d	18 22	18 26	18 32	18 36		18 42	18 46	18 56	19 06	19 16	19 26		19 36	19 46	19 56		20 06	20 16	20 26		20 36	20 46
Romford	d	18 24	18 28	18 34	18 38	18 36	18 44	18 48	18 58	19 08	19 18	19 28	19 28	19 38	19 48	19 58	19 53	20 08	20 18	20 28	20 28	20 38	20 48
Chadwell Heath	d		18 32		18 42			18 52	19 02	19 12	19 22	19 32		19 42	19 52	20 02		20 12	20 22	20 32		20 42	20 52
Goodmayes	d		18 34		18 44			18 54	19 04	19 14	19 24	19 34		19 44	19 54	20 04		20 14	20 24	20 34		20 44	20 54
Seven Kings	d		18 36		18 46			18 56	19 06	19 16	19 26	19 36		19 46	19 56	20 06		20 16	20 26	20 36		20 46	20 56
Ilford 2	d	18 32	18 39	18 42	18 49		18 52	18 59	19 09	19 19	19 29	19 39		19 49	19 59	20 09		20 19	20 29	20 39		20 49	20 59
Manor Park	d	18 35		18 45			18 55	19 02	19 12	19 22	19 32	19 42		19 52	20 02	20 12		20 22	20 32	20 42		20 52	21 02
Forest Gate	d	18 37		18 47			18 57	19 04	19 14	19 24	19 34	19 44		19 54	20 04	20 14		20 24	20 34	20 44		20 54	21 04
Maryland	d	18 39		18 49			18 59	19 06	19 16	19 26	19 36	19 46		19 56	20 06	20 16		20 26	20 36	20 46		20 56	21 06
Stratford 7 ⊖	d	18 42	18 45	18 52	18 55	18 46	19 02	19 09	19 19	19 29	19 39	19 49	19 37	19 59	20 09	20 19	20 01	20 29	20 39	20 49	20 37	20 59	21 09
London Liverpool Street 15 ⊖	a	18 54	18 57	19 04	19 07	18 56	19 14	19 19	19 27	19 37	19 47	19 57	19 45	20 07	20 17	20 27	20 10	20 37	20 47	20 57	20 45	21 07	21 17

Station		XR	LE 1 C	XR	XR	XR	XR	XR	XR	LE 1 C	XR	XR	LE 1 A	XR	XR	XR	XR	LE 1 B	XR	LE 1 D	XR
Shenfield 3	d	20 44	20 45	20 54	21 04	21 14	21 24	21 34	21 44	21 45	21 59	22 14	22 20	22 29	22 44	22 59	23 14	23 20	23 29	23 39	23 44
Brentwood	d	20 47		20 57	21 07	21 17	21 27	21 37	21 47		22 02	22 17		22 32	22 47	23 02	23 17		23 32		23 47
Harold Wood	d	20 52		21 02	21 12	21 22	21 32	21 42	21 52		22 07	22 22		22 37	22 52	23 07	23 22		23 37		23 52
Gidea Park 2	d	20 56		21 06	21 16	21 26	21 36	21 46	21 56		22 11	22 26		22 41	22 56	23 11	23 26		23 41		23 56
Romford	d	20 58	20 53	21 08	21 18	21 28	21 38	21 48	21 58	21 53	22 13	22 28	22 28	22 43	22 58	23 13	23 28	23 28	23 43	23 47	23 58
Chadwell Heath	d	21 02		21 12	21 22	21 32	21 42	21 52	22 02		22 17	22 32		22 47	23 02	23 17	23 32		23 47		00 02
Goodmayes	d	21 04		21 14	21 24	21 34	21 44	21 54	22 04		22 19	22 34		22 49	23 04	23 19	23 34		23 49		00 04
Seven Kings	d	21 06		21 16	21 26	21 36	21 46	21 56	22 06		22 21	22 36		22 51	23 06	23 21	23 36		23 51		00 06
Ilford 2	d	21 09		21 19	21 29	21 39	21 49	21 59	22 09		22 24	22 39		22 54	23 09	23 24	23 39		23 54		00 09
Manor Park	d	21 12		21 22	21 32	21 42	21 52	22 02	22 12		22 27	22 42		22 57	23 12	23 27	23 42		23 57		00 12
Forest Gate	d	21 14		21 24	21 34	21 44	21 54	22 04	22 14		22 30	22 44		22 59	23 14	23 31	23 44		23 59		00 14
Maryland	d	21 16		21 26	21 36	21 46	21 56	22 06	22 16		22 32	22 46		23 01	23 16	23 33	23 46		00 01		00 16
Stratford 7 ⊖	d	21 19	21 02	21 29	21 39	21 49	21 59	22 09	22 19	22 02	22 35	22 49	22 37	23 04	23 19	23 35	23 49	23 37	00 04	23 57	00 19
London Liverpool Street 15 ⊖	a	21 27	21 10	21 37	21 47	21 57	22 07	22 17	22 27	22 10	22 43	22 57	22 45	23 12	23 27	23 46	00 01	23 48	00 15	00 06	00 30

Saturdays
21 December to 16 May

Station		XR E	XR E	XR	XR	LE 1 F	XR	LE 1 C	XR	XR	XR	XR	XR	LE 1 C	XR	LE 1 F	XR	XR	XR	LE 1 A	XR	XR	XR
Shenfield 3	d			04 44	05 14	05 24	05 29	05 35	05 44	05 59	06 14	06 24	06 34	06 35	06 44	06 46	06 54	07 04	07 14	07 20	07 24	07 34	07 44
Brentwood	d			04 47	05 17		05 32		05 47	06 02	06 17	06 27	06 37		06 47		06 57	07 07	07 17		07 27	07 37	07 47
Harold Wood	d			04 52	05 22		05 37		05 52	06 07	06 22	06 32	06 42		06 52		07 02	07 12	07 22		07 32	07 42	07 52
Gidea Park 2	d			04 56	05 26		05 41		05 56	06 11	06 26	06 36	06 46		06 56		07 06	07 16	07 26		07 36	07 46	07 56
Romford	d			04 58	05 28	05 32	05 43	05 43	05 58	06 13	06 28	06 38	06 48	06 43	06 58	06 54	07 08	07 18	07 28	07 28	07 38	07 48	07 58
Chadwell Heath	d		00 02	05 02	05 32		05 47		06 02	06 17	06 32	06 42	06 52		07 02		07 12	07 22	07 32		07 42	07 52	08 02
Goodmayes	d		00 04	05 04	05 34		05 49		06 04	06 19	06 34	06 44	06 54		07 04		07 14	07 24	07 34		07 44	07 54	08 04
Seven Kings	d		00 06	05 06	05 36	05 37	05 51		06 06	06 21	06 36	06 46	06 56		07 06		07 16	07 26	07 36		07 46	07 56	08 06
Ilford 2	d		00 09	05 09	05 39		05 54		06 09	06 24	06 39	06 49	06 59		07 09		07 19	07 29	07 39		07 49	07 59	08 09
Manor Park	d		00 12	05 12	05 42		05 57		06 12	06 27	06 42	06 52	07 02		07 12		07 22	07 32	07 42		07 52	08 02	08 12
Forest Gate	d		00 14	05 14	05 44		05 59		06 14	06 29	06 44	06 54	07 04		07 14		07 24	07 34	07 44		07 54	08 04	08 14
Maryland	d	00 01	00 16	05 16	05 46		06 01		06 16	06 31	06 46	06 56	07 06		07 16		07 26	07 36	07 46		07 56	08 06	08 16
Stratford 7 ⊖	d	00 04	00 19	05 19	05 49	05 43	06 04	05 52	06 19	06 34	06 49	06 59	07 09	06 52	07 19	07 03	07 29	07 39	07 49	07 37	07 59	08 09	08 19
London Liverpool Street 15 ⊖	a	00 15	00 30	05 27	05 57	05 51	06 13	06 00	06 27	06 42	06 57	07 07	07 17	07 00	07 27	07 11	07 37	07 47	07 57	07 46	08 07	08 17	08 27

Station		LE 1 C	XR	XR	XR	LE 1 G	XR	XR	XR	LE 1 C	XR	XR	XR	LE 1 A	XR	XR	XR	LE 1 C	XR	XR	XR	XR	LE 1 A
Shenfield 3	d	07 45	07 54	08 04	08 14	08 20	08 24	08 34	08 44	08 45	08 54	09 04	09 14	09 20	09 24	09 34	09 44	09 45	09 54	10 04	10 14	10 24	10 27
Brentwood	d		07 57	08 07	08 17		08 27	08 37	08 47		08 57	09 07	09 17		09 27	09 37	09 47		09 57	10 07	10 17	10 27	
Harold Wood	d		08 02	08 12	08 22		08 32	08 42	08 52		09 02	09 12	09 22		09 32	09 42	09 52		10 02	10 12	10 22	10 32	
Gidea Park 2	d		08 06	08 16	08 26		08 36	08 46	08 56		09 06	09 16	09 26		09 36	09 46	09 56		10 06	10 16	10 26	10 36	
Romford	d	07 53	08 08	08 18	08 28	08 28	08 38	08 48	08 58	08 53	09 08	09 18	09 28	09 28	09 38	09 48	09 58	09 53	10 08	10 18	10 28	10 38	10 35
Chadwell Heath	d		08 12	08 22	08 32		08 42	08 52	09 02		09 12	09 22	09 32		09 42	09 52	10 02		10 12	10 22	10 32	10 42	
Goodmayes	d		08 14	08 24	08 34		08 44	08 54	09 04		09 14	09 24	09 34		09 44	09 54	10 04		10 14	10 24	10 34	10 44	
Seven Kings	d		08 16	08 26	08 36		08 46	08 56	09 06		09 16	09 26	09 36		09 46	09 56	10 06		10 16	10 26	10 36	10 46	
Ilford 2	d		08 19	08 29	08 39		08 49	08 59	09 09		09 19	09 29	09 39		09 49	09 59	10 09		10 19	10 29	10 39	10 49	
Manor Park	d		08 22	08 32	08 42		08 52	09 02	09 12		09 22	09 32	09 42		09 52	10 02	10 12		10 22	10 32	10 42	10 52	
Forest Gate	d		08 24	08 34	08 44		08 54	09 04	09 14		09 24	09 34	09 44		09 54	10 04	10 14		10 24	10 34	10 44	10 54	
Maryland	d		08 26	08 36	08 46		08 56	09 06	09 16		09 26	09 36	09 46		09 56	10 06	10 16		10 26	10 36	10 46	10 56	
Stratford 7 ⊖	d	08 02	08 29	08 39	08 49	08 37	08 59	09 09	09 19	09 02	09 29	09 39	09 49	09 37	09 59	10 09	10 19	10 02	10 29	10 39	10 49	10 59	10 45
London Liverpool Street 15 ⊖	a	08 10	08 37	08 47	08 57	08 46	09 07	09 17	09 27	09 10	09 37	09 47	09 57	09 46	10 07	10 17	10 27	10 10	10 37	10 47	10 57	11 07	10 53

A From Colchester Town
B From Ipswich
C From Southend Victoria
D From Southminster
E From Shenfield
F From Colchester
G From Harwich International

Table T005-R

Saturdays

21 December to 16 May

Shenfield - Ilford - London Liverpool Street

		XR	XR	LE [1] A	XR	XR	XR	LE [1] B	XR		XR	XR	LE [1] A	XR	XR	XR	LE [1] B	XR	XR	XR	LE [1] A	XR	XR
Shenfield [3]	d	10 34	10 44	10 45	10 54	11 04	11 14	11 20	11 24	and at the same minutes past each hour until	16 34	16 44	16 45	16 54	17 04	17 14	17 20	17 24	17 34	17 44	17 45	17 54	18 04
Brentwood	d	10 37	10 47		10 57	11 07	11 17		11 27		16 37	16 47		16 57	17 07	17 17		17 27	17 37	17 47		17 57	18 07
Harold Wood	d	10 42	10 52		11 02	11 12	11 22		11 32		16 42	16 52		17 02	17 12	17 22		17 32	17 42	17 52		18 02	18 12
Gidea Park [2]	d	10 46	10 56		11 06	11 16	11 26		11 36		16 46	16 56		17 06	17 16	17 26		17 36	17 46	17 56		18 06	18 16
Romford	d	10 48	10 58	10 53	11 08	11 18	11 28	11 28	11 38		16 48	16 58	16 53	17 08	17 18	17 28	17 28	17 38	17 48	17 58	17 53	18 08	18 18
Chadwell Heath	d	10 52	11 02		11 12	11 22	11 32		11 42		16 52	17 02		17 12	17 22	17 32		17 42	17 52	18 02		18 12	18 22
Goodmayes	d	10 54	11 04		11 14	11 24	11 34		11 44		16 54	17 04		17 14	17 24	17 34		17 44	17 54	18 04		18 14	18 24
Seven Kings	d	10 56	11 06		11 16	11 26	11 36		11 46		16 56	17 06		17 16	17 26	17 36		17 46	17 56	18 06		18 16	18 26
Ilford [2]	d	10 59	11 09		11 19	11 29	11 39		11 49		16 59	17 09		17 19	17 29	17 39		17 49	17 59	18 09		18 19	18 29
Manor Park	d	11 02	11 12		11 22	11 32	11 42		11 52		17 02	17 12		17 22	17 32	17 42		17 52	18 02	18 12		18 22	18 32
Forest Gate	d	11 04	11 14		11 24	11 34	11 44		11 54		17 04	17 14		17 24	17 34	17 44		17 54	18 04	18 14		18 24	18 34
Maryland	d	11 06	11 16		11 26	11 36	11 46		11 56		17 06	17 16		17 26	17 36	17 46		17 56	18 06	18 16		18 26	18 36
Stratford [7] ⊖	d	11 09	11 19	11 02	11 29	11 39	11 49	11 37	11 59		17 09	17 19	17 02	17 29	17 39	17 49	17 37	17 59	18 09	18 19	18 02	18 29	18 39
London Liverpool Street [15] ⊖	a	11 17	11 27	11 10	11 37	11 47	11 57	11 46	12 07		17 17	17 27	17 10	17 37	17 47	17 57	17 46	18 07	18 17	18 27	18 10	18 37	18 47

		XR	XR	LE [1] B	XR		XR	LE [1] A	XR	XR	XR	LE [1] B	XR	XR	XR		LE ◇[1] A	XR	XR	XR	LE [1] B	XR	XR	XR	LE ◇[1] A
Shenfield [3]	d	18 14	18 24	18 27	18 34		18 44	18 45	18 54	19 04	19 14	19 20	19 24	19 34	19 44		19 45	19 54	20 04	20 14	20 20	20 24	20 34	20 44	20 45
Brentwood	d	18 17	18 27		18 37		18 47		18 57	19 07	19 17		19 27	19 37	19 47			19 57	20 07	20 17		20 27	20 37	20 47	
Harold Wood	d	18 22	18 32		18 42		18 52		19 02	19 12	19 22		19 32	19 42	19 52			20 02	20 12	20 22		20 32	20 42	20 52	
Gidea Park [2]	d	18 26	18 36		18 46		18 56		19 06	19 16	19 26		19 36	19 46	19 56			20 06	20 16	20 26		20 36	20 46	20 56	
Romford	d	18 28	18 38	18 35	18 48		18 58	18 53	19 08	19 18	19 28	19 28	19 38	19 48	19 58		19 53	20 08	20 18	20 28	20 28	20 38	20 48	20 58	20 53
Chadwell Heath	d	18 32	18 42		18 52		19 02		19 12	19 22	19 32		19 42	19 52	20 02			20 12	20 22	20 32		20 42	20 52	21 02	
Goodmayes	d	18 34	18 44		18 54		19 04		19 14	19 24	19 34		19 44	19 54	20 04			20 14	20 24	20 34		20 44	20 54	21 04	
Seven Kings	d	18 36	18 46		18 56		19 06		19 16	19 26	19 36		19 46	19 56	20 06			20 16	20 26	20 36		20 46	20 56	21 06	
Ilford [2]	d	18 39	18 49		18 59		19 09		19 19	19 29	19 39		19 49	19 59	20 09			20 19	20 29	20 39		20 49	20 59	21 09	
Manor Park	d	18 42	18 52		19 02		19 12		19 22	19 32	19 42		19 52	20 02	20 12			20 22	20 32	20 42		20 52	21 02	21 12	
Forest Gate	d	18 44	18 54		19 04		19 14		19 24	19 34	19 44		19 54	20 04	20 14			20 24	20 34	20 44		20 54	21 04	21 14	
Maryland	d	18 46	18 56		19 06		19 16		19 26	19 36	19 46		19 56	20 06	20 16			20 26	20 36	20 46		20 56	21 06	21 16	
Stratford [7] ⊖	d	18 49	18 59	18 44	19 09		19 19	19 02	19 29	19 39	19 49	19 37	19 59	20 09	20 19		20 02	20 29	20 39	20 49	20 37	20 59	21 09	21 19	21 02
London Liverpool Street [15] ⊖	a	18 57	19 07	18 53	19 17		19 27	19 10	19 37	19 47	19 57	19 46	20 07	20 17	20 27		20 10	20 37	20 47	20 57	20 46	21 07	21 17	21 27	21 10

		XR	XR	LE [1] B	XR	XR	LE ◇[1] A	XR	XR	LE [1] B	XR		XR	LE [1] C	XR	LE [1] D	XR
Shenfield [3]	d	20 59	21 14	21 20	21 29	21 44	21 45	21 59	22 14	22 20	22 29	and every 15 minutes until	23 14	23 20	23 29	23 39	23 44
Brentwood	d	21 02	21 17		21 32	21 47		22 02	22 17		22 32		23 17		23 32		23 47
Harold Wood	d	21 07	21 22		21 37	21 52		22 07	22 22		22 37		23 22		23 37		23 52
Gidea Park [2]	d	21 11	21 26		21 41	21 56		22 11	22 26		22 41		23 26		23 41		23 56
Romford	d	21 13	21 28	21 28	21 43	21 58	21 53	22 13	22 28	22 28	22 43		23 28	23 28	23 43	23 47	23 58
Chadwell Heath	d	21 17	21 32		21 47	22 02		22 17	22 32		22 47		23 32		23 47		00 02
Goodmayes	d	21 19	21 34		21 49	22 04		22 19	22 34		22 49		23 34		23 49		00 04
Seven Kings	d	21 21	21 36		21 51	22 06		22 21	22 36		22 51		23 36		23 51		00 06
Ilford [2]	d	21 24	21 39		21 54	22 09		22 24	22 39		22 54		23 39		23 54		00 09
Manor Park	d	21 27	21 42		21 57	22 12		22 27	22 42		22 57		23 42		23 57		00 12
Forest Gate	d	21 29	21 44		21 59	22 14		22 29	22 44		22 59		23 44		23 59		00 14
Maryland	d	21 31	21 46		22 01	22 16		22 31	22 46		23 01		23 46		00 01		00 16
Stratford [7] ⊖	d	21 34	21 49	21 37	22 04	22 19	22 02	22 34	22 49	22 37	23 04		23 49	23 37	00 04	23 57	00 19
London Liverpool Street [15] ⊖	a	21 42	21 57	21 46	22 12	22 27	22 10	22 42	22 57	22 46	23 12		23 57	23 45	00 15	00 05	00 30

Sundays

15 December to 10 May

		XR E	XR E	XR		XR	XR	LE [1] A	XR	LE [1] F		XR	LE [1] A	XR	LE [1] G	XR	LE [1] A	XR	XR	LE [1] A		XR	XR	LE [1] A
Shenfield [3]	d				and every 15 minutes until		06 41	06 52	06 56	07 07		07 11	07 22	07 26	07 37	07 40	07 52	07 56	08 10	08 23		08 26	08 41	08 53
Brentwood	d						06 45		07 00			07 15		07 30		07 45		08 00	08 15			08 30	08 45	
Harold Wood	d						06 49		07 04			07 19		07 34		07 49		08 04	08 19			08 34	08 49	
Gidea Park [2]	d			05 52		06 37	06 52		07 07			07 22		07 37		07 52		08 07	08 22			08 37	08 52	
Romford	d			05 55		06 40	06 55	07 04	07 10	07 19		07 25	07 34	07 40	07 49	07 55	08 04	08 10	08 25	08 34		08 40	08 55	09 05
Chadwell Heath	d		00 02	05 59		06 44	06 59		07 14			07 29		07 44		07 59		08 14	08 29			08 44	08 59	
Goodmayes	d		00 04	06 01		06 46	07 01		07 16			07 31		07 46		08 01		08 16	08 31			08 46	09 01	
Seven Kings	d		00 06	06 03		06 48	07 03		07 18			07 33		07 48		08 03		08 18	08 33			08 48	09 03	
Ilford [2]	d		00 09	06 06		06 51	07 06		07 21			07 36		07 51		08 06		08 21	08 36			08 51	09 06	
Manor Park	d		00 12	06 09		06 54	07 09		07 24			07 39		07 54		08 09		08 24	08 39			08 54	09 09	
Forest Gate	d		00 14	06 11		06 56	07 11		07 26			07 41		07 56		08 11		08 26	08 41			08 56	09 11	
Maryland	d	00 01	00 16	06 13		06 58	07 13		07 28			07 43		07 58		08 13		08 28	08 43			08 58	09 13	
Stratford [7] ⊖	d	00 04	00 19	06 16		07 01	07 16	07 19	07 31	07 34		07 46	07 49	08 01	08 04	08 16	08 19	08 31	08 46	08 54		09 01	09 16	09 16
London Liverpool Street [15] ⊖	a	00 15	00 30	06 25		07 10	07 25	07 27	07 40	07 43		07 55	07 57	08 10	08 13	08 25	08 27	08 40	08 55	09 02		09 10	09 25	09 27

		XR	XR	XR	LE [1] A	XR	XR	LE ◇[1] A		XR	XR	LE [1] A	XR	XR	LE [1] A		XR	XR	LE [1] A	XR	XR
Shenfield [3]	d	08 56	09 11	09 26	09 29	09 41	09 56	09 59	and at the same minutes past each hour until	22 11	22 26	22 29	22 41	22 56	22 59		23 11	23 26	23 29	23 41	23 56
Brentwood	d	09 00	09 15	09 30		09 45	10 00			22 15	22 30		22 45	23 00			23 15	23 30		23 45	00 01
Harold Wood	d	09 04	09 19	09 34		09 49	10 04			22 19	22 34		22 49	23 04			23 19	23 34		23 49	00 04
Gidea Park [2]	d	09 07	09 22	09 37		09 52	10 07			22 22	22 37		22 52	23 07			23 22	23 37		23 52	00 07
Romford	d	09 10	09 25	09 40	09 38	09 55	10 10	10 08		22 25	22 40	22 38	22 55	23 10	23 08		23 25	23 40	23 37	23 55	00 10
Chadwell Heath	d	09 14	09 29	09 44		09 59	10 14			22 29	22 44		22 59	23 14			23 29	23 44		23 59	00 14
Goodmayes	d	09 16	09 31	09 46		10 01	10 16			22 31	22 46		23 01	23 16			23 31	23 46		00 01	00 16
Seven Kings	d	09 18	09 33	09 48		10 03	10 18			22 33	22 48		23 03	23 18			23 33	23 48		00 03	00 18
Ilford [2]	d	09 21	09 36	09 51		10 06	10 21			22 36	22 51		23 06	23 21			23 36	23 51		00 06	00 21
Manor Park	d	09 24	09 39	09 54		10 09	10 24			22 39	22 54		23 09	23 24			23 39	23 54		00 09	00 24
Forest Gate	d	09 26	09 41	09 56		10 11	10 26			22 41	22 56		23 11	23 26			23 41	23 56		00 11	00 26
Maryland	d	09 28	09 43	09 58		10 13	10 28			22 43	22 58		23 13	23 28			23 43	23 58		00 13	00 28
Stratford [7] ⊖	d	09 31	09 46	10 01	09 48	10 16	10 31	10 18		22 46	23 01	22 48	23 16	23 31	23 18		23 46	00 02	23 47	00 16	00 31
London Liverpool Street [15] ⊖	a	09 40	09 55	10 10	09 57	10 25	10 40	10 27		22 55	23 10	22 57	23 25	23 40	23 27		23 55	00 10	23 56	00 25	00 40

A From Southend Victoria
B From Colchester Town
C From Ipswich
D From Southminster
E not 15 December. From Shenfield
F From Chelmsford
G From Colchester

NRT DECEMBER 19 EDITION

Table T006-F

Mondays to Fridays

16 December to 15 May

London Liverpool Street - Shenfield - Wickford - Southminster and Southend

Miles	Miles			LE MX [1] A	LE MO [1] A	LE MX [1] A	LE MO [1] A	LE MO B	LE MO C	LE MX [1]	LE MX [1] B	LE MO A		LE MO	LE MX [1] B	LE MX [1]	LE [1]	LE ◇[1] D	LE [1]	LE [1]	LE [1]	LE ◇[1] D		LE [1]	LE [1] E
0	0	**London Liverpool Street** [15] ⊖	d					00 02	00 14	00 15	00 18			00 44	00 46	00 50		05 23		05 35	05 55	06 02			06 12
4	4	Stratford [7] ⊖ ⛴	d					00 09	00 21	00 22	00 25			00 51	00 53	00 57		05 30		05 42	06 02	06 09			06 20
12½	12½	Romford	d				00 01		00 36	00 32		←		01 05		01 08		05 38							
20¼	20¼	**Shenfield** [3]	a				00 16	00 31	00 49	00 44	00 47	00 49		01 19	01 16	01 20		05 47		06 01	06 18	06 24			06 36
—	—		d			00 09	00 16		00 49	00 45		00 49		01 19		01 20			05 55	06 03	06 19			06 30	
24¼	24¼	Billericay	d			00 15	00 22		→	00 51		00 55		01 25		01 26			06 01	06 09	06 25			06 36	
29	29	**Wickford** [2]	d		00 01	00 21	00 28			00 56		01 01		01 31		01 31	05 16		06 09	06 15	06 31			06 45	
—	31½	Battlesbridge	d														05 20		06 13					06 49	
—	34	South Woodham Ferrers	d														05 24		06 17					06 53	
—	37¼	North Fambridge	d														05 41		06 23					07 03	
—	40¼	Althorne	d														05 46		06 28					07 08	
—	43¼	Burnham-on-Crouch	d														05 51		06 33					07 13	
—	45½	**Southminster**	a														05 57		06 40					07 20	
33¼	—	Rayleigh	d		00 06	00 26	00 33			01 01		01 06		01 36		01 36				06 20	06 36				
36¼	—	Hockley	d	00 01	00 10	00 31	00 37			01 06		01 10		01 40		01 41				06 25	06 41				
38¾	—	Rochford	d	00 04	00 14	00 34	00 41			01 09		01 14		01 44		01 44				06 28	06 44				
39¾	—	Southend Airport ✈	d	00 07	00 16	00 37	00 43			01 12		01 16		01 46		01 47				06 31	06 47				
40¾	—	Prittlewell	d	00 10	00 19	00 40	00 46			01 16		01 19		01 49		01 50				06 35	06 50				
41½	—	**Southend Victoria**	a	00 18	00 27	00 48	00 54			01 23		01 27		01 57		01 58				06 38	06 54				

		LE [1]	LE [1]	LE [1] F	LE [1] G	LE [1]	LE [1]	LE [1] E		LE [1]	LE [1] H	LE ◇[1] D	LE [1]	LE [1]	LE [1] G	LE [1]	LE [1] E	LE [1]		LE [1] H	LE [1] H	LE [1]	LE [1]	LE ◇[1] D	LE [1]
London Liverpool Street [15] ⊖	d	06 15	06 35	06 38	06 48	06 50		07 02		07 05	07 08	07 17	07 20	07 33	07 36	07 40	07 46	07 57		08 00	08 06	08 13		08 16	08 32
Stratford [7] ⊖ ⛴	d	06 22	06 42	06 45	06 55	06 57		07 09		07 12	07 15	07 24	07 27	07 42	07 45		07 54	08 05		08 08	08 14	08 21		08 24	08 42
Romford	d										07 23														
Shenfield [3]	a	06 38	06 57	07 00	07 11	07 13		07 24		07 27	07 32	07 39	07 42	07 58	08 01		08 10	08 21		08 25	08 30	08 37		08 40	08 58
	d	06 39	06 59			07 14				07 29			07 43	07 58				08 22				08 39			08 59
Billericay	d	06 45	07 05			07 20				07 35			07 49	08 04				08 28				08 45			09 05
Wickford [2]	d	06 51	07 11			07 26	07 36			07 41			07 55	08 10		08 18		08 34				08 51	08 56		09 11
Battlesbridge	d						07 40									08 22							09 00		
South Woodham Ferrers	d						07 44									08 26							09 04		
North Fambridge	d						07 52									08 32							09 11		
Althorne	d						07 57									08 37							09 16		
Burnham-on-Crouch	d						08 02									08 42							09 21		
Southminster	a						08 08									08 48							09 27		
Rayleigh	d	06 56	07 16			07 31				07 46			08 00	08 15				08 39				08 56			09 16
Hockley	d	07 01	07 21			07 36				07 51			08 05	08 20				08 44				09 01			09 21
Rochford	d	07 04	07 24			07 39				07 54			08 08	08 23				08 47				09 04			09 24
Southend Airport ✈	d	07 07	07 27			07 42				07 57			08 11	08 26				08 50				09 07			09 27
Prittlewell	d	07 10	07 30			07 45				08 01			08 14	08 29				08 53				09 10			09 30
Southend Victoria	a	07 15	07 34			07 49				08 04			08 18	08 34				08 57				09 14			09 34

		LE [1] G	LE [1] E	LE [1]		LE [1]	LE [1] H	LE ◇[1]	LE ◇[1] D	LE ◇[1]	LE [1]	LE [1] G	LE [1] E	LE ◇[1]		LE [1] H	LE ◇[1]	LE [1]	LE ◇[1] D	LE [1] G	LE ◇[1]	LE [1] E	LE ◇[1]	LE [1]
London Liverpool Street [15] ⊖	d	08 36	08 48	08 55			09 02	09 13	09 18	09 34		09 38	09 48	09 55		10 02	10 13		10 18	10 34	10 38	10 46	10 52	
Stratford [7] ⊖ ⛴	d	08 45	08 55	09 02			09 09	09 21	09 25	09 42		09 45	09 55	10 02		10 09	10 20		10 25	10 41	10 45	10 53	10 59	
Romford	d											09 53					10 28			10 49				
Shenfield [3]	a	09 02	09 11	09 17			09 24	09 38	09 40	09 57		10 02	10 11	10 18		10 24	10 37		10 40	10 58	11 00	11 08	11 14	
	d			09 18				09 39		09 59				10 19			10 39				11 01		11 17	
Billericay	d			09 24				09 45		10 05				10 25			10 45				11 07		11 23	
Wickford [2]	d			09 31		09 36		09 51		10 11	10 16			10 31			10 51	10 56			11 13		11 30	11 36
Battlesbridge	d					09 40					10 20							11 00						11 40
South Woodham Ferrers	d					09 44					10 24							11 04						11 44
North Fambridge	d					09 51					10 31							11 11						11 51
Althorne	d					09 56					10 36							11 16						11 56
Burnham-on-Crouch	d					10 01					10 41							11 21						12 01
Southminster	a					10 07					10 47							11 27						12 07
Rayleigh	d			09 36				09 56		10 16				10 36			10 56				11 18		11 35	
Hockley	d			09 41				10 01		10 21				10 41			11 01				11 23		11 40	
Rochford	d			09 44				10 04		10 24				10 44			11 04				11 26		11 43	
Southend Airport ✈	d			09 47				10 07		10 27				10 47			11 07				11 29		11 46	
Prittlewell	d			09 50				10 10		10 30				10 50			11 10				11 32		11 49	
Southend Victoria	a			09 54				10 14		10 34				10 54			11 14				11 36		11 54	

		LE [1] H	LE ◇[1]	LE ◇[1] D	LE ◇[1]	LE [1]	LE [1] G	LE [1] E	LE ◇[1]	LE [1] H		LE ◇[1]	LE [1]	LE ◇[1] D	LE ◇[1]	LE [1] G	LE [1] E	LE ◇[1]	LE [1]	LE [1] H		LE ◇[1]	LE ◇[1] D	LE ◇[1]	LE [1]
London Liverpool Street [15] ⊖	d	11 04	11 13	11 18	11 35		11 38	11 48	11 55	12 02		12 13		12 18	12 35	12 38	12 48	12 55		13 02		13 13	13 18	13 35	
Stratford [7] ⊖ ⛴	d	11 11	11 20	11 25	11 42		11 45	11 55	12 02	12 09		12 20		12 25	12 42	12 45	12 55	13 02		13 09		13 20	13 25	13 42	
Romford	d		11 28				11 53					12 28				12 53						13 28			
Shenfield [3]	a	11 26	11 37	11 41	11 57		12 02	12 11	12 17	12 24		12 37		12 40	12 57	13 02	13 11	13 18		13 24		13 37	13 40	13 57	
	d		11 39		11 59				12 19			12 39			12 59			13 19				13 39		13 59	
Billericay	d		11 45		12 05				12 25			12 45			13 05			13 25				13 45		14 05	
Wickford [2]	d		11 51		12 11	12 16			12 31			12 51	12 56		13 11			13 31	13 36			13 51		14 11	14 16
Battlesbridge	d					12 20							13 00						13 40						14 20
South Woodham Ferrers	d					12 24							13 04						13 44						14 24
North Fambridge	d					12 31							13 11						13 51						14 31
Althorne	d					12 36							13 16						13 56						14 36
Burnham-on-Crouch	d					12 41							13 21						14 01						14 41
Southminster	a					12 47							13 27						14 07						14 47
Rayleigh	d		11 56		12 16				12 36			12 56			13 16			13 36				13 56		14 16	
Hockley	d		12 01		12 21				12 41			13 01			13 21			13 41				14 01		14 21	
Rochford	d		12 04		12 24				12 44			13 04			13 24			13 44				14 04		14 24	
Southend Airport ✈	d		12 07		12 27				12 47			13 07			13 27			13 47				14 07		14 27	
Prittlewell	d		12 10		12 30				12 50			13 10			13 30			13 51				14 10		14 30	
Southend Victoria	a		12 14		12 34				12 54			13 14			13 34			13 54				14 14		14 34	

A From London Liverpool Street
B To Colchester
C To Southend Victoria
D To Clacton-on-Sea
E To Braintree
F To Harwich Town
G To Colchester Town
H To Ipswich

16 December to 15 May

London Liverpool Street - Shenfield - Wickford - Southminster and Southend

Station		LE 1 A	LE 1 B	LE ◇1	LE 1 C	LE 1	LE 1	LE ◇1 D	LE 1	LE 1 A	LE 1 B	LE 1	LE 1	LE 1 C	LE 1	LE ◇1 D	LE 1	LE 1	LE 1 A	LE 1 B	LE 1	LE ◇1 C	LE 1
London Liverpool Street 15 ⊖	d	13 38	13 48	13 55	14 02	14 13		14 18	14 35	14 38	14 48	14 55		15 02	15 13	15 18	15 35		15 38	15 48	15 55	16 02	16 10
Stratford 7 ⊖	d	13 45	13 55	14 02	14 09	14 20		14 25	14 42	14 45	14 55	15 02		15 09	15 20	15 25	15 42		15 45	15 55	16 02	16 09	16 18
Romford	d	13 53				14 28				14 53					15 28				15 53				
Shenfield 3	a	14 02	14 11	14 18	14 24	14 37		14 40	14 57	15 02	15 11	15 17		15 24	15 37	15 40	15 57		16 02	16 11	16 17	16 25	16 34
	d			14 19		14 39			14 59			15 19			15 39		15 59				16 19		16 34
Billericay	d			14 25		14 45			15 05			15 25			15 45		16 05				16 25		16 41
Wickford 2	d			14 31		14 51	14 56		15 11			15 31	15 36		15 51		16 11	16 14			16 31		16 48
Battlesbridge	d						15 00						15 40					16 18					
South Woodham Ferrers	d						15 04						15 44					16 22					
North Fambridge	d						15 11						15 51					16 29					
Althorne	d						15 16						15 56					16 34					
Burnham-on-Crouch	d						15 21						16 01					16 39					
Southminster	a						15 27						16 07					16 45					
Rayleigh	d			14 36		14 56			15 16			15 36			15 56		16 16				16 36		16 53
Hockley	d			14 41		15 01			15 21			15 41			16 01		16 21				16 41		16 57
Rochford	d			14 44		15 04			15 24			15 44			16 04		16 24				16 44		17 01
Southend Airport ✈	d			14 47		15 07			15 27			15 47			16 07		16 27				16 47		17 03
Prittlewell	d			14 50		15 10			15 30			15 50			16 10		16 31				16 50		17 06
Southend Victoria	a			14 54		15 14			15 34			15 54			16 14		16 34				16 54		17 15

Station		LE ◇1 D	LE 1 E	LE 1	LE 1	LE ◇1 C	LE 1 B	LE 1	LE 1 E	LE 1	LE ◇1 F	LE 1	LE 1	LE 1 B	LE 1	LE 1	LE 1	LE 1 A	LE 1	LE 1	LE 1 B	LE 1
London Liverpool Street 15 ⊖	d	16 14	16 17	16 24		16 32	16 34	16 40	16 47	16 54	17 02	17 04	17 15	17 20	17 22	17 25	17 34	17 40	17 45	17 54	18 00	18 02
Stratford 7 ⊖	d	16 22	16 25	16 32			16 42	16 48	16 55	17 02	17 10	17 13	17 23	17 29	17 32	17 34	17 43		17 53	18 03	18 09	18 12
Romford	d																					
Shenfield 3	a	16 38	16 41	16 48		16 54	16 58	17 04	17 11	17 18	17 26	17 29	17 39	17 45		17 50	17 59	18 05	18 09	18 19	18 25	
	d			16 48				17 04		17 19		17 30	17 39			17 52	18 00		18 09	18 20		
Billericay	d			16 55				17 11		17 26		17 37	17 46			17 58	18 06		18 16	18 26		
Wickford 2	d			17 02	17 06			17 18		17 33		17 44	17 53		18 00	18 05	18 13		18 23	18 33		18 41
Battlesbridge	d				17 10										18 04							18 45
South Woodham Ferrers	d				17 14										18 08							18 49
North Fambridge	d				17 21										18 14							18 55
Althorne	d				17 26										18 19							19 00
Burnham-on-Crouch	d				17 31										18 24							19 05
Southminster	a				17 37										18 32							19 14
Rayleigh	d			17 07				17 23		17 38		17 49	17 58			18 10	18 18		18 28	18 38		
Hockley	d			17 11				17 27		17 42		17 53	18 02			18 15	18 23		18 32	18 43		
Rochford	d			17 15				17 31		17 46		17 57	18 06			18 18	18 26		18 36	18 46		
Southend Airport ✈	d			17 17				17 33		17 48		17 59	18 08			18 21	18 29		18 38	18 49		
Prittlewell	d			17 20				17 36		17 51		18 02	18 11			18 24	18 32		18 41	18 52		
Southend Victoria	a			17 26				17 42		17 57		18 08	18 17			18 30	18 38		18 47	18 58		

Station		LE 1	LE 1	LE 1 A	LE 1	LE ◇1 D	LE 1	LE 1	LE 1	LE 1	LE 1 B	LE 1	LE ◇1 D	LE ◇1	LE 1	LE 1 A	LE 1 B	LE ◇1	LE ◇1 C	LE ◇1	LE 1	LE ◇1 D	LE ◇1
London Liverpool Street 15 ⊖	d	18 05	18 17	18 20	18 25	18 35	18 37	18 41	18 45	18 52	19 04	19 13	19 18	19 35		19 38	19 48	19 55	20 02	20 13		20 18	20 35
Stratford 7 ⊖	d	18 14	18 25	18 28	18 33	18 43	18 46	18 50	18 53	18 59	19 11	19 21	19 25	19 42		19 45	19 55	20 03	20 09	20 20		20 25	20 42
Romford	d																			20 28			20 50
Shenfield 3	a	18 31	18 42	18 45	18 49	18 59	19 02		19 09	19 15	19 27	19 38	19 40	19 57		20 00	20 11	20 18	20 24	20 37		20 40	20 59
	d	18 31	18 43		18 50		19 02		19 10	19 15		19 38		19 58				20 19		20 39			20 59
Billericay	d	18 38	18 49		18 57		19 09		19 17	19 22		19 44		20 04				20 25		20 45			21 05
Wickford 2	d	18 45	18 56		19 04		19 16	19 20	19 24	19 29		19 51		20 10	20 16			20 31		20 51	20 56		21 12
Battlesbridge	d							19 24							20 20						21 00		
South Woodham Ferrers	d							19 28							20 24						21 04		
North Fambridge	d							19 35							20 31						21 11		
Althorne	d							19 40							20 36						21 16		
Burnham-on-Crouch	d							19 45							20 41						21 21		
Southminster	a							19 53							20 47						21 27		
Rayleigh	d	18 50	19 01		19 09		19 21		19 29	19 34		19 56		20 15				20 36		20 56			21 17
Hockley	d	18 55	19 06		19 13		19 25		19 33	19 39		20 00		20 20				20 41		21 01			21 21
Rochford	d	18 58	19 09		19 17		19 29		19 37	19 43		20 04		20 23				20 44		21 04			21 25
Southend Airport ✈	d	19 01	19 12		19 19		19 31		19 39	19 46		20 07		20 26				20 47		21 07			21 27
Prittlewell	d	19 04	19 15		19 22		19 34		19 42	19 49		20 10		20 29				20 50		21 10			21 30
Southend Victoria	a	19 10	19 21		19 28		19 40		19 47	19 55		20 14		20 35				20 54		21 14			21 34

Station		LE 1 A	LE 1 B	LE ◇1	LE 1	LE 1 G	LE ◇1	LE ◇1 D	LE ◇1	LE 1	LE 1 A	LE 1 B	LE ◇1	LE 1 H	LE ◇1	LE 1	LE ◇1 D	LE 1 H	LE ◇1	LE 1 C	LE 1	LE ◇1 D
London Liverpool Street 15 ⊖	d	20 38	20 48	20 55		21 02	21 13	21 18	21 35		21 38	21 48	21 55	22 02	22 13		22 18	22 38	22 45	23 02	23 15	23 18
Stratford 7 ⊖	d	20 45	20 55	21 02		21 09	21 20	21 25	21 42		21 45	21 55	22 02	22 09	22 20		22 25	22 45	22 52	23 09	23 22	23 25
Romford	d						21 28				21 53				22 28							
Shenfield 3	a	21 01	21 11	21 17		21 24	21 37	21 40	21 57		22 02	22 11	22 17	22 24	22 37		22 40	23 00	23 07	23 25	23 38	23 40
	d			21 19			21 39		21 59				22 19		22 39				23 09		23 39	
Billericay	d			21 25			21 45		22 05				22 25		22 45				23 15		23 45	
Wickford 2	d			21 31	21 36		21 51		22 11	22 16			22 31		22 51	22 56			23 21		23 51	
Battlesbridge	d				21 40					22 20						23 00						
South Woodham Ferrers	d				21 44					22 24						23 04						
North Fambridge	d				21 51					22 31						23 11						
Althorne	d				21 56					22 36						23 16						
Burnham-on-Crouch	d				22 01					22 41						23 21						
Southminster	a				22 07					22 47						23 27						
Rayleigh	d			21 36			21 56		22 16				22 36		22 56				23 26		23 56	
Hockley	d			21 41			22 01		22 21				22 41		23 01				23 31		00 01	
Rochford	d			21 44			22 04		22 24				22 44		23 04				23 34		00 04	
Southend Airport ✈	d			21 47			22 07		22 27				22 47		23 07				23 37		00 07	
Prittlewell	d			21 50			22 10		22 30				22 50		23 10				23 40		00 10	
Southend Victoria	a			21 54			22 14		22 34				22 54		23 14				23 48		00 18	

A To Colchester Town
B To Braintree
C To Ipswich
D To Clacton-on-Sea
E To Witham
F To Norwich
G To Harwich International
H To Colchester

16 December to 15 May

London Liverpool Street - Shenfield - Wickford - Southminster and Southend

Station		LE 1	LE 1 A
London Liverpool Street 15 ⊖	d	23 45	23 48
Stratford 7 ⊖	d	23 52	23 55
Romford	d		
Shenfield 3	a	00 07	00 10
	d	00 09	
Billericay	d	00 15	
Wickford 2	d	00 21	
Battlesbridge	d		
South Woodham Ferrers	d		
North Fambridge	d		
Althorne	d		
Burnham-on-Crouch	d		
Southminster	a		
Rayleigh	d	00 26	
Hockley	d	00 31	
Rochford	d	00 34	
Southend Airport ✈	d	00 37	
Prittlewell	d	00 40	
Southend Victoria	a	00 48	

Saturdays

21 December to 16 May

Station		LE 1 B	LE 1 B	LE 1	LE 1 A	LE 1 A	LE 1	LE 1 C	LE 1	LE 1	LE 1	LE 1 C	LE 1	LE 1	LE ◇1 D	LE 1	LE 1 E	LE 1 F	LE 1	LE 1	LE 1 C	LE 1	LE ◇1 D
London Liverpool Street 15 ⊖	d			00 15	00 18	00 46	00 50	05 34			05 36	06 02	06 05		06 18	06 35	06 38	06 48	06 55		07 02	07 13	07 18
Stratford 7 ⊖	d			00 22	00 25	00 53	00 57	05 41			05 43	06 09	06 12		06 25	06 42	06 45	06 55	07 02		07 09	07 20	07 25
Romford	d			00 32			01 08	05 49									06 53					07 28	
Shenfield 3	a			00 45	00 47	01 16	01 20	05 58			06 01	06 24	06 27		06 40	06 57	07 02	07 11	07 17		07 24	07 37	07 41
	d		00 09	00 45			01 20				06 03		06 29			06 59			07 19			07 39	
Billericay	d		00 15	00 51			01 26				06 09		06 35			07 05			07 25			07 45	
Wickford 2	d		00 21	00 56			01 31		05 36	06 12	06 15		06 41	06 56		07 11			07 31	07 36		07 51	
Battlesbridge	d								05 40	06 16				07 00						07 40			
South Woodham Ferrers	d								05 44	06 20				07 04						07 44			
North Fambridge	d								05 51	06 31				07 11						07 51			
Althorne	d								05 56	06 36				07 16						07 56			
Burnham-on-Crouch	d								06 01	06 41				07 21						08 01			
Southminster	a								06 07	06 47				07 27						08 07			
Rayleigh	d		00 26	01 01			01 36				06 20		06 46			07 16			07 36			07 56	
Hockley	d	00 01	00 31	01 06			01 41				06 25		06 51			07 21			07 41			08 01	
Rochford	d	00 04	00 34	01 09			01 44				06 28		06 54			07 24			07 44			08 04	
Southend Airport ✈	d	00 07	00 37	01 12			01 47				06 31		06 57			07 27			07 47			08 07	
Prittlewell	d	00 10	00 40	01 16			01 50				06 34		07 00			07 30			07 50			08 10	
Southend Victoria	a	00 18	00 48	01 23			01 58				06 38		07 04			07 34			07 54			08 14	

Station		LE 1	LE 1	LE 1 G	LE 1 F	LE 1	LE 1 C	LE 1	LE 1	LE ◇1 D	LE 1	LE 1 G	LE 1 F	LE 1	LE 1	LE 1 C	LE ◇1	LE ◇1 D	LE ◇1	LE 1	LE 1 G	LE 1 F	LE ◇1
London Liverpool Street 15 ⊖	d	07 35		07 38	07 48	07 55	08 02	08 13		08 18	08 35	08 38	08 48	08 55		09 02	09 13	09 18	09 35		09 38	09 48	09 55
Stratford 7 ⊖	d	07 42		07 45	07 55	08 02	08 09	08 20		08 25	08 42	08 45	08 55	09 02		09 09	09 20	09 25	09 42		09 45	09 55	10 02
Romford	d			07 53				08 28				08 53					09 28				09 53		
Shenfield 3	a	07 57		08 02	08 11	08 17	08 24	08 38		08 41	08 57	09 02	09 11	09 17		09 24	09 37	09 41	09 57		10 02	10 11	10 17
	d	07 59				08 19		08 39			08 59			09 19			09 39		09 59				10 19
Billericay	d	08 05				08 25		08 45			09 05			09 25			09 45		10 05				10 25
Wickford 2	d	08 11	08 16			08 31		08 51	08 56		09 11			09 31	09 36		09 51		10 11	10 16			10 31
Battlesbridge	d		08 20						09 00						09 40					10 20			
South Woodham Ferrers	d		08 24						09 04						09 44					10 24			
North Fambridge	d		08 31						09 11						09 51					10 31			
Althorne	d		08 36						09 16						09 56					10 36			
Burnham-on-Crouch	d		08 41						09 21						10 01					10 41			
Southminster	a		08 47						09 27						10 07					10 47			
Rayleigh	d	08 16				08 36		08 56			09 16			09 36			09 56		10 16				10 36
Hockley	d	08 21				08 41		09 01			09 21			09 41			10 01		10 21				10 41
Rochford	d	08 24				08 44		09 04			09 24			09 44			10 04		10 24				10 44
Southend Airport ✈	d	08 27				08 47		09 07			09 27			09 47			10 07		10 27				10 47
Prittlewell	d	08 30				08 50		09 10			09 30			09 50			10 10		10 30				10 50
Southend Victoria	a	08 34				08 54		09 14			09 34			09 54			10 14		10 34				10 54

Station		LE 1 C	LE ◇1	LE 1	LE ◇1 D	LE 1 G	LE ◇1	LE 1 F	LE ◇1	LE 1	LE 1 C	LE ◇1	LE ◇1 D	LE ◇1	LE 1	LE 1 G	LE 1 F	LE ◇1	LE 1 C	LE ◇1	LE 1	LE ◇1 D
London Liverpool Street 15 ⊖	d	10 02	10 13		10 18	10 34	10 38	10 46	10 53		11 04	11 13	11 18	11 35		11 38	11 48	11 55	12 02	12 13		12 18
Stratford 7 ⊖	d	10 09	10 20		10 25	10 41	10 45	10 53	11 00		11 11	11 20	11 25	11 42		11 45	11 55	12 02	12 09	12 20		12 25
Romford	d		10 28			10 49						11 28				11 53				12 28		
Shenfield 3	a	10 24	10 37		10 41	10 58	11 00	11 08	11 17		11 26	11 37	11 41	11 57		12 02	12 11	12 17	12 24	12 37		12 41
	d		10 39				11 01		11 19			11 39		11 59				12 19		12 39		
Billericay	d		10 45				11 07		11 25			11 45		12 05				12 25		12 45		
Wickford 2	d		10 51	10 56			11 13		11 31	11 36		11 51		12 11	12 16			12 31		12 51	12 56	
Battlesbridge	d			11 00						11 40					12 20						13 00	
South Woodham Ferrers	d			11 04						11 44					12 24						13 04	
North Fambridge	d			11 11						11 51					12 31						13 11	
Althorne	d			11 16						11 56					12 36						13 16	
Burnham-on-Crouch	d			11 21						12 01					12 41						13 21	
Southminster	a			11 27						12 07					12 47						13 27	
Rayleigh	d		10 56				11 18		11 36			11 56		12 16				12 36		12 56		
Hockley	d		11 01				11 23		11 41			12 01		12 21				12 41		13 01		
Rochford	d		11 04				11 26		11 44			12 04		12 24				12 44		13 04		
Southend Airport ✈	d		11 07				11 29		11 47			12 07		12 27				12 47		13 07		
Prittlewell	d		11 10				11 32		11 50			12 10		12 30				12 50		13 10		
Southend Victoria	a		11 14				11 36		11 54			12 14		12 34				12 54		13 14		

A To Colchester
B From London Liverpool Street
C To Ipswich
D To Clacton-on-Sea
E To Harwich International
F To Braintree
G To Colchester Town

Table T006-F

Saturdays
21 December to 16 May

London Liverpool Street - Shenfield - Wickford - Southminster and Southend

Station		LE ◇1	LE 1	LE 1	LE ◇1	LE 1	LE 1	LE ◇1	LE ◇1	LE ◇1	LE 1	LE 1	LE 1	LE ◇1	LE 1	LE 1	LE 1	LE ◇1	LE 1	LE 1	LE 1	LE 1	LE 1
			A	B			C		D			A	B		C			D		A	B		
London Liverpool Street 15 ⊖	d	12 35	12 38	12 48	12 55		13 02	13 13	13 18	13 35		13 38	13 48	13 55	14 02	14 13		14 18	14 35	14 38	14 48	14 55	
Stratford 7 ⊖	d	12 42	12 45	12 55	13 02		13 09	13 20	13 25	13 42		13 45	13 55	14 02	14 09	14 20		14 25	14 42	14 45	14 55	15 02	
Romford	d		12 53					13 28				13 53				14 28				14 53			
Shenfield 3	a	12 57	13 02	13 11	13 17		13 24	13 37	13 41	13 57		14 02	14 11	14 17	14 24	14 37		14 41	14 58	15 02	15 11	15 17	
	d	12 59			13 19			13 39		13 59				14 19		14 39			14 59			15 19	
Billericay	d	13 05			13 25			13 45		14 05				14 25		14 45			15 05			15 25	
Wickford 2	d	13 11			13 31	13 36		13 51		14 11	14 16			14 31		14 51	14 56		15 11			15 31	15 36
Battlesbridge	d					13 40					14 20						15 00						15 40
South Woodham Ferrers	d					13 44					14 24						15 04						15 44
North Fambridge	d					13 51					14 31						15 11						15 51
Althorne	d					13 56					14 36						15 16						15 56
Burnham-on-Crouch	d					14 01					14 41						15 21						16 01
Southminster	a					14 07					14 47						15 27						16 07
Rayleigh	d	13 16			13 36			13 56		14 16				14 36		14 56			15 16			15 36	
Hockley	d	13 21			13 41			14 01		14 21				14 41		15 01			15 21			15 41	
Rochford	d	13 24			13 44			14 04		14 24				14 44		15 04			15 24			15 44	
Southend Airport ✈	d	13 27			13 47			14 07		14 27				14 47		15 07			15 27			15 47	
Prittlewell	d	13 30			13 50			14 10		14 30				14 50		15 10			15 30			15 50	
Southend Victoria	a	13 34			13 54			14 14		14 34				14 54		15 14			15 34			15 54	

Station		LE 1	LE 1	LE ◇1	LE 1	LE 1	LE 1	LE 1	LE 1	LE 1	LE 1	LE 1	LE ◇1	LE 1	LE 1	LE 1	LE 1	LE 1	LE ◇1	LE 1	LE ◇1	LE 1
		C		D			A	B		C			D		A	B			C		D	
London Liverpool Street 15 ⊖	d	15 02	15 13	15 18	15 35		15 38	15 48	15 55	16 02	16 13		16 18	16 35	16 38	16 48	16 55		17 02	17 13	17 18	17 35
Stratford 7 ⊖	d	15 09	15 20	15 25	15 42		15 45	15 55	16 02	16 09	16 20		16 25	16 42	16 45	16 55	17 03		17 09	17 21	17 25	17 43
Romford	d		15 28				15 53				16 28				16 53					17 30		
Shenfield 3	a	15 24	15 37	15 41	15 57		16 02	16 11	16 17	16 24	16 37		16 41	16 57	17 02	17 11	17 19		17 25	17 39	17 41	17 59
	d		15 39		15 59				16 19		16 39			16 59			17 19			17 39		17 59
Billericay	d		15 45		16 05				16 25		16 45			17 05			17 25			17 45		18 05
Wickford 2	d		15 51		16 11	16 16			16 31		16 51	16 56		17 11			17 31	17 36		17 51		18 11
Battlesbridge	d					16 20						17 00						17 40				
South Woodham Ferrers	d					16 24						17 04						17 44				
North Fambridge	d					16 31						17 11						17 51				
Althorne	d					16 36						17 16						17 56				
Burnham-on-Crouch	d					16 41						17 21						18 01				
Southminster	a					16 47						17 27						18 07				
Rayleigh	d		15 56		16 16				16 36		16 56			17 16			17 36			17 56		18 16
Hockley	d		16 01		16 21				16 41		17 01			17 21			17 41			18 01		18 21
Rochford	d		16 04		16 24				16 44		17 04			17 24			17 44			18 04		18 24
Southend Airport ✈	d		16 07		16 27				16 47		17 07			17 27			17 47			18 07		18 27
Prittlewell	d		16 10		16 30				16 50		17 10			17 30			17 50			18 10		18 30
Southend Victoria	a		16 14		16 34				16 54		17 14			17 34			17 54			18 14		18 34

Station		LE 1	LE 1	LE 1	LE 1	LE ◇1	LE 1	LE 1	LE ◇1	LE 1	LE 1	LE 1	LE 1	LE 1	LE ◇1	LE ◇1	LE ◇1	LE 1	LE ◇1	LE 1	LE 1	LE 1	LE ◇1
			A	B		C			D	A		B			C		D	E			A	B	
London Liverpool Street 15 ⊖	d		17 38	17 48	17 55	18 02	18 13		18 18	18 34	18 38	18 46	18 53		19 04	19 13	19 18	19 32	19 35		19 38	19 48	19 55
Stratford 7 ⊖	d		17 45	17 55	18 03	18 09	18 21		18 25	18 41	18 45	18 53	19 00		19 11	19 20	19 25	19 39	19 43		19 46	19 55	20 02
Romford	d		17 54				18 30			18 50						19 28					19 54		
Shenfield 3	a		18 03	18 11	18 19	18 25	18 39		18 41	18 59	19 01	19 08	19 17		19 26	19 37	19 41	19 56	19 59		20 03	20 11	20 17
	d				18 19		18 39				19 01		19 19			19 39			19 59				20 19
Billericay	d				18 25		18 45				19 07		19 25			19 45			20 05				20 25
Wickford 2	d	18 16			18 31		18 51	18 56			19 13		19 31	19 36		19 51			20 12	20 16			20 31
Battlesbridge	d	18 20						19 00						19 40						20 20			
South Woodham Ferrers	d	18 24						19 04						19 44						20 24			
North Fambridge	d	18 31						19 11						19 51						20 31			
Althorne	d	18 36						19 16						19 56						20 36			
Burnham-on-Crouch	d	18 41						19 21						20 01						20 41			
Southminster	a	18 47						19 27						20 07						20 47			
Rayleigh	d				18 36		18 56				19 18		19 36			19 56			20 17				20 36
Hockley	d				18 41		19 01				19 23		19 41			20 01			20 21				20 41
Rochford	d				18 44		19 04				19 26		19 44			20 04			20 25				20 44
Southend Airport ✈	d				18 47		19 07				19 29		19 47			20 07			20 28				20 47
Prittlewell	d				18 50		19 10				19 32		19 50			20 10			20 31				20 50
Southend Victoria	a				18 54		19 14				19 36		19 54			20 14			20 35				20 54

Station		LE 1	LE ◇1	LE 1	LE ◇1	LE ◇1	LE 1	LE 1	LE ◇1	LE 1	LE 1	LE ◇1	LE ◇1	LE ◇1	LE 1	LE 1	LE 1	LE ◇1	LE 1	LE ◇1	LE 1	LE ◇1	LE
		C			D		A	B			E		D			A	B		F			D	F
London Liverpool Street 15 ⊖	d	20 02	20 13		20 18	20 35	20 38	20 48	20 55		21 02	21 13	21 18	21 35		21 38	21 48	21 55	22 02	22 13		22 18	22 38
Stratford 7 ⊖	d	20 09	20 20		20 25	20 42	20 45	20 55	21 02		21 09	21 20	21 25	21 42		21 45	21 55	22 02	22 09	22 20		22 25	22 45
Romford	d		20 28				20 53					21 28				21 53				22 28			
Shenfield 3	a	20 24	20 37		20 41	20 58	21 02	21 11	21 17		21 24	21 37	21 41	21 57		22 02	22 11	22 17	22 24	22 37		22 41	23 00
	d		20 39			20 59			21 19			21 39		21 59				22 19		22 39			
Billericay	d		20 45			21 05			21 25			21 45		22 05				22 25		22 45			
Wickford 2	d		20 51	20 56		21 11			21 31	21 36		21 51		22 11	22 16			22 31		22 51	22 56		
Battlesbridge	d			21 00						21 40					22 20						23 00		
South Woodham Ferrers	d			21 04						21 44					22 24						23 04		
North Fambridge	d			21 11						21 51					22 31						23 11		
Althorne	d			21 16						21 56					22 36						23 16		
Burnham-on-Crouch	d			21 21						22 01					22 41						23 21		
Southminster	a			21 27						22 07					22 47						23 27		
Rayleigh	d		20 56			21 16			21 36			21 56		22 16				22 36		22 56			
Hockley	d		21 01			21 21			21 41			22 01		22 21				22 41		23 01			
Rochford	d		21 04			21 24			21 44			22 04		22 24				22 44		23 04			
Southend Airport ✈	d		21 07			21 27			21 47			22 07		22 27				22 47		23 07			
Prittlewell	d		21 10			21 30			21 50			22 10		22 30				22 50		23 10			
Southend Victoria	a		21 14			21 34			21 54			22 14		22 34				22 54		23 14			

A To Colchester Town
B To Braintree
C To Ipswich
D To Clacton-on-Sea
E To Harwich International
F To Colchester

NRT DECEMBER 19 EDITION

Table T006-F

Saturdays
21 December to 16 May

London Liverpool Street - Shenfield - Wickford - Southminster and Southend

Station		LE	LE	LE	LE	LE	LE
			A		B		C
London Liverpool Street 15 ⊖	d	22 45	23 02	23 15	23 18	23 45	23 48
Stratford 7 ⊖	d	22 52	23 09	23 22	23 25	23 52	23 55
Romford	d						
Shenfield 3	a	23 08	23 25	23 38	23 40	00 08	00 11
	d	23 09		23 39		00 09	
Billericay	d	23 15		23 45		00 15	
Wickford 2	d	23 21		23 51		00 21	
Battlesbridge	d						
South Woodham Ferrers	d						
North Fambridge	d						
Althorne	d						
Burnham-on-Crouch	d						
Southminster	a						
Rayleigh	d	23 26		23 56		00 26	
Hockley	d	23 31		00 01		00 31	
Rochford	d	23 34		00 04		00 34	
Southend Airport ✈	d	23 37		00 07		00 37	
Prittlewell	d	23 40		00 10		00 40	
Southend Victoria	a	23 48		00 18		00 48	

Sundays
15 December to 10 May

Station		LE	LE	LE 1	LE 1	LE 1	LE 1	LE 1	LE 1	LE 1	LE 1	LE 1	LE 1	LE 1	LE 1	LE 1	LE 1	LE ◇1	LE 1	LE ◇1	LE ◇1	
		D	D		C						E	A			B		A			B		
London Liverpool Street 15 ⊖	d			00 15	00 18	00 50		07 14		07 44	07 57	08 00	08 15		08 30	08 45	09 08	09 23		09 38	09 53	
Stratford 7 ⊖	d			00 22	00 25	00 57		07 21		07 51	08 04	08 07	08 22		08 37	08 52	09 15	09 30		09 45	10 00	
Romford	d			00 32		01 08		07 32		08 02		08 20	08 33			09 03		09 39			10 09	
Shenfield 3	a			00 44	00 47	01 20		07 45		08 15	08 31	08 34	08 46		09 03	09 16	09 31	09 48		10 01	10 18	
	d		00 09	00 45		01 20		07 46		08 16			08 47			09 17		09 48			10 18	and at
Billericay	d		00 15	00 51		01 26		07 52		08 22			08 53			09 23		09 54			10 24	the same
Wickford 2	d		00 21	00 56		01 31	07 30	07 58	08 06	08 28			08 59	09 06		09 29		10 01	10 06		10 31	minutes
Battlesbridge	d						07 34		08 10					09 10					10 10			past
South Woodham Ferrers	d						07 38		08 14					09 14					10 14			each
North Fambridge	d						07 44		08 21					09 21					10 21			hour until
Althorne	d						07 49		08 26					09 26					10 26			
Burnham-on-Crouch	d						07 54		08 31					09 31					10 31			
Southminster	a						08 00		08 37					09 37					10 37			
Rayleigh	d		00 26	01 01		01 36		08 03		08 33			09 04			09 34		10 06			10 36	
Hockley	d	00 01	00 31	01 06		01 41		08 08		08 38			09 09			09 39		10 10			10 40	
Rochford	d	00 04	00 34	01 09		01 44		08 11		08 41			09 12			09 42		10 14			10 44	
Southend Airport ✈	d	00 07	00 37	01 12		01 47		08 14		08 44			09 15			09 45		10 16			10 46	
Prittlewell	d	00 10	00 40	01 15		01 50		08 16		08 46			09 17			09 47		10 19			10 49	
Southend Victoria	a	00 18	00 48	01 23		01 58		08 21		08 51			09 21			09 52		10 24			10 54	

Station		LE 1	LE ◇1	LE 1	LE ◇1	LE ◇1	LE 1	LE 1	LE ◇1	LE 1	LE ◇1	LE ◇1	LE 1	LE ◇1	LE 1	LE ◇1	LE ◇1	LE 1	LE 1	LE ◇1	LE ◇1	LE 1	LE 1
		A			B		E	A			B		A			B		A		B		A	
London Liverpool Street 15 ⊖	d	19 08	19 23		19 38	19 53	20 00	20 08	20 23		20 38	20 53	21 08	21 23		21 38	21 53	22 08	22 23	22 38	22 53	23 08	23 23
Stratford 7 ⊖	d	19 15	19 30		19 45	20 00	20 07	20 15	20 30		20 45	21 00	21 15	21 30		21 45	22 00	22 15	22 30	22 45	23 00	23 15	23 30
Romford	d		19 39			20 09			20 39			21 09		21 39			22 09		22 39		23 09		23 39
Shenfield 3	a	19 31	19 48		20 01	20 18	20 23	20 31	20 48		21 01	21 18	21 31	21 48		22 01	22 18	22 31	22 48	23 01	23 18	23 31	23 48
	d		19 48			20 18			20 48			21 18		21 48			22 18		22 48		23 18		23 48
Billericay	d		19 54			20 24			20 54			21 24		21 54			22 24		22 54		23 24		23 54
Wickford 2	d		20 01	20 06		20 31			21 01	21 06		21 31		22 01	22 06		22 31		23 01		23 31		00 01
Battlesbridge	d			20 10						21 10					22 10								
South Woodham Ferrers	d			20 14						21 14					22 14								
North Fambridge	d			20 21						21 21					22 21								
Althorne	d			20 26						21 26					22 26								
Burnham-on-Crouch	d			20 31						21 31					22 31								
Southminster	a			20 37						21 37					22 37								
Rayleigh	d		20 06			20 36			21 06			21 36		22 06			22 36		23 06		23 36		00 06
Hockley	d		20 10			20 40			21 10			21 40		22 10			22 40		23 10		23 40		00 10
Rochford	d		20 14			20 44			21 14			21 44		22 14			22 44		23 14		23 44		00 14
Southend Airport ✈	d		20 16			20 46			21 16			21 46		22 16			22 46		23 16		23 46		00 16
Prittlewell	d		20 19			20 49			21 19			21 49		22 19			22 49		23 19		23 49		00 19
Southend Victoria	a		20 24			20 54			21 24			21 54		22 24			22 54		23 27		23 57		00 27

Station		LE 1	LE 1
		C	
London Liverpool Street 15 ⊖	d	23 32	23 42
Stratford 7 ⊖	d	23 39	23 49
Romford	d		00 01
Shenfield 3	a	23 57	00 16
	d		00 16
Billericay	d		00 22
Wickford 2	d		00 28
Battlesbridge	d		
South Woodham Ferrers	d		
North Fambridge	d		
Althorne	d		
Burnham-on-Crouch	d		
Southminster	a		
Rayleigh	d		00 33
Hockley	d		00 37
Rochford	d		00 41
Southend Airport ✈	d		00 43
Prittlewell	d		00 46
Southend Victoria	a		00 54

A To Ipswich
B To Clacton-on-Sea
C To Colchester
D not 15 December. From London Liverpool Street
E To Harwich International

Southend and Southminster - Wickford - Shenfield - London Liverpool Street

Miles	Miles			LE ■	LE ■	LE ■ A	LE ■	LE ■ A	LE ■	LE ■	LE ■	LE ◇■ B	LE ■	LE ■ C	LE ■	LE ◇■ B	LE ■	LE ■	LE ■ D	LE ■	LE ■ E	LE ■	LE ■
0	—	Southend Victoria	d	04 00	04 30		05 00		05 20		05 40		06 00		06 11			06 26		06 40		06 50	
0¾	—	Prittlewell	d	04 02	04 32		05 02		05 22		05 42		06 02		06 13			06 28		06 42		06 52	
1¾	—	Southend Airport	d	04 05	04 35		05 05		05 25		05 45		06 05		06 16			06 31		06 45		06 55	
2¾	—	Rochford	d	04 08	04 38		05 08		05 28		05 48		06 08		06 19			06 34		06 48		06 58	
5¼	—	Hockley	d	04 12	04 42		05 12		05 32		05 52		06 12		06 23			06 38		06 52		07 02	
8½	—	Rayleigh	d	04 16	04 46		05 16		05 36		05 56		06 16		06 27			06 42		06 56		07 06	
—	0	Southminster	d							05 26							06 07						06 47
—	2¾	Burnham-on-Crouch	d							05 30							06 11						06 51
—	5¼	Althorne	d							05 35							06 16						06 56
—	8¼	North Fambridge	d							05 41							06 24						07 02
—	11½	South Woodham Ferrers	d							05 46							06 30						07 09
—	14	Battlesbridge	d							05 50							06 34						07 13
12½	16½	Wickford	d	04 21	04 51		05 21		05 41	05a56	06 01		06 21		06 32		06 40	06 47		07 01		07 11	07 19
17¼	21¼	Billericay	d	04 27	04 57		05 27		05 47		06 07		06 27		06 39		06 46	06 53		07 08		07 18	07 26
—	—	Shenfield	a	04 38	05 08		05 35		05 55		06 15		06 35		06 45		06 53	07 01		07 14		07 24	07 32
21¼	25¼	Shenfield	d	04 38	05 08	05 24	05 35	05 53	05 55		06 15	06 25	06 35	06 42	06 45	06 50	06 53	07 01	07 08	07 14	07 19	07 24	07 32
29	33	Romford	d			05 32																	
37½	41½	Stratford	d	04 58	05 28	05 45	05 50	06 08	06 11		06 31	06 40	06 50	06s59	07s03	07s07	07s10	07s20	07s24	07s32	07s36	07s42	07s50
41½	45½	London Liverpool Street	a	05 06	05 37	05 53	05 58	06 16	06 19		06 40	06 48	06 58	07 09	07 14	07 18	07 21	07 31	07 35	07 42	07 46	07 52	08 01

		LE ■	LE ■ C	LE ◇■ B	LE ■	LE ■ C	LE ■	LE ■ F	LE ■	LE ◇■ B	LE ■	LE ■	LE ■ F	LE ■ G	LE ■	LE ■ B	LE ■	LE ■ F	LE ■	LE ■ E	LE ■ B	LE ■	LE ■
Southend Victoria	d	07 03			07 13		07 23		07 32		07 42				07 52		08 03		08 12				08 30
Prittlewell	d	07 05			07 15		07 25		07 34		07 44				07 54		08 05		08 14				08 32
Southend Airport	d	07 08			07 18		07 28		07 37		07 47				07 57		08 08		08 17				08 35
Rochford	d	07 11			07 21		07 31		07 40		07 50				08 00		08 11		08 20				08 38
Hockley	d	07 15			07 25		07 35		07 44		07 54				08 04		08 15		08 24				08 42
Rayleigh	d	07 19			07 29		07 39		07 48		07 58				08 08		08 19		08 28				08 46
Southminster	d											07 36										08 16	
Burnham-on-Crouch	d											07 40										08 20	
Althorne	d											07 45										08 25	
North Fambridge	d											07 51										08 32	
South Woodham Ferrers	d											07 58										08 38	
Battlesbridge	d																					08 42	
Wickford	d	07 24			07 34		07 44		07 53		08 03	08 07			08 13		08 24		08 33			08 47	08 51
Billericay	d	07 31			07 41		07 51		08 00		08 10	08 14			08 20		08 31		08 40			08 54	08 58
Shenfield	a				07 47		07 57		08 06		08 16				08 26		08 37		08 46			09 00	09 04
Shenfield	d		07 39	07 41	07 47	07 50	07 57	08 01	08 06	08 09	08 16		08 21	08 24	08 26	08 29	08 37	08 42	08 46	08 51	08 55	09 00	09 04
Romford	d																		08 55				
Stratford	d	07s53	07s56	07s59	08s05	08s08	08s16	08s19	08s24	08s26	08s34	08s36	08s39	08s41	08s44	08s46	08s57	09s00	09s06	09s09		09s18	09s22
London Liverpool Street	a	08 03	08 07	08 09	08 15	08 19	08 26	08 30	08 36	08 38	08 46	08 48	08 50	08 54	08 56	08 58	09 08	09 11	09 16	09 19	09 21	09 28	09 33

		LE ■ H	LE ■ C	LE ◇■ I	LE ■	LE ■	LE ■ E	LE ■	LE ■ D	LE ■	LE ■	LE ◇■ B	LE ■	LE ◇■ J	LE ■ E	LE ■	LE ■	LE ■ J	LE ■	LE ◇■ B	LE ■ D	LE ■
Southend Victoria	d				08 52			09 10		09 30			09 48			10 10			10 30			10 50
Prittlewell	d				08 54			09 12		09 32			09 50			10 12			10 32			10 52
Southend Airport	d				08 57			09 15		09 35			09 53			10 15			10 35			10 55
Rochford	d				09 00			09 18		09 38			09 56			10 18			10 38			10 58
Hockley	d				09 04			09 22		09 42			10 00			10 22			10 42			11 02
Rayleigh	d				09 08			09 26		09 46			10 04			10 26			10 46			11 06
Southminster	d					08 56					09 36						10 16					
Burnham-on-Crouch	d					09 00					09 40						10 20					
Althorne	d					09 05					09 45						10 25					
North Fambridge	d					09 11					09 51						10 31					
South Woodham Ferrers	d					09 16					09 56						10 36					
Battlesbridge	d					09 20					10 00						10 40					
Wickford	d				09 13	09a26		09 31		09 51	10a06		10 09			10 32	10a46		10 51			11 11
Billericay	d				09 20			09 37		09 57			10 15			10 38			10 57			11 17
Shenfield	a				09 27			09 45		10 05			10 23			10 46			11 05			11 25
Shenfield	d	09 09	09 21	09 25	09 27		09 38	09 46	09 51	10 05		10 08	10 23	10 29	10 36	10 46		10 51	11 05	11 08	11 20	11 25
Romford	d							09 55								10 55					11 28	
Stratford	d	09s26	09s38	09s42	09s45		09 54	10 04	10 07	10 20		10 27	10 38		10 51	11 05		11 08	11 20	11 23	11 37	11 40
London Liverpool Street	a	09 36	09 50	09 54	09 56		10 03	10 12	10 17	10 28		10 35	10 46	10 51	11 00	11 13		11 16	11 28	11 33	11 45	11 48

		LE ■	LE ■ E	LE ■	LE ■ J	LE ■	LE ■	LE ◇■ B	LE ■ D	LE ■	LE ■ E	LE ◇■	LE ■	LE ■ J	LE ◇■	LE ◇■ B	LE ■ D	LE ◇■	LE ■	LE ■ E	LE ◇■	LE ■ J	LE ◇■
Southend Victoria	d			11 10		11 30				11 50		12 10			12 30			12 50			13 10		13 30
Prittlewell	d			11 12		11 32				11 52		12 12			12 32			12 52			13 12		13 32
Southend Airport	d			11 15		11 35				11 55		12 15			12 35			12 55			13 15		13 35
Rochford	d			11 18		11 38				11 58		12 18			12 38			12 58			13 18		13 38
Hockley	d			11 22		11 42				12 02		12 22			12 42			13 02			13 22		13 42
Rayleigh	d			11 26		11 46				12 06		12 26			12 46			13 06			13 26		13 46
Southminster	d	10 56					11 36						12 16						12 56				
Burnham-on-Crouch	d	11 00					11 40						12 20						13 00				
Althorne	d	11 05					11 45						12 25						13 05				
North Fambridge	d	11 11					11 51						12 31						13 11				
South Woodham Ferrers	d	11 16					11 56						12 36						13 16				
Battlesbridge	d	11 20					12 00						12 40						13 20				
Wickford	d	11a26		11 31		11 51	12a06			12 11		12 31	12a46		12 51			13 11	13a26		13 31		13 51
Billericay	d			11 37		11 57				12 17		12 37			12 57			13 17			13 37		13 57
Shenfield	a			11 45		12 05				12 25		12 45			13 05			13 25			13 45		14 05
Shenfield	d		11 38	11 45	11 51	12 05		12 08	12 20	12 25	12 38	12 45		12 51	13 05	13 08	13 20	13 25		13 38	13 45	13 51	14 05
Romford	d			11 53					12 28			12 53					13 28				13 53		
Stratford	d		11 52	12 02	12 06	12 20		12 23	12 37	12 40	12 52	13 01		13 06	13 20	13 23	13 37	13 40		13 53	14 02	14 06	14 19
London Liverpool Street	a		12 01	12 10	12 14	12 28		12 31	12 45	12 48	13 01	13 10		13 14	13 28	13 31	13 45	13 48		14 03	14 10	14 14	14 28

A From Colchester
B From Clacton-on-Sea
C From Witham
D From Colchester Town
E From Braintree
F From Chelmsford
G From Harwich International
H From Harwich Town
I From Walton-on-the-Naze
J From Ipswich

Table T006-R

Mondays to Fridays

16 December to 15 May

Southend and Southminster - Wickford - Shenfield - London Liverpool Street

		LE ■	LE ◇■ A	LE ■ B	LE ◇■	LE ■ C	LE ◇■	LE ■	LE ■ D	LE ◇■	LE ◇■ A	LE ■ B	LE ◇■	LE ■	LE ■ C	LE ◇■	LE ■ D	LE ◇■	LE ■	LE ◇■ A	LE ■ B	LE ◇■	LE ■ C
Southend Victoria	d				13 50		14 10			14 30			14 50			15 10		15 30				15 50	
Prittlewell	d				13 52		14 12			14 32			14 52			15 12		15 32				15 52	
Southend Airport	d				13 55		14 15			14 35			14 55			15 15		15 35				15 55	
Rochford	d				13 58		14 18			14 38			14 58			15 18		15 38				15 58	
Hockley	d				14 02		14 22			14 42			15 02			15 22		15 42				16 02	
Rayleigh	d				14 06		14 26			14 46			15 06			15 26		15 46				16 06	
Southminster	d	13 36						14 16						14 56					15 36				
Burnham-on-Crouch	d	13 40						14 20						15 00					15 40				
Althorne	d	13 45						14 25						15 05					15 45				
North Fambridge	d	13 51						14 31						15 11					15 51				
South Woodham Ferrers	d	13 56						14 36						15 16					15 56				
Battlesbridge	d	14 00						14 40						15 20					16 00				
Wickford	d	14a06			14 11		14 31	14a46		14 51			15 11	15a26		15 31		15 51	16a06			16 11	
Billericay	d				14 17		14 37			14 57			15 17			15 37		15 57				16 17	
Shenfield	a				14 25		14 45			15 05			15 25			15 45		16 05				16 25	
Shenfield	d		14 08	14 20	14 25	14 38	14 45		14 51	15 05	15 08	15 20	15 25		15 38	15 45	15 51	16 05		16 08	16 20	16 25	16 40
Romford	d			14 28			14 53					15 28				15 53							
Stratford	d		14 23	14 37	14 40	14 53	15 02		15 06	15 20	15 23	15 37	15 40		15 53	16 02	16 06	16 20		16 23	16 35	16 40	16 55
London Liverpool Street	a		14 31	14 47	14 50	15 01	15 10		15 14	15 29	15 31	15 45	15 48		16 01	16 11	16 14	16 28		16 31	16 44	16 48	17 03

		LE ◇■	LE ■	LE ■ D	LE ◇■	LE ◇■ A	LE ■ B	LE ◇■	LE ■ E	LE ■ C	LE ◇■	LE ■	LE ■ D	LE ◇■	LE ◇■ A	LE ◇■	LE ■ C	LE ◇■	LE ■ B	LE ◇■	LE ■	LE ■ F
Southend Victoria	d	16 10			16 30			16 50			17 10			17 25		17 35		17 50		18 03		
Prittlewell	d	16 12			16 32			16 52			17 12			17 27		17 37		17 52		18 05		
Southend Airport	d	16 15			16 35			16 55			17 15			17 30		17 40		17 55		18 08		
Rochford	d	16 18			16 38			16 58			17 18			17 33		17 43		17 58		18 11		
Hockley	d	16 22			16 42			17 02			17 22			17 37		17 47		18 02		18 15		
Rayleigh	d	16 26			16 46			17 06			17 26			17 41		17 51		18 06		18 19		
Southminster	d		16 14									17 06									17 56	
Burnham-on-Crouch	d		16 18									17 10									18 00	
Althorne	d		16 23									17 15									18 05	
North Fambridge	d		16 29									17 21									18 14	
South Woodham Ferrers	d		16 34									17 26									18 19	
Battlesbridge	d		16 38									17 30									18 23	
Wickford	d	16 31	16a44		16 51			17 11			17 31	17 37		17 46		17 56		18 11		18 24	18a29	
Billericay	d	16 37			16 57			17 17			17 37			17 52		18 02		18 17		18 30		
Shenfield	a	16 45			17 05			17 25			17 45	17 48		18 00		18 10		18 25		18 37		
Shenfield	d	16 45		16 51	17 05	17 08	17 22	17 25	17 28	17 38	17 46	17 49	17 51	18 00	18 07	18 13	18 22	18 25	18 28	18 37		18 40
Romford	d																		18 36			
Stratford	d	17 00		17 07	17 20	17 23	17 37	17 40	17 43	17 53	18 01	18 09	18 07	18 15		18 29	18 37	18 40	18 46	18 52		18 55
London Liverpool Street	a	17 13		17 16	17 29	17 34	17 46	17 49	17 53	18 03	18 11	18 19	18 18	18 24	18 34	18 37	18 45	18 48	18 56	19 00		19 03

		LE ■ D	LE ◇■	LE ◇■	LE ◇■ A	LE ■ C	LE ■ D	LE ◇■	LE ■	LE ■ E	LE ◇■	LE ■ D	LE ◇■	LE ■	LE ◇■ A	LE ■ B	LE ◇■	LE ■ D	LE ■	LE ■	LE ■ C	LE ■ E	LE ■
Southend Victoria	d		18 20	18 30				18 50			19 10		19 30				19 50		20 10				20 30
Prittlewell	d		18 22	18 32				18 52			19 12		19 32				19 52		20 12				20 32
Southend Airport	d		18 25	18 35				18 55			19 15		19 35				19 55		20 15				20 35
Rochford	d		18 28	18 38				18 58			19 18		19 38				19 58		20 18				20 38
Hockley	d		18 32	18 42				19 02			19 22		19 42				20 02		20 22				20 42
Rayleigh	d		18 36	18 46				19 06			19 26		19 46				20 06		20 26				20 46
Southminster	d								18 36					19 19						20 16			
Burnham-on-Crouch	d								18 40					19 23						20 20			
Althorne	d								18 45					19 28						20 25			
North Fambridge	d								18 59					19 39						20 31			
South Woodham Ferrers	d								19 04					19 44						20 36			
Battlesbridge	d								19 08					19 48						20 40			
Wickford	d		18 41	18 51				19 11	19 17		19 31		19 51	19 55			20 11		20 31	20a46			20 51
Billericay	d		18 47	18 57				19 17	19 23		19 37		19 57				20 17		20 37				20 57
Shenfield	a		18 55	19 05				19 25	19 36		19 45		20 05	20 08			20 25		20 45				21 05
Shenfield	d	18 51	18 57	19 05	19 08	19 13	19 20	19 25		19 38	19 45	19 51	20 05		20 08	20 20	20 25	20 38	20 45		20 47	20 53	21 05
Romford	d						19 28				19 53					20 28			20 53				
Stratford	d	19 06	19 12	19 20	19 23	19 28	19 37	19 40		19 53	20 01	20 06	20 20		20 23	20 37	20 40	20 53	21 02			21 08	21 20
London Liverpool Street	a	19 14	19 20	19 28	19 33	19 36	19 45	19 48		20 01	20 10	20 14	20 28		20 31	20 45	20 51	21 01	21 10		21 12	21 16	21 28

		LE ◇■ A	LE ■	LE ■	LE ■ B	LE ■ C	LE ■	LE ■ G	LE ■	LE ■	LE ◇■ A	LE ■ B	LE ■	LE ■	LE ■ C	LE ■ B	LE ■	LE ◇■ A	LE ■ D	LE ■	LE ◇■ H	LE ■
Southend Victoria	d		20 50				21 10		21 30				22 00				22 30			23 00		
Prittlewell	d		20 52				21 12		21 32				22 02				22 32			23 02		
Southend Airport	d		20 55				21 15		21 35				22 05				22 35			23 05		
Rochford	d		20 58				21 18		21 38				22 08				22 38			23 08		
Hockley	d		21 02				21 22		21 42				22 12				22 42			23 12		
Rayleigh	d		21 06				21 26		21 46				22 16				22 46			23 16		
Southminster	d			20 56						21 36				22 16								22 56
Burnham-on-Crouch	d			21 00						21 40				22 20								23 00
Althorne	d			21 05						21 45				22 25								23 05
North Fambridge	d			21 11						21 51				22 31								23 11
South Woodham Ferrers	d			21 16						21 56				22 36								23 16
Battlesbridge	d			21 20						22 00				22 40								23 20
Wickford	d		21 11	21a26			21 31		21 51	22a07			22 21	22a46			22 51			23 21		23 26
Billericay	d		21 17				21 37		21 57				22 27				22 57			23 27		23 32
Shenfield	a		21 25				21 45		22 05				22 35				23 05			23 35		23 39
Shenfield	d	21 08	21 25		21 27	21 38	21 45	21 51	22 05		22 08	22 20	22 35		22 38	22 51	23 05	23 08	23 20	23 35	23 37	23 39
Romford	d						21 53					22 28							23 28			23 47
Stratford	d	21 23	21 40		21 43	21 53	22 02	22 06	22 20		22 23	22 37	22 50		22 52	23s06	23 19	23 22	23 37	23 50	23s53	23 57
London Liverpool Street	a	21 31	21 48		21 51	22 01	22 10	22 14	22 28		22 31	22 45	22 58		23 01	23 14	23 28	23 31	23 48	00 01	00 03	00 06

A From Clacton-on-Sea
B From Colchester Town
C From Braintree
D From Ipswich
E From Colchester
F From Witham
G From Harwich International
H From Norwich

Table T006-R

Saturdays

21 December to 16 May

Southend and Southminster - Wickford - Shenfield - London Liverpool Street

	LE	LE	LE A	LE	LE A	LE	LE A	LE	LE	LE A	LE	LE ◇ B	LE C	LE	LE	LE D	LE	LE E	LE	LE	LE ◇ B	LE F
Southend Victoria d	04 00	04 30		05 00		05 30		06 00			06 30			06 50			07 10		07 30			
Prittlewell d	04 02	04 32		05 02		05 32		06 02			06 32			06 52			07 12		07 32			
Southend Airport ✈ d	04 05	04 35		05 05		05 35		06 05			06 35			06 55			07 15		07 35			
Rochford d	04 08	04 38		05 08		05 38		06 08			06 38			06 58			07 18		07 38			
Hockley d	04 12	04 42		05 12		05 42		06 12			06 42			07 02			07 22		07 42			
Rayleigh d	04 16	04 46		05 16		05 46		06 16			06 46			07 06			07 26		07 46			
Southminster d									06 16						06 56					07 36		
Burnham-on-Crouch d									06 20						07 00					07 40		
Althorne d									06 25						07 05					07 45		
North Fambridge d									06 31						07 11					07 51		
South Woodham Ferrers d									06 36						07 16					07 56		
Battlesbridge d									06 40						07 20					08 00		
Wickford 2 d	04 21	04 51		05 21		05 51		06 21	06a46		06 51			07 11	07a26		07 31		07 51	08a06		
Billericay d	04 27	04 57		05 27		05 57		06 27			06 57			07 17			07 37		07 57			
Shenfield a	04 38	05 08		05 35		06 05		06 35			07 05			07 25			07 45		08 05			
Shenfield 3 d	04 38	05 08	05 24	05 35	05 53	06 05	06 24	06 35		06 46	07 05	07 08	07 20	07 25		07 38	07 45	07 51	08 05		08 08	08 20
Romford d			05 32	05 43				06 43		06 54			07 28				07 53					08 28
Stratford 7 ⊖ ⛴ d	04 58	05 26	05 43	05 52	06 08	06 20	06 39	06 52		07 03	07 20	07 23	07 37	07 40		07 53	08 02	08 06	08 20		08 23	08 37
London Liverpool Street 15 ⊖ a	05 06	05 34	05 51	06 00	06 16	06 28	06 47	07 00		07 11	07 28	07 31	07 46	07 49		08 01	08 10	08 14	08 28		08 31	08 46

	LE	LE D	LE	LE	LE E	LE	LE ◇ B	LE C	LE	LE	LE D	LE	LE ◇ E	LE	LE	LE ◇ B	LE	LE C	LE D	LE	LE	LE ◇ E
Southend Victoria d	07 50		08 10			08 30			08 50			09 10		09 30			09 50			10 10		
Prittlewell d	07 52		08 12			08 32			08 52			09 12		09 32			09 52			10 12		
Southend Airport ✈ d	07 55		08 15			08 35			08 55			09 15		09 35			09 55			10 15		
Rochford d	07 58		08 18			08 38			08 58			09 18		09 38			09 58			10 18		
Hockley d	08 02		08 22			08 42			09 02			09 22		09 42			10 02			10 22		
Rayleigh d	08 06		08 26			08 46			09 06			09 26		09 46			10 06			10 26		
Southminster d				08 16						08 56					09 36						10 16	
Burnham-on-Crouch d				08 20						09 00					09 40						10 20	
Althorne d				08 25						09 05					09 45						10 25	
North Fambridge d				08 31						09 11					09 51						10 31	
South Woodham Ferrers d				08 36						09 16					09 56						10 36	
Battlesbridge d				08 40						09 20					10 00						10 40	
Wickford 2 d	08 11		08 31	08a46		08 51			09 11	09a26		09 31		09 51	10a06		10 11			10 31	10a46	
Billericay d	08 17		08 37			08 57			09 17			09 37		09 57			10 17			10 37		
Shenfield a	08 25		08 45			09 05			09 25			09 45		10 04			10 24			10 45		
Shenfield 3 d	08 25	08 38	08 45		08 51	09 05	09 08	09 20	09 25		09 38	09 45	09 51	10 04		10 08	10 24	10 27	10 38	10 45		10 52
Romford d			08 53					09 28				09 53						10 35		10 53		
Stratford 7 ⊖ ⛴ d	08 40	08 53	09 02		09 06	09 20	09 23	09 37	09 40		09 53	10 02	10 06	10 19		10 27	10 40	10 45	10 54	11 02		11 07
London Liverpool Street 15 ⊖ a	08 49	09 01	09 10		09 14	09 28	09 31	09 46	09 49		10 01	10 10	10 14	10 28		10 35	10 49	10 53	11 02	11 10		11 15

	LE	LE ◇ B	LE C	LE	LE	LE D	LE ◇	LE ◇ E	LE ◇	LE	LE ◇ B	LE C	LE ◇	LE D	LE ◇	LE	LE E	LE ◇	LE ◇ B	LE C	LE ◇
Southend Victoria d	10 30			10 50			11 10		11 30				11 50		12 10			12 30			12 50
Prittlewell d	10 32			10 52			11 12		11 32				11 52		12 12			12 32			12 52
Southend Airport ✈ d	10 35			10 55			11 15		11 35				11 55		12 15			12 35			12 55
Rochford d	10 38			10 58			11 18		11 38				11 58		12 18			12 38			12 58
Hockley d	10 42			11 02			11 22		11 42				12 02		12 22			12 42			13 02
Rayleigh d	10 46			11 06			11 26		11 46				12 06		12 26			12 46			13 06
Southminster d					10 56					11 36						12 16					
Burnham-on-Crouch d					11 00					11 40						12 20					
Althorne d					11 05					11 45						12 25					
North Fambridge d					11 11					11 51						12 31					
South Woodham Ferrers d					11 16					11 56						12 36					
Battlesbridge d					11 20					12 00						12 40					
Wickford 2 d	10 51			11 11	11a26		11 31		11 51	12a06			12 11		12 31	12a46		12 51			13 11
Billericay d	10 57			11 17			11 37		11 57				12 17		12 37			12 57			13 17
Shenfield a	11 05			11 25			11 45		12 05				12 25		12 45			13 05			13 25
Shenfield 3 d	11 05	11 08	11 20	11 25		11 38	11 45	11 51	12 05		12 08	12 20	12 25	12 38	12 45		12 51	13 05	13 08	13 20	13 25
Romford d			11 28				11 53					12 28			12 53					13 28	
Stratford 7 ⊖ ⛴ d	11 20	11 23	11 37	11 40		11 53	12 02	12 06	12 20		12 23	12 37	12 40	12 53	13 02		13 06	13 20	13 23	13 37	13 40
London Liverpool Street 15 ⊖ a	11 28	11 31	11 46	11 49		12 01	12 10	12 14	12 28		12 31	12 46	12 49	13 01	13 10		13 14	13 28	13 31	13 46	13 49

	LE	LE D	LE ◇	LE E	LE ◇	LE	LE ◇ B	LE C	LE ◇	LE D	LE ◇	LE	LE E	LE ◇	LE ◇ B	LE C	LE ◇	LE	LE D	LE ◇	LE E	LE ◇
Southend Victoria d			13 10		13 30				13 50		14 10			14 30			14 50			15 10		15 30
Prittlewell d			13 12		13 32				13 52		14 12			14 32			14 52			15 12		15 32
Southend Airport ✈ d			13 15		13 35				13 55		14 15			14 35			14 55			15 15		15 35
Rochford d			13 18		13 38				13 58		14 18			14 38			14 58			15 18		15 38
Hockley d			13 22		13 42				14 02		14 22			14 42			15 02			15 22		15 42
Rayleigh d			13 26		13 46				14 06		14 26			14 46			15 06			15 26		15 46
Southminster d	12 56					13 36						14 16						14 56				
Burnham-on-Crouch d	13 00					13 40						14 20						15 00				
Althorne d	13 05					13 45						14 25						15 05				
North Fambridge d	13 11					13 51						14 31						15 11				
South Woodham Ferrers d	13 16					13 56						14 36						15 16				
Battlesbridge d	13 20					14 00						14 40						15 20				
Wickford 2 d	13a26		13 31		13 51	14a06			14 11		14 31	14a46		14 51			15 11	15a26		15 31		15 51
Billericay d			13 37		13 57				14 17		14 37			14 57			15 17			15 37		15 57
Shenfield a			13 45		14 05				14 25		14 45			15 05			15 25			15 45		16 05
Shenfield 3 d		13 38	13 45	13 51	14 05		14 08	14 20	14 25	14 38	14 45		14 51	15 05	15 08	15 20	15 25		15 38	15 45	15 51	16 05
Romford d			13 53					14 28			14 53					15 28				15 53		
Stratford 7 ⊖ ⛴ d		13 53	14 02	14 06	14 20		14 23	14 37	14 40	14 53	15 02		15 06	15 20	15 23	15 37	15 40		15 53	16 02	16 06	16 20
London Liverpool Street 15 ⊖ a		14 01	14 10	14 14	14 28		14 31	14 46	14 50	15 01	15 10		15 14	15 28	15 31	15 46	15 49		16 01	16 10	16 14	16 28

A From Colchester
B From Clacton-on-Sea
C From Colchester Town
D From Braintree
E From Ipswich
F From Harwich International

NRT DECEMBER 19 EDITION

Table T006-R

Saturdays

21 December to 16 May

Southend and Southminster - Wickford - Shenfield - London Liverpool Street

	LE	LE ◇ A	LE B	LE ◇	LE C	LE	LE	LE D	LE	LE ◇ A	LE B	LE	LE	LE C	LE	LE D	LE	LE	LE ◇ A	LE	LE B
Southend Victoria d				15 50		16 10			16 30			16 50			17 10		17 30			17 50	
Prittlewell d				15 52		16 12			16 32			16 52			17 12		17 32			17 52	
Southend Airport ✈ d				15 55		16 15			16 35			16 55			17 15		17 35			17 55	
Rochford d				15 58		16 18			16 38			16 58			17 18		17 38			17 58	
Hockley d				16 02		16 22			16 42			17 02			17 22		17 42			18 02	
Rayleigh d				16 06		16 26			16 46			17 06			17 26		17 46			18 06	
Southminster d	15 36						16 16						16 56					17 36			
Burnham-on-Crouch d	15 40						16 20						17 00					17 40			
Althorne d	15 45						16 25						17 05					17 45			
North Fambridge d	15 51						16 31						17 11					17 51			
South Woodham Ferrers d	15 56						16 36						17 16					17 56			
Battlesbridge d	16 00						16 40						17 20					18 00			
Wickford 2 d	16a06			16 11		16 31	16a46		16 51			17 11	17a26		17 31		17 51	18a06		18 11	
Billericay d				16 17		16 37			16 57			17 17			17 37		17 57			18 17	
Shenfield a				16 25		16 45			17 05			17 25			17 44		18 04			18 25	
Shenfield 3 d		16 08	16 20	16 25	16 38	16 45		16 51	17 05	17 08	17 20	17 25		17 38	17 45	17 51	18 04		18 08	18 25	18 27
Romford d			16 28			16 53					17 28				17 53						18 35
Stratford 7 ⊖ ⛴ d		16 23	16 37	16 40	16 53	17 02		17 06	17 20	17 23	17 37	17 40		17 53	18 02	18 06	18 19		18 27	18 40	18 44
London Liverpool Street 15 ⊖ a		16 31	16 46	16 49	17 01	17 10		17 14	17 28	17 31	17 46	17 49		18 01	18 10	18 14	18 28		18 35	18 50	18 53

	LE C	LE	LE	LE D	LE	LE ◇ A	LE B	LE	LE	LE C	LE ◇	LE D	LE ◇	LE	LE ◇ A	LE B	LE ◇	LE C	LE ◇	LE	LE D	LE ◇
Southend Victoria d		18 10			18 30			18 50			19 10		19 30				19 50		20 10			20 30
Prittlewell d		18 12			18 32			18 52			19 12		19 32				19 52		20 12			20 32
Southend Airport ✈ d		18 15			18 35			18 55			19 15		19 35				19 55		20 15			20 35
Rochford d		18 18			18 38			18 58			19 18		19 38				19 58		20 18			20 38
Hockley d		18 22			18 42			19 02			19 22		19 42				20 02		20 22			20 42
Rayleigh d		18 26			18 46			19 06			19 26		19 46				20 06		20 26			20 46
Southminster d			18 16						18 56					19 36						20 16		
Burnham-on-Crouch d			18 20						19 00					19 40						20 20		
Althorne d			18 25						19 05					19 45						20 25		
North Fambridge d			18 31						19 11					19 51						20 31		
South Woodham Ferrers d			18 36						19 16					19 56						20 36		
Battlesbridge d			18 40						19 20					20 00						20 40		
Wickford 2 d		18 31	18a46		18 51			19 11	19a26		19 31		19 51	20a06			20 11		20 31	20a46		20 51
Billericay d		18 37			18 57			19 17			19 37		19 57				20 17		20 37			20 57
Shenfield a		18 45			19 05			19 25			19 45		20 05				20 25		20 45			21 05
Shenfield 3 d	18 38	18 45		18 52	19 05	19 08	19 20	19 25		19 38	19 45	19 51	20 05		20 08	20 20	20 25	20 38	20 45		20 51	21 05
Romford d		18 53					19 28				19 53					20 28			20 53			
Stratford 7 ⊖ ⛴ d	18 54	19 02		19 07	19 20	19 23	19 37	19 40		19 53	20 02	20 06	20 20		20 23	20 37	20 40	20 53	21 02		21 06	21 20
London Liverpool Street 15 ⊖ a	19 03	19 10		19 15	19 28	19 33	19 46	19 49		20 01	20 10	20 14	20 28		20 31	20 46	20 49	21 01	21 10		21 14	21 28

	LE ◇ A	LE B	LE ◇	LE	LE C	LE ◇	LE E	LE ◇	LE	LE ◇ A	LE B	LE ◇	LE	LE C	LE D	LE ◇	LE ◇ A	LE D	LE	LE ◇ F	LE
Southend Victoria d			20 50			21 10		21 30				22 00				22 30			23 00		
Prittlewell d			20 52			21 12		21 32				22 02				22 32			23 02		
Southend Airport ✈ d			20 55			21 15		21 35				22 05				22 35			23 05		
Rochford d			20 58			21 18		21 38				22 08				22 38			23 08		
Hockley d			21 02			21 22		21 42				22 12				22 42			23 12		
Rayleigh d			21 06			21 26		21 46				22 16				22 46			23 16		
Southminster d				20 56					21 36				22 16								22 56
Burnham-on-Crouch d				21 00					21 40				22 20								23 00
Althorne d				21 05					21 45				22 25								23 05
North Fambridge d				21 11					21 51				22 31								23 11
South Woodham Ferrers d				21 16					21 56				22 36								23 16
Battlesbridge d				21 20					22 00				22 40								23 20
Wickford 2 d			21 11	21a26		21 31		21 51	22a06			22 21	22a46			22 51			23 21		23 26
Billericay d			21 17			21 37		21 57				22 27				22 57			23 27		23 32
Shenfield a			21 25			21 45		22 05				22 35				23 05			23 35		23 39
Shenfield 3 d	21 08	21 20	21 25		21 38	21 45	21 51	22 05		22 08	22 20	22 35		22 38	22 51	23 05	23 08	23 20	23 35	23 37	23 39
Romford d		21 28				21 53					22 28							23 28			23 47
Stratford 7 ⊖ ⛴ d	21 23	21 37	21 40		21 53	22 02	22 06	22 20		22 23	22 37	22 50		22 53	23 06	23 20	23 23	23 37	23 50	23s53	23 57
London Liverpool Street 15 ⊖ a	21 34	21 46	21 51		22 01	22 10	22 14	22 28		22 31	22 46	22 58		23 01	23 14	23 28	23 31	23 45	23 58	00 03	00 05

A From Clacton-on-Sea
B From Colchester Town
C From Braintree
D From Ipswich
E From Harwich International
F From Norwich

Table T006-R

Sundays
15 December to 10 May

Southend and Southminster - Wickford - Shenfield - London Liverpool Street

		LE	LE	LE	LE	LE	LE	LE	LE	LE	LE	LE	LE	LE	LE	LE	LE	LE	
		1	1	1	1	1	1	1	1	1	◇1	1	1	1	1	◇1	◇1	1	
			A		B		B	C			D		E			D		E	
Southend Victoria	d	06 14		06 44		07 14			07 48			08 19		08 54			09 24		and at the same minutes past each hour until
Prittlewell	d	06 16		06 46		07 16			07 50			08 21		08 56			09 26		
Southend Airport ✈	d	06 19		06 49		07 19			07 53			08 24		08 59			09 29		
Rochford	d	06 22		06 52		07 22			07 56			08 27		09 02			09 32		
Hockley	d	06 26		06 56		07 26			08 00			08 31		09 06			09 36		
Rayleigh	d	06 30		07 00		07 30			08 04			08 35		09 10			09 40		
Southminster	d									08 06					09 06				
Burnham-on-Crouch	d									08 10					09 10				
Althorne	d									08 15					09 15				
North Fambridge	d									08 21					09 21				
South Woodham Ferrers	d									08 26					09 26				
Battlesbridge	d									08 30					09 30				
Wickford 2	d	06 35		07 05		07 35			08 09	08a36		08 40		09 15	09a36		09 45		
Billericay	d	06 41		07 11		07 41			08 15			08 46		09 21			09 51		
Shenfield	a	06 52		07 22		07 52			08 23			08 53		09 28			09 58		
Shenfield 3	d	06 52	07 07	07 22	07 37	07 52	08 07	08 17	08 23		08 37	08 53	09 12	09 29		09 42	09 59	10 12	
Romford	d	07 04	07 19	07 34	07 49	08 04			08 34			09 05		09 38			10 08		
Stratford 7 ⊖ ⛴	d	07 19	07 34	07 49	08 04	08 19	08 34	08s48	08 54		09 04	09 16	09 27	09 48		09 58	10 18	10 28	
London Liverpool Street 15 ⊖	a	07 27	07 43	07 57	08 13	08 27	08 43	08 58	09 02		09 13	09 27	09 37	09 57		10 07	10 27	10 37	

		LE	LE	LE	LE	LE	LE	LE	LE	LE	LE	LE	LE	LE	LE	LE	LE	LE	LE	LE
		◇1	1	◇1	◇1	1	1	◇1	1	◇1	◇1	1	1	1	◇1	1	1	1	1	◇1
				D		E	C			D		E			D		E			F
Southend Victoria	d	19 54			20 24			20 54			21 24		21 54			22 24			22 54	
Prittlewell	d	19 56			20 26			20 56			21 26		21 56			22 26			22 56	
Southend Airport ✈	d	19 59			20 29			20 59			21 29		21 59			22 29			22 59	
Rochford	d	20 02			20 32			21 02			21 32		22 02			22 32			23 02	
Hockley	d	20 06			20 36			21 06			21 36		22 06			22 36			23 06	
Rayleigh	d	20 10			20 40			21 10			21 40		22 10			22 40			23 10	
Southminster	d		20 06						21 06					22 06				22 42		
Burnham-on-Crouch	d		20 10						21 10					22 10				22 46		
Althorne	d		20 15						21 15					22 15				22 51		
North Fambridge	d		20 21						21 21					22 21				22 57		
South Woodham Ferrers	d		20 26						21 26					22 26				23 02		
Battlesbridge	d		20 30						21 30					22 30				23 06		
Wickford 2	d	20 15	20a36		20 45			21 15	21a36		21 45		22 15	22a36		22 45		23 12	23 16	
Billericay	d	20 21			20 51			21 21			21 51		22 21			22 51			23 22	
Shenfield	a	20 28			20 58			21 28			21 58		22 28			22 58		23 23	23 29	
Shenfield 3	d	20 29		20 42	20 59	21 12	21 21	21 29		21 42	21 59	22 12	22 29		22 42	22 59	23 12		23 29	23 37
Romford	d	20 38			21 08			21 38			22 08		22 38			23 08			23 37	
Stratford 7 ⊖ ⛴	d	20 48		20 58	21 18	21 28	21s37	21 48		21 58	22 18	22 28	22 48		22 58	23 18	23 28		23 47	23s55
London Liverpool Street 15 ⊖	a	20 57		21 07	21 27	21 37	21 46	21 57		22 07	22 27	22 37	22 57		23 07	23 27	23 37		23 56	00 06

A From Chelmsford
B From Colchester
C From Harwich International
D From Clacton-on-Sea
E From Ipswich
F From Norwich

Table T010-F

Mondays to Fridays
16 December to 15 May

Marks Tey - Sudbury

Miles			LE	LE	LE	LE	LE	LE	LE	LE	LE	LE	LE	LE	LE	LE	LE	LE	LE	LE	LE
0	Colchester 4	d																			
5	**Marks Tey** 2	d	06 01	06 52	07 39	08 22	09 09	10 01	11 01	12 02	13 01	14 01	15 01	16 01	17 08	18 05	19 14	20 08	21 01	22 01	23 01
8½	Chappel & Wakes Colne	d	06 07	06 58		08 28	09 15	10 07	11 07	12 08	13 07	14 07	15 07	16 07	17 14	18 11	19 20	20 14	21 07	22 07	23 07
11¾	Bures	d	06 13	07 04		08 34	09 21	10 13	11 13	12 14	13 13	14 13	15 13	16 13	17 20	18 17	19 26	20 20	21 13	22 13	23 13
16¾	**Sudbury**	a	06 21	07 12	07 55	08 42	09 29	10 21	11 21	12 22	13 21	14 21	15 21	16 21	17 28	18 25	19 34	20 28	21 21	22 21	23 21

Saturdays
21 December to 16 May

		LE	LE	LE	LE	LE	LE	LE	LE	LE	LE	LE	LE	LE	LE	LE	LE	LE	LE
Colchester 4	d	05 50																	
Marks Tey 2	d	06 01	07 01	08 01	09 01	10 01	11 01	12 01	13 01	14 01	15 01	16 01	17 01	18 01	19 01	20 01	21 01	22 01	23 01
Chappel & Wakes Colne	d	06 07	07 07	08 07	09 07	10 07	11 07	12 07	13 07	14 07	15 07	16 07	17 07	18 07	19 07	20 07	21 07	22 07	23 07
Bures	d	06 13	07 13	08 13	09 13	10 13	11 13	12 13	13 13	14 13	15 13	16 13	17 13	18 13	19 13	20 13	21 13	22 13	23 13
Sudbury	a	06 21	07 21	08 21	09 21	10 21	11 21	12 21	13 21	14 21	15 21	16 21	17 21	18 21	19 21	20 21	21 21	22 21	23 21

Sundays
15 December to 10 May

		LE	LE	LE	LE	LE	LE	LE	LE	LE	LE	LE	LE	LE	LE	LE	LE
Colchester 4	d	07 01															
Marks Tey 2	d	07 16	08 16	09 16	10 16	11 16	12 16	13 16	14 16	15 16	16 16	17 16	18 16	19 16	20 16	21 16	22 16
Chappel & Wakes Colne	d	07 22	08 22	09 22	10 22	11 22	12 22	13 22	14 22	15 22	16 22	17 22	18 22	19 22	20 22	21 22	22 22
Bures	d	07 28	08 28	09 28	10 28	11 28	12 28	13 28	14 28	15 28	16 28	17 28	18 28	19 28	20 28	21 28	22 28
Sudbury	a	07 36	08 36	09 36	10 36	11 36	12 36	13 36	14 36	15 36	16 36	17 36	18 36	19 36	20 36	21 36	22 36

NRT DECEMBER 19 EDITION

Table T010-R

Mondays to Fridays
16 December to 15 May

Sudbury - Marks Tey

Miles			LE	LE	LE	LE	LE	LE	LE	LE	LE	LE	LE	LE	LE	LE	LE	LE	LE	LE	LE	LE
0	**Sudbury**	d	05 30	06 29	07 16	07 59	08 46	09 33	10 26	11 26	12 26	13 26	14 26	15 26	16 32	17 32	18 37	19 38	20 32	21 26	22 26	23 26
5	Bures	d	05 37	06 36	07 23	08 06	08 53	09 40	10 33	11 33	12 33	13 33	14 33	15 33	16 39	17 39	18 44	19 45	20 39	21 33	22 33	23 33
8¼	Chappel & Wakes Colne	d	05 43	06 42	07 29	08 12	08 59	09 46	10 39	11 39	12 39	13 39	14 39	15 39	16 45	17 45	18 50	19 51	20 45	21 39	22 39	23 39
11¾	**Marks Tey** 2	a	05 49	06 48	07 35	08 18	09 05	09 52	10 45	11 45	12 45	13 45	14 45	15 45	16 51	17 51	18 56	19 57	20 51	21 45	22 45	23 45
16¾	Colchester 4	a																				23 55

Saturdays
21 December to 16 May

		LE	LE	LE	LE	LE	LE	LE	LE	LE	LE	LE	LE	LE	LE	LE	LE	LE	LE
Sudbury	d	06 26	07 26	08 26	09 26	10 26	11 26	12 26	13 26	14 26	15 26	16 26	17 26	18 26	19 26	20 26	21 26	22 26	23 26
Bures	d	06 33	07 33	08 33	09 33	10 33	11 33	12 33	13 33	14 33	15 33	16 33	17 33	18 33	19 33	20 33	21 33	22 33	23 33
Chappel & Wakes Colne	d	06 39	07 39	08 39	09 39	10 39	11 39	12 39	13 39	14 39	15 39	16 39	17 39	18 39	19 39	20 39	21 39	22 39	23 39
Marks Tey 2	a	06 45	07 45	08 45	09 45	10 45	11 45	12 45	13 45	14 45	15 45	16 45	17 45	18 45	19 45	20 45	21 45	22 45	23 45
Colchester 4	a																		00 01

Sundays
15 December to 10 May

		LE	LE	LE	LE	LE	LE	LE	LE	LE	LE	LE	LE	LE	LE	LE	LE
Sudbury	d	07 42	08 42	09 42	10 42	11 42	12 42	13 42	14 42	15 42	16 42	17 42	18 42	19 42	20 42	21 42	22 42
Bures	d	07 49	08 49	09 49	10 49	11 49	12 49	13 49	14 49	15 49	16 49	17 49	18 49	19 49	20 49	21 49	22 49
Chappel & Wakes Colne	d	07 55	08 55	09 55	10 55	11 55	12 55	13 55	14 55	15 55	16 55	17 55	18 55	19 55	20 55	21 55	22 55
Marks Tey 2	a	08 01	09 01	10 01	11 01	12 01	13 01	14 01	15 01	16 01	17 01	18 01	19 01	20 01	21 01	22 01	23 01
Colchester 4	a																23 10

Table T011-F

Mondays to Fridays
16 December to 15 May

London - Chelmsford, Colchester, Walton-on-Naze, Clacton, Harwich, Ipswich and Norwich

Miles	Miles	Miles	Miles	Miles			LE MX 1 A	LE MX 1	LE MO 1 A	LE MO	LE MX 1	LE MX 1	LE B	LE 1	LE C	LE B	LE 1	LE 1	LE 1	LE 1	LE 1	LE 1	LE 1	LE B
0	—	—	—	—	**London Liverpool Street** 15 ⊖	d				00 02	00 18	00 46												
4	—	—	—	—	Stratford 7 ⊖	d				00 09	00 25	00 53												
12¼	—	—	—	—	Romford	d																		
20¼	—	—	—	—	Shenfield 3	d				00 32	00 47	01 16												
23½	—	—	—	—	Ingatestone	d				00 36	00 52	01 20												
29¾	—	—	—	—	**Chelmsford**	d			00 07	00 43	00 59	01 27												
36	—	—	—	—	Hatfield Peverel	d				00 49	01 05													
38½	0	—	—	—	**Witham** 2	d		00 07	00 17	00 56	01 11	01 38		05 21										
—	3	—	—	—	White Notley	d		00 14						05 28										
—	4¼	—	—	—	Cressing	d		00 16						05 30										
—	5½	—	—	—	Braintree Freeport	d		00 19						05 33										
—	6¼	—	—	—	**Braintree**	a		00 23						05 37										
42¼	—	—	—	—	Kelvedon	d				01 00	01 16													
46½	—	—	—	—	Marks Tey 2	d			00 25	01 06	01 21													
51¾	0	0	—	—	**Colchester** 4	a			00 39	01 20	01 35	01 57												
—	—	—	—	—		d	00 04								05 40				06 10	06 15		06 20		
—	—	2¼	—	—	Colchester Town	a																06 27		
—	—	—	—	—		d																		
—	2¾	3¼	—	—	Hythe	d																		
—	—	5¾	—	—	Wivenhoe	d																		
—	—	7½	—	—	Alresford (Essex)	d																		
—	—	9¾	—	—	Great Bentley	d																		
—	—	12½	—	—	Weeley	d																		
—	—	14¾	0	—	Thorpe-le-Soken 1	a																		
—	—	—	—	—		d												06 02					06 30	
—	—	—	4¾	—	**Clacton-on-Sea**	a																		
—	—	17¼	—	—	Kirby Cross	d												06 10					06 38	
—	—	18½	—	—	Frinton-on-Sea	d												06 13					06 41	
—	—	19¾	—	—	**Walton-on-the-Naze**	a												06 17					06 45	
59½	—	—	—	0	Manningtree 8	d	00 12								05 49		05 58		06 18	06 23				
—	0	—	—	1¾	Mistley	d											06 02		06 22					
—	—	—	—	5¼	Wrabness	d											06 07		06 27					
—	—	—	—	9½	Harwich International	d											06 15		06 36					
—	—	—	—	10¾	Dovercourt	d											06 18		06 39					
—	—	—	—	11¼	**Harwich Town**	a											06 20		06 41					
68¾	10½	—	—	—	**Ipswich**	a	00 30								06 00					06 34				
—	—	—	—	—		d							05 10		06 00	06 16					06 39			06 54
77	—	—	—	—	Needham Market	d							05 20			06 25								07 03
80¼	—	—	—	—	Stowmarket	d							05a26		06a11	06a30					06 50			07a08
95	—	—	—	—	Diss	d															07 03			
115	—	—	—	—	**Norwich**	a															07 24			

		LE 1 D	LE ◇1	LE 1 E	LE ◇1	LE 1	LE ◇1	LE 1	LE 1	LE 1	LE ◇1	LE 1	LE 1	LE 1	LE 1	LE C	LE ◇1	LE 1 F	LE 1	LE G	LE 1	LE ◇1
London Liverpool Street 15 ⊖	d		05 23		06 00		06 02	06 12			06 25			06 38	06 48		07 00		07 02		07 08	07 17
Stratford 7 ⊖	d		05 30				06 09	06 20			06u33			06 45	06 55				07 09		07 15	07 24
Romford	d		05 38																		07 23	
Shenfield 3	d	05 45	05 48				06 25	06 36						07 01	07 11		07u22		07 25		07 33	07 40
Ingatestone	d		05 52					06 40							07 15							07 44
Chelmsford	d		05 59		06 30		06 34	06 47			06 58			07 10	07 22				07 34		07 42	07 52
Hatfield Peverel	d		06 05	←				06 53											07 40			
Witham 2	d	06 16	06 12	06 16			06 45	07 03			07 09			07 21	07 33				07 48		07 53	08 03
White Notley	d	→		06 23				07 10											07 55			
Cressing	d			06 25				07 12											07 57			
Braintree Freeport	d			06 28				07 15											08 00			
Braintree	a			06 32				07 19											08 04			
Kelvedon	d		06 16				06 49							07 25							07 57	
Marks Tey 2	d		06 22				06 55							07 31	07 40						08 03	08 11
Colchester 4	a		06 29		06 49		07 02				07 22			07 38	07 47		07 50				08 10	08 18
	d		06 30		06 50		07 02		07 10		07 23		07 26	07 43	07 48		07 51	07 56			08 10	08 19
Colchester Town	a												07 34		07 56			08 03				
	d												07 38					08 07				
Hythe	d						07 07						07 42					08 11				08 23
Wivenhoe	d		06 37				07 11						07 46					08 15				08 27
Alresford (Essex)	d						07 14											08 19				
Great Bentley	d						07 18											08 23				
Weeley	d						07 22											08 26				
Thorpe-le-Soken 1	a		06 50				07 28						07 57					08 31				08 38
	d		06 50			06 57	07 28					07 37	07 57					08 40				08 38
Clacton-on-Sea	a		06 59				07 37						08 06					→				08 47
Kirby Cross	d					07 05						07 45										
Frinton-on-Sea	d					07 08						07 48										
Walton-on-the-Naze	a					07 12						07 52										
Manningtree 8	d				06 58				07 18	07 24	07 31			07 51			07 59				08 18	
Mistley	d									07 28				07 55						08 02		
Wrabness	d									07 33				08 01								
Harwich International	d									07 41				08 10								
Dovercourt	d									07 44				08 13								
Harwich Town	a									07 46				08 15								
Ipswich	a				07 10				07 30		07 42						08 11			08 18	08 31	
	d				07 12						07 44					08 03	08 12			08 21		
Needham Market	d																			08 29		
Stowmarket	d				07 23						07 55					08a15	08 23			08a34		
Diss	d				07 35						08 08						08 36					
Norwich	a				07 55						08 27						08 56					

A From London Liverpool Street
B To Cambridge
C To Peterborough
D To Braintree
E From Shenfield
F To Walton-on-the-Naze
G From Harwich International to Cambridge

NRT DECEMBER 19 EDITION

Table T011-F

Mondays to Fridays
16 December to 15 May

London - Chelmsford, Colchester, Walton-on-Naze, Clacton, Harwich, Ipswich and Norwich

		LE 1 A	LE ◇1 ☕	LE 1	LE 1		LE ◇1 ☕	LE 1	LE 1	LE B	LE 1	LE ◇1	LE 1	LE ◇1 ☕	LE 1		LE 1	LE C	LE ◇1 ☕	LE B	LE 1 D	LE 1	LE ◇1
London Liverpool Street 15 ⊖	d		07 30	07 36	07 46		07 55		08 00		08 06	08 16		08 30	08 36		08 48		09 00			09 02	09 18
Stratford 7 ⊖	d			07 45	07 54				08 08		08 14	08 24		08u38	08 45		08 55					09 09	09 25
Romford	d																						
Shenfield 3	d			08 01	08 11				08 25		08 30	08 41			09 03		09 11					09 25	09 41
Ingatestone	d			08 05							08 34	08 45					09 15						09 45
Chelmsford	d		08 02	08 12	08 20				08 34		08 41	08 52		09 03	09 12		09 22					09 34	09 52
Hatfield Peverel	d			08 19							08 47											09 40	
Witham 2	d			08 25	08 35	08 38			08 45		08 54	09 03			09 23		09 35					09 47	10 03
White Notley	d				08 42												09 42						
Cressing	d				08 44												09 44						
Braintree Freeport	d				08 47												09 47						
Braintree	a				08 51												09 51						
Kelvedon	d			08 29							08 58				09 27							09 51	
Marks Tey 2	d			08 35							09 04	09 10			09 33							09 57	
Colchester 4	a		08 21	08 42		08 53	08 45		08 57		09 11	09 17		09 23	09 40				09 46			10 04	10 15
	d		08 23	08 43		08 56	08 47		08 57		09 11	09 18	09 21	09 23	09 44	09 51			09 47		09 57	10 04	10 16
Colchester Town	a			08 51		09 03							09 28		09 52						10 04		
	d					09 07															10 08		
Hythe	d					09 11															10 12		
Wivenhoe	d					09 15						09 25									10 16		10 23
Alresford (Essex)	d					09 19															10 20		
Great Bentley	d					09 23															10 24		
Weeley	d	←				09 26															10 27		
Thorpe-le-Soken 1	a	08 31				09 31						09 36									10 32		10 36
	d	08 40				09 38						09 36									10 38		10 36
Clacton-on-Sea	a											09 45									→		10 45
Kirby Cross	d	08 45				09 43																	
Frinton-on-Sea	d	08 48				09 46																	
Walton-on-the-Naze	a	08 52				09 50																	
Manningtree 8	d		08 31				08 55	09 00			09 19			09 31		10 00			09 55			10 12	
Mistley	d							09 04								10 04							
Wrabness	d							09 09								10 09							
Harwich International	d							09 17								10 17							
Dovercourt	d							09 20								10 20							
Harwich Town	a							09 22								10 22							
Ipswich	a		08 43				09 07		09 16		09 31			09 43					10 06			10 25	
	d		08 44				09 08			09 20				09 44				10 01	10 08	10 20			
Needham Market	d									09 29										10 29			
Stowmarket	d		08 55							09a34				09 55				10a12		10a34			
Diss	d		09 08				09 29							10 08					10 29				
Norwich	a		09 27				09 48							10 27					10 51				

		LE 1 A	LE 1	LE ◇1 ☕	LE 1	LE 1	LE ◇1 ☕	LE B	LE 1	LE 1 D	LE 1	LE ◇1	LE 1 A	LE 1	LE ◇1 ☕	LE 1	LE 1	LE ▪	LE C	LE ◇1 ☕	LE B	LE 1
London Liverpool Street 15 ⊖	d			09 30	09 38	09 48	10 00				10 02	10 18			10 30	10 34	10 46	11 00		11 02		
Stratford 7 ⊖	d			09u38	09 45	09 55					10 09	10 25			10u38	10 41	10 53					
Romford	d				09 53											10 49						
Shenfield 3	d				10 03	10 11					10 25	10 41				10 59	11 08					
Ingatestone	d					10 15						10 45					11 13					
Chelmsford	d			10 03	10 12	10 22					10 34	10 52			11 03	11 08	11 20					
Hatfield Peverel	d										10 40											
Witham 2	d				10 23	10 34					10 47	11 03				11 20	11 34					
White Notley	d					10 41											11 41					
Cressing	d					10 43											11 43					
Braintree Freeport	d					10 46											11 46					
Braintree	a					10 50											11 50					
Kelvedon	d				10 27						10 51					11 24						
Marks Tey 2	d				10 33						10 57					11 30						
Colchester 4	a			10 22	10 40		10 46				11 04	11 15			11 22	11 37				11 47		
	d		10 20	10 23	10 41		10 47			10 56	11 04	11 16		11 20	11 23	11 39				11 48		
Colchester Town	a		10 27		10 49					11 03				11 27		11 47						
	d									11 07												
Hythe	d									11 11												
Wivenhoe	d									11 15		11 23										
Alresford (Essex)	d									11 19												
Great Bentley	d									11 23												
Weeley	d	←								11 26			←									
Thorpe-le-Soken 1	a	10 32								11 31		11 35	11 31									
	d	10 38								11 37		11 35	11 37									
Clacton-on-Sea	a									→		11 44										
Kirby Cross	d	10 43											11 42									
Frinton-on-Sea	d	10 46											11 45									
Walton-on-the-Naze	a	10 50											11 49									
Manningtree 8	d			10 31			10 55		11 00		11 12				11 31					11 56		12 01
Mistley	d								11 04													12 05
Wrabness	d								11 09													12 10
Harwich International	d								11 17													12 18
Dovercourt	d								11 20													12 21
Harwich Town	a								11 22													12 23
Ipswich	a			10 43			11 07				11 26				11 43			11 55		12 08		
	d			10 44			11 08	11 20							11 43			11 55	12 01	12 09	12 20	
Needham Market	d							11 29													12 29	
Stowmarket	d			10 55				11a34							11 54				12a12		12a34	
Diss	d			11 08			11 29								12 07					12 30		
Norwich	a			11 27			11 50								12 27			12 30		12 51		

A From Colchester
B To Cambridge
C To Peterborough
D To Walton-on-the-Naze

London - Chelmsford, Colchester, Walton-on-Naze, Clacton, Harwich, Ipswich and Norwich

Station		LE 1 A	LE 1	LE ◇1	LE 1 B	LE 1	LE ◇1 🍴	LE 1	LE 1		LE ◇1 🍴	LE C	LE 1	LE 1 A	LE 1	LE ◇1	LE 1 B	LE 1	LE ◇1 🍴		LE 1	LE 1	LE D	LE ◇1 🍴	LE C
London Liverpool Street 15 ⊖	d		11 04	11 18			11 30	11 38	11 48		12 00				12 02	12 18			12 30		12 38	12 48		13 00	
Stratford 7 ⊖ ⛴	d		11 11	11 25			11u38	11 45	11 55						12 09	12 25			12u38		12 45	12 55			
Romford	d							11 53													12 53				
Shenfield 3	d		11 27	11 41				12 03	12 11						12 25	12 41					13 03	13 11			
Ingatestone	d			11 45					12 15							12 45						13 15			
Chelmsford	d		11 36	11 52			12 03	12 12	12 22						12 34	12 52			13 03		13 12	13 22			
Hatfield Peverel	d		11 42												12 40										
Witham 2	d		11 49	12 03				12 23	12 34						12 47	13 03					13 23	13 34			
White Notley	d								12 41													13 41			
Cressing	d								12 43													13 43			
Braintree Freeport	d								12 46													13 46			
Braintree	a								12 50													13 50			
Kelvedon	d		11 53					12 27							12 51						13 27				
Marks Tey 2	d		11 59					12 33							12 57						13 33				
Colchester 4	a		12 06	12 15			12 22	12 40			12 46				13 04	13 15			13 22		13 40			13 46	
	d	11 56	12 06	12 16		12 20	12 23	12 41			12 47			12 56	13 04	13 16		13 20	13 23		13 41			13 47	
Colchester Town	a	12 03				12 27		12 49						13 03				13 27			13 49				
	d	12 07												13 07											
Hythe	d	12 11												13 11											
Wivenhoe	d	12 15		12 23										13 15		13 23									
Alresford (Essex)	d	12 19												13 19											
Great Bentley	d	12 23												13 23											
Weeley	d	12 26			←									13 26			←								
Thorpe-le-Soken 1	a	12 31		12 35	12 31									13 31		13 35	13 31								
	d	12 37		12 35	12 37									13 37		13 35	13 37								
Clacton-on-Sea	a	→		12 44										→		13 44									
Kirby Cross	d				12 42												13 42								
Frinton-on-Sea	d				12 45												13 45								
Walton-on-the-Naze	a				12 49												13 49								
Manningtree 5	d		12 14				12 31				12 55		13 00		13 12				13 31					13 55	
Mistley	d												13 04												
Wrabness	d												13 09												
Harwich International	d												13 17												
Dovercourt	d												13 20												
Harwich Town	a												13 22												
Ipswich	a		12 27				12 43				13 07				13 25				13 43					14 07	
	d						12 44				13 08	13 20							13 44				13 58	14 08	14 20
Needham Market	d											13 29													14 29
Stowmarket	d						12 55					13a34							13 55				14a09		14a34
Diss	d						13 08				13 29								14 08					14 29	
Norwich	a						13 27				13 50								14 27					14 50	

Station		LE 1	LE 1 A	LE 1	LE ◇1		LE 1 B	LE 1	LE ◇1 🍴	LE 1	LE 1	LE ◇1 🍴	LE C	LE 1	LE 1 A		LE 1	LE ◇1	LE 1 B	LE 1	LE ◇1 🍴	LE 1	LE 1	LE D	LE ◇1 🍴
London Liverpool Street 15 ⊖	d			13 02	13 18				13 30	13 38	13 48	14 00					14 02	14 18			14 30	14 38	14 48		15 00
Stratford 7 ⊖ ⛴	d			13 09	13 25				13u38	13 45	13 55						14 09	14 25			14u38	14 45	14 55		
Romford	d									13 53												14 53			
Shenfield 3	d			13 25	13 41					14 03	14 11						14 25	14 41				15 03	15 11		
Ingatestone	d				13 45						14 15							14 45					15 15		
Chelmsford	d			13 34	13 52				14 03	14 12	14 22						14 34	14 52			15 03	15 12	15 22		
Hatfield Peverel	d			13 40													14 40								
Witham 2	d			13 47	14 03					14 23	14 34						14 47	15 03				15 23	15 35		
White Notley	d										14 41												15 42		
Cressing	d										14 43												15 44		
Braintree Freeport	d										14 46												15 47		
Braintree	a										14 50												15 51		
Kelvedon	d			13 51						14 27							14 51					15 27			
Marks Tey 2	d			13 57						14 33							14 57					15 33			
Colchester 4	a			14 04	14 15				14 22	14 40		14 46					15 04	15 15			15 22	15 40			15 46
	d		13 56	14 04	14 16			14 20	14 23	14 41		14 47			14 56		15 04	15 16		15 20	15 23	15 41			15 47
Colchester Town	a		14 03					14 27		14 49					15 03					15 27		15 49			
	d		14 07												15 07										
Hythe	d		14 11												15 11										
Wivenhoe	d		14 15		14 23										15 15			15 23							
Alresford (Essex)	d		14 19												15 19										
Great Bentley	d		14 23												15 23										
Weeley	d		14 26				←								15 26				←						
Thorpe-le-Soken 1	a		14 31		14 35		14 31								15 31			15 35	15 31						
	d		14 37		14 35		14 37								15 37			15 35	15 37						
Clacton-on-Sea	a		→		14 44										→			15 44							
Kirby Cross	d						14 42												15 42						
Frinton-on-Sea	d						14 45												15 45						
Walton-on-the-Naze	a						14 49												15 49						
Manningtree 5	d	14 00		14 12					14 31			14 55		15 00			15 12				15 31				15 55
Mistley	d	14 04												15 04											
Wrabness	d	14 09												15 09											
Harwich International	d	14 17												15 17											
Dovercourt	d	14 20												15 20											
Harwich Town	a	14 22												15 22											
Ipswich	a			14 25					14 43			15 07					15 25				15 43				16 07
	d								14 44			15 08	15 20								15 44			16 00	16 08
Needham Market	d												15 29												
Stowmarket	d								14 55				15a34								15 55			16a12	
Diss	d								15 08			15 29									16 08				16 30
Norwich	a								15 27			15 48									16 27				16 50

A To Walton-on-the-Naze
B From Colchester
C To Cambridge
D To Peterborough

Table T011-F

Mondays to Fridays

16 December to 15 May

London - Chelmsford, Colchester, Walton-on-Naze, Clacton, Harwich, Ipswich and Norwich

Station		LE A	LE 1	LE 1 B	LE 1	LE 1	LE ◇1	LE 1 C	LE 1	LE ■1 🍴		LE 1	LE 1	LE 1	LE ■1 🍴	LE A	LE 1	LE 1 B	LE ◇1	LE 1		LE 1	LE ◇1	LE 1 C
London Liverpool Street 15 ⊖	d				15 02		15 18			15 30			15 38	15 48	16 00				16 02				16 14	
Stratford 7 ⊖ ⛴	d				15 09		15 25						15 45	15 55					16 09				16 22	
Romford	d												15 53											
Shenfield 3	d				15 25		15 41						16 03	16 11					16 25				16 38	
Ingatestone	d						15 45					15 58		16 15										
Chelmsford	d				15 34		15 52			16 00		16 05	16 12	16 22					16 35				16 48	
Hatfield Peverel	d				15 40							16 11							16 41					
Witham 2	d				15 47		16 03					16 18	16 23	16 35					16 47					
White Notley	d													16 42										
Cressing	d													16 44										
Braintree Freeport	d													16 47										
Braintree	a													16 51										
Kelvedon	d				15 51							16 22	16 27						16 52				16 59	
Marks Tey 2	d				15 57							16 28	16 33						16 57				17 05	
Colchester 4	a				16 04		16 15			16 21		16 36	16 40		16 46				17 04				17 12	
	d			15 56	16 04	16 14	16 16		16 20	16 21			16 41		16 47			16 56	17 05			17 09	17 13	
Colchester Town	a			16 03					16 27				16 49					17 03				17 16		
	d			16 07														17 07						
Hythe	d			16 11														17 11					17 17	
Wivenhoe	d			16 15			16 23											17 15					17 21	
Alresford (Essex)	d			16 19														17 19						
Great Bentley	d			16 23														17 23						
Weeley	d			16 26				←										17 26						←
Thorpe-le-Soken 1	a			16 31			16 35	16 31										17 31					17 35	17 31
	d			16 37			16 35	16 37										17 37					17 35	17 37
Clacton-on-Sea	a			→			16 44											→					17 46	
Kirby Cross	d							16 42																17 42
Frinton-on-Sea	d							16 45																17 45
Walton-on-the-Naze	a							16 49																17 49
Manningtree 5	d		16 00		16 12	16 23				16 29					16 55		17 00		17 13	17 24				
Mistley	d		16 04			16 27											17 04			17 28				
Wrabness	d		16 09			16 32											17 09			17 33				
Harwich International	d		16 17			16 41											17 17			17 41				
Dovercourt	d		16 20			16 44											17 20			17 44				
Harwich Town	a		16 22			16 46											17 22			17 46				
Ipswich	a				16 25					16 40					17 07				17 29					
	d	16 20								16 41					17 08	17 20								
Needham Market	d	16 29														17 29								
Stowmarket	d	16a34								16 52					17 19	17a34								
Diss	d									17 05					17 32									
Norwich	a									17 24					17 53									

Station		LE 1	LE ■1 🍴	LE D	LE 1 B	LE ◇1	LE 1		LE 1 C	LE ◇1		LE 1 B	LE 1	LE ■1 E 🍴	LE A	LE ◇1	LE 1 C		LE ◇1		LE 1	LE 1	LE 1	LE ■1 🍴	LE 1
London Liverpool Street 15 ⊖	d	16 17	16 30			16 32	16 34			16 44			16 47	17 00		17 02			17 08		17 12	17 18	17 20	17 30	
Stratford 7 ⊖ ⛴	d	16 25					16 42			16 52			16 55			17 10			17 16		17 20	17 26	17 29		
Romford	d																								
Shenfield 3	d	16 41				16 54	16 58						17 11			17 26							17 45		
Ingatestone	d	16 46											17 16										17 49		
Chelmsford	d	16 53				17 04	17 08			17 15			17 23			17 36			17 40		17 44	17 50	17 57		
Hatfield Peverel	d						17 14															17 56			
Witham 2	d	17a06				17 12	17 21						17a36			17 46			17 50			18a06	18 10		
White Notley	d						17 28																18 17		
Cressing	d						17 30																18 19		
Braintree Freeport	d						17 33																18 22		
Braintree	a						17 39																18 28		
Kelvedon	d									17 27									17 55		17 58				
Marks Tey 2	d									17 32						17 54			18 00						
Colchester 4	a		17 16			17 26				17 40						18 01			18 08		18 11				
	d		17 17		17 24	17 27				17 44	17 47	17 56				18 01			18 11	18 16	18 12				
Colchester Town	a				17 33							18 03								18 26					
	d				17 37							18 07													
Hythe	d				17 41							18 11							18 16						
Wivenhoe	d				17 45					17 51		18 15							18 20						
Alresford (Essex)	d				17 49					17 55		18 19							18 24						
Great Bentley	d				17 53					17 59		18 23							18 28						
Weeley	d				17 56				←			18 26					←								
Thorpe-le-Soken 1	a				18 01				18 01	18 06		18 31					18 31		18 35						
	d				18 10				18 10	18 06		18 38					18 38		18 35						
Clacton-on-Sea	a				→					18 17		→							18 46						
Kirby Cross	d								18 15								18 43								
Frinton-on-Sea	d								18 18								18 46								
Walton-on-the-Naze	a								18 22								18 50								
Manningtree 5	d					17 35					17 57					18 09					18 20			18 27	18 35
Mistley	d										18 01														18 39
Wrabness	d										18 06														18 44
Harwich International	d										18 15														18 52
Dovercourt	d										18 18														18 55
Harwich Town	a										18 22														18 57
Ipswich	a		17 34			17 49								17 59		18 20					18 35			18 37	
	d		17 36	17 41										18 00	18 17	18 25								18 39	
Needham Market	d			17 51											18 26										
Stowmarket	d		17 47	17a56											18a31	18 36								18 50	
Diss	d		18 00											18 21		18 48								19 04	
Norwich	a		18 22											18 42		19 09								19 25	

A To Cambridge
B To Walton-on-the-Naze
C From Colchester
D To Peterborough
E The East Anglian

Table T011-F

Mondays to Fridays
16 December to 15 May

London - Chelmsford, Colchester, Walton-on-Naze, Clacton, Harwich, Ipswich and Norwich

Station		LE ◇1	LE 1	LE 1	LE 1 A	LE 1 B	LE 1 🍴	LE 1 C	LE ◇1	LE 1	LE D	LE 1	LE 1 E	LE 1 🍴	LE 1 F	LE ◇1	LE 1 C	LE 1	LE 1	LE 1 G	LE 1	
London Liverpool Street 15 ⊖	d	17 32	17 38			17 40	17 50		17 52			17 58	18 00	18 10		18 12		18 14			18 20	
Stratford 7 ⊖ ⛴	d	17 40	17 46						18 00			18 06	18 09			18 20		18 23			18 28	
Romford	d																					
Shenfield 3	d					18 05							18 25								18 45	
Ingatestone	d					18 09							18 29					18 42				
Chelmsford	d	18 05	18 12			18 17			18 25				18 37			18 46		18 50			18 55	
Hatfield Peverel	d		18 18					←				18 35					←	18 56				
Witham 2	d	18 15				18 31		18 31	18 36			18 41	19 01			18 58	19 01				19 09	
White Notley	d					→							→				19 08					
Cressing	d																19 10					
Braintree Freeport	d																19 13					
Braintree	a																19 19					
Kelvedon	d		18 25					18 37				18 46						19 05				
Marks Tey 2	d	18 23							18 46							19 05					19 18	
Colchester 4	a	18 30	18 36				18 42	18 48	18 53			18 56		19 00		19 12		19 16			19 26	
	d	18 30	18 36		18 41		18 43	18 49	18 54			18 57		19 02	19 08	19 13					19 29	19 34
Colchester Town	a							18 59							19 15					←		19 45
	d														19 19							
Hythe	d				18 45				18 58						19 23	19 17				19 23	19 34	
Wivenhoe	d	18 38			18 49				19 02						→	19 21				19 27	19 38	
Alresford (Essex)	d				18 53															19 31	19 42	
Great Bentley	d				18 57															19 35	19 46	
Weeley	d				19 00															19 38	19 49	
Thorpe-le-Soken 1	a	18 51			19 05				19 13							19 32				19 43	19 54	
	d	18 51		18 56	19 05				19 13							19 32			19 37	19 43	20 00	
Clacton-on-Sea	a	19 02			19 14				19 24							19 43				19 52		
Kirby Cross	d			19 04															19 42		20 05	
Frinton-on-Sea	d			19 07															19 45		20 08	
Walton-on-the-Naze	a			19 11															19 49		20 14	
Manningtree 5	d		18 45				18 52			19 02		19 05		19 11								
Mistley	d									19 06												
Wrabness	d									19 11												
Harwich International	d		19a03							19 19												
Dovercourt	d									19 22												
Harwich Town	a									19 24												
Ipswich	a						19 02					19 19		19 21								
	d						19 04				19 13			19 23								
Needham Market	d										19 22											
Stowmarket	d						19 16				19a27			19 34								
Diss	d						19 30							19 47								
Norwich	a						19 50							20 09								

A From Manningtree
B To Colchester Town
C From London Liverpool Street
D To Cambridge
E To Braintree
F To Clacton-on-Sea
G From Colchester

NRT DECEMBER 19 EDITION

Table T011-F

Mondays to Fridays
16 December to 15 May

London - Chelmsford, Colchester, Walton-on-Naze, Clacton, Harwich, Ipswich and Norwich

Station		LE 1 🍴	LE 1	LE 1	LE ◇1	LE ◇1	LE 1 A	LE	LE B	LE 1 🍴	LE C	LE 1	LE 1	LE 1 D	LE 1 E	LE ◇1	LE ◇1	LE 1 F	LE 1 🍴	LE 1 G	LE 1	LE 1	LE 1
London Liverpool Street 15 ⊖	d	18 30			18 32	18 35	18 48	19 00		19 02		19 04				19 10	19 18		19 30		19 32		19 38
Stratford 7 ⊖ ⛴	d				18 40	18 43	18 56					19 11				19 17	19 25				19 39		19 45
Romford	d																						
Shenfield 3	d					18 59						19 27					19 41						20 01
Ingatestone	d					19 04											19 45						
Chelmsford	d				19 03	19 11	19 19					19 37				19 41	19 52				20 02		20 10
Hatfield Peverel	d					19 17									←	19 47							20 16
Witham 2	d				19 14	19 23	19 37					19 49			19 37	19 53	20 03				20 13		20 23
White Notley	d						→					19 56											
Cressing	d											19 58											
Braintree Freeport	d											20 01											
Braintree	a											20 05											
Kelvedon	d				19 18										19 43	19 58							20 27
Marks Tey 2	d					19 31									19 49	20 03							20 33
Colchester 4	a	19 19			19 30	19 38				19 47					19 56	20 10	20 15		20 19		20 25		20 40
	d	19 19		19 20	19 30	19 39				19 48				19 56	19 57	20 11	20 16		20 20	20 20	20 25		20 41
Colchester Town	a			19 27										20 03						20 27			20 49
	d													20 07									
Hythe	d					19 43								20 11									
Wivenhoe	d					19 47								20 15			20 23						
Alresford (Essex)	d													20 19									
Great Bentley	d													20 23									
Weeley	d													20 26				←					
Thorpe-le-Soken 1	a					19 58								20 31			20 35	20 31					
	d					19 58								20 37			20 35	20 37					
Clacton-on-Sea	a					20 11								→			20 44						
Kirby Cross	d																	20 42					
Frinton-on-Sea	d																	20 45					
Walton-on-the-Naze	a																	20 49					
Manningtree 5	d	19 28	19 35		19 38					19 56			20 00		20 05	20 19			20 28		20 34	20 38	
Mistley	d		19 39										20 04									20 42	
Wrabness	d		19 44										20 09									20 47	
Harwich International	d		19 52										20 17		20a24						20a54	20 55	
Dovercourt	d		19 55										20 20									20 58	
Harwich Town	a		19 57										20 22									21 00	
Ipswich	a	19 40			19 53			19 55		20 08						20 31			20 40				
	d	19 40						19 55	20 01	20 09	20 21								20 41				
Needham Market	d										20 30												
Stowmarket	d	19 52							20a12	20 21	20a35								20 52				
Diss	d	20 05								20 34									21 05				
Norwich	a	20 27						20 30		20 53									21 24				

Station		LE 1	LE ◇	LE C	LE 1 H	LE 1	LE 1 D	LE ◇1	LE ◇1	LE 1 F	LE 1	LE ◇1 🍴	LE 1	LE 1	LE I	LE ◇1 🍴	LE J	LE 1	LE 1 D	LE 1	LE ◇1	LE 1 F
London Liverpool Street 15 ⊖	d	19 48	20 00					20 02	20 18			20 30	20 38	20 48		21 00				21 02	21 18	
Stratford 7 ⊖ ⛴	d	19 55						20 09	20 25			20u38	20 45	20 55						21 09	21 25	
Romford	d																					
Shenfield 3	d	20 11						20 25	20 41				21 03	21 11						21 25	21 41	
Ingatestone	d	20 15							20 45					21 15							21 45	
Chelmsford	d	20 22						20 34	20 52			21 03	21 12	21 22						21 34	21 52	
Hatfield Peverel	d							20 40												21 40		
Witham 2	d	20 34						20 47	21 03				21 23	21 34						21 47	22 03	
White Notley	d	20 41												21 41								
Cressing	d	20 43												21 43								
Braintree Freeport	d	20 46												21 46								
Braintree	a	20 50												21 50								
Kelvedon	d							20 51					21 27							21 51		
Marks Tey 2	d							20 57					21 33							21 57		
Colchester 4	a		20 46					21 04	21 15			21 22	21 40			21 46				22 04	22 15	
	d		20 47				20 56	21 04	21 16		21 20	21 23	21 41			21 47			21 56	22 04	22 16	
Colchester Town	a						21 03				21 27		21 49						22 03			
	d						21 07												22 07			
Hythe	d						21 11												22 11			
Wivenhoe	d						21 15		21 23										22 15		22 23	
Alresford (Essex)	d						21 19												22 19			
Great Bentley	d						21 23												22 23			
Weeley	d						21 26			←									22 26			←
Thorpe-le-Soken 1	a						21 31		21 35	21 31									22 31		22 35	22 31
	d				20 54		21 37		21 35	21 37									22 37		22 35	22 37
Clacton-on-Sea	a				21 03		→		21 44										→		22 44	
Kirby Cross	d									21 42												22 42
Frinton-on-Sea	d									21 45												22 45
Walton-on-the-Naze	a									21 49												22 49
Manningtree 5	d		20 55			21 00		21 12				21 32				21 56		22 00		22 12		
Mistley	d					21 04												22 04				
Wrabness	d					21 09												22 09				
Harwich International	d					21 17									21 38			22 17		22a28		
Dovercourt	d					21 20												22 20				
Harwich Town	a					21 22												22 22				
Ipswich	a		21 07					21 25				21 43			22 04	22 07						
	d		21 08	21 17								21 45				22 09	22 19					
Needham Market	d			21 27													22 29					
Stowmarket	d		21 19	21a33								21 56				22 20	22a35					
Diss	d		21 32									22 09				22 33						
Norwich	a		21 51									22 29				22 53						

A To Harwich International
B To Peterborough
C To Cambridge
D To Walton-on-the-Naze
E From London Liverpool Street
F From Colchester
G From Harwich International
H From Walton-on-the-Naze
I To Lowestoft
J To Bury St Edmunds

Table T011-F

London - Chelmsford, Colchester, Walton-on-Naze, Clacton, Harwich, Ipswich and Norwich

Mondays to Fridays
16 December to 15 May

		LE ◇1 ⊏	LE 1	LE 1	LE 1	LE 1	LE 1 A	LE 1 B	LE 1	LE ◇1	LE 1 C	LE ◇1 ⊏	LE 1	LE 1	LE 1	LE 1	LE ◇1	LE ◇1 ⊏	LE 1
London Liverpool Street 15 ⊖	d	21 30	21 38	21 48	22 00				22 02	22 18		22 30		22 38		23 02	23 18	23 30	23 48
Stratford 7 ⊖ ⇌	d	21u38	21 45	21 55					22 09	22 25		22u38		22 45		23 09	23 25	23u38	23 55
Romford	d		21 53																
Shenfield 3	d		22 03	22 11					22 25	22 41				23 01		23 25	23 41		00 11
Ingatestone	d			22 15						22 45				23 05			23 45		00 15
Chelmsford	d	22 03	22 12	22 22	22 28				22 34	22 52		23 03		23 12		23 34	23 52	00 03	00 22
Hatfield Peverel	d								22 40							23 40			00 28
Witham 2	d		22 23	22 34					22 47	23 03				23 23	23 25	23 47	00 03		00 35
White Notley	d			22 41											23 32				
Cressing	d			22 43											23 34				
Braintree Freeport	d			22 46											23 37				
Braintree	a			22 50											23 41				
Kelvedon	d		22 27						22 51					23 27		23 51			00 39
Marks Tey 2	d		22 33						22 57					23 33		23 57			00 45
Colchester 4	a	22 22	22 40		22 47				23 05	23 15		23 22		23 47		00 04	00 15	00 22	00 59
	d	22 23	22 41		22 47			22 56		23 16		23 23				00 04	00 16	00 23	
Colchester Town	a		22 49					23 03											
	d							23 07											
Hythe	d							23 11											
Wivenhoe	d							23 15		23 23							00 23		
Alresford (Essex)	d							23 19									00 27		
Great Bentley	d							23 23									00 31		
Weeley	d							23 26			←								
Thorpe-le-Soken 1	a							23 31		23 35	23 31						00 38		
	d						23 16	23 37		23 35	23 37						00 38		
Clacton-on-Sea	a						23 25	→		23 44							00 53		
Kirby Cross	d										23 42								
Frinton-on-Sea	d										23 45								
Walton-on-the-Naze	a										23 49								
Manningtree 5	d	22 32			22 55	23 00						23 32	23 36			00 12		00 32	
Mistley	d					23 04							23 40						
Wrabness	d					23 09							23 45						
Harwich International	d					23 17							23 53						
Dovercourt	d					23 20							23 56						
Harwich Town	a					23 22							23 58						
Ipswich	a	22 44			23 08							23 44				00 30		00 44	
	d	22 45										23 45						00 45	
Needham Market	d																		
Stowmarket	d	22 57										23 57						00 57	
Diss	d	23 11										00 11						01 11	
Norwich	a	23 30										00 30						01 36	

Saturdays
21 December to 16 May

		LE 1 D	LE 1	LE 1	LE 1	LE E	LE 1	LE F	LE E	LE 1	LE 1	LE 1	LE 1	LE ◇1	LE 1	LE 1 G	LE 1	LE E	LE 1 B	LE 1	LE ◇1	LE 1 C	LE ◇1
London Liverpool Street 15 ⊖	d			00 18	00 46								05 34							06 02	06 18		06 30
Stratford 7 ⊖ ⇌	d			00 25	00 53								05 41							06 09	06 25		06u38
Romford	d												05 49										
Shenfield 3	d			00 47	01 16								05 59							06 25	06 41		
Ingatestone	d			00 52	01 20								06 03								06 45		
Chelmsford	d			00 59	01 27								06 10							06 34	06 52		07 03
Hatfield Peverel	d			01 05									06 16							06 40			
Witham 2	d		00 07	01 11	01 38		05 34						06 23		06 34					06 47	07 03		
White Notley	d		00 14				05 41								06 41								
Cressing	d		00 16				05 43								06 43								
Braintree Freeport	d		00 19				05 46								06 46								
Braintree	a		00 23				05 50								06 50								
Kelvedon	d			01 16									06 27							06 51			
Marks Tey 2	d			01 21									06 33							06 57			
Colchester 4	a			01 35	01 57								06 40							07 04	07 15		07 22
	d	00 04						05 40		05 53	06 10	06 20	06 40						06 56	07 04	07 16		07 23
Colchester Town	a											06 27							07 03				
	d																		07 07				
Hythe	d																		07 11				
Wivenhoe	d																		07 15		07 24		
Alresford (Essex)	d																		07 19				
Great Bentley	d																		07 23				
Weeley	d																		07 26			←	
Thorpe-le-Soken 1	a																		07 31		07 35	07 31	
	d															06 37			07 37		07 35	07 37	
Clacton-on-Sea	a																		→		07 44		
Kirby Cross	d															06 42						07 42	
Frinton-on-Sea	d															06 45						07 45	
Walton-on-the-Naze	a															06 49						07 49	
Manningtree 5	d	00 12						05 49		06 01	06 18		06 48				07 00			07 12			07 31
Mistley	d									06 05							07 04						
Wrabness	d									06 10							07 09						
Harwich International	d									06 18							07 17						
Dovercourt	d									06 21							07 20						
Harwich Town	a									06 23							07 22						
Ipswich	a	00 30						05 59			06 30		07 00							07 25			07 43
	d					05 10		06 00	06 16					07 10				07 20					07 44
Needham Market	d					05 20			06 25									07 29					
Stowmarket	d					05a26		06a11	06a30					07 21				07a34					07 55
Diss	d													07 34									08 08
Norwich	a													07 53									08 27

A From Walton-on-the-Naze
B To Walton-on-the-Naze
C From Colchester
D From London Liverpool Street
E To Cambridge
F To Peterborough
G From Clacton-on-Sea

Table T011-F

London - Chelmsford, Colchester, Walton-on-Naze, Clacton, Harwich, Ipswich and Norwich

Saturdays
21 December to 16 May

		LE 1	LE 1	LE 1	LE A	LE ◇1	LE 1 B	LE C	LE 1	LE 1	LE ◇1	LE 1 D	LE 1	LE ◇1 ⊏	LE 1	LE 1	LE ◇1 ⊏	LE E	LE 1	LE 1 B	LE 1	LE ◇1	LE 1 D
London Liverpool Street 15 ⊖	d	06 38		06 48		07 00				07 02	07 18			07 30	07 38	07 48	08 00				08 02	08 18	
Stratford 7 ⊖ ⇌	d	06 45		06 55						07 09	07 25			07u38	07 45	07 55					08 09	08 25	
Romford	d	06 53													07 53								
Shenfield 3	d	07 03		07 11						07 25	07 41				08 03	08 11					08 25	08 41	
Ingatestone	d			07 15							07 45					08 15						08 45	
Chelmsford	d	07 12		07 22						07 34	07 52			08 03	08 12	08 22					08 34	08 52	
Hatfield Peverel	d									07 40											08 40		
Witham 2	d	07 23		07 34						07 47	08 03				08 23	08 34					08 47	09 03	
White Notley	d			07 41												08 41							
Cressing	d			07 43												08 43							
Braintree Freeport	d			07 46												08 46							
Braintree	a			07 50												08 50							
Kelvedon	d	07 27								07 51					08 27						08 51		
Marks Tey 2	d	07 33								07 57					08 33						08 57		
Colchester 4	a	07 40				07 47				08 04	08 15			08 22	08 40		08 46				09 04	09 15	
	d	07 40	07 44			07 47	07 56			08 04	08 16		08 20	08 23	08 41		08 47			08 56	09 04	09 16	
Colchester Town	a		07 51				08 03						08 27		08 49					09 03			
	d						08 07													09 07			
Hythe	d						08 11													09 11			
Wivenhoe	d						08 15				08 24									09 15		09 24	
Alresford (Essex)	d						08 19													09 19			
Great Bentley	d						08 23													09 23			
Weeley	d						08 26					←								09 26			←
Thorpe-le-Soken 1	a						08 31				08 35	08 31								09 31		09 35	09 31
	d						08 37				08 35	08 37								09 37		09 35	09 37
Clacton-on-Sea	a						→				08 44									→		09 44	
Kirby Cross	d											08 42											09 42
Frinton-on-Sea	d											08 45											09 45
Walton-on-the-Naze	a											08 49											09 49
Manningtree 5	d	07 48				07 55			08 00	08 12				08 31			08 55		09 00		09 12		
Mistley	d							08 02	08 04										09 04				
Wrabness	d								08 09										09 09				
Harwich International	d	08a09							08 17										09 17				
Dovercourt	d								08 20										09 20				
Harwich Town	a								08 22										09 22				
Ipswich	a					08 07		08 18		08 25				08 43			09 07				09 25		
	d				08 00	08 08		08 21						08 44			09 08	09 20					
Needham Market	d							08 29										09 29					
Stowmarket	d				08a11			08a34						08 55				09a34					
Diss	d					08 29								09 08			09 29						
Norwich	a					08 50								09 27			09 50						

		LE 1	LE ◇1 ⊏	LE 1	LE 1	LE A	LE ◇1 ⊏	LE E	LE 1	LE 1 B	LE 1	LE ◇1	LE 1 D	LE 1	LE ◇1 ⊏	LE 1	LE 1	LE ◇1 ⊏	LE E	LE 1	LE 1 B	LE 1
London Liverpool Street 15 ⊖	d		08 30	08 38	08 48		09 00				09 02	09 18			09 30	09 38	09 48	10 00				10 02
Stratford 7 ⊖ ⇌	d		08u38	08 45	08 55						09 09	09 25			09u38	09 45	09 55					10 09
Romford	d			08 53												09 53						
Shenfield 3	d			09 03	09 11						09 25	09 41				10 03	10 11					10 25
Ingatestone	d				09 15							09 45					10 15					
Chelmsford	d		09 03	09 12	09 22						09 34	09 52			10 03	10 12	10 22					10 34
Hatfield Peverel	d										09 40											10 40
Witham 2	d			09 23	09 34						09 47	10 03				10 23	10 34					10 47
White Notley	d				09 41												10 41					
Cressing	d				09 43												10 43					
Braintree Freeport	d				09 46												10 46					
Braintree	a				09 50												10 50					
Kelvedon	d			09 27							09 51					10 27						10 51
Marks Tey 2	d			09 33							09 57					10 33						10 57
Colchester 4	a		09 22	09 40			09 46				10 04	10 15			10 22	10 40		10 46				11 04
	d	09 20	09 23	09 41			09 47		09 51	09 56	10 04	10 16		10 20	10 23	10 41		10 47			10 56	11 04
Colchester Town	a	09 27		09 49						10 03				10 27		10 49					11 03	
	d									10 07											11 07	
Hythe	d									10 11											11 11	
Wivenhoe	d									10 15		10 24									11 15	
Alresford (Essex)	d									10 19											11 19	
Great Bentley	d									10 23											11 23	
Weeley	d									10 26			←								11 26	
Thorpe-le-Soken 1	a									10 31		10 35	10 31								11 31	
	d									10 37		10 35	10 37								11 37	
Clacton-on-Sea	a									→		10 44									→	
Kirby Cross	d												10 42									
Frinton-on-Sea	d												10 45									
Walton-on-the-Naze	a												10 49									
Manningtree 5	d		09 31				09 55		10 00		10 12				10 31			10 55		11 01		11 12
Mistley	d								10 04											11 05		
Wrabness	d								10 09											11 10		
Harwich International	d								10 17											11 18		
Dovercourt	d								10 20											11 21		
Harwich Town	a								10 22											11 23		
Ipswich	a		09 43				10 07				10 25				10 43			11 07				11 25
	d		09 44			09 58	10 08	10 20							10 44			11 08	11 20			
Needham Market	d							10 29											11 29			
Stowmarket	d		09 55			10a09		10a34							10 55				11a34			
Diss	d		10 08				10 29								11 08			11 29				
Norwich	a		10 27				10 50								11 27			11 50				

A To Peterborough
B To Walton-on-the-Naze
C From Harwich International to Cambridge
D From Colchester
E To Cambridge

Table T011-F

Saturdays

21 December to 16 May

London - Chelmsford, Colchester, Walton-on-Naze, Clacton, Harwich, Ipswich and Norwich

		LE	LE	LE	LE	LE	LE	LE		LE	LE	LE	LE	LE	LE	LE	LE	LE		LE	LE	LE	LE	LE	LE
		◇1	1	1	◇1	1	1	1			◇1		1	1	1	◇1	1	1		◇1	1	1	◇1		1
			A							B		C		D			A							C	
					☕						☕									☕			☕		
London Liverpool Street 15 ⊖	d	10 18			10 30	10 34	10 46	11 00			11 02				11 04	11 18				11 30	11 38	11 48	12 00		
Stratford 7 ⊖	d	10 25			10u38	10 41	10 53								11 11	11 25				11u38	11 45	11 55			
Romford	d					10 49															11 53				
Shenfield 3	d	10 41				10 59	11 08								11 27	11 41					12 03	12 11			
Ingatestone	d	10 45					11 13									11 45						12 15			
Chelmsford	d	10 52			11 02	11 08	11 20								11 36	11 52				12 03	12 12	12 22			
Hatfield Peverel	d														11 42										
Witham 2	d	11 03				11 20	11 34								11 49	12 03					12 23	12 34			
White Notley	d						11 41															12 41			
Cressing	d						11 43															12 43			
Braintree Freeport	d						11 46															12 46			
Braintree	a						11 50															12 50			
Kelvedon	d					11 24									11 53						12 27				
Marks Tey 2	d					11 30									11 59						12 33				
Colchester 4	a	11 15			11 22	11 37					11 47				12 06	12 15				12 22	12 40		12 46		
	d	11 16		11 20	11 22	11 41					11 48			11 56	12 06	12 16		12 20		12 23	12 41		12 47		
Colchester Town	a			11 27		11 49								12 03				12 27			12 49				
	d													12 07											
Hythe	d													12 11											
Wivenhoe	d	11 24												12 15		12 24									
Alresford (Essex)	d													12 19											
Great Bentley	d													12 23											
Weeley	d		←											12 26			←								
Thorpe-le-Soken 1	a	11 35	11 31											12 31		12 35	12 31								
	d	11 35	11 37											12 37		12 35	12 37								
Clacton-on-Sea	a	11 44												→		12 44									
Kirby Cross	d		11 42														12 42								
Frinton-on-Sea	d		11 45														12 45								
Walton-on-the-Naze	a		11 49														12 49								
Manningtree 5	d				11 31						11 56		12 01		12 14					12 31			12 55		13 00
Mistley	d												12 05												13 04
Wrabness	d												12 10												13 09
Harwich International	d												12 18												13 17
Dovercourt	d												12 21												13 20
Harwich Town	a												12 23												13 22
Ipswich	a				11 43			11 55			12 07				12 27					12 43			13 07		
	d				11 43			11 55		12 01	12 09	12 20								12 44			13 08	13 20	
Needham Market	d											12 29												13 29	
Stowmarket	d				11 54					12a12		12a34								12 55				13a34	
Diss	d				12 07						12 30									13 08			13 29		
Norwich	a				12 27			12 30			12 52									13 27			13 50		

		LE	LE	LE		LE	LE	LE	LE	LE	LE	LE	LE	LE		LE	LE	LE	LE	LE	LE	LE	LE	LE	
		1	1	◇1		1	1	◇1	1	1		◇1		1		1	1	◇1	1	1	◇1	1	1	◇1	
		D				A					B		C			D			A						
								☕				☕									☕			☕	
London Liverpool Street 15 ⊖	d		12 02	12 18				12 30	12 38	12 48		13 00					13 02	13 18			13 30	13 38	13 48	14 00	
Stratford 7 ⊖	d		12 09	12 25				12u38	12 45	12 55							13 09	13 25			13u38	13 45	13 55		
Romford	d								12 53													13 53			
Shenfield 3	d		12 25	12 41					13 03	13 11							13 25	13 41				14 03	14 11		
Ingatestone	d			12 45						13 15								13 45					14 15		
Chelmsford	d		12 34	12 52				13 03	13 12	13 22							13 34	13 52			14 03	14 12	14 22		
Hatfield Peverel	d		12 40														13 40								
Witham 2	d		12 47	13 03					13 23	13 34							13 47	14 03				14 23	14 34		
White Notley	d									13 41													14 41		
Cressing	d									13 43													14 43		
Braintree Freeport	d									13 46													14 46		
Braintree	a									13 50													14 50		
Kelvedon	d		12 51						13 27								13 51					14 27			
Marks Tey 2	d		12 57						13 33								13 57					14 33			
Colchester 4	a		13 04	13 15				13 22	13 40			13 46					14 04	14 15			14 22	14 40		14 46	
	d	12 56	13 04	13 16			13 20	13 23	13 41			13 47				13 56	14 04	14 16		14 20	14 23	14 41		14 47	
Colchester Town	a	13 03					13 27		13 49							14 03				14 27		14 49			
	d	13 07														14 07									
Hythe	d	13 11														14 11									
Wivenhoe	d	13 15		13 24												14 15		14 24							
Alresford (Essex)	d	13 19														14 19									
Great Bentley	d	13 23														14 23									
Weeley	d	13 26				←										14 26			←						
Thorpe-le-Soken 1	a	13 31		13 35		13 31										14 31		14 35	14 31						
	d	13 37		13 35		13 37										14 37		14 35	14 37						
Clacton-on-Sea	a	→		13 44												→		14 44							
Kirby Cross	d					13 42													14 42						
Frinton-on-Sea	d					13 45													14 45						
Walton-on-the-Naze	a					13 49													14 49						
Manningtree 5	d		13 12					13 31				13 55		14 00			14 12				14 31			14 55	
Mistley	d													14 04											
Wrabness	d													14 09											
Harwich International	d													14 17											
Dovercourt	d													14 20											
Harwich Town	a													14 22											
Ipswich	a		13 25					13 43				14 07					14 25				14 43			15 07	
	d							13 44			13 58	14 08	14 20								14 44			15 08	
Needham Market	d												14 29												
Stowmarket	d							13 55			14a09		14a34								14 55				
Diss	d							14 08				14 29									15 08			15 29	
Norwich	a							14 27				14 50									15 27			15 48	

A From Colchester
B To Peterborough
C To Cambridge
D To Walton-on-the-Naze

Table T011-F

Saturdays

21 December to 16 May

London - Chelmsford, Colchester, Walton-on-Naze, Clacton, Harwich, Ipswich and Norwich

		LE	LE	LE	LE	LE	LE	LE	LE	LE		LE	LE	LE	LE	LE	LE	LE	LE	LE		LE	LE	LE	LE
			1	1	1	◇1	1	1	◇1	1		1		◇1		1	1	1	◇1	1		1	◇1	1	1
		A		B			C						D		A		B			C					
									☕					☕									☕		
London Liverpool Street 15 ⊖	d				14 02	14 18			14 30	14 38		14 48		15 00				15 02	15 18				15 30	15 38	15 48
Stratford 7 ⊖	d				14 09	14 25			14u38	14 45		14 55						15 09	15 25				15u38	15 45	15 55
Romford	d									14 53														15 53	
Shenfield 3	d				14 25	14 41				15 03		15 11						15 25	15 41					16 03	16 11
Ingatestone	d					14 45						15 15							15 45						16 15
Chelmsford	d				14 34	14 52			15 03	15 12		15 22						15 34	15 52				16 03	16 12	16 22
Hatfield Peverel	d				14 40													15 40							
Witham 2	d				14 47	15 03				15 23		15 34						15 47	16 03					16 23	16 34
White Notley	d											15 41													16 41
Cressing	d											15 43													16 43
Braintree Freeport	d											15 46													16 46
Braintree	a											15 50													16 50
Kelvedon	d				14 51					15 27								15 51						16 27	
Marks Tey 2	d				14 57					15 33								15 57						16 33	
Colchester 4	a				15 04	15 15			15 23	15 40				15 46				16 04	16 15				16 22	16 40	
	d			14 56	15 04	15 16		15 20	15 23	15 41				15 47			15 56	16 04	16 16			16 20	16 23	16 41	
Colchester Town	a			15 03				15 27		15 49							16 03					16 27		16 49	
	d			15 07													16 07								
Hythe	d			15 11													16 11								
Wivenhoe	d			15 15		15 24											16 15		16 24						
Alresford (Essex)	d			15 19													16 19								
Great Bentley	d			15 23													16 23								
Weeley	d			15 26			←										16 26			←					
Thorpe-le-Soken 1	a			15 31		15 35	15 31										16 31		16 35	16 31					
	d			15 37		15 35	15 37										16 37		16 35	16 37					
Clacton-on-Sea	a			→		15 44											→		16 44						
Kirby Cross	d						15 42													16 42					
Frinton-on-Sea	d						15 45													16 45					
Walton-on-the-Naze	a						15 49													16 49					
Manningtree 5	d		15 00		15 12				15 31					15 55		16 00		16 12					16 31		
Mistley	d		15 04													16 04									
Wrabness	d		15 09													16 09									
Harwich International	d		15 17													16 17									
Dovercourt	d		15 20													16 20									
Harwich Town	a		15 22													16 22									
Ipswich	a				15 26				15 43					16 07				16 25					16 43		
	d	15 20							15 44				15 58	16 08	16 20								16 44		
Needham Market	d	15 29													16 29										
Stowmarket	d	15a34							15 55				16a09		16a34								16 55		
Diss	d								16 08					16 29									17 08		
Norwich	a								16 27					16 50									17 27		

		LE	LE	LE	LE	LE		LE	LE	LE	LE	LE	LE	LE	LE	LE		LE	LE	LE	LE	LE	LE	LE	LE
		◇1		1	1	1		◇1	1	1	◇1	1	1		◇1			1	1	◇1	◇1	1	1	◇1	1
			A		B				C					D		A			B			C			
		☕									☕				☕									☕	
London Liverpool Street 15 ⊖	d	16 00				16 02		16 18			16 30	16 38	16 48		17 00					17 02	17 18			17 30	17 38
Stratford 7 ⊖	d					16 09		16 25			16u38	16 45	16 55							17 09	17 25			17u38	17 45
Romford	d											16 53													17 54
Shenfield 3	d					16 25		16 41				17 03	17 11							17 25	17 41				18 03
Ingatestone	d							16 45					17 15								17 45				
Chelmsford	d					16 34		16 52			17 03	17 12	17 22							17 34	17 52			18 03	18 12
Hatfield Peverel	d					16 40														17 40					
Witham 2	d					16 47		17 03				17 23	17 34							17 47	18 03				18 23
White Notley	d												17 41												
Cressing	d												17 43												
Braintree Freeport	d												17 46												
Braintree	a												17 50												
Kelvedon	d					16 51						17 27								17 51					18 27
Marks Tey 2	d					16 57						17 33								17 57					18 33
Colchester 4	a	16 46				17 04		17 15			17 22	17 40			17 46					18 04	18 15			18 22	18 40
	d	16 47			16 56	17 04		17 16		17 20	17 23	17 41			17 47			17 51	17 56	18 04	18 16		18 20	18 23	18 41
Colchester Town	a				17 03					17 27		17 49							18 03				18 27		18 49
	d				17 07														18 07						
Hythe	d				17 11														18 11						
Wivenhoe	d				17 15			17 24											18 15		18 24				
Alresford (Essex)	d				17 19														18 19						
Great Bentley	d				17 23														18 23						
Weeley	d				17 26				←										18 26			←			
Thorpe-le-Soken 1	a				17 31			17 35	17 31										18 31		18 35	18 31			
	d				17 37			17 35	17 37										18 37		18 35	18 37			
Clacton-on-Sea	a				→			17 44											→		18 44				
Kirby Cross	d								17 42													18 42			
Frinton-on-Sea	d								17 45													18 45			
Walton-on-the-Naze	a								17 49													18 49			
Manningtree 5	d	16 55		17 00		17 12					17 31				17 55			18 00		18 12				18 31	
Mistley	d			17 04														18 04							
Wrabness	d			17 09														18 09							
Harwich International	d			17 17														18 17							
Dovercourt	d			17 20														18 20							
Harwich Town	a			17 22														18 22							
Ipswich	a	17 07				17 25					17 43				18 07					18 25				18 43	
	d	17 08	17 20								17 44			17 58	18 08	18 20								18 44	
Needham Market	d		17 29													18 29									
Stowmarket	d	17 19	17a34								17 55			18a09		18a34								18 55	
Diss	d	17 32									18 08				18 29									19 08	
Norwich	a	17 51									18 27				18 50									19 27	

A To Cambridge
B To Walton-on-the-Naze
C From Colchester
D To Peterborough

Table T011-F

Saturdays
21 December to 16 May

London - Chelmsford, Colchester, Walton-on-Naze, Clacton, Harwich, Ipswich and Norwich

Station		LE ■	LE ◇■ 🍴	LE A	LE ■	LE ■ B	LE ◇■	LE ◇■	LE ■ C	LE ■	LE ◇■ 🍴	LE ■	LE ■	LE ■	LE D	LE ◇■ 🍴	LE A	LE ■	LE ■ B	LE ◇■	LE ◇■	LE ■ C
London Liverpool Street 15 ⊖	d	17 48	18 00				18 02	18 18			18 30	18 34	18 46	19 00		19 02				19 04	19 18	
Stratford 7 ⊖	d	17 55					18 09	18 25			18u38	18 41	18 53							19 11	19 25	
Romford	d											18 50										
Shenfield 3	d	18 11					18 25	18 41				18 59	19 08							19 27	19 41	
Ingatestone	d	18 15						18 45					19 13								19 45	
Chelmsford	d	18 22					18 34	18 52			19 02	19 08	19 20							19 36	19 52	
Hatfield Peverel	d						18 40													19 42		
Witham 2	d	18 34					18 47	19 03				19 20	19 34							19 49	20 03	
White Notley	d	18 41											19 41									
Cressing	d	18 43											19 43									
Braintree Freeport	d	18 46											19 46									
Braintree	a	18 50											19 50									
Kelvedon	d						18 51					19 24								19 53		
Marks Tey 2	d						18 57					19 30								19 59		
Colchester 4	a		18 46				19 04	19 15			19 22	19 37				19 47				20 06	20 15	
	d		18 47			18 56	19 04	19 16		19 20	19 22	19 41				19 48			19 56	20 06	20 16	
Colchester Town	a					19 03				19 27		19 49							20 03			
	d					19 07													20 07			
Hythe	d					19 11													20 11			
Wivenhoe	d					19 15		19 24											20 15		20 24	
Alresford (Essex)	d					19 19													20 19			
Great Bentley	d					19 23													20 23			
Weeley	d					19 26			←										20 26			←
Thorpe-le-Soken 1	a					19 31		19 35	19 31										20 31		20 35	20 31
	d					19 37		19 35	19 37										20 37		20 35	20 37
Clacton-on-Sea	a					→		19 44											→		20 44	
Kirby Cross	d								19 42													20 42
Frinton-on-Sea	d								19 45													20 45
Walton-on-the-Naze	a								19 49													20 49
Manningtree 5	d		18 55		19 00		19 12				19 31					19 56		20 01		20 14		
Mistley	d				19 04													20 05				
Wrabness	d				19 09													20 10				
Harwich International	d				19 17													20 18				
Dovercourt	d				19 20													20 21				
Harwich Town	a				19 22													20 23				
Ipswich	a		19 07				19 24				19 43			19 55		20 08				20 27		
	d		19 08	19 20							19 43			19 55	20 01	20 09	20 20					
Needham Market	d			19 29													20 29					
Stowmarket	d			19a34							19 54				20a12		20a34					
Diss	d		19 29								20 07					20 30						
Norwich	a		19 50								20 27			20 30		20 51						

Station		LE ■	LE ◇■ 🍴	LE ■	LE ■	LE ■	LE ◇	LE A	LE ■	LE ■ B	LE ■	LE ◇■	LE ■ C	LE ■	LE ◇■ 🍴	LE ■	LE ■	LE E	LE ◇■	LE F	LE ■	LE ■ B	LE ■
London Liverpool Street 15 ⊖	d		19 30	19 32	19 38	19 48	20 00				20 02	20 18			20 30	20 38	20 48		21 00				21 02
Stratford 7 ⊖	d		19u38	19 39	19 46	19 55					20 09	20 25			20u38	20 45	20 55						21 09
Romford	d				19 54											20 53							
Shenfield 3	d			19 57	20 04	20 11					20 25	20 41				21 03	21 11						21 25
Ingatestone	d					20 15						20 45					21 15						
Chelmsford	d		20 03	20 07	20 13	20 22					20 34	20 52			21 03	21 12	21 22						21 34
Hatfield Peverel	d										20 40												21 40
Witham 2	d			20 20	20 24	20 34					20 47	21 03				21 23	21 34						21 47
White Notley	d					20 41											21 41						
Cressing	d					20 43											21 43						
Braintree Freeport	d					20 46											21 46						
Braintree	a					20 50											21 50						
Kelvedon	d				20 28						20 51					21 27							21 51
Marks Tey 2	d				20 34						20 57					21 33							21 57
Colchester 4	a		20 22	20 32	20 41		20 46				21 04	21 15			21 22	21 40			21 46				22 04
	d	20 20	20 23	20 32	20 42		20 47			20 56	21 04	21 16		21 20	21 23	21 41			21 48			21 56	22 04
Colchester Town	a	20 27			20 50					21 03				21 27		21 49						22 03	
	d									21 07												22 07	
Hythe	d									21 11												22 11	
Wivenhoe	d									21 15		21 24										22 15	
Alresford (Essex)	d									21 19												22 19	
Great Bentley	d									21 23												22 23	
Weeley	d									21 26			←									22 26	
Thorpe-le-Soken 1	a									21 31		21 35	21 31									22 31	
	d									21 37		21 35	21 37									22 37	
Clacton-on-Sea	a									→		21 44										→	
Kirby Cross	d												21 42										
Frinton-on-Sea	d												21 45										
Walton-on-the-Naze	a												21 49										
Manningtree 5	d		20 31	20 40			20 55		21 00		21 12				21 32				21 56		22 00		22 12
Mistley	d								21 04												22 04		
Wrabness	d								21 09												22 09		
Harwich International	d			20a56					21 17									21 38			22 17		22a28
Dovercourt	d								21 20												22 20		
Harwich Town	a								21 22												22 22		
Ipswich	a		20 43				21 07				21 25				21 43			22 05	22 08				
	d		20 44				21 08	21 17							21 45					22 19			
Needham Market	d							21 27												22 29			
Stowmarket	d		20 55					21a33							21 56					22a35			
Diss	d		21 08				21 29								22 09								
Norwich	a		21 27				21 50								22 29								

A To Cambridge
B To Walton-on-the-Naze
C From Colchester
D To Peterborough
E To Lowestoft
F To Bury St Edmunds

Table T011-F

Saturdays
21 December to 16 May

London - Chelmsford, Colchester, Walton-on-Naze, Clacton, Harwich, Ipswich and Norwich

Station		LE ◇■	LE ■ A	LE ◇■ 🍴	LE ■	LE ■	LE ■	LE ■	LE ■ B	LE ■ C	LE ■	LE ◇■	LE ■ A	LE ◇■ 🍴	LE ■	LE	LE ■	LE	LE	LE ◇■ 🍴	LE
London Liverpool Street 15 ⊖	d	21 18		21 30	21 38	21 48	22 00				22 02	22 18		22 30		22 38		23 02	23 18	23 30	23 48
Stratford 7 ⊖	d	21 25		21u38	21 45	21 55					22 09	22 25		22u38		22 45		23 09	23 25	23u38	23 55
Romford	d				21 53																
Shenfield 3	d	21 41			22 03	22 11					22 25	22 41				23 01		23 25	23 41		00 11
Ingatestone	d	21 45				22 15						22 45				23 05			23 45		00 16
Chelmsford	d	21 52		22 03	22 12	22 22	22 28				22 34	22 52		23 03		23 12		23 35	23 52	00 03	00 23
Hatfield Peverel	d										22 40							23 41			00 29
Witham 2	d	22 03			22 23	22 34					22 47	23 03				23 23	23 25	23 47	00 03		00 35
White Notley	d					22 41											23 32				
Cressing	d					22 43											23 34				
Braintree Freeport	d					22 46											23 37				
Braintree	a					22 50											23 41				
Kelvedon	d				22 27						22 51					23 27		23 52			00 40
Marks Tey 2	d				22 33						22 57					23 33		23 57			00 45
Colchester 4	a	22 15		22 22	22 40		22 47				23 05	23 15		23 22		23 47		00 04	00 15	00 22	00 59
	d	22 16		22 23	22 41		22 48			22 56		23 16		23 23				00 05	00 16	00 23	
Colchester Town	a				22 49					23 03											
	d									23 07											
Hythe	d									23 11									00 20		
Wivenhoe	d	22 24								23 15		23 24							00 24		
Alresford (Essex)	d									23 19									00 28		
Great Bentley	d									23 23									00 32		
Weeley	d		←							23 26			←								
Thorpe-le-Soken 1	a	22 35	22 31							23 31		23 35	23 31						00 39		
	d	22 35	22 37						23 16	23 37		23 35	23 37						00 39		
Clacton-on-Sea	a	22 44							23 25	→		23 44							00 54		
Kirby Cross	d		22 42										23 42								
Frinton-on-Sea	d		22 45										23 45								
Walton-on-the-Naze	a		22 49										23 49								
Manningtree 5	d			22 32			22 56	23 00						23 32	23 36			00 13		00 32	
Mistley	d							23 04							23 40						
Wrabness	d							23 09							23 45						
Harwich International	d							23 17							23 53						
Dovercourt	d							23 20							23 56						
Harwich Town	a							23 22							23 58						
Ipswich	a			22 44			23 08							23 44				00 30		00 44	
	d			22 45										23 45						00 45	
Needham Market	d																				
Stowmarket	d			22 57										23 57						00 57	
Diss	d			23 11										00 11						01 11	
Norwich	a			23 30										00 36						01 36	

Sundays
15 December to 10 May

Station		LE D	LE ■	LE ■	LE E	LE ■	LE E	LE ■	LE ■	LE ■	LE ■	LE ■	LE ■	LE E	LE ■	LE ■	LE ■	LE ◇■	LE F	LE E	LE ■	LE ■	LE ■
London Liverpool Street 15 ⊖	d			00 18											07 57	08 00		08 27				08 30	
Stratford 7 ⊖	d			00 25											08 04	08 07						08 37	
Romford	d															08 20							
Shenfield 3	d			00 47											08 31	08 34						09 04	
Ingatestone	d			00 52												08 39							
Chelmsford	d			00 59											08 42	08 46						09 13	
Hatfield Peverel	d			01 05												08 52							
Witham 2	d		00 09	01 11				07 35				08 25			08 53	08 58						09 24	09 27
White Notley	d		00 16					07 42				08 32											09 34
Cressing	d		00 18					07 44				08 34											09 36
Braintree Freeport	d		00 21					07 47				08 37											09 39
Braintree	a		00 25					07 51				08 41											09 43
Kelvedon	d			01 16												09 03							
Marks Tey 2	d			01 21												09 08						09 31	
Colchester 4	a			01 35											09 05	09 15		09 27				09 39	
	d	00 05				07 30			08 13		08 18		08 37		09 05	09 16		09 28	09 32			09 39	
Colchester Town	a																						
	d																						
Hythe	d												08 42									09 44	
Wivenhoe	d												08 46									09 48	
Alresford (Essex)	d												08 49									09 51	
Great Bentley	d												08 53									09 55	
Weeley	d																						
Thorpe-le-Soken 1	a												09 00									10 02	
	d												09 00								09 02	10 02	
Clacton-on-Sea	a												09 09									10 12	
Kirby Cross	d																				09 07		
Frinton-on-Sea	d																				09 10		
Walton-on-the-Naze	a																				09 14		
Manningtree 5	d	00 13				07 38			08 21		08 26				09 14	09 24	09 26		09 40				
Mistley	d										08 30						09 30						
Wrabness	d										08 35						09 35						
Harwich International	d										08 43			08 50	09a30		09 43						
Dovercourt	d										08 46						09 46						
Harwich Town	a										08 48						09 48						
Ipswich	a	00 30				07 50			08 33					09 14		09 36		09 45	09 51				
	d				07 34		08 20			08 46				09 20				09 46	09 55	10 20			
Needham Market	d				07 44		08 29							09 29						10 29			
Stowmarket	d				07a49		08a35			08 57				09a35				09 57	10a07	10a35			
Diss	d									09 10								10 10					
Norwich	a									09 30								10 30					

A From Colchester
B From Walton-on-the-Naze
C To Walton-on-the-Naze
D not 15 December. From London Liverpool Street
E To Cambridge
F To Peterborough

Table T011-F

Sundays

15 December to 10 May

London - Chelmsford, Colchester, Walton-on-Naze, Clacton, Harwich, Ipswich and Norwich

		LE ■	LE ■	LE ◇■ 🍴	LE A	LE ■	LE ◇■	LE ■	LE ■	LE ■	LE ◇■ 🍴	LE ■	LE ◇■	LE ■	LE B	LE ◇■	LE A	LE ■	LE ■	LE ◇■ 🍴	LE A	LE ■	LE ◇■
London Liverpool Street 15 ⊖	d	09 08		09 30			09 38		10 08		10 30		10 38			11 00		11 08		11 30			11 38
Stratford 7 ⊖	d	09 15		09u38			09 45		10 15		10u38		10 45					11 15		11u38			11 45
Romford	d																						
Shenfield 3	d	09 32					10 02		10 32				11 02					11 32					12 02
Ingatestone	d	09 36							10 36									11 36					
Chelmsford	d	09 43					10 11		10 43				11 11					11 43					12 11
Hatfield Peverel	d	09 49							10 49									11 49					
Witham 2	d	09 56					10 22	10 25	10 56				11 22	11 25				11 56					12 22
White Notley	d							10 32						11 32									
Cressing	d							10 34						11 34									
Braintree Freeport	d							10 37						11 37									
Braintree	a							10 41						11 41									
Kelvedon	d	10 00							11 00									12 00					
Marks Tey 2	d	10 06					10 29		11 06				11 29					12 06					12 29
Colchester 4	a	10 13		10 19			10 37		11 13		11 19		11 37			11 45		12 13		12 19			12 37
	d	10 13		10 20			10 37		11 13		11 20		11 37			11 47		12 13		12 20			12 37
Colchester Town	a																						
	d																						
Hythe	d						10 42						11 42										12 42
Wivenhoe	d						10 46						11 46										12 46
Alresford (Essex)	d						10 49						11 49										12 49
Great Bentley	d						10 53						11 53										12 53
Weeley	d																						
Thorpe-le-Soken 1	a						11 00						12 00										13 00
	d					10 04	11 00					11 02	12 00									12 02	13 00
Clacton-on-Sea	a						11 10						12 10										13 10
Kirby Cross	d					10 09						11 07										12 07	
Frinton-on-Sea	d					10 12						11 10										12 10	
Walton-on-the-Naze	a					10 16						11 14										12 14	
Manningtree 5	d	10 21	10 26	10 29					11 21	11 26	11 29							12 21	12 26	12 29			
Mistley	d		10 30							11 30									12 30				
Wrabness	d		10 35							11 35									12 35				
Harwich International	d		10 43							11 43									12 43				
Dovercourt	d		10 46							11 46									12 46				
Harwich Town	a		10 48							11 48									12 48				
Ipswich	a	10 35		10 40					11 35		11 40					12 03		12 35		12 40			
	d			10 41	11 20						11 41				11 55	12 05	12 20			12 41	13 20		
Needham Market	d				11 29												12 29				13 29		
Stowmarket	d			10 53	11a35						11 53				12a07	12 17	12a35			12 53	13a35		
Diss	d			11 06							12 06					12 30				13 06			
Norwich	a			11 27							12 27					12 52				13 27			

		LE ■	LE ■	LE ■	LE ◇■ 🍴	LE ■	LE ◇■	LE ■	LE B	LE ■	LE A	LE ■	LE ■	LE ◇■ 🍴	LE A	LE ◇■	LE ■	LE ■	LE ■	LE ◇■ 🍴	LE ■	LE ◇■
London Liverpool Street 15 ⊖	d		12 08		12 30		12 38					13 08		13 30		13 38		14 08		14 30		14 38
Stratford 7 ⊖	d		12 15		12u38		12 45					13 15		13u38		13 45		14 15		14u38		14 45
Romford	d																					
Shenfield 3	d		12 32				13 02					13 32				14 02		14 32				15 02
Ingatestone	d		12 36									13 36						14 36				
Chelmsford	d		12 43				13 11					13 43				14 11		14 43				15 11
Hatfield Peverel	d		12 49									13 49						14 49				
Witham 2	d	12 25	12 56				13 22	13 25				13 56				14 22	14 25	14 56				15 22
White Notley	d	12 32						13 32									14 32					
Cressing	d	12 34						13 34									14 34					
Braintree Freeport	d	12 37						13 37									14 37					
Braintree	a	12 41						13 41									14 41					
Kelvedon	d		13 00									14 00						15 00				
Marks Tey 2	d		13 06				13 29					14 06				14 29		15 06				15 29
Colchester 4	a		13 13		13 19		13 37					14 13		14 19		14 37		15 13		15 19		15 37
	d		13 13		13 20		13 37					14 13		14 20		14 37		15 13		15 20		15 37
Colchester Town	a																					
	d																					
Hythe	d						13 42									14 42						15 42
Wivenhoe	d						13 46									14 46						15 46
Alresford (Essex)	d						13 49									14 49						15 49
Great Bentley	d						13 53									14 53						15 53
Weeley	d																					
Thorpe-le-Soken 1	a						14 00									15 00						16 00
	d					13 02	14 00			14 02						15 00					15 02	16 00
Clacton-on-Sea	a						14 10									15 10						16 10
Kirby Cross	d					13 07				14 07											15 07	
Frinton-on-Sea	d					13 10				14 10											15 10	
Walton-on-the-Naze	a					13 14				14 14											15 14	
Manningtree 5	d		13 21	13 26	13 29							14 21	14 26	14 29				15 21	15 26	15 29		
Mistley	d			13 30									14 30						15 30			
Wrabness	d			13 35									14 35						15 35			
Harwich International	d			13 43									14 43						15 43			
Dovercourt	d			13 46									14 46						15 46			
Harwich Town	a			13 48									14 48						15 48			
Ipswich	a		13 34		13 40							14 34		14 39				15 36		15 40		
	d				13 41				13 55		14 20			14 41	15 20					15 41		
Needham Market	d										14 29				15 29							
Stowmarket	d				13 53				14a07		14a35			14 52	15a35					15 53		
Diss	d				14 06									15 05						16 06		
Norwich	a				14 27									15 29						16 27		

A To Cambridge

B To Peterborough

Table T011-F

Sundays

15 December to 10 May

London - Chelmsford, Colchester, Walton-on-Naze, Clacton, Harwich, Ipswich and Norwich

		LE ■	LE A	LE ■	LE B	LE ■	LE ■	LE ◇■ 🍴	LE B	LE ◇■	LE ■	LE ■	LE ■	LE ◇■ 🍴	LE ■	LE ◇■	LE ■	LE A	LE ■	LE B	LE ■	LE ■	LE ◇■ 🍴
London Liverpool Street 15 ⊖	d					15 08		15 30		15 38		16 08		16 30		16 38					17 08		17 30
Stratford 7 ⊖	d					15 15		15u38		15 45		16 15		16u38		16 45					17 15		17u38
Romford	d																						
Shenfield 3	d					15 32				16 02		16 32				17 02					17 32		
Ingatestone	d					15 36						16 36									17 36		
Chelmsford	d					15 43				16 11		16 43				17 11					17 43		
Hatfield Peverel	d					15 49						16 49									17 49		
Witham 2	d	15 25				15 56				16 22	16 25	16 56				17 22	17 25				17 56		
White Notley	d	15 32									16 32						17 32						
Cressing	d	15 34									16 34						17 34						
Braintree Freeport	d	15 37									16 37						17 37						
Braintree	a	15 41									16 41						17 41						
Kelvedon	d					16 00						17 00									18 00		
Marks Tey 2	d					16 06				16 29		17 06				17 29					18 06		
Colchester 4	a					16 13		16 19		16 37		17 13		17 19		17 37					18 13		18 19
	d					16 13		16 20		16 37		17 13		17 20		17 37					18 13		18 20
Colchester Town	a																						
	d																						
Hythe	d									16 42						17 42							
Wivenhoe	d									16 46						17 46							
Alresford (Essex)	d									16 49						17 49							
Great Bentley	d									16 53						17 53							
Weeley	d																						
Thorpe-le-Soken 1	a									17 00						18 00							
	d			16 02						17 00					17 02	18 00			18 02				
Clacton-on-Sea	a									17 10						18 10							
Kirby Cross	d			16 07											17 07				18 07				
Frinton-on-Sea	d			16 10											17 10				18 10				
Walton-on-the-Naze	a			16 14											17 14				18 14				
Manningtree 5	d					16 21	16 26	16 29				17 21	17 26	17 29							18 21	18 26	18 29
Mistley	d						16 30						17 30									18 30	
Wrabness	d						16 35						17 35									18 35	
Harwich International	d						16 43						17 43									18 43	
Dovercourt	d						16 46						17 46									18 46	
Harwich Town	a						16 48						17 48									18 48	
Ipswich	a					16 34		16 40				17 35		17 40							18 34		18 40
	d		15 55		16 20			16 41	17 20					17 41				17 55		18 20			18 41
Needham Market	d				16 29				17 29											18 29			
Stowmarket	d		16a07		16a35			16 53	17a35					17 53				18a07		18a35			18 53
Diss	d							17 06						18 06									19 06
Norwich	a							17 27						18 28									19 27

		LE ◇■	LE ■	LE ◇	LE B	LE ■	LE ■	LE ◇■ 🍴	LE ■	LE ◇■	LE ■	LE ◇■ 🍴	LE ■	LE ■	LE ◇■ 🍴	LE B	LE ■	LE ◇■	LE ■	LE ■	LE ■	LE ■
London Liverpool Street 15 ⊖	d	17 38		18 00		18 08		18 30		18 38		19 00	19 08		19 30			19 38		20 00	20 08	
Stratford 7 ⊖	d	17 45				18 15		18u38		18 45			19 15		19u38			19 45		20 07	20 15	
Romford	d																					
Shenfield 3	d	18 02				18 32				19 02			19 32					20 02		20 23	20 32	
Ingatestone	d					18 36							19 36								20 36	
Chelmsford	d	18 11				18 43				19 11			19 43					20 11		20 33	20 43	
Hatfield Peverel	d					18 49							19 49								20 49	
Witham 2	d	18 22	18 25			18 56				19 22	19 25		19 56					20 22	20 25	20 43	20 56	
White Notley	d		18 32								19 32								20 32			
Cressing	d		18 34								19 34								20 34			
Braintree Freeport	d		18 37								19 37								20 37			
Braintree	a		18 41								19 41								20 41			
Kelvedon	d					19 00							20 00								21 00	
Marks Tey 2	d	18 29				19 06				19 29			20 06					20 29			21 06	
Colchester 4	a	18 37		18 45		19 13		19 19		19 37		19 45	20 13		20 19			20 37		20 55	21 13	
	d	18 37		18 47		19 13		19 20		19 37		19 47	20 13		20 20			20 37		20 56	21 13	
Colchester Town	a																					
	d																					
Hythe	d	18 42								19 42								20 42				
Wivenhoe	d	18 46								19 46								20 46				
Alresford (Essex)	d	18 49								19 49								20 49				
Great Bentley	d	18 53								19 53								20 53				
Weeley	d																					
Thorpe-le-Soken 1	a	19 00								20 00								21 00				
	d	19 00							19 02	20 00							20 02	21 00				
Clacton-on-Sea	a	19 10								20 10								21 10				
Kirby Cross	d								19 07								20 07					
Frinton-on-Sea	d								19 10								20 10					
Walton-on-the-Naze	a								19 14								20 14					
Manningtree 5	d					19 21	19 26	19 29				19 56	20 21	20 26	20 29					21 04	21 21	21 26
Mistley	d						19 30							20 30								21 30
Wrabness	d						19 35							20 35								21 35
Harwich International	d						19 43							20 43						21a24		21 43
Dovercourt	d						19 46							20 46								21 46
Harwich Town	a						19 48							20 48								21 48
Ipswich	a			19 03		19 34		19 40				20 06	20 34		20 40						21 34	
	d			19 05	19 20			19 41				20 08			20 41	21 05						
Needham Market	d				19 29											21 14						
Stowmarket	d			19 16	19a35			19 53				20 19			20 53	21a20						
Diss	d			19 29				20 06				20 32			21 06							
Norwich	a			19 51				20 27				20 54			21 27							

A To Peterborough

B To Cambridge

Table T011-F

Sundays

15 December to 10 May

London - Chelmsford, Colchester, Walton-on-Naze, Clacton, Harwich, Ipswich and Norwich

		LE	LE	LE	LE	LE	LE	LE	LE	LE	LE	LE	LE	LE	LE	LE	LE	LE	LE	LE
		◇1 ⊏	1	◇1	1		1	1	◇1 ⊏	1	◇1	1	1	◇1 ⊏	1	◇1	1	1	◇1	1
London Liverpool Street 15 ⊖	d	20 30		20 38			21 08		21 30		21 38		22 08	22 30		22 38		23 08	23 30	23 32
Stratford 7 ⊖	d	20u38		20 45			21 15		21u38		21 45		22 15	22u38		22 45		23 15		23 39
Romford	d																			
Shenfield 3	d			21 02			21 32				22 02		22 32			23 02		23 32		23 57
Ingatestone	d						21 36						22 36					23 36		
Chelmsford	d			21 11			21 43				22 11		22 43			23 11		23 43		00 07
Hatfield Peverel	d						21 49						22 49					23 49		
Witham 2	d			21 22	21 25		21 56				22 22	22 25	22 56			23 22	23 25	23 56		00 17
White Notley	d				21 32							22 32					23 32			
Cressing	d				21 34							22 34					23 34			
Braintree Freeport	d				21 37							22 37					23 37			
Braintree	a				21 41							22 41					23 41			
Kelvedon	d						22 00						23 00					23 59		
Marks Tey 2	d			21 29			22 06				22 29		23 06			23 29		00 06		00 25
Colchester 4	a	21 19		21 37			22 13		22 19		22 37		23 13	23 19		23 37		00 13	00 22	00 39
	d	21 20		21 37			22 13		22 20		22 37		23 13	23 20		23 37		00 13	00 26	
Colchester Town	a																			
	d																			
Hythe	d			21 42							22 42					23 42				
Wivenhoe	d			21 46							22 46					23 46				
Alresford (Essex)	d			21 49							22 49					23 49				
Great Bentley	d			21 53							22 53					23 53				
Weeley	d																			
Thorpe-le-Soken 1	a			22 00							23 00					23 59				
	d		21 02	22 00						22 02	23 00				23 02	23 59				
Clacton-on-Sea	a			22 10							23 10					00 15				
Kirby Cross	d		21 07							22 07					23 07					
Frinton-on-Sea	d		21 10							22 10					23 10					
Walton-on-the-Naze	a		21 14							22 14					23 14					
Manningtree 5	d	21 29					22 21	22 26	22 30				23 21	23 30				00 21	00 36	
Mistley	d							22 30												
Wrabness	d							22 35												
Harwich International	d					21 38		22 43												
Dovercourt	d							22 46												
Harwich Town	a							22 48												
Ipswich	a	21 40				22 05	22 34		22 40				23 34	23 40				00 39	00 46	
	d	21 41							22 42					23 42					00 48	
Needham Market	d																			
Stowmarket	d	21 53							22 54					23 54					01 00	
Diss	d	22 06							23 07					00 07					01 13	
Norwich	a	22 27							23 30					00 27					01 38	

Table T011-R

Mondays to Fridays

16 December to 15 May

Norwich, Ipswich, Harwich, Clacton, Walton-on-Naze, Colchester and Chelmsford - London

Miles	Miles	Miles	Miles	Miles			LE MX	LE	LE	LE	LE	LE	LE	LE	LE	LE	LE	LE	LE	LE	LE	LE	LE
							1	1	1	◇1	1	1	◇1	◇	1	1	◇1	1	A	1	1	1 ⊏	◇1
0	—	—	—	—	**Norwich**	d								05 00								05 30	
20	—	—	—	—	Diss	d								05 18								05 48	
34¼	—	—	—	—	Stowmarket	d								05 30					05 51			06 00	
38	—	—	—	—	Needham Market	d													05 56				
46¼	—	—	0	—	**Ipswich**	a								05 42					06 07			06 12	
—	—	—	—	—		d				05 12				05 44				06 00				06 14	
—	0	—	—	—	**Harwich Town**	d					05 24												
—	0½	—	—	—	Dovercourt	d					05 26												
—	1¾	—	—	—	Harwich International	d					05 29												
—	5½	—	—	—	Wrabness	d					05 35												
—	9½	—	10½	—	Mistley	d					05 41												
55½	11¼	—	—	—	Manningtree 5	d				05 24	05a46			05 54				06 11				06 24	
—	—	0	—	—	**Walton-on-the-Naze**	d									05 33					06 03			
—	—	1¼	—	—	Frinton-on-Sea	d									05 36					06 06			
—	—	2½	—	—	Kirby Cross	d									05 39					06 09			
—	—	—	0	—	**Clacton-on-Sea**	d							05 20				05 40						06 10
—	—	5	4¾	—	Thorpe-le-Soken 1	a							05 28		05 45		05 48			06 15			06 18
—	—	—	—	—		d							05 28				05 48						06 18
—	—	7¼	—	—	Weeley	d											05 52						
—	—	10	—	—	Great Bentley	d											05 56						
—	—	12¼	—	—	Alresford (Essex)	d											06 00						
—	—	14	—	—	Wivenhoe	d							05 38				06 04						06 29
—	—	16½	—	—	Hythe	d											06 08						06 33
—	—	18	—	—	Colchester Town	a																	
—	—	—	—	—		d															06 19		
63¼	—	19¾	—	—	**Colchester** 4	a				05 33			05 46	06 03			06 14	06 20			06 26	06 33	06 39
—	—	—	—	—		d		04 43	05 12	05 34			05 47	06 05			06 15	06 20			06 27	06 35	06 40
68¼	—	—	—	—	Marks Tey 2	d		04 49	05 18				05 53					06 26			06 33		
72¾	—	—	—	—	Kelvedon	d		04 54	05 23				05 59				06 25	06 32					06 50
—	—	—	—	0	**Braintree**	d	00 27					05 43											
—	—	—	—	0¾	Braintree Freeport	d	00 29					05 45											
—	—	—	—	2	Cressing	d	00 32					05 48											
—	—	—	—	3¼	White Notley	d	00 35					05 51											
76½	—	—	—	6¼	**Witham** 2	d	00a43	05 00	05 29	05 48		06a00	06 05			06 18	06 31	06 38			06 47		
79	—	—	—	—	Hatfield Peverel	d		05 04	05 33							06 22							
85¼	—	—	—	—	**Chelmsford**	d		05 11	05 40	05 58			06 14			06 29	06 40	06 47			06 56		07 03
91½	—	—	—	—	Ingatestone	d		05 18	05 47							06 36					07 03		
94¾	—	—	—	—	Shenfield 3	a		05 23	05 52				06 24			06 42	06 50				07 08		
102¾	—	—	—	—	Romford	a		05 32															
111	—	—	—	—	Stratford 7 ⊖	a		05 45	06 08	06s23			06 40	06s45		06s59	07s07				07s24	07s16	07s28
115	—	—	—	—	**London Liverpool Street** 15 ⊖	a		05 53	06 16	06 34			06 48	06 54		07 09	07 18	07 23			07 35	07 27	07 38

		LE	LE	LE	LE	LE	LE	LE	LE	LE	LE	LE	LE	LE	LE	LE	LE	LE	LE	LE	LE	LE
		1	1	1	1	1 ⊏	1	1	1	◇1	◇1	A	1	B	1	◇1	1 ⊏	1	1	1	1	◇1
Norwich	d					06 00											06 24					
Diss	d					06 18											06 42					
Stowmarket	d					06 30						06 42					06 54					
Needham Market	d											06 47										
Ipswich	a					06 42						06 58					07 06					
	d		06 29			06 44					06 52			06 59			07 08					
Harwich Town	d			06 24									06 52									
Dovercourt	d			06 26									06 54									
Harwich International	d			06 29									06 57	07a26								
Wrabness	d			06 35									07 03									
Mistley	d			06 41									07 09									
Manningtree 5	d		06 39	06a46		06 54					07 02		07a14				07 18					
Walton-on-the-Naze	d							06 31											06 58			
Frinton-on-Sea	d							06 34											07 01			
Kirby Cross	d							06 37											07 04			
Clacton-on-Sea	d						06 28			06 38						06 47		06 51				07 05
Thorpe-le-Soken 1	a						06 36	06 43		06 46						06 55		06 59	07 10			07 13
	d						06 36			06 46						06 55		06 59				07 13
Weeley	d						06 40											07 03				
Great Bentley	d						06 43											07 06				
Alresford (Essex)	d						06 47											07 10				
Wivenhoe	d						06 51			06 57						07 06		07 14				07 24
Hythe	d						06 55			07 01						07 10		07 18				
Colchester Town	a						06 59											07 22				
	d				06 47		07 03											07 27				
Colchester 4	a		06 48		06 54	07 03	07 13			07 07	07 12					07 16	07 28	07 36				07 32
	d		06 49		06 55	07 05				07 08	07 13					07 17	07 30					07 33
Marks Tey 2	d		06 55		07 01						07 19					07 23						
Kelvedon	d		07 00							07 18						07 29						07 43
Braintree	d	06 40																			07 26	
Braintree Freeport	d	06 42																			07 28	
Cressing	d	06 45																			07 31	
White Notley	d	06 48																			07 34	
Witham 2	d	06 57	07 06		07 10				07 17						07 29	07 35					07 43	07 50
Hatfield Peverel	d	07 02													07 33						07 48	
Chelmsford	d	07 09			07 19				07 27	07 31	07 35				07 40					07 49	07 55	07 59
Ingatestone	d								07 33		07 42									07 56		
Shenfield 3	a	07 19							07 39	07 41					07 50					08 01		08 09
Romford	a																					
Stratford 7 ⊖	a	07s36	07s39		07s45				07s56	07s59	08s02				08s08	08s10				08s19	08s21	08s26
London Liverpool Street 15 ⊖	a	07 46	07 50		07 56	07 58			08 07	08 09	08 13				08 19	08 22	08 24			08 30	08 32	08 38

A From Bury St Edmunds

B From Lowestoft

Table T011-R

Mondays to Fridays

16 December to 15 May

Norwich, Ipswich, Harwich, Clacton, Walton-on-Naze, Colchester and Chelmsford - London

Station		LE ◇1	LE 1	LE 1	LE R 1 🍴	LE 1	LE 1	LE ◇1	LE R 1 🍴	LE A	LE 1	LE 1	LE 1	LE 1	LE R 1 B 🍴	LE 1	LE 1	LE ◇1	LE 1	LE 1	LE ◇1 C	LE ◇1	LE R 1 🍴
Norwich	d				06 48				07 05						07 40								08 00
Diss	d				07 06				07 23						07 58								08 17
Stowmarket	d	07 03			07 18				07 35	07 45								08 10					08 29
Needham Market	d									07 50													
Ipswich	a	07 16			07 30				07 47	08 01					08 18			08 24					08 41
	d	07 17			07 32			07 38	07 49						08 20			08 26					08 43
Harwich Town	d					07 16										07 58			08 28				
Dovercourt	d					07 18										08 00			08 30				
Harwich International	d			07 15		07 21										08 03			08 33				
Wrabness	d					07 27										08 09			08 39				
Mistley	d					07 33										08 15			08 45				
Manningtree 5	d	07 27		07 31	07 43	07 38		07 49	07 59							08 20		08 36	08a50				08 53
Walton-on-the-Naze	d																08 00				07 38		
Frinton-on-Sea	d																08 03				07 41		
Kirby Cross	d																08 06				07 44		
Clacton-on-Sea	d						07 16							07 45								08 11	
Thorpe-le-Soken 1	a						07 24							07 53			08 11				07 50	08 19	
	d						07 24							07 53			08 12				07 58	08 19	
Weeley	d						07 28														08 02	08 23	
Great Bentley	d						07 31														08 05	08 26	
Alresford (Essex)	d						07 35														08 09	08 30	
Wivenhoe	d						07 39							08 03			08 22				08 13	08 34	
Hythe	d						07 43										08 26				08 17	08 38	
Colchester Town	a																				08 21		
	d												08 00								08 32		
Colchester 4	a	07 37		07 41		07 47	07 50	07 58	08 08				08 09	08 16		08 29	08 35	08 45			08 40	08 46	09 02
	d	07 38		07 42		07 54		07 59	08 10				08 18			08 37		08 45			08 48		09 03
Marks Tey 2	d	07 44		07 48				08 05					08 24								08 54		
Kelvedon	d	07 49				08 04		08 10					08 30								09 00		
Braintree	d											08 12											
Braintree Freeport	d											08 14											
Cressing	d											08 17											
White Notley	d											08 20											
Witham 2	d	07 55		08 03		08 10		08 16				08 28	08 36			08 50				08 58	09 06		
Hatfield Peverel	d			08 07								08 32								09 02			
Chelmsford	d		08 09	08 14		08 19					08 30	08 39	08 45			08 59		09 04		09 09	09 15		09 21
Ingatestone	d		08 16								08 37	08 46								09 16			
Shenfield 3	a		08 21	08 24		08 29					08 42	08 51	08 55			09 09				09 21	09 25		
Romford	a																						
Stratford 7 ⊖ ⛴	a	08s29	08s39	08s41		08s46		08s49	08s53		09s00	09s09				09s26		09s29		09s38	09s42		09s49
London Liverpool Street 15 ⊖	a	08 40	08 50	08 54	08 42	08 58		09 01	09 04		09 11	09 19	09 21		09 24	09 36		09 39		09 50	09 54		10 00

Station		LE 1	LE 1	LE ◇1	LE A	LE R 1 🍴	LE 1 D	LE ◇1	LE ◇1	LE E	LE R	LE 1	LE 1 F	LE 1	LE R 1 🍴	LE 1	LE 1	LE 1	LE A	LE ◇1 🍴	LE 1	LE 1 D
Norwich	d					08 30					09 00				09 03					09 30		
Diss	d					08 47									09 21					09 47		
Stowmarket	d				08 45					09 12					09 33				09 48			
Needham Market	d				08 50														09 53			
Ipswich	a				09 03	09 08				09 26	09 33				09 45				10 04	10 08		
	d			08 58		09 09			09 23		09 33				09 47			09 52		10 09		
Harwich Town	d													09 28							10 28	
Dovercourt	d													09 30							10 30	
Harwich International	d													09 33							10 33	
Wrabness	d													09 39							10 39	
Mistley	d													09 45							10 45	
Manningtree 5	d			09 08		09 19			09 33					09 50				10 03		10 19	10a50	
Walton-on-the-Naze	d						09 00															10 00
Frinton-on-Sea	d						09 03															10 03
Kirby Cross	d						09 06															10 06
Clacton-on-Sea	d							09 05					←									
Thorpe-le-Soken 1	a						09 12	09 13					09 12									10 12
	d						09 17	09 13					09 17									10 17
Weeley	d						→						09 21									→
Great Bentley	d												09 24									
Alresford (Essex)	d												09 28									
Wivenhoe	d							09 23					09 32									
Hythe	d												09 36									
Colchester Town	a												09 40									
	d		08 58									09 35	09 44			10 00						
Colchester 4	a		09 05	09 17		09 28		09 31	09 42			09 43	09 53	09 59	10 02	10 08		10 12		10 28		
	d		09 07	09 17		09 30		09 33	09 50						10 04			10 12		10 30		
Marks Tey 2	d		09 13						09 56									10 18				
Kelvedon	d		09 19						10 01									10 24				
Braintree	d	09 00															10 00					
Braintree Freeport	d	09 02															10 02					
Cressing	d	09 05															10 05					
White Notley	d	09 08															10 08					
Witham 2	d	09 16	09 29					09 45	10 07								10 16	10 29				
Hatfield Peverel	d		09 33															10 33				
Chelmsford	d	09 26	09 40					09 54	10 16						10 21		10 26	10 40				
Ingatestone	d	09 32						10 01	10 23													
Shenfield 3	a	09 38	09 50					10 07	10 28								10 36	10 51				
Romford	a																					
Stratford 7 ⊖ ⛴	a	09 54	10 07	10 01				10 27							10s47		10 51	11 08				
London Liverpool Street 15 ⊖	a	10 03	10 17	10 10		10 21		10 35	10 51		10 30				10 56		11 00	11 16		11 19		

A From Cambridge
B The East Anglian
C ◇ from Colchester
D To Colchester
E From Peterborough
F From Walton-on-the-Naze

Table T011-R

Mondays to Fridays

16 December to 15 May

Norwich, Ipswich, Harwich, Clacton, Walton-on-Naze, Colchester and Chelmsford - London

Station		LE ◇1	LE 1	LE 1 A	LE ◇1 🍴	LE 1	LE 1	LE 1	LE B	LE ◇1 🍴	LE C	LE 1	LE 1 D	LE ◇1	LE 1	LE 1 A	LE ◇1 🍴	LE 1	LE 1	LE 1	LE B	LE ◇1 🍴	LE 1
Norwich	d				10 00					10 30							11 00					11 30	
Diss	d				10 17					10 47							11 17					11 47	
Stowmarket	d				10 29				10 48		11 14						11 29				11 47		
Needham Market	d								10 53												11 52		
Ipswich	a				10 41				11 03	11 08	11 28						11 41				12 02	12 08	
	d				10 43			10 52		11 09							11 43			11 48		12 09	
Harwich Town	d											11 28											12 28
Dovercourt	d											11 30											12 30
Harwich International	d											11 33											12 33
Wrabness	d											11 39											12 39
Mistley	d											11 45											12 45
Manningtree 5	d				10 53			11 02		11 19		11a50					11 53			11 58		12 19	12a50
Walton-on-the-Naze	d												11 00										
Frinton-on-Sea	d												11 03										
Kirby Cross	d												11 06										
Clacton-on-Sea	d	10 05		←										11 05		←							
Thorpe-le-Soken 1	a	10 13		10 12									11 12	11 13		11 12							
	d	10 13		10 17									11 17	11 13		11 17							
Weeley	d			10 21									→			11 21							
Great Bentley	d			10 24												11 24							
Alresford (Essex)	d			10 28												11 28							
Wivenhoe	d	10 23		10 32										11 23		11 32							
Hythe	d			10 36												11 36							
Colchester Town	a			10 40												11 40							
	d		10 35	10 44		11 00									11 35	11 44		12 00					
Colchester 4	a	10 31	10 42	10 52	11 02	11 07		11 11		11 28				11 31	11 42	11 52	12 02	12 07		12 07		12 28	
	d	10 33	10 43		11 03			11 12		11 30				11 33	11 43		12 03			12 12		12 30	
Marks Tey 2	d		10 49					11 18							11 49					12 18			
Kelvedon	d		10 54					11 23							11 54					12 23			
Braintree	d						11 00												12 00				
Braintree Freeport	d						11 02												12 02				
Cressing	d						11 05												12 05				
White Notley	d						11 08												12 08				
Witham 2	d	10 46	11 00				11 16	11 29						11 46	12 00				12 16	12 29			
Hatfield Peverel	d							11 33												12 33			
Chelmsford	d	10 56	11 09		11 21		11 26	11 40						11 56	12 09		12 21		12 26	12 40			
Ingatestone	d	11 02					11 32							12 02					12 32				
Shenfield 3	a	11 08	11 19				11 38	11 50						12 08	12 19				12 38	12 50			
Romford	a		11 28												12 28								
Stratford 7 ⊖ ⛴	a	11 23	11 37		11s46		11 52	12 06						12 23	12 37		12s46		12 52	13 06			
London Liverpool Street 15 ⊖	a	11 33	11 45		11 55		12 01	12 14		12 19				12 31	12 45		12 55		13 01	13 14		13 19	

Station		LE 1 D	LE ◇1	LE 1	LE 1 A	LE ◇1 🍴		LE 1	LE 1	LE 1	LE B	LE ◇1 🍴	LE C	LE 1	LE 1 D	LE ◇1	LE 1	LE 1 A	LE ◇1 🍴	LE 1	LE 1	LE 1	LE B	LE ◇1 🍴
Norwich	d					12 00						12 30							13 00					13 30
Diss	d					12 17						12 47							13 17					13 47
Stowmarket	d					12 29					12 47		13 14						13 29				13 47	
Needham Market	d										12 52												13 52	
Ipswich	a					12 41					13 02	13 08	13 28						13 41				14 02	14 08
	d					12 43				12 52		13 09							13 43			13 52		14 09
Harwich Town	d													13 28										
Dovercourt	d													13 30										
Harwich International	d													13 33										
Wrabness	d													13 39										
Mistley	d													13 45										
Manningtree 5	d					12 53				13 02		13 19		13a50					13 53			14 02		14 19
Walton-on-the-Naze	d	12 00													13 00									
Frinton-on-Sea	d	12 03													13 03									
Kirby Cross	d	12 06													13 06									
Clacton-on-Sea	d		12 05		←											13 05		←						
Thorpe-le-Soken 1	a	12 12	12 13		12 12										13 12	13 13		13 12						
	d	12 17	12 13		12 17										13 17	13 13		13 17						
Weeley	d	→			12 21										→			13 21						
Great Bentley	d				12 24													13 24						
Alresford (Essex)	d				12 28													13 28						
Wivenhoe	d		12 23		12 32											13 23		13 32						
Hythe	d				12 36													13 36						
Colchester Town	a				12 40													13 40						
	d			12 35	12 44			13 00									13 35	13 44		14 00				
Colchester 4	a		12 31	12 42	12 52	13 02		13 07		13 12		13 28				13 31	13 42	13 52	14 02	14 07		14 12		14 28
	d		12 33	12 43		13 03				13 12		13 30				13 33	13 43		14 03			14 12		14 30
Marks Tey 2	d			12 49						13 18							13 49					14 18		
Kelvedon	d			12 54						13 23							13 54					14 23		
Braintree	d								13 00												14 00			
Braintree Freeport	d								13 02												14 02			
Cressing	d								13 05												14 05			
White Notley	d								13 08												14 08			
Witham 2	d		12 46	13 00					13 16	13 29						13 46	14 00				14 16	14 29		
Hatfield Peverel	d									13 33												14 33		
Chelmsford	d		12 56	13 09		13 21			13 26	13 40						13 56	14 09		14 21		14 26	14 40		
Ingatestone	d		13 02						13 32							14 02					14 32			
Shenfield 3	a		13 08	13 19					13 38	13 51						14 08	14 19				14 38	14 51		
Romford	a			13 28													14 28							
Stratford 7 ⊖ ⛴	a		13 23	13 37		13s46			13 53	14 06						14 23	14 37		14s46		14 53	15 06		
London Liverpool Street 15 ⊖	a		13 31	13 45		13 55			14 03	14 14		14 19				14 31	14 47		14 55		15 01	15 14		15 19

A From Walton-on-the-Naze
B From Cambridge
C From Peterborough
D To Colchester

Table T011-R

Mondays to Fridays
16 December to 15 May

Norwich, Ipswich, Harwich, Clacton, Walton-on-Naze, Colchester and Chelmsford - London

		LE ■	LE ■ A	LE ◇■	LE ■	LE ■ B	LE ◇■ ⊡	LE ■	LE ■	LE ■	LE C	LE ◇■ ⊡	LE D	LE ■	LE ■ A	LE ◇■	LE ■	LE ■ B	LE ◇■ ⊡	LE ■	LE ■	LE ■
Norwich	d						14 00					14 30							15 00			
Diss	d						14 17					14 47							15 17			
Stowmarket	d						14 29				14 47		15 14						15 29			
Needham Market	d										14 52											
Ipswich	a						14 41				15 02	15 08	15 28						15 41			
	d						14 43			14 52		15 09							15 43			15 52
Harwich Town	d	14 28												15 28								
Dovercourt	d	14 30												15 30								
Harwich International	d	14 33												15 33								
Wrabness	d	14 39												15 39								
Mistley	d	14 45												15 45								
Manningtree ■	d	14a50					14 53			15 02		15 19		15a50					15 53			16 02
Walton-on-the-Naze	d		14 00												15 00							
Frinton-on-Sea	d		14 03												15 03							
Kirby Cross	d		14 06												15 06							
Clacton-on-Sea	d			14 05		←										15 05		←				
Thorpe-le-Soken ■	a		14 12	14 13		14 12									15 12	15 13		15 12				
	d		14 17	14 13		14 17									15 17	15 13		15 17				
Weeley	d		→			14 21									→			15 21				
Great Bentley	d					14 24												15 24				
Alresford (Essex)	d					14 28												15 28				
Wivenhoe	d			14 23		14 32										15 23		15 32				
Hythe	d					14 36												15 36				
Colchester Town	a					14 40												15 40				
	d				14 35	14 44		15 00									15 35	15 44		16 00		
Colchester ■	a			14 31	14 42	14 52	15 02	15 07		15 11		15 28				15 31	15 42	15 52	16 02	16 07		16 11
	d			14 33	14 43		15 03			15 12		15 30				15 33	15 43		16 03			16 12
Marks Tey ■	d				14 49					15 18							15 49					16 18
Kelvedon	d				14 54					15 23							15 54					16 23
Braintree	d								15 00												16 00	
Braintree Freeport	d								15 02												16 02	
Cressing	d								15 05												16 05	
White Notley	d								15 08												16 08	
Witham ■	d			14 46	15 00				15 16	15 29						15 46	16 00				16 17	16 29
Hatfield Peverel	d									15 33												16 33
Chelmsford	d			14 56	15 09		15 21		15 26	15 40						15 55	16 09		16 21		16 27	16 40
Ingatestone	d			15 02					15 32							16 02					16 34	
Shenfield ■	a			15 08	15 19				15 38	15 50						16 07	16 19				16 39	16 51
Romford	a				15 28																	
Stratford ■ ⊖ ⛴	a			15 23	15 37		15s46		15 53	16 06						16 23	16 35		16s46		16 55	17 07
London Liverpool Street ■ ⊖	a			15 31	15 45		15 55		16 01	16 14		16 17				16 31	16 44		16 57		17 03	17 16

		LE C	LE ◇■ ⊡	LE ■	LE ■ A	LE ◇■	LE ■	LE ■	LE ■ B	LE ◇■ ⊡	LE ■	LE ■	LE ■	LE C	LE ■	LE ◇■ ⊡	LE D	LE ■	LE ■	LE ■ A	LE ◇■	LE ■	LE ■
Norwich	d		15 30							16 00						16 30		17 00					
Diss	d		15 47							16 17						16 47							
Stowmarket	d	15 47								16 29				16 47			17 14						
Needham Market	d	15 52												16 52									
Ipswich	a	16 04	16 08							16 41				17 02		17 08	17 28	17 33					
	d		16 09							16 43			16 52			17 09		17 33					
Harwich Town	d			16 28											16 53				17 27				
Dovercourt	d			16 30											16 55				17 29				
Harwich International	d			16 33											16 58				17 32				
Wrabness	d			16 39											17 04				17 38				
Mistley	d			16 45											17 10				17 44				
Manningtree ■	d		16 19	16a50						16 53			17 02		17a15	17 19			17a49				
Walton-on-the-Naze	d				16 00															17 00			
Frinton-on-Sea	d				16 03															17 03			
Kirby Cross	d				16 06															17 06			
Clacton-on-Sea	d					16 05			←												17 05		
Thorpe-le-Soken ■	a				16 12	16 13			16 12											17 12	17 13		
	d				16 17	16 13			16 17											17 17	17 13		
Weeley	d				→				16 21											→			
Great Bentley	d								16 24														
Alresford (Essex)	d								16 28														
Wivenhoe	d					16 23			16 32												17 23		
Hythe	d								16 36														
Colchester Town	a								16 40														
	d						16 35		16 44		16 56												17 30
Colchester ■	a		16 28			16 31	16 42		16 54	17 02	17 05		17 11			17 28					17 31		17 37
	d		16 30			16 33	16 43	16 53		17 03			17 12			17 30					17 33		17 50
Marks Tey ■	d							16 59					17 18										17 56
Kelvedon	d						16 52						17 23										18 02
Braintree	d											17 00										17 44	
Braintree Freeport	d											17 02										17 46	
Cressing	d											17 05										17 49	
White Notley	d											17 08										17 52	
Witham ■	d					16 46	16 58	17 08				17 16	17 29								17 46	18 00	18 07
Hatfield Peverel	d						17 02						17 33										18 11
Chelmsford	d					16 56	17 09	17 17		17 21		17 26	17 40								17 56	18 09	18 18
Ingatestone	d					17 02						17 32										18 16	
Shenfield ■	a					17 08	17 19	17 27				17 38	17 50								18 06	18 21	18 28
Romford	a																						18 36
Stratford ■ ⊖ ⛴	a					17 23	17 37	17 43		17s46		17 53	18 07									18 37	18 46
London Liverpool Street ■ ⊖	a		17 19			17 34	17 46	17 53		17 58		18 03	18 18			18 21		18 30			18 34	18 45	18 56

A To Colchester
B From Walton-on-the-Naze
C From Cambridge
D From Peterborough

Table T011-R

Mondays to Fridays
16 December to 15 May

Norwich, Ipswich, Harwich, Clacton, Walton-on-Naze, Colchester and Chelmsford - London

		LE ■ A	LE ■ B	LE ◇■ ⊡	LE C	LE ■	LE ■ D	LE ■ E	LE ◇■ ⊡	LE ■	LE ■ F	LE ◇■	LE ■	LE ■	LE ■	LE ■ A	LE ■ B	LE ■	LE ■	LE ◇■ ⊡	LE ■ G	LE ■
Norwich	d			17 03					17 30											18 00		
Diss	d			17 22					17 47											18 17		
Stowmarket	d			17 34	17 48				17 59											18 29		
Needham Market	d				17 53																	
Ipswich	a			17 46	18 03				18 11											18 41		
	d		17 40	17 48					18 13						18 22					18 43		
Harwich Town	d									18 00									18 26			
Dovercourt	d									18 02									18 28			
Harwich International	d									18 05									18 31			
Wrabness	d									18 11									18 37			
Mistley	d									18 17									18 43			
Manningtree ■	d		17 51					18 14		18a22					18 33				18a48	18 53		
Walton-on-the-Naze	d										17 57											18 34
Frinton-on-Sea	d										18 00											18 37
Kirby Cross	d										18 03											18 43
Clacton-on-Sea	d	←										18 05				←		18 22				
Thorpe-le-Soken ■	a	17 12									18 09	18 13				18 09		18 30				18 49
	d	17 17									18 17	18 13				18 17		18 30				
Weeley	d	17 21									→					18 21						
Great Bentley	d	17 24														18 24						
Alresford (Essex)	d	17 28														18 28						
Wivenhoe	d	17 32										18 23				18 32		18 40				
Hythe	d	17 36														18 36		18 44				
Colchester Town	a	17 40					←									18 40		18 48				
	d	17 44											18 32			18 44		18 52				
Colchester ■	a	17 52	18 00	18 03			18 00	18 24	18 28			18 33	18 39		18 42	18 52		19 00		19 02		
	d		18 12	18 05			18 12		18 30			18 33			18 43		18 55			19 03		
Marks Tey ■	d		→				18 18								18 49		19 01					
Kelvedon	d						18 23								18 54							
Braintree	d													18 33								
Braintree Freeport	d													18 36								
Cressing	d													18 39								
White Notley	d													18 42								
Witham ■	d					18 18	18 29					18 46		18 51	19 00		19 16					
Hatfield Peverel	d						18 33							18 55							←	
Chelmsford	d			18 22		18 28	18 40					18 56		19 02	19 09		19 26			19 21	19 26	
Ingatestone	d					18 34						19 02					→				19 32	
Shenfield ■	a					18 40	18 50					19 08		19 12	19 19						19 38	
Romford	a														19 28							
Stratford ■ ⊖ ⛴	a			18s49		18 55	19 06					19 23		19 28	19 37					19s46	19 53	
London Liverpool Street ■ ⊖	a			18 58		19 03	19 14		19 17			19 33		19 36	19 45					19 55	20 01	

		LE ■	LE C	LE ■	LE ◇■ ⊡	LE ■	LE H	LE ■	LE ■ F	LE ◇■	LE ■	LE ■	LE ■ A	LE ■ B	LE ■	LE ◇■ ⊡	LE ■ D	LE C	LE ■	LE ■	LE ■	LE ◇■	LE ■
Norwich	d				18 30											19 00						19 30	
Diss	d				18 47											19 17						19 47	
Stowmarket	d		18 48				19 14									19 29		19 47					
Needham Market	d		18 53															19 52					
Ipswich	a		19 03		19 08		19 28									19 41		20 04				20 10	
	d	18 49			19 09									19 35		19 43						20 10	
Harwich Town	d					19 03									19 28								20 05
Dovercourt	d					19 05									19 30								20 07
Harwich International	d					19 08									19 33								20 10
Wrabness	d					19 14									19 39								20 16
Mistley	d					19 20									19 45								20 22
Manningtree ■	d	18 59			19 19	19a25								19 45	19a50	19 53						20 20	20a27
Walton-on-the-Naze	d								18 57		19 18												
Frinton-on-Sea	d								19 00		19 21												
Kirby Cross	d								19 03		19 24												
Clacton-on-Sea	d									19 02			←										
Thorpe-le-Soken ■	a								19 09	19 10	19 30		19 09										
	d								19 15	19 10			19 15										
Weeley	d								→				19 19										
Great Bentley	d												19 22										
Alresford (Essex)	d												19 26										
Wivenhoe	d									19 23			19 30										
Hythe	d												19 34										
Colchester Town	a												19 38										
	d			19 08								19 35	19 42						20 00				
Colchester ■	a	19 08		19 15	19 28					19 31		19 42	19 50	19 54		20 02			20 07			20 29	
	d	19 12			19 30					19 33		19 43		19 55		20 03					20 12	20 30	
Marks Tey ■	d	19 18										19 49		20 01							20 18		
Kelvedon	d	19 23										19 54									20 23		
Braintree	d							19 25												20 11			
Braintree Freeport	d							19 27												20 13			
Cressing	d							19 30												20 16			
White Notley	d							19 33												20 19			
Witham ■	d	19 29						19 42		19 46		20 00		20 16						20 27	20 31		
Hatfield Peverel	d	19 33															←				20 35		
Chelmsford	d	19 40						19 51		19 56		20 09		20 26		20 21	20 26			20 36	20 42		
Ingatestone	d									20 02				→			20 32						
Shenfield ■	a	19 50								20 08		20 19					20 38			20 46	20 52		
Romford	a											20 28											
Stratford ■ ⊖ ⛴	a	20 06						20 15		20 23		20 37				20s46	20 53				21 08		
London Liverpool Street ■ ⊖	a	20 14			20 20			20 23		20 31		20 45				20 55	21 01			21 12	21 16	21 19	

A From Walton-on-the-Naze
B To London Liverpool Street
C From Cambridge
D From Ipswich
E To Clacton-on-Sea
F To Colchester
G From Colchester
H From Peterborough

Table T011-R

Mondays to Fridays
16 December to 15 May

Norwich, Ipswich, Harwich, Clacton, Walton-on-Naze, Colchester and Chelmsford - London

		LE	LE	LE	LE	LE		LE	LE	LE	LE	LE	LE	LE	LE	LE		LE	LE	LE	LE	LE	LE	LE	LE
		1	◇1	1	1	1		1	1	◇1	1	1	1		◇1	1		◇1	1	1		1	1	◇1	
		A		B				C						D		A					E	C			D
										⊡														⊡	
Norwich	d									20 00					20 30									21 00	
Diss	d									20 17					20 47									21 17	
Stowmarket	d									20 29				20 47							21 14			21 29	21 47
Needham Market	d													20 52											21 52
Ipswich	a									20 41				21 02	21 08						21 28			21 41	22 02
	d					20 22				20 43				21 03	21 09						21 28			21 43	
Harwich Town	d								20 28										21 04				21 28		
Dovercourt	d								20 30										21 06				21 30		
Harwich International	d								20 33				20 45	21a29					21 09				21 33		
Wrabness	d								20 39										21 15				21 39		
Mistley	d								20 45										21 21				21 45		
Manningtree 5	d					20 32			20a50	20 53			20 58		21 19				21 26		21 38		21a50	21 53	
Walton-on-the-Naze	d	19 56		20 33												21 00									
Frinton-on-Sea	d	19 59		20 36												21 03									
Kirby Cross	d	20 06		20 42												21 06									
Clacton-on-Sea	d		20 05					←										21 05				←			
Thorpe-le-Soken 1	a	20 12	20 13	20 48				20 12								21 12		21 13				21 12			
	d	20 17	20 13					20 17								21 17		21 13				21 17			
Weeley	d	→						20 21								→						21 21			
Great Bentley	d							20 24														21 24			
Alresford (Essex)	d							20 28														21 28			
Wivenhoe	d		20 23					20 32										21 23				21 32			
Hythe	d							20 36														21 36			
Colchester Town	a							20 40														21 40			
	d				20 35			20 44			21 00									21 35		21 44			
Colchester 4	a		20 31		20 42	20 45		20 52		21 02	21 07		21 07		21 28			21 31	21 35	21 42	21 51	21 52		22 02	
	d		20 33		20 50					21 03			21 12		21 30			21 33		21 43				22 03	
Marks Tey 2	d				20 56								21 18							21 49					
Kelvedon	d				21 01								21 23							21 54					
Braintree	d											21 00													
Braintree Freeport	d											21 02													
Cressing	d											21 05													
White Notley	d											21 08													
Witham 2	d		20 46		21 07							21 16	21 29					21 46		22 00					
Hatfield Peverel	d												21 33												
Chelmsford	d		20 56		21 16					21 21		21 26	21 40					21 56		22 09				22 21	
Ingatestone	d		21 02									21 32						22 02							
Shenfield 3	a		21 08		21 26							21 38	21 50					22 08		22 19					
Romford	a																			22 28					
Stratford 7 ⊖	a		21 23		21 43					21s46		21 53	22 06					22 23		22 37				22s46	
London Liverpool Street 15 ⊖	a		21 31		21 51					21 55		22 01	22 14		22 19			22 31		22 45				22 55	

		LE		LE	LE	LE	LE	LE	LE	LE	LE	LE		LE	LE	LE	LE	LE	LE	LE	LE	LE
		1		1	1	1	◇1	1	1	1	1	◇1			1	1	1		1		1	1
		F				A			C					D		B		E		D		
Norwich	d											22 00							23 05			
Diss	d											22 17							23 23			
Stowmarket	d											22 29		22 47				23 08	23 36	23 48		
Needham Market	d													22 52						23 53		
Ipswich	a											22 41		23 02				23 21	23 49	00 04		
	d							22 23				22 43						23 22				
Harwich Town	d									22 28											23 28	
Dovercourt	d									22 30											23 30	
Harwich International	d									22 33											23 33	
Wrabness	d									22 39											23 39	
Mistley	d									22 45											23 45	
Manningtree 5	d							22 33		22a50		22 53						23 32			23 50	
Walton-on-the-Naze	d					22 00										23 00						
Frinton-on-Sea	d					22 03										23 03						
Kirby Cross	d					22 06										23 06						
Clacton-on-Sea	d						22 05		←								23 05					
Thorpe-le-Soken 1	a					22 12	22 13		22 12							23 12	23 13					
	d					22 17	22 13		22 17								23 13					
Weeley	d					→			22 21								23 17					
Great Bentley	d								22 24								23 20					
Alresford (Essex)	d								22 28								23 24					
Wivenhoe	d						22 23		22 32								23 28					
Hythe	d								22 36								23 32					
Colchester Town	a								22 40													
	d	22 00			22 00				22 44						23 00							
Colchester 4	a	22 07			22 07		22 31	22 42	22 52			23 02			23 07		23 38	23 42			23 59	
	d				22 12		22 33	22 43				23 03										
Marks Tey 2	d				22 18			22 49														
Kelvedon	d				22 23			22 54														
Braintree	d			22 00							22 56											23 45
Braintree Freeport	d			22 02							22 58											23 47
Cressing	d			22 05							23 01											23 50
White Notley	d			22 08							23 04											23 53
Witham 2	d			22 16	22 29		22 46	23 00			23a12	23 16										00a01
Hatfield Peverel	d				22 33																	
Chelmsford	d			22 26	22 40		22 56	23 09				23 25										
Ingatestone	d			22 32			23 02															
Shenfield 3	a			22 38	22 50		23 08	23 19				23 36										
Romford	a							23 28														
Stratford 7 ⊖	a			22 52	23s06		23 22	23 37				23s53										
London Liverpool Street 15 ⊖	a			23 01	23 14		23 31	23 48				00 03										

A To Colchester
B To Clacton-on-Sea
C From Walton-on-the-Naze
D From Cambridge
E From Peterborough
F To Colchester C.S.D.

Table T011-R

Saturdays
21 December to 16 May

Norwich, Ipswich, Harwich, Clacton, Walton-on-Naze, Colchester and Chelmsford - London

		LE	LE	LE	LE	LE	LE	LE	LE	LE		LE	LE	LE	LE	LE	LE	LE	LE	LE		LE	LE	LE	LE
		1	1	1	1		1	◇	1	1		◇1	1	1	◇1	1	1	1	◇1	1		1			◇1
						A								B		C		D						E	
												⊡							⊡						⊡
Norwich	d							05 00				05 30							06 00						06 30
Diss	d							05 17				05 47							06 17						06 47
Stowmarket	d							05 29											06 29					06 46	
Needham Market	d																							06 51	
Ipswich	a							05 41				06 08							06 41					07 02	07 08
	d							05 43				06 09							06 43			06 52	06 59		07 09
Harwich Town	d												06 28												
Dovercourt	d												06 30												
Harwich International	d												06 33										07a27		
Wrabness	d												06 39												
Mistley	d												06 45												
Manningtree 5	d							05 53				06 19	06a50						06 53			07 02			07 19
Walton-on-the-Naze	d													06 00											
Frinton-on-Sea	d													06 03											
Kirby Cross	d													06 06											
Clacton-on-Sea	d						05 30								06 05	06 24		←							
Thorpe-le-Soken 1	a						05 38							06 12	06 13	06 32		06 12							
	d						05 38							06 17	06 13			06 17							
Weeley	d													→				06 21							
Great Bentley	d																	06 24							
Alresford (Essex)	d																	06 28							
Wivenhoe	d						05 48								06 24			06 32							
Hythe	d																	06 36							
Colchester Town	a																	06 40							
	d																06 35	06 44							
Colchester 4	a						05 57	06 02				06 28			06 32		06 42	06 52	07 02			07 11			07 28
	d		04 43	05 12	05 43	05 50		06 03		06 07		06 30			06 33		06 43		07 03			07 12			07 30
Marks Tey 2	d		04 49	05 18	05 49	05a57				06 13							06 49					07 18			
Kelvedon	d		04 54	05 23	05 54					06 18							06 54					07 23			
Braintree	d	00 27							06 00											07 00					
Braintree Freeport	d	00 29							06 02											07 02					
Cressing	d	00 32							06 05											07 05					
White Notley	d	00 35							06 08											07 08					
Witham 2	d	00a43	05 00	05 29	06 00				06a16	06 24					06 46		07 00			07 16		07 29			
Hatfield Peverel	d		05 04	05 33	06 04					06 28												07 33			
Chelmsford	d		05 11	05 40	06 11			06 21		06 35					06 56		07 09		07 21	07 26		07 40			
Ingatestone	d		05 18	05 47	06 18										07 02					07 32					
Shenfield 3	a		05 23	05 52	06 23					06 45					07 08		07 19			07 38		07 50			
Romford	a		05 32							06 54							07 28								
Stratford 7 ⊖	a		05 43	06 08	06 39			06s46		07 03					07 23		07 37		07s46	07 53		08 06			
London Liverpool Street 15 ⊖	a		05 51	06 16	06 47			06 55		07 11		07 19			07 31		07 46		07 55	08 01		08 14			08 19

		LE	LE	LE	LE	LE		LE	LE	LE	LE	LE	LE	LE	LE	LE		LE	LE	LE	LE	LE	LE	LE	LE
		1	◇1	1	1	1		◇1	1	1	1		◇1	1	1	◇1		1	1	■ 1	1	1	1	◇1	
		B			D							F			B				D						F
								⊡					⊡							⊡					
Norwich	d							07 00					07 30							08 00					
Diss	d							07 17					07 47							08 17					
Stowmarket	d							07 29				07 45								08 29					08 47
Needham Market	d											07 50													08 52
Ipswich	a							07 41				08 02	08 08							08 41					09 02
	d							07 43			07 52		08 09							08 43				08 52	
Harwich Town	d					07 28								08 28											
Dovercourt	d					07 30								08 30											
Harwich International	d			07 20		07 33								08 33											
Wrabness	d					07 39								08 39											
Mistley	d					07 45								08 45											
Manningtree 5	d			07 33		07a50		07 53			08 02		08 19	08a50						08 53				09 02	
Walton-on-the-Naze	d	07 00													08 00										
Frinton-on-Sea	d	07 03													08 03										
Kirby Cross	d	07 06													08 06										
Clacton-on-Sea	d		07 05		←											08 05			←						
Thorpe-le-Soken 1	a	07 12	07 13		07 12										08 12	08 13			08 12						
	d	07 17	07 13		07 17										08 17	08 13			08 17						
Weeley	d	→			07 21										→				08 21						
Great Bentley	d				07 24														08 24						
Alresford (Essex)	d				07 28														08 28						
Wivenhoe	d		07 24		07 32											08 24			08 32						
Hythe	d				07 36														08 36						
Colchester Town	a				07 40														08 40						
	d				07 44				08 00									08 35	08 44			09 00			
Colchester 4	a		07 32	07 42	07 52			08 02	08 07		08 11		08 28			08 32		08 42	08 52			09 07		09 11	
	d		07 33	07 43				08 03			08 12		08 30			08 33		08 43			09 03			09 12	
Marks Tey 2	d			07 49							08 18							08 49						09 18	
Kelvedon	d			07 54							08 23							08 54						09 23	
Braintree	d									08 00													09 00		
Braintree Freeport	d									08 02													09 02		
Cressing	d									08 05													09 05		
White Notley	d									08 08													09 08		
Witham 2	d		07 46	08 00						08 16	08 29					08 46		09 00					09 16	09 29	
Hatfield Peverel	d										08 33													09 33	
Chelmsford	d		07 56	08 09				08 21		08 26	08 40					08 56		09 09			09 20		09 26	09 40	
Ingatestone	d		08 02							08 32						09 02							09 32		
Shenfield 3	a		08 08	08 19						08 38	08 50					09 08		09 19					09 38	09 50	
Romford	a			08 28														09 28							
Stratford 7 ⊖	a		08 23	08 37				08s46		08 53	09 06					09 23		09 37		09s43	09 44		09 53	10 06	
London Liverpool Street 15 ⊖	a		08 31	08 46				08 55		09 01	09 14		09 19			09 31		09 46		09 52	09 54		10 01	10 14	

A To Sudbury
B To Colchester
C To Walton-on-the-Naze
D From Walton-on-the-Naze
E From Bury St Edmunds
F From Cambridge

Table T011-R

Saturdays

21 December to 16 May

Norwich, Ipswich, Harwich, Clacton, Walton-on-Naze, Colchester and Chelmsford - London

		LE	LE	LE	LE	LE	LE	LE	LE	LE	LE	LE	LE	LE	LE	LE	LE	LE	LE	LE	LE	LE
		◇1		■	1	◇1	1	1	1	◇1	1	1	◇1		■1	1	1	◇1	1	1	■1	1
			A		B			C						D			B			C		
		⊡								⊡					⊡						⊡	
Norwich	d	08 30		09 00						09 04					09 30						10 00	
Diss	d	08 47								09 21					09 47						10 17	
Stowmarket	d		09 14							09 33				09 47							10 29	
Needham Market	d													09 52								
Ipswich	a	09 08	09 28	09 33						09 45				10 02	10 08						10 41	
	d	09 09		09 33						09 47			09 52		10 09						10 43	
Harwich Town	d								09 28							10 28						
Dovercourt	d								09 30							10 30						
Harwich International	d								09 33							10 33						
Wrabness	d								09 39							10 39						
Mistley	d								09 45							10 45						
Manningtree 5	d	09 19							09 50				10 03		10 19	10a50					10 53	
Walton-on-the-Naze	d				09 00												10 00					
Frinton-on-Sea	d				09 03												10 03					
Kirby Cross	d				09 06												10 06					
Clacton-on-Sea	d					09 05		←										10 05		←		
Thorpe-le-Soken 1	a				09 12	09 13		09 12									10 12	10 13		10 12		
	d				09 17	09 13		09 17									10 17	10 13		10 17		
Weeley	d				→			09 21									→			10 21		
Great Bentley	d							09 24												10 24		
Alresford (Essex)	d							09 28												10 28		
Wivenhoe	d					09 24		09 32										10 24		10 32		
Hythe	d							09 36												10 36		
Colchester Town	a							09 40												10 40		
	d						09 35	09 44			10 00								10 35	10 44		
Colchester 4	a	09 28				09 32	09 42	09 52	09 59	10 02	10 07		10 12		10 28			10 32	10 42	10 52		
	d	09 30				09 33	09 50			10 04			10 13		10 30			10 33	10 43			11 03
Marks Tey 2	d						09 56						10 19						10 49			
Kelvedon	d						10 01						10 24						10 54			
Braintree	d											10 00										
Braintree Freeport	d											10 02										
Cressing	d											10 05										
White Notley	d											10 08										
Witham 2	d					09 46	10 07					10 16	10 30					10 46	11 00			
Hatfield Peverel	d												10 34									
Chelmsford	d					09 55	10 16			10 23		10 26	10 41					10 56	11 09			11 20
Ingatestone	d					10 01						10 33						11 02				
Shenfield 3	a					10 07	10 27					10 38	10 51					11 08	11 19			
Romford	a						10 35												11 28			
Stratford 7 ⊖ ⛴	a					10 27	10 45			10s47		10 54	11 07					11 23	11 37		11s43	11 46
London Liverpool Street 15 ⊖	a	10 19		10 30		10 35	10 53			10 56		11 02	11 15		11 19			11 31	11 46		11 52	11 55

		LE	LE	LE	LE	LE	LE	LE	LE	LE	LE	LE	LE	LE	LE	LE	LE	LE	LE	LE	LE	LE	LE
		1	1	◇1		◇1		1	1	◇1	1	1	◇1	1	1	1		◇1	1	1	◇1	1	1
					D		A		B			C					D			B			C
						⊡							⊡					⊡					
Norwich	d					10 30							11 00					11 30					
Diss	d					10 47							11 17					11 47					
Stowmarket	d				10 47		11 14						11 29				11 47						
Needham Market	d				10 52												11 52						
Ipswich	a				11 02	11 08	11 28						11 41				12 02	12 08					
	d			10 52		11 09							11 43			11 50		12 09					
Harwich Town	d							11 28											12 28				
Dovercourt	d							11 30											12 30				
Harwich International	d							11 33											12 33				
Wrabness	d							11 39											12 39				
Mistley	d							11 45											12 45				
Manningtree 5	d			11 02		11 19		11a50					11 53			12 02		12 19	12a50				
Walton-on-the-Naze	d								11 00											12 00			
Frinton-on-Sea	d								11 03											12 03			
Kirby Cross	d								11 06											12 06			
Clacton-on-Sea	d									11 05		←									12 05		←
Thorpe-le-Soken 1	a								11 12	11 13		11 12								12 12	12 13		12 12
	d								11 17	11 13		11 17								12 17	12 13		12 17
Weeley	d								→			11 21								→			12 21
Great Bentley	d											11 24											12 24
Alresford (Essex)	d											11 28											12 28
Wivenhoe	d									11 24		11 32									12 24		12 32
Hythe	d											11 36											12 36
Colchester Town	a											11 40											12 40
	d	11 00									11 35	11 44		12 00								12 35	12 44
Colchester 4	a	11 07		11 12		11 28				11 32	11 42	11 52	12 02	12 07		12 11		12 28			12 32	12 42	12 52
	d			11 12		11 30				11 33	11 43		12 03			12 12		12 30			12 33	12 43	
Marks Tey 2	d			11 18							11 49					12 18						12 49	
Kelvedon	d			11 23							11 54					12 23						12 54	
Braintree	d		11 00												12 00								
Braintree Freeport	d		11 02												12 02								
Cressing	d		11 05												12 05								
White Notley	d		11 08												12 08								
Witham 2	d		11 16	11 29						11 46	12 00				12 16	12 29					12 46	13 00	
Hatfield Peverel	d			11 33												12 33							
Chelmsford	d		11 26	11 40						11 56	12 09		12 21		12 26	12 40					12 56	13 09	
Ingatestone	d		11 32							12 02					12 32						13 02		
Shenfield 3	a		11 38	11 51						12 08	12 19				12 38	12 50					13 08	13 19	
Romford	a										12 28											13 28	
Stratford 7 ⊖ ⛴	a		11 53	12 06						12 23	12 37		12s46		12 53	13 06					13 23	13 37	
London Liverpool Street 15 ⊖	a		12 01	12 14		12 19				12 31	12 46		12 55		13 01	13 14		13 19			13 31	13 46	

A From Peterborough
B To Colchester
C From Walton-on-the-Naze
D From Cambridge

Table T011-R

Saturdays

21 December to 16 May

Norwich, Ipswich, Harwich, Clacton, Walton-on-Naze, Colchester and Chelmsford - London

		LE	LE	LE	LE	LE	LE	LE	LE	LE	LE	LE	LE	LE	LE	LE	LE	LE	LE	LE	LE	LE
		◇1	1	1	1		◇1		1	1	◇1	1	1	◇1	1	1	1		◇1	1	1	◇1
						A		B		C			D					A			C	
		⊡					⊡							⊡					⊡			
Norwich	d	12 00					12 30							13 00					13 30			
Diss	d	12 17					12 47							13 17					13 47			
Stowmarket	d	12 29				12 47		13 14						13 29				13 47				
Needham Market	d					12 52												13 52				
Ipswich	a	12 41				13 02	13 08	13 28						13 41				14 02	14 08			
	d	12 43			12 52		13 09							13 43			13 52		14 09			
Harwich Town	d								13 28											14 28		
Dovercourt	d								13 30											14 30		
Harwich International	d								13 33											14 33		
Wrabness	d								13 39											14 39		
Mistley	d								13 45											14 45		
Manningtree 5	d	12 53			13 02		13 19		13a50					13 53			14 02		14 19	14a50		
Walton-on-the-Naze	d									13 00											14 00	
Frinton-on-Sea	d									13 03											14 03	
Kirby Cross	d									13 06											14 06	
Clacton-on-Sea	d										13 05		←									14 05
Thorpe-le-Soken 1	a									13 12	13 13		13 12								14 12	14 13
	d									13 17	13 13		13 17								14 17	14 13
Weeley	d									→			13 21								→	
Great Bentley	d												13 24									
Alresford (Essex)	d												13 28									
Wivenhoe	d										13 24		13 32									14 24
Hythe	d												13 36									
Colchester Town	a												13 40									
	d		13 00									13 35	13 44		14 00							
Colchester 4	a	13 02	13 07		13 11		13 28				13 32	13 42	13 52	14 02	14 07		14 11		14 28			14 32
	d	13 03			13 12		13 30				13 33	13 43		14 03			14 12		14 30			14 33
Marks Tey 2	d				13 18							13 49					14 18					
Kelvedon	d				13 23							13 54					14 23					
Braintree	d			13 00												14 00						
Braintree Freeport	d			13 02												14 02						
Cressing	d			13 05												14 05						
White Notley	d			13 08												14 08						
Witham 2	d			13 16	13 29						13 46	14 00				14 16	14 29					14 46
Hatfield Peverel	d				13 33												14 33					
Chelmsford	d	13 21		13 26	13 40						13 56	14 09		14 21		14 26	14 40					14 56
Ingatestone	d			13 32							14 02					14 32						15 02
Shenfield 3	a			13 38	13 50						14 08	14 19				14 38	14 50					15 08
Romford	a											14 28										
Stratford 7 ⊖ ⛴	a	13s46		13 53	14 06						14 23	14 37		14s46		14 53	15 06					15 23
London Liverpool Street 15 ⊖	a	13 55		14 01	14 14		14 19				14 31	14 46		14 55		15 01	15 14		15 19			15 31

		LE	LE	LE	LE	LE	LE	LE	LE	LE	LE	LE	LE	LE	LE	LE	LE	LE	LE	LE	LE	LE	LE
		1	1	◇1	1	1	1		◇1		1	1	◇1	1	1	◇1	1	1	1		◇1	1	1
			D					A		B		C			D					A			C
				⊡					⊡							⊡					⊡		
Norwich	d			14 00					14 30							15 00					15 30		
Diss	d			14 17					14 47							15 17					15 47		
Stowmarket	d			14 29				14 47		15 14						15 29				15 47			
Needham Market	d							14 52												15 52			
Ipswich	a			14 41				15 02	15 08	15 29						15 41				16 02	16 08		
	d			14 43			14 52		15 09							15 43			15 52		16 09		
Harwich Town	d										15 28											16 28	
Dovercourt	d										15 30											16 30	
Harwich International	d										15 33											16 33	
Wrabness	d										15 39											16 39	
Mistley	d										15 45											16 45	
Manningtree 5	d			14 53			15 02		15 19		15a50					15 53			16 02		16 19	16a50	
Walton-on-the-Naze	d											15 00											16 00
Frinton-on-Sea	d											15 03											16 03
Kirby Cross	d											15 06											16 06
Clacton-on-Sea	d		←										15 05		←								
Thorpe-le-Soken 1	a		14 12									15 12	15 13		15 12								16 12
	d		14 17									15 17	15 13		15 17								16 17
Weeley	d		14 21									→			15 21								→
Great Bentley	d		14 24												15 24								
Alresford (Essex)	d		14 28												15 28								
Wivenhoe	d		14 32										15 24		15 32								
Hythe	d		14 36												15 36								
Colchester Town	a		14 40												15 40								
	d	14 35	14 44		15 00									15 35	15 44		16 00						
Colchester 4	a	14 42	14 52	15 02	15 07		15 11		15 28				15 32	15 42	15 52	16 02	16 07		16 11		16 28		
	d	14 43		15 03			15 12		15 30				15 33	15 43		16 03			16 12		16 30		
Marks Tey 2	d	14 49					15 18							15 49					16 18				
Kelvedon	d	14 54					15 23							15 54					16 23				
Braintree	d					15 00												16 00					
Braintree Freeport	d					15 02												16 02					
Cressing	d					15 05												16 05					
White Notley	d					15 08												16 08					
Witham 2	d	15 00				15 16	15 29						15 46	16 00				16 16	16 29				
Hatfield Peverel	d						15 33												16 33				
Chelmsford	d	15 09		15 21		15 26	15 40						15 56	16 09		16 21		16 26	16 40				
Ingatestone	d					15 32							16 02					16 32					
Shenfield 3	a	15 19				15 38	15 50						16 08	16 19				16 38	16 50				
Romford	a	15 28												16 28									
Stratford 7 ⊖ ⛴	a	15 37		15s46		15 53	16 06						16 23	16 37		16s46		16 53	17 06				
London Liverpool Street 15 ⊖	a	15 46		15 55		16 01	16 14		16 19				16 31	16 46		16 55		17 01	17 14		17 19		

A From Cambridge
B From Peterborough
C To Colchester
D From Walton-on-the-Naze

Table T011-R

Saturdays

21 December to 16 May

Norwich, Ipswich, Harwich, Clacton, Walton-on-Naze, Colchester and Chelmsford - London

		LE ◇1	LE 1	LE 1 A	LE ◇1 ⊡	LE 1	LE 1	LE 1	LE B	LE ◇1 ⊡	LE C	LE	LE 1 D	LE ◇1	LE 1	LE 1 A	LE 1	LE ◇1 ⊡	LE 1	LE 1	LE 1	LE B	LE ◇1 ⊡
Norwich	d				16 00					16 30		17 00						17 04					17 30
Diss	d				16 17					16 47								17 21					17 47
Stowmarket	d				16 29				16 47		17 14							17 33				17 49	17 59
Needham Market	d								16 52													17 54	
Ipswich	a				16 41				17 02	17 08	17 28	17 33						17 45				18 03	18 11
	d				16 43			16 52		17 09		17 33						17 47			17 52		18 13
Harwich Town	d																17 28						
Dovercourt	d																17 30						
Harwich International	d																17 33						
Wrabness	d																17 39						
Mistley	d																17 45						
Manningtree 5	d				16 53			17 02		17 19							17 50				18 03		
Walton-on-the-Naze	d												17 00										
Frinton-on-Sea	d												17 03										
Kirby Cross	d												17 06										
Clacton-on-Sea	d	16 05		←										17 05		←							
Thorpe-le-Soken 1	a	16 13		16 12									17 12	17 13		17 12							
	d	16 13		16 17									17 17	17 13		17 17							
Weeley	d			16 21									→			17 21							
Great Bentley	d			16 24												17 24							
Alresford (Essex)	d			16 28												17 28							
Wivenhoe	d	16 24		16 32										17 24		17 32							
Hythe	d			16 36												17 36							
Colchester Town	a			16 40												17 40							
	d		16 35	16 44		17 00									17 35	17 44			18 00				
Colchester 4	a	16 32	16 42	16 52	17 02	17 07		17 11		17 28				17 32	17 42	17 52	17 59	18 02	18 07		18 12		18 28
	d	16 33	16 43		17 03			17 12		17 30				17 33	17 50			18 04			18 13		18 30
Marks Tey 2	d		16 49					17 18							17 56						18 19		
Kelvedon	d		16 54					17 23							18 01						18 24		
Braintree	d						17 00													18 00			
Braintree Freeport	d						17 02													18 02			
Cressing	d						17 05													18 05			
White Notley	d						17 08													18 08			
Witham 2	d	16 46	17 00				17 16	17 29						17 46	18 07					18 16	18 30		
Hatfield Peverel	d							17 33													18 34		
Chelmsford	d	16 56	17 09		17 21		17 26	17 40						17 55	18 16			18 21		18 26	18 41		
Ingatestone	d	17 02					17 32							18 01						18 33			
Shenfield 3	a	17 08	17 19				17 38	17 50						18 07	18 26					18 38	18 51		
Romford	a		17 28												18 35								
Stratford 7 ⊖	a	17 23	17 37		17s46		17 53	18 06						18 27	18 44			18s47		18 54	19 07		
London Liverpool Street 15 ⊖	a	17 31	17 46		17 55		18 01	18 14		18 19		18 30		18 35	18 53			18 56		19 03	19 15		19 19

		LE 1	LE 1 D	LE ◇1	LE 1	LE 1 A	LE ◇1 ⊡	LE 1	LE 1	LE 1	LE B	LE ◇1 ⊡	LE C	LE 1	LE 1 D	LE ◇1	LE 1	LE 1 A	LE ◇1 ⊡	LE 1	LE 1	LE 1
Norwich	d						18 00					18 30							19 00			
Diss	d						18 17					18 47							19 17			
Stowmarket	d						18 29				18 49		19 14						19 29			
Needham Market	d										18 54											
Ipswich	a						18 41				19 03	19 08	19 28						19 41			
	d						18 43			18 52		19 09							19 43			19 50
Harwich Town	d	18 28												19 28								
Dovercourt	d	18 30												19 30								
Harwich International	d	18 33												19 33								
Wrabness	d	18 39												19 39								
Mistley	d	18 45												19 45								
Manningtree 5	d	18a50					18 53			19 02		19 19		19a50					19 53			20 02
Walton-on-the-Naze	d		18 00												19 00							
Frinton-on-Sea	d		18 03												19 03							
Kirby Cross	d		18 06												19 06							
Clacton-on-Sea	d			18 05		←										19 05		←				
Thorpe-le-Soken 1	a		18 12	18 13		18 12									19 12	19 13		19 12				
	d		18 17	18 13		18 17									19 17	19 13		19 17				
Weeley	d		→			18 21									→			19 21				
Great Bentley	d					18 24												19 24				
Alresford (Essex)	d					18 28												19 28				
Wivenhoe	d			18 24		18 32										19 24		19 32				
Hythe	d					18 36												19 36				
Colchester Town	a					18 40												19 40				
	d				18 35	18 44		19 00									19 35	19 44		20 00		
Colchester 4	a			18 32	18 42	18 52	19 02	19 07		19 11		19 28				19 32	19 42	19 52	20 02	20 07		20 11
	d			18 33	18 43		19 03			19 12		19 30				19 33	19 43		20 03			20 12
Marks Tey 2	d				18 49					19 18							19 49					20 18
Kelvedon	d				18 54					19 23							19 54					20 23
Braintree	d								19 00												20 00	
Braintree Freeport	d								19 02												20 02	
Cressing	d								19 05												20 05	
White Notley	d								19 08												20 08	
Witham 2	d			18 46	19 00				19 16	19 29						19 46	20 00				20 16	20 29
Hatfield Peverel	d									19 33												20 33
Chelmsford	d			18 56	19 09		19 21		19 26	19 40						19 56	20 09		20 21		20 26	20 40
Ingatestone	d			19 02					19 32							20 02					20 32	
Shenfield 3	a			19 08	19 19				19 38	19 50						20 08	20 19				20 38	20 50
Romford	a				19 28												20 28					
Stratford 7 ⊖	a			19 23	19 37		19s46		19 53	20 06						20 23	20 37		20s46		20 53	21 06
London Liverpool Street 15 ⊖	a			19 33	19 46		19 55		20 01	20 14		20 19				20 31	20 46		20 55		21 01	21 14

A From Walton-on-the-Naze
B From Cambridge
C From Peterborough
D To Colchester

Table T011-R

Saturdays

21 December to 16 May

Norwich, Ipswich, Harwich, Clacton, Walton-on-Naze, Colchester and Chelmsford - London

		LE A	LE 1	LE 1	LE 1 B	LE ◇1	LE 1	LE 1 C	LE ◇1 ⊡	LE 1	LE 1	LE 1	LE A	LE 1	LE 1 B	LE ◇1	LE 1	LE ◇ D	LE 1 C	LE 1	LE ◇1 ⊡	LE 1	LE 1
Norwich	d								20 00												21 00		
Diss	d								20 17												21 17		
Stowmarket	d	19 47							20 29				20 46					21 14			21 29		
Needham Market	d	19 52											20 51										
Ipswich	a	20 02							20 41				21 01					21 28			21 41		
	d		20 09						20 43				21 01	21 09				21 28			21 43		
Harwich Town	d			20 28																21 28			
Dovercourt	d			20 30																21 30			
Harwich International	d			20 33								20 45	21a29							21 33			
Wrabness	d			20 39																21 39			
Mistley	d			20 45																21 45			
Manningtree 5	d		20 19	20a50					20 53			20 58		21 19				21 38		21a50	21 53		
Walton-on-the-Naze	d				20 00										21 00								
Frinton-on-Sea	d				20 03										21 03								
Kirby Cross	d				20 06										21 06								
Clacton-on-Sea	d					20 05		←								21 05			←				
Thorpe-le-Soken 1	a				20 12	20 13		20 12							21 12	21 13			21 12				
	d				20 17	20 13		20 17							21 17	21 13			21 17				
Weeley	d				→			20 21							→				21 21				
Great Bentley	d							20 24											21 24				
Alresford (Essex)	d							20 28											21 28				
Wivenhoe	d					20 24		20 32								21 24			21 32				
Hythe	d							20 36											21 36				
Colchester Town	a							20 40											21 40				
	d						20 35	20 44		21 00							21 35		21 44			22 00	
Colchester 4	a		20 29			20 32	20 42	20 52	21 02	21 07		21 07		21 28		21 32	21 42	21 48	21 52		22 02	22 07	
	d		20 30			20 33	20 43		21 03			21 12		21 30		21 33	21 43				22 03		
Marks Tey 2	d						20 49					21 18					21 49						
Kelvedon	d						20 54					21 23					21 54						
Braintree	d										21 00												22 00
Braintree Freeport	d										21 02												22 02
Cressing	d										21 05												22 05
White Notley	d										21 08												22 08
Witham 2	d					20 46	21 00				21 16	21 29				21 46	22 00						22 16
Hatfield Peverel	d											21 33											
Chelmsford	d					20 56	21 09		21 21		21 26	21 40				21 56	22 09				22 21		22 26
Ingatestone	d					21 02					21 32					22 02							22 32
Shenfield 3	a					21 08	21 19				21 38	21 50				22 08	22 19						22 38
Romford	a						21 28										22 28						
Stratford 7 ⊖	a					21 23	21 37		21s46		21 53	22 06				22 23	22 37				22s46		22 53
London Liverpool Street 15 ⊖	a		21 17			21 34	21 46		21 55		22 01	22 14		22 17		22 31	22 46				22 55		23 01

		LE 1	LE A	LE 1 B	LE ◇1	LE 1	LE 1 C	LE 1	LE 1	LE ◇1	LE A	LE 1	LE 1 E	LE 1	LE 1	LE F	LE 1	LE A	LE 1	LE 1
Norwich	d									22 00							23 05			
Diss	d									22 17							23 23			
Stowmarket	d		21 47							22 29	22 46					23 10	23 36	23 51		
Needham Market	d		21 52								22 51							23 56		
Ipswich	a		22 02							22 41	23 03					23 23	23 49	00 08		
	d	21 52				22 23				22 43				23 15		23 23				
Harwich Town	d							22 28											23 28	
Dovercourt	d							22 30											23 30	
Harwich International	d							22 33											23 33	
Wrabness	d							22 39											23 39	
Mistley	d							22 45											23 45	
Manningtree 5	d	22 02				22 33		22a50		22 53				23 25		23 32			23 50	
Walton-on-the-Naze	d			22 00									23 00							
Frinton-on-Sea	d			22 03									23 03							
Kirby Cross	d			22 06									23 06							
Clacton-on-Sea	d				22 05		←								23 05					
Thorpe-le-Soken 1	a			22 12	22 13		22 12						23 12		23 13					
	d			22 17	22 13		22 17								23 13					
Weeley	d			→			22 21								23 17					
Great Bentley	d						22 24								23 20					
Alresford (Essex)	d						22 28								23 24					
Wivenhoe	d				22 24		22 32								23 28					
Hythe	d						22 36								23 32					
Colchester Town	a						22 40													
	d						22 44					23 00								
Colchester 4	a	22 11			22 32	22 42	22 52			23 02		23 07		23 35	23 38	23 42			23 59	
	d	22 12			22 33	22 43				23 03										
Marks Tey 2	d	22 18				22 49														
Kelvedon	d	22 23				22 54														
Braintree	d								22 56											23 47
Braintree Freeport	d								22 58											23 49
Cressing	d								23 01											23 52
White Notley	d								23 04											23 55
Witham 2	d	22 29			22 46	23 00			23a12	23 16										00a03
Hatfield Peverel	d	22 33																		
Chelmsford	d	22 40			22 56	23 09				23 25										
Ingatestone	d				23 02															
Shenfield 3	a	22 50			23 08	23 19				23 36										
Romford	a					23 28														
Stratford 7 ⊖	a	23 06			23 23	23 37				23s53										
London Liverpool Street 15 ⊖	a	23 14			23 31	23 45				00 03										

A From Cambridge
B To Colchester
C From Walton-on-the-Naze
D From Peterborough. ◇ from Ipswich
E To Clacton-on-Sea
F From Peterborough

Table T011-R

Sundays

15 December to 10 May

Norwich, Ipswich, Harwich, Clacton, Walton-on-Naze, Colchester and Chelmsford - London

		LE ■	LE ■	LE ■	LE A	LE ■	LE ■	LE ◇■ ⊏P	LE ■	LE ■		LE ◇■	LE ■	LE ◇■ ⊏P	LE ■	LE ■	LE ■	LE ◇■	LE ◇	LE ■		LE ◇■ ⊏P	LE ■	LE ■	LE ■
Norwich	d							06 52						08 00					08 20			09 00			
Diss	d							07 09						08 17					08 38			09 17			
Stowmarket	d							07 21						08 29					08 50			09 29			
Needham Market	d																								
Ipswich	a							07 33						08 41					09 02			09 41			
	d							07 35	08 01				08 09	08 43					09 04	09 09		09 43			
Harwich Town	d															08 53								09 53	
Dovercourt	d															08 55								09 55	
Harwich International	d						07 20		08a26							08 58								09 58	
Wrabness	d															09 04								10 04	
Mistley	d															09 10								10 10	
Manningtree ■	d						07 33	07 45					08 19	08 53		09a15				09 19		09 53		10a15	
Walton-on-the-Naze	d														08 29								09 29		
Frinton-on-Sea	d														08 32								09 32		
Kirby Cross	d														08 35								09 35		
Clacton-on-Sea	d											07 32						08 36							
Thorpe-le-Soken ■	a											07 40			08 41			08 44					09 41		
	d											07 40						08 44							
Weeley	d																								
Great Bentley	d											07 45						08 49							
Alresford (Essex)	d											07 49						08 53							
Wivenhoe	d											07 53						08 57							
Hythe	d											07 57						09 01							
Colchester Town	a																								
	d																								
Colchester ■	a						07 42	07 54				08 03	08 29	09 02				09 07	09 19	09 29		10 02			
	d			06 51	07 01	07 21	07 42	07 55				08 03	08 30	09 03				09 07	09 22	09 30		10 03			
Marks Tey ■	d			06 57	07a14	07 27						08 09	08 36					09 13		09 36					
Kelvedon	d			07 02		07 32							08 41							09 41					
Braintree	d	00 31								07 58							09 00								10 00
Braintree Freeport	d	00 33								08 00							09 02								10 02
Cressing	d	00 36								08 03							09 05								10 05
White Notley	d	00 39								08 06							09 08								10 08
Witham ■	d	00a47		07 08		07 38	07 55			08a14		08 18	08 47				09a16	09 22		09 47					10a16
Hatfield Peverel	d			07 12		07 42							08 51							09 51					
Chelmsford	d		06 55	07 19		07 49	08 04					08 27	08 59					09 31		09 59					
Ingatestone	d		07 02	07 26		07 56							09 05							10 05					
Shenfield ■	a		07 07	07 37		08 07	08 14					08 37	09 11					09 41		10 11					
Romford	a		07 18	07 48																					
Stratford ■ ⊖	a		07 33	08 03		08 33	08s48					09 03	09 27	09s44				09 58		10 28		10s44			
London Liverpool Street ■ ⊖	a		07 43	08 13		08 43	08 58	09 00				09 13	09 37	09 55				10 07	10 10	10 37		10 55			

		LE ◇■	LE ■	LE B	LE ◇■ ⊏P	LE B		LE ■	LE ■	LE ■	LE ◇■	LE ■	LE ◇■ ⊏P	LE B	LE ■	LE ■		LE ■	LE ◇■	LE ■	LE ◇■ ⊏P	LE B	LE ■	LE ■	LE ■
Norwich	d				10 00								11 00								12 00				
Diss	d				10 17								11 17								12 17				
Stowmarket	d			10 08	10 29	10 47							11 29	11 47							12 29	12 47			
Needham Market	d			10 13		10 52								11 52								12 52			
Ipswich	a			10 24	10 41	11 02							11 41	12 02							12 41	13 02			
	d		10 09		10 43							11 09	11 43							12 09	12 43				
Harwich Town	d								10 53							11 53								12 53	
Dovercourt	d								10 55							11 55								12 55	
Harwich International	d								10 58							11 58								12 58	
Wrabness	d								11 04							12 04								13 04	
Mistley	d								11 10							12 10								13 10	
Manningtree ■	d		10 19		10 53				11a15			11 19	11 53			12a15				12 19	12 53			13a15	
Walton-on-the-Naze	d							10 29							11 29								12 29		
Frinton-on-Sea	d							10 32							11 32								12 32		
Kirby Cross	d							10 35							11 35								12 35		
Clacton-on-Sea	d	09 36									10 36								11 36						
Thorpe-le-Soken ■	a	09 44						10 41			10 44				11 41				11 44				12 41		
	d	09 44									10 44								11 44						
Weeley	d																								
Great Bentley	d	09 49									10 49								11 49						
Alresford (Essex)	d	09 53									10 53								11 53						
Wivenhoe	d	09 57									10 57								11 57						
Hythe	d	10 01									11 01								12 01						
Colchester Town	a																								
	d																								
Colchester ■	a	10 07	10 29		11 02						11 07	11 29	12 02						12 07	12 29	13 02				
	d	10 07	10 30		11 03						11 07	11 30	12 03						12 07	12 30	13 03				
Marks Tey ■	d	10 13	10 36								11 13	11 36							12 13	12 36					
Kelvedon	d		10 41									11 41								12 41					
Braintree	d									11 00								12 00							13 00
Braintree Freeport	d									11 02								12 02							13 02
Cressing	d									11 05								12 05							13 05
White Notley	d									11 08								12 08							13 08
Witham ■	d	10 22	10 47							11a16	11 22	11 47						12a16	12 22	12 47					13a16
Hatfield Peverel	d		10 51									11 51								12 51					
Chelmsford	d	10 31	10 59								11 31	11 59							12 31	12 59					
Ingatestone	d		11 05									12 05								13 05					
Shenfield ■	a	10 41	11 11								11 41	12 11							12 41	13 11					
Romford	a																								
Stratford ■ ⊖	a	10 58	11 28		11s44						11 58	12 28	12s44						12 58	13 28	13s44				
London Liverpool Street ■ ⊖	a	11 07	11 37		11 55						12 07	12 37	12 55						13 07	13 37	13 55				

A To Sudbury
B From Cambridge

Table T011-R

Sundays

15 December to 10 May

Norwich, Ipswich, Harwich, Clacton, Walton-on-Naze, Colchester and Chelmsford - London

		LE ◇■		LE ■	LE A	LE ◇■ ⊏P	LE B	LE ■	LE ■	LE ■	LE ◇■	LE ■		LE ◇■ ⊏P	LE B	LE ■	LE ■	LE ■	LE ◇■	LE ■	LE A	LE ◇■ ⊏P		LE B	LE ■
Norwich	d					13 00								14 00								15 00			
Diss	d					13 17								14 17								15 17			
Stowmarket	d				13 11	13 29	13 48							14 29	14 47						15 14	15 29		15 47	
Needham Market	d						13 53								14 52									15 52	
Ipswich	a				13 25	13 41	14 02							14 41	15 02						15 27	15 41		16 02	
	d			13 09		13 43						14 09		14 43						15 09		15 43			
Harwich Town	d								13 53								14 53								
Dovercourt	d								13 55								14 55								
Harwich International	d								13 58								14 58								
Wrabness	d								14 04								15 04								
Mistley	d								14 10								15 10								
Manningtree ■	d			13 19		13 53			14a15			14 19		14 53			15a15			15 19		15 53			
Walton-on-the-Naze	d							13 29								14 29									15 29
Frinton-on-Sea	d							13 32								14 32									15 32
Kirby Cross	d							13 35								14 35									15 35
Clacton-on-Sea	d	12 36									13 36								14 36						
Thorpe-le-Soken ■	a	12 44						13 41			13 44					14 41			14 44						15 41
	d	12 44									13 44								14 44						
Weeley	d																								
Great Bentley	d	12 49									13 49								14 49						
Alresford (Essex)	d	12 53									13 53								14 53						
Wivenhoe	d	12 57									13 57								14 57						
Hythe	d	13 01									14 01								15 01						
Colchester Town	a																								
	d																								
Colchester ■	a	13 07		13 29		14 02					14 07	14 29		15 02					15 07	15 29		16 02			
	d	13 07		13 30		14 03					14 07	14 30		15 03					15 07	15 30		16 03			
Marks Tey ■	d	13 13		13 36							14 13	14 36							15 13	15 36					
Kelvedon	d			13 41								14 41								15 41					
Braintree	d									14 00								15 00							
Braintree Freeport	d									14 02								15 02							
Cressing	d									14 05								15 05							
White Notley	d									14 08								15 08							
Witham ■	d	13 22		13 47						14a16	14 22	14 48						15a16	15 22	15 47					
Hatfield Peverel	d			13 51								14 52								15 51					
Chelmsford	d	13 31		13 59							14 31	14 59							15 31	15 59					
Ingatestone	d			14 05								15 05								16 05					
Shenfield ■	a	13 41		14 11							14 41	15 11							15 41	16 11					
Romford	a																								
Stratford ■ ⊖	a	13 58		14 28		14s44					14 58	15 28		15s44					15 58	16 28		16s44			
London Liverpool Street ■ ⊖	a	14 07		14 37		14 55					15 07	15 37		15 55					16 07	16 37		16 55			

		LE ■	LE ■	LE ◇■	LE ◇■	LE ■	LE ■ ■ ⊏P	LE B		LE ■	LE ■	LE ■	LE ◇■	LE ◇■ ⊏P	LE ■	LE A	LE ◇■ ⊏P	LE B		LE ■	LE ■	LE ■	LE ◇■	LE ■	LE ◇■ ⊏P
Norwich	d				15 22		16 00							16 20			17 00								18 00
Diss	d				15 40		16 17							16 38			17 17								18 17
Stowmarket	d				15 53		16 29	16 47						16 52		17 11	17 29	17 47							18 29
Needham Market	d							16 52										17 52							
Ipswich	a				16 05		16 41	17 02						17 05		17 25	17 41	18 02							18 41
	d				16 07	16 09	16 43							17 07	17 09		17 43							18 09	18 43
Harwich Town	d	15 53									16 53										17 53				
Dovercourt	d	15 55									16 55										17 55				
Harwich International	d	15 58									16 58										17 58				
Wrabness	d	16 04									17 04										18 04				
Mistley	d	16 10									17 10										18 10				
Manningtree ■	d	16a15				16 20	16 53				17a15				17 20		17 53				18a15			18 19	18 53
Walton-on-the-Naze	d									16 29										17 29					
Frinton-on-Sea	d									16 32										17 32					
Kirby Cross	d									16 35										17 35					
Clacton-on-Sea	d			15 36									16 36										17 36		
Thorpe-le-Soken ■	a			15 44						16 41			16 44							17 41			17 44		
	d			15 44									16 44										17 44		
Weeley	d																								
Great Bentley	d			15 49									16 49										17 49		
Alresford (Essex)	d			15 53									16 53										17 53		
Wivenhoe	d			15 57									16 57										17 57		
Hythe	d			16 01									17 01										18 01		
Colchester Town	a																								
	d																								
Colchester ■	a			16 07	16 22	16 29	17 02						17 07	17 22	17 29		18 02						18 07	18 29	19 02
	d			16 07	16 24	16 30	17 03						17 07	17 24	17 30		18 03						18 07	18 30	19 03
Marks Tey ■	d			16 13		16 36							17 13		17 36								18 13	18 36	
Kelvedon	d					16 41									17 41									18 41	
Braintree	d		16 00									17 00										18 00			
Braintree Freeport	d		16 02									17 02										18 02			
Cressing	d		16 05									17 05										18 05			
White Notley	d		16 08									17 08										18 08			
Witham ■	d		16a16	16 22		16 47						17a16	17 22		17 47							18a16	18 22	18 47	
Hatfield Peverel	d					16 51									17 51									18 51	
Chelmsford	d			16 31		16 59							17 31		17 59								18 31	18 59	
Ingatestone	d					17 05									18 05									19 05	
Shenfield ■	a			16 41		17 11							17 41		18 11								18 41	19 11	
Romford	a																								
Stratford ■ ⊖	a			16 58		17 28	17s44						17 58		18 28		18s44						18 58	19 28	19s44
London Liverpool Street ■ ⊖	a			17 07	17 12	17 37	17 55						18 07	18 12	18 37		18 55						19 07	19 37	19 55

A From Peterborough
B From Cambridge

Table T011-R

Sundays
15 December to 10 May

Norwich, Ipswich, Harwich, Clacton, Walton-on-Naze, Colchester and Chelmsford - London

		LE	LE	LE		LE	LE	LE	LE	LE	LE	LE	LE	LE		LE	LE	LE	LE	LE	LE	LE	LE	LE
			1	1		1	◇1	1		◇1		1	1	1		◇1	1	1	1	◇1	1		1	◇1
		A							B		A											A		
Norwich	d									19 00										20 00				
Diss	d									19 17										20 17				
Stowmarket	d	18 47							19 11	19 29	19 47									20 29		20 46		
Needham Market	d	18 52									19 52											20 51		
Ipswich	a	19 02							19 25	19 41	20 02									20 41		21 03		
	d							19 09	19 25	19 43							20 09			20 43		21 03		
Harwich Town	d			18 53									19 53								20 53			
Dovercourt	d			18 55									19 55								20 55			
Harwich International	d			18 58									19 58						20 30		20 58	21a29		
Wrabness	d			19 04									20 04								21 04			
Mistley	d			19 10									20 10								21 10			
Manningtree 5	d			19a15				19 19	19 34	19 53			20a15				20 19		20 43	20 53	21a15			
Walton-on-the-Naze	d		18 29									19 29						20 29						
Frinton-on-Sea	d		18 32									19 32						20 32						
Kirby Cross	d		18 35									19 35						20 35						
Clacton-on-Sea	d						18 36									19 36								20 36
Thorpe-le-Soken 1	a		18 41				18 44					19 41				19 44		20 41						20 44
	d						18 44									19 44								20 44
Weeley	d																							
Great Bentley	d						18 49									19 49								20 49
Alresford (Essex)	d						18 53									19 53								20 53
Wivenhoe	d						18 57									19 57								20 57
Hythe	d						19 01									20 01								21 01
Colchester Town	a																							
	d																							
Colchester 4	a						19 07	19 29	19 44	20 02						20 07	20 29		20 52	21 02				21 07
	d						19 07	19 30		20 03						20 07	20 30		20 52	21 03				21 07
Marks Tey 2	d						19 13	19 36								20 13	20 36							21 13
Kelvedon	d							19 41									20 41							
Braintree	d					19 00								20 00									21 00	
Braintree Freeport	d					19 02								20 02									21 02	
Cressing	d					19 05								20 05									21 05	
White Notley	d					19 08								20 08									21 08	
Witham 2	d					19a16	19 22	19 47						20a16		20 22	20 47						21a16	21 22
Hatfield Peverel	d							19 51									20 51							
Chelmsford	d						19 31	19 59								20 31	20 59		21 10					21 31
Ingatestone	d							20 05									21 05							
Shenfield 3	a						19 41	20 11								20 41	21 11		21 20					21 41
Romford	a																							
Stratford 7 ⊖ ⇌	a						19 58	20 28		20s44						20 58	21 28		21s37	21s44				21 58
London Liverpool Street 15 ⊖	a						20 07	20 37		20 55						21 07	21 37		21 46	21 55				22 07

		LE	LE	LE	LE	LE	LE	LE	LE	LE		LE	LE	LE	LE	LE	LE	LE
		1		◇1		1	1	1	◇1	1		1	1	1	◇1	1	1	
			B		A													A
Norwich	d			21 00											22 00		23 05	
Diss	d			21 17											22 17		23 23	
Stowmarket	d		21 11	21 29	21 48										22 29		23 36	23 55
Needham Market	d				21 53													23 59
Ipswich	a		21 25	21 41	22 03										22 41		23 51	00 10
	d	21 09	21 25	21 43						22 09					22 43			
Harwich Town	d						21 53									22 53		
Dovercourt	d						21 55									22 55		
Harwich International	d						21 58									22 58		
Wrabness	d						22 04									23 04		
Mistley	d						22 10									23 10		
Manningtree 5	d	21 19	21 34	21 53			22a15			22 19					22 53	23 15		
Walton-on-the-Naze	d					21 29						22 18						
Frinton-on-Sea	d					21 32						22 21						
Kirby Cross	d					21 35						22 24						
Clacton-on-Sea	d								21 36				22 23					
Thorpe-le-Soken 1	a					21 41			21 44			22 30	22 31					
	d								21 44				22 31					
Weeley	d																	
Great Bentley	d								21 49									
Alresford (Essex)	d								21 53									
Wivenhoe	d								21 57				22 41					
Hythe	d								22 01				22 45					
Colchester Town	a																	
	d																	
Colchester 4	a	21 29	21 44	22 02					22 07	22 29			22 51		23 02	23 24		
	d	21 30		22 03					22 07	22 30					23 03			
Marks Tey 2	d	21 36							22 13	22 36								
Kelvedon	d	21 41								22 41								
Braintree	d							22 00						22 56				
Braintree Freeport	d							22 02						22 58				
Cressing	d							22 05						23 01				
White Notley	d							22 08						23 04				
Witham 2	d	21 47						22a16	22 22	22 47				23a12	23 16			
Hatfield Peverel	d	21 51								22 51								
Chelmsford	d	21 59							22 31	22 59					23 25			
Ingatestone	d	22 05								23 05								
Shenfield 3	a	22 11							22 41	23 11					23 36			
Romford	a																	
Stratford 7 ⊖ ⇌	a	22 28		22s44					22 58	23 28					23s55			
London Liverpool Street 15 ⊖	a	22 37		22 55					23 07	23 37					00 06			

A From Cambridge
B From Peterborough

Table T013-F

Mondays to Fridays
16 December to 15 May

Ipswich - Felixstowe and Lowestoft

Miles	Miles			LE	LE	LE	LE	LE	LE	LE	LE	LE		LE	LE	LE	LE	LE	LE	LE	LE	LE		LE	LE
—	—	Harwich International	d																						
0	—	**Ipswich**	d	05 04	06 04	06 20		07 14	07 35	08 25	08 57	09 17		09 58	10 17	10 58	11 17	11 58	12 17	12 58	13 17	13 58		14 17	14 58
3½	0	Westerfield	d	05 10	06 10	06 26		07 20	07 41	08 31	09 03			10 04		11 04		12 04		13 04		14 04			15 04
—	2½	Derby Road	d	05 15	06 15			07 25		08 36	09 08			10 09		11 09		12 09		13 09		14 09			15 09
—	10½	Trimley	d	05 24	06 24			07 34		08 45	09 17			10 18		11 18		12 18		13 18		14 18			15 18
—	12¼	**Felixstowe**	a	05 30	06 30			07 40		08 51	09 23			10 24		11 24		12 24		13 24		14 24			15 24
10¼	—	Woodbridge	d			06 37			07 53			09 32			10 32		11 32		12 32		13 32			14 32	
11½	—	Melton	d			06 41			07 57			09 36			10 36		11 36		12 36		13 36			14 36	
15¾	—	Wickham Market	d			06 48			08 04			09 43			10 43		11 43		12 43		13 43			14 43	
22½	—	Saxmundham	d			06a58	07 44		08 15			09 54			10 54		11 54		12 54		13 54			14 54	
26¾	—	Darsham	d				07 50		08 21			10 00			11 00		12 00		13 00		14 00			15 00	
32	—	Halesworth	d				08 00		08 31			10 10			11 10		12 10		13 10		14 10			15 10	
36	—	Brampton (Suffolk)	d				08x06		08x37			10x16			11x16		12x16		13x16		14x16			15x16	
40¼	—	Beccles	d				08 15		08 46			10 25			11 25		12 25		13 25		14 25			15 25	
46¾	—	Oulton Broad South	d				08 25		08 56			10 35			11 35		12 35		13 35		14 35			15 36	
49	—	**Lowestoft**	a				08 33		09 06			10 43			11 43		12 43		13 43		14 43			15 43	

		LE	LE	LE	LE	LE	LE	LE		LE	LE	LE	LE	LE	LE	LE	LE
Harwich International	d															21 38	
Ipswich	d	15 17	15 54	15 58	16 58	17 17	17 58	18 13		18 58	19 17	19 58	20 17	20 58	21 17	22 17	22 28
Westerfield	d		16 00	16 04	17 04		18 04	18 19		19 04		20 04		21 04			22 34
Derby Road	d			16 09	17 09		18 09			19 09		20 09		21 09			22 39
Trimley	d			16 18	17 18		18 18			19 18		20 18		21 18			22 48
Felixstowe	a			16 24	17 24		18 24			19 24		20 24		21 24			22 57
Woodbridge	d	15 32	16 18			17 32		18 30			19 32		20 32		21 32	22 32	
Melton	d	15 36	16 22			17 36		18 34			19 36		20 36		21 36	22 36	
Wickham Market	d	15 43	16 29			17 43		18 40			19 43		20 43		21 43	22 43	
Saxmundham	d	15 54	16 40			17 54		18 51			19 54		20 54		21 54	22 54	
Darsham	d	16 00	16 46			18 00		18 58			20 00		21 00		22 00	23 00	
Halesworth	d	16 10	16 56			18 10		19 07			20 10		21 10		22 10	23 10	
Brampton (Suffolk)	d	16x16	17x02			18x16		19x14			20x16		21x16		22x16	23x16	
Beccles	d	16 25	17 18			18 25		19 25			20 25		21 25		22 25	23 25	
Oulton Broad South	d	16 35	17 28			18 35		19 35			20 35		21 35		22 35	23 35	
Lowestoft	a	16 43	17 36			18 43		19 43			20 43		21 43		22 43	23 43	

Saturdays
21 December to 16 May

		LE	LE	LE	LE	LE	LE	LE	LE	LE		LE	LE	LE	LE	LE	LE	LE	LE	LE		LE	LE	LE	LE
Harwich International	d																								
Ipswich	d	05 58	06 58	07 17	07 58	08 17	08 58	09 17	09 58	10 17		10 58	11 17	11 58	12 17	12 58	13 17	13 58	14 17	14 58		15 17	15 58	16 17	16 58
Westerfield	d	06 04	07 04		08 04		09 04		10 04			11 05		12 04		13 04		14 04		15 04			16 04		17 04
Derby Road	d	06 09	07 09		08 09		09 09		10 09			11 10		12 09		13 09		14 09		15 09			16 09		17 09
Trimley	d	06 18	07 18		08 18		09 18		10 18			11 19		12 18		13 18		14 18		15 18			16 18		17 18
Felixstowe	a	06 24	07 24		08 24		09 24		10 24			11 24		12 24		13 24		14 24		15 24			16 24		17 24
Woodbridge	d			07 32		08 32		09 32		10 32			11 32		12 32		13 32		14 32			15 32		16 32	
Melton	d			07 36		08 36		09 36		10 36			11 36		12 36		13 36		14 36			15 36		16 36	
Wickham Market	d			07 43		08 43		09 43		10 43			11 43		12 43		13 43		14 43			15 43		16 43	
Saxmundham	d			07 54		08 54		09 54		10 54			11 54		12 54		13 54		14 54			15 54		16 54	
Darsham	d			08 00		09 00		10 00		11 00			12 00		13 00		14 00		15 00			16 00		17 00	
Halesworth	d			08 10		09 10		10 10		11 10			12 10		13 10		14 10		15 10			16 10		17 10	
Brampton (Suffolk)	d			08x16		09x16		10x16		11x16			12x16		13x16		14x16		15x16			16x16		17x16	
Beccles	d			08 25		09 25		10 25		11 25			12 25		13 25		14 25		15 25			16 25		17 25	
Oulton Broad South	d			08 35		09 35		10 35		11 35			12 35		13 35		14 35		15 35			16 35		17 41	
Lowestoft	a			08 43		09 43		10 43		11 43			12 43		13 43		14 43		15 43			16 43		17 51	

		LE	LE	LE	LE	LE		LE	LE	LE	LE	LE	LE
Harwich International	d											21 38	
Ipswich	d	17 17	17 58	18 17	18 58	19 17		19 58	20 17	20 58	21 17	22 17	22 28
Westerfield	d		18 04		19 04			20 04		21 04			22 34
Derby Road	d		18 09		19 09			20 09		21 09			22 39
Trimley	d		18 18		19 18			20 18		21 18			22 48
Felixstowe	a		18 24		19 24			20 24		21 24			22 53
Woodbridge	d	17 32		18 32		19 32			20 32		21 32	22 32	
Melton	d	17 36		18 36		19 36			20 36		21 36	22 36	
Wickham Market	d	17 43		18 43		19 43			20 43		21 43	22 43	
Saxmundham	d	17 54		18 54		19 54			20 54		21 54	22 54	
Darsham	d	18 00		19 00		20 00			21 00		22 00	23 00	
Halesworth	d	18 10		19 10		20 10			21 10		22 10	23 10	
Brampton (Suffolk)	d	18x16		19x16		20x16			21x16		22x16	23x16	
Beccles	d	18 25		19 25		20 25			21 25		22 25	23 25	
Oulton Broad South	d	18 35		19 35		20 35			21 35		22 35	23 35	
Lowestoft	a	18 43		19 43		20 43			21 43		22 43	23 43	

Sundays
15 December to 10 May

		LE	LE	LE	LE	LE	LE	LE	LE	LE		LE	LE	LE	LE	LE	LE	LE	LE	LE		LE	LE	LE	LE	LE	LE
Harwich International	d																										
Ipswich	d	09 55	10 08	10 55	11 10	11 55	12 08	12 55	13 10	13 55		14 08	14 55	15 10	15 55	16 08	16 55	17 10	17 55	18 08		18 55	19 08	19 55	20 11	21 08	22 02
Westerfield	d	10 01	10 14	11 01		12 01	12 14	13 01		14 01		14 14	15 01		16 01	16 14	17 01		18 01	18 14		19 01	19 14	20 01		21 14	22 08
Derby Road	d	10 06		11 06		12 06		13 06		14 06			15 06		16 06		17 06		18 06			19 06		20 06			
Trimley	d	10 15		11 15		12 15		13 15		14 15			15 15		16 15		17 15		18 15			19 15		20 15			
Felixstowe	a	10 21		11 21		12 21		13 21		14 21			15 21		16 21		17 21		18 21			19 21		20 21			
Woodbridge	d		10 25		11 25		12 25		13 25			14 25		15 25		16 25		17 25		18 25			19 25		20 26	21 25	22 19
Melton	d		10 29		11 29		12 29		13 29			14 29		15 29		16 29		17 29		18 29			19 29		20 30	21 29	22 23
Wickham Market	d		10 36		11 36		12 36		13 36			14 36		15 36		16 36		17 36		18 36			19 36		20 37	21 36	22 29
Saxmundham	d		10 47		11 47		12 47		13 47			14 47		15 47		16 47		17 47		18 47			19 47		20 48	21 47	22 40
Darsham	d		10 53		11 53		12 53		13 53			14 53		15 53		16 53		17 53		18 53			19 53		20 54	21 53	22 46
Halesworth	d		11 03		12 03		13 03		14 03			15 03		16 03		17 03		18 03		19 03			20 03		21 04	22 03	22 56
Brampton (Suffolk)	d		11x09		12x09		13x09		14x09			15x09		16x09		17x09		18x09		19x09			20x09		21x10	22x09	23x02
Beccles	d		11 18		12 18		13 18		14 18			15 18		16 18		17 18		18 18		19 18			20 18		21 19	22 18	23 11
Oulton Broad South	d		11 28		12 28		13 28		14 28			15 28		16 28		17 28		18 28		19 28			20 28		21 29	22 28	23 21
Lowestoft	a		11 36		12 36		13 36		14 36			15 36		16 36		17 36		18 36		19 36			20 36		21 37	22 36	23 30

Table T013-R

Mondays to Fridays

16 December to 15 May

Lowestoft and Felixstowe - Ipswich

Miles	Miles			LE	LE	LE	LE	LE	LE	LE	LE	LE	LE	LE	LE	LE	LE	LE	LE	LE	LE	LE	LE
0	—	**Lowestoft**	d		05 25		06 14	06 41		07 27			09 07		10 07		11 07		12 07		13 07		14 07
2¼	—	Oulton Broad South	d		05 31		06 20	06 47		07 33			09 13		10 13		11 13		12 13		13 13		14 13
8½	—	Beccles	d		05 41		06 30	06 57		07 43			09 25		10 25		11 25		12 25		13 25		14 25
13	—	Brampton (Suffolk)	d		05x49		06x38	07x05		07x51			09x33		10x33		11x33		12x33		13x33		14x33
17	—	Halesworth	d		05 56		06 45	07 12		07 58			09 41		10 41		11 41		12 41		13 41		14 41
22¼	—	Darsham	d		06 05		06 54	07 21		08 07			09 49		10 49		11 49		12 49		13 49		14 49
26½	—	Saxmundham	d		06 12		07 02	07 28		08 15			09 56		10 56		11 56		12 56		13 56		14 56
33¾	—	Wickham Market	d		06 22		07 12	07 38		08 25			10 06		11 06		12 06		13 06		14 06		15 06
37¼	—	Melton	d		06 29		07 19	07 45		08 32			10 12		11 12		12 12		13 12		14 12		15 12
38¾	—	Woodbridge	d		06 35		07 25	07 51		08 38			10 18		11 18		12 18		13 18		14 18		15 18
—	0	**Felixstowe**	d	05 34		06 36			07 47		08 54	09 28		10 28		11 28		12 28		13 28		14 28	
—	1¾	Trimley	d	05 37		06 39			07 50		08 57	09 31		10 31		11 31		12 31		13 31		14 31	
—	9¾	Derby Road	d	05 47		06 49			08 00		09 09	09 41		10 41		11 41		12 41		13 41		14 41	
45½	12½	Westerfield	d	05 52	06 46	06 54	07 35	08 01	08 05	08 49	09 14	09 46		10 46		11 46		12 46		13 46		14 46	
49	—	**Ipswich**	a	06 01	06 53	07 02	07 44	08 09	08 14	08 56	09 24	09 54	10 36	10 54	11 36	11 54	12 36	12 54	13 36	13 54	14 36	14 54	15 36
—	—	Harwich International	a		07 26																		

		LE	LE	LE	LE	LE	LE	LE	LE	LE	LE	LE	LE	LE	LE	LE	LE
Lowestoft	d		15 07		16 07		17 02		18 07		19 07		20 07		21 07		
Oulton Broad South	d		15 13		16 13		17 08		18 13		19 13		20 13		21 13		
Beccles	d		15 25		16 25		17 25		18 25		19 25		20 25		21 25		
Brampton (Suffolk)	d		15x33		16x33		17x33		18x33		19x33		20x33		21x33		
Halesworth	d		15 41		16 41		17 41		18 41		19 41		20 41		21 41		
Darsham	d		15 49		16 49		17 49		18 49		19 49		20 49		21 49		
Saxmundham	d		15 56		17 06		17 56		18 56		19 56		20 56		21 56		
Wickham Market	d		16 06		17 16		18 06		19 06		20 06		21 06		22 06		
Melton	d		16 12		17 22		18 12		19 12		20 12		21 12		22 12		
Woodbridge	d		16 18		17 28		18 18		19 18		20 18		21 18		22 18		
Felixstowe	d	15 28		16 28		17 28		18 28		19 28		20 28		21 28			23 01
Trimley	d	15 31		16 31		17 31		18 31		19 31		20 31		21 31			23 04
Derby Road	d	15 41		16 41		17 41		18 41		19 41		20 41		21 41			23 14
Westerfield	d	15 46		16 46		17 46		18 46		19 46		20 46		21 46	22 29		23 19
Ipswich	a	15 54	16 36	16 54	17 46	17 53	18 36	18 54	19 36	19 54	20 37	20 54	21 36	21 54	22 36		23 27
Harwich International	a																

Saturdays

21 December to 16 May

		LE	LE	LE	LE	LE	LE	LE	LE	LE	LE	LE	LE	LE	LE	LE	LE	LE	LE	LE	LE	LE	LE
Lowestoft	d		06 07		07 07		08 07		09 07		10 07		11 07		12 07		13 07		14 07		15 07		16 07
Oulton Broad South	d		06 13		07 13		08 13		09 13		10 13		11 13		12 13		13 13		14 13		15 13		16 13
Beccles	d		06 25		07 25		08 25		09 25		10 25		11 25		12 25		13 25		14 25		15 25		16 25
Brampton (Suffolk)	d		06x33		07x33		08x33		09x33		10x33		11x33		12x33		13x33		14x33		15x33		16x33
Halesworth	d		06 41		07 41		08 41		09 41		10 41		11 41		12 41		13 41		14 41		15 41		16 41
Darsham	d		06 49		07 49		08 49		09 49		10 49		11 49		12 49		13 49		14 49		15 49		16 49
Saxmundham	d		06 56		07 56		08 56		09 56		10 56		11 56		12 56		13 56		14 56		15 56		16 56
Wickham Market	d		07 06		08 06		09 06		10 06		11 06		12 06		13 06		14 06		15 06		16 06		17 06
Melton	d		07 12		08 12		09 12		10 12		11 12		12 12		13 12		14 12		15 12		16 12		17 12
Woodbridge	d		07 18		08 18		09 18		10 18		11 18		12 18		13 18		14 18		15 18		16 18		17 18
Felixstowe	d	06 28		07 28		08 28		09 28		10 28		11 28		12 28		13 28		14 28		15 28		16 28	
Trimley	d	06 31		07 31		08 31		09 31		10 31		11 31		12 31		13 31		14 31		15 31		16 31	
Derby Road	d	06 41		07 41		08 41		09 41		10 41		11 41		12 41		13 41		14 41		15 41		16 41	
Westerfield	d	06 46		07 46		08 46		09 46		10 46		11 46		12 46		13 46		14 46		15 46		16 46	
Ipswich	a	06 54	07 36	07 54	08 36	08 54	09 36	09 54	10 36	10 54	11 36	11 54	12 36	12 54	13 36	13 54	14 36	14 54	15 36	15 54	16 36	16 54	17 36
Harwich International	a																						

		LE	LE	LE	LE	LE	LE	LE	LE	LE	LE	LE
Lowestoft	d		17 07		18 07		19 07		20 07		21 07	
Oulton Broad South	d		17 13		18 13		19 13		20 13		21 13	
Beccles	d		17 25		18 25		19 25		20 25		21 25	
Brampton (Suffolk)	d		17x33		18x33		19x33		20x33		21x33	
Halesworth	d		17 41		18 41		19 41		20 41		21 41	
Darsham	d		17 49		18 49		19 49		20 49		21 49	
Saxmundham	d		17 56		18 56		19 56		20 56		21 56	
Wickham Market	d		18 06		19 06		20 06		21 06		22 06	
Melton	d		18 12		19 12		20 12		21 12		22 12	
Woodbridge	d		18 18		19 18		20 18		21 18		22 18	
Felixstowe	d	17 28		18 28		19 28		20 28		21 28		22 58
Trimley	d	17 31		18 31		19 31		20 31		21 31		23 01
Derby Road	d	17 41		18 41		19 41		20 41		21 41		23 11
Westerfield	d	17 46		18 46		19 46		20 46		21 46	22 29	23 16
Ipswich	a	17 54	18 36	18 54	19 36	19 54	20 36	20 54	21 36	21 54	22 36	23 25
Harwich International	a											

Sundays

15 December to 10 May

		LE	LE	LE	LE	LE	LE	LE	LE	LE	LE	LE	LE	LE	LE	LE	LE	LE	LE	LE	LE	LE	LE	LE	LE
Lowestoft	d	08 05	09 05		10 05		11 00		12 00		13 00		14 00		15 00		16 00		17 00		18 00		19 00		20 00
Oulton Broad South	d	08 11	09 11		10 11		11 06		12 06		13 06		14 06		15 06		16 06		17 06		18 06		19 06		20 06
Beccles	d	08 21	09 21		10 21		11 21		12 21		13 21		14 21		15 21		16 21		17 21		18 21		19 21		20 21
Brampton (Suffolk)	d	08x29	09x29		10x29		11x29		12x29		13x29		14x29		15x29		16x29		17x29		18x29		19x29		20x29
Halesworth	d	08 36	09 36		10 36		11 36		12 36		13 36		14 36		15 36		16 36		17 36		18 36		19 36		20 36
Darsham	d	08 44	09 44		10 44		11 44		12 44		13 44		14 44		15 44		16 44		17 44		18 44		19 44		20 44
Saxmundham	d	08 52	09 52		10 52		11 52		12 52		13 52		14 52		15 52		16 52		17 52		18 52		19 52		20 52
Wickham Market	d	09 01	10 01		11 01		12 01		13 01		14 01		15 01		16 01		17 01		18 01		19 01		20 01		21 01
Melton	d	09 08	10 08		11 08		12 08		13 08		14 08		15 08		16 08		17 08		18 08		19 08		20 08		21 08
Woodbridge	d	09 14	10 14		11 14		12 14		13 14		14 14		15 14		16 14		17 14		18 14		19 14		20 14		21 14
Felixstowe	d			10 25		11 25		12 25		13 25		14 25		15 25		16 25		17 25		18 25		19 25		20 25	
Trimley	d			10 28		11 28		12 28		13 28		14 28		15 28		16 28		17 28		18 28		19 28		20 28	
Derby Road	d			10 38		11 38		12 38		13 38		14 38		15 38		16 38		17 38		18 38		19 38		20 38	
Westerfield	d	09 24		10 43	11 24	11 43		12 43	13 24	13 43		14 43	15 24	15 43		16 43	17 24	17 43	18 24	18 43	19 24	19 43		20 43	21 24
Ipswich	a	09 32	10 32	10 50	11 32	11 50	12 32	12 50	13 32	13 50	14 32	14 51	15 32	15 50	16 32	16 50	17 32	17 50	18 32	18 50	19 32	19 50	20 32	20 50	21 32
Harwich International	a																								

Table T014-F

Mondays to Fridays

16 December to 15 May

Ipswich - Bury St. Edmunds, Cambridge, Ely and Peterborough

Miles	Miles	Miles			LE	LE	LE	LE	LE	LE	LE	LE	LE	LE	LE	LE	LE	LE	LE	LE	LE	LE	LE
—	—	—	Colchester	d		05 40																	
—	—	—	Manningtree	d		05 49																	
—	—	0	Harwich International	d						07 50													
0	0	18	**Ipswich**	d	05 10	06 00	06 16	06 54	08 03	08 21	09 20	10 01	10 20	11 20	12 01	12 20	13 20	13 58	14 20	15 20	16 00	16 20	17 20
8½	—	—	Needham Market	d	05 20		06 25	07 03		08 29	09 29		10 29	11 29		12 29	13 29		14 29	15 29		16 29	17 29
12	12	—	Stowmarket	d	05 26	06 12	06 31	07 09	08 16	08 35	09 38	10 13	10 35	11 35	12 13	12 35	13 35	14 11	14 35	15 35	16 12	16 35	17 35
17¾	—	—	Elmswell	d	05 35		06 39	07 17		08 44	09 46		10 43	11 43		12 43	13 43		14 43	15 43		16 43	17 43
22¼	—	—	Thurston	d	05 41		06 45	07 23		08 50	09 52		10 49	11 49		12 49	13 49		14 49	15 49		16 49	17 49
26½	26½	—	**Bury St Edmunds**	a	05 48	06 28	06 51	07 29	08 32	08 56	09 58	10 29	10 55	11 55	12 30	12 55	13 55	14 27	14 55	15 55	16 29	16 55	17 55
—	—	—	**Bury St Edmunds**	d	05 49	06 29	06 54	07 33	08 33	08 58	10 00	10 30	10 57	11 57	12 31	12 57	13 57	14 29	14 57	15 57	16 29	16 57	17 57
36	—	—	Kennett	d	06 00		07 04	07 43			10 10			12 07			14 07			16 07		17 07	18 10
41	—	—	Newmarket	d	06 09		07 15	07 52		09 18	10 20		11 18	12 19		13 18	14 19		15 18	16 19		17 19	18 19
44¾	—	—	Dullingham	d	06 14		07 20	08 00		09 23			11 23			13 23			15 23				
55½	—	—	**Cambridge**	a	06 33		07 40	08 19		09 42	10 42		11 41	12 41		13 41	14 41		15 41	16 41		17 42	18 41
—	51	—	**Ely** 6	a		06 56			08 59			10 58			12 58			14 58			16 58		
				d		06 57			08 59			10 58			12 58			14 58			16 58		
—	60¾	—	Manea	a		07 07			09 10			11 09			13 09			15 09			17 09		
—	66½	—	March	a		07 15			09 17			11 16			13 16			15 16			17 16		
—	74¼	—	Whittlesea	a		07 26			09 29			11 28			13 28			15 28			17 28		
—	81¼	—	**Peterborough** 8	a		07 38			09 40			11 39			13 39			15 39			17 39		

		LE	LE	LE	LE	LE	LE	LE
Colchester	d							
Manningtree	d							
Harwich International	d							
Ipswich	d	17 41	18 17	19 13	20 01	20 21	21 17	22 19
Needham Market	d	17 51	18 26	19 22		20 30	21 27	22 29
Stowmarket	d	17 58	18 32	19 28	20 13	20 36	21 33	22 35
Elmswell	d	18 07	18 40	19 36		20 45	21 42	22 44
Thurston	d	18 14	18 46	19 42		20 51	21 48	22 50
Bury St Edmunds	a	18 20	18 52	19 48	20 29	20 57	21 55	22 57
Bury St Edmunds	d	18 27	18 57	19 57	20 30	20 58	21 56	
Kennett	d	18 38		20 07			22 07	
Newmarket	d		19 18	20 19		21 18	22 20	
Dullingham	d		19 23			21 24	22 25	
Cambridge	a		19 41	20 42		21 42	22 42	
Ely 6	a	18 56			20 59			
	d	18 58			21 01			
Manea	a	19 09			21 10			
March	a	19 16			21 18			
Whittlesea	a	19 28			21 30			
Peterborough 8	a	19 39			21 40			

Saturdays

21 December to 16 May

		LE	LE	LE	LE	LE	LE	LE	LE	LE	LE	LE	LE	LE	LE	LE	LE	LE	LE	LE	LE	LE	LE
Colchester	d		05 40																				
Manningtree	d		05 49																				
Harwich International	d						07 50																
Ipswich	d	05 10	06 00	06 16	07 20	08 00	08 21	09 20	09 58	10 20	11 20	12 01	12 20	13 20	13 58	14 20	15 20	15 58	16 20	17 20	17 58	18 20	19 20
Needham Market	d	05 20		06 25	07 29		08 29	09 29		10 29	11 29		12 29	13 29		14 29	15 29		16 29	17 29		18 29	19 29
Stowmarket	d	05 26	06 12	06 31	07 35	08 12	08 35	09 35	10 11	10 35	11 35	12 13	12 35	13 35	14 11	14 35	15 35	16 11	16 35	17 35	18 11	18 35	19 35
Elmswell	d	05 35		06 39	07 43		08 44	09 43		10 43	11 43		12 43	13 43		14 43	15 43		16 43	17 43		18 43	19 43
Thurston	d	05 41		06 45	07 49		08 50	09 49		10 49	11 49		12 49	13 49		14 49	15 49		16 49	17 49		18 49	19 49
Bury St Edmunds	a	05 48	06 28	06 52	07 55	08 28	08 56	09 55	10 27	10 55	11 55	12 30	12 55	13 55	14 27	14 55	15 55	16 27	16 55	17 55	18 27	18 55	19 55
Bury St Edmunds	d	05 49	06 29	06 54	07 57	08 29	08 57	09 57	10 29	10 57	11 57	12 31	12 57	13 57	14 29	14 57	15 57	16 29	16 57	17 57	18 29	18 57	19 57
Kennett	d	06 00		07 06	08 07			10 07			12 08			14 07			16 07		17 09	18 07			20 07
Newmarket	d	06 09		07 16	08 19		09 18	10 19		11 18	12 19		13 18	14 19		15 18	16 19		17 19	18 19		19 18	20 19
Dullingham	d	06 14		07 21	08 24		09 23			11 23			13 23			15 23						19 23	
Cambridge	a	06 32		07 40	08 40		09 40	10 40		11 40	12 40		13 40	14 40		15 40	16 40		17 40	18 40		19 40	20 40
Ely 6	a		06 57			08 58			10 58			12 58			14 58			16 58			18 58		
	d		06 58			08 58			10 58			12 58			14 58			16 58			18 58		
Manea	a		07 09			09 09			11 09			13 09			15 09			17 09			19 09		
March	a		07 16			09 16			11 16			13 16			15 16			17 16			19 16		
Whittlesea	a		07 28			09 28			11 28			13 28			15 28			17 28			19 28		
Peterborough 8	a		07 39			09 39			11 39			13 39			15 39			17 39			19 39		

		LE	LE	LE	LE
Colchester	d				
Manningtree	d				
Harwich International	d				
Ipswich	d	20 01	20 20	21 17	22 19
Needham Market	d		20 29	21 27	22 29
Stowmarket	d	20 13	20 35	21 33	22 35
Elmswell	d		20 43	21 42	22 44
Thurston	d		20 49	21 48	22 50
Bury St Edmunds	a	20 30	20 55	21 55	22 57
Bury St Edmunds	d	20 31	20 57	21 56	
Kennett	d			22 07	
Newmarket	d		21 18	22 19	
Dullingham	d		21 23	22 25	
Cambridge	a		21 40	22 42	
Ely 6	a	20 58			
	d	20 58			
Manea	a	21 09			
March	a	21 16			
Whittlesea	a	21 28			
Peterborough 8	a	21 39			

For complete service between Ely and Peterborough refer to Table T017

For complete service between Colchester and Stowmarket refer to Table T011

Table T014-F

Sundays
15 December to 10 May

Ipswich - Bury St. Edmunds, Cambridge, Ely and Peterborough

		LE	LE	LE	LE	LE	LE	LE	LE	LE	LE	LE	LE	LE	LE	LE	LE	LE	LE	LE
Colchester	d				09 32															
Manningtree	d				09 40															
Harwich International	d			08 50																
Ipswich	d	07 34	08 20	09 20	09 55	10 20	11 20	11 55	12 20	13 20	13 55	14 20	15 20	15 55	16 20	17 20	17 55	18 20	19 20	21 05
Needham Market	d	07 44	08 29	09 29		10 29	11 29		12 29	13 29		14 29	15 29		16 29	17 29		18 29	19 29	21 14
Stowmarket	d	07 49	08 35	09 35	10 07	10 35	11 35	12 07	12 35	13 35	14 07	14 35	15 35	16 07	16 35	17 35	18 07	18 35	19 35	21 20
Elmswell	d	07 58	08 44	09 44		10 44	11 44		12 44	13 44		14 44	15 44		16 44	17 44		18 44	19 44	21 29
Thurston	d	08 04	08 50	09 50		10 50	11 50		12 50	13 50		14 50	15 50		16 50	17 50		18 50	19 50	21 35
Bury St Edmunds	a	08 11	08 57	09 57	10 24	10 57	11 57	12 24	12 57	13 57	14 24	14 57	15 57	16 24	16 57	17 57	18 24	18 57	19 57	21 42
Bury St Edmunds	d	08 11	08 58	09 57	10 25	10 58	11 57	12 25	12 58	13 57	14 25	14 58	15 57	16 25	16 58	17 57	18 25	18 58	19 57	21 42
Kennett	d	08 22		10 08			12 08			14 08			16 08			18 08			20 08	21 53
Newmarket	d	08 31	09 17	10 17		11 17	12 17		13 18	14 17		15 17	16 17		17 17	18 17		19 17	20 17	22 01
Dullingham	d	08 36		10 22			12 22			14 22			16 22			18 22			20 22	22 06
Cambridge	a	08 54	09 40	10 40		11 40	12 40		13 40	14 40		15 40	16 40		17 40	18 40		19 40	20 40	22 25
Ely 6	a				10 52			12 52			14 52			16 52			18 52			
	d				10 52			12 52			14 52			16 52			18 52			
Manea	a																			
March	a				11 08			13 08			15 08			17 08			19 08			
Whittlesea	a				11 20			13 20			15 20			17 20			19 20			
Peterborough 8	a				11 31			13 31			15 31			17 31			19 31			

For complete service between Ely and Peterborough refer to Table T017

For complete service between Colchester and Stowmarket refer to Table T011

AVAILABLE FROM MP Middleton Press

Table T014-R

Mondays to Fridays
16 December to 15 May

Peterborough, Ely, Cambridge and Bury St. Edmunds - Ipswich

Miles	Miles	Miles			LE	LE	LE	LE	LE	LE	LE	LE	LE	LE	LE	LE	LE	LE	LE	LE	LE	LE	LE
0	—	—	**Peterborough** 8	d					07 49			09 50			11 50			13 50			15 50		
7	—	—	Whittlesea	d					07 57			09 58			11 58			13 58			15 58		
14¾	—	—	March	d					08 08			10 09			12 09			14 09			16 09		
20½	—	—	Manea	d					08 16			10 17			12 17			14 17			16 17		
30¼	—	—	**Ely** 6	a					08 29			10 31			12 31			14 31			16 31		
—	—	—		d					08 30			10 32			12 32			14 32			16 32		
—	0	—	**Cambridge**	d			06 42	07 44		08 47	09 47		10 47	11 47		12 47	13 47		14 47	15 47		16 47	17 47
—	11¼	—	Dullingham	d				08 00			10 04			12 03			14 03			16 03		17 03	18 03
—	14½	—	Newmarket	d			07 02	08 05		09 07	10 09		11 07	12 08		13 07	14 08		15 07	16 08		17 08	18 08
—	19½	—	Kennett	d			07 10			09 15			11 15			13 15			15 15			17 16	18 16
54¾	29¼	—	**Bury St Edmunds**	a			07 21	08 23	08 56	09 26	10 27	10 58	11 26	12 26	12 58	13 26	14 26	14 58	15 26	16 26	16 58	17 27	18 27
—	—	—	**Bury St Edmunds**	d	05 31	06 22	07 24	08 24	08 56	09 26	10 27	10 58	11 26	12 26	12 58	13 26	14 26	14 58	15 26	16 26	16 58	17 28	18 28
—	33¼	—	Thurston	d	05 37	06 28	07 30	08 30		09 32	10 33		11 32	12 32		13 32	14 32		15 32	16 32		17 34	18 34
—	37¾	—	Elmswell	d	05 43	06 34	07 36	08 36		09 38	10 39		11 38	12 38		13 38	14 38		15 38	16 38		17 40	18 40
69¼	43¾	—	Stowmarket	d	05 51	06 42	07 45	08 45	09 12	09 48	10 48	11 14	11 47	12 47	13 14	13 47	14 47	15 14	15 47	16 47	17 14	17 48	18 48
—	47¼	—	Needham Market	d	05 56	06 47	07 50	08 50		09 53	10 53		11 52	12 52		13 52	14 52		15 52	16 52		17 53	18 53
81¼	55¾	0	**Ipswich**	a	06 07	06 58	08 01	09 03	09 26	10 04	11 03	11 28	12 02	13 02	13 28	14 02	15 02	15 28	16 04	17 02	17 28	18 03	19 03
—	—	18	Harwich International	a																			
—	—	—	Manningtree	a																			
—	—	—	Colchester	a																			

		LE	LE	LE	LE	LE	LE	LE	LE
Peterborough 8	d	17 50			19 50			21 45	
Whittlesea	d	17 58			19 58			21 53	
March	d	18 09			20 09			22 04	
Manea	d	18 17			20 17			22 12	
Ely 6	a	18 31			20 31			22 25	
	d	18 31			20 31			22 26	
Cambridge	d		18 47	19 47		20 47	21 47		22 47
Dullingham	d			20 03			22 03		23 03
Newmarket	d		19 07	20 08		21 07	22 08		23 08
Kennett	d		19 15			21 15			23 16
Bury St Edmunds	a	18 57	19 26	20 26	20 58	21 26	22 26	22 52	23 27
Bury St Edmunds	d	18 58	19 26	20 26	20 58	21 26	22 26	22 52	23 28
Thurston	d		19 32	20 32		21 32	22 32		23 34
Elmswell	d		19 38	20 38		21 38	22 38		23 40
Stowmarket	d	19 14	19 47	20 47	21 14	21 47	22 47	23 08	23 48
Needham Market	d		19 52	20 52		21 52	22 52		23 53
Ipswich	a	19 28	20 04	21 02	21 28	22 02	23 02	23 21	00 04
Harwich International	a			21 29					
Manningtree	a				21 37			23 31	
Colchester	a				21 51			23 42	

Saturdays
21 December to 16 May

		LE	LE	LE	LE	LE	LE	LE	LE	LE	LE	LE	LE	LE	LE	LE	LE	LE	LE	LE	LE	LE	LE ◇ A
Peterborough 8	d				07 50			09 50			11 50			13 50			15 50			17 50			19 50
Whittlesea	d				07 58			09 58			11 58			13 58			15 58			17 58			19 58
March	d				08 09			10 09			12 09			14 09			16 09			18 09			20 09
Manea	d				08 17			10 17			12 17			14 17			16 17			18 17			20 17
Ely 6	a				08 31			10 31			12 31			14 31			16 31			18 31			20 32
	d				08 32			10 32			12 32			14 32			16 32			18 32			20 32
Cambridge	d		06 42	07 47		08 47	09 47		10 47	11 47		12 47	13 47		14 47	15 47		16 47	17 47		18 47	19 47	
Dullingham	d			08 03			10 03			12 03			14 03			16 03		17 03	18 03			20 03	
Newmarket	d		07 02	08 08		09 07	10 08		11 07	12 08		13 07	14 08		15 07	16 08		17 08	18 08		19 07	20 08	
Kennett	d		07 10			09 15			11 15			13 15			15 15			17 16	18 16		19 15		
Bury St Edmunds	a		07 23	08 25	08 58	09 26	10 25	10 58	11 26	12 25	12 58	13 26	14 25	14 58	15 26	16 25	16 58	17 27	18 27	18 58	19 26	20 25	20 58
Bury St Edmunds	d	06 23	07 23	08 26	08 58	09 26	10 26	10 58	11 26	12 26	12 58	13 26	14 26	14 58	15 26	16 26	16 58	17 28	18 28	18 58	19 26	20 26	20 58
Thurston	d	06 29	07 30	08 32		09 32	10 32		11 32	12 32		13 32	14 32		15 32	16 32		17 34	18 34		19 32	20 32	
Elmswell	d	06 36	07 36	08 38		09 38	10 38		11 38	12 38		13 38	14 38		15 38	16 38		17 40	18 40		19 38	20 38	
Stowmarket	d	06 46	07 45	08 47	09 14	09 47	10 47	11 14	11 47	12 47	13 14	13 47	14 47	15 14	15 47	16 47	17 14	17 49	18 49	19 14	19 47	20 46	21 14
Needham Market	d	06 51	07 50	08 52		09 52	10 52		11 52	12 52		13 52	14 52		15 52	16 52		17 54	18 54		19 52	20 51	
Ipswich	a	07 02	08 02	09 02	09 28	10 02	11 02	11 28	12 02	13 02	13 28	14 02	15 02	15 29	16 02	17 02	17 28	18 03	19 03	19 28	20 02	21 01	21 28
Harwich International	a																					21 29	
Manningtree	a																						21 37
Colchester	a																						21 48

A ◇ from Ipswich

For complete service between Ely and Peterborough refer to Table T017

For complete service between Colchester and Stowmarket refer to Table T011

Table T014-R

Saturdays

21 December to 16 May

Peterborough, Ely, Cambridge and Bury St. Edmunds - Ipswich

		LE	LE	LE	LE
Peterborough ■	d			21 47	
Whittlesea	d			21 55	
March	d			22 06	
Manea	d			22 14	
Ely ■	a			22 27	
	d			22 28	
Cambridge	d	20 47	21 47		22 47
Dullingham	d		22 03		23 03
Newmarket	d	21 07	22 08		23 08
Kennett	d	21 15			23 16
Bury St Edmunds	a	21 26	22 25	22 54	23 29
Bury St Edmunds	d	21 26	22 26	22 54	23 29
Thurston	d	21 32	22 32		23 35
Elmswell	d	21 38	22 38		23 42
Stowmarket	d	21 47	22 46	23 10	23 51
Needham Market	d	21 52	22 51		23 56
Ipswich	a	22 02	23 03	23 23	00 08
Harwich International	a				
Manningtree	a			23 31	
Colchester	a			23 42	

Sundays

15 December to 10 May

		LE	LE	LE	LE	LE	LE	LE	LE	LE	LE	LE	LE	LE	LE	LE	LE	LE	LE	LE
Peterborough ■	d					11 47			13 50			15 47			17 45			19 47		
Whittlesea	d					11 55			13 58			15 55			17 53			19 55		
March	d					12 06			14 09			16 06			18 04			20 06		
Manea	d																			
Ely ■	a					12 25			14 31			16 25			18 23			20 25		
	d					12 28			14 32			16 28			18 29			20 28		
Cambridge	d	09 00	09 46	10 45	11 46		12 46	13 46		14 45	15 46		16 45	17 46		18 45	19 46		20 46	22 52
Dullingham	d	09 22		11 01			13 02			15 01			17 01			19 01			21 02	23 08
Newmarket	d	09 27	10 06	11 06	12 06		13 07	14 06		15 06	16 06		17 06	18 06		19 06	20 06		21 07	23 13
Kennett	d	09 36		11 14			13 15			15 14			17 14			19 14			21 15	23 21
Bury St Edmunds	a	09 47	10 23	11 25	12 23	12 54	13 26	14 23	14 58	15 25	16 23	16 54	17 25	18 23	18 55	19 25	20 23	20 55	21 26	23 32
Bury St Edmunds	d	09 47	10 26	11 26	12 26	12 55	13 27	14 26	14 58	15 26	16 26	16 55	17 26	18 26	18 55	19 26	20 25	20 55	21 27	23 33
Thurston	d	09 53	10 32	11 32	12 32		13 33	14 32		15 32	16 32		17 32	18 32		19 32	20 31		21 33	23 39
Elmswell	d	09 59	10 38	11 38	12 38		13 39	14 38		15 38	16 38		17 38	18 38		19 38	20 37		21 39	23 45
Stowmarket	d	10 08	10 47	11 47	12 47	13 11	13 48	14 47	15 14	15 47	16 47	17 11	17 47	18 47	19 11	19 47	20 46	21 11	21 48	23 55
Needham Market	d	10 13	10 52	11 52	12 52		13 53	14 52		15 52	16 52		17 52	18 52		19 52	20 51		21 53	23 59
Ipswich	a	10 24	11 02	12 02	13 02	13 25	14 02	15 02	15 27	16 02	17 02	17 25	18 02	19 02	19 25	20 02	21 03	21 25	22 03	00 10
Harwich International	a																21 29			
Manningtree	a														19 34			21 34		
Colchester	a														19 44			21 44		

For complete service between Ely and Peterborough refer to Table T017

For complete service between Colchester and Stowmarket refer to Table T011

Table T015-F

Mondays to Fridays

16 December to 14 February

Norwich - Great Yarmouth and Lowestoft

Miles	Miles	Miles			LE	LE	LE	LE	LE	LE	LE	LE	LE	LE	LE	LE	LE	LE	LE	LE	LE	LE	LE
—	—	—	London Liverpool Street ■ ⊖	d																			
0	0	0	**Norwich**	d	05 06	05 36	06 11	06 27	06 45	06 52	07 43	07 55	08 09	08 37	08 55	09 36	10 05	10 36	10 58	11 36	12 05	12 36	12 55
4¾	4¾	4¾	Brundall Gardens	d		05 43	06 18			06 59		08 02		08 44		09 43		10 43		11 43		12 43	
5¾	5¾	5¾	Brundall	d	05 15	05 46	06 21	06 36	06 54	07 02	07 52	08 05		08 47		09 46	10 14	10 46		11 46	12 14	12 46	
8	—	—	Lingwood	d			06 26			07 07	07 57		08 21	08 52		09 51		10 51		11 51		12 51	
10½	—	—	Acle	d			06 35			07 12	08 02		08 28	08 59		09 56		10 56		11 57		12 56	
—	7¾	7¾	Buckenham	d																			
—	10	10	Cantley	d		05 52			07 00			08 11					10 20				12 20		
—	12¼	12¼	Reedham (Norfolk)	d		05 57		06 44	07 04			08 16					10 24				12 24		
—	16	—	Berney Arms	d																			
18¼	20½	—	**Great Yarmouth**	a	05 33		06 48			07 26	08 15		08 42	09 12		10 09		11 09		12 09		13 09	
—	—	16¼	Haddiscoe	d		06 05			07 13			08 24					10 33				12 33		
—	—	18	Somerleyton	d		06 09			07 17			08 28					10 37				12 37		
—	—	22	Oulton Broad North	d		06 16		07 00	07 23			08 35			09 25		10 43		11 28		12 43		13 25
—	—	23½	**Lowestoft**	a		06 22		07 07	07 30			08 41			09 32		10 50		11 35		12 50		13 32

		LE	LE	LE	LE	LE	LE	LE	LE	LE	LE	LE	LE	LE	LE	LE	LE	LE	LE	LE	LE	LE	LE
London Liverpool Street ■ ⊖	d																						
Norwich	d	13 36	14 05	14 40	14 55	15 36	15 50	16 40	16 58	17 06	17 36	17 50	18 04	18 40	19 02	19 40	20 05	20 38	21 05	21 40	22 05	22 40	23 00
Brundall Gardens	d	13 43		14 47		15 43		16 47		17 13	17 43		18 11	18 47		19 47		20 45		21 47			
Brundall	d	13 46	14 14	14 50		15 46	15 59	16 50	17 07	17 16	17 46	17 59	18 14	18 50	19 11	19 50	20 14	20 48	21 14	21 50	22 14	22 49	23 09
Lingwood	d	13 51		14 55		15 51		16 55		17 21	17 51		18 19	18 55		19 55		20 53		21 55			23 14
Acle	d	13 56		15 00		15 56		17 00		17 28	17 58		18 28	19 01		20 00		20 58		22 00			23 18
Buckenham	d																						
Cantley	d		14 20		15 07		16 05		17 13			18 05			19 17		20 20		21 20		22 20	22 55	
Reedham (Norfolk)	d		14 24		15 12		16 09		17 17			18 09			19 21		20 24		21 24		22 24	22 59	
Berney Arms	d																						
Great Yarmouth	a	14 09		15 13		16 09		17 13		17 41	18 11		18 41	19 14		20 13		21 13		22 13			23 31
Haddiscoe	d		14 33				16 18		17 26			18 18			19 30		20 33		21 33		22 33	23 08	
Somerleyton	d		14 37				16 22		17 30			18 22			19 34		20 37		21 37		22 37	23 12	
Oulton Broad North	d		14 43		15 28		16 28		17 36			18 28			19 43		20 43		21 43		22 43	23 18	
Lowestoft	a		14 50		15 37		16 35		17 43			18 35			19 50		20 50		21 50		22 52	23 25	

Mondays to Fridays

17 February to 15 May

		LE	LE	LE	LE	LE	LE	LE	LE	LE	LE	LE	LE	LE	LE	LE	LE	LE	LE	LE	LE	LE	LE
London Liverpool Street ■ ⊖	d																						
Norwich	d	05 06	05 36	06 11	06 27	06 45	06 52	07 36	07 55	08 09	08 37	08 55	09 36	10 05	10 36	10 58	11 36	12 05	12 36	12 55	13 36	14 05	14 40
Brundall Gardens	d		05 43	06 18			06 59		08 02		08 44		09 43		10 43		11 43		12 43		13 43		14 47
Brundall	d	05 15	05 46	06 21	06 36	06 54	07 02	07 45	08 05		08 47		09 46	10 14	10 46		11 46	12 14	12 46		13 46	14 14	14 50
Lingwood	d			06 26			07 07			08 21	08 52		09 51		10 51				12 51		13 51		14 55
Acle	d			06 35			07 12			08 28	08 59		09 56		10 56				12 56		13 56		15 00
Buckenham	d																						
Cantley	d		05 52			07 00		07 51	08 11					10 20			11 52	12 20				14 20	
Reedham (Norfolk)	d		05 57		06 44	07 04		07 55	08 16					10 24			11 57	12 24				14 24	
Berney Arms	d							08x01									12x03						
Great Yarmouth	a	05 40		06 48			07 26	08 12		08 42	09 12		10 09		11 09		12 13		13 09		14 09		15 13
Haddiscoe	d		06 05			07 13			08 24					10 33				12 33				14 33	
Somerleyton	d		06 09			07 17			08 28					10 37				12 37				14 37	
Oulton Broad North	d		06 16		07 00	07 23			08 35			09 25		10 43		11 28		12 43		13 25		14 43	
Lowestoft	a		06 22		07 07	07 30			08 41			09 32		10 50		11 35		12 50		13 32		14 50	

		LE	LE	LE	LE	LE	LE	LE	LE	LE	LE	LE	LE	LE	LE	LE	LE	LE	LE	LE
London Liverpool Street ■ ⊖	d																			
Norwich	d	14 55	15 36	15 50	16 40	16 58	17 06	17 36	17 50	18 04	18 40	19 02	19 40	20 05	20 38	21 05	21 40	22 05	22 40	23 00
Brundall Gardens	d		15 43		16 47		17 13	17 43		18 11	18 47		19 47		20 45		21 47			
Brundall	d		15 46	15 59	16 50	17 07	17 16	17 46	17 59	18 14	18 50	19 11	19 50	20 14	20 48	21 14	21 50	22 14	22 49	23 09
Lingwood	d		15 51		16 55		17 21	17 51		18 19	18 55		19 55		20 53		21 55			23 14
Acle	d		15 56		17 00		17 28	17 56		18 28	19 00		20 00		20 58		22 00			23 18
Buckenham	d																			
Cantley	d	15 07		16 05		17 13			18 05			19 17		20 20		21 20		22 20	22 55	
Reedham (Norfolk)	d	15 12		16 09		17 17			18 09			19 21		20 24		21 24		22 24	22 59	
Berney Arms	d																			
Great Yarmouth	a		16 09		17 13		17 41	18 09		18 41	19 13		20 13		21 13		22 13			23 31
Haddiscoe	d			16 18		17 26			18 18			19 30		20 33		21 33		22 33	23 08	
Somerleyton	d			16 22		17 30			18 22			19 34		20 37		21 37		22 37	23 12	
Oulton Broad North	d	15 28		16 28		17 36			18 28			19 43		20 43		21 43		22 43	23 18	
Lowestoft	a	15 37		16 35		17 43			18 35			19 50		20 50		21 50		22 52	23 25	

Saturdays

21 December to 15 February

		LE	LE	LE	LE	LE	LE	LE	LE	LE	LE	LE	LE	LE	LE	LE	LE	LE	LE	LE	LE	LE	LE
London Liverpool Street ■ ⊖	d																						
Norwich	d	05 32	05 40	06 36	06 50	07 06	07 36	07 50	08 09	08 36	08 55	09 36	10 05	10 36	10 58	11 36	12 05	12 36	12 58	13 36	14 05	14 36	14 58
Brundall Gardens	d		05 47	06 43		07 13		07 57		08 43		09 43		10 43		11 43		12 43		13 43		14 43	
Brundall	d	05 41	05 50	06 46	06 59	07 16	07 45	08 00		08 46		09 46	10 14	10 46		11 46	12 14	12 46		13 46	14 14	14 46	
Lingwood	d	05 46		06 51		07 21	07 50		08 21	08 51		09 51		10 51		11 51		12 51		13 51		14 51	
Acle	d	05 50		06 56		07 29	07 56		08 28	08 59		09 56		10 56		11 58		12 56		13 56		14 56	
Buckenham	d												10x18										
Cantley	d		05 56		07 05			08 06					10 22				12 20				14 20		15 11
Reedham (Norfolk)	d		06 01		07 09			08 11					10 26				12 24				14 24		15 16
Berney Arms	d																						
Great Yarmouth	a	06 04		07 09		07 42	08 09		08 41	09 12		10 09		11 09		12 11		13 09		14 09		15 09	
Haddiscoe	d		06 09		07 18			08 19					10 35				12 33				14 33		
Somerleyton	d		06 13		07 22			08 23					10 39				12 37				14 37		
Oulton Broad North	d		06 20		07 28			08 30			09 25		10 45		11 28		12 43		13 28		14 43		15 32
Lowestoft	a		06 26		07 35			08 36			09 32		10 52		11 35		12 50		13 35		14 50		15 38

Table T015-F

Saturdays

21 December to 15 February

Norwich - Great Yarmouth and Lowestoft

	LE	LE	LE	LE	LE	LE	LE	LE	LE	LE	LE	LE	LE	LE	LE	LE	LE	LE
London Liverpool Street ⊖ d																		
Norwich d	15 36	15 50	16 40	16 57	17 06	17 36	17 50	18 06	18 40	19 05	19 33	20 05	20 40	21 05	21 40	22 05	22 40	23 00
Brundall Gardens d	15 43		16 47		17 13	17 43		18 13	18 47		19 40		20 47		21 47			
Brundall d	15 46	15 59	16 50	17 06	17 16	17 46	17 59	18 16	18 50	19 14	19 43	20 14	20 50	21 14	21 50	22 14	22 49	23 09
Lingwood d	15 51		16 55		17 21	17 51		18 21	18 55		19 48		20 55		21 55			23 14
Acle d	15 56		17 00		17 28	17 58		18 29	19 00		19 53		21 00		22 00			23 18
Buckenham d																		
Cantley d		16 05		17 12			18 05			19 20		20 20		21 20		22 20	22 55	
Reedham (Norfolk) d		16 09		17 16			18 09			19 24		20 24		21 24		22 24	22 59	
Berney Arms d																		
Great Yarmouth a	16 09		17 13		17 41	18 10		18 42	19 13		20 06		21 13		22 13			23 31
Haddiscoe d		16 18		17 25			18 18			19 33		20 33		21 33		22 33	23 08	
Somerleyton d		16 22		17 29			18 22			19 37		20 37		21 37		22 37	23 12	
Oulton Broad North d		16 28		17 35			18 28			19 43		20 43		21 43		22 43	23 18	
Lowestoft a		16 35		17 42			18 35			19 50		20 50		21 50		22 50	23 25	

Saturdays

22 February to 16 May

	LE	LE	LE	LE	LE	LE	LE	LE	LE	LE	LE	LE	LE	LE	LE	LE	LE	LE	LE	LE	LE	LE
London Liverpool Street ⊖ d																						
Norwich d	05 32	05 40	06 36	06 50	07 06	07 36	07 50	08 09	08 36	08 55	09 36	10 05	10 36	10 58	11 36	12 05	12 36	12 58	13 36	14 05	14 36	14 58
Brundall Gardens d		05 47	06 43		07 13		07 57		08 43		09 43		10 43		11 43		12 43		13 43		14 43	
Brundall d	05 41	05 50	06 46	06 59	07 16	07 45	08 00		08 46		09 46	10 14	10 46		11 46	12 14	12 46		13 46	14 14	14 46	
Lingwood d			06 51		07 21			08 21	08 51		09 51		10 51				12 51		13 51		14 51	
Acle d			06 56		07 29			08 28	08 59		09 56		10 56				12 56		13 56		14 56	
Buckenham d												10x18										
Cantley d		05 56		07 05		07 51	08 06					10 22			11 52	12 20				14 20		15 11
Reedham (Norfolk) d	05 49	06 01		07 09		07 55	08 11					10 26			11 57	12 24				14 24		15 16
Berney Arms d						08x01									12x03							
Great Yarmouth a	06 04		07 09		07 42	08 12		08 41	09 12		10 09		11 09		12 13		13 09		14 09		15 09	
Haddiscoe d		06 09		07 18			08 19					10 35				12 33				14 33		
Somerleyton d		06 13		07 22			08 23					10 39				12 37				14 37		
Oulton Broad North d		06 20		07 28			08 30			09 25		10 45		11 28		12 43		13 28		14 43		15 32
Lowestoft a		06 26		07 35			08 36			09 32		10 52		11 35		12 50		13 35		14 50		15 38

	LE	LE	LE	LE	LE	LE	LE	LE	LE	LE	LE	LE	LE	LE	LE	LE	LE	LE
London Liverpool Street ⊖ d																		
Norwich d	15 36	15 50	16 40	16 57	17 06	17 36	17 50	18 06	18 40	19 05	19 33	20 05	20 40	21 05	21 40	22 05	22 40	23 00
Brundall Gardens d	15 43		16 47		17 13	17 43		18 13	18 47		19 40		20 47		21 47			
Brundall d	15 46	15 59	16 50	17 06	17 16	17 46	17 59	18 16	18 50	19 14	19 43	20 14	20 50	21 14	21 50	22 14	22 49	23 09
Lingwood d	15 51		16 55		17 21	17 51		18 21	18 55		19 48		20 55		21 55			23 14
Acle d	15 56		17 00		17 28	17 56		18 29	19 00		19 53		21 00		22 00			23 18
Buckenham d																		
Cantley d		16 05		17 12			18 05			19 20		20 20		21 20		22 20	22 55	
Reedham (Norfolk) d		16 09		17 16			18 09			19 24		20 24		21 24		22 24	22 59	
Berney Arms d																		
Great Yarmouth a	16 09		17 13		17 41	18 09		18 42	19 13		20 06		21 13		22 13			23 31
Haddiscoe d		16 18		17 25			18 18			19 33		20 33		21 33		22 33	23 08	
Somerleyton d		16 22		17 29			18 22			19 37		20 37		21 37		22 37	23 12	
Oulton Broad North d		16 28		17 35			18 28			19 43		20 43		21 43		22 43	23 18	
Lowestoft a		16 35		17 42			18 35			19 50		20 50		21 50		22 50	23 25	

Sundays

15 December to 16 February

	LE	LE	LE	LE	LE	LE	LE	LE	LE	LE	LE	LE	LE	LE	LE	LE	LE	LE	LE	LE	LE	LE
London Liverpool Street ⊖ d																						
Norwich d	07 25	07 36	08 05	08 45	09 05	09 36	10 05	10 45	11 05	11 36	12 05	12 45	13 05	13 36	14 05	14 45	15 05	15 36	16 05	16 45	17 05	17 36
Brundall Gardens d				08 52				10 52				12 52				14 52				16 52		
Brundall d		07 45	08 14	08 55		09 45	10 14	10 55		11 45	12 14	12 55		13 45	14 14	14 55		15 45	16 14	16 55		17 45
Lingwood d		07 50		09 00		09 50		11 00		11 50		13 00		13 50		15 00		15 50		17 00		17 50
Acle d		07 54		09 05		09 54		11 05		11 54		13 05		13 54		15 05		15 54		17 05		17 54
Buckenham d			08x18				10x18				12x18				14x18				16x18			
Cantley d			08 22				10 20				12 20				14 20				16 22			
Reedham (Norfolk) d			08 24				10 24				12 24				14 24				16 26			
Berney Arms d																						
Great Yarmouth a		08 08		09 18		10 07		11 18		12 08		13 18		14 08		15 18		16 08		17 18		18 08
Haddiscoe d			08 33				10 33				12 33				14 33				16 35			
Somerleyton d			08 37				10 37				12 37				14 37				16 39			
Oulton Broad North d	07 55		08 43		09 36		10 43		11 36		12 43		13 36		14 43		15 36		16 45		17 36	
Lowestoft a	08 00		08 50		09 42		10 50		11 43		12 50		13 43		14 50		15 43		16 52		17 43	

	LE	LE	LE	LE	LE	LE	LE	LE	LE
London Liverpool Street ⊖ d									
Norwich d	18 05	18 45	19 05	19 36	20 05	20 45	20 58	21 36	22 36
Brundall Gardens d		18 52				20 52			22 43
Brundall d	18 14	18 55		19 45	20 14	20 55	21 07	21 45	22 46
Lingwood d		19 00		19 50		21 00		21 50	22 51
Acle d		19 05		19 54		21 05		21 54	22 56
Buckenham d									
Cantley d	18 20				20 20		21 13		
Reedham (Norfolk) d	18 24				20 24		21 17		
Berney Arms d									
Great Yarmouth a		19 18		20 08		21 18		22 08	23 09
Haddiscoe d	18 33				20 33		21 26		
Somerleyton d	18 37				20 37		21 30		
Oulton Broad North d	18 43		19 36		20 43		21 36		
Lowestoft a	18 50		19 43		20 50		21 43		

Table T015-F

Sundays

23 February to 29 March

Norwich - Great Yarmouth and Lowestoft

	LE	LE	LE	LE	LE	LE	LE	LE	LE	LE	LE	LE	LE	LE	LE	LE	LE	LE	LE	LE	LE	LE
London Liverpool Street ⊖ d																						
Norwich d	07 25	07 36	08 05	08 45	09 05	09 36	10 05	10 45	11 05	11 36	12 05	12 45	13 05	13 36	14 05	14 45	15 05	15 36	16 05	16 45	17 05	17 36
Brundall Gardens d				08 52				10 52				12 52				14 52				16 52		
Brundall d		07 45	08 14	08 55		09 45	10 14	10 55		11 45	12 14	12 55		13 45	14 14	14 55		15 45	16 14	16 55		17 45
Lingwood d				09 00				11 00				13 00				15 00				17 00		
Acle d				09 05				11 05				13 05				15 05				17 05		
Buckenham d						09x49				11x49								15x49	16x18			
Cantley d		07 51	08 20			09 53	10 20			11 53	12 20			13 51	14 20			15 53	16 22			17 51
Reedham (Norfolk) d		07 55	08 24			09 57	10 24			11 57	12 24			13 55	14 24			15 57	16 26			17 55
Berney Arms d		08x01				10x03				12x03				14x01								
Great Yarmouth a		08 12		09 18		10 14		11 18		12 14		13 18		14 12		15 18		16 14		17 18		18 10
Haddiscoe d			08 33				10 33				12 33				14 33				16 35			
Somerleyton d			08 37				10 37				12 37				14 37				16 39			
Oulton Broad North d	07 55		08 43		09 36		10 43		11 36		12 43		13 36		14 43		15 36		16 45		17 36	
Lowestoft a	08 00		08 50		09 42		10 50		11 43		12 50		13 43		14 50		15 43		16 52		17 43	

	LE	LE	LE	LE	LE	LE	LE	LE	LE
London Liverpool Street ⊖ d									
Norwich d	18 05	18 45	19 05	19 36	20 05	20 45	20 58	21 36	22 36
Brundall Gardens d		18 52				20 52			22 43
Brundall d	18 14	18 55		19 45	20 14	20 55	21 07	21 45	22 46
Lingwood d		19 00				21 00			22 51
Acle d		19 05				21 05			22 56
Buckenham d									
Cantley d	18 20			19 51	20 20		21 13	21 51	
Reedham (Norfolk) d	18 24			19 55	20 24		21 17	21 55	
Berney Arms d									
Great Yarmouth a		19 18		20 10		21 18		22 10	23 09
Haddiscoe d	18 33				20 33		21 26		
Somerleyton d	18 37				20 37		21 30		
Oulton Broad North d	18 43		19 36		20 43		21 36		
Lowestoft a	18 50		19 43		20 50		21 43		

Sundays

5 April to 10 May

	LE	LE	LE	LE	LE	LE	LE	LE	LE	LE	LE	LE	LE	LE	LE	LE	LE	LE	LE	LE	LE	LE
London Liverpool Street ⊖ d																						
Norwich d	07 25	07 36	08 05	08 45	09 05	09 36	10 05	10 45	11 05	11 36	12 05	12 45	13 05	13 36	14 05	14 45	15 05	15 36	16 05	16 45	17 05	17 36
Brundall Gardens d				08 52				10 52				12 52				14 52				16 52		
Brundall d		07 45	08 14	08 55		09 45	10 14	10 55		11 45	12 14	12 55		13 45	14 14	14 55		15 45	16 14	16 55		17 45
Lingwood d				09 00				11 00				13 00				15 00				17 00		
Acle d				09 05				11 05				13 05				15 05				17 05		
Buckenham d						09x49				11x49								15x49	16x18			
Cantley d		07 51	08 20			09 53	10 20			11 53	12 20			13 51	14 20			15 53	16 22			17 51
Reedham (Norfolk) d		07 55	08 24			09 57	10 24			11 57	12 24			13 55	14 24			15 57	16 26			17 55
Berney Arms d		08x01				10x03				12x03				14x01				16x03				
Great Yarmouth a		08 12		09 18		10 14		11 18		12 14		13 18		14 12		15 18		16 14		17 18		18 10
Haddiscoe d			08 33				10 33				12 33				14 33				16 35			
Somerleyton d			08 37				10 37				12 37				14 37				16 39			
Oulton Broad North d	07 55		08 43		09 36		10 43		11 36		12 43		13 36		14 43		15 36		16 45		17 36	
Lowestoft a	08 00		08 50		09 42		10 50		11 43		12 50		13 43		14 50		15 43		16 52		17 43	

	LE	LE	LE	LE	LE	LE	LE	LE	LE
London Liverpool Street ⊖ d									
Norwich d	18 05	18 45	19 05	19 36	20 05	20 45	20 58	21 36	22 36
Brundall Gardens d		18 52				20 52			22 43
Brundall d	18 14	18 55		19 45	20 14	20 55	21 07	21 45	22 46
Lingwood d		19 00				21 00			22 51
Acle d		19 05				21 05			22 56
Buckenham d									
Cantley d	18 20			19 51	20 20		21 13	21 51	
Reedham (Norfolk) d	18 24			19 55	20 24		21 17	21 55	
Berney Arms d									
Great Yarmouth a		19 18		20 10		21 18		22 10	23 09
Haddiscoe d	18 33				20 33		21 26		
Somerleyton d	18 37				20 37		21 30		
Oulton Broad North d	18 43		19 36		20 43		21 36		
Lowestoft a	18 50		19 43		20 50		21 43		

Table T015-R

Lowestoft and Great Yarmouth - Norwich

Mondays to Fridays
16 December to 14 February

Miles	Miles	Miles			LE	LE	LE	LE	LE	LE	LE	LE		LE	LE	LE	LE	LE	LE	LE	LE	LE		LE	LE
0	—	—	**Lowestoft**	d		05 42		06 35			07 33	07 48				08 50		09 48		10 57		11 48			12 57
1½	—	—	Oulton Broad North	d		05 47		06 39			07 38	07 54				08 55		09 53		11 02		11 53			13 02
5½	—	—	Somerleyton	d		05 53		06 45			07 44					09 01		09 59				11 59			
7¼	—	—	Haddiscoe	d		05 57		06 49			07 48					09 05		10 03				12 03			
—	0	0	**Great Yarmouth**	d	05 43		06 24		06 58	07 30				08 17	08 47		09 17		10 17		11 17			12 17	
—	—	4½	Berney Arms	d																					
11¼	—	8¼	Reedham (Norfolk)	d		06 06		06 58			07 57	08 11				09 14		10 12				12 12			
13½	—	10½	Cantley	d		06 10		07 02			08 01	08 15				09 18		10 16				12 16			
15¼	—	12¾	Buckenham	d																					
—	8	—	Acle	d	05 54		06 35		07 13	07 41				08 28	08 58		09 28		10 28		11 28			12 28	
—	10½	—	Lingwood	d	05 59		06 40		07 17	07 46				08 33	09 03		09 33		10 33		11 33			12 33	
17¾	12¾	14¾	Brundall	d	06 03	06 17	06 44	07 09	07 22	07 50	08 08			08 37		09 25	09 37	10 23	10 37		11 39	12 23		12 37	
18¼	13¾	15¾	Brundall Gardens	d	06 06		06 47		07 24	07 53				08 40			09 40		10 40		11 42			12 40	
23½	18½	20½	**Norwich**	a	06 15	06 27	06 57	07 20	07 35	08 05	08 18	08 32		08 50	09 19	09 35	09 50	10 33	10 50	11 35	11 51	12 33		12 50	13 33
—	—	—	London Liverpool Street 15 ⊖	a																					

		LE	LE	LE	LE	LE	LE	LE		LE	LE	LE	LE	LE	LE	LE	LE	LE		LE	LE	LE	LE	LE	LE
Lowestoft	d		13 48		14 57		15 48			16 48			17 48			18 48		19 55			20 57		21 48		22 48
Oulton Broad North	d		13 53		15 02		15 53			16 53			17 53			18 53		20 00			21 02		21 53		22 53
Somerleyton	d		13 59				15 59			16 59			17 59			18 59		20 06					21 59		22 59
Haddiscoe	d		14 03				16 03			17 03			18 03			19 03		20 10					22 03		23 03
Great Yarmouth	d	13 17		14 17		15 17		16 17			17 17	17 47		18 17	18 47		19 17			20 17		21 17		22 17	
Berney Arms	d																								
Reedham (Norfolk)	d		14 12				16 12			17 12			18 12			19 12		20 19					22 12		23 12
Cantley	d		14 16				16 17			17 16			18 16			19 16		20 23					22 16		23 16
Buckenham	d																								
Acle	d	13 28		14 28		15 33		16 28			17 28	17 58		18 28	19 02		19 28			20 28		21 28		22 28	
Lingwood	d	13 33		14 33		15 38		16 33			17 33	18 03		18 33	19 06		19 33			20 33		21 33		22 33	
Brundall	d	13 37	14 23	14 37		15 42	16 23	16 37		17 23	17 37	18 12	18 23	18 38	19 12	19 23	19 37	20 30		20 37		21 37	22 23	22 37	23 23
Brundall Gardens	d	13 40		14 40		15 45		16 40			17 40			18 41			19 40			20 40		21 40		22 40	
Norwich	a	13 50	14 33	14 50	15 33	15 55	16 39	16 50		17 33	17 50	18 23	18 33	18 50	19 25	19 33	19 50	20 43		20 50	21 33	21 52	22 32	22 50	23 33
London Liverpool Street 15 ⊖	a																								

		LE	LE
Lowestoft	d		23 30
Oulton Broad North	d		23 35
Somerleyton	d		
Haddiscoe	d		
Great Yarmouth	d	23 34	
Berney Arms	d		
Reedham (Norfolk)	d		23 52
Cantley	d		23 56
Buckenham	d		
Acle	d	23 45	
Lingwood	d	23 50	
Brundall	d	23 55	00 03
Brundall Gardens	d		
Norwich	a	00 07	00 17
London Liverpool Street 15 ⊖	a		

Mondays to Fridays
17 February to 27 March

		LE	LE	LE	LE	LE	LE	LE	LE	LE		LE	LE	LE	LE	LE	LE	LE	LE	LE		LE	LE	LE	LE
Lowestoft	d		05 42		06 35			07 33	07 48				08 50		09 48		10 57		11 48			12 57		13 48	
Oulton Broad North	d		05 47		06 39			07 38	07 54				08 55		09 53		11 02		11 53			13 02		13 53	
Somerleyton	d		05 53		06 45			07 44					09 01		09 59				11 59					13 59	
Haddiscoe	d		05 57		06 49			07 48					09 05		10 03				12 03					14 03	
Great Yarmouth	d	05 43		06 24		06 58	07 30			08 17		08 47		09 17		10 17		11 17		12 17			13 17		14 17
Berney Arms	d																								
Reedham (Norfolk)	d		06 06		06 58			07 57	08 11				09 14		10 12				12 12					14 12	
Cantley	d		06 10		07 02			08 01	08 15				09 18		10 16				12 16					14 16	
Buckenham	d																								
Acle	d	05 54		06 35		07 13	07 41			08 28		08 58		09 28		10 28		11 28		12 28			13 28		14 28
Lingwood	d	05 59		06 40		07 17	07 46			08 33		09 03		09 33		10 33		11 33		12 33			13 33		14 33
Brundall	d	06 03	06 17	06 44	07 09	07 22	07 50	08 08		08 37			09 25	09 37	10 23	10 37		11 39	12 23	12 37			13 37	14 23	14 37
Brundall Gardens	d	06 06		06 47		07 24	07 53			08 40				09 40		10 40		11 42		12 40			13 40		14 40
Norwich	a	06 15	06 27	06 57	07 20	07 35	08 05	08 18	08 32	08 50		09 19	09 35	09 50	10 33	10 50	11 35	11 51	12 33	12 50		13 33	13 50	14 33	14 50
London Liverpool Street 15 ⊖	a																								

		LE	LE	LE	LE	LE		LE	LE	LE	LE	LE	LE	LE	LE	LE		LE	LE	LE	LE	LE	LE	LE
Lowestoft	d	14 57		15 48		16 48				17 48			18 48		19 55			20 57		21 48		22 48		23 30
Oulton Broad North	d	15 02		15 53		16 53				17 53			18 53		20 00			21 02		21 53		22 53		23 35
Somerleyton	d			15 59		16 59				17 59			18 59		20 06					21 59		22 59		
Haddiscoe	d			16 03		17 03				18 03			19 03		20 10					22 03		23 03		
Great Yarmouth	d		15 17		16 17			17 17	17 47		18 17	18 47		19 17		20 17			21 17		22 17		23 34	
Berney Arms	d		15x24																					
Reedham (Norfolk)	d		15 32	16 12		17 12			18 01	18 12		19 01	19 12		20 19					22 12		23 12	23 47	23 52
Cantley	d		15 36	16 17		17 16			18 05	18 16		19 05	19 16		20 23					22 16		23 16		23 56
Buckenham	d																							
Acle	d				16 28			17 28			18 28			19 28		20 28			21 28		22 28			
Lingwood	d				16 33			17 33			18 33			19 33		20 33			21 33		22 33			
Brundall	d		15 42	16 23	16 37	17 23		17 37	18 12	18 23	18 38	19 12	19 23	19 37	20 30	20 37			21 37	22 23	22 37	23 23	23 55	00 03
Brundall Gardens	d		15 45		16 40			17 40			18 41			19 40		20 40			21 40		22 40			
Norwich	a	15 33	15 55	16 39	16 50	17 33		17 50	18 23	18 33	18 50	19 25	19 33	19 50	20 43	20 50		21 33	21 52	22 32	22 50	23 33	00 07	00 17
London Liverpool Street 15 ⊖	a																							

Table T015-R

Lowestoft and Great Yarmouth - Norwich

Mondays to Fridays
30 March to 15 May

		LE	LE	LE	LE	LE		LE	LE	LE	LE	LE	LE	LE	LE	LE		LE	LE	LE	LE	LE	LE	LE	LE
Lowestoft	d		05 42		06 35				07 33	07 48			08 50		09 48			10 57		11 48		12 57		13 48	
Oulton Broad North	d		05 47		06 39				07 38	07 54			08 55		09 53			11 02		11 53		13 02		13 53	
Somerleyton	d		05 53		06 45				07 44				09 01		09 59					11 59				13 59	
Haddiscoe	d		05 57		06 49				07 48				09 05		10 03					12 03				14 03	
Great Yarmouth	d	05 43		06 24		06 58		07 30			08 17	08 47		09 17		10 17			11 17		12 17		13 17		14 17
Berney Arms	d																								
Reedham (Norfolk)	d		06 06		06 58				07 57	08 11			09 14		10 12					12 12				14 12	
Cantley	d		06 10		07 02				08 01	08 15			09 18		10 16					12 16				14 16	
Buckenham	d																								
Acle	d	05 54		06 35		07 13		07 41			08 28	08 58		09 28		10 28			11 28		12 28		13 28		14 28
Lingwood	d	05 59		06 40		07 17		07 46			08 33	09 03		09 33		10 33			11 33		12 33		13 33		14 33
Brundall	d	06 03	06 17	06 44	07 09	07 22		07 50	08 08		08 37		09 25	09 37	10 23	10 37			11 39	12 23	12 37		13 37	14 23	14 37
Brundall Gardens	d	06 06		06 47		07 24		07 53			08 40			09 40		10 40			11 42		12 40		13 40		14 40
Norwich	a	06 15	06 27	06 57	07 20	07 35		08 05	08 18	08 32	08 50	09 19	09 35	09 50	10 33	10 50		11 35	11 51	12 33	12 50	13 33	13 50	14 33	14 50
London Liverpool Street 15 ⊖	a																								

		LE		LE	LE	LE	LE	LE	LE	LE	LE	LE		LE	LE	LE	LE	LE	LE	LE	LE	LE		LE	LE
Lowestoft	d	14 57			15 48		16 48			17 48				18 48		19 55		20 57		21 48		22 48			23 30
Oulton Broad North	d	15 02			15 53		16 53			17 53				18 53		20 00		21 02		21 53		22 53			23 35
Somerleyton	d				15 59		16 59			17 59				18 59		20 06				21 59		22 59			
Haddiscoe	d				16 03		17 03			18 03				19 03		20 10				22 03		23 03			
Great Yarmouth	d			15 17		16 17		17 17	17 47		18 17	18 47			19 17		20 17		21 17		22 17			23 34	
Berney Arms	d			15x24					17x54																
Reedham (Norfolk)	d			15 32	16 12		17 12		18 01	18 12		19 01		19 12		20 19				22 12		23 12		23 47	23 52
Cantley	d			15 36	16 17		17 16		18 05	18 16		19 05		19 16		20 23				22 16		23 16			23 56
Buckenham	d																								
Acle	d					16 28		17 28			18 28				19 28		20 28		21 28		22 28				
Lingwood	d					16 33		17 33			18 33				19 33		20 33		21 33		22 33				
Brundall	d			15 42	16 23	16 37	17 23	17 37	18 12	18 23	18 38	19 12		19 23	19 37	20 30	20 37		21 37	22 23	22 37	23 23		23 55	00 03
Brundall Gardens	d			15 45		16 40		17 40			18 41				19 40		20 40		21 40		22 40				
Norwich	a	15 33		15 55	16 39	16 50	17 33	17 50	18 23	18 33	18 50	19 25		19 33	19 50	20 43	20 50	21 33	21 52	22 32	22 50	23 33		00 07	00 17
London Liverpool Street 15 ⊖	a																								

Saturdays
21 December to 15 February

		LE	LE	LE	LE	LE	LE	LE	LE	LE		LE	LE	LE	LE	LE	LE	LE	LE	LE		LE	LE	LE	LE
Lowestoft	d		06 38			07 40			08 48			09 48		10 57		11 48		12 57		13 48			14 57		15 48
Oulton Broad North	d		06 43			07 45			08 53			09 53		11 02		11 53		13 02		13 53			15 02		15 53
Somerleyton	d		06 49			07 51			08 59			09 59				11 59				13 59					15 59
Haddiscoe	d		06 53			07 55			09 03			10 03				12 03				14 03					16 03
Great Yarmouth	d	06 15		07 17	07 45		08 17	08 47		09 17			10 17		11 17		12 17		13 17			14 17		15 17	
Berney Arms	d																								
Reedham (Norfolk)	d		07 02			08 04			09 12			10 12				12 12				14 12					16 12
Cantley	d		07 06			08 08			09 16			10 16				12 16				14 16					16 16
Buckenham	d																								16x20
Acle	d	06 26		07 28	07 56		08 28	08 58		09 28			10 28		11 28		12 28		13 28			14 28		15 33	
Lingwood	d	06 31		07 33	08 01		08 33	09 03		09 33			10 33		11 33		12 33		13 33			14 33		15 38	
Brundall	d	06 35	07 13	07 37	08 05	08 15	08 37		09 23	09 37		10 23	10 37		11 37	12 23	12 37		13 37	14 23		14 37		15 42	16 23
Brundall Gardens	d	06 38		07 40	08 08		08 40			09 40			10 40		11 40		12 40		13 40			14 40		15 45	
Norwich	a	06 48	07 24	07 50	08 18	08 25	08 50	09 17	09 33	09 52		10 33	10 50	11 33	11 52	12 33	12 50	13 33	13 51	14 33		14 50	15 33	15 55	16 34
London Liverpool Street 15 ⊖	a																								

		LE	LE	LE	LE	LE		LE	LE	LE	LE	LE	LE	LE	LE	LE		LE	LE	LE	LE
Lowestoft	d		16 48			17 48				18 48		19 55		20 57		21 48			22 48		23 30
Oulton Broad North	d		16 53			17 53				18 53		20 00		21 02		21 53			22 53		23 35
Somerleyton	d		16 59			17 59				18 59		20 06				21 59			22 59		
Haddiscoe	d		17 03			18 03				19 03		20 10				22 03			23 03		
Great Yarmouth	d	16 17		17 17	17 47			18 17	18 47		19 17		20 17		21 17			22 17		23 34	
Berney Arms	d																				
Reedham (Norfolk)	d		17 12			18 12				19 12		20 19				22 12			23 12		23 52
Cantley	d		17 16			18 16				19 16		20 23				22 16			23 16		23 56
Buckenham	d																				
Acle	d	16 28		17 28	17 58			18 28	19 02		19 28		20 28		21 28			22 28		23 45	
Lingwood	d	16 33		17 33	18 03			18 33	19 06		19 33		20 33		21 33			22 33		23 50	
Brundall	d	16 37	17 23	17 37	18 12	18 23		18 37	19 12	19 23	19 37	20 30	20 37		21 37	22 23		22 37	23 23	23 55	00 03
Brundall Gardens	d	16 40		17 40				18 40			19 40		20 40		21 40			22 40			
Norwich	a	16 50	17 33	17 50	18 23	18 33		18 50	19 23	19 33	19 50	20 40	20 50	21 33	21 50	22 34		22 50	23 33	00 07	00 14
London Liverpool Street 15 ⊖	a																				

Saturdays
22 February to 28 March

		LE	LE	LE	LE	LE	LE	LE	LE	LE		LE	LE	LE	LE	LE	LE	LE	LE	LE		LE	LE	LE	LE
Lowestoft	d		06 38			07 40			08 48			09 48		10 57		11 48		12 57		13 48			14 57		15 48
Oulton Broad North	d		06 43			07 45			08 53			09 53		11 02		11 53		13 02		13 53			15 02		15 53
Somerleyton	d		06 49			07 51			08 59			09 59				11 59				13 59					15 59
Haddiscoe	d		06 53			07 55			09 03			10 03				12 03				14 03					16 03
Great Yarmouth	d	06 15		07 17	07 45		08 17	08 47		09 17			10 17		11 17		12 17		13 17			14 17		15 12	
Berney Arms	d																							15x19	
Reedham (Norfolk)	d		07 02			08 04			09 12			10 12				12 12				14 12				15 27	16 12
Cantley	d		07 06			08 08			09 16			10 16				12 16				14 16				15 31	16 16
Buckenham	d																								16x20
Acle	d	06 26		07 28	07 56		08 28	08 58		09 28			10 28		11 28		12 28		13 28			14 28			
Lingwood	d	06 31		07 33	08 01		08 33	09 03		09 33			10 33		11 33		12 33		13 33			14 33			
Brundall	d	06 35	07 13	07 37	08 05	08 15	08 37		09 23	09 37		10 23	10 37		11 37	12 23	12 37		13 37	14 23		14 37		15 37	16 23
Brundall Gardens	d	06 38		07 40	08 08		08 40			09 40			10 40		11 40		12 40		13 40			14 40		15 40	
Norwich	a	06 48	07 24	07 50	08 18	08 25	08 50	09 17	09 33	09 52		10 33	10 50	11 33	11 52	12 33	12 50	13 33	13 51	14 33		14 50	15 33	15 50	16 34
London Liverpool Street 15 ⊖	a																								

Table T015-R

Lowestoft and Great Yarmouth - Norwich

Saturdays

22 February to 28 March

		LE	LE	LE	LE	LE	LE	LE	LE	LE	LE	LE	LE	LE	LE	LE	LE	LE	LE
Lowestoft	d		16 48			17 48			18 48		19 55		20 57		21 48		22 48		23 30
Oulton Broad North	d		16 53			17 53			18 53		20 00		21 02		21 53		22 53		23 35
Somerleyton	d		16 59			17 59			18 59		20 06				21 59		22 59		
Haddiscoe	d		17 03			18 03			19 03		20 10				22 03		23 03		
Great Yarmouth	d	16 17		17 17	17 47		18 17	18 47		19 17		20 17		21 17		22 17		23 34	
Berney Arms	d																		
Reedham (Norfolk)	d		17 12		18 01	18 12		19 01	19 12		20 19				22 12		23 12	23 47	23 52
Cantley	d		17 16		18 05	18 16		19 05	19 16		20 23				22 16		23 16		23 56
Buckenham	d																		
Acle	d	16 28		17 28			18 28			19 28		20 28		21 28		22 28			
Lingwood	d	16 33		17 33			18 33			19 33		20 33		21 33		22 33			
Brundall	d	16 37	17 23	17 37	18 12	18 23	18 37	19 12	19 23	19 37	20 30	20 37		21 37	22 23	22 37	23 23	23 55	00 03
Brundall Gardens	d	16 40		17 40			18 40			19 40		20 40		21 40		22 40			
Norwich	a	16 50	17 33	17 50	18 23	18 33	18 50	19 23	19 33	19 50	20 40	20 50	21 33	21 50	22 34	22 50	23 33	00 07	00 14
London Liverpool Street 15 ⊖	a																		

Saturdays

4 April to 16 May

		LE	LE	LE	LE	LE	LE	LE	LE	LE	LE	LE	LE	LE	LE	LE	LE	LE	LE	LE	LE	LE	LE
Lowestoft	d		06 38			07 40			08 48		09 48		10 57		11 48		12 57		13 48		14 57		15 48
Oulton Broad North	d		06 43			07 45			08 53		09 53		11 02		11 53		13 02		13 53		15 02		15 53
Somerleyton	d		06 49			07 51			08 59		09 59				11 59				13 59				15 59
Haddiscoe	d		06 53			07 55			09 03		10 03				12 03				14 03				16 03
Great Yarmouth	d	06 15		07 17	07 45		08 17	08 47		09 17		10 17		11 17		12 17		13 17		14 17		15 12	
Berney Arms	d																					15x19	
Reedham (Norfolk)	d		07 02			08 04			09 12		10 12				12 12				14 12			15 27	16 12
Cantley	d		07 06			08 08			09 16		10 16				12 16				14 16			15 31	16 16
Buckenham	d																						16x20
Acle	d	06 26		07 28	07 56		08 28	08 58		09 28		10 28		11 28		12 28		13 28		14 28			
Lingwood	d	06 31		07 33	08 01		08 33	09 03		09 33		10 33		11 33		12 33		13 33		14 33			
Brundall	d	06 35	07 13	07 37	08 05	08 15	08 37		09 23	09 37	10 23	10 37		11 37	12 23	12 37		13 37	14 23	14 37		15 37	16 23
Brundall Gardens	d	06 38		07 40	08 08		08 40			09 40		10 40		11 40		12 40		13 40		14 40		15 40	
Norwich	a	06 48	07 24	07 50	08 18	08 25	08 50	09 17	09 33	09 52	10 33	10 50	11 33	11 52	12 33	12 50	13 33	13 51	14 33	14 50	15 33	15 50	16 34
London Liverpool Street 15 ⊖	a																						

		LE	LE	LE	LE	LE	LE	LE	LE	LE	LE	LE	LE	LE	LE	LE	LE	LE	LE
Lowestoft	d		16 48			17 48			18 48		19 55		20 57		21 48		22 48		23 30
Oulton Broad North	d		16 53			17 53			18 53		20 00		21 02		21 53		22 53		23 35
Somerleyton	d		16 59			17 59			18 59		20 06				21 59		22 59		
Haddiscoe	d		17 03			18 03			19 03		20 10				22 03		23 03		
Great Yarmouth	d	16 17		17 17	17 47		18 17	18 47		19 17		20 17		21 17		22 17		23 34	
Berney Arms	d				17x54														
Reedham (Norfolk)	d		17 12		18 01	18 12		19 01	19 12		20 19				22 12		23 12	23 47	23 52
Cantley	d		17 16		18 05	18 16		19 05	19 16		20 23				22 16		23 16		23 56
Buckenham	d																		
Acle	d	16 28		17 28			18 28			19 28		20 28		21 28		22 28			
Lingwood	d	16 33		17 33			18 33			19 33		20 33		21 33		22 33			
Brundall	d	16 37	17 23	17 37	18 12	18 23	18 37	19 12	19 23	19 37	20 30	20 37		21 37	22 23	22 37	23 23	23 55	00 03
Brundall Gardens	d	16 40		17 40			18 40			19 40		20 40		21 40		22 40			
Norwich	a	16 50	17 33	17 50	18 23	18 33	18 50	19 23	19 33	19 50	20 40	20 50	21 33	21 50	22 34	22 50	23 33	00 07	00 14
London Liverpool Street 15 ⊖	a																		

Sundays

15 December to 16 February

		LE	LE	LE	LE	LE	LE	LE	LE	LE	LE	LE	LE	LE	LE	LE	LE	LE	LE	LE	LE	LE	LE
Lowestoft	d		08 58		09 46		11 05		11 46		13 05		13 46		15 05		15 46		17 05		17 46		19 05
Oulton Broad North	d		09 03		09 51		11 10		11 51		13 10		13 51		15 10		15 51		17 10		17 51		19 10
Somerleyton	d				09 57				11 57				13 57				15 57				17 57		
Haddiscoe	d				10 01				12 01				14 01				16 01				18 01		
Great Yarmouth	d	08 21		09 22		10 22		11 22		12 22		13 22		14 22		15 22		16 22		17 22		18 20	
Berney Arms	d																						
Reedham (Norfolk)	d		09 19		10 10				12 10				14 10				16 10				18 10		
Cantley	d		09 23		10 14				12 14				14 14				16 14				18 14		
Buckenham	d				10x18				12x18								16x18						
Acle	d	08 32		09 33		10 33		11 33		12 33		13 33		14 33		15 33		16 33		17 33		18 31	
Lingwood	d	08 37		09 38		10 38		11 38		12 38		13 38		14 38		15 38		16 38		17 38		18 36	
Brundall	d	08 42	09 29	09 42	10 21	10 43		11 42	12 21	12 43		13 42	14 21	14 42		15 42	16 21	16 41		17 42	18 21	18 40	
Brundall Gardens	d			09 45				11 45				13 45				15 45				17 45			
Norwich	a	08 53	09 40	09 55	10 31	10 54	11 40	11 55	12 31	12 54	13 40	13 55	14 31	14 53	15 40	15 55	16 31	16 55	17 40	17 55	18 31	18 51	19 40
London Liverpool Street 15 ⊖	a																						

		LE	LE	LE	LE	LE	LE	LE	LE	LE
Lowestoft	d		19 46		21 05		21 46			23 35
Oulton Broad North	d		19 51		21 10		21 51			23 40
Somerleyton	d		19 57				21 57			
Haddiscoe	d		20 01				22 01			
Great Yarmouth	d	19 22		20 22		21 22		22 22	23 22	
Berney Arms	d									
Reedham (Norfolk)	d		20 10				22 10			23 55
Cantley	d		20 14				22 14			23 59
Buckenham	d									
Acle	d	19 33		20 33		21 33		22 33	23 33	
Lingwood	d	19 38		20 38		21 38		22 38	23 38	
Brundall	d	19 42	20 21	20 40		21 42	22 21	22 40	23 40	00 04
Brundall Gardens	d	19 45				21 45			23 43	
Norwich	a	19 55	20 31	20 53	21 40	21 55	22 31	22 53	23 54	00 15
London Liverpool Street 15 ⊖	a									

Table T015-R

Lowestoft and Great Yarmouth - Norwich

Sundays

23 February to 29 March

		LE	LE	LE	LE	LE	LE	LE	LE	LE	LE	LE	LE	LE	LE	LE	LE	LE	LE	LE	LE	LE	LE
Lowestoft	d		08 58		09 46		11 05		11 46		13 05		13 46		15 05		15 46		17 05		17 46		19 05
Oulton Broad North	d		09 03		09 51		11 10		11 51		13 10		13 51		15 10		15 51		17 10		17 51		19 10
Somerleyton	d				09 57				11 57				13 57				15 57				17 57		
Haddiscoe	d				10 01				12 01				14 01				16 01				18 01		
Great Yarmouth	d	08 17		09 22		10 17		11 22		12 17		13 22		14 17		15 22		16 17		17 22		18 17	
Berney Arms	d	08x24				10x24				12x24				14x24									
Reedham (Norfolk)	d	08 31	09 19		10 10	10 31			12 10	12 31			14 10	14 31			16 10	16 31			18 10	18 30	
Cantley	d	08 35	09 23		10 14	10 35			12 14	12 35			14 14	14 35			16 14	16 35			18 14	18 34	
Buckenham	d				10x18	10x39				12x39								16x39					
Acle	d			09 33				11 33				13 33				15 33				17 33			
Lingwood	d			09 38				11 38				13 38				15 38				17 38			
Brundall	d	08 42	09 29	09 42	10 21	10 43		11 42	12 21	12 43		13 42	14 21	14 42		15 42	16 21	16 43		17 42	18 21	18 40	
Brundall Gardens	d			09 45				11 45				13 45				15 45				17 45			
Norwich	a	08 53	09 40	09 55	10 31	10 54	11 40	11 55	12 31	12 54	13 40	13 55	14 31	14 53	15 40	15 55	16 31	16 55	17 40	17 55	18 31	18 51	19 40
London Liverpool Street 15 ⊖	a																						

		LE	LE	LE	LE	LE	LE	LE	LE	LE
Lowestoft	d		19 46		21 05		21 46			23 35
Oulton Broad North	d		19 51		21 10		21 51			23 40
Somerleyton	d		19 57				21 57			
Haddiscoe	d		20 01				22 01			
Great Yarmouth	d	19 22		20 17		21 22		22 17	23 17	
Berney Arms	d									
Reedham (Norfolk)	d		20 10	20 30			22 10	22 30	23 30	23 55
Cantley	d		20 14	20 34			22 14	22 34	23 34	
Buckenham	d									
Acle	d	19 33				21 33				
Lingwood	d	19 38				21 38				
Brundall	d	19 42	20 21	20 40		21 42	22 21	22 40	23 40	00 04
Brundall Gardens	d	19 45				21 45			23 43	
Norwich	a	19 55	20 31	20 53	21 40	21 55	22 31	22 52	23 53	00 13
London Liverpool Street 15 ⊖	a									

Sundays

5 April to 10 May

		LE	LE	LE	LE	LE	LE	LE	LE	LE	LE	LE	LE	LE	LE	LE	LE	LE	LE	LE	LE	LE	LE
Lowestoft	d		08 58		09 46		11 05		11 46		13 05		13 46		15 05		15 46		17 05		17 46		19 05
Oulton Broad North	d		09 03		09 51		11 10		11 51		13 10		13 51		15 10		15 51		17 10		17 51		19 10
Somerleyton	d				09 57				11 57				13 57				15 57				17 57		
Haddiscoe	d				10 01				12 01				14 01				16 01				18 01		
Great Yarmouth	d	08 17		09 22		10 17		11 22		12 17		13 22		14 17		15 22		16 17		17 22		18 17	
Berney Arms	d	08x24				10x24				12x24				14x24				16x24					
Reedham (Norfolk)	d	08 31	09 19		10 10	10 31			12 10	12 31			14 10	14 31			16 10	16 31			18 10	18 30	
Cantley	d	08 35	09 23		10 14	10 35			12 14	12 35			14 14	14 35			16 14	16 35			18 14	18 34	
Buckenham	d				10x18	10x39				12x39								16x39					
Acle	d			09 33				11 33				13 33				15 33				17 33			
Lingwood	d			09 38				11 38				13 38				15 38				17 38			
Brundall	d	08 42	09 29	09 42	10 21	10 43		11 42	12 21	12 43		13 42	14 21	14 42		15 42	16 21	16 43		17 42	18 21	18 40	
Brundall Gardens	d			09 45				11 45				13 45				15 45				17 45			
Norwich	a	08 53	09 40	09 55	10 31	10 54	11 40	11 55	12 31	12 54	13 40	13 55	14 31	14 53	15 40	15 55	16 31	16 55	17 40	17 55	18 31	18 51	19 40
London Liverpool Street 15 ⊖	a																						

		LE	LE	LE	LE	LE	LE	LE	LE	LE
Lowestoft	d		19 46		21 05		21 46			23 35
Oulton Broad North	d		19 51		21 10		21 51			23 40
Somerleyton	d		19 57				21 57			
Haddiscoe	d		20 01				22 01			
Great Yarmouth	d	19 22		20 17		21 22		22 17	23 17	
Berney Arms	d									
Reedham (Norfolk)	d		20 10	20 30			22 10	22 30	23 30	23 55
Cantley	d		20 14	20 34			22 14	22 34	23 34	
Buckenham	d									
Acle	d	19 33				21 33				
Lingwood	d	19 38				21 38				
Brundall	d	19 42	20 21	20 40		21 42	22 21	22 40	23 40	00 04
Brundall Gardens	d	19 45				21 45			23 43	
Norwich	a	19 55	20 31	20 53	21 40	21 55	22 31	22 52	23 53	00 13
London Liverpool Street 15 ⊖	a									

Table T016-F

Norwich - Cromer and Sheringham

Mondays to Fridays
16 December to 15 May

Miles			LE	LE	LE	LE	LE	LE	LE	LE	LE	LE	LE	LE	LE	LE	LE	LE	LE FX	LE FO
0	**Norwich**	d	05 10	05 40	07 15	08 21	09 45	10 45	11 45	12 45	13 45	14 45	15 45	16 45	17 45	18 55	19 55	21 15	22 45	23 05
6	Salhouse	d		05 50	07 25	08 31	09 55		11 55		13 55		15 55	16 55	17 55		20 05	21 25	22 55	23 15
8¾	Hoveton & Wroxham	d	05 23	05 55	07 30	08 36	10 00	10 59	12 00	12 59	14 00	14 59	16 00	17 00	18 00	19 09	20 10	21 30	23 00	23 20
13	Worstead	d		06 02	07 37	08 43		11 05		13 05		15 05	16 07	17 07	18 07	19 15	20 17	21 37	23 07	23 27
—	**North Walsham**	a	05 33	06 07	07 42	08 48	10 10	11 11	12 10	13 11	14 10	15 11	16 12	17 12	18 12	19 21	20 22	21 42	23 12	23 32
16	**North Walsham**	d	05 34	06 10	07 45	08 51	10 13	11 13	12 13	13 13	14 13	15 14	16 15	17 15	18 18	19 21	20 25	21 43	23 13	23 33
19¾	Gunton	d		06 16	07 51	08 57	10 19		12 19		14 19		16 21	17 21	18 24	19 27	20 31	21 49	23 19	23 39
23½	Roughton Road	d		06 23	07 57	09 03	10 25		12 25		14 25		16 27	17 27	18 30	19 34	20 37	21 55	23 25	23 45
—	**Cromer**	a	05 49	06 28	08 03	09 09	10 31	11 28	12 31	13 28	14 31	15 29	16 33	17 33	18 36	19 40	20 43	22 01	23 31	23 51
26½	**Cromer**	d	05 56	06 39	08 06	09 12	10 34	11 32	12 34	13 32	14 34	15 33	16 36	17 36	18 39	19 43	20 46	22 04	23 34	23 54
28¾	West Runton	d	06 00	06 44	08 11	09 17	10 39	11 36	12 39	13 36	14 39	15 37	16 41	17 41	18 44	19 48	20 51	22 09	23 39	23 59
30½	**Sheringham**	a	06 07	06 49	08 16	09 22	10 44	11 42	12 44	13 42	14 44	15 43	16 46	17 46	18 49	19 53	20 56	22 14	23 44	00 04

Saturdays
21 December to 16 May

		LE	LE	LE	LE	LE	LE	LE	LE	LE	LE	LE	LE	LE	LE	LE	LE	LE
Norwich	d	05 20	05 45	07 15	08 21	09 45	10 45	11 45	12 45	13 45	14 45	15 45	16 45	17 45	18 55	19 55	21 15	23 05
Salhouse	d		05 55	07 25	08 31	09 55		11 55		13 55		15 55	16 55	17 55		20 05	21 25	23 15
Hoveton & Wroxham	d	05 33	06 00	07 30	08 36	10 00	10 59	12 00	12 59	14 00	14 59	16 00	17 00	18 00	19 09	20 10	21 30	23 20
Worstead	d		06 07	07 37	08 43		11 05		13 05		15 05	16 07	17 07	18 07	19 15	20 17	21 37	23 27
North Walsham	a	05 43	06 12	07 42	08 48	10 10	11 11	12 10	13 11	14 10	15 11	16 12	17 12	18 12	19 21	20 22	21 42	23 32
North Walsham	d	05 44	06 13	07 45	08 51	10 13	11 13	12 13	13 13	14 13	15 14	16 15	17 15	18 18	19 21	20 25	21 43	23 33
Gunton	d		06 19	07 51	08 57	10 19		12 19		14 19		16 21	17 21	18 24	19 27	20 31	21 49	23 39
Roughton Road	d		06 25	07 57	09 03	10 25		12 25		14 25		16 27	17 27	18 30	19 34	20 37	21 55	23 45
Cromer	a	05 59	06 31	08 03	09 09	10 31	11 28	12 31	13 28	14 31	15 29	16 33	17 33	18 36	19 40	20 43	22 01	23 51
Cromer	d	06 02	06 36	08 06	09 12	10 34	11 32	12 34	13 32	14 34	15 33	16 36	17 36	18 39	19 43	20 46	22 04	23 54
West Runton	d	06 07	06 40	08 11	09 17	10 39	11 36	12 39	13 36	14 39	15 37	16 41	17 41	18 44	19 48	20 51	22 09	23 59
Sheringham	a	06 12	06 46	08 16	09 22	10 44	11 42	12 44	13 42	14 44	15 43	16 46	17 46	18 49	19 53	20 56	22 14	00 04

Sundays
15 December to 10 May

		LE	LE	LE	LE	LE	LE	LE	LE	LE	LE	LE	LE	LE
Norwich	d	08 36	09 45	10 36	11 45	12 36	13 45	14 36	15 45	16 36	17 45	18 36	19 45	20 36
Salhouse	d	08 46		10 46		12 46		14 46		16 46		18 46		20 46
Hoveton & Wroxham	d	08 51	09 59	10 51	11 59	12 51	13 59	14 51	15 59	16 51	17 59	18 51	19 59	20 51
Worstead	d	08 58		10 58		12 58		14 58		16 58		18 58		20 58
North Walsham	a	09 03	10 09	11 03	12 09	13 03	14 09	15 03	16 09	17 03	18 09	19 03	20 09	21 03
North Walsham	d	09 04	10 11	11 06	12 11	13 06	14 11	15 06	16 11	17 06	18 11	19 06	20 11	21 06
Gunton	d	09 10		11 12		13 12		15 12		17 12		19 12		21 12
Roughton Road	d	09 16		11 18		13 18		15 18		17 18		19 18		21 18
Cromer	a	09 22	10 26	11 24	12 26	13 24	14 26	15 24	16 26	17 24	18 26	19 24	20 26	21 24
Cromer	d	09 25	10 30	11 27	12 30	13 27	14 30	15 27	16 30	17 27	18 30	19 27	20 30	21 27
West Runton	d	09 30		11 32		13 32		15 32		17 32		19 32		21 32
Sheringham	a	09 36	10 38	11 38	12 38	13 38	14 38	15 38	16 38	17 38	18 38	19 38	20 38	21 38

Table T016-R

Sheringham and Cromer - Norwich

Mondays to Fridays
16 December to 15 May

Miles			LE	LE	LE	LE	LE	LE	LE	LE	LE	LE	LE	LE	LE	LE	LE	LE	LE	LE FX
0	**Sheringham**	d		06 31	07 16	08 22	09 44	10 47	11 44	12 47	13 44	14 47	15 46	16 49	17 49	18 52	19 56	21 10	22 17	23 47
1¾	West Runton	d		06 35	07 20	08 26	09 48	10 51	11 48	12 51	13 48	14 51	15 50	16 53	17 53	18 56	20 00	21 14	22 21	23 51
—	**Cromer**	a		06 39	07 24	08 30	09 52	10 55	11 52	12 55	13 52	14 55	15 54	16 57	17 57	19 00	20 04	21 18	22 25	23 55
4	**Cromer**	d	05 53	06 42	07 27	08 33	09 55	10 58	11 55	12 58	13 55	14 58	15 57	17 00	18 00	19 03	20 07	21 21	22 28	23 58
7	Roughton Road	d	05 58	06 48	07 33	08 39	10 01		12 01		14 01	15 04	16 03		18 06		20 13	21 27	22 34	
10½	Gunton	d	06 04	06 54	07 39	08 45	10 07		12 07		14 07		16 09		18 12		20 19	21 33	22 40	
—	**North Walsham**	a	06 09	07 00	07 45	08 51	10 13	11 13	12 13	13 13	14 13	15 14	16 15	17 15	18 18	19 18	20 25	21 39	22 46	00 13
14½	**North Walsham**	d	06 11	07 00	07 45	08 51	10 13	11 14	12 13	13 14	14 13	15 14	16 15	17 15	18 18	19 21	20 25	21 43	22 46	00 13
17½	Worstead	d	06 16	07 05	07 50	08 56	10 18		12 18		14 18		16 20		18 23		20 30	21 48	22 51	
21½	Hoveton & Wroxham	d	06 23	07 12	07 57	09 03	10 25	11 24	12 25	13 24	14 25	15 24	16 27	17 25	18 30	19 31	20 37	21 55	22 58	00 22
24½	Salhouse	d	06 27	07 17	08 02	09 08		11 28		13 28		15 29	16 32		18 34		20 42	21 59	23 03	
30½	**Norwich**	a	06 40	07 29	08 14	09 23	10 41	11 41	12 41	13 41	14 41	15 41	16 45	17 41	18 47	19 46	20 55	22 12	23 15	00 37

Saturdays
21 December to 16 May

		LE	LE	LE	LE	LE	LE	LE	LE	LE	LE	LE	LE	LE	LE	LE	LE	LE
Sheringham	d	00 07	06 21	07 16	08 22	09 44	10 47	11 44	12 47	13 44	14 47	15 46	16 49	17 49	18 52	19 56	21 10	22 17
West Runton	d	00 11	06 25	07 20	08 26	09 48	10 51	11 48	12 51	13 48	14 51	15 50	16 53	17 53	18 56	20 00	21 14	22 21
Cromer	a	00 15	06 29	07 24	08 30	09 52	10 55	11 52	12 55	13 52	14 55	15 54	16 57	17 57	19 00	20 04	21 18	22 25
Cromer	d	00 18	06 32	07 27	08 33	09 55	10 58	11 55	12 58	13 55	14 58	15 57	17 00	18 00	19 03	20 07	21 21	22 28
Roughton Road	d		06 38	07 33	08 39	10 01		12 01		14 01	15 04	16 03		18 06		20 13	21 27	22 34
Gunton	d		06 44	07 39	08 45	10 07		12 07		14 07		16 09		18 12		20 19	21 33	22 40
North Walsham	a	00 33	06 50	07 45	08 51	10 13	11 13	12 13	13 13	14 13	15 14	16 15	17 15	18 18	19 18	20 25	21 39	22 46
North Walsham	d	00 33	06 50	07 45	08 51	10 13	11 14	12 13	13 14	14 13	15 14	16 15	17 15	18 18	19 21	20 25	21 43	22 46
Worstead	d		06 55	07 50	08 56	10 18		12 18		14 18		16 20		18 23		20 30	21 48	22 51
Hoveton & Wroxham	d	00 42	07 02	07 57	09 03	10 25	11 24	12 25	13 24	14 25	15 24	16 27	17 25	18 30	19 31	20 37	21 55	22 58
Salhouse	d		07 07	08 02	09 08		11 28		13 28		15 29	16 32		18 35		20 42	21 59	23 03
Norwich	a	00 57	07 20	08 14	09 23	10 41	11 41	12 41	13 41	14 41	15 41	16 44	17 44	18 47	19 46	20 55	22 12	23 15

Sundays
15 December to 10 May

		LE	LE	LE	LE	LE	LE	LE	LE	LE	LE	LE	LE	LE	LE
Sheringham	d	00 07	09 42	10 41	11 42	12 41	13 42	14 41	15 42	16 41	17 42	18 41	19 42	20 41	21 42
West Runton	d	00 11	09 46		11 46		13 46		15 46		17 46		19 46		21 46
Cromer	a	00 15	09 50	10 47	11 50	12 47	13 50	14 47	15 50	16 47	17 50	18 47	19 50	20 47	21 50
Cromer	d	00 18	09 53	10 51	11 53	12 51	13 53	14 51	15 53	16 51	17 53	18 51	19 53	20 51	21 53
Roughton Road	d		09 59		11 59		13 59		15 59		17 59		19 59		21 59
Gunton	d		10 05		12 05		14 05		16 05		18 05		20 05		22 05
North Walsham	a	00 33	10 11	11 06	12 11	13 06	14 11	15 06	16 11	17 06	18 11	19 06	20 11	21 06	22 11
North Walsham	d	00 33	10 12	11 06	12 12	13 06	14 12	15 06	16 12	17 06	18 12	19 06	20 12	21 06	22 12
Worstead	d		10 17		12 17		14 17		16 17		18 17		20 17		22 17
Hoveton & Wroxham	d	00 42	10 24	11 16	12 24	13 16	14 24	15 16	16 24	17 16	18 24	19 16	20 24	21 16	22 24
Salhouse	d		10 28		12 28		14 28		16 28		18 28		20 28		22 28
Norwich	a	00 57	10 40	11 31	12 40	13 31	14 40	15 31	16 40	17 31	18 40	19 31	20 40	21 31	22 40

Table T017-F

Mondays to Fridays
16 December to 15 May

London and Cambridge - Ely, Kings Lynn, Peterborough and Norwich

Miles	Miles	Miles			GN MX	GN MO	GN MX	LE MX	LE MO	XC	XC	LE	LE	GN	EM	GN	LE	LE	EM	XC	LE	LE	LE
—	—	—	London Liverpool Street ⊖	d														06 00			06 25		07 00
—	—	0	London Kings Cross ⊖	d												05 42							
—	0	—	Stansted Airport ✈	d							05 27									06 12			
0	24¼	58	Cambridge	a							05 55					06 30				06 44			
—	—	—		d		00 04	00 08			05 15	05 57		06 02	06 14		06 35				06 57		07 00	
2¼	26¾	60¼	Cambridge North	d		00 08	00 13						06 06	06 18		06 39						07 04	
5¼	—	63¼	Waterbeach	d		00 12	00 17							06 22		06 44							
—	—	—	Ipswich	d				00 45	00 48			06 39					06 00	07 12			07 44		08 12
14¾	39¼	72¾	Ely	a		00 22	00 26			05 29	06 11		06 18	06 33		06 53	06 56			07 11		07 16	
—	—	—		d		00 22	00 27			05 30	06 12		06 19	06 33	06 51	06 54	06 57		07 08	07 12		07 17	
—	—	78¾	Littleport	d	00 06	00 29	00 34							06 41		07 01							
—	—	88½	Downham Market	d	00 15	00 38	00 43							06 50		07 17							
—	—	93¼	Watlington	d	00 21	00 44	00 49							06 56		07 23							
—	—	99¼	Kings Lynn	a	00 29	00 52	00 57							07 04		07 32							
—	—	—		d																			
—	49	—	Manea	d							06 23						07 08						
—	54¼	—	March	d						05 46	06 30				07 07		07 15			07 28			
—	62½	—	Whittlesea	d						05 58	06 42						07 27			07 40			
—	69¼	—	Peterborough	a						06 08	06 52				07 25		07 38			07 50			
21½	—	—	Shippea Hill	d																		07x26	
26¾	—	—	Lakenheath	d																			
30¾	—	—	Brandon	d									06 35						07 25			07 36	
38	—	—	Thetford	d									06 44						07 33			07 45	
45¾	—	—	Harling Road	d									06 52									07 53	
48¾	—	—	Eccles Road	d									06 57									07 58	
52¼	—	—	Attleborough	d									07 03						07 47			08 04	
55¾	—	—	Spooner Row	d																		08x09	
58¾	—	—	Wymondham	d									07 10						07 54			08 13	
68¼	—	—	Norwich	a				01 36	01 38			07 24	07 25					07 55	08 13		08 27	08 30	08 56

		GN	LE	EM	GN	XC	EM	GN	LE	EM	GN	LE	LE	LE	LE	LE	XC	GN	LE	LE	LE	LE	EM
London Liverpool Street ⊖	d												07 08	07 28	07 30	07 55				07 58	08 00	08 06	
London Kings Cross ⊖	d				06 42			07 12			07 42							08 12					
Stansted Airport ✈	d					07 21											08 21						
Cambridge	a				07 30	07 55		08 04			08 30			08 54			08 58	09 01		09 27			
	d	07 10	07 22		07 35	08 01		08 12	08 19		08 35			08 55			09 01	09 06	09 12	09 29			
Cambridge North	d	07 14	07 26		07 39			08 18	08 23		08 39			09a00				09 10	09 16	09a34			
Waterbeach	d	07 18			07 44			08 22			08 44												
Ipswich	d											08 03	08a31		08 44	09 08					09a16	09a31	
Ely	a	07 28	07 39		07 53	08 15		08 32	08 35		08 55	08 59					09 15	09 22	09 28				
	d	07 28		07 44	08 02	08 16	08 16	08 32	08 35	08 51	08 55	08 59					09 16		09 28				09 49
Littleport	d	07 36			08 11			08 39			09 03												
Downham Market	d	07 49			08 21			08 48			09 19												
Watlington	d	07 55			08 27			08 54			09 25												
Kings Lynn	a	08 04			08 35			09 02			09 34												
	d																						
Manea	d											09 10											
March	d			08 00		08 32				09 07		09 18					09 32						
Whittlesea	d			08 12								09 29											
Peterborough	a			08 22		08 50				09 25		09 40					09 50						
Shippea Hill	d																						
Lakenheath	d																						
Brandon	d								08 51										09 44				
Thetford	d						08 38		09 01										09 53				10 10
Harling Road	d																						
Eccles Road	d																						
Attleborough	d						08 52		09 16										10 08				
Spooner Row	d								09 21														
Wymondham	d						09 00		09 25										10 15				
Norwich	a						09 15		09 40						09 27	09 48			10 30				10 45

		EM	GN	LE	LE	XC	EM	GN	LE	EM	LE	GN	LE	LE	LE	LE	LE	XC	EM	GN	LE	LE	LE
London Liverpool Street ⊖	d			08 28	08 30						08 58			09 00	09 02	09 28	09 30				09 58	10 00	10 02
London Kings Cross ⊖	d		08 42					09 12				09 42								10 12			
Stansted Airport ✈	d					09 21												10 27					
Cambridge	a		09 30	09 54		09 57		10 03			10 10	10 30				10 51		10 56		11 00	11 09		
	d		09 35	09 55		10 00		10 05	10 13		10 20	10 36				10 53		11 01		11 04	11 13		
Cambridge North	d		09 39	10a00				10 09	10 17		10a25	10 40				10a58				11 08	11a18		
Waterbeach	d		09 44									10 44											
Ipswich	d				09 44								10 01	10 08	10a25		10 44					11 08	11a26
Ely	a		09 54			10 14		10 24	10 29			10 55	10 58					11 15		11 23			
	d	09 51	09 56			10 16	10 19		10 29	10 50		10 55	10 58					11 16	11 22				
Littleport	d		10 04									11 04											
Downham Market	d		10 17									11 17											
Watlington	d		10 23									11 23											
Kings Lynn	a		10 31									11 31											
	d																						
Manea	d												11 09										
March	d					10 32							11 17					11 32					
Whittlesea	d												11 28										
Peterborough	a	10 26				10 50				11 27			11 39					11 50					
Shippea Hill	d																						
Lakenheath	d																						
Brandon	d								10 45														
Thetford	d						10 40		10 54										11 43				
Harling Road	d																						
Eccles Road	d																						
Attleborough	d								11 09														
Spooner Row	d																						
Wymondham	d								11 16														
Norwich	a				10 27		11 12		11 37					10 51			11 27		12 15			11 50	

NRT DECEMBER 19 EDITION

Table T017-F

Mondays to Fridays
16 December to 15 May

London and Cambridge - Ely, Kings Lynn, Peterborough and Norwich

		LE	EM	GN	LE	LE	XC	EM	GN	LE	LE	LE	LE	EM	GN	LE	LE	LE	LE	XC	EM	GN
London Liverpool Street ⊖	d				10 28	10 30				10 58	11 00	11 02					11 04	11 28	11 30			
London Kings Cross ⊖	d			10 42					11 12						11 42							12 12
Stansted Airport ✈	d	10 48					11 27						11 48							12 27		
Cambridge	a	11 19		11 32	11 51		11 56		12 01	12 09			12 19		12 31			12 51		12 56		13 00
	d	11 20		11 37	11 53		12 01		12 04	12 13			12 20		12 36			12 53		13 01		13 04
Cambridge North	d	11 24		11 40	11a58				12 08	12a18			12 24		12 40			12a58				13 08
Waterbeach	d			11 45											12 44							
Ipswich	d					11 43					11 55	12 09				12 01	12a27		12 44			
Ely	a	11 36		11 55			12 15		12 23				12 36		12 55	12 58				13 15		13 23
	d	11 36	11 51	11 56			12 16	12 16					12 36	12 49	12 55	12 58				13 16	13 18	
Littleport	d			12 04											13 04							
Downham Market	d			12 17											13 17							
Watlington	d			12 23											13 23							
Kings Lynn	a			12 31											13 31							
	d																					
Manea	d															13 09						
March	d		12 08				12 32									13 17				13 32		
Whittlesea	d															13 28						
Peterborough	a		12 24				12 50							13 23		13 39				13 50		
Shippea Hill	d																					
Lakenheath	d																					
Brandon	d	11 52											12 52									
Thetford	d	12 01						12 38					13 01								13 40	
Harling Road	d																					
Eccles Road	d																					
Attleborough	d	12 16											13 16									
Spooner Row	d																					
Wymondham	d	12 23											13 23									
Norwich	a	12 43				12 27		13 13			12 30	12 51	13 39						13 27		14 13	

		LE	LE	LE	LE	EM	GN	LE	LE	XC	EM	GN	LE	LE	LE	EM	GN	LE	LE	LE	LE	XC	EM
London Liverpool Street ⊖	d	11 58	12 00	12 02				12 28	12 30				12 58	13 00					13 02	13 28	13 30		
London Kings Cross ⊖	d						12 42					13 12					13 42						
Stansted Airport ✈	d				12 48					13 27					13 48							14 27	
Cambridge	a	13 09			13 19		13 30	13 51		13 56		14 00	14 09		14 19		14 30			14 51		14 56	
	d	13 13			13 20		13 36	13 53		14 01		14 04	14 13		14 20		14 36			14 53		15 01	
Cambridge North	d	13a18			13 24		13 40	13a58				14 08	14a18		14 24		14 40			14a58			
Waterbeach	d						13 45										14 44						
Ipswich	d		13 08	13a25					13 44					14 08				13 58	14a25		14 44		
Ely	a				13 36		13 55			14 15		14 23			14 36		14 55	14 58				15 15	
	d				13 37	13 51	13 56			14 16	14 16				14 36	14 49	14 55	14 58				15 16	15 18
Littleport	d						14 05										15 04						
Downham Market	d						14 17										15 17						
Watlington	d						14 23										15 23						
Kings Lynn	a						14 31										15 31						
	d																						
Manea	d																	15 09					
March	d									14 32								15 17				15 32	
Whittlesea	d																	15 28					
Peterborough	a					14 25				14 50						15 30		15 39				15 50	
Shippea Hill	d																						
Lakenheath	d																						
Brandon	d				13 53										14 52								
Thetford	d				14 02						14 38				15 01								15 39
Harling Road	d																						
Eccles Road	d																						
Attleborough	d				14 17										15 16								
Spooner Row	d																						
Wymondham	d				14 24										15 23								
Norwich	a		13 50		14 42				14 27		15 11			14 50	15 42						15 27		16 15

Table T017-F

London and Cambridge - Ely, Kings Lynn, Peterborough and Norwich

Mondays to Fridays

16 December to 15 May

		GN	LE	LE	LE	LE	EM	GN	GN	LE	LE	LE	XC	EM	GN	LE	GN	LE	EM	GN	LE	LE	LE
		1	◇1	◇1	1		◇	1	1	1	◇1	◇1	◇1	◇	1		1	◇1	◇	1		◇1	1
London Liverpool Street 15 ⊖	d		13 58	14 00	14 02						14 28	14 30						14 58				15 00	15 02
London Kings Cross 15 ⊖	d	14 12							14 42						15 12					15 42			
Stansted Airport ✈	d					14 48							15 27			15 37							
Cambridge	a	15 00	15 09			15 19			15 30		15 51		15 56		16 02	16 15		16 27		16 30			
	d	15 04	15 13			15 20		15 30	15 35	15 44	15 53		16 01		16 04	16 16	16 20	16 29		16 36			
Cambridge North	d	15 08	15a20			15 24		15 34	15 39	15 48	15a58				16 08	16 21		16a34		16 40			
Waterbeach	d							15 39	15 43	15 53							16 27			16 44			
Ipswich	d			15 08	15a25							15 44									16 00	16 08	16a25
Ely 6	a	15 23				15 36		15 49	15 53	16 03			16 15		16 23	16 32	16 36			16 55	16 58		
	d					15 36	15 48		15 55				16 16	16 18		16 33	16 37		16 50	16 55	16 58		
Littleport	d								16 04								16 44			17 04			
Downham Market	d								16 17								16 53			17 17			
Watlington	d								16 23								16 59			17 23			
Kings Lynn	a								16 31								17 07			17 31			
	d																						
Manea	d																				17 09		
March	d												16 32								17 17		
Whittlesea	d																				17 28		
Peterborough 8	a						16 25						16 50						17 24		17 39		
Shippea Hill	d																						
Lakenheath	d																						
Brandon	d					15 52										16 49							
Thetford	d					16 01								16 40		16 57							
Harling Road	d																						
Eccles Road	d																						
Attleborough	d					16 16										17 12							
Spooner Row	d																						
Wymondham	d					16 23										17 20							
Norwich	a			15 48		16 39						16 27		17 14		17 37						16 50	

		LE	LE	XC	EM	GN	LE	LE	LE	LE	LE	LE	LE	EM	GN		LE	XC	EM	GN	LE		LE
		◇1	1	◇1	◇	1	◇1	1	◇1	1	◇1	1 A		◇	1		◇1	◇1	◇	1	◇1 B		1
London Liverpool Street 15 ⊖	d	15 28	15 30				15 58	16 00	16 02	16 30	16 32	17 00					17 02				17 07		17 12
London Kings Cross 15 ⊖	d					16 12									16 39					17 09			
Stansted Airport ✈	d			16 27									16 48					17 27					
Cambridge	a	16 51		16 56		17 04	17 21						17 28		17 33			17 56		18 05	18 17		
	d	16 53		17 01		17 06	17 21						17 29		17 38	17 44		18 01		18 07	18 19	18 26	
Cambridge North	d	16a58				17 10	17 26						17 34		17 43	17 49				18 11		18a33	
Waterbeach	d												17 38		17 48	17 53					18 25		
Ipswich	d		16 41					17 08	17a29	17 36	17a49	18 00					18 25						18a35
Ely 6	a			17 15		17 23	17 39						17 47		17 58	18 05		18 15		18 24	18 34		
	d			17 16	17 18								17 48	17 52	17 59			18 16	18 22		18 35		
Littleport	d														18 08						18 42		
Downham Market	d														18 17						18 52		
Watlington	d														18 23						18 58		
Kings Lynn	a														18 31						19 09		
	d																						
Manea	d																	18 27					
March	d			17 32														18 34					
Whittlesea	d																						
Peterborough 8	a			17 50										18 25				18 52					
Shippea Hill	d																						
Lakenheath	d																						
Brandon	d												18 04										
Thetford	d				17 40								18 12						18 43				
Harling Road	d																						
Eccles Road	d																						
Attleborough	d												18 27										
Spooner Row	d																						
Wymondham	d												18 35										
Norwich	a		17 24		18 13			17 53		18 22		18 42	18 49				19 09		19 16				

A The East Anglian

B The Fenman

Table T017-F

London and Cambridge - Ely, Kings Lynn, Peterborough and Norwich

Mondays to Fridays

16 December to 15 May

		LE	LE	EM	LE	GN		LE	LE	LE	XC	EM	GN	LE	EM	LE		LE	LE	LE	GN	LE	LE
		1		◇		1		◇1	1	1	◇1	◇	1		◇	◇1		1	1	◇1	1	1	
London Liverpool Street 15 ⊖	d	17 30						17 37	17 50	17 58						18 07		18 10	18 30	18 32		18 37	19 00
London Kings Cross 15 ⊖	d					17 39							18 09								18 39		
Stansted Airport ✈	d		17 56								18 21												
Cambridge	a		18 29			18 32		18 49			18 56		19 03			19 17					19 32	19 49	
	d		18 30			18 37	18 44	18 51			19 01		19 08	19 25		19 21	19 28				19 41	19 51	
Cambridge North	d		18 35			18 41	18 48	18a58					19 12	19 29			19a35				19 45	19a59	
Waterbeach	d		18 39			18 46										19 28					19 50		
Ipswich	d	18 39			17 41				19 04	19a19								19 23	19 40	19a53			19 55
Ely 6	a		18 48		18 56	18 55	19 03				19 15		19 25	19 42		19 38					20 00		
	d		18 49	18 52	18 58	18 56					19 16	19 24	19 31	19 44	19 52	19 38					20 02		
Littleport	d					19 04										19 46					20 09		
Downham Market	d					19 13							19 47			19 57					20 19		
Watlington	d					19 19							19 53			20 03					20 25		
Kings Lynn	a					19 28							20 01			20 14					20 33		
	d																						
Manea	d				19 09																		
March	d			19 08	19 17						19 32												
Whittlesea	d				19 28																		
Peterborough 8	a			19 26	19 39						19 50				20 25								
Shippea Hill	d																						
Lakenheath	d																						
Brandon	d		19 05											20 00									
Thetford	d		19 13									19 45		20 09									
Harling Road	d																						
Eccles Road	d																						
Attleborough	d		19 28											20 24									
Spooner Row	d																						
Wymondham	d		19 36											20 31									
Norwich	a	19 25	19 52						19 50			20 19		20 45				20 09	20 27				20 30

		LE	XC	EM	GN	LE	LE	GN	LE	LE	LE	LE	LE	LE	XC	GN	LE	GN	LE	LE	LE	EM
		1	◇1	◇	1	◇1		1		◇1	◇1	1	◇	◇1	◇1	1		1	◇1	◇1	◇1	◇
London Liverpool Street 15 ⊖	d	19 02				19 07				19 10	19 28	19 30	20 00	20 02					20 28	20 30	21 00	
London Kings Cross 15 ⊖	d				19 12			19 39								20 09		20 39				
Stansted Airport ✈	d		19 21												20 21							
Cambridge	a		19 56		20 05	20 15		20 33			20 55				21 00	21 03		21 32	21 51			
	d		20 01		20 07	20 16	20 20	20 38			20 57				21 02	21 08	21 20	21 37	21 53			
Cambridge North	d				20 11		20 24	20 42			21a01					21 12	21 24	21 41	21a58			
Waterbeach	d					20 22		20 47								21 17		21 46				
Ipswich	d	20 09							20 01	20a31		20 41	21 08	21a25						21 45	22 09	
Ely 6	a		20 15		20 24	20 32	20 36	20 57	20 59						21 16	21 27	21 36	21 56				
	d		20 16	20 18		20 32	20 36	20 58	21 01						21 17	21 29	21 36	21 57				22 17
Littleport	d					20 39		21 06								21 36		22 05				
Downham Market	d					20 49		21 18								21 47		22 17				
Watlington	d					20 55		21 23								21 53		22 23				
Kings Lynn	a					21 07		21 32								22 01		22 31				
	d																					
Manea	d								21 10													
March	d		20 32						21 19						21 33							
Whittlesea	d								21 30													
Peterborough 8	a		20 50						21 40						21 51							
Shippea Hill	d																					
Lakenheath	d																					
Brandon	d						20 52										21 52					
Thetford	d			20 38			21 01										22 01					22 39
Harling Road	d																					
Eccles Road	d																					
Attleborough	d						21 16										22 16					22 53
Spooner Row	d																					
Wymondham	d						21 23										22 23					23 00
Norwich	a	20 53		21 13			21 37					21 24	21 51				22 37			22 29	22 53	23 18

Table T017-F

Mondays to Fridays
16 December to 15 May

London and Cambridge - Ely, Kings Lynn, Peterborough and Norwich

		GN	GN	LE	LE	LE	LE	LE	GN	GN	LE	LE	LE	GN	LE
		1	1		◇1	◇1 🚌		1	1	1	◇1	◇1 🚌	1	1	◇1 🚌
London Liverpool Street 15 ⊖	d				21 28	21 30		22 00			22 28	22 30	23 02		23 30
London Kings Cross 15 ⊖	d	21 09	21 39						22 09	22 39				23 09	
Stansted Airport ✈	d			22 10			←								
Cambridge	a	22 03	22 33	22 45	22 51		22 45		23 04	23 33	23 51			00 03	
	d	22 08	22 38	22 57	22 52		22 57		23 09	23 38	23 53			00 08	
Cambridge North	d	22 12	22 42	→	22a58		23 01		23 13	23 42	23a58			00 13	
Waterbeach	d	22 17	22 47						23 17	23 47				00 17	
Ipswich	d					22 45		23a08				23 45	00a30		00 45
Ely 6	a	22 27	22 57				23 13		23 28	23 57				00 26	
	d		22 58				23 13			23 58				00 27	
Littleport	d		23 06							00 06				00 34	
Downham Market	d		23 17							00 15				00 43	
Watlington	d		23 23							00 21				00 49	
Kings Lynn	a		23 31							00 29				00 57	
	d														
Manea	d														
March	d														
Whittlesea	d														
Peterborough 6	a														
Shippea Hill	d														
Lakenheath	d														
Brandon	d						23 29								
Thetford	d						23 38								
Harling Road	d														
Eccles Road	d														
Attleborough	d						23 53								
Spooner Row	d														
Wymondham	d						23 59								
Norwich	a					23 30	00 14					00 30			01 36

Saturdays
21 December to 16 May

		GN	GN	LE	XC	XC	LE	EM	GN	LE	LE	LE	LE	EM	XC	GN	LE	LE	LE	EM	GN	LE	LE
		1	1	◇1 🚌	◇1	◇1		◇	1	◇1		1	◇1	◇	◇1	1	◇1	1		◇	1	◇1	◇1
London Liverpool Street 15 ⊖	d									05 20		05 34					05 58	06 02				06 28	06 30
London Kings Cross 15 ⊖	d								05 42												06 42		
Stansted Airport ✈	d					05 27									06 27				06 48				
Cambridge	a					05 55			06 30	06 51					06 56		07 07		07 19		07 30	07 51	
	d		00 08		05 15	05 57	06 05		06 35	06 53					06 58	07 13	07 16		07 20		07 35	07 53	
Cambridge North	d		00 13				06 09		06 38	06a58						07 19	07a20		07 25		07 38	07a58	
Waterbeach	d		00 17						06 44												07 44		
Ipswich	d			00 45							06 00	07a00	07 10					07a25					07 44
Ely 6	a		00 26		05 29	06 11	06 22		06 53		06 57				07 12	07 31			07 37		07 54		
	d		00 27		05 30	06 12	06 22	06 51	06 54		06 58			07 06	07 13				07 38	07 48	07 55		
Littleport	d	00 06	00 34						07 04												08 04		
Downham Market	d	00 15	00 43						07 17												08 17		
Watlington	d	00 21	00 49						07 23												08 23		
Kings Lynn	a	00 29	00 57						07 31												08 31		
	d																						
Manea	d					06 23					07 09												
March	d				05 46	06 30		07 07			07 17				07 29					08 04			
Whittlesea	d				05 58	06 42					07 28				07 41					08 14			
Peterborough 6	a				06 08	06 52		07 25			07 39				07 51					08 27			
Shippea Hill	d																		07x47				
Lakenheath	d																						
Brandon	d						06 38							07 22					07 57				
Thetford	d						06 47							07 30					08 05				
Harling Road	d						06 55												08 13				
Eccles Road	d						06 59												08 18				
Attleborough	d						07 05							07 44					08 23				
Spooner Row	d																						
Wymondham	d						07 12							07 51					08 31				
Norwich	a			01 36			07 26						07 53	08 13					08 45				08 27

NRT DECEMBER 19 EDITION

Table T017-F

Saturdays
21 December to 16 May

London and Cambridge - Ely, Kings Lynn, Peterborough and Norwich

		XC	EM	GN	LE	LE	LE	EM	GN	LE	LE	LE	LE	XC	GN	LE	LE	LE	EM	EM	LE	GN
		◇1	◇	1	◇1	◇1		◇	1		1	◇1	◇1 🚌	◇1	1	◇1	◇1 🚌	1	◇	◇		1
London Liverpool Street 15 ⊖	d				06 58	07 00					07 02	07 28	07 30			07 58	08 00	08 02				
London Kings Cross 15 ⊖	d			07 12					07 42						08 12							08 42
Stansted Airport ✈	d	07 27					07 48							08 27							08 48	
Cambridge	a	07 57		08 00	08 09		08 19		08 30			08 51		08 56	09 00	09 09					09 19	09 30
	d	08 01		08 04	08 13		08 20		08 35			08 53		09 01	09 04	09 13					09 30	09 35
Cambridge North	d			08 08	08a18		08 24		08 38			08a58			09 08	09a18					09 34	09 38
Waterbeach	d								08 44													09 44
Ipswich	d					08 08				08 00	08a25		08 44				09 08	09a25				
Ely 6	a	08 15		08 23			08 36		08 54	08 58				09 15	09 23						09 47	09 55
	d	08 16	08 16				08 36	08 48	08 55	08 58				09 16					09 44	09 46	09 51	09 56
Littleport	d								09 04													10 04
Downham Market	d								09 17													10 22
Watlington	d								09 23													10 28
Kings Lynn	a								09 31													10 36
	d																					
Manea	d									09 09												
March	d	08 32						09 05		09 17				09 32								
Whittlesea	d									09 28												
Peterborough 6	a	08 50						09 22		09 39				09 50						10 21		
Shippea Hill	d																					
Lakenheath	d																					
Brandon	d						08 52														10 08	
Thetford	d		08 37				09 01												10 07		10 17	
Harling Road	d																					
Eccles Road	d																					
Attleborough	d		08 51				09 16														10 32	
Spooner Row	d						09x21															
Wymondham	d		08 58				09 26														10 39	
Norwich	a		09 15			08 50	09 40						09 27				09 50		10 43		10 53	

		LE	LE	XC	EM	GN	LE	LE	LE	EM	GN	LE	LE	LE	LE	XC	EM	GN	LE	LE	LE	LE	EM
		◇1	◇1 🚌	◇1	◇	1	◇1	◇1 🚌		◇	1		1	◇1	◇1 🚌	◇1 🍴	◇	1	◇1	◇1 🚌	1		◇
London Liverpool Street 15 ⊖	d	08 28	08 30				08 58	09 00					09 02	09 28	09 30				09 58	10 00	10 02		
London Kings Cross 15 ⊖	d					09 12					09 42							10 13					
Stansted Airport ✈	d			09 27					09 48							10 27						10 48	
Cambridge	a	09 51		09 56		10 00	10 09		10 19		10 30			10 51		10 56		11 00	11 09			11 19	
	d	09 53		10 01		10 04	10 13		10 26		10 35			10 53		11 01		11 04	11 13			11 20	
Cambridge North	d	09a58				10 08	10a18		10 30		10 38			10a58				11 08	11a18			11 24	
Waterbeach	d										10 44												
Ipswich	d		09 44					10 08				09 58	10a25		10 44					11 08	11a25		
Ely 6	a			10 15		10 23			10 42		10 54	10 58				11 15		11 23				11 36	
	d			10 16	10 22				10 42	10 48	10 55	10 58				11 16	11 16					11 36	11 48
Littleport	d										11 04												
Downham Market	d										11 17												
Watlington	d										11 23												
Kings Lynn	a										11 31												
	d																						
Manea	d											11 09											
March	d			10 32								11 17				11 32							12 05
Whittlesea	d											11 28											
Peterborough 6	a			10 50						11 20		11 39				11 50							12 21
Shippea Hill	d																						
Lakenheath	d																						
Brandon	d								10 58													11 52	
Thetford	d				10 43				11 07								11 37					12 01	
Harling Road	d																						
Eccles Road	d																						
Attleborough	d								11 22													12 16	
Spooner Row	d																						
Wymondham	d								11 29													12 24	
Norwich	a		10 27		11 15			10 50	11 43						11 27		12 13			11 50		12 43	

Table T017-F

London and Cambridge - Ely, Kings Lynn, Peterborough and Norwich

Saturdays
21 December to 16 May

		GN	LE	LE	XC	EM	GN	LE	LE	LE		LE	EM	GN	LE	LE	LE	LE	XC	EM		GN	LE	LE	LE
		1	◇1	◇1	◇1	◇	1	◇1	1	◇1			◇	1		1	◇1	◇1	◇1	◇		1	◇1	◇1	1
London Liverpool Street ⊖	d		10 28	10 30				10 58	11 00	11 02						11 04	11 28	11 30					11 58	12 00	12 02
London Kings Cross ⊖	d	10 42					11 12							11 42								12 12			
Stansted Airport ✈	d				11 27							11 48							12 27						
Cambridge	a	11 30	11 51		11 56		12 00	12 09				12 19		12 30			12 51		12 56			13 00	13 09		
	d	11 35	11 53		12 01		12 04	12 13				12 20		12 35			12 53		13 01			13 04	13 13		
Cambridge North	d	11 38	11a58				12 08	12a18				12 24		12 38			12a58					13 08	13a18		
Waterbeach	d	11 44												12 44											
Ipswich	d			11 43					11 55	12 09					12 01	12a27		12 44						13 08	13a25
Ely	a	11 54			12 15		12 23					12 36		12 54	12 58				13 15			13 23			
	d	11 55			12 16	12 16						12 36	12 51	12 55	12 58				13 16	13 22					
Littleport	d	12 04												13 04											
Downham Market	d	12 17												13 17											
Watlington	d	12 23												13 23											
Kings Lynn	a	12 31												13 31											
	d																								
Manea	d														13 09										
March	d				12 32										13 17				13 32						
Whittlesea	d														13 28										
Peterborough	a				12 50								13 26		13 39				13 50						
Shippea Hill	d																								
Lakenheath	d																								
Brandon	d											12 52													
Thetford	d					12 38						13 01								13 43					
Harling Road	d																								
Eccles Road	d																								
Attleborough	d											13 16													
Spooner Row	d																								
Wymondham	d											13 24													
Norwich	a			12 27		13 13			12 30	12 52		13 39						13 27		14 12				13 50	

		LE	EM	GN	LE	LE		XC	EM	GN	LE	LE	LE	EM	GN	LE		LE	LE	LE	XC	EM	GN	LE	LE
			◇	1	◇1	◇1		◇1	◇	1	◇1	◇1		◇	1			1	◇1	◇1	◇1	◇	1	◇1	◇1
London Liverpool Street ⊖	d				12 28	12 30					12 58	13 00						13 02	13 28	13 30				13 58	14 00
London Kings Cross ⊖	d			12 42						13 12					13 42								14 12		
Stansted Airport ✈	d	12 48						13 27					13 48								14 27				
Cambridge	a	13 19		13 30	13 51			13 56		14 00	14 09		14 19		14 30				14 51		14 56		15 00	15 09	
	d	13 20		13 35	13 53			14 01		14 04	14 13		14 20		14 35				14 53		15 01		15 04	15 13	
Cambridge North	d	13 24		13 38	13a58					14 08	14a18		14 24		14 38				14a58				15 08	15a18	
Waterbeach	d			13 44											14 44										
Ipswich	d					13 44						14 08				13 58		14a25		14 44					15 08
Ely	a	13 36		13 54				14 15		14 23			14 36		14 54	14 58					15 15		15 23		
	d	13 36	13 48	13 55				14 16	14 16				14 36	14 50	14 55	14 58					15 16	15 19			
Littleport	d			14 04											15 04										
Downham Market	d			14 17											15 17										
Watlington	d			14 23											15 23										
Kings Lynn	a			14 31											15 31										
	d																								
Manea	d															15 09									
March	d							14 32								15 17					15 32				
Whittlesea	d															15 28									
Peterborough	a		14 25					14 50						15 23		15 39					15 50				
Shippea Hill	d																								
Lakenheath	d																								
Brandon	d	13 52											14 52												
Thetford	d	14 01							14 37				15 01									15 40			
Harling Road	d																								
Eccles Road	d																								
Attleborough	d	14 16											15 16												
Spooner Row	d																								
Wymondham	d	14 24											15 24												
Norwich	a	14 39				14 27			15 13			14 50	15 39							15 27		16 12			15 48

Table T017-F

London and Cambridge - Ely, Kings Lynn, Peterborough and Norwich

Saturdays
21 December to 16 May

		LE	LE	EM	GN	LE	LE	XC		EM	GN	LE	LE	LE	EM	GN	LE	LE		LE	LE	XC	EM	GN	LE
		1		◇	1	◇1	◇1	◇1		◇	1	◇1	◇1		◇	1		1		◇1	◇1	◇1	◇	1	◇1
London Liverpool Street ⊖	d	14 02				14 28	14 30					14 58	15 00					15 02		15 28	15 30				15 58
London Kings Cross ⊖	d				14 42						15 12					15 42								16 12	
Stansted Airport ✈	d		14 48					15 27						15 48								16 27			
Cambridge	a		15 19		15 30	15 51		15 56			16 00	16 09		16 19		16 30				16 51		16 56		17 00	17 09
	d		15 20		15 35	15 53		16 01			16 04	16 13		16 20		16 35				16 53		17 01		17 04	17 13
Cambridge North	d		15 24		15 38	15a58					16 08	16a18		16 24		16 38				16a58				17 08	17a18
Waterbeach	d				15 44											16 44									
Ipswich	d	15a26					15 44						16 08				15 58	16a25			16 44				
Ely	a		15 36		15 54			16 15			16 23			16 35		16 54	16 58					17 15		17 23	
	d		15 36	15 47	15 55			16 16		16 22				16 35	16 47	16 55	16 58					17 16	17 17		
Littleport	d				16 04											17 04									
Downham Market	d				16 17											17 17									
Watlington	d				16 23											17 23									
Kings Lynn	a				16 31											17 31									
	d																								
Manea	d																17 09								
March	d							16 32									17 17					17 32			
Whittlesea	d																17 28								
Peterborough	a			16 25				16 50							17 23		17 39					17 50			
Shippea Hill	d																								
Lakenheath	d		15x49																						
Brandon	d		15 55											16 52											
Thetford	d		16 03							16 44				17 01									17 38		
Harling Road	d																								
Eccles Road	d																								
Attleborough	d		16 18											17 16											
Spooner Row	d																								
Wymondham	d		16 26											17 24											
Norwich	a		16 40				16 27			17 12			16 50	17 40							17 27		18 14		

		LE	LE	LE		EM	GN	LE	LE	XC	EM	GN	LE	LE		LE	EM	GN	LE	LE	LE	LE	XC	EM	
		◇1	1			◇	1	◇1	◇1	◇1	◇	1	◇1	◇1			◇	1		◇1	◇1	◇1	◇1	◇	
London Liverpool Street ⊖	d	16 00	16 02					16 28	16 30				16 58	17 00						17 02	17 28	17 30			
London Kings Cross ⊖	d						16 42					17 12						17 42							
Stansted Airport ✈	d			16 48						17 27						17 48							18 27		
Cambridge	a			17 19			17 30	17 51		17 56		18 00	18 09			18 19		18 30			18 51		18 56		
	d			17 20			17 35	17 53		18 01		18 04	18 13			18 20		18 35			18 53		19 01		
Cambridge North	d			17 24			17 38	17a58				18 08	18a18			18 24		18 38			18a58				
Waterbeach	d						17 44											18 44							
Ipswich	d	17 08	17a25						17 44					18 08					17 58	18a25		18 44			
Ely	a			17 36			17 54			18 15		18 23				18 36		18 54	18 58				19 15		
	d			17 36		17 47	17 56			18 16	18 16					18 36	18 48	18 55	18 58				19 16	19 22	
Littleport	d						18 05											19 04							
Downham Market	d						18 17											19 17							
Watlington	d						18 23											19 23							
Kings Lynn	a						18 31											19 31							
	d																								
Manea	d									18 27									19 09						
March	d									18 34							19 05		19 17				19 32		
Whittlesea	d																		19 28						
Peterborough	a					18 23				18 52							19 24		19 39				19 50		
Shippea Hill	d																								
Lakenheath	d																								
Brandon	d			17 52												18 52									
Thetford	d			18 01							18 37					19 01								19 43	
Harling Road	d																								
Eccles Road	d																								
Attleborough	d			18 16												19 16									
Spooner Row	d																								
Wymondham	d			18 24												19 23									
Norwich	a	17 51		18 39					18 27		19 13			18 50		19 37						19 27		20 16	

Table T017-F

Saturdays

21 December to 16 May

London and Cambridge - Ely, Kings Lynn, Peterborough and Norwich

		GN	LE	LE	LE	LE		EM	GN	LE	LE	XC	EM	GN	LE	LE		LE	LE	GN	LE	LE	LE	LE	GN
		1	◇1	◇1	◇1			◇	1	◇1	◇1	◇1	◇	1	◇1	■		◇1		1		◇1	◇1	◇1	1
London Liverpool Street 15 ⊖	d		17 58	18 00	18 02					18 28	18 30				18 58	19 00		19 02				19 04	19 28	19 30	
London Kings Cross 15 ⊖	d	18 12							18 42					19 12						19 42					20 12
Stansted Airport ✈	d					18 48						19 27							19 48						
Cambridge	a	19 00	19 09			19 19			19 30	19 51		19 56		20 00	20 09				20 19	20 30			20 51		21 04
	d	19 04	19 13			19 20			19 35	19 53		20 01		20 04	20 13				20 20	20 35			20 53		21 05
Cambridge North	d	19 08	19a18			19 25			19 38	19a58				20 08	20a18				20 24	20 38			20a58		21 09
Waterbeach	d								19 44											20 44					
Ipswich	d			19 08	19a24						19 43					19 55		20 09			20 01	20a27		20 44	
Ely 6	a	19 20				19 37			19 54			20 15		20 21					20 36	20 54	20 58				21 21
	d	19 25				19 37		19 48	19 55			20 16	20 16	20 23					20 36	20 55	20 58				21 25
Littleport	d	19 34							20 04											21 04					21 33
Downham Market	d	19 46							20 17					20 46						21 17					21 46
Watlington	d	19 52							20 23											21 23					21 52
Kings Lynn	a	20 00							20 31					21 00						21 31					22 00
	d																								
Manea	d																				21 09				
March	d											20 32									21 17				
Whittlesea	d																				21 28				
Peterborough 8	a							20 23				20 50									21 39				
Shippea Hill	d																								
Lakenheath	d																								
Brandon	d					19 53													20 52						
Thetford	d					20 02							20 38						21 01						
Harling Road	d																								
Eccles Road	d																								
Attleborough	d					20 17													21 16						
Spooner Row	d																								
Wymondham	d					20 24													21 23						
Norwich	a			19 50		20 38					20 27		21 13			20 30		20 51	21 37					21 27	

		LE		LE	LE	LE	GN	LE	LE	EM	GN	LE		LE	GN	LE	LE	LE	LE	GN	GN	LE		LE	LE
		◇1		◇	1		1	◇1	◇1	◇	1	◇1		◇1	1		◇1	◇1	1	1	1	◇1		◇1	
London Liverpool Street 15 ⊖	d	19 58		20 00	20 02			20 28	20 30			20 58		21 00			21 28	21 30	22 00			22 28		22 30	23 02
London Kings Cross 15 ⊖	d						20 42				21 12				21 42					22 12	22 42				
Stansted Airport ✈	d					20 48										22 10									
Cambridge	a	21 09				21 19	21 32	21 51			22 04	22 09			22 30	22 43	22 51			23 04	23 30	23 51			
	d	21 13				21 20	21 37	21 53			22 05	22 13			22 35	22 55	22 59			23 05	23 35	23 52			
Cambridge North	d	21a18				21 24	21 41	21a58			22 09	22a18			22 38	22 59	23a04			23 09	23 38	23a57			
Waterbeach	d						21 46								22 44						23 44				
Ipswich	d			21 08	21a25				21 45					22a08				22 45	23a08					23 45	00a30
Ely 6	a					21 35	21 56				22 23				22 54	23 11				23 23	23 54				
	d					21 36	21 57			22 17					22 55	23 11					23 55				
Littleport	d						22 05								23 02						00 03				
Downham Market	d						22 17								23 11						00 12				
Watlington	d						22 23								23 17						00 18				
Kings Lynn	a						22 31								23 25						00 26				
	d																								
Manea	d																								
March	d																								
Whittlesea	d																								
Peterborough 8	a																								
Shippea Hill	d																								
Lakenheath	d																								
Brandon	d					21 53										23 27									
Thetford	d					22 01				22 38						23 36									
Harling Road	d																								
Eccles Road	d																								
Attleborough	d					22 16				22 52						23 51									
Spooner Row	d																								
Wymondham	d					22 24				22 59						23 58									
Norwich	a			21 50		22 38			22 29	23 19						00 12		23 30						00 36	

NRT DECEMBER 19 EDITION

Table T017-F

Saturdays

21 December to 16 May

London and Cambridge - Ely, Kings Lynn, Peterborough and Norwich

		GN	LE
		1	◇1
London Liverpool Street 15 ⊖	d		23 30
London Kings Cross 15 ⊖	d	23 12	
Stansted Airport ✈	d		
Cambridge	a	00 04	
	d	00 08	
Cambridge North	d	00 13	
Waterbeach	d	00 17	
Ipswich	d		00 45
Ely 6	a	00 26	
	d	00 27	
Littleport	d	00 34	
Downham Market	d	00 43	
Watlington	d	00 49	
Kings Lynn	a	00 57	
	d		
Manea	d		
March	d		
Whittlesea	d		
Peterborough 8	a		
Shippea Hill	d		
Lakenheath	d		
Brandon	d		
Thetford	d		
Harling Road	d		
Eccles Road	d		
Attleborough	d		
Spooner Row	d		
Wymondham	d		
Norwich	a		01 36

Sundays

15 December to 10 May

		GN	GN	LE	LE	LE	GN	LE	LE	LE		LE	GN	LE	LE	LE	LE	LE	LE	XC		GN	LE	LE	LE
		1	1	◇1	1	◇	1	◇1	1	◇1		◇1	1	◇1		1	◇1	◇1		◇1		1	◇1	1	◇1
London Liverpool Street 15 ⊖	d							07 42	08 00	08 27		08 28		08 57		09 08	09 28	09 30					09 57	10 08	10 28
London Kings Cross 15 ⊖	d						07 53						09 11									10 11			
Stansted Airport ✈	d					08 18													10 09	10 27					
Cambridge	a					08 49	08 58	09 19				09 41	09 59	10 19			10 41		10 45	10 55		10 58	11 19		11 41
	d		00 08			08 50	09 04	09 20				09 42	10 04	10 20			10 42		10 50	11 01		11 04	11 20		11 42
Cambridge North	d		00 13			08 55	09 08	09a25				09a47	10 08	10a28			10a47		10 54			11 08	11a28		11a48
Waterbeach	d		00 17				09 12						10 12									11 12			
Ipswich	d			00 45	08 46				09a36	09 46					09 55	10a35		10 41						11a35	
Ely 6	a		00 26			09 07	09 22						10 22		10 52				11 07	11 15		11 22			
	d		00 27			09 07	09 22						10 22		10 52				11 07	11 16		11 22			
Littleport	d	00 03	00 34				09 29						10 29									11 29			
Downham Market	d	00 12	00 43				09 38						10 38									11 38			
Watlington	d	00 18	00 49				09 44						10 44									11 44			
Kings Lynn	a	00 26	00 57				09 52						10 52									11 52			
	d																								
Manea	d																								
March	d														11 09					11 32					
Whittlesea	d														11 20										
Peterborough 8	a														11 31					11 50					
Shippea Hill	d																								
Lakenheath	d					09x20													11x20						
Brandon	d					09 26													11 26						
Thetford	d					09 34													11 34						
Harling Road	d																								
Eccles Road	d																								
Attleborough	d					09 49													11 49						
Spooner Row	d																								
Wymondham	d					09 57													11 57						
Norwich	a			01 36	09 30	10 13				10 30								11 27	12 13						

Table T017-F

Sundays

15 December to 10 May

London and Cambridge - Ely, Kings Lynn, Peterborough and Norwich

	LE ◇■	EM ◇	LE	XC ◇■	GN ■	LE ◇■	LE	LE ◇■	LE ■	LE ◇■	LE ◇■	LE	XC ◇■	GN ■	LE ◇■	LE ■	LE ◇■	LE ◇■	LE	XC ◇■	EM ◇
London Liverpool Street ⊖ d	10 30					10 57		11 00	11 08	11 28	11 30				11 57	12 08	12 28	12 30			
London Kings Cross ⊖ d					11 11									12 11							
Stansted Airport ✈ d			11 09	11 27								12 09	12 27						13 09	13 27	
Cambridge a			11 45	11 55	11 58	12 19				12 41		12 45	12 55	12 58	13 19		13 41		13 45	13 55	
d			11 50	12 01	12 04	12 20				12 42		12 50	13 01	13 04	13 20		13 42		13 50	14 01	
Cambridge North d			11 54		12 08	12a28				12a47		12 54		13 08	13a28		13a47		13 54		
Waterbeach d					12 12									13 12							
Ipswich d	11 41						11 55	12 05	12a35		12 41					13a34		13 41			
Ely ■ a			12 07	12 15	12 22		12 52					13 07	13 15	13 22					14 07	14 15	
d		11 39	12 07	12 16	12 22		12 52					13 07	13 16	13 22					14 07	14 16	14 19
Littleport d					12 29									13 29							
Downham Market d					12 38									13 38							
Watlington d					12 44									13 44							
Kings Lynn a					12 52									13 52							
d																					
Manea d																					
March d				12 32			13 09						13 32							14 32	
Whittlesea d							13 20														
Peterborough ■ a		12 11		12 50			13 31						13 50							14 50	
Shippea Hill d																					
Lakenheath d												13x20									
Brandon d			12 23									13 26							14 23		14 35
Thetford d			12 32									13 34							14 32		14 43
Harling Road d																					
Eccles Road d																					
Attleborough d			12 47									13 49							14 47		14 57
Spooner Row d																					
Wymondham d			12 54									13 57							14 54		15 07
Norwich a	12 27		13 12					12 52			13 27	14 13						14 27	15 13		15 23

	GN ■	LE ◇■	EM ◇	LE	LE ■	LE ◇■	LE ◇■	LE	XC ◇■	GN ■	LE ◇■	LE ■	LE ◇■	LE ◇■	EM ◇	EM ◇	LE	XC ◇■	GN ■	LE ◇■	EM ◇	LE
London Liverpool Street ⊖ d		12 57			13 08	13 28	13 30				13 57	14 08	14 28	14 30						14 57		
London Kings Cross ⊖ d	13 11									14 11									15 11			
Stansted Airport ✈ d								14 09	14 27								15 09	15 27				
Cambridge a	13 58	14 19				14 41		14 45	14 55	14 58	15 19		15 41				15 45	15 55	15 58	16 19		
d	14 04	14 20				14 42		14 50	15 01	15 04	15 20		15 42				15 50	16 01	16 04	16 20		
Cambridge North d	14 08	14a28				14a47		14 54		15 08	15a28		15a47				15 54		16 08	16a28		
Waterbeach d	14 12									15 12									16 12			
Ipswich d				13 55	14a34		14 41					15a36		15 41								15 55
Ely ■ a	14 22			14 52				15 07	15 15	15 22							16 07	16 15	16 22			16 52
d	14 22		14 40	14 52				15 07	15 16	15 22					15 40	15 46	16 07	16 16	16 22		16 34	16 52
Littleport d	14 29									15 29									16 29			
Downham Market d	14 38									15 38									16 38			
Watlington d	14 44									15 44									16 44			
Kings Lynn a	14 52									15 52									16 52			
d																						
Manea d																						
March d				15 09					15 32							16 03		16 32				17 09
Whittlesea d				15 20																		17 20
Peterborough ■ a			15 13	15 31					15 50							16 20		16 50				17 31
Shippea Hill d																						
Lakenheath d																	16x20					
Brandon d								15 23									16 26					
Thetford d								15 32							16 01		16 34				16 55	
Harling Road d																						
Eccles Road d																						
Attleborough d								15 47									16 49					
Spooner Row d																						
Wymondham d								15 54									16 57					
Norwich a							15 29	16 13						16 27	16 35		17 13				17 26	

	LE ■	LE ◇■	LE ◇■	LE	XC ◇■	GN ■	LE ◇■	LE ■	LE ◇■	LE ◇■	EM ◇	EM ◇	LE	XC ◇■	GN ■	LE ◇■	LE ■	LE ◇■	LE ◇■	EM ◇	EM ◇
London Liverpool Street ⊖ d	15 08	15 28	15 30				15 57	16 08	16 28	16 30						16 57	17 08	17 28	17 30		
London Kings Cross ⊖ d						16 11									17 11						
Stansted Airport ✈ d				16 09	16 27								17 09	17 27							
Cambridge a		16 41		16 45	16 55	16 58	17 19		17 41				17 45	17 55	17 58	18 19		18 41			
d		16 42		16 50	17 01	17 04	17 20		17 42				17 50	18 01	18 04	18 20		18 42			
Cambridge North d		16a47		16 54		17 08	17a28		17a47				17 54		18 08	18a28		18a47			
Waterbeach d						17 12									18 12						
Ipswich d	16a34		16 41					17a35		17 41							18a34		18 41		
Ely ■ a				17 07	17 15	17 22							18 07	18 15	18 22						
d				17 07	17 16	17 22					17 36	17 49	18 07	18 16	18 22					18 35	18 47
Littleport d						17 29									18 30						
Downham Market d						17 38									18 39						
Watlington d						17 44									18 44						
Kings Lynn a						17 52									18 53						
d																					
Manea d																					
March d					17 32									18 32							
Whittlesea d																					
Peterborough ■ a					17 50							18 20		18 50							19 20
Shippea Hill d																					
Lakenheath d																					
Brandon d				17 23									18 23								
Thetford d				17 32							17 57		18 32							18 56	
Harling Road d																					
Eccles Road d																					
Attleborough d				17 47									18 47								
Spooner Row d																					
Wymondham d				17 54									18 54								
Norwich a			17 27	18 13						18 28	18 30		19 13						19 27	19 28	

Table T017-F

Sundays

15 December to 10 May

London and Cambridge - Ely, Kings Lynn, Peterborough and Norwich

	LE	LE	XC ◇■	GN ■	LE ◇■	LE ◇	LE ■	LE ◇■	EM ◇	LE ◇■	EM ◇	LE	XC ◇■	GN ■	LE ◇■	LE ◇■	LE ■	LE ◇■	LE ◇■	EM ◇	LE	GN ■
London Liverpool Street ⊖ d					17 57	18 00	18 08	18 28		18 30					18 57	19 00	19 08	19 28	19 30			
London Kings Cross ⊖ d				18 11										19 11								20 11
Stansted Airport ✈ d		18 09	18 27									19 09	19 27								20 09	
Cambridge a		18 45	18 55	18 58	19 19			19 41				19 45	19 55	20 00	20 19			20 41			20 45	20 58
d		18 50	19 01	19 04	19 20			19 42				19 50	20 01	20 05	20 20			20 42			20 50	21 04
Cambridge North d		18 54		19 08	19a28			19a47				19 54		20 09	20a28			20a47			20 54	21 08
Waterbeach d				19 12										20 13								21 12
Ipswich d	17 55					19 05	19a34			19 41						20 08	20a34		20 41			
Ely ■ a	18 52	19 07	19 15	19 22								20 07	20 15	20 23							21 07	21 22
d	18 52	19 07	19 16	19 22					19 30		19 49	20 07	20 16	20 23						20 35	21 07	21 22
Littleport d				19 29										20 30								21 29
Downham Market d				19 38										20 39								21 38
Watlington d				19 44										20 45								21 44
Kings Lynn a				19 52										20 53								21 52
d																						
Manea d																						
March d	19 09		19 32										20 32									
Whittlesea d	19 20																					
Peterborough ■ a	19 31		19 50								20 23		20 50									
Shippea Hill d																						
Lakenheath d																						
Brandon d		19 23										20 23									21 23	
Thetford d		19 32							19 52			20 32								20 56	21 32	
Harling Road d																						
Eccles Road d																						
Attleborough d		19 47										20 47								21 10	21 47	
Spooner Row d																						
Wymondham d		19 54										20 54								21 17	21 54	
Norwich a		20 13				19 51			20 26	20 27		21 10				20 54			21 27	21 37	22 13	

	LE ◇■	LE ■	LE ◇■	EM ◇	LE	GN ■	LE ◇■	LE ■	EM ◇	LE ◇■	GN ■	LE ◇■	LE ■	LE ◇■	LE ■	GN ■	LE ◇■
London Liverpool Street ⊖ d	19 57	20 08	20 30				20 57	21 08		21 30		21 57	22 08	22 30	23 08		23 30
London Kings Cross ⊖ d						21 11					22 11					23 11	
Stansted Airport ✈ d					21 11												
Cambridge a	21 19				21 49	21 58	22 19				22 58	23 19				00 02	
d	21 20				21 50	22 04	22 20				23 04	23 20				00 04	
Cambridge North d	21a28				21 55	22 08	22a25				23 08	23a25				00 08	
Waterbeach d						22 12					23 12					00 12	
Ipswich d		21a34	21 41					22a34		22 42			23a34	23 42	00a39		00 48
Ely ■ a					22 07	22 22					23 22					00 22	
d				21 44	22 07	22 22			22 30		23 22					00 22	
Littleport d						22 29					23 29					00 29	
Downham Market d						22 38					23 38					00 38	
Watlington d						22 44					23 44					00 44	
Kings Lynn a						22 52					23 52					00 52	
d																	
Manea d																	
March d																	
Whittlesea d																	
Peterborough ■ a				22 16													
Shippea Hill d																	
Lakenheath d																	
Brandon d					22 23												
Thetford d					22 32				22 51								
Harling Road d																	
Eccles Road d																	
Attleborough d					22 47				23 05								
Spooner Row d																	
Wymondham d					22 54				23 12								
Norwich a			22 27		23 13				23 25	23 30				00 27			01 38

Table T017-R

Mondays to Fridays
16 December to 15 May

Norwich, Peterborough, Kings Lynn and Ely - Cambridge and London

Miles	Miles	Miles			GN	LE	LE	LE	LE	LE	GN	LE	GN	GN	EM	LE	LE	LE	LE	LE	EM	GN	GN
					1	◇1	◇	1	◇1	1 ⊡	1		1	1	◇	1	1 ⊡	◇1	1 ⊡	◇1 A	◇	1	1
0	—	—	**Norwich**	d			05 00			05 30		05 33			05 50		06 00		06 24				
10	—	—	Wymondham	d								05 45			06 03								
12¾	—	—	Spooner Row	d																			
16	—	—	Attleborough	d								05 52			06 10								
19½	—	—	Eccles Road	d																			
22¾	—	—	Harling Road	d																			
30½	—	—	Thetford	d								06 06			06 24								
37½	—	—	Brandon	d								06 14											
41½	—	—	Lakenheath	d																			
46½	—	—	Shippea Hill	a																			
—	0	—	**Peterborough** 8	d																	06 28		
—	7	—	Whittlesea	d																			
—	15	—	March	d																	06 44		
—	20¾	—	Manea	a																			
—	—	0	**Kings Lynn**	a																			
—	—	—		d	04 43				05 17		05 40		06 09							06 17		06 40	
—	—	6	Watlington	d	04 50				05 24		05 47		06 17							06 25		06 47	
—	—	10¾	Downham Market	d	04 57				05 31		05 54		06 24							06 32		06 54	
—	—	21	Littleport	a	05 06				05 40		06 03									06 41		07 03	
53¾	30½	26½	**Ely** 6	a	05 15				05 49		06 12	06 31	06 42		06 46					06 49	07 02	07 12	
				d	05 15				05 50		06 12	06 32	06 42	06 45						06 50		07 12	07 15
—	—	—	Ipswich	d		05 12	05 44	06 00		06 14						06 29	06 44	06 52	07 08				
—	—	36	Waterbeach	d	05 25				05 59		06 22			06 56						06 59		07 22	
66	43	39	Cambridge North	d	05 30				06 04		06 27	06 44	06 55							07 04			07 29
68¾	45¼	41¼	**Cambridge**	a	05 34				06 10		06 34	06 52	07 00	07 03						07 10		07 30	07 34
—	—	—		d	05 40				06 18		06 40		07 09							07 17		07 39	
—	69¾	—	**Stansted Airport** ✈	a																			
—	—	99¼	**London Kings Cross** 15 ⊖	a	06 32						07 32		08 02									08 34	
—	—	—	**London Liverpool Street** 15 ⊖	a		06 34	06 54	07 23	07 25	07 27						07 50	07 58	08 13	08 24	08 25			

		LE	LE	LE	LE	EM	GN	GN	XC	LE	LE	LE	EM	GN	LE	LE	LE	GN	EM	XC	LE	LE	LE
		◇1	◇1		1 ⊡	◇	1	1	◇1	◇1	1 ⊡	◇1	◇	1			1 B ⊡	1	◇	◇1 ⊤	◇1	1 ⊡	◇1
Norwich	d			06 33	06 48	06 51					07 05					07 33	07 40		07 57			08 00	
Wymondham	d			06 45												07 45							
Spooner Row	d																						
Attleborough	d			06 52												07 52							
Eccles Road	d																						
Harling Road	d																						
Thetford	d			07 06		07 19										08 06			08 24				
Brandon	d			07 14												08 14							
Lakenheath	d																						
Shippea Hill	a																						
Peterborough 8	d								07 13				07 38		07 49					08 19			
Whittlesea	d								07 21						07 57								
March	d								07 32				07 54		08 08					08 34			
Manea	a								07 39						08 15								
Kings Lynn	a																						
	d						07 05	07 16						07 48				08 12					
Watlington	d						07 12							07 56				08 19					
Downham Market	d						07 19	07 28						08 03				08 26					
Littleport	a						07 28							08 12				08 35					
Ely 6	a			07 31		07 40	07 37	07 44	07 53				08 12	08 25	08 29	08 32		08 44	08 47	08 52			
	d		07 29	07 33			07 41	07 46	07 53			08 00		08 25	08 30	08 33		08 45		08 54			
Ipswich	d	07 17			07 32					07 38	07 49				09a26		08 20				08 26	08 43	08 58
Waterbeach	d						07 51					08 09		08 35				08 55					
Cambridge North	d		07 41	07 47				07 58				08 14		08 40		08 45		09 00					
Cambridge	a		07 47	07 53			07 59	08 03	08 08			08 20		08 44		08 51		09 04		09 12			
	d		07 51				08 09		08 11			08 21		08 49				09 10		09 14			
Stansted Airport ✈	a								08 41											09 44			
London Kings Cross 15 ⊖	a						09 04							09 46				10 05					
London Liverpool Street 15 ⊖	a	08 40	09 21		08 42					09 01	09 04	09 50					09 24				09 39	10 00	10 10

A The Fenman

B The East Anglian

NRT DECEMBER 19 EDITION

Table T017-R

Mondays to Fridays
16 December to 15 May

Norwich, Peterborough, Kings Lynn and Ely - Cambridge and London

		LE	LE	GN	LE	EM	EM	LE	LE	LE	LE	LE	GN	XC	GN	EM	LE	GN	LE	LE	LE	EM
		1 ⊡	◇1	1		◇	◇		◇1	1 ⊡	◇1	1	1	◇1 ⊤	1	◇	◇1	1		◇1 ⊡		◇
Norwich	d	08 30			08 33		08 56	09 00		09 03									09 27	09 30		09 57
Wymondham	d				08 45														09 39			
Spooner Row	d																					
Attleborough	d				08 52														09 46			
Eccles Road	d																					
Harling Road	d																					
Thetford	d				09 06		09 24												10 00			10 24
Brandon	d				09 14														10 08			
Lakenheath	d																					
Shippea Hill	a																					
Peterborough 8	d					09 03								09 19		09 40					09 50	
Whittlesea	d																				09 58	
March	d													09 34							10 09	
Manea	a																				10 16	
Kings Lynn	a																					
	d			08 44									09 10					09 44				
Watlington	d			08 51									09 17					09 51				
Downham Market	d			08 58									09 28					09 58				
Littleport	a			09 07									09 37					10 07				
Ely 6	a			09 16	09 31	09 41	09 45						09 48	09 52		10 13		10 16	10 27		10 31	10 46
	d			09 17	09 31								09 48	09 53				10 17	10 27		10 32	
Ipswich	d	09 09						09 33	09 23	09 47		09 52								10 09	11a28	
Waterbeach	d			09 26									09 58					10 26				
Cambridge North	d		09 11	09 31	09 44						09 53		10 03		←		10 13	10 31	10 39			
Cambridge	a		09 17	09 36	09 49						09 59		10 07	10 10	10 07		10 19	10 36	10 45			
	d		09 20	09 41	09 50						10 03		10 14	10 11	10 14		10 20	10 44	10 48			
Stansted Airport ✈	a				10 24								↦	10 41					11 24			
London Kings Cross 15 ⊖	a			10 34											11 05			11 34				
London Liverpool Street 15 ⊖	a	10 21	10 45					10 30	10 51	10 56	11 15	11 16					11 45			11 19		

		LE	LE	LE	LE	GN	XC	GN	LE	GN	EM	LE	EM	LE	LE	LE	GN	XC	GN	EM	LE	GN	LE
		◇1 ⊡	1	◇1	◇1 ⊡	1	◇1 ⊤	1	◇1	1	◇		◇	◇1 ⊡	1	◇1	1	◇1 ⊤	1	◇	◇1	1	
Norwich	d	10 00			10 30							10 33	10 57	11 00									11 27
Wymondham	d											10 45											11 39
Spooner Row	d																						
Attleborough	d											10 52											11 46
Eccles Road	d																						
Harling Road	d																						
Thetford	d											11 06	11 24										12 00
Brandon	d											11 14											12 08
Lakenheath	d																						
Shippea Hill	a																						
Peterborough 8	d						10 19				10 45							11 19		11 41			
Whittlesea	d																						
March	d						10 34											11 34					
Manea	a																						
Kings Lynn	a																						
	d									10 44												11 44	
Watlington	d									10 51												11 51	
Downham Market	d									10 58												11 58	
Littleport	a									11 07												12 07	
Ely 6	a						10 52			11 16	11 19	11 31	11 46					11 53		12 13		12 16	12 25
	d					10 47	10 53			11 17		11 31					11 47	11 54				12 17	12 27
Ipswich	d	10 43	10 52		11 09									11 43	11 48								
Waterbeach	d									11 26												12 26	
Cambridge North	d			10 53		11 01		←	11 13	11 31		11 44				11 53	12 01		←		12 13	12 31	12 39
Cambridge	a			10 59		11 05	11 08	11 05	11 19	11 36		11 49				11 59	12 05	12 09	12 05		12 19	12 37	12 44
	d			11 03		11 14	11 11	11 14	11 20	11 44		11 50				12 03	12 14	12 11	12 14		12 20	12 44	12 48
Stansted Airport ✈	a					↦	11 41					12 24					↦	12 41					13 24
London Kings Cross 15 ⊖	a							12 02		12 35									13 03			13 33	
London Liverpool Street 15 ⊖	a	11 55	12 14	12 15	12 19				12 45					12 55	13 14	13 15					13 45		

Norwich, Peterborough, Kings Lynn and Ely - Cambridge and London

		LE	LE	EM	LE	LE	LE	LE	GN	XC		GN	EM	LE	GN	LE	EM	LE	LE	LE		GN	XC	GN	EM
		◇■		◇	◇■	■	◇■	◇■	■	◇■		■	◇	◇■	■		◇	◇■	■	◇■		■	◇■	■	◇
Norwich	d	11 30		11 57	12 00			12 30								12 33	12 57	13 00							
Wymondham	d															12 45									
Spooner Row	d																								
Attleborough	d															12 52									
Eccles Road	d																								
Harling Road	d																								
Thetford	d			12 24												13 06	13 24								
Brandon	d															13 14									
Lakenheath	d																								
Shippea Hill	a																								
Peterborough ■	d		11 50							12 19			12 42										13 19		13 41
Whittlesea	d		11 58																						
March	d		12 09							12 34													13 34		
Manea	a		12 16																						
Kings Lynn	a																								
	d														12 44										
Watlington	d														12 51										
Downham Market	d														12 58										
Littleport	a														13 07										
Ely ■	a		12 31	12 45						12 52			13 14		13 17	13 31	13 46						13 53		14 13
	d		12 32						12 47	12 53					13 17	13 31						13 47	13 53		
Ipswich	d	12 09	13a28		12 43	12 52		13 09										13 43	13 52						
Waterbeach	d														13 26										
Cambridge North	d						12 53		13 01			←		13 13	13 31	13 44				13 53		14 01		←	
Cambridge	a						12 59		13 05	13 08		13 05		13 19	13 37	13 49				13 59		14 05	14 08	14 05	
	d						13 03		13 14	13 11		13 14		13 20	13 44	13 50				14 03		14 14	14 11	14 14	
Stansted Airport ✈	a								→	13 41						14 24						→	14 41		
London Kings Cross ⊖	a											14 03			14 33									15 02	
London Liverpool Street ⊖	a	13 19			13 55	14 14	14 15	14 19						14 45				14 55	15 14	15 15					

		LE	GN	LE	LE	LE		EM	LE	LE	LE	GN	XC	GN	EM	LE		GN	LE	LE	EM	LE	LE	LE	GN
		◇■	■		◇■			◇	◇■	■	◇■	■	◇■	■	◇	◇■		■		◇■	◇	◇■	◇■	■	■
Norwich	d			13 27	13 30			13 57	14 00										14 27	14 30	14 57	15 00			
Wymondham	d			13 39															14 39						
Spooner Row	d																								
Attleborough	d			13 46															14 46						
Eccles Road	d																								
Harling Road	d																								
Thetford	d			14 00				14 24											15 00		15 24				
Brandon	d			14 08															15 08						
Lakenheath	d																								
Shippea Hill	a																								
Peterborough ■	d					13 50							14 19		14 41										
Whittlesea	d					13 58																			
March	d					14 09							14 34												
Manea	a					14 16																			
Kings Lynn	a																								
	d		13 44															14 44							
Watlington	d		13 51															14 51							
Downham Market	d		13 58															14 58							
Littleport	a		14 07															15 07							
Ely ■	a		14 16	14 25		14 31		14 45					14 52		15 14			15 17	15 27		15 45				
	d		14 17	14 26		14 32						14 47	14 53					15 17	15 27						15 45
Ipswich	d				14 09	15a28			14 43	14 52										15 09		15 43		15 52	
Waterbeach	d		14 26															15 26							
Cambridge North	d	14 13	14 31	14 38							14 53	15 01		←		15 13		15 31	15 39				15 43		16 00
Cambridge	a	14 19	14 36	14 44							14 59	15 05	15 08	15 05		15 19		15 37	15 45				15 49		16 05
	d	14 20	14 44	14 48							15 03	15 14	15 11	15 14		15 20		15 44	15 47				15 50		16 14
Stansted Airport ✈	a			15 31								→	15 41						16 24						→
London Kings Cross ⊖	a		15 33											16 02				16 33							
London Liverpool Street ⊖	a	15 45			15 19				15 55	16 14	16 15					16 46				16 17		16 57	17 16	17 16	

		XC		GN	EM	LE	GN	LE	LE	LE	EM	LE		LE	GN	XC	EM	LE	LE	GN	LE	LE		GN	GN
		◇■		■	◇	◇■	■		◇■		◇	◇■		◇■	■	◇■	◇	■	◇■	■		◇■		■	■
Norwich	d							15 27	15 30		15 48	16 00									16 27	16 30			
Wymondham	d							15 39													16 39				
Spooner Row	d																				16x43				
Attleborough	d							15 46			16 05										16 48				
Eccles Road	d										16 10														
Harling Road	d										16 14														
Thetford	d							16 00			16 23										17 02				
Brandon	d							16 08													17 10				
Lakenheath	d																								
Shippea Hill	a																								
Peterborough ■	d	15 19			15 40					15 50						16 19	16 41								
Whittlesea	d									15 58															
March	d	15 34								16 09						16 34									
Manea	a									16 16															
Kings Lynn	a																								
	d						15 44													16 44					17 15
Watlington	d						15 51													16 51					
Downham Market	d						15 58													16 58					17 29
Littleport	a						16 07													17 07					
Ely ■	a	15 53			16 13		16 17	16 27		16 31	16 45					16 53	17 13			17 17	17 27				17 45
	d	15 53					16 17	16 27		16 32					16 47	16 54				17 17	17 27			17 42	17 46
Ipswich	d								16 09	17a28		16 43						16 52				17 09			
Waterbeach	d						16 26													17 26					17 55
Cambridge North	d			←		16 13	16 31	16 39						16 43	17 01				17 13	17 31	17 39			17 55	
Cambridge	a	16 08		16 05		16 19	16 37	16 45						16 49	17 05	17 09			17 19	17 37	17 47			17 59	18 02
	d	16 11		16 14		16 20	16 44	16 47						16 50	17 08	17 11			17 20	17 43				18 08	
Stansted Airport ✈	a	16 41						17 24								17 41									
London Kings Cross ⊖	a			17 03			17 32								18 03					18 33				19 05	
London Liverpool Street ⊖	a					17 44			17 19			17 58		18 16				18 18	18 46			18 21			

Table T017-R

Mondays to Fridays

16 December to 15 May

Norwich, Peterborough, Kings Lynn and Ely - Cambridge and London

		EM	LE	LE	XC	LE	GN	EM		LE	LE	LE	LE	EM	XC	GN	LE	LE		LE	LE	GN	EM	LE	LE
		◇	■	◇■	◇■	■	■	◇			◇■		◇■	◇	◇■	■	■	◇■		■	◇■	■	◇		◇■
Norwich	d	16 56	17 00	17 03								17 27	17 30	17 54				18 00						18 27	18 30
Wymondham	d	17 09										17 39		18 06										18 39	
Spooner Row	d																								
Attleborough	d											17 47		18 13										18 46	
Eccles Road	d											17 52													
Harling Road	d											17 57													
Thetford	d	17 27										18 07		18 27										19 00	
Brandon	d											18 15												19 08	
Lakenheath	d																								
Shippea Hill	a																								
Peterborough ■	d				17 19			17 44		17 50					18 18								18 45		
Whittlesea	d				17 27					17 58															
March	d				17 38					18 09					18 33								19 00		
Manea	a				17 45					18 16															
Kings Lynn	a																								
	d						17 44															18 40			
Watlington	d						17 51															18 47			
Downham Market	d						17 58															18 54			
Littleport	a						18 07															19 03			
Ely ■	a	17 48			17 59		18 16	18 19		18 31		18 36		18 48	18 51							19 16	19 19	19 26	
	d				18 00		18 17			18 31		18 37			18 52	18 57						19 17		19 26	
Ipswich	d		17 33	17 48		17 40				19a28			18 13				18 22	18 43		18 49					19 09
Waterbeach	d						18 27															19 27			
Cambridge North	d						18 32				18 42	18 49				19 09					19 13	19 32		19 38	
Cambridge	a				18 15		18 36				18 48	18 56			19 07	19 13					19 19	19 36		19 44	
	d				18 17		18 44				18 50				19 11	19 14					19 20	19 44			
Stansted Airport ✈	a				18 54										19 41										
London Kings Cross ⊖	a						19 35									20 02						20 33			
London Liverpool Street ⊖	a		18 30	18 58		19 14					20 15		19 17				19 45	19 55		20 14	20 45				20 20

		XC	EM	LE		LE	LE	GN	XC	GN	EM	LE	GN	LE		LE	LE	LE	LE	LE	GN	XC	GN	LE	
		◇■	◇	◇■		■	◇■	■	◇■	■	◇	◇■	■			◇■	◇■	◇■	◇■		■	◇■	■	◇■	
Norwich	d		18 57	19 00										19 27		19 30	20 00		20 30						
Wymondham	d													19 39											
Spooner Row	d																								
Attleborough	d													19 46											
Eccles Road	d																								
Harling Road	d																								
Thetford	d		19 24											20 00											
Brandon	d													20 08											
Lakenheath	d																								
Shippea Hill	a																								
Peterborough ■	d	19 00							19 19		19 42									19 50		20 19			
Whittlesea	d																			19 58					
March	d	19 15							19 34											20 09		20 34			
Manea	a																			20 16					
Kings Lynn	a																								
	d												19 44												
Watlington	d												19 51												
Downham Market	d												19 58												
Littleport	a												20 07												
Ely ■	a	19 33	19 47						19 53		20 15		20 18	20 27						20 31		20 52			
	d	19 34						19 47	19 53				20 18	20 27						20 31	20 49	20 53			
Ipswich	d			19 43		19 35										20 10	20 43		21 09	21a28					
Waterbeach	d												20 28												
Cambridge North	d						19 52	20 01		←		20 13	20 33	20 39				20 53			21 01		←	21 13	
Cambridge	a	19 50					19 58	20 05	20 08	20 05		20 19	20 38	20 45				20 59			21 05	21 08	21 05	21 19	
	d						20 03	20 14	20 11	20 14		20 20	20 44	20 48				21 03			21 14	21 11	21 14	21 20	
Stansted Airport ✈	a							→	20 41					21 24							→	21 41			
London Kings Cross ⊖	a									21 02			21 33										22 03		
London Liverpool Street ⊖	a			20 55		21 01	21 14					21 44				21 19	21 55	22 15	22 19					22 45	

Table T017-R

Mondays to Fridays
16 December to 15 May

Norwich, Peterborough, Kings Lynn and Ely - Cambridge and London

		GN	LE	LE	LE	GN	XC	GN	EM		LE	LE	GN	LE	LE	LE	GN	XC	GN		LE	LE			
Norwich	d		21 00									21 15		22 00							22 40	23 05			
Wymondham	d											21 27									22 52				
Spooner Row	d																								
Attleborough	d											21 34									22 59				
Eccles Road	d																								
Harling Road	d																								
Thetford	d											21 48									23 13				
Brandon	d											21 56									23 21				
Lakenheath	d																								
Shippea Hill	a																								
Peterborough	d						21 19		21 39						21 45			22 19							
Whittlesea	d														21 53										
March	d						21 34								22 04			22 34							
Manea	a														22 11										
Kings Lynn	a																								
	d	20 44											21 44						22 44						
Watlington	d	20 51											21 51						22 51						
Downham Market	d	20 59											21 58						22 58						
Littleport	a	21 08											22 07						23 07						
Ely	a	21 16					21 52		22 13			22 13	22 16		22 25			22 52	23 16		23 38				
	d	21 17				21 47	21 53					22 14	22 17		22 26		22 46	22 53	23 17		23 38				
Ipswich	d		21 43		22 23									22 43	23a21							23a49			
Waterbeach	d	21 26											22 26						23 26						
Cambridge North	d	21 31		21 53		22 00		←			22 13	22 26	22 31			22 43	23 01		23 31		23 51				
Cambridge	a	21 35		21 59		22 05	22 08	22 05			22 19	22 32	22 36			22 49	23 06	23 09	23 38		23 58				
	d	21 44		22 03		22 14	22 11	22 14			22 20		22 44			22 50	23 14								
Stansted Airport	a					→	22 41																		
London Kings Cross	a	22 32						23 03					23 34				00 08								
London Liverpool Street	a		22 55	23 15	23 48						23 48			00 03		00 18									

Saturdays
21 December to 16 May

		LE	GN	GN	LE	GN	LE	LE	EM	GN		LE	EM	LE	LE	GN	LE	LE	EM	LE		LE	LE	GN	XC
Norwich	d	05 00					05 27	05 30	05 50			06 00					06 27	06 30	06 53	07 00					
Wymondham	d						05 39		06 02								06 39								
Spooner Row	d																								
Attleborough	d						05 46		06 09								06 46								
Eccles Road	d																								
Harling Road	d																								
Thetford	d						06 00		06 23								07 00		07 20						
Brandon	d						06 08										07 08								
Lakenheath	d																								
Shippea Hill	a																								
Peterborough	d												06 27												07 13
Whittlesea	d																								07 21
March	d												06 43												07 32
Manea	a																								07 39
Kings Lynn	a																								
	d					05 44										06 44									
Watlington	d					05 51										06 51									
Downham Market	d					05 58										06 58									
Littleport	a					06 07										07 07									
Ely	a					06 16	06 26		06 44				07 03			07 16	07 25		07 41						07 53
	d		05 12	05 47		06 17	06 27			06 47						07 17	07 26							07 47	07 53
Ipswich	d	05 43						06 09				06 43		06 52				07 09		07 43		07 52			
Waterbeach	d		05 21			06 27										07 27									
Cambridge North	d		05 26	06 00	06 13	06 32	06 39			07 01					07 13	07 32	07 39						07 53	08 01	
Cambridge	a		05 31	06 05	06 19	06 37	06 47			07 06					07 19	07 36	07 44						07 59	08 05	08 08
	d		05 37	06 14	06 20	06 44	06 51			07 14					07 20	07 44	07 48						08 03	08 14	08 11
Stansted Airport	a						07 24										08 24							→	08 41
London Kings Cross	a		06 33	07 03		07 32				08 03						08 33									
London Liverpool Street	a	06 55			07 45			07 19				07 55		08 14	08 45			08 19		08 55		09 14	09 15		

NRT DECEMBER 19 EDITION

Table T017-R

Saturdays
21 December to 16 May

Norwich, Peterborough, Kings Lynn and Ely - Cambridge and London

		GN		EM	LE	GN	LE	LE	LE	EM	LE	LE		LE	GN	XC	GN	LE	GN	LE	LE	EM		LE	GN
Norwich	d						07 27	07 30		07 57	08 00									08 27	08 30				
Wymondham	d						07 39													08 39					
Spooner Row	d																								
Attleborough	d						07 46													08 46					
Eccles Road	d																								
Harling Road	d																								
Thetford	d						08 00			08 24										09 00					
Brandon	d						08 08													09 08					
Lakenheath	d																								
Shippea Hill	a																								
Peterborough	d			07 35					07 50							08 19						09 00			
Whittlesea	d								07 58																
March	d			07 53					08 09							08 34									
Manea	a								08 16																
Kings Lynn	a																								
	d					07 44													08 44						09 13
Watlington	d					07 51													08 51						
Downham Market	d					07 58													08 58						09 25
Littleport	a					08 07													09 07						
Ely	a			08 13		08 16	08 26		08 31	08 45						08 52			09 16	09 25		09 35			09 42
	d					08 17	08 27		08 32						08 47	08 53			09 17	09 27					09 47
Ipswich	d							08 09	09a28		08 43	08 52									09 09				
Waterbeach	d					08 27													09 27						
Cambridge North	d	←			08 13	08 32	08 39							08 53	09 01		←	09 13	09 32	09 39				09 53	10 01
Cambridge	a	08 05			08 19	08 37	08 44							08 59	09 05	09 08	09 05	09 19	09 37	09 44				09 59	10 05
	d	08 14			08 20	08 44	08 48							09 03	09 14	09 11	09 14	09 20	09 44	09 48				10 03	10 14
Stansted Airport	a						09 24								→	09 41				10 24					→
London Kings Cross	a	09 03				09 33											10 05		10 33						
London Liverpool Street	a				09 45			09 19			09 52	10 14		10 15				10 45			10 19			11 15	

		EM	LE	LE	XC	GN	LE	LE		GN	GN	EM	LE	LE	LE	LE	GN	EM		LE	XC	GN	LE	LE	EM
Norwich	d	08 56	09 00	09 04									09 27	09 30				09 57		10 00					
Wymondham	d												09 39												
Spooner Row	d																								
Attleborough	d												09 46												
Eccles Road	d																								
Harling Road	d																								
Thetford	d	09 24											10 00					10 24							
Brandon	d												10 08												
Lakenheath	d																								
Shippea Hill	a																								
Peterborough	d				09 19							09 45			09 50						10 19				10 40
Whittlesea	d														09 58										
March	d				09 34										10 09						10 34				
Manea	a														10 16										
Kings Lynn	a																								
	d										09 44						10 13								
Watlington	d										09 51														
Downham Market	d										09 58						10 25								
Littleport	a										10 07														
Ely	a	09 45			09 52						10 16	10 19	10 26		10 31		10 42	10 45			10 52				11 13
	d				09 53					10 12	10 17		10 27		10 32		10 47				10 53				
Ipswich	d		09 33	09 47			09 52							10 09	11a28					10 43			10 52		
Waterbeach	d										10 27														
Cambridge North	d					←		10 13		10 24	10 32		10 39			10 53	11 01					←		11 13	
Cambridge	a				10 08	10 05		10 19		10 30	10 37		10 44			10 59	11 05				11 08	11 05		11 19	
	d				10 11	10 14		10 20		10 44			10 48			11 03	11 14				11 11	11 14		11 20	
Stansted Airport	a				10 41								11 24				→				11 41				
London Kings Cross	a					11 03				11 33												12 05			
London Liverpool Street	a		10 30	10 56			11 15	11 45						11 19		12 15				11 52			12 14	12 45	

Table T017-R

Saturdays
21 December to 16 May

Norwich, Peterborough, Kings Lynn and Ely - Cambridge and London

		GN	GN	LE	LE	EM	LE	LE	LE	GN		XC	GN	EM	LE	GN	LE	LE	LE	EM		LE	LE	LE	LE
		1	1		◇1	◇	◇1	1	◇1	1		◇1	1	◇	◇1	1		◇1		◇		◇1	1	◇1	◇1
Norwich	d			10 27	10 30	10 57	11 00										11 27	11 30		11 57		12 00			12 30
Wymondham	d			10 39													11 39								
Spooner Row	d																								
Attleborough	d			10 46													11 46								
Eccles Road	d																								
Harling Road	d																								
Thetford	d			11 00		11 24											12 00			12 24					
Brandon	d			11 08													12 08								
Lakenheath	d			11x13																					
Shippea Hill	a																								
Peterborough 8	d											11 19		11 41					11 50						
Whittlesea	d																		11 58						
March	d											11 34							12 09						
Manea	a																		12 16						
Kings Lynn	a																								
	d		10 44													11 44									
Watlington	d		10 51													11 51									
Downham Market	d		10 58													11 58									
Littleport	a		11 07													12 07									
Ely 8	a		11 16	11 27		11 46						11 52		12 13		12 16	12 25		12 31	12 45					
	d	11 12	11 17	11 27						11 47		11 53				12 17	12 27		12 32						
Ipswich	d				11 09		11 43	11 50										12 09	13a28			12 43	12 52		13 09
Waterbeach	d		11 27													12 27									
Cambridge North	d	11 24	11 32	11 40					11 53	12 01			←		12 13	12 32	12 39							12 53	
Cambridge	a	11 30	11 37	11 45					11 59	12 05		12 08	12 05		12 19	12 37	12 44							12 59	
	d	11 44		11 48					12 03	12 14		12 11	12 14		12 20	12 44	12 48							13 03	
Stansted Airport ✈	a			12 24						→		12 41					13 24								
London Kings Cross 15 ⊖	a	12 35											13 03			13 33									
London Liverpool Street 15 ⊖	a				12 19		12 55	13 14	13 15						13 45			13 19				13 55	14 14	14 15	14 19

		GN	XC	GN	LE	GN		EM	LE	EM	LE	LE	LE	GN	XC	GN		EM	LE	GN	LE	LE	LE	EM	LE
		1	◇1	1	◇1	1		◇		◇	◇1	1	◇1	1	◇1	1		◇	◇1	1		◇1		◇	◇1
Norwich	d								12 33	12 57	13 00										13 27	13 30		13 57	14 00
Wymondham	d								12 45												13 39				
Spooner Row	d																								
Attleborough	d								12 52												13 46				
Eccles Road	d																								
Harling Road	d																								
Thetford	d								13 06	13 24											14 00			14 24	
Brandon	d								13 14												14 08				
Lakenheath	d																								
Shippea Hill	a																								
Peterborough 8	d		12 19					12 44							13 19			13 40					13 50		
Whittlesea	d																						13 58		
March	d		12 34												13 34								14 09		
Manea	a																						14 16		
Kings Lynn	a																								
	d					12 44														13 44					
Watlington	d					12 51														13 51					
Downham Market	d					12 58														13 58					
Littleport	a					13 07														14 07					
Ely 8	a		12 52			13 16		13 19	13 31	13 45					13 52			14 13		14 16	14 25		14 31	14 45	
	d	12 47	12 53			13 17			13 31					13 47	13 53					14 17	14 27		14 32		
Ipswich	d										13 43	13 52										14 09	15a29		14 43
Waterbeach	d					13 27														14 27					
Cambridge North	d	13 01		←	13 13	13 32			13 44				13 53	14 01		←			14 13	14 32	14 39				
Cambridge	a	13 05	13 08	13 05	13 19	13 37			13 49				13 59	14 05	14 08	14 05			14 19	14 37	14 44				
	d	13 14	13 11	13 14	13 20	13 44			13 51				14 03	14 14	14 11	14 14			14 20	14 44	14 48				
Stansted Airport ✈	a	→	13 41						14 24					→	14 41						15 24				
London Kings Cross 15 ⊖	a			14 03		14 32										15 03				15 33					
London Liverpool Street 15 ⊖	a				14 45						14 55	15 14	15 15						15 45			15 19			15 55

		LE		LE	GN	XC	GN	EM	LE	GN	LE	LE		EM	LE	LE	LE	GN	XC	GN	LE	GN		EM	LE
		1		◇1	1	◇1	1	◇	◇1	1		◇1		◇	◇1	1	◇1	1	◇1	1	◇1	1		◇	
Norwich	d										14 27	14 30		14 57	15 00										15 20
Wymondham	d										14 39														15 32
Spooner Row	d																								
Attleborough	d										14 46														15 39
Eccles Road	d																								15 44
Harling Road	d																								15 48
Thetford	d										15 00			15 24											15 57
Brandon	d										15 08														16 05
Lakenheath	d																								
Shippea Hill	a																								16x13
Peterborough 8	d					14 19		14 41											15 19					15 45	
Whittlesea	d																								
March	d					14 34													15 34						
Manea	a																								
Kings Lynn	a																								
	d									14 44												15 44			
Watlington	d									14 51												15 51			
Downham Market	d									14 58												15 58			
Littleport	a									15 07												16 07			
Ely 8	a					14 52		15 14		15 17	15 28			15 45					15 52			16 16		16 19	16 25
	d				14 47	14 53				15 18	15 28							15 47	15 53			16 17			16 26
Ipswich	d	14 52										15 09			15 43	15 52									
Waterbeach	d									15 28												16 27			
Cambridge North	d			14 53	15 01		←		15 13	15 33	15 41						15 53	16 01		←	16 13	16 32			16 38
Cambridge	a			14 59	15 05	15 08	15 05		15 19	15 37	15 46						15 59	16 05	16 08	16 05	16 19	16 37			16 43
	d			15 03	15 14	15 11	15 14		15 20	15 44	15 48						16 03	16 14	16 11	16 14	16 20	16 44			16 48
Stansted Airport ✈	a				→	15 41					16 24							→	16 41						17 24
London Kings Cross 15 ⊖	a						16 03			16 35										17 04		17 33			
London Liverpool Street 15 ⊖	a	16 14		16 15					16 45			16 19			16 55	17 14	17 15				17 45				

Table T017-R

Saturdays
21 December to 16 May

Norwich, Peterborough, Kings Lynn and Ely - Cambridge and London

		LE	LE	EM	LE	LE	LE	GN		XC	GN	EM	LE	GN	LE	LE	EM	LE		LE	LE	LE	GN	XC	EM
		◇1		◇	◇1	1	◇1	1		◇1	1	◇	◇1	1		◇1	◇	1		◇1	1	◇1	1	◇1	◇
Norwich	d	15 30		15 52	16 00										16 27	16 30	16 54	17 00		17 04					
Wymondham	d														16 39		17 06								
Spooner Row	d																								
Attleborough	d			16 09											16 46										
Eccles Road	d																								
Harling Road	d																								
Thetford	d			16 23											17 00		17 24								
Brandon	d														17 08										
Lakenheath	d																								
Shippea Hill	a																								
Peterborough 8	d		15 50							16 19		16 39												17 19	17 40
Whittlesea	d		15 58																					17 27	
March	d		16 09							16 34														17 38	
Manea	a		16 16																					17 45	
Kings Lynn	a																								
	d													16 44											
Watlington	d													16 51											
Downham Market	d													16 58											
Littleport	a													17 07											
Ely 8	a		16 31	16 45						16 52		17 13		17 16	17 25		17 45							17 59	18 13
	d		16 32					16 47		16 53				17 17	17 27								17 47	18 00	
Ipswich	d	16 09	17a28		16 43	16 52										17 09		17 33		17 47	17 52				
Waterbeach	d													17 27											
Cambridge North	d						16 53	17 01			←		17 13	17 32	17 39							17 53	18 01		
Cambridge	a						16 59	17 05		17 08	17 05		17 19	17 37	17 44							17 59	18 06	18 15	
	d						17 03	17 14		17 11	17 14		17 20	17 44	17 48							18 03	18 14	18 17	
Stansted Airport ✈	a							→		17 41					18 24									18 52	
London Kings Cross 15 ⊖	a										18 03			18 34									19 03		
London Liverpool Street 15 ⊖	a	17 19			17 55	18 14	18 15						18 45			18 19		18 30		18 56	19 15	19 15			

		LE	GN	LE		LE	LE	EM	LE	LE	LE	GN	XC	GN		LE	GN	EM	LE	LE	EM	LE	LE	LE	
		◇1	1			◇1		◇	◇1	1	◇1	1	◇1	1		◇1	1	◇		◇1	◇	◇1	1	◇1	
Norwich	d			17 20		17 30		17 50	18 00										18 27	18 30	18 57	19 00			
Wymondham	d			17 32				18 02											18 39						
Spooner Row	d			17x36																					
Attleborough	d			17 41				18 09											18 46						
Eccles Road	d			17 46																					
Harling Road	d			17 50																					
Thetford	d			18 00				18 23											19 00		19 24				
Brandon	d			18 08															19 08						
Lakenheath	d																								
Shippea Hill	a																								
Peterborough 8	d						17 50						18 19					18 44							
Whittlesea	d						17 58																		
March	d						18 09						18 34					19 01							
Manea	a						18 16																		
Kings Lynn	a																								
	d		17 44														18 44								
Watlington	d		17 51														18 51								
Downham Market	d		17 58														18 58								
Littleport	a		18 07														19 07								
Ely 8	a		18 16	18 25			18 31	18 45					18 52				19 16	19 19	19 26		19 45				
	d		18 17	18 27			18 32					18 47	18 53				19 17		19 27						
Ipswich	d					18 13	19a28		18 43	18 52										19 09		19 43	19 50		
Waterbeach	d		18 27														19 27								
Cambridge North	d	18 13	18 32	18 39							18 53	19 01		←		19 13	19 32		19 39					19 53	
Cambridge	a	18 19	18 37	18 44							18 59	19 05	19 08	19 05		19 19	19 37		19 44					19 59	
	d	18 20	18 44	18 48							19 03	19 14	19 11	19 14		19 20	19 44		19 48					20 03	
Stansted Airport ✈	a			19 24								→	19 41						20 24						
London Kings Cross 15 ⊖	a		19 35											20 03			20 33								
London Liverpool Street 15 ⊖	a	19 45				19 19			19 55	20 14	20 15					20 45				20 19		20 55	21 14	21 15	

Table T017-R

Saturdays
21 December to 16 May

Norwich, Peterborough, Kings Lynn and Ely - Cambridge and London

		LE	GN	XC	GN	EM		LE	GN	LE	LE	LE	LE	LE	GN	XC		GN	LE	GN	LE	LE	LE	LE	GN
		1	1	◇1	1	◇		◇1	1		◇1	◇1	1		1	◇1		1	◇1	1	◇1	1	◇1	1	1
											⊏P										⊏P				
Norwich	d									19 27	20 00										21 00				
Wymondham	d									19 39															
Spooner Row	d																								
Attleborough	d									19 46															
Eccles Road	d																								
Harling Road	d																								
Thetford	d									20 00															
Brandon	d									20 08															
Lakenheath	d																								
Shippea Hill	a																								
Peterborough ■	d			19 19		19 41								19 50		20 19									
Whittlesea	d													19 58											
March	d			19 34										20 09		20 34									
Manea	a													20 16											
Kings Lynn	a																								
	d								19 44											20 44					
Watlington	d								19 51											20 51					
Downham Market	d								19 58											20 58					
Littleport	a								20 07											21 07					
Ely ■	a			19 52		20 14			20 17	20 26				20 32		20 52				21 16					
	d		19 47	19 53					20 17	20 27				20 32	20 47	20 53				21 17					21 47
Ipswich	d	20 09									20 43		21 09	21a28							21 43	21 52		22 23	
Waterbeach	d								20 27											21 27					
Cambridge North	d		20 01		←			20 13	20 32	20 39		20 53			21 01			←	21 13	21 32			21 53		22 01
Cambridge	a		20 05	20 08	20 05			20 19	20 37	20 44		20 59			21 05	21 08		21 05	21 19	21 37			21 59		22 05
	d		20 14	20 11	20 14			20 20	20 44	20 48		21 03			21 14	21 11		21 14	21 20	21 44			22 03		22 14
Stansted Airport ✈	a		→	20 41						21 24					→	21 41									→
London Kings Cross ■ ⊖	a				21 03				21 33									22 03		22 33					
London Liverpool Street ■ ⊖	a	21 17						21 45			21 55	22 15	22 17						22 45		22 55	23 14	23 15	23 45	

		XC		GN	LE	LE	EM	GN	LE	LE	LE	XC		GN	GN	LE	LE
		◇1		1	◇1		◇	1	◇1		◇1	◇1		1	1	1	1
Norwich	d					21 10			22 00							22 40	23 05
Wymondham	d					21 22										22 52	
Spooner Row	d																
Attleborough	d					21 29										22 59	
Eccles Road	d																
Harling Road	d																
Thetford	d					21 43										23 13	
Brandon	d					21 51										23 21	
Lakenheath	d																
Shippea Hill	a																
Peterborough ■	d	21 19					21 40			21 47		22 14					
Whittlesea	d									21 55							
March	d	21 34								22 06		22 30					
Manea	a									22 13							
Kings Lynn	a																
	d							21 44							22 57		
Watlington	d							21 51							23 04		
Downham Market	d							21 58							23 11		
Littleport	a							22 07							23 20		
Ely ■	a	21 52				22 10	22 13	22 16		22 27		22 48			23 28	23 38	
	d	21 53				22 10		22 17		22 28		22 48		22 52	23 29	23 38	
Ipswich	d								22 43	23a23							23a49
Waterbeach	d							22 27							23 38		
Cambridge North	d			←	22 13	22 23		22 32			22 43			23 05	23 43	23 51	
Cambridge	a	22 08		22 05	22 19	22 28		22 37			22 49	23 03		23 09	23 49	23 59	
	d	22 11		22 14	22 20			22 44			22 50			23 14			
Stansted Airport ✈	a	22 41															
London Kings Cross ■ ⊖	a			23 03				23 35						00 08			
London Liverpool Street ■ ⊖	a				23 45				00 03		00 14						

NRT DECEMBER 19 EDITION

Table T017-R

Sundays
15 December to 10 May

Norwich, Peterborough, Kings Lynn and Ely - Cambridge and London

		LE	LE	LE	LE	GN		LE	LE	LE	GN	LE	LE	LE	LE	LE		GN	LE	EM	LE	LE	LE	LE	GN
		◇1	1	◇1	◇	1		1	◇1	◇1	1		1	◇1	◇1	◇1		1		◇	1	◇1	◇1	◇1	1
		⊏P		⊏P					⊏P						⊏P								⊏P		
Norwich	d	06 52		08 00	08 20				09 00			09 03			10 00				10 03	10 47			11 00		
Wymondham	d											09 15							10 15						
Spooner Row	d																								
Attleborough	d											09 22							10 22						
Eccles Road	d																								
Harling Road	d																								
Thetford	d											09 36							10 36	11 14					
Brandon	d											09 44							10 44						
Lakenheath	d											09x49													
Shippea Hill	a																								
Peterborough ■	d																								
Whittlesea	d																								
March	d																								
Manea	a																								
Kings Lynn	a																								
	d					08 26					09 26							10 26							11 26
Watlington	d					08 33					09 33							10 33							11 33
Downham Market	d					08 40					09 40							10 40							11 40
Littleport	a					08 49					09 49							10 49							11 49
Ely ■	a					08 57					09 57	10 03						10 57	11 01	11 35					11 57
	d					08 57					09 57	10 03						10 57	11 03						11 57
Ipswich	d	07 35	08 09	08 43	09 04			09 09	09 43				10 09		10 43						11 09		11 43		
Waterbeach	d					09 07					10 07							11 07							12 07
Cambridge North	d					09 12				09 42	10 12	10 16		10 23		10 42		11 12	11 16			11 23		11 42	12 12
Cambridge	a					09 16				09 48	10 16	10 21		10 29		10 48		11 16	11 24			11 29		11 48	12 16
	d					09 22				09 50	10 22	10 25		10 31		10 50		11 22	11 25			11 31		11 50	12 22
Stansted Airport ✈	a											11 05							12 05						
London Kings Cross ■ ⊖	a					10 09					11 09							12 09							13 09
London Liverpool Street ■ ⊖	a	09 00	09 37	09 55	10 10			10 37	10 55	11 14			11 37	11 43	11 55	12 14					12 37	12 43	12 55	13 14	

		LE		LE	LE	LE	LE	LE	LE	GN	LE	LE		LE	LE	XC	GN	LE	EM	LE	LE	EM		LE	LE
				1	◇1	◇1	◇1	1		1		◇1		◇1	◇1	◇1	1		◇	1		◇		◇1	◇1
						⊏P								⊏P		⊥o									⊏P
Norwich	d	11 03				12 00					12 03			13 00				13 03				13 47			14 00
Wymondham	d	11 15									12 15							13 15							
Spooner Row	d																								
Attleborough	d	11 22									12 22							13 22							
Eccles Road	d																								
Harling Road	d																								
Thetford	d	11 36									12 36							13 36				14 14			
Brandon	d	11 44									12 44							13 44							
Lakenheath	d	11x49																							
Shippea Hill	a																								
Peterborough ■	d								11 47							13 19			13 43		13 50				
Whittlesea	d								11 55												13 58				
March	d								12 06							13 34					14 09				
Manea	a																								
Kings Lynn	a																								
	d									12 26							13 26								
Watlington	d									12 33							13 33								
Downham Market	d									12 40							13 40								
Littleport	a									12 49							13 49								
Ely ■	a	12 03							12 25	12 57	13 01					13 52	13 57	14 01	14 16		14 31	14 35			
	d	12 03							12 28	12 57	13 03					13 53	13 57	14 03			14 32				
Ipswich	d			12 09		12 43		13 09	13a25					13 43						14 09	15a27				14 43
Waterbeach	d									13 07							14 07								
Cambridge North	d	12 16			12 23		12 42			13 12	13 16	13 23			13 42		14 12	14 16						14 23	
Cambridge	a	12 21			12 29		12 48			13 16	13 21	13 29			13 48	14 08	14 16	14 21						14 29	
	d	12 25			12 31		12 50			13 22	13 25	13 31			13 50	14 15	14 22	14 25						14 31	
Stansted Airport ✈	a	13 05									14 05					14 45		15 05							
London Kings Cross ■ ⊖	a									14 09							15 10								
London Liverpool Street ■ ⊖	a			13 37	13 43	13 55	14 14	14 37				14 43		14 55	15 14					15 37				15 43	15 55

Table T017-R

Sundays

15 December to 10 May

Norwich, Peterborough, Kings Lynn and Ely - Cambridge and London

		LE ◇1	XC ◇1	GN 1		LE	EM ◇	EM ◇	LE 1	LE ◇1	LE ◇1	LE ◇1	XC ◇1	GN 1		LE	LE ◇1	LE 1	LE	EM ◇	EM ◇	LE ◇1	LE 1	LE ◇1	
Norwich	d					14 03		14 53			15 00					15 03	15 22				15 54		16 00		
Wymondham	d					14 15										15 15									
Spooner Row	d																								
Attleborough	d					14 22										15 22									
Eccles Road	d																								
Harling Road	d																								
Thetford	d					14 36		15 20								15 36					16 21				
Brandon	d					14 44										15 44									
Lakenheath	d															15x49									
Shippea Hill	a																								
Peterborough 8	d		14 19				14 58						15 19						15 47	15 58	17a12				
Whittlesea	d																		15 55						
March	d		14 34										15 34						16 06						
Manea	a																								
Kings Lynn	a																								
	d			14 26										15 26											
Watlington	d			14 33										15 33											
Downham Market	d			14 40										15 40											
Littleport	a			14 49										15 49											
Ely 8	a		14 52	14 57		15 01	15 31	15 41					15 52	15 57		16 03			16 25	16 31					
	d		14 53	14 57		15 03							15 53	15 57		16 03			16 28						
Ipswich	d								15 09		15 43						16 07	16 09	17a25				16 43		
Waterbeach	d			15 07										16 07											
Cambridge North	d	14 42		15 12		15 16				15 23		15 42		16 12		16 16						16 23		16 42	
Cambridge	a	14 48	15 08	15 16		15 21				15 29		15 48	16 08	16 16		16 21						16 29		16 48	
	d	14 50	15 15	15 22		15 25				15 31		15 50	16 15	16 22		16 25						16 31		16 50	
Stansted Airport ✈	a		15 45			16 05							16 45			17 05									
London Kings Cross 15 ⊖	a			16 10										17 11											
London Liverpool Street 15 ⊖	a	16 14							16 37	16 43	16 55	17 14					17 12	17 37				17 43	17 55	18 14	

		XC ◇1	GN 1	LE	LE ◇1	EM ◇	EM ◇	LE 1	LE ◇1	LE ◇1		LE ◇1	XC ◇1	GN 1	LE	LE 1	LE ◇1	LE	GN 1	EM ◇		EM ◇	LE ◇1	LE ◇1	LE 1
Norwich	d			16 03	16 20		16 54			17 00					17 03							17 54	18 00		
Wymondham	d			16 15											17 15										
Spooner Row	d																								
Attleborough	d			16 22											17 22										
Eccles Road	d																								
Harling Road	d																								
Thetford	d			16 36			17 21								17 36							18 21			
Brandon	d			16 44											17 44										
Lakenheath	d																								
Shippea Hill	a																								
Peterborough 8	d	16 19				16 59							17 19					17 45		17 57					
Whittlesea	d																	17 53							
March	d	16 34											17 34					18 04		18 13					
Manea	a																								
Kings Lynn	a																								
	d		16 26											17 26					17 54						
Watlington	d		16 33											17 33					18 01						
Downham Market	d		16 40											17 40					18 08						
Littleport	a		16 49											17 49					18 17						
Ely 8	a	16 52	16 57	17 01		17 32	17 44						17 52	17 57	18 01			18 23	18 25	18 31		18 43			
	d	16 53	16 57	17 03									17 53	17 57	18 03			18 29	18 26						
Ipswich	d				17 07			17 09		17 43						18 09		→					18 43		19 09
Waterbeach	d		17 07											18 07											
Cambridge North	d		17 12	17 16					17 23			17 42		18 12	18 16		18 23		18 38					18 42	
Cambridge	a	17 08	17 16	17 21					17 29			17 48	18 08	18 16	18 21		18 29		18 42					18 48	
	d	17 15	17 22	17 25					17 31			17 50	18 15	18 22	18 25		18 31		18 43					18 50	
Stansted Airport ✈	a	17 45		18 05									18 45		19 05										
London Kings Cross 15 ⊖	a		18 10											19 12					19 36						
London Liverpool Street 15 ⊖	a				18 12			18 37	18 43	18 55		19 14				19 37	19 43						19 55	20 14	20 37

Table T017-R

Sundays

15 December to 10 May

Norwich, Peterborough, Kings Lynn and Ely - Cambridge and London

		LE		XC ◇1	GN 1	LE	EM ◇	EM ◇	LE ◇1	LE ◇1	LE ◇1	XC ◇1		GN 1	LE	LE 1	LE ◇1	LE ◇1	LE ◇1	LE 1	LE	EM ◇		XC ◇1	GN 1
Norwich	d					18 03		18 56		19 00					19 03			20 00							
Wymondham	d					18 15									19 15										
Spooner Row	d																								
Attleborough	d					18 22									19 22										
Eccles Road	d																								
Harling Road	d																								
Thetford	d					18 36		19 23							19 36										
Brandon	d					18 44									19 44										
Lakenheath	d																								
Shippea Hill	a																								
Peterborough 8	d			18 19			18 49					19 19									19 47	19 57		20 19	
Whittlesea	d																				19 55				
March	d			18 34								19 34									20 06			20 34	
Manea	a																								
Kings Lynn	a																								
	d				18 26									19 26											20 26
Watlington	d				18 33									19 33											20 33
Downham Market	d				18 40									19 40											20 40
Littleport	a	←			18 49									19 49											20 49
Ely 8	a	18 23		18 52	18 57	19 01	19 22	19 45				19 52		19 57	20 01						20 25	20 32		20 52	20 57
	d	18 29		18 53	18 57	19 03						19 53		19 57	20 03						20 28			20 53	20 57
Ipswich	d	19a25								19 43						20 09		20 43		21 09	21a25				
Waterbeach	d				19 07									20 07											21 07
Cambridge North	d				19 12	19 16			19 23		19 42			20 12	20 16		20 23		20 42						21 12
Cambridge	a			19 08	19 16	19 21			19 29		19 48	20 08		20 16	20 21		20 29		20 48					21 08	21 16
	d			19 15	19 22	19 25			19 31		19 50	20 15		20 22	20 25		20 31		20 50					21 13	21 22
Stansted Airport ✈	a			19 45		20 05						20 45			21 05									21 45	
London Kings Cross 15 ⊖	a				20 10									21 09											22 10
London Liverpool Street 15 ⊖	a								20 43	20 55	21 14					21 37	21 43	21 55	22 14	22 37					

		LE	EM ◇	LE ◇1	LE ◇1	XC ◇1	GN 1	EM ◇		LE 1	LE ◇1	XC ◇1	GN 1	LE	LE 1
Norwich	d	20 03	20 52		21 00						22 00			22 03	23 05
Wymondham	d	20 15												22 15	
Spooner Row	d														
Attleborough	d	20 22												22 22	
Eccles Road	d														
Harling Road	d														
Thetford	d	20 36	21 19											22 36	
Brandon	d	20 44												22 44	
Lakenheath	d														
Shippea Hill	a														
Peterborough 8	d					21 19		21 54				22 17			
Whittlesea	d														
March	d					21 34						22 32			
Manea	a														
Kings Lynn	a														
	d						21 26						22 26		
Watlington	d						21 33						22 33		
Downham Market	d						21 40						22 40		
Littleport	a						21 49						22 49		
Ely 8	a	21 01	21 40			21 52	21 57	22 27				22 50	22 57	23 01	
	d	21 03				21 53	21 57					22 51	22 57	23 03	
Ipswich	d				21 43					22 09	22 43				23a51
Waterbeach	d						22 07						23 07		
Cambridge North	d	21 16		21 23			22 12						23 12	23 16	
Cambridge	a	21 21		21 29		22 08	22 16					23 06	23 16	23 20	
	d	21 25		21 31		22 15	22 22						23 20		
Stansted Airport ✈	a	22 05				22 45									
London Kings Cross 15 ⊖	a						23 16						00 49		
London Liverpool Street 15 ⊖	a			22 43	22 55					23 37	00 06				

Table T018-F

Mondays to Fridays

16 December to 15 May

Peterborough - Sleaford, Lincoln and Doncaster

Miles	Miles			EM A	NT	NT ◇ B	EM C	EM	EM	NT ◇ B	EM	NT ◇ B		EM	NT ◇ B	EM	NT ◇ B	EM	EM	NT ◇ B	EM	NT ◇ B		EM	NT ◇ B
0	—	**Peterborough** 8	d	06 32				07 30						08 33		09 35			10 40		11 50			12 41	
16½	—	Spalding	d	06a53				07a51						08 54		09 56			11 01		12 13			13 02	
35½	—	Sleaford	a											09 18		10 20			11 25		12 38			13 26	
—	—		d				06 53		07 43		08 40			09 18		10 21			11 25		12 42			13 26	
40	—	Ruskington	d				07 02		07 51		08 49			09 28		10 29			11 34		12 50			13 35	
47½	—	Metheringham	d				07 12		08 01		08 59			09 37		10 38			11 43		12 59			13 44	
56¾	—	**Lincoln**	a				07 25		08 15		09 13			09 53		10 53			11 57		13 14			14 03	
—	—		d		06 43	07 23				08 26	09 15	09 30			10 30		11 30	11 54		12 29	13 15	13 30			14 30
62¾	—	Saxilby	d		06 52	07 32				08 35	09 23	09 39			10 39		11 39	12 02		12 39	13 23	13 39			14 39
72¼	0	Gainsborough Lea Road	d		07 04	07 44				08 47	09 35	09 51			10 51		11 51	12 15		12 51	13 35	13 51			14 51
—	32¾	Sheffield 7	a		08 04	08 42				09 42		10 42			11 42		12 42			13 40		14 42			15 42
93½	51½	**Doncaster** 7	a								10 03							12 45			14 04				

		EM	NT ◇ B	NT ◇ B	EM ◇	NT ◇ B	EM	NT ◇ B		EM	EM	EM	NT ◇ B	EM	NT	EM	NT	EM		NT
Peterborough 8	d	13 41			15 11		16 25			17 32		18 36						20 30		
Spalding	d	14 04			15 32		16 46			17a55		18a59						20a51		
Sleaford	a	14 29			15 56		17 15													
	d	14 29			16 14		17 16				17 56			19 00		20 05				
Ruskington	d	14 37			16 22		17 24				18 04			19 08		20 13				
Metheringham	d	14 46			16 32		17 34				18 14			19 17		20 22				
Lincoln	a	15 00			16 45		17 48				18 29			19 32		20 39				
	d		15 30	16 30		17 23		18 24			18 31		19 26	19 32	20 19		21 29			22 44
Saxilby	d		15 39	16 39		17 31		18 32			18 39		19 35	19 41	20 27		21 37			22 52
Gainsborough Lea Road	d		15 51	16 51		17 44		18 45			18 55		19 48	19 53	20 40		21 50			23 05
Sheffield 7	a		16 42	17 42		18 42		19 42					20 42		21 38		22 48			00 03
Doncaster 7	a										19 25			20 21						

Saturdays

21 December to 16 May

		EM A	NT	NT ◇ B	EM C	EM	EM	NT ◇ B	EM	NT ◇ B		EM	NT ◇ B	EM	NT ◇ B	EM	NT ◇ B	EM	NT ◇ B	EM		EM	NT ◇ B	EM	NT ◇ B
Peterborough 8	d	06 30				07 30						08 33		09 32				11 52		12 42					
Spalding	d	06a52				07a52						08 54		09 53				12 13		13 03					
Sleaford	a											09 17		10 20				12 39		13 27					
	d				06 53		07 43					09 19		10 20				12 41		13 27					
Ruskington	d				07 02		07 51					09 28		10 28				12 49		13 36					
Metheringham	d				07 12		08 01					09 37		10 37				12 58		13 46					
Lincoln	a				07 25		08 15					09 56		10 53				13 14		14 03					
	d		06 43	07 23				08 26	09 15	09 30			10 30		11 30	11 54	12 29		13 30			14 10	14 30	15 10	15 30
Saxilby	d		06 52	07 32				08 35	09 23	09 39			10 39		11 39	12 02	12 39		13 39			14 18	14 38	15 18	15 39
Gainsborough Lea Road	d		07 04	07 44				08 47	09 35	09 51			10 51		11 51	12 15	12 51		13 51			14 30	14 51	15 30	15 51
Sheffield 7	a		08 04	08 41				09 42		10 42			11 42		12 42		13 40		14 42				15 42		16 42
Doncaster 7	a								10 05							12 43						14 58		16 00	

		NT ◇ B	EM ◇	NT ◇ B	EM	NT ◇ B		EM	EM	NT ◇ B	EM	EM	NT	EM	NT	EM		NT
Peterborough 8	d		15 11		16 25			17 32			18 36					20 30		
Spalding	d		15 32		16 47			17a55			18a58					20a52		
Sleaford	a		16 00		17 17													
	d		16 14		17 19				17 54			19 00		20 10				
Ruskington	d		16 22		17 27				18 02			19 08		20 18				
Metheringham	d		16 32		17 37				18 12			19 17		20 27				
Lincoln	a		16 47		17 51				18 27			19 32		20 44				
	d	16 30		17 23		18 24				19 26		19 32	20 19		21 29			22 44
Saxilby	d	16 39		17 31		18 32				19 35		19 41	20 27		21 37			22 52
Gainsborough Lea Road	d	16 51		17 44		18 45				19 48		19 53	20 40		21 50			23 05
Sheffield 7	a	17 42		18 42		19 42				20 41			21 38		22 48			00 03
Doncaster 7	a											20 21						

Sundays

15 December to 10 May

		NT ◇ D	NT ◇ D	NT ◇ D	NT ◇ D	NT ◇ D	NT	NT ◇	NT	NT ◇		NT	NT ◇	NT	NT
Peterborough 8	d														
Spalding	d														
Sleaford	a														
	d														
Ruskington	d														
Metheringham	d														
Lincoln	a														
	d	10 14	11 14	12 14	13 14	14 14	15 12	16 12	17 15	18 12		19 19	20 17	21 20	21 51
Saxilby	d	10 23	11 23	12 23	13 23	14 23	15 21	16 21	17 24	18 23		19 28	20 26	21 29	22 00
Gainsborough Lea Road	d	10 35	11 35	12 35	13 35	14 35	15 33	16 35	17 36	18 37		19 40	20 38	21 41	22 12
Sheffield 7	a	11 34	12 34	13 34	14 36	15 35	16 31	17 33	18 36	19 33		20 40	21 35	22 41	23 12
Doncaster 7	a														

A From Nottingham
B To Leeds
C To Leicester
D To Huddersfield

For connections from London Kings Cross refer to Table T025

NRT DECEMBER 19 EDITION

Table T018-R

Mondays to Fridays

16 December to 15 May

Doncaster, Lincoln and Sleaford - Peterborough

Miles	Miles			EM	EM	EM	NT	NT ◇	EM	EM A		NT ◇ B	EM	NT ◇ B	EM	NT ◇ B	EM	EM	NT ◇ B	EM		NT ◇ B	EM C	NT ◇ B	EM
0	0	**Doncaster** 7	d					06 03										10 24							13 01
—	18¾	Sheffield 7	d				05 45	06 35				07 37		08 37		09 37			10 37			11 37		12 37	
21¼	51½	Gainsborough Lea Road	d				06 39	07 34				08 24		09 24		10 30		10 48	11 24			12 24		13 24	13 30
30¾	—	Saxilby	d				06 51	07 46				08 36		09 36		10 42		11 00	11 36			12 36		13 36	13 43
36¾	—	**Lincoln**	a				07 07	07 57				08 47		09 48		10 55		11 17	11 49			12 48		13 49	13 53
—	—		d	06 17		07 05				08 00			09 11		10 18		11 10			12 10			13 30		
46¼	—	Metheringham	d			07 18				08 12			09 23		10 31		11 23			12 22			13 43		
53½	—	Ruskington	d			07 27				08 21			09 32		10 41		11 32			12 31			13 52		
58	—	Sleaford	a	06 46		07 37				08 31			09 42		10 50		11 42			12 41			14 02		
—	—		d							08 35			09 43		10 51		11 42			12 42			14 03		
77	—	Spalding	d		07 00				08 00	09 00			10 07		11 13		12 04			13 07			14 25		
93½	—	**Peterborough** 8	a		07 22				08 20	09 23			10 31		11 34		12 26			13 28			14 46		

		EM	NT ◇ B	EM	EM	NT ◇ B		EM ◇ C	NT ◇ B	EM D	NT ◇ B	EM	NT ◇ B	EM	EM	NT ◇ B		EM	EM E	NT ◇ B	EM	EM	NT	EM F
Doncaster 7	d				14 27													19 39				20 36		
Sheffield 7	d		13 37			14 37			15 37		16 37		17 37			18 37				19 38			20 53	
Gainsborough Lea Road	d		14 24		14 55	15 25			16 24		17 33		18 33			19 38		20 02		20 33		21 00	21 48	
Saxilby	d		14 36		15 07	15 37			16 36		17 45		18 45			19 50		20 13		20 44		21 12	21 59	
Lincoln	a		14 48		15 17	15 48			16 49		17 56		18 57			20 06		20 24		20 58		21 25	22 11	
	d	14 41		15 12				16 00		17 18		18 10		19 15					20 48					
Metheringham	d	14 54		15 25				16 13		17 33		18 23		19 28					21 01					
Ruskington	d	15 03		15 34				16 22		17 43		18 32		19 37					21 10					
Sleaford	a	15 13		15 44				16 33		17 52		18 42		19 47					21 19					
	d	15 16						16 34																
Spalding	d	15 38						16 56							18 08						19 59			21 03
Peterborough 8	a	15 59						17 18							18 28						20 22			21 25

Saturdays

21 December to 16 May

		EM	EM	NT	NT ◇	EM	EM A	NT ◇ B	NT ◇ B	EM		NT ◇ B	EM	EM	NT ◇ B	NT ◇ B	EM C	NT ◇ B	EM	EM		NT ◇ B	NT ◇ B	EM	EM ◇ C
Doncaster 7	d				06 00									10 24					13 05					15 07	
Sheffield 7	d			05 45	06 35			07 37	08 37			09 37			10 37	11 37		12 37				13 37	14 37		
Gainsborough Lea Road	d			06 39	07 34			08 24	09 24			10 30		10 48	11 24	12 24		13 24	13 30			14 24	15 25	15 31	
Saxilby	d			06 51	07 46			08 36	09 36			10 42		10 59	11 36	12 36		13 36	13 42			14 36	15 37	15 43	
Lincoln	a			07 07	08 01			08 47	09 48			10 55		11 10	11 49	12 48		13 49	13 54			14 48	15 48	15 58	
	d		07 05				08 01			10 18			11 10				13 33			14 41					16 01
Metheringham	d		07 18				08 14			10 31			11 23				13 46			14 54					16 14
Ruskington	d		07 27				08 23			10 41			11 32				13 55			15 03					16 23
Sleaford	a		07 37				08 32			10 50			11 42				14 05			15 13					16 34
	d						08 35			10 51			11 42				14 06			15 16					16 34
Spalding	d	07 00				08 05	09 00			11 19			12 04				14 29			15 38					16 57
Peterborough 8	a	07 22				08 27	09 24			11 43			12 28				14 51			16 02					17 23

		NT ◇ B	EM	EM	NT ◇ B	EM		NT ◇ B	EM	EM	NT ◇ B	EM E	NT ◇ B	EM	EM	NT		EM F
Doncaster 7	d			16 27											20 33			
Sheffield 7	d	15 37			16 37			17 37			18 37		19 38			20 53		
Gainsborough Lea Road	d	16 24		16 52	17 33			18 33			19 38		20 33		20 56	21 48		
Saxilby	d	16 36		17 03	17 45			18 45			19 50		20 44		21 09	21 59		
Lincoln	a	16 49		17 19	17 56			18 57			20 06		20 58		21 24	22 11		
	d		17 15			18 10			19 05			20 49						
Metheringham	d		17 28			18 23			19 18			21 02						
Ruskington	d		17 37			18 32			19 27			21 11						
Sleaford	a		17 47			18 42			19 37			21 20						
	d																	
Spalding	d									18 08				19 59				21 03
Peterborough 8	a									18 31				20 22				21 25

Sundays

15 December to 10 May

		NT ◇	NT	NT ◇	NT	NT ◇ G	NT ◇ G	NT ◇ G	NT ◇ G	NT ◇ G		NT ◇ G	NT	NT ◇	NT	NT ◇
Doncaster 7	d															
Sheffield 7	d	08 45	09 41	10 41	11 41	12 41	13 36	14 41	15 42	16 37		17 38	18 42	19 34	20 20	21 23
Gainsborough Lea Road	d	09 34	10 37	11 32	12 37	13 33	14 31	15 33	16 33	17 34		18 30	19 39	20 25	21 16	22 20
Saxilby	d	09 46	10 49	11 44	12 49	13 45	14 43	15 45	16 45	17 46		18 42	19 51	20 37	21 28	22 32
Lincoln	a	09 57	11 00	11 56	13 00	13 56	14 55	15 57	16 57	17 58		18 54	20 04	20 49	21 41	22 45
	d															
Metheringham	d															
Ruskington	d															
Sleaford	a															
	d															
Spalding	d															
Peterborough 8	a															

A From Nottingham
B From Leeds
C From Newark North Gate
D From Leicester
E To Boston
F To Nottingham
G From Huddersfield

For connections to London Kings Cross refer to Table T025

Table T019-F

Nottingham and Grantham - Skegness

Mondays to Fridays
16 December to 15 May

Miles	Miles			EM	EM	EM	EM	EM	EM	EM	EM	EM	EM	EM	EM	EM	EM	EM	EM	EM	EM	EM	EM
				A	◇	◇	◇	◇	◇ B	◇ C	◇	◇ D	◇	◇ D	◇	◇ D	◇	◇ D	◇	◇ D	◇	◇ D	◇
0	—	**Nottingham** 8 ⇌	d	05 07		05 50	06 41	07 35	07 52	08 35	08 45	09 34	09 55	10 34	10 45	11 34	11 45	12 34	12 45	13 34	13 45	14 34	14 45
4½	—	Netherfield	d								08 51												
5	—	Radcliffe (Notts)	d				06 51				08 56								12 55				14 55
8½	—	Bingham	d	05 21		06 04	06 57	07 49			09 02		10 09		11 00		11 59		13 01		13 59		15 01
10¾	—	Aslockton	d	05 25				07 53			09 06				11 04						14 03		
14½	—	Elton & Orston	d																				
15	0	Bottesford	d	05 32		06 13	07 05	07 59			09 12				11 10				13 09				15 09
22½	—	**Grantham** 7	a	05 46		06 27	07 19	08 12	08 23	09 06	09 26	10 06		11 07	11 23	12 10	12 19	13 07	13 23	14 05	14 23	15 07	15 22
—	—		d			06 31	07 23	08 16			09 32				11 27		12 25		13 27		14 27		15 26
34	12½	Ancaster	d					08 34											13 44				
37¾	—	Rauceby	d				07 45	08 40															
40	—	**Sleaford**	d			07 00	07 50	08 45			10 01		10 44		11 53		12 50		13 54		14 52		15 52
44½	—	Heckington	d			07 07	07 57	08 52			10 08		10 51		12 00		12 57		14 01		14 59		15 59
49½	—	Swineshead	d				08 04																16 05
52¾	—	Hubberts Bridge	d				08 09																16 10
56½	—	**Boston**	d		06 25	07 25	08 18	09 12			10 25		11 11		12 19		13 15		14 21		15 17		16 20
73¾	—	Thorpe Culvert	d			07 47																	
75¼	—	Wainfleet	d		06 49	07 51	08 42	09 36			10 49		11 35		12 44		13 40		14 46		15 42		16 45
77	—	Havenhouse	d			07 55																	
80½	—	**Skegness**	a		07 03	08 05	08 56	09 49			11 00		11 50		12 58		13 54		15 00		15 56		16 59

		EM	EM	EM	EM	EM	EM	EM	EM	EM	EM	EM
		◇ D	◇	◇ D	◇	◇ D	◇	◇ D	◇	◇ D	E	◇
Nottingham 8 ⇌	d	15 34	15 45	16 35	16 45	17 34	17 44	18 37	18 44	20 34		20 51
Netherfield	d		15 51		16 51		17 50					
Radcliffe (Notts)	d		15 56		16 56		17 55					21 01
Bingham	d		16 02		17 02	17 48	18 01		18 58			21 07
Aslockton	d		16 06		17 06	17 52	18 05		19 03			21 11
Elton & Orston	d				17 10							
Bottesford	d		16 12		17 14		18 12		19 10			21 17
Grantham 7	a	16 08	16 25	17 06	17 28	18 09	18 25	19 07	19 23	21 07		21 32
	d		16 29		17 32		18 29		19 26			21 38
Ancaster	d				17 49				19 44			
Rauceby	d				17 55				19 50			
Sleaford	d		16 55		18 00		18 55		19 55		21 20	22 03
Heckington	d		17 02		18 07		19 02		20 02		21 28	22 10
Swineshead	d											
Hubberts Bridge	d											
Boston	d		17 21		18 26		19 21		20 18		21a53	22a29
Thorpe Culvert	d		17 43									
Wainfleet	d		17 48		18 50		19 46		20 43			
Havenhouse	d		17 51									
Skegness	a		18 00		19 05		19 59		20 57			

Saturdays
21 December to 16 May

		EM	EM	EM	EM	EM	EM	EM	EM	EM	EM	EM	EM	EM	EM	EM	EM	EM	EM	EM	EM	EM	EM
		A	◇	◇	◇	◇	◇ C	◇ C	◇	◇ D	◇	◇ D	◇	◇ D	◇	◇ D	◇	◇ D	◇	◇ D	◇	◇ D	◇
Nottingham 8 ⇌	d	05 07		05 50	06 41	07 31	07 45	08 35	08 40	09 34	09 55	10 34	10 45	11 34	11 45	12 34	12 45	13 34	13 45	14 34	14 45	15 34	15 45
Netherfield	d								08 48														15 51
Radcliffe (Notts)	d								08 52								12 55						15 56
Bingham	d	05 21		06 04	06 55	07 45			08 58		10 09		10 59		11 59		13 01		13 59		14 59		16 02
Aslockton	d	05 25				07 49			09 02				11 03						14 03				16 06
Elton & Orston	d																						
Bottesford	d	05 32		06 13	07 04	07 56			09 09				11 09				13 09				15 08		16 12
Grantham 7	a	05 46		06 27	07 18	08 09	08 15	09 06	09 23	10 06		11 05	11 23	12 05	12 19	13 06	13 25	14 05	14 23	15 05	15 22	16 06	16 25
	d			06 31	07 24	08 17			09 30				11 27		12 25		13 29		14 27		15 26		16 29
Ancaster	d					08 34																	
Rauceby	d					08 40																	
Sleaford	d			07 00	07 50	08 46			09 56		10 44		11 53		12 50		13 55		14 52		15 52		16 55
Heckington	d			07 07	07 57	08 53			10 03		10 51		12 00		12 57		14 02		14 59		15 59		17 02
Swineshead	d				08 03																16 05		
Hubberts Bridge	d				08 08																16 10		
Boston	d		06 25	07 25	08 17	09 11			10 22		11 11		12 19		13 15		14 21		15 17		16 20		17 21
Thorpe Culvert	d			07 47																			17 43
Wainfleet	d		06 49	07 51	08 42	09 35			10 47		11 35		12 44		13 40		14 46		15 42		16 45		17 48
Havenhouse	d			07 55																			17 51
Skegness	a		07 03	08 05	08 55	09 48			11 00		11 50		12 58		13 54		15 00		15 56		16 59		18 00

A To Spalding
B From Mansfield Woodhouse to Norwich
C To Norwich
D From Liverpool Lime Street to Norwich
E From Lincoln

For connections from London Kings Cross refer to Table T026

Table T019-F

Nottingham and Grantham - Skegness

Saturdays
21 December to 16 May

		EM	EM	EM	EM	EM	EM	EM	EM	EM
		◇ A	◇	◇ A	◇	◇ A	◇	◇ A	B	
Nottingham 8 ⇌	d	16 34	16 45	17 34	17 44	18 37	18 45	20 35		20 51
Netherfield	d		16 51		17 50					
Radcliffe (Notts)	d		16 56		17 55					21 01
Bingham	d		17 02	17 48	18 01		18 59			21 07
Aslockton	d		17 06	17 52	18 05		19 03			21 11
Elton & Orston	d		17 10							
Bottesford	d		17 14		18 12		19 10			21 17
Grantham 7	a	17 04	17 28	18 09	18 25	19 08	19 23	21 07		21 31
	d		17 32		18 29		19 26			21 36
Ancaster	d		17 49				19 44			
Rauceby	d		17 55				19 50			
Sleaford	d		18 00		18 55		19 55		21 21	22 01
Heckington	d		18 07		19 02		20 02		21 29	22 08
Swineshead	d									
Hubberts Bridge	d									
Boston	d		18 26		19 21		20 18		21a53	22a29
Thorpe Culvert	d									
Wainfleet	d		18 50		19 46		20 42			
Havenhouse	d									
Skegness	a		19 05		19 59		20 57			

Sundays
15 December to 10 May

		EM	EM	EM	EM	EM	EM	EM	EM	EM	EM	EM	EM	EM	EM	EM	EM	EM
						◇	◇ C	◇	◇ D	◇ E	◇	◇ A	◇	◇ A	◇ A		◇ A	◇ A
Nottingham 8 ⇌	d	08 15	09 15	10 00	11 15	11 57	12 40		13 47	14 45	14 56	15 50	16 23	16 45	17 36	18 31	18 46	20 45
Netherfield	d												16 29		17 42			
Radcliffe (Notts)	d												16 34		17 46			
Bingham	d	08 29	09 29	10 14	11 29	12 11	12 54				15 10		16 40		17 52	18 45	19 00	20 59
Aslockton	d												16 44		17 56			
Elton & Orston	d																	
Bottesford	d												16 50		18 03			
Grantham 7	a	08 49	09 50	10 35	11 50	12 29	13 13		14 20	15 16	15 31	16 20	17 06	17 15	18 16	19 08	19 21	21 18
	d					12 33		13 50			15 36		17 10			19 13		
Ancaster	d																	
Rauceby	d																	
Sleaford	d					12 59		14 16			16 02		17 38			19 41		
Heckington	d					13 06		14 23			16 09		17 45			19 48		
Swineshead	d																	
Hubberts Bridge	d																	
Boston	d					13 24		14 45			16 29		18 04			20a09		
Thorpe Culvert	d																	
Wainfleet	d					13 49		15 09			16 53		18 29					
Havenhouse	d																	
Skegness	a					14 00		15 24			17 08		18 40					

A From Liverpool Lime Street to Norwich
B From Lincoln
C To Norwich
D From Sheffield to Norwich
E From Manchester Piccadilly to Norwich

For connections from London Kings Cross refer to Table T026

Table T019-R

Skegness - Grantham and Nottingham

Mondays to Fridays
16 December to 15 May

Miles	Miles			EM	EM	EM	EM	EM	EM	EM	EM	EM	EM	EM	EM	EM	EM	EM	EM	EM	EM	EM	EM
				◇	◇	◇	◇	◇	◇	◇	◇	◇	◇	◇	◇	◇	◇	◇	◇	◇	◇	◇	◇
						A		A		A		A		A		A		A		A		A	
0	—	**Skegness**	d				07 09		08 10		09 06		10 15		11 15		12 15		13 15		14 15		15 09
3¼	—	Havenhouse	d				07 15																
5	—	Wainfleet	d				07 19		08 18		09 14		10 23		11 23		12 23		13 23		14 23		15 17
7	—	Thorpe Culvert	d				07 23																
23¾	—	**Boston**	d		06 13		07 46		08 45		09 41		10 50		11 50		12 50		13 50		14 50		15 44
27½	—	Hubberts Bridge	d				07 52																15 50
30¾	—	Swineshead	d				07 57																15 55
35¾	—	Heckington	d		06 27		08 02		08 59		09 55		11 04		12 04		13 04		14 04		15 04		16 01
40¼	—	**Sleaford**	d		06 35		08 11		09 07		10 03		11 12		12 12		13 13		14 13		15 12		16 10
42½	—	Rauceby	d		06 39		08 15																16 14
46¼	0	Ancaster	d		06 45		08 21						11 21										16 20
57¾	—	**Grantham** 7	a		07 04		08 42		09 38		10 31		11 42		12 41		13 42		14 42		15 41		16 41
—	—		d	06 10	07 10	07 58	08 45	08 56	09 44	09 58	10 36	11 00	11 45	12 02	12 45	12 59	13 48	13 58	14 45	14 58	15 45	16 03	16 45
65¼	12¾	Bottesford	d	06 21	07 21	08 11			09 55				11 56				13 56				15 56		
67¾	—	Elton & Orston	d	06 25																			
69½	—	Aslockton	d	06 29	07 27	08 18	09 00				10 51				13 00				15 00		16 02		
71¾	—	Bingham	d	06 33	07 31	08 22	09 05		10 03		10 56		12 04		13 04		14 07		15 05		16 07		17 02
75¼	—	Radcliffe (Notts)	d	06 39	07 37	08 28			10 08				12 10						15 10				
77	—	Netherfield	d		07 42	08 33																	
80¼	—	**Nottingham** 8	a	06 54	07 53	08 40	09 20	09 27	10 20	10 35	11 13	11 34	12 22	12 35	13 23	13 36	14 24	14 35	15 23	15 34	16 25	16 35	17 20

		EM	EM	EM	EM	EM	EM	EM	EM	EM	EM	EM
		◇	◇	◇	◇	◇	◇	◇	◇	◇	◇	◇
		A		A		B		C		C		
Skegness	d		16 11		17 30		18 14		19 14		20 15	21 02
Havenhouse	d		16 17									
Wainfleet	d		16 21		17 38		18 22		19 22		20 23	21 10
Thorpe Culvert	d		16 25									
Boston	d		16 48		18 05		18 48		19 49		20 50	21 37
Hubberts Bridge	d											
Swineshead	d											
Heckington	d		17 04		18 19		19 04		20 05		21 04	21 51
Sleaford	d		17 13		18 27		19 13		20 13		21 18	22 00
Rauceby	d											
Ancaster	d											
Grantham 7	a		17 42				19 41		20 40		21 45	
	d	16 58	17 45	17 58		18 57	19 45	19 59	20 44	21 00	21 49	
Bottesford	d		17 56				19 56				22 00	
Elton & Orston	d											
Aslockton	d		18 02				20 02				22 06	
Bingham	d		18 07		19 03	19 17	20 06		21 01		22 10	22 35
Radcliffe (Notts)	d						20 12		21 07			
Netherfield	d						20 16					
Nottingham 8	a	17 35	18 22	18 31	19 21	19 35	20 25	20 31	21 20	21 36	22 26	22 53

Saturdays
21 December to 16 May

		EM	EM	EM	EM	EM	EM	EM	EM	EM	EM	EM	EM	EM	EM	EM	EM	EM	EM	EM	EM	EM	EM
				◇	◇	◇	◇	◇	◇	◇	◇	◇	◇	◇	◇	◇	◇	◇	◇	◇	◇	◇	◇
				A		A		A		A		A		A		A		A		A		A	
Skegness	d				07 09		08 15		09 15		10 15		11 15		12 15		13 15		14 15		15 09		16 11
Havenhouse	d				07 15																		16 17
Wainfleet	d				07 19		08 23		09 23		10 23		11 23		12 23		13 23		14 23		15 17		16 21
Thorpe Culvert	d				07 23																		16 25
Boston	d		06 13		07 46		08 50		09 50		10 50		11 50		12 50		13 50		14 50		15 44		16 48
Hubberts Bridge	d				07 52																15 50		
Swineshead	d				07 57																15 55		
Heckington	d		06 27		08 02		09 04		10 05		11 04		12 04		13 04		14 04		15 04		16 01		17 04
Sleaford	d		06 35		08 11		09 12		10 14		11 12		12 12		13 12		14 13		15 12		16 10		17 13
Rauceby	d		06 39		08 15																16 14		
Ancaster	d		06 45		08 21						11 21										16 20		
Grantham 7	a		07 07		08 42		09 41		10 43		11 42		12 41		13 41		14 42		15 41		16 41		17 42
	d	06 10	07 10	07 58	08 45	09 00	09 45	09 56	10 46	10 55	11 45	11 56	12 45	12 57	13 47	13 58	14 45	14 56	15 45	15 57	16 45	16 58	17 45
Bottesford	d	06 21	07 21	08 11			09 56				11 56				13 56				15 56				17 56
Elton & Orston	d	06 25																					
Aslockton	d	06 29	07 27	08 17	09 00				11 01				13 00				15 00						18 02
Bingham	d	06 33	07 32	08 22	09 05		10 04		11 06		12 04		13 04		14 06		15 05		16 04		17 02		18 07
Radcliffe (Notts)	d	06 39	07 37	08 27							12 10												
Netherfield	d		07 42	08 32																			
Nottingham 8	a	06 54	07 52	08 39	09 20	09 37	10 21	10 35	11 23	11 36	12 22	12 36	13 23	13 35	14 24	14 33	15 23	15 35	16 22	16 35	17 20	17 35	18 22

A From Norwich to Liverpool Lime Street B From Norwich to Manchester Piccadilly C From Norwich

For connections to London Kings Cross refer to Table T026

NRT DECEMBER 19 EDITION

Table T019-R

Skegness - Grantham and Nottingham

Saturdays
21 December to 16 May

		EM	EM	EM	EM	EM	EM	EM	EM	EM	EM
		◇	◇	◇	◇	◇	◇	◇	◇		◇
		A		B		C		C		D	
Skegness	d		17 24		18 14		19 19		20 15		21 02
Havenhouse	d										
Wainfleet	d		17 32		18 22		19 27		20 23		21 10
Thorpe Culvert	d										
Boston	d		17 59		18 49		19 54		20 50		21 37
Hubberts Bridge	d										
Swineshead	d										
Heckington	d		18 13		19 04		20 10		21 04		21 51
Sleaford	d		18 21		19 13		20 18		21 12		22 00
Rauceby	d										
Ancaster	d										
Grantham 7	a				19 41		20 45		21 42		
	d	17 59		18 58	19 45	20 03	20 48	20 58	21 46	22 02	
Bottesford	d				19 56				21 57		
Elton & Orston	d										
Aslockton	d				20 02				22 03		
Bingham	d		18 59	19 15	20 06		21 05		22 07		22 35
Radcliffe (Notts)	d				20 12						
Netherfield	d				20 16						
Nottingham 8	a	18 30	19 21	19 31	20 24	20 36	21 24	21 32	22 24	22 32	22 54

Sundays
15 December to 10 May

		EM	EM	EM	EM	EM	EM	EM	EM	EM	EM	EM	EM	EM	EM	EM	EM	EM	EM
						◇		◇	◇	◇	◇		◇	◇		◇	◇	◇	◇
				E		A		F		A	A		B	B		C		C	C
Skegness	d								14 10			16 10			18 07		19 15		
Havenhouse	d																		
Wainfleet	d								14 18			16 18			18 15		19 23		
Thorpe Culvert	d																		
Boston	d						12 13		14 45			16 45			18 42		19 50		
Hubberts Bridge	d																		
Swineshead	d																		
Heckington	d						12 27		14 59			16 59			18 56		20 04		
Sleaford	d						12 35		15 07			17 07			19 04		20 12		
Rauceby	d																		
Ancaster	d																		
Grantham 7	a						13 04		15 35			17 41			19 32		20 41		
	d	09 00	10 01	10 45	12 01	12 52		15 09	15 40	15 55	16 58	17 45	17 55	18 59	19 36	19 57	20 45	21 02	22 55
Bottesford	d					13 03													
Elton & Orston	d																		
Aslockton	d					13 09													
Bingham	d	09 17	10 18	11 02	12 18	13 13			15 57			18 02	18 12		19 53		21 02		
Radcliffe (Notts)	d					13 19													
Netherfield	d					13 23													
Nottingham 8	a	09 33	10 37	11 19	12 36	13 30		15 39	16 16	16 24	17 31	18 20	18 27	19 33	20 11	20 31	21 20	21 34	23 28

A From Norwich to Liverpool Lime Street
B From Norwich to Manchester Piccadilly
C From Norwich
D From Spalding
E To Matlock
F From Peterborough to Liverpool Lime Street

For connections to London Kings Cross refer to Table T026

Table T020-F

Mondays to Fridays

16 December to 15 May

London - Chingford

Miles			LO MO	LO MX	LO MO	LO MX	LO MO	LO MX	LO MX	LO MO	LO MX	LO	LO	LO	LO	LO	LO	LO	LO	LO	LO	LO
0	**London Liverpool Street** 15 ⊖	d	00 03	00 03	00 18	00 18	00 33	00 33	00 48	01 03	01 03	06 03	06 33	06 48	07 03	07 18	07 33	07 48	08 05	08 18	08 35	08 48
1¼	Bethnal Green	d	00 06	00 06	00 21	00 21	00 36	00 36	.	.	.	06 06	06 36	06 51	07 06	07 21	07 36	07 51	.	08 21	.	08 51
3	Hackney Downs	d	00 10	00 10	00 25	00 25	00 40	00 40	00 55	01 10	01 10	06 10	06 40	06 55	07 10	07 25	07 40	07 55	08 12	08 25	08 42	08 55
4	Clapton	d	00 13	00 13	00 28	00 28	00 43	00 43	00 58	01 13	01 13	06 13	06 43	06 58	07 13	07 28	07 43	07 58	08 15	08 28	08 45	08 58
5¾	St James Street	d	00 16	00 16	00 32	00 32	00 47	00 47	01 02	01 17	01 17	06 16	06 46	07 01	07 17	07 32	07 47	08 02	08 18	08 31	08 48	09 01
6¼	Walthamstow Central ⊖	d	00 18	00 18	00 34	00 34	00 49	00 49	01 04	01 19	01 19	06 18	06 48	07 03	07 19	07 34	07 49	08 04	08 20	08 33	08 50	09 03
7	Wood Street	d	00 20	00 20	00 36	00 36	00 51	00 51	01 06	01 21	01 21	06 20	06 50	07 05	07 21	07 36	07 51	08 06	08 22	08 35	08 52	09 05
8½	Highams Park	d	00 23	00 23	00 39	00 39	00 54	00 54	01 09	01 24	01 24	06 23	06 53	07 08	07 24	07 39	07 54	08 09	08 25	08 38	08 55	09 08
10½	**Chingford**	a	00 29	00 30	00 44	00 45	00 59	01 00	01 15	01 29	01 30	06 30	07 00	07 17	07 30	07 45	08 02	08 15	08 32	08 45	09 02	09 17

		LO	LO	LO	LO		LO	LO	LO	LO	LO	LO	LO	LO	LO	LO	LO	LO	LO	LO	LO	LO
London Liverpool Street 15 ⊖	d	09 03	09 18	09 33	09 48	and at	15 03	15 18	15 33	15 48	16 03	16 18	16 33	16 48	17 03	17 18	17 33	17 48	18 03	18 18	18 33	18 48
Bethnal Green	d	09 06	09 21	09 36	09 51	the same	15 06	15 21	15 36	15 51	16 06	16 21	16 36	16 51	.	17 21	.	17 51	.	18 21	.	18 51
Hackney Downs	d	09 10	09 25	09 40	09 55	minutes	15 10	15 25	15 40	15 55	16 10	16 25	16 40	16 55	17 10	17 25	17 40	17 55	18 10	18 25	18 40	18 55
Clapton	d	09 13	09 28	09 43	09 58	past	15 13	15 28	15 43	15 58	16 13	16 28	16 43	16 58	17 12	17 28	17 42	17 58	18 12	18 28	18 42	18 58
St James Street	d	09 16	09 31	09 46	10 01	each	15 16	15 31	15 46	16 01	16 16	16 31	16 46	17 01	17 16	17 31	17 46	18 01	18 16	18 31	18 46	19 01
Walthamstow Central ⊖	d	09 18	09 33	09 48	10 03	hour until	15 18	15 33	15 48	16 03	16 19	16 34	16 49	17 04	17 18	17 34	17 48	18 04	18 18	18 34	18 48	19 04
Wood Street	d	09 20	09 35	09 50	10 05		15 20	15 35	15 50	16 05	16 21	16 36	16 51	17 06	17 20	17 36	17 50	18 06	18 20	18 36	18 50	19 06
Highams Park	d	09 23	09 38	09 53	10 08		15 23	15 38	15 53	16 08	16 24	16 39	16 54	17 09	17 23	17 39	17 53	18 09	18 23	18 39	18 53	19 09
Chingford	a	09 30	09 45	10 00	10 15		15 30	15 45	16 00	16 15	16 32	16 47	17 02	17 17	17 32	17 47	18 02	18 17	18 32	18 47	19 02	19 17

		LO	LO	LO	LO	LO	LO	LO	LO	LO	LO	LO	LO	LO	LO	LO	LO	LO	LO	LO	LO
London Liverpool Street 15 ⊖	d	19 03	19 18	19 33	19 48	20 03	20 18	20 33	20 48	21 03	21 18	21 33	21 48	22 03	22 18	22 33	22 48	23 03	23 18	23 33	23 48
Bethnal Green	d	.	19 21	19 36	19 51	20 06	20 21	20 36	20 51	21 06	21 21	21 36	21 51	22 06	22 21	22 36	22 51	23 06	23 21	23 36	23 51
Hackney Downs	d	19 10	19 25	19 40	19 55	20 10	20 25	20 40	20 55	21 10	21 25	21 40	21 55	22 10	22 25	22 40	22 55	23 10	23 25	23 40	23 55
Clapton	d	19 12	19 28	19 43	19 58	20 13	20 28	20 43	20 58	21 13	21 28	21 43	21 58	22 13	22 28	22 43	22 58	23 13	23 28	23 43	23 58
St James Street	d	19 16	19 31	19 46	20 01	20 16	20 31	20 46	21 01	21 16	21 31	21 46	22 01	22 16	22 31	22 46	23 01	23 16	23 31	23 46	00 01
Walthamstow Central ⊖	d	19 18	19 33	19 48	20 03	20 18	20 33	20 48	21 03	21 18	21 33	21 48	22 03	22 18	22 33	22 48	23 03	23 18	23 33	23 48	00 03
Wood Street	d	19 20	19 35	19 50	20 05	20 20	20 35	20 50	21 05	21 20	21 35	21 50	22 05	22 20	22 35	22 50	23 05	23 20	23 35	23 50	00 05
Highams Park	d	19 23	19 38	19 53	20 08	20 23	20 38	20 53	21 08	21 23	21 38	21 53	22 08	22 23	22 38	22 53	23 08	23 23	23 38	23 53	00 08
Chingford	a	19 30	19 45	20 00	20 16	20 30	20 45	21 00	21 15	21 30	21 45	22 00	22 15	22 30	22 45	23 00	23 15	23 30	23 45	00 00	00 15

Saturdays

21 December to 16 May

		LO	LO	LO	LO	LO	LO	LO	LO	LO	LO		LO	LO	LO	LO	LO	LO
London Liverpool Street 15 ⊖	d	00 03	00 18	00 33	00 48	01 03	06 03	06 33	06 48	07 03	07 18	and at	22 33	22 48	23 03	23 18	23 33	23 48
Bethnal Green	d	00 06	00 21	00 36	.	.	06 06	06 36	06 51	07 06	07 21	the same	22 36	22 51	23 06	23 21	23 36	23 51
Hackney Downs	d	00 10	00 25	00 40	00 55	01 10	06 10	06 40	06 55	07 10	07 25	minutes	22 40	22 55	23 10	23 25	23 40	23 55
Clapton	d	00 13	00 28	00 43	00 58	01 13	06 13	06 43	06 58	07 13	07 28	past	22 43	22 58	23 13	23 28	23 43	23 58
St James Street	d	00 16	00 32	00 47	01 02	01 17	06 16	06 46	07 01	07 16	07 31	each	22 46	23 01	23 16	23 31	23 46	00 01
Walthamstow Central ⊖	d	00 18	00 34	00 49	01 04	01 19	06 18	06 48	07 03	07 18	07 33	hour until	22 48	23 03	23 18	23 33	23 48	00 03
Wood Street	d	00 20	00 36	00 51	01 06	01 21	06 20	06 50	07 05	07 20	07 35		22 50	23 05	23 20	23 35	23 50	00 05
Highams Park	d	00 23	00 39	00 54	01 09	01 24	06 23	06 53	07 08	07 23	07 38		22 53	23 08	23 23	23 38	23 53	00 08
Chingford	a	00 30	00 45	01 00	01 15	01 30	06 30	07 00	07 15	07 30	07 45		23 00	23 15	23 30	23 45	23 59	00 15

Sundays

15 December to 10 May

		LO	LO	LO	LO	LO	LO	LO	LO	LO	LO	LO	LO	LO	LO	LO		LO	LO	LO	LO	LO
London Liverpool Street 15 ⊖	d	00 03	00 18	00 33	00 48	01 03	07 33	08 03	08 18	08 33	08 48	09 03	09 18	09 33	09 48	10 03	and at	22 18	22 33	22 48	23 03	23 18
Bethnal Green	d	00 06	00 21	00 36	.	.	.	.	.	.	.	.	09 21	09 36	09 51	10 06	the same	22 21	22 36	22 51	23 06	23 21
Hackney Downs	d	00 10	00 25	00 40	00 55	01 10	07 40	08 10	08 25	08 40	08 55	09 10	09 25	09 40	09 55	10 10	minutes	22 25	22 40	22 55	23 10	23 25
Clapton	d	00 13	00 28	00 43	00 58	01 13	07 43	08 13	08 28	08 43	08 58	09 13	09 28	09 43	09 58	10 13	past	22 28	22 43	22 58	23 13	23 28
St James Street	d	00 16	00 32	00 47	01 02	01 17	07 46	08 16	08 31	08 46	09 01	09 16	09 31	09 46	10 01	10 16	each	22 31	22 46	23 01	23 16	23 31
Walthamstow Central ⊖	d	00 18	00 34	00 49	01 04	01 19	07 48	08 18	08 33	08 48	09 03	09 18	09 33	09 48	10 03	10 18	hour until	22 33	22 48	23 03	23 18	23 33
Wood Street	d	00 20	00 36	00 51	01 06	01 21	07 50	08 20	08 35	08 50	09 05	09 20	09 35	09 50	10 05	10 20		22 35	22 50	23 05	23 20	23 35
Highams Park	d	00 23	00 39	00 54	01 09	01 24	07 53	08 23	08 38	08 53	09 08	09 23	09 38	09 53	10 08	10 23		22 38	22 53	23 08	23 23	23 38
Chingford	a	00 30	00 45	01 00	01 15	01 30	07 59	08 29	08 44	08 59	09 14	09 29	09 44	09 59	10 14	10 29		22 44	22 59	23 14	23 29	23 44

		LO	LO
London Liverpool Street 15 ⊖	d	23 33	23 48
Bethnal Green	d	23 36	23 51
Hackney Downs	d	23 40	23 55
Clapton	d	23 43	23 58
St James Street	d	23 46	00 01
Walthamstow Central ⊖	d	23 48	00 03
Wood Street	d	23 50	00 05
Highams Park	d	23 53	00 08
Chingford	a	23 59	00 14

Table T020-R

Mondays to Fridays

16 December to 15 May

Chingford - London

Miles			LO	LO	LO	LO	LO	LO	LO	LO	LO	LO	LO	LO	LO	LO	LO	LO	LO	LO
0	**Chingford**	d	05 10	05 25	05 40	05 55	06 10	06 29	06 44	06 59	07 14	07 29	07 44	07 59	08 14	08 29	08 44	08 57	09 12	09 27
2	Highams Park	d	05 14	05 29	05 44	05 59	06 14	06 33	06 48	07 03	07 18	07 33	07 48	08 03	08 18	08 33	08 48	09 01	09 16	09 31
3½	Wood Street	d	05 17	05 32	05 47	06 02	06 17	06 36	06 51	07 06	07 21	07 36	07 51	08 06	08 21	08 36	08 51	09 04	09 19	09 34
4¼	Walthamstow Central ⊖	d	05 19	05 34	05 49	06 04	06 19	06 39	06 54	07 09	07 24	07 39	07 54	08 09	08 24	08 39	08 54	09 07	09 22	09 37
4¾	St James Street	d	05 21	05 36	05 51	06 06	06 21	06 42	06 56	07 12	07 26	07 42	07 56	08 12	08 26	08 42	08 56	09 10	09 25	09 40
6½	Clapton	d	05 24	05 39	05 54	06 09	06 24	06 45	07 00	07 15	07 30	07 45	08 00	08 15	08 30	08 45	09 00	09 13	09 28	09 43
7½	Hackney Downs	d	05 28	05 43	05 58	06 13	06 28	06 49	07 03	07 18	07 33	07 48	08 03	08 18	08 33	08 48	09 03	09 17	09 32	09 47
9¼	Bethnal Green	d	05 32	05 47	06 02	06 17	06 32	06 53	07 07	.	07 37	.	08 07	.	08 37	.	09 07	09 21	09 36	09 51
10½	**London Liverpool Street** 15 ⊖	a	05 37	05 52	06 07	06 22	06 37	06 59	07 11	07 26	07 44	07 56	08 14	08 29	08 44	08 59	09 14	09 27	09 42	09 57

		LO	LO	LO	LO		LO	LO	LO	LO	LO	LO	LO	LO	LO	LO	LO	LO	LO	LO	LO	LO
Chingford	d	09 40	09 55	10 10	10 25	and at	15 40	15 55	16 10	16 25	16 40	16 55	17 10	17 25	17 39	17 55	18 09	18 25	18 39	18 55	19 09	19 25
Highams Park	d	09 44	09 59	10 14	10 29	the same	15 44	15 59	16 14	16 29	16 44	16 59	17 14	17 29	17 43	17 59	18 13	18 29	18 43	18 59	19 13	19 29
Wood Street	d	09 47	10 02	10 17	10 32	minutes	15 47	16 02	16 17	16 32	16 47	17 02	17 17	17 32	17 46	18 02	18 16	18 32	18 46	19 02	19 16	19 32
Walthamstow Central ⊖	d	09 49	10 04	10 19	10 34	past	15 49	16 04	16 19	16 34	16 49	17 04	17 19	17 34	17 48	18 04	18 18	18 34	18 48	19 04	19 18	19 34
St James Street	d	09 51	10 06	10 21	10 36	each	15 51	16 06	16 21	16 36	16 51	17 06	17 21	17 36	17 50	18 06	18 20	18 36	18 50	19 06	19 20	19 36
Clapton	d	09 54	10 09	10 24	10 39	hour until	15 54	16 09	16 24	16 39	16 54	17 09	17 24	17 39	17 55	18 09	18 24	18 39	18 54	19 09	19 24	19 39
Hackney Downs	d	09 58	10 13	10 28	10 43		15 58	16 13	16 28	16 43	16 58	17 13	17 28	17 43	17 58	18 13	18 27	18 43	18 57	19 13	19 27	19 43
Bethnal Green	d	10 02	10 17	10 32	10 47		16 02	16 17	16 32	16 47	17 02	17 17	17 32	17 47	18 02	18 17	18 31	18 47	19 01	19 17	19 31	19 47
London Liverpool Street 15 ⊖	a	10 07	10 22	10 37	10 52		16 07	16 22	16 37	16 52	17 07	17 22	17 37	17 55	18 06	18 25	18 36	18 52	19 06	19 25	19 36	19 55

		LO	LO	LO	LO		LO	LO	LO	LO
Chingford	d	19 40	19 55	20 10	20 25	and at	22 40	22 55	23 10	23 25
Highams Park	d	19 44	19 59	20 14	20 29	the same	22 44	22 59	23 14	23 29
Wood Street	d	19 47	20 02	20 17	20 32	minutes	22 47	23 02	23 17	23 32
Walthamstow Central ⊖	d	19 49	20 04	20 19	20 34	past	22 49	23 04	23 19	23 34
St James Street	d	19 51	20 06	20 21	20 36	each	22 51	23 06	23 21	23 36
Clapton	d	19 54	20 09	20 24	20 39	hour until	22 54	23 09	23 24	23 39
Hackney Downs	d	19 58	20 13	20 28	20 43		22 58	23 13	23 28	23 43
Bethnal Green	d	20 02	20 17	20 32	20 47		23 02	23 17	23 32	23 47
London Liverpool Street 15 ⊖	a	20 07	20 22	20 37	20 52		23 07	23 22	23 37	23 52

Saturdays

21 December to 16 May

		LO	LO	LO	LO		LO	LO	LO	LO	LO	LO
Chingford	d	05 10	05 25	05 40	05 55	and at	22 10	22 25	22 40	22 55	23 10	23 25
Highams Park	d	05 14	05 29	05 44	05 59	the same	22 14	22 29	22 44	22 59	23 14	23 29
Wood Street	d	05 17	05 32	05 47	06 02	minutes	22 17	22 32	22 47	23 02	23 17	23 32
Walthamstow Central ⊖	d	05 19	05 34	05 49	06 04	past	22 19	22 34	22 49	23 04	23 19	23 34
St James Street	d	05 21	05 36	05 51	06 06	each	22 21	22 36	22 51	23 06	23 21	23 36
Clapton	d	05 24	05 39	05 54	06 09	hour until	22 24	22 39	22 54	23 09	23 24	23 39
Hackney Downs	d	05 28	05 43	05 58	06 13		22 28	22 43	22 58	23 13	23 28	23 43
Bethnal Green	d	05 32	05 47	06 02	06 17		22 32	22 47	23 02	23 17	23 32	23 47
London Liverpool Street 15 ⊖	a	05 36	05 51	06 06	06 21		22 36	22 51	23 06	23 21	23 36	23 51

Sundays

15 December to 10 May

		LO	LO	LO	LO	LO	LO	LO	LO	LO	LO	LO	LO	LO		LO	LO	LO	LO	LO	LO
Chingford	d	06 40	06 55	07 10	07 25	07 40	07 55	08 10	08 25	08 40	08 55	09 10	09 25	09 40	and at	21 55	22 10	22 25	22 40	22 55	23 10
Highams Park	d	06 44	06 59	07 14	07 29	07 44	07 59	08 14	08 29	08 44	08 59	09 14	09 29	09 44	the same	21 59	22 14	22 29	22 44	22 59	23 14
Wood Street	d	06 47	07 02	07 17	07 32	07 47	08 02	08 17	08 32	08 47	09 02	09 17	09 32	09 47	minutes	22 02	22 17	22 32	22 47	23 02	23 17
Walthamstow Central ⊖	d	06 49	07 04	07 19	07 34	07 49	08 04	08 19	08 34	08 49	09 04	09 19	09 34	09 49	past	22 04	22 19	22 34	22 49	23 04	23 19
St James Street	d	06 51	07 06	07 21	07 36	07 51	08 06	08 21	08 36	08 51	09 06	09 21	09 36	09 51	each	22 06	22 21	22 36	22 51	23 06	23 21
Clapton	d	06 54	07 09	07 24	07 39	07 54	08 09	08 24	08 39	08 54	09 09	09 24	09 39	09 54	hour until	22 09	22 24	22 39	22 54	23 09	23 24
Hackney Downs	d	06 58	07 13	07 28	07 43	07 58	08 13	08 28	08 43	08 58	09 13	09 28	09 43	09 58		22 13	22 28	22 43	22 58	23 13	23 28
Bethnal Green	d	.	.	.	.	.	.	.	.	.	09 17	09 32	09 47	10 02		22 17	22 32	22 47	23 02	23 17	23 32
London Liverpool Street 15 ⊖	a	07 06	07 21	07 36	07 51	08 06	08 21	08 36	08 51	09 06	09 21	09 36	09 51	10 06		22 21	22 36	22 51	23 06	23 21	23 36

Table T021-F

Mondays to Fridays

16 December to 15 May

London - Cheshunt (via Seven Sisters) and Enfield Town

Miles	Miles			LO MX	LO	LO	LO	LO	LO	LO	LO	LO	LO	LO	LO	LO	LO	LO	LO	LO	LO	LO	LO
0	0	**London Liverpool Street** 15 ⊖	d	00 01	05 45	06 00	06 15	06 21	06 36	06 45	06 51	07 07	07 15	07 21	07 36	07 45	07 51	08 00	08 07	08 15	08 30	08 38	08 45
1¼	1¼	Bethnal Green	d	00 03	05 48	06 03	.	06 24	06 39	.	06 54	07 10	.	07 24	07 39	.	07 54	.	08 10	08 18	08 33	.	08 48
1¾	1¾	Cambridge Heath	d	00 05	05 50	06 05	.	06 26	06 41	.	06 56	07 12	.	07 26	07 41	.	07 56	.	08 12	08 20	08 35	08 43	08 50
2½	2½	London Fields	d	00 07	05 52	06 07	.	06 28	06 43	.	06 58	07 14	.	07 28	07 43	.	07 58	.	08 14	08 22	08 37	08 45	08 52
3	3	Hackney Downs	d	00 09	05 54	06 09	06 22	06 30	06 45	06 52	07 00	07 16	07 22	07 30	07 45	07 52	08 00	08 07	08 16	08 24	08 39	08 47	08 54
3¾	3¾	Rectory Road	d	00 12	05 57	06 12	.	06 33	06 48	06 55	07 03	07 19	07 25	07 33	07 48	07 55	08 03	.	08 19	08 27	08 42	08 49	08 57
4½	4½	Stoke Newington	d	00 13	05 58	06 13	.	06 34	06 49	06 56	07 04	07 20	07 26	07 34	07 49	07 56	08 04	.	08 20	08 28	08 43	08 51	08 58
5	5	Stamford Hill	d	00 15	06 00	06 15	.	06 36	06 51	06 58	07 06	07 22	07 28	07 36	07 51	07 58	08 06	.	08 22	08 30	08 45	08 53	09 00
5½	5½	Seven Sisters ⊖	d	00 17	06 03	06 18	06 27	06 39	06 54	07 01	07 09	07 25	07 31	07 39	07 54	08 01	08 09	08 16	08 25	08 33	08 48	08 55	09 03
6¼	6¼	Bruce Grove	d	00 19	06 05	06 20	.	06 41	06 56	07 03	07 11	07 27	07 33	07 41	07 56	08 03	08 11	.	08 27	08 35	08 50	08 57	09 05
7¼	7¼	White Hart Lane	d	00 21	06 07	06 22	.	06 43	06 58	07 05	07 13	07 29	07 35	07 43	07 58	08 05	08 13	.	08 29	08 37	08 52	08 59	09 07
8	8	Silver Street	d	00 23	06 09	06 24	.	06 45	07 00	07 07	07 15	07 31	07 37	07 45	08 00	08 07	08 15	.	08 31	08 39	08 54	09 01	09 09
8½	8½	Edmonton Green	d	00 25	06 11	06 26	06 32	06 47	07 02	07 09	07 17	07 33	07 39	07 47	08 02	08 09	08 17	08 21	08 33	08 41	08 56	09 03	09 11
—	9¾	Bush Hill Park	d	00 28	.	06 29	.	06 50	.	07 12	07 20	.	07 42	07 50	.	08 12	08 20	.	08 36	.	08 59	.	09 14
—	10¾	**Enfield Town**	a	00 34	.	06 33	.	06 54	.	07 18	07 24	.	07 48	07 54	.	08 18	08 24	.	08 42	.	09 05	.	09 20
10½	—	Southbury	d	.	06 14	.	06 36	.	07 05	.	.	07 36	.	.	08 05	.	.	08 24	.	08 47	.	09 07	.
12¼	—	Turkey Street	d	.	06 17	.	06 39	.	07 08	.	.	07 39	.	.	08 08	.	.	08 27	.	08 50	.	09 10	.
13½	—	Theobalds Grove	d	.	06 20	.	06 41	.	07 11	.	.	07 42	.	.	08 11	.	.	08 30	.	08 52	.	09 12	.
14½	—	**Cheshunt**	a	.	06 24	.	06 50	.	07 15	.	.	07 50	.	.	08 19	.	.	08 39	.	08 58	.	09 17	.

		LO	LO	LO	LO	LO		LO	LO	LO	LO	LO	LO	LO	LE A	LO	LO	LO	LE A	LO	LO	LO
London Liverpool Street 15 ⊖	d	09 00	09 15	09 30	09 45	10 00	and at the same minutes past each hour until	15 15	15 30	15 45	16 00	16 15	16 21	16 30	16 41	16 45	16 52	17 00	17 11	17 15	17 22	17 30
Bethnal Green	d	09 03	09 18	09 33	09 48	10 03		15 18	15 33	15 48	16 03	16 18	.	16 33	.	16 48	.	17 03	.	17 18	.	17 33
Cambridge Heath	d	09 05	09 20	09 35	09 50	10 05		15 20	15 35	15 50	16 05	16 20	16 26	16 35	.	16 50	16 57	17 05	.	17 20	17 27	17 35
London Fields	d	09 07	09 22	09 37	09 52	10 07		15 22	15 37	15 52	16 07	16 22	16 28	16 37	.	16 52	16 59	17 07	.	17 22	17 29	17 37
Hackney Downs	d	09 09	09 24	09 39	09 54	10 09		15 24	15 39	15 54	16 09	16 24	16 30	16 39	16 48	16 54	17 01	17 09	17 18	17 24	17 31	17 39
Rectory Road	d	09 12	09 27	09 42	09 57	10 12		15 27	15 42	15 57	16 12	16 27	16 32	16 42	.	16 57	17 03	17 12	.	17 27	17 33	17 42
Stoke Newington	d	09 13	09 28	09 43	09 58	10 13		15 28	15 43	15 58	16 13	16 28	16 34	16 43	.	16 58	17 05	17 13	.	17 28	17 35	17 43
Stamford Hill	d	09 15	09 30	09 45	10 00	10 15		15 30	15 45	16 00	16 15	16 30	.	16 45	.	17 00	.	17 15	.	17 30	.	17 45
Seven Sisters ⊖	d	09 18	09 33	09 48	10 03	10 18		15 33	15 48	16 03	16 18	16 33	16 37	16 48	16 54	17 03	17 09	17 18	17 24	17 33	17 39	17 48
Bruce Grove	d	09 20	09 35	09 50	10 05	10 20		15 35	15 50	16 05	16 20	16 35	16 39	16 50	.	17 05	17 11	17 20	.	17 35	17 41	17 50
White Hart Lane	d	09 22	09 37	09 52	10 07	10 22		15 37	15 52	16 07	16 22	16 37	16 41	16 52	.	17 07	17 13	17 22	.	17 37	17 43	17 52
Silver Street	d	09 24	09 39	09 54	10 09	10 24		15 39	15 54	16 09	16 24	16 39	16 43	16 54	.	17 09	17 15	17 24	.	17 39	17 45	17 54
Edmonton Green	d	09 26	09 41	09 56	10 11	10 26		15 41	15 56	16 11	16 26	16 41	16 46	16 56	17 00	17 11	17 17	17 26	17 30	17 41	17 47	17 56
Bush Hill Park	d	09 29	.	09 59	.	10 29		.	15 59	.	16 29	16 44	.	16 59	.	17 14	.	17 29	.	17 44	.	17 59
Enfield Town	a	09 35	.	10 03	.	10 33		.	16 03	.	16 33	16 50	.	17 05	.	17 20	.	17 33	.	17 50	.	18 05
Southbury	d	.	09 44	.	10 14	.		15 44	.	16 14	.	.	16 49	.	.	.	17 21	.	.	.	17 51	.
Turkey Street	d	.	09 47	.	10 17	.		15 47	.	16 17	.	.	16 52	.	.	.	17 24	.	.	.	17 54	.
Theobalds Grove	d	.	09 50	.	10 20	.		15 50	.	16 20	.	.	16 55	.	.	.	17 26	.	.	.	17 56	.
Cheshunt	a	.	09 54	.	10 24	.		15 54	.	16 24	.	.	17 00	.	17 09	.	17 31	.	17 39	.	18 05	.

		LE A	LO	LO	LO	LE A	LO	LO	LO	LE A	LO	LO	LO	LO	LO	LO	LO	LO	LO	LO	LO	LO	LO
London Liverpool Street 15 ⊖	d	17 41	17 45	17 52	18 00	18 11	18 15	18 22	18 30	18 41	18 45	19 00	19 15	19 22	19 30	19 45	20 00	20 15	20 30	20 45	21 00	21 15	21 30
Bethnal Green	d	.	17 48	.	18 03	.	18 18	.	18 33	.	18 48	19 03	19 18	.	19 33	19 48	20 03	20 18	20 33	20 48	21 03	21 18	21 33
Cambridge Heath	d	.	17 50	17 57	18 05	.	18 20	18 27	18 35	.	18 50	19 05	19 20	.	19 35	19 50	20 05	20 20	20 35	20 50	21 05	21 20	21 35
London Fields	d	.	17 52	17 59	18 07	.	18 22	18 29	18 37	.	18 52	19 07	19 22	19 28	19 37	19 52	20 07	20 22	20 37	20 52	21 07	21 22	21 37
Hackney Downs	d	17 48	17 54	18 01	18 09	18 18	18 24	18 31	18 39	18 48	18 54	19 09	19 24	19 30	19 39	19 54	20 09	20 24	20 39	20 54	21 09	21 24	21 39
Rectory Road	d	.	17 57	18 03	18 12	.	18 27	18 33	18 42	.	18 57	19 12	19 27	19 32	19 42	19 57	20 12	20 27	20 42	20 57	21 12	21 27	21 42
Stoke Newington	d	.	17 58	18 05	18 13	.	18 28	18 35	18 43	.	18 58	19 13	19 28	19 34	19 43	19 58	20 13	20 28	20 43	20 58	21 13	21 28	21 43
Stamford Hill	d	.	18 00	.	18 15	.	18 30	.	18 45	.	19 00	19 15	19 30	.	19 45	20 00	20 15	20 30	20 45	21 00	21 15	21 30	21 45
Seven Sisters ⊖	d	17 54	18 03	18 09	18 18	18 24	18 33	18 39	18 48	18 54	19 03	19 18	19 33	19 37	19 48	20 03	20 18	20 33	20 48	21 03	21 18	21 33	21 48
Bruce Grove	d	.	18 05	18 11	18 20	.	18 35	18 41	18 50	.	19 05	19 20	19 35	19 39	19 50	20 05	20 20	20 35	20 50	21 05	21 20	21 35	21 50
White Hart Lane	d	.	18 07	18 13	18 22	.	18 37	18 43	18 52	.	19 07	19 22	19 37	19 41	19 52	20 07	20 22	20 37	20 52	21 07	21 22	21 37	21 52
Silver Street	d	.	18 09	18 15	18 24	.	18 39	18 45	18 54	.	19 09	19 24	19 39	19 43	19 54	20 09	20 24	20 39	20 54	21 09	21 24	21 39	21 54
Edmonton Green	d	18 00	18 11	18 17	18 26	18 30	18 41	18 47	18 56	19 00	19 11	19 26	19 41	19 45	19 56	20 11	20 26	20 41	20 56	21 11	21 26	21 41	21 56
Bush Hill Park	d	.	18 14	.	18 29	.	18 44	.	18 59	.	.	19 29	.	19 48	19 59	.	20 29	.	20 59	.	21 29	.	21 59
Enfield Town	a	.	18 20	.	18 35	.	18 50	.	19 05	.	.	19 35	.	19 55	20 03	.	20 33	.	21 03	.	21 33	.	22 03
Southbury	d	.	.	18 21	.	.	.	18 51	.	.	19 15	.	19 44	.	.	20 14	.	20 44	.	21 14	.	21 44	.
Turkey Street	d	.	.	18 24	.	.	.	18 54	.	.	19 18	.	19 47	.	.	20 17	.	20 47	.	21 17	.	21 47	.
Theobalds Grove	d	.	.	18 26	.	.	.	18 56	.	.	19 20	.	19 50	.	.	20 20	.	20 50	.	21 20	.	21 50	.
Cheshunt	a	18 09	.	18 31	.	18 39	.	19 01	.	19 09	19 28	.	19 58	.	.	20 28	.	20 54	.	21 24	.	21 54	.

		LO	LO	LO	LO	LO	LO	LO	LO	LO
London Liverpool Street 15 ⊖	d	21 45	22 00	22 15	22 30	22 45	23 00	23 15	23 30	23 45
Bethnal Green	d	21 48	22 03	22 18	22 33	22 48	23 03	23 18	23 33	23 48
Cambridge Heath	d	21 50	22 05	22 20	22 35	22 50	23 05	23 20	23 35	23 50
London Fields	d	21 52	22 07	22 22	22 37	22 52	23 07	23 22	23 37	23 52
Hackney Downs	d	21 54	22 09	22 24	22 39	22 54	23 09	23 24	23 39	23 54
Rectory Road	d	21 57	22 12	22 27	22 42	22 57	23 12	23 27	23 42	23 57
Stoke Newington	d	21 58	22 13	22 28	22 43	22 58	23 13	23 28	23 43	23 58
Stamford Hill	d	22 00	22 15	22 30	22 45	23 00	23 15	23 30	23 45	23 59
Seven Sisters ⊖	d	22 03	22 18	22 33	22 48	23 03	23 18	23 33	23 48	00 03
Bruce Grove	d	22 05	22 20	22 35	22 50	23 05	23 20	23 35	23 50	00 05
White Hart Lane	d	22 07	22 22	22 37	22 52	23 07	23 22	23 37	23 52	00 07
Silver Street	d	22 09	22 24	22 39	22 54	23 09	23 24	23 39	23 54	00 09
Edmonton Green	d	22 11	22 26	22 41	22 56	23 11	23 26	23 41	23 56	00 11
Bush Hill Park	d	.	22 29	.	22 59	.	23 29	.	23 59	.
Enfield Town	a	.	22 33	.	23 03	.	23 33	.	00 03	.
Southbury	d	22 14	.	22 44	.	23 14	.	23 44	.	00 14
Turkey Street	d	22 17	.	22 47	.	23 17	.	23 47	.	00 17
Theobalds Grove	d	22 20	.	22 50	.	23 20	.	23 50	.	00 20
Cheshunt	a	22 24	.	22 54	.	23 24	.	23 54	.	00 24

A To Hertford East

Table T021-F

Saturdays

21 December to 16 May

London - Cheshunt (via Seven Sisters) and Enfield Town

		LO	LO	LO	LO	LO	LO	LO		LO	LO	LO	LO	LO
London Liverpool Street 15 ⊖	d	00 01	05 15	05 30	05 45	06 00	06 15	06 30	and at the same minutes past each hour until	22 45	23 00	23 15	23 30	23 45
Bethnal Green	d	00 03	05 18	.	05 48	06 03	06 18	06 33		22 48	23 03	23 18	23 33	23 48
Cambridge Heath	d	00 05	05 20	.	05 50	06 05	06 20	06 35		22 50	23 05	23 20	23 35	23 50
London Fields	d	00 07	05 22	.	05 52	06 07	06 22	06 37		22 52	23 07	23 22	23 37	23 52
Hackney Downs	d	00 09	05 24	05 38	05 54	06 09	06 24	06 39		22 54	23 09	23 24	23 39	23 54
Rectory Road	d	00 12	05 27	.	05 57	06 12	06 27	06 42		22 57	23 12	23 27	23 42	23 57
Stoke Newington	d	00 13	05 28	.	05 58	06 13	06 28	06 43		22 58	23 13	23 28	23 43	23 58
Stamford Hill	d	00 15	05 30	.	06 00	06 15	06 30	06 45		23 00	23 15	23 30	23 45	23 59
Seven Sisters ⊖	d	00 17	05 33	05 48	06 03	06 18	06 33	06 48		23 03	23 18	23 33	23 48	00 03
Bruce Grove	d	00 19	05 35	05 50	06 05	06 20	06 35	06 50		23 05	23 20	23 35	23 50	00 05
White Hart Lane	d	00 21	05 37	05 52	06 07	06 22	06 37	06 52		23 07	23 22	23 37	23 52	00 07
Silver Street	d	00 23	05 39	05 54	06 09	06 24	06 39	06 54		23 09	23 24	23 39	23 54	00 09
Edmonton Green	d	00 25	05 41	05 56	06 11	06 26	06 41	06 56		23 11	23 26	23 41	23 56	00 11
Bush Hill Park	d	00 28	.	05 59	.	06 29	.	06 59		.	23 29	.	23 59	.
Enfield Town	a	00 34	.	06 03	.	06 33	.	07 03		.	23 33	.	00 03	.
Southbury	d	.	05 44	.	06 14	.	06 44	.		23 14	.	23 44	.	00 14
Turkey Street	d	.	05 47	.	06 17	.	06 47	.		23 17	.	23 47	.	00 17
Theobalds Grove	d	.	05 50	.	06 20	.	06 50	.		23 20	.	23 50	.	00 20
Cheshunt	a	.	05 54	.	06 24	.	06 54	.		23 24	.	23 54	.	00 24

Sundays

15 December to 10 May

		LO	LO	LO	LO	LO	LO	LO	LO	LO	LO	LO	LO		LO	LO	LO	LO	LO	LO
London Liverpool Street 15 ⊖	d	00 01	07 30	07 45	08 00	08 15	08 30	08 45	09 00	09 15	09 30	09 45	10 00	and at the same minutes past each hour until	22 15	22 30	22 45	23 00	23 15	23 30
Bethnal Green	d	00 03	.	.	.	.	.	.	.	09 18	09 33	09 48	10 03		22 18	22 33	22 48	23 03	23 18	23 33
Cambridge Heath	d	00 05	.	.	.	.	.	.	.	09 20	09 35	09 50	10 05		22 20	22 35	22 50	23 05	23 20	23 35
London Fields	d	00 07	.	.	.	.	.	.	.	09 22	09 37	09 52	10 07		22 22	22 37	22 52	23 07	23 22	23 37
Hackney Downs	d	00 09	07 39	07 54	08 09	08 24	08 39	08 54	09 09	09 24	09 39	09 54	10 09		22 24	22 39	22 54	23 09	23 24	23 39
Rectory Road	d	00 12	07 42	07 57	08 12	08 27	08 42	08 57	09 12	09 27	09 42	09 57	10 12		22 27	22 42	22 57	23 12	23 27	23 42
Stoke Newington	d	00 13	07 43	07 58	08 13	08 28	08 43	08 58	09 13	09 28	09 43	09 58	10 13		22 28	22 43	22 58	23 13	23 28	23 43
Stamford Hill	d	00 15	07 45	08 00	08 15	08 30	08 45	09 00	09 15	09 30	09 45	10 00	10 15		22 30	22 45	23 00	23 15	23 30	23 45
Seven Sisters ⊖	d	00 18	07 48	08 03	08 18	08 33	08 48	09 03	09 18	09 33	09 48	10 03	10 18		22 33	22 48	23 03	23 18	23 33	23 48
Bruce Grove	d	00 20	07 50	08 05	08 20	08 35	08 50	09 05	09 20	09 35	09 50	10 05	10 20		22 35	22 50	23 05	23 20	23 35	23 50
White Hart Lane	d	00 22	07 52	08 07	08 22	08 37	08 52	09 07	09 22	09 37	09 52	10 07	10 22		22 37	22 52	23 07	23 22	23 37	23 52
Silver Street	d	00 24	07 54	08 09	08 24	08 39	08 54	09 09	09 24	09 39	09 54	10 09	10 24		22 39	22 54	23 09	23 24	23 39	23 54
Edmonton Green	d	00 26	07 56	08 11	08 26	08 41	08 56	09 11	09 26	09 41	09 56	10 11	10 26		22 41	22 56	23 11	23 26	23 41	23 56
Bush Hill Park	d	00 29	07 59	.	08 29	.	08 59	.	09 29	.	09 59	.	10 29		.	22 59	.	23 29	.	23 59
Enfield Town	a	00 33	08 03	.	08 33	.	09 03	.	09 33	.	10 03	.	10 33		.	23 03	.	23 33	.	00 03
Southbury	d	.	.	08 14	.	08 44	.	09 14	.	09 44	.	10 14	.		22 44	.	23 14	.	23 44	.
Turkey Street	d	.	.	08 17	.	08 47	.	09 17	.	09 47	.	10 17	.		22 47	.	23 17	.	23 47	.
Theobalds Grove	d	.	.	08 20	.	08 50	.	09 20	.	09 50	.	10 20	.		22 50	.	23 20	.	23 50	.
Cheshunt	a	.	.	08 24	.	08 54	.	09 24	.	09 54	.	10 24	.		22 54	.	23 24	.	23 54	.

Table T021-R

Cheshunt (via Seven Sisters) and Enfield Town - London

Mondays to Fridays
16 December to 15 May

Miles	Miles		LO	LO	LO	LO	LO	LO	LE A	LO	LO	LO	LE A	LO	LO	LO	LE A	LO	LO	LO	LE A	LO
0	—	**Cheshunt** d	05 16		06 01			06 33	06 47		06 52		07 17		07 22		07 47		07 52		08 17	
1	—	Theobalds Grove d	05 19		06 04			06 36			06 55				07 25				07 55			
2¼	—	Turkey Street d	05 21		06 06			06 38			06 57				07 27				07 57			
4	—	Southbury d	05 24		06 09			06 41			07 00				07 30				08 00			
—	0	**Enfield Town** d		05 52		06 18	06 33			06 53		07 08		07 23		07 38		07 53		08 08		08 23
—	1	Bush Hill Park d		05 55		06 21	06 36			06 56		07 11		07 26		07 41		07 56		08 11		08 26
6	2¼	Edmonton Green d	05 28	05 58	06 13	06 24	06 39	06 45	06 55	06 59	07 04	07 14	07 25	07 29	07 34	07 44	07 55	07 59	08 04	08 14	08 25	08 29
6½	2¾	Silver Street d	05 30	06 00	06 15	06 26	06 41	06 47		07 01	07 06	07 16		07 31	07 36	07 46		08 01	08 06	08 16		08 31
7¼	3½	White Hart Lane d	05 32	06 02	06 17	06 28	06 43	06 49		07 03	07 08	07 18		07 33	07 38	07 48		08 03	08 08	08 18		08 33
8¼	4½	Bruce Grove d	05 34	06 04	06 19	06 30	06 45	06 51		07 05	07 10	07 20		07 35	07 40	07 50		08 05	08 10	08 20		08 35
9	5¼	Seven Sisters ⊖ d	05 36	06 06	06 21	06 33	06 48	06 54	07 02	07 08	07 13	07 23	07 32	07 38	07 43	07 53	08 02	08 08	08 13	08 23	08 32	08 38
9½	5¾	Stamford Hill d	05 38	06 08	06 23	06 35	06 50	06 56		07 10		07 25		07 40		07 55		08 10		08 25		08 40
10¼	6½	Stoke Newington d	05 40	06 10	06 25	06 37	06 52	06 58		07 12	07 16	07 27		07 42	07 46	07 57		08 12	08 16	08 27		08 42
10¾	7	Rectory Road d	05 42	06 12	06 27	06 39	06 54	07 00		07 14	07 18	07 29		07 44	07 48	07 59		08 14	08 18	08 29		08 43
11½	7¾	Hackney Downs d	05 45	06 15	06 30	06 43	06 58	07 04	07 08	07 18	07 22	07 33	07 38	07 48	07 52	08 03	08 08	08 18	08 22	08 33	08 38	08 48
12	8¼	London Fields d	05 47	06 17	06 32	06 45	07 00	07 06		07 20	07 24	07 35		07 50	07 54	08 05		08 20	08 24	08 35		08 50
12¾	9	Cambridge Heath d	05 49	06 19	06 34	06 47	07 02	07 08		07 22		07 37		07 52		08 07		08 22		08 37		08 52
13¼	9½	Bethnal Green d	05 51	06 21	06 36	06 49		07 10		07 24		07 39		07 54		08 09		08 24		08 39		08 54
14¼	10½	**London Liverpool Street** 15 ⊖ a	05 55	06 26	06 40	06 56	07 11	07 16	07 18	07 31	07 31	07 46	07 48	08 01	08 05	08 16	08 18	08 31	08 35	08 46	08 48	09 01

	LO	LO	LO	LO	LO	LO	LO	LO	LO	LO	LO	LO	LO	LO	LO	LO	LO	LO	LO	LO	LO	LO
Cheshunt d	08 22		08 43			09 07		09 31		10 01		10 31		11 01		11 31		12 01		12 31		13 01
Theobalds Grove d	08 25		08 46			09 10		09 34		10 04		10 34		11 04		11 34		12 04		12 34		13 04
Turkey Street d	08 27		08 48			09 12		09 36		10 06		10 36		11 06		11 36		12 06		12 36		13 06
Southbury d	08 30		08 51			09 15		09 39		10 09		10 39		11 09		11 39		12 09		12 39		13 09
Enfield Town d		08 38		08 53	09 08		09 23		09 52		10 22		10 52		11 22		11 52		12 22		12 52	
Bush Hill Park d		08 41		08 56	09 11		09 26		09 55		10 25		10 55		11 25		11 55		12 25		12 55	
Edmonton Green d	08 34	08 44	08 55	08 59	09 14	09 19	09 29	09 43	09 58	10 13	10 28	10 43	10 58	11 13	11 28	11 43	11 58	12 13	12 28	12 43	12 58	13 13
Silver Street d	08 36	08 46		09 01	09 16	09 21	09 31	09 45	10 00	10 15	10 30	10 45	11 00	11 15	11 30	11 45	12 00	12 15	12 30	12 45	13 00	13 15
White Hart Lane d	08 38	08 48		09 03	09 18	09 23	09 33	09 47	10 02	10 17	10 32	10 47	11 02	11 17	11 32	11 47	12 02	12 17	12 32	12 47	13 02	13 17
Bruce Grove d	08 40	08 50		09 05	09 20	09 25	09 35	09 49	10 04	10 19	10 34	10 49	11 04	11 19	11 34	11 49	12 04	12 19	12 34	12 49	13 04	13 19
Seven Sisters ⊖ d	08 43	08 53	09 02	09 08	09 23	09 28	09 38	09 51	10 06	10 21	10 36	10 51	11 06	11 21	11 36	11 51	12 06	12 21	12 36	12 51	13 06	13 21
Stamford Hill d		08 55		09 10	09 25		09 40	09 53	10 08	10 23	10 38	10 53	11 08	11 23	11 38	11 53	12 08	12 23	12 38	12 53	13 08	13 23
Stoke Newington d	08 46	08 57		09 12	09 27	09 31	09 42	09 55	10 10	10 25	10 40	10 55	11 10	11 25	11 40	11 55	12 10	12 25	12 40	12 55	13 10	13 25
Rectory Road d	08 48	08 59		09 14	09 29	09 33	09 44	09 57	10 12	10 27	10 42	10 57	11 12	11 27	11 42	11 57	12 12	12 27	12 42	12 57	13 12	13 27
Hackney Downs d	08 52	09 03	09 08	09 18	09 33	09 37	09 48	10 00	10 15	10 30	10 45	11 00	11 15	11 30	11 45	12 00	12 15	12 30	12 45	13 00	13 15	13 30
London Fields d	08 54	09 05		09 20	09 35	09 39	09 50	10 02	10 17	10 32	10 47	11 02	11 17	11 32	11 47	12 02	12 17	12 32	12 47	13 02	13 17	13 32
Cambridge Heath d		09 07		09 22	09 37		09 52	10 04	10 19	10 34	10 49	11 04	11 19	11 34	11 49	12 04	12 19	12 34	12 49	13 04	13 19	13 34
Bethnal Green d		09 09		09 24	09 39		09 54	10 06	10 21	10 36	10 51	11 06	11 21	11 36	11 51	12 06	12 21	12 36	12 51	13 06	13 21	13 36
London Liverpool Street 15 ⊖ a	09 05	09 16	09 22	09 31	09 46	09 46	10 01	10 10	10 26	10 40	10 56	11 14	11 26	11 40	11 56	12 10	12 26	12 40	12 56	13 10	13 26	13 40

	LO	LO	LO	LO	LO	LO	LO	LO	LO	LO	LO	LO	LO	LO	LO	LO	LO	LO	LO	LO	LO
Cheshunt d		13 31		14 01		14 31		15 01		15 31		16 01		16 31			17 06			17 40	
Theobalds Grove d		13 34		14 04		14 34		15 04		15 34		16 04		16 34			17 09			17 43	
Turkey Street d		13 36		14 06		14 36		15 06		15 36		16 06		16 36			17 11			17 45	
Southbury d		13 39		14 09		14 39		15 09		15 39		16 09		16 39			17 14			17 48	
Enfield Town d	13 22		13 52		14 22		14 52		15 22		15 52		16 22		16 51	17 06		17 21	17 36		17 51
Bush Hill Park d	13 25		13 55		14 25		14 55		15 25		15 55		16 25		16 54	17 09		17 24	17 39		17 54
Edmonton Green d	13 28	13 43	13 58	14 13	14 28	14 43	14 58	15 13	15 28	15 43	15 58	16 13	16 28	16 43	16 57	17 12	17 18	17 27	17 42	17 52	17 57
Silver Street d	13 30	13 45	14 00	14 15	14 30	14 45	15 00	15 15	15 30	15 45	16 00	16 15	16 30	16 45	16 59	17 14	17 20	17 29	17 44		17 59
White Hart Lane d	13 32	13 47	14 02	14 17	14 32	14 47	15 02	15 17	15 32	15 47	16 02	16 17	16 32	16 47	17 01	17 16	17 22	17 31	17 46		18 01
Bruce Grove d	13 34	13 49	14 04	14 19	14 34	14 49	15 04	15 19	15 34	15 49	16 04	16 19	16 34	16 49	17 03	17 18	17 24	17 33	17 48		18 03
Seven Sisters ⊖ d	13 36	13 51	14 06	14 21	14 36	14 51	15 06	15 21	15 36	15 51	16 06	16 21	16 36	16 51	17 05	17 20	17 27	17 35	17 50	17 58	18 05
Stamford Hill d	13 38	13 53	14 08	14 23	14 38	14 53	15 08	15 23	15 38	15 53	16 08	16 23	16 38	16 53	17 07	17 22		17 37	17 52		18 07
Stoke Newington d	13 40	13 55	14 10	14 25	14 40	14 55	15 10	15 25	15 40	15 55	16 10	16 25	16 40	16 55	17 09	17 24	17 30	17 39	17 54	18 01	18 09
Rectory Road d	13 42	13 57	14 12	14 27	14 42	14 57	15 12	15 27	15 42	15 57	16 12	16 27	16 42	16 57	17 11	17 26		17 41	17 56		18 11
Hackney Downs d	13 45	14 00	14 15	14 30	14 45	15 00	15 15	15 30	15 45	16 00	16 15	16 30	16 45	17 00	17 14	17 29	17 33	17 44	17 59	18 04	18 14
London Fields d	13 47	14 02	14 17	14 32	14 47	15 02	15 17	15 32	15 47	16 02	16 17	16 32	16 47	17 02	17 16	17 31		17 46	18 01		18 16
Cambridge Heath d	13 49	14 04	14 19	14 34	14 49	15 04	15 19	15 34	15 49	16 04	16 19	16 34	16 49	17 04	17 18	17 33		17 48	18 03		18 18
Bethnal Green d	13 51	14 06	14 21	14 36	14 51	15 06	15 21	15 36	15 51	16 06	16 21	16 36	16 51	17 06	17 20	17 35		17 50	18 05		18 20
London Liverpool Street 15 ⊖ a	13 56	14 10	14 26	14 44	14 56	15 10	15 26	15 40	15 56	16 14	16 26	16 40	16 56	17 10	17 25	17 40	17 45	17 55	18 11	18 19	18 25

	LO	LO	LO	LO	LO	LO	LO	LO	LO	LO	LO	LO		LO	LO	LO	LO	LO	LO	LE ◇1 B	LE A
Cheshunt d		18 10			18 40			19 10		19 31		20 01			22 31		23 01		23 31	23 52	23 59
Theobalds Grove d		18 13			18 43			19 13		19 34		20 04			22 34		23 04		23 34		
Turkey Street d		18 15			18 45			19 15		19 36		20 06			22 36		23 06		23 36		
Southbury d		18 18			18 48			19 18		19 39		20 09			22 39		23 09		23 39		
Enfield Town d	18 06		18 21	18 36		18 51	19 06		19 22		19 52		and at	22 22		22 52		23 22			
Bush Hill Park d	18 09		18 24	18 39		18 54	19 09		19 25		19 55		the same	22 25		22 55		23 25			
Edmonton Green d	18 12	18 22	18 27	18 42	18 52	18 57	19 12	19 22	19 28	19 43	19 58	20 13	minutes	22 28	22 43	22 58	23 13	23 28	23 43		
Silver Street d	18 14		18 29	18 44		18 59	19 14		19 30	19 45	20 00	20 15	past	22 30	22 45	23 00	23 15	23 30	23 45		
White Hart Lane d	18 16		18 31	18 46		19 01	19 16		19 32	19 47	20 02	20 17	each	22 32	22 47	23 02	23 17	23 32	23 47		
Bruce Grove d	18 18		18 33	18 48		19 03	19 18		19 34	19 49	20 04	20 19	hour until	22 34	22 49	23 04	23 19	23 34	23 49		
Seven Sisters ⊖ d	18 20	18 28	18 35	18 50	18 58	19 05	19 20	19 28	19 36	19 51	20 06	20 21		22 36	22 51	23 06	23 21	23 36	23 51	00 04	00 12
Stamford Hill d	18 22		18 37	18 52		19 07	19 22		19 38	19 53	20 08	20 23		22 38	22 53	23 08	23 23	23 38	23 53		
Stoke Newington d	18 24	18 31	18 39	18 54	19 01	19 09	19 24	19 31	19 40	19 55	20 10	20 25		22 40	22 55	23 10	23 25	23 40	23 55		
Rectory Road d	18 26		18 41	18 56		19 11	19 26		19 42	19 57	20 12	20 27		22 42	22 57	23 12	23 27	23 42	23 57		
Hackney Downs d	18 29	18 34	18 44	18 59	19 04	19 14	19 29	19 34	19 45	20 00	20 15	20 30		22 45	23 00	23 15	23 30	23 45	23 59		00 17
London Fields d	18 31		18 46	19 01		19 16	19 31		19 47	20 02	20 17	20 32		22 47	23 02	23 17	23 32	23 47	00 02		
Cambridge Heath d	18 33		18 48	19 03		19 18	19 33		19 49	20 04	20 19	20 34		22 49	23 04	23 19	23 34	23 49	00 04		
Bethnal Green d	18 35		18 50	19 05		19 20	19 35		19 51	20 06	20 21	20 36		22 51	23 06	23 21	23 36	23 51	00 06		
London Liverpool Street 15 ⊖ a	18 40	18 49	18 55	19 10	19 19	19 25	19 40	19 49	19 56	20 10	20 26	20 40		22 56	23 10	23 26	23 40	23 56	00 10	00 18	00 26

A From Hertford East   B From Cambridge North

Table T021-R

Cheshunt (via Seven Sisters) and Enfield Town - London

Saturdays
21 December to 16 May

	LO	LE ◇1 A	LO	LO	LO	LO		LO	LO	LO	LO	LO	LO	LO	LO
Cheshunt d	05 16	05 30	06 01		06 31			22 01		22 31		23 01		23 31	
Theobalds Grove d	05 19		06 04		06 34			22 04		22 34		23 04		23 34	
Turkey Street d	05 21		06 06		06 36			22 06		22 36		23 06		23 36	
Southbury d	05 24		06 09		06 39			22 09		22 39		23 09		23 39	
Enfield Town d				06 22		06 52	and at		22 22		22 52		23 22		23 52
Bush Hill Park d				06 25		06 55	the same		22 25		22 55		23 25		23 55
Edmonton Green d	05 28		06 13	06 28	06 43	06 58	minutes	22 13	22 28	22 43	22 58	23 13	23 28	23 43	23 58
Silver Street d	05 30		06 15	06 30	06 45	07 00	past	22 15	22 30	22 45	23 00	23 15	23 30	23 45	23 59
White Hart Lane d	05 32		06 17	06 32	06 47	07 02	each	22 17	22 32	22 47	23 02	23 17	23 32	23 47	00 02
Bruce Grove d	05 34		06 19	06 34	06 49	07 04	hour until	22 19	22 34	22 49	23 04	23 19	23 34	23 49	00 04
Seven Sisters ⊖ d	05 36	05 42	06 21	06 36	06 51	07 06		22 21	22 36	22 51	23 06	23 21	23 36	23 51	00 06
Stamford Hill d	05 38		06 23	06 38	06 53	07 08		22 23	22 38	22 53	23 08	23 23	23 38	23 53	00 08
Stoke Newington d	05 40		06 25	06 40	06 55	07 10		22 25	22 40	22 55	23 10	23 25	23 40	23 55	00 10
Rectory Road d	05 42		06 27	06 42	06 57	07 12		22 27	22 42	22 57	23 12	23 27	23 42	23 57	00 12
Hackney Downs d	05 45		06 30	06 45	07 00	07 15		22 30	22 45	23 00	23 15	23 30	23 45	23 59	00 15
London Fields d	05 47		06 32	06 47	07 02	07 17		22 32	22 47	23 02	23 17	23 32	23 47	00 02	00 17
Cambridge Heath d	05 49		06 34	06 49	07 04	07 19		22 34	22 49	23 04	23 19	23 34	23 49	00 04	00 19
Bethnal Green d	05 51		06 36	06 51	07 06	07 21		22 36	22 51	23 06	23 21	23 36	23 51	00 06	00 21
London Liverpool Street 15 ⊖ a	05 55	05 57	06 40	06 55	07 10	07 25		22 40	22 55	23 10	23 25	23 40	23 55	00 10	00 25

Sundays
15 December to 10 May

	LO	LO	LO	LO	LO	LO	LO	LO	LO	LO		LO	LO	LO	LO	LO	LO	LO
Cheshunt d	07 31		08 01		08 31		09 01		09 31			22 01		22 31		23 01		23 31
Theobalds Grove d	07 34		08 04		08 34		09 04		09 34			22 04		22 34		23 04		23 34
Turkey Street d	07 36		08 06		08 36		09 06		09 36			22 06		22 36		23 06		23 36
Southbury d	07 39		08 09		08 39		09 09		09 39			22 09		22 39		23 09		23 39
Enfield Town d		07 52		08 22		08 52		09 22		09 52			22 22		22 52		23 22	
Bush Hill Park d		07 55		08 25		08 55		09 25		09 55	and at		22 25		22 55		23 25	
Edmonton Green d	07 43	07 58	08 13	08 28	08 43	08 58	09 13	09 28	09 43	09 58	the same	22 13	22 28	22 43	22 58	23 13	23 28	23 43
Silver Street d	07 45	08 00	08 15	08 30	08 45	09 00	09 15	09 30	09 45	10 00	minutes	22 15	22 30	22 45	23 00	23 15	23 30	23 45
White Hart Lane d	07 47	08 02	08 17	08 32	08 47	09 02	09 17	09 32	09 47	10 02	past	22 17	22 32	22 47	23 02	23 17	23 32	23 47
Bruce Grove d	07 49	08 04	08 19	08 34	08 49	09 04	09 19	09 34	09 49	10 04	each	22 19	22 34	22 49	23 04	23 19	23 34	23 49
Seven Sisters ⊖ d	07 51	08 06	08 21	08 36	08 51	09 06	09 21	09 36	09 51	10 06	hour until	22 21	22 36	22 51	23 06	23 21	23 36	23 51
Stamford Hill d	07 53	08 08	08 23	08 38	08 53	09 08	09 23	09 38	09 53	10 08		22 23	22 38	22 53	23 08	23 23	23 38	23 53
Stoke Newington d	07 55	08 10	08 25	08 40	08 55	09 10	09 25	09 40	09 55	10 10		22 25	22 40	22 55	23 10	23 25	23 40	23 55
Rectory Road d	07 57	08 12	08 27	08 42	08 57	09 12	09 27	09 42	09 57	10 12		22 27	22 42	22 57	23 12	23 27	23 42	23 57
Hackney Downs d	08 00	08 15	08 30	08 45	09 00	09 15	09 30	09 45	10 00	10 15		22 30	22 45	23 00	23 15	23 30	23 45	23 59
London Fields d							09 32	09 47	10 02	10 17		22 32	22 47	23 02	23 17	23 32	23 47	00 02
Cambridge Heath d							09 34	09 49	10 04	10 19		22 34	22 49	23 04	23 19	23 34	23 49	00 04
Bethnal Green d							09 36	09 51	10 06	10 21		22 36	22 51	23 06	23 21	23 36	23 51	00 06
London Liverpool Street 15 ⊖ a	08 10	08 25	08 40	08 55	09 10	09 25	09 40	09 55	10 10	10 25		22 40	22 55	23 10	23 25	23 41	23 55	00 10

A From Cambridge

Table T022-F

Mondays to Fridays

16 December to 15 May

London - Broxbourne, Hertford East, Bishops Stortford, Stansted Airport, Cambridge and Cambridge North

Miles	Miles	Miles			LE MO ■ A	LE MO B	LE MX A	LE MX A	LE MO ■ A	LE MO ◇■ A	LE MX ◇■ A	LE ■ A	LE MFO ■		LE MFO ■	XC ◇■ C	LE MTh FO	LE TWO	LE	LE ■	XC ◇■ C	LE ■	LE ◇■		LE ■
0	—	—	**London Liverpool Street** 15 ⊖	d									03 40		04 10		04 40	04 40		05 10		05 25	05 28		05 40
3	—	—	Hackney Downs	d																					
—	0	0	Stratford 7 ⊖	d																					
—	—	2¼	Lea Bridge	d																					
—	6¾	—	Seven Sisters ⊖	d																					
6	—	4¼	Tottenham Hale ⊖	d								00 10					04 52	04 59		05 22		05 37	05 40		05 52
7	—	5¼	Northumberland Park	d																					
7¾	—	6	Meridian Water	d																					
10	—	—	Ponders End	d			00 01																		
10¾	—	—	Brimsdown	d			00 03																		
11¾	—	—	Enfield Lock	d			00 06																		
12¾	—	—	Waltham Cross	d			00 08																		
14	—	12¼	Cheshunt	d			00 11					00 18					05 00	05 07					05 48		
17¼	—	15½	**Broxbourne** 3	a			00 16					00 23					05 05	05 12					05 53		
—	0	—	**Broxbourne** 3	d		00 03	00 16					00 23					05 05	05 12	05 40				05 53		
—	1¾	—	Rye House	d		00 06	00 20												05 43						
—	3	—	St Margarets (Herts)	d		00 09	00 23												05 46						
—	5	—	Ware	d		00 13	00 27												05 50						
—	7	—	**Hertford East**	a		00 19	00 32												05 56						
20	—	18½	Roydon	d								00 27											05 57		
22¾	—	21	Harlow Town	d							00 01	00 31					05 11	05 18		05 38		05 53	06 01		
24½	—	22¾	Harlow Mill	d							00 04	00 34											06 04		
26¾	—	25	Sawbridgeworth	d					00 04		00 08	00 38								05 43			06 08		
30¼	—	28½	**Bishops Stortford**	a					00 11		00 14	00 44					05 20	05 27		05 49		06 02	06 14		06 17
30¼	—	28½	**Bishops Stortford**	d	00 03			00 04			00 14						05 20	05 27		05 50		06 03	06 14		06 18
33¾	0	—	Stansted Mountfitchet	d							00 18						05 24	05 31					06 18		06 23
—	—	—	**Stansted Airport** ✈	a	00 12			00 13					04 30		04 57		05 39	05 39		06 00		06 12			06 29
—	3¾	—	**Stansted Airport** ✈	d												05 27					06 12				
35½	8¼	—	Elsenham	d							00 22												06 22		
40	—	—	Newport (Essex)	d							00 27												06 27		
41¾	—	—	Audley End	d							00 30					05 41					06 27		06 30		
45¾	—	—	Great Chesterford	d						00 05	00 35												06 35		
49	—	—	Whittlesford Parkway	d						00 10	00 40												06 40		
52½	—	—	Shelford	d						00 14	00 44												06 44		
55¾	—	—	**Cambridge**	a						00 20	00 51					05 55					06 44		06 55		
—	—	—		d																					
58	—	—	**Cambridge North**	a																					

		LE WX	LE WO	LE	LE D	LE ■	LE ◇■	LE A	LE ■		LE	LE	XC ◇■ C	LE ◇■ E	LE ■	LE ■	LE ◇■ A	LE	LE		LE	LE ■	LE ◇■	LE	LE
London Liverpool Street 15 ⊖	d	05 42	05 42		05 52	05 55	05 58		06 10		06 12	06 25		06 28		06 40			06 42			06 55	06 58	07 10	07 12
Hackney Downs	d	05 48	05 49								06 18								06 48						07 18
Stratford 7 ⊖	d			05 46	06 03										06 36			06 44			06 49				
Lea Bridge	d			05 52	06 09													06 50			06 55				
Seven Sisters ⊖	d							←																	
Tottenham Hale ⊖	d	05 55	05 55	05 56	06 16	06 07	06 10	06 16	06 22		06 25	06 37		06 40	06 45	06 52		06 54	06 55		07 00	07 07	07 10	07 22	07 25
Northumberland Park	d			05 58	→			06 18							06 48			06 56							
Meridian Water	d			06a01				06 20										06a59							
Ponders End	d	05 59	05 59								06 29										07 04				07 29
Brimsdown	d	06 02	06 02								06 32										07 07				07 32
Enfield Lock	d	06 04	06 04					06 25			06 34								07 01						07 34
Waltham Cross	d	06 07	06 07								06 37								07 04						07 37
Cheshunt	d	06 09	06 09				06 18	06 29			06 39			06 51	06 55		←		07 06		07 11		07 21		07 39
Broxbourne 3	a	06 15	06 15				06 23	06 34			06 45			06 56	07 00		06 56		07 12		07 17		07 26		07 45
Broxbourne 3	d	06 15	06 15				06 25	06 38			06 45			07 04	07 00		07 04		07 15				07 26		07 45
Rye House	d	06 18	06 18					06 41			06 48			→					07 18						07 48
St Margarets (Herts)	d	06 21	06 21					06 44			06 51								07 21						07 51
Ware	d	06 25	06 25					06 48			06 55								07 25						07 55
Hertford East	a	06 31	06 31					06 54			07 01								07 31						08 02
Roydon	d						06 29										07 10						07 30		
Harlow Town	d					06 26	06 33					06 55					07 14					07 25	07 34		
Harlow Mill	d						06 36										07 17						07 37		
Sawbridgeworth	d						06 39										07 20						07 41		
Bishops Stortford	a					06 35	06 45		06 49						07 14	07 17	07 26						07 47	07 50	
Bishops Stortford	d					06 35	06 46		06 50							07 18	07 28						07 47	07 51	
Stansted Mountfitchet	d						06 50										07 32					07 36	07 51		
Stansted Airport ✈	a					06 44			06 59			07 12				07 30						07 43		08 00	
Stansted Airport ✈	d												07 21												
Elsenham	d						06 54										07 36						07 55		
Newport (Essex)	d						06 59										07 41						08 00		
Audley End	d						07 02						07 41				07 45						08 03		
Great Chesterford	d						07 07										07 50						08 08		
Whittlesford Parkway	d						07 12										07 55						08 13		
Shelford	d						07 16										08 00						08 17		
Cambridge	a						07 24						07 55				08 09						08 24		
	d																								
Cambridge North	a																								

A From London Liverpool Street
B From Stratford
C To Birmingham New Street
D To Hertford East
E To Cambridge

Table T022-F

Mondays to Fridays

16 December to 15 May

London - Broxbourne, Hertford East, Bishops Stortford, Stansted Airport, Cambridge and Cambridge North

		LE	LE ■	LE	LE ◇■		LE ■	XC ◇■ A	LE ■	LE	LE	LE ■	LE ■	LE ◇■	LE ◇■		LE ■	LE ■	LE	LE	LE ■	LE ◇■ B	LE ◇■	LE ◇■ C	LE ■
London Liverpool Street 15 ⊖	d		07 23	07 25	07 28				07 40	07 42		07 53	07 55	07 58	08 03			08 10	08 12		08 25	08 28	08 33		
Hackney Downs	d									07 48									08 18						
Stratford 7 ⊖	d	07 17					07 34				07 47						08 04			08 17					08 34
Lea Bridge	d	07 23					07 40				07 53						08 10			08 23					08 40
Seven Sisters ⊖	d																								
Tottenham Hale ⊖	d	07 27		07 37	07 41		07 47		07 52	07 55	07 57		08 07	08 11	08 15		08 18	08 22	08 25	08 27	08 37	08 40	08 45		08 48
Northumberland Park	d	07 29					07 49				07 59						08 20			08 29					08 50
Meridian Water	d	07a32					07 51				08a02									08a32					08 52
Ponders End	d									07 59									08 29						
Brimsdown	d									08 02									08 32						
Enfield Lock	d									08 04							08 26		08 34						
Waltham Cross	d									08 07									08 37						
Cheshunt	d				07 51		07 58			08 09				08 21			08 29		08 39			08 48			08 59
Broxbourne 3	a		07 48		07 56		08 04			08 15		08 18		08 25			08 35		08 45			08 53			09 05
Broxbourne 3	d				07 56		08 09			08 15				08 25			08 39		08 45			08 53			09 09
Rye House	d									08 18									08 48						
St Margarets (Herts)	d									08 21									08 51						
Ware	d									08 25									08 55						
Hertford East	a									08 32									09 02						
Roydon	d				08 00		08 14										08 43					08 57			09 13
Harlow Town	d			07 56	08 04		08 19						08 26	08 36			08 47				08 55	09 05			09 17
Harlow Mill	d				08 07		08 22										08 50								09 20
Sawbridgeworth	d				08 11		08 25							08 42			08 54					09 11		←	09 24
Bishops Stortford	a				08 17		08 32		08 20					08 47			09 02	08 51				09 17		09 17	09 32
Bishops Stortford	d				08 17				08 21					08 47				08 51				09 17		09 17	
Stansted Mountfitchet	d				08 21								08 37	08 51								→		09 21	
Stansted Airport ✈	a			08 13					08 30				08 45					09 01			09 14				
Stansted Airport ✈	d							08 21																	
Elsenham	d				08 25									08 55										09 25	
Newport (Essex)	d				08 30									09 00										09 30	
Audley End	d				08 33			08 41						09 03									09 23	09 33	
Great Chesterford	d				08 38									09 08										09 38	
Whittlesford Parkway	d				08 43									09 13										09 43	
Shelford	d				08 47									09 17										09 47	
Cambridge	a				08 54			08 58						09 27	09 07								09 39	09 54	
	d				08 55									09 29										09 55	
Cambridge North	a				09 00									09 34										10 00	

			XC ◇■ A	LE	LE	LE	LE ■	LE ◇■	LE ■	LE ■	LE		LE	LE	LE ◇■	LE ■	LE	XC ◇■ A	LE	LE	LE ■		LE ◇■	LE ■	LE D
London Liverpool Street 15 ⊖	d			08 40	08 42		08 55	08 58		09 10	09 12			09 25	09 28		09 40		09 42		09 55		09 58		
Hackney Downs	d				08 48						09 18								09 48						
Stratford 7 ⊖	d					08 47			09 00				09 17			09 30				09 47				10 00	
Lea Bridge	d					08 53			09 06				09 23			09 36				09 53				10 06	
Seven Sisters ⊖	d																								
Tottenham Hale ⊖	d			08 52	08 55	08 57	09 07	09 10	09 14	09 22	09 25		09 27	09 37	09 40	09 44	09 52		09 55	09 57	10 07		10 10	10 13	
Northumberland Park	d					08 59			09 16				09 29			09 46				09 59				10 15	
Meridian Water	d					09a02							09a32			09 48				10a02					
Ponders End	d				08 59						09 29								09 59						
Brimsdown	d				09 02						09 32								10 02						
Enfield Lock	d				09 04				09 22		09 34								10 04					10 21	
Waltham Cross	d				09 07						09 37					09 54			10 07						
Cheshunt	d				09 09			09 18	09 25		09 39				09 48	09 56			10 09				10 18	10 25	
Broxbourne 3	a				09 15			09 23	09 31		09 45				09 53	10 02			10 15				10 23	10 30	
Broxbourne 3	d				09 15			09 23	09 34		09 45				09 53	10 05			10 15				10 23	10 34	
Rye House	d				09 18						09 48								10 18						
St Margarets (Herts)	d				09 21						09 51								10 21						
Ware	d				09 25						09 55								10 25						
Hertford East	a				09 32						10 01								10 31						
Roydon	d								09 39						09 57									10 39	
Harlow Town	d						09 25	09 29	09 43					09 55	10 01	10 12					10 25		10 29	10 43	
Harlow Mill	d								09 46						10 04									10 46	
Sawbridgeworth	d								09 49						10 08	10 17								10 49	
Bishops Stortford	a			09 20				09 38	09 56	09 45					10 14	10 23	10 17						10 38	10 56	
Bishops Stortford	d			09 21				09 39		09 45					10 14		10 18						10 39		
Stansted Mountfitchet	d						09 37								10 18						10 36				
Stansted Airport ✈	a			09 30			09 47			09 55				10 12			10 27				10 44				
Stansted Airport ✈	d		09 21															10 27							10 48
Elsenham	d														10 22										
Newport (Essex)	d														10 27										
Audley End	d		09 41					09 51							10 30			10 41					10 51		11 02
Great Chesterford	d														10 35										
Whittlesford Parkway	d							09 58							10 40								10 58		11 09
Shelford	d														10 44										
Cambridge	a		09 57					10 10							10 51			10 56					11 09		11 19
	d							10 20							10 53								11 13		11 20
Cambridge North	a							10 25							10 58								11 18		11 24

A To Birmingham New Street
B To Cambridge North
C From London Liverpool Street
D To Norwich

Table T022-F

Mondays to Fridays

16 December to 15 May

London - Broxbourne, Hertford East, Bishops Stortford, Stansted Airport, Cambridge and Cambridge North

		LE ■	LE	LE	LE ■	LE ◇■	LE ■		LE ■	XC ◇■ A	LE	LE	LE	LE ◇■	LE ■	LE B	LE ■		LE	LE	LE ■	LE ◇■	LE ■	LE	XC ◇■ A
London Liverpool Street 15 ⊖	d	10 10	10 12		10 25	10 28			10 40		10 42		10 55	10 58			11 10		11 12		11 25	11 28		11 40	
Hackney Downs	d		10 18								10 48								11 18						
Stratford 7 ⊖	d			10 16			10 30					10 46			11 00					11 16			11 30		
Lea Bridge	d			10 22			10 36					10 52			11 06					11 22			11 36		
Seven Sisters ⊖	d																								
Tottenham Hale ⊖	d	10 22	10 25	10 26	10 37	10 40	10 43		10 52		10 55	10 56	11 07	11 10	11 13		11 22		11 25	11 26	11 37	11 40	11 43	11 52	
Northumberland Park	d			10 28								10 58			11 15					11 28					
Meridian Water	d			10a31								11a01								11a31					
Ponders End	d		10 29								10 59								11 29						
Brimsdown	d		10 32								11 02								11 32						
Enfield Lock	d		10 34								11 04				11 21				11 34						
Waltham Cross	d		10 37				10 50				11 07								11 37				11 50		
Cheshunt	d		10 39			10 48	10 52				11 09			11 18	11 25				11 39			11 48	11 52		
Broxbourne 3	a		10 45			10 53	10 58				11 15			11 23	11 30				11 45			11 53	11 58		
Broxbourne 3	d		10 45			10 53	10 58				11 15			11 23	11 34				11 45			11 53	11 58		
Rye House	d		10 48								11 18								11 48						
St Margarets (Herts)	d		10 51								11 21								11 51						
Ware	d		10 55								11 25								11 55						
Hertford East	a		11 01								11 31								12 01						
Roydon	d					10 57									11 39							11 57			
Harlow Town	d				10 55	11 01	11 11						11 25	11 29	11 43						11 55	12 01	12 11		
Harlow Mill	d					11 04									11 46							12 04			
Sawbridgeworth	d					11 08	11 17								11 49							12 08	12 17		
Bishops Stortford	a	10 45				11 14	11 23		11 17					11 38	11 56		11 45					12 14	12 23	12 17	
Bishops Stortford	d	10 45				11 14			11 18					11 39			11 45					12 14		12 18	
Stansted Mountfitchet	d					11 18							11 36									12 18			
Stansted Airport ✈	a	10 57			11 13				11 27				11 44				11 57				12 12			12 27	
Stansted Airport ✈	d									11 27						11 48									12 27
Elsenham	d					11 22																12 22			
Newport (Essex)	d					11 27																12 27			
Audley End	d					11 30				11 41				11 51		12 02						12 30			12 41
Great Chesterford	d					11 35																12 35			
Whittlesford Parkway	d					11 40								11 58		12 09						12 40			
Shelford	d					11 44																12 44			
Cambridge	a					11 51				11 56				12 09		12 19						12 51			12 56
	d					11 53								12 13		12 20						12 53			
Cambridge North	a					11 58								12 18		12 24						12 58			

		LE	LE		LE	LE ◇■	LE ■	LE B	LE ■	LE	LE	LE ■	LE ◇■		LE ■	LE ■	XC ◇■ A	LE	LE	LE ■	LE ◇■	LE ■	LE B		LE
London Liverpool Street 15 ⊖	d	11 42			11 55	11 58			12 10	12 12		12 25	12 28			12 40		12 42		12 55	12 58				13 10
Hackney Downs	d	11 48								12 18								12 48							
Stratford 7 ⊖	d		11 46				12 00				12 16				12 30				12 46			13 00			
Lea Bridge	d		11 52				12 06				12 22				12 36				12 52			13 06			
Seven Sisters ⊖	d																								
Tottenham Hale ⊖	d	11 55	11 56		12 07	12 10	12 13		12 22	12 25	12 26	12 37	12 40		12 43	12 52		12 55	12 56	13 07	13 10	13 13			13 22
Northumberland Park	d		11 58				12 15				12 28								12 58			13 15			
Meridian Water	d		12a01								12a31								13a01						
Ponders End	d	11 59								12 29								12 59							
Brimsdown	d	12 02								12 32								13 02							
Enfield Lock	d	12 04					12 21			12 34								13 04				13 21			
Waltham Cross	d	12 07								12 37					12 50			13 07							
Cheshunt	d	12 09				12 18	12 25			12 39			12 48		12 52			13 09			13 18	13 25			
Broxbourne 3	a	12 15				12 23	12 30			12 45			12 53		12 58			13 15			13 23	13 30			
Broxbourne 3	d	12 15				12 23	12 34			12 45			12 53		12 58			13 15			13 23	13 34			
Rye House	d	12 18								12 48								13 18							
St Margarets (Herts)	d	12 21								12 51								13 21							
Ware	d	12 25								12 55								13 25							
Hertford East	a	12 31								13 01								13 31							
Roydon	d						12 39						12 57									13 39			
Harlow Town	d				12 25	12 29	12 43					12 55	13 01		13 11					13 25	13 29	13 43			
Harlow Mill	d						12 46						13 04									13 46			
Sawbridgeworth	d						12 49						13 08		13 17							13 49			
Bishops Stortford	a					12 38	12 56		12 45				13 14		13 23	13 17					13 38	13 56			13 45
Bishops Stortford	d					12 39			12 45				13 14			13 18					13 39				13 45
Stansted Mountfitchet	d				12 36								13 18							13 36					
Stansted Airport ✈	a				12 44				12 57			13 12				13 27				13 44					13 57
Stansted Airport ✈	d							12 48									13 27						13 48		
Elsenham	d												13 22												
Newport (Essex)	d												13 27												
Audley End	d					12 51		13 02					13 30				13 41				13 51		14 02		
Great Chesterford	d												13 35												
Whittlesford Parkway	d					12 58		13 09					13 40								13 58		14 09		
Shelford	d												13 44												
Cambridge	a					13 09		13 19					13 51				13 56				14 09		14 19		
	d					13 13		13 20					13 53								14 13		14 20		
Cambridge North	a					13 18		13 24					13 58								14 18		14 24		

A To Birmingham New Street

B To Norwich

Table T022-F

Mondays to Fridays

16 December to 15 May

London - Broxbourne, Hertford East, Bishops Stortford, Stansted Airport, Cambridge and Cambridge North

		LE	LE	LE ■	LE ◇■	LE ■	LE ■	XC ◇■ A	LE		LE	LE	LE ◇■	LE ■	LE B	LE	LE	LE	LE ■		LE ◇■	LE ■	LE ■	XC ◇■ A	LE
London Liverpool Street 15 ⊖	d	13 12		13 25	13 28		13 40		13 42			13 55	13 58			14 10	14 12		14 25		14 28		14 40		14 42
Hackney Downs	d	13 18							13 48								14 18								14 48
Stratford 7 ⊖	d		13 16			13 30					13 46			14 00				14 16				14 30			
Lea Bridge	d		13 22			13 36					13 52			14 06				14 22				14 36			
Seven Sisters ⊖	d																								
Tottenham Hale ⊖	d	13 25	13 26	13 37	13 40	13 43	13 52		13 55		13 56	14 07	14 10	14 13		14 22	14 25	14 26	14 37		14 40	14 43	14 52		14 55
Northumberland Park	d		13 28								13 58			14 15				14 28							
Meridian Water	d		13a31								14a01							14a31							
Ponders End	d	13 29							13 59								14 29								14 59
Brimsdown	d	13 32							14 02								14 32								15 02
Enfield Lock	d	13 34							14 04					14 21			14 34								15 04
Waltham Cross	d	13 37				13 50			14 07								14 37					14 50			15 07
Cheshunt	d	13 39			13 48	13 52			14 09				14 18	14 25			14 39				14 48	14 52			15 09
Broxbourne 3	a	13 45			13 53	13 58			14 15				14 23	14 30			14 45				14 53	14 58			15 15
Broxbourne 3	d	13 45			13 53	13 58			14 15				14 23	14 34			14 45				14 53	14 58			15 15
Rye House	d	13 48							14 18								14 48								15 18
St Margarets (Herts)	d	13 51							14 21								14 51								15 21
Ware	d	13 55							14 25								14 55								15 25
Hertford East	a	14 01							14 31								15 01								15 31
Roydon	d				13 57									14 39							14 57				
Harlow Town	d			13 55	14 01	14 11						14 25	14 29	14 43					14 55		15 01	15 11			
Harlow Mill	d				14 04									14 46							15 04				
Sawbridgeworth	d				14 08	14 17								14 49							15 08	15 17			
Bishops Stortford	a				14 14	14 23	14 17						14 38	14 56		14 45					15 14	15 23	15 17		
Bishops Stortford	d				14 14		14 18						14 39			14 45					15 14		15 18		
Stansted Mountfitchet	d				14 18							14 36									15 18				
Stansted Airport ✈	a			14 12			14 27					14 44				14 57			15 13				15 27		
Stansted Airport ✈	d							14 27							14 48									15 27	
Elsenham	d				14 22																15 22				
Newport (Essex)	d				14 27																15 27				
Audley End	d				14 30			14 41					14 51		15 02						15 30			15 41	
Great Chesterford	d				14 35																15 35				
Whittlesford Parkway	d				14 40								14 58		15 09						15 40				
Shelford	d				14 44																15 44				
Cambridge	a				14 51			14 56					15 09		15 19						15 51			15 56	
	d				14 53								15 13		15 20						15 53				
Cambridge North	a				14 58								15 20		15 24						15 58				

		LE	LE B	LE ■	LE ◇■		LE ■	LE ■	LE	LE	LE	LE ◇■	LE ■	LE ■	XC ◇■ A		LE	LE	LE ■	LE ◇■ C	LE ■	LE B	LE	LE	LE
London Liverpool Street 15 ⊖	d			14 55	14 58			15 10	15 12		15 25	15 28		15 40			15 42		15 55	15 58			16 10	16 12	
Hackney Downs	d								15 18								15 48							16 19	
Stratford 7 ⊖	d	14 46					15 00			15 16			15 30					15 46			16 00				16 16
Lea Bridge	d	14 52					15 06			15 22			15 36					15 52			16 06				16 22
Seven Sisters ⊖	d																								
Tottenham Hale ⊖	d	14 56		15 07	15 10		15 13	15 22	15 25	15 26	15 37	15 40	15 43	15 52			15 55	15 56	16 07	16 10	16 13		16 22	16 25	16 26
Northumberland Park	d	14 58					15 15			15 28								15 58			16 15				16 28
Meridian Water	d	15a01								15a31								16a01			16 17				16a31
Ponders End	d								15 29								15 59							16 30	
Brimsdown	d								15 32								16 02							16 32	
Enfield Lock	d						15 21		15 34								16 04				16 22			16 35	
Waltham Cross	d								15 37				15 50				16 07							16 37	
Cheshunt	d				15 18		15 25		15 39			15 48	15 52				16 09			16 18	16 26			16 40	
Broxbourne 3	a				15 23		15 30		15 45			15 53	15 58				16 15			16 23	16 31			16 45	
Broxbourne 3	d				15 23		15 34		15 45			15 53	15 58				16 15			16 23	16 35			16 46	
Rye House	d								15 48								16 18							16 49	
St Margarets (Herts)	d								15 51								16 21							16 52	
Ware	d								15 55								16 25							16 56	
Hertford East	a								16 01								16 31							17 04	
Roydon	d						15 39					15 57								16 27	16 39				
Harlow Town	d			15 25	15 29		15 43				15 55	16 01	16 11						16 25	16 31	16 43				
Harlow Mill	d						15 46					16 04								16 34	16 46				
Sawbridgeworth	d						15 49					16 08	16 17							16 38	16 50				
Bishops Stortford	a				15 38		15 56	15 45				16 14	16 23	16 17						16 44	16 58		16 47		
Bishops Stortford	d				15 42			15 46				16 14		16 18						16 44			16 48		
Stansted Mountfitchet	d			15 36	15 47							16 18							16 36	16 48					
Stansted Airport ✈	a			15 44				15 56			16 12			16 27					16 44				17 02		
Stansted Airport ✈	d		15 37												16 27							16 48			
Elsenham	d				15 52							16 22								16 52					
Newport (Essex)	d				15 58							16 27								16 57					
Audley End	d		15 56		16 02							16 30			16 41					17 00		17 05			
Great Chesterford	d				16 08							16 35								17 05					
Whittlesford Parkway	d		16 04		16 13							16 40								17 10		17 15			
Shelford	d				16 18							16 44								17 14					
Cambridge	a		16 15		16 27							16 51			16 56					17 21		17 28			
	d		16 16		16 29							16 53								17 21		17 29			
Cambridge North	a		16 20		16 34							16 58								17 25		17 33			

A To Birmingham New Street

B To Norwich

C To Ely

Table T022-F

Mondays to Fridays

16 December to 15 May

London - Broxbourne, Hertford East, Bishops Stortford, Stansted Airport, Cambridge and Cambridge North

Station			LE	LE ■	LE ■	XC ◇■ A	LE ■	LE B	LE ◇■	LE C	LE ■ D		LE ■	LE	LE	LE ◇■ E	LE F	LE ■	LE ■ G	LE B	LE ◇■		LE C	LE	LE ■
London Liverpool Street [15] ⊖	d		16 25	16 28			16 39	16 41	16 43				16 54	16 56		17 07		17 09		17 11	17 13				17 24
Hackney Downs	d							16 48						17 03						17 18					
Stratford [7] ⊖	d				16 30						16 47				17 00									17 17	
Lea Bridge	d				16 36						16 53				17 06									17 23	
Seven Sisters ⊖	d							16 54												17 24					
Tottenham Hale ⊖	d		16 37	16 40	16 43		16 52		16 55		16 58		17 06	17 10	17 10	17 19		17 22			17 25			17 28	17 36
Northumberland Park	d														17 12									17 31	
Meridian Water	d														17a15									17 33	
Ponders End	d				16 48						17 03														
Brimsdown	d				16 50									17 15											
Enfield Lock	d				16 53						17 07			17 18										17 38	
Waltham Cross	d				16 55					←	17 10			17 21									←	17 40	
Cheshunt	d				16 58			17 09	17 04	17 09	17 13			17 24						17 39	17 34		17 39	17 43	
Broxbourne [3]	a			16 53	17 03			→	17 10	17 15	17 18			17 31						→	17 39		17 45	17 48	
Broxbourne [3]	d			16 53	17 04				17 10	17 15	17 23										17 40		17 45	17 52	
Rye House	d									17 19													17 49	17 55	
St Margarets (Herts)	d									17 22													17 52	17 58	
Ware	d									17 26													17 56	18 02	
Hertford East	a									17 33													18 03	18 10	
Roydon	d								17 14		17 28								←		17 44				
Harlow Town	d		16 56	17 00	17 13				17 18		17 43		17 26					17 40	17 43		17 48				17 56
Harlow Mill	d								17 21		→								17 46		17 51				
Sawbridgeworth	d			17 05					17 25										17 50		17 55				
Bishops Stortford	a		17 05	17 11	17 25		17 17		17 31				17 35			17 43			17 58		18 01				18 05
Bishops Stortford	d		17 05	17 12			17 18		17 31				17 35			17 44					18 01				18 05
Stansted Mountfitchet	d			17 16					17 36									17 52			18 06				
Stansted Airport ✈	a		17 17				17 29						17 47					18 02							18 17
Stansted Airport ✈	d					17 27											17 56								
Elsenham	d								17 39												18 09				
Newport (Essex)	d								17 45												18 15				
Audley End	d			17 26		17 41			17 48							17 56	18 11				18 18				
Great Chesterford	d								17 53												18 23				
Whittlesford Parkway	d			17 33					17 57							18 04	18 19				18 28				
Shelford	d								18 02												18 32				
Cambridge	a			17 45		17 56			18 11							18 17	18 29				18 41				
	d															18 26	18 30								
Cambridge North	a															18 33	18 34								

Station		LE	LE ◇■	XC ◇■ A	LE	LE B	LE ◇■		LE C	LE ■ D	LE ■	LE	LE	LE ◇■ H	LE ■	LE ■ G	LE B		LE ◇■	LE C	LE	LE	LE	LE ■	XC ◇■ A
London Liverpool Street [15] ⊖	d	17 26	17 37		17 39	17 41	17 43				17 54	17 56		18 07	18 09		18 11		18 13			18 24	18 26	18 37	
Hackney Downs	d	17 33				17 48						18 03					18 18						18 33		
Stratford [7] ⊖	d									17 47			18 00								18 17				
Lea Bridge	d									17 53			18 06								18 23				
Seven Sisters ⊖	d					17 54											18 24								
Tottenham Hale ⊖	d	17 39	17 49		17 52		17 55			17 59	18 06	18 10	18 10	18 19	18 22				18 25		18 28	18 36	18 39	18 49	
Northumberland Park	d												18 12								18 31				
Meridian Water	d												18a15								18 33				
Ponders End	d	17 44								18 04													18 44		
Brimsdown	d	17 46										18 15											18 46		
Enfield Lock	d	17 49								18 08		18 18									18 38		18 49		
Waltham Cross	d	17 51							←	18 10		18 21								←	18 40		18 51		
Cheshunt	d	17 54				18 09	18 04		18 09	18 13		18 24					18 39		18 34	18 39	18 43		18 54		
Broxbourne [3]	a	18 01				→	18 09		18 15	18 18		18 31					→		18 39	18 45	18 48		19 01		
Broxbourne [3]	d						18 10		18 15	18 23									18 40	18 45	18 52				
Rye House	d								18 19											18 49	18 55				
St Margarets (Herts)	d								18 22											18 52	18 58				
Ware	d								18 26											18 56	19 02				
Hertford East	a								18 33											19 03	19 10				
Roydon	d						18 14			18 28						←			18 44						
Harlow Town	d				18 10		18 18			18 43	18 26				18 40	18 43			18 48			18 56			
Harlow Mill	d						18 21			→						18 46			18 51						
Sawbridgeworth	d				18 15		18 25									18 50			18 55						
Bishops Stortford	a		18 13				18 31				18 35			18 43		18 58			19 01			19 05		19 13	
Bishops Stortford	d		18 14				18 31				18 35			18 44					19 01			19 05		19 14	
Stansted Mountfitchet	d						18 36								18 52				19 06						
Stansted Airport ✈	a				18 32						18 47				19 01							19 17			
Stansted Airport ✈	d			18 21																					19 21
Elsenham	d						18 39												19 09						
Newport (Essex)	d						18 45												19 15						
Audley End	d		18 26	18 41			18 48							18 56					19 18					19 26	19 41
Great Chesterford	d						18 53												19 23						
Whittlesford Parkway	d		18 34				18 58							19 04					19 28					19 34	
Shelford	d						19 02												19 32						
Cambridge	a		18 49	18 56			19 14							19 17					19 41					19 49	19 56
	d		18 51											19 28										19 51	
Cambridge North	a		18 58											19 35										19 59	

A To Birmingham New Street
B To Hertford East
C From London Liverpool Street
D To Bishops Stortford
E The Fenman. ■ ◇ to Cambridge
F To Norwich
G From Stratford
H ■ ◇ to Cambridge

Table T022-F

Mondays to Fridays

16 December to 15 May

London - Broxbourne, Hertford East, Bishops Stortford, Stansted Airport, Cambridge and Cambridge North

Station		LE	LE A		LE ◇■	LE B	LE ■ C	LE ■	LE	LE	LE ◇■ D	LE ■	LE ■ E		LE ◇■	LE	LE ■	LE ◇■	LE ■	XC ◇■ F	LE ■	LE	LE		LE ■
London Liverpool Street [15] ⊖	d	18 39	18 41		18 43			18 54	18 56		19 07	19 09			19 11	19 13	19 25	19 28			19 40	19 42			19 55
Hackney Downs	d		18 48						19 03							19 19						19 48			
Stratford [7] ⊖	d						18 47			19 00									19 30				19 46		
Lea Bridge	d						18 53			19 06									19 36				19 52		
Seven Sisters ⊖	d		18 54																						
Tottenham Hale ⊖	d	18 52			18 55		18 58	19 06	19 09	19 10	19 19	19 22			19 25	19 28	19 37	19 40	19 43		19 52	19 55	19 56		20 07
Northumberland Park	d						19 01			19 12									19 45				19 58		
Meridian Water	d						19 03			19a15									19 47				20a01		
Ponders End	d								19 14							19 32						19 59			
Brimsdown	d								19 16							19 35						20 02			
Enfield Lock	d						19 08		19 19							19 37						20 04			
Waltham Cross	d					←	19 10		19 21							19 40			19 53			20 07			
Cheshunt	d		19 09		19 04	19 09	19 13		19 24						19 34	19 42		19 49	19 55			20 09			
Broxbourne [3]	a		→		19 09	19 15	19 18		19 31						19 39	19 48		19 55	20 01			20 15			
Broxbourne [3]	d				19 10	19 15	19 23		19 36						19 40	19 48		19 55	20 04			20 15			
Rye House	d					19 19			19 39							19 51						20 18			
St Margarets (Herts)	d					19 22			19 42							19 54						20 21			
Ware	d					19 26			19 47							19 58						20 25			
Hertford East	a					19 33			19 54							20 04						20 31			
Roydon	d				19 14		19 28						←		19 44			20 00	20 09						
Harlow Town	d	19 10			19 18		19 43	19 26				19 40	19 43		19 48		19 58	20 04	20 13						20 25
Harlow Mill	d				19 21		→						19 46		19 51			20 07	20 16						
Sawbridgeworth	d	19 15			19 25								19 50		19 55			20 10	20 19						
Bishops Stortford	a				19 31			19 35				19 49	19 56		20 01			20 16	20 28		20 20				
Bishops Stortford	d				19 31			19 35				19 49			20 01			20 17			20 21				
Stansted Mountfitchet	d				19 36							19 53			20 06			20 21							20 36
Stansted Airport ✈	a	19 32						19 47				20 00					20 15				20 30				20 44
Stansted Airport ✈	d																			20 21					
Elsenham	d				19 39										20 09			20 25							
Newport (Essex)	d				19 45										20 15			20 30							
Audley End	d				19 48						19 56				20 18			20 33		20 41					
Great Chesterford	d				19 53										20 23			20 38							
Whittlesford Parkway	d				19 58						20 03				20 28			20 43							
Shelford	d				20 02										20 32			20 47							
Cambridge	a				20 11						20 15				20 40			20 55		21 00					
	d																	20 57							
Cambridge North	a																	21 01							

Station		LE ◇■	LE ■	LE ■	LE	LE	LE ■	LE ◇■	LE ■		LE	XC ■	LE	LE	LE	LE ◇■	LE ■	LE ■	LE G		LE	LE	LE ■	LE ◇■	LE ■
London Liverpool Street [15] ⊖	d	19 58		20 10	20 12		20 25	20 28			20 40		20 42		20 55	20 58		21 10			21 12		21 25	21 28	
Hackney Downs	d				20 18								20 48								21 18				
Stratford [7] ⊖	d		20 00			20 16			20 30					20 46			21 00					21 16			21 30
Lea Bridge	d		20 06			20 22			20 36					20 52			21 06					21 22			21 36
Seven Sisters ⊖	d																								
Tottenham Hale ⊖	d	20 10	20 13	20 22	20 25	20 26	20 37	20 40	20 43		20 52		20 55	20 56	21 07	21 10	21 13	21 22			21 25	21 26	21 37	21 40	21 43
Northumberland Park	d		20 15			20 28								20 58			21 15					21 28			
Meridian Water	d					20a31								21a01								21a31			
Ponders End	d				20 29								20 59								21 29				
Brimsdown	d				20 32								21 02								21 32				
Enfield Lock	d		20 21		20 34								21 04				21 21				21 34				
Waltham Cross	d				20 37				20 50				21 07								21 37				21 50
Cheshunt	d	20 18	20 25		20 39			20 48	20 52				21 09			21 18	21 25				21 39			21 48	21 52
Broxbourne [3]	a	20 23	20 30		20 45			20 53	20 58				21 15			21 23	21 30				21 45			21 53	21 58
Broxbourne [3]	d	20 23	20 34		20 45			20 53	20 58				21 15			21 23	21 34				21 45			21 53	21 58
Rye House	d				20 48								21 18								21 48				
St Margarets (Herts)	d				20 51								21 21								21 51				
Ware	d				20 55								21 25								21 55				
Hertford East	a				21 01								21 31								22 01				
Roydon	d		20 39					20 57									21 39							21 57	
Harlow Town	d	20 29	20 43				20 55	21 01	21 11						21 25	21 29	21 43						21 55	22 01	22 11
Harlow Mill	d		20 46					21 04									21 46							22 04	
Sawbridgeworth	d	20 34	20 49					21 08	21 17							21 34	21 49							22 08	22 17
Bishops Stortford	a	20 40	20 56	20 45				21 14	21 23		21 17					21 40	21 56	21 45						22 14	22 23
Bishops Stortford	d	20 40		20 45				21 14			21 18					21 40		21 45						22 14	
Stansted Mountfitchet	d							21 18							21 36									22 18	
Stansted Airport ✈	a			20 55			21 12				21 27				21 44			21 57					22 14		
Stansted Airport ✈	d											21 27							22 10						
Elsenham	d							21 22																22 22	
Newport (Essex)	d							21 27																22 27	
Audley End	d	20 52						21 30				21 41				21 52			22 23					22 30	
Great Chesterford	d							21 35																22 35	
Whittlesford Parkway	d	21 00						21 40								22 00			22 31					22 40	
Shelford	d							21 44																22 44	
Cambridge	a	21 09						21 51				21 56				22 09			22 45					22 51	
	d							21 53											22 57					22 52	
Cambridge North	a							21 58											23 01					22 58	

A To Hertford East
B From London Liverpool Street
C To Bishops Stortford
D To Kings Lynn
E From Stratford
F To Birmingham New Street
G To Norwich

Table T022-F

Mondays to Fridays
16 December to 15 May

London - Broxbourne, Hertford East, Bishops Stortford, Stansted Airport, Cambridge and Cambridge North

	LE 1	XC 1	LE	LE	LE 1	LE ◇1	LE 1	LE 1	XC 1	LE	LE	LE 1	LE ◇1	LE 1	LE 1	LE	LE	LE	LE ◇1	LE 1	LE	LE
London Liverpool Street 15 ⊖ d	21 40		21 42		21 55	21 58		22 10		22 12		22 25	22 28		22 40	22 42		22 55	22 58		23 12	23 25
Hackney Downs d			21 48							22 18						22 48					23 18	
Stratford 7 ⊖ d				21 46			22 00				22 16			22 30			22 46			23 00		
Lea Bridge d				21 52			22 06				22 22			22 36			22 52			23 06		
Seven Sisters ⊖ d																						
Tottenham Hale ⊖ d	21 52		21 55	21 56	22 07	22 10	22 13	22 22		22 25	22 26	22 37	22 40	22 43	22 52	22 55	22 56	23 07	23 10	23 13	23 25	23 37
Northumberland Park d				21 58			22 15				22 28						22 58			23 15		
Meridian Water d				22a01							22a31						23a01					
Ponders End d			21 59							22 29						22 59					23 29	
Brimsdown d			22 02							22 32						23 02					23 32	
Enfield Lock d			22 04				22 21			22 34						23 04				23 21	23 34	
Waltham Cross d			22 07							22 37				22 50		23 07					23 37	
Cheshunt d			22 09			22 18	22 25			22 39			22 48	22 52		23 09			23 18	23 25	23 39	
Broxbourne 3 a			22 15			22 23	22 30			22 45			22 53	22 58		23 15			23 23	23 30	23 45	
Broxbourne 3 d			22 15			22 23	22 34			22 45			22 53	22 59		23 15			23 23	23 30	23 45	
Rye House d			22 18							22 48						23 18					23 48	
St Margarets (Herts) d			22 21							22 51						23 21					23 51	
Ware d			22 25							22 55						23 25					23 55	
Hertford East a			22 31							23 01						23 31					00 01	
Roydon d							22 39						22 57							23 34		
Harlow Town d					22 25	22 29	22 43					22 55	23 01	23 11				23 25	23 29	23 38		23 55
Harlow Mill d							22 46						23 04							23 41		
Sawbridgeworth d						22 34	22 49						23 08	23 17					23 34	23 45		
Bishops Stortford a	22 17					22 40	22 56	22 45					23 14	23 23	23 17				23 40	23 51		00 04
Bishops Stortford d	22 18					22 40		22 45					23 14		23 18				23 40			00 04
Stansted Mountfitchet d					22 36								23 18					23 37				
Stansted Airport ✈ a	22 27				22 44			22 55				23 12			23 30			23 44				00 13
Stansted Airport ✈ d		22 27							22 57													
Elsenham d													23 22									
Newport (Essex) d													23 27									
Audley End d		22 41				22 52			23 10				23 30						23 52			
Great Chesterford d													23 35									
Whittlesford Parkway d						23 00							23 40						23 59			
Shelford d													23 44									
Cambridge a		22 56				23 09			23 26				23 51						00 09			
d													23 53									
Cambridge North a													23 58									

	LE ◇1	LE	LE FX 1	LE FO 1
London Liverpool Street 15 ⊖ d	23 28	23 42	23 58	23 58
Hackney Downs d		23 48		
Stratford 7 ⊖ d				
Lea Bridge d				
Seven Sisters ⊖ d				
Tottenham Hale ⊖ d	23 40	23 54	00 10	00 10
Northumberland Park d		23 57		
Meridian Water d				
Ponders End d		00 01		
Brimsdown d		00 03		
Enfield Lock d		00 06		
Waltham Cross d		00 08		
Cheshunt d	23 48	00 11	00 18	00 18
Broxbourne 3 a	23 53	00 16	00 23	00 23
Broxbourne 3 d	23 53	00 16	00 23	00 23
Rye House d		00 20		
St Margarets (Herts) d		00 23		
Ware d		00 27		
Hertford East a		00 32		
Roydon d	23 57		00 27	00 27
Harlow Town d	00 01		00 31	00 31
Harlow Mill d	00 04		00 34	00 34
Sawbridgeworth d	00 08		00 38	00 38
Bishops Stortford a	00 14		00 44	00 44
Bishops Stortford d	00 14			00 44
Stansted Mountfitchet d	00 18			00 48
Stansted Airport ✈ a				
Stansted Airport ✈ d				
Elsenham d	00 22			00 52
Newport (Essex) d	00 27			00 57
Audley End d	00 30			01 00
Great Chesterford d	00 35			01 05
Whittlesford Parkway d	00 40			01 10
Shelford d	00 44			
Cambridge a	00 51			01 19
d				
Cambridge North a				

Table T022-F

Saturdays
21 December to 16 May

London - Broxbourne, Hertford East, Bishops Stortford, Stansted Airport, Cambridge and Cambridge North

	LE A	LE A	LE ◇1 A	LE 1 A	LE 1	LE 1	XC ◇1 B	LE	LE 1	LE ◇1 C	LE 1	LE ◇1 A	LE 1	XC ◇1 B	LE	LE 1 D	LE 1	LE ◇1	LE 1 A	LE E	LE 1	LE
London Liverpool Street 15 ⊖ d					03 40	04 10		04 40	05 10	05 20	05 25		05 40		05 42	05 51	05 55	05 58			06 10	06 12
Hackney Downs d															05 48							06 18
Stratford 7 ⊖ d										05 29						06 00						
Lea Bridge d										05 35						06 06						
Seven Sisters ⊖ d												←							←			
Tottenham Hale ⊖ d				00 10				04 52	05 22	05 40	05 37	05 40	05 52		05 55	06 13	06 07	06 10	06 13		06 22	06 25
Northumberland Park d										→						→			06 15			
Meridian Water d																						
Ponders End d	00 01														05 59							06 29
Brimsdown d	00 03														06 02							06 32
Enfield Lock d	00 06														06 04				06 21			06 34
Waltham Cross d	00 08														06 07							06 37
Cheshunt d	00 11			00 18				05 00				05 48			06 09			06 18	06 25			06 39
Broxbourne 3 a	00 16			00 23				05 05				05 53			06 15			06 23	06 30			06 45
Broxbourne 3 d	00 16			00 23				05 05				05 53			06 15			06 23	06 34			06 45
Rye House d	00 20														06 18							06 48
St Margarets (Herts) d	00 23														06 21							06 51
Ware d	00 27														06 25							06 55
Hertford East a	00 32														06 31							07 01
Roydon d				00 27								05 57							06 39			
Harlow Town d			00 01	00 31				05 11	05 38		05 53	06 01					06 24	06 29	06 43			
Harlow Mill d			00 04	00 34								06 04							06 46			
Sawbridgeworth d			00 08	00 38					05 43			06 08							06 49			
Bishops Stortford a			00 14	00 44				05 20	05 49		06 02	06 14	06 17				06 33	06 38	06 56		06 45	
Bishops Stortford d		00 04	00 14	00 44				05 20	05 50		06 02	06 14	06 18				06 33	06 39			06 45	
Stansted Mountfitchet d			00 18	00 48				05 24			06 06	06 18					06 37					
Stansted Airport ✈ a		00 13			04 30	05 00		05 39	05 59		06 13		06 27				06 44				06 57	
Stansted Airport ✈ d							05 27							06 27						06 48		
Elsenham d			00 22	00 52								06 22										
Newport (Essex) d			00 27	00 57								06 27										
Audley End d			00 30	01 00			05 41					06 30		06 41				06 51		07 02		
Great Chesterford d			00 35	01 05								06 35										
Whittlesford Parkway d			00 40	01 10								06 40						06 58		07 10		
Shelford d			00 44									06 44										
Cambridge a			00 51	01 19			05 55					06 51		06 56				07 07		07 19		
d												06 53						07 16		07 20		
Cambridge North a												06 58						07 20		07 24		

	LE	LE 1 D	LE	LE ◇1	LE 1 A	LE 1	XC ◇1 B	LE	LE	LE 1	LE ◇1	LE 1	LE E	LE	LE	LE	LE	LE ◇1	LE 1	LE 1	XC ◇1 B	LE
London Liverpool Street 15 ⊖ d		06 21	06 25	06 28		06 40		06 42		06 55	06 58			07 10	07 12		07 25	07 28		07 40		07 42
Hackney Downs d								06 48							07 18							07 48
Stratford 7 ⊖ d	06 16	06 30							06 46			07 00				07 16			07 30			
Lea Bridge d	06 22	06 36							06 52			07 06				07 22			07 36			
Seven Sisters ⊖ d					←																	
Tottenham Hale ⊖ d	06 26	06 43	06 37	06 40	06 43	06 52		06 55	06 56	07 07	07 10	07 13		07 22	07 25	07 26	07 37	07 40	07 43	07 52		07 55
Northumberland Park d	06 28	→							06 58			07 15				07 28						
Meridian Water d	06a31								07a01							07a31						
Ponders End d								06 59							07 29							07 59
Brimsdown d								07 02							07 32							08 02
Enfield Lock d								07 04				07 21			07 34							08 04
Waltham Cross d					06 50			07 07							07 37				07 50			08 07
Cheshunt d				06 48	06 52			07 09			07 18	07 25			07 39			07 48	07 52			08 09
Broxbourne 3 a				06 53	06 58			07 15			07 23	07 30			07 45			07 53	07 58			08 15
Broxbourne 3 d				06 53	06 58			07 15			07 23	07 34			07 45			07 53	07 58			08 15
Rye House d								07 18							07 48							08 18
St Margarets (Herts) d								07 21							07 51							08 21
Ware d								07 25							07 55							08 25
Hertford East a								07 31							08 01							08 31
Roydon d				06 57								07 39						07 57				
Harlow Town d			06 55	07 01	07 11					07 25	07 29	07 43					07 55	08 01	08 11			
Harlow Mill d				07 04								07 46						08 04				
Sawbridgeworth d				07 08	07 17							07 49						08 08	08 17			
Bishops Stortford a				07 14	07 23	07 17					07 38	07 56		07 45				08 14	08 23	08 17		
Bishops Stortford d				07 14		07 18					07 39			07 45				08 14		08 18		
Stansted Mountfitchet d				07 18						07 36								08 18				
Stansted Airport ✈ a			07 13			07 27				07 44				07 57			08 13			08 27		
Stansted Airport ✈ d							07 27						07 48								08 27	
Elsenham d				07 22														08 22				
Newport (Essex) d				07 27														08 27				
Audley End d				07 30			07 41				07 51		08 02					08 30			08 41	
Great Chesterford d				07 35														08 35				
Whittlesford Parkway d				07 40							07 58		08 10					08 40				
Shelford d				07 44														08 44				
Cambridge a				07 51			07 57				08 09		08 19					08 51			08 56	
d				07 53							08 13		08 20					08 53				
Cambridge North a				07 58							08 18		08 24					08 58				

A From London Liverpool Street
B To Birmingham New Street
C To Cambridge North
D To Bishops Stortford
E To Norwich

Table T022-F

Saturdays

21 December to 16 May

London - Broxbourne, Hertford East, Bishops Stortford, Stansted Airport, Cambridge and Cambridge North

		LE		LE ■	LE ◇■	LE ■	LE A	LE ■	LE	LE	LE ■	LE ◇■		LE ■	LE	XC ◇■ B	LE	LE	LE ■	LE ◇■	LE ■	LE A		LE ■	LE
London Liverpool Street [15] ⊖	d			07 55	07 58			08 10	08 12		08 25	08 28			08 40		08 42		08 55	08 58				09 10	09 12
Hackney Downs	d								08 18								08 48								09 18
Stratford [7] ⊖	d	07 46				08 00				08 16				08 30				08 46			09 00				
Lea Bridge	d	07 52				08 06				08 22				08 36				08 52			09 06				
Seven Sisters ⊖	d																								
Tottenham Hale ⊖	d	07 56		08 07	08 10	08 13		08 22	08 25	08 26	08 37	08 40		08 43	08 52		08 55	08 56	09 07	09 10	09 13			09 22	09 25
Northumberland Park	d	07 58				08 15				08 28								08 58			09 15				
Meridian Water	d	08a01								08a31								09a01							
Ponders End	d								08 29								08 59								09 29
Brimsdown	d								08 32								09 02								09 32
Enfield Lock	d					08 21			08 34								09 04				09 21				09 34
Waltham Cross	d								08 37					08 50			09 07								09 37
Cheshunt	d				08 18	08 25			08 39			08 48		08 52			09 09			09 18	09 25				09 39
Broxbourne [3]	a				08 23	08 30			08 45			08 53		08 58			09 15			09 23	09 30				09 45
Broxbourne [3]	d				08 23	08 34			08 45			08 53		08 58			09 15			09 23	09 34				09 45
Rye House	d								08 48								09 18								09 48
St Margarets (Herts)	d								08 51								09 21								09 51
Ware	d								08 55								09 25								09 55
Hertford East	a								09 01								09 31								10 01
Roydon	d					08 39						08 57									09 39				
Harlow Town	d			08 25	08 29	08 43					08 55	09 01		09 11					09 25	09 29	09 43				
Harlow Mill	d					08 46						09 04									09 46				
Sawbridgeworth	d					08 49						09 08		09 17							09 49				
Bishops Stortford	a				08 38	08 56		08 45				09 14		09 23	09 17					09 38	09 56			09 45	
Bishops Stortford	d				08 39			08 45				09 14			09 18					09 39				09 45	
Stansted Mountfitchet	d			08 36								09 18							09 36						
Stansted Airport ✈	a			08 44				08 57			09 14				09 27				09 44					09 57	
Stansted Airport ✈	d						08 48									09 27						09 48			
Elsenham	d											09 22													
Newport (Essex)	d											09 27													
Audley End	d				08 51		09 02					09 30				09 41				09 51		10 02			
Great Chesterford	d											09 35													
Whittlesford Parkway	d				08 58		09 10					09 40								09 58		10 10			
Shelford	d											09 44													
Cambridge	a				09 09		09 19					09 51				09 56				10 09		10 19			
	d				09 13		09 30					09 53								10 13		10 26			
Cambridge North	a				09 18		09 34					09 58								10 18		10 30			

		LE	LE	LE ◇■	LE ■	LE	XC ◇■ B	LE		LE	LE ■	LE ◇■	LE ■	LE A	LE ■	LE	LE	LE ■		LE ◇■	LE ■	LE ■	XC ◇■ B	LE	LE
London Liverpool Street [15] ⊖	d		09 25	09 28		09 40		09 42			09 55	09 58			10 10	10 12		10 25		10 28		10 40		10 42	
Hackney Downs	d							09 48								10 18								10 48	
Stratford [7] ⊖	d	09 16			09 30					09 46			10 00				10 16				10 30				10 46
Lea Bridge	d	09 22			09 36					09 52			10 06				10 22				10 36				10 52
Seven Sisters ⊖	d																								
Tottenham Hale ⊖	d	09 26	09 37	09 40	09 43	09 52		09 55		09 56	10 07	10 10	10 13		10 22	10 25	10 26	10 37		10 40	10 43	10 52		10 55	10 56
Northumberland Park	d	09 28								09 58			10 15				10 28								10 58
Meridian Water	d	09a31								10a01							10a31								11a01
Ponders End	d							09 59								10 29								10 59	
Brimsdown	d							10 02								10 32								11 02	
Enfield Lock	d							10 04					10 21			10 34								11 04	
Waltham Cross	d				09 50			10 07								10 37					10 50			11 07	
Cheshunt	d			09 48	09 52			10 09				10 18	10 25			10 39				10 48	10 52			11 09	
Broxbourne [3]	a			09 53	09 58			10 15				10 23	10 30			10 45				10 53	10 58			11 15	
Broxbourne [3]	d			09 53	09 58			10 15				10 23	10 34			10 45				10 53	10 58			11 15	
Rye House	d							10 18								10 48								11 18	
St Margarets (Herts)	d							10 21								10 51								11 21	
Ware	d							10 25								10 55								11 25	
Hertford East	a							10 31								11 01								11 31	
Roydon	d			09 57									10 39							10 57					
Harlow Town	d		09 55	10 01	10 11						10 25	10 29	10 43					10 55		11 01	11 11				
Harlow Mill	d			10 04									10 46							11 04					
Sawbridgeworth	d			10 08	10 17								10 49							11 08	11 17				
Bishops Stortford	a			10 14	10 23	10 17						10 38	10 56		10 45					11 14	11 23	11 17			
Bishops Stortford	d			10 14		10 18						10 39			10 45					11 14		11 18			
Stansted Mountfitchet	d			10 18							10 36									11 18					
Stansted Airport ✈	a		10 14			10 27					10 44				10 57			11 14				11 27			
Stansted Airport ✈	d						10 27							10 48									11 27		
Elsenham	d			10 22																11 22					
Newport (Essex)	d			10 27																11 27					
Audley End	d			10 30			10 41					10 51		11 02						11 30			11 41		
Great Chesterford	d			10 35																11 35					
Whittlesford Parkway	d			10 40								10 58		11 10						11 40					
Shelford	d			10 44																11 44					
Cambridge	a			10 51			10 56					11 09		11 19						11 51			11 56		
	d			10 53								11 13		11 20						11 53					
Cambridge North	a			10 58								11 18		11 24						11 58					

A To Norwich
B To Birmingham New Street

Table T022-F

Saturdays

21 December to 16 May

London - Broxbourne, Hertford East, Bishops Stortford, Stansted Airport, Cambridge and Cambridge North

		LE	LE ◇■	LE ■		LE A	LE ■	LE	LE	LE ■	LE ◇■	LE ■	LE	XC ◇■ B		LE	LE	LE	LE ◇■	LE ■	LE A	LE ■	LE	LE	
London Liverpool Street [15] ⊖	d	10 55	10 58				11 10	11 12		11 25	11 28		11 40			11 42		11 55	11 58			12 10	12 12		
Hackney Downs	d							11 18								11 48							12 18		
Stratford [7] ⊖	d			11 00					11 16			11 30					11 46			12 00				12 16	
Lea Bridge	d			11 06					11 22			11 36					11 52			12 06				12 22	
Seven Sisters ⊖	d																								
Tottenham Hale ⊖	d	11 07	11 10	11 13			11 22	11 25	11 26	11 37	11 40	11 43	11 52			11 55	11 56	12 07	12 10	12 13		12 22	12 25	12 26	
Northumberland Park	d			11 15					11 28								11 58			12 15				12 28	
Meridian Water	d								11a31								12a01							12a31	
Ponders End	d							11 29								11 59							12 29		
Brimsdown	d							11 32								12 02							12 32		
Enfield Lock	d			11 21				11 34								12 04				12 21			12 34		
Waltham Cross	d							11 37				11 50				12 07							12 37		
Cheshunt	d		11 18	11 25				11 39			11 48	11 52				12 09			12 18	12 25			12 39		
Broxbourne [3]	a		11 23	11 30				11 45			11 53	11 58				12 15			12 23	12 30			12 45		
Broxbourne [3]	d		11 23	11 34				11 45			11 53	11 58				12 15			12 23	12 34			12 45		
Rye House	d							11 48								12 18							12 48		
St Margarets (Herts)	d							11 51								12 21							12 51		
Ware	d							11 55								12 25							12 55		
Hertford East	a							12 01								12 31							13 01		
Roydon	d			11 39							11 57									12 39					
Harlow Town	d	11 25	11 29	11 43						11 55	12 01	12 11						12 25	12 29	12 43					
Harlow Mill	d			11 46							12 04									12 46					
Sawbridgeworth	d			11 49							12 08	12 17								12 49					
Bishops Stortford	a		11 38	11 56			11 45				12 14	12 23	12 17						12 38	12 56		12 45			
Bishops Stortford	d		11 39				11 45				12 14		12 18						12 39			12 45			
Stansted Mountfitchet	d	11 36									12 18							12 36							
Stansted Airport ✈	a	11 44					11 57			12 14			12 27					12 44				12 57			
Stansted Airport ✈	d					11 48								12 27							12 48				
Elsenham	d										12 22														
Newport (Essex)	d										12 27														
Audley End	d		11 51			12 02					12 30			12 41					12 51		13 02				
Great Chesterford	d										12 35														
Whittlesford Parkway	d		11 58			12 10					12 40								12 58		13 10				
Shelford	d										12 44														
Cambridge	a		12 09			12 19					12 51			12 56					13 09		13 19				
	d		12 13			12 20					12 53								13 13		13 20				
Cambridge North	a		12 18			12 24					12 58								13 18		13 24				

		LE ■	LE ◇■	LE ■	LE ■	XC ◇■ B	LE	LE	LE ■	LE ◇■		LE ■	LE A	LE	LE	LE	LE ■	LE ◇■	LE ■	LE ■		XC ◇■ B	LE	LE	LE
London Liverpool Street [15] ⊖	d	12 25	12 28		12 40		12 42		12 55	12 58				13 10	13 12		13 25	13 28		13 40			13 42		13 55
Hackney Downs	d						12 48								13 18								13 48		
Stratford [7] ⊖	d			12 30				12 46				13 00				13 16			13 30					13 46	
Lea Bridge	d			12 36				12 52				13 06				13 22			13 36					13 52	
Seven Sisters ⊖	d																								
Tottenham Hale ⊖	d	12 37	12 40	12 43	12 52		12 55	12 56	13 07	13 10		13 13		13 22	13 25	13 26	13 37	13 40	13 43	13 52			13 55	13 56	14 07
Northumberland Park	d							12 58				13 15				13 28								13 58	
Meridian Water	d							13a01								13a31								14a01	
Ponders End	d						12 59								13 29								13 59		
Brimsdown	d						13 02								13 32								14 02		
Enfield Lock	d						13 04					13 21			13 34								14 04		
Waltham Cross	d			12 50			13 07								13 37				13 50				14 07		
Cheshunt	d		12 48	12 52			13 09			13 18		13 25			13 39			13 48	13 52				14 09		
Broxbourne [3]	a		12 53	12 58			13 15			13 23		13 30			13 45			13 53	13 58				14 15		
Broxbourne [3]	d		12 53	12 58			13 15			13 23		13 34			13 45			13 53	13 58				14 15		
Rye House	d						13 18								13 48								14 18		
St Margarets (Herts)	d						13 21								13 51								14 21		
Ware	d						13 25								13 55								14 25		
Hertford East	a						13 31								14 01								14 31		
Roydon	d		12 57									13 39						13 57							
Harlow Town	d	12 55	13 01	13 11					13 25	13 29		13 43					13 55	14 01	14 11						14 25
Harlow Mill	d		13 04									13 46						14 04							
Sawbridgeworth	d		13 08	13 17								13 49						14 08	14 17						
Bishops Stortford	a		13 14	13 23	13 17					13 38		13 56		13 45				14 14	14 23	14 17					
Bishops Stortford	d		13 14		13 18					13 39				13 45				14 14		14 18					
Stansted Mountfitchet	d		13 18						13 36									14 18							14 36
Stansted Airport ✈	a	13 14			13 27				13 44					13 57			14 14			14 27					14 44
Stansted Airport ✈	d					13 27							13 48									14 27			
Elsenham	d		13 22															14 22							
Newport (Essex)	d		13 27															14 27							
Audley End	d		13 30			13 41				13 51			14 02					14 30				14 41			
Great Chesterford	d		13 35															14 35							
Whittlesford Parkway	d		13 40							13 58			14 10					14 40							
Shelford	d		13 44															14 44							
Cambridge	a		13 51			13 56				14 09			14 19					14 51				14 56			
	d		13 53							14 13			14 20					14 53							
Cambridge North	a		13 58							14 18			14 24					14 58							

A To Norwich
B To Birmingham New Street

Table T022-F

Saturdays

21 December to 16 May

London - Broxbourne, Hertford East, Bishops Stortford, Stansted Airport, Cambridge and Cambridge North

		LE ◇1	LE 1	LE A	LE	LE	LE	LE 1	LE ◇1	LE 1	LE 1	XC ◇1 B	LE	LE	LE 1	LE ◇1	LE 1	LE A	LE 1	LE	LE	LE	LE ◇1
London Liverpool Street 15 ⊖	d	13 58			14 10	14 12		14 25	14 28		14 40		14 42		14 55	14 58			15 10	15 12		15 25	15 28
Hackney Downs	d					14 18							14 48							15 18			
Stratford 7 ⊖	d		14 00				14 16			14 30				14 46			15 00				15 16		
Lea Bridge	d		14 06				14 22			14 36				14 52			15 06				15 22		
Seven Sisters ⊖	d																						
Tottenham Hale ⊖	d	14 10	14 13		14 22	14 25	14 26	14 37	14 40	14 43	14 52		14 55	14 56	15 07	15 10	15 13		15 22	15 25	15 26	15 37	15 40
Northumberland Park	d		14 15				14 28							14 58			15 15				15 28		
Meridian Water	d						14a31							15a01							15a31		
Ponders End	d					14 29							14 59							15 29			
Brimsdown	d					14 32							15 02							15 32			
Enfield Lock	d		14 21			14 34							15 04				15 21			15 34			
Waltham Cross	d					14 37				14 50			15 07							15 37			
Cheshunt	d	14 18	14 25			14 39			14 48	14 52			15 09			15 18	15 25			15 39			15 48
Broxbourne 3	a	14 23	14 30			14 45			14 53	14 58			15 15			15 23	15 30			15 45			15 53
Broxbourne 3	d	14 23	14 34			14 45			14 53	14 58			15 15			15 23	15 34			15 45			15 53
Rye House	d					14 48							15 18							15 48			
St Margarets (Herts)	d					14 51							15 21							15 51			
Ware	d					14 55							15 25							15 55			
Hertford East	a					15 01							15 31							16 01			
Roydon	d		14 39						14 57								15 39						15 57
Harlow Town	d	14 29	14 43					14 55	15 01	15 11					15 25	15 29	15 43					15 55	16 01
Harlow Mill	d		14 46						15 04								15 46						16 04
Sawbridgeworth	d		14 49						15 08	15 17							15 49						16 08
Bishops Stortford	a	14 38	14 56		14 45				15 14	15 23	15 17					15 38	15 56		15 45				16 14
Bishops Stortford	d	14 39			14 45				15 14		15 18					15 39			15 45				16 14
Stansted Mountfitchet	d								15 18						15 36								16 18
Stansted Airport ✈	a				14 57			15 14			15 27				15 44				15 57			16 14	
Stansted Airport ✈	d			14 48								15 27						15 48					
Elsenham	d								15 22														16 22
Newport (Essex)	d								15 27														16 27
Audley End	d	14 51		15 02					15 30			15 41				15 51		16 02					16 30
Great Chesterford	d								15 35														16 35
Whittlesford Parkway	d	14 58		15 10					15 40							15 58		16 10					16 40
Shelford	d								15 44														16 44
Cambridge	a	15 09		15 19					15 51			15 56				16 09		16 19					16 51
	d	15 13		15 20					15 53							16 13		16 20					16 53
Cambridge North	a	15 18		15 24					15 58							16 18		16 24					16 58

		LE 1	LE 1	XC ◇1 B	LE	LE	LE 1	LE ◇1	LE 1	LE A	LE	LE	LE	LE	LE ◇1	LE 1	LE 1	XC ◇1 B	LE	LE	LE 1	LE ◇1
London Liverpool Street 15 ⊖	d		15 40		15 42		15 55	15 58			16 10	16 12		16 25	16 28		16 40		16 42		16 55	16 58
Hackney Downs	d				15 48							16 18							16 48			
Stratford 7 ⊖	d	15 30				15 46			16 00				16 16			16 30				16 46		
Lea Bridge	d	15 36				15 52			16 06				16 22			16 36				16 52		
Seven Sisters ⊖	d																					
Tottenham Hale ⊖	d	15 43	15 52		15 55	15 56	16 07	16 10	16 13		16 22	16 25	16 26	16 37	16 40	16 43	16 52		16 55	16 56	17 07	17 10
Northumberland Park	d					15 58			16 15				16 28							16 58		
Meridian Water	d					16a01							16a31							17a01		
Ponders End	d				15 59							16 29							16 59			
Brimsdown	d				16 02							16 32							17 02			
Enfield Lock	d				16 04				16 21			16 34							17 04			
Waltham Cross	d	15 50			16 07							16 37				16 50			17 07			
Cheshunt	d	15 52			16 09			16 18	16 25			16 39			16 48	16 52			17 09			17 18
Broxbourne 3	a	15 58			16 15			16 23	16 30			16 45			16 53	16 58			17 15			17 23
Broxbourne 3	d	15 58			16 15			16 23	16 34			16 45			16 53	16 58			17 15			17 23
Rye House	d				16 18							16 48							17 18			
St Margarets (Herts)	d				16 21							16 51							17 21			
Ware	d				16 25							16 55							17 25			
Hertford East	a				16 31							17 01							17 31			
Roydon	d								16 39						16 57							
Harlow Town	d	16 11					16 25	16 29	16 43					16 55	17 01	17 11					17 25	17 29
Harlow Mill	d								16 46						17 04							
Sawbridgeworth	d	16 17							16 49						17 08	17 17						
Bishops Stortford	a	16 23	16 17					16 38	16 56		16 45				17 14	17 23	17 17					17 38
Bishops Stortford	d		16 18					16 39			16 45				17 14		17 18					17 39
Stansted Mountfitchet	d						16 36								17 18						17 36	
Stansted Airport ✈	a		16 27				16 44				16 57			17 14			17 27				17 44	
Stansted Airport ✈	d			16 27						16 48								17 27				
Elsenham	d														17 22							
Newport (Essex)	d														17 27							
Audley End	d			16 41				16 51		17 02					17 30			17 41				17 51
Great Chesterford	d														17 35							
Whittlesford Parkway	d							16 58		17 10					17 40							17 58
Shelford	d														17 44							
Cambridge	a			16 56				17 09		17 19					17 51			17 56				18 09
	d							17 13		17 20					17 53							18 13
Cambridge North	a							17 18		17 24					17 58							18 18

A To Norwich

B To Birmingham New Street

Table T022-F

Saturdays

21 December to 16 May

London - Broxbourne, Hertford East, Bishops Stortford, Stansted Airport, Cambridge and Cambridge North

		LE 1	LE A	LE 1	LE	LE	LE 1	LE ◇1	LE 1	LE	XC ◇1 B	LE	LE	LE 1	LE ◇1	LE 1	LE A	LE 1	LE	LE	LE	LE ◇1	LE 1
London Liverpool Street 15 ⊖	d			17 10	17 12		17 25	17 28		17 40		17 42		17 55	17 58			18 10	18 12		18 25	18 28	
Hackney Downs	d				17 18							17 48							18 18				
Stratford 7 ⊖	d	17 00				17 16			17 30				17 46			18 00				18 16			18 30
Lea Bridge	d	17 06				17 22			17 36				17 52			18 06				18 22			18 36
Seven Sisters ⊖	d																						
Tottenham Hale ⊖	d	17 13		17 22	17 25	17 26	17 37	17 40	17 43	17 52		17 55	17 56	18 07	18 10	18 13		18 22	18 25	18 26	18 37	18 40	18 43
Northumberland Park	d	17 15				17 28							17 58			18 15				18 28			
Meridian Water	d					17a31							18a01							18a31			
Ponders End	d				17 29							17 59							18 29				
Brimsdown	d				17 32							18 02							18 32				
Enfield Lock	d	17 21			17 34							18 04				18 21			18 34				
Waltham Cross	d				17 37				17 50			18 07							18 37				18 50
Cheshunt	d	17 25			17 39			17 48	17 52			18 09			18 18	18 25			18 39			18 48	18 52
Broxbourne 3	a	17 30			17 45			17 53	17 58			18 15			18 23	18 30			18 45			18 53	18 58
Broxbourne 3	d	17 34			17 45			17 53	17 58			18 15			18 23	18 34			18 45			18 53	18 58
Rye House	d				17 48							18 18							18 48				
St Margarets (Herts)	d				17 51							18 21							18 51				
Ware	d				17 55							18 25							18 55				
Hertford East	a				18 01							18 31							19 01				
Roydon	d	17 39						17 57								18 39						18 57	
Harlow Town	d	17 43					17 55	18 01	18 11					18 25	18 29	18 43					18 55	19 01	19 11
Harlow Mill	d	17 46						18 04								18 46						19 04	
Sawbridgeworth	d	17 49						18 08	18 17							18 49						19 08	19 17
Bishops Stortford	a	17 56		17 45				18 14	18 23	18 17					18 38	18 56		18 45				19 14	19 23
Bishops Stortford	d			17 45				18 14		18 18					18 39			18 45				19 14	
Stansted Mountfitchet	d							18 18						18 36								19 18	
Stansted Airport ✈	a			17 57			18 14			18 27				18 43				18 57			19 14		
Stansted Airport ✈	d		17 48								18 27						18 48						
Elsenham	d							18 22														19 22	
Newport (Essex)	d							18 27														19 27	
Audley End	d		18 02					18 30			18 41				18 51		19 02					19 30	
Great Chesterford	d							18 35														19 35	
Whittlesford Parkway	d		18 10					18 40							18 58		19 10					19 40	
Shelford	d							18 44														19 44	
Cambridge	a		18 19					18 51			18 56				19 09		19 19					19 51	
	d		18 20					18 53							19 13		19 20					19 53	
Cambridge North	a		18 24					18 58							19 18		19 24					19 58	

		LE	XC ◇1 B	LE	LE	LE 1	LE ◇1	LE 1	LE A	LE 1	LE	LE	LE 1	LE ◇1	LE 1	LE 1	XC 1	LE	LE	LE 1	LE ◇1	LE 1
London Liverpool Street 15 ⊖	d	18 40		18 42		18 55	18 58			19 10	19 12		19 25	19 28		19 40		19 42		19 55	19 58	
Hackney Downs	d			18 48							19 18							19 48				
Stratford 7 ⊖	d				18 46			19 00				19 16			19 30				19 46			20 00
Lea Bridge	d				18 52			19 06				19 22			19 36				19 52			20 06
Seven Sisters ⊖	d																					
Tottenham Hale ⊖	d	18 52		18 55	18 56	19 07	19 10	19 13		19 22	19 25	19 26	19 37	19 40	19 43	19 52		19 55	19 56	20 07	20 10	20 13
Northumberland Park	d				18 58			19 15				19 28							19 58			20 15
Meridian Water	d				19a01							19a31							20a01			
Ponders End	d			18 59							19 29							19 59				
Brimsdown	d			19 02							19 32							20 02				
Enfield Lock	d			19 04				19 21			19 34							20 04				20 21
Waltham Cross	d			19 07							19 37				19 50			20 07				
Cheshunt	d			19 09			19 18	19 25			19 39			19 48	19 52			20 09			20 18	20 25
Broxbourne 3	a			19 15			19 23	19 30			19 45			19 53	19 58			20 15			20 23	20 30
Broxbourne 3	d			19 15			19 23	19 34			19 45			19 53	19 58			20 15			20 23	20 34
Rye House	d			19 18							19 48							20 18				
St Margarets (Herts)	d			19 21							19 51							20 21				
Ware	d			19 25							19 55							20 25				
Hertford East	a			19 31							20 01							20 31				
Roydon	d							19 39						19 57								20 39
Harlow Town	d					19 25	19 29	19 43					19 55	20 01	20 11					20 25	20 29	20 43
Harlow Mill	d							19 46						20 04								20 46
Sawbridgeworth	d							19 49						20 08	20 17							20 49
Bishops Stortford	a	19 17					19 38	19 56		19 45				20 14	20 23	20 17					20 38	20 56
Bishops Stortford	d	19 18					19 39			19 45				20 14		20 18					20 39	
Stansted Mountfitchet	d					19 36								20 18						20 36		
Stansted Airport ✈	a	19 27				19 44				19 57			20 14			20 27				20 44		
Stansted Airport ✈	d		19 27						19 48								20 27					
Elsenham	d													20 22								
Newport (Essex)	d													20 27								
Audley End	d		19 41				19 51		20 02					20 30			20 41				20 51	
Great Chesterford	d													20 35								
Whittlesford Parkway	d						19 58		20 10					20 40							20 58	
Shelford	d													20 44								
Cambridge	a		19 56				20 09		20 19					20 51			20 58				21 09	
	d						20 13		20 20					20 53							21 13	
Cambridge North	a						20 18		20 24					20 58							21 18	

A To Norwich

B To Birmingham New Street

Table T022-F

Saturdays
21 December to 16 May

London - Broxbourne, Hertford East, Bishops Stortford, Stansted Airport, Cambridge and Cambridge North

		LE	LE	LE	LE	LE	LE	LE	LE	XC
		A	■			■	◇■	■		■
London Liverpool Street ⊖	d		20 10	20 12		20 25	20 28		20 40	
Hackney Downs	d			20 18						
Stratford	d				20 16			20 30		
Lea Bridge	d				20 22			20 36		
Seven Sisters ⊖	d									
Tottenham Hale ⊖	d		20 22	20 25	20 26	20 37	20 40	20 43	20 52	
Northumberland Park	d				20 28					
Meridian Water	d				20a31					
Ponders End	d			20 29						
Brimsdown	d			20 32						
Enfield Lock	d			20 34						
Waltham Cross	d			20 37				20 50		
Cheshunt	d			20 39			20 48	20 52		
Broxbourne	a			20 45			20 53	20 58		
Broxbourne	d			20 45			20 53	20 58		
Rye House	d			20 48						
St Margarets (Herts)	d			20 51						
Ware	d			20 55						
Hertford East	a			21 01						
Roydon	d						20 57			
Harlow Town	d					20 55	21 01	21 11		
Harlow Mill	d						21 04			
Sawbridgeworth	d						21 08	21 17		
Bishops Stortford	a		20 45				21 14	21 23	21 17	
Bishops Stortford	d		20 45				21 14		21 18	
Stansted Mountfitchet	d						21 18			
Stansted Airport ✈	a		20 57			21 14			21 27	
Stansted Airport ✈	d	20 43								21 27
Elsenham	d						21 22			
Newport (Essex)	d						21 27			
Audley End	d	21 02					21 30			21 41
Great Chesterford	d						21 35			
Whittlesford Parkway	d	21 10					21 40			
Shelford	d						21 44			
Cambridge	a	21 19					21 51			21 56
Cambridge	d	21 20					21 53			
Cambridge North	a	21 24					21 58			

		LE	LE	LE	LE	LE	LE	LE	LE	LE	LE	LE	LE	LE
					◇■	■	■	A			■	◇■	■	■
London Liverpool Street ⊖	d	20 42		20 55	20 58		21 10		21 12		21 25	21 28		21 40
Hackney Downs	d	20 48							21 18					
Stratford	d		20 46			21 00				21 16			21 30	
Lea Bridge	d		20 52			21 06				21 22			21 36	
Seven Sisters ⊖	d													
Tottenham Hale ⊖	d	20 55	20 56	21 07	21 10	21 13	21 22		21 25	21 26	21 37	21 40	21 43	21 52
Northumberland Park	d		20 58			21 15				21 28				
Meridian Water	d		21a01							21a31				
Ponders End	d	20 59							21 29					
Brimsdown	d	21 02							21 32					
Enfield Lock	d	21 04				21 21			21 34					
Waltham Cross	d	21 07							21 37				21 50	
Cheshunt	d	21 09			21 18	21 25			21 39			21 48	21 52	
Broxbourne	a	21 15			21 23	21 30			21 45			21 53	21 58	
Broxbourne	d	21 15			21 23	21 34			21 45			21 53	21 58	
Rye House	d	21 18							21 48					
St Margarets (Herts)	d	21 21							21 51					
Ware	d	21 25							21 55					
Hertford East	a	21 31							22 01					
Roydon	d					21 39						21 57		
Harlow Town	d			21 25	21 29	21 43					21 55	22 01	22 11	
Harlow Mill	d					21 46						22 04		
Sawbridgeworth	d					21 49						22 08	22 17	
Bishops Stortford	a				21 38	21 56	21 45					22 14	22 23	22 17
Bishops Stortford	d				21 39		21 45					22 14		22 18
Stansted Mountfitchet	d			21 36								22 18		
Stansted Airport ✈	a			21 44			21 55				22 14			22 27
Stansted Airport ✈	d							22 10						
Elsenham	d											22 22		
Newport (Essex)	d											22 27		
Audley End	d				21 51			22 25				22 30		
Great Chesterford	d											22 35		
Whittlesford Parkway	d				21 58			22 33				22 40		
Shelford	d											22 44		
Cambridge	a				22 09			22 43				22 51		
Cambridge	d				22 13			22 55				22 59		
Cambridge North	a				22 18			22 59				23 04		

		XC	LE	LE	LE	LE	LE	LE	LE	LE	LE	LE
		■			■	◇■	■	■			■	◇■
London Liverpool Street ⊖	d		21 42		21 55	21 58		22 10	22 12		22 25	22 28
Hackney Downs	d		21 48						22 18			
Stratford	d			21 46			22 00			22 16		
Lea Bridge	d			21 52			22 06			22 22		
Seven Sisters ⊖	d											
Tottenham Hale ⊖	d		21 55	21 56	22 07	22 10	22 13	22 22	22 25	22 26	22 37	22 40
Northumberland Park	d			21 58			22 15			22 28		
Meridian Water	d			22a01						22a31		
Ponders End	d		21 59						22 29			
Brimsdown	d		22 02						22 32			
Enfield Lock	d		22 04				22 21		22 34			
Waltham Cross	d		22 07						22 37			
Cheshunt	d		22 09			22 18	22 25		22 39			22 48
Broxbourne	a		22 15			22 23	22 30		22 45			22 53
Broxbourne	d		22 15			22 23	22 34		22 45			22 53
Rye House	d		22 18						22 48			
St Margarets (Herts)	d		22 21						22 51			
Ware	d		22 25						22 55			
Hertford East	a		22 31						23 01			
Roydon	d						22 39					22 57
Harlow Town	d				22 25	22 29	22 43				22 55	23 01
Harlow Mill	d						22 46					23 04
Sawbridgeworth	d						22 49					23 08
Bishops Stortford	a					22 38	22 56	22 45				23 14
Bishops Stortford	d					22 39		22 45				23 14
Stansted Mountfitchet	d				22 36							23 18
Stansted Airport ✈	a				22 44			22 55			23 12	
Stansted Airport ✈	d	22 27										
Elsenham	d											23 22
Newport (Essex)	d											23 27
Audley End	d	22 41				22 51						23 30
Great Chesterford	d											23 35
Whittlesford Parkway	d					22 58						23 40
Shelford	d											23 44
Cambridge	a	22 58				23 08						23 51
Cambridge	d											23 52
Cambridge North	a											23 57

		LE	LE	XC	LE	LE	LE	LE	LE	LE	LE	LE
		■	■	■				◇■	■			◇■
London Liverpool Street ⊖	d		22 40		22 42		22 55	22 58		23 12	23 25	23 28
Hackney Downs	d				22 48					23 18		
Stratford	d	22 30				22 46			23 00			
Lea Bridge	d	22 36				22 52			23 06			
Seven Sisters ⊖	d											
Tottenham Hale ⊖	d	22 43	22 52		22 55	22 56	23 07	23 10	23 13	23 25	23 37	23 40
Northumberland Park	d					22 58			23 15			
Meridian Water	d					23a01						
Ponders End	d				22 59					23 29		
Brimsdown	d				23 02					23 32		
Enfield Lock	d				23 04				23 21	23 34		
Waltham Cross	d	22 50			23 07					23 37		
Cheshunt	d	22 52			23 09			23 18	23 25	23 39		23 48
Broxbourne	a	22 58			23 15			23 23	23 30	23 45		23 53
Broxbourne	d	22 58			23 15			23 23	23 30	23 45		23 53
Rye House	d				23 18					23 48		
St Margarets (Herts)	d				23 21					23 51		
Ware	d				23 25					23 55		
Hertford East	a				23 31					00 01		
Roydon	d								23 34			23 57
Harlow Town	d	23 11					23 25	23 29	23 38		23 55	00 01
Harlow Mill	d								23 41			00 04
Sawbridgeworth	d	23 17							23 45			00 08
Bishops Stortford	a	23 23	23 17					23 38	23 51		00 04	00 14
Bishops Stortford	d		23 18					23 39			00 04	00 14
Stansted Mountfitchet	d						23 36					00 18
Stansted Airport ✈	a		23 27				23 43				00 13	
Stansted Airport ✈	d			23 27								
Elsenham	d											00 22
Newport (Essex)	d											00 27
Audley End	d			23 41				23 51				00 30
Great Chesterford	d											00 35
Whittlesford Parkway	d							23 58				00 40
Shelford	d											00 44
Cambridge	a			23 58				00 08				00 51
Cambridge	d											
Cambridge North	a											

A To Norwich

NRT DECEMBER 19 EDITION

Table T022-F

Saturdays
21 December to 16 May

London - Broxbourne, Hertford East, Bishops Stortford, Stansted Airport, Cambridge and Cambridge North

		LE	LE
			■
London Liverpool Street ⊖	d	23 42	23 58
Hackney Downs	d	23 49	
Stratford	d		
Lea Bridge	d		
Seven Sisters ⊖	d		
Tottenham Hale ⊖	d	23 55	00 10
Northumberland Park	d	23 58	
Meridian Water	d		
Ponders End	d	00 02	
Brimsdown	d	00 04	
Enfield Lock	d	00 07	
Waltham Cross	d	00 09	
Cheshunt	d	00 12	00 18
Broxbourne	a	00 17	00 23
Broxbourne	d	00 17	00 23
Rye House	d	00 21	
St Margarets (Herts)	d	00 24	
Ware	d	00 28	
Hertford East	a	00 33	
Roydon	d		00 27
Harlow Town	d		00 31
Harlow Mill	d		00 34
Sawbridgeworth	d		00 38
Bishops Stortford	a		00 44
Bishops Stortford	d		00 44
Stansted Mountfitchet	d		00 48
Stansted Airport ✈	a		
Stansted Airport ✈	d		
Elsenham	d		00 52
Newport (Essex)	d		00 57
Audley End	d		01 00
Great Chesterford	d		01 05
Whittlesford Parkway	d		01 10
Shelford	d		
Cambridge	a		01 19
Cambridge	d		
Cambridge North	a		

Sundays
15 December to 10 May

		LE	LE	LE	LE	LE	LE	LE	LE	LE	LE
				◇■	■			■	■	■	■
		A	A	A	A						
London Liverpool Street ⊖	d					04 10	04 40	05 10	05 40	06 10	06 25
Hackney Downs	d										
Stratford	d										
Lea Bridge	d										
Seven Sisters ⊖	d										
Tottenham Hale ⊖	d				00 10		04 52	05 22	05 52	06 22	06 37
Northumberland Park	d										
Meridian Water	d										
Ponders End	d	00 02									
Brimsdown	d	00 04									
Enfield Lock	d	00 07									
Waltham Cross	d	00 09									
Cheshunt	d	00 12			00 18				06 00		
Broxbourne	a	00 17			00 23				06 05		
Broxbourne	d	00 17			00 23				06 05		
Rye House	d	00 21									
St Margarets (Herts)	d	00 24									
Ware	d	00 28									
Hertford East	a	00 33									
Roydon	d				00 27						
Harlow Town	d			00 01	00 31		05 08	05 38	06 11		06 53
Harlow Mill	d			00 04	00 34						
Sawbridgeworth	d			00 08	00 38						
Bishops Stortford	a			00 14	00 44		05 17	05 47	06 20	06 45	
Bishops Stortford	d		00 04	00 14	00 44		05 18	05 48	06 21	06 46	
Stansted Mountfitchet	d			00 18	00 48		05 22				07 04
Stansted Airport ✈	a		00 13			04 58	05 34	05 57	06 30	06 55	07 12
Stansted Airport ✈	d										
Elsenham	d			00 22	00 52						
Newport (Essex)	d			00 27	00 57						
Audley End	d			00 30	01 00						
Great Chesterford	d			00 35	01 05						
Whittlesford Parkway	d			00 40	01 10						
Shelford	d			00 44							
Cambridge	a			00 51	01 19						
Cambridge	d										
Cambridge North	a										

		LE	LE	LE	LE	LE	LE	LE	LE	LE	LE	LE	LE
			■		■	◇	■		◇■	■	◇■	■	■
						B			C		D		E
London Liverpool Street ⊖	d	06 40	06 55	07 10	07 25		07 40		07 42	07 55		08 10	
Hackney Downs	d								07 48				
Stratford	d												
Lea Bridge	d												
Seven Sisters ⊖	d												
Tottenham Hale ⊖	d	06 52	07 07	07 22	07 37		07 52		07 55	08 07		08 22	
Northumberland Park	d												
Meridian Water	d												
Ponders End	d								07 59				
Brimsdown	d								08 02				
Enfield Lock	d								08 04				
Waltham Cross	d								08 07				
Cheshunt	d								08 09				
Broxbourne	a								08 15				
Broxbourne	d							08 10	08 23				
Rye House	d							08 13					
St Margarets (Herts)	d							08 16					
Ware	d							08 20					
Hertford East	a							08 27					
Roydon	d								08 27		←		
Harlow Town	d		07 23		07 53				08 31 →	08 23	08 31		
Harlow Mill	d										08 34		
Sawbridgeworth	d										08 38		
Bishops Stortford	a	07 15		07 45			08 15				08 44	08 47	
Bishops Stortford	d	07 16		07 46			08 16				08 44	08 48	
Stansted Mountfitchet	d				08 04						08 48		
Stansted Airport ✈	a	07 25	07 40	07 55	08 12		08 27			08 40		08 57	
Stansted Airport ✈	d					08 18							09 09 →
Elsenham	d										08 52		
Newport (Essex)	d										08 57		
Audley End	d					08 33					09 00		
Great Chesterford	d										09 05		
Whittlesford Parkway	d					08 41					09 10		
Shelford	d												
Cambridge	a					08 49					09 19		
Cambridge	d					08 50					09 20		
Cambridge North	a					08 54					09 25		

A not 15 December. From London Liverpool Street
B To Norwich
C To Cambridge North
D From London Liverpool Street
E To Cambridge

Table T022-F

Sundays

15 December to 10 May

London - Broxbourne, Hertford East, Bishops Stortford, Stansted Airport, Cambridge and Cambridge North

Station		LE	LE ■	LE ◇■	LE ■	LE ■		LE	LE	LE	LE ◇■	LE ■	LE A	LE	LE	LE		LE ◇■	LE A	LE ■	XC ◇■ B	LE	LE	LE ■	LE ◇■
London Liverpool Street 15 ⊖	d		08 25	08 28		08 40				08 55	08 57	09 10				09 25		09 28		09 40				09 55	09 57
Hackney Downs	d										09 03														10 03
Stratford 7 ⊖	d	08 14						08 44	08 54					09 14	09 24							09 44	09 54		
Lea Bridge	d	08 20						08 50	09 00					09 20	09 30							09 50	10 00		
Seven Sisters ⊖	d																								
Tottenham Hale ⊖	d	08 25	08 37	08 40		08 52		08 55	09 04	09 07	09 10	09 22		09 25	09 34	09 37		09 40		09 52		09 55	10 04	10 07	10 10
Northumberland Park	d								09 06						09 36								10 06		
Meridian Water	d								09a09						09a39								10a09		
Ponders End	d	08 29						08 59						09 29								09 59			
Brimsdown	d	08 32						09 02						09 32								10 02			
Enfield Lock	d	08 34						09 04						09 34								10 04			
Waltham Cross	d	08 37						09 07						09 37								10 07			
Cheshunt	d	08 39		08 48				09 09			09 18			09 39				09 48				10 09			10 18
Broxbourne 3	a	08 45		08 53				09 15			09 23			09 45				09 53				10 15			10 23
Broxbourne 3	d	08 45		08 53				09 15			09 23			09 45				09 53				10 15			10 23
Rye House	d	08 48						09 18						09 48								10 18			
St Margarets (Herts)	d	08 51						09 21						09 51								10 21			
Ware	d	08 55						09 25						09 55								10 25			
Hertford East	a	09 01						09 31						10 01								10 31			
Roydon	d										09 27														10 27
Harlow Town	d		08 55	08 59						09 25	09 31					09 55		09 59						10 25	10 31
Harlow Mill	d										09 34														10 34
Sawbridgeworth	d			09 04							09 38							10 04							10 38
Bishops Stortford	a			09 10		09 15					09 44	09 47						10 10		10 15					10 44
Bishops Stortford	d			09 10		09 16					09 44	09 48						10 10		10 15					10 44
Stansted Mountfitchet	d		09 06								09 48					10 06									10 48
Stansted Airport ✈	a		09 13		←	09 25				09 42		09 57				10 13			←	10 25				10 42	
Stansted Airport ✈	d				09 09								10 09						10 09		10 27				
Elsenham	d										09 52		→												10 52
Newport (Essex)	d										09 57														10 57
Audley End	d			09 22	09 26						10 00							10 22	10 26		10 41				11 00
Great Chesterford	d										10 05														11 05
Whittlesford Parkway	d			09 30	09 34						10 10							10 30	10 34						11 10
Shelford	d			09 34														10 34							
Cambridge	a			09 41	09 45						10 19							10 41	10 45		10 55				11 19
	d			09 42							10 20							10 42	10 50						11 20
Cambridge North	a			09 47							10 28							10 47	10 54						11 28

Station		LE ■		LE A	LE	LE	LE ■	LE ◇■	LE A	LE ■	XC ◇■ B	LE		LE	LE	LE ◇■	LE	LE A	LE	LE	LE ■	LE ◇■		LE A	LE
London Liverpool Street 15 ⊖	d	10 10					10 25	10 28		10 40					10 55	10 57	11 10				11 25	11 28			11 40
Hackney Downs	d															11 03									
Stratford 7 ⊖	d				10 14	10 24						10 44		10 54					11 14	11 24					
Lea Bridge	d				10 20	10 30						10 50		11 00					11 20	11 30					
Seven Sisters ⊖	d																								
Tottenham Hale ⊖	d	10 22			10 25	10 34	10 37	10 40		10 52		10 55		11 04	11 07	11 10	11 22		11 25	11 34	11 37	11 40			11 52
Northumberland Park	d					10 36								11 06						11 36					
Meridian Water	d					10a39								11a09						11a39					
Ponders End	d				10 29							10 59							11 29						
Brimsdown	d				10 32							11 02							11 32						
Enfield Lock	d				10 34							11 04							11 34						
Waltham Cross	d				10 37							11 07							11 37						
Cheshunt	d				10 39			10 48				11 09				11 18			11 39			11 48			
Broxbourne 3	a				10 45			10 53				11 15				11 23			11 45			11 53			
Broxbourne 3	d				10 45			10 53				11 15				11 23			11 45			11 53			
Rye House	d				10 48							11 18							11 48						
St Margarets (Herts)	d				10 51							11 21							11 51						
Ware	d				10 55							11 25							11 55						
Hertford East	a				11 01							11 31							12 01						
Roydon	d															11 27									
Harlow Town	d						10 55	10 59							11 25	11 31					11 55	11 59			
Harlow Mill	d															11 34									
Sawbridgeworth	d							11 04								11 38						12 04			
Bishops Stortford	a	10 47						11 10		11 15						11 44	11 47					12 10			12 15
Bishops Stortford	d	10 48						11 10		11 15						11 44	11 48					12 10			12 15
Stansted Mountfitchet	d						11 06									11 48					12 06				
Stansted Airport ✈	a	10 57					11 13		←	11 25					11 42		11 57				12 13			←	12 25
Stansted Airport ✈	d			11 09					11 09		11 27							12 09						12 09	
Elsenham	d			→												11 52		→							
Newport (Essex)	d															11 57									
Audley End	d							11 22	11 26		11 41					12 00						12 22		12 26	
Great Chesterford	d															12 05									
Whittlesford Parkway	d							11 30	11 34							12 10						12 30		12 34	
Shelford	d							11 34														12 34			
Cambridge	a							11 41	11 45		11 55					12 19						12 41		12 45	
	d							11 42	11 50							12 20						12 42		12 50	
Cambridge North	a							11 48	11 54							12 28						12 47		12 54	

A To Norwich B To Birmingham New Street

Table T022-F

Sundays

15 December to 10 May

London - Broxbourne, Hertford East, Bishops Stortford, Stansted Airport, Cambridge and Cambridge North

Station		XC ◇■ A	LE	LE	LE ■	LE ◇■	LE ■	LE B		LE	LE	LE ■	LE ◇■	LE B	LE ■	XC ◇■ A	LE	LE		LE ■	LE ◇■	LE	LE B	LE	LE
London Liverpool Street 15 ⊖	d				11 55	11 57	12 10					12 25	12 28		12 40					12 55	12 57	13 10			
Hackney Downs	d					12 03															13 03				
Stratford 7 ⊖	d		11 44	11 54						12 14	12 24						12 44	12 54						13 14	13 24
Lea Bridge	d		11 50	12 00						12 20	12 30						12 50	13 00						13 20	13 30
Seven Sisters ⊖	d																								
Tottenham Hale ⊖	d		11 55	12 04	12 07	12 10	12 22			12 25	12 34	12 37	12 40		12 52		12 55	13 04		13 07	13 10	13 22		13 25	13 34
Northumberland Park	d			12 06							12 36							13 06							13 36
Meridian Water	d			12a09							12a39							13a09							13a39
Ponders End	d		11 59							12 29							12 59							13 29	
Brimsdown	d		12 02							12 32							13 02							13 32	
Enfield Lock	d		12 04							12 34							13 04							13 34	
Waltham Cross	d		12 07							12 37							13 07							13 37	
Cheshunt	d		12 09			12 18				12 39			12 48				13 09				13 18			13 39	
Broxbourne 3	a		12 15			12 23				12 45			12 53				13 15				13 23			13 45	
Broxbourne 3	d		12 15			12 23				12 45			12 53				13 15				13 23			13 45	
Rye House	d		12 18							12 48							13 18							13 48	
St Margarets (Herts)	d		12 21							12 51							13 21							13 51	
Ware	d		12 25							12 55							13 25							13 55	
Hertford East	a		12 31							13 01							13 31							14 01	
Roydon	d					12 27															13 27				
Harlow Town	d				12 25	12 31						12 55	12 59							13 25	13 31				
Harlow Mill	d					12 34															13 34				
Sawbridgeworth	d					12 38							13 04								13 38				
Bishops Stortford	a					12 44	12 47						13 10		13 15						13 44	13 47			
Bishops Stortford	d					12 44	12 48						13 10		13 15						13 44	13 48			
Stansted Mountfitchet	d					12 48						13 06									13 48				
Stansted Airport ✈	a				12 42		12 57					13 13		←	13 25					13 42		13 57			
Stansted Airport ✈	d	12 27						13 09						13 09		13 27							14 09		
Elsenham	d					12 52		→													13 52		→		
Newport (Essex)	d					12 57															13 57				
Audley End	d	12 41				13 00							13 22	13 26		13 41					14 00				
Great Chesterford	d					13 05															14 05				
Whittlesford Parkway	d					13 10							13 30	13 34							14 10				
Shelford	d												13 34												
Cambridge	a	12 55				13 19							13 41	13 45		13 55					14 19				
	d					13 20							13 42	13 50							14 20				
Cambridge North	a					13 28							13 47	13 54							14 28				

Station		LE	LE ◇■	LE B		LE ■	XC ◇■ A	LE	LE	LE	LE ◇■	LE ■	LE B	LE		LE	LE ■	LE ◇■	LE B	LE ■	XC ◇■ A 🍴	LE	LE	LE ■	
London Liverpool Street 15 ⊖	d	13 25	13 28			13 40				13 55	13 57	14 10					14 25	14 28		14 40				14 55	
Hackney Downs	d										14 03														
Stratford 7 ⊖	d							13 44	13 54					14 14		14 24						14 44	14 54		
Lea Bridge	d							13 50	14 00					14 20		14 30						14 50	15 00		
Seven Sisters ⊖	d																								
Tottenham Hale ⊖	d	13 37	13 40			13 52		13 55	14 04	14 07	14 10	14 22		14 25		14 34	14 37	14 40		14 52		14 55	15 04	15 07	
Northumberland Park	d								14 06							14 36							15 06		
Meridian Water	d								14a09							14a39							15a09		
Ponders End	d							13 59						14 29								14 59			
Brimsdown	d							14 02						14 32								15 02			
Enfield Lock	d							14 04						14 34								15 04			
Waltham Cross	d							14 07						14 37								15 07			
Cheshunt	d		13 48					14 09			14 18			14 39				14 48				15 09			
Broxbourne 3	a		13 53					14 15			14 23			14 45				14 53				15 15			
Broxbourne 3	d		13 53					14 15			14 23			14 45				14 53				15 15			
Rye House	d							14 18						14 48								15 18			
St Margarets (Herts)	d							14 21						14 51								15 21			
Ware	d							14 25						14 55								15 25			
Hertford East	a							14 31						15 01								15 31			
Roydon	d										14 27														
Harlow Town	d	13 55	13 59							14 25	14 31						14 55	14 59						15 25	
Harlow Mill	d										14 34														
Sawbridgeworth	d		14 04								14 38							15 04							
Bishops Stortford	a		14 10			14 15					14 44	14 47						15 10		15 15					
Bishops Stortford	d		14 10			14 15					14 44	14 48						15 10		15 15					
Stansted Mountfitchet	d	14 06									14 48						15 06								
Stansted Airport ✈	a	14 13		←		14 25				14 42		14 57					15 13		←	15 25				15 42	
Stansted Airport ✈	d			14 09			14 27						15 09						15 09		15 27				
Elsenham	d										14 52		→												
Newport (Essex)	d										14 57														
Audley End	d		14 22	14 26			14 41				15 00							15 22	15 26		15 41				
Great Chesterford	d										15 05														
Whittlesford Parkway	d		14 30	14 34							15 10							15 30	15 34						
Shelford	d		14 34															15 34							
Cambridge	a		14 41	14 45			14 55				15 19							15 41	15 45		15 55				
	d		14 42	14 50							15 20							15 42	15 50						
Cambridge North	a		14 47	14 54							15 28							15 47	15 54						

A To Birmingham New Street B To Norwich

Table T022-F

Sundays

15 December to 10 May

London - Broxbourne, Hertford East, Bishops Stortford, Stansted Airport, Cambridge and Cambridge North

		LE ◇1	LE 1	LE	LE	LE	LE	LE ◇1	LE	LE	XC ◇1	LE	LE	LE 1	LE ◇1	LE	LE	LE	LE	LE 1	LE ◇1	LE	LE 1
				A					A		B ⌶						A					A	
London Liverpool Street [15] ⊖	d	14 57	15 10				15 25	15 28		15 40				15 55	15 57	16 10				16 25	16 28		16 40
Hackney Downs	d	15 03													16 03								
Stratford [7] ⊖	d				15 14	15 24						15 44	15 54					16 14	16 24				
Lea Bridge	d				15 20	15 30						15 50	16 00					16 20	16 30				
Seven Sisters ⊖	d																						
Tottenham Hale ⊖	d	15 10	15 22		15 25	15 34	15 37	15 40		15 52		15 55	16 04	16 07	16 10	16 22		16 25	16 34	16 37	16 40		16 52
Northumberland Park	d					15 36							16 06						16 36				
Meridian Water	d					15a39							16a09						16a39				
Ponders End	d				15 29							15 59						16 29					
Brimsdown	d				15 32							16 02						16 32					
Enfield Lock	d				15 34							16 04						16 34					
Waltham Cross	d				15 37							16 07						16 37					
Cheshunt	d	15 18			15 39			15 48				16 09			16 18			16 39			16 48		
Broxbourne [3]	a	15 23			15 45			15 53				16 15			16 23			16 45			16 53		
Broxbourne [3]	d	15 23			15 45			15 53				16 15			16 23			16 45			16 53		
Rye House	d				15 48							16 18						16 48					
St Margarets (Herts)	d				15 51							16 21						16 51					
Ware	d				15 55							16 25						16 55					
Hertford East	a				16 01							16 31						17 01					
Roydon	d	15 27													16 27								
Harlow Town	d	15 31					15 55	15 59						16 25	16 31					16 55	16 59		
Harlow Mill	d	15 34													16 34								
Sawbridgeworth	d	15 38						16 04							16 38						17 04		
Bishops Stortford	a	15 44	15 47					16 10		16 15					16 44	16 47					17 10		17 15
Bishops Stortford	d	15 44	15 48					16 10		16 15					16 44	16 48					17 10		17 15
Stansted Mountfitchet	d	15 48					16 06								16 48					17 06			
Stansted Airport ✈	a		15 57				16 13		←	16 25				16 42		16 57				17 13		←	17 25
Stansted Airport ✈	d			16 09					16 09		16 27						17 09					17 09	
Elsenham	d	15 52		→											16 52		→						
Newport (Essex)	d	15 57													16 57								
Audley End	d	16 00						16 22	16 26		16 41				17 00						17 22	17 26	
Great Chesterford	d	16 05													17 05								
Whittlesford Parkway	d	16 10						16 30	16 34						17 10						17 30	17 34	
Shelford	d							16 34													17 34		
Cambridge	a	16 19						16 41	16 45		16 55				17 19						17 41	17 45	
	d	16 20						16 42	16 50						17 20						17 42	17 50	
Cambridge North	a	16 28						16 47	16 54						17 28						17 47	17 54	

		XC ◇1	LE	LE	LE 1	LE ◇1	LE 1	LE	LE	LE	LE 1	LE ◇1	LE	LE	XC ◇1	LE	LE	LE 1	LE ◇1	LE 1	LE	LE	LE
		B ⌶						A					A		B						A		
London Liverpool Street [15] ⊖	d				16 55	16 57	17 10				17 25	17 28		17 40				17 55	17 57	18 10			
Hackney Downs	d					17 03													18 03				
Stratford [7] ⊖	d		16 44	16 54					17 14	17 24						17 44	17 54					18 14	18 24
Lea Bridge	d		16 50	17 00					17 20	17 30						17 50	18 00					18 20	18 30
Seven Sisters ⊖	d																						
Tottenham Hale ⊖	d		16 55	17 04	17 07	17 10	17 22		17 25	17 34	17 37	17 40		17 52		17 55	18 04	18 07	18 10	18 22		18 25	18 34
Northumberland Park	d			17 06						17 36							18 06						18 36
Meridian Water	d			17a09						17a39							18a09						18a39
Ponders End	d		16 59						17 29							17 59						18 29	
Brimsdown	d		17 02						17 32							18 02						18 32	
Enfield Lock	d		17 04						17 34							18 04						18 34	
Waltham Cross	d		17 07						17 37							18 07						18 37	
Cheshunt	d		17 09			17 18			17 39			17 48				18 09			18 18			18 39	
Broxbourne [3]	a		17 15			17 23			17 45			17 53				18 15			18 23			18 45	
Broxbourne [3]	d		17 15			17 23			17 45			17 53				18 15			18 23			18 45	
Rye House	d		17 18						17 48							18 18						18 48	
St Margarets (Herts)	d		17 21						17 51							18 21						18 51	
Ware	d		17 25						17 55							18 25						18 55	
Hertford East	a		17 31						18 01							18 31						19 01	
Roydon	d					17 27													18 27				
Harlow Town	d				17 25	17 31					17 55	17 59						18 25	18 31				
Harlow Mill	d					17 34													18 34				
Sawbridgeworth	d					17 38						18 04							18 38				
Bishops Stortford	a					17 44	17 47					18 10		18 15					18 44	18 47			
Bishops Stortford	d					17 44	17 48					18 10		18 15					18 44	18 48			
Stansted Mountfitchet	d					17 48					18 06								18 48				
Stansted Airport ✈	a				17 42		17 57				18 13		←	18 25				18 42		18 57			
Stansted Airport ✈	d	17 27						18 09					18 09		18 27						19 09		
Elsenham	d					17 52		→											18 52		→		
Newport (Essex)	d					17 57													18 57				
Audley End	d	17 41				18 00						18 22	18 26		18 41				19 00				
Great Chesterford	d					18 05													19 05				
Whittlesford Parkway	d					18 10						18 30	18 34						19 10				
Shelford	d											18 34											
Cambridge	a	17 55				18 19						18 41	18 45		18 55				19 19				
	d					18 20						18 42	18 50						19 20				
Cambridge North	a					18 28						18 47	18 54						19 28				

A To Norwich B To Birmingham New Street

NRT DECEMBER 19 EDITION

Table T022-F

Sundays

15 December to 10 May

London - Broxbourne, Hertford East, Bishops Stortford, Stansted Airport, Cambridge and Cambridge North

		LE	LE ◇1	LE	LE 1	XC ◇1	LE	LE	LE 1	LE ◇1	LE 1	LE	LE	LE	LE 1	LE ◇1	LE	LE 1	XC 1	LE	LE	LE
				A		B						A					A					
London Liverpool Street [15] ⊖	d	18 25	18 28		18 40				18 55	18 57	19 10				19 25	19 28		19 40				19 55
Hackney Downs	d									19 03												
Stratford [7] ⊖	d						18 44	18 54					19 14	19 24						19 44	19 54	
Lea Bridge	d						18 50	19 00					19 20	19 30						19 50	20 00	
Seven Sisters ⊖	d																					
Tottenham Hale ⊖	d	18 37	18 40		18 52		18 55	19 04	19 07	19 10	19 22		19 25	19 34	19 37	19 40		19 52		19 55	20 04	20 07
Northumberland Park	d							19 06						19 36							20 06	
Meridian Water	d							19a09						19a39							20a09	
Ponders End	d						18 59						19 29							19 59		
Brimsdown	d						19 02						19 32							20 02		
Enfield Lock	d						19 04						19 34							20 04		
Waltham Cross	d						19 07						19 37							20 07		
Cheshunt	d		18 48				19 09			19 18			19 39			19 48				20 09		
Broxbourne [3]	a		18 53				19 15			19 23			19 45			19 53				20 15		
Broxbourne [3]	d		18 53				19 15			19 23			19 45			19 53				20 15		
Rye House	d						19 18						19 48							20 18		
St Margarets (Herts)	d						19 21						19 51							20 21		
Ware	d						19 25						19 55							20 25		
Hertford East	a						19 31						20 01							20 31		
Roydon	d									19 27												
Harlow Town	d	18 55	18 59						19 25	19 31					19 55	19 59						20 25
Harlow Mill	d									19 34												
Sawbridgeworth	d		19 04							19 38						20 04						
Bishops Stortford	a		19 10		19 15					19 44	19 47					20 10		20 15				
Bishops Stortford	d		19 10		19 15					19 44	19 48					20 10		20 15				
Stansted Mountfitchet	d	19 06								19 48					20 06							
Stansted Airport ✈	a	19 13		←	19 25				19 42		19 57				20 13		←	20 25				20 42
Stansted Airport ✈	d			19 09		19 27						20 09					20 09		20 27			
Elsenham	d									19 52		→										
Newport (Essex)	d									19 57												
Audley End	d		19 22	19 26		19 41				20 00						20 22	20 26		20 41			
Great Chesterford	d									20 05												
Whittlesford Parkway	d		19 30	19 34						20 10						20 30	20 34					
Shelford	d		19 34													20 34						
Cambridge	a		19 41	19 45		19 55				20 19						20 41	20 45		20 55			
	d		19 42	19 50						20 20						20 42	20 50					
Cambridge North	a		19 47	19 54						20 28						20 47	20 54					

		LE ◇1	LE 1	XC 1	LE	LE	LE	LE 1	LE ◇1	LE	LE	LE	LE	LE 1	LE ◇1	LE 1	LE	LE	LE	LE 1	LE ◇1	LE	LE 1
							A			A							C						
London Liverpool Street [15] ⊖	d	19 57	20 10					20 25	20 28		20 40			20 55	20 57	21 10				21 25	21 28		21 40
Hackney Downs	d	20 03													21 03								
Stratford [7] ⊖	d				20 14	20 24						20 44	20 54					21 14	21 24				
Lea Bridge	d				20 20	20 30						20 50	21 00					21 20	21 30				
Seven Sisters ⊖	d																						
Tottenham Hale ⊖	d	20 10	20 22		20 25	20 34		20 37	20 40		20 52	20 55	21 04	21 07	21 10	21 22		21 25	21 34	21 37	21 40		21 52
Northumberland Park	d					20 36							21 06						21 36				
Meridian Water	d					20a39							21a09						21a39				
Ponders End	d				20 29							20 59						21 29					
Brimsdown	d				20 32							21 02						21 32					
Enfield Lock	d				20 34							21 04						21 34					
Waltham Cross	d				20 37							21 07						21 37					
Cheshunt	d	20 18			20 39				20 48			21 09			21 18			21 39			21 48		
Broxbourne [3]	a	20 23			20 45				20 53			21 15			21 23			21 45			21 53		
Broxbourne [3]	d	20 23			20 45				20 53			21 15			21 23			21 45			21 53		
Rye House	d				20 48							21 18						21 48					
St Margarets (Herts)	d				20 51							21 21						21 51					
Ware	d				20 55							21 25						21 55					
Hertford East	a				21 01							21 31						22 01					
Roydon	d	20 27													21 27								
Harlow Town	d	20 31						20 55	20 59					21 25	21 31					21 55	21 59		
Harlow Mill	d	20 34													21 34								
Sawbridgeworth	d	20 38							21 04						21 38						22 04		
Bishops Stortford	a	20 44	20 47						21 10		21 15				21 44	21 47					22 10		22 15
Bishops Stortford	d	20 44	20 48						21 10		21 15				21 44	21 48					22 10		22 15
Stansted Mountfitchet	d	20 48						21 06							21 48					22 06			
Stansted Airport ✈	a		20 57					21 15		←	21 28			21 42		21 57				22 13		←	22 25
Stansted Airport ✈	d			21 04			21 11			21 11							22 09					22 09	
Elsenham	d	20 52					→								21 52		→						
Newport (Essex)	d	20 57													21 57								
Audley End	d	21 00		21 18					21 22	21 33					22 00						22 22	22 26	
Great Chesterford	d	21 05													22 05								
Whittlesford Parkway	d	21 10							21 30	21 41					22 10						22 30	22 34	
Shelford	d								21 34												22 34		
Cambridge	a	21 19		21 33					21 41	21 49					22 19						22 41	22 44	
	d	21 20								21 50					22 20								
Cambridge North	a	21 28								21 54					22 25								

A To Norwich B To Birmingham New Street C To Cambridge

Table T022-F

Sundays
15 December to 10 May

London - Broxbourne, Hertford East, Bishops Stortford, Stansted Airport, Cambridge and Cambridge North

		XC ■	LE	LE	LE ■	LE ◇■	LE	XC ■	LE	LE	LE ■	LE ◇■	LE ■	LE	LE	LE ◇■	LE ■	LE ■	LE	LE ■
London Liverpool Street 15 ⊖	d				21 55	21 57	22 10				22 25	22 28	22 40		22 55	22 57	23 25	23 28		23 58
Hackney Downs	d					22 03										23 03				
Stratford 7 ⊖	d		21 44	21 54					22 14	22 24				22 44					23 32	
Lea Bridge	d		21 50	22 00					22 20	22 30				22 50					23 38	
Seven Sisters ⊖	d																			
Tottenham Hale ⊖	d		21 55	22 04	22 07	22 10	22 22		22 25	22 34	22 37	22 40	22 52	22 55	23 07	23 10	23 37	23 40	23 43	00 10
Northumberland Park	d			22 06						22 36										
Meridian Water	d			22a09						22a39										
Ponders End	d		21 59						22 29					22 59					23 47	
Brimsdown	d		22 02						22 32					23 02					23 50	
Enfield Lock	d		22 04						22 34					23 04					23 52	
Waltham Cross	d		22 07						22 37					23 07					23 55	
Cheshunt	d		22 09			22 18			22 39			22 48		23 09		23 18		23 48	23 57	00 18
Broxbourne 3	a		22 15			22 23			22 45			22 53		23 15		23 23		23 53	00 03	00 23
Broxbourne 3	d		22 15			22 23			22 45			22 53		23 15		23 23		23 53	00 03	00 23
Rye House	d		22 18						22 48					23 18					00 06	
St Margarets (Herts)	d		22 21						22 51					23 21					00 09	
Ware	d		22 25						22 55					23 25					00 13	
Hertford East	a		22 31						23 01					23 31					00 19	
Roydon	d					22 27										23 27				00 27
Harlow Town	d				22 25	22 31					22 55	22 59			23 25	23 31	23 53	23 59		00 31
Harlow Mill	d					22 34										23 34				00 34
Sawbridgeworth	d					22 38						23 04				23 38		00 04		00 38
Bishops Stortford	a					22 44	22 47					23 10	23 15			23 44	00 02	00 11		00 44
Bishops Stortford	d					22 44	22 48					23 10	23 15			23 44	00 03			
Stansted Mountfitchet	d					22 48					23 06					23 48				
Stansted Airport ✈	a				22 42		22 57				23 13		23 25		23 42		00 12			
Stansted Airport ✈	d	22 27						23 04												
Elsenham	d					22 52										23 52				
Newport (Essex)	d					22 57										23 57				
Audley End	d	22 41				23 00		23 20				23 23				23 59				
Great Chesterford	d					23 05										00 05				
Whittlesford Parkway	d					23 10						23 31				00 10				
Shelford	d											23 35				00 14				
Cambridge	a	22 55				23 19		23 36				23 42				00 20				
	d					23 20														
Cambridge North	a					23 25														

AVAILABLE FROM MP Middleton Press

Table T022-R

Mondays to Fridays
16 December to 15 May

Cambridge North, Cambridge, Stansted Airport, Bishops Stortford, Hertford East and Broxbourne - London

Miles	Miles	Miles			LE MX ◇■ A	LE ■ B	LE MX C	LE MO ■ B	LE MX ■ B	LE MX ■	LE B	LE	XC ■	LE ◇■	LE	LE ■ D	LE MFO ■	LE TW ThO ■	LE ■ E	XC ■	LE	LE ◇■	LE ■
0	—	—	**Cambridge North**	d																			
2¼	—	—	**Cambridge**	a																			
—	—	—		d									04 44	04 48						05 17		05 20	05 31
5½	—	—	Shelford	d																			05 36
9	—	—	Whittlesford Parkway	d										04 55								05 28	05 41
12¼	—	—	Great Chesterford	d																		05 32	
16¼	—	—	Audley End	d									04 59	05 03						05 34		05 38	05 49
18	—	—	Newport (Essex)	d																		05 41	
22½	0	—	Elsenham	d																		05 46	
—	—	—	**Stansted Airport** ✈	a									05 14							05 49			
—	4½	—	**Stansted Airport** ✈	d								00 30					05 30						
24¾	8¼	—	Stansted Mountfitchet	d																		05 50	
27¾	—	0	**Bishops Stortford**	a								00 39		05 16			05 39					05 56	06 02
27¾	—	0	**Bishops Stortford**	d							00 08	00 39		05 16		05 30	05 39	05 39				05 56	06 02
31¼	—	3½	Sawbridgeworth	d										05 21		05 35						06 01	06 07
33½	—	5¾	Harlow Mill	d										05 24		05 38							06 10
35¼	—	7½	Harlow Town	d					00 01		00 16	00 47		05 27		05 41	05 47	05 47				06 06	06 13
38	—	10¼	Roydon	d										05 31		05 45						06 10	
—	0	—	**Hertford East**	d						00 07					05 25								
—	2	—	Ware	d											05 29								
—	4	—	St Margarets (Herts)	d											05 33								
—	5¼	—	Rye House	d											05 36				←				
40¾	—	13¼	**Broxbourne** 3	a						00 19				05 36	05 40	05 50	05 53	05 53	05 50			06 14	06 20
—	7	—	**Broxbourne** 3	d						00 19				05 36	05 40	05 56	05 53	05 53	05 56			06 15	06 20
44	—	16¼	Cheshunt	d										05 41	05 44	→	05 57	05 57	06 01			06 19	
45¼	—	—	Waltham Cross	d											05 47				06 03				
46¼	—	—	Enfield Lock	d											05 49				06 06				
47¼	—	—	Brimsdown	d											05 52				06 08				
48	—	—	Ponders End	d											05 54				06 10				
50¼	—	22¼	Meridian Water	d											05 57				06 14		06 22		
51	—	23½	Northumberland Park	d											05 59				06 16		06 24		
52	—	24¼	Tottenham Hale ⊖	d										05 49	06 03		06 07	06 07	06 19		06 27	06 28	06 31
—	0	—	Seven Sisters ⊖	d	00 04	00 08	00 12	00 21	00 21														
—	—	26¼	Lea Bridge	d															06 23		06 30		
—	6¾	28½	Stratford 7 ⊖	a															06 32		06 37		06 45
55	—	—	Hackney Downs	d			00 17								06 08								
58	—	—	**London Liverpool Street** 15 ⊖	a	00 18	00 22	00 26	00 35	00 36	00 49	00 51	01 21		06 03	06 18		06 23	06 23				06 43	

		LE	LE	LE ◇■	LE ■	LE	LE	LE ◇■	LE ■ F	LE ■	LE ◇■ G	LE	LE ■ E	LE ■	LE	LE	LE ◇■	LE ■	XC ■	LE ◇■	LE	LE	LE ■
Cambridge North	d										06 04												
Cambridge	a										06 10												
	d			05 48				05 51			06 18						06 21		06 35	06 47			
Shelford	d							05 56									06 26						
Whittlesford Parkway	d			05 55				06 00			06 25						06 30			06 55			
Great Chesterford	d							06 04									06 34						
Audley End	d			06 04				06 10			06 34						06 40		06 50	07 04			
Newport (Essex)	d							06 13									06 43						
Elsenham	d							06 19									06 49						
Stansted Airport ✈	a																		07 09				
Stansted Airport ✈	d	06 00			06 15					06 30				06 43				07 00					07 13
Stansted Mountfitchet	d	06 06						06 22		06 36							06 52						
Bishops Stortford	a	06 10		06 17	06 24			06 28		06 40	06 47			06 52			06 58	07 09		07 17			07 22
Bishops Stortford	d	06 10		06 18	06 24			06 29	06 33	06 41	06 47			06 52			06 58	07 09		07 17			07 22
Sawbridgeworth	d							06 33	06 38								07 03	07 14					
Harlow Mill	d							06 37	06 41								07 06						
Harlow Town	d	06 17		06 27	06 32			06 40	06 45	06 49				07 01	06 56		07 10	07 19					07 31
Roydon	d							06 44							07 00		07 14						
Hertford East	d		06 06				06 27									06 57							
Ware	d		06 10				06 31									07 01							
St Margarets (Herts)	d		06 14				06 35									07 05							
Rye House	d		06 17				06 38									07 08							
Broxbourne 3	a		06 22	06 34			06 43	06 48	06 52						07 05	07 13	07 18						
Broxbourne 3	d		06 26	06 34		06 39	06 43	06 49	07 00						07 09	07 13	07 18					07 30	
Cheshunt	d		06 30			06 44	06 47	06 53						07 10	07 14	07 17	07 23						07 40
Waltham Cross	d		06 33			06 46			07 06						07 17							07 36	
Enfield Lock	d		06 35			06 49			07 09						07 20							07 39	
Brimsdown	d		06 38			06 51			07 12						07 23							07 42	
Ponders End	d		06 40						07 14													07 44	
Meridian Water	d											07 08									07 38		
Northumberland Park	d					06 56						07 10	←								07 40		
Tottenham Hale ⊖	d	06 34	06 45	06 49	06 51	06 59		07 02	07 20	07 05	07 08	07 13	07 20	07 23	07 29		07 32	07 35		07 38	07 43	07 50	07 53
Seven Sisters ⊖	d						07 02		→							07 32							
Lea Bridge	d					07 03						07 16			07 33						07 46		
Stratford 7 ⊖	a					07 13						07 23			07 43						07 53		
Hackney Downs	d		06 52				07 08						07 26			07 38						07 56	
London Liverpool Street 15 ⊖	a	06 49	07 02	07 05	07 08		07 18	07 20		07 23	07 25		07 38	07 41		07 48	07 50	07 53		07 55		08 08	08 10

A From Cambridge North
B From Stansted Airport
C From Hertford East
D To Stratford
E From Bishops Stortford
F To London Liverpool Street
G From Kings Lynn

Table T022-R

Mondays to Fridays
16 December to 15 May

Cambridge North, Cambridge, Stansted Airport, Bishops Stortford, Hertford East and Broxbourne - London

Station	LE	LE	LE ◇1	LE A	LE 1 B	LE	LE ◇1 C	LE	LE D	LE 1	LE 1 E	LE	LE ◇1	LE 1	XC 1	LE ◇1	LE	LE	LE	LE	LE ◇1 F
Cambridge North d							07 04														07 41
Cambridge a							07 10														07 47
Cambridge d			06 51				07 17						07 20		07 35	07 47					07 51
Shelford d			06 56										07 26								07 56
Whittlesford Parkway d			07 00				07 25						07 30			07 55					08 00
Great Chesterford d			07 04										07 34								08 04
Audley End d			07 10				07 34						07 40		07 50	08 04					08 10
Newport (Essex) d			07 13										07 43								08 13
Elsenham d			07 19										07 49								08 19
Stansted Airport ✈ a															08 09						
Stansted Airport ✈ d						07 30				07 42				08 00					08 15		
Stansted Mountfitchet d			07 22							07 48			07 52								08 22
Bishops Stortford a			07 28			07 39	07 47			07 52			07 58	08 09		08 17			08 24		08 28
Bishops Stortford d			07 28		07 33	07 40	07 47			07 53			07 58	08 09		08 17			08 24		08 28
Sawbridgeworth d			07 33		07 38								08 03	08 14							08 33
Harlow Mill d			07 36		07 41								08 06								08 36
Harlow Town d			07 40		07 56	07 48				08 01			08 10	08 19					08 32		08 40
Roydon d			07 44		08 00								08 14								08 44
Hertford East d	07 17	07 27										07 57								08 17	
Ware d	07 21	07 31										08 01								08 21	
St Margarets (Herts) d	07 25	07 35										08 05								08 25	
Rye House d	07 28	07 38										08 08								08 28	
Broxbourne 3 a	07 33	07 43	07 48		08 05							08 13	08 18							08 36	08 48
Broxbourne 3 d	07 39	07 43	07 48	08 00	08 09						←	08 13	08 18					08 30		08 39	08 48
Cheshunt d	07 43	07 47	07 53		08 14	07 57				08 10	08 14	08 17	08 23					08 35		08 44	08 53
Waltham Cross d	07 46			08 06	→						08 17							08 37		08 46	
Enfield Lock d	07 48			08 09							08 20							08 40		08 49	
Brimsdown d	07 51			08 12							08 23							08 42		08 51	
Ponders End d				08 14														08 44			
Meridian Water d	07 56							08 08									08 38				
Northumberland Park d								08 10	←								08 40			08 56	
Tottenham Hale ⊖ d	07 59		08 02	08 20		08 05	08 08	08 13	08 20	08 23	08 29		08 32	08 35		08 38	08 43	08 50	08 53	08 59	09 02
Seven Sisters ⊖ d		08 02		→								08 32									
Lea Bridge d	08 03							08 16			08 33						08 46			09 03	
Stratford 7 ⊖ a	08 13							08 23			08 43						08 53			09 13	
Hackney Downs d		08 08							08 26			08 38						08 56			
London Liverpool Street 15 ⊖ a		08 18	08 20			08 23	08 25		08 37	08 40		08 48	08 50	08 53		08 55		09 07	09 09		09 21

Station	LE	XC ◇1 G	LE	LE	LE 1 B	LE ◇1	LE 1	LE 1 E	LE ◇1 F	LE 1	LE	LE	LE 1	LE 1	LE ◇1	LE 1	XC ◇1 G	LE	LE	LE	LE 1	LE ◇1
Cambridge North d									08 14													09 11
Cambridge a									08 20													09 17
Cambridge d		08 11				08 18			08 21						08 48		09 14					09 20
Shelford d									08 26						08 53							09 25
Whittlesford Parkway d						08 25			08 31						09 00							09 30
Great Chesterford d									08 35						09 04							09 34
Audley End d		08 26				08 34			08 40						09 10		09 29					09 40
Newport (Essex) d									08 43						09 13							09 43
Elsenham d									08 49						09 19							09 49
Stansted Airport ✈ a		08 41															09 44					
Stansted Airport ✈ d	08 30						08 45			09 00			09 15			09 30				09 45		
Stansted Mountfitchet d							08 51		08 53				09 21		09 24							09 52
Bishops Stortford a	08 39					08 48			08 58	09 09					09 29	09 39						09 58
Bishops Stortford d	08 39				08 43	08 49			08 58	09 09				09 13	09 29	09 39					09 47	09 58
Sawbridgeworth d					08 48				09 03					09 18	09 33						09 52	10 03
Harlow Mill d									09 06					09 21	09 37							10 06
Harlow Town d					08 53	08 57	09 02		09 10				09 32	09 24	09 40					10 00	10 05	10 09
Roydon d									09 14					09 28								10 13
Hertford East d				08 39								09 09							09 39			
Ware d				08 43								09 13							09 43			
St Margarets (Herts) d				08 47								09 17							09 47			
Rye House d				08 50				←				09 20							09 50			
Broxbourne 3 a				08 55	09 00	09 03		09 00	09 18			09 25		09 33	09 46				09 55		10 11	10 17
Broxbourne 3 d				08 55	09 09	09 04		09 09	09 18			09 25		09 39	09 46				09 55		10 12	10 17
Cheshunt d				09 00	→			09 14	09 23			09 30		09 43	09 50				09 59		10 16	10 21
Waltham Cross d				09 02				09 16				09 32							10 01		10 19	
Enfield Lock d				09 05				09 19				09 35		09 47					10 04			
Brimsdown d				09 07								09 37							10 06			
Ponders End d				09 09								09 39							10 08			
Meridian Water d			09 08					09 24			09 38			09 52				10 08				
Northumberland Park d			09 10					09 26			09 40			09 54				10 10				
Tottenham Hale ⊖ d	09 05		09 13	09 15		09 19	09 21	09 29	09 32	09 35	09 43	09 45	09 48	09 57	10 00	10 03		10 13	10 14	10 17	10 27	10 30
Seven Sisters ⊖ d																						
Lea Bridge d			09 16					09 33			09 46			10 01				10 16			10 31	
Stratford 7 ⊖ a			09 23					09 43			09 53			10 08				10 23			10 40	
Hackney Downs d				09 21								09 51							10 20			
London Liverpool Street 15 ⊖ a	09 23			09 33		09 35	09 39		09 50	09 53		10 01	10 03		10 15	10 17			10 28	10 31		10 45

A To London Liverpool Street
B To Stratford
C From Kings Lynn. The Fenman
D From Broxbourne
E From Bishops Stortford
F From Ely
G From Birmingham New Street

NRT DECEMBER 19 EDITION

Table T022-R

Mondays to Fridays
16 December to 15 May

Cambridge North, Cambridge, Stansted Airport, Bishops Stortford, Hertford East and Broxbourne - London

Station	LE 1	LE	LE	LE 1	LE A	LE 1	LE ◇1	LE	XC ◇1 B	LE	LE	LE	LE 1	LE ◇1	LE 1	LE	LE	LE 1	LE A	LE 1	LE ◇1	LE 1
Cambridge North d					09 44		09 53							10 13					10 39		10 53	
Cambridge a					09 49		09 59							10 19					10 45		10 59	
Cambridge d					09 50		10 03		10 11					10 20					10 48		11 03	
Shelford d														10 25								
Whittlesford Parkway d					09 58		10 11							10 30					10 57		11 11	
Great Chesterford d														10 34								
Audley End d					10 07		10 19		10 26					10 40					11 06		11 19	
Newport (Essex) d														10 43								
Elsenham d														10 49								
Stansted Airport ✈ a					10 24				10 41										11 24			
Stansted Airport ✈ d	10 00			10 15				10 30				10 45			11 00			11 15				11 30
Stansted Mountfitchet d				10 21										10 52				11 21				
Bishops Stortford a	10 09						10 32	10 39						10 58	11 09						11 32	11 39
Bishops Stortford d	10 09					10 15	10 32	10 39					10 47	10 58	11 09					11 15	11 32	11 39
Sawbridgeworth d						10 20							10 52	11 03						11 20		
Harlow Mill d						10 23								11 06						11 23		
Harlow Town d				10 32		10 26	10 40					11 00	11 05	11 09				11 32		11 26	11 40	
Roydon d						10 30								11 13						11 30		
Hertford East d			10 09								10 39						11 09					
Ware d			10 13								10 43						11 13					
St Margarets (Herts) d			10 17								10 47						11 17					
Rye House d			10 20								10 50						11 20					
Broxbourne 3 a			10 25			10 35	10 46				10 55		11 11	11 17			11 25			11 35	11 46	
Broxbourne 3 d			10 25			10 39	10 46				10 55		11 12	11 17			11 25			11 39	11 46	
Cheshunt d			10 29			10 44	10 50				10 59		11 16	11 21			11 29			11 44	11 50	
Waltham Cross d			10 31								11 01		11 19				11 31					
Enfield Lock d			10 34			10 47					11 04						11 34			11 47		
Brimsdown d			10 36								11 06						11 36					
Ponders End d			10 38								11 08						11 38					
Meridian Water d		10 38								11 08						11 38						
Northumberland Park d		10 40				10 53				11 10						11 40				11 53		
Tottenham Hale ⊖ d	10 33	10 43	10 44	10 48		10 56	11 00	11 03		11 13	11 14	11 17	11 27	11 31	11 33	11 43	11 44	11 48		11 56	12 01	12 03
Seven Sisters ⊖ d																						
Lea Bridge d		10 46				11 00				11 16			11 31			11 46				12 00		
Stratford 7 ⊖ a		10 53				11 10				11 23			11 40			11 53				12 10		
Hackney Downs d			10 50								11 20						11 50					
London Liverpool Street 15 ⊖ a	10 47		10 58	11 02			11 15	11 17			11 30	11 32		11 45	11 47		12 00	12 02			12 15	12 17

Station	XC ◇1 C	LE	LE	LE 1	LE 1	LE ◇1	LE	LE	LE	LE 1	LE A	LE 1	LE ◇1	LE 1	XC ◇1 B	LE	LE	LE	LE 1	LE ◇1	LE
Cambridge North d						11 13					11 44		11 53							12 13	
Cambridge a						11 19					11 49		11 59							12 19	
Cambridge d	11 11					11 20					11 50		12 03		12 11					12 20	
Shelford d						11 25														12 25	
Whittlesford Parkway d						11 30					11 58		12 11							12 30	
Great Chesterford d						11 34														12 34	
Audley End d	11 26					11 40					12 07		12 19		12 26					12 40	
Newport (Essex) d						11 43														12 43	
Elsenham d						11 49														12 49	
Stansted Airport ✈ a	11 41										12 24				12 41						
Stansted Airport ✈ d				11 45			12 00			12 15				12 30				12 45			13 00
Stansted Mountfitchet d						11 52				12 21										12 52	
Bishops Stortford a						11 58	12 09						12 32	12 39						12 58	13 09
Bishops Stortford d					11 47	11 58	12 09					12 15	12 32	12 39					12 47	12 58	13 09
Sawbridgeworth d					11 52	12 03						12 20							12 52	13 03	
Harlow Mill d						12 06						12 23								13 06	
Harlow Town d				12 00	12 05	12 09				12 32		12 26	12 40					13 00	13 05	13 09	
Roydon d						12 13						12 30								13 13	
Hertford East d			11 39						12 09								12 39				
Ware d			11 43						12 13								12 43				
St Margarets (Herts) d			11 47						12 17								12 47				
Rye House d			11 50						12 20								12 50				
Broxbourne 3 a			11 55		12 11	12 17			12 25			12 35	12 46				12 55		13 11	13 17	
Broxbourne 3 d			11 55		12 12	12 17			12 25			12 39	12 46				12 55		13 12	13 17	
Cheshunt d			11 59		12 16	12 21			12 29			12 44	12 50				12 59		13 16	13 21	
Waltham Cross d			12 01		12 19				12 31								13 01		13 19		
Enfield Lock d			12 04						12 34			12 47					13 04				
Brimsdown d			12 06						12 36								13 06				
Ponders End d			12 08						12 38								13 08				
Meridian Water d		12 08						12 38								13 08					
Northumberland Park d		12 10						12 40				12 53				13 10					
Tottenham Hale ⊖ d		12 13	12 14	12 17	12 27	12 31	12 33	12 43	12 44	12 48		12 56	13 01	13 03		13 13	13 14	13 17	13 27	13 30	13 33
Seven Sisters ⊖ d																					
Lea Bridge d		12 16			12 31			12 46				13 00				13 16			13 31		
Stratford 7 ⊖ a		12 23			12 40			12 53				13 10				13 23			13 40		
Hackney Downs d			12 20						12 50								13 20				
London Liverpool Street 15 ⊖ a			12 30	12 32		12 45	12 47		13 00	13 02			13 15	13 17			13 28	13 31		13 45	13 47

A From Norwich
B From Birmingham New Street
C From Bristol Temple Meads

Table T022-R

Mondays to Fridays
16 December to 15 May

Cambridge North, Cambridge, Stansted Airport, Bishops Stortford, Hertford East and Broxbourne - London

	LE	LE	LE ■	LE A	LE ■	LE ◇■	LE ■	XC ◇■ B	LE	LE	LE ■	LE ■	LE ◇■	LE ■	LE	LE	LE	LE A	LE ■	LE ◇■	LE ■	XC ◇■ B
Cambridge North d				12 39		12 53							13 13					13 44		13 53		
Cambridge a				12 44		12 59							13 19					13 49		13 59		
d				12 48		13 03		13 11					13 20					13 50		14 03		14 11
Shelford d													13 25									
Whittlesford Parkway d				12 57		13 11							13 30					13 58		14 11		
Great Chesterford d													13 34									
Audley End d				13 06		13 19		13 26					13 40					14 07		14 19		14 26
Newport (Essex) d													13 43									
Elsenham d													13 49									
Stansted Airport ✈ a				13 24				13 41										14 24				14 41
Stansted Airport ✈ d			13 15				13 30				13 45			14 00			14 15				14 30	
Stansted Mountfitchet d			13 21										13 52				14 21					
Bishops Stortford a						13 32	13 39						13 58	14 09						14 32	14 39	
Bishops Stortford d					13 15	13 32	13 39					13 47	13 58	14 09					14 15	14 32	14 39	
Sawbridgeworth d					13 20							13 52	14 03						14 20			
Harlow Mill d					13 23								14 06						14 23			
Harlow Town d			13 32		13 26	13 40					14 00	14 05	14 09				14 32		14 26	14 40		
Roydon d					13 30								14 13						14 30			
Hertford East d		13 09								13 39						14 09						
Ware d		13 13								13 43						14 13						
St Margarets (Herts) d		13 17								13 47						14 17						
Rye House d		13 20								13 50						14 20						
Broxbourne 3 a		13 25			13 35	13 46				13 55		14 11	14 17			14 25			14 35	14 46		
Broxbourne 3 d		13 25			13 39	13 46				13 55		14 12	14 17			14 25			14 39	14 46		
Cheshunt d		13 29			13 44	13 50				13 59		14 16	14 21			14 29			14 44	14 50		
Waltham Cross d		13 31								14 01		14 19				14 31						
Enfield Lock d		13 34			13 47					14 04						14 34			14 47			
Brimsdown d		13 36								14 06						14 36						
Ponders End d		13 38								14 08						14 38						
Meridian Water d	13 38								14 08						14 38							
Northumberland Park d	13 40				13 53				14 10						14 40				14 53			
Tottenham Hale ⊖ d	13 43	13 44	13 48		13 56	14 00	14 03		14 13	14 14	14 17	14 27	14 30	14 33	14 43	14 44	14 48		14 56	15 01	15 03	
Seven Sisters ⊖ d																						
Lea Bridge d	13 46				14 00				14 16			14 31			14 46				15 00			
Stratford 7 ⊖ a	13 53				14 10				14 23			14 40			14 53				15 10			
Hackney Downs d		13 50								14 20						14 50						
London Liverpool Street 15 ⊖ a		13 58	14 02			14 15	14 17			14 28	14 31		14 45	14 47		14 58	15 02			15 15	15 17	

	LE	LE	LE ■	LE ■	LE ◇■	LE	LE	LE	LE	LE ■	LE ■ C	LE A	LE ◇■	LE ■	XC ◇■ B	LE	LE	LE ■	LE ■	LE ◇■	LE ■
Cambridge North d					14 13							14 38	14 53							15 13	
Cambridge a					14 19							14 44	14 59							15 19	
d					14 20							14 48	15 03		15 11					15 20	
Shelford d					14 25															15 25	
Whittlesford Parkway d					14 30							14 57	15 11							15 30	
Great Chesterford d					14 34															15 34	
Audley End d					14 40							15 06	15 19		15 26					15 40	
Newport (Essex) d					14 43															15 43	
Elsenham d					14 49															15 49	
Stansted Airport ✈ a												15 31		←	15 41						
Stansted Airport ✈ d			14 45			15 00			15 15		15 30			15 30				15 45			16 00
Stansted Mountfitchet d					14 52				15 21		→									15 52	
Bishops Stortford a					14 58	15 09							15 32	15 39						15 58	16 09
Bishops Stortford d				14 47	14 58	15 09				15 15			15 32	15 39					15 47	15 58	16 09
Sawbridgeworth d				14 52	15 03					15 20									15 52	16 03	
Harlow Mill d					15 06					15 23										16 06	
Harlow Town d			15 00	15 05	15 09				15 32	15 26			15 40					16 00	16 03	16 09	
Roydon d					15 13					15 30										16 13	
Hertford East d		14 39						15 09									15 39				
Ware d		14 43						15 13									15 43				
St Margarets (Herts) d		14 47						15 17									15 47				
Rye House d		14 50						15 20									15 50				
Broxbourne 3 a		14 55		15 11	15 17			15 25		15 35			15 46				15 55		16 10	16 17	
Broxbourne 3 d		14 55		15 12	15 17			15 25		15 39			15 46				15 55		16 10	16 17	
Cheshunt d		14 59		15 16	15 21			15 29		15 44			15 50				15 59		16 14	16 21	
Waltham Cross d		15 01		15 19				15 31									16 01		16 16		
Enfield Lock d		15 04						15 34		15 47							16 04				
Brimsdown d		15 06						15 36									16 06				
Ponders End d		15 08						15 38									16 08				
Meridian Water d	15 08						15 38			15 52						16 08					
Northumberland Park d	15 10						15 40			15 54						16 10			16 23		
Tottenham Hale ⊖ d	15 13	15 14	15 17	15 27	15 31	15 33	15 43	15 44	15 48	15 58			16 01	16 04		16 13	16 14	16 17	16 27	16 30	16 33
Seven Sisters ⊖ d																					
Lea Bridge d	15 16			15 31			15 46			16 02						16 16			16 31		
Stratford 7 ⊖ a	15 23			15 40			15 53			16 10						16 23			16 38		
Hackney Downs d		15 20						15 50									16 20				
London Liverpool Street 15 ⊖ a		15 28	15 31		15 45	15 47		15 58	16 02				16 15	16 18			16 31	16 33		16 46	16 48

A From Norwich
B From Birmingham New Street
C To London Liverpool Street

Table T022-R

Mondays to Fridays
16 December to 15 May

Cambridge North, Cambridge, Stansted Airport, Bishops Stortford, Hertford East and Broxbourne - London

	LE	LE	LE ■	LE A	LE ■	LE ◇■	LE	XC ◇■ B	LE	LE ■	LE ■	LE ◇■	LE ◇■	LE ■	LE	LE	LE ■	LE	LE A	LE ■	LE ◇■	LE
Cambridge North d				15 39		15 43						16 13							16 39		16 43	
Cambridge a				15 45		15 49						16 19							16 45		16 49	
d				15 47		15 50		16 11				16 20	16 35						16 47		16 50	
Shelford d						15 55						16 25									16 56	
Whittlesford Parkway d				15 56		16 00						16 30	16 43						16 56		17 00	
Great Chesterford d						16 04						16 34									17 04	
Audley End d				16 05		16 10		16 26				16 40	16 52						17 05		17 10	
Newport (Essex) d						16 13						16 43									17 13	
Elsenham d						16 19						16 49									17 19	
Stansted Airport ✈ a				16 24				16 41											17 24			
Stansted Airport ✈ d			16 15				16 30			16 45				17 00				17 15				17 30
Stansted Mountfitchet d			16 21			16 24						16 52						17 21			17 24	
Bishops Stortford a						16 30	16 39					16 58	17 05	17 09							17 30	17 39
Bishops Stortford d					16 15	16 30	16 39				16 43	16 58	17 05	17 09						17 15	17 30	17 39
Sawbridgeworth d					16 20						16 48	17 03								17 20	17 35	
Harlow Mill d					16 23						16 51									17 23	17 38	
Harlow Town d			16 32		16 26	16 38				17 00	16 54	17 08						17 32		17 26	17 41	
Roydon d					16 30						16 58									17 30		
Hertford East d		16 09							16 39							17 09						
Ware d		16 13							16 43							17 13						
St Margarets (Herts) d		16 17							16 47							17 17						
Rye House d		16 20							16 50							17 20						
Broxbourne 3 a		16 25			16 35	16 44			16 56		17 03	17 14				17 26				17 35	17 47	
Broxbourne 3 d		16 25			16 39	16 44			16 56		17 07	17 14				17 26	17 35			17 40	17 47	
Cheshunt d		16 29			16 44	16 48			17 00		17 12	17 18				17 30				17 44	17 51	
Waltham Cross d		16 31							17 02		17 14					17 33						
Enfield Lock d		16 34			16 47				17 05							17 35				17 48		
Brimsdown d		16 36							17 07							17 38						
Ponders End d		16 38							17 09							17 40						
Meridian Water d	16 38				16 52										17 36					17 53		
Northumberland Park d	16 40				16 54						17 21				17 38					17 55		
Tottenham Hale ⊖ d	16 43	16 44	16 48		16 58	17 01	17 04		17 15	17 18	17 24	17 27	17 30	17 33	17 41	17 46		17 51		17 58	18 01	18 04
Seven Sisters ⊖ d																						
Lea Bridge d	16 46				17 02						17 28				17 44					18 02		
Stratford 7 ⊖ a	16 53				17 09						17 36				17 51					18 09		
Hackney Downs d		16 50							17 21							17 51						
London Liverpool Street 15 ⊖ a		16 59	17 02			17 16	17 18		17 30	17 32		17 44	17 46	17 48		18 00	18 02	18 08			18 16	18 18

	XC ◇■ B	LE	LE ■	LE ■	LE ■	LE ◇■	LE ■	LE	LE	LE ■	LE ■	LE ■	LE	LE ◇■	LE ■	LE	LE ■	LE	XC ◇■ B	LE	LE ◇■	LE ■
Cambridge North d						17 13																
Cambridge a						17 19																
d	17 11					17 20								17 51					18 17		18 20	
Shelford d						17 25								17 55							18 26	
Whittlesford Parkway d						17 30								18 00							18 30	
Great Chesterford d						17 34								18 04							18 34	
Audley End d	17 26					17 40								18 10					18 35		18 40	
Newport (Essex) d						17 43								18 13							18 43	
Elsenham d						17 49								18 19							18 49	
Stansted Airport ✈ a	17 41																		18 54			
Stansted Airport ✈ d				17 45			18 00				18 15				18 30			18 45				19 00
Stansted Mountfitchet d						17 52					18 21			18 24							18 52	
Bishops Stortford a						17 58	18 10							18 29	18 39						18 58	19 09
Bishops Stortford d					17 47	17 58	18 10					18 15		18 30	18 39						18 58	19 09
Sawbridgeworth d					17 52	18 03						18 20		18 35							19 03	
Harlow Mill d						18 06						18 23									19 06	
Harlow Town d				18 00	17 57	18 09					18 32	18 26		18 40				19 00			19 09	
Roydon d						18 13						18 30									19 13	
Hertford East d		17 39							18 09				18 25			18 39						
Ware d		17 43							18 13				18 29			18 43						
St Margarets (Herts) d		17 47							18 17				18 33			18 47						
Rye House d		17 50							18 20				18 36			18 50						
Broxbourne 3 a		17 56			18 04	18 17			18 26			18 35	18 43	18 46		18 56					19 17	
Broxbourne 3 d		17 56	18 05		18 10	18 17			18 26	18 35		18 40		18 46		18 56	19 05			19 10	19 17	
Cheshunt d		18 00			18 14	18 21			18 30			18 44		18 50		19 00				19 14	19 21	
Waltham Cross d		18 02			18 17				18 32							19 02				19 17		
Enfield Lock d		18 05							18 35			18 48				19 05						
Brimsdown d		18 07							18 37							19 07						
Ponders End d		18 09							18 39							19 09						
Meridian Water d								18 36				18 53										
Northumberland Park d					18 23			18 38				18 55								19 23		
Tottenham Hale ⊖ d		18 15		18 21	18 27	18 30	18 33	18 41	18 45		18 51	18 58		19 01	19 04	19 15		19 21		19 27	19 30	19 33
Seven Sisters ⊖ d																						
Lea Bridge d					18 31			18 44				19 02								19 31		
Stratford 7 ⊖ a					18 38			18 51				19 09								19 38		
Hackney Downs d		18 21							18 51							19 21						
London Liverpool Street 15 ⊖ a		18 29	18 31	18 38		18 46	18 48		18 59	19 01	19 08			19 16	19 18	19 29	19 31	19 38			19 45	19 47

A From Norwich
B From Birmingham New Street

Table T022-R

Mondays to Fridays

16 December to 15 May

Cambridge North, Cambridge, Stansted Airport, Bishops Stortford, Hertford East and Broxbourne - London

		LE		LE	LE 1	LE 1	LE	LE ◇1	LE	XC ◇1 A	LE	LE		LE	LE	LE ◇1	LE 1	LE	LE	LE 1	LE 1	LE ◇1		LE 1	XC ◇1 A
Cambridge North	d							18 42								19 13						19 52			
Cambridge	a							18 48								19 19						19 58			
	d							18 50		19 11						19 20						20 03			20 11
Shelford	d							18 55								19 26									
Whittlesford Parkway	d							19 00								19 30						20 11			
Great Chesterford	d							19 04								19 34									
Audley End	d							19 10		19 26						19 40						20 19			20 26
Newport (Essex)	d							19 13								19 43									
Elsenham	d							19 19								19 49									
Stansted Airport ✈	a									19 41															20 41
Stansted Airport ✈	d				19 15				19 30					19 45			20 00			20 15				20 30	
Stansted Mountfitchet	d				19 21			19 24								19 52				20 21					
Bishops Stortford	a							19 29	19 39							19 58	20 09					20 32		20 39	
Bishops Stortford	d					19 15		19 30	19 39							19 58	20 09				20 15	20 32		20 39	
Sawbridgeworth	d					19 20		19 35								20 03					20 20				
Harlow Mill	d					19 23										20 06					20 23				
Harlow Town	d				19 32	19 26		19 40						20 00		20 09				20 32	20 26	20 40			
Roydon	d					19 30										20 13					20 30				
Hertford East	d			19 09			19 25					19 39							20 10						
Ware	d			19 13			19 29					19 43							20 14						
St Margarets (Herts)	d			19 17			19 33					19 47							20 18						
Rye House	d			19 20			19 36					19 50							20 21						
Broxbourne 3	a			19 26		19 35	19 42	19 46				19 55				20 17			20 25		20 35	20 46			
Broxbourne 3	d			19 26		19 39		19 46				19 55			20 12	20 17			20 25		20 39	20 46			
Cheshunt	d			19 30		19 43		19 50				19 59			20 16	20 21			20 29		20 44	20 50			
Waltham Cross	d			19 32								20 01			20 19				20 32						
Enfield Lock	d			19 35		19 47						20 04							20 34		20 47				
Brimsdown	d			19 37								20 06							20 37						
Ponders End	d			19 39								20 08							20 39						
Meridian Water	d	19 36				19 52					20 08							20 38							
Northumberland Park	d	19 38				19 54					20 10							20 40			20 53				
Tottenham Hale ⊖	d	19 41		19 45	19 48	19 57		20 00	20 03		20 13	20 14		20 17	20 27	20 30	20 33	20 43	20 44	20 48	20 56	21 00		21 03	
Seven Sisters ⊖	d																								
Lea Bridge	d	19 44				20 01					20 16				20 31			20 46			21 00				
Stratford 7 ⊖	a	19 51				20 10					20 23				20 38			20 53			21 10				
Hackney Downs	d			19 51								20 20							20 50						
London Liverpool Street 15 ⊖	a			19 59	20 03			20 15	20 17			20 31		20 33		20 45	20 47		20 59	21 01		21 14		21 17	

		LE	LE	LE 1	LE 1	LE ◇1	LE 1	LE		LE	LE 1	LE B	LE 1	LE ◇1	LE 1	XC ◇1 A	LE	LE		LE	LE 1	LE ◇1	LE	LE	LE
Cambridge North	d					20 13						20 39		20 53								21 13			
Cambridge	a					20 19						20 45		20 59								21 19			
	d					20 20						20 48		21 03		21 11						21 20			
Shelford	d					20 25																21 25			
Whittlesford Parkway	d					20 30						20 57		21 11								21 30			
Great Chesterford	d					20 34																21 34			
Audley End	d					20 40						21 06		21 19		21 26						21 40			
Newport (Essex)	d					20 43																21 43			
Elsenham	d					20 49																21 49			
Stansted Airport ✈	a											21 24				21 41									
Stansted Airport ✈	d			20 45			21 00				21 15				21 30					21 45			22 00		
Stansted Mountfitchet	d					20 52					21 21											21 52			
Bishops Stortford	a					20 58	21 09							21 32	21 39							21 58	22 09		
Bishops Stortford	d				20 47	20 58	21 09						21 15	21 32	21 39						21 47	21 58	22 09		
Sawbridgeworth	d				20 52	21 03							21 20								21 52	22 03			
Harlow Mill	d					21 06							21 23									22 06			
Harlow Town	d			21 00	20 57	21 09					21 32		21 26	21 40						22 00	22 05	22 09			
Roydon	d					21 13							21 30									22 13			
Hertford East	d		20 39							21 09								21 39							22 09
Ware	d		20 43							21 13								21 43							22 13
St Margarets (Herts)	d		20 47							21 17								21 47							22 17
Rye House	d		20 50							21 20								21 50							22 20
Broxbourne 3	a		20 55		21 04	21 17				21 25			21 35	21 46				21 55			22 11	22 17			22 25
Broxbourne 3	d		20 55		21 07	21 17				21 25			21 39	21 46				21 55			22 12	22 17			22 25
Cheshunt	d		20 59		21 12	21 21				21 29			21 44	21 50				21 59			22 16	22 21			22 29
Waltham Cross	d		21 01		21 14					21 31								22 01			22 19				22 31
Enfield Lock	d		21 04							21 34			21 47					22 04							22 34
Brimsdown	d		21 06							21 36								22 06							22 36
Ponders End	d		21 08							21 38								22 08							22 38
Meridian Water	d	21 08						21 38									22 08							22 38	
Northumberland Park	d	21 10						21 40					21 53				22 10							22 40	
Tottenham Hale ⊖	d	21 13	21 14	21 17	21 23	21 30	21 33	21 43		21 44	21 48		21 56	22 01	22 03		22 13	22 14		22 17	22 27	22 31	22 33	22 43	22 44
Seven Sisters ⊖	d																								
Lea Bridge	d	21 15			21 27			21 46					22 00				22 16				22 31			22 46	
Stratford 7 ⊖	a	21 23			21 40			21 53					22 10				22 23				22 40			22 53	
Hackney Downs	d		21 20							21 50								22 20							22 50
London Liverpool Street 15 ⊖	a		21 28	21 31		21 44	21 47			21 58	22 02			22 15	22 17			22 28		22 31		22 45	22 47		22 58

A From Birmingham New Street
B From Norwich

NRT DECEMBER 19 EDITION

Table T022-R

Mondays to Fridays

16 December to 15 May

Cambridge North, Cambridge, Stansted Airport, Bishops Stortford, Hertford East and Broxbourne - London

		LE 1	LE 1	LE ◇1		LE 1	XC ◇1 A	LE	LE	LE 1	LE ◇1	LE 1	LE	LE 1		LE ◇1	LE 1	LE FO 1	LE	LE 1	LE				
Cambridge North	d			21 53							22 13					22 43									
Cambridge	a			21 59							22 19					22 49									
	d			22 03			22 11				22 20					22 50		23 26							
Shelford	d										22 25					22 55		23 31							
Whittlesford Parkway	d			22 11							22 30					23 00		23 36							
Great Chesterford	d										22 34					23 04		23 40							
Audley End	d			22 19			22 26				22 40					23 10		23 45							
Newport (Essex)	d										22 43					23 13		23 48							
Elsenham	d										22 49					23 19		23 54							
Stansted Airport ✈	a						22 41																		
Stansted Airport ✈	d	22 15				22 30				22 45		23 00		23 15			23 30			23 45	23 59				
Stansted Mountfitchet	d	22 21									22 52			23 21		23 24		23 58							
Bishops Stortford	a			22 32		22 39					22 58	23 09				23 29	23 39	00 03			00 08				
Bishops Stortford	d		22 15	22 32		22 39					22 58	23 09				23 29	23 39				00 08				
Sawbridgeworth	d		22 20								23 03					23 33									
Harlow Mill	d		22 23								23 06					23 37									
Harlow Town	d	22 32	22 26	22 40						23 00	23 09			23 33		23 40				00 01	00 16				
Roydon	d		22 30								23 13					23 44									
Hertford East	d								22 39				23 09						23 39						
Ware	d								22 43				23 13						23 43						
St Margarets (Herts)	d								22 47				23 17						23 47						
Rye House	d								22 50				23 20						23 50						
Broxbourne 3	a		22 35	22 46					22 55		23 17		23 25			23 48			23 55						
Broxbourne 3	d		22 39	22 46					22 55		23 17		23 25			23 48			23 55						
Cheshunt	d		22 44	22 50					22 59		23 21		23 29			23 52			23 59						
Waltham Cross	d								23 01				23 31												
Enfield Lock	d		22 47						23 04				23 34												
Brimsdown	d								23 06				23 36												
Ponders End	d								23 08				23 38												
Meridian Water	d							23 08																	
Northumberland Park	d		22 53					23 10																	
Tottenham Hale ⊖	d	22 48	22 56	23 01		23 03		23 13	23 14	23 17	23 30	23 33	23 44	23 48											
Seven Sisters ⊖	d															00 04	00 08		00 12	00 21					
Lea Bridge	d		23 00					23 16																	
Stratford 7 ⊖	a		23 09					23 23																	
Hackney Downs	d								23 20				23 50						00 17						
London Liverpool Street 15 ⊖	a	23 02		23 15		23 17			23 28	23 33	23 48	23 50	23 58	00 02		00 18	00 22		00 26	00 36	00 51				

Saturdays

21 December to 16 May

		LE ◇1 B	LE 1 C	LE D	LE 1 C	LE 1	LE C	LE	LE ◇1	XC 1		LE 1	LE 1	LE	LE 1	LE ◇1	LE	XC 1	LE	LE		LE 1	LE 1	LE ◇1	LE 1
Cambridge North	d																								
Cambridge	a																								
	d								04 38	04 51						05 21		05 40						06 04	
Shelford	d															05 26									
Whittlesford Parkway	d								04 45							05 30								06 11	
Great Chesterford	d															05 34									
Audley End	d								04 53							05 40		05 55						06 19	
Newport (Essex)	d															05 43									
Elsenham	d															05 49									
Stansted Airport ✈	a									05 17								06 10							
Stansted Airport ✈	d							00 30					05 30				06 00					06 15			06 30
Stansted Mountfitchet	d															05 52						06 21			
Bishops Stortford	a							00 39	05 06				05 39			05 58	06 09							06 32	06 39
Bishops Stortford	d						00 08	00 39	05 07			05 14	05 39		05 47	05 58	06 09						06 15	06 32	06 39
Sawbridgeworth	d								05 11			05 19			05 52	06 03							06 20		
Harlow Mill	d								05 15			05 22				06 06							06 23		
Harlow Town	d				00 01		00 16	00 47	05 18			05 25			06 05	06 09						06 32	06 26	06 40	
Roydon	d								05 22			05 29				06 13							06 30		
Hertford East	d					00 07														06 09					
Ware	d																			06 13					
St Margarets (Herts)	d																			06 17					
Rye House	d																			06 20					
Broxbourne 3	a					00 19			05 26			05 33			06 11	06 17				06 25			06 35	06 46	
Broxbourne 3	d					00 19			05 26			05 33		05 55	06 12	06 17				06 25			06 39	06 46	
Cheshunt	d								05 30			05 37		05 59	06 16	06 21				06 29			06 44	06 50	
Waltham Cross	d											05 40		06 01	06 19					06 31					
Enfield Lock	d											05 42		06 04						06 34			06 47		
Brimsdown	d											05 45		06 06						06 36					
Ponders End	d											05 47		06 08						06 38					
Meridian Water	d																		06 38						
Northumberland Park	d											05 51							06 40				06 53		
Tottenham Hale ⊖	d											05 55	06 01	06 14	06 27	06 30	06 33		06 43	06 44		06 48	06 56	07 00	07 03
Seven Sisters ⊖	d	00 04	00 08	00 12	00 21				05 42																
Lea Bridge	d											05 59			06 31				06 46				07 00		
Stratford 7 ⊖	a											06 05			06 40				06 53				07 10		
Hackney Downs	d			00 17										06 20						06 50					
London Liverpool Street 15 ⊖	a	00 18	00 22	00 26	00 36	00 49	00 51	01 21	05 57			06 14	06 15	06 28		06 45	06 47			06 58		07 01		07 15	07 17

A From Birmingham New Street
B From Cambridge North
C From Stansted Airport
D From Hertford East

Table T022-R

Saturdays
21 December to 16 May

Cambridge North, Cambridge, Stansted Airport, Bishops Stortford, Hertford East and Broxbourne - London

		LE ■	LE	LE	LE ■	LE ■	LE ◇■	LE ■	XC ■	LE	LE	LE ■	LE A	LE ■	LE ◇■	LE	LE	LE	LE ■	LE ■	LE ◇■	LE ■	XC ■
Cambridge North	d						06 13						06 39								07 13		
Cambridge	a						06 19						06 47								07 19		
	d	06 10					06 20		06 40				06 51		07 03						07 20		07 40
Shelford	d						06 25														07 25		
Whittlesford Parkway	d	06 18					06 30						06 59		07 11						07 30		
Great Chesterford	d						06 34														07 34		
Audley End	d	06 26					06 40		06 55				07 08		07 19						07 40		07 55
Newport (Essex)	d						06 43														07 43		
Elsenham	d						06 49														07 49		
Stansted Airport ✈	a	06 41							07 10				07 24										08 10
Stansted Airport ✈	d				06 45			07 00				07 15				07 30			07 45			08 00	
Stansted Mountfitchet	d						06 52					07 21									07 52		
Bishops Stortford	a						06 58	07 09							07 32	07 39					07 58	08 09	
Bishops Stortford	d					06 47	06 58	07 09						07 15	07 32	07 39				07 47	07 58	08 09	
Sawbridgeworth	d					06 52	07 03							07 20						07 52	08 03		
Harlow Mill	d						07 06							07 23							08 06		
Harlow Town	d				07 00	07 03	07 09					07 32		07 26	07 40				08 02	08 05	08 09		
Roydon	d						07 13							07 30							08 13		
Hertford East	d			06 39							07 09							07 39					
Ware	d			06 43							07 13							07 43					
St Margarets (Herts)	d			06 47							07 17							07 47					
Rye House	d			06 50							07 20							07 50					
Broxbourne ■	a			06 55		07 10	07 17				07 25			07 35	07 46			07 55		08 11	08 17		
Broxbourne ■	d			06 55		07 12	07 17				07 25			07 39	07 46			07 55		08 12	08 17		
Cheshunt	d			06 59		07 16	07 21				07 29			07 44	07 50			07 59		08 16	08 21		
Waltham Cross	d			07 01		07 19					07 31							08 01		08 19			
Enfield Lock	d			07 04							07 34			07 47				08 04					
Brimsdown	d			07 06							07 36							08 06					
Ponders End	d			07 08							07 38							08 08					
Meridian Water	d		07 08							07 38							08 08						
Northumberland Park	d		07 10							07 40				07 53			08 10						
Tottenham Hale ⊖	d		07 13	07 14	07 17	07 27	07 30	07 33		07 43	07 44	07 48		07 56	08 00	08 03	08 13	08 14	08 17	08 27	08 30	08 33	
Seven Sisters ⊖	d																						
Lea Bridge	d		07 16			07 31				07 46				08 00			08 16			08 31			
Stratford ■ ⊖	a		07 23			07 40				07 53				08 10			08 23			08 40			
Hackney Downs	d			07 20							07 50							08 20					
London Liverpool Street ■ ⊖	a			07 28	07 31		07 45	07 47			07 58	08 02			08 15	08 17		08 28	08 31		08 45	08 47	

		LE	LE	LE	LE A	LE ■	LE ◇■	LE	XC ◇■ B	LE	LE	LE ■	LE ■	LE ◇■	LE ■	LE	LE	LE ■	LE A	LE ■	LE ◇■	LE ■
Cambridge North	d				07 39		07 53							08 13					08 39		08 53	
Cambridge	a				07 44		07 59							08 19					08 44		08 59	
	d				07 48		08 03		08 11					08 20					08 48		09 03	
Shelford	d													08 25								
Whittlesford Parkway	d				07 57		08 11							08 30					08 57		09 11	
Great Chesterford	d													08 34								
Audley End	d				08 07		08 19		08 26					08 40					09 07		09 19	
Newport (Essex)	d													08 43								
Elsenham	d													08 49								
Stansted Airport ✈	a				08 24				08 41										09 24			
Stansted Airport ✈	d			08 15				08 30				08 45			09 00			09 15				09 30
Stansted Mountfitchet	d			08 21										08 52				09 21				
Bishops Stortford	a						08 32	08 39						08 58	09 09						09 32	09 39
Bishops Stortford	d					08 15	08 32	08 39					08 47	08 58	09 09					09 15	09 32	09 39
Sawbridgeworth	d					08 20							08 52	09 03						09 20		
Harlow Mill	d					08 23								09 06						09 23		
Harlow Town	d			08 32		08 26	08 40					09 00	09 05	09 09				09 32		09 26	09 40	
Roydon	d					08 30								09 13						09 30		
Hertford East	d		08 09								08 39						09 09					
Ware	d		08 13								08 43						09 13					
St Margarets (Herts)	d		08 17								08 47						09 17					
Rye House	d		08 20								08 50						09 20					
Broxbourne ■	a		08 25			08 35	08 46				08 55		09 11	09 17			09 25			09 35	09 46	
Broxbourne ■	d		08 25			08 39	08 46				08 55		09 12	09 17			09 25			09 39	09 46	
Cheshunt	d		08 29			08 44	08 50				08 59		09 16	09 21			09 29			09 44	09 50	
Waltham Cross	d		08 31								09 01		09 19				09 31					
Enfield Lock	d		08 34			08 47					09 04						09 34			09 47		
Brimsdown	d		08 36								09 06						09 36					
Ponders End	d		08 38								09 08						09 38					
Meridian Water	d	08 38								09 08						09 38						
Northumberland Park	d	08 40				08 53				09 10						09 40				09 53		
Tottenham Hale ⊖	d	08 43	08 44	08 48		08 56	09 00	09 03		09 13	09 14	09 17	09 27	09 30	09 33	09 43	09 44	09 48		09 56	10 00	10 03
Seven Sisters ⊖	d																					
Lea Bridge	d	08 46				09 00				09 16			09 31			09 46				10 00		
Stratford ■ ⊖	a	08 53				09 10				09 23			09 40			09 53				10 10		
Hackney Downs	d		08 50								09 20						09 50					
London Liverpool Street ■ ⊖	a		08 58	09 02			09 15	09 17			09 28	09 31		09 45	09 47		09 58	10 02			10 15	10 17

A From Norwich

B From Birmingham New Street

Table T022-R

Saturdays
21 December to 16 May

Cambridge North, Cambridge, Stansted Airport, Bishops Stortford, Hertford East and Broxbourne - London

		XC ◇■ A	LE	LE	LE	LE ■	LE ◇■	LE ■	LE	LE	LE ■	LE B	LE ■	LE ◇■	LE	XC ◇■ A	LE	LE	LE	LE ■	LE ◇■	LE ■	LE
Cambridge North	d						09 13					09 39		09 53							10 13		
Cambridge	a						09 19					09 44		09 59							10 19		
	d	09 11					09 20					09 48		10 03		10 11					10 20		
Shelford	d						09 25														10 25		
Whittlesford Parkway	d						09 30					09 57		10 11							10 30		
Great Chesterford	d						09 34														10 34		
Audley End	d	09 26					09 40					10 07		10 19		10 26					10 40		
Newport (Essex)	d						09 43														10 43		
Elsenham	d						09 49														10 49		
Stansted Airport ✈	a	09 41										10 24				10 41							
Stansted Airport ✈	d				09 45			10 00			10 15				10 30				10 45			11 00	
Stansted Mountfitchet	d						09 52				10 21										10 52		
Bishops Stortford	a						09 58	10 09						10 32	10 39						10 58	11 09	
Bishops Stortford	d					09 47	09 58	10 09					10 15	10 32	10 39					10 47	10 58	11 09	
Sawbridgeworth	d					09 52	10 03						10 20							10 52	11 03		
Harlow Mill	d						10 06						10 23								11 06		
Harlow Town	d				10 00	10 05	10 09				10 32		10 26	10 40					11 00	11 05	11 09		
Roydon	d						10 13						10 30								11 13		
Hertford East	d			09 39						10 09								10 39					
Ware	d			09 43						10 13								10 43					
St Margarets (Herts)	d			09 47						10 17								10 47					
Rye House	d			09 50						10 20								10 50					
Broxbourne ■	a			09 55		10 11	10 17			10 25			10 35	10 46				10 55		11 11	11 17		
Broxbourne ■	d			09 55		10 12	10 17			10 25			10 39	10 46				10 55		11 12	11 17		
Cheshunt	d			09 59		10 16	10 21			10 29			10 44	10 50				10 59		11 16	11 21		
Waltham Cross	d			10 01		10 19				10 31								11 01		11 19			
Enfield Lock	d			10 04						10 34			10 47					11 04					
Brimsdown	d			10 06						10 36								11 06					
Ponders End	d			10 08						10 38								11 08					
Meridian Water	d		10 08						10 38								11 08						11 38
Northumberland Park	d		10 10						10 40				10 53				11 10						11 40
Tottenham Hale ⊖	d		10 13	10 14	10 17	10 27	10 30	10 33	10 43	10 44	10 48		10 56	11 00	11 03		11 13	11 14	11 17	11 27	11 31	11 33	11 43
Seven Sisters ⊖	d																						
Lea Bridge	d		10 16			10 31			10 46				11 00				11 16			11 31			11 46
Stratford ■ ⊖	a		10 23			10 40			10 53				11 10				11 23			11 40			11 53
Hackney Downs	d			10 20						10 50								11 20					
London Liverpool Street ■ ⊖	a			10 28	10 31		10 45	10 47		10 58	11 02			11 15	11 17			11 28	11 31		11 45	11 47	

		LE	LE ■	LE B	LE ■	LE ◇■	LE ■	XC ◇■ C	LE	LE	LE ■	LE ■	LE ◇■	LE	LE	LE	LE ■	LE B	LE ■	LE ◇■	LE ■	XC ◇■ A
Cambridge North	d			10 39		10 53							11 13					11 40		11 53		
Cambridge	a			10 44		10 59							11 19					11 45		11 59		
	d			10 48		11 03		11 11					11 20					11 48		12 03		12 11
Shelford	d												11 25									
Whittlesford Parkway	d			10 57		11 11							11 30					11 57		12 11		
Great Chesterford	d												11 34									
Audley End	d			11 07		11 19		11 26					11 40					12 07		12 19		12 26
Newport (Essex)	d												11 43									
Elsenham	d												11 49									
Stansted Airport ✈	a			11 24				11 41										12 24				12 41
Stansted Airport ✈	d		11 15				11 30				11 45			12 00			12 15				12 30	
Stansted Mountfitchet	d		11 21										11 52				12 21					
Bishops Stortford	a					11 32	11 39						11 58	12 09						12 32	12 39	
Bishops Stortford	d				11 15	11 32	11 39					11 47	11 58	12 09					12 15	12 32	12 39	
Sawbridgeworth	d				11 20							11 52	12 03						12 20			
Harlow Mill	d				11 23								12 06						12 23			
Harlow Town	d		11 32		11 26	11 40					12 00	12 05	12 09				12 32		12 26	12 40		
Roydon	d				11 30								12 13						12 30			
Hertford East	d	11 09								11 39						12 09						
Ware	d	11 13								11 43						12 13						
St Margarets (Herts)	d	11 17								11 47						12 17						
Rye House	d	11 20								11 50						12 20						
Broxbourne ■	a	11 25			11 35	11 46				11 55		12 11	12 17			12 25			12 35	12 46		
Broxbourne ■	d	11 25			11 39	11 46				11 55		12 12	12 17			12 25			12 39	12 46		
Cheshunt	d	11 29			11 44	11 50				11 59		12 16	12 21			12 29			12 44	12 50		
Waltham Cross	d	11 31								12 01		12 19				12 31						
Enfield Lock	d	11 34			11 47					12 04						12 34			12 47			
Brimsdown	d	11 36								12 06						12 36						
Ponders End	d	11 38								12 08						12 38						
Meridian Water	d								12 08						12 38							
Northumberland Park	d				11 53				12 10						12 40				12 53			
Tottenham Hale ⊖	d	11 44	11 48		11 56	12 00	12 03		12 13	12 14	12 17	12 27	12 31	12 33	12 43	12 44	12 48		12 56	13 00	13 03	
Seven Sisters ⊖	d																					
Lea Bridge	d				12 00				12 16			12 31			12 46				13 00			
Stratford ■ ⊖	a				12 10				12 23			12 40			12 53				13 10			
Hackney Downs	d	11 50								12 20						12 50						
London Liverpool Street ■ ⊖	a	11 58	12 02			12 15	12 17			12 28	12 31		12 45	12 47		12 58	13 02			13 15	13 17	

A From Birmingham New Street

B From Norwich

C From Gloucester

Table T022-R

Saturdays

21 December to 16 May

Cambridge North, Cambridge, Stansted Airport, Bishops Stortford, Hertford East and Broxbourne - London

		LE	LE	LE	LE ■	LE ◇■	LE	LE	LE	LE ■		LE A	LE ■	LE ◇■	LE ■	XC ◇■ B	LE	LE	LE ■	LE ■		LE ◇■	LE ■	LE	LE
Cambridge North	d					12 13						12 39		12 53								13 13			
Cambridge	a					12 19						12 44		12 59								13 19			
	d					12 20						12 48		13 03		13 11						13 20			
Shelford	d					12 25																13 25			
Whittlesford Parkway	d					12 30						12 57		13 11								13 30			
Great Chesterford	d					12 34																13 34			
Audley End	d					12 40						13 07		13 19		13 26						13 40			
Newport (Essex)	d					12 43																13 43			
Elsenham	d					12 49																13 49			
Stansted Airport ✈	a											13 24				13 41									
Stansted Airport ✈	d			12 45			13 00			13 15					13 30				13 45				14 00		
Stansted Mountfitchet	d					12 52				13 21												13 52			
Bishops Stortford	a					12 58	13 09							13 32	13 39							13 58	14 09		
Bishops Stortford	d				12 47	12 58	13 09						13 15	13 32	13 39					13 47		13 58	14 09		
Sawbridgeworth	d				12 52	13 03							13 20							13 52		14 03			
Harlow Mill	d					13 06							13 23									14 06			
Harlow Town	d			13 00	13 05	13 09				13 32			13 26	13 40					14 00	14 05		14 09			
Roydon	d					13 13							13 30									14 13			
Hertford East	d		12 39						13 09									13 39							14 09
Ware	d		12 43						13 13									13 43							14 13
St Margarets (Herts)	d		12 47						13 17									13 47							14 17
Rye House	d		12 50						13 20									13 50							14 20
Broxbourne ■	a		12 55		13 11	13 17			13 25				13 35	13 46				13 55		14 11		14 17			14 25
Broxbourne ■	d		12 55		13 12	13 17			13 25				13 39	13 46				13 55		14 12		14 17			14 25
Cheshunt	d		12 59		13 16	13 21			13 29				13 44	13 50				13 59		14 16		14 21			14 29
Waltham Cross	d		13 01		13 19				13 31									14 01		14 19					14 31
Enfield Lock	d		13 04						13 34				13 47					14 04							14 34
Brimsdown	d		13 06						13 36									14 06							14 36
Ponders End	d		13 08						13 38									14 08							14 38
Meridian Water	d	13 08						13 38									14 08							14 38	
Northumberland Park	d	13 10						13 40					13 53				14 10							14 40	
Tottenham Hale ⊖	d	13 13	13 14	13 17	13 27	13 31	13 33	13 43	13 44	13 48			13 56	14 00	14 03		14 13	14 14	14 17	14 27		14 30	14 33	14 43	14 44
Seven Sisters ⊖	d																								
Lea Bridge	d	13 16			13 31			13 46					14 00				14 16			14 31				14 46	
Stratford ■ ⊖	a	13 23			13 40			13 53					14 10				14 23			14 40				14 53	
Hackney Downs	d		13 20						13 50									14 20							14 50
London Liverpool Street ■ ⊖	a		13 28	13 31		13 45	13 47		13 58	14 02				14 15	14 17			14 28	14 31			14 45	14 47		14 58

		LE	LE A	LE ■	LE ◇■	LE ■		XC ◇■ B	LE	LE	LE ■	LE ■	LE ◇■	LE	LE	LE		LE	LE A	LE ■	LE ◇■	LE ■	XC ◇■ B	LE	LE
Cambridge North	d		13 44		13 53								14 13						14 39		14 53				
Cambridge	a		13 49		13 59								14 19						14 44		14 59				
	d		13 51		14 03			14 11					14 20						14 48		15 03		15 11		
Shelford	d												14 25												
Whittlesford Parkway	d		13 59		14 11								14 30						14 57		15 11				
Great Chesterford	d												14 34												
Audley End	d		14 08		14 19			14 26					14 40						15 07		15 19		15 26		
Newport (Essex)	d												14 43												
Elsenham	d												14 49												
Stansted Airport ✈	a		14 24					14 41											15 24				15 41		
Stansted Airport ✈	d	14 15				14 30					14 45			15 00				15 15				15 30			
Stansted Mountfitchet	d	14 21											14 52					15 21							
Bishops Stortford	a				14 32	14 39							14 58	15 09							15 32	15 39			
Bishops Stortford	d			14 15	14 32	14 39						14 47	14 58	15 09						15 15	15 32	15 39			
Sawbridgeworth	d			14 20								14 52	15 03							15 20					
Harlow Mill	d			14 23									15 06							15 23					
Harlow Town	d	14 32		14 26	14 40						15 00	15 05	15 09					15 32		15 26	15 40				
Roydon	d			14 30									15 13							15 30					
Hertford East	d									14 39						15 09									15 39
Ware	d									14 43						15 13									15 43
St Margarets (Herts)	d									14 47						15 17									15 47
Rye House	d									14 50						15 20									15 50
Broxbourne ■	a			14 35	14 46					14 55		15 11	15 17			15 25				15 35	15 46				15 55
Broxbourne ■	d			14 39	14 46					14 55		15 12	15 17			15 25				15 39	15 46				15 55
Cheshunt	d			14 44	14 50					14 59		15 16	15 21			15 29				15 44	15 50				15 59
Waltham Cross	d									15 01		15 19				15 31									16 01
Enfield Lock	d			14 47						15 04						15 34				15 47					16 04
Brimsdown	d									15 06						15 36									16 06
Ponders End	d									15 08						15 38									16 08
Meridian Water	d								15 08						15 38									16 08	
Northumberland Park	d			14 53					15 10						15 40					15 53				16 10	
Tottenham Hale ⊖	d	14 48		14 56	15 01	15 03			15 13	15 14	15 17	15 27	15 30	15 33	15 43	15 44		15 48		15 56	16 01	16 03		16 13	16 14
Seven Sisters ⊖	d																								
Lea Bridge	d			15 00					15 16			15 31			15 46					16 00				16 16	
Stratford ■ ⊖	a			15 10					15 23			15 40			15 53					16 10				16 23	
Hackney Downs	d									15 20						15 50									16 20
London Liverpool Street ■ ⊖	a	15 02			15 15	15 17				15 28	15 31		15 45	15 47		15 58		16 02			16 15	16 17			16 28

A From Norwich
B From Birmingham New Street

NRT DECEMBER 19 EDITION

Table T022-R

Saturdays

21 December to 16 May

Cambridge North, Cambridge, Stansted Airport, Bishops Stortford, Hertford East and Broxbourne - London

		LE ■		LE ■	LE ◇■	LE ■	LE	LE	LE ■	LE A	LE ■	LE ◇■		LE	XC ◇■ B	LE	LE	LE ■	LE ■	LE ◇■	LE ■	LE		LE	LE
Cambridge North	d				15 13					15 41		15 53								16 13					
Cambridge	a				15 19					15 46		15 59								16 19					
	d				15 20					15 48		16 03			16 11					16 20					
Shelford	d				15 25															16 25					
Whittlesford Parkway	d				15 30					15 57		16 11								16 30					
Great Chesterford	d				15 34															16 34					
Audley End	d				15 40					16 07		16 19			16 26					16 40					
Newport (Essex)	d				15 43															16 43					
Elsenham	d				15 49															16 49					
Stansted Airport ✈	a									16 24					16 41										
Stansted Airport ✈	d	15 45				16 00			16 15					16 30				16 45			17 00				17 15
Stansted Mountfitchet	d				15 52				16 21											16 52					17 21
Bishops Stortford	a				15 58	16 09						16 32		16 39						16 58	17 09				
Bishops Stortford	d			15 47	15 58	16 09					16 15	16 32		16 39					16 47	16 58	17 09				
Sawbridgeworth	d			15 52	16 03						16 20								16 52	17 03					
Harlow Mill	d				16 06						16 23									17 06					
Harlow Town	d	16 00		16 05	16 09				16 32		16 26	16 40						17 00	17 05	17 09					17 32
Roydon	d				16 13						16 30									17 13					
Hertford East	d							16 09									16 39							17 09	
Ware	d							16 13									16 43							17 13	
St Margarets (Herts)	d							16 17									16 47							17 17	
Rye House	d							16 20									16 50							17 20	
Broxbourne ■	a			16 11	16 17			16 25			16 35	16 46					16 55		17 11	17 17				17 25	
Broxbourne ■	d			16 12	16 17			16 25			16 39	16 46					16 55		17 12	17 17				17 25	
Cheshunt	d			16 16	16 21			16 29			16 44	16 50					16 59		17 16	17 21				17 29	
Waltham Cross	d			16 19				16 31									17 01		17 19					17 31	
Enfield Lock	d							16 34			16 47						17 04							17 34	
Brimsdown	d							16 36									17 06							17 36	
Ponders End	d							16 38									17 08							17 38	
Meridian Water	d						16 38									17 08						17 38			
Northumberland Park	d						16 40				16 53					17 10						17 40			
Tottenham Hale ⊖	d	16 17		16 27	16 30	16 33	16 43	16 44	16 48		16 56	17 01		17 03		17 13	17 14	17 17	17 27	17 30	17 33	17 43		17 44	17 48
Seven Sisters ⊖	d																								
Lea Bridge	d			16 31			16 46				17 00					17 16			17 31			17 46			
Stratford ■ ⊖	a			16 40			16 53				17 10					17 23			17 40			17 53			
Hackney Downs	d							16 50									17 20							17 50	
London Liverpool Street ■ ⊖	a	16 31			16 45	16 47		16 58	17 02			17 15		17 17			17 28	17 31		17 45	17 47			17 58	18 02

		LE A	LE ■	LE ◇■	LE	XC ◇■ B	LE	LE		LE ■	LE ■	LE ◇■	LE ■	LE	LE	LE ■	LE A	LE ■		LE ◇■	LE ■	LE	LE	LE	XC ◇■ B
Cambridge North	d	16 38		16 53								17 13					17 39			17 53					
Cambridge	a	16 43		16 59								17 19					17 44			17 59					
	d	16 48		17 03		17 11						17 20					17 48			18 03					18 17
Shelford	d											17 25													
Whittlesford Parkway	d	16 57		17 11								17 30					17 57			18 11					
Great Chesterford	d											17 34													
Audley End	d	17 07		17 19		17 26						17 40					18 07			18 19					18 32
Newport (Essex)	d											17 43													
Elsenham	d											17 49													
Stansted Airport ✈	a	17 24				17 41											18 24								18 52
Stansted Airport ✈	d				17 30					17 45			18 00			18 15					18 30			18 45	
Stansted Mountfitchet	d											17 52				18 21									
Bishops Stortford	a			17 32	17 39							17 58	18 09							18 32	18 39				
Bishops Stortford	d		17 15	17 32	17 39						17 47	17 58	18 09					18 15		18 32	18 39				
Sawbridgeworth	d		17 20								17 52	18 03						18 20							
Harlow Mill	d		17 23									18 06						18 23							
Harlow Town	d		17 26	17 40						18 00	18 05	18 09				18 32		18 26		18 40				19 00	
Roydon	d		17 30									18 13						18 30							
Hertford East	d							17 39							18 09								18 39		
Ware	d							17 43							18 13								18 43		
St Margarets (Herts)	d							17 47							18 17								18 47		
Rye House	d							17 50							18 20								18 50		
Broxbourne ■	a		17 35	17 46				17 55			18 11	18 17			18 25			18 35		18 46			18 55		
Broxbourne ■	d		17 39	17 46				17 55			18 12	18 17			18 25			18 39		18 46			18 55		
Cheshunt	d		17 44	17 50				17 59			18 16	18 21			18 29			18 44		18 50			18 59		
Waltham Cross	d							18 01			18 19				18 31								19 01		
Enfield Lock	d		17 47					18 04							18 34			18 47					19 04		
Brimsdown	d							18 06							18 36								19 06		
Ponders End	d							18 08							18 38								19 08		
Meridian Water	d						18 08							18 38								19 08			
Northumberland Park	d		17 53				18 10							18 40				18 53				19 10			
Tottenham Hale ⊖	d		17 56	18 01	18 03		18 13	18 14		18 17	18 27	18 30	18 33	18 43	18 44	18 48		18 56		19 00	19 03	19 13	19 14	19 17	
Seven Sisters ⊖	d																								
Lea Bridge	d		18 00				18 16				18 31			18 46				19 00				19 16			
Stratford ■ ⊖	a		18 10				18 23				18 40			18 53				19 10				19 23			
Hackney Downs	d							18 20							18 50								19 20		
London Liverpool Street ■ ⊖	a			18 15	18 17			18 28		18 31		18 45	18 47		18 58	19 02				19 15	19 17		19 28	19 31	

A From Norwich
B From Birmingham New Street

Table T022-R

Saturdays
21 December to 16 May

Cambridge North, Cambridge, Stansted Airport, Bishops Stortford, Hertford East and Broxbourne - London

		LE 1	LE ◇1	LE 1	LE	LE	LE 1	LE A	LE 1	LE ◇1	LE	XC ◇1 B	LE	LE	LE	LE 1	LE ◇1	LE 1	LE	LE	LE 1	LE A
Cambridge North	d		18 13					18 39		18 53							19 13					19 39
Cambridge	a		18 19					18 44		18 59							19 19					19 44
	d		18 20					18 48		19 03		19 11					19 20					19 48
Shelford	d		18 26														19 25					
Whittlesford Parkway	d		18 30					18 57		19 11							19 30					19 57
Great Chesterford	d		18 34														19 34					
Audley End	d		18 40					19 07		19 19		19 26					19 40					20 07
Newport (Essex)	d		18 43														19 43					
Elsenham	d		18 49														19 49					
Stansted Airport ✈	a							19 24				19 41										20 24
Stansted Airport ✈	d			19 00			19 15				19 30				19 45			20 00			20 15	
Stansted Mountfitchet	d		18 52				19 21										19 52				20 21	
Bishops Stortford	a		18 58	19 09						19 32	19 39						19 58	20 09				
Bishops Stortford	d	18 47	18 58	19 09					19 15	19 32	19 39					19 47	19 58	20 09				
Sawbridgeworth	d	18 52	19 03						19 20							19 52	20 03					
Harlow Mill	d		19 06						19 23								20 06					
Harlow Town	d	19 05	19 09				19 32		19 26	19 40					20 00	20 05	20 09				20 32	
Roydon	d		19 13						19 30								20 13					
Hertford East	d					19 09								19 39						20 09		
Ware	d					19 13								19 43						20 13		
St Margarets (Herts)	d					19 17								19 47						20 17		
Rye House	d					19 20								19 50						20 20		
Broxbourne 8	a	19 11	19 17			19 25			19 35	19 46				19 55		20 11	20 17			20 25		
Broxbourne 8	d	19 12	19 17			19 25			19 39	19 46				19 55		20 12	20 17			20 25		
Cheshunt	d	19 16	19 21			19 29			19 44	19 50				19 59		20 16	20 21			20 29		
Waltham Cross	d	19 19				19 31								20 01		20 19				20 31		
Enfield Lock	d					19 34			19 47					20 04						20 34		
Brimsdown	d					19 36								20 06						20 36		
Ponders End	d					19 38								20 08						20 38		
Meridian Water	d				19 38								20 08						20 38			
Northumberland Park	d				19 40				19 53				20 10						20 40			
Tottenham Hale ⊖	d	19 27	19 30	19 33	19 43	19 44	19 48		19 56	20 00	20 03		20 13	20 14	20 17	20 27	20 30	20 33	20 43	20 44	20 48	
Seven Sisters ⊖	d																					
Lea Bridge	d	19 31			19 46				20 00				20 16			20 31			20 46			
Stratford 7 ⊖	a	19 40			19 53				20 10				20 23			20 40			20 53			
Hackney Downs	d					19 50								20 20						20 50		
London Liverpool Street 15 ⊖	a		19 45	19 47		19 58	20 03			20 15	20 17			20 28	20 31		20 45	20 47		20 58	21 02	

		LE 1	LE ◇1	LE 1	XC ◇1 B	LE	LE	LE 1	LE 1	LE ◇1	LE 1	LE	LE	LE 1	LE A	LE 1	LE ◇1	LE 1	XC ◇1 B	LE	LE	LE	LE 1
Cambridge North	d		19 53							20 13					20 39		20 53						
Cambridge	a		19 59							20 19					20 44		20 59						
	d		20 03		20 11					20 20					20 48		21 03		21 11				
Shelford	d									20 25													
Whittlesford Parkway	d		20 11							20 30					20 57		21 11						
Great Chesterford	d									20 34													
Audley End	d		20 19		20 26					20 40					21 07		21 19		21 26				
Newport (Essex)	d									20 43													
Elsenham	d									20 49													
Stansted Airport ✈	a				20 41										21 24				21 41				
Stansted Airport ✈	d			20 30				20 45			21 00			21 15				21 30				21 45	
Stansted Mountfitchet	d									20 52				21 21									
Bishops Stortford	a		20 32	20 39						20 58	21 09						21 32	21 39					
Bishops Stortford	d	20 15	20 32	20 39					20 47	20 58	21 09					21 15	21 32	21 39					21 47
Sawbridgeworth	d	20 20							20 52	21 03						21 20							21 52
Harlow Mill	d	20 23								21 06						21 23							
Harlow Town	d	20 26	20 40					21 00	21 05	21 09				21 32		21 26	21 40					22 00	22 05
Roydon	d	20 30								21 13						21 30							
Hertford East	d						20 39						21 09								21 39		
Ware	d						20 43						21 13								21 43		
St Margarets (Herts)	d						20 47						21 17								21 47		
Rye House	d						20 50						21 20								21 50		
Broxbourne 8	a	20 35	20 46				20 55		21 11	21 17			21 25			21 35	21 46				21 55		22 11
Broxbourne 8	d	20 39	20 46				20 55		21 12	21 17			21 25			21 39	21 46				21 55		22 12
Cheshunt	d	20 44	20 50				20 59		21 16	21 21			21 29			21 44	21 50				21 59		22 16
Waltham Cross	d						21 01		21 19				21 31								22 01		22 19
Enfield Lock	d	20 47					21 04						21 34			21 47					22 04		
Brimsdown	d						21 06						21 36								22 06		
Ponders End	d						21 08						21 38								22 08		
Meridian Water	d					21 08						21 38								22 08			
Northumberland Park	d	20 53				21 10						21 40				21 53				22 10			
Tottenham Hale ⊖	d	20 56	21 00	21 03		21 13	21 14	21 17	21 27	21 30	21 33	21 43	21 44	21 48		21 56	22 00	22 03		22 13	22 14	22 17	22 27
Seven Sisters ⊖	d																						
Lea Bridge	d	21 00				21 16			21 31			21 46				22 00				22 16			22 31
Stratford 7 ⊖	a	21 10				21 23			21 40			21 53				22 10				22 23			22 40
Hackney Downs	d						21 20						21 50								22 20		
London Liverpool Street 15 ⊖	a		21 15	21 17			21 28	21 31		21 45	21 47		21 58	22 02			22 15	22 17			22 28	22 31	

A From Norwich
B From Birmingham New Street

Table T022-R

Saturdays
21 December to 16 May

Cambridge North, Cambridge, Stansted Airport, Bishops Stortford, Hertford East and Broxbourne - London

		LE ◇1	LE	LE	LE	LE 1	LE 1	LE ◇1	LE 1	XC ◇1 A	LE	LE	LE 1	LE ◇1	LE 1	LE	LE 1	LE ◇1	LE 1	LE 1	LE	LE 1	LE
Cambridge North	d	21 13						21 53						22 13				22 43					
Cambridge	a	21 19						21 59						22 19				22 49					
	d	21 20						22 03		22 11				22 20				22 50		23 25			
Shelford	d	21 25												22 25				22 55		23 30			
Whittlesford Parkway	d	21 30						22 11						22 30				23 00		23 34			
Great Chesterford	d	21 34												22 34				23 04		23 38			
Audley End	d	21 40						22 19		22 26				22 40				23 10		23 44			
Newport (Essex)	d	21 43												22 43				23 13		23 47			
Elsenham	d	21 49												22 49				23 19		23 53			
Stansted Airport ✈	a									22 41													
Stansted Airport ✈	d		22 00			22 15			22 30				22 45		23 00		23 15		23 30			23 45	23 59
Stansted Mountfitchet	d	21 52				22 21								22 52			23 21	23 24		23 57			
Bishops Stortford	a	21 58	22 09					22 32	22 39					22 58	23 09			23 29	23 39	00 02			00 08
Bishops Stortford	d	21 58	22 09				22 15	22 32	22 39					22 58	23 09			23 29	23 39				00 08
Sawbridgeworth	d	22 03					22 20							23 03				23 33					
Harlow Mill	d	22 06					22 23							23 06				23 37					
Harlow Town	d	22 09				22 32	22 26	22 40					23 00	23 09			23 32	23 40				23 59	00 16
Roydon	d	22 13					22 30							23 13				23 44					
Hertford East	d				22 09							22 39				23 09					23 39		
Ware	d				22 13							22 43				23 13					23 43		
St Margarets (Herts)	d				22 17							22 47				23 17					23 47		
Rye House	d				22 20							22 50				23 20					23 50		
Broxbourne 8	a	22 17			22 25		22 35	22 46				22 55		23 17		23 25		23 48			23 55		
Broxbourne 8	d	22 17			22 25		22 39	22 46				22 55		23 17		23 25		23 48			23 55		
Cheshunt	d	22 21			22 29		22 44	22 50				22 59		23 21		23 29		23 52			23 59		
Waltham Cross	d				22 31							23 01				23 31					00 01		
Enfield Lock	d				22 34		22 47					23 04				23 34					00 04		
Brimsdown	d				22 36							23 06				23 36					00 06		
Ponders End	d				22 38							23 08				23 38					00 08		
Meridian Water	d			22 38							23 08												
Northumberland Park	d			22 40			22 53				23 10												
Tottenham Hale ⊖	d	22 30	22 33	22 43	22 44	22 48	22 56	23 00	23 03		23 13	23 14	23 17	23 30	23 33	23 44	23 48	00 01	00 04		00 14	00 17	
Seven Sisters ⊖	d																						
Lea Bridge	d			22 46			23 00				23 16												
Stratford 7 ⊖	a			22 53			23 10				23 22												
Hackney Downs	d				22 50							23 20				23 50					00 20		
London Liverpool Street 15 ⊖	a	22 45	22 47		22 58	23 02		23 15	23 17			23 28	23 31	23 45	23 47	23 58	00 02	00 14	00 17		00 28	00 31	00 51

Sundays
15 December to 10 May

		LE ◇1 B	LE 1 C	LE D	LE	LE 1 C	LE C	LE	LE	LE	LE 1	LE 1	LE 1	LE 1	LE 1	LE 1	LE	LE	LE	LE ◇1	LE 1	LE	LE
Cambridge North	d																						
Cambridge	a																						
	d																			07 31		07 39	
Shelford	d																						
Whittlesford Parkway	d																			07 39		07 46	
Great Chesterford	d																						
Audley End	d																			07 47		07 55	
Newport (Essex)	d																						
Elsenham	d																						
Stansted Airport ✈	a																					08 09	
Stansted Airport ✈	d							00 30	05 30	06 00	06 30		07 00	07 15		07 30		07 45			08 00		
Stansted Mountfitchet	d																	07 51					
Bishops Stortford	a							00 39	05 40	06 09	06 39		07 09			07 39				08 00	08 09		
Bishops Stortford	d						00 08	00 39	05 41	06 09	06 39	06 42	07 09		07 26	07 39				08 00	08 09		
Sawbridgeworth	d											06 46			07 30					08 05			
Harlow Mill	d														07 34								
Harlow Town	d						00 16	00 47	05 49	06 17	06 47	06 51	07 17	07 30	07 37			08 02		08 10			
Roydon	d														07 41								
Hertford East	d				00 07												07 39						08 09
Ware	d																07 43						08 13
St Margarets (Herts)	d																07 47						08 17
Rye House	d																07 50						08 20
Broxbourne 8	a				00 19							06 57			07 45		07 55			08 16			08 25
Broxbourne 8	d											06 57			07 45		07 55			08 16			08 25
Cheshunt	d											07 01			07 49		07 59			08 20			08 29
Waltham Cross	d			00 01								07 04					08 01						08 31
Enfield Lock	d			00 04								07 06					08 04						08 34
Brimsdown	d			00 06								07 09					08 06						08 36
Ponders End	d			00 08								07 11					08 08						08 38
Meridian Water	d																		08 15				
Northumberland Park	d																		08 17				
Tottenham Hale ⊖	d	00 01	00 04	00 14		00 17			06 06	06 33	07 03	07 17	07 33	07 46	07 58	08 01	08 14	08 17	08 20	08 29	08 32		08 44
Seven Sisters ⊖	d																						
Lea Bridge	d																08 18		08 23				08 48
Stratford 7 ⊖	a														08 08		08 25		08 30				08 55
Hackney Downs	d			00 20								07 22											
London Liverpool Street 15 ⊖	a	00 14	00 17	00 28		00 31	00 51	01 21	06 19	06 46	07 16	07 31	07 46	08 00		08 14		08 31		08 43	08 46		

A From Birmingham New Street
B not 15 December. From Cambridge North
C not 15 December. From Stansted Airport
D not 15 December. From Hertford East

Table T022-R

Sundays
15 December to 10 May

Cambridge North, Cambridge, Stansted Airport, Bishops Stortford, Hertford East and Broxbourne - London

		LE	LE	LE ◇1	LE 1	LE	LE 1	LE	LE 1 A	LE 1	LE ◇1	LE 1	LE	LE 1	LE	LE ◇1	LE 1	XC 1	LE	LE 1	LE	LE A	LE
Cambridge North	d																						
Cambridge	a																						
	d			07 50						08 25	08 31					08 50		09 15					09 25
Shelford	d			07 56												08 56							
Whittlesford Parkway	d			08 00						08 34	08 39					09 00							09 34
Great Chesterford	d			08 04												09 04							
Audley End	d			08 10						08 43	08 47					09 10		09 30					09 43
Newport (Essex)	d			08 13												09 13							
Elsenham	d			08 19												09 19							
Stansted Airport ✈	a									09 05		←						09 45					10 05
Stansted Airport ✈	d	08 15			08 30		08 45		09 00			09 00		09 15			09 30			09 45		10 00	
Stansted Mountfitchet	d			08 22			08 51		→							09 22				09 51		→	
Bishops Stortford	a			08 28	08 39						09 00	09 09				09 28	09 39						
Bishops Stortford	d			08 28	08 39						09 00	09 09				09 28	09 39						
Sawbridgeworth	d			08 32							09 05					09 32							
Harlow Mill	d			08 36												09 36							
Harlow Town	d	08 30		08 39			09 02				09 10			09 30		09 39				10 02			
Roydon	d			08 43												09 43							
Hertford East	d					08 39							09 09						09 39				
Ware	d					08 43							09 13						09 43				
St Margarets (Herts)	d					08 47							09 17						09 47				
Rye House	d					08 50							09 20						09 50				
Broxbourne 3	a			08 47		08 55					09 16		09 25			09 47			09 55				
Broxbourne 3	d			08 47		08 55					09 16		09 25			09 47			09 55				
Cheshunt	d			08 51		08 59					09 20		09 29			09 51			09 59				
Waltham Cross	d					09 01							09 31						10 01				
Enfield Lock	d					09 04							09 34						10 04				
Brimsdown	d					09 06							09 36						10 06				
Ponders End	d					09 08							09 38						10 08				
Meridian Water	d		08 45					09 15							09 45						10 15		
Northumberland Park	d		08 47					09 17							09 47						10 17		
Tottenham Hale ⊖	d	08 47	08 50	09 00	09 03	09 14	09 17	09 20			09 29	09 32	09 44	09 47	09 50	10 00	10 03		10 14	10 17	10 20		
Seven Sisters ⊖	d																						
Lea Bridge	d		08 53			09 18		09 23					09 48		09 53				10 18		10 23		
Stratford 7 ⊖	a		09 00			09 25		09 30					09 55		10 00				10 25		10 30		
Hackney Downs	d			09 05												10 05							
London Liverpool Street 15 ⊖	a	09 01		09 14	09 16		09 31				09 43	09 46		10 01		10 14	10 16			10 31			

		LE ◇1	LE	LE	LE 1	LE	LE ◇1	LE	XC 1	LE	LE 1	LE	LE 1 A	LE B	LE ◇1	LE 1	LE	LE 1	LE	LE ◇1	LE 1	XC 1
Cambridge North	d						09 42							10 16	10 23					10 42		
Cambridge	a						09 48							10 21	10 29					10 48		
	d	09 31					09 50		10 15					10 25	10 31					10 50		11 15
Shelford	d						09 56													10 56		
Whittlesford Parkway	d	09 39					10 00							10 34	10 39					11 00		
Great Chesterford	d						10 04													11 04		
Audley End	d	09 47					10 10		10 30					10 43	10 47					11 10		11 30
Newport (Essex)	d						10 13													11 13		
Elsenham	d						10 19													11 19		
Stansted Airport ✈	a		←						10 45					11 05		←						11 45
Stansted Airport ✈	d		10 00		10 15			10 30			10 45		11 00			11 00		11 15			11 30	
Stansted Mountfitchet	d						10 22				10 51		→							11 22		
Bishops Stortford	a	10 00	10 09				10 28	10 39							11 00	11 09				11 28	11 39	
Bishops Stortford	d	10 00	10 09				10 28	10 39							11 00	11 09				11 28	11 39	
Sawbridgeworth	d	10 05					10 32								11 05					11 32		
Harlow Mill	d						10 36													11 36		
Harlow Town	d	10 10			10 30		10 39				11 02				11 10			11 30		11 39		
Roydon	d						10 43													11 43		
Hertford East	d			10 09						10 39							11 09					
Ware	d			10 13						10 43							11 13					
St Margarets (Herts)	d			10 17						10 47							11 17					
Rye House	d			10 20						10 50							11 20					
Broxbourne 3	a	10 16		10 25			10 47			10 55					11 16		11 25			11 47		
Broxbourne 3	d	10 16		10 25			10 47			10 55					11 16		11 25			11 47		
Cheshunt	d	10 20		10 29			10 51			10 59					11 20		11 29			11 51		
Waltham Cross	d			10 31						11 01							11 31					
Enfield Lock	d			10 34						11 04							11 34					
Brimsdown	d			10 36						11 06							11 36					
Ponders End	d			10 38						11 08							11 38					
Meridian Water	d					10 45						11 15							11 45			
Northumberland Park	d					10 47						11 17							11 47			
Tottenham Hale ⊖	d	10 29	10 32	10 44	10 47	10 50	11 00	11 03		11 14	11 17	11 20			11 29	11 32	11 44	11 47	11 50	12 00	12 03	
Seven Sisters ⊖	d																					
Lea Bridge	d			10 48		10 53				11 18		11 23					11 48		11 53			
Stratford 7 ⊖	a			10 55		11 00				11 25		11 30					11 55		12 00			
Hackney Downs	d						11 05													12 05		
London Liverpool Street 15 ⊖	a	10 43	10 46		11 01		11 14	11 16			11 31				11 43	11 46		12 01		12 14	12 16	

A To London Liverpool Street
B From Norwich

NRT DECEMBER 19 EDITION

Table T022-R

Sundays
15 December to 10 May

Cambridge North, Cambridge, Stansted Airport, Bishops Stortford, Hertford East and Broxbourne - London

		LE	LE 1	LE	LE A	LE B	LE ◇1	LE	LE	LE	LE	LE ◇1	LE 1	XC 1	LE	LE	LE	LE 1 A	LE B	LE ◇1	LE 1	LE	LE 1
Cambridge North	d					11 16	11 23					11 42							12 16	12 23			
Cambridge	a					11 24	11 29					11 48							12 21	12 29			
	d					11 25	11 31					11 50		12 15					12 25	12 31			
Shelford	d											11 56											
Whittlesford Parkway	d					11 34	11 39					12 00							12 34	12 39			
Great Chesterford	d											12 04											
Audley End	d					11 43	11 47					12 10		12 30					12 43	12 47			
Newport (Essex)	d											12 13											
Elsenham	d											12 19											
Stansted Airport ✈	a					12 05		←						12 45					13 05		←		
Stansted Airport ✈	d		11 45		12 00			12 00		12 15			12 30			12 45		13 00			13 00		13 15
Stansted Mountfitchet	d		11 51		→							12 22				12 51		→					
Bishops Stortford	a						12 00	12 09				12 28	12 39							13 00	13 09		
Bishops Stortford	d						12 00	12 09				12 28	12 39							13 00	13 09		
Sawbridgeworth	d						12 05					12 32								13 05			
Harlow Mill	d											12 36											
Harlow Town	d		12 02				12 10			12 30		12 39				13 02				13 10			13 30
Roydon	d											12 43											
Hertford East	d	11 39							12 09						12 39							13 09	
Ware	d	11 43							12 13						12 43							13 13	
St Margarets (Herts)	d	11 47							12 17						12 47							13 17	
Rye House	d	11 50							12 20						12 50							13 20	
Broxbourne 3	a	11 55					12 16		12 25			12 47			12 55					13 16		13 25	
Broxbourne 3	d	11 55					12 16		12 25			12 47			12 55					13 16		13 25	
Cheshunt	d	11 59					12 20		12 29			12 51			12 59					13 20		13 29	
Waltham Cross	d	12 01							12 31						13 01							13 31	
Enfield Lock	d	12 04							12 34						13 04							13 34	
Brimsdown	d	12 06							12 36						13 06							13 36	
Ponders End	d	12 08							12 38						13 08							13 38	
Meridian Water	d			12 15							12 45						13 15						
Northumberland Park	d			12 17							12 47						13 17						
Tottenham Hale ⊖	d	12 14	12 17	12 20			12 29	12 32	12 44	12 47	12 50	13 00	13 03		13 14	13 17	13 20			13 29	13 32	13 44	13 47
Seven Sisters ⊖	d																						
Lea Bridge	d	12 18		12 23					12 48		12 53				13 18		13 23					13 48	
Stratford 7 ⊖	a	12 25		12 30					12 55		13 00				13 25		13 30					13 55	
Hackney Downs	d											13 05											
London Liverpool Street 15 ⊖	a		12 31				12 43	12 46		13 01		13 14	13 16			13 31				13 43	13 46		14 01

		LE	LE ◇1	LE 1	XC 1	LE	LE 1	LE	LE 1 A	LE B	LE ◇1	LE 1	LE	LE	LE	LE ◇1	LE	XC ◇1 C	LE	LE 1	LE	LE A
Cambridge North	d		12 42							13 16	13 23					13 42						
Cambridge	a		12 48							13 21	13 29					13 48						
	d		12 50		13 15					13 25	13 31					13 50		14 15				
Shelford	d		12 56													13 56						
Whittlesford Parkway	d		13 00							13 34	13 39					14 00						
Great Chesterford	d		13 04													14 04						
Audley End	d		13 10		13 30					13 43	13 47					14 10		14 30				
Newport (Essex)	d		13 13													14 13						
Elsenham	d		13 19													14 19						
Stansted Airport ✈	a				13 45					14 05		←						14 45				
Stansted Airport ✈	d			13 30			13 45		14 00			14 00		14 15			14 30			14 45		15 00
Stansted Mountfitchet	d		13 22				13 51		→							14 22				14 51		→
Bishops Stortford	a		13 28	13 39							14 00	14 09				14 28	14 39					
Bishops Stortford	d		13 28	13 39							14 00	14 09				14 28	14 39					
Sawbridgeworth	d		13 32								14 05					14 32						
Harlow Mill	d		13 36													14 36						
Harlow Town	d		13 39				14 02				14 10			14 30		14 39				15 02		
Roydon	d		13 43													14 43						
Hertford East	d					13 39							14 09						14 39			
Ware	d					13 43							14 13						14 43			
St Margarets (Herts)	d					13 47							14 17						14 47			
Rye House	d					13 50							14 20						14 50			
Broxbourne 3	a		13 47			13 55					14 16		14 25			14 47			14 55			
Broxbourne 3	d		13 47			13 55					14 16		14 25			14 47			14 55			
Cheshunt	d		13 51			13 59					14 20		14 29			14 51			14 59			
Waltham Cross	d					14 01							14 31						15 01			
Enfield Lock	d					14 04							14 34						15 04			
Brimsdown	d					14 06							14 36						15 06			
Ponders End	d					14 08							14 38						15 08			
Meridian Water	d	13 45						14 15							14 45						15 15	
Northumberland Park	d	13 47						14 17							14 47						15 17	
Tottenham Hale ⊖	d	13 50	14 00	14 03		14 14	14 17	14 20			14 29	14 32	14 44	14 47	14 50	15 00	15 03		15 14	15 17	15 20	
Seven Sisters ⊖	d																					
Lea Bridge	d	13 53				14 18		14 23					14 48		14 53				15 18		15 23	
Stratford 7 ⊖	a	14 00				14 25		14 30					14 55		15 00				15 25		15 30	
Hackney Downs	d		14 05													15 05						
London Liverpool Street 15 ⊖	a		14 14	14 16			14 31				14 43	14 46		15 01		15 14	15 16			15 31		

A To London Liverpool Street
B From Norwich
C From Birmingham New Street

Table T022-R

Sundays
15 December to 10 May

Cambridge North, Cambridge, Stansted Airport, Bishops Stortford, Hertford East and Broxbourne - London

Station		LE A	LE ◇1	LE	LE	LE 1	LE	LE ◇1	LE 1	XC ◇1 B	LE	LE 1	LE	LE 1 C	LE A	LE ◇1	LE 1	LE	LE 1	LE	LE ◇1	LE	XC ◇1 B
Cambridge North	d	14 16	14 23					14 42							15 16	15 23					15 42		
Cambridge	a	14 21	14 29					14 48							15 21	15 29					15 48		
	d	14 25	14 31					14 50		15 15					15 25	15 31					15 50		16 15
Shelford	d							14 56													15 56		
Whittlesford Parkway	d	14 34	14 39					15 00							15 34	15 39					16 00		
Great Chesterford	d							15 04													16 04		
Audley End	d	14 43	14 47					15 10		15 30					15 43	15 47					16 10		16 30
Newport (Essex)	d							15 13													16 13		
Elsenham	d							15 19													16 19		
Stansted Airport ✈	a	15 05		←						15 45					16 05		←						16 45
Stansted Airport ✈	d			15 00		15 15			15 30			15 45		16 00			16 00		16 15			16 30	
Stansted Mountfitchet	d							15 22				15 51		→							16 22		
Bishops Stortford	a		15 00	15 09				15 28	15 39							16 00	16 09				16 28	16 39	
Bishops Stortford	d		15 00	15 09				15 28	15 39							16 00	16 09				16 28	16 39	
Sawbridgeworth	d		15 05					15 32								16 05					16 32		
Harlow Mill	d							15 36													16 36		
Harlow Town	d		15 10			15 30		15 39				16 02				16 10			16 30		16 39		
Roydon	d							15 43													16 43		
Hertford East	d				15 09						15 39							16 09					
Ware	d				15 13						15 43							16 13					
St Margarets (Herts)	d				15 17						15 47							16 17					
Rye House	d				15 20						15 50							16 20					
Broxbourne 3	a		15 16		15 25			15 47			15 55					16 16		16 25			16 47		
Broxbourne 3	d		15 16		15 25			15 47			15 55					16 16		16 25			16 47		
Cheshunt	d		15 20		15 29			15 51			15 59					16 20		16 29			16 51		
Waltham Cross	d				15 31						16 01							16 31					
Enfield Lock	d				15 34						16 04							16 34					
Brimsdown	d				15 36						16 06							16 36					
Ponders End	d				15 38						16 08							16 38					
Meridian Water	d						15 45						16 15							16 45			
Northumberland Park	d						15 47						16 17							16 47			
Tottenham Hale ⊖	d		15 29	15 32	15 44	15 47	15 50	16 00	16 03		16 14	16 17	16 20			16 29	16 32	16 44	16 47	16 50	17 00	17 03	
Seven Sisters ⊖	d																						
Lea Bridge	d				15 48		15 53				16 18		16 23					16 48		16 53			
Stratford 7 ⊖	a				15 55		16 00				16 25		16 30					16 55		17 00			
Hackney Downs	d							16 05													17 05		
London Liverpool Street 15 ⊖	a		15 43	15 46		16 01		16 14	16 16			16 31				16 43	16 46		17 01		17 14	17 16	

Station		LE	LE	LE	LE 1 C	LE A	LE ◇1	LE 1	LE	LE	LE	LE ◇1	LE 1	XC ◇1 B	LE	LE 1	LE	LE 1 C	LE A	LE ◇1	LE 1	LE	LE 1
Cambridge North	d					16 16	16 23					16 42							17 16	17 23			
Cambridge	a					16 21	16 29					16 48							17 21	17 29			
	d					16 25	16 31					16 50		17 15					17 25	17 31			
Shelford	d											16 56											
Whittlesford Parkway	d					16 34	16 39					17 00							17 34	17 39			
Great Chesterford	d											17 04											
Audley End	d					16 43	16 47					17 10		17 30					17 43	17 47			
Newport (Essex)	d											17 13											
Elsenham	d											17 19											
Stansted Airport ✈	a					17 05		←						17 45					18 05		←		
Stansted Airport ✈	d		16 45		17 00			17 00		17 15			17 30			17 45		18 00			18 00		18 15
Stansted Mountfitchet	d		16 51		→							17 22				17 51		→					
Bishops Stortford	a						17 00	17 09				17 28	17 39							18 00	18 09		
Bishops Stortford	d						17 00	17 09				17 28	17 39							18 00	18 09		
Sawbridgeworth	d						17 05					17 32								18 05			
Harlow Mill	d											17 36											
Harlow Town	d		17 02				17 10			17 30		17 39				18 02				18 10			18 30
Roydon	d											17 43											
Hertford East	d	16 39							17 09						17 39							18 09	
Ware	d	16 43							17 13						17 43							18 13	
St Margarets (Herts)	d	16 47							17 17						17 47							18 17	
Rye House	d	16 50							17 20						17 50							18 20	
Broxbourne 3	a	16 55					17 16		17 25			17 47			17 55					18 16		18 25	
Broxbourne 3	d	16 55					17 16		17 25			17 47			17 55					18 16		18 25	
Cheshunt	d	16 59					17 20		17 29			17 51			17 59					18 20		18 29	
Waltham Cross	d	17 01							17 31						18 01							18 31	
Enfield Lock	d	17 04							17 34						18 04							18 34	
Brimsdown	d	17 06							17 36						18 06							18 36	
Ponders End	d	17 08							17 38						18 08							18 38	
Meridian Water	d			17 15							17 45						18 15						
Northumberland Park	d			17 17							17 47						18 17						
Tottenham Hale ⊖	d	17 14	17 17	17 20			17 29	17 32	17 44	17 47	17 50	18 00	18 03		18 14	18 17	18 20			18 29	18 32	18 44	18 47
Seven Sisters ⊖	d																						
Lea Bridge	d	17 18		17 23					17 48		17 53				18 18		18 23					18 48	
Stratford 7 ⊖	a	17 25		17 30					17 55		18 00				18 25		18 30					18 55	
Hackney Downs	d											18 05											
London Liverpool Street 15 ⊖	a		17 31				17 43	17 46		18 01		18 14	18 16			18 31				18 43	18 46		19 01

A From Norwich B From Birmingham New Street C To London Liverpool Street

Table T022-R

Sundays
15 December to 10 May

Cambridge North, Cambridge, Stansted Airport, Bishops Stortford, Hertford East and Broxbourne - London

Station		LE	LE ◇1	LE 1	XC ◇1 A	LE	LE	LE	LE 1 B	LE C	LE ◇1	LE 1	LE	LE 1	LE	LE ◇1	LE	XC ◇1 A	LE	LE 1	LE	LE 1 B
Cambridge North	d		17 42							18 16	18 23					18 42						
Cambridge	a		17 48							18 21	18 29					18 48						
	d		17 50		18 15					18 25	18 31					18 50		19 15				
Shelford	d		17 56													18 56						
Whittlesford Parkway	d		18 00							18 34	18 39					19 00						
Great Chesterford	d		18 04													19 04						
Audley End	d		18 10		18 30					18 43	18 47					19 10		19 30				
Newport (Essex)	d		18 13													19 13						
Elsenham	d		18 19													19 19						
Stansted Airport ✈	a				18 45					19 05		←						19 45				
Stansted Airport ✈	d			18 30			18 45		19 00			19 00		19 15			19 30			19 45		20 00
Stansted Mountfitchet	d		18 22				18 51		→							19 22				19 51		→
Bishops Stortford	a		18 28	18 39							19 00	19 09				19 28	19 39					
Bishops Stortford	d		18 28	18 39							19 00	19 09				19 28	19 39					
Sawbridgeworth	d		18 32								19 05					19 32						
Harlow Mill	d		18 36													19 36						
Harlow Town	d		18 39				19 02				19 10			19 30		19 39				20 02		
Roydon	d		18 43													19 43						
Hertford East	d					18 39							19 09						19 39			
Ware	d					18 43							19 13						19 43			
St Margarets (Herts)	d					18 47							19 17						19 47			
Rye House	d					18 50							19 20						19 50			
Broxbourne 3	a		18 47			18 55					19 16		19 25			19 47			19 55			
Broxbourne 3	d		18 47			18 55					19 16		19 25			19 47			19 55			
Cheshunt	d		18 51			18 59					19 20		19 29			19 51			19 59			
Waltham Cross	d					19 01							19 31						20 01			
Enfield Lock	d					19 04							19 34						20 04			
Brimsdown	d					19 06							19 36						20 06			
Ponders End	d					19 08							19 38						20 08			
Meridian Water	d	18 45						19 15							19 45						20 15	
Northumberland Park	d	18 47						19 17							19 47						20 17	
Tottenham Hale ⊖	d	18 50	19 00	19 03		19 14	19 17	19 20			19 29	19 32	19 44	19 47	19 50	20 00	20 03		20 14	20 17	20 20	
Seven Sisters ⊖	d																					
Lea Bridge	d	18 53				19 18		19 23					19 48		19 53				20 18		20 23	
Stratford 7 ⊖	a	19 00				19 25		19 30					19 55		20 00				20 25		20 30	
Hackney Downs	d		19 05													20 05						
London Liverpool Street 15 ⊖	a		19 14	19 16			19 31				19 43	19 46		20 01		20 14	20 16			20 31		

Station		LE C	LE ◇1	LE 1	LE	LE 1	LE	LE ◇1	LE 1	XC ◇1 A	LE	LE 1	LE	LE B	LE C	LE ◇1	LE	LE	LE 1	LE	LE ◇1	LE 1	XC ◇1 A
Cambridge North	d	19 16	19 23					19 42							20 16	20 23					20 42		
Cambridge	a	19 21	19 29					19 48							20 21	20 29					20 48		
	d	19 25	19 31					19 50		20 15					20 25	20 31					20 50		21 13
Shelford	d							19 56													20 56		
Whittlesford Parkway	d	19 34	19 39					20 00							20 34	20 39					21 00		
Great Chesterford	d							20 04													21 04		
Audley End	d	19 43	19 47					20 10		20 30					20 43	20 47					21 10		21 30
Newport (Essex)	d							20 13													21 13		
Elsenham	d							20 19													21 19		
Stansted Airport ✈	a	20 05		←						20 45					21 05		←						21 45
Stansted Airport ✈	d			20 00		20 15			20 30			20 45		21 00			21 00		21 15			21 30	
Stansted Mountfitchet	d							20 22				20 51		→							21 22		
Bishops Stortford	a		20 00	20 09				20 28	20 39							21 00	21 09				21 28	21 39	
Bishops Stortford	d		20 00	20 09				20 28	20 39							21 00	21 09				21 28	21 39	
Sawbridgeworth	d		20 05					20 32								21 05					21 32		
Harlow Mill	d							20 36													21 36		
Harlow Town	d		20 10			20 30		20 39				21 02				21 10			21 30		21 39		
Roydon	d							20 43													21 43		
Hertford East	d				20 09						20 39							21 09					
Ware	d				20 13						20 43							21 13					
St Margarets (Herts)	d				20 17						20 47							21 17					
Rye House	d				20 20						20 50							21 20					
Broxbourne 3	a		20 16		20 25			20 47			20 55					21 16		21 25			21 47		
Broxbourne 3	d		20 16		20 25			20 47			20 55					21 16		21 25			21 47		
Cheshunt	d		20 20		20 29			20 51			20 59					21 20		21 29			21 51		
Waltham Cross	d				20 31						21 01							21 31					
Enfield Lock	d				20 34						21 04							21 34					
Brimsdown	d				20 36						21 06							21 36					
Ponders End	d				20 38						21 08							21 38					
Meridian Water	d						20 45						21 15							21 45			
Northumberland Park	d						20 47						21 17							21 47			
Tottenham Hale ⊖	d		20 29	20 32	20 44	20 47	20 50	21 00	21 03		21 14	21 17	21 20			21 29	21 32	21 44	21 47	21 50	22 00	22 03	
Seven Sisters ⊖	d																						
Lea Bridge	d				20 48		20 53				21 18		21 23					21 48		21 53			
Stratford 7 ⊖	a				20 55		21 00				21 25		21 30					21 55		22 00			
Hackney Downs	d							21 05													22 05		
London Liverpool Street 15 ⊖	a		20 43	20 46		21 01		21 14	21 16			21 31				21 43	21 46		22 01		22 14	22 16	

A From Birmingham New Street B To London Liverpool Street C From Norwich

Table T022-R

Sundays

15 December to 10 May

Cambridge North, Cambridge, Stansted Airport, Bishops Stortford, Hertford East and Broxbourne - London

		LE	LE	LE	LE ■	LE	LE ◇■	LE ■	LE	LE ■	LE	LE ■	LE ■	XC ◇■	LE	LE ■	LE ◇■	LE ■	LE ■	LE	LE ■	LE ■
					A	B								C								
Cambridge North	d					21 16	21 23					21 42							22 42			
Cambridge	a					21 21	21 29					21 49							22 48			
	d					21 25	21 31					21 50		22 15			22 32		22 50			
Shelford	d											21 56							22 56			
Whittlesford Parkway	d					21 34	21 39					22 00					22 39		23 00			
Great Chesterford	d											22 04							23 04			
Audley End	d					21 43	21 47					22 10		22 30			22 47		23 10			
Newport (Essex)	d											22 13							23 13			
Elsenham	d											22 19							23 19			
Stansted Airport ✈	a					22 05		←						22 45								
Stansted Airport ✈	d		21 45		22 00			22 00		22 15			22 30			22 45		23 00		23 15	23 30	23 45
Stansted Mountfitchet	d		21 51		→							22 22				22 51			23 22			
Bishops Stortford	a						22 00	22 09				22 28	22 39				23 00	23 09	23 28		23 39	
Bishops Stortford	d						22 00	22 09				22 28	22 39				23 00	23 09			23 39	
Sawbridgeworth	d						22 05					22 32					23 05					
Harlow Mill	d											22 36										
Harlow Town	d		22 02				22 10			22 30		22 39				23 02	23 10			23 30	23 47	23 59
Roydon	d											22 43										
Hertford East	d	21 39							22 09						22 39							
Ware	d	21 43							22 13						22 43							
St Margarets (Herts)	d	21 47							22 17						22 47							
Rye House	d	21 50							22 20						22 50							
Broxbourne ■	a	21 55					22 16		22 25			22 47			22 55		23 16					
Broxbourne ■	d	21 55					22 16		22 25			22 47			22 55		23 16					
Cheshunt	d	21 59					22 20		22 29			22 51			22 59		23 20					
Waltham Cross	d	22 01							22 31						23 01							
Enfield Lock	d	22 04							22 34						23 04							
Brimsdown	d	22 06							22 36						23 06							
Ponders End	d	22 08							22 38						23 08							
Meridian Water	d			22 15							22 45											
Northumberland Park	d			22 17							22 47											
Tottenham Hale ⊖	d	22 14	22 17	22 20			22 29	22 32	22 44	22 47	22 50	23 00	23 03		23 14	23 17	23 29	23 32		23 46		
Seven Sisters ⊖	d																				00 08	00 21
Lea Bridge	d	22 18		22 23							22 53	23 04			23 18							
Stratford ■ ⊖	a	22 25		22 30							23 00	23 11			23 25							
Hackney Downs	d								22 50													
London Liverpool Street [15] ⊖	a		22 31				22 43	22 46	22 58	23 01			23 16			23 31	23 43	23 46		23 59	00 22	00 35

		LE
Cambridge North	d	
Cambridge	a	
	d	
Shelford	d	
Whittlesford Parkway	d	
Great Chesterford	d	
Audley End	d	
Newport (Essex)	d	
Elsenham	d	
Stansted Airport ✈	a	
Stansted Airport ✈	d	23 59
Stansted Mountfitchet	d	
Bishops Stortford	a	00 03
Bishops Stortford	d	00 03
Sawbridgeworth	d	
Harlow Mill	d	
Harlow Town	d	00 16
Roydon	d	
Hertford East	d	
Ware	d	
St Margarets (Herts)	d	
Rye House	d	
Broxbourne ■	a	
Broxbourne ■	d	
Cheshunt	d	
Waltham Cross	d	
Enfield Lock	d	
Brimsdown	d	
Ponders End	d	
Meridian Water	d	
Northumberland Park	d	
Tottenham Hale ⊖	d	
Seven Sisters ⊖	d	
Lea Bridge	d	
Stratford ■ ⊖	a	
Hackney Downs	d	
London Liverpool Street [15] ⊖	a	00 5

A To London Liverpool Street B From Norwich C From Birmingham New Street

Table T024-F

Mondays to Fridays

16 December to 15 May

London - Welwyn Garden City and Hertford North

Miles	Miles			GN MX	TL MX ■	TL MO ■	GN MO	GN MX	GN MX	GN MO A	GN MO B	GN MX	TL MX ■	GN MO A	GN MO B	TL MO ■	GN MX	GN MO A	GN MO B	GN MX	TL MX ■	GN MO ■	TL MX ■
—	—	London Bridge	d																				
—	—	London Blackfriars	d																		00 37		
—	—	City Thameslink	d																				
—	—	Farringdon	d																		00 41		
—	—	St Pancras International	d																		00 46		
0	—	London Kings Cross [15] ⊖	d			00 02			00 01		00 05	00 16	00 23		00 24	00 32	00 36		00 39	00 40		01 02	01 05
—	—	Finsbury Park	a			00 07			00 06		00 12	00 22	00 28		00 29	00 37	00 42		00 44	00 46	00 52	01 08	01 10
—	0	Moorgate ⊖	d											00 17				00 27					
—	0½	Old Street ⊖	d							00 01				00 19				00 29					
—	1¾	Essex Road	d							00 04				00 22				00 32					
—	2¼	Highbury & Islington ⊖	d							00 06				00 25				00 35					
—	2¾	Drayton Park	d							00 09				00 27				00 37					
2½	3½	Finsbury Park ⊖	a							00 11				00 30				00 40					
—	—	Finsbury Park	d		00 02	00 09			00 11	00 12	00 13	00 23	00 29	00 31	00 31	00 39	00 43	00 42	00 46	00 47	00 54	01 09	01 11
3½	4½	Harringay	d					00 01	00 14	00 14	00 15	00 26		00 33	00 33			00 44	00 48	00 49			
4	5	Hornsey	d				00 01	00 03	00 16	00 16	00 17	00 28		00 35	00 35			00 46	00 50	00 51			
5	6	Alexandra Palace	d				00 05	00 07	00 19	00 19	00 20	00 31		00 39	00 39		00 47	00 49	00 53	00 55		01 14	
6½	—	New Southgate	d						00 22	00 22	00 23							00 52	00 56				
8½	—	Oakleigh Park	d						00 25	00 26	00 27							00 56	01 00				
9¼	—	New Barnet	d						00 28	00 28	00 29						00 53	00 58	01 02				
10½	—	Hadley Wood	d						00 31	00 31	00 32						00 56	01 01	01 05				
12¾	—	Potters Bar	d		00 17	00 20			00 35	00 35	00 36		00 42			00 50	01 00	01 05	01 09				01 22
14½	—	Brookmans Park	d						00 38	00 38	00 39							01 08	01 12				
15½	—	Welham Green	d						00 41	00 41	00 42							01 11	01 15				
17¾	—	Hatfield	d		00 23	00 26			00 44	00 44	00 45		00 48			00 56	01 06	01 14	01 18				01 28
20¼	—	Welwyn Garden City ■	d		00 28	00 31			00a49	00a51	00a52		00 58			01 01	01a11	01a21	01a25		01 15		01 34
22	—	Welwyn North	d		00 31	00 35							01 01			01s04							01 37
25	—	Knebworth	d		00 35	00 39							01 05			01s08							01 41
—	6¾	Bowes Park	d				00 07	00 09				00 34		00 41	00 41					00 58			
—	7¾	Palmers Green	d	00 01			00 10	00 12				00 36		00 44	00 44					01 01		01 17	
—	8¾	Winchmore Hill	d	00 04			00 13	00 15				00 39		00 47	00 47					01 04		01 19	
—	9½	Grange Park	d	00 06			00 15	00 17				00 41		00 49	00 49					01 06			
—	10¼	Enfield Chase	d	00 08			00 17	00 19				00 43		00 51	00 51					01 08		01 22	
—	11	Gordon Hill	d	00 11			00 20	00 22				00 46		00 54	00 54					01 11		01 24	
—	12½	Crews Hill	d	00 14			00 23	00 25				00 49		00 57	00 57					01 14			
—	14¼	Cuffley	d	00 17			00 26	00 28				00 52		01 00	01 00					01 17		01 28	
—	17¾	Bayford	d	00 21			00 30	00 33				00 56		01 04	01 04					01 22			
—	20¾	Hertford North	a	00 27			00 35	00 37				01 02		01 10	01 10					01 26		01 35	
—	25	Watton-at-Stone	a				00 42	00 44												01 33			
27½	30	Stevenage ■	a		00 39	00 43	00 50	00 51					01 09			01 12				01 40	01 23	01 46	01 45

		GN MX	TL MO ■	TL MX	GN	GN	TL ■	GN	TL ■	GN	GN	TL ■	GN	TL	GN	GN	TL ■	GN	GN	TL	GN	GN	GN
London Bridge	d																						
London Blackfriars	d																						
City Thameslink	d																						
Farringdon	d																						
St Pancras International	d																						
London Kings Cross [15] ⊖	d	01 10	01 32	01 40	05 06	05 21	05 25		05 56			06 21		06 30			06 51			07 06			
Finsbury Park	a	01 15	01 37	01 47	05 12	05 27	05 30		06 01			06 26		06 36			06 57			07 15			
Moorgate ⊖	d							05 37		05 57	06 07		06 17		06 27	06 37		06 45	06 52		07 00	07 05	07 10
Old Street ⊖	d							05 39		05 59	06 09		06 19		06 29	06 39		06 47	06 54		07 02	07 07	07 12
Essex Road	d							05 42		06 02	06 12		06 22		06 32	06 42		06 50	06 57		07 05	07 10	07 15
Highbury & Islington ⊖	d							05 45		06 05	06 15		06 25		06 35	06 45		06 53	07 00		07 08	07 13	07 18
Drayton Park	d							05 47		06 07	06 17		06 27		06 37	06 47		06 55	07 02		07 10	07 15	07 20
Finsbury Park ⊖	a							05 50		06 10	06 20		06 30		06 40	06 50		06 58	07 05		07 12	07 18	07 22
Finsbury Park	d	01 16	01 39	01 48	05 13	05 27	05 33	05 53	06 02	06 13	06 23	06 30	06 33	06 37	06 43	06 53	07 01	07 00	07 05	07 15	07 15	07 18	07 23
Harringay	d	01 18			05 16	05 30		05 56		06 16	06 26				06 46	06 56			07 08				07 26
Hornsey	d	01 20			05 18	05 32		05 58		06 18	06 28				06 48	06 58			07 10				07 28
Alexandra Palace	d	01 24	01 43	01 53	05 21	05 35		06 01		06 21	06 31		06 37		06 51	07 01		07 07	07 14		07 21	07 23	07 31
New Southgate	d		01 46	01 56						06 24				06 45	06 54					07 21	07 24		
Oakleigh Park	d		01 49	01 59						06 28				06 48	06 58					07 24	07 28		
New Barnet	d		01 51	02 02						06 30			06 43	06 51	07 00			07 13		07 27	07 30		
Hadley Wood	d		01 54	02 04						06 33					07 03						07 33		
Potters Bar	d		01 58	02 08			05 45		06 13	06 37		06 42	06 48	06 56	07 07		07 13	07 18		07 32	07 37		
Brookmans Park	d												06 51					07 21					
Welham Green	d												06 54					07 24					
Hatfield	d		02 04	02 14			05 51		06 19	06 43		06 48	06 57	07 02	07 13		07 18	07 27		07 38	07 43		
Welwyn Garden City ■	d		02 09	02a20			05 56		06 24	06a48		06 56	07a02	07a06	07a18		07 26	07a32		07a42	07a48		
Welwyn North	d		02s12				06 00		06 27			07 00					07 30						
Knebworth	d		02s16				06 04		06 31			07 04					07 34						
Bowes Park	d	01 26				05 38		06 04			06 34					07 04						07 26	
Palmers Green	d	01 29			05 25	05 40		06 06			06 36					07 06			07 17			07 28	07 35
Winchmore Hill	d	01 32			05 27	05 43		06 09			06 39					07 09			07 20			07 31	07 38
Grange Park	d	01 34				05 45		06 11			06 41					07 11						07 33	
Enfield Chase	d	01 36			05 30	05 48		06 13			06 43					07 13			07 24			07 35	07 41
Gordon Hill	d	01 38			05 33	05 51		06 16			06 46					07 16			07a27			07 38	07a44
Crews Hill	d				05 36	05 54		06 19			06 49					07 19						07 41	
Cuffley	d	01 43			05 39	05 57		06 22			06 52					07 22						07 44	
Bayford	d				05 43	06 01		06 27			06 57					07 26						07 48	
Hertford North	a	01 52			05 49	06 06		06 32			07 01					07 31						07 54	
Watton-at-Stone	a					06 13		06 39			07 13					07 39							
Stevenage ■	a		02 20				06 08		06 37			07 08					07 38						

A until 17 February B from 24 February

See Table 025 for fast trains between London and Stevenage

Table T024-F

Mondays to Fridays

16 December to 15 May

London - Welwyn Garden City and Hertford North

Station		TL [1]	GN	GN	GN	TL	GN	GN	GN	TL [1]	GN	GN	TL	GN	GN	GN	TL [1]	GN	GN	GN	TL	GN
London Bridge	d																					
London Blackfriars	d																					
City Thameslink	d																					
Farringdon	d																					
St Pancras International	d																					
London Kings Cross [15] ⊖	d	07 21				07 36				07 51			08 06				08 21				08 36	
Finsbury Park	a	07 27				07 45				07 57			08 15				08 27				08 45	
Moorgate ⊖	d		07 15	07 20	07 25		07 30	07 35	07 40		07 50	07 55		08 00	08 05	08 10		08 15	08 20	08 25		08 30
Old Street ⊖	d		07 17	07 22	07 27		07 32	07 37	07 42		07 52	07 57		08 02	08 07	08 12		08 17	08 22	08 27		08 32
Essex Road	d		07 20	07 25	07 30		07 35	07 40	07 45		07 55	08 00		08 05	08 10	08 15		08 20	08 25	08 30		08 35
Highbury & Islington ⊖	d		07 23	07 28	07 33		07 38	07 43	07 48		07 58	08 03		08 08	08 13	08 18		08 23	08 28	08 33		08 38
Drayton Park	d		07 25	07 30	07 35		07 40	07 45	07 50		08 00	08 05		08 10	08 15	08 20		08 25	08 30	08 35		08 40
Finsbury Park ⊖	a		07 28	07 33	07 38		07 42	07 48	07 53		08 03	08 08		08 13	08 18	08 23		08 28	08 33	08 38		08 42
Finsbury Park	d	07 31	07 30	07 33	07 38	07 45	07 45	07 48	07 53	08 01	08 03	08 08	08 15	08 15	08 18	08 23	08 31	08 30	08 33	08 38	08 45	08 45
Harringay	d			07 36	07 41				07 56			08 11				08 26			08 36	08 41		
Hornsey	d			07 38	07 43				07 58			08 13				08 28			08 38	08 43		
Alexandra Palace	d		07 37	07 41	07 47		07 51	07 54	08 01		08 07	08 17		08 21	08 24	08 31		08 37	08 41	08 47		08 51
New Southgate	d					07 51	07 54						08 21	08 24							08 51	08 54
Oakleigh Park	d					07 54	07 58						08 24	08 28							08 54	08 58
New Barnet	d		07 43			07 57	08 00				08 13		08 27	08 30				08 43			08 57	09 00
Hadley Wood	d						08 03							08 33								09 03
Potters Bar	d	07 43	07 48			08 02	08 07			08 13	08 18		08 32	08 37			08 43	08 48			09 02	09 07
Brookmans Park	d		07 51								08 21							08 51				
Welham Green	d		07 54								08 24							08 54				
Hatfield	d	07 48	07 57			08 08	08 13			08 18	08 27		08 38	08 43			08 48	08 57			09 08	09 13
Welwyn Garden City [4]	d	07 56	08a02			08a12	08a18			08 26	08a32		08a42	08a48			08 56	09a02			09a12	09a18
Welwyn North	d	08 00								08 30							09 00					
Knebworth	d	08 04								08 34							09 04					
Bowes Park	d				07 50							08 20								08 50		
Palmers Green	d			07 45	07 52			07 58	08 05			08 22			08 28	08 35			08 45	08 52		
Winchmore Hill	d			07 48	07 55			08 01	08 08			08 25			08 31	08 38			08 48	08 55		
Grange Park	d				07 57							08 27								08 57		
Enfield Chase	d			07 51	08 00			08 04	08 11			08 30			08 34	08 41			08 51	09 00		
Gordon Hill	d			07 54	08a03			08 07	08 15			08a33			08 37	08a44			08 54	09a03		
Crews Hill	d							08 10							08 40							
Cuffley	d			07 58				08 13	08 19						08 43				08 58			
Bayford	d							08 17							08 47							
Hertford North	a			08 06				08 23	08 28						08 53				09 06			
Watton-at-Stone	a			08 13					08 35										09 13			
Stevenage [4]	a	08 08								08 38							09 08					

Station		GN	GN	TL [1]	GN	GN	TL	GN	GN	TL [1]	GN	GN	GN	GN	TL [1]	GN	GN	GN	GN	TL [1]	GN	GN	GN
London Bridge	d																						
London Blackfriars	d																						
City Thameslink	d																						
Farringdon	d																						
St Pancras International	d																						
London Kings Cross [15] ⊖	d			08 51			09 06			09 21					09 51					10 21			
Finsbury Park	a			08 57			09 15			09 27					09 56					10 27			
Moorgate ⊖	d	08 35	08 40		08 45	08 55		09 00	09 10		09 20	09 25	09 30	09 40		09 50	09 55	10 00	10 10		10 20	10 25	10 30
Old Street ⊖	d	08 37	08 42		08 47	08 57		09 02	09 12		09 22	09 27	09 32	09 42		09 52	09 57	10 02	10 12		10 22	10 27	10 32
Essex Road	d	08 40	08 45		08 50	09 00		09 05	09 15		09 25	09 30	09 35	09 45		09 55	10 00	10 05	10 15		10 25	10 30	10 35
Highbury & Islington ⊖	d	08 43	08 48		08 53	09 03		09 08	09 18		09 28	09 33	09 38	09 48		09 58	10 03	10 08	10 18		10 28	10 33	10 38
Drayton Park	d	08 45	08 50		08 55	09 05		09 10	09 20		09 30	09 35	09 40	09 50		10 00	10 05	10 10	10 20		10 30	10 35	10 40
Finsbury Park ⊖	a	08 48	08 53		08 58	09 08		09 12	09 23		09 33	09 38	09 43	09 53		10 03	10 08	10 13	10 23		10 33	10 38	10 43
Finsbury Park	d	08 48	08 53	09 01	09 00	09 09	09 15	09 15	09 24	09 31	09 33	09 39	09 44	09 54	10 00	10 03	10 09	10 14	10 24	10 31	10 33	10 39	10 44
Harringay	d		08 56			09 11			09 26			09 41	09 46	09 56			10 11	10 16	10 26			10 41	10 46
Hornsey	d		08 58			09 13			09 28			09 43	09 48	09 58			10 13	10 18	10 28			10 43	10 48
Alexandra Palace	d	08 53	09 01		09 07	09 17		09 21	09 32		09 38	09 47	09 51	10 02		10 08	10 17	10 21	10 32		10 38	10 47	10 51
New Southgate	d						09 21	09 24			09 41		09 54			10 11		10 24			10 41		10 54
Oakleigh Park	d						09 24	09 28			09 44		09 58			10 14		10 28			10 44		10 58
New Barnet	d				09 13		09 27	09 30			09 46		10 00			10 16		10 30			10 46		11 00
Hadley Wood	d							09 33			09 49		10 03			10 19		10 33			10 49		11 03
Potters Bar	d			09 13	09 18		09 32	09 37		09 43	09 53		10 07		10 13	10 23		10 37		10 43	10 53		11 07
Brookmans Park	d				09 21						09 56					10 26					10 56		
Welham Green	d				09 24						09 59					10 29					10 59		
Hatfield	d			09 18	09 27		09 38	09 43		09 48	10 02		10 13		10 18	10 32		10 43		10 48	11 02		11 13
Welwyn Garden City [4]	d			09 26	09a32		09a42	09a48		09 56	10a07		10a18		10 26	10a37		10a48		10 56	11a07		11a18
Welwyn North	d			09 30						10 00					10 30					11 01			
Knebworth	d			09 34						10 04					10 34					11 05			
Bowes Park	d					09 19			09 34			09 49		10 04			10 19		10 34			10 49	
Palmers Green	d	08 57	09 05			09 22			09 37			09 52		10 07			10 22		10 37			10 52	
Winchmore Hill	d	09 00	09 08			09 25			09 40			09 55		10 10			10 25		10 40			10 55	
Grange Park	d					09 27			09 42			09 57		10 12			10 27		10 42			10 57	
Enfield Chase	d	09 04	09 11			09 29			09 44			09 59		10 14			10 29		10 44			10 59	
Gordon Hill	d	09 07	09 15			09 32			09 47			10 02		10 17			10 32		10 47			11 02	
Crews Hill	d	09 10				09 35						10 05					10 35					11 05	
Cuffley	d	09 13	09 19			09 38			09 52			10 08		10 22			10 38		10 52			11 08	
Bayford	d	09 17				09 42						10 12					10 42					11 12	
Hertford North	a	09 23	09 28			09 48			09 59			10 18		10 29			10 48		10 59			11 18	
Watton-at-Stone	a		09 35						10 11					10 41					11 11				
Stevenage [4]	a			09 38						10 08					10 38					11 09			

See Table 025 for fast trains between London and Stevenage

Table T024-F

Mondays to Fridays

16 December to 15 May

London - Welwyn Garden City and Hertford North

Station		GN	TL [1]	GN	GN	GN	GN	TL [1]	GN	GN	GN	GN	TL [1]	GN	GN	GN	GN	TL [1]	GN	GN	GN	GN	TL [1]
London Bridge	d																						
London Blackfriars	d																						
City Thameslink	d																						
Farringdon	d																						
St Pancras International	d																						
London Kings Cross [15] ⊖	d		10 51					11 21					11 51					12 21					12 51
Finsbury Park	a		10 57					11 27					11 57					12 27					12 57
Moorgate ⊖	d	10 40		10 50	10 55	11 00	11 10		11 20	11 25	11 30	11 40		11 50	11 55	12 00	12 10		12 20	12 25	12 30	12 40	
Old Street ⊖	d	10 42		10 52	10 57	11 02	11 12		11 22	11 27	11 32	11 42		11 52	11 57	12 02	12 12		12 22	12 27	12 32	12 42	
Essex Road	d	10 45		10 55	11 00	11 05	11 15		11 25	11 30	11 35	11 45		11 55	12 00	12 05	12 15		12 25	12 30	12 35	12 45	
Highbury & Islington ⊖	d	10 48		10 58	11 03	11 08	11 18		11 28	11 33	11 38	11 48		11 58	12 03	12 08	12 18		12 28	12 33	12 38	12 48	
Drayton Park	d	10 50		11 00	11 05	11 10	11 20		11 30	11 35	11 40	11 50		12 00	12 05	12 10	12 20		12 30	12 35	12 40	12 50	
Finsbury Park ⊖	a	10 53		11 03	11 08	11 13	11 23		11 33	11 38	11 43	11 53		12 03	12 08	12 13	12 23		12 33	12 38	12 43	12 53	
Finsbury Park	d	10 54	11 01	11 03	11 09	11 14	11 24	11 31	11 33	11 39	11 44	11 54	12 01	12 03	12 09	12 14	12 24	12 31	12 33	12 39	12 44	12 54	13 01
Harringay	d	10 56			11 11	11 16	11 26			11 41	11 46	11 56			12 11	12 16	12 26			12 41	12 46	12 56	
Hornsey	d	10 58			11 13	11 18	11 28			11 43	11 48	11 58			12 13	12 18	12 28			12 43	12 48	12 58	
Alexandra Palace	d	11 02		11 08	11 17	11 21	11 32		11 38	11 47	11 51	12 02		12 08	12 17	12 21	12 32		12 38	12 47	12 51	13 02	
New Southgate	d			11 11		11 24			11 41		11 54			12 11		12 24			12 41		12 54		
Oakleigh Park	d			11 14		11 28			11 44		11 58			12 14		12 28			12 44		12 58		
New Barnet	d			11 16		11 30			11 46		12 00			12 16		12 30			12 46		13 00		
Hadley Wood	d			11 19		11 33			11 49		12 03			12 19		12 33			12 49		13 03		
Potters Bar	d		11 13	11 23		11 37		11 43	11 53		12 07		12 13	12 23		12 37		12 43	12 53		13 07		13 13
Brookmans Park	d			11 26					11 56					12 26					12 56				
Welham Green	d			11 29					11 59					12 29					12 59				
Hatfield	d		11 18	11 32		11 43		11 48	12 02		12 13		12 18	12 32		12 43		12 48	13 02		13 13		13 18
Welwyn Garden City [4]	d		11 26	11a37		11a48		11 56	12a07		12a18		12 26	12a37		12a48		12 56	13a07		13a18		13 26
Welwyn North	d		11 30					12 00					12 30					13 00					13 30
Knebworth	d		11 34					12 04					12 34					13 04					13 34
Bowes Park	d	11 04			11 19		11 34			11 49		12 04			12 19		12 34			12 49		13 04	
Palmers Green	d	11 07			11 22		11 37			11 52		12 07			12 22		12 37			12 52		13 07	
Winchmore Hill	d	11 10			11 25		11 40			11 55		12 10			12 25		12 40			12 55		13 10	
Grange Park	d	11 12			11 27		11 42			11 57		12 12			12 27		12 42			12 57		13 12	
Enfield Chase	d	11 14			11 29		11 44			11 59		12 14			12 29		12 44			12 59		13 14	
Gordon Hill	d	11 17			11 32		11 47			12 02		12 17			12 32		12 47			13 02		13 17	
Crews Hill	d				11 35					12 05					12 35					13 05			
Cuffley	d	11 22			11 38		11 52			12 08		12 22			12 38		12 52			13 08		13 22	
Bayford	d				11 42					12 12					12 42					13 12			
Hertford North	a	11 29			11 48		11 59			12 18		12 29			12 48		12 59			13 18		13 29	
Watton-at-Stone	a	11 41					12 11					12 41					13 11					13 41	
Stevenage [4]	a		11 38					12 08					12 38					13 08					13 38

Station		GN	GN	GN	GN	TL [1]	GN	GN	GN	GN	TL [1]	GN	GN	GN	GN	TL [1]	GN	GN	GN	GN	TL [1]	GN
London Bridge	d																					
London Blackfriars	d																					
City Thameslink	d																					
Farringdon	d																					
St Pancras International	d																					
London Kings Cross [15] ⊖	d					13 21					13 51					14 21					14 51	
Finsbury Park	a					13 27					13 57					14 27					14 57	
Moorgate ⊖	d	12 50	12 55	13 00	13 10		13 20	13 25	13 30	13 40		13 50	13 55	14 00	14 10		14 20	14 25	14 30	14 40		14 50
Old Street ⊖	d	12 52	12 57	13 02	13 12		13 22	13 27	13 32	13 42		13 52	13 57	14 02	14 12		14 22	14 27	14 32	14 42		14 52
Essex Road	d	12 55	13 00	13 05	13 15		13 25	13 30	13 35	13 45		13 55	14 00	14 05	14 15		14 25	14 30	14 35	14 45		14 55
Highbury & Islington ⊖	d	12 58	13 03	13 08	13 18		13 28	13 33	13 38	13 48		13 58	14 03	14 08	14 18		14 28	14 33	14 38	14 48		14 58
Drayton Park	d	13 00	13 05	13 10	13 20		13 30	13 35	13 40	13 50		14 00	14 05	14 10	14 20		14 30	14 35	14 40	14 50		15 00
Finsbury Park ⊖	a	13 03	13 08	13 13	13 23		13 33	13 38	13 43	13 53		14 03	14 08	14 13	14 23		14 33	14 38	14 43	14 53		15 03
Finsbury Park	d	13 03	13 09	13 14	13 24	13 31	13 33	13 39	13 44	13 54	14 01	14 03	14 09	14 14	14 24	14 31	14 33	14 39	14 44	14 54	15 01	15 03
Harringay	d		13 11	13 16	13 26			13 41	13 46	13 56			14 11	14 16	14 26			14 41	14 46	14 56		
Hornsey	d		13 13	13 18	13 28			13 43	13 48	13 58			14 13	14 18	14 28			14 43	14 48	14 58		
Alexandra Palace	d	13 08	13 17	13 21	13 32		13 38	13 47	13 51	14 02		14 08	14 17	14 21	14 32		14 38	14 47	14 51	15 02		15 08
New Southgate	d	13 11		13 24			13 41		13 54			14 11		14 24			14 41		14 54			15 11
Oakleigh Park	d	13 14		13 28			13 44		13 58			14 14		14 28			14 44		14 58			15 14
New Barnet	d	13 16		13 30			13 46		14 00			14 16		14 30			14 46		15 00			15 16
Hadley Wood	d	13 19		13 33			13 49		14 03			14 19		14 33			14 49		15 03			15 19
Potters Bar	d	13 23		13 37		13 43	13 53		14 07		14 13	14 23		14 37		14 43	14 53		15 07		15 13	15 23
Brookmans Park	d	13 26					13 56					14 26					14 56					15 26
Welham Green	d	13 29					13 59					14 29					14 59					15 29
Hatfield	d	13 32		13 43		13 48	14 02		14 13		14 18	14 32		14 43		14 48	15 02		15 13		15 18	15 32
Welwyn Garden City [4]	d	13a37		13a48		13 56	14a07		14a18		14 26	14a37		14a48		14 56	15a07		15a18		15 26	15a37
Welwyn North	d					14 00					14 30					15 00					15 30	
Knebworth	d					14 04					14 34					15 04					15 34	
Bowes Park	d		13 19		13 34			13 49		14 04			14 19		14 34			14 49		15 04		
Palmers Green	d		13 22		13 37			13 52		14 07			14 22		14 37			14 52		15 07		
Winchmore Hill	d		13 25		13 40			13 55		14 10			14 25		14 40			14 55		15 10		
Grange Park	d		13 27		13 42			13 57		14 12			14 27		14 42			14 57		15 12		
Enfield Chase	d		13 29		13 44			13 59		14 14			14 29		14 44			14 59		15 14		
Gordon Hill	d		13 32		13 47			14 02		14 17			14 32		14 47			15 02		15 17		
Crews Hill	d		13 35					14 05					14 35					15 05				
Cuffley	d		13 38		13 52			14 08		14 22			14 38		14 52			15 08		15 22		
Bayford	d		13 42					14 12					14 42					15 12				
Hertford North	a		13 48		13 59			14 18		14 29			14 48		14 59			15 18		15 29		
Watton-at-Stone	a				14 11					14 41					15 11					15 41		
Stevenage [4]	a					14 09					14 38					15 08					15 38	

See Table 025 for fast trains between London and Stevenage

Table T024-F

Mondays to Fridays

16 December to 15 May

London - Welwyn Garden City and Hertford North

Station		GN	GN	GN	TL 1	GN	GN	GN	GN	TL 1	GN	GN	GN	GN	TL 1	GN	GN	GN	TL	GN	GN	GN 1	TL 1
London Bridge	d																						
London Blackfriars	d																						
City Thameslink	d																						
Farringdon	d																						
St Pancras International	d																						
London Kings Cross 15 ⊖	d				15 21					15 51					16 21				16 36			16 54	16 51
Finsbury Park	a				15 27					15 57					16 27				16 42				16 57
Moorgate ⊖	d	14 55	15 00	15 10		15 20	15 25	15 30	15 40		15 50	15 55	16 00	16 10		16 15	16 20	16 25		16 30	16 40		
Old Street ⊖	d	14 57	15 02	15 12		15 22	15 27	15 32	15 42		15 52	15 57	16 03	16 13		16 18	16 23	16 28		16 33	16 43		
Essex Road	d	15 00	15 05	15 15		15 25	15 30	15 35	15 45		15 55	16 00	16 06	16 16		16 21	16 26	16 31		16 36	16 46		
Highbury & Islington ⊖	d	15 03	15 08	15 18		15 28	15 33	15 38	15 48		15 58	16 03	16 08	16 18		16 23	16 28	16 33		16 38	16 48		
Drayton Park	d	15 05	15 10	15 20		15 30	15 35	15 40	15 50		16 00	16 05	16 11	16 21		16 26	16 31	16 36		16 41	16 51		
Finsbury Park ⊖	a	15 08	15 13	15 23		15 33	15 38	15 43	15 53		16 03	16 08	16 13	16 23		16 28	16 33	16 38		16 43	16 53		
Finsbury Park	d	15 09	15 14	15 24	15 31	15 33	15 39	15 44	15 54	16 01	16 03	16 09	16 15	16 24	16 31	16 30	16 34	16 39	16 45	16 45	16 54		17 01
Harringay	d	15 11	15 16	15 26			15 41	15 46	15 56			16 11	16 17	16 26			16 36	16 41			16 56		
Hornsey	d	15 13	15 18	15 28			15 43	15 48	15 58			16 13	16 19	16 28			16 38	16 43			16 58		
Alexandra Palace	d	15 17	15 21	15 32		15 38	15 47	15 51	16 02		16 08	16 17	16 22	16 32		16 37	16 42	16 47		16 52	17 02		
New Southgate	d		15 24			15 41		15 54			16 11		16 25			16 40			16 52	16 55			
Oakleigh Park	d		15 28			15 44		15 58			16 14		16 29			16 44			16 55	16 59			
New Barnet	d		15 30			15 46		16 00			16 16		16 31			16 46			16 57	17 01			
Hadley Wood	d		15 33			15 49		16 03			16 19		16 34			16 49				17 04			
Potters Bar	d		15 37		15 43	15 53		16 07		16 13	16 23		16 38		16 43	16 53			17 02	17 08			17 13
Brookmans Park	d					15 56					16 26		16 41			16 56				17 11			
Welham Green	d					15 59					16 29		16 44			16 59				17 14			
Hatfield	d		15 43		15 48	16 02		16 13		16 18	16 32		16 47		16 51	17 02			17 08	17 17			17 21
Welwyn Garden City 4	d		15a48		15 56	16a07		16a18		16 26	16a37		16a52		16 56	17a07			17a12	17a22			17 26
Welwyn North	d				16 00					16 30					17 00							17 11	17 30
Knebworth	d				16 04					16 34					17 04							17a15	17 34
Bowes Park	d	15 19		15 34			15 49		16 04			16 19		16 34				16 49			17 04		
Palmers Green	d	15 22		15 37			15 52		16 07			16 22		16 37			16 46	16 52			17 07		
Winchmore Hill	d	15 25		15 40			15 55		16 10			16 25		16 40			16 49	16 55			17 10		
Grange Park	d	15 27		15 42			15 57		16 12			16 27		16 42				16 57			17 12		
Enfield Chase	d	15 29		15 44			15 59		16 14			16 29		16 45			16 52	17 00			17 15		
Gordon Hill	d	15 32		15 47			16 02		16 17			16 32		16 47			16 55	17a03			17 17		
Crews Hill	d	15 35					16 05					16 35					16 58						
Cuffley	d	15 38		15 52			16 08		16 22			16 38		16 52			17 01				17 22		
Bayford	d	15 42					16 12					16 42					17 05						
Hertford North	a	15 48		15 59			16 18		16 29			16 48		17 01			17 10				17 31		
Watton-at-Stone	a			16 11					16 37								17 17						
Stevenage 4	a				16 08					16 38					17 09								17 39

Station		GN	GN	GN	TL	GN	GN	GN	GN 1	TL 1	GN	GN	GN	TL	GN	GN	GN	GN 1	TL 1	GN	GN	GN
London Bridge	d																					
London Blackfriars	d																					
City Thameslink	d																					
Farringdon	d																					
St Pancras International	d																					
London Kings Cross 15 ⊖	d				17 06				17 24	17 21				17 36				17 54	17 51			
Finsbury Park	a				17 12					17 27				17 42					17 57			
Moorgate ⊖	d	16 45	16 50	16 55		17 00	17 05	17 09			17 15	17 20	17 25		17 30	17 35	17 40			17 45	17 50	17 55
Old Street ⊖	d	16 48	16 53	16 58		17 03	17 08	17 12			17 18	17 23	17 28		17 33	17 38	17 43			17 48	17 53	17 58
Essex Road	d	16 51	16 56	17 01		17 06	17 11	17 15			17 21	17 26	17 31		17 36	17 41	17 46			17 51	17 56	18 01
Highbury & Islington ⊖	d	16 53	16 58	17 03		17 08	17 13	17 17			17 23	17 28	17 33		17 38	17 43	17 48			17 53	17 58	18 03
Drayton Park	d	16 56	17 01	17 06		17 11	17 16	17 20			17 26	17 31	17 36		17 41	17 46	17 51			17 56	18 01	18 06
Finsbury Park ⊖	a	16 58	17 03	17 08		17 13	17 18	17 22			17 28	17 33	17 38		17 43	17 48	17 53			17 58	18 03	18 08
Finsbury Park	d	17 00	17 04	17 09	17 15	17 15	17 19	17 23		17 31	17 30	17 34	17 39	17 45	17 45	17 49	17 54		18 01	18 00	18 04	18 09
Harringay	d		17 06	17 11				17 25				17 36	17 41				17 56				18 06	18 11
Hornsey	d		17 08	17 13				17 27				17 38	17 43				17 58				18 08	18 13
Alexandra Palace	d	17 07	17 12	17 17		17 22	17 24	17 31			17 37	17 42	17 47		17 52	17 55	18 02			18 07	18 12	18 17
New Southgate	d	17 10			17 22	17 25					17 40			17 52	17 55					18 10		
Oakleigh Park	d	17 14			17 25	17 29					17 44			17 55	17 59					18 14		
New Barnet	d	17 16			17 27	17 31					17 46			17 57	18 01					18 16		
Hadley Wood	d	17 19				17 34					17 49				18 04					18 19		
Potters Bar	d	17 23			17 32	17 38				17 43	17 53			18 02	18 08				18 13	18 23		
Brookmans Park	d	17 26				17 41					17 56				18 11					18 26		
Welham Green	d	17 29				17 44					17 59				18 14					18 29		
Hatfield	d	17 32			17 38	17 47				17 51	18 02			18 08	18 17				18 21	18 32		
Welwyn Garden City 4	d	17a37			17a42	17a52				17 56	18a07			18a12	18a22				18 26	18a37		
Welwyn North	d								17 41	18 00								18 11	18 30			
Knebworth	d								17a45	18 04								18a15	18 34			
Bowes Park	d			17 19				17 33					17 49				18 04					18 19
Palmers Green	d		17 16	17 22			17 28	17 36				17 46	17 52			17 59	18 07				18 16	18 22
Winchmore Hill	d		17 19	17 25			17 31	17 39				17 49	17 55			18 02	18 10				18 19	18 25
Grange Park	d			17 27				17 41					17 57				18 12					18 27
Enfield Chase	d		17 22	17 30			17 34	17 44				17 52	18 00			18 05	18 15				18 22	18 30
Gordon Hill	d		17 25	17a33			17 37	17a47				17 55	18a03			18 08	18 17				18 25	18a33
Crews Hill	d		17 28									17 58									18 28	
Cuffley	d		17 31				17 42					18 01				18 13	18 22				18 31	
Bayford	d		17 35									18 05									18 35	
Hertford North	a		17 40				17 51					18 10				18 22	18 31				18 40	
Watton-at-Stone	a		17 47									18 17									18 47	
Stevenage 4	a									18 09									18 39			

See Table 025 for fast trains between London and Stevenage

NRT DECEMBER 19 EDITION

Table T024-F

Mondays to Fridays

16 December to 15 May

London - Welwyn Garden City and Hertford North

Station		TL	GN	GN	GN	GN 1	TL 1	GN	GN	GN	TL	GN	GN	GN 1	TL 1	GN	GN	GN	TL	GN	GN	TL 1	GN
London Bridge	d																						
London Blackfriars	d																						
City Thameslink	d																						
Farringdon	d																						
St Pancras International	d																						
London Kings Cross 15 ⊖	d	18 07				18 24	18 21				18 36			18 54	18 51				19 06			19 21	
Finsbury Park	a	18 12					18 27				18 42				18 57				19 15			19 28	
Moorgate ⊖	d		18 00	18 05	18 10			18 15	18 20	18 25		18 32	18 40			18 45	18 50	18 55		19 00	19 10		19 15
Old Street ⊖	d		18 03	18 08	18 13			18 18	18 23	18 28		18 35	18 43			18 48	18 53	18 58		19 03	19 12		19 17
Essex Road	d		18 06	18 11	18 16			18 21	18 26	18 31		18 38	18 46			18 51	18 56	19 01		19 06	19 15		19 20
Highbury & Islington ⊖	d		18 08	18 13	18 18			18 23	18 28	18 33		18 40	18 48			18 53	18 58	19 03		19 08	19 18		19 23
Drayton Park	d		18 11	18 16	18 21			18 26	18 31	18 36		18 43	18 51			18 56	19 01	19 05		19 11	19 20		19 25
Finsbury Park ⊖	a		18 13	18 18	18 23			18 28	18 33	18 38		18 45	18 53			18 58	19 03	19 08		19 13	19 23		19 28
Finsbury Park	d	18 15	18 15	18 19	18 24		18 31	18 30	18 34	18 39	18 45	18 46	18 54		19 01	19 00	19 04	19 09	19 15	19 18	19 24	19 31	19 30
Harringay	d				18 26				18 36	18 41			18 56				19 06	19 11			19 26		
Hornsey	d				18 28				18 38	18 43			18 58				19 08	19 13			19 28		
Alexandra Palace	d		18 22	18 25	18 32			18 37	18 42	18 47		18 52	19 02			19 07	19 12	19 17		19 22	19 32		19 37
New Southgate	d	18 22	18 25					18 40			18 52	18 55				19 10			19 22	19 25			19 40
Oakleigh Park	d	18 25	18 29					18 44			18 55	18 59				19 14			19 25	19 29			19 44
New Barnet	d	18 27	18 31					18 46			18 57	19 01				19 16			19 27	19 31			19 46
Hadley Wood	d		18 34					18 49				19 04				19 19				19 34			19 49
Potters Bar	d	18 32	18 38				18 43	18 53			19 02	19 08			19 13	19 23			19 32	19 38		19 45	19 53
Brookmans Park	d		18 41					18 56				19 11				19 26							19 56
Welham Green	d		18 44					18 59				19 14				19 29							19 59
Hatfield	d	18 38	18 47				18 51	19 02			19 08	19 17			19 21	19 32			19 38	19 44		19 50	20 02
Welwyn Garden City 4	d	18a42	18a52				18 56	19a07			19a12	19a22			19 26	19a37			19a42	19a49		19 56	20a07
Welwyn North	d					18 41	19 00							19 11	19 30							20 00	
Knebworth	d					18a45	19 04							19a15	19 34							20 04	
Bowes Park	d				18 34					18 49			19 04					19 19			19 34		
Palmers Green	d			18 29	18 37				18 46	18 52			19 07				19 16	19 22			19 37		
Winchmore Hill	d			18 32	18 40				18 49	18 55			19 10				19 19	19 25			19 40		
Grange Park	d				18 42					18 57			19 12					19 27			19 42		
Enfield Chase	d			18 35	18 45				18 52	19 00			19 15				19 22	19 30			19 44		
Gordon Hill	d			18 38	18 47				18 55	19 03			19 17				19 25	19a33			19 47		
Crews Hill	d								18 58	19 06							19 28						
Cuffley	d			18 43	18 52				19 01	19 09			19 22				19 31				19 52		
Bayford	d								19 05	19 13							19 35						
Hertford North	a			18 52	19 01				19 10	19 19			19 31				19 40				19 59		
Watton-at-Stone	a								19 17								19 47				20 11		
Stevenage 4	a						19 09								19 38							20 08	

Station		GN	GN	GN	TL 1	GN	GN	GN	GN	TL 1	GN	GN	GN	GN	TL 1	GN	GN	GN	GN	TL 1	GN	GN	GN
London Bridge	d																						
London Blackfriars	d																						
City Thameslink	d																						
Farringdon	d																						
St Pancras International	d																						
London Kings Cross 15 ⊖	d				19 51					20 21					20 51					21 21			
Finsbury Park	a				19 57					20 27					20 57					21 27			
Moorgate ⊖	d	19 25	19 30	19 40		19 50	19 55	20 00	20 10		20 20	20 25	20 30	20 40		20 50	20 55	21 00	21 10		21 20	21 25	21 30
Old Street ⊖	d	19 27	19 33	19 42		19 52	19 57	20 02	20 12		20 22	20 27	20 32	20 42		20 52	20 57	21 02	21 12		21 22	21 27	21 32
Essex Road	d	19 30	19 36	19 45		19 55	20 00	20 05	20 15		20 25	20 30	20 35	20 45		20 55	21 00	21 05	21 15		21 25	21 30	21 35
Highbury & Islington ⊖	d	19 33	19 38	19 48		19 58	20 03	20 08	20 18		20 28	20 33	20 38	20 48		20 58	21 03	21 08	21 18		21 28	21 33	21 38
Drayton Park	d	19 35	19 41	19 50		20 00	20 05	20 10	20 20		20 30	20 35	20 40	20 50		21 00	21 05	21 10	21 20		21 30	21 35	21 40
Finsbury Park ⊖	a	19 38	19 43	19 53		20 03	20 08	20 13	20 23		20 33	20 38	20 43	20 53		21 03	21 08	21 13	21 23		21 33	21 38	21 43
Finsbury Park	d	19 39	19 44	19 54	20 01	20 03	20 09	20 14	20 24	20 31	20 33	20 39	20 44	20 54	21 01	21 03	21 09	21 14	21 24	21 31	21 33	21 39	21 44
Harringay	d	19 41	19 46	19 56			20 11	20 16	20 26			20 41	20 46	20 56			21 11	21 16	21 26			21 41	21 46
Hornsey	d	19 43	19 48	19 58			20 13	20 18	20 28			20 43	20 48	20 58			21 13	21 18	21 28			21 43	21 48
Alexandra Palace	d	19 47	19 51	20 02		20 08	20 17	20 21	20 32		20 38	20 47	20 51	21 02		21 08	21 17	21 21	21 32		21 38	21 47	21 51
New Southgate	d		19 54			20 11		20 24			20 41		20 54			21 11		21 24			21 41		21 54
Oakleigh Park	d		19 58			20 14		20 28			20 44		20 58			21 14		21 28			21 44		21 58
New Barnet	d		20 00			20 16		20 30			20 46		21 00			21 16		21 30			21 46		22 00
Hadley Wood	d		20 03			20 19		20 33			20 49		21 03			21 19		21 33			21 49		22 03
Potters Bar	d		20 07		20 13	20 23		20 37		20 43	20 53		21 07		21 13	21 23		21 37		21 43	21 53		22 07
Brookmans Park	d					20 26					20 56					21 26					21 56		
Welham Green	d					20 29					20 59					21 29					21 59		
Hatfield	d		20 13		20 18	20 32		20 43		20 48	21 02		21 13		21 18	21 32		21 43		21 48	22 02		22 13
Welwyn Garden City 4	d		20a18		20 26	20a37		20a48		20 56	21a07		21a18		21 26	21a37		21a48		21 56	22a07		22a18
Welwyn North	d				20 30					21 00					21 30					22 00			
Knebworth	d				20 34					21 04					21 34					22 04			
Bowes Park	d	19 49		20 04			20 19		20 34			20 49		21 04			21 19		21 34			21 49	
Palmers Green	d	19 52		20 07			20 22		20 37			20 52		21 07			21 22		21 37			21 52	
Winchmore Hill	d	19 55		20 10			20 25		20 40			20 55		21 10			21 25		21 40			21 55	
Grange Park	d	19 57		20 12			20 27		20 42			20 57		21 12			21 27		21 42			21 57	
Enfield Chase	d	19 59		20 14			20 29		20 44			20 59		21 14			21 29		21 44			21 59	
Gordon Hill	d	20 02		20 17			20 32		20 47			21 01		21 16			21 31		21 47			22 01	
Crews Hill	d	20 05					20 35					21 04					21 34					22 04	
Cuffley	d	20 08		20 22			20 38		20 52			21 08		21 21			21 38		21 52			22 08	
Bayford	d	20 12					20 42					21 12					21 42					22 12	
Hertford North	a	20 18		20 29			20 48		20 59			21 18		21 29			21 48		21 59			22 20	
Watton-at-Stone	a			20 37					21 11										22 11				
Stevenage 4	a				20 38					21 08					21 38					22 08			

See Table 025 for fast trains between London and Stevenage

Table T024-F

Mondays to Fridays
16 December to 15 May

London - Welwyn Garden City and Hertford North

		GN	TL 1	GN	GN	GN	TL 1	GN	GN	GN	TL 1	GN	GN	GN	TL 1	GN	GN	GN	TL 1
London Bridge	d																		
London Blackfriars	d																		
City Thameslink	d																		
Farringdon	d																		
St Pancras International	d																		
London Kings Cross 15 ⊖	d		21 51	22 01	22 12	22 21	22 25	22 31	22 42	22 51	22 55	23 01	23 12	23 21	23 25	23 31	23 42	23 51	23 55
Finsbury Park	a		21 57	22 06	22 18	22 27	22 31	22 36	22 47	22 57	23 01	23 06	23 18	23 28	23 31	23 36	23 47	23 57	00 01
Moorgate ⊖	d	21 40																	
Old Street ⊖	d	21 42																	
Essex Road	d	21 45																	
Highbury & Islington ⊖	d	21 48																	
Drayton Park	d	21 50																	
Finsbury Park ⊖	a	21 53																	
Finsbury Park	d	21 54	22 01	22 07	22 18	22 28	22 32	22 37	22 48	22 58	23 02	23 07	23 19	23 29	23 33	23 37	23 48	23 58	00 02
Harringay	d	21 56		22 10	22 21	22 30		22 40	22 51	23 00		23 10	23 21	23 31		23 40	23 51	00 01	
Hornsey	d	21 58		22 12	22 23	22 32		22 42	22 53	23 02		23 12	23 23	23 33		23 42	23 53	00 03	
Alexandra Palace	d	22 02		22 15	22 26	22 36		22 45	22 56	23 06		23 15	23 27	23 37		23 45	23 56	00 07	
New Southgate	d			22 18				22 48				23 18				23 48			
Oakleigh Park	d			22 21				22 51				23 21				23 51			
New Barnet	d			22 24				22 54				23 24				23 54			
Hadley Wood	d			22 27				22 57				23 27				23 57			
Potters Bar	d		22 13	22 31			22 46	23 01			23 16	23 31			23 45	00 02			00 17
Brookmans Park	d			22 34				23 04				23 34				00 05			
Welham Green	d			22 36				23 06				23 36				00 07			
Hatfield	d		22 18	22 40			22 52	23 10			23 22	23 40			23 51	00 11			00 23
Welwyn Garden City 4	d		22 26	22a45			22 57	23a15			23 27	23a45			23 57	00a16			00 28
Welwyn North	d		22 30				23 00				23 31				00 01				00 31
Knebworth	d		22 34				23 04				23 35				00 05				00 35
Bowes Park	d	22 04			22 29	22 38			22 59	23 08			23 30	23 39			23 59	00 09	
Palmers Green	d	22 07			22 31	22 41			23 01	23 11			23 32	23 42			00 01	00 12	
Winchmore Hill	d	22 10			22 34	22 44			23 04	23 14			23 35	23 45			00 04	00 15	
Grange Park	d	22 12			22 36	22 46			23 06	23 16			23 37	23 47			00 06	00 17	
Enfield Chase	d	22 14			22 38	22 48			23 08	23 18			23 39	23 49			00 08	00 19	
Gordon Hill	d	22 17			22 41	22 51			23 11	23 21			23 42	23 52			00 11	00 22	
Crews Hill	d				22 44				23 14				23 45				00 14	00 25	
Cuffley	d	22 22			22 47	22 56			23 17	23 26			23 48	23 57			00 17	00 28	
Bayford	d				22 51				23 21				23 52				00 21	00 33	
Hertford North	a	22 29			22 57	23 03			23 27	23 33			23 58	00 04			00 27	00 37	
Watton-at-Stone	a	22 41				23 11				23 40				00 17				00 44	
Stevenage 4	a		22 38				23 10				23 40			00 25	00 09			00 51	00 39

Saturdays
21 December to 15 February

		GN	TL 1	GN	GN	GN	TL 1	GN	GN	TL 1	TL 1	GN	TL	GN	GN	TL 1	GN	TL 1	GN	GN	TL 1	GN	GN
London Bridge	d																						
London Blackfriars	d									00 37													
City Thameslink	d																						
Farringdon	d									00 41													
St Pancras International	d									00 46													
London Kings Cross 15 ⊖	d				00 01	00 16	00 23	00 36	00 40		01 05	01 10	01 40	05 06	05 21	05 28		05 56	06 05		06 28		
Finsbury Park	a				00 06	00 22	00 28	00 42	00 46	00 52	01 10	01 15	01 47	05 12	05 26	05 33		06 01	06 10		06 33		
Moorgate ⊖	d																05 43			06 13		06 28	06 43
Old Street ⊖	d																05 45			06 15		06 30	06 45
Essex Road	d																05 48			06 18		06 33	06 48
Highbury & Islington ⊖	d																05 51			06 21		06 36	06 51
Drayton Park	d																05 53			06 23		06 38	06 53
Finsbury Park ⊖	a																05 56			06 26		06 41	06 56
Finsbury Park	d		00 02		00 11	00 23	00 29	00 43	00 47	00 54	01 11	01 16	01 48	05 13	05 27	05 34	05 57	06 02	06 12	06 27	06 34	06 42	06 57
Harringay	d			00 01	00 14	00 26			00 49			01 18		05 16	05 30		05 59		06 14	06 29		06 44	06 59
Hornsey	d			00 03	00 16	00 28			00 51			01 20		05 18	05 32		06 01		06 16	06 31		06 46	07 01
Alexandra Palace	d			00 07	00 19	00 31		00 47	00 55			01 24	01 53	05 21	05 35		06 05		06 20	06 35		06 49	07 05
New Southgate	d				00 22								01 56						06 23			06 52	
Oakleigh Park	d				00 25								01 59						06 26			06 56	
New Barnet	d				00 28			00 53					02 02						06 29			06 58	
Hadley Wood	d				00 31			00 56					02 04						06 32			07 01	
Potters Bar	d		00 17		00 35		00 42	01 00			01 22		02 08			05 45		06 14	06 36		06 45	07 05	
Brookmans Park	d				00 38														06 39			07 08	
Welham Green	d				00 41														06 41			07 11	
Hatfield	d		00 23		00 44		00 48	01 06			01 28		02 14			05 51		06 19	06 45		06 51	07 14	
Welwyn Garden City 4	d		00 28		00a49		00 58	01a11		01 15	01 34		02a20			05 56		06 24	06a50		06 56	07a19	
Welwyn North	d		00 31				01 01				01 37					06 00		06 27			07 00		
Knebworth	d		00 35				01 05				01 41					06 04		06 32			07 04		
Bowes Park	d			00 09		00 34			00 58			01 26			05 38		06 07			06 37			07 07
Palmers Green	d	00 01		00 12		00 36			01 01			01 29		05 25	05 40		06 10			06 40			07 10
Winchmore Hill	d	00 04		00 15		00 39			01 04			01 32		05 27	05 43		06 13			06 43			07 13
Grange Park	d	00 06		00 17		00 41			01 06			01 34			05 45		06 15			06 45			07 15
Enfield Chase	d	00 08		00 19		00 43			01 08			01 36		05 30	05 48		06 17			06 47			07 17
Gordon Hill	d	00 11		00 22		00 46			01 11			01 38		05 33	05 51		06 20			06 50			07 20
Crews Hill	d	00 14		00 25		00 49			01 14					05 36	05 54		06 23			06 53			07 23
Cuffley	d	00 17		00 28		00 52			01 17			01 43		05 39	05 57		06 26			06 56			07 26
Bayford	d	00 21		00 33		00 56			01 22					05 43	06 01		06 30			07 00			07 30
Hertford North	a	00 27		00 37		01 02			01 26			01 52		05 49	06 06		06 35			07 05			07 35
Watton-at-Stone	a			00 44					01 33						06 12		06 43			07 12			07 43
Stevenage 4	a		00 39	00 51			01 09		01 40	01 23	01 45				06 20	06 08		06 37		07 20	07 08		

See Table 025 for fast trains between London and Stevenage

Table T024-F

Saturdays
21 December to 15 February

London - Welwyn Garden City and Hertford North

		TL 1	GN	GN	TL 1	GN	GN	TL 1	GN	GN	TL 1	GN	GN	TL 1	GN	GN	TL 1	GN	GN	TL 1	GN	GN	TL 1
London Bridge	d																						
London Blackfriars	d																						
City Thameslink	d																						
Farringdon	d																						
St Pancras International	d																						
London Kings Cross 15 ⊖	d	06 58			07 28			07 58			08 28			08 58			09 28			09 58			10 28
Finsbury Park	a	07 03			07 33			08 03			08 33			09 03			09 33			10 03			10 33
Moorgate ⊖	d		06 58	07 13		07 28	07 43		07 58	08 13		08 28	08 43		08 58	09 13		09 28	09 43		09 58	10 13	
Old Street ⊖	d		07 00	07 15		07 30	07 45		08 00	08 15		08 30	08 45		09 00	09 15		09 30	09 45		10 00	10 15	
Essex Road	d		07 03	07 18		07 33	07 48		08 03	08 18		08 33	08 48		09 03	09 18		09 33	09 48		10 03	10 18	
Highbury & Islington ⊖	d		07 06	07 21		07 36	07 51		08 06	08 21		08 36	08 51		09 06	09 21		09 36	09 51		10 06	10 21	
Drayton Park	d		07 08	07 23		07 38	07 53		08 08	08 23		08 38	08 53		09 08	09 23		09 38	09 53		10 08	10 23	
Finsbury Park ⊖	a		07 11	07 26		07 41	07 56		08 11	08 26		08 41	08 56		09 11	09 26		09 41	09 56		10 11	10 26	
Finsbury Park	d	07 04	07 12	07 27	07 34	07 42	07 57	08 04	08 12	08 27	08 34	08 42	08 57	09 04	09 12	09 27	09 34	09 42	09 57	10 04	10 12	10 27	10 34
Harringay	d		07 14	07 29		07 44	07 59		08 14	08 29		08 44	08 59		09 14	09 29		09 44	09 59		10 14	10 29	
Hornsey	d		07 16	07 31		07 46	08 01		08 16	08 31		08 46	09 01		09 16	09 31		09 46	10 01		10 16	10 31	
Alexandra Palace	d		07 19	07 35		07 49	08 05		08 19	08 35		08 49	09 05		09 19	09 35		09 49	10 05		10 19	10 35	
New Southgate	d		07 22			07 52			08 22			08 52			09 22			09 52			10 22		
Oakleigh Park	d		07 26			07 56			08 26			08 56			09 26			09 56			10 26		
New Barnet	d		07 28			07 58			08 28			08 58			09 28			09 58			10 28		
Hadley Wood	d		07 31			08 01			08 31			09 01			09 31			10 01			10 31		
Potters Bar	d	07 15	07 35		07 45	08 05		08 15	08 35		08 45	09 05		09 15	09 35		09 45	10 05		10 15	10 35		10 45
Brookmans Park	d		07 38			08 08			08 38			09 08			09 38			10 08			10 38		
Welham Green	d		07 41			08 11			08 41			09 11			09 41			10 11			10 41		
Hatfield	d	07 21	07 44		07 51	08 14		08 21	08 44		08 51	09 14		09 21	09 44		09 51	10 14		10 21	10 44		10 51
Welwyn Garden City 4	d	07 26	07a49		07 56	08a19		08 26	08a49		08 56	09a19		09 26	09a49		09 56	10a19		10 26	10a49		10 56
Welwyn North	d	07 30			08 00			08 30			09 00			09 31			10 00			10 30			11 00
Knebworth	d	07 34			08 04			08 34			09 04			09 34			10 04			10 34			11 04
Bowes Park	d			07 37			08 07			08 37			09 07			09 37			10 07			10 37	
Palmers Green	d			07 40			08 10			08 40			09 10			09 40			10 10			10 40	
Winchmore Hill	d			07 43			08 13			08 43			09 13			09 43			10 13			10 43	
Grange Park	d			07 45			08 15			08 45			09 15			09 45			10 15			10 45	
Enfield Chase	d			07 47			08 17			08 47			09 17			09 47			10 17			10 47	
Gordon Hill	d			07 50			08 20			08 50			09 20			09 50			10 20			10 50	
Crews Hill	d			07 53			08 23			08 53			09 23			09 53			10 23			10 53	
Cuffley	d			07 56			08 26			08 56			09 26			09 56			10 26			10 56	
Bayford	d			08 00			08 30			09 00			09 30			10 00			10 30			11 00	
Hertford North	a			08 05			08 35			09 05			09 35			10 05			10 35			11 05	
Watton-at-Stone	a			08 12			08 43			09 12			09 43			10 12			10 43			11 12	
Stevenage 4	a	07 38		08 20	08 08			08 38		09 20	09 08			09 38		10 20	10 08			10 38		11 20	11 08

		GN	GN	TL 1	GN	GN	TL 1	GN	GN	TL 1	GN	GN	TL 1	GN	GN	TL 1	GN	GN	TL 1	GN	GN	TL 1
London Bridge	d																					
London Blackfriars	d																					
City Thameslink	d																					
Farringdon	d																					
St Pancras International	d																					
London Kings Cross 15 ⊖	d			10 58			11 28			11 58			12 28			12 58			13 28			13 58
Finsbury Park	a			11 03			11 33			12 03			12 33			13 03			13 33			14 03
Moorgate ⊖	d	10 28	10 43		10 58	11 13		11 28	11 43		11 58	12 13		12 28	12 43		12 58	13 13		13 28	13 43	
Old Street ⊖	d	10 30	10 45		11 00	11 15		11 30	11 45		12 00	12 15		12 30	12 45		13 00	13 15		13 30	13 45	
Essex Road	d	10 33	10 48		11 03	11 18		11 33	11 48		12 03	12 18		12 33	12 48		13 03	13 18		13 33	13 48	
Highbury & Islington ⊖	d	10 36	10 51		11 06	11 21		11 36	11 51		12 06	12 21		12 36	12 51		13 06	13 21		13 36	13 51	
Drayton Park	d	10 38	10 53		11 08	11 23		11 38	11 53		12 08	12 23		12 38	12 53		13 08	13 23		13 38	13 53	
Finsbury Park ⊖	a	10 41	10 56		11 11	11 26		11 41	11 56		12 11	12 26		12 41	12 56		13 11	13 26		13 41	13 56	
Finsbury Park	d	10 42	10 57	11 04	11 12	11 27	11 34	11 42	11 57	12 04	12 12	12 27	12 34	12 42	12 57	13 04	13 12	13 27	13 34	13 42	13 57	14 04
Harringay	d	10 44	10 59		11 14	11 29		11 44	11 59		12 14	12 29		12 44	12 59		13 14	13 29		13 44	13 59	
Hornsey	d	10 46	11 01		11 16	11 31		11 46	12 01		12 16	12 31		12 46	13 01		13 16	13 31		13 46	14 01	
Alexandra Palace	d	10 49	11 05		11 19	11 35		11 49	12 05		12 19	12 35		12 49	13 05		13 19	13 35		13 49	14 05	
New Southgate	d	10 52			11 22			11 52			12 22			12 52			13 22			13 52		
Oakleigh Park	d	10 56			11 26			11 56			12 26			12 56			13 26			13 56		
New Barnet	d	10 58			11 28			11 58			12 28			12 58			13 28			13 58		
Hadley Wood	d	11 01			11 31			12 01			12 31			13 01			13 31			14 01		
Potters Bar	d	11 05		11 15	11 35		11 45	12 05		12 15	12 35		12 45	13 05		13 15	13 35		13 45	14 05		14 15
Brookmans Park	d	11 08			11 38			12 08			12 38			13 08			13 38			14 08		
Welham Green	d	11 11			11 41			12 11			12 41			13 11			13 41			14 11		
Hatfield	d	11 14		11 21	11 44		11 51	12 14		12 21	12 44		12 51	13 14		13 21	13 44		13 51	14 14		14 21
Welwyn Garden City 4	d	11a19		11 26	11a49		11 56	12a19		12 26	12a49		12 56	13a19		13 26	13a49		13 56	14a19		14 26
Welwyn North	d			11 31			12 00			12 30			13 00			13 30			14 00			14 30
Knebworth	d			11 34			12 04			12 34			13 04			13 34			14 04			14 34
Bowes Park	d		11 07			11 37			12 07			12 37			13 07			13 37			14 07	
Palmers Green	d		11 10			11 40			12 10			12 40			13 10			13 40			14 10	
Winchmore Hill	d		11 13			11 43			12 13			12 43			13 13			13 43			14 13	
Grange Park	d		11 15			11 45			12 15			12 45			13 15			13 45			14 15	
Enfield Chase	d		11 17			11 47			12 17			12 47			13 17			13 47			14 17	
Gordon Hill	d		11 20			11 50			12 20			12 50			13 20			13 50			14 20	
Crews Hill	d		11 23			11 53			12 23			12 53			13 23			13 53			14 23	
Cuffley	d		11 26			11 56			12 26			12 56			13 26			13 56			14 26	
Bayford	d		11 30			12 00			12 30			13 00			13 30			14 00			14 30	
Hertford North	a		11 35			12 05			12 35			13 05			13 35			14 05			14 35	
Watton-at-Stone	a		11 43			12 12			12 43			13 12			13 43			14 12			14 43	
Stevenage 4	a			11 38		12 20	12 08			12 38		13 21	13 08			13 38		14 20	14 08			14 38

See Table 025 for fast trains between London and Stevenage

Table T024-F

Saturdays

21 December to 15 February

London - Welwyn Garden City and Hertford North

		GN	GN	TL	GN	GN	TL	GN	GN	TL	GN	GN	TL	GN	GN	TL	GN	GN	TL	
London Bridge	d																			
London Blackfriars	d																			
City Thameslink	d																			
Farringdon	d																			
St Pancras International	d																			
London Kings Cross 15 ⊖	d			14 28			14 58			15 28			15 58			16 28			16 58	
Finsbury Park	a			14 33			15 03			15 33			16 03			16 33			17 03	
Moorgate ⊖	d	13 58	14 13		14 28	14 43		14 58	15 13		15 28	15 43		15 58	16 13		16 28	16 43		
Old Street ⊖	d	14 00	14 15		14 30	14 45		15 00	15 15		15 30	15 45		16 00	16 15		16 30	16 45		
Essex Road	d	14 03	14 18		14 33	14 48		15 03	15 18		15 33	15 48		16 03	16 18		16 33	16 48		
Highbury & Islington ⊖	d	14 06	14 21		14 36	14 51		15 06	15 21		15 36	15 51		16 06	16 21		16 36	16 51		
Drayton Park	d	14 08	14 23		14 38	14 53		15 08	15 23		15 38	15 53		16 08	16 23		16 38	16 53		
Finsbury Park ⊖	a	14 11	14 26		14 41	14 56		15 11	15 26		15 41	15 56		16 11	16 26		16 41	16 56		
Finsbury Park	d	14 12	14 27	14 34	14 42	14 57	15 04	15 12	15 27	15 34	15 42	15 57	16 04	16 12	16 27	16 34	16 42	16 57	17 04	
Harringay	d	14 14	14 29		14 44	14 59		15 14	15 29		15 44	15 59		16 14	16 29		16 44	16 59		
Hornsey	d	14 16	14 31		14 46	15 01		15 16	15 31		15 46	16 01		16 16	16 31		16 46	17 01		and at the same minutes past each hour until
Alexandra Palace	d	14 19	14 35		14 49	15 05		15 19	15 35		15 49	16 05		16 19	16 35		16 49	17 05		
New Southgate	d	14 22			14 52			15 22			15 52			16 22			16 52			
Oakleigh Park	d	14 26			14 56			15 26			15 56			16 26			16 56			
New Barnet	d	14 28			14 58			15 28			15 58			16 28			16 58			
Hadley Wood	d	14 31			15 01			15 31			16 01			16 31			17 01			
Potters Bar	d	14 35		14 45	15 05		15 15	15 35		15 45	16 05		16 15	16 35		16 45	17 05		17 15	
Brookmans Park	d	14 38			15 08			15 38			16 08			16 38			17 08			
Welham Green	d	14 41			15 11			15 41			16 11			16 41			17 11			
Hatfield	d	14 44		14 51	15 14		15 21	15 44		15 51	16 14		16 21	16 44		16 51	17 14		17 21	
Welwyn Garden City 4	d	14a49		14 56	15a19		15 26	15a49		15 56	16a19		16 26	16a49		16 56	17a19		17 26	
Welwyn North	d			15 00			15 30			16 00			16 31			17 00			17 30	
Knebworth	d			15 04			15 34			16 04			16 35			17 04			17 34	
Bowes Park	d		14 37			15 07			15 37			16 07			16 37			17 07		
Palmers Green	d		14 40			15 10			15 40			16 10			16 40			17 10		
Winchmore Hill	d		14 43			15 13			15 43			16 13			16 43			17 13		
Grange Park	d		14 45			15 15			15 45			16 15			16 45			17 15		
Enfield Chase	d		14 47			15 17			15 47			16 17			16 47			17 17		
Gordon Hill	d		14 50			15 20			15 50			16 20			16 50			17 20		
Crews Hill	d		14 53			15 23			15 53			16 23			16 53			17 23		
Cuffley	d		14 56			15 26			15 56			16 26			16 56			17 26		
Bayford	d		15 00			15 30			16 00			16 30			17 00			17 30		
Hertford North	a		15 05			15 35			16 05			16 35			17 05			17 35		
Watton-at-Stone	a		15 12			15 43			16 12			16 43			17 12			17 43		
Stevenage 4	a		15 20	15 08			15 38		16 20	16 08			16 38		17 20	17 08			17 38	

		GN	GN	TL	GN	GN	TL	GN	GN	TL	GN	GN	TL	GN
London Bridge	d													
London Blackfriars	d													
City Thameslink	d													
Farringdon	d													
St Pancras International	d													
London Kings Cross 15 ⊖	d			22 28			22 58			23 28			23 54	
Finsbury Park	a			22 33			23 03			23 33			00 01	
Moorgate ⊖	d	21 58	22 13		22 28	22 43		22 58	23 13		23 28	23 43		23 58
Old Street ⊖	d	22 00	22 15		22 30	22 45		23 00	23 15		23 30	23 45		00 01
Essex Road	d	22 03	22 18		22 33	22 48		23 03	23 18		23 33	23 48		00 04
Highbury & Islington ⊖	d	22 06	22 21		22 36	22 51		23 06	23 21		23 36	23 51		00 07
Drayton Park	d	22 08	22 23		22 38	22 53		23 08	23 23		23 38	23 53		00 09
Finsbury Park ⊖	a	22 11	22 26		22 41	22 56		23 11	23 26		23 41	23 56		00 12
Finsbury Park	d	22 12	22 27	22 34	22 42	22 57	23 04	23 12	23 27	23 34	23 42	23 57	00 03	00 12
Harringay	d	22 14	22 29		22 44	22 59		23 14	23 29		23 44	23 59		00 15
Hornsey	d	22 16	22 31		22 46	23 01		23 16	23 31		23 46	00 01		00 17
Alexandra Palace	d	22 19	22 35		22 49	23 05		23 19	23 35		23 49	00 05		00 19
New Southgate	d	22 22			22 52			23 22			23 52			00 22
Oakleigh Park	d	22 26			22 56			23 26			23 56			00 26
New Barnet	d	22 28			22 58			23 28			23 58			00 28
Hadley Wood	d	22 31			23 01			23 31			00 01			00 31
Potters Bar	d	22 35		22 45	23 05		23 15	23 35		23 45	00 05		00 16	00 35
Brookmans Park	d	22 38			23 08			23 38			00 08			00 38
Welham Green	d	22 41			23 11			23 41			00 11			00 41
Hatfield	d	22 44		22 51	23 14		23 21	23 44		23 51	00 14		00 23	00 44
Welwyn Garden City 4	d	22a49		22 56	23a19		23 26	23a49		23 56	00a19		00 28	00a49
Welwyn North	d			23 00			23 30			00 01			00 31	
Knebworth	d			23 04			23 34			00 05			00 36	
Bowes Park	d		22 37			23 07			23 37			00 07		
Palmers Green	d		22 40			23 10			23 40			00 10		
Winchmore Hill	d		22 43			23 13			23 43			00 13		
Grange Park	d		22 45			23 15			23 45			00 15		
Enfield Chase	d		22 47			23 17			23 47			00 17		
Gordon Hill	d		22 50			23 20			23 50			00 20		
Crews Hill	d		22 53			23 23			23 53			00 23		
Cuffley	d		22 56			23 26			23 56			00 26		
Bayford	d		23 00			23 30			00 01			00 30		
Hertford North	a		23 05			23 35			00 07			00 35		
Watton-at-Stone	a		23 12			23 43						00 41		
Stevenage 4	a		23 20	23 08			23 38			00 09		00 48	00 39	

See Table 025 for fast trains between London and Stevenage

Table T024-F

Saturdays

22 February to 16 May

London - Welwyn Garden City and Hertford North

		GN	TL	GN	GN	GN	TL	GN	GN	TL	TL	GN	TL	GN	GN	TL	GN	TL	GN	GN	TL	GN	GN
London Bridge	d																						
London Blackfriars	d									00 37													
City Thameslink	d																						
Farringdon	d									00 41													
St Pancras International	d									00 46													
London Kings Cross 15 ⊖	d				00 01	00 16	00 23	00 36	00 40		01 05	01 10	01 40	05 06	05 21	05 28	05 51	05 56	06 05	06 21	06 28	06 31	06 51
Finsbury Park	a				00 06	00 22	00 28	00 42	00 46	00 52	01 10	01 15	01 47	05 12	05 26	05 33	05 56	06 01	06 10	06 26	06 33	06 37	06 57
Moorgate ⊖	d																						
Old Street ⊖	d																						
Essex Road	d																						
Highbury & Islington ⊖	d																						
Drayton Park	d																						
Finsbury Park ⊖	a																						
Finsbury Park	d		00 02		00 11	00 23	00 29	00 43	00 47	00 54	01 11	01 16	01 48	05 13	05 27	05 34	05 57	06 02	06 12	06 27	06 34	06 38	06 57
Harringay	d			00 01	00 14	00 26			00 49			01 18		05 16	05 30		06 00		06 14	06 30		06 41	07 00
Hornsey	d			00 03	00 16	00 28			00 51			01 20		05 18	05 32		06 02		06 16	06 32		06 43	07 02
Alexandra Palace	d			00 07	00 19	00 31		00 47	00 55			01 24	01 53	05 21	05 35		06 05		06 20	06 35		06 46	07 05
New Southgate	d				00 22								01 56						06 23			06 49	
Oakleigh Park	d				00 25								01 59						06 26			06 52	
New Barnet	d				00 28			00 53					02 02						06 29			06 55	
Hadley Wood	d				00 31			00 56					02 04						06 32			06 58	
Potters Bar	d		00 17		00 35		00 42	01 00			01 22		02 08			05 45		06 14	06 36		06 45	07 02	
Brookmans Park	d				00 38														06 39			07 05	
Welham Green	d				00 41														06 41			07 07	
Hatfield	d		00 23		00 44		00 48	01 06			01 28		02 14			05 51		06 19	06 45		06 51	07 11	
Welwyn Garden City 4	d		00 28		00a49		00 58	01a11		01 15	01 34		02a20			05 56		06 24	06a50		06 56	07a16	
Welwyn North	d		00 31				01 01				01 37					06 00		06 27			07 00		
Knebworth	d		00 35				01 05				01 41					06 04		06 32			07 04		
Bowes Park	d			00 09		00 34			00 58			01 26			05 38		06 08			06 38			07 08
Palmers Green	d	00 01		00 12		00 36			01 01			01 29		05 25	05 40		06 10			06 40			07 10
Winchmore Hill	d	00 04		00 15		00 39			01 04			01 32		05 27	05 43		06 13			06 43			07 13
Grange Park	d	00 06		00 17		00 41			01 06			01 34			05 45		06 15			06 45			07 15
Enfield Chase	d	00 08		00 19		00 43			01 08			01 36		05 30	05 48		06 18			06 48			07 18
Gordon Hill	d	00 11		00 22		00 46			01 11			01 38		05 33	05 51		06 20			06 50			07 20
Crews Hill	d	00 14		00 25		00 49			01 14					05 36	05 54		06 23			06 53			07 23
Cuffley	d	00 17		00 28		00 52			01 17			01 43		05 39	05 57		06 26			06 56			07 26
Bayford	d	00 21		00 33		00 56			01 22					05 43	06 01		06 31			07 01			07 31
Hertford North	a	00 27		00 37		01 02			01 26			01 52		05 49	06 06		06 36			07 06			07 36
Watton-at-Stone	a			00 44					01 33						06 12		06 43			07 12			07 43
Stevenage 4	a		00 39	00 51			01 09		01 40	01 23	01 45				06 20	06 08		06 37		07 20	07 08		

		TL	GN	GN	TL	GN	GN	TL	GN	GN	TL	GN	GN	TL	GN	GN	TL	GN	GN	TL	GN	GN	TL
London Bridge	d																						
London Blackfriars	d																						
City Thameslink	d																						
Farringdon	d																						
St Pancras International	d																						
London Kings Cross 15 ⊖	d	06 58	07 01	07 21	07 28	07 31	07 51	07 58	08 01	08 21	08 28	08 31	08 51	08 58	09 01	09 21	09 28	09 31	09 51	09 58	10 01	10 21	10 28
Finsbury Park	a	07 03	07 07	07 27	07 33	07 37	07 57	08 03	08 07	08 27	08 33	08 37	08 57	09 03	09 07	09 27	09 33	09 37	09 57	10 03	10 07	10 27	10 33
Moorgate ⊖	d																						
Old Street ⊖	d																						
Essex Road	d																						
Highbury & Islington ⊖	d																						
Drayton Park	d																						
Finsbury Park ⊖	a																						
Finsbury Park	d	07 04	07 08	07 27	07 34	07 38	07 57	08 04	08 08	08 27	08 34	08 38	08 57	09 04	09 08	09 27	09 34	09 38	09 57	10 04	10 08	10 27	10 34
Harringay	d		07 11	07 30		07 41	08 00		08 11	08 30		08 41	09 00		09 11	09 30		09 41	10 00		10 11	10 30	
Hornsey	d		07 13	07 32		07 43	08 02		08 13	08 32		08 43	09 02		09 13	09 32		09 43	10 02		10 13	10 32	
Alexandra Palace	d		07 16	07 35		07 46	08 05		08 16	08 35		08 46	09 05		09 16	09 35		09 46	10 05		10 16	10 35	
New Southgate	d		07 19			07 49			08 19			08 49			09 19			09 49			10 19		
Oakleigh Park	d		07 22			07 52			08 22			08 52			09 22			09 52			10 22		
New Barnet	d		07 25			07 55			08 25			08 55			09 25			09 55			10 25		
Hadley Wood	d		07 28			07 58			08 28			08 58			09 28			09 58			10 28		
Potters Bar	d	07 15	07 32		07 45	08 02		08 15	08 32		08 45	09 02		09 15	09 32		09 45	10 02		10 15	10 32		10 45
Brookmans Park	d		07 35			08 05			08 35			09 05			09 35			10 05			10 35		
Welham Green	d		07 37			08 07			08 37			09 07			09 37			10 07			10 37		
Hatfield	d	07 21	07 41		07 51	08 11		08 21	08 41		08 51	09 11		09 21	09 41		09 51	10 11		10 21	10 41		10 51
Welwyn Garden City 4	d	07 26	07a46		07 56	08a16		08 26	08a46		08 56	09a16		09 26	09a46		09 56	10a16		10 26	10a46		10 56
Welwyn North	d	07 30			08 00			08 30			09 00			09 31			10 00			10 30			11 00
Knebworth	d	07 34			08 04			08 34			09 04			09 34			10 04			10 34			11 04
Bowes Park	d			07 38			08 08			08 38			09 08			09 38			10 08			10 38	
Palmers Green	d			07 40			08 10			08 40			09 10			09 40			10 10			10 40	
Winchmore Hill	d			07 43			08 13			08 43			09 13			09 43			10 13			10 43	
Grange Park	d			07 45			08 15			08 45			09 15			09 45			10 15			10 45	
Enfield Chase	d			07 48			08 18			08 48			09 18			09 48			10 18			10 48	
Gordon Hill	d			07 50			08 20			08 50			09 20			09 50			10 20			10 50	
Crews Hill	d			07 53			08 23			08 53			09 23			09 53			10 23			10 53	
Cuffley	d			07 56			08 26			08 56			09 26			09 56			10 26			10 56	
Bayford	d			08 01			08 31			09 01			09 31			10 01			10 31			11 01	
Hertford North	a			08 06			08 36			09 06			09 36			10 06			10 36			11 06	
Watton-at-Stone	a			08 12			08 43			09 12			09 43			10 12			10 43			11 12	
Stevenage 4	a	07 38		08 20	08 08			08 38		09 20	09 08			09 38		10 20	10 08			10 38		11 20	11 08

See Table 025 for fast trains between London and Stevenage

Table T024-F

Saturdays
22 February to 16 May

London - Welwyn Garden City and Hertford North

		GN		GN	TL 1	GN	GN	TL 1	GN	GN	TL 1	GN		GN	TL 1	GN	GN	TL 1	GN	GN	TL 1	GN		GN	TL 1
London Bridge	d																								
London Blackfriars	d																								
City Thameslink	d																								
Farringdon	d																								
St Pancras International	d																								
London Kings Cross 15 ⊖	d	10 31		10 51	10 58	11 01	11 21	11 28	11 31	11 51	11 58	12 01		12 21	12 28	12 31	12 51	12 58	13 01	13 21	13 28	13 31		13 51	13 58
Finsbury Park	a	10 37		10 57	11 03	11 07	11 27	11 33	11 37	11 57	12 03	12 07		12 27	12 33	12 37	12 57	13 03	13 07	13 27	13 33	13 37		13 57	14 03
Moorgate ⊖	d																								
Old Street ⊖	d																								
Essex Road	d																								
Highbury & Islington ⊖	d																								
Drayton Park	d																								
Finsbury Park ⊖	a																								
Finsbury Park	d	10 38		10 57	11 04	11 08	11 27	11 34	11 38	11 57	12 04	12 08		12 27	12 34	12 38	12 57	13 04	13 08	13 27	13 34	13 38		13 57	14 04
Harringay	d	10 41		11 00		11 11	11 30		11 41	12 00		12 11		12 30		12 41	13 00		13 11	13 30		13 41		14 00	
Hornsey	d	10 43		11 02		11 13	11 32		11 43	12 02		12 13		12 32		12 43	13 02		13 13	13 32		13 43		14 02	
Alexandra Palace	d	10 46		11 05		11 16	11 35		11 46	12 05		12 16		12 35		12 46	13 05		13 16	13 35		13 46		14 05	
New Southgate	d	10 49				11 19			11 49			12 19				12 49			13 19			13 49			
Oakleigh Park	d	10 52				11 22			11 52			12 22				12 52			13 22			13 52			
New Barnet	d	10 55				11 25			11 55			12 25				12 55			13 25			13 55			
Hadley Wood	d	10 58				11 28			11 58			12 28				12 58			13 28			13 58			
Potters Bar	d	11 02			11 15	11 32		11 45	12 02		12 15	12 32			12 45	13 02		13 15	13 32		13 45	14 02			14 15
Brookmans Park	d	11 05				11 35			12 05			12 35				13 05			13 35			14 05			
Welham Green	d	11 07				11 37			12 07			12 37				13 07			13 37			14 07			
Hatfield	d	11 11			11 21	11 41		11 51	12 11		12 21	12 41			12 51	13 11		13 21	13 41		13 51	14 11			14 21
Welwyn Garden City 4	d	11a16			11 26	11a46		11 56	12a16		12 26	12a46			12 56	13a16		13 26	13a46		13 56	14a16			14 26
Welwyn North	d				11 31			12 00			12 30				13 00			13 30			14 00				14 30
Knebworth	d				11 34			12 04			12 34				13 04			13 34			14 04				14 34
Bowes Park	d			11 08			11 38			12 08				12 38			13 08			13 38				14 08	
Palmers Green	d			11 10			11 40			12 10				12 40			13 10			13 40				14 10	
Winchmore Hill	d			11 13			11 43			12 13				12 43			13 13			13 43				14 13	
Grange Park	d			11 15			11 45			12 15				12 45			13 15			13 45				14 15	
Enfield Chase	d			11 18			11 48			12 18				12 48			13 18			13 48				14 18	
Gordon Hill	d			11 20			11 50			12 20				12 50			13 20			13 50				14 20	
Crews Hill	d			11 23			11 53			12 23				12 53			13 23			13 53				14 23	
Cuffley	d			11 26			11 56			12 26				12 56			13 26			13 56				14 26	
Bayford	d			11 31			12 01			12 31				13 01			13 31			14 01				14 31	
Hertford North	a			11 36			12 06			12 36				13 06			13 36			14 06				14 36	
Watton-at-Stone	a			11 43			12 12			12 43				13 12			13 43			14 12				14 43	
Stevenage 4	a				11 38		12 20	12 08			12 38			13 21	13 08			13 38		14 20	14 08				14 38

		GN	GN	TL 1	GN	GN	TL 1	GN		GN	TL 1	GN	GN	TL 1	GN	GN	TL 1	GN	GN	TL 1	
London Bridge	d																				
London Blackfriars	d																				
City Thameslink	d																				
Farringdon	d																				
St Pancras International	d																				
London Kings Cross 15 ⊖	d	14 01	14 21	14 28	14 31	14 51	14 58	15 01		15 21	15 28	15 31	15 51	15 58	16 01	16 21	16 28	16 31	16 51	16 58	
Finsbury Park	a	14 07	14 27	14 33	14 37	14 57	15 03	15 07		15 27	15 33	15 37	15 57	16 03	16 07	16 27	16 33	16 37	16 57	17 03	
Moorgate ⊖	d																				
Old Street ⊖	d																				
Essex Road	d																				
Highbury & Islington ⊖	d																				
Drayton Park	d																				
Finsbury Park ⊖	a																				
Finsbury Park	d	14 08	14 27	14 34	14 38	14 57	15 04	15 08		15 27	15 34	15 38	15 57	16 04	16 08	16 27	16 34	16 38	16 57	17 04	
Harringay	d	14 11	14 30		14 41	15 00		15 11		15 30		15 41	16 00		16 11	16 30		16 41	17 00		
Hornsey	d	14 13	14 32		14 43	15 02		15 13		15 32		15 43	16 02		16 13	16 32		16 43	17 02		and at the same minutes past each hour until
Alexandra Palace	d	14 16	14 35		14 46	15 05		15 16		15 35		15 46	16 05		16 16	16 35		16 46	17 05		
New Southgate	d	14 19			14 49			15 19				15 49			16 19			16 49			
Oakleigh Park	d	14 22			14 52			15 22				15 52			16 22			16 52			
New Barnet	d	14 25			14 55			15 25				15 55			16 25			16 55			
Hadley Wood	d	14 28			14 58			15 28				15 58			16 28			16 58			
Potters Bar	d	14 32		14 45	15 02		15 15	15 32			15 45	16 02		16 15	16 32		16 45	17 02		17 15	
Brookmans Park	d	14 35			15 05			15 35				16 05			16 35			17 05			
Welham Green	d	14 37			15 07			15 37				16 07			16 37			17 07			
Hatfield	d	14 41		14 51	15 11		15 21	15 41			15 51	16 11		16 21	16 41		16 51	17 11		17 21	
Welwyn Garden City 4	d	14a46		14 56	15a16		15 26	15a46			15 56	16a16		16 26	16a46		16 56	17a16		17 26	
Welwyn North	d			15 00			15 30				16 00			16 31			17 00			17 30	
Knebworth	d			15 04			15 34				16 04			16 35			17 04			17 34	
Bowes Park	d		14 38			15 08				15 38			16 08			16 38			17 08		
Palmers Green	d		14 40			15 10				15 40			16 10			16 40			17 10		
Winchmore Hill	d		14 43			15 13				15 43			16 13			16 43			17 13		
Grange Park	d		14 45			15 15				15 45			16 15			16 45			17 15		
Enfield Chase	d		14 48			15 18				15 48			16 18			16 48			17 18		
Gordon Hill	d		14 50			15 20				15 50			16 20			16 50			17 20		
Crews Hill	d		14 53			15 23				15 53			16 23			16 53			17 23		
Cuffley	d		14 56			15 26				15 56			16 26			16 56			17 26		
Bayford	d		15 01			15 31				16 01			16 31			17 01			17 31		
Hertford North	a		15 06			15 36				16 06			16 36			17 06			17 36		
Watton-at-Stone	a		15 12			15 43				16 12			16 43			17 12			17 43		
Stevenage 4	a		15 20	15 08			15 38			16 20	16 08			16 38		17 20	17 08			17 38	

See Table 025 for fast trains between London and Stevenage

Table T024-F

Saturdays
22 February to 16 May

London - Welwyn Garden City and Hertford North

		GN	GN	TL 1	GN	GN	TL 1		GN	GN	TL 1	GN	GN	TL 1
London Bridge	d													
London Blackfriars	d													
City Thameslink	d													
Farringdon	d													
St Pancras International	d													
London Kings Cross 15 ⊖	d	22 01	22 21	22 28	22 31	22 51	22 58		23 01	23 21	23 28	23 31	23 51	23 54
Finsbury Park	a	22 07	22 27	22 33	22 37	22 57	23 03		23 07	23 27	23 33	23 37	23 57	00 01
Moorgate ⊖	d													
Old Street ⊖	d													
Essex Road	d													
Highbury & Islington ⊖	d													
Drayton Park	d													
Finsbury Park ⊖	a													
Finsbury Park	d	22 08	22 27	22 34	22 38	22 57	23 04		23 08	23 27	23 34	23 38	23 58	00 03
Harringay	d	22 11	22 30		22 41	23 00			23 11	23 30		23 41	00 01	
Hornsey	d	22 13	22 32		22 43	23 02			23 13	23 32		23 43	00 03	
Alexandra Palace	d	22 16	22 35		22 46	23 05			23 16	23 35		23 46	00 06	
New Southgate	d	22 19			22 49				23 19			23 49		
Oakleigh Park	d	22 22			22 52				23 22			23 52		
New Barnet	d	22 25			22 55				23 25			23 55		
Hadley Wood	d	22 28			22 58				23 28			23 58		
Potters Bar	d	22 32		22 45	23 02		23 15		23 32		23 45	00 02		00 16
Brookmans Park	d	22 35			23 05				23 35			00 05		
Welham Green	d	22 37			23 07				23 37			00 07		
Hatfield	d	22 41		22 51	23 11		23 21		23 41		23 51	00 11		00 23
Welwyn Garden City 4	d	22a46		22 56	23a16		23 26		23a46		23 56	00a16		00 28
Welwyn North	d			23 00			23 30				00 01			00 31
Knebworth	d			23 04			23 34				00 05			00 36
Bowes Park	d		22 38			23 08				23 38			00 08	
Palmers Green	d		22 40			23 10				23 40			00 11	
Winchmore Hill	d		22 43			23 13				23 43			00 14	
Grange Park	d		22 45			23 15				23 45			00 16	
Enfield Chase	d		22 48			23 18				23 48			00 18	
Gordon Hill	d		22 50			23 20				23 50			00 21	
Crews Hill	d		22 53			23 23				23 53			00 24	
Cuffley	d		22 56			23 26				23 56			00 27	
Bayford	d		23 01			23 31				00 01			00 31	
Hertford North	a		23 06			23 36				00 07			00 36	
Watton-at-Stone	a		23 12			23 43							00 42	
Stevenage 4	a		23 20	23 08			23 38				00 09		00 49	00 39

Sundays
15 December to 16 February

		TL 1	GN	GN	TL 1	GN	GN	TL 1	TL 1	GN		GN	GN	GN	GN	GN	TL 1	GN	GN	GN		GN
London Bridge	d																					
London Blackfriars	d							00 37														
City Thameslink	d																					
Farringdon	d							00 41														
St Pancras International	d							00 46														
London Kings Cross 15 ⊖	d				00 23				01 05	01 10		01 40	05 50	06 20	06 35	06 50	07 02					
Finsbury Park	a				00 28			00 52	01 10	01 15		01 45	05 55	06 25	06 41	06 55	07 07					
Moorgate ⊖	d					00 17	00 27											07 00	07 15	07 28		07 45
Old Street ⊖	d			00 01		00 19	00 29											07 02	07 17	07 30		07 47
Essex Road	d			00 04		00 22	00 32											07 05	07 20	07 33		07 50
Highbury & Islington ⊖	d			00 07		00 25	00 35											07 08	07 23	07 36		07 53
Drayton Park	d			00 09		00 27	00 37											07 10	07 25	07 38		07 55
Finsbury Park ⊖	a			00 12		00 30	00 40											07 13	07 28	07 41		07 58
Finsbury Park	d	00 03		00 12	00 29	00 32	00 41	00 54	01 11	01 16		01 46	05 57	06 27	06 42	06 57	07 08	07 14	07 29	07 44		07 59
Harringay	d			00 15		00 34				01 18			05 59	06 29	06 44	06 59		07 16	07 31	07 46		08 01
Hornsey	d		00 01	00 17		00 36				01 20			06 01	06 31	06 46	07 01		07 18	07 33	07 48		08 03
Alexandra Palace	d		00 05	00 19		00 40	00 45			01 24		01 51	06 05	06 35	06 49	07 05		07 21	07 37	07 51		08 07
New Southgate	d			00 22								01 54			06 52			07 24		07 54		
Oakleigh Park	d			00 26								01 57			06 56			07 28		07 58		
New Barnet	d			00 28			00 51					01 59			06 58			07 30		08 00		
Hadley Wood	d			00 31			00 54					02 02			07 01			07 33		08 03		
Potters Bar	d	00 16		00 35	00 42		00 58		01 22			02 06			07 05		07 19	07 37		08 07		
Brookmans Park	d			00 38											07 08			07 40		08 10		
Welham Green	d			00 41											07 11			07 43		08 13		
Hatfield	d	00 23		00 44	00 48		01 04		01 28			02 12			07 14		07 25	07 46		08 16		
Welwyn Garden City 4	d	00 28		00a49	00 59		01a09	01 15	01 34			02a19			07a21		07 31	07a53		08a21		
Welwyn North	d	00 31			01 02				01 37								07 35					
Knebworth	d	00 36			01 06				01 41								07 39					
Bowes Park	d		00 07			00 42				01 26			06 07	06 37		07 07			07 39			08 09
Palmers Green	d		00 10			00 45				01 29			06 10	06 40		07 10			07 42			08 12
Winchmore Hill	d		00 13			00 48				01 32			06 13	06 43		07 13			07 45			08 15
Grange Park	d		00 15			00 50				01 34			06 15	06 45		07 15			07 47			08 17
Enfield Chase	d		00 17			00 53				01 36			06 17	06 47		07 17			07 49			08 19
Gordon Hill	d		00 20			00 55				01 38			06 20	06 50		07 20			07 52			08 22
Crews Hill	d		00 23			00 58							06 23	06 53		07 23			07 55			08 25
Cuffley	d		00 26			01 02				01 43			06 26	06 56		07 26			07 58			08 28
Bayford	d		00 30			01 06							06 30	07 00		07 30			08 02			08 32
Hertford North	a		00 35			01 11				01 52			06 36	07 05		07 35			08 07			08 37
Watton-at-Stone	a		00 41			01 18								07 12		07 42			08 14			08 44
Stevenage 4	a	00 39	00 48		01 10	01 27		01 23	01 45					07 20		07 50	07 43		08 22			08 52

See Table 025 for fast trains between London and Stevenage

Table T024-F

London - Welwyn Garden City and Hertford North

Sundays
15 December to 16 February

Station		TL [1]	GN	GN	GN	GN		TL [1]	GN	GN	GN	GN	TL [1]	GN	GN	TL [1]	GN	GN	TL [1]	GN	GN	TL [1]
London Bridge	d																					
London Blackfriars	d																					
City Thameslink	d																					
Farringdon	d																					
St Pancras International	d																					
London Kings Cross [15] ⊖	d	08 02						15 02					16 02			16 32			17 02			17 32
Finsbury Park	a	08 07						15 07					16 07			16 37			17 07			17 37
Moorgate ⊖	d		07 58	08 13	08 28	08 43			14 58	15 13	15 28	15 43		15 58	16 13		16 28	16 43		16 58	17 13	
Old Street ⊖	d		08 00	08 15	08 30	08 45			15 00	15 15	15 30	15 45		16 00	16 15		16 30	16 45		17 00	17 15	
Essex Road	d		08 03	08 18	08 33	08 48			15 03	15 18	15 33	15 48		16 03	16 18		16 33	16 48		17 03	17 18	
Highbury & Islington ⊖	d		08 06	08 21	08 36	08 51			15 06	15 21	15 36	15 51		16 06	16 21		16 36	16 51		17 06	17 21	
Drayton Park	d		08 08	08 23	08 38	08 53			15 08	15 23	15 38	15 53		16 08	16 23		16 38	16 53		17 08	17 23	
Finsbury Park ⊖	a		08 11	08 26	08 41	08 56			15 11	15 26	15 41	15 56		16 11	16 26		16 41	16 56		17 11	17 26	
Finsbury Park	d	08 08	08 12	08 27	08 42	08 57		15 08	15 12	15 27	15 42	15 57	16 08	16 12	16 27	16 38	16 42	16 57	17 08	17 12	17 27	17 38
Harringay	d		08 14	08 29	08 44	08 59			15 14	15 29	15 44	15 59		16 14	16 29		16 44	16 59		17 14	17 29	
Hornsey	d		08 16	08 31	08 46	09 01	and at		15 16	15 31	15 46	16 01		16 16	16 31		16 46	17 01		17 16	17 31	
Alexandra Palace	d		08 19	08 35	08 49	09 05	the same		15 19	15 35	15 49	16 05		16 19	16 35		16 49	17 05		17 19	17 35	
New Southgate	d		08 22		08 52		minutes		15 22		15 52			16 22			16 52			17 22		
Oakleigh Park	d		08 26		08 56		past		15 26		15 56			16 26			16 56			17 26		
New Barnet	d		08 28		08 58		each		15 28		15 58			16 28			16 58			17 28		
Hadley Wood	d		08 31		09 01		hour until		15 31		16 01			16 31			17 01			17 31		
Potters Bar	d	08 19	08 35		09 05			15 19	15 35		16 05		16 19	16 35		16 49	17 05		17 19	17 35		17 49
Brookmans Park	d		08 38		09 08				15 38		16 08			16 38			17 08			17 38		
Welham Green	d		08 41		09 11				15 41		16 11			16 41			17 11			17 41		
Hatfield	d	08 25	08 44		09 14			15 25	15 44		16 14		16 25	16 44		16 55	17 14		17 25	17 44		17 55
Welwyn Garden City [4]	d	08 31	08a49		09a19			15 31	15a49		16a19		16 31	16a49		17 01	17a19		17 31	17a49		18 01
Welwyn North	d	08 35						15 35					16 35			17 05			17 35			18 05
Knebworth	d	08 39						15 39					16 39			17 09			17 39			18 09
Bowes Park	d			08 37		09 07				15 37		16 07			16 37			17 07			17 37	
Palmers Green	d			08 40		09 10				15 40		16 10			16 40			17 10			17 40	
Winchmore Hill	d			08 43		09 13				15 43		16 13			16 43			17 13			17 43	
Grange Park	d			08 45		09 15				15 45		16 15			16 45			17 15			17 45	
Enfield Chase	d			08 47		09 17				15 47		16 17			16 47			17 17			17 47	
Gordon Hill	d			08 50		09 20				15 50		16 20			16 50			17 20			17 50	
Crews Hill	d			08 53		09 23				15 53		16 23			16 53			17 23			17 53	
Cuffley	d			08 56		09 26				15 56		16 26			16 56			17 26			17 56	
Bayford	d			09 00		09 30				16 00		16 30			17 00			17 30			18 00	
Hertford North	a			09 05		09 35				16 05		16 35			17 05			17 35			18 05	
Watton-at-Stone	a			09 12		09 42				16 12		16 42			17 12			17 42			18 12	
Stevenage [4]	a	08 43		09 20		09 50		15 43		16 20		16 50	16 43		17 20	17 13		17 50	17 43		18 20	18 13

Station		GN	GN	TL [1]	GN	GN	TL [1]	GN	GN	TL [1]	GN	GN	GN	GN	TL [1]	GN	GN	GN	GN	TL [1]	GN	GN	GN
London Bridge	d																						
London Blackfriars	d																						
City Thameslink	d																						
Farringdon	d																						
St Pancras International	d																						
London Kings Cross [15] ⊖	d			18 02			18 32			19 02					20 02					21 02			
Finsbury Park	a			18 07			18 37			19 07					20 07					21 07			
Moorgate ⊖	d	17 28	17 43		17 58	18 13		18 28	18 43		18 58	19 13	19 28	19 43		19 58	20 13	20 28	20 43		20 58	21 13	21 28
Old Street ⊖	d	17 30	17 45		18 00	18 15		18 30	18 45		19 00	19 15	19 30	19 45		20 00	20 15	20 30	20 45		21 00	21 15	21 30
Essex Road	d	17 33	17 48		18 03	18 18		18 33	18 48		19 03	19 18	19 33	19 48		20 03	20 18	20 33	20 48		21 03	21 18	21 33
Highbury & Islington ⊖	d	17 36	17 51		18 06	18 21		18 36	18 51		19 06	19 21	19 36	19 51		20 06	20 21	20 36	20 51		21 06	21 21	21 36
Drayton Park	d	17 38	17 53		18 08	18 23		18 38	18 53		19 08	19 23	19 38	19 53		20 08	20 23	20 38	20 53		21 08	21 23	21 38
Finsbury Park ⊖	a	17 41	17 56		18 11	18 26		18 41	18 56		19 11	19 26	19 41	19 56		20 11	20 26	20 41	20 56		21 11	21 26	21 41
Finsbury Park	d	17 42	17 57	18 08	18 12	18 27	18 38	18 42	18 57	19 08	19 12	19 27	19 42	19 57	20 08	20 12	20 27	20 42	20 57	21 08	21 12	21 27	21 42
Harringay	d	17 44	17 59		18 14	18 29		18 44	18 59		19 14	19 29	19 44	19 59		20 14	20 29	20 44	20 59		21 14	21 29	21 44
Hornsey	d	17 46	18 01		18 16	18 31		18 46	19 01		19 16	19 31	19 46	20 01		20 16	20 31	20 46	21 01		21 16	21 31	21 46
Alexandra Palace	d	17 49	18 05		18 19	18 35		18 49	19 05		19 19	19 35	19 49	20 05		20 19	20 35	20 49	21 05		21 19	21 35	21 49
New Southgate	d	17 52			18 22			18 52			19 22		19 52			20 22		20 52			21 22		21 52
Oakleigh Park	d	17 56			18 26			18 56			19 26		19 56			20 26		20 56			21 26		21 56
New Barnet	d	17 58			18 28			18 58			19 28		19 58			20 28		20 58			21 28		21 58
Hadley Wood	d	18 01			18 31			19 01			19 31		20 01			20 31		21 01			21 31		22 01
Potters Bar	d	18 05		18 19	18 35		18 49	19 05		19 19	19 35		20 05		20 19	20 35		21 05		21 19	21 35		22 05
Brookmans Park	d	18 08			18 38			19 08			19 38		20 08			20 38		21 08			21 38		22 08
Welham Green	d	18 11			18 41			19 11			19 41		20 11			20 41		21 11			21 41		22 11
Hatfield	d	18 14		18 25	18 44		18 55	19 14		19 26	19 44		20 14		20 26	20 44		21 14		21 25	21 44		22 14
Welwyn Garden City [4]	d	18a19		18 31	18a49		19 01	19a19		19 31	19a49		20a19		20 31	20a49		21a19		21 31	21a49		22a19
Welwyn North	d			18 35			19 05			19 35					20 35					21 35			
Knebworth	d			18 39			19 09			19 39					20 39					21 39			
Bowes Park	d		18 07			18 37			19 07			19 37		20 07			20 37		21 07			21 37	
Palmers Green	d		18 10			18 40			19 10			19 40		20 10			20 40		21 10			21 40	
Winchmore Hill	d		18 13			18 43			19 13			19 43		20 13			20 43		21 13			21 43	
Grange Park	d		18 15			18 45			19 15			19 45		20 15			20 45		21 15			21 45	
Enfield Chase	d		18 17			18 47			19 17			19 47		20 17			20 47		21 17			21 47	
Gordon Hill	d		18 20			18 50			19 20			19 50		20 20			20 50		21 20			21 50	
Crews Hill	d		18 23			18 53			19 23			19 53		20 23			20 53		21 23			21 53	
Cuffley	d		18 26			18 56			19 26			19 56		20 26			20 56		21 26			21 56	
Bayford	d		18 30			19 00			19 30			20 00		20 30			21 00		21 30			22 00	
Hertford North	a		18 35			19 05			19 35			20 05		20 35			21 05		21 35			22 05	
Watton-at-Stone	a		18 42			19 12			19 42			20 12		20 42			21 12		21 42			22 12	
Stevenage [4]	a		18 50	18 43		19 20	19 13		19 50	19 43		20 20		20 50	20 43		21 20		21 50	21 43		22 20	

See Table 025 for fast trains between London and Stevenage

Table T024-F

London - Welwyn Garden City and Hertford North

Sundays
15 December to 16 February

Station		GN	TL [1]	GN	GN	GN	GN	TL [1]	GN	GN	GN	GN	GN
London Bridge	d												
London Blackfriars	d												
City Thameslink	d												
Farringdon	d												
St Pancras International	d												
London Kings Cross [15] ⊖	d		22 02					23 02					
Finsbury Park	a		22 07					23 07					
Moorgate ⊖	d	21 43		21 58	22 13	22 28	22 43		22 58	23 13	23 28	23 43	23 58
Old Street ⊖	d	21 45		22 00	22 15	22 30	22 45		23 00	23 15	23 30	23 45	00 01
Essex Road	d	21 48		22 03	22 18	22 33	22 48		23 03	23 18	23 33	23 48	00 04
Highbury & Islington ⊖	d	21 51		22 06	22 21	22 36	22 51		23 06	23 21	23 36	23 51	00 06
Drayton Park	d	21 53		22 08	22 23	22 38	22 53		23 08	23 23	23 38	23 53	00 09
Finsbury Park ⊖	a	21 56		22 11	22 26	22 41	22 56		23 11	23 26	23 41	23 56	00 11
Finsbury Park	d	21 57	22 08	22 12	22 27	22 42	22 57	23 09	23 12	23 27	23 42	23 57	00 12
Harringay	d	21 59		22 14	22 29	22 44	22 59		23 14	23 29	23 44	23 59	00 14
Hornsey	d	22 01		22 16	22 31	22 46	23 01		23 16	23 31	23 46	00 01	00 16
Alexandra Palace	d	22 05		22 19	22 35	22 49	23 05		23 19	23 35	23 49	00 05	00 19
New Southgate	d			22 22		22 52			23 22		23 52		00 22
Oakleigh Park	d			22 26		22 56			23 26		23 56		00 26
New Barnet	d			22 28		22 58			23 28		23 58		00 28
Hadley Wood	d			22 31		23 01			23 31		00 01		00 31
Potters Bar	d		22 19	22 35		23 05		23 20	23 35		00 05		00 35
Brookmans Park	d			22 38		23 08			23 38		00 08		00 38
Welham Green	d			22 41		23 11			23 41		00 11		00 41
Hatfield	d		22 25	22 44		23 14		23 26	23 44		00 14		00 44
Welwyn Garden City [4]	d		22 31	22a49		23a19		23 31	23a49		00a21		00a51
Welwyn North	d		22 35					23 35					
Knebworth	d		22 39					23 39					
Bowes Park	d	22 07			22 37		23 07			23 37		00 07	
Palmers Green	d	22 10			22 40		23 10			23 40		00 10	
Winchmore Hill	d	22 13			22 43		23 13			23 43		00 13	
Grange Park	d	22 15			22 45		23 15			23 45		00 15	
Enfield Chase	d	22 17			22 47		23 17			23 47		00 17	
Gordon Hill	d	22 20			22 50		23 20			23 50		00 20	
Crews Hill	d	22 23			22 53		23 23			23 53		00 23	
Cuffley	d	22 26			22 56		23 26			23 56		00 26	
Bayford	d	22 30			23 00		23 30			00 01		00 30	
Hertford North	a	22 35			23 05		23 35			00 06		00 35	
Watton-at-Stone	a	22 42			23 12		23 42					00 42	
Stevenage [4]	a	22 50	22 43		23 20		23 52	23 43				00 50	

Sundays
23 February to 10 May

Station		TL [1]	GN	GN	TL [1]	GN	GN	TL [1]	TL [1]	GN	GN	GN	GN	GN	GN	TL [1]	GN	GN	GN	GN
London Bridge	d																			
London Blackfriars	d							00 37												
City Thameslink	d																			
Farringdon	d							00 41												
St Pancras International	d							00 46												
London Kings Cross [15] ⊖	d			00 03	00 23	00 26	00 35		01 05	01 10	01 40	05 50	06 20	06 35	06 50	07 02	07 07	07 20	07 38	07 50
Finsbury Park	a			00 08	00 28	00 32	00 42	00 52	01 10	01 15	01 45	05 55	06 25	06 41	06 55	07 07	07 12	07 25	07 44	07 55
Moorgate ⊖	d																			
Old Street ⊖	d																			
Essex Road	d																			
Highbury & Islington ⊖	d																			
Drayton Park	d																			
Finsbury Park ⊖	a																			
Finsbury Park	d	00 03		00 11	00 29	00 33	00 42	00 54	01 11	01 16	01 46	05 57	06 27	06 42	06 57	07 08	07 14	07 29	07 44	07 59
Harringay	d		00 01	00 15		00 35				01 18		05 59	06 29	06 44	06 59		07 16	07 31	07 46	08 01
Hornsey	d		00 03	00 17		00 37				01 20		06 01	06 31	06 46	07 01		07 18	07 33	07 48	08 03
Alexandra Palace	d		00 06	00 19		00 41	00 47			01 24	01 51	06 05	06 35	06 49	07 05		07 21	07 37	07 51	08 07
New Southgate	d			00 22							01 54			06 52			07 24		07 54	
Oakleigh Park	d			00 26							01 57			06 56			07 28		07 58	
New Barnet	d			00 28			00 53				01 59			06 58			07 30		08 00	
Hadley Wood	d			00 31			00 56				02 02			07 01			07 33		08 03	
Potters Bar	d	00 16		00 35	00 42		01 00		01 22		02 06			07 05		07 19	07 37		08 07	
Brookmans Park	d			00 38										07 08			07 40		08 10	
Welham Green	d			00 41										07 11			07 43		08 13	
Hatfield	d	00 23		00 44	00 48		01 06		01 28		02 12			07 14		07 25	07 46		08 16	
Welwyn Garden City [4]	d	00 28		00a49	00 59		01a11	01 15	01 34		02a19			07a21		07 31	07a53		08a22	
Welwyn North	d	00 31			01 02				01 37							07 35				
Knebworth	d	00 36			01 06				01 41							07 39				
Bowes Park	d		00 08			00 43				01 26		06 07	06 37		07 07			07 39		08 09
Palmers Green	d		00 11			00 46				01 29		06 10	06 40		07 10			07 42		08 12
Winchmore Hill	d		00 14			00 49				01 32		06 13	06 43		07 13			07 45		08 15
Grange Park	d		00 16			00 51				01 34		06 15	06 45		07 15			07 47		08 17
Enfield Chase	d		00 18			00 54				01 36		06 17	06 47		07 17			07 49		08 19
Gordon Hill	d		00 21			00 56				01 38		06 20	06 50		07 20			07 52		08 22
Crews Hill	d		00 24			00 59						06 23	06 53		07 23			07 55		08 25
Cuffley	d		00 27			01 03				01 43		06 26	06 56		07 26			07 58		08 28
Bayford	d		00 31			01 07						06 30	07 00		07 30			08 02		08 32
Hertford North	a		00 36			01 12				01 52		06 36	07 05		07 35			08 07		08 37
Watton-at-Stone	a		00 42			01 18							07 12		07 42			08 14		08 44
Stevenage [4]	a	00 39	00 49		01 10	01 27		01 23	01 45				07 20		07 50	07 43		08 22		08 52

See Table 025 for fast trains between London and Stevenage

Table T024-F

Sundays

23 February to 10 May

London - Welwyn Garden City and Hertford North

		TL 1	GN	GN	GN	GN		TL 1	GN	GN	GN	GN		TL 1	GN	GN	GN	GN	TL 1	GN	GN	GN		GN
London Bridge	d																							
London Blackfriars	d																							
City Thameslink	d																							
Farringdon	d																							
St Pancras International	d																							
London Kings Cross 15 ⊖	d	08 02	08 05	08 20	08 35	08 50		13 02	13 05	13 20	13 35	13 50		14 02	14 05	14 20	14 37	14 50	15 02	15 05	15 20	15 35		15 50
Finsbury Park	a	08 07	08 11	08 25	08 40	08 55		13 07	13 11	13 25	13 40	13 55		14 07	14 11	14 25	14 43	14 55	15 07	15 11	15 25	15 40		15 55
Moorgate ⊖	d																							
Old Street ⊖	d																							
Essex Road	d																							
Highbury & Islington ⊖	d																							
Drayton Park	d																							
Finsbury Park ⊖	a																							
Finsbury Park	d	08 08	08 12	08 27	08 42	08 57		13 08	13 12	13 27	13 42	13 57		14 08	14 12	14 27	14 43	14 57	15 08	15 12	15 27	15 42		15 57
Harringay	d		08 15	08 29	08 45	08 59			13 15	13 29	13 45	13 59			14 15	14 29	14 46	14 59		15 15	15 29	15 45		15 59
Hornsey	d		08 17	08 31	08 47	09 01	and at		13 17	13 31	13 47	14 01			14 17	14 31	14 48	15 01		15 17	15 31	15 47		16 01
Alexandra Palace	d		08 20	08 35	08 50	09 05	the same		13 20	13 35	13 50	14 05			14 20	14 35	14 51	15 05		15 20	15 35	15 50		16 05
New Southgate	d		08 23		08 53		minutes		13 23		13 53				14 23		14 54			15 23		15 53		
Oakleigh Park	d		08 26		08 56		past		13 26		13 56				14 26		14 57			15 26		15 56		
New Barnet	d		08 29		08 59		each		13 29		13 59				14 29		15 00			15 29		15 59		
Hadley Wood	d		08 32		09 02		hour until		13 32		14 02				14 32		15 03			15 32		16 02		
Potters Bar	d	08 19	08 36		09 06			13 19	13 36		14 06			14 19	14 36		15 07		15 19	15 36		16 06		
Brookmans Park	d		08 39		09 09				13 39		14 09				14 39		15 10			15 39		16 09		
Welham Green	d		08 41		09 11				13 41		14 11				14 41		15 12			15 41		16 11		
Hatfield	d	08 25	08 45		09 15			13 25	13 45		14 15			14 25	14 45		15 16		15 25	15 45		16 15		
Welwyn Garden City 4	d	08 31	08a50		09a20			13 31	13a50		14a20			14 31	14a50		15a21		15 31	15a50		16a20		
Welwyn North	d	08 35						13 35						14 35					15 35					
Knebworth	d	08 39						13 39						14 39					15 39					
Bowes Park	d			08 37		09 07				13 37		14 07				14 37		15 07			15 37			16 07
Palmers Green	d			08 40		09 10				13 40		14 10				14 40		15 10			15 40			16 10
Winchmore Hill	d			08 43		09 13				13 43		14 13				14 43		15 13			15 43			16 13
Grange Park	d			08 45		09 15				13 45		14 15				14 45		15 15			15 45			16 15
Enfield Chase	d			08 47		09 17				13 47		14 17				14 47		15 17			15 47			16 17
Gordon Hill	d			08 50		09 20				13 50		14 20				14 50		15 20			15 50			16 20
Crews Hill	d			08 53		09 23				13 53		14 23				14 53		15 23			15 53			16 23
Cuffley	d			08 56		09 26				13 56		14 26				14 56		15 26			15 56			16 26
Bayford	d			09 00		09 30				14 00		14 30				15 00		15 30			16 00			16 30
Hertford North	a			09 05		09 35				14 05		14 35				15 05		15 35			16 05			16 35
Watton-at-Stone	a			09 12		09 42				14 12		14 42				15 12		15 42			16 12			16 42
Stevenage 4	a	08 43		09 20		09 50		13 43		14 20		14 50		14 43		15 20		15 50	15 43		16 20			16 50

		TL 1	GN	GN	TL 1	GN	GN	TL 1	GN		GN	TL 1	GN	GN	TL 1	GN	GN	TL 1	GN		GN	TL 1	GN	GN	GN
London Bridge	d																								
London Blackfriars	d																								
City Thameslink	d																								
Farringdon	d																								
St Pancras International	d																								
London Kings Cross 15 ⊖	d	16 02	16 05	16 20	16 32	16 35	16 50	17 02	17 05		17 20	17 32	17 35	17 50	18 02	18 05	18 20	18 32	18 35		18 50	19 02	19 05	19 20	19 35
Finsbury Park	a	16 07	16 11	16 25	16 37	16 41	16 55	17 07	17 11		17 25	17 37	17 41	17 55	18 07	18 11	18 25	18 37	18 41		18 55	19 07	19 11	19 25	19 41
Moorgate ⊖	d																								
Old Street ⊖	d																								
Essex Road	d																								
Highbury & Islington ⊖	d																								
Drayton Park	d																								
Finsbury Park ⊖	a																								
Finsbury Park	d	16 08	16 12	16 27	16 38	16 42	16 57	17 08	17 12		17 27	17 38	17 42	17 57	18 08	18 12	18 27	18 38	18 42		18 57	19 08	19 12	19 27	19 42
Harringay	d		16 15	16 29		16 45	16 59		17 15		17 29		17 45	17 59		18 15	18 29		18 45		18 59		19 15	19 29	19 45
Hornsey	d		16 17	16 31		16 47	17 01		17 17		17 31		17 47	18 01		18 17	18 31		18 47		19 01		19 17	19 31	19 47
Alexandra Palace	d		16 20	16 35		16 50	17 05		17 20		17 35		17 50	18 05		18 20	18 35		18 50		19 05		19 20	19 35	19 50
New Southgate	d		16 23			16 53			17 23				17 53			18 23			18 53				19 23		19 53
Oakleigh Park	d		16 26			16 56			17 26				17 56			18 26			18 56				19 26		19 56
New Barnet	d		16 29			16 59			17 29				17 59			18 29			18 59				19 29		19 59
Hadley Wood	d		16 32			17 02			17 32				18 02			18 32			19 02				19 32		20 02
Potters Bar	d	16 19	16 36		16 49	17 06		17 19	17 36			17 49	18 06		18 19	18 36		18 49	19 06			19 19	19 36		20 06
Brookmans Park	d		16 39			17 09			17 39				18 09			18 39			19 09				19 39		20 09
Welham Green	d		16 41			17 11			17 41				18 11			18 41			19 11				19 41		20 11
Hatfield	d	16 25	16 45		16 55	17 15		17 25	17 45			17 55	18 15		18 25	18 45		18 55	19 15			19 26	19 45		20 15
Welwyn Garden City 4	d	16 31	16a50		17 01	17a20		17 31	17a50			18 01	18a20		18 31	18a50		19 01	19a20			19 31	19a50		20a20
Welwyn North	d	16 35			17 05			17 35				18 05			18 35			19 05				19 35			
Knebworth	d	16 39			17 09			17 39				18 09			18 39			19 09				19 39			
Bowes Park	d			16 37			17 07				17 37			18 07			18 37				19 07			19 37	
Palmers Green	d			16 40			17 10				17 40			18 10			18 40				19 10			19 40	
Winchmore Hill	d			16 43			17 13				17 43			18 13			18 43				19 13			19 43	
Grange Park	d			16 45			17 15				17 45			18 15			18 45				19 15			19 45	
Enfield Chase	d			16 47			17 17				17 47			18 17			18 47				19 17			19 47	
Gordon Hill	d			16 50			17 20				17 50			18 20			18 50				19 20			19 50	
Crews Hill	d			16 53			17 23				17 53			18 23			18 53				19 23			19 53	
Cuffley	d			16 56			17 26				17 56			18 26			18 56				19 26			19 56	
Bayford	d			17 00			17 30				18 00			18 30			19 00				19 30			20 00	
Hertford North	a			17 05			17 35				18 05			18 35			19 05				19 35			20 05	
Watton-at-Stone	a			17 12			17 42				18 12			18 42			19 12				19 42			20 12	
Stevenage 4	a	16 43		17 20	17 13		17 50	17 43			18 20	18 13		18 50	18 43		19 20	19 13			19 50	19 43		20 20	

See Table 025 for fast trains between London and Stevenage

Table T024-F

Sundays

23 February to 10 May

London - Welwyn Garden City and Hertford North

		GN	TL 1	GN	GN		GN	GN	TL 1	GN	GN	GN	GN	TL 1	GN		GN	GN	GN	TL 1	GN	GN	GN	GN
London Bridge	d																							
London Blackfriars	d																							
City Thameslink	d																							
Farringdon	d																							
St Pancras International	d																							
London Kings Cross 15 ⊖	d	19 50	20 02	20 05	20 20		20 35	20 50	21 02	21 05	21 20	21 35	21 50	22 02	22 05		22 20	22 35	22 50	23 02	23 05	23 20	23 35	23 50
Finsbury Park	a	19 55	20 07	20 11	20 25		20 40	20 55	21 07	21 11	21 25	21 40	21 55	22 07	22 11		22 25	22 40	22 55	23 07	23 12	23 25	23 40	23 55
Moorgate ⊖	d																							
Old Street ⊖	d																							
Essex Road	d																							
Highbury & Islington ⊖	d																							
Drayton Park	d																							
Finsbury Park ⊖	a																							
Finsbury Park	d	19 57	20 08	20 12	20 27		20 42	20 57	21 08	21 12	21 27	21 42	21 57	22 08	22 12		22 27	22 42	22 57	23 09	23 13	23 27	23 42	23 57
Harringay	d	19 59		20 15	20 29		20 45	20 59		21 15	21 29	21 45	21 59		22 15		22 29	22 45	22 59		23 15	23 29	23 45	23 59
Hornsey	d	20 01		20 17	20 31		20 47	21 01		21 17	21 31	21 47	22 01		22 17		22 31	22 47	23 01		23 17	23 31	23 47	00 01
Alexandra Palace	d	20 05		20 20	20 35		20 50	21 05		21 20	21 35	21 50	22 05		22 20		22 35	22 50	23 05		23 20	23 35	23 50	00 05
New Southgate	d			20 23			20 53			21 23		21 53			22 23			22 53			23 23		23 53	
Oakleigh Park	d			20 26			20 56			21 26		21 56			22 26			22 56			23 27		23 56	
New Barnet	d			20 29			20 59			21 29		21 59			22 29			22 59			23 29		23 59	
Hadley Wood	d			20 32			21 02			21 32		22 02			22 32			23 02			23 32		00 02	
Potters Bar	d		20 19	20 36			21 06		21 19	21 36		22 06		22 19	22 36			23 06		23 20	23 36		00 06	
Brookmans Park	d			20 39			21 09			21 39		22 09			22 39			23 09			23 39		00 09	
Welham Green	d			20 41			21 11			21 41		22 11			22 41			23 11			23 42		00 11	
Hatfield	d		20 26	20 45			21 15		21 25	21 45		22 15		22 25	22 45			23 15		23 26	23 45		00 15	
Welwyn Garden City 4	d		20 31	20a50			21a20		21 31	21a50		22a20		22 31	22a50			23a20		23 31	23a50		00a22	
Welwyn North	d		20 35						21 35					22 35						23 35				
Knebworth	d		20 39						21 39					22 39						23 39				
Bowes Park	d	20 07			20 37			21 07			21 37		22 07				22 37		23 07			23 37		00 07
Palmers Green	d	20 10			20 40			21 10			21 40		22 10				22 40		23 10			23 40		00 10
Winchmore Hill	d	20 13			20 43			21 13			21 43		22 13				22 43		23 13			23 43		00 13
Grange Park	d	20 15			20 45			21 15			21 45		22 15				22 45		23 15			23 45		00 15
Enfield Chase	d	20 17			20 47			21 17			21 47		22 17				22 47		23 17			23 47		00 17
Gordon Hill	d	20 20			20 50			21 20			21 50		22 20				22 50		23 20			23 50		00 20
Crews Hill	d	20 23			20 53			21 23			21 53		22 23				22 53		23 23			23 53		00 23
Cuffley	d	20 26			20 56			21 26			21 56		22 26				22 56		23 26			23 56		00 26
Bayford	d	20 30			21 00			21 30			22 00		22 30				23 00		23 30			00 01		00 30
Hertford North	a	20 35			21 05			21 35			22 05		22 35				23 05		23 35			00 06		00 35
Watton-at-Stone	a	20 42			21 12			21 42			22 12		22 42				23 12		23 42					00 42
Stevenage 4	a	20 50	20 43		21 20			21 50	21 43		22 20		22 50	22 43			23 20		23 54	23 43				00 50

See Table 025 for fast trains between London and Stevenage

Table T024-R

Mondays to Fridays

16 December to 15 May

Hertford North and Welwyn Garden City - London

Miles	Miles			GN MO A	GN MX	GN MO B	GN MO A	GN MO A	TL MX ■	GN MX	GN MO B	GN MO A	GN MO A	GN MO ■	GN MO A	TL MX ■	GN	GN	TL	GN	GN	GN	TL ■
—	—	Stevenage	d											00 07		00 16		04 22				05 02	05 06
—	12¼	Watton-at-Stone	d																			05 09	
16½	—	Hertford North	d															04 33				05 15	
—	19½	Bayford	d																			05 20	
—	23	Cuffley	d															04 40				05 24	
—	24¾	Crews Hill	d																			05 27	
—	26¼	Gordon Hill	d															04 45				05 31	
—	27	Enfield Chase	d							00 01	00 02		00 02					04 47				05 33	
—	27¾	Grange Park	d							00 03	00 04		00 04									05 35	
—	28½	Winchmore Hill	d							00 05	00 06		00 06					04 50				05 37	
—	29½	Palmers Green	d							00 08	00 09		00 09					04 53				05 40	
—	30½	Bowes Park	a							00 10	00 11		00 11									05 42	
9¾	—	Knebworth	d											00 11		00 19							05 09
12¾	—	Welwyn North	d											00 15		00 23							05 13
14½	—	Welwyn Garden City ■	d											00 19		00 28	04 00		05 00				05 18
17	—	Hatfield	d											00 23		00 31	04 04		05 05				05 21
19¼	—	Welham Green	d														04 08						
20¼	—	Brookmans Park	d														04 10						
22	—	Potters Bar	d						00 02					00 29		00 38	04 14		05 11				05 28
24¼	—	Hadley Wood	d														04 17						
25½	—	New Barnet	d														04 20		05 16				
26¼	—	Oakleigh Park	d														04 22		05 18				
28¼	—	New Southgate	a														04 25		05 21				
29¾	31¼	Alexandra Palace	d							00 13	00 14		00 14				04 30	04 57				05 45	
30¾	32¼	Hornsey	d			00 01	00 01			00 16	00 17		00 17				04 32	04 59				05 48	
31¼	32¾	Harringay	d			00 03	00 03			00 18	00 19		00 19				04 34	05 01				05 50	
32¼	33¾	Finsbury Park ⊖	a			00 06	00 06		00 15	00 20	00 24		00 24	00 39		00 51	04 39	05 04	05 29			05 52	05 41
—	—	Finsbury Park	d				00 06						00 25							05 41		05 55	
—	34½	Drayton Park	d				00 09	00 09				00 27	00 28		00 37					05 44	05 47	05 58	
—	35	Highbury & Islington ⊖	d				00 12						00 31							05 46		06 01	
—	35½	Essex Road	d				00 14						00 33							05 48		06 03	
—	36¾	Old Street ⊖	d	00 02			00 17						00 36							05 52		06 06	
—	37¼	Moorgate ⊖	a	00 06			00 21						00 40							05 56		06 10	
—	—	Finsbury Park	d		00 03	00 07		00a11	00 15	00 21	00 25	00a30		00 40	00a40	00 51	04 40	05 05	05 30		05a50		05 41
34¾	—	London Kings Cross ■ ⊖	a		00 11	00 13			00 21	00 27	00 31			00 49		00 57	04 46	05 13	05 36				05 47
—	—	St Pancras International	d																				
—	—	Farringdon	d																				
—	—	City Thameslink	d																				
—	—	London Blackfriars	a																				
—	—	London Bridge	a																				

		TL ■	GN	TL	GN	GN	GN	GN	GN	GN	TL ■	TL	GN	GN	GN	GN	GN	GN	GN	TL ■	GN	GN ■	TL
Stevenage	d	05 13								05 32	05 40								06 06	06 10			
Watton-at-Stone	d									05 39									06 13				
Hertford North	d					05 33				05 48				06 00			06 10		06 20				
Bayford	d					05 38				05 52							06 15						
Cuffley	d					05 42				05 57				06 07			06 19		06 27				
Crews Hill	d					05 45				06 00							06 22						
Gordon Hill	d					05 49				06 03				06 14			06 26		06 33				
Enfield Chase	d					05 51				06 05				06 16			06 28		06 35				
Grange Park	d					05 53				06 07				06 18			06 30						
Winchmore Hill	d					05 55				06 10				06 20			06 33		06 39				
Palmers Green	d					05 58				06 12				06 23			06 36		06 42				
Bowes Park	a					06 00				06 15				06 25			06 38						
Knebworth	d										05 43									06 13		06 28	
Welwyn North	d										05 47									06 17		06 32	
Welwyn Garden City ■	d	05 22	05 24	05 32				05 38			05 52	06 02			06 08					06 22	06 24		06 32
Hatfield	d		05 29	05 37				05 43			05 55	06 07			06 13					06 25	06 29		06 37
Welham Green	d		05 32					05 47							06 17						06 33		
Brookmans Park	d		05 35					05 49							06 19						06 35		
Potters Bar	d		05 38	05 43				05 53			06 02	06 13			06 23					06 32	06 39		06 43
Hadley Wood	d		05 42					05 56							06 26								06 46
New Barnet	d		05 45	05 48				05 59				06 18			06 29						06 44		06 49
Oakleigh Park	d		05 47	05 50				06 01				06 20			06 31								06 51
New Southgate	a		05 50	05 53				06 04				06 23			06 34								06 54
Alexandra Palace	d		05 53			06 03		06 10		06 18				06 28	06 38		06 41		06 46		06 50		
Hornsey	d		05 56			06 06				06 20				06 31			06 44		06 49		06 53		
Harringay	d		05 58			06 08				06 22				06 33			06 46		06 51		06 55		
Finsbury Park ⊖	a	05 35	06 00	05 59		06 10		06 14		06 25	06 13	06 28		06 35	06 42		06 48		06 53	06 43	06 57		07 00
Finsbury Park	d		06 01			06 11		06 16		06 26				06 36	06 43		06 49		06 54		06 59		
Drayton Park	d		06 04		06 07	06 14	06 17	06 19	06 27	06 29			06 37	06 39	06 46	06 47	06 52	06 55	06 57		07 02		
Highbury & Islington ⊖	d		06 07			06 17		06 22		06 31				06 42	06 49		06 54		06 59		07 04		
Essex Road	d		06 09			06 19		06 24		06 33				06 44	06 51		06 56		07 01		07 06		
Old Street ⊖	d		06 12			06 22		06 27		06 37				06 47	06 54		07 00		07 05		07 10		
Moorgate ⊖	a		06 16			06 26		06 31		06 41				06 51	06 58		07 04		07 09		07 14		
Finsbury Park	d	05 37		06 00	06a10		06a20		06a30		06 14	06 29	06a40			06a50		06a58		06 44			07 01
London Kings Cross ■ ⊖	a			06 06							06 20	06 35								06 50		06 52	07 07
St Pancras International	d	05 45																					
Farringdon	d	05 49																					
City Thameslink	d	05 51																					
London Blackfriars	a	05 53																					
London Bridge	a																						

A until 17 February

B from 24 February

See Table 025 for fast trains between London and Stevenage

NRT DECEMBER 19 EDITION

Table T024-R

Mondays to Fridays

16 December to 15 May

Hertford North and Welwyn Garden City - London

		GN	GN	GN	GN	GN	GN	TL ■	GN ■	GN	GN	GN	GN	GN	TL	GN	GN	GN	GN	GN	GN	TL ■
Stevenage	d							06 40														07 10
Watton-at-Stone	d										06 35											
Hertford North	d		06 28		06 32						06 42								07 02			
Bayford	d				06 37														07 07			
Cuffley	d		06 36		06 41						06 49								07 11			
Crews Hill	d				06 44														07 14			
Gordon Hill	d		06 41		06 48						06 55						07 11		07 18			
Enfield Chase	d		06 43		06 50						06 57						07 13		07 20			
Grange Park	d		06 45								06 59						07 15					
Winchmore Hill	d		06 48		06 54						07 02						07 18		07 24			
Palmers Green	d		06 51		06 57						07 05						07 21		07 27			
Bowes Park	a		06 53								07 07						07 23					
Knebworth	d							06 43	06 58													07 13
Welwyn North	d							06 47	07 02													07 17
Welwyn Garden City ■	d						06 38	06 52						06 54	07 02						07 08	07 22
Hatfield	d						06 43	06 55						06 59	07 07						07 13	07 25
Welham Green	d						06 47							07 02							07 17	
Brookmans Park	d						06 49							07 05							07 19	
Potters Bar	d						06 53	07 02						07 08	07 13						07 23	07 32
Hadley Wood	d						06 56								07 16						07 26	
New Barnet	d						06 59							07 13	07 19						07 29	
Oakleigh Park	d						07 01							07 15	07 21						07 31	
New Southgate	a						07 04							07 18	07 24						07 34	
Alexandra Palace	d		06 57		07 01		07 08				07 11			07 22			07 27		07 31		07 38	
Hornsey	d				07 04						07 14			07 24					07 34			
Harringay	d				07 06						07 16			07 26					07 36			
Finsbury Park ⊖	a		07 02		07 08		07 12	07 13			07 18			07 29	07 32		07 33		07 38		07 42	07 43
Finsbury Park	d		07 04		07 09		07 14				07 19			07 30			07 34		07 39		07 44	
Drayton Park	d	07 02	07 07	07 10	07 12	07 15	07 17			07 20	07 22	07 25	07 30	07 33		07 35	07 37	07 40	07 42	07 45	07 47	
Highbury & Islington ⊖	d		07 09		07 14		07 19				07 24			07 35			07 39		07 44		07 49	
Essex Road	d		07 11		07 16		07 21				07 26			07 37			07 41		07 46		07 51	
Old Street ⊖	d		07 15		07 20		07 25				07 30			07 40			07 45		07 50		07 55	
Moorgate ⊖	a		07 19		07 24		07 29				07 34			07 44			07 49		07 54		07 59	
Finsbury Park	d	07a05		07a12		07a18		07 14		07a22		07a28	07a33		07 32	07a38		07a42		07a48		07 44
London Kings Cross ■ ⊖	a							07 20	07 21						07 38							07 50
St Pancras International	d																					
Farringdon	d																					
City Thameslink	d																					
London Blackfriars	a																					
London Bridge	a																					

		GN ■	GN	GN	GN	GN	GN	TL	GN	GN	GN	GN	GN	GN	TL ■	GN ■	GN	GN	GN	GN	GN	GN	TL
Stevenage	d														07 40								
Watton-at-Stone	d			07 05																07 37			
Hertford North	d			07 11	07 15							07 32								07 44			
Bayford	d				07 20							07 37								07 48			
Cuffley	d			07 18	07 24							07 41								07 53			
Crews Hill	d				07 27							07 44								07 56			
Gordon Hill	d			07 24	07 31					07 41		07 48						07 55		08 00			
Enfield Chase	d			07 27	07 33					07 43		07 50						07 57		08 02			
Grange Park	d			07 29	07 35					07 45								07 59		08 04			
Winchmore Hill	d			07 32	07 38					07 48		07 54						08 02		08 07			
Palmers Green	d			07 35	07 41					07 51		07 57						08 05		08 10			
Bowes Park	a			07 37	07 43					07 53								08 07		08 12			
Knebworth	d	07 28													07 43	07 57							
Welwyn North	d	07 32													07 47	08 01							
Welwyn Garden City ■	d						07 24	07 32						07 38	07 52							07 54	08 02
Hatfield	d						07 29	07 37						07 43	07 55							07 59	08 07
Welham Green	d						07 32							07 47								08 02	
Brookmans Park	d						07 35							07 49								08 05	
Potters Bar	d						07 38	07 43						07 53	08 02							08 08	08 13
Hadley Wood	d							07 46						07 56									08 16
New Barnet	d						07 43	07 49						07 59								08 13	08 19
Oakleigh Park	d						07 45	07 51						08 01								08 15	08 21
New Southgate	a						07 48	07 54						08 04								08 18	08 24
Alexandra Palace	d			07 41	07 46		07 52			07 57		08 01		08 08				08 11		08 16		08 22	
Hornsey	d			07 44	07 49		07 54					08 04						08 14		08 19		08 24	
Harringay	d			07 46	07 51		07 56					08 06						08 16		08 21		08 26	
Finsbury Park ⊖	a			07 48	07 53		07 59	08 02		08 03		08 08		08 12	08 13			08 18		08 23		08 29	08 32
Finsbury Park	d			07 49	07 54		08 00			08 04		08 09		08 14				08 19		08 24		08 30	
Drayton Park	d		07 50	07 52	07 57	08 00	08 03		08 05	08 07	08 10	08 12	08 15	08 17			08 20	08 22	08 25	08 27	08 30	08 33	
Highbury & Islington ⊖	d			07 54	07 59		08 05			08 09		08 14		08 19				08 24		08 29		08 35	
Essex Road	d			07 56	08 01		08 07			08 11		08 16		08 21				08 26		08 31		08 37	
Old Street ⊖	d			08 00	08 05		08 10			08 15		08 20		08 25				08 30		08 35		08 40	
Moorgate ⊖	a			08 04	08 09		08 14			08 19		08 24		08 29				08 34		08 39		08 44	
Finsbury Park	d		07a53			08a03		08 02	08a08		08a13		08a18		08 14		08a23		08a28		08a33		08 32
London Kings Cross ■ ⊖	a	07 51						08 08							08 21	08 21							08 38
St Pancras International	d																						
Farringdon	d																						
City Thameslink	d																						
London Blackfriars	a																						
London Bridge	a																						

See Table 025 for fast trains between London and Stevenage

Table T024-R

Mondays to Fridays

16 December to 15 May

Hertford North and Welwyn Garden City - London

		GN	GN	GN		GN	GN	GN	TL 1	GN 1	GN	GN	GN	GN		TL	GN	GN	GN	GN	GN	TL 1	GN 1	GN
Stevenage	d								08 10													08 40		
Watton-at-Stone	d											08 05												
Hertford North	d					08 02						08 12								08 32				
Bayford	d					08 07														08 37				
Cuffley	d					08 11						08 19								08 41				
Crews Hill	d					08 14														08 44				
Gordon Hill	d		08 11			08 18						08 25						08 41		08 48				
Enfield Chase	d		08 13			08 20						08 27						08 43		08 50				
Grange Park	d		08 15									08 29						08 45						
Winchmore Hill	d		08 18			08 24						08 32						08 48		08 54				
Palmers Green	d		08 21			08 27						08 35						08 51		08 57				
Bowes Park	a		08 23									08 37						08 53						
Knebworth	d								08 13	08 28												08 43	08 58	
Welwyn North	d								08 17	08 33												08 47		
Welwyn Garden City 4	d							08 08	08 22					08 24		08 32					08 38	08 52		
Hatfield	d							08 13	08 25					08 29		08 37					08 43	08 55		
Welham Green	d							08 17						08 32							08 47			
Brookmans Park	d							08 19						08 35							08 49			
Potters Bar	d							08 23	08 32					08 38		08 43					08 53	09 02		
Hadley Wood	d							08 26								08 46					08 56			
New Barnet	d							08 29						08 43		08 49					08 59			
Oakleigh Park	d							08 31						08 45		08 51					09 01			
New Southgate	a							08 34						08 48		08 54					09 04			
Alexandra Palace	d		08 27			08 31		08 38				08 41		08 52				08 57		09 01	09 08			
Hornsey	d					08 34						08 44		08 54						09 04				
Harringay	d					08 36						08 46		08 56						09 06				
Finsbury Park ⊖	a		08 33			08 38		08 42	08 43			08 48		08 59		09 02		09 03		09 08	09 12	09 13		
Finsbury Park	d		08 34			08 39		08 44				08 49		09 00				09 04		09 09	09 14			
Drayton Park	d	08 35	08 37	08 40		08 42	08 45	08 47			08 50	08 52	08 55	09 03			09 05	09 07	09 10	09 12	09 17			09 20
Highbury & Islington ⊖	d		08 39			08 44		08 49				08 54		09 05				09 09		09 14	09 19			
Essex Road	d		08 41			08 46		08 51				08 56		09 07				09 11		09 16	09 21			
Old Street ⊖	d		08 45			08 50		08 55				09 00		09 10				09 15		09 20	09 25			
Moorgate ⊖	a		08 49			08 54		08 59				09 04		09 14				09 19		09 24	09 29			
Finsbury Park	d	08a38		08a42			08a48		08 44		08a53		08a58			09 02	09a08		09a12			09 18		09a23
London Kings Cross 15 ⊖	a								08 50	08 52						09 08						09 25	09 20	
St Pancras International	d																							
Farringdon	d																							
City Thameslink	d																							
London Blackfriars	a																							
London Bridge	a																							

		GN	GN	GN	GN	TL	GN	GN	GN	GN		GN	TL 1	GN	GN	GN	GN	GN	GN	GN		GN	TL 1	GN	GN
Stevenage	d												09 06										09 40		
Watton-at-Stone	d		08 37												09 10										09 40
Hertford North	d		08 44							09 02					09 17					09 30					09 47
Bayford	d		08 49							09 07										09 35					
Cuffley	d		08 53							09 11					09 25					09 39					09 55
Crews Hill	d		08 56							09 14										09 42					
Gordon Hill	d	08 55	09 00					09 11		09 18					09 31					09 46					10 01
Enfield Chase	d	08 57	09 02					09 13		09 20					09 33					09 48					10 03
Grange Park	d	08 59	09 04					09 15							09 35					09 50					10 05
Winchmore Hill	d	09 02	09 07					09 18		09 24					09 37					09 52					10 07
Palmers Green	d	09 05	09 10					09 21		09 27					09 40					09 55					10 10
Bowes Park	a	09 07	09 12					09 23							09 42					09 57					10 12
Knebworth	d												09 09										09 43		
Welwyn North	d												09 13										09 47		
Welwyn Garden City 4	d				08 54	09 02						09 08	09 22					09 24				09 38	09 52		
Hatfield	d				08 59	09 07						09 13	09 25					09 29				09 43	09 55		
Welham Green	d				09 02							09 17						09 33				09 47			
Brookmans Park	d				09 05							09 19						09 36				09 49			
Potters Bar	d				09 08	09 13						09 23	09 32					09 40				09 53	10 02		
Hadley Wood	d					09 16						09 26						09 44				09 56			
New Barnet	d				09 13	09 19						09 29						09 47				09 59			
Oakleigh Park	d				09 15	09 21						09 31						09 49				10 01			
New Southgate	a				09 18	09 24						09 34						09 52				10 04			
Alexandra Palace	d	09 11	09 16		09 22			09 27		09 31		09 38			09 45			09 55		10 00		10 08			10 15
Hornsey	d	09 14	09 19		09 24					09 34					09 48			09 58		10 03					10 18
Harringay	d	09 16	09 21		09 26					09 36					09 50			10 00		10 05					10 20
Finsbury Park ⊖	a	09 18	09 23		09 29	09 30		09 33		09 38		09 42	09 43		09 52			10 02		10 07		10 12	10 13		10 22
Finsbury Park	d	09 19	09 24		09 30			09 34		09 39		09 44			09 53			10 03		10 08		10 13			10 23
Drayton Park	d	09 22	09 27	09 30	09 33		09 35	09 37	09 40	09 42		09 47		09 50	09 56	10 00	10 05	10 06	10 10	10 11		10 16		10 20	10 26
Highbury & Islington ⊖	d	09 24	09 29		09 35			09 39		09 44		09 49			09 59			10 09		10 14		10 19			10 29
Essex Road	d	09 26	09 31		09 37			09 41		09 46		09 51			10 01			10 11		10 16		10 21			10 31
Old Street ⊖	d	09 30	09 35		09 40			09 45		09 50		09 55			10 04			10 14		10 19		10 24			10 34
Moorgate ⊖	a	09 34	09 39		09 44			09 49		09 54		09 59			10 08			10 18		10 23		10 28			10 38
Finsbury Park	d			09a33		09 30	09a38		09a43				09 44	09a53		10a03	10a08		10a13				10 17	10a23	
London Kings Cross 15 ⊖	a					09 38							09 50										10 25		
St Pancras International	d																								
Farringdon	d																								
City Thameslink	d																								
London Blackfriars	a																								
London Bridge	a																								

See Table 025 for fast trains between London and Stevenage

Table T024-R

Mondays to Fridays

16 December to 15 May

Hertford North and Welwyn Garden City - London

		GN	GN	GN	GN	GN		GN	TL 1	GN	GN	GN	GN	GN	GN	GN		GN	TL 1	GN	GN	GN	GN	GN	GN
Stevenage	d								10 10										10 40						
Watton-at-Stone	d										10 10										10 40				
Hertford North	d					10 00					10 17					10 30					10 47				
Bayford	d					10 05										10 35									
Cuffley	d					10 09					10 25					10 39					10 55				
Crews Hill	d					10 12										10 42									
Gordon Hill	d					10 16					10 31					10 46					11 01				
Enfield Chase	d					10 18					10 33					10 48					11 03				
Grange Park	d					10 20					10 35					10 50					11 05				
Winchmore Hill	d					10 22					10 37					10 52					11 07				
Palmers Green	d					10 25					10 40					10 55					11 10				
Bowes Park	a					10 27					10 42					10 57					11 12				
Knebworth	d								10 13										10 43						
Welwyn North	d								10 17										10 47						
Welwyn Garden City 4	d			09 58				10 09	10 22					10 28				10 39	10 52					10 58	
Hatfield	d			10 03				10 13	10 25					10 33				10 43	10 55					11 03	
Welham Green	d							10 17										10 47							
Brookmans Park	d							10 19										10 49							
Potters Bar	d			10 10				10 23	10 32					10 40				10 53	11 02					11 10	
Hadley Wood	d			10 14				10 26						10 44				10 56						11 14	
New Barnet	d			10 17				10 29						10 47				10 59						11 17	
Oakleigh Park	d			10 19				10 31						10 49				11 01						11 19	
New Southgate	a			10 22				10 34						10 52				11 04						11 22	
Alexandra Palace	d			10 25		10 30		10 38			10 45			10 55		11 00		11 08			11 15			11 25	
Hornsey	d			10 28		10 33					10 48			10 58		11 03					11 18			11 28	
Harringay	d			10 30		10 35					10 50			11 00		11 05					11 20			11 30	
Finsbury Park ⊖	a			10 32		10 37		10 42	10 43		10 52			11 02		11 07		11 12	11 13		11 22			11 32	
Finsbury Park	d			10 33		10 38		10 43			10 53			11 03		11 08		11 13			11 23			11 33	
Drayton Park	d	10 30	10 35	10 36	10 40	10 41		10 46		10 50	10 56	11 00	11 05	11 06	11 10	11 11		11 16		11 20	11 26	11 30	11 35	11 36	11 40
Highbury & Islington ⊖	d			10 39		10 44		10 49			10 59			11 09		11 14		11 19			11 29			11 39	
Essex Road	d			10 41		10 46		10 51			11 01			11 11		11 16		11 21			11 31			11 41	
Old Street ⊖	d			10 44		10 49		10 54			11 04			11 14		11 19		11 24			11 34			11 44	
Moorgate ⊖	a			10 48		10 53		10 58			11 08			11 18		11 23		11 28			11 38			11 48	
Finsbury Park	d	10a33	10a38		10a43				10 44	10a53		11a03	11a08		11a13				11 14	11a23		11a33	11a38		11a43
London Kings Cross 15 ⊖	a								10 50										11 20						
St Pancras International	d																								
Farringdon	d																								
City Thameslink	d																								
London Blackfriars	a																								
London Bridge	a																								

		GN		GN	TL 1	GN	GN	GN	GN	GN	GN	GN		GN	TL 1	GN	GN	GN	GN	GN	GN	GN		GN	TL 1
Stevenage	d				11 10										11 40										12 10
Watton-at-Stone	d						11 10										11 40								
Hertford North	d	11 00					11 17					11 30					11 47					12 00			
Bayford	d	11 05										11 35										12 05			
Cuffley	d	11 09					11 25					11 39					11 55					12 09			
Crews Hill	d	11 12										11 42										12 12			
Gordon Hill	d	11 16					11 31					11 46					12 01					12 16			
Enfield Chase	d	11 18					11 33					11 48					12 03					12 18			
Grange Park	d	11 20					11 35					11 50					12 05					12 20			
Winchmore Hill	d	11 22					11 37					11 52					12 07					12 22			
Palmers Green	d	11 25					11 40					11 55					12 10					12 25			
Bowes Park	a	11 27					11 42					11 57					12 12					12 27			
Knebworth	d				11 13										11 43										12 13
Welwyn North	d				11 17										11 47										12 17
Welwyn Garden City 4	d			11 09	11 22					11 28				11 39	11 52					11 58				12 09	12 22
Hatfield	d			11 13	11 25					11 33				11 43	11 55					12 03				12 13	12 25
Welham Green	d			11 17										11 47										12 17	
Brookmans Park	d			11 19										11 49										12 19	
Potters Bar	d			11 23	11 32					11 40				11 53	12 02					12 10				12 23	12 32
Hadley Wood	d			11 26						11 44				11 56						12 14				12 26	
New Barnet	d			11 29						11 47				11 59						12 17				12 29	
Oakleigh Park	d			11 31						11 49				12 01						12 19				12 31	
New Southgate	a			11 34						11 52				12 04						12 22				12 34	
Alexandra Palace	d	11 31		11 38			11 45			11 55		12 00		12 08			12 15			12 25		12 30		12 38	
Hornsey	d	11 34					11 48			11 58		12 03					12 18			12 28		12 33			
Harringay	d	11 36					11 50			12 00		12 05					12 20			12 30		12 35			
Finsbury Park ⊖	a	11 38		11 42	11 43		11 52			12 02		12 07		12 12	12 13		12 22			12 32		12 37		12 42	12 43
Finsbury Park	d	11 39		11 43			11 53			12 03		12 08		12 13			12 23			12 33		12 38		12 43	
Drayton Park	d	11 42		11 46		11 50	11 56	12 00	12 05	12 06	12 10	12 11		12 16		12 20	12 26	12 30	12 35	12 36	12 40	12 41		12 46	
Highbury & Islington ⊖	d	11 45		11 49			11 59			12 09		12 14		12 19			12 29			12 39		12 44		12 49	
Essex Road	d	11 47		11 51			12 01			12 11		12 16		12 21			12 31			12 41		12 46		12 51	
Old Street ⊖	d	11 50		11 54			12 04			12 14		12 19		12 24			12 34			12 44		12 49		12 54	
Moorgate ⊖	a	11 54		11 58			12 08			12 18		12 23		12 28			12 38			12 48		12 53		12 58	
Finsbury Park	d				11 44	11a53		12a03	12a08		12a13				12 14	12a23		12a33	12a38		12a43				12 44
London Kings Cross 15 ⊖	a				11 50										12 20										12 50
St Pancras International	d																								
Farringdon	d																								
City Thameslink	d																								
London Blackfriars	a																								
London Bridge	a																								

See Table 025 for fast trains between London and Stevenage

Table T024-R

Mondays to Fridays

16 December to 15 May

Hertford North and Welwyn Garden City - London

		GN	GN	GN	GN	GN	GN	GN	GN	TL 1	GN	GN	GN	GN	GN	GN	GN	GN	TL 1	GN	GN	GN	GN
Stevenage	d									12 40									13 08				
Watton-at-Stone	d		12 10									12 40									13 10		
Hertford North	d		12 17					12 30				12 47					13 00				13 17		
Bayford	d							12 35									13 05						
Cuffley	d		12 25					12 39				12 55					13 09				13 25		
Crews Hill	d							12 42									13 12						
Gordon Hill	d		12 31					12 46				13 01					13 16				13 31		
Enfield Chase	d		12 33					12 48				13 03					13 18				13 33		
Grange Park	d		12 35					12 50				13 05					13 20				13 35		
Winchmore Hill	d		12 37					12 52				13 07					13 22				13 37		
Palmers Green	d		12 40					12 55				13 10					13 25				13 40		
Bowes Park	a		12 42					12 57				13 12					13 27				13 42		
Knebworth	d									12 43									13 13				
Welwyn North	d									12 47									13 17				
Welwyn Garden City 4	d					12 28			12 39	12 52					12 58			13 09	13 22				
Hatfield	d					12 33			12 43	12 55					13 03			13 13	13 25				
Welham Green	d								12 47									13 17					
Brookmans Park	d								12 49									13 19					
Potters Bar	d					12 40			12 53	13 02					13 10			13 23	13 32				
Hadley Wood	d					12 44			12 56						13 14			13 26					
New Barnet	d					12 47			12 59						13 17			13 29					
Oakleigh Park	d					12 49			13 01						13 19			13 31					
New Southgate	a					12 52			13 04						13 22			13 34					
Alexandra Palace	d		12 45			12 55		13 00	13 08			13 15			13 25		13 30	13 38			13 45		
Hornsey	d		12 48			12 58		13 03				13 18			13 28		13 33				13 48		
Harringay	d		12 50			13 00		13 05				13 20			13 30		13 35				13 50		
Finsbury Park ⊖	a		12 52			13 02		13 07	13 12	13 13		13 22			13 32		13 37	13 42	13 43		13 52		
Finsbury Park	d		12 53			13 03		13 08	13 13			13 23			13 33		13 38	13 43			13 53		
Drayton Park	d	12 50	12 56	13 00	13 05	13 06	13 10	13 11	13 16		13 20	13 26	13 30	13 35	13 36	13 40	13 41	13 46		13 50	13 56	14 00	14 05
Highbury & Islington ⊖	d		12 59			13 09		13 14	13 19			13 29			13 39		13 44	13 49			13 59		
Essex Road	d		13 01			13 11		13 16	13 21			13 31			13 41		13 46	13 51			14 01		
Old Street ⊖	d		13 04			13 14		13 19	13 24			13 34			13 44		13 49	13 54			14 04		
Moorgate ⊖	a		13 08			13 18		13 23	13 28			13 38			13 48		13 53	13 58			14 08		
Finsbury Park	d	12a53		13a03	13a08		13a13			13 14	13a23		13a33	13a38		13a43			13 44	13a53		14a03	14a08
London Kings Cross 15 ⊖	a									13 20									13 50				
St Pancras International	d																						
Farringdon	d																						
City Thameslink	d																						
London Blackfriars	a																						
London Bridge	a																						

		GN	GN	GN	GN	TL 1	GN	GN	GN	GN	GN	GN	GN	GN	TL 1	GN	GN	GN	GN	GN	GN	GN
Stevenage	d					13 40									14 10							
Watton-at-Stone	d							13 40									14 10					
Hertford North	d			13 30				13 47					14 00				14 17					14 30
Bayford	d			13 35									14 05									14 35
Cuffley	d			13 39				13 55					14 09				14 25					14 39
Crews Hill	d			13 42									14 12									14 42
Gordon Hill	d			13 46				14 01					14 16				14 31					14 46
Enfield Chase	d			13 48				14 03					14 18				14 33					14 48
Grange Park	d			13 50				14 05					14 20				14 35					14 50
Winchmore Hill	d			13 52				14 07					14 22				14 37					14 52
Palmers Green	d			13 55				14 10					14 25				14 40					14 55
Bowes Park	a			13 57				14 12					14 27				14 42					14 57
Knebworth	d					13 43									14 13							
Welwyn North	d					13 47									14 17							
Welwyn Garden City 4	d	13 28			13 39	13 52					13 58			14 09	14 22					14 28		
Hatfield	d	13 33			13 43	13 55					14 03			14 13	14 25					14 33		
Welham Green	d				13 47									14 17								
Brookmans Park	d				13 49									14 19								
Potters Bar	d	13 40			13 53	14 02					14 10			14 23	14 32					14 40		
Hadley Wood	d	13 44			13 56						14 14			14 26						14 44		
New Barnet	d	13 47			13 59						14 17			14 29						14 47		
Oakleigh Park	d	13 49			14 01						14 19			14 31						14 49		
New Southgate	a	13 52			14 04						14 22			14 34						14 52		
Alexandra Palace	d	13 55		14 00	14 08			14 15			14 25		14 30	14 38			14 45			14 55		15 00
Hornsey	d	13 58		14 03				14 18			14 28		14 33				14 48			14 58		15 03
Harringay	d	14 00		14 05				14 20			14 30		14 35				14 50			15 00		15 05
Finsbury Park ⊖	a	14 02		14 07	14 13	14 13		14 22			14 32		14 37	14 42	14 43		14 52			15 02		15 07
Finsbury Park	d	14 03		14 08	14 13			14 23			14 33		14 38	14 43			14 53			15 03		15 08
Drayton Park	d	14 06	14 10	14 11	14 16		14 20	14 26	14 30	14 35	14 36	14 40	14 41	14 46		14 50	14 56	15 00	15 05	15 06	15 10	15 11
Highbury & Islington ⊖	d	14 09		14 14	14 19			14 29			14 39		14 44	14 49			14 59			15 09		15 14
Essex Road	d	14 11		14 16	14 21			14 31			14 41		14 46	14 51			15 01			15 11		15 16
Old Street ⊖	d	14 14		14 19	14 24			14 34			14 44		14 49	14 54			15 04			15 14		15 19
Moorgate ⊖	a	14 18		14 23	14 28			14 38			14 48		14 53	14 58			15 08			15 18		15 23
Finsbury Park	d		14a13			14 14	14a23		14a33	14a38		14a43			14 44	14a53		15a03	15a08		15a13	
London Kings Cross 15 ⊖	a					14 20									14 50							
St Pancras International	d																					
Farringdon	d																					
City Thameslink	d																					
London Blackfriars	a																					
London Bridge	a																					

See Table 025 for fast trains between London and Stevenage

Table T024-R

Mondays to Fridays

16 December to 15 May

Hertford North and Welwyn Garden City - London

		GN	TL 1	GN	GN	GN	GN	GN	GN	GN	GN	TL 1	GN	GN	GN	GN	GN	GN	GN	GN	GN	TL 1	GN
Stevenage	d		14 40									15 10										15 40	
Watton-at-Stone	d				14 40									15 10									
Hertford North	d				14 47					15 00				15 17					15 30				
Bayford	d									15 05									15 35				
Cuffley	d				14 55					15 09				15 25					15 39				
Crews Hill	d									15 12									15 42				
Gordon Hill	d				15 01					15 16				15 31					15 46				
Enfield Chase	d				15 03					15 18				15 33					15 48				
Grange Park	d				15 05					15 20				15 35					15 50				
Winchmore Hill	d				15 07					15 22				15 37					15 52				
Palmers Green	d				15 10					15 25				15 40					15 55				
Bowes Park	a				15 12					15 27				15 42					15 57				
Knebworth	d		14 43									15 13										15 43	
Welwyn North	d		14 47									15 17										15 47	
Welwyn Garden City 4	d	14 39	14 52					14 58			15 09	15 22						15 28			15 39	15 52	
Hatfield	d	14 43	14 55					15 03			15 13	15 25						15 33			15 43	15 55	
Welham Green	d	14 47									15 17										15 47		
Brookmans Park	d	14 49									15 19										15 49		
Potters Bar	d	14 53	15 02					15 10			15 23	15 32						15 40			15 53	16 02	
Hadley Wood	d	14 56						15 14			15 26							15 44			15 56		
New Barnet	d	14 59						15 17			15 29							15 47			15 59		
Oakleigh Park	d	15 01						15 19			15 31							15 49			16 01		
New Southgate	a	15 04						15 22			15 34							15 52			16 04		
Alexandra Palace	d	15 08			15 15			15 25		15 30	15 38			15 45				15 55	16 00		16 08		
Hornsey	d				15 18			15 28		15 33				15 48				15 58	16 03				
Harringay	d				15 20			15 30		15 35				15 50				16 00	16 05				
Finsbury Park ⊖	a	15 12	15 13		15 22			15 32		15 37	15 42	15 43		15 52				16 02	16 07		16 12	16 13	
Finsbury Park	d	15 13			15 23			15 33		15 38	15 43			15 53		15 58		16 03	16 08		16 13		
Drayton Park	d	15 16		15 20	15 26	15 30	15 35	15 36	15 40	15 41	15 46		15 50	15 56	16 00	16 01	16 05	16 06	16 11	16 11	16 16		16 21
Highbury & Islington ⊖	d	15 19			15 29			15 39		15 44	15 49			15 59		16 03		16 09	16 14		16 19		
Essex Road	d	15 21			15 31			15 41		15 46	15 51			16 01		16 05		16 11	16 16		16 21		
Old Street ⊖	d	15 24			15 34			15 44		15 49	15 54			16 04		16 09		16 14	16 19		16 24		
Moorgate ⊖	a	15 28			15 38			15 48		15 53	15 58			16 08		16 13		16 18	16 23		16 28		
Finsbury Park	d		15 14	15a23		15a33	15a38		15a43			15 44	15a53		16a03		16a08			16a13		16 14	16a23
London Kings Cross 15 ⊖	a		15 20									15 50										16 20	
St Pancras International	d																						
Farringdon	d																						
City Thameslink	d																						
London Blackfriars	a																						
London Bridge	a																						

		GN	GN	GN	GN	GN	GN	GN	GN	GN	TL 1	GN	GN	GN	GN	GN	GN	GN	GN	GN	GN	GN	TL 1
Stevenage	d										16 10												16 40
Watton-at-Stone	d	15 40												16 07									
Hertford North	d	15 47						16 00						16 14		16 26							
Bayford	d							16 05						16 19									
Cuffley	d	15 55						16 09						16 23		16 33							
Crews Hill	d							16 12						16 26									
Gordon Hill	d	16 01						16 16						16 30		16 38							
Enfield Chase	d	16 03						16 18						16 32		16 40							
Grange Park	d	16 05						16 20						16 34		16 42							
Winchmore Hill	d	16 07						16 22						16 37		16 45							
Palmers Green	d	16 10						16 25						16 39		16 47							
Bowes Park	a	16 12						16 27						16 42		16 50							
Knebworth	d										16 13												16 43
Welwyn North	d										16 17												16 47
Welwyn Garden City 4	d					15 58				16 09	16 22							16 28		16 32		16 43	16 52
Hatfield	d					16 03				16 13	16 25							16 33		16 36		16 48	16 55
Welham Green	d									16 17										16 40		16 51	
Brookmans Park	d									16 19										16 42		16 54	
Potters Bar	d					16 10				16 23	16 32							16 40		16 46		16 57	17 02
Hadley Wood	d					16 14				16 26								16 44		16 49			
New Barnet	d					16 17				16 29								16 47		16 52		17 02	
Oakleigh Park	d					16 19				16 31								16 49		16 54			
New Southgate	a					16 22				16 34								16 52		16 57			
Alexandra Palace	d	16 15				16 25		16 30		16 38				16 45		16 53		16 55		17 01		17 08	
Hornsey	d	16 18				16 28		16 33						16 48				16 58		17 03			
Harringay	d	16 20				16 30		16 35						16 50				17 00		17 05			
Finsbury Park ⊖	a	16 22				16 32		16 37		16 42	16 43			16 52		16 57		17 02		17 08		17 12	17 14
Finsbury Park	d	16 23		16 28		16 33		16 38		16 43		16 48		16 53		16 58		17 03		17 08		17 13	
Drayton Park	d	16 26	16 26	16 31	16 31	16 36	16 36	16 41	16 41	16 46		16 51	16 51	16 56	16 56	17 01	17 01	17 06	17 06	17 11	17 11	17 16	
Highbury & Islington ⊖	d	16 29		16 33		16 39		16 44		16 49		16 53		16 59		17 04		17 09		17 14		17 19	
Essex Road	d	16 31		16 35		16 41		16 46		16 51		16 55		17 01		17 06		17 11		17 16		17 21	
Old Street ⊖	d	16 34		16 39		16 44		16 49		16 54		16 59		17 04		17 09		17 14		17 19		17 24	
Moorgate ⊖	a	16 38		16 43		16 48		16 53		16 58		17 03		17 08		17 13		17 18		17 23		17 28	
Finsbury Park	d		16a28		16a33		16a38		16a43		16 44		16a53		16a58		17a03		17a08		17a13		17 14
London Kings Cross 15 ⊖	a										16 50												17 20
St Pancras International	d																						
Farringdon	d																						
City Thameslink	d																						
London Blackfriars	a																						
London Bridge	a																						

See Table 025 for fast trains between London and Stevenage

Table T024-R

Mondays to Fridays
16 December to 15 May

Hertford North and Welwyn Garden City - London

		GN		GN	GN	GN	GN	GN	TL	GN	GN	GN		GN	GN	GN	TL [1]	GN	GN	GN	GN	GN		GN	TL
Stevenage	d																17 10								
Watton-at-Stone	d				16 33										16 59										
Hertford North	d				16 40		16 56								17 06					17 11					
Bayford	d				16 44															17 15					
Cuffley	d				16 49		17 03								17 13					17 20					
Crews Hill	d				16 52															17 23					
Gordon Hill	d				16 56		17 08					17 12			17 20					17 26		17 39			
Enfield Chase	d				16 58		17 10					17 14			17 22					17 28		17 41			
Grange Park	d				17 00							17 16								17 30					
Winchmore Hill	d				17 02		17 13					17 19			17 25					17 33		17 44			
Palmers Green	d				17 05		17 16					17 21			17 28					17 35		17 46			
Bowes Park	a				17 07							17 24								17 38					
Knebworth	d																17 13								
Welwyn North	d																17 17								
Welwyn Garden City [4]	d							16 58	17 02							17 13	17 22							17 28	17 32
Hatfield	d								17 07							17 18	17 25								17 37
Welham Green	d															17 21									
Brookmans Park	d															17 24									
Potters Bar	d							17 08	17 13							17 27	17 32							17 38	17 43
Hadley Wood	d							17 11																17 41	
New Barnet	d							17 14	17 18							17 32								17 44	17 48
Oakleigh Park	d							17 16	17 20															17 46	17 50
New Southgate	a							17 19	17 23															17 49	17 53
Alexandra Palace	d				17 12		17 20	17 23				17 27			17 32	17 38				17 42		17 50		17 53	
Hornsey	d				17 14							17 29			17 34					17 44					
Harringay	d				17 16							17 31			17 36					17 46					
Finsbury Park ⊖	a				17 19		17 24	17 27	17 29			17 34			17 39	17 42	17 44			17 49		17 54		17 57	17 59
Finsbury Park	d				17 19		17 24	17 28				17 34			17 39	17 43				17 49		17 54		17 58	
Drayton Park	d	17 16		17 20	17 22	17 26	17 27	17 31		17 31	17 36	17 37		17 41	17 42	17 46		17 46	17 51	17 52	17 56	17 57		18 01	
Highbury & Islington ⊖	d				17 25		17 30	17 34				17 40			17 45	17 49				17 55		18 00		18 04	
Essex Road	d				17 27		17 32	17 36				17 42			17 47	17 51				17 57		18 02		18 06	
Old Street ⊖	d				17 30		17 35	17 39				17 45			17 50	17 54				18 00		18 05		18 09	
Moorgate ⊖	a				17 34		17 39	17 43				17 49			17 54	17 58				18 04		18 09		18 13	
Finsbury Park	d	17a18		17a22		17a28			17 29	17a33	17a38			17a43			17 44	17a48	17a53		17a58				17 59
London Kings Cross [15] ⊖	a								17 35								17 50								18 06
St Pancras International	d																								
Farringdon	d																								
City Thameslink	d																								
London Blackfriars	a																								
London Bridge	a																								

		GN	GN	GN	GN	GN	GN	TL [1]		GN	GN	GN	GN	GN	TL	GN	GN	GN		GN	GN	GN	TL [1]	GN	GN
Stevenage	d							17 40															18 10		
Watton-at-Stone	d											17 38													18 10
Hertford North	d			17 37								17 44								18 03					18 17
Bayford	d			17 41																18 07					
Cuffley	d			17 46								17 52								18 12					18 25
Crews Hill	d											17 55								18 15					
Gordon Hill	d			17 50		17 54						17 58						18 12		18 20					18 30
Enfield Chase	d					17 56						18 00						18 14		18 22					18 32
Grange Park	d											18 02						18 16							18 34
Winchmore Hill	d					17 59						18 04						18 18		18 25					18 36
Palmers Green	d					18 01						18 07						18 21		18 28					18 39
Bowes Park	a											18 09						18 23							18 41
Knebworth	d							17 43															18 13		
Welwyn North	d							17 47															18 17		
Welwyn Garden City [4]	d						17 43	17 52						17 58	18 02							18 13	18 22		
Hatfield	d						17 48	17 55							18 07							18 18	18 25		
Welham Green	d						17 51															18 21			
Brookmans Park	d						17 54															18 24			
Potters Bar	d						17 57	18 02						18 08	18 13							18 27	18 32		
Hadley Wood	d													18 11											
New Barnet	d						18 02							18 14	18 18							18 32			
Oakleigh Park	d													18 16	18 20										
New Southgate	a													18 19	18 23										
Alexandra Palace	d			17 57		18 05	18 09					18 12		18 23				18 27		18 32		18 38			18 46
Hornsey	d			17 59								18 15						18 29		18 34					18 48
Harringay	d			18 01								18 17						18 31		18 36					18 50
Finsbury Park ⊖	a			18 04		18 09	18 13	18 14				18 19		18 27	18 29			18 34		18 39		18 42	18 44		18 53
Finsbury Park	d			18 04		18 09	18 13					18 20		18 28				18 34		18 39		18 43			18 53
Drayton Park	d	18 01	18 06	18 07	18 11	18 12	18 16			18 16	18 21	18 23	18 26	18 31		18 31	18 36	18 37		18 42	18 43	18 46		18 51	18 56
Highbury & Islington ⊖	d			18 10		18 15	18 19					18 26		18 34				18 40		18 45		18 49			18 59
Essex Road	d			18 12		18 17	18 21					18 28		18 36				18 42		18 47		18 51			19 01
Old Street ⊖	d			18 15		18 20	18 24					18 31		18 39				18 45		18 50		18 54			19 04
Moorgate ⊖	a			18 19		18 24	18 28					18 35		18 43				18 49		18 54		18 58			19 08
Finsbury Park	d	18a03	18a08		18a13			18 14		18a18	18a23		18a28		18 33	18a33	18a38				18a45		18 44	18a53	
London Kings Cross [15] ⊖	a							18 20							18 41								18 50		
St Pancras International	d																								
Farringdon	d																								
City Thameslink	d																								
London Blackfriars	a																								
London Bridge	a																								

See Table 025 for fast trains between London and Stevenage

Table T024-R

Mondays to Fridays
16 December to 15 May

Hertford North and Welwyn Garden City - London

		GN	GN	TL		GN	GN	GN	GN	GN	TL [1]	GN	GN	GN		GN	GN	GN	GN	GN	TL [1]	GN	GN	GN	
Stevenage	d										18 40										19 10				
Watton-at-Stone	d													18 40									19 10		
Hertford North	d							18 30						18 47				19 00					19 16		
Bayford	d							18 35										19 05							
Cuffley	d							18 39						18 55				19 09					19 24		
Crews Hill	d							18 42										19 12							
Gordon Hill	d							18 46						19 00				19 16					19 30		
Enfield Chase	d							18 48						19 02				19 18					19 32		
Grange Park	d							18 50						19 04				19 20					19 34		
Winchmore Hill	d							18 52						19 06				19 22					19 36		
Palmers Green	d							18 55						19 09				19 25					19 39		
Bowes Park	a							18 57						19 11				19 27					19 41		
Knebworth	d										18 43										19 13				
Welwyn North	d										18 47										19 17				
Welwyn Garden City [4]	d		18 28	18 32						18 43	18 52					18 58				19 13	19 22				
Hatfield	d			18 37						18 48	18 55									19 18	19 25				
Welham Green	d									18 51										19 21					
Brookmans Park	d									18 54										19 24					
Potters Bar	d		18 38	18 43						18 57	19 02					19 08				19 27	19 32				
Hadley Wood	d		18 41													19 11									
New Barnet	d		18 44	18 48						19 02						19 14				19 32					
Oakleigh Park	d		18 46	18 50												19 16									
New Southgate	a		18 49	18 53												19 19									
Alexandra Palace	d		18 53					19 00		19 08				19 15		19 23		19 30		19 38			19 45		
Hornsey	d							19 03						19 18				19 33					19 48		
Harringay	d							19 05						19 20				19 35					19 50		
Finsbury Park ⊖	a		18 57	19 01				19 07		19 12	19 14			19 22		19 27		19 37		19 42	19 44		19 52		
Finsbury Park	d		18 58					19 08		19 13				19 23		19 28		19 38		19 43			19 53		
Drayton Park	d	18 56	19 01			19 01	19 05	19 11	19 11	19 16		19 20	19 25	19 26		19 31	19 35	19 41	19 41	19 46		19 50	19 56	20 00	
Highbury & Islington ⊖	d		19 03					19 14		19 19				19 29		19 34		19 44		19 49			19 59		
Essex Road	d		19 06					19 16		19 21				19 31		19 36		19 46		19 51			20 01		
Old Street ⊖	d		19 09					19 19		19 24				19 34		19 39		19 49		19 54			20 04		
Moorgate ⊖	a		19 13					19 23		19 28				19 38		19 43		19 53		19 58			20 08		
Finsbury Park	d	18a58		19 03		19a03	19a08		19a13		19 14	19a23	19a28				19a38		19a43		19 44	19a53		20a03	
London Kings Cross [15] ⊖	a			19 10							19 20										19 50				
St Pancras International	d																								
Farringdon	d																								
City Thameslink	d																								
London Blackfriars	a																								
London Bridge	a																								

		GN	GN	GN	GN	GN	TL [1]	GN	GN	GN		GN	GN	GN	GN	GN	TL [1]	GN	GN	GN		GN	GN	GN	GN
Stevenage	d						19 40										20 10								
Watton-at-Stone	d								19 40										20 10						
Hertford North	d				19 30				19 47						20 00				20 17						20 30
Bayford	d				19 35										20 05										20 35
Cuffley	d				19 39				19 55						20 09				20 25						20 39
Crews Hill	d				19 42										20 12										20 42
Gordon Hill	d				19 46				20 01						20 16				20 31						20 46
Enfield Chase	d				19 48				20 03						20 18				20 33						20 48
Grange Park	d				19 50				20 05						20 20				20 35						20 50
Winchmore Hill	d				19 52				20 07						20 22				20 37						20 52
Palmers Green	d				19 55				20 10						20 25				20 40						20 55
Bowes Park	a				19 57				20 12						20 27				20 42						20 57
Knebworth	d						19 43										20 13								
Welwyn North	d						19 47										20 17								
Welwyn Garden City [4]	d	19 28				19 43	19 52						19 58			20 08	20 22						20 28		
Hatfield	d					19 48	19 55						20 03			20 13	20 25						20 33		
Welham Green	d					19 51										20 17									
Brookmans Park	d					19 54										20 19									
Potters Bar	d	19 38				19 57	20 02						20 10			20 23	20 32						20 40		
Hadley Wood	d	19 41											20 14			20 26							20 44		
New Barnet	d	19 44				20 02							20 17			20 29							20 47		
Oakleigh Park	d	19 46											20 19			20 31							20 49		
New Southgate	a	19 49											20 22			20 34							20 52		
Alexandra Palace	d	19 53			20 00	20 08			20 15				20 25		20 30	20 38			20 45				20 55		21 00
Hornsey	d				20 03				20 18				20 28		20 33				20 48				20 58		21 03
Harringay	d				20 05				20 20				20 30		20 35				20 50				21 00		21 05
Finsbury Park ⊖	a	19 57			20 07	20 12	20 14		20 22				20 32		20 37	20 42	20 43		20 52				21 02		21 07
Finsbury Park	d	19 58			20 08	20 13			20 23				20 33		20 38	20 43			20 53				21 03		21 08
Drayton Park	d	20 01	20 05	20 10	20 11	20 16		20 20	20 26	20 30		20 35	20 36	20 40	20 41	20 46		20 50	20 56	21 00		21 05	21 06	21 10	21 11
Highbury & Islington ⊖	d	20 04			20 14	20 19			20 29				20 39		20 44	20 49			20 59				21 09		21 14
Essex Road	d	20 06			20 16	20 21			20 31				20 41		20 46	20 51			21 01				21 11		21 16
Old Street ⊖	d	20 09			20 19	20 24			20 34				20 44		20 49	20 54			21 04				21 14		21 19
Moorgate ⊖	a	20 13			20 23	20 28			20 38				20 48		20 53	20 58			21 08				21 18		21 23
Finsbury Park	d		20a08	20a13			20 14	20a23		20a33		20a38		20a43			20 44	20a53		21a03		21a08		21a13	
London Kings Cross [15] ⊖	a						20 20										20 50								
St Pancras International	d																								
Farringdon	d																								
City Thameslink	d																								
London Blackfriars	a																								
London Bridge	a																								

See Table 025 for fast trains between London and Stevenage

Table T024-R

Mondays to Fridays

16 December to 15 May

Hertford North and Welwyn Garden City - London

		GN	TL 1	GN	GN	GN		GN	GN	GN	GN	TL 1	GN	GN	GN	GN		TL 1	GN	GN	GN	TL 1	GN	GN	GN
Stevenage	d		20 40									21 10						21 40				22 10			
Watton-at-Stone	d				20 40									21 10					21 40						
Hertford North	d				20 47				21 00					21 21	21 30				21 51	22 00			22 21	22 30	
Bayford	d								21 05						21 35					22 05				22 35	
Cuffley	d				20 55				21 09					21 28	21 39				21 58	22 09			22 28	22 39	
Crews Hill	d								21 12						21 42					22 12				22 42	
Gordon Hill	d				21 01				21 16					21 34	21 46				22 04	22 16			22 34	22 46	
Enfield Chase	d				21 03				21 18					21 36	21 48				22 06	22 18			22 36	22 48	
Grange Park	d				21 05				21 20					21 38	21 50				22 08	22 20			22 38	22 50	
Winchmore Hill	d				21 07				21 22					21 41	21 52				22 11	22 22			22 41	22 52	
Palmers Green	d				21 10				21 25					21 43	21 55				22 13	22 25			22 43	22 55	
Bowes Park	a				21 12				21 27					21 46	21 57				22 16	22 27			22 46	22 57	
Knebworth	d		20 43									21 13						21 43				22 13			
Welwyn North	d		20 47									21 17						21 47				22 17			
Welwyn Garden City 4	d	20 39	20 52								21 09	21 22				21 39		21 52			22 09	22 22			22 38
Hatfield	d	20 43	20 55								21 13	21 25				21 43		21 55			22 13	22 25			22 43
Welham Green	d	20 47									21 17					21 47					22 17				22 47
Brookmans Park	d	20 49									21 19					21 49					22 19				22 49
Potters Bar	d	20 53	21 02								21 23	21 32				21 53		22 02			22 23	22 32			22 53
Hadley Wood	d	20 56									21 26					21 56					22 26				22 56
New Barnet	d	20 59									21 29					21 59					22 29				22 59
Oakleigh Park	d	21 01									21 31					22 01					22 31				23 01
New Southgate	a	21 04									21 34					22 04					22 34				23 04
Alexandra Palace	d	21 08			21 15				21 30		21 39			21 49	22 00	22 09			22 19	22 30	22 39		22 49	23 00	23 09
Hornsey	d				21 18				21 33		21 42			21 51	22 03	22 12			22 21	22 33	22 42		22 51	23 03	23 12
Harringay	d				21 20				21 35		21 45			21 53	22 05	22 15			22 23	22 35	22 45		22 53	23 05	23 15
Finsbury Park ⊖	a	21 12	21 13		21 22				21 37		21 47	21 43		21 56	22 07	22 17		22 13	22 26	22 37	22 47	22 43	22 56	23 07	23 17
Finsbury Park	d	21 13			21 23																				
Drayton Park	d	21 16		21 20	21 26	21 30		21 35		21 40			21 50												
Highbury & Islington ⊖	d	21 19			21 29																				
Essex Road	d	21 21			21 31																				
Old Street ⊖	d	21 24			21 34																				
Moorgate ⊖	a	21 28			21 38																				
Finsbury Park	d		21 14	21a23		21a33		21a38	21 40	21a43	21 48	21 44	21a53	21 58	22 10	22 18		22 14	22 28	22 40	22 48	22 44	22 58	23 10	23 18
London Kings Cross 15 ⊖	a		21 20						21 47		21 55	21 53		22 06	22 17	22 25		22 20	22 35	22 47	22 55	22 51	23 06	23 17	23 25
St Pancras International	d																								
Farringdon	d																								
City Thameslink	d																								
London Blackfriars	a																								
London Bridge	a																								

		TL 1		GN	GN	TL 1	GN	GN	GN	GN (bus)	TL 1
Stevenage	d	22 40				23 10				23 28	23 40
Watton-at-Stone	d			22 40			23 10		23 35		
Hertford North	d			22 48			23 18		23 43	23s50	
Bayford	d			22 52			23 22		23 47	00s01	
Cuffley	d			22 57			23 27		23 52	00s11	
Crews Hill	d			23 00			23 30		23 55	00s17	
Gordon Hill	d			23 04			23 34		23 59	00s25	
Enfield Chase	d			23 06			23 36		00 01	00s31	
Grange Park	d			23 08			23 38		00 03	00s36	
Winchmore Hill	d			23 11			23 41		00 05	00s42	
Palmers Green	d			23 13			23 43		00 08	00s50	
Bowes Park	a			23 16			23 46		00 10	01 00	
Knebworth	d	22 43				23 14					23 43
Welwyn North	d	22 47				23 18					23 47
Welwyn Garden City 4	d	22 52			23 08	23 22		23 24			23 52
Hatfield	d	22 55			23 13	23 26		23 29			23 55
Welham Green	d				23 17			23 33			
Brookmans Park	d				23 19			23 35			
Potters Bar	d	23 02			23 23	23 32		23 39			00 02
Hadley Wood	d				23 26			23 42			
New Barnet	d				23 29			23 45			
Oakleigh Park	d				23 31			23 47			
New Southgate	a				23 34			23 50			
Alexandra Palace	d			23 19	23 39		23 49	23 53	00 13		
Hornsey	d			23 21	23 42		23 51	23 56	00 16		
Harringay	d			23 23	23 45		23 53	23 58	00 18		
Finsbury Park ⊖	a	23 13		23 26	23 47	23 43	23 56	00 01	00 20		00 15
Finsbury Park	d										
Drayton Park	d										
Highbury & Islington ⊖	d										
Essex Road	d										
Old Street ⊖	d										
Moorgate ⊖	a										
Finsbury Park	d	23 14		23 28	23 48	23 44	23 57	00 03	00 21		00 15
London Kings Cross 15 ⊖	a	23 20		23 37	23 55	23 50	00 05	00 11	00 27		00 21
St Pancras International	d										
Farringdon	d										
City Thameslink	d										
London Blackfriars	a										
London Bridge	a										

See Table 025 for fast trains between London and Stevenage

NRT DECEMBER 19 EDITION

Table T024-R

Saturdays

21 December to 15 February

Hertford North and Welwyn Garden City - London

		GN	TL 1	GN	TL 1	GN	GN	GN	GN	GN		TL 1	TL 1	GN	GN	GN	TL 1	GN	GN	TL 1		GN	GN	GN	GN
Stevenage	d				00 16		04 22			04 58		05 04	05 11			05 28	05 40			06 10					
Watton-at-Stone	d									05 05						05 35									
Hertford North	d						04 33			05 13						05 43							06 13		
Bayford	d									05 17						05 47							06 17		
Cuffley	d						04 40			05 22						05 52							06 22		
Crews Hill	d									05 25						05 55							06 25		
Gordon Hill	d						04 45			05 28						05 58							06 28		
Enfield Chase	d			00 01			04 47			05 31						06 01							06 31		
Grange Park	d			00 03						05 33						06 03							06 33		
Winchmore Hill	d			00 05			04 50			05 35						06 05							06 35		
Palmers Green	d			00 08			04 53			05 38						06 08							06 38		
Bowes Park	a			00 10						05 40						06 10							06 40		
Knebworth	d				00 19							05 07					05 43			06 13					
Welwyn North	d				00 23							05 11					05 47			06 17					
Welwyn Garden City 4	d				00 28	04 00		05 00				05 16	05 20	05 28			05 52		05 58	06 22					06 28
Hatfield	d				00 31	04 04		05 05				05 19		05 33			05 55		06 03	06 25					06 33
Welham Green	d					04 08								05 37					06 07						06 37
Brookmans Park	d					04 10								05 39					06 09						06 39
Potters Bar	d		00 02		00 38	04 14		05 12				05 26		05 43			06 02		06 13	06 32					06 43
Hadley Wood	d					04 17								05 46					06 16						06 46
New Barnet	d					04 20		05 17						05 49					06 19						06 49
Oakleigh Park	d					04 22		05 19						05 51					06 21						06 51
New Southgate	a					04 25		05 22						05 54					06 24						06 54
Alexandra Palace	d			00 13		04 30	04 57			05 43				05 58		06 13			06 28				06 43		06 58
Hornsey	d			00 16		04 32	04 59			05 46				06 01		06 16			06 31				06 46		07 01
Harringay	d			00 18		04 34	05 01			05 48				06 03		06 18			06 33				06 48		07 03
Finsbury Park ⊖	a		00 15	00 20	00 51	04 39	05 04	05 30		05 50		05 39	05 34	06 05		06 20	06 13		06 35	06 44			06 50		07 05
Finsbury Park	d									05 52				06 07		06 22			06 37				06 52		07 07
Drayton Park	d								05 53	05 55				06 10	06 23	06 25		06 38	06 40			06 53	06 55	07 08	07 10
Highbury & Islington ⊖	d									05 58				06 13		06 28			06 43				06 58		07 13
Essex Road	d									06 00				06 15		06 30			06 45				07 00		07 15
Old Street ⊖	d									06 03				06 18		06 33			06 48				07 03		07 18
Moorgate ⊖	a									06 07				06 22		06 37			06 52				07 07		07 22
Finsbury Park	d	00 03	00 15	00 21	00 51	04 40	05 05	05 31	05a56			05 39	05 35		06a26		06 14	06a41		06 45		06a56		07a11	
London Kings Cross 15 ⊖	a	00 11	00 21	00 27	00 57	04 46	05 13	05 37				05 46					06 20			06 50					
St Pancras International	d												05 45												
Farringdon	d												05 49												
City Thameslink	d																								
London Blackfriars	a												05 53												
London Bridge	a																								

		GN	GN	TL 1	GN	GN	TL 1	GN	GN	GN	GN	GN	GN	TL 1		GN	GN	TL 1	GN	GN	GN	GN	GN	GN
Stevenage	d		06 28	06 40			07 10						07 28	07 40				10 10						10 28
Watton-at-Stone	d		06 35						07 05				07 35							10 05				10 35
Hertford North	d		06 43						07 13				07 43							10 13				10 43
Bayford	d		06 47						07 17				07 47							10 17				10 47
Cuffley	d		06 52						07 22				07 52							10 22				10 52
Crews Hill	d		06 55						07 25				07 55							10 25				10 55
Gordon Hill	d		06 58						07 28				07 58							10 28				10 58
Enfield Chase	d		07 01						07 31				08 01							10 31				11 01
Grange Park	d		07 03						07 33				08 03							10 33				11 03
Winchmore Hill	d		07 05						07 35				08 05							10 35				11 05
Palmers Green	d		07 08						07 38				08 08							10 38				11 08
Bowes Park	a		07 10						07 40				08 10							10 40				11 10
Knebworth	d			06 43			07 13							07 43				10 13						
Welwyn North	d			06 47			07 17							07 47				10 17						
Welwyn Garden City 4	d			06 52		06 58	07 22				07 28			07 52			09 58	10 22				10 28		
Hatfield	d			06 55		07 03	07 25				07 33			07 55	and at the same minutes past each hour until		10 03	10 25				10 33		
Welham Green	d					07 07					07 37						10 07					10 37		
Brookmans Park	d					07 09					07 39						10 09					10 39		
Potters Bar	d			07 02		07 13	07 32				07 43			08 02			10 13	10 32				10 43		
Hadley Wood	d					07 16					07 46						10 16					10 46		
New Barnet	d					07 19					07 49						10 19					10 49		
Oakleigh Park	d					07 21					07 51						10 21					10 51		
New Southgate	a					07 24					07 54						10 24					10 54		
Alexandra Palace	d		07 13			07 28			07 43		07 58		08 13				10 28			10 43		10 58		11 13
Hornsey	d		07 16			07 31			07 46		08 01		08 16				10 31			10 46		11 01		11 16
Harringay	d		07 18			07 33			07 48		08 03		08 18				10 33			10 48		11 03		11 18
Finsbury Park ⊖	a		07 20	07 14		07 35	07 44		07 50		08 05		08 20	08 13			10 35	10 44		10 50		11 05		11 20
Finsbury Park	d		07 22			07 37			07 52		08 07		08 22				10 37			10 52		11 07		11 22
Drayton Park	d	07 23	07 25		07 38	07 40		07 53	07 55	08 08	08 10	08 23	08 25			10 38	10 40		10 53	10 55	11 08	11 10	11 23	11 25
Highbury & Islington ⊖	d		07 28			07 43			07 58		08 13		08 28				10 43			10 58		11 13		11 28
Essex Road	d		07 30			07 45			08 00		08 15		08 30				10 45			11 00		11 15		11 30
Old Street ⊖	d		07 33			07 48			08 03		08 18		08 33				10 48			11 03		11 18		11 33
Moorgate ⊖	a		07 37			07 52			08 07		08 22		08 37				10 52			11 07		11 22		11 37
Finsbury Park	d	07a26		07 15	07a41		07 45	07a56		08a11		08a26		08 14		10a41		10 45	10a56		11a11		11a26	
London Kings Cross 15 ⊖	a			07 20			07 50							08 20				10 50						
St Pancras International	d																							
Farringdon	d																							
City Thameslink	d																							
London Blackfriars	a																							
London Bridge	a																							

See Table 025 for fast trains between London and Stevenage

Table T024-R

Saturdays

21 December to 15 February

Hertford North and Welwyn Garden City - London

		TL 1		GN	GN	TL 1	GN	GN	GN	GN	GN	GN		TL 1	GN	GN	TL 1	GN	GN	GN	GN	GN		GN	TL 1
Stevenage	d	10 40				11 10						11 28		11 40			12 10							12 28	12 40
Watton-at-Stone	d							11 05				11 35							12 05					12 35	
Hertford North	d							11 13				11 43							12 13					12 43	
Bayford	d							11 17				11 47							12 17					12 47	
Cuffley	d							11 22				11 52							12 22					12 52	
Crews Hill	d							11 25				11 55							12 25					12 55	
Gordon Hill	d							11 28				11 58							12 28					12 58	
Enfield Chase	d							11 31				12 01							12 31					13 01	
Grange Park	d							11 33				12 03							12 33					13 03	
Winchmore Hill	d							11 35				12 05							12 35					13 05	
Palmers Green	d							11 38				12 08							12 38					13 08	
Bowes Park	a							11 40				12 10							12 40					13 10	
Knebworth	d	10 43				11 13								11 43			12 13								12 43
Welwyn North	d	10 47				11 17								11 47			12 19								12 47
Welwyn Garden City 4	d	10 52			10 58	11 22				11 28				11 53		11 58	12 23				12 28				12 52
Hatfield	d	10 55			11 03	11 25				11 33				11 55		12 03	12 26				12 33				12 55
Welham Green	d				11 07					11 37						12 07					12 37				
Brookmans Park	d				11 09					11 39						12 09					12 39				
Potters Bar	d	11 02			11 13	11 32				11 43				12 02		12 13	12 33				12 43				13 02
Hadley Wood	d				11 16					11 46						12 16					12 46				
New Barnet	d				11 19					11 49						12 19					12 49				
Oakleigh Park	d				11 21					11 51						12 21					12 51				
New Southgate	a				11 24					11 54						12 24					12 54				
Alexandra Palace	d				11 28			11 43		11 58		12 13				12 28			12 43		12 58			13 13	
Hornsey	d				11 31			11 46		12 01		12 16				12 31			12 46		13 01			13 16	
Harringay	d				11 33			11 48		12 03		12 18				12 33			12 48		13 03			13 18	
Finsbury Park ⊖	a	11 13			11 35	11 44		11 50		12 05		12 20		12 13		12 35	12 44		12 50		13 05			13 20	13 13
Finsbury Park	d				11 37			11 52		12 07		12 22				12 37			12 52		13 07			13 22	
Drayton Park	d			11 38	11 40		11 53	11 55	12 08	12 10	12 23	12 25			12 38	12 40		12 53	12 55	13 08	13 10	13 23		13 25	
Highbury & Islington ⊖	d				11 43			11 58		12 13		12 28				12 43			12 58		13 13			13 28	
Essex Road	d				11 45			12 00		12 15		12 30				12 45			13 00		13 15			13 30	
Old Street ⊖	d				11 48			12 03		12 18		12 33				12 48			13 03		13 18			13 33	
Moorgate ⊖	a				11 52			12 07		12 22		12 37				12 52			13 07		13 22			13 37	
Finsbury Park	d	11 14		11a41		11 45	11a56		12a11		12a26			12 14	12a41		12 45	12a56		13a11		13a26			13 14
London Kings Cross 15 ⊖	a	11 20				11 50								12 20			12 50								13 20
St Pancras International	d																								
Farringdon	d																								
City Thameslink	d																								
London Blackfriars	a																								
London Bridge	a																								

		GN	GN	TL 1	GN	GN	GN	GN		GN	GN	TL 1	GN	GN	TL 1	GN	GN	GN		GN	GN	GN	TL 1	GN	GN
Stevenage	d			13 10							13 28	13 40			14 10							14 28	14 40		
Watton-at-Stone	d					13 05					13 35						14 05					14 35			
Hertford North	d					13 13					13 43						14 13					14 43			
Bayford	d					13 17					13 47						14 17					14 47			
Cuffley	d					13 22					13 52						14 22					14 52			
Crews Hill	d					13 25					13 55						14 25					14 55			
Gordon Hill	d					13 28					13 58						14 28					14 58			
Enfield Chase	d					13 31					14 01						14 31					15 01			
Grange Park	d					13 33					14 03						14 33					15 03			
Winchmore Hill	d					13 35					14 05						14 35					15 05			
Palmers Green	d					13 38					14 08						14 38					15 08			
Bowes Park	a					13 40					14 10						14 40					15 10			
Knebworth	d			13 13								13 43			14 13								14 43		
Welwyn North	d			13 17								13 47			14 17								14 47		
Welwyn Garden City 4	d		12 58	13 22				13 28				13 52		13 58	14 22					14 28			14 52		14 58
Hatfield	d		13 03	13 25				13 33				13 55		14 03	14 25					14 33			14 55		15 03
Welham Green	d		13 07					13 37						14 07						14 37					15 07
Brookmans Park	d		13 09					13 39						14 09						14 39					15 09
Potters Bar	d		13 13	13 32				13 43				14 02		14 13	14 32					14 43			15 02		15 13
Hadley Wood	d		13 16					13 46						14 16						14 46					15 16
New Barnet	d		13 19					13 49						14 19						14 49					15 19
Oakleigh Park	d		13 21					13 51						14 21						14 51					15 21
New Southgate	a		13 24					13 54						14 24						14 54					15 24
Alexandra Palace	d		13 28			13 43		13 58			14 13			14 28			14 43			14 58		15 13			15 28
Hornsey	d		13 31			13 46		14 01			14 16			14 31			14 46			15 01		15 16			15 31
Harringay	d		13 33			13 48		14 03			14 18			14 33			14 48			15 03		15 18			15 33
Finsbury Park ⊖	a		13 35	13 44		13 50		14 05			14 20	14 13		14 35	14 44		14 50			15 05		15 20	15 13		15 35
Finsbury Park	d		13 37			13 52		14 07			14 22			14 37			14 52			15 07		15 22			15 37
Drayton Park	d	13 38	13 40		13 53	13 55	14 08	14 10		14 23	14 25		14 38	14 40		14 53	14 55	15 08		15 10	15 23	15 25		15 38	15 40
Highbury & Islington ⊖	d		13 43			13 58		14 13			14 28			14 43			14 58			15 13		15 28			15 43
Essex Road	d		13 45			14 00		14 15			14 30			14 45			15 00			15 15		15 30			15 45
Old Street ⊖	d		13 48			14 03		14 18			14 33			14 48			15 03			15 18		15 33			15 48
Moorgate ⊖	a		13 52			14 07		14 22			14 37			14 52			15 07			15 22		15 37			15 52
Finsbury Park	d	13a41		13 45	13a56		14a11			14a26		14 14	14a41		14 45	14a56		15a11			15a26		15 14	15a41	
London Kings Cross 15 ⊖	a			13 50								14 20			14 50								15 20		
St Pancras International	d																								
Farringdon	d																								
City Thameslink	d																								
London Blackfriars	a																								
London Bridge	a																								

See Table 025 for fast trains between London and Stevenage

Table T024-R

Saturdays

21 December to 15 February

Hertford North and Welwyn Garden City - London

		TL 1	GN	GN		GN	GN	GN	GN	TL 1	GN	GN	TL 1	GN		GN	GN	GN	GN	GN	TL 1	GN	GN	TL 1	
Stevenage	d	15 10							15 28	15 40			16 10							16 28	16 40			17 10	
Watton-at-Stone	d			15 05					15 35							16 05				16 35					
Hertford North	d			15 13					15 43							16 13				16 43					
Bayford	d			15 17					15 47							16 17				16 47					
Cuffley	d			15 22					15 52							16 22				16 52					
Crews Hill	d			15 25					15 55							16 25				16 55					
Gordon Hill	d			15 28					15 58							16 28				16 58					
Enfield Chase	d			15 31					16 01							16 31				17 01					
Grange Park	d			15 33					16 03							16 33				17 03					
Winchmore Hill	d			15 35					16 05							16 35				17 05					
Palmers Green	d			15 38					16 08							16 38				17 08					
Bowes Park	a			15 40					16 10							16 40				17 10					
Knebworth	d	15 13								15 43			16 13								16 43			17 13	
Welwyn North	d	15 17								15 47			16 19								16 48			17 17	
Welwyn Garden City 4	d	15 22					15 28			15 52		15 58	16 22					16 28			16 53		16 58	17 22	
Hatfield	d	15 25					15 33			15 55		16 03	16 26					16 33			16 56		17 03	17 25	
Welham Green	d						15 37					16 07						16 37					17 07		
Brookmans Park	d						15 39					16 09						16 39					17 09		
Potters Bar	d	15 32					15 43			16 02		16 13	16 32					16 43			17 02		17 13	17 32	
Hadley Wood	d						15 46					16 16						16 46					17 16		
New Barnet	d						15 49					16 19						16 49					17 19		
Oakleigh Park	d						15 51					16 21						16 51					17 21		
New Southgate	a						15 54					16 24						16 54					17 24		
Alexandra Palace	d			15 43			15 58		16 13			16 28				16 43		16 58		17 13			17 28		
Hornsey	d			15 46			16 01		16 16			16 31				16 46		17 01		17 16			17 31		
Harringay	d			15 48			16 03		16 18			16 33				16 48		17 03		17 18			17 33		
Finsbury Park ⊖	a	15 43		15 50			16 05		16 20	16 13		16 35	16 44			16 50		17 05		17 20	17 13		17 35	17 44	
Finsbury Park	d			15 52			16 07		16 22			16 37				16 52		17 07		17 22			17 37		
Drayton Park	d		15 53	15 55		16 08	16 10	16 23	16 25		16 38	16 40		16 53		16 55	17 08	17 10	17 23	17 25		17 38	17 40		
Highbury & Islington ⊖	d			15 58			16 13		16 28			16 43				16 58		17 13		17 28			17 43		
Essex Road	d			16 00			16 15		16 30			16 45				17 00		17 15		17 30			17 45		
Old Street ⊖	d			16 03			16 18		16 33			16 48				17 03		17 18		17 33			17 48		
Moorgate ⊖	a			16 07			16 22		16 37			16 52				17 07		17 22		17 37			17 52		
Finsbury Park	d	15 44	15a56			16a11		16a26		16 14	16a41		16 45	16a56			17a11		17a26		17 14	17a41		17 45	
London Kings Cross 15 ⊖	a	15 50								16 20			16 50								17 20			17 50	
St Pancras International	d																								
Farringdon	d																								
City Thameslink	d																								
London Blackfriars	a																								
London Bridge	a																								

		GN	GN	GN	GN	GN	GN	TL 1	GN	GN		TL 1	GN	GN	GN	GN	GN	GN	TL 1	GN		GN	TL 1	GN	GN
Stevenage	d						17 28	17 40				18 10						18 28	18 40				19 10		
Watton-at-Stone	d		17 05				17 35							18 05				18 35							19 05
Hertford North	d		17 13				17 43							18 13				18 43							19 13
Bayford	d		17 17				17 47							18 17				18 47							19 17
Cuffley	d		17 22				17 52							18 22				18 52							19 22
Crews Hill	d		17 25				17 55							18 25				18 55							19 25
Gordon Hill	d		17 28				17 58							18 28				18 58							19 28
Enfield Chase	d		17 31				18 01							18 31				19 01							19 31
Grange Park	d		17 33				18 03							18 33				19 03							19 33
Winchmore Hill	d		17 35				18 05							18 35				19 05							19 35
Palmers Green	d		17 38				18 08							18 38				19 08							19 38
Bowes Park	a		17 40				18 10							18 40				19 10							19 40
Knebworth	d							17 43				18 13							18 43				19 13		
Welwyn North	d							17 47				18 18							18 47				19 18		
Welwyn Garden City 4	d				17 28			17 52		17 58		18 23				18 28			18 52			18 58	19 23		
Hatfield	d				17 33			17 55		18 03		18 26				18 33			18 55			19 03	19 27		
Welham Green	d				17 37					18 07						18 37						19 07			
Brookmans Park	d				17 39					18 09						18 39						19 09			
Potters Bar	d				17 43			18 02		18 13		18 32				18 43			19 02			19 13	19 33		
Hadley Wood	d				17 46					18 16						18 46						19 16			
New Barnet	d				17 49					18 19						18 49						19 19			
Oakleigh Park	d				17 51					18 21						18 51						19 21			
New Southgate	a				17 54					18 24						18 54						19 24			
Alexandra Palace	d		17 43		17 58		18 13			18 28				18 43		18 58		19 13				19 28			19 43
Hornsey	d		17 46		18 01		18 16			18 31				18 46		19 01		19 16				19 31			19 46
Harringay	d		17 48		18 03		18 18			18 33				18 48		19 03		19 18				19 33			19 48
Finsbury Park ⊖	a		17 50		18 05		18 20	18 13		18 35		18 44		18 50		19 05		19 20	19 13			19 35	19 44		19 50
Finsbury Park	d		17 52		18 07		18 22			18 37				18 52		19 07		19 22				19 37			19 52
Drayton Park	d	17 53	17 55	18 08	18 10	18 23	18 25		18 38	18 40			18 53	18 55	19 08	19 10	19 23	19 25		19 38		19 40		19 53	19 55
Highbury & Islington ⊖	d		17 58		18 13		18 28			18 43				18 58		19 13		19 28				19 43			19 58
Essex Road	d		18 00		18 15		18 30			18 45				19 00		19 15		19 30				19 45			20 00
Old Street ⊖	d		18 03		18 18		18 33			18 48				19 03		19 18		19 33				19 48			20 03
Moorgate ⊖	a		18 07		18 22		18 37			18 52				19 07		19 22		19 37				19 52			20 07
Finsbury Park	d	17a56		18a11		18a26		18 14	18a41			18 45	18a56		19a11		19a26		19 14	19a41			19 45	19a56	
London Kings Cross 15 ⊖	a							18 20				18 50							19 20				19 50		
St Pancras International	d																								
Farringdon	d																								
City Thameslink	d																								
London Blackfriars	a																								
London Bridge	a																								

See Table 025 for fast trains between London and Stevenage

Table T024-R

Saturdays

21 December to 15 February

Hertford North and Welwyn Garden City - London

Station		GN	GN	GN	GN	TL 1		GN	GN	TL 1	GN	GN	GN	GN	GN	GN		TL 1	GN	GN	TL 1	GN	GN	GN	GN
Stevenage	d				19 28	19 40				20 10						20 28		20 40			21 10				
Watton-at-Stone	d				19 35							20 05				20 35							21 05		
Hertford North	d				19 43							20 13				20 43							21 13		
Bayford	d				19 47							20 17				20 47							21 17		
Cuffley	d				19 52							20 22				20 52							21 22		
Crews Hill	d				19 55							20 25				20 55							21 25		
Gordon Hill	d				19 58							20 28				20 58							21 28		
Enfield Chase	d				20 01							20 31				21 01							21 31		
Grange Park	d				20 03							20 33				21 03							21 33		
Winchmore Hill	d				20 05							20 35				21 05							21 35		
Palmers Green	d				20 08							20 38				21 08							21 38		
Bowes Park	a				20 10							20 40				21 10							21 40		
Knebworth	d					19 43				20 13								20 43			21 13				
Welwyn North	d					19 47				20 17								20 47			21 17				
Welwyn Garden City 4	d		19 28			19 52			19 58	20 22				20 28				20 52		20 58	21 22				21 28
Hatfield	d		19 33			19 55			20 03	20 25				20 33				20 55		21 03	21 25				21 33
Welham Green	d		19 37						20 07					20 37						21 07					21 37
Brookmans Park	d		19 39						20 09					20 39						21 09					21 39
Potters Bar	d		19 43			20 02			20 13	20 32				20 43				21 02		21 13	21 32				21 43
Hadley Wood	d		19 46						20 16					20 46						21 16					21 46
New Barnet	d		19 49						20 19					20 49						21 19					21 49
Oakleigh Park	d		19 51						20 21					20 51						21 21					21 51
New Southgate	a		19 54						20 24					20 54						21 24					21 54
Alexandra Palace	d		19 58		20 13				20 28			20 43		20 58		21 13				21 28			21 43		21 58
Hornsey	d		20 01		20 16				20 31			20 46		21 01		21 16				21 31			21 46		22 01
Harringay	d		20 03		20 18				20 33			20 48		21 03		21 18				21 33			21 48		22 03
Finsbury Park ⊖	a		20 05		20 20	20 13			20 35	20 44		20 50		21 05		21 20		21 13		21 35	21 44		21 50		22 05
Finsbury Park	d		20 07		20 22				20 37			20 52		21 07		21 22				21 37			21 52		22 07
Drayton Park	d	20 08	20 10	20 23	20 25			20 38	20 40		20 53	20 55	21 08	21 10	21 23	21 25			21 38	21 40		21 53	21 55	22 08	22 10
Highbury & Islington ⊖	d		20 13		20 28				20 43			20 58		21 13		21 28				21 43			21 58		22 13
Essex Road	d		20 15		20 30				20 45			21 00		21 15		21 30				21 45			22 00		22 15
Old Street ⊖	d		20 18		20 33				20 48			21 03		21 18		21 33				21 48			22 03		22 18
Moorgate ⊖	a		20 22		20 37				20 52			21 07		21 22		21 37				21 52			22 07		22 22
Finsbury Park	d	20a11		20a26		20 14		20a41		20 45	20a56		21a11		21a26			21 14	21a41		21 45	21a56		22a11	
London Kings Cross 15 ⊖	a					20 20				20 50								21 20			21 50				
St Pancras International	d																								
Farringdon	d																								
City Thameslink	d																								
London Blackfriars	a																								
London Bridge	a																								

Station		GN		GN	TL 1	GN	GN	TL 1	GN	GN	GN	GN		GN	GN	TL 1	GN	GN	TL 1	GN	GN	GN		GN	TL 1
Stevenage	d			21 28	21 40			22 10							22 28	22 40			23 10					23 28	23 40
Watton-at-Stone	d			21 35						22 05					22 35						23 05			23 35	
Hertford North	d			21 43						22 13					22 43						23 13			23 43	
Bayford	d			21 47						22 17					22 47						23 17			23 47	
Cuffley	d			21 52						22 22					22 52						23 22			23 52	
Crews Hill	d			21 55						22 25					22 55						23 25			23 55	
Gordon Hill	d			21 58						22 28					22 58						23 28			23 58	
Enfield Chase	d			22 01						22 31					23 01						23 31			00 01	
Grange Park	d			22 03						22 33					23 03						23 33			00 03	
Winchmore Hill	d			22 05						22 35					23 05						23 35			00 05	
Palmers Green	d			22 08						22 38					23 08						23 38			00 08	
Bowes Park	a			22 10						22 40					23 10						23 40			00 10	
Knebworth	d				21 43			22 13								22 43			23 13						23 43
Welwyn North	d				21 47			22 17								22 47			23 17						23 47
Welwyn Garden City 4	d				21 52		21 58	22 22				22 28				22 52		22 58	23 22			23 28			23 52
Hatfield	d				21 55		22 03	22 25				22 33				22 55		23 03	23 25			23 33			23 55
Welham Green	d						22 07					22 37						23 07				23 37			
Brookmans Park	d						22 09					22 39						23 09				23 39			
Potters Bar	d				22 02		22 13	22 32				22 43				23 02		23 13	23 32			23 43			00 02
Hadley Wood	d						22 16					22 46						23 16				23 46			
New Barnet	d						22 19					22 49						23 19				23 49			
Oakleigh Park	d						22 21					22 51						23 21				23 51			
New Southgate	a						22 24					22 54						23 24				23 54			
Alexandra Palace	d			22 13			22 28			22 43		22 58			23 13			23 28			23 43	23 58		00 13	
Hornsey	d			22 16			22 31			22 46		23 01			23 16			23 31			23 46	00 01		00 16	
Harringay	d			22 18			22 33			22 48		23 03			23 18			23 33			23 48	00 03		00 18	
Finsbury Park ⊖	a			22 20	22 13		22 35	22 44		22 50		23 05			23 20	23 13		23 35	23 43		23 50	00 06		00 20	00 17
Finsbury Park	d			22 22			22 37			22 52		23 07			23 22			23 37			23 51	00 06		00 22	
Drayton Park	d	22 23		22 25		22 38	22 40		22 53	22 55	23 08	23 10		23 23	23 25		23 38	23 40		23 53	23 54	00 09		00 25	
Highbury & Islington ⊖	d			22 28			22 43			22 58		23 13			23 28			23 43			23 57	00 12		00 28	
Essex Road	d			22 30			22 45			23 00		23 15			23 30			23 45			23 59	00 14		00 30	
Old Street ⊖	d			22 33			22 48			23 03		23 18			23 33			23 48			00 02	00 17		00 33	
Moorgate ⊖	a			22 37			22 52			23 07		23 22			23 37			23 52			00 06	00 21		00 37	
Finsbury Park	d	22a26			22 14	22a41		22 45	22a56		23a11			23a26		23 14	23a41		23 44	23a56					00 18
London Kings Cross 15 ⊖	a				22 20			22 50								23 20			23 50						00 27
St Pancras International	d																								
Farringdon	d																								
City Thameslink	d																								
London Blackfriars	a																								
London Bridge	a																								

See Table 025 for fast trains between London and Stevenage

Table T024-R

Saturdays

22 February to 16 May

Hertford North and Welwyn Garden City - London

Station		GN	TL 1	GN	TL 1	GN	GN	GN	GN	TL 1		TL 1	GN	GN	TL 1	GN	TL 1	GN	GN	GN		TL 1	GN	TL 1	GN
Stevenage	d				00 16		04 22		04 58	05 04		05 11		05 30	05 40		06 10			06 30		06 40		07 10	
Watton-at-Stone	d								05 05					05 39						06 39					07 09
Hertford North	d						04 33		05 13					05 48				06 18		06 48					07 18
Bayford	d								05 17					05 52				06 22		06 52					07 22
Cuffley	d						04 40		05 22					05 57				06 27		06 57					07 27
Crews Hill	d								05 25					06 00				06 30		07 00					07 30
Gordon Hill	d						04 45		05 28					06 03				06 33		07 03					07 33
Enfield Chase	d			00 01			04 47		05 31					06 06				06 36		07 06					07 36
Grange Park	d			00 03					05 33					06 08				06 38		07 08					07 38
Winchmore Hill	d			00 05			04 50		05 35					06 10				06 40		07 10					07 40
Palmers Green	d			00 08			04 53		05 38					06 13				06 43		07 13					07 43
Bowes Park	a			00 10					05 40					06 15				06 45		07 15					07 45
Knebworth	d				00 19					05 07					05 43		06 13					06 43		07 13	
Welwyn North	d				00 23					05 11					05 47		06 17					06 47		07 17	
Welwyn Garden City 4	d				00 28	04 00		05 00		05 16		05 20	05 38		05 52	06 08	06 22		06 38			06 52	07 08	07 22	
Hatfield	d				00 31	04 04		05 05		05 19			05 43		05 55	06 13	06 25		06 43			06 55	07 13	07 25	
Welham Green	d					04 08							05 47			06 17			06 47				07 17		
Brookmans Park	d					04 10							05 49			06 19			06 49				07 19		
Potters Bar	d		00 02		00 38	04 14		05 12		05 26			05 53		06 02	06 23	06 32		06 53			07 02	07 23	07 32	
Hadley Wood	d					04 17							05 56			06 26			06 56				07 26		
New Barnet	d					04 20		05 17					05 59			06 29			06 59				07 29		
Oakleigh Park	d					04 22		05 19					06 01			06 31			07 01				07 31		
New Southgate	a					04 25		05 22					06 04			06 34			07 04				07 34		
Alexandra Palace	d			00 13		04 30	04 57		05 43				06 09	06 18		06 39		06 48	07 09	07 18			07 39		07 48
Hornsey	d			00 16		04 32	04 59		05 46				06 12	06 21		06 42		06 51	07 12	07 21			07 42		07 51
Harringay	d			00 18		04 34	05 01		05 48				06 15	06 23		06 45		06 53	07 15	07 23			07 45		07 53
Finsbury Park ⊖	a		00 15	00 20	00 51	04 39	05 04	05 30	05 50	05 39		05 34	06 17	06 25	06 13	06 48	06 44	06 55	07 18	07 25		07 14	07 48	07 44	07 55
Finsbury Park	d																								
Drayton Park	d																								
Highbury & Islington ⊖	d																								
Essex Road	d																								
Old Street ⊖	d																								
Moorgate ⊖	a																								
Finsbury Park	d	00 03	00 15	00 21	00 51	04 40	05 05	05 31	05 53	05 39		05 35	06 19	06 28	06 14	06 48	06 45	06 58	07 19	07 28		07 15	07 48	07 45	07 58
London Kings Cross 15 ⊖	a	00 11	00 21	00 27	00 57	04 46	05 13	05 37	06 01	05 46			06 25	06 36	06 20	06 55	06 50	07 06	07 25	07 35		07 20	07 55	07 50	08 06
St Pancras International	d											05 45													
Farringdon	d											05 49													
City Thameslink	d																								
London Blackfriars	a											05 53													
London Bridge	a																								

Station		GN	GN	TL 1	GN	TL 1		GN	GN	GN	TL 1	GN	TL 1	GN	GN	GN		TL 1	GN	TL 1	GN	GN	GN	TL 1	GN
Stevenage	d		07 30	07 40		08 10				08 30	08 40		09 10			09 30		09 40		10 10			10 30	10 40	
Watton-at-Stone	d		07 39					08 09		08 39				09 09		09 39					10 09		10 39		
Hertford North	d		07 48					08 18		08 48				09 18		09 48					10 18		10 48		
Bayford	d		07 52					08 22		08 52				09 22		09 52					10 22		10 52		
Cuffley	d		07 57					08 27		08 57				09 27		09 57					10 27		10 57		
Crews Hill	d		08 00					08 30		09 00				09 30		10 00					10 30		11 00		
Gordon Hill	d		08 03					08 33		09 03				09 33		10 03					10 33		11 03		
Enfield Chase	d		08 06					08 36		09 06				09 36		10 06					10 36		11 06		
Grange Park	d		08 08					08 38		09 08				09 38		10 08					10 38		11 08		
Winchmore Hill	d		08 10					08 40		09 10				09 40		10 10					10 40		11 10		
Palmers Green	d		08 13					08 43		09 13				09 43		10 13					10 43		11 13		
Bowes Park	a		08 15					08 45		09 15				09 45		10 15					10 45		11 15		
Knebworth	d			07 43		08 13					08 43		09 13					09 43		10 13				10 43	
Welwyn North	d			07 47		08 17					08 47		09 17					09 47		10 17				10 47	
Welwyn Garden City 4	d	07 38		07 52	08 08	08 22			08 38		08 52	09 08	09 22		09 38			09 52	10 08	10 22		10 38		10 52	11 08
Hatfield	d	07 43		07 55	08 13	08 25			08 43		08 55	09 13	09 25		09 43			09 55	10 13	10 25		10 43		10 55	11 13
Welham Green	d	07 47			08 17				08 47			09 17			09 47				10 17			10 47			11 17
Brookmans Park	d	07 49			08 19				08 49			09 19			09 49				10 19			10 49			11 19
Potters Bar	d	07 53		08 02	08 23	08 32			08 53		09 02	09 23	09 32		09 53			10 02	10 23	10 32		10 53		11 02	11 23
Hadley Wood	d	07 56			08 26				08 56			09 26			09 56				10 26			10 56			11 26
New Barnet	d	07 59			08 29				08 59			09 29			09 59				10 29			10 59			11 29
Oakleigh Park	d	08 01			08 31				09 01			09 31			10 01				10 31			11 01			11 31
New Southgate	a	08 04			08 34				09 04			09 34			10 04				10 34			11 04			11 34
Alexandra Palace	d	08 09	08 18		08 39			08 48	09 09	09 18		09 39		09 48	10 09	10 18			10 39		10 48	11 09	11 18		11 39
Hornsey	d	08 12	08 21		08 42			08 51	09 12	09 21		09 42		09 51	10 12	10 21			10 42		10 51	11 12	11 21		11 42
Harringay	d	08 15	08 23		08 45			08 53	09 15	09 23		09 45		09 53	10 15	10 23			10 45		10 53	11 15	11 23		11 45
Finsbury Park ⊖	a	08 17	08 25	08 13	08 48	08 44		08 55	09 17	09 25	09 13	09 48	09 44	09 55	10 17	10 25		10 13	10 47	10 44	10 55	11 17	11 25	11 13	11 47
Finsbury Park	d																								
Drayton Park	d																								
Highbury & Islington ⊖	d																								
Essex Road	d																								
Old Street ⊖	d																								
Moorgate ⊖	a																								
Finsbury Park	d	08 19	08 28	08 14	08 48	08 45		08 58	09 19	09 28	09 14	09 48	09 45	09 58	10 19	10 28		10 14	10 48	10 45	10 58	11 19	11 28	11 14	11 48
London Kings Cross 15 ⊖	a	08 25	08 36	08 20	08 55	08 50		09 06	09 25	09 36	09 20	09 55	09 50	10 08	10 25	10 36		10 20	10 55	10 50	11 06	11 25	11 36	11 20	11 55
St Pancras International	d																								
Farringdon	d																								
City Thameslink	d																								
London Blackfriars	a																								
London Bridge	a																								

See Table 025 for fast trains between London and Stevenage

Table T024-R

Saturdays

22 February to 16 May

Hertford North and Welwyn Garden City - London

		TL 1		GN	GN	GN	TL 1	GN	TL 1	GN	GN	GN		TL 1	GN	TL 1	GN	GN	GN	TL 1	GN	TL 1		GN	GN
Stevenage	d	11 10				11 30	11 40		12 10			12 30		12 40		13 10			13 30	13 40		14 10			
Watton-at-Stone	d			11 09		11 39				12 09		12 39					13 09		13 39					14 09	
Hertford North	d			11 18		11 48				12 18		12 48					13 18		13 48					14 18	
Bayford	d			11 22		11 52				12 22		12 52					13 22		13 52					14 22	
Cuffley	d			11 27		11 57				12 27		12 57					13 27		13 57					14 27	
Crews Hill	d			11 30		12 00				12 30		13 00					13 30		14 00					14 30	
Gordon Hill	d			11 33		12 03				12 33		13 03					13 33		14 03					14 33	
Enfield Chase	d			11 36		12 06				12 36		13 06					13 36		14 06					14 36	
Grange Park	d			11 38		12 08				12 38		13 08					13 38		14 08					14 38	
Winchmore Hill	d			11 40		12 10				12 40		13 10					13 40		14 10					14 40	
Palmers Green	d			11 43		12 13				12 43		13 13					13 43		14 13					14 43	
Bowes Park	a			11 45		12 15				12 45		13 15					13 45		14 15					14 45	
Knebworth	d	11 13					11 43		12 13					12 43		13 13				13 43		14 13			
Welwyn North	d	11 17					11 47		12 19					12 47		13 17				13 47		14 17			
Welwyn Garden City 4	d	11 22			11 38		11 53	12 08	12 23		12 38			12 52	13 08	13 22		13 38		13 52	14 08	14 22			14 38
Hatfield	d	11 25			11 43		11 55	12 13	12 26		12 43			12 55	13 13	13 25		13 43		13 55	14 13	14 25			14 43
Welham Green	d				11 47			12 17			12 47				13 17			13 47			14 17				14 47
Brookmans Park	d				11 49			12 19			12 49				13 19			13 49			14 19				14 49
Potters Bar	d	11 32			11 53		12 02	12 23	12 33		12 53			13 02	13 23	13 32		13 53		14 02	14 23	14 32			14 53
Hadley Wood	d				11 56			12 26			12 56				13 26			13 56			14 26				14 56
New Barnet	d				11 59			12 29			12 59				13 29			13 59			14 29				14 59
Oakleigh Park	d				12 01			12 31			13 01				13 31			14 01			14 31				15 01
New Southgate	a				12 04			12 34			13 04				13 34			14 04			14 34				15 04
Alexandra Palace	d			11 48	12 09	12 18		12 39		12 48	13 09	13 18			13 39		13 48	14 09	14 18		14 39			14 48	15 09
Hornsey	d			11 51	12 12	12 21		12 42		12 51	13 12	13 21			13 42		13 51	14 12	14 21		14 42			14 51	15 12
Harringay	d			11 53	12 15	12 23		12 45		12 53	13 15	13 23			13 45		13 53	14 15	14 23		14 45			14 53	15 15
Finsbury Park ⊖	a	11 44		11 55	12 17	12 25	12 13	12 47	12 44	12 55	13 17	13 25		13 13	13 48	13 44	13 55	14 17	14 25	14 13	14 47	14 44		14 55	15 17
Finsbury Park	d																								
Drayton Park	d																								
Highbury & Islington ⊖	d																								
Essex Road	d																								
Old Street ⊖	d																								
Moorgate ⊖	a																								
Finsbury Park	d	11 45		12 00	12 19	12 29	12 14	12 48	12 45	12 58	13 19	13 28		13 14	13 49	13 45	13 58	14 19	14 28	14 14	14 48	14 45		14 58	15 19
London Kings Cross 15 ⊖	a	11 50		12 08	12 25	12 38	12 20	12 55	12 50	13 06	13 25	13 36		13 20	13 55	13 50	14 06	14 25	14 35	14 20	14 55	14 50		15 06	15 25
St Pancras International	d																								
Farringdon	d																								
City Thameslink	d																								
London Blackfriars	a																								
London Bridge	a																								

		GN	TL 1	GN	TL 1	GN	GN	GN		TL 1	GN	TL 1	GN	GN	GN	TL 1	GN	TL 1		GN	GN	GN	TL 1	GN	TL 1
Stevenage	d	14 30	14 40		15 10			15 30		15 40		16 10			16 30	16 40		17 10				17 30	17 40		18 10
Watton-at-Stone	d	14 39				15 09		15 39					16 09		16 39					17 09		17 39			
Hertford North	d	14 48				15 18		15 48					16 18		16 48					17 18		17 48			
Bayford	d	14 52				15 22		15 52					16 22		16 52					17 22		17 52			
Cuffley	d	14 57				15 27		15 57					16 27		16 57					17 27		17 57			
Crews Hill	d	15 00				15 30		16 00					16 30		17 00					17 30		18 00			
Gordon Hill	d	15 03				15 33		16 03					16 33		17 03					17 33		18 03			
Enfield Chase	d	15 06				15 36		16 06					16 36		17 06					17 36		18 06			
Grange Park	d	15 08				15 38		16 08					16 38		17 08					17 38		18 08			
Winchmore Hill	d	15 10				15 40		16 10					16 40		17 10					17 40		18 10			
Palmers Green	d	15 13				15 43		16 13					16 43		17 13					17 43		18 13			
Bowes Park	a	15 15				15 45		16 15					16 45		17 15					17 45		18 15			
Knebworth	d		14 43		15 13					15 43		16 13				16 43		17 13					17 43		18 13
Welwyn North	d		14 47		15 17					15 47		16 19				16 48		17 17					17 47		18 18
Welwyn Garden City 4	d		14 52	15 08	15 22		15 38			15 52	16 08	16 22		16 38		16 53	17 08	17 22			17 38		17 52	18 08	18 23
Hatfield	d		14 55	15 13	15 25		15 43			15 55	16 13	16 26		16 43		16 56	17 13	17 25			17 43		17 55	18 13	18 26
Welham Green	d			15 17			15 47				16 17			16 47			17 17				17 47			18 17	
Brookmans Park	d			15 19			15 49				16 19			16 49			17 19				17 49			18 19	
Potters Bar	d		15 02	15 23	15 32		15 53			16 02	16 23	16 32		16 53		17 02	17 23	17 32			17 53		18 02	18 23	18 32
Hadley Wood	d			15 26			15 56				16 26			16 56			17 26				17 56			18 26	
New Barnet	d			15 29			15 59				16 29			16 59			17 29				17 59			18 29	
Oakleigh Park	d			15 31			16 01				16 31			17 01			17 31				18 01			18 31	
New Southgate	a			15 34			16 04				16 34			17 04			17 34				18 04			18 34	
Alexandra Palace	d	15 18		15 39		15 48	16 09	16 18			16 39		16 48	17 09	17 18		17 39			17 48	18 09	18 18		18 39	
Hornsey	d	15 21		15 42		15 51	16 12	16 21			16 42		16 51	17 12	17 21		17 42			17 51	18 12	18 21		18 42	
Harringay	d	15 23		15 45		15 53	16 15	16 23			16 45		16 53	17 15	17 23		17 45			17 53	18 15	18 23		18 45	
Finsbury Park ⊖	a	15 25	15 13	15 47	15 43	15 55	16 17	16 25		16 13	16 48	16 44	16 55	17 17	17 25	17 13	17 48	17 44		17 55	18 17	18 25	18 13	18 48	18 44
Finsbury Park	d																								
Drayton Park	d																								
Highbury & Islington ⊖	d																								
Essex Road	d																								
Old Street ⊖	d																								
Moorgate ⊖	a																								
Finsbury Park	d	15 28	15 14	15 48	15 44	15 58	16 19	16 30		16 14	16 48	16 45	16 58	17 19	17 28	17 14	17 48	17 45		17 58	18 19	18 28	18 14	18 48	18 45
London Kings Cross 15 ⊖	a	15 36	15 20	15 55	15 50	16 06	16 25	16 38		16 20	16 55	16 50	17 07	17 25	17 36	17 20	17 55	17 50		18 06	18 25	18 37	18 20	18 55	18 50
St Pancras International	d																								
Farringdon	d																								
City Thameslink	d																								
London Blackfriars	a																								
London Bridge	a																								

See Table 025 for fast trains between London and Stevenage

Table T024-R

Saturdays

22 February to 16 May

Hertford North and Welwyn Garden City - London

		GN	GN	GN		TL 1	GN	TL 1	GN	GN	GN	TL 1	GN	TL 1		GN	GN	GN	TL 1	GN	TL 1	GN	GN	GN
Stevenage	d			18 30		18 40		19 10			19 30	19 40		20 10				20 30	20 40		21 10			21 30
Watton-at-Stone	d	18 09		18 39					19 09		19 39					20 09		20 39				21 09		21 39
Hertford North	d	18 18		18 48					19 18		19 48					20 18		20 48				21 18		21 48
Bayford	d	18 22		18 52					19 22		19 52					20 22		20 52				21 22		21 52
Cuffley	d	18 27		18 57					19 27		19 57					20 27		20 57				21 27		21 57
Crews Hill	d	18 30		19 00					19 30		20 00					20 30		21 00				21 30		22 00
Gordon Hill	d	18 33		19 03					19 33		20 03					20 33		21 03				21 33		22 03
Enfield Chase	d	18 36		19 06					19 36		20 06					20 36		21 06				21 36		22 06
Grange Park	d	18 38		19 08					19 38		20 08					20 38		21 08				21 38		22 08
Winchmore Hill	d	18 40		19 10					19 40		20 10					20 40		21 10				21 40		22 10
Palmers Green	d	18 43		19 13					19 43		20 13					20 43		21 13				21 43		22 13
Bowes Park	a	18 45		19 15					19 45		20 15					20 45		21 15				21 45		22 15
Knebworth	d					18 43		19 13				19 43		20 13					20 43		21 13			
Welwyn North	d					18 47		19 18				19 47		20 17					20 47		21 17			
Welwyn Garden City 4	d		18 38			18 52	19 08	19 23		19 38		19 52	20 08	20 22			20 38		20 52	21 08	21 22		21 38	
Hatfield	d		18 43			18 55	19 13	19 27		19 43		19 55	20 13	20 25			20 43		20 55	21 13	21 25		21 43	
Welham Green	d		18 47				19 17			19 47			20 17				20 47			21 17			21 47	
Brookmans Park	d		18 49				19 19			19 49			20 19				20 49			21 19			21 49	
Potters Bar	d		18 53			19 02	19 23	19 33		19 53		20 02	20 23	20 32			20 53		21 02	21 23	21 32		21 53	
Hadley Wood	d		18 56				19 26			19 56			20 26				20 56			21 26			21 56	
New Barnet	d		18 59				19 29			19 59			20 29				20 59			21 29			21 59	
Oakleigh Park	d		19 01				19 31			20 01			20 31				21 01			21 31			22 01	
New Southgate	a		19 04				19 34			20 04			20 34				21 04			21 34			22 04	
Alexandra Palace	d	18 48	19 09	19 18			19 39		19 48	20 09	20 18		20 39			20 48	21 09	21 18		21 39		21 48	22 09	22 18
Hornsey	d	18 51	19 12	19 21			19 42		19 51	20 12	20 21		20 42			20 51	21 12	21 21		21 42		21 51	22 12	22 21
Harringay	d	18 53	19 15	19 23			19 45		19 53	20 15	20 23		20 45			20 53	21 15	21 23		21 45		21 53	22 15	22 23
Finsbury Park ⊖	a	18 55	19 17	19 25		19 13	19 48	19 44	19 55	20 17	20 25	20 13	20 47	20 44		20 55	21 17	21 25	21 13	21 48	21 44	21 55	22 17	22 25
Finsbury Park	d																							
Drayton Park	d																							
Highbury & Islington ⊖	d																							
Essex Road	d																							
Old Street ⊖	d																							
Moorgate ⊖	a																							
Finsbury Park	d	18 58	19 19	19 30		19 14	19 48	19 45	19 58	20 19	20 28	20 14	20 48	20 45		20 58	21 19	21 28	21 14	21 49	21 45	21 58	22 19	22 28
London Kings Cross 15 ⊖	a	19 06	19 25	19 38		19 20	19 55	19 50	20 06	20 25	20 36	20 20	20 55	20 50		21 06	21 25	21 36	21 20	21 55	21 50	22 06	22 25	22 36
St Pancras International	d																							
Farringdon	d																							
City Thameslink	d																							
London Blackfriars	a																							
London Bridge	a																							

		TL 1	GN	TL 1	GN	GN	GN	TL 1	GN	TL 1		GN	GN	GN	TL 1
Stevenage	d	21 40		22 10			22 30	22 40		23 10				23 28	23 40
Watton-at-Stone	d				22 09		22 39					23 05		23 35	
Hertford North	d				22 18		22 48					23 13		23 43	
Bayford	d				22 22		22 52					23 17		23 47	
Cuffley	d				22 27		22 57					23 22		23 52	
Crews Hill	d				22 30		23 00					23 25		23 55	
Gordon Hill	d				22 33		23 03					23 28		23 58	
Enfield Chase	d				22 36		23 06					23 31		00 01	
Grange Park	d				22 38		23 08					23 33		00 03	
Winchmore Hill	d				22 40		23 10					23 35		00 05	
Palmers Green	d				22 43		23 13					23 38		00 08	
Bowes Park	a				22 45		23 15					23 40		00 10	
Knebworth	d	21 43		22 13				22 43		23 13					23 43
Welwyn North	d	21 47		22 17				22 47		23 17					23 47
Welwyn Garden City 4	d	21 52	22 08	22 22		22 38		22 52	22 58	23 22			23 28		23 52
Hatfield	d	21 55	22 13	22 25		22 43		22 55	23 03	23 25			23 33		23 55
Welham Green	d		22 17			22 47			23 07				23 37		
Brookmans Park	d		22 19			22 49			23 09				23 39		
Potters Bar	d	22 02	22 23	22 32		22 53		23 02	23 13	23 32			23 43		00 02
Hadley Wood	d		22 26			22 56			23 16				23 46		
New Barnet	d		22 29			22 59			23 19				23 49		
Oakleigh Park	d		22 31			23 01			23 21				23 51		
New Southgate	a		22 34			23 04			23 24				23 54		
Alexandra Palace	d		22 39		22 48	23 09	23 18		23 28			23 43	23 58	00 13	
Hornsey	d		22 42		22 51	23 12	23 21		23 31			23 46	00 01	00 16	
Harringay	d		22 45		22 53	23 15	23 23		23 33			23 48	00 03	00 18	
Finsbury Park ⊖	a	22 13	22 48	22 44	22 55	23 17	23 25	23 13	23 35	23 43		23 50	00 06	00 21	00 17
Finsbury Park	d														
Drayton Park	d														
Highbury & Islington ⊖	d														
Essex Road	d														
Old Street ⊖	d														
Moorgate ⊖	a														
Finsbury Park	d	22 14	22 49	22 45	22 58	23 19	23 30	23 14	23 38	23 44		23 53	00 07	00 23	00 18
London Kings Cross 15 ⊖	a	22 20	22 55	22 50	23 06	23 25	23 38	23 20	23 47	23 50		00 02	00 13	00 30	00 27
St Pancras International	d														
Farringdon	d														
City Thameslink	d														
London Blackfriars	a														
London Bridge	a														

See Table 025 for fast trains between London and Stevenage

Table T024-R

Sundays

15 December to 16 February

Hertford North and Welwyn Garden City - London

		GN	GN	GN	TL 1	GN	GN	GN	TL 1	GN		GN	GN	TL 1	GN	GN	GN	GN	GN	GN		GN	GN	GN	GN
Stevenage	d								00 16					06 40					06 58						07 28
Watton-at-Stone	d																		07 05						07 35
Hertford North	d									06 13						06 43			07 11						07 43
Bayford	d									06 17						06 47			07 15						07 47
Cuffley	d									06 22						06 52			07 20						07 52
Crews Hill	d									06 25						06 55			07 23						07 55
Gordon Hill	d									06 28						06 58			07 26						07 58
Enfield Chase	d					00 01				06 31						07 01			07 29						08 01
Grange Park	d					00 03				06 33						07 03			07 31						08 03
Winchmore Hill	d					00 05				06 35						07 05			07 33						08 05
Palmers Green	d					00 08				06 38						07 08			07 36						08 08
Bowes Park	a					00 10				06 40						07 10			07 38						08 10
Knebworth	d								00 19					06 44											
Welwyn North	d								00 23					06 48											
Welwyn Garden City 4	d								00 28			06 26		06 53				06 56					07 27		
Hatfield	d								00 31			06 31		06 57				07 01					07 32		
Welham Green	d											06 35						07 05					07 35		
Brookmans Park	d											06 37						07 07					07 38		
Potters Bar	d				00 02				00 38			06 41		07 03				07 11					07 41		
Hadley Wood	d											06 44						07 14					07 45		
New Barnet	d											06 47						07 17					07 48		
Oakleigh Park	d											06 49						07 19					07 50		
New Southgate	a											06 52						07 22					07 53		
Alexandra Palace	d					00 13				06 43		06 56				07 13		07 26	07 41				07 56		08 13
Hornsey	d		00 01			00 16				06 46		06 59				07 16		07 29	07 44				07 59		08 16
Harringay	d		00 03			00 18				06 48		07 01				07 18		07 31	07 46				08 01		08 18
Finsbury Park ⊖	a		00 06		00 17	00 20			00 51	06 53		07 06		07 13		07 23		07 36	07 51				08 06		08 20
Finsbury Park	d		00 06			00 22				06 54		07 07				07 24		07 37	07 52				08 07		08 22
Drayton Park	d		00 09	00 09		00 25	00 27	00 37		06 57		07 10	07 10		07 25	07 27	07 38	07 40	07 55	07 55		08 08	08 10	08 23	08 25
Highbury & Islington ⊖	d		00 12			00 28				07 00		07 13				07 30		07 43	07 58				08 13		08 28
Essex Road	d		00 14			00 30				07 02		07 15				07 32		07 45	08 00				08 15		08 30
Old Street ⊖	d	00 02	00 17			00 33				07 05		07 18				07 35		07 48	08 03				08 18		08 33
Moorgate ⊖	a	00 06	00 21			00 37				07 09		07 22				07 39		07 52	08 07				08 22		08 37
Finsbury Park	d			00a12	00 18		00a30	00a40	00 51				07a13	07 14	07a28		07a41			07a58		08a11		08a26	
London Kings Cross 15 ⊖	a				00 27				00 57					07 23											
St Pancras International	d																								
Farringdon	d																								
City Thameslink	d																								
London Blackfriars	a																								
London Bridge	a																								

		TL 1	GN	GN	GN	GN		GN	GN	GN	GN	TL 1	GN	GN	GN	GN		TL 1	GN	GN	GN	GN	TL 1	GN	GN
Stevenage	d	07 42				07 58					08 28	08 40				08 58		09 10				09 28	09 40		
Watton-at-Stone	d					08 05					08 35					09 05						09 35			
Hertford North	d					08 13					08 43					09 13						09 43			
Bayford	d					08 17					08 47					09 17						09 47			
Cuffley	d					08 22					08 52					09 22						09 52			
Crews Hill	d					08 25					08 55					09 25						09 55			
Gordon Hill	d					08 28					08 58					09 28						09 58			
Enfield Chase	d					08 31					09 01					09 31						10 01			
Grange Park	d					08 33					09 03					09 33						10 03			
Winchmore Hill	d					08 35					09 05					09 35						10 05			
Palmers Green	d					08 38					09 08					09 38						10 08			
Bowes Park	a					08 40					09 10					09 40						10 10			
Knebworth	d	07 46										08 43						09 14					09 44		
Welwyn North	d	07 50										08 47						09 17					09 47		
Welwyn Garden City 4	d	07 56		07 59					08 28			08 52		08 58				09 22		09 28			09 52		09 58
Hatfield	d	08 00		08 04					08 33			08 56		09 03				09 26		09 33			09 56		10 03
Welham Green	d			08 08					08 37					09 07						09 37					10 07
Brookmans Park	d			08 10					08 39					09 09						09 39					10 09
Potters Bar	d	08 06		08 14					08 43			09 02		09 13				09 32		09 43			10 02		10 13
Hadley Wood	d			08 17					08 46					09 16						09 46					10 16
New Barnet	d			08 20					08 49					09 19						09 49					10 19
Oakleigh Park	d			08 22					08 51					09 21						09 51					10 21
New Southgate	a			08 25					08 54					09 24						09 54					10 24
Alexandra Palace	d			08 29		08 43			08 58		09 13			09 28		09 43				09 58		10 13			10 28
Hornsey	d			08 32		08 46			09 01		09 16			09 31		09 46				10 01		10 16			10 31
Harringay	d			08 34		08 48			09 03		09 18			09 33		09 48				10 03		10 18			10 33
Finsbury Park ⊖	a	08 15		08 36		08 50			09 05		09 20	09 13		09 35		09 50		09 42		10 05		10 20	10 12		10 35
Finsbury Park	d			08 37		08 52			09 07		09 22			09 37		09 52				10 07		10 22			10 37
Drayton Park	d		08 38	08 40	08 53	08 55		09 08	09 10	09 23	09 25		09 38	09 40	09 53	09 55			10 08	10 10	10 23	10 25		10 38	10 40
Highbury & Islington ⊖	d			08 43		08 58			09 13		09 28			09 43		09 58				10 13		10 28			10 43
Essex Road	d			08 45		09 00			09 15		09 30			09 45		10 00				10 15		10 30			10 45
Old Street ⊖	d			08 48		09 03			09 18		09 33			09 48		10 03				10 18		10 33			10 48
Moorgate ⊖	a			08 52		09 07			09 22		09 37			09 52		10 07				10 22		10 37			10 52
Finsbury Park	d	08 16	08a41		08a56			09a11		09a26		09 13	09a41		09a56			09 43	10a11		10a26		10 13	10a41	
London Kings Cross 15 ⊖	a	08 22										09 21						09 49					10 19		
St Pancras International	d																								
Farringdon	d																								
City Thameslink	d																								
London Blackfriars	a																								
London Bridge	a																								

See Table 025 for fast trains between London and Stevenage

NRT DECEMBER 19 EDITION

Table T024-R

Sundays

15 December to 16 February

Hertford North and Welwyn Garden City - London

		GN		GN	TL 1	GN	GN	GN	GN	TL 1	GN	GN		GN	GN	TL 1	GN	GN	GN	GN	TL 1	GN		GN	GN
Stevenage	d			09 58	10 10				10 28	10 40					10 58	11 10				11 28	11 40				
Watton-at-Stone	d			10 05					10 35						11 05					11 35					
Hertford North	d			10 13					10 43						11 13					11 43					
Bayford	d			10 17					10 47						11 17					11 47					
Cuffley	d			10 22					10 52						11 22					11 52					
Crews Hill	d			10 25					10 55						11 25					11 55					
Gordon Hill	d			10 28					10 58						11 28					11 58					
Enfield Chase	d			10 31					11 01						11 31					12 01					
Grange Park	d			10 33					11 03						11 33					12 03					
Winchmore Hill	d			10 35					11 05						11 35					12 05					
Palmers Green	d			10 38					11 08						11 38					12 08					
Bowes Park	a			10 40					11 10						11 40					12 10					
Knebworth	d				10 14					10 44						11 14					11 44				
Welwyn North	d				10 17					10 47						11 19					11 47				
Welwyn Garden City 4	d				10 22		10 28			10 52		10 58				11 23		11 28			11 52			11 58	
Hatfield	d				10 26		10 33			10 56		11 03				11 27		11 33			11 56			12 03	
Welham Green	d						10 37					11 07						11 37						12 07	
Brookmans Park	d						10 39					11 09						11 39						12 09	
Potters Bar	d				10 32		10 43			11 02		11 13				11 32		11 43			12 02			12 13	
Hadley Wood	d						10 46					11 16						11 46						12 16	
New Barnet	d						10 49					11 19						11 49						12 19	
Oakleigh Park	d						10 51					11 21						11 51						12 21	
New Southgate	a						10 54					11 24						11 54						12 24	
Alexandra Palace	d			10 43			10 58		11 13			11 28			11 43			11 58		12 13				12 28	
Hornsey	d			10 46			11 01		11 16			11 31			11 46			12 01		12 16				12 31	
Harringay	d			10 48			11 03		11 18			11 33			11 48			12 03		12 18				12 33	
Finsbury Park ⊖	a			10 50	10 42		11 05		11 20	11 12		11 35			11 50	11 43		12 05		12 20	12 12			12 35	
Finsbury Park	d			10 52			11 07		11 22			11 37			11 52			12 07		12 22				12 37	
Drayton Park	d	10 53		10 55		11 08	11 10	11 23	11 25		11 38	11 40		11 53	11 55		12 08	12 10	12 23	12 25		12 38		12 40	12 53
Highbury & Islington ⊖	d			10 58			11 13		11 28			11 43			11 58			12 13		12 28				12 43	
Essex Road	d			11 00			11 15		11 30			11 45			12 00			12 15		12 30				12 45	
Old Street ⊖	d			11 03			11 18		11 33			11 48			12 03			12 18		12 33				12 48	
Moorgate ⊖	a			11 07			11 22		11 37			11 52			12 07			12 22		12 37				12 52	
Finsbury Park	d	10a56			10 43	11a11		11a26		11 13	11a41			11a56		11 44	12a11		12a26		12 13	12a41			12a56
London Kings Cross 15 ⊖	a				10 49					11 19						11 51					12 19				
St Pancras International	d																								
Farringdon	d																								
City Thameslink	d																								
London Blackfriars	a																								
London Bridge	a																								

		GN	GN	GN	GN	GN	TL 1	GN		GN	GN	GN	GN	GN	GN	GN	TL 1	GN		GN	GN	GN	GN	GN	GN
Stevenage	d	11 58				12 28	12 40					12 58				13 28	13 40					13 58			
Watton-at-Stone	d	12 05				12 35						13 05				13 35						14 05			
Hertford North	d	12 13				12 43						13 13				13 43						14 13			
Bayford	d	12 17				12 47						13 17				13 47						14 17			
Cuffley	d	12 22				12 52						13 22				13 52						14 22			
Crews Hill	d	12 25				12 55						13 25				13 55						14 25			
Gordon Hill	d	12 28				12 58						13 28				13 58						14 28			
Enfield Chase	d	12 31				13 01						13 31				14 01						14 31			
Grange Park	d	12 33				13 03						13 33				14 03						14 33			
Winchmore Hill	d	12 35				13 05						13 35				14 05						14 35			
Palmers Green	d	12 38				13 08						13 38				14 08						14 38			
Bowes Park	a	12 40				13 10						13 40				14 10						14 40			
Knebworth	d						12 44										13 44								
Welwyn North	d						12 47										13 47								
Welwyn Garden City 4	d			12 28			12 52			12 58				13 28			13 52			13 58				14 28	
Hatfield	d			12 33			12 56			13 03				13 33			13 56			14 03				14 33	
Welham Green	d			12 37						13 07				13 37						14 07				14 37	
Brookmans Park	d			12 39						13 09				13 39						14 09				14 39	
Potters Bar	d			12 43			13 02			13 13				13 43			14 02			14 13				14 43	
Hadley Wood	d			12 46						13 16				13 46						14 16				14 46	
New Barnet	d			12 49						13 19				13 49						14 19				14 49	
Oakleigh Park	d			12 51						13 21				13 51						14 21				14 51	
New Southgate	a			12 54						13 24				13 54						14 24				14 54	
Alexandra Palace	d	12 43		12 58		13 13				13 28		13 43		13 58		14 13				14 28		14 43		14 58	
Hornsey	d	12 46		13 01		13 16				13 31		13 46		14 01		14 16				14 31		14 46		15 01	
Harringay	d	12 48		13 03		13 18				13 33		13 48		14 03		14 18				14 33		14 48		15 03	
Finsbury Park ⊖	a	12 50		13 05		13 20	13 12			13 35		13 50		14 05		14 20	14 12			14 35		14 50		15 05	
Finsbury Park	d	12 52		13 07		13 22				13 37		13 52		14 07		14 22				14 37		14 52		15 07	
Drayton Park	d	12 55	13 08	13 10	13 23	13 25		13 38		13 40	13 53	13 55	14 08	14 10	14 23	14 25		14 38		14 40	14 53	14 55	15 08	15 10	15 23
Highbury & Islington ⊖	d	12 58		13 13		13 28				13 43		13 58		14 13		14 28				14 43		14 58		15 13	
Essex Road	d	13 00		13 15		13 30				13 45		14 00		14 15		14 30				14 45		15 00		15 15	
Old Street ⊖	d	13 03		13 18		13 33				13 48		14 03		14 18		14 33				14 48		15 03		15 18	
Moorgate ⊖	a	13 07		13 22		13 37				13 52		14 07		14 22		14 37				14 52		15 07		15 22	
Finsbury Park	d		13a11		13a26		13 13	13a41			13a56		14a11		14a26		14 13	14a41			14a56		15a11		15a26
London Kings Cross 15 ⊖	a						13 19										14 19								
St Pancras International	d																								
Farringdon	d																								
City Thameslink	d																								
London Blackfriars	a																								
London Bridge	a																								

See Table 025 for fast trains between London and Stevenage

Table T024-R

Sundays

15 December to 16 February

Hertford North and Welwyn Garden City - London

		GN	TL 1	GN	GN	GN	GN	GN	GN	GN	GN	TL 1	GN	GN	GN	GN	GN	GN	GN	GN	TL 1	GN
Stevenage	d	14 28	14 40				14 58				15 28	15 40				15 58				16 28	16 40	
Watton-at-Stone	d	14 35					15 05				15 35					16 05				16 35		
Hertford North	d	14 43					15 13				15 43					16 13				16 43		
Bayford	d	14 47					15 17				15 47					16 17				16 47		
Cuffley	d	14 52					15 22				15 52					16 22				16 52		
Crews Hill	d	14 55					15 25				15 55					16 25				16 55		
Gordon Hill	d	14 58					15 28				15 58					16 28				16 58		
Enfield Chase	d	15 01					15 31				16 01					16 31				17 01		
Grange Park	d	15 03					15 33				16 03					16 33				17 03		
Winchmore Hill	d	15 05					15 35				16 05					16 35				17 05		
Palmers Green	d	15 08					15 38				16 08					16 38				17 08		
Bowes Park	a	15 10					15 40				16 10					16 40				17 10		
Knebworth	d		14 44									15 44									16 44	
Welwyn North	d		14 47									15 47									16 47	
Welwyn Garden City 4	d		14 52		14 58				15 28			15 52		15 58				16 28			16 52	
Hatfield	d		14 56		15 03				15 33			15 56		16 03				16 33			16 56	
Welham Green	d				15 07				15 37					16 07				16 37				
Brookmans Park	d				15 09				15 39					16 09				16 39				
Potters Bar	d		15 02		15 13				15 43			16 02		16 13				16 43			17 02	
Hadley Wood	d				15 16				15 46					16 16				16 46				
New Barnet	d				15 19				15 49					16 19				16 49				
Oakleigh Park	d				15 21				15 51					16 21				16 51				
New Southgate	a				15 24				15 54					16 24				16 54				
Alexandra Palace	d	15 13			15 28		15 43		15 58		16 13			16 28		16 43		16 58		17 13		
Hornsey	d	15 16			15 31		15 46		16 01		16 16			16 31		16 46		17 01		17 16		
Harringay	d	15 18			15 33		15 48		16 03		16 18			16 33		16 48		17 03		17 18		
Finsbury Park ⊖	a	15 20	15 12		15 35		15 50		16 05		16 20	16 12		16 35		16 50		17 05		17 20	17 12	
Finsbury Park	d	15 22			15 37		15 52		16 07		16 22			16 37		16 52		17 07		17 22		
Drayton Park	d	15 25		15 38	15 40	15 53	15 55	16 08	16 10	16 23	16 25		16 38	16 40	16 53	16 55	17 08	17 10	17 23	17 25		17 38
Highbury & Islington ⊖	d	15 28			15 43		15 58		16 13		16 28			16 43		16 58		17 13		17 28		
Essex Road	d	15 30			15 45		16 00		16 15		16 30			16 45		17 00		17 15		17 30		
Old Street ⊖	d	15 33			15 48		16 03		16 18		16 33			16 48		17 03		17 18		17 33		
Moorgate ⊖	a	15 37			15 52		16 07		16 22		16 37			16 52		17 07		17 22		17 37		
Finsbury Park	d		15 13	15a41		15a56		16a11		16a26		16 13	16a41		16a56		17a11		17a26		17 13	17a41
London Kings Cross 15 ⊖	a		15 20									16 19									17 19	
St Pancras International	d																					
Farringdon	d																					
City Thameslink	d																					
London Blackfriars	a																					
London Bridge	a																					

		GN	GN	GN	GN	GN	GN	GN	TL 1	GN	GN	GN	GN	GN	GN	GN	GN	TL 1	GN	GN	GN	GN	GN
Stevenage	d			16 58				17 28	17 40				17 58				18 28	18 40				18 58	
Watton-at-Stone	d			17 05				17 35					18 05				18 35					19 05	
Hertford North	d			17 13				17 43					18 13				18 43					19 13	
Bayford	d			17 17				17 47					18 17				18 47					19 17	
Cuffley	d			17 22				17 52					18 22				18 52					19 22	
Crews Hill	d			17 25				17 55					18 25				18 55					19 25	
Gordon Hill	d			17 28				17 58					18 28				18 58					19 28	
Enfield Chase	d			17 31				18 01					18 31				19 01					19 31	
Grange Park	d			17 33				18 03					18 33				19 03					19 33	
Winchmore Hill	d			17 35				18 05					18 35				19 05					19 35	
Palmers Green	d			17 38				18 08					18 38				19 08					19 38	
Bowes Park	a			17 40				18 10					18 40				19 10					19 40	
Knebworth	d								17 44									18 44					
Welwyn North	d								17 47									18 47					
Welwyn Garden City 4	d	16 58				17 28			17 52		17 58				18 28			18 52		18 58			
Hatfield	d	17 03				17 33			17 56		18 03				18 33			18 56		19 03			
Welham Green	d	17 07				17 37					18 07				18 37					19 07			
Brookmans Park	d	17 09				17 39					18 09				18 39					19 09			
Potters Bar	d	17 13				17 43			18 02		18 13				18 43			19 02		19 13			
Hadley Wood	d	17 16				17 46					18 16				18 46					19 16			
New Barnet	d	17 19				17 49					18 19				18 49					19 19			
Oakleigh Park	d	17 21				17 51					18 21				18 51					19 21			
New Southgate	a	17 24				17 54					18 24				18 54					19 24			
Alexandra Palace	d	17 28		17 43		17 58		18 13			18 28		18 43		18 58		19 13			19 28		19 43	
Hornsey	d	17 31		17 46		18 01		18 16			18 31		18 46		19 01		19 16			19 31		19 46	
Harringay	d	17 33		17 48		18 03		18 18			18 33		18 48		19 03		19 18			19 33		19 48	
Finsbury Park ⊖	a	17 35		17 50		18 05		18 20	18 12		18 35		18 50		19 05		19 20	19 12		19 35		19 50	
Finsbury Park	d	17 37		17 52		18 07		18 22			18 37		18 52		19 07		19 21			19 37		19 52	
Drayton Park	d	17 40	17 53	17 55	18 08	18 10	18 23	18 25		18 38	18 40	18 53	18 55	19 08	19 10	19 23	19 25		19 38	19 40	19 53	19 55	20 08
Highbury & Islington ⊖	d	17 43		17 58		18 13		18 28			18 43		18 58		19 13		19 28			19 43		19 58	
Essex Road	d	17 45		18 00		18 15		18 30			18 45		19 00		19 15		19 30			19 45		20 00	
Old Street ⊖	d	17 48		18 03		18 18		18 33			18 48		19 03		19 18		19 33			19 48		20 03	
Moorgate ⊖	a	17 52		18 07		18 22		18 37			18 52		19 07		19 22		19 37			19 52		20 07	
Finsbury Park	d		17a56		18a11		18a26		18 13	18a41		18a56		19a11		19a26		19 13	19a41		19a56		20a11
London Kings Cross 15 ⊖	a								18 19									19 19					
St Pancras International	d																						
Farringdon	d																						
City Thameslink	d																						
London Blackfriars	a																						
London Bridge	a																						

See Table 025 for fast trains between London and Stevenage

Table T024-R

Sundays

15 December to 16 February

Hertford North and Welwyn Garden City - London

		GN	GN	GN	TL 1	GN	GN	GN	GN	GN	GN	GN	GN	TL 1	GN	GN	GN	GN	GN	GN	GN	GN	TL 1
Stevenage	d			19 28	19 40				19 58				20 28	20 40				20 58				21 28	21 40
Watton-at-Stone	d			19 35					20 05				20 35					21 05				21 35	
Hertford North	d			19 43					20 13				20 43					21 13				21 43	
Bayford	d			19 47					20 17				20 47					21 17				21 47	
Cuffley	d			19 52					20 22				20 52					21 22				21 52	
Crews Hill	d			19 55					20 25				20 55					21 25				21 55	
Gordon Hill	d			19 58					20 28				20 58					21 28				21 58	
Enfield Chase	d			20 01					20 31				21 01					21 31				22 01	
Grange Park	d			20 03					20 33				21 03					21 33				22 03	
Winchmore Hill	d			20 05					20 35				21 05					21 35				22 05	
Palmers Green	d			20 08					20 38				21 08					21 38				22 08	
Bowes Park	a			20 10					20 40				21 10					21 40				22 10	
Knebworth	d				19 44									20 44									21 44
Welwyn North	d				19 47									20 48									21 48
Welwyn Garden City 4	d	19 28			19 52		19 58				20 28			20 52		20 58				21 28			21 52
Hatfield	d	19 33			19 56		20 03				20 33			20 56		21 03				21 33			21 56
Welham Green	d	19 37					20 07				20 37					21 07				21 37			
Brookmans Park	d	19 39					20 09				20 39					21 09				21 39			
Potters Bar	d	19 43			20 02		20 13				20 43			21 02		21 13				21 43			22 02
Hadley Wood	d	19 46					20 16				20 46					21 16				21 46			
New Barnet	d	19 49					20 19				20 49					21 19				21 49			
Oakleigh Park	d	19 51					20 21				20 51					21 21				21 51			
New Southgate	a	19 54					20 24				20 54					21 24				21 54			
Alexandra Palace	d	19 58		20 13			20 28		20 43		20 58		21 13			21 28		21 43		21 58		22 13	
Hornsey	d	20 01		20 16			20 31		20 46		21 01		21 16			21 31		21 46		22 01		22 16	
Harringay	d	20 03		20 18			20 33		20 48		21 03		21 18			21 33		21 48		22 03		22 18	
Finsbury Park ⊖	a	20 05		20 20	20 12		20 35		20 50		21 05		21 20	21 12		21 35		21 50		22 05		22 20	22 13
Finsbury Park	d	20 07		20 22			20 37		20 52		21 07		21 22			21 37		21 52		22 07		22 22	
Drayton Park	d	20 10	20 23	20 25		20 38	20 40	20 53	20 55	21 08	21 10	21 23	21 25		21 38	21 40	21 53	21 55	22 08	22 10	22 23	22 25	
Highbury & Islington ⊖	d	20 13		20 28			20 43		20 58		21 13		21 28			21 43		21 58		22 12		22 28	
Essex Road	d	20 15		20 30			20 45		21 00		21 15		21 30			21 45		22 00		22 14		22 30	
Old Street ⊖	d	20 18		20 33			20 48		21 03		21 18		21 33			21 48		22 03		22 18		22 33	
Moorgate ⊖	a	20 22		20 37			20 52		21 07		21 22		21 37			21 52		22 07		22 22		22 37	
Finsbury Park	d		20a26		20 13	20a41		20a56		21a11		21a26		21 13	21a41		21a56		22a11		22a26		22 13
London Kings Cross 15 ⊖	a				20 19									21 19									22 21
St Pancras International	d																						
Farringdon	d																						
City Thameslink	d																						
London Blackfriars	a																						
London Bridge	a																						

		GN	GN	GN	GN	GN	GN	GN	GN	TL 1	GN	GN	GN	GN	GN	GN
Stevenage	d				21 58				22 28	22 40				22 58		23 28
Watton-at-Stone	d				22 05				22 35					23 05		23 35
Hertford North	d				22 13				22 43					23 13		23 43
Bayford	d				22 17				22 47					23 17		23 47
Cuffley	d				22 22				22 52					23 22		23 52
Crews Hill	d				22 25				22 55					23 25		23 55
Gordon Hill	d				22 28				22 58					23 28		23 58
Enfield Chase	d				22 31				23 01					23 31		00 02
Grange Park	d				22 33				23 03					23 33		00 04
Winchmore Hill	d				22 35				23 05					23 35		00 06
Palmers Green	d				22 38				23 08					23 38		00 09
Bowes Park	a				22 40				23 10					23 40		00 11
Knebworth	d									22 44						
Welwyn North	d									22 48						
Welwyn Garden City 4	d		21 58				22 28			22 52		22 58			23 28	
Hatfield	d		22 03				22 33			22 56		23 03			23 33	
Welham Green	d		22 07				22 37					23 07			23 37	
Brookmans Park	d		22 09				22 39					23 09			23 39	
Potters Bar	d		22 13				22 43			23 02		23 13			23 43	
Hadley Wood	d		22 16				22 46					23 16			23 46	
New Barnet	d		22 19				22 49					23 19			23 49	
Oakleigh Park	d		22 21				22 51					23 21			23 51	
New Southgate	a		22 24				22 54					23 24			23 54	
Alexandra Palace	d		22 28		22 43		22 58		23 13			23 28		23 43	23 58	00 14
Hornsey	d		22 31		22 46		23 01		23 16			23 31		23 46	00 01	00 17
Harringay	d		22 33		22 48		23 03		23 18			23 33		23 48	00 03	00 19
Finsbury Park ⊖	a		22 35		22 50		23 05		23 20	23 13		23 35		23 50	00 06	00 24
Finsbury Park	d		22 37		22 52		23 07		23 22			23 37		23 51	00 06	00 25
Drayton Park	d	22 38	22 40	22 53	22 55	23 08	23 10	23 23	23 25		23 38	23 40	23 53	23 54	00 09	00 28
Highbury & Islington ⊖	d		22 43		22 58		23 13		23 28			23 43		23 57	00 12	00 31
Essex Road	d		22 45		23 00		23 15		23 30			23 45		23 59	00 14	00 33
Old Street ⊖	d		22 48		23 03		23 18		23 33			23 48		00 02	00 17	00 36
Moorgate ⊖	a		22 52		23 07		23 22		23 37			23 52		00 06	00 21	00 40
Finsbury Park	d	22a41		22a56		23a11		23a26		23 13	23a41		23a56			
London Kings Cross 15 ⊖	a									23 21						
St Pancras International	d															
Farringdon	d															
City Thameslink	d															
London Blackfriars	a															
London Bridge	a															

See Table 025 for fast trains between London and Stevenage

Table T024-R

Sundays

23 February to 10 May

Hertford North and Welwyn Garden City - London

		GN	TL 1	GN	TL 1	GN	GN	TL 1	GN	GN		GN	GN	GN	TL 1	GN	GN	GN	GN	TL 1		GN	GN	TL 1	GN
Stevenage	d				00 16			06 40				06 58		07 28	07 42		07 58		08 28	08 40			08 58	09 10	
Watton-at-Stone	d											07 05		07 35			08 05		08 35				09 05		
Hertford North	d					06 13			06 43			07 11		07 43			08 13		08 43				09 13		
Bayford	d					06 17			06 47			07 15		07 47			08 17		08 47				09 17		
Cuffley	d					06 22			06 52			07 20		07 52			08 22		08 52				09 22		
Crews Hill	d					06 25			06 55			07 23		07 55			08 25		08 55				09 25		
Gordon Hill	d					06 28			06 58			07 26		07 58			08 28		08 58				09 28		
Enfield Chase	d			00 01		06 31			07 01			07 29		08 01			08 31		09 01				09 31		
Grange Park	d			00 03		06 33			07 03			07 31		08 03			08 33		09 03				09 33		
Winchmore Hill	d			00 05		06 35			07 05			07 33		08 05			08 35		09 05				09 35		
Palmers Green	d			00 08		06 38			07 08			07 36		08 08			08 38		09 08				09 38		
Bowes Park	a			00 10		06 40			07 10			07 38		08 10			08 40		09 10				09 40		
Knebworth	d				00 19			06 44							07 46					08 43				09 14	
Welwyn North	d				00 23			06 48							07 50					08 47				09 17	
Welwyn Garden City 4	d				00 28		06 26	06 53		06 56			07 27		07 56	07 59		08 28		08 52		08 58		09 22	09 28
Hatfield	d				00 31		06 31	06 57		07 01			07 32		08 00	08 04		08 33		08 56		09 03		09 26	09 33
Welham Green	d						06 35			07 05			07 35			08 08		08 37				09 07			09 37
Brookmans Park	d						06 37			07 07			07 38			08 10		08 39				09 09			09 39
Potters Bar	d		00 02		00 38		06 41	07 03		07 11			07 41		08 06	08 14		08 43		09 02		09 13		09 32	09 43
Hadley Wood	d						06 44			07 14			07 45			08 17		08 46				09 16			09 46
New Barnet	d						06 47			07 17			07 48			08 20		08 49				09 19			09 49
Oakleigh Park	d						06 49			07 19			07 50			08 22		08 51				09 21			09 51
New Southgate	a						06 52			07 22			07 53			08 25		08 54				09 24			09 54
Alexandra Palace	d			00 13		06 43	06 56		07 13	07 26		07 41	07 56	08 13		08 29	08 43	08 58	09 13			09 28	09 43		09 58
Hornsey	d	00 01		00 16		06 46	06 59		07 16	07 29		07 44	07 59	08 16		08 32	08 46	09 01	09 16			09 31	09 46		10 01
Harringay	d	00 03		00 18		06 48	07 01		07 18	07 31		07 46	08 01	08 18		08 34	08 48	09 03	09 18			09 33	09 48		10 03
Finsbury Park ⊖	a	00 06	00 17	00 21	00 51	06 53	07 06	07 13	07 23	07 36		07 51	08 06	08 20	08 15	08 36	08 50	09 05	09 20	09 13		09 35	09 50	09 42	10 05
Finsbury Park	d																								
Drayton Park	d																								
Highbury & Islington ⊖	d																								
Essex Road	d																								
Old Street ⊖	d																								
Moorgate ⊖	a																								
Finsbury Park	d	00 07	00 18	00 23	00 51	06 54	07 07	07 14	07 24	07 37		07 52	08 07	08 21	08 16	08 37	08 51	09 06	09 21	09 13		09 36	09 51	09 43	10 06
London Kings Cross 15 ⊖	a	00 13	00 27	00 30	00 57	07 01	07 14	07 23	07 31	07 44		07 59	08 14	08 27	08 22	08 44	08 58	09 12	09 27	09 21		09 43	09 58	09 49	10 12
St Pancras International	d																								
Farringdon	d																								
City Thameslink	d																								
London Blackfriars	a																								
London Bridge	a																								

		GN	TL 1	GN	GN	TL 1		GN	GN	TL 1	GN	GN	TL 1	GN	GN	TL 1		GN	GN	GN	GN	TL 1	GN	GN	GN
Stevenage	d	09 28	09 40		09 58	10 10			10 28	10 40		10 58	11 10		11 28	11 40			11 58		12 28	12 40		12 58	
Watton-at-Stone	d	09 35			10 05				10 35			11 05			11 35				12 05		12 35			13 05	
Hertford North	d	09 43			10 13				10 43			11 13			11 43				12 13		12 43			13 13	
Bayford	d	09 47			10 17				10 47			11 17			11 47				12 17		12 47			13 17	
Cuffley	d	09 52			10 22				10 52			11 22			11 52				12 22		12 52			13 22	
Crews Hill	d	09 55			10 25				10 55			11 25			11 55				12 25		12 55			13 25	
Gordon Hill	d	09 58			10 28				10 58			11 28			11 58				12 28		12 58			13 28	
Enfield Chase	d	10 01			10 31				11 01			11 31			12 01				12 31		13 01			13 31	
Grange Park	d	10 03			10 33				11 03			11 33			12 03				12 33		13 03			13 33	
Winchmore Hill	d	10 05			10 35				11 05			11 35			12 05				12 35		13 05			13 35	
Palmers Green	d	10 08			10 38				11 08			11 38			12 08				12 38		13 08			13 38	
Bowes Park	a	10 10			10 40				11 10			11 40			12 10				12 40		13 10			13 40	
Knebworth	d		09 44			10 14				10 44			11 14			11 44						12 44			
Welwyn North	d		09 47			10 17				10 47			11 19			11 47						12 47			
Welwyn Garden City 4	d		09 52	09 58		10 22		10 28		10 52	10 58		11 23	11 28		11 52		11 58		12 28		12 52	12 58		13 28
Hatfield	d		09 56	10 03		10 26		10 33		10 56	11 03		11 27	11 33		11 56		12 03		12 33		12 56	13 03		13 33
Welham Green	d			10 07				10 37			11 07			11 37				12 07		12 37			13 07		13 37
Brookmans Park	d			10 09				10 39			11 09			11 39				12 09		12 39			13 09		13 39
Potters Bar	d		10 02	10 13		10 32		10 43		11 02	11 13		11 32	11 43		12 02		12 13		12 43		13 02	13 13		13 43
Hadley Wood	d			10 16				10 46			11 16			11 46				12 16		12 46			13 16		13 46
New Barnet	d			10 19				10 49			11 19			11 49				12 19		12 49			13 19		13 49
Oakleigh Park	d			10 21				10 51			11 21			11 51				12 21		12 51			13 21		13 51
New Southgate	a			10 24				10 54			11 24			11 54				12 24		12 54			13 24		13 54
Alexandra Palace	d	10 13		10 28	10 43			10 58	11 13		11 28	11 43		11 58	12 13			12 28	12 43	12 58	13 13		13 28	13 43	13 58
Hornsey	d	10 16		10 31	10 46			11 01	11 16		11 31	11 46		12 01	12 16			12 31	12 46	13 01	13 16		13 31	13 46	14 01
Harringay	d	10 18		10 33	10 48			11 03	11 18		11 33	11 48		12 03	12 18			12 33	12 48	13 03	13 18		13 33	13 48	14 03
Finsbury Park ⊖	a	10 20	10 12	10 35	10 50	10 42		11 05	11 20	11 12	11 35	11 50	11 43	12 05	12 20	12 12		12 35	12 50	13 05	13 20	13 12	13 35	13 50	14 05
Finsbury Park	d																								
Drayton Park	d																								
Highbury & Islington ⊖	d																								
Essex Road	d																								
Old Street ⊖	d																								
Moorgate ⊖	a																								
Finsbury Park	d	10 21	10 13	10 36	10 51	10 43		11 06	11 21	11 13	11 36	11 51	11 44	12 06	12 21	12 13		12 36	12 51	13 06	13 21	13 13	13 36	13 51	14 06
London Kings Cross 15 ⊖	a	10 27	10 19	10 43	10 58	10 49		11 12	11 27	11 19	11 43	11 58	11 51	12 12	12 28	12 19		12 43	12 58	13 12	13 28	13 19	13 43	13 58	14 12
St Pancras International	d																								
Farringdon	d																								
City Thameslink	d																								
London Blackfriars	a																								
London Bridge	a																								

See Table 025 for fast trains between London and Stevenage

NRT DECEMBER 19 EDITION

Table T024-R

Sundays

23 February to 10 May

Hertford North and Welwyn Garden City - London

		GN		TL 1	GN	GN	GN	GN	TL 1	GN	GN	GN		GN	TL 1	GN	GN	GN	GN	TL 1	GN	GN		GN	GN
Stevenage	d	13 28		13 40		13 58		14 28	14 40		14 58			15 28	15 40		15 58		16 28	16 40		16 58			17 28
Watton-at-Stone	d	13 35				14 05		14 35			15 05			15 35			16 05		16 35			17 05			17 35
Hertford North	d	13 43				14 13		14 43			15 13			15 43			16 13		16 43			17 13			17 43
Bayford	d	13 47				14 17		14 47			15 17			15 47			16 17		16 47			17 17			17 47
Cuffley	d	13 52				14 22		14 52			15 22			15 52			16 22		16 52			17 22			17 52
Crews Hill	d	13 55				14 25		14 55			15 25			15 55			16 25		16 55			17 25			17 55
Gordon Hill	d	13 58				14 28		14 58			15 28			15 58			16 28		16 58			17 28			17 58
Enfield Chase	d	14 01				14 31		15 01			15 31			16 01			16 31		17 01			17 31			18 01
Grange Park	d	14 03				14 33		15 03			15 33			16 03			16 33		17 03			17 33			18 03
Winchmore Hill	d	14 05				14 35		15 05			15 35			16 05			16 35		17 05			17 35			18 05
Palmers Green	d	14 08				14 38		15 08			15 38			16 08			16 38		17 08			17 38			18 08
Bowes Park	a	14 10				14 40		15 10			15 40			16 10			16 40		17 10			17 40			18 10
Knebworth	d			13 44					14 44						15 44					16 44					
Welwyn North	d			13 47					14 47						15 47					16 47					
Welwyn Garden City 4	d			13 52	13 58		14 28		14 52	14 58		15 28			15 52	15 58		16 28		16 52	16 58			17 28	
Hatfield	d			13 56	14 03		14 33		14 56	15 03		15 33			15 56	16 03		16 33		16 56	17 03			17 33	
Welham Green	d				14 07		14 37			15 07		15 37				16 07		16 37			17 07			17 37	
Brookmans Park	d				14 09		14 39			15 09		15 39				16 09		16 39			17 09			17 39	
Potters Bar	d			14 02	14 13		14 43		15 02	15 13		15 43			16 02	16 13		16 43		17 02	17 13			17 43	
Hadley Wood	d				14 16		14 46			15 16		15 46				16 16		16 46			17 16			17 46	
New Barnet	d				14 19		14 49			15 19		15 49				16 19		16 49			17 19			17 49	
Oakleigh Park	d				14 21		14 51			15 21		15 51				16 21		16 51			17 21			17 51	
New Southgate	a				14 24		14 54			15 24		15 54				16 24		16 54			17 24			17 54	
Alexandra Palace	d	14 13			14 28	14 43	14 58	15 13		15 28	15 43	15 58		16 13		16 28	16 43	16 58	17 13		17 28	17 43		17 58	18 13
Hornsey	d	14 16			14 31	14 46	15 01	15 16		15 31	15 46	16 01		16 16		16 31	16 46	17 01	17 16		17 31	17 46		18 01	18 16
Harringay	d	14 18			14 33	14 48	15 03	15 18		15 33	15 48	16 03		16 18		16 33	16 48	17 03	17 18		17 33	17 48		18 03	18 18
Finsbury Park ⊖	a	14 20		14 12	14 35	14 50	15 05	15 20	15 12	15 35	15 50	16 05		16 20	16 12	16 35	16 50	17 05	17 20	17 12	17 35	17 50		18 05	18 20
Finsbury Park	d																								
Drayton Park	d																								
Highbury & Islington ⊖	d																								
Essex Road	d																								
Old Street ⊖	d																								
Moorgate ⊖	a																								
Finsbury Park	d	14 21		14 13	14 36	14 51	15 06	15 21	15 13	15 36	15 51	16 06		16 21	16 13	16 36	16 51	17 06	17 21	17 13	17 36	17 51		18 06	18 21
London Kings Cross 15 ⊖	a	14 28		14 19	14 43	14 58	15 12	15 28	15 20	15 42	15 58	16 12		16 28	16 19	16 42	16 58	17 12	17 29	17 19	17 43	17 58		18 12	18 29
St Pancras International	d																								
Farringdon	d																								
City Thameslink	d																								
London Blackfriars	a																								
London Bridge	a																								

		TL 1	GN	GN	GN	GN	TL 1	GN		GN	GN	GN	TL 1	GN	GN	GN	GN	TL 1		GN	GN	GN	GN	TL 1	GN
Stevenage	d	17 40		17 58		18 28	18 40			18 58		19 28	19 40		19 58		20 28	20 40			20 58		21 28	21 40	
Watton-at-Stone	d			18 05		18 35				19 05		19 35			20 05		20 35				21 05		21 35		
Hertford North	d			18 13		18 43				19 13		19 43			20 13		20 43				21 13		21 43		
Bayford	d			18 17		18 47				19 17		19 47			20 17		20 47				21 17		21 47		
Cuffley	d			18 22		18 52				19 22		19 52			20 22		20 52				21 22		21 52		
Crews Hill	d			18 25		18 55				19 25		19 55			20 25		20 55				21 25		21 55		
Gordon Hill	d			18 28		18 58				19 28		19 58			20 28		20 58				21 28		21 58		
Enfield Chase	d			18 31		19 01				19 31		20 01			20 31		21 01				21 31		22 01		
Grange Park	d			18 33		19 03				19 33		20 03			20 33		21 03				21 33		22 03		
Winchmore Hill	d			18 35		19 05				19 35		20 05			20 35		21 05				21 35		22 05		
Palmers Green	d			18 38		19 08				19 38		20 08			20 38		21 08				21 38		22 08		
Bowes Park	a			18 40		19 10				19 40		20 10			20 40		21 10				21 40		22 10		
Knebworth	d	17 44					18 44						19 44					20 44						21 44	
Welwyn North	d	17 47					18 47						19 47					20 48						21 48	
Welwyn Garden City 4	d	17 52	17 58		18 28		18 52	18 58			19 28		19 52	19 58		20 28		20 52		20 58		21 28		21 52	21 58
Hatfield	d	17 56	18 03		18 33		18 56	19 03			19 33		19 56	20 03		20 33		20 56		21 03		21 33		21 56	22 03
Welham Green	d		18 07		18 37			19 07			19 37			20 07		20 37				21 07		21 37			22 07
Brookmans Park	d		18 09		18 39			19 09			19 39			20 09		20 39				21 09		21 39			22 09
Potters Bar	d	18 02	18 13		18 43		19 02	19 13			19 43		20 02	20 13		20 43		21 02		21 13		21 43		22 02	22 13
Hadley Wood	d		18 16		18 46			19 16			19 46			20 16		20 46				21 16		21 46			22 16
New Barnet	d		18 19		18 49			19 19			19 49			20 19		20 49				21 19		21 49			22 19
Oakleigh Park	d		18 21		18 51			19 21			19 51			20 21		20 51				21 21		21 51			22 21
New Southgate	a		18 24		18 54			19 24			19 54			20 24		20 54				21 24		21 54			22 24
Alexandra Palace	d		18 28	18 43	18 58	19 13		19 28		19 43	19 58	20 13		20 28	20 43	20 58	21 13			21 28	21 43	21 58	22 13		22 28
Hornsey	d		18 31	18 46	19 01	19 16		19 31		19 46	20 01	20 16		20 31	20 46	21 01	21 16			21 31	21 46	22 01	22 16		22 31
Harringay	d		18 33	18 48	19 03	19 18		19 33		19 48	20 03	20 18		20 33	20 48	21 03	21 18			21 33	21 48	22 03	22 18		22 33
Finsbury Park ⊖	a	18 12	18 35	18 50	19 05	19 20	19 12	19 35		19 50	20 05	20 20	20 12	20 35	20 50	21 05	21 20	21 12		21 35	21 50	22 05	22 20	22 13	22 35
Finsbury Park	d																								
Drayton Park	d																								
Highbury & Islington ⊖	d																								
Essex Road	d																								
Old Street ⊖	d																								
Moorgate ⊖	a																								
Finsbury Park	d	18 13	18 36	18 51	19 06	19 21	19 13	19 36		19 51	20 06	20 21	20 13	20 36	20 51	21 06	21 21	21 13		21 36	21 51	22 06	22 21	22 13	22 36
London Kings Cross 15 ⊖	a	18 19	18 42	18 58	19 12	19 28	19 19	19 43		19 58	20 12	20 28	20 19	20 43	20 58	21 12	21 28	21 19		21 43	21 58	22 13	22 28	22 21	22 43
St Pancras International	d																								
Farringdon	d																								
City Thameslink	d																								
London Blackfriars	a																								
London Bridge	a																								

See Table 025 for fast trains between London and Stevenage

Table T024-R

Sundays

23 February to 10 May

Hertford North and Welwyn Garden City - London

		GN	GN	GN		TL 1	GN	GN	GN	GN
Stevenage	d	21 58		22 28		22 40		22 58		23 28
Watton-at-Stone	d	22 05		22 35				23 05		23 35
Hertford North	d	22 13		22 43				23 13		23 43
Bayford	d	22 17		22 47				23 17		23 47
Cuffley	d	22 22		22 52				23 22		23 52
Crews Hill	d	22 25		22 55				23 25		23 55
Gordon Hill	d	22 28		22 58				23 28		23 58
Enfield Chase	d	22 31		23 01				23 31		00 02
Grange Park	d	22 33		23 03				23 33		00 04
Winchmore Hill	d	22 35		23 05				23 35		00 06
Palmers Green	d	22 38		23 08				23 38		00 09
Bowes Park	a	22 40		23 10				23 40		00 11
Knebworth	d					22 44				
Welwyn North	d					22 48				
Welwyn Garden City 4	d		22 28			22 52	22 58		23 28	
Hatfield	d		22 33			22 56	23 03		23 33	
Welham Green	d		22 37				23 07		23 37	
Brookmans Park	d		22 39				23 09		23 39	
Potters Bar	d		22 43			23 02	23 13		23 43	
Hadley Wood	d		22 46				23 16		23 46	
New Barnet	d		22 49				23 19		23 49	
Oakleigh Park	d		22 51				23 21		23 51	
New Southgate	a		22 54				23 24		23 54	
Alexandra Palace	d	22 43	22 58	23 13			23 28	23 43	23 58	00 14
Hornsey	d	22 46	23 01	23 16			23 31	23 46	00 01	00 17
Harringay	d	22 48	23 03	23 18			23 33	23 48	00 03	00 19
Finsbury Park ⊖	a	22 50	23 05	23 20		23 13	23 35	23 50	00 06	00 24
Finsbury Park	d									
Drayton Park	d									
Highbury & Islington ⊖	d									
Essex Road	d									
Old Street ⊖	d									
Moorgate ⊖	a									
Finsbury Park	d	22 51	23 06	23 21		23 13	23 36	23 51	00 07	00 25
London Kings Cross 15 ⊖	a	22 58	23 12	23 27		23 21	23 42	23 59	00 13	00 31
St Pancras International	d									
Farringdon	d									
City Thameslink	d									
London Blackfriars	a									
London Bridge	a									

See Table 025 for fast trains between London and Stevenage

Table T025-F

Mondays to Fridays

16 December to 15 May

Brighton, Gatwick Airport, Maidstone East and London - Stevenage, Cambridge, Kings Lynn and Peterborough

Miles	Miles			GN MX 1	TL MX 1	TL MO 1	GN MX 1	GN MO 1	GN MX 1	TL MO 1	GN MX 1	TL MX 1		TL MX 1	TL MX 1	TL MX 1	TL MO 1	TL MX 1	GN MX 1	TL MX 1	TL MO 1	TL MX 1		GN 1	GN MO 1
—	—	Brighton	d																						
—	—	Gatwick Airport	d																						
—	—	East Croydon	d																				00 09			
—	—	Maidstone East	d																						
—	—	**London Bridge**	d																						
—	—	London Blackfriars	d																				00 37			
—	—	City Thameslink	d																						
—	—	Farringdon	d																				00 41			
—	—	St Pancras International	d																				00 46			
0	0	London Kings Cross 15 ⊖	d														00 02	00 23	00 32		00 32				01 02
2½	2½	Finsbury Park ⊖	d													00 02	00 09	00 29	00 39	←	00 39	00 54			01 09
12¾	12¾	Potters Bar	d													00 17	00 20	00 42		00 42	00 50				
17¾	17¾	Hatfield	d													00 23	00 26	→		00 48	00 56				
20¼	20¼	Welwyn Garden City 4	d													00 28	00 31			00 58	01 01	01 15			
22	22	**Welwyn North**	d											00 01		00 31	00 35			01 01	01s04				
25	25	**Knebworth**	d											00 05		00 35	00 39			01 05	01s08				
27½	27½	**Stevenage 4**	d									00 03		00 09	00 14	00 40	00 44		01 04	01 10	01 13	01 24			01 46
31¾	31¾	**Hitchin 3**	d									00 08		00 14	00 22	00 48	00 52		01 13	01 18	01 23	01 32			→
34¾	—	**Letchworth Garden City**	d								00 10	00 14		00 20		00 54	00 58		01s18	01 24					
36¾	—	**Baldock**	d									00 17		00 23		00 57	01 01		01s21	01 27					
41	—	**Ashwell & Morden**	d							00 04				00 27		01 01	01 06			01 31					
45	—	**Royston**	d							00 09	00 19	00 25		00 32		01 06	01 11		01s29	01a37					
48	—	**Meldreth**	d							00 13				00 36		01 10	01 15								
50	—	**Shepreth**	d							00 16				00 39		01 13	01 18								
51	—	**Foxton**	d							00 19				00 41		01 15	01 21								
58	—	Cambridge	a							00 30	00 35	00 41		00 54		01 25	01 32		01 44						
—	—	Cambridge	d					00 04	00 08															06 14	
60¼	—	Cambridge North	d					00 08	00 13															06 18	
63¼	—	Waterbeach	d					00 12	00 17															06 22	
72¾	—	Ely	d					00 22	00 27															06 33	
78¼	—	**Littleport**	d				00 06	00 29	00 34															06 41	
88½	—	**Downham Market**	d				00 15	00 38	00 43															06 50	
93¼	—	**Watlington**	d				00 21	00 44	00 49															06 56	
99¼	—	**Kings Lynn**	a				00 29	00 52	00 57															07 04	
—	37	**Arlesey**	d			00 01									00 27						01s28	01 37			
—	41	**Biggleswade**	d		00 01	00 06									00 32						01s33	01 43			
—	44	**Sandy**	d		00 05	00 10									00 36						01s37	01 46			
—	51½	**St Neots**	d		00 12	00 17									00 43						01s45	01 54			
—	58¾	**Huntingdon**	d	00 04	00 20	00 24									00 51						01s56	02 01			
—	76¼	Peterborough 8	a	00 22	00 37	00 42									01 09						02 12	02 19			

		TL MX 1	GN MO 1	TL MO 1	TL MX 1	TL MO 1	TL 1	TL 1		TL 1	TL 1	GN 1	TL 1	GN 1	TL 1	GR 1	TL 1	TL 1		GR 1	TL 1	TL 1	TL 1	GR 1	GN 1
Brighton	d																								
Gatwick Airport	d																								
East Croydon	d																								
Maidstone East	d																								
London Bridge	d																								
London Blackfriars	d																								
City Thameslink	d																								
Farringdon	d																								
St Pancras International	d																								
London Kings Cross 15 ⊖	d	01 05		01 32	01 36		05 03	05 18		05 25	05 33	05 42			05 48	05 55	05 56	06 03		06 15		06 18	06 21	06 33	06 42
Finsbury Park ⊖	d	01 11		01 39	01 44	←	05 09	05 24		05 33	05 42		←		05 54		06 02	06 11			←	06 24	06 30		
Potters Bar	d	01 22		01 58		01 58				05 45			05 45				06 13				06 13		06 42		
Hatfield	d	01 28		→		02 04				→			05 51				→				06 19		→		
Welwyn Garden City 4	d	01 34				02 09							05 56								06 24				
Welwyn North	d	01 37				02s12							06 00								06 27				
Knebworth	d	01 41	←			02s16							06 04								06 31				
Stevenage 4	d	01 46	01 46		02 12	02 21	05 34	05 49			06 03		06 08		06 14	06 17		06 32		06 37	06 38	06 44		06 55	
Hitchin 3	d	01 54	01 56		02 20	02 31	05 42	05 58			06 08		06 14		06 20			06 38			06 44	06 50			
Letchworth Garden City	d	02 00	02s01				05 48				06 14		06 22					06 44			06 49				
Baldock	d	02 03	02s04				05 51				06 17		06 25					06 47			06 53				
Ashwell & Morden	d	02 07	02s09										06 30					06 52			06 57				
Royston	d	02a13	02a15				05 59				06 25		06 36					06 57			07 02				
Meldreth	d												06 40								07 06				
Shepreth	d												06 43								07 09				
Foxton	d												06 45								07 11				
Cambridge	a						06 14				06 41	06 30	06 57					07 13			07 23				07 30
Cambridge	d											06 35		07 10											07 35
Cambridge North	d											06 39		07 14											07 39
Waterbeach	d											06 44		07 18											07 44
Ely	d											06 54		07 28											08 02
Littleport	d											07 01		07 36											08 11
Downham Market	d											07 17		07 49											08 21
Watlington	d											07 23		07 55											08 27
Kings Lynn	a											07 32		08 04											08 35
Arlesey	d				02 25			06 03							06 25							06 55			
Biggleswade	d				02 31	02s39		06 08							06 30							07 00			
Sandy	d				02 34			06 12							06 34							07 04			
St Neots	d				02 42	02s49		06 19							06 41							07 11			
Huntingdon	d				02 49	03s00		06 27							06 49							07 19			
Peterborough 8	a				03 07	03 16		06 42							07 09	06 46				07 06		07 34		07 24	

Please refer to Table T024 for the service from Moorgate to Stevenage via Hertford North

Table T025-F

Mondays to Fridays

16 December to 15 May

Brighton, Gatwick Airport, Maidstone East and London - Stevenage, Cambridge, Kings Lynn and Peterborough

		TL	TL	TL	TL	TL	GR	GN	TL	TL	TL	TL	TL	TL	GN	TL	TL	TL	TL	GN	TL	TL
Brighton	d	05 06							05 38					06 05							06 37	
Gatwick Airport	d	05 46		05 49	06 13				06 16		←	06 43		06 46			←	07 13			07 16	
East Croydon	d	06 01		06 16	06 46				06 31		06 46	07 16		07 01			07 16	07 46			07 31	
Maidstone East	d				↦							↦						↦				
London Bridge	d	06 16		06 31					06 46		07 01			07 16			07 31				07 46	
London Blackfriars	d	06 22		06 37					06 52		07 07			07 22			07 37				07 52	
City Thameslink	d	06 24		06 39					06 54		07 09			07 24			07 39				07 54	
Farringdon	d	06 26		06 41					06 56		07 11			07 26			07 41				07 56	
St Pancras International	d	06 31		06 46					07 01		07 16			07 31			07 46				08 01	
London Kings Cross ⊖	d					06 51	07 06	07 12					07 21		07 42				07 51	08 12		
Finsbury Park ⊖	d	06 42	←	06 54		07 01			07 12	←	07 24		07 31	07 42		←	07 54		08 01		08 12	←
Potters Bar	d		06 42			07 13				07 13			07 43			07 43			08 13			08 13
Hatfield	d		06 48			↦				07 18			↦			07 48			↦			08 18
Welwyn Garden City	d		06 56							07 26						07 56						08 26
Welwyn North	d		07 00							07 30						08 00						08 30
Knebworth	d		07 04							07 34						08 04						08 34
Stevenage	d	07 03	07 08	07 14			07 28		07 33	07 38	07 44			08 02		08 08	08 14				08 33	08 38
Hitchin	d	07 08	07 14	07 20					07 38	07 44	07 50			08 07		08 14	08 20				08 38	08 44
Letchworth Garden City	d	07 14	07 19						07 44	07 49				08 13		08 19					08 44	08 49
Baldock	d	07 17	07 23						07 47	07 53				08 16		08 22					08 47	08 53
Ashwell & Morden	d		07 27						07 52	07 57						08 27					08 52	08 57
Royston	d	07 25	07 32					07 48	07 57	08 02				08a24		08 32					08 57	09 02
Meldreth	d		07 36							08 06						08 36						09 06
Shepreth	d		07 39							08 09						08 39						09 09
Foxton	d		07 41							08 11						08 41						09 11
Cambridge	a	07 43	07 51					08 04	08 12	08 21					08 30	08 51				09 01	09 11	09 21
Cambridge	d							08 12							08 35					09 06		
Cambridge North	d							08 18							08 39					09 10		
Waterbeach	d							08 22							08 44							
Ely	d							08 32							08 55					09a22		
Littleport	d							08 39							09 03							
Downham Market	d							08 48							09 19							
Watlington	d							08 54							09 25							
Kings Lynn	a							09 02							09 34							
Arlesey	d			07 25							07 55						08 25					
Biggleswade	d			07 30							08 00						08 30					
Sandy	d			07 34							08 04						08 34					
St Neots	d			07 41							08 11						08 41					
Huntingdon	d			07 49							08 19						08 49					
Peterborough	a			08 06			07 57				08 40						09 05					

		TL	TL	TL	GN	TL	TL	TL	TL	TL	GR	GN	TL	TL	TL	TL	TL	GN	TL	TL	TL	TL	GR
Brighton	d					07 07							07 37						08 07				
Gatwick Airport	d	←	07 43			07 46		←	08 13				08 16		←	08 43			08 46		←		
East Croydon	d	07 46	08 16			08 01		08 16	08 46				08 31		08 46	09 16			09 01		09 16		
Maidstone East	d		↦						↦							↦							
London Bridge	d	08 01				08 16		08 31					08 46		09 01				09 16		09 31		
London Blackfriars	d	08 07				08 22		08 37					08 52		09 07				09 22		09 37		
City Thameslink	d	08 09				08 24		08 39					08 54		09 09				09 24		09 39		
Farringdon	d	08 11				08 26		08 41					08 56		09 11				09 26		09 41		
St Pancras International	d	08 16				08 31		08 46					09 01		09 16				09 31		09 46		
London Kings Cross ⊖	d			08 21	08 42					08 51	09 06	09 12					09 21	09 42				09 51	10 06
Finsbury Park ⊖	d	08 24		08 31		08 42	←	08 54		09 01			09 12	←	09 24		09 31		09 42	←	09 54	10 00	
Potters Bar	d			08 43			08 43			09 13				09 13			09 43			09 43		10 13	
Hatfield	d			↦			08 48			↦				09 18			↦			09 48		↦	
Welwyn Garden City	d						08 56							09 26						09 56			
Welwyn North	d						09 00							09 30						10 00			
Knebworth	d						09 04							09 34						10 04			
Stevenage	d	08 44				09 03	09 08	09 14			09 28		09 33	09 38	09 44				10 03	10 08	10 14		10 28
Hitchin	d	08 50				09 08	09 14	09 20					09 38	09 44	09 50				10 08	10 14	10 20		
Letchworth Garden City	d					09 14	09 19						09 44	09 49					10 14	10 19			
Baldock	d					09 17	09 23						09 47	09 53					10 17	10 23			
Ashwell & Morden	d						09 27						09 52	09 57						10 27			
Royston	d					09 25	09 32					09 48	09 57	10 02					10 25	10 32			
Meldreth	d						09 36							10 06						10 36			
Shepreth	d						09 39							10 09						10 39			
Foxton	d						09 41							10 11						10 41			
Cambridge	a				09 30	09 42	09 51					10 03	10 12	10 21				10 30	10 40	10 54			
Cambridge	d				09 35							10 05						10 36					
Cambridge North	d				09 39							10 09						10 40					
Waterbeach	d				09 44													10 44					
Ely	d				09 56							10a24						10 55					
Littleport	d				10 04													11 04					
Downham Market	d				10 17													11 17					
Watlington	d				10 23													11 23					
Kings Lynn	a				10 31													11 31					
Arlesey	d	08 55						09 25							09 55						10 25		
Biggleswade	d	09 00						09 30							10 00						10 30		
Sandy	d	09 04						09 34							10 04						10 34		
St Neots	d	09 11						09 41							10 11						10 41		
Huntingdon	d	09 19						09 49							10 19						10 49		
Peterborough	a	09 35						10 05			09 57				10 40						11 05		10 57

Please refer to Table T024 for the service from Moorgate to Stevenage via Hertford North

NRT DECEMBER 19 EDITION

Table T025-F

Mondays to Fridays

16 December to 15 May

Brighton, Gatwick Airport, Maidstone East and London - Stevenage, Cambridge, Kings Lynn and Peterborough

		GN	TL	TL	TL	TL	GN	TL	TL	TL	TL	GR	GN	TL	TL	TL	TL	GN	TL	TL	TL	TL	GR
Brighton	d		08 37					09 08						09 38					10 08				
Gatwick Airport	d		09 16		09 19			09 46		09 49				10 17		10 19			10 46		10 49		
East Croydon	d		09 31		09 45			10 01		10 15				10 32		10 45			11 01		11 15		
Maidstone East	d																						
London Bridge	d		09 46		10 01			10 16		10 31				10 46		11 01			11 16		11 31		
London Blackfriars	d		09 52		10 07			10 22		10 37				10 52		11 07			11 22		11 37		
City Thameslink	d		09 54		10 09			10 24		10 39				10 54		11 09			11 24		11 39		
Farringdon	d		09 56		10 11			10 26		10 41				10 56		11 11			11 26		11 41		
St Pancras International	d		10 01		10 16			10 31		10 46				11 01		11 16			11 31		11 46		
London Kings Cross ⊖	d	10 12				10 21	10 42				10 51	11 06	11 12				11 21	11 42				11 51	12 06
Finsbury Park ⊖	d		10 12	←	10 24	10 31		10 42	←	10 54	11 01			11 12	←	11 24	11 31		11 42	←	11 54	12 01	
Potters Bar	d			10 13		10 43			10 43		11 13				11 13		11 43			11 43		12 13	
Hatfield	d			10 18		↦			10 48		↦				11 18		↦			11 48		↦	
Welwyn Garden City	d			10 26					10 56						11 26					11 56			
Welwyn North	d			10 30					11 01						11 30					12 00			
Knebworth	d			10 34					11 05						11 34					12 04			
Stevenage	d		10 33	10 38	10 44			11 03	11 10	11 14		11 28		11 33	11 38	11 44			12 03	12 08	12 14		12 28
Hitchin	d		10 38	10 44	10 50			11 08	11 18	11 20				11 38	11 44	11 50			12 08	12 14	12 20		
Letchworth Garden City	d		10 44	10 49				11 14	11a24					11 44	11 50				12 14	12 19			
Baldock	d		10 47	10 53				11 17						11 47	11 53				12 17	12 23			
Ashwell & Morden	d		10 52	10 57										11 52	11 57					12 27			
Royston	d		10 57	11 02				11 25						11 57	12 02				12 25	12 32			
Meldreth	d			11 06											12 06					12 36			
Shepreth	d			11 09											12 09					12 39			
Foxton	d			11 11											12 11					12 44			
Cambridge	a	11 00	11 11	11 22			11 32	11 40					12 01	12 11	12 22			12 31	12 40	12 54			
Cambridge	d	11 04					11 37						12 04					12 36					
Cambridge North	d	11 08					11 40						12 08					12 40					
Waterbeach	d						11 45											12 44					
Ely	d	11a23					11 56						12a23					12 55					
Littleport	d						12 04											13 04					
Downham Market	d						12 17											13 17					
Watlington	d						12 23											13 23					
Kings Lynn	a						12 31											13 31					
Arlesey	d				10 55					11 25						11 55					12 25		
Biggleswade	d				11 00					11 30						12 00					12 30		
Sandy	d				11 04					11 34						12 04					12 34		
St Neots	d				11 11					11 41						12 11					12 41		
Huntingdon	d				11 19					11 49						12 19					12 49		
Peterborough	a				11 39					12 05		11 57				12 39					13 05		12 58

		GN	TL	TL	TL	TL	GN	TL	TL	TL	TL	GR	GN	TL	TL	TL	TL	GN	TL	TL	TL	TL
Brighton	d		10 38					11 08						11 38					12 08			
Gatwick Airport	d		11 16		11 19			11 46		11 49				12 16		12 19			12 46		12 49	
East Croydon	d		11 31		11 45			12 01		12 15				12 31		12 45			13 01		13 15	
Maidstone East	d																					
London Bridge	d		11 46		12 01			12 16		12 31				12 46		13 01			13 16		13 31	
London Blackfriars	d		11 52		12 07			12 22		12 37				12 52		13 07			13 22		13 37	
City Thameslink	d		11 54		12 09			12 24		12 39				12 54		13 09			13 24		13 39	
Farringdon	d		11 56		12 11			12 26		12 41				12 56		13 11			13 26		13 41	
St Pancras International	d		12 01		12 16			12 31		12 46				13 01		13 16			13 31		13 46	
London Kings Cross ⊖	d	12 12				12 21	12 42				12 51	13 06	13 12				13 21	13 42				13 51
Finsbury Park ⊖	d		12 12	←	12 24	12 31		12 42	←	12 54	13 01			13 12	←	13 24	13 31		13 42	←	13 54	14 01
Potters Bar	d			12 13		12 43			12 43		13 13				13 13		13 43			13 43		14 13
Hatfield	d			12 18		↦			12 48		↦				13 18		↦			13 48		↦
Welwyn Garden City	d			12 26					12 56						13 26					13 56		
Welwyn North	d			12 30					13 00						13 30					14 00		
Knebworth	d			12 34					13 04						13 34					14 04		
Stevenage	d		12 33	12 38	12 44			13 03	13 08	13 14		13 28		13 33	13 38	13 44			14 03	14 10	14 14	
Hitchin	d		12 38	12 44	12 50			13 08	13 14	13 20				13 38	13 44	13 50			14 08	14 16	14 20	
Letchworth Garden City	d		12 44	12 49				13 14	13 19					13 44	13 49				14 14	14 21		
Baldock	d		12 47	12 53				13 17	13 23					13 47	13 53				14 17	14 25		
Ashwell & Morden	d		12 52	12 57					13 27					13 52	13 57					14 29		
Royston	d		12 57	13 02				13 25	13 32					13 57	14 02				14 25	14 34		
Meldreth	d			13 06					13 36						14 06					14 38		
Shepreth	d			13 09					13 39						14 09					14 41		
Foxton	d			13 11					13 41						14 11					14 43		
Cambridge	a	13 00	13 11	13 22			13 30	13 40	13 54				14 00	14 11	14 22			14 30	14 40	14 54		
Cambridge	d	13 04					13 36						14 04					14 36				
Cambridge North	d	13 08					13 40						14 08					14 40				
Waterbeach	d						13 45											14 44				
Ely	d	13a23					13 56						14a23					14 55				
Littleport	d						14 05											15 04				
Downham Market	d						14 17											15 17				
Watlington	d						14 23											15 23				
Kings Lynn	a						14 31											15 31				
Arlesey	d				12 55					13 25						13 55					14 25	
Biggleswade	d				13 00					13 30						14 00					14 30	
Sandy	d				13 04					13 34						14 04					14 34	
St Neots	d				13 11					13 41						14 11					14 41	
Huntingdon	d				13 19					13 49						14 19					14 49	
Peterborough	a				13 39					14 05		13 59				14 39					15 07	

Please refer to Table T024 for the service from Moorgate to Stevenage via Hertford North

Table T025-F

Mondays to Fridays

16 December to 15 May

Brighton, Gatwick Airport, Maidstone East and London - Stevenage, Cambridge, Kings Lynn and Peterborough

		GR	GN	TL	TL	GN	TL	TL	GN	TL	TL	TL	TL	GR	GN	TL	GN	TL	TL	TL	GN	TL	TL
Brighton	d			12 38						13 08						13 38						14 08	
Gatwick Airport	d			13 16			13 19			13 46		13 49				14 16			14 19			14 46	
East Croydon	d			13 31			13 45			14 01		14 15				14 31			14 45			15 01	
Maidstone East	d																						
London Bridge	d			13 46			14 01			14 16		14 31				14 46			15 01			15 16	
London Blackfriars	d			13 52			14 07			14 22		14 37				14 52			15 07			15 22	
City Thameslink	d			13 54			14 09			14 24		14 39				14 54			15 09			15 24	
Farringdon	d			13 56			14 11			14 26		14 41				14 56			15 11			15 26	
St Pancras International	d			14 01			14 16			14 31		14 46				15 01			15 16			15 31	
London Kings Cross	d	14 06	14 12					14 21	14 42				14 51	15 06	15 12					15 21	15 42		
Finsbury Park	d			14 12	←		14 24	14 31		14 42	←	14 54	15 01			15 12		←	15 24	15 31		15 42	←
Potters Bar	d				14 13			14 43			14 43		15 13					15 13		15 43			15 43
Hatfield	d				14 18			→			14 48		→					15 18		→			15 48
Welwyn Garden City	d				14 26						14 56							15 26					15 56
Welwyn North	d				14 30						15 00							15 30					16 00
Knebworth	d				14 34						15 04							15 34					16 04
Stevenage	d	14 28		14 33	14 38		14 44			15 03	15 08	15 14		15 28		15 33		15 38	15 44			16 03	16 08
Hitchin	d			14 38	14 44		14 50			15 08	15 14	15 20				15 38		15 44	15 50			16 08	16 14
Letchworth Garden City	d			14 44	14 49					15 14	15 19					15 44		15 49				16 14	16 19
Baldock	d			14 47	14 53					15 17	15 23					15 47		15 53				16 17	16 23
Ashwell & Morden	d			14 52	14 57						15 27					15 52		15 57					16 27
Royston	d			14 57	15 02					15 25	15 32					15 57		16 02				16 25	16 32
Meldreth	d				15 06						15 36							16 06					16 36
Shepreth	d				15 09						15 39							16 09					16 39
Foxton	d				15 11						15 41							16 11					16 41
Cambridge	a		15 00	15 11	15 22				15 30	15 40	15 54				16 02	16 11		16 23			16 30	16 40	16 54
Cambridge	d		15 04			15 30			15 35						16 04		16 20				16 36		
Cambridge North	d		15 08			15 34			15 39						16 08						16 40		
Waterbeach	d					15 39			15 43								16 27				16 44		
Ely	d		15a23			15a49			15 55						16a23		16 37				16 55		
Littleport	d								16 04								16 44				17 04		
Downham Market	d								16 17								16 53				17 17		
Watlington	d								16 23								16 59				17 23		
Kings Lynn	a								16 31								17 07				17 31		
Arlesey	d						14 55					15 25							15 55				
Biggleswade	d						15 00					15 30							16 00				
Sandy	d						15 04					15 34							16 04				
St Neots	d						15 11					15 42							16 11				
Huntingdon	d						15 19					15 48							16 19				
Peterborough	a	14 57					15 39					16 05		15 57					16 39				

		TL	TL	GR	GN	TL	TL	TL	TL	GN		TL	GN	TL	TL	TL	GN	GN	TL	GN	TL	TL
Brighton	d					14 38						15 08							15 38			
Gatwick Airport	d	14 49				15 16		15 19				15 46			15 49				16 16			16 19
East Croydon	d	15 15				15 31		15 45				16 01			16 15				16 31			16 45
Maidstone East	d																					
London Bridge	d	15 31				15 46		16 01				16 16			16 31				16 46			17 01
London Blackfriars	d	15 37				15 52		16 07				16 22			16 37				16 52			17 07
City Thameslink	d	15 39				15 54		16 09				16 24			16 39				16 54			17 09
Farringdon	d	15 41				15 56		16 11				16 26			16 41				16 56			17 11
St Pancras International	d	15 46				16 01		16 16				16 31			16 46				17 01			17 16
London Kings Cross	d		15 51	16 06	16 12				16 21	16 39			16 42			16 51	16 54	17 09		17 12		
Finsbury Park	d	15 54	16 01			16 12	←	16 24	16 31			16 39		←	16 54	17 01			17 09		←	17 24
Potters Bar	d		16 13				16 13		16 43					16 43		17 13					17 13	
Hatfield	d		→				16 18		→					16 51		→					17 21	
Welwyn Garden City	d						16 26							16 56							17 26	
Welwyn North	d						16 30							17 00			17 11				17 30	
Knebworth	d						16 34							17 04			17 16				17 34	
Stevenage	d	16 14		16 28		16 33	16 38	16 44				17 00	17 05	17 10	17 14				17 30	17 35	17 40	17 44
Hitchin	d	16 20				16 38	16 44	16 50				17 06		17 15	17 20		17 25		17 36		17 45	17 50
Letchworth Garden City	d				16 40	16 44	16 49			17 08		17 12		17 21			17 31	17 38	17 42		17 51	
Baldock	d					16 47	16 53					17 15		17 24			17a35		17 45		17 54	
Ashwell & Morden	d					16 52	16 57					17 20		17 29					17 50		17 59	
Royston	d				16 50	16 57	17 02			17 18		17 25		17 34				17 48	17 55		18 04	
Meldreth	d						17 06							17 37							18 07	
Shepreth	d						17 09							17 40							18 10	
Foxton	d						17 11							17 42							18 12	
Cambridge	a				17 04	17 11	17 24			17 33		17 40		17 54				18 05	18 12		18 23	
Cambridge	d				17 06					17 38	17 44							18 07				
Cambridge North	d				17 10					17 43	17 49							18 11				
Waterbeach	d									17 48	17 53											
Ely	d				17a23					17 59	18a05							18a24				
Littleport	d									18 08												
Downham Market	d									18 17												
Watlington	d									18 23												
Kings Lynn	a									18 31												
Arlesey	d	16 25						16 55							17 25							17 55
Biggleswade	d	16 30						17 00					17 18		17 30					17 48		18 00
Sandy	d	16 34						17 04							17 34							18 03
St Neots	d	16 41						17 11					17 28		17 41					17 58		18 11
Huntingdon	d	16 49						17 19					17 36		17 49					18 06		18 18
Peterborough	a	17 05		16 57				17 35					17 53		18 05					18 22		18 34

Please refer to Table T024 for the service from Moorgate to Stevenage via Hertford North

Table T025-F

Mondays to Fridays

16 December to 15 May

Brighton, Gatwick Airport, Maidstone East and London - Stevenage, Cambridge, Kings Lynn and Peterborough

		TL	GN	GN		TL	GN	TL	TL	TL	GN	GN	TL	GN	TL	TL	TL	GN	GN	TL	GN	TL	TL
Brighton	d					16 08							16 38							17 08			
Gatwick Airport	d					16 46			16 49				17 16			17 19				17 46			17 49
East Croydon	d					17 01			17 15				17 31			17 45				18 01			18 15
Maidstone East	d																						
London Bridge	d					17 16			17 31				17 46			18 01				18 16			18 31
London Blackfriars	d					17 22			17 37				17 52			18 07				18 22			18 37
City Thameslink	d					17 24			17 39				17 54			18 09				18 24			18 39
Farringdon	d					17 26			17 41				17 56			18 11				18 26			18 41
St Pancras International	d					17 31			17 46				18 01			18 16				18 31			18 46
London Kings Cross	d	17 21	17 24	17 39			17 42			17 51	17 54	18 09		18 12			18 21	18 24	18 39		18 42		
Finsbury Park	d	17 31				17 39		←	17 54	18 01			18 09		←	18 24	18 31			18 39		←	18 54
Potters Bar	d	17 43						17 43		18 13					18 13		18 43					18 43	
Hatfield	d	→						17 51		→					18 21		→					18 51	
Welwyn Garden City	d							17 56							18 26							18 56	
Welwyn North	d		17 41					18 00			18 11				18 30			18 41				19 00	
Knebworth	d		17 46					18 04			18 16				18 34			18 46				19 04	
Stevenage	d					18 00	18 05	18 10	18 14				18 30	18 35	18 40	18 44				19 00	19 05	19 10	19 14
Hitchin	d		17 55			18 06		18 15	18 20		18 25		18 36		18 45	18 50		18 55		19 06		19 15	19 20
Letchworth Garden City	d		18 01	18 08		18 12		18 21			18 31	18 38	18 42		18 51			19 01	19 07	19 12		19 21	
Baldock	d		18a05			18 15		18 24			18a35		18 45		18 54			19a05		19 15		19 24	
Ashwell & Morden	d					18 20		18 29					18 50		18 59					19 20		19 29	
Royston	d			18 17		18 25		18 34				18 48	18 55		19 04				19 17	19 25		19 34	
Meldreth	d							18 37							19 07							19 37	
Shepreth	d							18 40							19 10							19 40	
Foxton	d							18 42							19 12							19 42	
Cambridge	a			18 32		18 43		18 53				19 03	19 10		19 23				19 32	19 42		19 53	
Cambridge	d			18 37	18 44							19 08							19 41				
Cambridge North	d			18 41	18 48							19 12							19 45				
Waterbeach	d			18 46															19 50				
Ely	d			18 56	19a03							19 31							20 02				
Littleport	d			19 04															20 09				
Downham Market	d			19 13								19 47							20 19				
Watlington	d			19 19								19 53							20 25				
Kings Lynn	a			19 28								20 01							20 33				
Arlesey	d								18 25							18 55							19 25
Biggleswade	d						18 18		18 30					18 48		19 00					19 18		19 30
Sandy	d								18 34							19 04							19 34
St Neots	d						18 28		18 41					18 58		19 11					19 28		19 41
Huntingdon	d						18 36		18 49					19 06		19 19					19 36		19 49
Peterborough	a						18 53		19 05					19 22		19 41					19 53		20 05

		TL	GN	GR	GN	TL	TL	GN	TL	TL	GN	TL	TL	TL	TL	GN	GN	TL	GN	TL	TL	TL	GR
Brighton	d					17 38						18 08						18 38					
Gatwick Airport	d					18 16			18 19			18 46		18 49				19 16			19 19		
East Croydon	d					18 31			18 45			19 01		19 15				19 31			19 45		
Maidstone East	d																						
London Bridge	d					18 46			19 01			19 16		19 31				19 46			20 01		
London Blackfriars	d					18 52			19 07			19 22		19 37				19 52			20 07		
City Thameslink	d					18 54			19 09			19 24		19 39				19 54			20 09		
Farringdon	d					18 56			19 11			19 26		19 41				19 56			20 11		
St Pancras International	d					19 01			19 16			19 31		19 46				20 01			20 16		
London Kings Cross	d	18 51	18 54	19 06	19 12			19 18		19 21	19 39				19 51	19 57	20 09		20 12			20 21	20 33
Finsbury Park	d	19 01				19 12	←		19 24	19 31		19 39	←	19 53	20 01			20 09		←	20 24	20 31	
Potters Bar	d	19 13					19 13			19 45			19 45		20 13					20 13		20 43	
Hatfield	d	→					19 21			→			19 50		→					20 18		→	
Welwyn Garden City	d						19 26						19 56							20 26			
Welwyn North	d		19 11				19 30						20 00							20 30			
Knebworth	d		19 16				19 34						20 04			20 16				20 34			
Stevenage	d			19 28		19 33	19 38		19 44			20 00	20 08	20 14				20 30	20 34	20 38	20 44		20 55
Hitchin	d		19 25			19 38	19 44		19 50			20 06	20 14	20 20		20 25		20 36		20 44	20 50		
Letchworth Garden City	d		19 32		19 40	19 44	19 49				20 08	20 12	20 19			20 31	20 38	20 42		20 49			
Baldock	d		19a35			19 47	19 53					20 15	20 23			20a35		20 45		20 53			
Ashwell & Morden	d					19 52	19 57						20 27					20 50		20 57			
Royston	d				19 50	19 57	20 02				20 18	20 23	20 32				20 48	20 55		21 02			
Meldreth	d						20 06						20 36							21 06			
Shepreth	d						20 09						20 39							21 09			
Foxton	d						20 11						20 41							21 11			
Cambridge	a				20 05	20 11	20 21				20 33	20 43	20 51				21 03	21 14		21 21			
Cambridge	d				20 07						20 38						21 08						
Cambridge North	d				20 11						20 42						21 12						
Waterbeach	d										20 47						21 17						
Ely	d				20a24						20 58						21 29						
Littleport	d										21 06						21 36						
Downham Market	d										21 18						21 47						
Watlington	d										21 23						21 53						
Kings Lynn	a										21 32						22 01						
Arlesey	d								19 55					20 25							20 55		
Biggleswade	d							19 48	20 00					20 30					20 46		21 00		
Sandy	d								20 04					20 34							21 04		
St Neots	d							19 58	20 11					20 41					20 55		21 11		
Huntingdon	d							20 06	20 19					20 49					21 03		21 19		
Peterborough	a			19 58				20 22	20 35					21 05					21 22		21 35		21 25

Please refer to Table T024 for the service from Moorgate to Stevenage via Hertford North

Table T025-F

Mondays to Fridays

16 December to 15 May

Brighton, Gatwick Airport, Maidstone East and London - Stevenage, Cambridge, Kings Lynn and Peterborough

		GN	TL	TL	TL	TL	GN	GR	GN	GN	TL	TL	TL	GR	GN	TL	TL	TL	TL	GN	GN	GN
		1	1	1	1	1	1	1 ☕	1	1	1	1	1	1 ☕	1	1	1	1	1	1	1	1
Brighton	d		19 08													20 08						
Gatwick Airport	d		19 46		19 49							20 19				20 46		20 49				
East Croydon	d		20 01		20 15							20 45				21 01		21 15				
Maidstone East	d																					
London Bridge	d		20 16		20 31							21 01				21 16		21 31				
London Blackfriars	d		20 22		20 37							21 07				21 22		21 37				
City Thameslink	d		20 24		20 39							21 09				21 24		21 39				
Farringdon	d		20 26		20 41							21 11				21 26		21 41				
St Pancras International	d		20 31		20 46							21 16				21 31		21 46				
London Kings Cross 15 ⊖	d	20 39				20 51	20 54	21 00	21 09	21 12	←		21 21	21 33	21 39				21 51	21 54	22 09	22 12
Finsbury Park ⊖	d		20 39	←	20 54	21 01					21 01	21 24	21 31			21 39	←	21 54	22 01			
Potters Bar	d			20 43		→					21 13		21 43				21 43		→			
Hatfield	d			20 48							21 18		→				21 48					
Welwyn Garden City 4	d			20 56							21 26						21 56					
Welwyn North	d			21 00							21 30						22 00					
Knebworth	d			21 04			21 14				21 34						22 04			22 14		
Stevenage 4	d		21 00	21 08	21 14			21 22		21 34	21 38	21 44		21 56		22 00	22 08	22 14				22 34
Hitchin 4	d		21 06	21 14	21 20		21 25				21 44	21 50				22 06	22 14	22 20		22 24		
Letchworth Garden City	d	21 08	21 12	21 19			21 31		21 38		21 49				22 08	22 12	22 19			22a30	22 38	
Baldock	d		21 15	21 23			21a35				21 53					22 15	22 23					
Ashwell & Morden	d		21 20	21 27							21 57					22 20	22 27					
Royston	d	21 17	21 25	21 32					21 48		22 02				22 18	22 25	22 32				22 48	
Meldreth	d			21 36							22 06						22 36					
Shepreth	d			21 39							22 09						22 39					
Foxton	d			21 41							22 11						22 41					
Cambridge	a	21 32	21 40	21 54					22 03		22 21				22 33	22 40	22 54				23 04	
Cambridge	d	21 37							22 08						22 38						23 09	
Cambridge North	d	21 41							22 12						22 42						23 13	
Waterbeach	d	21 46							22 17						22 47						23 17	
Ely	d	21 57							22a27						22 58						23a28	
Littleport	d	22 05													23 06							
Downham Market	d	22 17													23 17							
Watlington	d	22 23													23 23							
Kings Lynn	a	22 31													23 31							
Arlesey	d				21 25							21 55						22 25				
Biggleswade	d				21 30				21 46			22 00						22 30				22 46
Sandy	d				21 34							22 04						22 34				
St Neots	d				21 41				21 55			22 11						22 41				22 55
Huntingdon	d				21 49				22 03			22 19						22 49				23 03
Peterborough 8	a				22 05			21 51	22 19			22 35		22 25				23 05				23 19

		TL	TL	TL	GN	TL	TL	TL	TL	GN	GN	TL	TL	TL	GN	TL	TL	TL	TL	TL
		1	1	1	1	1	1	1	1	1	1	1	1	1	1	1	1	1	1	1
Brighton	d					21 08										22 08				
Gatwick Airport	d		21 19			21 46		21 49					22 19			22 46		22 49		23 35
East Croydon	d		21 45			22 01		22 15					22 45			23 01		23 15		00 09
Maidstone East	d																			
London Bridge	d		22 01			22 16		22 31					23 01			23 16		23 31		
London Blackfriars	d		22 07			22 22		22 37					23 07			23 22		23 37		00 37
City Thameslink	d		22 09			22 24		22 39												
Farringdon	d		22 11			22 26		22 41					23 11			23 26		23 41		00 41
St Pancras International	d		22 16			22 31		22 46					23 16			23 31		23 46		00 46
London Kings Cross 15 ⊖	d	←		22 25	22 39				22 55	23 09	23 12	←		23 25	23 42				23 55	
Finsbury Park ⊖	d	22 01	22 24	22 32		22 41	←	22 54	23 02			23 02	23 24	23 33		23 42	←	23 54	00 02	00 54
Potters Bar	d	22 13		22 46			22 46		→			23 16		23 45			23 45		00 17	
Hatfield	d	22 18		→			22 52					23 22		→			23 51		00 23	
Welwyn Garden City 4	d	22 26					22 57					23 27					23 57		00 28	01 15
Welwyn North	d	22 30					23 00					23 31					00 01		00 31	
Knebworth	d	22 34					23 04					23 35					00 05		00 35	
Stevenage 4	d	22 38	22 44			23 01	23 10	23 14			23 35	23 40	23 45			00 03	00 09	00 14	00 40	01 24
Hitchin 4	d	22 44	22 50			23 07	23 16	23 20				23 45	23 50			00 08	00 14	00 22	00 48	01 32
Letchworth Garden City	d	22 49			23 09	23 13	23 21			23 38		23 51			00 10	00 14	00 20		00 54	
Baldock	d	22 53				23 16	23 24					23 54				00 17	00 23		00 57	
Ashwell & Morden	d	22 57				23 21	23 29					23 58					00 27		01 01	
Royston	d	23 02			23 18	23 26	23 34			23 48		00a04			00 19	00 25	00 32		01 06	
Meldreth	d	23 06					23 37										00 36		01 10	
Shepreth	d	23 09					23 40										00 39		01 13	
Foxton	d	23 11					23 42										00 41		01 15	
Cambridge	a	23 22			23 33	23 41	23 54			00 03					00 35	00 41	00 54		01 25	
Cambridge	d				23 38					00 08										
Cambridge North	d				23 42					00 13										
Waterbeach	d				23 47					00 17										
Ely	d				23 58					00 27										
Littleport	d				00 06					00 34										
Downham Market	d				00 15					00 43										
Watlington	d				00 21					00 49										
Kings Lynn	a				00 29					00 57										
Arlesey	d		22 55					23 25					23 55					00 27		01 37
Biggleswade	d		23 00					23 30			23 47		00 01					00 32		01 43
Sandy	d		23 04					23 34					00 05					00 36		01 46
St Neots	d		23 11					23 41			23 56		00 12					00 43		01 54
Huntingdon	d		23 19					23 49			00 04		00 20					00 51		02 01
Peterborough 8	a		23 37					00 07			00 22		00 37					01 09		02 19

Please refer to Table T024 for the service from Moorgate to Stevenage via Hertford North

Table T025-F

Saturdays

21 December to 16 May

Brighton, Gatwick Airport, Maidstone East and London - Stevenage, Cambridge, Kings Lynn and Peterborough

		GN	TL	GN	GN	GN	TL	TL	TL	TL	TL	GN	TL	TL	TL	TL	TL	TL	TL	TL	GN	TL	GN
		1	1	1	1	1	1	1	1	1	1	1	1	1	1	1	1	1	1	1	1	1	1
Brighton	d																						
Gatwick Airport	d																						
East Croydon	d													00 09									
Maidstone East	d																						
London Bridge	d																						
London Blackfriars	d													00 37									
City Thameslink	d																						
Farringdon	d													00 41									
St Pancras International	d													00 46									
London Kings Cross 15 ⊖	d										00 23	00 32			01 05	01 36	05 03	05 14	05 28	05 33	05 42		
Finsbury Park ⊖	d									00 02	00 29	00 39	←	00 54	01 11	01 44	05 09	05 20	05 34	05 42		←	
Potters Bar	d									00 17	00 42		00 42		01 22				05 45			05 45	
Hatfield	d									00 23	→		00 48		01 28				→			05 51	
Welwyn Garden City 4	d									00 28			00 58	01 15	01 34							05 56	
Welwyn North	d							00 01		00 31			01 01		01 37							06 00	
Knebworth	d							00 05		00 35			01 05		01 41							06 04	
Stevenage 4	d						00 03	00 09	00 14	00 40		01 04	01 10	01 24	01 46	02 12	05 34	05 45		06 03		06 08	
Hitchin 4	d						00 08	00 14	00 22	00 48		01 13	01 18	01 32	01 54	02 20	05 42	05 54		06 08		06 14	
Letchworth Garden City	d					00 10	00 14	00 20		00 54		01s18	01 24		02 00		05 48			06 14		06 19	
Baldock	d						00 17	00 23		00 57		01s21	01 27		02 03		05 51			06 17		06 23	
Ashwell & Morden	d							00 27		01 01			01 31		02 07							06 27	
Royston	d					00 19	00 25	00 32		01 06		01s29	01a37		02a13		05 59			06 25		06 32	
Meldreth	d							00 36		01 10												06 36	
Shepreth	d							00 39		01 13												06 39	
Foxton	d							00 41		01 15												06 41	
Cambridge	a					00 35	00 41	00 54		01 25		01 44					06 14			06 40	06 30	06 54	
Cambridge	d				00 08																06 35		07 13
Cambridge North	d				00 13																06 38		07 19
Waterbeach	d				00 17																06 44		
Ely	d				00 27																06 54		07a31
Littleport	d			00 06	00 34																07 04		
Downham Market	d			00 15	00 43																07 17		
Watlington	d			00 21	00 49																07 23		
Kings Lynn	a			00 29	00 57																07 31		
Arlesey	d								00 27					01 37		02 25		05 58					
Biggleswade	d		00 01						00 32					01 43		02 31		06 05					
Sandy	d		00 05						00 36					01 46		02 34		06 09					
St Neots	d		00 12						00 43					01 54		02 42		06 17					
Huntingdon	d	00 04	00 20						00 51					02 01		02 49		06 25					
Peterborough 8	a	00 22	00 37						01 09					02 19		03 07		06 41					

		TL	GR	TL	GR	TL	TL	GR	GN	TL	TL	TL	TL	GR	TL	TL	GN	TL	GN	TL	TL	TL	TL
		1	1 ☕	1	1 ☕	1	1	1 ☕	1	1	1	1	1	1 ☕	1	1	1	1	1	1	1	1	1
Brighton	d									05 06										06 08			
Gatwick Airport	d									05 46		05 49				06 19				06 46		06 49	
East Croydon	d									06 01		06 15				06 45				07 01		07 15	
Maidstone East	d																						
London Bridge	d									06 16		06 31				07 01				07 16		07 31	
London Blackfriars	d									06 22		06 37				07 07				07 22		07 37	
City Thameslink	d																						
Farringdon	d									06 26		06 41				07 11				07 26		07 41	
St Pancras International	d									06 31		06 46				07 16				07 31		07 46	
London Kings Cross 15 ⊖	d	05 48	05 55	05 56	06 15	06 16	06 28	06 30	06 42				06 58	07 06	←		07 12	07 28	07 42				07 58
Finsbury Park ⊖	d	05 54		06 02		06 22	06 34			06 42	←	06 54	07 04		07 04	07 24		07 34		07 42	←	07 54	08 04
Potters Bar	d			06 14			06 45				06 45		→		07 15			07 45			07 45		08 15
Hatfield	d			06 19			→				06 51				07 21			→			07 51		08 21
Welwyn Garden City 4	d			06 24							06 56				07 26						07 56		08 26
Welwyn North	d			06 27							07 00				07 30						08 00		08 30
Knebworth	d			06 32							07 04				07 34						08 04		08 34
Stevenage 4	d	06 14	06 17	06 38	06 38	06 42		06 52		07 03	07 08	07 14		07 28	07 38	07 44				08 03	08 08	08 14	08 38
Hitchin 4	d	06 20		06 44		06 48				07 08	07 14	07 20			07 44	07 50				08 08	08 14	08 20	08 44
Letchworth Garden City	d			06 50						07 14	07 19				07 50					08 14	08 19		08 50
Baldock	d			06 53						07 17	07 23				07 53					08 17	08 23		08 53
Ashwell & Morden	d			06 57							07 27				07 57						08 27		08 57
Royston	d			07a03						07 25	07 32				08a03					08 25	08 32		09a03
Meldreth	d										07 36										08 36		
Shepreth	d										07 39										08 39		
Foxton	d										07 41										08 41		
Cambridge	a								07 30	07 40	07 54						08 00		08 30	08 40	08 54		
Cambridge	d								07 35								08 04		08 35				
Cambridge North	d								07 38								08 08		08 38				
Waterbeach	d								07 44										08 44				
Ely	d								07 55								08a23		08 55				
Littleport	d								08 04										09 04				
Downham Market	d								08 17										09 17				
Watlington	d								08 23										09 23				
Kings Lynn	a								08 31										09 31				
Arlesey	d	06 25				06 53						07 25				07 55						08 25	
Biggleswade	d	06 30				06 59						07 30				08 00						08 30	
Sandy	d	06 34				07 03						07 34				08 04						08 34	
St Neots	d	06 41				07 11						07 41				08 11						08 41	
Huntingdon	d	06 49				07 19						07 49				08 19						08 49	
Peterborough 8	a	07 04	06 46		07 07	07 35		07 21				08 05		07 57		08 39						09 08	

Please refer to Table T024 for the service from Moorgate to Stevenage via Hertford North

Table T025-F

Saturdays

21 December to 16 May

Brighton, Gatwick Airport, Maidstone East and London - Stevenage, Cambridge, Kings Lynn and Peterborough

Station		TL	GN	TL	GN	TL	TL	TL	TL	GR	TL	TL	GN	TL	GN	TL	TL	TL	TL	GR	TL	TL
Brighton	d					07 08										08 08						
Gatwick Airport	d	07 19				07 46		07 49				08 19				08 46		08 49				09 19
East Croydon	d	07 45				08 01		08 15				08 45				09 01		09 15				09 45
Maidstone East	d																					
London Bridge	d	08 01				08 16		08 31				09 01				09 16		09 31				10 01
London Blackfriars	d	08 07				08 22		08 37				09 07				09 22		09 37				10 07
City Thameslink	d											09 09				09 24		09 39				10 09
Farringdon	d	08 11				08 26		08 41				09 11				09 26		09 41				10 11
St Pancras International	d	08 16				08 31		08 46				09 16				09 31		09 46				10 16
London Kings Cross 15 ⊖	d		08 12	08 28	08 42				08 58	09 06	←		09 12	09 28	09 42				09 58	10 06	←	
Finsbury Park ⊖	d	08 24		08 34		08 42	←	08 54	09 04		09 04	09 24		09 34		09 42	←	09 54	10 04		10 04	10 24
Potters Bar	d			08 45			08 45		→		09 15			09 45			09 45		→		10 15	
Hatfield	d			→			08 51				09 21			→			09 51				10 21	
Welwyn Garden City 4	d						08 56				09 26						09 56				10 26	
Welwyn North	d						09 00				09 31						10 00				10 30	
Knebworth	d						09 04				09 34						10 04				10 34	
Stevenage 4	d	08 44				09 03	09 08	09 14		09 29	09 38	09 44				10 03	10 08	10 14		10 29	10 38	10 44
Hitchin 4	d	08 50				09 08	09 14	09 20			09 44	09 50				10 08	10 14	10 20			10 44	10 50
Letchworth Garden City	d					09 14	09 19				09 50					10 14	10 19				10 50	
Baldock	d					09 17	09 23				09 53					10 17	10 23				10 53	
Ashwell & Morden	d						09 27				09 57						10 27				10 57	
Royston	d					09 25	09 32				10a04					10 25	10 32				11a03	
Meldreth	d						09 36										10 36					
Shepreth	d						09 39										10 39					
Foxton	d						09 41										10 41					
Cambridge	a		09 00		09 30	09 40	09 54						10 00		10 30	10 40	10 54					
Cambridge	d		09 04		09 35								10 04		10 35							
Cambridge North	d		09 08		09 38								10 08		10 38							
Waterbeach	d				09 44										10 44							
Ely	d		09a23		09 56								10a23		10 55							
Littleport	d				10 04										11 04							
Downham Market	d				10 22										11 17							
Watlington	d				10 28										11 23							
Kings Lynn	a				10 36										11 31							
Arlesey	d	08 55						09 25				09 55						10 25				10 55
Biggleswade	d	09 00						09 30				10 00						10 30				11 00
Sandy	d	09 04						09 34				10 04						10 34				11 04
St Neots	d	09 11						09 41				10 11						10 41				11 11
Huntingdon	d	09 19						09 49				10 19						10 49				11 19
Peterborough 8	a	09 36						10 05		09 58		10 40						11 05		10 58		11 39

Station		GN	TL	GN	TL	TL	TL	TL	GR	TL	TL	GN	TL	GN	TL	TL	TL	TL	GR	TL	TL	GN	TL
Brighton	d				09 08										10 08								
Gatwick Airport	d				09 46		09 49				10 19				10 46		10 49				11 19		
East Croydon	d				10 01		10 15				10 45				11 01		11 15				11 45		
Maidstone East	d																						
London Bridge	d				10 16		10 31				11 01				11 16		11 31				12 01		
London Blackfriars	d				10 22		10 37				11 07				11 22		11 37				12 07		
City Thameslink	d				10 24		10 39				11 09				11 24		11 39				12 09		
Farringdon	d				10 26		10 41				11 11				11 26		11 41				12 11		
St Pancras International	d				10 31		10 46				11 16				11 31		11 46				12 16		
London Kings Cross 15 ⊖	d	10 13	10 28	10 42				10 58	11 06	←		11 12	11 28	11 42				11 58	12 06	←		12 12	12 28
Finsbury Park ⊖	d		10 34		10 42	←	10 54	11 04		11 04	11 24		11 34		11 42	←	11 54	12 04		12 04	12 24		12 34
Potters Bar	d		10 45			10 45		→		11 15			11 45			11 45		→		12 15			12 45
Hatfield	d		→			10 51				11 21			→			11 51				12 21			→
Welwyn Garden City 4	d					10 56				11 26						11 56				12 26			
Welwyn North	d					11 00				11 31						12 00				12 30			
Knebworth	d					11 04				11 34						12 04				12 34			
Stevenage 4	d				11 03	11 08	11 14		11 28	11 38	11 44				12 03	12 08	12 14		12 28	12 38	12 44		
Hitchin 4	d				11 08	11 14	11 20			11 44	11 50				12 08	12 14	12 20			12 44	12 50		
Letchworth Garden City	d				11 14	11 19				11 50					12 14	12 19				12 50			
Baldock	d				11 17	11 23				11 53					12 17	12 23				12 53			
Ashwell & Morden	d					11 27				11 57						12 27				12 57			
Royston	d				11 25	11 32				12a04					12 25	12 32				13a03			
Meldreth	d					11 36										12 36							
Shepreth	d					11 39										12 39							
Foxton	d					11 41										12 41							
Cambridge	a	11 00		11 30	11 40	11 54						12 00		12 30	12 40	12 54						13 00	
Cambridge	d	11 04		11 35								12 04		12 35								13 04	
Cambridge North	d	11 08		11 38								12 08		12 38								13 08	
Waterbeach	d			11 44										12 44									
Ely	d	11a23		11 55								12a23		12 55								13a23	
Littleport	d			12 04										13 04									
Downham Market	d			12 17										13 17									
Watlington	d			12 23										13 23									
Kings Lynn	a			12 31										13 31									
Arlesey	d						11 25				11 55						12 25				12 55		
Biggleswade	d						11 30				12 00						12 30				13 00		
Sandy	d						11 34				12 04						12 34				13 04		
St Neots	d						11 41				12 11						12 41				13 11		
Huntingdon	d						11 49				12 19						12 49				13 19		
Peterborough 8	a						12 05		11 57		12 39						13 05		12 58		13 39		

Please refer to Table T024 for the service from Moorgate to Stevenage via Hertford North

Table T025-F

Saturdays

21 December to 16 May

Brighton, Gatwick Airport, Maidstone East and London - Stevenage, Cambridge, Kings Lynn and Peterborough

Station		GN	TL	TL	TL	TL	TL	GN	TL	GN	TL	TL	TL	TL	GR	TL	TL	GN	TL	GN	TL	TL
Brighton	d		11 08								12 08										13 08	
Gatwick Airport	d		11 46		11 49		12 19				12 46		12 49				13 19				13 46	
East Croydon	d		12 01		12 15		12 45				13 01		13 15				13 45				14 01	
Maidstone East	d																					
London Bridge	d		12 16		12 31		13 01				13 16		13 31				14 01				14 16	
London Blackfriars	d		12 22		12 37		13 07				13 22		13 37				14 07				14 22	
City Thameslink	d		12 24		12 39		13 09				13 24		13 39				14 09				14 24	
Farringdon	d		12 26		12 41		13 11				13 26		13 41				14 11				14 26	
St Pancras International	d		12 31		12 46		13 16				13 31		13 46				14 16				14 31	
London Kings Cross 15 ⊖	d	12 42				12 58		13 12	13 28	13 42				13 58	14 06	←		14 12	14 28	14 42		
Finsbury Park ⊖	d		12 42	←	12 54	13 04	13 24		13 34		13 42	←	13 54	14 04		14 04	14 24		14 34		14 42	←
Potters Bar	d			12 45		13 15			13 45			13 45		→		14 15			14 45			14 45
Hatfield	d			12 51		13 21			→			13 51				14 21			→			14 51
Welwyn Garden City 4	d			12 56		13 26						13 56				14 26						14 56
Welwyn North	d			13 00		13 30						14 00				14 30						15 00
Knebworth	d			13 04		13 34						14 04				14 34						15 04
Stevenage 4	d		13 03	13 08	13 14	13 38	13 44				14 03	14 08	14 14		14 28	14 38	14 44				15 03	15 08
Hitchin 4	d		13 08	13 14	13 20	13 44	13 50				14 08	14 14	14 20			14 44	14 50				15 08	15 14
Letchworth Garden City	d		13 14	13 19		13 50					14 14	14 19				14 50					15 14	15 19
Baldock	d		13 17	13 23		13 53					14 17	14 23				14 53					15 17	15 23
Ashwell & Morden	d			13 27		13 57						14 27				14 57						15 27
Royston	d		13 25	13 32		14a03					14 25	14 32				15a03					15 25	15 32
Meldreth	d			13 36								14 36										15 36
Shepreth	d			13 39								14 39										15 39
Foxton	d			13 41								14 41										15 41
Cambridge	a	13 30	13 40	13 54				14 00		14 30	14 40	14 54						15 00		15 30	15 40	15 54
Cambridge	d	13 35						14 04		14 35								15 04		15 35		
Cambridge North	d	13 38						14 08		14 38								15 08		15 38		
Waterbeach	d	13 44								14 44										15 44		
Ely	d	13 55						14a23		14 55								15a23		15 55		
Littleport	d	14 04								15 04										16 04		
Downham Market	d	14 17								15 17										16 17		
Watlington	d	14 23								15 23										16 23		
Kings Lynn	a	14 31								15 31										16 31		
Arlesey	d				13 25		13 55						14 25				14 55					
Biggleswade	d				13 30		14 00						14 30				15 00					
Sandy	d				13 34		14 04						14 34				15 04					
St Neots	d				13 41		14 11						14 41				15 11					
Huntingdon	d				13 49		14 19						14 49				15 19					
Peterborough 8	a				14 05		14 40						15 05		14 57		15 39					

Station		TL	TL	GR	TL	TL	GN	TL	GN	TL	TL	TL	TL	GR	TL	TL	GN	TL	GN	GN	TL	TL	TL
Brighton	d									14 08											15 08		
Gatwick Airport	d	13 49				14 19				14 46		14 49				15 19					15 46		15 49
East Croydon	d	14 15				14 45				15 01		15 15				15 45					16 01		16 15
Maidstone East	d																						
London Bridge	d	14 31				15 01				15 16		15 31				16 01					16 16		16 31
London Blackfriars	d	14 37				15 07				15 22		15 37				16 07					16 22		16 37
City Thameslink	d	14 39				15 09				15 24		15 39				16 09					16 24		16 39
Farringdon	d	14 41				15 11				15 26		15 41				16 11					16 26		16 41
St Pancras International	d	14 46				15 16				15 31		15 46				16 16					16 31		16 46
London Kings Cross 15 ⊖	d		14 58	15 06	←		15 12	15 28	15 42				15 58	16 06	←		16 12	16 28	16 36	16 42			
Finsbury Park ⊖	d	14 54	15 04		15 04	15 24		15 34		15 42	←	15 54	16 04		16 04	16 24		16 34			16 42	←	16 54
Potters Bar	d		→		15 15			15 45			15 45		→		16 15			16 45				16 45	
Hatfield	d				15 21			→			15 51				16 21			→				16 51	
Welwyn Garden City 4	d				15 26						15 56				16 26							16 56	
Welwyn North	d				15 30						16 00				16 31							17 00	
Knebworth	d				15 34						16 04				16 35							17 04	
Stevenage 4	d	15 14		15 28	15 38	15 44				16 03	16 08	16 14		16 28	16 39	16 44					17 03	17 08	17 14
Hitchin 4	d	15 20			15 44	15 50				16 08	16 14	16 20			16 45	16 50					17 08	17 14	17 20
Letchworth Garden City	d				15 50					16 14	16 19				16 50						17 14	17 19	
Baldock	d				15 53					16 17	16 23				16 53						17 17	17 23	
Ashwell & Morden	d				15 57						16 27				16 58							17 27	
Royston	d				16a03					16 25	16 32				17a03						17 25	17 32	
Meldreth	d										16 36											17 36	
Shepreth	d										16 39											17 39	
Foxton	d										16 41											17 41	
Cambridge	a						16 00		16 30	16 40	16 54						17 00			17 30	17 40	17 54	
Cambridge	d						16 04		16 35								17 04			17 35			
Cambridge North	d						16 08		16 38								17 08			17 38			
Waterbeach	d								16 44											17 44			
Ely	d						16a23		16 55								17a23			17 56			
Littleport	d								17 04											18 05			
Downham Market	d								17 17											18 17			
Watlington	d								17 23											18 23			
Kings Lynn	a								17 31											18 31			
Arlesey	d	15 25				15 55						16 25				16 55							17 25
Biggleswade	d	15 30				16 00						16 30				17 00			17 09				17 30
Sandy	d	15 34				16 04						16 34				17 04							17 34
St Neots	d	15 41				16 11						16 41				17 11			17 19				17 41
Huntingdon	d	15 49				16 19						16 49				17 19			17 27				17 49
Peterborough 8	a	16 07		15 57		16 40						17 05		17 00		17 34			17 43				18 04

Please refer to Table T024 for the service from Moorgate to Stevenage via Hertford North

Table T025-F

Saturdays

21 December to 16 May

Brighton, Gatwick Airport, Maidstone East and London - Stevenage, Cambridge, Kings Lynn and Peterborough

		TL	TL	GN	TL	GN	GN	TL	TL	TL	TL	TL	GN	TL	GN	GN	TL	TL	TL	TL	GR	TL	TL
Brighton	d							16 08									17 08						
Gatwick Airport	d		16 19					16 46		16 49		17 19					17 46		17 49				18 19
East Croydon	d		16 45					17 01		17 15		17 45					18 01		18 15				18 45
Maidstone East	d																						
London Bridge	d		17 01					17 16		17 31		18 01					18 16		18 31				19 01
London Blackfriars	d		17 07					17 22		17 37		18 07					18 22		18 37				19 07
City Thameslink	d		17 09					17 24		17 39		18 09					18 24		18 39				19 09
Farringdon	d		17 11					17 26		17 41		18 11					18 26		18 41				19 11
St Pancras International	d		17 16					17 31		17 46		18 16					18 31		18 46				19 16
London Kings Cross	d	16 58		17 12	17 28	17 36	17 42				17 58		18 12	18 28	18 36	18 42				18 58	19 06	←	
Finsbury Park	d	17 04	17 24		17 34			17 42	←	17 54	18 04	18 24		18 34			18 42	←	18 54	19 04		19 04	19 24
Potters Bar	d	17 15			17 45				17 45		18 15			18 45				18 45		→		19 15	
Hatfield	d	17 21			→				17 51		18 21			→				18 51				19 21	
Welwyn Garden City	d	17 26							17 56		18 26							18 56				19 26	
Welwyn North	d	17 30							18 00		18 30							19 00				19 30	
Knebworth	d	17 34							18 04		18 34							19 04				19 34	
Stevenage	d	17 38	17 44					18 03	18 08	18 14	18 38	18 44					19 03	19 08	19 14		19 28	19 38	19 44
Hitchin	d	17 44	17 50					18 08	18 14	18 20	18 44	18 50					19 08	19 14	19 20			19 44	19 50
Letchworth Garden City	d	17 50						18 14	18 19		18 50						19 14	19 19				19 50	
Baldock	d	17 53						18 17	18 23		18 53						19 17	19 23				19 53	
Ashwell & Morden	d	17 57							18 27		18 57							19 27				19 57	
Royston	d	18a03						18 25	18 32		19a03						19 25	19 32				20a03	
Meldreth	d								18 36									19 36					
Shepreth	d								18 39									19 39					
Foxton	d								18 41									19 41					
Cambridge	a			18 00			18 30	18 40	18 54				19 00			19 30	19 40	19 54					
Cambridge	d			18 04			18 35						19 04			19 35							
Cambridge North	d			18 08			18 38						19 08			19 38							
Waterbeach	d						18 44									19 44							
Ely	d			18a23			18 55						19 25			19 55							
Littleport	d						19 04						19 34			20 04							
Downham Market	d						19 17						19 46			20 17							
Watlington	d						19 23						19 52			20 23							
Kings Lynn	a						19 31						20 00			20 31							
Arlesey	d		17 55							18 25		18 55							19 25				19 55
Biggleswade	d		18 00			18 09				18 30		19 00			19 09				19 30				20 00
Sandy	d		18 04							18 34		19 04							19 34				20 04
St Neots	d		18 11			18 19				18 41		19 11			19 19				19 41				20 11
Huntingdon	d		18 19			18 27				18 49		19 19			19 27				19 49				20 19
Peterborough	a		18 37			18 43				19 05		19 34			19 43				20 04		19 57		20 40

		GN	TL	GN	TL	TL	TL	TL	TL	GN	TL	TL	GN	TL	TL	TL	TL	TL	GN	TL	TL	GN
Brighton	d				18 08									19 08								
Gatwick Airport	d				18 46		18 49		19 19					19 46		19 49		20 19				
East Croydon	d				19 01		19 15		19 45					20 01		20 15		20 45				
Maidstone East	d																					
London Bridge	d				19 16		19 31		20 01					20 16		20 31		21 01				
London Blackfriars	d				19 22		19 37		20 07					20 22		20 37		21 07				
City Thameslink	d				19 24		19 39		20 09					20 24		20 39						
Farringdon	d				19 26		19 41		20 11					20 26		20 41		21 11				
St Pancras International	d				19 31		19 46		20 16					20 31		20 46		21 16				
London Kings Cross	d	19 12	19 28	19 42				19 58		20 12		20 28	20 42				20 58		21 12		21 28	21 42
Finsbury Park	d		19 34		19 42	←	19 54	20 04	20 24			20 34		20 42	←	20 54	21 04	21 24			21 34	
Potters Bar	d		19 45			19 45		20 15				20 45			20 45		21 15				21 45	
Hatfield	d		→			19 51		20 21				→			20 51		21 21				→	
Welwyn Garden City	d					19 56		20 26							20 56		21 26					
Welwyn North	d					20 00		20 30							21 00		21 30					
Knebworth	d					20 04		20 34							21 04		21 34					
Stevenage	d				20 03	20 08	20 14	20 38	20 44					21 03	21 08	21 14	21 38	21 44				
Hitchin	d				20 08	20 14	20 20	20 44	20 50		←			21 08	21 14	21 20	21 44	21 50		←		
Letchworth Garden City	d				20 14	20 19		20 50		20 40	20 50		21 10	21 14	21 19		21 50		21 40	21 50		
Baldock	d				20 17	20 23		→			20 53			21 17	21 23		→			21 53		
Ashwell & Morden	d					20 27					20 57				21 27					21 57		
Royston	d				20 25	20 32				20 49	21a03			21 25	21 32				21 49	22a03		
Meldreth	d					20 36									21 36							
Shepreth	d					20 39									21 39							
Foxton	d					20 41									21 41							
Cambridge	a	20 00		20 30	20 40	20 54				21 04			21 32	21 40	21 54				22 04			22 30
Cambridge	d	20 04		20 35						21 05			21 37						22 05			22 35
Cambridge North	d	20 08		20 38						21 09			21 41						22 09			22 38
Waterbeach	d			20 44									21 46									22 44
Ely	d	20 23		20 55						21 25			21 57						22a23			22 55
Littleport	d			21 04						21 33			22 05									23 02
Downham Market	d	20 46		21 17						21 46			22 17									23 11
Watlington	d			21 23						21 52			22 23									23 17
Kings Lynn	a	21 00		21 31						22 00			22 31									23 25
Arlesey	d						20 25		20 55							21 25		21 55				
Biggleswade	d						20 30		21 00							21 30		22 00				
Sandy	d						20 34		21 04							21 34		22 04				
St Neots	d						20 41		21 11							21 41		22 11				
Huntingdon	d						20 49		21 19							21 49		22 19				
Peterborough	a						21 04		21 34							22 05		22 39				

Please refer to Table T024 for the service from Moorgate to Stevenage via Hertford North

NRT DECEMBER 19 EDITION

Table T025-F

Saturdays

21 December to 16 May

Brighton, Gatwick Airport, Maidstone East and London - Stevenage, Cambridge, Kings Lynn and Peterborough

		TL	TL	TL	TL	TL	GN	TL	TL	GN	TL	TL	TL	TL	TL	GN	TL	TL	GN	TL	TL	TL	TL
Brighton	d	20 08									21 08									22 08			
Gatwick Airport	d	20 46		20 49		21 19					21 46		21 49		22 19					22 46		22 49	
East Croydon	d	21 01		21 15		21 45					22 01		22 16		22 46					23 01		23 15	
Maidstone East	d																						
London Bridge	d	21 16		21 31		22 01					22 16		22 31		23 01					23 16		23 31	
London Blackfriars	d	21 22		21 37		22 07					22 22		22 37		23 07					23 22		23 37	
City Thameslink	d																						
Farringdon	d	21 26		21 41		22 11					22 26		22 41		23 11					23 26		23 41	
St Pancras International	d	21 31		21 46		22 16					22 31		22 46		23 16					23 31		23 46	
London Kings Cross	d				21 58		22 12		22 28	22 42				22 58		23 12		23 28	23 42				23 54
Finsbury Park	d	21 42	←	21 54	22 04	22 24			22 34		22 42	←	22 54	23 04	23 24			23 34		23 42	←	23 54	00 03
Potters Bar	d		21 45		22 15				22 45			22 45		23 15				23 45			23 45		00 16
Hatfield	d		21 51		22 21				→			22 51		23 21				→			23 51		00 23
Welwyn Garden City	d		21 56		22 26							22 56		23 26							23 56		00 28
Welwyn North	d		22 00		22 30							23 00		23 30							00 01		00 31
Knebworth	d		22 04		22 34							23 04		23 34							00 05		00 36
Stevenage	d	22 03	22 08	22 14	22 38	22 44					23 03	23 08	23 14	23 38	23 44					00 03	00 09	00 14	00 40
Hitchin	d	22 08	22 14	22 20	22 44	22 50		←			23 08	23 14	23 20	23 44	23 50		←			00 08	00 17	00 22	00 49
Letchworth Garden City	d	22 14	22 19		22 50		22 40	22 50			23 14	23 19		23 50		23 39	23 50		00 10	00 14	00 23		00 54
Baldock	d	22 17	22 23		→			22 53			23 17	23 23		→			23 53			00 17	00 26		00 57
Ashwell & Morden	d		22 27					22 57				23 27					23 57				00 30		01 02
Royston	d	22 25	22 32				22 49	23a03			23 25	23 32				23 49	00a03		00 19	00 25	00 35		01 08
Meldreth	d		22 36									23 36									00 39		01 12
Shepreth	d		22 39									23 39									00 42		01 15
Foxton	d		22 41									23 41									00 44		01 17
Cambridge	a	22 40	22 54				23 04			23 30	23 40	23 54				00 04			00 34	00 41	00 54		01 28
Cambridge	d						23 05			23 35						00 08							
Cambridge North	d						23 09			23 38						00 13							
Waterbeach	d									23 44						00 17							
Ely	d						23a23			23 55						00 27							
Littleport	d									00 03						00 34							
Downham Market	d									00 12						00 43							
Watlington	d									00 18						00 49							
Kings Lynn	a									00 26						00 57							
Arlesey	d			22 25		22 55							23 25		23 55							00 27	
Biggleswade	d			22 30		23 00							23 30		00 01							00 33	
Sandy	d			22 34		23 04							23 34		00 05							00 36	
St Neots	d			22 41		23 11							23 41		00 12							00 43	
Huntingdon	d			22 49		23 19							23 49		00 20							00 51	
Peterborough	a			23 05		23 37							00 07		00 39							01 09	

		TL A	TL B
Brighton	d		
Gatwick Airport	d	23 34	23 34
East Croydon	d	00 10	00 10
Maidstone East	d		
London Bridge	d		
London Blackfriars	d	00 37	00 37
City Thameslink	d		
Farringdon	d	00 41	00 41
St Pancras International	d	00 46	00 46
London Kings Cross	d		
Finsbury Park	d	00 54	00 54
Potters Bar	d		
Hatfield	d		
Welwyn Garden City	d	01 15	01 15
Welwyn North	d		
Knebworth	d		
Stevenage	d	01 24	01 24
Hitchin	d	01a32	01 32
Letchworth Garden City	d		
Baldock	d		
Ashwell & Morden	d		
Royston	d		
Meldreth	d		
Shepreth	d		
Foxton	d		
Cambridge	a		
Cambridge	d		
Cambridge North	d		
Waterbeach	d		
Ely	d		
Littleport	d		
Downham Market	d		
Watlington	d		
Kings Lynn	a		
Arlesey	d		01 37
Biggleswade	d		01 42
Sandy	d		01 45
St Neots	d		01 53
Huntingdon	d		02 01
Peterborough	a		02 21

A from 22 February until 28 March

B until 15 February, from 4 April

Please refer to Table T024 for the service from Moorgate to Stevenage via Hertford North

Table T025-F

Sundays

15 December to 10 May

Brighton, Gatwick Airport, Maidstone East and London - Stevenage, Cambridge, Kings Lynn and Peterborough

		TL A	GN A	GN A	GN A	TL A	TL A	TL A	TL A	GN	TL	GN	TL	TL B	TL C	GN B (bus)	TL	TL	TL	TL	GN	TL	TL
Brighton	d																						
Gatwick Airport	d																						
East Croydon	d													00 10	00 10								
Maidstone East	d																						
London Bridge	d													00 37	00 37								
London Blackfriars	d																						
City Thameslink	d																						
Farringdon	d													00 41	00 41								
St Pancras International	d													00 46	00 46								
London Kings Cross ⊖	d									00 12	00 23	00 32					01 05	06 31	07 02	07 35	07 53	08 02	08 13
Finsbury Park ⊖	d								00 03	00 20	00 29	00 38	←	00 54	00 54		01 11	06 38	07 08	07 41	07 59	08 08	08 19
Potters Bar	d								00 16		00 42		00 42				01 22		07 19			08 19	
Hatfield	d								00 23		→		00 48				01 28		07 25			→	
Welwyn Garden City	d								00 28				00 59	01 15	01 15		01 34		07 31				
Welwyn North	d						00 01		00 31				01 02				01 37		07 35				
Knebworth	d						00 05		00 36				01 06				01 41		07 39				
Stevenage	d					00 03	00 09	00 14	00 40	00 56		01 05	01 11	01 24	01 24		01 46	07 03	07 44	08 07	08 20		08 40
Hitchin	d					00 08	00 17	00 22	00 49	01 02		01 13	01 19	01a32	01 32	01 40	01 54	07 13	07 52	08 16	08 26		08 45
Letchworth Garden City	d				00 10	00 14	00 23		00 54			01s18	01a25				02a00	07 18	07 58		08 32		
Baldock	d					00 17	00 26		00 57			01s22						07 22	08 01		08 35		
Ashwell & Morden	d						00 30		01 02										08 06				
Royston	d				00 19	00 25	00 35		01 08			01s30						07 30	08 11		08 44		
Meldreth	d						00 39		01 12										08 14				
Shepreth	d						00 42		01 15										08 17				
Foxton	d						00 44		01 17										08 19				
Cambridge	a				00 34	00 41	00 54		01 28			01 45						07 45	08 30		08 58		
Cambridge	d			00 08																	09 04		
Cambridge North	d			00 13																	09 08		
Waterbeach	d			00 17																	09 12		
Ely	d			00 27																	09 22		
Littleport	d		00 03	00 34																	09 29		
Downham Market	d		00 12	00 43																	09 38		
Watlington	d		00 18	00 49																	09 44		
Kings Lynn	a		00 26	00 57																	09 52		
Arlesey	d							00 27		01 07					01 37	01 58				08 22			08 50
Biggleswade	d	00 01						00 33		01 12					01 42	02 18				08 27			08 55
Sandy	d	00 05						00 36		01 16					01 45	02 28				08 31			08 59
St Neots	d	00 12						00 43		01 23					01 53	02 48				08 39			09 06
Huntingdon	d	00 20						00 51		01 31					02 01	03 18				08 47			09 13
Peterborough	a	00 39						01 09		01 49					02 21	03 58				09 04			09 29

		TL	TL	TL	GR	GN	TL	TL	GR	TL	TL	GN	TL	TL	TL	TL	GR	GN	TL	TL	TL	TL	GN
Brighton	d																						
Gatwick Airport	d									08 46					09 46						10 46		
East Croydon	d									09 07					10 07						11 07		
Maidstone East	d																						
London Bridge	d									09 25					10 25						11 25		
London Blackfriars	d									09 31					10 31						11 31		
City Thameslink	d																						
Farringdon	d									09 35					10 35						11 35		
St Pancras International	d									09 40					10 40						11 40		
London Kings Cross ⊖	d		08 39	09 02	09 03	09 11	09 13		09 33		10 02	10 11	10 13			11 02	11 03	11 11	11 13			12 02	12 11
Finsbury Park ⊖	d	←	08 46	09 08			09 19	←		09 47	10 08		10 19	←	10 47	11 08			11 19	←	11 47	12 08	
Potters Bar	d	08 19		09 19				09 19			10 19			10 19		11 19				11 19		12 19	
Hatfield	d	08 25		→				09 25			→			10 25		→				11 25		→	
Welwyn Garden City	d	08 31						09 31						10 31						11 31			
Welwyn North	d	08 35						09 35						10 35						11 35			
Knebworth	d	08 39						09 39						10 39						11 39			
Stevenage	d	08 44	09 06		09 25		09 40	09 44	09 55	10 07			10 40	10 44	11 07		11 25		11 40	11 44	12 07		
Hitchin	d	08 50	09 12				09 45	09 50		10 13			10 45	10 50	11 13				11 45	11 50	12 13		
Letchworth Garden City	d	08 56	09 18					09 56		10 18				10 56	11 18					11 56	12 18		
Baldock	d	08 59	09 22					09 59		10 22				10 59	11 22					11 59	12 22		
Ashwell & Morden	d	09 04						10 04						11 04						12 04			
Royston	d	09 09	09 30					10 09		10 30				11 09	11 30					12 09	12 30		
Meldreth	d	09 12						10 12						11 12						12 12			
Shepreth	d	09 15						10 15						11 15						12 15			
Foxton	d	09 17						10 17						11 17						12 17			
Cambridge	a	09 28	09 47			09 59		10 28		10 48		10 58		11 28	11 48			11 58		12 28	12 48		12 58
Cambridge	d					10 04						11 04						12 04					13 04
Cambridge North	d					10 08						11 08						12 08					13 08
Waterbeach	d					10 12						11 12						12 12					13 12
Ely	d					10 22						11 22						12 22					13 22
Littleport	d					10 29						11 29						12 29					13 29
Downham Market	d					10 38						11 38						12 38					13 38
Watlington	d					10 44						11 44						12 44					13 44
Kings Lynn	a					10 52						11 52						12 52					13 52
Arlesey	d						09 50						10 50						11 50				
Biggleswade	d						09 55						10 55						11 55				
Sandy	d						09 59						10 59						11 59				
St Neots	d						10 06						11 06						12 06				
Huntingdon	d						10 13						11 13						12 13				
Peterborough	a				09 54		10 29		10 24				11 29				11 54		12 29				

A not 15 December
B from 23 February until 29 March
C from 22 December until 16 February, from 5 April

Please refer to Table T024 for the service from Moorgate to Stevenage via Hertford North

Table T025-F

Sundays

15 December to 10 May

Brighton, Gatwick Airport, Maidstone East and London - Stevenage, Cambridge, Kings Lynn and Peterborough

		TL	TL	TL	TL	GR	GN	TL	TL	GR	TL	TL	GN	TL	TL	TL	TL	GR	GN	TL	TL	GR
Brighton	d																					
Gatwick Airport	d			11 46							12 46					13 46						
East Croydon	d			12 07							13 07					14 07						
Maidstone East	d																					
London Bridge	d			12 25							13 25					14 25						
London Blackfriars	d			12 31							13 31					14 31						
City Thameslink	d																					
Farringdon	d			12 35							13 35					14 35						
St Pancras International	d			12 40							13 40					14 40						
London Kings Cross ⊖	d	12 14			13 02	13 03	13 11	13 13		13 33		14 02	14 11	14 13			15 02	15 03	15 11	15 13		15 33
Finsbury Park ⊖	d	12 20	←	12 46	13 08			13 19	←		13 47	14 08		14 19	←	14 47	15 08			15 19	←	
Potters Bar	d		12 19		13 19				13 19			14 19			14 19		15 19				15 19	
Hatfield	d		12 25		→				13 25			→			14 25		→				15 25	
Welwyn Garden City	d		12 31						13 31						14 31						15 31	
Welwyn North	d		12 35						13 35						14 35						15 35	
Knebworth	d		12 39						13 39						14 39						15 39	
Stevenage	d	12 40	12 44	13 07		13 25		13 40	13 44	13 55	14 07			14 40	14 44	15 07		15 25		15 40	15 44	15 55
Hitchin	d	12 45	12 50	13 13				13 45	13 50		14 13			14 45	14 50	15 13				15 45	15 50	
Letchworth Garden City	d		12 56	13 18					13 56		14 18				14 56	15 18					15 56	
Baldock	d		12 59	13 22					13 59		14 22				14 59	15 22					15 59	
Ashwell & Morden	d		13 04						14 04						15 04						16 04	
Royston	d		13 09	13 30					14 09		14 30				15 09	15 30					16 09	
Meldreth	d		13 12						14 12						15 12						16 12	
Shepreth	d		13 15						14 15						15 15						16 15	
Foxton	d		13 17						14 17						15 17						16 17	
Cambridge	a		13 28	13 48			13 58		14 28		14 48		14 58		15 28	15 48			15 58		16 28	
Cambridge	d						14 04						15 04						16 04			
Cambridge North	d						14 08						15 08						16 08			
Waterbeach	d						14 12						15 12						16 12			
Ely	d						14 22						15 22						16 22			
Littleport	d						14 29						15 29						16 29			
Downham Market	d						14 38						15 38						16 38			
Watlington	d						14 44						15 44						16 44			
Kings Lynn	a						14 52						15 52						16 52			
Arlesey	d	12 50						13 50						14 50						15 50		
Biggleswade	d	12 55						13 55						14 55						15 55		
Sandy	d	12 59						13 59						14 59						15 59		
St Neots	d	13 06						14 06						15 06						16 06		
Huntingdon	d	13 13						14 13						15 13						16 13		
Peterborough	a	13 29				13 54		14 29		14 24				15 29				15 54		16 29		16 24

		TL	TL	GN	TL	TL	TL	TL	TL	GN	TL	GN	TL	TL	TL	TL	TL	GN	TL	GN	TL	TL	TL
Brighton	d																						
Gatwick Airport	d	14 46						15 46								16 46							
East Croydon	d	15 07						16 07								17 07							
Maidstone East	d																						
London Bridge	d	15 25						16 25								17 25							
London Blackfriars	d	15 31						16 31								17 31							
City Thameslink	d																						
Farringdon	d	15 35						16 35								17 35							
St Pancras International	d	15 40						16 40								17 40							
London Kings Cross ⊖	d		16 02	16 11	16 13		16 32			16 55	17 02	17 11	17 13		17 32			17 55	18 02	18 11	18 13		18 32
Finsbury Park ⊖	d	15 47	16 08		16 19	←	16 38	16 47	←		17 08		17 19	←	17 38	17 46	←		18 08		18 19	←	18 38
Potters Bar	d		16 19			16 19	16 49		16 49		17 19			17 19	17 49		17 49		18 19			18 19	18 49
Hatfield	d		→			16 25	→		16 55		→			17 25	→		17 55		→			18 25	→
Welwyn Garden City	d					16 31			17 01					17 31			18 01					18 31	
Welwyn North	d					16 35			17 05					17 35			18 05					18 35	
Knebworth	d					16 39			17 09					17 39			18 09					18 39	
Stevenage	d	16 07			16 40	16 44		17 07	17 14				17 40	17 44		18 07	18 14				18 40	18 44	
Hitchin	d	16 13			16 45	16 50		17 13	17 21				17 45	17 50		18 13	18 20				18 45	18 50	
Letchworth Garden City	d	16 18				16 56		17 18	17a27					17 56		18 18	18a27					18 56	
Baldock	d	16 22				16 59		17 22						17 59		18 22						18 59	
Ashwell & Morden	d					17 04								18 04								19 04	
Royston	d	16 30				17 09		17 30						18 09		18 30						19 09	
Meldreth	d					17 12								18 12								19 12	
Shepreth	d					17 15								18 15								19 15	
Foxton	d					17 17								18 17								19 17	
Cambridge	a	16 48		16 58		17 28		17 48				17 58		18 28		18 48				18 58		19 28	
Cambridge	d			17 04								18 04								19 04			
Cambridge North	d			17 08								18 08								19 08			
Waterbeach	d			17 12								18 12								19 12			
Ely	d			17 22								18 22								19 22			
Littleport	d			17 29								18 30								19 29			
Downham Market	d			17 38								18 39								19 38			
Watlington	d			17 44								18 44								19 44			
Kings Lynn	a			17 52								18 53								19 52			
Arlesey	d				16 50								17 50								18 50		
Biggleswade	d				16 55					17 26			17 55					18 25			18 55		
Sandy	d				16 59								17 59								18 59		
St Neots	d				17 06					17 36			18 06					18 35			19 06		
Huntingdon	d				17 13					17 43			18 13					18 42			19 13		
Peterborough	a				17 29					18 01			18 29					18 59			19 29		

Please refer to Table T024 for the service from Moorgate to Stevenage via Hertford North

Table T025-F

Sundays
15 December to 10 May

Brighton, Gatwick Airport, Maidstone East and London - Stevenage, Cambridge, Kings Lynn and Peterborough

		TL	TL	GN	TL	GR	GN	TL	TL	GR	TL	TL	GN	TL	TL	GR	TL	TL	GN	TL	TL	GR
Brighton	d																					
Gatwick Airport	d	17 46									18 46						19 46					
East Croydon	d	18 07									19 07						20 07					
Maidstone East	d																					
London Bridge	d	18 25									19 25						20 25					
London Blackfriars	d	18 31									19 31						20 31					
City Thameslink	d																					
Farringdon	d	18 35									19 35						20 35					
St Pancras International	d	18 40									19 40						20 40					
London Kings Cross 15 ⊖	d			18 55	19 02	19 06	19 11	19 13		19 35		20 02	20 11	20 13		20 35		21 02	21 11	21 13		21 35
Finsbury Park ⊖	d	18 47	←		19 08			19 19	←		19 47	20 08		20 19	←		20 47	21 08		21 19	←	
Potters Bar	d		18 49		19 19				19 19			20 19			20 19			21 19			21 19	
Hatfield	d		18 55		→				19 26			→			20 26			→			21 25	
Welwyn Garden City 4	d		19 01						19 31						20 31						21 31	
Welwyn North	d		19 05						19 35						20 35						21 35	
Knebworth	d		19 09						19 39						20 39						21 39	
Stevenage 4	d	19 07	19 14			19 29		19 40	19 44	19 57	20 07			20 40	20 44	20 57	21 07			21 40	21 44	21 57
Hitchin 4	d	19 13	19 20					19 45	19 50		20 13			20 45	20 50		21 13			21 45	21 50	
Letchworth Garden City	d	19 18	19a27						19 56		20 18				20 56		21 18				21 56	
Baldock	d	19 22							19 59		20 22				20 59		21 22				21 59	
Ashwell & Morden	d								20 04						21 04						22 04	
Royston	d	19 30							20 09		20 30				21 09		21 30				22 09	
Meldreth	d								20 13						21 13						22 12	
Shepreth	d								20 16						21 16						22 15	
Foxton	d								20 19						21 19						22 17	
Cambridge	a	19 48					20 00		20 30		20 48		20 58		21 30		21 45		21 58		22 28	
Cambridge	d						20 05						21 04						22 04			
Cambridge North	d						20 09						21 08						22 08			
Waterbeach	d						20 13						21 12						22 12			
Ely	d						20 23						21 22						22 22			
Littleport	d						20 30						21 29						22 29			
Downham Market	d						20 39						21 38						22 38			
Watlington	d						20 45						21 44						22 44			
Kings Lynn	a						20 53						21 52						22 52			
Arlesey	d							19 50						20 50						21 50		
Biggleswade	d			19 26				19 55						20 55						21 55		
Sandy	d							19 59						20 59						21 59		
St Neots	d			19 36				20 06						21 06						22 06		
Huntingdon	d			19 43				20 13						21 13						22 13		
Peterborough 8	a			20 01		19 58		20 29		20 26				21 29		21 26				22 29		22 26

		TL	TL	GN	TL	TL	TL	TL	GN	TL	TL
Brighton	d										
Gatwick Airport	d	20 46					21 46				
East Croydon	d	21 07					22 07				
Maidstone East	d										
London Bridge	d	21 25					22 25				
London Blackfriars	d	21 31					22 31				
City Thameslink	d										
Farringdon	d	21 35					22 35				
St Pancras International	d	21 40					22 40				
London Kings Cross 15 ⊖	d		22 02	22 11	22 13			23 02	23 11	←	23 23
Finsbury Park ⊖	d	21 47	22 08		22 19	←	22 47	23 09		23 09	23 31
Potters Bar	d		22 19			22 19				23 20	
Hatfield	d		→			22 25		→		23 26	
Welwyn Garden City 4	d					22 31				23 31	
Welwyn North	d					22 35				23 35	
Knebworth	d					22 39				23 39	
Stevenage 4	d	22 08			22 39	22 44	23 08			23 44	23 51
Hitchin 4	d	22 13			22 44	22 50	23 13			23 50	23 56
Letchworth Garden City	d	22 19				22 56	23 19		23 38	23 56	
Baldock	d	22 22				22 59	23 22			23 59	
Ashwell & Morden	d					23 04				00 04	
Royston	d	22 30				23 09	23 30		23 48	00 09	
Meldreth	d					23 12				00 13	
Shepreth	d					23 15				00 16	
Foxton	d					23 17				00 19	
Cambridge	a	22 48		22 58		23 28	23 45		00 02	00 30	
Cambridge	d			23 04					00 04		
Cambridge North	d			23 08					00 08		
Waterbeach	d			23 12					00 12		
Ely	d			23 22					00 22		
Littleport	d			23 29					00 29		
Downham Market	d			23 38					00 38		
Watlington	d			23 44					00 44		
Kings Lynn	a			23 52					00 52		
Arlesey	d				22 49						00 01
Biggleswade	d				22 54						00 06
Sandy	d				22 58						00 10
St Neots	d				23 05						00 17
Huntingdon	d				23 12						00 24
Peterborough 8	a				23 30						00 42

Please refer to Table T024 for the service from Moorgate to Stevenage via Hertford North

NRT DECEMBER 19 EDITION

Table T025-R

Mondays to Fridays
16 December to 15 May

Peterborough, Kings Lynn, Cambridge and Stevenage - London, Maidstone East, Gatwick Airport and Brighton

Miles	Miles			TL MX	GN MO	TL MX	GN MO	TL MX	TL MX	TL	GN	GN	TL	TL	TL	TL	GN	TL	TL	TL	TL	GN	TL
0	—	Peterborough 8	d							03 24				04 20					04 54				
17½	—	**Huntingdon**	d							03 39				04 35					05 11				
24¾	—	**St Neots**	d							03 46				04 42					05 18				
32¼	—	**Sandy**	d							03 54				04 50					05 26				
35¼	—	**Biggleswade**	d							03 58				04 54					05 30				
39¼	—	**Arlesey**	a							04 02				04 58					05 34				
—	—	**Kings Lynn**	d																				
—	—	**Watlington**	d																				
—	—	**Downham Market**	d																				
—	—	**Littleport**	d																				
—	—	Ely	d																				
—	—	Waterbeach	d																				
—	—	Cambridge North	d																				
—	0	Cambridge	a																				
—	—	Cambridge	d													04 54					05 24		05 27
—	7	**Foxton**	d																				05 36
—	8	**Shepreth**	d																				05 38
—	10	**Meldreth**	d																				05 41
—	13	**Royston**	d						00 09							05 09		05 17			05 38		05 46
—	17	**Ashwell & Morden**	d															05 21			05 43		05 50
—	21¼	**Baldock**	d					00 03	00 17							05 17		05 26			05 48		05 55
—	23¼	**Letchworth Garden City**	a					00 06	00 20							05 20		05 29			05 51		05 59
44½	26	**Hitchin 4**	d		00 01	00 06		00 10	00 28	04 11			05 00	05 07		05 26		05 34	05 41		05 56		06 04
48¾	30¼	**Stevenage 4**	d		00 07	00 12	←	00 16	00 34	04 17	04 22	05 02	05 06	05 13		05 32	05 32	05 40	05 47	←	06 02	06 06	06 10
51¼	33	**Knebworth**	d		00 11		00 11	00 19					05 09					05 43		05 43			06 13
54¼	36	**Welwyn North**	d		→		00 15	00 23					05 13					→		05 47			→
56	37¾	Welwyn Garden City 4	d				00 19	00 28					05 18	05 22	←					05 52			
58½	40¼	Hatfield	d				00 23	00 31					05 21		05 21					05 55			
63½	45¼	Potters Bar	d	00 02			00 29	00 38					→		05 28					06 02			
73¾	55½	Finsbury Park ⊖	a	00 15		00 38	00 39	00 51	01 00	04 45	05 04	05 52		05 35	05 41	05 51	06 25		06 07	06 13	06 21	06 53	
76¼	58	London Kings Cross 15 ⊖	a	00 21		00 45	00 49	00 57	01 06	04 51	05 13				05 47					06 20			
—	—	St Pancras International	a											05 44		05 59			06 14		06 29		
—	—	Farringdon	a											05 49		06 04			06 19		06 34		
—	—	City Thameslink	a											05 51		06 06			06 21		06 36		
—	—	London Blackfriars	a											05 53		06 08			06 23		06 38		
—	—	**London Bridge**	a											05 59		06 14			06 29		06 44		
—	—	Maidstone East	a																				
—	—	East Croydon	a											06 16		06 28			06 46		06 59		
—	—	Gatwick Airport	a											06 50		06 44			07 19		07 14		
—	—	Brighton	a													07 22					07 49		

		GN	TL	GN	TL	GN	TL	TL	TL	GN	GN	TL	GN	TL	TL	GN	TL	GN	TL	GN	TL	TL
Peterborough 8	d		05 24	05 42					05 54		06 05						06 24	06 36				
Huntingdon	d		05 41	05 56					06 11		06 20						06 41	06 50				
St Neots	d		05 48	06 04					06 18		06 28						06 48	06 59				
Sandy	d		05 56						06 26								06 56					
Biggleswade	d		06 00	06 14					06 30		06 38						07 00	07 08				
Arlesey	a		06 05						06 35								07 05					
Kings Lynn	d	04 43														05 40						
Watlington	d	04 50														05 47						
Downham Market	d	04 57														05 54						
Littleport	d	05 07														06 04						
Ely	d	05 15														06 12						
Waterbeach	d	05 25														06 22						
Cambridge North	d	05 30														06 27						
Cambridge	a	05 34														06 34						
Cambridge	d	05 40					05 54	05 57		06 10				06 24	06 27	06 40					06 54	06 57
Foxton	d							06 06							06 36							07 06
Shepreth	d							06 08							06 38							07 08
Meldreth	d							06 11							06 41							07 11
Royston	d	05 54					06 08	06 16		06 24			06 34	06 38	06 47	06 54					07 08	07 16
Ashwell & Morden	d						06 13	06 20						06 43	06 51						07 13	07 20
Baldock	d					06 12	06 18	06 25					06 42	06 48	06 56					07 12	07 18	07 25
Letchworth Garden City	a	06 04				06 15	06 21	06 28		06 34			06 45	06 51	06 59	07 04				07 15	07 21	07 28
Hitchin 4	d		06 11			06 20	06 26	06 34	06 41				06 50	06 56	07 04		07 11			07 20	07 26	07 34
Stevenage 4	d		06 17		←		06 32	06 40	06 47		06 49	←		07 02	07 10		07 17	07 20	←		07 32	07 40
Knebworth	d				06 13	06 28		06 43				06 43	06 58		07 13				07 13	07 28		07 43
Welwyn North	d				06 17	06 32		→				06 47	07 02		→				07 17	07 32		→
Welwyn Garden City 4	d				06 22							06 52							07 22			
Hatfield	d				06 25							06 55							07 25			
Potters Bar	d				06 32							07 02							07 32			
Finsbury Park ⊖	a		06 37		06 43		06 51		07 07			07 13		07 21			07 37		07 43		07 51	
London Kings Cross 15 ⊖	a	06 32		06 44	06 50	06 52				07 02	07 14	07 20	07 21			07 32		07 44	07 50	07 51		
St Pancras International	a		06 44				06 59		07 14					07 29			07 44				07 59	
Farringdon	a		06 49				07 04		07 19					07 34			07 49				08 04	
City Thameslink	a		06 51				07 06		07 21					07 36			07 51				08 06	
London Blackfriars	a		06 53				07 08		07 23					07 38			07 53				08 08	
London Bridge	a		06 59				07 14		07 29					07 44			07 59				08 14	
Maidstone East	a																					
East Croydon	a		07 16				07 29		07 46					08 00			08 16				08 29	
Gatwick Airport	a		07 46				07 44		08 16					08 15			08 45				08 44	
Brighton	a						08 19							08 50							09 20	

Please refer to Table T024 for the service from Moorgate to Stevenage via Hertford North

Table T025-R

Peterborough, Kings Lynn, Cambridge and Stevenage - London, Maidstone East, Gatwick Airport and Brighton

Mondays to Fridays
16 December to 15 May

		GN	GN	TL	GN	GN	TL	GN	TL	TL	GN	GN	TL	GN	TL	GN	TL	TL	GN	GN	TL	GN	GN
Peterborough	d			06 54	07 05	07 14							07 24	07 35							07 54	08 04	
Huntingdon	d			07 11	07 20	07 30							07 41	07 49							08 11	08 20	
St Neots	d			07 18	07 28	07 39							07 48	07 57							08 18	08 28	
Sandy	d			07 26									07 56								08 26		
Biggleswade	d			07 30	07 38								08 00	08 08							08 30	08 39	
Arlesey	a			07 35									08 05								08 35		
Kings Lynn	d	06 09									06 40								07 05	07 16			
Watlington	d	06 17									06 47								07 12				
Downham Market	d	06 24									06 54								07 19	07 28			
Littleport	d										07 04								07 29				
Ely	d	06 42	06 45								07 12	07 15							07 41	07 46			
Waterbeach	d		06 56								07 22								07 51				
Cambridge North	d	06 55										07 29								07 58			
Cambridge	a	07 00	07 03								07 30	07 34							07 59	08 03			
Cambridge	d	07 09							07 24	07 27	07 39						07 54	07 57	08 09				
Foxton	d									07 36								08 06					
Shepreth	d									07 38								08 08					
Meldreth	d									07 41								08 11					
Royston	d	07 24							07 38	07 46	07 54						08 08	08 16	08 24				
Ashwell & Morden	d								07 43	07 50							08 13	08 20					
Baldock	d							07 42	07 48	07 55						08 12	08 18	08 25					08 42
Letchworth Garden City	a	07 33						07 45	07 51	07 58	08 03					08 15	08 21	08 28	08 33				08 45
Hitchin	d			07 41				07 50	07 56	08 04			08 11			08 20	08 26	08 34			08 41		08 50
Stevenage	d			07 47	07 51		←		08 02	08 10			08 17	08 21	←		08 32	08 40			08 47	08 53	
Knebworth	d						07 43	07 57		08 13					08 13	08 28		08 43					08 58
Welwyn North	d						07 47	08 01		→					08 17	08 33		08 47					
Welwyn Garden City	d						07 52								08 22			→					
Hatfield	d						07 55								08 25								
Potters Bar	d						08 02								08 32								
Finsbury Park	a			08 07			08 13		08 21				08 37		08 43		08 51				09 07		
London Kings Cross	a	08 02			08 14	08 18	08 21	08 21			08 34			08 46	08 50	08 52			09 04			09 18	09 20
St Pancras International	a			08 14					08 29				08 44				08 59				09 14		
Farringdon	a			08 19					08 34				08 49				09 04				09 19		
City Thameslink	a			08 21					08 36				08 51				09 06				09 21		
London Blackfriars	a			08 23					08 38				08 53				09 08				09 23		
London Bridge	a			08 29					08 44				08 59				09 14				09 29		
Maidstone East	a																						
East Croydon	a			08 46					08 58				09 14				09 28				09 44		
Gatwick Airport	a			09 15					09 14				09 43				09 44				10 13		
Brighton	a								09 49								10 19						

		TL	TL	TL	TL	GR	TL	GR	TL	TL	GN	TL	TL	TL	GN	TL	GN	TL	TL	GR	TL	GN
Peterborough	d				08 23	08 29				←						08 56	09 17					
Huntingdon	d				08 38					08 38						09 12	09 32					
St Neots	d				→					08 45						09 20	09 40					
Sandy	d									08 53						09 27						
Biggleswade	d									08 57						09 31	09 49					
Arlesey	a									09 01						09 35						
Kings Lynn	d										07 48				08 12							08 44
Watlington	d										07 56				08 19							08 51
Downham Market	d										08 03				08 26							08 58
Littleport	d										08 13				08 36							09 08
Ely	d										08 25				08 45							09 17
Waterbeach	d										08 35				08 55							09 26
Cambridge North	d										08 40				09 00							09 31
Cambridge	a								←		08 44				09 04							09 36
Cambridge	d			08 25					08 25		08 49		08 54	08 58	09 10				09 24		09 27	09 41
Foxton	d			→					08 34					09 06							09 36	
Shepreth	d								08 36					09 08							09 38	
Meldreth	d						←		08 39					09 11							09 41	
Royston	d		08 38				08 38		08 44		09 05		09 09	09 18	09 26				09 38		09 46	
Ashwell & Morden	d		→				08 43		08 48		09 10			09 22					09 43		09 50	
Baldock	d						08 48		08 53				09 17	09 27					09 48		09 55	
Letchworth Garden City	a						08 51		08 56		09 16		09 20	09 30					09 51		09 58	10 03
Hitchin	d						08 56		09 00	09 07			09 24	09 34		09 41			09 56		10 04	
Stevenage	d					08 59	09 02	09 05	09 06	09 13		←	09 30	09 40		09 47		←	10 02	10 07	10 10	
Knebworth	d	←							09 09			09 09		09 43				09 43			10 13	
Welwyn North	d	08 47							→			09 13		→				09 47			→	
Welwyn Garden City	d	08 52										09 22						09 52				
Hatfield	d	08 55										09 25						09 55				
Potters Bar	d	09 02										09 32						10 02				
Finsbury Park	a	09 13					09 22			09 33		09 43	09 50			10 07		10 13	10 21			
London Kings Cross	a	09 25				09 26		09 31			09 46	09 50			10 05		10 20	10 25		10 31		10 34
St Pancras International	a						09 29			09 44			09 59			10 14			10 29			
Farringdon	a						09 34			09 49			10 04			10 19			10 34			
City Thameslink	a						09 36			09 51			10 06			10 21			10 36			
London Blackfriars	a						09 38			09 53			10 08			10 23			10 38			
London Bridge	a						09 44			09 59			10 14			10 29			10 44			
Maidstone East	a																					
East Croydon	a						09 58			10 14			10 28			10 44			10 58			
Gatwick Airport	a						10 14			10 43			10 44			11 12			11 14			
Brighton	a						10 49						11 19						11 49			

Please refer to Table T024 for the service from Moorgate to Stevenage via Hertford North

Table T025-R

Peterborough, Kings Lynn, Cambridge and Stevenage - London, Maidstone East, Gatwick Airport and Brighton

Mondays to Fridays
16 December to 15 May

		TL	TL	TL	TL	GN	TL	TL	TL	GR	TL	GN	TL	TL	TL	TL	GN	TL	TL	TL	TL	TL	GR
Peterborough	d	09 26					09 54						10 24					10 54				11 23	11 29
Huntingdon	d	09 41					10 11						10 41					11 11				11 41	
St Neots	d	09 48					10 18						10 48					11 18				→	
Sandy	d	09 56					10 26						10 56					11 26					
Biggleswade	d	10 00					10 30						11 00					11 30					
Arlesey	a	10 05					10 34						11 04					11 34					
Kings Lynn	d					09 10						09 44											
Watlington	d					09 17						09 51											
Downham Market	d					09 28						09 58											
Littleport	d					09 38						10 08											
Ely	d					09 48						10 17					10 47						
Waterbeach	d					09 58						10 26											
Cambridge North	d					10 03						10 31					11 01						
Cambridge	a					10 07						10 36					11 05						
Cambridge	d			09 54	09 58	10 14			10 24		10 27	10 44			10 54	10 57	11 14			11 24	11 27		
Foxton	d				10 07						10 36					11 06					→		
Shepreth	d				10 09						10 38					11 08							
Meldreth	d				10 12						10 41					11 11							
Royston	d			10 09	10 17				10 38		10 47				11 09	11 17				11 38			
Ashwell & Morden	d				10 21				10 43		10 51					11 21				→			
Baldock	d			10 17	10 26				10 48		10 56				11 17	11 26							
Letchworth Garden City	a			10 20	10 29				10 51		10 59				11 20	11 29							
Hitchin	d	10 11		10 26	10 34		10 41		10 56		11 04		11 11		11 26	11 34		11 41					
Stevenage	d	10 17	←	10 32	10 40		10 47	←	11 02	11 04	11 10		11 17	←	11 32	11 40		11 47	←				11 58
Knebworth	d		10 13		10 43			10 43			11 13			11 13		11 43			11 43				
Welwyn North	d		10 17		→			10 47			→			11 17		→			11 47				
Welwyn Garden City	d		10 22					10 52						11 22					11 52				
Hatfield	d		10 25					10 55						11 25					11 55				
Potters Bar	d		10 32					11 02						11 32					12 02				
Finsbury Park	a	10 37	10 43	10 51			11 07	11 13	11 21				11 37	11 43	11 51			12 06	12 13				
London Kings Cross	a		10 50			11 05		11 20		11 31		11 34		11 50			12 02		12 20				12 23
St Pancras International	a	10 44		10 59			11 14		11 29				11 44		11 59			12 14					
Farringdon	a	10 49		11 04			11 19		11 34				11 49		12 04			12 19					
City Thameslink	a	10 51		11 06			11 21		11 36				11 51		12 06			12 21					
London Blackfriars	a	10 53		11 08			11 23		11 38				11 53		12 08			12 23					
London Bridge	a	10 59		11 14			11 29		11 44				11 59		12 14			12 29					
Maidstone East	a																						
East Croydon	a	11 14		11 28			11 44		11 58				12 14		12 28			12 44					
Gatwick Airport	a	11 43		11 44			12 13		12 14				12 43		12 44			13 13					
Brighton	a			12 19					12 49						13 19								

		TL	GR	TL	TL	GN	TL	TL	TL	GN	TL	TL	TL	TL	TL	GR	TL	GR	TL	TL	GN	TL
Peterborough	d				←						11 54				12 24	12 30				←		
Huntingdon	d				11 41						12 11				12 41					12 41		
St Neots	d				11 48						12 18				→					12 48		
Sandy	d				11 56						12 26									12 56		
Biggleswade	d				12 00						12 30									13 00		
Arlesey	a				12 04						12 34									13 04		
Kings Lynn	d					10 44															11 44	
Watlington	d					10 51															11 51	
Downham Market	d					10 58															11 58	
Littleport	d					11 08															12 08	
Ely	d					11 17				11 47											12 17	
Waterbeach	d					11 26															12 26	
Cambridge North	d					11 31				12 01											12 31	
Cambridge	a			←		11 36				12 05											12 37	
Cambridge	d			11 27		11 44		11 54	11 57	12 14			12 24								12 44	
Foxton	d			11 36					12 06													
Shepreth	d			11 38					12 08													
Meldreth	d	←		11 41					12 11													
Royston	d	11 38		11 47				12 09	12 17				12 38									
Ashwell & Morden	d	11 43		11 51					12 21				12 43									
Baldock	d	11 47		11 56				12 17	12 26				12 48									
Letchworth Garden City	a	11 50		11 59				12 20	12 29				12 51						←			
Hitchin	d	11 55		12 04	12 11			12 26	12 34		12 41		12 56	13 00			←		13 00	13 11		
Stevenage	d	12 01	12 03	12 10	12 17		←	12 32	12 40		12 47	←	13 02	→		12 59	13 02	13 04	13 08	13 17		←
Knebworth	d			12 13			12 13		12 43			12 43	→						13 13			13 13
Welwyn North	d			→			12 17		→			12 47							→			13 17
Welwyn Garden City	d						12 22					12 52										13 22
Hatfield	d						12 25					12 55										13 25
Potters Bar	d						12 32					13 02										13 32
Finsbury Park	a	12 20			12 37		12 43	12 51			13 07	13 13					13 21			13 37		13 43
London Kings Cross	a		12 30			12 35	12 50			13 03		13 20				13 23		13 31			13 33	13 50
St Pancras International	a	12 29			12 44			12 59			13 14						13 29			13 44		
Farringdon	a	12 34			12 49			13 04			13 19						13 34			13 49		
City Thameslink	a	12 36			12 51			13 06			13 21						13 36			13 51		
London Blackfriars	a	12 38			12 53			13 08			13 23						13 38			13 53		
London Bridge	a	12 44			12 59			13 14			13 29						13 44			13 59		
Maidstone East	a																					
East Croydon	a	12 58			13 14			13 28			13 44						13 58			14 14		
Gatwick Airport	a	13 14			13 43			13 44			14 13						14 14			14 43		
Brighton	a	13 49						14 19									14 49					

Please refer to Table T024 for the service from Moorgate to Stevenage via Hertford North

Table T025-R

Mondays to Fridays

16 December to 15 May

Peterborough, Kings Lynn, Cambridge and Stevenage - London, Maidstone East, Gatwick Airport and Brighton

Station		TL	TL	GN	TL	TL	TL	TL	TL	GR	TL	GR	TL	TL	GN	TL	TL	TL	GN	TL	TL	TL	TL
Peterborough	d				12 54				13 24	13 29				←						13 54			
Huntingdon	d				13 11				13 41					13 41						14 11			
St Neots	d				13 18				→					13 48						14 18			
Sandy	d				13 26									13 56						14 26			
Biggleswade	d				13 30									14 00						14 30			
Arlesey	a				13 34									14 04						14 34			
Kings Lynn	d														12 44								
Watlington	d														12 51								
Downham Market	d														12 58								
Littleport	d														13 08								
Ely	d			12 47											13 17				13 47				
Waterbeach	d														13 26								
Cambridge North	d			13 01											13 31				14 01				
Cambridge	a			13 05									←		13 37				14 05				
Cambridge	d	12 54	12 57	13 14			13 24	13 27					13 27		13 44		13 54	13 57	14 14			14 24	14 27
Foxton	d		13 06					→					13 36					14 06					→
Shepreth	d		13 08										13 38					14 08					
Meldreth	d		13 11								←		13 41					14 11					
Royston	d	13 09	13 17				13 38				13 38		13 47				14 09	14 17				14 38	
Ashwell & Morden	d		13 21				→				13 43		13 51					14 21				→	
Baldock	d	13 17	13 26								13 48		13 56				14 17	14 26					
Letchworth Garden City	a	13 20	13 29								13 51		13 59				14 20	14 29					
Hitchin	d	13 26	13 34		13 41						13 56		14 04	14 11			14 26	14 34		14 41			
Stevenage	d	13 32	13 40		13 47	←				13 59	14 02	14 04	14 10	14 17		←	14 32	14 40		14 47	←		
Knebworth	d		13 43			13 43							14 13			14 13		14 43			14 43		
Welwyn North	d		→			13 47							→			14 17		→			14 47		
Welwyn Garden City	d					13 52										14 22					14 52		
Hatfield	d					13 55										14 25					14 55		
Potters Bar	d					14 02										14 32					15 02		
Finsbury Park	a	13 51			14 07	14 13					14 21			14 37		14 43	14 51			15 07	15 13		
London Kings Cross	a			14 03		14 20				14 23		14 31			14 33	14 50			15 02		15 20		
St Pancras International	a	13 59			14 14						14 29			14 44			14 59			15 14			
Farringdon	a	14 04			14 19						14 34			14 49			15 04			15 19			
City Thameslink	a	14 06			14 21						14 36			14 51			15 06			15 21			
London Blackfriars	a	14 08			14 23						14 38			14 53			15 08			15 23			
London Bridge	a	14 14			14 29						14 44			14 59			15 14			15 29			
Maidstone East	a																						
East Croydon	a	14 28			14 44						14 58			15 14			15 28			15 44			
Gatwick Airport	a	14 44			15 13						15 14			15 43			15 44			16 13			
Brighton	a	15 19									15 49						16 19						

Station		TL	GR	TL	GR	TL	TL	GN	TL	TL	TL	GN	TL	TL	TL	TL	TL	GR	TL	GN	GR	TL	TL
Peterborough	d	14 24	14 29				←						14 54				15 24	15 30					←
Huntingdon	d	14 41					14 41						15 11				15 41						15 41
St Neots	d	→					14 48						15 18				→						15 48
Sandy	d						14 56						15 26										15 56
Biggleswade	d						15 00						15 30										16 00
Arlesey	a						15 04						15 34										16 04
Kings Lynn	d							13 44												14 44			
Watlington	d							13 51												14 51			
Downham Market	d							13 58												14 58			
Littleport	d							14 07												15 08			
Ely	d							14 17				14 47								15 17			
Waterbeach	d							14 26												15 26			
Cambridge North	d							14 31				15 01								15 31			
Cambridge	a					←		14 36				15 05								15 37			
Cambridge	d					14 27		14 44		14 54	14 57	15 14			15 24	15 27				15 44		←	
Foxton	d					14 36					15 06					15 36						15 36	
Shepreth	d					14 38					15 08					→						15 38	
Meldreth	d			←		14 41					15 11								←			15 41	
Royston	d			14 38		14 47				15 09	15 17				15 38				15 38			15 47	
Ashwell & Morden	d			14 43		14 51					15 21				→				15 43			15 51	
Baldock	d			14 48		14 56				15 17	15 26								15 48			15 56	
Letchworth Garden City	a			14 51		14 59				15 20	15 29								15 51			15 59	
Hitchin	d			14 56		15 04	15 11			15 26	15 34		15 41						15 56			16 04	16 11
Stevenage	d		14 59	15 02	15 04	15 10	15 17		←	15 32	15 40		15 47	←				15 59	16 02		16 04	16 10	16 17
Knebworth	d					15 13			15 13		15 43			15 43								16 13	
Welwyn North	d					→			15 17		→			15 47								→	
Welwyn Garden City	d								15 22					15 52									
Hatfield	d								15 25					15 55									
Potters Bar	d								15 32					16 02									
Finsbury Park	a			15 21			15 37		15 43	15 51			16 07	16 13					16 21				16 37
London Kings Cross	a		15 23		15 31			15 33	15 50			16 02		16 20				16 23		16 33	16 33		
St Pancras International	a			15 29			15 44			15 59			16 14						16 29				16 44
Farringdon	a			15 34			15 49			16 04			16 19						16 34				16 49
City Thameslink	a			15 36			15 51			16 06			16 21						16 36				16 51
London Blackfriars	a			15 38			15 53			16 08			16 23						16 38				16 53
London Bridge	a			15 44			15 59			16 14			16 29						16 44				16 59
Maidstone East	a																						
East Croydon	a			15 58			16 14			16 29			16 44						16 59				17 14
Gatwick Airport	a			16 14			16 43			16 44			17 15						17 14				17 45
Brighton	a			16 49						17 21									17 51				

Please refer to Table T024 for the service from Moorgate to Stevenage via Hertford North

NRT DECEMBER 19 EDITION

Table T025-R

Mondays to Fridays

16 December to 15 May

Peterborough, Kings Lynn, Cambridge and Stevenage - London, Maidstone East, Gatwick Airport and Brighton

Station		TL	TL	TL	GN	TL	TL	TL	TL	TL	GR	TL	GR	TL	TL	GN	TL	TL	TL	GN	TL	TL
Peterborough	d					15 54				16 24	16 30				←						16 53	
Huntingdon	d					16 11				16 41					16 41						17 11	
St Neots	d					16 18				→					16 48						17 18	
Sandy	d					16 26									16 56						17 26	
Biggleswade	d					16 30									17 00						17 30	
Arlesey	a					16 34									17 04						17 34	
Kings Lynn	d															15 44						
Watlington	d															15 51						
Downham Market	d															15 58						
Littleport	d															16 08						
Ely	d				15 45											16 17				16 47		
Waterbeach	d															16 26						
Cambridge North	d				16 00											16 31				17 01		
Cambridge	a				16 05									←		16 37				17 05		
Cambridge	d		15 54	15 57	16 14			16 24	16 27					16 27		16 44		16 54	16 57	17 08		
Foxton	d			16 06					→					16 36					17 06			
Shepreth	d			16 08										16 38					17 08			
Meldreth	d			16 11								←		16 41					17 11			
Royston	d		16 09	16 17				16 38				16 38		16 47				17 09	17 16	17 23		
Ashwell & Morden	d			16 21				→				16 43		16 51					17 20			
Baldock	d		16 17	16 26								16 48		16 56				17 17	17 25			
Letchworth Garden City	a		16 20	16 29								16 51		16 59				17 20	17 28	17 33		
Hitchin	d		16 26	16 34		16 41						16 56		17 04	17 11			17 26	17 34		17 41	
Stevenage	d	←	16 32	16 40		16 47	←				16 59	17 02	17 04	17 10	17 17		←	17 32	17 40		17 47	←
Knebworth	d	16 13		16 43			16 43							17 13			17 13		17 43			17 43
Welwyn North	d	16 17		→			16 47							→			17 17		→			17 47
Welwyn Garden City	d	16 22					16 52										17 22					17 52
Hatfield	d	16 25					16 55										17 25					17 55
Potters Bar	d	16 32					17 02										17 32					18 02
Finsbury Park	a	16 43	16 51			17 07	17 14					17 21			17 37		17 44	17 51			18 07	18 14
London Kings Cross	a	16 50			17 03		17 20				17 23		17 31			17 32	17 50			18 03		18 20
St Pancras International	a		16 59			17 14						17 29			17 44			17 59			18 14	
Farringdon	a		17 04			17 19						17 34			17 49			18 04			18 19	
City Thameslink	a		17 06			17 21						17 36			17 51			18 06			18 21	
London Blackfriars	a		17 08			17 23						17 38			17 53			18 08			18 23	
London Bridge	a		17 14			17 29						17 44			17 59			18 14			18 29	
Maidstone East	a																					
East Croydon	a		17 29			17 45						17 59			18 14			18 29			18 44	
Gatwick Airport	a		17 44			18 15						18 14			18 45			18 44			19 15	
Brighton	a		18 21									18 51						19 21				

Station		TL	TL	TL	GR	TL	GR	TL	TL	GN	TL	TL	TL	GN	GN	TL	TL	TL	TL	TL	GR	TL	GR
Peterborough	d			17 24	17 30				←							17 54				18 24	18 29		
Huntingdon	d			17 41					17 41							18 11				18 41			
St Neots	d			→					17 48							18 18				→			
Sandy	d								17 56							18 26							
Biggleswade	d								18 00							18 30							
Arlesey	a								18 04							18 34							
Kings Lynn	d									16 44					17 15								
Watlington	d									16 51													
Downham Market	d									16 58					17 29								
Littleport	d									17 08													
Ely	d									17 17				17 42	17 46								
Waterbeach	d									17 26					17 55								
Cambridge North	d									17 31				17 55									
Cambridge	a							←		17 37				17 59	18 02								
Cambridge	d	17 25	17 29					17 29		17 43		17 54	17 57	18 08				18 23	18 26				
Foxton	d		→					17 38					18 06						→				
Shepreth	d							17 40					18 08										
Meldreth	d					←		17 43					18 11									←	
Royston	d	17 39				17 39		17 48				18 09	18 16	18 23				18 38				18 38	
Ashwell & Morden	d	→				17 44		17 52					18 20					→				18 43	
Baldock	d					17 48		17 57				18 17	18 25									18 48	
Letchworth Garden City	a					17 51		18 00				18 21	18 28	18 33								18 51	
Hitchin	d					17 56		18 04	18 11			18 26	18 34			18 41						18 56	
Stevenage	d				17 59	18 02	18 05	18 10	18 17		←	18 32	18 40			18 47	←				18 59	19 02	19 07
Knebworth	d							18 13			18 13		18 43				18 43						
Welwyn North	d							→			18 17		→				18 47						
Welwyn Garden City	d										18 22						18 52						
Hatfield	d										18 25						18 55						
Potters Bar	d										18 32						19 02						
Finsbury Park	a					18 21			18 36		18 44	18 51				19 07	19 14					19 21	
London Kings Cross	a				18 25		18 31			18 33	18 50			19 05			19 20				19 23		19 32
St Pancras International	a					18 29			18 44			18 59				19 14						19 29	
Farringdon	a					18 34			18 49			19 04				19 19						19 34	
City Thameslink	a					18 36			18 51			19 06				19 21						19 36	
London Blackfriars	a					18 38			18 53			19 08				19 23						19 38	
London Bridge	a					18 44			18 59			19 14				19 29						19 44	
Maidstone East	a																						
East Croydon	a					18 59			19 14			19 29				19 44						19 58	
Gatwick Airport	a					19 14			19 45			19 44				20 14						20 14	
Brighton	a					19 51						20 19										20 49	

Please refer to Table T024 for the service from Moorgate to Stevenage via Hertford North

Table T025-R

Mondays to Fridays
16 December to 15 May

Peterborough, Kings Lynn, Cambridge and Stevenage - London, Maidstone East, Gatwick Airport and Brighton

		TL	TL	GN	TL	GN	TL	TL	TL	GN	TL	TL	TL	GR	GR	TL	TL	GN	GN	GR	TL	GR
		1	1	1	1	1	1	1	1	1	1	1	1	1	1	1	1	1	1	1	1	1
Peterborough 8	d		←			18 32			18 52				19 24	19 30			←		19 42	19 50		
Huntingdon	d		18 41						19 11				19 41				19 41		19 56			
St Neots	d		18 48						19 18				→				19 48		20 04			
Sandy	d		18 56						19 26								19 56					
Biggleswade	d		19 00						19 30								20 00		20 15			
Arlesey	a		19 04						19 34								20 04					
Kings Lynn	d			17 44														18 40				
Watlington	d			17 51														18 47				
Downham Market	d			17 58														18 54				
Littleport	d			18 08														19 04				
Ely	d			18 17						18 57								19 17				
Waterbeach	d			18 27														19 27				
Cambridge North	d			18 32						19 09								19 32				
Cambridge	a	←		18 36						19 13						←		19 36				
Cambridge	d	18 26		18 44			18 53	18 57		19 14		19 26				19 26		19 44				
Foxton	d	18 36						19 06				→				19 35						
Shepreth	d	18 38						19 08								19 38						
Meldreth	d	18 41						19 11								19 41						
Royston	d	18 47					19 09	19 17								19 47						
Ashwell & Morden	d	18 51						19 21								19 51						
Baldock	d	18 56					19 17	19 26								19 56						
Letchworth Garden City	a	18 59					19 20	19 29								19 59						
Hitchin 4	d	19 04	19 11				19 26	19 34	19 41							20 04	20 11					
Stevenage 4	d	19 10	19 17		←	19 23	19 32	19 40	19 47		←			19 59	20 03	20 10	20 17			20 20	←	20 29
Knebworth	d	19 13			19 13			19 43			19 43					20 13					20 13	
Welwyn North	d	→			19 17			→			19 47					→					20 17	
Welwyn Garden City 4	d				19 22						19 52										20 22	
Hatfield	d				19 25						19 55										20 25	
Potters Bar	d				19 32						20 02										20 32	
Finsbury Park ⊖	a		19 37		19 44		19 51		20 07		20 14						20 36				20 43	
London Kings Cross 15 ⊖	a			19 35	19 50	19 50				20 02	20 20			20 23	20 27			20 33	20 47	20 46	20 50	20 53
St Pancras International	a		19 44				19 59		20 14								20 44					
Farringdon	a		19 49				20 04		20 19								20 49					
City Thameslink	a		19 51				20 06		20 21								20 51					
London Blackfriars	a		19 53				20 08		20 23								20 53					
London Bridge	a		19 59				20 14		20 29								20 59					
Maidstone East	a																					
East Croydon	a		20 14				20 28		20 44								21 14					
Gatwick Airport	a		20 43				20 44		21 13								21 43					
Brighton	a						21 19															

		TL	TL	GN	TL	TL	GN	GR	TL	GN	TL	GR	TL	TL	TL	TL	GN	TL	GR	TL	TL	TL	TL
		1	1	1	1	1	1	1	1	1	1	1	1	1	1	1	1	1	1	1	1	1	1
Peterborough 8	d				19 54		20 18				20 24	20 46	←					20 54	21 16	←			21 24
Huntingdon	d				20 11		20 32				20 41		20 41					21 11		21 11			21 41
St Neots	d				20 18		20 40				→		20 48					→		21 18			→
Sandy	d				20 26								20 56							21 26			
Biggleswade	d				20 30		20 50						21 00							21 30			
Arlesey	a				20 34								21 04							21 34			
Kings Lynn	d									19 44													
Watlington	d									19 51													
Downham Market	d									19 58													
Littleport	d									20 08													
Ely	d			19 47						20 18							20 49						
Waterbeach	d									20 28													
Cambridge North	d			20 01						20 33							21 01						
Cambridge	a			20 05						20 38							21 05						
Cambridge	d	19 54	19 57	20 14					20 27	20 44					20 54	20 57	21 14					21 27	
Foxton	d		20 06						20 36							21 06						→	
Shepreth	d		20 08						20 38							21 08							
Meldreth	d		20 11						20 41							21 11							
Royston	d	20 09	20 17						20 47						21 08	21 17							
Ashwell & Morden	d		20 21						20 51							21 21							
Baldock	d	20 17	20 26						20 56						21 16	21 26							
Letchworth Garden City	a	20 20	20 29						20 59						21 19	21 29							
Hitchin 4	d	20 26	20 34		20 41				21 04				21 11		21 24	21 34				21 41			
Stevenage 4	d	20 32	20 40		20 47	←		21 06	21 10			21 15	21 17	←	21 30	21 40			21 45	21 47	←		
Knebworth	d		20 43			20 43			21 13					21 13		21 43					21 43		
Welwyn North	d		→			20 47			→					21 17		→					21 47		
Welwyn Garden City 4	d					20 52								21 22							21 52		
Hatfield	d					20 55								21 25							21 55		
Potters Bar	d					21 02								21 32							22 02		
Finsbury Park ⊖	a	20 51			21 07	21 13							21 36	21 43	21 49					22 06	22 13		
London Kings Cross 15 ⊖	a			21 02		21 20	21 22	21 31		21 33		21 39		21 53			22 03		22 10		22 20		
St Pancras International	a	20 59			21 14								21 44		21 59					22 14			
Farringdon	a	21 04			21 19								21 49		22 04					22 19			
City Thameslink	a	21 06			21 21								21 51		22 06					22 21			
London Blackfriars	a	21 08			21 23								21 53		22 08					22 23			
London Bridge	a	21 14			21 29								21 59		22 14					22 29			
Maidstone East	a																						
East Croydon	a	21 28			21 44								22 14		22 28					22 44			
Gatwick Airport	a	21 44			22 13								22 43		22 44					23 12			
Brighton	a	22 20													23 19								

Please refer to Table T024 for the service from Moorgate to Stevenage via Hertford North

Table T025-R

Mondays to Fridays
16 December to 15 May

Peterborough, Kings Lynn, Cambridge and Stevenage - London, Maidstone East, Gatwick Airport and Brighton

		GR	TL	TL	GN	GN	TL	TL	TL	GN	TL	GR	TL	TL	TL	TL	GR	TL	GN	TL	TL	TL	TL
		1	1	1	1	1	1	1	1	1	1	1	1	1	1	1	1	1	1	1	1	1	1
Peterborough 8	d	21 28		←		21 41					21 54	22 16	←			22 24	22 39			←			
Huntingdon	d			21 41		21 55					22 11		22 11			22 41				22 41			
St Neots	d			21 48		22 03					→		22 18			→				22 48			
Sandy	d			21 56									22 26							22 56			
Biggleswade	d			22 00		22 14							22 30							23 00			
Arlesey	a			22 04									22 34							23 04			
Kings Lynn	d				20 44														21 44				
Watlington	d				20 51														21 51				
Downham Market	d				20 59														21 58				
Littleport	d				21 08														22 08				
Ely	d				21 17					21 47									22 17				
Waterbeach	d				21 26														22 26				
Cambridge North	d				21 31					22 00									22 31				
Cambridge	a		←		21 35					22 05								←	22 36				
Cambridge	d		21 27		21 44			21 54	21 57	22 14					22 27			22 27	22 44			22 54	22 57
Foxton	d		21 36						22 06						→			22 36					23 06
Shepreth	d		21 38						22 08									22 38					23 08
Meldreth	d		21 41						22 11									22 41					23 11
Royston	d		21 47					22 09	22 17									22 47				23 09	23 17
Ashwell & Morden	d		21 51						22 21									22 51					23 21
Baldock	d		21 56					22 17	22 26									22 56				23 17	23 26
Letchworth Garden City	a		21 59					22 20	22 29									22 59				23 20	23 29
Hitchin 4	d		22 04	22 10				22 26	22 34				22 41					23 04		23 11		23 26	23 34
Stevenage 4	d	21 59	22 10	22 16		22 26	←	22 32	22 40			22 45	22 47	←			23 08	23 10		23 17	←	23 32	23 40
Knebworth	d		22 13				22 13		22 43					22 43				23 14			23 14		23 43
Welwyn North	d		→				22 17		→					22 47				→			23 18		→
Welwyn Garden City 4	d						22 22							22 52							23 22		
Hatfield	d						22 25							22 55							23 26		
Potters Bar	d						22 32							23 02							23 32		
Finsbury Park ⊖	a			22 36			22 43	22 51					23 06	23 13						23 36	23 43	23 51	
London Kings Cross 15 ⊖	a	22 25			22 32	22 48	22 51			23 03		23 09		23 20			23 32		23 34	23 44	23 50	23 58	
St Pancras International	a			22 44				22 59					23 14										
Farringdon	a			22 49				23 04					23 19										
City Thameslink	a			22 51																			
London Blackfriars	a			22 53				23 08					23 23										
London Bridge	a			22 59				23 14					23 29										
Maidstone East	a																						
East Croydon	a			23 15				23 28					23 44										
Gatwick Airport	a			23 41				23 47					00 12										
Brighton	a							00 23															

		GN	TL	TL	TL	TL	GN	TL
		1	1	1	1	1	1	1
Peterborough 8	d		22 54		23 20			
Huntingdon	d		23 11		23 35			
St Neots	d		23 18		23 42			
Sandy	d		23 26		23 50			
Biggleswade	d		23 30		23 53			
Arlesey	a		23 34		23 58			
Kings Lynn	d						22 44	
Watlington	d						22 51	
Downham Market	d						22 58	
Littleport	d						23 08	
Ely	d	22 46					23 17	
Waterbeach	d						23 26	
Cambridge North	d	23 01					23 31	
Cambridge	a	23 06					23 38	
Cambridge	d	23 14				23 35		23 54
Foxton	d					23 44		
Shepreth	d					23 46		
Meldreth	d					23 49		
Royston	d					23 54		00 09
Ashwell & Morden	d					23 58		
Baldock	d					00 03		00 17
Letchworth Garden City	a					00 06		00 20
Hitchin 4	d		23 44		00 06	00 10		00 28
Stevenage 4	d		23 50	←	00 12	00 16		00 34
Knebworth	d			23 43		00 19		
Welwyn North	d			23 47		00 23		
Welwyn Garden City 4	d			23 52		00 28		
Hatfield	d			23 55		00 31		
Potters Bar	d			00 02		00 38		
Finsbury Park ⊖	a		00 10	00 15	00 38	00 51		01 00
London Kings Cross 15 ⊖	a	00 08	00 18	00 21	00 45	00 57		01 06
St Pancras International	a							
Farringdon	a							
City Thameslink	a							
London Blackfriars	a							
London Bridge	a							
Maidstone East	a							
East Croydon	a							
Gatwick Airport	a							
Brighton	a							

Please refer to Table T024 for the service from Moorgate to Stevenage via Hertford North

Table T025-R

Saturdays
21 December to 16 May

Peterborough, Kings Lynn, Cambridge and Stevenage - London, Maidstone East, Gatwick Airport and Brighton

		TL	TL	TL	TL	TL	GN	GN	GN	TL	TL	TL	GN	GN	GN	TL	TL	TL	TL	TL	GN	GN	TL
		1	1	1	1	1		A	B	1	1	1	B	A	B	1	1	1	1	1	1	B	1
Peterborough	d					03 24					04 18							04 54					05 24
Huntingdon	d					03 39					04 33							05 11					05 41
St Neots	d					03 46					04 40							05 18					05 48
Sandy	d					03 54					04 48							05 26					05 56
Biggleswade	d					03 58					04 52							05 30					06 00
Arlesey	a					04 02					04 56							05 34					06 04
Kings Lynn	d																						
Watlington	d																						
Downham Market	d																						
Littleport	d																						
Ely	d																				05 12		
Waterbeach	d																				05 21		
Cambridge North	d																				05 26		
Cambridge	a																				05 31		
Cambridge	d															04 54				05 27	05 37		
Foxton	d																			05 36			
Shepreth	d																			05 38			
Meldreth	d																			05 41			
Royston	d				00 09											05 09	05 17			05 47	05 54		
Ashwell & Morden	d																05 21			05 51			
Baldock	d			00 03	00 17											05 17	05 26			05 56			
Letchworth Garden City	a			00 06	00 20											05 20	05 29			05 59	06 03		
Hitchin	d		00 06	00 10	00 28	04 11				04 58	05 05					05 26	05 34	05 41		06 04			06 11
Stevenage	d		00 12	00 16	00 34	04 17	04 22	04 58	04 58	05 04	05 11			05 28	05 30	05 32	05 40	05 47	←	06 10			06 17
Knebworth	d			00 19						05 07							05 43		05 43	06 13			
Welwyn North	d			00 23						05 11							→		05 47	→			
Welwyn Garden City	d			00 28						05 16	05 20	←							05 52				
Hatfield	d			00 31						05 19		05 19							05 55				
Potters Bar	d	00 02		00 38						→		05 26	←						06 02			←	
Finsbury Park ⊖	a	00 15	00 38	00 51	01 00	04 45	05 04	05 50	05 50		05 34	05 39	05 50	06 20	06 25	05 51		06 06	06 13			06 25	06 36
London Kings Cross ⊖	a	00 21	00 45	00 57	01 06	04 51	05 13		→			05 46	06 01		→				06 20		06 33	06 36	
St Pancras International	a										05 44					05 59		06 14					06 44
Farringdon	a										05 49					06 04		06 19					06 49
City Thameslink	a																						
London Blackfriars	a										05 53					06 08		06 23					06 53
London Bridge	a										05 59					06 14		06 29					06 59
Maidstone East	a																						
East Croydon	a										06 14					06 28		06 44					07 14
Gatwick Airport	a										06 50					06 44		07 12					07 42
Brighton	a															07 22							

		TL	GN	GN	TL	TL	GN	TL	TL	TL	GN	GN	TL	TL	GN	GN	TL	TL	GN	TL	TL	TL	GN
		1	A	B	1	1	1	1	1	1	1	B	1	1	A	B	1	1	1	1	1	1	1
Peterborough	d							05 54					06 24							06 54			
Huntingdon	d							06 11					06 41							07 11			
St Neots	d							06 18					06 48							07 18			
Sandy	d							06 26					06 56							07 26			
Biggleswade	d							06 30					07 00							07 30			
Arlesey	a							06 34					07 04							07 34			
Kings Lynn	d										05 44												06 44
Watlington	d										05 51												06 51
Downham Market	d										05 58												06 58
Littleport	d										06 08												07 08
Ely	d						05 47				06 17								06 47				07 17
Waterbeach	d										06 27												07 27
Cambridge North	d						06 00				06 32								07 01				07 32
Cambridge	a						06 05				06 37								07 06				07 36
Cambridge	d				05 54	05 59	06 14			06 27	06 44						06 54		07 14			07 27	07 44
Foxton	d					06 08				06 36												07 36	
Shepreth	d					06 10				06 38												07 38	
Meldreth	d					06 13				06 41												07 41	
Royston	d				06 09	06 18				06 47							07 09	07 17				07 47	
Ashwell & Morden	d					06 22				06 51								07 21				07 51	
Baldock	d				06 17	06 27				06 56							07 17	07 26				07 56	
Letchworth Garden City	a				06 20	06 30				06 59							07 20	07 29				07 59	
Hitchin	d				06 26	06 34		06 41		07 04			07 11				07 26	07 34		07 41		08 04	
Stevenage	d	←	06 28	06 30	06 32	06 40		06 47	←	07 10			07 17	←	07 28	07 30	07 32	07 40		07 47	←	08 10	
Knebworth	d	06 13				06 43			06 43	07 13				07 13				07 43			07 43	08 13	
Welwyn North	d	06 17				→			06 47	→				07 17				→			07 47	→	
Welwyn Garden City	d	06 22							06 52					07 22							07 52		
Hatfield	d	06 25							06 55					07 25							07 55		
Potters Bar	d	06 32							07 02			←		07 32							08 02		
Finsbury Park ⊖	a	06 44	07 20	07 25	06 51			07 06	07 14			07 25	07 36	07 44	08 20	08 25	07 51			08 07	08 13		
London Kings Cross ⊖	a	06 50		→			07 03		07 20		07 32	07 35		07 50		→			08 03		08 20		08 33
St Pancras International	a				06 59			07 14					07 44				07 59			08 14			
Farringdon	a				07 04			07 19					07 49				08 04			08 19			
City Thameslink	a																						
London Blackfriars	a				07 08			07 23					07 53				08 08			08 23			
London Bridge	a				07 14			07 29					07 59				08 14			08 29			
Maidstone East	a																						
East Croydon	a				07 28			07 44					08 14				08 28			08 44			
Gatwick Airport	a				07 44			08 12					08 42				08 44			09 12			
Brighton	a				08 19												09 19						

A until 15 February **B** from 22 February

Please refer to Table T024 for the service from Moorgate to Stevenage via Hertford North

NRT DECEMBER 19 EDITION

Table T025-R

Saturdays
21 December to 16 May

Peterborough, Kings Lynn, Cambridge and Stevenage - London, Maidstone East, Gatwick Airport and Brighton

		GN	TL	TL	GN	GN	TL	TL	GN	TL	GN	TL	TL	TL	GR	GR	GN	GN	TL	TL	TL	GN
		A	1	1	B	A	1	1	1	1	1	1	1	1	1	1	1	A	1	1	1	B
Peterborough	d		07 24							07 54	08 04			08 24	08 29					←		
Huntingdon	d		07 41							08 11	08 20			08 41						08 41		
St Neots	d		07 48							08 18	08 28			→						08 48		
Sandy	d		07 56							08 26										08 56		
Biggleswade	d		08 00							08 30	08 38									09 00		
Arlesey	a		08 04							08 34										09 04		
Kings Lynn	d																07 44					
Watlington	d																07 51					
Downham Market	d																07 58					
Littleport	d																08 08					
Ely	d								07 47								08 17					
Waterbeach	d																08 27					
Cambridge North	d								08 01								08 32					
Cambridge	a								08 05								08 37					
Cambridge	d						07 54		08 14				08 27				08 44		←			
Foxton	d												08 36						08 36			
Shepreth	d												→						08 38			
Meldreth	d																		08 41			
Royston	d						08 09	08 17											08 47			
Ashwell & Morden	d							08 21											08 51			
Baldock	d						08 17	08 26											08 56			
Letchworth Garden City	a						08 20	08 29											08 59			
Hitchin	d		08 11				08 26	08 34		08 41									09 04	09 11		
Stevenage	d		08 17	←	08 28	08 30	08 32	08 40		08 47		←			08 59	09 04			09 10	09 17	←	09 28
Knebworth	d			08 13				08 43				08 43							09 13		09 13	
Welwyn North	d			08 17				→				08 47							→		09 17	
Welwyn Garden City	d			08 22								08 52									09 22	
Hatfield	d			08 25								08 55									09 25	
Potters Bar	d	←		08 32								09 02						←			09 32	
Finsbury Park ⊖	a	08 25	08 37	08 44	09 20	09 25	08 51			09 07		09 13						09 25		09 37	09 44	10 20
London Kings Cross ⊖	a	08 36		08 50		→			09 03		09 17	09 20			09 23	09 31	09 33	09 36			09 50	
St Pancras International	a		08 44				08 59			09 14										09 44		
Farringdon	a		08 49				09 04			09 19										09 49		
City Thameslink	a						09 06			09 21										09 51		
London Blackfriars	a		08 53				09 08			09 23										09 53		
London Bridge	a		08 59				09 14			09 29										09 59		
Maidstone East	a																					
East Croydon	a		09 14				09 28			09 44										10 14		
Gatwick Airport	a		09 42				09 44			10 12										10 42		
Brighton	a						10 19															

		GN	TL	TL	GN	TL	GN	TL	GR	TL	GN	GN	TL	TL	GN	GN	TL	TL	GN	TL	GN	TL	GR
		A	1	1	1	1	1	1	1	1	1	A	1	1	B	A	1	1	1	1	1	1	1
Peterborough	d					08 54	09 04						09 24							09 54	10 04		
Huntingdon	d					09 11	09 20						09 41							10 11	10 20		
St Neots	d					09 18	09 28						09 48							10 18	10 28		
Sandy	d					09 26							09 56							10 26			
Biggleswade	d					09 30	09 39						10 00							10 30	10 38		
Arlesey	a					09 34							10 04							10 34			
Kings Lynn	d										08 44								09 13				
Watlington	d										08 51												
Downham Market	d										08 58								09 25				
Littleport	d										09 08												
Ely	d				08 47						09 17								09 47				
Waterbeach	d										09 27												
Cambridge North	d				09 01						09 32								10 01				
Cambridge	a				09 05						09 37								10 05				
Cambridge	d		08 54		09 14					09 27	09 44						09 54		10 14				
Foxton	d									09 36													
Shepreth	d									09 38													
Meldreth	d									09 41													
Royston	d		09 09	09 17						09 47							10 09	10 17					
Ashwell & Morden	d			09 21						09 51								10 21					
Baldock	d		09 17	09 26						09 56							10 17	10 26					
Letchworth Garden City	a		09 20	09 29						09 59							10 20	10 29					
Hitchin	d		09 26	09 34		09 41				10 04			10 11				10 26	10 34		10 41			
Stevenage	d	09 30	09 32	09 40		09 47		←	10 06	10 10			10 17	←	10 28	10 30	10 32	10 40		10 47		←	11 05
Knebworth	d			09 43				09 43		10 13				10 13				10 43				10 43	
Welwyn North	d			→				09 47		→				10 17				→				10 47	
Welwyn Garden City	d							09 52						10 22								10 52	
Hatfield	d							09 55						10 25								10 55	
Potters Bar	d							10 02				←		10 32								11 02	
Finsbury Park ⊖	a	10 25	09 51			10 07		10 13				10 25	10 37	10 44	11 20	11 25	10 51			11 07		11 13	
London Kings Cross ⊖	a	→			10 05		10 17	10 20	10 31		10 33	10 36		10 50		→			11 03		11 15	11 20	11 31
St Pancras International	a		09 59			10 14							10 44				10 59			11 14			
Farringdon	a		10 04			10 19							10 49				11 04			11 19			
City Thameslink	a		10 06			10 21							10 51				11 06			11 21			
London Blackfriars	a		10 08			10 23							10 53				11 08			11 23			
London Bridge	a		10 14			10 29							10 59				11 14			11 29			
Maidstone East	a																						
East Croydon	a		10 28			10 44							11 14				11 28			11 44			
Gatwick Airport	a		10 44			11 12							11 42				11 44			12 12			
Brighton	a		11 19														12 19						

A from 22 February **B** until 15 February

Table T025-R

Saturdays

21 December to 16 May

Peterborough, Kings Lynn, Cambridge and Stevenage - London, Maidstone East, Gatwick Airport and Brighton

		TL	GN	GN	GN	TL	TL	GN	GN	TL	TL	GN	TL	TL	TL	TL	GR	GR	GN	GN	GN	TL
		1	1	1		1	1			1	1	1	1	1	1	1	1	1	1	1		1
					A			B	A												A	
Peterborough 8	d					10 24							10 53			11 24	11 35					
Huntingdon	d					10 41							11 11			11 41						
St Neots	d					10 48							11 18			→						
Sandy	d					10 56							11 26									
Biggleswade	d					11 00							11 30									
Arlesey	a					11 04							11 34									
Kings Lynn	d			09 44								10 13								10 44		
Watlington	d			09 51																10 51		
Downham Market	d			09 58								10 25								10 58		
Littleport	d			10 08																11 08		
Ely	d		10 12	10 17								10 47							11 12	11 17		
Waterbeach	d			10 27																11 27		
Cambridge North	d		10 24	10 32								11 01							11 24	11 32		
Cambridge	a		10 30	10 37								11 05							11 30	11 37		
Cambridge	d	10 27	10 44							10 54		11 14			11 27				11 44			←
Foxton	d	10 36													11 36							11 36
Shepreth	d	10 38													→							11 38
Meldreth	d	10 41																				11 41
Royston	d	10 47								11 09	11 17											11 47
Ashwell & Morden	d	10 51									11 21											11 51
Baldock	d	10 56								11 17	11 26											11 56
Letchworth Garden City	a	10 59								11 20	11 29											11 59
Hitchin 4	d	11 04				11 11				11 25	11 34		11 41									12 04
Stevenage 4	d	11 10				11 17	←	11 28	11 30	11 31	11 40		11 47	←			12 04	12 08				12 10
Knebworth	d	11 13					11 13				11 43			11 43								12 13
Welwyn North	d	→					11 17				→			11 47								→
Welwyn Garden City 4	d						11 22							11 53								
Hatfield	d						11 25							11 55								
Potters Bar	d				←		11 32							12 02							←	
Finsbury Park ⊖	a				11 25	11 37	11 44	12 20	12 25	11 51			12 07	12 13							12 25	
London Kings Cross 15 ⊖	a		11 33		11 36		11 50		→			12 05		12 20			12 31	12 34	12 35		12 38	
St Pancras International	a					11 44				11 59			12 14									
Farringdon	a					11 49				12 04			12 19									
City Thameslink	a					11 51				12 06			12 21									
London Blackfriars	a					11 53				12 08			12 23									
London Bridge	a					11 59				12 14			12 29									
Maidstone East	a																					
East Croydon	a					12 14				12 28			12 44									
Gatwick Airport	a					12 42				12 44			13 12									
Brighton	a									13 19												

A from 22 February **B** until 15 February

Please refer to Table T024 for the service from Moorgate to Stevenage via Hertford North

Table T025-R

Saturdays

21 December to 16 May

Peterborough, Kings Lynn, Cambridge and Stevenage - London, Maidstone East, Gatwick Airport and Brighton

		TL	TL	GN	GN	TL	TL	GN	TL	TL	TL	TL	GR	GR	GN	GN	TL	TL	TL	GN	GN	TL	TL
		1	1			1	1	1	1	1	1	1	1	1	1		1	1	1			1	1
				A	B											B				A	B		
Peterborough 8	d	←							11 54			12 24	12 30					←					
Huntingdon	d	11 41							12 11			12 41						12 41					
St Neots	d	11 48							12 18			→						12 48					
Sandy	d	11 56							12 26									12 56					
Biggleswade	d	12 00							12 30									13 00					
Arlesey	a	12 04							12 34									13 04					
Kings Lynn	d														11 44								
Watlington	d														11 51								
Downham Market	d														11 58								
Littleport	d														12 08								
Ely	d							11 47							12 17								
Waterbeach	d														12 27								
Cambridge North	d							12 01							12 32								
Cambridge	a							12 05							12 37								
Cambridge	d					11 54		12 14			12 27				12 44		←					12 54	
Foxton	d										12 36						12 36						
Shepreth	d										→						12 38						
Meldreth	d																12 41						
Royston	d					12 09	12 17										12 47					13 09	13 17
Ashwell & Morden	d						12 21										12 51						13 21
Baldock	d					12 17	12 26										12 56					13 17	13 26
Letchworth Garden City	a					12 20	12 29										12 59					13 20	13 29
Hitchin 4	d	12 11				12 26	12 34		12 41								13 04	13 11				13 26	13 34
Stevenage 4	d	12 17	←	12 28	12 30	12 32	12 40		12 47	←			12 59	13 04			13 10	13 17	←	13 28	13 30	13 32	13 40
Knebworth	d		12 13				12 43			12 43							13 13		13 13				13 43
Welwyn North	d		12 19				→			12 47							→		13 17				→
Welwyn Garden City 4	d		12 23							12 52									13 22				
Hatfield	d		12 26							12 55									13 25				
Potters Bar	d		12 33							13 02						←			13 32				
Finsbury Park ⊖	a	12 36	12 44	13 20	13 25	12 51			13 07	13 13						13 25		13 37	13 44	14 20	14 25	13 51	
London Kings Cross 15 ⊖	a		12 50		→			13 03		13 20			13 24	13 31	13 33	13 36			13 50		→		
St Pancras International	a	12 44				12 59			13 14									13 44				13 59	
Farringdon	a	12 49				13 04			13 19									13 49				14 04	
City Thameslink	a	12 51				13 06			13 21									13 51				14 06	
London Blackfriars	a	12 53				13 08			13 23									13 53				14 08	
London Bridge	a	12 59				13 14			13 29									13 59				14 14	
Maidstone East	a																						
East Croydon	a	13 14				13 28			13 44									14 14				14 28	
Gatwick Airport	a	13 42				13 44			14 12									14 42				14 44	
Brighton	a					14 19																15 19	

		GN	TL	TL	TL	TL	GR	GR	GN	GN	TL	TL	TL	GN	GN	TL	TL	GN	TL	TL	TL	TL
		1	1	1	1	1	1	1	1		1	1	1			1	1	1	1	1	1	1
										B				A	B							
Peterborough 8	d		12 54			13 24	13 30					←							13 54			14 24
Huntingdon	d		13 11			13 41						13 41							14 11			14 41
St Neots	d		13 18			→						13 48							14 18			→
Sandy	d		13 26									13 56							14 26			
Biggleswade	d		13 30									14 00							14 30			
Arlesey	a		13 34									14 04							14 34			
Kings Lynn	d								12 44													
Watlington	d								12 51													
Downham Market	d								12 58													
Littleport	d								13 08													
Ely	d	12 47							13 17									13 47				
Waterbeach	d								13 27													
Cambridge North	d	13 01							13 32									14 01				
Cambridge	a	13 05							13 37									14 05				
Cambridge	d	13 14			13 27				13 44		←					13 54		14 14			14 27	
Foxton	d				13 36						13 36										14 36	
Shepreth	d				→						13 38										→	
Meldreth	d										13 41											
Royston	d										13 47					14 09	14 17					
Ashwell & Morden	d										13 51						14 21					
Baldock	d										13 56					14 17	14 26					
Letchworth Garden City	a										13 59					14 20	14 29					
Hitchin 4	d		13 41								14 04	14 11				14 26	14 34		14 41			
Stevenage 4	d		13 47	←			13 59	14 04			14 10	14 17	←	14 28	14 30	14 32	14 40		14 47	←		
Knebworth	d			13 43							14 13		14 13				14 43			14 43		
Welwyn North	d			13 47							→		14 17				→			14 47		
Welwyn Garden City 4	d			13 52									14 22							14 52		
Hatfield	d			13 55									14 25							14 55		
Potters Bar	d			14 02						←			14 32							15 02		
Finsbury Park ⊖	a		14 06	14 13						14 25		14 37	14 44	15 20	15 25	14 51			15 06	15 13		
London Kings Cross 15 ⊖	a	14 03		14 20			14 23	14 31	14 32	14 35			14 50		→			15 03		15 20		
St Pancras International	a		14 14									14 44				14 59			15 14			
Farringdon	a		14 19									14 49				15 04			15 19			
City Thameslink	a		14 21									14 51				15 06			15 21			
London Blackfriars	a		14 23									14 53				15 08			15 23			
London Bridge	a		14 29									14 59				15 14			15 29			
Maidstone East	a																					
East Croydon	a		14 44									15 14				15 28			15 44			
Gatwick Airport	a		15 12									15 42				15 44			16 12			
Brighton	a															16 19						

A until 15 February **B** from 22 February

Table T025-R

Saturdays

21 December to 16 May

Peterborough, Kings Lynn, Cambridge and Stevenage - London, Maidstone East, Gatwick Airport and Brighton

		GR	GR	GN	GN	TL	TL	TL	GN	GN	TL	TL	GN	TL	TL	TL	TL	GR	GR	GN	GN	TL	TL
		■	■															■	■				
		1	1	1		1	1	1			1	1	1	1	1	1	1	1	1	1		1	1
					A				B	A											A		
		🍴	🍴															🍴	🍴				
Peterborough 8	d	14 29					←							14 54			15 24	15 34					←
Huntingdon	d						14 41							15 11			15 41						15 41
St Neots	d						14 48							15 18			→						15 48
Sandy	d						14 56							15 26									15 56
Biggleswade	d						15 00							15 30									16 00
Arlesey	a						15 04							15 34									16 04
Kings Lynn	d			13 44																14 44			
Watlington	d			13 51																14 51			
Downham Market	d			13 58																14 58			
Littleport	d			14 08																15 08			
Ely	d			14 17									14 47							15 18			
Waterbeach	d			14 27																15 28			
Cambridge North	d			14 32									15 01							15 33			
Cambridge	a			14 37									15 05							15 37			
Cambridge	d			14 44		←					14 54		15 14			15 27				15 44		←	
Foxton	d					14 36										15 36						15 36	
Shepreth	d					14 38										→						15 38	
Meldreth	d					14 41																15 41	
Royston	d					14 47					15 09	15 17										15 47	
Ashwell & Morden	d					14 51						15 21										15 51	
Baldock	d					14 56					15 17	15 26										15 56	
Letchworth Garden City	a					14 59					15 20	15 29										15 59	
Hitchin 4	d					15 04	15 11				15 26	15 34		15 41								16 04	16 11
Stevenage 4	d	14 59	15 04			15 10	15 17	←	15 28	15 30	15 31	15 40		15 47	←			16 03	16 08			16 10	16 17
Knebworth	d					15 13		15 13				15 43			15 43							16 13	
Welwyn North	d					→		15 17				→			15 47							→	
Welwyn Garden City 4	d							15 22							15 52								
Hatfield	d							15 25							15 55								
Potters Bar	d				←			15 32							16 02						←		
Finsbury Park ⊖	a				15 25		15 37	15 43	16 20	16 25	15 51			16 07	16 13						16 25		16 36
London Kings Cross 15 ⊖	a	15 23	15 31	15 33	15 36			15 50		→			16 03		16 20			16 31	16 34	16 35	16 38		
St Pancras International	a						15 44				15 59			16 14									16 44
Farringdon	a						15 49				16 04			16 19									16 49
City Thameslink	a						15 51				16 06			16 21									16 51
London Blackfriars	a						15 53				16 08			16 23									16 53
London Bridge	a						15 59				16 14			16 29									16 59
Maidstone East	a																						
East Croydon	a						16 14				16 28			16 44									17 14
Gatwick Airport	a						16 42				16 44			17 12									17 42
Brighton	a										17 19												

		TL	GN	GN	TL	TL	GN	TL	TL	TL	TL	GR	GR	GN	GN	TL	TL	TL	GN	GN	TL	TL
												■	■									
		1			1	1	1	1	1	1	1	1	1	1		1	1	1			1	1
			B	A											A				B	A		
												🍴	🍴									
Peterborough 8	d							15 54			16 24	16 29					←					
Huntingdon	d							16 11			16 41						16 41					
St Neots	d							16 18			→						16 48					
Sandy	d							16 26									16 56					
Biggleswade	d							16 30									17 00					
Arlesey	a							16 34									17 04					
Kings Lynn	d													15 44								
Watlington	d													15 51								
Downham Market	d													15 58								
Littleport	d													16 08								
Ely	d						15 47							16 17								
Waterbeach	d													16 27								
Cambridge North	d						16 01							16 32								
Cambridge	a						16 05							16 37								
Cambridge	d				15 54		16 14			16 27				16 44		←					16 54	
Foxton	d									16 36						16 36						
Shepreth	d									→						16 38						
Meldreth	d															16 41						
Royston	d				16 09	16 17										16 47					17 09	17 17
Ashwell & Morden	d					16 21										16 51						17 21
Baldock	d				16 17	16 26										16 56					17 17	17 26
Letchworth Garden City	a				16 20	16 29										16 59					17 20	17 29
Hitchin 4	d				16 26	16 34		16 41								17 04	17 11				17 26	17 34
Stevenage 4	d	←	16 28	16 30	16 32	16 40		16 47	←			16 59	17 04			17 10	17 17	←	17 28	17 30	17 32	17 40
Knebworth	d	16 13				16 43			16 43							17 13		17 13				17 43
Welwyn North	d	16 19				→			16 48							→		17 17				→
Welwyn Garden City 4	d	16 22							16 53									17 22				
Hatfield	d	16 26							16 56									17 25				
Potters Bar	d	16 32							17 02						←			17 32				
Finsbury Park ⊖	a	16 44	17 20	17 25	16 51			17 06	17 13						17 25		17 37	17 44	18 20	18 25	17 51	
London Kings Cross 15 ⊖	a	16 50		→			17 04		17 20			17 23	17 31	17 33	17 36			17 50		→		
St Pancras International	a				16 59			17 14									17 44				17 59	
Farringdon	a				17 04			17 19									17 49				18 04	
City Thameslink	a				17 06			17 21									17 51				18 06	
London Blackfriars	a				17 08			17 23									17 53				18 08	
London Bridge	a				17 14			17 29									17 59				18 14	
Maidstone East	a																					
East Croydon	a				17 28			17 44									18 14				18 28	
Gatwick Airport	a				17 44			18 12									18 42				18 44	
Brighton	a				18 19																19 19	

A from 22 February
B until 15 February

NRT DECEMBER 19 EDITION

Table T025-R

Saturdays

21 December to 16 May

Peterborough, Kings Lynn, Cambridge and Stevenage - London, Maidstone East, Gatwick Airport and Brighton

		GN	TL	TL	TL	TL	GR	GR	GN	GN	TL	TL	TL	GN	GN	TL	TL	GN	TL	TL	TL	TL	GR
							■	■															■
		1	1	1	1	1	1	1	1		1	1	1			1	1	1	1	1	1	1	1
										A				B	A								
							🍴	🍴															🍴
Peterborough 8	d		16 54			17 24	17 34					←							17 56			18 24	18 29
Huntingdon	d		17 11			17 41						17 41							18 12			18 41	
St Neots	d		17 18			→						17 48							18 19			→	
Sandy	d		17 26									17 56							18 27				
Biggleswade	d		17 30									18 00							18 31				
Arlesey	a		17 34									18 04							18 35				
Kings Lynn	d								16 44														
Watlington	d								16 51														
Downham Market	d								16 58														
Littleport	d								17 08														
Ely	d	16 47							17 17									17 47					
Waterbeach	d								17 27														
Cambridge North	d	17 01							17 32									18 01					
Cambridge	a	17 05							17 37									18 06					
Cambridge	d	17 14			17 27				17 44		←					17 54		18 14			18 27		
Foxton	d				17 36						17 36										18 36		
Shepreth	d				→						17 38										→		
Meldreth	d										17 41												
Royston	d										17 47					18 09	18 17						
Ashwell & Morden	d										17 51						18 21						
Baldock	d										17 56					18 17	18 26						
Letchworth Garden City	a										17 59					18 20	18 29						
Hitchin 4	d		17 41								18 04	18 11				18 26	18 34		18 41				
Stevenage 4	d		17 47	←			18 03	18 08			18 10	18 17	←	18 28	18 30	18 32	18 40		18 47	←			18 59
Knebworth	d			17 43							18 13		18 13				18 43			18 43			
Welwyn North	d			17 47							→		18 18				→			18 47			
Welwyn Garden City 4	d			17 52									18 23							18 52			
Hatfield	d			17 55									18 26							18 55			
Potters Bar	d			18 02						←			18 32							19 02			
Finsbury Park ⊖	a		18 07	18 13						18 25		18 36	18 44	19 20	19 25	18 51			19 07	19 13			
London Kings Cross 15 ⊖	a	18 03		18 20			18 29	18 32	18 34	18 37			18 50		→			19 03		19 20			19 23
St Pancras International	a		18 14									18 44				18 59			19 14				
Farringdon	a		18 19									18 49				19 04			19 19				
City Thameslink	a		18 21									18 51				19 06			19 21				
London Blackfriars	a		18 23									18 53				19 08			19 23				
London Bridge	a		18 29									18 59				19 14			19 29				
Maidstone East	a																						
East Croydon	a		18 44									19 14				19 28			19 44				
Gatwick Airport	a		19 12									19 42				19 44			20 12				
Brighton	a															20 19							

		GR	GN	GN	TL	TL	TL	GN	GN	TL	TL	GN	TL	TL	TL	TL	GR	GR	GN	GN	TL	TL	GR
		■															■	■					■
		1	1		1	1	1			1	1	1	1	1	1	1	1	1	1		1	1	1
				A				B	A											A			
		🍴															🍴	🍴					🍴
Peterborough 8	d					←							18 54			19 24	19 30					←	19 50
Huntingdon	d					18 41							19 11			19 41						19 41	
St Neots	d					18 48							19 18			→						19 48	
Sandy	d					18 56							19 26									19 56	
Biggleswade	d					19 00							19 30									20 00	
Arlesey	a					19 04							19 34									20 04	
Kings Lynn	d		17 44																18 44				
Watlington	d		17 51																18 51				
Downham Market	d		17 58																18 58				
Littleport	d		18 08																19 08				
Ely	d		18 17									18 47							19 17				
Waterbeach	d		18 27																19 27				
Cambridge North	d		18 32									19 01							19 32				
Cambridge	a		18 37									19 05							19 37				
Cambridge	d		18 44		←					18 54		19 14			19 27				19 44		←		
Foxton	d				18 36										19 36						19 36		
Shepreth	d				18 38										→						19 38		
Meldreth	d				18 41																19 41		
Royston	d				18 47					19 09	19 17										19 47		
Ashwell & Morden	d				18 51						19 21										19 51		
Baldock	d				18 56					19 17	19 26										19 56		
Letchworth Garden City	a				18 59					19 20	19 29										19 59		
Hitchin 4	d				19 04	19 11				19 26	19 34		19 41								20 04	20 11	
Stevenage 4	d	19 09			19 10	19 17	←	19 28	19 30	19 32	19 40		19 47	←			19 59	20 05			20 10	20 17	20 20
Knebworth	d				19 13		19 13				19 43			19 43							20 13		
Welwyn North	d				→		19 18				→			19 47							→		
Welwyn Garden City 4	d						19 23							19 52									
Hatfield	d						19 27							19 55									
Potters Bar	d			←			19 33							20 02						←			
Finsbury Park ⊖	a			19 25		19 36	19 44	20 20	20 25	19 51			20 06	20 13						20 25		20 36	
London Kings Cross 15 ⊖	a	19 33	19 35	19 38			19 50		→			20 03		20 20			20 23	20 31	20 33	20 36			20 46
St Pancras International	a					19 44				19 59			20 14									20 44	
Farringdon	a					19 49				20 04			20 19									20 49	
City Thameslink	a					19 51				20 06			20 21									20 51	
London Blackfriars	a					19 53				20 08			20 23									20 53	
London Bridge	a					19 59				20 14			20 29									20 59	
Maidstone East	a																						
East Croydon	a					20 14				20 28			20 44									21 14	
Gatwick Airport	a					20 42				20 44			21 12									21 42	
Brighton	a									21 19													

A from 22 February
B until 15 February

Table T025-R

Saturdays
21 December to 16 May

Peterborough, Kings Lynn, Cambridge and Stevenage - London, Maidstone East, Gatwick Airport and Brighton

		TL		GN	GR	GN	TL	TL	GN	TL	TL	GR		TL	GN	GN	TL	GR	TL	GN	GN	TL		TL	GN
				A		B										B				A	B				
Peterborough	d									19 54							20 24	20 51							
Huntingdon	d									20 11							20 41								
St Neots	d									20 18							20 48								
Sandy	d									20 26							20 56								
Biggleswade	d									20 30							21 00								
Arlesey	a									20 34							21 04								
Kings Lynn	d														19 44										
Watlington	d														19 51										
Downham Market	d														19 58										
Littleport	d														20 08										
Ely	d								19 47						20 17										20 47
Waterbeach	d														20 27										
Cambridge North	d								20 01						20 32										21 01
Cambridge	a								20 05						20 37										21 05
Cambridge	d						19 54		20 14					20 27	20 44							20 54			21 14
Foxton	d													20 36											
Shepreth	d													20 38											
Meldreth	d													20 41											
Royston	d						20 09	20 17						20 47								21 09		21 17	
Ashwell & Morden	d							20 21						20 51										21 21	
Baldock	d						20 17	20 26						20 56								21 17		21 26	
Letchworth Garden City	a						20 20	20 29						20 59								21 20		21 29	
Hitchin	d						20 26	20 34		20 41				21 04			21 11					21 26		21 34	
Stevenage	d	←		20 28	20 29	20 30	20 32	20 40		20 47	←	21 04		21 10			21 17	21 20	←	21 28	21 30	21 32		21 40	
Knebworth	d	20 13						20 43			20 43			21 13					21 13					21 43	
Welwyn North	d	20 17						→			20 47			→					21 17					→	
Welwyn Garden City	d	20 22									20 52								21 22						
Hatfield	d	20 25									20 55								21 25						
Potters Bar	d	20 32									21 02					←			21 32						
Finsbury Park ⊖	a	20 44		21 20		21 25	20 51			21 07	21 13					21 25	21 36		21 44	22 20	22 25	21 51			
London Kings Cross ⊖	a	20 50			20 53	→			21 03		21 20	21 31			21 33	21 36		21 44	21 50		→				22 03
St Pancras International	a						20 59			21 14							21 44					21 59			
Farringdon	a						21 04			21 19							21 49					22 04			
City Thameslink	a																								
London Blackfriars	a						21 08			21 23							21 53					22 08			
London Bridge	a						21 14			21 29							21 59					22 14			
Maidstone East	a																								
East Croydon	a						21 28			21 44							22 14					22 28			
Gatwick Airport	a						21 44			22 12							22 42					22 44			
Brighton	a						22 19															23 19			

		TL	GR	TL	TL	TL	GR	GN		GN	TL	TL	TL	GN	GN	TL	TL	GN		TL	TL	TL	GN	GN	TL
										B				A	B									B	
Peterborough	d	20 54	21 18			21 24	21 28					←								21 54					22 24
Huntingdon	d	21 11				21 41						21 41								22 11					22 41
St Neots	d	21 18				→						21 48								22 18					22 48
Sandy	d	21 26										21 56								22 26					22 56
Biggleswade	d	21 30										22 00								22 30					23 00
Arlesey	a	21 34										22 04								22 34					23 04
Kings Lynn	d							20 44															21 44		
Watlington	d							20 51															21 51		
Downham Market	d							20 58															21 58		
Littleport	d							21 08															22 08		
Ely	d							21 17										21 47					22 17		
Waterbeach	d							21 27															22 27		
Cambridge North	d							21 32										22 01					22 32		
Cambridge	a							21 37										22 05					22 37		
Cambridge	d				21 27			21 44			←					21 54		22 14				22 27	22 44		
Foxton	d				21 36						21 36											22 36			
Shepreth	d				→						21 38											22 38			
Meldreth	d										21 41											22 41			
Royston	d										21 47					22 09	22 17					22 47			
Ashwell & Morden	d										21 51						22 21					22 51			
Baldock	d										21 56					22 18	22 26					22 56			
Letchworth Garden City	a										21 59					22 21	22 29					22 59			
Hitchin	d	21 41									22 04	22 11				22 26	22 34			22 41		23 04			23 11
Stevenage	d	21 47	21 48	←			21 59				22 10	22 17	←	22 28	22 30	22 32	22 40			22 47	←	23 10			23 17
Knebworth	d			21 43							22 13		22 13				22 43				22 43	23 13			
Welwyn North	d			21 47							→		22 17				→				22 47	→			
Welwyn Garden City	d			21 52									22 22								22 52				
Hatfield	d			21 55									22 25								22 55				
Potters Bar	d			22 02						←			22 32								23 02			←	
Finsbury Park ⊖	a	22 06		22 13						22 25		22 36	22 44	23 20	23 25	22 52				23 06	23 13			23 25	23 36
London Kings Cross ⊖	a		22 16	22 20			22 24	22 33		22 36			22 50		→			23 03			23 20		23 35	23 38	23 44
St Pancras International	a	22 14										22 44				22 59				23 14					
Farringdon	a	22 19										22 49				23 04				23 19					
City Thameslink	a																								
London Blackfriars	a	22 23										22 53				23 08				23 23					
London Bridge	a	22 29										22 59				23 14				23 29					
Maidstone East	a																								
East Croydon	a	22 44										23 14				23 28				23 44					
Gatwick Airport	a	23 12										23 42				23 47				00 12					
Brighton	a															00 23									

A until 15 February
B from 22 February

Table T025-R

Saturdays
21 December to 16 May

Peterborough, Kings Lynn, Cambridge and Stevenage - London, Maidstone East, Gatwick Airport and Brighton

		TL	GN	GN		TL	TL	GN	TL	TL	GN	TL	TL	GN		TL
			A	B							B					
Peterborough	d								22 54			23 20				
Huntingdon	d								23 11			23 35				
St Neots	d								23 18			23 42				
Sandy	d								23 26			23 50				
Biggleswade	d								23 30			23 53				
Arlesey	a								23 34			23 58				
Kings Lynn	d													22 57		
Watlington	d													23 04		
Downham Market	d													23 11		
Littleport	d													23 20		
Ely	d							22 52						23 29		
Waterbeach	d													23 38		
Cambridge North	d							23 05						23 43		
Cambridge	a							23 09						23 49		
Cambridge	d					22 54		23 14					23 35			23 54
Foxton	d												23 44			
Shepreth	d												23 46			
Meldreth	d												23 49			
Royston	d					23 09	23 17						23 54			00 09
Ashwell & Morden	d						23 21						23 58			
Baldock	d					23 17	23 26						00 03			00 17
Letchworth Garden City	a					23 20	23 29						00 06			00 20
Hitchin	d					23 26	23 34		23 44			00 07	00 10			00 26
Stevenage	d	←	23 28	23 28		23 32	23 40		23 50	←		00 13	00 16			00 32
Knebworth	d	23 13					23 43			23 43			00 19			
Welwyn North	d	23 17					→			23 47			00 23			
Welwyn Garden City	d	23 22								23 52			00 28			
Hatfield	d	23 25								23 55			00 31			
Potters Bar	d	23 32								00 02	←		00 38			
Finsbury Park ⊖	a	23 43	00 20	00 21		23 51			00 13	00 17	00 21	00 39	00 51			00 58
London Kings Cross ⊖	a	23 50		→		23 59		00 08	00 22	00 27	00 30	00 45	00 57			01 05
St Pancras International	a															
Farringdon	a															
City Thameslink	a															
London Blackfriars	a															
London Bridge	a															
Maidstone East	a															
East Croydon	a															
Gatwick Airport	a															
Brighton	a															

A until 15 February
B from 22 February

Please refer to Table T024 for the service from Moorgate to Stevenage via Hertford North

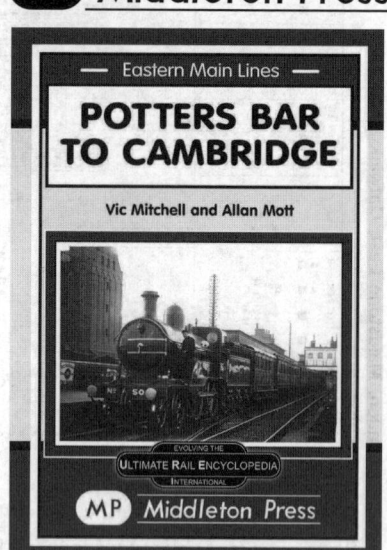

AVAILABLE FROM
MP Middleton Press
Eastern Main Lines
POTTERS BAR TO CAMBRIDGE
Vic Mitchell and Allan Mott
EVOLVING THE ULTIMATE RAIL ENCYCLOPEDIA INTERNATIONAL
MP Middleton Press

Table T025-R

Sundays

15 December to 10 May

Peterborough, Kings Lynn, Cambridge and Stevenage - London, Maidstone East, Gatwick Airport and Brighton

		TL	TL	TL	TL	GN	TL	GN	TL	GN	GN	TL	GN	GN	GN	GN	TL	GN	TL	TL	GN	GN	GN
		1	1	1	1		1		1			1					1		1	1			
		A	A	A	A	B bus	B	B bus	C	D	E		B bus	E	D	E	B	B bus	C		E	D	E
Peterborough 8	d					04 05		05 05	05 45									06 05	06 45				
Huntingdon	d					04 45		05 45	06 00				←					06 45	07 01				
St Neots	d					05 15		06 15	06 08				06 15					07 15	07 08				
Sandy	d					05 35		→	06 15				06 35					→	07 16				
Biggleswade	d					05 45			06 19				06 45						07 20				
Arlesey	a					06 05			06 24				07 05						07 24				
Kings Lynn	d																						
Watlington	d																						
Downham Market	d																						
Littleport	d																						
Ely	d																						
Waterbeach	d																						
Cambridge North	d																						
Cambridge	a																						
Cambridge	d											06 41								06 55			
Foxton	d																			07 05			
Shepreth	d																			07 08			
Meldreth	d																			07 11			
Royston	d				00 09							06 55								07 16			
Ashwell & Morden	d																			07 21			
Baldock	d			00 03	00 17							07 03								07 26			
Letchworth Garden City	a			00 06	00 20							07 06								07 29			
Hitchin 4	d		00 07	00 10	00 26	06a23	06 34		06 34			07 11	07a23				07 32		07 32	07 36			
Stevenage 4	d		00 13	00 16	00 32		06 40		06 40	06 58	06 58	07 17			07 28	07 28	07 38		07 38	07 42		07 58	07 58
Knebworth	d			00 19			06 44		06 44											07 46			
Welwyn North	d			00 23			06 48		06 48											07 50			
Welwyn Garden City 4	d			00 28			06 53		06 53											07 56			
Hatfield	d			00 31			06 57		06 57											08 00			
Potters Bar	d	00 02		00 38			07 03		07 03					←						08 06	←		
Finsbury Park ⊖	a	00 17	00 39	00 51	00 58		07 13		07 13	07 51	07 51	07 41		07 51	08 20	08 20	08 00		08 00	08 15	08 20	08 50	08 50
London Kings Cross 15 ⊖	a	00 27	00 45	00 57	01 05		07 23		07 23		→	07 50		07 59		→	08 09		08 09	08 22	08 27		→
St Pancras International	a																						
Farringdon	a																						
City Thameslink	a																						
London Blackfriars	a																						
London Bridge	a																						
Maidstone East	a																						
East Croydon	a																						
Gatwick Airport	a																						
Brighton	a																						

		TL	GN	GN	GN	GN	TL	TL	GN	GN	GN	GN	TL	TL	GN	GN	GN	TL	TL	GR	GN	GN
		1					1	1	1				1	1				1	1	R 1	1	1
			B bus	E	D	E				E	D	E			E	D	E			catering		
Peterborough 8	d						07 45											08 45		09 11		09 15
Huntingdon	d		←				08 01											09 01				09 29
St Neots	d		07 15				08 08											09 08				09 37
Sandy	d		07 35				08 16											09 16				
Biggleswade	d		07 45				08 20											09 20				09 46
Arlesey	a		08 05				08 24											09 24				
Kings Lynn	d																				08 26	
Watlington	d																				08 33	
Downham Market	d																				08 40	
Littleport	d																				08 49	
Ely	d																				08 57	
Waterbeach	d																				09 07	
Cambridge North	d																				09 12	
Cambridge	a																				09 16	
Cambridge	d	07 28						07 55	08 21				08 28						08 55		09 22	
Foxton	d							08 05											09 04			
Shepreth	d							08 08											09 06			
Meldreth	d							08 11											09 09			
Royston	d	07 43						08 16					08 43						09 15			
Ashwell & Morden	d							08 21											09 19			
Baldock	d	07 50						08 26					08 50						09 24			
Letchworth Garden City	a	07 53						08 29					08 53						09 27			
Hitchin 4	d	07 59	08a23				08 30	08 34					08 59	09 04				09 30	09 34			
Stevenage 4	d	08 05			08 28	08 28	08 36	08 40			08 58	08 58	09 05	09 10		09 28	09 28	09 36	09 40	09 41		
Knebworth	d							08 43						09 14					09 44			
Welwyn North	d							08 47						09 17					09 47			
Welwyn Garden City 4	d							08 52						09 22					09 52			
Hatfield	d							08 56						09 26					09 56			
Potters Bar	d			←				09 02		←				09 32	←				10 02			
Finsbury Park ⊖	a	08 24		08 50	09 20	09 20	08 55	09 13		09 20	09 50	09 50	09 24	09 42	09 50	10 20	10 20	09 56	10 12			
London Kings Cross 15 ⊖	a	08 31		08 58		→	09 03	09 21	09 09	09 27		→		09 49	09 58		→	10 03	10 19	10 06	10 09	10 17
St Pancras International	a												09 34									
Farringdon	a												09 39									
City Thameslink	a																					
London Blackfriars	a												09 43									
London Bridge	a												09 50									
Maidstone East	a																					
East Croydon	a												10 07									
Gatwick Airport	a												10 27									
Brighton	a																					

A not 15 December
B from 23 February until 29 March
C until 16 February, from 5 April
D until 16 February
E from 23 February

NRT DECEMBER 19 EDITION

Table T025-R

Sundays

15 December to 10 May

Peterborough, Kings Lynn, Cambridge and Stevenage - London, Maidstone East, Gatwick Airport and Brighton

		GN	GN	GN	TL	TL	GN	GN	GN	TL	TL	GN	GN	GN	GN	GN	TL	GR	TL	GR	GN	GN	GN
					1	1				1	1	1	1				1	R 1	1	R 1			
		A	B	A			A	B	A					A	B	A		catering		catering	A	B	A
Peterborough 8	d									09 45			10 15					10 36		10 42			
Huntingdon	d									10 01			10 29										
St Neots	d									10 08			10 37										
Sandy	d									10 16													
Biggleswade	d									10 20			10 46										
Arlesey	a									10 24													
Kings Lynn	d											09 26											
Watlington	d											09 33											
Downham Market	d											09 40											
Littleport	d											09 49											
Ely	d											09 57											
Waterbeach	d											10 07											
Cambridge North	d											10 12											
Cambridge	a											10 16											
Cambridge	d				09 28						09 55	10 22					10 28						
Foxton	d										10 04												
Shepreth	d										10 06												
Meldreth	d										10 09												
Royston	d				09 43						10 15						10 43						
Ashwell & Morden	d										10 19												
Baldock	d				09 50						10 24						10 50						
Letchworth Garden City	a				09 53						10 27						10 53						
Hitchin 4	d				09 59	10 04				10 30	10 34						10 59		11 04				
Stevenage 4	d		09 58	09 58	10 05	10 10		10 28	10 28	10 36	10 40				10 58	10 58	11 05	11 06	11 10	11 11		11 28	11 28
Knebworth	d					10 14					10 44								11 14				
Welwyn North	d					10 17					10 47								11 19				
Welwyn Garden City 4	d					10 22					10 52								11 23				
Hatfield	d					10 26					10 56								11 27				
Potters Bar	d	←				10 32	←				11 02			←					11 32		←		
Finsbury Park ⊖	a	10 20	10 50	10 50	10 24	10 42	10 50	11 20	11 20	10 56	11 12			11 20	11 50	11 50	11 24		11 43		11 50	12 20	12 20
London Kings Cross 15 ⊖	a	10 27		→		10 49	10 58		→	11 03	11 19	11 09	11 18	11 27		→		11 33	11 51	11 36	11 58		→
St Pancras International	a				10 34												11 34						
Farringdon	a				10 39												11 39						
City Thameslink	a																						
London Blackfriars	a				10 43												11 43						
London Bridge	a				10 50												11 50						
Maidstone East	a																						
East Croydon	a				11 07												12 07						
Gatwick Airport	a				11 27												12 27						
Brighton	a																						

		TL	TL	GN	GN	GN	GN	GN	TL	GN	TL	GR	GN	GN	TL	TL	GN	GN	GN	GN	TL	GR
		1	1	1	1				1		1	R 1			1	1	1				1	R 1
						A	B	A		A		catering	A	B				A	B	A		catering
Peterborough 8	d	10 45			11 15						11 45	11 59			←							12 39
Huntingdon	d	11 01			11 29						12 01				12 01							
St Neots	d	11 08			11 37						→				12 08							
Sandy	d	11 16													12 16							
Biggleswade	d	11 20			11 46										12 20							
Arlesey	a	11 24													12 24							
Kings Lynn	d			10 26													11 26					
Watlington	d			10 33													11 33					
Downham Market	d			10 40													11 40					
Littleport	d			10 49													11 49					
Ely	d			10 57													11 57					
Waterbeach	d			11 07													12 07					
Cambridge North	d			11 12													12 12					
Cambridge	a			11 16													12 16					
Cambridge	d		10 55	11 22					11 28							11 55	12 22				12 28	
Foxton	d		11 04													12 04						
Shepreth	d		11 06													12 06						
Meldreth	d		11 09													12 09						
Royston	d		11 15						11 43							12 15					12 43	
Ashwell & Morden	d		11 19													12 19						
Baldock	d		11 24						11 50							12 24					12 50	
Letchworth Garden City	a		11 27						11 53							12 27					12 53	
Hitchin 4	d	11 30	11 34						11 59						12 30	12 34					12 59	
Stevenage 4	d	11 36	11 40				11 58	11 58	12 05	12 28		12 28		12 28	12 36	12 40			12 58	12 58	13 05	13 08
Knebworth	d		11 44													12 44						
Welwyn North	d		11 47													12 47						
Welwyn Garden City 4	d		11 52													12 52						
Hatfield	d		11 56													12 56						
Potters Bar	d		12 02			←							←			13 02		←				
Finsbury Park ⊖	a	11 56	12 12			12 20	12 50	12 50	12 24	13 20			12 50	13 20	12 56	13 12		13 20	13 50	13 50	13 24	
London Kings Cross 15 ⊖	a	12 03	12 19	12 09	12 17	12 28		→		→		12 52	12 58		13 03	13 19	13 09	13 28		→		13 33
St Pancras International	a								12 34												13 34	
Farringdon	a								12 39												13 39	
City Thameslink	a																					
London Blackfriars	a								12 43												13 43	
London Bridge	a								12 50												13 50	
Maidstone East	a																					
East Croydon	a								13 07												14 07	
Gatwick Airport	a								13 27												14 27	
Brighton	a																					

A from 23 February
B until 16 February

Table T025-R

Sundays
15 December to 10 May

Peterborough, Kings Lynn, Cambridge and Stevenage - London, Maidstone East, Gatwick Airport and Brighton

		GN	GN	GN	TL	TL	GN	GR	GN	GN		GN	TL	GN	GN	GN	TL	TL	GN	GN		GN	GN	GR	TL
		A	B	A					A	B		A		A	B	A				A		B	A		
Peterborough	d				12 45			13 23									13 45							14 34	
Huntingdon	d				13 01												14 01								
St Neots	d				13 08												14 08								
Sandy	d				13 16												14 16								
Biggleswade	d				13 20												14 20								
Arlesey	a				13 24												14 24								
Kings Lynn	d						12 26												13 26						
Watlington	d						12 33												13 33						
Downham Market	d						12 40												13 40						
Littleport	d						12 49												13 49						
Ely	d						12 57												13 57						
Waterbeach	d						13 07												14 07						
Cambridge North	d						13 12												14 12						
Cambridge	a						13 16												14 16						
Cambridge	d					12 55	13 22						13 28					13 55	14 22						14 28
Foxton	d					13 04												14 04							
Shepreth	d					13 06												14 06							
Meldreth	d					13 09												14 09							
Royston	d					13 15							13 43					14 15							14 43
Ashwell & Morden	d					13 19												14 19							
Baldock	d					13 24							13 50					14 24							14 50
Letchworth Garden City	a					13 27							13 53					14 27							14 53
Hitchin	d				13 30	13 34							13 59				14 30	14 34							14 59
Stevenage	d		13 28	13 28	13 36	13 40		13 53		13 58		13 58	14 05		14 28	14 28	14 36	14 40				14 58	14 58	15 03	15 05
Knebworth	d					13 44												14 44							
Welwyn North	d					13 47												14 47							
Welwyn Garden City	d					13 52												14 52							
Hatfield	d					13 56												14 56							
Potters Bar	d	←				14 02			←					←				15 02		←					
Finsbury Park ⊖	a	13 50	14 20	14 20	13 56	14 12			14 20	14 50		14 50	14 24	14 50	15 20	15 20	14 56	15 12		15 20		15 50	15 50		15 25
London Kings Cross ⊖	a	13 58		→	14 03	14 19	14 09	14 18	14 28			→		14 58		→	15 03	15 20	15 10	15 28			→	15 27	
St Pancras International	a												14 34												15 34
Farringdon	a												14 39												15 39
City Thameslink	a																								
London Blackfriars	a												14 43												15 43
London Bridge	a												14 50												15 50
Maidstone East	a																								
East Croydon	a												15 07												16 07
Gatwick Airport	a												15 27												16 27
Brighton	a																								

		GN	GN	GN	TL	TL		GN	GR	GN	GN	GN	TL	GN	GN	GN		TL	TL	GN	GN	GN	GN	GR	TL
		A	B	A						A	B	A		A	B	A					A	B	A		
Peterborough	d				14 45				15 23									15 45						16 34	
Huntingdon	d				15 01													16 01							
St Neots	d				15 08													16 08							
Sandy	d				15 16													16 16							
Biggleswade	d				15 20													16 20							
Arlesey	a				15 24													16 24							
Kings Lynn	d							14 26												15 26					
Watlington	d							14 33												15 33					
Downham Market	d							14 40												15 40					
Littleport	d							14 49												15 49					
Ely	d							14 57												15 57					
Waterbeach	d							15 07												16 07					
Cambridge North	d							15 12												16 12					
Cambridge	a							15 16												16 16					
Cambridge	d					14 55		15 22					15 28						15 55	16 22					16 28
Foxton	d					15 04													16 04						
Shepreth	d					15 06													16 06						
Meldreth	d					15 09													16 09						
Royston	d					15 15							15 43						16 15						16 43
Ashwell & Morden	d					15 19													16 19						
Baldock	d					15 24							15 50						16 24						16 50
Letchworth Garden City	a					15 27							15 53						16 27						16 53
Hitchin	d				15 30	15 34							15 59					16 30	16 34						16 59
Stevenage	d		15 28	15 28	15 36	15 40			15 53		15 58	15 58	16 05		16 28	16 28		16 36	16 40			16 58	16 58	17 03	17 05
Knebworth	d					15 44													16 44						
Welwyn North	d					15 47													16 47						
Welwyn Garden City	d					15 52													16 52						
Hatfield	d					15 56													16 56						
Potters Bar	d	←				16 02				←				←					17 02		←				
Finsbury Park ⊖	a	15 50	16 20	16 20	15 56	16 12				16 20	16 50	16 50	16 25	16 50	17 20	17 20		16 56	17 12		17 20	17 50	17 50		17 25
London Kings Cross ⊖	a	15 58		→	16 03	16 19		16 10	16 18	16 28		→		16 58		→		17 03	17 19	17 11	17 29		→	17 28	
St Pancras International	a												16 34												17 34
Farringdon	a												16 39												17 39
City Thameslink	a																								
London Blackfriars	a												16 43												17 43
London Bridge	a												16 50												17 50
Maidstone East	a																								
East Croydon	a												17 07												18 07
Gatwick Airport	a												17 27												18 27
Brighton	a																								

A from 23 February
B until 16 February

Please refer to Table T024 for the service from Moorgate to Stevenage via Hertford North

Table T025-R

Sundays
15 December to 10 May

Peterborough, Kings Lynn, Cambridge and Stevenage - London, Maidstone East, Gatwick Airport and Brighton

		GN		GN	GN	TL	TL	GN	GN	GN	GN	GR		TL	GN	GN	GN	TL	GR	TL	TL	GN		GN	GN
		A		B	A				A	B	A				A	B	A							A	B
Peterborough	d					16 45												17 45	18 04	←					
Huntingdon	d					17 01												18 01		18 01					
St Neots	d					17 08												→		18 08					
Sandy	d					17 16														18 16					
Biggleswade	d					17 20														18 20					
Arlesey	a					17 24														18 24					
Kings Lynn	d							16 26														17 26			
Watlington	d							16 33														17 33			
Downham Market	d							16 40														17 40			
Littleport	d							16 49														17 49			
Ely	d							16 57														17 57			
Waterbeach	d							17 07														18 07			
Cambridge North	d							17 12														18 12			
Cambridge	a							17 16														18 16			
Cambridge	d						16 55	17 22						17 28							17 55	18 22			
Foxton	d						17 04														18 04				
Shepreth	d						17 06														18 06				
Meldreth	d						17 09														18 09				
Royston	d						17 15							17 43							18 15				
Ashwell & Morden	d						17 19														18 19				
Baldock	d						17 24							17 50							18 24				
Letchworth Garden City	a						17 27							17 53							18 27				
Hitchin	d					17 30	17 34							17 59						18 30	18 34				
Stevenage	d			17 28	17 28	17 36	17 40			17 58	17 58	18 04		18 05		18 28	18 28		18 33	18 36	18 40				18 58
Knebworth	d						17 44														18 44				
Welwyn North	d						17 47														18 47				
Welwyn Garden City	d						17 52														18 52				
Hatfield	d						17 56														18 56				
Potters Bar	d	←					18 02		←						←						19 02			←	
Finsbury Park ⊖	a	17 50		18 20	18 20	17 56	18 12		18 20	18 50	18 50			18 27	18 50	19 20	19 20			18 55	19 12			19 20	19 50
London Kings Cross ⊖	a	17 58			→	18 03	18 19	18 10	18 29		→	18 29			18 58		→		18 59	19 02	19 19	19 12		19 28	
St Pancras International	a													18 34											
Farringdon	a													18 39											
City Thameslink	a																								
London Blackfriars	a													18 43											
London Bridge	a													18 50											
Maidstone East	a																								
East Croydon	a													19 07											
Gatwick Airport	a													19 27											
Brighton	a																								

		GN	TL	GR	GN	GN	GN	GN		TL	GR	TL	TL	GN	GN	GN	GN	GR		TL	GN	GN	GN	TL	TL
		A				A	B	A							A	B	A				A	B	A		
Peterborough	d									18 45	19 03	←												19 45	
Huntingdon	d									19 01		19 01												20 01	
St Neots	d									→		19 08												20 08	
Sandy	d											19 16												20 16	
Biggleswade	d											19 20												20 20	
Arlesey	a											19 24												20 24	
Kings Lynn	d				17 54									18 26											
Watlington	d				18 01									18 33											
Downham Market	d				18 08									18 40											
Littleport	d				18 17									18 49											
Ely	d				18 26									18 57											
Waterbeach	d													19 07											
Cambridge North	d				18 38									19 12											
Cambridge	a				18 42									19 16											
Cambridge	d		18 28		18 43								18 55	19 22						19 28					19 55
Foxton	d												19 04												20 04
Shepreth	d												19 06												20 06
Meldreth	d												19 09												20 09
Royston	d		18 43										19 15							19 43					20 15
Ashwell & Morden	d												19 19												20 19
Baldock	d		18 50										19 24							19 50					20 24
Letchworth Garden City	a		18 53										19 27							19 53					20 27
Hitchin	d		18 59									19 30	19 34							19 59				20 30	20 34
Stevenage	d	18 58	19 05	19 10			19 28	19 28			19 32	19 36	19 40			19 58	19 58	20 03		20 05		20 28	20 28	20 36	20 40
Knebworth	d												19 44												20 44
Welwyn North	d												19 47												20 48
Welwyn Garden City	d												19 52												20 52
Hatfield	d												19 56												20 56
Potters Bar	d					←							20 02		←						←				21 02
Finsbury Park ⊖	a	19 50	19 24			19 50	20 20	20 20				19 55	20 12		20 20	20 50	20 50			20 26	20 50	21 20	21 20	20 55	21 12
London Kings Cross ⊖	a	→		19 34	19 36	19 58		→			19 57	20 03	20 19	20 10	20 28		→	20 27			20 58		→	21 03	21 19
St Pancras International	a		19 34																	20 34					
Farringdon	a		19 39																	20 39					
City Thameslink	a																								
London Blackfriars	a		19 43																	20 43					
London Bridge	a		19 50																	20 50					
Maidstone East	a																								
East Croydon	a		20 07																	21 07					
Gatwick Airport	a		20 27																	21 27					
Brighton	a																								

A from 23 February
B until 16 February

Please refer to Table T024 for the service from Moorgate to Stevenage via Hertford North

Table T025-R

Sundays

15 December to 10 May

Peterborough, Kings Lynn, Cambridge and Stevenage - London, Maidstone East, Gatwick Airport and Brighton

Station		GN	GN	GN	GN	TL	GR	GN	GN	GN	TL	TL	GN	GN	GN	GN	TL	GN	GN	GN	TL	TL
		■	A	B	A	■	■	A	B	A	■	■	■	A	B	A	■	A	B	A	■	■
Peterborough ■	d										20 45										21 45	
Huntingdon	d										21 01										22 01	
St Neots	d										21 08										22 08	
Sandy	d										21 16										22 16	
Biggleswade	d										21 20										22 20	
Arlesey	a										21 24										22 24	
Kings Lynn	d	19 26											20 26									
Watlington	d	19 33											20 33									
Downham Market	d	19 40											20 40									
Littleport	d	19 49											20 49									
Ely	d	19 57											20 57									
Waterbeach	d	20 07											21 07									
Cambridge North	d	20 12											21 12									
Cambridge	a	20 16											21 16									
Cambridge	d	20 22				20 28						20 55	21 22				21 28					21 55
Foxton	d											21 05										22 05
Shepreth	d											21 08										22 08
Meldreth	d											21 11										22 11
Royston	d					20 43						21 16					21 43					22 16
Ashwell & Morden	d											21 21										22 21
Baldock	d					20 50						21 26					21 50					22 26
Letchworth Garden City	a					20 53						21 29					21 53					22 29
Hitchin ■	d					20 59					21 30	21 34					21 59				22 30	22 34
Stevenage ■	d			20 58	20 58	21 05	21 09		21 28	21 28	21 36	21 40			21 58	21 58	22 05		22 28	22 28	22 36	22 40
Knebworth	d											21 44										22 44
Welwyn North	d											21 48										22 48
Welwyn Garden City ■	d											21 52										22 52
Hatfield	d											21 56										22 56
Potters Bar	d		←					←				22 02		←				←				23 02
Finsbury Park ⊖	a		21 20	21 50	21 50	21 24		21 50	22 20	22 20	21 56	22 13		22 20	22 50	22 50	22 24	22 50	23 20	23 20	22 56	23 13
London Kings Cross ■ ⊖	a	21 09	21 28		→		21 33	21 58		→	22 03	22 21	22 10	22 28		→		22 58		→	23 03	23 21
St Pancras International	a					21 34											22 34					
Farringdon	a					21 39											22 39					
City Thameslink	a																					
London Blackfriars	a					21 43											22 43					
London Bridge	a					21 50											22 50					
Maidstone East	a																					
East Croydon	a					22 07											23 07					
Gatwick Airport	a					22 26											23 35					
Brighton	a																					

Station		GR	GN	GR	GN	GN	GN	TL	GN	GN	GN	TL	GN	GN
		■	■	■	A	B	A	■	A	B	A	■	A	■
Peterborough ■	d	22 15		22 24								22 45		
Huntingdon	d											23 01		
St Neots	d											23 08		
Sandy	d											23 16		
Biggleswade	d											23 20		
Arlesey	a											23 24		
Kings Lynn	d		21 26											22 26
Watlington	d		21 33											22 33
Downham Market	d		21 40											22 40
Littleport	d		21 49											22 49
Ely	d		21 57											22 57
Waterbeach	d		22 07											23 07
Cambridge North	d		22 12											23 12
Cambridge	a		22 16											23 16
Cambridge	d		22 22					22 28						23 20
Foxton	d													23 30
Shepreth	d													23 33
Meldreth	d													23 36
Royston	d							22 43						23 41
Ashwell & Morden	d													23 46
Baldock	d							22 50						23 51
Letchworth Garden City	a							22 53						23 54
Hitchin ■	d							22 59				23 30		00 01
Stevenage ■	d	22 45		22 53		22 58	22 58	23 05		23 28	23 28	23 36		00 07
Knebworth	d													00 11
Welwyn North	d													00 15
Welwyn Garden City ■	d													00 19
Hatfield	d													00 23
Potters Bar	d				←				←				←	00 29
Finsbury Park ⊖	a				23 20	23 50	23 50	23 24	23 50	00 24	00 24	23 56	00 24	00 39
London Kings Cross ■ ⊖	a	23 10	23 16	23 17	23 27		→	23 31	23 59		→	00 03	00 31	00 49
St Pancras International	a													
Farringdon	a													
City Thameslink	a													
London Blackfriars	a													
London Bridge	a													
Maidstone East	a													
East Croydon	a													
Gatwick Airport	a													
Brighton	a													

A from 23 February
B until 16 February

Please refer to Table T024 for the service from Moorgate to Stevenage via Hertford North

NRT DECEMBER 19 EDITION

Table T026-F

Mondays to Fridays

16 December to 15 May

London - Humberside, Yorkshire, North East England and Scotland

Miles	Miles	Miles	Station		GR MO	TP MO	GR MX	TP MX	GR MO	GR MX	TP	XC	XC	TP	GR	XC	TP	XC	GR	TP	TP	TP	XC
					■ A	◇■ B	■ A	◇■ B	■ A	■ A	◇■ C	◇■	◇■ D	◇■	■	◇■ E	◇■ F	◇■ G	■	◇■ H	◇■ F	◇■ B	◇■ I
0	—	—	London Kings Cross ■ ⊖	d																			
27½	—	—	Stevenage ■	d																			
76¼	—	—	Peterborough ■	a																			
—	—	—	Norwich	d																			
—	—	—	Peterborough ■	d																			
105¼	—	—	Grantham ■	a																			
—	—	—		d																			
120	—	—	Newark North Gate ■	a																			
—	—	—		d																			
—	—	—	Lincoln	a																			
138½	—	—	Retford ■	d																			
156	0	—	Doncaster ■	a																			
—	—	—	Selby	a																			
—	—	—	Hull	a																			
—	—	—	Sheffield ■	a																			
—	—	—	Pontefract Monkhill	a																			
—	—	—	Wakefield Kirkgate ■	a																			
—	19¾	—	Wakefield Westgate ■	d																			
—	29¾	—	Leeds ■	a																			
—	—	—	Mirfield	a																			
—	—	—	Brighouse	a																			
—	—	—	Halifax	a																			
—	—	—	Shipley	a																			
—	—	—	Bradford Forster Square	a																			
—	—	—	Bradford Interchange	a																			
—	—	—	Keighley	a																			
—	—	—	Skipton	a																			
—	—	—	Doncaster ■	d															06 10				07 03
188½	—	—	York ■	a															06 30				07 24
—	—	—	Scarborough	a																			
—	—	—	Harrogate	a																			
—	—	—	Leeds ■	d												05 43	05 52	←		06 15	06 42	06 51	
—	—	—	York ■	d					00 12	00 41	05 05					06 27	06 19	06 27	06 35	06 39	07 07	07 22	07 31
210¾	—	—	Thirsk	d							05 28					→				06 56			
218½	—	—	Northallerton	d					00s45	01s09	05 36								06 55	07 05	07 29		
232½	—	—	Darlington ■	a					00s59	01s23	05 57						06 45	06 53	07 07		07 41	07 48	07 58
—	—	—	Eaglescliffe	a																			
—	—	—	Middlesbrough	a							06 34									07 35			
—	—	—	Darlington ■	d				00 01									06 47	06 55	07 09		07 42	07 50	07 59
254½	—	—	Durham	d	00 07	00 11	00 14	00 25	01s17	01s42							07 03	07 13	07 27		07 59	08 06	08 17
260¼	—	—	Chester-le-Street	d		00 17		00 33									07 10				08 05		
268½	—	—	Newcastle ■	a	00 38	00 43	00 43	00 59	01 50	02 15							07 19	07 30	07 40		08 17	08 19	08 31
—	—	—	Hartlepool	a																			
—	—	—	Sunderland	a																			
—	—	—	Newcastle ■	d										05 53	06 22		07 21	07 35	07 42			08 21	
285	—	—	Morpeth	a										06 07	06 36		07 34	07 47				08 34	
303¼	—	—	Alnmouth for Alnwick	a										06 21	06 53				08 08				
335½	—	—	Berwick-upon-Tweed	a										06 42	07 17			08 20	08 31				
363¾	—	—	Dunbar 238	a											07 41				08 54				
393	—	0	Edinburgh ■ 238	a										07 30	08 07		08 51	09 03	09 21			09 53	
—	—	—		d								06 25	07 27					09 12					
394¼	—	1¼	Haymarket 238	d									07 32					09 16					
437¼	—	—	Motherwell	a								07 04	08 14					09 54					
450¼	—	—	Glasgow Central ■	a								07 21	08 31					10 15					
—	—	—	Stirling	a																			
—	—	—	Perth	a																			
185¾	—	—	Inverness	a																			
—	—	13¼	Inverkeithing	a																			
—	—	26	Kirkcaldy	a																			
—	—	51	Leuchars ■	a																			
—	—	59¼	Dundee	a																			
—	—	76¼	Arbroath	a																			
—	—	90	Montrose	a																			
—	—	114¼	Stonehaven	a																			
—	—	130½	Aberdeen	a																			

A From London Kings Cross
B From Liverpool Lime Street
C To Redcar Central
D From Dunbar
E To Glasgow Central
F From Manchester Airport
G From Leeds. ⚒ to Edinburgh
H From Manchester Victoria to Redcar Central
I From Derby

Table T026-F

Mondays to Fridays

16 December to 15 May

London - Humberside, Yorkshire, North East England and Scotland

Station		GR	TP	GR	TP	TP	XC	GR	GR	TP	GR	EM	EM	XC	GR	TP	TP	XC	GR	GR	HT	GR	TP
			A		B	C	D			A		MO E	MX E	D		B	C	D					A
London Kings Cross	d							05 55	06 15		06 33				07 00				07 03	07 06	07 27	07 30	
Stevenage	d							06 17	06 37		06 55									07 28			
Peterborough	a							06 46	07 06		07 24				07 46				07 49	07 57		08 16	
Norwich	d											05 50	05 50										
Peterborough	d							06 47	07 08		07 25	07 29	07 29		07 48				07 53	07 58		08 18	
Grantham	a							07 05	07 26		07 43	07 57	07 57							08 16	08 26		
	d							07 06	07 27		07 44	07 58	07 58							08 17	08 27		
Newark North Gate	a							07 18	07 39											08 29		08 45	
	d							07 19	07 41											08 30		08 46	
Lincoln	a																						
Retford	d							07 34	07 56											08 45	08 51		
Doncaster	a							07 48	08 10		08 16								08 42	09 02	09 05	09 10	
Selby	a																				09 22		
Hull	a																				10 00		
Sheffield	a											09 37	09 38										
Pontefract Monkhill	a																						
Wakefield Kirkgate	a																						
Wakefield Westgate	d						07 47	08 07			08 36							08 49	09 01				
Leeds	a						08 03	08 22			08 52							09 02	09 16				
Mirfield	a																						
Brighouse	a																						
Halifax	a																						
Shipley	a																						
Bradford Forster Square	a																						
Bradford Interchange	a																						
Keighley	a																						
Skipton	a																						
Doncaster	d								08 11					08 19						09 04		09 12	
York	a								08 32					08 40	08 51					09 27		09 32	
Scarborough	a																						
Harrogate	a																						
Leeds	d	07 08	07 14		07 42	07 51	08 08			08 14						08 42	08 51	09 08					09 14
York	d	07 35	07 39		08 07	08 21	08 31		08 34	08 39				08 42	08 55	09 07	09 21	09 31				09 35	09 39
Thirsk	d		07 56							08 56													09 56
Northallerton	d		08 05		08 26				08 55	09 06						09 26							10 07
Darlington	a	08 03			08 37	08 47	08 58		09 07					09 14	09 22	09 37	09 47	09 58				10 04	
Eaglescliffe	a																						
Middlesbrough	a		08 35							09 36													10 37
Darlington	d	08 05			08 39	08 49	08 59		09 09					09 15	09 24	09 39	09 49	10 00				10 07	
Durham	d	08 23			08 55	09 05	09 17		09 27					09 32		09 55	10 05	10 17				10 24	
Chester-le-Street	d				09 02																		
Newcastle	a	08 37			09 12	09 18	09 29		09 40					09 45	09 51	10 11	10 19	10 29				10 39	
Hartlepool	a																						
Sunderland	a																						
Newcastle	d	08 42		08 56		09 21	09 33		09 47						09 54		10 21	10 35				10 42	
Morpeth	a	08 55				09 33											10 34						
Alnmouth for Alnwick	a						09 57															11 07	
Berwick-upon-Tweed	a	09 30		09 38			10 19								10 36								
Dunbar 238	a	09 54																11 38					
Edinburgh 238	a	10 20		10 31		10 52	11 06		11 12						11 22		11 50	12 04				12 10	
	d	10 28					11 11																
Haymarket 238	d	10 33					11 15																
Motherwell	a						11 54																
Glasgow Central	a						12 11																
Stirling	a																						
Perth	a																						
Inverness	a																						
Inverkeithing	a	10 47																					
Kirkcaldy	a	11 04																					
Leuchars	a	11 28																					
Dundee	a	11 44																					
Arbroath	a	12 01																					
Montrose	a	12 17																					
Stonehaven	a	12 41																					
Aberdeen	a	13 02																					

A From Manchester Airport to Redcar Central
B From Manchester Airport
C From Liverpool Lime Street
D From Birmingham New Street
E To Liverpool Lime Street

Table T026-F

Mondays to Fridays

16 December to 15 May

London - Humberside, Yorkshire, North East England and Scotland

Station		GR	EM	XC	GR	TP	TP	XC	GR	GR	GC	XC	GR	TP	GR	EM	XC	GR	TP	XC	TP	XC	GR
			A	B		C	D	E				F		G		A	H		C	I	D	J	
London Kings Cross	d	07 33			08 00				08 03	08 06	08 27		08 30		08 33			09 00					09 03
Stevenage	d	07 55													08 56								
Peterborough	a								08 49	08 53			09 16					09 46					09 49
Norwich	d		06 51													07 57							
Peterborough	d		08 25						08 51	08 54			09 18			09 27		09 48					09 52
Grantham	a	08 40	08 55							09 13					09 40	09 55							
	d	08 41	08 56							09 14					09 41	09 58							
Newark North Gate	a									09 27			09 45										
	d									09 29			09 46										
Lincoln	a									09 55													
Retford	d																						
Doncaster	a	09 13							09 40				10 09		10 13								10 40
Selby	a																						
Hull	a																						
Sheffield	a		10 37													11 37							
Pontefract Monkhill	a																						
Wakefield Kirkgate	a																						
Wakefield Westgate	d	09 32						09 47	10 01						10 32							10 46	11 01
Leeds	a	09 45						10 00	10 16						10 47							11 01	11 16
Mirfield	a																						
Brighouse	a																						
Halifax	a																						
Shipley	a																						
Bradford Forster Square	a																						
Bradford Interchange	a																						
Keighley	a																						
Skipton	a																						
Doncaster	d			09 19									10 10				10 19			10 53			
York	a			09 40	09 50						10 20		10 32				10 40	10 51		11 15			
Scarborough	a																						
Harrogate	a	10 19										←											
Leeds	d					09 42	09 51	10 08				10 08		10 14					10 42		10 51	11 08	
York	d			09 42	09 54	10 07	10 21	→			10 25	10 31	10 35	10 39			10 42	10 54	11 07	11 17	11 21	11 31	
Thirsk	d										10 42			10 56									
Northallerton	d					10 26					10 59		10 55	11 07					11 26				
Darlington	a			10 12	10 22	10 37	10 47					10 59	11 07				11 14	11 22	11 37	11 43	11 48	11 59	
Eaglescliffe	a										11 15												
Middlesbrough	a													11 37									
Darlington	d			10 13	10 23	10 39	10 49					11 00	11 09				11 16	11 23	11 39	11 44	11 49	12 00	
Durham	d			10 30		10 55	11 05					11 17	11 27				11 33		11 55	12 01	12 06	12 17	
Chester-le-Street	d					11 02																	
Newcastle	a			10 43	10 50	11 13	11 19					11 29	11 40				11 46	11 50	12 11	12 14	12 18	12 29	
Hartlepool	a										11 35												
Sunderland	a										12 02												
Newcastle	d				10 52		11 21					11 32	11 44					11 52			12 21	12 36	
Morpeth	a						11 34					11 45									12 34		
Alnmouth for Alnwick	a																						
Berwick-upon-Tweed	a				11 35							12 18						12 35					
Dunbar 238	a																					13 41	
Edinburgh 238	a				12 20		12 51					13 02	13 09					13 20			13 50	14 07	
	d											13 11											
Haymarket 238	d											13 16											
Motherwell	a											13 54											
Glasgow Central	a											14 12											
Stirling	a																						
Perth	a																						
Inverness	a																						
Inverkeithing	a																						
Kirkcaldy	a																						
Leuchars	a																						
Dundee	a																						
Arbroath	a																						
Montrose	a																						
Stonehaven	a																						
Aberdeen	a																						

A To Liverpool Lime Street
B From Birmingham New Street
C From Manchester Airport
D From Liverpool Lime Street
E From Bath Spa to Glasgow Central
F From Bath Spa
G From Manchester Airport to Redcar Central
H From Guildford
I From Reading
J From Plymouth

Table T026-F

Mondays to Fridays

16 December to 15 May

London - Humberside, Yorkshire, North East England and Scotland

Station		GR	GR	TP	GR	HT	EM	GR	TP	XC	TP	XC	GR	GR	GR	TP	GR	EM	GC	GR	TP	TP
				A			B		C	D	E	F				A		B			C	E
London Kings Cross	d	09 06	09 30		09 33	09 48		10 00					10 03	10 06	10 30		10 33		10 57	11 00		
Stevenage	d	09 28			09 56									10 28			10 56					
Peterborough	a	09 57	10 16										10 50	10 57	11 16							
Norwich	d						08 56											09 57				
Peterborough	d	09 59	10 18				10 28						10 51	11 01	11 18			11 28				
Grantham	a	10 18			10 40	10 49	10 58							11 20			11 40	12 01				
	d	10 20			10 41	10 50	11 00							11 21			11 41	12 02				
Newark North Gate	a	10 32	10 45											11 34	11 45							
	d	10 33	10 46											11 36	11 46							
Lincoln	a													12 02								
Retford	d	10 49				11 11																
Doncaster	a	11 03	11 09		11 13	11 26							11 40		12 09		12 13		12 27			
Selby	a					11 43																
Hull	a					12 18																
Sheffield	a						12 37											13 37				
Pontefract Monkhill	a																		12 57			
Wakefield Kirkgate	a																		13 14			
Wakefield Westgate	d				11 32							11 46	12 01				12 32					
Leeds	a				11 46							12 01	12 16				12 48					
Mirfield	a																		13 27			
Brighouse	a																		13 35			
Halifax	a																		13 47			
Shipley	a																					
Bradford Forster Square	a																					
Bradford Interchange	a																		14 03			
Keighley	a																					
Skipton	a																					
Doncaster	d	11 05	11 10							11 54					12 10							
York	a	11 30	11 32					11 52		12 15					12 31					12 51		
Scarborough	a																					
Harrogate	a				12 19																	
Leeds	d			11 14					11 42		11 51	12 08				12 14					12 42	12 51
York	d		11 35	11 39				11 55	12 07	12 17	12 22	12 32			12 35	12 39				12 54	13 07	13 20
Thirsk	d			11 56												12 56						
Northallerton	d			12 05					12 26						12 55	13 05					13 26	
Darlington	a		12 04					12 22	12 37	12 43	12 48	12 59			13 07					13 21	13 37	13 46
Eaglescliffe	a																					
Middlesbrough	a			12 35												13 35						
Darlington	d		12 06					12 24	12 39	12 44	12 50	13 00			13 09					13 23	13 39	13 48
Durham	d		12 24						12 55	13 01	13 06	13 17			13 27						13 55	14 04
Chester-le-Street	d								13 02													
Newcastle	a		12 37					12 50	13 13	13 16	13 19	13 29			13 40					13 49	14 10	14 19
Hartlepool	a																					
Sunderland	a																					
Newcastle	d		12 39					12 54			13 21	13 35			13 45					13 52		14 21
Morpeth	a		12 53								13 34											14 34
Alnmouth for Alnwick	a		13 09									13 59										
Berwick-upon-Tweed	a							13 37				14 21								14 34		
Dunbar 238	a																					
Edinburgh 238	a		14 13					14 21			14 49	15 08			15 16					15 19		15 49
	d							14 29				15 12										
Haymarket 238	d							14 34				15 17										
Motherwell	a											15 54										
Glasgow Central	a											16 12										
Stirling	a																					
Perth	a																					
Inverness	a																					
Inverkeithing	a							14 49														
Kirkcaldy	a							15 06														
Leuchars	a							15 31														
Dundee	a							15 46														
Arbroath	a							16 05														
Montrose	a							16 21														
Stonehaven	a							16 45														
Aberdeen	a							17 04														

A From Manchester Airport to Redcar Central
B To Liverpool Lime Street
C From Manchester Airport
D From Southampton Central
E From Liverpool Lime Street
F From Plymouth

Table T026-F

Mondays to Fridays

16 December to 15 May

London - Humberside, Yorkshire, North East England and Scotland

Station		XC	GR	GR	GC	XC	GR	TP	GR	XC	HT	EM	GR	TP	TP	XC	GR	GR	GR	TP	GR	EM	XC
		A				B		C		D		E		F	G	H				C		E	I
London Kings Cross	d		11 03	11 06	11 27		11 30		11 33		11 48		12 00				12 03	12 06	12 30		12 33		
Stevenage	d			11 28					11 56									12 28			12 56		
Peterborough	a		11 50	11 57			12 16										12 50	12 58	13 16				
Norwich	d											10 57										11 57	
Peterborough	d		11 53	11 59			12 18					12 26					12 52	13 01	13 18			13 26	
Grantham	a			12 18					12 40		12 49	12 58						13 20			13 40	13 56	
	d			12 19					12 41		12 50	12 59						13 21			13 41	13 58	
Newark North Gate	a			12 31			12 45											13 34	13 45				
	d			12 32			12 46											13 36	13 46				
Lincoln	a																	14 02					
Retford	d			12 47							13 11												
Doncaster	a		12 40	13 03			13 09		13 13		13 26						13 40		14 09		14 13		
Selby	a										13 43												
Hull	a										14 18												
Sheffield	a											14 37										15 37	
Pontefract Monkhill	a																						
Wakefield Kirkgate	a																						
Wakefield Westgate	d	12 46	13 01						13 32							13 47	14 01				14 32		
Leeds	a	13 00	13 16						13 46							14 00	14 16				14 48		
Mirfield	a																						
Brighouse	a																						
Halifax	a																						
Shipley	a																						
Bradford Forster Square	a																						
Bradford Interchange	a																						
Keighley	a																						
Skipton	a																						
Doncaster	d			13 05			13 10			13 19									14 11				14 17
York	a			13 29	13 20		13 32			13 40			13 52						14 32				14 39
Scarborough	a																						
Harrogate	a					←			14 19														
Leeds	d	13 08				13 08		13 14						13 42	13 51	14 08				14 14			
York	d	→			13 23	13 31	13 35	13 39		13 42			13 55	14 07	14 21	14 31			14 35	14 39			14 42
Thirsk	d				13 40			13 56												14 56			
Northallerton	d				13 49			14 07											14 55	15 07			
Darlington	a					14 02	14 07			14 12			14 22	14 37	14 47	14 59			15 07				15 13
Eaglescliffe	a				14 04																		
Middlesbrough	a							14 37												15 37			
Darlington	d					14 03	14 08			14 13			14 24	14 38	14 49	15 00			15 09				15 14
Durham	d					14 20	14 26			14 30				14 55	15 05	15 17			15 27				15 31
Chester-le-Street	d													15 01									
Newcastle	a					14 32	14 39			14 43			14 50	15 13	15 18	15 29			15 40				15 45
Hartlepool	a				14 23																		
Sunderland	a				14 51																		
Newcastle	d					14 35	14 43						14 55		15 21	15 37			15 45				
Morpeth	a					14 47									15 33								
Alnmouth for Alnwick	a						15 08									16 01							
Berwick-upon-Tweed	a												15 38			16 23							
Dunbar 238	a					15 40																	
Edinburgh 238	a					16 06	16 15						16 22		16 48	17 05			17 14				
	d												16 34			17 12							
Haymarket 238	d												16 39			17 17							
Motherwell	a															17 55							
Glasgow Central	a															18 11							
Stirling	a												17 16										
Perth	a												17 53										
Inverness	a												20 06										
Inverkeithing	a																						
Kirkcaldy	a																						
Leuchars	a																						
Dundee	a																						
Arbroath	a																						
Montrose	a																						
Stonehaven	a																						
Aberdeen	a																						

A From Plymouth to Edinburgh
B From Plymouth
C From Manchester Airport to Redcar Central
D From Reading
E To Liverpool Lime Street
F From Manchester Airport
G From Liverpool Lime Street
H From Penzance
I From Southampton Central

Table T026-F

Mondays to Fridays

16 December to 15 May

London - Humberside, Yorkshire, North East England and Scotland

Station		GC	GR	TP	TP	XC	GR	GR	GR	TP	GR	XC	HT	EM	GR	TP	TP	XC	GR	GR	GR	TP
				A	B	C				D		E		F		A	B	G				D
London Kings Cross	d	12 57	13 00				13 03	13 06	13 30		13 33		13 48		14 00				14 03	14 06	14 30	
Stevenage	d							13 28			13 56									14 28		
Peterborough	a		13 46				13 49	13 59	14 17										14 50	14 57	15 17	
Norwich	d													12 57								
Peterborough	d		13 48				13 52	14 00	14 18					14 26					14 51	14 59	15 19	
Grantham	a							14 19			14 40		14 49	14 57						15 18		
	d							14 21			14 42		14 50	14 58						15 19		
Newark North Gate	a							14 33	14 45											15 32	15 46	
	d							14 34	14 46											15 34	15 47	
Lincoln	a																			16 01		
Retford	d							14 49					15 13									
Doncaster	a						14 39	15 03	15 09		15 13		15 26						15 40		16 10	
Selby	a												15 43									
Hull	a												16 25									
Sheffield	a													16 37								
Pontefract Monkhill	a																					
Wakefield Kirkgate	a																					
Wakefield Westgate	d					14 47	15 01				15 32							15 47	16 00			
Leeds	a					15 00	15 16				15 46							16 00	16 16			
Mirfield	a																					
Brighouse	a																					
Halifax	a																					
Shipley	a																					
Bradford Forster Square	a																					
Bradford Interchange	a																					
Keighley	a																					
Skipton	a																					
Doncaster	d							15 05	15 11			15 19									16 11	
York	a	14 49	14 51					15 29	15 31			15 40			15 52						16 32	
Scarborough	a																					
Harrogate	a										16 19											
Leeds	d			14 42	14 51	15 08				15 14						15 42	15 51	16 08				16 14
York	d	14 51	14 54	15 07	15 22	15 32			15 35	15 39		15 42			15 55	16 07	16 19	16 31			16 35	16 39
Thirsk	d	15 14								15 56												16 56
Northallerton	d	15 27		15 26					15 55	16 07						16 26					16 55	17 07
Darlington	a		15 21	15 37	15 48	15 59			16 07			16 13			16 22	16 37	16 47	16 58			17 07	
Eaglescliffe	a	15 43																				
Middlesbrough	a									16 37												17 37
Darlington	d		15 23	15 39	15 50	16 01			16 09			16 14			16 24	16 39	16 49	17 00			17 09	
Durham	d			15 55	16 06	16 18			16 26			16 31				17 00	17 05	17 17			17 27	
Chester-le-Street	d			16 02												17 07						
Newcastle	a		15 49	16 13	16 19	16 32			16 39			16 44			16 50	17 18	17 18	17 29			17 40	
Hartlepool	a	16 11																				
Sunderland	a	16 38																				
Newcastle	d		15 52		16 21	16 35			16 42						16 56		17 20	17 37			17 49	
Morpeth	a				16 34	16 48			16 55								17 33					
Alnmouth for Alnwick	a					17 03			17 10									18 01				
Berwick-upon-Tweed	a		16 34												17 39			18 23				
Dunbar 238	a					17 44																
Edinburgh 238	a		17 23		17 52	18 07			18 18						18 22		18 52	19 07			19 13	
	d					18 11									18 33			19 11				
Haymarket 238	d					18 17									18 38			19 16				
Motherwell	a																	19 54				
Glasgow Central	a																	20 15				
Stirling	a																					
Perth	a																					
Inverness	a																					
Inverkeithing	a					18 29									18 53							
Kirkcaldy	a					18 45									19 11							
Leuchars	a					19 19									19 39							
Dundee	a					19 33									19 54							
Arbroath	a					19 51									20 13							
Montrose	a					20 05									20 30							
Stonehaven	a					20 26									20 54							
Aberdeen	a					20 44									21 15							

A From Manchester Airport
B From Liverpool Lime Street
C From Plymouth. to Edinburgh
D From Manchester Airport to Redcar Central
E From Reading
F To Liverpool Lime Street
G From Penzance. to Edinburgh

Table T026-F

Mondays to Fridays

16 December to 15 May

London - Humberside, Yorkshire, North East England and Scotland

Station		GR	EM	XC	GC	GR	TP	XC	TP	XC	GR	GR	GR	TP	GR	HT	EM	GR	TP	TP	XC	GR	GR
			A	B			C	D	E	F				G		H	A		C	E	I		
London Kings Cross	d	14 33			14 48	15 00					15 03	15 06	15 30		15 33	15 48		16 00				16 03	16 06
Stevenage	d	14 56										15 28			15 56								16 28
Peterborough	a										15 50	15 57	16 16									16 50	16 57
Norwich	d		13 57														14 57						
Peterborough	d		15 30								15 51	15 59	16 18				16 27					16 52	17 01
Grantham	a	15 41	16 00									16 18			16 40	16 49	16 57						17 20
	d	15 42	16 03									16 19			16 41	16 50	16 58						17 21
Newark North Gate	a											16 31	16 45										17 34
	d											16 33	16 46										17 36
Lincoln	a																						18 02
Retford	d											16 48				17 12							
Doncaster	a	16 14			16 20						16 40	17 02	17 09		17 16	17 26						17 39	
Selby	a															17 43							
Hull	a															18 23							
Sheffield	a		17 38														18 37						
Pontefract Monkhill	a				16 52																		
Wakefield Kirkgate	a				17 13																		
Wakefield Westgate	d	16 33								16 47	17 01				17 35						17 47	18 01	
Leeds	a	16 51								17 01	17 16				17 49						18 00	18 16	
Mirfield	a				17 25																		
Brighouse	a				17 33																		
Halifax	a				17 46																		
Shipley	a																						
Bradford Forster Square	a																						
Bradford Interchange	a				18 01																		
Keighley	a																						
Skipton	a																						
Doncaster	d			16 19				16 54				17 04	17 10										
York	a			16 40		16 51		17 14				17 27	17 31					17 51					
Scarborough	a																						
Harrogate	a														18 32								
Leeds	d						16 42		16 51	17 07				17 13					17 42	17 51	18 08		
York	d			16 42		16 55	17 07	17 16	17 21	17 31			17 34	17 39				17 55	18 07	18 22	18 32		
Thirsk	d													17 56									
Northallerton	d						17 26						17 55	18 05					18 26				
Darlington	a			17 13		17 22	17 37	17 42	17 47	17 59			18 07					18 22	18 37	18 48	19 00		
Eaglescliffe	a																						
Middlesbrough	a													18 35									
Darlington	d			17 14		17 24	17 39	17 43	17 49	18 00			18 09					18 24	18 39	18 50	19 01		
Durham	d			17 31			17 55	18 00	18 05	18 16			18 27						18 55	19 06	19 20		
Chester-le-Street	d																		19 02				
Newcastle	a			17 43		17 50	18 10	18 13	18 18	18 32			18 41					18 50	19 13	19 19	19 33		
Hartlepool	a																						
Sunderland	a																						
Newcastle	d					17 53			18 21	18 35			18 44					18 53		19 21	19 35		
Morpeth	a								18 34	18 49										19 34			
Alnmouth for Alnwick	a												19 09								20 01		
Berwick-upon-Tweed	a					18 37				19 22								19 36			20 25		
Dunbar 238	a									19 45													
Edinburgh 238	a					19 19			20 08	20 10			20 14					20 20		20 54	21 09		
	d					19 25				20 14			20 19					20 32			21 14		
Haymarket 238	d					19 30				20 19			20 24					20 37			21 19		
Motherwell	a												21 02								21 59		
Glasgow Central	a												21 26								22 21		
Stirling	a					20 16																	
Perth	a																						
Inverness	a																						
Inverkeithing	a									20 32								20 51					
Kirkcaldy	a																	21 09					
Leuchars	a									21 28								21 37					
Dundee	a									21 43								21 53					
Arbroath	a																	22 10					
Montrose	a																	22 26					
Stonehaven	a																	22 50					
Aberdeen	a																	23 11					

A To Liverpool Lime Street
B From Southampton Central
C From Manchester Airport
D From Reading
E From Liverpool Lime Street
F From Penzance. to Edinburgh
G From Manchester Airport to Redcar Central
H To Beverley
I From Plymouth. to Edinburgh

Table T026-F

Mondays to Fridays

16 December to 15 May

London - Humberside, Yorkshire, North East England and Scotland

		GC	GR	TP	XC	GR	EM	GC	GR	XC	TP	TP	XC	GR	GR	GR	XC	TP	GR	EM	XC	TP	TP
				A	B		C			D	E	F	G				H	A		I	J	K	L
London Kings Cross ⊖	d	16 27	16 30			16 33		16 48	17 00					17 03	17 18	17 30			17 33				
Stevenage	d					16 55													17 55				
Peterborough	a		17 16											17 50	18 07	18 17							
Norwich	d						15 48													16 56			
Peterborough	d		17 18				17 26							17 51	18 09	18 19				18 26			
Grantham	a					17 40	17 58								18 28				18 41	18 54			
	d					17 41	17 58								18 29				18 42	18 57			
Newark North Gate	a		17 45												18 41	18 46							
	d		17 46												18 42	18 47							
Lincoln	a																						
Retford	d					18 04																	
Doncaster	a	18 03	18 10			18 18								18 40	19 04				19 14				
Selby	a														19 27								
Hull	a														20 05								
Sheffield	a						19 37													20 35			
Pontefract Monkhill	a																						
Wakefield Kirkgate	a	18 26																					
Wakefield Westgate	d				18 20	18 36							18 51	19 01					19 33				
Leeds	a				18 36	18 52							19 05	19 17					19 48				
Mirfield	a	18 43																					
Brighouse	a	18 53																					
Halifax	a	19 05																					
Shipley	a																						
Bradford Forster Square	a																						
Bradford Interchange	a	19 21																					
Keighley	a																						
Skipton	a																						
Doncaster	d		18 12																		19 20		
York	a		18 32					18 39	18 49							19 27					19 41		
Scarborough	a																						
Harrogate	a									←							←		20 32				
Leeds	d			18 14	18 38					18 38	18 42	18 51	19 07				19 07	19 14				19 42	19 51
York	d		18 35	18 39	→			18 42	18 55	19 05	19 07	19 17	→			19 30	19 34	19 39			19 42	20 07	20 16
Thirsk	d			18 56				19 01										19 57				→	→
Northallerton	d		18 56	19 05				19 10			19 26							20 07					
Darlington	a		19 09						19 23	19 32	19 37	19 43				19 58	20 04				20 13		
Eaglescliffe	a							19 27															
Middlesbrough	a			19 35														20 37					
Darlington	d		19 10						19 25	19 33	19 39	19 45				20 00	20 05				20 14		
Durham	d		19 28							19 49	19 55	20 01				20 18	20 22				20 31		
Chester-le-Street	d																						
Newcastle	a		19 41						19 51	20 02	20 10	20 14				20 31	20 36				20 44		
Hartlepool	a							19 46															
Sunderland	a							20 21															
Newcastle	d		19 44						19 54	20 03		20 16				20 33	20 39						
Morpeth	a		19 57									20 29					20 52						
Alnmouth for Alnwick	a									20 28						20 58							
Berwick-upon-Tweed	a								20 37								21 26						
Dunbar 238	a															21 42	21 49						
Edinburgh 238	a		21 14						21 22	21 29		21 57				22 08	22 14						
	d																						
Haymarket 238	d																						
Motherwell	a																						
Glasgow Central	a																						
Stirling	a																						
Perth	a																						
Inverness	a																						
Inverkeithing	a																						
Kirkcaldy	a																						
Leuchars	a																						
Dundee	a																						
Arbroath	a																						
Montrose	a																						
Stonehaven	a																						
Aberdeen	a																						

A From Manchester Airport to Redcar Central
B From Southampton Central to Edinburgh
C To Liverpool Lime Street
D From Southampton Central. ⌶ to Newcastle
E From Manchester Airport
F From Liverpool Lime Street
G From Plymouth to Edinburgh
H From Plymouth. ⌶ to Newcastle
I To Manchester Piccadilly
J From Reading
K From Manchester Airport to Newcastle
L From Liverpool Lime Street to Edinburgh

NRT DECEMBER 19 EDITION

Table T026-F

Mondays to Fridays

16 December to 15 May

London - Humberside, Yorkshire, North East England and Scotland

		XC	GR	GR	TP	TP	GR	GR	XC	GR	TP	GR	XC	HT	EM	GR	XC	GR	GR	XC	TP	GC
		A			B	C			D		E		F	G	H		I			J	K	
London Kings Cross ⊖	d		17 48	18 00			18 03	18 18		18 30		18 33		18 48		19 00		19 03	19 06			19 27
Stevenage	d											18 55							19 28			
Peterborough	a		18 36				18 50	19 07		19 16								19 49	19 58			
Norwich	d														17 54							
Peterborough	d		18 38				18 55	19 09		19 18					19 26			19 52	20 00			
Grantham	a		19 04					19 27				19 40		19 52	19 58				20 19			
	d		19 05					19 28				19 42		19 52					20 20			
Newark North Gate	a						19 22			19 45									20 34			
	d						19 24			19 47									20 36			
Lincoln	a																		21 03			
Retford	d		19 28									20 05		20 13								
Doncaster	a		19 42				19 48			20 11		20 20		20 27				20 40				
Selby	a													20 47								
Hull	a													21 24								
Sheffield	a																					
Pontefract Monkhill	a																					
Wakefield Kirkgate	a																					
Wakefield Westgate	d	19 49	20 02				20 07					20 40					20 48	21 01				
Leeds	a	20 05	20 17				20 21					20 54					21 02	21 17				
Mirfield	a																					
Brighouse	a																					
Halifax	a																					
Shipley	a											21s18										
Bradford Forster Square	a											21 29										
Bradford Interchange	a																					
Keighley	a						21s01															
Skipton	a						21 19															
Doncaster	d									20 12			20 20							20 54		
York	a			19 47				20 16		20 33			20 41			20 54				21 15		21 20
Scarborough	a																					
Harrogate	a								←													
Leeds	d	20 08			←	←			20 08		20 14										20 51	
York	d	→		19 52	20 07	20 16		20 19	20 32	20 35	20 39		20 46			20 57				21 17	21 20	21 22
Thirsk	d										20 56											21 38
Northallerton	d				20 26			20 38			21 05											21 47
Darlington	a			20 20	20 37	20 43		20 51	20 58	21 03			21 12			21 25				21 43	21 46	
Eaglescliffe	a																					22 02
Middlesbrough	a										21 35											
Darlington	d			20 22	20 39	20 45		20 52	21 00	21 04			21 13			21 26				21 44	21 48	
Durham	d				20 55	21 01		21 10	21 16	21 22			21 30							22 01	22 04	
Chester-le-Street	d				21 02																	
Newcastle	a			20 48	21 15	21 14		21 25	21 29	21 35			21 44			21 53				22 14	22 19	
Hartlepool	a																					22 22
Sunderland	a																					22 52
Newcastle	d			20 51		21 16			21 35	21 38						21 55						
Morpeth	a					21 31				21 51												
Alnmouth for Alnwick	a								22 00	22 07												
Berwick-upon-Tweed	a			21 34												22 38						
Dunbar 238	a																					
Edinburgh 238	a			22 22		22 49			23 03	23 16						23 31						
	d																					
Haymarket 238	d																					
Motherwell	a																					
Glasgow Central	a																					
Stirling	a																					
Perth	a																					
Inverness	a																					
Inverkeithing	a																					
Kirkcaldy	a																					
Leuchars	a																					
Dundee	a																					
Arbroath	a																					
Montrose	a																					
Stonehaven	a																					
Aberdeen	a																					

A From Plymouth to Edinburgh
B From Manchester Airport
C From Liverpool Lime Street
D From Plymouth. ⌶ to Newcastle
E From Manchester Airport to Redcar Central
F From Southampton Central
G To Beverley
H To Nottingham
I From Plymouth
J From Reading
K From Liverpool Lime Street. ⌶ from York

Table T026-F

London - Humberside, Yorkshire, North East England and Scotland

Mondays to Fridays

16 December to 15 May

		GR FO	GR FX	TP A	GR	EM B	GC		GR	TP C	XC D	EM E	GR	HT	EM E	GR	EM E		XC D	TP F	GR	TP G	GR	GR	GR	GR	
London Kings Cross 15 ⊖	d	19 30	19 30		19 33		19 54		20 00				20 03	20 30		20 33					21 00		21 33	22 00	23 00	23 33	
Stevenage 4	d				19 55											20 55					21 22		21 56				
Peterborough 8	a	20 16	20 16										20 50			21 25					21 51		22 25	22 47	23s44	00s16	
Norwich	d					18 57																					
Peterborough 8	d	20 18	20 18			20 27							20 52			21 26					21 53		22 28	22 49			
Grantham 7	a				20 40	20 58								21 29		21 44							22 47	23 08	00s12	00s45	
	d				20 41									21 30		21 45							22 48	23 09			
Newark North Gate 7	a	20 45	20 45										21 19			21 57					22 20		23 00	23 21	00s24	00s57	
	d	20 46	20 46										21 20			21 58					22 21		23 02	23 23			
Lincoln	a																										
Retford 10	d													21 53									23 17				
Doncaster 7	a	21 09	21 09		21 13		21 21						21 43	22 06		22 22					22 44		23 36	23 51	00s57	01s24	
Selby	a													22 23													
Hull	a													23 00													
Sheffield 7	a																										
Pontefract Monkhill	a																										
Wakefield Kirkgate 4	a						21 50																				
Wakefield Westgate 7	d				21 31						21 47	21 59	22 06		22 34	22 41	22 49		22 55				23 55				
Leeds 10	a				21 47						22 02	22 20	22 21		22 49	22 57	23 06		23 08				00 10			02 36	
Mirfield	a						22 02																				
Brighouse	a						22 10																				
Halifax	a						22 25																				
Shipley	a																										
Bradford Forster Square	a																										
Bradford Interchange	a						22 41																				
Keighley	a																										
Skipton	a																										
Doncaster 7	d	21 10	21 10																		22 49			23 52			
York 8	a	21 31	21 31						21 48												23 09			00 38	01 33		
Scarborough	a																										
Harrogate	a																										
Leeds 10	d			21 14						21 51										22 42							
York 8	d	21 33	21 33	21 39					21 53	22 21										23 08	23 12			00 41			
Thirsk	d			21 56																23 31							
Northallerton	d	21 53	21 53	22 05						22 40										23 39	23 43			01s09			
Darlington 7	a	22 05	22 05						22 21	22 51										23 51	23 55			01s23			
Eaglescliffe	a																										
Middlesbrough	a			22 35																		←					
Darlington 7	d	22 07	22 07						22 23	22 53										00 01	23 57	00 01					
Durham	d	22 24	22 24						22 41	23 09										→	00 14	00 25		01s42			
Chester-le-Street	d									23 16												00 33					
Newcastle 8	a	22 39	22 39						22 54	23 26											00 43	00 59		02 15			
Hartlepool	a																										
Sunderland	a								23 23																		
Newcastle 8	d	22 40																									
Morpeth	a	22 53																									
Alnmouth for Alnwick	a	23 09																									
Berwick-upon-Tweed	a	23 33																									
Dunbar 238	a																										
Edinburgh 10 238	a	00 28																									
	d																										
Haymarket 238	d																										
Motherwell	a																										
Glasgow Central 15	a																										
Stirling	a																										
Perth	a																										
Inverness	a																										
Inverkeithing	a																										
Kirkcaldy	a																										
Leuchars 3	a																										
Dundee	a																										
Arbroath	a																										
Montrose	a																										
Stonehaven	a																										
Aberdeen	a																										

A From Manchester Airport to Redcar Central
B To Nottingham
C From Liverpool Lime Street. from York
D From Plymouth
E From St Pancras International
F From Liverpool Lime Street to Newcastle
G From Liverpool Lime Street

Table T026-F

London - Humberside, Yorkshire, North East England and Scotland

Saturdays

21 December to 16 May

		GR A	TP B	GR A	TP C	XC	XC	TP	GR	TP D		XC	GR	TP E	TP D	TP B	GR	TP F	XC G	TP D		TP B	XC H	GR	GR
London Kings Cross 15 ⊖	d																							05 55	06 15
Stevenage 4	d																							06 17	06 38
Peterborough 8	a																							06 46	07 07
Norwich	d																								
Peterborough 8	d																							06 47	07 09
Grantham 7	a																							07 05	07 27
	d																							07 06	07 28
Newark North Gate 7	a																							07 18	07 40
	d																							07 19	07 41
Lincoln	a																								
Retford 10	d																							07 34	07 56
Doncaster 7	a																							07 48	08 10
Selby	a																								
Hull	a																								
Sheffield 7	a																								
Pontefract Monkhill	a																								
Wakefield Kirkgate 4	a																								
Wakefield Westgate 7	d																						07 47	08 07	
Leeds 10	a																						08 01	08 22	
Mirfield	a																								
Brighouse	a																								
Halifax	a																								
Shipley	a																								
Bradford Forster Square	a																								
Bradford Interchange	a																								
Keighley	a																								
Skipton	a																								
Doncaster 7	d												06 10						07 18						08 12
York 8	a												06 30						07 41						08 32
Scarborough	a																								
Harrogate	a																								
Leeds 10	d									05 52				06 15	06 42	06 51	07 08	07 14		07 42		07 51	08 08		
York 8	d			00 41	05 05					06 19			06 35	06 39	07 07	07 22	07 35	07 39	07 51	08 07		08 21	08 31		08 35
Thirsk	d				05 28									06 56				07 56							
Northallerton	d			01s09	05 36								06 55	07 05	07 28			08 05		08 26					08 54
Darlington 7	a			01s23	05 57					06 45			07 07		07 40	07 48	08 03		08 17	08 37		08 47	08 59		09 07
Eaglescliffe	a																								
Middlesbrough	a				06 34									07 35				08 35							
Darlington 7	d		00 01							06 47			07 09		07 41	07 50	08 05		08 18	08 39		08 49	09 00		09 08
Durham	d	00 14	00 25	01s42						07 03			07 27		07 57	08 06	08 23		08 35	08 55		09 05	09 17		09 26
Chester-le-Street	d		00 33							07 10					08 03					09 02					
Newcastle 8	a	00 43	00 59	02 15						07 19			07 40		08 16	08 19	08 37		08 48	09 12		09 18	09 29		09 39
Hartlepool	a																								
Sunderland	a																								
Newcastle 8	d							05 53	06 20	07 21		07 38	07 42			08 21	08 42					09 21	09 33		09 46
Morpeth	a							06 07	06 33	07 34		07 50				08 34	08 55					09 33			
Alnmouth for Alnwick	a							06 21	06 50				08 08										09 57		
Berwick-upon-Tweed	a							06 42	07 15			08 23	08 31				09 30						10 19		
Dunbar 238	a								07 39				08 53				09 54								
Edinburgh 10 238	a							07 30	08 07	08 59		09 07	09 19			09 53	10 23					10 56	11 03		11 09
	d					06 22	07 26					09 12					10 28						11 11		
Haymarket 238	d						07 31					09 16					10 33						11 16		
Motherwell	a					07 05	08 13					09 54											11 54		
Glasgow Central 15	a					07 22	08 30					10 14											12 12		
Stirling	a																								
Perth	a																								
Inverness	a																								
Inverkeithing	a																10 47								
Kirkcaldy	a																11 04								
Leuchars 3	a																11 28								
Dundee	a																11 44								
Arbroath	a																12 01								
Montrose	a																12 17								
Stonehaven	a																12 41								
Aberdeen	a																13 02								

A From London Kings Cross
B From Liverpool Lime Street
C To Redcar Central
D From Manchester Airport
E From Manchester Victoria to Redcar Central
F From Manchester Airport to Redcar Central
G From Derby
H From Birmingham New Street

Table T026-F

Saturdays

21 December to 16 May

London - Humberside, Yorkshire, North East England and Scotland

Station		TP	GR	EM	XC	GR		TP	TP	XC	GR	GR	HT	GR	TP	GR		EM	XC	GC	GR	TP	TP	XC	GR
		◇1 A	1	◇ B	◇1 C	1		◇1 D	◇1 E	◇1 C	1	1	◇1	1	◇1 A	1		◇ B	◇1 C	1	1	◇1 D	◇1 E	◇1 F	1
London Kings Cross 15 ⊖	d		06 30			07 00					07 03	07 06	07 27	07 30		07 35				07 48	08 00				08 03
Stevenage 4	d		06 52									07 28				07 57									
Peterborough 8	a		07 21			07 46					07 51	07 57		08 16											08 49
Norwich	d			05 50														06 53							
Peterborough 8	d		07 23	07 27		07 48					07 53	07 58		08 18				08 29							08 51
Grantham 7	a		07 41	07 55								08 16	08 26			08 40		08 59							
	d		07 42	07 58								08 17	08 27			08 42		09 00							
Newark North Gate 7	a											08 29		08 45											
	d											08 30		08 46											
Lincoln	a																								
Retford 10	d											08 45	08 51												
Doncaster 7	a		08 16								08 39	09 02	09 05	09 10		09 13									09 41
Selby	a												09 22												
Hull	a												10 00												
Sheffield 7	a			09 37														10 37							
Pontefract Monkhill	a																								
Wakefield Kirkgate 4	a																								
Wakefield Westgate 7	d		08 36							08 49	09 01					09 32								09 47	10 01
Leeds 10	a		08 52							09 02	09 16					09 45								10 00	10 16
Mirfield	a																								
Brighouse	a																								
Halifax	a																								
Shipley	a																								
Bradford Forster Square	a																								
Bradford Interchange	a																								
Keighley	a																								
Skipton	a																								
Doncaster 7	d				08 19							09 04		09 12					09 19						
York 8	a				08 40	08 52						09 27		09 32					09 40	09 44	09 52				
Scarborough	a																								
Harrogate	a															10 19									
Leeds 10	d	08 14						08 42	08 51	09 08					09 14							09 42	09 51	10 08	
York 8	d	08 39			08 42	08 55		09 07	09 21	09 31				09 35	09 39				09 42	09 49	09 54	10 07	10 21	10 31	
Thirsk	d	08 56													09 56					10 06					
Northallerton	d	09 06						09 26							10 07					10 17		10 26			
Darlington 7	a				09 14	09 22		09 37	09 47	09 58				10 03					10 12		10 22	10 37	10 47	10 59	
Eaglescliffe	a																			10 36					
Middlesbrough	a	09 36													10 37										
Darlington 7	d				09 15	09 24		09 39	09 49	10 00				10 06					10 13		10 23	10 39	10 49	11 00	
Durham	d				09 32			09 55	10 05	10 17				10 23					10 30			10 55	11 05	11 17	
Chester-le-Street	d																					11 02			
Newcastle 8	a				09 45	09 51		10 11	10 19	10 29				10 38					10 43		10 50	11 13	11 19	11 29	
Hartlepool	a																			10 56					
Sunderland	a																			11 26					
Newcastle 8	d					09 54			10 21	10 35				10 41							10 54		11 21	11 33	
Morpeth	a								10 34														11 34	11 45	
Alnmouth for Alnwick	a													11 06											
Berwick-upon-Tweed	a					10 36															11 37			12 18	
Dunbar 238	a									11 38															
Edinburgh 10 238	a					11 28			11 54	12 05				12 09							12 26		12 56	13 05	
	d																							13 11	
Haymarket 238	d																							13 15	
Motherwell	a																							13 54	
Glasgow Central 15	a																							14 12	
Stirling	a																								
Perth	a																								
Inverness	a																								
Inverkeithing	a																								
Kirkcaldy	a																								
Leuchars 3	a																								
Dundee	a																								
Arbroath	a																								
Montrose	a																								
Stonehaven	a																								
Aberdeen	a																								

A From Manchester Airport to Redcar Central
B To Liverpool Lime Street
C From Birmingham New Street
D From Manchester Airport
E From Liverpool Lime Street
F From Bristol Temple Meads

Table T026-F

Saturdays

21 December to 16 May

London - Humberside, Yorkshire, North East England and Scotland

Station		GR		GR	TP	GR	EM	XC	GR	TP	TP	XC		GR	GR	GR	TP	GR	XC	HT	EM	GR		TP	XC
		1		1	◇1 A	1	◇ B	◇1 C	1	◇1 D	◇1 E	◇1 F		1	1	1	◇1 A	1	◇1 G	◇1	◇ B	1		◇1 D	◇1 H
London Kings Cross 15 ⊖	d	08 06		08 30		08 33			09 00					09 03	09 06	09 30		09 33		09 48		10 00			
Stevenage 4	d					08 55									09 29			09 56							
Peterborough 8	a	08 53		09 16					09 46					09 50	09 58	10 16									
Norwich	d						07 57														08 56				
Peterborough 8	d	08 54		09 18			09 28		09 48					09 52	10 01	10 18					10 22				
Grantham 7	a	09 13				09 40	09 56								10 20			10 40		10 48	10 54				
	d	09 14				09 41	09 56								10 21			10 41		10 49	10 55				
Newark North Gate 7	a	09 27		09 45											10 33	10 45									
	d	09 29		09 46											10 34	10 46									
Lincoln	a	09 55																							
Retford 10	d														10 49					11 11					
Doncaster 7	a			10 09		10 13								10 39	11 03	11 09		11 13		11 24					
Selby	a																			11 43					
Hull	a																			12 18					
Sheffield 7	a						11 37														12 37				
Pontefract Monkhill	a																								
Wakefield Kirkgate 4	a																								
Wakefield Westgate 7	d					10 32						10 46		11 01				11 32							
Leeds 10	a					10 47						11 00		11 16				11 46							
Mirfield	a																								
Brighouse	a																								
Halifax	a																								
Shipley	a																								
Bradford Forster Square	a																								
Bradford Interchange	a																								
Keighley	a																								
Skipton	a																								
Doncaster 7	d			10 10				10 19							11 05	11 10			11 19						11 53
York 8	a			10 32				10 40	10 51						11 29	11 32			11 40			11 52			12 15
Scarborough	a																								
Harrogate	a																	12 19							
Leeds 10	d				10 14					10 42	10 51	11 08					11 14							11 42	
York 8	d			10 35	10 39			10 42	10 54	11 07	11 21	11 31				11 35	11 39		11 42			11 55		12 07	12 17
Thirsk	d				10 56												11 56								
Northallerton	d			10 55	11 07					11 26							12 07							12 26	
Darlington 7	a			11 07				11 14	11 22	11 37	11 48	11 59				12 04			12 11			12 22		12 37	12 43
Eaglescliffe	a																								
Middlesbrough	a				11 37												12 37								
Darlington 7	d			11 09				11 16	11 23	11 39	11 49	12 00				12 06			12 12			12 24		12 39	12 44
Durham	d			11 27				11 33		11 55	12 06	12 17				12 24			12 29					12 55	13 01
Chester-le-Street	d																							13 02	
Newcastle 8	a			11 40				11 46	11 50	12 11	12 18	12 30				12 37			12 42			12 50		13 13	13 16
Hartlepool	a																								
Sunderland	a																								
Newcastle 8	d			11 44					11 52		12 21	12 36				12 39						12 54			
Morpeth	a										12 34					12 53									
Alnmouth for Alnwick	a															13 07									
Berwick-upon-Tweed	a								12 35													13 37			
Dunbar 238	a											13 38													
Edinburgh 10 238	a			13 09					13 27		13 57	14 05				14 10						14 25			
	d																					14 29			
Haymarket 238	d																					14 34			
Motherwell	a																								
Glasgow Central 15	a																								
Stirling	a																								
Perth	a																								
Inverness	a																								
Inverkeithing	a																					14 49			
Kirkcaldy	a																					15 06			
Leuchars 3	a																					15 31			
Dundee	a																					15 46			
Arbroath	a																					16 04			
Montrose	a																					16 21			
Stonehaven	a																					16 45			
Aberdeen	a																					17 06			

A From Manchester Airport to Redcar Central
B To Liverpool Lime Street
C From Guildford
D From Manchester Airport
E From Liverpool Lime Street
F From Plymouth
G From Bournemouth
H From Southampton Central

Table T026-F

London - Humberside, Yorkshire, North East England and Scotland

		TP	XC	GR	GR	GR	TP	GR	EM	GC	GR	TP	XC	TP	XC	GR	GR	GC	XC	GR	TP	GR	HT
		A	B				C		D			E	F	A	G				B		C		
London Kings Cross 15 ⊖	d			10 03	10 06	10 30		10 35		10 48	11 00					11 03	11 06	11 27		11 30		11 35	11 48
Stevenage 4	d				10 29			10 57									11 28					11 57	
Peterborough 8	a			10 50	10 58	11 16										11 50	11 57			12 16			
Norwich	d								09 57														
Peterborough 8	d			10 53	10 59	11 18			11 23							11 53	11 59			12 18			
Grantham 7	a				11 18			11 41	11 55								12 17					12 40	12 48
	d				11 20			11 42	11 56								12 18					12 41	12 49
Newark North Gate 7	a				11 33	11 45											12 30			12 45			
	d				11 35	11 46											12 31			12 46			
Lincoln	a				12 01																		
Retford 10	d																12 46						13 11
Doncaster 7	a			11 41		12 09		12 14		12 18						12 40	13 02			13 09		13 15	13 24
Selby	a																						13 43
Hull	a																						14 25
Sheffield 7	a								13 37														
Pontefract Monkhill	a																						
Wakefield Kirkgate 4	a									12 49													
Wakefield Westgate 7	d		11 46	12 01				12 34							12 47	13 01						13 33	
Leeds 10	a		12 00	12 16				12 49							13 00	13 16						13 47	
Mirfield	a									13 01													
Brighouse	a									13 09													
Halifax	a									13 20													
Shipley	a																						
Bradford Forster Square	a																						
Bradford Interchange	a									13 37													
Keighley	a																						
Skipton	a																						
Doncaster 7	d					12 10							12 54				13 05			13 10			
York 8	a					12 31					12 51		13 15				13 29	13 19		13 31			
Scarborough	a																						
Harrogate	a																		←			14 19	
Leeds 10	d	11 51	12 08				12 14					12 42		12 51	13 08				13 08		13 14		
York 8	d	12 22	12 31			12 35	12 39				12 54	13 07	13 17	13 20	→			13 23	13 31	13 35	13 39		
Thirsk	d						12 56											13 40			13 56		
Northallerton	d					12 55	13 05					13 26						13 49			14 05		
Darlington 7	a	12 48	12 59			13 07					13 21	13 37	13 43	13 46					14 02	14 07			
Eaglescliffe	a																	14 04					
Middlesbrough	a						13 35														14 35		
Darlington 7	d	12 50	13 00			13 09					13 23	13 39	13 44	13 48					14 03	14 08			
Durham	d	13 06	13 17			13 27						13 55	14 01	14 04					14 20	14 26			
Chester-le-Street	d																						
Newcastle 8	a	13 19	13 29			13 40					13 49	14 10	14 14	14 19					14 32	14 39			
Hartlepool	a																	14 23					
Sunderland	a																	14 51					
Newcastle 8	d	13 21	13 35			13 45					13 52			14 21					14 35	14 42			
Morpeth	a	13 34												14 34					14 47				
Alnmouth for Alnwick	a		13 59																	15 07			
Berwick-upon-Tweed	a		14 21								14 34												
Dunbar 238	a																		15 40				
Edinburgh 10 238	a	14 54	15 03			15 09					15 27			15 54					16 06	16 17			
	d		15 12																				
Haymarket 238	d		15 16																				
Motherwell	a		15 54																				
Glasgow Central 15	a		16 12																				
Stirling	a																						
Perth	a																						
Inverness	a																						
Inverkeithing	a																						
Kirkcaldy	a																						
Leuchars 8	a																						
Dundee	a																						
Arbroath	a																						
Montrose	a																						
Stonehaven	a																						
Aberdeen	a																						

A From Liverpool Lime Street
B From Plymouth
C From Manchester Airport to Redcar Central
D To Liverpool Lime Street
E From Manchester Airport
F From Reading
G From Plymouth to Edinburgh

Table T026-F

London - Humberside, Yorkshire, North East England and Scotland

		EM	GR	TP	XC	TP	XC	GR	GR	GR	TP	GR	EM	GR	TP	XC	TP	XC	GR	GR	GC	XC
		A		B	C	D	E				F		A		B	G	H	I				J
London Kings Cross 15 ⊖	d		12 00					12 03	12 06	12 30		12 35		13 00					13 03	13 06	13 18	
Stevenage 4	d								12 28			12 57										
Peterborough 8	a							12 50	12 58	13 16				13 46					13 49	13 53		
Norwich	d	10 57											11 57									
Peterborough 8	d	12 24						12 51	13 01	13 18			13 28	13 48					13 52	13 56		
Grantham 7	a	12 57							13 20			13 40	13 56							14 15		
	d	12 57							13 21			13 41	13 58							14 16		
Newark North Gate 7	a								13 34	13 45										14 28		
	d								13 36	13 47										14 33		
Lincoln	a								14 02													
Retford 10	d																			14 49		
Doncaster 7	a							13 41		14 10		14 14							14 40	15 03		
Selby	a																					
Hull	a																					
Sheffield 7	a	14 37											15 37									
Pontefract Monkhill	a																					
Wakefield Kirkgate 4	a																					
Wakefield Westgate 7	d						13 46	14 01				14 33						14 47	15 01			
Leeds 10	a						14 02	14 16				14 48						15 00	15 16			
Mirfield	a																					
Brighouse	a																					
Halifax	a																					
Shipley	a																					
Bradford Forster Square	a																					
Bradford Interchange	a																					
Keighley	a																					
Skipton	a																					
Doncaster 7	d				13 54					14 11						14 54				15 05		
York 8	a		13 52		14 14					14 32				14 51		15 15				15 29	15 09	
Scarborough	a																					
Harrogate	a																					
Leeds 10	d			13 42		13 51	14 08				14 14				14 42		14 51	15 08				←
York 8	d		13 55	14 07	14 16	14 21	14 32			14 35	14 39			14 54	15 07	15 17	15 22	→			15 14	15 17
Thirsk	d										14 56					→	→				15 37	
Northallerton	d									14 55	15 05				15 26						15 46	
Darlington 7	a		14 22	14 37	14 42	14 47	14 59			15 08				15 21	15 37							15 43
Eaglescliffe	a																				16 01	
Middlesbrough	a										15 35											
Darlington 7	d		14 24	14 38	14 43	14 49	15 00			15 09				15 23	15 39							15 44
Durham	d			14 55	15 00	15 05	15 18			15 27					15 55							16 01
Chester-le-Street	d			15 01											16 02							
Newcastle 8	a		14 50	15 13	15 15	15 18	15 31			15 40				15 49	16 13							16 14
Hartlepool	a																				16 22	
Sunderland	a																				16 51	
Newcastle 8	d		14 55			15 21	15 35			15 45				15 59								
Morpeth	a					15 33																
Alnmouth for Alnwick	a						15 59															
Berwick-upon-Tweed	a		15 38				16 21							16 41								
Dunbar 238	a																					
Edinburgh 10 238	a		16 25			16 55	17 05			17 10				17 30								
	d		16 34				17 10															
Haymarket 238	d		16 39				17 16															
Motherwell	a						17 54															
Glasgow Central 15	a						18 11															
Stirling	a		17 16																			
Perth	a		17 53																			
Inverness	a		20 06																			
Inverkeithing	a																					
Kirkcaldy	a																					
Leuchars 8	a																					
Dundee	a																					
Arbroath	a																					
Montrose	a																					
Stonehaven	a																					
Aberdeen	a																					

A To Liverpool Lime Street
B From Manchester Airport
C From Southampton Central
D From Liverpool Lime Street
E From Penzance. to Edinburgh
F From Manchester Airport to Redcar Central
G From Reading to Newcastle
H From Liverpool Lime Street to Edinburgh
I From Plymouth to Aberdeen
J From Reading

Table T026-F

Saturdays

21 December to 16 May

London - Humberside, Yorkshire, North East England and Scotland

		TP	XC	GR	TP	GR	EM	GR	TP	TP	XC	GR	GR	GR	TP	GR	XC	HT	EM	GR	TP	TP	XC
		◇■	◇■	■	◇■	■	◇	■	◇■	◇■	◇■	■	■	■	◇■	■	◇■	◇■	◇	■	◇■	◇■	◇■
		A	B		C		D		E	A	F				C		G		D		E	A	B
London Kings Cross 15 ⊖	d			13 30		13 35		14 00				14 03	14 06	14 30		14 35		14 48		15 00			
Stevenage 4	d					13 58							14 28			14 57							
Peterborough 8	a			14 16								14 50	14 57	15 16									
Norwich	d						12 57												13 57				
Peterborough 8	d			14 18			14 26					14 53	14 59	15 18					15 24				
Grantham 7	a					14 40	14 55						15 18			15 41		15 49	15 55				
	d					14 41	14 56						15 19			15 42		15 50	15 57				
Newark North Gate 7	a			14 45									15 32	15 45									
	d			14 46									15 36	15 46									
Lincoln	a												16 06										
Retford 10	d																	16 11					
Doncaster 7	a			15 09		15 13						15 40		16 09		16 14		16 25					
Selby	a																	16 41					
Hull	a																	17 25					
Sheffield 7	a						16 37												17 34				
Pontefract Monkhill	a																						
Wakefield Kirkgate 4	a																						
Wakefield Westgate 7	d					15 31					15 46	16 01				16 33							16 46
Leeds 10	a					15 46					16 01	16 16				16 51							17 00
Mirfield	a																						
Brighouse	a																						
Halifax	a																						
Shipley	a																						
Bradford Forster Square	a																						
Bradford Interchange	a																						
Keighley	a																						
Skipton	a																						
Doncaster 7	d			15 10										16 10			16 19						
York 8	a			15 31				15 52						16 32			16 40			16 51			
Scarborough	a																						
Harrogate	a		←			16 19																	
Leeds 10	d	←	15 08		15 14				15 42	15 51	16 08				16 14						16 42	16 51	17 08
York 8	d	15 22	15 32	15 35	15 39			15 55	16 07	16 19	16 32			16 35	16 39		16 42			16 55	17 07	17 21	17 31
Thirsk	d				15 56										16 56								
Northallerton	d			15 55	16 05				16 26					16 55	17 07						17 26		
Darlington 7	a	15 48	15 59	16 07				16 22	16 37	16 47	16 58			17 08			17 13			17 22	17 37	17 47	17 59
Eaglescliffe	a																						
Middlesbrough	a				16 35										17 37								
Darlington 7	d	15 50	16 01	16 09				16 24	16 39	16 49	17 00			17 09			17 14			17 24	17 39	17 49	18 00
Durham	d	16 06	16 18	16 26					16 55	17 05	17 17			17 27			17 31				17 55	18 05	18 16
Chester-le-Street	d								17 02														
Newcastle 8 ⛴	a	16 19	16 30	16 39				16 50	17 13	17 18	17 29			17 40			17 44			17 50	18 10	18 18	18 33
Hartlepool	a																						
Sunderland ⛴	a																						
Newcastle 8 ⛴	d	16 21	16 35	16 42				16 58		17 20	17 35			17 44						17 53		18 21	18 40
Morpeth	a	16 34	16 48	16 55						17 33												18 34	
Alnmouth for Alnwick	a		17 03	17 10							17 59												
Berwick-upon-Tweed	a							17 43			18 20									18 37			19 22
Dunbar 238	a		17 44																				19 45
Edinburgh 10 238 ⛴	a	17 57	18 06	18 15				18 31		18 56	19 02			19 10						19 28		20 04	20 08
	d		18 12					18 35			19 10												20 12
Haymarket 238 ⛴	d		18 16					18 40			19 15												20 17
Motherwell	a										19 53												
Glasgow Central 15	a										20 15												
Stirling	a																						
Perth	a																						
Inverness	a																						
Inverkeithing	a		18 29					18 56															20 31
Kirkcaldy	a		18 43					19 13															20 51
Leuchars 3	a		19 14					19 41															21 26
Dundee	a		19 28					19 57															21 43
Arbroath	a		19 48					20 14															
Montrose	a		20 02					20 30															
Stonehaven	a		20 23					20 54															
Aberdeen	a		20 42					21 16															

A From Liverpool Lime Street
B From Plymouth. ⚒ to Edinburgh
C From Manchester Airport to Redcar Central
D To Liverpool Lime Street
E From Manchester Airport
F From Penzance. ⚒ to Edinburgh
G From Southampton Central

Table T026-F

Saturdays

21 December to 16 May

London - Humberside, Yorkshire, North East England and Scotland

		GR	GR	GR	TP	GR	EM	GC	XC	GR	TP	TP	XC	GR	GR	GC	GR	TP	XC	GR	EM	GC	GR
		■	■	■	◇■	■	◇	■	◇■	■	◇■	◇■	◇■	■	■	■	■	◇■	◇■	■	◇	■	■
					A		B		C		D	E	F					A	G		B		
London Kings Cross 15 ⊖	d	15 03	15 06	15 30		15 35		15 48		16 00				16 03	16 06	16 27	16 30			16 33		16 48	17 00
Stevenage 4	d		15 28			15 57									16 28					16 55			
Peterborough 8	a	15 50	15 57	16 16										16 51	17 00		17 17						
Norwich	d						14 57														15 52		
Peterborough 8	d	15 54	15 59	16 18			16 27							16 54	17 01		17 18				17 25		
Grantham 7	a		16 17			16 41	16 57								17 20					17 41	17 57		
	d		16 18			16 42	16 58								17 22					17 42	17 59		
Newark North Gate 7	a		16 30	16 45											17 35		17 46						
	d		16 32	16 46											17 36		17 47						
Lincoln	a														18 03								
Retford 10	d		16 47																	18 05			
Doncaster 7	a	16 42	17 01	17 09		17 14		17 18						17 40		18 03	18 10			18 19			
Selby	a																						
Hull	a																						
Sheffield 7	a						18 34														19 37		
Pontefract Monkhill	a																						
Wakefield Kirkgate 4	a							17 44								18 26							
Wakefield Westgate 7	d	17 01				17 35							17 48	18 01					18 20	18 38			
Leeds 10	a	17 16				17 49							18 01	18 16					18 36	18 53			
Mirfield	a							17 58								18 43							
Brighouse	a							18 09								18 53							
Halifax	a							18 21								19 05							
Shipley	a																						
Bradford Forster Square	a																						
Bradford Interchange	a							18 40								19 21							
Keighley	a																						
Skipton	a																						
Doncaster 7	d		17 02	17 10					17 19								18 12						
York 8	a		17 25	17 31					17 42	17 51							18 33					18 40	18 49
Scarborough	a																						
Harrogate	a					18 32																	
Leeds 10	d				17 13						17 42	17 51	18 08					18 14	18 38				
York 8	d			17 34	17 39				17 47	17 56	18 07	18 22	18 31				18 35	18 39	→			18 42	18 55
Thirsk	d				17 56													18 56				19 00	
Northallerton	d			17 55	18 05						18 26						18 56	19 05				19 09	
Darlington 7	a			18 07					18 17	18 23	18 37	18 48	19 00				19 09						19 24
Eaglescliffe	a																					19 27	
Middlesbrough	a				18 35													19 35					
Darlington 7	d			18 09					18 18	18 25	18 39	18 50	19 01				19 10						19 26
Durham	d			18 27					18 35		18 55	19 06	19 20				19 28						
Chester-le-Street	d										19 02												
Newcastle 8 ⛴	a			18 41					18 47	18 51	19 13	19 19	19 33				19 41						19 52
Hartlepool	a																					19 46	
Sunderland ⛴	a																					20 21	
Newcastle 8 ⛴	d			18 44						18 54		19 21	19 35				19 44						19 55
Morpeth	a											19 34					19 57						
Alnmouth for Alnwick	a			19 09									20 01										
Berwick-upon-Tweed	a									19 36			20 25										20 37
Dunbar 238	a																						
Edinburgh 10 238 ⛴	a			20 14						20 21		20 54	21 09				21 14						21 22
	d												21 12										
Haymarket 238 ⛴	d												21 17										
Motherwell	a												21 56										
Glasgow Central 15	a												22 20										
Stirling	a																						
Perth	a																						
Inverness	a																						
Inverkeithing	a																						
Kirkcaldy	a																						
Leuchars 3	a																						
Dundee	a																						
Arbroath	a																						
Montrose	a																						
Stonehaven	a																						
Aberdeen	a																						

A From Manchester Airport to Redcar Central
B To Liverpool Lime Street
C From Reading
D From Manchester Airport
E From Liverpool Lime Street
F From Plymouth. ⚒ to Edinburgh
G From Southampton Central to Newcastle

Table T026-F

Saturdays

21 December to 16 May

London - Humberside, Yorkshire, North East England and Scotland

		XC	TP	TP	XC	GR	GR	GR	XC	TP	GR	XC	HT	EM	GR	TP	XC	TP	XC	GR	GR	GR
		A	B	C	D				E	F		G	H	I		B	A	C	E			
London Kings Cross ⊖	d					17 03	17 18	17 30			17 33		17 48		18 00					18 03	18 18	18 30
Stevenage	d										17 55											
Peterborough	a					17 50	18 07	18 17												18 50	19 08	19 16
Norwich	d													16 54								
Peterborough	d					17 52	18 09	18 18						18 26						18 51	19 10	19 18
Grantham	a						18 28				18 41		18 49	18 55							19 28	
	d						18 29				18 42		18 50	18 58							19 29	
Newark North Gate	a						18 41	18 46												19 18		19 45
	d						18 42	18 47												19 22		19 47
Lincoln	a																					
Retford	d												19 12								19 52	
Doncaster	a					18 40	19 04				19 14		19 25							19 47	20 06	20 11
Selby	a						19 27						19 42									
Hull	a						20 05						20 18									
Sheffield	a													20 29								
Pontefract Monkhill	a																					
Wakefield Kirkgate	a																					
Wakefield Westgate	d				18 50	19 01					19 33								19 49	20 07	20 25	
Leeds	a				19 03	19 17					19 50								20 05	20 20	20 41	
Mirfield	a																					
Brighouse	a																					
Halifax	a																					
Shipley	a																					
Bradford Forster Square	a																					
Bradford Interchange	a																					
Keighley	a																			21s00		
Skipton	a																			21 18		
Doncaster	d											19 19					19 54					20 12
York	a							19 28				19 41			19 51		20 15					20 33
Scarborough	a																					
Harrogate	a	←							←													
Leeds	d	18 38	18 42	18 51	19 07				19 07	19 14						19 42		19 51	20 08			
York	d	19 05	19 07	19 22	→			19 30	19 34	19 39		19 42			19 53	20 07	20 17	20 22	20 32			20 35
Thirsk	d									19 56												
Northallerton	d		19 26							20 07						20 26						20 55
Darlington	a	19 32	19 37	19 48				19 58	20 04			20 13			20 22	20 37	20 43	20 48	20 59			21 07
Eaglescliffe	a																					
Middlesbrough	a									20 37												
Darlington	d	19 33	19 39	19 50				19 59	20 05			20 14			20 23	20 39	20 44	20 50	21 00			21 09
Durham	d	19 49	19 55	20 06				20 17	20 22			20 31				20 55	21 01	21 06	21 17			21 27
Chester-le-Street	d															21 02						
Newcastle	a	20 02	20 12	20 21				20 31	20 35			20 44			20 50	21 15	21 16	21 21	21 29			21 42
Hartlepool	a																					
Sunderland	a																					
Newcastle	d							20 33	20 38						20 52				21 34			
Morpeth	a								20 50						21 06							
Alnmouth for Alnwick	a														21 23				21 59			
Berwick-upon-Tweed	a								21 23						21 47							
Dunbar 238	a								21 45						22 11							
Edinburgh 238	a							21 58	22 08						22 38				23 00			
	d																					
Haymarket 238	d																					
Motherwell	a																					
Glasgow Central	a																					
Stirling	a																					
Perth	a																					
Inverness	a																					
Inverkeithing	a																					
Kirkcaldy	a																					
Leuchars	a																					
Dundee	a																					
Arbroath	a																					
Montrose	a																					
Stonehaven	a																					
Aberdeen	a																					

A From Southampton Central
B From Manchester Airport
C From Liverpool Lime Street
D From Plymouth to Edinburgh
E From Plymouth. ⚒ to Newcastle
F From Manchester Airport to Redcar Central
G From Reading
H To Beverley
I To Manchester Piccadilly

Table T026-F

Saturdays

21 December to 16 May

London - Humberside, Yorkshire, North East England and Scotland

		TP	GR	EM	GR	TP	XC	GR	GR	GC	GR	TP	GR	XC	HT	EM	GC	GR	TP	XC	EM	GR	GR
		A		B		C	D					E		F		B			C	G	H		
London Kings Cross ⊖	d		18 33		19 00			19 03	19 06	19 27	19 30		19 33		19 48		19 57	20 00				20 03	20 30
Stevenage	d		18 55						19 28				19 55										
Peterborough	a							19 49	19 57		20 16							20 46				20 50	21 17
Norwich	d			17 50												18 57							
Peterborough	d			19 30				19 51	19 59		20 18					20 26		20 48				20 52	21 18
Grantham	a		19 41	19 57					20 18				20 40		20 51	20 58						21 11	21 37
	d		19 42						20 21				20 41		20 52							21 12	21 38
Newark North Gate	a								20 34		20 45							21 15					21 50
	d								20 36		20 46							21 16					21 51
Lincoln	a								21 03														
Retford	d		20 06												21 14								22 07
Doncaster	a		20 21					20 39			21 10		21 13		21 27		21 32	21 39				21 44	22 21
Selby	a														21 44								
Hull	a														22 20								
Sheffield	a																						
Pontefract Monkhill	a																21 57						
Wakefield Kirkgate	a																22 20						
Wakefield Westgate	d		20 40				20 48	21 01					21 31							21 48	21 58	22 06	22 42
Leeds	a		20 54				21 02	21 17					21 45							22 02	22 14	22 21	22 57
Mirfield	a																22 31						
Brighouse	a																22 40						
Halifax	a																22 53						
Shipley	a												22s09										
Bradford Forster Square	a												22 20										
Bradford Interchange	a																23 09						
Keighley	a																						
Skipton	a																						
Doncaster	d										21 12			21 18				21 40					
York	a				20 48					21 20	21 33			21 41				22 02					
Scarborough	a																						
Harrogate	a		21 35																				
Leeds	d	20 14				20 51	21 09					21 14							21 51				
York	d	20 39			20 54	21 20	21a46			21 23	21 35	21 39		21 46				22 05	22 21				
Thirsk	d	20 56								21 38		21 56											
Northallerton	d	21 05								21 47	21 55	22 07							22 40				
Darlington	a				21 21	21 46					22 07			22 13				22 32	22 51				
Eaglescliffe	a									22 02													
Middlesbrough	a	21 35										22 40											
Darlington	d				21 23	21 48					22 09			22 14				22 34	22 53				
Durham	d					22 04					22 26			22 33				22 51	23 09				
Chester-le-Street	d																		23 16				
Newcastle	a				21 52	22 19					22 41			22 46				23 06	23 26				
Hartlepool	a									22 22													
Sunderland	a									22 52													
Newcastle	d																						
Morpeth	a																						
Alnmouth for Alnwick	a																						
Berwick-upon-Tweed	a																						
Dunbar 238	a																						
Edinburgh 238	a																						
	d																						
Haymarket 238	d																						
Motherwell	a																						
Glasgow Central	a																						
Stirling	a																						
Perth	a																						
Inverness	a																						
Inverkeithing	a																						
Kirkcaldy	a																						
Leuchars	a																						
Dundee	a																						
Arbroath	a																						
Montrose	a																						
Stonehaven	a																						
Aberdeen	a																						

A From Manchester Airport to Redcar Central
B To Nottingham
C From Liverpool Lime Street. ⚒ from York
D From Plymouth. ⚒ to Leeds
E From Manchester Airport
F From Reading
G From Plymouth
H From St Pancras International

Table T026-F

Saturdays
21 December to 16 May

London - Humberside, Yorkshire, North East England and Scotland

Station		EM	GR	TP	EM	XC	GR
			◇1	◇1	◇1	◇1	1
		A		B	C	D	
London Kings Cross 15 ⊖	d		21 00				22 00
Stevenage 4	d						
Peterborough 8	a		21 47				22 46
Norwich	d						
Peterborough 8	d	21 27	21 48				22 48
Grantham 7	a	22 00					23 06
	d						23 07
Newark North Gate 7	a						23 19
	d						23 20
Lincoln	a						
Retford 10	d						23 34
Doncaster 7	a						23 48
Selby	a						
Hull	a						
Sheffield 7	a						
Pontefract Monkhill	a						
Wakefield Kirkgate 4	a						
Wakefield Westgate 7	d				22 49	23 13	00 07
Leeds 10	a				23 07	23 26	00 22
Mirfield	a						
Brighouse	a						
Halifax	a						
Shipley	a						
Bradford Forster Square	a						
Bradford Interchange	a						
Keighley	a						
Skipton	a						
Doncaster 7	d						
York 8	a		22 56				
Scarborough	a						
Harrogate	a						
Leeds 10	d			22 42			
York 8	d		22 58	23 08			
Thirsk	d						
Northallerton	d		23 19	23 27			
Darlington 7	a		23 32	23 38			
Eaglescliffe	a						
Middlesbrough	a						
Darlington 7	d		23 33	23 40			
Durham	d		23 51	23 56			
Chester-le-Street	d			00 03			
Newcastle 8	a		00 06	00 14			
Hartlepool	a						
Sunderland	a						
Newcastle 8	d						
Morpeth	a						
Alnmouth for Alnwick	a						
Berwick-upon-Tweed	a						
Dunbar 238	a						
Edinburgh 10 238	a						
	d						
Haymarket 238	d						
Motherwell	a						
Glasgow Central 15	a						
Stirling	a						
Perth	a						
Inverness	a						
Inverkeithing	a						
Kirkcaldy	a						
Leuchars 3	a						
Dundee	a						
Arbroath	a						
Montrose	a						
Stonehaven	a						
Aberdeen	a						

A From Spalding to Nottingham
B From Liverpool Lime Street
C From St Pancras International
D From Plymouth

Table T026-F

Sundays
15 December to 10 May

London - Humberside, Yorkshire, North East England and Scotland

Station		TP	GR	XC	GR	TP	TP	XC	GR	GR	TP	TP	XC	GR	TP	TP	XC	GR	TP	TP	XC	GR	TP
		◇1	1	◇1	1	◇1	◇1	◇1	1	1	◇1	◇1	◇1	1	◇1	◇1	◇1	1	◇1	◇1	◇1	1	◇1
		A	B			C	D					E				E				F	G		H
London Kings Cross 15 ⊖	d																					08 48	
Stevenage 4	d																						
Peterborough 8	a																						
Norwich	d																						
Peterborough 8	d																						
Grantham 7	a																						
	d																						
Newark North Gate 7	a																						
	d																						
Lincoln	a																						
Retford 10	d																						
Doncaster 7	a																						
Selby	a																						
Hull	a																						
Sheffield 7	a																						
Pontefract Monkhill	a																						
Wakefield Kirkgate 4	a																						
Wakefield Westgate 7	d		00 07																		09 47		
Leeds 10	a		00 22																		10 02		
Mirfield	a																						
Brighouse	a																						
Halifax	a																						
Shipley	a																						
Bradford Forster Square	a																						
Bradford Interchange	a																						
Keighley	a																						
Skipton	a																						
Doncaster 7	d																	09 37					
York 8	a																	09 57				10 34	
Scarborough	a																						
Harrogate	a																						
Leeds 10	d													08 30			09 18			09 51	10 09		10 14
York 8	d										08 21	08 39		09 00	09 19	09 39	09 44	10 00	10 07	10 22	10 33	10 37	10 41
Thirsk	d											08 56				09 56							10 58
Northallerton	d											09 07		09 21		10 07			10 26				11 11
Darlington 7	a										08 47			09 33	09 45		10 10	10 27	10 37	10 49	10 59	11 04	
Eaglescliffe	a																						
Middlesbrough	a											09 37				10 37							11 41
Darlington 7	d										08 49			09 35	09 47		10 11	10 29	10 39	10 51	11 00	11 06	
Durham	d										09 05			09 54	10 03		10 28	10 46	10 55		11 17	11 24	
Chester-le-Street	d	00 03													10 10				11 02				
Newcastle 8	a	00 14									09 18			10 09	10 19		10 40	10 59	11 13	11 19	11 29	11 37	
Hartlepool	a																						
Sunderland	a																						
Newcastle 8	d								08 45	09 15	09 20		09 45	10 12	10 21		10 42	11 02		11 21	11 31	11 40	
Morpeth	a								08 58		09 33		09 57	10 25	10 34					11 34	11 43	11 53	
Alnmouth for Alnwick	a								09 14				10 12	10 42									
Berwick-upon-Tweed	a								09 38	09 57				11 06			11 24	11 44			12 16		
Dunbar 238	a								10 01					11 32									
Edinburgh 10 238	a								10 28	10 45	11 03		11 12	11 58	12 07		12 08	12 29		13 00	13 00	13 08	
	d			08 04	09 10	09 13	09 15	10 23									12 17				13 13		
Haymarket 238	d			08 09	09 15	09a16	09a18										12 21				13 18		
Motherwell	a							11 03									12 59				13 55		
Glasgow Central 15	a							11 28									13 19				14 14		
Stirling	a																						
Perth	a																						
Inverness	a																						
Inverkeithing	a			08 24	09 31																		
Kirkcaldy	a			08 39	09 48																		
Leuchars 3	a			09 04	10 13																		
Dundee	a			09 18	10 28																		
Arbroath	a			09 35	10 46																		
Montrose	a			09 49	11 02																		
Stonehaven	a			10 10	11 26																		
Aberdeen	a			10 28	11 47																		

A not 15 December. From Liverpool Lime Street
B not 15 December. From London Kings Cross
C until 5 January, from 23 February until 29 March. To Manchester Airport
D from 12 January until 16 February, from 5 April. To Manchester Airport
E To Redcar Central
F From Liverpool Lime Street
G From Sheffield. to Edinburgh
H From Manchester Victoria to Redcar Central

Table T026-F

Sundays
15 December to 10 May

London - Humberside, Yorkshire, North East England and Scotland

Station		GR	TP	TP	TP	XC	GR	GR	XC	GR	GR	TP	GC	GR	TP	GR	TP	XC	GR	GR	HT	TP	GR
			A	B	C	D			E			F		G	H		C	I				F	
London Kings Cross	d	09 00					09 03	09 22		09 30	09 33		09 50	10 00		10 03			10 07	10 30	10 49		11 00
Stevenage	d						09 25				09 55												
Peterborough	a						09 54	10 08		10 16	10 24					10 50			10 54	11 16			
Norwich	d																						
Peterborough	d						09 55	10 10		10 18	10 25					10 51			10 57	11 18			
Grantham	a						10 13				10 44								11 15		11 48		
	d						10 14				10 45								11 16		11 49		
Newark North Gate	a						10 26				10 58								11 28	11 45			
	d						10 27				11 03								11 30	11 46			
Lincoln	a										11 29												
Retford	d									10 56											12 11		
Doncaster	a						10 50	10 56		11 10						11 38			11 53	12 09	12 27		
Selby	a																				12 44		
Hull	a																				13 20		
Sheffield	a																						
Pontefract Monkhill	a																						
Wakefield Kirkgate	a																						
Wakefield Westgate	d					10 46	11 10											11 46	12 12				
Leeds	a					10 59	11 24											11 59	12 28				
Mirfield	a																						
Brighouse	a																						
Halifax	a																						
Shipley	a																						
Bradford Forster Square	a																						
Bradford Interchange	a																						
Keighley	a																						
Skipton	a																						
Doncaster	d							10 58		11 11						11 43				12 10			
York	a	10 46						11 18		11 32			11 40	11 47		12 03				12 31			12 46
Scarborough	a																						
Harrogate	a						11 56		←														
Leeds	d			10 42	10 51	11 07			11 07			11 14			11 42		11 51	12 08				12 14	
York	d	10 50	11 07	11 07	11 18	→		11 21	11 31	11 34		11 39	11 42	11 55	12 06	12 09	12 22	12 32		12 35		12 39	12 51
Thirsk	d												11 59									12 56	
Northallerton	d		11 26	11 26								12 01	12 07							12 55		13 05	
Darlington	a	11 17	11 37	11 37				11 49	11 57	12 02				12 23	12 33	12 38	12 48	12 58		13 07			13 18
Eaglescliffe	a												12 24										
Middlesbrough	a											12 31										13 35	
Darlington	d	11 19	11 39	11 39				11 50	11 58	12 03				12 24	12 34	12 39	12 50	12 59		13 09			13 20
Durham	d		11 55	11 55	12 00			12 11	12 15	12 21					12 51	12 57	13 06	13 16		13 26			
Chester-le-Street	d														12 57								
Newcastle	a	11 45	12 10	12 10	12 13			12 26	12 27	12 34				12 51	13 07	13 10	13 21	13 28		13 39			13 46
Hartlepool	a												12 44										
Sunderland	a												13 09										
Newcastle	d	11 52			12 14				12 30	12 38				12 53		13 15	13 24	13 31		13 42			13 49
Morpeth	a				12 27												13 36						
Alnmouth for Alnwick	a									13 03								13 55					
Berwick-upon-Tweed	a	12 34												13 37				14 16					14 31
Dunbar 238	a								13 35	13 46													
Edinburgh 238	a	13 19			13 57				13 58	14 18				14 20		14 38	14 59	15 00		15 08			15 16
	d													14 33				15 10					
Haymarket 238	d													14 39				15 14					
Motherwell	a																	15 55					
Glasgow Central	a																	16 12					
Stirling	a																						
Perth	a																						
Inverness	a																						
Inverkeithing	a													14 53									
Kirkcaldy	a													15 10									
Leuchars	a													15 34									
Dundee	a													15 50									
Arbroath	a													16 07									
Montrose	a													16 23									
Stonehaven	a													16 47									
Aberdeen	a													17 08									

A from 23 February until 29 March
B until 16 February, from 5 April. From Manchester Airport
C From Liverpool Lime Street
D From Birmingham New Street to Edinburgh
E From Birmingham New Street
F From Manchester Victoria to Redcar Central
G The Northern Lights
H From Manchester Airport
I From Birmingham New Street. to Edinburgh

Table T026-F

Sundays
15 December to 10 May

London - Humberside, Yorkshire, North East England and Scotland

Station		TP	TP	XC	GR	GR	TP	XC	EM	GR	TP	GR	EM	GC	TP	GR	TP	TP	XC	GR	GR	XC
		A	B	C			B	D	E		F		G		H	I	J	F	K			D
London Kings Cross	d				11 03	11 22				11 30		11 33		11 50		12 00				12 03	12 22	
Stevenage	d				11 25							11 55										
Peterborough	a				11 54					12 16										12 50	13 09	
Norwich	d								10 47													
Peterborough	d				11 55				12 16	12 18			←							12 51	13 11	
Grantham	a				12 13	12 23			12 46			12 41	12 46							13 09		
	d				12 14	12 24			12 52			12 42	12 52							13 10		
Newark North Gate	a				12 26				→			12 55								13 22		
	d				12 27							12 58								13 23		
Lincoln	a											13 25										
Retford	d									12 56												
Doncaster	a				12 50					13 10				13 19						13 46	13 57	
Selby	a																					
Hull	a																					
Sheffield	a												14 34									
Pontefract Monkhill	a																					
Wakefield Kirkgate	a													13 44								
Wakefield Westgate	d			12 46	13 10														13 46	14 05		
Leeds	a			13 00	13 24														14 00	14 20		
Mirfield	a													13 57								
Brighouse	a													14 05								
Halifax	a													14 20								
Shipley	a																					
Bradford Forster Square	a																					
Bradford Interchange	a													14 37								
Keighley	a																					
Skipton	a																					
Doncaster	d									13 11											13 59	
York	a					13 12				13 32						13 47					14 19	
Scarborough	a																					
Harrogate	a				13 58			←														←
Leeds	d	12 41	12 51	13 06			←	13 06							13 14		13 45	13 51	14 07			14 07
York	d	13 06	13 20	→		13 15	13 20	13 30		13 34					13 39	13 50	14 11	14 16	→		14 22	14 30
Thirsk	d		→												13 56							
Northallerton	d	13 25				13 34					←				14 05							
Darlington	a	13 37				13 47	14 07	13 57		14 02	14 07					14 18	14 38	14 43			14 48	14 57
Eaglescliffe	a						→															
Middlesbrough	a														14 35							
Darlington	d	13 38				13 48		13 58		14 03	14 09					14 19	14 39	14 44			14 50	14 58
Durham	d	13 55				14 06		14 15		14 21	14 26						14 56	15 01			15 08	15 15
Chester-le-Street	d																15 02					
Newcastle	a	14 08				14 19		14 27		14 34	14 38					14 46	15 13	15 14			15 23	15 27
Hartlepool	a																					
Sunderland	a																					
Newcastle	d					14 23		14 29		14 37	14 41					14 50		15 21				15 29
Morpeth	a					14 36		14 43			14 54							15 34				
Alnmouth for Alnwick	a									15 02												15 53
Berwick-upon-Tweed	a															15 35						16 14
Dunbar 238	a							15 36														
Edinburgh 238	a					15 56		15 59		16 08	16 15					16 18		16 56				16 57
	d															16 32						17 11
Haymarket 238	d															16 37						17 15
Motherwell	a																					17 52
Glasgow Central	a																					18 13
Stirling	a															17 16						
Perth	a															17 53						
Inverness	a															20 09						
Inverkeithing	a																					
Kirkcaldy	a																					
Leuchars	a																					
Dundee	a																					
Arbroath	a																					
Montrose	a																					
Stonehaven	a																					
Aberdeen	a																					

A From Manchester Piccadilly
B From Liverpool Lime Street to Edinburgh
C From Bristol Temple Meads to Edinburgh
D From Bristol Temple Meads
E To Liverpool Lime Street
F From Liverpool Lime Street
G From Norwich to Liverpool Lime Street
H From Manchester Airport to Redcar Central
I The Highland Chieftain
J From Manchester Airport
K From Bristol Temple Meads to Glasgow Central

Table T026-F

Sundays

15 December to 10 May

London - Humberside, Yorkshire, North East England and Scotland

		GR	TP A	GR	XC B	HT	GR	TP C	TP D	XC E	GR	GR	TP A	TP F	TP G	XC H	GR	GC	TP A	EM I	XC B	GR	TP C
London Kings Cross ⊖	d	12 30		12 33		12 48	13 00				13 03	13 30					13 33	13 48				14 00	
Stevenage	d			12 56							13 25						13 55						
Peterborough	a	13 16									13 54	14 16					14 24						
Norwich	d																						
Peterborough	d	13 18									13 55	14 18					14 26			14 31			
Grantham	a			13 41		13 47					14 13						14 46			15 07			
	d			13 43		13 48					14 15						14 52			15 09			
Newark North Gate	a	13 45									14 27												
	d	13 46									14 28												
Lincoln	a																						
Retford	d					14 10						14 56					15 20						
Doncaster	a	14 09		14 19		14 24					14 51	15 10					15 34						
Selby	a					14 41																	
Hull	a					15 18																	
Sheffield	a																			16 35			
Pontefract Monkhill	a																						
Wakefield Kirkgate	a																						
Wakefield Westgate	d			14 38						14 47	15 11					15 46	16 01						
Leeds	a			14 54						15 00	15 24					16 00	16 17						
Mirfield	a																						
Brighouse	a																						
Halifax	a																						
Shipley	a																						
Bradford Forster Square	a																						
Bradford Interchange	a																						
Keighley	a																						
Skipton	a																						
Doncaster	d	14 10			14 19							15 11									15 20		
York	a	14 31			14 40		14 49					15 32						15 37			15 41	15 47	
Scarborough	a																						
Harrogate	a										15 55												
Leeds	d		14 12					14 44	14 51	15 07			15 13	15 42	15 51	16 07			←				←
York	d	14 33	14 36		14 50		14 53	15 07	15 22	15 31		15 34	15 41	16 07	16 20	→		15 38	15 41		15 45	15 53	16 07
Thirsk	d		14 54										→	→	→			15 55	16 04				
Northallerton	d	14 53	15 02															16 07					16 26
Darlington	a	15 06			15 16		15 21	15 37		15 57		16 02									16 11	16 20	16 37
Eaglescliffe	a																	16 23					
Middlesbrough	a		15 35																16 40				
Darlington	d	15 07			15 17		15 22	15 39		15 58		16 03									16 12	16 22	16 39
Durham	d	15 25			15 34			15 55	16 06	16 15		16 21									16 29		16 55
Chester-le-Street	d																						17 02
Newcastle	a	15 38			15 46		15 50	16 10	16 19	16 27		16 34									16 42	16 48	17 13
Hartlepool	a																	16 45					
Sunderland	a																	17 10					
Newcastle	d	15 45					15 53		16 21	16 29		16 38										16 52	
Morpeth	a								16 34														
Alnmouth for Alnwick	a									16 55		17 03											
Berwick-upon-Tweed	a						16 35															17 35	
Dunbar 238	a									17 37													
Edinburgh 238	a	17 09					17 20		17 57	17 59		18 08										18 18	
	d									18 13												18 36	
Haymarket 238	d									18 18												18 41	
Motherwell	a																						
Glasgow Central	a																						
Stirling	a																						
Perth	a																						
Inverness	a																						
Inverkeithing	a									18 30												18 54	
Kirkcaldy	a									18 45												19 11	
Leuchars	a									19 16												19 36	
Dundee	a									19 30												19 51	
Arbroath	a									19 50												20 09	
Montrose	a									20 04												20 25	
Stonehaven	a									20 25												20 49	
Aberdeen	a									20 43												21 10	

A From Manchester Airport to Redcar Central
B From Birmingham New Street
C From Manchester Airport
D From Liverpool Lime Street
E From Plymouth. ⚲ to Edinburgh
F From Manchester Airport to Newcastle
G From Liverpool Lime Street to Edinburgh
H From Plymouth to Glasgow Central
I To Liverpool Lime Street

Table T026-F

Sundays

15 December to 10 May

London - Humberside, Yorkshire, North East England and Scotland

		TP A	XC B	GR	GR	GR	HT C	EM D	TP E	XC F	GR	TP G	TP A	XC H	GR	GR	TP E	XC I	EM D	GR	EM J	GC
London Kings Cross ⊖	d			14 03	14 30	14 35	14 48				15 00				15 03	15 30				15 33		15 50
Stevenage	d					14 57									15 25					15 55		
Peterborough	a			14 50	15 16										15 54	16 17				16 24		
Norwich	d							13 47											14 53			
Peterborough	d			14 52	15 18			15 23							15 55	16 18			16 24	16 25	←	
Grantham	a			15 10			15 48	15 53							16 13	16 37			16 56	16 46	16 56	
	d			15 11			15 49	15 55							16 14	16 38			16 58	16 51	16 58	
Newark North Gate	a			15 23	15 45	15 50									16 26				→	17 04		
	d			15 24	15 46	15 54									16 27					17 06		
Lincoln	a					16 22														17 37		
Retford	d						16 10								16 42							
Doncaster	a			15 47	16 09		16 26								16 56	17 10						17 18
Selby	a						16 46															
Hull	a						17 21															
Sheffield	a							17 39													18 33	
Pontefract Monkhill	a																					
Wakefield Kirkgate	a																					17 49
Wakefield Westgate	d			16 08										16 46	17 15							
Leeds	a			16 23										16 59	17 28							
Mirfield	a																					18 02
Brighouse	a																					18 10
Halifax	a																					18 22
Shipley	a																					
Bradford Forster Square	a																					
Bradford Interchange	a																					18 37
Keighley	a																					
Skipton	a																					
Doncaster	d				16 10					16 16						17 12		17 19				
York	a				16 31					16 37	16 47					17 33		17 40				
Scarborough	a																					
Harrogate	a		←												17 59							
Leeds	d	←	16 07						16 13			16 42	16 52	17 07			17 14					
York	d	16 20	16 30		16 33				16 39	16 44	16 52	17 07	17 19	17 31		17 35	17 39	17 43				
Thirsk	d								16 56								17 56					
Northallerton	d				16 54				17 07			17 26					18 05					
Darlington	a	16 47	16 57		17 05					17 10	17 19	17 37	17 45	17 57		18 03		18 09				
Eaglescliffe	a																					
Middlesbrough	a								17 37								18 35					
Darlington	d	16 48	16 58		17 07					17 11	17 21	17 39	17 47	17 58		18 04		18 11				
Durham	d	17 05	17 14		17 25					17 28		17 55	18 03	18 15		18 22		18 27				
Chester-le-Street	d																					
Newcastle	a	17 17	17 27		17 39					17 41	17 47	18 10	18 16	18 27		18 35		18 41				
Hartlepool	a																					
Sunderland	a																					
Newcastle	d	17 21	17 28		17 43						17 50		18 18	18 29		18 38						
Morpeth	a	17 34	17 41										18 31									
Alnmouth for Alnwick	a		17 55													19 04						
Berwick-upon-Tweed	a		18 17								18 33			19 11								
Dunbar 238	a													19 34								
Edinburgh 238	a	18 57	18 59		19 08						19 18		19 58	19 59		20 09						
	d		19 18																			
Haymarket 238	d		19 23																			
Motherwell	a		20 01																			
Glasgow Central	a		20 20																			
Stirling	a																					
Perth	a																					
Inverness	a																					
Inverkeithing	a																					
Kirkcaldy	a																					
Leuchars	a																					
Dundee	a																					
Arbroath	a																					
Montrose	a																					
Stonehaven	a																					
Aberdeen	a																					

A From Liverpool Lime Street
B From Plymouth. ⚲ to Edinburgh
C not from 5 January until 12 January
D To Liverpool Lime Street
E From Manchester Airport to Redcar Central
F From Guildford
G From Manchester Airport
H From Penzance
I From Reading
J From Norwich to Liverpool Lime Street

Table T026-F

Sundays 15 December to 10 May

London - Humberside, Yorkshire, North East England and Scotland

Station		GR	TP	TP	XC	EM	GR	GR	TP	TP	TP	XC	GR	EM	GC	GR	TP	TP	XC	XC	GR	GR	GR
			A	B	C	D			E	F	G	H		I			A	B	J	K			
London Kings Cross 15 ⊖	d	16 00					16 05	16 30					16 35		16 53	17 00					17 05	17 22	17 30
Stevenage 4	d												16 57										
Peterborough 8	a						16 51	17 16													17 51		18 16
Norwich	d													15 54									
Peterborough 8	d						16 53	17 18						17 19							17 53		18 18
Grantham 7	a						17 11						17 40	17 49								18 24	18 36
	d						17 12						17 41	17 55								18 26	18 37
Newark North Gate 7	a						17 24	17 45													18 20	18 38	
	d						17 26	17 46													18 21	18 39	
Lincoln	a																						
Retford 10	d												18 04										
Doncaster 7	a						17 49	18 09					18 18								18 44	19 03	19 08
Selby	a																					19 22	
Hull	a																					20 02	
Sheffield 7	a													19 31									
Pontefract Monkhill	a																						
Wakefield Kirkgate 4	a																						
Wakefield Westgate 7	d				17 47	18 01	18 10					18 33	18 39							18 47	19 04		
Leeds 10	a				18 01	18 16	18 26					18 47	18 55							19 01	19 19		
Mirfield	a																						
Brighouse	a																						
Halifax	a																						
Shipley	a																						
Bradford Forster Square	a																						
Bradford Interchange	a																						
Keighley	a																						
Skipton	a																						
Doncaster 7	d							18 10															19 10
York 8	a	17 46						18 32							18 40	18 47							19 32
Scarborough	a																						
Harrogate	a																		←		19 58		
Leeds 10	d		17 42	17 51	18 07				18 14	18 42	18 52	18 56					←	←	18 56	19 08			
York 8	d	17 49	18 07	18 20	18 31			18 35	18 39	19 07	19 17	→			18 41	18 50	19 07	19 17	19 22	19 32			19 37
Thirsk	d								18 56	→	→				19 00								
Northallerton	d		18 26					18 55	19 07						19 11		19 26						
Darlington 7	a	18 19	18 37	18 47	18 59			19 07								19 17	19 37	19 43	19 48	19 59			20 04
Eaglescliffe	a														19 30								
Middlesbrough	a								19 37														
Darlington 7	d	18 20	18 39	18 48	19 00			19 09								19 19	19 39	19 45	19 50	20 00			20 07
Durham	d		18 55	19 05	19 17			19 26									19 55	20 01	20 07	20 17			20 25
Chester-le-Street	d		19 02																				
Newcastle 8	a	18 47	19 13	19 17	19 30			19 39								19 46	20 10	20 14	20 20	20 29			20 38
Hartlepool	a														19 50								
Sunderland	a														20 21								
Newcastle 8	d	18 50		19 21	19 32			19 42								19 51		20 16		20 37			20 41
Morpeth	a			19 34				19 55										20 29		20 49			20 54
Alnmouth for Alnwick	a				19 57																		21 10
Berwick-upon-Tweed	a	19 32			20 20											20 34				21 22			
Dunbar 238	a							20 48												21 44			
Edinburgh 10 238	a	20 19		20 57	21 03			21 12								21 19		21 57		22 06			22 15
	d				21 12			21 22															
Haymarket 238	d				21 17			21 26															
Motherwell	a				21 55			22 04															
Glasgow Central 15	a				22 12			22 26															
Stirling	a																						
Perth	a																						
Inverness	a																						
Inverkeithing	a																						
Kirkcaldy	a																						
Leuchars 3	a																						
Dundee	a																						
Arbroath	a																						
Montrose	a																						
Stonehaven	a																						
Aberdeen	a																						

A From Manchester Airport
B From Liverpool Lime Street
C From Plymouth. ⌶ to Edinburgh
D From St Pancras International
E From Manchester Airport to Redcar Central
F From Manchester Airport to Newcastle
G From Liverpool Lime Street to Edinburgh
H From Reading to Newcastle
I To Manchester Piccadilly
J From Reading
K From Plymouth

Table T026-F

Sundays 15 December to 10 May

London - Humberside, Yorkshire, North East England and Scotland

Station		TP	GR	XC	HT	EM	GR	TP	TP	XC	GR	GC	TP	GR	XC	GR	TP	GR	EM	XC	GC	GR	TP
		A		B	C	D		E	F	G			H		I		A		J	K			L
London Kings Cross 15 ⊖	d		17 35		17 48		18 00				18 03	18 22		18 27		18 30		18 35			18 53	19 00	
Stevenage 4	d		17 57		18u09													18 57					
Peterborough 8	a						18 46				18 50												
Norwich	d					16 54													17 54				
Peterborough 8	d					18 26	18 48				18 52								19 22				
Grantham 7	a		18 41		18 51	18 57												19 39	19 52				
	d		18 43		18 52	18 59												19 41					
Newark North Gate 7	a										19 19					19 45							
	d										19 21					19 46							
Lincoln	a																						
Retford 10	d				19 14													20 04					
Doncaster 7	a		19 14		19 27						19 48					20 09		20 18			20 24		
Selby	a				19 44																		
Hull	a				20 19																		
Sheffield 7	a					20 30																	
Pontefract Monkhill	a																						
Wakefield Kirkgate 4	a																				21 00		
Wakefield Westgate 7	d		19 34							19 52	20 08							20 39					
Leeds 10	a		19 49							20 07	20 21							20 52					
Mirfield	a																				21 12		
Brighouse	a																				21 21		
Halifax	a																				21 33		
Shipley	a																						
Bradford Forster Square	a																						
Bradford Interchange	a																				21 48		
Keighley	a																	21s19					
Skipton	a																	21 36					
Doncaster 7	d			19 22												20 10				20 19			
York 8	a			19 43			19 54					20 10		20 18		20 32				20 42		20 47	
Scarborough	a																						
Harrogate	a										21 02				←								
Leeds 10	d	19 14						19 42	19 51	20 09			←		20 09		20 14						20 52
York 8	d	19 41		19 54			19 59	20 07	20 21	→		20 12	20 21	20 24	20 32	20 36	20 39			20 44		20 52	21 22
Thirsk	d	19 58							→			20 29					20 56						
Northallerton	d	20 07						20 26				20 43				20 56	21 06						
Darlington 7	a			20 20			20 26	20 37					20 47	20 53	21 00	21 08				21 13		21 20	21 48
Eaglescliffe	a											21 00											
Middlesbrough	a	20 37															21 36						
Darlington 7	d			20 21			20 28	20 39					20 50	20 55	21 01	21 10				21 14		21 22	21 50
Durham	d			20 38				20 55					21 06	21 12	21 18	21 27				21 32			22 06
Chester-le-Street	d							21 02															
Newcastle 8	a			20 50			20 55	21 13					21 21	21 27	21 31	21 40				21 45		21 50	22 21
Hartlepool	a											21 21											
Sunderland	a											21 51											
Newcastle 8	d			20 56			21 00								21 34	21 45						21 52	
Morpeth	a																					22 06	
Alnmouth for Alnwick	a														21 59							22 23	
Berwick-upon-Tweed	a						21 42									22 27						22 47	
Dunbar 238	a																					23 11	
Edinburgh 10 238	a			22 18			22 27								23 03	23 12						23 38	
	d																						
Haymarket 238	d																						
Motherwell	a																						
Glasgow Central 15	a																						
Stirling	a																						
Perth	a																						
Inverness	a																						
Inverkeithing	a																						
Kirkcaldy	a																						
Leuchars 3	a																						
Dundee	a																						
Arbroath	a																						
Montrose	a																						
Stonehaven	a																						
Aberdeen	a																						

A From Manchester Airport to Redcar Central
B From Reading. ⌶ to Newcastle
C To Beverley
D To Manchester Piccadilly
E From Manchester Airport
F From Liverpool Lime Street to Newcastle
G From Plymouth to Edinburgh
H From Liverpool Lime Street
I From Plymouth. ⌶ to Newcastle
J To Nottingham
K From Reading
L From Liverpool Lime Street. ⌶ from York

Table T026-F

Sundays
15 December to 10 May

London - Humberside, Yorkshire, North East England and Scotland

		XC	TP	GR	GR	GC	GR	XC	EM	GR	HT	EM	GR	TP	XC	GR	GR	GR	TP	XC	GR	EM
		A	B					C	D			E		F	G				H	I		E
London Kings Cross 15 ⊖	d			19 03	19 06	19 22	19 30			19 35	19 52		20 00			20 05	20 35	21 00			21 05	
Stevenage 4	d				19 29					19 57							20 57					
Peterborough 8	a			19 50	19 58		20 17			20 26			20 46			20 52	21 26	21 46			21 52	
Norwich	d											18 56										20 52
Peterborough 8	d			19 51	20 01		20 18			20 27		20 30	20 48			20 53	21 27	21 48			21 53	22 23
Grantham 7	a				20 20					20 45	20 51	21 00					21 45					22 53
	d				20 22					20 47	20 52						21 46					
Newark North Gate 7	a			20 18	20 36		20 46										21 58				22 20	
	d			20 19	20 37		20 47										21 59				22 21	
Lincoln	a				21 03																	
Retford 10	d										21 14					21 32						
Doncaster 7	a			20 42		20 58	21 11			21 18	21 27					21 47	22 22				22 48	
Selby	a										21 44											
Hull	a										22 20											
Sheffield 7 ⛴	a																					
Pontefract Monkhill	a																					
Wakefield Kirkgate 4	a					21 23																
Wakefield Westgate 7	d	20 48		21 03					21 33	21 39					21 49	22 06	22 41			22 49	23 10	
Leeds 10	a	21 02		21 19					21 49	21 54					22 02	22 21	22 58			23 02	23 26	
Mirfield	a					21 38																
Brighouse	a					21 45																
Halifax	a					21 57																
Shipley	a																					
Bradford Forster Square	a																					
Bradford Interchange	a					22 13																
Keighley	a																					
Skipton	a																					
Doncaster 7	d						21 16	21 23														
York 8	a						21 37	21 44					21 53					22 57				
Scarborough	a																					
Harrogate	a																					
Leeds 10	d	21 08	21 14											21 51					22 43			
York 8	d	21a31	21 39				21 39	21 46					21 56	22 22				23 02	23 09			
Thirsk	d		21 56																23 32			
Northallerton	d		22 07										22 30	22 41				23 37	23 40			
Darlington 7	a						22 19	22 24					22 42	22 52				23 48	23 52			
Eaglescliffe	a																					
Middlesbrough	a		22 37																			
Darlington 7	d						22 20	22 25					22 43	22 54				23 50	23 54			
Durham	d						22 38	22 42					23 01	23 12				00 07	00 11			
Chester-le-Street	d													23 19					00 17			
Newcastle 8 ⛴	a						23 09	23 10					23 32	23 44				00 38	00 43			
Hartlepool	a																					
Sunderland ⛴	a																					
Newcastle 8 ⛴	d																					
Morpeth	a																					
Alnmouth for Alnwick	a																					
Berwick-upon-Tweed	a																					
Dunbar 238	a																					
Edinburgh 10 238 ⛴	a																					
	d																					
Haymarket 238 ⛴	d																					
Motherwell	a																					
Glasgow Central 15	a																					
Stirling	a																					
Perth	a																					
Inverness	a																					
Inverkeithing	a																					
Kirkcaldy	a																					
Leuchars 3	a																					
Dundee	a																					
Arbroath	a																					
Montrose	a																					
Stonehaven	a																					
Aberdeen	a																					

A From Plymouth. ⚒ to Leeds
B From Manchester Airport to Redcar Central
C From Reading
D From St Pancras International
E To Nottingham
F From Liverpool Lime Street. ⚒ from York
G From Plymouth
H From Liverpool Lime Street
I From Penzance

Table T026-F

Sundays
15 December to 10 May

London - Humberside, Yorkshire, North East England and Scotland

		EM	GR	GR	GR	GR
		A				
London Kings Cross 15 ⊖	d		21 35	22 00	22 05	22 35
Stevenage 4	d		21 57			
Peterborough 8	a		22 26	22 47	22 51	23s25
Norwich	d					
Peterborough 8	d		22 27	22 48	22 53	
Grantham 7	a		22 46		23 11	23s46
	d		22 48		23 12	
Newark North Gate 7	a		23 00		23 24	23s58
	d		23 01		23 25	
Lincoln	a					
Retford 10	d		23 17			
Doncaster 7	a		23 35	23 41	23 53	00s28
Selby	a					
Hull	a					
Sheffield 7 ⛴	a					
Pontefract Monkhill	a					
Wakefield Kirkgate 4	a					
Wakefield Westgate 7	d	23 53	23 59			
Leeds 10	a	00 08	00 14			01 33
Mirfield	a					
Brighouse	a					
Halifax	a					
Shipley	a					
Bradford Forster Square	a					
Bradford Interchange	a					
Keighley	a					
Skipton	a					
Doncaster 7	d			23 43	23 54	
York 8	a			00 08	00 19	
Scarborough	a					
Harrogate	a					
Leeds 10	d					
York 8	d			00 12		
Thirsk	d					
Northallerton	d			00s45		
Darlington 7	a			00s59		
Eaglescliffe	a					
Middlesbrough	a					
Darlington 7	d					
Durham	d			01s17		
Chester-le-Street	d					
Newcastle 8 ⛴	a			01 50		
Hartlepool	a					
Sunderland ⛴	a					
Newcastle 8 ⛴	d					
Morpeth	a					
Alnmouth for Alnwick	a					
Berwick-upon-Tweed	a					
Dunbar 238	a					
Edinburgh 10 238 ⛴	a					
	d					
Haymarket 238 ⛴	d					
Motherwell	a					
Glasgow Central 15	a					
Stirling	a					
Perth	a					
Inverness	a					
Inverkeithing	a					
Kirkcaldy	a					
Leuchars 3	a					
Dundee	a					
Arbroath	a					
Montrose	a					
Stonehaven	a					
Aberdeen	a					

A From St Pancras International

Table T026-R

Mondays to Fridays

16 December to 15 May

Scotland, North East England, Yorkshire and Humberside - London

Miles	Miles	Miles			TP MX	TP MX	XC MX	TP MO	TP MX	GR	EM	EM MO	GR		HT	EM	GR	GR	GR	TP	TP	GR	GR		GR
					A	B	C	D	D		E	F				G				H	D				I
—	—	0	**Aberdeen**	d																					
—	—	16¼	Stonehaven	d																					
—	—	40½	Montrose	d																					
—	—	54¼	Arbroath	d																					
—	—	71¼	**Dundee**	d																					
—	—	79½	Leuchars 3	d																					
—	—	104½	Kirkcaldy	d																					
—	—	117¼	Inverkeithing	a																					
—	—	—	**Inverness**	d																					
—	—	—	Perth	d																					
—	—	—	**Stirling**	a																					
0	—	—	**Glasgow Central 15**	d																					
12¾	—	—	Motherwell	a																					
56	—	129¼	Haymarket 238	d			00 06																		
57¼	—	130½	**Edinburgh 10** 238	a			00 10																		
—	—	—		d																					
86½	—	—	Dunbar 238	d																					
114¾	—	—	**Berwick-upon-Tweed**	d																					
147	—	—	Alnmouth for Alnwick	d																					
165¼	—	—	Morpeth	d	00 01																				
181¾	—	—	**Newcastle 8**	a	00 27																				
—	—	—	**Sunderland**	d																					
—	—	—	Hartlepool	d																					
—	—	—	**Newcastle 8**	d				00 08	00 08									04 44		05 06		05 26			
190	—	—	Chester-le-Street	d																					
195¾	—	—	**Durham**	d				00 21	00 21									04 59		05 18		05 39			
217¾	—	—	**Darlington 7**	a				00 38	00 38									05 15		05 35		05 56			
—	—	—	**Middlesbrough**	d																	05 12				
—	—	—	Eaglescliffe	a																					
—	—	—	**Darlington 7**	d				00 40	00 40									05 17		05 36		05 58			
231¾	—	—	Northallerton	d														05 28			05 41	06 09			
239½	—	—	Thirsk	d		00 03															05 51				
—	—	—	**York 8**	a		00 29		01 36	01 36									05 57		06 02	06 09	06 29			
—	—	—	Leeds	a				02 05	02 18											06 28	06 42				
—	—	—		d																					
—	—	—	Harrogate	d																					
—	—	—	Scarborough	a																					
—	—	—	York	d						04 40								05 59				06 31			
294¼	—	—	**Doncaster 7**	a						05 05								06 21				06 53			
—	—	—	**Skipton**	d																					
—	—	—	Keighley	d																					
—	—	—	**Bradford Interchange**	d																					
—	—	—	Bradford Forster Square	d																					06 30
—	—	—	Shipley	d																					06u37
—	—	—	**Halifax**	d																					
—	—	—	Brighouse	d																					
—	—	—	Mirfield	d																					
—	0	—	**Leeds 10**	d									05 05			05 19	05 30		06 05				06 40		07 00
—	10	—	**Wakefield Westgate 7**	d									05 18			05 32	05 43		06 18				06 53		07 13
—	—	—	Wakefield Kirkgate 4	d																					
—	—	—	Pontefract Monkhill	d																					
—	—	—	Sheffield 7	d																					
—	—	—	**Hull**	d											04 57										
—	—	—	Selby	a																					
—	29¾	—	**Doncaster 7**	d						05 07			05 37		05 54	05a57	06 02	06 22	06 37			06 54	07 14		
311¾	—	—	**Retford 10**	d									05 51		06 08				06 51						
—	—	—	**Lincoln**	d																					
330¼	—	—	**Newark North Gate 7**	a						05 34			06 05				06 24	06 45	07 05				07 36		
—	—	—		d						05 36			06 06				06 26	06 46	07 06				07 37		
344¾	—	—	**Grantham 7**	a						05 47			06 17		06 31		06 37	06 57	07 17			07 25			
—	—	—		d						05 49	05 51	05 56	06 18		06 32		06 38	06 58	07 18			07 26			
374	—	—	**Peterborough 8**	a						06 09	06 22	06 26	06 38				06 58	07 18	07 39			07 46			
—	—	—	Norwich	d																					
—	—	—	**Peterborough 8**	d						06 10			06 40				07 00	07 19	07 40			07 49			
422¾	—	—	**Stevenage 4**	d																					
450¼	—	—	**London Kings Cross 15** ⊖	a						07 01			07 30		07 59		07 49	08 10	08 31			08 39	08 51		08 59

A From Edinburgh
B From Redcar Central
C From Aberdeen
D To Manchester Airport
E until 3 April, MX from 7 April. From Nottingham to Spalding
F from 6 April. From Nottingham to Spalding
G To St Pancras International
H To Liverpool Lime Street. from York
I West Riding Limited

Table T026-R

Mondays to Fridays

16 December to 15 May

Scotland, North East England, Yorkshire and Humberside - London

		GR	TP	TP	HT	XC	GR	GR	GR		EM	GR	GR	XC	TP	GR	EM	TP MX	TP MO		GR	TP MX	TP MO	GC	TP
			A	B	C	D					E	F		G	H		I	A	A		J	K	K		B
Aberdeen	d																								
Stonehaven	d																								
Montrose	d																								
Arbroath	d																								
Dundee	d																								
Leuchars 3	d																								
Kirkcaldy	d																								
Inverkeithing	a																								
Inverness	d																								
Perth	d																								
Stirling	a																								
Glasgow Central 15	d																								
Motherwell	a																								
Haymarket 238	d																								
Edinburgh 10 238	a																								
	d																	05 14	05 17		05 40				
Dunbar 238	d																	05 45	05 45						
Berwick-upon-Tweed	d															06 00									
Alnmouth for Alnwick	d															06 21									
Morpeth	d															06 38		06 43	06 43						
Newcastle 8	a															06 52		06 57	06 57		07 02				
Sunderland	d	05 40																							
Hartlepool	d																					←	←		
Newcastle 8	d	05 59	06 06			06 24			06 30					06 40	06 41	06 55		07 09	07 09		07 05	07 09	07 09		
Chester-le-Street	d														06 52			→	→						
Durham	d	06 12	06 18			06 37			06 43					06 52	06 59	07 08						07 21	07 21		
Darlington 7	a	06 30	06 35			06 53			07 01					07 09	07 16	07 26									
Middlesbrough	d			06 21																					07 20
Eaglescliffe	a																								
Darlington 7	d	06 32	06 36			06 55			07 02					07 10	07 17	07 32									
Northallerton	d			06 50					07 14						07 28										07 50
Thirsk	d			06 59																					07 59
York 8	a	06 59	07 02	07 17		07 21			07 34					07 37	07 47	07 59						08 02	08 02		08 17
Leeds	a		07 28	07 42										08 08	08 12							08 28	08 28		08 42
	d																								
Harrogate	d																								
Scarborough	a																								
York	d	07 01				07 28			07 37							08 02									
Doncaster 7	a					07 51																			
Skipton	d												06 55												
Keighley	d												07u07												
Bradford Interchange	d																							06 55	
Bradford Forster Square	d																								
Shipley	d												07u18												
Halifax	d																							07 10	
Brighouse	d																							07 20	
Mirfield	d																							07 26	
Leeds 10	d							07 15					07 41	08 11											
Wakefield Westgate 7	d							07 28					07 54	08 23											
Wakefield Kirkgate 4	d																							07 40	
Pontefract Monkhill	d																							07 59	
Sheffield 7	d					08a15								08a55											
Hull	d				06 26							06 58													
Selby	a				07 00							07 32													
Doncaster 7	d				07 21			07 47				07 55	08 14											08 31	
Retford 10	d				07 41											08 35									
Lincoln	d						07 30																		
Newark North Gate 7	a						07 55					08 20	08 38												
	d						07 58					08 21	08 39												
Grantham 7	a				08 02			08 17				08 33													
	d				08 03			08 18			08 27	08 33					09 10								
Peterborough 8	a	08 09					08 27		08 43		08 58		09 06				09 36								
Norwich	d										10a45						11a12								
Peterborough 8	d	08 12					08 29		08 44				09 08												
Stevenage 4	d						08 59	09 05																	
London Kings Cross 15 ⊖	a	09 09			09 14		09 26	09 31	09 37			09 51	10 00			10 03					09 40			10 09	

A To Liverpool Lime Street
B From Redcar Central to Manchester Airport
C From Beverley
D To Reading
E From Mansfield Woodhouse
F The Hull Executive
G To Plymouth
H To Manchester Airport
I From Nottingham
J The Flying Scotsman
K From Edinburgh to Liverpool Lime Street

Table T026-R

Mondays to Fridays
16 December to 15 May

Scotland, North East England, Yorkshire and Humberside - London

Station		GC	GR	GR	XC A	GR	XC B	TP C	GR D	TP E	TP F	HT G	GC	EM H	GR	GR	XC I	GR	XC J	TP C	GR	GR	TP E
Aberdeen	d																						
Stonehaven	d																						
Montrose	d																						
Arbroath	d																						
Dundee	d																						
Leuchars	d																						
Kirkcaldy	d																						
Inverkeithing	a																						
Inverness	d																						
Perth	d																						
Stirling	a																						
Glasgow Central	d																		06 01				
Motherwell	a																		06 15				
Haymarket 238	d								06 13										06 57				
Edinburgh 238	a								06 17										07 01				
	d			05 48			06 06		06 24	06 27						06 56	07 00		07 10		07 30		
Dunbar 238	d			06 10															07 32				
Berwick-upon-Tweed	d			06 34			06 50		07 08								07 43				08 12		
Alnmouth for Alnwick	d			06 56			07 11										08 03						
Morpeth	d			07 12						07 44							08 18						
Newcastle	a			07 26			07 38		07 52	07 58						08 24	08 32		08 38		08 55		
Sunderland	d	06 43																					
Hartlepool	d	07 05																					
Newcastle	d			07 29	07 35		07 40	07 43	07 59	08 06						08 27	08 35		08 40	08 43	08 58		09 06
Chester-le-Street	d							07 52												08 52			
Durham	d			07 43	07 47		07 53	07 59		08 18						08 40	08 48		08 54	08 59			09 18
Darlington	a			08 00	08 05		08 10	08 16	08 27	08 35						08 57	09 04		09 10	09 16	09 26		09 35
Middlesbrough	d										08 20												
Eaglescliffe	a	07 34																					
Darlington	d			08 02	08 06		08 12	08 17	08 28	08 36						08 59	09 06		09 12	09 17	09 27		09 36
Northallerton	d	07 55						08 28			08 50					09 10							
Thirsk	d	08 03									08 59												
York	a	08 21		08 29	08 32		08 41	08 47	08 55	09 02	09 17					09 30	09 33		09 39	09 48	09 54		10 02
Leeds	a						09 08	09 12		09 27	09 43								10 07	10 12			10 27
	d																						
Harrogate	d		07 34																				
Scarborough	a																						
York	d	08 22		08 31	08 35				08 58							09 32	09 37				09 57	10 02	
Doncaster	a			08 54	08 56											09 54	09 59					10 23	
Skipton	d																						
Keighley	d																						
Bradford Interchange	d												07 56										
Bradford Forster Square	d																						
Shipley	d																						
Halifax	d												08 10										
Brighouse	d												08 24										
Mirfield	d												08 32										
Leeds	d		08 15			08 45	09 11								09 15			09 45	10 11				
Wakefield Westgate	d		08 30			08 59	09 23								09 29			09 58	10 23				
Wakefield Kirkgate	d												08 55										
Pontefract Monkhill	d																						
Sheffield	d				09a22		09a54							08 38			10a22		10a55				
Hull	d											08 24											
Selby	a											08 58											
Doncaster	d		08 49	08 56		09 19						09 24	09 30		09 48	09 55		10 18				10 25	
Retford	d											09 38										10 39	
Lincoln	d																						
Newark North Gate	a			09 19												10 18						10 53	
	d			09 20												10 19						10 55	
Grantham	a		09 19									09 59		10 06	10 18							11 06	
	d		09 21									10 00		10 11	10 19							11 07	
Peterborough	a			09 48		10 08								10 42		10 46		11 08				11 27	
Norwich	d													12a15									
Peterborough	d			09 50		10 10										10 49		11 10				11 29	
Stevenage	d		10 07												11 04							11 58	
London Kings Cross ⊖	a	10 14	10 31	10 39		11 01			10 49			11 09	11 17		11 31	11 39		11 59			11 49	12 23	

A To Southampton Central
B To Plymouth
C To Manchester Airport
D not 16 December. From Stirling
E To Liverpool Lime Street
F From Redcar Central to Manchester Airport
G From Beverley
H From Liverpool Lime Street
I To Reading
J To Plymouth. 🍴 from Edinburgh

NRT DECEMBER 19 EDITION

Table T026-R

Mondays to Fridays
16 December to 15 May

Scotland, North East England, Yorkshire and Humberside - London

Station		TP A	EM B	GR	GC	GR	TP C	XC D	GR	XC E	TP C	GR	TP F	TP A	HT	GR	EM B	GR	GR	XC G	GC	GR
Aberdeen	d																					
Stonehaven	d																					
Montrose	d																					
Arbroath	d																					
Dundee	d									06 33												
Leuchars	d									06 46												
Kirkcaldy	d									07 22												
Inverkeithing	a									07 38												
Inverness	d																					
Perth	d																					
Stirling	a																					
Glasgow Central	d					06 48	07 10															
Motherwell	a					07 03	07 25															
Haymarket 238	d					07 48				08 00												
Edinburgh 238	a					07 52				08 04												
	d					08 00				08 08	08 10	08 30							09 00			
Dunbar 238	d																					
Berwick-upon-Tweed	d									08 51		09 12										
Alnmouth for Alnwick	d					09 00																
Morpeth	d									09 24	09 29											
Newcastle	a					09 27				09 39	09 44	09 56							10 24			
Sunderland	d				08 44																	
Hartlepool	d				09 08																	
Newcastle	d					09 29		09 35		09 41	09 47	09 58	10 06						10 26	10 35		
Chester-le-Street	d																					
Durham	d					09 43		09 49		09 55	09 59		10 18						10 39	10 47		
Darlington	a					10 00		10 06		10 11	10 16	10 26	10 35						10 57	11 04		
Middlesbrough	d	09 21												10 21								
Eaglescliffe	a				09 39																	
Darlington	d					10 02		10 07		10 12	10 17	10 28	10 36						10 59	11 06		
Northallerton	d	09 50			09 59						10 28			10 50					11 10			
Thirsk	d	09 59			10 08									10 59								
York	a	10 17			10 24	10 29		10 33		10 39	10 47	10 55	11 02	11 17					11 30	11 33		
Leeds	a	10 42								11 07	11 12		11 27	11 42								
	d																					
Harrogate	d			09 36																		
Scarborough	a																					
York	d				10 26	10 32		10 35				10 57							11 32	11 36		
Doncaster	a					10 54		10 58											11 54	11 58		
Skipton	d																					
Keighley	d																					
Bradford Interchange	d																				10 22	
Bradford Forster Square	d																					
Shipley	d																					
Halifax	d																				10 36	
Brighouse	d																				10 47	
Mirfield	d																				10 54	
Leeds	d			10 15					10 45	11 11								11 15				11 45
Wakefield Westgate	d			10 28					10 58	11 23								11 28				11 58
Wakefield Kirkgate	d																				11 14	
Pontefract Monkhill	d																				11 34	
Sheffield	d		09 38					11a21		11a54							10 37			12a21		
Hull	d														10 33							
Selby	a														11 07							
Doncaster	d			10 47		10 57			11 19						11 24			11 47	11 55		12 04	12 19
Retford	d														11 39							
Lincoln	d															11 27						
Newark North Gate	a					11 19										11 51			12 18			
	d					11 21										11 56			12 19			
Grantham	a		11 07	11 17											11 59	12 07	12 10	12 17				
	d		11 10	11 18											12 00	12 08	12 12	12 18				
Peterborough	a		11 39			11 48			12 07							12 28	12 40		12 46			13 07
Norwich	d		13a13														14a13					
Peterborough	d					11 50			12 10							12 30			12 48			13 10
Stevenage	d			12 03												12 59		13 04				
London Kings Cross ⊖	a			12 30	12 32	12 40			13 01			12 49			13 08	13 23		13 31	13 39		13 44	14 01

A From Redcar Central to Manchester Airport
B From Liverpool Lime Street
C To Manchester Airport
D To Southampton Central
E To Plymouth. 🍴 from Edinburgh
F To Liverpool Lime Street
G To Reading

Table T026-R

Mondays to Fridays

16 December to 15 May

Scotland, North East England, Yorkshire and Humberside - London

Station		XC	TP	GR	GR	TP	TP		EM	GR	GR	XC	GR	XC	TP	TP	TP		GR	TP	TP	HT	GR	EM	GR
		◇1 A ✠	◇1 B ✠	■1 ⊐	■1 ⊐	◇1 C ✠	◇1 D ✠		◇ E	■1 ⊐	■1 ⊐	◇1 F ✠	■1 ⊐	◇1 G ✠	◇1 B ✠	◇1 B ✠	◇1 C ✠		■1 ⊐	◇1 H ✠	◇1 D ✠	◇1 ⊠	■1 ⊐	◇ E	■1 ⊐
Aberdeen	d																		07 52						
Stonehaven	d																		08 10						
Montrose	d																		08 33						
Arbroath	d																		08 49						
Dundee	d																		09 08						
Leuchars 3	d																		09 22						
Kirkcaldy	d																		09 47						
Inverkeithing	a																		10 02						
Inverness	d																								
Perth	d																								
Stirling	a																								
Glasgow Central 15	d	07 48												09 00		09 06									
Motherwell	a	08 03												09 14		09 22									
Haymarket 238	d	08 51												09 54					10 20						
Edinburgh 10 238	a	08 55												10 00					10 25						
	d	09 07		09 30		09 33					10 00			10 10			10 21		10 30						
Dunbar 238	d	09 28																							
Berwick-upon-Tweed	d	09 52		10 12										10 51					11 12						
Alnmouth for Alnwick	d	10 12									11 00														
Morpeth	d					10 48								11 22			11 33								
Newcastle 8	a	10 39		10 55		11 02					11 27			11 36			11 53		11 56						
Sunderland	d																								
Hartlepool	d																			←					
Newcastle 8	d	10 42	10 47	10 58		11 05					11 29	11 35		11 39	11 43		12 06		11 58	12 06					
Chester-le-Street	d														11 52		→								
Durham	d	10 54	10 59			11 17					11 43	11 49		11 53	11 59					12 18					
Darlington 7	a	11 11	11 16	11 26		11 33					12 00	12 06		12 11	12 16				12 26	12 35					
Middlesbrough	d						11 21														12 21				
Eaglescliffe	a																								
Darlington 7	d	11 12	11 17	11 27		11 34					12 02	12 07		12 12	12 17				12 28	12 36					
Northallerton	d		11 28				11 50								12 28						12 50				
Thirsk	d						11 59														12 59				
York 8	a	11 38	11 47	11 54		12 01	12 17				12 29	12 33		12 39	12 47				12 55	13 02	13 17				
Leeds	a	12 09	12 12			12 27	12 42							13 08	13 12					13 27	13 43				
	d																								
Harrogate	d									11 36															
Scarborough	a																								
York	d			11 58	12 02						12 32	12 35							12 57						
Doncaster 7	a				12 24						12 54	12 58													
Skipton	d																								
Keighley	d																								
Bradford Interchange	d																								
Bradford Forster Square	d																								
Shipley	d																								
Halifax	d																								
Brighouse	d																								
Mirfield	d																								
Leeds 10	d	12 11								12 15			12 45	13 11											13 15
Wakefield Westgate 7	d	12 23								12 28			12 58	13 23											13 28
Wakefield Kirkgate 4	d																								
Pontefract Monkhill	d																								
Sheffield 7	d	12a55							11 38			13a21		13a54										12 38	
Hull	d																					12 33			
Selby	a																					13 07			
Doncaster 7	d				12 25					12 47	12 57		13 19									13 25			13 47
Retford 10	d				12 40																	13 39			
Lincoln	d																						13 24		
Newark North Gate 7	a				12 54						13 19												13 48		
	d				12 55						13 21												13 54		
Grantham 7	a				13 06				13 07	13 17												13 59	14 05	14 05	14 17
	d				13 07				13 09	13 18												14 00	14 06	14 11	14 18
Peterborough 8	a				13 28				13 39		13 48		14 08										14 27	14 39	
Norwich	d								15a11															16a15	
Peterborough 8	d				13 29						13 50		14 10										14 29		
Stevenage 4	d				13 59					14 04													14 59		15 04
London Kings Cross 15 ⊖	a			13 49	14 23					14 31	14 39		15 01						14 50			15 09	15 23		15 31

A To Plymouth. ✠ from Edinburgh
B To Manchester Airport
C To Liverpool Lime Street
D From Redcar Central to Manchester Airport
E From Liverpool Lime Street
F To Southampton Central
G To Penzance. ✠ from Edinburgh
H From Edinburgh to Liverpool Lime Street

Table T026-R

Mondays to Fridays

16 December to 15 May

Scotland, North East England, Yorkshire and Humberside - London

Station		GR	XC		GR	XC	TP	GR	GC	GR	TP	TP	EM		GR	GR	XC	GR	XC	TP	GR	TP	TP		TP
		■1 ⊐	◇1 A ✠		■1 ⊐	■◇1 B ✠	◇1 C ✠	■1 D ⊐	■1 ⊐	■1 ⊐	◇1 E ✠	◇1 F ✠	◇ G		■1 ⊐	■1 ⊐	◇1 H ✠	■1 ⊐	◇1 I ✠	◇1 C ✠	■1 ⊐	◇1 C ✠	◇1 E ✠		◇1 F ✠
Aberdeen	d					08 20															09 52				
Stonehaven	d					08 37															10 10				
Montrose	d					08 59															10 33				
Arbroath	d					09 14															10 49				
Dundee	d					09 33															11 08				
Leuchars 3	d					09 46															11 24				
Kirkcaldy	d					10 18															11 49				
Inverkeithing	a					10 33															12 04				
Inverness	d							07 55																	
Perth	d							09 58																	
Stirling	a							10 30																	
Glasgow Central 15	d																		11 00			11 08			
Motherwell	a																		11 14			11 23			
Haymarket 238	d					10 50		11 17											11 57		12 22				
Edinburgh 10 238	a					10 54		11 21											12 02		12 26				
	d	11 00				11 06		11 30			11 33					12 00			12 08		12 30		12 33		
Dunbar 238	d					11 28																			
Berwick-upon-Tweed	d					11 51													12 50		13 13				
Alnmouth for Alnwick	d					12 12										13 00									
Morpeth	d										12 46								13 21				13 49		
Newcastle 8	a	12 24				12 38		12 53			13 00					13 27			13 35		13 56		14 03		
Sunderland	d								12 30																
Hartlepool	d								12 55																
Newcastle 8	d	12 27	12 35			12 42	12 45	12 56			13 06					13 29	13 35		13 39	13 43	13 59		14 06		
Chester-le-Street	d																			13 51					
Durham	d	12 40	12 48			12 54	12 59				13 18					13 43	13 48		13 53	13 58			14 18		
Darlington 7	a	12 58	13 04			13 11	13 16	13 24			13 35					14 00	14 05		14 10	14 16	14 27		14 35		
Middlesbrough	d											13 21													14 21
Eaglescliffe	a								13 13																
Darlington 7	d	13 00	13 06			13 12	13 17	13 27			13 36					14 02	14 06		14 11	14 17	14 28		14 36		
Northallerton	d	13 11					13 28		13 33			13 50								14 28					14 50
Thirsk	d								13 43			13 59													14 59
York 8	a	13 31	13 33			13 38	13 48	13 54	13 59		14 02	14 17				14 29	14 33		14 38	14 47	14 55		15 02		15 17
Leeds	a					14 07	14 13				14 27	14 42							15 07	15 12			15 27		15 42
	d																								
Harrogate	d														13 36										
Scarborough	a																								
York	d	13 33	13 35					13 58	14 06	14 02						14 32	14 35				14 58				
Doncaster 7	a	13 55	13 58							14 23						14 54	14 58								
Skipton	d																								
Keighley	d																								
Bradford Interchange	d																								
Bradford Forster Square	d																								
Shipley	d																								
Halifax	d																								
Brighouse	d																								
Mirfield	d																								
Leeds 10	d				13 45	14 11									14 15			14 45	15 11						
Wakefield Westgate 7	d				13 58	14 23									14 28			14 58	15 23						
Wakefield Kirkgate 4	d																								
Pontefract Monkhill	d																								
Sheffield 7	d		14a22			14a55							13 37				15a21		15a55						
Hull	d																								
Selby	a																								
Doncaster 7	d	13 56			14 19					14 26					14 47	14 56		15 19							
Retford 10	d									14 41															
Lincoln	d																								
Newark North Gate 7	a	14 19								14 55						15 18									
	d	14 20								14 56						15 20									
Grantham 7	a									15 07			15 07		15 17										
	d									15 08			15 11		15 18										
Peterborough 8	a	14 48			15 08					15 28			15 38			15 48		16 08							
Norwich	d												17a14												
Peterborough 8	d	14 50			15 10					15 30						15 49		16 10							
Stevenage 4	d									15 59					16 04										
London Kings Cross 15 ⊖	a	15 41			16 01			15 50	16 08	16 23					16 33	16 39		17 01			16 50				

A To Reading
B To Penzance. ◇ from Edinburgh ■ to Edinburgh
C To Manchester Airport
D The Highland Chieftain
E To Liverpool Lime Street
F From Redcar Central to Manchester Airport
G From Liverpool Lime Street
H To Guildford
I To Penzance

Table T026-R

Mondays to Fridays

16 December to 15 May

Scotland, North East England, Yorkshire and Humberside - London

Station		GR	EM	GR	GR	XC	HT	GR	XC	TP	TP	GR	TP	GC	GR	EM	GR	XC	TP	GR	GR	XC	TP
			◇ A			◇ B	◇		◇ C	◇ D	◇ E		◇ F			◇ A		◇ B	◇ G			◇ C	◇ D
Aberdeen	d																						
Stonehaven	d																						
Montrose	d																						
Arbroath	d																						
Dundee	d																						
Leuchars	d																						
Kirkcaldy	d																						
Inverkeithing	a																						
Inverness	d																						
Perth	d																						
Stirling	a																						
Glasgow Central	d																					13 00	
Motherwell	a																					13 16	
Haymarket 238	d																					13 55	
Edinburgh 238	a																					13 59	
	d				13 00				13 08		13 19	13 30								14 00		14 09	
Dunbar 238	d								13 30														
Berwick-upon-Tweed	d											14 13										14 50	
Alnmouth for Alnwick	d								14 13											15 00			
Morpeth	d										14 32									15 15			
Newcastle	a				14 23				14 40		14 50	14 56								15 30		15 37	
Sunderland	d																						
Hartlepool	d												←										
Newcastle	d				14 26	14 36			14 42	14 47	15 03	14 59	15 03					15 15		15 32		15 39	15 43
Chester-le-Street	d										→												15 52
Durham	d				14 39	14 48			14 55	14 59			15 15					15 28		15 45		15 51	15 59
Darlington	a				14 57	15 05			15 12	15 16		15 26	15 32					15 44		16 03		16 08	16 16
Middlesbrough	d																		15 21				
Eaglescliffe	a																						
Darlington	d				14 59	15 06			15 13	15 17		15 27	15 33					15 45		16 04		16 09	16 17
Northallerton	d				15 10					15 28									15 50				
Thirsk	d																		15 59				
York	a				15 30	15 33			15 40	15 47		15 54	15 59					16 11	16 17	16 31		16 35	16 48
Leeds	a								16 07	16 12			16 27					16 38	16 42			17 07	17 12
	d																						
Harrogate	d																15 36						
Scarborough	a																						
York	d				15 32	15 36						15 57			16 03					16 34			
Doncaster	a				15 55	15 59									16 25					16 55			
Skipton	d																						
Keighley	d																						
Bradford Interchange	d													14 50									
Bradford Forster Square	d																						
Shipley	d																						
Halifax	d													15 03									
Brighouse	d													15 17									
Mirfield	d													15 24									
Leeds	d			15 15				15 45	16 11								16 15	16 41			16 45	17 11	
Wakefield Westgate	d			15 28				15 58	16 23								16 28	16 53			16 58	17 23	
Wakefield Kirkgate	d													15 39									
Pontefract Monkhill	d													15 55									
Sheffield	d		14 38			16a22			16a54							15 37		17a21				17a54	
Hull	d						15 08																
Selby	a						15 42																
Doncaster	d			15 47	15 56		16 05	16 17						16 22	16 26		16 47			16 57	17 18		
Retford	d						16 19								16 41								
Lincoln	d	15 27																					
Newark North Gate	a	15 51			16 19										16 55					17 19			
	d	15 56			16 20										16 56					17 20			
Grantham	a	16 07	16 08	16 17			16 39								17 07	17 06	17 17						
	d	16 08	16 11	16 18			16 40								17 08	17 11	17 19						
Peterborough	a	16 28	16 39		16 48			17 08							17 28	17 42				17 49	18 07		
Norwich	d		18a13													19a16							
Peterborough	d	16 30			16 49			17 10							17 30					17 50	18 09		
Stevenage	d	16 59		17 04											17 59		18 05						
London Kings Cross	a	17 23		17 31	17 40		17 47	18 01				17 51		18 07	18 25		18 31			18 39	19 01		

A From Liverpool Lime Street
B To Reading
C To Plymouth
D To Manchester Airport
E To Liverpool Lime Street
F From Edinburgh to Liverpool Lime Street
G From Redcar Central to Manchester Airport

Table T026-R

Mondays to Fridays

16 December to 15 May

Scotland, North East England, Yorkshire and Humberside - London

Station		TP	GR	GC	TP	TP	GR	EM	GR	GR	XC	HT	GR	XC	TP	GR	GR	TP	TP	EM	GR	GR	XC
		◇ A			◇ B	◇ C		◇ D			◇ E	◇		◇ F	◇ A			◇ B	◇ C	◇ D			◇ G
Aberdeen	d																						
Stonehaven	d																						
Montrose	d																						
Arbroath	d																						
Dundee	d																						
Leuchars	d																						
Kirkcaldy	d																						
Inverkeithing	a																						
Inverness	d																						
Perth	d																						
Stirling	a																						
Glasgow Central	d	13 08																					
Motherwell	a	13 23																					
Haymarket 238	d																						
Edinburgh 238	a																						
	d		14 30		14 33					15 00				15 08		15 30		15 33				16 00	
Dunbar 238	d													15 29									
Berwick-upon-Tweed	d		15 12													16 12							
Alnmouth for Alnwick	d																						
Morpeth	d				15 47													16 48					
Newcastle	a		15 56		16 02					16 23				16 33		16 56		17 03				17 22	
Sunderland	d			15 30																			
Hartlepool	d			15 54																			
Newcastle	d		15 59		16 06					16 27	16 35			16 39	16 43	16 59		17 06				17 27	17 32
Chester-le-Street	d														16 52								17 41
Durham	d				16 18					16 40	16 48			16 53	16 59			17 18				17 40	17 48
Darlington	a		16 26		16 35					16 57	17 04			17 10	17 15	17 27		17 35				17 57	18 05
Middlesbrough	d					16 21													17 21				
Eaglescliffe	a			16 13																			
Darlington	d		16 28		16 36					16 59	17 06			17 12	17 17	17 28		17 36				17 59	18 06
Northallerton	d			16 33		16 50				17 10					17 28				17 50			18 10	
Thirsk	d			16 43		16 59													17 59				
York	a		16 56	17 00	17 02	17 17				17 30	17 33			17 39	17 47	17 54		18 02	18 17			18 30	18 33
Leeds	a				17 27	17 42								18 07	18 12			18 27	18 42				
	d																						
Harrogate	d																				17 36		
Scarborough	a																						
York	d		16 58	17 06						17 32	17 36					17 58	18 02					18 32	18 36
Doncaster	a									17 54	17 58						18 24					18 54	18 59
Skipton	d																						
Keighley	d																						
Bradford Interchange	d																						
Bradford Forster Square	d																						
Shipley	d																						
Halifax	d																						
Brighouse	d																						
Mirfield	d																						
Leeds	d								17 14				17 45	18 11							18 15		
Wakefield Westgate	d								17 27				17 58	18 23							18 28		
Wakefield Kirkgate	d																						
Pontefract Monkhill	d																						
Sheffield	d							16 37			18a22			18a54						17 43			19a22
Hull	d											17 08											
Selby	a											17 43											
Doncaster	d								17 46	17 56		18 02	18 19				18 25				18 47	18 55	
Retford	d								18 00			18 16					18 40						
Lincoln	d						17 27																
Newark North Gate	a						17 51			18 18							18 54					19 18	
	d						17 54			18 20							18 55					19 19	
Grantham	a						18 05	18 09	18 22			18 36					19 06			19 07	19 17		
	d						18 06	18 11	18 23			18 37					19 08			19 10	19 19		
Peterborough	a						18 27	18 38		18 47			19 08				19 28			19 40		19 47	
Norwich	d							20a19												21a13			
Peterborough	d						18 29			18 49			19 10				19 30					19 50	
Stevenage	d						18 59		19 07								19 59				20 03	20 20	
London Kings Cross	a		18 49	19 07			19 23		19 32	19 40		19 47	20 01			19 55	20 23				20 27	20 46	

A To Manchester Airport
B To Liverpool Lime Street
C From Redcar Central to Manchester Airport
D From Liverpool Lime Street
E To Reading
F To Plymouth
G To Southampton Central

Table T026-R

Mondays to Fridays
16 December to 15 May

Scotland, North East England, Yorkshire and Humberside - London

Station		GR	XC	TP	TP	GR	TP	GC	GR	TP	GR	XC	HT	GR	XC	TP	GR	TP	TP	GR	EM	XC
		■1	◇1	◇1	◇1	■1	◇1	■1	■1	◇1	■1	◇1	◇1	■1	◇1	◇1	■1	◇1	◇1	■1	◇	◇1
			A	B	B		C			D		E			F	G		C	H		I	E
Aberdeen	d																14 52					
Stonehaven	d																15 10					
Montrose	d																15 33					
Arbroath	d																15 49					
Dundee	d																16 08					
Leuchars 3	d																16 22					
Kirkcaldy	d																16 48					
Inverkeithing	a																17 03					
Inverness	d																					
Perth	d																					
Stirling	a																					
Glasgow Central 15	d		15 00		15 08																	
Motherwell	a		15 15		15 23																	
Haymarket 238	d		15 57														17 22					
Edinburgh 10 238	a		16 02														17 26					
	d		16 08			16 30	16 33				17 00				17 07		17 30	17 32				
Dunbar 238	d														17 29		17 52					
Berwick-upon-Tweed	d					17 12									17 52		18 16					
Alnmouth for Alnwick	d		17 07								18 00											
Morpeth	d		17 21				17 48								18 24			18 52				
Newcastle 8	a		17 36			17 55	18 04				18 27				18 38		19 00	19 06				
Sunderland	d							17 30														
Hartlepool	d							17 56														
Newcastle 8	d		17 39	17 43		17 58	18 07				18 29	18 35			18 40	18 43	19 02	19 09				19 35
Chester-le-Street	d			17 52												18 52						
Durham	d		17 54	17 59			18 19				18 42	18 48			18 54	19 00		19 21				19 49
Darlington 7	a		18 11	18 16		18 25	18 36				19 00	19 06			19 11	19 16	19 30					20 06
Middlesbrough	d									18 21									19 21			
Eaglescliffe	a							18 16														
Darlington 7	d		18 12	18 17		18 26	18 37				19 01	19 07			19 12	19 17	19 32					20 07
Northallerton	d			18 28				18 41		18 50						19 28			19 50			
Thirsk	d							18 51		18 59									19 59			
York 8	a		18 39	18 47		18 53	19 03	19 09		19 17	19 28	19 33			19 38	19 47	19 59	20 02	20 17			20 33
Leeds	a		19 07	19 12			19 28			19 42					20 07	20 12		20 27	20 43			
	d																					
Harrogate	d																					
Scarborough	a																					
York	d					18 58		19 12			19 31	19 36					20 01					20 36
Doncaster 7	a										19 52	19 58					20 23					20 59
Skipton	d																					
Keighley	d																					
Bradford Interchange	d																					
Bradford Forster Square	d																					
Shipley	d																					
Halifax	d																					
Brighouse	d																					
Mirfield	d																					
Leeds 10	d	18 45	19 11						19 16					19 45	20 10							
Wakefield Westgate 7	d	18 58	19 23						19 29					19 58	20 23							
Wakefield Kirkgate 4	d																					
Pontefract Monkhill	d																					
Sheffield 7	d		19a55									20a21			20a54						19 37	21a25
Hull	d												19 08									
Selby	a												19 43									
Doncaster 7	d	19 19							19 48		19 54		20 04	20 17			20 27					
Retford 10	d												20 18									
Lincoln	d																			20 25		
Newark North Gate 7	a										20 16									20 49		
	d										20 17									20 51		
Grantham 7	a								20 18				20 39							21 02	21 07	
	d								20 20				20 40							21 04	21 10	
Peterborough 8	a	20 08									20 45			21 05			21 14			21 25	21 37	
Norwich	d																				23a18	
Peterborough 8	d	20 10									20 46			21 07			21 16			21 28		
Stevenage 4	d					20 29			21 06		21 15						21 45			21 59		
London Kings Cross 15 ⊖	a	20 59				20 53		21 07	21 31		21 39		21 50	21 59			22 10			22 25		

A To Bristol Temple Meads
B To Manchester Airport
C To Liverpool Lime Street
D From Redcar Central to Manchester Airport
E To Birmingham New Street
F To Bristol Temple Meads. ⚲ to Leeds
G To Manchester Victoria
H From Redcar Central to Manchester Victoria
I From Liverpool Lime Street

Table T026-R

Mondays to Fridays
16 December to 15 May

Scotland, North East England, Yorkshire and Humberside - London

Station		GR	XC	TP	TP	GR	GR	TP	TP	TP	GR	XC	TP	TP	GR	GR FO	TP	XC	XC	TP
		■1	◇1	◇1	◇1	■1	■1	◇1	◇1	◇1	■1	◇1	◇1	◇1	■1	■1	◇1	◇1	◇1	◇1
			A	B	C			D	C	D			E	D						D
Aberdeen	d														18 18				21 35	
Stonehaven	d														18 36				21 52	
Montrose	d														18 59				22 13	
Arbroath	d														19 15				22 28	
Dundee	d														19 34				22 49	
Leuchars 3	d														19 48				23 02	
Kirkcaldy	d														20 13				23 36	
Inverkeithing	a														20 28				23 50	
Inverness	d																			
Perth	d																			
Stirling	a																			
Glasgow Central 15	d		17 00	17 08								19 00						21 05		
Motherwell	a		17 15	17 24								19 15						21 22		
Haymarket 238	d		17 58									19 55			20 46				00 06	
Edinburgh 10 238	a		18 03									19 59			20 50			22 22	00 10	
	d		18 08		18 11		18 30		19 30		19 36	20 03	20 30		21 00	22 00	22 14			
Dunbar 238	d		18 30				18 54					20 24			21 24	22 22	22 51			
Berwick-upon-Tweed	d		18 54				19 20				20 18	20 48			21 48	22 46	23 15			
Alnmouth for Alnwick	d		19 14				19 43		20 31		20 40	21 09			22 11	23 09	23 35			
Morpeth	d				19 33		20 00		20 45		20 57		21 45		22 28	23 26	00 01			
Newcastle 8	a		19 40		19 47		20 14		20 59		21 12	21 35	21 59		22 42	23 54	00 27			
Sunderland	d																			
Hartlepool	d																			
Newcastle 8	d		19 42		20 06		20 17		21 02		21 15	21 36	22 01		22 45					
Chester-le-Street	d								21 11											
Durham	d		19 55		20 18		20 30		21 18		21 29	21 50	22 14		22 59					
Darlington 7	a		20 11		20 35		20 48		21 35		21 46	22 08	22 30		23 19					
Middlesbrough	d							20 21		21 21				22 21						23 22
Eaglescliffe	a																			
Darlington 7	d		20 13		20 36		20 49		21 36		21 48	22 09	22 32		23 20					
Northallerton	d							20 54		21 50	21 59		22 43	22 50	23s46					23 54
Thirsk	d							21 05		21 59				22 59						00 03
York 8	a		20 40		21 02		21 16	21 25	22 02	22 19	22 20	22 35	23 02	23 19	00 14					00 29
Leeds	a		21 07		21 27				22 26				23 28		00 45					
	d																			
Harrogate	d																			
Scarborough	a																			
York	d						21 19				22 25									
Doncaster 7	a						21 40				22 46									
Skipton	d																			
Keighley	d																			
Bradford Interchange	d																			
Bradford Forster Square	d																			
Shipley	d																			
Halifax	d																			
Brighouse	d																			
Mirfield	d																			
Leeds 10	d	20 45	21 11																	
Wakefield Westgate 7	d	20 58	21 23																	
Wakefield Kirkgate 4	d																			
Pontefract Monkhill	d																			
Sheffield 7	d		21a54																	
Hull	d					20 29														
Selby	a					21 03														
Doncaster 7	d	21 17				21a23	21 42				22 48									
Retford 10	d	21 32									23 02									
Lincoln	d																			
Newark North Gate 7	a						22 04				23 16									
	d						22 05				23 17									
Grantham 7	a	21 54					22 16				23 28									
	d	21 55					22 17				23 29									
Peterborough 8	a	22 15					22 37				23 55									
Norwich	d																			
Peterborough 8	d	22 16					22 39				23 56									
Stevenage 4	d	22 45					23 08				00s37									
London Kings Cross 15 ⊖	a	23 09					23 32				01 13									

A To Birmingham New Street. ⚲ to Leeds
B To Manchester Airport
C To Liverpool Lime Street. ⚲ from York
D From Redcar Central
E To Manchester Airport. ⚲ from York

Table T026-R

Saturdays

21 December to 16 May

Scotland, North East England, Yorkshire and Humberside - London

		TP	TP	XC	TP	GR	EM	GR	GR	GR		GR	TP	TP	GR	HT	GR	GR	GR	TP		TP	XC	GR	GR
		A	B	C	D		E						F	D		G		H		I		J	K		
Aberdeen	d																								
Stonehaven	d																								
Montrose	d																								
Arbroath	d																								
Dundee	d																								
Leuchars	d																								
Kirkcaldy	d																								
Inverkeithing	a																								
Inverness	d																								
Perth	d																								
Stirling	a																								
Glasgow Central	d																								
Motherwell	a																								
Haymarket 238	d			00 06																					
Edinburgh 238	a			00 10																					
	d																								
Dunbar 238	d																								
Berwick-upon-Tweed	d																								
Alnmouth for Alnwick	d																								
Morpeth	d	00 01																							
Newcastle	a	00 27																							
Sunderland	d																								
Hartlepool	d																								
Newcastle	d				00 08					04 44			05 06		05 26				05 59	06 06			06 23		
Chester-le-Street	d																								
Durham	d				00 21					04 59			05 18		05 39				06 12	06 18			06 36		
Darlington	a				00 38					05 15			05 35		05 56				06 30	06 35			06 52		
Middlesbrough	d													05 19								06 21			
Eaglescliffe	a																								
Darlington	d				00 40					05 17			05 36		05 58				06 32	06 36			06 54		
Northallerton	d									05 28				05 50	06 09							06 50			
Thirsk	d		00 03											05 58								06 59			
York	a		00 29		01 36					05 57			06 02	06 16	06 29				06 59	07 02		07 17	07 21		
Leeds	a				02 18								06 28	06 42						07 28		07 42			
	d																								
Harrogate	d																								
Scarborough	a																								
York	d					04 40				05 59					06 31				07 01				07 28		
Doncaster	a					05 04				06 21					06 53								07 49		
Skipton	d																								
Keighley	d																								
Bradford Interchange	d																								
Bradford Forster Square	d																	06 30							
Shipley	d																	06u37							
Halifax	d																								
Brighouse	d																								
Mirfield	d																								
Leeds	d							05 05	05 30			06 05					06 40	07 00							07 15
Wakefield Westgate	d							05 18	05 43			06 18					06 53	07 13							07 28
Wakefield Kirkgate	d																								
Pontefract Monkhill	d																								
Sheffield	d																						08a15		
Hull	d															06 17									
Selby	a															06 51									
Doncaster	d					05 07		05 37	06 03	06 22		06 37			06 54	07 10	07 14								07 47
Retford	d							05 51				06 51													
Lincoln	d																							07 30	
Newark North Gate	a					05 34		06 05	06 26	06 45		07 05					07 36							07 56	
	d					05 35		06 06	06 27	06 46		07 06					07 37							07 57	
Grantham	a					05 46		06 17	06 39	06 57		07 17			07 25	07 39									08 17
	d					05 48	05 51	06 18	06 40	06 58		07 18			07 26	07 40									08 18
Peterborough	a					06 08	06 25	06 38	07 00	07 18		07 39			07 46				08 10					08 27	
Norwich	d																								
Peterborough	d					06 10		06 39	07 03	07 19		07 40			07 49				08 20					08 29	
Stevenage	d																							08 59	09 04
London Kings Cross	a					07 00		07 30	07 53	08 10		08 30			08 39	08 47	08 53	09 01	09 10					09 23	09 31

A From Edinburgh
B From Redcar Central
C From Aberdeen
D To Manchester Airport
E From Nottingham to Spalding
F To Liverpool Lime Street. ⚒ from York
G From Beverley
H West Riding Limited
I To Liverpool Lime Street
J From Redcar Central to Manchester Airport
K To Reading

NRT DECEMBER 19 EDITION

Table T026-R

Saturdays

21 December to 16 May

Scotland, North East England, Yorkshire and Humberside - London

		GR	EM	GR	GR	XC		TP	GR	TP	GC	TP	GC	EM	GR	GR		XC	GR	XC	TP	GR	TP	TP	HT
			A	B		C		D		E		F		A				G		H	D		E	F	
Aberdeen	d																								
Stonehaven	d																								
Montrose	d																								
Arbroath	d																								
Dundee	d																								
Leuchars	d																								
Kirkcaldy	d																								
Inverkeithing	a																								
Inverness	d																								
Perth	d																								
Stirling	a																								
Glasgow Central	d																								
Motherwell	a																								
Haymarket 238	d																								
Edinburgh 238	a																								
	d									05 14						05 48				06 06		06 24	06 27		
Dunbar 238	d									05 45						06 10									
Berwick-upon-Tweed	d															06 34				06 49		07 08			
Alnmouth for Alnwick	d															06 56				07 10					
Morpeth	d									06 43						07 12							07 44		
Newcastle	a									06 57						07 26				07 37		07 55	08 02		
Sunderland	d												06 43												
Hartlepool	d												07 08												
Newcastle	d	06 30				06 40		06 41	06 55	07 09						07 29		07 35		07 39	07 43	07 58	08 06		
Chester-le-Street	d							06 52													07 52				
Durham	d	06 43				06 52		06 59	07 08	07 21						07 43		07 47		07 53	07 59		08 18		
Darlington	a	07 01				07 09		07 16	07 25							08 00		08 05		08 10	08 16	08 26	08 35		
Middlesbrough	d											07 20												08 20	
Eaglescliffe	a												07 34												
Darlington	d	07 02				07 10		07 17	07 27							08 02		08 06		08 11	08 17	08 28	08 36		
Northallerton	d	07 14						07 28				07 50	07 55								08 28			08 50	
Thirsk	d											07 59	08 04											08 59	
York	a	07 34				07 37		07 47	07 54	08 02		08 17	08 21			08 29		08 32		08 41	08 47	08 54	09 02	09 17	
Leeds	a					08 07		08 12		08 28		08 42								09 08	09 12		09 27	09 43	
	d																								
Harrogate	d														07 35										
Scarborough	a																								
York	d	07 38							07 57				08 22			08 31		08 35				08 57			
Doncaster	a															08 54		08 56							
Skipton	d				06 55																				
Keighley	d				07u09																				
Bradford Interchange	d										06 55														
Bradford Forster Square	d																								
Shipley	d				07u19																				
Halifax	d										07 10														
Brighouse	d										07 20														
Mirfield	d										07 27														
Leeds	d				07 40	08 11									08 15				08 45	09 11					
Wakefield Westgate	d					08 23									08 30				08 59	09 23					
Wakefield Kirkgate	d										07 40														
Pontefract Monkhill	d										07 59														
Sheffield	d					08a54												09a22		09a54					
Hull	d			06 58																					08 24
Selby	a			07 32																					08 58
Doncaster	d			07 58	08 10						08 31				08 49	08 56			09 19						09 25
Retford	d								08 29																09 41
Lincoln	d																								
Newark North Gate	a			08 24	08 32											09 19									
	d			08 25	08 33											09 20									
Grantham	a			08 36											09 19										10 01
	d		08 20	08 38										09 10	09 21										10 02
Peterborough	a	08 42	08 55	08 58	09 01									09 36		09 48			10 08						
Norwich	d		10a43											11a15											
Peterborough	d	08 50		09 00	09 03											09 50			10 09						
Stevenage	d														10 06										
London Kings Cross	a	09 39		09 49	09 55				10 01		10 11		10 18		10 31	10 39			10 59			10 49			11 08

A From Nottingham
B The Hull Executive
C To Plymouth. ⚒ from Leeds
D To Manchester Airport
E To Liverpool Lime Street
F From Redcar Central to Manchester Airport
G To Southampton Central
H To Plymouth

Table T026-R

Saturdays

21 December to 16 May

Scotland, North East England, Yorkshire and Humberside - London

Station		EM		GR	GR	GR	EM	XC	XC	TP	GR	GC		GC	GR	GR	TP	TP	GR	TP	XC	GR		XC	TP
		A					A	B	C	D							E	F		D	G			C	D
Aberdeen	d																								
Stonehaven	d																								
Montrose	d																								
Arbroath	d																								
Dundee	d																							06 33	
Leuchars	d																							06 46	
Kirkcaldy	d																							07 22	
Inverkeithing	a																							07 37	
Inverness	d																								
Perth	d																								
Stirling	a																								
Glasgow Central	d								06 01										06 48	07 10					
Motherwell	a								06 15										07 03	07 25					
Haymarket 238	d								06 57										07 48					07 59	
Edinburgh 238	a								07 01										07 52					08 03	
	d				06 55			07 00	07 07		07 30								08 00					08 08	08 10
Dunbar 238	d								07 29																
Berwick-upon-Tweed	d							07 43			08 12													08 51	
Alnmouth for Alnwick	d							08 03											09 01					09 12	
Morpeth	d							08 18																	09 29
Newcastle	a				08 24			08 32	08 38		08 55								09 27					09 39	09 45
Sunderland	d													08 28											
Hartlepool	d													08 53											
Newcastle	d				08 27			08 35	08 40	08 43	08 58						09 06		09 30		09 35			09 41	09 47
Chester-le-Street	d									08 52															
Durham	d				08 40			08 48	08 54	08 59							09 18		09 43		09 49			09 54	09 59
Darlington	a				08 57			09 04	09 10	09 16	09 26						09 35		10 01		10 06			10 11	10 16
Middlesbrough	d																	09 21							
Eaglescliffe	a													09 11											
Darlington	d				08 59			09 06	09 12	09 17	09 27						09 36		10 02		10 07			10 12	10 17
Northallerton	d				09 10									09 33				09 50							10 28
Thirsk	d													09 42				09 59							
York	a				09 30			09 33	09 39	09 48	09 54			09 59			10 02	10 17	10 29		10 33			10 39	10 47
Leeds	a								10 07	10 12							10 27	10 42						11 07	11 12
	d																								
Harrogate	d															09 36									
Scarborough	a																								
York	d				09 32			09 37			09 57			10 09	10 04				10 32		10 35				
Doncaster	a				09 54			09 59							10 27				10 53		10 58				
Skipton	d																								
Keighley	d																								
Bradford Interchange	d											08 44													
Bradford Forster Square	d																								
Shipley	d																								
Halifax	d											08 57													
Brighouse	d											09 13													
Mirfield	d											09 20													
Leeds	d			09 15		09 45			10 11							10 15						10 45		11 11	
Wakefield Westgate	d			09 29		09 58			10 23							10 28						10 58		11 23	
Wakefield Kirkgate	d											09 40													
Pontefract Monkhill	d											09 57													
Sheffield	d	08 37					09 37	10a22	10a54												11a21			11a54	
Hull	d																								
Selby	a																								
Doncaster	d			09 48	09 55	10 18						10 25			10 31	10 47			10 57			11 19			
Retford	d														10 47										
Lincoln	d																								
Newark North Gate	a				10 18										11 01				11 20						
	d				10 19										11 02				11 21						
Grantham	a	10 06		10 19			11 05								11 13	11 17									
	d	10 11		10 20			11 05								11 14	11 18									
Peterborough	a	10 38			10 47	11 07	11 36								11 34				11 49			12 09			
Norwich	d	12a13					13a13																		
Peterborough	d				10 49	11 10									11 35				11 51			12 11			
Stevenage	d			11 05											12 04	12 08									
London Kings Cross	a			11 31	11 39	12 03					11 48	11 58		12 08	12 31	12 34			12 46			13 00			

A From Liverpool Lime Street
B To Reading
C To Plymouth. from Edinburgh
D To Manchester Airport
E To Liverpool Lime Street
F From Redcar Central to Manchester Airport
G To Southampton Central

Table T026-R

Saturdays

21 December to 16 May

Scotland, North East England, Yorkshire and Humberside - London

Station		GR	TP	TP	HT	GR	EM	GR		GR	XC	GC	GR	XC	TP	TP	GR	GR		TP	TP	EM	GR	GR	XC
			A	B			C				D			E	A	F				A	B	C			G
Aberdeen	d																								
Stonehaven	d																								
Montrose	d																								
Arbroath	d																								
Dundee	d																								
Leuchars	d																								
Kirkcaldy	d																								
Inverkeithing	a																								
Inverness	d																								
Perth	d																								
Stirling	a																								
Glasgow Central	d													07 48	08 05										
Motherwell	a													08 03	08 26										
Haymarket 238	d													08 52											
Edinburgh 238	a													08 56											
	d	08 30								09 00				09 08			09 30			09 33				10 00	
Dunbar 238	d													09 29											
Berwick-upon-Tweed	d	09 12												09 53			10 12								
Alnmouth for Alnwick	d																							11 00	
Morpeth	d																			10 48					
Newcastle	a	09 56								10 24				10 36			10 56			11 02				11 27	
Sunderland	d																								
Hartlepool	d																								
Newcastle	d	09 59	10 06							10 26	10 35			10 41		10 47	10 58			11 05				11 29	11 35
Chester-le-Street	d																								
Durham	d		10 18							10 39	10 47			10 54		10 59				11 17				11 43	11 49
Darlington	a	10 27	10 35							10 57	11 04			11 10		11 16	11 26			11 33				12 00	12 06
Middlesbrough	d			10 21																	11 21				
Eaglescliffe	a																								
Darlington	d	10 29	10 36							10 59	11 06			11 11		11 17	11 28			11 34				12 02	12 07
Northallerton	d			10 50						11 10						11 28					11 50				
Thirsk	d			10 59																	11 59				
York	a	10 56	11 02	11 17						11 30	11 33			11 37		11 47	11 55			12 01	12 17			12 29	12 33
Leeds	a		11 27	11 42										12 07		12 12				12 27	12 42				
	d																								
Harrogate	d																						11 36		
Scarborough	a																								
York	d	10 59								11 32	11 36						11 58	12 03						12 31	12 35
Doncaster	a									11 54	11 58							12 25						12 53	12 58
Skipton	d																								
Keighley	d																								
Bradford Interchange	d											10 22													
Bradford Forster Square	d																								
Shipley	d																								
Halifax	d											10 36													
Brighouse	d											10 47													
Mirfield	d											10 55													
Leeds	d							11 15					11 45	12 11									12 15		
Wakefield Westgate	d							11 29					11 58	12 23									12 28		
Wakefield Kirkgate	d											11 14													
Pontefract Monkhill	d											11 32													
Sheffield	d						10 37				12a21			12a55								11 38			13a21
Hull	d				10 33																				
Selby	a				11 07																				
Doncaster	d				11 25			11 48		11 55		12 04	12 18					12 26					12 47	12 55	
Retford	d				11 39													12 41							
Lincoln	d					11 27																			
Newark North Gate	a					11 51				12 18								12 55						13 17	
	d					11 56				12 19								12 56						13 19	
Grantham	a				12 00	12 07	12 05	12 18										13 07				13 06	13 17		
	d				12 01	12 08	12 13	12 19										13 08				13 11	13 18		
Peterborough	a					12 28	12 40			12 46			13 07					13 28				13 38		13 46	
Norwich	d						14a12															15a13			
Peterborough	d					12 30				12 48			13 10					13 30						13 50	
Stevenage	d					12 59		13 04										13 59					14 04		
London Kings Cross	a	12 52			13 08	13 24		13 31		13 39		13 44	14 01				13 49	14 23					14 31	14 39	

A To Liverpool Lime Street
B From Redcar Central to Manchester Airport
C From Liverpool Lime Street
D To Reading
E To Plymouth. from Edinburgh
F To Manchester Airport
G To Southampton Central

Table T026-R

Saturdays

21 December to 16 May

Scotland, North East England, Yorkshire and Humberside - London

		GR	XC	TP	TP	TP	GR	TP	TP	GR	EM	GR	GR	XC	GR	XC	GC	TP	GR	TP	TP	HT
		■1	◇1	◇1	◇1	◇1	■1	◇1	◇1	■1	◇	■1	■1	◇1	■1	◇1	■1	◇1	■1	◇1	◇1	◇1
			A	B	B	C		D	E		F			G		A		B	H	C	E	
Aberdeen	d						07 52									08 20						
Stonehaven	d						08 10									08 37						
Montrose	d						08 33									08 59						
Arbroath	d						08 49									09 14						
Dundee	d						09 08									09 33						
Leuchars 3	d						09 22									09 46						
Kirkcaldy	d						09 47									10 18						
Inverkeithing	a						10 02									10 33						
Inverness	d																		07 55			
Perth	d																		09 58			
Stirling	a																		10 30			
Glasgow Central 15	d		09 00		09 07																	
Motherwell	a		09 14		09 22																	
Haymarket 238	d		09 58				10 21									10 50			11 14			
Edinburgh 10 238	a		10 03				10 26									10 54			11 19			
	d		10 06			10 16	10 30						11 00			11 08			11 30	11 33		
Dunbar 238	d															11 29						
Berwick-upon-Tweed	d		10 48				11 12									11 53						
Alnmouth for Alnwick	d							←								12 13						
Morpeth	d		11 22			11 48		11 48												12 46		
Newcastle 8	a		11 36			→	11 56	12 02					12 23			12 40			12 53	13 00		
Sunderland	d																12 18					
Hartlepool	d																12 42					
Newcastle 8	d		11 39	11 43			11 58	12 06					12 27	12 35		12 42		12 45	12 56	13 06		
Chester-le-Street	d			11 52																		
Durham	d		11 54	11 59				12 18					12 40	12 48		12 54		12 59		13 18		
Darlington 7	a		12 11	12 16			12 26	12 35					12 58	13 04		13 11		13 16	13 24	13 35		
Middlesbrough	d								12 21												13 21	
Eaglescliffe	a																13 01					
Darlington 7	d		12 12	12 17			12 28	12 36					13 00	13 06		13 12		13 17	13 25	13 36		
Northallerton	d			12 28					12 50				13 11				13 20	13 28			13 50	
Thirsk	d								12 59								13 29				13 59	
York 8	a		12 39	12 47			12 55	13 02	13 17				13 31	13 34		13 41	13 46	13 48	13 55	14 02	14 17	
Leeds	a		13 08	13 12				13 27	13 43							14 07		14 13		14 27	14 42	
	d																					
Harrogate	d																					
Scarborough	a																					
York	d						12 57						13 33	13 35			13 51		13 57			
Doncaster 7	a												13 55	13 58								
Skipton	d																					
Keighley	d																					
Bradford Interchange	d																					
Bradford Forster Square	d																					
Shipley	d																					
Halifax	d																					
Brighouse	d																					
Mirfield	d																					
Leeds 10	d	12 45	13 11									13 15			13 45	14 11						
Wakefield Westgate 7	d	12 58	13 23									13 28			13 58	14 23						
Wakefield Kirkgate 4	d																					
Pontefract Monkhill	d																					
Sheffield 7	d		13a54								12 38			14a22		14a54						
Hull	d																					13 31
Selby	a																					14 05
Doncaster 7	d	13 18										13 47	13 56		14 18							14 25
Retford 10	d																					14 39
Lincoln	d									13 24												
Newark North Gate 7	a									13 48			14 19									
	d									13 54			14 20									
Grantham 7	a									14 05	14 05	14 17										15 00
	d									14 06	14 11	14 18										15 01
Peterborough 8	a	14 07								14 27	14 40		14 47		15 07							
Norwich	d										16a12											
Peterborough 8	d	14 10								14 29			14 49		15 10							
Stevenage 4	d									14 59		15 04										
London Kings Cross 15 ⊖	a	15 01					14 51			15 23		15 31	15 39		16 00		15 44		15 50			16 09

A To Penzance
B To Manchester Airport
C To Liverpool Lime Street
D From Edinburgh to Liverpool Lime Street
E From Redcar Central to Manchester Airport
F From Liverpool Lime Street
G To Reading
H The Highland Chieftain

NRT DECEMBER 19 EDITION

Table T026-R

Saturdays

21 December to 16 May

Scotland, North East England, Yorkshire and Humberside - London

		EM	GR	GR	GR	XC	GR	XC	TP	GR	TP	TP	TP	GR	EM	GR	GR	XC	GR	XC	TP	TP	GR
		◇	■1	■1	■1	◇1	■1	◇1	◇1	■1	◇1	◇1	◇1	■1	◇	■1	■1	◇1	■1	◇1	◇1	◇1	■1
		A				B		C	D		D	E	F		A			G		H	D	E	
Aberdeen	d									09 52													
Stonehaven	d									10 10													
Montrose	d									10 33													
Arbroath	d									10 49													
Dundee	d									11 08													
Leuchars 3	d									11 24													
Kirkcaldy	d									11 49													
Inverkeithing	a									12 04													
Inverness	d																						
Perth	d																						
Stirling	a																						
Glasgow Central 15	d							11 00			11 08												
Motherwell	a							11 14			11 23												
Haymarket 238	d							11 54		12 22													
Edinburgh 10 238	a							12 01		12 26													
	d				12 00			12 06		12 30		12 33					13 00			13 09		13 19	13 30
Dunbar 238	d																			13 30			
Berwick-upon-Tweed	d							12 47		13 13													14 13
Alnmouth for Alnwick	d				13 00															14 12			
Morpeth	d							13 20				13 49										14 37	
Newcastle 8	a				13 27			13 34		13 56		14 03					14 23			14 39		14 52	14 56
Sunderland	d																						
Hartlepool	d																						
Newcastle 8	d				13 29	13 35		13 39	13 43	13 59		14 06					14 26	14 36		14 42	14 47	15 03	14 59
Chester-le-Street	d								13 51													→	
Durham	d				13 43	13 48		13 54	13 58			14 18					14 39	14 48		14 54	14 59		
Darlington 7	a				14 00	14 05		14 10	14 16	14 27		14 35					14 57	15 05		15 11	15 16		15 26
Middlesbrough	d												14 21										
Eaglescliffe	a																						
Darlington 7	d				14 02	14 06		14 11	14 17	14 28		14 36					14 59	15 06		15 12	15 17		15 27
Northallerton	d								14 28				14 50				15 10				15 28		
Thirsk	d												14 59										
York 8	a				14 29	14 33		14 38	14 47	14 55		15 02	15 17				15 30	15 33		15 38	15 47		15 54
Leeds	a							15 07	15 12			15 27	15 42							16 07	16 12		
	d																						
Harrogate	d			13 36																			
Scarborough	a																						
York	d		14 05		14 32	14 35				14 58							15 32	15 36					15 57
Doncaster 7	a		14 28		14 53	14 58											15 54	15 59					
Skipton	d																						
Keighley	d																						
Bradford Interchange	d																						
Bradford Forster Square	d																						
Shipley	d																						
Halifax	d																						
Brighouse	d																						
Mirfield	d																						
Leeds 10	d			14 15			14 45	15 11								15 15			15 45	16 11			
Wakefield Westgate 7	d			14 28			14 58	15 23								15 28			15 58	16 23			
Wakefield Kirkgate 4	d																						
Pontefract Monkhill	d																						
Sheffield 7	d	13 38				15a21		15a55							14 38			16a22		16a54			
Hull	d																						
Selby	a																						
Doncaster 7	d		14 30	14 47	14 55		15 19									15 47	15 55		16 19				
Retford 10	d		14 46																				
Lincoln	d													15 24									
Newark North Gate 7	a		15 00		15 17									15 48			16 18						
	d		15 01		15 18									15 54			16 19						
Grantham 7	a	15 05	15 12	15 17										16 05	16 06	16 18							
	d	15 06	15 13	15 18										16 06	16 08	16 19							
Peterborough 8	a	15 41	15 33		15 46		16 10							16 26	16 39		16 47		17 08				
Norwich	d	17a12													18a14								
Peterborough 8	d		15 34		15 51		16 12							16 29			16 50		17 10				
Stevenage 4	d		16 03	16 08										16 59		17 04							
London Kings Cross 15 ⊖	a		16 31	16 34	16 46		17 01			16 52				17 23		17 31	17 39		18 01				17 49

A From Liverpool Lime Street
B To Guildford
C To Penzance
D To Manchester Airport
E To Liverpool Lime Street
F From Redcar Central to Manchester Airport
G To Reading
H To Plymouth

Table T026-R

Saturdays

21 December to 16 May

Scotland, North East England, Yorkshire and Humberside - London

		TP	HT	EM	GR	GR	XC	TP	GR	GC	GR	XC	TP	TP	GR	GC	TP	TP	GR	EM	GR	GR	XC
		◇■	◇■	◇	■	■	◇■	◇■	■	■	■	◇■	◇■	◇■	■	■	◇■	◇■	■	◇	■	■	◇■
		A		B			C	D				E	F	F			G	D		B			C
		✕	⊠		R	R	✕	✕	R	R	R	✕	✕	✕	R	R	✕	✕	R		R	R	✕
Aberdeen	d																						
Stonehaven	d																						
Montrose	d																						
Arbroath	d																						
Dundee	d																						
Leuchars 3	d																						
Kirkcaldy	d																						
Inverkeithing	a																						
Inverness	d																						
Perth	d																						
Stirling	a																						
Glasgow Central 15	d											13 00		13 08									
Motherwell	a											13 16		13 23									
Haymarket 238	d											13 58											
Edinburgh 10 238	a											14 03											
	d								14 00			14 07			14 30		14 33					15 00	
Dunbar 238	d																						
Berwick-upon-Tweed	d											14 48			15 11								
Alnmouth for Alnwick	d								15 00														
Morpeth	d								15 15			15 22					15 47						
Newcastle 8	a								15 30			15 36			15 55		16 01					16 23	
Sunderland	d															15 29							
Hartlepool	d	←														15 53							
Newcastle 8	d	15 03					15 11		15 32			15 39	15 43		15 57		16 06					16 27	16 35
Chester-le-Street	d												15 52										
Durham	d	15 15					15 24		15 45			15 51	15 59				16 18					16 40	16 48
Darlington 7	a	15 32					15 40		16 03			16 08	16 16		16 24		16 35					16 57	17 04
Middlesbrough	d							15 21										16 21					
Eaglescliffe	a															16 12							
Darlington 7	d	15 33					15 41		16 04			16 09	16 17		16 26		16 36					16 59	17 06
Northallerton	d							15 50								16 33		16 50				17 10	
Thirsk	d							15 59								16 43		16 59					
York 8	a	15 59					16 11	16 17	16 31			16 39	16 48		16 54	16 59	17 02	17 17				17 30	17 33
Leeds	a	16 27					16 38	16 42				17 07	17 12				17 27	17 42					
	d																						
Harrogate	d					15 36																	
Scarborough	a																						
York	d				16 02				16 34						16 58	17 06						17 32	17 36
Doncaster 7	a				16 27				16 55													17 54	17 58
Skipton	d																						
Keighley	d																						
Bradford Interchange	d									15 22													
Bradford Forster Square	d																						
Shipley	d																						
Halifax	d									15 35													
Brighouse	d									15 48													
Mirfield	d									15 56													
Leeds 10	d					16 15	16 41				16 45	17 11									17 14		
Wakefield Westgate 7	d					16 28	16 53				16 58	17 23									17 27		
Wakefield Kirkgate 4	d									16 14													
Pontefract Monkhill	d									16 33													
Sheffield 7	d			15 38			17a21					17a54								16 38			18a22
Hull	d		15 31																				
Selby	a		16 05																				
Doncaster 7	d		16 24		16 28	16 49			16 57	17 08	17 20										17 46	17 55	
Retford 10	d		16 38		16 43																18 00		
Lincoln	d																		17 27				
Newark North Gate 7	a				16 57				17 19										17 51			18 18	
	d				16 58				17 21										17 54			18 19	
Grantham 7	a		16 59	17 04	17 09	17 19													18 05	18 09	18 22		
	d		17 00	17 06	17 10	17 21													18 06	18 11	18 23		
Peterborough 8	a			17 36	17 32				17 48		18 09								18 27	18 38		18 48	
Norwich	d			19a13																20a16			
Peterborough 8	d				17 34				17 51		18 10								18 29			18 51	
Stevenage 4	d				18 03	18 08													18 59		19 09		
London Kings Cross 15 ⊖	a		18 09		18 29	18 32			18 46	18 47	19 01				18 52	19 09			19 23		19 33	19 46	

A From Edinburgh to Liverpool Lime Street
B From Liverpool Lime Street
C To Reading
D From Redcar Central to Manchester Airport
E To Plymouth
F To Manchester Airport
G To Liverpool Lime Street

Table T026-R

Saturdays

21 December to 16 May

Scotland, North East England, Yorkshire and Humberside - London

		GR	XC	TP	GR	GR	TP	TP	EM	GR	GR	XC	GR	XC	TP	TP	TP	GR	GC	TP	TP	HT
		■	◇■	◇■	■	■	◇■	◇■	◇	■	■	◇■	■	◇■	◇■	◇■	◇■	■	■	◇■	◇■	◇■
			A	B			C	D	E			F		G	B	B	C			H	D	
		R	✕	✕	R	R	✕	✕		R	R	✕	R	✕	✕	✕	✕	R	R	✕		⊠
Aberdeen	d																					
Stonehaven	d																					
Montrose	d																					
Arbroath	d																					
Dundee	d																					
Leuchars 3	d																					
Kirkcaldy	d																					
Inverkeithing	a																					
Inverness	d																					
Perth	d																					
Stirling	a																					
Glasgow Central 15	d													15 00		15 09						
Motherwell	a													15 15		15 23						
Haymarket 238	d													15 57								
Edinburgh 10 238	a													16 03								
	d		15 08		15 30		15 33				16 00			16 06			16 21	16 30				
Dunbar 238	d		15 29																			
Berwick-upon-Tweed	d				16 12													17 12				
Alnmouth for Alnwick	d													17 06						←		
Morpeth	d						16 48							17 20			17 48			17 48		
Newcastle 8	a		16 33		16 56		17 03				17 23			17 34			→	17 55		18 04		
Sunderland	d																		17 29			
Hartlepool	d																		17 54			
Newcastle 8	d		16 39	16 43	16 59		17 06				17 27	17 32		17 39	17 43			17 58		18 07		
Chester-le-Street	d			16 52								17 41			17 52							
Durham	d		16 53	16 59			17 18				17 40	17 48		17 54	17 59					18 19		
Darlington 7	a		17 11	17 15	17 26		17 35				17 57	18 05		18 11	18 16			18 25		18 36		
Middlesbrough	d							17 21													18 21	
Eaglescliffe	a																		18 13			
Darlington 7	d		17 12	17 17	17 27		17 36				17 59	18 06		18 12	18 17			18 26		18 37		
Northallerton	d			17 28				17 50			18 10				18 28				18 32		18 50	
Thirsk	d							17 59											18 43		18 59	
York 8	a		17 39	17 47	17 54		18 02	18 17			18 30	18 33		18 39	18 47			18 54	18 59	19 03	19 17	
Leeds	a		18 07	18 12			18 27	18 42						19 07	19 12					19 28	19 42	
	d																					
Harrogate	d									17 36												
Scarborough	a																					
York	d				17 58	18 02					18 32	18 36						18 57	19 02			
Doncaster 7	a					18 23					18 54	18 59										
Skipton	d																					
Keighley	d																					
Bradford Interchange	d																					
Bradford Forster Square	d																					
Shipley	d																					
Halifax	d																					
Brighouse	d																					
Mirfield	d																					
Leeds 10	d	17 45	18 11							18 15			18 45	19 11								
Wakefield Westgate 7	d	17 58	18 23							18 28			18 58	19 23								
Wakefield Kirkgate 4	d																					
Pontefract Monkhill	d																					
Sheffield 7	d		18a54						17 41			19a22		19a54								
Hull	d																					18 36
Selby	a																					19 10
Doncaster 7	d	18 19				18 25				18 47	18 55		19 23									19 28
Retford 10	d					18 39																19 42
Lincoln	d																					
Newark North Gate 7	a					18 53					19 18											
	d					18 55					19 19											
Grantham 7	a					19 06			19 08	19 18												20 03
	d					19 07			19 10	19 19												20 04
Peterborough 8	a	19 08				19 27			19 39		19 47		20 13									
Norwich	d								21a13													
Peterborough 8	d	19 10				19 30					19 50		20 15									
Stevenage 4	d					19 59				20 05	20 20							20 29				
London Kings Cross 15 ⊖	a	20 01			19 49	20 23				20 31	20 46		21 09					20 53	20 59			21 15

A To Plymouth
B To Manchester Airport
C To Liverpool Lime Street
D From Redcar Central to Manchester Airport
E From Liverpool Lime Street
F To Southampton Central
G To Bristol Temple Meads
H From Edinburgh to Liverpool Lime Street

Table T026-R

Saturdays
21 December to 16 May

Scotland, North East England, Yorkshire and Humberside - London

Station		GR	GR	XC	GR	XC	TP	GR	TP	TP	GR	EM	GR	XC	XC	TP	GR	TP	TP	GR	TP	XC	GR
				A		B	C		D	E		F		A	B	G		H	I		H		
Aberdeen	d							14 52															
Stonehaven	d							15 10															
Montrose	d							15 33															
Arbroath	d							15 49															
Dundee	d							16 08															
Leuchars	d							16 23															
Kirkcaldy	d							16 48															
Inverkeithing	a							17 03															
Inverness	d																						
Perth	d																						
Stirling	a																						
Glasgow Central	d														17 00	17 08						19 00	
Motherwell	a														17 14	17 23						19 14	
Haymarket 238	d							17 21							17 58							19 53	
Edinburgh 238	a							17 26							18 03							20 00	
	d		17 00			17 08		17 30	17 32						18 07		18 30	18 33		19 00	19 30		20 00
Dunbar 238	d					17 31		17 52							18 30					19 21			20 22
Berwick-upon-Tweed	d					17 54		18 16							18 53		19 12			19 46			20 47
Alnmouth for Alnwick	d		18 00												19 14					20 08	20 31		21 09
Morpeth	d								18 52									19 47		20 25	20 45		21 26
Newcastle	a		18 26			18 37		19 00	19 06						19 40		19 57	20 01		20 41	20 59		21 43
Sunderland	d																						
Hartlepool	d																						
Newcastle	d		18 29	18 36		18 40	18 43	19 02	19 09					19 35	19 45			20 06		20 43	21 02		
Chester-le-Street	d						18 52														21 11		
Durham	d		18 42	18 49		18 54	19 00		19 21					19 49	19 57			20 18		20 58	21 18		
Darlington	a		19 00	19 06		19 11	19 16	19 30						20 06	20 14			20 35		21 15	21 35		
Middlesbrough	d									19 21									20 21				
Eaglescliffe	a																						
Darlington	d		19 01	19 07		19 12	19 17	19 32						20 07	20 15			20 36		21 18	21 36		
Northallerton	d						19 28			19 50									20 54	21 31			
Thirsk	d									19 59									21 05				
York	a		19 28	19 33		19 38	19 47	19 59	20 02	20 17				20 33	20 41			21 02	21 25	21 55	22 02		
Leeds	a					20 07	20 12		20 27	20 43					21 08			21 27			22 27		
	d																						
Harrogate	d																						
Scarborough	a																						
York	d		19 31	19 36				20 01						20 35						21 57			
Doncaster	a		19 52	19 58				20 23						20 57						22 21			
Skipton	d																						
Keighley	d																						
Bradford Interchange	d																						
Bradford Forster Square	d																						
Shipley	d																						
Halifax	d																						
Brighouse	d																						
Mirfield	d																						
Leeds	d	19 16			19 45	20 10							20 15		21 11								
Wakefield Westgate	d	19 29			19 58	20 23							20 28		21 23								
Wakefield Kirkgate	d																						
Pontefract Monkhill	d																						
Sheffield	d			20a21		20a54						19 37		21a21	21a53								
Hull	d																						
Selby	a																						
Doncaster	d	19 48	19 54		20 17			20 25					20 48										
Retford	d												21 02										
Lincoln	d										20 25												
Newark North Gate	a		20 16								20 49		21 16										
	d		20 19								20 51		21 17										
Grantham	a	20 18									21 02	21 07	21 28										
	d	20 19									21 04	21 08	21 29										
Peterborough	a		20 46		21 04			21 15			21 25	21 39	21 49										
Norwich	d											23a19											
Peterborough	d		20 51		21 05			21 18			21 28		21 50										
Stevenage	d	21 04	21 20					21 48			21 59												
London Kings Cross	a	21 31	21 44		21 54			22 16			22 24		22 39										

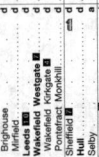

A To Birmingham New Street
B To Birmingham New Street. ⚌ to Leeds
C To Manchester Victoria
D To Liverpool Lime Street
E From Redcar Central to Manchester Victoria
F From Liverpool Lime Street
G To Manchester Airport
H To Liverpool Lime Street. ⚌ from York
I From Redcar Central

NRT DECEMBER 19 EDITION

Table T026-R

Saturdays
21 December to 16 May

Scotland, North East England, Yorkshire and Humberside - London

Station		XC	TP	XC	TP	TP	TP	TP
			A		B		A	
Aberdeen	d			21 35				
Stonehaven	d			21 52				
Montrose	d			22 13				
Arbroath	d			22 28				
Dundee	d			22 49				
Leuchars	d			23 02				
Kirkcaldy	d			23 34				
Inverkeithing	a			23 48				
Inverness	d							
Perth	d							
Stirling	a							
Glasgow Central	d	21 05						
Motherwell	a							
Haymarket 238	d	21 56		00 04				
Edinburgh 238	a	22 00		00 08				
	d							
Dunbar 238	d							
Berwick-upon-Tweed	d							
Alnmouth for Alnwick	d							
Morpeth	d							
Newcastle	a							
Sunderland	d							
Hartlepool	d							
Newcastle	d				22 00	22 00		22 30
Chester-le-Street	d							22 40
Durham	d				22 15	22 15		22a46
Darlington	a				22 32	22 32		
Middlesbrough	d		21 21				22 21	
Eaglescliffe	a							
Darlington	d				22 33	22 33		
Northallerton	d		21 50		22 44	22 44	22 50	
Thirsk	d		21 59				22 59	
York	a		22 19		23 03	23 03	23 19	
Leeds	a				23 27			
	d							
Harrogate	d							
Scarborough	a							
York	d							
Doncaster	a							
Skipton	d							
Keighley	d							
Bradford Interchange	d							
Bradford Forster Square	d							
Shipley	d							
Halifax	d							
Brighouse	d							
Mirfield	d							
Leeds	d							
Wakefield Westgate	d							
Wakefield Kirkgate	d							
Pontefract Monkhill	d							
Sheffield	d							
Hull	d							
Selby	a							
Doncaster	d							
Retford	d							
Lincoln	d							
Newark North Gate	a							
	d							
Grantham	a							
	d							
Peterborough	a							
Norwich	d							
Peterborough	d							
Stevenage	d							
London Kings Cross	a							

A From Redcar Central
B until 15 February, from 4 April. To Manchester Airport

Table T026-R

Sundays

15 December to 10 May

Scotland, North East England, Yorkshire and Humberside - London

Station		XC	GC	GR	GR	TP	GC	GC	GR	GR	XC	GR	TP	GR	TP	HT	GR	GR	XC	GR	TP	TP	GR
		A				B	C	D			E		F		G				E		F	G	
Aberdeen	d																						
Stonehaven	d																						
Montrose	d																						
Arbroath	d																						
Dundee	d																						
Leuchars	d																						
Kirkcaldy	d																						
Inverkeithing	a																						
Inverness	d																						
Perth	d																						
Stirling	a																						
Glasgow Central	d																						
Motherwell	a																						
Haymarket 238	d	00 04																					
Edinburgh 238	a	00 08																					
	d																						
Dunbar 238	d																						
Berwick-upon-Tweed	d																						
Alnmouth for Alnwick	d																						
Morpeth	d																						
Newcastle	a																						
Sunderland	d																						
Hartlepool	d																						
Newcastle	d					07 49			07 54				08 06	08 25	08 47		08 55				09 03		09 25
Chester-le-Street	d																						
Durham	d					08 01			08 08				08 18	08 38	08 59		09 08				09 15		09 38
Darlington	a					08 18			08 26				08 35	08 55	09 16		09 26				09 32		09 55
Middlesbrough	d																					09 29	
Eaglescliffe	a																						
Darlington	d					08 19			08 27				08 36	08 57	09 17		09 28				09 33		09 57
Northallerton	d														09 28								10 08
Thirsk	d																						
York	a					08 45			08 54				09 02	09 25	09 47		09 55				10 01	10 17	10 28
Leeds	a					09 12							09 27		10 12						10 27	10 43	
	d																						
Harrogate	d																			09 15			
Scarborough	a																						
York	d			08 00					08 58					09 27			09 57		09 36				10 30
Doncaster	a			08 21																			10 52
Skipton	d																						
Keighley	d																						
Bradford Interchange	d						07 57	08 10															
Bradford Forster Square	d																						
Shipley	d																						
Halifax	d		07 34				08 11																
Brighouse	d		07 54				08 21																
Mirfield	d		08 11				08 28																
Leeds	d				08 05					08 40	09 00	09 05						09 40	10 01	10 05			
Wakefield Westgate	d				08 18					08 55	09 12	09 18						09 53	10 14	10 18			
Wakefield Kirkgate	d		08a36				08 45	08 45															
Pontefract Monkhill	d																						
Sheffield	d																						
Hull	d															08 59							
Selby	a															09 33							
Doncaster	d			08 23	08 37		09 11	09 11		09 20	09a29	09 38				09 59			10a31	10 37			10 53
Retford	d				08 51											10 13		10 20		10 52			
Lincoln	d																						
Newark North Gate	a				09 05							10 01		10 07				10 34		11 06			11 16
	d				09 07							10 02		10 08				10 40		11 07			11 17
Grantham	a				09 18							10 13		10 19		10 34				11 18			
	d				09 19							10 15		10 20		10 35				11 20			
Peterborough	a			09 10	09 39				10 03	10 07		10 35		10 40			11 03	11 07		11 40			11 44
Norwich	d																						
Peterborough	d			09 11	09 42				10 05	10 11		10 36		10 42			11 04	11 09		11 42			11 51
Stevenage	d			09 41								11 06		11 11									
London Kings Cross ⊖	a			10 06	10 33		10 40	10 40	10 54	11 08		11 33		11 36		11 39	11 53	11 58		12 33			12 40

A not 15 December. From Aberdeen
B To Manchester Piccadilly
C until 16 February, from 5 April
D from 23 February until 29 March
E To Plymouth
F To Liverpool Lime Street
G To Manchester Airport

Table T026-R

Sundays

15 December to 10 May

Scotland, North East England, Yorkshire and Humberside - London

Station		TP	GR	XC	TP	GC	GR	GR	GR	TP	TP	GR	HT	GR	GR	XC	TP	EM	TP	GR	TP	TP	GR
		A		B	C					A	D		E			B	C	F	A		G	D	
Aberdeen	d																						
Stonehaven	d																						
Montrose	d																						
Arbroath	d																						
Dundee	d																						
Leuchars	d																						
Kirkcaldy	d																						
Inverkeithing	a																						
Inverness	d																						
Perth	d																						
Stirling	a																						
Glasgow Central	d	10 13																					
Motherwell	a	10 29																					
Haymarket 238	d																						
Edinburgh 238	a																						
	d											09 00				09 08			09 20	09 30			10 00
Dunbar 238	d																						
Berwick-upon-Tweed	d															09 51				10 13			
Alnmouth for Alnwick	d																						11 00
Morpeth	d																		10 30				
Newcastle	a											10 23				10 35			10 44	10 56			11 27
Sunderland	d					09 23																	
Hartlepool	d					09 47															←		
Newcastle	d			09 35	09 43			10 00		10 06		10 27				10 39	10 47		11 06	10 59	11 06		11 29
Chester-le-Street	d				09 52														→				
Durham	d			09 47	09 59					10 18		10 41				10 53	10 59				11 18		11 42
Darlington	a			10 04	10 16			10 27		10 35		10 58				11 09	11 16			11 27	11 35		12 00
Middlesbrough	d										10 18											11 18	
Eaglescliffe	a					10 06																	
Darlington	d			10 05	10 17			10 28		10 36		11 00				11 10	11 17			11 28	11 36		12 01
Northallerton	d					10 25					10 48	11 12					11 28					11 48	
Thirsk	d					10 34					10 56											11 56	
York	a			10 31	10 48	10 51		10 55		11 02	11 14	11 31				11 38	11 47			11 55	12 02	12 14	12 28
Leeds	a			10 58	11 12					11 27	11 42					12 08	12 12				12 27	12 43	
	d																						
Harrogate	d														11 15								
Scarborough	a																						
York	d					10 54		10 58				11 34								11 58			12 31
Doncaster	a											11 55											12 52
Skipton	d																						
Keighley	d																						
Bradford Interchange	d																						
Bradford Forster Square	d																						
Shipley	d																						
Halifax	d																						
Brighouse	d																						
Mirfield	d																						
Leeds	d		10 45	11 00					11 05						12 05	12 11							
Wakefield Westgate	d		10 58	11 12					11 18						12 18	12 24							
Wakefield Kirkgate	d																						
Pontefract Monkhill	d																						
Sheffield	d															12a53							
Hull	d												11 12										
Selby	a												11 46										
Doncaster	d		11 17	11a28					11 39			11 57	12 04		12 37								12 54
Retford	d		11 34									12 11	12 18										
Lincoln	d						10 55							12 23									
Newark North Gate	a						11 19		12 01					12 47	13 00								13 16
	d						11 21		12 03					12 49	13 01								13 18
Grantham	a						11 32		12 14				12 38	13 00	13 12								
	d						11 33		12 15				12 39	13 01	13 13			13 15					
Peterborough	a						11 53	12 02	12 36			12 50		13 22	13 33			13 41					13 46
Norwich	d																	15a23					
Peterborough	d						11 59	12 06	12 39			12 51		13 23	13 34								13 50
Stevenage	d						12 28		13 08					13 53									
London Kings Cross ⊖	a		12 59			12 42	12 52	12 55	13 33			13 40	13 42	14 18	14 23					13 49			14 39

A To Liverpool Lime Street
B To Plymouth
C To Manchester Airport
D From Redcar Central to Manchester Airport
E From Beverley
F From Nottingham
G From Edinburgh to Liverpool Lime Street

Table T026-R

Sundays

15 December to 10 May

Scotland, North East England, Yorkshire and Humberside - London

		GC	GR	EM	XC	TP	TP	GR	TP	TP	GR	GR	GR	EM	XC	GC	TP	GR	GR	TP	TP	GR
					A	B	C		D	E				F	G		B			C	E	
Aberdeen	d																					
Stonehaven	d																					
Montrose	d																					
Arbroath	d																					
Dundee	d																					
Leuchars	d																					
Kirkcaldy	d																					
Inverkeithing	a																					
Inverness	d																					
Perth	d																					
Stirling	a																					
Glasgow Central	d																					
Motherwell	a																					
Haymarket 238	d																					
Edinburgh 238	a																					
	d				10 08		10 20	10 30			11 00				11 05			11 20	11 30	11 33		
Dunbar 238	d														11 26							
Berwick-upon-Tweed	d							11 12							11 50				12 12			
Alnmouth for Alnwick	d				11 07										12 10							
Morpeth	d				11 22		11 33											12 34		12 48		
Newcastle	a				11 36		11 47	11 56			12 23				12 36			12 48	12 56	13 02		
Sunderland	d															12 12						
Hartlepool	d								←							12 36						
Newcastle	d				11 40	11 43	12 05	11 58	12 05		12 25				12 40		12 46	12 51	12 59	13 05		13 15
Chester-le-Street	d					11 53	→															
Durham	d				11 52	12 00			12 17		12 39				12 53		12 59	13 05		13 17		13 28
Darlington	a				12 09	12 16		12 25	12 34		12 57				13 09		13 16	13 23	13 28	13 34		13 46
Middlesbrough	d									12 18											13 18	
Eaglescliffe	a															12 56						
Darlington	d				12 10	12 18		12 27	12 35		12 58				13 10		13 17	13 24	13 29	13 35		13 47
Northallerton	d					12 29				12 48	13 10					13 15	13 28				13 48	14 00
Thirsk	d									12 56						13 27					13 56	
York	a				12 36	12 48		12 54	13 01	13 14	13 29				13 36	13 44	13 47	13 53	13 57	14 02	14 14	14 21
Leeds	a				13 08	13 13			13 28	13 43					14 08		14 12			14 27	14 43	
	d																					
Harrogate	d												13 15									
Scarborough	a																					
York	d							12 56			13 32					13 47		13 56	14 00			14 24
Doncaster	a										13 53											14 45
Skipton	d																					
Keighley	d																					
Bradford Interchange	d	12 05																				
Bradford Forster Square	d																					
Shipley	d																					
Halifax	d	12 19																				
Brighouse	d	12 30																				
Mirfield	d	12 39																				
Leeds	d		13 05		13 11								14 05		14 11							
Wakefield Westgate	d		13 18		13 24								14 18		14 23							
Wakefield Kirkgate	d	12 56																				
Pontefract Monkhill	d																					
Sheffield	d			12 43	13a54									13 48	14a51							
Hull	d																					
Selby	a																					
Doncaster	d	13 21	13 37								13 55		14 37									14 48
Retford	d										14 09											
Lincoln	d											14 20										
Newark North Gate	a		13 59									14 44	14 59									
	d		14 00									14 46	15 00									
Grantham	a		14 11	14 20								14 57	15 11	15 16								
	d		14 12	14 22								14 58	15 12	15 20								
Peterborough	a		14 32	14 51							14 48	15 19	15 32	15 51								15 36
Norwich	d			16a35										17a26								
Peterborough	d		14 34								14 51	15 23	15 34									15 38
Stevenage	d		15 03									15 53										
London Kings Cross	a	14 54	15 27					14 45			15 40	16 18	16 23			15 41		15 47	15 51			16 27

A To Penzance
B To Manchester Airport
C To Liverpool Lime Street
D From Edinburgh to Liverpool Lime Street
E From Redcar Central to Manchester Airport
F From Manchester Piccadilly
G To Plymouth

NRT DECEMBER 19 EDITION

Table T026-R

Sundays

15 December to 10 May

Scotland, North East England, Yorkshire and Humberside - London

		GR	XC	HT	GR	XC	TP	TP	GR	TP	GR	HT	GR	TP	GR	GR	EM	XC	XC	TP	GC	TP	GR
			A	B	B	C	D	D		E	F		G	H			I	A	J	D		D	
Aberdeen	d										09 47												
Stonehaven	d										10 05												
Montrose	d										10 28												
Arbroath	d										10 44												
Dundee	d										11 04												
Leuchars	d										11 18												
Kirkcaldy	d										11 43												
Inverkeithing	a										11 58												
Inverness	d																						
Perth	d																						
Stirling	a																						
Glasgow Central	d					10 55		11 05											12 02	13 06			
Motherwell	a					11 13		11 24											12 17	13 24			
Haymarket 238	d					11 53					12 18								12 56				
Edinburgh 238	a					11 57					12 22								13 01				
	d	12 00				12 08			12 20	12 24	12 30					13 00			13 08				13 20
Dunbar 238	d																		13 29				
Berwick-upon-Tweed	d					12 49					13 13					13 43							
Alnmouth for Alnwick	d	13 00																	14 11				
Morpeth	d								13 33	13 38													
Newcastle	a	13 27				13 34			13 47	13 53	13 56					14 26			14 37				14 45
Sunderland	d																				14 12		
Hartlepool	d																				14 39		
Newcastle	d	13 29	13 36			13 40	13 43		13 50	13 56	13 59				14 16	14 31		14 36	14 41			14 47	14 51
Chester-le-Street	d						13 52																
Durham	d	13 42	13 48			13 53	13 59		14 03	14 08					14 29			14 48	14 53			14 59	15 04
Darlington	a	14 00	14 05			14 09	14 15			14 25	14 29				14 47	14 59		15 05	15 10			15 16	15 21
Middlesbrough	d													14 15									
Eaglescliffe	a																				14 57		
Darlington	d	14 01	14 06			14 10	14 16			14 26	14 31				14 49	15 00		15 06	15 10			15 17	15 23
Northallerton	d													14 47	15 02						15 18	15 29	
Thirsk	d													14 55							15 27		
York	a	14 28	14 32			14 39	14 43		14 47	14 53	14 58			15 13	15 21	15 27		15 32	15 40		15 44	15 48	15 53
Leeds	a					15 07	15 11			15 27				15 43					16 07			16 12	
	d																						
Harrogate	d																						
Scarborough	a																						
York	d	14 31	14 35						14 50		15 00				15 24	15 30		15 35			15 48		15 57
Doncaster	a	14 52	14 56												15 45	15 52		15 57					
Skipton	d																						
Keighley	d																						
Bradford Interchange	d																						
Bradford Forster Square	d																						
Shipley	d																						
Halifax	d																						
Brighouse	d																						
Mirfield	d																						
Leeds	d				15 05	15 11							←						16 11				
Wakefield Westgate	d				15 18	15 23							15 18						16 23				
Wakefield Kirkgate	d				→																		
Pontefract Monkhill	d																						
Sheffield	d		15a22			15a53						←					14 41	16a20	16a52				
Hull	d			14 36								14 36											
Selby	a			→								15 10											
Doncaster	d	14 54										15 28	15 37		15 47	15 53							
Retford	d											15 42				16 08							
Lincoln	d																						
Newark North Gate	a	15 16											15 59		16 09								
	d	15 18											16 00		16 10								
Grantham	a								15 39			16 05	16 11				16 20						
	d								15 40			16 06	16 12				16 22						
Peterborough	a	15 46											16 32		16 39	16 48	16 52						
Norwich	d																18a30						
Peterborough	d	15 51											16 34		16 42	16 51							
Stevenage	d											16s51	17 03										
London Kings Cross	a	16 40							16 44		16 51	17 14	17 28		17 36	17 41					17 42		17 48

A To Reading
B To London Kings Cross
C To Penzance. ✕ from Edinburgh
D To Manchester Airport
E To Liverpool Lime Street
F The Northern Lights
G From Leeds
H From Redcar Central to Manchester Airport
I From Liverpool Lime Street
J To Plymouth

Table T026-R

Sundays
15 December to 10 May

Scotland, North East England, Yorkshire and Humberside - London

		GR	TP	GC	GR	TP	EM	XC	GR	GC	GR	GR	XC	TP	TP	GR	TP	HT	GR	TP	GR	EM
		A	B			C	D	E					F	G	B		H			C		D
Aberdeen	d												11 10			11 47						
Stonehaven	d												11 27			12 05						
Montrose	d												11 49			12 28						
Arbroath	d												12 04			12 44						
Dundee	d												12 22			13 03						
Leuchars 3	d												12 35			13 18						
Kirkcaldy	d												13 08			13 44						
Inverkeithing	a												13 22			14 02						
Inverness	d	09 40																				
Perth	d	12 01																				
Stirling	a	12 35																				
Glasgow Central 15	d																					
Motherwell	a																					
Haymarket 238	d	13 13											13 39			14 21						
Edinburgh 10 238	a	13 19											13 43			14 26						
	d	13 30	13 33					13 55	14 00				14 08		14 21	14 30					14 50	
Dunbar 238	d																					
Berwick-upon-Tweed	d	14 13						14 36					14 49								15 32	
Alnmouth for Alnwick	d								15 00													
Morpeth	d		14 49										15 20		15 31							
Newcastle 8	a	14 56	15 03					15 19	15 28				15 35		15 44	15 53					16 15	
Sunderland	d																					
Hartlepool	d																←					
Newcastle 8	d	14 59	15 05					15 25	15 31				15 40	15 43	16 00	15 56	16 00		16 06		16 18	
Chester-le-Street	d													15 52	→							
Durham	d		15 18					15 38	15 44				15 52	15 59			16 15		16 20		16 31	
Darlington 7	a	15 27	15 34					15 56	16 01				16 09	16 16		16 24	16 31		16 37		16 47	
Middlesbrough	d					15 18														16 18		
Eaglescliffe	a																					
Darlington 7	d	15 28	15 36					15 57	16 03				16 10	16 17		16 25	16 33		16 39		16 49	
Northallerton	d					15 48								16 28					16 51			
Thirsk	d					15 56														16 55		
York 8	a	15 58	16 02			16 14		16 23	16 30				16 36	16 47		16 52	16 59		17 10	17 16	17 19	
Leeds	a		16 28			16 43							17 09	17 12			17 28			17 44		
	d																					
Harrogate	d				15 36																	
Scarborough	a																					
York	d	16 01						16 25	16 32							16 59			17 13		17 23	
Doncaster 7	a							16 48	16 54										17 34			
Skipton	d																					
Keighley	d																					
Bradford Interchange	d			15 08						15 59												
Bradford Forster Square	d																					
Shipley	d																					
Halifax	d			15 21						16 12												
Brighouse	d			15 36						16 22												
Mirfield	d			15 45						16 30												
Leeds 10	d				16 16							16 45	17 12									
Wakefield Westgate 7	d				16 29							16 58	17 24									
Wakefield Kirkgate 4	d			16 02						16 44												
Pontefract Monkhill	d																					
Sheffield 7	d						15 39	17a19					17a53									16 43
Hull	d																	16 21				
Selby	a																	17 02				
Doncaster 7	d			16 27	16 48				16 55	17 13		17 19						17 27	17 36			
Retford 10	d																	17 41				
Lincoln	d										16 50											
Newark North Gate 7	a								17 18		17 16	17 43									18 03	
	d								17 19		17 23	17 44									18 04	
Grantham 7	a				17 18		17 15				17 34							18 01	18 06			18 16
	d				17 19		17 21				17 35							18 02	18 07			18 17
Peterborough 8	a						17 50		17 47		18 03	18 12									18 31	18 46
Norwich	d						19a28															20a26
Peterborough 8	d								17 51		18 04	18 14									18 33	
Stevenage 4	d				18 04						18 33							18s46				
London Kings Cross 15 ⊖	a	17 53		17 56	18 29				18 40	18 44	18 59	19 05				18 50		19 10	19 18		19 22	

A The Highland Chieftain
B To Liverpool Lime Street
C From Redcar Central to Manchester Airport
D From Liverpool Lime Street
E To Reading
F To Plymouth. ⚒ from Edinburgh
G To Manchester Airport
H From Edinburgh to Liverpool Lime Street

Table T026-R

Sundays
15 December to 10 May

Scotland, North East England, Yorkshire and Humberside - London

		GR	GR	XC	GR	GR	XC	TP	TP	GR	TP	GR	TP	GR	EM	XC	GR	XC	TP	TP	GR	GR	TP
				A			B	C	D		E		F		G	H		I	C	C			D
Aberdeen	d																					13 47	
Stonehaven	d																					14 05	
Montrose	d																					14 28	
Arbroath	d																					14 44	
Dundee	d																					15 03	
Leuchars 3	d																					15 17	
Kirkcaldy	d																					15 43	
Inverkeithing	a																					15 58	
Inverness	d																						
Perth	d																						
Stirling	a																						
Glasgow Central 15	d						13 48											14 55		15 05			
Motherwell	a						14 02											15 13		15 24			
Haymarket 238	d						14 42											15 52				16 20	
Edinburgh 10 238	a						14 47											15 57				16 24	
	d		15 00				15 08		15 20	15 30				16 00				16 08			16 20	16 30	16 34
Dunbar 238	d						15 29																
Berwick-upon-Tweed	d									16 12												17 13	
Alnmouth for Alnwick	d													17 00				17 08					
Morpeth	d						16 22		16 30									17 22			17 33		17 48
Newcastle 8	a		16 23				16 36		16 44	16 55				17 27				17 36			17 47	17 56	18 02
Sunderland	d																						
Hartlepool	d										←												
Newcastle 8	d		16 26	16 35			16 40	16 43	17 06	17 01	17 06			17 29		17 35		17 40	17 43		17 52	18 00	18 04
Chester-le-Street	d							16 52	→										17 52				
Durham	d		16 40	16 47			16 52	16 59			17 18			17 42		17 48		17 53	17 59				18 17
Darlington 7	a		16 59	17 04			17 09	17 16		17 28	17 35			18 00		18 05		18 10	18 15		18 20	18 28	18 33
Middlesbrough	d												17 18										
Eaglescliffe	a																						
Darlington 7	d		17 00	17 05			17 10	17 17		17 29	17 36			18 01		18 06		18 11	18 17		18 21	18 30	18 35
Northallerton	d												17 48						18 28		18 33		
Thirsk	d												17 56										
York 8	a		17 27	17 31			17 40	17 48		17 56	18 02		18 14	18 28		18 33		18 41	18 47		18 52	18 58	19 02
Leeds	a						18 10	18 12			18 27		18 43					19 08	19 13				19 27
	d																						
Harrogate	d					17 05											18 02						
Scarborough	a																						
York	d		17 30	17 35						17 59				18 31		18 35					18 55	19 01	
Doncaster 7	a		17 52	17 57										18 52		18 57							
Skipton	d																						
Keighley	d																						
Bradford Interchange	d																						
Bradford Forster Square	d																						
Shipley	d																						
Halifax	d																						
Brighouse	d																						
Mirfield	d																						
Leeds 10	d	17 16				17 47	18 11					18 15					18 45	19 12					
Wakefield Westgate 7	d	17 29				18 00	18 23					18 28					18 59	19 24					
Wakefield Kirkgate 4	d																						
Pontefract Monkhill	d																						
Sheffield 7	d			18a20			18a53								17 40	19a20		19a53					
Hull	d																						
Selby	a																						
Doncaster 7	d	17 48	17 57			18 18						18 47		18 55			19 21						
Retford 10	d	18 02																					
Lincoln	d				18 00																		
Newark North Gate 7	a				18 24	18 43								19 17			19 45						
	d				18 25	18 44								19 19			19 46						
Grantham 7	a	18 24	18 29		18 36							19 17			19 21						19 43		
	d	18 25	18 31		18 37							19 18			19 23						19 44		
Peterborough 8	a		18 51		18 57	19 12								19 46	19 56		20 14						
Norwich	d														21a37								
Peterborough 8	d		18 52		19 03	19 14								19 51			20 15						
Stevenage 4	d	19 10			19 32							20 03											
London Kings Cross 15 ⊖	a	19 34	19 42		19 57	20 05				19 47		20 27		20 40			21 07				20 48	20 53	

A To Reading
B To Plymouth. ⚒ from Edinburgh
C To Manchester Airport
D To Liverpool Lime Street
E From Edinburgh to Liverpool Lime Street
F From Redcar Central to Manchester Airport
G From Liverpool Lime Street
H To Guildford
I To Bristol Temple Meads. ⚒ from Edinburgh

Table T026-R

Sundays
15 December to 10 May

Scotland, North East England, Yorkshire and Humberside - London

		TP	HT	GR	XC	GR	GR	XC	GC	TP	TP	GR	GR	TP	TP	EM	XC	GR	GR	XC	TP	TP	TP
		◇1	◇1	■ 1	◇1	■ 1	■ 1	◇1	■ 1	◇1	◇1	■ 1	■ 1	◇1	◇1	◇	◇1	■ 1	■ 1	◇1	◇1	◇1	◇1
		A			B		C	D		E	F		G	H	I	J	B			K	L	F	F
			⊠	🍴	🛒	🍴	🍴	🛒	🍴	🛒	🛒	🍴	🍴	🛒				🍴	🍴	🛒	🛒	🛒	
Aberdeen	d																						
Stonehaven	d																						
Montrose	d																						
Arbroath	d																						
Dundee	d																						
Leuchars 8	d																						
Kirkcaldy	d																						
Inverkeithing	a																						
Inverness	d																						
Perth	d																						
Stirling	a																						
Glasgow Central 15	d																			16 55	17 04	18 47	
Motherwell	a																			17 12	17 19	19 03	
Haymarket 238 ⛴	d																			17 51			
Edinburgh 10 238 ⛴	a																			17 56			
	d					17 00		17 08			17 19	17 30						18 00		18 06			18 20
Dunbar 238	d							17 29				17 52								18 28			
Berwick-upon-Tweed	d							17 53				18 16								18 52			
Alnmouth for Alnwick	d																	19 01					
Morpeth	d										18 30									19 23			19 30
Newcastle 8 ⛴	a					18 23		18 36			18 44	18 59						19 28		19 38			19 44
Sunderland ⛴	d								18 12														
Hartlepool	d								18 36					←									
Newcastle 8 ⛴	d				18 25	18 29		18 39		18 43	19 06	19 02		19 06			19 26	19 30		19 41			20 06
Chester-le-Street	d									18 52	→												→
Durham	d				18 37	18 42		18 52		18 59				19 18			19 39	19 44		19 53			
Darlington 7	a				18 55	19 00		19 08		19 16		19 28		19 35			19 55	20 01		20 10			
Middlesbrough	d	18 15													19 19								
Eaglescliffe	a								18 55														
Darlington 7	d				18 56	19 01		19 09		19 17		19 29		19 36			19 56	20 03		20 10			
Northallerton	d	18 44				19 13			19 20	19 28					19 50								
Thirsk	d	18 53							19 29						19 58								
York 8	a	19 11			19 22	19 32		19 36	19 46	19 50		19 57		20 02	20 16		20 24	20 30		20 37			
Leeds	a	19 43						20 08		20 14				20 27	20 43					21 08			
	d																						
Harrogate	d																						
Scarborough	a																						
York	d				19 24	19 35			19 49			20 00					20 26	20 32					
Doncaster 7	a				19 50	19 56											20 48	20 54					
Skipton	d																						
Keighley	d																						
Bradford Interchange	d																						
Bradford Forster Square	d																						
Shipley	d																						
Halifax	d																						
Brighouse	d																						
Mirfield	d																						
Leeds 10	d			19 16			19 46	20 11					←						20 45	21 11			
Wakefield Westgate 7	d			19 29			19 59	20 23					19 59						20 58	21 23			
Wakefield Kirkgate 4	d						→																
Pontefract Monkhill	d																						
Sheffield 7 ⛴	d				20a16			20a52								19 40	21a13			21a52			
Hull	d		18 47																				
Selby	a		19 21																				
Doncaster 7	d		19 40	19 48		19 58							20 20					20 55	21 17				
Retford 10	d		19 54	20 02															21 31				
Lincoln	d																						
Newark North Gate 7	a					20 20							20 44					21 18					
	d					20 21							20 45					21 19					
Grantham 7	a		20 14	20 24								20 48				21 18			21 53				
	d		20 15	20 25								20 49				21 20			21 54				
Peterborough 8	a					20 49						21 09	21 13			21 52		21 47	22 14				
Norwich	d															23a25							
Peterborough 8	d					20 51						21 10	21 14					21 50	22 15				
Stevenage 4	d			21 09															22 45				
London Kings Cross 15 ⊖	a		21 19	21 33		21 40			21 43			21 59	22 07					22 39	23 10				

A From Redcar Central to Manchester Airport
B To Birmingham New Street
C To London Kings Cross
D To Bristol Temple Meads. 🛒 to Leeds
E To Manchester Victoria
F To Liverpool Lime Street
G From Leeds
H From Edinburgh to Liverpool Lime Street
I From Redcar Central to Manchester Victoria
J From Liverpool Lime Street
K To Birmingham New Street. 🛒 from Edinburgh to Leeds
L To Manchester Airport

NRT DECEMBER 19 EDITION

Table T026-R

Sundays
15 December to 10 May

Scotland, North East England, Yorkshire and Humberside - London

		GR	TP	TP	GR	TP	TP	GR	XC	TP	TP	GR	GR	XC	XC	TP	CS	TP
		■ 1	◇1	◇1	■ 1	◇1	◇1	■ 1	◇1	◇1	◇1	■ 1	■ 1	◇1	◇1	◇1	B	◇1
			A	B		C	B	D		E	F	G				B	H	B
		🍴	🛒		🍴	🛒		🍴		🛒	🛒	🍴	🍴			🛒	🛏 ✕	🛒
Aberdeen	d														21 30			
Stonehaven	d														21 47			
Montrose	d														22 08			
Arbroath	d														22 23			
Dundee	d														22 41			
Leuchars 8	d														22 54			
Kirkcaldy	d														23 26			
Inverkeithing	a														23 40			
Inverness	d																	
Perth	d																	
Stirling	a																	
Glasgow Central 15	d								19 00	19 15				20 58			23 15	
Motherwell	a								19 14	19 31				21 17			23 30	
Haymarket 238 ⛴	d								19 59					22 04	23 57			
Edinburgh 10 238 ⛴	a								20 04					22 08	00 01			
	d	18 30			19 00	19 30		20 00	20 18		20 30		21 00					
Dunbar 238	d				19 22			20 23	20 40				21 23					
Berwick-upon-Tweed	d	19 13			19 46			20 47	21 04				21 47					
Alnmouth for Alnwick	d							21 10					22 10					
Morpeth	d					20 40		21 27			21 40							
Newcastle 8 ⛴	a	19 56			20 30	20 55		21 41	21 48		21 55		22 38					
Sunderland ⛴	d																	
Hartlepool	d		←															
Newcastle 8 ⛴	d	20 00	20 06		20 32	21 02		21 44			22 01							
Chester-le-Street	d					21 11												
Durham	d		20 18		20 46	21 18		21 58			22 14							
Darlington 7	a	20 27	20 35		21 03	21 35		22 16			22 30							
Middlesbrough	d			20 22			21 19									22 19		23 19
Eaglescliffe	a																	
Darlington 7	d	20 29	20 36		21 05	21 36		22 17			22 32	←						
Northallerton	d			20 53			21 50	22 31			22 43	22 31				22 50		
Thirsk	d			21 01			21 58	→								22 58		
York 8	a	20 56	21 02	21 21	21 32	22 02	22 18				23 02	23 05				23 18		00 18
Leeds	a		21 27			22 27					23 27	23 35						
	d																	
Harrogate	d																	
Scarborough	a																	
York	d	21 00			21 35													
Doncaster 7	a	21 21			21 56													
Skipton	d																	
Keighley	d																	
Bradford Interchange	d																	
Bradford Forster Square	d																	
Shipley	d																	
Halifax	d																	
Brighouse	d																	
Mirfield	d																	
Leeds 10	d																	
Wakefield Westgate 7	d																	
Wakefield Kirkgate 4	d																	
Pontefract Monkhill	d																	
Sheffield 7 ⛴	d																	
Hull	d																	
Selby	a																	
Doncaster 7	d	21 26			21 58													
Retford 10	d																	
Lincoln	d																	
Newark North Gate 7	a	21 48			22 20													
	d	21 50			22 21													
Grantham 7	a	22 01			22 32													
	d	22 02			22 33													
Peterborough 8	a	22 22			22 53													
Norwich	d																	
Peterborough 8	d	22 24			22 55													
Stevenage 4	d	22 53			23s33													
London Kings Cross 15 ⊖	a	23 17			23 58													

A From Edinburgh to Liverpool Lime Street. 🛒 from York
B From Redcar Central
C To Liverpool Lime Street. 🛒 from York
D To Leeds
E To Manchester Airport
F To Manchester Airport. 🛒 from York
G From Edinburgh
H until 29 March. To London Euston

Table T027-F

Nottingham - Newark - Lincoln - Cleethorpes

Mondays to Fridays
16 December to 15 May

Miles	Miles			EM	EM	EM	EM	EM	EM	EM	EM	GR	EM	EM	EM	EM	EM	EM	GR	EM	EM	EM	EM
						A				B	◇ C	■ 1 D	E	C			E	C	■ 1 D	E	C		E
0	—	**Nottingham** ■	d		05 54	06 53		07 56		08 12	08 51		09 28	09 49			10 29	10 49		11 29	11 51		12 29
3	—	Carlton	d		06 01	06 59		08 02		08 19	08 58			09 55				10 56			11 58		
5	—	Burton Joyce	d		06 04	07 02		08 06						09 59							12 02		
9¼	—	Lowdham	d		06 09	07 07		08 10		08 27	09 04			10 04				11 02			12 06		
10	—	Thurgarton	d		06 13	07 11		08 14						10 08							12 10		
11	—	Bleasby	d		06 16	07 14		08 17						10 11							12 14		
12¼	—	Fiskerton	d		06 20	07 17		08 21			09 11			10 15				11 09			12 17		
13¾	—	Rolleston	d		06 22	07 19		08 23						10 17							12 20		
17¼	—	**Newark Castle**	d		06 30	07 27		08a30		08 40	09a20		09 52	10a25			10 51	11a19		11 53	12a29		12 53
—	0	**Newark North Gate** ■	a																				
—	—		d				07 42		08 31			09 29			09 57	10 50			11 36			12 06	
22¼	5	Collingham	d		06 39	07 35	07 51		08 40	08 49					10 05		11 04			12 01		12 15	13 02
25	—	Swinderby	d		06 43		07 56		08 45								11 09					12 19	
29¾	—	Hykeham	d		06 50	07 44	08 02		08 51	08 57					10 14		11 15			12 10		12 26	13 11
33¾	—	**Lincoln**	a		07 02	07 56	08 12		09 02	09 08		09 55	10 17		10 23	11 14	11 26		12 02	12 21		12 36	13 23
—	—		d	05 57			08 15								10 25							12 38	
48½	—	Market Rasen	d	06 13			08 32								10 42							12 54	
63½	—	Barnetby	a	06 30			08 49								10 58							13 10	
69½	—	Habrough	a	06 40			08 59								11 08							13 20	
77½	—	**Grimsby Town**	a	06 55			09 12								11 22							13 35	
80¾	—	**Cleethorpes**	a																				

		EM	EM	GR	EM	EM	EM	EM	EM	EM	GR	EM	EM	EM	EM	EM	EM	GR	EM	EM	EM	EM	EM
		C	A	■ 1 D	E		C	E	C	◇ A	■ 1 D	E	C		F	C		■ 1 D	E		E	C	
Nottingham ■	d	12 50			13 29		13 49	14 29	14 50			15 29	15 49		16 27	16 50			17 26	17 50	18 17	18 51	
Carlton	d	12 56					13 55		14 59				15 55			16 56			17 32		18 23	18 58	
Burton Joyce	d								15 02							17 00			17 36		18 27		
Lowdham	d	13 03					14 02		15 07				16 02		16 38	17 05			17 40	18 01	18 31		
Thurgarton	d								15 10							17 09					18 35		
Bleasby	d								15 14							17 12					18 39		
Fiskerton	d	13 10					14 09		15 17				16 09			17 16			17 47		18 42	19 10	
Rolleston	d								15 20							17 18					18 45		
Newark Castle	d	13a20			13 52		14a17	14 53	15a29			15 53	16a17		16 53	17a26			17 56	18 18	18 53	19a19	
Newark North Gate ■	a																						
	d		13 02	13 36						15 28	15 34			16 46			17 23	17 36					19 35
Collingham	d		13 11		14 00			15 04		15 37		16 02			17 02		17 31		18 05	18 27	19 02		19 44
Swinderby	d				14 04							16 07							18 09	18 32	19 06		
Hykeham	d				14 10			15 13		15 46		16 13		17 03			17 40		18 16	18 39	19 12		
Lincoln	a		13 30	14 02	14 23			15 22		15 55	16 01	16 23		17 13	17 18		17 54	18 02	18 28	18 49	19 22		20 00
	d					14 35								17 22									20 02
Market Rasen	d					14 52								17 39									20 19
Barnetby	a					15 08								17 55									20 35
Habrough	a					15 18								18 05									20 44
Grimsby Town	a					15 32								18 18									20 56
Cleethorpes	a																						21 04

		EM	EM	EM	GR	EM	EM
		E		◇ 1 G	■ 1 D	E	
Nottingham ■	d	19 19		20 00		21 20	22 26
Carlton	d	19 25				21 28	22 32
Burton Joyce	d	19 29					22 35
Lowdham	d	19 33		20 11		21 34	22 40
Thurgarton	d	19 37					
Bleasby	d	19 41					22 45
Fiskerton	d	19 44				21 41	22 49
Rolleston	d	19 47					
Newark Castle	d	19 54		20 24		21 53	22 57
Newark North Gate ■	a						23 06
	d		20 04		20 36		23 10
Collingham	d	20 03	20 13	20 32		22 01	23 19
Swinderby	d						23 23
Hykeham	d	20 11				22 10	23 30
Lincoln	a	20 21	20 29	20 52	21 03	22 20	23 40
	d						
Market Rasen	d						
Barnetby	a						
Habrough	a						
Grimsby Town	a						
Cleethorpes	a						

A To Peterborough
B From Worksop
C From Matlock
D From London Kings Cross
E From Leicester
F From Leicester to Sleaford
G From St Pancras International

For connections from London Kings Cross refer to Table T026

Table T027-F

Nottingham - Newark - Lincoln - Cleethorpes

Saturdays
21 December to 16 May

		EM	EM	EM	EM	EM	EM	EM	EM	GR	EM	EM	EM	EM	EM	EM	GR	EM	EM	EM	EM	EM	EM
				A					B	■ 1 C		D	B		D	B	■ 1 C	D	B		D	B	A
Nottingham ■	d		05 55	06 53		07 58		08 11	08 54			09 22	09 49		10 29	10 54		11 29	11 53		12 29	12 49	
Carlton	d		06 01	06 59		08 04			09 00			09 28	09 55			11 00			11 59			12 55	
Burton Joyce	d		06 05	07 03		08 08							09 59						12 03				
Lowdham	d		06 10	07 07		08 12			09 07			09 34	10 04			11 08			12 08			13 02	
Thurgarton	d		06 14	07 11		08 16							10 08						12 12				
Bleasby	d		06 17	07 14		08 19							10 11						12 15				
Fiskerton	d		06 20	07 18		08 22			09 14			09 42	10 15			11 15			12 19			13 09	
Rolleston	d		06 22	07 20		08 24							10 17			11 17			12 21				
Newark Castle	d		06 30	07 26		08a32		08 42	09a22			09 51	10a25		10 51	11a25		11 55	12a30		12 53	13a18	
Newark North Gate ■	a																						
	d						08 20			09 29	09 46			10 49			11 35			12 05			13 02
Collingham	d		06 40	07 39			08 29	08 51			09 54	10 01			11 04			12 06		12 15	13 03		13 11
Swinderby	d		06 44				08 34								11 08					12 19			
Hykeham	d		06 50	07 47			08 41	09 00				10 10			11 15			12 15		12 26	13 12		
Lincoln	a		07 03	07 58			08 55	09 09		09 55	10 10	10 19		11 14	11 25		12 01	12 26		12 36	13 22		13 30
	d	05 40			08 08						10 15									12 36			
Market Rasen	d	05 56			08 25						10 32									12 54			
Barnetby	a	06 13			08 49						10 48									13 10			
Habrough	a	06 23			08 59						10 57									13 20			
Grimsby Town	a	06 41			09 12						11 11									13 34			
Cleethorpes	a																						

		GR	EM	EM	EM	EM	EM	EM	GR	EM	EM	EM	EM	EM	GR	EM	EM	EM	EM	EM	EM	EM
		■ 1 C	D		B	D	B	◇ A	■ 1 C	D	B	D		B	■ 1 C	D	B		D	B	◇ 1 E	
Nottingham ■	d		13 29		13 48	14 19	14 50			15 28	15 51	16 21		16 48		17 31	17 47		18 17	18 57	19 29	
Carlton	d				13 55		14 56				15 57			16 55			17 53			19 04		
Burton Joyce	d						15 00							16 59			17 57					
Lowdham	d				14 02		15 04				16 05			17 03			18 02		18 30		19 40	
Thurgarton	d						15 08							17 07			18 06					
Bleasby	d						15 12							17 11			18 09					
Fiskerton	d				14 09		15 15				16 12			17 14			18 13			19 16		
Rolleston	d						15 18							17 17			18 15					
Newark Castle	d		13 51		14a18	14 42	15a26			15 54	16a20	16 43		17a25		17 53	18a23		18 43	19a25	19 53	
Newark North Gate ■	a																					
	d	13 36						15 28	15 36						17 36			18 06				20 30
Collingham	d		14 02			14 52		15 38		16 02		16 52				18 02		18 15	18 54		20 08	20 39
Swinderby	d		14 06							16 07						18 06			19 01			
Hykeham	d		14 12			15 00				16 13						18 12			19 10			
Lincoln	a	14 02	14 24			15 11		15 56	16 06	16 25		17 08			18 03	18 24		18 33	19 23		20 26	20 54
	d			14 52									17 22					18 34				20 56
Market Rasen	d			15 10									17 38					18 51				21a13
Barnetby	a			15 26									17 54					19 07				
Habrough	a			15 36									18 02					19 17				
Grimsby Town	a			15 50									18 18					19 33				
Cleethorpes	a																					

		GR	EM	EM
		■ 1 C	D	D
Nottingham ■	d		20 30	21 24
Carlton	d		20 36	21 30
Burton Joyce	d			21 34
Lowdham	d		20 41	21 38
Thurgarton	d			
Bleasby	d			21 43
Fiskerton	d		20 51	21 47
Rolleston	d			
Newark Castle	d		21 04	21 57
Newark North Gate ■	a			22 06
	d	20 36		22 09
Collingham	d		21 12	22 18
Swinderby	d			22 22
Hykeham	d		21 21	22 28
Lincoln	a	21 03	21 32	22 40
	d			
Market Rasen	d			
Barnetby	a			
Habrough	a			
Grimsby Town	a			
Cleethorpes	a			

A To Peterborough
B From Matlock
C From London Kings Cross
D From Leicester
E From St Pancras International

For connections from London Kings Cross refer to Table T026

Table T027-F

Sundays
15 December to 10 May

Nottingham - Newark - Lincoln - Cleethorpes

		EM	EM	GR	EM	EM	EM	GR	EM	EM	EM	GR	EM	EM	EM	GR	EM	EM	EM	EM	EM	GR	EM
				R 1 A ☕				R 1 A ☕				R 1 A ☕				R 1 A ☕						R 1 A ☕	
Nottingham [8]	d	09 30	10 30			11 30	12 30			13 30	14 35		15 30		16 33			17 27	18 36		19 35		20 39
Carlton	d	09 36				11 36					14 41							17 33					
Burton Joyce	d	09 40				11 40					14 45							17 36					
Lowdham	d	09 44	10 41			11 44	12 41			13 41	14 49		15 41		16 44			17 40	18 46		19 45		20 49
Thurgarton	d	09 48				11 48					14 53							17 44					
Bleasby	d	09 51				11 51					14 57							17 47					
Fiskerton	d	09 56				11 55					15 00							17 51					
Rolleston	d	09 58				11 57					15 03							17 53					
Newark Castle	d	10 06	10 55			12 06	12 53			13 54	15 13		15 56		16 59			18 01	19 02		19 58		21 03
Newark North Gate [7]	a																		19 12				
	d			11 03	11 40			12 58	13 35			15 54		16 45		17 06	17 55		19 28	19 53		20 37	
Collingham	d	10 17			11 48	12 17			13 43		15 26		16 08	16 53	17 08		18 04	18 11	19 37		20 07		21 12
Swinderby	d	10 22				12 22					15 31			16 58	17 12			18 15	19 42		20 12		21 17
Hykeham	d	10 28				12 28					15 37			17 04	17 18			18 21	19 48		20 18		21 23
Lincoln	a	10 40	11 24	11 29	12 07	12 40	13 19	13 25	14 02	14 24	15 50	16 22	16 26	17 16	17 31	17 37	18 20	18 33	19 57	20 19	20 30	21 03	21 35
	d																						
Market Rasen	d																						
Barnetby	a																						
Habrough	a																						
Grimsby Town	a																						
Cleethorpes	a																						

		EM	EM
Nottingham [8]	d		22 28
Carlton	d		22 34
Burton Joyce	d		22 37
Lowdham	d		22 42
Thurgarton	d		22 46
Bleasby	d		22 49
Fiskerton	d		22 52
Rolleston	d		22 54
Newark Castle	d		23 03
Newark North Gate [7]	a		23 13
	d	22 10	23 17
Collingham	d	22 19	23 25
Swinderby	d		23 30
Hykeham	d		23 36
Lincoln	a	22 37	23 48
	d		
Market Rasen	d		
Barnetby	a		
Habrough	a		
Grimsby Town	a		
Cleethorpes	a		

A From London Kings Cross

For connections from London Kings Cross refer to Table T026

Table T027-R

Mondays to Fridays
16 December to 15 May

Cleethorpes - Lincoln - Newark - Nottingham

Miles	Miles			EM	EM	EM	EM	EM	EM	GR	EM	EM	EM	EM	EM	EM	EM	EM	EM	EM	EM	GR	EM
					A			◇1 B ✕	A	R 1 C ☕	D		A	E	A		E	A	◇	E	A	R 1 C ☕	
0	—	**Cleethorpes**	d				05 49																
3¼	—	**Grimsby Town**	d				05 56					07 03							09 20				
11¼	—	Habrough	d				06 06					07 13							09 30				
17¾	—	Barnetby	d				06 16					07 22							09 39				
32¼	—	Market Rasen	d				06 32					07 39							09 55				
47	—	**Lincoln**	a				06 51					07 57							10 14				
—	—		d	05 26		06 46	06 54	07 04		07 30	07 35	07 59		08 36		09 10	09 37		10 16	10 36		11 27	11 35
51	—	Hykeham	d	05 34		06 53	07 01				07 43			08 44			09 45			10 44			
55¾	—	Swinderby	d	05 40			07 07				07 49			08 50			09 51			10 50			
58½	0	Collingham	d	05 45		07 03	07 12	07 20			07 54	08 15		08 55		09 29	09 56		10 31	10 55			
—	5	**Newark North Gate [7]**	a	05 55			07 22			07 55		08 24				09 39			10 40			11 51	12 00
—	—		d	05 59																			
63½	—	**Newark Castle**	d	06 08	06 42	07 14		07 30	07 39		08 06		08 41	09 07	09 37		10 07	10 47		11 06	11 39		
67	—	Rolleston	d	06 15	06 48				07 46						09 44						11 46		
68	—	Fiskerton	d	06 17	06 51				07 48		08 13		08 48		09 46			10 54			11 48		
69¾	—	Bleasby	d	06 21	06 55				07 52						09 50						11 52		
70¾	—	Thurgarton	d	06 25	06 58				07 55						09 53						11 55		
71½	—	Lowdham	d	06 29	07 02			07 43	08 00		08 20		08 56		09 58			11 02			12 00		
75¾	—	Burton Joyce	d	06 34	07 06				08 04				09 00		10 02						12 04		
77¾	—	Carlton	d	06 38	07 11				08 08				09 05		10 06			11 08			12 08		
80¾	—	**Nottingham [8]**	a	06 47	07 18	07 40		07 56	08 17		08 32		09 13	09 30	10 14		10 30	11 16		11 30	12 16		

		EM	EM	EM	EM	EM	GR	EM	EM	EM	EM	EM	GR	EM	EM	EM	EM	EM	EM	GR	EM	EM	EM
		E	A		E	A	R 1 C ☕	E	A	E	A		R 1 C ☕	E	A		E	A		R 1 C ☕	E		E
Cleethorpes	d																						
Grimsby Town	d			11 28								13 52							15 47				
Habrough	d			11 38								14 02							15 57				
Barnetby	d			11 47								14 11							16 07				
Market Rasen	d			12 03								14 27							16 23				
Lincoln	a			12 22								14 47							16 42				
	d	11 40		12 23	12 34		13 24	13 37		14 36		14 49	15 27	15 36		15 42	16 34		16 43	17 27	17 30	18 18	18 35
Hykeham	d				12 42			13 45		14 44				15 44			16 42				17 38	18 26	18 42
Swinderby	d				12 48					14 50				15 50			16 48				17 44		
Collingham	d			12 40	12 53			13 55		14 55		15 05		15 55			16 53		16 59		17 49	18 36	18 52
Newark North Gate [7]	a			12 50			13 48					15 14	15 51			16 11			17 11	17 51		18 46	
	d																						
Newark Castle	d	12 06	12 47		13 05	13 47		14 07	14 39	15 06	15 47			16 07	16 40		17 04	17 39			17 59		19 03
Rolleston	d								14 46						16 47			17 46			18 05		
Fiskerton	d		12 54			13 54			14 48		15 54				16 49			17 48			18 07		19 10
Bleasby	d								14 52						16 53			17 52			18 11		
Thurgarton	d								14 55						16 56			17 55			18 14		
Lowdham	d		13 02			14 02			15 00		16 02				17 01		17 16	18 00			18 18		19 17
Burton Joyce	d								15 04						17 05			18 04			18 22		
Carlton	d		13 08			14 08			15 08		16 08				17 09		17 23	18 08			18 26		19 23
Nottingham [8]	a	12 30	13 16		13 30	14 16		14 30	15 16	15 30	16 16			16 30	17 17		17 29	18 16			18 34		19 30

		EM	EM	GR	EM	EM	EM	EM
			A	R 1 C ☕				
Cleethorpes	d						21 17	
Grimsby Town	d	18 28					21 24	
Habrough	d	18 38					21 35	
Barnetby	d	18 47					21 44	
Market Rasen	d	19 02					22 00	
Lincoln	a	19 21					22 19	
	d	19 23		20 25	20 31	21 40		22 26
Hykeham	d	19 31			20 38	21 49		22 34
Swinderby	d	19 37						22 40
Collingham	d	19 44			20 48	21 58		22 45
Newark North Gate [7]	a	19 53		20 49				
	d							
Newark Castle	d		19 47		20 58	22 07		22 54
Rolleston	d							
Fiskerton	d		19 54		21 04	22 17		23 01
Bleasby	d							23 05
Thurgarton	d							
Lowdham	d		20 02		21 11	22 25		23 10
Burton Joyce	d							23 14
Carlton	d		20 08		21 17	22 32		23 18
Nottingham [8]	a		20 16		21 27	22 39		23 28

A To Matlock
B To St Pancras International
C To London Kings Cross
D From Sleaford to Leicester
E To Leicester

For connections to London Kings Cross refer to Table T026

Table T027-R

Saturdays

21 December to 16 May

Cleethorpes - Lincoln - Newark - Nottingham

		EM	EM	EM	GR	EM		EM	EM	EM	EM	EM	EM	EM	EM	EM		EM	GR	EM	EM	EM	EM	EM	EM
			◇ A	B	C	D		B		E	B		E	B	◇	E		B	C		E	B		E	B
Cleethorpes	d																								
Grimsby Town	d								06 50						09 20								11 28		
Habrough	d								07 00						09 30								11 38		
Barnetby	d								07 09						09 39								11 47		
Market Rasen	d								07 26						09 55								12 03		
Lincoln	a								07 44						10 14								12 22		
	d	05 26	07 04		07 30	07 35			07 46	08 37		09 12	09 36		10 15	10 36			11 27	11 35	11 40		12 23	12 36	
Hykeham	d	05 33				07 44				08 44			09 43			10 43								12 44	
Swinderby	d	05 39				07 50				08 50			09 50			10 49								12 50	
Collingham	d	05 44	07 19			07 55			08 02	08 55		09 27	09 54		10 32	10 54							12 40	12 54	
Newark North Gate 7	a	05 55			07 56				08 12			09 39			10 44				11 51	12 00			12 52		
	d	05 59																							
Newark Castle	d	06 10	07 29	07 41		08 05		08 43		09 06	09 38		10 06	10 47		11 04		11 39			12 04	12 47		13 05	13 49
Rolleston	d	06 16		07 47							09 45							11 46							
Fiskerton	d	06 18		07 50				08 50			09 47			10 54		11 11		11 48				12 54			13 56
Bleasby	d	06 22		07 54				08 55			09 51							11 52							
Thurgarton	d	06 25		07 57							09 54							11 55							
Lowdham	d	06 29	07 42	08 01				09 00			09 59			11 02		11 18		12 00				13 02			14 04
Burton Joyce	d	06 34		08 06							10 03							12 04							
Carlton	d	06 37		08 10				09 07			10 07			11 08		11 24		12 08				13 08			14 10
Nottingham 8	a	06 47	07 57	08 17		08 28		09 17		09 32	10 15		10 30	11 16		11 31		12 16			12 27	13 16		13 29	14 18

		GR		EM	EM	EM	EM	EM	GR	EM	EM	EM		EM	EM	GR	EM	EM	EM	EM	EM	EM		GR	EM
		C		E	B	E	B		C	E	B	E		B		C	E	B	E	B				C	
Cleethorpes	d																								
Grimsby Town	d							13 52							16 00						18 28				19 45
Habrough	d							14 02							16 10						18 38				19 55
Barnetby	d							14 11							16 19						18 47				20 04
Market Rasen	d							14 27							16 35						19 02				20 20
Lincoln	a							14 47							16 53						19 21				20 39
	d	13 24		13 37		14 33		14 49	15 24	15 27		16 35			16 55	17 27	17 30		18 31		19 23	19 39		20 25	
Hykeham	d			13 44		14 40				15 34		16 43					17 37		18 38		19 30				
Swinderby	d									15 40		16 49					17 43				19 36				
Collingham	d			13 54		14 52		15 05		15 47		16 54			17 11		17 48		18 48		19 41				
Newark North Gate 7	a	13 48						15 14	15 48						17 21	17 51					19 51			20 49	
	d																								
Newark Castle	d			14 05	14 39	15 04	15 47			15 59	16 38	17 04		17 39			17 58	18 47	19 00	19 47		20 04			
Rolleston	d				14 46						16 45			17 46			18 04								
Fiskerton	d				14 48		15 54			16 06	16 47			17 48			18 06	18 54		19 54					
Bleasby	d				14 52						16 51			17 52			18 09								
Thurgarton	d				14 55						16 54			17 55			18 12								
Lowdham	d				15 00		16 02			16 12	16 59	17 17		18 00			18 17	19 02		20 02		20 17			
Burton Joyce	d				15 04						17 03			18 04			18 21								
Carlton	d				15 08		16 08			16 19	17 07			18 08			18 24	19 08		20 08					
Nottingham 8	a			14 28	15 16	15 30	16 16			16 27	17 15	17 30		18 16			18 33	19 16	19 24	20 16		20 30			

		EM
Cleethorpes	d	
Grimsby Town	d	
Habrough	d	
Barnetby	d	
Market Rasen	d	
Lincoln	a	
	d	20 45
Hykeham	d	
Swinderby	d	
Collingham	d	21 00
Newark North Gate 7	a	
	d	
Newark Castle	d	21 10
Rolleston	d	
Fiskerton	d	
Bleasby	d	
Thurgarton	d	
Lowdham	d	21 23
Burton Joyce	d	
Carlton	d	
Nottingham 8	a	21 37

A To St Pancras International
B To Matlock
C To London Kings Cross
D From Sleaford to Leicester
E To Leicester

For connections to London Kings Cross refer to Table T026

Table T027-R

Sundays

15 December to 10 May

Cleethorpes - Lincoln - Newark - Nottingham

		EM	EM	GR	EM	EM		EM	GR	EM	EM	GR	EM	EM	EM	EM		GR	EM	EM	GR	EM	EM	EM	EM
				A					A			A						A			A				
Cleethorpes	d																								
Grimsby Town	d																								
Habrough	d																								
Barnetby	d																								
Market Rasen	d																								
Lincoln	a																								
	d	08 47	09 59	10 55	11 05	11 10		11 56	12 23	12 45	13 01	14 20	14 23	15 08	15 44	16 15		16 50	16 56	17 09	18 00	18 05	19 03	19 22	20 05
Hykeham	d	08 54				11 18							14 30	15 15		16 22			17 03			18 12	19 10		20 12
Swinderby	d	09 01				11 24							14 37	15 21		16 29			17 09			18 18	19 17		20 18
Collingham	d	09 05			11 20	11 29				12 59			14 41	15 26	15 59	16 33			17 14	17 24		18 23	19 21		20 23
Newark North Gate 7	a	09 15		11 19	11 30				12 47	13 10		14 44		15 36	16 09			17 16		17 34	18 24			19 46	
	d	09 18												15 39											
Newark Castle	d	09 29	10 24			11 42		12 24			13 29		14 54	15 50		16 46			17 24			18 34	19 33		20 35
Rolleston	d	09 35				11 48							15 01			16 52						18 40			
Fiskerton	d	09 37				11 50							15 03			16 54						18 42			
Bleasby	d	09 41				11 54							15 07			16 58						18 46			
Thurgarton	d	09 44				11 57							15 10			17 01						18 49			
Lowdham	d	09 48	10 37			12 01		12 40			13 42		15 14	16 02		17 06			17 36			18 53	19 45		20 47
Burton Joyce	d	09 52				12 06							15 18			17 10						18 57			
Carlton	d	09 56				12 09							15 22			17 14						19 01			
Nottingham 8	a	10 08	10 53			12 21		12 57			13 57		15 33	16 20		17 26			17 53			19 11	20 05		21 02

		EM		EM	EM
Cleethorpes	d				
Grimsby Town	d				
Habrough	d				
Barnetby	d				
Market Rasen	d				
Lincoln	a				
	d	21 00		21 26	22 10
Hykeham	d	21 07		21 34	22 17
Swinderby	d	21 13		21 40	22 23
Collingham	d	21 18		21 45	22 28
Newark North Gate 7	a	21 27		21 55	
	d	21 30			
Newark Castle	d	21 40			22 38
Rolleston	d				22 44
Fiskerton	d				22 46
Bleasby	d				22 50
Thurgarton	d				22 53
Lowdham	d	21 52			22 57
Burton Joyce	d				23 01
Carlton	d				23 05
Nottingham 8	a	22 09			23 15

A To London Kings Cross

For connections to London Kings Cross refer to Table T026

Table T028-F

Mondays to Fridays
16 December to 15 May

Cleethorpes - Barton-on-Humber - Barnetby - Gainsborough Central

Miles	Miles			TP ◇1 A	EM B	NT	NT BHX	TP ◇1 A	EM B	NT	NT BHX	TP ◇1 A	TP ◇1 A	NT	NT BHX	EM ◇ B	TP ◇1 A	TP ◇1 A	NT	NT BHX	EM B	TP ◇1 A	TP ◇1 A
0	0	**Cleethorpes**	d	05 05	05 49	05 59		06 26		06 58		07 29	08 26	08 56			09 26	10 26	10 55			11 26	12 26
1½	1½	New Clee	d			06x02				07x01				08x59					10x58				
2¼	2¼	Grimsby Docks	d			06 05				07 04				09 02					11 01				
3¼	3¼	**Grimsby Town**	a	05 12	05 55	06 07		06 33		07 06		07 36	08 33	09 04			09 33	10 33	11 03			11 33	12 33
—	—		d	05 13	05 56	06 08		06 34	07 03	07 07		07 37	08 34	09 05		09 20	09 34	10 34	11 04		11 28	11 34	12 34
5¼	5¼	Great Coates	d			06 12				07 11				09 09					11 08				
6½	6½	Healing	d			06 15				07 14				09 12					11 11				
7½	7½	Stallingborough	d			06 18				07 17				09 15					11 14				
11¼	11¼	Habrough	d	05 23	06 06	06 24		06 44	07 13	07 25		07 47	08 44	09 21		09 30	09 44	10 44	11 20		11 38	11 44	12 44
13	—	Ulceby	d							07 29				09 25					11 24				
15½	—	Thornton Abbey	d			06 33				07 34				09 30					11 29				
17¼	—	Goxhill	d			06 36				07 37				09 33					11 32				
19¼	—	New Holland	d			06 41				07 42				09 38					11 37				
20¾	—	Barrow Haven	d			06 44				07 45				09 41					11 40				
22¾	—	**Barton-on-Humber**	a			06 50				07 51				09 47					11 46				
—	—	Barton-on-Humber	d				07 28				07 58				10 03					12 03			
—	—	Hull Paragon Interchange	a				08 00				08 30				10 35					12 35			
—	17¾	**Barnetby**	a	05 31	06 15			06 52	07 22			07 55	08 52			09 39	09 52	10 52			11 47	11 52	12 52
—	—		d																				
—	21½	Brigg	d																				
—	27¾	Kirton Lindsey	d																				
—	38	Gainsborough Central	a																				
—	—		d																				
—	48	**Retford**	a																				

		NT	NT BHX	TP ◇1 A	EM B	TP ◇1 A	NT	NT BHX	TP ◇1 A	EM B	TP ◇1 A	NT	NT BHX	TP ◇1 A	EM B	TP ◇1 A	NT	TP ◇1 C	TP ◇1 A	NT BHX	NT	EM D	TP ◇1 E
Cleethorpes	d	12 55		13 26		14 26	14 55		15 26		16 26	16 55		17 26		18 26	19 00	19 26	20 26		21 04	21 17	21 26
New Clee	d	12x58					14x58					16x58					19x03				21x07		
Grimsby Docks	d	13 01					15 01					17 01					19 06				21 10		
Grimsby Town	a	13 03		13 33		14 33	15 03		15 33		16 33	17 03		17 33		18 33	19 08	19 33	20 33		21 12	21 23	21 33
	d	13 04		13 34	13 52	14 34	15 04		15 34	15 47	16 34	17 04		17 34	18 28	18 34	19 09	19 34	20 34		21 13	21 24	21 34
Great Coates	d	13 08					15 08					17 08					19 13				21 17		
Healing	d	13 11					15 11					17 11					19 16				21 20		
Stallingborough	d	13 14					15 14					17 14					19 19				21 23		
Habrough	d	13 20		13 44	14 02	14 44	15 20		15 44	15 57	16 44	17 20		17 44	18 38	18 44	19 26	19 44	20 44		21 29	21 35	21 44
Ulceby	d	13 24					15 24					17 24					19 29						
Thornton Abbey	d	13 29					15 29					17 29					19 34				21 38		
Goxhill	d	13 32					15 32					17 32					19 38				21 41		
New Holland	d	13 37					15 37					17 37					19 43				21 46		
Barrow Haven	d	13 40					15 40					17 40					19 46				21 49		
Barton-on-Humber	a	13 46					15 46					17 46					19 51				21 55		
Barton-on-Humber	d		14 03					16 03					18 03							20 52			
Hull Paragon Interchange	a		14 35					16 35					18 35							21 17			
Barnetby	a			13 52	14 11	14 52			15 52	16 06	16 52			17 52	18 46	18 52		19 52	20 52			21 44	21 52
	d																						
Brigg	d																						
Kirton Lindsey	d																						
Gainsborough Central	a																						
	d																						
Retford	a																						

Saturdays
21 December to 16 May

		TP ◇1 A	NT	NT	TP ◇1 A	EM B	NT	NT	TP ◇1 A	TP ◇1 A	NT	NT	EM ◇ B	TP ◇1 A	TP ◇1 A	NT	NT	NT ◇	EM B	TP ◇1 A	TP ◇1 A	NT	NT
Cleethorpes	d	05 05	05 59		06 26		06 58		07 29	08 26	08 56			09 26	10 26	10 55		11 14		11 26	12 26	12 55	
New Clee	d		06x02				07x01				08x59					10x58						12x58	
Grimsby Docks	d		06 05				07 04				09 02					11 01						13 01	
Grimsby Town	a	05 12	06 07		06 33		07 06		07 36	08 33	09 04			09 33	10 33	11 03		11 20		11 33	12 33	13 03	
	d	05 13	06 08		06 34	06 50	07 07		07 37	08 34	09 05		09 20	09 34	10 34	11 04		11 21	11 28	11 34	12 34	13 04	
Great Coates	d		06 12				07 12				09 09					11 08						13 08	
Healing	d		06 15				07 15				09 12					11 11						13 11	
Stallingborough	d		06 18				07 18				09 15					11 14						13 14	
Habrough	d	05 23	06 24		06 44	07 00	07 24		07 47	08 44	09 21		09 30	09 44	10 44	11 20		11 31	11 38	11 44	12 44	13 20	
Ulceby	d						07 28				09 25					11 24						13 24	
Thornton Abbey	d		06 33				07 33				09 30					11 29						13 29	
Goxhill	d		06 36				07 36				09 33					11 32						13 32	
New Holland	d		06 41				07 41				09 38					11 37						13 37	
Barrow Haven	d		06 44				07 44				09 41					11 40						13 40	
Barton-on-Humber	a		06 50				07 50				09 47					11 46						13 46	
Barton-on-Humber	d			06 50				07 58				10 03					12 03						14 03
Hull Paragon Interchange	a			07 17				08 30				10 35					12 35						14 35
Barnetby	a	05 31			06 52	07 09			07 55	08 52			09 39	09 52	10 52			11 40	11 47	11 52	12 52		
	d																	11 42					
Brigg	d																	11 48					
Kirton Lindsey	d																	11 56					
Gainsborough Central	a																	12 09					
	d																						
Retford	a																	12 27					

A To Manchester Airport
B To Newark North Gate
C To Manchester Piccadilly
D To Lincoln
E To Sheffield

For Hull, Doncaster, Meadowhall, Sheffield, Manchester and Manchester Airport refer to Table T029

Table T028-F

Saturdays
21 December to 16 May

Cleethorpes - Barton-on-Humber - Barnetby - Gainsborough Central

		TP ◇1 A	EM B	TP ◇1 A	NT	NT ◇	TP ◇1 A	EM B	TP ◇1 A	NT	NT	TP ◇1 A	EM B	TP ◇1 A	NT	NT ◇ C	TP ◇1 D	EM E	TP ◇1 A	NT	NT	NT
Cleethorpes	d	13 26		14 26	14 55	15 11	15 26		16 26	16 55		17 26		18 26	18 56	19 17	19 26		20 26		21 04	
New Clee	d				14x58					16x58					18x59						21x07	
Grimsby Docks	d				15 01					17 01					19 02						21 10	
Grimsby Town	a	13 33		14 33	15 03	15 17	15 33		16 33	17 03		17 33		18 33	19 04	19 23	19 33		20 33		21 12	
	d	13 34	13 52	14 34	15 04	15 18	15 34	16 00	16 34	17 04		17 34	18 28	18 34	19 05	19 24	19 34	19 45	20 34		21 13	
Great Coates	d				15 08					17 08					19 09						21 17	
Healing	d				15 11					17 11					19 12						21 20	
Stallingborough	d				15 14					17 14					19 15						21 23	
Habrough	d	13 44	14 02	14 44	15 20	15 27	15 44	16 10	16 44	17 20		17 44	18 38	18 44	19 21	19 33	19 44	19 55	20 44		21 29	
Ulceby	d				15 24					17 24					19 25							
Thornton Abbey	d				15 29					17 29					19 30						21 38	
Goxhill	d				15 32					17 32					19 33						21 41	
New Holland	d				15 37					17 37					19 38						21 46	
Barrow Haven	d				15 40					17 40					19 41						21 49	
Barton-on-Humber	a				15 46					17 46					19 47						21 55	
Barton-on-Humber	d										18 03									20 52		22 55
Hull Paragon Interchange	a										18 35									21 17		23 23
Barnetby	a	13 52	14 11	14 52		15 36	15 52	16 19	16 52			17 52	18 46	18 52		19 42	19 52	20 04	20 52			
	d					15 38										19 43						
Brigg	d					15 43										19 48						
Kirton Lindsey	d					15 52										19 57						
Gainsborough Central	a					16 10										20 15						
	d																					
Retford	a					16 31										20 31						

Sundays
15 December to 10 May

		TP ◇1 A		TP ◇1 A	TP ◇1 A	TP ◇1 A	TP ◇1 A	TP ◇1 D	TP ◇1 F
Cleethorpes	d	09 26		16 26	17 27	18 29	19 26	20 26	21 16
New Clee	d								
Grimsby Docks	d								
Grimsby Town	a	09 33		16 33	17 34	18 36	19 33	20 33	21 23
	d	09 34		16 34	17 35	18 37	19 34	20 34	21 24
Great Coates	d								
Healing	d								
Stallingborough	d								
Habrough	d	09 44	and hourly until	16 44	17 45	18 47	19 44	20 44	21 34
Ulceby	d								
Thornton Abbey	d								
Goxhill	d								
New Holland	d								
Barrow Haven	d								
Barton-on-Humber	a								
Barton-on-Humber	d								
Hull Paragon Interchange	a								
Barnetby	a	09 52		16 52	17 53	18 55	19 52	20 52	21 42
	d								
Brigg	d								
Kirton Lindsey	d								
Gainsborough Central	a								
	d								
Retford	a								

A To Manchester Airport
B To Newark North Gate
C To Sheffield. via Retford
D To Manchester Piccadilly
E To Lincoln
F To Sheffield

For Hull, Doncaster, Meadowhall, Sheffield, Manchester and Manchester Airport refer to Table T029

Table T028-R

Mondays to Fridays

16 December to 15 May

Gainsborough Central - Barnetby - Barton-on-Humber - Cleethorpes

Miles	Miles			NT BHX 🚌	EM A	TP ◇1 B	NT	NT BHX 🚌	NT	TP ◇1 C		EM D	NT BHX 🚌	TP ◇1 C	NT	TP ◇1 C	EM D	NT BHX 🚌	TP ◇1 C	NT		TP ◇1 C	NT BHX 🚌	EM D	TP ◇1 C
—	0	**Retford**	d																						
—	10	Gainsborough Central	a																						
—	—		d																						
—	20¼	Kirton Lindsey	d																						
—	26½	Brigg	d																						
—	30¾	**Barnetby**	a																						
—	—		d		06 31	06 36				08 16		08 50		09 21		10 20	10 59		11 18			12 18		13 11	13 18
—	—	Hull Paragon Interchange	d	06 20				07 15					09 10					11 10					13 10		
—	—	Barton-on-Humber	a	06 54				07 46					09 41					11 41					13 41		
0	—	**Barton-on-Humber**	d				06 58		07 56						09 50					11 50					
2	—	Barrow Haven	d				07 03		08 01						09 55					11 55					
3½	—	New Holland	d				07 07		08 05						09 59					11 59					
5½	—	Goxhill	d				07 12		08 10						10 04					12 04					
7¼	—	Thornton Abbey	d				07 16		08 14						10 08					12 08					
9¾	—	Ulceby	d				07 21		08 19						10 13					12 13					
11½	36¾	Habrough	d		06 40	06 48	07 25		08 23	08 28		08 59		09 29	10 17	10 28	11 08		11 26	12 17		12 26		13 20	13 26
15¼	—	Stallingborough	d				07 31		08 28						10 23					12 23					
16¼	—	Healing	d				07 34		08 31						10 26					12 26					
17½	—	Great Coates	d				07 37		08 34						10 29					12 29					
19½	44¾	**Grimsby Town**	a		06 55	07 02	07 41		08 39	08 44		09 12		09 41	10 34	10 41	11 22		11 41	12 34		12 39		13 35	13 41
—	—		d			07 07	07 41		08 39	08 45				09 42	10 34	10 42			11 42	12 34		12 40			13 42
20½	—	Grimsby Docks	d				07 44		08 42						10 37					12 37					
21¼	—	New Clee	d						08x44						10x39					12x39					
22¾	48	**Cleethorpes**	a			07 16	07 50		08 48	08 53				09 54	10 44	10 53			11 53	12 43		12 51			13 51

		NT	TP ◇1 C	EM A	NT BHX 🚌	TP ◇1 C		NT	TP ◇1 C	NT BHX 🚌	TP ◇1 C	EM D	NT	TP ◇1 C	NT BHX 🚌	TP ◇1 C		TP ◇1 C	NT	EM D	TP ◇1 C	NT 🚌	NT	TP ◇1 C	TP ◇1 C
Retford	d																								
Gainsborough Central	a																								
	d																								
Kirton Lindsey	d																								
Brigg	d																								
Barnetby	a																								
	d		14 18	15 09		15 18			16 18		17 18	17 56		18 18		19 18		20 18		20 35	21 18			22 28	23 26
Hull Paragon Interchange	d				15 10					17 00					19 10							21 20			
Barton-on-Humber	a				15 41					17 31					19 41							21 44			
Barton-on-Humber	d	13 50						15 50					17 55						20 01				22 02		
Barrow Haven	d	13 55						15 55					18 00						20 07				22 07		
New Holland	d	13 59						15 59					18 04						20 11				22 11		
Goxhill	d	14 04						16 04					18 09						20 16				22 17		
Thornton Abbey	d	14 08						16 08					18 13						20 20				22 20		
Ulceby	d	14 13						16 13					18 18						20 25				22 25		
Habrough	d	14 17	14 26	15 18		15 26		16 17	16 26		17 26	18 05	18 22	18 28		19 27			20 31	20 44	21 26		22 30	22 36	23 35
Stallingborough	d	14 23						16 23					18 28						20 36				22 36		
Healing	d	14 26						16 26					18 31						20 39				22 38		
Great Coates	d	14 29						16 29					18 34						20 42				22 41		
Grimsby Town	a	14 34	14 39	15 32		15 41		16 34	16 39		17 41	18 18	18 39	18 41		19 42		20 39	20 47	20 56	21 39		22 46	22 51	23 48
	d	14 34	14 40			15 42		16 34	16 40		17 42		18 39	18 42		19 43		20 40	20 48	20 57	21 40		22 47	22 52	23 49
Grimsby Docks	d	14 37						16 37					18 42						20 50				22 49		
New Clee	d	14x39						16x39					18x44						20x52				22x51		
Cleethorpes	a	14 44	14 51			15 51		16 43	16 51		17 51		18 48	18 54		19 54		20 51	20 56	21 04	21 51		22 55	23 04	00 01

A From Lincoln
B From Sheffield
C From Manchester Airport
D From Newark North Gate

For Hull, Doncaster, Meadowhall, Sheffield, Manchester and Manchester Airport refer to Table T029

Table T028-R

Saturdays

21 December to 16 May

Gainsborough Central - Barnetby - Barton-on-Humber - Cleethorpes

		EM A	NT 🚌	TP ◇1 B	NT	NT 🚌		NT	TP ◇1 C	EM A	NT 🚌	TP ◇1 C	NT ◇ D	NT	TP ◇1 C	EM E		NT 🚌	TP ◇1 C	NT	TP ◇1 C	NT 🚌	EM E	TP ◇1 C	NT ◇ D
Retford	d												08 37												12 39
Gainsborough Central	a																								
	d												08 54												12 59
Kirton Lindsey	d												09 07												13 12
Brigg	d												09 20												13 20
Barnetby	a												09 31												13 31
	d	06 14		06 36					08 16	08 50		09 21	09 32		10 20	10 48			11 18		12 18		13 11	13 18	13 32
Hull Paragon Interchange	d		06 20			07 15					09 10							11 10				13 10			
Barton-on-Humber	a		06 54			07 46					09 41							11 41				13 41			
Barton-on-Humber	d				06 56			07 56						09 50						11 50					
Barrow Haven	d				07 01			08 01						09 55						11 55					
New Holland	d				07 05			08 05						09 59						11 59					
Goxhill	d				07 10			08 10						10 04						12 04					
Thornton Abbey	d				07 14			08 14						10 08						12 08					
Ulceby	d				07 19			08 19						10 13						12 13					
Habrough	d	06 26		06 48	07 23			08 23	08 28	08 59		09 29	09 41	10 17	10 28	10 57			11 26	12 17	12 26		13 20	13 26	13 40
Stallingborough	d				07 29			08 29						10 23						12 23					
Healing	d				07 32			08 32						10 26						12 26					
Great Coates	d				07 35			08 35						10 29						12 29					
Grimsby Town	a	06 41		07 02	07 40			08 40	08 44	09 12		09 41	09 54	10 34	10 41	11 11			11 41	12 34	12 39		13 34	13 41	13 53
	d			07 07	07 41			08 40	08 45			09 42	09 55	10 34	10 42				11 42	12 34	12 40			13 42	13 54
Grimsby Docks	d				07 44			08 43						10 37						12 37					
New Clee	d				07x46			08x45						10x39						12x39					
Cleethorpes	a			07 16	07 50			08 49	08 53			09 54	10 04	10 44	10 53				11 53	12 43	12 51			13 51	14 03

		NT		TP ◇1 C	NT 🚌	TP ◇1 C	EM A	NT	TP ◇1 C	NT 🚌	TP ◇1 C	NT ◇		EM A	NT	TP ◇1 C	EM D	NT 🚌	TP ◇1 C	TP ◇1 C	NT	TP ◇1 C		NT 🚌	NT
Retford	d											16 41													
Gainsborough Central	a																								
	d											16 58													
Kirton Lindsey	d											17 12													
Brigg	d											17 24													
Barnetby	a											17 34													
	d			14 18		15 18	15 27		16 18		17 18	17 35		17 54		18 18	19 08		19 18	20 18		21 18			
Hull Paragon Interchange	d				15 10					17 00								19 10						21 20	
Barton-on-Humber	a				15 41					17 31								19 41						21 44	
Barton-on-Humber	d	13 50						15 50							17 55						20 01				22 02
Barrow Haven	d	13 55						15 55							18 00						20 07				22 07
New Holland	d	13 59						15 59							18 04						20 11				22 11
Goxhill	d	14 04						16 04							18 09						20 16				22 16
Thornton Abbey	d	14 08						16 08							18 13						20 20				22 20
Ulceby	d	14 13						16 13							18 18						20 25				22 25
Habrough	d	14 17		14 26		15 26	15 37	16 17	16 26		17 26	17 43		18 03	18 22	18 28	19 17		19 27		20 31	21 26			22 30
Stallingborough	d	14 23						16 23							18 28						20 36				22 35
Healing	d	14 26						16 26							18 31						20 39				22 38
Great Coates	d	14 29						16 29							18 34						20 42				22 41
Grimsby Town	a	14 34		14 39		15 41	15 50	16 34	16 39		17 41	17 57		18 18	18 39	18 41	19 33		19 42	20 39	20 47	21 39			22 46
	d	14 34		14 40		15 42		16 34	16 40		17 42	17 58			18 39	18 42			19 43	20 40	20 48	21 40			22 47
Grimsby Docks	d	14 37						16 37							18 42						20 50				22 49
New Clee	d	14x39						16x39							18x44						20x52				22x51
Cleethorpes	a	14 43		14 51		15 51		16 43	16 51		17 51	18 08			18 48	18 54			19 54	20 51	20 56	21 51			22 55

		TP ◇1 C	TP ◇1 C
Retford	d		
Gainsborough Central	a		
	d		
Kirton Lindsey	d		
Brigg	d		
Barnetby	a		
	d	22 28	23 26
Hull Paragon Interchange	d		
Barton-on-Humber	a		
Barton-on-Humber	d		
Barrow Haven	d		
New Holland	d		
Goxhill	d		
Thornton Abbey	d		
Ulceby	d		
Habrough	d	22 36	23 35
Stallingborough	d		
Healing	d		
Great Coates	d		
Grimsby Town	a	22 51	23 48
	d	22 52	23 49
Grimsby Docks	d		
New Clee	d		
Cleethorpes	a	23 04	00 01

A From Lincoln
B From Sheffield
C From Manchester Airport
D From Newark North Gate

For Hull, Doncaster, Meadowhall, Sheffield, Manchester and Manchester Airport refer to Table T029

Table T028-R

Sundays
15 December to 10 May

Gainsborough Central - Barnetby - Barton-on-Humber - Cleethorpes

		TP	TP	TP	TP	TP	TP	TP	TP	TP		TP	TP	TP	TP	TP
		◇1	◇1	◇1	◇1	◇1	◇1	◇1	◇1	◇1		◇1	◇1	◇1	◇1	◇1
		A	A	A	A	A	A	A	A	A		A	A	A	A	A
Retford	d															
Gainsborough Central	a															
	d															
Kirton Lindsey	d															
Brigg	d															
Barnetby	a															
	d	10 18	11 19	12 19	13 17	14 17	15 17	16 18	17 17	18 17		19 17	20 17	21 17	22 17	23 19
Hull Paragon Interchange	d															
Barton-on-Humber	a															
Barton-on-Humber	d															
Barrow Haven	d															
New Holland	d															
Goxhill	d															
Thornton Abbey	d															
Ulceby	d															
Habrough	d	10 27	11 28	12 28	13 26	14 26	15 26	16 27	17 28	18 26		19 26		21 26	22 26	23 28
Stallingborough	d															
Healing	d															
Great Coates	d															
Grimsby Town	a	10 40	11 43	12 41	13 41	14 41	15 41	16 40	17 43	18 39		19 41	20 39	21 39	22 39	23 43
	d	10 41	11 44	12 42	13 42	14 42	15 42	16 41	17 44	18 40		19 42	20 40	21 40	22 40	23 44
Grimsby Docks	d															
New Clee	d															
Cleethorpes	a	10 53	11 53	12 53	13 51	14 51	15 51	16 51	17 53	18 51		19 51	20 49	21 51	22 51	23 53

A From Manchester Airport

For Hull, Doncaster, Meadowhall, Sheffield, Manchester and Manchester Airport refer to Table T029

AVAILABLE FROM MP Middleton Press

NRT DECEMBER 19 EDITION

Table T029-F

Mondays to Saturdays
16 December to 16 May

Manchester Airport, Manchester, Sheffield and Meadowhall - Doncaster and Hull

Miles	Miles	Miles	Miles			NT MX	TP	NT	TP	NT	NT	TP	NT	NT	NT	NT	NT	NT	NT SX	NT		TP	NT	NT SO	NT
						◇	◇1		◇1	◇		◇1		◇		■ ◇	◇					◇1			
						A	B	C		C		D		D		E	C						F		C
0	—	—	—	**Manchester Airport** 85	d																				
9¾	—	—	—	**Manchester Piccadilly** 10	d																	05 15			
15¾	—	—	—	Stockport 78	d																				
52½	—	—	—	**Sheffield** 7	a																				
—	—	—	—		d			05 15	05 21		05 25					05 42		05 48	06 05					06 07	06 16
56	—	—	—	**Meadowhall**	d			05 21			05 31					05 48		05 54	06 11					06 13	06 22
58¾	—	—	—	Rotherham Central	d			05 28			05 37							06 00	06 18					06 20	06 28
63¼	—	—	—	Swinton (S.Yorks)	d			05a38			05 46							06 09	06 26					06 28	06a38
64½	—	—	—	Mexborough	d						05 49							06 12	06 29					06 31	
66¾	—	—	—	Conisbrough	d						05 53							06 16	06 33					06 35	
—	—	—	—	London Kings Cross	d																				
71½	—	—	—	**Doncaster** 7	a				05 51		06 02					06 11		06 25	06 42					06 44	
—	—	—	—	York 8 26	a																				
—	0	0	0	**Doncaster** 31	d				05 53	05 58					06 11	06 14	06 31		06 43				06 44	06 45	
—	—	—	1¾	Bentley (S.Yorks) 31	a					06 01					06 15		06 34		06 47					06 49	
—	—	—	4	Adwick 31	a					06 05					06 20		06 38		06 52					06 54	
75½	—	4	—	Kirk Sandall	d											06 20							06 50		
78¼	—	6¾	—	Hatfield & Stainforth	d											06 24							06 55		
—	—	9¾	—	Thorne South	d																		07 00		
—	—	15¾	—	Crowle	d																		07 08		
—	—	19½	—	Althorpe	d																		07 14		
—	—	23	—	**Scunthorpe**	a				06 18														07 22		
—	—	—	—		d				06 19																
—	—	34	—	Barnetby 28	d				06 36																
—	—	41	—	Habrough 28	d				06 48																
—	—	49	—	**Grimsby Town** 28	a				07 02																
—	—	—	—		d				07 07																
—	—	52	—	**Cleethorpes** 28	a				07 16																
81¼	—	—	—	Thorne North	d											06 30									
88¾	—	—	—	Goole	d											06 39									
92¼	—	—	—	Saltmarshe	d											06 44									
—	—	—	—	York 8 33	d								05 36							06 15					
—	18¼	—	—	**Selby**	a								05 59							06 49		07 07			
—	—	—	—		d							05 55	05 59	06 28						06 50		07 08			
—	24½	—	—	Wressle	d																				
—	27	—	—	Howden	d															06 59					
—	30	—	—	Eastrington	d																				
95½	32¼	—	—	Gilberdyke	d											06 51				07 08					
98	34¾	—	—	Broomfleet	d											06 55				07 13					
102	38¾	—	—	Brough	d	00 03	00 11					06 12		06 51		07 01				07 19		07 27			
105	41¾	—	—	Ferriby	d											07 06				07 23					
107¾	44½	—	—	Hessle	d											07 10				07 28					
112	49¼	—	—	**Hull**	a	00 17	00 26					06 28	06 30	07 04		07 21				07 38		07 42			

A From Sheffield
B From Manchester Piccadilly
C To Leeds
D From Leeds
E To Scarborough. ◇ to Thorne North ■ from Thorne North
F From Selby

For services between Barnetby, Habrough, Grimsby Town and Cleethorpes, refer to Table T028

Table T029-F

Mondays to Saturdays

16 December to 16 May

Manchester Airport, Manchester, Sheffield and Meadowhall - Doncaster and Hull

	NT ◇ A	NT B	NT SX C	XC SX ◇1 D	NT ◇ E	NT	NT SX F	NT G	XC SO ◇1 D	NT ◇ H	NT ◇ A	TP ◇1 I	NT SO	NT SX	NT ◇ E	NT J	TP ◇1	NT	NT K	NT SX A	NT SO A	XC SO ◇1 L
Manchester Airport 85 d																	05 54					
Manchester Piccadilly 10 d																	06 15					
Stockport 78 d																	06 26					
Sheffield 7 a							←										07 06					
d		06 27	06 27	06 33					06 52	06 55						07 01	07 08			07 12	07 15	07 21
Meadowhall d		06 33	06 33				06 33			07 03						07 07	07 15		←	07 21	07 21	
Rotherham Central d		06 39	→				06 39									07 19			07 19	07 28	07 28	
Swinton (S.Yorks) d		06 48					06 48									→			07 29	07a38	07a38	
Mexborough d		06 52					06 52												07 33			
Conisbrough d		06 56					06 56												07 37			
London Kings Cross d																						
Doncaster 7 a		07 05		06 59			07 05		07 15	07 22							07 32		07 46			
York 8 26 a				07 24					07 41													08 29
Doncaster 31 d	06 54					07 06	07 11	07 11		07 24	07 28						07 33	07 42	07 53			
Bentley (S.Yorks) 31 a	06 58						07 14	07 14			07 31								07 57			
Adwick 31 a	07 01						07 19	07 19			07 35								08 02			
Kirk Sandall d						07 12												07 48				
Hatfield & Stainforth d						07 17												07 53				
Thorne South d																		07 58				
Crowle d																		08 07				
Althorpe d																		08 13				
Scunthorpe a																	08 00	08 21				
d																	08 00					
Barnetby 28 d																	08 16					
Habrough 28 d																	08 28					
Grimsby Town 28 a																	08 44					
d																	08 45					
Cleethorpes 28 a																	08 53					
Thorne North d						07 23																
Goole d						07 32				07 46												
Saltmarshe d						07 37																
York 8 33 d													07 32	07 32								
Selby a													07 58	08 00								
d					07 27							07 54	08 00	08 01	08 27							
Wressle d													08 08	08 08								
Howden d												08 04	08 13	08 13								
Eastrington d													08 18	08 18								
Gilberdyke d						07 44							08 23	08 24								
Broomfleet d						07 48																
Brough d					07 45	07 54				08 02		08 18	08 31	08 32	08 45							
Ferriby d						07 59							08 36	08 36								
Hessle d						08 03							08 40	08 41								
Hull a					07 59	08 13				08 15		08 34	08 49	08 50	08 59							

A To Leeds
B SO until 8 February, from 15 February
C until 14 February. To Adwick
D From Derby to Newcastle
E From Halifax
F until 14 February. From Sheffield
G SO until 8 February, from 15 February. From Hull
H To Scarborough
I From Liverpool Lime Street
J To Adwick
K From Sheffield
L From Birmingham New Street to Glasgow Central

For services between Barnetby, Habrough, Grimsby Town and Cleethorpes, refer to Table T028

Table T029-F

Mondays to Saturdays

16 December to 16 May

Manchester Airport, Manchester, Sheffield and Meadowhall - Doncaster and Hull

	XC SX ◇1 A 🚲	NT SX ◇	NT SO ◇	NT ◇ B	NT	NT	XC SX ◇1 C 🚲	XC SO ◇1 C 🚲	NT SO ◇ D	NT ◇ E	NT ◇ B	NT	TP ◇1 F 🚲	NT	TP ◇1 🚲	NT B	NT ◇	HT ◇1 ⊠	XC ◇1 G 🚲	NT	XC SX ◇1 C 🚲	XC SO ◇1 C 🚲
Manchester Airport 85 d													06 53									
Manchester Piccadilly 10 d													07 18		07 30							
Stockport 78 d													07 28									
Sheffield 7 a													08 10									
d	07 21	07 24	07 25			07 31	07 50	07 52	07 55	07 57		08 07	08 11			08 16			08 22	08 32	08 50	08 50
Meadowhall d		07 30	07 31			07 37				08 03		08 13	08 17			08 22				08 38		
Rotherham Central d		07 36	07 37			07 44						08 19				08 28				08 44		
Swinton (S.Yorks) d		07 48	07 48			07 52						08 30				08a39				08 52		
Mexborough d						07 56						08 33								08 56		
Conisbrough d						08 00						08 37								09 00		
London Kings Cross d																		07 27				
Doncaster 7 a						08 09	08 14	08 14		08 22		08 46	08 36					09 05		09 08	09 15	09 17
York 8 26 a	08 30	08 48	08 49				08 40	08 40											09 30		09 40	09 40
Doncaster 31 d				07 59	08 05	08 10				08 24	08 26		08 38	08 44				09 07				
Bentley (S.Yorks) 31 a				08 02		08 13					08 29											
Adwick 31 a				08 07		08 18					08 33											
Kirk Sandall d					08 11									08 50								
Hatfield & Stainforth d					08 16									08 55								
Thorne South d														09 00								
Crowle d														09 09								
Althorpe d														09 15								
Scunthorpe a													09 05	09 23								
d													09 06									
Barnetby 28 d									09 32				09 21									
Habrough 28 d									09 41				09 29									
Grimsby Town 28 a									09 54				09 41									
d									09 55				09 42									
Cleethorpes 28 a									10 04				09 54									
Thorne North d					08 22																	
Goole d					08 33					08 42												
Saltmarshe d																						
York 8 33 d																	08 45					
Selby a															08 55		09 14	09 22				
d															08 56		09 14	09 23				
Wressle d																						
Howden d																	09 24	09 33				
Eastrington d																						
Gilberdyke d					08 46												09 32					
Broomfleet d																						
Brough d					08 54					09 00					09 15		09 40	09 46				
Ferriby d					08 59																	
Hessle d					09 03																	
Hull a					09 12					09 15					09 30		09 54	10 00				

A From Birmingham New Street to Glasgow Central
B To Leeds
C From Birmingham New Street to Newcastle
D via Retford
E To Scarborough
F 🚲 to Sheffield
G From Birmingham New Street to Edinburgh

For services between Barnetby, Habrough, Grimsby Town and Cleethorpes, refer to Table T028

Table T029-F

Mondays to Saturdays

16 December to 16 May

Manchester Airport, Manchester, Sheffield and Meadowhall - Doncaster and Hull

	NT ◇ A	NT ◇ B	NT	NT ◇ C	NT D	TP ◇1 ⊼	NT	NT E	TP ◇1 ⊼	NT SX C	NT SO C	NT ◇ F	XC ◇1 G ⊼	EM SO ◇1 H ⊼	NT SO	NT SX	XC ◇1 I ⊼	NT ◇ A	NT	NT SX ◇ B	NT ◇ C	NT SO ◇ B
Manchester Airport 85 d						07 53																
Manchester Piccadilly 10 d						08 19			08 30													
Stockport 78 d						08 28																
Sheffield 7 a						09 09																
d		08 56			09 06	09 11				09 15	09 15		09 21	09 29	09 29	09 32	09 51			09 57		09 59
Meadowhall d		09 02			09 11	09 17		←		09 21	09 21				09 35	09 38				10 03		10 05
Rotherham Central d					09 18			09 18		09 28	09 29				09 44	09 44						
Swinton (S.Yorks) d					→			09 28		09a38	09a38				09 52	09 52						
Mexborough d								09 32							09 56	09 56						
Conisbrough d								09 36							10 00	10 00						
London Kings Cross d																						
Doncaster 7 a		09 22				09 37		09 45						09 58	10 10	10 10	10 15			10 22		10 26
York 8 26 a													10 30	10 23			10 40					
Doncaster 31 d		09 24		09 26		09 39	09 42	09 50											10 05	10 24	10 26	10 28
Bentley (S.Yorks) 31 a				09 29				09 54													10 29	
Adwick 31 a				09 33				09 59													10 33	
Kirk Sandall d							09 48												10 11			
Hatfield & Stainforth d							09 53												10 16			
Thorne South d							09 58															
Crowle d							10 07															
Althorpe d							10 13															
Scunthorpe a						10 04	10 21															
d						10 05																
Barnetby 28 d						10 20																
Habrough 28 d						10 28																
Grimsby Town 28 a						10 41																
d						10 42																
Cleethorpes 28 a						10 53																
Thorne North d																			10 22			
Goole d		09 42	09 53																10 35	10 47		10 49
Saltmarshe d																						
York 8 33 d												09 45										
Selby a									09 57			10 14										
d	09 31								09 57			10 14						10 27				
Wressle d																						
Howden d												10 24										
Eastrington d																						
Gilberdyke d			10 02									10 32							10 45			
Broomfleet d																						
Brough d	09 52	09 58	10 10						10 16			10 40						10 46	10 53	11 03		11 05
Ferriby d			10 15																10 57			
Hessle d			10 20																11 02			
Hull a	10 05	10 12	10 29						10 34			10 54						10 59	11 11	11 16		11 18

A From Halifax
B To Scarborough
C To Leeds
D To Adwick
E From Sheffield
F To Bridlington
G From Bath Spa to Glasgow Central
H From St Pancras International
I From Guildford to Newcastle

For services between Barnetby, Habrough, Grimsby Town and Cleethorpes, refer to Table T028

NRT DECEMBER 19 EDITION

Table T029-F

Mondays to Saturdays

16 December to 16 May

Manchester Airport, Manchester, Sheffield and Meadowhall - Doncaster and Hull

	NT A	TP ◇1 B ⊼	NT	NT C	TP SO ◇1 ⊼	TP SX ◇1 ⊼	NT D	NT ◇ E	XC ◇1 F ⊼	XC SX ◇1 G ⊼	NT	XC SO ◇1 H ⊼	NT ◇ I	NT	NT ◇ J	NT ◇ D	HT SO ◇1 ⊠	HT SX ◇1 ⊠	NT A	TP ◇1 B ⊼	NT	NT C
Manchester Airport 85 d		08 53																		09 53		
Manchester Piccadilly 10 d		09 18			09 30	09 35														10 18		
Stockport 78 d		09 28																		10 28		
Sheffield 7 a		10 09																		11 08		
d	10 05	10 11					10 15		10 21	10 29	10 32	10 51			10 57				11 05	11 10		
Meadowhall d	10 11	10 17		←			10 21				10 38				11 03				11 11	11 17		←
Rotherham Central d	10 19			10 19			10 28				10 44								11 19			11 19
Swinton (S.Yorks) d	→			10 28			10a36				10 52								→			11 28
Mexborough d				10 32							10 56											11 32
Conisbrough d				10 36							11 00											11 36
London Kings Cross d																	09 48	09 48				
Doncaster 7 a		10 35		10 45						10 52	11 09	11 14			11 22		11 24	11 26		11 35		11 45
York 8 26 a									11 30	11 15		11 40										
Doncaster 31 d		10 37	10 42	10 47										11 05	11 24	11 26	11 26	11 28		11 37	11 42	11 47
Bentley (S.Yorks) 31 a				10 51												11 29						11 51
Adwick 31 a				10 56												11 33						11 56
Kirk Sandall d			10 48											11 11							11 48	
Hatfield & Stainforth d			10 53											11 16							11 53	
Thorne South d			10 58																		11 58	
Crowle d			11 07																		12 07	
Althorpe d			11 13																		12 13	
Scunthorpe a		11 02	11 21																	12 02	12 21	
d		11 03																		12 03		
Barnetby 28 d		11 18																		12 18		
Habrough 28 d		11 26																		12 26		
Grimsby Town 28 a		11 41																		12 39		
d		11 42																		12 40		
Cleethorpes 28 a		11 53																		12 51		
Thorne North d														11 22								
Goole d														11 31	11 42							
Saltmarshe d														11 36								
York 8 33 d								10 45														
Selby a					10 56	10 56		11 14									11 43	11 43				
d					10 56	10 56		11 14					11 27				11 43	11 43				
Wressle d																						
Howden d								11 24									11 53	11 53				
Eastrington d																						
Gilberdyke d								11 32						11 43								
Broomfleet d														11 47								
Brough d					11 15	11 15		11 40					11 46	11 53	11 59		12 05	12 05				
Ferriby d														11 57								
Hessle d														12 02								
Hull a					11 30	11 30		11 54					11 59	12 11	12 14		12 18	12 18				

A To Adwick
B ⊼ to Sheffield
C From Sheffield
D To Leeds
E To Bridlington
F From Plymouth to Edinburgh
G From Reading to Newcastle
H From Bournemouth to Newcastle
I From Halifax
J To Scarborough

For services between Barnetby, Habrough, Grimsby Town and Cleethorpes, refer to Table T028

Table T029-F

Mondays to Saturdays

16 December to 16 May

Manchester Airport, Manchester, Sheffield and Meadowhall - Doncaster and Hull

	TP SX ◇1 🍴	TP SO ◇1 🍴	NT A	NT ◇ B	XC SO ◇1 C 🍴	XC SX ◇1 C 🍴	XC SO ◇1 D 🍴	XC SX ◇1 D 🍴	NT	NT SO ◇	NT SX ◇	NT SO ◇ E	NT ◇ F	NT	NT ◇ G	NT ◇ A	NT H	TP ◇1 I 🍴	NT	NT J	TP ◇1 🍴	NT A
Manchester Airport 85 ✈ d																		10 53				
Manchester Piccadilly 10 d	10 30	10 35																11 18			11 35	
Stockport 78 d																		11 28				
Sheffield 7 a																		12 08				
d			11 15		11 21	11 21	11 29	11 29	11 32	11 41	11 41	11 54			11 57		12 05	12 11				12 15
Meadowhall d			11 21						11 38	11 47	11 47				12 03		12 11	12 17		←		12 21
Rotherham Central d			11 28						11 44	11 55	11 57						12 19			12 19		12 28
Swinton (S.Yorks) d			11a38						11 52	12 03	12 06						→			12 28		12a38
Mexborough d									11 56											12 32		
Conisbrough d									12 00											12 36		
London Kings Cross d																						
Doncaster 7 a							11 52	11 53	12 09						12 22			12 35		12 45		
York 8 26 a					12 30	12 31	12 15	12 15		12 56	13 05											
Doncaster 31 d														12 05	12 24	12 26		12 37	12 42	12 47		
Bentley (S.Yorks) 31 a																12 29				12 51		
Adwick 31 a																12 33				12 56		
Kirk Sandall d														12 11					12 48			
Hatfield & Stainforth d														12 16					12 53			
Thorne South d																			12 58			
Crowle d																			13 07			
Althorpe d																			13 13			
Scunthorpe a																		13 02	13 21			
d																		13 03				
Barnetby 28 d												13 32						13 18				
Habrough 28 d												13 40						13 26				
Grimsby Town 28 a												13 53						13 41				
d												13 54						13 42				
Cleethorpes 28 a												14 03						13 51				
Thorne North d														12 22								
Goole d														12 31	12 44							
Saltmarshe d																						
York 8 33 d				11 45																		
Selby a	11 56	11 56		12 14																	12 56	
d	11 56	11 56		12 14									12 27								12 56	
Wressle d																						
Howden d				12 24																		
Eastrington d																						
Gilberdyke d				12 32										12 45								
Broomfleet d																						
Brough d	12 15	12 15		12 40									12 46	12 53	13 03						13 15	
Ferriby d														12 57								
Hessle d														13 02								
Hull a	12 30	12 30		12 54									12 59	13 12	13 16						13 32	

A To Leeds
B To Bridlington
C From Plymouth to Glasgow Central
D From Southampton Central to Newcastle
E via Retford
F From Halifax
G To Scarborough
H To Adwick
I 🍴 to Sheffield
J From Sheffield

For services between Barnetby, Habrough, Grimsby Town and Cleethorpes, refer to Table T028

Table T029-F

Mondays to Saturdays

16 December to 16 May

Manchester Airport, Manchester, Sheffield and Meadowhall - Doncaster and Hull

	NT ◇ A	XC ◇1 B 🍴	XC SO ◇1 C 🍴	NT	XC SX ◇1 C 🍴	NT ◇ D	NT	NT ◇ E	HT SO ◇1 ⊠	NT ◇ F	HT SX ◇1 ⊠	NT G	TP ◇1 H 🍴	NT	NT I	TP ◇1 🍴	NT F	NT ◇ A	XC ◇1 J 🍴	XC SO ◇1 K 🍴	NT	XC SX ◇1 K 🍴
Manchester Airport 85 ✈ d													11 53									
Manchester Piccadilly 10 d													12 18			12 35						
Stockport 78 d													12 28									
Sheffield 7 a													13 08									
d		12 21	12 29	12 32	12 51			12 57				13 05	13 11				13 15		13 21	13 29	13 32	13 46
Meadowhall d				12 38				13 03				13 11	13 17		←		13 21				13 38	
Rotherham Central d				12 44								13 19			13 19		13 28				13 44	
Swinton (S.Yorks) d				12 52								→			13 28		13a38				13 52	
Mexborough d				12 56											13 32						13 56	
Conisbrough d				13 00											13 36						14 00	
London Kings Cross d									11 48		11 48											
Doncaster 7 a			12 53	13 09	13 16			13 22	13 24		13 26		13 35		13 45					13 53	14 10	14 14
York 8 26 a		13 30	13 15		13 40														14 30	14 14		14 39
Doncaster 31 d							13 05	13 24	13 26	13 27	13 28		13 37	13 42	13 47							
Bentley (S.Yorks) 31 a										13 30					13 51							
Adwick 31 a										13 34					13 56							
Kirk Sandall d							13 11							13 48								
Hatfield & Stainforth d							13 16							13 53								
Thorne South d														13 58								
Crowle d														14 07								
Althorpe d														14 13								
Scunthorpe a													14 02	14 21								
d													14 03									
Barnetby 28 d													14 18									
Habrough 28 d													14 26									
Grimsby Town 28 a													14 39									
d													14 40									
Cleethorpes 28 a													14 51									
Thorne North d							13 22															
Goole d							13 31	13 43														
Saltmarshe d																						
York 8 33 d	12 42																	13 45				
Selby a	13 15								13 43		13 43					13 56		14 14				
d	13 15					13 27			13 46		13 43					13 56		14 15				
Wressle d																						
Howden d	13 25								13 55		13 53							14 25				
Eastrington d																						
Gilberdyke d	13 33						13 45											14 32				
Broomfleet d																						
Brough d	13 41					13 46	13 53	14 00	14 09		14 05					14 15		14 40				
Ferriby d							13 57															
Hessle d							14 02															
Hull a	13 55					13 59	14 11	14 14	14 25		14 18					14 30		14 54				

A To Bridlington
B From Plymouth to Edinburgh
C From Reading to Newcastle
D From Halifax
E To Scarborough
F To Leeds
G To Adwick
H 🍴 to Sheffield
I From Sheffield
J From Penzance to Glasgow Central
K From Southampton Central to Newcastle

For services between Barnetby, Habrough, Grimsby Town and Cleethorpes, refer to Table T028

Table T029-F

Mondays to Saturdays

16 December to 16 May

Manchester Airport, Manchester, Sheffield and Meadowhall - Doncaster and Hull

		NT	NT	NT	NT	NT	TP	NT	NT	TP	NT	NT	XC	XC SO	NT	XC SX	NT	NT	NT	NT	HT SX	NT	TP
		◇ A		◇ B	◇ C	D	◇1 E		F	◇1	◇ C	◇ G	◇1 H	◇1 I		◇1 I	◇ A		◇ B	◇ C	◇1	D	◇1 E
Manchester Airport 85	d						12 53																13 53
Manchester Piccadilly 10	d						13 18			13 35													14 18
Stockport 78	d						13 28																14 28
Sheffield 7	a						14 08																15 08
	d			13 57		14 05	14 11				14 15		14 21	14 29	14 32	14 51			14 57			15 05	15 11
Meadowhall	d			14 02		14 11	14 17		←		14 21				14 38				15 03			15 11	15 17
Rotherham Central	d					14 19			14 19		14 28				14 44							15 19	
Swinton (S.Yorks)	d					→			14 28		14a38				14 52							→	
Mexborough	d								14 32						14 56								
Conisbrough	d								14 36						15 00								
London Kings Cross	d																				13 48		
Doncaster 7	a			14 22			14 35		14 45					14 53	15 10	15 15			15 22		15 26		15 35
York 8 26	a												15 30	15 15		15 40							
Doncaster 31	d		14 05	14 24	14 26		14 37	14 42	14 47									15 05	15 24	15 26	15 28		15 37
Bentley (S.Yorks) 31	a				14 29				14 51											15 29			
Adwick 31	a				14 33				14 56											15 33			
Kirk Sandall	d		14 11					14 48										15 11					
Hatfield & Stainforth	d		14 16					14 53										15 16					
Thorne South	d							14 58															
Crowle	d							15 07															
Althorpe	d							15 13															
Scunthorpe	a						15 02	15 21															16 02
	d						15 03																16 03
Barnetby 28	d						15 18																16 18
Habrough 28	d						15 26																16 26
Grimsby Town 28	a						15 41																16 39
	d						15 42																16 40
Cleethorpes 28	a						15 51																16 51
Thorne North	d		14 22															15 22					
Goole	d		14 31	14 44														15 31	15 47				
Saltmarshe	d																						
York 8 33	d											14 46											
Selby	a									14 56		15 14									15 43		
	d	14 27								14 56		15 14					15 27				15 43		
Wressle	d																						
Howden	d											15 24									15 54		
Eastrington	d																						
Gilberdyke	d		14 44									15 32						15 44					
Broomfleet	d																						
Brough	d	14 46	14 52	15 01						15 15		15 40					15 46	15 52	16 02		16 08		
Ferriby	d		14 56															15 56					
Hessle	d		15 01															16 01					
Hull	a	14 59	15 12	15 15						15 31		15 54					15 59	16 12	16 15		16 25		

A From Halifax
B To Scarborough
C To Leeds
D To Adwick
E to Sheffield
F From Sheffield
G To Bridlington
H From Plymouth to Aberdeen
I From Reading to Newcastle

For services between Barnetby, Habrough, Grimsby Town and Cleethorpes, refer to Table T028

Table T029-F

Mondays to Saturdays

16 December to 16 May

Manchester Airport, Manchester, Sheffield and Meadowhall - Doncaster and Hull

		NT	NT	TP	NT	NT	XC	NT	NT SX	NT SO	XC SX	XC SO	NT SO	NT	NT	NT SO	NT SX	HT SO	NT	NT	TP	NT	NT
			A	◇1	B	◇ C	◇1 D		◇	◇	1 E	◇1 E	◇ F	◇ G		◇ H	◇ H	◇1	◇ B	I	◇1 J		A
Manchester Airport 85	d																				14 53		
Manchester Piccadilly 10	d			14 35																	15 18		
Stockport 78	d																				15 28		
Sheffield 7	a																				16 08		
	d				15 15		15 21	15 32	15 40	15 41	15 51	15 51	15 54			15 57	15 57			16 05	16 11		
Meadowhall	d		←		15 21			15 38	15 48	15 47						16 03	16 03			16 11	16 17		←
Rotherham Central	d		15 19		15 28			15 44	15 56	15 56										16 19			16 19
Swinton (S.Yorks)	d		15 28		15a36			15 52	16 07	16 06										→			16 28
Mexborough	d		15 32					15 56															16 32
Conisbrough	d		15 36					16 00															16 36
London Kings Cross	d																	14 48					
Doncaster 7	a		15 45					16 10			16 15	16 17				16 22	16 22	16 25			16 35		16 45
York 8 26	a						16 30		17 00	16 58	16 40	16 40											
Doncaster 31	d	15 42	15 47												16 05	16 24	16 25	16 26	16 27		16 37	16 42	16 47
Bentley (S.Yorks) 31	a		15 51																16 30				16 51
Adwick 31	a		15 56																16 34				16 56
Kirk Sandall	d	15 48													16 11							16 48	
Hatfield & Stainforth	d	15 53													16 16							16 53	
Thorne South	d	15 58																				16 58	
Crowle	d	16 07																				17 07	
Althorpe	d	16 13																				17 13	
Scunthorpe	a	16 21																			17 02	17 20	
	d																				17 03		
Barnetby 28	d												17 35								17 18		
Habrough 28	d												17 43								17 26		
Grimsby Town 28	a												17 57								17 41		
	d												17 58								17 42		
Cleethorpes 28	a												18 08								17 51		
Thorne North	d														16 22								
Goole	d														16 31	16 43	16 43						
Saltmarshe	d														16 36								
York 8 33	d					15 46																	
Selby	a			15 55		16 17												16 41					
	d			15 55		16 18								16 27				16 42					
Wressle	d																						
Howden	d					16 28												16 51					
Eastrington	d																						
Gilberdyke	d					16 36									16 45								
Broomfleet	d																						
Brough	d			16 14		16 44								16 47	16 53	16 59	16 59	17 08					
Ferriby	d														16 57								
Hessle	d														17 02								
Hull	a			16 31		16 57								17 01	17 12	17 15	17 15	17 25					

A From Sheffield
B To Leeds
C To Bridlington
D From Penzance to Glasgow Central
E From Southampton Central to Newcastle
F via Retford
G From Halifax
H To Scarborough
I To Adwick
J to Sheffield

For services between Barnetby, Habrough, Grimsby Town and Cleethorpes, refer to Table T028

Table T029-F

Mondays to Saturdays

16 December to 16 May

Manchester Airport, Manchester, Sheffield and Meadowhall - Doncaster and Hull

	TP ◇1 ✠	NT A	NT ◇ B		XC ◇1 C ✠	XC SX ◇1 D ✠	NT	XC SO ◇1 D ✠	NT ◇ E	NT	NT ◇ F	NT ◇ A	HT SX ◇1 G ⊠	NT H	TP ◇1 I ✠	NT	NT J	TP ◇1 ✠	NT A		NT ◇ B	XC SO ◇1 K ✠	XC SX ◇1 K ✠	NT
Manchester Airport 85 ✈ d															15 53									
Manchester Piccadilly 10 d	15 35														16 18			16 30						
Stockport 78 d															16 28									
Sheffield 7 a															17 09									
d		16 15			16 21	16 29	16 32	16 51			16 57			17 05	17 11				17 15			17 21	17 21	17 32
Meadowhall d		16 21					16 38				17 05			17 11	17 17		←		17 21					17 38
Rotherham Central d		16 28					16 44							17 19			17 19		17 28					17 44
Swinton (S.Yorks) d		16a38					16 52							→			17 28		17a38					17 52
Mexborough d							16 56										17 32							17 56
Conisbrough d							17 00										17 36							18 00
London Kings Cross d													15 48											
Doncaster 7 a						16 53	17 10	17 13			17 24		17 26		17 35		17 45							18 10
York 8 26 a					17 30	17 14		17 42														18 30	18 31	
Doncaster 31 d										17 05	17 26	17 26	17 28		17 37	17 42	17 48							
Bentley (S.Yorks) 31 a												17 29					17 52							
Adwick 31 a												17 33					17 57							
Kirk Sandall d										17 11						17 48								
Hatfield & Stainforth d										17 16						17 53								
Thorne South d																17 58								
Crowle d																18 07								
Althorpe d																18 13								
Scunthorpe a															18 02	18 21								
d															18 03									
Barnetby 28 d															18 18									
Habrough 28 d															18 28									
Grimsby Town 28 a															18 41									
d															18 42									
Cleethorpes 28 a															18 54									
Thorne North d										17 22														
Goole d										17 33	17 47													
Saltmarshe d																								
York 8 33 d			16 45																		17 45			
Selby a	16 59		17 14										17 43					17 59			18 15			
d	16 59		17 14						17 27				17 43					17 59			18 16			
Wressle d			17 22																					
Howden d			17 27										17 53					18 09			18 26			
Eastrington d																								
Gilberdyke d			17 35							17 46											18 34			
Broomfleet d																								
Brough d	17 18		17 43						17 49	17 55	18 03		18 07					18 22			18 42			
Ferriby d										17 59														
Hessle d										18 04														
Hull a	17 34		17 56						18 02	18 13	18 17		18 23					18 37			18 55			

A To Leeds
B To Bridlington
C From Penzance to Dundee
D From Reading to Newcastle
E From Halifax
F To Scarborough
G To Beverley
H To Adwick
I ✠ to Sheffield
J From Sheffield
K From Plymouth to Glasgow Central

For services between Barnetby, Habrough, Grimsby Town and Cleethorpes, refer to Table T028

Table T029-F

Mondays to Saturdays

16 December to 16 May

Manchester Airport, Manchester, Sheffield and Meadowhall - Doncaster and Hull

	XC ◇1 A ✠	NT ◇ B	NT SO		NT SX	NT ◇ C	NT ◇ D	NT E	TP ◇1 F ✠	NT	NT G	TP ◇1 ✠	NT H	NT ◇ I	XC ◇1 J ✠	NT	XC SO ◇1 K ✠	XC SX ◇1 K ✠	NT ◇ B		NT ◇ I	HT SO ◇1 L ⊠	NT ◇ D	NT
Manchester Airport 85 ✈ d									16 53															
Manchester Piccadilly 10 d									17 18			17 30												
Stockport 78 d									17 28															
Sheffield 7 a									18 10															
d	17 51					17 57		18 05	18 11				18 15		18 21	18 30	18 51	18 51			18 57			
Meadowhall d						18 03		18 11	18 17		←		18 21			18 38					19 03			
Rotherham Central d								18 18			18 18		18 28			18 44								
Swinton (S.Yorks) d								→			18 29		18a38			18 52								
Mexborough d											18 33					18 56								
Conisbrough d											18 37					19 00								
London Kings Cross d																						17 48		
Doncaster 7 a						18 23			18 35		18 46					19 09	19 13	19 17			19 22	19 25		
York 8 26 a	19 04														19 30		19 41	19 41						
Doncaster 31 d			18 05		18 05	18 25	18 28		18 37	18 42	18 48										19 24	19 27	19 28	
Bentley (S.Yorks) 31 a							18 31				18 52												19 31	
Adwick 31 a							18 35				18 57												19 35	
Kirk Sandall d			18 11		18 11					18 48														
Hatfield & Stainforth d			18 16		18 16					18 53														
Thorne South d										18 58														
Crowle d										19 07														
Althorpe d										19 13														
Scunthorpe a									19 03	19 21														
d									19 03															
Barnetby 28 d									19 18															
Habrough 28 d									19 27															
Grimsby Town 28 a									19 42															
d									19 43															
Cleethorpes 28 a									19 54															
Thorne North d			18 22		18 22	18 37																		
Goole d			18 31		18 31	18 46															19 42			19 53
Saltmarshe d																								19 57
York 8 33 d														18 45										
Selby a												18 58		19 14								19 42		
d		18 27										18 59		19 14					19 35			19 42		
Wressle d																								
Howden d														19 24								19 52		
Eastrington d																								
Gilberdyke d			18 44		18 45									19 32										
Broomfleet d																								
Brough d		18 46	18 52		18 53	19 04						19 18		19 40							20 00	20 05		20 11
Ferriby d			18 57		18 57																			20 15
Hessle d			19 02		19 02																			20 19
Hull a		18 59	19 12		19 12	19 17						19 33		19 54					20 06		20 13	20 18		20 28

A From Southampton Central to Newcastle
B From Halifax
C To Scarborough
D To Leeds
E To Adwick
F ✠ to Sheffield
G From Sheffield
H SX until 14 February, from 17 February. To Leeds
I To Bridlington
J From Plymouth to Edinburgh
K From Reading to Newcastle
L To Beverley

For services between Barnetby, Habrough, Grimsby Town and Cleethorpes, refer to Table T028

Table T029-F

Mondays to Saturdays

16 December to 16 May

Manchester Airport, Manchester, Sheffield and Meadowhall - Doncaster and Hull

		NT	TP	NT		NT	TP	NT	NT	XC	XC	NT	XC	NT	NT	NT	NT	HT	NT	TP		NT	NT	TP	TP
											SO		SX					SX						SX	SO
			◇1				◇1		◇	◇1	◇1		◇1	◇		◇	◇	◇1		◇1				◇1	◇1
		A	B			C		D	E	F	G		G	H			D	I	A				C		
			🍴				🍴			🍴	🍴		🍴					⊠							
Manchester Airport 85	d		17 53																	18 53					
Manchester Piccadilly 10	d		18 18				18 30													19 18				19 30	19 35
Stockport 78	d		18 28																	19 28					
Sheffield 7	a		19 08																	20 08					
	d	19 05	19 11					19 15		19 21	19 29	19 32	19 51			19 57			20 05	20 11					
Meadowhall	d	19 13	19 17			←		19 21				19 38				20 03			20 11	20 17			←		
Rotherham Central	d	19 19				19 19		19 28				19 44							20 19				20 19		
Swinton (S.Yorks)	d	→				19 29		19a38				19 52							→				20 28		
Mexborough	d					19 32						19 56											20 31		
Conisbrough	d					19 36						20 00											20 35		
London Kings Cross	d																	18 48							
Doncaster 7	a		19 37			19 45					19 53	20 10	20 13			20 22		20 27		20 35			20 44		
York 8 26	a									20 30	20 15		20 41												
Doncaster 31	d		19 39	19 42		19 54									20 05	20 24	20 28	20 28		20 37		20 42	20 48		
Bentley (S.Yorks) 31	a					19 58											20 31						20 52		
Adwick 31	a					20 03											20 35						20 57		
Kirk Sandall	d			19 49											20 11							20 48			
Hatfield & Stainforth	d			19 54											20 16							20 53			
Thorne South	d			19 59																		20 58			
Crowle	d			20 08																		21 07			
Althorpe	d			20 14																		21 13			
Scunthorpe	a		20 02	20 22																21 02		21 21			
	d		20 03																	21 03					
Barnetby 28	d		20 18																	21 18					
Habrough 28	d																			21 26					
Grimsby Town 28	a		20 39																	21 39					
	d		20 40																	21 40					
Cleethorpes 28	a		20 51																	21 51					
Thorne North	d														20 22										
Goole	d														20 31										
Saltmarshe	d																								
York 8 33	d								19 41																
Selby	a						19 56		20 10							20 40		20 47						20 56	20 56
	d						19 56		20 10					20 27		20 41		20 49						20 56	20 57
Wressle	d								20 18																
Howden	d								20 23									20 59						21 06	21 07
Eastrington	d																								
Gilberdyke	d								20 31						20 45										
Broomfleet	d														20 49										
Brough	d						20 17		20 39					20 46	20 55	21 01		21 11						21 19	21 20
Ferriby	d														20 59										
Hessle	d														21 04										
Hull	a						20 34		20 52					20 59	21 13	21 16		21 24						21 34	21 35

A To Adwick
B 🍴 to Sheffield
C From Sheffield
D To Leeds
E To Bridlington
F From Plymouth to Edinburgh
G From Southampton Central to Newcastle
H From Halifax
I To Beverley

For services between Barnetby, Habrough, Grimsby Town and Cleethorpes, refer to Table T028

Table T029-F

Mondays to Saturdays

16 December to 16 May

Manchester Airport, Manchester, Sheffield and Meadowhall - Doncaster and Hull

		NT	NT	XC		XC	NT	XC	NT	NT	NT	HT	NT	NT	TP	NT	TP	NT	NT	NT		HT	NT	XC	NT
				SO		SX		SO				SO										SX		SX	
			◇	◇1		◇1		◇1	◇	◇	◇	◇1			◇1		◇1		◇			◇1	◇	◇1	◇
		A		B		C		C	D	E	A			F		G		A					D	H	
						🍴		🍴				⊠										⊠			
Manchester Airport 85	d														19 53										
Manchester Piccadilly 10	d														20 18		20 35								
Stockport 78	d														20 28										
Sheffield 7	a														21 08										
	d	20 15		20 21		20 29	20 32	20 50		20 57				21 05	21 11			21 15						21 52	21 57
Meadowhall	d	20 21					20 38			21 03				21 11	21 17			21 21							22 03
Rotherham Central	d	20 28					20 44							21 19	21 23	←		21 29							
Swinton (S.Yorks)	d	20a38					20 52							21 28		21 28		21a40							
Mexborough	d						20 56							→		21 38									
Conisbrough	d						21 00									21 42									
London Kings Cross	d											19 48										20 30			
Doncaster 7	a					20 53	21 09	21 17		21 22		21 27			21 47	21 52						22 06		22 28	22 22
York 8 26	a			21 46		21 15		21 41																→	
Doncaster 31	d									21 24	21 28	21 29			21 47	21 53				21 54		22 08			22 25
Bentley (S.Yorks) 31	a										21 31					21 56									
Adwick 31	a										21 35					22 01									
Kirk Sandall	d																			22 00					
Hatfield & Stainforth	d																			22 05					
Thorne South	d																			22 10					
Crowle	d																			22 19					
Althorpe	d																			22 25					
Scunthorpe	a														22 12					22 33					
	d														22 13										
Barnetby 28	d														22 28										
Habrough 28	d														22 36										
Grimsby Town 28	a														22 51										
	d														22 52										
Cleethorpes 28	a														23 04										
Thorne North	d																								
Goole	d									21 43			21 51												22 44
Saltmarshe	d												21 55												22 48
York 8 33	d		20 45																21 44						
Selby	a		21 14									21 44					21 56		22 14			22 23			
	d		21 14						21 27			21 45					21 56		22 14			22 23	22 32		
Wressle	d																								
Howden	d		21 23									21 54					22 06		22 24			22 33			
Eastrington	d		21 28																						
Gilberdyke	d												22 04						22 32						22 54
Broomfleet	d																								
Brough	d		21 38						21 46	21 58		22 06	22 13				22 19		22 40			22 47	22 52		23 02
Ferriby	d		21 43										22 17												
Hessle	d		21 48										22 22												
Hull	a		21 57						22 02	22 13		22 20	22 31				22 36		22 53			23 00	23 05		23 16

A To Leeds
B From Plymouth
C From Reading to Newcastle
D From Halifax
E To Bridlington
F To Adwick
G From Sheffield
H From Southampton Central to York

For services between Barnetby, Habrough, Grimsby Town and Cleethorpes, refer to Table T028

Table T029-F

Mondays to Saturdays

16 December to 16 May

Manchester Airport, Manchester, Sheffield and Meadowhall - Doncaster and Hull

	NT ◇ A	XC SO ◇1 B	XC SX ◇1 B	NT C		TP ◇1	NT D	TP ◇1	NT E	XC SO ◇1 F	NT	NT ◇ A	NT SO ◇ G	NT SX ◇ G	NT SO ◇	NT SX ◇	NT	TP SO ◇1	TP SX ◇1	NT SX A		TP SX ◇1	TP SO ◇1	NT
Manchester Airport 85 d						20 53												21 53	21 53					
Manchester Piccadilly 10 d						21 18		21 35										22 17	22 20			22 32	22 34	
Stockport 78 d						21 28																		
Sheffield 7 a						22 08												23 07	23 09					
d		22 03		22 07		22 11			22{15	22 25					22 59	22 59	23 05	23 09	23 12	23 15				23 27
Meadowhall d				22 13		22 17	←		22{21						23 05	23 05	23 11			23 21				23 33
Rotherham Central d				22 19			22 19		22{28								23 18			23 28				23 39
Swinton (S.Yorks) d				→			22 29		22a41								23 27			23a36				23 48
Mexborough d							22 33										23 30							23 51
Conisbrough d							22 37										23 34							23 55
London Kings Cross d			←																					
Doncaster 7 a		22 26	22 28			22 35	22 46			22 50					23 25	23 25	23 43	23 35	23 53					00 04
York 8 26 a		22 47	22 51																					
Doncaster 31 d	22 32					22 38	22 47					23 24			23 28	23 28								
Bentley (S.Yorks) 31 a	22 35						22 51					23 27												
Adwick 31 a	22 39						22 55					23 31												
Kirk Sandall d						22 43																		
Hatfield & Stainforth d						22 48																		
Thorne South d						22 52																		
Crowle d						23 01																		
Althorpe d						23 06																		
Scunthorpe a						23 11																		
d						23 12																		
Barnetby 28 d						23 26																		
Habrough 28 d						23 35																		
Grimsby Town 28 a						23 48																		
d						23 49																		
Cleethorpes 28 a						00 01																		
Thorne North d																								
Goole d															23 47	23 47								
Saltmarshe d																								
York 8 33 d											22 47													
Selby a								23 02			23 17											23 51	23 52	
d								23 02			23 18		23 27	23 31								23 52	23 53	
Wressle d																								
Howden d											23 27													
Eastrington d																								
Gilberdyke d											23 34													
Broomfleet d																								
Brough d								23 21			23 42		23 48	23 51	00 02	00 03						00 11	00 12	
Ferriby d											23 46													
Hessle d											23 51													
Hull a								23 36			00 03		00 03	00 04	00 15	00 17						00 26	00 27	

A To Leeds
B From Southampton Central
C To Adwick
D From Sheffield
E SX until 14 February, from 17 February. To Leeds
F From Plymouth to Leeds
G From Halifax

For services between Barnetby, Habrough, Grimsby Town and Cleethorpes, refer to Table T028

Table T029-F

Sundays

15 December to 16 February

Manchester Airport, Manchester, Sheffield and Meadowhall - Doncaster and Hull

	NT ◇ A	TP ◇1 B	NT ◇ C	TP ◇1 D ✠	NT	NT C	NT ◇ E		NT ◇ C	NT	NT	TP ◇1 ✠	XC ◇1 F ✠	NT ◇ E	NT C	NT	NT G	NT	NT ◇ C	NT	TP ◇1 ✠	XC ◇1 H ✠	TP ◇1 I ✠	
Manchester Airport 85 d												07 51									08 46			
Manchester Piccadilly 10 d												08 13									09 10			
Stockport 78 d												08 23									09 19			
Sheffield 7 a												09 08									10 08			
d					08 06	08 27	08 36				09 06	09 10	09 21	09 25	09 35		10 02			10 06	10 10	10 21		
Meadowhall d					08 12	08 33	08 43				09 12	09 16		09 31	09 41		10a07			10 12	10 16			
Rotherham Central d					08 18	08 39					09 18				09 48					10 18				
Swinton (S.Yorks) d					08 26	08a47					09 28				09a56					10 28				
Mexborough d					08 29						09 31									10 31				
Conisbrough d					08 33						09 35									10 35				
London Kings Cross d																								
Doncaster 7 a					08 43		09 03				09 45	09 36		09 50						10 45	10 36			
York 8 26 a													10 31									11 29		
Doncaster 31 d			08 25		08 46		09 05		09 25			09 38		09 52				10 16	10 25		10 38			
Bentley (S.Yorks) 31 a			08 28						09 28										10 28					
Adwick 31 a			08 32						09 32										10 32					
Kirk Sandall d					08 52													10 22						
Hatfield & Stainforth d					08 57													10 27						
Thorne South d																								
Crowle d																								
Althorpe d																								
Scunthorpe a												10 03									11 03			
d												10 04									11 04			
Barnetby 28 d												10 18									11 19			
Habrough 28 d												10 27									11 28			
Grimsby Town 28 a												10 40									11 43			
d												10 41									11 44			
Cleethorpes 28 a												10 53									11 53			
Thorne North d					09 03													10 32						
Goole d					09 12		09 24							10 11				10 41						
Saltmarshe d																								
York 8 33 d										08 51						10 01								
Selby a										09 21						10 20								
d				09 00						09 21						10 21							11 00	
Wressle d																								
Howden d										09 31						10 29								
Eastrington d																								
Gilberdyke d					09 23													10 50						
Broomfleet d																								
Brough d	00{02	00{12		09 19	09 31		09 38			09 44				10 26		10 42		10 58					11 19	
Ferriby d																		11 03						
Hessle d																		11 07						
Hull a	00{15	00{27		09 34	09 45		09 52			09 58				10 40		10 55		11 17					11 37	

A not 15 December. From Sheffield
B not 15 December. From Manchester Piccadilly
C To Leeds
D From Leeds
E To Scarborough
F To Glasgow Central
G From Retford
H From Birmingham New Street to Edinburgh
I From Liverpool Lime Street

For services between Barnetby, Habrough, Grimsby Town and Cleethorpes, refer to Table T028

Table T029-F

Sundays

15 December to 16 February

Manchester Airport, Manchester, Sheffield and Meadowhall - Doncaster and Hull

Station		NT ◇ A	NT B	NT	NT	NT ◇ B	NT	TP ◇1		TP ◇1	NT	XC ◇1 C	NT B	EM ◇1 D	NT ◇ A	NT	NT ◇ B	HT ◇1	NT	TP ◇1	TP ◇1	XC ◇1 E	NT ◇ A	NT B
Manchester Airport 85	d							09 56												10 55				
Manchester Piccadilly 10	d							10 14		10 35										11 19	11 35			
Stockport 78	d							10 23												11 29				
Sheffield 7	a							11 05												12 09				
	d	10 25	10 30				11 06	11 10				11 21	11 24	11 31	11 34				12 06	12 10		12 21	12 25	12 31
Meadowhall	d	10 31	10 36				11 12	11 16					11 30		11 41				12 12	12 16			12 31	12 37
Rotherham Central	d		10 42				11 18						11 39						12 18					12 43
Swinton (S.Yorks)	d		10a50				11 27						11a53						12 28					12a51
Mexborough	d						11 31												12 31					
Conisbrough	d						11 35												12 35					
London Kings Cross	d																	10 49						
Doncaster 7	a	10 50					11 44	11 36						11 54	12 00			12 27	12 45	12 34			12 50	
York 8 26	a											12 30		12 19								13 28		
Doncaster 31	d	10 54			11 15	11 25		11 39							12 03	12 13	12 25	12 29		12 37			12 55	
Bentley (S.Yorks) 31	a					11 28											12 28							
Adwick 31	a					11 32											12 32							
Kirk Sandall	d				11 21											12 19								
Hatfield & Stainforth	d				11 26											12 24								
Thorne South	d																							
Crowle	d																							
Althorpe	d																							
Scunthorpe	a							12 04												13 02				
	d							12 05												13 03				
Barnetby 28	d							12 19												13 17				
Habrough 28	d							12 28												13 26				
Grimsby Town 28	a							12 41												13 41				
	d							12 42												13 42				
Cleethorpes 28	a							12 53												13 51				
Thorne North	d				11 31											12 29								
Goole	d	11 17			11 40										12 25	12 38							13 19	
Saltmarshe	d																							
York 8 33	d			10 49							11 54													
Selby	a			11 18						11 59	12 13							12 44			13 00			
	d			11 18						11 59	12 15							12 44			13 00			
Wressle	d																							
Howden	d			11 27							12 23							12 54						
Eastrington	d																							
Gilberdyke	d				11 49											12 47								
Broomfleet	d																							
Brough	d	11 32		11 39	11 57					12 18	12 36				12 42	12 55		13 07			13 19		13 35	
Ferriby	d																							
Hessle	d																							
Hull	a	11 46		11 57	12 11					12 35	12 49				12 56	13 12		13 20			13 36		13 48	

A To Scarborough
B To Leeds
C From Birmingham New Street to Glasgow Central
D From Leicester
E From Bristol Temple Meads to Edinburgh

For services between Barnetby, Habrough, Grimsby Town and Cleethorpes, refer to Table T028

Table T029-F

Sundays

15 December to 16 February

Manchester Airport, Manchester, Sheffield and Meadowhall - Doncaster and Hull

Station		NT	NT	NT ◇ A	NT	TP ◇1	TP ◇1	XC ◇1 B		NT ◇ C	NT A	NT	XC ◇1 D	NT	NT ◇ A	HT ◇1	NT	TP ◇1	TP ◇1	XC ◇1 E	NT ◇ C	NT A	NT	NT
Manchester Airport 85	d					11 56												12 56						
Manchester Piccadilly 10	d					12 19	12 35											13 20	13 35					
Stockport 78	d					12 28												13 29						
Sheffield 7	a					13 08												14 09						
	d				13 06	13 10		13 21		13 24	13 31		13 52				14 06	14 10		14 21	14 25	14 31		
Meadowhall	d				13 12	13 16				13 31	13 37						14 12	14 16			14 31	14 37		
Rotherham Central	d				13 18						13 43						14 18					14 43		
Swinton (S.Yorks)	d				13 27						13a51						14 27					14a51		
Mexborough	d				13 31												14 31							
Conisbrough	d				13 35												14 35							
London Kings Cross	d															12 48								
Doncaster 7	a				13 44	13 34				13 50			14 14			14 24	14 44	14 34			14 51			
York 8 26	a							14 29					14 40							15 29				
Doncaster 31	d		13 15	13 25		13 37				13 52				14 15	14 25	14 26		14 37			15 00			15 15
Bentley (S.Yorks) 31	a			13 28											14 28									
Adwick 31	a			13 32											14 32									
Kirk Sandall	d		13 21											14 21										15 21
Hatfield & Stainforth	d		13 26											14 26										15 26
Thorne South	d																							
Crowle	d																							
Althorpe	d																							
Scunthorpe	a					14 02												15 02						
	d					14 03												15 03						
Barnetby 28	d					14 17												15 17						
Habrough 28	d					14 26												15 26						
Grimsby Town 28	a					14 41												15 41						
	d					14 42												15 42						
Cleethorpes 28	a					14 51												15 51						
Thorne North	d		13 31											14 31										15 31
Goole	d		13 40							14 16				14 40							15 19			15 40
Saltmarshe	d																							
York 8 33	d	12 50										13 51											14 54	
Selby	a	13 20					14 00					14 19				14 41			15 00				15 14	
	d	13 21					14 00					14 20				14 42			15 00				15 16	
Wressle	d																							
Howden	d	13 29										14 29				14 52							15 24	
Eastrington	d																							
Gilberdyke	d		13 49											14 49										15 49
Broomfleet	d																							
Brough	d	13 42	13 57				14 19			14 34		14 42		14 57		15 05			15 19		15 34		15 41	15 57
Ferriby	d																							
Hessle	d																							
Hull	a	13 55	14 11				14 36			14 48		14 55		15 11		15 18			15 36		15 48		15 55	16 11

A To Leeds
B From Bristol Temple Meads to Glasgow Central
C To Scarborough
D From Birmingham New Street to Newcastle
E From Plymouth to Aberdeen

For services between Barnetby, Habrough, Grimsby Town and Cleethorpes, refer to Table T028

Table T029-F

Sundays

15 December to 16 February

Manchester Airport, Manchester, Sheffield and Meadowhall - Doncaster and Hull

Station		XC ◇1 A	NT ◇ B	NT	TP ◇1	TP ◇1	XC ◇1 C	NT ◇ D	NT B	NT	XC ◇1 E	NT	NT ◇ B	HT ◇1 F	NT	TP ◇1	TP ◇1	NT ◇ G	XC ◇1 H	NT ◇ D	NT B	NT	XC ◇1 I
Manchester Airport 85	d				13 56											14 56							
Manchester Piccadilly 10	d				14 19	14 35										15 18	15 35						
Stockport 78	d				14 28											15 28							
Sheffield 7	a				15 08											16 08							
	d	14 52		15 06	15 10		15 21	15 25	15 31		15 50				16 06	16 10		16 13	16 21	16 25	16 31		16 52
Meadowhall	d			15 12	15 16			15 31	15 37						16 12	16 16		16 20		16 32	16 37		
Rotherham Central	d			15 19					15 43						16 18			16 28			16 43		
Swinton (S.Yorks)	d			15 28					15a51						16 28			16 38			16a51		
Mexborough	d			15 31											16 31								
Conisbrough	d			15 35											16 35								
London Kings Cross	d													14 48									
Doncaster 7	a	15 18		15 44	15 35			15 50			16 12			16 26	16 45	16 34				16 54			17 14
York 8 26	a	15 41					16 29				16 37							17 36	17 29				17 40
Doncaster 31	d		15 25		15 38			15 52				16 15	16 25	16 31		16 37				16 55			
Bentley (S.Yorks) 31	a		15 28										16 28										
Adwick 31	a		15 32										16 32										
Kirk Sandall	d											16 21											
Hatfield & Stainforth	d											16 26											
Thorne South	d																						
Crowle	d																						
Althorpe	d																						
Scunthorpe	a				16 03											17 02							
	d				16 04											17 03							
Barnetby 28	d				16 18											17 17							
Habrough 28	d				16 27											17 28							
Grimsby Town 28	a				16 40											17 43							
	d				16 41											17 44							
Cleethorpes 28	a				16 51											17 53							
Thorne North	d											16 31											
Goole	d							16 16				16 40								17 16			
Saltmarshe	d																						
York 8 33	d									15 51												16 51	
Selby	a					16 00				16 20				16 46			17 00					17 20	
	d					16 00				16 20				16 46			17 00					17 20	
Wressle	d																						
Howden	d									16 29				16 56								17 29	
Eastrington	d																						
Gilberdyke	d											16 49											
Broomfleet	d																						
Brough	d					16 19		16 35		16 41		16 57		17 08			17 19			17 34		17 41	
Ferriby	d																						
Hessle	d																						
Hull	a					16 36		16 48		16 55		17 12		17 21			17 36			17 48		17 54	

A From Birmingham New Street to Newcastle
B To Leeds
C From Plymouth to Glasgow Central
D To Scarborough
E From Guildford to Newcastle
F not from 5 January until 12 January
G via Pontefract Baghill
H From Penzance to Edinburgh
I From Reading to Newcastle

For services between Barnetby, Habrough, Grimsby Town and Cleethorpes, refer to Table T028

Table T029-F

Sundays

15 December to 16 February

Manchester Airport, Manchester, Sheffield and Meadowhall - Doncaster and Hull

Station		NT	NT ◇ A	NT	TP ◇1	TP ◇1	NT	XC ◇1 B	NT ◇ C	NT	NT A	XC ◇1 D	NT ◇ A	NT	TP ◇1	TP ◇1	XC ◇1 E	NT ◇ F	NT A	NT	GR 1	NT	XC ◇1 G
Manchester Airport 85	d				15 56										16 56								
Manchester Piccadilly 10	d				16 19	16 35									17 19	17 35							
Stockport 78	d				16 28										17 28								
Sheffield 7	a				17 08										18 09								
	d			17 06	17 10			17 21	17 25		17 30	17 52		18 06	18 11		18 21	18 25	18 31				18 52
Meadowhall	d			17 12	17 16				17 31		17 36			18 12	18 17			18 31	18 37				
Rotherham Central	d			17 18							17 42			18 18					18 43				
Swinton (S.Yorks)	d			17 27							17a52			18 27					18a51				
Mexborough	d			17 31										18 31									
Conisbrough	d			17 35										18 35									
London Kings Cross	d																				17 22		
Doncaster 7	a			17 44	17 34				17 50			18 14		18 45	18 35			18 50			19 03		19 14
York 8 26	a							18 29				19 18					19 30						19 43
Doncaster 31	d	17 15	17 25		17 37				18 02	18 15			18 25		18 37			18 52			19 05	19 15	
Bentley (S.Yorks) 31	a		17 28										18 28										
Adwick 31	a		17 32										18 32										
Kirk Sandall	d	17 21								18 21												19 21	
Hatfield & Stainforth	d	17 26								18 26												19 26	
Thorne South	d																						
Crowle	d																						
Althorpe	d																						
Scunthorpe	a				18 02										19 02								
	d				18 03										19 03								
Barnetby 28	d				18 17										19 17								
Habrough 28	d				18 26										19 26								
Grimsby Town 28	a				18 39										19 41								
	d				18 40										19 42								
Cleethorpes 28	a				18 51										19 51								
Thorne North	d	17 31								18 31												19 31	
Goole	d	17 40							18 24	18 40								19 16				19 40	
Saltmarshe	d																						
York 8 33	d						17 51													18 49			
Selby	a					18 00	18 11									19 00				19 17	19 22		
	d					18 00	18 12									19 00				19 18	19 26		
Wressle	d																						
Howden	d					18 10	18 20													19 27			
Eastrington	d																						
Gilberdyke	d	17 49								18 49												19 49	
Broomfleet	d																						
Brough	d	17 57				18 23	18 33		18 39	18 57						19 19		19 34		19 40	19 47	19 57	
Ferriby	d																						
Hessle	d																						
Hull	a	18 11				18 39	18 46		18 52	19 14						19 36		19 48		19 53	20 02	20 11	

A To Leeds
B From Plymouth to Glasgow Central
C To Scarborough
D From Reading to Newcastle
E From Plymouth to Edinburgh
F To Bridlington
G From Reading to Edinburgh

For services between Barnetby, Habrough, Grimsby Town and Cleethorpes, refer to Table T028

Table T029-F

Sundays

15 December to 16 February

Manchester Airport, Manchester, Sheffield and Meadowhall - Doncaster and Hull

	HT	NT	NT	NT	TP	TP	XC	NT	NT	NT	XC	NT	NT	NT	TP	TP	XC	NT	NT	NT	NT	XC
	◇■	◇	◇		◇■	◇■	◇■	◇			◇■		◇		◇■	◇■	◇■	◇				◇■
	A ⊠	B	C		🍴	🍴	D 🍴	E	B		F		B				G		B			F
Manchester Airport 85 ✈ d					17 56										18 56							
Manchester Piccadilly 10 d					18 19	18 35									19 19	19 35						
Stockport 78 d					18 28										19 28							
Sheffield 7 a					19 09										20 09							
d			19 00	19 06	19 11		19 21	19 25	19 31		19 52			20 06	20 11		20 22	20 25	20 31			20 54
Meadowhall d			19 06	19 12	19 17			19 31	19 37					20 12	20 17			20 31	20 37			
Rotherham Central d			19 12	19 18					19 43					20 20					20 47			
Swinton (S.Yorks) d			19 20	19 28					19a51					20 29					20a55			
Mexborough d				19 32										20 32								
Conisbrough d				19 36										20 36								
London Kings Cross d	17 48																					
Doncaster 7 a	19 27			19 45	19 35			19 50			20 14			20 46	20 35			20 50				21 20
York 8 26 a			20 16				20 30				20 42						21 31					21 44
Doncaster 31 d	19 29	19 29			19 37			19 51				20 15	20 25		20 37			20 52			21 15	
Bentley (S.Yorks) 31 a		19 32											20 28									
Adwick 31 a		19 36											20 32									
Kirk Sandall d												20 21									21 21	
Hatfield & Stainforth d												20 26									21 26	
Thorne South d																						
Crowle d																						
Althorpe d																						
Scunthorpe a					20 02										21 02							
d					20 03										21 03							
Barnetby 28 d					20 17										21 17							
Habrough 28 d															21 26							
Grimsby Town 28 a					20 39										21 39							
d					20 40										21 40							
Cleethorpes 28 a					20 49										21 51							
Thorne North d												20 31									21 31	
Goole d								20 16				20 40						21 16			21 40	
Saltmarshe d																						
York 8 33 d										19 56										20 52		
Selby a	19 44					20 00				20 15						21 00				21 11		
d	19 44					20 00				20 18						21 00				21 14		
Wressle d																						
Howden d	19 54									20 26						21 10				21 22		
Eastrington d																						
Gilberdyke d												20 49								21 32	21 49	
Broomfleet d																						
Brough d	20 06					20 19		20 35		20 41		20 57				21 23		21 34		21 39	21 57	
Ferriby d																				21 44		
Hessle d																				21 48		
Hull a	20 19					20 34		20 49		20 54		21 11				21 38		21 48		21 57	22 16	

A To Beverley
B To Leeds
C via Pontefract Baghill
D From Plymouth to Edinburgh
E To Bridlington
F From Reading to Newcastle
G From Plymouth

For services between Barnetby, Habrough, Grimsby Town and Cleethorpes, refer to Table T028

Table T029-F

Sundays

15 December to 16 February

Manchester Airport, Manchester, Sheffield and Meadowhall - Doncaster and Hull

	NT	HT	NT	TP	TP	NT	NT	NT	NT	NT	TP	NT	TP	NT	NT	TP	NT	TP
	◇	◇■		◇■	◇■	◇			◇		◇■		◇■	◇		◇■		◇■
	A	⊠						A	A						A			
Manchester Airport 85 ✈ d				19 56							20 55					21 56		
Manchester Piccadilly 10 d				20 18	20 35						21 19		21 35			22 19		22 35
Stockport 78 d				20 28							21 28					22 27		
Sheffield 7 a				21 09							22 11					23 09		
d			21 06	21 11		21 25		21 31		22 08	22 12			22 25	22 32	23 11	23 30	
Meadowhall d			21 12	21 17		21 31		21 37		22 14	22 18			22 31	22 38		23 36	
Rotherham Central d			21 18					21 44		22 20					22 44		23 42	
Swinton (S.Yorks) d			21 28					21a52		22 30					22a53		23 51	
Mexborough d			21 32							22 33							23 54	
Conisbrough d			21 36							22 37							23 58	
London Kings Cross d		19 52																
Doncaster 7 a		21 27	21 45	21 35		21 50				22 47	22 36			22 50		23 42	00 06	
York 8 26 a																		
Doncaster 31 d	21 25	21 29		21 37		21 52	22 15		22 28		22 39			22 52				
Bentley (S.Yorks) 31 a	21 28								22 31									
Adwick 31 a	21 32								22 35									
Kirk Sandall d							22 21											
Hatfield & Stainforth d							22 26											
Thorne South d																		
Crowle d																		
Althorpe d																		
Scunthorpe a				22 02							23 04							
d				22 03							23 05							
Barnetby 28 d				22 17							23 19							
Habrough 28 d				22 26							23 28							
Grimsby Town 28 a				22 39							23 43							
d				22 40							23 44							
Cleethorpes 28 a				22 51							23 53							
Thorne North d							22 31											
Goole d						22 16	22 40							23 15				
Saltmarshe d																		
York 8 33 d												22 19						
Selby a		21 44			22 00							22 38	23 02					23 51
d		21 45			22 00							22 39	23 03					23 52
Wressle d																		
Howden d		21 55			22 10							22 47						
Eastrington d																		
Gilberdyke d							22 49					22 55		23 26				
Broomfleet d																		
Brough d		22 07			22 23	22 34	22 57					23 03	23 22	23 34				00 11
Ferriby d												23 08		23 39				
Hessle d												23 12		23 43				
Hull a		22 20			22 38	22 48	23 11					23 21	23 37	23 52				00 26

A To Leeds

For services between Barnetby, Habrough, Grimsby Town and Cleethorpes, refer to Table T028

Table T029-F

Sundays
23 February to 29 March

Manchester Airport, Manchester, Sheffield and Meadowhall - Doncaster and Hull

	NT	TP	NT	TP	NT	NT	NT		NT	NT	NT	TP	XC	NT	NT	NT	NT	NT	NT	NT	TP	XC	TP
	◇	◇■1	◇	◇■1			◇		◇			◇■1	◇■1	◇				◇			◇■1	◇■1	◇■1
	A	B	C	D		C	E		C				F	E	C		G		C			H	I
				⊼								⊼	⊼								⊼	⊼	⊼
Manchester Airport 85 d																							
Manchester Piccadilly 10 d												08 13									09 10		
Stockport 78 d												08 23									09 19		
Sheffield 7 a												09 08									10 08		
d					08 06	08 27	08 36				09 06	09 10	09 21	09 25	09 35		10 02			10 06	10 10	10 21	
Meadowhall d					08 12	08 33	08 43				09 12	09 16		09 31	09 41		10a07			10 12	10 16		
Rotherham Central d					08 18	08 39					09 18				09 48					10 18			
Swinton (S.Yorks) d					08 26	08a47					09 28				09a56					10 28			
Mexborough d					08 29						09 31									10 31			
Conisbrough d					08 33						09 35									10 35			
London Kings Cross d																							
Doncaster 7 a					08 43		09 03				09 45	09 36		09 50						10 45	10 36		
York 8 26 a													10 31									11 29	
Doncaster 31 d			08 25		08 46		09 05		09 25			09 38		09 52				10 16	10 25		10 38		
Bentley (S.Yorks) 31 a			08 28						09 28										10 28				
Adwick 31 a			08 32						09 32										10 32				
Kirk Sandall d					08 52													10 22					
Hatfield & Stainforth d					08 57													10 27					
Thorne South d																							
Crowle d																							
Althorpe d																							
Scunthorpe a												10 03									11 03		
d												10 04									11 04		
Barnetby 28 d												10 18									11 19		
Habrough 28 d												10 27									11 28		
Grimsby Town 28 a												10 40									11 43		
d												10 41									11 44		
Cleethorpes 28 a												10 53									11 53		
Thorne North d					09 03													10 32					
Goole d					09 12		09 24							10 11				10 41					
Saltmarshe d																							
York 8 33 d										08 51						10 01							
Selby a										09 21						10 20							
d				09 00						09 21						10 21							11 00
Wressle d																							
Howden d										09 31						10 29							
Eastrington d																							
Gilberdyke d					09 23													10 50					
Broomfleet d																							
Brough d	00 02	00 12		09 19	09 31		09 38			09 44				10 26		10 42		10 58					11 19
Ferriby d																		11 03					
Hessle d																		11 07					
Hull a	00 15	00 27		09 34	09 45		09 52			09 58				10 40		10 55		11 17					11 37

A From Sheffield
B From Manchester Piccadilly
C To Leeds
D From Leeds
E To Scarborough
F To Glasgow Central
G From Retford
H From Birmingham New Street to Edinburgh
I From Liverpool Lime Street

For services between Barnetby, Habrough, Grimsby Town and Cleethorpes, refer to Table T028

Table T029-F

Sundays
23 February to 29 March

Manchester Airport, Manchester, Sheffield and Meadowhall - Doncaster and Hull

	NT	NT	NT	NT	NT	NT	TP		TP	NT	XC	NT	EM	NT	NT	NT	HT	NT	TP	TP	XC	NT	NT
	◇				◇		◇■1		◇■1		◇■1		◇■1	◇		◇	◇■1		◇■1	◇■1	◇■1	◇	
	A	B			B						C	B	D	A		B					E	A	B
							⊼		⊼		⊼		⊡				⊠		⊼	⊼	⊼		
Manchester Airport 85 d							09 56												10 55				
Manchester Piccadilly 10 d							10 14		10 35										11 19	11 35			
Stockport 78 d							10 23												11 29				
Sheffield 7 a							11 05												12 09				
d	10 25	10 30				11 06	11 10				11 21	11 24	11 31	11 34				12 06	12 10		12 21	12 25	12 31
Meadowhall d	10 31	10 36				11 12	11 16					11 30		11 41				12 12	12 16			12 31	12 37
Rotherham Central d		10 42				11 18						11 39						12 18					12 43
Swinton (S.Yorks) d		10a50				11 27						11a53						12 28					12a51
Mexborough d						11 31												12 31					
Conisbrough d						11 35												12 35					
London Kings Cross d																	10 49						
Doncaster 7 a	10 50					11 44	11 36						11 54	12 00			12 27	12 45	12 34			12 50	
York 8 26 a											12 30		12 19								13 28		
Doncaster 31 d	10 54			11 15	11 25		11 39							12 03	12 13	12 25	12 29		12 37			12 55	
Bentley (S.Yorks) 31 a					11 28											12 28							
Adwick 31 a					11 32											12 32							
Kirk Sandall d				11 21											12 19								
Hatfield & Stainforth d				11 26											12 24								
Thorne South d																							
Crowle d																							
Althorpe d																							
Scunthorpe a							12 04												13 02				
d							12 05												13 03				
Barnetby 28 d							12 19												13 17				
Habrough 28 d							12 28												13 26				
Grimsby Town 28 a							12 41												13 41				
d							12 42												13 42				
Cleethorpes 28 a							12 53												13 51				
Thorne North d				11 31											12 29								
Goole d	11 17			11 40										12 25	12 38							13 19	
Saltmarshe d																							
York 8 33 d			10 49							11 54													
Selby a			11 18						11 59	12 13							12 44			13 00			
d			11 18						11 59	12 15							12 44			13 00			
Wressle d																							
Howden d			11 27							12 23							12 54						
Eastrington d																							
Gilberdyke d				11 49											12 47								
Broomfleet d																							
Brough d	11 32		11 39	11 57					12 18	12 36				12 42	12 55		13 07			13 19		13 35	
Ferriby d																							
Hessle d																							
Hull a	11 46		11 57	12 11					12 35	12 49				12 56	13 12		13 20			13 36		13 48	

A To Scarborough
B To Leeds
C From Birmingham New Street to Glasgow Central
D From Leicester
E From Bristol Temple Meads to Edinburgh

For services between Barnetby, Habrough, Grimsby Town and Cleethorpes, refer to Table T028

Table T029-F

Sundays

23 February to 29 March

Manchester Airport, Manchester, Sheffield and Meadowhall - Doncaster and Hull

		NT	NT	NT	NT	TP	TP	XC	NT	NT	NT	XC	NT	NT	HT	NT	TP	TP	XC	NT	NT	NT	NT
				◇ A		◇1 🛒	◇1 🛒	◇1 B 🛒	◇ C	A		◇1 D 🛒		◇ A	◇1 ⊠		◇1 🛒	◇1 🛒	◇1 E 🛒	◇ C	A		
Manchester Airport 85 ✈	d					11 56											12 56						
Manchester Piccadilly 10	d					12 19	12 35										13 20	13 35					
Stockport 78	d					12 28											13 29						
Sheffield 7	a					13 08											14 09						
	d				13 06	13 10		13 21	13 24	13 31		13 52				14 06	14 10		14 21	14 25	14 31		
Meadowhall	d				13 12	13 16			13 31	13 37						14 12	14 16			14 31	14 37		
Rotherham Central	d				13 18					13 43						14 18					14 43		
Swinton (S.Yorks)	d				13 27					13a51						14 27					14a51		
Mexborough	d				13 31											14 31							
Conisbrough	d				13 35											14 35							
London Kings Cross	d														12 48								
Doncaster 7	a				13 44	13 34			13 50			14 14			14 24	14 44	14 34			14 51			
York 8 26	a							14 29				14 40							15 29				
Doncaster 31	d		13 15	13 25		13 37			13 52				14 15	14 25	14 26		14 37			15 00			15 15
Bentley (S.Yorks) 31	a			13 28										14 28									
Adwick 31	a			13 32										14 32									
Kirk Sandall	d		13 21										14 21										15 21
Hatfield & Stainforth	d		13 26										14 26										15 26
Thorne South	d																						
Crowle	d																						
Althorpe	d																						
Scunthorpe	a					14 02											15 02						
	d					14 03											15 03						
Barnetby 28	d					14 17											15 17						
Habrough 28	d					14 26											15 26						
Grimsby Town 28	a					14 41											15 41						
	d					14 42											15 42						
Cleethorpes 28	a					14 51											15 51						
Thorne North	d		13 31										14 31										15 31
Goole	d		13 40						14 16				14 40							15 19			15 40
Saltmarshe	d																						
York 8 33	d	12 50									13 51											14 54	
Selby	a	13 20					14 00				14 19				14 41			15 00				15 14	
	d	13 21					14 00				14 20				14 42			15 00				15 16	
Wressle	d																						
Howden	d	13 29									14 29				14 52							15 24	
Eastrington	d																						
Gilberdyke	d		13 49										14 49										15 49
Broomfleet	d																						
Brough	d	13 42	13 57				14 19		14 34		14 42		14 57		15 05			15 19		15 34		15 41	15 57
Ferriby	d																						
Hessle	d																						
Hull	a	13 55	14 11				14 36		14 48		14 55		15 11		15 18			15 36		15 48		15 55	16 11

A To Leeds
B From Bristol Temple Meads to Glasgow Central
C To Scarborough
D From Birmingham New Street to Newcastle
E From Plymouth to Aberdeen

For services between Barnetby, Habrough, Grimsby Town and Cleethorpes, refer to Table T028

Table T029-F

Sundays

23 February to 29 March

Manchester Airport, Manchester, Sheffield and Meadowhall - Doncaster and Hull

		XC	NT	NT	TP	TP	XC	NT	NT	NT	XC	NT	NT	HT	NT	TP	TP	NT	XC	NT	NT	NT	XC
		◇1 A 🛒	◇ B		◇1 🛒	◇1 🛒	◇1 C 🛒	◇ D	B		◇1 E 🛒		◇ B	◇1 ⊠		◇1 🛒	◇1 🛒	◇ F	◇1 G 🛒	◇ D	B		◇1 H 🛒
Manchester Airport 85 ✈	d				13 56											14 56							
Manchester Piccadilly 10	d				14 19	14 35										15 18	15 35						
Stockport 78	d				14 28											15 28							
Sheffield 7	a				15 08											16 08							
	d	14 52		15 06	15 10		15 21	15 25	15 31		15 50				16 06	16 10		16 13	16 21	16 25	16 31		16 52
Meadowhall	d			15 12	15 16			15 31	15 37						16 12	16 16		16 20		16 32	16 37		
Rotherham Central	d			15 19					15 43						16 18			16 28			16 43		
Swinton (S.Yorks)	d			15 28					15a51						16 28			16 38			16a51		
Mexborough	d			15 31											16 31								
Conisbrough	d			15 35											16 35								
London Kings Cross	d													14 48									
Doncaster 7	a	15 18		15 44	15 35			15 50			16 12			16 26	16 45	16 34				16 54			17 14
York 8 26	a	15 41					16 29				16 37							17 36	17 29				17 40
Doncaster 31	d		15 25		15 38			15 52				16 15	16 25	16 31		16 37				16 55			
Bentley (S.Yorks) 31	a		15 28										16 28										
Adwick 31	a		15 32										16 32										
Kirk Sandall	d											16 21											
Hatfield & Stainforth	d											16 26											
Thorne South	d																						
Crowle	d																						
Althorpe	d																						
Scunthorpe	a				16 03											17 02							
	d				16 04											17 03							
Barnetby 28	d				16 18											17 17							
Habrough 28	d				16 27											17 28							
Grimsby Town 28	a				16 40											17 43							
	d				16 41											17 44							
Cleethorpes 28	a				16 51											17 53							
Thorne North	d											16 31											
Goole	d							16 16				16 40								17 16			
Saltmarshe	d																						
York 8 33	d									15 51												16 51	
Selby	a					16 00				16 20				16 46			17 00					17 20	
	d					16 00				16 20				16 46			17 00					17 20	
Wressle	d																						
Howden	d									16 29				16 56								17 29	
Eastrington	d																						
Gilberdyke	d											16 49											
Broomfleet	d																						
Brough	d					16 19		16 35		16 41		16 57		17 08			17 19			17 34		17 41	
Ferriby	d																						
Hessle	d																						
Hull	a					16 36		16 48		16 55		17 12		17 21			17 36			17 48		17 54	

A From Birmingham New Street to Newcastle
B To Leeds
C From Plymouth to Glasgow Central
D To Scarborough
E From Guildford to Newcastle
F via Pontefract Baghill
G From Penzance to Edinburgh
H From Reading to Newcastle

For services between Barnetby, Habrough, Grimsby Town and Cleethorpes, refer to Table T028

Table T029-F

Sundays

23 February to 29 March

Manchester Airport, Manchester, Sheffield and Meadowhall - Doncaster and Hull

		NT	NT	NT	TP	TP	NT	XC	NT	NT	NT	XC	NT	NT	TP	TP	XC	NT	NT	NT	GR	NT	XC
			◇		◇[1]	◇[1]		◇[1]	◇			◇[1]	◇		◇[1]	◇[1]	◇[1]	◇			[1]		◇[1]
			A					B	C		A	D	A				E	F	A				G
					🍴	🍴		🍴				🍴			🍴	🍴	🍴				🍴		🍴
Manchester Airport 85 ✈ 🚋	d				15 56										16 56								
Manchester Piccadilly [10] 🚋	d				16 19	16 35									17 19	17 35							
Stockport 78	d				16 28										17 28								
Sheffield [7] 🚋	a				17 08										18 09								
	d			17 06	17 10			17 21	17 25		17 30	17 52		18 06	18 11		18 21	18 25	18 31				18 52
Meadowhall 🚋	d			17 12	17 16				17 31		17 36			18 12	18 17			18 31	18 37				
Rotherham Central	d			17 18							17 42			18 18					18 43				
Swinton (S.Yorks)	d			17 27							17a52			18 27					18a51				
Mexborough	d			17 31										18 31									
Conisbrough	d			17 35										18 35									
London Kings Cross	d																				17 22		
Doncaster [7]	a			17 44	17 34				17 50			18 14		18 45	18 35			18 50			19 03		19 14
York [8] 26	a							18 29				19 18					19 30						19 43
Doncaster 31	d	17 15	17 25		17 37				18 02	18 15			18 25		18 37			18 52			19 05	19 15	
Bentley (S.Yorks) 31	a		17 28										18 28										
Adwick 31	a		17 32										18 32										
Kirk Sandall	d	17 21								18 21												19 21	
Hatfield & Stainforth	d	17 26								18 26												19 26	
Thorne South	d																						
Crowle	d																						
Althorpe	d																						
Scunthorpe	a				18 02										19 02								
	d				18 03										19 03								
Barnetby 28	d				18 17										19 17								
Habrough 28	d				18 26										19 26								
Grimsby Town 28	a				18 39										19 41								
	d				18 40										19 42								
Cleethorpes 28	a				18 51										19 51								
Thorne North	d	17 31								18 31												19 31	
Goole	d	17 40							18 24	18 40								19 16				19 40	
Saltmarshe	d																						
York [8] 33	d						17 51													18 49			
Selby	a					18 00	18 11									19 00				19 17	19 22		
	d					18 00	18 12									19 00				19 18	19 26		
Wressle	d																						
Howden	d					18 10	18 20													19 27			
Eastrington	d																						
Gilberdyke	d	17 49								18 49												19 49	
Broomfleet	d																						
Brough	d	17 57				18 23	18 33		18 39	18 57						19 19		19 34		19 40	19 47	19 57	
Ferriby	d																						
Hessle	d																						
Hull	a	18 11				18 39	18 46		18 52	19 14						19 36		19 48		19 53	20 02	20 11	

A To Leeds
B From Plymouth to Glasgow Central
C To Scarborough
D From Reading to Newcastle
E From Plymouth to Edinburgh
F To Bridlington
G From Reading to Edinburgh

For services between Barnetby, Habrough, Grimsby Town and Cleethorpes, refer to Table T028

Table T029-F

Sundays

23 February to 29 March

Manchester Airport, Manchester, Sheffield and Meadowhall - Doncaster and Hull

		HT	NT	NT	NT	TP	TP	XC	NT	NT	NT	XC	NT	NT	NT	TP	TP	XC	NT	NT	NT	NT	XC
		◇[1]	◇	◇		◇[1]	◇[1]	◇[1]	◇			◇[1]		◇		◇[1]	◇[1]	◇[1]	◇				◇[1]
		A	B	C				D	E	B		F		B				G		B			F
		⊠				🍴	🍴	🍴															
Manchester Airport 85 ✈ 🚋	d					17 56										18 56							
Manchester Piccadilly [10] 🚋	d					18 19	18 35									19 19	19 35						
Stockport 78	d					18 28										19 28							
Sheffield [7] 🚋	a					19 09										20 09							
	d			19 00	19 06	19 11		19 21	19 25	19 31		19 52			20 06	20 11		20 22	20 25	20 31			20 54
Meadowhall 🚋	d			19 06	19 12	19 17			19 31	19 37					20 12	20 17			20 31	20 37			
Rotherham Central	d			19 12	19 18					19 43					20 20					20 47			
Swinton (S.Yorks)	d			19 20	19 28					19a51					20 29					20a55			
Mexborough	d				19 32										20 32								
Conisbrough	d				19 36										20 36								
London Kings Cross	d	17 48																					
Doncaster [7]	a	19 27			19 45	19 35			19 50			20 14			20 46	20 35			20 50				21 20
York [8] 26	a			20 16				20 30				20 42						21 31					21 44
Doncaster 31	d	19 29	19 29			19 37			19 51				20 15	20 25		20 37			20 52			21 15	
Bentley (S.Yorks) 31	a		19 32											20 28									
Adwick 31	a		19 36											20 32									
Kirk Sandall	d												20 21									21 21	
Hatfield & Stainforth	d												20 26									21 26	
Thorne South	d																						
Crowle	d																						
Althorpe	d																						
Scunthorpe	a					20 02										21 02							
	d					20 03										21 03							
Barnetby 28	d					20 17										21 17							
Habrough 28	d															21 26							
Grimsby Town 28	a					20 39										21 39							
	d					20 40										21 40							
Cleethorpes 28	a					20 49										21 51							
Thorne North	d												20 31									21 31	
Goole	d								20 16				20 40						21 16			21 40	
Saltmarshe	d																						
York [8] 33	d										19 56										20 52		
Selby	a	19 44					20 00				20 15						21 00				21 11		
	d	19 44					20 00				20 18						21 00				21 14		
Wressle	d																						
Howden	d	19 54									20 26						21 10				21 22		
Eastrington	d																						
Gilberdyke	d												20 49								21 32	21 49	
Broomfleet	d																						
Brough	d	20 06					20 19		20 35		20 41		20 57				21 23		21 34		21 39	21 57	
Ferriby	d																				21 44		
Hessle	d																				21 48		
Hull	a	20 19					20 34		20 49		20 54		21 11				21 38		21 48		21 57	22 16	

A To Beverley
B To Leeds
C via Pontefract Baghill
D From Plymouth to Edinburgh
E To Bridlington
F From Reading to Newcastle
G From Plymouth

For services between Barnetby, Habrough, Grimsby Town and Cleethorpes, refer to Table T028

Table T029-F

Sundays
23 February to 29 March

Manchester Airport, Manchester, Sheffield and Meadowhall - Doncaster and Hull

	NT	HT	NT	TP	TP	NT	NT	NT	NT	NT	TP	NT		TP	NT	NT	TP	NT	TP
	◇	◇1		◇1	◇1	◇			◇		◇1			◇1	◇		◇1		◇1
	A							A	A							A			
		⊠																	
Manchester Airport 85 ✈ d				19 56							20 55						21 56		
Manchester Piccadilly 10 d				20 18	20 35						21 19			21 35			22 19		22 35
Stockport 78 d				20 28							21 28						22 27		
Sheffield 7 a				21 09							22 11						23 09		
d			21 06	21 11		21 25		21 31		22 08	22 12				22 25	22 32	23 11	23 30	
Meadowhall d			21 12	21 17		21 31		21 37		22 14	22 18				22 31	22 38		23 36	
Rotherham Central d			21 18					21 44		22 20						22 44		23 42	
Swinton (S.Yorks) d			21 28					21a52		22 30						22a53		23 51	
Mexborough d			21 32							22 33								23 54	
Conisbrough d			21 36							22 37								23 58	
London Kings Cross d		19 52																	
Doncaster 7 a		21 27	21 45	21 35		21 50				22 47	22 36				22 50		23 42	00 06	
York 8 26 a																			
Doncaster 31 d	21 25	21 29		21 37		21 52	22 15		22 28		22 39				22 52				
Bentley (S.Yorks) 31 a	21 28								22 31										
Adwick 31 a	21 32								22 35										
Kirk Sandall d							22 21												
Hatfield & Stainforth d							22 26												
Thorne South d																			
Crowle d																			
Althorpe d																			
Scunthorpe a				22 02							23 04								
d				22 03							23 05								
Barnetby 28 d				22 17							23 19								
Habrough 28 d				22 26							23 28								
Grimsby Town 28 a				22 39							23 43								
d				22 40							23 44								
Cleethorpes 28 a				22 51							23 53								
Thorne North d							22 31												
Goole d						22 16	22 40								23 15				
Saltmarshe d																			
York 8 33 d												22 19							
Selby a		21 44			22 00							22 38		23 02					23 51
d		21 45			22 00							22 39		23 03					23 52
Wressle d																			
Howden d		21 55			22 10							22 47							
Eastrington d																			
Gilberdyke d							22 49					22 55			23 26				
Broomfleet d																			
Brough d		22 07			22 23	22 34	22 57					23 03		23 22	23 34				00 11
Ferriby d												23 08			23 39				
Hessle d												23 12			23 43				
Hull a		22 20			22 38	22 48	23 11					23 21		23 37	23 52				00 26

A To Leeds

For services between Barnetby, Habrough, Grimsby Town and Cleethorpes, refer to Table T028

NRT DECEMBER 19 EDITION

Table T029-F

Sundays
5 April to 10 May

Manchester Airport, Manchester, Sheffield and Meadowhall - Doncaster and Hull

	NT	TP	NT	TP	NT	NT	NT		NT	NT	NT	TP	XC	NT	NT	NT	NT	NT	NT	NT	TP	XC	TP
	◇	◇1	◇	◇1			◇		◇			◇1	◇1	◇					◇		◇1	◇1	◇1
	A	B	C	D		C	E		C				F	E	C		G		C			H	I
				🍴								🍴	🍴								🍴	🍴	🍴
Manchester Airport 85 ✈ d												07 51									08 46		
Manchester Piccadilly 10 d												08 13									09 10		
Stockport 78 d												08 23									09 19		
Sheffield 7 a												09 08									10 08		
d					08 06	08 27	08 36				09 06	09 10	09 21	09 25	09 35		10 02			10 06	10 10	10 21	
Meadowhall d					08 12	08 33	08 43				09 12	09 16		09 31	09 41		10a07			10 12	10 16		
Rotherham Central d					08 18	08 39					09 18				09 48					10 18			
Swinton (S.Yorks) d					08 26	08a47					09 28				09a56					10 28			
Mexborough d					08 29						09 31									10 31			
Conisbrough d					08 33						09 35									10 35			
London Kings Cross d																							
Doncaster 7 a					08 43		09 03				09 45	09 36		09 50						10 45	10 36		
York 8 26 a													10 31									11 29	
Doncaster 31 d			08 25		08 46		09 05		09 25			09 38		09 52				10 16	10 25		10 38		
Bentley (S.Yorks) 31 a			08 28						09 28										10 28				
Adwick 31 a			08 32						09 32										10 32				
Kirk Sandall d					08 52													10 22					
Hatfield & Stainforth d					08 57													10 27					
Thorne South d																							
Crowle d																							
Althorpe d																							
Scunthorpe a												10 03									11 03		
d												10 04									11 04		
Barnetby 28 d												10 18									11 19		
Habrough 28 d												10 27									11 28		
Grimsby Town 28 a												10 40									11 43		
d												10 41									11 44		
Cleethorpes 28 a												10 53									11 53		
Thorne North d					09 03													10 32					
Goole d					09 12		09 24							10 11				10 41					
Saltmarshe d																							
York 8 33 d										08 51						10 01							
Selby a										09 21						10 20							
d				09 00						09 21						10 21							11 00
Wressle d																							
Howden d										09 31						10 29							
Eastrington d																							
Gilberdyke d					09 23													10 50					
Broomfleet d																							
Brough d	00 02	00 12		09 19	09 31		09 38			09 44				10 26		10 42		10 58					11 19
Ferriby d																		11 03					
Hessle d																		11 07					
Hull a	00 15	00 27		09 34	09 45		09 52			09 58				10 40		10 55		11 17					11 37

A From Sheffield
B From Manchester Piccadilly
C To Leeds
D From Leeds
E To Scarborough
F To Glasgow Central
G From Retford
H From Birmingham New Street to Edinburgh
I From Liverpool Lime Street

For services between Barnetby, Habrough, Grimsby Town and Cleethorpes, refer to Table T028

Table T029-F

Sundays
5 April to 10 May

Manchester Airport, Manchester, Sheffield and Meadowhall - Doncaster and Hull

		NT	NT	NT	NT	NT	NT	TP	TP	NT	XC	NT	EM	NT	NT	NT	HT	NT	TP	TP	XC	NT	NT
		◇				◇		◇1	◇1		◇1		◇1	◇		◇	◇1		◇1	◇1	◇1	◇	
		A	B			B					C	B	D	A		B					E	A	B
Manchester Airport	85 d							09 56											10 55				
Manchester Piccadilly	d							10 14	10 35										11 19	11 35			
Stockport	78 d							10 23											11 29				
Sheffield	a							11 05											12 09				
	d	10 25	10 30				11 06	11 10				11 21	11 24	11 31	11 34				12 06	12 10		12 21	12 25	12 31
Meadowhall	d	10 31	10 36				11 12	11 16					11 30		11 41				12 12	12 16			12 31	12 37
Rotherham Central	d		10 42				11 18						11 39						12 18					12 43
Swinton (S.Yorks)	d		10a50				11 27						11a53						12 28					12a51
Mexborough	d						11 31												12 31					
Conisbrough	d						11 35												12 35					
London Kings Cross	d																	10 49						
Doncaster	a	10 50					11 44	11 36						11 54	12 00			12 27	12 45	12 34			12 50	
York	26 a											12 30		12 19								13 28		
Doncaster	31 d	10 54			11 15	11 25		11 39							12 03	12 13	12 25	12 29		12 37			12 55	
Bentley (S.Yorks)	31 a					11 28											12 28							
Adwick	31 a					11 32											12 32							
Kirk Sandall	d				11 21											12 19								
Hatfield & Stainforth	d				11 26											12 24								
Thorne South	d																							
Crowle	d																							
Althorpe	d																							
Scunthorpe	a							12 04												13 02				
	d							12 05												13 03				
Barnetby	28 d							12 19												13 17				
Habrough	28 d							12 28												13 26				
Grimsby Town	28 a							12 41												13 41				
	d							12 42												13 42				
Cleethorpes	28 a							12 53												13 51				
Thorne North	d				11 31											12 29								
Goole	d	11 17			11 40										12 25	12 38							13 19	
Saltmarshe	d																							
York	33 d			10 49							11 54													
Selby	a			11 18						11 59	12 13							12 44			13 00			
	d			11 18						11 59	12 15							12 44			13 00			
Wressle	d																							
Howden	d			11 27							12 23							12 54						
Eastrington	d																							
Gilberdyke	d				11 49											12 47								
Broomfleet	d																							
Brough	d	11 32		11 39	11 57					12 18	12 36				12 42	12 55		13 07			13 19		13 35	
Ferriby	d																							
Hessle	d																							
Hull	a	11 46		11 57	12 11					12 35	12 49				12 56	13 12		13 20			13 36		13 48	

A To Scarborough
B To Leeds
C From Birmingham New Street to Glasgow Central
D From Leicester
E From Bristol Temple Meads to Edinburgh

For services between Barnetby, Habrough, Grimsby Town and Cleethorpes, refer to Table T028

Table T029-F

Sundays
5 April to 10 May

Manchester Airport, Manchester, Sheffield and Meadowhall - Doncaster and Hull

		NT	NT	NT	NT	TP	TP	XC	NT	NT	NT	XC	NT	NT	HT	NT	TP	TP	XC	NT	NT	NT	NT
				◇		◇1	◇1	◇1	◇			◇1		◇	◇1		◇1	◇1	◇1	◇			
				A				B	C	A		D		A					E	C	A		
Manchester Airport	85 d					11 56											12 56						
Manchester Piccadilly	d					12 19	12 35										13 20	13 35					
Stockport	78 d					12 28											13 29						
Sheffield	a					13 08											14 09						
	d				13 06	13 10		13 21	13 24	13 31		13 52				14 06	14 10		14 21	14 25	14 31		
Meadowhall	d				13 12	13 16			13 31	13 37						14 12	14 16			14 31	14 37		
Rotherham Central	d				13 18					13 43						14 18					14 43		
Swinton (S.Yorks)	d				13 27					13a51						14 27					14a51		
Mexborough	d				13 31											14 31							
Conisbrough	d				13 35											14 35							
London Kings Cross	d														12 48								
Doncaster	a				13 44	13 34			13 50			14 14			14 24	14 44	14 34			14 51			
York	26 a							14 29				14 40							15 29				
Doncaster	31 d		13 15	13 25		13 37			13 52				14 15	14 25	14 26		14 37			15 00			15 15
Bentley (S.Yorks)	31 a			13 28										14 28									
Adwick	31 a			13 32										14 32									
Kirk Sandall	d		13 21										14 21										15 21
Hatfield & Stainforth	d		13 26										14 26										15 26
Thorne South	d																						
Crowle	d																						
Althorpe	d																						
Scunthorpe	a					14 02											15 02						
	d					14 03											15 03						
Barnetby	28 d					14 17											15 17						
Habrough	28 d					14 26											15 26						
Grimsby Town	28 a					14 41											15 41						
	d					14 42											15 42						
Cleethorpes	28 a					14 51											15 51						
Thorne North	d		13 31										14 31										15 31
Goole	d		13 40						14 16				14 40							15 19			15 40
Saltmarshe	d																						
York	33 d	12 50									13 51											14 54	
Selby	a	13 20					14 00				14 19				14 41			15 00				15 14	
	d	13 21					14 00				14 20				14 42			15 00				15 16	
Wressle	d																						
Howden	d	13 29									14 29				14 52							15 24	
Eastrington	d																						
Gilberdyke	d		13 49										14 49										15 49
Broomfleet	d																						
Brough	d	13 42	13 57				14 19		14 34		14 42		14 57		15 05			15 19		15 34		15 41	15 57
Ferriby	d																						
Hessle	d																						
Hull	a	13 55	14 11				14 36		14 48		14 55		15 11		15 18			15 36		15 48		15 55	16 11

A To Leeds
B From Bristol Temple Meads to Glasgow Central
C To Scarborough
D From Birmingham New Street to Newcastle
E From Plymouth to Aberdeen

For services between Barnetby, Habrough, Grimsby Town and Cleethorpes, refer to Table T028

Table T029-F

Sundays
5 April to 10 May

Manchester Airport, Manchester, Sheffield and Meadowhall - Doncaster and Hull

		XC ◇1 A ✠	NT ◇ B	NT	TP ◇1 ✠	TP ◇1 ✠	XC ◇1 C ✠	NT ◇ D	NT B	NT	XC ◇1 E ✠	NT	NT ◇ B	HT ◇1 ⊠	NT	TP ◇1 ✠	TP ◇1 ✠	NT ◇ F	XC ◇1 G ✠	NT ◇ D	NT B	NT	XC ◇1 H ✠
Manchester Airport 85	d				13 56											14 56							
Manchester Piccadilly 10	d				14 19	14 35										15 18	15 35						
Stockport 78	d				14 28											15 28							
Sheffield 7	a				15 08											16 08							
	d	14 52		15 06	15 10		15 21	15 25	15 31		15 50				16 06	16 10		16 13	16 21	16 25	16 31		16 52
Meadowhall	d			15 12	15 16			15 31	15 37						16 12	16 16		16 20		16 32	16 37		
Rotherham Central	d			15 19					15 43						16 18			16 28			16 43		
Swinton (S.Yorks)	d			15 28					15a51						16 28			16 38			16a51		
Mexborough	d			15 31											16 31								
Conisbrough	d			15 35											16 35								
London Kings Cross	d													14 48									
Doncaster 7	a	15 18		15 44	15 35			15 50			16 12			16 26	16 45	16 34				16 54			17 14
York 8 26	a	15 41					16 29				16 37							17 36	17 29				17 40
Doncaster 31	d		15 25		15 38			15 52				16 15	16 25	16 31		16 37				16 55			
Bentley (S.Yorks) 31	a		15 28										16 28										
Adwick 31	a		15 32										16 32										
Kirk Sandall	d											16 21											
Hatfield & Stainforth	d											16 26											
Thorne South	d																						
Crowle	d																						
Althorpe	d																						
Scunthorpe	a				16 03											17 02							
	d				16 04											17 03							
Barnetby 28	d				16 18											17 17							
Habrough 28	d				16 27											17 28							
Grimsby Town 28	a				16 40											17 43							
	d				16 41											17 44							
Cleethorpes 28	a				16 51											17 53							
Thorne North	d											16 31											
Goole	d							16 16				16 40								17 16			
Saltmarshe	d																						
York 8 33	d									15 51												16 51	
Selby	a					16 00				16 20				16 46			17 00					17 20	
	d					16 00				16 20				16 46			17 00					17 20	
Wressle	d																						
Howden	d									16 29				16 56								17 29	
Eastrington	d																						
Gilberdyke	d											16 49											
Broomfleet	d																						
Brough	d					16 19		16 35		16 41		16 57		17 08			17 19			17 34		17 41	
Ferriby	d																						
Hessle	d																						
Hull	a					16 36		16 48		16 55		17 12		17 21			17 36			17 48		17 54	

A From Birmingham New Street to Newcastle
B To Leeds
C From Plymouth to Glasgow Central
D To Scarborough
E From Guildford to Newcastle
F via Pontefract Baghill
G From Penzance to Edinburgh
H From Reading to Newcastle

For services between Barnetby, Habrough, Grimsby Town and Cleethorpes, refer to Table T028

NRT DECEMBER 19 EDITION

Table T029-F

Sundays
5 April to 10 May

Manchester Airport, Manchester, Sheffield and Meadowhall - Doncaster and Hull

		NT	NT ◇ A	NT	TP ◇1 ✠	TP ◇1 ✠	NT	XC ◇1 B ✠	NT ◇ C	NT	NT A	XC ◇1 D ✠	NT ◇ A	NT	TP ◇1 ✠	TP ◇1 ✠	XC ◇1 E ✠	NT ◇ F	NT A	NT	GR 1	NT	XC ◇1 G ✠
Manchester Airport 85	d				15 56										16 56								
Manchester Piccadilly 10	d				16 19	16 35									17 19	17 35							
Stockport 78	d				16 28										17 28								
Sheffield 7	a				17 08										18 09								
	d			17 06	17 10			17 21	17 25		17 30	17 52		18 06	18 11		18 21	18 25	18 31				18 52
Meadowhall	d			17 12	17 16				17 31		17 36			18 12	18 17			18 31	18 37				
Rotherham Central	d			17 18							17 42			18 18					18 43				
Swinton (S.Yorks)	d			17 27							17a52			18 27					18a51				
Mexborough	d			17 31										18 31									
Conisbrough	d			17 35										18 35									
London Kings Cross	d																				17 22		
Doncaster 7	a			17 44	17 34				17 50			18 14		18 45	18 35			18 50			19 03		19 14
York 8 26	a							18 29				19 18					19 30						19 43
Doncaster 31	d	17 15	17 25		17 37				18 02	18 15			18 25		18 37			18 52			19 05	19 15	
Bentley (S.Yorks) 31	a		17 28										18 28										
Adwick 31	a		17 32										18 32										
Kirk Sandall	d	17 21								18 21												19 21	
Hatfield & Stainforth	d	17 26								18 26												19 26	
Thorne South	d																						
Crowle	d																						
Althorpe	d																						
Scunthorpe	a				18 02										19 02								
	d				18 03										19 03								
Barnetby 28	d				18 17										19 17								
Habrough 28	d				18 26										19 26								
Grimsby Town 28	a				18 39										19 41								
	d				18 40										19 42								
Cleethorpes 28	a				18 51										19 51								
Thorne North	d	17 31								18 31												19 31	
Goole	d	17 40							18 24	18 40								19 16				19 40	
Saltmarshe	d																						
York 8 33	d						17 51													18 49			
Selby	a					18 00	18 11									19 00				19 17	19 22		
	d					18 00	18 12									19 00				19 18	19 26		
Wressle	d																						
Howden	d					18 10	18 20													19 27			
Eastrington	d																						
Gilberdyke	d	17 49								18 49												19 49	
Broomfleet	d																						
Brough	d	17 57				18 23	18 33		18 39	18 57						19 19		19 34		19 40	19 47	19 57	
Ferriby	d																						
Hessle	d																						
Hull	a	18 11				18 39	18 46		18 52	19 14						19 36		19 48		19 53	20 02	20 11	

A To Leeds
B From Plymouth to Glasgow Central
C To Scarborough
D From Reading to Newcastle
E From Plymouth to Edinburgh
F To Bridlington
G From Reading to Edinburgh

For services between Barnetby, Habrough, Grimsby Town and Cleethorpes, refer to Table T028

Table T029-F

Sundays

5 April to 10 May

Manchester Airport, Manchester, Sheffield and Meadowhall - Doncaster and Hull

	HT	NT	NT	NT	TP	TP	XC		NT	NT	NT	XC	NT	NT	NT	TP	TP	XC	NT	NT	NT	NT	XC
	◇■ A ⊠	◇ B	◇ C		◇■ ℋ	◇■ ℋ	◇■ D ℋ		◇ E	B		◇■ F		◇ B		◇■	◇■	◇■ G	◇	B			◇■ F
Manchester Airport 85 d					17 56											18 56							
Manchester Piccadilly d					18 19	18 35										19 19	19 35						
Stockport 78 d					18 28											19 28							
Sheffield a					19 09											20 09							
d			19 00	19 06	19 11		19 21		19 25	19 31		19 52			20 06	20 11		20 22	20 25	20 31			20 54
Meadowhall d			19 06	19 12	19 17				19 31	19 37					20 12	20 17			20 31	20 37			
Rotherham Central d			19 12	19 18						19 43					20 20					20 47			
Swinton (S.Yorks) d			19 20	19 28						19a51					20 29					20a55			
Mexborough d				19 32											20 32								
Conisbrough d				19 36											20 36								
London Kings Cross d	17 48																						
Doncaster a	19 27			19 45	19 35				19 50			20 14			20 46	20 35			20 50				21 20
York 26 a			20 16				20 30					20 42						21 31					21 44
Doncaster 31 d	19 29	19 29			19 37				19 51				20 15	20 25		20 37			20 52			21 15	
Bentley (S.Yorks) 31 a		19 32												20 28									
Adwick 31 a		19 36												20 32									
Kirk Sandall d													20 21									21 21	
Hatfield & Stainforth d													20 26									21 26	
Thorne South d																							
Crowle d																							
Althorpe d																							
Scunthorpe a					20 02											21 02							
d					20 03											21 03							
Barnetby 28 d					20 17											21 17							
Habrough 28 d																21 26							
Grimsby Town 28 a					20 39											21 39							
d					20 40											21 40							
Cleethorpes 28 a					20 49											21 51							
Thorne North d													20 31									21 31	
Goole d									20 16				20 40						21 16			21 40	
Saltmarshe d																							
York 33 d											19 56										20 52		
Selby a	19 44					20 00					20 15						21 00				21 11		
d	19 44					20 00					20 18						21 00				21 14		
Wressle d																							
Howden d	19 54										20 26						21 10				21 22		
Eastrington d																							
Gilberdyke d													20 49								21 32	21 49	
Broomfleet d																							
Brough d	20 06					20 19			20 35		20 41		20 57				21 23		21 34		21 39	21 57	
Ferriby d																					21 44		
Hessle d																					21 48		
Hull a	20 19					20 34			20 49		20 54		21 11				21 38		21 48		21 57	22 16	

A To Beverley
B To Leeds
C via Pontefract Baghill
D From Plymouth to Edinburgh
E To Bridlington
F From Reading to Newcastle
G From Plymouth

For services between Barnetby, Habrough, Grimsby Town and Cleethorpes, refer to Table T028

Table T029-F

Sundays

5 April to 10 May

Manchester Airport, Manchester, Sheffield and Meadowhall - Doncaster and Hull

	NT	HT	NT	TP	TP	NT	NT	NT	NT	NT	TP	NT		TP	NT	NT	TP	NT	TP
	◇ A	◇■ ⊠		◇■	◇■	◇		A	◇ A		◇■			◇■	◇	A	◇■		◇■
Manchester Airport 85 d				19 56							20 55						21 56		
Manchester Piccadilly d				20 18	20 35						21 19			21 35			22 19		22 35
Stockport 78 d				20 28							21 28						22 27		
Sheffield a				21 09							22 11						23 09		
d			21 06	21 11		21 25		21 31		22 08	22 12				22 25	22 32	23 11	23 30	
Meadowhall d			21 12	21 17		21 31		21 37		22 14	22 18				22 31	22 38		23 36	
Rotherham Central d			21 18					21 44		22 20						22 44		23 42	
Swinton (S.Yorks) d			21 28					21a52		22 30						22a53		23 51	
Mexborough d			21 32							22 33								23 54	
Conisbrough d			21 36							22 37								23 58	
London Kings Cross d		19 52																	
Doncaster a		21 27	21 45	21 35		21 50				22 47	22 36				22 50		23 42	00 06	
York 26 a																			
Doncaster 31 d	21 25	21 29		21 37		21 52	22 15		22 28		22 39				22 52				
Bentley (S.Yorks) 31 a	21 28								22 31										
Adwick 31 a	21 32								22 35										
Kirk Sandall d							22 21												
Hatfield & Stainforth d							22 26												
Thorne South d																			
Crowle d																			
Althorpe d																			
Scunthorpe a				22 02							23 04								
d				22 03							23 05								
Barnetby 28 d				22 17							23 19								
Habrough 28 d				22 26							23 28								
Grimsby Town 28 a				22 39							23 43								
d				22 40							23 44								
Cleethorpes 28 a				22 51							23 53								
Thorne North d							22 31												
Goole d						22 16	22 40								23 15				
Saltmarshe d																			
York 33 d												22 19							
Selby a		21 44			22 00							22 38		23 02					23 51
d		21 45			22 00							22 39		23 03					23 52
Wressle d																			
Howden d		21 55			22 10							22 47							
Eastrington d																			
Gilberdyke d							22 49					22 55			23 26				
Broomfleet d																			
Brough d		22 07			22 23	22 34	22 57					23 03		23 22	23 34				00 11
Ferriby d												23 08			23 39				
Hessle d												23 12			23 43				
Hull a		22 20			22 38	22 48	23 11					23 21		23 37	23 52				00 26

A To Leeds

For services between Barnetby, Habrough, Grimsby Town and Cleethorpes, refer to Table T028

Table T029-R

Mondays to Saturdays

16 December to 16 May

Hull - Doncaster - Meadowhall, Sheffield, Manchester and Manchester Airport

Miles	Miles	Miles	Miles			NT MX	NT MX	NT MX	NT MX	TP	HT SX	TP SO	TP SX	EM SX	NT SO	NT SX		NT	NT	NT SX	NT SO	TP	NT	NT	NT
							◇			◇1	◇1	◇1	◇1	◇1	◇	◇			◇			◇1			
						A	B	A	C		⊠			D ⊠	E	E				C	C	F ⊥			G
0	0	—	—	**Hull**	d						04 57	05 06	05 06						05 16					05 30	
4¾	4¾	—	—	Hessle	d																			05 37	
7½	7½	—	—	Ferriby	d																			05 42	
10½	10½	—	—	Brough	d						05 09	05 18	05 18						05 28					05 47	
14½	14½	—	—	Broomfleet	d																				
17	17	—	—	Gilberdyke	d							05 25	05 25						05 36						
—	19¼	—	—	Eastrington	d																				
—	22¼	—	—	Howden	d							05 32	05 32												
—	25	—	—	Wressle	d																				
—	31	—	—	**Selby**	a							05 42	05 42												
—	—	—	—		d							05 42	05 42												06 15
—	—	—	—	York [8] 33	a																				
20¾	—	—	—	Saltmarshe	d														05 42						
23¾	—	—	—	Goole	d														05 48					06 01	
31	—	—	—	Thorne North	d																			06 10	
—	—	0	—	**Cleethorpes** 28	d																	05 05			
—	—	3	—	**Grimsby Town** 28	d																	05 13			
—	—	11	—	Habrough 28	d																	05 23			
—	—	18	—	Barnetby 28	d																	05 32			
—	—	29	—	**Scunthorpe**	a																	05 47			
—	—	—	—		d																	05 47			
—	—	32½	—	Althorpe	d																	05 52			
—	—	36¼	—	Crowle	d																	05 58			
—	—	42¼	—	Thorne South	d																	06 06			
34¼	—	45¼	—	Hatfield & Stainforth	d																	06 12		06 16	
37	—	48	—	Kirk Sandall	d																			06 20	
—	—	—	0	Adwick 31	d																				
—	—	—	2¼	Bentley (S.Yorks) 31	d																				
41	49¼	52	4	**Doncaster [7]** 31	a						05 43								06 10			06 24		06 29	06 36
—	—	—	—	London Kings Cross [15] ⊖26	a						07 59														
—	—	—	—	York [8] 26	d																				
—	—	—	—	**Doncaster [7]**	d					05 36				05 59	06 00	06 03		06 06	06 12			06 25	06 34		
45¾	—	—	—	Conisbrough	d													06 13					06 41		
48	—	—	—	Mexborough	d													06 18					06 46		
49¾	—	—	—	Swinton (S.Yorks)	d				00 04									06 21		06 30	06 33		06 49		
53¾	—	—	—	Rotherham Central	d				00 13									06 29		06 41	06 42	06 46	06 58		
56½	—	—	—	**Meadowhall** ⇌	d	00 04	00 08	00 12	00 19	05 57								06 37	06 33	06 50	06 50	06 54	07 10		
60	—	—	—	**Sheffield [7]** ⇌	a	00 13	00 17	00 21	00 28	06 08				06 23	06 26	06 32		06 46	06 44	07 00	07 00	07 05	07 18		
—	—	—	—		d					06 09												07 07			
96¾	—	—	—	Stockport 78	a					06 53												07 52			
102¾	—	—	—	**Manchester Piccadilly [10]** ⇌	a					07 02		07 11	07 17									08 02			
112½	—	—	—	**Manchester Airport** 85 ✈⇌	a					07 27												08 26			

A From Doncaster
B From Hull
C From Leeds
D From Leeds to St Pancras International
E To Lincoln
F ⊥ from Sheffield
G To Scunthorpe

For services between Barnetby, Habrough, Grimsby Town and Cleethorpes, refer to Table T028

Table T029-R

Mondays to Saturdays

16 December to 16 May

Hull - Doncaster - Meadowhall, Sheffield, Manchester and Manchester Airport

		XC	NT	NT	NT	TP SX	TP SO	NT	HT SO	NT SX	NT SO	HT SX	NT	XC SO	XC SX	NT		NT	NT	TP	NT	GR SX	GR SO	TP	NT
		◇1				◇1	◇1	◇	◇1			◇1	◇	◇1	◇1					◇1		■ 1	■ 1	◇1	◇
		A ⊥						B	C ⊠			C ⊠		D	D	E						F ⊓	F ⊓	⊥	B
Hull	d		05 45		05 53	06 04	06 04	06 10	06 17	06 19	06 22	06 26	06 31								06 43	06 58	06 58	07 05	07 15
Hessle	d				06 00																06 50				
Ferriby	d				06 05																06 55				
Brough	d		05 57		06 10	06 16	06 16	06 22	06 29	06 30	06 33	06 38	06 43								07 00	07 12	07 12	07 17	07 27
Broomfleet	d																				07 06				
Gilberdyke	d		06 05		06 18					06 38	06 41										07 10				
Eastrington	d		06 09																						
Howden	d		06 14						06 40	06 45	06 48	06 50												07 29	
Wressle	d		06 18																						
Selby	a		06 27			06 36	06 36	06 43	06 51	06 56	06 58	07 00										07 32	07 32	07 39	07 47
	d		06 27			06 37	06 37		06 51	06 57	06 59	07 01										07 35	07 35	07 40	
York [8] 33	a		06 59							07 34	07 35														
Saltmarshe	d				06 23																07 15				
Goole	d				06 31								06 58								07 21				
Thorne North	d				06 40																07 29				
Cleethorpes 28	d																			06 26					
Grimsby Town 28	d																			06 34					
Habrough 28	d																			06 44					
Barnetby 28	d																			06 53					
Scunthorpe	a																			07 08					
	d																		06 48	07 08					
Althorpe	d																		06 53						
Crowle	d																		07 00						
Thorne South	d																		07 08						
Hatfield & Stainforth	d				06 45														07 14		07 35				
Kirk Sandall	d				06 50														07 18		07 40				
Adwick 31	d			06 45														07 16							
Bentley (S.Yorks) 31	d			06 49														07 20							
Doncaster [7] 31	a			06 54	07 00				07 08			07 16	07 19					07 25	07 28	07 38	07 49	07 51	07 53		
London Kings Cross [15] ⊖26	a								08 47			09 14										09 51	09 49		
York [8] 26	d	06 24												06 12	06 45										
Doncaster [7]	d	06 47		06 55									07 20					07 26		07 42					
Conisbrough	d			07 03														07 34							
Mexborough	d			07 07														07 39							
Swinton (S.Yorks)	d			07 10												07 34		07 42							
Rotherham Central	d			07 19												07 44		07 56							
Meadowhall ⇌	d			07 31									07 38			07 50		08 03		07 59					
Sheffield [7] ⇌	a	07 12		07 39									07 47	07 51	07 51	07 57		08 10		08 06					
	d																			08 08					
Stockport 78	a																			08 52					
Manchester Piccadilly [10] ⇌	a					08 13	08 14													09 02				09 14	
Manchester Airport 85 ✈⇌	a																			09 25					

A To Southampton Central
B To Halifax
C From Beverley
D To Plymouth
E From Leeds
F The Hull Executive

For services between Barnetby, Habrough, Grimsby Town and Cleethorpes, refer to Table T028

Table T029-R

Mondays to Saturdays
16 December to 16 May

Hull - Doncaster - Meadowhall, Sheffield, Manchester and Manchester Airport

	XC	NT	NT	XC	XC	NT	NT	NT	NT	NT	TP	NT	TP	TP	NT		XC	XC	NT	HT	HT	NT	HT	HT
				SO	SX			SO	SX				SO	SX			SX	SO		SX	SO		SX	SO
	◇		◇	◇1	◇1						◇1		◇1	◇1	◇		◇1	◇1		◇1	◇1	◇	◇1	◇1
	A		B	C	C			D	D		E				F		G	G		H	I	J	B	K
					✠						✠						✠	✠		⊠	⊠		⊠	⊠
Hull d			07 19				07 50					07 53	08 07	08 07	08 15					08 24	08 24	08 28		
Hessle d												08 00												
Ferriby d												08 05												
Brough d			07 33				08 02					08 10	08 19	08 19	08 27					08 36	08 36	08 41		
Broomfleet d												08 15												
Gilberdyke d							08 09					08 20												
Eastrington d							08 13																	
Howden d							08 18													08 47	08 47			
Wressle d																								
Selby a							08 29						08 38	08 38	08 47					08 58	08 58			
d							08 29						08 40	08 40						09 01	09 01			
York 8 33 a							09 02																	
Saltmarshe d																								
Goole d			07 49									08 28										08 56		
Thorne North d			07 57									08 37												
Cleethorpes 28 d											07 29													
Grimsby Town 28 d											07 37													
Habrough 28 d											07 47													
Barnetby 28 d											07 56													
Scunthorpe a											08 11													
d						07 48					08 11													
Althorpe d						07 53																		
Crowle d						08 00																		
Thorne South d						08 08																		
Hatfield & Stainforth d						08 14						08 43												
Kirk Sandall d						08 18						08 47												
Adwick 31 d		07 49								08 21									08 48					
Bentley (S.Yorks) 31 d		07 53								08 25									08 52				←	←
Doncaster 7 31 a		07 58	08 19			08 28				08 30	08 41	08 57							08 59	09 22	09 24	09 19	09 22	09 24
London Kings Cross 15 ⊖26 a																				→	→		11 09	11 08
York 8 26 d	07 28			07 44	07 44												08 35	08 35						
Doncaster 7 d	07 52	08 00	08 22							08 32	08 42						08 57	08 58	09 03			09 20		
Conisbrough d		08 11								08 39									09 12					
Mexborough d		08 15								08 44									09 17					
Swinton (S.Yorks) d		08 20						08 36	08 36	08 47									09 20					
Rotherham Central d		08 28						08 45	08 45	08 57									09 28					
Meadowhall d		08 34	08 40					08 51	08 51	09 06	09 02								09 34			09 38		
Sheffield 7 a	08 15	08 44	08 48	08 54	08 55			09 00	09 01	09 14	09 09						09 22	09 22	09 44			09 49		
d											09 11													
Stockport 78 a											09 53													
Manchester Piccadilly 10 a											10 02		10 04	10 11										
Manchester Airport 85 a											10 25													

A From Newcastle to Reading
B From Beverley
C From Newcastle to Plymouth
D From Leeds
E ✠ from Sheffield
F To Halifax
G From Newcastle to Southampton Central
H From Beverley to London Kings Cross
I To London Kings Cross
J From Scarborough
K From Hull

For services between Barnetby, Habrough, Grimsby Town and Cleethorpes, refer to Table T028

Table T029-R

Mondays to Saturdays
16 December to 16 May

Hull - Doncaster - Meadowhall, Sheffield, Manchester and Manchester Airport

	XC	NT	NT	NT	NT	TP	NT	TP	NT	XC	NT	NT	NT	XC	XC		NT	NT	NT	NT	TP	NT	TP	NT
														SO	SX									
	◇1	◇				◇1		◇1	◇	◇1	◇		◇	◇1	◇1						◇1		◇1	◇
	A	B		C		D			E	F			B	G	G			H	C		D			E
	✠					✠				✠				✠	✠						✠			
Hull d		08 50					08 53	09 08	09 15				09 25					09 50				09 53	10 08	10 15
Hessle d							09 00															10 00		
Ferriby d							09 05															10 05		
Brough d		09 02					09 10	09 20	09 27				09 37					10 02				10 10	10 20	10 27
Broomfleet d																								
Gilberdyke d		09 09					09 18											10 09				10 17		
Eastrington d																								
Howden d		09 16																10 16						
Wressle d		09 21																						
Selby a		09 29						09 39	09 47									10 27					10 39	10 47
d		09 30						09 40										10 27					10 40	
York 8 33 a		10 01																11 02						
Saltmarshe d							09 23																	
Goole d							09 28						09 54									10 28		
Thorne North d							09 37															10 37		
Cleethorpes 28 d						08 26															09 26			
Grimsby Town 28 d						08 34															09 34			
Habrough 28 d						08 44															09 44			
Barnetby 28 d						08 53															09 53			
Scunthorpe a						09 08															10 08			
d			08 52			09 08											09 48				10 08			
Althorpe d			08 57														09 53							
Crowle d			09 04														10 00							
Thorne South d			09 12														10 08							
Hatfield & Stainforth d			09 18				09 43										10 14					10 43		
Kirk Sandall d			09 22				09 47										10 18					10 47		
Adwick 31 d					09 25															10 24				
Bentley (S.Yorks) 31 d					09 29															10 28				
Doncaster 7 31 a			09 32		09 34	09 38	10 00						10 19				10 28			10 33	10 38	10 57		
London Kings Cross 15 ⊖26 a																								
York 8 26 d	08 44									09 37	09 15			09 44	09 44									
Doncaster 7 d					09 35	09 42				10 00		10 04	10 21							10 35	10 42			
Conisbrough d					09 42							10 11								10 42				
Mexborough d					09 47							10 16								10 47				
Swinton (S.Yorks) d				09 37	09 50						10 10	10 19							10 36	10 50				
Rotherham Central d				09 45	09 59						10 19	10 28							10 45	10 58				
Meadowhall d				09 51	10 06	10 02					10 24	10 34	10 41						10 51	11 06	11 02			
Sheffield 7 a	09 54			10 01	10 14	10 09				10 22	10 33	10 44	10 50	10 54	10 55				11 01	11 14	11 09			
d						10 11															11 11			
Stockport 78 a						10 52															11 52			
Manchester Piccadilly 10 a						11 02		11 04													12 02		12 04	
Manchester Airport 85 a						11 25															12 25			

A From Edinburgh to Plymouth
B From Bridlington
C From Leeds
D ✠ from Sheffield
E To Halifax
F From Edinburgh to Reading
G From Glasgow Central to Plymouth
H From Scarborough

For services between Barnetby, Habrough, Grimsby Town and Cleethorpes, refer to Table T028

Table T029-R

Mondays to Saturdays
16 December to 16 May

Hull - Doncaster - Meadowhall, Sheffield, Manchester and Manchester Airport

		XC	NT	NT	HT SX	HT SO	XC SO	XC SX	NT	NT	NT	NT	TP	NT	TP	NT	XC	NT	NT	XC	NT	NT SX	NT SO	NT
		◇1 A 🛒		◇ B	◇1 ☒	◇1 ☒	◇1 C 🛒	◇1 C 🛒		◇ D	E		◇1 F 🛒		◇1	◇ G	◇1 H 🛒		◇ B	◇1 I 🛒		◇ D	◇ D	E
Hull	d			10 25	10 33	10 33				10 50				10 53	11 06	11 15			11 25			11 50	11 50	
Hessle	d													11 00										
Ferriby	d													11 05										
Brough	d			10 37	10 45	10 45				11 02				11 10	11 18	11 27			11 37			12 02	12 02	
Broomfleet	d																							
Gilberdyke	d									11 09				11 17								12 09	12 09	
Eastrington	d									11 13														
Howden	d				10 56	10 56				11 18												12 16	12 16	
Wressle	d																							
Selby	a				11 07	11 07				11 29					11 37	11 47						12 27	12 27	
	d				11 07	11 07				11 29					11 38							12 27	12 27	
York 8	33 a									12 03												12 48	12 49	
Saltmarshe	d													11 23										
Goole	d			10 54										11 28					11 54					
Thorne North	d													11 37										
Cleethorpes	28 d												10 26											
Grimsby Town	28 d												10 34											
Habrough	28 d												10 44											
Barnetby	28 d												10 53											
Scunthorpe	a												11 08											
	d								10 48				11 08								11 48			
Althorpe	d								10 53												11 53			
Crowle	d								11 00												12 00			
Thorne South	d								11 08												12 08			
Hatfield & Stainforth	d								11 14					11 43							12 14			
Kirk Sandall	d								11 18					11 47							12 18			
Adwick	31 d											11 24												
Bentley (S.Yorks)	31 d											11 28												
Doncaster 7	31 a			11 19	11 22	11 24			11 28			11 33	11 37	11 57					12 19		12 28			
London Kings Cross 15	⊖26 a				13 08	13 08																		
York 8	26 d	10 35					10 43	10 44									11 36			11 44				
Doncaster 7	d	10 59	11 04	11 21								11 35	11 42				11 59	12 03	12 21					
Conisbrough	d		11 11									11 42						12 10						
Mexborough	d		11 16									11 47						12 15						
Swinton (S.Yorks)	d		11 19								11 36	11 50						12 18						12 36
Rotherham Central	d		11 28								11 44	11 58						12 28						12 45
Meadowhall	d		11 34	11 38							11 51	12 06	12 02					12 34	12 41					12 51
Sheffield 7	a	11 21	11 44	11 49			11 54	11 54			12 01	12 14	12 08				12 21	12 44	12 50	12 55				13 01
	d												12 11											
Stockport	78 a												12 52											
Manchester Piccadilly 10	a												13 02		13 04									
Manchester Airport	85 a												13 25											

A From Newcastle to Southampton Central
B From Scarborough
C From Dundee to Plymouth
D From Bridlington
E From Leeds
F 🛒 from Sheffield
G To Halifax
H From Newcastle to Reading
I From Glasgow Central to Plymouth

For services between Barnetby, Habrough, Grimsby Town and Cleethorpes, refer to Table T028

Table T029-R

Mondays to Saturdays
16 December to 16 May

Hull - Doncaster - Meadowhall, Sheffield, Manchester and Manchester Airport

		NT	TP	NT	TP	NT	XC	NT	NT	HT SX	XC	NT	NT	NT	NT	TP	NT	TP	NT	XC	NT	NT	NT	HT SO
			◇1 A 🛒		◇1	◇ B	◇1 C 🛒		◇ D	◇1 ☒	◇1 E 🛒		◇ F	G		◇1 A 🛒		◇1	◇ B	◇1 H 🛒	◇		◇ D	◇1 ☒
Hull	d			11 53	12 08	12 15			12 25	12 33			12 50				12 53	13 08	13 15				13 25	13 31
Hessle	d			12 00													13 00							
Ferriby	d			12 05													13 05							
Brough	d			12 10	12 20	12 27			12 37	12 45			13 02				13 10	13 20	13 27				13 37	13 43
Broomfleet	d			12 15																				
Gilberdyke	d			12 20									13 09				13 18							
Eastrington	d																							
Howden	d									12 56			13 16											13 54
Wressle	d												13 21											
Selby	a				12 40	12 47				13 07			13 29					13 39	13 47					14 05
	d				12 41					13 07			13 30					13 40						14 08
York 8	33 a												14 00											
Saltmarshe	d																13 23							
Goole	d			12 28					12 54								13 28						13 54	
Thorne North	d			12 37													13 37							
Cleethorpes	28 d		11 26													12 26								
Grimsby Town	28 d		11 34													12 34								
Habrough	28 d		11 44													12 44								
Barnetby	28 d		11 53													12 53								
Scunthorpe	a		12 08													13 08								
	d		12 08									12 48				13 08								
Althorpe	d											12 53												
Crowle	d											13 00												
Thorne South	d											13 08												
Hatfield & Stainforth	d			12 43								13 14					13 43							
Kirk Sandall	d			12 47								13 18					13 47							
Adwick	31 d	12 24													13 24									
Bentley (S.Yorks)	31 d	12 28													13 28									
Doncaster 7	31 a	12 33	12 38	12 57					13 19	13 23		13 28			13 33	13 38	13 57						14 19	14 24
London Kings Cross 15	⊖26 a									15 09														16 09
York 8	26 d						12 35				12 44									13 35	13 15			
Doncaster 7	d	12 35	12 42				12 59	13 04	13 21						13 35	13 42				14 00		14 05	14 21	
Conisbrough	d	12 42						13 12							13 42							14 12		
Mexborough	d	12 47						13 16							13 47							14 17		
Swinton (S.Yorks)	d	12 50						13 19						13 36	13 50						14 11	14 20		
Rotherham Central	d	12 58						13 28						13 45	13 58						14 19	14 28		
Meadowhall	d	13 06	13 02					13 34	13 38					13 51	14 06	14 02					14 24	14 34	14 38	
Sheffield 7	a	13 14	13 08				13 21	13 44	13 49		13 54			14 01	14 14	14 08				14 22	14 32	14 44	14 49	
	d		13 11													14 11								
Stockport	78 a		13 52													14 52								
Manchester Piccadilly 10	a		14 02		14 04											15 02		15 04						
Manchester Airport	85 a		14 25													15 25								

A 🛒 from Sheffield
B To Halifax
C From Newcastle to Southampton Central
D From Scarborough
E From Glasgow Central to Penzance
F From Bridlington
G From Leeds
H From Newcastle to Reading

For services between Barnetby, Habrough, Grimsby Town and Cleethorpes, refer to Table T028

Table T029-R

Mondays to Saturdays

16 December to 16 May

Hull - Doncaster - Meadowhall, Sheffield, Manchester and Manchester Airport

		XC SO ◇1 A 🛒	XC SX ◇1 A 🛒	NT	NT B	NT	TP ◇1 C 🛒	NT	TP SO ◇1	TP SX ◇1	NT ◇ D	XC ◇1 E 🛒	NT	NT ◇ F	XC ◇1 G 🛒	NT	NT B	NT	TP ◇1 C 🛒	NT	XC ◇1 H 🛒	NT	NT ◇ I	TP SX ◇1
Hull	d							13 53	14 07	14 07	14 15			14 25						14 42			14 50	15 03
Hessle	d							14 00												14 49				
Ferriby	d							14 05												15 01				
Brough	d							14 10	14 20	14 20	14 27			14 37						15 06			15 02	15 15
Broomfleet	d							14 15																
Gilberdyke	d							14 20												15 14			15 09	
Eastrington	d																							
Howden	d																						15 16	
Wressle	d																							
Selby	a								14 39	14 39	14 48												15 27	15 34
	d								14 40	14 40													15 27	15 36
York 8 33	a																						16 01	
Saltmarshe	d																			15 20				
Goole	d							14 28						14 54						15 28				
Thorne North	d							14 37												15 37				
Cleethorpes 28	d						13 26												14 26					
Grimsby Town 28	d						13 34												14 34					
Habrough 28	d						13 44												14 44					
Barnetby 28	d						13 53												14 53					
Scunthorpe	a						14 08												15 08					
	d			13 48			14 08									14 48			15 08					
Althorpe	d			13 53												14 53								
Crowle	d			14 00												15 00								
Thorne South	d			14 08												15 08								
Hatfield & Stainforth	d			14 14				14 44								15 14				15 43				
Kirk Sandall	d			14 18				14 48								15 18				15 47				
Adwick 31	d					14 24												15 24						
Bentley (S.Yorks) 31	d					14 28												15 28						
Doncaster 7 31	a			14 28		14 33	14 38	14 57						15 19		15 28		15 33	15 38	15 57				
London Kings Cross 15 ⊖26	a																							
York 8 26	d	13 44	13 44									14 35			14 44						15 36			
Doncaster 7	d					14 35	14 42					14 59	15 04	15 21				15 35	15 42		16 00	16 04		
Conisbrough	d					14 42							15 12					15 42				16 12		
Mexborough	d					14 47							15 16					15 47				16 16		
Swinton (S.Yorks)	d				14 36	14 50							15 19				15 36	15 50				16 19		
Rotherham Central	d				14 44	14 58							15 28				15 45	15 57				16 28		
Meadowhall ⇌	d				14 52	15 06	15 02						15 34	15 41			15 51	16 06	16 02			16 34		
Sheffield 7 ⇌	a	14 54	14 55		15 01	15 14	15 08					15 21	15 44	15 50	15 55		16 01	16 14	16 08		16 22	16 44		
	d						15 11												16 11					
Stockport 78	a						15 52												16 52					
Manchester Piccadilly 10 ⇌	a						16 02		16 04	16 14									17 02					17 14
Manchester Airport 85 ✈⇌	a						16 25												17 25					

A From Aberdeen to Penzance
B From Leeds
C 🛒 from Sheffield
D To Halifax
E From Newcastle to Guildford
F From Scarborough
G From Glasgow Central to Penzance
H From Newcastle to Reading
I From Bridlington

For services between Barnetby, Habrough, Grimsby Town and Cleethorpes, refer to Table T028

Table T029-R

Mondays to Saturdays

16 December to 16 May

Hull - Doncaster - Meadowhall, Sheffield, Manchester and Manchester Airport

		TP SO ◇1	HT SX ◇1 ⊠	NT SO ◇ A	NT SX ◇ A	NT ◇ B	HT SO ◇1 ⊠	XC ◇1 C 🛒	NT	NT ◇ D	NT E	NT	TP ◇1 F 🛒	NT	TP ◇1	XC ◇1 G 🛒	NT ◇ A	NT	NT ◇ B	XC ◇1 H 🛒	NT	NT ◇ D	NT E	NT
Hull	d	15 08	15 08	15 15	15 16	15 25	15 31			15 50				15 53	16 08		16 15		16 25			16 50		
Hessle	d													16 00										
Ferriby	d													16 05										
Brough	d	15 20	15 20	15 27	15 28	15 37	15 43			16 02				16 10	16 20		16 27		16 37			17 02		
Broomfleet	d													16 15										
Gilberdyke	d									16 09				16 20								17 10		
Eastrington	d																					17 14		
Howden	d		15 31				15 55			16 16												17 19		
Wressle	d																							
Selby	a	15 39	15 42	15 46	15 48		16 05			16 27					16 39		16 47					17 29		
	d	15 40	15 43				16 06			16 27					16 40							17 30		
York 8 33	a									16 49												18 01		
Saltmarshe	d																							
Goole	d					15 54								16 29					16 55					
Thorne North	d													16 37										
Cleethorpes 28	d												15 26											
Grimsby Town 28	d												15 34											
Habrough 28	d												15 44											
Barnetby 28	d												15 53											
Scunthorpe	a												16 08											
	d								15 48				16 08								16 48			
Althorpe	d								15 53												16 53			
Crowle	d								16 00												17 00			
Thorne South	d								16 08												17 08			
Hatfield & Stainforth	d								16 14					16 43							17 14			
Kirk Sandall	d								16 18					16 48							17 18			
Adwick 31	d											16 24												17 24
Bentley (S.Yorks) 31	d											16 28												17 28
Doncaster 7 31	a		16 03			16 19	16 23		16 28			16 33	16 38	16 57					17 19		17 28			17 33
London Kings Cross 15 ⊖26	a		17 47				18 09																	
York 8 26	d							15 44								16 13				16 44				
Doncaster 7	d					16 21						16 35	16 42					17 04	17 21					17 35
Conisbrough	d											16 42						17 12						17 43
Mexborough	d											16 47						17 16						17 48
Swinton (S.Yorks)	d										16 36	16 50						17 19					17 35	17 51
Rotherham Central	d										16 45	16 58						17 28					17 46	17 58
Meadowhall ⇌	d					16 38					16 51	17 06	17 02					17 34	17 38				17 51	18 06
Sheffield 7 ⇌	a					16 49		16 54			17 01	17 14	17 08			17 21		17 44	17 49	17 54			18 01	18 14
	d												17 11											
Stockport 78	a												17 52											
Manchester Piccadilly 10 ⇌	a	17 16											18 02		18 11									
Manchester Airport 85 ✈⇌	a												18 25											

A To Halifax
B From Scarborough
C From Edinburgh to Plymouth
D From Bridlington
E From Leeds
F 🛒 from Sheffield
G From Newcastle to Reading
H From Glasgow Central to Plymouth

For services between Barnetby, Habrough, Grimsby Town and Cleethorpes, refer to Table T028

Table T029-R

Mondays to Saturdays

16 December to 16 May

Hull - Doncaster - Meadowhall, Sheffield, Manchester and Manchester Airport

Station		TP ◇1 A	NT	TP SX ◇1	TP SO ◇1	HT SX ◇1	NT ◇ B	XC ◇1 C	NT ◇	NT	EM SO ◇1 D	NT ◇ E	XC ◇1 F	NT	NT G	NT		TP ◇1	NT	XC ◇1 H	NT	NT ◇ I	TP ◇1	NT ◇ B	NT ◇ E
Hull	d		16 53	17 03	17 08	17 08	17 15					17 25							17 40			17 50	18 08	18 15	18 25
Hessle	d		17 00																17 47			17 57			
Ferriby	d		17 05																17 52			18 02			
Brough	d		17 10	17 15	17 20	17 21	17 27					17 37							17 57			18 07	18 20	18 27	18 37
Broomfleet	d																		18 02						
Gilberdyke	d		17 18																18 07			18 14			
Eastrington	d																								
Howden	d					17 33																18 21			
Wressle	d																								
Selby	a			17 37	17 39	17 43	17 47															18 32	18 39	18 47	
	d			17 37	17 40	17 44																18 32	18 40		
York 8 33	a																					19 04			
Saltmarshe	d		17 23																18 12						
Goole	d		17 28									17 54							18 20						18 54
Thorne North	d		17 37																18 28						
Cleethorpes 28	d	16 26																17 26							
Grimsby Town 28	d	16 34																17 34							
Habrough 28	d	16 44																17 44							
Barnetby 28	d	16 53																17 53							
Scunthorpe	a	17 08																18 08							
	d	17 08												17 48				18 08							
Althorpe	d													17 53											
Crowle	d													18 00											
Thorne South	d													18 08											
Hatfield & Stainforth	d		17 43											18 14					18 34						
Kirk Sandall	d		17 48											18 18					18 39						
Adwick 31	d															18 24									
Bentley (S.Yorks) 31	d															18 28									
Doncaster 7 31	a	17 38	17 57			18 00						18 19		18 28		18 33		18 38	18 48						19 18
London Kings Cross 15 ⊖26	a					19 47																			
York 8 26	d							17 36	17 15		17 50		17 44							18 36					
Doncaster 7	d	17 42						18 00		18 04	18 13	18 21				18 35		18 42		19 00	19 04				19 20
Conisbrough	d									18 12						18 42					19 12				
Mexborough	d									18 16						18 47					19 16				
Swinton (S.Yorks)	d								18 10	18 20					18 36	18 50					19 19				
Rotherham Central	d								18 18	18 28					18 45	18 58					19 28				
Meadowhall	d	18 02							18 24	18 34		18 38			18 51	19 06		19 02			19 34				19 38
Sheffield 7	a	18 08						18 22	18 32	18 44	18 38	18 49	18 54		19 01	19 14		19 09		19 22	19 44				19 49
	d	18 11																19 11							
Stockport 78	a	18 52																19 52							
Manchester Piccadilly 10	a	19 03		19 14	19 11													20 02					20 04		
Manchester Airport 85	a	19 25																20 25							

A from Sheffield
B To Halifax
C From Newcastle to Reading
D To St Pancras International
E From Scarborough
F From Edinburgh to Plymouth
G From Leeds
H From Newcastle to Southampton Central
I From Bridlington

For services between Barnetby, Habrough, Grimsby Town and Cleethorpes, refer to Table T028

NRT DECEMBER 19 EDITION

Table T029-R

Mondays to Saturdays

16 December to 16 May

Hull - Doncaster - Meadowhall, Sheffield, Manchester and Manchester Airport

Station		HT SO ◇1	XC SO ◇1 A	XC SX ◇1 A	NT	NT ◇ B	NT C	NT	TP ◇1	NT	TP SX ◇1	TP SO ◇1	XC ◇1 D	NT	HT SX ◇1	NT ◇ E		NT ◇ F	XC ◇1 G	NT	NT ◇ B	NT C	NT	TP SO ◇1	TP SX ◇1
Hull	d	18 36				18 50				18 53	19 03	19 08			19 08	19 15		19 25			19 50				
Hessle	d									19 00															
Ferriby	d									19 05															
Brough	d	18 48				19 02				19 10	19 15	19 20			19 20	19 27		19 37			20 02				
Broomfleet	d																								
Gilberdyke	d					19 09				19 18											20 09				
Eastrington	d																								
Howden	d	18 59				19 16									19 33						20 16				
Wressle	d					19 21																			
Selby	a	19 10				19 29					19 37	19 40			19 43	19 49					20 27				
	d	19 11				19 31					19 38	19 40			19 45						20 27				
York 8 33	a					20 03															21 01				
Saltmarshe	d									19 23															
Goole	d									19 28								19 54							
Thorne North	d									19 37															
Cleethorpes 28	d								18 26															19 26	19 26
Grimsby Town 28	d								18 34															19 34	19 34
Habrough 28	d								18 44															19 44	19 44
Barnetby 28	d								18 53															19 53	19 53
Scunthorpe	a								19 08															20 08	20 08
	d				18 48				19 08											19 48				20 08	20 08
Althorpe	d				18 53															19 53					
Crowle	d				19 00															20 00					
Thorne South	d				19 08															20 08					
Hatfield & Stainforth	d				19 14					19 43										20 14					
Kirk Sandall	d				19 18					19 47										20 18					
Adwick 31	d							19 24															20 24		
Bentley (S.Yorks) 31	d							19 28															20 28		
Doncaster 7 31	a	19 27			19 28			19 33	19 41	19 57					20 03			20 19		20 28			20 33	20 38	20 38
London Kings Cross 15 ⊖26	a	21 15													21 50										
York 8 26	d		18 44	18 44									19 36						19 44						
Doncaster 7	d							19 35	19 42				19 59	20 06				20 21					20 35	20 42	20 42
Conisbrough	d							19 43						20 14									20 42		
Mexborough	d							19 47						20 18									20 47		
Swinton (S.Yorks)	d						19 36	19 50						20 21								20 36	20 50		
Rotherham Central	d						19 45	19 58						20 30								20 45	20 59		
Meadowhall	d						19 51	20 06	20 02					20 36				20 38				20 54	21 08	21 04	21 04
Sheffield 7	a		19 54	19 55			20 01	20 14	20 09				20 21	20 44				20 49	20 54			21 04	21 17	21 09	21 09
	d								20 11															21 11	21 11
Stockport 78	a								20 52															21 52	21 52
Manchester Piccadilly 10	a								21 02		21 15	21 04												22 04	22 08
Manchester Airport 85	a								21 25																

A From Glasgow Central to Bristol Temple Meads
B From Bridlington
C From Leeds
D From Newcastle to Birmingham New Street
E To Halifax
F From Scarborough
G From Edinburgh to Bristol Temple Meads

For services between Barnetby, Habrough, Grimsby Town and Cleethorpes, refer to Table T028

Table T029-R

Mondays to Saturdays

16 December to 16 May

Hull - Doncaster - Meadowhall, Sheffield, Manchester and Manchester Airport

		NT	TP	NT	XC SO	XC SX	NT	NT	GR SX	XC SO	XC SX	NT	NT	NT	TP	NT	NT	TP	NT SO	NT SX	NT	NT SO	NT SX	NT
			◇1	◇	◇1	◇1		◇	1	◇1	◇1				◇1		◇	◇1	◇	◇	◇	◇	◇	
				A	B	B		C		D	D		E				F	G	A	A		C	C	
Hull	d	19 55	20 08	20 15				20 25	20 29							20 42	20 50	21 08	21 15	21 15		21 26	21 26	
Hessle	d	20 02														20 49	20 57							
Ferriby	d	20 07														20 53	21 02							
Brough	d	20 12	20 20	20 27				20 37	20 42							20 58	21 07	21 20	21 27	21 27		21 38	21 38	
Broomfleet	d																							
Gilberdyke	d	20 19														21 06	21 14							
Eastrington	d																							
Howden	d																21 21							
Wressle	d																							
Selby	a		20 39	20 47				20 57	21 03								21 32	21 39	21 46	21 47				
	d		20 41					20 57	21 04								21 32							
York 8 33	a																22 08							
Saltmarshe	d																							
Goole	d	20 29														21 16						21 53	21 53	
Thorne North	d	20 38														21 25								
Cleethorpes 28	d														20 26									
Grimsby Town 28	d														20 34									
Habrough 28	d														20 44									
Barnetby 28	d														20 53									
Scunthorpe	a														21 08									
	d											20 48			21 08									21 48
Althorpe	d											20 53												21 53
Crowle	d											21 00												22 00
Thorne South	d											21 08												22 08
Hatfield & Stainforth	d	20 44										21 14				21 31								22 14
Kirk Sandall	d	20 48										21 18				21 35								22 18
Adwick 31	d													21 24										
Bentley (S.Yorks) 31	d													21 28										
Doncaster 7 31	a	20 58						21 18	21 23			21 28		21 33	21 38	21 44						22 15	22 15	22 30
London Kings Cross 15 ⊖26	a																							
York 8 26	d				20 35	20 36				20 45	20 44													
Doncaster 7	d				20 59	21 01	21 04	21 21						21 35	21 43						21 51	22 17	22 17	
Conisbrough	d						21 11							21 42										
Mexborough	d						21 16							21 47										
Swinton (S.Yorks)	d						21 19						21 36	21 50										
Rotherham Central	d						21 29						21 44	21 58										
Meadowhall ⇌	d						21 35	21 38					21 51	22 06	22 02						22 10	22 34	22 36	
Sheffield 7 ⇌	a				21 21	21 25	21 45	21 49		21 53	21 54		21 59	22 14	22 08						22 19	22 44	22 45	
	d														22 10									
Stockport 78	a														22 52									
Manchester Piccadilly 10 ⇌	a		22 10												23 02									
Manchester Airport 85 ✈⇌	a														23 25									

A To Halifax
B From Newcastle to Birmingham New Street
C From Scarborough
D From Glasgow Central to Birmingham New Street
E From Leeds
F From Bridlington
G To Liverpool Lime Street

For services between Barnetby, Habrough, Grimsby Town and Cleethorpes, refer to Table T028

Table T029-R

Mondays to Saturdays

16 December to 16 May

Hull - Doncaster - Meadowhall, Sheffield, Manchester and Manchester Airport

		NT	TP SX	TP SO	NT	NT	NT	NT	TP SX	NT	NT SO	NT SX	NT SO	NT	NT	NT	TP	NT
		◇	◇1	◇1	◇	◇			◇1						◇		◇1	
		A			B	C	D				D	D	D				C	
Hull	d	21 50	22 08	22 08	22 15	22 30									22 45	22 51	23 08	
Hessle	d	21 57														22 58		
Ferriby	d	22 02														23 02		
Brough	d	22 07	22 20	22 20	22 27	22 42									22 57	23 07	23 20	
Broomfleet	d																	
Gilberdyke	d	22 14													23 04	23 14		
Eastrington	d																	
Howden	d	22 21				22 54												
Wressle	d																	
Selby	a	22 32	22 39	22 39	22 47	23 04											23 39	
	d	22 32	22 40	22 40														
York 8 33	a	23 07																
Saltmarshe	d																	
Goole	d														23 13	23 23		
Thorne North	d														23 21	23 31		
Cleethorpes 28	d								21 26									
Grimsby Town 28	d								21 34									
Habrough 28	d								21 44									
Barnetby 28	d								21 53									
Scunthorpe	a								22 08									
	d								22 08	22 48								
Althorpe	d									22 53								
Crowle	d									23 00								
Thorne South	d									23 08								
Hatfield & Stainforth	d									23 14					23 26	23 36		
Kirk Sandall	d									23 18					23 30	23 40		
Adwick 31	d							22 23										
Bentley (S.Yorks) 31	d							22 27										
Doncaster 7 31	a							22 34	22 38	23 28					23 39	23 48		
London Kings Cross 15 ⊖26	a																	
York 8 26	d																	
Doncaster 7	d							22 37	22 44					23 35	23 43			23 49
Conisbrough	d							22 45						23 42				
Mexborough	d							22 49						23 47				
Swinton (S.Yorks)	d						22 41	22 52			23 01	23 18	23 31	23 50				
Rotherham Central	d						22 50	23 00			23 10	23 28	23 40	23 57				
Meadowhall ⇌	d						22 56	23 06			23 15	23 34	23 47	00 04	00 08			00 12
Sheffield 7 ⇌	a						23 04	23 14	23 18		23 25	23 41	23 55	00 13	00 17			00 21
	d																	
Stockport 78	a																	
Manchester Piccadilly 10 ⇌	a		00 11	00 14														
Manchester Airport 85 ✈⇌	a																	

A From Bridlington
B To Halifax
C To Leeds
D From Leeds

For services between Barnetby, Habrough, Grimsby Town and Cleethorpes, refer to Table T028

Table T029-R

Sundays

15 December to 29 March

Hull - Doncaster - Meadowhall, Sheffield, Manchester and Manchester Airport

	NT A	NT ◇ B	NT A	NT	TP ◇1	NT	NT	NT C	XC ◇1 D ✠	NT	NT	TP ◇1	HT ◇1 ☒	TP ◇1	NT C	NT ◇	XC ◇1 E ✠	NT	TP ◇1	NT	TP ◇1	NT C
Hull d					08 08	08 31					08 45		08 59	09 08		09 27				09 59	10 08	
Hessle d											08 52											
Ferriby d											08 57											
Brough d					08 20	08 43					09 02		09 11	09 20		09 39				10 11	10 20	
Broomfleet d																						
Gilberdyke d						08 50					09 10									10 19		
Eastrington d																						
Howden d						08 57							09 23									
Wressle d																						
Selby a					08 39	09 08							09 33	09 39							10 39	
Selby d					08 41	09 08							09 35	09 40							10 40	
York 8 33 a						09 42																
Saltmarshe d																						
Goole d										09 00	09 18					09 54				10 28		
Thorne North d										09 09	09 27					10 03				10 36		
Cleethorpes 28 d																			09 26			
Grimsby Town 28 d																			09 34			
Habrough 28 d																			09 44			
Barnetby 28 d																			09 53			
Scunthorpe a																			10 08			
Scunthorpe d																			10 09			
Althorpe d																						
Crowle d																						
Thorne South d																						
Hatfield & Stainforth d										09 14										10 42		
Kirk Sandall d										09 19										10 47		
Adwick 31 d																						
Bentley (S.Yorks) 31 d																						
Doncaster 7 31 a										09 29	09 43		09 56			10 19			10 39	10 57		
London Kings Cross 15 ⊖26 a													11 39									
York 8 26 d																	09 36					
Doncaster 7 d				08 07			09 03		09 31	09 37		09 45				10 21	10 32	10 35	10 43			
Conisbrough d				08 14			09 10			09 45								10 42				
Mexborough d				08 19			09 15			09 50								10 47				
Swinton (S.Yorks) d				08 22			09 18	09 32		09 53					10 09			10 50				11 21
Rotherham Central d				08 31			09 26	09 40		10 04					10 22			10 59				11 29
Meadowhall d	00 04	00 08	00 12	08 37			09 33	09 45		10 10		10 05			10 27	10 39		11 07	11 02			11 37
Sheffield 7 a	00 13	00 17	00 21	08 45			09 41	09 53	09 56	10 18		10 12			10 36	10 49	10 54	11 15	11 10			11 45
Sheffield 7 d												10 14							11 11			
Stockport 78 a												10 55							11 56			
Manchester Piccadilly 10 a					10 12							11 06		11 09					12 10		12 12	
Manchester Airport 85 ✈ a												11 26							12 31			

A not 15 December. From Doncaster
B not 15 December. From Hull
C From Leeds
D From Leeds to Plymouth
E To Plymouth

For services between Barnetby, Habrough, Grimsby Town and Cleethorpes, refer to Table T028

NRT DECEMBER 19 EDITION

Table T029-R

Sundays

15 December to 29 March

Hull - Doncaster - Meadowhall, Sheffield, Manchester and Manchester Airport

	NT ◇ A	XC ◇1 B ✠	NT	TP ◇1	NT	NT	TP ◇1	HT ◇1 C ☒	NT ◇	XC ◇1 D ✠	NT	NT E	NT	TP ◇1	NT	TP ◇1	NT ◇	XC ◇1 F ✠	NT	NT E	NT	TP ◇1
Hull d	10 29				10 39	10 57	11 04	11 12	11 25		11 31				11 59	12 06	12 29		12 34			
Hessle d																						
Ferriby d																						
Brough d	10 41				10 51	11 09	11 16	11 24	11 37		11 43				12 11	12 18	12 41		12 47			
Broomfleet d																						
Gilberdyke d						11 17					11 50				12 19							
Eastrington d																						
Howden d					11 03			11 35			11 57								12 59			
Wressle d																						
Selby a					11 13		11 35	11 46			12 08					12 39			13 09			
Selby d					11 14		11 36	11 46			12 08					12 40			13 10			
York 8 33 a					11 45						12 29								13 40			
Saltmarshe d																						
Goole d	10 56					11 26			11 54						12 28		12 56					
Thorne North d						11 34									12 36							
Cleethorpes 28 d				10 26										11 26								12 26
Grimsby Town 28 d				10 34										11 34								12 34
Habrough 28 d				10 44										11 44								12 44
Barnetby 28 d				10 53										11 53								12 53
Scunthorpe a				11 08										12 08								13 08
Scunthorpe d				11 08										12 08								13 08
Althorpe d																						
Crowle d																						
Thorne South d																						
Hatfield & Stainforth d						11 40									12 42							
Kirk Sandall d						11 45									12 47							
Adwick 31 d																						
Bentley (S.Yorks) 31 d																						
Doncaster 7 31 a	11 19			11 38		11 55		12 02	12 17					12 38	12 57		13 21					13 38
London Kings Cross 15 ⊖26 a								13 42														
York 8 26 d		10 34								11 41								12 45				
Doncaster 7 d	11 22	11 30	11 34	11 43					12 19				12 33	12 43			13 23				13 33	13 44
Conisbrough d			11 41										12 40								13 40	
Mexborough d			11 46										12 45								13 45	
Swinton (S.Yorks) d			11 49									12 34	12 48							13 35	13 48	
Rotherham Central d			11 59									12 45	12 58							13 46	13 59	
Meadowhall d	11 44		12 06	12 02					12 37			12 51	13 05	13 01			13 41			13 52	14 06	14 02
Sheffield 7 a	11 51	11 54	12 13	12 08					12 46	12 53		12 58	13 12	13 08			13 49	13 54		13 59	14 13	14 09
Sheffield 7 d				12 11										13 10								14 11
Stockport 78 a				12 52										13 54								14 53
Manchester Piccadilly 10 a				13 04			13 10							14 03		14 09						15 03
Manchester Airport 85 ✈ a				13 26										14 25								15 25

A From Bridlington
B From Newcastle to Plymouth
C From Beverley
D From Edinburgh to Plymouth
E From Leeds
F From Edinburgh to Penzance

For services between Barnetby, Habrough, Grimsby Town and Cleethorpes, refer to Table T028

Table T029-R

Sundays

15 December to 29 March

Hull - Doncaster - Meadowhall, Sheffield, Manchester and Manchester Airport

	NT	TP	NT	XC	NT	NT	NT	TP	NT	TP	XC	NT	NT	HT	XC	NT	NT	TP	NT	TP	XC	NT
		◇■	◇	◇■				◇■		◇■	◇■		◇	◇■	◇■			◇■		◇■	◇■	◇
			A	B		C					D		A		E	C					D	A
				✠							✠			☒	✠						✠	
Hull d	12 57	13 04	13 29		13 35				13 57	14 06		14 23	14 29	14 36					14 57	15 06		15 29
Hessle d																						
Ferriby d																						
Brough d	13 09	13 16	13 41		13 47				14 09	14 18		14 35	14 41	14 48					15 09	15 18		15 41
Broomfleet d																						
Gilberdyke d	13 17								14 17										15 17			
Eastrington d																						
Howden d					13 59							14 47		14 59								
Wressle d																						
Selby a		13 37			14 09					14 37		14 57		15 10						15 37		
d		13 38			14 10					14 38		14 58		15 10						15 38		
York ■ 33 a					14 29							15 27										
Saltmarshe d																						
Goole d	13 26		13 56						14 26				14 56						15 26			15 56
Thorne North d	13 34								14 34										15 34			
Cleethorpes 28 d								13 26										14 26				
Grimsby Town 28 d								13 34										14 34				
Habrough 28 d								13 44										14 44				
Barnetby 28 d								13 53										14 53				
Scunthorpe a								14 08										15 08				
d								14 08										15 08				
Althorpe d																						
Crowle d																						
Thorne South d																						
Hatfield & Stainforth d	13 40								14 40										15 40			
Kirk Sandall d	13 45								14 45										15 45			
Adwick 31 d																						
Bentley (S.Yorks) 31 d																						
Doncaster ■ 31 a	13 55		14 19					14 38	14 55				15 19	15 27				15 38	15 55			16 19
London Kings Cross ■ ⊖26 a														17 14								
York ■ 26 d				13 45							14 35				14 44						15 35	
Doncaster ■ d			14 21				14 33	14 44			15 00		15 21				15 30	15 43			15 58	16 22
Conisbrough d							14 40										15 37					
Mexborough d							14 45										15 42					
Swinton (S.Yorks) d						14 34	14 48									15 34	15 48					
Rotherham Central d						14 44	14 59									15 44	15 59					
Meadowhall 🚋 d			14 39			14 49	15 06	15 02					15 39			15 50	16 06	16 02				16 40
Sheffield ■ 🚋 a			14 48	14 51		14 57	15 14	15 09			15 22		15 48		15 53	15 58	16 13	16 08			16 20	16 49
d								15 11										16 10				
Stockport 78 a								15 53										16 53				
Manchester Piccadilly ■ 🚋 a		15 09						16 02		16 09								17 02		17 09		
Manchester Airport 85 ✈🚋 a								16 25										17 25				

A From Scarborough
B From Edinburgh to Plymouth
C From Leeds
D From Newcastle to Reading
E From Glasgow Central to Penzance

For services between Barnetby, Habrough, Grimsby Town and Cleethorpes, refer to Table T028

Table T029-R

Sundays

15 December to 29 March

Hull - Doncaster - Meadowhall, Sheffield, Manchester and Manchester Airport

	XC	NT	NT	NT	TP	XC	NT	TP	HT	NT	HT	XC	NT	NT	NT	TP	NT	TP	XC	EM	NT	XC
	◇■				◇■	◇■		◇■	◇■	◇	◇■	◇■				◇■		◇■	◇■	◇■	◇	◇■
	A		B			C			D	E	F	G		B					H	I	E	A
	✠					✠			☒		☒	✠							✠	🍴		✠
Hull d		15 35					15 54	16 06	16 21	16 29			16 35				16 57	17 06			17 29	
Hessle d							16 01															
Ferriby d							16 06															
Brough d		15 47					16 11	16 18	16 34	16 41			16 47				17 09	17 18			17 41	
Broomfleet d																						
Gilberdyke d							16 19										17 17					
Eastrington d																						
Howden d		15 59							16 49				16 59									
Wressle d																						
Selby a		16 09						16 38	17 02				17 09					17 37				
d		16 10						16 39	17 04				17 10					17 38				
York ■ 33 a		16 42											17 43									
Saltmarshe d																						
Goole d							16 27			16 56							17 26				17 56	
Thorne North d							16 36										17 34					
Cleethorpes 28 d					15 26											16 26						
Grimsby Town 28 d					15 34											16 34						
Habrough 28 d					15 44											16 44						
Barnetby 28 d					15 53											16 53						
Scunthorpe a					16 08											17 08						
d					16 08											17 08						
Althorpe d																						
Crowle d																						
Thorne South d																						
Hatfield & Stainforth d							16 42										17 40					
Kirk Sandall d							16 47										17 45					
Adwick 31 d																						
Bentley (S.Yorks) 31 d																						
Doncaster ■ 31 a					16 38		16 57		17 25	17 19	← 17 25					17 38	17 55				18 19	
London Kings Cross ■ ⊖26 a									→		19 10											
York ■ 26 d	15 44					16 25						16 44							17 35	17 48		17 44
Doncaster ■ d				16 35	16 44	16 51				17 21					17 33	17 43			17 58	18 13	18 22	
Conisbrough d				16 42											17 40							
Mexborough d				16 47											17 45							
Swinton (S.Yorks) d			16 34	16 50										17 34	17 48							
Rotherham Central d			16 43	16 59										17 43	17 56							
Meadowhall 🚋 d			16 49	17 06	17 02					17 39				17 51	18 04	18 00					18 40	
Sheffield ■ 🚋 a	16 52		16 56	17 14	17 09	17 19				17 48		17 53		17 58	18 11	18 07			18 20	18 40	18 49	18 53
d					17 10											18 11						
Stockport 78 a					17 53											18 53						
Manchester Piccadilly ■ 🚋 a					18 03			18 09								19 03		19 09				
Manchester Airport 85 ✈🚋 a					18 25											19 25						

A From Glasgow Central to Plymouth
B From Leeds
C From Edinburgh to Reading
D To London Kings Cross
E From Scarborough
F From Hull
G From Aberdeen to Plymouth
H From Newcastle to Reading
I To St Pancras International

For services between Barnetby, Habrough, Grimsby Town and Cleethorpes, refer to Table T028

Table T029-R

Sundays
15 December to 29 March

Hull - Doncaster - Meadowhall, Sheffield, Manchester and Manchester Airport

Station		NT	NT A	NT	TP ◇1	NT	NT ◇	TP ◇1	XC ◇1 B	NT ◇ C	XC ◇1 D	NT	HT ◇1 ⊠	NT A	NT	TP ◇1	XC ◇1 E	NT	TP ◇1	NT ◇ C	XC ◇1 F	NT	NT A
Hull	d	17 35				17 57		18 06		18 29		18 35	18 47					18 57	19 04	19 29		19 35	
Hessle	d																						
Ferriby	d																						
Brough	d	17 47				18 09		18 18		18 41		18 47	18 59					19 09	19 16	19 41		19 47	
Broomfleet	d																						
Gilberdyke	d					18 17												19 17					
Eastrington	d																						
Howden	d	17 59										18 59	19 10									19 59	
Wressle	d																						
Selby	a	18 09						18 37				19 09	19 21						19 37			20 09	
	d	18 10						18 38				19 10	19 22						19 38			20 10	
York 8 33	a	18 37										19 43										20 39	
Saltmarshe	d																						
Goole	d					18 26				18 56								19 26		19 56			
Thorne North	d					18 34												19 34					
Cleethorpes 28	d				17 27											18 29							
Grimsby Town 28	d				17 35											18 37							
Habrough 28	d				17 45											18 47							
Barnetby 28	d				17 54											18 56							
Scunthorpe	a				18 09											19 08							
	d				18 09											19 08							
Althorpe	d																						
Crowle	d																						
Thorne South	d																						
Hatfield & Stainforth	d					18 40												19 40					
Kirk Sandall	d					18 45												19 45					
Adwick 31	d																						
Bentley (S.Yorks) 31	d																						
Doncaster 7 31	a				18 39	18 55				19 19			19 38			19 41		19 55		20 19			
London Kings Cross 15 ⊖26	a												21 19										
York 8 26	d						18 02		18 35		18 45						19 24				19 45		
Doncaster 7	d			18 29	18 44				18 58	19 21					19 33	19 42	19 54			20 21			
Conisbrough	d			18 36											19 40								
Mexborough	d			18 43											19 45								
Swinton (S.Yorks)	d		18 37	18 48			18 55							19 34	19 48								20 34
Rotherham Central	d		18 46	18 55			19 03							19 44	19 57								20 46
Meadowhall	d		18 52	19 06	19 02		19 09			19 39				19 52	20 05	20 01				20 39			20 51
Sheffield 7	a		18 59	19 12	19 09		19 19		19 20	19 48	19 53			19 59	20 11	20 08	20 16			20 47	20 52		20 59
	d				19 11											20 11							
Stockport 78	a				19 53											20 53							
Manchester Piccadilly 10	a				20 03			20 09								21 04			21 09				
Manchester Airport 85	a				20 25											21 25							

Station		NT	TP ◇1	XC ◇1 E	NT	TP ◇1	NT	NT ◇ C	XC ◇1 G	TP ◇1 H	NT A	NT ◇ I	NT	TP ◇1	NT ◇ C	NT	NT A	TP ◇1	NT	NT	TP ◇1	NT	TP ◇1 J	NT A
Hull	d				19 54	20 06	20 21	20 29		21 06					21 29	21 35				21 57	22 06	22 52	23 04	
Hessle	d				20 01																	22 59		
Ferriby	d				20 06																	23 04		
Brough	d				20 11	20 18	20 33	20 41		21 18					21 41	21 47				22 09	22 18	23 09	23 16	
Broomfleet	d																							
Gilberdyke	d				20 19															22 17		23 17		
Eastrington	d																							
Howden	d						20 45									21 59								
Wressle	d																							
Selby	a					20 38	20 55			21 37						22 09					22 37		23 35	
	d					20 39	21 01									22 10					22 38			
York 8 33	a						21 26									22 43								
Saltmarshe	d																							
Goole	d				20 27			20 56							21 56					22 26		23 25		
Thorne North	d				20 36															22 34		23 34		
Cleethorpes 28	d		19 26											20 26				21 16						
Grimsby Town 28	d		19 34											20 34				21 24						
Habrough 28	d		19 44											20 44				21 34						
Barnetby 28	d		19 53											20 53				21 43						
Scunthorpe	a		20 08											21 08				21 58						
	d		20 08											21 08				21 58						
Althorpe	d																							
Crowle	d																							
Thorne South	d																							
Hatfield & Stainforth	d				20 42															22 40		23 40		
Kirk Sandall	d				20 47															22 45		23 45		
Adwick 31	d																							
Bentley (S.Yorks) 31	d																							
Doncaster 7 31	a		20 38		20 57			21 19						21 41	22 19			22 28		22 55		23 55		
London Kings Cross 15 ⊖26	a																							
York 8 26	d			20 26					20 45			20 48												
Doncaster 7	d	20 28	20 43	20 51				21 21					21 33	21 44	22 21			22 29	22 40					
Conisbrough	d	20 35											21 40						22 47					
Mexborough	d	20 40											21 45						22 52					
Swinton (S.Yorks)	d	20 43									21 34	21 45	21 49				22 34		22 55					23 23
Rotherham Central	d	20 52									21 44		22 00				22 43		23 04					23 31
Meadowhall	d	20 58	21 02					21 39			21 52	21 56	22 07	22 03	22 42		22 49		23 11					23 37
Sheffield 7	a	21 05	21 08	21 13				21 49	21 52		21 59	22 03	22 13	22 10	22 50		22 56	23 00	23 20					23 45
	d		21 11											22 13										
Stockport 78	a		21 56											23 03										
Manchester Piccadilly 10	a		22 05			22 07								23 19							00 11			
Manchester Airport 85	a		22 25																					

A From Leeds
B From Newcastle to Guildford
C From Scarborough
D From Glasgow Central to Bristol Temple Meads
E From Newcastle to Birmingham New Street
F From Edinburgh to Bristol Temple Meads
G From Glasgow Central to Birmingham New Street
H To Liverpool Lime Street
I via Pontefract Baghill
J To Leeds

Table T029-R

Sundays
5 April to 10 May

Hull - Doncaster - Meadowhall, Sheffield, Manchester and Manchester Airport

Station		NT A	NT ◇ B	NT A	NT	TP ◇1	NT	NT	NT C	XC ◇1 D	NT	NT	HT ◇1 ⊠	TP ◇1	TP ◇1	NT C	NT ◇	XC ◇1 E	NT	TP ◇1	NT	TP ◇1	NT C	NT ◇ F
Hull	d					08 08	08 31					08 45	08 59	09 08			09 27				09 59	10 08		10 29
Hessle	d											08 52												
Ferriby	d											08 57												
Brough	d					08 20	08 43					09 02	09 11	09 20			09 39				10 11	10 20		10 41
Broomfleet	d																							
Gilberdyke	d						08 50					09 10									10 19			
Eastrington	d																							
Howden	d						08 57						09 23											
Wressle	d																							
Selby	a					08 39	09 08						09 33	09 39								10 39		
	d					08 41	09 08						09 35	09 40								10 40		
York 8 33	a						09 42																	
Saltmarshe	d																							
Goole	d										09 00	09 18					09 54				10 28			10 56
Thorne North	d										09 09	09 27					10 03				10 36			
Cleethorpes 28	d																			09 26				
Grimsby Town 28	d																			09 34				
Habrough 28	d																			09 44				
Barnetby 28	d																			09 53				
Scunthorpe	a																			10 08				
	d																			10 09				
Althorpe	d																							
Crowle	d																							
Thorne South	d																							
Hatfield & Stainforth	d										09 14										10 42			
Kirk Sandall	d										09 19										10 47			
Adwick 31	d																							
Bentley (S.Yorks) 31	d																							
Doncaster 7 31	a										09 29	09 43	09 56				10 19			10 39	10 57			11 19
London Kings Cross 15 ⊖26	a												11 39											
York 8 26	d																	09 36						
Doncaster 7	d				08 07			09 03		09 31	09 37				09 45		10 21	10 32	10 35	10 43				11 22
Conisbrough	d				08 14			09 10			09 45								10 42					
Mexborough	d				08 19			09 15			09 50								10 47					
Swinton (S.Yorks)	d				08 22			09 18	09 32		09 53					10 09			10 50				11 21	
Rotherham Central	d				08 31			09 26	09 40		10 04					10 22			10 59				11 29	
Meadowhall	d	00 04	00 08	00 12	08 37			09 33	09 45		10 10				10 05	10 27	10 39		11 07	11 02			11 37	11 44
Sheffield 7	a	00 13	00 17	00 21	08 45			09 41	09 53	09 56	10 18				10 12	10 36	10 49	10 54	11 15	11 10			11 45	11 51
	d														10 14					11 11				
Stockport 78	a														10 55					11 56				
Manchester Piccadilly 10	a					10 12								11 05	11 06					12 10		12 09		
Manchester Airport 85	a														11 26					12 31				

A From Doncaster
B From Hull
C From Leeds
D From Leeds to Plymouth
E To Plymouth
F From Bridlington

For services between Barnetby, Habrough, Grimsby Town and Cleethorpes, refer to Table T028

Table T029-R

Sundays
5 April to 10 May

Hull - Doncaster - Meadowhall, Sheffield, Manchester and Manchester Airport

	XC	NT	TP	NT	NT	TP	HT	NT	XC	NT	NT	NT	TP	NT	TP		NT	XC	NT	NT	NT	TP	NT	TP
	◇1		◇1			◇1	◇1	◇	◇1				◇1		◇1		◇	◇1				◇1		◇1
	A						B		C		D							E		D				
	🍴						⊠		🍴									🍴						
Hull d				10 39	10 57	11 04	11 12	11 25		11 31				11 59	12 06		12 29		12 34				12 57	13 04
Hessle d																								
Ferriby d																								
Brough d				10 51	11 09	11 16	11 24	11 37		11 43				12 11	12 18		12 41		12 47				13 09	13 16
Broomfleet d																								
Gilberdyke d					11 17					11 50				12 19									13 17	
Eastrington d																								
Howden d				11 03			11 35			11 57									12 59					
Wressle d																								
Selby a				11 13		11 35	11 46			12 08					12 39				13 09					13 37
d				11 14		11 36	11 46			12 08					12 40				13 10					13 38
York 8 33 a				11 45						12 29									13 40					
Saltmarshe d																								
Goole d					11 26			11 54						12 28			12 56						13 26	
Thorne North d					11 34									12 36									13 34	
Cleethorpes 28 d			10 26										11 26									12 26		
Grimsby Town 28 d			10 34										11 34									12 34		
Habrough 28 d			10 44										11 44									12 44		
Barnetby 28 d			10 53										11 53									12 53		
Scunthorpe a			11 08										12 08									13 08		
d			11 08										12 08									13 08		
Althorpe d																								
Crowle d																								
Thorne South d																								
Hatfield & Stainforth d					11 40									12 42									13 40	
Kirk Sandall d					11 45									12 47									13 45	
Adwick 31 d																								
Bentley (S.Yorks) 31 d																								
Doncaster 7 31 a			11 38		11 55		12 02	12 17					12 38	12 57			13 21					13 38	13 55	
London Kings Cross 15 ⊖26 a							13 42																	
York 8 26 d	10 34								11 41									12 45						
Doncaster 7 d	11 30	11 34	11 43					12 19				12 33	12 43				13 23				13 33	13 44		
Conisbrough d		11 41										12 40									13 40			
Mexborough d		11 46										12 45									13 45			
Swinton (S.Yorks) d		11 49									12 34	12 48								13 35	13 48			
Rotherham Central d		11 59									12 45	12 58								13 46	13 59			
Meadowhall d		12 06	12 02					12 37			12 51	13 05	13 01				13 41			13 52	14 06	14 02		
Sheffield 7 a	11 54	12 13	12 08					12 46	12 53		12 58	13 12	13 08				13 49	13 54		13 59	14 13	14 09		
d			12 11										13 10									14 11		
Stockport 78 a			12 52										13 54									14 53		
Manchester Piccadilly 10 a			13 04			13 10							14 03		14 09							15 03		15 09
Manchester Airport 85 a			13 26										14 25									15 25		

	NT	XC	NT	NT	NT	TP	NT		TP	XC	NT	NT	HT	XC	NT	NT	TP	NT	TP	XC	NT	XC	NT	
	◇	◇1				◇1			◇1	◇1		◇	◇1	◇1			◇1		◇1	◇1	◇	◇1		
	F	C		D						G		F		H	D					G	F	I		
		🍴								🍴			⊠	🍴						🍴		🍴		
Hull d	13 29		13 35				13 57		14 06		14 23	14 29	14 36					14 57	15 06		15 29		15 35	
Hessle d																								
Ferriby d																								
Brough d	13 41		13 47				14 09		14 18		14 35	14 41	14 48					15 09	15 18		15 41		15 47	
Broomfleet d																								
Gilberdyke d							14 17											15 17						
Eastrington d																								
Howden d			13 59								14 47		14 59										15 59	
Wressle d																								
Selby a			14 09						14 37		14 57		15 10						15 37				16 09	
d			14 10						14 38		14 58		15 10						15 38				16 10	
York 8 33 a			14 29								15 27												16 42	
Saltmarshe d																								
Goole d	13 56						14 26					14 56						15 26			15 56			
Thorne North d							14 34											15 34						
Cleethorpes 28 d						13 26											14 26							
Grimsby Town 28 d						13 34											14 34							
Habrough 28 d						13 44											14 44							
Barnetby 28 d						13 53											14 53							
Scunthorpe a						14 08											15 08							
d						14 08											15 08							
Althorpe d																								
Crowle d																								
Thorne South d																								
Hatfield & Stainforth d							14 40											15 40						
Kirk Sandall d							14 45											15 45						
Adwick 31 d																								
Bentley (S.Yorks) 31 d																								
Doncaster 7 31 a	14 19					14 38	14 55					15 19	15 27				15 38	15 55			16 19			
London Kings Cross 15 ⊖26 a													17 14											
York 8 26 d		13 45								14 35				14 44						15 35		15 44		
Doncaster 7 d	14 21				14 33	14 44				15 00		15 21				15 30	15 43			15 58	16 22			
Conisbrough d					14 40											15 37								
Mexborough d					14 45											15 42								
Swinton (S.Yorks) d				14 34	14 48										15 34	15 48								
Rotherham Central d				14 44	14 59										15 44	15 59								
Meadowhall d	14 39			14 49	15 06	15 02						15 39			15 50	16 06	16 02				16 40			
Sheffield 7 a	14 48	14 51		14 57	15 14	15 09				15 22		15 48		15 53	15 58	16 13	16 08			16 20	16 49	16 52		
d						15 11											16 10							
Stockport 78 a						15 53											16 53							
Manchester Piccadilly 10 a						16 02			16 09								17 02		17 09					
Manchester Airport 85 a						16 25											17 25							

A From Newcastle to Plymouth
B From Beverley
C From Edinburgh to Plymouth
D From Leeds
E From Edinburgh to Penzance
F From Scarborough
G From Newcastle to Reading
H From Glasgow Central to Penzance
I From Glasgow Central to Plymouth

Table T029-R

Sundays
5 April to 10 May

Hull - Doncaster - Meadowhall, Sheffield, Manchester and Manchester Airport

	NT	NT	TP	XC	NT	TP	HT	NT	HT	XC	NT	NT	NT	TP	NT		TP	XC	EM	NT	XC	NT	NT	NT
			◇1	◇1		◇1	◇1	◇	◇1	◇1				◇1			◇1	◇1	◇1	◇	◇1			
	A			B			C	D	E	F		A						G	H	D	I		A	
				🍴			⊠		⊠	🍴								🍴	🍴		🍴			
Hull d					15 54	16 06	16 21	16 29			16 35				16 57		17 06			17 29		17 35		
Hessle d					16 01																			
Ferriby d					16 06																			
Brough d					16 11	16 18	16 34	16 41			16 47				17 09		17 18			17 41		17 47		
Broomfleet d																								
Gilberdyke d					16 19										17 17									
Eastrington d																								
Howden d							16 49				16 59											17 59		
Wressle d																								
Selby a						16 38	17 02				17 09						17 37					18 09		
d						16 39	17 04				17 10						17 38					18 10		
York 8 33 a											17 43											18 37		
Saltmarshe d																								
Goole d					16 27			16 56							17 26					17 56				
Thorne North d					16 36										17 34									
Cleethorpes 28 d			15 26											16 26										
Grimsby Town 28 d			15 34											16 34										
Habrough 28 d			15 44											16 44										
Barnetby 28 d			15 53											16 53										
Scunthorpe a			16 08											17 08										
d			16 08											17 08										
Althorpe d																								
Crowle d																								
Thorne South d																								
Hatfield & Stainforth d					16 42										17 40									
Kirk Sandall d					16 47										17 45									
Adwick 31 d																								
Bentley (S.Yorks) 31 d									←															
Doncaster 7 31 a			16 38		16 57		17 25	17 19	17 25					17 38	17 55					18 19				
London Kings Cross 15 ⊖26 a							→		19 10															
York 8 26 d				16 25						16 44								17 35	17 48		17 44			
Doncaster 7 d		16 35	16 44	16 51				17 21					17 33	17 43				17 58	18 13	18 22				18 29
Conisbrough d		16 42											17 40											18 36
Mexborough d		16 47											17 45											18 43
Swinton (S.Yorks) d	16 34	16 50										17 34	17 48										18 37	18 48
Rotherham Central d	16 43	16 59										17 43	17 56										18 46	18 55
Meadowhall d	16 49	17 06	17 02					17 39				17 51	18 04	18 00						18 40			18 52	19 06
Sheffield 7 a	16 56	17 14	17 09	17 19				17 48		17 53		17 58	18 11	18 07				18 20	18 40	18 49	18 53		18 59	19 12
d			17 10											18 11										
Stockport 78 a			17 53											18 53										
Manchester Piccadilly 10 a			18 03			18 09								19 03			19 09							
Manchester Airport 85 a			18 25											19 25										

A From Leeds
B From Edinburgh to Reading
C To London Kings Cross
D From Scarborough
E From Hull
F From Aberdeen to Plymouth
G From Newcastle to Reading
H To St Pancras International
I From Glasgow Central to Plymouth

For services between Barnetby, Habrough, Grimsby Town and Cleethorpes, refer to Table T028

Table T029-R

Sundays
5 April to 10 May

Hull - Doncaster - Meadowhall, Sheffield, Manchester and Manchester Airport

Station		TP ◇1	NT	NT ◇	TP ◇1	XC ◇1 A 🍴	NT ◇ B	XC ◇1 C 🍴	NT	HT ◇1 ⊠	NT D	NT	TP ◇1	XC ◇1 E 🍴	NT	TP ◇1		NT ◇ B	XC ◇1 F	NT	NT D	NT	TP ◇1	XC ◇1 E	NT
Hull	d		17 57		18 06		18 29		18 35	18 47					18 57	19 04		19 29		19 35					19 54
Hessle	d																								20 01
Ferriby	d																								20 06
Brough	d		18 09		18 18		18 41		18 47	18 59					19 09	19 16		19 41		19 47					20 11
Broomfleet	d																								
Gilberdyke	d		18 17												19 17										20 19
Eastrington	d																								
Howden	d								18 59	19 10										19 59					
Wressle	d																								
Selby	a				18 37				19 09	19 21						19 37				20 09					
	d				18 38				19 10	19 22						19 38				20 10					
York 8	33 a								19 43											20 39					
Saltmarshe	d																								
Goole	d		18 26				18 56								19 26			19 56							20 27
Thorne North	d		18 34												19 34										20 36
Cleethorpes	28 d	17 27											18 29										19 26		
Grimsby Town	28 d	17 35											18 37										19 34		
Habrough	28 d	17 45											18 47										19 44		
Barnetby	28 d	17 54											18 56										19 53		
Scunthorpe	a	18 09											19 08										20 08		
	d	18 09											19 08										20 08		
Althorpe	d																								
Crowle	d																								
Thorne South	d																								
Hatfield & Stainforth	d		18 40												19 40										20 42
Kirk Sandall	d		18 45												19 45										20 47
Adwick	31 d																								
Bentley (S.Yorks)	31 d																								
Doncaster 7	31 a	18 39	18 55				19 19			19 38			19 41		19 55			20 19					20 38		20 57
London Kings Cross 15	⊖26 a									21 19															
York 8	26 d			18 02		18 35		18 45						19 24					19 45					20 26	
Doncaster 7	d	18 44				18 58	19 21					19 33	19 42	19 54				20 21				20 28	20 43	20 51	
Conisbrough	d											19 40										20 35			
Mexborough	d											19 45										20 40			
Swinton (S.Yorks)	d			18 55							19 34	19 48									20 34	20 43			
Rotherham Central	d			19 03							19 44	19 57									20 46	20 52			
Meadowhall	⇌ d	19 02		19 09			19 39				19 52	20 05	20 01					20 39			20 51	20 58	21 02		
Sheffield 7	⇌ a	19 09		19 19		19 20	19 48	19 53			19 59	20 11	20 08	20 16				20 47	20 52		20 59	21 05	21 08	21 13	
	d	19 11											20 11										21 11		
Stockport	78 a	19 53											20 53										21 56		
Manchester Piccadilly 10	⇌ a	20 03			20 09								21 04			21 09							22 05		
Manchester Airport	85 ✈⇌ a	20 25											21 25										22 25		

Station		TP ◇1	NT	NT ◇ B	XC ◇1 G	TP ◇1 H	NT D	NT ◇ I		NT	TP ◇1	NT ◇ B	NT	NT D	TP ◇1	NT	NT	TP ◇1	NT	TP ◇1 J	NT D
Hull	d	20 06	20 21	20 29		21 06						21 29	21 35				21 57	22 06	22 52	23 04	
Hessle	d																		22 59		
Ferriby	d																		23 04		
Brough	d	20 18	20 33	20 41		21 18						21 41	21 47				22 09	22 18	23 09	23 16	
Broomfleet	d																				
Gilberdyke	d																22 17		23 17		
Eastrington	d																				
Howden	d		20 45										21 59								
Wressle	d																				
Selby	a	20 38	20 55			21 37							22 09					22 37		23 35	
	d	20 39	21 01										22 10					22 38			
York 8	33 a		21 26										22 43								
Saltmarshe	d																				
Goole	d			20 56								21 56					22 26		23 25		
Thorne North	d																22 34		23 34		
Cleethorpes	28 d										20 26				21 16						
Grimsby Town	28 d										20 34				21 24						
Habrough	28 d										20 44				21 34						
Barnetby	28 d										20 53				21 43						
Scunthorpe	a										21 08				21 58						
	d										21 08				21 58						
Althorpe	d																				
Crowle	d																				
Thorne South	d																				
Hatfield & Stainforth	d																22 40		23 40		
Kirk Sandall	d																22 45		23 45		
Adwick	31 d																				
Bentley (S.Yorks)	31 d																				
Doncaster 7	31 a			21 19							21 41	22 19			22 28		22 55		23 55		
London Kings Cross 15	⊖26 a																				
York 8	26 d				20 45			20 48													
Doncaster 7	d			21 21						21 33	21 44	22 21			22 29	22 40					
Conisbrough	d									21 40						22 47					
Mexborough	d									21 45						22 52					
Swinton (S.Yorks)	d						21 34	21 45		21 49				22 34		22 55					23 23
Rotherham Central	d						21 44			22 00				22 43		23 04					23 31
Meadowhall	⇌ d			21 39			21 52	21 56		22 07	22 03	22 42		22 49		23 11					23 37
Sheffield 7	⇌ a			21 49	21 52		21 59	22 03		22 13	22 10	22 50		22 56	23 00	23 20					23 45
	d										22 13										
Stockport	78 a										23 03										
Manchester Piccadilly 10	⇌ a	22 07									23 19							00 11			
Manchester Airport	85 ✈⇌ a																				

A From Newcastle to Guildford
B From Scarborough
C From Glasgow Central to Bristol Temple Meads
D From Leeds
E From Newcastle to Birmingham New Street
F From Edinburgh to Bristol Temple Meads
G From Glasgow Central to Birmingham New Street
H To Liverpool Lime Street
I via Pontefract Baghill
J To Leeds

Table T030-F

Mondays to Fridays
16 December to 15 May

Lincoln - Retford - Sheffield

Miles	Station		NT ◇ A	NT ◇ B	NT	NT ◇ B	NT	NT ◇ B	NT	NT ◇ B	NT		NT ◇ B	NT	NT ◇ B	NT	NT ◇ B	NT	NT ◇ B		NT	NT ◇ B		NT
0	**Lincoln**	18 d			06 43	07 23		08 26		09 30			10 30		11 30		12 29		13 30	and at the same minutes past each hour until		16 30		
6	Saxilby	18 d			06 52	07 32		08 35		09 39			10 39		11 39		12 39		13 39			16 39		
15½	Gainsborough Lea Road	18 d			07 04	07 44		08 47		09 51			10 51		11 51		12 51		13 51			16 51		
—	Gainsborough Central	d					08 16		09 16		10 16			11 16		12 12		13 16			16 16			17 16
25	**Retford 10**	a			07 17	07 57	08 31	09 00	09 31	10 06	10 31		11 06	11 31	12 06	12 27	13 06	13 31	14 06		16 31	17 06		17 31
—		d	06 13	06 56	07 17	07 57	08 31	09 00	09 31	10 06	10 31		11 06	11 31	12 06	12 31	13 06	13 31	14 06		16 31	17 06		17 31
32¾	Worksop	d	06 25	07 09	07 29	08 08	08 43	09 11	09 43	10 18	10 43		11 18	11 43	12 18	12 43	13 18	13 43	14 18		16 43	17 18		17 42
34¾	Shireoaks	d	06 30	07 13	07 34	08 12	08 47	09 16	09 47		10 47			11 47		12 47		13 47			16 47			17 47
37¾	Kiveton Park	d	06 35	07 19	07 39	08 18	08 53	09 21	09 53		10 53			11 53		12 53		13 53			16 53			17 53
39	Kiveton Bridge	d	06 38	07 22	07 42	08 21	08 56	09 24	09 56		10 56			11 56		12 56		13 56			16 56			17 56
43¼	Woodhouse	d	06 44	07 29	07 49	08 27	09 02		10 02		11 02			12 02		13 02		14 02			17 02			18 03
46¼	Darnall	d	06 49	07 35	07 56	08 32	09 08		10 08		11 08			12 08		13 08		14 08			17 08			18 08
48½	**Sheffield 7**	⇌ a	06 56	07 43	08 04	08 42	09 17	09 42	10 17	10 42	11 17		11 42	12 17	12 42	13 17	13 40	14 17	14 42		17 17	17 42		18 17
—	Meadowhall	34 a		07 53		08 50		09 50		10 50			11 50		12 50		13 50		14 50			17 50		

Station		NT ◇ B	NT	NT ◇ B	NT	NT ◇ B	NT	NT	NT		NT	NT
Lincoln	18 d	17 23		18 24		19 26	20 19	21 29				22 44
Saxilby	18 d	17 31		18 32		19 35	20 27	21 37				22 52
Gainsborough Lea Road	18 d	17 44		18 45		19 48	20 40	21 50				23 05
Gainsborough Central	d		18 16		19 12							
Retford 10	a	17 56	18 31	18 57	19 27	20 01	20 52	22 02				23 17
	d	17 57	18 31	18 58	19 27	20 01	20 53	22 04	22 51			23 18
Worksop	d	18 08	18 46	19 09	19 39	20 12	21 05	22 16	23 03		23 21	23 30
Shireoaks	d	18 12	18 50	19 13	19 43	20 17	21 09	22 20	23 08		23 25	23 34
Kiveton Park	d	18 18	18 56	19 19	19 49	20 22	21 15	22 26	23 13		23 30	23 40
Kiveton Bridge	d	18 21	18 59	19 22	19 52	20 25	21 18	22 29	23 16		23 34	23 43
Woodhouse	d	18 27	19 06	19 28	19 59		21 24	22 35	23 23		23 40	23 52
Darnall	d	18 32	19 12	19 33	20 04		21 29	22 40	23 28		23 46	23 57
Sheffield 7	⇌ a	18 42	19 25	19 42	20 12	20 42	21 38	22 48	23 36		23 57	00 03
Meadowhall	34 a	18 50		19 50		20 50						

Saturdays
21 December to 16 May

Station		NT ◇ A	NT ◇ B	NT	NT ◇ B	NT	NT ◇ B	NT	NT ◇ B	NT		NT ◇ B	NT	NT ◇ B	NT ◇ C	NT ◇ B	NT	NT ◇ B	NT	NT ◇ B		NT	NT ◇ B	NT ◇ C	NT ◇ B
Lincoln	18 d			06 43	07 23		08 26		09 30			10 30		11 30		12 29		13 30		14 30			15 30		16 30
Saxilby	18 d			06 52	07 32		08 35		09 39			10 39		11 39		12 39		13 39		14 38			15 39		16 39
Gainsborough Lea Road	18 d			07 04	07 44		08 47		09 51			10 51		11 51		12 51		13 51		14 51			15 51		16 51
Gainsborough Central	d					08 16		09 16		10 16			11 16		12 12		13 16		14 16			15 16		16 16	
Retford 10	a			07 17	07 57	08 31	09 00	09 31	10 06	10 31		11 06	11 31	12 06		13 06	13 31	14 06	14 31	15 06		15 31	16 06		17 06
	d	06 13	06 55	07 17	07 57	08 31	09 00	09 31	10 06	10 31		11 06	11 31	12 06		13 06	13 31	14 06	14 31	15 07		15 31	16 06		17 06
Worksop	d	06 25	07 08	07 29	08 08	08 43	09 11	09 43	10 18	10 43		11 18	11 43	12 18	12 43	13 18	13 43	14 18	14 43	15 18		15 43	16 18	16 43	17 18
Shireoaks	d	06 30	07 12	07 34	08 12	08 47	09 16	09 47		10 47			11 47		12 47		13 47		14 47			15 47		16 47	
Kiveton Park	d	06 35	07 18	07 39	08 18	08 53	09 21	09 53		10 53			11 53		12 53		13 53		14 53			15 53		16 53	
Kiveton Bridge	d	06 38	07 21	07 42	08 21	08 56	09 24	09 56		10 56			11 56		12 56		13 56		14 56			15 56		16 56	
Woodhouse	d	06 44	07 28	07 49	08 27	09 02		10 02		11 02			12 02		13 02		14 02		15 02			16 02		17 02	
Darnall	d	06 49	07 33	07 56	08 32	09 08		10 08		11 08			12 08		13 08		14 08		15 08			16 08		17 08	
Sheffield 7	⇌ a	06 56	07 41	08 04	08 41	09 17	09 42	10 17	10 42	11 17		11 42	12 17	12 42	13 17	13 40	14 17	14 42	15 17	15 42		16 17	16 42	17 17	17 42
Meadowhall	34 a		07 52		08 50		09 50		10 50			11 50		12 50		13 50		14 50		15 50			16 50		17 50

Station		NT	NT ◇ B	NT	NT ◇ B	NT		NT ◇ B	NT ◇ C	NT	NT	NT	NT	NT
Lincoln	18 d		17 23		18 24			19 26		20 19	21 29			22 44
Saxilby	18 d		17 31		18 32			19 35		20 27	21 37			22 52
Gainsborough Lea Road	18 d		17 44		18 45			19 48		20 40	21 50			23 05
Gainsborough Central	d	17 16		18 16		19 12			20 15					
Retford 10	a	17 31	17 56	18 31	18 57	19 27		20 01	20 31	20 52	22 02			23 17
	d	17 31	17 57	18 31	18 58	19 27		20 01	20 32	20 53	22 04	22 51		23 18
Worksop	d	17 42	18 08	18 46	19 09	19 39		20 12	20 43	21 05	22 16	23 03	23 21	23 30
Shireoaks	d	17 47	18 12	18 50	19 13	19 43		20 17	20 47	21 09	22 20	23 08	23 25	23 34
Kiveton Park	d	17 53	18 18	18 56	19 19	19 49		20 22	20 53	21 15	22 26	23 13	23 30	23 40
Kiveton Bridge	d	17 56	18 21	18 59	19 22	19 52		20 25	20 56	21 18	22 29	23 16	23 34	23 43
Woodhouse	d	18 03	18 27	19 06	19 28	19 59			21 02	21 24	22 35	23 23	23 40	23 52
Darnall	d	18 08	18 32	19 12	19 33	20 04			21 08	21 29	22 40	23 28	23 46	23 57
Sheffield 7	⇌ a	18 17	18 42	19 24	19 42	20 12		20 41	21 15	21 38	22 48	23 36	23 57	00 03
Meadowhall	34 a		18 50		19 50			20 50						

A To Nottingham
B To Leeds
C From Cleethorpes, via Retford

For connections from London Kings Cross refer to Table T026

Table T030-F

Sundays

15 December to 10 May

Lincoln - Retford - Sheffield

		NT	NT ◇ A	NT ◇ A	NT ◇ A	NT ◇ A	NT	NT ◇ A	NT	NT ◇	NT	NT ◇	NT	NT ◇	NT	NT
Lincoln	18 d		10 14	11 14	12 14	13 14		14 14	15 12	16 12	17 15	18 12	19 19	20 17	21 20	21 51
Saxilby	18 d		10 23	11 23	12 23	13 23		14 23	15 21	16 21	17 24	18 23	19 28	20 26	21 29	22 00
Gainsborough Lea Road	18 d		10 35	11 35	12 35	13 35		14 35	15 33	16 33	17 36	18 37	19 40	20 38	21 41	22 12
Gainsborough Central	d															
Retford [10]	a		10 49	11 49	12 49	13 50		14 49	15 47	16 47	17 50	18 51	19 54	20 53	21 55	22 26
	d	09 12	10 50	11 50	12 50	13 50	14 14	14 50	15 48	16 48	17 51	18 52	19 55	20 53	21 56	22 27
Worksop	d	09 26	11 02	12 02	13 02	14 02	14 28	15 02	15 59	17 00	18 03	19 04	20 07	21 05	22 07	22 38
Shireoaks	d	09 30	11 07	12 06	13 06	14 07	14 33	15 06	16 04	17 04	18 07		20 11		22 12	22 43
Kiveton Park	d	09 36	11 12	12 12	13 12	14 12	14 38	15 12	16 09	17 10	18 13	19 12	20 17	21 14	22 17	22 49
Kiveton Bridge	d	09 39	11 15	12 15	13 15	14 15	14 41	15 15	16 12	17 13	18 16	19 15	20 20	21 17	22 21	22 52
Woodhouse	d	09 45	11 22	12 22	13 21	14 22	14 48	15 21	16 19	17 19	18 22		20 26		22 27	22 58
Darnall	d	09 51				14 27		15 27		17 25	18 28		20 32		22 33	23 04
Sheffield [7]	a	09 59	11 34	12 34	13 34	14 36	15 01	15 35	16 31	17 33	18 36	19 33	20 40	21 35	22 41	23 12
Meadowhall	34 a	10 07	11 45	12 44	13 44	14 44		15 45								

A To Huddersfield

For connections from London Kings Cross refer to Table T026

SUNDAY RETURN TIMES

NRT DECEMBER 19 EDITION

Table T030-R

Sundays

15 December to 10 May

Sheffield - Retford - Lincoln

		NT ◇	NT	NT ◇	NT	NT ◇ A	NT	NT ◇ A	NT ◇ A	NT ◇ A	NT ◇ A	NT ◇ A	NT	NT ◇	NT	NT ◇
Meadowhall	34 d					12 27		13 19	14 27	15 21	16 26	17 21				
Sheffield [7]	d	08 45	09 41	10 41	11 41	12 41	13 14	13 36	14 41	15 42	16 37	17 38	18 42	19 34	20 20	21 23
Darnall	d		09 46		11 46		13 19				16 43		18 47		20 26	21 28
Woodhouse	d		09 52		11 51		13 25				16 48		18 53		20 31	21 34
Kiveton Bridge	d		09 58	10 55	11 58	12 55	13 31	13 52	14 55	15 56	16 55	17 52	18 59	19 48	20 37	21 40
Kiveton Park	d		10 02	10 58	12 01	12 58	13 35	13 57	14 58	15 59	16 58	17 55	19 03	19 51	20 41	21 44
Shireoaks	d		10 07		12 06		13 40				17 03		19 08		20 46	21 49
Worksop	d	09 08	10 12	11 06	12 11	13 07	13 45	14 06	15 07	16 08	17 08	18 05	19 13	20 00	20 51	21 54
Retford [10]	a	09 18	10 22	11 16	12 21	13 17	13 59	14 16	15 17	16 18	17 18	18 15	19 23	20 10	21 01	22 04
	d	09 19	10 22	11 17	12 22	13 18		14 16	15 18	16 18	17 19	18 15	19 24	20 10	21 01	22 05
Gainsborough Central	d															
Gainsborough Lea Road	18 a	09 33	10 36	11 31	12 36	13 32		14 31	15 32	16 33	17 33	18 30	19 38	20 25	21 15	22 19
Saxilby	18 a	09 46	10 49	11 44	12 49	13 45		14 43	15 45	16 45	17 46	18 42	19 51	20 37	21 28	22 32
Lincoln	18 a	09 57	11 00	11 56	13 00	13 56		14 55	15 57	16 57	17 58	18 54	20 04	20 49	21 41	22 45

A From Huddersfield

For connections to London Kings Cross refer to Table T026

Table T030-R

Mondays to Fridays

16 December to 15 May

Sheffield - Retford - Lincoln

Miles			NT	NT	EM	NT ◇ A	NT B	NT ◇ C	NT	NT ◇ C	NT	NT ◇ C	NT	NT ◇ C	NT	NT ◇ C	NT	NT ◇ C	NT	NT ◇ C	NT	NT ◇ C	NT
—	Meadowhall	34 d					06 40	07 27		08 27		09 27		10 27		11 27		12 27		13 27		14 27	
0	**Sheffield [7]**	d	05 45	06 10		06 35	06 58	07 37	07 55	08 37	08 53	09 37	09 54	10 37	10 54	11 37	11 54	12 37	12 54	13 37	13 54	14 37	14 54
2¼	Darnall	d	05 50			06 44	07 04		08 00		08 58		09 59		10 59		11 59		12 59		13 59		14 59
5¼	Woodhouse	d	05 55			06 49	07 09		08 06		09 04		10 05		11 05		12 05		13 05		14 05		15 05
9½	Kiveton Bridge	d	06 02			06 56	07 16		08 12		09 10		10 11		11 11		12 11		13 11		14 11		15 11
10¾	Kiveton Park	d	06 05	06 25		06 59	07 19		08 16		09 14		10 15		11 15		12 15		13 15		14 15		15 15
13¾	Shireoaks	d	06 09			07 04	07 24		08 20		09 18		10 19		11 19		12 19		13 19		14 19		15 19
15¾	Worksop	d	06 14	06 34	06 56	07 09	07 29	07 59	08 25	08 59	09 23	09 59	10 24	10 59	11 24	11 59	12 24	12 59	13 24	13 59	14 24	14 59	15 24
23½	**Retford [10]**	a	06 23	06 49		07 19	07 39	08 09	08 35	09 08	09 33	10 08	10 34	11 08	11 34	12 08	12 34	13 08	13 34	14 08	14 34	15 09	15 34
—		d	06 24			07 19	07 39	08 09	08 36	09 09	09 34	10 09	10 35	11 09	11 35	12 09	12 35	13 09	13 35	14 09	14 35	15 10	15 35
—	Gainsborough Central	d					07a55		08a51		09a49		10a52		11a51		12a50		13a50		14a50		15a50
33	Gainsborough Lea Road	18 a	06 39			07 34		08 24		09 23		10 30		11 24		12 23		13 24		14 24		15 24	
42½	Saxilby	18 a	06 51			07 46		08 36		09 35		10 42		11 36		12 35		13 36		14 36		15 36	
48½	**Lincoln**	18 a	07 07		09 08	07 57		08 47		09 48		10 55		11 49		12 48		13 49		14 48		15 48	

		NT ◇ C	NT	NT ◇ C	NT	NT ◇ C	NT	NT ◇ C	NT ◇ C	NT	NT
Meadowhall	34 d	15 27		16 27		17 27		18 27	19 28		
Sheffield [7]	d	15 37	15 54	16 37	16 54	17 37	17 54	18 37	19 38	20 53	21 43
Darnall	d		15 59	16 43	16 59	17 43	17 59	18 45	19 43	20 58	21 48
Woodhouse	d		16 05	16 48	17 05	17 48	18 05	18 51	19 48	21 03	21 54
Kiveton Bridge	d		16 11	16 55	17 11	17 55	18 11	18 57	19 55	21 10	22 00
Kiveton Park	d		16 15	16 58	17 15	17 58	18 15	19 01	19 58	21 13	22 04
Shireoaks	d		16 19	17 03	17 19	18 03	18 19	19 07	20 03	21 18	22 09
Worksop	d	15 59	16 24	17 08	17 24	18 08	18 24	19 13	20 08	21 23	22 14
Retford [10]	a	16 08	16 34	17 17	17 34	18 18	18 34	19 23	20 17	21 32	22 28
	d	16 09	16 35	17 18	17 35	18 18	18 35	19 23	20 18	21 33	
Gainsborough Central	d		16a50		17a50		18a50				
Gainsborough Lea Road	18 a	16 24		17 32		18 33		19 38	20 33	21 47	
Saxilby	18 a	16 36		17 44		18 45		19 50	20 44	21 59	
Lincoln	18 a	16 49		17 56		18 57		20 06	20 58	22 11	

Saturdays

21 December to 16 May

		NT	NT	NT ◇ A	NT B	NT ◇ C	NT ◇ D	NT ◇ C	NT	NT ◇ C	NT	NT ◇ C	NT	NT ◇ C	NT ◇ D	NT ◇ C	NT	NT ◇ C	NT	NT ◇ C	NT	NT ◇ C	NT ◇ D
Meadowhall	34 d				06 40	07 27		08 27		09 27		10 27		11 27		12 27		13 27		14 27		15 27	
Sheffield [7]	d	05 45	06 13	06 35	06 58	07 37	07 55	08 37	08 53	09 37	09 54	10 37	10 54	11 37	11 54	12 37	12 54	13 37	13 54	14 37	14 54	15 37	15 54
Darnall	d	05 50		06 43	07 04		08 00		08 58		09 59		10 59		11 59		12 59		13 59		14 59		16 00
Woodhouse	d	05 55		06 49	07 09		08 06		09 04		10 05		11 05		12 05		13 05		14 05		15 05		16 05
Kiveton Bridge	d	06 02		06 56	07 16		08 12		09 10		10 11		11 11		12 11		13 11		14 11		15 11		16 12
Kiveton Park	d	06 05	06 28	06 59	07 19		08 16		09 14		10 15		11 15		12 15		13 15		14 15		15 15		16 15
Shireoaks	d	06 09		07 04	07 24		08 20		09 18		10 19		11 19		12 19		13 19		14 19		15 19		16 20
Worksop	d	06 14	06 36	07 09	07 29	07 59	08 25	08 59	09 23	09 59	10 24	10 59	11 24	11 59	12 24	12 59	13 24	13 59	14 24	14 59	15 24	15 59	16 25
Retford [10]	a	06 23	06 52	07 19	07 39	08 09		09 08	09 33	10 08	10 34	11 08	11 34	12 08		13 08	13 34	14 08	14 34	15 09	15 34	16 08	
	d	06 24		07 19	07 39	08 09		09 09	09 34	10 09	10 35	11 09	11 35	12 09		13 09	13 35	14 09	14 35	15 10	15 35	16 09	
Gainsborough Central	d				07a55		08a54		09a49		10a52		11a51		12a58		13a50		14a50		15a50		16a58
Gainsborough Lea Road	18 a	06 39		07 34		08 24		09 23		10 30		11 24		12 23		13 24		14 24		15 24		16 24	
Saxilby	18 a	06 51		07 46		08 36		09 35		10 42		11 36		12 35		13 36		14 36		15 36		16 36	
Lincoln	18 a	07 07		08 01		08 47		09 48		10 55		11 49		12 48		13 49		14 48		15 48		16 49	

		NT ◇ C	NT	NT ◇ C	NT	NT ◇ C	NT ◇ C	NT	NT
Meadowhall	34 d	16 27		17 27		18 27	19 28		
Sheffield [7]	d	16 37	16 54	17 37	17 54	18 37	19 38	20 53	21 43
Darnall	d	16 43	16 59	17 43	17 59	18 45	19 43	20 58	21 48
Woodhouse	d	16 48	17 05	17 48	18 05	18 51	19 48	21 03	21 54
Kiveton Bridge	d	16 55	17 11	17 55	18 11	18 57	19 55	21 10	22 00
Kiveton Park	d	16 58	17 15	17 58	18 15	19 01	19 58	21 13	22 04
Shireoaks	d	17 03	17 19	18 03	18 19	19 07	20 03	21 18	22 09
Worksop	d	17 08	17 24	18 08	18 24	19 13	20 08	21 23	22 14
Retford [10]	a	17 17	17 34	18 18	18 34	19 23	20 17	21 32	22 28
	d	17 18	17 35	18 18	18 35	19 23	20 18	21 33	
Gainsborough Central	d		17a50		18a50				
Gainsborough Lea Road	18 a	17 32		18 33		19 38	20 33	21 47	
Saxilby	18 a	17 44		18 45		19 50	20 44	21 59	
Lincoln	18 a	17 56		18 57		20 06	20 58	22 11	

A From Doncaster
B From Barnsley
C From Leeds
D To Cleethorpes. via Retford

For connections to London Kings Cross refer to Table T026

← See Sunday times, left.

Table T031-F

Mondays to Fridays

16 December to 15 May

Sheffield, Doncaster and Wakefield - Leeds

Miles	Miles	Station		NT MX ◇	NT MX	NT	NT	NT ◇	NT	NT ◇	NT	NT	NT	NT ◇	NT ◇	NT A	NT B	NT ◇	NT ◇	NT	NT	NT	NT ◇	XC ◇1
—	0	**Sheffield 7** 29	d			05 15	05 28				06 02	06 05	06 16	06 19		06 27		06 44		07 01	07 04	07 12	07 18	07 21
—	3¼	Meadowhall 29	d			05 21	05 34				06 08	06 11	06 22	06 25		06 33		06 51		07 07	07 10	07 21	07 24	
—	6¼	Rotherham Central 29	d			05 28						06 18	06 28			06 39				07 19		07 28		
—	10¾	Swinton (S.Yorks) 29	d			05 38						06 26	06 38			06 48				07 29		07 38		
—	13	Bolton-upon-Dearne	d			05 43							06 43									07 43		
—	14¼	Goldthorpe	d			05 46							06 46									07 46		
—	15	Thurnscoe	d			05 49							06 49									07 49		
—	18½	Moorthorpe	d			05 55							06 55									08 00		
0	—	**Doncaster 7**	d					05 58	06 11	06 31		06 43			06 54	07 11	07 11		07 28	07 53				
1¾	—	Bentley (S.Yorks)	d					06 01	06 15	06 34		06 47			06 58	07 14	07 14		07 31	07 57				
4	—	Adwick	a					06 05	06 20	06 38		06 52			07 01	07 19	07 19		07 35	08 02				
—	—		d					06 05		06 38					07 01				07 35					
8¾	—	South Elmsall	d					06 12		06 43					07 07				07 40					
13¼	22¼	Fitzwilliam	d			06 01		06 18		06 48			07 01		07 13				07 45			08 06		
18	27	Sandal & Agbrigg	d			06 08		06 24		06 54			07 08		07 18				07 51			08 12		
19¾	28¾	**Wakefield Westgate 7** 32,39	a			06 12		06 28		06 58			07 12		07 23				07 55			08 16		07 46
—	—		d	00 01	00 13	06 14		06 29		06 59			07 14		07 23				07 56			08 17		07 47
—	—	Pontefract Monkhill 32	d																→			→		
—	—	Wakefield Kirkgate 4 32,34,39	a				06 15				06 48			06 54				07 22			07 50		07 57	
—	—		d				06 15				06 49			06 55				07 23			07 51		07 57	
22¼	31¼	Outwood	d	00 04	00 18	06 19		06 34		07 03			07 19		07 28									
29¼	38¼	**Leeds 10** 32,34	a	00 17	00 30	06 31	06 44	06 47		07 17	07 25		07 31	07 16	07 39			07 43			08 26		08 17	08 03

Station		NT ◇	GR ■1	NT	NT ◇	NT	NT ◇	GR ■1	NT	NT	NT ◇	XC ◇1	NT ◇	GR ■1	NT	NT ◇	GR ■1	NT	NT ◇	NT	NT	NT ◇	XC ◇1	NT ◇
Sheffield 7 29	d					07 31	07 47		08 04	08 16	08 19	08 22				08 45		09 03		09 06	09 15	09 18	09 21	
Meadowhall 29	d					07 37	07 54		08 10	08 22	08 25					08 51		09 09		09 11	09 21	09 24		
Rotherham Central 29	d					07 44				08 28										09 18	09 28			
Swinton (S.Yorks) 29	d					07 52				08 39										09 28	09 38			
Bolton-upon-Dearne	d									08 44											09 43			
Goldthorpe	d									08 47											09 46			
Thurnscoe	d									08 50											09 49			
Moorthorpe	d									08 55											09 55			
Doncaster 7	d		07 50		07 59	08 10		08 17					08 26	08 43			09 15		09 26	09 50				
Bentley (S.Yorks)	d				08 03	08 13							08 29						09 29	09 54				
Adwick	a				08 07	08 18							08 33						09 33	09 59				
	d				08 07								08 33						09 33					
South Elmsall	d				08 12								08 40						09 39					
Fitzwilliam	d				08 17					09 01			08 46						09 45		10 01			
Sandal & Agbrigg	d	←		←	08 23					09 08			08 51		←				09 51		10 08			←
Wakefield Westgate 7 32,39	a	07 55	08 06	08 16	08 27			08 34		09 12		08 48	08 55	08 59	09 12		09 31		09 55		10 12		09 46	09 55
	d	07 56	08 07	08 17	08 28			08 36		09 14		08 49	08 56	09 01	09 14		09 32		09 55		10 14		09 47	09 55
Pontefract Monkhill 32	d									→									→		→			
Wakefield Kirkgate 4 32,34,39	a						08 23		08 49		08 55					09 24		09 49				09 55		
	d						08 24		08 50		08 56					09 25		09 49				09 55		
Outwood	d	08 00		08 22	08 32								09 00		09 19									10 00
Leeds 10 32,34	a	08 12	08 22	08 34	08 44		08 44	08 52	09 24		09 14	09 02	09 12	09 16	09 31	09 44	09 45	10 25			10 14	10 00	10 11	

Station		GR ■1	NT	NT ◇	GR ■1	NT	NT ◇	NT	NT	NT ◇	XC ◇1	NT ◇	GR ■1	NT	NT ◇	GR ■1	NT	NT ◇	NT	NT	NT ◇	XC ◇1	NT ◇
Sheffield 7 29	d			09 45		10 02		10 05	10 15	10 18	10 21				10 45		11 02		11 05	11 15	11 18	11 21	
Meadowhall 29	d			09 51		10 08		10 11	10 21	10 24					10 51		11 08		11 11	11 21	11 24		
Rotherham Central 29	d							10 19	10 28										11 19	11 28			
Swinton (S.Yorks) 29	d							10 28	10 36										11 28	11 38			
Bolton-upon-Dearne	d								10 41											11 43			
Goldthorpe	d								10 44											11 46			
Thurnscoe	d								10 47											11 49			
Moorthorpe	d								10 53											11 55			
Doncaster 7	d	09 44			10 15		10 26	10 47					10 43			11 15		11 26	11 47				
Bentley (S.Yorks)	d						10 29	10 51										11 29	11 51				
Adwick	a						10 33	10 56										11 33	11 56				
	d						10 33											11 33					
South Elmsall	d						10 39											11 39					
Fitzwilliam	d						10 45		11 00									11 45		12 01			
Sandal & Agbrigg	d		←				10 50		11 08			←		←				11 50		12 08			←
Wakefield Westgate 7 32,39	a	10 00	10 12		10 31		10 54		11 12		10 45	10 54	11 00	11 12		11 31		11 54		12 12		11 45	11 54
	d	10 01	10 14		10 32		10 55		11 14		10 46	10 55	11 01	11 14		11 32		11 55		12 14		11 46	11 55
Pontefract Monkhill 32	d						→		→									→		→			
Wakefield Kirkgate 4 32,34,39	a			10 24		10 48				10 55					11 24		11 48				11 55		
	d			10 24		10 49				10 55					11 24		11 49				11 55		
Outwood	d		10 19									10 59		11 19									11 59
Leeds 10 32,34	a	10 16	10 31	10 44	10 47	11 25				11 14	11 01	11 11	11 16	11 31	11 44	11 46	12 25				12 14	12 01	12 11

A until 14 February   B from 17 February

NRT DECEMBER 19 EDITION

Table T031-F

Mondays to Fridays

16 December to 15 May

Sheffield, Doncaster and Wakefield - Leeds

Station		GR ■1	NT	NT ◇	GR ■1	NT	NT ◇	GC ■1	NT	NT	NT ◇	XC ◇1	NT ◇	GR ■1	NT	NT ◇	GR ■1	NT	NT ◇	NT	NT	NT ◇	XC ◇1
Sheffield 7 29	d			11 45		12 02			12 05	12 15	12 18	12 21				12 45		13 02		13 05	13 15	13 18	13 21
Meadowhall 29	d			11 51		12 08			12 11	12 21	12 24					12 51		13 08		13 11	13 21	13 24	
Rotherham Central 29	d								12 19	12 28										13 19	13 28		
Swinton (S.Yorks) 29	d								12 28	12 38										13 28	13 38		
Bolton-upon-Dearne	d									12 43											13 43		
Goldthorpe	d									12 46											13 46		
Thurnscoe	d									12 49											13 49		
Moorthorpe	d									12 55											13 55		
Doncaster 7	d	11 43			12 15		12 26	12 35	12 47					12 43			13 15		13 27	13 47			
Bentley (S.Yorks)	d						12 29		12 51										13 30	13 51			
Adwick	a						12 33		12 56										13 34	13 56			
	d						12 33												13 34				
South Elmsall	d						12 39												13 39				
Fitzwilliam	d						12 45			13 01									13 45		14 01		
Sandal & Agbrigg	d		←				12 50			13 08			←		←				13 50		14 08		
Wakefield Westgate 7 32,39	a	11 59	12 12		12 31		12 54			13 12		12 45	12 54	13 00	13 12		13 31		13 54		14 12		13 46
	d	12 01	12 14		12 32		12 55			13 14		12 46	12 55	13 01	13 14		13 32		13 55		14 14		13 47
Pontefract Monkhill 32	d						→	12 58		→									→		→		
Wakefield Kirkgate 4 32,34,39	a			12 24		12 48		13 14			12 55					13 24		13 50				13 55	
	d			12 24		12 49					12 55					13 24		13 50				13 55	
Outwood	d		12 19										12 59		13 19								
Leeds 10 32,34	a	12 16	12 31	12 44	12 48	13 25					13 14	13 00	13 11	13 16	13 31	13 44	13 46	14 25				14 14	14 00

Station		NT ◇	GR ■1	NT	NT ◇	GR ■1	NT	NT ◇	NT	NT	NT ◇	XC ◇1	NT ◇	GR ■1	NT	NT ◇	GR ■1	NT	NT ◇	NT	NT	NT ◇	XC ◇1	NT ◇
Sheffield 7 29	d				13 43		14 02		14 05	14 15	14 18	14 21				14 45		15 02		15 05	15 15	15 18	15 21	
Meadowhall 29	d				13 51		14 08		14 11	14 21	14 24					14 51		15 08		15 11	15 21	15 24		
Rotherham Central 29	d								14 19	14 28										15 19	15 28			
Swinton (S.Yorks) 29	d								14 28	14 38										15 28	15 36			
Bolton-upon-Dearne	d									14 43											15 40			
Goldthorpe	d									14 46											15 43			
Thurnscoe	d									14 49											15 46			
Moorthorpe	d									14 55											15 52			
Doncaster 7	d		13 43			14 15		14 26	14 47					14 43			15 15		15 26	15 47				
Bentley (S.Yorks)	d							14 29	14 51										15 29	15 51				
Adwick	a							14 33	14 56										15 33	15 56				
	d							14 33											15 33					
South Elmsall	d							14 39											15 39					
Fitzwilliam	d							14 45		15 01									15 45		16 00			
Sandal & Agbrigg	d	←		←				14 50		15 08			←		←				15 50		16 07			←
Wakefield Westgate 7 32,39	a	13 54	13 59	14 12		14 31		14 54		15 12		14 46	14 54	14 59	15 12		15 31		15 54		16 12		15 46	15 54
	d	13 55	14 01	14 14		14 32		14 55		15 14		14 47	14 55	15 01	15 14		15 32		15 55		16 14		15 47	15 55
Pontefract Monkhill 32	d							→		→									→		→			
Wakefield Kirkgate 4 32,34,39	a				14 24		14 48				14 55					15 24		15 48				15 55		
	d				14 24		14 49				14 55					15 24		15 49				15 55		
Outwood	d	13 59		14 19									14 59		15 19									15 59
Leeds 10 32,34	a	14 11	14 16	14 31	14 44	14 48	15 25				15 14	15 00	15 11	15 16	15 31	15 44	15 46	16 25				16 14	16 00	16 11

Station		GR ■1	NT	NT ◇	GR ■1	NT	GC ■1	NT ◇	NT	NT	NT ◇	XC ◇1	NT ◇	GR ■1	NT	NT ◇	GR ■1	NT	NT ◇	NT	NT	NT ◇	XC ◇1
Sheffield 7 29	d			15 45		16 02			16 05	16 15	16 18	16 21				16 45		17 02		17 05	17 15	17 18	17 21
Meadowhall 29	d			15 51		16 08			16 11	16 21	16 24					16 51		17 08		17 11	17 21	17 24	
Rotherham Central 29	d								16 19	16 28										17 19	17 28		
Swinton (S.Yorks) 29	d								16 28	16 38										17 28	17 38		
Bolton-upon-Dearne	d									16 43											17 43		
Goldthorpe	d									16 46											17 46		
Thurnscoe	d									16 49											17 49		
Moorthorpe	d									16 55											17 55		
Doncaster 7	d	15 43			16 15		16 23	16 27	16 47					16 43			17 17		17 26	17 48			
Bentley (S.Yorks)	d							16 30	16 51										17 29	17 52			
Adwick	a							16 34	16 56										17 33	17 57			
	d							16 34											17 33				
South Elmsall	d							16 39											17 39				
Fitzwilliam	d							16 45		17 01									17 45		18 01		
Sandal & Agbrigg	d		←					16 50		17 08			←		←				17 50		18 08		
Wakefield Westgate 7 32,39	a	15 59	16 12		16 31			16 54		17 12		16 46	16 54	16 59	17 12		17 33		17 54		18 12		17 46
	d	16 00	16 14		16 33			16 55		17 14		16 47	16 55	17 01	17 14		17 35		17 55		18 14		17 47
Pontefract Monkhill 32	d						16 54	→		→									→		→		
Wakefield Kirkgate 4 32,34,39	a			16 23		16 48	17 13				16 55					17 24		17 48				17 55	
	d			16 24		16 49					16 55					17 24		17 49				17 55	
Outwood	d		16 19										16 59		17 19								
Leeds 10 32,34	a	16 16	16 31	16 44	16 51	17 25					17 14	17 01	17 11	17 16	17 31	17 44	17 49	18 25				18 14	18 00

Table T031-F

Mondays to Fridays
16 December to 15 May

Sheffield, Doncaster and Wakefield - Leeds

Station			NT	GR	NT	NT	XC	GC	GR	NT	NT	NT	NT	NT	XC	NT	GR	NT	NT	GR	NT	NT	NT	NT
			◇	1		◇	◇1	1	1		◇			◇	◇1	◇	1		◇	1		◇		
Sheffield 7	29	d				17 45	17 51			18 02		18 05	18 15	18 18	18 21				18 45		19 02		19 05	19 15
Meadowhall	29	d				17 51				18 08		18 11	18 21	18 24					18 51		19 08		19 13	19 21
Rotherham Central	29	d										18 18	18 28										19 19	19 28
Swinton (S.Yorks)	29	d										18 29	18 38										19 29	19 38
Bolton-upon-Dearne		d											18 43											19 43
Goldthorpe		d											18 46											19 46
Thurnscoe		d											18 49											19 49
Moorthorpe		d											18 55											19 55
Doncaster 7		d		17 41				18 04	18 19		18 28	18 48					18 43			19 16		19 28	19 54	
Bentley (S.Yorks)		d									18 31	18 52										19 31	19 58	
Adwick		a									18 35	18 57										19 35	20 03	
		d									18 35											19 35		
South Elmsall		d									18 40											19 40		
Fitzwilliam		d									18 46		19 01									19 45		20 07
Sandal & Agbrigg		d	←		←						18 51		19 08			←		←				19 51		20 14
Wakefield Westgate 7	32,39	a	17 54	17 59	18 12		18 18		18 35		18 55		19 12		18 48	18 55	19 00	19 12		19 32		19 55		20 18
		d	17 55	18 01	18 14		18 20		18 36		18 56		19 14		18 51	18 56	19 01	19 14		19 33		19 55		20 19
Pontefract Monkhill	32	d									→		→									→		→
Wakefield Kirkgate 4	32,34,39	a				18 24		18 26		18 48				18 55					19 24		19 48			
		d				18 24				18 49				18 55					19 24		19 49			
Outwood		d	17 59		18 19											19 00		19 19						
Leeds 10	32,34	a	18 12	18 16	18 31	18 44	18 36		18 52	19 24				19 14	19 05	19 13	19 17	19 31	19 44	19 48	20 25			

Station			NT	XC	NT	GR	GR	NT	NT	GR	NT FX	NT FO	NT	NT	NT	NT	XC	NT	GR	NT	NT	GR	NT	GC	NT
			◇	◇1	◇	1	1		◇	1			◇			◇	◇1	◇	1		◇	1		1	◇
Sheffield 7	29	d	19 18	19 21					19 45		20 02	20 02		20 05	20 15	20 18	20 21				20 45		21 02		
Meadowhall	29	d	19 24						19 51		20 08	20 08		20 11	20 21	20 24					20 51		21 08		
Rotherham Central	29	d												20 19	20 28										
Swinton (S.Yorks)	29	d												20 28	20 38										
Bolton-upon-Dearne		d													20 43										
Goldthorpe		d													20 46										
Thurnscoe		d													20 49										
Moorthorpe		d													20 55										
Doncaster 7		d				19 44	19 50			20 22			20 28	20 48					20 42			21 14		21 22	21 28
Bentley (S.Yorks)		d											20 31	20 52											21 31
Adwick		a											20 35	20 57											21 35
		d											20 35												21 35
South Elmsall		d											20 40												21 40
Fitzwilliam		d											20 45		21 01										21 45
Sandal & Agbrigg		d			←			←					20 51		21 08			←		←					21 51
Wakefield Westgate 7	32,39	a		19 46	19 55	20 01	20 06	20 18		20 38			20 55		21 12		20 47	20 55	20 59	21 12		21 30			21 55
		d		19 49	19 55	20 02	20 07	20 19		20 40			20 55		21 13		20 48	20 55	21 01	21 13		21 31			21 55
Pontefract Monkhill	32	d											→		→										→
Wakefield Kirkgate 4	32,34,39	a	19 55						20 24		20 48	20 48				20 55					21 24		21 48	21 50	
		d	19 55						20 24		20 49	20 49				20 55					21 24		21 49		
Outwood		d			20 00			20 24										21 00		21 18					
Leeds 10	32,34	a	20 15	20 05	20 12	20 17	20 21	20 36	20 44	20 54	21 25	21 26				21 14	21 02	21 13	21 17	21 30	21 44	21 47	22 25		

Station			NT	NT	NT	XC	NT	EM	GR	NT	EM	GR	NT	NT	NT	NT	EM	XC	NT	NT	NT	GR	NT	NT FX
					◇	◇1	◇	◇1	1		◇1	1	◇			◇	◇1	◇1	◇			1	◇	
Sheffield 7	29	d	21 05	21 15	21 18	21 23		21 26			22 04			22 07	22 15	22 18	22 21	22 24			22 31			23 15
Meadowhall	29	d	21 11	21 21	21 24									22 13	22 21	22 24					22 37			23 21
Rotherham Central	29	d	21 19	21 29										22 19	22 28									23 28
Swinton (S.Yorks)	29	d	21 28	21 40										22 29	22 41									23 36
Bolton-upon-Dearne		d		21 45											22 45									23 40
Goldthorpe		d		21 47											22 49									23 43
Thurnscoe		d		21 50											22 52									23 46
Moorthorpe		d		21 56											22 58									23 52
Doncaster 7		d	21 53						21 45			22 23	22 32	22 47								23 37	23 24	
Bentley (S.Yorks)		d	21 56										22 35	22 51									23 27	
Adwick		a	22 01										22 39	22 55									23 31	
		d											22 39										23 31	
South Elmsall		d											22 45										23 36	
Fitzwilliam		d		22 01									22 51		23 05								23 50	23 59
Sandal & Agbrigg		d		22 08			←			←			22 56		23 11				←	←			23 56	
Wakefield Westgate 7	32,39	a		22 12		21 46	21 55	21 57	22 05	22 12	22 33	22 39	23 00		23 15		22 48	22 53	23 00	23 15		23 54	23 59	00 12
		d		22 12		21 47	21 55	21 59	22 06	22 12	22 34	22 41	23 01		23 16		22 49	22 55	23 01	23 16		23 55	00 01	00 13
Pontefract Monkhill	32	d		→									→		→									
Wakefield Kirkgate 4	32,34,39	a			21 55											22 55					23 17			
		d			21 55											22 55					23 18			
Outwood		d					22 00			22 18									23 05	23 21			00 04	00 18
Leeds 10	32,34	a			22 14	22 02	22 12	22 20	22 21	22 29	22 49	22 57				23 14	23 06	23 08	23 18	23 34	23 58	00 10	00 17	00 30

Table T031-F

Mondays to Fridays
16 December to 15 May

Sheffield, Doncaster and Wakefield - Leeds

Station			NT FO	NT
Sheffield 7	29	d	23 15	23 18
Meadowhall	29	d	23 21	23 24
Rotherham Central	29	d	23 28	
Swinton (S.Yorks)	29	d	23 36	
Bolton-upon-Dearne		d	23 40	
Goldthorpe		d	23 43	
Thurnscoe		d	23 46	
Moorthorpe		d	23 52	
Doncaster 7		d		
Bentley (S.Yorks)		d		
Adwick		a		
		d		
South Elmsall		d		
Fitzwilliam		d	23 59	
Sandal & Agbrigg		d		
Wakefield Westgate 7	32,39	a		
		d		
Pontefract Monkhill	32	d		
Wakefield Kirkgate 4	32,34,39	a		00 04
		d		
Outwood		d		
Leeds 10	32,34	a	00 30	

Saturdays
21 December to 16 May

Station			NT	NT	NT	NT	NT	NT	NT	NT	NT	NT	NT	NT	NT	NT	NT	NT	NT	NT	XC	NT	GR	NT	NT
			◇			◇		◇				◇	◇	◇		◇				◇	◇1	◇	1		◇
Sheffield 7	29	d		05 15	05 28				06 04	06 07	06 16	06 19		06 44			07 01	07 04	07 15	07 18	07 21				
Meadowhall	29	d		05 21	05 34				06 10	06 13	06 22	06 25		06 51			07 07	07 10	07 21	07 25					
Rotherham Central	29	d		05 28						06 20	06 28						07 19		07 28						
Swinton (S.Yorks)	29	d		05 38						06 28	06 38						07 29		07 38						
Bolton-upon-Dearne		d		05 43							06 43								07 43						
Goldthorpe		d		05 46							06 46								07 46						
Thurnscoe		d		05 49							06 49								07 49						
Moorthorpe		d		05 55							06 55								07 58						
Doncaster 7		d				05 58	06 11	06 31		06 45			06 54		07 11	07 28	07 53						07 50		07 59
Bentley (S.Yorks)		d				06 01	06 15	06 34		06 49			06 58		07 14	07 31	07 57								08 03
Adwick		a				06 05	06 20	06 38		06 54			07 01		07 19	07 35	08 02								08 07
		d				06 05		06 38					07 01			07 35									08 07
South Elmsall		d				06 12		06 43					07 07			07 40									08 12
Fitzwilliam		d		06 01		06 18		06 48			07 01		07 13			07 45			08 06						08 17
Sandal & Agbrigg		d		06 08		06 24		06 54			07 08		07 18			07 51			08 13			←		←	08 23
Wakefield Westgate 7	32,39	a		06 12		06 28		06 58			07 12		07 23			07 55			08 18		07 46	07 55	08 06	08 18	08 27
		d	00 01	06 14		06 29		06 59			07 14		07 23			07 56			08 18		07 47	07 56	08 07	08 18	08 28
Pontefract Monkhill	32	d														→			→						
Wakefield Kirkgate 4	32,34,39	a			06 15				06 49			06 54		07 22				07 50		07 57					
		d			06 15				06 50			06 55		07 23				07 51		07 57					
Outwood		d	00 04	06 19		06 34		07 03			07 19		07 28									08 00		08 23	08 32
Leeds 10	32,34	a	00 17	06 31	06 44	06 47		07 17	07 25		07 31	07 16	07 39	07 43				08 26		08 17	08 01	08 12	08 22	08 36	08 44

Station			NT	NT	GR	NT	NT	NT	XC	NT	GR	NT	NT	GR	NT	NT	NT	NT	NT	XC	NT	GR	NT	NT
				◇	1			◇	◇1	◇	1		◇	1		◇			◇	◇1	◇	1		◇
Sheffield 7	29	d	07 31	07 47		08 04	08 16	08 19	08 22				08 45		09 03		09 06	09 15	09 18	09 21				09 45
Meadowhall	29	d	07 37	07 54		08 10	08 22	08 25					08 51		09 09		09 11	09 21	09 24					09 52
Rotherham Central	29	d	07 44				08 28										09 18	09 29						
Swinton (S.Yorks)	29	d	07 52				08 39										09 28	09 38						
Bolton-upon-Dearne		d					08 44											09 43						
Goldthorpe		d					08 47											09 46						
Thurnscoe		d					08 50											09 49						
Moorthorpe		d					08 55											09 55						
Doncaster 7		d	08 10		08 18					08 26	08 43			09 15		09 26	09 50					09 44		
Bentley (S.Yorks)		d	08 13							08 29						09 29	09 54							
Adwick		a	08 18							08 33						09 33	09 59							
		d								08 33						09 33								
South Elmsall		d								08 40						09 39								
Fitzwilliam		d					09 01			08 46						09 45		10 01						
Sandal & Agbrigg		d					09 08			08 51		←				09 51		10 08			←		←	
Wakefield Westgate 7	32,39	a			08 34		09 12		08 48	08 55	08 59	09 12		09 31		09 55		10 12		09 46	09 55	10 00	10 12	
		d			08 36		09 14		08 49	08 56	09 01	09 14		09 32		09 55		10 14		09 47	09 55	10 01	10 14	
Pontefract Monkhill	32	d					→									→		→						
Wakefield Kirkgate 4	32,34,39	a		08 23		08 49		08 56					09 23		09 49				09 55					10 24
		d		08 24		08 50		08 57					09 24		09 49				09 55					10 24
Outwood		d								09 00		09 19									10 00		10 19	
Leeds 10	32,34	a		08 44	08 52	09 24		09 14	09 02	09 12	09 16	09 31	09 44	09 45	10 24				10 14	10 00	10 11	10 16	10 31	10 44

Table T031-F

Saturdays

21 December to 16 May

Sheffield, Doncaster and Wakefield - Leeds

	GR	NT	NT	NT	NT	NT	XC	NT	GR	NT	NT	GR	NT	NT	NT	NT	NT	XC	NT	GR	NT	NT
			◇			◇	◇	◇			◇			◇			◇	◇	◇			◇
Sheffield 29 d		10 02		10 05	10 15	10 18	10 21				10 45		11 02		11 05	11 15	11 18	11 21				11 45
Meadowhall 29 d		10 08		10 11	10 21	10 24					10 51		11 08		11 11	11 21	11 24					11 51
Rotherham Central 29 d				10 19	10 28										11 19	11 28						
Swinton (S.Yorks) 29 d				10 28	10 36										11 28	11 38						
Bolton-upon-Dearne d					10 41											11 43						
Goldthorpe d					10 44											11 46						
Thurnscoe d					10 47											11 49						
Moorthorpe d					10 53											11 55						
Doncaster d	10 15		10 26	10 47					10 42			11 15		11 26	11 47					11 43		
Bentley (S.Yorks) d			10 29	10 51										11 29	11 51							
Adwick a			10 33	10 56										11 33	11 56							
d			10 33											11 33								
South Elmsall d			10 39											11 39								
Fitzwilliam d			10 45		11 00									11 45		12 01						
Sandal & Agbrigg d			10 50		11 08			←		←				11 50		12 08			←		←	
Wakefield Westgate 32,39 a	10 31		10 54		11 12		10 45	10 54	11 00	11 12		11 31		11 54		12 12		11 45	11 54	12 00	12 12	
d	10 32		10 55		11 14		10 46	10 55	11 01	11 14		11 32		11 55		12 14		11 46	11 55	12 01	12 14	
Pontefract Monkhill 32 d			→		→									→		→						
Wakefield Kirkgate 32,34,39 a		10 48				10 55					11 24		11 48				11 55					12 24
d		10 49				10 55					11 24		11 49				11 55					12 24
Outwood d								10 59		11 19									11 59		12 19	
Leeds 32,34 a	10 47	11 25				11 14	11 00	11 11	11 16	11 31	11 44	11 46	12 25				12 14	12 00	12 11	12 16	12 31	12 44

	GR	NT	GC	NT	NT	NT	NT	XC	NT	GR	NT	NT	GR	NT	NT	NT	NT	NT	XC	NT	GR	NT	NT
				◇			◇	◇	◇			◇			◇			◇	◇	◇			◇
Sheffield 29 d		12 02			12 05	12 15	12 18	12 21				12 45		13 02		13 05	13 15	13 18	13 21				13 43
Meadowhall 29 d		12 08			12 11	12 21	12 24					12 51		13 08		13 11	13 21	13 24					13 51
Rotherham Central 29 d					12 19	12 28										13 19	13 28						
Swinton (S.Yorks) 29 d					12 28	12 38										13 28	13 38						
Bolton-upon-Dearne d						12 43											13 43						
Goldthorpe d						12 46											13 46						
Thurnscoe d						12 49											13 49						
Moorthorpe d						12 55											13 55						
Doncaster d	12 16		12 22	12 26	12 47					12 43			13 16		13 27	13 47					13 43		
Bentley (S.Yorks) d				12 29	12 51										13 30	13 51							
Adwick a				12 33	12 56										13 34	13 56							
d				12 33											13 34								
South Elmsall d				12 39											13 39								
Fitzwilliam d				12 45		13 01									13 45		14 01						
Sandal & Agbrigg d				12 50		13 08			←		←				13 50		14 08			←		←	
Wakefield Westgate 32,39 a	12 32			12 54		13 12		12 46	12 54	13 00	13 12		13 32		13 54		14 12		13 45	13 54	13 59	14 12	
d	12 34			12 55		13 14		12 47	12 55	13 01	13 14		13 33		13 55		14 14		13 46	13 55	14 01	14 14	
Pontefract Monkhill 32 d				→		→									→		→						
Wakefield Kirkgate 32,34,39 a		12 48	12 49				12 55					13 24		13 50				13 55					14 24
d		12 49					12 55					13 24		13 50				13 55					14 24
Outwood d									12 59		13 19									13 59		14 19	
Leeds 32,34 a	12 49	13 25					13 14	13 00	13 11	13 16	13 31	13 44	13 47	14 25				14 14	14 02	14 11	14 16	14 31	14 44

	GR	NT	NT	NT	NT	NT	XC	NT	GR	NT	NT	GR	NT	NT	NT	NT	NT	XC	NT	GR	NT	NT
			◇			◇	◇	◇			◇			◇			◇	◇	◇			◇
Sheffield 29 d		14 02		14 05	14 15	14 18	14 21				14 45		15 02		15 05	15 15	15 18	15 21				15 45
Meadowhall 29 d		14 08		14 11	14 21	14 24					14 51		15 08		15 11	15 21	15 24					15 51
Rotherham Central 29 d				14 19	14 28										15 19	15 28						
Swinton (S.Yorks) 29 d				14 28	14 38										15 28	15 36						
Bolton-upon-Dearne d					14 43											15 40						
Goldthorpe d					14 46											15 43						
Thurnscoe d					14 49											15 46						
Moorthorpe d					14 55											15 52						
Doncaster d	14 16		14 26	14 47					14 43			15 14		15 26	15 47					15 43		
Bentley (S.Yorks) d			14 29	14 51										15 29	15 51							
Adwick a			14 33	14 56										15 33	15 56							
d			14 33											15 33								
South Elmsall d			14 39											15 39								
Fitzwilliam d			14 45		15 01									15 45		16 00						
Sandal & Agbrigg d			14 50		15 08			←		←				15 50		16 07			←		←	
Wakefield Westgate 32,39 a	14 32		14 54		15 12		14 46	14 54	14 59	15 12		15 30		15 54		16 12		15 45	15 54	15 59	16 12	
d	14 33		14 55		15 14		14 47	14 55	15 01	15 14		15 31		15 55		16 14		15 46	15 55	16 01	16 14	
Pontefract Monkhill 32 d			→		→									→		→						
Wakefield Kirkgate 32,34,39 a		14 48				14 55					15 24		15 48				15 55					16 24
d		14 49				14 55					15 24		15 49				15 55					16 24
Outwood d								14 59		15 19									15 59		16 19	
Leeds 32,34 a	14 48	15 25				15 14	15 00	15 11	15 16	15 31	15 44	15 46	16 25				16 14	16 01	16 11	16 16	16 31	16 44

Table T031-F

Saturdays

21 December to 16 May

Sheffield, Doncaster and Wakefield - Leeds

	GR	NT	NT	NT	NT	NT	XC	NT	GR	NT	NT	GR	GC	NT	NT	NT	NT	NT	XC	NT	GR	NT
			◇			◇	◇	◇			◇				◇			◇	◇	◇		
Sheffield 29 d		16 02		16 05	16 15	16 18	16 21				16 45			17 02		17 05	17 15	17 18	17 21			
Meadowhall 29 d		16 08		16 11	16 21	16 24					16 51			17 08		17 11	17 21	17 24				
Rotherham Central 29 d				16 19	16 28											17 19	17 28					
Swinton (S.Yorks) 29 d				16 28	16 38											17 28	17 38					
Bolton-upon-Dearne d					16 43												17 43					
Goldthorpe d					16 46												17 46					
Thurnscoe d					16 49												17 49					
Moorthorpe d					16 55												17 55					
Doncaster d	16 15		16 27	16 47					16 44			17 16	17 22		17 26	17 48					17 42	
Bentley (S.Yorks) d			16 30	16 51											17 29	17 52						
Adwick a			16 34	16 56											17 33	17 57						
d			16 34												17 33							
South Elmsall d			16 39												17 39							
Fitzwilliam d			16 45		17 01										17 45		18 01					
Sandal & Agbrigg d			16 50		17 08			←		←					17 50		18 08			←		←
Wakefield Westgate 32,39 a	16 32		16 54		17 12		16 45	16 54	17 00	17 12		17 34			17 54		18 12		17 47	17 54	17 59	18 12
d	16 33		16 55		17 14		16 46	16 55	17 01	17 14		17 35			17 55		18 14		17 48	17 55	18 01	18 14
Pontefract Monkhill 32 d			→		→										→		→					
Wakefield Kirkgate 32,34,39 a		16 48				16 55					17 24		17 44	17 48				17 55				
d		16 49				16 55					17 24			17 49				17 55				
Outwood d								16 59		17 19										17 59		18 19
Leeds 32,34 a	16 51	17 25				17 14	17 00	17 11	17 16	17 31	17 44	17 49		18 25				18 14	18 01	18 12	18 16	18 31

	NT	XC	GC	GR	NT	NT	NT	NT	NT	XC	NT	GR	NT	NT	GR	NT	NT	NT	NT	NT	XC	NT	GR
	◇	◇				◇		A	◇	◇	◇		A	◇			◇			◇	◇	◇	
Sheffield 29 d	17 45	17 51			18 02		18 05	18 15	18 18	18 21				18 45		19 02		19 05	19 15	19 18	19 21		
Meadowhall 29 d	17 51				18 08		18 11	18 21	18 24					18 51		19 08		19 13	19 21	19 24			
Rotherham Central 29 d							18 18	18 28										19 19	19 28				
Swinton (S.Yorks) 29 d							18 29	18 38										19 29	19 38				
Bolton-upon-Dearne d								18 43											19 43				
Goldthorpe d								18 46											19 46				
Thurnscoe d								18 49											19 49				
Moorthorpe d								18 55											19 55				
Doncaster d			18 05	18 20		18 28	18 48					18 43			19 16		19 28	19 54					19 50
Bentley (S.Yorks) d						18 31	18 52										19 31	19 58					
Adwick a						18 35	18 57										19 35	20 03					
d						18 35											19 35						
South Elmsall d						18 40											19 40						
Fitzwilliam d						18 46		19 01									19 45		20 07				
Sandal & Agbrigg d						18 51		19 08			←		←				19 51		20 14			←	
Wakefield Westgate 32,39 a		18 18		18 36		18 55		19 12		18 49	18 55	19 00	19 12		19 32		19 55		20 18		19 46	19 55	20 06
d		18 20		18 38		18 56		19 14		18 50	18 56	19 01	19 14		19 33		19 55		20 19		19 49	19 55	20 07
Pontefract Monkhill 32 d						→		→									→		→				
Wakefield Kirkgate 32,34,39 a	18 24		18 26		18 48				18 55					19 24		19 48				19 55			
d	18 24				18 49				18 55					19 24		19 49				19 55			
Outwood d											19 00		19 19									20 00	
Leeds 32,34 a	18 44	18 36		18 53	19 24				19 14	19 03	19 13	19 17	19 31	19 44	19 50	20 25				20 15	20 05	20 12	20 20

	NT	GR	NT	GR	NT	NT	NT	NT	NT	XC	NT	GR	NT	NT	GR	NT	NT	GC	NT	NT	NT	XC
			◇			◇			◇	◇	◇			◇			◇				◇	◇
Sheffield 29 d			19 45		20 02		20 05	20 15	20 18	20 21				20 45		21 02			21 05	21 15	21 18	21 21
Meadowhall 29 d			19 51		20 08		20 11	20 21	20 24					20 51		21 08			21 11	21 21	21 24	
Rotherham Central 29 d							20 19	20 28											21 19	21 29		
Swinton (S.Yorks) 29 d							20 28	20 38											21 28	21 40		
Bolton-upon-Dearne d								20 43												21 45		
Goldthorpe d								20 46												21 47		
Thurnscoe d								20 49												21 50		
Moorthorpe d								20 55												21 56		
Doncaster d		20 07		20 22		20 28	20 48					20 42			21 14		21 28	21 34	21 53			
Bentley (S.Yorks) d						20 31	20 52										21 31		21 56			
Adwick a						20 35	20 57										21 35		22 01			
d						20 35											21 35					
South Elmsall d						20 40											21 40					
Fitzwilliam d						20 45		21 01									21 45			22 01		
Sandal & Agbrigg d	←					20 51		21 08			←		←				21 51			22 08		
Wakefield Westgate 32,39 a	20 18	20 23		20 39		20 55		21 12		20 47	20 55	20 59	21 12		21 30		21 55			22 12		21 47
d	20 19	20 25		20 40		20 55		21 13		20 48	20 55	21 01	21 13		21 31		21 55			22 12		21 48
Pontefract Monkhill 32 d						→		→									→	22 03		→		
Wakefield Kirkgate 32,34,39 a			20 24		20 48				20 55					21 24		21 48		22 20			21 55	
d			20 24		20 49				20 55					21 24		21 49					21 55	
Outwood d	20 24										21 00		21 18									
Leeds 32,34 a	20 36	20 41	20 44	20 54	21 25				21 14	21 02	21 13	21 17	21 30	21 44	21 45	22 25					22 14	22 02

A from 22 February

Table T031-F

Sheffield, Doncaster and Wakefield - Leeds

Saturdays
21 December to 16 May

Station		NT	EM	GR	NT	GR	NT	NT	NT	NT	EM	NT	XC	NT	NT	NT	GR
									A					A			
Sheffield 29	d		21 26					22 07	22 15	22 18	22 21		22 25		22 31		
Meadowhall 29	d							22 13	22 21	22 24					22 37		
Rotherham Central 29	d							22 19	22 28								
Swinton (S.Yorks) 29	d							22 29	22 41								
Bolton-upon-Dearne	d								22 45								
Goldthorpe	d								22 49								
Thurnscoe	d								22 52								
Moorthorpe	d								22 58								
Doncaster	d			21 45		22 23	22 32	22 47					22 55			23 24	23 50
Bentley (S.Yorks)	d						22 35	22 51								23 27	
Adwick	a						22 39	22 55								23 31	
	d						22 39									23 31	
South Elmsall	d						22 45									23 36	
Fitzwilliam	d						22 51		23 12							23 41	
Sandal & Agbrigg	d	←			←		22 56		23 19			←		←		23 47	
Wakefield Westgate 32,39	a	21 55	21 57	22 05	22 12	22 40	23 00		23 23		22 48	23 00	23 12	23 23		23 51	00 06
	d	21 55	21 58	22 06	22 12	22 42	23 01		23 24		22 49	23 01	23 13	23 24		23 51	00 07
Pontefract Monkhill 32	d						→		→								
Wakefield Kirkgate 32,34,39	a									22 55					23 17		
	d									22 55					23 18		
Outwood	d	22 00			22 18							23 05		23 29		23 57	
Leeds 32,34	a	22 12	22 14	22 21	22 29	22 57				23 14	23 07	23 18	23 26	23 41	23 59	00 09	00 22

Sundays
15 December to 10 May

Station		GR	NT	NT	NT	NT	XC	NT	NT	NT	XC	NT	GR	NT	NT	NT	XC	NT	GR	NT	NT	XC	NT	GR
		B																						
Sheffield 29	d			08 27	08 39	09 17	09 21		09 35	10 17	10 21			10 30	10 51	11 16	11 21			11 24	12 16	12 21		
Meadowhall 29	d			08 33	08 45	09 23			09 41	10 23				10 36	10 57	11 22				11 30	12 23			
Rotherham Central 29	d			08 39					09 48					10 42						11 39				
Swinton (S.Yorks) 29	d			08 47					09 56					10 50						11 53				
Bolton-upon-Dearne	d			08 52					10 00					10 55						11 57				
Goldthorpe	d			08 54					10 03					10 57						12 00				
Thurnscoe	d			08 57					10 06					11 00						12 03				
Moorthorpe	d			09 02					10 11					11 05						12 08				
Doncaster	d		08 25					09 25				10 25	10 52					11 25	11 55				12 25	12 52
Bentley (S.Yorks)	d		08 28					09 28				10 28						11 28					12 28	
Adwick	a		08 32					09 32				10 32						11 32					12 32	
	d		08 32					09 32				10 32						11 32					12 32	
South Elmsall	d		08 39					09 39				10 39						11 39					12 39	
Fitzwilliam	d		08 45	09 09				09 45	10 17			10 45		11 12				11 45		12 14			12 45	
Sandal & Agbrigg	d		08 51	09 15				09 51	10 23			10 51		11 18				11 51		12 20			12 51	
Wakefield Westgate 32,39	a		08 55	09 19			09 45	09 55	10 27		10 45	10 55	11 08	11 22			11 45	11 55	12 11	12 24		12 45	12 55	13 08
	d	00 07	08 55	09 20			09 47	09 56	10 28		10 46	10 56	11 10	11 22			11 46	11 56	12 12	12 25		12 46	12 56	13 10
Pontefract Monkhill 32	d																							
Wakefield Kirkgate 32,34,39	a				09 22	09 57				10 53					11 29	11 51					13 02			
	d				09 23	09 59				10 53					11 30	11 52					13 02			
Outwood	d		09 00	09 25				10 01	10 33			11 01		11 27				12 01		12 30			13 01	
Leeds 32,34	a	00 22	09 13	09 39	09 56	10 24	10 02	10 13	10 44	11 13	10 59	11 13	11 24	11 42	12 06	12 11	11 59	12 13	12 28	12 42	13 22	13 00	13 13	13 24

Station		NT	NT	GC	NT	XC	NT	GR	NT	GR	NT	XC	NT	GR	NT	NT	NT	XC	NT	GR	GR	NT	NT
Sheffield 29	d	12 31	12 44		13 17	13 21			13 31		14 17	14 21			14 31	14 44	15 17	15 21				15 31	16 17
Meadowhall 29	d	12 37	12 50		13 23				13 37		14 23				14 37	14 50	15 23					15 37	16 23
Rotherham Central 29	d	12 43							13 43						14 43							15 43	
Swinton (S.Yorks) 29	d	12 51							13 51						14 51							15 51	
Bolton-upon-Dearne	d	12 55							13 56						14 56							15 56	
Goldthorpe	d	12 58							13 58						14 58							15 58	
Thurnscoe	d	13 01							14 01						15 01							16 01	
Moorthorpe	d	13 06							14 06						15 06							16 09	
Doncaster	d			13 21			13 25	13 48		14 20			14 25	14 54					15 25	15 36	15 50		
Bentley (S.Yorks)	d						13 28						14 28						15 28				
Adwick	a						13 32						14 32						15 32				
	d						13 32						14 32						15 32				
South Elmsall	d						13 39						14 38						15 38				
Fitzwilliam	d	13 12					13 45		14 13				14 45		15 13				15 45			16 15	
Sandal & Agbrigg	d	13 18					13 51		14 19				14 51		15 19				15 51			16 21	
Wakefield Westgate 32,39	a	13 22				13 45	13 55	14 04	14 23	14 37		14 45	14 55	15 10	15 23			15 45	15 55	15 59	16 06	16 25	
	d	13 23				13 46	13 56	14 05	14 23	14 38		14 47	14 56	15 11	15 23			15 46	15 56	16 01	16 08	16 26	
Pontefract Monkhill 32	d																						
Wakefield Kirkgate 32,34,39	a		13 29	13 44	13 55						14 55					15 28	15 52						16 56
	d		13 29		13 56						14 56					15 29	15 55						16 57
Outwood	d	13 28					14 01		14 28				15 01		15 28				16 01			16 31	
Leeds 32,34	a	13 42	14 04		14 18	14 00	14 13	14 20	14 43	14 54	15 17	15 00	15 13	15 24	15 44	16 04	16 15	16 00	16 13	16 17	16 23	16 44	17 17

A from 22 February

B not 15 December

Table T031-F

Sheffield, Doncaster and Wakefield - Leeds

Sundays
15 December to 10 May

Station		XC	NT	GR	NT	NT	GC	NT	XC	NT	NT	EM	GR	NT	XC	GR	NT	XC	NT	GR	NT	GR	NT
Sheffield 29	d	16 21			16 31	16 44		17 17	17 21		17 30	17 34			17 52		18 17	18 21			18 31		18 45
Meadowhall 29	d				16 37	16 50		17 23			17 36						18 23				18 37		18 51
Rotherham Central 29	d				16 43						17 42										18 43		
Swinton (S.Yorks) 29	d				16 51						17 52										18 51		
Bolton-upon-Dearne	d				16 56						17 57										18 56		
Goldthorpe	d				16 58						18 00										18 58		
Thurnscoe	d				17 01						18 03										19 01		
Moorthorpe	d				17 08						18 08										19 06		
Doncaster	d		16 25	16 58			17 22			17 25			17 52		18 17	18 21			18 25	18 45		19 16	
Bentley (S.Yorks)	d		16 28							17 28									18 28				
Adwick	a		16 32							17 32									18 32				
	d		16 32							17 32									18 32				
South Elmsall	d		16 39							17 38									18 38				
Fitzwilliam	d		16 45		17 14					17 44	18 14								18 44		19 13		
Sandal & Agbrigg	d		16 51		17 20					17 50	18 20			←					18 50		19 19		
Wakefield Westgate 32,39	a	16 45	16 55	17 14	17 24				17 46	17 54	18 24	18 00	18 08	18 24	18 32	18 37		18 45	18 54	19 03	19 23	19 32	
	d	16 46	16 56	17 15	17 25				17 47	17 55	18 25	18 01	18 10	18 25	18 33	18 39		18 47	18 55	19 04	19 23	19 34	
Pontefract Monkhill 32	d										→												
Wakefield Kirkgate 32,34,39	a					17 28	17 49	17 52									18 52						19 28
	d					17 29		17 53									18 53						19 29
Outwood	d		17 01		17 30					17 59				18 30					19 00		19 29		
Leeds 32,34	a	16 59	17 13	17 28	17 43	18 04		18 17	18 01	18 13		18 16	18 26	18 43	18 47	18 55	19 15	19 01	19 13	19 19	19 43	19 49	20 04

Station		NT	XC	NT	GR	NT	GR	NT	XC	NT	GC	GR	NT	GC	EM	GR	NT	XC	NT	GR	NT	GR	XC	NT
Sheffield 29	d	19 16	19 21			19 31		20 17	20 22				20 31		21 03		21 17	21 21			21 31		22 21	
Meadowhall 29	d	19 23				19 37		20 23					20 37				21 23				21 37			
Rotherham Central 29	d					19 43							20 47								21 44			
Swinton (S.Yorks) 29	d					19 51							20 55								21 52			
Bolton-upon-Dearne	d					19 56							21 00								21 56			
Goldthorpe	d					19 58							21 02								21 59			
Thurnscoe	d					20 01							21 05								22 02			
Moorthorpe	d					20 06							21 10								22 07			
Doncaster	d			19 29	19 50		20 20			20 25	20 39	20 44		21 00		21 21			21 25	21 48		22 24		22 28
Bentley (S.Yorks)	d			19 32						20 28									21 28					22 31
Adwick	a			19 36						20 32									21 32					22 35
	d			19 36						20 32									21 32					22 35
South Elmsall	d			19 42						20 39									21 39					22 41
Fitzwilliam	d			19 47		20 13				20 46			21 18						21 46		22 13			22 47
Sandal & Agbrigg	d			19 53		20 19				20 52			21 24						21 51		22 19			22 52
Wakefield Westgate 32,39	a		19 49	19 57	20 06	20 23	20 38		20 47	20 56		21 02	21 28		21 32	21 37		21 48	21 55	22 05	22 23	22 40	22 48	22 56
	d		19 52	19 57	20 08	20 25	20 39		20 48	20 56		21 03	21 28		21 33	21 39		21 49	21 56	22 06	22 24	22 41	22 49	22 57
Pontefract Monkhill 32	d																							
Wakefield Kirkgate 32,34,39	a	19 52						20 52			21 00			21 23			21 52							
	d	19 53						20 53									21 53							
Outwood	d			20 02		20 30				21 01			21 33						22 00		22 29			23 01
Leeds 32,34	a	20 15	20 07	20 15	20 21	20 44	20 52	21 14	21 02	21 13		21 19	21 45		21 49	21 54	22 15	22 02	22 12	22 21	22 45	22 58	23 02	23 13

Station		GR	NT	NT	EM	GR
Sheffield 29	d		22 32	22 44	23 26	
Meadowhall 29	d		22 38	22 50		
Rotherham Central 29	d		22 44			
Swinton (S.Yorks) 29	d		22 53			
Bolton-upon-Dearne	d		22 57			
Goldthorpe	d		23 00			
Thurnscoe	d		23 03			
Moorthorpe	d		23 08			
Doncaster	d	22 50				23 37
Bentley (S.Yorks)	d					
Adwick	a					
	d					
South Elmsall	d					
Fitzwilliam	d		23 14			
Sandal & Agbrigg	d		23 20			
Wakefield Westgate 32,39	a	23 08	23 24		23 52	23 57
	d	23 10	23 25		23 53	23 59
Pontefract Monkhill 32	d					
Wakefield Kirkgate 32,34,39	a			23 31		
	d			23 32		
Outwood	d		23 30			
Leeds 32,34	a	23 26	23 45	00 07	00 08	00 14

Table T031-R

Mondays to Fridays

16 December to 15 May

Leeds - Wakefield, Doncaster and Sheffield

Miles	Miles			NT	GR	EM	GR	NT	NT	GR	XC	NT		NT	NT	EM	NT	NT	GR	NT	GR	NT	XC	NT	GR
				MX																	A				
0	0	**Leeds** 32,34	d		05 05	05 19	05 30	05 34	05 54	06 05	06 11			06 25	06 32	06 34	06 38		06 40	06 47	07 00	07 03	07 10		07 15
7½	7½	Outwood	d					05 45						06 33				←		06 58					
—	—	Wakefield Kirkgate 32,34,39	a						06 26						07 02		06 55	07 02				07 22			
—	—		d						06 27						07 03		06 56	07 03				07 23			
—	—	Pontefract Monkhill	d												→										
10	10	**Wakefield Westgate** 32,39	a		05 17	05 31	05 42	05 49		06 17	06 22			06 37		06 45			06 52	07 02	07 12		07 22		07 27
—	—		d		05 18	05 32	05 43	05 50		06 18	06 23			06 37		06 47			06 53	07 02			07 23		07 28
11¾	11¾	Sandal & Agbrigg	d					05 53						06 40						07 06					
16½	16½	Fitzwilliam	d					06 01						06 46						07 13					
21	—	South Elmsall	d											06 51											
25¼	—	Adwick	a											06 56											
—	—		d	00 05								06 45		06 57										07 16	
28	—	Bentley (S.Yorks)	d	00 09								06 49		07 01										07 20	
29¾	—	**Doncaster**	a	00 15	05 35	05 57	06 00			06 35		06 54		07 08					07 12					07 25	07 45
—	20¼	Moorthorpe	d					06 15												07 19					
—	23¾	Thurnscoe	d					06 21												07 25					
—	24½	Goldthorpe	d					06 23												07 27					
—	25¾	Bolton-upon-Dearne	d					06 26												07 30					
—	28	Swinton (S.Yorks) 29	a					06 30				07 10								07 34				07 42	
—	32½	Rotherham Central 29	a					06 40				07 18								07 43				07 49	
—	35¼	Meadowhall 29	a					06 50	07 06			07 24					07 26	07 43		07 49		07 52		08 02	
—	38¾	**Sheffield** 29	a			06 23		07 00	07 15		06 51	07 39				07 22	07 34	07 54		07 57		08 00	07 51	08 10	

		NT	NT	GC		NT	NT	NT	NT	GR	NT	NT	XC	NT	GR	NT	NT	GC	NT	NT		NT	NT	GR	NT
Leeds 32,34	d		07 22			07 32	07 38			07 41	07 48	08 04	08 11		08 15		08 22		08 32	08 38				08 45	08 48
Outwood	d		07 31						←		07 59						08 31						←		09 00
Wakefield Kirkgate 32,34,39	a					08 02	07 54		08 02			08 21							09 02	08 54			09 02		
	d			07 40		08 03	07 55		08 03			08 22						08 55	09 03	08 55			09 03		
Pontefract Monkhill	d			07 59		→													→						
Wakefield Westgate 32,39	a		07 35							07 53	08 03		08 22		08 28		08 35							08 57	09 04
	d		07 35							07 54	08 03		08 23		08 30		08 35							08 59	09 04
Sandal & Agbrigg	d		07 39								08 07						08 39								09 08
Fitzwilliam	d		07 45								08 14						08 46								09 15
South Elmsall	d		07 50														08 51								
Adwick	a		07 56														08 56								
	d	07 49	07 56											08 21		08 48	08 57								
Bentley (S.Yorks)	d	07 53	08 00											08 25		08 52	09 01								
Doncaster	a	07 58	08 07	08 28						08 11				08 30	08 47	08 59	09 07	09 24						09 16	
Moorthorpe	d										08 20														09 21
Thurnscoe	d										08 26														09 27
Goldthorpe	d										08 29														09 30
Bolton-upon-Dearne	d										08 32														09 33
Swinton (S.Yorks) 29	a	08 20									08 36			08 47		09 20									09 37
Rotherham Central 29	a	08 28						←			08 45			08 54		09 28						←			09 45
Meadowhall 29	a	08 34					08 26	08 34	08 43		08 51	08 53		09 05		09 34				09 26		09 34	09 42		09 51
Sheffield 29	a	→					08 34	08 44	08 51		09 01	09 04	08 55	09 14		→				09 34		09 44	09 51		10 01

		NT	XC	NT	GR	NT	NT	NT	NT	NT	GR	NT		NT	XC	NT	GR	NT	NT	NT	NT	GR	NT	GC	NT
Leeds 32,34	d	09 09	09 11		09 15	09 21		09 32	09 38		09 45	09 48		10 09	10 11		10 15	10 21	10 32	10 38		10 45	10 48		11 09
Outwood	d					09 30				←		09 59						10 30			←		10 59		
Wakefield Kirkgate 32,34,39	a	09 25						10 02	09 54	10 02				10 25					11 02	10 54	11 02				11 25
	d	09 26						10 03	09 55	10 03				10 26					11 03	10 55	11 03			11 14	11 26
Pontefract Monkhill	d							→											→					11 34	
Wakefield Westgate 32,39	a		09 22		09 27	09 34					09 57	10 03			10 22		10 27	10 34				10 57	11 03		
	d		09 23		09 29	09 34					09 58	10 03			10 23		10 28	10 34				10 58	11 03		
Sandal & Agbrigg	d					09 38						10 07						10 38					11 07		
Fitzwilliam	d					09 45						10 14						10 45					11 14		
South Elmsall	d					09 50												10 50							
Adwick	a					09 56												10 55							
	d			09 25		09 56										10 24		10 56							
Bentley (S.Yorks)	d			09 29		10 00										10 28		11 00							
Doncaster	a			09 34	09 46	10 06					10 16					10 33	10 45	11 06				11 15		12 00	
Moorthorpe	d						09 59					10 20											11 20		
Thurnscoe	d											10 26											11 26		
Goldthorpe	d											10 29											11 29		
Bolton-upon-Dearne	d											10 32											11 32		
Swinton (S.Yorks) 29	a			09 50			10 08					10 36				10 50							11 36		
Rotherham Central 29	a			09 58			10 18					10 45				10 57							11 44		
Meadowhall 29	a	09 56		10 05			10 24		10 26	10 42		10 51		10 56		11 05				11 26	11 42		11 51		11 56
Sheffield 29	a	10 04	09 54	10 14			10 33		10 34	10 52		11 01		11 04	10 55	11 14				11 34	11 51		12 01		12 04

A West Riding Limited

NRT DECEMBER 19 EDITION

Table T031-R

Mondays to Fridays

16 December to 15 May

Leeds - Wakefield, Doncaster and Sheffield

		XC	NT	GR	NT	NT	NT	NT	GR	NT	NT	XC		NT	GR	NT	NT	NT	NT	GR	NT	NT	XC	NT	GR
Leeds 32,34	d	11 11		11 15	11 21	11 32	11 38		11 45	11 48	12 09	12 11			12 15	12 21	12 32	12 38		12 45	12 48	13 09	13 11		13 15
Outwood	d				11 30			←		11 59						12 30			←		12 59				
Wakefield Kirkgate 32,34,39	a					12 02	11 54	12 02			12 25						13 02	12 54	13 02			13 25			
	d					12 03	11 55	12 03			12 26						13 03	12 55	13 03			13 26			
Pontefract Monkhill	d					→											→								
Wakefield Westgate 32,39	a	11 22		11 27	11 34				11 57	12 03		12 22			12 27	12 34				12 57	13 03		13 22		13 27
	d	11 23		11 28	11 34				11 58	12 03		12 23			12 28	12 34				12 58	13 03		13 23		13 28
Sandal & Agbrigg	d				11 38					12 07						12 38					13 07				
Fitzwilliam	d				11 44					12 14						12 44					13 14				
South Elmsall	d				11 50											12 50									
Adwick	a				11 55											12 55									
	d		11 24		11 56									12 24		12 56								13 24	
Bentley (S.Yorks)	d		11 28		12 00									12 28		13 00								13 28	
Doncaster	a		11 33	11 45	12 06				12 15					12 33	12 45	13 06				13 16				13 33	13 45
Moorthorpe	d									12 20											13 20				
Thurnscoe	d									12 26											13 26				
Goldthorpe	d									12 29											13 29				
Bolton-upon-Dearne	d									12 32											13 32				
Swinton (S.Yorks) 29	a		11 50							12 36				12 50							13 36			13 50	
Rotherham Central 29	a		11 57							12 45				12 57							13 45			13 57	
Meadowhall 29	a		12 05				12 26	12 42		12 51	12 56			13 05				13 26	13 42		13 51	13 56		14 05	
Sheffield 29	a	11 54	12 14				12 34	12 52		13 01	13 04	12 55		13 14				13 34	13 51		14 01	14 04	13 54	14 14	

		NT	NT	NT		NT	NT	GR	NT	NT	XC	NT	GR	NT	NT	NT	NT	GR	NT	NT		XC	NT	GR	NT
Leeds 32,34	d	13 21		13 32		13 38		13 45	13 48	14 09	14 11		14 15	14 21	14 32	14 38		14 45	14 48	15 09		15 11		15 15	15 21
Outwood	d	13 30					←		13 59					14 30			←		14 59						15 30
Wakefield Kirkgate 32,34,39	a			14 02		13 54	14 02			14 25					15 02	14 54	15 02			15 25					
	d			14 03		13 55	14 03			14 26					15 03	14 55	15 03			15 26					
Pontefract Monkhill	d			→											→										
Wakefield Westgate 32,39	a	13 34						13 57	14 03		14 22		14 27	14 34				14 57	15 03			15 22		15 27	15 34
	d	13 34						13 58	14 03		14 23		14 28	14 35				14 58	15 03			15 23		15 28	15 35
Sandal & Agbrigg	d	13 38							14 07					14 38					15 07						15 38
Fitzwilliam	d	13 44							14 14					14 45					15 14						15 45
South Elmsall	d	13 50												14 50											15 50
Adwick	a	13 55												14 55											15 55
	d	13 56										14 24		14 56									15 24		15 56
Bentley (S.Yorks)	d	14 00										14 28		15 00									15 28		16 00
Doncaster	a	14 06						14 15				14 33	14 45	15 06				15 15					15 33	15 45	16 06
Moorthorpe	d		13 58						14 20										15 20						
Thurnscoe	d								14 26										15 26						
Goldthorpe	d								14 29										15 29						
Bolton-upon-Dearne	d								14 32										15 32						
Swinton (S.Yorks) 29	a		14 09						14 36			14 50							15 36				15 50		
Rotherham Central 29	a		14 18						14 44			14 57							15 45				15 57		
Meadowhall 29	a		14 24			14 26	14 42		14 51	14 56		15 05				15 26	15 42		15 51	15 56			16 05		
Sheffield 29	a		14 32			14 34	14 51		15 01	15 04	14 55	15 14				15 34	15 52		16 01	16 04		15 55	16 14		

		GC	NT	NT	NT	GR	NT	NT	XC	NT	GR	NT		NT	NT	XC	NT	GR	NT	NT	XC	NT	GR	NT	NT
Leeds 32,34	d		15 32	15 38		15 45	15 48	16 09	16 11		16 15	16 21		16 32	16 38	16 41		16 45	16 48	17 09	17 11		17 14	17 22	
Outwood	d				←		15 59					16 30					←		17 00					17 31	
Wakefield Kirkgate 32,34,39	a		16 02	15 54	16 02			16 25						17 02	16 54		17 02			17 26					
	d	15 39	16 03	15 55	16 03			16 26						17 03	16 55		17 03			17 27					
Pontefract Monkhill	d	15 55	→											→											
Wakefield Westgate 32,39	a					15 57	16 03		16 22		16 27	16 34				16 52		16 57	17 04		17 22		17 26	17 35	
	d					15 58	16 03		16 23		16 28	16 34				16 53		16 58	17 04		17 23		17 27	17 35	
Sandal & Agbrigg	d						16 07					16 38							17 08					17 39	
Fitzwilliam	d						16 14					16 44							17 14					17 45	
South Elmsall	d											16 49												17 50	
Adwick	a											16 55												17 56	
	d									16 24		16 55										17 24		17 56	
Bentley (S.Yorks)	d									16 28		16 59										17 28		18 00	
Doncaster	a	16 17				16 15				16 33	16 45	17 06						17 16				17 33	17 44	18 07	
Moorthorpe	d						16 20												17 20						17 57
Thurnscoe	d						16 26												17 26						
Goldthorpe	d						16 29												17 28						
Bolton-upon-Dearne	d						16 32												17 31						
Swinton (S.Yorks) 29	a						16 36			16 50									17 35			17 51			18 06
Rotherham Central 29	a						16 45			16 57									17 45			17 58			18 18
Meadowhall 29	a			16 26	16 42		16 51	16 56		17 05					17 26		17 42		17 51	17 56		18 05			18 24
Sheffield 29	a			16 34	16 51		17 01	17 04	16 54	17 14					17 34	17 21	17 51		18 01	18 04	17 54	18 14			18 32

Table T031-R

Leeds - Wakefield, Doncaster and Sheffield

Mondays to Fridays

16 December to 15 May

	NT	NT	NT	GR	NT	NT	NT	NT	XC	NT	GR	NT	NT	NT	NT	GR	NT	NT	XC	NT	GR	NT	NT
		◇		■1 🍴			◇	◇	◇■1 🍴		■1 🍴	◇		◇		■1 🍴		◇	◇■1 🍴		■1 🍴	◇	
Leeds 10 32,34 d	17 32	17 38		17 45	17 48		17 57	18 03	18 11		18 15	18 22	18 32	18 38		18 45	18 48	19 03	19 11		19 16	19 22	19 32
Outwood d			←		17 59		18 06					18 31			←		18 59					19 31	
Wakefield Kirkgate 4 32,34,39 a	18 02	17 54	18 02						18 21				19 02	18 56	19 02			19 20					20 02
d	18 03	17 55	18 03						18 22				19 03	18 57	19 03			19 21					20 03
Pontefract Monkhill d	→												→										
Wakefield Westgate 7 32,39 a				17 57	18 03		18 10		18 22		18 27	18 35				18 57	19 03		19 22		19 28	19 35	
d				17 58	18 03		18 10		18 23		18 28	18 35				18 58	19 03		19 23		19 29	19 35	
Sandal & Agbrigg d					18 07		18 14					18 39					19 07					19 39	
Fitzwilliam d					18 14		18 20					18 45					19 14					19 45	
South Elmsall d							18 25					18 50										19 50	
Adwick a							18 31					18 56										19 56	
d						18 24	18 31					18 56								19 24		19 56	
Bentley (S.Yorks) d						18 28	18 35					19 00								19 28		20 00	
Doncaster 7 a				18 16		18 33	18 42				18 45	19 07				19 17				19 33	19 46	20 07	
Moorthorpe d					18 20												19 20						
Thurnscoe d					18 26												19 26						
Goldthorpe d					18 29												19 29						
Bolton-upon-Dearne d					18 32												19 32						
Swinton (S.Yorks) 29 a					18 36	18 50											19 36			19 50			
Rotherham Central 29 a					18 45	18 57				←							19 45			19 57			
Meadowhall 29 a		18 26	18 42		18 51	19 05		18 52		19 05				19 27	19 42		19 51	19 51		20 05			20 42
Sheffield 7 29 a		18 34	18 51		19 01	→		19 04	18 54	19 14				19 35	19 51		20 01	20 04	19 55	20 14			20 51

	GR	NT	NT	XC	NT	NT	NT	GR	NT	NT	XC	NT	NT	NT	NT	NT	NT	NT	NT	NT	NT	NT
	■1 🍴		◇	◇■1		◇		■1 🍴		◇	◇■1		◇		◇				◇			
Leeds 10 32,34 d	19 45	19 48	20 04	20 10		20 22	20 32	20 45	20 48	21 04	21 11		21 22	21 32	21 37		21 48		22 22	22 30	22 32	23 02
Outwood d		19 59				20 31			20 59				21 31			←	21 59		22 31	22 41		
Wakefield Kirkgate 4 32,34,39 a			20 21				21 02			21 20				22 02	21 53	22 02					23 02	23 33
d			20 22				21 03			21 21				22 03	21 53	22 03					23 03	23 34
Pontefract Monkhill d														→								
Wakefield Westgate 7 32,39 a	19 57	20 03		20 21		20 35		20 57	21 03		21 22		21 35				22 03		22 35	22 45		
d	19 58	20 03		20 23		20 35		20 58	21 03		21 23		21 35				22 03		22 35	22 45		
Sandal & Agbrigg d		20 07				20 39			21 07				21 39				22 07		22 39	22 49		
Fitzwilliam d		20 14				20 45			21 14				21 45				22 14		22 45	22 56		
South Elmsall d						20 50							21 50						22 50			
Adwick a						20 56							21 56						22 56			
d					20 24	20 56						21 24	21 56					22 23	22 56			
Bentley (S.Yorks) d					20 28	21 00						21 28	22 00					22 27	23 00			
Doncaster 7 a	20 15				20 33	21 07		21 15				21 33	22 07					22 34	23 07			
Moorthorpe d		20 20							21 20								22 26			23 02		
Thurnscoe d		20 26							21 26								22 32			23 08		
Goldthorpe d		20 29							21 29								22 34			23 11		
Bolton-upon-Dearne d		20 32							21 32								22 37			23 14		
Swinton (S.Yorks) 29 a		20 36			20 50				21 36			21 50					22 41	22 52		23 18		
Rotherham Central 29 a		20 45			20 57				21 44			21 57					22 49	22 59		23 27		
Meadowhall 29 a		20 51	20 51		21 07		21 42		21 51	21 53		22 05			22 25	22 42	22 55	23 05		23 33	23 42	00 13
Sheffield 7 29 a		21 04	21 01	20 54	21 17		21 51		21 59	22 02	21 54	22 14			22 40	22 51	23 04	23 14		23 41	23 51	00 24

	NT	NT
		◇
Leeds 10 32,34 d	23 11	23 31
Outwood d	23 22	23 40
Wakefield Kirkgate 4 32,34,39 a		
d		
Pontefract Monkhill d		
Wakefield Westgate 7 32,39 a	23 26	23 44
d	23 26	23 44
Sandal & Agbrigg d	23 30	23 48
Fitzwilliam d	23 37	23 54
South Elmsall d		23 59
Adwick a		00 05
d		00 05
Bentley (S.Yorks) d		00 09
Doncaster 7 a		00 15
Moorthorpe d	23 45	
Thurnscoe d	23 51	
Goldthorpe d	23 53	
Bolton-upon-Deame d	23 56	
Swinton (S.Yorks) 29 a	00 01	
Rotherham Central 29 a	00 12	
Meadowhall 29 a	00 19	
Sheffield 7 29 a	00 28	

Table T031-R

Leeds - Wakefield, Doncaster and Sheffield

Saturdays

21 December to 16 May

	NT	GR	GR	NT	NT	GR	XC	NT	NT	NT	EM	NT	NT	GR	NT	GR	NT	XC	NT	GR	NT	NT
	◇	■1 🍴	■1 🍴			■1 🍴	◇■1 🍴		◇		◇■1 ⊠	◇		■1 🍴		■1 A 🍴	◇	◇■1 🍴		■1 🍴		◇
Leeds 10 32,34 d		05 05	05 30	05 34	05 54	06 05	06 11		06 25	06 32	06 34	06 38		06 40	06 47	07 00	07 03	07 11		07 15		07 22
Outwood d				05 45					06 33				←		06 58							07 31
Wakefield Kirkgate 4 32,34,39 a					06 26					07 02		06 55	07 02				07 21					
d					06 27					07 03		06 56	07 03				07 22					
Pontefract Monkhill d										→												
Wakefield Westgate 7 32,39 a		05 17	05 42	05 49		06 17	06 22		06 37		06 45			06 52	07 02	07 12		07 22		07 27		07 35
d		05 18	05 43	05 50		06 18	06 23		06 37		06 46			06 53	07 02			07 23		07 28		07 35
Sandal & Agbrigg d				05 53					06 40						07 06							07 39
Fitzwilliam d				06 01					06 46						07 13							07 45
South Elmsall d									06 51													07 50
Adwick a									06 56													07 56
d	00 05							06 45	06 57										07 16		07 49	07 56
Bentley (S.Yorks) d	00 09							06 49	07 01										07 20		07 53	08 00
Doncaster 7 a	00 15	05 35	06 00			06 35		06 54	07 08					07 12					07 25	07 45	07 58	08 07
Moorthorpe d				06 15											07 19							
Thurnscoe d				06 21											07 25							
Goldthorpe d				06 23											07 27							
Bolton-upon-Dearne d				06 26											07 30							
Swinton (S.Yorks) 29 a				06 33				07 10							07 34				07 42		08 20	
Rotherham Central 29 a				06 41				07 18							07 43				07 49		08 28	
Meadowhall 29 a				06 48	07 06			07 24				07 26	07 43		07 49		07 52		08 02		08 34	
Sheffield 7 29 a				07 00	07 15		06 51	07 39			07 24	07 34	07 55		07 57		08 00	07 51	08 10		→	

	GC	NT	NT	EM	NT	NT	NT	NT	XC	NT	GR	NT	NT	NT	NT	NT	NT	GR	NT	NT	XC	NT	GR
	■1 🍴		◇	◇■1 🍴				◇	◇■1 🍴		■1 🍴		◇		◇			■1 🍴		◇	◇■1 🍴		■1 🍴
Leeds 10 32,34 d		07 32	07 38	07 40			07 48	08 04	08 11		08 15		08 22	08 32	08 38			08 45	08 48	09 09	09 11		09 15
Outwood d						←	07 59						08 31				←		09 00				
Wakefield Kirkgate 4 32,34,39 a		08 02	07 54			08 02		08 21						09 02	08 54		09 02			09 25			
d	07 40	08 03	07 55			08 03		08 22						09 03	08 55		09 03			09 26			
Pontefract Monkhill d	07 59	→												→									
Wakefield Westgate 7 32,39 a				07 51			08 03		08 22		08 28		08 35					08 57	09 04		09 22		09 27
d				07 53			08 03		08 23		08 30		08 35					08 59	09 04		09 23		09 29
Sandal & Agbrigg d							08 07						08 39						09 08				
Fitzwilliam d							08 14						08 46						09 15				
South Elmsall d													08 51										
Adwick a													08 56										
d										08 21		08 48	08 57									09 25	
Bentley (S.Yorks) d										08 25		08 52	09 01									09 29	
Doncaster 7 a	08 28									08 30	08 47	08 59	09 07					09 16				09 34	09 46
Moorthorpe d							08 20												09 21				
Thurnscoe d							08 26												09 27				
Goldthorpe d							08 29												09 30				
Bolton-upon-Dearne d							08 32												09 33				
Swinton (S.Yorks) 29 a							08 36			08 47		09 20							09 37			09 50	
Rotherham Central 29 a					←		08 45			08 54		09 28				←			09 45			09 58	
Meadowhall 29 a			08 26		08 34	08 42	08 51	08 53		09 05		09 34			09 26	09 34	09 42		09 51	09 56		10 05	
Sheffield 7 29 a			08 34	08 25	08 44	08 50	09 00	09 04	08 54	09 14		→			09 34	09 44	09 51		10 01	10 04	09 54	10 14	

	NT	GC	NT	NT	NT	NT	GR	NT	NT	XC	NT	GR	NT	NT	NT	NT	GR	NT	GC	NT	XC	NT
	◇	■1 🍴	◇		◇		■1 🍴		◇	◇■1 🍴		■1 🍴	◇		◇		■1 🍴		■1 🍴	◇	◇■1 🍴	
Leeds 10 32,34 d	09 21			09 32	09 38		09 45	09 48	10 09	10 11		10 15	10 21	10 32	10 38		10 45	10 48		11 09	11 11	
Outwood d	09 30					←		09 59					10 30			←		10 59				
Wakefield Kirkgate 4 32,34,39 a				10 02	09 54	10 02			10 25					11 02	10 54	11 02				11 25		
d		09 40		10 03	09 55	10 03			10 26					11 03	10 55	11 03			11 14	11 26		
Pontefract Monkhill d		09 57		→										→					11 32			
Wakefield Westgate 7 32,39 a	09 34						09 57	10 03		10 22		10 27	10 34				10 57	11 03			11 22	
d	09 34						09 58	10 03		10 23		10 28	10 34				10 58	11 03			11 23	
Sandal & Agbrigg d	09 38							10 07					10 38					11 07				
Fitzwilliam d	09 45							10 14					10 45					11 14				
South Elmsall d	09 50												10 50									
Adwick a	09 56												10 55									
d	09 56										10 24		10 56									11 24
Bentley (S.Yorks) d	10 00										10 28		11 00									11 28
Doncaster 7 a	10 06	10 23					10 15				10 33	10 45	11 06				11 16		12 01			11 33
Moorthorpe d			09 59					10 20										11 20				
Thurnscoe d								10 26										11 26				
Goldthorpe d								10 29										11 29				
Bolton-upon-Dearne d								10 32										11 32				
Swinton (S.Yorks) 29 a			10 08					10 36			10 50							11 36				11 50
Rotherham Central 29 a			10 18					10 45			10 57							11 44				11 57
Meadowhall 29 a			10 24		10 26	10 42		10 51	10 56		11 05				11 26	11 42		11 51		11 56		12 05
Sheffield 7 29 a			10 33		10 34	10 52		11 01	11 04	10 54	11 14				11 34	11 51		12 01		12 04	11 54	12 14

A West Riding Limited

Table T031-R

Saturdays

21 December to 16 May

Leeds - Wakefield, Doncaster and Sheffield

Station			GR	NT	NT	NT	NT	GR	NT	NT	XC	NT	GR	NT	NT	NT	NT	GR	NT	NT	XC	NT	GR	NT
			■ 1 ⊡		◇		◇	■ 1 ⊡		◇	◇1 ⊼		■ 1 ⊡	◇		◇		■ 1 ⊡		◇	◇1 ⊼		■ 1 ⊡	◇
Leeds 10	32,34	d	11 15	11 21	11 32	11 38		11 45	11 48	12 09	12 11		12 15	12 21	12 32	12 38		12 45	12 48	13 09	13 11		13 15	13 21
Outwood		d		11 30			←		11 59					12 30			←		12 59					13 30
Wakefield Kirkgate 4	32,34,39	a			12 02	11 54	12 02			12 25					13 02	12 54	13 02			13 25				
		d			12 03	11 55	12 03			12 26					13 03	12 55	13 03			13 26				
Pontefract Monkhill		d			→										→									
Wakefield Westgate 7	32,39	a	11 28	11 34				11 57	12 03		12 22		12 27	12 34				12 57	13 03		13 22		13 27	13 34
		d	11 29	11 34				11 58	12 03		12 23		12 28	12 34				12 58	13 03		13 23		13 28	13 34
Sandal & Agbrigg		d		11 38					12 07					12 38					13 07					13 38
Fitzwilliam		d		11 44					12 14					12 44					13 14					13 44
South Elmsall		d		11 50										12 50										13 50
Adwick		a		11 55										12 55										13 55
		d		11 56								12 24		12 56								13 24		13 56
Bentley (S.Yorks)		d		12 00								12 28		13 00								13 28		14 00
Doncaster 7		a	11 46	12 06				12 15				12 33	12 45	13 06				13 16				13 33	13 45	14 06
Moorthorpe		d							12 20										13 20					
Thurnscoe		d							12 26										13 26					
Goldthorpe		d							12 29										13 29					
Bolton-upon-Dearne		d							12 32										13 32					
Swinton (S.Yorks)	29	a							12 36			12 50							13 36			13 50		
Rotherham Central	29	a							12 45			12 57							13 45			13 57		
Meadowhall	29	a				12 26	12 42		12 51	12 56		13 05				13 26	13 42		13 51	13 56		14 05		
Sheffield 7	29	a				12 34	12 52		13 01	13 04	12 55	13 14				13 34	13 51		14 01	14 04	13 54	14 14		

Station			NT	NT	NT	NT	GR	NT	NT	XC	NT	GR	NT	NT	NT	NT	GR	NT	NT	XC	NT	GR	NT	NT	NT
			◇		◇		■ 1 ⊡		◇	◇1 ⊼		■ 1 ⊡	◇		◇		■ 1 ⊡		◇	◇1 ⊼		■ 1 ⊡	◇		◇
Leeds 10	32,34	d		13 32	13 38		13 45	13 48	14 09	14 11		14 15	14 21	14 32	14 38		14 45	14 48	15 09	15 11		15 15	15 21	15 32	15 38
Outwood		d				←		13 59					14 30			←		14 59					15 30		
Wakefield Kirkgate 4	32,34,39	a		14 02	13 54	14 02			14 25					15 02	14 54	15 02			15 25					16 02	15 54
		d		14 03	13 55	14 03			14 26					15 03	14 55	15 03			15 26					16 03	15 55
Pontefract Monkhill		d		→										→										→	
Wakefield Westgate 7	32,39	a					13 57	14 03		14 22		14 27	14 34				14 57	15 03		15 22		15 27	15 34		
		d					13 58	14 03		14 23		14 28	14 35				14 58	15 03		15 23		15 28	15 35		
Sandal & Agbrigg		d						14 07					14 38					15 07					15 38		
Fitzwilliam		d						14 14					14 45					15 14					15 45		
South Elmsall		d											14 50										15 50		
Adwick		a											14 55										15 55		
		d									14 24		14 56								15 24		15 56		
Bentley (S.Yorks)		d									14 28		15 00								15 28		16 00		
Doncaster 7		a					14 15				14 33	14 45	15 06				15 15				15 33	15 45	16 06		
Moorthorpe		d	13 58					14 20										15 20							
Thurnscoe		d						14 26										15 26							
Goldthorpe		d						14 29										15 29							
Bolton-upon-Dearne		d						14 32										15 32							
Swinton (S.Yorks)	29	a	14 09					14 36			14 50							15 36			15 50				
Rotherham Central	29	a	14 18					14 44			14 57							15 45			15 57				
Meadowhall	29	a	14 24		14 26	14 42		14 51	14 56		15 05				15 26	15 42		15 51	15 56		16 05				16 26
Sheffield 7	29	a	14 32		14 34	14 51		15 01	15 04	14 54	15 14				15 34	15 52		16 01	16 04	15 55	16 14				16 34

Station			NT	GR	NT	GC	NT	XC	NT	GR	NT	NT	NT	XC	NT	GR	NT	NT	XC	NT	GR	NT	NT	NT
				■ 1 ⊡		■ 1 ⊡	◇	◇1 ⊼		■ 1 ⊡	◇		◇	◇1 ⊼		■ 1 ⊡		◇	◇1 ⊼		■ 1 ⊡	◇	◇	
Leeds 10	32,34	d		15 45	15 48		16 09	16 11		16 15	16 21	16 32	16 38	16 41		16 45	16 48	17 09	17 11		17 14	17 22		17 32
Outwood		d	←		15 59						16 30				←		17 00					17 31		
Wakefield Kirkgate 4	32,34,39	a	16 02				16 25					17 02	16 54		17 02			17 26						18 02
		d	16 03			16 14	16 26					17 03	16 55		17 03			17 27						18 03
Pontefract Monkhill		d				16 33						→												→
Wakefield Westgate 7	32,39	a		15 57	16 03			16 22		16 27	16 34			16 52		16 57	17 04		17 22		17 26	17 35		
		d		15 58	16 03			16 23		16 28	16 34			16 53		16 58	17 04		17 23		17 27	17 35		
Sandal & Agbrigg		d			16 07						16 38						17 08					17 39		
Fitzwilliam		d			16 14						16 44						17 14					17 45		
South Elmsall		d									16 49											17 50		
Adwick		a									16 55											17 56		
		d							16 24		16 55									17 24		17 56		
Bentley (S.Yorks)		d							16 28		16 59									17 28		18 00		
Doncaster 7		a		16 16		17 06			16 33	16 45	17 06					17 16				17 33	17 44	18 07		
Moorthorpe		d			16 20												17 20						17 57	
Thurnscoe		d			16 26												17 26							
Goldthorpe		d			16 29												17 28							
Bolton-upon-Dearne		d			16 32												17 31							
Swinton (S.Yorks)	29	a			16 36				16 50								17 35			17 51			18 06	
Rotherham Central	29	a			16 45				16 57								17 45			17 58			18 18	
Meadowhall	29	a	16 42		16 51		16 56		17 05				17 26		17 42		17 51	17 56		18 05			18 24	
Sheffield 7	29	a	16 51		17 01		17 04	16 54	17 14				17 34	17 21	17 51		18 01	18 04	17 54	18 14			18 32	

Table T031-R

Saturdays

21 December to 16 May

Leeds - Wakefield, Doncaster and Sheffield

Station			NT	NT	GR	NT	NT	NT	NT	XC	NT	GR	NT	NT	NT	NT	GR	NT	NT	XC	NT	GR	NT	NT
			◇		■ 1 ⊡			◇	◇	◇1 ⊼		■ 1 ⊡	◇		◇		■ 1 ⊡		◇	◇1 ⊼		■ 1 ⊡	◇	
Leeds 10	32,34	d	17 38		17 45	17 48		17 57	18 03	18 11		18 15	18 22	18 32	18 38		18 45	18 48	19 03	19 11		19 16	19 22	19 32
Outwood		d		←		17 59		18 06					18 31			←		18 59					19 31	
Wakefield Kirkgate 4	32,34,39	a	17 54	18 02					18 21					19 02	18 56	19 02			19 20					20 02
		d	17 55	18 03					18 22					19 03	18 57	19 03			19 21					20 03
Pontefract Monkhill		d												→										
Wakefield Westgate 7	32,39	a			17 57	18 03		18 10		18 22		18 27	18 35				18 57	19 03		19 22		19 28	19 35	
		d			17 58	18 03		18 10		18 23		18 28	18 35				18 58	19 03		19 23		19 29	19 35	
Sandal & Agbrigg		d				18 07		18 14					18 39					19 07					19 39	
Fitzwilliam		d				18 14		18 20					18 45					19 14					19 45	
South Elmsall		d						18 25					18 50										19 50	
Adwick		a						18 31					18 56										19 56	
		d					18 24	18 31					18 56								19 24		19 56	
Bentley (S.Yorks)		d					18 28	18 35					19 00								19 28		20 00	
Doncaster 7		a			18 16		18 33	18 42				18 46	19 07				19 15				19 33	19 46	20 07	
Moorthorpe		d				18 20												19 20						
Thurnscoe		d				18 26												19 26						
Goldthorpe		d				18 29												19 29						
Bolton-upon-Dearne		d				18 32												19 32						
Swinton (S.Yorks)	29	a				18 36	18 50											19 36			19 50			
Rotherham Central	29	a				18 45	18 57				←							19 45			19 57			
Meadowhall	29	a	18 26	18 42		18 51	19 05		18 52		19 05				19 27	19 42		19 51	19 51		20 05			20 42
Sheffield 7	29	a	18 34	18 51		19 01	→		19 04	18 54	19 14				19 35	19 51		20 01	20 04	19 54	20 14			20 51

Station			GR	NT	NT	XC	NT	GR	NT	NT	NT	NT	XC	NT	NT	NT	NT	NT	NT	NT	NT	NT	NT	NT	NT
			■ 1 ⊡		◇	◇1		■ 1 ⊡	◇			◇	◇1		◇		◇					◇			◇
Leeds 10	32,34	d	19 45	19 48	20 04	20 10		20 15	20 22	20 32	20 48	21 04	21 11		21 22	21 32	21 37		21 48		22 15	22 22	22 32	22 44	23 31
Outwood		d		19 59					20 31		20 59				21 31			←	21 59		22 26	22 31		22 55	23 40
Wakefield Kirkgate 4	32,34,39	a			20 21					21 02		21 20				22 02	21 53	22 02					23 02		
		d			20 22					21 03		21 21				22 03	21 53	22 03					23 03		
Pontefract Monkhill		d														→									
Wakefield Westgate 7	32,39	a	19 57	20 03		20 21		20 27	20 35		21 03		21 22		21 35				22 03		22 30	22 35		22 59	23 44
		d	19 58	20 03		20 23		20 28	20 35		21 03		21 23		21 35				22 03		22 30	22 35		22 59	23 44
Sandal & Agbrigg		d		20 07					20 39		21 07				21 39				22 07		22 34	22 39		23 03	23 48
Fitzwilliam		d		20 14					20 45		21 14				21 45				22 14		22 40	22 45		23 09	23 54
South Elmsall		d							20 50						21 50							22 50			23 59
Adwick		a							20 56						21 56							22 56			00 05
		d					20 24		20 56					21 24	21 56					22 23		22 56			00 05
Bentley (S.Yorks)		d					20 28		21 00					21 28	22 00					22 27		23 00			00 09
Doncaster 7		a	20 15				20 33	20 46	21 07					21 33	22 07					22 34		23 07			00 15
Moorthorpe		d		20 20							21 20								22 26		22 46			23 16	
Thurnscoe		d		20 26							21 26								22 32		22 52			23 22	
Goldthorpe		d		20 29							21 29								22 34		22 54			23 24	
Bolton-upon-Dearne		d		20 32							21 32								22 37		22 57			23 27	
Swinton (S.Yorks)	29	a		20 36			20 50				21 36			21 50					22 41	22 52	23 01			23 31	
Rotherham Central	29	a		20 45			20 57				21 44			21 57					22 49	22 59	23 09			23 39	
Meadowhall	29	a		20 51	20 51		21 07			21 42	21 51	21 51		22 05			22 25	22 42	22 55	23 05	23 15		23 42	23 45	
Sheffield 7	29	a		21 04	21 01	20 54	21 17			21 51	21 59	22 02	21 53	22 14			22 40	22 51	23 04	23 14	23 25		23 51	23 55	

Sundays

15 December to 10 May

Station			NT	GR	XC	NT	GC	NT	GR	NT	XC	GR	NT	NT	NT	GR	EM	XC	GR	NT	NT	NT	NT	GR	EM
			◇ A	■ 1 ⊡	◇1 ⊼	◇	■ 1 ⊡		■ 1 ⊡		◇1 ⊼	■ 1 ⊡	◇	◇		■ 1 ⊡	◇1 ⊡	◇1 ⊼	■ 1 ⊡	◇		◇		■ 1 ⊡	◇1 ⊡
Leeds 10	32,34	d		08 05	08 10	08 21		08 33	08 40	08 46	09 00	09 05	09 09	09 20	09 25	09 40	09 50	10 01	10 05	10 09	10 18	10 20	10 31	10 45	10 50
Outwood		d				08 30				08 57				09 29								10 29	10 42		
Wakefield Kirkgate 4	32,34,39	a						09 02					09 25							10 25	10 47				
		d					08 45	09 03					09 25							10 25	10 47				
Pontefract Monkhill		d																							
Wakefield Westgate 7	32,39	a		08 17	08 22	08 34			08 52	09 01	09 11	09 17		09 33	09 38	09 52	10 01	10 12	10 17			10 33	10 46	10 57	11 01
		d		08 18	08 23	08 34			08 55	09 01	09 12	09 18		09 33	09 39		10 02	10 14	10 18			10 33	10 47	10 58	11 03
Sandal & Agbrigg		d				08 38				09 05				09 37								10 37	10 51		
Fitzwilliam		d				08 44				09 11				09 43	09 47							10 43	10 57		
South Elmsall		d				08 49								09 48								10 48			
Adwick		a				08 55								09 54								10 54			
		d	00 05			08 55								09 54								10 54			
Bentley (S.Yorks)		d	00 09			08 59								09 58								10 58			
Doncaster 7		a	00 15	08 35		09 07	09 09		09 14		09 29	09 37		10 05				10 31	10 35			11 06		11 16	
Moorthorpe		d								09 17					09 53								11 04		
Thurnscoe		d								09 23					09 59								11 10		
Goldthorpe		d								09 25					10 01								11 12		
Bolton-upon-Dearne		d								09 28					10 04								11 15		
Swinton (S.Yorks)	29	a								09 32					10 08								11 19		
Rotherham Central	29	a								09 39					10 17								11 29		
Meadowhall	29	a						09 41		09 45			09 56		10 27					10 56	11 29		11 37		
Sheffield 7	29	a			08 52			09 50		09 53	09 56		10 03		10 36		10 30	10 54		11 03	11 38		11 45		11 41

A not 15 December

Table T031-R

Sundays
15 December to 10 May

Leeds - Wakefield, Doncaster and Sheffield

Station		XC	GR	NT	NT	NT	GR	NT	XC	NT	NT	NT	GC
		◇1	1	◇	◇		1	◇	◇1		◇		1
Leeds 32,34	d	11 00	11 05	11 09	11 21	11 48	12 05	12 09	12 11	12 17	12 21	12 48	
Outwood	d				11 30	11 59					12 30	12 59	
Wakefield Kirkgate 32,34,39	a			11 25				12 25		12 46			
	d			11 25				12 25		12 46			12 56
Pontefract Monkhill	d												
Wakefield Westgate 32,39	a	11 11	11 17		11 34	12 03	12 17		12 22		12 34	13 03	
	d	11 12	11 18		11 34	12 03	12 18		12 24		12 34	13 03	
Sandal & Agbrigg	d				11 38	12 07					12 38	13 07	
Fitzwilliam	d				11 44	12 13					12 44	13 13	
South Elmsall	d				11 49						12 49		
Adwick	a				11 55						12 55		
	d				11 55						12 55		
Bentley (S.Yorks)	d				11 59						12 59		
Doncaster	a	11 28	11 35		12 08		12 35				13 08		13 19
Moorthorpe	d					12 19						13 19	
Thurnscoe	d					12 25						13 25	
Goldthorpe	d					12 27						13 27	
Bolton-upon-Dearne	d					12 30						13 30	
Swinton (S.Yorks) 29	a					12 34						13 34	
Rotherham Central 29	a					12 42						13 44	
Meadowhall 29	a			11 56		12 50		12 56		13 30		13 51	
Sheffield 29	a	11 54		12 03		12 58		13 03	12 53	13 38		13 59	

Station		GR	NT	XC		NT	NT	GR	NT	XC	NT	NT	EM
		1	◇	◇1		◇		1	◇	◇1		◇	◇1
Leeds 32,34	d	13 05	13 09	13 11		13 21	13 48	14 05	14 09	14 11	14 17	14 21	14 34
Outwood	d					13 30	13 59					14 30	
Wakefield Kirkgate 32,34,39	a		13 25						14 25		14 46		
	d		13 25						14 25		14 46		
Pontefract Monkhill	d												
Wakefield Westgate 32,39	a	13 17		13 22		13 34	14 03	14 17		14 22		14 34	14 45
	d	13 18		13 24		13 34	14 03	14 18		14 23		14 34	14 47
Sandal & Agbrigg	d					13 38	14 07					14 38	
Fitzwilliam	d					13 44	14 13					14 44	
South Elmsall	d					13 49						14 49	
Adwick	a					13 55						14 55	
	d					13 55						14 55	
Bentley (S.Yorks)	d					13 59						14 59	
Doncaster	a	13 35				14 08		14 35				15 08	
Moorthorpe	d						14 19						
Thurnscoe	d						14 25						
Goldthorpe	d						14 27						
Bolton-upon-Dearne	d						14 30						
Swinton (S.Yorks) 29	a						14 34						
Rotherham Central 29	a						14 43						
Meadowhall 29	a		13 56				14 49		14 56		15 31		
Sheffield 29	a		14 03	13 54			14 57		15 03	14 51	15 39		15 18

Station		NT	GR	NT	XC	NT	NT	GC		NT	XC	GR	GC
			1	◇	◇1	◇		1		◇	◇1	1	1
Leeds 32,34	d	14 46	15 05	15 09	15 11	15 21	15 42			16 09	16 11	16 16	
Outwood	d	14 59				15 30	15 53						
Wakefield Kirkgate 32,34,39	a			15 25						16 25			
	d			15 25				16 02		16 25			16 44
Pontefract Monkhill	d												
Wakefield Westgate 32,39	a	15 03	15 17		15 22	15 34	15 57				16 22	16 28	
	d	15 03	15 18		15 23	15 34	15 57				16 23	16 29	
Sandal & Agbrigg	d	15 07				15 38	16 01						
Fitzwilliam	d	15 13				15 44	16 07						
South Elmsall	d					15 49							
Adwick	a					15 55							
	d					15 55							
Bentley (S.Yorks)	d					15 59							
Doncaster	a		15 35			16 08		16 25				16 46	17 11
Moorthorpe	d	15 19					16 13						
Thurnscoe	d	15 25					16 19						
Goldthorpe	d	15 27					16 21						
Bolton-upon-Dearne	d	15 30					16 29						
Swinton (S.Yorks) 29	a	15 34					16 33						
Rotherham Central 29	a	15 43					16 42						
Meadowhall 29	a	15 50		15 56			16 48			16 56			
Sheffield 29	a	15 58		16 03	15 53		16 56			17 05	16 52		

Station		NT	NT	GR	NT	NT	XC	GR	NT	GR	NT	NT
			◇	1		◇	◇1	1	◇	1		◇
Leeds 32,34	d	16 17	16 21	16 45	16 48	17 09	17 12	17 16	17 21	17 47	17 49	18 09
Outwood	d		16 30		16 59				17 30		18 01	
Wakefield Kirkgate 32,34,39	a	16 48				17 25						18 25
	d	16 48				17 26						18 26
Pontefract Monkhill	d											
Wakefield Westgate 32,39	a		16 34	16 57	17 03		17 23	17 28	17 34	17 59	18 05	
	d		16 34	16 58	17 03		17 24	17 29	17 34	18 00	18 06	
Sandal & Agbrigg	d		16 38		17 07				17 38		18 09	
Fitzwilliam	d		16 44		17 13				17 44		18 16	
South Elmsall	d		16 49						17 49			
Adwick	a		16 55						17 55			
	d		16 55						17 55			
Bentley (S.Yorks)	d		16 59						17 59			
Doncaster	a		17 08	17 16				17 46	18 08	18 16		
Moorthorpe	d				17 19						18 22	
Thurnscoe	d				17 25						18 28	
Goldthorpe	d				17 27						18 30	
Bolton-upon-Dearne	d				17 30						18 33	
Swinton (S.Yorks) 29	a				17 34						18 37	
Rotherham Central 29	a				17 43						18 45	
Meadowhall 29	a	17 30			17 50	17 56					18 51	18 55
Sheffield 29	a	17 40			17 58	18 03	17 53				18 59	19 03

Station		XC	NT	NT	GR	NT	GR	NT	NT	XC	GR	NT	GR
		◇1	◇		1	◇	1		◇	◇1	1	◇	1
Leeds 32,34	d	18 11		18 14	18 15	18 21	18 45	18 48	19 09	19 12	19 16	19 22	19 46
Outwood	d					18 30		18 59				19 31	
Wakefield Kirkgate 32,34,39	a			18 48					19 25				
	d			18 48					19 25				
Pontefract Monkhill	d												
Wakefield Westgate 32,39	a	18 22			18 27	18 34	18 57	19 03		19 23	19 28	19 35	19 58
	d	18 23			18 28	18 34	18 59	19 03		19 24	19 29	19 35	19 59
Sandal & Agbrigg	d					18 38		19 07				19 39	
Fitzwilliam	d					18 44		19 13				19 45	
South Elmsall	d					18 49						19 50	
Adwick	a					18 55						19 56	
	d					18 55						19 56	
Bentley (S.Yorks)	d					18 59						20 00	
Doncaster	a				18 45	19 07	19 17				19 46	20 09	20 17
Moorthorpe	d		18 44					19 19					
Thurnscoe	d							19 25					
Goldthorpe	d							19 27					
Bolton-upon-Dearne	d							19 30					
Swinton (S.Yorks) 29	a		18 55					19 34					
Rotherham Central 29	a		19 02					19 44					
Meadowhall 29	a		19 09	19 35				19 51	19 56				
Sheffield 29	a	18 53	19 19	19 43				19 59	20 03	19 53			

Station		NT	NT	XC		NT	NT	GR	NT	NT	NT	XC	NT
			◇	◇1			◇	1		◇ A	◇	◇1	◇
Leeds 32,34	d	19 48	20 09	20 11		20 17	20 21	20 45	20 48		21 09	21 11	21 21
Outwood	d	19 59					20 30		20 59				21 30
Wakefield Kirkgate 32,34,39	a		20 25			20 46					21 29		
	d		20 25			20 46					21 30		
Pontefract Monkhill	d												
Wakefield Westgate 32,39	a	20 03		20 22			20 34	20 57	21 03			21 22	21 34
	d	20 03		20 23			20 34	20 58	21 03			21 23	21 34
Sandal & Agbrigg	d	20 07					20 38		21 07				21 38
Fitzwilliam	d	20 13					20 44		21 13				21 44
South Elmsall	d						20 49						21 49
Adwick	a						20 55						21 55
	d						20 55						21 55
Bentley (S.Yorks)	d						20 59						21 59
Doncaster	a						21 07	21 15					22 08
Moorthorpe	d	20 19							21 19	21 36			
Thurnscoe	d	20 25							21 25				
Goldthorpe	d	20 27							21 27				
Bolton-upon-Dearne	d	20 30							21 30				
Swinton (S.Yorks) 29	a	20 34							21 34	21 45			
Rotherham Central 29	a	20 42							21 43				
Meadowhall 29	a	20 51	20 55			21 28			21 51	21 55	21 59		
Sheffield 29	a	20 59	21 03	20 52		21 38			21 59	22 03	22 07	21 52	

A via Pontefract Baghill

Table T031-R

Sundays
15 December to 10 May

Leeds - Wakefield, Doncaster and Sheffield

Station		NT	NT		NT	NT	NT
			◇				◇
Leeds 32,34	d	21 46	22 09		22 18	22 37	22 45
Outwood	d	21 59				22 48	22 54
Wakefield Kirkgate 32,34,39	a		22 25		22 47		
	d		22 25		22 47		
Pontefract Monkhill	d						
Wakefield Westgate 32,39	a	22 03				22 52	22 58
	d	22 03				22 52	22 58
Sandal & Agbrigg	d	22 07				22 55	23 02
Fitzwilliam	d	22 13				23 02	23 08
South Elmsall	d						23 13
Adwick	a						23 19
	d						23 19
Bentley (S.Yorks)	d						23 23
Doncaster	a						23 31
Moorthorpe	d	22 19				23 08	
Thurnscoe	d	22 25				23 14	
Goldthorpe	d	22 27				23 16	
Bolton-upon-Dearne	d	22 30				23 19	
Swinton (S.Yorks) 29	a	22 34				23 23	
Rotherham Central 29	a	22 43				23 31	
Meadowhall 29	a	22 48	22 55		23 26	23 37	
Sheffield 29	a	22 56	23 03		23 35	23 45	

AVAILABLE FROM MP Middleton Press

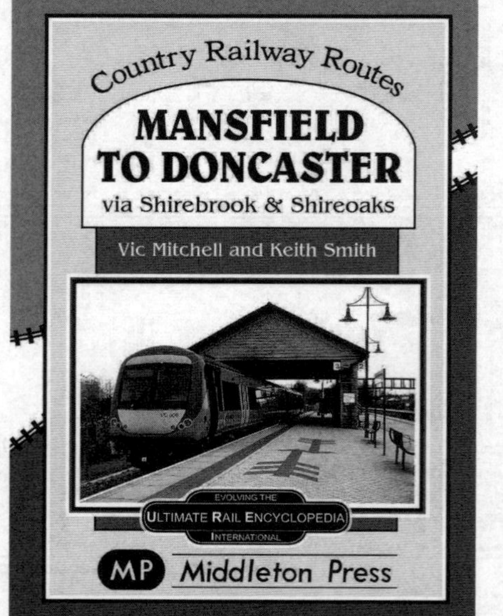

Table T032-F

Mondays to Fridays
16 December to 15 May

Bradford, Leeds and Wakefield - Pontefract, Knottingley and Goole

Miles	Miles		NT	NT	NT	NT	NT	NT	NT	NT	GC	NT	NT	NT	NT	NT	GC	NT	NT	NT	NT	NT
					A	B		A		B			A		B			A		B		A
—	—	Bradford Interchange 41 d									06 55						07 56					
—	—	Halifax 41 d									07 10						08 10					
—	—	Brighouse 41 d									07 20						08 24					
—	—	Mirfield d				06 12				07 12	07 26				08 12		08 32			09 12		
0	—	**Leeds** 31 d	05 24	05 47	05 54		06 15	06 32	06 58			07 30	07 32	07 58		08 29		08 32	08 58		09 29	09 32
6	—	Woodlesford d		05 57	06 03			06 41	07 07				07 41	08 07				08 41	09 07			09 41
10¾	—	Castleford a		06 05	06 12	06 40		06 49	07 16	07 40			07 49	08 16	08 40			08 49	09 16	09 40		09 49
—	—	d		06 08	06 14			06 52	07 18				07 52	08 18				08 52	09 18			09 52
12¼	—	Glasshoughton d		06 13					07 23					08 23					09 23			
—	0	**Wakefield Westgate** 31,39 d	05 38				06 34					07 43				08 42					09 42	
—	—	**Wakefield Kirkgate** 31,34,39 a	05 41		06 26		06 37	07 02			07 39	07 46	08 02			08 45	08 52	09 02			09 45	10 02
—	—	d	05 42				06 37				07 40	07 47				08 46	08 55				09 46	
—	5¼	Streethouse d	05 51				06 46					07 55				08 54					09 54	
—	7	Featherstone d	05 55				06 50					07 59				08 58					09 58	
—	9	Pontefract Tanshelf d	05 59				06 54					08 03				09 02					10 02	
14	9¾	**Pontefract Monkhill** a	06 01	06 17			06 56		07 28		07 58	08 06		08 28		09 05			09 28		10 05	
—	—	d	06 02	06 18			06 57		07 28		07 59	08 06		08 28		09 05			09 28		10 05	
—	—	London Kings Cross ⊖26 a									10 09						11 17					
16	—	**Knottingley** a	06 08	06 24			07 02		07 34			08 12		08 34		09 11			09 34		10 11	
—	—	d																				
20¼	—	Whitley Bridge d																				
22	—	Hensall d																				
25¾	—	Snaith d																				
28½	—	Rawcliffe d																				
32½	—	**Goole** a																				

	NT	NT	NT	NT	NT	GC	NT	NT	NT	NT		NT	NT	NT	NT	NT	GC	NT	NT	NT	NT	NT
		B		A			B		A			B		A		B			A		B	
Bradford Interchange 41 d						10 22											14 50					
Halifax 41 d						10 36											15 03					
Brighouse 41 d						10 47											15 17					
Mirfield d		10 12				10 54	11 12					14 12				15 12	15 24				16 12	
Leeds 31 d	09 58		10 29	10 32	10 58			11 29	11 32	11 58			14 29	14 32	14 58			15 29	15 32	15 58		16 29
Woodlesford d	10 07			10 41	11 07				11 41	12 07				14 41	15 07				15 41	16 07		
Castleford a	10 16	10 40		10 49	11 16		11 40		11 49	12 16	and at the same minutes past each hour until	14 40		14 49	15 16	15 40			15 49	16 16	16 40	
d	10 18			10 52	11 18				11 52	12 18				14 52	15 18				15 52	16 18		
Glasshoughton d	10 23				11 23					12 23					15 23					16 23		
Wakefield Westgate 31,39 d			10 42					11 42					14 42					15 42				16 42
Wakefield Kirkgate 31,34,39 a			10 45	11 02		11 13		11 45	12 02				14 45	15 02			15 38	15 45	16 02			16 45
d			10 46			11 14		11 46					14 46				15 39	15 46				16 46
Streethouse d			10 54					11 54					14 54					15 54				16 54
Featherstone d			10 58					11 58					14 58					15 58				16 58
Pontefract Tanshelf d			11 02					12 02					15 02					16 02				17 02
Pontefract Monkhill a	10 28		11 05		11 28	11 32		12 05		12 28			15 05		15 28		15 54	16 05		16 28		17 05
d	10 28		11 05		11 28	11 34		12 05		12 28			15 05		15 28		15 55	16 05		16 28		17 05
London Kings Cross ⊖26 a						13 44											18 07					
Knottingley a	10 34		11 11		11 34			12 11		12 34			15 11		15 34			16 11		16 34		17 11
d																						
Whitley Bridge d																						
Hensall d																						
Snaith d																						
Rawcliffe d																						
Goole a																						

	NT	NT	NT	NT	NT	NT	NT	NT	NT	NT	NT	NT	NT	NT	NT	NT	NT	NT	NT	NT	NT
	A		B		A		B		A		B		A		B		A		B		A
Bradford Interchange 41 d																					
Halifax 41 d																					
Brighouse 41 d																					
Mirfield d			17 12				18 12				19 12				20 12				21 12		
Leeds 31 d	16 32	16 58		17 29	17 32	17 58		18 29	18 32	18 58		19 29	19 32	19 58		20 29	20 32	20 58		21 29	21 32
Woodlesford d	16 41	17 07			17 41	18 07			18 41	19 07			19 41	20 07			20 41	21 07			21 41
Castleford a	16 49	17 16	17 40		17 49	18 16	18 40		18 49	19 16	19 40		19 49	20 16	20 41		20 49	21 16	21 40		21 49
d	16 52	17 18			17 52	18 18			18 52	19 18			19 52	20 18			20 52	21 18			21 52
Glasshoughton d		17 23				18 23				19 23				20 23				21 23			
Wakefield Westgate 31,39 d				17 42				18 42				19 42				20 42				21 42	
Wakefield Kirkgate 31,34,39 a	17 02			17 45	18 02			18 45	19 02			19 45	20 02			20 45	21 02			21 45	22 02
d				17 46				18 46				19 46				20 46				21 46	
Streethouse d				17 54				18 54				19 54				20 54				21 54	
Featherstone d				17 58				18 58				19 58				20 58				21 58	
Pontefract Tanshelf d				18 02				19 02				20 02				21 02				22 02	
Pontefract Monkhill a		17 28		18 05		18 30		19 05		19 28		20 05		20 28		21 05		21 30		22 05	
d		17 28		18 05		18 30		19 05		19 28		20 05		20 28		21 05		21 30		22 05	
London Kings Cross ⊖26 a																					
Knottingley a		17 34		18 11		18 35		19 11		19 34		20 11		20 34		21 11		21 37		22 11	
d						18 36															
Whitley Bridge d						18 42															
Hensall d						18 47															
Snaith d						18 53															
Rawcliffe d						18 58															
Goole a						19 08															

A To Sheffield
B From Huddersfield

NRT DECEMBER 19 EDITION

Table T032-F

Mondays to Fridays
16 December to 15 May

Bradford, Leeds and Wakefield - Pontefract, Knottingley and Goole

	NT	NT	NT	NT	NT	NT
		A	B		B	
Bradford Interchange 41 d						
Halifax 41 d						
Brighouse 41 d						
Mirfield d		22 12				
Leeds 31 d	22 03		22 32	22 50	23 02	23 18
Woodlesford d	22 12		22 41		23 11	23 29
Castleford a	22 21	22 40	22 49		23 20	23 38
d	22 23		22 52		23 22	23 40
Glasshoughton d	22 28					23 45
Wakefield Westgate 31,39 d				23 04		
Wakefield Kirkgate 31,34,39 a			23 02	23 07	23 33	
d				23 08		
Streethouse d				23 16		
Featherstone d				23 20		
Pontefract Tanshelf d				23 24		
Pontefract Monkhill a	22 33			23 27		23 49
d	22 33			23 27		23 49
London Kings Cross ⊖26 a						
Knottingley a	22 39			23 32		23 55
d						
Whitley Bridge d						
Hensall d						
Snaith d						
Rawcliffe d						
Goole a						

Saturdays
21 December to 16 May

	NT	NT	NT	NT	NT	NT	NT	NT	GC	NT	NT	NT	NT	NT	NT	NT	NT	GC	NT	NT	NT	NT
			B	A		B		A			B		A		B		A			B		A
Bradford Interchange 41 d									06 55									08 44				
Halifax 41 d									07 10									08 57				
Brighouse 41 d									07 20									09 13				
Mirfield d				06 12				07 12	07 27				08 12				09 12	09 20				10 12
Leeds 31 d	05 24	05 47	05 54		06 15	06 32	06 58			07 30	07 32	07 58		08 29	08 32	08 58			09 29	09 32	09 58	
Woodlesford d		05 57	06 03			06 41	07 07				07 41	08 07			08 41	09 07				09 41	10 07	
Castleford a		06 05	06 12	06 40		06 49	07 16	07 40			07 49	08 16	08 40		08 49	09 16	09 40			09 49	10 16	10 40
d		06 08	06 14			06 52	07 18				07 52	08 18			08 52	09 18				09 52	10 18	
Glasshoughton d		06 13					07 23					08 23				09 23					10 23	
Wakefield Westgate 31,39 d	05 38				06 34					07 43				08 42					09 42			
Wakefield Kirkgate 31,34,39 a	05 41		06 26		06 37	07 02			07 39	07 46	08 02			08 45	09 02			09 39	09 45	10 02		
d	05 42				06 37				07 40	07 47				08 46				09 40	09 46			
Streethouse d	05 51				06 46					07 55				08 54					09 54			
Featherstone d	05 55				06 50					07 59				08 58					09 58			
Pontefract Tanshelf d	05 59				06 54					08 03				09 02					10 02			
Pontefract Monkhill a	06 01	06 17			06 56		07 28		07 58	08 06		08 28		09 05		09 28		09 55	10 05		10 28	
d	06 02	06 18			06 57		07 28		07 59	08 06		08 28		09 05		09 28		09 57	10 05		10 28	
London Kings Cross ⊖26 a									10 11									11 58				
Knottingley a	06 08	06 24			07 02		07 34			08 12		08 34		09 11		09 34			10 11		10 34	
d																						
Whitley Bridge d																						
Hensall d																						
Snaith d																						
Rawcliffe d																						
Goole a																						

	NT	NT	NT	GC	NT	NT	NT	NT		NT	NT	NT	NT	GC	NT	NT	NT	NT	NT	NT	NT	NT
		B			A		B			A		B			A		B		A		B	
Bradford Interchange 41 d				10 22										15 22								
Halifax 41 d				10 36										15 35								
Brighouse 41 d				10 47										15 48								
Mirfield d				10 55	11 12					15 12				15 56	16 12				17 12			
Leeds 31 d	10 29	10 32	10 58			11 29	11 32	11 58			15 29	15 32	15 58			16 29	16 32	16 58		17 29	17 32	17 58
Woodlesford d		10 41	11 07				11 41	12 07				15 41	16 07				16 41	17 07			17 41	18 07
Castleford a		10 49	11 16		11 40		11 49	12 16	and at the same minutes past each hour until	15 40		15 49	16 16		16 40		16 49	17 16	17 40		17 49	18 16
d		10 52	11 18				11 52	12 18				15 52	16 18				16 52	17 18			17 52	18 18
Glasshoughton d			11 23					12 23					16 23					17 23				18 23
Wakefield Westgate 31,39 d	10 42					11 42					15 42					16 42				17 42		
Wakefield Kirkgate 31,34,39 a	10 45	11 02		11 11		11 45	12 02				15 45	16 02		16 11		16 45	17 02			17 45	18 02	
d	10 46			11 14		11 46					15 46			16 14		16 46				17 46		
Streethouse d	10 54					11 54					15 54					16 54				17 54		
Featherstone d	10 58					11 58					15 58					16 58				17 58		
Pontefract Tanshelf d	11 02					12 02					16 02					17 02				18 02		
Pontefract Monkhill a	11 05		11 28	11 30		12 05		12 28			16 05		16 28	16 32		17 05		17 28		18 05		18 30
d	11 05		11 28	11 32		12 05		12 28			16 05		16 28	16 33		17 05		17 28		18 05		18 30
London Kings Cross ⊖26 a				13 44										18 47								
Knottingley a	11 11		11 34			12 11		12 34			16 11		16 34			17 11		17 34		18 11		18 35
d																						18 36
Whitley Bridge d																						18 42
Hensall d																						18 47
Snaith d																						18 53
Rawcliffe d																						18 58
Goole a																						19 08

A From Huddersfield
B To Sheffield

Table T032-F

Saturdays
21 December to 16 May

Bradford, Leeds and Wakefield - Pontefract, Knottingley and Goole

		NT A	NT	NT B	NT	NT A	NT	NT B	NT	NT A	NT	NT B	NT	NT A	NT	NT B	NT	NT A	NT B	NT	NT
Bradford Interchange 41	d																				
Halifax 41	d																				
Brighouse 41	d																				
Mirfield	d	18 12				19 12				20 12				21 12				22 12			
Leeds 10 31	d		18 29	18 32	18 58		19 29	19 32	19 58		20 29	20 32	20 58		21 29	21 32	22 03		22 32	22 50	23 00
Woodlesford	d			18 41	19 07			19 41	20 07			20 41	21 07			21 41	22 12		22 41		23 09
Castleford	a	18 40		18 49	19 16	19 40		19 49	20 16	20 41		20 49	21 16	21 40		21 49	22 21	22 40	22 49		23 18
	d			18 52	19 18			19 52	20 18			20 52	21 18			21 52	22 23		22 52		
Glasshoughton	d				19 23				20 23				21 23				22 28				
Wakefield Westgate 7 31,39	d		18 42				19 42				20 42				21 42					23 04	
Wakefield Kirkgate 4 31,34,39	a		18 45	19 02			19 45	20 02			20 45	21 02			21 45	22 02			23 02	23 07	
	d		18 46				19 46				20 46				21 46					23 08	
Streethouse	d		18 54				19 54				20 54				21 54					23 16	
Featherstone	d		18 58				19 58				20 58				21 58					23 20	
Pontefract Tanshelf	d		19 02				20 02				21 02				22 02					23 24	
Pontefract Monkhill	a		19 05		19 28		20 05		20 28		21 05		21 30		22 05		22 33			23 27	
	d		19 05		19 28		20 05		20 28		21 05		21 30		22 05		22 33			23 27	
London Kings Cross 15 ⊖26	a																				
Knottingley	a		19 11		19 34		20 11		20 34		21 11		21 37		22 11		22 39			23 32	
	d																				
Whitley Bridge	d																				
Hensall	d																				
Snaith	d																				
Rawcliffe	d																				
Goole	a																				

Sundays
15 December to 10 May

		GC ◼ 1 C ☕	GC ◼ 1 D ☕	NT B	NT	NT	NT B	NT	NT	NT B	NT	GC ◼ 1 ☕	NT	NT B	NT	GC ◼ 1 ☕	NT	GC ◼ 1 ☕	NT B	NT	NT	NT B	NT
Bradford Interchange 41	d	07 57	08 10									12 05				15 08		15 59					
Halifax 41	d	08 11										12 19				15 21		16 12					
Brighouse 41	d	08 21										12 30				15 36		16 22					
Mirfield	d	08 28										12 39				15 45		16 30					
Leeds 10 31	d			08 33	08 52	09 12	10 18	10 25	11 17	12 17	12 26		13 17	14 17	14 25		15 17		16 17	16 26	17 17	18 14	18 25
Woodlesford	d			08 41		09 21	10 26		11 26	12 25			13 26	14 25			15 26		16 25		17 26	18 22	
Castleford	a			08 50		09 29	10 34		11 34	12 33			13 34	14 33			15 34		16 33		17 34	18 31	
	d			08 52		09 32	10 37		11 37	12 36			13 37	14 36			15 37		16 37		17 37	18 38	
Glasshoughton	d					09 37			11 42				13 42				15 42				17 42		
Wakefield Westgate 7 31,39	d				09 06			10 39			12 40				14 39					16 47			18 39
Wakefield Kirkgate 4 31,34,39	a	08 44	08 45	09 02	09 10		10 47	10 42		12 46	12 43	12 55		14 46	14 42	16 01		16 43	16 48	16 51		18 48	18 42
	d	08 45	08 45		09 12			10 42			12 43	12 56			14 42	16 02		16 44		16 52			18 42
Streethouse	d				09 20			10 49			12 50				14 49					16 59			18 49
Featherstone	d				09 24			10 53			12 54				14 53					17 03			18 53
Pontefract Tanshelf	d				09 28			10 57			12 58				14 57					17 06			18 57
Pontefract Monkhill	a				09 31	09 43		10 59	11 46		13 00		13 46		14 59		15 46			17 09	17 46		18 59
	d				09 31	09 43		11 00	11 46		13 01		13 46		15 00		15 46			17 09	17 46		19 00
London Kings Cross 15 ⊖26	a	10 40	10 40									14 54				17 56		18 44					
Knottingley	a				09 36	09 49		11 05	11 52		13 06		13 52		15 05		15 52			17 14	17 52		19 05
	d																						
Whitley Bridge	d																						
Hensall	d																						
Snaith	d																						
Rawcliffe	d																						
Goole	a																						

		NT	NT B	NT	NT	NT B	NT
Bradford Interchange 41	d						
Halifax 41	d						
Brighouse 41	d						
Mirfield	d						
Leeds 10 31	d	19 17	20 17	20 25	21 17	22 18	22 25
Woodlesford	d	19 25	20 25		21 25	22 26	
Castleford	a	19 33	20 33		21 33	22 34	
	d	19 36	20 36		21 36	22 37	
Glasshoughton	d	19 40			21 40		
Wakefield Westgate 7 31,39	d			20 39			22 39
Wakefield Kirkgate 4 31,34,39	a		20 46	20 42		22 47	22 42
	d			20 43			22 42
Streethouse	d			20 50			22 49
Featherstone	d			20 54			22 53
Pontefract Tanshelf	d			20 57			22 57
Pontefract Monkhill	a	19 45		21 00	21 45		22 59
	d	19 45		21 00	21 45		23 00
London Kings Cross 15 ⊖26	a						
Knottingley	a	19 51		21 06	21 51		23 05
	d						
Whitley Bridge	d						
Hensall	d						
Snaith	d						
Rawcliffe	d						
Goole	a						

A From Huddersfield
B To Sheffield
C until 16 February, from 5 April
D from 23 February until 29 March

Table T032-R

Mondays to Fridays
16 December to 15 May

Goole, Knottingley and Pontefract - Wakefield and Leeds, Bradford

Miles	Miles			TP ◇1 A	NT B	NT	NT C	NT B	NT ◇ B	NT	NT D	NT	NT ◇ E	NT	NT B	NT	NT	NT D	NT ◇ F	NT	NT B	NT	NT D
0	—	**Goole**	d																	07 42			
4	—	Rawcliffe	d																	07 50			
6¾	—	Snaith	d																	07 55			
10½	—	Hensall	d																	08 02			
12¼	—	Whitley Bridge	d																	08 05			
16½	—	**Knottingley**	a																	08 12			
—	—		d			06 14				06 40				07 15		07 30	07 48			08 13		08 40	
—	—	London Kings Cross 15 ⊖26	d																				
18½	0	**Pontefract Monkhill**	a			06 18				06 44				07 19		07 34	07 52			08 17		08 44	
—	—		d			06 18				06 45				07 19		07 35	07 53			08 17		08 45	
—	0¾	Pontefract Tanshelf	d							06 47						07 37						08 47	
—	2¾	Featherstone	d							06 52						07 42						08 52	
—	4½	Streethouse	d							06 55						07 45						08 55	
—	8¾	**Wakefield Kirkgate** 4 31,34,39	a							07 06						07 58						09 06	
—	—		d	05 24	06 15		06 20	06 49	06 55	07 07	07 10		07 23		07 51	07 59		08 10	08 24		08 50	09 07	09 10
—	9¾	**Wakefield Westgate** 7 31,39	a							07 10						08 02						09 09	
20	—	Glasshoughton	d			06 23								07 24			08 03			08 22			
21½	—	Castleford	a			06 28		07 01						07 29	08 01		08 08			08 27	09 01		
—	—		d			06 31		07 04				07 11		07 32	08 04		08 11			08 30	09 04		
26½	—	Woodlesford	d		06 28	06 40		07 13				07 20		07 41	08 13		08 23			08 39	09 13		
32½	—	**Leeds** 10 31	a		06 44	06 53		07 25	07 16	07 25		07 38	07 43	07 53	08 26	08 17	08 35		08 44	08 52	09 24	09 25	
—	—	Mirfield	a	05 36			06 34				07 23							08 23					09 23
—	—	Brighouse 41	a																				
—	—	Halifax 41	a																				
—	—	**Bradford Interchange** 41	a																				

		NT ◇ G	NT	NT B	NT	NT D	NT ◇ G	NT	NT B	NT	NT D	NT ◇ G	NT	NT B	NT	NT D	NT ◇ G	NT	NT B	NT	NT D	GC ◼ 1 ☕	NT ◇ G
Goole	d																						
Rawcliffe	d																						
Snaith	d																						
Hensall	d																						
Whitley Bridge	d																						
Knottingley	a																						
	d		09 16		09 40			10 16		10 40			11 16		11 40			12 16		12 40			
London Kings Cross 15 ⊖26	d																					10 57	
Pontefract Monkhill	a		09 20		09 44			10 20		10 44			11 20		11 44			12 20		12 44		12 57	
	d		09 20		09 45			10 20		10 45			11 20		11 45			12 20		12 45		12 58	
Pontefract Tanshelf	d				09 47					10 47					11 47					12 47			
Featherstone	d				09 52					10 52					11 52					12 52			
Streethouse	d				09 55					10 55					11 55					12 55			
Wakefield Kirkgate 4 31,34,39	a				10 06					11 06					12 06					13 06		13 14	
	d	09 25		09 49	10 07	10 10	10 24		10 49	11 07	11 10	11 24		11 49	12 07	12 10	12 24		12 49	13 07	13 10	13 15	13 24
Wakefield Westgate 7 31,39	a				10 09					11 09					12 09					13 09			
Glasshoughton	d		09 25					10 25					11 25					12 25					
Castleford	a		09 30	10 01				10 30	11 01				11 30	12 01				12 30	13 01				
	d		09 33	10 04				10 33	11 04				11 33	12 04				12 33	13 04				
Woodlesford	d		09 42	10 13				10 42	11 13				11 42	12 13				12 42	13 13				
Leeds 10 31	a	09 44	09 52	10 25	10 25		10 44	10 53	11 25	11 26		11 44	11 53	12 25	12 25		12 44	12 53	13 25	13 25			13 44
Mirfield	a					10 23					11 23					12 23					13 23	13 27	
Brighouse 41	a																					13 35	
Halifax 41	a																					13 47	
Bradford Interchange 41	a																					14 03	

		NT	NT B	NT	NT D	NT ◇ G	NT	NT B	NT	NT D	NT ◇ G	NT	NT B	NT	NT D	NT ◇ G	NT	NT B	NT	NT D	GC ◼ 1 ☕	NT ◇ G
Goole	d																					
Rawcliffe	d																					
Snaith	d																					
Hensall	d																					
Whitley Bridge	d																					
Knottingley	a																					
	d	13 16		13 40			14 16		14 40			15 16		15 40			16 16		16 40			
London Kings Cross 15 ⊖26	d																				14 48	
Pontefract Monkhill	a	13 20		13 44			14 20		14 44			15 20		15 44			16 20		16 44		16 52	
	d	13 20		13 45			14 20		14 45			15 20		15 45			16 20		16 45		16 54	
Pontefract Tanshelf	d			13 47					14 47					15 47					16 47			
Featherstone	d			13 52					14 52					15 52					16 52			
Streethouse	d			13 55					14 55					15 55					16 55			
Wakefield Kirkgate 4 31,34,39	a			14 06					15 06					16 06					17 06		17 13	
	d		13 50	14 07	14 10	14 24		14 49	15 07	15 10	15 24		15 49	16 07	16 10	16 24		16 49	17 07	17 10	17 14	17 24
Wakefield Westgate 7 31,39	a			14 09					15 09					16 09					17 09			
Glasshoughton	d	13 25					14 25					15 25					16 25					
Castleford	a	13 30	14 01				14 30	15 01				15 30	16 01				16 30	17 01				
	d	13 33	14 04				14 33	15 04				15 33	16 04				16 33	17 04				
Woodlesford	d	13 42	14 13				14 42	15 13				15 42	16 13				16 42	17 13				
Leeds 10 31	a	13 53	14 25	14 25		14 44	14 53	15 25	15 25		15 44	15 53	16 25	16 25		16 44	16 53	17 25	17 25			17 44
Mirfield	a				14 23					15 23					16 23					17 23	17 25	
Brighouse 41	a																				17 33	
Halifax 41	a																				17 46	
Bradford Interchange 41	a																				18 01	

A To Manchester Piccadilly
B From Sheffield
C To Huddersfield
D From Castleford to Huddersfield
E From Chesterfield
F From Retford
G From Lincoln

Table T032-R

Mondays to Fridays

16 December to 15 May

Goole, Knottingley and Pontefract - Wakefield and Leeds, Bradford

		NT	NT	NT	NT	NT	GC	NT	NT	NT	NT	NT	NT	NT	NT	NT	NT	NT	NT FX	NT FO	NT	NT	NT
			A		B	◇ C	■ 1		A		B	◇ C		A		B	◇ C		A	A		B	◇ C
Goole	d																	19 43					
Rawcliffe	d																	19 51					
Snaith	d																	19 56					
Hensall	d																	20 03					
Whitley Bridge	d																	20 06					
Knottingley	a																	20 13					
	d	17 16		17 40				18 16		18 40			19 16		19 40			20 16			20 40		
London Kings Cross 15 ⊖26	d						16 27																
Pontefract Monkhill	a	17 20		17 44				18 20		18 44			19 20		19 44			20 20			20 44		
	d	17 20		17 45				18 20		18 45			19 20		19 45			20 20			20 45		
Pontefract Tanshelf	d			17 47						18 47					19 47						20 47		
Featherstone	d			17 52						18 52					19 52						20 52		
Streethouse	d			17 55						18 55					19 55						20 55		
Wakefield Kirkgate 4 31,34,39	a			18 06			18 26			19 06					20 06						21 06		
	d		17 49	18 07	18 10	18 24	18 31		18 49	19 07	19 10	19 24		19 49	20 07	20 10	20 24		20 49	20 49	21 07	21 10	21 24
Wakefield Westgate 7 31,39	a			18 09						19 09					20 11						21 09		
Glasshoughton	d	17 25						18 25					19 25					20 25					
Castleford	a	17 30	18 01					18 30	19 01				19 30	20 01				20 30	21 01	21 01			
	d	17 33	18 04					18 33	19 04				19 33	20 04				20 33	21 04	21 04			
Woodlesford	d	17 42	18 13					18 42	19 13				19 42	20 13				20 42	21 13	21 13			
Leeds 10 31	a	17 53	18 25	18 25		18 44		18 53	19 24	19 24		19 44	19 53	20 25	20 27		20 44	20 52	21 25	21 26	21 25		21 44
Mirfield	a				18 23		18 43				19 23					20 23						21 23	
Brighouse 41	a						18 53																
Halifax 41	a						19 05																
Bradford Interchange 41	a						19 21																

		NT	NT	GC	NT	NT	NT	NT	NT	NT	NT
			A	■ 1	B			B			A
Goole	d										
Rawcliffe	d										
Snaith	d										
Hensall	d										
Whitley Bridge	d										
Knottingley	a										
	d	21 16				21 45	22 16		22 47	23 09	
London Kings Cross 15 ⊖26	d			19 54							
Pontefract Monkhill	a	21 20				21 49	22 20		22 51	23 13	
	d	21 20				21 50	22 20		22 52	23 14	
Pontefract Tanshelf	d					21 52			22 54		
Featherstone	d					21 57			22 59		
Streethouse	d					22 00			23 02		
Wakefield Kirkgate 4 31,34,39	a			21 50		22 14			23 13		
	d		21 49	21 51	22 10	22 14		23 11	23 14		23 18
Wakefield Westgate 7 31,39	a					22 18			23 17		
Glasshoughton	d	21 25					22 25			23 19	
Castleford	a	21 30	22 01				22 30			23 24	23 32
	d	21 33	22 04				22 33			23 26	23 34
Woodlesford	d	21 42	22 13				22 42			23 36	23 43
Leeds 10 31	a	21 53	22 25				22 53			23 47	23 58
Mirfield	a			22 02	22 23			23 25			
Brighouse 41	a			22 10							
Halifax 41	a			22 25							
Bradford Interchange 41	a			22 41							

Saturdays

21 December to 16 May

		TP	NT	NT	NT	NT	NT	NT	NT	NT	NT	NT	NT	NT	NT	NT	NT	NT	NT	NT	NT	NT	NT
		◇1 D	A		E	A	◇ A		B		◇ F		A			B	◇ G		A		B	◇ C	
Goole	d																	07 42					
Rawcliffe	d																	07 50					
Snaith	d																	07 55					
Hensall	d																	08 02					
Whitley Bridge	d																	08 05					
Knottingley	a																	08 12					
	d			06 14				06 40				07 15		07 30	07 48			08 13		08 40			09 16
London Kings Cross 15 ⊖26	d																						
Pontefract Monkhill	a			06 18				06 44				07 19		07 34	07 52			08 17		08 44			09 20
	d			06 18				06 45				07 19		07 35	07 53			08 17		08 45			09 20
Pontefract Tanshelf	d							06 47						07 37						08 47			
Featherstone	d							06 52						07 42						08 52			
Streethouse	d							06 55						07 45						08 55			
Wakefield Kirkgate 4 31,34,39	a							07 06						07 58						09 06			
	d	05 24	06 15		06 20	06 50	06 55	07 07	07 10		07 23		07 51	07 59		08 10	08 24		08 50	09 07	09 10	09 24	
Wakefield Westgate 7 31,39	a							07 10						08 02						09 09			
Glasshoughton	d			06 23								07 24			08 03			08 22					09 25
Castleford	a			06 28		07 01						07 29	08 01		08 08			08 27	09 01				09 30
	d			06 31		07 04				07 11		07 32	08 04		08 11			08 30	09 04				09 33
Woodlesford	d		06 28	06 40		07 13				07 24		07 41	08 13		08 23			08 39	09 13				09 42
Leeds 10 31	a		06 44	06 53		07 25	07 16	07 25		07 38	07 43	07 53	08 26	08 17	08 35		08 44	08 52	09 24	09 25		09 44	09 52
Mirfield	a	05 36			06 34				07 23							08 23					09 23		
Brighouse 41	a																						
Halifax 41	a																						
Bradford Interchange 41	a																						

A From Sheffield
B From Castleford to Huddersfield
C From Lincoln
D To Manchester Piccadilly
E To Huddersfield
F From Chesterfield
G From Retford

NRT DECEMBER 19 EDITION

Table T032-R

Saturdays

21 December to 16 May

Goole, Knottingley and Pontefract - Wakefield and Leeds, Bradford

		NT	NT	NT	NT	NT	NT	NT	NT	NT	NT	NT	NT	NT	NT	NT	NT	GC	NT	NT	NT	NT	NT
		A		B	◇ C		A		B	◇ C		A		B	◇ C		A	■ 1		B	◇ C		A
Goole	d																						
Rawcliffe	d																						
Snaith	d																						
Hensall	d																						
Whitley Bridge	d																						
Knottingley	a																						
	d		09 40			10 16		10 40			11 16		11 40			12 16			12 40			13 16	
London Kings Cross 15 ⊖26	d																	10 48					
Pontefract Monkhill	a		09 44			10 20		10 44			11 20		11 44			12 20			12 44			13 20	
	d		09 45			10 20		10 45			11 20		11 45			12 20			12 45			13 20	
Pontefract Tanshelf	d		09 47					10 47					11 47						12 47				
Featherstone	d		09 52					10 52					11 52						12 52				
Streethouse	d		09 55					10 55					11 55						12 55				
Wakefield Kirkgate 4 31,34,39	a		10 06					11 06					12 06					12 49	13 06				
	d	09 49	10 07	10 10	10 24		10 49	11 07	11 10	11 24		11 49	12 07	12 10	12 24		12 49	12 50	13 07	13 10	13 24		13 50
Wakefield Westgate 7 31,39	a		10 09					11 09					12 09						13 09				
Glasshoughton	d					10 25					11 25					12 25						13 25	
Castleford	a	10 01				10 30	11 01				11 30	12 01				12 30	13 01					13 30	14 01
	d	10 04				10 33	11 04				11 33	12 04				12 33	13 04					13 33	14 04
Woodlesford	d	10 13				10 42	11 13				11 42	12 13				12 42	13 13					13 42	14 13
Leeds 10 31	a	10 24	10 25		10 44	10 53	11 25	11 26		11 44	11 53	12 25	12 25		12 44	12 53	13 25		13 25		13 44	13 53	14 25
Mirfield	a			10 23					11 23					12 23				13 01		13 23			
Brighouse 41	a																	13 09					
Halifax 41	a																	13 20					
Bradford Interchange 41	a																	13 37					

		NT	NT	NT	NT	NT	NT	NT	NT	NT	NT	NT	NT	NT	NT	NT	NT	NT	NT	GC	NT	NT
			B	◇ C		A		B	◇ C		A		B	◇ C		A		B	◇ C	■ 1		A
Goole	d																					
Rawcliffe	d																					
Snaith	d																					
Hensall	d																					
Whitley Bridge	d																					
Knottingley	a																					
	d	13 40			14 16		14 40			15 16		15 40			16 16		16 40				17 16	
London Kings Cross 15 ⊖26	d																			15 48		
Pontefract Monkhill	a	13 44			14 20		14 44			15 20		15 44			16 20		16 44				17 20	
	d	13 45			14 20		14 45			15 20		15 45			16 20		16 45				17 20	
Pontefract Tanshelf	d	13 47					14 47					15 47					16 47					
Featherstone	d	13 52					14 52					15 52					16 52					
Streethouse	d	13 55					14 55					15 55					16 55					
Wakefield Kirkgate 4 31,34,39	a	14 06					15 06					16 06					17 06			17 44		
	d	14 07	14 10	14 24		14 49	15 07	15 10	15 24		15 49	16 07	16 10	16 24		16 49	17 07	17 10	17 24	17 47		17 49
Wakefield Westgate 7 31,39	a	14 09					15 09					16 09					17 09					
Glasshoughton	d				14 25					15 25					16 25						17 25	
Castleford	a				14 30	15 01				15 30	16 01				16 30	17 01					17 30	18 01
	d				14 33	15 04				15 33	16 04				16 33	17 04					17 33	18 04
Woodlesford	d				14 42	15 13				15 42	16 13				16 42	17 13					17 42	18 13
Leeds 10 31	a	14 25		14 44	14 53	15 25	15 25		15 44	15 53	16 25	16 25		16 44	16 53	17 25	17 25		17 44		17 53	18 25
Mirfield	a		14 23					15 23					16 23					17 23		17 58		
Brighouse 41	a																			18 09		
Halifax 41	a																			18 21		
Bradford Interchange 41	a																			18 40		

		NT	NT	NT	GC	NT	NT	NT	NT	NT	NT	NT	NT	NT	NT	NT	NT	NT	NT	NT	NT	NT	NT
			B	◇ C	■ 1		A		B	◇ C		A		B	◇ C		A		B	◇ C		A	B
Goole	d															19 44							
Rawcliffe	d															19 52							
Snaith	d															19 57							
Hensall	d															20 04							
Whitley Bridge	d															20 07							
Knottingley	a															20 14							
	d	17 40				18 16		18 40			19 16		19 40			20 16		20 40			21 16		
London Kings Cross 15 ⊖26	d				16 27																		
Pontefract Monkhill	a	17 44				18 20		18 44			19 20		19 44			20 20		20 44			21 20		
	d	17 45				18 20		18 45			19 20		19 45			20 20		20 45			21 20		
Pontefract Tanshelf	d	17 47						18 47					19 47					20 47					
Featherstone	d	17 52						18 52					19 52					20 52					
Streethouse	d	17 55						18 55					19 55					20 55					
Wakefield Kirkgate 4 31,34,39	a	18 06			18 26			19 06					20 06					21 06					
	d	18 07	18 10	18 24	18 31		18 49	19 07	19 10	19 24		19 49	20 07	20 10	20 24		20 49	21 07	21 10	21 24		21 49	22 10
Wakefield Westgate 7 31,39	a	18 09						19 09					20 11					21 09					
Glasshoughton	d					18 25					19 25					20 25					21 25		
Castleford	a					18 30	19 01				19 30	20 01				20 30	21 01				21 30	22 01	
	d					18 33	19 04				19 33	20 04				20 33	21 04				21 33	22 04	
Woodlesford	d					18 42	19 13				19 42	20 13				20 42	21 13				21 42	22 13	
Leeds 10 31	a	18 25		18 44		18 53	19 24	19 24		19 44	19 53	20 25	20 27		20 44	20 52	21 25	21 25		21 44	21 53	22 25	
Mirfield	a		18 23		18 43				19 23					20 23					21 23				22 23
Brighouse 41	a				18 53																		
Halifax 41	a				19 05																		
Bradford Interchange 41	a				19 21																		

A From Sheffield
B From Castleford to Huddersfield
C From Lincoln

Table T032-R

Saturdays
21 December to 16 May

Goole, Knottingley and Pontefract - Wakefield and Leeds, Bradford

	NT	GC	NT	NT	NT	NT	NT
		■ 1		A			B
Goole d							
Rawcliffe d							
Snaith d							
Hensall d							
Whitley Bridge d							
Knottingley a							
d	21 45		22 16		22 47	23 09	
London Kings Cross 15 ⊖26 d		19 57					
Pontefract Monkhill a	21 49	21 57	22 20		22 51	23 13	
d	21 50	22 03	22 20		22 52	23 14	
Pontefract Tanshelf d	21 52				22 54		
Featherstone d	21 57				22 59		
Streethouse d	22 00				23 02		
Wakefield Kirkgate 4 31,34,39 a	22 14	22 20			23 13		
d	22 14	22 21		23 11	23 14		23 18
Wakefield Westgate 7 31,39 a	22 18				23 17		
Glasshoughton d			22 25			23 19	
Castleford a			22 30			23 24	23 30
d			22 33			23 26	23 32
Woodlesford d			22 42			23 36	23 41
Leeds 10 31 a			22 53			23 47	23 59
Mirfield a		22 31		23 25			
Brighouse 41 a		22 40					
Halifax 41 a		22 53					
Bradford Interchange 41 a		23 09					

Sundays
15 December to 10 May

	NT	NT	NT	NT	NT	NT	NT	NT	NT	NT	GC	NT	NT	NT	NT	NT	NT	GC	NT	NT	NT	GC
	B		◇ B			B			B		■ 1		B			B		■ 1		B		■ 1
Goole d																						
Rawcliffe d																						
Snaith d																						
Hensall d																						
Whitley Bridge d																						
Knottingley a																						
d		09 22		09 42	10 30		11 12	12 30		13 10		14 30		15 12	16 30		17 20		18 30		19 12	
London Kings Cross 15 ⊖26 d											11 50							15 50				18 53
Pontefract Monkhill a		09 26		09 46	10 34		11 16	12 34		13 14		14 34		15 16	16 34		17 24		18 34		19 16	
d		09 26		09 46	10 34		11 16	12 34		13 14		14 34		15 16	16 34		17 24		18 34		19 16	
Pontefract Tanshelf d				09 49			11 19			13 17				15 19			17 27				19 19	
Featherstone d				09 53			11 22			13 20				15 22			17 30				19 22	
Streethouse d				09 56			11 26			13 24				15 26			17 34				19 26	
Wakefield Kirkgate 4 31,34,39 a				10 06			11 35			13 33	13 44			15 36			17 43	17 49			19 36	21 00
d	09 23		09 59	10 08		11 30	11 36		13 29	13 35	13 45		15 29	15 37		17 29	17 46	17 51		19 29	19 37	21 00
Wakefield Westgate 7 31,39 a				10 11			11 39			13 39				15 39			17 50				19 39	
Glasshoughton d		09 33			10 39			12 39				14 39			16 39				18 39			
Castleford a	09 33	09 39			10 43	11 40		12 43	13 39			14 43	15 39		16 43	17 40			18 43	19 40		
d	09 36	09 42			10 46	11 43		12 46	13 42			14 46	15 42		16 46	17 42			18 46	19 42		
Woodlesford d	09 45	09 51			10 55	11 52		12 55	13 51			14 55	15 51		16 55	17 51			18 55	19 51		
Leeds 10 31 a	09 56	10 01	10 24	10 27	11 05	12 06	11 56	13 05	14 04	13 54		15 05	16 04	15 56	17 05	18 04	18 06		19 05	20 04	19 54	
Mirfield a											13 57							18 02				21 12
Brighouse 41 a											14 05							18 10				21 21
Halifax 41 a											14 20							18 22				21 33
Bradford Interchange 41 a											14 37							18 37				21 48

	GC	NT	NT	NT	NT
	■ 1			B	
Goole d					
Rawcliffe d					
Snaith d					
Hensall d					
Whitley Bridge d					
Knottingley a					
d		20 30	21 12		22 30
London Kings Cross 15 ⊖26 d	19 22				
Pontefract Monkhill a		20 34	21 16		22 34
d		20 34	21 16		22 34
Pontefract Tanshelf d			21 19		
Featherstone d			21 22		
Streethouse d			21 26		
Wakefield Kirkgate 4 31,34,39 a	21 23		21 36		
d	21 24		21 37		
Wakefield Westgate 7 31,39 a			21 40		
Glasshoughton d		20 39			22 39
Castleford a		20 43			22 43
d		20 46		21 45	22 46
Woodlesford d		20 55		21 54	22 55
Leeds 10 31 a		21 05	21 57	22 07	23 05
Mirfield a	21 38				
Brighouse 41 a	21 45				
Halifax 41 a	21 57				
Bradford Interchange 41 a	22 13				

A From Castleford to Huddersfield
B From Sheffield

Table T033-F

Mondays to Fridays
16 December to 15 May

Sheffield and Selby - York

Local services only

Miles	Miles		NT MO	NT	NT	NT	NT	NT	NT	NT	NT	NT	NT	NT	NT	NT	NT	NT	NT	NT	NT	NT
			◇ A		B		C		◇		◇ A	◇ D	◇ A	E	◇ A	◇ D	◇ A	◇ D	◇ A	◇	◇ D	◇ A
0	—	**Sheffield** 7 29,31 d							07 24											11 41		
3½	—	Meadowhall 29,31 d							07 30											11 47		
6¼	—	Rotherham Central 29,31 d							07 36											11 57		
10¾	—	Swinton (S.Yorks) 29,31 d							07 48											12 06		
18½	—	Moorthorpe 31 d							08 04											12 16		
25½	—	Pontefract Baghill d							08 12											12 24		
—	—	Hull 29 d		05 45		06 19				07 50		08 50		09 50		10 50		11 50			12 50	
—	0	**Selby** d		06 27		06 57		07 56		08 29		09 30		10 27		11 29		12 27			13 30	
33¾	8¼	Sherburn-in-Elmet d		06 41		07 10		08 09	08 27	08 43		09 43		10 41		11 41				12 42	13 41	
36	10½	Church Fenton d	00 04	06 45	06 49	07 15		08 14	08 31	08 47	08 49	09 48	09 49	10 45	10 49	11 45	11 49		12 49	12 49	13 46	13 49
38	12½	Ulleskelf d				07 19	08 08		08 36											12 54		
46½	21	**York** 8 29 a	00 16	06 59	07 02	07 34	08 19	08 27	08 48	09 02	09 01	10 01	09 59	11 02	10 59	12 03	12 00	12 48	13 01	13 05	14 00	14 00

	NT	NT	NT	NT	NT	NT	NT	NT	NT	NT	NT	NT	NT	NT	NT	NT	NT	NT	NT	NT	NT	NT
	◇ A	◇ D	◇ A	◇ D	◇	◇ A	◇ D	◇ A	B	◇ A	◇ D	◇ A	◇ D	◇ D	◇ A	B	◇ A	◇ D	◇ D	◇ A	◇ A	
Sheffield 7 29,31 d					15 40																	
Meadowhall 29,31 d					15 48																	
Rotherham Central 29,31 d					15 56																	
Swinton (S.Yorks) 29,31 d					16 07																	
Moorthorpe 31 d					16 17																	
Pontefract Baghill d					16 25																	
Hull 29 d		14 50		15 50			16 50				17 50		18 50	19 50				20 50	21 50			
Selby d		15 27		16 27			17 30				18 32		19 31	20 27				21 32	22 32			23 44
Sherburn-in-Elmet d		15 41			16 40		17 43				18 46		19 44	20 41				21 46	22 46			
Church Fenton d	14 49	15 45	15 49		16 44	16 49	17 48	17 52		18 49	18 50	19 49	19 49	20 45	20 49		21 49	21 50	22 50	22 51	23 49	
Ulleskelf d					16 48				18 08							21 44						
York 8 29 a	15 00	16 01	15 59	16 49	17 00	17 00	18 01	18 02	18 19	19 00	19 04	20 00	20 03	21 01	21 00	21 56	22 00	22 08	23 07	23 02	00 01	00 08

Saturdays
21 December to 16 May

	NT	NT	NT	NT	NT	NT	NT	NT	NT	NT	NT	NT	NT	NT	NT	NT	NT	NT	NT	NT	NT	NT
		B		C	F	◇		◇ A	◇ D	◇ A	E	◇ A	◇ D	◇ A	◇ D	◇	◇ A	◇ D	◇ A	◇ A	◇ D	◇ A
Sheffield 7 29,31 d						07 25										11 41						
Meadowhall 29,31 d						07 31										11 47						
Rotherham Central 29,31 d						07 37										11 55						
Swinton (S.Yorks) 29,31 d						07 48										12 03						
Moorthorpe 31 d						08 04										12 13						
Pontefract Baghill d						08 12										12 21						
Hull 29 d	05 45		06 22				07 50		08 50		09 50		10 50		11 50			12 50			14 50	
Selby d	06 27		06 59		07 56		08 29		09 30		10 27		11 29		12 27			13 30			15 27	
Sherburn-in-Elmet d	06 41		07 12		08 09	08 27	08 43		09 43		10 41		11 41			12 36		13 41			15 41	
Church Fenton d	06 45	06 49	07 17		08 14	08 31	08 47	08 49	09 48	09 49	10 45	10 49	11 45	11 49		12 40	12 49	13 46	13 49	14 49	15 45	15 49
Ulleskelf d			07 21	08 08		08 36																
York 8 29 a	06 59	07 02	07 35	08 19	08 27	08 49	09 02	09 01	10 01	09 59	11 02	10 59	12 03	12 00	12 49	12 56	13 01	14 00	14 00	14 59	16 01	15 59

	NT	NT	NT	NT	NT	NT	NT	NT	NT	NT	NT	NT	NT	NT	NT	NT	NT	NT
	◇ D	◇	◇ A	◇ D	◇ A	B	◇ A	◇ D	◇ A	◇ D	◇ D	◇ A	B	◇ A	◇ D	◇ D	◇ A	◇ A
Sheffield 7 29,31 d		15 41																
Meadowhall 29,31 d		15 47																
Rotherham Central 29,31 d		15 56																
Swinton (S.Yorks) 29,31 d		16 06																
Moorthorpe 31 d		16 16																
Pontefract Baghill d		16 24																
Hull 29 d	15 50			16 50				17 50		18 50	19 50				20 50	21 50		
Selby d	16 27			17 30				18 32		19 31	20 27				21 32	22 32		
Sherburn-in-Elmet d		16 39		17 43				18 46		19 44	20 41				21 46	22 46		
Church Fenton d		16 43	16 49	17 48	17 52		18 49	18 50	19 49	19 49	20 45	20 49		21 49	21 50	22 50	22 51	23 46
Ulleskelf d						18 08							21 44					
York 8 29 a	16 49	16 58	17 00	18 01	18 02	18 19	19 00	19 04	20 00	20 03	21 01	21 02	21 56	22 00	22 08	23 07	23 02	23 57

Sundays
15 December to 10 May

	NT	NT	NT	NT	NT	NT	NT	NT	NT	NT	NT	NT	NT	NT	NT	NT	NT	NT	NT	NT	NT	NT
		B		◇ G	◇ H		◇ A		◇ A		◇ A		◇ A		◇ A		◇ A	◇ I		◇ A		◇ A
Sheffield 7 29,31 d																		16 13				
Meadowhall 29,31 d																		16 20				
Rotherham Central 29,31 d																		16 28				
Swinton (S.Yorks) 29,31 d																		16 38				
Moorthorpe 31 d																		16 53				
Pontefract Baghill d																		17 01				
Hull 29 d			08 31			10 39		11 31		12 34		13 35		14 23		15 35			16 35		17 35	
Selby d	08 15		09 08			11 14		12 08		13 10		14 10		14 58		16 10			17 10		18 10	
Sherburn-in-Elmet d	08 28		09 25			11 27				13 23				15 10		16 25		17 15	17 26			
Church Fenton d	08 32	08 38		09 58	11 01	11 31	12 00		13 00		13 57		14 56	15 14	16 00		17 00	17 20	17 31	18 00		19 00
Ulleskelf d			09 31							13 29						16 31		17 24				
York 8 29 a	08 44	08 51	09 42	10 11	11 13	11 45	12 14	12 29	13 12	13 40	14 10	14 29	15 09	15 27	16 13	16 42	17 13	17 36	17 43	18 14	18 37	19 13

A From Blackpool North
B From Leeds
C From Hebden Bridge
D From Bridlington
E From Scarborough
F from 22 February
G From Halifax
H From Blackburn
I via Pontefract Baghill

Table T033-F

Sundays
15 December to 10 May

Sheffield and Selby - York

Local services only

Station			NT	NT ◇ A	NT ◇ B	NT	NT ◇ B	NT	NT ◇ B	NT	NT ◇ B	NT
Sheffield [7]	29,31	d		19 00								
Meadowhall	29,31	d		19 06								
Rotherham Central	29,31	d		19 12								
Swinton (S.Yorks)	29,31	d		19 20								
Moorthorpe	31	d		19 29								
Pontefract Baghill		d		19 37								
Hull	29	d	18 35			19 35		20 21		21 35		
Selby		d	19 10			20 10		21 01		22 10		22 45
Sherburn-in-Elmet		d	19 26	19 52		20 23				22 26		22 57
Church Fenton		d		19 56	20 00	20 28	20 59		21 59	22 30	23 01	23 01
Ulleskelf		d	19 32	20 00								
York [8]	29	a	19 43	20 16	20 13	20 39	21 11	21 26	22 12	22 43	23 14	23 15

A via Pontefract Baghill
B From Blackpool North

SUNDAY RETURN TIMES

Table T033-R

Sundays
15 December to 10 May

York - Selby and Sheffield

Local services only

Station			NT	NT ◇ A	NT	NT ◇ A	NT	NT ◇ A	NT	NT ◇ A	NT	NT ◇ A	NT	NT ◇ A	NT	NT ◇ A	NT	NT ◇ A	NT	NT ◇ A	NT	NT ◇	NT ◇ A	NT
York [8]	29	d	08 51	09 21	10 01	10 08	10 49	11 21	11 54	12 21	12 50	13 21	13 51	14 21	14 54	15 21	15 51	16 21	16 51	17 21	17 51	18 02	18 21	18 49
Ulleskelf		d	09 01				10 58				13 00						16 00					18 12		
Church Fenton		a	09 04	09 32		10 19	11 01	11 33		12 32	13 04	13 32	14 02	14 32		15 32	16 03	16 32	17 02	17 32		18 16	18 32	19 00
		d	09 05				11 01				13 04		14 02				16 03		17 02			18 19		19 00
Sherburn-in-Elmet		d	09 09				11 05				13 08		14 06				16 07		17 06			18 22		19 04
Selby		a	09 21		10 20		11 18		12 13		13 20		14 19		15 14		16 20		17 20		18 11			19 17
Hull	29	a	09 58		10 55		11 57		12 49		13 55		14 55		15 55		16 55		17 54		18 46			19 53
Pontefract Baghill		d																				18 34		
Moorthorpe	31	a																				18 44		
Swinton (S.Yorks)	29,31	a																				18 55		
Rotherham Central	29,31	a																				19 02		
Meadowhall	29,31	a																				19 09		
Sheffield [7]	29,31	a																				19 19		

Station			NT ◇ A	NT	NT ◇ A	NT ◇ B	NT	NT ◇ A	NT	NT
York [8]	29	d	19 21	19 56	20 21	20 48	20 52	21 21	21 51	22 19
Ulleskelf		d				20 58			22 00	
Church Fenton		a	19 32		20 32	21 02		21 32	22 03	
		d				21 02			22 04	
Sherburn-in-Elmet		d				21 06			22 07	
Selby		a		20 15			21 11		22 22	22 38
Hull	29	a		20 54			21 57			23 21
Pontefract Baghill		d				21 24				
Moorthorpe	31	a				21 36				
Swinton (S.Yorks)	29,31	a				21 45				
Rotherham Central	29,31	a								
Meadowhall	29,31	a				21 55				
Sheffield [7]	29,31	a				22 03				

A To Blackpool North
B via Pontefract Baghill

Table T033-R

Mondays to Fridays
16 December to 15 May

York - Selby and Sheffield

Local services only

Miles	Miles	Station			NT ◇ A	NT	NT	NT ◇ A	NT	NT ◇ A	NT	NT B	NT ◇ A	NT ◇	NT ◇	NT ◇ A	NT ◇ C	NT ◇ A	NT ◇ C	NT ◇ A	NT ◇ C	NT ◇ A	NT ◇ C	NT ◇
0	0	**York [8]**	29	d	05 19	05 36	05 40	06 12	06 15	07 13	07 32	07 47	08 23	08 45	09 15	09 23	09 45	10 23	10 45	11 23	11 45	12 23	12 42	13 15
8¾	8¾	Ulleskelf		d					06 25	07 21		07 57			09 26									13 25
10¾	10¾	Church Fenton		a	05 29			06 22	06 29	07 25	07 43	08 01	08 33	08 56	09 30	09 33	09 56	10 33		11 33	11 56	12 33		13 29
—	—			d					06 30		07 44			08 57	09 31		09 57				11 57			13 29
12¾	12¾	Sherburn-in-Elmet		d					06 34		07 48			09 01	09 35		10 01				12 01			13 33
—	21	**Selby**		a		05 59	06 06		06 49		08 00			09 14			10 14		11 14		12 14		13 15	
—	—	Hull	29	a		06 30			07 38		08 50			09 54			10 54		11 54		12 54		13 55	
21½	—	Pontefract Baghill		d											09 48									13 46
28¼	—	Moorthorpe	31	a											09 59									13 57
36	—	Swinton (S.Yorks)	29,31	a											10 08									14 09
40½	—	Rotherham Central	29,31	a											10 18									14 18
43¼	—	Meadowhall	29,31	a											10 24									14 24
46¾	—	**Sheffield [7]**	29,31	a											10 33									14 32

Station			NT ◇ A	NT ◇ C	NT ◇ A	NT ◇ C	NT ◇ A	NT ◇ C	NT ◇ A	NT ◇ C	NT ◇	NT ◇ A	NT ◇ C	NT ◇ A	NT ◇ C	NT ◇ A	NT ◇ C	NT ◇ A	NT ◇	NT B	NT ◇ A	NT ◇	NT ◇ D	NT
York [8]	29	d	13 23	13 45	14 23	14 46	15 23	15 46	16 23	16 45	17 15	17 23	17 45	18 22	18 45	19 23	19 41	20 23	20 45	21 08	21 23	21 44	22 19	22 47
Ulleskelf		d						15 56			17 25													22 56
Church Fenton		a	13 33	13 56	14 33		15 33	16 00	16 33	16 56	17 29	17 33	17 58	18 32	18 56	19 33	19 52	20 33	20 56	21 18	21 33	21 55	22 29	23 00
		d		13 57				16 00		16 57	17 29		17 58		18 57		19 53		20 57			21 56		23 00
Sherburn-in-Elmet		d		14 01				16 05		17 01	17 33		18 03		19 01		19 57		21 01			22 00		23 04
Selby		a		14 14		15 14		16 17		17 14			18 15		19 14		20 10		21 14			22 14		23 17
Hull	29	a		14 54		15 54		16 57		17 56			18 55		19 54		20 52		21 57			22 53		00 03
Pontefract Baghill		d									17 46													
Moorthorpe	31	a									17 57													
Swinton (S.Yorks)	29,31	a									18 06													
Rotherham Central	29,31	a									18 18													
Meadowhall	29,31	a									18 24													
Sheffield [7]	29,31	a									18 32													

Station			NT B	NT
York [8]	29	d	23 13	23 19
Ulleskelf		d		
Church Fenton		a	23 29	
		d		
Sherburn-in-Elmet		d		
Selby		a		23 40
Hull	29	a		
Pontefract Baghill		d		
Moorthorpe	31	a		
Swinton (S.Yorks)	29,31	a		
Rotherham Central	29,31	a		
Meadowhall	29,31	a		
Sheffield [7]	29,31	a		

Saturdays
21 December to 16 May

Station			NT ◇ A	NT	NT	NT ◇ A	NT	NT ◇ A	NT	NT B	NT ◇ A	NT ◇	NT ◇	NT ◇ A	NT ◇ C	NT ◇ A	NT ◇ C	NT ◇ A	NT ◇ C	NT ◇ A	NT ◇ C	NT ◇	NT ◇ A	NT ◇ C
York [8]	29	d	05 19	05 36	05 40	06 12	06 15	07 13	07 32	07 47	08 23	08 45	09 15	09 23	09 45	10 23	10 45	11 23	11 45	12 23	12 42	13 15	13 23	13 45
Ulleskelf		d					06 25	07 21		07 57			09 26									13 25		
Church Fenton		a	05 29			06 22	06 29	07 25	07 43	08 01	08 33	08 56	09 30	09 33	09 56	10 33		11 33	11 56	12 33		13 29	13 33	13 56
		d					06 30		07 43			08 57	09 31		09 57				11 57			13 29		13 57
Sherburn-in-Elmet		d					06 34		07 47			09 01	09 35		10 01				12 01			13 33		14 01
Selby		a		05 59	06 06		06 49		07 58			09 14			10 14		11 14		12 14		13 15			14 14
Hull	29	a		06 30			07 38		08 49			09 54			10 54		11 54		12 54		13 55			14 54
Pontefract Baghill		d											09 48									13 46		
Moorthorpe	31	a											09 59									13 57		
Swinton (S.Yorks)	29,31	a											10 08									14 09		
Rotherham Central	29,31	a											10 18									14 18		
Meadowhall	29,31	a											10 24									14 24		
Sheffield [7]	29,31	a											10 33									14 32		

Station			NT ◇ A	NT ◇ C	NT ◇ A	NT ◇ C	NT ◇ A	NT ◇ C	NT ◇	NT ◇ A	NT ◇ C	NT ◇ A	NT ◇ C	NT ◇ A	NT ◇ C	NT ◇ A	NT ◇	NT B	NT ◇ A	NT ◇	NT ◇ D	NT	NT B
York [8]	29	d	14 23	14 46	15 23	15 46	16 23	16 45	17 15	17 23	17 45	18 22	18 45	19 23	19 41	20 23	20 45	21 08	21 23	21 44	22 19	22 47	23 13
Ulleskelf		d				15 56			17 25													22 56	
Church Fenton		a	14 33		15 33	16 00	16 33	16 56	17 29	17 33	17 58	18 32	18 56	19 33	19 52	20 33	20 56	21 18	21 33	21 55	22 29	23 00	23 29
		d				16 00		16 57	17 29		17 58		18 57		19 53		20 57			21 56		23 00	
Sherburn-in-Elmet		d				16 05		17 01	17 33		18 03		19 01		19 57		21 01			22 00		23 04	
Selby		a		15 14		16 17		17 14			18 15		19 14		20 10		21 14			22 14		23 17	
Hull	29	a		15 54		16 57		17 56			18 55		19 54		20 52		21 57			22 53		00 03	
Pontefract Baghill		d							17 46														
Moorthorpe	31	a							17 57														
Swinton (S.Yorks)	29,31	a							18 06														
Rotherham Central	29,31	a							18 18														
Meadowhall	29,31	a							18 24														
Sheffield [7]	29,31	a							18 32														

A To Blackpool North
B To Leeds
C To Bridlington
D To Blackburn

← See Sunday times, left.

Table T034-F

Mondays to Fridays

16 December to 15 May

Nottingham and Sheffield - Barnsley - Huddersfield and Leeds

Miles	Miles		NT MX ◇ A	NT	NT	NT B	NT	NT	NT ◇ C	NT B	NT	NT D	NT	NT E	NT	NT ◇	NT B	NT	NT ◇	NT ◇ C	NT E	NT D
0	—	**Nottingham 8** ⇌ d																				
—	—	Ilkeston d																				
12	—	Langley Mill d																				
18¼	—	Alfreton d																				
28¼	—	Chesterfield d																	06 25			
33½	—	Dronfield d	00 02																06 32			
40½	0	**Sheffield 7** 29,31 ⇌ a	00 15																06 42			
—	—	d		05 15	05 18	05 25	05 28	05 37	05 42	05 48	05 51		06 02	06 05	06 16	06 19	06 27	06 30	06 44	06 55	07 01	
44	3½	**Meadowhall 4** 29,31 ⇌ a		05 20	05 23	05 30	05 33	05 42	05 47	05 53	05 56		06 07	06 10	06 21	06 24	06 32	06 35	06 49	07 02	07 06	
—	—	d		05 21	05 24		05 34	05 43			05 57		06 08		06 22	06 25		06 36	06 51			
47¾	7¼	Chapeltown d			05 30		05 40	05 49					06 14					06 42				
51	10½	Elsecar d			05 35		05 46	05 55					06 20					06 48				
52½	12	Wombwell d			05 39		05 49	05 58					06 23					06 51				
56½	16	**Barnsley** a			05 45		05 57	06 04			06 12		06 29			06 39		06 58	07 06			
—	—	d					05 57	06 05					06 30			06 39		07 01	07 06			
—	19	Dodworth d						06 11										07 07				
—	20¼	Silkstone Common d						06 14										07 10				
—	23½	Penistone d						06 20										07 17				
—	27½	Denby Dale d						06 27										07 24				
—	29¾	Shepley d						06 32										07 29				
—	30¾	Stocksmoor d						06 35										07 32				
—	32¼	Brockholes d						06 39										07 36				
—	33¾	Honley d						06 41										07 38				
—	34¾	Berry Brow d						06 44										07 41				
—	35¾	Lockwood d						06 47										07 44				
—	37	**Huddersfield** a						06 51										07 48				
60	—	Darton d					06 02						06 35									
67½	—	**Wakefield Kirkgate 4** 31 a					06 15						06 48			06 54			07 22			
—	—	d					06 15					06 28	06 49			06 55			07 23			07 28
70½	—	Normanton d					06 21					06 34	06 55			06 59			07 27			07 34
74	—	Castleford 32 a										06 40	07 01									07 40
78¾	—	Woodlesford 32 a					06 28						07 13									
84¾	—	**Leeds 10** 31,32 a		06 31			06 44						07 25		07 31	07 16			07 43			

	NT	TP ◇1 F	NT	NT ◇	EM ◇ G	NT ◇ H	NT E	NT	NT ◇ I	NT ◇ C	EM ◇1 J	NT D	NT	NT B	TP ◇1 F	NT	NT ◇	NT B	NT	EM ◇ G	NT ◇ K	NT D
Nottingham 8 ⇌ d				06 16	06 35												07 18			07 45		
Ilkeston d				06 28													07 30			07 59		
Langley Mill d				06 35													07 37					
Alfreton d				06 43	06 56												07 45			08 10		
Chesterfield d				06 53	07 06						07 42						07 57			08 20		
Dronfield d				07 00	07 14						07 49						08 04			08 27		
Sheffield 7 29,31 ⇌ a				07 10	07 24						08 00						08 15			08 39		
d	07 04	07 08	07 12	07 18		07 24	07 31	07 35	07 47	07 57			08 04	08 07	08 11	08 16	08 19	08 32	08 35		08 45	
Meadowhall 4 29,31 ⇌ a	07 09	07 14	07 18	07 23		07 29	07 37	07 40	07 53	08 02			08 09	08 12	08 17	08 21	08 24	08 37	08 40		08 50	
d	07 10		07 21	07 24				07 41	07 54				08 10			08 22	08 25		08 41		08 51	
Chapeltown d	07 17							07 47					08 16						08 47			
Elsecar d	07 23							07 53					08 22						08 53			
Wombwell d	07 26							07 56					08 25						08 56			
Barnsley a	07 32			07 41				08 02	08 08				08 31				08 40		09 02		09 09	
d	07 33			07 42				08 03	08 08				08 32				08 40		09 03		09 09	
Dodworth d								08 09											09 09			
Silkstone Common d								08 12											09 12			
Penistone d								08 19											09 19			
Denby Dale d								08 26											09 26			
Shepley d								08 31											09 31			
Stocksmoor d								08 34											09 34			
Brockholes d								08 38											09 38			
Honley d								08 40											09 40			
Berry Brow d								08 43											09 43			
Lockwood d								08 46											09 46			
Huddersfield a								08 50											09 50			
Darton d	07 38												08 37									
Wakefield Kirkgate 4 31 a	07 50			07 57					08 23				08 49				08 55				09 24	
d	07 51			07 57					08 24			08 29	08 50				08 56				09 25	09 28
Normanton d	07 56								08 29			08 34	08 56									09 34
Castleford 32 a	08 01											08 40	09 01									09 40
Woodlesford 32 a	08 13												09 13									
Leeds 10 31,32 a	08 26		08 34	08 17					08 44				09 24			09 31	09 14				09 44	

A From Nottingham
B To Doncaster
C To Scarborough
D From Huddersfield
E To Adwick
F From Manchester Airport to Cleethorpes
G To Liverpool Lime Street
H To York
I From Retford
J From Derby
K From Lincoln

Table T034-F

Mondays to Fridays

16 December to 15 May

Nottingham and Sheffield - Barnsley - Huddersfield and Leeds

	NT ◇ A	NT	NT B	TP ◇1 C	NT	NT ◇	NT D	NT	EM MO ◇ E	EM MX ◇ E	NT ◇ F	NT G	NT ◇ A	NT	NT B	TP ◇1 C	NT	NT ◇	NT D	NT	EM ◇ E
Nottingham 8 ⇌ d						08 17			08 47	08 47								09 17			09 47
Ilkeston d						08 29												09 29			
Langley Mill d						08 36												09 36			
Alfreton d						08 44			09 08	09 08								09 44			10 08
Chesterfield d						08 55			09 20	09 20								09 55			10 21
Dronfield d						09 02												10 02			
Sheffield 7 29,31 ⇌ a						09 13			09 37	09 38								10 13			10 37
d	08 56	09 03	09 06	09 11	09 15	09 18	09 32	09 35			09 45		09 57	10 02	10 05	10 11	10 15	10 18	10 32	10 35	
Meadowhall 4 29,31 ⇌ a	09 01	09 09	09 11	09 16	09 20	09 23	09 37	09 40			09 50		10 02	10 07	10 10	10 16	10 20	10 23	10 37	10 40	
d		09 09			09 21	09 24		09 41			09 51			10 08			10 21	10 24		10 41	
Chapeltown d		09 15						09 47						10 14						10 47	
Elsecar d		09 21						09 53						10 20						10 53	
Wombwell d		09 25						09 56						10 23						10 56	
Barnsley a		09 31				09 39		10 02			10 09			10 29				10 39		11 02	
d		09 31				09 40		10 03			10 09			10 30				10 40		11 03	
Dodworth d								10 09												11 09	
Silkstone Common d								10 12												11 12	
Penistone d								10 19												11 19	
Denby Dale d								10 26												11 26	
Shepley d								10 31												11 31	
Stocksmoor d								10 34												11 34	
Brockholes d								10 38												11 38	
Honley d								10 40												11 40	
Berry Brow d								10 43												11 43	
Lockwood d								10 46												11 46	
Huddersfield a								10 50												11 50	
Darton d		09 36												10 35							
Wakefield Kirkgate 4 31 a		09 49				09 55					10 24			10 48				10 55			
d		09 49				09 55					10 24	10 28		10 49				10 55			
Normanton d		09 56										10 34		10 56							
Castleford 32 a		10 01										10 40		11 01							
Woodlesford 32 a		10 13												11 13							
Leeds 10 31,32 a		10 25			10 31	10 14					10 44			11 25			11 31	11 14			

	NT ◇ F	NT G	NT ◇ A	NT	NT B	TP ◇1 C	NT	NT ◇	NT D	NT	EM ◇ E	NT ◇ H	NT ◇ F	NT G	NT ◇ A	NT	NT B	TP ◇1 C	NT	NT ◇	NT D	NT
Nottingham 8 ⇌ d								10 17			10 51									11 17		
Ilkeston d								10 29												11 29		
Langley Mill d								10 36												11 36		
Alfreton d								10 44			11 12									11 44		
Chesterfield d								10 55			11 22									11 55		
Dronfield d								11 02												12 02		
Sheffield 7 29,31 ⇌ a								11 13			11 37									12 13		
d	10 45		10 57	11 02	11 05	11 10	11 15	11 18	11 32	11 35		11 41	11 45		11 57	12 02	12 05	12 11	12 15	12 18	12 32	12 35
Meadowhall 4 29,31 ⇌ a	10 50		11 02	11 07	11 10	11 16	11 20	11 23	11 37	11 40		11 46	11 50		12 02	12 07	12 10	12 16	12 20	12 23	12 37	12 40
d	10 51			11 08			11 21	11 24		11 41			11 51			12 08			12 21	12 24		12 41
Chapeltown d				11 14						11 47						12 14						12 47
Elsecar d				11 20						11 53						12 20						12 53
Wombwell d				11 23						11 56						12 23						12 56
Barnsley a	11 09			11 29				11 39		12 02			12 09			12 29				12 39		13 02
d	11 09			11 30				11 40		12 03			12 09			12 30				12 40		13 03
Dodworth d										12 09												13 09
Silkstone Common d										12 12												13 12
Penistone d										12 18												13 19
Denby Dale d										12 25												13 26
Shepley d										12 30												13 31
Stocksmoor d										12 33												13 34
Brockholes d										12 37												13 38
Honley d										12 39												13 40
Berry Brow d										12 42												13 43
Lockwood d										12 45												13 46
Huddersfield a										12 49												13 50
Darton d				11 35												12 35						
Wakefield Kirkgate 4 31 a	11 24			11 48				11 55					12 24			12 48				12 55		
d	11 24	11 28		11 49				11 55					12 24	12 28		12 49				12 55		
Normanton d		11 34		11 56										12 34		12 56						
Castleford 32 a		11 40		12 01										12 40		13 01						
Woodlesford 32 a				12 13												13 13						
Leeds 10 31,32 a	11 44			12 25			12 31	12 14					12 44			13 25			13 31	13 14		

A To Scarborough
B To Adwick
C From Manchester Airport to Cleethorpes
D To Doncaster
E From Norwich to Liverpool Lime Street
F From Lincoln
G From Huddersfield
H To York

Table T034-F

Mondays to Fridays

16 December to 15 May

Nottingham and Sheffield - Barnsley - Huddersfield and Leeds

		EM	NT	NT	NT	NT		NT	TP	NT	NT	NT	NT	EM	NT	NT		NT	NT	NT	TP	NT	NT	NT	NT
		◇ A	◇ B	C	◇ D			E	◇1 F		◇	G		◇ A	◇ B	C		◇ D		E	◇1 F		◇	G	
Nottingham 8	d	11 47									12 17			12 47									13 17		
Ilkeston	d										12 29			13 00									13 29		
Langley Mill	d										12 36												13 36		
Alfreton	d	12 08									12 44			13 10									13 44		
Chesterfield	d	12 22									12 55			13 21									13 55		
Dronfield	d										13 02												14 02		
Sheffield 7 29,31	a	12 37									13 13			13 37									14 13		
	d		12 45		12 57	13 02		13 05	13 11	13 15	13 18	13 32	13 35		13 43			13 57	14 02	14 05	14 11	14 15	14 18	14 32	14 35
Meadowhall 4 29,31	a		12 50		13 02	13 07		13 10	13 16	13 20	13 23	13 37	13 40		13 50			14 02	14 07	14 10	14 16	14 20	14 23	14 37	14 40
	d		12 51			13 08				13 21	13 24		13 41		13 51				14 08			14 21	14 24		14 41
Chapeltown	d					13 14							13 47						14 14						14 47
Elsecar	d					13 20							13 53						14 20						14 53
Wombwell	d					13 23							13 56						14 23						14 56
Barnsley	a		13 09			13 29					13 39		14 02		14 09				14 29				14 39		15 02
	d		13 09			13 30					13 40		14 03		14 09				14 30				14 40		15 03
Dodworth	d												14 09												15 09
Silkstone Common	d												14 12												15 12
Penistone	d												14 19												15 19
Denby Dale	d												14 26												15 26
Shepley	d												14 31												15 31
Stocksmoor	d												14 34												15 34
Brockholes	d												14 38												15 38
Honley	d												14 40												15 40
Berry Brow	d												14 43												15 43
Lockwood	d												14 46												15 46
Huddersfield	a												14 50												15 50
Darton	d					13 35													14 35						
Wakefield Kirkgate 4 31	a		13 24			13 50					13 55				14 24				14 48				14 55		
	d		13 24	13 28		13 50					13 55				14 24	14 28			14 49				14 55		
Normanton	d			13 34		13 56										14 34			14 56						
Castleford 32	a			13 40		14 01										14 40			15 01						
Woodlesford 32	a					14 13													15 13						
Leeds 10 31,32	a		13 44			14 25				14 31	14 14				14 44				15 25			15 31	15 14		

		EM		NT	NT	NT	NT	NT	TP	NT	NT	NT		NT	EM	NT	NT	NT	NT	NT	NT	TP		NT	NT
		◇ A		◇ B	C	◇ D		E	◇1 F		◇	G			◇ A	◇ H	◇ B	C	◇ D		E	◇1 F			◇
Nottingham 8	d	13 47									14 17				14 47										15 17
Ilkeston	d										14 29														15 29
Langley Mill	d										14 36														15 36
Alfreton	d	14 10									14 44				15 08										15 44
Chesterfield	d	14 20									14 55				15 21										15 55
Dronfield	d										15 02														16 02
Sheffield 7 29,31	a	14 37									15 13				15 37										16 13
	d			14 45		14 57	15 02	15 05	15 11	15 15	15 18	15 32		15 35		15 40	15 45		15 57	16 02	16 05	16 11		16 15	16 18
Meadowhall 4 29,31	a			14 50		15 02	15 07	15 10	15 16	15 20	15 23	15 37		15 40		15 47	15 50		16 02	16 07	16 10	16 16		16 20	16 23
	d			14 51			15 08			15 21	15 24			15 41			15 51			16 08				16 21	16 24
Chapeltown	d						15 14							15 47						16 14					
Elsecar	d						15 20							15 53						16 20					
Wombwell	d						15 23							15 56						16 23					
Barnsley	a			15 09			15 29				15 39			16 02			16 08			16 29					16 39
	d			15 09			15 30				15 40			16 03			16 09			16 30					16 40
Dodworth	d													16 09											
Silkstone Common	d													16 12											
Penistone	d													16 19											
Denby Dale	d													16 26											
Shepley	d													16 31											
Stocksmoor	d													16 34											
Brockholes	d													16 38											
Honley	d													16 40											
Berry Brow	d													16 43											
Lockwood	d													16 46											
Huddersfield	a													16 50											
Darton	d						15 35													16 35					
Wakefield Kirkgate 4 31	a			15 24			15 48				15 55						16 23			16 48					16 55
	d			15 24	15 28		15 49				15 55						16 24	16 28		16 49					16 55
Normanton	d				15 34		15 56											16 34		16 56					
Castleford 32	a				15 40		16 01											16 40		17 01					
Woodlesford 32	a						16 13													17 13					
Leeds 10 31,32	a			15 44			16 25			16 31	16 14						16 44			17 25				17 31	17 14

A From Norwich to Liverpool Lime Street
B From Lincoln
C From Huddersfield
D To Scarborough
E To Adwick
F From Manchester Airport to Cleethorpes
G To Doncaster
H To York

Table T034-F

Mondays to Fridays

16 December to 15 May

Nottingham and Sheffield - Barnsley - Huddersfield and Leeds

		NT	NT	EM	NT	NT	NT	NT		NT	TP	NT	NT	NT	NT	EM	NT	NT		NT	NT	NT	TP	NT	NT
		A		◇ B	◇ C	D	◇ E			F	◇1 G		◇	A		◇ B	◇ C	D		◇ E		F	◇1 G		◇
Nottingham 8	d			15 47									16 17			16 47									17 17
Ilkeston	d			16 00									16 29												17 29
Langley Mill	d												16 36												17 36
Alfreton	d			16 10									16 44			17 08									17 44
Chesterfield	d			16 21									16 55			17 20									17 55
Dronfield	d												17 02												18 02
Sheffield 7 29,31	a			16 37									17 13			17 38									18 13
	d	16 32	16 35		16 45		16 57	17 02		17 05	17 11	17 15	17 18	17 32	17 35		17 45			17 57	18 02	18 05	18 11	18 15	18 18
Meadowhall 4 29,31	a	16 37	16 40		16 50		17 02	17 07		17 10	17 16	17 20	17 23	17 37	17 40		17 50			18 02	18 07	18 10	18 17	18 20	18 23
	d		16 41		16 51			17 08				17 21	17 24		17 41		17 51				18 08			18 21	18 24
Chapeltown	d		16 47					17 14							17 47						18 14				
Elsecar	d		16 53					17 20							17 53						18 20				
Wombwell	d		16 56					17 23							17 56						18 23				
Barnsley	a		17 02		17 09			17 29					17 39		18 02		18 09				18 29				18 39
	d		17 03		17 09			17 30					17 40		18 03		18 09				18 30				18 40
Dodworth	d		17 09												18 09										
Silkstone Common	d		17 12												18 13										
Penistone	d		17 19												18 23										
Denby Dale	d		17 26												18 29										
Shepley	d		17 31												18 34										
Stocksmoor	d		17 33												18 37										
Brockholes	d		17 37												18 41										
Honley	d		17 40												18 43										
Berry Brow	d		17 43												18 46										
Lockwood	d		17 45												18 49										
Huddersfield	a		17 50												18 54										
Darton	d							17 35													18 35				
Wakefield Kirkgate 4 31	a				17 24			17 48					17 55				18 24				18 48				18 55
	d				17 24	17 28		17 49					17 55				18 24	18 28			18 49				18 55
Normanton	d					17 34		17 56										18 34			18 56				
Castleford 32	a					17 40		18 01										18 40			19 01				
Woodlesford 32	a							18 13													19 13				
Leeds 10 31,32	a				17 44			18 25				18 31	18 14				18 44				19 24			19 31	19 14

		NT	NT	EM		NT	NT	NT	NT	NT	TP	NT	NT	NT		NT	EM	NT	NT	NT	NT	NT	NT	TP	
																					FX	FO			
		A		◇ B		◇ C	D	◇ H		F	◇1 G		◇	A			◇ B	◇ C	D	◇ I			F	◇1 G	
Nottingham 8	d			17 47									18 17				18 47								
Ilkeston	d												18 29												
Langley Mill	d			18 03									18 36												
Alfreton	d			18 11									18 44				19 08								
Chesterfield	d			18 21									18 55				19 21								
Dronfield	d												19 02												
Sheffield 7 29,31	a			18 37									19 13				19 37								
	d	18 30	18 35			18 45		18 57	19 02	19 05	19 11	19 15	19 18	19 32		19 35		19 45		19 57	20 02	20 02	20 05	20 11	
Meadowhall 4 29,31	a	18 35	18 40			18 50		19 02	19 07	19 12	19 16	19 20	19 23	19 37		19 40		19 50		20 02	20 07	20 07	20 10	20 16	
	d		18 41			18 51			19 08			19 21	19 24			19 41		19 51			20 08	20 08			
Chapeltown	d		18 47						19 14							19 47					20 14	20 14			
Elsecar	d		18 53						19 20							19 53					20 20	20 20			
Wombwell	d		18 56						19 23							19 56					20 23	20 23			
Barnsley	a		19 02			19 09			19 29				19 39			20 02		20 09			20 29	20 29			
	d		19 03			19 09			19 30				19 40			20 03		20 09			20 30	20 30			
Dodworth	d		19 09													20 09									
Silkstone Common	d		19 12													20 12									
Penistone	d		19 19													20 19									
Denby Dale	d		19 26													20 26									
Shepley	d		19 31													20 31									
Stocksmoor	d		19 34													20 34									
Brockholes	d		19 38													20 38									
Honley	d		19 40													20 40									
Berry Brow	d		19 43													20 43									
Lockwood	d		19 46													20 46									
Huddersfield	a		19 50													20 50									
Darton	d								19 35												20 35	20 35			
Wakefield Kirkgate 4 31	a					19 24			19 48				19 55					20 24			20 48	20 48			
	d					19 24	19 28		19 49				19 55					20 24	20 28		20 49	20 49			
Normanton	d						19 34		19 56										20 34		20 56	20 56			
Castleford 32	a						19 40		20 01										20 41		21 01	21 01			
Woodlesford 32	a								20 13												21 13	21 13			
Leeds 10 31,32	a					19 44			20 25			20 36	20 15					20 44			21 25	21 26			

A To Doncaster
B From Norwich to Liverpool Lime Street
C From Lincoln
D From Huddersfield
E To Scarborough
F To Adwick
G From Manchester Airport to Cleethorpes
H To Bridlington
I To Hull

Table T034-F

Mondays to Fridays
16 December to 15 May

Nottingham and Sheffield - Barnsley - Huddersfield and Leeds

		NT	NT	NT	EM	NT	NT	NT	NT	NT	NT	TP	NT	NT	NT	EM	NT	NT	EM	NT	TP	NT	NT
			◇	A	◇ B		◇ C	D	◇ E		F	◇1 G		◇	D	◇1 H		◇ I	◇1 H	F	◇1 G		◇
Nottingham	d		19 17		19 40									20 17		20 33			21 08				21 12
Ilkeston	d		19 29											20 29									21 29
Langley Mill	d		19 36											20 36		20 49			21 25				21 36
Alfreton	d		19 44		20 09									20 44		20 57			21 33				21 44
Chesterfield	d		19 55		20 20									20 55		21 10			21 44				21 55
Dronfield	d		20 02											21 02									22 02
Sheffield 29,31	a		20 13		20 35									21 13		21 24			21 59				22 14
	d	20 15	20 18	20 32		20 35	20 45		20 57	21 02	21 05	21 11	21 15	21 18		21 26	21 35	21 57	22 04	22 07	22 11	22 15	22 18
Meadowhall 29,31	a	20 20	20 23	20 37		20 40	20 50		21 02	21 07	21 10	21 16	21 20	21 23			21 40	22 02		22 12	22 16	22 20	22 23
	d	20 21	20 24			20 41	20 51			21 08			21 21	21 24			21 41					22 21	22 24
Chapeltown	d					20 47				21 14							21 47						
Elsecar	d					20 53				21 20							21 53						
Wombwell	d					20 56				21 23							21 56						
Barnsley	a		20 39			21 02	21 09			21 29				21 39			22 02						22 39
	d		20 40			21 03	21 09			21 30				21 40			22 03						22 40
Dodworth	d					21 09											22 09						
Silkstone Common	d					21 12											22 12						
Penistone	d					21 19											22 19						
Denby Dale	d					21 26											22 26						
Shepley	d					21 31											22 31						
Stocksmoor	d					21 34											22 34						
Brockholes	d					21 38											22 38						
Honley	d					21 40											22 40						
Berry Brow	d					21 43											22 43						
Lockwood	d					21 46											22 46						
Huddersfield	a					21 50											22 50						
Darton	d									21 35													
Wakefield Kirkgate 31	a		20 55				21 24			21 48				21 55									22 55
	d		20 55				21 24	21 28		21 49				21 55	22 28								22 55
Normanton	d							21 34		21 56					22 34								
Castleford 32	a							21 40		22 01					22 40								
Woodlesford 32	a									22 13													
Leeds 31,32	a	21 30	21 14				21 44			22 25			22 29	22 14		22 20			22 49			23 34	23 14

		NT	NT	NT	NT	NT	NT	NT	NT
				◇ I	A			A	◇
Nottingham	d								23 18
Ilkeston	d								23 30
Langley Mill	d								23 36
Alfreton	d								23 44
Chesterfield	d								23 54
Dronfield	d								00 02
Sheffield 29,31	a								00 15
	d	22 31	22 38	22 59	23 05	23 15	23 18	23 27	
Meadowhall 29,31	a	22 36	22 43	23 04	23 10	23 20	23 23	23 32	
	d	22 37	22 44			23 21	23 24		
Chapeltown	d	22 43	22 51				23 30		
Elsecar	d	22 48	22 57				23 35		
Wombwell	d	22 52	23 01				23 39		
Barnsley	a	22 59	23 07				23 46		
	d	22 59	23 07				23 46		
Dodworth	d		23 13						
Silkstone Common	d		23 17						
Penistone	d		23 26						
Denby Dale	d		23 33						
Shepley	d		23 38						
Stocksmoor	d		23 40						
Brockholes	d		23 44						
Honley	d		23 47						
Berry Brow	d		23 50						
Lockwood	d		23 52						
Huddersfield	a		23 57						
Darton	d	23 04					23 51		
Wakefield Kirkgate 31	a	23 17					00 04		
	d	23 18							
Normanton	d	23 22							
Castleford 32	a	23 32							
Woodlesford 32	a	23 43							
Leeds 31,32	a	23 58				00 30			

A To Doncaster
B From Norwich to Manchester Piccadilly
C From Lincoln
D From Huddersfield
E To Bridlington
F To Adwick
G From Manchester Airport to Cleethorpes
H From St Pancras International
I To Hull

Table T034-F

Saturdays
21 December to 16 May

Nottingham and Sheffield - Barnsley - Huddersfield and Leeds

		NT	NT	NT	NT	NT	NT	NT	NT	NT	NT	NT	NT	NT	NT	NT	NT	NT	NT	NT	NT	NT	TP
		◇ A			B			◇ C	B		D		E		◇	B		◇	◇ C	E	D		◇1 F
Nottingham	d																						
Ilkeston	d																						
Langley Mill	d																						
Alfreton	d																						
Chesterfield	d																	06 25					
Dronfield	d	00 02																06 32					
Sheffield 29,31	a	00 15																06 42					
	d		05 15	05 18	05 25	05 28	05 37	05 42	05 48	05 51		06 04	06 07	06 16	06 19	06 27	06 30	06 44	06 55	07 01		07 04	07 08
Meadowhall 29,31	a		05 20	05 23	05 30	05 33	05 42	05 47	05 53	05 56		06 09	06 12	06 21	06 24	06 32	06 35	06 49	07 02	07 06		07 09	07 14
	d		05 21	05 24		05 34	05 43			05 57		06 10		06 22	06 25		06 36	06 51				07 10	
Chapeltown	d			05 30		05 40	05 49					06 16					06 42					07 17	
Elsecar	d			05 35		05 46	05 55					06 22					06 48					07 23	
Wombwell	d			05 39		05 49	05 58					06 25					06 51					07 26	
Barnsley	a			05 45		05 57	06 04			06 12		06 31			06 39		06 58	07 06				07 32	
	d					05 57	06 05					06 32			06 39		07 01	07 06				07 33	
Dodworth	d						06 11										07 07						
Silkstone Common	d						06 14										07 10						
Penistone	d						06 20										07 17						
Denby Dale	d						06 27										07 24						
Shepley	d						06 32										07 29						
Stocksmoor	d						06 35										07 32						
Brockholes	d						06 39										07 36						
Honley	d						06 41										07 38						
Berry Brow	d						06 44										07 41						
Lockwood	d						06 47										07 44						
Huddersfield	a						06 51										07 48						
Darton	d					06 02						06 37										07 38	
Wakefield Kirkgate 31	a					06 15						06 49			06 54			07 22				07 50	
	d					06 15					06 28	06 50			06 55			07 23			07 28	07 51	
Normanton	d					06 21					06 34	06 55			06 59			07 27			07 34	07 56	
Castleford 32	a										06 40	07 01									07 40	08 01	
Woodlesford 32	a					06 28						07 13										08 13	
Leeds 31,32	a		06 31			06 44						07 25		07 31	07 16			07 43				08 26	

		NT	NT	NT	EM	NT	NT	NT	NT	NT	NT	EM	NT	TP	NT	NT	NT	NT	EM	NT	NT	NT	NT
			◇	◇ G	◇ H	E		◇ I	◇ C	D		◇1 J	B	◇1 F		◇	B		◇ H	◇ K	D	◇ C	
Nottingham	d		06 17		06 40											07 18			07 46				
Ilkeston	d		06 29													07 30			07 59				
Langley Mill	d		06 36													07 37							
Alfreton	d		06 44		07 01											07 45			08 09				
Chesterfield	d		06 54		07 11							07 49				07 57			08 20				
Dronfield	d		07 01		07 18							07 56				08 04			08 26				
Sheffield 29,31	a		07 11		07 28							08 07				08 15			08 37				
	d	07 15	07 18	07 25		07 31	07 35	07 47	07 57		08 04		08 07	08 11	08 16	08 19	08 32	08 35		08 45		08 56	09 03
Meadowhall 29,31	a	07 20	07 23	07 30		07 37	07 40	07 52	08 02		08 09		08 12	08 17	08 21	08 24	08 37	08 40		08 50		09 01	09 09
	d	07 21	07 25				07 41	07 54			08 10				08 22	08 25		08 41		08 51			09 09
Chapeltown	d						07 47				08 16							08 47					09 15
Elsecar	d						07 53				08 22							08 53					09 21
Wombwell	d						07 56				08 25							08 56					09 25
Barnsley	a		07 41				08 02	08 08			08 31					08 40		09 02		09 09			09 31
	d		07 42				08 03	08 08			08 32					08 41		09 03		09 09			09 31
Dodworth	d						08 09											09 09					
Silkstone Common	d						08 12											09 12					
Penistone	d						08 19											09 19					
Denby Dale	d						08 26											09 26					
Shepley	d						08 31											09 31					
Stocksmoor	d						08 34											09 34					
Brockholes	d						08 38											09 38					
Honley	d						08 40											09 40					
Berry Brow	d						08 43											09 43					
Lockwood	d						08 46											09 46					
Huddersfield	a						08 50											09 50					
Darton	d										08 37												09 36
Wakefield Kirkgate 31	a		07 57					08 23			08 49					08 56				09 23			09 49
	d		07 57					08 24		08 29	08 50					08 57				09 24	09 28		09 49
Normanton	d							08 29		08 34	08 56										09 34		09 56
Castleford 32	a									08 40	09 01										09 40		10 01
Woodlesford 32	a										09 13												10 13
Leeds 31,32	a	08 36	08 17					08 44			09 24				09 31	09 14				09 44			10 24

A From Nottingham
B To Doncaster
C To Scarborough
D From Huddersfield
E To Adwick
F From Manchester Airport to Cleethorpes
G To York
H To Liverpool Lime Street
I From Retford
J From Derby
K From Lincoln

Table T034-F

Saturdays

21 December to 16 May

Nottingham and Sheffield - Barnsley - Huddersfield and Leeds

		NT A	TP ◇1 B	NT	NT ◇	NT C	NT	EM ◇ D	NT ◇ E	NT F	NT ◇ G	NT	NT A	TP ◇1 B	NT	NT ◇	NT C	NT	EM ◇ D	NT ◇ E	NT F	NT ◇ G
Nottingham 6	d				08 17			08 48								09 17			09 47			
Ilkeston	d				08 29											09 29						
Langley Mill	d				08 36											09 36						
Alfreton	d				08 44			09 09								09 44			10 08			
Chesterfield	d				08 55			09 20								09 55			10 20			
Dronfield	d				09 02											10 02						
Sheffield 7 29,31	a				09 13			09 37								10 13			10 37			
	d	09 06	09 11	09 15	09 18	09 29	09 35		09 45		09 59	10 02	10 05	10 11	10 15	10 18	10 32	10 35		10 45		10 57
Meadowhall 4 29,31	a	09 11	09 17	09 20	09 23	09 34	09 40		09 50		10 04	10 07	10 10	10 16	10 20	10 23	10 37	10 40		10 50		11 02
	d			09 21	09 24		09 41		09 52			10 08			10 21	10 24		10 41		10 51		
Chapeltown	d						09 47					10 14						10 47				
Elsecar	d						09 53					10 20						10 53				
Wombwell	d						09 56					10 23						10 56				
Barnsley	a				09 39		10 02		10 09			10 29				10 39		11 02		11 09		
	d				09 40		10 03		10 09			10 30				10 40		11 03		11 09		
Dodworth	d						10 09											11 09				
Silkstone Common	d						10 12											11 12				
Penistone	d						10 19											11 19				
Denby Dale	d						10 26											11 26				
Shepley	d						10 31											11 31				
Stocksmoor	d						10 34											11 34				
Brockholes	d						10 38											11 38				
Honley	d						10 40											11 40				
Berry Brow	d						10 43											11 43				
Lockwood	d						10 46											11 46				
Huddersfield	a						10 50											11 50				
Darton	d											10 35										
Wakefield Kirkgate 4 31	a				09 55				10 24			10 48				10 55				11 24		
	d				09 55				10 24	10 28		10 49				10 55				11 24	11 28	
Normanton	d									10 34		10 56									11 34	
Castleford 32	a									10 40		11 01									11 40	
Woodlesford 32	a											11 13										
Leeds 10 31,32	a			10 31	10 14				10 44			11 25			11 31	11 14				11 44		

		NT	NT A	TP ◇1 B	NT	NT ◇	NT C	NT	EM ◇ D	NT ◇ H	NT ◇ E	NT F	NT ◇ G	NT	NT A	TP ◇1 B	NT	NT ◇	NT C	NT	EM ◇ D	NT ◇ E	NT F
Nottingham 6	d					10 17			10 47									11 17			11 47		
Ilkeston	d					10 29												11 29					
Langley Mill	d					10 36												11 36					
Alfreton	d					10 44			11 08									11 44			12 08		
Chesterfield	d					10 55			11 20									11 55			12 20		
Dronfield	d					11 02												12 02					
Sheffield 7 29,31	a					11 13			11 37									12 13			12 37		
	d	11 02	11 05	11 10	11 15	11 18	11 32	11 35		11 41	11 45		11 57	12 02	12 05	12 11	12 15	12 18	12 32	12 35		12 45	
Meadowhall 4 29,31	a	11 07	11 10	11 16	11 20	11 23	11 37	11 40		11 46	11 50		12 02	12 07	12 10	12 16	12 20	12 23	12 37	12 40		12 50	
	d	11 08			11 21	11 24		11 41			11 51			12 08			12 21	12 24		12 41		12 51	
Chapeltown	d	11 14						11 47						12 14						12 47			
Elsecar	d	11 20						11 53						12 20						12 53			
Wombwell	d	11 23						11 56						12 23						12 56			
Barnsley	a	11 29				11 39		12 02			12 09			12 29				12 39		13 02		13 09	
	d	11 30				11 40		12 03			12 09			12 30				12 40		13 03		13 09	
Dodworth	d							12 09												13 09			
Silkstone Common	d							12 12												13 12			
Penistone	d							12 18												13 19			
Denby Dale	d							12 25												13 26			
Shepley	d							12 30												13 31			
Stocksmoor	d							12 33												13 34			
Brockholes	d							12 37												13 38			
Honley	d							12 39												13 40			
Berry Brow	d							12 42												13 43			
Lockwood	d							12 45												13 46			
Huddersfield	a							12 49												13 50			
Darton	d	11 35												12 35									
Wakefield Kirkgate 4 31	a	11 48				11 55					12 24			12 48				12 55				13 24	
	d	11 49				11 55					12 24	12 28		12 49				12 55				13 24	13 28
Normanton	d	11 56										12 34		12 56									13 34
Castleford 32	a	12 01										12 40		13 01									13 40
Woodlesford 32	a	12 13												13 13									
Leeds 10 31,32	a	12 25			12 31	12 14					12 44			13 25			13 31	13 14				13 44	

A To Adwick
B From Manchester Airport to Cleethorpes
C To Doncaster
D From Norwich to Liverpool Lime Street
E From Lincoln
F From Huddersfield
G To Scarborough
H To York

NRT DECEMBER 19 EDITION

Table T034-F

Saturdays

21 December to 16 May

Nottingham and Sheffield - Barnsley - Huddersfield and Leeds

		NT ◇ A	NT	NT B	TP ◇1 C	NT	NT ◇	NT D	NT	EM ◇ E	NT ◇ F	NT G	NT ◇ A	NT	NT B	TP ◇1 C	NT	NT ◇	NT D	NT	EM ◇ E	NT ◇ F
Nottingham 6	d						12 17			12 47								13 17			13 47	
Ilkeston	d						12 29			13 00								13 29				
Langley Mill	d						12 36											13 36				
Alfreton	d						12 44			13 10								13 44			14 08	
Chesterfield	d						12 55			13 22								13 55			14 20	
Dronfield	d						13 02											14 02				
Sheffield 7 29,31	a						13 13			13 37								14 13			14 37	
	d	12 57	13 02	13 05	13 11	13 15	13 18	13 32	13 35		13 43		13 57	14 02	14 05	14 11	14 15	14 18	14 32	14 35		14 45
Meadowhall 4 29,31	a	13 02	13 07	13 10	13 16	13 20	13 23	13 37	13 40		13 50		14 02	14 07	14 10	14 16	14 20	14 23	14 37	14 40		14 50
	d		13 08			13 21	13 24		13 41		13 51			14 08			14 21	14 24		14 41		14 51
Chapeltown	d		13 14						13 47					14 14						14 47		
Elsecar	d		13 20						13 53					14 20						14 53		
Wombwell	d		13 23						13 56					14 23						14 56		
Barnsley	a		13 29				13 39		14 02		14 09			14 29				14 39		15 02		15 09
	d		13 30				13 40		14 03		14 09			14 30				14 40		15 03		15 09
Dodworth	d								14 09											15 09		
Silkstone Common	d								14 12											15 12		
Penistone	d								14 19											15 19		
Denby Dale	d								14 26											15 26		
Shepley	d								14 31											15 31		
Stocksmoor	d								14 34											15 34		
Brockholes	d								14 38											15 38		
Honley	d								14 40											15 40		
Berry Brow	d								14 43											15 43		
Lockwood	d								14 46											15 46		
Huddersfield	a								14 50											15 50		
Darton	d		13 35											14 35								
Wakefield Kirkgate 4 31	a		13 50				13 55				14 24			14 48				14 55				15 24
	d		13 50				13 55				14 24	14 28		14 49				14 55				15 24
Normanton	d		13 56									14 34		14 56								
Castleford 32	a		14 01									14 40		15 01								
Woodlesford 32	a		14 13											15 13								
Leeds 10 31,32	a		14 25			14 31	14 14				14 44			15 25			15 31	15 14				15 44

		NT G	NT ◇ A	NT	NT B	TP ◇1 C	NT	NT ◇	NT D	NT	EM ◇ E	NT ◇ H	NT ◇ F	NT G	NT ◇ A	NT	NT B	TP ◇1 C	NT	NT ◇	NT D	NT	EM ◇ E
Nottingham 6	d							14 17			14 47									15 17			15 47
Ilkeston	d							14 29												15 29			16 00
Langley Mill	d							14 36												15 36			
Alfreton	d							14 44			15 08									15 44			16 10
Chesterfield	d							14 55			15 20									15 55			16 21
Dronfield	d							15 02												16 02			
Sheffield 7 29,31	a							15 13			15 37									16 13			16 37
	d		14 57	15 02	15 05	15 11	15 15	15 18	15 32	15 35		15 41	15 45		15 57	16 02	16 05	16 11	16 15	16 18	16 32	16 35	
Meadowhall 4 29,31	a		15 02	15 07	15 10	15 16	15 20	15 23	15 37	15 40		15 46	15 50		16 02	16 07	16 10	16 16	16 20	16 23	16 37	16 40	
	d			15 08			15 21	15 24		15 41			15 51			16 08			16 21	16 24		16 41	
Chapeltown	d			15 14						15 47						16 14						16 47	
Elsecar	d			15 20						15 53						16 20						16 53	
Wombwell	d			15 23						15 56						16 23						16 56	
Barnsley	a			15 29				15 39		16 02			16 09			16 29				16 39		17 02	
	d			15 30				15 40		16 03			16 09			16 30				16 40		17 03	
Dodworth	d									16 09												17 09	
Silkstone Common	d									16 12												17 12	
Penistone	d									16 19												17 19	
Denby Dale	d									16 26												17 26	
Shepley	d									16 31												17 31	
Stocksmoor	d									16 34												17 33	
Brockholes	d									16 38												17 37	
Honley	d									16 40												17 40	
Berry Brow	d									16 43												17 43	
Lockwood	d									16 46												17 45	
Huddersfield	a									16 50												17 50	
Darton	d			15 35												16 35							
Wakefield Kirkgate 4 31	a			15 48				15 55					16 24			16 48				16 55			
	d	15 28		15 49				15 55					16 24	16 28		16 49				16 55			
Normanton	d	15 34		15 56										16 34		16 56							
Castleford 32	a	15 40		16 01										16 40		17 01							
Woodlesford 32	a			16 13												17 13							
Leeds 10 31,32	a			16 25			16 31	16 14					16 44			17 25			17 31	17 14			

A To Scarborough
B To Adwick
C From Manchester Airport to Cleethorpes
D To Doncaster
E From Norwich to Liverpool Lime Street
F From Lincoln
G From Huddersfield
H To York

Table T034-F

Saturdays

21 December to 16 May

Nottingham and Sheffield - Barnsley - Huddersfield and Leeds

		NT ◇ A	NT B	NT ◇ C	NT	NT D		TP ◇1 E	NT	NT ◇	NT F	EM ◇ G	NT	NT ◇ A	NT B	NT ◇ C		NT	NT D	TP ◇1 E	NT H	NT ◇	NT F	EM ◇ G	NT
Nottingham 8	d									16 17		16 44										17 17		17 44	
Ilkeston	d									16 29												17 29			
Langley Mill	d									16 36												17 36		18 00	
Alfreton	d									16 44		17 05										17 44		18 08	
Chesterfield	d									16 55		17 15										17 55		18 18	
Dronfield	d									17 02												18 02			
Sheffield 7 29,31	a									17 13		17 34										18 13		18 34	
	d	16 45		16 57	17 02	17 05		17 11	17 15	17 18	17 32		17 35	17 45		17 57		18 02	18 05	18 11	18 15	18 18	18 30		18 35
Meadowhall 4 29,31	a	16 50		17 02	17 07	17 10		17 16	17 20	17 23	17 37		17 40	17 50		18 02		18 07	18 10	18 17	18 20	18 23	18 35		18 40
	d	16 51			17 08				17 21	17 24			17 41	17 51				18 08			18 21	18 24			18 41
Chapeltown	d				17 14								17 47					18 14							18 47
Elsecar	d				17 20								17 53					18 20							18 53
Wombwell	d				17 23								17 56					18 23							18 56
Barnsley	a	17 09			17 29					17 39			18 02	18 09				18 29				18 39			19 02
	d	17 09			17 30					17 40			18 03	18 09				18 30				18 40			19 03
Dodworth	d												18 09												19 09
Silkstone Common	d												18 13												19 12
Penistone	d												18 23												19 19
Denby Dale	d												18 29												19 26
Shepley	d												18 34												19 31
Stocksmoor	d												18 37												19 34
Brockholes	d												18 41												19 38
Honley	d												18 43												19 40
Berry Brow	d												18 46												19 43
Lockwood	d												18 49												19 46
Huddersfield	a												18 54												19 50
Darton	d				17 35													18 35							
Wakefield Kirkgate 4 31	a	17 24			17 48					17 55				18 24				18 48				18 55			
	d	17 24	17 28		17 49					17 55				18 24	18 28			18 49				18 55			
Normanton	d		17 34		17 56										18 34			18 56							
Castleford 32	a		17 40		18 01										18 40			19 01							
Woodlesford 32	a				18 13													19 13							
Leeds 10 31,32	a	17 44			18 25				18 31	18 14				18 44				19 24			19 31	19 14			

		NT ◇ A		NT B	NT ◇ I	NT	NT D	TP ◇1 E	NT	NT ◇	NT F	NT		EM ◇ G	NT ◇ A	NT B	NT ◇ J	NT	NT D	TP ◇1 E	NT	NT ◇		EM ◇ K	NT F
Nottingham 8	d									18 17				18 47								19 17		19 39	
Ilkeston	d									18 29												19 29			
Langley Mill	d									18 36												19 36			
Alfreton	d									18 44				19 08								19 44		20 01	
Chesterfield	d									18 55				19 21								19 55		20 11	
Dronfield	d									19 02												20 02			
Sheffield 7 29,31	a									19 13				19 37								20 13		20 29	
	d	18 45			18 57	19 02	19 05	19 11	19 15	19 18	19 32	19 35			19 45		19 57	20 02	20 05	20 11	20 15	20 18			20 32
Meadowhall 4 29,31	a	18 50			19 02	19 07	19 12	19 16	19 20	19 23	19 37	19 40			19 50		20 02	20 07	20 10	20 16	20 20	20 23			20 37
	d	18 51				19 08			19 21	19 24		19 41			19 51			20 08			20 21	20 24			
Chapeltown	d					19 14						19 47						20 14							
Elsecar	d					19 20						19 53						20 20							
Wombwell	d					19 23						19 56						20 23							
Barnsley	a	19 09				19 29				19 39		20 02			20 09			20 29				20 39			
	d	19 09				19 30				19 40		20 03			20 09			20 30				20 40			
Dodworth	d											20 09													
Silkstone Common	d											20 12													
Penistone	d											20 19													
Denby Dale	d											20 26													
Shepley	d											20 31													
Stocksmoor	d											20 34													
Brockholes	d											20 38													
Honley	d											20 40													
Berry Brow	d											20 43													
Lockwood	d											20 46													
Huddersfield	a											20 50													
Darton	d					19 35												20 35							
Wakefield Kirkgate 4 31	a	19 24				19 48				19 55					20 24			20 48				20 55			
	d	19 24		19 28		19 49				19 55					20 24	20 28		20 49				20 55			
Normanton	d			19 34		19 56										20 34		20 56							
Castleford 32	a			19 40		20 01										20 41		21 01							
Woodlesford 32	a					20 13												21 13							
Leeds 10 31,32	a	19 44				20 25			20 36	20 15					20 44			21 25			21 30	21 14			

A From Lincoln
B From Huddersfield
C To Scarborough
D To Adwick
E From Manchester Airport to Cleethorpes
F To Doncaster
G From Norwich to Liverpool Lime Street
H from 22 February
I To Bridlington
J To Hull
K From Norwich to Manchester Piccadilly

Table T034-F

Saturdays

21 December to 16 May

Nottingham and Sheffield - Barnsley - Huddersfield and Leeds

		NT	NT ◇ A	NT B	NT ◇ C	NT	NT D	TP ◇1 E		NT	NT ◇	NT B	EM ◇1 F	NT	NT ◇ G	NT D	TP ◇1 E	NT H		NT ◇	NT	NT	NT ◇ G	NT I	NT I
Nottingham 8	d										20 17		20 24							21 12					
Ilkeston	d										20 29									21 29					
Langley Mill	d										20 36		20 43							21 36					
Alfreton	d										20 44		20 51							21 44					
Chesterfield	d										20 55		21 09							21 55					
Dronfield	d										21 02									22 02					
Sheffield 7 29,31	a										21 13		21 24							22 13					
	d	20 35	20 45		20 57	21 02	21 05	21 11		21 15	21 18		21 26	21 35	21 57	22 07	22 11	22 15		22 18	22 31	22 38	22 59	23 05	23 27
Meadowhall 4 29,31	a	20 40	20 50		21 02	21 07	21 10	21 16		21 20	21 23			21 40	22 02	22 12	22 16	22 20		22 23	22 36	22 43	23 04	23 10	23 32
	d	20 41	20 51			21 08				21 21	21 24			21 41				22 21		22 24	22 37	22 44			
Chapeltown	d	20 47				21 14								21 47							22 43	22 51			
Elsecar	d	20 53				21 20								21 53							22 48	22 57			
Wombwell	d	20 56				21 23								21 56							22 52	23 01			
Barnsley	a	21 02	21 09			21 29					21 39			22 02						22 39	22 59	23 07			
	d	21 03	21 09			21 30					21 40			22 03						22 40	22 59	23 07			
Dodworth	d	21 09												22 09								23 13			
Silkstone Common	d	21 12												22 12								23 17			
Penistone	d	21 19												22 19								23 26			
Denby Dale	d	21 26												22 26								23 33			
Shepley	d	21 31												22 31								23 38			
Stocksmoor	d	21 34												22 34								23 40			
Brockholes	d	21 38												22 38								23 44			
Honley	d	21 40												22 40								23 47			
Berry Brow	d	21 43												22 43								23 50			
Lockwood	d	21 46												22 46								23 52			
Huddersfield	a	21 50												22 50								23 57			
Darton	d					21 35															23 04				
Wakefield Kirkgate 4 31	a		21 24			21 48					21 55									22 55	23 17				
	d		21 24	21 28		21 49					21 55	22 28								22 55	23 18				
Normanton	d			21 34		21 56						22 34									23 22				
Castleford 32	a			21 40		22 01						22 40									23 30				
Woodlesford 32	a					22 13															23 41				
Leeds 10 31,32	a		21 44			22 25				22 29	22 14		22 14					23 41		23 14	23 59				

		NT ◇
Nottingham 8	d	23 18
Ilkeston	d	23 30
Langley Mill	d	23 36
Alfreton	d	23 44
Chesterfield	d	23 54
Dronfield	d	00 02
Sheffield 7 29,31	a	00 15
	d	
Meadowhall 4 29,31	a	
	d	
Chapeltown	d	
Elsecar	d	
Wombwell	d	
Barnsley	a	
	d	
Dodworth	d	
Silkstone Common	d	
Penistone	d	
Denby Dale	d	
Shepley	d	
Stocksmoor	d	
Brockholes	d	
Honley	d	
Berry Brow	d	
Lockwood	d	
Huddersfield	a	
Darton	d	
Wakefield Kirkgate 4 31	a	
	d	
Normanton	d	
Castleford 32	a	
Woodlesford 32	a	
Leeds 10 31,32	a	

A From Lincoln
B From Huddersfield
C To Bridlington
D To Adwick
E From Manchester Airport to Cleethorpes
F From St Pancras International
G To Hull
H from 22 February
I To Doncaster

Table T034-F

Sundays
15 December to 10 May

Nottingham and Sheffield - Barnsley - Huddersfield and Leeds

		NT ◇ A	NT B	NT	NT ◇ C	NT	NT D	TP ◇1 E ✠	NT ◇	NT ◇ C	NT	NT	NT F	NT D	TP ◇1 E ✠	NT ◇ G	NT ◇ C	NT	EM ◇ H	NT	NT	NT D	TP ◇1 E ✠
Nottingham [8]	d															09 18			09 47				
Ilkeston	d															09 33							
Langley Mill	d															09 38							
Alfreton	d															09 46			10 05				
Chesterfield	d															09 56			10 18				
Dronfield	d	00 02														10 03			10 25				
Sheffield [7] 29,31	a	00 15														10 16			10 37				
	d		08 06	08 27	08 36	08 39	09 06	09 10	09 17	09 25	09 35	09 38	10 02	10 06	10 10	10 17	10 25	10 30		10 38	10 51	11 06	11 10
Meadowhall [4] 29,31	a		08 11	08 32	08 41	08 44	09 11	09 15	09 22	09 30	09 40	09 44	10 07	10 11	10 15	10 23	10 30	10 35		10 43	10 56	11 11	11 15
	d			08 33		08 45			09 23		09 41	09 45				10 23		10 36		10 45	10 57		
Chapeltown	d					08 51						09 51								10 51			
Elsecar	d					08 57						09 57								10 56			
Wombwell	d					09 00						10 00								11 00			
Barnsley	a					09 06			09 37			10 06				10 37				11 05	11 11		
	d					09 06			09 38			10 06				10 38				11 06	11 12		
Dodworth	d											10 12								11 12			
Silkstone Common	d											10 16								11 16			
Penistone	d											10 23								11 23			
Denby Dale	d											10 30								11 29			
Shepley	d											10 35								11 34			
Stocksmoor	d											10 37								11 37			
Brockholes	d											10 41								11 41			
Honley	d											10 44								11 43			
Berry Brow	d											10 47								11 46			
Lockwood	d											10 49								11 49			
Huddersfield	a											10 54								11 54			
Darton	d					09 11			09 43												11 17		
Wakefield Kirkgate [4] 31	a					09 22			09 57							10 53					11 29		
	d					09 23			09 59							10 53					11 30		
Normanton	d					09 28			10 04												11 35		
Castleford 32	a					09 33															11 40		
Woodlesford 32	a					09 45															11 52		
Leeds [10] 31,32	a			09 39		09 56			10 24		10 44					11 13		11 42			12 06		

		NT ◇	NT	NT ◇ C	EM ◇ H	NT ◇ I	NT D	TP ◇1 E ✠	NT ◇	NT ◇ C	NT	EM ◇ H	NT ◇ I	NT	NT D	TP ◇1 E ✠	NT ◇	NT ◇ C	NT	EM ◇ H	NT ◇ I	NT D	TP ◇1 E ✠
Nottingham [8]	d	10 17			10 48				11 18			11 44					12 19			12 40			
Ilkeston	d	10 30							11 31			11 56					12 32						
Langley Mill	d	10 35							11 36								12 37			12 56			
Alfreton	d	10 43			11 09				11 44			12 08					12 45			13 04			
Chesterfield	d	10 54			11 19				11 55			12 18					12 56			13 17			
Dronfield	d	11 01							12 02								13 03						
Sheffield [7] 29,31	a	11 13			11 35				12 14			12 35					13 15			13 33			
	d	11 16	11 24	11 34		11 38	12 06	12 10	12 16	12 25	12 31		12 39	12 44	13 06	13 10	13 17	13 24	13 31		13 39	14 06	14 10
Meadowhall [4] 29,31	a	11 21	11 29	11 41		11 45	12 11	12 16	12 22	12 30	12 36		12 44	12 49	13 11	13 15	13 22	13 29	13 36		13 44	14 11	14 16
	d	11 22	11 30			11 45			12 23		12 37		12 45	12 50			13 23		13 37		13 45		
Chapeltown	d					11 51							12 51	12 56							13 51		
Elsecar	d					11 57							12 56	13 02							13 56		
Wombwell	d					12 00							13 00	13 06							14 00		
Barnsley	a	11 36				12 06			12 37				13 05	13 12			13 37				14 05		
	d	11 36				12 06			12 37				13 06	13 12			13 37				14 06		
Dodworth	d					12 12							13 12								14 12		
Silkstone Common	d					12 16							13 16								14 16		
Penistone	d					12 23							13 23								14 23		
Denby Dale	d					12 30							13 29								14 29		
Shepley	d					12 35							13 34								14 34		
Stocksmoor	d					12 37							13 37								14 37		
Brockholes	d					12 41							13 41								14 41		
Honley	d					12 44							13 43								14 43		
Berry Brow	d					12 47							13 46								14 46		
Lockwood	d					12 49							13 49								14 49		
Huddersfield	a					12 55							13 54								14 54		
Darton	d													13 17									
Wakefield Kirkgate [4] 31	a	11 51							13 02					13 29			13 55						
	d	11 52							13 02					13 29			13 56						
Normanton	d													13 34									
Castleford 32	a													13 39									
Woodlesford 32	a													13 51									
Leeds [10] 31,32	a	12 11	12 42						13 22		13 42			14 04			14 18		14 43				

A not 15 December. From Nottingham
B To Hull
C To Scarborough
D To Doncaster
E From Manchester Airport to Cleethorpes
F From Retford
G To Carlisle
H To Liverpool Lime Street
I From Lincoln

Table T034-F

Sundays
15 December to 10 May

Nottingham and Sheffield - Barnsley - Huddersfield and Leeds

		NT ◇	NT ◇ A	NT	EM ◇ B	NT ◇ C	NT	NT D	TP ◇1 E ✠	NT ◇	NT ◇ A	NT	EM ◇ F	NT ◇ C	NT D	TP ◇1 E ✠	NT ◇ G	NT ◇	NT ◇ A	NT	EM ◇ H	NT
Nottingham [8]	d	13 19			13 42					14 19			14 47					15 20			15 47	
Ilkeston	d	13 32								14 32								15 33				
Langley Mill	d	13 37			13 58					14 37			15 03					15 38				
Alfreton	d	13 45			14 06					14 45			15 11					15 46			16 08	
Chesterfield	d	13 56			14 16					14 56			15 21					15 57			16 18	
Dronfield	d	14 03								15 03								16 04				
Sheffield [7] 29,31	a	14 15			14 34					15 15			15 39					16 14			16 35	
	d	14 17	14 25	14 31		14 39	14 44	15 06	15 10	15 17	15 25	15 31		15 39	16 06	16 10	16 13	16 17	16 25	16 31		16 39
Meadowhall [4] 29,31	a	14 22	14 30	14 36		14 44	14 49	15 11	15 15	15 22	15 30	15 36		15 45	16 11	16 16	16 20	16 22	16 30	16 36		16 44
	d	14 23		14 37		14 45	14 50			15 23		15 37		15 45				16 23		16 37		16 45
Chapeltown	d						14 56							15 51								
Elsecar	d						15 02							15 57								
Wombwell	d						15 06							16 00								
Barnsley	a	14 37				14 59	15 11			15 37				16 06				16 37				16 59
	d	14 37				15 02	15 12			15 37				16 06				16 37				17 02
Dodworth	d					15 08								16 12								17 08
Silkstone Common	d					15 12								16 16								17 12
Penistone	d					15 19								16 22								17 19
Denby Dale	d					15 25								16 29								17 25
Shepley	d					15 30								16 34								17 30
Stocksmoor	d					15 33								16 36								17 33
Brockholes	d					15 37								16 40								17 37
Honley	d					15 40								16 43								17 40
Berry Brow	d					15 43								16 46								17 42
Lockwood	d					15 45								16 48								17 45
Huddersfield	a					15 50								16 54								17 51
Darton	d						15 17															
Wakefield Kirkgate [4] 31	a	14 55					15 28			15 52								16 56				
	d	14 56					15 29			15 55								16 57				
Normanton	d						15 34															
Castleford 32	a						15 39															
Woodlesford 32	a						15 51															
Leeds [10] 31,32	a	15 17		15 44			16 04			16 15		16 44						17 17		17 43		

		NT	NT D	TP ◇1 E ✠	NT ◇	NT ◇ A	NT	EM ◇ B	NT	NT D	TP ◇1 E ✠	NT ◇	NT ◇ I	NT	EM ◇ B	NT	NT	NT ◇ G	NT D	TP ◇1 E ✠	NT ◇	NT ◇ I	EM ◇ J
Nottingham [8]	d				16 19			16 42				17 19			17 39						18 19		18 40
Ilkeston	d				16 32			16 57				17 32									18 32		
Langley Mill	d				16 37			17 03				17 37			17 57						18 37		18 56
Alfreton	d				16 45			17 11				17 45			18 05						18 45		19 04
Chesterfield	d				16 56			17 22				17 56			18 16						18 56		19 15
Dronfield	d				17 03							18 03									19 03		
Sheffield [7] 29,31	a				17 15			17 39				18 15			18 33						19 14		19 31
	d	16 44	17 06	17 10	17 17	17 25	17 30		17 42	18 06	18 11	18 17	18 25	18 31		18 39	18 45	19 00	19 06	19 11	19 16	19 25	
Meadowhall [4] 29,31	a	16 49	17 11	17 15	17 22	17 30	17 35		17 47	18 11	18 16	18 22	18 30	18 36		18 44	18 50	19 05	19 11	19 16	19 22	19 30	
	d	16 50			17 23		17 36		17 48			18 23		18 37		18 45	18 51				19 23		
Chapeltown	d	16 56							17 54								18 57						
Elsecar	d	17 02							17 59								19 02						
Wombwell	d	17 06							18 03								19 06						
Barnsley	a	17 11			17 37				18 08			18 37				18 59	19 11				19 37		
	d	17 12			17 37				18 09			18 37				19 05	19 12				19 37		
Dodworth	d								18 15							19 11							
Silkstone Common	d								18 19							19 15							
Penistone	d								18 25							19 22							
Denby Dale	d								18 31							19 28							
Shepley	d								18 36							19 33							
Stocksmoor	d								18 39							19 36							
Brockholes	d								18 43							19 40							
Honley	d								18 45							19 43							
Berry Brow	d								18 48							19 46							
Lockwood	d								18 51							19 48							
Huddersfield	a								18 56							19 52							
Darton	d	17 17															19 17						
Wakefield Kirkgate [4] 31	a	17 28			17 52							18 52					19 28				19 52		
	d	17 29			17 53							18 53					19 29				19 53		
Normanton	d	17 34															19 34						
Castleford 32	a	17 40															19 40						
Woodlesford 32	a	17 51															19 51						
Leeds [10] 31,32	a	18 04			18 17		18 43					19 15		19 43			20 04				20 15		

A To Scarborough
B From Norwich to Liverpool Lime Street
C From Lincoln
D To Doncaster
E From Manchester Airport to Cleethorpes
F To Liverpool Lime Street
G To York, via Pontefract Baghill
H From Peterborough to Liverpool Lime Street
I To Bridlington
J From Norwich to Manchester Piccadilly

Table T034-F

Sundays

15 December to 10 May

Nottingham and Sheffield - Barnsley - Huddersfield and Leeds

		NT	NT	NT	TP	NT	NT	EM	NT	NT	NT	TP	NT	NT	NT	NT	NT	TP	NT	NT	NT	NT
					◇■	◇	◇	◇				◇■	◇	◇				◇■	◇		◇	
				A	B		C	D			A	B		C			A	B	C			A
Nottingham ■	d					19 19		19 42					20 11								21 33	
Ilkeston	d					19 32							20 24								21 52	
Langley Mill	d					19 37							20 29								21 57	
Alfreton	d					19 45		20 03					20 37								22 05	
Chesterfield	d					19 56		20 13					20 48								22 16	
Dronfield	d					20 03							20 55								22 23	
Sheffield ■ 29,31	a					20 15		20 30					21 07								22 34	
	d	19 31	19 39	20 06	20 11	20 17	20 25		20 31	20 48	21 06	21 11	21 17	21 25	21 31	21 44	22 08	22 12	22 25	22 32	22 44	23 30
Meadowhall ■ 29,31	a	19 36	19 44	20 11	20 16	20 22	20 30		20 37	20 53	21 11	21 16	21 22	21 30	21 36	21 50	22 13	22 18	22 30	22 37	22 49	23 35
	d	19 37	19 45			20 23			20 37	20 54			21 23		21 37	21 50				22 38	22 50	
Chapeltown	d		19 51							21 00						21 56					22 56	
Elsecar	d		19 56							21 05						22 02					23 01	
Wombwell	d		20 00							21 09						22 05					23 05	
Barnsley	a		20 05			20 37				21 14			21 37			22 11					23 11	
	d		20 06			20 37				21 15			21 37								23 12	
Dodworth	d		20 12																			
Silkstone Common	d		20 16																			
Penistone	d		20 23																			
Denby Dale	d		20 29																			
Shepley	d		20 34																			
Stocksmoor	d		20 37																			
Brockholes	d		20 41																			
Honley	d		20 43																			
Berry Brow	d		20 46																			
Lockwood	d		20 49																			
Huddersfield	a		20 53																			
Darton	d									21 20											23 17	
Wakefield Kirkgate ■ 31	a					20 52							21 52								23 31	
	d					20 53							21 53								23 32	
Normanton	d									21 37											23 37	
Castleford 32	a									21 42											23 42	
Woodlesford 32	a									21 54											23 54	
Leeds ■ 31,32	a	20 44				21 14			21 45	22 07			22 15		22 45					23 45	00 07	

		NT
		◇
Nottingham ■	d	22 33
Ilkeston	d	22 52
Langley Mill	d	22 57
Alfreton	d	23 05
Chesterfield	d	23 16
Dronfield	d	23 23
Sheffield ■ 29,31	a	23 35
	d	
Meadowhall ■ 29,31	a	
	d	
Chapeltown	d	
Elsecar	d	
Wombwell	d	
Barnsley	a	
	d	
Dodworth	d	
Silkstone Common	d	
Penistone	d	
Denby Dale	d	
Shepley	d	
Stocksmoor	d	
Brockholes	d	
Honley	d	
Berry Brow	d	
Lockwood	d	
Huddersfield	a	
Darton	d	
Wakefield Kirkgate ■ 31	a	
	d	
Normanton	d	
Castleford 32	a	
Woodlesford 32	a	
Leeds ■ 31,32	a	

A To Doncaster
B From Manchester Airport to Cleethorpes
C To Hull
D From Norwich to Manchester Piccadilly

Table T034-R

Mondays to Fridays

16 December to 15 May

Leeds and Huddersfield - Barnsley - Sheffield and Nottingham

Miles	Miles			EM MO	EM MX	NT MX	NT MX	NT MX	NT MX	NT MX	NT	NT	NT	TP	NT	NT	NT	NT	NT	NT	TP	NT	NT
				◇	◇		◇				◇		◇	◇■		◇				◇	◇■		
				A	A	B	C	B	D	D				E		C	B	F		G	H		B
0	—	**Leeds** ■ 31,32	d																05 34			05 54	
6	—	Woodlesford 32	d																			06 03	
10¾	—	Castleford 32	d																			06 14	
14¼	—	Normanton	d																			06 21	
17¼	—	Wakefield Kirkgate ■ 31	a																			06 26	
—	—		d																			06 27	
24¾	—	Darton	d																			06 37	
—	0	**Huddersfield**	d																				
—	1¼	Lockwood	d																				
—	2¼	Berry Brow	d																				
—	3¼	Honley	d																				
—	4¼	Brockholes	d																				
—	6¼	Stocksmoor	d																				
—	7¼	Shepley	d																				
—	9½	Denby Dale	d																				
—	13½	Penistone	d																				
—	16¾	Silkstone Common	d																				
—	18	Dodworth	d																				
28¼	21	**Barnsley**	a																			06 44	
—	—		d									05 23			05 52			06 20				06 45	
32¼	25	Wombwell	d									05 28			05 57			06 25				06 50	
33¾	26½	Elsecar	d						00 03			05 32			06 01			06 29				06 54	
37	29¾	Chapeltown	d						00 08			05 37			06 06			06 34				07 00	
40¾	33½	**Meadowhall** 29,31	a						00 13			05 43			06 11			06 40	06 50			07 06	
—	—		d			00 04	00 08	00 12	00 15	00 19		05 43		05 57	06 12	06 33	06 37	06 40	06 50		06 54	07 07	07 10
44¼	37	**Sheffield** ■ 29,31	a			00 13	00 17	00 21	00 24	00 28		05 53		06 08	06 20	06 44	06 46	06 48	07 00		07 05	07 15	07 18
—	—		d								05 15		06 03							07 02			
51¼	—	Dronfield	d								05 24		06 13							07 11			
56½	—	Chesterfield	d		00 02						05 30		06 19							07 17			
66½	—	Alfreton	d								05 46		06 29							07 28			
72¾	—	Langley Mill	d	00 02							05 53		06 36							07 35			
—	—	Ilkeston	d								05 58		06 41							07 40			
84¾	—	**Nottingham**	a	00 23	00 45						06 11		07 00							07 53			

		NT	EM	NT	NT	NT	NT	NT	NT	NT	TP	NT	NT	NT	NT	EM	NT	NT	NT	NT	NT	TP	NT
			◇■		◇		◇			◇	◇■				◇	◇		◇			◇	◇■	
		I	J		K	L	C	D			H	L		I	K	M	L	N	D			H	L
Leeds ■ 31,32	d	06 32	06 34		06 38				06 47	07 03				07 32	07 38					07 48	08 04		
Woodlesford 32	d	06 41												07 41									
Castleford 32	d	06 52												07 52									
Normanton	d	06 57						←						07 57					←				
Wakefield Kirkgate ■ 31	a	07 02			06 55			07 02		07 22				08 02	07 54				08 02		08 21		
	d	07 03			06 56			07 03		07 23				08 03	07 55				08 03		08 22		
Darton	d	→						07 14						→					08 14				
Huddersfield	d			06 13									07 12										
Lockwood	d			06 16									07 15										
Berry Brow	d			06 19									07 18										
Honley	d			06 22									07 21										
Brockholes	d			06 25									07 24										
Stocksmoor	d			06 29									07 28										
Shepley	d			06 31									07 30										
Denby Dale	d			06 36									07 35										
Penistone	d			06 44									07 43										
Silkstone Common	d			06 49									07 48										
Dodworth	d			06 53									07 52										
Barnsley	a			07 00	07 11			07 21		07 38			07 59		08 09				08 21		08 37		
	d			07 01	07 13			07 22		07 39			08 00		08 11				08 22		08 38		
Wombwell	d			07 06				07 27					08 05						08 27				
Elsecar	d			07 10				07 31					08 09						08 31				
Chapeltown	d			07 16				07 37					08 15						08 37				
Meadowhall 29,31	a			07 21	07 26			07 43	07 49	07 52			08 20		08 26				08 43	08 51	08 53		
	d			07 22	07 27	07 31	07 38	07 47	07 50	07 53	07 59	08 03	08 21		08 27		08 34	08 40	08 43	08 51	08 57	09 02	09 06
Sheffield ■ 29,31	a		07 22	07 29	07 34	07 39	07 47	07 54	07 57	08 00	08 06	08 10	08 28		08 34		08 44	08 48	08 51	09 01	09 04	09 09	09 14
	d		07 28							08 03						08 38					09 06		
Dronfield	d									08 13											09 16		
Chesterfield	d		07 42							08 20						08 54					09 22		
Alfreton	d		07 53							08 33						09 05					09 33		
Langley Mill	d		08 01							08 41											09 40		
Ilkeston	d									08 46											09 45		
Nottingham	a		08 24							08 59						09 27					09 59		

A From Liverpool Lime Street
B From Doncaster
C From Hull
D From Leeds
E From Doncaster to Manchester Airport
F To Gainsborough Central
G From Retford
H From Cleethorpes to Manchester Airport
I To Sheffield
J To St Pancras International
K To Lincoln
L From Adwick
M From Liverpool Lime Street to Norwich
N From Beverley

Table T034-R

Mondays to Fridays

16 December to 15 May

Leeds and Huddersfield - Barnsley - Sheffield and Nottingham

Station		NT	NT	NT	EM	NT	NT	NT	NT	NT	TP	NT	NT	NT	NT	NT	EM	NT	NT	NT	NT	NT
			A	◇ B	◇ C	D	◇ E	F		◇	◇1 G	D		◇ H	A	◇ B	◇ C	I	◇ J	F		◇
Leeds [10]	31,32 d		08 32	08 38					08 48	09 09					09 32	09 38					09 48	10 09
Woodlesford	32 d		08 41												09 41							
Castleford	32 d		08 52												09 52							
Normanton	d		08 57					←							09 57					←		
Wakefield Kirkgate [4]	31 a		09 02	08 54				09 02		09 25					10 02	09 54				10 02		10 25
	d		09 03	08 55				09 03		09 26					10 03	09 55				10 03		10 26
Darton	d		→					09 14							→					10 14		
Huddersfield	d	08 12											09 12									
Lockwood	d	08 15											09 15									
Berry Brow	d	08 18											09 18									
Honley	d	08 21											09 21									
Brockholes	d	08 24											09 24									
Stocksmoor	d	08 28											09 28									
Shepley	d	08 30											09 30									
Denby Dale	d	08 35											09 35									
Penistone	d	08 43											09 43									
Silkstone Common	d	08 48											09 48									
Dodworth	d	08 52											09 52									
Barnsley	a	08 59		09 09				09 21		09 41			09 59			10 10				10 21		10 41
	d	09 00		09 11				09 22		09 42			10 00			10 12				10 22		10 42
Wombwell	d	09 05						09 27					10 05							10 27		
Elsecar	d	09 09						09 31					10 09							10 31		
Chapeltown	d	09 15						09 37					10 15							10 37		
Meadowhall	29,31 a	09 20		09 26				09 42	09 51	09 56			10 20			10 26				10 42	10 51	10 56
	d	09 21		09 27		09 34	09 38	09 43	09 51	09 57	10 02	10 06	10 21	10 24		10 27		10 34	10 41	10 44	10 51	10 57
Sheffield [7]	29,31 a	09 28		09 34		09 44	09 49	09 51	10 01	10 04	10 09	10 14	10 28	10 33		10 34		10 44	10 50	10 52	11 01	11 04
	d				09 38					10 06							10 37					11 06
Dronfield	d									10 16												11 16
Chesterfield	d				09 52					10 22							10 54					11 22
Alfreton	d				10 02					10 32							11 05					11 32
Langley Mill	d									10 40												11 40
Ilkeston	d				10 12					10 45												11 45
Nottingham	a				10 27					10 58							11 26					11 58

Station		TP	NT	NT	NT	NT	EM	NT	NT	NT	NT	NT	TP	NT	NT	NT	NT	EM	NT	NT	NT	NT	NT
		◇1 G	D		A	◇ B	◇ C	I	◇ E	F		◇	◇1 G	D		A	◇ B	◇ C	I	◇ E	F		◇
Leeds [10]	31,32 d				10 32	10 38					10 48	11 09				11 32	11 38					11 48	12 09
Woodlesford	32 d				10 41											11 41							
Castleford	32 d				10 52											11 52							
Normanton	d				10 57					←						11 57					←		
Wakefield Kirkgate [4]	31 a				11 02	10 54				11 02		11 25				12 02	11 54				12 02		12 25
	d				11 03	10 55				11 03		11 26				12 03	11 55				12 03		12 26
Darton	d				→					11 14						→					12 14		
Huddersfield	d			10 12											11 12								
Lockwood	d			10 15											11 15								
Berry Brow	d			10 18											11 18								
Honley	d			10 21											11 21								
Brockholes	d			10 24											11 24								
Stocksmoor	d			10 28											11 28								
Shepley	d			10 30											11 30								
Denby Dale	d			10 35											11 35								
Penistone	d			10 43											11 43								
Silkstone Common	d			10 48											11 48								
Dodworth	d			10 52											11 52								
Barnsley	a			10 59		11 09				11 21		11 41			11 59		12 09				12 21		12 41
	d			11 00		11 11				11 22		11 42			12 00		12 11				12 22		12 42
Wombwell	d			11 05						11 27					12 05						12 27		
Elsecar	d			11 09						11 31					12 09						12 31		
Chapeltown	d			11 15						11 37					12 15						12 37		
Meadowhall	29,31 a			11 20		11 26				11 42	11 51	11 56			12 20		12 26				12 42	12 51	12 56
	d	11 02	11 06	11 21		11 27		11 34	11 38	11 43	11 51	11 57	12 02	12 06	12 21		12 27		12 34	12 41	12 44	12 51	12 57
Sheffield [7]	29,31 a	11 09	11 14	11 28		11 34		11 44	11 49	11 51	12 01	12 04	12 08	12 14	12 28		12 34		12 44	12 50	12 52	13 01	13 04
	d						11 38					12 06						12 38					13 06
Dronfield	d											12 16											13 16
Chesterfield	d						11 54					12 22						12 52					13 22
Alfreton	d						12 05					12 32						13 03					13 32
Langley Mill	d											12 40											13 40
Ilkeston	d											12 45											13 45
Nottingham	a						12 29					12 58						13 27					13 58

A To Sheffield
B To Lincoln
C From Liverpool Lime Street to Norwich
D From Adwick
E From Scarborough
F From Leeds
G From Cleethorpes to Manchester Airport
H From York
I From Doncaster
J From Bridlington

Table T034-R

Mondays to Fridays

16 December to 15 May

Leeds and Huddersfield - Barnsley - Sheffield and Nottingham

Station		TP	NT	NT	NT	NT	EM	NT	NT	NT	NT	NT	TP	NT	NT	NT	NT	NT	EM	NT	NT	NT	NT
		◇1 A	B		C	◇ D	◇ E	F	◇ G	H		◇	◇1 A	B		◇ I	C	◇ D	◇ E	F	◇ G	H	
Leeds [10]	31,32 d				12 32	12 38					12 48	13 09					13 32	13 38					13 48
Woodlesford	32 d				12 41												13 41						
Castleford	32 d				12 52												13 52						
Normanton	d				12 57					←							13 57					←	
Wakefield Kirkgate [4]	31 a				13 02	12 54				13 02		13 25					14 02	13 54				14 02	
	d				13 03	12 55				13 03		13 26					14 03	13 55				14 03	
Darton	d				→					13 14							→					14 14	
Huddersfield	d			12 12											13 12								
Lockwood	d			12 15											13 15								
Berry Brow	d			12 18											13 18								
Honley	d			12 21											13 21								
Brockholes	d			12 24											13 24								
Stocksmoor	d			12 28											13 28								
Shepley	d			12 30											13 30								
Denby Dale	d			12 35											13 35								
Penistone	d			12 43											13 43								
Silkstone Common	d			12 48											13 48								
Dodworth	d			12 52											13 52								
Barnsley	a			12 59		13 09				13 21		13 41			13 59			14 09				14 21	
	d			13 00		13 11				13 22		13 42			14 00			14 11				14 22	
Wombwell	d			13 05						13 27					14 05							14 27	
Elsecar	d			13 09						13 31					14 09							14 31	
Chapeltown	d			13 15						13 37					14 15							14 37	
Meadowhall	29,31 a			13 20		13 26				13 42	13 51	13 56			14 20			14 26				14 42	14 51
	d	13 02	13 06	13 21		13 27		13 34	13 38	13 43	13 51	13 57	14 02	14 06	14 21	14 24		14 27		14 34	14 38	14 43	14 52
Sheffield [7]	29,31 a	13 08	13 14	13 28		13 34		13 44	13 49	13 51	14 01	14 04	14 08	14 14	14 28	14 32		14 34		14 44	14 49	14 51	15 01
	d						13 37					14 06							14 38				
Dronfield	d											14 16											
Chesterfield	d						13 52					14 22							14 52				
Alfreton	d						14 03					14 32							15 03				
Langley Mill	d											14 40											
Ilkeston	d											14 45							15 13				
Nottingham	a						14 27					14 58							15 28				

Station		NT	TP	NT	NT	NT	NT	EM	NT	NT	NT	NT	NT	TP	NT	NT	NT	NT	EM	NT	NT	NT
		◇	◇1 A	B		C	◇ D	◇ E	F	◇ G	H		◇	◇1 A	B		C	◇ D	◇ E	F	◇ G	H
Leeds [10]	31,32 d	14 09				14 32	14 38					14 48	15 09				15 32	15 38				
Woodlesford	32 d					14 41											15 41					
Castleford	32 d					14 52											15 52					
Normanton	d					14 57					←						15 57					←
Wakefield Kirkgate [4]	31 a	14 25				15 02	14 54				15 02		15 25				16 02	15 54				16 02
	d	14 26				15 03	14 55				15 03		15 26				16 03	15 55				16 03
Darton	d					→					15 14						→					16 14
Huddersfield	d				14 12											15 12						
Lockwood	d				14 15											15 15						
Berry Brow	d				14 18											15 18						
Honley	d				14 21											15 21						
Brockholes	d				14 24											15 24						
Stocksmoor	d				14 28											15 28						
Shepley	d				14 30											15 30						
Denby Dale	d				14 35											15 35						
Penistone	d				14 43											15 43						
Silkstone Common	d				14 48											15 48						
Dodworth	d				14 52											15 52						
Barnsley	a	14 41			14 59		15 09				15 21		15 41			15 59		16 09				16 21
	d	14 42			15 00		15 11				15 22		15 42			16 00		16 11				16 22
Wombwell	d				15 05						15 27					16 05						16 27
Elsecar	d				15 09						15 31					16 09						16 31
Chapeltown	d				15 15						15 37					16 15						16 37
Meadowhall	29,31 a	14 56			15 20		15 26				15 42	15 51	15 56			16 20		16 26				16 42
	d	14 57	15 02	15 06	15 21		15 27		15 34	15 41	15 44	15 51	15 57	16 02	16 06	16 21		16 27		16 34	16 38	16 43
Sheffield [7]	29,31 a	15 04	15 08	15 14	15 28		15 34		15 44	15 50	15 52	16 01	16 04	16 08	16 14	16 28		16 34		16 44	16 49	16 51
	d	15 06						15 37					16 06						16 37			
Dronfield	d	15 16											16 16						16 48			
Chesterfield	d	15 22						15 53					16 22						16 53			
Alfreton	d	15 32						16 05					16 32						17 04			
Langley Mill	d	15 40											16 40									
Ilkeston	d	15 45											16 45									
Nottingham	a	15 58						16 27					16 58						17 27			

A From Cleethorpes to Manchester Airport
B From Adwick
C To Sheffield
D To Lincoln
E From Liverpool Lime Street to Norwich
F From Doncaster
G From Scarborough
H From Leeds
I From York

Table T034-R

Mondays to Fridays
16 December to 15 May

Leeds and Huddersfield - Barnsley - Sheffield and Nottingham

	NT	NT	TP	NT	NT	NT	NT		EM	NT	NT	NT	NT	NT	TP	NT	NT		NT	NT	NT	NT	NT	NT
		◇	◇1				◇		◇		◇			◇	◇1				◇		◇		◇	
			A	B		C	D		E	F	G	H			A	B			I	C	D	F	G	H
Leeds 10 31,32 d	15 48	16 09				16 32	16 38						16 48	17 09						17 32	17 38			
Woodlesford 32 d						16 41														17 41				
Castleford 32 d						16 52														17 52				
Normanton d						16 57						←		17 21						17 57				←
Wakefield Kirkgate 4 31 a		16 25				17 02	16 54					17 02		17 26						18 02	17 54			18 02
d		16 26				17 03	16 55					17 03		17 27						18 03	17 55			18 03
Darton d						→						17 14								→				18 14
Huddersfield d					16 12												17 12							
Lockwood d					16 15												17 15							
Berry Brow d					16 18												17 18							
Honley d					16 21												17 21							
Brockholes d					16 24												17 24							
Stocksmoor d					16 28												17 28							
Shepley d					16 30												17 30							
Denby Dale d					16 35												17 35							
Penistone d					16 43												17 43							
Silkstone Common d					16 48												17 48							
Dodworth d					16 52												17 52							
Barnsley a		16 41			16 59		17 09					17 21		17 42			17 59				18 09			18 21
d		16 42			17 00		17 11					17 22		17 43			18 00				18 11			18 22
Wombwell d					17 05							17 27					18 05							18 27
Elsecar d					17 09							17 31					18 09							18 31
Chapeltown d					17 15							17 37					18 15							18 37
Meadowhall 29,31 a	16 51	16 56			17 20		17 26					17 42	17 51	17 56			18 20				18 26			18 42
d	16 51	16 57	17 02	17 06	17 21		17 27			17 34	17 38	17 43	17 51	17 57	18 02	18 06	18 21		18 24		18 27	18 34	18 38	18 43
Sheffield 7 29,31 a	17 01	17 04	17 08	17 14	17 28		17 34			17 44	17 49	17 51	18 01	18 04	18 08	18 14	18 28		18 32		18 34	18 44	18 49	18 51
d		17 06							17 43					18 06										
Dronfield d		17 16							17 54					18 16										
Chesterfield d		17 22							18 01					18 22										
Alfreton d		17 32							18 11					18 32										
Langley Mill d		17 40												18 40										
Ilkeston d		17 45												18 45										
Nottingham a		17 58							18 31					18 58										

	EM	NT	NT		TP	NT	NT	NT	NT	NT	EM	NT	NT		NT	NT	NT	TP	NT	NT	EM	NT	NT
	◇		◇		◇1					◇	◇		◇				◇	◇1			◇		◇
	J				A	B			C	D	E	F	G		H			A	B		J	F	G
Leeds 10 31,32 d		17 48	18 03						18 32	18 38						18 48	19 03						
Woodlesford 32 d									18 41														
Castleford 32 d									18 52														
Normanton d									18 57	18 51					←								
Wakefield Kirkgate 4 31 a			18 21						19 02	18 56					19 02		19 20						
d			18 22						19 03	18 57					19 03		19 21						
Darton d									→						19 14								
Huddersfield d							17 51	18 13												19 12			
Lockwood d							17 54	18 16												19 15			
Berry Brow d							17 57	18 19												19 18			
Honley d							18 00	18 22												19 21			
Brockholes d							18 03	18 25												19 24			
Stocksmoor d							18 07	18 29												19 28			
Shepley d							18 09	18 31												19 30			
Denby Dale d							18 14	18 39												19 35			
Penistone d							18 27	18 46												19 43			
Silkstone Common d							18 32	18 52												19 48			
Dodworth d							18 36	18 55												19 52			
Barnsley a			18 37				18 44	19 02		19 12					19 21		19 36			19 59			
d			18 38				18 45	19 02		19 13					19 22		19 37			20 00			
Wombwell d							18 50	19 08							19 27					20 05			
Elsecar d							18 54	19 12							19 31					20 09			
Chapeltown d							19 00	19 17							19 37					20 15			
Meadowhall 29,31 a		18 51	18 52				19 07	19 23		19 27					19 42	19 51	19 51			20 20			
d		18 51	18 57		19 02	19 06	19 09	19 23		19 28		19 34	19 38		19 43	19 51	19 57	20 02	20 06	20 21		20 36	20 38
Sheffield 7 29,31 a		19 01	19 04		19 09	19 14	19 17	19 32		19 35		19 44	19 49		19 51	20 01	20 04	20 09	20 14	20 28		20 44	20 49
d	18 51		19 06								19 37						20 06				20 41		
Dronfield d			19 16														20 16						
Chesterfield d	19 07		19 22								19 52						20 22				20 56		
Alfreton d	19 19		19 32								20 03						20 32				21 08		
Langley Mill d			19 40														20 40						
Ilkeston d			19 45														20 45						
Nottingham a	19 40		19 58								20 27						20 59				21 34		

A From Cleethorpes to Manchester Airport
B From Adwick
C To Sheffield
D To Lincoln
E From Liverpool Lime Street to Norwich
F From Doncaster
G From Scarborough
H From Leeds
I From York
J From Liverpool Lime Street

Table T034-R

Mondays to Fridays
16 December to 15 May

Leeds and Huddersfield - Barnsley - Sheffield and Nottingham

	NT	NT	NT	NT	TP	NT	NT	EM	NT		NT	NT	NT	NT	TP	NT	NT	NT	NT		NT	NT	NT	NT
			◇		◇1			◇			◇			◇	◇1		◇				◇	◇		
		A		B	C	D		E	F		G				H	D	F		A			G	B	
Leeds 10 31,32 d	19 32	19 48	20 04									20 32	20 48	21 04					21 32		21 37			21 48
Woodlesford 32 d	19 41											20 41							21 41					
Castleford 32 d	19 52											20 52							21 52					
Normanton d	19 57											20 57							21 57				←	
Wakefield Kirkgate 4 31 a	20 02		20 21									21 02		21 20					22 02		21 53		22 02	
d	20 03		20 22									21 03		21 21					22 03		21 53		22 03	
Darton d	20 14											21 14							→				22 14	
Huddersfield d							20 12											21 12						
Lockwood d							20 15											21 15						
Berry Brow d							20 18											21 18						
Honley d							20 21											21 21						
Brockholes d							20 24											21 24						
Stocksmoor d							20 28											21 28						
Shepley d							20 30											21 30						
Denby Dale d							20 35											21 35						
Penistone d							20 43											21 43						
Silkstone Common d							20 48											21 48						
Dodworth d							20 52											21 52						
Barnsley a	20 21		20 37				20 59					21 21		21 36				21 59			22 09		22 21	
d	20 22		20 38				21 00					21 22		21 37				22 00			22 11		22 22	
Wombwell d	20 27						21 05					21 27						22 05					22 27	
Elsecar d	20 31						21 09					21 31						22 09					22 31	
Chapeltown d	20 37			←			21 15					21 37						22 15					22 37	
Meadowhall 29,31 a	20 42	20 51	20 51	20 51			21 20					21 42	21 51	21 53				22 20			22 25		22 42	22 55
d	20 43	20 54	20 51	20 54	21 04	21 08	21 21		21 35		21 38	21 43	21 51	21 55	22 02	22 06	22 10	22 21			22 30	22 36	22 43	22 56
Sheffield 7 29,31 a	20 51	→	21 01	21 04	21 09	21 17	21 29		21 45		21 49	21 51	21 59	22 02	22 08	22 14	22 19	22 28			22 40	22 45	22 51	23 04
d			21 04					21 37						22 04										
Dronfield d			21 14					21 49						22 14										
Chesterfield d			21 20					21 55						22 20										
Alfreton d								22 05						22 31										
Langley Mill d								22 13						22 38										
Ilkeston d								22 18						22 43										
Nottingham a			22 00					22 31						22 57										

	NT	EM	NT	NT	NT		NT	NT
		◇						
	D	E						
Leeds 10 31,32 d			22 30	22 32			23 02	23 11
Woodlesford 32 d				22 41			23 11	
Castleford 32 d				22 52			23 22	
Normanton d				22 57			23 28	
Wakefield Kirkgate 4 31 a				23 02			23 33	
d				23 03			23 34	
Darton d				23 14			23 44	
Huddersfield d					22 50			
Lockwood d					22 53			
Berry Brow d					22 56			
Honley d					22 59			
Brockholes d					23 02			
Stocksmoor d					23 06			
Shepley d					23 08			
Denby Dale d					23 13			
Penistone d					23 23			
Silkstone Common d					23 29			
Dodworth d					23 32			
Barnsley a				23 21	23 39		23 51	
d				23 22	23 39		23 52	
Wombwell d				23 27	23 44		23 57	
Elsecar d				23 31	23 48		00 03	
Chapeltown d				23 37	23 53		00 08	
Meadowhall 29,31 a			23 33	23 42	23 59		00 13	00 19
d	23 06		23 34	23 43	23 59		00 15	00 19
Sheffield 7 29,31 a	23 14		23 41	23 51	00 08		00 24	00 28
d		23 38						
Dronfield d								
Chesterfield d		00 02						
Alfreton d								
Langley Mill d								
Ilkeston d								
Nottingham a		00 45						

A To Sheffield
B From Leeds
C From Cleethorpes to Manchester Piccadilly
D From Adwick
E From Liverpool Lime Street
F From Doncaster
G From Scarborough
H From Cleethorpes to Manchester Airport

Table T034-R

Saturdays

21 December to 16 May

Leeds and Huddersfield - Barnsley - Sheffield and Nottingham

Station		EM	NT	NT	NT	NT	NT	NT	NT	NT	TP	NT	NT	NT	NT	NT	NT	TP	NT	NT	NT	EM	NT
		◇		◇				◇		◇	◇1		◇				◇	◇1				◇1	
		A	B	C	B	D	D				E		C	B	F		G	H		B	I	J	
Leeds [10] 31,32	d															05 34			05 54		06 32	06 34	
Woodlesford 32	d																		06 03		06 41		
Castleford 32	d																		06 14		06 52		
Normanton	d																		06 21		06 57		
Wakefield Kirkgate [4] 31	a																		06 26		07 02		
	d																		06 27		07 03		
Darton	d																		06 37		→		
Huddersfield	d																						06 13
Lockwood	d																						06 16
Berry Brow	d																						06 19
Honley	d																						06 22
Brockholes	d																						06 25
Stocksmoor	d																						06 29
Shepley	d																						06 31
Denby Dale	d																						06 36
Penistone	d																						06 44
Silkstone Common	d																						06 49
Dodworth	d																						06 53
Barnsley	a																		06 44				07 00
	d								05 23			05 52			06 20				06 45				07 01
Wombwell	d								05 28			05 57			06 25				06 50				07 06
Elsecar	d					00 03			05 32			06 01			06 29				06 54				07 10
Chapeltown	d					00 08			05 37			06 06			06 34				07 00				07 16
Meadowhall 29,31	a					00 13			05 43			06 11			06 40	06 48			07 06				07 21
	d		00 04	00 08	00 12	00 15	00 19		05 43		05 57	06 12	06 33	06 37	06 40	06 50		06 54	07 07	07 10			07 22
Sheffield [7] 29,31	a		00 13	00 17	00 21	00 24	00 28		05 53		06 08	06 20	06 44	06 46	06 48	07 00		07 05	07 15	07 18		07 24	07 29
	d							05 15		06 01							07 02					07 37	
Dronfield	d							05 24		06 13							07 11						
Chesterfield	d	00 02						05 30		06 19							07 17					07 50	
Alfreton	d							05 45		06 29							07 28					08 01	
Langley Mill	d							05 53		06 36							07 35					08 09	
Ilkeston	d							05 58		06 41							07 40						
Nottingham	a	00 45						06 11		07 00							07 53					08 25	

Station		NT	NT	NT	NT	NT	NT	TP	NT	NT	NT	NT	EM	EM	NT	NT	NT	NT	NT	TP	NT	NT	NT
		◇		◇			◇	◇1				◇	◇1	◇		◇			◇	◇1			
		K	L	C	D			H	L		I	K	J	M	L	N	D			H	L		I
Leeds [10] 31,32	d	06 38				06 47	07 03				07 32	07 38	07 40					07 48	08 04				08 32
Woodlesford 32	d										07 41												08 41
Castleford 32	d										07 52												08 52
Normanton	d				←						07 57						←						08 57
Wakefield Kirkgate [4] 31	a	06 55			07 02		07 21				08 02	07 54					08 02		08 21				09 02
	d	06 56			07 03		07 22				08 03	07 55					08 03		08 22				09 03
Darton	d				07 14						→						08 14						→
Huddersfield	d									07 12												08 12	
Lockwood	d									07 15												08 15	
Berry Brow	d									07 18												08 18	
Honley	d									07 21												08 21	
Brockholes	d									07 24												08 24	
Stocksmoor	d									07 28												08 28	
Shepley	d									07 30												08 30	
Denby Dale	d									07 35												08 35	
Penistone	d									07 43												08 43	
Silkstone Common	d									07 48												08 48	
Dodworth	d									07 52												08 52	
Barnsley	a	07 11			07 21		07 37			07 59		08 09					08 21		08 37			08 59	
	d	07 13			07 22		07 38			08 00		08 11					08 22		08 38			09 00	
Wombwell	d				07 27					08 05							08 27					09 05	
Elsecar	d				07 31					08 09							08 31					09 09	
Chapeltown	d				07 37					08 15							08 37					09 15	
Meadowhall 29,31	a	07 26			07 43	07 49	07 52			08 20		08 26					08 42	08 51	08 53			09 20	
	d	07 27	07 31	07 38	07 47	07 50	07 53	07 59	08 03	08 21		08 27			08 34	08 40	08 43	08 51	08 57	09 02	09 06	09 21	
Sheffield [7] 29,31	a	07 34	07 39	07 47	07 55	07 57	08 00	08 06	08 10	08 28		08 34	08 25		08 44	08 48	08 50	09 00	09 04	09 09	09 14	09 28	
	d						08 03						08 34	08 37					09 06				
Dronfield	d						08 13												09 16				
Chesterfield	d						08 19						08 47	08 52					09 22				
Alfreton	d						08 29						08 57	09 03					09 33				
Langley Mill	d						08 37												09 40				
Ilkeston	d						08 42												09 45				
Nottingham	a						08 55						09 19	09 27					09 59				

A From Liverpool Lime Street
B From Doncaster
C From Hull
D From Leeds
E From Doncaster to Manchester Airport
F To Gainsborough Central
G From Retford
H From Cleethorpes to Manchester Airport
I To Sheffield
J To St Pancras International
K To Lincoln
L From Adwick
M From Liverpool Lime Street to Norwich
N From Beverley

Table T034-R

Saturdays

21 December to 16 May

Leeds and Huddersfield - Barnsley - Sheffield and Nottingham

Station		NT	EM	NT	NT	NT	NT	NT	TP	NT	NT	NT	NT	NT	EM	NT	NT	NT	NT	NT	TP	NT
		◇	◇		◇			◇	◇1			◇		◇	◇		◇			◇	◇1	
		A	B	C	D	E			F	C		G	H	A	B	I	J	E			F	C
Leeds [10] 31,32	d	08 38					08 48	09 09					09 32	09 38					09 48	10 09		
Woodlesford 32	d												09 41									
Castleford 32	d												09 52									
Normanton	d					←							09 57					←				
Wakefield Kirkgate [4] 31	a	08 54				09 02		09 25					10 02	09 54				10 02		10 25		
	d	08 55				09 03		09 26					10 03	09 55				10 03		10 26		
Darton	d					09 14							→					10 14				
Huddersfield	d										09 12											
Lockwood	d										09 15											
Berry Brow	d										09 18											
Honley	d										09 21											
Brockholes	d										09 24											
Stocksmoor	d										09 28											
Shepley	d										09 30											
Denby Dale	d										09 35											
Penistone	d										09 43											
Silkstone Common	d										09 48											
Dodworth	d										09 52											
Barnsley	a	09 09				09 21		09 41			09 59			10 10				10 21		10 41		
	d	09 11				09 22		09 42			10 00			10 12				10 22		10 42		
Wombwell	d					09 27					10 05							10 27				
Elsecar	d					09 31					10 09							10 31				
Chapeltown	d					09 37					10 15							10 37				
Meadowhall 29,31	a	09 26				09 42	09 51	09 56			10 20			10 26				10 42	10 51	10 56		
	d	09 27		09 34	09 38	09 43	09 51	09 57	10 02	10 06	10 21	10 24		10 27		10 34	10 41	10 44	10 51	10 57	11 02	11 06
Sheffield [7] 29,31	a	09 34		09 44	09 49	09 51	10 01	10 04	10 09	10 14	10 28	10 33		10 34		10 44	10 50	10 52	11 01	11 04	11 09	11 14
	d		09 37					10 06							10 37					11 06		
Dronfield	d							10 16												11 16		
Chesterfield	d		09 52					10 22							10 52					11 22		
Alfreton	d		10 03					10 32							11 02					11 32		
Langley Mill	d							10 40												11 40		
Ilkeston	d							10 45												11 45		
Nottingham	a		10 27					10 58							11 27					11 58		

Station		NT	NT	NT	EM	NT	NT	NT	NT	NT	TP	NT	NT	NT	NT	EM	NT	NT	NT	NT	NT	TP	NT
				◇	◇		◇			◇	◇1				◇	◇		◇			◇	◇1	
			H	A	B	I	D	E			F	C		H	A	B	I	D	E			F	C
Leeds [10] 31,32	d		10 32	10 38					10 48	11 09				11 32	11 38					11 48	12 09		
Woodlesford 32	d		10 41											11 41									
Castleford 32	d		10 52											11 52									
Normanton	d		10 57					←						11 57					←				
Wakefield Kirkgate [4] 31	a		11 02	10 54				11 02		11 25				12 02	11 54				12 02		12 25		
	d		11 03	10 55				11 03		11 26				12 03	11 55				12 03		12 26		
Darton	d		→					11 14						→					12 14				
Huddersfield	d	10 12											11 12										
Lockwood	d	10 15											11 15										
Berry Brow	d	10 18											11 18										
Honley	d	10 21											11 21										
Brockholes	d	10 24											11 24										
Stocksmoor	d	10 28											11 28										
Shepley	d	10 30											11 30										
Denby Dale	d	10 35											11 35										
Penistone	d	10 43											11 43										
Silkstone Common	d	10 48											11 48										
Dodworth	d	10 52											11 52										
Barnsley	a	10 59		11 09				11 21		11 41			11 59		12 09				12 21		12 41		
	d	11 00		11 11				11 22		11 42			12 00		12 11				12 22		12 42		
Wombwell	d	11 05						11 27					12 05						12 27				
Elsecar	d	11 09						11 31					12 09						12 31				
Chapeltown	d	11 15						11 37					12 15						12 37				
Meadowhall 29,31	a	11 20		11 26				11 42	11 51	11 56			12 20		12 26				12 42	12 51	12 56		
	d	11 21		11 27		11 34	11 38	11 43	11 51	11 57	12 02	12 06	12 21		12 27		12 34	12 41	12 44	12 51	12 57	13 02	13 06
Sheffield [7] 29,31	a	11 28		11 34		11 44	11 49	11 51	12 01	12 04	12 08	12 14	12 28		12 34		12 44	12 50	12 52	13 01	13 04	13 08	13 14
	d				11 38					12 06						12 38					13 06		
Dronfield	d									12 16											13 16		
Chesterfield	d				11 52					12 22						12 52					13 22		
Alfreton	d				12 03					12 32						13 02					13 32		
Langley Mill	d									12 40											13 40		
Ilkeston	d				12 13					12 45						13 12					13 45		
Nottingham	a				12 27					12 58						13 27					13 58		

A To Lincoln
B From Liverpool Lime Street to Norwich
C From Adwick
D From Scarborough
E From Leeds
F From Cleethorpes to Manchester Airport
G From York
H To Sheffield
I From Doncaster
J From Bridlington

Table T034-R

Saturdays

21 December to 16 May

Leeds and Huddersfield - Barnsley - Sheffield and Nottingham

Station		NT	NT A	NT ◇ B	EM ◇ C	NT D	NT ◇ E	NT F	NT	NT ◇	TP ◇1 G	NT H	NT	NT ◇ I	NT A	NT ◇ B	EM ◇ C	NT D	NT ◇ E	NT F	NT	NT ◇
Leeds 10 31,32	d		12 32	12 38					12 48	13 09					13 32	13 38					13 48	14 09
Woodlesford 32	d		12 41												13 41							
Castleford 32	d		12 52												13 52							
Normanton	d		12 57					←							13 57					←		
Wakefield Kirkgate 4 31	a		13 02	12 54				13 02		13 25					14 02	13 54				14 02		14 25
	d		13 03	12 55				13 03		13 26					14 03	13 55				14 03		14 26
Darton	d		→					13 14							→					14 14		
Huddersfield	d	12 12											13 12									
Lockwood	d	12 15											13 15									
Berry Brow	d	12 18											13 18									
Honley	d	12 21											13 21									
Brockholes	d	12 24											13 24									
Stocksmoor	d	12 28											13 28									
Shepley	d	12 30											13 30									
Denby Dale	d	12 35											13 35									
Penistone	d	12 43											13 43									
Silkstone Common	d	12 48											13 48									
Dodworth	d	12 52											13 52									
Barnsley	a	12 59		13 09				13 21		13 41			13 59			14 09				14 21		14 41
	d	13 00		13 11				13 22		13 42			14 00			14 11				14 22		14 42
Wombwell	d	13 05						13 27					14 05							14 27		
Elsecar	d	13 09						13 31					14 09							14 31		
Chapeltown	d	13 15						13 37					14 15							14 37		
Meadowhall 29,31	a	13 20		13 26				13 42	13 51	13 56			14 20			14 26				14 42	14 51	14 56
	d	13 21		13 27		13 34	13 38	13 43	13 51	13 57	14 02	14 06	14 21	14 24		14 27		14 34	14 38	14 43	14 52	14 57
Sheffield 7 29,31	a	13 28		13 34		13 44	13 49	13 51	14 01	14 04	14 08	14 14	14 28	14 32		14 34		14 44	14 49	14 51	15 01	15 04
	d				13 38					14 06							14 38					15 06
Dronfield	d									14 16												15 16
Chesterfield	d				13 54					14 22							14 54					15 22
Alfreton	d				14 04					14 32							15 04					15 32
Langley Mill	d									14 40												15 40
Ilkeston	d									14 45												15 45
Nottingham	a				14 27					14 58							15 27					15 58

Station		TP ◇1 G	NT H	NT	NT A	NT ◇ B	EM ◇ C	NT D	NT ◇ E	NT F	NT	NT ◇	TP ◇1 G	NT H	NT	NT A	NT ◇ B	EM ◇ C	NT D	NT ◇ E	NT F	NT	NT ◇
Leeds 10 31,32	d				14 32	14 38					14 48	15 09				15 32	15 38					15 48	16 09
Woodlesford 32	d				14 41											15 41							
Castleford 32	d				14 52											15 52							
Normanton	d				14 57					←						15 57					←		
Wakefield Kirkgate 4 31	a				15 02	14 54				15 02		15 25				16 02	15 54				16 02		16 25
	d				15 03	14 55				15 03		15 26				16 03	15 55				16 03		16 26
Darton	d				→					15 14						→					16 14		
Huddersfield	d			14 12											15 12								
Lockwood	d			14 15											15 15								
Berry Brow	d			14 18											15 18								
Honley	d			14 21											15 21								
Brockholes	d			14 24											15 24								
Stocksmoor	d			14 28											15 28								
Shepley	d			14 30											15 30								
Denby Dale	d			14 35											15 35								
Penistone	d			14 43											15 43								
Silkstone Common	d			14 48											15 48								
Dodworth	d			14 52											15 52								
Barnsley	a			14 59		15 09				15 21		15 41			15 59		16 09				16 21		16 41
	d			15 00		15 11				15 22		15 42			16 00		16 11				16 22		16 42
Wombwell	d			15 05						15 27					16 05						16 27		
Elsecar	d			15 09						15 31					16 09						16 31		
Chapeltown	d			15 15						15 37					16 15						16 37		
Meadowhall 29,31	a			15 20		15 26				15 42	15 51	15 56			16 20		16 26				16 42	16 51	16 56
	d	15 02	15 06	15 21		15 27		15 34	15 41	15 44	15 51	15 57	16 02	16 06	16 21		16 27		16 34	16 38	16 43	16 51	16 57
Sheffield 7 29,31	a	15 08	15 14	15 28		15 34		15 44	15 50	15 52	16 01	16 04	16 08	16 14	16 28		16 34		16 44	16 49	16 51	17 01	17 04
	d						15 38					16 06						16 38					17 06
Dronfield	d											16 16						16 48					17 16
Chesterfield	d						15 53					16 22						16 54					17 22
Alfreton	d						16 04					16 32						17 05					17 32
Langley Mill	d											16 40											17 40
Ilkeston	d											16 45											17 45
Nottingham	a						16 27					16 58						17 27					17 58

A To Sheffield
B To Lincoln
C From Liverpool Lime Street to Norwich
D From Doncaster
E From Scarborough
F From Leeds
G From Cleethorpes to Manchester Airport
H From Adwick
I From York

Table T034-R

Saturdays

21 December to 16 May

Leeds and Huddersfield - Barnsley - Sheffield and Nottingham

Station		TP ◇1 A	NT B	NT	NT C	NT ◇ D	EM ◇ E	NT F	NT ◇ G	NT H	NT	NT ◇	TP ◇1 A	NT B	NT	NT ◇ I	NT C	NT ◇ D	EM ◇ J	NT F	NT ◇ G	NT H	NT
Leeds 10 31,32	d				16 32	16 38					16 48	17 09					17 32	17 38					17 48
Woodlesford 32	d				16 41												17 41						
Castleford 32	d				16 52												17 52						
Normanton	d				16 57					←		17 21					17 57					←	
Wakefield Kirkgate 4 31	a				17 02	16 54				17 02		17 26					18 02	17 54				18 02	
	d				17 03	16 55				17 03		17 27					18 03	17 55				18 03	
Darton	d				→					17 14							→					18 14	
Huddersfield	d			16 12											17 12								
Lockwood	d			16 15											17 15								
Berry Brow	d			16 18											17 18								
Honley	d			16 21											17 21								
Brockholes	d			16 24											17 24								
Stocksmoor	d			16 28											17 28								
Shepley	d			16 30											17 30								
Denby Dale	d			16 35											17 35								
Penistone	d			16 43											17 43								
Silkstone Common	d			16 48											17 48								
Dodworth	d			16 52											17 52								
Barnsley	a			16 59		17 09				17 21		17 42			17 59			18 09				18 21	
	d			17 00		17 11				17 22		17 43			18 00			18 11				18 22	
Wombwell	d			17 05						17 27					18 05							18 27	
Elsecar	d			17 09						17 31					18 09							18 31	
Chapeltown	d			17 15						17 37					18 15							18 37	
Meadowhall 29,31	a			17 20		17 26				17 42	17 51	17 56			18 20			18 26				18 42	18 51
	d	17 02	17 06	17 21		17 27		17 34	17 38	17 43	17 51	17 57	18 02	18 06	18 21	18 24		18 27		18 34	18 38	18 43	18 51
Sheffield 7 29,31	a	17 08	17 14	17 28		17 34		17 44	17 49	17 51	18 01	18 04	18 08	18 14	18 28	18 32		18 34		18 44	18 49	18 51	19 01
	d						17 41					18 06							18 40				
Dronfield	d						17 51					18 16											
Chesterfield	d						17 57					18 22							18 58				
Alfreton	d						18 08					18 32							19 09				
Langley Mill	d											18 40											
Ilkeston	d											18 45											
Nottingham	a						18 29					18 58							19 29				

Station		NT ◇	TP ◇1 A	NT B	NT	NT	NT C	NT ◇ D	EM ◇ E	NT F	NT ◇ G	NT H	NT	NT ◇	TP ◇1 A	NT B	NT	EM ◇ J	NT F	NT ◇ G	NT	NT C
Leeds 10 31,32	d	18 03					18 32	18 38					18 48	19 03							19 32	19 48
Woodlesford 32	d						18 41														19 41	
Castleford 32	d						18 52														19 52	
Normanton	d						18 57	18 51				←									19 57	
Wakefield Kirkgate 4 31	a	18 21					19 02	18 56				19 02		19 20							20 02	
	d	18 22					19 03	18 57				19 03		19 21							20 03	
Darton	d						→					19 14									20 14	
Huddersfield	d				17 51	18 13											19 12					
Lockwood	d				17 54	18 16											19 15					
Berry Brow	d				17 57	18 19											19 18					
Honley	d				18 00	18 22											19 21					
Brockholes	d				18 03	18 25											19 24					
Stocksmoor	d				18 07	18 29											19 28					
Shepley	d				18 09	18 31											19 30					
Denby Dale	d				18 14	18 39											19 35					
Penistone	d				18 27	18 46											19 43					
Silkstone Common	d				18 32	18 52											19 48					
Dodworth	d				18 36	18 55											19 52					
Barnsley	a	18 37			18 44	19 02		19 12				19 21		19 36			19 59				20 21	
	d	18 38			18 45	19 02		19 13				19 22		19 37			20 00				20 22	
Wombwell	d				18 50	19 08						19 27					20 05				20 27	
Elsecar	d				18 54	19 12						19 31					20 09				20 31	
Chapeltown	d				19 00	19 17						19 37					20 15				20 37	
Meadowhall 29,31	a	18 52			19 07	19 23		19 27				19 42	19 51	19 51			20 20				20 42	20 51
	d	18 57	19 02	19 06	19 09	19 23		19 28		19 34	19 38	19 43	19 51	19 57	20 02	20 06	20 21		20 36	20 38	20 43	20 54
Sheffield 7 29,31	a	19 04	19 09	19 14	19 17	19 32		19 35		19 44	19 49	19 51	20 01	20 04	20 09	20 14	20 28		20 44	20 49	20 51	→
	d	19 06							19 37					20 06				20 39				
Dronfield	d	19 16												20 16								
Chesterfield	d	19 22							19 53					20 22				20 54				
Alfreton	d	19 32							20 04					20 32				21 05				
Langley Mill	d	19 40												20 40								
Ilkeston	d	19 45												20 45								
Nottingham	a	19 58							20 28					20 59				21 33				

A From Cleethorpes to Manchester Airport
B From Adwick
C To Sheffield
D To Lincoln
E From Liverpool Lime Street to Norwich
F From Doncaster
G From Scarborough
H From Leeds
I From York
J From Liverpool Lime Street

Table T034-R

Saturdays

21 December to 16 May

Leeds and Huddersfield - Barnsley - Sheffield and Nottingham

			NT ◇	NT A	TP ◇■ B	NT C	NT	EM ◇ D	NT E	NT ◇ F	NT	NT	NT ◇	TP ◇■ G	NT C	NT ◇ E	NT	NT H	NT ◇	EM ◇ D	NT ◇ F	NT A	NT	NT C
Leeds [10]	31,32	d	20 04								20 32	20 48	21 04					21 32	21 37				21 48	
Woodlesford	32	d									20 41							21 41						
Castleford	32	d									20 52							21 52						
Normanton		d									20 57							21 57				←		
Wakefield Kirkgate [4]	31	a	20 21								21 02		21 20					22 02	21 53			22 02		
		d	20 22								21 03		21 21					22 03	21 53			22 03		
Darton		d									21 14							→				22 14		
Huddersfield		d					20 12										21 12							
Lockwood		d					20 15										21 15							
Berry Brow		d					20 18										21 18							
Honley		d					20 21										21 21							
Brockholes		d					20 24										21 24							
Stocksmoor		d					20 28										21 28							
Shepley		d					20 30										21 30							
Denby Dale		d					20 35										21 35							
Penistone		d					20 43										21 43							
Silkstone Common		d					20 48										21 48							
Dodworth		d					20 52										21 52							
Barnsley		a	20 37				20 59				21 21		21 36				21 59		22 09			22 21		
		d	20 38				21 00				21 22		21 37				22 00		22 11			22 22		
Wombwell		d					21 05				21 27						22 05					22 27		
Elsecar		d					21 09				21 31						22 09					22 31		
Chapeltown		d		←			21 15				21 37						22 15					22 37		
Meadowhall	29,31	a	20 51	20 51			21 20				21 42	21 51	21 51				22 20		22 25			22 42	22 55	
		d	20 51	20 54	21 04	21 08	21 21		21 35	21 38	21 43	21 51	21 54	22 02	22 06	22 10	22 21		22 30		22 34	22 43	22 56	23 06
Sheffield [7]	29,31	a	21 01	21 04	21 09	21 17	21 29		21 45	21 49	21 51	21 59	22 02	22 08	22 14	22 19	22 28		22 40		22 44	22 51	23 04	23 14
		d	21 04					21 38					22 04							22 42				
Dronfield		d	21 14					21 49					22 14											
Chesterfield		d	21 20					21 54					22 20							22 56				
Alfreton		d						22 05					22 31							23 07				
Langley Mill		d						22 13					22 38											
Ilkeston		d						22 18					22 43											
Nottingham		a	22 00					22 34					22 57							23 28				

			NT	EM ◇ D	NT	NT	NT
Leeds [10]	31,32	d	22 15		22 32	22 44	
Woodlesford	32	d			22 41		
Castleford	32	d			22 52		
Normanton		d			22 57		
Wakefield Kirkgate [4]	31	a			23 02		
		d			23 03		
Darton		d			23 14		
Huddersfield		d					22 50
Lockwood		d					22 53
Berry Brow		d					22 56
Honley		d					22 59
Brockholes		d					23 02
Stocksmoor		d					23 06
Shepley		d					23 08
Denby Dale		d					23 13
Penistone		d					23 23
Silkstone Common		d					23 29
Dodworth		d					23 32
Barnsley		a			23 21		23 39
		d			23 22		23 39
Wombwell		d			23 27		23 44
Elsecar		d			23 31		23 48
Chapeltown		d			23 37		23 53
Meadowhall	29,31	a	23 15		23 42	23 45	23 59
		d	23 15		23 43	23 47	23 59
Sheffield [7]	29,31	a	23 25		23 51	23 55	00 08
		d		23 38			
Dronfield		d					
Chesterfield		d		23 53			
Alfreton		d					
Langley Mill		d					
Ilkeston		d					
Nottingham		a		00 29			

A From Leeds
B From Cleethorpes to Manchester Piccadilly
C From Adwick
D From Liverpool Lime Street
E From Doncaster
F From Scarborough
G From Cleethorpes to Manchester Airport
H To Sheffield

Table T034-R

Sundays

15 December to 10 May

Leeds and Huddersfield - Barnsley - Sheffield and Nottingham

			NT A	NT ◇ B	NT A	NT C	NT ◇	NT C	NT	NT	NT ◇	TP ◇■ D	NT E	NT	NT	EM ◇■ F	NT ◇ G	NT ◇	TP ◇■ H	NT C	NT	NT	NT	NT ◇ I
Leeds [10]	31,32	d							08 33	08 46	09 09				09 25	09 50		10 09				10 18	10 31	
Woodlesford	32	d							08 41													10 26		
Castleford	32	d							08 52													10 37		
Normanton		d							08 58													10 42		
Wakefield Kirkgate [4]	31	a							09 02		09 25							10 25				10 47		
		d							09 03		09 25							10 25				10 47		
Darton		d							09 14													11 01		
Huddersfield		d												09 10							10 15			
Lockwood		d												09 13							10 18			
Berry Brow		d												09 16							10 21			
Honley		d												09 19							10 24			
Brockholes		d												09 22							10 27			
Stocksmoor		d												09 26							10 31			
Shepley		d												09 28							10 34			
Denby Dale		d												09 33							10 39			
Penistone		d												09 41							10 46			
Silkstone Common		d												09 46							10 52			
Dodworth		d												09 50							10 55			
Barnsley		a							09 20		09 41			09 57				10 41			11 02	11 08		
		d							09 20		09 42			09 58				10 42			11 02	11 08		
Wombwell		d							09 25					10 03								11 14		
Elsecar		d							09 29					10 07								11 18		
Chapeltown		d							09 34					10 12								11 23		
Meadowhall	29,31	a							09 41	09 45	09 56			10 17	10 27			10 56			11 18	11 29	11 37	
		d	00 04	00 08	00 12	08 37		09 33	09 41	09 45	09 56	10 05	10 10	10 18	10 27		10 39	10 56	11 02	11 07	11 19	11 29	11 37	11 44
Sheffield [7]	29,31	a	00 13	00 17	00 21	08 45		09 41	09 50	09 53	10 03	10 12	10 18	10 27	10 36	10 30	10 49	11 03	11 10	11 15	11 27	11 38	11 45	11 51
		d					09 05				10 06					10 35		11 06						
Dronfield		d					09 15				10 16							11 16						
Chesterfield		d					09 21				10 22					10 48		11 22						
Alfreton		d					09 32				10 32							11 32						
Langley Mill		d					09 39				10 40							11 40						
Ilkeston		d					09 44				10 45							11 45						
Nottingham		a					10 00				11 00					11 21		12 00						

			NT ◇	TP ◇■ H	NT C	NT ◇ J	EM ◇ K	NT ◇ G	NT	NT ◇	TP ◇■ H	NT C	NT ◇ J	NT	EM ◇ L	NT ◇ G	NT	NT ◇	TP ◇■ H	NT C	NT ◇ J	EM ◇ M	NT ◇ N	NT
Leeds [10]	31,32	d	11 09						11 48	12 09				12 17			12 48	13 09						13 48
Woodlesford	32	d												12 25										
Castleford	32	d												12 36										
Normanton		d												12 41										
Wakefield Kirkgate [4]	31	a	11 25							12 25				12 46				13 25						
		d	11 25							12 25				12 46				13 25						
Darton		d												13 00										
Huddersfield		d				11 19							12 15								13 19			
Lockwood		d				11 22							12 18								13 22			
Berry Brow		d				11 25							12 21								13 25			
Honley		d				11 28							12 24								13 28			
Brockholes		d				11 31							12 27								13 31			
Stocksmoor		d				11 35							12 31								13 35			
Shepley		d				11 37							12 33								13 37			
Denby Dale		d				11 42							12 38								13 42			
Penistone		d				11 50							12 46								13 50			
Silkstone Common		d				11 55							12 51								13 55			
Dodworth		d				11 59							12 55								13 59			
Barnsley		a	11 41			12 06				12 41			13 02	13 08				13 41			14 06			
		d	11 42			12 07				12 42			13 03	13 08				13 42			14 07			
Wombwell		d				12 12								13 13							14 12			
Elsecar		d				12 16								13 18							14 16			
Chapeltown		d				12 21								13 23							14 21			
Meadowhall	29,31	a	11 56			12 26			12 50	12 56			13 17	13 30			13 51	13 56			14 26			14 49
		d	11 56	12 02	12 06	12 27		12 37	12 51	12 56	13 01	13 05	13 19	13 30		13 41	13 52	13 56	14 02	14 06	14 27		14 39	14 49
Sheffield [7]	29,31	a	12 03	12 08	12 13	12 37		12 46	12 58	13 03	13 08	13 12	13 30	13 38		13 49	13 59	14 03	14 09	14 13	14 38		14 48	14 57
		d	12 06				12 43			13 06					13 48			14 06				14 41		
Dronfield		d	12 16							13 16								14 16						
Chesterfield		d	12 22				12 57			13 22					14 02			14 22				14 55		
Alfreton		d	12 32				13 08			13 32					14 12			14 32				15 08		
Langley Mill		d	12 40							13 40								14 40				15 15		
Ilkeston		d	12 45							13 45					14 22			14 45						
Nottingham		a	13 00				13 34			14 00					14 35			15 00				15 32		

A not 15 December. From Doncaster
B not 15 December. From Hull
C From Doncaster
D From Doncaster to Manchester Airport
E From Goole
F To St Pancras International
G From Hull
H From Cleethorpes to Manchester Airport
I From Bridlington
J To Lincoln
K To Norwich
L From Manchester Piccadilly to Norwich
M From Liverpool Lime Street to Norwich
N From Scarborough

Table T034-R

Sundays

15 December to 10 May

Leeds and Huddersfield - Barnsley - Sheffield and Nottingham

	NT ◇	TP ◇1 A	NT B	NT ◇ C	EM ◇ D	NT	NT ◇ E	NT	NT ◇	TP ◇1 A	NT B	NT ◇ C	EM ◇ D	NT ◇ E	NT	NT ◇	TP ◇1 A	NT B	NT ◇ C	EM ◇ D	NT
Leeds [10] 31,32 d	14 09					14 17		14 46	15 09						15 42	16 09					16 17
Woodlesford 32 d						14 25															16 25
Castleford 32 d						14 36															16 37
Normanton d						14 41															16 42
Wakefield Kirkgate [4] 31 a	14 25					14 46			15 25							16 25					16 48
d	14 25					14 46			15 25							16 25					16 48
Darton d						15 00															17 02
Huddersfield d				14 15								15 15							16 15		
Lockwood d				14 18								15 18							16 18		
Berry Brow d				14 21								15 21							16 21		
Honley d				14 24								15 24							16 24		
Brockholes d				14 27								15 27							16 27		
Stocksmoor d				14 31								15 31							16 31		
Shepley d				14 33								15 33							16 33		
Denby Dale d				14 38								15 38							16 38		
Penistone d				14 46								15 46							16 46		
Silkstone Common d				14 51								15 51							16 51		
Dodworth d				14 55								15 55							16 55		
Barnsley a	14 41			15 02		15 08			15 41			16 02				16 41			17 02		17 09
d	14 42			15 03		15 11			15 42			16 03				16 42			17 03		17 09
Wombwell d						15 16						16 08									17 14
Elsecar d						15 20						16 12									17 18
Chapeltown d						15 25						16 17									17 23
Meadowhall 29,31 a	14 56			15 17		15 31		15 50	15 56			16 22			16 48	16 56			17 17		17 30
d	14 56	15 02	15 06	15 21		15 32	15 39	15 50	15 56	16 02	16 06	16 26		16 40	16 49	16 56	17 02	17 06	17 21		17 31
Sheffield [7] 29,31 a	15 03	15 09	15 14	15 29		15 39	15 48	15 58	16 03	16 08	16 13	16 34		16 49	16 56	17 05	17 09	17 14	17 29		17 40
d	15 06				15 39				16 06				16 43			17 06				17 40	
Dronfield d	15 16								16 16							17 16					
Chesterfield d	15 22				15 53				16 22				16 57			17 22				17 54	
Alfreton d	15 32				16 04				16 32				17 07			17 32				18 05	
Langley Mill d	15 40				16 11				16 40				17 15			17 40				18 12	
Ilkeston d	15 45								16 45							17 45				18 17	
Nottingham a	16 00				16 28				17 00				17 30			18 00				18 34	

	NT ◇ E	NT	NT ◇	TP ◇1 A	NT B	NT	EM ◇ F	NT ◇ E	NT	NT ◇ G	TP ◇1 A	NT B	NT ◇ H	NT	EM ◇ D	NT	NT ◇ E	NT	NT ◇	TP ◇1 A	NT B	NT
Leeds [10] 31,32 d		16 48	17 09						17 49	18 09						18 14		18 48	19 09			
Woodlesford 32 d																18 22						
Castleford 32 d																18 38						
Normanton d																18 43						
Wakefield Kirkgate [4] 31 a			17 25							18 25						18 48			19 25			
d			17 26							18 26						18 48			19 25			
Darton d																19 06						
Huddersfield d						17 15								18 15								19 15
Lockwood d						17 18								18 18								19 18
Berry Brow d						17 21								18 21								19 21
Honley d						17 24								18 24								19 24
Brockholes d						17 27								18 27								19 27
Stocksmoor d						17 31								18 34								19 31
Shepley d						17 33								18 36								19 33
Denby Dale d						17 38								18 41								19 38
Penistone d						17 46								18 49								19 46
Silkstone Common d						17 51								18 54								19 51
Dodworth d						17 55								18 58								19 55
Barnsley a			17 41			18 02				18 42				19 05		19 14			19 41			20 02
d			17 42			18 03				18 42				19 06		19 14			19 42			20 03
Wombwell d						18 08										19 19						20 08
Elsecar d						18 12										19 23						20 12
Chapeltown d						18 17										19 28						20 17
Meadowhall 29,31 a		17 50	17 56			18 23			18 51	18 55				19 20		19 35		19 51	19 56			20 22
d	17 39	17 51	17 56	18 00	18 04	18 26		18 40	18 52	18 56	19 02	19 06	19 09	19 20		19 36	19 39	19 52	19 56	20 01	20 05	20 23
Sheffield [7] 29,31 a	17 48	17 58	18 03	18 07	18 11	18 33		18 49	18 59	19 03	19 09	19 12	19 19	19 29		19 43	19 48	19 59	20 03	20 08	20 11	20 32
d			18 06				18 40			19 06					19 40				20 06			
Dronfield d			18 16							19 16									20 16			
Chesterfield d			18 22				18 54			19 22					19 54				20 22			
Alfreton d			18 32				19 05			19 32					20 05				20 32			
Langley Mill d			18 40				19 12			19 40					20 12				20 40			
Ilkeston d			18 45							19 45									20 45			
Nottingham a			19 00				19 33			20 00					20 30				21 00			

A From Cleethorpes to Manchester Airport
B From Doncaster
C To Lincoln
D From Liverpool Lime Street to Norwich
E From Scarborough
F From Liverpool Lime Street
G From Carlisle
H From York

Table T034-R

Sundays

15 December to 10 May

Leeds and Huddersfield - Barnsley - Sheffield and Nottingham

	EM ◇ A	NT ◇ B	NT	NT ◇	NT C	TP ◇1 D	EM ◇ A	NT	NT ◇ B	NT	NT ◇ E	NT ◇	TP ◇1 F	NT C	NT	NT ◇ B	NT	NT ◇	NT C	EM ◇ A	NT
Leeds [10] 31,32 d			19 48	20 09				20 17		20 48		21 09					21 46	22 09			22 18
Woodlesford 32 d								20 25													22 26
Castleford 32 d								20 36													22 37
Normanton d								20 41													22 42
Wakefield Kirkgate [4] 31 a				20 25				20 46				21 29						22 25			22 47
d				20 25				20 46				21 30						22 25			22 47
Darton d								21 00													22 58
Huddersfield d																					
Lockwood d																					
Berry Brow d																					
Honley d																					
Brockholes d																					
Stocksmoor d																					
Shepley d																					
Denby Dale d																					
Penistone d																					
Silkstone Common d																					
Dodworth d																					
Barnsley a				20 41				21 07				21 46						22 41			23 05
d				20 42				21 07				21 46			22 18			22 42			23 05
Wombwell d								21 12							22 24						23 10
Elsecar d								21 16							22 28						23 14
Chapeltown d								21 21							22 33						23 19
Meadowhall 29,31 a			20 51	20 55				21 28		21 51		21 59			22 38		22 48	22 55			23 26
d		20 39	20 51	20 55	20 58	21 02		21 31	21 39	21 52	21 56	22 00	22 03	22 07	22 39	22 42	22 49	22 55	23 11		23 26
Sheffield [7] 29,31 a		20 47	20 59	21 03	21 05	21 08		21 38	21 49	21 59	22 03	22 07	22 10	22 13	22 49	22 50	22 56	23 03	23 20		23 35
d	20 40			21 06			21 38					22 08								23 30	
Dronfield d				21 16			21 50					22 18									
Chesterfield d	20 54			21 22			21 56					22 24								23 44	
Alfreton d	21 05			21 32			22 06					22 35								23 55	
Langley Mill d	21 12			21 40			22 14					22 42								00 02	
Ilkeston d				21 45								22 47									
Nottingham a	21 33			22 00			22 36					23 05								00 23	

	NT
Leeds [10] 31,32 d	22 37
Woodlesford 32 d	
Castleford 32 d	
Normanton d	
Wakefield Kirkgate [4] 31 a	
d	
Darton d	
Huddersfield d	
Lockwood d	
Berry Brow d	
Honley d	
Brockholes d	
Stocksmoor d	
Shepley d	
Denby Dale d	
Penistone d	
Silkstone Common d	
Dodworth d	
Barnsley a	
d	
Wombwell d	
Elsecar d	
Chapeltown d	
Meadowhall 29,31 a	23 37
d	23 37
Sheffield [7] 29,31 a	23 45
d	
Dronfield d	
Chesterfield d	
Alfreton d	
Langley Mill d	
Ilkeston d	
Nottingham a	

A From Liverpool Lime Street
B From Scarborough
C From Doncaster
D From Cleethorpes to Manchester Airport
E From York, via Pontefract Baghill
F From Cleethorpes to Manchester Piccadilly

Table T035-F

York - Harrogate - Leeds

Mondays to Fridays

16 December to 15 May

Miles	Station		NT	NT	NT	NT	NT	NT	GR	NT	NT	NT	NT	NT	NT	NT	GR	NT	NT	NT	NT	NT	NT
									A ☕								A ☕			◇			◇
0	York 8	40 d						06 49					07 56			08 47		09 11			10 11		
3	Poppleton	d						06 54					08 01			08 53		09 16			10 16		
8¾	Hammerton	d						07 02					08 09			09 01		09 24			10 24		
10¼	Cattal	d						07 05					08 12			09 05		09 27			10 27		
16¾	**Knaresborough**	a						07 13					08 20			09 13		09 35			10 35		
—		d				06 55		07 14		07 37		08 06	08 21		09 05	09 13		09 36		10 06	10 36		11 06
18¼	Starbeck	d				06 58		07 17		07 40		08 09	08 25		09 08	09 17		09 39		10 09	10 39		11 09
20½	**Harrogate**	a				07 03		07 22		07 45		08 14	08 29		09 13	09 21		09 44		10 14	10 49		11 14
—		d	06 03	06 32	06 55	07 04	07 13	07 23	07 34	07 46	08 05	08 15	08 31		09 13	09 23	09 36	09 45	10 02	10 15	10 50	11 02	11 15
21½	Hornbeam Park	d	06 05	06 34	06 57	07 07	07 16	07 26		07 49	08 07	08 18	08 34		09 16	09 25		09 48	10 04	10 18	10 53	11 04	11 18
23¾	Pannal	d	06 10	06 40	07 02	07 12		07 31		07 54	08 12	08 23	08 39		09 21	09 31		09 53		10 23	10 58		11 23
27	Weeton	d	06 15	06 45	07 07	07 17		07 36		07 59	08 17	08 28	08 44		09 26	09 36		09 58		10 28	11 03		11 28
33	Horsforth	d	06 24	06 53	07 16	07 26	07 36	07 45	07 53	08 08	08 26	08 36	08 52	09 07	09 35	09 44	09 54	10 07	10 20	10 37	11 12	11 20	11 37
35¾	Headingley	d	06 28	06 58		07 30		07 49		08 12	08 30	08 41	08 57	09 11	09 39	09 49		10 11		10 41	11 16		11 41
36½	Burley Park	d	06 31	07 00		07 33		07 52		08 14	08 33	08 43	08 59	09 13	09 42	09 51		10 14		10 44	11 19		11 44
38¾	**Leeds 10**	40 a	06 40	07 10	07 28	07 42	07 50	08 02	08 04	08 24	08 41	08 55	09 08	09 20	09 51	10 00	10 05	10 22	10 33	10 53	11 27	11 33	11 53

Station		GR	NT	NT	NT	NT	NT	NT	GR	NT	NT	NT	NT	NT	NT	GR	NT	NT	NT	NT	NT	NT	GR
		A ☕			◇			◇	A ☕			◇			◇	A ☕			◇				A ☕
York 8	40 d		11 11			12 11				13 11			14 11				15 11			16 11			
Poppleton	d		11 16			12 16				13 16			14 16				15 16			16 16			
Hammerton	d		11 24			12 24				13 24			14 24				15 24			16 24			
Cattal	d		11 27			12 32				13 27			14 32				15 27			16 32			
Knaresborough	a		11 35			12 40				13 35			14 40				15 35			16 40			
	d		11 36		12 06	12 40		13 06		13 36		14 06	14 40		15 06		15 36		16 06	16 40		17 06	
Starbeck	d		11 39		12 09	12 44		13 09		13 39		14 09	14 44		15 09		15 39		16 09	16 44		17 09	
Harrogate	a		11 44		12 14	12 48		13 14		13 44		14 14	14 48		15 14		15 44		16 14	16 48		17 14	
	d	11 36	11 45	12 02	12 15	12 50	13 02	13 15	13 36	13 45	14 02	14 15	14 50	15 02	15 15	15 36	15 45	16 02	16 15	16 50	17 02	17 15	17 36
Hornbeam Park	d		11 48	12 04	12 18	12 52	13 04	13 18		13 48	14 04	14 18	14 52	15 04	15 18		15 48	16 04	16 18	16 52	17 04	17 18	
Pannal	d		11 53		12 23	12 58		13 23		13 53		14 23	14 58		15 23		15 53		16 23	16 58		17 23	
Weeton	d		11 58		12 28	13 03		13 28		13 58		14 28	15 03		15 28		15 58		16 28	17 03		17 28	
Horsforth	d		12 07	12 20	12 37	13 11	13 20	13 37		14 07	14 20	14 37	15 11	15 20	15 37		16 07	16 20	16 37	17 11	17 20	17 37	
Headingley	d		12 11		12 41	13 16		13 41		14 11		14 41	15 16		15 41		16 11		16 41	17 16		17 41	
Burley Park	d		12 14		12 44	13 18		13 44		14 14		14 44	15 18		15 44		16 14		16 44	17 18		17 43	
Leeds 10	40 a	12 07	12 23	12 32	12 53	13 28	13 33	13 53	14 06	14 23	14 32	14 53	15 28	15 33	15 53	16 07	16 22	16 32	16 53	17 27	17 33	17 53	18 06

Station		NT	NT	NT	NT	NT	NT	NT	NT	NT	NT	NT
York 8	40 d	17 11		17 42	18 11		19 11		20 11	21 11	22 11	22 44
Poppleton	d	17 16		17 49	18 16		19 16		20 16	21 16	22 16	22 49
Hammerton	d	17 24		17 57	18 24		19 24		20 24	21 24	22 24	22 57
Cattal	d	17 27		18 00	18 28		19 27		20 27	21 27	22 27	23 00
Knaresborough	a	17 35		18 08	18 36		19 35		20 35	21 35	22 35	23 08
	d	17 36		18 09	18 37	19 06	19 36	20 06	20 36	21 36	22 36	23 09
Starbeck	d	17 39		18 12	18 40	19 09	19 39	20 09	20 39	21 39	22 39	23 12
Harrogate	a	17 44		18 17	18 45	19 14	19 44	20 14	20 44	21 44	22 44	23 17
	d	17 45	18 07	18 18	18 46	19 15	19 45	20 15	20 45	21 47	22 45	23 18
Hornbeam Park	d	17 48	18 09	18 21	18 49	19 18	19 48	20 18	20 48	21 50	22 48	23 21
Pannal	d	17 53	18 14	18 26	18 54	19 23	19 53	20 23	20 53	21 55	22 53	23 26
Weeton	d	17 58	18 19	18 31	18 59	19 28	19 58	20 28	20 58	22 00	22 58	23 31
Horsforth	d	18 07	18 27	18 41	19 08	19 37	20 07	20 37	21 07	22 09	23 07	23 40
Headingley	d	18 11	18 31		19 12	19 41	20 11	20 41	21 11	22 13	23 11	23 44
Burley Park	d	18 14	18 34		19 15	19 44	20 14	20 44	21 14	22 16	23 14	23 47
Leeds 10	40 a	18 22	18 41	18 54	19 23	19 53	20 23	20 53	21 23	22 24	23 22	23 57

Saturdays

21 December to 16 May

Station		NT	NT	NT	NT	NT	NT	GR	NT	NT	NT	NT	NT	NT	NT	GR	NT	NT	NT	NT	NT	NT	GR
								A ☕								A ☕			◇			◇	A ☕
York 8	40 d						06 49					07 56			08 47		09 11			10 11			
Poppleton	d						06 54					08 01			08 53		09 16			10 16			
Hammerton	d						07 02					08 09			09 01		09 24			10 24			
Cattal	d						07 05					08 12			09 05		09 27			10 27			
Knaresborough	a						07 13					08 20			09 13		09 35			10 35			
	d				06 55		07 14		07 37		08 06	08 21		09 05	09 13		09 36		10 06	10 36		11 06	
Starbeck	d				06 58		07 17		07 40		08 09	08 25		09 08	09 17		09 39		10 09	10 39		11 09	
Harrogate	a				07 03		07 22		07 45		08 14	08 29		09 13	09 21		09 44		10 14	10 49		11 14	
	d	06 03	06 32	06 55	07 04	07 13	07 23	07 35	07 46	08 05	08 15	08 31		09 13	09 23	09 36	09 45	10 02	10 15	10 50	11 02	11 15	11 36
Hornbeam Park	d	06 05	06 34	06 57	07 07	07 16	07 26		07 49	08 07	08 18	08 34		09 16	09 25		09 48	10 04	10 18	10 53	11 04	11 18	
Pannal	d	06 10	06 40	07 02	07 12		07 31		07 54	08 12	08 23	08 39		09 21	09 31		09 53		10 23	10 58		11 23	
Weeton	d	06 15	06 45	07 07	07 17		07 36		07 59	08 17	08 28	08 44		09 26	09 36		09 58		10 28	11 03		11 28	
Horsforth	d	06 24	06 53	07 16	07 26	07 36	07 45	07 54	08 08	08 26	08 36	08 52	09 07	09 35	09 44	09 54	10 07	10 20	10 37	11 12	11 20	11 37	
Headingley	d	06 28	06 58		07 30		07 49		08 12	08 30	08 41	08 57	09 11	09 39	09 49		10 11		10 41	11 16		11 41	
Burley Park	d	06 31	07 00		07 33		07 52		08 14	08 33	08 43	08 59	09 13	09 42	09 51		10 14		10 44	11 19		11 44	
Leeds 10	40 a	06 40	07 10	07 28	07 42	07 50	08 02	08 07	08 24	08 41	08 55	09 08	09 20	09 51	10 00	10 05	10 22	10 33	10 53	11 27	11 33	11 53	12 07

A To London Kings Cross

Table T035-F

York - Harrogate - Leeds

Saturdays

21 December to 16 May

Station		NT	NT	NT	NT	NT	NT	GR	NT	NT	NT	NT	NT	NT	GR	NT	NT	NT	NT	NT	NT	GR
				◇			◇	A ☕			◇			◇	A ☕			◇				A ☕
York 8	40 d	11 11			12 11				13 11			14 11				15 11			16 11			
Poppleton	d	11 16			12 16				13 16			14 16				15 16			16 16			
Hammerton	d	11 24			12 24				13 24			14 24				15 24			16 24			
Cattal	d	11 27			12 32				13 27			14 32				15 27			16 32			
Knaresborough	a	11 35			12 40				13 35			14 40				15 35			16 40			
	d	11 36		12 06	12 40		13 06		13 36		14 06	14 40		15 06		15 36		16 06	16 40		17 06	
Starbeck	d	11 39		12 09	12 44		13 09		13 39		14 09	14 44		15 09		15 39		16 09	16 44		17 09	
Harrogate	a	11 44		12 14	12 48		13 14		13 44		14 14	14 48		15 14		15 44		16 14	16 48		17 14	
	d	11 45	12 02	12 15	12 50	13 02	13 15	13 36	13 45	14 02	14 15	14 50	15 02	15 15	15 36	15 45	16 02	16 15	16 50	17 02	17 15	17 36
Hornbeam Park	d	11 48	12 04	12 18	12 52	13 04	13 18		13 48	14 04	14 18	14 52	15 04	15 18		15 48	16 04	16 18	16 52	17 04	17 18	
Pannal	d	11 53		12 23	12 58		13 23		13 53		14 23	14 58		15 23		15 53		16 23	16 58		17 23	
Weeton	d	11 58		12 28	13 03		13 28		13 58		14 28	15 03		15 28		15 58		16 28	17 03		17 28	
Horsforth	d	12 07	12 20	12 37	13 11	13 20	13 37		14 07	14 20	14 37	15 11	15 20	15 37		16 07	16 20	16 37	17 11	17 20	17 37	
Headingley	d	12 11		12 41	13 16		13 41		14 11		14 41	15 16		15 41		16 11		16 41	17 16		17 41	
Burley Park	d	12 14		12 44	13 18		13 44		14 14		14 44	15 18		15 44		16 14		16 44	17 18		17 43	
Leeds 10	40 a	12 23	12 32	12 53	13 28	13 33	13 53	14 06	14 23	14 32	14 53	15 28	15 33	15 53	16 07	16 22	16 32	16 53	17 27	17 33	17 53	18 06

Station		NT	NT	NT	NT	NT	NT	NT	NT	NT	NT	NT
York 8	40 d	17 11		17 42	18 11		19 11		20 11	21 11	22 11	22 44
Poppleton	d	17 16		17 49	18 16		19 16		20 16	21 16	22 16	22 49
Hammerton	d	17 24		17 57	18 24		19 24		20 24	21 24	22 24	22 57
Cattal	d	17 27		18 00	18 28		19 27		20 27	21 27	22 27	23 00
Knaresborough	a	17 35		18 08	18 36		19 35		20 35	21 35	22 35	23 08
	d	17 36		18 09	18 37	19 06	19 36	20 06	20 36	21 36	22 36	23 09
Starbeck	d	17 39		18 12	18 40	19 09	19 39	20 09	20 39	21 39	22 39	23 12
Harrogate	a	17 44		18 17	18 45	19 14	19 44	20 14	20 44	21 44	22 44	23 17
	d	17 45	18 07	18 18	18 46	19 15	19 45	20 15	20 45	21 47	22 45	23 18
Hornbeam Park	d	17 48	18 09	18 21	18 49	19 18	19 48	20 18	20 48	21 50	22 48	23 21
Pannal	d	17 53	18 14	18 26	18 54	19 23	19 53	20 23	20 53	21 55	22 53	23 26
Weeton	d	17 58	18 19	18 31	18 59	19 28	19 58	20 28	20 58	22 00	22 58	23 31
Horsforth	d	18 07	18 27	18 41	19 08	19 37	20 07	20 37	21 07	22 09	23 07	23 40
Headingley	d	18 11	18 31		19 12	19 41	20 11	20 41	21 11	22 13	23 11	23 44
Burley Park	d	18 14	18 34		19 15	19 44	20 14	20 44	21 14	22 16	23 14	23 47
Leeds 10	40 a	18 22	18 41	18 54	19 23	19 53	20 23	20 53	21 23	22 24	23 22	23 57

Sundays

15 December to 10 May

Station		GR	NT	NT	NT	NT	GR	NT	NT	NT	NT	GR	NT	NT	NT	NT	NT	GR	NT	NT	NT	GR	NT
		A ☕					A ☕					A ☕						A ☕				A ☕	
York 8	40 d							10 47		11 47			12 47		13 47		14 47			15 47			16 47
Poppleton	d							10 52		11 52			12 52		13 52		14 52			15 52			16 52
Hammerton	d							11 00		12 00			13 00		14 00		15 00			16 00			17 00
Cattal	d							11 03		12 03			13 03		14 04		15 03			16 04			17 03
Knaresborough	a							11 11		12 11			13 11		14 12		15 11			16 12			17 11
	d					10 42		11 12	11 42	12 12	12 42		13 12	13 42	14 12	14 42	15 12		15 42	16 12	16 42		17 12
Starbeck	d					10 45		11 15	11 45	12 15	12 45		13 16	13 45	14 16	14 45	15 15		15 45	16 16	16 45		17 15
Harrogate	a					10 50		11 20	11 50	12 21	12 50		13 20	13 50	14 21	14 50	15 20		15 50	16 22	16 50		17 20
	d	09 15	09 22	09 52	10 22	10 51	11 15	11 21	11 51	12 22	12 51	13 15	13 22	13 51	14 23	14 51	15 21	15 36	15 51	16 23	16 51	17 05	17 21
Hornbeam Park	d		09 24	09 54	10 24	10 54		11 24	11 54	12 25	12 54		13 24	13 54	14 25	14 54	15 24		15 54	16 26	16 54		17 24
Pannal	d		09 30	10 00	10 30	10 59		11 29	11 59	12 30	12 59		13 30	13 59	14 31	14 59	15 29		15 59	16 31	16 59		17 29
Weeton	d		09 35	10 05	10 35	11 04		11 34	12 04	12 35	13 04		13 35	14 04	14 36	15 04	15 34		16 04	16 36	17 04		17 34
Horsforth	d	09 33	09 43	10 13	10 43	11 13	11 33	11 43	12 13	12 44	13 13		13 43	14 13	14 44	15 13	15 43		16 13	16 45	17 13		17 43
Headingley	d		09 48	10 18	10 48	11 17		11 47	12 17	12 48	13 17		13 48	14 17	14 49	15 17	15 47		16 17	16 49	17 17		17 47
Burley Park	d		09 50	10 20	10 50	11 21		11 50	12 20	12 51	13 20		13 50	14 20	14 51	15 20	15 50		16 20	16 52	17 20		17 50
Leeds 10	40 a	09 46	10 00	10 30	11 00	11 30	11 46	12 00	12 29	13 01	13 29	13 46	14 00	14 29	15 01	15 29	16 00	16 05	16 29	17 02	17 29	17 34	18 00

Station		NT	GR	NT	NT	NT	NT	NT	NT	NT	NT	NT
			A ☕									
York 8	40 d			17 47		18 47		19 47		20 47	21 43	
Poppleton	d			17 52		18 52		19 52		20 52	21 47	
Hammerton	d			18 00		19 00		20 00		21 00	21 55	
Cattal	d			18 04		19 03		20 04		21 03	21 59	
Knaresborough	a			18 12		19 12		20 12		21 11	22 07	
	d	17 42		18 12	18 42	19 12	19 42	20 12	20 42	21 12	22 07	
Starbeck	d	17 45		18 16	18 45	19 15	19 45	20 16	20 45	21 15	22 11	
Harrogate	a	17 50		18 22	18 50	19 20	19 50	20 21	20 50	21 20	22 15	
	d	17 51	18 02	18 23	18 51	19 21	19 51	20 23	20 51	21 21	22 17	23 12
Hornbeam Park	d	17 54		18 26	18 54	19 24	19 54	20 25	20 54	21 24	22 19	23 15
Pannal	d	17 59		18 31	18 59	19 29	19 59	20 31	20 59	21 29	22 25	23 20
Weeton	d	18 04		18 36	19 04	19 34	20 04	20 36	21 04	21 34	22 30	23 25
Horsforth	d	18 13		18 45	19 13	19 43	20 13	20 44	21 13	21 43	22 38	23 34
Headingley	d	18 17		18 49	19 17	19 47	20 17	20 49	21 17	21 47	22 43	23 38
Burley Park	d	18 20		18 52	19 20	19 50	20 20	20 51	21 20	21 50	22 45	23 42
Leeds 10	40 a	18 29	18 31	19 02	19 29	20 00	20 29	21 01	21 29	22 00	22 56	23 51

A To London Kings Cross

Table T035-R

Leeds - Harrogate - York

Mondays to Fridays
16 December to 15 May

Miles	Station		NT MX A	NT	NT	NT	NT	NT	NT	NT	NT	NT	NT ◇	NT	NT	GR ■1 B ⊡	NT ◇	NT	NT	NT ◇	NT	NT	GR ■1 B ⊡
0	**Leeds 10**	40 d		06 05	06 23	06 33	07 00	07 15	07 45	08 09	08 29	08 48	08 59	09 15	09 29	09 53	09 59	10 15	10 29	10 59	11 15	11 35	11 53
2¼	Burley Park	d		06 10		06 38	07 05	07 20	07 50	08 14	08 34	08 52	09 04		09 34		10 04		10 34	11 04		11 40	
3	Headingley	d		06 13		06 41	07 08	07 23	07 53	08 17	08 37	08 55	09 07		09 37		10 07		10 37	11 07		11 43	
5¾	Horsforth	d		06 18	06 33	06 47	07 13	07 28	07 58	08 22	08 42	09a01	09 12	09 24	09 42		10 12	10 24	10 42	11 12	11 24	11 49	
11¾	Weeton	d		06 26		06 55	07 21	07 36	08 06		08 50		09 20		09 50		10 20		10 50	11 20		11 57	
15	Pannal	d	00 05	06 32		07 01	07 27	07 42	08 12	08 34	08 56		09 26		09 56		10 26		10 56	11 26		12 03	
17¼	Hornbeam Park	d	00 10	06 37		07 06	07 32	07 47	08 17	08 39	09 01		09 31	09 40	10 01		10 31	10 40	11 01	11 31	11 40	12 08	
18¾	**Harrogate**	a	00 16	06 40	06 51	07 09	07 38	07 50	08 20	08 42	09 04		09 34	09 45	10 04	10 19	10 35	10 45	11 04	11 34	11 45	12 11	12 19
—		d		06 42		07 10	07 40	07 52	08 22	08 44	09 07		09 36		10 06		10 37		11 06	11 36		12 12	
20¾	Starbeck	d		06 46		07 15	07 44	07 56	08 26	08 48	09 11		09 40		10 10		10 41		11 10	11 40		12 17	
22	**Knaresborough**	a		06 51		07 19	07 51	08 01	08 31	08 55	09 16		09 47		10 15		10 48		11 15	11 47		12 21	
—		d		06 51		07 20		08 01	08 31		09 16				10 15				11 15			12 22	
28½	Cattal	d		06 59		07 28		08 09	08 39		09 24				10 23				11 23			12 30	
30	Hammerton	d		07 05		07 32		08 13	08 43		09 28				10 27				11 27			12 34	
35¾	Poppleton	d		07 12		07 39		08 21	08 51		09 36				10 35				11 35			12 41	
38¾	**York 8**	40 a		07 21		07 46		08 29	09 01		09 46				10 46				11 46			12 52	

Station		NT ◇	NT	NT	NT ◇	NT	NT	GR ■1 B ⊡	NT ◇	NT	NT	NT ◇	NT	NT	GR ■1 B ⊡	NT ◇	NT	NT	NT	NT	NT	NT
Leeds 10	40 d	11 59	12 15	12 29	12 59	13 15	13 35	13 53	13 59	14 15	14 29	14 59	15 15	15 35	15 53	15 59	16 15	16 29	16 45	16 59	17 09	17 32
Burley Park	d	12 04		12 34	13 04		13 40		14 04		14 34	15 04		15 40		16 04		16 34	16 50	17 04	17 14	17 37
Headingley	d	12 07		12 37	13 07		13 43		14 07		14 37	15 07		15 43		16 07		16 37	16 52	17 07	17 17	17 40
Horsforth	d	12 12	12 24	12 42	13 12	13 24	13 49		14 12	14 24	14 42	15 12	15 24	15 49		16 12	16 24	16 42	16a59	17 12	17 22	17 45
Weeton	d	12 20		12 50	13 20		13 57		14 20		14 50	15 20		15 57		16 20		16 50		17 20	17 30	17 53
Pannal	d	12 26		12 56	13 26		14 03		14 26		14 56	15 26		16 03		16 26		16 56		17 26	17 36	17 59
Hornbeam Park	d	12 31	12 40	13 01	13 31	13 40	14 08		14 31	14 40	15 01	15 31	15 40	16 08		16 31	16 40	17 01		17 31	17 41	18 04
Harrogate	a	12 34	12 45	13 04	13 34	13 45	14 11	14 19	14 34	14 46	15 04	15 34	15 46	16 11	16 19	16 34	16 46	17 04		17 34	17 44	18 07
	d	12 36		13 06	13 36		14 12		14 36		15 06	15 36		16 12		16 36		17 06		17 36	17 49	18 09
Starbeck	d	12 40		13 10	13 40		14 17		14 40		15 10	15 40		16 17		16 40		17 10		17 40	17 53	18 13
Knaresborough	a	12 47		13 15	13 47		14 21		14 47		15 15	15 47		16 21		16 47		17 15		17 47	17 58	18 18
	d			13 15			14 22				15 15			16 22				17 15				18 18
Cattal	d			13 23			14 30				15 23			16 30				17 23				18 26
Hammerton	d			13 27			14 34				15 27			16 34				17 27				18 30
Poppleton	d			13 35			14 41				15 35			16 41				17 35				18 38
York 8	40 a			13 45			14 52				15 46			16 52				17 50				18 51

Station		NT	NT	GR ■1 B ⊡	NT	NT	NT	NT	GR ■1 B ⊡	NT	NT	NT	NT
Leeds 10	40 d	17 39	17 49	18 00	18 09	18 29	19 01	19 29	20 01	20 30	21 29	22 39	23 39
Burley Park	d	17 44	17 54		18 14	18 34	19 06	19 34		20 35	21 34	22 44	23 44
Headingley	d	17 47	17 57		18 17	18 37	19 09	19 37		20 38	21 37	22 47	23 46
Horsforth	d	17 52	18 02	18 10	18 22	18 42	19 14	19 42	20 11	20 43	21 42	22 52	23 52
Weeton	d	18 00	18 10		18 30	18 50	19 22	19 50		20 51	21 50	23 00	23 59
Pannal	d	18 06	18 16		18 36	18 56	19 28	19 56		20 57	21 56	23 06	00 05
Hornbeam Park	d	18 11	18 21		18 41	19 01	19 33	20 01		21 02	22 01	23 11	00 10
Harrogate	a	18 14	18 24	18 32	18 46	19 04	19 36	20 04	20 32	21 05	22 04	23 17	00 16
	d	18 16	18 26		18 51	19 06	19 38	20 06		21 07	22 06		
Starbeck	d	18 20	18 30		18 55	19 10	19 42	20 10		21 11	22 10		
Knaresborough	a	18 27	18 35		19 02	19 15	19 49	20 15		21 16	22 15		
	d		18 39			19 15		20 15		21 16	22 15		
Cattal	d		18 47			19 23		20 23		21 24	22 23		
Hammerton	d		18 51			19 27		20 27		21 28	22 27		
Poppleton	d		18 59			19 35		20 35		21 36	22 35		
York 8	40 a		19 06			19 45		20 48		21 47	22 47		

Saturdays
21 December to 16 May

Station		NT A	NT	NT	NT	NT	NT	NT	NT	NT	NT	NT ◇	NT	NT	GR ■1 B ⊡	NT ◇	NT	NT	NT ◇	NT	NT	GR ■1 B ⊡	NT ◇
Leeds 10	40 d		06 05	06 23	06 33	07 00	07 15	07 45	08 09	08 29	08 48	08 59	09 15	09 29	09 53	09 59	10 15	10 29	10 59	11 15	11 35	11 53	11 59
Burley Park	d		06 10		06 38	07 05	07 20	07 50	08 14	08 34	08 52	09 04		09 34		10 04		10 34	11 04		11 40		12 04
Headingley	d		06 13		06 41	07 08	07 23	07 53	08 17	08 37	08 55	09 07		09 37		10 07		10 37	11 07		11 43		12 07
Horsforth	d		06 18	06 33	06 47	07 13	07 28	07 58	08 22	08 42	09a01	09 12	09 24	09 42		10 12	10 24	10 42	11 12	11 24	11 49		12 12
Weeton	d		06 26		06 55	07 21	07 36	08 06		08 50		09 20		09 50		10 20		10 50	11 20		11 57		12 20
Pannal	d	00 05	06 32		07 01	07 27	07 42	08 12	08 34	08 56		09 26		09 56		10 26		10 56	11 26		12 03		12 26
Hornbeam Park	d	00 10	06 37		07 06	07 32	07 47	08 17	08 39	09 01		09 31	09 40	10 01		10 31	10 40	11 01	11 31	11 40	12 08		12 31
Harrogate	a	00 16	06 40	06 51	07 09	07 38	07 50	08 20	08 42	09 04		09 34	09 45	10 04	10 19	10 35	10 45	11 04	11 34	11 45	12 11	12 19	12 34
	d		06 42		07 10	07 40	07 52	08 22	08 44	09 07		09 36		10 06		10 37		11 06	11 36		12 12		12 36
Starbeck	d		06 46		07 15	07 44	07 56	08 26	08 48	09 11		09 40		10 10		10 41		11 10	11 40		12 17		12 40
Knaresborough	a		06 51		07 19	07 51	08 01	08 31	08 55	09 16		09 47		10 15		10 48		11 15	11 47		12 21		12 47
	d		06 51		07 20		08 01	08 31		09 16				10 15				11 15			12 22		
Cattal	d		06 59		07 28		08 09	08 39		09 24				10 23				11 23			12 30		
Hammerton	d		07 05		07 32		08 13	08 43		09 28				10 27				11 27			12 34		
Poppleton	d		07 13		07 39		08 21	08 51		09 36				10 35				11 35			12 41		
York 8	40 a		07 20		07 46		08 29	08 59		09 46				10 45				11 46			12 52		

A From Leeds B From London Kings Cross

Table T035-R

Leeds - Harrogate - York

Saturdays
21 December to 16 May

Station		NT	NT	NT ◇	NT	NT	GR ■1 A ⊡	NT ◇	NT	NT	NT ◇	NT	NT	GR ■1 A ⊡	NT ◇	NT	NT	NT	NT	NT	NT	NT
Leeds 10	40 d	12 15	12 29	12 59	13 15	13 35	13 53	13 59	14 15	14 29	14 59	15 15	15 35	15 53	15 59	16 15	16 29	16 45	16 59	17 09	17 32	17 39
Burley Park	d		12 34	13 04		13 40		14 04		14 34	15 04		15 40		16 04		16 34	16 50	17 04	17 14	17 37	17 44
Headingley	d		12 37	13 07		13 43		14 07		14 37	15 07		15 43		16 07		16 37	16 52	17 07	17 17	17 40	17 47
Horsforth	d	12 24	12 42	13 12	13 24	13 49		14 12	14 24	14 42	15 12	15 24	15 49		16 12	16 24	16 42	16a59	17 12	17 22	17 45	17 52
Weeton	d		12 50	13 20		13 57		14 20		14 50	15 20		15 57		16 20		16 50		17 20	17 30	17 53	18 00
Pannal	d		12 56	13 26		14 03		14 26		14 56	15 26		16 03		16 26		16 56		17 26	17 36	17 59	18 06
Hornbeam Park	d	12 40	13 01	13 31	13 40	14 08		14 31	14 40	15 01	15 31	15 40	16 08		16 31	16 40	17 01		17 31	17 41	18 04	18 11
Harrogate	a	12 45	13 04	13 34	13 45	14 11	14 19	14 34	14 46	15 04	15 34	15 46	16 11	16 19	16 34	16 46	17 04		17 34	17 44	18 07	18 14
	d		13 06	13 36		14 12		14 36		15 06	15 36		16 12		16 36		17 06		17 36	17 49	18 09	18 16
Starbeck	d		13 10	13 40		14 17		14 40		15 10	15 40		16 17		16 40		17 10		17 40	17 53	18 13	18 20
Knaresborough	a		13 15	13 47		14 21		14 47		15 15	15 47		16 21		16 47		17 15		17 47	17 58	18 18	18 27
	d		13 15			14 22				15 15			16 22				17 15				18 18	
Cattal	d		13 23			14 30				15 23			16 30				17 23				18 26	
Hammerton	d		13 27			14 34				15 27			16 34				17 27				18 30	
Poppleton	d		13 35			14 41				15 35			16 41				17 35				18 38	
York 8	40 a		13 45			14 52				15 46			16 52				17 51				18 51	

Station		NT	GR ■1 A ⊡	NT	NT	NT	NT	NT	GR ■1 A ⊡	NT	NT	NT
Leeds 10	40 d	17 49	18 00	18 09	18 29	19 01	19 29	20 30	21 05	21 29	22 39	23 39
Burley Park	d	17 54		18 14	18 34	19 06	19 34	20 35		21 34	22 44	23 44
Headingley	d	17 57		18 17	18 37	19 09	19 37	20 38		21 37	22 47	23 46
Horsforth	d	18 02	18 10	18 22	18 42	19 14	19 42	20 43	21 14	21 42	22 52	23 52
Weeton	d	18 10		18 30	18 50	19 22	19 50	20 51		21 50	23 00	23 59
Pannal	d	18 16		18 36	18 56	19 28	19 56	20 57		21 56	23 06	00 05
Hornbeam Park	d	18 21		18 41	19 01	19 33	20 01	21 02		22 01	23 11	00 10
Harrogate	a	18 24	18 32	18 46	19 04	19 36	20 04	21 05	21 35	22 04	23 17	00 16
	d	18 26		18 51	19 06	19 38	20 06	21 07		22 06		
Starbeck	d	18 30		18 55	19 10	19 42	20 10	21 11		22 10		
Knaresborough	a	18 35		19 02	19 15	19 49	20 15	21 16		22 15		
	d	18 39			19 15		20 15	21 16		22 15		
Cattal	d	18 47			19 23		20 23	21 24		22 23		
Hammerton	d	18 51			19 27		20 27	21 28		22 27		
Poppleton	d	18 59			19 35		20 35	21 36		22 35		
York 8	40 a	19 06			19 45		20 48	21 47		22 47		

Sundays
15 December to 10 May

Station		NT B	NT	NT	NT	NT	GR ■1 A ⊡	NT	NT	NT	NT	GR ■1 A ⊡	NT	NT	NT	NT	GR ■1 A ⊡	NT	NT	NT	NT	GR ■1 A ⊡	NT
Leeds 10	40 d		09 02	10 05	10 35	11 05	11 30	11 36	12 05	12 36	13 05	13 32	13 36	14 05	14 36	15 05	15 29	15 36	16 05	16 36	17 05	17 33	17 36
Burley Park	d		09 10	10 10	10 41	11 10		11 41	12 10	12 41	13 10		13 41	14 10	14 41	15 10		15 41	16 10	16 41	17 10		17 41
Headingley	d		09 13	10 13	10 44	11 13		11 44	12 13	12 44	13 13		13 44	14 13	14 44	15 13		15 44	16 13	16 44	17 13		17 44
Horsforth	d		09 18	10 18	10 49	11 18		11 49	12 18	12 49	13 18		13 49	14 18	14 49	15 18		15 49	16 18	16 50	17 18		17 49
Weeton	d		09 26	10 26	10 57	11 26		11 57	12 26	12 57	13 26		13 57	14 26	14 57	15 26		15 57	16 26	16 58	17 26		17 57
Pannal	d	00 05	09 32	10 32	11 03	11 32		12 03	12 32	13 03	13 32		14 03	14 32	15 03	15 32		16 03	16 32	17 04	17 32		18 03
Hornbeam Park	d	00 10	09 38	10 38	11 09	11 38		12 09	12 38	13 09	13 38		14 09	14 38	15 09	15 38		16 09	16 38	17 09	17 38		18 09
Harrogate	a	00 16	09 41	10 41	11 12	11 41	11 56	12 12	12 41	13 12	13 41	13 58	14 12	14 41	15 12	15 41	15 55	16 12	16 41	17 12	17 41	17 59	18 12
	d		09 42	10 42	11 13	11 42		12 13	12 42	13 13	13 42		14 13	14 42	15 13	15 42		16 13	16 42	17 14	17 42		18 13
Starbeck	d		09 47	10 47	11 18	11 47		12 18	12 47	13 18	13 47		14 18	14 47	15 18	15 47		16 18	16 47	17 18	17 47		18 18
Knaresborough	a		09 51	10 51	11 24	11 51		12 24	12 51	13 24	13 51		14 24	14 51	15 24	15 51		16 24	16 51	17 25	17 51		18 24
	d		09 52	10 52		11 52			12 52		13 52			14 52		15 52			16 52		17 52		
Cattal	d		10 00	11 00		12 00			13 00		14 00			15 00		16 00			17 00		18 00		
Hammerton	d		10 04	11 04		12 04			13 04		14 04			15 04		16 04			17 04		18 04		
Poppleton	d		10 11	11 12		12 11			13 11		14 11			15 11		16 11			17 11		18 11		
York 8	40 a		10 21	11 20		12 20			13 20		14 22			15 20		16 20			17 20		18 21		

Station		NT	NT	NT	GR ■1 A ⊡	NT	NT	GR ■1 A ⊡	NT	NT	NT	NT
Leeds 10	40 d	18 05	18 36	19 05	19 26	19 36	20 05	20 31	21 05	21 36	22 27	23 15
Burley Park	d	18 10	18 41	19 10		19 41	20 10		21 10	21 41	22 32	23 20
Headingley	d	18 13	18 44	19 13		19 44	20 13		21 13	21 44	22 35	23 23
Horsforth	d	18 18	18 49	19 18	19 36	19 49	20 18	20 41	21 18	21 49	22 40	23 28
Weeton	d	18 26	18 57	19 26		19 57	20 26		21 26	21 57	22 48	23 36
Pannal	d	18 32	19 03	19 32		20 03	20 32		21 32	22 03	22 54	23 42
Hornbeam Park	d	18 38	19 09	19 38		20 09	20 38		21 38	22 09	23 00	23 48
Harrogate	a	18 41	19 12	19 41	19 58	20 12	20 41	21 02	21 41	22 12	23 06	23 54
	d	18 42	19 13	19 42		20 13	20 42		21 42	22 13		
Starbeck	d	18 47	19 18	19 47		20 18	20 47		21 47	22 18		
Knaresborough	a	18 51	19 24	19 51		20 24	20 51		21 51	22 24		
	d	18 52		19 52			20 52		21 52			
Cattal	d	19 00		20 00			21 00		22 00			
Hammerton	d	19 04		20 04			21 04		22 04			
Poppleton	d	19 15		20 11			21 11		22 11			
York 8	40 a	19 29		20 21			21 20		22 20			

A From London Kings Cross B not 15 December. From Leeds

Table T036-F

Mondays to Fridays

16 December to 15 May

Leeds and Bradford - Skipton

Miles	Miles				NT ◇ A 🛒	NT	NT	NT	NT	NT	NT ◇ B	NT	NT	NT ◇ A 🛒	NT	NT	NT ◇ C	NT	NT	NT	NT	NT ◇ A 🛒	NT	NT
0	—	**Leeds** 10	37	d	05 17		06 26		06 56		07 20	07 23		07 48	07 52		08 18	08 25		08 54		09 19	09 26	
4¼	—	Kirkstall Forge		d																09 00				
7¾	—	Apperley Bridge		d																				
—	0	**Bradford Forster Square**	37	d		06 03		06 41		07 11			07 41			08 11			08 41		09 07			09 41
—	1¾	Frizinghall	37	d		06 06		06 44		07 14			07 44			08 14			08 44		09 10			09 44
10¾	2¾	Shipley	37	a	05 29	06 10	06 42	06 48	07 08	07 18	07 32	07 37	07 48	08 00	08 04	08 18	08 31	08 37	08 49	09 07	09 14	09 32	09 37	09 48
—	—			d	05 30	06 11	06 42	06 49	07 09	07 19	07 33	07 38	07 49	08 01	08 06	08 19	08 32	08 38	08 49	09 08	09 15	09 32	09 38	09 49
11½	—	Saltaire		d	05 32	06 13	06 45	06 52	07 11	07 22		07 40	07 52		08 08	08 22		08 40	08 52	09 10	09 18		09 40	09 52
13¾	—	Bingley		d	05 37	06 17	06 49	06 56	07 14	07 26	07 38	07 44	07 56	08 06	08 12	08 26	08 37	08 44	08 56	09 14	09 22	09 37	09 44	09 56
14½	—	Crossflatts		d	05 39	06 19	06 51	06 58	07 16	07 28		07 47	07 58		08 15	08 28		08 47	08 59	09 17	09 24		09 47	09 58
17	—	Keighley		d	05 44	06 24	06 56	07 03	07 21	07 33	07 43	07 51	08 03	08 11	08 19	08 33	08 42	08 51	09 03	09 21	09 29	09 42	09 51	10 03
20	—	Steeton & Silsden		d	05 48	06 28	07 00	07 07	07 25	07 37		07 56	08 07		08 24	08 37		08 56	09 08	09 26	09 33		09 56	10 07
23¼	—	Cononley		d	05 53	06 32	07 05	07 12	07 29	07 42		08 00	08 12		08 28	08 42		09 00	09 12	09 30	09 38		10 00	10 12
26¼	—	**Skipton**		a	06 00	06 41	07 13	07 20	07 38	07 50	07 58	08 08	08 20	08 24	08 36	08 50	08 55	09 09	09 21	09 39	09 46	09 57	10 09	10 20

			NT	NT	NT ◇ C	NT	NT	NT ◇ A 🛒	NT	NT	NT	NT	NT	NT	NT ◇ C	NT	NT	NT	NT	NT ◇ A 🛒	NT	NT	NT	NT
Leeds 10	37	d	09 56		10 18	10 26		10 49	10 56		11 26		11 56		12 18	12 26		12 56		13 18	13 26		13 56	
Kirkstall Forge		d																						
Apperley Bridge		d																						
Bradford Forster Square	37	d		10 11			10 41			11 11		11 41		12 11			12 41		13 11			13 41		14 11
Frizinghall	37	d		10 14			10 44			11 14		11 44		12 14			12 44		13 14			13 44		14 14
Shipley	37	a	10 08	10 18	10 32	10 37	10 48	11 02	11 08	11 18	11 38	11 48	12 08	12 18	12 32	12 37	12 48	13 07	13 18	13 32	13 37	13 48	14 08	14 18
		d	10 08	10 19	10 33	10 38	10 49	11 03	11 09	11 19	11 38	11 49	12 08	12 19	12 33	12 38	12 49	13 08	13 19	13 33	13 38	13 49	14 08	14 19
Saltaire		d	10 11	10 22		10 40	10 52		11 12	11 22	11 41	11 52	12 11	12 22		12 40	12 52	13 10	13 22		13 40	13 52	14 11	14 22
Bingley		d	10 15	10 26	10 37	10 44	10 56	11 07	11 16	11 26	11 45	11 56	12 15	12 26	12 37	12 44	12 56	13 14	13 26	13 37	13 44	13 56	14 15	14 26
Crossflatts		d	10 17	10 28		10 47	10 58		11 19	11 28	11 47	11 58	12 17	12 28		12 47	12 58	13 17	13 28		13 47	13 58	14 17	14 28
Keighley		d	10 22	10 33	10 43	10 51	11 03	11 13	11 24	11 33	11 52	12 03	12 22	12 33	12 43	12 51	13 03	13 21	13 33	13 43	13 51	14 03	14 22	14 33
Steeton & Silsden		d	10 26	10 37		10 56	11 07		11 29	11 37	11 56	12 07	12 26	12 37		12 56	13 07	13 26	13 37		13 56	14 07	14 26	14 37
Cononley		d	10 31	10 42		11 00	11 12		11 34	11 42	12 01	12 12	12 31	12 42		13 00	13 12	13 30	13 42		14 00	14 12	14 31	14 42
Skipton		a	10 39	10 50	10 55	11 09	11 20	11 25	11 42	11 50	12 09	12 21	12 39	12 51	12 56	13 09	13 20	13 39	13 50	13 55	14 09	14 21	14 39	14 51

			NT ◇ C	NT	NT	NT	NT	NT ◇ A 🛒	NT	NT	NT	NT	NT	NT	NT ◇ A 🛒	NT	NT	NT	NT ◇ C	NT	NT	NT	NT
Leeds 10	37	d	14 18	14 26		14 56		15 18	15 26		15 56		16 26		16 48	16 56		17 18	17 26		17 41	17 54	
Kirkstall Forge		d																17 26			17 48		
Apperley Bridge		d																					
Bradford Forster Square	37	d			14 41		15 11			15 41		16 11		16 41			17 11			17 41			18 11
Frizinghall	37	d			14 44		15 14			15 44		16 14		16 44			17 14			17 44			18 14
Shipley	37	a	14 32	14 37	14 48	15 08	15 18	15 32	15 37	15 48	16 08	16 18	16 37	16 48	17 01	17 07	17 18	17 33	17 38	17 48	17 55	18 07	18 18
		d	14 33	14 38	14 49	15 08	15 19	15 33	15 38	15 49	16 08	16 19	16 38	16 49	17 02	17 08	17 19	17 33	17 40	17 49	17 55	18 08	18 19
Saltaire		d		14 40	14 52	15 11	15 22		15 40	15 52	16 11	16 22	16 40	16 52		17 10	17 22	17 36		17 52	17 58	18 10	18 22
Bingley		d	14 38	14 44	14 56	15 15	15 26	15 37	15 44	15 56	16 15	16 26	16 44	16 56	17 07	17 14	17 26	17 40	17 45	17 56	18 02	18 14	18 26
Crossflatts		d		14 47	14 58	15 17	15 28		15 47	15 58	16 17	16 28	16 47	16 58		17 17	17 28	17 42		17 58	18 04	18 17	18 28
Keighley		d	14 43	14 51	15 03	15 22	15 33	15 43	15 51	16 03	16 22	16 33	16 51	17 03	17 13	17 21	17 33	17 47	17 52	18 03	18 09	18 21	18 33
Steeton & Silsden		d		14 56	15 07	15 26	15 37		15 56	16 07	16 26	16 37	16 56	17 07		17 26	17 37	17 51	17 56	18 07	18 13	18 26	18 37
Cononley		d		15 00	15 12	15 31	15 42		16 00	16 12	16 31	16 42	17 00	17 12		17 30	17 42	17 56		18 12	18 18	18 30	18 42
Skipton		a	14 57	15 09	15 20	15 39	15 50	15 55	16 09	16 20	16 39	16 50	17 09	17 20	17 25	17 39	17 50	18 04	18 08	18 20	18 26	18 39	18 50

			NT ◇ A 🛒	NT	NT	NT	NT	NT ◇ B	NT	NT	NT D 🛒	NT	NT	NT	GR ■ 1 E 🍴	NT	NT	NT	NT	NT	NT	NT	NT	NT
Leeds 10	37	d	18 18	18 26		18 55		19 18	19 26		19 49	19 56		20 25	20 39		20 56		21 26	21 56		22 26	22 56	
Kirkstall Forge		d							19 33			20 03		20 33			21 03		21 33	22 02		22 33		
Apperley Bridge		d							19 37			20 07		20 37			21 07		21 37			22 37		
Bradford Forster Square	37	d			18 41		19 11			19 41			20 11			20 48		21 11			22 11			23 11
Frizinghall	37	d			18 44		19 14			19 44			20 14			20 51		21 14			22 14			23 14
Shipley	37	a	18 32	18 37	18 48	19 08	19 18	19 31	19 42	19 48	20 02	20 12	20 18	20 42		20 55	21 11	21 18	21 42	22 09	22 18	22 42	23 07	23 18
		d	18 32	18 38	18 49	19 09	19 19	19 32	19 42	19 49	20 02	20 12	20 19	20 42		20 56	21 12	21 19	21 42	22 10	22 19	22 42	23 08	23 19
Saltaire		d		18 40	18 52	19 12	19 22		19 45	19 52		20 15	20 22	20 45		20 59	21 14	21 22	21 45	22 12	22 22	22 45	23 10	23 22
Bingley		d	18 37	18 44	18 56	19 16	19 26	19 37	19 49	19 56	20 07	20 19	20 26	20 49		21 03	21 18	21 26	21 49	22 16	22 26	22 49	23 14	23 26
Crossflatts		d		18 47	18 58	19 18	19 28		19 51	19 58		20 21	20 28	20 51		21 05	21 21	21 28	21 51	22 19	22 28	22 51	23 17	23 28
Keighley		d	18 42	18 51	19 03	19 23	19 33	19 43	19 56	20 03	20 12	20 26	20 33	20 56	21s01	21 10	21 25	21 33	21 56	22 23	22 33	22 56	23 21	23 33
Steeton & Silsden		d		18 56	19 07	19 27	19 37		20 00	20 07		20 30	20 37	21 00		21 14	21 30	21 37	22 00	22 28	22 37	23 00	23 26	23 37
Cononley		d		19 00	19 12	19 32	19 42		20 05	20 12		20 35	20 42	21 05		21 19	21 34	21 42	22 05	22 32	22 42	23 05	23 30	23 42
Skipton		a	18 55	19 09	19 22	19 40	19 50	19 57	20 13	20 20	20 26	20 43	20 50	21 13	21 19	21 27	21 43	21 50	22 13	22 41	22 50	23 13	23 38	23 50

			NT
Leeds 10	37	d	23 20
Kirkstall Forge		d	23 27
Apperley Bridge		d	23 31
Bradford Forster Square	37	d	
Frizinghall	37	d	
Shipley	37	a	23 36
		d	23 36
Saltaire		d	23 38
Bingley		d	23 42
Crossflatts		d	23 44
Keighley		d	23 49
Steeton & Silsden		d	23 53
Cononley		d	23 57
Skipton		a	00 05

A To Carlisle
B To Lancaster
C To Morecambe
D To Ribblehead
E From London Kings Cross

Table T036-F

Saturdays

21 December to 16 May

Leeds and Bradford - Skipton

			NT	NT ◇ A 🛒	NT	NT	NT	NT	NT ◇ B	NT	NT	NT ◇ A 🛒	NT	NT	NT ◇ C	NT	NT	NT	NT	NT ◇ A 🛒	NT	NT	NT	NT
Leeds 10	37	d		06 20	06 26		06 56		07 20	07 23		07 48	07 52		08 18	08 25		08 54		09 19	09 26		09 56	
Kirkstall Forge		d																09 00						
Apperley Bridge		d																						
Bradford Forster Square	37	d	06 03			06 41		07 11			07 41			08 11			08 41		09 07			09 41		10 11
Frizinghall	37	d	06 06			06 44		07 14			07 44			08 14			08 44		09 10			09 44		10 14
Shipley	37	a	06 10	06 32	06 42	06 48	07 08	07 18	07 32	07 37	07 48	08 00	08 04	08 18	08 31	08 37	08 49	09 07	09 14	09 31	09 37	09 48	10 08	10 18
		d	06 11	06 33	06 42	06 49	07 09	07 19	07 33	07 38	07 49	08 01	08 06	08 19	08 32	08 38	08 49	09 08	09 15	09 32	09 38	09 49	10 08	10 19
Saltaire		d	06 13	06 35	06 45	06 52	07 11	07 22		07 40	07 52		08 08	08 22		08 40	08 52	09 10	09 18		09 40	09 52	10 11	10 22
Bingley		d	06 17	06 40	06 49	06 56	07 14	07 26	07 38	07 44	07 56	08 06	08 12	08 26	08 37	08 44	08 56	09 14	09 22	09 37	09 44	09 56	10 15	10 26
Crossflatts		d	06 19	06 42	06 51	06 58	07 16	07 28		07 47	07 58		08 15	08 28		08 47	08 59	09 17	09 24		09 47	09 58	10 17	10 28
Keighley		d	06 24	06 47	06 56	07 03	07 21	07 33	07 43	07 51	08 03	08 11	08 19	08 33	08 42	08 51	09 03	09 21	09 29	09 42	09 51	10 03	10 22	10 33
Steeton & Silsden		d	06 28	06 51	07 00	07 07	07 25	07 37		07 56	08 07		08 24	08 37		08 56	09 08	09 26	09 33		09 56	10 07	10 26	10 37
Cononley		d	06 32	06 56	07 05	07 12	07 29	07 42		08 00	08 12		08 28	08 42		09 00	09 12	09 30	09 38		10 00	10 12	10 31	10 42
Skipton		a	06 41	07 03	07 13	07 20	07 38	07 50	07 58	08 08	08 20	08 24	08 36	08 50	08 55	09 09	09 21	09 39	09 46	09 57	10 09	10 20	10 39	10 50

			NT ◇ C	NT	NT	NT ◇ A 🛒	NT	NT	NT	NT	NT	NT	NT ◇ C	NT	NT	NT	NT	NT ◇ A 🛒	NT	NT	NT	NT	NT ◇ C
Leeds 10	37	d	10 18	10 26		10 49	10 56		11 26		11 56		12 18	12 26		12 56		13 18	13 26		13 56		14 18
Kirkstall Forge		d																					
Apperley Bridge		d																					
Bradford Forster Square	37	d			10 41			11 11		11 41		12 11			12 41		13 11			13 41		14 11	
Frizinghall	37	d			10 44			11 14		11 44		12 14			12 44		13 14			13 44		14 14	
Shipley	37	a	10 32	10 37	10 48	11 01	11 08	11 18	11 38	11 48	12 08	12 18	12 32	12 37	12 48	13 07	13 18	13 32	13 37	13 48	14 08	14 18	14 32
		d	10 33	10 38	10 49	11 03	11 09	11 19	11 38	11 49	12 08	12 19	12 33	12 38	12 49	13 08	13 19	13 33	13 38	13 49	14 08	14 19	14 33
Saltaire		d		10 40	10 52		11 12	11 22	11 41	11 52	12 11	12 22		12 40	12 52	13 10	13 22		13 40	13 52	14 11	14 22	
Bingley		d	10 37	10 44	10 56	11 07	11 16	11 26	11 45	11 56	12 15	12 26	12 37	12 44	12 56	13 14	13 26	13 37	13 44	13 56	14 15	14 26	14 38
Crossflatts		d		10 47	10 58		11 19	11 28	11 47	11 58	12 17	12 28		12 47	12 58	13 17	13 28		13 47	13 58	14 17	14 28	
Keighley		d	10 43	10 51	11 03	11 13	11 24	11 33	11 52	12 03	12 22	12 33	12 43	12 51	13 03	13 21	13 33	13 43	13 51	14 03	14 22	14 33	14 43
Steeton & Silsden		d		10 56	11 07		11 29	11 37	11 56	12 07	12 26	12 37		12 56	13 07	13 26	13 37		13 56	14 07	14 26	14 37	
Cononley		d		11 00	11 12		11 34	11 42	12 01	12 12	12 31	12 42		13 00	13 12	13 30	13 42		14 00	14 12	14 31	14 42	
Skipton		a	10 55	11 09	11 20	11 25	11 42	11 50	12 09	12 21	12 39	12 51	12 56	13 09	13 20	13 39	13 50	13 55	14 09	14 21	14 39	14 51	14 57

			NT	NT	NT	NT	NT ◇ A 🛒	NT	NT	NT	NT	NT	NT	NT ◇ A 🛒	NT	NT	NT	NT ◇ C	NT	NT	NT	NT	NT ◇ A 🛒	NT
Leeds 10	37	d	14 26		14 56		15 18	15 26		15 56		16 26		16 48	16 56		17 18	17 26		17 41	17 54		18 18	18 26
Kirkstall Forge		d															17 26			17 48				
Apperley Bridge		d																						
Bradford Forster Square	37	d		14 41		15 11			15 41		16 11		16 41			17 11			17 41			18 11		
Frizinghall	37	d		14 44		15 14			15 44		16 14		16 44			17 14			17 44			18 14		
Shipley	37	a	14 37	14 48	15 08	15 18	15 32	15 37	15 48	16 08	16 18	16 37	16 48	17 01	17 07	17 18	17 33	17 38	17 48	17 55	18 07	18 18	18 32	18 37
		d	14 38	14 49	15 08	15 19	15 33	15 38	15 49	16 08	16 19	16 38	16 49	17 02	17 08	17 19	17 33	17 40	17 49	17 55	18 08	18 19	18 32	18 38
Saltaire		d	14 40	14 52	15 11	15 22		15 40	15 52	16 11	16 22	16 40	16 52		17 10	17 22	17 36		17 52	17 58	18 10	18 22		18 40
Bingley		d	14 44	14 56	15 15	15 26	15 37	15 44	15 56	16 15	16 26	16 44	16 56	17 07	17 14	17 26	17 40	17 45	17 56	18 02	18 14	18 26	18 37	18 44
Crossflatts		d	14 47	14 58	15 17	15 28		15 47	15 58	16 17	16 28	16 47	16 58		17 17	17 28	17 42		17 58	18 04	18 17	18 28		18 47
Keighley		d	14 51	15 03	15 22	15 33	15 43	15 51	16 03	16 22	16 33	16 51	17 03	17 13	17 21	17 33	17 47	17 52	18 03	18 09	18 21	18 33	18 42	18 51
Steeton & Silsden		d	14 56	15 07	15 26	15 37		15 56	16 07	16 26	16 37	16 56	17 07		17 26	17 37	17 51	17 56	18 07	18 13	18 26	18 37		18 56
Cononley		d	15 00	15 12	15 31	15 42		16 00	16 12	16 31	16 42	17 00	17 12		17 30	17 42	17 56		18 12	18 18	18 30	18 42		19 00
Skipton		a	15 09	15 20	15 39	15 50	15 55	16 09	16 20	16 39	16 50	17 09	17 20	17 25	17 39	17 50	18 04	18 07	18 20	18 26	18 39	18 50	18 55	19 09

			NT	NT	NT	NT ◇ B	NT	NT	NT D 🛒	NT	NT	NT	GR ■ 1 E 🍴	NT	NT	NT	NT	NT	NT	NT	NT	NT	NT
Leeds 10	37	d		18 55		19 18	19 26		19 49	19 56		20 25	20 39		20 56		21 26	21 52		22 26	22 56		23 20
Kirkstall Forge		d					19 33			20 03		20 33			21 03		21 33	21 58		22 33			23 27
Apperley Bridge		d					19 37			20 07		20 37			21 07		21 37			22 37			23 31
Bradford Forster Square	37	d	18 41		19 11			19 41			20 11			20 48		21 11			22 11			23 11	
Frizinghall	37	d	18 44		19 14			19 44			20 14			20 51		21 14			22 14			23 14	
Shipley	37	a	18 48	19 08	19 18	19 31	19 42	19 48	20 02	20 12	20 18	20 42		20 55	21 11	21 18	21 42	22 05	22 18	22 42	23 07	23 18	23 36
		d	18 49	19 09	19 19	19 32	19 42	19 49	20 02	20 12	20 19	20 42		20 56	21 12	21 19	21 42	22 06	22 19	22 42	23 08	23 19	23 36
Saltaire		d	18 52	19 12	19 22		19 45	19 52		20 15	20 22	20 45		20 59	21 14	21 22	21 45	22 08	22 22	22 45	23 10	23 22	23 38
Bingley		d	18 56	19 16	19 26	19 37	19 49	19 56	20 07	20 19	20 26	20 49		21 03	21 18	21 26	21 49	22 12	22 26	22 49	23 14	23 26	23 42
Crossflatts		d	18 58	19 18	19 28		19 51	19 58		20 21	20 28	20 51		21 05	21 21	21 28	21 51	22 15	22 28	22 51	23 17	23 28	23 44
Keighley		d	19 03	19 23	19 33	19 43	19 56	20 03	20 12	20 26	20 33	20 56	21s00	21 10	21 25	21 33	21 56	22 19	22 33	22 56	23 21	23 33	23 49
Steeton & Silsden		d	19 07	19 27	19 37		20 00	20 07		20 30	20 37	21 00		21 14	21 30	21 37	22 00	22 24	22 37	23 00	23 26	23 37	23 53
Cononley		d	19 12	19 32	19 42		20 05	20 12		20 35	20 42	21 05		21 19	21 34	21 42	22 05	22 28	22 42	23 05	23 30	23 42	23 57
Skipton		a	19 22	19 40	19 50	19 57	20 13	20 20	20 26	20 43	20 50	21 13	21 18	21 27	21 43	21 50	22 13	22 37	22 50	23 13	23 38	23 50	00 05

A To Carlisle
B To Lancaster
C To Morecambe
D To Ribblehead
E From London Kings Cross

Table T036-F

Leeds and Bradford - Skipton

Sundays

15 December to 10 May

		NT	NT	NT	NT	NT	NT	NT	NT	NT	NT	NT	NT	NT	NT	NT	NT	NT	NT	NT	NT	NT	NT
		◇ A	◇ B			◇ C		◇ D				◇ B			◇ A			◇ B			◇ A	
Leeds	37 d	08 32	08 59		10 16	10 32		11 16	11 26		11 57	12 16	12 28		13 16	13 32		14 16	14 24		15 16	15 32	
Kirkstall Forge	d																						
Apperley Bridge	d																						
Bradford Forster Square	37 d			09 48			10 48			11 48				12 48			13 48			14 48			15 48
Frizinghall	37 d			09 51			10 51			11 51				12 51			13 51			14 51			15 51
Shipley	37 a	08 44	09 12	09 55	10 27	10 45	10 55	11 27	11 37	11 55	12 08	12 27	12 40	12 55	13 27	13 44	13 55	14 27	14 36	14 55	15 27	15 44	15 55
	d	08 45	09 13	09 56	10 28	10 45	10 56	11 29	11 38	11 56	12 10	12 28	12 41	12 56	13 28	13 45	13 56	14 28	14 37	14 56	15 28	15 45	15 56
Saltaire	d	08 47	09 15	09 59	10 30		10 59		11 40	11 59		12 30		12 59	13 30		13 59	14 30		14 59	15 30		15 59
Bingley	d	08 52	09 20	10 03	10 34	10 50	11 03	11 34	11 44	12 03	12 14	12 34	12 45	13 03	13 34	13 49	14 03	14 34	14 42	15 03	15 34	15 49	16 03
Crossflatts	d	08 54	09 22	10 05	10 36		11 05		11 46	12 05		12 36		13 05	13 36		14 05	14 36		15 05	15 36		16 05
Keighley	d	08 59	09 27	10 09	10 41	10 55	11 09	11 39	11 51	12 09	12 19	12 41	12 51	13 09	13 41	13 55	14 09	14 41	14 47	15 09	15 41	15 55	16 09
Steeton & Silsden	d	09 03	09 31	10 13	10 45		11 13		11 55	12 13		12 45		13 13	13 45		14 13	14 45		15 13	15 45		16 13
Cononley	d	09 08	09 36	10 18	10 49		11 18		11 59	12 18		12 49		13 18	13 49		14 18	14 49		15 18	15 49		16 18
Skipton	a	09 15	09 43	10 26	10 56	11 08	11 26	11 52	12 06	12 26	12 32	12 58	13 03	13 26	13 56	14 07	14 26	14 57	15 02	15 26	15 58	16 08	16 26

		NT	NT	NT	NT	NT	NT	NT	NT	NT	NT	NT	NT	NT	GR	NT	NT	NT	NT	NT
			◇ B			◇ A				◇ B					■ 1 E					
Leeds	37 d	16 12	16 23		17 16	17 32		18 16		18 52	19 16		20 16		21 00	21 16		22 20		23 23
Kirkstall Forge	d																			
Apperley Bridge	d																			
Bradford Forster Square	37 d			16 48			17 48		18 48			19 48		20 48			21 48		22 48	
Frizinghall	37 d			16 51			17 51		18 51			19 51		20 51			21 51		22 51	
Shipley	37 a	16 23	16 35	16 55	17 27	17 44	17 55	18 28	18 55	19 04	19 27	19 55	20 27	20 55		21 27	21 55	22 31	22 55	23 34
	d	16 24	16 37	16 56	17 28	17 45	17 56	18 28	18 56	19 05	19 28	19 56	20 28	20 56		21 28	21 56	22 32	22 56	23 35
Saltaire	d	16 26		16 59	17 30		17 59	18 31	18 59		19 30	19 59	20 30	20 59		21 30	21 59	22 34	22 59	23 37
Bingley	d	16 30	16 41	17 03	17 34	17 49	18 03	18 35	19 03	19 09	19 34	20 03	20 34	21 03		21 34	22 03	22 38	23 03	23 41
Crossflatts	d	16 32		17 05	17 36		18 05	18 37	19 05		19 36	20 05	20 36	21 05		21 36	22 05	22 40	23 05	23 43
Keighley	d	16 37	16 47	17 09	17 40	17 55	18 09	18 41	19 09	19 16	19 41	20 09	20 41	21 09	21s19	21 41	22 09	22 45	23 09	23 48
Steeton & Silsden	d	16 41		17 13	17 44		18 13	18 45	19 13		19 45	20 13	20 45	21 13		21 45	22 13	22 49	23 13	23 52
Cononley	d	16 45		17 18	17 49		18 18	18 50	19 18		19 49	20 18	20 49	21 18		21 49	22 18	22 53	23 18	23 56
Skipton	a	16 54	17 01	17 26	17 58	18 08	18 26	18 58	19 26	19 33	19 58	20 26	20 58	21 26	21 36	21 58	22 26	23 02	23 26	00 04

A To Morecambe
B To Carlisle
C To Heysham Harbour
D From Nottingham to Carlisle
E From London Kings Cross

Table T036-R

Skipton - Bradford and Leeds

Mondays to Fridays

16 December to 15 May

Miles	Miles			NT	NT	NT	NT	NT	GR	NT	NT	NT	NT	NT	NT	NT	NT	NT	NT	NT	NT	NT	NT
									■ 1 A							◇ B	◇ C						
0	—	**Skipton**	d	05 45	06 04	06 18	06 34	06 40	06 55	07 01	07 09	07 17	07 30	07 36	07 44	07 55	08 05	08 09	08 15	08 34	08 45	09 04	09 17
3	—	Cononley	d	05 50	06 09	06 23	06 39	06 45		07 06	07 14	07 22	07 35	07 41	07 49			08 14	08 20	08 39	08 52	09 09	09 22
6¼	—	Steeton & Silsden	d	05 55	06 14	06 28	06 44	06 50		07 11	07 19	07 27	07 40	07 46	07 54		08 12	08 19	08 25	08 44	08 57	09 14	09 27
9¼	—	Keighley	d	05 59	06 18	06 32	06 48	06 54	07u07	07 15	07 23	07 31	07 44	07 50	07 58	08 05	08 17	08 24	08 30	08 48	09 01	09 18	09 31
11¾	—	Crossflatts	d	06 03	06 22	06 36	06 52	06 58		07 19	07 27	07 35	07 48	07 54	08 02			08 28	08 34	08 52	09 05	09 22	09 35
12½	—	Bingley	d	06 06	06 25	06 39	06 55	07 01		07 22	07 30	07 38	07 51	07 57	08 05	08 10	08 22	08 31	08 37	08 55	09 08	09 25	09 38
14¾	—	Saltaire	d	06 10	06 29	06 43	06 59	07 05		07 26	07 34	07 42	07 55	08 01	08 09			08 35	08 41	08 59	09 12	09 29	09 42
15½	0	Shipley	a	06 12	06 31	06 46	07 02	07 07		07 28	07 37	07 44	07 57	08 04	08 11	08 15	08 26	08 37	08 44	09 01	09 14	09 31	09 44
—	—		d	06 13	06 32	06 46	07 03	07 08	07u18	07 29	07 37	07 45	07 58	08 04	08 12	08 15	08 27	08 38	08 44	09 02	09 15	09 32	09 45
—	1	Frizinghall	37 d		06 35		07 08				07 41			08 08					08 48	09 05		09 35	
—	2¾	**Bradford Forster Square**	37 a		06 41		07 14				07 47			08 14					08 54	09 11		09 41	
18½	—	Apperley Bridge	d									07 49											
22	—	Kirkstall Forge	d																				
26¼	—	**Leeds**	37 a	06 27		07 02		07 22	07 33	07 44		08 00	08 13		08 28	08 33	08 41	08 55			09 29		10 01

		NT	NT	NT	NT	NT	NT	NT	NT	NT	NT	NT	NT	NT	NT	NT	NT	NT	NT	NT	NT	NT	NT
						◇ B			◇ C					◇ D					◇ B				
Skipton	d	09 34	09 47	10 04	10 17	10 25	10 34	10 47	10 59	11 04	11 17	11 34	11 47	11 59	12 04	12 17	12 34	12 47	12 56	13 04	13 17	13 34	13 47
Cononley	d	09 39	09 52	10 09	10 22		10 39	10 52		11 09	11 22	11 39	11 52		12 09	12 22	12 39	12 52		13 10	13 22	13 39	13 52
Steeton & Silsden	d	09 44	09 57	10 14	10 27		10 44	10 57		11 14	11 27	11 44	11 57		12 14	12 27	12 44	12 57		13 14	13 27	13 44	13 57
Keighley	d	09 48	10 01	10 18	10 31	10 38	10 48	11 01	11 09	11 18	11 31	11 48	12 01	12 09	12 18	12 31	12 48	13 01	13 09	13 19	13 31	13 48	14 01
Crossflatts	d	09 52	10 05	10 22	10 35		10 52	11 05		11 22	11 35	11 52	12 05		12 22	12 35	12 52	13 05		13 23	13 35	13 52	14 05
Bingley	d	09 55	10 08	10 25	10 38	10 45	10 55	11 08	11 14	11 25	11 38	11 55	12 08	12 14	12 25	12 38	12 55	13 08	13 14	13 25	13 38	13 55	14 08
Saltaire	d	09 59	10 12	10 29	10 42		10 59	11 12		11 29	11 42	11 59	12 12		12 29	12 42	12 59	13 12		13 30	13 42	13 59	14 12
Shipley	a	10 01	10 14	10 31	10 44	10 49	11 01	11 14	11 19	11 31	11 44	12 01	12 14	12 18	12 32	12 44	13 01	13 14	13 20	13 32	13 44	14 01	14 14
	d	10 02	10 15	10 32	10 45	10 50	11 02	11 15	11 19	11 32	11 45	12 02	12 15	12 19	12 32	12 45	13 02	13 15	13 20	13 33	13 45	14 02	14 15
Frizinghall	37 d	10 05		10 35			11 05			11 35		12 05			12 36		13 05			13 36		14 05	
Bradford Forster Square	37 a	10 11		10 41			11 11			11 41		12 11			12 42		13 11			13 42		14 11	
Apperley Bridge	d																						
Kirkstall Forge	d																						
Leeds	37 a		10 29		10 59	11 08		11 32	11 38		12 00		12 30	12 38		12 59		13 31	13 38		14 00		14 30

		NT	NT	NT	NT	NT	NT	NT	NT	NT	NT	NT	NT	NT	NT	NT	NT	NT	NT	NT	NT	NT
		◇ D							◇ B			◇ D					◇ B					
Skipton	d	13 59	14 04	14 17	14 34	14 47	15 04	15 17	15 29	15 34	15 47	16 00	16 04	16 17	16 34	16 47	16 59	17 04	17 17	17 34	17 47	18 03
Cononley	d		14 09	14 22	14 39	14 52	15 09	15 22		15 39	15 52		16 09	16 22	16 39	16 52		17 09	17 22	17 39	17 52	18 08
Steeton & Silsden	d		14 14	14 27	14 44	14 57	15 14	15 27		15 44	15 57		16 14	16 27	16 44	16 57		17 14	17 27	17 44	17 57	18 13
Keighley	d	14 09	14 18	14 31	14 48	15 01	15 18	15 31	15 41	15 48	16 01	16 10	16 18	16 31	16 48	17 01	17 09	17 18	17 31	17 48	18 01	18 17
Crossflatts	d		14 22	14 35	14 52	15 05	15 22	15 35		15 52	16 05		16 22	16 35	16 52	17 05		17 22	17 35	17 52	18 05	18 21
Bingley	d	14 14	14 25	14 38	14 55	15 08	15 25	15 38	15 46	15 55	16 08	16 15	16 25	16 38	16 55	17 08	17 14	17 25	17 38	17 55	18 08	18 24
Saltaire	d		14 29	14 42	14 59	15 12	15 29	15 42		15 59	16 12		16 29	16 42	16 59	17 12		17 29	17 42	17 59	18 12	18 28
Shipley	a	14 19	14 31	14 44	15 01	15 14	15 31	15 44	15 50	16 01	16 14	16 19	16 32	16 44	17 01	17 14	17 19	17 31	17 44	18 01	18 14	18 30
	d	14 20	14 32	14 45	15 02	15 15	15 32	15 45	15 51	16 02	16 15	16 20	16 32	16 45	17 02	17 15	17 20	17 32	17 45	18 02	18 15	18 32
Frizinghall	37 d		14 35		15 05		15 35			16 05			16 36		17 05			17 35		18 05		18 35
Bradford Forster Square	37 a		14 41		15 11		15 41			16 11			16 42		17 11			17 41		18 11		18 41
Apperley Bridge	d																					
Kirkstall Forge	d																					
Leeds	37 a	14 37		14 59		15 31		15 59	16 05		16 29	16 39		16 59		17 31	17 39		18 01		18 29	

		NT	NT	NT	NT	NT	NT	NT	NT	NT	NT	NT	NT	NT	NT	NT	NT	NT	NT	NT	NT	NT	NT
			◇ B			◇ D							◇ B					◇ D		◇ B	E		
Skipton	d	18 17	18 29	18 41	18 47	18 59	19 04	19 17	19 34	19 47	20 04	20 17	20 29	20 34	20 47	21 17	21 33	21 43	21 48	22 11	22 26	22 34	22 49
Cononley	d	18 22		18 46	18 52		19 09	19 22	19 39	19 53	20 09	20 22		20 39	20 52	21 22	21 38		21 53		22 31	22 39	22 54
Steeton & Silsden	d	18 27		18 51	18 57		19 14	19 27	19 44	19 58	20 14	20 27		20 44	20 57	21 27	21 43		21 58		22 36	22 44	22 59
Keighley	d	18 31	18 39	18 55	19 01	19 09	19 18	19 31	19 48	20 02	20 18	20 31	20 39	20 48	21 01	21 31	21 47	21 55	22 02	22 21	22 41	22 48	23 03
Crossflatts	d	18 35		18 59	19 05		19 22	19 35	19 52	20 06	20 22	20 35		20 52	21 05	21 35	21 51		22 06		22 45	22 52	23 07
Bingley	d	18 38	18 44	19 02	19 08	19 14	19 25	19 38	19 55	20 09	20 25	20 38	20 44	20 55	21 08	21 38	21 54	22 00	22 09	22 26	22 47	22 55	23 10
Saltaire	d	18 42		19 06	19 12		19 29	19 42	19 59	20 13	20 29	20 42		20 59	21 12	21 42	21 58		22 13		22 51	22 59	23 14
Shipley	a	18 44	18 50	19 09	19 14	19 19	19 32	19 44	20 01	20 15	20 32	20 44	20 50	21 02	21 14	21 44	22 00	22 05	22 15	22 31	22 54	23 02	23 16
	d	18 45	18 50	19 09	19 15	19 20	19 32	19 46	20 02	20 16	20 32	20 45	20 51	21 02	21 15	21 45	22 01	22 06	22 16	22 31	22 55	23 02	23 17
Frizinghall	37 d			19 13			19 36		20 05		20 36			21 06			22 04					23 06	
Bradford Forster Square	37 a			19 19			19 42		20 11		20 42			21 12			22 10					23 12	
Apperley Bridge	d									20 21		20 49			21 19	21 49			22 20				23 21
Kirkstall Forge	d											20 54			21 24	21 54			22 25				23 26
Leeds	37 a	18 59	19 08		19 29	19 38		20 01		20 32		21 02	21 06		21 32	22 02		22 22	22 34	22 48	23 12		23 34

A To London Kings Cross
B From Carlisle
C From Lancaster
D From Morecambe
E From Ribblehead

Table T036-R

Saturdays
21 December to 16 May

Skipton - Bradford and Leeds

		NT	NT	NT	NT	NT	GR	NT	NT	NT	NT	NT	NT	NT	NT	NT	NT	NT	NT	NT	NT	NT	NT
							A							B	◇ C								
Skipton	d	05 45	06 04	06 18	06 34	06 40	06 55	07 01	07 09	07 17	07 30	07 36	07 44	07 55	08 05	08 09	08 15	08 34	08 45	09 04	09 17	09 34	09 47
Cononley	d	05 50	06 09	06 23	06 39	06 45		07 06	07 14	07 22	07 35	07 41	07 49			08 14	08 20	08 39	08 52	09 09	09 22	09 39	09 52
Steeton & Silsden	d	05 55	06 14	06 28	06 44	06 50		07 11	07 19	07 27	07 40	07 46	07 54	08 03	08 12	08 19	08 25	08 44	08 57	09 14	09 27	09 44	09 57
Keighley	d	05 59	06 18	06 32	06 48	06 54	07u09	07 15	07 23	07 31	07 44	07 50	07 58	08 08	08 17	08 24	08 30	08 48	09 01	09 18	09 31	09 48	10 01
Crossflatts	d	06 03	06 22	06 36	06 52	06 58		07 19	07 27	07 35	07 48	07 54	08 02			08 28	08 34	08 52	09 05	09 22	09 35	09 52	10 05
Bingley	d	06 06	06 25	06 39	06 55	07 01		07 22	07 30	07 38	07 51	07 57	08 05	08 13	08 22	08 31	08 37	08 55	09 08	09 25	09 38	09 55	10 08
Saltaire	d	06 10	06 29	06 43	06 59	07 05		07 26	07 34	07 42	07 55	08 01	08 09			08 35	08 41	08 59	09 12	09 29	09 42	09 59	10 12
Shipley	a	06 12	06 31	06 46	07 02	07 07		07 28	07 37	07 44	07 57	08 04	08 11	08 18	08 26	08 37	08 44	09 01	09 14	09 31	09 44	10 01	10 14
	d	06 13	06 32	06 46	07 03	07 08	07u19	07 29	07 37	07 45	07 58	08 04	08 12	08 19	08 27	08 38	08 44	09 02	09 15	09 32	09 45	10 02	10 15
Frizinghall 37	d		06 35		07 08				07 41			08 08					08 48	09 05		09 35		10 05	
Bradford Forster Square 37	a		06 41		07 14				07 47			08 14					08 54	09 11		09 41		10 11	
Apperley Bridge	d									07 49													
Kirkstall Forge	d																						
Leeds 10 37	a	06 27		07 02		07 22	07 33	07 44		08 00	08 13		08 28	08 35	08 41	08 55			09 29		10 01		10 29

		NT	NT	NT	NT	NT	NT	NT	NT	NT	NT	NT	NT	NT	NT	NT	NT	NT	NT	NT	NT	NT
		◇ D					◇ C			◇ D			◇ E					◇ D				
Skipton	d	09 56	10 04	10 17	10 34	10 47	10 59	11 04	11 17	11 28	11 34	11 47	11 59	12 04	12 17	12 34	12 47	12 56	13 04	13 17	13 34	13 47
Cononley	d		10 09	10 22	10 39	10 52		11 09	11 22		11 39	11 52		12 09	12 22	12 39	12 52		13 10	13 22	13 39	13 52
Steeton & Silsden	d		10 14	10 27	10 44	10 57		11 14	11 27		11 44	11 57		12 14	12 27	12 44	12 57		13 14	13 27	13 44	13 57
Keighley	d	10 09	10 18	10 31	10 48	11 01	11 09	11 18	11 31	11 38	11 48	12 01	12 09	12 18	12 31	12 48	13 01	13 09	13 19	13 31	13 48	14 01
Crossflatts	d		10 22	10 35	10 52	11 05		11 22	11 35		11 52	12 05		12 22	12 35	12 52	13 05		13 23	13 35	13 52	14 05
Bingley	d	10 13	10 25	10 38	10 55	11 08	11 14	11 25	11 38	11 45	11 55	12 08	12 14	12 25	12 38	12 55	13 08	13 14	13 25	13 38	13 55	14 08
Saltaire	d		10 29	10 42	10 59	11 12		11 29	11 42		11 59	12 12		12 29	12 42	12 59	13 12		13 30	13 42	13 59	14 12
Shipley	a	10 19	10 31	10 44	11 01	11 14	11 19	11 31	11 44	11 49	12 01	12 14	12 18	12 32	12 44	13 01	13 14	13 20	13 32	13 44	14 01	14 14
	d	10 19	10 32	10 45	11 02	11 15	11 19	11 32	11 45	11 50	12 02	12 15	12 19	12 32	12 45	13 02	13 15	13 20	13 33	13 45	14 02	14 15
Frizinghall 37	d		10 35		11 05			11 35			12 05			12 36		13 05			13 36		14 05	
Bradford Forster Square 37	a		10 41		11 11			11 41			12 11			12 42		13 11			13 42		14 11	
Apperley Bridge	d																					
Kirkstall Forge	d																					
Leeds 10 37	a	10 37		10 59		11 32	11 38		12 00	12 04		12 30	12 38		12 59		13 31	13 38		14 00		14 30

		NT	NT	NT	NT	NT	NT	NT	NT	NT	NT	NT	NT	NT	NT	NT	NT	NT	NT	NT	NT	NT	NT
		◇ E							◇ D			◇ E					◇ D						
Skipton	d	13 59	14 04	14 17	14 34	14 47	15 04	15 17	15 29	15 34	15 47	15 59	16 04	16 17	16 34	16 47	16 59	17 04	17 17	17 34	17 47	18 03	18 17
Cononley	d		14 09	14 22	14 39	14 52	15 09	15 22		15 39	15 52		16 09	16 22	16 39	16 52		17 09	17 22	17 39	17 52	18 08	18 22
Steeton & Silsden	d		14 14	14 27	14 44	14 57	15 14	15 27		15 44	15 57		16 14	16 27	16 44	16 57		17 14	17 27	17 44	17 57	18 13	18 27
Keighley	d	14 09	14 18	14 31	14 48	15 01	15 18	15 31	15 41	15 48	16 01	16 09	16 18	16 31	16 48	17 01	17 09	17 18	17 31	17 48	18 01	18 17	18 31
Crossflatts	d		14 22	14 35	14 52	15 05	15 22	15 35		15 52	16 05		16 22	16 35	16 52	17 05		17 22	17 35	17 52	18 05	18 21	18 35
Bingley	d	14 14	14 25	14 38	14 55	15 08	15 25	15 38	15 46	15 55	16 08	16 14	16 25	16 38	16 55	17 08	17 14	17 25	17 38	17 55	18 08	18 24	18 38
Saltaire	d		14 29	14 42	14 59	15 12	15 29	15 42		15 59	16 12		16 29	16 42	16 59	17 12		17 29	17 42	17 59	18 12	18 28	18 42
Shipley	a	14 19	14 31	14 44	15 01	15 14	15 31	15 44	15 50	16 01	16 14	16 19	16 32	16 44	17 01	17 14	17 19	17 31	17 44	18 01	18 14	18 30	18 44
	d	14 20	14 32	14 45	15 02	15 15	15 32	15 45	15 51	16 02	16 15	16 20	16 32	16 45	17 02	17 15	17 20	17 32	17 45	18 02	18 15	18 32	18 45
Frizinghall 37	d		14 35		15 05		15 35			16 05			16 36		17 05			17 35		18 05		18 35	
Bradford Forster Square 37	a		14 41		15 11		15 41			16 11			16 42		17 11			17 41		18 11		18 41	
Apperley Bridge	d																						
Kirkstall Forge	d																						
Leeds 10 37	a	14 37		14 59		15 31		15 59	16 05		16 29	16 39		16 59		17 31	17 39		18 01		18 29		18 59

		NT	NT	NT	NT	NT	NT	NT	NT	NT	NT	NT	NT	NT	NT	NT	NT	NT	NT	NT	NT	NT
		◇ D			◇ E							◇ D					◇ E		◇ D	B		
Skipton	d	18 29	18 41	18 47	18 59	19 04	19 17	19 34	19 47	20 04	20 17	20 29	20 34	20 47	21 17	21 33	21 43	21 48	22 11	22 26	22 34	22 49
Cononley	d		18 46	18 52		19 09	19 22	19 39	19 53	20 09	20 22		20 39	20 52	21 22	21 38		21 53		22 31	22 39	22 54
Steeton & Silsden	d		18 51	18 57		19 14	19 27	19 44	19 58	20 14	20 27		20 44	20 57	21 27	21 43		21 58		22 36	22 44	22 59
Keighley	d	18 39	18 55	19 01	19 09	19 18	19 31	19 48	20 02	20 18	20 31	20 39	20 48	21 01	21 31	21 47	21 55	22 02	22 21	22 41	22 48	23 03
Crossflatts	d		18 59	19 05		19 22	19 35	19 52	20 06	20 22	20 35		20 52	21 05	21 35	21 51		22 06		22 45	22 52	23 07
Bingley	d	18 44	19 02	19 08	19 14	19 25	19 38	19 55	20 09	20 25	20 38	20 44	20 55	21 08	21 38	21 54	22 00	22 09	22 26	22 47	22 55	23 10
Saltaire	d		19 06	19 12		19 29	19 42	19 59	20 13	20 29	20 42		20 59	21 12	21 42	21 58		22 13		22 51	22 59	23 14
Shipley	a	18 50	19 09	19 14	19 19	19 32	19 44	20 01	20 15	20 32	20 44	20 50	21 02	21 14	21 44	22 00	22 05	22 15	22 30	22 54	23 02	23 16
	d	18 50	19 09	19 15	19 20	19 32	19 46	20 02	20 16	20 32	20 45	20 51	21 02	21 15	21 45	22 01	22 06	22 16	22 31	22 54	23 02	23 17
Frizinghall 37	d		19 13			19 36		20 05		20 36			21 06			22 04				23 06		
Bradford Forster Square 37	a		19 19			19 42		20 11		20 42			21 12			22 10				23 12		
Apperley Bridge	d								20 21		20 49			21 19	21 49			22 20				23 21
Kirkstall Forge	d										20 54			21 24	21 54			22 25				23 26
Leeds 10 37	a	19 08		19 29	19 38		20 01		20 32		21 02	21 09		21 32	22 02		22 22	22 34	22 48	23 11		23 34

A To London Kings Cross
B From Ribblehead
C From Lancaster
D From Carlisle
E From Morecambe

NRT DECEMBER 19 EDITION

Table T036-R

Sundays
15 December to 10 May

Skipton - Bradford and Leeds

		NT	NT	NT	NT	NT	NT	NT	NT	NT	NT	NT	NT	NT	NT	NT	NT	NT	NT	NT	NT	NT	NT
										◇ A			◇ B					◇ A		◇ C			
Skipton	d	08 32	08 42	09 12	09 42	10 12	10 30	10 42	11 12	11 30	11 42	12 12	12 22	12 42	13 12	13 42	14 12	14 30	14 42	14 58	15 12	15 42	16 07
Cononley	d	08 37	08 47	09 17	09 47	10 17		10 47	11 17		11 47	12 17		12 47	13 17	13 47	14 17		14 47		15 17	15 47	
Steeton & Silsden	d	08 42	08 52	09 22	09 52	10 22		10 52	11 22		11 52	12 22		12 52	13 22	13 52	14 22		14 52		15 22	15 52	
Keighley	d	08 46	08 56	09 26	09 56	10 26	10 40	10 56	11 26	11 40	11 56	12 26	12 32	12 56	13 26	13 56	14 26	14 40	14 56	15 08	15 26	15 56	16 17
Crossflatts	d	08 50	09 00	09 30	10 00	10 30		11 00	11 30		12 00	12 30		13 00	13 30	14 00	14 30		15 00		15 30	16 00	
Bingley	d	08 53	09 03	09 33	10 03	10 33	10 44	11 03	11 33	11 44	12 03	12 33	12 38	13 03	13 33	14 03	14 33	14 44	15 03	15 12	15 33	16 03	16 21
Saltaire	d	08 57	09 07	09 37	10 07	10 37		11 07	11 37		12 07	12 37		13 07	13 37	14 07	14 37		15 07		15 37	16 07	
Shipley	a	08 59	09 10	09 39	10 10	10 39	10 49	11 10	11 39	11 49	12 10	12 39	12 45	13 10	13 39	14 10	14 39	14 49	15 10	15 17	15 39	16 10	16 26
	d	09 00	09 10	09 40	10 10	10 40	10 49	11 10	11 40	11 49	12 10	12 40	12 48	13 10	13 40	14 10	14 40	14 49	15 10	15 17	15 40	16 10	16 26
Frizinghall 37	d		09 14		10 14			11 14			12 14			13 14		14 14			15 14			16 14	
Bradford Forster Square 37	a		09 20		10 20			11 20			12 20			13 20		14 20			15 20			16 20	
Apperley Bridge	d																						
Kirkstall Forge	d																						
Leeds 10 37	a	09 14		09 54		10 54	11 06		11 54	12 06		12 54	13 07		13 54		14 54	15 09		15 37	15 54		16 43

		NT	NT	NT	NT	NT	NT	NT	NT	NT	NT	NT	NT	NT	NT	NT	NT	NT	NT	NT	NT	NT
				◇ B		◇ D		◇ A			◇ B		◇ A				◇ A		◇ B			
Skipton	d	16 12	16 42	17 06	17 14	17 23	17 42	17 58	18 12	18 42	19 05	19 12	19 30	19 42	20 12	20 42	21 17	21 22	21 33	21 42	22 12	23 12
Cononley	d	16 17	16 47		17 19		17 47		18 17	18 47		19 17		19 47	20 17	20 47		21 27		21 47	22 17	23 18
Steeton & Silsden	d	16 22	16 52		17 24		17 52		18 22	18 52		19 22		19 52	20 22	20 52		21 32		21 52	22 22	23 22
Keighley	d	16 26	16 56	17 16	17 28	17 33	17 56	18 08	18 26	18 56	19 15	19 26	19 40	19 56	20 26	20 56	21 27	21 36	21 43	21 56	22 26	23 27
Crossflatts	d	16 30	17 00		17 32		18 00		18 30	19 00		19 30		20 00	20 30	21 00		21 40		22 00	22 30	23 32
Bingley	d	16 33	17 03	17 21	17 35	17 40	18 03	18 13	18 33	19 03	19 20	19 33	19 45	20 03	20 33	21 03	21 32	21 43	21 48	22 03	22 33	23 34
Saltaire	d	16 37	17 07		17 39		18 07		18 37	19 07		19 37		20 07	20 37	21 07		21 47		22 07	22 37	23 39
Shipley	a	16 39	17 10	17 25	17 41	17 46	18 10	18 17	18 39	19 10	19 24	19 39	19 49	20 10	20 39	21 10	21 36	21 49	21 53	22 10	22 39	23 42
	d	16 40	17 10	17 26	17 42	17 47	18 10	18 18	18 40	19 10	19 25	19 40	19 50	20 10	20 40	21 10	21 38	21 49	21 54	22 10	22 39	23 42
Frizinghall 37	d		17 14				18 14			19 14				20 14		21 14				22 14		
Bradford Forster Square 37	a		17 20				18 20			19 20				20 20		21 20				22 20		
Apperley Bridge	d																					
Kirkstall Forge	d																					
Leeds 10 37	a	16 54		17 45	17 56	18 05		18 32	18 54		19 45	19 54	20 08		20 54		21 55	22 05	22 10		22 54	23 57

A From Carlisle
B From Morecambe
C From Heysham Harbour
D From Carlisle to Nottingham

Table T037-F

Mondays to Fridays
16 December to 15 May

Leeds - Shipley and Bradford

Miles	Miles			NT	NT ◇	NT ◇	NT	NT	NT ◇	NT ◇	NT ◇	NT		NT	NT	NT	NT ◇	NT	NT	NT	NT ◇	NT		NT ◇	NT ◇
0	0	**Leeds 10**	d	05 01	05 12	05 17		05 22	05 42	05 57	06 12			06 26	06 27	06 30	06 42		06 56		06 57	07 11		07 12	07 20
4¼	—	Kirkstall Forge	d													06 37						07 17			
7¾	—	Apperley Bridge	d													06 41						07 22			
10¼	—	**Shipley**	a			05 29								06 42		06 45			07 08			07 26			07 32
—	—		d				06 13					06 32				06 46		07 03		07 14		07 26			
11¾	—	Frizinghall	d				06 16					06 35				06 48		07 08		07 17		07 29			
—	4	Bramley	d	05 09	05 18			05 30	05 49		06 18				06 35		06 49							07 18	
—	5¾	New Pudsey	d	05 14	05 22			05 35	05 53	06 06	06 22				06 40		06 53				07 07			07 22	
—	9½	**Bradford Interchange**	a	05 22	05 30			05 43	06 01	06 14	06 30				06 48		07 01				07 15			07 30	
13½	—	**Bradford Forster Square**	a				06 22					06 41				06 55		07 14		07 23		07 36			

		NT	NT	NT	NT ◇	NT	NT ◇	NT ◇		NT	NT	NT	NT ◇	NT	NT ◇	NT ◇	NT	NT		NT ◇	NT ◇	NT	NT	NT	NT
Leeds 10	d		07 23		07 27	07 41	07 42	07 48			07 52		07 55	08 12	08 12	08 18	08 25			08 27	08 42		08 42		08 54
Kirkstall Forge	d					07 47								08 18									08 49		09 00
Apperley Bridge	d					07 51								08 23									08 53		
Shipley	a		07 37			07 56		08 00			08 04			08 27		08 31	08 37						08 57		09 07
	d	07 37		07 44		07 56				08 04		08 11		08 27				08 44				08 49	08 58	09 02	
Frizinghall	d	07 41		07 47		07 59				08 08		08 14		08 30				08 48				08 52	09 00	09 05	
Bramley	d				07 35		07 49								08 18					08 35	08 49				
New Pudsey	d				07 40		07 53						08 04		08 22					08 40	08 53				
Bradford Interchange	a				07 48		08 01						08 12		08 30					08 48	09 01				
Bradford Forster Square	a	07 47		07 53		08 06				08 14		08 20		08 38				08 54				08 57	09 07	09 11	

		NT	NT ◇	NT		NT ◇	NT ◇	NT	NT	NT	NT ◇	NT	NT ◇	NT		NT	NT	NT ◇	NT	NT ◇	NT ◇	NT	NT	NT	
Leeds 10	d		08 57	09 12		09 12	09 19		09 26		09 27	09 42	09 42			09 56		09 57	10 12	10 12	10 18		10 26		
Kirkstall Forge	d			09 18								09 49							10 19						
Apperley Bridge	d			09 23								09 53							10 23						
Shipley	a			09 27			09 32		09 37			09 57				10 08			10 27		10 32		10 37		
	d	09 14		09 28				09 32		09 44		09 58		10 02			10 14		10 28			10 32		10 44	
Frizinghall	d	09 17		09 30				09 35		09 47		10 00		10 05			10 17		10 30			10 35		10 47	
Bramley	d					09 18					09 35		09 49							10 18					
New Pudsey	d		09 06			09 22					09 40		09 53					10 06		10 22					
Bradford Interchange	a		09 14			09 30					09 48		10 01					10 15		10 30					
Bradford Forster Square	a	09 23		09 37				09 41		09 53		10 07		10 11			10 23		10 37			10 41		10 53	

		NT ◇	NT	NT ◇	NT ◇	NT	NT	NT	NT ◇	NT		NT ◇	NT	NT	NT	NT ◇	NT	NT ◇	NT	NT		NT	NT ◇	NT	NT ◇
Leeds 10	d	10 27	10 42	10 42	10 49		10 56		10 57	11 12		11 12		11 26		11 27	11 42	11 42		11 56			11 57	12 12	12 12
Kirkstall Forge	d		10 49							11 19							11 49							12 19	
Apperley Bridge	d		10 53							11 23							11 53							12 23	
Shipley	a		10 57		11 02		11 08			11 27				11 38			11 57			12 08				12 27	
	d		10 58			11 02		11 14		11 28			11 32		11 44		11 58		12 02			12 14		12 28	
Frizinghall	d		11 00			11 05		11 17		11 30			11 35		11 47		12 00		12 05			12 17		12 30	
Bramley	d	10 35		10 49								11 18				11 35		11 49							12 18
New Pudsey	d	10 40		10 53					11 06			11 22				11 40		11 53					12 06		12 22
Bradford Interchange	a	10 48		11 01					11 14			11 30				11 48		12 01					12 14		12 30
Bradford Forster Square	a		11 07			11 11		11 23		11 37			11 41		11 53		12 07		12 11			12 23		12 37	

		NT ◇	NT	NT	NT	NT ◇		NT	NT ◇	NT	NT	NT	NT ◇	NT	NT ◇	NT ◇		NT	NT	NT	NT ◇	NT	NT ◇	NT	NT
Leeds 10	d	12 18		12 26		12 27		12 42	12 42		12 56		12 57	13 12	13 12	13 18			13 26		13 27	13 42	13 42		13 56
Kirkstall Forge	d							12 49						13 19								13 49			
Apperley Bridge	d							12 53						13 23								13 53			
Shipley	a	12 32		12 37				12 57			13 07			13 27		13 32			13 37			13 57			14 08
	d		12 32		12 44			12 58		13 02		13 14		13 28				13 33		13 44		13 58		14 02	
Frizinghall	d		12 36		12 47			13 00		13 05		13 17		13 30				13 36		13 47		14 00		14 05	
Bramley	d					12 35			12 49						13 18						13 35		13 49		
New Pudsey	d					12 40			12 53				13 07		13 22						13 40		13 53		
Bradford Interchange	a					12 48			13 01				13 15		13 30						13 48		14 01		
Bradford Forster Square	a		12 42		12 53			13 07		13 11		13 23		13 37				13 42		13 53		14 07		14 11	

		NT		NT ◇	NT	NT ◇	NT ◇	NT	NT	NT	NT ◇	NT		NT ◇	NT	NT	NT	NT ◇	NT	NT ◇	NT ◇	NT		NT	NT
Leeds 10	d			13 57	14 12	14 12	14 18		14 26		14 27	14 42		14 42		14 56		14 57	15 12	15 12	15 18			15 26	
Kirkstall Forge	d				14 19							14 49							15 19						
Apperley Bridge	d				14 23							14 53							15 23						
Shipley	a				14 27		14 32		14 37			14 57				15 08			15 27		15 32			15 37	
	d	14 14			14 28			14 32		14 44		14 58			15 02		15 14		15 28			15 32			15 44
Frizinghall	d	14 17			14 30			14 35		14 47		15 00			15 05		15 17		15 30			15 35			15 47
Bramley	d					14 18					14 35			14 49						15 18					
New Pudsey	d			14 06		14 22					14 40			14 53				15 06		15 22					
Bradford Interchange	a			14 15		14 30					14 48			15 01				15 15		15 30					
Bradford Forster Square	a	14 23			14 37			14 41		14 53		15 07			15 11		15 23		15 37			15 41			15 53

Table T037-F

Mondays to Fridays
16 December to 15 May

Leeds - Shipley and Bradford

		NT ◇	NT	NT ◇		NT	NT	NT	NT ◇	NT	NT ◇	NT	NT	NT		NT ◇	NT	NT ◇	NT ◇	NT	NT	NT	NT ◇	NT	
Leeds 10	d	15 27	15 42	15 42			15 56		15 57	16 12	16 12		16 26			16 27	16 42	16 42	16 48		16 56		16 57	17 12	
Kirkstall Forge	d		15 49							16 19							16 49								
Apperley Bridge	d		15 53							16 23							16 53							17 21	
Shipley	a		15 57				16 08			16 27			16 37				16 57		17 01		17 07			17 25	
	d		15 58			16 02		16 14		16 28		16 32		16 44			16 58			17 02		17 14		17 26	
Frizinghall	d		16 00			16 05		16 17		16 30		16 36		16 47			17 00			17 05		17 17		17 29	
Bramley	d	15 35		15 49							16 18					16 35		16 49							
New Pudsey	d	15 40		15 53					16 06		16 22					16 40		16 53					17 06		
Bradford Interchange	a	15 48		16 01					16 15		16 30					16 48		17 01					17 15		
Bradford Forster Square	a		16 07			16 11		16 23		16 37		16 42		16 53			17 07			17 11		17 23		17 36	

		NT ◇	NT	NT	NT ◇	NT	NT ◇	NT	NT	NT		NT ◇	NT	NT	NT ◇	NT	NT ◇	NT ◇	NT	NT		NT	NT ◇	NT ◇	NT
Leeds 10	d	17 12		17 18	17 26		17 27	17 35	17 41			17 42	17 54		17 57	18 12	18 12	18 18		18 26			18 27	18 42	18 43
Kirkstall Forge	d			17 26					17 48							18 19									18 50
Apperley Bridge	d							17 46								18 23									18 54
Shipley	a			17 33	17 38			17 50	17 55				18 07			18 27		18 32		18 37					18 58
	d		17 32			17 44		17 51		18 02				18 15		18 28			18 32			18 44			18 59
Frizinghall	d		17 35			17 47		17 53		18 05				18 17		18 30			18 35			18 47			19 01
Bramley	d	17 18					17 35					17 49					18 18						18 35	18 49	
New Pudsey	d	17 22					17 40					17 53			18 06		18 22						18 40	18 53	
Bradford Interchange	a	17 30					17 48					18 01			18 15		18 30						18 48	19 01	
Bradford Forster Square	a		17 41			17 53		18 00		18 11				18 23		18 37			18 41			18 53			19 08

		NT	NT	NT ◇	NT ◇	NT		NT	NT ◇	NT	NT	NT	NT ◇	NT ◇	NT	NT		NT	NT	NT ◇	NT ◇	NT	NT	NT	NT ◇
Leeds 10	d	18 55		18 57	19 12			19 12	19 18		19 26		19 27	19 40	19 49			19 56		19 57	20 12		20 25		20 27
Kirkstall Forge	d							19 18			19 33							20 03					20 33		
Apperley Bridge	d							19 23			19 37							20 07					20 37		
Shipley	a	19 08						19 27	19 31		19 42				20 02			20 12					20 42		
	d		19 09			19 14		19 28		19 32		19 46				20 02			20 16			20 32		20 48	
Frizinghall	d		19 13			19 17		19 30		19 36		19 49				20 05			20 19			20 36		20 51	
Bramley	d				19 18								19 35	19 47							20 18				20 35
New Pudsey	d			19 06	19 22								19 40	19 51						20 07	20 22				20 40
Bradford Interchange	a			19 15	19 30								19 48	19 59						20 15	20 30				20 48
Bradford Forster Square	a		19 19			19 23		19 37		19 42		19 55				20 11			20 25			20 42		20 58	

		NT ◇		NT	NT	NT	NT ◇	GR	NT ◇	NT	NT	NT ◇		NT ◇	NT	NT	NT	NT ◇	NT ◇	NT	NT	NT ◇		NT ◇	NT
Leeds 10	d	20 42			20 56		20 57	21 07	21 12	21 26		21 27		21 42		21 56		21 57	22 12	22 26		22 27		22 42	
Kirkstall Forge	d				21 03					21 33						22 02				22 33					
Apperley Bridge	d				21 07					21 37										22 37					
Shipley	a				21 11			21s18		21 42						22 09				22 42					
	d			21 02		21 14					21 48				22 01		22 15				22 48				23 02
Frizinghall	d			21 06		21 17					21 51				22 04		22 17				22 51				23 06
Bramley	d	20 49							21 18			21 35		21 49					22 18			22 36		22 49	
New Pudsey	d	20 53					21 07		21 22			21 40		21 53				22 06	22 22			22 40		22 53	
Bradford Interchange	a	21 01					21 15		21 30			21 48		22 01				22 15	22 30			22 49		23 01	
Bradford Forster Square	a			21 12		21 23		21 29			21 58				22 10		22 23				22 58				23 12

		NT	NT	NT ◇	NT	NT ◇
Leeds 10	d	22 56		22 57	23 20	23 27
Kirkstall Forge	d				23 27	
Apperley Bridge	d				23 31	
Shipley	a	23 07			23 36	
	d		23 14			
Frizinghall	d		23 17			
Bramley	d					23 35
New Pudsey	d			23 06		23 40
Bradford Interchange	a			23 15		23 48
Bradford Forster Square	a		23 23			

Saturdays
21 December to 16 May

		NT	NT ◇	NT	NT ◇	NT ◇	NT ◇	NT	NT ◇	NT		NT	NT	NT	NT ◇	NT	NT	NT	NT ◇	NT		NT ◇	NT ◇	NT	NT
Leeds 10	d	05 01	05 12	05 22	05 42	05 57	06 12		06 20			06 26	06 27	06 30	06 42		06 56		06 57	07 11		07 12	07 20		07 23
Kirkstall Forge	d													06 37						07 17					
Apperley Bridge	d													06 41						07 22					
Shipley	a								06 32			06 42		06 45			07 08			07 26			07 32		07 37
	d							06 13		06 32				06 46		07 03		07 14		07 26				07 37	
Frizinghall	d							06 16		06 35				06 48		07 08		07 17		07 29				07 41	
Bramley	d	05 09	05 18	05 30	05 49		06 18						06 35		06 49							07 18			
New Pudsey	d	05 14	05 22	05 35	05 53	06 06	06 22						06 40		06 53				07 07			07 22			
Bradford Interchange	a	05 22	05 30	05 43	06 01	06 14	06 30						06 48		07 01				07 15			07 30			
Bradford Forster Square	a							06 22		06 41				06 55		07 14		07 23		07 36				07 47	

Table T037-F

Saturdays

21 December to 16 May

Leeds - Shipley and Bradford

		NT		NT	NT	NT	NT	NT	NT	NT	NT	NT		NT	NT	NT	NT	NT	NT	NT	NT	NT		NT	NT
				◇		◇	◇ 🍴				◇			◇	◇			◇	◇						
Leeds 10	d			07 27	07 41	07 42	07 48		07 52		07 55	08 12		08 12	08 18	08 25		08 27	08 42		08 42			08 54	
Kirkstall Forge	d				07 47							08 18									08 49			09 00	
Apperley Bridge	d				07 51							08 23									08 53				
Shipley	a				07 56		08 00		08 04			08 27			08 31	08 37					08 57			09 07	
	d	07 44			07 56			08 04		08 11		08 27					08 44			08 49	08 58	09 02			09 14
Frizinghall	d	07 47			07 59			08 08		08 14		08 30					08 48			08 52	09 00	09 05			09 17
Bramley	d			07 35		07 49								08 18				08 35	08 49						
New Pudsey	d			07 40		07 53					08 04			08 22				08 40	08 53						
Bradford Interchange	a			07 48		08 01					08 12			08 30				08 48	09 01						
Bradford Forster Square	a	07 53			08 06			08 14		08 20		08 38					08 54			08 57	09 07	09 11			09 23

		NT	NT	NT	NT	NT	NT	NT		NT	NT	NT	NT	NT	NT	NT	NT	NT		NT	NT	NT	NT	NT	NT
		◇		◇	◇ 🍴					◇		◇				◇		◇		◇				◇	
Leeds 10	d	08 57	09 12	09 12	09 19		09 26			09 27	09 42	09 42		09 56		09 57	10 12	10 12		10 18		10 26		10 27	10 42
Kirkstall Forge	d		09 18								09 49						10 19								10 49
Apperley Bridge	d		09 23								09 53						10 23								10 53
Shipley	a		09 27		09 31		09 37				09 57			10 08			10 27			10 32		10 37			10 57
	d		09 28			09 32		09 44			09 58		10 02		10 14		10 28				10 32		10 44		10 58
Frizinghall	d		09 30			09 35		09 47			10 00		10 05		10 17		10 30				10 35		10 47		11 00
Bramley	d			09 18						09 35		09 49						10 18						10 35	
New Pudsey	d	09 06		09 22						09 40		09 53				10 06		10 22						10 40	
Bradford Interchange	a	09 14		09 30						09 48		10 01				10 15		10 30						10 48	
Bradford Forster Square	a		09 37			09 41		09 53			10 07		10 11		10 23		10 37				10 41		10 53		11 07

		NT	NT	NT		NT	NT	NT	NT	NT	NT	NT	NT	NT		NT	NT	NT	NT	NT	NT	NT	NT	NT	
		◇	◇ 🍴					◇		◇				◇			◇				◇		◇	◇	
Leeds 10	d	10 42	10 49			10 56		10 57	11 12	11 12		11 26		11 27		11 42	11 42		11 56		11 57	12 12	12 12	12 18	
Kirkstall Forge	d								11 19							11 49						12 19			
Apperley Bridge	d								11 23							11 53						12 23			
Shipley	a		11 01			11 08			11 27			11 38				11 57			12 08			12 27		12 32	
	d			11 02			11 14		11 28		11 32		11 44			11 58		12 02		12 14		12 28			
Frizinghall	d			11 05			11 17		11 30		11 35		11 47			12 00		12 05		12 17		12 30			
Bramley	d	10 49								11 18				11 35			11 49						12 18		
New Pudsey	d	10 53						11 06		11 22				11 40			11 53				12 06		12 22		
Bradford Interchange	a	11 01						11 14		11 30				11 48			12 01				12 14		12 30		
Bradford Forster Square	a			11 11			11 23		11 37		11 41		11 53			12 07		12 11		12 23		12 37			

		NT	NT	NT	NT	NT	NT	NT	NT	NT		NT	NT	NT	NT	NT	NT	NT	NT	NT		NT	NT	NT	NT
					◇		◇					◇		◇	◇ 🍴				◇			◇			
Leeds 10	d		12 26		12 27	12 42	12 42		12 56			12 57	13 12	13 12	13 18		13 26		13 27	13 42		13 42		13 56	
Kirkstall Forge	d					12 49							13 19							13 49					
Apperley Bridge	d					12 53							13 23							13 53					
Shipley	a		12 37			12 57			13 07				13 27		13 32		13 37			13 57				14 08	
	d	12 32		12 44		12 58		13 02		13 14			13 28			13 33		13 44		13 58			14 02		14 14
Frizinghall	d	12 36		12 47		13 00		13 05		13 17			13 30			13 36		13 47		14 00			14 05		14 17
Bramley	d				12 35		12 49							13 18					13 35			13 49			
New Pudsey	d				12 40		12 53					13 06		13 22					13 40			13 53			
Bradford Interchange	a				12 48		13 01					13 15		13 30					13 48			14 01			
Bradford Forster Square	a	12 42		12 53		13 07		13 11		13 23			13 37			13 42		13 53		14 07			14 11		14 23

		NT	NT	NT	NT	NT		NT	NT	NT	NT	NT	NT	NT	NT	NT		NT	NT	NT	NT	NT	NT	NT	NT
		◇		◇	◇					◇		◇				◇			◇	◇ 🍴				◇	
Leeds 10	d	13 57	14 12	14 12	14 18			14 26		14 27	14 42	14 42		14 56		14 57		15 12	15 12	15 18		15 26		15 27	15 42
Kirkstall Forge	d		14 19								14 49							15 19							15 49
Apperley Bridge	d		14 23								14 53							15 23							15 53
Shipley	a		14 27		14 32			14 37			14 57			15 08				15 27		15 32		15 37			15 57
	d		14 28			14 32			14 44		14 58		15 02		15 14			15 28			15 32		15 44		15 58
Frizinghall	d		14 30			14 35			14 47		15 00		15 05		15 17			15 30			15 35		15 47		16 00
Bramley	d			14 18						14 35		14 49							15 18					15 35	
New Pudsey	d	14 06		14 22						14 40		14 53				15 06			15 22					15 40	
Bradford Interchange	a	14 15		14 30						14 48		15 01				15 15			15 30					15 48	
Bradford Forster Square	a		14 37			14 41			14 53		15 07		15 11		15 23			15 37			15 41		15 53		16 07

		NT		NT	NT	NT	NT	NT	NT	NT	NT	NT		NT	NT	NT	NT	NT	NT	NT	NT	NT		NT	NT
		◇					◇		◇					◇		◇	◇ 🍴				◇			◇	
Leeds 10	d	15 42			15 56		15 57	16 12	16 12		16 26			16 27	16 42	16 42	16 48		16 56		16 57	17 12		17 12	
Kirkstall Forge	d							16 19							16 49										
Apperley Bridge	d							16 23							16 53							17 21			
Shipley	a				16 08			16 27			16 37				16 57		17 01		17 07			17 25			
	d			16 02		16 14		16 28		16 32		16 44			16 58			17 02		17 14		17 26			17 32
Frizinghall	d			16 05		16 17		16 30		16 36		16 47			17 00			17 05		17 17		17 29			17 35
Bramley	d	15 49							16 18					16 35		16 49								17 18	
New Pudsey	d	15 53					16 07		16 22					16 40		16 53					17 06			17 22	
Bradford Interchange	a	16 01					16 15		16 30					16 48		17 01					17 15			17 30	
Bradford Forster Square	a			16 11		16 23		16 37		16 42		16 53			17 07			17 11		17 23		17 36			17 41

Table T037-F

Saturdays

21 December to 16 May

Leeds - Shipley and Bradford

		NT	NT	NT		NT	NT	NT	NT	NT	NT	NT	NT	NT		NT	NT	NT	NT	NT	NT	NT	NT	NT	
			◇			◇				◇			◇			◇	◇ 🍴				◇	◇			
Leeds 10	d	17 18	17 26			17 27	17 35	17 41		17 42	17 54		17 57	18 12		18 12	18 18		18 26		18 27	18 42	18 43	18 55	
Kirkstall Forge	d	17 26						17 48						18 19									18 50		
Apperley Bridge	d						17 46							18 23									18 54		
Shipley	a	17 33	17 38				17 50	17 55			18 07			18 27			18 32		18 37				18 58	19 08	
	d			17 44			17 51		18 02			18 15		18 28				18 32		18 44			18 59		
Frizinghall	d			17 47			17 53		18 05			18 17		18 30				18 35		18 47			19 01		
Bramley	d					17 35				17 49						18 18					18 35	18 49			
New Pudsey	d					17 40				17 53			18 06			18 22					18 40	18 53			
Bradford Interchange	a					17 48				18 01			18 15			18 30					18 48	19 01			
Bradford Forster Square	a			17 53			18 00		18 11			18 23		18 37				18 41		18 53			19 08		

		NT	NT	NT	NT	NT	NT	NT	NT	NT		NT	NT	NT	NT	NT	NT	NT	NT	NT		NT	NT	NT	NT
			◇	◇			◇					◇	◇	🍴				◇	◇					◇	◇
Leeds 10	d		18 57	19 12		19 12	19 18		19 26			19 27	19 40	19 49		19 56		19 57	20 12			20 25		20 27	20 42
Kirkstall Forge	d					19 18			19 33							20 03						20 33			
Apperley Bridge	d					19 23			19 37							20 07						20 37			
Shipley	a					19 27	19 31		19 42					20 02		20 12						20 42			
	d	19 09			19 14	19 28		19 32		19 46					20 02		20 16			20 32			20 48		
Frizinghall	d	19 13			19 17	19 30		19 36		19 49					20 05		20 19			20 36			20 51		
Bramley	d			19 18								19 35	19 47						20 18					20 35	20 49
New Pudsey	d		19 06	19 22								19 40	19 51					20 07	20 22					20 40	20 53
Bradford Interchange	a		19 15	19 30								19 48	19 59					20 15	20 30					20 48	21 01
Bradford Forster Square	a	19 19			19 23	19 37		19 42		19 55					20 11		20 25			20 42			20 58		

		NT	NT	NT	NT	NT		NT	NT	NT	NT	NT	NT	NT	GR	NT		NT	NT	NT	NT	NT	NT	NT	NT
					◇	◇				◇	◇			◇	■ 1 🍴			◇			◇	◇			
Leeds 10	d		20 56		20 57	21 12		21 26		21 27	21 42		21 52	21 57	21 58			22 12	22 26		22 27	22 42		22 56	
Kirkstall Forge	d		21 03					21 33					21 58						22 33						
Apperley Bridge	d		21 07					21 37											22 37						
Shipley	a		21 11					21 42					22 05		22s09				22 42					23 07	
	d	21 02		21 14					21 48			22 01				22 15				22 48			23 02		23 14
Frizinghall	d	21 06		21 17					21 51			22 04				22 17				22 51			23 06		23 17
Bramley	d					21 18				21 35	21 49							22 18			22 36	22 49			
New Pudsey	d				21 06	21 22				21 40	21 53			22 06				22 22			22 40	22 53			
Bradford Interchange	a				21 15	21 30				21 48	22 01			22 15				22 30			22 49	23 01			
Bradford Forster Square	a	21 12		21 23					21 58			22 10			22 20	22 23				22 58			23 12		23 23

		NT		NT	NT
		◇			◇
Leeds 10	d	22 57		23 20	23 27
Kirkstall Forge	d			23 27	
Apperley Bridge	d			23 31	
Shipley	a			23 36	
	d				
Frizinghall	d				
Bramley	d				23 35
New Pudsey	d	23 07			23 40
Bradford Interchange	a	23 15			23 49
Bradford Forster Square	a				

Sundays

15 December to 10 May

		NT	NT	NT	NT	NT	NT	NT	NT	NT		NT	NT	NT	NT	NT	NT	NT	NT	NT		NT	NT	NT	NT
			◇		◇			◇		◇				◇		◇				◇			◇		
Leeds 10	d	07 58	08 18	08 29	08 32	08 36		08 59		09 19		09 29	09 41	09 52		10 15		10 16	10 29	10 32		10 41	10 49		
Kirkstall Forge	d					08 43							09 48									10 48			
Apperley Bridge	d					08 47							09 52									10 52			
Shipley	a				08 44	08 51		09 12					09 57					10 27		10 45		10 56			
	d					08 52	09 10		09 17				09 57		10 10		10 16					10 57		11 10	11 16
Frizinghall	d					08 54	09 14		09 19				10 00		10 14		10 19					10 59		11 14	11 19
Bramley	d	08 06	08 26	08 41						09 27		09 37				10 25			10 37						
New Pudsey	d	08 10	08 30	08 45						09 31		09 41		10 02		10 31			10 41				10 59		
Bradford Interchange	a	08 19	08 38	08 54						09 39		09 50		10 10		10 39			10 50				11 07		
Bradford Forster Square	a					09 01	09 20		09 25				10 07		10 20		10 25					11 06		11 20	11 24

		NT	NT	NT	NT	NT		NT	NT	NT	NT	NT	NT	NT	NT	NT		NT	NT	NT	NT	NT	NT	NT	NT
		◇	◇					◇					◇	◇				◇				◇		◇	
Leeds 10	d	11 16	11 18	11 26	11 29	11 41		11 57	11 57			12 16	12 18	12 28	12 29	12 41		12 57			13 16	13 18	13 29	13 32	13 41
Kirkstall Forge	d					11 48										12 48									13 48
Apperley Bridge	d					11 52										12 52									13 52
Shipley	a	11 27		11 37		11 56			12 08			12 27		12 40		12 56					13 27			13 44	13 56
	d					11 57				12 10	12 16					12 57			13 10	13 16					13 57
Frizinghall	d					11 59				12 14	12 19					12 59			13 14	13 19					13 59
Bramley	d		11 26		11 37								12 27		12 37							13 27	13 37		
New Pudsey	d		11 30		11 41			12 06					12 31		12 41			13 06				13 31	13 41		
Bradford Interchange	a		11 38		11 50			12 15					12 39		12 50			13 15				13 39	13 50		
Bradford Forster Square	a					12 06				12 20	12 25					13 06			13 20	13 25					14 06

Table T037-F

Sundays
15 December to 10 May

Leeds - Shipley and Bradford

		NT ◇	NT	NT	NT	NT ◇	NT ◇	NT	NT	NT ◇	NT	NT	NT	NT ◇	NT	NT ◇	NT	NT ◇	NT	NT	NT	NT ◇	NT ◇
Leeds 10	d	13 57			14 16	14 19	14 24	14 29	14 41	14 56			15 16	15 18	15 29	15 32	15 41	15 57			16 12	16 19	16 23
Kirkstall Forge	d								14 48								15 48						
Apperley Bridge	d								14 52								15 52						
Shipley	a				14 27		14 36		14 56				15 27			15 44	15 56				16 23		16 35
	d		14 10	14 16					14 57		15 10	15 16					15 57		16 10	16 16			
Frizinghall	d		14 14	14 19					14 59		15 14	15 19					15 59		16 14	16 19			
Bramley	d					14 27		14 37						15 26	15 37							16 27	
New Pudsey	d	14 06				14 31		14 41		15 05				15 30	15 41			16 07				16 31	
Bradford Interchange	a	14 17				14 39		14 50		15 14				15 38	15 50			16 15				16 39	
Bradford Forster Square	a		14 20	14 25					15 06		15 20	15 25					16 06		16 20	16 25			

		NT	NT	NT ◇	NT	NT	NT	NT ◇	NT	NT ◇	NT	NT ◇	NT	NT	NT	NT ◇	NT	NT	NT ◇	NT	NT ◇	NT
Leeds 10	d	16 31	16 41	16 56			17 16	17 18	17 29	17 32	17 45	17 56			18 16	18 18	18 29	18 41	18 52		18 56	
Kirkstall Forge	d		16 48								17 52							18 48				
Apperley Bridge	d		16 52								17 56							18 52				
Shipley	a		16 56				17 27			17 44	18 00				18 28			18 56	19 04			
	d		16 57		17 10	17 17					18 01		18 10	18 16				18 57		19 10		19 16
Frizinghall	d		16 59		17 14	17 20					18 03		18 14	18 19				18 59		19 14		19 19
Bramley	d	16 39						17 27	17 37							18 27	18 37					
New Pudsey	d	16 43		17 05				17 31	17 41			18 05				18 31	18 41				19 05	
Bradford Interchange	a	16 52		17 14				17 39	17 50			18 15				18 39	18 50				19 15	
Bradford Forster Square	a		17 06		17 20	17 26					18 10		18 20	18 25				19 06		19 20		19 25

		NT	NT ◇	NT	NT	NT ◇	NT	NT	NT	NT ◇	NT	NT	NT ◇	NT	NT	NT	NT ◇	NT	NT	NT ◇	NT	NT ◇	NT
Leeds 10	d	19 16	19 19	19 29	19 42	19 56			20 16	20 18	20 29	20 41	20 56			21 16	21 18	21 32	21 42	21 56		22 11	
Kirkstall Forge	d				19 49							20 48							21 49				
Apperley Bridge	d				19 53							20 52							21 53				
Shipley	a	19 27			19 57				20 27			20 56				21 27			21 59				
	d				19 58		20 10	20 18				20 57		21 10	21 17				21 59		22 10		22 16
Frizinghall	d				20 00		20 14	20 20				20 59		21 14	21 19				22 02		22 14		22 19
Bramley	d		19 27	19 37						20 27	20 37						21 27	21 40				22 20	
New Pudsey	d		19 31	19 41		20 05				20 31	20 41		21 06				21 31	21 44		22 05		22 25	
Bradford Interchange	a		19 39	19 50		20 14				20 39	20 50		21 14				21 39	21 53		22 15		22 34	
Bradford Forster Square	a				20 07		20 20	20 26				21 06		21 20	21 25				22 08		22 20		22 25

		NT	NT	NT	NT ◇	NT
Leeds 10	d	22 20	22 31	22 41	23 19	23 23
Kirkstall Forge	d			22 48		
Apperley Bridge	d			22 52		
Shipley	a	22 31		22 56		23 34
	d			22 57		
Frizinghall	d			22 59		
Bramley	d		22 39		23 27	
New Pudsey	d		22 43		23 31	
Bradford Interchange	a		22 52		23 39	
Bradford Forster Square	a			23 07		

Table T037-R

Mondays to Fridays
16 December to 15 May

Bradford and Shipley - Leeds

Miles	Miles			NT MX ◇	NT MO ◇	NT MX ◇	NT	NT	NT	NT	NT	GR 1 A	NT ◇	NT	NT	NT	NT	NT	NT ◇	NT ◇	NT	GR 1	NT
0	—	**Bradford Forster Square**	d				05 46	05 58	06 03			06 30			06 41	06 46	06 55				07 11		07 16
—	0	**Bradford Interchange**	d		00 01	00 27					06 18		06 31						07 01	07 07			
—	3½	New Pudsey	d	00 02	00 10						06 26		06 39						07 10	07 16			
—	5½	Bramley	d	00 05	00 13						06 30		06 43						07 13				
1¾	—	Frizinghall	d				05 49	06 01	06 06						06 44	06 49	06 58				07 14		07 19
2¾	—	**Shipley**	a				05 53	06 05	06 10						06 48	06 53	07 02				07 18		07 23
—	—		d					06 06		06 13		06u37		06 46			07 02	07 08				07u18	
5¾	—	Apperley Bridge	d					06 10									07 07						
9¼	—	Kirkstall Forge	d					06 15									07 11						
13½	9½	**Leeds** 10	a	00 14	00 21	00 46		06 24		06 27	06 39	06 52	06 52	07 02			07 20	07 22	07 23	07 31		07 33	

		NT	NT	NT ◇	NT	NT ◇	NT	NT	NT	NT	NT	NT ◇	NT	NT ◇	NT	NT ◇	NT	NT	NT ◇	NT ◇	NT ◇	NT	NT
Bradford Forster Square	d				07 30			07 41		07 47			07 54				08 11	08 16					08 31
Bradford Interchange	d	07 21		07 29		07 37			07 43			07 53		08 07						08 20	08 30		
New Pudsey	d	07 31		07 38		07 45			07 53			08 02		08 16						08 29	08 39		
Bramley	d			07 42		07 49			07 58			08 05								08 32	08 43		
Frizinghall	d				07 33			07 44		07 50			07 57				08 14	08 19					08 36
Shipley	a				07 37			07 48		07 54			08 01				08 18	08 23					08 41
	d		07 29		07 37		07 45				07 58		08 02		08 12	08 15			08 27			08 38	08 42
Apperley Bridge	d				07 42		07 49						08 06										08 46
Kirkstall Forge	d				07 47								08 11										08 51
Leeds 10	a	07 41	07 44	07 49	07 55	08 00	08 00		08 07		08 13	08 14	08 19	08 26	08 28	08 33			08 41	08 41	08 53	08 55	08 59

		NT	NT	NT ◇	NT	NT ◇	NT	NT	NT	NT ◇	NT ◇	NT	NT	NT	NT	NT ◇	NT	NT ◇	NT	NT	NT	NT ◇
Bradford Forster Square	d	08 41	08 46		09 00		09 07		09 16			09 30		09 41	09 46		10 00			10 11	10 16	
Bradford Interchange	d			09 02		09 07				09 21	09 30					09 53		10 07				10 23
New Pudsey	d			09 10		09 16				09 30	09 39					10 01		10 16				10 31
Bramley	d			09 13						09 33	09 43					10 04						10 34
Frizinghall	d	08 44	08 49		09 03		09 10		09 19			09 33		09 44	09 49		10 03			10 14	10 19	
Shipley	a	08 49	08 53		09 07		09 14		09 23			09 37		09 48	09 53		10 07			10 18	10 23	
	d				09 08			09 15				09 38	09 45				10 07		10 15			
Apperley Bridge	d				09 12							09 42					10 12					
Kirkstall Forge	d				09 17							09 47					10 17					
Leeds 10	a			09 22	09 26	09 27		09 29		09 43	09 52	09 57	10 01			10 13	10 26	10 27	10 29			10 43

		NT ◇	NT	NT	NT	NT ◇	NT	NT ◇	NT	NT ◇	NT	NT	NT ◇	NT	NT ◇	NT ◇	NT	NT	NT	NT	NT ◇	NT	NT ◇
Bradford Forster Square	d		10 30		10 41		10 46		11 00			11 11		11 16			11 30		11 41	11 46		12 00	
Bradford Interchange	d	10 30						10 53		11 07					11 21	11 31					11 56		12 07
New Pudsey	d	10 39						11 01		11 16					11 30	11 40					12 05		12 16
Bramley	d	10 43						11 04							11 33	11 44					12 08		
Frizinghall	d		10 33		10 44		10 49		11 03			11 14		11 19			11 34		11 44	11 49		12 03	
Shipley	a		10 37		10 48		10 53		11 07			11 18		11 23			11 38		11 48	11 53		12 07	
	d		10 38	10 45		10 50			11 07		11 15		11 19				11 38	11 45				12 08	
Apperley Bridge	d		10 42						11 12								11 43					12 12	
Kirkstall Forge	d		10 47						11 17								11 48					12 17	
Leeds 10	a	10 52	10 56	10 59		11 08		11 13	11 25	11 27	11 32		11 38		11 42	11 52	11 56	12 00			12 18	12 26	12 27

		NT	NT	NT ◇	NT	NT ◇	NT ◇	NT	NT	NT	NT	NT ◇	NT	NT ◇	NT	NT	NT ◇	NT	NT ◇	NT ◇	NT	NT
Bradford Forster Square	d		12 11		12 16			12 30		12 41	12 46		13 00			13 11		13 16			13 30	
Bradford Interchange	d					12 21	12 31					12 57		13 07					13 22	13 31		
New Pudsey	d					12 30	12 40					13 06		13 16					13 30	13 40		
Bramley	d					12 33	12 44					13 09							13 34	13 44		
Frizinghall	d		12 14		12 19			12 33		12 44	12 49		13 03			13 14		13 19			13 33	
Shipley	a		12 18		12 23			12 37		12 48	12 53		13 07			13 18		13 23			13 37	
	d	12 15		12 19				12 38	12 45				13 08		13 15		13 20				13 38	13 45
Apperley Bridge	d							12 42					13 12								13 42	
Kirkstall Forge	d							12 47					13 17								13 47	
Leeds 10	a	12 30		12 38		12 42	12 52	12 56	12 59			13 18	13 26	13 27	13 31		13 38		13 43	13 52	13 56	14 00

		NT	NT	NT ◇	NT	NT ◇	NT	NT	NT ◇	NT	NT ◇	NT ◇	NT	NT	NT	NT	NT ◇	NT	NT ◇	NT	NT	NT	NT ◇
Bradford Forster Square	d	13 41	13 46		14 00			14 11		14 16			14 30		14 41	14 46		15 00			15 11	15 16	
Bradford Interchange	d			13 56		14 08					14 21	14 30					14 52		15 07				15 21
New Pudsey	d			14 04		14 17					14 30	14 39					15 00		15 16				15 30
Bramley	d			14 07							14 33	14 43					15 04						15 34
Frizinghall	d	13 44	13 49		14 03			14 14		14 19			14 33		14 44	14 49		15 03			15 14	15 19	
Shipley	a	13 48	13 53		14 07			14 18		14 23			14 37		14 48	14 53		15 07			15 18	15 23	
	d				14 08		14 15		14 20				14 38	14 45				15 08		15 15			
Apperley Bridge	d				14 12								14 42					15 12					
Kirkstall Forge	d				14 17								14 47					15 17					
Leeds 10	a			14 18	14 25	14 27	14 30		14 37		14 42	14 52	14 56	14 59			15 13	15 25	15 27	15 31			15 43

A West Riding Limited

Table T037-R

Mondays to Fridays

16 December to 15 May

Bradford and Shipley - Leeds

		NT ◇		NT	NT	NT	NT ◇ 🚲	NT	NT ◇	NT	NT ◇	NT		NT	NT ◇	NT	NT ◇	NT ◇	NT	NT	NT	NT		NT ◇	NT
Bradford Forster Square	d			15 30		15 41		15 46		16 00				16 11		16 16			16 30		16 41	16 46			17 00
Bradford Interchange	d	15 30							15 57		16 07						16 21	16 30						16 55	
New Pudsey	d	15 39							16 05		16 16						16 30	16 39						17 04	
Bramley	d	15 43							16 08								16 33	16 43						17 07	
Frizinghall	d			15 33		15 44		15 49		16 03				16 14		16 19			16 33		16 44	16 49			17 03
Shipley	a			15 37		15 48		15 53		16 07				16 18		16 23			16 37		16 48	16 53			17 07
	d			15 38	15 45		15 51			16 08		16 15			16 20				16 38	16 45					17 08
Apperley Bridge	d			15 42						16 12									16 42						17 12
Kirkstall Forge	d			15 47						16 17									16 47						17 17
Leeds 10	a	15 52		15 56	15 59		16 05		16 18	16 25	16 27	16 29			16 39		16 42	16 52	16 56	16 59				17 19	17 25

		NT ◇	NT	NT	NT ◇ 🚲	NT	NT ◇	NT ◇		NT	NT	NT	NT	NT ◇	NT	NT ◇	NT	NT		NT	NT ◇	NT ◇	NT	NT	NT
Bradford Forster Square	d			17 11		17 16				17 30		17 41	17 49		18 00			18 11		18 16			18 30		18 41
Bradford Interchange	d	17 07					17 22	17 30						17 59		18 07					18 25	18 31			
New Pudsey	d	17 16					17 31	17 39						18 07		18 16					18 33	18 40			
Bramley	d						17 34	17 43						18 11							18 36	18 44			
Frizinghall	d			17 14		17 19				17 33		17 44	17 52		18 03			18 14		18 19			18 33		18 44
Shipley	a			17 18		17 23				17 37		17 48	17 56		18 07			18 18		18 23			18 37		18 48
	d		17 15		17 20					17 38	17 45				18 08		18 15						18 38	18 45	
Apperley Bridge	d									17 42					18 12								18 42		
Kirkstall Forge	d									17 47					18 17								18 47		
Leeds 10	a	17 29	17 31		17 39		17 43	17 52		17 57	18 01			18 21	18 26	18 27	18 29				18 43	18 52	18 57	18 59	

		NT ◇ 🚲	NT	NT ◇		NT	NT ◇	NT	NT	NT ◇	NT	NT ◇	NT ◇	NT		NT	NT	NT	NT ◇	NT ◇	NT	NT	NT	NT ◇	
Bradford Forster Square	d		18 46			19 00			19 11		19 16			19 30			19 41	19 46				20 11	20 16		
Bradford Interchange	d			18 58			19 07					19 26	19 31						19 58	20 07				20 21	
New Pudsey	d			19 07			19 16					19 35	19 40						20 07	20 16				20 29	
Bramley	d			19 10								19 38	19 44						20 10					20 35	
Frizinghall	d		18 49			19 03			19 14		19 19			19 33			19 44	19 49				20 14	20 19		
Shipley	a		18 53			19 07			19 18		19 23			19 37			19 48	19 53				20 18	20 23		
	d	18 50				19 08		19 15		19 20				19 38		19 46					20 16				
Apperley Bridge	d					19 12								19 42							20 21				
Kirkstall Forge	d					19 17								19 47											
Leeds 10	a	19 08		19 19		19 25	19 27	19 29		19 38		19 47	19 53	19 56		20 01			20 19	20 26	20 32			20 43	

		NT ◇	NT	NT	NT ◇ 🚲	NT	NT ◇	NT ◇	NT	NT		NT	NT ◇	NT	NT ◇	NT	NT ◇	NT ◇	NT ◇	NT		NT	NT	NT ◇	NT ◇ 🚲
Bradford Forster Square	d		20 30			20 48				21 11		21 16		21 28								22 11	22 16		
Bradford Interchange	d	20 30					20 53	21 07					21 22		21 31		21 53		22 07					22 22	
New Pudsey	d	20 39					21 01	21 16					21 30		21 39		22 01		22 16					22 31	
Bramley	d	20 43					21 04						21 34		21 43		22 04							22 34	
Frizinghall	d		20 33			20 51				21 14		21 19		21 31								22 14	22 19		
Shipley	a		20 37			20 55				21 18		21 23		21 35								22 18	22 23		
	d			20 45	20 51				21 15							21 45		22 06		22 16					22 31
Apperley Bridge	d			20 49					21 19							21 49				22 20					
Kirkstall Forge	d			20 54					21 24							21 54				22 25					
Leeds 10	a	20 52		21 02	21 06		21 14	21 28	21 32				21 43		21 53	22 02	22 13	22 22	22 27	22 34				22 45	22 48

		NT	NT ◇	NT 🚲	NT ◇	NT ◇		NT	NT	NT	NT	NT	NT ◇
Bradford Forster Square	d	22 25							23 11	23 16			
Bradford Interchange	d		22 35		22 53	23 07					23 27	23 34	23 53
New Pudsey	d		22 43		23 01	23 16					23 37	23 42	00 02
Bramley	d		22 47		23 04						23 41	23 46	00 05
Frizinghall	d	22 28							23 14	23 19			
Shipley	a	22 32							23 18	23 23			
	d			22 55				23 17					
Apperley Bridge	d							23 21					
Kirkstall Forge	d							23 26					
Leeds 10	a		22 57	23 12	23 13	23 26		23 34			23 50	23 55	00 14

Saturdays

21 December to 16 May

		NT ◇	NT ◇	NT	NT	NT	NT	NT	GR ■ 1 A	NT ◇		NT	NT	NT	NT	NT	NT ◇	NT ◇	NT	GR ■ 1		NT	NT	NT	NT ◇
Bradford Forster Square	d			05 46	05 58	06 03			06 30				06 41	06 46	06 55				07 11			07 16			
Bradford Interchange	d		00 27					06 18		06 31							07 01	07 07					07 21		07 29
New Pudsey	d	00 02						06 26		06 39							07 10	07 16					07 31		07 38
Bramley	d	00 05						06 30		06 43							07 13								07 42
Frizinghall	d			05 49	06 01	06 06							06 44	06 49	06 58				07 14			07 19			
Shipley	a			05 53	06 05	06 10							06 48	06 53	07 02				07 18			07 23			
	d				06 06		06 13		06u37			06 46			07 02	07 08				07u19				07 29	
Apperley Bridge	d				06 10										07 07										
Kirkstall Forge	d				06 15										07 11										
Leeds 10	a	00 14	00 46		06 24		06 27	06 39	06 52	06 52		07 02			07 20	07 22	07 23	07 31		07 33			07 41	07 44	07 49

A West Riding Limited

Table T037-R

Saturdays

21 December to 16 May

Bradford and Shipley - Leeds

		NT		NT ◇	NT	NT	NT	NT	NT ◇	NT	NT ◇	NT		NT	NT	NT	NT ◇	NT ◇	NT ◇	NT	NT	NT		NT	NT ◇
Bradford Forster Square	d	07 30				07 41	07 47			07 54				08 11		08 16					08 31	08 41		08 46	
Bradford Interchange	d			07 37					07 53		08 07							08 20	08 30						09 02
New Pudsey	d			07 45					08 02		08 16							08 29	08 39						09 10
Bramley	d			07 49					08 05									08 32	08 43						09 13
Frizinghall	d	07 33				07 44	07 50			07 57				08 14		08 19					08 36	08 44		08 49	
Shipley	a	07 37				07 48	07 54			08 01				08 18		08 23					08 41	08 49		08 53	
	d	07 37			07 45			07 58		08 02		08 12			08 19		08 27			08 38	08 42				
Apperley Bridge	d	07 42			07 49					08 06											08 46				
Kirkstall Forge	d	07 47								08 11											08 51				
Leeds 10	a	07 55		08 00	08 00			08 13	08 14	08 19	08 26	08 28			08 35		08 41	08 41	08 53	08 55	08 59				09 22

		NT	NT ◇	NT	NT	NT	NT ◇	NT ◇		NT	NT	NT	NT	NT ◇	NT	NT ◇	NT	NT		NT ◇ 🚲	NT	NT ◇	NT ◇	NT	NT
Bradford Forster Square	d	09 00		09 07		09 16				09 30		09 41	09 46		10 00			10 11			10 16			10 30	
Bradford Interchange	d		09 07				09 22	09 30						09 53		10 07						10 22	10 30		
New Pudsey	d		09 16				09 31	09 39						10 01		10 16						10 30	10 39		
Bramley	d						09 34	09 43						10 04								10 34	10 43		
Frizinghall	d	09 03		09 10		09 19				09 33		09 44	09 49		10 03			10 14			10 19			10 33	
Shipley	a	09 07		09 14		09 23				09 37		09 48	09 53		10 07			10 18			10 23			10 37	
	d	09 08			09 15					09 38	09 45				10 07		10 15			10 19				10 38	10 45
Apperley Bridge	d	09 12								09 42					10 12									10 42	
Kirkstall Forge	d	09 17								09 47					10 17									10 47	
Leeds 10	a	09 26	09 27		09 29		09 43	09 52		09 57	10 01			10 13	10 26	10 27	10 29			10 37		10 43	10 52	10 56	10 59

		NT	NT	NT ◇		NT	NT ◇	NT	NT	NT ◇	NT	NT ◇	NT ◇	NT		NT	NT	NT ◇ 🚲	NT	NT ◇	NT	NT ◇	NT	NT	
Bradford Forster Square	d	10 41	10 46			11 00			11 11		11 16			11 30			11 41		11 46		12 00			12 11	
Bradford Interchange	d			10 53			11 07					11 21	11 31							11 56		12 07			
New Pudsey	d			11 01			11 16					11 30	11 40							12 05		12 16			
Bramley	d			11 04								11 33	11 44							12 08					
Frizinghall	d	10 44	10 49			11 03			11 14		11 19			11 34			11 44		11 49		12 03			12 14	
Shipley	a	10 48	10 53			11 07			11 18		11 23			11 38			11 48		11 53		12 07			12 18	
	d					11 07		11 15		11 19				11 38		11 45		11 50			12 08		12 15		
Apperley Bridge	d					11 12								11 43							12 12				
Kirkstall Forge	d					11 17								11 48							12 17				
Leeds 10	a			11 13		11 25	11 27	11 32		11 38		11 42	11 52	11 56		12 00		12 04		12 18	12 26	12 27	12 30		

		NT ◇	NT	NT ◇	NT ◇	NT	NT	NT	NT	NT ◇		NT	NT ◇	NT	NT	NT ◇ 🚲	NT	NT ◇	NT ◇	NT		NT	NT	NT	NT ◇
Bradford Forster Square	d		12 16			12 30		12 41	12 46			13 00			13 11		13 16			13 30			13 41	13 46	
Bradford Interchange	d			12 21	12 31					12 57			13 07					13 21	13 31						13 56
New Pudsey	d			12 30	12 40					13 06			13 16					13 30	13 40						14 04
Bramley	d			12 33	12 44					13 09								13 33	13 44						14 07
Frizinghall	d		12 19			12 33		12 44	12 49			13 03			13 14		13 19			13 33			13 44	13 49	
Shipley	a		12 23			12 37		12 48	12 53			13 07			13 18		13 23			13 37			13 48	13 53	
	d	12 19				12 38	12 45					13 08		13 15		13 20				13 38		13 45			
Apperley Bridge	d					12 42						13 12								13 42					
Kirkstall Forge	d					12 47						13 17								13 47					
Leeds 10	a	12 38		12 42	12 52	12 56	12 59			13 18		13 26	13 27	13 31		13 38		13 42	13 52	13 56		14 00			14 18

		NT	NT ◇	NT	NT	NT ◇		NT	NT ◇	NT ◇	NT	NT	NT	NT	NT ◇	NT		NT ◇	NT	NT	NT	NT ◇	NT ◇	NT	NT
Bradford Forster Square	d	14 00			14 11			14 16			14 30		14 41	14 46		15 00				15 11	15 16			15 30	
Bradford Interchange	d		14 07						14 21	14 30					14 52			15 07				15 24	15 30		
New Pudsey	d		14 16						14 30	14 39					15 00			15 16				15 32	15 39		
Bramley	d								14 33	14 43					15 04							15 36	15 43		
Frizinghall	d	14 03			14 14			14 19			14 33		14 44	14 49		15 03				15 14	15 19			15 33	
Shipley	a	14 07			14 18			14 23			14 37		14 48	14 53		15 07				15 18	15 23			15 37	
	d	14 08		14 15		14 20					14 38	14 45				15 08			15 15					15 38	15 45
Apperley Bridge	d	14 12									14 42					15 12								15 42	
Kirkstall Forge	d	14 17									14 47					15 17								15 47	
Leeds 10	a	14 25	14 27	14 30		14 37			14 42	14 52	14 56	14 59			15 13	15 25		15 27	15 31			15 45	15 52	15 56	15 59

		NT		NT ◇ 🚲	NT	NT ◇	NT	NT ◇	NT	NT	NT ◇	NT		NT ◇	NT ◇	NT	NT	NT	NT	NT ◇	NT	NT ◇		NT	NT
Bradford Forster Square	d	15 41			15 46		16 00			16 11		16 16				16 30		16 41	16 46		17 00				17 11
Bradford Interchange	d					15 57		16 07						16 21	16 30					16 55		17 07			
New Pudsey	d					16 05		16 16						16 30	16 39					17 04		17 16			
Bramley	d					16 08								16 33	16 43					17 07					
Frizinghall	d	15 44			15 49		16 03			16 14		16 19				16 33		16 44	16 49		17 03				17 14
Shipley	a	15 48			15 53		16 07			16 18		16 23				16 37		16 48	16 53		17 07				17 18
	d			15 51			16 08		16 15		16 20					16 38	16 45				17 08			17 15	
Apperley Bridge	d						16 12									16 42					17 12				
Kirkstall Forge	d						16 17									16 47					17 17				
Leeds 10	a			16 05		16 18	16 25	16 27	16 29		16 39			16 43	16 52	16 56	16 59			17 19	17 25	17 28		17 31	

Table T037-R

Bradford and Shipley - Leeds

Saturdays

21 December to 16 May

		NT	NT	NT	NT	NT	NT	NT	NT	NT	NT	NT	NT	NT	NT	NT	NT	NT	NT	NT	NT	NT
		◇ H		◇	◇					◇		◇				◇	◇				◇ H	
Bradford Forster Square	d		17 16			17 30		17 41	17 49		18 00			18 11	18 16			18 30		18 41		18 46
Bradford Interchange	d			17 22	17 30					17 59		18 07				18 25	18 31					
New Pudsey	d			17 31	17 39					18 07		18 16				18 33	18 40					
Bramley	d			17 34	17 43					18 11						18 36	18 44					
Frizinghall	d		17 19			17 33		17 44	17 52		18 03			18 14	18 19			18 33		18 44		18 49
Shipley	a		17 23			17 37		17 48	17 56		18 07			18 18	18 23			18 37		18 48		18 53
	d	17 20				17 38	17 45				18 08		18 15					18 38	18 45		18 50	
Apperley Bridge	d					17 42					18 12							18 42				
Kirkstall Forge	d					17 47					18 17							18 47				
Leeds	a	17 39		17 43	17 52	17 57	18 01			18 21	18 26	18 27	18 29			18 45	18 52	18 57	18 59		19 08	

		NT	NT	NT	NT	NT	NT	NT	NT	NT	NT	NT	NT	NT	NT	NT	NT	NT	NT	NT	NT	NT	NT
		◇		◇			◇		◇	◇					◇	◇				◇	◇		
Bradford Forster Square	d		19 00			19 11		19 16			19 30		19 41	19 46				20 11	20 16			20 30	
Bradford Interchange	d	18 58		19 07					19 26	19 31					19 58	20 07				20 21	20 30		
New Pudsey	d	19 07		19 16					19 35	19 40					20 07	20 16				20 30	20 39		
Bramley	d	19 10							19 38	19 44					20 10					20 33	20 43		
Frizinghall	d		19 03			19 14		19 19			19 33		19 44	19 49				20 14	20 19			20 33	
Shipley	a		19 07			19 18		19 23			19 37		19 48	19 53				20 18	20 23			20 37	
	d		19 08		19 15		19 20				19 38	19 46					20 16						20 45
Apperley Bridge	d		19 12								19 42						20 21						20 49
Kirkstall Forge	d		19 17								19 47												20 54
Leeds	a	19 19	19 25	19 27	19 29		19 38		19 47	19 53	19 56	20 01			20 19	20 26	20 32			20 43	20 52		21 02

		NT	NT	NT	NT	NT	NT	NT	NT	NT	NT	NT	NT	NT	NT	NT	NT	NT	NT	NT	NT	NT	NT
		◇ H		◇	◇				◇		◇		◇	◇	◇				◇	◇ H		◇	H
Bradford Forster Square	d		20 48				21 11	21 16		21 28							22 11	22 16			22 25		
Bradford Interchange	d			20 53	21 07				21 22		21 31		21 53		22 07				22 21			22 30	
New Pudsey	d			21 01	21 16				21 30		21 39		22 01		22 16				22 30			22 39	
Bramley	d			21 04					21 34		21 43		22 04						22 33			22 43	
Frizinghall	d		20 51				21 14	21 19		21 31							22 14	22 19			22 28		
Shipley	a		20 55				21 18	21 23		21 35							22 18	22 23			22 32		
	d	20 51				21 15						21 45		22 06		22 16				22 31			22 54
Apperley Bridge	d					21 19						21 49				22 20							
Kirkstall Forge	d					21 24						21 54				22 25							
Leeds	a	21 09		21 14	21 28	21 32			21 43		21 53	22 02	22 13	22 22	22 26	22 34			22 42	22 48		22 52	23 11

		NT	NT	NT	NT	NT	NT	NT	NT
		◇	◇				A		◇
Bradford Forster Square	d				23 11	23 16			
Bradford Interchange	d	22 53	23 04				23 27	23 34	23 53
New Pudsey	d	23 01	23 13				23 37	23 42	00 02
Bramley	d	23 04					23 41	23 46	00 05
Frizinghall	d				23 14	23 19			
Shipley	a				23 18	23 23			
	d			23 17					
Apperley Bridge	d			23 21					
Kirkstall Forge	d			23 26					
Leeds	a	23 13	23 23	23 34			23 50	23 55	00 14

Sundays

15 December to 10 May

		NT	NT	NT	NT	NT	NT	NT	NT	NT	NT	NT	NT	NT	NT	NT	NT	NT	NT	NT	NT	NT	NT
		◇		◇						◇	◇							◇	◇				
Bradford Forster Square	d				09 13		09 38		09 48			10 13		10 38			10 48			11 13		11 38	
Bradford Interchange	d			09 14				09 44		10 00	10 13				10 44			10 59	11 18				11 44
New Pudsey	d	00 02		09 23				09 53		10 09	10 22				10 53			11 08	11 26				11 53
Bramley	d	00 05						09 56		10 13					10 56			11 11					11 56
Frizinghall	d				09 16		09 41		09 51			10 16		10 41			10 51			11 16		11 41	
Shipley	a				09 20		09 45		09 55			10 20		10 45			10 55			11 20		11 45	
	d		09 00		09 21	09 40						10 21	10 40			10 49				11 21	11 40		
Apperley Bridge	d				09 26							10 26								11 26			
Kirkstall Forge	d				09 31							10 31								11 32			
Leeds	a	00 14	09 14	09 35	09 39	09 54		10 04		10 21	10 32	10 40	10 54		11 04	11 06		11 19	11 38	11 40	11 54		12 04

		NT	NT	NT	NT	NT	NT	NT	NT	NT	NT	NT	NT	NT	NT	NT	NT	NT	NT	NT	NT	NT	NT
		◇		◇	◇					◇		◇	◇						◇	◇			
Bradford Forster Square	d		11 48			12 13		12 38			12 48			13 13		13 38		13 48			14 13		14 38
Bradford Interchange	d			11 59	12 16				12 44			12 59	13 13				13 44		13 59	14 11			
New Pudsey	d			12 08	12 26				12 53			13 08	13 22				13 53		14 08	14 20			
Bramley	d			12 12					12 56			13 11					13 58		14 11				
Frizinghall	d		11 51			12 16		12 41			12 51			13 16		13 41		13 51			14 16		14 41
Shipley	a		11 55			12 20		12 45			12 55			13 20		13 45		13 55			14 20		14 45
	d	11 49				12 21	12 40			12 48				13 20	13 40						14 21	14 40	
Apperley Bridge	d					12 26								13 25							14 26		
Kirkstall Forge	d					12 31								13 30							14 31		
Leeds	a	12 06		12 20	12 36	12 40	12 54		13 04	13 07		13 19	13 33	13 39	13 54		14 06		14 20	14 31	14 40	14 54	

A from 22 February

Table T037-R

Bradford and Shipley - Leeds

Sundays

15 December to 10 May

		NT	NT	NT	NT	NT	NT	NT	NT	NT	NT	NT	NT	NT	NT	NT	NT	NT	NT	NT	NT	NT	NT
			◇		◇	◇	◇						◇	◇							◇	◇	
Bradford Forster Square	d			14 48				15 13		15 38		15 48			16 13			16 38		16 48			17 13
Bradford Interchange	d	14 44			15 02	15 14					15 44		15 59	16 13					16 44		16 59	17 13	
New Pudsey	d	14 53			15 11	15 23					15 53		16 10	16 22					16 53		17 08	17 22	
Bramley	d	14 56			15 15						15 56		16 15						16 56		17 11		
Frizinghall	d			14 51				15 16		15 41		15 51			16 16			16 41		16 51			17 16
Shipley	a			14 55				15 20		15 45		15 55			16 20			16 45		16 55			17 20
	d		14 49				15 17	15 21	15 40						16 21	16 26	16 40						17 21
Apperley Bridge	d							15 26							16 26								17 26
Kirkstall Forge	d							15 31							16 31								17 31
Leeds	a	15 04	15 09		15 23	15 35	15 37	15 40	15 54		16 04		16 25	16 33	16 40	16 43	16 54		17 04		17 19	17 33	17 40

		NT	NT	NT	NT	NT	NT	NT	NT	NT	NT	NT	NT	NT	NT	NT	NT	NT	NT	NT	NT	NT
		◇			◇			◇	◇	◇						◇	◇		◇			
Bradford Forster Square	d			17 38			17 48				18 14		18 38		18 48			19 13			19 38	
Bradford Interchange	d					17 44		17 59		18 14				18 45		18 59	19 14					19 44
New Pudsey	d					17 53		18 08		18 23				18 54		19 08	19 22					19 53
Bramley	d					17 56		18 11						18 57		19 13						19 56
Frizinghall	d			17 41			17 51				18 17		18 41		18 51			19 16			19 41	
Shipley	a			17 45			17 55				18 21		18 45		18 55			19 20			19 45	
	d	17 26	17 42		17 47				18 18		18 22	18 40						19 21	19 25	19 40		
Apperley Bridge	d										18 27							19 26				
Kirkstall Forge	d										18 32							19 31				
Leeds	a	17 45	17 56		18 05	18 06		18 19	18 32	18 35	18 41	18 54		19 05		19 23	19 32	19 40	19 45	19 54		20 03

		NT	NT	NT	NT	NT	NT	NT	NT	NT	NT	NT	NT	NT	NT	NT	NT	NT	NT	NT	NT	NT	NT
		◇		◇	◇						◇	◇		◇				◇		◇		◇	
Bradford Forster Square	d		19 48			20 13		20 38		20 48			21 13		21 38				21 48		22 13		
Bradford Interchange	d			19 59	20 13				20 44		21 00	21 13				21 44				22 00		22 20	
New Pudsey	d			20 10	20 22				20 53		21 10	21 22				21 53				22 09		22 28	
Bramley	d			20 13					20 56		21 14					21 56				22 12			
Frizinghall	d		19 51			20 16		20 41		20 51			21 16		21 41				21 51		22 16		
Shipley	a		19 55			20 20		20 45		20 55			21 20		21 45				21 55		22 20		
	d	19 50				20 21	20 40						21 21	21 38			21 49	21 54			22 21		22 39
Apperley Bridge	d					20 26							21 26								22 26		
Kirkstall Forge	d					20 31							21 31								22 31		
Leeds	a	20 08		20 21	20 33	20 40	20 54		21 04		21 24	21 33	21 40	21 55		22 04	22 05	22 10		22 24	22 40	22 41	22 54

		NT	NT	NT	NT	NT	NT	NT	NT
					◇	◇			
Bradford Forster Square	d	22 38		22 48			23 15		
Bradford Interchange	d		22 46		22 59	23 14			23 44
New Pudsey	d		22 57		23 08	23 22			23 53
Bramley	d		23 01		23 11				23 56
Frizinghall	d	22 41		22 51			23 18		
Shipley	a	22 45		22 55			23 22		
	d						23 23	23 42	
Apperley Bridge	d						23 29		
Kirkstall Forge	d						23 35		
Leeds	a		23 10		23 22	23 34	23 44	23 57	00 04

Table T038-F

Mondays to Fridays
16 December to 15 May

Leeds and Bradford - Ilkley

Miles	Miles			NT	NT	NT	NT	NT	NT	NT	NT	NT		NT	NT	NT	NT	NT	NT	NT	NT	NT		NT	NT
0	—	**Leeds**	37 d		06 00	06 38		07 03		07 29	07 34			07 58		08 32		09 03		09 33		10 03			10 33
4¼	—	Kirkstall Forge	37 d																						
—	0	**Bradford Forster Square**	37 d	05 46			06 46		07 16			07 47			08 16		08 46		09 16		09 46			10 16	
—	1¾	Frizinghall	37 d	05 49			06 49		07 19			07 50			08 19		08 49		09 19		09 49			10 19	
—	2¾	Shipley	37 d	05 53			06 53		07 24			07 55			08 23		08 53		09 23		09 53			10 23	
—	4¼	Baildon	d	05 56			06 56		07 27			07 58			08 26		08 56		09 26		09 56			10 26	
10¾	7½	Guiseley	d	06 02	06 12	06 50	07 02	07 15	07 32	07 41	07 48	08 04		08 10	08 32	08 45	09 02	09 15	09 32	09 45	10 02	10 15		10 32	10 45
11½	8¾	Menston	d	06 05	06 15	06 53	07 05	07 18	07 35	07 44	07 52	08 07		08 13	08 35	08 48	09 05	09 18	09 35	09 48	10 05	10 18		10 35	10 48
13	10¼	Burley-in-Wharfedale	d	06 08	06 18	06 56	07 08	07 21	07 38	07 47	07 56	08 10		08 18	08 38	08 51	09 08	09 21	09 38	09 51	10 08	10 21		10 38	10 51
15¼	12½	Ben Rhydding	d	06 11	06 21	06 59	07 11	07 24	07 42	07 50	07 59	08 14		08 21	08 41	08 55	09 11	09 24	09 41	09 54	10 11	10 24		10 41	10 54
16¾	13½	**Ilkley**	a	06 15	06 28	07 06	07 16	07 31	07 46	07 57	08 05	08 18		08 27	08 47	09 02	09 17	09 31	09 47	10 01	10 17	10 31		10 47	11 01

		NT	NT	NT	NT	NT	NT	NT		NT	NT	NT	NT	NT	NT	NT	NT	NT		NT	NT	NT	NT	NT	NT
Leeds	37 d		11 03		11 33		12 03			12 33		13 03		13 33		14 03		14 33			15 03		15 33		16 03
Kirkstall Forge	37 d																								
Bradford Forster Square	37 d	10 46		11 16		11 46		12 16			12 46		13 16		13 46		14 16			14 46		15 16		15 46	
Frizinghall	37 d	10 49		11 19		11 49		12 19			12 49		13 19		13 49		14 19			14 49		15 19		15 49	
Shipley	37 d	10 53		11 23		11 53		12 23			12 53		13 23		13 53		14 23			14 53		15 23		15 53	
Baildon	d	10 56		11 26		11 56		12 26			12 56		13 26		13 56		14 26			14 56		15 26		15 56	
Guiseley	d	11 02	11 15	11 32	11 45	12 02	12 15	12 32		12 45	13 02	13 15	13 32	13 45	14 02	14 15	14 32	14 45		15 02	15 15	15 32	15 45	16 02	16 15
Menston	d	11 05	11 18	11 35	11 48	12 05	12 18	12 35		12 48	13 05	13 18	13 35	13 48	14 05	14 18	14 35	14 48		15 05	15 18	15 35	15 48	16 05	16 18
Burley-in-Wharfedale	d	11 08	11 21	11 38	11 51	12 08	12 21	12 38		12 51	13 08	13 21	13 38	13 51	14 08	14 21	14 38	14 51		15 08	15 21	15 38	15 51	16 08	16 21
Ben Rhydding	d	11 11	11 24	11 41	11 54	12 11	12 24	12 41		12 54	13 11	13 24	13 41	13 54	14 11	14 24	14 41	14 54		15 11	15 24	15 41	15 54	16 11	16 24
Ilkley	a	11 17	11 31	11 47	12 00	12 17	12 31	12 47		13 00	13 17	13 31	13 47	14 01	14 17	14 31	14 47	15 01		15 17	15 31	15 47	16 01	16 18	16 31

		NT	NT	NT		NT	NT	NT	NT	NT	NT	NT	NT	NT		NT	NT	NT	NT	NT	NT	NT	NT	NT	
Leeds	37 d		16 33			17 02	17 15		17 32	17 46		18 04		18 34			19 04		19 33		20 04		20 33	21 03	
Kirkstall Forge	37 d																								
Bradford Forster Square	37 d	16 16		16 46				17 16			17 49		18 16			18 46		19 16		19 46		20 16			
Frizinghall	37 d	16 19		16 49				17 19			17 52		18 19			18 49		19 19		19 49		20 19			
Shipley	37 d	16 23		16 53				17 24			17 56		18 23			18 54		19 24		19 53		20 23			
Baildon	d	16 26		16 56				17 27			17 59		18 26			18 57		19 27		19 56		20 26			
Guiseley	d	16 32	16 45	17 02		17 15	17 28	17 35	17 45	17 59	18 09	18 16	18 32	18 46		19 03	19 16	19 33	19 45	20 02	20 16	20 32	20 45	21 15	
Menston	d	16 35	16 48	17 05		17 18	17 31	17 38	17 49	18 02	18 12	18 19	18 35	18 49		19 06	19 19	19 36	19 48	20 05	20 19	20 35	20 48	21 18	
Burley-in-Wharfedale	d	16 38	16 51	17 08		17 21	17 34	17 41	17 53	18 05	18 15	18 23	18 38	18 52		19 09	19 22	19 39	19 51	20 08	20 22	20 38	20 51	21 21	
Ben Rhydding	d	16 41	16 54	17 11		17 24	17 37	17 45	17 57	18 09	18 18	18 27	18 41	18 55		19 12	19 25	19 42	19 54	20 11	20 25	20 41	20 54	21 24	
Ilkley	a	16 48	17 01	17 17		17 31	17 44	17 50	18 04	18 16	18 24	18 34	18 47	19 02		19 18	19 32	19 49	20 01	20 17	20 32	20 47	21 01	21 31	

		NT	NT	NT	NT	NT	NT
Leeds	37 d		21 33		22 33		23 34
Kirkstall Forge	37 d						
Bradford Forster Square	37 d	21 16		22 16		23 16	
Frizinghall	37 d	21 19		22 19		23 19	
Shipley	37 d	21 23		22 23		23 24	
Baildon	d	21 26		22 26		23 27	
Guiseley	d	21 32	21 45	22 32	22 45	23 32	23 46
Menston	d	21 35	21 48	22 35	22 48	23 35	23 49
Burley-in-Wharfedale	d	21 37	21 51	22 38	22 51	23 38	23 52
Ben Rhydding	d	21 41	21 54	22 41	22 54	23 42	23 55
Ilkley	a	21 46	22 01	22 47	23 01	23 47	00 02

Saturdays
21 December to 16 May

		NT	NT	NT	NT	NT	NT	NT	NT	NT		NT	NT	NT	NT	NT	NT	NT	NT	NT		NT	NT	NT	NT
Leeds	37 d		06 00	06 38		07 03		07 29	07 34			07 58		08 32		09 03		09 33		10 03			10 33		11 03
Kirkstall Forge	37 d																								
Bradford Forster Square	37 d	05 46			06 46		07 16			07 47			08 16		08 46		09 16		09 46			10 16		10 46	
Frizinghall	37 d	05 49			06 49		07 19			07 50			08 19		08 49		09 19		09 49			10 19		10 49	
Shipley	37 d	05 53			06 53		07 24			07 55			08 23		08 53		09 23		09 53			10 23		10 53	
Baildon	d	05 56			06 56		07 27			07 58			08 26		08 56		09 26		09 56			10 26		10 56	
Guiseley	d	06 02	06 12	06 50	07 02	07 15	07 32	07 41	07 48	08 04		08 10	08 32	08 45	09 02	09 15	09 32	09 45	10 02	10 15		10 32	10 45	11 02	11 15
Menston	d	06 05	06 15	06 53	07 05	07 18	07 35	07 44	07 52	08 07		08 13	08 35	08 48	09 05	09 18	09 35	09 48	10 05	10 18		10 35	10 48	11 05	11 18
Burley-in-Wharfedale	d	06 08	06 18	06 56	07 08	07 21	07 38	07 47	07 56	08 10		08 18	08 38	08 51	09 08	09 21	09 38	09 51	10 08	10 21		10 38	10 51	11 08	11 21
Ben Rhydding	d	06 11	06 21	06 59	07 11	07 24	07 42	07 50	07 59	08 14		08 21	08 41	08 55	09 11	09 24	09 41	09 54	10 11	10 24		10 41	10 54	11 11	11 24
Ilkley	a	06 15	06 28	07 06	07 16	07 31	07 46	07 57	08 05	08 18		08 27	08 47	09 02	09 17	09 31	09 47	10 01	10 17	10 31		10 47	11 01	11 17	11 31

		NT	NT	NT	NT	NT		NT	NT	NT	NT	NT	NT	NT	NT	NT		NT	NT	NT	NT	NT	NT	NT	NT
Leeds	37 d		11 33		12 03			12 33		13 03		13 33		14 03		14 33			15 03		15 33		16 03		16 33
Kirkstall Forge	37 d																								
Bradford Forster Square	37 d	11 16		11 46		12 16			12 46		13 16		13 46		14 16			14 46		15 16		15 46		16 16	
Frizinghall	37 d	11 19		11 49		12 19			12 49		13 19		13 49		14 19			14 49		15 19		15 49		16 19	
Shipley	37 d	11 23		11 53		12 23			12 53		13 23		13 53		14 23			14 53		15 23		15 53		16 23	
Baildon	d	11 26		11 56		12 26			12 56		13 26		13 56		14 26			14 56		15 26		15 56		16 26	
Guiseley	d	11 32	11 45	12 02	12 15	12 32		12 45	13 02	13 15	13 32	13 45	14 02	14 15	14 32	14 45		15 02	15 15	15 32	15 45	16 02	16 15	16 32	16 45
Menston	d	11 35	11 48	12 05	12 18	12 35		12 48	13 05	13 18	13 35	13 48	14 05	14 18	14 35	14 48		15 05	15 18	15 35	15 48	16 05	16 18	16 35	16 48
Burley-in-Wharfedale	d	11 38	11 51	12 08	12 21	12 38		12 51	13 08	13 21	13 38	13 51	14 08	14 21	14 38	14 51		15 08	15 21	15 38	15 51	16 08	16 21	16 38	16 51
Ben Rhydding	d	11 41	11 54	12 11	12 24	12 41		12 54	13 11	13 24	13 41	13 54	14 11	14 24	14 41	14 54		15 11	15 24	15 41	15 54	16 11	16 24	16 41	16 54
Ilkley	a	11 47	12 00	12 17	12 31	12 47		13 00	13 17	13 31	13 47	14 01	14 17	14 31	14 47	15 01		15 17	15 31	15 47	16 01	16 18	16 31	16 48	17 01

		NT		NT	NT	NT	NT	NT	NT	NT	NT	NT		NT	NT	NT	NT	NT	NT	NT	NT	NT		NT	NT
Leeds	37 d			17 02	17 15		17 32	17 46		18 04		18 34			19 04		19 33		20 04		20 33	21 03			21 33
Kirkstall Forge	37 d																								
Bradford Forster Square	37 d	16 46				17 16			17 49		18 16			18 46		19 16		19 46		20 16				21 16	
Frizinghall	37 d	16 49				17 19			17 52		18 19			18 49		19 19		19 49		20 19				21 19	
Shipley	37 d	16 53				17 24			17 56		18 23			18 54		19 24		19 53		20 23				21 23	
Baildon	d	16 56				17 27			17 59		18 26			18 57		19 27		19 56		20 26				21 26	
Guiseley	d	17 02		17 15	17 28	17 35	17 45	17 59	18 09	18 16	18 32	18 46		19 03	19 16	19 33	19 45	20 02	20 16	20 32	20 45	21 15		21 32	21 45
Menston	d	17 05		17 18	17 31	17 38	17 49	18 02	18 12	18 19	18 35	18 49		19 06	19 19	19 36	19 48	20 05	20 19	20 35	20 48	21 18		21 35	21 48
Burley-in-Wharfedale	d	17 08		17 21	17 34	17 41	17 53	18 05	18 15	18 23	18 38	18 52		19 09	19 22	19 39	19 51	20 08	20 22	20 38	20 51	21 21		21 37	21 51
Ben Rhydding	d	17 11		17 24	17 37	17 45	17 57	18 09	18 18	18 27	18 41	18 55		19 12	19 25	19 42	19 54	20 11	20 25	20 41	20 54	21 24		21 41	21 54
Ilkley	a	17 17		17 31	17 44	17 50	18 04	18 16	18 24	18 34	18 47	19 02		19 18	19 32	19 49	20 01	20 17	20 32	20 47	21 01	21 31		21 46	22 01

NRT DECEMBER 19 EDITION

Table T038-F

Saturdays
21 December to 16 May

Leeds and Bradford - Ilkley

		NT	NT	NT		NT
Leeds	37 d		22 33			23 34
Kirkstall Forge	37 d					
Bradford Forster Square	37 d	22 16		23 16		
Frizinghall	37 d	22 19		23 19		
Shipley	37 d	22 23		23 24		
Baildon	d	22 26		23 27		
Guiseley	d	22 32	22 45	23 32		23 46
Menston	d	22 35	22 48	23 35		23 49
Burley-in-Wharfedale	d	22 38	22 51	23 38		23 52
Ben Rhydding	d	22 41	22 54	23 42		23 55
Ilkley	a	22 47	23 01	23 47		00 02

Sundays
15 December to 10 May

		NT	NT	NT		NT	NT	NT	NT	NT	NT		NT	NT		NT	NT	NT	NT	NT	NT
Leeds	37 d	09 15		10 12			15 12		16 16		17 12			20 12			21 11		22 12		23 18
Kirkstall Forge	37 d				and at							and at									
Bradford Forster Square	37 d		09 38		the same	14 38		15 38		16 38		the same	19 38			20 38		21 38		22 38	
Frizinghall	37 d		09 41		minutes	14 41		15 41		16 41		minutes	19 41			20 41		21 41		22 41	
Shipley	37 d		09 45		past	14 45		15 45		16 45		past	19 45			20 45		21 45		22 45	
Baildon	d		09 48		each	14 48		15 48		16 48		each	19 48			20 48		21 48		22 48	
Guiseley	d	09 26	09 54	10 24	hour until	14 54	15 24	15 54	16 28	16 54	17 24	hour until	19 54	20 24		20 54	21 23	21 54	22 24	22 54	23 30
Menston	d	09 29	09 57	10 27		14 57	15 27	15 57	16 31	16 57	17 27		19 57	20 27		20 57	21 26	21 57	22 27	22 57	23 33
Burley-in-Wharfedale	d	09 32	10 00	10 30		15 00	15 30	16 00	16 34	17 00	17 30		20 00	20 30		21 00	21 29	22 00	22 30	23 00	23 36
Ben Rhydding	d	09 36	10 03	10 33		15 03	15 33	16 03	16 37	17 03	17 33		20 03	20 33		21 03	21 32	22 03	22 33	23 03	23 39
Ilkley	a	09 41	10 09	10 40		15 09	15 40	16 09	16 44	17 09	17 40		20 09	20 40		21 09	21 39	22 09	22 40	23 09	23 46

AVAILABLE FROM MP Middleton Press

Table T038-R

Ilkley - Bradford and Leeds

Mondays to Fridays

16 December to 15 May

Miles	Miles			NT	NT	NT	NT	NT	NT	NT	NT	NT	NT	NT	NT	NT	NT	NT	NT	NT	NT	NT	NT
0	0	**Ilkley**	d	05 50	06 02	06 40	06 51	07 09	07 21	07 37	07 48	07 55	08 08	08 18	08 24	08 40	08 51	09 10	09 21	09 40	09 51	10 10	10 21
1	1	Ben Rhydding	d	05 52	06 04	06 42	06 53	07 11	07 23	07 39	07 50	07 57	08 10	08 20	08 26	08 42	08 53	09 12	09 23	09 42	09 53	10 12	10 23
3¼	3¼	Burley-in-Wharfedale	d	05 57	06 09	06 47	06 58	07 16	07 28	07 44	07 55	08 02	08 15	08 25	08 32	08 47	08 58	09 17	09 28	09 47	09 58	10 17	10 28
4¾	4¾	Menston	d	06 01	06 13	06 51	07 02	07 20	07 31	07 48	07 59	08 06	08 19	08 29	08 36	08 51	09 02	09 21	09 32	09 51	10 02	10 21	10 32
6	6	Guiseley	d	06 04	06 16	06 54	07 05	07 23	07 35	07 52	08 02	08 09	08 22	08 32	08 39	08 54	09 05	09 24	09 35	09 54	10 05	10 24	10 35
—	9¼	Baildon	d	06 10			07 11		07 41		08 08				08 45		09 11		09 41		10 11		10 41
—	10¾	Shipley	37 a	06 13			07 14		07 44		08 11				08 48		09 14		09 44		10 14		10 44
—	11¾	Frizinghall	37 a	06 16			07 17		07 47		08 14				08 52		09 17		09 47		10 17		10 47
—	13½	**Bradford Forster Square**	37 a	06 22			07 23		07 53		08 20				08 57		09 23		09 53		10 23		10 53
12	—	Kirkstall Forge	37 d																				
16¼	—	**Leeds** 10	37 a		06 31	07 10		07 37		08 05		08 25	08 37	08 47		09 09		09 38		10 08		10 38	

		NT	NT	NT	NT	NT	NT	NT	NT	NT	NT	NT	NT	NT	NT	NT	NT	NT	NT	NT	NT	NT	NT
Ilkley	d	10 40	10 51	11 10	11 21	11 40	11 51	12 10	12 21	12 41	12 51	13 10	13 21	13 40	13 51	14 10	14 21	14 40	14 51	15 10	15 21	15 40	15 51
Ben Rhydding	d	10 42	10 53	11 12	11 23	11 42	11 53	12 12	12 23	12 43	12 54	13 12	13 23	13 42	13 53	14 12	14 23	14 42	14 53	15 12	15 23	15 42	15 53
Burley-in-Wharfedale	d	10 47	10 58	11 17	11 28	11 47	11 58	12 18	12 28	12 48	12 59	13 17	13 28	13 47	13 58	14 17	14 28	14 47	14 58	15 17	15 28	15 47	15 58
Menston	d	10 51	11 02	11 21	11 32	11 51	12 02	12 21	12 32	12 51	13 02	13 21	13 32	13 51	14 02	14 21	14 32	14 51	15 02	15 21	15 32	15 51	16 02
Guiseley	d	10 54	11 05	11 24	11 35	11 54	12 05	12 25	12 35	12 55	13 05	13 24	13 35	13 54	14 05	14 24	14 35	14 54	15 05	15 24	15 35	15 54	16 05
Baildon	d		11 11		11 41		12 11		12 41		13 11		13 41		14 11		14 41		15 11		15 41		16 11
Shipley	37 a		11 14		11 44		12 14		12 44		13 14		13 44		14 14		14 44		15 14		15 44		16 14
Frizinghall	37 a		11 17		11 47		12 17		12 47		13 17		13 47		14 17		14 47		15 17		15 47		16 17
Bradford Forster Square	37 a		11 23		11 53		12 23		12 53		13 23		13 53		14 23		14 53		15 23		15 53		16 23
Kirkstall Forge	37 d																						
Leeds 10	37 a	11 11		11 41		12 09		12 41		13 08		13 41		14 09		14 41		15 08		15 38		16 11	

		NT	NT	NT	NT	NT	NT	NT	NT	NT	NT	NT	NT	NT	NT	NT	NT	NT	NT	NT	NT	NT
Ilkley	d	16 10	16 21	16 40	16 51	17 12	17 21	17 43	17 51	18 04	18 11	18 21	18 40	18 51	19 11	19 23	19 40	19 53	20 10	20 40	20 51	21 10
Ben Rhydding	d	16 12	16 23	16 42	16 53	17 14	17 23	17 45	17 53	18 06	18 13	18 23	18 42	18 53	19 13	19 25	19 42	19 55	20 12	20 42	20 53	21 12
Burley-in-Wharfedale	d	16 17	16 28	16 47	16 58	17 19	17 28	17 50	17 58	18 11	18 18	18 28	18 47	18 58	19 18	19 30	19 47	20 00	20 17	20 47	20 58	21 17
Menston	d	16 21	16 32	16 51	17 02	17 23	17 32	17 54	18 02	18 15	18 22	18 32	18 51	19 02	19 22	19 34	19 51	20 04	20 21	20 51	21 02	21 21
Guiseley	d	16 24	16 35	16 54	17 05	17 27	17 35	17 58	18 06	18 18	18 25	18 35	18 54	19 05	19 25	19 37	19 54	20 07	20 24	20 54	21 05	21 24
Baildon	d		16 41		17 11		17 41		18 11			18 41		19 11		19 43		20 13			21 11	
Shipley	37 a		16 44		17 14		17 44		18 14			18 44		19 14		19 46		20 16			21 14	
Frizinghall	37 a		16 47		17 17		17 47		18 17			18 47		19 17		19 49		20 19			21 17	
Bradford Forster Square	37 a		16 53		17 23		17 53		18 23			18 53		19 23		19 55		20 25			21 23	
Kirkstall Forge	37 d																					
Leeds 10	37 a	16 41		17 08		17 41		18 12		18 38	18 39		19 12		19 40		20 09		20 38	21 09		21 38

		NT	NT	NT	NT	NT
Ilkley	d	21 37	21 51	22 10	22 51	23 18
Ben Rhydding	d	21 39	21 53	22 12	22 53	23 20
Burley-in-Wharfedale	d	21 44	21 58	22 17	22 58	23 25
Menston	d	21 48	22 02	22 21	23 02	23 29
Guiseley	d	21 51	22 05	22 24	23 05	23 32
Baildon	d		22 11		23 11	
Shipley	37 a		22 14		23 14	
Frizinghall	37 a		22 17		23 17	
Bradford Forster Square	37 a		22 23		23 23	
Kirkstall Forge	37 d					
Leeds 10	37 a	22 07		22 38		23 46

Saturdays

21 December to 16 May

		NT	NT	NT	NT	NT	NT	NT	NT	NT	NT	NT	NT	NT	NT	NT	NT	NT	NT	NT	NT	NT	NT
Ilkley	d	05 50	06 02	06 40	06 51	07 09	07 21	07 37	07 48	07 55	08 08	08 18	08 24	08 40	08 51	09 10	09 21	09 40	09 51	10 10	10 21	10 40	10 51
Ben Rhydding	d	05 52	06 04	06 42	06 53	07 11	07 23	07 39	07 50	07 57	08 10	08 20	08 26	08 42	08 53	09 12	09 23	09 42	09 53	10 12	10 23	10 42	10 53
Burley-in-Wharfedale	d	05 57	06 09	06 47	06 58	07 16	07 28	07 44	07 55	08 02	08 15	08 25	08 32	08 47	08 58	09 17	09 28	09 47	09 58	10 17	10 28	10 47	10 58
Menston	d	06 01	06 13	06 51	07 02	07 20	07 31	07 48	07 59	08 06	08 19	08 29	08 36	08 51	09 02	09 21	09 32	09 51	10 02	10 21	10 32	10 51	11 02
Guiseley	d	06 04	06 16	06 54	07 05	07 23	07 35	07 52	08 02	08 09	08 22	08 32	08 39	08 54	09 05	09 24	09 35	09 54	10 05	10 24	10 35	10 54	11 05
Baildon	d	06 10			07 11		07 41		08 08				08 45		09 11		09 41		10 11		10 41		11 11
Shipley	37 a	06 13			07 14		07 44		08 11				08 48		09 14		09 44		10 14		10 44		11 14
Frizinghall	37 a	06 16			07 17		07 47		08 14				08 52		09 17		09 47		10 17		10 47		11 17
Bradford Forster Square	37 a	06 22			07 23		07 53		08 20				08 57		09 23		09 53		10 23		10 53		11 23
Kirkstall Forge	37 d																						
Leeds 10	37 a		06 31	07 10		07 37		08 05		08 25	08 37	08 47		09 09		09 38		10 08		10 38		11 11	

		NT	NT	NT	NT	NT	NT	NT	NT	NT	NT	NT	NT	NT	NT	NT	NT	NT	NT	NT	NT	NT	NT
Ilkley	d	11 10	11 21	11 40	11 51	12 10	12 21	12 41	12 51	13 10	13 21	13 40	13 51	14 10	14 21	14 40	14 51	15 10	15 21	15 40	15 51	16 10	16 21
Ben Rhydding	d	11 12	11 23	11 42	11 53	12 12	12 23	12 43	12 54	13 12	13 23	13 42	13 53	14 12	14 23	14 42	14 53	15 12	15 23	15 42	15 53	16 12	16 23
Burley-in-Wharfedale	d	11 17	11 28	11 47	11 58	12 18	12 28	12 48	12 59	13 17	13 28	13 47	13 58	14 17	14 28	14 47	14 58	15 17	15 28	15 47	15 58	16 17	16 28
Menston	d	11 21	11 32	11 51	12 02	12 21	12 32	12 51	13 02	13 21	13 32	13 51	14 02	14 21	14 32	14 51	15 02	15 21	15 32	15 51	16 02	16 21	16 32
Guiseley	d	11 24	11 35	11 54	12 05	12 25	12 35	12 55	13 05	13 24	13 35	13 54	14 05	14 24	14 35	14 54	15 05	15 24	15 35	15 54	16 05	16 24	16 35
Baildon	d		11 41		12 11		12 41		13 11		13 41		14 11		14 41		15 11		15 41		16 11		16 41
Shipley	37 a		11 44		12 14		12 44		13 14		13 44		14 14		14 44		15 14		15 44		16 14		16 44
Frizinghall	37 a		11 47		12 17		12 47		13 17		13 47		14 17		14 47		15 17		15 47		16 17		16 47
Bradford Forster Square	37 a		11 53		12 23		12 53		13 23		13 53		14 23		14 53		15 23		15 53		16 23		16 53
Kirkstall Forge	37 d																						
Leeds 10	37 a	11 41		12 09		12 41		13 08		13 41		14 09		14 41		15 08		15 38		16 11		16 41	

		NT	NT	NT	NT	NT	NT	NT	NT	NT	NT	NT	NT	NT	NT	NT	NT	NT	NT	NT	NT	NT
Ilkley	d	16 40	16 51	17 12	17 21	17 43	17 51	18 04	18 11	18 21	18 40	18 51	19 11	19 23	19 40	19 53	20 10	20 40	20 51	21 10	21 37	21 51
Ben Rhydding	d	16 42	16 53	17 14	17 23	17 45	17 53	18 06	18 13	18 23	18 42	18 53	19 13	19 25	19 42	19 55	20 12	20 42	20 53	21 12	21 39	21 53
Burley-in-Wharfedale	d	16 47	16 58	17 19	17 28	17 50	17 58	18 11	18 18	18 28	18 47	18 58	19 18	19 30	19 47	20 00	20 17	20 47	20 58	21 17	21 44	21 58
Menston	d	16 51	17 02	17 23	17 32	17 54	18 02	18 15	18 22	18 32	18 51	19 02	19 22	19 34	19 51	20 04	20 21	20 51	21 02	21 21	21 48	22 02
Guiseley	d	16 54	17 05	17 27	17 35	17 58	18 06	18 18	18 25	18 35	18 54	19 05	19 25	19 37	19 54	20 07	20 24	20 54	21 05	21 24	21 51	22 05
Baildon	d		17 11		17 41		18 11			18 41		19 11		19 43		20 13			21 11			22 11
Shipley	37 a		17 14		17 44		18 14			18 44		19 14		19 46		20 16			21 14			22 14
Frizinghall	37 a		17 17		17 47		18 17			18 47		19 17		19 49		20 19			21 17			22 17
Bradford Forster Square	37 a		17 23		17 53		18 23			18 53		19 23		19 55		20 25			21 23			22 23
Kirkstall Forge	37 d																					
Leeds 10	37 a	17 08		17 41		18 12		18 38	18 39		19 12		19 40		20 09		20 38	21 09		21 38	22 07	

Table T038-R

Ilkley - Bradford and Leeds

Saturdays

21 December to 16 May

		NT	NT	NT
Ilkley	d	22 10	22 51	23 18
Ben Rhydding	d	22 12	22 53	23 20
Burley-in-Wharfedale	d	22 17	22 58	23 25
Menston	d	22 21	23 02	23 29
Guiseley	d	22 24	23 05	23 32
Baildon	d		23 11	
Shipley	37 a		23 14	
Frizinghall	37 a		23 17	
Bradford Forster Square	37 a		23 23	
Kirkstall Forge	37 d			
Leeds 10	37 a	22 38		23 46

Sundays

15 December to 10 May

		NT	NT	NT	NT	NT	NT	NT	NT		NT	NT	NT	NT	NT	NT	NT	NT	NT	NT	NT	NT
Ilkley	d	08 30	08 53	09 21	09 53	10 21	10 53	11 21	11 53	and at the same minutes past each hour until	15 21	15 53	16 21	16 53	17 21	17 53	18 21	18 53	19 21	19 53	20 21	20 53
Ben Rhydding	d	08 32	08 55	09 23	09 55	10 23	10 55	11 23	11 55		15 23	15 55	16 23	16 55	17 23	17 55	18 23	18 55	19 23	19 55	20 23	20 55
Burley-in-Wharfedale	d	08 37	09 00	09 28	10 00	10 28	11 00	11 28	12 00		15 28	16 00	16 28	17 00	17 28	18 00	18 28	19 00	19 28	20 00	20 28	21 00
Menston	d	08 41	09 04	09 32	10 04	10 32	11 04	11 32	12 04		15 32	16 04	16 32	17 04	17 32	18 04	18 32	19 04	19 32	20 04	20 32	21 04
Guiseley	d	08 44	09 07	09 35	10 07	10 35	11 07	11 35	12 07		15 35	16 07	16 35	17 07	17 35	18 07	18 35	19 07	19 35	20 07	20 35	21 07
Baildon	d		09 13		10 13		11 13		12 13			16 13		17 14		18 13		19 13		20 14		21 13
Shipley	37 a		09 16		10 16		11 16		12 16			16 16		17 17		18 16		19 16		20 17		21 16
Frizinghall	37 a		09 19		10 19		11 19		12 19			16 19		17 20		18 19		19 19		20 20		21 19
Bradford Forster Square	37 a		09 25		10 25		11 24		12 25			16 25		17 26		18 25		19 25		20 26		21 25
Kirkstall Forge	37 d																					
Leeds 10	37 a	08 59		09 51		10 50		11 50			15 50		16 50		17 51		18 50		19 49		20 50	

		NT	NT	NT	NT
Ilkley	d	21 21	21 53	22 21	23 21
Ben Rhydding	d	21 23	21 55	22 23	23 23
Burley-in-Wharfedale	d	21 28	22 00	22 28	23 28
Menston	d	21 32	22 04	22 32	23 32
Guiseley	d	21 35	22 07	22 35	23 35
Baildon	d		22 13		
Shipley	37 a		22 16		
Frizinghall	37 a		22 19		
Bradford Forster Square	37 a		22 25		
Kirkstall Forge	37 d				
Leeds 10	37 a	21 52		22 50	23 52

Table T039-F

Mondays to Saturdays
16 December to 15 February

Liverpool, Manchester Airport and Manchester - Huddersfield - Wakefield, Leeds, Hull, York, Scarborough, Middlesbrough, Newcastle and Edinburgh

Miles	Miles	Miles			TP MX ◇1	TP MO ◇1	TP MX ◇1	TP MO ◇1	TP MX ◇1	TP MO ◇1	TP MX ◇1	TP MO ◇1	TP MX ◇1	TP MO ◇1	TP SO ◇1	TP MSX ◇1	TP MO ◇1	TP MSX ◇1	TP SO ◇1		TP ◇1	TP SO ◇1	TP MO ◇1	TP MSX ◇1	TP SO ◇1
0	—	—	**Liverpool Lime Street** 10	90 d																					
—	—	—	Lea Green	90 d																					
—	—	—	Newton-le-Willows	90 d																					
—	0	—	**Manchester Airport**	d													00 38	00 38	00 38						
—	—	—	Gatley	d																					
—	10	—	**Manchester Piccadilly** 10	a													00 51	00 51	00 52						
—	—	—		d													00 53	00 53	01 03			02 42	02 42	02 42	
—	11	—	**Manchester Oxford Road**	d																					
32	—	—	**Manchester Victoria**	a																					
—	—	—		d											00 05	00 05									
—	—	—	Ashton-under-Lyne	d																					
39	—	—	**Stalybridge**	a																					
—	—	—		d									00 05												
—	—	—	Mossley (Grtr Manchester)	d																					
—	—	—	Greenfield	d																					
—	—	—	Marsden	d		00 04	00 05																		
—	—	—	Slaithwaite	d		00 08	00 09																		←
57	—	—	**Huddersfield**	a		00 14	00 16						00 24		00 32	01 01			01 32			03 15	03 33	03 33	03 15
—	—	—		d								00 19	00 25	00 27	00 34	01 12			01 33			03 51	03 50	03 50	03 51
—	—	—	Deighton	d																		→			
—	—	—	**Mirfield**	d							00 03														
—	—	—	Wakefield Kirkgate	a																					
—	—	—	Normanton	a																					
—	—	—	Castleford	a																					
—	—	—	Ravensthorpe	d						00 02	00 08														
65	—	—	**Dewsbury**	a						00 04	00 10	00s27	00 33												
—	—	—		d					00 02	00 09	00 10		00 34												
—	—	—	Batley	d						00 12	00 13														
—	—	—	Morley	d						00 17	00 18														
—	—	—	Cottingley	d						00 21	00 22														
74	—	—	**Leeds** 10	a					00 15	00 29	00 29	00 41	00 47	01 03	01 11	01 31	02 06	02 06	02 08				04 09	04 09	04 30
—	—	—		d				00 22	00 29			00 46	00 53	01 06	01 13	01 43	02 11	02 19	02 19				04 20	04 20	04 32
—	—	—	Cross Gates	40 d																					
—	—	—	Garforth	40 d																					
—	—	—	South Milford	40 d																					
—	—	—	Selby	29,40 d																					
—	—	—	Howden	29 a																					
—	—	—	Brough	29 a																					
—	—	0	**Hull**	29 a																					
99	—	—	**York** 8	26 a				01 02	01 10			01 26	01 29	01 32	01 39	02 27	02 39	02 58	02 58				04 45	05 00	04 57
—	—	—		d																					
—	—	—	Malton	d																					
—	—	—	Seamer	43 a																					
—	—	54	**Scarborough**	43 a																					
—	—	—	Thirsk	26 d																					
—	—	—	Northallerton	26 d																					
—	—	—	Yarm	a																					
—	—	—	Thornaby	44 a																					
—	—	100	**Middlesbrough**	44 a																					
—	—	—	Redcar Central	44 a																					
143	—	—	**Darlington**	26 a																					
—	—	—		d	00 01																				
—	—	—	Durham	26 a	00 19																				
—	—	—	Chester-le-Street	26 a	00 32																				
179	—	—	**Newcastle** 8	26 a	00 59																				
—	—	—		d																	05 53				
—	—	—	Morpeth	26 a																	06 07				
220	—	—	**Edinburgh**	26 a																	07 30				

Table T039-F

Mondays to Saturdays
16 December to 15 February

Liverpool, Manchester Airport and Manchester - Huddersfield - Wakefield, Leeds, Hull, York, Scarborough, Middlesbrough, Newcastle and Edinburgh

		TP ◇1	TP ◇1	TP ◇1	TP ◇1	TP ◇1	TP ◇1	NT	TP ◇1	TP SO ◇1	TP SX ◇1		NT ◇	TP SX ◇1	TP SO ◇1	NT	TP SO ◇1	TP SX ◇1	TP ◇1	TP SO ◇1	TP SX ◇1	TP ◇1	NT	TP ◇1	NT
Liverpool Lime Street 10	90 d													05 20	05 20										
Lea Green	90 d													05 32	05 32										
Newton-le-Willows	90 d													05 39	05 39										
Manchester Airport	d									05 19	05 19						05 37	05 37							
Gatley	d																								
Manchester Piccadilly 10	a									05 33	05 33						05 56	05 56							
	d								05 15	05 34	05 34						05 57	05 57	06 00					06 27	
Manchester Oxford Road	d									05 40	05 40						06 01	06 01							
Manchester Victoria	a									05 45	05 45			05 58	05 58		06 06	06 10							
	d				05 00					05 45	05 45		05 45	06 00	06 00		06 15	06 15					06 26		
Ashton-under-Lyne	d																						06 36		
Stalybridge	a																		06 12				06 40	06 41	
	d																		06 12					06 42	
Mossley (Grtr Manchester)	d																		06 17						
Greenfield	d																		06 22						
Marsden	d																		06 30						
Slaithwaite	d																		06 34	←	←	←			
Huddersfield	a								06 11	06 16	06 16			06 28	06 28		06 45	06 45	06 41	06 45	06 45	06 41		06 59	
	d						05 49	06 03	06 14	06 17	06 17			06 30	06 30		06 46	06 46	06 49	06 46	06 46	06 49		07 00	07 03
Deighton	d						05 53	06 07									→	→	→			06 53			07 07
Mirfield	d						05 57	06 12								06 39						06 57			07 12
Wakefield Kirkgate	a							06 28																	07 28
Normanton	a							06 34																	07 34
Castleford	a							06 40																	07 40
Ravensthorpe	d						06 01									06 42						07 01			
Dewsbury	a						06 04			06 26	06 26					06 45				06 56	06 56	07 04			
	d						06 09			06 27	06 27					06 46				06 57	06 57	07 09			
Batley	d						06 12									06 49						07 12			
Morley	d						06 17									06 55						07 17			
Cottingley	d						06 21									06 58						07 21			
Leeds 10	a				06 12		06 29		06 33	06 40	06 40		07 23	06 49	06 49	07 08				07 10	07 10	07 29		07 22	
	d		05 35		06 15				06 36	06 42	06 42			06 51	06 51					07 14	07 14			07 27	
Cross Gates	40 d																								
Garforth	40 d																							07 36	
South Milford	40 d																								
Selby	29,40 d		05 55						07 08																
Howden	29 a																								
Brough	29 a		06 12						07 26																
Hull	29 a		06 28						07 42																
York 8	26 a				06 37					07 05	07 05			07 14	07 17					07 36	07 36			07 58	
	d	05 05		06 04	06 39	07 02				07 07	07 07			07 22	07 22					07 39	07 39			08 03	
Malton	d			06 29		07 27																		08 28	
Seamer	43 a			06 45		07 44																		08 44	
Scarborough	43 a			06 55		07 53																		08 52	
Thirsk	26 d	05 28			06 56															07 56	07 56				
Northallerton	26 d	05 36			07 05					07 28	07 29									08 05	08 05				
Yarm	a				07 17															08 17	08 17				
Thornaby	44 a	06 27			07 27															08 28	08 28				
Middlesbrough	44 a	06 34			07 35															08 35	08 35				
Redcar Central	44 a	06 47			07 50															08 48	08 48				
Darlington	26 a									07 40	07 41			07 48	07 48										
	d									07 41	07 42			07 50	07 50										
Durham	26 a									07 57	07 58			08 05	08 05										
Chester-le-Street	26 a									08 03	08 04														
Newcastle 8	26 a									08 16	08 17			08 19	08 19										
	d													08 21	08 21										
Morpeth	26 a													08 34	08 34										
Edinburgh	26 a													09 53	09 53										

Table T039-F

Mondays to Saturdays
16 December to 15 February

Liverpool, Manchester Airport and Manchester - Huddersfield - Wakefield, Leeds, Hull, York, Scarborough, Middlesbrough, Newcastle and Edinburgh

Station			NT	TP		NT	NT	NT	TP	TP	NT	TP	TP	NT	TP	TP	TP	TP	NT	TP		NT	TP	NT	TP	NT
			SO			SX			SO	SX		SX	SO													
			◇	◇1		◇	◇	◇	◇1	◇1		◇1 🚲	◇1 🚲	◇	◇1 🚲	◇1	◇1	◇1 🚲		◇1 🚲			◇1 🚲	◇	◇1 🚲	
Liverpool Lime Street [10]	90	d		05 52								06 24	06 24							06 54						
Lea Green	90	d		06 06																07 06						
Newton-le-Willows	90	d		06 12								06 41	06 41													
Manchester Airport ✈		d							06 10	06 15					06 35			07 07							07 10	
Gatley		d													06 41											
Manchester Piccadilly [10]		a							06 32	06 32					06 54			07 25							07 33	
		d							06 34	06 34					06 56	06 58		07 26					07 30		07 34	
Manchester Oxford Road		d							06 38	06 38					06 59			07a28							07 38	
Manchester Victoria		a		06 31					06 45	06 45		06 59	06 59		07 11					07 29					07 43	
		d	06 31	06 32		06 32	06 37	06 42	06 45	06 45	06 52	07 00	07 00		07 15				07 23	07 30				07 36	07 45	07 53
Ashton-under-Lyne		d									07 02								07 33							08 03
Stalybridge		a		06 44							07 06					07 13			07 37	07 41			07 43			08 07
		d		06 44												07 13				07 42			07 45			
Mossley (Grtr Manchester)		d		06 49												07 18							07 49			
Greenfield		d		06 53												07 22							07 53			
Marsden		d		07 01												07 30							08 01			
Slaithwaite		d		07 05												07 34							08 05			
Huddersfield		a		07 11					07 16	07 16		07 28	07 28		07 45	07 41				08 00			08 11		08 16	
		d		07 12					07 17	07 17		07 30	07 30		07 46		07 49			08 00		08 03	08 12		08 17	
Deighton		d												←			07 53					08 07				
Mirfield		d					07 40							07 40			07 57					08 12		08 39		
Wakefield Kirkgate		a					→															08 28		→		
Normanton		a																				08 34				
Castleford		a																				08 40				
Ravensthorpe		d															08 01									
Dewsbury		a							07 26	07 26				07 45	07 56		08 04								08 26	
		d							07 27	07 27				07 45	07 57		08 09								08 27	
Batley		d												07 48			08 12									
Morley		d												07 54			08 17									
Cottingley		d												07 58			08 21									
Leeds [10]		a	08 00	07 31		08 00		08 14	07 40	07 40		07 49	07 49	08 06	08 10		08 29			08 22			08 31		08 40	
		d		07 34					07 42	07 42		07 51	07 51		08 14					08 27			08 34		08 42	
Cross Gates	40	d																								
Garforth	40	d																		08 36						
South Milford	40	d																								
Selby	29,40	d		07 54																			08 56			
Howden	29	a		08 03																						
Brough	29	a		08 17																			09 15			
Hull	29	a		08 34																			09 30			
York [8]	26	a							08 05	08 05		08 18	08 18		08 36					08 54					09 05	
		d							08 07	08 07		08 21	08 21		08 39					09 00					09 07	
Malton		d																		09 25						
Seamer	43	a																		09 41						
Scarborough	43	a																		09 49						
Thirsk	26	d													08 56											
Northallerton	26	d							08 26	08 26					09 06										09 26	
Yarm		a													09 18											
Thornaby	44	a													09 28											
Middlesbrough	44	a													09 36											
Redcar Central	44	a													09 49											
Darlington	26	a							08 37	08 37		08 47	08 47												09 37	
		d							08 39	08 39		08 49	08 49												09 39	
Durham	26	a							08 54	08 54		09 04	09 04												09 54	
Chester-le-Street	26	a							09 01	09 01																
Newcastle [8]	26	a							09 12	09 12		09 18	09 18												10 11	
		d										09 21	09 21													
Morpeth	26	a										09 33	09 33													
Edinburgh	26	a										10 52	10 56													

Table T039-F

Mondays to Saturdays
16 December to 15 February

Liverpool, Manchester Airport and Manchester - Huddersfield - Wakefield, Leeds, Hull, York, Scarborough, Middlesbrough, Newcastle and Edinburgh

Station			NT	TP	TP	NT	TP	TP	TP	TP	NT	GC		TP	NT	TP	NT	TP	NT	NT	TP	TP	NT	GC	TP	TP
				SX	SO		SO		SX			SO									SX	SO		SX		
			◇	◇1 🚲	◇1 🚲	◇	◇1 🚲	◇1	◇1 🚲	◇1		1 ☕		◇1 🚲		◇1 🚲	◇	◇1 🚲		◇	◇1 🚲	◇1 🚲	◇	1 ☕	◇1 🚲	◇1
Liverpool Lime Street [10]	90	d		07 24	07 24									07 54							08 24	08 24				
Lea Green	90	d												08 07												
Newton-le-Willows	90	d		07 41	07 41																08 41	08 41				
Manchester Airport ✈		d					07 35		07 47									08 10							08 35	
Gatley		d					07 41		07 53																08 41	
Manchester Piccadilly [10]		a					07 54		08 03									08 33							08 54	
		d					07 56	08 00	08 05							08 30		08 35							08 56	08 58
Manchester Oxford Road		d					07 59		08 08									08 38							09 00	
Manchester Victoria		a		07 59	07 59		08 11		08 14					08 29				08 45			08 59	08 59			09 12	
		d	07 57	08 00	08 00		08 15		08 15		08 21			08 30			08 37	08 45	08 52	08 56	09 00	09 00			09 15	
Ashton-under-Lyne		d									08 31								09 02							
Stalybridge		a						08 13			08 35			08 41		08 44			09 06							09 12
		d						08 13						08 42		08 45										09 13
Mossley (Grtr Manchester)		d						08 18								08 49										09 17
Greenfield		d						08 23								08 53										09 22
Marsden		d						08 31								09 01										09 30
Slaithwaite		d						08 35								09 05										09 34
Huddersfield		a		08 28	08 28		08 45	08 42	08 45					09 00		09 11		09 16			09 28	09 28			09 45	09 41
		d		08 30	08 30		08 46		08 46	08 49				09 01	09 03	09 12		09 17			09 30	09 30			09 46	
Deighton		d				←				08 53					09 07								←			
Mirfield		d				08 39				08 57					09 12		09 39						09 39			
Wakefield Kirkgate		a													09 28		→									
Normanton		a													09 34											
Castleford		a													09 40											
Ravensthorpe		d				08 42				09 01																
Dewsbury		a				08 45	08 56		08 56	09 04								09 26					09 44		09 56	
		d				08 46	08 57		08 57	09 09								09 27					09 44		09 57	
Batley		d				08 49				09 12													09 47			
Morley		d				08 55				09 17													09 53			
Cottingley		d								09 21																
Leeds [10]		a	09 22	08 49	08 49	09 04	09 10		09 10	09 29				09 22		09 31		09 40		10 13	09 49	09 49	10 04		10 10	
		d		08 51	08 51		09 14		09 14					09 27		09 34		09 42			09 51	09 51			10 14	
Cross Gates	40	d																								
Garforth	40	d												09 36												
South Milford	40	d																								
Selby	29,40	d														09 57										
Howden	29	a																								
Brough	29	a														10 16										
Hull	29	a														10 34										
York [8]	26	a		09 14	09 14		09 36		09 36					09 55				10 04			10 14	10 14			10 36	
		d		09 21	09 21		09 39		09 39			09 49		10 00				10 07			10 21	10 21		10 25	10 39	
Malton		d												10 25												
Seamer	43	a												10 42												
Scarborough	43	a												10 52												
Thirsk	26	d					09 56		09 56			10 06												10 42	10 56	
Northallerton	26	d					10 07		10 07			10a16						10 26						10a58	11 07	
Yarm		a					10 20		10 20																11 20	
Thornaby	44	a					10 30		10 30																11 30	
Middlesbrough	44	a					10 37		10 37																11 37	
Redcar Central	44	a					10 50		10 50																11 50	
Darlington	26	a		09 47	09 47													10 37			10 47	10 47				
		d		09 49	09 49													10 39			10 49	10 49				
Durham	26	a		10 04	10 04													10 54			11 04	11 04				
Chester-le-Street	26	a																11 01								
Newcastle [8]	26	a		10 19	10 19													11 13			11 19	11 19				
		d		10 21	10 21																11 21	11 21				
Morpeth	26	a		10 34	10 34																11 34	11 34				
Edinburgh	26	a		11 50	11 54																12 51	12 56				

Table T039-F

Mondays to Saturdays

16 December to 15 February

Liverpool, Manchester Airport and Manchester - Huddersfield - Wakefield, Leeds, Hull, York, Scarborough, Middlesbrough, Newcastle and Edinburgh

Station			TP	TP		NT	TP	NT	TP	NT	TP	TP	TP	NT	NT	TP	TP	NT	TP	TP		TP	TP	NT	TP	NT
									SO			SX				SX	SO		SX	SO						
			◇1	◇1			◇1		◇1	◇	◇1	◇1	◇1		◇	◇1	◇1	◇	◇1	◇1		◇1	◇1		◇1	
				⊼			⊼		⊼		⊼	⊼	⊼			⊼	⊼		⊼	⊼					⊼	
Liverpool Lime Street 10	90	d					08 54									09 24	09 24								09 53	
Lea Green	90	d					09 06																		10 06	
Newton-le-Willows	90	d														09 41	09 41									
Manchester Airport		d		09 07							09 10								09 36	09 40						
Gatley		d																	09 42	09 46						
Manchester Piccadilly 10		a		09 25							09 33		←						09 55	09 55						
		d		09 26					09 30		09 34	09 35							09 57	09 57		09 58				
Manchester Oxford Road		d		09a28							09 38		09 38						10 00	10 00						
Manchester Victoria		a					09 29				→		09 44			09 59	09 59		10 11	10 11					10 29	
		d				09 23	09 30			09 37			09 45	09 52	09 56	10 00	10 00		10 15	10 15				10 23	10 30	
Ashton-under-Lyne		d				09 33								10 02										10 33		
Stalybridge		a				09 37	09 41		09 42			09 50		10 06								10 12		10 37	10 41	
		d					09 42		09 46			09 50										10 12			10 42	
Mossley (Grtr Manchester)		d																				10 17				
Greenfield		d																				10 22				
Marsden		d																				10 30				
Slaithwaite		d																				10 34				
Huddersfield		a					10 00		10 05			10 08	10 16			10 28	10 28		10 44	10 44		10 41			11 00	
		d	09 49				10 01	10 03	10 12			10 12	10 17			10 30	10 30		10 45	10 45			10 49		11 01	11 03
Deighton		d	09 53					10 07										←					10 53			11 07
Mirfield		d	09 57					10 12		10 39								10 39					10 59			11 12
Wakefield Kirkgate		a						10 28		→																11 28
Normanton		a						10 34																		11 34
Castleford		a						10 40																		11 40
Ravensthorpe		d	10 01																				11 02			
Dewsbury		a	10 04										10 26					10 44	10 56	10 56			11 05			
		d	10 09										10 27					10 44	10 57	10 57			11 09			
Batley		d	10 12															10 47					11 12			
Morley		d	10 17															10 53					11 17			
Cottingley		d	10 21																				11 21			
Leeds 10		a	10 29				10 21		10 31			10 31	10 40		11 13	10 49	10 49	11 03	11 10	11 10			11 29		11 21	
		d					10 27		10 34			10 34	10 42			10 51	10 51		11 14	11 14					11 27	
Cross Gates	40	d																								
Garforth	40	d					10 36																		11 36	
South Milford	40	d																								
Selby	29,40	d							10 56			10 56														
Howden	29	a																								
Brough	29	a							11 15			11 15														
Hull	29	a							11 30			11 30														
York 8	26	a					10 55						11 05			11 15	11 15		11 36	11 36					11 57	
		d					11 00						11 07			11 21	11 21		11 39	11 39					12 00	
Malton		d					11 25																		12 25	
Seamer	43	a					11 41																		12 41	
Scarborough	43	a					11 51																		12 51	
Thirsk	26	d																	11 56	11 56						
Northallerton	26	d											11 26						12 05	12 07						
Yarm		a																	12 17	12 20						
Thornaby	44	a																	12 27	12 30						
Middlesbrough	44	a																	12 35	12 37						
Redcar Central	44	a																	12 48	12 50						
Darlington	26	a											11 37			11 48	11 48									
		d											11 39			11 49	11 49									
Durham	26	a											11 54			12 05	12 05									
Chester-le-Street	26	a																								
Newcastle 8	26	a											12 11			12 18	12 18									
		d														12 21	12 21									
Morpeth	26	a														12 34	12 34									
Edinburgh	26	a														13 50	13 57									

Table T039-F

Mondays to Saturdays

16 December to 15 February

Liverpool, Manchester Airport and Manchester - Huddersfield - Wakefield, Leeds, Hull, York, Scarborough, Middlesbrough, Newcastle and Edinburgh

Station			TP	NT	TP	TP	TP	TP	TP	NT	NT	TP		TP	NT	TP	TP	TP	TP	NT	TP	NT	NT	TP	TP	TP
			SX		SO	SX	SO	SO	SX			SX		SO												
			◇1	◇	◇1	◇1	◇1	◇1	◇1		◇	◇1		◇1	◇	◇1	◇1	◇1	◇1		◇1		◇	◇1	◇1	◇1
			⊼		⊼	⊼	⊼	⊼	⊼			⊼		⊼		⊼			⊼		⊼			⊼	⊼	⊼
Liverpool Lime Street 10	90	d										10 24		10 24							10 54					
Lea Green	90	d																			11 06					
Newton-le-Willows	90	d										10 41		10 41												
Manchester Airport		d			10 10	10 10										10 40			11 07					11 10		
Gatley		d														10 46										
Manchester Piccadilly 10		a			10 33	10 33		←	←							10 55			11 25					11 33		←
		d	10 30		10 34	10 34	10 35									10 57	10 58		11 26					11 34	11 35	
Manchester Oxford Road		d			10 38	10 38		10 38	10 38							11 00			11a28					11 38		11 38
Manchester Victoria		a			→	→		10 44	10 44			10 59		10 59		11 11					11 29			→		11 44
		d		10 37				10 44	10 45	10 52	10 55	11 00		11 00		11 15				11 23	11 30		11 34			11 45
Ashton-under-Lyne		d								11 02										11 33						
Stalybridge		a	10 42				10 50			11 06							11 12			11 37	11 42				11 50	
		d	10 50				10 50										11 12				11 42				11 50	
Mossley (Grtr Manchester)		d															11 17									
Greenfield		d															11 22									
Marsden		d															11 30									
Slaithwaite		d															11 34									
Huddersfield		a	11 08				11 08	11 16	11 16			11 28		11 28		11 45	11 41				12 00				12 08	12 16
		d	11 12				11 12	11 17	11 17			11 30		11 30		11 46		11 49			12 01	12 03			12 12	12 17
Deighton		d													←			11 53				12 07				
Mirfield		d		11 39											11 39			11 57				12 12	12 39			
Wakefield Kirkgate		a		→																		12 28	→			
Normanton		a																				12 34				
Castleford		a																				12 40				
Ravensthorpe		d																12 01								
Dewsbury		a						11 26	11 26						11 44	11 56		12 04								12 26
		d						11 27	11 27						11 44	11 57		12 09								12 27
Batley		d													11 47			12 12								
Morley		d													11 53			12 17								
Cottingley		d																12 21								
Leeds 10		a	11 31				11 31	11 40	11 40		12 18	11 49		11 49	12 03	12 10		12 29			12 21				12 31	12 40
		d	11 34				11 34	11 42	11 42			11 51		11 51		12 14					12 27				12 34	12 42
Cross Gates	40	d																								
Garforth	40	d																			12 36					
South Milford	40	d																								
Selby	29,40	d	11 56				11 56																		12 56	
Howden	29	a																								
Brough	29	a	12 15				12 15																		13 15	
Hull	29	a	12 30				12 30																		13 32	
York 8	26	a						12 05	12 05			12 14		12 14		12 36					12 55					13 05
		d						12 07	12 07			12 22		12 22		12 39					13 00					13 07
Malton		d																			13 25					
Seamer	43	a																			13 41					
Scarborough	43	a																			13 51					
Thirsk	26	d														12 56										
Northallerton	26	d						12 26	12 26							13 05										13 26
Yarm		a														13 18										
Thornaby	44	a														13 28										
Middlesbrough	44	a														13 35										
Redcar Central	44	a														13 49										
Darlington	26	a						12 37	12 37			12 48		12 48												13 37
		d						12 39	12 39			12 50		12 50												13 39
Durham	26	a						12 54	12 54			13 05		13 05												13 54
Chester-le-Street	26	a						13 01	13 01																	
Newcastle 8	26	a						13 13	13 13			13 19		13 19												14 10
		d										13 21		13 21												
Morpeth	26	a										13 34		13 34												
Edinburgh	26	a										14 49		14 54												

Table T039-F

Mondays to Saturdays
16 December to 15 February

Liverpool, Manchester Airport and Manchester - Huddersfield - Wakefield, Leeds, Hull, York, Scarborough, Middlesbrough, Newcastle and Edinburgh

			NT	NT		TP SX	TP SO	NT	GC	TP SO	TP SX	TP	TP	NT	TP	NT	NT	TP	TP	TP		NT	NT	TP SX	TP SO	NT
				◇		◇1	◇1	◇	1	◇1	◇1	◇1	◇1		◇1		◇	◇1	◇1	◇1			◇	◇1	◇1	◇
Liverpool Lime Street 10	90	d				11 24	11 24								11 54									12 24	12 24	
Lea Green	90	d													12 06											
Newton-le-Willows	90	d				11 41	11 42																	12 41	12 41	
Manchester Airport		d								11 40	11 40							12 10								
Gatley		d								11 46	11 46															
Manchester Piccadilly 10		a								11 55	11 55							12 33		←						
		d								11 57	11 57	11 58						12 34	12 35							
Manchester Oxford Road		d								12 00	12 00							12 38		12 38						
Manchester Victoria		a				11 59	11 59			12 10	12 10				12 29			→		12 44				12 59	12 59	
		d	11 52	11 55		12 00	12 00			12 15	12 15			12 23	12 30		12 37			12 45		12 52	12 56	13 00	13 00	
Ashton-under-Lyne		d	12 02											12 33								13 02				
Stalybridge		a	12 06									12 12		12 37	12 41				12 50			13 06				
		d										12 12			12 42				12 50							
Mossley (Grtr Manchester)		d										12 17														
Greenfield		d										12 22														
Marsden		d										12 30														
Slaithwaite		d										12 34														
Huddersfield		a				12 28	12 28			12 45	12 45	12 41			13 00				13 08	13 16				13 28	13 28	
		d				12 30	12 30			12 46	12 46		12 49		13 01	13 03			13 12	13 17				13 30	13 30	
Deighton		d						←					12 53			13 07										←
Mirfield		d						12 39					12 57			13 12	13 39									13 39
Wakefield Kirkgate		a														13 28	→									
Normanton		a														13 34										
Castleford		a														13 40										
Ravensthorpe		d											13 01													
Dewsbury		a						12 44		12 56	12 56		13 04							13 26						13 44
		d						12 44		12 57	12 57		13 09							13 27						13 44
Batley		d						12 47					13 12													13 47
Morley		d						12 53					13 17													13 53
Cottingley		d											13 21													
Leeds 10		a		13 18		12 49	12 49	13 03		13 10	13 10		13 29		13 21				13 31	13 40			14 18	13 49	13 49	14 03
		d				12 51	12 51			13 14	13 14				13 27				13 34	13 42				13 51	13 51	
Cross Gates	40	d																								
Garforth	40	d													13 36											
South Milford	40	d																								
Selby	29,40	d																	13 56							
Howden	29	a																								
Brough	29	a																	14 15							
Hull	29	a																	14 30							
York 8	26	a				13 14	13 14			13 36	13 36				13 55					14 05				14 14	14 14	
		d				13 20	13 20		13 23	13 39	13 39				14 00					14 07				14 21	14 21	
Malton		d													14 25											
Seamer	43	a													14 41											
Scarborough	43	a													14 51											
Thirsk	26	d							13 40	13 56	13 56															
Northallerton	26	d							13a48	14 05	14 07															
Yarm		a								14 17	14 20															
Thornaby	44	a								14 27	14 30															
Middlesbrough	44	a								14 35	14 37															
Redcar Central	44	a								14 48	14 50															
Darlington	26	a				13 46	13 46													14 37				14 47	14 47	
		d				13 48	13 48													14 38				14 49	14 49	
Durham	26	a				14 03	14 03													14 54				15 04	15 04	
Chester-le-Street	26	a																		15 00						
Newcastle 8	26	a				14 19	14 19													15 13				15 18	15 18	
		d				14 21	14 21																	15 21	15 21	
Morpeth	26	a				14 34	14 34																	15 33	15 33	
Edinburgh	26	a				15 49	15 54																	16 48	16 55	

Table T039-F

Mondays to Saturdays
16 December to 15 February

Liverpool, Manchester Airport and Manchester - Huddersfield - Wakefield, Leeds, Hull, York, Scarborough, Middlesbrough, Newcastle and Edinburgh

			TP SO	TP SX	TP	TP	TP	NT	GC SX	TP	NT	NT		TP	TP	TP	GC SO	NT	NT	TP SX	TP SO	NT	TP SO	TP SX	TP	TP
			◇1	◇1	◇1	◇1	◇1		1	◇1		◇		◇1	◇1	◇1	1		◇	◇1	◇1	◇	◇1	◇1	◇1	◇1
Liverpool Lime Street 10	90	d								12 54										13 24	13 24					
Lea Green	90	d								13 06																
Newton-le-Willows	90	d																		13 41	13 41					
Manchester Airport		d	12 40	12 40			13 07							13 10									13 40	13 40		
Gatley		d	12 46	12 46																			13 46	13 46		
Manchester Piccadilly 10		a	12 55	12 55			13 25							13 33		←							13 55	13 55		
		d	12 57	12 57	12 58		13 26							13 34	13 35								13 57	13 57	13 58	
Manchester Oxford Road		d	13 00	13 00			13a28							13 38		13 38							14 00	14 00		
Manchester Victoria		a	13 10	13 13						13 29				→		13 44				13 59	13 59		14 10	14 10		
		d	13 15	13 15				13 22		13 30		13 37				13 45		13 52	13 55	14 00	14 00		14 15	14 15		
Ashton-under-Lyne		d						13 32										14 02								
Stalybridge		a			13 12			13 36		13 41					13 50			14 06							14 12	
		d			13 13					13 42					13 50										14 12	
Mossley (Grtr Manchester)		d			13 18																				14 17	
Greenfield		d			13 22																				14 22	
Marsden		d			13 30																				14 30	
Slaithwaite		d			13 34																				14 34	
Huddersfield		a	13 45	13 45	13 41					14 00					14 08	14 16				14 28	14 28		14 45	14 45	14 41	
		d	13 46	13 46		13 49				14 01	14 03				14 12	14 17				14 30	14 30		14 46	14 46		14 49
Deighton		d				13 53					14 07											←				14 53
Mirfield		d				13 57					14 12	14 39										14 39				14 57
Wakefield Kirkgate		a									14 28	→														
Normanton		a									14 34															
Castleford		a									14 40															
Ravensthorpe		d				14 01																				15 01
Dewsbury		a	13 56	13 56		14 04										14 26						14 44	14 56	14 56		15 04
		d	13 57	13 57		14 09										14 27						14 44	14 57	14 57		15 09
Batley		d				14 12																14 47				15 12
Morley		d				14 17																14 53				15 17
Cottingley		d				14 21																				15 21
Leeds 10		a	14 10	14 10		14 29				14 21					14 31	14 40			15 13	14 49	14 49	15 03	15 10	15 10		15 29
		d	14 14	14 14						14 27					14 34	14 42				14 51	14 51		15 14	15 14		
Cross Gates	40	d																								
Garforth	40	d								14 36																
South Milford	40	d																								
Selby	29,40	d													14 56											
Howden	29	a																								
Brough	29	a													15 15											
Hull	29	a													15 31											
York 8	26	a	14 36	14 36						14 55						15 05				15 14	15 14		15 36	15 36		
		d	14 39	14 39					14 51	15 00						15 07	15 14			15 22	15 22		15 39	15 39		
Malton		d								15 25																
Seamer	43	a								15 41																
Scarborough	43	a								15 51																
Thirsk	26	d	14 56	14 56					15 14								15 37						15 56	15 56		
Northallerton	26	d	15 05	15 07					15a25							15 26	15a45						16 05	16 07		
Yarm		a	15 17	15 20																			16 17	16 20		
Thornaby	44	a	15 27	15 30																			16 27	16 30		
Middlesbrough	44	a	15 35	15 37																			16 35	16 37		
Redcar Central	44	a	15 48	15 50																			16 48	16 50		
Darlington	26	a														15 37				15 48	15 48					
		d														15 39				15 50	15 50					
Durham	26	a														15 54				16 05	16 05					
Chester-le-Street	26	a														16 01										
Newcastle 8	26	a														16 13				16 19	16 19					
		d																		16 21	16 21					
Morpeth	26	a																		16 34	16 34					
Edinburgh	26	a																		17 52	17 57					

Table T039-F

Mondays to Saturdays

16 December to 15 February

Liverpool, Manchester Airport and Manchester - Huddersfield - Wakefield, Leeds, Hull, York, Scarborough, Middlesbrough, Newcastle and Edinburgh

Station			NT	TP		NT	NT	TP SO	TP SX	TP	TP SO	TP SX	NT	NT	TP SX	TP SO	NT	TP	TP	TP		TP	NT	TP	NT	NT
				◇1 ⊼			◇	◇1 ⊼	◇1 ⊼	◇1 ⊼	◇1 ⊼	◇1 ⊼		◇	◇1 ⊼	◇1 ⊼	◇	◇1 ⊼	◇1	◇1		◇1 ⊼		◇1 ⊼		◇
Liverpool Lime Street 10	90	d		13 54											14 24	14 24								14 54		
Lea Green	90	d		14 06																				15 06		
Newton-le-Willows	90	d													14 41	14 41										
Manchester Airport		d						14 10	14 10									14 40				15 07				
Gatley		d																14 46								
Manchester Piccadilly 10		a						14 33	14 33		←	←						14 55				15 25				
		d						14 34	14 34	14 35								14 57	14 58			15 26				
Manchester Oxford Road		d						14 38	14 38		14 38	14 38						15 00				15a28				
Manchester Victoria		a		14 29				→	→		14 44	14 44			14 59	14 59		15 11						15 29		
		d	14 23	14 30			14 36				14 45	14 45	14 52	14 56	15 00	15 00		15 15					15 23	15 30		15 36
Ashton-under-Lyne		d	14 33										15 02										15 33			
Stalybridge		a	14 37	14 41						14 50			15 06						15 12				15 37	15 41		
		d		14 42						14 50									15 12					15 42		
Mossley (Grtr Manchester)		d																	15 17							
Greenfield		d																	15 22							
Marsden		d																	15 30							
Slaithwaite		d																	15 34							
Huddersfield		a		15 00						15 08	15 14	15 14			15 28	15 28		15 45	15 41					16 00		
		d		15 01		15 03				15 09	15 15	15 15			15 29	15 29		15 46		15 49				16 01	16 03	
Deighton		d				15 07											←			15 53					16 07	
Mirfield		d				15 12	15 38										15 38			15 59					16 12	16 38
Wakefield Kirkgate		a				15 28	→																		16 28	→
Normanton		a				15 34																			16 34	
Castleford		a				15 40																			16 40	
Ravensthorpe		d																		16 03						
Dewsbury		a									15 26	15 26					15 43	15 56		16 06						
		d									15 27	15 27					15 43	15 57		16 09						
Batley		d															15 46			16 12						
Morley		d															15 52			16 17						
Cottingley		d																		16 21						
Leeds 10		a		15 21						15 31	15 40	15 40		16 18	15 49	15 49	16 02	16 10		16 29				16 20		
		d		15 27						15 33	15 42	15 42			15 51	15 51		16 14						16 27		
Cross Gates	40	d																								
Garforth	40	d		15 36																				16 36		
South Milford	40	d																								
Selby	29,40	d								15 55																
Howden	29	a																								
Brough	29	a								16 14																
Hull	29	a								16 31																
York 8	26	a		15 55							16 05	16 05			16 14	16 14		16 36						16 55		
		d		16 00							16 07	16 07			16 19	16 19		16 39						17 00		
Malton		d		16 25																				17 25		
Seamer	43	a		16 41																				17 41		
Scarborough	43	a		16 51																				17 51		
Thirsk	26	d																16 56								
Northallerton	26	d									16 26	16 26						17 07								
Yarm		a																17 20								
Thornaby	44	a																17 30								
Middlesbrough	44	a																17 37								
Redcar Central	44	a																17 50								
Darlington	26	a									16 37	16 37			16 47	16 47										
		d									16 39	16 39			16 49	16 49										
Durham	26	a									16 54	16 59			17 05	17 04										
Chester-le-Street	26	a									17 01	17 06														
Newcastle 8	26	a									17 13	17 18			17 18	17 18										
		d													17 20	17 20										
Morpeth	26	a													17 33	17 33										
Edinburgh	26	a													18 52	18 56										

Table T039-F

Mondays to Saturdays

16 December to 15 February

Liverpool, Manchester Airport and Manchester - Huddersfield - Wakefield, Leeds, Hull, York, Scarborough, Middlesbrough, Newcastle and Edinburgh

Station			TP	TP	TP	NT	NT SO	NT SX	TP SO	TP SX	NT	TP		TP	TP	NT	TP	NT	TP	NT	TP	NT	NT	TP	NT	TP SX
			◇1 ⊼	◇1 ⊼	◇1 ⊼		◇	◇	◇1 ⊼	◇1 ⊼	◇	◇1 ⊼		◇1	◇1		◇1 ⊼		◇1 ⊼	◇	◇1 ⊼		◇	◇1 ⊼	◇	◇1 ⊼
Liverpool Lime Street 10	90	d							15 24	15 24							15 54							16 24		
Lea Green	90	d															16 06									
Newton-le-Willows	90	d							15 41	15 41														16 41		
Manchester Airport		d	15 10									15 40									16 10					16 34
Gatley		d										15 46														16 40
Manchester Piccadilly 10		a	15 33		←							15 55									16 33					16 55
		d	15 34	15 35								15 57		15 58					16 30		16 34					16 57
Manchester Oxford Road		d	15 38		15 38							16 00									16 38					17 00
Manchester Victoria		a	→		15 44				15 59	15 59		16 10					16 29				16 44			16 59		17 10
		d			15 45	15 52	15 54	15 56	16 00	16 00		16 15				16 23	16 30			16 37	16 45	16 52	16 56	17 00		17 15
Ashton-under-Lyne		d				16 02										16 33						17 02				
Stalybridge		a		15 50		16 06								16 12		16 37	16 41		16 43			17 06				
		d		15 50										16 12			16 42		16 45							
Mossley (Grtr Manchester)		d												16 17					16 49							
Greenfield		d												16 22					16 53							
Marsden		d												16 30					17 01							
Slaithwaite		d												16 34					17 05							
Huddersfield		a		16 08	16 16				16 28	16 28		16 45		16 41			17 00		17 11		17 16			17 28		17 45
		d		16 12	16 17				16 30	16 30		16 46			16 49		17 01	17 03	17 12		17 17			17 30		17 46
Deighton		d									←				16 53			17 07							←	
Mirfield		d									16 38				16 57			17 12		17 39					17 39	
Wakefield Kirkgate		a																17 28		→						
Normanton		a																17 34								
Castleford		a																17 40								
Ravensthorpe		d													17 01											
Dewsbury		a			16 26						16 43	16 56			17 04						17 26				17 44	17 56
		d			16 27						16 44	16 57			17 09						17 27				17 44	17 57
Batley		d									16 47				17 12										17 47	
Morley		d									16 53				17 17										17 53	
Cottingley		d													17 21											
Leeds 10		a		16 31	16 40		17 19	17 19	16 49	16 49	17 04	17 10			17 29		17 21		17 31		17 40		18 21	17 49	18 03	18 10
		d		16 34	16 42				16 51	16 51		17 13					17 27		17 34		17 42			17 51		18 14
Cross Gates	40	d		16 40															17 41							
Garforth	40	d		16 45													17 36		17 45							
South Milford	40	d																								
Selby	29,40	d		16 59															17 59							
Howden	29	a																	18 08							
Brough	29	a		17 18															18 21							
Hull	29	a		17 34															18 37							
York 8	26	a			17 05				17 14	17 14		17 35					17 55				18 05			18 18		18 36
		d			17 07				17 21	17 21		17 39					18 00				18 07			18 22		18 39
Malton		d															18 25									
Seamer	43	a															18 42									
Scarborough	43	a															18 52									
Thirsk	26	d										17 56														18 56
Northallerton	26	d			17 26							18 05									18 26					19 05
Yarm		a										18 17														19 17
Thornaby	44	a										18 27														19 27
Middlesbrough	44	a										18 35														19 35
Redcar Central	44	a										18 48														19 48
Darlington	26	a			17 37				17 47	17 47											18 37			18 48		
		d			17 39				17 49	17 49											18 39			18 50		
Durham	26	a			17 54				18 04	18 04											18 54			19 05		
Chester-le-Street	26	a																			19 01					
Newcastle 8	26	a			18 10				18 18	18 18											19 13			19 19		
		d							18 21	18 21														19 21		
Morpeth	26	a							18 34	18 34														19 34		
Edinburgh	26	a							20 04	20 08														20 54		

Table T039-F

Mondays to Saturdays
16 December to 15 February

Liverpool, Manchester Airport and Manchester - Huddersfield - Wakefield, Leeds, Hull, York, Scarborough, Middlesbrough, Newcastle and Edinburgh

			TP SO	TP		TP	TP	NT	GC SO	GC SX	TP	NT	TP	NT	TP SX	TP SO	NT	NT	TP SX	TP SO		NT	TP SX	TP SO	TP SX	TP
			◇■ 🍴	◇■		◇■	◇■ 🍴		■ ■ 🍽	■ ■ 🍽	◇■ 🍴		◇■ 🍴	◇	◇■ 🍴	◇■ 🍴		◇	◇■ 🍴	◇■ 🍴		◇	◇■ 🍴	◇■ 🍴	◇■ 🍴	◇■
Liverpool Lime Street ■	90	d									16 54								17 24	17 24						
Lea Green	90	d									17 06															
Newton-le-Willows	90	d																	17 41	17 41						
Manchester Airport ✈		d	16 40				17 07								17 10	17 10							17 34	17 40		
Gatley		d	16 46																				17 42	17 46	←	
Manchester Piccadilly ■		a	16 55				17 25								17 33	17 33							17 56	17 56	17 56	
		d	16 57	16 58			17 27						17 30		17 35	17 35							17 58	17 57	17 58	18 00
Manchester Oxford Road		d	17 00				17a29								17 38	17 38							→	18 01	18 01	
Manchester Victoria		a	17 10								17 29				17 44	17 44			17 58	17 59				18 11	18 13	
		d	17 15					17 23			17 30			17 37	17 45	17 45	17 52	17 56	18 00	18 00				18 15	18 15	
Ashton-under-Lyne		d						17 33									18 02									
Stalybridge		a		17 12				17 37			17 41		17 45				18 06									18 13
		d		17 12							17 42		17 45													18 13
Mossley (Grtr Manchester)		d		17 17									17 50													18 18
Greenfield		d		17 22									17 54													18 22
Marsden		d		17 30									18 02													18 30
Slaithwaite		d		17 34									18 05													18 34
Huddersfield		a	17 45	17 40							18 00		18 11		18 16	18 16			18 28	18 28				18 45	18 45	18 41
		d	17 46			17 49					18 01	18 03	18 12		18 17	18 17			18 30	18 30				18 46	18 46	
Deighton		d				17 53						18 07										←				
Mirfield		d				17 57						18 12		18 38								18 38				
Wakefield Kirkgate		a										18 28		→												
Normanton		a										18 34														
Castleford		a										18 40														
Ravensthorpe		d				18 01																				
Dewsbury		a	17 56			18 04									18 26	18 26						18 43		18 56	18 56	
		d	17 57			18 09									18 27	18 27						18 44		18 57	18 57	
Batley		d				18 12																18 47				
Morley		d				18 17																18 53				
Cottingley		d				18 21																				
Leeds ■		a	18 10			18 29					18 21		18 31		18 40	18 40		19 19	18 49	18 49		19 02		19 10	19 10	
		d	18 14								18 27		18 34		18 42	18 42			18 51	18 51				19 14	19 14	
Cross Gates	40	d											18 40													
Garforth	40	d									18 36		18 45													
South Milford	40	d																								
Selby	29,40	d											18 59													
Howden	29	a																								
Brough	29	a											19 17													
Hull	29	a											19 33													
York ■	26	a	18 36								18 55				19 05	19 05			19 14	19 14				19 36	19 36	
		d	18 39						18 42	18 42	19 00				19 07	19 07			19 17	19 22				19 39	19 39	
Malton		d									19 25															
Seamer	43	a									19 41															
Scarborough	43	a									19 51															
Thirsk	26	d	18 56						19 00	19 01														19 56	19 57	
Northallerton	26	d	19 05						19a08	19a09					19 26	19 26								20 07	20 07	
Yarm		a	19 17																					20 20	20 20	
Thornaby	44	a	19 27																					20 30	20 30	
Middlesbrough	44	a	19 35																					20 37	20 37	
Redcar Central	44	a	19 48																					20 51	20 51	
Darlington	26	a													19 37	19 37			19 43	19 48						
		d													19 39	19 39			19 45	19 50						
Durham	26	a													19 54	19 54			20 00	20 05						
Chester-le-Street	26	a																								
Newcastle ■	26	a													20 10	20 12			20 14	20 21						
		d																	20 16							
Morpeth	26	a																	20 29							
Edinburgh	26	a																	21 57							

Table T039-F

Mondays to Saturdays
16 December to 15 February

Liverpool, Manchester Airport and Manchester - Huddersfield - Wakefield, Leeds, Hull, York, Scarborough, Middlesbrough, Newcastle and Edinburgh

			TP	NT	TP	NT	TP	NT	TP	NT	NT	TP SX		TP SO	NT	TP SX	TP SO	TP	TP	TP SX	NT SX	NT	TP	NT	TP SX	NT
			◇■		◇■ 🍴		◇■ 🍴	◇	◇■ 🍴		◇	◇■ 🍴		◇■ 🍴	◇	◇■	◇■	◇■	◇■	◇■ 🍴	◇		◇■		◇■	◇
Liverpool Lime Street ■	90	d			17 54							18 24		18 24									18 54			
Lea Green	90	d			18 06																		19 06			
Newton-le-Willows	90	d										18 42		18 41												
Manchester Airport ✈		d							18 10							18 37	18 40			19 07						
Gatley		d														18 43	18 46									
Manchester Piccadilly ■		a							18 33							18 55	18 55			19 25						
		d					18 30		18 34							18 57	18 57	19 00		19 26					19 30	
Manchester Oxford Road		d							18 38							19 00	19 00			19a28						
Manchester Victoria		a			18 29				18 44			18 59		18 59		19 11	19 11						19 29			
		d		18 23	18 30			18 37	18 45	18 52	18 56	19 00		19 00		19 15	19 15				19 21	19 24	19 30			19 36
Ashton-under-Lyne		d		18 33						19 02												19 33				
Stalybridge		a		18 37	18 41		18 43			19 06								19 13				19 38	19 41		19 42	
		d			18 42		18 45											19 13					19 42		19 50	
Mossley (Grtr Manchester)		d					18 49											19 18								
Greenfield		d					18 53											19 22								
Marsden		d					19 01											19 30								
Slaithwaite		d					19 05											19 34								
Huddersfield		a			19 00		19 11		19 16			19 28		19 28		19 45	19 45	19 41					20 00		20 08	
		d	18 49		19 01	19 03	19 12		19 17			19 30		19 30		19 46	19 46		19 49				20 01	20 03	20 12	
Deighton		d	18 53			19 07									←				19 53					20 07		
Mirfield		d	18 57			19 12		19 39							19 39				19 57					20 12		20 39
Wakefield Kirkgate		a				19 28		→																20 28		→
Normanton		a				19 34																		20 34		
Castleford		a				19 40																		20 41		
Ravensthorpe		d	19 01																20 01							
Dewsbury		a	19 04						19 26						19 44	19 55	19 55		20 04							
		d	19 09						19 27						19 44	19 56	19 56		20 09							
Batley		d	19 12												19 47				20 12							
Morley		d	19 17												19 53				20 17							
Cottingley		d	19 21																20 21							
Leeds ■		a	19 29		19 21		19 31		19 40		20 19	19 49		19 49	20 03	20 09	20 09		20 30		20 43		20 23		20 31	
		d			19 27		19 34		19 42			19 51		19 51		20 14	20 14						20 27		20 33	
Cross Gates	40	d																								
Garforth	40	d			19 36																		20 36			
South Milford	40	d																								
Selby	29,40	d					19 56																		20 56	
Howden	29	a																							21 05	
Brough	29	a					20 16																		21 18	
Hull	29	a					20 34																		21 34	
York ■	26	a			19 55				20 05			20 14		20 14		20 36	20 36						20 57			
		d			20 00				20 07			20 16		20 22		20 39	20 39						21 00			
Malton		d			20 25																		21 25			
Seamer	43	a			20 41																		21 41			
Scarborough	43	a			20 51																		21 51			
Thirsk	26	d														20 56	20 56									
Northallerton	26	d							20 26							21 05	21 05									
Yarm		a														21 18	21 18									
Thornaby	44	a														21 28	21 28									
Middlesbrough	44	a														21 35	21 35									
Redcar Central	44	a														21 48	21 48									
Darlington	26	a							20 37			20 43		20 48												
		d							20 39			20 45		20 50												
Durham	26	a							20 54			21 00		21 05												
Chester-le-Street	26	a							21 01																	
Newcastle ■	26	a							21 15			21 14		21 21												
		d										21 16														
Morpeth	26	a										21 31														
Edinburgh	26	a										22 49														

Table T039-F

Mondays to Saturdays

16 December to 15 February

Liverpool, Manchester Airport and Manchester - Huddersfield - Wakefield, Leeds, Hull, York, Scarborough, Middlesbrough, Newcastle and Edinburgh

			TP	TP SO		TP	NT	NT	TP	NT	GC SX	GC SO	TP SO	TP	TP SX	TP SO	NT	TP	TP	NT		NT	TP	TP	TP	NT
			◇1	◇1		◇1		◇	◇1 A ✠	◇	■ ■ R	■ ■ R	◇1	◇1	◇1	◇1		◇1	◇1			◇	◇1	◇1	◇1	
Liverpool Lime Street 10	90	d							19 25										19 54							
Lea Green	90	d																	20 06							
Newton-le-Willows	90	d							19 41																	
Manchester Airport ✈		d	19 10										19 36		19 38								20 10			
Gatley		d											19 42		19 44											
Manchester Piccadilly 10		a	19 33			←							19 54		19 57								20 33		←	
		d	19 34	19 35									19 55	19 58	19 59								20 34	20 35		
Manchester Oxford Road		d	19 38			19 38							19 59		20 02	←							20 38		20 38	
Manchester Victoria		a	→			19 44			19 59				20 10		20 14	20 10			20 29				→		20 44	
		d				19 45	19 52	19 56	20 00				20 15		20 15	20 15	20 22		20 30			20 37			20 45	20 52
Ashton-under-Lyne		d					20 02						→				20 32									21 02
Stalybridge		a		19 50			20 06							20 12			20 36		20 41					20 50		21 07
		d		19 50										20 13					20 42					20 50		
Mossley (Grtr Manchester)		d												20 18												
Greenfield		d												20 22												
Marsden		d												20 30												
Slaithwaite		d												20 34												
Huddersfield		a		20 08		20 16			20 29					20 41	20 45	20 45			21 00					21 08	21 16	
		d		20 12		20 17			20 30						20 46	20 46		20 49	21 01	21 03				21 12	21 17	
Deighton		d								←								20 53		21 07						
Mirfield		d								20 39								20 57		21 12		21 39				
Wakefield Kirkgate		a																		21 28		→				
Normanton		a																		21 34						
Castleford		a																		21 40						
Ravensthorpe		d																21 01								
Dewsbury		a				20 26				20 44					20 56	20 56		21 04							21 26	
		d				20 27				20 44					20 57	20 57		21 09							21 27	
Batley		d								20 47								21 12								
Morley		d								20 53								21 17								
Cottingley		d																21 21								
Leeds 10		a		20 31		20 40		21 14	20 49	21 04					21 10	21 10		21 29	21 22					21 31	21 40	
		d		20 33		20 42			20 51						21 14	21 14			21 27					21 34	21 42	
Cross Gates	40	d																								
Garforth	40	d																	21 36							
South Milford	40	d																								
Selby	29,40	d		20 57																				21 56		
Howden	29	a		21 06																				22 05		
Brough	29	a		21 19																				22 18		
Hull	29	a		21 35																				22 36		
York 8	26	a				21 06			21 14						21 36	21 36			21 55						22 07	
		d				21 15			21 20		21 22	21 23			21 39	21 39			22 00							
Malton		d				21 39													22 25							
Seamer	43	a				21 56													22 41							
Scarborough	43	a				22 03													22 51							
Thirsk	26	d									21 38	21 38			21 56	21 56										
Northallerton	26	d									21a46	21a46			22 05	22 07										
Yarm		a													22 17	22 20										
Thornaby	44	a													22 27	22 30										
Middlesbrough	44	a													22 35	22 40										
Redcar Central	44	a													22 48											
Darlington	26	a							21 46																	
		d							21 48																	
Durham	26	a							22 03																	
Chester-le-Street	26	a																								
Newcastle 8	26	a							22 19																	
		d																								
Morpeth	26	a																								
Edinburgh	26	a																								

A ✠ from York

Table T039-F

Mondays to Saturdays

16 December to 15 February

Liverpool, Manchester Airport and Manchester - Huddersfield - Wakefield, Leeds, Hull, York, Scarborough, Middlesbrough, Newcastle and Edinburgh

			NT	TP SX	TP SO	NT	TP	TP SX	TP	TP	NT	NT		TP SO	TP SX	TP SO	TP SX	NT	NT	TP	TP	TP	TP SX	TP SO	NT	TP SO
			◇	◇1 A ✠	◇1 A ✠	◇	◇1	◇1 ✠	◇1	◇1				◇1	◇1	◇1	◇1	◇		◇1	◇1	◇1	◇1	◇1		◇1
Liverpool Lime Street 10	90	d		20 24	20 24											21 08	21 08									22 06
Lea Green	90	d														21 20	21 20									22 19
Newton-le-Willows	90	d		20 40	20 40											21 27	21 27									22 25
Manchester Airport ✈		d						21 06												21 35						
Gatley		d																		21 41						
Manchester Piccadilly 10		a						21 20												21 53						
		d					20 58	21 22						21 35	21 35					21 55	21 58		22 32	22 34		
Manchester Oxford Road		d						21a24												21 58						
Manchester Victoria		a		20 59	20 59											21 45	21 45			22 11						22 45
		d	20 56	21 00	21 00				21 15		21 23					21 45	21 45	21 56	22 08	22 14					22 36	22 45
Ashton-under-Lyne		d									21 33								22 18						22 47	
Stalybridge		a					21 12				21 37			21 50	21 50	21 57	21 57		22 22		22 14		22 49	22 50	22 51	22 57
		d					21 13							21 50	21 50	21 58	21 58				22 14		22 50	22 50		22 58
Mossley (Grtr Manchester)		d					21 18														22 19					
Greenfield		d					21 23														22 23					
Marsden		d					21 31														22 31					
Slaithwaite		d					21 35														22 35					
Huddersfield		a		21 27	21 27		21 42		21 46					22 08	22 08	22 16	22 16			22 45	22 42		23 08	23 09		23 16
		d		21 29	21 29				21 47	21 51		22 03		22 12	22 12	22 17	22 17			22 46		22 52	23 12	23 12		23 17
Deighton		d				←				21 55		22 07										22 56				
Mirfield		d				21 39				21 59		22 12										23 00				
Wakefield Kirkgate		a										22 28														
Normanton		a										22 34														
Castleford		a										22 40														
Ravensthorpe		d								22 03												23 04				
Dewsbury		a				21 44			21 56	22 06						22 26	22 26			22 56		23 07				23 26
		d				21 45			21 57	22 08						22 27	22 27			22 57		23 09				23 27
Batley		d				21 48				22 11												23 12				
Morley		d				21 54				22 16												23 17				
Cottingley		d								22 20												23 21				
Leeds 10		a	22 13	21 48	21 49	22 05			22 12	22 28				22 35	22 36	22 40	22 40	23 13		23 10		23 29	23 31	23 31		23 40
		d		21 51	21 51				22 14					22 37	22 37	22 42	22 42			23 13			23 33	23 34		23 42
Cross Gates	40	d																								
Garforth	40	d																								
South Milford	40	d												22 53	22 53											
Selby	29,40	d												23 02	23 02								23 52	23 53		
Howden	29	a																								
Brough	29	a												23 21	23 21								00 10	00 11		
Hull	29	a												23 36	23 36								00 26	00 27		
York 8	26	a		22 13	22 14				22 36							23 07	23 07			23 40						00 10
		d		22 21	22 21				22 41							23 08	23 08									
Malton		d							23 05																	
Seamer	43	a							23 22																	
Scarborough	43	a							23 31																	
Thirsk	26	d															23 31									
Northallerton	26	d		22 40	22 40											23 27	23 39									
Yarm		a																								
Thornaby	44	a																								
Middlesbrough	44	a																								
Redcar Central	44	a																								
Darlington	26	a		22 51	22 51											23 38	23 51									
		d		22 53	22 53											23 40	00 01									
Durham	26	a		23 08	23 08											23 55	00 19									
Chester-le-Street	26	a		23 15	23 15											00 02	00 32									
Newcastle 8	26	a		23 26	23 26											00 14	00 59									
		d																								
Morpeth	26	a																								
Edinburgh	26	a																								

A ✠ from York

Table T039-F

Mondays to Saturdays
16 December to 15 February

Liverpool, Manchester Airport and Manchester - Huddersfield - Wakefield, Leeds, Hull, York, Scarborough, Middlesbrough, Newcastle and Edinburgh

	TP SX	NT		TP SX	TP	TP SO	TP SO	TP SX	TP SO	TP SX	TP SX	TP SO	NT SX	NT	TP	TP SO	TP SX	TP SO		TP FO	TP FSX
	◇1	◇		◇1	◇1	◇1	◇1	◇1	◇1	◇1	◇1	◇1	◇		◇1	◇1	◇1	◇1		◇1	◇1
Liverpool Lime Street 10 90 d	22 06															23 08	23 08				
Lea Green 90 d	22 19															23 20	23 23				
Newton-le-Willows 90 d	22 25															23 27	23 31				
Manchester Airport d				22 39		22 40				23 10								23 40		23 40	23 40
Gatley d																					
Manchester Piccadilly 10 a				22 56		22 59		←		23 24								23 53		23 54	23 54
d				22 58	23 00	23 01				23 26					23 35			23 55		23 55	23 55
Manchester Oxford Road d				23 06		23 05		23 06		23a28								23 58		23 59	23 59
Manchester Victoria a	22 45			→		23 11		23 13								23 45	23 50	00 04		00 04	00 04
d	22 46	22 56				23 15		23 15					23 19	23 29		23 45	23 53	00 04		00 05	00 05
Ashton-under-Lyne d														23 39							
Stalybridge a	22 57				23 13									23 43	23 47	23 58	00 04				
d	22 58				23 14										23 47	23 59	00 05				
Mossley (Grtr Manchester) d					23 18										23 52						
Greenfield d					23 22										23 57						
Marsden d					23 30										00 05						
Slaithwaite d					23 34										00 09						
Huddersfield a	23 16				23 40	23 45		23 50	←						00 16	00 19	00 24	00 32		00 32	01 01
d	23 17				23 41	23 46	23 50	23 51			23 54					00 20	00 25	00 34		00 34	01 12
Deighton d					23 44		23 54		23 54		23 58										
Mirfield d					23 49		→		23 58		00 03										
Wakefield Kirkgate a					00 04																
Normanton a																					
Castleford a																					
Ravensthorpe d									00 03		00 08	←									
Dewsbury a	23 26					23 56		00 01	00 06		00 10	00 06				00 29	00 33				
d	23 27					23 57		00 02	00 11		00 10	00 11				00 30	00 34				
Batley d									→		00 13	00 14									
Morley d											00 18	00 19									
Cottingley d											00 22	00 23									
Leeds 10 a	23 40	00 14				00 10		00 15			00 29	00 31	00 46			00 43	00 47	00 53		01 11	01 31
d	23 42					00 22		00 29								00 48	00 53	01 05		01 13	01 43
Cross Gates 40 d																					
Garforth 40 d																					
South Milford 40 d																					
Selby 29,40 d																					
Howden 29 a																					
Brough 29 a																					
Hull 29 a																					
York 8 26 a	00 10					01 02		01 10								01 25	01 29	01 44		01 39	02 27
d																					
Malton d																					
Seamer 43 a																					
Scarborough 43 a																					
Thirsk 26 d																					
Northallerton 26 d																					
Yarm a																					
Thornaby 44 a																					
Middlesbrough 44 a																					
Redcar Central 44 a																					
Darlington 26 a																					
d																					
Durham 26 a																					
Chester-le-Street 26 a																					
Newcastle 8 26 a																					
d																					
Morpeth 26 a																					
Edinburgh 26 a																					

Table T039-F

Mondays to Saturdays
17 February to 28 March

Liverpool, Manchester Airport and Manchester - Huddersfield - Wakefield, Leeds, Hull, York, Scarborough, Middlesbrough, Newcastle and Edinburgh

	TP MX	TP MO	TP MX	TP MO	TP MX	TP MO	TP MX	TP MO	TP MX	TP MO	TP SO	TP MSX	TP MO	TP MSX	TP SO		TP	TP SO	TP MO	TP MSX	TP SO	TP	TP	TP
	◇1	◇1	◇1	◇1	◇1	◇1	◇1	◇1	◇1	◇1	◇1	◇1	◇1	◇1	◇1		◇1	◇1	◇1	◇1	◇1	◇1	◇1	◇1
Liverpool Lime Street 10 90 d																								
Lea Green 90 d																								
Newton-le-Willows 90 d																								
Manchester Airport d													00 38	00 38	00 38									
Gatley d																								
Manchester Piccadilly 10 a													00 51	00 51	00 52									
d													00 53	00 53	01 03			02 42	02 42	02 42				
Manchester Oxford Road d																								
Manchester Victoria a																								
d											00 05	00 05												
Ashton-under-Lyne d																								
Stalybridge a																								
d									00 05															
Mossley (Grtr Manchester) d																								
Greenfield d																								
Marsden d		00 04	00 05																					
Slaithwaite d		00 08	00 09																		←			
Huddersfield a		00 14	00 16						00 24		00 32	01 01			01 32			03 15	03 33	03 33	03 15			
d								00 19	00 25	00 27	00 34	01 12			01 33			03 51	03 50	03 50	03 51			
Deighton d																		→						
Mirfield d							00 03																	
Wakefield Kirkgate a																								
Normanton a																								
Castleford a																								
Ravensthorpe d						00 02	00 08																	
Dewsbury a						00 04	00 10	00s27	00 33															
d					00 02	00 09	00 10		00 34															
Batley d						00 12	00 13																	
Morley d						00 17	00 18																	
Cottingley d						00 21	00 22																	
Leeds 10 a					00 15	00 29	00 29	00 41	00 47	01 03	01 11	01 31	02 06	02 06	02 08				04 09	04 09	04 30			
d				00 22	00 29			00 46	00 53	01 06	01 13	01 43	02 11	02 19	02 19				04 20	04 20	04 32		05 35	
Cross Gates 40 d																								
Garforth 40 d																								
South Milford 40 d																								
Selby 29,40 d																							05 55	
Howden 29 a																								
Brough 29 a																							06 12	
Hull 29 a																							06 28	
York 8 26 a				01 02	01 10			01 26	01 29	01 32	01 39	02 27	02 39	02 58	02 58				04 45	05 00	04 57			
d																						05 05		06 04
Malton d																								06 29
Seamer 43 a																								06 45
Scarborough 43 a																								06 55
Thirsk 26 d																						05 28		
Northallerton 26 d																						05 36		
Yarm a																								
Thornaby 44 a																						06 27		
Middlesbrough 44 a																						06 34		
Redcar Central 44 a																						06 47		
Darlington 26 a																								
d	00 01																							
Durham 26 a	00 19																							
Chester-le-Street 26 a	00 32																							
Newcastle 8 26 a	00 59																							
d																	05 53							
Morpeth 26 a																	06 07							
Edinburgh 26 a																	07 30							

Table T039-F

Mondays to Saturdays

17 February to 28 March

Liverpool, Manchester Airport and Manchester - Huddersfield - Wakefield, Leeds, Hull, York, Scarborough, Middlesbrough, Newcastle and Edinburgh

Station		TP	TP	TP	NT	TP	TP SO	TP SX	NT	TP SX	TP SO	NT	TP SO	TP SX	TP	TP SO	TP SX	TP	NT	TP	NT	NT SO	TP
		◇1 🛒	◇1	◇1		◇1	◇1 🛒	◇1 🛒	◇	◇1 🛒	◇1 🛒		◇1	◇1	◇1	◇1	◇1	◇1		◇1		◇	◇1
Liverpool Lime Street 10	90 d									05 20	05 20												05 52
Lea Green	90 d									05 32	05 32												06 06
Newton-le-Willows	90 d									05 39	05 39												06 12
Manchester Airport	d						05 19	05 19					05 37	05 37									
Gatley	d																						
Manchester Piccadilly 10	a						05 33	05 33					05 56	05 56									
	d					05 15	05 34	05 34					05 57	05 57	06 00					06 27			
Manchester Oxford Road	d						05 40	05 40					06 01	06 01									
Manchester Victoria	a						05 45	05 45		05 58	05 58		06 06	06 10									06 31
	d	05 00					05 45	05 45	05 45	06 00	06 00		06 15	06 15					06 26			06 31	06 32
Ashton-under-Lyne	d																		06 36				
Stalybridge	a														06 12				06 40	06 41			06 44
	d														06 12					06 42			06 44
Mossley (Grtr Manchester)	d														06 17								06 49
Greenfield	d														06 22								06 53
Marsden	d														06 30								07 01
Slaithwaite	d														06 34	←	←	←					07 05
Huddersfield	a					06 11	06 16	06 16		06 28	06 28		06 45	06 45	06 41	06 45	06 45	06 41		06 59			07 11
	d			05 49	06 03	06 14	06 17	06 17		06 30	06 30		06 46	06 46	06 49	06 46	06 46	06 49		07 00	07 03		07 12
Deighton	d			05 53	06 07								→	→	→			06 53			07 07		
Mirfield	d			05 57	06 12							06 39						06 57			07 12		
Wakefield Kirkgate	a				06 28																07 28		
Normanton	a				06 34																07 34		
Castleford	a				06 40																07 40		
Ravensthorpe	d			06 01								06 42						07 01					
Dewsbury	a			06 04			06 26	06 26				06 45				06 56	06 56	07 04					
	d			06 09			06 27	06 27				06 46				06 57	06 57	07 09					
Batley	d			06 12								06 49						07 12					
Morley	d			06 17								06 55						07 17					
Cottingley	d			06 21								06 58						07 21					
Leeds 10	a	06 12		06 29		06 33	06 40	06 40	07 23	06 49	06 49	07 08				07 10	07 10	07 29		07 22		08 00	07 31
	d	06 15				06 36	06 42	06 42		06 51	06 51					07 14	07 14			07 27			07 34
Cross Gates	40 d																						
Garforth	40 d																			07 36			
South Milford	40 d																						
Selby	29,40 d					07 08																	07 54
Howden	29 a																						08 03
Brough	29 a					07 26																	08 17
Hull	29 a					07 42																	08 34
York 8	26 a	06 37					07 05	07 05		07 14	07 17					07 36	07 36			07 58			
	d	06 39	07 02				07 07	07 07		07 22	07 22					07 39	07 39			08 03			
Malton	d		07 27																	08 28			
Seamer	43 a		07 44																	08 44			
Scarborough	43 a		07 53																	08 52			
Thirsk	26 d	06 56														07 56	07 56						
Northallerton	26 d	07 05					07 28	07 29								08 05	08 05						
Yarm	a	07 17														08 17	08 17						
Thornaby	44 a	07 27														08 28	08 28						
Middlesbrough	44 a	07 35														08 35	08 35						
Redcar Central	44 a	07 50														08 48	08 48						
Darlington	26 a						07 40	07 41		07 48	07 48												
	d						07 41	07 42		07 50	07 50												
Durham	26 a						07 57	07 58		08 05	08 05												
Chester-le-Street	26 a						08 03	08 04															
Newcastle 8	26 a						08 16	08 17		08 19	08 19												
	d									08 21	08 21												
Morpeth	26 a									08 34	08 34												
Edinburgh	26 a									09 53	09 53												

Table T039-F

Mondays to Saturdays

17 February to 28 March

Liverpool, Manchester Airport and Manchester - Huddersfield - Wakefield, Leeds, Hull, York, Scarborough, Middlesbrough, Newcastle and Edinburgh

Station		NT SX	NT	NT	TP SO	TP SX	NT	TP SX	TP SO	NT	TP	TP	TP	TP	NT	TP	NT	TP	NT	TP	NT	NT	TP SX	TP SO
		◇	◇	◇	◇1	◇1		◇1 🛒	◇1 🛒	◇	◇1 🛒	◇1	◇1	◇1 🛒		◇1 🛒		◇1 🛒	◇	◇1 🛒		◇	◇1 🛒	◇1 🛒
Liverpool Lime Street 10	90 d							06 24	06 24							06 54							07 24	07 24
Lea Green	90 d															07 06								
Newton-le-Willows	90 d							06 41	06 41														07 41	07 41
Manchester Airport	d				06 10	06 15					06 35			07 07						07 10				
Gatley	d										06 41													
Manchester Piccadilly 10	a				06 32	06 32					06 54			07 25						07 33				
	d				06 34	06 34					06 56	06 58		07 26				07 30		07 34				
Manchester Oxford Road	d				06 38	06 38					06 59			07a28						07 38				
Manchester Victoria	a				06 45	06 45		06 59	06 59		07 11					07 29				07 43			07 59	07 59
	d	06 32	06 37	06 42	06 45	06 45	06 52	07 00	07 00		07 15				07 23	07 30			07 36	07 45	07 53	07 57	08 00	08 00
Ashton-under-Lyne	d						07 02								07 33						08 03			
Stalybridge	a						07 06					07 13			07 37	07 41		07 43			08 07			
	d											07 13				07 42		07 45						
Mossley (Grtr Manchester)	d											07 18						07 49						
Greenfield	d											07 22						07 53						
Marsden	d											07 30						08 01						
Slaithwaite	d											07 34						08 05						
Huddersfield	a				07 16	07 16		07 28	07 28		07 45	07 41				08 00		08 11		08 16			08 28	08 28
	d				07 17	07 17		07 30	07 30		07 46		07 49			08 00	08 03	08 12		08 17			08 30	08 30
Deighton	d									←			07 53				08 07							
Mirfield	d		07 40							07 40			07 57				08 12		08 39					
Wakefield Kirkgate	a		→														08 28		→					
Normanton	a																08 34							
Castleford	a																08 40							
Ravensthorpe	d												08 01											
Dewsbury	a				07 26	07 26				07 45	07 56		08 04							08 26				
	d				07 27	07 27				07 45	07 57		08 09							08 27				
Batley	d									07 48			08 12											
Morley	d									07 54			08 17											
Cottingley	d									07 58			08 21											
Leeds 10	a	08 00		08 14	07 40	07 40		07 49	07 49	08 06	08 10		08 29			08 22		08 31		08 40		09 22	08 49	08 49
	d				07 42	07 42		07 51	07 51		08 14					08 27		08 34		08 42			08 51	08 51
Cross Gates	40 d																							
Garforth	40 d															08 36								
South Milford	40 d																							
Selby	29,40 d																	08 56						
Howden	29 a																							
Brough	29 a																	09 15						
Hull	29 a																	09 30						
York 8	26 a				08 05	08 05		08 18	08 18		08 36					08 54				09 05			09 14	09 14
	d				08 07	08 07		08 21	08 21		08 39					09 00				09 07			09 21	09 21
Malton	d															09 25								
Seamer	43 a															09 41								
Scarborough	43 a															09 49								
Thirsk	26 d										08 56													
Northallerton	26 d				08 26	08 26					09 06									09 26				
Yarm	a										09 18													
Thornaby	44 a										09 28													
Middlesbrough	44 a										09 36													
Redcar Central	44 a										09 49													
Darlington	26 a				08 37	08 37		08 47	08 47											09 37			09 47	09 47
	d				08 39	08 39		08 49	08 49											09 39			09 49	09 49
Durham	26 a				08 54	08 54		09 04	09 04											09 54			10 04	10 04
Chester-le-Street	26 a				09 01	09 01																		
Newcastle 8	26 a				09 12	09 12		09 18	09 18											10 11			10 19	10 19
	d							09 21	09 21														10 21	10 21
Morpeth	26 a							09 33	09 33														10 34	10 34
Edinburgh	26 a							10 52	10 56														11 50	11 54

Table T039-F

Mondays to Saturdays

17 February to 28 March

Liverpool, Manchester Airport and Manchester - Huddersfield - Wakefield, Leeds, Hull, York, Scarborough, Middlesbrough, Newcastle and Edinburgh

			NT	TP SO	TP	TP SX	TP	NT	GC SO	TP	NT	TP	NT	TP	NT	NT	TP SX	TP SO	NT	GC SX	TP	TP	TP	TP
			◇	◇1 ✕	◇1	◇1 ✕	◇1		■ 1	◇1 ✕		◇1 ✕	◇	◇1 ✕		◇	◇1 ✕	◇1 ✕	◇	■ 1	◇1 ✕	◇1	◇1	◇1 ✕
Liverpool Lime Street 10	90	d								07 54							08 24	08 24						
Lea Green	90	d								08 07														
Newton-le-Willows	90	d															08 41	08 41						
Manchester Airport		d		07 35		07 47								08 10							08 35			09 07
Gatley		d		07 41		07 53															08 41			
Manchester Piccadilly 10		a		07 54		08 03								08 33							08 54			09 25
		d		07 56	08 00	08 05						08 30		08 35							08 56	08 58		09 26
Manchester Oxford Road		d		07 59		08 08								08 38							09 00			09a28
Manchester Victoria		a		08 11		08 14				08 29				08 45			08 59	08 59			09 12			
		d		08 15		08 15		08 21		08 30			08 37	08 45	08 52	08 56	09 00	09 00			09 15			
Ashton-under-Lyne		d						08 31							09 02									
Stalybridge		a			08 13			08 35		08 41		08 44			09 06							09 12		
		d			08 13					08 42		08 45										09 13		
Mossley (Grtr Manchester)		d			08 18							08 49										09 17		
Greenfield		d			08 23							08 53										09 22		
Marsden		d			08 31							09 01										09 30		
Slaithwaite		d			08 35							09 05										09 34		
Huddersfield		a		08 45	08 42	08 45				09 00		09 11		09 16			09 28	09 28			09 45	09 41		
		d		08 46		08 46	08 49			09 01	09 03	09 12		09 17			09 30	09 30			09 46		09 49	
Deighton		d	←				08 53				09 07								←				09 53	
Mirfield		d	08 39				08 57				09 12		09 39						09 39				09 57	
Wakefield Kirkgate		a									09 28		→											
Normanton		a									09 34													
Castleford		a									09 40													
Ravensthorpe		d	08 42				09 01																10 01	
Dewsbury		a	08 45	08 56		08 56	09 04							09 26					09 44		09 56		10 04	
		d	08 46	08 57		08 57	09 09							09 27					09 44		09 57		10 09	
Batley		d	08 49				09 12												09 47				10 12	
Morley		d	08 55				09 17												09 53				10 17	
Cottingley		d					09 21																10 21	
Leeds 10		a	09 04	09 10		09 10	09 29			09 22		09 31		09 40		10 13	09 49	09 49	10 04		10 10		10 29	
		d		09 14		09 14				09 27		09 34		09 42			09 51	09 51			10 14			
Cross Gates	40	d																						
Garforth	40	d								09 36														
South Milford	40	d																						
Selby	29,40	d										09 57												
Howden	29	a																						
Brough	29	a										10 16												
Hull	29	a										10 34												
York 8	26	a		09 36		09 36				09 55				10 04			10 14	10 14			10 36			
		d		09 39		09 39			09 49	10 00				10 07			10 21	10 21		10 25	10 39			
Malton		d								10 25														
Seamer	43	a								10 42														
Scarborough	43	a								10 52														
Thirsk	26	d		09 56		09 56			10 06											10 42	10 56			
Northallerton	26	d		10 07		10 07			10a16					10 26						10a58	11 07			
Yarm		a		10 20		10 20															11 20			
Thornaby	44	a		10 30		10 30															11 30			
Middlesbrough	44	a		10 37		10 37															11 37			
Redcar Central	44	a		10 50		10 50															11 50			
Darlington	26	a												10 37			10 47	10 47						
		d												10 39			10 49	10 49						
Durham	26	a												10 54			11 04	11 04						
Chester-le-Street	26	a												11 01										
Newcastle 8	26	a												11 13			11 19	11 19						
		d															11 21	11 21						
Morpeth	26	a															11 34	11 34						
Edinburgh	26	a															12 51	12 56						

Table T039-F

Mondays to Saturdays

17 February to 28 March

Liverpool, Manchester Airport and Manchester - Huddersfield - Wakefield, Leeds, Hull, York, Scarborough, Middlesbrough, Newcastle and Edinburgh

			NT	TP	NT	TP SO	NT	TP	TP SX	TP	NT	NT	TP SX	TP SO	NT	TP SX	TP SO	TP	TP	NT	TP	NT	TP SX	NT	TP SO
				◇1 ✕		◇1 ✕	◇	◇1 ✕	◇1 ✕	◇1 ✕		◇	◇1 ✕	◇1 ✕	◇	◇1 ✕	◇1 ✕	◇1	◇1		◇1 ✕		◇1 ✕	◇	◇1 ✕
Liverpool Lime Street 10	90	d		08 54									09 24	09 24							09 53				
Lea Green	90	d		09 06																	10 06				
Newton-le-Willows	90	d											09 41	09 41											
Manchester Airport		d						09 10								09 36	09 40								10 10
Gatley		d														09 42	09 46								
Manchester Piccadilly 10		a						09 33		←						09 55	09 55								10 33
		d				09 30		09 34	09 35							09 57	09 57	09 58					10 30		10 34
Manchester Oxford Road		d						09 38		09 38						10 00	10 00								10 38
Manchester Victoria		a		09 29				→		09 44			09 59	09 59		10 11	10 11				10 29				→
		d	09 23	09 30			09 37			09 45	09 52	09 56	10 00	10 00		10 15	10 15			10 23	10 30			10 37	
Ashton-under-Lyne		d	09 33								10 02									10 33					
Stalybridge		a	09 37	09 41		09 42			09 50		10 06							10 12		10 37	10 41		10 42		
		d		09 42		09 46			09 50									10 12			10 42		10 50		
Mossley (Grtr Manchester)		d																10 17							
Greenfield		d																10 22							
Marsden		d																10 30							
Slaithwaite		d																10 34							
Huddersfield		a		10 00		10 05			10 08	10 16			10 28	10 28		10 44	10 44	10 41			11 00		11 08		
		d		10 01	10 03	10 12			10 12	10 17			10 30	10 30		10 45	10 45		10 49		11 01	11 03	11 12		
Deighton		d			10 07										←				10 53			11 07			
Mirfield		d			10 12		10 39								10 39				10 59			11 12		11 39	
Wakefield Kirkgate		a			10 28		→															11 28		→	
Normanton		a			10 34																	11 34			
Castleford		a			10 40																	11 40			
Ravensthorpe		d																	11 02						
Dewsbury		a								10 26					10 44	10 56	10 56		11 05						
		d								10 27					10 44	10 57	10 57		11 09						
Batley		d													10 47				11 12						
Morley		d													10 53				11 17						
Cottingley		d																	11 21						
Leeds 10		a		10 21		10 31			10 31	10 40		11 13	10 49	10 49	11 03	11 10	11 10		11 29		11 21		11 31		
		d		10 27		10 34			10 34	10 42			10 51	10 51		11 14	11 14				11 27		11 34		
Cross Gates	40	d																							
Garforth	40	d		10 36																	11 36				
South Milford	40	d																							
Selby	29,40	d				10 56			10 56														11 56		
Howden	29	a																							
Brough	29	a				11 15			11 15														12 15		
Hull	29	a				11 30			11 30														12 30		
York 8	26	a		10 55						11 05			11 15	11 15		11 36	11 36				11 57				
		d		11 00						11 07			11 21	11 21		11 39	11 39				12 00				
Malton		d		11 25																	12 25				
Seamer	43	a		11 41																	12 41				
Scarborough	43	a		11 51																	12 51				
Thirsk	26	d														11 56	11 56								
Northallerton	26	d								11 26						12 05	12 07								
Yarm		a														12 17	12 20								
Thornaby	44	a														12 27	12 30								
Middlesbrough	44	a														12 35	12 37								
Redcar Central	44	a														12 48	12 50								
Darlington	26	a								11 37			11 48	11 48											
		d								11 39			11 49	11 49											
Durham	26	a								11 54			12 05	12 05											
Chester-le-Street	26	a																							
Newcastle 8	26	a								12 11			12 18	12 18											
		d											12 21	12 21											
Morpeth	26	a											12 34	12 34											
Edinburgh	26	a											13 50	13 57											

Table T039-F

Mondays to Saturdays
17 February to 28 March

Liverpool, Manchester Airport and Manchester - Huddersfield - Wakefield, Leeds, Hull, York, Scarborough, Middlesbrough, Newcastle and Edinburgh

Station		TP	TP	TP	TP	NT	NT	TP		TP	NT	TP	TP	TP	TP	NT	TP	NT	NT	TP	TP	TP	NT	NT
		SX	SO	SO	SX			SX		SO														
		◇1	◇1	◇1	◇1		◇	◇1		◇1	◇	◇1	◇1	◇1	◇1		◇1		◇	◇1	◇1	◇1		◇
		⊼	⊼	⊼	⊼			⊼		⊼		⊼			⊼		⊼			⊼	⊼	⊼		
Liverpool Lime Street 10	90 d							10 24		10 24							10 54							
Lea Green	90 d																11 06							
Newton-le-Willows	90 d							10 41		10 41														
Manchester Airport	d	10 10										10 40			11 07					11 10				
Gatley	d											10 46												
Manchester Piccadilly 10	a	10 33		←	←							10 55			11 25					11 33		←		
	d	10 34	10 35									10 57	10 58		11 26					11 34	11 35			
Manchester Oxford Road	d	10 38		10 38	10 38							11 00			11a28					11 38		11 38		
Manchester Victoria	a	→		10 44	10 44			10 59		10 59		11 11					11 29			→		11 44		
	d			10 44	10 45	10 52	10 55	11 00		11 00		11 15				11 23	11 30		11 34			11 45	11 52	11 55
Ashton-under-Lyne	d					11 02										11 33							12 02	
Stalybridge	a		10 50			11 06							11 12			11 37	11 42				11 50		12 06	
	d		10 50										11 12				11 42				11 50			
Mossley (Grtr Manchester)	d												11 17											
Greenfield	d												11 22											
Marsden	d												11 30											
Slaithwaite	d												11 34											
Huddersfield	a		11 08	11 16	11 16			11 28		11 28		11 45	11 41				12 00				12 08	12 16		
	d		11 12	11 17	11 17			11 30		11 30		11 46		11 49			12 01	12 03			12 12	12 17		
Deighton	d										←			11 53				12 07						
Mirfield	d										11 39			11 57				12 12	12 39					
Wakefield Kirkgate	a																	12 28	→					
Normanton	a																	12 34						
Castleford	a																	12 40						
Ravensthorpe	d													12 01										
Dewsbury	a			11 26	11 26						11 44	11 56		12 04								12 26		
	d			11 27	11 27						11 44	11 57		12 09								12 27		
Batley	d										11 47			12 12										
Morley	d										11 53			12 17										
Cottingley	d													12 21										
Leeds 10	a		11 31	11 40	11 40		12 18	11 49		11 49	12 03	12 10		12 29			12 21				12 31	12 40		13 18
	d		11 34	11 42	11 42			11 51		11 51		12 14					12 27				12 34	12 42		
Cross Gates	40 d																							
Garforth	40 d																12 36							
South Milford	40 d																							
Selby	29,40 d		11 56																		12 56			
Howden	29 a																							
Brough	29 a		12 15																		13 15			
Hull	29 a		12 30																		13 32			
York 8	26 a			12 05	12 05			12 14		12 14		12 36					12 55					13 05		
	d			12 07	12 07			12 22		12 22		12 39					13 00					13 07		
Malton	d																13 25							
Seamer	43 a																13 41							
Scarborough	43 a																13 51							
Thirsk	26 d											12 56												
Northallerton	26 d			12 26	12 26							13 05										13 26		
Yarm	a											13 18												
Thornaby	44 a											13 28												
Middlesbrough	44 a											13 35												
Redcar Central	44 a											13 49												
Darlington	26 a			12 37	12 37			12 48		12 48												13 37		
	d			12 39	12 39			12 50		12 50												13 39		
Durham	26 a			12 54	12 54			13 05		13 05												13 54		
Chester-le-Street	26 a			13 01	13 01																			
Newcastle 8	26 a			13 13	13 13			13 19		13 19												14 10		
	d							13 21		13 21														
Morpeth	26 a							13 34		13 34														
Edinburgh	26 a							14 49		14 54														

NRT DECEMBER 19 EDITION

Table T039-F

Mondays to Saturdays
17 February to 28 March

Liverpool, Manchester Airport and Manchester - Huddersfield - Wakefield, Leeds, Hull, York, Scarborough, Middlesbrough, Newcastle and Edinburgh

Station		TP	TP	NT	GC	TP	TP	TP	TP	NT	TP	NT	NT	TP	TP	TP		NT	NT	TP	TP	NT	TP	TP	TP
		SX	SO			SO	SX													SX	SO		SO	SX	
		◇1	◇1	◇	1	◇1	◇1	◇1	◇1		◇1		◇	◇1	◇1	◇1			◇	◇1	◇1	◇	◇1	◇1	◇1
		⊼	⊼		⊡	⊼	⊼				⊼			⊼	⊼	⊼				⊼	⊼		⊼	⊼	
Liverpool Lime Street 10	90 d	11 24	11 24								11 54									12 24	12 24				
Lea Green	90 d										12 06														
Newton-le-Willows	90 d	11 41	11 42																	12 41	12 41				
Manchester Airport	d					11 40	11 40							12 10									12 40	12 40	
Gatley	d					11 46	11 46																12 46	12 46	
Manchester Piccadilly 10	a					11 55	11 55							12 33		←							12 55	12 55	
	d					11 57	11 57	11 58						12 34	12 35								12 57	12 57	12 58
Manchester Oxford Road	d					12 00	12 00							12 38		12 38							13 00	13 00	
Manchester Victoria	a	11 59	11 59			12 10	12 10				12 29			→		12 44				12 59	12 59		13 10	13 13	
	d	12 00	12 00			12 15	12 15			12 23	12 30		12 37			12 45		12 52	12 56	13 00	13 00		13 15	13 15	
Ashton-under-Lyne	d									12 33								13 02							
Stalybridge	a							12 12		12 37	12 41				12 50			13 06							13 12
	d							12 12			12 42				12 50										13 13
Mossley (Grtr Manchester)	d							12 17																	13 18
Greenfield	d							12 22																	13 22
Marsden	d							12 30																	13 30
Slaithwaite	d							12 34																	13 34
Huddersfield	a	12 28	12 28			12 45	12 45	12 41			13 00				13 08	13 16				13 28	13 28		13 45	13 45	13 41
	d	12 30	12 30			12 46	12 46		12 49		13 01	13 03			13 12	13 17				13 30	13 30		13 46	13 46	
Deighton	d			←					12 53			13 07										←			
Mirfield	d			12 39					12 57			13 12	13 39									13 39			
Wakefield Kirkgate	a											13 28	→												
Normanton	a											13 34													
Castleford	a											13 40													
Ravensthorpe	d								13 01																
Dewsbury	a			12 44		12 56	12 56		13 04							13 26						13 44	13 56	13 56	
	d			12 44		12 57	12 57		13 09							13 27						13 44	13 57	13 57	
Batley	d			12 47					13 12													13 47			
Morley	d			12 53					13 17													13 53			
Cottingley	d								13 21																
Leeds 10	a	12 49	12 49	13 03		13 10	13 10		13 29		13 21				13 31	13 40			14 18	13 49	13 49	14 03	14 10	14 10	
	d	12 51	12 51			13 14	13 14				13 27				13 34	13 42				13 51	13 51		14 14	14 14	
Cross Gates	40 d																								
Garforth	40 d										13 36														
South Milford	40 d																								
Selby	29,40 d														13 56										
Howden	29 a																								
Brough	29 a														14 15										
Hull	29 a														14 30										
York 8	26 a	13 14	13 14			13 36	13 36				13 55					14 05				14 14	14 14		14 36	14 36	
	d	13 20	13 20		13 23	13 39	13 39				14 00					14 07				14 21	14 21		14 39	14 39	
Malton	d										14 25														
Seamer	43 a										14 41														
Scarborough	43 a										14 51														
Thirsk	26 d				13 40	13 56	13 56																14 56	14 56	
Northallerton	26 d				13a48	14 05	14 07																15 05	15 07	
Yarm	a					14 17	14 20																15 17	15 20	
Thornaby	44 a					14 27	14 30																15 27	15 30	
Middlesbrough	44 a					14 35	14 37																15 35	15 37	
Redcar Central	44 a					14 48	14 50																15 48	15 50	
Darlington	26 a	13 46	13 46													14 37				14 47	14 47				
	d	13 48	13 48													14 38				14 49	14 49				
Durham	26 a	14 03	14 03													14 54				15 04	15 04				
Chester-le-Street	26 a															15 00									
Newcastle 8	26 a	14 19	14 19													15 13				15 18	15 18				
	d	14 21	14 21																	15 21	15 21				
Morpeth	26 a	14 34	14 34																	15 33	15 33				
Edinburgh	26 a	15 49	15 54																	16 48	16 55				

Table T039-F

Mondays to Saturdays
17 February to 28 March

Liverpool, Manchester Airport and Manchester - Huddersfield - Wakefield, Leeds, Hull, York, Scarborough, Middlesbrough, Newcastle and Edinburgh

		TP	TP	NT	GC	TP	NT	NT	TP	TP	TP	GC	NT	NT	TP	TP	NT	TP	TP	TP	TP	NT	TP
					SX							SO			SX	SO		SO	SX				
		◇1	◇1 ⊼		R 1 ⊏	◇1 ⊼		◇	◇1 ⊼	◇1 ⊼	◇1 ⊼	R 1 ⊏		◇	◇1 ⊼	◇1 ⊼	◇	◇1 ⊼	◇1 ⊼	◇1	◇1		◇1 ⊼
Liverpool Lime Street 10	90 d					12 54									13 24	13 24							13 54
Lea Green	90 d					13 06																	14 06
Newton-le-Willows	90 d														13 41	13 41							
Manchester Airport	d		13 07						13 10									13 40	13 40				
Gatley	d																	13 46	13 46				
Manchester Piccadilly 10	a		13 25						13 33		←							13 55	13 55				
	d		13 26						13 34	13 35								13 57	13 57	13 58			
Manchester Oxford Road	d		13a28						13 38		13 38							14 00	14 00				
Manchester Victoria	a					13 29			→		13 44				13 59	13 59		14 10	14 10				14 29
	d			13 22		13 30		13 37			13 45		13 52	13 55	14 00	14 00		14 15	14 15			14 23	14 30
Ashton-under-Lyne	d			13 32									14 02									14 33	
Stalybridge	a			13 36		13 41				13 50			14 06							14 12		14 37	14 41
	d					13 42				13 50										14 12			14 42
Mossley (Grtr Manchester)	d																			14 17			
Greenfield	d																			14 22			
Marsden	d																			14 30			
Slaithwaite	d																			14 34			
Huddersfield	a					14 00				14 08	14 16				14 28	14 28		14 45	14 45	14 41			15 00
	d	13 49				14 01	14 03			14 12	14 17				14 30	14 30		14 46	14 46		14 49		15 01
Deighton	d	13 53					14 07										←				14 53		
Mirfield	d	13 57					14 12	14 39									14 39				14 57		
Wakefield Kirkgate	a						14 28	→															
Normanton	a						14 34																
Castleford	a						14 40																
Ravensthorpe	d	14 01																			15 01		
Dewsbury	a	14 04									14 26						14 44	14 56	14 56		15 04		
	d	14 09									14 27						14 44	14 57	14 57		15 09		
Batley	d	14 12															14 47				15 12		
Morley	d	14 17															14 53				15 17		
Cottingley	d	14 21																			15 21		
Leeds 10	a	14 29				14 21				14 31	14 40			15 13	14 49	14 49	15 03	15 10	15 10		15 29		15 21
	d					14 27				14 34	14 42				14 51	14 51		15 14	15 14				15 27
Cross Gates	40 d																						
Garforth	40 d					14 36																	15 36
South Milford	40 d																						
Selby	29,40 d									14 56													
Howden	29 a																						
Brough	29 a									15 15													
Hull	29 a									15 31													
York 8	26 a					14 55					15 05				15 14	15 14		15 36	15 36				15 55
	d				14 51	15 00					15 07	15 14			15 22	15 22		15 39	15 39				16 00
Malton	d					15 25																	16 25
Seamer	43 a					15 41																	16 41
Scarborough	43 a					15 51																	16 51
Thirsk	26 d				15 14							15 37						15 56	15 56				
Northallerton	26 d				15a25						15 26	15a45						16 05	16 07				
Yarm	a																	16 17	16 20				
Thornaby	44 a																	16 27	16 30				
Middlesbrough	44 a																	16 35	16 37				
Redcar Central	44 a																	16 48	16 50				
Darlington	26 a										15 37				15 48	15 48							
	d										15 39				15 50	15 50							
Durham	26 a										15 54				16 05	16 05							
Chester-le-Street	26 a										16 01												
Newcastle 8	26 a										16 13				16 19	16 19							
	d														16 21	16 21							
Morpeth	26 a														16 34	16 34							
Edinburgh	26 a														17 52	17 57							

Table T039-F

Mondays to Saturdays
17 February to 28 March

Liverpool, Manchester Airport and Manchester - Huddersfield - Wakefield, Leeds, Hull, York, Scarborough, Middlesbrough, Newcastle and Edinburgh

		NT	NT	TP	TP	TP	TP	TP	NT	NT	TP	TP	NT	TP	TP	TP	TP	NT	TP	NT	NT	TP	TP	TP
				SO	SX		SO	SX			SX	SO												
			◇	◇1 ⊼	◇1 ⊼	◇1 ⊼	◇1 ⊼	◇1 ⊼		◇	◇1 ⊼	◇1 ⊼	◇	◇1 ⊼	◇1	◇1	◇1 ⊼		◇1 ⊼		◇	◇1 ⊼	◇1 ⊼	◇1 ⊼
Liverpool Lime Street 10	90 d										14 24	14 24							14 54					
Lea Green	90 d																		15 06					
Newton-le-Willows	90 d										14 41	14 41												
Manchester Airport	d			14 10	14 10									14 40			15 07					15 10		
Gatley	d													14 46										
Manchester Piccadilly 10	a			14 33	14 33		←	←						14 55			15 25					15 33		←
	d			14 34	14 34	14 35								14 57	14 58		15 26					15 34	15 35	
Manchester Oxford Road	d			14 38	14 38		14 38	14 38						15 00			15a28					15 38		15 38
Manchester Victoria	a			→	→		14 44	14 44			14 59	14 59		15 11					15 29			→		15 44
	d		14 36				14 45	14 45	14 52	14 56	15 00	15 00		15 15				15 23	15 30		15 36			15 45
Ashton-under-Lyne	d								15 02									15 33						
Stalybridge	a					14 50			15 06						15 12			15 37	15 41				15 50	
	d					14 50									15 12				15 42				15 50	
Mossley (Grtr Manchester)	d														15 17									
Greenfield	d														15 22									
Marsden	d														15 30									
Slaithwaite	d														15 34									
Huddersfield	a					15 08	15 14	15 14			15 28	15 28		15 45	15 41				16 00				16 08	16 16
	d	15 03				15 09	15 15	15 15			15 29	15 29		15 46		15 49			16 01	16 03			16 12	16 17
Deighton	d	15 07											←			15 53				16 07				
Mirfield	d	15 12	15 38										15 38			15 59				16 12	16 38			
Wakefield Kirkgate	a	15 28	→																	16 28	→			
Normanton	a	15 34																		16 34				
Castleford	a	15 40																		16 40				
Ravensthorpe	d															16 03								
Dewsbury	a						15 26	15 26					15 43	15 56		16 06								16 26
	d						15 27	15 27					15 43	15 57		16 09								16 27
Batley	d												15 46			16 12								
Morley	d												15 52			16 17								
Cottingley	d															16 21								
Leeds 10	a					15 31	15 40	15 40		16 18	15 49	15 49	16 02	16 10		16 29			16 20				16 31	16 40
	d					15 33	15 42	15 42			15 51	15 51		16 14					16 27				16 34	16 42
Cross Gates	40 d																						16 40	
Garforth	40 d																		16 36				16 45	
South Milford	40 d																							
Selby	29,40 d					15 55																	16 59	
Howden	29 a																							
Brough	29 a					16 14																	17 18	
Hull	29 a					16 31																	17 34	
York 8	26 a						16 05	16 05			16 14	16 14		16 36					16 55					17 05
	d						16 07	16 07			16 19	16 19		16 39					17 00					17 07
Malton	d																		17 25					
Seamer	43 a																		17 41					
Scarborough	43 a																		17 51					
Thirsk	26 d													16 56										
Northallerton	26 d						16 26	16 26						17 07										17 26
Yarm	a													17 20										
Thornaby	44 a													17 30										
Middlesbrough	44 a													17 37										
Redcar Central	44 a													17 50										
Darlington	26 a						16 37	16 37			16 47	16 47												17 37
	d						16 39	16 39			16 49	16 49												17 39
Durham	26 a						16 54	16 59			17 05	17 04												17 54
Chester-le-Street	26 a						17 01	17 06																
Newcastle 8	26 a						17 13	17 18			17 18	17 18												18 10
	d										17 20	17 20												
Morpeth	26 a										17 33	17 33												
Edinburgh	26 a										18 52	18 56												

Table T039-F

Mondays to Saturdays

17 February to 28 March

Liverpool, Manchester Airport and Manchester - Huddersfield - Wakefield, Leeds, Hull, York, Scarborough, Middlesbrough, Newcastle and Edinburgh

		NT	NT SO	NT SX	TP SO	TP SX	NT	TP		TP	TP	NT	TP	NT	TP	NT	TP	NT	NT	TP	NT	TP SX	TP SO	TP
			◇	◇	◇1 🛒	◇1 🛒	◇	◇1 🛒		◇1	◇1		◇1 🛒		◇1 🛒	◇	◇1 🛒		◇	◇1 🛒	◇	◇1 🛒	◇1 🛒	◇1
Liverpool Lime Street 10 90	d				15 24	15 24							15 54							16 24				
Lea Green 90	d												16 06											
Newton-le-Willows 90	d				15 41	15 41														16 41				
Manchester Airport	d							15 40									16 10					16 34	16 40	
Gatley	d							15 46														16 40	16 46	
Manchester Piccadilly 10	a							15 55									16 33					16 55	16 55	
	d							15 57		15 58					16 30		16 34					16 57	16 57	16 58
Manchester Oxford Road	d							16 00									16 38					17 00	17 00	
Manchester Victoria	a				15 59	15 59		16 10					16 29				16 44			16 59		17 10	17 10	
	d	15 52	15 54	15 56	16 00	16 00		16 15				16 23	16 30			16 37	16 45	16 52	16 56	17 00		17 15	17 15	
Ashton-under-Lyne	d	16 02										16 33						17 02						
Stalybridge	a	16 06								16 12		16 37	16 41		16 43			17 06						17 12
	d									16 12			16 42		16 45									17 12
Mossley (Grtr Manchester)	d									16 17					16 49									17 17
Greenfield	d									16 22					16 53									17 22
Marsden	d									16 30					17 01									17 30
Slaithwaite	d									16 34					17 05									17 34
Huddersfield	a				16 28	16 28		16 45		16 41			17 00		17 11		17 16			17 28		17 45	17 45	17 40
	d				16 30	16 30		16 46			16 49		17 01	17 03	17 12		17 17			17 30		17 46	17 46	
Deighton	d						←				16 53			17 07							←			
Mirfield	d						16 38				16 57			17 12		17 39					17 39			
Wakefield Kirkgate	a													17 28		→								
Normanton	a													17 34										
Castleford	a													17 40										
Ravensthorpe	d										17 01													
Dewsbury	a						16 43	16 56			17 04						17 26				17 44	17 56	17 56	
	d						16 44	16 57			17 09						17 27				17 44	17 57	17 57	
Batley	d						16 47				17 12										17 47			
Morley	d						16 53				17 17										17 53			
Cottingley	d										17 21													
Leeds 10	a		17 19	17 19	16 49	16 49	17 04	17 10			17 29		17 21		17 31		17 40		18 21	17 49	18 03	18 10	18 10	
	d				16 51	16 51		17 13					17 27		17 34		17 42			17 51		18 14	18 14	
Cross Gates 40	d														17 41									
Garforth 40	d												17 36		17 45									
South Milford 40	d																							
Selby 29,40	d														17 59									
Howden 29	a														18 08									
Brough 29	a														18 21									
Hull 29	a														18 37									
York 8 26	a				17 14	17 14		17 35					17 55				18 05			18 18		18 36	18 36	
	d				17 21	17 21		17 39					18 00				18 07			18 22		18 39	18 39	
Malton	d												18 25											
Seamer 43	a												18 42											
Scarborough 43	a												18 52											
Thirsk 26	d							17 56														18 56	18 56	
Northallerton 26	d							18 05									18 26					19 05	19 05	
Yarm	a							18 17														19 17	19 17	
Thornaby 44	a							18 27														19 27	19 27	
Middlesbrough 44	a							18 35														19 35	19 35	
Redcar Central 44	a							18 48														19 48	19 48	
Darlington 26	a				17 47	17 47											18 37			18 48				
	d				17 49	17 49											18 39			18 50				
Durham 26	a				18 04	18 04											18 54			19 05				
Chester-le-Street 26	a																19 01							
Newcastle 8 26	a				18 18	18 18											19 13			19 19				
	d				18 21	18 21														19 21				
Morpeth 26	a				18 34	18 34														19 34				
Edinburgh 26	a				20 04	20 08														20 54				

NRT DECEMBER 19 EDITION

Table T039-F

Mondays to Saturdays

17 February to 28 March

Liverpool, Manchester Airport and Manchester - Huddersfield - Wakefield, Leeds, Hull, York, Scarborough, Middlesbrough, Newcastle and Edinburgh

		TP	TP	NT	GC SO	GC SX	TP	NT	TP	NT	TP SX	TP SO	NT	NT	TP SX	TP SO		NT	TP SX	TP SO	TP SX	TP	TP	NT	TP
		◇1	◇1 🛒		1 ☕	1 ☕	◇1 🛒		◇1 🛒	◇	◇1 🛒	◇1 🛒		◇	◇1 🛒	◇1 🛒		◇	◇1 🛒	◇1 🛒	◇1 🛒	◇1	◇1		◇1 🛒
Liverpool Lime Street 10 90	d						16 54								17 24	17 24									17 54
Lea Green 90	d						17 06																		18 06
Newton-le-Willows 90	d														17 41	17 41									
Manchester Airport	d		17 07								17 10	17 10							17 34	17 40					
Gatley	d																		17 42	17 46	←				
Manchester Piccadilly 10	a		17 25								17 33	17 33							17 56	17 56	17 56				
	d		17 27						17 30		17 35	17 35							17 58	17 57	17 58	18 00			
Manchester Oxford Road	d		17a29								17 38	17 38							→	18 01	18 01				
Manchester Victoria	a						17 29				17 44	17 44			17 58	17 59				18 11	18 13				18 29
	d			17 23			17 30			17 37	17 45	17 45	17 52	17 56	18 00	18 00				18 15	18 15			18 23	18 30
Ashton-under-Lyne	d			17 33									18 02											18 33	
Stalybridge	a			17 37			17 41		17 45				18 06									18 13		18 37	18 41
	d						17 42		17 45													18 13			18 42
Mossley (Grtr Manchester)	d								17 50													18 18			
Greenfield	d								17 54													18 22			
Marsden	d								18 02													18 30			
Slaithwaite	d								18 05													18 34			
Huddersfield	a						18 00		18 11		18 16	18 16			18 28	18 28				18 45	18 45	18 41			19 00
	d	17 49					18 01	18 03	18 12		18 17	18 17			18 30	18 30				18 46	18 46		18 49		19 01
Deighton	d	17 53						18 07										←					18 53		
Mirfield	d	17 57						18 12		18 38								18 38					18 57		
Wakefield Kirkgate	a							18 28		→															
Normanton	a							18 34																	
Castleford	a							18 40																	
Ravensthorpe	d	18 01																					19 01		
Dewsbury	a	18 04									18 26	18 26						18 43		18 56	18 56		19 04		
	d	18 09									18 27	18 27						18 44		18 57	18 57		19 09		
Batley	d	18 12																18 47					19 12		
Morley	d	18 17																18 53					19 17		
Cottingley	d	18 21																					19 21		
Leeds 10	a	18 29					18 21		18 31		18 40	18 40		19 19	18 49	18 49		19 02		19 10	19 10		19 29		19 21
	d						18 27		18 34		18 42	18 42			18 51	18 51				19 14	19 14				19 27
Cross Gates 40	d								18 40																
Garforth 40	d						18 36		18 45																19 36
South Milford 40	d																								
Selby 29,40	d								18 59																
Howden 29	a																								
Brough 29	a								19 17																
Hull 29	a								19 33																
York 8 26	a						18 55				19 05	19 05			19 14	19 14				19 36	19 36				19 55
	d				18 42	18 42	19 00				19 07	19 07			19 17	19 22				19 39	19 39				20 00
Malton	d						19 25																		20 25
Seamer 43	a						19 41																		20 41
Scarborough 43	a						19 51																		20 51
Thirsk 26	d				19 00	19 01														19 56	19 57				
Northallerton 26	d				19a08	19a09					19 26	19 26								20 07	20 07				
Yarm	a																			20 20	20 20				
Thornaby 44	a																			20 30	20 30				
Middlesbrough 44	a																			20 37	20 37				
Redcar Central 44	a																			20 51	20 51				
Darlington 26	a										19 37	19 37			19 43	19 48									
	d										19 39	19 39			19 45	19 50									
Durham 26	a										19 54	19 54			20 00	20 05									
Chester-le-Street 26	a																								
Newcastle 8 26	a										20 10	20 12			20 14	20 21									
	d														20 16										
Morpeth 26	a														20 29										
Edinburgh 26	a														21 57										

Table T039-F

Mondays to Saturdays
17 February to 28 March

Liverpool, Manchester Airport and Manchester - Huddersfield - Wakefield, Leeds, Hull, York, Scarborough, Middlesbrough, Newcastle and Edinburgh

Station		NT	TP	NT	TP	NT	NT	TP SX	TP SO	NT	TP SX	TP SO	TP	TP	TP SX	NT SX	NT	TP	NT	TP SX	NT	TP	TP SO
			◇1 ✠	◇	◇1 ✠		◇	◇1 ✠	◇1 ✠	◇	◇1	◇1	◇1	◇1	◇1 ✠	◇		◇1		◇1	◇	◇1	◇1
Liverpool Lime Street 10	90 d							18 24	18 24									18 54					
Lea Green	90 d																	19 06					
Newton-le-Willows	90 d							18 42	18 41														
Manchester Airport	d				18 10						18 37	18 40			19 07							19 10	
Gatley	d										18 43	18 46											
Manchester Piccadilly 10	a				18 33						18 55	18 55			19 25							19 33	
	d		18 30		18 34						18 57	18 57	19 00		19 26					19 30		19 34	19 35
Manchester Oxford Road	d				18 38						19 00	19 00			19a28							19 38	
Manchester Victoria	a				18 44			18 59	18 59		19 11	19 11						19 29				→	
	d			18 37	18 45	18 52	18 56	19 00	19 00		19 15	19 15				19 21	19 24	19 30			19 36		
Ashton-under-Lyne	d					19 02											19 33						
Stalybridge	a		18 43			19 06							19 13				19 38	19 41		19 42			19 50
	d		18 45										19 13					19 42		19 50			19 50
Mossley (Grtr Manchester)	d		18 49										19 18										
Greenfield	d		18 53										19 22										
Marsden	d		19 01										19 30										
Slaithwaite	d		19 05										19 34										
Huddersfield	a		19 11		19 16			19 28	19 28		19 45	19 45	19 41					20 00		20 08			20 08
	d	19 03	19 12		19 17			19 30	19 30		19 46	19 46		19 49				20 01	20 03	20 12			20 12
Deighton	d	19 07								←				19 53					20 07				
Mirfield	d	19 12		19 39						19 39				19 57					20 12		20 39		
Wakefield Kirkgate	a	19 28		→															20 28		→		
Normanton	a	19 34																	20 34				
Castleford	a	19 40																	20 41				
Ravensthorpe	d													20 01									
Dewsbury	a				19 26					19 44	19 55	19 55		20 04									
	d				19 27					19 44	19 56	19 56		20 09									
Batley	d									19 47				20 12									
Morley	d									19 53				20 17									
Cottingley	d													20 21									
Leeds 10	a		19 31		19 40		20 19	19 49	19 49	20 03	20 09	20 09		20 30		20 43		20 23		20 31			20 31
	d		19 34		19 42			19 51	19 51		20 14	20 14						20 27		20 33			20 33
Cross Gates	40 d																						
Garforth	40 d																	20 36					
South Milford	40 d																						
Selby	29,40 d		19 56																	20 56			20 57
Howden	29 a																			21 05			21 06
Brough	29 a		20 16																	21 18			21 19
Hull	29 a		20 34																	21 34			21 35
York 8	26 a				20 05			20 14	20 14		20 36	20 36						20 57					
	d				20 07			20 16	20 22		20 39	20 39						21 00					
Malton	d																	21 25					
Seamer	43 a																	21 41					
Scarborough	43 a																	21 51					
Thirsk	26 d										20 56	20 56											
Northallerton	26 d				20 26						21 05	21 05											
Yarm	a										21 18	21 18											
Thornaby	44 a										21 28	21 28											
Middlesbrough	44 a										21 35	21 35											
Redcar Central	44 a										21 48	21 48											
Darlington	26 a				20 37			20 43	20 48														
	d				20 39			20 45	20 50														
Durham	26 a				20 54			21 00	21 05														
Chester-le-Street	26 a				21 01																		
Newcastle 8	26 a				21 15			21 14	21 21														
	d							21 16															
Morpeth	26 a							21 31															
Edinburgh	26 a							22 49															

Table T039-F

Mondays to Saturdays
17 February to 28 March

Liverpool, Manchester Airport and Manchester - Huddersfield - Wakefield, Leeds, Hull, York, Scarborough, Middlesbrough, Newcastle and Edinburgh

Station		TP	NT	NT	TP	NT	GC SX	GC SO	TP SO	TP	TP SX	TP SO	NT	TP	TP	NT	NT	TP	TP	TP	NT	NT	TP SX	TP SO
		◇1		◇	◇1 A ✠	◇	1 ⊏	1 ⊏	◇1	◇1	◇1	◇1		◇1	◇1		◇	◇1	◇1	◇1		◇	◇1 A ✠	◇1 A ✠
Liverpool Lime Street 10	90 d				19 25										19 54								20 24	20 24
Lea Green	90 d														20 06									
Newton-le-Willows	90 d				19 41																		20 40	20 40
Manchester Airport	d								19 36		19 38							20 10						
Gatley	d								19 42		19 44													
Manchester Piccadilly 10	a	←							19 54		19 57							20 33		←				
	d								19 55	19 58	19 59							20 34	20 35					
Manchester Oxford Road	d	19 38							19 59		20 02	←						20 38		20 38				
Manchester Victoria	a	19 44			19 59				20 10		20 14	20 10			20 29			→		20 44			20 59	20 59
	d	19 45	19 52	19 56	20 00				20 15		20 15	20 15	20 22		20 30		20 37			20 45	20 52	20 56	21 00	21 00
Ashton-under-Lyne	d		20 02						→				20 32								21 02			
Stalybridge	a		20 06							20 12			20 36		20 41				20 50		21 07			
	d									20 13					20 42				20 50					
Mossley (Grtr Manchester)	d									20 18														
Greenfield	d									20 22														
Marsden	d									20 30														
Slaithwaite	d									20 34														
Huddersfield	a	20 16			20 29					20 41	20 45	20 45			21 00				21 08	21 16			21 27	21 27
	d	20 17			20 30						20 46	20 46		20 49	21 01	21 03			21 12	21 17			21 29	21 29
Deighton	d					←								20 53		21 07								
Mirfield	d					20 39								20 57		21 12	21 39							
Wakefield Kirkgate	a															21 28	→							
Normanton	a															21 34								
Castleford	a															21 40								
Ravensthorpe	d													21 01										
Dewsbury	a	20 26				20 44					20 56	20 56		21 04						21 26				
	d	20 27				20 44					20 57	20 57		21 09						21 27				
Batley	d					20 47								21 12										
Morley	d					20 53								21 17										
Cottingley	d													21 21										
Leeds 10	a	20 40		21 14	20 49	21 04					21 10	21 10		21 29	21 22				21 31	21 40		22 13	21 48	21 49
	d	20 42			20 51						21 14	21 14			21 27				21 34	21 42			21 51	21 51
Cross Gates	40 d																							
Garforth	40 d														21 36									
South Milford	40 d																							
Selby	29,40 d																		21 56					
Howden	29 a																		22 05					
Brough	29 a																		22 18					
Hull	29 a																		22 36					
York 8	26 a	21 06			21 14						21 36	21 36			21 55					22 07			22 13	22 14
	d	21 15			21 20		21 22	21 23			21 39	21 39			22 00								22 21	22 21
Malton	d	21 39													22 25									
Seamer	43 a	21 56													22 41									
Scarborough	43 a	22 03													22 51									
Thirsk	26 d						21 38	21 38			21 56	21 56												
Northallerton	26 d						21a46	21a46			22 05	22 07											22 40	22 40
Yarm	a										22 17	22 20												
Thornaby	44 a										22 27	22 30												
Middlesbrough	44 a										22 35	22 40												
Redcar Central	44 a										22 48													
Darlington	26 a				21 46																		22 51	22 51
	d				21 48																		22 53	22 53
Durham	26 a				22 03																		23 08	23 08
Chester-le-Street	26 a																						23 15	23 15
Newcastle 8	26 a				22 19																		23 26	23 26
	d																							
Morpeth	26 a																							
Edinburgh	26 a																							

A ✠ from York

Table T039-F

Mondays to Saturdays

17 February to 28 March

Liverpool, Manchester Airport and Manchester - Huddersfield - Wakefield, Leeds, Hull, York, Scarborough, Middlesbrough, Newcastle and Edinburgh

	NT ◇	TP ◇1	TP SX ◇1 (trolley)	TP ◇1	TP ◇1	NT	NT		TP SO ◇1	TP SX ◇1	TP SO ◇1	TP SX ◇1	NT ◇	NT	TP ◇1	TP ◇1	TP ◇1	TP SX ◇1	TP SO ◇1	NT	TP SO ◇1	TP SX ◇1	NT ◇
Liverpool Lime Street 90 d											21 08	21 08									22 06	22 06	
Lea Green 90 d											21 20	21 20									22 19	22 19	
Newton-le-Willows 90 d											21 27	21 27									22 25	22 25	
Manchester Airport d			21 06												21 35								
Gatley d															21 41								
Manchester Piccadilly a			21 20												21 53								
d		20 58	21 22						21 35	21 35					21 55	21 58		22 32	22 34				
Manchester Oxford Road d			21a24												21 58								
Manchester Victoria a											21 45	21 45			22 11						22 45	22 45	
d				21 15		21 23					21 45	21 45	21 56	22 08	22 14					22 36	22 45	22 46	22 56
Ashton-under-Lyne d						21 33								22 18						22 47			
Stalybridge a		21 12				21 37			21 50	21 50	21 57	21 57		22 22		22 14		22 49	22 50	22 51	22 57	22 57	
d		21 13							21 50	21 50	21 58	21 58				22 14		22 50	22 50		22 58	22 58	
Mossley (Grtr Manchester) d		21 18														22 19							
Greenfield d		21 23														22 23							
Marsden d		21 31														22 31							
Slaithwaite d		21 35														22 35							
Huddersfield a		21 42		21 46					22 08	22 08	22 16	22 16			22 45	22 42		23 08	23 09		23 16	23 16	
d				21 47	21 51		22 03		22 12	22 12	22 17	22 17			22 46		22 52	23 12	23 12		23 17	23 17	
Deighton d	←				21 55		22 07										22 56						
Mirfield d	21 39				21 59		22 12										23 00						
Wakefield Kirkgate a							22 28																
Normanton a							22 34																
Castleford a							22 40																
Ravensthorpe d					22 03												23 04						
Dewsbury a	21 44			21 56	22 06						22 26	22 26			22 56		23 07				23 26	23 26	
d	21 45			21 57	22 08						22 27	22 27			22 57		23 09				23 27	23 27	
Batley d	21 48				22 11												23 12						
Morley d	21 54				22 16												23 17						
Cottingley d					22 20												23 21						
Leeds a	22 05			22 12	22 28				22 35	22 36	22 40	22 40	23 13		23 10		23 29	23 31	23 31		23 40	23 40	00 14
d				22 14					22 37	22 37	22 42	22 42			23 13			23 33	23 34		23 42	23 42	
Cross Gates 40 d																							
Garforth 40 d																							
South Milford 40 d									22 53	22 53													
Selby 29,40 d									23 02	23 02								23 52	23 53				
Howden 29 a																							
Brough 29 a									23 21	23 21								00 10	00 11				
Hull 29 a									23 36	23 36								00 26	00 27				
York 26 a				22 36							23 07	23 07			23 40						00 10	00 10	
d				22 41							23 08	23 08											
Malton d				23 05																			
Seamer 43 a				23 22																			
Scarborough 43 a				23 31																			
Thirsk 26 d												23 31											
Northallerton 26 d											23 27	23 39											
Yarm a																							
Thornaby 44 a																							
Middlesbrough 44 a																							
Redcar Central 44 a																							
Darlington 26 a											23 38	23 51											
d											23 40	00 01											
Durham 26 a											23 55	00 19											
Chester-le-Street 26 a											00 02	00 32											
Newcastle 26 a											00 14	00 59											
d																							
Morpeth 26 a																							
Edinburgh 26 a																							

Table T039-F

Mondays to Saturdays

17 February to 28 March

Liverpool, Manchester Airport and Manchester - Huddersfield - Wakefield, Leeds, Hull, York, Scarborough, Middlesbrough, Newcastle and Edinburgh

	TP SX ◇1	TP ◇1	TP SO ◇1	TP SO 🚌	TP SX ◇1	TP SX ◇1	TP SX ◇1 (trolley)	NT SX ◇	TP SO 🚌	NT	TP SX ◇1	TP SO 🚌	TP SX ◇1	TP SO 🚌	TP FO ◇1		TP SO 🚌	TP FSX ◇1	TP SO 🚌	TP FSX ◇1
Liverpool Lime Street 90 d													23 08							
Lea Green 90 d													23 23							
Newton-le-Willows 90 d													23 31							
Manchester Airport d	22 39		22 40				23 10							23 20	23 40			23 40		
Gatley d																				
Manchester Piccadilly a	22 56		22 59		←		23 24							23 45	23 54			23 54		
d	22 58	23 00	23 01				23 26				23 35	23 35		23 45	23 55			23 55		
Manchester Oxford Road d	23 06		23 05		23 06		23a28								23 59			23 59		
Manchester Victoria a	→		23 11		23 13								23 50		00 04			00 04		
d			23 15		23 15			23 19		23 29			23 53		00 05			00 05		
Ashton-under-Lyne d										23 39										
Stalybridge a		23 13								23 43	23 47	23 59	00 04							
d		23 14									23 47	23 59	00 05							
Mossley (Grtr Manchester) d		23 18									23 52	00 17								
Greenfield d		23 22									23 57	00 33								
Marsden d		23 30									00 05	01 00								
Slaithwaite d		23 34									00 09	01 10					←			
Huddersfield a		23 40	23 45		23 50				←		00 16	01 30	00 24	00 45	00 32		00 45	01 01		
d		23 41		23 50	23 51	23 54							00 25	00 45	00 34		00 45	01 12		
Deighton d		23 44		23 59		23 58			23 59					→						
Mirfield d		23 49		→		00 03			00 09											
Wakefield Kirkgate a		00 04																		
Normanton a																				
Castleford a																				
Ravensthorpe d						00 08			00 14											
Dewsbury a					00 01	00 10			00 22				00 33				01 10			
d					00 02	00 10			00 22				00 34				01 10			
Batley d						00 13			00 30											
Morley d						00 18			00 42											
Cottingley d						00 22			00 52										←	←
Leeds a					00 15	00 29		00 46	01 07				00 47		01 11		01 35	01 31	01 35	01 31
d					00 29								00 53		01 13		01 35	01 43	01 35	01 43
Cross Gates 40 d																	→	→		
Garforth 40 d																				
South Milford 40 d																				
Selby 29,40 d																				
Howden 29 a																				
Brough 29 a																				
Hull 29 a																				
York 26 a					01 10								01 29		01 39				02 25	02 27
d																				
Malton d																				
Seamer 43 a																				
Scarborough 43 a																				
Thirsk 26 d																				
Northallerton 26 d																				
Yarm a																				
Thornaby 44 a																				
Middlesbrough 44 a																				
Redcar Central 44 a																				
Darlington 26 a																				
d																				
Durham 26 a																				
Chester-le-Street 26 a																				
Newcastle 26 a																				
d																				
Morpeth 26 a																				
Edinburgh 26 a																				

Table T039-F

Mondays to Saturdays
30 March to 16 May

Liverpool, Manchester Airport and Manchester - Huddersfield - Wakefield, Leeds, Hull, York, Scarborough, Middlesbrough, Newcastle and Edinburgh

		TP	TP	TP	TP	TP	TP	TP	TP	TP	TP	TP	TP	TP	TP	TP		TP	TP	TP	TP	TP	TP	TP	TP
		MX	MO	MX	MO	MX	MO	MX	MO	MX	MO	SO	MSX	MO	MSX	SO			SO	MO	MSX	SO			
		◇1	◇1	◇1	◇1	◇1	◇1	◇1	◇1	◇1	◇1	◇1	◇1	◇1	◇1	◇1		◇1 🛒	◇1	◇1	◇1	◇1	◇1	◇1	◇1
Liverpool Lime Street 10	90 d																								
Lea Green	90 d																								
Newton-le-Willows	90 d																								
Manchester Airport ⇌✈	d													00 38	00 38	00 38									
Gatley	d																								
Manchester Piccadilly 10 ⇌	a													00 51	00 51	00 52									
	d													00 53	00 53	01 03			02 42	02 42	02 42				
Manchester Oxford Road	d																								
Manchester Victoria ⇌	a																								
	d											00 05	00 05												
Ashton-under-Lyne ⇌	d																								
Stalybridge	a																								
	d									00 05															
Mossley (Grtr Manchester)	d																								
Greenfield	d																								
Marsden	d		00 04	00 05																					
Slaithwaite	d		00 08	00 09																		←			
Huddersfield	a		00 14	00 16						00 24		00 32	01 01			01 32			03 15	03 33	03 33	03 15			
	d								00 19	00 25	00 27	00 34	01 12			01 33			03 51	03 50	03 50	03 51			
Deighton	d																		→						
Mirfield	d							00 03																	
Wakefield Kirkgate	a																								
Normanton	a																								
Castleford	a																								
Ravensthorpe	d						00 02	00 08																	
Dewsbury	a						00 04	00 10	00s27	00 33															
	d					00 02	00 09	00 10		00 34															
Batley	d						00 12	00 13																	
Morley	d						00 17	00 18																	
Cottingley	d						00 21	00 22																	
Leeds 10	a					00 15	00 29	00 29	00 41	00 47	01 03	01 11	01 31	02 06	02 06	02 08				04 09	04 09	04 30			
	d				00 22	00 29			00 46	00 53	01 06	01 13	01 43	02 11	02 19	02 19				04 20	04 20	04 32		05 35	
Cross Gates	40 d																								
Garforth	40 d																								
South Milford	40 d																								
Selby	29,40 d																							05 55	
Howden	29 a																								
Brough	29 a																							06 12	
Hull	29 a																							06 28	
York 8	26 a				01 02	01 10			01 26	01 29	01 32	01 39	02 27	02 39	02 58	02 58				04 45	05 00	04 57			
	d																						05 05		06 04
Malton	d																								06 29
Seamer	43 a																								06 45
Scarborough	43 a																								06 55
Thirsk	26 d																						05 28		
Northallerton	26 d																						05 36		
Yarm	a																								
Thornaby	44 a																						06 27		
Middlesbrough	44 a																						06 34		
Redcar Central	44 a																						06 47		
Darlington	26 a																								
	d	00 01																							
Durham	26 a	00 19																							
Chester-le-Street	26 a	00 32																							
Newcastle 8	26 ⇌ a	00 59																							
	d																	05 53							
Morpeth	26 a																	06 07							
Edinburgh	26 a																	07 30							

Table T039-F

Mondays to Saturdays
30 March to 16 May

Liverpool, Manchester Airport and Manchester - Huddersfield - Wakefield, Leeds, Hull, York, Scarborough, Middlesbrough, Newcastle and Edinburgh

		TP	TP	TP	NT	TP	TP	TP		NT	TP	TP	NT	TP	TP	TP	TP	TP	TP	NT	TP	NT	NT	TP	
							SO	SX			SX	SO		SO	SX		SO	SX					SO		
		◇1 🛒	◇1	◇1		◇1	◇1 🛒	◇1 🛒		◇	◇1 🛒	◇1 🛒		◇1	◇1	◇1	◇1	◇1	◇1		◇1		◇	◇1	
Liverpool Lime Street 10	90 d										05 20	05 20												05 52	
Lea Green	90 d										05 32	05 32												06 06	
Newton-le-Willows	90 d										05 39	05 39												06 12	
Manchester Airport ⇌✈	d						05 19	05 19						05 37	05 37										
Gatley	d																								
Manchester Piccadilly 10 ⇌	a						05 33	05 33						05 56	05 56										
	d					05 15	05 34	05 34						05 57	05 57	06 00					06 27				
Manchester Oxford Road	d						05 40	05 40						06 01	06 01										
Manchester Victoria ⇌	a						05 45	05 45			05 58	05 58		06 06	06 10									06 31	
	d	05 00					05 45	05 45		05 45	06 00	06 00		06 15	06 15					06 26			06 31	06 32	
Ashton-under-Lyne ⇌	d																			06 36					
Stalybridge	a															06 12				06 40	06 41			06 44	
	d															06 12					06 42			06 44	
Mossley (Grtr Manchester)	d															06 17								06 49	
Greenfield	d															06 22								06 53	
Marsden	d															06 30								07 01	
Slaithwaite	d															06 34	←	←	←					07 05	
Huddersfield	a					06 11	06 16	06 16			06 28	06 28		06 45	06 45	06 41	06 45	06 45	06 41		06 59			07 11	
	d			05 49	06 03	06 14	06 17	06 17			06 30	06 30		06 46	06 46	06 49	06 46	06 46	06 49		07 00	07 03		07 12	
Deighton	d			05 53	06 07									→	→	→			06 53			07 07			
Mirfield	d			05 57	06 12								06 39						06 57			07 12			
Wakefield Kirkgate	a				06 28																	07 28			
Normanton	a				06 34																	07 34			
Castleford	a				06 40																	07 40			
Ravensthorpe	d			06 01									06 42						07 01						
Dewsbury	a			06 04			06 26	06 26					06 45				06 56	06 56	07 04						
	d			06 09			06 27	06 27					06 46				06 57	06 57	07 09						
Batley	d			06 12									06 49						07 12						
Morley	d			06 17									06 55						07 17						
Cottingley	d			06 21									06 58						07 21						
Leeds 10	a	06 12		06 29		06 33	06 40	06 40		07 23	06 49	06 49	07 08				07 10	07 10	07 29		07 22		08 00	07 31	
	d	06 15				06 36	06 42	06 42			06 51	06 51					07 14	07 14			07 27			07 34	
Cross Gates	40 d																								
Garforth	40 d																				07 36				
South Milford	40 d																								
Selby	29,40 d					07 08																		07 54	
Howden	29 a																							08 03	
Brough	29 a					07 26																		08 17	
Hull	29 a					07 42																		08 34	
York 8	26 a	06 37					07 05	07 05			07 14	07 17					07 36	07 36			07 58				
	d	06 39	07 02				07 07	07 07			07 22	07 22					07 39	07 39			08 03				
Malton	d		07 27																		08 28				
Seamer	43 a		07 44																		08 44				
Scarborough	43 a		07 53																		08 52				
Thirsk	26 d	06 56															07 56	07 56							
Northallerton	26 d	07 05					07 28	07 29									08 05	08 05							
Yarm	a	07 17															08 17	08 17							
Thornaby	44 a	07 27															08 28	08 28							
Middlesbrough	44 a	07 35															08 35	08 35							
Redcar Central	44 a	07 50															08 48	08 48							
Darlington	26 a						07 40	07 41			07 48	07 48													
	d						07 41	07 42			07 50	07 50													
Durham	26 a						07 57	07 58			08 05	08 05													
Chester-le-Street	26 a						08 03	08 04																	
Newcastle 8	26 ⇌ a						08 16	08 17			08 19	08 19													
	d										08 21	08 21													
Morpeth	26 a										08 34	08 34													
Edinburgh	26 a										09 53	09 53													

Table T039-F

Mondays to Saturdays
30 March to 16 May

Liverpool, Manchester Airport and Manchester - Huddersfield - Wakefield, Leeds, Hull, York, Scarborough, Middlesbrough, Newcastle and Edinburgh

		NT	NT	NT	TP	TP	NT	TP	TP	NT	TP	TP	TP	TP	NT	TP		NT	TP	NT	TP	NT	NT	TP	TP
		SX			SO	SX		SX	SO															SX	SO
		◇	◇	◇	◇1	◇1		◇1 🛒	◇1 🛒	◇	◇1 🛒	◇1	◇1	◇1 🛒		◇1 🛒			◇1 🛒	◇	◇1 🛒		◇	◇1 🛒	◇1 🛒
Liverpool Lime Street 10	90 d							06 24	06 24							06 54								07 24	07 24
Lea Green	90 d															07 06									
Newton-le-Willows	90 d							06 41	06 41															07 41	07 41
Manchester Airport	d				06 10	06 15					06 35			07 07							07 10				
Gatley	d										06 41														
Manchester Piccadilly 10	a				06 32	06 32					06 54			07 25							07 33				
	d				06 34	06 34					06 56	06 58		07 26					07 30		07 34				
Manchester Oxford Road	d				06 38	06 38					06 59			07a28							07 38				
Manchester Victoria	a				06 45	06 45		06 59	06 59		07 11					07 29					07 43			07 59	07 59
	d	06 32	06 37	06 42	06 45	06 45	06 52	07 00	07 00		07 15				07 23	07 30				07 36	07 45	07 53	07 57	08 00	08 00
Ashton-under-Lyne	d						07 02								07 33							08 03			
Stalybridge	a						07 06					07 13			07 37	07 41			07 43			08 07			
	d											07 13				07 42			07 45						
Mossley (Grtr Manchester)	d											07 18							07 49						
Greenfield	d											07 22							07 53						
Marsden	d											07 30							08 01						
Slaithwaite	d											07 34							08 05						
Huddersfield	a				07 16	07 16		07 28	07 28		07 45	07 41				08 00			08 11		08 16			08 28	08 28
	d				07 17	07 17		07 30	07 30		07 46		07 49			08 00		08 03	08 12		08 17			08 30	08 30
Deighton	d									←			07 53					08 07							
Mirfield	d		07 40							07 40			07 57					08 12		08 39					
Wakefield Kirkgate	a		→															08 28		→					
Normanton	a																	08 34							
Castleford	a																	08 40							
Ravensthorpe	d												08 01												
Dewsbury	a				07 26	07 26				07 45	07 56		08 04								08 26				
	d				07 27	07 27				07 45	07 57		08 09								08 27				
Batley	d									07 48			08 12												
Morley	d									07 54			08 17												
Cottingley	d									07 58			08 21												
Leeds 10	a	08 00		08 14	07 40	07 40		07 49	07 49	08 06	08 10		08 29			08 22			08 31		08 40		09 22	08 49	08 49
	d				07 42	07 42		07 51	07 51		08 14					08 27			08 34		08 42			08 51	08 51
Cross Gates	40 d																								
Garforth	40 d															08 36									
South Milford	40 d																								
Selby	29,40 d																		08 56						
Howden	29 a																								
Brough	29 a																		09 15						
Hull	29 a																		09 30						
York 8	26 a				08 05	08 05		08 18	08 18		08 36					08 54					09 05			09 14	09 14
	d				08 07	08 07		08 21	08 21		08 39					09 00					09 07			09 21	09 21
Malton	d															09 25									
Seamer	43 a															09 41									
Scarborough	43 a															09 49									
Thirsk	26 d										08 56														
Northallerton	26 d				08 26	08 26					09 06										09 26				
Yarm	a										09 18														
Thornaby	44 a										09 28														
Middlesbrough	44 a										09 36														
Redcar Central	44 a										09 49														
Darlington	26 a				08 37	08 37		08 47	08 47												09 37			09 47	09 47
	d				08 39	08 39		08 49	08 49												09 39			09 49	09 49
Durham	26 a				08 54	08 54		09 04	09 04												09 54			10 04	10 04
Chester-le-Street	26 a				09 01	09 01																			
Newcastle 8	26 a				09 12	09 12		09 18	09 18												10 11			10 19	10 19
	d							09 21	09 21															10 21	10 21
Morpeth	26 a							09 33	09 33															10 34	10 34
Edinburgh	26 a							10 52	10 56															11 50	11 54

NRT DECEMBER 19 EDITION

Table T039-F

Mondays to Saturdays
30 March to 16 May

Liverpool, Manchester Airport and Manchester - Huddersfield - Wakefield, Leeds, Hull, York, Scarborough, Middlesbrough, Newcastle and Edinburgh

		NT	TP	TP	TP	TP	NT	GC		TP	NT	TP	NT	TP	NT	NT	TP	TP	NT	GC	TP	TP	TP	TP
			SO		SX			SO									SX	SO		SX				
		◇	◇1 🛒	◇1	◇1 🛒	◇1		1		◇1 🛒		◇1 🛒	◇	◇1 🛒		◇	◇1 🛒	◇1 🛒	◇	1	◇1 🛒	◇1	◇1	◇1 🛒
Liverpool Lime Street 10	90 d									07 54							08 24	08 24						
Lea Green	90 d									08 07														
Newton-le-Willows	90 d																08 41	08 41						
Manchester Airport	d		07 35		07 47									08 10							08 35			09 07
Gatley	d		07 41		07 53																08 41			
Manchester Piccadilly 10	a		07 54		08 03									08 33							08 54			09 25
	d		07 56	08 00	08 05							08 30		08 35							08 56	08 58		09 26
Manchester Oxford Road	d		07 59		08 08									08 38							09 00			09a28
Manchester Victoria	a		08 11		08 14					08 29				08 45			08 59	08 59			09 12			
	d		08 15		08 15		08 21			08 30			08 37	08 45	08 52	08 56	09 00	09 00			09 15			
Ashton-under-Lyne	d						08 31								09 02									
Stalybridge	a			08 13			08 35			08 41		08 44			09 06							09 12		
	d			08 13						08 42		08 45										09 13		
Mossley (Grtr Manchester)	d			08 18								08 49										09 17		
Greenfield	d			08 23								08 53										09 22		
Marsden	d			08 31								09 01										09 30		
Slaithwaite	d			08 35								09 05										09 34		
Huddersfield	a		08 45	08 42	08 45					09 00		09 11		09 16			09 28	09 28			09 45	09 41		
	d		08 46		08 46	08 49				09 01	09 03	09 12		09 17			09 30	09 30			09 46		09 49	
Deighton	d	←				08 53					09 07								←				09 53	
Mirfield	d	08 39				08 57					09 12		09 39						09 39				09 57	
Wakefield Kirkgate	a										09 28		→											
Normanton	a										09 34													
Castleford	a										09 40													
Ravensthorpe	d	08 42				09 01																	10 01	
Dewsbury	a	08 45	08 56		08 56	09 04								09 26					09 44		09 56		10 04	
	d	08 46	08 57		08 57	09 09								09 27					09 44		09 57		10 09	
Batley	d	08 49				09 12													09 47				10 12	
Morley	d	08 55				09 17													09 53				10 17	
Cottingley	d					09 21																	10 21	
Leeds 10	a	09 04	09 10		09 10	09 29				09 22		09 31		09 40		10 13	09 49	09 49	10 04		10 10		10 29	
	d		09 14		09 14					09 27		09 34		09 42			09 51	09 51			10 14			
Cross Gates	40 d																							
Garforth	40 d									09 36														
South Milford	40 d																							
Selby	29,40 d											09 57												
Howden	29 a																							
Brough	29 a											10 16												
Hull	29 a											10 34												
York 8	26 a		09 36		09 36					09 55				10 04			10 14	10 14			10 36			
	d		09 39		09 39			09 49		10 00				10 07			10 21	10 21		10 25	10 39			
Malton	d									10 25														
Seamer	43 a									10 42														
Scarborough	43 a									10 52														
Thirsk	26 d		09 56		09 56			10 06												10 42	10 56			
Northallerton	26 d		10 07		10 07			10a16						10 26						10a58	11 07			
Yarm	a		10 20		10 20																11 20			
Thornaby	44 a		10 30		10 30																11 30			
Middlesbrough	44 a		10 37		10 37																11 37			
Redcar Central	44 a		10 50		10 50																11 50			
Darlington	26 a													10 37			10 47	10 47						
	d													10 39			10 49	10 49						
Durham	26 a													10 54			11 04	11 04						
Chester-le-Street	26 a													11 01										
Newcastle 8	26 a													11 13			11 19	11 19						
	d																11 21	11 21						
Morpeth	26 a																11 34	11 34						
Edinburgh	26 a																12 51	12 56						

Table T039-F

Mondays to Saturdays

30 March to 16 May

Liverpool, Manchester Airport and Manchester - Huddersfield - Wakefield, Leeds, Hull, York, Scarborough, Middlesbrough, Newcastle and Edinburgh

		NT	TP	NT	TP	NT	TP	TP	TP	NT	NT	TP	TP	NT	TP	TP		TP	TP	NT	TP	NT	TP	NT	TP
					SO			SX				SX	SO		SX	SO							SX		SO
			◇1 ⚲		◇1 ⚲	◇	◇1 ⚲	◇1 ⚲	◇1 ⚲		◇	◇1 ⚲	◇1 ⚲	◇	◇1 ⚲	◇1 ⚲		◇1	◇1		◇1 ⚲		◇1 ⚲	◇	◇1 ⚲
Liverpool Lime Street 10	90 d		08 54									09 24	09 24								09 53				
Lea Green	90 d		09 06																		10 06				
Newton-le-Willows	90 d											09 41	09 41												
Manchester Airport ✈	d						09 10								09 36	09 40									10 10
Gatley	d														09 42	09 46									
Manchester Piccadilly 10	a						09 33		←						09 55	09 55									10 33
	d				09 30		09 34	09 35							09 57	09 57		09 58					10 30		10 34
Manchester Oxford Road	d						09 38		09 38						10 00	10 00									10 38
Manchester Victoria	a		09 29				→		09 44			09 59	09 59		10 11	10 11					10 29				→
	d	09 23	09 30			09 37			09 45	09 52	09 56	10 00	10 00		10 15	10 15				10 23	10 30			10 37	
Ashton-under-Lyne	d	09 33								10 02										10 33					
Stalybridge	a	09 37	09 41		09 42			09 50		10 06								10 12		10 37	10 41		10 42		
	d		09 42		09 46			09 50										10 12			10 42		10 50		
Mossley (Grtr Manchester)	d																	10 17							
Greenfield	d																	10 22							
Marsden	d																	10 30							
Slaithwaite	d																	10 34							
Huddersfield	a		10 00		10 05			10 08	10 16			10 28	10 28		10 44	10 44		10 41			11 00		11 08		
	d		10 01	10 03	10 12			10 12	10 17			10 30	10 30		10 45	10 45			10 49		11 01	11 03	11 12		
Deighton	d			10 07										←					10 53			11 07			
Mirfield	d			10 12		10 39								10 39					10 59			11 12		11 39	
Wakefield Kirkgate	a			10 28		→																11 28		→	
Normanton	a			10 34																		11 34			
Castleford	a			10 40																		11 40			
Ravensthorpe	d																		11 02						
Dewsbury	a								10 26					10 44	10 56	10 56			11 05						
	d								10 27					10 44	10 57	10 57			11 09						
Batley	d													10 47					11 12						
Morley	d													10 53					11 17						
Cottingley	d																		11 21						
Leeds 10	a		10 21		10 31			10 31	10 40		11 13	10 49	10 49	11 03	11 10	11 10			11 29		11 21		11 31		
	d		10 27		10 34			10 34	10 42			10 51	10 51		11 14	11 14					11 27		11 34		
Cross Gates	40 d																								
Garforth	40 d		10 36																		11 36				
South Milford	40 d																								
Selby	29,40 d				10 56			10 56															11 56		
Howden	29 a																								
Brough	29 a				11 15			11 15															12 15		
Hull	29 a				11 30			11 30															12 30		
York 8	26 a		10 55						11 05			11 15	11 15		11 36	11 36					11 57				
	d		11 00						11 07			11 21	11 21		11 39	11 39					12 00				
Malton	d		11 25																		12 25				
Seamer	43 a		11 41																		12 41				
Scarborough	43 a		11 51																		12 51				
Thirsk	26 d														11 56	11 56									
Northallerton	26 d								11 26						12 05	12 07									
Yarm	a														12 17	12 20									
Thornaby	44 a														12 27	12 30									
Middlesbrough	44 a														12 35	12 37									
Redcar Central	44 a														12 48	12 50									
Darlington	26 a								11 37			11 48	11 48												
	d								11 39			11 49	11 49												
Durham	26 a								11 54			12 05	12 05												
Chester-le-Street	26 a																								
Newcastle 8	26 a								12 11			12 18	12 18												
	d											12 21	12 21												
Morpeth	26 a											12 34	12 34												
Edinburgh	26 a											13 50	13 57												

Table T039-F

Mondays to Saturdays

30 March to 16 May

Liverpool, Manchester Airport and Manchester - Huddersfield - Wakefield, Leeds, Hull, York, Scarborough, Middlesbrough, Newcastle and Edinburgh

		TP	TP	TP	TP	NT	NT	TP		TP	NT	TP	TP	TP	TP	NT	TP	NT	NT	TP	TP	TP	NT	NT	
		SX	SO	SO	SX			SX		SO															
		◇1 ⚲	◇1 ⚲	◇1 ⚲	◇1 ⚲		◇	◇1 ⚲		◇1 ⚲	◇	◇1 ⚲	◇1	◇1	◇1 ⚲		◇1 ⚲		◇	◇1 ⚲	◇1 ⚲	◇1 ⚲		◇	
Liverpool Lime Street 10	90 d							10 24		10 24							10 54								
Lea Green	90 d																11 06								
Newton-le-Willows	90 d							10 41		10 41															
Manchester Airport ✈	d	10 10										10 40			11 07					11 10					
Gatley	d											10 46													
Manchester Piccadilly 10	a	10 33		←	←							10 55			11 25					11 33		←			
	d	10 34	10 35									10 57	10 58		11 26					11 34	11 35				
Manchester Oxford Road	d	10 38		10 38	10 38							11 00			11a28					11 38		11 38			
Manchester Victoria	a	→		10 44	10 44			10 59		10 59		11 11					11 29			→		11 44			
	d			10 44	10 45	10 52	10 55	11 00		11 00		11 15				11 23	11 30		11 34			11 45	11 52	11 55	
Ashton-under-Lyne	d					11 02										11 33							12 02		
Stalybridge	a		10 50			11 06							11 12			11 37	11 42				11 50		12 06		
	d		10 50										11 12				11 42				11 50				
Mossley (Grtr Manchester)	d												11 17												
Greenfield	d												11 22												
Marsden	d												11 30												
Slaithwaite	d												11 34												
Huddersfield	a		11 08	11 16	11 16			11 28		11 28		11 45	11 41				12 00				12 08	12 16			
	d		11 12	11 17	11 17			11 30		11 30		11 46		11 49			12 01	12 03			12 12	12 17			
Deighton	d										←			11 53				12 07							
Mirfield	d										11 39			11 57				12 12	12 39						
Wakefield Kirkgate	a																	12 28	→						
Normanton	a																	12 34							
Castleford	a																	12 40							
Ravensthorpe	d													12 01											
Dewsbury	a			11 26	11 26						11 44	11 56		12 04								12 26			
	d			11 27	11 27						11 44	11 57		12 09								12 27			
Batley	d										11 47			12 12											
Morley	d										11 53			12 17											
Cottingley	d													12 21											
Leeds 10	a		11 31	11 40	11 40		12 18	11 49		11 49	12 03	12 10		12 29			12 21				12 31	12 40		13 18	
	d		11 34	11 42	11 42			11 51		11 51		12 14					12 27				12 34	12 42			
Cross Gates	40 d																								
Garforth	40 d																12 36								
South Milford	40 d																								
Selby	29,40 d		11 56																		12 56				
Howden	29 a																								
Brough	29 a		12 15																		13 15				
Hull	29 a		12 30																		13 32				
York 8	26 a			12 05	12 05			12 14		12 14		12 36					12 55					13 05			
	d			12 07	12 07			12 22		12 22		12 39					13 00					13 07			
Malton	d																13 25								
Seamer	43 a																13 41								
Scarborough	43 a																13 51								
Thirsk	26 d											12 56													
Northallerton	26 d			12 26	12 26							13 05										13 26			
Yarm	a											13 18													
Thornaby	44 a											13 28													
Middlesbrough	44 a											13 35													
Redcar Central	44 a											13 49													
Darlington	26 a			12 37	12 37			12 48		12 48												13 37			
	d			12 39	12 39			12 50		12 50												13 39			
Durham	26 a			12 54	12 54			13 05		13 05												13 54			
Chester-le-Street	26 a			13 01	13 01																				
Newcastle 8	26 a			13 13	13 13			13 19		13 19												14 10			
	d							13 21		13 21															
Morpeth	26 a							13 34		13 34															
Edinburgh	26 a							14 49		14 54															

Table T039-F

Mondays to Saturdays
30 March to 16 May

Liverpool, Manchester Airport and Manchester - Huddersfield - Wakefield, Leeds, Hull, York, Scarborough, Middlesbrough, Newcastle and Edinburgh

		TP	TP	NT	GC	TP	TP	TP	TP	NT	TP	NT	NT	TP	TP	TP		NT	NT	TP	TP	NT	TP	TP	TP
		SX	SO			SO	SX													SX	SO		SO	SX	
		◇1 🛒	◇1 🛒	◇	■ 1 🍴	◇1 🛒	◇1 🛒	◇1	◇1		◇1 🛒		◇	◇1 🛒	◇1 🛒	◇1 🛒			◇	◇1 🛒	◇1 🛒	◇	◇1 🛒	◇1 🛒	◇1
Liverpool Lime Street 10	90 d	11 24	11 24								11 54									12 24	12 24				
Lea Green	90 d										12 06														
Newton-le-Willows	90 d	11 41	11 42																	12 41	12 41				
Manchester Airport	d					11 40	11 40							12 10									12 40	12 40	
Gatley	d					11 46	11 46																12 46	12 46	
Manchester Piccadilly 10	a					11 55	11 55							12 33		←							12 55	12 55	
	d					11 57	11 57	11 58						12 34	12 35								12 57	12 57	12 58
Manchester Oxford Road	d					12 00	12 00							12 38		12 38							13 00	13 00	
Manchester Victoria	a	11 59	11 59			12 10	12 10				12 29			→		12 44				12 59	12 59		13 10	13 13	
	d	12 00	12 00			12 15	12 15			12 23	12 30		12 37			12 45		12 52	12 56	13 00	13 00		13 15	13 15	
Ashton-under-Lyne	d									12 33								13 02							
Stalybridge	a							12 12		12 37	12 41				12 50			13 06							13 12
	d							12 12			12 42				12 50										13 13
Mossley (Grtr Manchester)	d							12 17																	13 18
Greenfield	d							12 22																	13 22
Marsden	d							12 30																	13 30
Slaithwaite	d							12 34																	13 34
Huddersfield	a	12 28	12 28			12 45	12 45	12 41			13 00				13 08	13 16				13 28	13 28		13 45	13 45	13 41
	d	12 30	12 30			12 46	12 46		12 49		13 01	13 03			13 12	13 17				13 30	13 30		13 46	13 46	
Deighton	d			←					12 53			13 07										←			
Mirfield	d			12 39					12 57			13 12	13 39									13 39			
Wakefield Kirkgate	a											13 28	→												
Normanton	a											13 34													
Castleford	a											13 40													
Ravensthorpe	d								13 01																
Dewsbury	a			12 44		12 56	12 56		13 04							13 26						13 44	13 56	13 56	
	d			12 44		12 57	12 57		13 09							13 27						13 44	13 57	13 57	
Batley	d			12 47					13 12													13 47			
Morley	d			12 53					13 17													13 53			
Cottingley	d								13 21																
Leeds 10	a	12 49	12 49	13 03		13 10	13 10		13 29		13 21				13 31	13 40			14 18	13 49	13 49	14 03	14 10	14 10	
	d	12 51	12 51			13 14	13 14				13 27				13 34	13 42				13 51	13 51		14 14	14 14	
Cross Gates	40 d																								
Garforth	40 d										13 36														
South Milford	40 d																								
Selby	29,40 d														13 56										
Howden	29 a																								
Brough	29 a														14 15										
Hull	29 a														14 30										
York 8	26 a	13 14	13 14			13 36	13 36				13 55					14 05				14 14	14 14		14 36	14 36	
	d	13 20	13 20		13 23	13 39	13 39				14 00					14 07				14 21	14 21		14 39	14 39	
Malton	d										14 25														
Seamer	43 a										14 41														
Scarborough	43 a										14 51														
Thirsk	26 d				13 40	13 56	13 56																14 56	14 56	
Northallerton	26 d				13a48	14 05	14 07																15 05	15 07	
Yarm	a					14 17	14 20																15 17	15 20	
Thornaby	44 a					14 27	14 30																15 27	15 30	
Middlesbrough	44 a					14 35	14 37																15 35	15 37	
Redcar Central	44 a					14 48	14 50																15 48	15 50	
Darlington	26 a	13 46	13 46													14 37				14 47	14 47				
	d	13 48	13 48													14 38				14 49	14 49				
Durham	26 a	14 03	14 03													14 54				15 04	15 04				
Chester-le-Street	26 a															15 00									
Newcastle 8	26 a	14 19	14 19													15 13				15 18	15 18				
	d	14 21	14 21																	15 21	15 21				
Morpeth	26 a	14 34	14 34																	15 33	15 33				
Edinburgh	26 a	15 49	15 54																	16 48	16 55				

Table T039-F

Mondays to Saturdays
30 March to 16 May

Liverpool, Manchester Airport and Manchester - Huddersfield - Wakefield, Leeds, Hull, York, Scarborough, Middlesbrough, Newcastle and Edinburgh

		TP	TP	NT	GC	TP	NT	NT		TP	TP	TP	GC	NT	NT	TP	TP	NT	TP	TP	TP	TP	NT	TP
					SX								SO			SX	SO		SO	SX				
		◇1	◇1 🛒		■ 1 🍴	◇1 🛒		◇		◇1 🛒	◇1 🛒	◇1 🛒	■ 1 🍴		◇	◇1 🛒	◇1 🛒	◇	◇1 🛒	◇1 🛒	◇1	◇1		◇1 🛒
Liverpool Lime Street 10	90 d					12 54										13 24	13 24							13 54
Lea Green	90 d					13 06																		14 06
Newton-le-Willows	90 d															13 41	13 41							
Manchester Airport	d		13 07							13 10									13 40	13 40				
Gatley	d																		13 46	13 46				
Manchester Piccadilly 10	a		13 25							13 33		←							13 55	13 55				
	d		13 26							13 34	13 35								13 57	13 57	13 58			
Manchester Oxford Road	d		13a28							13 38		13 38							14 00	14 00				
Manchester Victoria	a					13 29				→		13 44				13 59	13 59		14 10	14 10				14 29
	d			13 22		13 30		13 37				13 45		13 52	13 55	14 00	14 00		14 15	14 15			14 23	14 30
Ashton-under-Lyne	d			13 32										14 02									14 33	
Stalybridge	a			13 36		13 41					13 50			14 06							14 12		14 37	14 41
	d					13 42					13 50										14 12			14 42
Mossley (Grtr Manchester)	d																				14 17			
Greenfield	d																				14 22			
Marsden	d																				14 30			
Slaithwaite	d																				14 34			
Huddersfield	a					14 00					14 08	14 16				14 28	14 28		14 45	14 45	14 41			15 00
	d	13 49				14 01	14 03				14 12	14 17				14 30	14 30		14 46	14 46		14 49		15 01
Deighton	d	13 53					14 07											←				14 53		
Mirfield	d	13 57					14 12	14 39										14 39				14 57		
Wakefield Kirkgate	a						14 28	→																
Normanton	a						14 34																	
Castleford	a						14 40																	
Ravensthorpe	d	14 01																				15 01		
Dewsbury	a	14 04										14 26						14 44	14 56	14 56		15 04		
	d	14 09										14 27						14 44	14 57	14 57		15 09		
Batley	d	14 12																14 47				15 12		
Morley	d	14 17																14 53				15 17		
Cottingley	d	14 21																				15 21		
Leeds 10	a	14 29				14 21					14 31	14 40			15 13	14 49	14 49	15 03	15 10	15 10		15 29		15 21
	d					14 27					14 34	14 42				14 51	14 51		15 14	15 14				15 27
Cross Gates	40 d																							
Garforth	40 d					14 36																		15 36
South Milford	40 d																							
Selby	29,40 d										14 56													
Howden	29 a																							
Brough	29 a										15 15													
Hull	29 a										15 31													
York 8	26 a					14 55						15 05				15 14	15 14		15 36	15 36				15 55
	d				14 51	15 00						15 07	15 14			15 22	15 22		15 39	15 39				16 00
Malton	d					15 25																		16 25
Seamer	43 a					15 41																		16 41
Scarborough	43 a					15 51																		16 51
Thirsk	26 d				15 14								15 37						15 56	15 56				
Northallerton	26 d				15a25							15 26	15a45						16 05	16 07				
Yarm	a																		16 17	16 20				
Thornaby	44 a																		16 27	16 30				
Middlesbrough	44 a																		16 35	16 37				
Redcar Central	44 a																		16 48	16 50				
Darlington	26 a											15 37				15 48	15 48							
	d											15 39				15 50	15 50							
Durham	26 a											15 54				16 05	16 05							
Chester-le-Street	26 a											16 01												
Newcastle 8	26 a											16 13				16 19	16 19							
	d															16 21	16 21							
Morpeth	26 a															16 34	16 34							
Edinburgh	26 a															17 52	17 57							

Table T039-F

Mondays to Saturdays
30 March to 16 May

Liverpool, Manchester Airport and Manchester - Huddersfield - Wakefield, Leeds, Hull, York, Scarborough, Middlesbrough, Newcastle and Edinburgh

Station			NT	NT ◇	TP SO ◇1 ✠	TP SX ◇1 ✠	TP ◇1 ✠	TP SO ◇1 ✠	TP SX ◇1 ✠	NT	NT ◇	TP SX ◇1 ✠	TP SO ◇1 ✠	NT ◇	TP ◇1 ✠	TP ◇1	TP ◇1	TP ◇1 ✠	NT	TP ◇1 ✠	NT	NT ◇	TP ◇1 ✠	TP ◇1 ✠	TP ◇1 ✠
Liverpool Lime Street 10	90	d										14 24	14 24							14 54					
Lea Green	90	d																		15 06					
Newton-le-Willows	90	d										14 41	14 41												
Manchester Airport		d			14 10	14 10									14 40			15 07					15 10		
Gatley		d													14 46										
Manchester Piccadilly 10		a			14 33	14 33		←	←						14 55			15 25					15 33		←
		d			14 34	14 34	14 35								14 57	14 58		15 26					15 34	15 35	
Manchester Oxford Road		d			14 38	14 38		14 38	14 38						15 00			15a28					15 38		15 38
Manchester Victoria		a			→	→		14 44	14 44			14 59	14 59		15 11					15 29			→		15 44
		d		14 36				14 45	14 45	14 52	14 56	15 00	15 00		15 15				15 23	15 30		15 36			15 45
Ashton-under-Lyne		d								15 02									15 33						
Stalybridge		a					14 50			15 06						15 12			15 37	15 41				15 50	
		d					14 50									15 12				15 42				15 50	
Mossley (Grtr Manchester)		d														15 17									
Greenfield		d														15 22									
Marsden		d														15 30									
Slaithwaite		d														15 34									
Huddersfield		a					15 08	15 14	15 14			15 28	15 28		15 45	15 41				16 00				16 08	16 16
		d	15 03				15 09	15 15	15 15			15 29	15 29		15 46		15 49			16 01	16 03			16 12	16 17
Deighton		d	15 07											←			15 53				16 07				
Mirfield		d	15 12	15 38										15 38			15 59				16 12	16 38			
Wakefield Kirkgate		a	15 28	→																	16 28	→			
Normanton		a	15 34																		16 34				
Castleford		a	15 40																		16 40				
Ravensthorpe		d															16 03								
Dewsbury		a						15 26	15 26					15 43	15 56		16 06								16 26
		d						15 27	15 27					15 43	15 57		16 09								16 27
Batley		d												15 46			16 12								
Morley		d												15 52			16 17								
Cottingley		d															16 21								
Leeds 10		a					15 31	15 40	15 40		16 18	15 49	15 49	16 02	16 10		16 29			16 20				16 31	16 40
		d					15 33	15 42	15 42			15 51	15 51		16 14					16 27				16 34	16 42
Cross Gates	40	d																						16 40	
Garforth	40	d																		16 36				16 45	
South Milford	40	d																							
Selby	29,40	d					15 55																	16 59	
Howden	29	a																							
Brough	29	a					16 14																	17 18	
Hull	29	a					16 31																	17 34	
York 8	26	a						16 05	16 05			16 14	16 14		16 36					16 55					17 05
		d						16 07	16 07			16 19	16 19		16 39					17 00					17 07
Malton		d																		17 25					
Seamer	43	a																		17 41					
Scarborough	43	a																		17 51					
Thirsk	26	d													16 56										
Northallerton	26	d						16 26	16 26						17 07										17 26
Yarm		a													17 20										
Thornaby	44	a													17 30										
Middlesbrough	44	a													17 37										
Redcar Central	44	a													17 50										
Darlington	26	a						16 37	16 37			16 47	16 47												17 37
		d						16 39	16 39			16 49	16 49												17 39
Durham	26	a						16 54	16 59			17 05	17 04												17 54
Chester-le-Street	26	a						17 01	17 06																
Newcastle 8	26	a						17 13	17 18			17 18	17 18												18 10
		d										17 20	17 20												
Morpeth	26	a										17 33	17 33												
Edinburgh	26	a										18 52	18 56												

Table T039-F

Mondays to Saturdays
30 March to 16 May

Liverpool, Manchester Airport and Manchester - Huddersfield - Wakefield, Leeds, Hull, York, Scarborough, Middlesbrough, Newcastle and Edinburgh

Station			NT	NT SO ◇	NT SX ◇	TP SO ◇1 ✠	TP SX ◇1 ✠	NT ◇	TP ◇1 ✠	TP ◇1	TP ◇1	NT	TP ◇1 ✠	NT	TP ◇1 ✠	NT ◇	TP ◇1 ✠	NT	NT ◇	TP ◇1 ✠	NT ◇	TP SX ◇1 ✠	TP SO ◇1 ✠	TP ◇1
Liverpool Lime Street 10	90	d				15 24	15 24						15 54							16 24				
Lea Green	90	d											16 06											
Newton-le-Willows	90	d				15 41	15 41													16 41				
Manchester Airport		d							15 40								16 10					16 34	16 40	
Gatley		d							15 46													16 40	16 46	
Manchester Piccadilly 10		a							15 55								16 33					16 55	16 55	
		d							15 57	15 58					16 30		16 34					16 57	16 57	16 58
Manchester Oxford Road		d							16 00								16 38					17 00	17 00	
Manchester Victoria		a				15 59	15 59		16 10				16 29				16 44			16 59		17 10	17 10	
		d	15 52	15 54	15 56	16 00	16 00		16 15			16 23	16 30			16 37	16 45	16 52	16 56	17 00		17 15	17 15	
Ashton-under-Lyne		d	16 02									16 33						17 02						
Stalybridge		a	16 06							16 12		16 37	16 41		16 43			17 06						17 12
		d								16 12			16 42		16 45									17 12
Mossley (Grtr Manchester)		d								16 17					16 49									17 17
Greenfield		d								16 22					16 53									17 22
Marsden		d								16 30					17 01									17 30
Slaithwaite		d								16 34					17 05									17 34
Huddersfield		a				16 28	16 28		16 45	16 41			17 00		17 11		17 16			17 28		17 45	17 45	17 40
		d				16 30	16 30		16 46		16 49		17 01	17 03	17 12		17 17			17 30		17 46	17 46	
Deighton		d						←			16 53			17 07							←			
Mirfield		d						16 38			16 57			17 12		17 39					17 39			
Wakefield Kirkgate		a												17 28		→								
Normanton		a												17 34										
Castleford		a												17 40										
Ravensthorpe		d									17 01													
Dewsbury		a						16 43	16 56		17 04						17 26				17 44	17 56	17 56	
		d						16 44	16 57		17 09						17 27				17 44	17 57	17 57	
Batley		d						16 47			17 12										17 47			
Morley		d						16 53			17 17										17 53			
Cottingley		d									17 21													
Leeds 10		a		17 19	17 19	16 49	16 49	17 04	17 10		17 29		17 21		17 31		17 40		18 21	17 49	18 03	18 10	18 10	
		d				16 51	16 51		17 13				17 27		17 34		17 42			17 51		18 14	18 14	
Cross Gates	40	d													17 41									
Garforth	40	d											17 36		17 45									
South Milford	40	d																						
Selby	29,40	d													17 59									
Howden	29	a													18 08									
Brough	29	a													18 21									
Hull	29	a													18 37									
York 8	26	a				17 14	17 14		17 35				17 55				18 05			18 18		18 36	18 36	
		d				17 21	17 21		17 39				18 00				18 07			18 22		18 39	18 39	
Malton		d											18 25											
Seamer	43	a											18 42											
Scarborough	43	a											18 52											
Thirsk	26	d							17 56													18 56	18 56	
Northallerton	26	d							18 05								18 26					19 05	19 05	
Yarm		a							18 17													19 17	19 17	
Thornaby	44	a							18 27													19 27	19 27	
Middlesbrough	44	a							18 35													19 35	19 35	
Redcar Central	44	a							18 48													19 48	19 48	
Darlington	26	a				17 47	17 47										18 37			18 48				
		d				17 49	17 49										18 39			18 50				
Durham	26	a				18 04	18 04										18 54			19 05				
Chester-le-Street	26	a															19 01							
Newcastle 8	26	a				18 18	18 18										19 13			19 19				
		d				18 21	18 21													19 21				
Morpeth	26	a				18 34	18 34													19 34				
Edinburgh	26	a				20 04	20 08													20 54				

Table T039-F

Mondays to Saturdays
30 March to 16 May

Liverpool, Manchester Airport and Manchester - Huddersfield - Wakefield, Leeds, Hull, York, Scarborough, Middlesbrough, Newcastle and Edinburgh

			TP	TP	NT	GC	GC	TP	NT	TP	NT	TP	TP	NT	NT	TP	TP		NT	TP	TP	TP	TP	TP	NT	TP
						SO	SX					SX	SO			SX	SO			SX	SO	SX				
			◇1	◇1 ✕		■ 1 ⊡	■ 1 ⊡	◇1 ✕		◇1 ✕	◇	◇1 ✕	◇1 ✕		◇	◇1 ✕	◇1 ✕		◇	◇1 ✕	◇1 ✕	◇1 ✕	◇1	◇1		◇1 ✕
Liverpool Lime Street 10	90	d						16 54								17 24	17 24									17 54
Lea Green	90	d						17 06																		18 06
Newton-le-Willows	90	d														17 41	17 41									
Manchester Airport		d		17 07								17 10	17 10							17 34	17 40					
Gatley		d																		17 42	17 46	←				
Manchester Piccadilly 10		a		17 25								17 33	17 33							17 56	17 56	17 56				
		d		17 27						17 30		17 35	17 35							17 58	17 57	17 58	18 00			
Manchester Oxford Road		d		17a29								17 38	17 38							→	18 01	18 01				
Manchester Victoria		a						17 29				17 44	17 44			17 58	17 59				18 11	18 13				18 29
		d			17 23			17 30			17 37	17 45	17 45	17 52	17 56	18 00	18 00				18 15	18 15			18 23	18 30
Ashton-under-Lyne		d			17 33									18 02											18 33	
Stalybridge		a			17 37			17 41		17 45				18 06									18 13		18 37	18 41
		d						17 42		17 45													18 13			18 42
Mossley (Grtr Manchester)		d								17 50													18 18			
Greenfield		d								17 54													18 22			
Marsden		d								18 02													18 30			
Slaithwaite		d								18 05													18 34			
Huddersfield		a						18 00		18 11		18 16	18 16			18 28	18 28				18 45	18 45	18 41			19 00
		d	17 49					18 01	18 03	18 12		18 17	18 17			18 30	18 30				18 46	18 46		18 49		19 01
Deighton		d	17 53						18 07										←					18 53		
Mirfield		d	17 57						18 12		18 38								18 38					18 57		
Wakefield Kirkgate		a							18 28		→															
Normanton		a							18 34																	
Castleford		a							18 40																	
Ravensthorpe		d	18 01																					19 01		
Dewsbury		a	18 04									18 26	18 26						18 43		18 56	18 56		19 04		
		d	18 09									18 27	18 27						18 44		18 57	18 57		19 09		
Batley		d	18 12																18 47					19 12		
Morley		d	18 17																18 53					19 17		
Cottingley		d	18 21																					19 21		
Leeds 10		a	18 29					18 21		18 31		18 40	18 40		19 19	18 49	18 49		19 02		19 10	19 10		19 29		19 21
		d						18 27		18 34		18 42	18 42			18 51	18 51				19 14	19 14				19 27
Cross Gates	40	d								18 40																
Garforth	40	d						18 36		18 45																19 36
South Milford	40	d																								
Selby	29,40	d								18 59																
Howden	29	a																								
Brough	29	a								19 17																
Hull	29	a								19 33																
York 8	26	a						18 55				19 05	19 05			19 14	19 14				19 36	19 36				19 55
		d				18 42	18 42	19 00				19 07	19 07			19 17	19 22				19 39	19 39				20 00
Malton		d						19 25																		20 25
Seamer	43	a						19 41																		20 41
Scarborough	43	a						19 51																		20 51
Thirsk	26	d				19 00	19 01														19 56	19 57				
Northallerton	26	d				19a08	19a09					19 26	19 26								20 07	20 07				
Yarm		a																			20 20	20 20				
Thornaby	44	a																			20 30	20 30				
Middlesbrough	44	a																			20 37	20 37				
Redcar Central	44	a																			20 51	20 51				
Darlington	26	a										19 37	19 37			19 43	19 48									
		d										19 39	19 39			19 45	19 50									
Durham	26	a										19 54	19 54			20 00	20 05									
Chester-le-Street	26	a																								
Newcastle 8	26	a										20 10	20 12			20 14	20 21									
		d														20 16										
Morpeth	26	a														20 29										
Edinburgh	26	a														21 57										

NRT DECEMBER 19 EDITION

Table T039-F

Mondays to Saturdays
30 March to 16 May

Liverpool, Manchester Airport and Manchester - Huddersfield - Wakefield, Leeds, Hull, York, Scarborough, Middlesbrough, Newcastle and Edinburgh

			NT	TP	NT	TP	NT	NT	TP		TP	NT	TP	TP	TP	TP	TP	NT	NT	TP	NT	TP	NT	TP	TP
									SX		SO		SX	SO			SX	SX				SX			SO
				◇1 ✕	◇	◇1 ✕		◇	◇1 ✕		◇1 ✕	◇	◇1	◇1	◇1	◇1	◇1 ✕	◇		◇1		◇1	◇	◇1	◇1
Liverpool Lime Street 10	90	d							18 24		18 24									18 54					
Lea Green	90	d																		19 06					
Newton-le-Willows	90	d							18 42		18 41														
Manchester Airport		d				18 10							18 37	18 40			19 07							19 10	
Gatley		d											18 43	18 46											
Manchester Piccadilly 10		a				18 33							18 55	18 55			19 25							19 33	
		d		18 30		18 34							18 57	18 57	19 00		19 26					19 30		19 34	19 35
Manchester Oxford Road		d				18 38							19 00	19 00			19a28							19 38	
Manchester Victoria		a				18 44			18 59		18 59		19 11	19 11						19 29				→	
		d			18 37	18 45	18 52	18 56	19 00		19 00		19 15	19 15				19 21	19 24	19 30			19 36		
Ashton-under-Lyne		d					19 02												19 33						
Stalybridge		a		18 43			19 06								19 13				19 38	19 41		19 42			19 50
		d		18 45											19 13					19 42		19 50			19 50
Mossley (Grtr Manchester)		d		18 49											19 18										
Greenfield		d		18 53											19 22										
Marsden		d		19 01											19 30										
Slaithwaite		d		19 05											19 34										
Huddersfield		a		19 11		19 16			19 28		19 28		19 45	19 45	19 41					20 00		20 08			20 08
		d	19 03	19 12		19 17			19 30		19 30		19 46	19 46		19 49				20 01	20 03	20 12			20 12
Deighton		d	19 07									←				19 53					20 07				
Mirfield		d	19 12		19 39							19 39				19 57					20 12		20 39		
Wakefield Kirkgate		a	19 28		→																20 28		→		
Normanton		a	19 34																		20 34				
Castleford		a	19 40																		20 41				
Ravensthorpe		d														20 01									
Dewsbury		a				19 26						19 44	19 55	19 55		20 04									
		d				19 27						19 44	19 56	19 56		20 09									
Batley		d										19 47				20 12									
Morley		d										19 53				20 17									
Cottingley		d														20 21									
Leeds 10		a		19 31		19 40		20 19	19 49		19 49	20 03	20 09	20 09		20 30		20 43		20 23		20 31			20 31
		d		19 34		19 42			19 51		19 51		20 14	20 14						20 27		20 33			20 33
Cross Gates	40	d																							
Garforth	40	d																		20 36					
South Milford	40	d																							
Selby	29,40	d		19 56																		20 56			20 57
Howden	29	a																				21 05			21 06
Brough	29	a		20 16																		21 18			21 19
Hull	29	a		20 34																		21 34			21 35
York 8	26	a				20 05			20 14		20 14		20 36	20 36						20 57					
		d				20 07			20 16		20 22		20 39	20 39						21 00					
Malton		d																		21 25					
Seamer	43	a																		21 41					
Scarborough	43	a																		21 51					
Thirsk	26	d											20 56	20 56											
Northallerton	26	d				20 26							21 05	21 05											
Yarm		a											21 18	21 18											
Thornaby	44	a											21 28	21 28											
Middlesbrough	44	a											21 35	21 35											
Redcar Central	44	a											21 48	21 48											
Darlington	26	a				20 37			20 43		20 48														
		d				20 39			20 45		20 50														
Durham	26	a				20 54			21 00		21 05														
Chester-le-Street	26	a				21 01																			
Newcastle 8	26	a				21 15			21 14		21 21														
		d							21 16																
Morpeth	26	a							21 31																
Edinburgh	26	a							22 49																

Table T039-F

Mondays to Saturdays
30 March to 16 May

Liverpool, Manchester Airport and Manchester - Huddersfield - Wakefield, Leeds, Hull, York, Scarborough, Middlesbrough, Newcastle and Edinburgh

	TP	NT	NT	TP	NT	GC	GC	TP	TP	TP	TP	NT	TP	TP	NT	NT	TP	TP	TP	NT	NT	TP	TP
						SX	SO	SO		SX	SO											SX	SO
	◇1		◇	◇1	◇	1	1	◇1	◇1	◇1	◇1		◇1	◇1		◇	◇1	◇1	◇1		◇	◇1	◇1
				A 🛒																		A 🛒	A 🛒
Liverpool Lime Street 10 90 d				19 25										19 54								20 24	20 24
Lea Green 90 d														20 06									
Newton-le-Willows 90 d				19 41																		20 40	20 40
Manchester Airport ✈ d								19 36		19 38							20 10						
Gatley d								19 42		19 44													
Manchester Piccadilly 10 a	←							19 54		19 57							20 33		←				
d								19 55	19 58	19 59							20 34	20 35					
Manchester Oxford Road d	19 38							19 59		20 02	←						20 38		20 38				
Manchester Victoria a	19 44			19 59				20 10		20 14	20 10			20 29			→		20 44			20 59	20 59
d	19 45	19 52	19 56	20 00				20 15		20 15	20 15	20 22		20 30		20 37			20 45	20 52	20 56	21 00	21 00
Ashton-under-Lyne d		20 02						→				20 32								21 02			
Stalybridge a		20 06							20 12			20 36		20 41				20 50		21 07			
d									20 13					20 42				20 50					
Mossley (Grtr Manchester) d									20 18														
Greenfield d									20 22														
Marsden d									20 30														
Slaithwaite d									20 34														
Huddersfield a	20 16			20 29					20 41	20 45	20 45			21 00				21 08	21 16			21 27	21 27
d	20 17			20 30						20 46	20 46		20 49	21 01	21 03			21 12	21 17			21 29	21 29
Deighton d					←								20 53		21 07								
Mirfield d					20 39								20 57		21 12	21 39							
Wakefield Kirkgate a															21 28	→							
Normanton a															21 34								
Castleford a															21 40								
Ravensthorpe d													21 01										
Dewsbury a	20 26				20 44					20 56	20 56		21 04						21 26				
d	20 27				20 44					20 57	20 57		21 09						21 27				
Batley d					20 47								21 12										
Morley d					20 53								21 17										
Cottingley d													21 21										
Leeds 10 a	20 40		21 14	20 49	21 04					21 10	21 10		21 29	21 22				21 31	21 40		22 13	21 48	21 49
d	20 42			20 51						21 14	21 14			21 27				21 34	21 42			21 51	21 51
Cross Gates 40 d																							
Garforth 40 d														21 36									
South Milford 40 d																							
Selby 29,40 d																		21 56					
Howden 29 a																		22 05					
Brough 29 a																		22 18					
Hull 29 a																		22 36					
York 8 26 a	21 06			21 14						21 36	21 36			21 55					22 07			22 13	22 14
d	21 15			21 20		21 22	21 23			21 39	21 39			22 00								22 21	22 21
Malton d	21 39													22 25									
Seamer 43 a	21 56													22 41									
Scarborough 43 a	22 03													22 51									
Thirsk 26 d						21 38	21 38			21 56	21 56												
Northallerton 26 d						21a46	21a46			22 05	22 07											22 40	22 40
Yarm a										22 17	22 20												
Thornaby 44 a										22 27	22 30												
Middlesbrough 44 a										22 35	22 40												
Redcar Central 44 a										22 48													
Darlington 26 a				21 46																		22 51	22 51
d				21 48																		22 53	22 53
Durham 26 a				22 03																		23 08	23 08
Chester-le-Street 26 a																						23 15	23 15
Newcastle 8 26 a				22 19																		23 26	23 26
d																							
Morpeth 26 a																							
Edinburgh 26 a																							

A 🛒 from York

Table T039-F

Mondays to Saturdays
30 March to 16 May

Liverpool, Manchester Airport and Manchester - Huddersfield - Wakefield, Leeds, Hull, York, Scarborough, Middlesbrough, Newcastle and Edinburgh

	NT	TP	TP	TP	TP	NT	NT	TP	TP	TP	TP	NT	NT	TP	TP	TP	TP	TP	NT	TP	TP	NT
			SX					SO	SX	SO	SX						SX	SO		SO	SX	
	◇	◇1	◇1	◇1	◇1			◇1	◇1	◇1	◇1	◇		◇1	◇1	◇1	◇1	◇1		◇1	◇1	◇
			🛒																			
Liverpool Lime Street 10 90 d										21 08	21 08									22 06	22 06	
Lea Green 90 d										21 20	21 20									22 19	22 19	
Newton-le-Willows 90 d										21 27	21 27									22 25	22 25	
Manchester Airport ✈ d			21 06											21 35								
Gatley d														21 41								
Manchester Piccadilly 10 a			21 20											21 53								
d		20 58	21 22					21 35	21 35					21 55	21 58		22 32	22 34				
Manchester Oxford Road d			21a24											21 58								
Manchester Victoria a										21 45	21 45			22 11						22 45	22 45	
d				21 15		21 23				21 45	21 45	21 56	22 08	22 14					22 36	22 45	22 46	22 56
Ashton-under-Lyne d						21 33							22 18						22 47			
Stalybridge a		21 12				21 37		21 50	21 50	21 57	21 57		22 22		22 14		22 49	22 50	22 51	22 57	22 57	
d		21 13						21 50	21 50	21 58	21 58				22 14		22 50	22 50		22 58	22 58	
Mossley (Grtr Manchester) d		21 18													22 19							
Greenfield d		21 23													22 23							
Marsden d		21 31													22 31							
Slaithwaite d		21 35													22 35							
Huddersfield a		21 42		21 46				22 08	22 08	22 16	22 16			22 45	22 42		23 08	23 09		23 16	23 16	
d				21 47	21 51		22 03	22 12	22 12	22 17	22 17			22 46		22 52	23 12	23 12		23 17	23 17	
Deighton d	←				21 55		22 07									22 56						
Mirfield d	21 39				21 59		22 12									23 00						
Wakefield Kirkgate a							22 28															
Normanton a							22 34															
Castleford a							22 40															
Ravensthorpe d					22 03											23 04						
Dewsbury a	21 44			21 56	22 06					22 26	22 26			22 56		23 07				23 26	23 26	
d	21 45			21 57	22 08					22 27	22 27			22 57		23 09				23 27	23 27	
Batley d	21 48				22 11											23 12						
Morley d	21 54				22 16											23 17						
Cottingley d					22 20											23 21						
Leeds 10 a	22 05			22 12	22 28			22 35	22 36	22 40	22 40	23 13		23 10		23 29	23 31	23 31		23 40	23 40	00 14
d				22 14				22 37	22 37	22 42	22 42			23 13			23 33	23 34		23 42	23 42	
Cross Gates 40 d																						
Garforth 40 d																						
South Milford 40 d								22 53	22 53													
Selby 29,40 d								23 02	23 02								23 52	23 53				
Howden 29 a																						
Brough 29 a								23 21	23 21								00 10	00 11				
Hull 29 a								23 36	23 36								00 26	00 27				
York 8 26 a				22 36						23 07	23 07			23 40						00 10	00 10	
d				22 41						23 08	23 08											
Malton d				23 05																		
Seamer 43 a				23 22																		
Scarborough 43 a				23 31																		
Thirsk 26 d											23 31											
Northallerton 26 d										23 27	23 39											
Yarm a																						
Thornaby 44 a																						
Middlesbrough 44 a																						
Redcar Central 44 a																						
Darlington 26 a										23 38	23 51											
d										23 40	00 01											
Durham 26 a										23 55	00 19											
Chester-le-Street 26 a										00 02	00 32											
Newcastle 8 26 a										00 14	00 59											
d																						
Morpeth 26 a																						
Edinburgh 26 a																						

Table T039-F

Mondays to Saturdays
30 March to 16 May

Liverpool, Manchester Airport and Manchester - Huddersfield - Wakefield, Leeds, Hull, York, Scarborough, Middlesbrough, Newcastle and Edinburgh

			TP	TP	TP	TP	TP	TP	TP	TP	TP	NT	NT	TP	TP	TP	TP	TP	TP
			SX		SO	SO	SX	SO	SX	SX	SO	SX			SO	SX	SO	FO	FSX
			◇1	◇1	◇1	◇1	◇1	◇1	◇1 ⊼	◇1	◇1	◇		◇1	◇1	◇1	◇1	◇1	◇1
Liverpool Lime Street 10	90	d													23 08	23 08			
Lea Green	90	d													23 20	23 23			
Newton-le-Willows	90	d													23 27	23 31			
Manchester Airport		d	22 39		22 40				23 10								23 40	23 40	23 40
Gatley		d																	
Manchester Piccadilly 10		a	22 56		22 59		←		23 24								23 53	23 54	23 54
		d	22 58	23 00	23 01				23 26					23 35			23 55	23 55	23 55
Manchester Oxford Road		d	23 06		23 05		23 06		23a28								23 58	23 59	23 59
Manchester Victoria		a	→		23 11		23 13								23 45	23 50	00 04	00 04	00 04
		d			23 15		23 15					23 19	23 29		23 45	23 53	00 04	00 05	00 05
Ashton-under-Lyne		d											23 39						
Stalybridge		a		23 13									23 43	23 47	23 58	00 04			
		d		23 14										23 47	23 59	00 05			
Mossley (Grtr Manchester)		d		23 18										23 52					
Greenfield		d		23 22										23 57					
Marsden		d		23 30										00 05					
Slaithwaite		d		23 34										00 09					
Huddersfield		a		23 40	23 45		23 50	←						00 16	00 19	00 24	00 32	00 32	01 01
		d		23 41	23 46	23 50	23 51			23 54					00 20	00 25	00 34	00 34	01 12
Deighton		d		23 44		23 54		23 54		23 58									
Mirfield		d		23 49		→		23 58		00 03									
Wakefield Kirkgate		a		00 04															
Normanton		a																	
Castleford		a																	
Ravensthorpe		d						00 03		00 08	←								
Dewsbury		a			23 56		00 01	00 06		00 10	00 06				00 29	00 33			
		d			23 57		00 02	00 11		00 10	00 11				00 30	00 34			
Batley		d						→		00 13	00 14								
Morley		d								00 18	00 19								
Cottingley		d								00 22	00 23								
Leeds 10		a			00 10		00 15			00 29	00 31	00 46			00 43	00 47	00 53	01 11	01 31
		d			00 22		00 29								00 48	00 53	00 56	01 13	01 43
Cross Gates	40	d																	
Garforth	40	d																	
South Milford	40	d																	
Selby	29,40	d																	
Howden	29	a																	
Brough	29	a																	
Hull	29	a																	
York 8	26	a			01 02		01 10								01 15	01 29	01 23	01 39	02 27
		d																	
Malton		d																	
Seamer	43	a																	
Scarborough	43	a																	
Thirsk	26	d																	
Northallerton	26	d																	
Yarm		a																	
Thornaby	44	a																	
Middlesbrough	44	a																	
Redcar Central	44	a																	
Darlington	26	a																	
		d																	
Durham	26	a																	
Chester-le-Street	26	a																	
Newcastle 8	26	a																	
		d																	
Morpeth	26	a																	
Edinburgh	26	a																	

NRT DECEMBER 19 EDITION

Table T039-F

Sundays
15 December to 16 February

Liverpool, Manchester Airport and Manchester - Huddersfield - Wakefield, Leeds, Hull, York, Scarborough, Middlesbrough, Newcastle and Edinburgh

			TP	TP	TP	TP	TP	TP	TP	TP	TP	TP	TP	TP	TP	TP	TP	TP	TP	TP	NT	TP	TP	TP	TP
			◇1	◇1	◇1	◇1	◇1	◇1	◇1	◇1	◇1	◇1	◇1	◇1	◇1	◇1	◇1	◇1	◇1	◇1		◇1	◇1	◇1	◇1
			A	A	A	A	A				⊼	⊼		⊼	⊼		⊼	⊼				⊼	B ⊼	C ⊼	B ⊼
Liverpool Lime Street 10	90	d																							
Lea Green	90	d																							
Newton-le-Willows	90	d																							
Manchester Airport		d						00 38	04 22		06 27						07 27						07⟆40	07⟆46	
Gatley		d																							←
Manchester Piccadilly 10		a						00 52	04 36		06 41						07 41						07⟆58	08⟆00	07⟆58
		d						01 03	04 40	05 45	06 45		07 00				07 44		08 00				08⟆22	08⟆05	08⟆22
Manchester Oxford Road		d																					→	08⟆09	
Manchester Victoria		a																						→	
		d					00⟆04														08 17				
Ashton-under-Lyne		d																			08 27				
Stalybridge		a									06 58		07 12				07 57		08 12		08 33				08⟆34
		d									06 59		07 12				07 58		08 12						08⟆41
Mossley (Grtr Manchester)		d											07 17						08 17						
Greenfield		d											07 22						08 22						
Marsden		d	00⟆05										07 30						08 30						
Slaithwaite		d	00⟆09										07 34						08 34						
Huddersfield		a	00⟆16				00⟆32	01 32	05 09	06 13	07 16		07 41				08 15		08 41						08⟆59
		d				00⟆20	00⟆34	01 33	05 10	06 14	07 17		07 49				08 16			08 49					09⟆01
Deighton		d											07 53							08 53					
Mirfield		d											07 57							08 57					
Wakefield Kirkgate		a																							
Normanton		a																							
Castleford		a																							
Ravensthorpe		d			00⟆03								08 01							09 01					
Dewsbury		a			00⟆06	00⟆29					07 26		08 04				08 25			09 04					
		d			00⟆11	00⟆30					07 27		08 09				08 26			09 09					
Batley		d			00⟆14								08 12							09 12					
Morley		d			00⟆19								08 17							09 17					
Cottingley		d			00⟆23								08 21							09 21					
Leeds 10		a			00⟆31	00⟆43	00⟆53	01 52	05 29	06 33	07 40		08 29				08 39			09 29					09⟆20
		d		00⟆22		00⟆48	01⟆05	02 03	05 33	06 38	07 42			08 35			08 41								09⟆22
Cross Gates	40	d																							
Garforth	40	d																							09⟆31
South Milford	40	d																							
Selby	29,40	d												09 00											
Howden	29	a																							
Brough	29	a												09 19											
Hull	29	a												09 34											
York 8	26	a		01⟆02		01⟆25	01⟆44	02 44	06 14	07 19	08 04						09 04								09⟆55
		d										08 21			08 39	09 00		09 19				09 39			10⟆00
Malton		d														09 25									10⟆25
Seamer	43	a														09 41									10⟆41
Scarborough	43	a														09 53									10⟆53
Thirsk	26	d													08 56							09 56			
Northallerton	26	d													09 07							10 07			
Yarm		a													09 20							10 20			
Thornaby	44	a													09 30							10 30			
Middlesbrough	44	a													09 37							10 37			
Redcar Central	44	a													09 50							10 52			
Darlington	26	a										08 47						09 45							
		d										08 49						09 47							
Durham	26	a										09 04						10 02							
Chester-le-Street	26	a																10 09							
Newcastle 8	26	a										09 18						10 19							
		d										09 20						10 21							
Morpeth	26	a										09 33						10 34							
Edinburgh	26	a										11 03						12 07							

A not 15 December **B** from 12 January **C** until 5 January

Table T039-F

Sundays

15 December to 16 February

Liverpool, Manchester Airport and Manchester - Huddersfield - Wakefield, Leeds, Hull, York, Scarborough, Middlesbrough, Newcastle and Edinburgh

	TP	TP	NT	TP	TP	TP	TP	NT	TP	TP	TP	TP	TP	NT	TP	TP	NT	TP	GC	TP	TP	TP
	◇1 A 🍴	◇1 A 🍴	◇	◇1 🍴	◇1 🍴	◇1 🍴	◇1		◇1 🍴	◇1	◇1 🍴	◇1 🍴	◇1 🍴	◇	◇1 🍴	◇1		◇1 🍴	■ 1 🍽	◇1	◇1 🍴	◇1 🍴
Liverpool Lime Street 10 90 d						08 12						08 54			09 23						09 55	
Lea Green 90 d						08 28						09 06									10 07	
Newton-le-Willows 90 d						08 34						09 12			09 39							
Manchester Airport d				09 05									09 14									
Gatley d																						
Manchester Piccadilly 10 a	←			09 20									09 32									
d		08 43		09 22							09 27		09 35									10 35
Manchester Oxford Road d	08 09			09a24									09 38									
Manchester Victoria a	08 14					08 55						09 31	09 44		09 57						10 29	
d	08 30		08 54			08 57	09 00	09 03	09 18			09 33	09 45	09 56	10 00	10 03	10 07	10 15			10 30	
Ashton-under-Lyne d								09 15									10 16					
Stalybridge a	08 40						09 11	09 19			09 40	09 43				10 14	10 23				10 41	10 51
d	08 41						09 12				09 41	09 51				10 15					10 42	10 51
Mossley (Grtr Manchester) d							09 16									10 19						
Greenfield d							09 21									10 23						
Marsden d							09 29									10 31						
Slaithwaite d							09 33									10 35						
Huddersfield a	08 59					09 28	09 40		09 44		09 59	10 08	10 16		10 28	10 42		10 44			10 59	11 09
d	09 01					09 30			09 45	09 49	10 01	10 12	10 17		10 30			10 45		10 49	11 01	11 12
Deighton d										09 53										10 53		
Mirfield d										09 57										10 57		
Wakefield Kirkgate a																						
Normanton a																						
Castleford a																						
Ravensthorpe d										10 01										11 01		
Dewsbury a									09 56	10 04			10 26					10 55		11 04		
d									09 57	10 09			10 27					10 56		11 09		
Batley d										10 12										11 12		
Morley d										10 17										11 17		
Cottingley d										10 21										11 21		
Leeds 10 a	09 20		10 21			09 49			10 10	10 29	10 21	10 31	10 40	11 19	10 49			11 09		11 29	11 21	11 31
d	09 22					09 51			10 14		10 22	10 34	10 42		10 51			11 14			11 23	11 34
Cross Gates 40 d																						
Garforth 40 d	09 31										10 31										11 32	
South Milford 40 d																						
Selby 29,40 d												11 00										11 59
Howden 29 a																						
Brough 29 a												11 19										12 18
Hull 29 a												11 37										12 35
York 8 26 a	09 55					10 14			10 36		10 54		11 05		11 15			11 36			11 48	
d	10 00				10 07	10 22			10 41		10 57		11 07		11 18			11 39	11 42		11 58	
Malton d	10 25										11 22										12 25	
Seamer 43 a	10 41										11 38										12 41	
Scarborough 43 a	10 53										11 50										12 53	
Thirsk 26 d									10 58										11 59			
Northallerton 26 d					10 26				11 11				11 26					12 01	12a06			
Yarm a									11 24									12 14				
Thornaby 44 a									11 34									12 24				
Middlesbrough 44 a									11 41									12 31				
Redcar Central 44 a									11 54									12 46				
Darlington 26 a					10 37	10 49							11 37									
d					10 39	10 51							11 39									
Durham 26 a					10 54								11 54		11 59							
Chester-le-Street 26 a					11 01																	
Newcastle 8 26 a					11 13	11 19							12 10		12 13							
d						11 21									12 14							
Morpeth 26 a						11 34									12 27							
Edinburgh 26 a		11 54				13 00									13 57							

A until 5 January

Table T039-F

Sundays

15 December to 16 February

Liverpool, Manchester Airport and Manchester - Huddersfield - Wakefield, Leeds, Hull, York, Scarborough, Middlesbrough, Newcastle and Edinburgh

	TP	NT	TP	TP	NT	TP	TP	TP	TP	TP	TP	NT	TP	TP	NT	TP	TP	TP	TP	TP	TP	TP	NT
	◇1 🍴	◇	◇1 🍴	◇1		◇1 🍴	◇1 🍴	◇1	◇1 🍴	◇1 🍴	◇1 🍴	◇	◇1 🍴	◇1		◇1 🍴	◇1	◇1 🍴	◇1 🍴	◇1 🍴	◇1 🍴	◇1 🍴	◇
Liverpool Lime Street 10 90 d			10 25						10 53				11 24					11 52					
Lea Green 90 d									11 05									12 05					
Newton-le-Willows 90 d			10 41										11 42										
Manchester Airport d	10 13					11 10										11 37				12 13			
Gatley d																11 43							
Manchester Piccadilly 10 a	10 34					11 23										11 59				12 33		←	
d	10 36			11 00		11 25				11 35	11 40			11 58		12 01				12 34	12 35		
Manchester Oxford Road d	10 39					11a27										12 05				12 38		12 38	
Manchester Victoria a	10 44		10 59						11 28				12 00			12 13		12 29		→		12 45	
d	10 45	10 56	11 00		11 07		11 15		11 30			11 56	12 01		12 07	12 15		12 30	12 31			12 45	12 57
Ashton-under-Lyne d					11 16										12 16								
Stalybridge a				11 12	11 23				11 40	11 51				12 12	12 23			12 41			12 51		
d				11 12					11 41	11 51				12 12				12 42			12 51		
Mossley (Grtr Manchester) d				11 17										12 17									
Greenfield d				11 22										12 22									
Marsden d				11 30										12 30									
Slaithwaite d				11 34										12 34									
Huddersfield a	11 16		11 28	11 41			11 45		11 59	12 09	12 16		12 28	12 41		12 45		12 59			13 09	13 16	
d	11 17		11 30				11 46	11 49	12 01	12 12	12 17		12 30			12 46	12 49	13 01			13 12	13 17	
Deighton d								11 53									12 53						
Mirfield d								11 57									12 57						
Wakefield Kirkgate a																							
Normanton a																							
Castleford a																							
Ravensthorpe d								12 01									13 01						
Dewsbury a	11 26						11 56	12 04			12 25					12 56	13 04					13 26	
d	11 26						11 57	12 09			12 26					12 57	13 09					13 27	
Batley d								12 12									13 12						
Morley d								12 17									13 17						
Cottingley d								12 21									13 21						
Leeds 10 a	11 39	12 20	11 49				12 10	12 29	12 21	12 31	12 39	13 19	12 49			13 10	13 29	13 20			13 31	13 40	14 20
d	11 42		11 51				12 14		12 22	12 34	12 41		12 51			13 14		13 22			13 34	13 45	
Cross Gates 40 d																							
Garforth 40 d									12 31									13 31					
South Milford 40 d																							
Selby 29,40 d										13 00											14 00		
Howden 29 a																							
Brough 29 a										13 19											14 19		
Hull 29 a										13 36											14 36		
York 8 26 a	12 04		12 14				12 36		12 52		13 05		13 15			13 36		13 52				14 10	
d	12 06		12 22				12 39		12 57		13 06		13 20			13 39		13 57				14 11	
Malton d									13 25									14 22					
Seamer 43 a									13 41									14 39					
Scarborough 43 a									13 53									14 51					
Thirsk 26 d							12 56									13 56							
Northallerton 26 d							13 05				13 25					14 05							
Yarm a							13 17									14 17							
Thornaby 44 a							13 27									14 27							
Middlesbrough 44 a							13 35									14 35							
Redcar Central 44 a							13 49									14 49							
Darlington 26 a	12 33		12 48								13 37		14 07									14 38	
d	12 34		12 50								13 38		14 09									14 39	
Durham 26 a	12 50		13 05								13 54		14 25									14 55	
Chester-le-Street 26 a	12 56																					15 01	
Newcastle 8 26 a	13 07		13 21								14 08		14 38									15 13	
d			13 24										14 41										
Morpeth 26 a			13 36										14 54										
Edinburgh 26 a			14 59										16 15						15 39				

Table T039-F

Sundays

15 December to 16 February

Liverpool, Manchester Airport and Manchester - Huddersfield - Wakefield, Leeds, Hull, York, Scarborough, Middlesbrough, Newcastle and Edinburgh

		TP	NT	TP	TP	TP	TP	TP	TP	TP	NT	TP	GC	NT	TP	TP	TP	TP	TP	TP	NT	TP	NT
		◇1 🍴		◇1 🍴	◇1	◇1	◇1 🍴	◇1 🍴	◇1 🍴	◇1 🍴	◇	◇1 🍴	■1 🍴		◇1 🍴	◇1	◇1	◇1 🍴	◇1 🍴	◇1 🍴	◇	◇1 🍴	
Liverpool Lime Street 10	90 d	12 24					12 52					13 25						13 52				14 25	
Lea Green	90 d						13 04											14 04					
Newton-le-Willows	90 d	12 40										13 41										14 41	
Manchester Airport	d			12 33				13 10		13 13					13 36					14 13			
Gatley	d			12 39											13 42								
Manchester Piccadilly 10	a			12 49				13 25		13 33					13 51					14 33			
	d			12 51	12 58			13 26	13 35	13 35					13 53	13 58			14 35	14 35			
Manchester Oxford Road	d			12 55				13a28		13 38					13 56					14 38			
Manchester Victoria	a	12 58		13 01			13 28			13 44		13 59			14 04			14 28		14 44		14 59	
	d	13 00	13 06	13 15			13 30			13 45	13 57	14 00		14 07	14 15			14 30		14 45	14 57	15 00	15 06
Ashton-under-Lyne	d		13 16											14 16									15 16
Stalybridge	a		13 22		13 12		13 40		13 51					14 23		14 12		14 40	14 51				15 22
	d				13 12		13 41		13 51							14 12		14 41	14 51				
Mossley (Grtr Manchester)	d				13 17											14 17							
Greenfield	d				13 22											14 22							
Marsden	d				13 30											14 30							
Slaithwaite	d				13 34											14 34							
Huddersfield	a	13 28		13 45	13 41		13 59		14 09	14 16		14 28			14 45	14 41		14 59	15 09	15 16		15 28	
	d	13 30		13 46		13 49	14 01		14 12	14 17		14 30			14 46		14 49	15 01	15 12	15 17		15 30	
Deighton	d					13 53											14 53						
Mirfield	d					13 57											14 57						
Wakefield Kirkgate	a																						
Normanton	a																						
Castleford	a																						
Ravensthorpe	d					14 01											15 01						
Dewsbury	a			13 56		14 04				14 26					14 56		15 04			15 26			
	d			13 57		14 09				14 27					14 57		15 09			15 27			
Batley	d					14 12											15 12						
Morley	d					14 17											15 17						
Cottingley	d					14 21											15 21						
Leeds 10	a	13 49		14 10		14 29	14 20		14 31	14 40	15 23	14 49			15 10		15 29	15 21	15 31	15 40	16 25	15 49	
	d	13 51		14 12			14 21		14 34	14 44		14 51			15 13			15 22	15 34	15 42		15 51	
Cross Gates	40 d																						
Garforth	40 d						14 30											15 31					
South Milford	40 d																						
Selby	29,40 d								15 00										16 00				
Howden	29 a																						
Brough	29 a								15 19										16 19				
Hull	29 a								15 36										16 36				
York 8	26 a	14 14		14 34			14 51			15 06		15 14			15 35			15 56		16 05		16 14	
	d	14 16		14 36			14 57			15 07		15 22	15 38		15 41			15 58		16 07		16 20	
Malton	d						15 25											16 25					
Seamer	43 a						15 41											16 41					
Scarborough	43 a						15 53											16 53					
Thirsk	26 d			14 54									15 55		16 04								
Northallerton	26 d			15 02									16a06							16 26			
Yarm	a			15 15											16 24								
Thornaby	44 a			15 27											16 34								
Middlesbrough	44 a			15 35											16 40								
Redcar Central	44 a			15 49											16 55								
Darlington	26 a	14 43								15 37										16 37		16 47	
	d	14 44								15 39										16 39		16 48	
Durham	26 a	15 00								15 55		16 05								16 54		17 04	
Chester-le-Street	26 a																			17 01			
Newcastle 8	26 a	15 14								16 10		16 19								17 13		17 17	
	d	15 21										16 21										17 21	
Morpeth	26 a	15 34										16 34										17 34	
Edinburgh	26 a	16 56										17 57										18 57	

Table T039-F

Sundays

15 December to 16 February

Liverpool, Manchester Airport and Manchester - Huddersfield - Wakefield, Leeds, Hull, York, Scarborough, Middlesbrough, Newcastle and Edinburgh

		TP	TP	TP	TP	TP	TP	TP	TP	NT	TP	NT	TP	TP	TP	TP	TP	TP	TP	NT	TP	NT	TP	TP
		◇1 🍴	◇1	◇1	◇1 🍴	◇1 🍴	◇1 🍴	◇1 🍴	◇1 🍴	◇	◇1 🍴		◇1 🍴	◇1	◇1	◇1 🍴	◇1 🍴	◇1 🍴	◇1 🍴	◇	◇1 🍴		◇1 🍴	◇1
Liverpool Lime Street 10	90 d				14 52						15 25					15 52					16 25			
Lea Green	90 d				15 04											16 04								
Newton-le-Willows	90 d										15 41										16 41			
Manchester Airport	d	14 36				15 10	15 13						15 36				16 13						16 36	
Gatley	d	14 42											15 42										16 42	
Manchester Piccadilly 10	a	14 51				15 25	15 33		←				15 51				16 33		←				16 51	
	d	14 53	14 58			15 26	15 34	15 35					15 53	15 58			16 34	16 35					16 53	16 58
Manchester Oxford Road	d	14 56				15a28	15 38		15 38				15 56				16 38		16 38				16 56	
Manchester Victoria	a	15 04			15 27		→		15 44		15 59		16 04			16 27	→		16 45		16 59		17 04	
	d	15 15			15 30				15 45	15 57	16 00	16 06	16 15			16 30			16 45	16 57	17 00	17 06	17 15	
Ashton-under-Lyne	d											16 16										17 16		
Stalybridge	a		15 12		15 41			15 51				16 22		16 12		16 40		16 51				17 22		17 12
	d		15 12		15 42			15 51						16 12		16 41		16 51						17 13
Mossley (Grtr Manchester)	d		15 17											16 17										17 17
Greenfield	d		15 22											16 22										17 22
Marsden	d		15 30											16 30										17 30
Slaithwaite	d		15 34											16 34										17 34
Huddersfield	a	15 45	15 41		16 00			16 09	16 16		16 28		16 45	16 41		16 59		17 09	17 16		17 28		17 45	17 41
	d	15 46		15 49	16 01			16 12	16 17		16 30		16 46		16 49	17 01		17 12	17 17		17 30		17 46	
Deighton	d			15 53											16 53									
Mirfield	d			15 57											16 57									
Wakefield Kirkgate	a																							
Normanton	a																							
Castleford	a																							
Ravensthorpe	d			16 01											17 01									
Dewsbury	a	15 56		16 04					16 26				16 56		17 04				17 26				17 56	
	d	15 57		16 09					16 27				16 57		17 09				17 27				17 57	
Batley	d			16 12											17 12									
Morley	d			16 17											17 17									
Cottingley	d			16 21											17 21									
Leeds 10	a	16 10		16 29	16 20			16 31	16 40	17 19	16 50		17 10		17 29	17 21		17 31	17 40	18 19	17 49		18 10	
	d	16 13			16 23			16 34	16 42		16 52		17 14			17 23		17 34	17 42		17 51		18 14	
Cross Gates	40 d							16 40										17 40						
Garforth	40 d				16 32			16 45								17 32		17 45						
South Milford	40 d																							
Selby	29,40 d							17 00										18 00						
Howden	29 a																	18 09						
Brough	29 a							17 19										18 22						
Hull	29 a							17 36										18 39						
York 8	26 a	16 35			16 53				17 05		17 15		17 36			17 53			18 05		18 15		18 36	
	d	16 39			16 58				17 07		17 19		17 39			17 58			18 07		18 20		18 39	
Malton	d				17 23											18 25								
Seamer	43 a				17 40											18 41								
Scarborough	43 a				17 52											18 53								
Thirsk	26 d	16 56											17 56										18 56	
Northallerton	26 d	17 07							17 26				18 05						18 26				19 07	
Yarm	a	17 20											18 17										19 20	
Thornaby	44 a	17 30											18 27										19 30	
Middlesbrough	44 a	17 37											18 35										19 37	
Redcar Central	44 a	17 52											18 49										19 52	
Darlington	26 a								17 37		17 45								18 37		18 47			
	d								17 39		17 47								18 39		18 48			
Durham	26 a								17 54		18 02								18 54		19 04			
Chester-le-Street	26 a																		19 01					
Newcastle 8	26 a								18 10		18 16								19 13		19 17			
	d										18 18										19 21			
Morpeth	26 a										18 31										19 34			
Edinburgh	26 a										19 58										20 57			

Table T039-F

Sundays
15 December to 16 February

Liverpool, Manchester Airport and Manchester - Huddersfield - Wakefield, Leeds, Hull, York, Scarborough, Middlesbrough, Newcastle and Edinburgh

		TP	TP	GC	TP	TP	TP	TP	NT	TP	NT	TP	TP	TP	TP	TP	TP	GC	NT	TP	NT	TP	TP
		◇1	◇1 trolley	■ 1 restaurant	◇1 trolley	◇1 trolley	◇1 trolley	◇1 trolley	◇	◇1 trolley		◇1 trolley	◇1	◇1	◇1 trolley	◇1 trolley	◇1 trolley	■ 1 restaurant	◇	◇1 trolley		◇1	◇1
Liverpool Lime Street 10	90 d				16 52					17 25					17 52					18 25			
Lea Green	90 d				17 04										18 04								
Newton-le-Willows	90 d									17 41										18 41			
Manchester Airport	d		17 10			17 13						17 36					18 13					18 36	
Gatley	d											17 42										18 42	
Manchester Piccadilly 10	a		17 25			17 33		←				17 51					18 33					18 51	
	d		17 26			17 34	17 35					17 53	17 58			18 35	18 35					18 53	18 58
Manchester Oxford Road	d		17a28			17 38		17 38				17 56					18 38					18 56	
Manchester Victoria	a				17 27	→		17 45		17 59		18 04			18 27		18 45			18 59		19 04	
	d				17 30			17 45	17 57	18 00	18 06	18 15			18 30		18 45		18 57	19 00	19 06	19 15	
Ashton-under-Lyne	d										18 16										19 16		
Stalybridge	a				17 40		17 51				18 22		18 12		18 40	18 51					19 22		19 12
	d				17 41		17 51						18 12		18 41	18 51							19 12
Mossley (Grtr Manchester)	d												18 17										19 17
Greenfield	d												18 22										19 22
Marsden	d												18 30										19 30
Slaithwaite	d												18 34										19 34
Huddersfield	a				17 59		18 09	18 16		18 28		18 45	18 41		18 59	19 09	19 16			19 28		19 45	19 41
	d	17 49			18 01		18 12	18 17		18 30		18 46		18 49	19 01	19 12	19 17			19 30		19 46	
Deighton	d	17 53												18 53									
Mirfield	d	17 57												18 57									
Wakefield Kirkgate	a																						
Normanton	a																						
Castleford	a																						
Ravensthorpe	d	18 01												19 01									
Dewsbury	a	18 04						18 26				18 56		19 04			19 26					19 56	
	d	18 09						18 27				18 57		19 09			19 27					19 57	
Batley	d	18 12												19 12									
Morley	d	18 17												19 17									
Cottingley	d	18 21												19 21									
Leeds 10	a	18 29			18 21		18 31	18 40	19 23	18 49		19 10		19 29	19 21	19 31	19 40		20 21	19 49		20 10	
	d				18 23		18 34	18 42		18 52		19 14			19 25	19 34	19 42			19 51		20 14	
Cross Gates	40 d						18 40																
Garforth	40 d				18 32		18 45								19 34								
South Milford	40 d																						
Selby	29,40 d						19 00									20 00							
Howden	29 a																						
Brough	29 a						19 19									20 19							
Hull	29 a						19 36									20 34							
York 8	26 a				18 53			19 05		19 14		19 36			19 55		20 05			20 17		20 36	
	d			18 41	18 58			19 07		19 17		19 41			20 00		20 07	20 12		20 21		20 39	
Malton	d				19 25										20 25								
Seamer	43 a				19 41										20 41								
Scarborough	43 a				19 53										20 53								
Thirsk	26 d			19 00								19 58						20 29				20 56	
Northallerton	26 d			19a10				19 26				20 07					20 26	20a42				21 06	
Yarm	a											20 20										21 19	
Thornaby	44 a											20 30										21 29	
Middlesbrough	44 a											20 37										21 36	
Redcar Central	44 a											20 51										21 51	
Darlington	26 a							19 37		19 43							20 37			20 47			
	d							19 39		19 45							20 39			20 50			
Durham	26 a							19 54		20 00							20 54			21 05			
Chester-le-Street	26 a																21 01						
Newcastle 8	26 a							20 10		20 14							21 13			21 21			
	d									20 16													
Morpeth	26 a									20 29													
Edinburgh	26 a									21 57													

Table T039-F

Sundays
15 December to 16 February

Liverpool, Manchester Airport and Manchester - Huddersfield - Wakefield, Leeds, Hull, York, Scarborough, Middlesbrough, Newcastle and Edinburgh

		TP	TP	TP	TP	TP	NT	TP	NT	TP	TP	TP	TP	TP	TP	NT	TP	TP	NT	TP	TP	TP	TP	TP
		◇1	◇1	◇1 trolley	◇1	◇1	◇	◇1 A trolley		◇1	◇1	◇1	◇1	◇1	◇1	◇	◇1 A trolley	◇1		◇1 trolley	◇1 trolley	◇1	◇1	◇1
Liverpool Lime Street 10	90 d		18 52					19 25					19 52				20 25							21 08
Lea Green	90 d		19 04										20 04											21 20
Newton-le-Willows	90 d							19 41									20 41							21 28
Manchester Airport	d			19 10		19 13				19 36					20 13					21 10				
Gatley	d									19 42														
Manchester Piccadilly 10	a			19 25		19 33				19 51					20 33					21 23				
	d			19 26	19 35	19 35				19 53	19 58			20 35	20 35			20 58		21 26			21 35	
Manchester Oxford Road	d			19a28		19 39				19 56					20 39					21a28				
Manchester Victoria	a		19 27			19 45		19 59		20 04			20 27		20 44		20 59							21 46
	d		19 30			19 45	19 57	20 00	20 06	20 15			20 30		20 45	20 57	21 00		21 07		21 15			21 47
Ashton-under-Lyne	d								20 16										21 16					
Stalybridge	a		19 40		19 51				20 22		20 12		20 40	20 50				21 12	21 23				21 50	21 58
	d		19 41		19 51						20 12		20 41	20 50				21 12					21 50	21 59
Mossley (Grtr Manchester)	d										20 17							21 17						
Greenfield	d										20 22							21 22						
Marsden	d										20 30							21 30						
Slaithwaite	d										20 34							21 34						
Huddersfield	a		19 59		20 09	20 16		20 28		20 45	20 41		20 59	21 08	21 16		21 28	21 41			21 45		22 08	22 17
	d	19 49	20 01		20 12	20 17		20 30		20 46		20 49	21 01	21 12	21 17		21 29				21 46	21 49	22 10	22 18
Deighton	d	19 53										20 53										21 53		
Mirfield	d	19 57										20 57										21 57		
Wakefield Kirkgate	a																							
Normanton	a																							
Castleford	a																							
Ravensthorpe	d	20 01										21 01										22 01		
Dewsbury	a	20 04				20 26				20 56		21 04			21 26						21 56	22 04		22 26
	d	20 09				20 27				20 57		21 09			21 27						21 57	22 09		22 27
Batley	d	20 12										21 12										22 12		
Morley	d	20 17										21 17										22 17		
Cottingley	d	20 21										21 21										22 21		
Leeds 10	a	20 29	20 21		20 31	20 40	21 24	20 49		21 10		21 29	21 21	21 31	21 40	22 24	21 48				22 10	22 29	22 31	22 40
	d		20 23		20 34	20 42		20 52		21 14			21 23	21 34	21 42		21 51				22 14		22 34	22 43
Cross Gates	40 d																							
Garforth	40 d		20 32										21 32											
South Milford	40 d																						22 53	
Selby	29,40 d				21 00									22 00									23 03	
Howden	29 a				21 09									22 09										
Brough	29 a				21 22									22 22									23 21	
Hull	29 a				21 38									22 38									23 37	
York 8	26 a		20 53			21 07		21 14		21 36			21 53		22 07		22 14				22 36			23 08
	d		20 58					21 22		21 39			21 58				22 22				22 45			23 09
Malton	d		21 23										22 23								23 10			
Seamer	43 a		21 40										22 40								23 26			
Scarborough	43 a		21 52										22 52								23 38			
Thirsk	26 d									21 56														23 32
Northallerton	26 d									22 07							22 41							23 40
Yarm	a									22 20														
Thornaby	44 a									22 30														
Middlesbrough	44 a									22 37														
Redcar Central	44 a									22 52														
Darlington	26 a							21 48									22 52							23 52
	d							21 50									22 54							23 54
Durham	26 a							22 05									23 11							00 10
Chester-le-Street	26 a																23 18							00 16
Newcastle 8	26 a							22 21									23 44							00 43
	d																							
Morpeth	26 a																							
Edinburgh	26 a																							

A trolley from York

Table T039-F

Sundays
15 December to 16 February

Liverpool, Manchester Airport and Manchester - Huddersfield - Wakefield, Leeds, Hull, York, Scarborough, Middlesbrough, Newcastle and Edinburgh

Station	Table		NT ◇	NT	TP ◇1	TP ◇1	TP ◇1	TP ◇1	TP ◇1	NT ◇	NT	TP ◇1	TP ◇1	TP ◇1	TP ◇1	TP ◇1	TP ◇1	TP ◇1
Liverpool Lime Street 10	90	d							22 07								23 08	
Lea Green	90	d							22 19								23 20	
Newton-le-Willows	90	d							22 26								23 27	
Manchester Airport		d			21 36							22 37			23 01			23 35
Gatley		d			21 42													
Manchester Piccadilly 10		a			21 51							22 50			23 14			23 47
		d			21 53	21 58		22 35				22 51	22 58		23 15	23 35		23 49
Manchester Oxford Road		d			21 56							22 55			23a17			23 52
Manchester Victoria		a			22 04				22 45			23 00					23 45	23 58
		d	21 57	22 07	22 15				22 45	22 57	23 06	23 15					23 45	23 58
Ashton-under-Lyne		d		22 17							23 16							
Stalybridge		a		22 23		22 14		22 50	22 57		23 22		23 13			23 47	23 57	
		d				22 14		22 50	22 58				23 13			23 47	23 58	
Mossley (Grtr Manchester)		d				22 19							23 18			23 52		
Greenfield		d				22 23							23 23			23 57		
Marsden		d				22 31							23 31			00 04		
Slaithwaite		d				22 35							23 35			00 08		
Huddersfield		a			22 45	22 42		23 08	23 16			23 45	23 42			00 14	00 18	00 26
		d			22 46		22 49	23 12	23 17			23 46		23 49			00 19	00 27
Deighton		d					22 53							23 53				
Mirfield		d					22 57							23 57				
Wakefield Kirkgate		a																
Normanton		a																
Castleford		a																
Ravensthorpe		d					23 01							00 02				
Dewsbury		a			22 56		23 04		23 26			23 56		00 04			00s27	
		d			22 57		23 09		23 27			23 57		00 09				
Batley		d					23 12							00 12				
Morley		d					23 17							00 17				
Cottingley		d					23 21							00 21				
Leeds 10		a	23 22		23 10		23 29	23 31	23 40	00 21		00 10		00 29			00 41	01 03
		d			23 14			23 33	23 42			00 22					00 46	01 06
Cross Gates	40	d																
Garforth	40	d																
South Milford	40	d																
Selby	29,40	d						23 52										
Howden	29	a																
Brough	29	a						00 10										
Hull	29	a						00 26										
York 8	26	a			23 41				00 10			01 02					01 26	01 32
		d																
Malton		d																
Seamer	43	a																
Scarborough	43	a																
Thirsk	26	d																
Northallerton	26	d																
Yarm		a																
Thornaby	44	a																
Middlesbrough	44	a																
Redcar Central	44	a																
Darlington	26	a																
		d																
Durham	26	a																
Chester-le-Street	26	a																
Newcastle 8	26	a																
		d																
Morpeth	26	a																
Edinburgh	26	a																

NRT DECEMBER 19 EDITION

Table T039-F

Sundays
23 February to 29 March

Liverpool, Manchester Airport and Manchester - Huddersfield - Wakefield, Leeds, Hull, York, Scarborough, Middlesbrough, Newcastle and Edinburgh

Station	Table		TP	TP	TP	TP	TP	TP	TP ◇1	TP	TP ◇1	TP	TP ◇1	TP ◇1	TP ◇	TP	TP	TP	NT	TP ◇1	TP ◇1	TP ◇1	TP ◇1	TP ◇1	NT ◇
Liverpool Lime Street 10	90	d																							
Lea Green	90	d																							
Newton-le-Willows	90	d																							
Manchester Airport		d					01 00	03 30		05 20		06 05					07 00				09 05				
Gatley		d																							
Manchester Piccadilly 10		a					01 25	03 55		05 45		06 30					07 25				09 20				
		d					01 25	03 55		05 45		06 30					07 25	08 00		08 43	09 22				
Manchester Oxford Road		d																			09a24				
Manchester Victoria		a																							
		d																	08 17						08 54
Ashton-under-Lyne		d																	08 27						
Stalybridge		a										06 55					07 50	08 25	08 33						
		d										06 55					07 50	08 25							
Mossley (Grtr Manchester)		d				00 17												08 32							
Greenfield		d				00 33												08 48							
Marsden		d				01 00												09 15							
Slaithwaite		d				01 10												09 25							
Huddersfield		a				01 30	02 25	04 55		06 45		07 40					08 35	09 45							
		d		00 01	00 45		02 25	04 55		06 45		07 40				08 15	08 35								
Deighton		d														08 24									
Mirfield		d	00 09													08 34									
Wakefield Kirkgate		a																							
Normanton		a																							
Castleford		a																							
Ravensthorpe		d	00 14													08 39									
Dewsbury		a	00 22	00 25	01 10					07 10		08 05				08 46									
		d	00 22	00 25	01 10					07 10		08 05				08 46									
Batley		d	00 30													08 54									
Morley		d	00 42													09 04									
Cottingley		d	00 52													09 14									
Leeds 10		a	01 07	00 50	01 35		03 00	05 30		07 35		08 30				09 29	09 10								10 21
		d		00 50	01 35		03 00	05 30		07 35			08 35		08 45									09 22	
Cross Gates	40	d																							
Garforth	40	d																						09 31	
South Milford	40	d																							
Selby	29,40	d											09 00												
Howden	29	a																							
Brough	29	a											09 19												
Hull	29	a											09 34												
York 8	26	a		01 40	02 25		03 50	06 20		08 25					09 07									09 55	
		d							08 21		08 39			09 00								09 19	09 39	10 00	
Malton		d												09 25										10 25	
Seamer	43	a												09 41										10 41	
Scarborough	43	a												09 53										10 53	
Thirsk	26	d									08 56												09 56		
Northallerton	26	d									09 07												10 07		
Yarm		a									09 20												10 20		
Thornaby	44	a									09 30												10 30		
Middlesbrough	44	a									09 37												10 37		
Redcar Central	44	a									09 50												10 52		
Darlington	26	a							08 47													09 45			
		d							08 49													09 47			
Durham	26	a							09 04													10 02			
Chester-le-Street	26	a																				10 09			
Newcastle 8	26	a							09 18													10 19			
		d							09 20													10 21			
Morpeth	26	a							09 33													10 34			
Edinburgh	26	a							11 03											11 54		12 07			

Table T039-F

Sundays
23 February to 29 March

Liverpool, Manchester Airport and Manchester - Huddersfield - Wakefield, Leeds, Hull, York, Scarborough, Middlesbrough, Newcastle and Edinburgh

Station			TP	TP	TP	NT	TP	TP	TP	TP	NT	TP	TP	NT	TP	GC	TP	TP	TP	TP	NT	TP	TP	NT
			◇1 ✕	◇1 ✕	◇1		◇1 ✕	◇1	◇1 ✕	◇1 ✕	◇	◇1 ✕	◇1 ✕		◇1 ✕	■ 1 ✕	◇1	◇1 ✕	◇1 ✕	◇1 ✕	◇	◇1 ✕	◇1	
Liverpool Lime Street 10	90	d		08 12						08 54			09 23					09 55				10 25		
Lea Green	90	d		08 28						09 06								10 07						
Newton-le-Willows	90	d		08 34						09 12			09 39									10 41		
Manchester Airport		d																		10 13				
Gatley		d																						
Manchester Piccadilly 10		a																		10 34				
		d							09 27										10 35	10 36			11 00	
Manchester Oxford Road		d																		10 39				
Manchester Victoria		a		08 55						09 31			09 57					10 29		10 44		10 59		
		d		08 57	09 00	09 03	09 18			09 33	09 56		10 00	10 07	10 15			10 30		10 45	10 56	11 00		11 07
Ashton-under-Lyne		d				09 15								10 16										11 16
Stalybridge		a			09 11	09 19			09 40	09 43				10 23				10 41	10 51				11 12	11 23
		d			09 12				09 41	09 51								10 42	10 51				11 12	
Mossley (Grtr Manchester)		d			09 16																		11 17	
Greenfield		d			09 21																		11 22	
Marsden		d			09 29																		11 30	
Slaithwaite		d			09 33																		11 34	
Huddersfield		a		09 28	09 40		09 44		09 59	10 08			10 28		10 44			10 59	11 09	11 16		11 28	11 41	
		d		09 30			09 45	09 49	10 01	10 12			10 30		10 45		10 49	11 01	11 12	11 17		11 30		
Deighton		d						09 53									10 53							
Mirfield		d						09 57									10 57							
Wakefield Kirkgate		a																						
Normanton		a																						
Castleford		a																						
Ravensthorpe		d						10 01									11 01							
Dewsbury		a					09 56	10 04							10 55		11 04			11 26				
		d					09 57	10 09							10 56		11 09			11 26				
Batley		d						10 12									11 12							
Morley		d						10 17									11 17							
Cottingley		d						10 21									11 21							
Leeds 10		a		09 49			10 10	10 29	10 21	10 31	11 19		10 49		11 09		11 29	11 21	11 31	11 39	12 20	11 49		
		d		09 51			10 14		10 22	10 34			10 51		11 14			11 23	11 34	11 42		11 51		
Cross Gates	40	d																						
Garforth	40	d							10 31									11 32						
South Milford	40	d																						
Selby	29,40	d								11 00									11 59					
Howden	29	a																						
Brough	29	a								11 19									12 18					
Hull	29	a								11 37									12 35					
York 8	26	a		10 14			10 36		10 54				11 15		11 36			11 48		12 04		12 14		
		d	10 07	10 22			10 41		10 57			11 07	11 18		11 39	11 42		11 58		12 06		12 22		
Malton		d							11 22									12 25						
Seamer	43	a							11 38									12 41						
Scarborough	43	a							11 50									12 53						
Thirsk	26	d					10 58									11 59								
Northallerton	26	d	10 26				11 11					11 26			12 01	12a06								
Yarm		a					11 24								12 14									
Thornaby	44	a					11 34								12 24									
Middlesbrough	44	a					11 41								12 31									
Redcar Central	44	a					11 54								12 46									
Darlington	26	a	10 37	10 49								11 37								12 33		12 48		
		d	10 39	10 51								11 39								12 34		12 50		
Durham	26	a	10 54									11 54	11 59							12 50		13 05		
Chester-le-Street	26	a	11 01																	12 56				
Newcastle 8	26	a	11 13	11 19								12 10	12 13							13 07		13 21		
		d		11 21									12 14									13 24		
Morpeth	26	a		11 34									12 27									13 36		
Edinburgh	26	a		13 00									13 57									14 59		

Table T039-F

Sundays
23 February to 29 March

Liverpool, Manchester Airport and Manchester - Huddersfield - Wakefield, Leeds, Hull, York, Scarborough, Middlesbrough, Newcastle and Edinburgh

Station			TP	TP	TP	TP	TP	TP	NT	TP	TP	NT	TP	TP	TP	TP	TP	TP	TP	NT	TP	NT	TP	TP	TP
			◇1 ✕	◇1 ✕	◇1	◇1 ✕	◇1 ✕	◇1 ✕	◇	◇1 ✕	◇1		◇1 ✕	◇1	◇1 ✕	◇1 ✕	◇1 ✕	◇1 ✕	◇1 ✕	◇	◇1 ✕		◇1 ✕	◇1	◇1
Liverpool Lime Street 10	90	d				10 53				11 24					11 52						12 24				
Lea Green	90	d				11 05									12 05										
Newton-le-Willows	90	d								11 42											12 40				
Manchester Airport		d	11 10										11 37				12 13						12 33		
Gatley		d											11 43										12 39		
Manchester Piccadilly 10		a	11 23										11 59				12 33		←				12 49		
		d	11 25				11 35	11 40			11 58		12 01				12 34	12 35					12 51	12 58	
Manchester Oxford Road		d	11a27										12 05				12 38		12 38				12 55		
Manchester Victoria		a				11 28				12 00			12 13		12 29		→		12 45		12 58		13 01		
		d		11 15		11 30			11 56	12 01		12 07	12 15		12 30	12 31			12 45	12 57	13 00	13 06	13 15		
Ashton-under-Lyne		d										12 16										13 16			
Stalybridge		a				11 40	11 51				12 12	12 23			12 41			12 51				13 22		13 12	
		d				11 41	11 51				12 12				12 42			12 51						13 12	
Mossley (Grtr Manchester)		d									12 17													13 17	
Greenfield		d									12 22													13 22	
Marsden		d									12 30													13 30	
Slaithwaite		d									12 34													13 34	
Huddersfield		a		11 45		11 59	12 09	12 16		12 28	12 41		12 45		12 59			13 09	13 16		13 28		13 45	13 41	
		d		11 46	11 49	12 01	12 12	12 17		12 30			12 46	12 49	13 01			13 12	13 17		13 30		13 46		13 49
Deighton		d			11 53									12 53											13 53
Mirfield		d			11 57									12 57											13 57
Wakefield Kirkgate		a																							
Normanton		a																							
Castleford		a																							
Ravensthorpe		d			12 01									13 01											14 01
Dewsbury		a		11 56	12 04			12 25					12 56	13 04					13 26				13 56		14 04
		d		11 57	12 09			12 26					12 57	13 09					13 27				13 57		14 09
Batley		d			12 12									13 12											14 12
Morley		d			12 17									13 17											14 17
Cottingley		d			12 21									13 21											14 21
Leeds 10		a		12 10	12 29	12 21	12 31	12 39	13 19	12 49			13 10	13 29	13 20			13 31	13 40	14 20	13 49		14 10		14 29
		d		12 14		12 22	12 34	12 41		12 51			13 14		13 22			13 34	13 45		13 51		14 12		
Cross Gates	40	d																							
Garforth	40	d				12 31									13 31										
South Milford	40	d																							
Selby	29,40	d					13 00											14 00							
Howden	29	a																							
Brough	29	a					13 19											14 19							
Hull	29	a					13 36											14 36							
York 8	26	a		12 36		12 52		13 05		13 15			13 36		13 52				14 10		14 14		14 34		
		d		12 39		12 57		13 06		13 20			13 39		13 57				14 11		14 16		14 36		
Malton		d				13 25									14 22										
Seamer	43	a				13 41									14 39										
Scarborough	43	a				13 53									14 51										
Thirsk	26	d		12 56									13 56										14 54		
Northallerton	26	d		13 05				13 25					14 05										15 02		
Yarm		a		13 17									14 17										15 15		
Thornaby	44	a		13 27									14 27										15 27		
Middlesbrough	44	a		13 35									14 35										15 35		
Redcar Central	44	a		13 49									14 49										15 49		
Darlington	26	a						13 37		14 07									14 38		14 43				
		d						13 38		14 09									14 39		14 44				
Durham	26	a						13 54		14 25									14 55		15 00				
Chester-le-Street	26	a																	15 01						
Newcastle 8	26	a						14 08		14 38									15 13		15 14				
		d								14 41											15 21				
Morpeth	26	a								14 54											15 34				
Edinburgh	26	a								16 15						15 39					16 56				

Table T039-F

Sundays
23 February to 29 March

Liverpool, Manchester Airport and Manchester - Huddersfield - Wakefield, Leeds, Hull, York, Scarborough, Middlesbrough, Newcastle and Edinburgh

		TP	TP	TP	TP	NT	TP	GC		NT	TP	TP	TP	TP	TP	TP	NT	TP	NT	TP	TP	TP	TP	TP
		◇1 ✠	◇1 ✠	◇1 ✠	◇1 ✠	◇	◇1 ✠	■ 1			◇1 ✠	◇1	◇1	◇1 ✠	◇1 ✠	◇1 ✠	◇	◇1 ✠		◇1 ✠	◇1	◇1	◇1 ✠	◇1 ✠
Liverpool Lime Street 10	90 d	12 52					13 25							13 52				14 25					14 52	
Lea Green	90 d	13 04												14 04									15 04	
Newton-le-Willows	90 d						13 41											14 41						
Manchester Airport	d		13 10		13 13						13 36					14 13				14 36				15 10
Gatley	d										13 42									14 42				
Manchester Piccadilly 10	a		13 25		13 33						13 51					14 33				14 51				15 25
	d		13 26	13 35	13 35						13 53	13 58			14 35	14 35				14 53	14 58			15 26
Manchester Oxford Road	d		13a28		13 38						13 56					14 38				14 56				15a28
Manchester Victoria	a	13 28			13 44		13 59				14 04			14 28		14 44		14 59		15 04			15 27	
	d	13 30			13 45	13 57	14 00			14 07	14 15			14 30		14 45	14 57	15 00	15 06	15 15			15 30	
Ashton-under-Lyne	d									14 16									15 16					
Stalybridge	a	13 40		13 51						14 23		14 12		14 40	14 51				15 22		15 12		15 41	
	d	13 41		13 51								14 12		14 41	14 51						15 12		15 42	
Mossley (Grtr Manchester)	d											14 17									15 17			
Greenfield	d											14 22									15 22			
Marsden	d											14 30									15 30			
Slaithwaite	d											14 34									15 34			
Huddersfield	a	13 59		14 09	14 16		14 28				14 45	14 41		14 59	15 09	15 16		15 28		15 45	15 41		16 00	
	d	14 01		14 12	14 17		14 30				14 46		14 49	15 01	15 12	15 17		15 30		15 46		15 49	16 01	
Deighton	d												14 53									15 53		
Mirfield	d												14 57									15 57		
Wakefield Kirkgate	a																							
Normanton	a																							
Castleford	a																							
Ravensthorpe	d												15 01									16 01		
Dewsbury	a				14 26						14 56		15 04			15 26				15 56		16 04		
	d				14 27						14 57		15 09			15 27				15 57		16 09		
Batley	d												15 12									16 12		
Morley	d												15 17									16 17		
Cottingley	d												15 21									16 21		
Leeds 10	a	14 20		14 31	14 40	15 23	14 49				15 10		15 29	15 21	15 31	15 40	16 25	15 49		16 10		16 29	16 20	
	d	14 21		14 34	14 44		14 51				15 13			15 22	15 34	15 42		15 51		16 13			16 23	
Cross Gates	40 d																							
Garforth	40 d	14 30												15 31									16 32	
South Milford	40 d																							
Selby	29,40 d			15 00											16 00									
Howden	29 a																							
Brough	29 a			15 19											16 19									
Hull	29 a			15 36											16 36									
York 8	26 a	14 51			15 06		15 14				15 35			15 56		16 05		16 14		16 35			16 53	
	d	14 57			15 07		15 22	15 38			15 41			15 58		16 07		16 20		16 39			16 58	
Malton	d	15 25												16 25									17 23	
Seamer	43 a	15 41												16 41									17 40	
Scarborough	43 a	15 53												16 53									17 52	
Thirsk	26 d							15 55			16 04									16 56				
Northallerton	26 d							16a06								16 26				17 07				
Yarm	a										16 24									17 20				
Thornaby	44 a										16 34									17 30				
Middlesbrough	44 a										16 40									17 37				
Redcar Central	44 a										16 55									17 52				
Darlington	26 a				15 37											16 37		16 47						
	d				15 39											16 39		16 48						
Durham	26 a				15 55		16 05									16 54		17 04						
Chester-le-Street	26 a															17 01								
Newcastle 8	26 a				16 10		16 19									17 13		17 17						
	d						16 21											17 21						
Morpeth	26 a						16 34											17 34						
Edinburgh	26 a						17 57											18 57						

NRT DECEMBER 19 EDITION

Table T039-F

Sundays
23 February to 29 March

Liverpool, Manchester Airport and Manchester - Huddersfield - Wakefield, Leeds, Hull, York, Scarborough, Middlesbrough, Newcastle and Edinburgh

		TP	TP	TP	NT	TP	NT	TP	TP	TP	TP	TP	TP	TP	NT	TP		NT	TP	TP	TP	TP	GC	TP	TP
		◇1 ✠	◇1 ✠	◇1 ✠	◇	◇1 ✠		◇1 ✠	◇1	◇1	◇1 ✠	◇1 ✠	◇1 ✠	◇1 ✠	◇	◇1 ✠			◇1 ✠	◇1	◇1	◇1 ✠	■ 1	◇1 ✠	◇1 ✠
Liverpool Lime Street 10	90 d					15 25					15 52					16 25								16 52	
Lea Green	90 d										16 04													17 04	
Newton-le-Willows	90 d					15 41										16 41									
Manchester Airport	d	15 13						15 36				16 13							16 36			17 10			17 13
Gatley	d							15 42											16 42						
Manchester Piccadilly 10	a	15 33		←				15 51				16 33		←					16 51			17 25			17 33
	d	15 34	15 35					15 53	15 58			16 34	16 35						16 53	16 58		17 26			17 34
Manchester Oxford Road	d	15 38		15 38				15 56				16 38		16 38					16 56			17a28			17 38
Manchester Victoria	a	→		15 44		15 59		16 04			16 27	→		16 45		16 59			17 04					17 27	→
	d			15 45	15 57	16 00	16 06	16 15			16 30			16 45	16 57	17 00		17 06	17 15					17 30	
Ashton-under-Lyne	d						16 16											17 16							
Stalybridge	a		15 51				16 22		16 12		16 40		16 51					17 22		17 12				17 40	
	d		15 51						16 12		16 41		16 51							17 13				17 41	
Mossley (Grtr Manchester)	d								16 17											17 17					
Greenfield	d								16 22											17 22					
Marsden	d								16 30											17 30					
Slaithwaite	d								16 34											17 34					
Huddersfield	a		16 09	16 16		16 28		16 45	16 41		16 59		17 09	17 16		17 28			17 45	17 41				17 59	
	d		16 12	16 17		16 30		16 46		16 49	17 01		17 12	17 17		17 30			17 46		17 49			18 01	
Deighton	d									16 53											17 53				
Mirfield	d									16 57											17 57				
Wakefield Kirkgate	a																								
Normanton	a																								
Castleford	a																								
Ravensthorpe	d									17 01											18 01				
Dewsbury	a			16 26				16 56		17 04				17 26					17 56		18 04				
	d			16 27				16 57		17 09				17 27					17 57		18 09				
Batley	d									17 12											18 12				
Morley	d									17 17											18 17				
Cottingley	d									17 21											18 21				
Leeds 10	a		16 31	16 40	17 19	16 50		17 10		17 29	17 21		17 31	17 40	18 19	17 49			18 10		18 29			18 21	
	d		16 34	16 42		16 52		17 14			17 23		17 34	17 42		17 51			18 14					18 23	
Cross Gates	40 d		16 40										17 40												
Garforth	40 d		16 45								17 32		17 45											18 32	
South Milford	40 d																								
Selby	29,40 d		17 00										18 00												
Howden	29 a												18 09												
Brough	29 a		17 19										18 22												
Hull	29 a		17 36										18 39												
York 8	26 a			17 05		17 15		17 36			17 53			18 05		18 15			18 36					18 53	
	d			17 07		17 19		17 39			17 58			18 07		18 20			18 39				18 41	18 58	
Malton	d										18 25													19 25	
Seamer	43 a										18 41													19 41	
Scarborough	43 a										18 53													19 53	
Thirsk	26 d							17 56											18 56				19 00		
Northallerton	26 d			17 26				18 05						18 26					19 07				19a10		
Yarm	a							18 17											19 20						
Thornaby	44 a							18 27											19 30						
Middlesbrough	44 a							18 35											19 37						
Redcar Central	44 a							18 49											19 52						
Darlington	26 a			17 37		17 45								18 37		18 47									
	d			17 39		17 47								18 39		18 48									
Durham	26 a			17 54		18 02								18 54		19 04									
Chester-le-Street	26 a													19 01											
Newcastle 8	26 a			18 10		18 16								19 13		19 17									
	d					18 18										19 21									
Morpeth	26 a					18 31										19 34									
Edinburgh	26 a					19 58										20 57									

Table T039-F

Sundays
23 February to 29 March

Liverpool, Manchester Airport and Manchester - Huddersfield - Wakefield, Leeds, Hull, York, Scarborough, Middlesbrough, Newcastle and Edinburgh

	TP	TP	NT	TP	NT	TP	TP	TP	TP	TP	TP	GC	NT	TP	NT	TP	TP	TP	TP	TP	TP	TP
	◇1 🛒	◇1 🛒	◇	◇1 🛒		◇1 🛒	◇1	◇1	◇1 🛒	◇1 🛒	◇1 🛒	■ 1 🍴	◇	◇1 🛒		◇1	◇1	◇1	◇1	◇1 🛒	◇1	◇1
Liverpool Lime Street 10 90 d				17 25					17 52					18 25					18 52			
Lea Green 90 d									18 04										19 04			
Newton-le-Willows 90 d				17 41										18 41								
Manchester Airport ✈ d						17 36					18 13					18 36				19 10		19 13
Gatley d						17 42										18 42						
Manchester Piccadilly 10 a		←				17 51					18 33					18 51				19 25		19 33
d	17 35					17 53	17 58			18 35	18 35					18 53	18 58			19 26	19 35	19 35
Manchester Oxford Road d		17 38				17 56					18 38					18 56				19a28		19 39
Manchester Victoria a		17 45		17 59		18 04			18 27		18 45			18 59		19 04			19 27			19 45
d		17 45	17 57	18 00	18 06	18 15			18 30		18 45		18 57	19 00	19 06	19 15			19 30			19 45
Ashton-under-Lyne d					18 16										19 16							
Stalybridge a	17 51				18 22		18 12		18 40	18 51					19 22		19 12		19 40		19 51	
d	17 51						18 12		18 41	18 51							19 12		19 41		19 51	
Mossley (Grtr Manchester) d							18 17										19 17					
Greenfield d							18 22										19 22					
Marsden d							18 30										19 30					
Slaithwaite d							18 34										19 34					
Huddersfield a	18 09	18 16		18 28		18 45	18 41		18 59	19 09	19 16			19 28		19 45	19 41		19 59		20 09	20 16
d	18 12	18 17		18 30		18 46		18 49	19 01	19 12	19 17			19 30		19 46		19 49	20 01		20 12	20 17
Deighton d								18 53										19 53				
Mirfield d								18 57										19 57				
Wakefield Kirkgate a																						
Normanton a																						
Castleford a																						
Ravensthorpe d								19 01										20 01				
Dewsbury a		18 26				18 56		19 04			19 26					19 56		20 04				20 26
d		18 27				18 57		19 09			19 27					19 57		20 09				20 27
Batley d								19 12										20 12				
Morley d								19 17										20 17				
Cottingley d								19 21										20 21				
Leeds 10 a	18 31	18 40	19 23	18 49		19 10		19 29	19 21	19 31	19 40		20 21	19 49		20 10		20 29	20 21		20 31	20 40
d	18 34	18 42		18 52		19 14			19 25	19 34	19 42			19 51		20 14			20 23		20 34	20 42
Cross Gates 40 d	18 40																					
Garforth 40 d	18 45								19 34										20 32			
South Milford 40 d																						
Selby 29,40 d	19 00									20 00											21 00	
Howden 29 a																					21 09	
Brough 29 a	19 19									20 19											21 22	
Hull 29 a	19 36									20 34											21 38	
York 8 26 a		19 05		19 14		19 36			19 55		20 05			20 17		20 36			20 53			21 07
d		19 07		19 17		19 41			20 00		20 07	20 12		20 21		20 39			20 58			
Malton d									20 25										21 23			
Seamer 43 a									20 41										21 40			
Scarborough 43 a									20 53										21 52			
Thirsk 26 d						19 58						20 29				20 56						
Northallerton 26 d		19 26				20 07					20 26	20a42				21 06						
Yarm a						20 20										21 19						
Thornaby 44 a						20 30										21 29						
Middlesbrough 44 a						20 37										21 36						
Redcar Central 44 a						20 51										21 51						
Darlington 26 a		19 37		19 43							20 37			20 47								
d		19 39		19 45							20 39			20 50								
Durham 26 a		19 54		20 00							20 54			21 05								
Chester-le-Street 26 a											21 01											
Newcastle 8 26 a		20 10		20 14							21 13			21 21								
d				20 16																		
Morpeth 26 a				20 29																		
Edinburgh 26 a				21 57																		

Table T039-F

Sundays
23 February to 29 March

Liverpool, Manchester Airport and Manchester - Huddersfield - Wakefield, Leeds, Hull, York, Scarborough, Middlesbrough, Newcastle and Edinburgh

	NT	TP	NT	TP	TP	TP	TP	TP	TP	NT	TP	TP	NT	TP	TP	TP	TP	TP	NT	NT	TP	TP	TP
	◇	◇1 A 🛒		◇1	◇1	◇1	◇1	◇1	◇1	◇	◇1 A 🛒	◇1		◇1 🛒	◇1 🛒	◇1	◇1	◇1	◇		◇1	◇1	◇1
Liverpool Lime Street 10 90 d		19 25					19 52				20 25							21 08					
Lea Green 90 d							20 04											21 20					
Newton-le-Willows 90 d		19 41									20 41							21 28					
Manchester Airport ✈ d				19 36					20 13					21 10							21 36		
Gatley d				19 42																	21 42		
Manchester Piccadilly 10 a				19 51					20 33					21 23							21 51		
d				19 53	19 58			20 35	20 35			20 58		21 26			21 35				21 53	21 58	
Manchester Oxford Road d				19 56					20 39					21a28							21 56		
Manchester Victoria a		19 59		20 04			20 27		20 44		20 59							21 46			22 04		
d	19 57	20 00	20 06	20 15			20 30		20 45	20 57	21 00		21 07		21 15			21 47	21 57	22 07	22 15		
Ashton-under-Lyne d			20 16										21 16							22 17			
Stalybridge a			20 22		20 12		20 40	20 50				21 12	21 23				21 50	21 58		22 23		22 14	
d					20 12		20 41	20 50				21 12					21 50	21 59				22 14	
Mossley (Grtr Manchester) d					20 17							21 17										22 19	
Greenfield d					20 22							21 22										22 23	
Marsden d					20 30							21 30										22 31	
Slaithwaite d					20 34							21 34										22 35	
Huddersfield a		20 28		20 45	20 41		20 59	21 08	21 16		21 28	21 41			21 45		22 08	22 17			22 45	22 42	
d		20 30		20 46		20 49	21 01	21 12	21 17		21 29				21 46	21 49	22 10	22 18			22 46		22 49
Deighton d						20 53										21 53							22 53
Mirfield d						20 57										21 57							22 57
Wakefield Kirkgate a																							
Normanton a																							
Castleford a																							
Ravensthorpe d						21 01										22 01							23 01
Dewsbury a				20 56		21 04			21 26						21 56	22 04		22 26			22 56		23 04
d				20 57		21 09			21 27						21 57	22 09		22 27			22 57		23 09
Batley d						21 12										22 12							23 12
Morley d						21 17										22 17							23 17
Cottingley d						21 21										22 21							23 21
Leeds 10 a	21 24	20 49		21 10		21 29	21 21	21 31	21 40	22 24	21 48				22 10	22 29	22 31	22 40	23 22		23 10		23 29
d		20 52		21 14			21 23	21 34	21 42		21 51				22 14		22 34	22 43			23 14		
Cross Gates 40 d																							
Garforth 40 d							21 32																
South Milford 40 d																	22 53						
Selby 29,40 d								22 00									23 03						
Howden 29 a								22 09															
Brough 29 a								22 22									23 21						
Hull 29 a								22 38									23 37						
York 8 26 a		21 14		21 36			21 53		22 07		22 14				22 36			23 08			23 41		
d		21 22		21 39			21 58				22 22				22 45			23 09					
Malton d							22 23								23 10								
Seamer 43 a							22 40								23 26								
Scarborough 43 a							22 52								23 38								
Thirsk 26 d				21 56														23 32					
Northallerton 26 d				22 07							22 41							23 40					
Yarm a				22 20																			
Thornaby 44 a				22 30																			
Middlesbrough 44 a				22 37																			
Redcar Central 44 a				22 52																			
Darlington 26 a		21 48									22 52							23 52					
d		21 50									22 54							23 54					
Durham 26 a		22 05									23 11							00 10					
Chester-le-Street 26 a											23 18							00 16					
Newcastle 8 26 a		22 21									23 44							00 43					
d																							
Morpeth 26 a																							
Edinburgh 26 a																							

A 🛒 from York

Table T039-F

Sundays
23 February to 29 March

Liverpool, Manchester Airport and Manchester - Huddersfield - Wakefield, Leeds, Hull, York, Scarborough, Middlesbrough, Newcastle and Edinburgh

Station			TP ◇1	TP ◇1	NT ◇	NT	TP ◇1	TP ◇1	TP ◇1	TP ◇1 🚲	TP ◇1	TP ◇1	TP ◇1
Liverpool Lime Street 10	90	d		22 07								23 08	
Lea Green	90	d		22 19								23 20	
Newton-le-Willows	90	d		22 26								23 27	
Manchester Airport ✈		d					22 37			23 01			23 35
Gatley		d											
Manchester Piccadilly 10		a					22 50			23 14			23 47
		d	22 35				22 51	22 58		23 15	23 35		23 49
Manchester Oxford Road		d					22 55			23a17			23 52
Manchester Victoria		a		22 45			23 00					23 45	23 58
		d		22 45	22 57	23 06	23 15					23 45	23 58
Ashton-under-Lyne		d				23 16							
Stalybridge		a	22 50	22 57		23 22		23 13			23 47	23 57	
		d	22 50	22 58				23 13			23 47	23 58	
Mossley (Grtr Manchester)		d						23 18			23 52		
Greenfield		d						23 23			23 57		
Marsden		d						23 31			00 04		
Slaithwaite		d						23 35			00 08		
Huddersfield		a	23 08	23 16			23 45	23 42			00 14	00 18	00 26
		d	23 12	23 17			23 46		23 49			00 19	00 27
Deighton		d							23 53				
Mirfield		d							23 57				
Wakefield Kirkgate		a											
Normanton		a											
Castleford		a											
Ravensthorpe		d							00 02				
Dewsbury		a		23 26			23 56		00 04			00s27	
		d		23 27			23 57		00 09				
Batley		d							00 12				
Morley		d							00 17				
Cottingley		d							00 21				
Leeds 10		a	23 31	23 40	00 21		00 10		00 29			00 41	01 03
		d	23 33	23 42			00 22					00 46	01 06
Cross Gates	40	d											
Garforth	40	d											
South Milford	40	d											
Selby	29,40	d	23 52										
Howden	29	a											
Brough	29	a	00 10										
Hull	29	a	00 26										
York 8	26	a		00 10			01 02					01 26	01 32
		d											
Malton		d											
Seamer	43	a											
Scarborough	43	a											
Thirsk	26	d											
Northallerton	26	d											
Yarm		a											
Thornaby	44	a											
Middlesbrough	44	a											
Redcar Central	44	a											
Darlington	26	a											
		d											
Durham	26	a											
Chester-le-Street	26	a											
Newcastle 8	26	a											
		d											
Morpeth	26	a											
Edinburgh	26	a											

Table T039-F

Sundays
5 April to 10 May

Liverpool, Manchester Airport and Manchester - Huddersfield - Wakefield, Leeds, Hull, York, Scarborough, Middlesbrough, Newcastle and Edinburgh

Station			TP ◇1	TP ◇1	TP ◇1	TP ◇1	TP ◇1	TP ◇1	TP ◇1	TP ◇1	TP ◇1 🚲	TP ◇1 🚲	TP ◇1	TP ◇1 🚲
Liverpool Lime Street 10	90	d												
Lea Green	90	d												
Newton-le-Willows	90	d												
Manchester Airport ✈		d						00 38	04 22		06 27			
Gatley		d												
Manchester Piccadilly 10		a						00 52	04 36		06 41			
		d						01 03	04 40	05 45	06 45		07 00	
Manchester Oxford Road		d												
Manchester Victoria		a												
		d					00 04							
Ashton-under-Lyne		d												
Stalybridge		a									06 58		07 12	
		d									06 59		07 12	
Mossley (Grtr Manchester)		d											07 17	
Greenfield		d											07 22	
Marsden		d	00 05										07 30	
Slaithwaite		d	00 09										07 34	
Huddersfield		a	00 16				00 32	01 32	05 09	06 13	07 16		07 41	
		d				00 20	00 34	01 33	05 10	06 14	07 17		07 49	
Deighton		d											07 53	
Mirfield		d											07 57	
Wakefield Kirkgate		a												
Normanton		a												
Castleford		a												
Ravensthorpe		d			00 03								08 01	
Dewsbury		a			00 06	00 29					07 26		08 04	
		d			00 11	00 30					07 27		08 09	
Batley		d			00 14								08 12	
Morley		d			00 19								08 17	
Cottingley		d			00 23								08 21	
Leeds 10		a			00 31	00 43	00 53	01 52	05 29	06 33	07 40		08 29	
		d		00 22		00 48	00 56	01 54	05 31	06 36	07 42			08 35
Cross Gates	40	d												
Garforth	40	d												
South Milford	40	d												
Selby	29,40	d												09 00
Howden	29	a												
Brough	29	a												09 19
Hull	29	a												09 34
York 8	26	a		01 02		01 15	01 23	02 21	05 58	07 03	08 04			
		d										08 21		
Malton		d												
Seamer	43	a												
Scarborough	43	a												
Thirsk	26	d												
Northallerton	26	d												
Yarm		a												
Thornaby	44	a												
Middlesbrough	44	a												
Redcar Central	44	a												
Darlington	26	a										08 47		
		d										08 49		
Durham	26	a										09 04		
Chester-le-Street	26	a												
Newcastle 8	26	a										09 18		
		d										09 20		
Morpeth	26	a										09 33		
Edinburgh	26	a										11 03		

Station			TP ◇1 🚲	TP ◇1	TP ◇1 🚲	TP ◇1 🚲	TP ◇1	TP ◇1	NT	TP ◇1 🚲	TP ◇1 🚲	NT ◇	TP ◇1 🚲
Liverpool Lime Street 10	90	d											
Lea Green	90	d											
Newton-le-Willows	90	d											
Manchester Airport ✈		d			07 27						07 56		09 05
Gatley		d											
Manchester Piccadilly 10		a			07 41						08 12		09 20
		d			07 44		08 00				08 19		09 22
Manchester Oxford Road		d									08 23		09a24
Manchester Victoria		a									08 28		
		d							08 17		08 30	08 54	
Ashton-under-Lyne		d							08 27				
Stalybridge		a			07 57		08 12		08 33		08 40		
		d			07 58		08 12				08 41		
Mossley (Grtr Manchester)		d					08 17						
Greenfield		d					08 22						
Marsden		d					08 30						
Slaithwaite		d					08 34						
Huddersfield		a			08 15		08 41				08 59		
		d			08 16			08 49			09 01		
Deighton		d						08 53					
Mirfield		d						08 57					
Wakefield Kirkgate		a											
Normanton		a											
Castleford		a											
Ravensthorpe		d						09 01					
Dewsbury		a			08 25			09 04					
		d			08 26			09 09					
Batley		d						09 12					
Morley		d						09 17					
Cottingley		d						09 21					
Leeds 10		a			08 39			09 29			09 20	10 21	
		d			08 41						09 22		
Cross Gates	40	d											
Garforth	40	d									09 31		
South Milford	40	d											
Selby	29,40	d											
Howden	29	a											
Brough	29	a											
Hull	29	a											
York 8	26	a			09 04						09 55		
		d	08 39	09 00		09 19				09 39	10 00		
Malton		d		09 25							10 25		
Seamer	43	a		09 41							10 41		
Scarborough	43	a		09 53							10 53		
Thirsk	26	d	08 56							09 56			
Northallerton	26	d	09 07							10 07			
Yarm		a	09 20							10 20			
Thornaby	44	a	09 30							10 30			
Middlesbrough	44	a	09 37							10 37			
Redcar Central	44	a	09 50							10 52			
Darlington	26	a				09 45							
		d				09 47							
Durham	26	a				10 02							
Chester-le-Street	26	a				10 09							
Newcastle 8	26	a				10 19							
		d				10 21							
Morpeth	26	a				10 34							
Edinburgh	26	a				12 07							

Table T039-F

Sundays
5 April to 10 May

Liverpool, Manchester Airport and Manchester - Huddersfield - Wakefield, Leeds, Hull, York, Scarborough, Middlesbrough, Newcastle and Edinburgh

Station		TP	TP	TP	NT	TP	TP	TP		TP	TP	NT	TP	TP	NT	TP	GC	TP	TP	TP	TP	NT	TP	TP
		◇■1 🍴	◇■1 🍴	◇■1		◇■1 🍴	◇■1	◇■1 🍴		◇■1 🍴	◇■1 🍴	◇	◇■1 🍴	◇■1		◇■1 🍴	■1	◇■1	◇■1 🍴	◇■1 🍴	◇■1 🍴	◇	◇■1 🍴	◇■1
Liverpool Lime Street	90 d		08 12							08 54			09 23						09 55				10 25	
Lea Green	90 d		08 28							09 06									10 07					
Newton-le-Willows	90 d		08 34							09 12			09 39										10 41	
Manchester Airport	d										09 14										10 13			
Gatley	d																							
Manchester Piccadilly	a										09 32										10 35			
	d							09 27			09 35									10 35	10 37			10 58
Manchester Oxford Road	d										09 38										10 40			
Manchester Victoria	a		08 55							09 31	09 44		09 57						10 29		10 45		10 59	
	d		08 57	09 00	09 03	09 18				09 33	09 45	09 56	10 00	10 03	10 07	10 15			10 30		10 46	10 56	11 00	
Ashton-under-Lyne	d				09 15										10 16									
Stalybridge	a			09 11	09 19			09 40		09 43				10 14	10 23				10 41	10 51				11 12
	d			09 12				09 41		09 51				10 15					10 42	10 51				11 12
Mossley (Grtr Manchester)	d			09 16										10 19										11 17
Greenfield	d			09 21										10 23										11 22
Marsden	d			09 29										10 31										11 30
Slaithwaite	d			09 33										10 35										11 34
Huddersfield	a		09 28	09 40		09 44		09 59		10 08	10 16		10 28	10 42		10 44			10 59	11 09	11 16		11 28	11 41
	d		09 30			09 45	09 49	10 01		10 12	10 17		10 30			10 45		10 49	11 01	11 12	11 17		11 30	
Deighton	d						09 53											10 53						
Mirfield	d						09 57											10 57						
Wakefield Kirkgate	a																							
Normanton	a																							
Castleford	a																							
Ravensthorpe	d						10 01											11 01						
Dewsbury	a					09 56	10 04				10 26					10 55		11 04			11 26			
	d					09 57	10 09				10 27					10 56		11 09			11 26			
Batley	d						10 12											11 12						
Morley	d						10 17											11 17						
Cottingley	d						10 21											11 21						
Leeds	a		09 49			10 10	10 29	10 21		10 31	10 40	11 19	10 49			11 09		11 29	11 21	11 31	11 39	12 20	11 49	
	d		09 51			10 14		10 22		10 34	10 42		10 51			11 14			11 23	11 34	11 42		11 51	
Cross Gates	40 d																							
Garforth	40 d							10 31											11 32					
South Milford	40 d																							
Selby	29,40 d									11 00										11 59				
Howden	29 a																							
Brough	29 a									11 19										12 18				
Hull	29 a									11 37										12 35				
York	26 a		10 14			10 36		10 54			11 05		11 15			11 36			11 48		12 04		12 14	
	d	10 07	10 22			10 41		10 57			11 07		11 18			11 39	11 42		11 58		12 06		12 22	
Malton	d							11 22											12 25					
Seamer	43 a							11 38											12 41					
Scarborough	43 a							11 50											12 53					
Thirsk	26 d					10 58											11 59							
Northallerton	26 d	10 26				11 11					11 26					12 01	12a06							
Yarm	a					11 24										12 14								
Thornaby	44 a					11 34										12 24								
Middlesbrough	44 a					11 41										12 31								
Redcar Central	44 a					11 54										12 46								
Darlington	26 a	10 37	10 49								11 37										12 33		12 48	
	d	10 39	10 51								11 39										12 34		12 50	
Durham	26 a	10 54									11 54		11 59								12 50		13 05	
Chester-le-Street	26 a	11 01																			12 56			
Newcastle	26 a	11 13	11 19								12 10		12 13								13 07		13 21	
	d		11 21										12 14										13 24	
Morpeth	26 a		11 34										12 27										13 36	
Edinburgh	26 a		13 00										13 57										14 59	

Table T039-F

Sundays
5 April to 10 May

Liverpool, Manchester Airport and Manchester - Huddersfield - Wakefield, Leeds, Hull, York, Scarborough, Middlesbrough, Newcastle and Edinburgh

Station		NT	TP	TP	TP	TP	TP	TP	NT	TP	TP	NT	TP	TP	TP	TP		TP	TP	TP	NT	TP	NT	TP	TP
			◇■1 🍴	◇■1 🍴	◇■1	◇■1 🍴	◇■1 🍴	◇■1 🍴	◇	◇■1 🍴	◇■1		◇■1 🍴	◇■1	◇■1 🍴	◇■1 🍴		◇■1 🍴	◇■1 🍴	◇■1 🍴	◇	◇■1 🍴		◇■1 🍴	◇■1
Liverpool Lime Street	90 d					10 53				11 24					11 52							12 24			
Lea Green	90 d					11 05									12 05										
Newton-le-Willows	90 d									11 42												12 40			
Manchester Airport	d		11 10										11 37					12 13						12 33	
Gatley	d												11 43											12 39	
Manchester Piccadilly	a		11 23										11 59					12 33		←				12 49	
	d		11 25				11 35	11 42			11 59		12 01					12 34	12 35					12 51	12 58
Manchester Oxford Road	d		11a27										12 05					12 38		12 38				12 55	
Manchester Victoria	a					11 28				12 00			12 13		12 29			→		12 45		12 58		13 01	
	d	11 07		11 15		11 30			11 56	12 01		12 07	12 15		12 30	12 31				12 45	12 57	13 00	13 06	13 15	
Ashton-under-Lyne	d	11 16										12 16											13 16		
Stalybridge	a	11 23				11 40	11 49				12 12	12 23			12 41				12 51				13 22		13 12
	d					11 41	11 49				12 12				12 42				12 51						13 12
Mossley (Grtr Manchester)	d										12 17														13 17
Greenfield	d										12 22														13 22
Marsden	d										12 30														13 30
Slaithwaite	d										12 34														13 34
Huddersfield	a			11 45		11 59	12 07	12 16		12 28	12 41		12 45		12 59				13 09	13 16		13 28		13 45	13 41
	d			11 46	11 49	12 01	12 12	12 17		12 30			12 46	12 49	13 01				13 12	13 17		13 30		13 46	
Deighton	d				11 53									12 53											
Mirfield	d				11 57									12 57											
Wakefield Kirkgate	a																								
Normanton	a																								
Castleford	a																								
Ravensthorpe	d				12 01									13 01											
Dewsbury	a			11 56	12 04			12 25					12 56	13 04						13 26				13 56	
	d			11 57	12 09			12 26					12 57	13 09						13 27				13 57	
Batley	d				12 12									13 12											
Morley	d				12 17									13 17											
Cottingley	d				12 21									13 21											
Leeds	a			12 10	12 29	12 21	12 31	12 39	13 19	12 49			13 10	13 29	13 20				13 31	13 40	14 20	13 49		14 10	
	d			12 14		12 22	12 34	12 41		12 51			13 14		13 22				13 34	13 45		13 51		14 12	
Cross Gates	40 d																								
Garforth	40 d					12 31									13 31										
South Milford	40 d																								
Selby	29,40 d						13 00												14 00						
Howden	29 a																								
Brough	29 a						13 19												14 19						
Hull	29 a						13 36												14 36						
York	26 a			12 36		12 52		13 05		13 15			13 36		13 52					14 10		14 14		14 34	
	d			12 39		12 57		13 06		13 20			13 39		13 57					14 11		14 16		14 36	
Malton	d					13 25									14 22										
Seamer	43 a					13 41									14 39										
Scarborough	43 a					13 53									14 51										
Thirsk	26 d			12 56									13 56											14 54	
Northallerton	26 d			13 05				13 25					14 05											15 02	
Yarm	a			13 17									14 17											15 15	
Thornaby	44 a			13 27									14 27											15 27	
Middlesbrough	44 a			13 35									14 35											15 35	
Redcar Central	44 a			13 49									14 49											15 49	
Darlington	26 a							13 37		14 07										14 38		14 43			
	d							13 38		14 09										14 39		14 44			
Durham	26 a							13 54		14 25										14 55		15 00			
Chester-le-Street	26 a																			15 01					
Newcastle	26 a							14 08		14 38										15 13		15 14			
	d									14 41												15 21			
Morpeth	26 a									14 54												15 34			
Edinburgh	26 a									16 15						15 39						16 56			

Table T039-F

Sundays
5 April to 10 May

Liverpool, Manchester Airport and Manchester - Huddersfield - Wakefield, Leeds, Hull, York, Scarborough, Middlesbrough, Newcastle and Edinburgh

		TP	TP	TP	TP	TP	NT	TP	GC	NT	TP	TP	TP	TP	TP	TP	NT	TP	NT	TP	TP	TP	TP
		◇1	◇1	◇1	◇1	◇1	◇	◇1	1		◇1	◇1	◇1	◇1	◇1	◇1	◇	◇1		◇1	◇1	◇1	◇1
Liverpool Lime Street 10	90 d		12 52					13 25						13 52				14 25					14 52
Lea Green	90 d		13 04											14 04									15 04
Newton-le-Willows	90 d							13 41										14 41					
Manchester Airport	d			13 10		13 13					13 36					14 13				14 36			
Gatley	d										13 42									14 42			
Manchester Piccadilly 10	a			13 25		13 33					13 51					14 33				14 51			
	d			13 26	13 35	13 35					13 53	13 58			14 35	14 35				14 53	14 58		
Manchester Oxford Road	d			13a28		13 38					13 56					14 38				14 56			
Manchester Victoria	a		13 28			13 44		13 59			14 04			14 28		14 44		14 59		15 04			15 27
	d		13 30			13 45	13 57	14 00		14 07	14 15			14 30		14 45	14 57	15 00	15 06	15 15			15 30
Ashton-under-Lyne	d									14 16									15 16				
Stalybridge	a		13 40		13 51					14 23		14 12		14 40	14 51				15 22		15 12		15 41
	d		13 41		13 51							14 12		14 41	14 51						15 12		15 42
Mossley (Grtr Manchester)	d											14 17									15 17		
Greenfield	d											14 22									15 22		
Marsden	d											14 30									15 30		
Slaithwaite	d											14 34									15 34		
Huddersfield	a		13 59		14 09	14 16		14 28			14 45	14 41		14 59	15 09	15 16		15 28		15 45	15 41		16 00
	d	13 49	14 01		14 12	14 17		14 30			14 46		14 49	15 01	15 12	15 17		15 30		15 46		15 49	16 01
Deighton	d	13 53											14 53									15 53	
Mirfield	d	13 57											14 57									15 57	
Wakefield Kirkgate	a																						
Normanton	a																						
Castleford	a																						
Ravensthorpe	d	14 01											15 01									16 01	
Dewsbury	a	14 04				14 26					14 56		15 04			15 26				15 56		16 04	
	d	14 09				14 27					14 57		15 09			15 27				15 57		16 09	
Batley	d	14 12											15 12									16 12	
Morley	d	14 17											15 17									16 17	
Cottingley	d	14 21											15 21									16 21	
Leeds 10	a	14 29	14 20		14 31	14 40	15 23	14 49			15 10		15 29	15 21	15 31	15 40	16 25	15 49		16 10		16 29	16 20
	d		14 21		14 34	14 44		14 51			15 13			15 22	15 34	15 42		15 51		16 13			16 23
Cross Gates	40 d																						
Garforth	40 d		14 30											15 31									16 32
South Milford	40 d																						
Selby	29,40 d				15 00										16 00								
Howden	29 a																						
Brough	29 a				15 19										16 19								
Hull	29 a				15 36										16 36								
York 8	26 a		14 51			15 06		15 14			15 35			15 56		16 05		16 14		16 35			16 53
	d		14 57			15 07		15 22	15 38		15 41			15 58		16 07		16 20		16 39			16 58
Malton	d		15 25											16 25									17 23
Seamer	43 a		15 41											16 41									17 40
Scarborough	43 a		15 53											16 53									17 52
Thirsk	26 d								15 55		16 04									16 56			
Northallerton	26 d								16a06							16 26				17 07			
Yarm	a										16 24									17 20			
Thornaby	44 a										16 34									17 30			
Middlesbrough	44 a										16 40									17 37			
Redcar Central	44 a										16 55									17 52			
Darlington	26 a					15 37										16 37		16 47					
	d					15 39										16 39		16 48					
Durham	26 a					15 55		16 05								16 54		17 04					
Chester-le-Street	26 a															17 01							
Newcastle 8	26 a					16 10		16 19								17 13		17 17					
	d							16 21										17 21					
Morpeth	26 a							16 34										17 34					
Edinburgh	26 a							17 57										18 57					

Table T039-F

Sundays
5 April to 10 May

Liverpool, Manchester Airport and Manchester - Huddersfield - Wakefield, Leeds, Hull, York, Scarborough, Middlesbrough, Newcastle and Edinburgh

		TP	TP	TP	TP	NT	TP	NT	TP	TP	TP	TP	TP	TP	TP	NT	TP	NT	TP	TP	TP	TP	GC	TP
		◇1	◇1	◇1	◇1	◇	◇1		◇1	◇1	◇1	◇1	◇1	◇1	◇1	◇	◇1		◇1	◇1	◇1	◇1	1	◇1
Liverpool Lime Street 10	90 d						15 25					15 52					16 25							16 52
Lea Green	90 d											16 04												17 04
Newton-le-Willows	90 d						15 41										16 41							
Manchester Airport	d	15 10	15 13						15 36				16 13						16 36			17 10		
Gatley	d								15 42										16 42					
Manchester Piccadilly 10	a	15 25	15 33		←				15 51				16 33		←				16 51			17 25		
	d	15 26	15 34	15 35					15 53	15 58			16 34	16 35					16 53	16 58		17 26		
Manchester Oxford Road	d	15a28	15 38		15 38				15 56				16 38		16 38				16 56			17a28		
Manchester Victoria	a		→		15 44		15 59		16 04			16 27	→		16 45		16 59		17 04					17 27
	d				15 45	15 57	16 00	16 06	16 15			16 30			16 45	16 57	17 00	17 06	17 15					17 30
Ashton-under-Lyne	d							16 16										17 16						
Stalybridge	a			15 51				16 22		16 12		16 40		16 51				17 22		17 12				17 40
	d			15 51						16 12		16 41		16 51						17 13				17 41
Mossley (Grtr Manchester)	d									16 17										17 17				
Greenfield	d									16 22										17 22				
Marsden	d									16 30										17 30				
Slaithwaite	d									16 34										17 34				
Huddersfield	a			16 09	16 16		16 28		16 45	16 41		16 59		17 09	17 16		17 28		17 45	17 41				17 59
	d			16 12	16 17		16 30		16 46		16 49	17 01		17 12	17 17		17 30		17 46		17 49			18 01
Deighton	d										16 53										17 53			
Mirfield	d										16 57										17 57			
Wakefield Kirkgate	a																							
Normanton	a																							
Castleford	a																							
Ravensthorpe	d										17 01										18 01			
Dewsbury	a				16 26				16 56		17 04				17 26				17 56		18 04			
	d				16 27				16 57		17 09				17 27				17 57		18 09			
Batley	d										17 12										18 12			
Morley	d										17 17										18 17			
Cottingley	d										17 21										18 21			
Leeds 10	a			16 31	16 40	17 19	16 50		17 10		17 29	17 21		17 31	17 40	18 19	17 49		18 10		18 29			18 21
	d			16 34	16 42		16 52		17 14			17 23		17 34	17 42		17 51		18 14					18 23
Cross Gates	40 d			16 40										17 40										
Garforth	40 d			16 45								17 32		17 45										18 32
South Milford	40 d																							
Selby	29,40 d			17 00										18 00										
Howden	29 a													18 09										
Brough	29 a			17 19										18 22										
Hull	29 a			17 36										18 39										
York 8	26 a				17 05		17 15		17 36			17 53			18 05		18 15		18 36					18 53
	d				17 07		17 19		17 39			17 58			18 07		18 20		18 39				18 41	18 58
Malton	d											18 25												19 25
Seamer	43 a											18 41												19 41
Scarborough	43 a											18 53												19 53
Thirsk	26 d								17 56										18 56				19 00	
Northallerton	26 d				17 26				18 05						18 26				19 07				19a10	
Yarm	a								18 17										19 20					
Thornaby	44 a								18 27										19 30					
Middlesbrough	44 a								18 35										19 37					
Redcar Central	44 a								18 49										19 52					
Darlington	26 a				17 37		17 45								18 37		18 47							
	d				17 39		17 47								18 39		18 48							
Durham	26 a				17 54		18 02								18 54		19 04							
Chester-le-Street	26 a														19 01									
Newcastle 8	26 a				18 10		18 16								19 13		19 17							
	d						18 18										19 21							
Morpeth	26 a						18 31										19 34							
Edinburgh	26 a						19 58										20 57							

Table T039-F

Sundays
5 April to 10 May

Liverpool, Manchester Airport and Manchester - Huddersfield - Wakefield, Leeds, Hull, York, Scarborough, Middlesbrough, Newcastle and Edinburgh

		TP	TP	TP	NT	TP	NT	TP		TP	TP	TP	TP	TP	GC	NT	TP	NT	TP	TP	TP	TP	TP	TP	
		◇1 ⊼	◇1 ⊼	◇1 ⊼	◇	◇1 ⊼		◇1 ⊼		◇1	◇1	◇1 ⊼	◇1 ⊼	◇1 ⊼	1 ⊡	◇	◇1 ⊼		◇1	◇1	◇1	◇1	◇1 ⊼	◇1	
Liverpool Lime Street 10	90 d					17 25						17 52					18 25				18 52				
Lea Green	90 d											18 04									19 04				
Newton-le-Willows	90 d					17 41											18 41								
Manchester Airport	d	17 13						17 36						18 13					18 36				19 10		
Gatley	d							17 42											18 42						
Manchester Piccadilly 10	a	17 33		←				17 51						18 33					18 51				19 25		
	d	17 34	17 35					17 53		17 58			18 35	18 35					18 53	18 58			19 26	19 35	
Manchester Oxford Road	d	17 38		17 38				17 56						18 38					18 56				19a28		
Manchester Victoria	a	→		17 45		17 59		18 04				18 27		18 45			18 59		19 04			19 27			
	d			17 45	17 57	18 00	18 06	18 15				18 30		18 45		18 57	19 00	19 06	19 15			19 30			
Ashton-under-Lyne	d						18 16											19 16							
Stalybridge	a		17 51				18 22			18 12		18 40	18 51					19 22		19 12		19 40		19 51	
	d		17 51							18 12		18 41	18 51							19 12		19 41		19 51	
Mossley (Grtr Manchester)	d									18 17										19 17					
Greenfield	d									18 22										19 22					
Marsden	d									18 30										19 30					
Slaithwaite	d									18 34										19 34					
Huddersfield	a		18 09	18 16		18 28		18 45		18 41		18 59	19 09	19 16			19 28		19 45	19 41		19 59		20 09	
	d		18 12	18 17		18 30		18 46			18 49	19 01	19 12	19 17			19 30		19 46		19 49	20 01		20 12	
Deighton	d										18 53										19 53				
Mirfield	d										18 57										19 57				
Wakefield Kirkgate	a																								
Normanton	a																								
Castleford	a																								
Ravensthorpe	d										19 01										20 01				
Dewsbury	a			18 26				18 56			19 04			19 26					19 56		20 04				
	d			18 27				18 57			19 09			19 27					19 57		20 09				
Batley	d										19 12										20 12				
Morley	d										19 17										20 17				
Cottingley	d										19 21										20 21				
Leeds 10	a		18 31	18 40	19 23	18 49		19 10			19 29	19 21	19 31	19 40		20 21	19 49		20 10		20 29	20 21		20 31	
	d		18 34	18 42		18 52		19 14				19 25	19 34	19 42			19 51		20 14			20 23		20 34	
Cross Gates	40 d		18 40																						
Garforth	40 d		18 45									19 34										20 32			
South Milford	40 d																								
Selby	29,40 d		19 00										20 00											21 00	
Howden	29 a																							21 09	
Brough	29 a		19 19										20 19											21 22	
Hull	29 a		19 36										20 34											21 38	
York 8	26 a			19 05		19 14		19 36				19 55		20 05			20 17		20 36			20 53			
	d			19 07		19 17		19 41				20 00		20 07	20 12		20 21		20 39			20 58			
Malton	d											20 25										21 23			
Seamer	43 a											20 41										21 40			
Scarborough	43 a											20 53										21 52			
Thirsk	26 d							19 58							20 29				20 56						
Northallerton	26 d			19 26				20 07						20 26	20a42				21 06						
Yarm	a							20 20											21 19						
Thornaby	44 a							20 30											21 29						
Middlesbrough	44 a							20 37											21 36						
Redcar Central	44 a							20 51											21 51						
Darlington	26 a			19 37		19 43								20 37			20 47								
	d			19 39		19 45								20 39			20 50								
Durham	26 a			19 54		20 00								20 54			21 05								
Chester-le-Street	26 a													21 01											
Newcastle 8	26 ⇌ a			20 10		20 14								21 13			21 21								
	d					20 16																			
Morpeth	26 a					20 29																			
Edinburgh	26 a					21 57																			

Table T039-F

Sundays
5 April to 10 May

Liverpool, Manchester Airport and Manchester - Huddersfield - Wakefield, Leeds, Hull, York, Scarborough, Middlesbrough, Newcastle and Edinburgh

		TP	NT	TP	NT	TP	TP	TP	TP	TP	TP	NT	TP	TP	NT	TP		TP	TP	TP	TP	NT	NT	TP	TP
		◇1	◇	◇1 A ⊼		◇1	◇1	◇1	◇1	◇1	◇1	◇	◇1 A ⊼	◇1		◇1 ⊼		◇1 ⊼	◇1	◇1	◇1	◇		◇1	◇1
Liverpool Lime Street 10	90 d			19 25					19 52				20 25								21 08				
Lea Green	90 d								20 04												21 20				
Newton-le-Willows	90 d			19 41									20 41								21 28				
Manchester Airport	d	19 13				19 36					20 13					21 10								21 36	
Gatley	d					19 42																		21 42	
Manchester Piccadilly 10	a	19 33				19 51					20 33					21 23								21 51	
	d	19 35				19 53	19 58			20 35	20 35			20 58		21 26				21 35				21 53	21 58
Manchester Oxford Road	d	19 39				19 56					20 39					21a28								21 56	
Manchester Victoria	a	19 45		19 59		20 04			20 27		20 44		20 59								21 46			22 04	
	d	19 45	19 57	20 00	20 06	20 15			20 30		20 45	20 57	21 00		21 07			21 15			21 47	21 57	22 07	22 15	
Ashton-under-Lyne	d				20 16										21 16								22 17		
Stalybridge	a				20 22		20 12		20 40	20 50				21 12	21 23					21 50	21 58		22 23		22 14
	d						20 12		20 41	20 50				21 12						21 50	21 59				22 14
Mossley (Grtr Manchester)	d						20 17							21 17											22 19
Greenfield	d						20 22							21 22											22 23
Marsden	d						20 30							21 30											22 31
Slaithwaite	d						20 34							21 34											22 35
Huddersfield	a	20 16		20 28		20 45	20 41		20 59	21 08	21 16		21 28	21 41				21 45		22 08	22 17			22 45	22 42
	d	20 17		20 30		20 46		20 49	21 01	21 12	21 17		21 29					21 46	21 49	22 10	22 18			22 46	
Deighton	d							20 53											21 53						
Mirfield	d							20 57											21 57						
Wakefield Kirkgate	a																								
Normanton	a																								
Castleford	a																								
Ravensthorpe	d							21 01											22 01						
Dewsbury	a	20 26				20 56		21 04			21 26							21 56	22 04		22 26			22 56	
	d	20 27				20 57		21 09			21 27							21 57	22 09		22 27			22 57	
Batley	d							21 12											22 12						
Morley	d							21 17											22 17						
Cottingley	d							21 21											22 21						
Leeds 10	a	20 40	21 24	20 49		21 10		21 29	21 21	21 31	21 40	22 24	21 48					22 10	22 29	22 31	22 40	23 22		23 10	
	d	20 42		20 52		21 14			21 23	21 34	21 42		21 51					22 14		22 34	22 43			23 14	
Cross Gates	40 d																								
Garforth	40 d								21 32																
South Milford	40 d																			22 53					
Selby	29,40 d									22 00										23 03					
Howden	29 a									22 09															
Brough	29 a									22 22										23 21					
Hull	29 a									22 38										23 37					
York 8	26 a	21 07		21 14		21 36			21 53		22 07		22 14					22 36			23 08			23 41	
	d			21 22		21 39			21 58				22 22					22 45			23 09				
Malton	d								22 23									23 10							
Seamer	43 a								22 40									23 26							
Scarborough	43 a								22 52									23 38							
Thirsk	26 d					21 56															23 32				
Northallerton	26 d					22 07							22 41								23 40				
Yarm	a					22 20																			
Thornaby	44 a					22 30																			
Middlesbrough	44 a					22 37																			
Redcar Central	44 a					22 52																			
Darlington	26 a			21 48									22 52								23 52				
	d			21 50									22 54								23 54				
Durham	26 a			22 05									23 11								00 10				
Chester-le-Street	26 a												23 18								00 16				
Newcastle 8	26 ⇌ a			22 21									23 44								00 43				
	d																								
Morpeth	26 a																								
Edinburgh	26 a																								

A ⊼ from York

Table T039-F

Sundays
5 April to 10 May

Liverpool, Manchester Airport and Manchester - Huddersfield - Wakefield, Leeds, Hull, York, Scarborough, Middlesbrough, Newcastle and Edinburgh

Station	Table		TP	TP	TP	NT	NT	TP	TP		TP	TP	TP	TP	TP
			◇1	◇1	◇1	◇		◇1	◇1		◇1	◇1	◇1	◇1	◇1
Liverpool Lime Street 10	90	d			22 07									23 08	
Lea Green	90	d			22 19									23 20	
Newton-le-Willows	90	d			22 26									23 27	
Manchester Airport		d						22 37				23 01			23 35
Gatley		d													
Manchester Piccadilly 10		a						22 50				23 14			23 47
		d		22 35				22 51	22 58			23 15	23 35		23 49
Manchester Oxford Road		d						22 55				23a17			23 52
Manchester Victoria		a			22 45			23 00						23 45	23 58
		d			22 45	22 57	23 06	23 15						23 45	23 58
Ashton-under-Lyne		d					23 16								
Stalybridge		a		22 50	22 57		23 22		23 13				23 47	23 57	
		d		22 50	22 58				23 13				23 47	23 58	
Mossley (Grtr Manchester)		d							23 18				23 52		
Greenfield		d							23 23				23 57		
Marsden		d							23 31				00 04		
Slaithwaite		d							23 35				00 08		
Huddersfield		a		23 08	23 16			23 45	23 42				00 14	00 18	00 26
		d	22 49	23 12	23 17			23 46			23 49			00 19	00 27
Deighton		d	22 53								23 53				
Mirfield		d	22 57								23 57				
Wakefield Kirkgate		a													
Normanton		a													
Castleford		a													
Ravensthorpe		d	23 01								00 02				
Dewsbury		a	23 04		23 26			23 56			00 04			00s27	
		d	23 09		23 27			23 57			00 09				
Batley		d	23 12								00 12				
Morley		d	23 17								00 17				
Cottingley		d	23 21								00 21				
Leeds 10		a	23 29	23 31	23 40	00 21		00 10			00 29			00 41	01 03
		d		23 33	23 42			00 22						00 46	01 06
Cross Gates	40	d													
Garforth	40	d													
South Milford	40	d													
Selby	29,40	d		23 52											
Howden	29	a													
Brough	29	a		00 10											
Hull	29	a		00 26											
York 8	26	a			00 10			01 02						01 26	01 32
		d													
Malton		d													
Seamer	43	a													
Scarborough	43	a													
Thirsk	26	d													
Northallerton	26	d													
Yarm		a													
Thornaby	44	a													
Middlesbrough	44	a													
Redcar Central	44	a													
Darlington	26	a													
		d													
Durham	26	a													
Chester-le-Street	26	a													
Newcastle 8	26	a													
		d													
Morpeth	26	a													
Edinburgh	26	a													

Table T039-R

Mondays to Saturdays
16 December to 15 February

Newcastle, Middlesborough, Scarborough, York, Hull, Leeds and Wakefield - Huddersfield - Manchester, Manchester Airport and Liverpool

Miles	Miles	Miles	Station	Table		TP	TP MX	TP MO	TP MX	TP MO	TP SO	TP MSX	TP SO	TP MO	TP MSX	TP MSX	TP SO	TP MO	TP MSX	TP SX		TP SO	TP SX	TP SO	TP SX	TP
						◇1	◇1	◇1	◇1	◇1	◇1	◇1	◇1	◇1	◇1	◇1	◇1	◇1	◇1	◇1		◇1	◇1	◇1	◇1	◇1
0	—	—	**Edinburgh**	26	d																					
—	—	—	Morpeth	26	d																					
41	—	—	**Newcastle 8**	26	a																					
—	—	—			d					00 08	00 08	00 08														
—	—	—	Chester-le-Street	26	d																					
—	—	—	Durham	26	d					00 21	00 21	00 21														
77	—	—	**Darlington 5**	26	a					00 38	00 38	00 38														
—	—	—			d					00 40	00 40	00 40														
—	—	—	Redcar Central	44	d																					
—	—	0	**Middlesbrough**	44	d																					
—	—	—	Thornaby	44	d																					
—	—	—	Yarm		d																					
—	—	—	Northallerton	26	d																					
—	—	—	Thirsk	26	d		00 03																			
—	—	46	**Scarborough**	43	d																					
—	—	—	Seamer	43	d																					
—	—	—	Malton		d																					
121	—	—	**York 8**	26	a		00 29			01 36	01 36	01 36														
—	—	—			d					01 38	01 38	01 38				02 47	02 52	02 52		03 40		03 40				04 27
—	—	100	**Hull**	29	d																					
—	—	—	Brough	29	d																					
—	—	—	Howden	29	d																					
—	—	—	Selby	29,40	d																					
—	—	—	South Milford	40	d																					
—	—	—	Garforth	40	d																					
—	—	—	Cross Gates	40	d														←							
146	—	—	**Leeds 10**		a					02 05	02 18	02 18				03 27	03 18	03 19	03 27	04 05		04 19				04 53
—	—	—			d			00 05	00 07	02 05	02 18	02 20				03 35	03 19	03 20	03 35	04 08		04 31				05 03
—	—	—	Cottingley		d											→										
—	—	—	Morley		d																					
—	—	—	Batley		d	00 02																				
155	—	—	**Dewsbury**		a	00 03																				
—	—	—			d	00 04																				
—	—	—	Ravensthorpe		d	00 07																				
—	—	—	Castleford		d																					
—	—	—	Normanton		d																					
—	—	—	Wakefield Kirkgate		d																					
—	—	—	**Mirfield**		d	00 11																				
—	—	—	Deighton		d	00 17							←													
163	—	—	**Huddersfield**		a	00 22				02 40	02 56	02 40	02 56				03 55	03 55	03 56	04 41		05 03				05 35
—	—	—			d					02 41	02 56	02 41	02 56				03 55	03 58	03 58	04 51		05 04				05 37
—	—	—	Slaithwaite		d						→															
—	—	—	Marsden		d																					
—	—	—	Greenfield		d																					
—	—	—	Mossley (Grtr Manchester)		d																					
181	—	—	**Stalybridge**		a																					
—	—	—			d																					
—	—	—	Ashton-under-Lyne		d																		←			
188	—	—	**Manchester Victoria**		a															05 35		05 34	05 35			06 09
—	—	—			d															05 39		05 37	05 39	05 54	05 54	06 10
—	0	—	**Manchester Oxford Road**		a									←	←					→		05 44	05 45			06 16
—	1	—	**Manchester Piccadilly**		a			01 23	01 06	03 41		03 41	03 29	03 41	03 41		04 27	04 56	04 56			05 49	05 49			06 20
—	—	—			d					03 43		03 43	03 34	03 43	03 43		04 34	04 57	04 57			05 50	05 50			06 20
—	—	—	Gatley		a					→		→										06 01	06 01			
—	11	—	**Manchester Airport**		a								03 51	03 59	03 59		04 52	05 13	05 13			06 13	06 13			06 41
—	—	—	Newton-le-Willows	90	a																			06 11	06 13	
—	—	—	Lea Green	90	a																			06 17	06 19	
220	—	—	**Liverpool Lime Street 10**	90	a																			06 32	06 34	

Table T039-R

Mondays to Saturdays

16 December to 15 February

Newcastle, Middlesborough, Scarborough, York, Hull, Leeds and Wakefield - Huddersfield - Manchester, Manchester Airport and Liverpool

Station			TP	NT	NT SO	NT SX	TP	NT	TP	NT	TP	TP SO		TP SX	NT	TP	NT	NT	TP	TP	TP SX	TP SO	TP	NT	TP SO	TP SX
			◇1		◇	◇	◇1	◇	◇1		◇1	◇1		◇1	◇	◇1		◇	◇1	◇1	◇1	◇1	◇1		◇1	◇1
												A		A					B							
												🛒		🛒					🛒						🛒	🛒
Edinburgh	26	d																								
Morpeth	26	d																								
Newcastle 8	26 ⛴	a																								
		d																	05 06							
Chester-le-Street	26	d																								
Durham	26	d																	05 18							
Darlington 5	26	a																	05 35							
		d																	05 36							
Redcar Central	44	d																								
Middlesbrough	44	d																			05 12	05 19				
Thornaby	44	d																			05 17	05 25				
Yarm		d																			05 25	05 33				
Northallerton	26	d																			05 41	05 50				
Thirsk	26	d																			05 51	05 58				
Scarborough	43	d																							05 34	05 34
Seamer	43	d																							05 40	05 40
Malton		d																							05 59	05 59
York 8	26	a																	06 02		06 09	06 16			06 24	06 24
		d							05 15		05 28					05 49			06 05		06 18	06 18			06 28	06 28
Hull	29	d										05 06		05 06												
Brough	29	d										05 18		05 18												
Howden	29	d										05 32		05 32												
Selby	29,40	d										05 42		05 42												
South Milford	40	d																								
Garforth	40	d									05 48														06 47	06 47
Cross Gates	40	d																								
Leeds 10		a							05 42		05 58	06 04		06 04		06 12			06 28		06 42	06 42			06 57	06 57
		d			05 12	05 12		05 19	05 45		06 00	06 07		06 07	06 12	06 15		06 17	06 30		06 45	06 45	06 47		07 00	07 00
Cottingley		d						05 25															06 52			
Morley		d						05 29										06 25					06 56			
Batley		d						05 34										06 30					07 01			
Dewsbury		a						05 37	05 55							06 26		06 33			06 55	06 55	07 03			
		d						05 38	05 57							06 27		06 34			06 57	06 57	07 04			
Ravensthorpe		d						05 41															07 07			
Castleford		d																								
Normanton		d																								
Wakefield Kirkgate		d					05 24																			
Mirfield		d					05 37	05 45										06 40					07 11			
Deighton		d					05 47																07 17			
Huddersfield		a					05 51		06 06		06 17	06 24		06 24		06 35			06 47		07 05	07 05	07 22		07 17	07 17
		d					05 54		06 08		06 18	06 25		06 25		06 36			06 48	06 53	07 08	07 08			07 18	07 18
Slaithwaite		d					06 01					06 32		06 32						07 00						
Marsden		d					06 06					06 37		06 37						07 05						
Greenfield		d					06 15					06 46		06 46						07 14						
Mossley (Grtr Manchester)		d					06 19					06 50		06 50						07 18						
Stalybridge		a					06 23				06 36	06 54		06 54						07 22					07 36	07 36
		d	06 00	06 03			06 23			06 30	06 37	06 54		06 54			07 00			07 22				07 32	07 37	07 37
Ashton-under-Lyne	⛴	d		06 07						06 34							07 04							07 36		
Manchester Victoria	⛴	a	06 14	06 18	06 30	06 31		06 53	06 38	06 46	06 50				07 30	07 09	07 15	07 52	07 22		07 38	07 38		07 46	07 52	07 52
		d	06 19						06 39		06 52					07 10			07 24		07 39	07 39			07 54	07 54
Manchester Oxford Road		a							06 47							07 16					07 45	07 45				
Manchester Piccadilly		a					06 38		06 53			07 11		07 17		07 20				07 39	07 49	07 49				
		d							06 55							07 21					07 50	07 50				
Gatley		a							07 03												08 01	08 01				
Manchester Airport	⛴✈	a							07 16							07 41					08 16	08 16				
Newton-le-Willows	90	a	06 38								07 08								07 40							
Lea Green	90	a	06 45								07 14														08 14	08 14
Liverpool Lime Street 10	90	a	07 03								07 30								08 00						08 33	08 36

A 🛒 from Leeds

B 🛒 from York

Table T039-R

Mondays to Saturdays

16 December to 15 February

Newcastle, Middlesborough, Scarborough, York, Hull, Leeds and Wakefield - Huddersfield - Manchester, Manchester Airport and Liverpool

Station			TP SX	TP SO		NT	NT	TP	NT	NT	TP	TP	TP SO	TP SX	TP	NT	TP	TP	NT	NT SX		NT SO	TP	NT	NT	TP SO
			◇1	◇1			◇	◇1		◇	◇1	◇1	◇1	◇1	◇1		◇1	◇1		◇		◇	◇1		◇	◇1
								🛒			🛒		🛒	🛒			🛒	🛒					🛒			🛒
Edinburgh	26	d																								05 14
Morpeth	26	d																								06 43
Newcastle 8	26 ⛴	a																								06 57
		d									06 06												06 41			07 09
Chester-le-Street	26	d																					06 52			
Durham	26	d									06 18												06 59			07 21
Darlington 5	26	a									06 35												07 16			
		d									06 36												07 17			
Redcar Central	44	d											06 07	06 07												
Middlesbrough	44	d											06 21	06 21												
Thornaby	44	d											06 27	06 27												
Yarm		d											06 35	06 35												
Northallerton	26	d											06 50	06 50									07 28			
Thirsk	26	d											06 59	06 59												
Scarborough	43	d															06 34									
Seamer	43	d															06 39									
Malton		d															06 58									
York 8	26	a									07 02		07 17	07 17			07 24						07 47			08 02
		d						06 49			07 05		07 19	07 19			07 27						07 50			08 04
Hull	29	d	06 04	06 04														07 05								
Brough	29	d	06 16	06 16														07 17								
Howden	29	d																07 29								
Selby	29,40	d	06 37	06 37														07 40								
South Milford	40	d																								
Garforth	40	d	06 52	06 52													07 43	07 55								
Cross Gates	40	d	06 57	06 57													07 48									
Leeds 10		a	07 04	07 04				07 13			07 28		07 42	07 42			07 56	08 04					08 12			08 28
		d	07 07	07 07			07 12	07 15		07 17	07 30		07 45	07 45	07 47		08 00	08 07		08 12		08 12	08 15		08 17	08 30
Cottingley		d													07 52											
Morley		d								07 25					07 56										08 25	
Batley		d								07 30					08 01										08 30	
Dewsbury		a						07 26		07 33			07 55	07 55	08 03								08 26		08 33	
		d						07 27		07 34			07 57	07 57	08 04								08 27		08 34	
Ravensthorpe		d													08 07											
Castleford		d				06 58													07 58							
Normanton		d				07 04													08 04							
Wakefield Kirkgate		d				07 10													08 10							
Mirfield		d				07 24				07 40					08 11				08 24						08 41	
Deighton		d				07 30									08 17				08 30							
Huddersfield		a	07 24	07 24		07 35		07 38			07 47		08 05	08 05	08 22		08 17	08 24	08 35				08 37			08 50
		d	07 25	07 25				07 39			07 48	07 53	08 08	08 08			08 18	08 25					08 38			08 50
Slaithwaite		d	07 32	07 32								08 00						08 32								
Marsden		d	07 37	07 37								08 05						08 37								
Greenfield		d	07 45	07 45								08 14						08 45								
Mossley (Grtr Manchester)		d	07 49	07 49								08 18						08 49								
Stalybridge		a	07 53	07 53								08 22					08 36	08 53								
		d	07 54	07 54					08 00			08 22				08 30	08 37	08 54						09 00		
Ashton-under-Lyne	⛴	d							08 04							08 34								09 04		
Manchester Victoria	⛴	a					08 42	08 08	08 15	08 53	08 20		08 38	08 38		08 45	08 50			09 40		09 45	09 08	09 15	09 54	09 21
		d						08 10			08 24		08 39	08 39			08 51						09 10			09 24
Manchester Oxford Road		a						08 15					08 45	08 45									09 15			
Manchester Piccadilly		a	08 13	08 14				08 20				08 39	08 49	08 49				09 14					09 19			
		d						08 21					08 51	08 51									09 20			
Gatley		a											09 01	09 01												
Manchester Airport	⛴✈	a						08 41					09 13	09 16									09 41			
Newton-le-Willows	90	a									08 40															09 40
Lea Green	90	a															09 16									
Liverpool Lime Street 10	90	a									09 02						09 32									10 00

Table T039-R

Mondays to Saturdays
16 December to 15 February

Newcastle, Middlesborough, Scarborough, York, Hull, Leeds and Wakefield - Huddersfield - Manchester, Manchester Airport and Liverpool

Station			TP MSX	TP MO	TP	TP	TP	GC SX	GC SO	NT	TP	TP SO		TP SX	NT	NT	TP	NT	NT	TP SX	TP SO	TP	TP	TP	NT	TP
			◇1	◇1	◇1	◇1	◇1	■ 1	■ 1		◇1	◇1		◇1		◇	◇1		◇	◇1	◇1	◇1	◇1	◇1		◇1
												A		A												
			☕	☕		☕		🍽	🍽		☕	☕		☕			☕			☕	☕		☕			☕
Edinburgh	26	d	05 14	05 17																06 27	06 27					
Morpeth	26	d	06 43	06 43																07 44	07 44					
Newcastle 8	26 ⛴	a	06 57	06 57																07 58	08 02					
		d	07 09	07 09													07 43			08 06	08 06					
Chester-le-Street	26	d															07 52									
Durham	26	d	07 21	07 21													07 59			08 18	08 18					
Darlington 5	26	a															08 16			08 35	08 35					
		d															08 17			08 36	08 36					
Redcar Central	44	d				07 06																	08 07			
Middlesbrough	44	d				07 20																	08 20			
Thornaby	44	d				07 26																	08 27			
Yarm		d				07 35																	08 35			
Northallerton	26	d				07 50		07 55	07 55								08 28						08 50			
Thirsk	26	d				07 59		08 03	08 04														08 59			
Scarborough	43	d									07 34															08 34
Seamer	43	d									07 40															08 40
Malton		d									07 59															08 59
York 8	26	a	08 02	08 02		08 17		08 21	08 21		08 24						08 47			09 02	09 02		09 17			09 24
		d	08 04	08 04		08 20					08 28						08 49			09 05	09 05		09 20			09 28
Hull	29	d										08 07		08 07												
Brough	29	d										08 19		08 19												
Howden	29	d																								
Selby	29,40	d										08 40		08 40												
South Milford	40	d																								
Garforth	40	d									08 45	08 55		08 55												09 46
Cross Gates	40	d									08 50															
Leeds 10		a	08 28	08 28		08 42					08 57	09 04		09 04			09 12			09 27	09 27		09 43			09 56
		d	08 30	08 30		08 45	08 47				09 00	09 07		09 07		09 12	09 15		09 17	09 30	09 30		09 45	09 48		10 00
Cottingley		d					08 52																	09 53		
Morley		d					08 56												09 26					09 57		
Batley		d					09 01												09 31					10 02		
Dewsbury		a				08 55	09 03										09 26		09 34				09 55	10 04		
		d				08 57	09 04										09 27		09 35				09 57	10 05		
Ravensthorpe		d					09 07																	10 08		
Castleford		d													08 58											
Normanton		d													09 04											
Wakefield Kirkgate		d													09 10											
Mirfield		d					09 11								09 24				09 42					10 12		
Deighton		d					09 17								09 30									10 18		
Huddersfield		a	08 50	08 50		09 05	09 22				09 17	09 24		09 24	09 35		09 37			09 47	09 47		10 05	10 23		10 17
		d	08 51	08 51	08 54	09 08					09 18	09 25		09 25			09 38			09 48	09 48	09 53	10 08			10 18
Slaithwaite		d			09 00																	10 00				
Marsden		d			09 05																	10 05				
Greenfield		d			09 14																	10 14				
Mossley (Grtr Manchester)		d			09 18																	10 18				
Stalybridge		a			09 22						09 36	09 43		09 43								10 22				10 36
		d			09 22					09 30	09 37	09 43		09 49				10 00				10 22			10 30	10 37
Ashton-under-Lyne	⛴	d								09 34								10 04							10 34	
Manchester Victoria	⛴	a	09 21	09 21		09 38				09 44	09 51					10 29	10 08	10 15	10 53	10 21	10 21		10 38		10 44	10 51
		d	09 24	09 24		09 39					09 54						10 10			10 24	10 24		10 39			10 54
Manchester Oxford Road		a				09 45											10 15						10 45			
Manchester Piccadilly		a			09 39	09 49						10 04		10 11			10 19					10 39	10 49			
		d				09 51											10 20						10 51			
Gatley		a				10 01																	11 01			
Manchester Airport	⛴✈	a				10 13											10 41						11 13			
Newton-le-Willows	90	a	09 40	09 40																10 40	10 40					
Lea Green	90	a									10 16															11 15
Liverpool Lime Street 10	90	a	10 00	10 00							10 32									10 59	10 59					11 33

A ☕ from Leeds

Table T039-R

Mondays to Saturdays
16 December to 15 February

Newcastle, Middlesborough, Scarborough, York, Hull, Leeds and Wakefield - Huddersfield - Manchester, Manchester Airport and Liverpool

Station			TP	NT		NT	TP	GC SO	NT	NT	TP	TP	NT	TP	TP	GC SX	NT	TP	TP	NT		NT	NT	NT	TP	TP
			◇1			◇	◇1	■ 1		◇	◇1	◇1	◇	◇1	◇1	■ 1		◇1	◇1				◇	◇	◇1	◇1
			A																A							
			☕				☕	🍽			☕			☕		🍽		☕	☕						☕	
Edinburgh	26	d																								
Morpeth	26	d																								
Newcastle 8	26 ⛴	a																								
		d					08 43				09 06														10 06	
Chester-le-Street	26	d					08 52																			
Durham	26	d					08 59				09 18														10 18	
Darlington 5	26	a					09 16				09 35														10 35	
		d					09 17				09 36														10 36	
Redcar Central	44	d												09 07												
Middlesbrough	44	d												09 21												
Thornaby	44	d												09 27												
Yarm		d												09 35												
Northallerton	26	d						09 33						09 50		09 59										
Thirsk	26	d						09 42						09 59		10 08										
Scarborough	43	d																09 34								
Seamer	43	d																09 40								
Malton		d																09 59								
York 8	26	a					09 48	09 59			10 02			10 17		10 24		10 24							11 02	
		d					09 49				10 05			10 20				10 29							11 05	
Hull	29	d	09 08																10 08							
Brough	29	d	09 20																10 20							
Howden	29	d																								
Selby	29,40	d	09 40																10 40							
South Milford	40	d																								
Garforth	40	d																10 46								
Cross Gates	40	d																								
Leeds 10		a	10 03				10 12				10 27			10 42				10 56	11 03						11 27	
		d	10 07			10 12	10 15			10 17	10 30		10 42	10 45	10 47			11 00	11 07				11 12	11 17	11 30	
Cottingley		d													10 52											
Morley		d								10 26					10 56									11 26		
Batley		d								10 31					11 01									11 31		
Dewsbury		a					10 26			10 34				10 55	11 03									11 34		
		d					10 27			10 35				10 57	11 04									11 35		
Ravensthorpe		d													11 07											
Castleford		d		09 58																		10 58				
Normanton		d		10 04																		11 04				
Wakefield Kirkgate		d		10 10																		11 10				
Mirfield		d		10 24						10 42					11 11							11 24		11 42		
Deighton		d		10 30											11 17							11 30				
Huddersfield		a	10 25	10 35			10 37				10 47			11 05	11 22			11 17	11 24			11 35			11 47	
		d	10 25				10 38				10 48	10 53		11 08				11 18	11 25						11 48	11 53
Slaithwaite		d										11 00														12 00
Marsden		d										11 05														12 05
Greenfield		d										11 14														12 14
Mossley (Grtr Manchester)		d										11 18														12 18
Stalybridge		a	10 43									11 22						11 36	11 43							12 22
		d	10 44						11 00			11 22					11 30	11 39	11 43	12 00						12 22
Ashton-under-Lyne	⛴	d							11 04								11 34			12 04						
Manchester Victoria	⛴	a				11 29	11 08		11 15	11 53	11 21		12 05	11 38			11 44	11 54		12 15			12 42	12 53	12 20	
		d					11 09				11 24			11 40				11 56							12 24	
Manchester Oxford Road		a					11 15							11 45												
Manchester Piccadilly		a	11 04				11 19					11 39		11 49					12 04							12 39
		d					11 20							11 51												
Gatley		a												12 01												
Manchester Airport	⛴✈	a					11 41							12 13												
Newton-le-Willows	90	a									11 40														12 40	
Lea Green	90	a																12 16								
Liverpool Lime Street 10	90	a									12 02							12 32							12 59	

A ☕ from Leeds

Table T039-R

Mondays to Saturdays
16 December to 15 February

Newcastle, Middlesborough, Scarborough, York, Hull, Leeds and Wakefield - Huddersfield - Manchester, Manchester Airport and Liverpool

	TP	TP	NT	TP	TP	NT	NT	TP	TP	NT	NT	NT	TP	TP	TP	TP	TP	NT	TP	TP	TP	NT	NT
								SX	SO		SX	SO	SX	SO					SX	SO			
	◇1 ⌶	◇1		◇1 ⌶	◇1 A ⌶		◇	◇1 ⌶	◇1 ⌶		◇	◇	◇1 ⌶	◇1 ⌶	◇1	◇1 ⌶	◇1		◇1 ⌶	◇1 ⌶	◇1 A ⌶		◇
Edinburgh 26 d													09 33	09 33									
Morpeth 26 d													10 48	10 48									
Newcastle 8 26 ⇌ a													11 02	11 02									
d								10 47	10 47				11 05	11 05									
Chester-le-Street 26 d																							
Durham 26 d								10 59	10 59				11 17	11 17									
Darlington 8 26 a								11 16	11 16				11 33	11 33									
d								11 17	11 17				11 34	11 34									
Redcar Central 44 d	10 07															11 07							
Middlesbrough 44 d	10 21															11 21							
Thornaby 44 d	10 27															11 27							
Yarm d	10 35															11 35							
Northallerton 26 d	10 50							11 28	11 28							11 50							
Thirsk 26 d	10 59															11 59							
Scarborough 43 d				10 34															11 34	11 34			
Seamer 43 d				10 40															11 40	11 40			
Malton d				10 59															11 58	11 58			
York 8 26 a	11 17			11 24				11 47	11 47				12 01	12 01		12 17			12 24	12 24			
d	11 20			11 28				11 49	11 50				12 04	12 04		12 20			12 28	12 28			
Hull 29 d					11 06																12 08		
Brough 29 d					11 18																12 20		
Howden 29 d																							
Selby 29,40 d					11 38																12 41		
South Milford 40 d																							
Garforth 40 d				11 46															12 46	12 46			
Cross Gates 40 d																							
Leeds 10 a	11 42			11 56	12 03			12 12	12 12				12 27	12 27		12 42			12 56	12 58	13 05		
d	11 45	11 47		12 00	12 07		12 12	12 15	12 15		12 17	12 17	12 30	12 30		12 45	12 47		13 00	13 00	13 07		13 12
Cottingley d		11 52															12 52						
Morley d		11 56									12 25	12 26					12 56						
Batley d		12 01									12 30	12 31					13 01						
Dewsbury a	11 55	12 03						12 26	12 26		12 33	12 34				12 55	13 03						
d	11 57	12 04						12 27	12 27		12 33	12 35				12 57	13 04						
Ravensthorpe d		12 07															13 07						
Castleford d						11 58																12 58	
Normanton d						12 04																13 04	
Wakefield Kirkgate d						12 10																13 10	
Mirfield d		12 11				12 24					12 40	12 45					13 11					13 24	
Deighton d		12 17				12 30											13 17					13 30	
Huddersfield a	12 05	12 22		12 17	12 24	12 35		12 37	12 37				12 47	12 47		13 05	13 22		13 17	13 17	13 24	13 35	
d	12 08			12 18	12 25			12 38	12 38				12 48	12 49	12 53	13 08			13 18	13 18	13 25		
Slaithwaite d															13 00								
Marsden d															13 05								
Greenfield d															13 14								
Mossley (Grtr Manchester) d															13 18								
Stalybridge a				12 36	12 43										13 22				13 36	13 36	13 43		
d			12 31	12 37	12 43					13 00					13 22			13 30	13 37	13 37	13 43		
Ashton-under-Lyne ⇌ d			12 35							13 04								13 34					
Manchester Victoria ⇌ a	12 38		12 45	12 50			13 46	13 08	13 08	13 15	13 54	13 54	13 21	13 21		13 38		13 44	13 50	13 50			14 29
d	12 39			12 54				13 10	13 10				13 24	13 24		13 39			13 54	13 54			
Manchester Oxford Road a	12 45							13 15	13 15							13 45							
Manchester Piccadilly a	12 49				13 04			13 20	13 20						13 39	13 49					14 04		
d	12 51							13 20	13 20							13 51							
Gatley a	13 01															14 01							
Manchester Airport ⇌✈ a	13 13							13 41	13 41							14 13							
Newton-le-Willows 90 a													13 40	13 40									
Lea Green 90 a				13 15															14 16	14 16			
Liverpool Lime Street 10 90 a				13 32									13 59	13 59					14 32	14 32			

A ⌶ from Leeds

Table T039-R

Mondays to Saturdays
16 December to 15 February

Newcastle, Middlesborough, Scarborough, York, Hull, Leeds and Wakefield - Huddersfield - Manchester, Manchester Airport and Liverpool

	TP	NT	NT	TP	TP	TP	NT	TP	TP	NT	TP	TP	GC	NT	NT	TP	GC	NT	NT	TP	TP	TP
				SX	SO								SO				SX					
	◇1 ⌶		◇	◇1 ⌶	◇1 ⌶	◇1	◇	◇1 ⌶	◇1		◇1 ⌶	◇1 A ⌶	■ 1 ⊏		◇	◇1 ⌶	■ 1 ⊏		◇	◇1 ⌶	◇1	◇1 ⌶
Edinburgh 26 d				10 21	10 16															11 33		
Morpeth 26 d				11 33	11 48															12 46		
Newcastle 8 26 ⇌ a				11 53	12 02															13 00		
d	11 43			12 06	12 06											12 45				13 06		
Chester-le-Street 26 d	11 52																					
Durham 26 d	11 59			12 18	12 18											12 59				13 18		
Darlington 8 26 a	12 16			12 35	12 35											13 16				13 35		
d	12 17			12 36	12 36											13 17				13 36		
Redcar Central 44 d								12 07														13 07
Middlesbrough 44 d								12 21														13 21
Thornaby 44 d								12 27														13 27
Yarm d								12 35														13 35
Northallerton 26 d	12 28							12 50					13 20			13 28	13 33					13 50
Thirsk 26 d								12 59					13 29				13 43					13 59
Scarborough 43 d											12 34											
Seamer 43 d											12 40											
Malton d											12 58											
York 8 26 a	12 47			13 02	13 02			13 17			13 24		13 46			13 48	13 59			14 02		14 17
d	12 49			13 04	13 05			13 20			13 28					13 50				14 05		14 20
Hull 29 d												13 08										
Brough 29 d												13 20										
Howden 29 d																						
Selby 29,40 d												13 40										
South Milford 40 d																						
Garforth 40 d											13 46											
Cross Gates 40 d																						
Leeds 10 a	13 12			13 27	13 27			13 43			13 56	14 03				14 13				14 27		14 42
d	13 15		13 17	13 30	13 30		13 42	13 45	13 47		14 00	14 07			14 12	14 15			14 17	14 30		14 45
Cottingley d									13 52													
Morley d			13 26						13 56										14 26			
Batley d			13 31						14 01										14 31			
Dewsbury a	13 26		13 34					13 55	14 03							14 26			14 34			14 55
d	13 27		13 35					13 57	14 04							14 27			14 35			14 57
Ravensthorpe d									14 07													
Castleford d														13 58								
Normanton d														14 04								
Wakefield Kirkgate d														14 10								
Mirfield d			13 42						14 11					14 24					14 42			
Deighton d									14 17					14 30								
Huddersfield a	13 37			13 47	13 47			14 05	14 22		14 17	14 24		14 35		14 37				14 47		15 05
d	13 38			13 48	13 48	13 53		14 08			14 18	14 24				14 38				14 48	14 53	15 08
Slaithwaite d						14 00															15 00	
Marsden d						14 05															15 05	
Greenfield d						14 14															15 14	
Mossley (Grtr Manchester) d						14 18															15 18	
Stalybridge a						14 22					14 36	14 42									15 22	
d		14 00				14 22				14 30	14 37	14 43						15 01			15 22	
Ashton-under-Lyne ⇌ d		14 04								14 34								15 05				
Manchester Victoria ⇌ a	14 08	14 16	14 53	14 20	14 20		15 06	14 38		14 44	14 50				15 29	15 08		15 16	15 53	15 21		15 38
d	14 10			14 24	14 24			14 40			14 54					15 10				15 24		15 40
Manchester Oxford Road a	14 15							14 45								15 15						15 45
Manchester Piccadilly a	14 19					14 39		14 49				15 04				15 19					15 39	15 49
d	14 20							14 51								15 20						15 51
Gatley a								15 01														16 01
Manchester Airport ⇌✈ a	14 41							15 13								15 41						16 13
Newton-le-Willows 90 a				14 40	14 40															15 40		
Lea Green 90 a											15 16											
Liverpool Lime Street 10 90 a				14 59	14 59						15 32									16 00		

A ⌶ from Leeds

Table T039-R

Mondays to Saturdays
16 December to 15 February

Newcastle, Middlesborough, Scarborough, York, Hull, Leeds and Wakefield - Huddersfield - Manchester, Manchester Airport and Liverpool

			TP	NT	TP	TP	TP	NT	NT	TP	TP	NT		NT	TP	TP	TP	NT	TP	TP	TP	NT	TP	TP	TP	NT
						SO	SX			SX	SO				SO	SX			SO	SX				SX	SO	
			◇1		◇1	◇1	◇1		◇	◇1	◇1			◇	◇1	◇1	◇1	◇	◇1	◇1	◇1		◇1	◇1	◇1	
						A	A																	A	A	
					✠	✠	✠			✠	✠				✠	✠			✠	✠			✠	✠	✠	
Edinburgh	26	d													12 33	12 33										
Morpeth	26	d													13 49	13 49										
Newcastle 8	26 ⇌	a													14 03	14 03										
		d								13 43	13 43				14 06	14 06										
Chester-le-Street	26	d								13 51	13 51															
Durham	26	d								13 58	13 58				14 18	14 18										
Darlington 5	26	a								14 16	14 16				14 35	14 35										
		d								14 17	14 17				14 36	14 36										
Redcar Central	44	d																	14 07	14 07						
Middlesbrough	44	d																	14 21	14 21						
Thornaby	44	d																	14 27	14 27						
Yarm		d																	14 35	14 35						
Northallerton	26	d								14 28	14 28								14 50	14 50						
Thirsk	26	d																	14 59	14 59						
Scarborough	43	d			13 34																		14 34			
Seamer	43	d			13 40																		14 40			
Malton		d			13 58																		14 58			
York 8	26	a			14 24					14 47	14 47				15 02	15 02			15 17	15 17			15 24			
		d			14 28					14 49	14 49				15 04	15 05			15 20	15 20			15 28			
Hull	29	d				14 07	14 07																	15 03	15 08	
Brough	29	d				14 20	14 20																	15 15	15 20	
Howden	29	d																								
Selby	29,40	d				14 40	14 40																	15 36	15 40	
South Milford	40	d																								
Garforth	40	d			14 46																		15 46			
Cross Gates	40	d																								
Leeds 10		a			14 56	15 03	15 03			15 12	15 12				15 27	15 27			15 42	15 42			15 56	16 03	16 03	
		d	14 47		15 00	15 07	15 07		15 12	15 15	15 15			15 17	15 30	15 30		15 42	15 45	15 45	15 47		16 00	16 07	16 07	
Cottingley		d	14 52																		15 52					
Morley		d	14 56											15 26							15 56					
Batley		d	15 01											15 31							16 01					
Dewsbury		a	15 03							15 26	15 26			15 34					15 55	15 55	16 03					
		d	15 04							15 27	15 27			15 35					15 57	15 57	16 04					
Ravensthorpe		d	15 07																		16 07					
Castleford		d						14 58																		15 58
Normanton		d						15 04																		16 04
Wakefield Kirkgate		d						15 10																		16 10
Mirfield		d	15 11					15 24						15 42							16 11					16 24
Deighton		d	15 17					15 30													16 17					16 30
Huddersfield		a	15 22		15 17	15 24	15 24	15 35		15 37	15 37				15 47	15 47			16 05	16 05	16 22		16 17	16 24	16 24	16 35
		d			15 18	15 25	15 25			15 38	15 38				15 48	15 48	15 53		16 08	16 08			16 18	16 25	16 25	
Slaithwaite		d															16 00							16 32	16 32	
Marsden		d															16 05							16 37	16 37	
Greenfield		d															16 14							16 45	16 45	
Mossley (Grtr Manchester)		d															16 18							16 49	16 49	
Stalybridge		a			15 36	15 43	15 43										16 22						16 36	16 53	16 53	
		d		15 30	15 37	15 43	15 50					16 00					16 22					16 29	16 37	16 54	16 54	
Ashton-under-Lyne	⇌	d		15 34								16 04										16 33				
Manchester Victoria	⇌	a		15 44	15 51				16 29	16 08	16 08	16 15		16 54	16 20	16 20		17 05	16 38	16 38		16 44	16 51			
		d			15 54					16 10	16 10				16 24	16 24			16 39	16 39			16 54			
Manchester Oxford Road		a								16 15	16 15								16 45	16 45						
Manchester Piccadilly		a				16 04	16 14			16 19	16 19						16 41		16 49	16 49				17 14	17 16	
		d								16 20	16 20								16 51	16 51						
Gatley		a																	17 01	17 01						
Manchester Airport	⇌✈	a								16 40	16 41								17 13	17 16						
Newton-le-Willows	90	a													16 41	16 40										
Lea Green	90	a			16 15																		17 16			
Liverpool Lime Street 10	90	a			16 32										17 01	16 59							17 32			

A ✠ from Leeds

NRT DECEMBER 19 EDITION

Table T039-R

Mondays to Saturdays
16 December to 15 February

Newcastle, Middlesborough, Scarborough, York, Hull, Leeds and Wakefield - Huddersfield - Manchester, Manchester Airport and Liverpool

			NT	TP		TP	NT	NT	TP	TP	TP	TP	TP	NT	TP	TP	NT	NT	TP	GC		GC	NT	NT	TP	TP
				SO		SX			SO	SX										SO		SX			SO	SX
																				■		■				
			◇	◇1		◇1		◇	◇1	◇1	◇1	◇1	◇1		◇1	◇1		◇	◇1	1		1		◇	◇1	◇1
																A										
				✠		✠			✠	✠		✠			✠	✠			✠	R		R			✠	✠
Edinburgh	26	d							13 19	13 19															14 33	14 33
Morpeth	26	d							14 37	14 32															15 47	15 47
Newcastle 8	26 ⇌	a							14 52	14 50															16 01	16 02
		d		14 47		14 47			15 03	15 03									15 43						16 06	16 06
Chester-le-Street	26	d																	15 52							
Durham	26	d		14 59		14 59			15 15	15 15									15 59						16 18	16 18
Darlington 5	26	a		15 16		15 16			15 32	15 32									16 16						16 35	16 35
		d		15 17		15 17			15 33	15 33									16 17						16 36	16 36
Redcar Central	44	d										15 07														
Middlesbrough	44	d										15 21														
Thornaby	44	d										15 27														
Yarm		d										15 35														
Northallerton	26	d		15 28		15 28						15 50								16 33		16 33				
Thirsk	26	d										15 59								16 43		16 43				
Scarborough	43	d													15 34											
Seamer	43	d													15 40											
Malton		d													15 58											
York 8	26	a		15 47		15 47			15 59	15 59		16 17			16 24				16 48	16 59		17 00			17 02	17 02
		d		15 49		15 50			16 01	16 01		16 20			16 28				16 49						17 04	17 04
Hull	29	d														16 08										
Brough	29	d														16 20										
Howden	29	d																								
Selby	29,40	d														16 40										
South Milford	40	d																								
Garforth	40	d													16 46											
Cross Gates	40	d																								
Leeds 10		a		16 12		16 12			16 27	16 27		16 42			16 57	17 03			17 12						17 27	17 27
		d	16 12	16 15		16 15		16 17	16 30	16 30		16 45	16 47		17 00	17 07		17 12	17 15					17 17	17 30	17 30
Cottingley		d											16 52											17 23		
Morley		d						16 25					16 56											17 27		
Batley		d						16 30					17 01											17 32		
Dewsbury		a		16 26		16 26		16 33				16 55	17 03						17 26					17 35		
		d		16 27		16 27		16 34				16 57	17 04						17 27					17 36		
Ravensthorpe		d						16 37					17 07													
Castleford		d															16 58									
Normanton		d															17 04									
Wakefield Kirkgate		d															17 10									
Mirfield		d						16 42					17 11				17 24							17 43		
Deighton		d											17 17				17 30									
Huddersfield		a		16 37		16 37			16 47	16 47		17 05	17 22		17 17	17 24	17 35		17 37						17 47	17 47
		d		16 38		16 38			16 48	16 48	16 53	17 08			17 21	17 25			17 38						17 48	17 48
Slaithwaite		d									17 00					17 32										
Marsden		d									17 05					17 37										
Greenfield		d									17 14					17 45										
Mossley (Grtr Manchester)		d									17 18					17 49										
Stalybridge		a									17 22				17 40	17 53										
		d					17 00				17 22			17 31	17 41	17 54							18 00			
Ashton-under-Lyne	⇌	d					17 04							17 35									18 04			
Manchester Victoria	⇌	a	17 34	17 08		17 08	17 15	17 53	17 20	17 20		17 38		17 45	17 54			18 44	18 08				18 15	18 53	18 22	18 22
		d		17 10		17 10			17 24	17 24		17 39			17 56				18 10						18 24	18 24
Manchester Oxford Road		a		17 15		17 15						17 45							18 15							
Manchester Piccadilly		a		17 19		17 19					17 39	17 49				18 11			18 19							
		d		17 20		17 20						17 51							18 20							
Gatley		a										18 01														
Manchester Airport	⇌✈	a		17 40		17 40						18 14							18 41							
Newton-le-Willows	90	a							17 40	17 40															18 40	18 40
Lea Green	90	a													18 16											
Liverpool Lime Street 10	90	a							17 59	18 02					18 33										19 01	19 01

A ✠ from Leeds

Table T039-R

Mondays to Saturdays

16 December to 15 February

Newcastle, Middlesborough, Scarborough, York, Hull, Leeds and Wakefield - Huddersfield - Manchester, Manchester Airport and Liverpool

			TP	TP	TP	NT	TP	TP	TP	TP	NT	NT	TP	NT	NT	TP	TP	TP	TP	TP	NT	TP	TP	NT	NT
							SO	SX	SX	SO						SX	SO								
			◇■	◇■	◇■		◇■	◇■	◇■	◇■		◇	◇■		◇	◇■	◇■	◇■	◇■	◇■		◇■	◇■		◇
				🍴			🍴	🍴	A 🍴	A 🍴			🍴			🍴	🍴		🍴				A 🍴		
Edinburgh	26	d														15 33	15 33								
Morpeth	26	d														16 48	16 48								
Newcastle ■	26 ⛴	a														17 03	17 03								
		d											16 43			17 06	17 06								
Chester-le-Street	26	d											16 52												
Durham	26	d											16 59			17 18	17 18								
Darlington ■	26	a											17 15			17 35	17 35								
		d											17 17			17 36	17 36								
Redcar Central	44	d		16 07															17 07						
Middlesbrough	44	d		16 21															17 21						
Thornaby	44	d		16 27															17 27						
Yarm		d		16 35															17 35						
Northallerton	26	d		16 50									17 28						17 50						
Thirsk	26	d		16 59															17 59						
Scarborough	43	d					16 34	16 34														17 34			
Seamer	43	d					16 40	16 40														17 40			
Malton		d					16 58	16 58														17 58			
York ■	26	a		17 17			17 24	17 25					17 47			18 02	18 02		18 17			18 24			
		d		17 20			17 28	17 28					17 49			18 05	18 05		18 18			18 28			
Hull	29	d							17 03	17 08													18 08		
Brough	29	d							17 15	17 20													18 20		
Howden	29	d																							
Selby	29,40	d							17 37	17 40													18 40		
South Milford	40	d																							
Garforth	40	d					17 46	17 46														18 45			
Cross Gates	40	d																							
Leeds ■		a		17 42			17 56	17 56	18 03	18 03			18 12			18 27	18 27		18 42			18 55	19 04		
		d		17 45	17 47		18 00	18 00	18 07	18 07		18 12	18 15		18 17	18 29	18 29		18 45	18 47		19 00	19 07		19 12
Cottingley		d			17 52															18 52					
Morley		d			17 56										18 25					18 56					
Batley		d			18 01										18 30					19 01					
Dewsbury		a		17 55	18 03								18 26		18 33				18 55	19 03					
		d		17 57	18 04								18 27		18 33				18 57	19 04					
Ravensthorpe		d			18 07															19 07					
Castleford		d									17 58													18 58	
Normanton		d									18 04													19 04	
Wakefield Kirkgate		d									18 10													19 10	
Mirfield		d			18 11						18 24				18 40					19 11				19 24	
Deighton		d			18 17						18 30									19 17				19 30	
Huddersfield		a		18 05	18 22		18 17	18 17	18 24	18 24	18 35		18 37			18 46	18 46		19 05	19 22		19 17	19 24	19 35	
		d	17 54	18 08			18 18	18 18	18 25	18 25			18 38			18 48	18 48	18 53	19 08			19 18	19 25		
Slaithwaite		d	18 01						18 32	18 32								19 00							
Marsden		d	18 06						18 37	18 37								19 05							
Greenfield		d	18 15						18 45	18 45								19 14							
Mossley (Grtr Manchester)		d	18 19						18 49	18 49								19 18							
Stalybridge		a	18 23				18 36	18 36	18 53	18 53								19 22				19 36	19 43		
		d	18 23			18 31	18 37	18 37	18 54	18 54				19 00				19 22			19 31	19 37	19 43		
Ashton-under-Lyne	⛴	d				18 35								19 04							19 35				
Manchester Victoria	⛴	a		18 38		18 47	18 52	18 52				19 29	19 08	19 15	19 53	19 20	19 20		19 38		19 46	19 50			20 29
		d		18 39			18 54	18 54					19 10			19 24	19 24		19 39			19 54			
Manchester Oxford Road		a		18 45									19 15						19 45						
Manchester Piccadilly		a	18 39	18 49					19 14	19 11			19 19					19 39	19 49				20 04		
		d		18 51									19 20						19 51						
Gatley		a		19 01															20 01						
Manchester Airport	⛴✈	a		19 16									19 42						20 13						
Newton-le-Willows	90	a														19 40	19 40					20 12			
Lea Green	90	a					19 17	19 17								19 47	19 47					20 19			
Liverpool Lime Street ■	90	a					19 33	19 33								20 03	20 05					20 35			

A 🍴 from Leeds

Table T039-R

Mondays to Saturdays

16 December to 15 February

Newcastle, Middlesborough, Scarborough, York, Hull, Leeds and Wakefield - Huddersfield - Manchester, Manchester Airport and Liverpool

			TP	GC	NT	NT	TP	TP	TP	GC	TP	TP	NT	TP	TP	TP	TP	TP	TP	NT	NT	TP	NT	NT
				SO			SO	SX		SX				SO	SX	SX	SO	SX	SX					
			◇■	■		◇	◇■	◇■	◇■	■	◇■	◇■		◇■	◇■	◇■	◇■	◇■	◇■		◇	◇■		◇
			🍴	⊏			🍴	🍴		⊏							A 🍴		🍴			🍴		
Edinburgh	26	d					16 21	16 33																
Morpeth	26	d					17 48	17 48																
Newcastle ■	26 ⛴	a					18 04	18 04																
		d	17 43				18 07	18 07														18 43		
Chester-le-Street	26	d	17 52																			18 52		
Durham	26	d	17 59				18 19	18 19														19 00		
Darlington ■	26	a	18 16				18 36	18 36														19 16		
		d	18 17				18 37	18 37														19 17		
Redcar Central	44	d									18 07													
Middlesbrough	44	d									18 21													
Thornaby	44	d									18 27													
Yarm		d									18 35													
Northallerton	26	d	18 28	18 32						18 41	18 50											19 28		
Thirsk	26	d		18 43						18 51	18 59													
Scarborough	43	d												18 34	18 34									
Seamer	43	d												18 40	18 40									
Malton		d												18 58	18 58									
York ■	26	a	18 47	18 59			19 03	19 03		19 09	19 17			19 24	19 24							19 47		
		d	18 49				19 06	19 06			19 20			19 28	19 28							19 49		
Hull	29	d														19 03	19 08							
Brough	29	d														19 15	19 20							
Howden	29	d																						
Selby	29,40	d														19 38	19 40							
South Milford	40	d																						
Garforth	40	d												19 46	19 46									
Cross Gates	40	d																	←					
Leeds ■		a	19 12				19 28	19 28			19 42			19 56	19 56	20 03	20 03		20 03			20 12		
		d	19 15			19 17	19 30	19 30			19 45	19 47		20 00	20 00	20 07	20 07		20 07		20 12	20 15		20 18
Cottingley		d										19 52				→								
Morley		d				19 25						19 56												20 26
Batley		d				19 30						20 01												20 31
Dewsbury		a	19 26			19 33					19 55	20 03										20 26		20 34
		d	19 27			19 34					19 57	20 04										20 27		20 35
Ravensthorpe		d										20 07												
Castleford		d																		19 58				
Normanton		d																		20 04				
Wakefield Kirkgate		d																		20 10				
Mirfield		d				19 41						20 11								20 24				20 42
Deighton		d										20 17								20 30				
Huddersfield		a	19 37				19 47	19 47			20 05	20 22		20 17	20 17		20 24		20 24	20 35		20 37		
		d	19 38				19 48	19 48	19 53		20 08			20 18	20 18		20 25		20 25			20 38		
Slaithwaite		d							20 00															
Marsden		d							20 05															
Greenfield		d							20 14															
Mossley (Grtr Manchester)		d							20 18									←						
Stalybridge		a							20 22					20 36	20 45		20 43	20 45	20 48					
		d			20 00				20 22				20 31	20 37	20 46		20 46	20 46	20 53				21 00	
Ashton-under-Lyne	⛴	d			20 04								20 35		→								21 04	
Manchester Victoria	⛴	a	20 09		20 15	20 53	20 21	20 21			20 38		20 46	20 52				21 01			21 46	21 11	21 14	21 54
		d	20 10				20 24	20 24			20 39													
Manchester Oxford Road		a	20 15								20 45													
Manchester Piccadilly		a	20 19						20 39		20 49						21 04		21 15					
		d	20 20								20 51													
Gatley		a									21 01													
Manchester Airport	⛴✈	a	20 40								21 11													
Newton-le-Willows	90	a																						
Lea Green	90	a																						
Liverpool Lime Street ■	90	a					20 56	20 56																

A 🍴 from Leeds

Table T039-R

Mondays to Saturdays
16 December to 15 February

Newcastle, Middlesborough, Scarborough, York, Hull, Leeds and Wakefield - Huddersfield - Manchester, Manchester Airport and Liverpool

Station			TP	TP	TP	NT	TP	TP	NT	TP	TP	TP		NT	NT	NT	NT	NT	TP	TP	TP	NT	NT	TP	TP	TP
			SO	SX						SX	SO			SX		SO			SO	SX					SO	SX
			◇1	◇1	◇1	◇	◇1	◇1		◇1	◇1	◇1					◇	◇	◇1	◇1	◇1		◇	◇1	◇1	◇1
			🛒	🛒								A 🛒							B 🛒	B 🛒						
Edinburgh	26	d	17 32	17 32															18 33	18 11						
Morpeth	26	d	18 52	18 52															19 47	19 33						
Newcastle 8	26	a	19 06	19 06															20 01	19 47						
		d	19 09	19 09															20 06	20 06						
Chester-le-Street	26	d																								
Durham	26	d	19 21	19 21															20 18	20 18						
Darlington 5	26	a																	20 35	20 35						
		d																	20 36	20 36						
Redcar Central	44	d					19 07																			
Middlesbrough	44	d					19 21																			
Thornaby	44	d					19 27																			
Yarm		d					19 35																			
Northallerton	26	d					19 50																			
Thirsk	26	d					19 59																			
Scarborough	43	d								19 34	19 34														20 34	20 34
Seamer	43	d								19 40	19 40														20 40	20 40
Malton		d								19 58	19 58														20 58	20 58
York 8	26	a	20 02	20 02			20 17			20 24	20 25								21 02	21 02					21 24	21 24
		d	20 05	20 05			20 20			20 28	20 28								21 05	21 05					21 28	21 28
Hull	29	d										20 08														
Brough	29	d										20 20														
Howden	29	d																								
Selby	29,40	d										20 41														
South Milford	40	d																								
Garforth	40	d								20 46	20 46														21 46	21 46
Cross Gates	40	d																								
Leeds 10		a	20 27	20 27			20 43			20 56	20 56	21 03							21 27	21 27					21 56	21 56
		d	20 30	20 30		20 42	20 45	20 47		21 00	21 00	21 07					21 12	21 17	21 30	21 30			21 42	21 47	22 00	22 00
Cottingley		d						20 52																21 52		
Morley		d						20 56										21 25						21 56		
Batley		d						21 01										21 30						22 01		
Dewsbury		a					20 55	21 03				21 17						21 33	21 41	21 41				22 03		
		d					20 57	21 04				21 18						21 34	21 42	21 42				22 04		
Ravensthorpe		d						21 07																22 07		
Castleford		d													20 58											
Normanton		d													21 04											
Wakefield Kirkgate		d													21 10											
Mirfield		d						21 11							21 24			21 41						22 11		
Deighton		d						21 17							21 30									22 17		
Huddersfield		a	20 47	20 47			21 05	21 22		21 17	21 17	21 26			21 35				21 50	21 50				22 22	22 17	22 17
		d	20 48	20 48	20 53		21 08			21 18	21 18	21 31							21 51	21 51	21 56				22 18	22 18
Slaithwaite		d			21 00																22 03					
Marsden		d			21 05																22 08					
Greenfield		d			21 14																22 17					
Mossley (Grtr Manchester)		d			21 18																22 21					
Stalybridge		a			21 22					21 39	21 39	21 51									22 25				22 39	22 39
		d			21 22				21 29	21 40	21 40	21 51		22 02		22 03					22 25	22 31			22 40	22 40
Ashton-under-Lyne		d							21 33					22 05		22 06						22 35				
Manchester Victoria		a	21 19	21 22		22 06	21 40		21 44	21 54	21 54			22 17		22 18	22 35	22 55	22 23	22 25		22 46	23 08		22 53	22 53
		d	21 24	21 24						21 56	21 56								22 24	22 26					22 55	22 55
Manchester Oxford Road		a								22 02	22 02														23 00	23 01
Manchester Piccadilly		a			21 39					22 06	22 06	22 10									22 44				23 04	23 05
		d								22 07	22 07														23 05	23 12
Gatley		a																								
Manchester Airport		a								22 22	22 22														23 20	23 28
Newton-le-Willows	90	a	21 40	21 40															22 40	22 46						
Lea Green	90	a	21 47	21 46															22 47	22 54						
Liverpool Lime Street 10	90	a	22 05	22 05															23 06	23 14						

A 🛒 from Leeds B 🛒 from York

Table T039-R

Mondays to Saturdays
16 December to 15 February

Newcastle, Middlesborough, Scarborough, York, Hull, Leeds and Wakefield - Huddersfield - Manchester, Manchester Airport and Liverpool

Station			TP	TP		NT	NT	NT	NT	NT	TP	TP	TP	TP	TP	NT	TP	TP	TP	TP		TP	TP	TP	NT	TP
						SO		SX				SX	SO	SX			SX	SO		SO		SX	SO	SX		SO
			◇1	◇1					◇		◇1	◇1	◇1	◇1	◇1	◇	◇1	◇1	◇1	◇1		◇1	◇1	◇1		◇1
				A 🛒								B 🛒	B 🛒	🛒								A 🛒	A 🛒	🛒		🛒
Edinburgh	26	d										19 30	19 30													
Morpeth	26	d										20 45	20 45													
Newcastle 8	26	a										20 59	20 59													
		d										21 02	21 02							22 00						22 00
Chester-le-Street	26	d										21 11	21 11													
Durham	26	d										21 18	21 18							22 15						22 15
Darlington 5	26	a										21 35	21 35							22 32						22 32
		d										21 36	21 36							22 33						22 33
Redcar Central	44	d	20 07												21 07											
Middlesbrough	44	d	20 21												21 21											
Thornaby	44	d	20 27												21 27											
Yarm		d	20 39												21 35											
Northallerton	26	d	20 54												21 50					22 44						22 44
Thirsk	26	d	21 05												21 59											
Scarborough	43	d																	21 34							
Seamer	43	d																	21 40							
Malton		d																	21 58							
York 8	26	a	21 25									22 02	22 02		22 19				22 24	23 03						23 03
		d										22 05	22 05						22 28							23 05
Hull	29	d		21 08																		22 08	22 08			
Brough	29	d		21 20																		22 20	22 20			
Howden	29	d																								
Selby	29,40	d		21 40																		22 40	22 40			
South Milford	40	d																								
Garforth	40	d																	22 47							
Cross Gates	40	d												←												
Leeds 10		a		22 03								22 26	22 27	22 26					22 58			23 03	23 03			23 27
		d		22 07					22 12	22 21		22 28	22 28	22 28		22 42	22 46	22 47	23 00			23 05	23 07			23 30
Cottingley		d										→					22 52	22 52								
Morley		d								22 29							22 56	22 56								
Batley		d								22 34							23 01	23 01						←		
Dewsbury		a		22 17						22 37			22 41	22 41			23 03	23 03				23 15		23 15		23 40
		d		22 18						22 38			22 42	22 42			23 04	23 04				23 18		23 18		23 41
Ravensthorpe		d															23 07	23 07				→				
Castleford		d					21 58																		22 58	
Normanton		d					22 04																		23 04	
Wakefield Kirkgate		d					22 10																		23 11	
Mirfield		d					22 24			22a44							23 11	23 11							23 25	
Deighton		d					22 30										23 18	23 18							23 31	
Huddersfield		a		22 26			22 35						22 50	22 50			23 22	23 22	23 17				23 24	23 26	23 36	23 50
		d		22 27							22 46		22 51	22 51					23 18				23 25	23 27		23 51
Slaithwaite		d									22 52												23 32	23 33		
Marsden		d									23 04												23 37	23 37		
Greenfield		d									23 13												23 46	23 46		
Mossley (Grtr Manchester)		d									23 17												23 50	23 50		
Stalybridge		a		22 45							23 21								23 36				23 54	23 54		
		d		22 46		23 00		23 03			23 24								23 37				23 54	23 54		
Ashton-under-Lyne		d				23 03		23 06																		
Manchester Victoria		a		23 00		23 14		23 16	23 37				23 23	23 23		00 11			23 50							
		d		23 02									23 24	23 25					23 52							
Manchester Oxford Road		a																	23 57							
Manchester Piccadilly		a									23 41								00 01				00 14	00 11		00 23
		d																	00 03							00 33
Gatley		a																								
Manchester Airport		a																	00 19							00 49
Newton-le-Willows	90	a											23 40	23 41												
Lea Green	90	a		23 23									23 47	23 47												
Liverpool Lime Street 10	90	a		23 43									00 05	00 05												

A 🛒 from Leeds B 🛒 from York

Table T039-R

Mondays to Saturdays

16 December to 15 February

Newcastle, Middlesborough, Scarborough, York, Hull, Leeds and Wakefield - Huddersfield - Manchester, Manchester Airport and Liverpool

			TP	TP SX	TP	TP SO	TP SO	TP	TP SX	TP WO	TP SX
			◇1	◇1	◇1	1	◇1	◇1	◇1	◇1	◇1
Edinburgh	26	d								22 12	
Morpeth	26	d									
Newcastle 8	26 ⇌	a									
		d				22 30					
Chester-le-Street	26	d				22 40					
Durham	26	d				22a46					
Darlington 5	26	a									
		d									
Redcar Central	44	d			22 07						23 07
Middlesbrough	44	d			22 21						23 22
Thornaby	44	d			22 27						23 28
Yarm		d			22 35						23 37
Northallerton	26	d			22 50						23 54
Thirsk	26	d			22 59						00 03
Scarborough	43	d		22 15			22 42		22 45		
Seamer	43	d		22 20			22 48		22 51		
Malton		d		22 39			23 06		23 11		
York 8	26	a		23 04	23 19		23 33		23 35		00 29
		d					23 37		23 39		
Hull	29	d						23 08			
Brough	29	d						23 20			
Howden	29	d									
Selby	29,40	d						23 40			
South Milford	40	d									
Garforth	40	d									
Cross Gates	40	d									
Leeds 10		a					00 02	00 04	00 06		
		d	23 47				00 07		00 07		
Cottingley		d	23 52								
Morley		d	23 56								
Batley		d	00 02								
Dewsbury		a	00 03								
		d	00 04								
Ravensthorpe		d	00 07								
Castleford		d									
Normanton		d									
Wakefield Kirkgate		d									
Mirfield		d	00 11								
Deighton		d	00 17								
Huddersfield		a	00 22								
		d									
Slaithwaite		d									
Marsden		d									
Greenfield		d									
Mossley (Grtr Manchester)		d									
Stalybridge		a									
		d									
Ashton-under-Lyne	⇌	d									
Manchester Victoria	⇌	a									
		d									
Manchester Oxford Road		a									
Manchester Piccadilly		a					00 56		01 06	01 42	
		d									
Gatley		a									
Manchester Airport	⇌✈	a									
Newton-le-Willows	90	a									
Lea Green	90	a									
Liverpool Lime Street 10	90	a									

Table T039-R

Mondays to Saturdays

17 February to 28 March

Newcastle, Middlesborough, Scarborough, York, Hull, Leeds and Wakefield - Huddersfield - Manchester, Manchester Airport and Liverpool

			TP	TP MX	TP MO	TP MX	TP MO	TP SO	TP MSX	TP SO	TP MO	TP MSX	TP MSX	TP SO	TP MO	TP MSX	TP SX		TP SO	TP SX	TP SO	TP SX	TP	TP	NT	NT SO
			◇1	◇1	◇1	◇1	◇1	◇1	◇1	◇1	◇1	◇1	◇1	◇1	◇1	◇1	◇1		◇1	◇1	◇1	◇1	◇1	◇1		◇
Edinburgh	26	d																								
Morpeth	26	d																								
Newcastle 8	26 ⇌	a																								
		d					00 08	00 08	00 08																	
Chester-le-Street	26	d																								
Durham	26	d					00 21	00 21	00 21																	
Darlington 5	26	a					00 38	00 38	00 38																	
		d					00 40	00 40	00 40																	
Redcar Central	44	d																								
Middlesbrough	44	d																								
Thornaby	44	d																								
Yarm		d																								
Northallerton	26	d																								
Thirsk	26	d		00 03																						
Scarborough	43	d																								
Seamer	43	d																								
Malton		d																								
York 8	26	a		00 29			01 36	01 36	01 36																	
		d					01 38	01 38	01 38				02 47	02 52	02 52		03 40		03 40				04 27			
Hull	29	d																								
Brough	29	d																								
Howden	29	d																								
Selby	29,40	d																								
South Milford	40	d																								
Garforth	40	d																								
Cross Gates	40	d														←										
Leeds 10		a					02 05	02 18	02 18				03 27	03 18	03 19	03 27	04 05		04 19				04 53			
		d			00 05	00 07	02 05	02 18	02 20				03 35	03 19	03 20	03 35	04 08		04 31				05 03			05 12
Cottingley		d											→													
Morley		d																								
Batley		d	00 02																							
Dewsbury		a	00 03																							
		d	00 04																							
Ravensthorpe		d	00 07																							
Castleford		d																								
Normanton		d																								
Wakefield Kirkgate		d																								
Mirfield		d	00 11																							
Deighton		d	00 17							←																
Huddersfield		a	00 22				02 40	02 56	02 40	02 56				03 55	03 55	03 56	04 41		05 03				05 35			
		d					02 41	02 56	02 41	02 56				03 55	03 58	03 58	04 51		05 04				05 37			
Slaithwaite		d						→																		
Marsden		d																								
Greenfield		d																								
Mossley (Grtr Manchester)		d																								
Stalybridge		a																								
		d																						06 00	06 03	
Ashton-under-Lyne	⇌	d																		←					06 07	
Manchester Victoria	⇌	a															05 35		05 34	05 35			06 09	06 14	06 18	06 30
		d															05 39		05 37	05 39	05 54	05 54	06 10	06 19		
Manchester Oxford Road		a									←	←					→		05 44	05 45			06 16			
Manchester Piccadilly		a			01 23	01 06	03 41		03 41	03 29	03 41	03 41		04 27	04 56	04 56			05 49	05 49			06 20			
		d					03 43		03 43	03 34	03 43	03 43		04 34	04 57	04 57			05 50	05 50			06 20			
Gatley		a					→		→										06 01	06 01						
Manchester Airport	⇌✈	a								03 51	03 59	03 59		04 52	05 13	05 13			06 13	06 13			06 41			
Newton-le-Willows	90	a																			06 11	06 13		06 38		
Lea Green	90	a																			06 17	06 19		06 45		
Liverpool Lime Street 10	90	a																			06 32	06 34		07 03		

Table T039-R

Mondays to Saturdays

17 February to 28 March

Newcastle, Middlesbrough, Scarborough, York, Hull, Leeds and Wakefield - Huddersfield - Manchester, Manchester Airport and Liverpool

	NT SX ◇	TP ◇1	NT ◇	TP ◇1	NT	TP ◇1	TP SO ◇1 A ✠		TP SX ◇1 A ✠	NT ◇	TP ◇1	NT	NT ◇	TP ◇1 B ✠	TP ◇1	TP SX ◇1	TP SO ◇1	TP ◇1	NT	TP SO ◇1 ✠	TP SX ◇1 ✠	TP SX ◇1	TP SO ◇1
Edinburgh 26 d																							
Morpeth 26 d																							
Newcastle 8 26 ⛴ a																							
d														05 06									
Chester-le-Street 26 d																							
Durham 26 d														05 18									
Darlington 5 26 a														05 35									
d														05 36									
Redcar Central 44 d																							
Middlesbrough 44 d																05 12	05 19						
Thornaby 44 d																05 17	05 25						
Yarm d																05 25	05 33						
Northallerton 26 d																05 41	05 50						
Thirsk 26 d																05 51	05 58						
Scarborough 43 d																				05 34	05 34		
Seamer 43 d																				05 40	05 40		
Malton d																				05 59	05 59		
York 8 26 a														06 02		06 09	06 16			06 24	06 24		
d				05 15		05 28					05 49			06 05		06 18	06 18			06 28	06 28		
Hull 29 d							05 06		05 06													06 04	06 04
Brough 29 d							05 18		05 18													06 16	06 16
Howden 29 d							05 32		05 32														
Selby 29,40 d							05 42		05 42													06 37	06 37
South Milford 40 d																							
Garforth 40 d						05 48														06 47	06 47	06 52	06 52
Cross Gates 40 d																						06 57	06 57
Leeds 10 a				05 42		05 58	06 04		06 04		06 12			06 28		06 42	06 42			06 57	06 57	07 04	07 04
d	05 12		05 19	05 45		06 00	06 07		06 07	06 12	06 15		06 17	06 30		06 45	06 45	06 47		07 00	07 00	07 07	07 07
Cottingley d			05 25															06 52					
Morley d			05 29										06 25					06 56					
Batley d			05 34										06 30					07 01					
Dewsbury a			05 37	05 55							06 26		06 33			06 55	06 55	07 03					
d			05 38	05 57							06 27		06 34			06 57	06 57	07 04					
Ravensthorpe d			05 41															07 07					
Castleford d																							
Normanton d																							
Wakefield Kirkgate d		05 24																					
Mirfield d		05 37	05 45										06 40					07 11					
Deighton d		05 47																07 17					
Huddersfield a		05 51		06 06		06 17	06 24		06 24		06 35			06 47		07 05	07 05	07 22		07 17	07 17	07 24	07 24
d		05 54		06 08		06 18	06 25		06 25		06 36			06 48	06 53	07 08	07 08			07 18	07 18	07 25	07 25
Slaithwaite d		06 01					06 32		06 32						07 00							07 32	07 32
Marsden d		06 06					06 37		06 37						07 05							07 37	07 37
Greenfield d		06 15					06 46		06 46						07 14							07 45	07 45
Mossley (Grtr Manchester) d		06 19					06 50		06 50						07 18							07 49	07 49
Stalybridge a		06 23				06 36	06 54		06 54						07 22					07 36	07 36	07 53	07 53
d		06 23			06 30	06 37	06 54		06 54			07 00			07 22				07 32	07 37	07 37	07 54	07 54
Ashton-under-Lyne ⛴ d					06 34							07 04							07 36				
Manchester Victoria ⛴ a	06 31		06 53	06 38	06 46	06 50				07 30	07 09	07 15	07 52	07 22		07 38	07 38		07 46	07 52	07 52		
d				06 39		06 52					07 10			07 24		07 39	07 39			07 54	07 54		
Manchester Oxford Road a				06 47							07 16					07 45	07 45						
Manchester Piccadilly a		06 38		06 53			07 11		07 17		07 20				07 39	07 49	07 49					08 13	08 14
d				06 55							07 21					07 50	07 50						
Gatley a				07 03												08 01	08 01						
Manchester Airport ⛴✈ a				07 16							07 41					08 16	08 16						
Newton-le-Willows 90 a						07 08								07 40									
Lea Green 90 a						07 14														08 14	08 14		
Liverpool Lime Street 10 90 a						07 30								08 00						08 33	08 36		

A ✠ from Leeds B ✠ from York

NRT DECEMBER 19 EDITION

Table T039-R

Mondays to Saturdays

17 February to 28 March

Newcastle, Middlesbrough, Scarborough, York, Hull, Leeds and Wakefield - Huddersfield - Manchester, Manchester Airport and Liverpool

	NT	NT ◇	TP ◇1 ✠	NT	NT ◇	TP ◇1 ✠	TP ◇1	TP SO ◇1 ✠	TP SX ◇1 ✠	TP ◇1	NT	TP ◇1 ✠	TP ◇1 ✠	NT	NT SX ◇		NT SO ◇	TP ◇1 ✠	NT	NT ◇	TP SO ◇1 ✠	TP MSX ◇1 ✠	TP MO ◇1 ✠	TP ◇1
Edinburgh 26 d																					05 14	05 14	05 17	
Morpeth 26 d																					06 43	06 43	06 43	
Newcastle 8 26 ⛴ a																					06 57	06 57	06 57	
d						06 06												06 41			07 09	07 09	07 09	
Chester-le-Street 26 d																		06 52						
Durham 26 d						06 18												06 59			07 21	07 21	07 21	
Darlington 5 26 a						06 35												07 16						
d						06 36												07 17						
Redcar Central 44 d								06 07	06 07															
Middlesbrough 44 d								06 21	06 21															
Thornaby 44 d								06 27	06 27															
Yarm d								06 35	06 35															
Northallerton 26 d								06 50	06 50									07 28						
Thirsk 26 d								06 59	06 59															
Scarborough 43 d												06 34												
Seamer 43 d												06 39												
Malton d												06 58												
York 8 26 a						07 02		07 17	07 17			07 24						07 47			08 02	08 02	08 02	
d			06 49			07 05		07 19	07 19			07 27						07 50			08 04	08 04	08 04	
Hull 29 d													07 05											
Brough 29 d													07 17											
Howden 29 d													07 29											
Selby 29,40 d													07 40											
South Milford 40 d																								
Garforth 40 d												07 43	07 55											
Cross Gates 40 d												07 48												
Leeds 10 a			07 13			07 28		07 42	07 42			07 56	08 04					08 12			08 28	08 28	08 28	
d		07 12	07 15		07 17	07 30		07 45	07 45	07 47		08 00	08 07		08 12		08 12	08 15		08 17	08 30	08 30	08 30	
Cottingley d										07 52														
Morley d					07 25					07 56										08 25				
Batley d					07 30					08 01										08 30				
Dewsbury a			07 26		07 33			07 55	07 55	08 03								08 26		08 33				
d			07 27		07 34			07 57	07 57	08 04								08 27		08 34				
Ravensthorpe d										08 07														
Castleford d	06 58													07 58										
Normanton d	07 04													08 04										
Wakefield Kirkgate d	07 10													08 10										
Mirfield d	07 24				07 40					08 11				08 24						08 41				
Deighton d	07 30									08 17				08 30										
Huddersfield a	07 35		07 38			07 47		08 05	08 05	08 22		08 17	08 24	08 35				08 37			08 50	08 50	08 50	
d			07 39			07 48	07 53	08 08	08 08			08 18	08 25					08 38			08 50	08 51	08 51	08 54
Slaithwaite d							08 00						08 32											09 00
Marsden d							08 05						08 37											09 05
Greenfield d							08 14						08 45											09 14
Mossley (Grtr Manchester) d							08 18						08 49											09 18
Stalybridge a							08 22					08 36	08 53											09 22
d				08 00			08 22				08 30	08 37	08 54						09 00					09 22
Ashton-under-Lyne ⛴ d				08 04							08 34								09 04					
Manchester Victoria ⛴ a		08 42	08 08	08 15	08 53	08 20		08 38	08 38		08 45	08 50			09 40		09 45	09 08	09 15	09 54	09 21	09 21	09 21	
d			08 10			08 24		08 39	08 39			08 51						09 10			09 24	09 24	09 24	
Manchester Oxford Road a			08 15					08 45	08 45									09 15						
Manchester Piccadilly a			08 20				08 39	08 49	08 49				09 14					09 19						09 39
d			08 21					08 51	08 51									09 20						
Gatley a								09 01	09 01															
Manchester Airport ⛴✈ a			08 41					09 13	09 16									09 41						
Newton-le-Willows 90 a						08 40															09 40	09 40	09 40	
Lea Green 90 a												09 16												
Liverpool Lime Street 10 90 a						09 02						09 32									10 00	10 00	10 00	

Table T039-R

Mondays to Saturdays
17 February to 28 March

Newcastle, Middlesborough, Scarborough, York, Hull, Leeds and Wakefield - Huddersfield - Manchester, Manchester Airport and Liverpool

	TP	TP	GC	GC	NT	TP	TP		TP	NT	NT	TP	NT	NT	TP	TP	TP	TP	TP	NT	TP	TP	NT
			SX	SO			SO		SX						SX	SO							
	◇1 🍴	◇1	■ 1 ⊐	■ 1 ⊐		◇1 🍴	◇1 A 🍴		◇1 A 🍴		◇	◇1 🍴		◇	◇1 🍴	◇1 🍴	◇1	◇1 🍴	◇1		◇1 🍴	◇1 A 🍴	
Edinburgh 26 d															06 27	06 27							
Morpeth 26 d															07 44	07 44							
Newcastle 8 26 ⛴ a															07 58	08 02							
d												07 43			08 06	08 06							
Chester-le-Street 26 d												07 52											
Durham 26 d												07 59			08 18	08 18							
Darlington 5 26 a												08 16			08 35	08 35							
d												08 17			08 36	08 36							
Redcar Central 44 d	07 06																	08 07					
Middlesbrough 44 d	07 20																	08 20					
Thornaby 44 d	07 26																	08 27					
Yarm d	07 35																	08 35					
Northallerton 26 d	07 50		07 55	07 55								08 28						08 50					
Thirsk 26 d	07 59		08 03	08 04														08 59					
Scarborough 43 d						07 34															08 34		
Seamer 43 d						07 40															08 40		
Malton d						07 59															08 59		
York 8 26 a	08 17		08 21	08 21		08 24						08 47			09 02	09 02		09 17			09 24		
d	08 20					08 28						08 49			09 05	09 05		09 20			09 28		
Hull 29 d							08 07		08 07													09 08	
Brough 29 d							08 19		08 19													09 20	
Howden 29 d																							
Selby 29,40 d							08 40		08 40													09 40	
South Milford 40 d																							
Garforth 40 d						08 45	08 55		08 55												09 46		
Cross Gates 40 d						08 50																	
Leeds 10 a	08 42					08 57	09 04		09 04			09 12			09 27	09 27		09 43			09 56	10 03	
d	08 45	08 47				09 00	09 07		09 07		09 12	09 15		09 17	09 30	09 30		09 45	09 48		10 00	10 07	
Cottingley d		08 52																	09 53				
Morley d		08 56												09 26					09 57				
Batley d		09 01												09 31					10 02				
Dewsbury a	08 55	09 03										09 26		09 34				09 55	10 04				
d	08 57	09 04										09 27		09 35				09 57	10 05				
Ravensthorpe d		09 07																	10 08				
Castleford d										08 58													09 58
Normanton d										09 04													10 04
Wakefield Kirkgate d										09 10													10 10
Mirfield d		09 11								09 24				09 42					10 12				10 24
Deighton d		09 17								09 30									10 18				10 30
Huddersfield a	09 05	09 22				09 17	09 24		09 24	09 35		09 37			09 47	09 47		10 05	10 23		10 17	10 25	10 35
d	09 08					09 18	09 25		09 25			09 38			09 48	09 48	09 53	10 08			10 18	10 25	
Slaithwaite d																	10 00						
Marsden d																	10 05						
Greenfield d																	10 14						
Mossley (Grtr Manchester) d																	10 18						
Stalybridge a						09 36	09 43		09 43								10 22				10 36	10 43	
d					09 30	09 37	09 43		09 49				10 00				10 22			10 30	10 37	10 44	
Ashton-under-Lyne ⛴ d					09 34								10 04							10 34			
Manchester Victoria ⛴ a	09 38				09 44	09 51					10 29	10 08	10 15	10 53	10 21	10 21		10 38		10 44	10 51		
d	09 39					09 54						10 10			10 24	10 24		10 39			10 54		
Manchester Oxford Road a	09 45											10 15						10 45					
Manchester Piccadilly a	09 49						10 04		10 11			10 19					10 39	10 49				11 04	
d	09 51											10 20						10 51					
Gatley a	10 01																	11 01					
Manchester Airport ⛴✈ a	10 13											10 41						11 13					
Newton-le-Willows 90 a															10 40	10 40							
Lea Green 90 a						10 16															11 15		
Liverpool Lime Street 10 90 a						10 32									10 59	10 59					11 33		

A 🍴 from Leeds

Table T039-R

Mondays to Saturdays
17 February to 28 March

Newcastle, Middlesborough, Scarborough, York, Hull, Leeds and Wakefield - Huddersfield - Manchester, Manchester Airport and Liverpool

	NT	TP	GC	NT	NT	TP	TP	NT	TP	TP	GC	NT	TP	TP	NT		NT	NT	NT	TP	TP	TP	TP	NT
			SO								SX													
	◇	◇1 🍴	■ 1 ⊐		◇	◇1 🍴	◇1	◇	◇1 🍴	◇1	■ 1 ⊐		◇1 🍴	◇1 A 🍴				◇	◇	◇1 🍴	◇1	◇1 🍴	◇1	
Edinburgh 26 d																								
Morpeth 26 d																								
Newcastle 8 26 ⛴ a																								
d		08 43				09 06														10 06				
Chester-le-Street 26 d		08 52																						
Durham 26 d		08 59				09 18														10 18				
Darlington 5 26 a		09 16				09 35														10 35				
d		09 17				09 36														10 36				
Redcar Central 44 d									09 07													10 07		
Middlesbrough 44 d									09 21													10 21		
Thornaby 44 d									09 27													10 27		
Yarm d									09 35													10 35		
Northallerton 26 d			09 33						09 50		09 59											10 50		
Thirsk 26 d			09 42						09 59		10 08											10 59		
Scarborough 43 d													09 34											
Seamer 43 d													09 40											
Malton d													09 59											
York 8 26 a		09 48	09 59			10 02			10 17		10 24		10 24							11 02		11 17		
d		09 49				10 05			10 20				10 29							11 05		11 20		
Hull 29 d														10 08										
Brough 29 d														10 20										
Howden 29 d																								
Selby 29,40 d														10 40										
South Milford 40 d																								
Garforth 40 d													10 46											
Cross Gates 40 d																								
Leeds 10 a		10 12				10 27			10 42				10 56	11 03						11 27		11 42		
d	10 12	10 15			10 17	10 30		10 42	10 45	10 47			11 00	11 07				11 12	11 17	11 30		11 45	11 47	
Cottingley d										10 52													11 52	
Morley d					10 26					10 56									11 26				11 56	
Batley d					10 31					11 01									11 31				12 01	
Dewsbury a		10 26			10 34				10 55	11 03									11 34			11 55	12 03	
d		10 27			10 35				10 57	11 04									11 35			11 57	12 04	
Ravensthorpe d										11 07													12 07	
Castleford d																	10 58							
Normanton d																	11 04							
Wakefield Kirkgate d																	11 10							
Mirfield d					10 42					11 11							11 24		11 42				12 11	
Deighton d										11 17							11 30						12 17	
Huddersfield a		10 37				10 47			11 05	11 22			11 17	11 24			11 35			11 47		12 05	12 22	
d		10 38				10 48	10 53		11 08				11 18	11 25						11 48	11 53	12 08		
Slaithwaite d							11 00														12 00			
Marsden d							11 05														12 05			
Greenfield d							11 14														12 14			
Mossley (Grtr Manchester) d							11 18														12 18			
Stalybridge a							11 22						11 36	11 43							12 22			
d				11 00			11 22					11 30	11 39	11 43	12 00						12 22			12 31
Ashton-under-Lyne ⛴ d				11 04								11 34			12 04									12 35
Manchester Victoria ⛴ a	11 29	11 08		11 15	11 53	11 21		12 05	11 38			11 44	11 54		12 15			12 42	12 53	12 20		12 38		12 45
d		11 09				11 24			11 40				11 56							12 24		12 39		
Manchester Oxford Road a		11 15							11 45													12 45		
Manchester Piccadilly a		11 19					11 39		11 49					12 04							12 39	12 49		
d		11 20							11 51													12 51		
Gatley a									12 01													13 01		
Manchester Airport ⛴✈ a		11 41							12 13													13 13		
Newton-le-Willows 90 a						11 40														12 40				
Lea Green 90 a													12 16											
Liverpool Lime Street 10 90 a						12 02							12 32							12 59				

A 🍴 from Leeds

Table T039-R

Mondays to Saturdays

17 February to 28 March

Newcastle, Middlesborough, Scarborough, York, Hull, Leeds and Wakefield - Huddersfield - Manchester, Manchester Airport and Liverpool

			TP	TP	NT	NT	TP SX	TP SO	NT	NT SX	NT SO	TP SX	TP SO	TP	TP	TP	NT	TP SX	TP SO	TP	NT	NT	TP	NT
			◇1 🛒	◇1 A 🛒		◇	◇1 🛒	◇1 🛒		◇	◇	◇1 🛒	◇1 🛒	◇1	◇1 🛒	◇1		◇1 🛒	◇1 🛒	◇1 A 🛒		◇	◇1 🛒	
Edinburgh	26	d										09 33	09 33											
Morpeth	26	d										10 48	10 48											
Newcastle 8	26 ⛴	a										11 02	11 02											
		d					10 47	10 47				11 05	11 05										11 43	
Chester-le-Street	26	d																					11 52	
Durham	26	d					10 59	10 59				11 17	11 17										11 59	
Darlington 8	26	a					11 16	11 16				11 33	11 33										12 16	
		d					11 17	11 17				11 34	11 34										12 17	
Redcar Central	44	d													11 07									
Middlesbrough	44	d													11 21									
Thornaby	44	d													11 27									
Yarm		d													11 35									
Northallerton	26	d					11 28	11 28							11 50								12 28	
Thirsk	26	d													11 59									
Scarborough	43	d	10 34															11 34	11 34					
Seamer	43	d	10 40															11 40	11 40					
Malton		d	10 59															11 58	11 58					
York 8	26	a	11 24				11 47	11 47				12 01	12 01		12 17			12 24	12 24				12 47	
		d	11 28				11 49	11 50				12 04	12 04		12 20			12 28	12 28				12 49	
Hull	29	d		11 06																12 08				
Brough	29	d		11 18																12 20				
Howden	29	d																						
Selby	29,40	d		11 38																12 41				
South Milford	40	d																						
Garforth	40	d	11 46															12 46	12 46					
Cross Gates	40	d																						
Leeds 10		a	11 56	12 03			12 12	12 12				12 27	12 27		12 42			12 56	12 58	13 05			13 12	
		d	12 00	12 07		12 12	12 15	12 15		12 17	12 17	12 30	12 30		12 45	12 47		13 00	13 00	13 07		13 12	13 15	
Cottingley		d														12 52								
Morley		d								12 25	12 26					12 56								
Batley		d								12 30	12 31					13 01								
Dewsbury		a					12 26	12 26		12 33	12 34				12 55	13 03							13 26	
		d					12 27	12 27		12 33	12 35				12 57	13 04							13 27	
Ravensthorpe		d														13 07								
Castleford		d			11 58																12 58			
Normanton		d			12 04																13 04			
Wakefield Kirkgate		d			12 10																13 10			
Mirfield		d			12 24					12 40	12 45					13 11					13 24			
Deighton		d			12 30											13 17					13 30			
Huddersfield		a	12 17	12 24	12 35		12 37	12 37				12 47	12 47		13 05	13 22		13 17	13 17	13 24	13 35		13 37	
		d	12 18	12 25			12 38	12 38				12 48	12 49	12 53	13 08			13 18	13 18	13 25			13 38	
Slaithwaite		d												13 00										
Marsden		d												13 05										
Greenfield		d												13 14										
Mossley (Grtr Manchester)		d												13 18										
Stalybridge		a	12 36	12 43										13 22				13 36	13 36	13 43				
		d	12 37	12 43					13 00					13 22			13 30	13 37	13 37	13 43				14 00
Ashton-under-Lyne	⛴	d							13 04								13 34							14 04
Manchester Victoria	⛴	a	12 50			13 46	13 08	13 08	13 15	13 54	13 54	13 21	13 21		13 38		13 44	13 50	13 50			14 29	14 08	14 16
		d	12 54				13 10	13 10				13 24	13 24		13 39			13 54	13 54				14 10	
Manchester Oxford Road		a					13 15	13 15							13 45								14 15	
Manchester Piccadilly		a		13 04			13 20	13 20						13 39	13 49					14 04			14 19	
		d					13 20	13 20							13 51								14 20	
Gatley		a													14 01									
Manchester Airport	⛴✈	a					13 41	13 41							14 13								14 41	
Newton-le-Willows	90	a										13 40	13 40											
Lea Green	90	a	13 15															14 16	14 16					
Liverpool Lime Street 10	90	a	13 32									13 59	13 59					14 32	14 32					

A 🛒 from Leeds

Table T039-R

Mondays to Saturdays

17 February to 28 March

Newcastle, Middlesborough, Scarborough, York, Hull, Leeds and Wakefield - Huddersfield - Manchester, Manchester Airport and Liverpool

			NT	TP SX	TP SO	TP	NT	TP	TP	NT	TP	TP	GC SO	NT	NT	TP	GC SX	NT	NT	TP	TP	TP	TP	NT	TP
			◇	◇1 🛒	◇1 🛒	◇1	◇	◇1 🛒	◇1		◇1 🛒	◇1 A 🛒	▪ 1 ⊏P		◇	◇1 🛒	▪ 1 ⊏P		◇	◇1 🛒	◇1	◇1 🛒	◇1		◇1 🛒
Edinburgh	26	d		10 21	10 16															11 33					
Morpeth	26	d		11 33	11 48															12 46					
Newcastle 8	26 ⛴	a		11 53	12 02															13 00					
		d		12 06	12 06											12 45				13 06					
Chester-le-Street	26	d																							
Durham	26	d		12 18	12 18											12 59				13 18					
Darlington 8	26	a		12 35	12 35											13 16				13 35					
		d		12 36	12 36											13 17				13 36					
Redcar Central	44	d						12 07														13 07			
Middlesbrough	44	d						12 21														13 21			
Thornaby	44	d						12 27														13 27			
Yarm		d						12 35														13 35			
Northallerton	26	d						12 50					13 20			13 28	13 33					13 50			
Thirsk	26	d						12 59					13 29				13 43					13 59			
Scarborough	43	d									12 34														13 34
Seamer	43	d									12 40														13 40
Malton		d									12 58														13 58
York 8	26	a		13 02	13 02			13 17			13 24		13 46			13 48	13 59			14 02		14 17			14 24
		d		13 04	13 05			13 20			13 28					13 50				14 05		14 20			14 28
Hull	29	d										13 08													
Brough	29	d										13 20													
Howden	29	d																							
Selby	29,40	d										13 40													
South Milford	40	d																							
Garforth	40	d									13 46														14 46
Cross Gates	40	d																							
Leeds 10		a		13 27	13 27			13 43			13 56	14 03				14 13				14 27		14 42			14 56
		d	13 17	13 30	13 30		13 42	13 45	13 47		14 00	14 07			14 12	14 15			14 17	14 30		14 45	14 47		15 00
Cottingley		d							13 52														14 52		
Morley		d	13 26						13 56										14 26				14 56		
Batley		d	13 31						14 01										14 31				15 01		
Dewsbury		a	13 34					13 55	14 03							14 26			14 34			14 55	15 03		
		d	13 35					13 57	14 04							14 27			14 35			14 57	15 04		
Ravensthorpe		d							14 07														15 07		
Castleford		d												13 58											
Normanton		d												14 04											
Wakefield Kirkgate		d												14 10											
Mirfield		d	13 42						14 11					14 24					14 42				15 11		
Deighton		d							14 17					14 30									15 17		
Huddersfield		a		13 47	13 47			14 05	14 22		14 17	14 24		14 35		14 37				14 47		15 05	15 22		15 17
		d		13 48	13 48	13 53		14 08			14 18	14 24				14 38				14 48	14 53	15 08			15 18
Slaithwaite		d				14 00															15 00				
Marsden		d				14 05															15 05				
Greenfield		d				14 14															15 14				
Mossley (Grtr Manchester)		d				14 18															15 18				
Stalybridge		a				14 22					14 36	14 42									15 22				15 36
		d				14 22				14 30	14 37	14 43						15 01			15 22			15 30	15 37
Ashton-under-Lyne	⛴	d								14 34								15 05						15 34	
Manchester Victoria	⛴	a	14 53	14 20	14 20		15 06	14 38		14 44	14 50				15 29	15 08		15 16	15 53	15 21		15 38		15 44	15 51
		d		14 24	14 24			14 40			14 54					15 10				15 24		15 40			15 54
Manchester Oxford Road		a						14 45								15 15						15 45			
Manchester Piccadilly		a				14 39		14 49				15 04				15 19					15 39	15 49			
		d						14 51								15 20						15 51			
Gatley		a						15 01														16 01			
Manchester Airport	⛴✈	a						15 13								15 41						16 13			
Newton-le-Willows	90	a		14 40	14 40															15 40					
Lea Green	90	a									15 16														16 15
Liverpool Lime Street 10	90	a		14 59	14 59						15 32									16 00					16 32

A 🛒 from Leeds

Table T039-R

Mondays to Saturdays
17 February to 28 March

Newcastle, Middlesborough, Scarborough, York, Hull, Leeds and Wakefield - Huddersfield - Manchester, Manchester Airport and Liverpool

Station		TP SO	TP SX	NT	NT	TP SX	TP SO	NT		NT	TP SO	TP SX	TP	NT	TP SO	TP SX	TP	NT	TP	TP SX	TP SO	NT	NT	TP SO
		◇1 A 🛒	◇1 A 🛒		◇	◇1 🛒	◇1 🛒			◇	◇1 🛒	◇1 🛒	◇1	◇	◇1 🛒	◇1 🛒	◇1		◇1 🛒	◇1 A 🛒	◇1 A 🛒		◇	◇1 🛒
Edinburgh	26 d										12 33	12 33												
Morpeth	26 d										13 49	13 49												
Newcastle 8	26 ⛴ a										14 03	14 03												
	d					13 43	13 43				14 06	14 06												14 47
Chester-le-Street	26 d					13 51	13 51																	
Durham	26 d					13 58	13 58				14 18	14 18												14 59
Darlington 8	26 a					14 16	14 16				14 35	14 35												15 16
	d					14 17	14 17				14 36	14 36												15 17
Redcar Central	44 d														14 07	14 07								
Middlesbrough	44 d														14 21	14 21								
Thornaby	44 d														14 27	14 27								
Yarm	d														14 35	14 35								
Northallerton	26 d					14 28	14 28								14 50	14 50								15 28
Thirsk	26 d														14 59	14 59								
Scarborough	43 d																		14 34					
Seamer	43 d																		14 40					
Malton	d																		14 58					
York 8	26 a					14 47	14 47				15 02	15 02			15 17	15 17			15 24					15 47
	d					14 49	14 49				15 04	15 05			15 20	15 20			15 28					15 49
Hull	29 d	14 07	14 07																	15 03	15 08			
Brough	29 d	14 20	14 20																	15 15	15 20			
Howden	29 d																							
Selby	29,40 d	14 40	14 40																	15 36	15 40			
South Milford	40 d																							
Garforth	40 d																		15 46					
Cross Gates	40 d																							
Leeds 10	a	15 03	15 03			15 12	15 12				15 27	15 27			15 42	15 42			15 56	16 03	16 03			16 12
	d	15 07	15 07		15 12	15 15	15 15			15 17	15 30	15 30		15 42	15 45	15 45	15 47		16 00	16 07	16 07		16 12	16 15
Cottingley	d																15 52							
Morley	d									15 26							15 56							
Batley	d									15 31							16 01							
Dewsbury	a					15 26	15 26			15 34					15 55	15 55	16 03							16 26
	d					15 27	15 27			15 35					15 57	15 57	16 04							16 27
Ravensthorpe	d																16 07							
Castleford	d			14 58																		15 58		
Normanton	d			15 04																		16 04		
Wakefield Kirkgate	d			15 10																		16 10		
Mirfield	d			15 24						15 42							16 11					16 24		
Deighton	d			15 30													16 17					16 30		
Huddersfield	a	15 24	15 24	15 35		15 37	15 37				15 47	15 47			16 05	16 05	16 22		16 17	16 24	16 24	16 35		16 37
	d	15 25	15 25			15 38	15 38				15 48	15 48	15 53		16 08	16 08			16 18	16 25	16 25			16 38
Slaithwaite	d												16 00							16 32	16 32			
Marsden	d												16 05							16 37	16 37			
Greenfield	d												16 14							16 45	16 45			
Mossley (Grtr Manchester)	d												16 18							16 49	16 49			
Stalybridge	a	15 43	15 43										16 22						16 36	16 53	16 53			
	d	15 43	15 50					16 00					16 22					16 29	16 37	16 54	16 54			
Ashton-under-Lyne	⛴ d							16 04										16 33						
Manchester Victoria	⛴ a				16 29	16 08	16 08	16 15		16 54	16 20	16 20		17 05	16 38	16 38		16 44	16 51				17 34	17 08
	d					16 10	16 10				16 24	16 24			16 39	16 39			16 54					17 10
Manchester Oxford Road	a					16 15	16 15								16 45	16 45								17 15
Manchester Piccadilly	a	16 04	16 14			16 19	16 19						16 41		16 49	16 49				17 14	17 16			17 19
	d					16 20	16 20								16 51	16 51								17 20
Gatley	a														17 01	17 01								
Manchester Airport	⛴✈ a					16 40	16 41								17 13	17 16								17 40
Newton-le-Willows	90 a										16 41	16 40												
Lea Green	90 a																		17 16					
Liverpool Lime Street 10	90 a										17 01	16 59							17 32					

A 🛒 from Leeds

Table T039-R

Mondays to Saturdays
17 February to 28 March

Newcastle, Middlesborough, Scarborough, York, Hull, Leeds and Wakefield - Huddersfield - Manchester, Manchester Airport and Liverpool

Station		TP SX	NT	NT	TP SO	TP SX	TP	TP	TP	NT	TP	TP	NT	NT	TP	GC SO		GC SX	NT	NT	TP SO	TP SX	TP	TP	TP
		◇1 🛒		◇	◇1 🛒	◇1 🛒	◇1	◇1 🛒	◇1		◇1 🛒	◇1 A 🛒		◇	◇1 🛒	■ 1 ⊡		■ 1 ⊡		◇	◇1 🛒	◇1 🛒	◇1	◇1 🛒	◇1
Edinburgh	26 d				13 19	13 19															14 33	14 33			
Morpeth	26 d				14 37	14 32															15 47	15 47			
Newcastle 8	26 ⛴ a				14 52	14 50															16 01	16 02			
	d	14 47			15 03	15 03									15 43						16 06	16 06			
Chester-le-Street	26 d														15 52										
Durham	26 d	14 59			15 15	15 15									15 59						16 18	16 18			
Darlington 8	26 a	15 16			15 32	15 32									16 16						16 35	16 35			
	d	15 17			15 33	15 33									16 17						16 36	16 36			
Redcar Central	44 d							15 07																16 07	
Middlesbrough	44 d							15 21																16 21	
Thornaby	44 d							15 27																16 27	
Yarm	d							15 35																16 35	
Northallerton	26 d	15 28						15 50								16 33		16 33						16 50	
Thirsk	26 d							15 59								16 43		16 43						16 59	
Scarborough	43 d										15 34														
Seamer	43 d										15 40														
Malton	d										15 58														
York 8	26 a	15 47			15 59	15 59		16 17			16 24				16 48	16 59		17 00			17 02	17 02		17 17	
	d	15 50			16 01	16 01		16 20			16 28				16 49						17 04	17 04		17 20	
Hull	29 d											16 08													
Brough	29 d											16 20													
Howden	29 d																								
Selby	29,40 d											16 40													
South Milford	40 d																								
Garforth	40 d										16 46														
Cross Gates	40 d																								
Leeds 10	a	16 12			16 27	16 27		16 42			16 57	17 03			17 12						17 27	17 27		17 42	
	d	16 15		16 17	16 30	16 30		16 45	16 47		17 00	17 07		17 12	17 15					17 17	17 30	17 30		17 45	17 47
Cottingley	d								16 52											17 23					17 52
Morley	d			16 25					16 56											17 27					17 56
Batley	d			16 30					17 01											17 32					18 01
Dewsbury	a	16 26		16 33				16 55	17 03						17 26					17 35				17 55	18 03
	d	16 27		16 34				16 57	17 04						17 27					17 36				17 57	18 04
Ravensthorpe	d			16 37					17 07																18 07
Castleford	d												16 58												
Normanton	d												17 04												
Wakefield Kirkgate	d												17 10												
Mirfield	d			16 42					17 11				17 24							17 43					18 11
Deighton	d								17 17				17 30												18 17
Huddersfield	a	16 37			16 47	16 47		17 05	17 22		17 17	17 24	17 35		17 37						17 47	17 47		18 05	18 22
	d	16 38			16 48	16 48	16 53	17 08			17 21	17 25			17 38						17 48	17 48	17 54	18 08	
Slaithwaite	d						17 00					17 32											18 01		
Marsden	d						17 05					17 37											18 06		
Greenfield	d						17 14					17 45											18 15		
Mossley (Grtr Manchester)	d						17 18					17 49											18 19		
Stalybridge	a						17 22				17 40	17 53											18 23		
	d		17 00				17 22			17 31	17 41	17 54							18 00				18 23		
Ashton-under-Lyne	⛴ d		17 04							17 35									18 04						
Manchester Victoria	⛴ a	17 08	17 15	17 53	17 20	17 20		17 38		17 45	17 54			18 44	18 08				18 15	18 53	18 22	18 22		18 38	
	d	17 10			17 24	17 24		17 39			17 56				18 10						18 24	18 24		18 39	
Manchester Oxford Road	a	17 15						17 45							18 15									18 45	
Manchester Piccadilly	a	17 19					17 39	17 49				18 11			18 19								18 39	18 49	
	d	17 20						17 51							18 20									18 51	
Gatley	a							18 01																19 01	
Manchester Airport	⛴✈ a	17 40						18 14							18 41									19 16	
Newton-le-Willows	90 a				17 40	17 40															18 40	18 40			
Lea Green	90 a										18 16														
Liverpool Lime Street 10	90 a				17 59	18 02					18 33										19 01	19 01			

A 🛒 from Leeds

Table T039-R

Mondays to Saturdays
17 February to 28 March

Newcastle, Middlesborough, Scarborough, York, Hull, Leeds and Wakefield - Huddersfield - Manchester, Manchester Airport and Liverpool

		NT	TP SO	TP SX	TP SX	TP SO	NT	NT	TP	NT	NT	TP SX	TP SO	TP	TP	TP	NT	TP	TP	NT	NT	TP	GC SO
			◇1	◇1	◇1	◇1		◇	◇1		◇	◇1	◇1	◇1	◇1	◇1		◇1	◇1		◇	◇1	1
			⊼	⊼	A ⊼	A ⊼			⊼			⊼	⊼		⊼				A ⊼			⊼	▭
Edinburgh 26	d											15 33	15 33										
Morpeth 26	d											16 48	16 48										
Newcastle 26	a											17 03	17 03										
	d								16 43			17 06	17 06									17 43	
Chester-le-Street 26	d								16 52													17 52	
Durham 26	d								16 59			17 18	17 18									17 59	
Darlington 26	a								17 15			17 35	17 35									18 16	
	d								17 17			17 36	17 36									18 17	
Redcar Central 44	d														17 07								
Middlesbrough 44	d														17 21								
Thornaby 44	d														17 27								
Yarm	d														17 35								
Northallerton 26	d								17 28						17 50							18 28	18 32
Thirsk 26	d														17 59								18 43
Scarborough 43	d		16 34	16 34														17 34					
Seamer 43	d		16 40	16 40														17 40					
Malton	d		16 58	16 58														17 58					
York 26	a		17 24	17 25					17 47			18 02	18 02		18 17			18 24				18 47	18 59
	d		17 28	17 28					17 49			18 05	18 05		18 18			18 28				18 49	
Hull 29	d				17 03	17 08													18 08				
Brough 29	d				17 15	17 20													18 20				
Howden 29	d																						
Selby 29,40	d				17 37	17 40													18 40				
South Milford 40	d																						
Garforth 40	d		17 46	17 46														18 45					
Cross Gates 40	d																						
Leeds	a		17 56	17 56	18 03	18 03			18 12			18 27	18 27		18 42			18 55	19 04			19 12	
	d		18 00	18 00	18 07	18 07		18 12	18 15		18 17	18 29	18 29		18 45	18 47		19 00	19 07		19 12	19 15	
Cottingley	d															18 52							
Morley	d										18 25					18 56							
Batley	d										18 30					19 01							
Dewsbury	a								18 26		18 33				18 55	19 03						19 26	
	d								18 27		18 33				18 57	19 04						19 27	
Ravensthorpe	d															19 07							
Castleford	d						17 58													18 58			
Normanton	d						18 04													19 04			
Wakefield Kirkgate	d						18 10													19 10			
Mirfield	d						18 24				18 40					19 11				19 24			
Deighton	d						18 30									19 17				19 30			
Huddersfield	a		18 17	18 17	18 24	18 24	18 35		18 37			18 46	18 46		19 05	19 22		19 17	19 24	19 35		19 37	
	d		18 18	18 18	18 25	18 25			18 38			18 48	18 48	18 53	19 08			19 18	19 25			19 38	
Slaithwaite	d				18 32	18 32								19 00									
Marsden	d				18 37	18 37								19 05									
Greenfield	d				18 45	18 45								19 14									
Mossley (Grtr Manchester)	d				18 49	18 49								19 18									
Stalybridge	a		18 36	18 36	18 53	18 53								19 22				19 36	19 43				
	d	18 31	18 37	18 37	18 54	18 54				19 00				19 22			19 31	19 37	19 43				
Ashton-under-Lyne	d	18 35								19 04							19 35						
Manchester Victoria	a	18 47	18 52	18 52				19 29	19 08	19 15	19 53	19 20	19 20		19 38		19 46	19 50			20 29	20 09	
	d		18 54	18 54					19 10			19 24	19 24		19 39			19 54				20 10	
Manchester Oxford Road	a								19 15						19 45							20 15	
Manchester Piccadilly	a				19 14	19 11			19 19					19 39	19 49				20 04			20 19	
	d								19 20						19 51							20 20	
Gatley	a														20 01								
Manchester Airport	a								19 42						20 13							20 40	
Newton-le-Willows 90	a											19 40	19 40					20 12					
Lea Green 90	a		19 17	19 17								19 47	19 47					20 19					
Liverpool Lime Street 90	a		19 33	19 33								20 03	20 05					20 35					

A ⊼ from Leeds

NRT DECEMBER 19 EDITION

Table T039-R

Mondays to Saturdays
17 February to 28 March

Newcastle, Middlesborough, Scarborough, York, Hull, Leeds and Wakefield - Huddersfield - Manchester, Manchester Airport and Liverpool

		NT	NT	TP SO	TP SX	TP	GC SX	TP	TP	NT	TP SO	TP SX	TP SX	TP SO	TP SX	TP SX	NT	NT	TP	NT	NT	TP SO	TP SX	TP
			◇	◇1	◇1	◇1	1	◇1	◇1		◇1	◇1	◇1	◇1	◇1	◇1		◇	◇1		◇	◇1	◇1	◇1
				⊼	⊼		▭							A ⊼		⊼			⊼			⊼	⊼	
Edinburgh 26	d			16 21	16 33																	17 32	17 32	
Morpeth 26	d			17 48	17 48																	18 52	18 52	
Newcastle 26	a			18 04	18 04																	19 06	19 06	
	d			18 07	18 07														18 43			19 09	19 09	
Chester-le-Street 26	d																		18 52					
Durham 26	d			18 19	18 19														19 00			19 21	19 21	
Darlington 26	a			18 36	18 36														19 16					
	d			18 37	18 37														19 17					
Redcar Central 44	d							18 07																
Middlesbrough 44	d							18 21																
Thornaby 44	d							18 27																
Yarm	d							18 35																
Northallerton 26	d						18 41	18 50											19 28					
Thirsk 26	d						18 51	18 59																
Scarborough 43	d										18 34	18 34												
Seamer 43	d										18 40	18 40												
Malton	d										18 58	18 58												
York 26	a			19 03	19 03		19 09	19 17			19 24	19 24							19 47			20 02	20 02	
	d			19 06	19 06			19 20			19 28	19 28							19 49			20 05	20 05	
Hull 29	d												19 03	19 08										
Brough 29	d												19 15	19 20										
Howden 29	d																							
Selby 29,40	d												19 38	19 40										
South Milford 40	d																							
Garforth 40	d										19 46	19 46												
Cross Gates 40	d															←								
Leeds	a			19 28	19 28			19 42			19 56	19 56	20 03	20 03		20 03			20 12			20 27	20 27	
	d		19 17	19 30	19 30			19 45	19 47		20 00	20 00	20 07	20 07		20 07		20 12	20 15		20 18	20 30	20 30	
Cottingley	d								19 52				→											
Morley	d		19 25						19 56												20 26			
Batley	d		19 30						20 01												20 31			
Dewsbury	a		19 33					19 55	20 03										20 26		20 34			
	d		19 34					19 57	20 04										20 27		20 35			
Ravensthorpe	d								20 07															
Castleford	d																19 58							
Normanton	d																20 04							
Wakefield Kirkgate	d																20 10							
Mirfield	d		19 41						20 11								20 24				20 42			
Deighton	d								20 17								20 30							
Huddersfield	a			19 47	19 47			20 05	20 22		20 17	20 17		20 24		20 24	20 35		20 37			20 47	20 47	
	d			19 48	19 48	19 53		20 08			20 18	20 18		20 25		20 25			20 38			20 48	20 48	20 53
Slaithwaite	d					20 00																		21 00
Marsden	d					20 05																		21 05
Greenfield	d					20 14																		21 14
Mossley (Grtr Manchester)	d					20 18									←									21 18
Stalybridge	a					20 22					20 36	20 45		20 43	20 45	20 48								21 22
	d	20 00				20 22				20 31	20 37	20 46		20 46	20 46	20 53				21 00				21 22
Ashton-under-Lyne	d	20 04								20 35		→								21 04				
Manchester Victoria	a	20 15	20 53	20 21	20 21			20 38		20 46	20 52				21 01			21 46	21 11	21 14	21 54	21 19	21 22	
	d			20 24	20 24			20 39														21 24	21 24	
Manchester Oxford Road	a							20 45																
Manchester Piccadilly	a					20 39		20 49						21 04		21 15								21 39
	d							20 51																
Gatley	a							21 01																
Manchester Airport	a							21 11																
Newton-le-Willows 90	a																					21 40	21 40	
Lea Green 90	a																					21 47	21 46	
Liverpool Lime Street 90	a			20 56	20 56																	22 05	22 05	

A ⊼ from Leeds

Table T039-R

Mondays to Saturdays

17 February to 28 March

Newcastle, Middlesborough, Scarborough, York, Hull, Leeds and Wakefield - Huddersfield - Manchester, Manchester Airport and Liverpool

		NT	TP	TP	NT	TP	TP	TP	NT	NT	NT	NT	NT	TP	TP	TP	NT	NT	TP	TP	TP	TP	TP
						SX	SO		SX		SO			SO	SX					SO	SX		
		◇	◇1	◇1		◇1	◇1	◇1				◇	◇	◇1	◇1	◇1		◇	◇1	◇1	◇1	◇1	◇1
								A						B	B								A
Edinburgh 26	d													18 33	18 11								
Morpeth 26	d													19 47	19 33								
Newcastle 26	a													20 01	19 47								
	d													20 06	20 06								
Chester-le-Street 26	d																						
Durham 26	d													20 18	20 18								
Darlington 26	a													20 35	20 35								
	d													20 36	20 36								
Redcar Central 44	d		19 07																			20 07	
Middlesbrough 44	d		19 21																			20 21	
Thornaby 44	d		19 27																			20 27	
Yarm	d		19 35																			20 39	
Northallerton 26	d		19 50																			20 54	
Thirsk 26	d		19 59																			21 05	
Scarborough 43	d					19 34	19 34													20 34	20 34		
Seamer 43	d					19 40	19 40													20 40	20 40		
Malton	d					19 58	19 58													20 58	20 58		
York 26	a		20 17			20 24	20 25							21 02	21 02					21 24	21 24	21 25	
	d		20 20			20 28	20 28							21 05	21 05					21 28	21 28		
Hull 29	d							20 08															21 08
Brough 29	d							20 20															21 20
Howden 29	d																						
Selby 29,40	d							20 41															21 40
South Milford 40	d																						
Garforth 40	d					20 46	20 46													21 46	21 46		
Cross Gates 40	d																						
Leeds 10	a		20 43			20 56	20 56	21 03						21 27	21 27					21 56	21 56		22 03
	d	20 42	20 45	20 47		21 00	21 00	21 07				21 12	21 17	21 30	21 30			21 42	21 47	22 00	22 00		22 07
Cottingley	d			20 52															21 52				
Morley	d			20 56									21 25						21 56				
Batley	d			21 01									21 30						22 01				
Dewsbury	a		20 55	21 03				21 17					21 33	21 41	21 41				22 03				22 17
	d		20 57	21 04				21 18					21 34	21 42	21 42				22 04				22 18
Ravensthorpe	d			21 07															22 07				
Castleford	d									20 58													
Normanton	d									21 04													
Wakefield Kirkgate	d									21 10													
Mirfield	d			21 11						21 24			21 41						22 11				
Deighton	d			21 17						21 30									22 17				
Huddersfield	a		21 05	21 22		21 17	21 17	21 26		21 35				21 50	21 50				22 22	22 17	22 17		22 26
	d		21 08			21 18	21 18	21 31						21 51	21 51	21 56				22 18	22 18		22 27
Slaithwaite	d															22 03							
Marsden	d															22 08							
Greenfield	d															22 17							
Mossley (Grtr Manchester)	d															22 21							
Stalybridge	a					21 39	21 39	21 51								22 25				22 39	22 39		22 45
	d				21 29	21 40	21 40	21 51	22 02		22 03					22 25	22 31			22 40	22 40		22 46
Ashton-under-Lyne	d				21 33				22 05		22 06						22 35						
Manchester Victoria	a	22 06	21 40		21 44	21 54	21 54		22 17		22 18	22 35	22 55	22 23	22 25		22 46	23 08		22 53	22 53		23 00
	d					21 56	21 56							22 24	22 26					22 55	22 55		23 02
Manchester Oxford Road	a					22 02	22 02													23 00	23 01		
Manchester Piccadilly	a					22 06	22 06	22 10								22 44				23 04	23 05		
	d					22 07	22 07													23 05	23 12		
Gatley	a																						
Manchester Airport	a					22 22	22 22													23 20	23 28		
Newton-le-Willows 90	a													22 40	22 46								
Lea Green 90	a													22 47	22 54								23 23
Liverpool Lime Street 10 90	a													23 06	23 14								23 43

A from Leeds B from York

Table T039-R

Mondays to Saturdays

17 February to 28 March

Newcastle, Middlesborough, Scarborough, York, Hull, Leeds and Wakefield - Huddersfield - Manchester, Manchester Airport and Liverpool

		NT	NT	NT	NT	NT	TP	TP	TP	TP	TP	NT	TP	TP	TP	TP	TP	TP	TP	TP	TP	NT	TP	TP
		SO		SX				SX	SO	SX			SX	SO		SO	SX	SO	SX	SO	SX		SO	SX
					◇		◇1	◇1	◇1	◇1	◇1	◇	◇1	◇1	◇1	◇1	◇1	1	◇1	◇1	◇1		◇1	◇1
								A	A										B	B				
Edinburgh 26	d							19 30	19 30															
Morpeth 26	d							20 45	20 45															
Newcastle 26	a							20 59	20 59															
	d							21 02	21 02							22 00		22 30						
Chester-le-Street 26	d							21 11	21 11									22 40						
Durham 26	d							21 18	21 18							22 15		22a46						
Darlington 26	a							21 35	21 35							22 32								
	d							21 36	21 36							22 33								
Redcar Central 44	d										21 07													
Middlesbrough 44	d										21 21													
Thornaby 44	d										21 27													
Yarm	d										21 35													
Northallerton 26	d										21 50					22 44								
Thirsk 26	d										21 59													
Scarborough 43	d														21 34		22 15						22 15	
Seamer 43	d														21 40		22 20						22 20	
Malton	d														21 58		22 39						22 39	
York 26	a							22 02	22 02		22 19				22 24	23 03	23 04						23 04	
	d							22 05	22 05						22 28								23 05	
Hull 29	d																		22 08	22 08				
Brough 29	d																		22 20	22 20				
Howden 29	d																							
Selby 29,40	d																		22 40	22 40				
South Milford 40	d																							
Garforth 40	d														22 47									
Cross Gates 40	d									←														
Leeds 10	a							22 26	22 27	22 26					22 58				23 03	23 03			23 27	
	d				22 12	22 21		22 28	22 28	22 28		22 42	22 46	22 47	23 00				23 05	23 07			23 30	23 47
Cottingley	d							→					22 52	22 52										23 52
Morley	d					22 29							22 56	22 56										23 56
Batley	d					22 34							23 01	23 01							←			00 02
Dewsbury	a					22 37			22 41	22 41			23 03	23 03					23 15		23 15		23 40	00 03
	d					22 38			22 42	22 42			23 04	23 04					23 18		23 18		23 41	00 04
Ravensthorpe	d												23 07	23 07					→					00 07
Castleford	d		21 58																			22 58		
Normanton	d		22 04																			23 04		
Wakefield Kirkgate	d		22 10																			23 11		
Mirfield	d		22 24			22a44							23 11	23 11								23 25		00 11
Deighton	d		22 30										23 18	23 18								23 31		00 17
Huddersfield	a		22 35						22 50	22 50			23 22	23 22	23 17					23 24	23 26	23 36	23 50	00 22
	d						22 46		22 51	22 51					23 18					23 25	23 27		23 51	
Slaithwaite	d						22 52													23 32	23 33			
Marsden	d						23 04													23 37	23 37			
Greenfield	d						23 13													23 46	23 46			
Mossley (Grtr Manchester)	d						23 17													23 50	23 50			
Stalybridge	a						23 21								23 36					23 54	23 54			
	d	23 00		23 03			23 24								23 37					23 54	23 54			
Ashton-under-Lyne	d	23 03		23 06																				
Manchester Victoria	a	23 14		23 16	23 37				23 23	23 23		00 11			23 50									
	d								23 24	23 25					23 52									
Manchester Oxford Road	a														23 57									
Manchester Piccadilly	a						23 41								00 01					00 14	00 11		00 25	
	d														00 03									
Gatley	a																							
Manchester Airport	a														00 19									
Newton-le-Willows 90	a								23 40	23 41														
Lea Green 90	a								23 47	23 47														
Liverpool Lime Street 10 90	a								00 05	00 05														

A from York B from Leeds

Table T039-R

Mondays to Saturdays

17 February to 28 March

Newcastle, Middlesborough, Scarborough, York, Hull, Leeds and Wakefield - Huddersfield - Manchester, Manchester Airport and Liverpool

Station			TP	TP SO	TP	TP SX	TP WO	TP SX
			◇1 🛒	◇1	◇1	◇1	◇1 🛒	◇1 🛒
Edinburgh	26	d					22 12	
Morpeth	26	d						
Newcastle 8	26 ⛴	a						
		d						
Chester-le-Street	26	d						
Durham	26	d						
Darlington 5	26	a						
		d						
Redcar Central	44	d	22 07					23 07
Middlesbrough	44	d	22 21					23 22
Thornaby	44	d	22 27					23 28
Yarm		d	22 35					23 37
Northallerton	26	d	22 50					23 54
Thirsk	26	d	22 59					00 03
Scarborough	43	d		22 45		22 45		
Seamer	43	d		22 51		22 51		
Malton		d		23 11		23 11		
York 8	26	a	23 19	23 35		23 35		00 29
		d				23 39		
Hull	29	d			23 08			
Brough	29	d			23 20			
Howden	29	d						
Selby	29,40	d			23 40			
South Milford	40	d						
Garforth	40	d						
Cross Gates	40	d						
Leeds 10		a			00 04	00 06		
		d				00 07		
Cottingley		d						
Morley		d						
Batley		d						
Dewsbury		a						
		d						
Ravensthorpe		d						
Castleford		d						
Normanton		d						
Wakefield Kirkgate		d						
Mirfield		d						
Deighton		d						
Huddersfield		a						
		d						
Slaithwaite		d						
Marsden		d						
Greenfield		d						
Mossley (Grtr Manchester)		d						
Stalybridge		a						
		d						
Ashton-under-Lyne	⛴	d						
Manchester Victoria	⛴	a						
		d						
Manchester Oxford Road		a						
Manchester Piccadilly		a				01 06	01 42	
		d						
Gatley		a						
Manchester Airport	⛴✈	a						
Newton-le-Willows	90	a						
Lea Green	90	a						
Liverpool Lime Street 10	90	a						

NRT DECEMBER 19 EDITION

Table T039-R

Mondays to Saturdays

30 March to 16 May

Newcastle, Middlesborough, Scarborough, York, Hull, Leeds and Wakefield - Huddersfield - Manchester, Manchester Airport and Liverpool

Station			TP	TP MX	TP MO	TP MX	TP MO	TP SO	TP MSX	TP SO	TP MO	TP MSX	TP MSX	TP SO	TP MO	TP MSX	TP SX		TP SO	TP SX	TP SO	TP SX	TP	TP	NT	NT SO
			◇1	◇1 🛒	◇1	◇1	◇1	◇1	◇1	◇1	◇1	◇1	◇1	◇1	◇1	◇1	◇1		◇1	◇1	◇1	◇1	◇1	◇1		◇
Edinburgh	26	d																								
Morpeth	26	d																								
Newcastle 8	26 ⛴	a																								
		d					00 08	00 08	00 08																	
Chester-le-Street	26	d																								
Durham	26	d					00 21	00 21	00 21																	
Darlington 5	26	a					00 38	00 38	00 38																	
		d					00 40	00 40	00 40																	
Redcar Central	44	d																								
Middlesbrough	44	d																								
Thornaby	44	d																								
Yarm		d																								
Northallerton	26	d																								
Thirsk	26	d		00 03																						
Scarborough	43	d																								
Seamer	43	d																								
Malton		d																								
York 8	26	a		00 29			01 36	01 36	01 36																	
		d					01 38	01 38	01 38				02 47	02 52	02 52		03 40		03 40				04 27			
Hull	29	d																								
Brough	29	d																								
Howden	29	d																								
Selby	29,40	d																								
South Milford	40	d																								
Garforth	40	d																								
Cross Gates	40	d														←										
Leeds 10		a					02 05	02 18	02 18				03 27	03 18	03 19	03 27	04 05		04 19				04 53			
		d			00 05	00 07	02 05	02 18	02 20				03 35	03 19	03 20	03 35	04 08		04 31				05 03			05 12
Cottingley		d											→													
Morley		d																								
Batley		d	00 02																							
Dewsbury		a	00 03																							
		d	00 04																							
Ravensthorpe		d	00 07																							
Castleford		d																								
Normanton		d																								
Wakefield Kirkgate		d																								
Mirfield		d	00 11																							
Deighton		d	00 17							←																
Huddersfield		a	00 22				02 40	02 56	02 40	02 56				03 55	03 55	03 56	04 41		05 03				05 35			
		d					02 41	02 56	02 41	02 56				03 55	03 58	03 58	04 51		05 04				05 37			
Slaithwaite		d						→																		
Marsden		d																								
Greenfield		d																								
Mossley (Grtr Manchester)		d																								
Stalybridge		a																								
		d																						06 00	06 03	
Ashton-under-Lyne	⛴	d																		←					06 07	
Manchester Victoria	⛴	a															05 35		05 34	05 35			06 09	06 14	06 18	06 30
		d															05 39		05 37	05 39	05 54	05 54	06 10	06 19		
Manchester Oxford Road		a									←	←					→		05 44	05 45			06 16			
Manchester Piccadilly		a			01 23	01 06	03 41		03 41	03 29	03 41	03 41		04 27	04 56	04 56			05 49	05 49			06 20			
		d					03 43		03 43	03 34	03 43	03 43		04 34	04 57	04 57			05 50	05 50			06 20			
Gatley		a					→		→										06 01	06 01						
Manchester Airport	⛴✈	a								03 51	03 59	03 59		04 52	05 13	05 13			06 13	06 13			06 41			
Newton-le-Willows	90	a																			06 11	06 13		06 38		
Lea Green	90	a																			06 17	06 19		06 45		
Liverpool Lime Street 10	90	a																			06 32	06 34		07 03		

Table T039-R

Mondays to Saturdays

30 March to 16 May

Newcastle, Middlesborough, Scarborough, York, Hull, Leeds and Wakefield - Huddersfield - Manchester, Manchester Airport and Liverpool

			NT SX ◇	TP ◇1	NT ◇	TP ◇1	NT	TP ◇1	TP SO ◇1 A 🛒	TP SX ◇1 A 🛒	NT ◇	TP ◇1	NT	NT ◇	TP ◇1 B 🛒	TP ◇1	TP SX ◇1	TP SO ◇1	TP ◇1	NT	TP SO ◇1 🛒	TP SX ◇1 🛒	TP SX ◇1	TP SO ◇1
Edinburgh	26	d																						
Morpeth	26	d																						
Newcastle 8	26 ⇌	a																						
		d													05 06									
Chester-le-Street	26	d																						
Durham	26	d													05 18									
Darlington 5	26	a													05 35									
		d													05 36									
Redcar Central	44	d																						
Middlesbrough	44	d															05 12	05 19						
Thornaby	44	d															05 17	05 25						
Yarm		d															05 25	05 33						
Northallerton	26	d															05 41	05 50						
Thirsk	26	d															05 51	05 58						
Scarborough	43	d																			05 34	05 34		
Seamer	43	d																			05 40	05 40		
Malton		d																			05 59	05 59		
York 8	26	a													06 02		06 09	06 16			06 24	06 24		
		d				05 15		05 28				05 49			06 05		06 18	06 18			06 28	06 28		
Hull	29	d							05 06	05 06													06 04	06 04
Brough	29	d							05 18	05 18													06 16	06 16
Howden	29	d							05 32	05 32														
Selby	29,40	d							05 42	05 42													06 37	06 37
South Milford	40	d																						
Garforth	40	d						05 48													06 47	06 47	06 52	06 52
Cross Gates	40	d																					06 57	06 57
Leeds 10		a				05 42		05 58	06 04	06 04		06 12			06 28		06 42	06 42			06 57	06 57	07 04	07 04
		d	05 12		05 19	05 45		06 00	06 07	06 07	06 12	06 15		06 17	06 30		06 45	06 45	06 47		07 00	07 00	07 07	07 07
Cottingley		d			05 25														06 52					
Morley		d			05 29									06 25					06 56					
Batley		d			05 34									06 30					07 01					
Dewsbury		a			05 37	05 55						06 26		06 33			06 55	06 55	07 03					
		d			05 38	05 57						06 27		06 34			06 57	06 57	07 04					
Ravensthorpe		d			05 41														07 07					
Castleford		d																						
Normanton		d																						
Wakefield Kirkgate		d		05 24																				
Mirfield		d		05 37	05 45									06 40					07 11					
Deighton		d		05 47															07 17					
Huddersfield		a		05 51		06 06		06 17	06 24	06 24		06 35			06 47		07 05	07 05	07 22		07 17	07 17	07 24	07 24
		d		05 54		06 08		06 18	06 25	06 25		06 36			06 48	06 53	07 08	07 08			07 18	07 18	07 25	07 25
Slaithwaite		d		06 01					06 32	06 32						07 00							07 32	07 32
Marsden		d		06 06					06 37	06 37						07 05							07 37	07 37
Greenfield		d		06 15					06 46	06 46						07 14							07 45	07 45
Mossley (Grtr Manchester)		d		06 19					06 50	06 50						07 18							07 49	07 49
Stalybridge		a		06 23				06 36	06 54	06 54						07 22					07 36	07 36	07 53	07 53
		d		06 23			06 30	06 37	06 54	06 54			07 00			07 22				07 32	07 37	07 37	07 54	07 54
Ashton-under-Lyne	⇌	d					06 34						07 04							07 36				
Manchester Victoria	⇌	a	06 31		06 53	06 38	06 46	06 50			07 30	07 09	07 15	07 52	07 22		07 38	07 38		07 46	07 52	07 52		
		d				06 39		06 52				07 10			07 24		07 39	07 39			07 54	07 54		
Manchester Oxford Road		a				06 47						07 16					07 45	07 45						
Manchester Piccadilly		a		06 38		06 53			07 11	07 17		07 20				07 39	07 49	07 49					08 13	08 14
		d				06 55						07 21					07 50	07 50						
Gatley		a				07 03											08 01	08 01						
Manchester Airport	⇌✈	a				07 16						07 41					08 16	08 16						
Newton-le-Willows	90	a						07 08							07 40									
Lea Green	90	a						07 14													08 14	08 14		
Liverpool Lime Street 10	90	a						07 30							08 00						08 33	08 36		

A 🛒 from Leeds

B 🛒 from York

Table T039-R

Mondays to Saturdays

30 March to 16 May

Newcastle, Middlesborough, Scarborough, York, Hull, Leeds and Wakefield - Huddersfield - Manchester, Manchester Airport and Liverpool

			NT	NT ◇	TP ◇1 🛒	NT	NT ◇	TP ◇1 🛒	TP ◇1	TP SO ◇1 🛒	TP SX ◇1 🛒	TP ◇1	NT	TP ◇1 🛒	TP ◇1 🛒	NT	NT SX ◇	NT SO ◇	TP ◇1 🛒	NT	NT ◇	TP SO ◇1 🛒	TP MSX ◇1 🛒	TP MO ◇1 🛒	TP ◇1
Edinburgh	26	d																				05 14	05 14	05 17	
Morpeth	26	d																				06 43	06 43	06 43	
Newcastle 8	26 ⇌	a																				06 57	06 57	06 57	
		d						06 06											06 41			07 09	07 09	07 09	
Chester-le-Street	26	d																	06 52						
Durham	26	d						06 18											06 59			07 21	07 21	07 21	
Darlington 5	26	a						06 35											07 16						
		d						06 36											07 17						
Redcar Central	44	d								06 07	06 07														
Middlesbrough	44	d								06 21	06 21														
Thornaby	44	d								06 27	06 27														
Yarm		d								06 35	06 35														
Northallerton	26	d								06 50	06 50								07 28						
Thirsk	26	d								06 59	06 59														
Scarborough	43	d												06 34											
Seamer	43	d												06 39											
Malton		d												06 58											
York 8	26	a						07 02		07 17	07 17			07 24					07 47			08 02	08 02	08 02	
		d			06 49			07 05		07 19	07 19			07 27					07 50			08 04	08 04	08 04	
Hull	29	d													07 05										
Brough	29	d													07 17										
Howden	29	d													07 29										
Selby	29,40	d													07 40										
South Milford	40	d																							
Garforth	40	d												07 43	07 55										
Cross Gates	40	d												07 48											
Leeds 10		a			07 13			07 28		07 42	07 42			07 56	08 04				08 12			08 28	08 28	08 28	
		d		07 12	07 15		07 17	07 30		07 45	07 45	07 47		08 00	08 07		08 12	08 12	08 15		08 17	08 30	08 30	08 30	
Cottingley		d										07 52													
Morley		d					07 25					07 56									08 25				
Batley		d					07 30					08 01									08 30				
Dewsbury		a			07 26		07 33			07 55	07 55	08 03							08 26		08 33				
		d			07 27		07 34			07 57	07 57	08 04							08 27		08 34				
Ravensthorpe		d										08 07													
Castleford		d	06 58													07 58									
Normanton		d	07 04													08 04									
Wakefield Kirkgate		d	07 10													08 10									
Mirfield		d	07 24				07 40					08 11				08 24					08 41				
Deighton		d	07 30									08 17				08 30									
Huddersfield		a	07 35		07 38			07 47		08 05	08 05	08 22		08 17	08 24	08 35			08 37			08 50	08 50	08 50	
		d			07 39			07 48	07 53	08 08	08 08			08 18	08 25				08 38			08 50	08 51	08 51	08 54
Slaithwaite		d							08 00						08 32										09 00
Marsden		d							08 05						08 37										09 05
Greenfield		d							08 14						08 45										09 14
Mossley (Grtr Manchester)		d							08 18						08 49										09 18
Stalybridge		a							08 22					08 36	08 53										09 22
		d				08 00			08 22				08 30	08 37	08 54					09 00					09 22
Ashton-under-Lyne	⇌	d				08 04							08 34							09 04					
Manchester Victoria	⇌	a		08 42	08 08	08 15	08 53	08 20		08 38	08 38		08 45	08 50			09 40	09 45	09 08	09 15	09 54	09 21	09 21	09 21	
		d			08 10			08 24		08 39	08 39			08 51					09 10			09 24	09 24	09 24	
Manchester Oxford Road		a			08 15					08 45	08 45								09 15						
Manchester Piccadilly		a			08 20				08 39	08 49	08 49				09 14				09 19						09 39
		d			08 21					08 51	08 51								09 20						
Gatley		a								09 01	09 01														
Manchester Airport	⇌✈	a			08 41					09 13	09 16								09 41						
Newton-le-Willows	90	a						08 40														09 40	09 40	09 40	
Lea Green	90	a												09 16											
Liverpool Lime Street 10	90	a						09 02						09 32								10 00	10 00	10 00	

Table T039-R

Mondays to Saturdays
30 March to 16 May

Newcastle, Middlesborough, Scarborough, York, Hull, Leeds and Wakefield - Huddersfield - Manchester, Manchester Airport and Liverpool

			TP	TP	GC SX	GC SO	NT	TP	TP SO	TP SX	NT	NT	TP	NT	NT	TP SX	TP SO	TP	TP	TP	NT	TP	TP	NT
			◇1 🛒	◇1	■ 1 ☕	■ 1 ☕		◇1 🛒	◇1 A 🛒	◇1 A 🛒		◇	◇1 🛒		◇	◇1 🛒	◇1 🛒	◇1	◇1 🛒	◇1		◇1 🛒	◇1 A 🛒	
Edinburgh	26	d														06 27	06 27							
Morpeth	26	d														07 44	07 44							
Newcastle 8	26 ⛴	a														07 58	08 02							
		d											07 43			08 06	08 06							
Chester-le-Street	26	d											07 52											
Durham	26	d											07 59			08 18	08 18							
Darlington 5	26	a											08 16			08 35	08 35							
		d											08 17			08 36	08 36							
Redcar Central	44	d	07 06																08 07					
Middlesbrough	44	d	07 20																08 20					
Thornaby	44	d	07 26																08 27					
Yarm		d	07 35																08 35					
Northallerton	26	d	07 50		07 55	07 55							08 28						08 50					
Thirsk	26	d	07 59		08 03	08 04													08 59					
Scarborough	43	d						07 34														08 34		
Seamer	43	d						07 40														08 40		
Malton		d						07 59														08 59		
York 8	26	a	08 17		08 21	08 21		08 24					08 47			09 02	09 02		09 17			09 24		
		d	08 20					08 28					08 49			09 05	09 05		09 20			09 28		
Hull	29	d							08 07	08 07													09 08	
Brough	29	d							08 19	08 19													09 20	
Howden	29	d																						
Selby	29,40	d							08 40	08 40													09 40	
South Milford	40	d																						
Garforth	40	d						08 45	08 55	08 55												09 46		
Cross Gates	40	d						08 50																
Leeds 10		a	08 42					08 57	09 04	09 04			09 12			09 27	09 27		09 43			09 56	10 03	
		d	08 45	08 47				09 00	09 07	09 07		09 12	09 15		09 17	09 30	09 30		09 45	09 48		10 00	10 07	
Cottingley		d		08 52																09 53				
Morley		d		08 56											09 26					09 57				
Batley		d		09 01											09 31					10 02				
Dewsbury		a	08 55	09 03									09 26		09 34				09 55	10 04				
		d	08 57	09 04									09 27		09 35				09 57	10 05				
Ravensthorpe		d		09 07																10 08				
Castleford		d									08 58													09 58
Normanton		d									09 04													10 04
Wakefield Kirkgate		d									09 10													10 10
Mirfield		d		09 11							09 24				09 42					10 12				10 24
Deighton		d		09 17							09 30									10 18				10 30
Huddersfield		a	09 05	09 22				09 17	09 24	09 24	09 35		09 37			09 47	09 47		10 05	10 23		10 17	10 25	10 35
		d	09 08					09 18	09 25	09 25			09 38			09 48	09 48	09 53	10 08			10 18	10 25	
Slaithwaite		d																10 00						
Marsden		d																10 05						
Greenfield		d																10 14						
Mossley (Grtr Manchester)		d																10 18						
Stalybridge		a						09 36	09 43	09 43								10 22				10 36	10 43	
		d					09 30	09 37	09 43	09 49				10 00				10 22			10 30	10 37	10 44	
Ashton-under-Lyne	⛴	d					09 34							10 04							10 34			
Manchester Victoria	⛴	a	09 38				09 44	09 51				10 29	10 08	10 15	10 53	10 21	10 21		10 38		10 44	10 51		
		d	09 39					09 54					10 10			10 24	10 24		10 39			10 54		
Manchester Oxford Road		a	09 45										10 15						10 45					
Manchester Piccadilly		a	09 49						10 04	10 11			10 19					10 39	10 49				11 04	
		d	09 51										10 20						10 51					
Gatley		a	10 01																11 01					
Manchester Airport	⛴✈	a	10 13										10 41						11 13					
Newton-le-Willows	90	a														10 40	10 40							
Lea Green	90	a						10 16														11 15		
Liverpool Lime Street 10	90	a						10 32								10 59	10 59					11 33		

A 🛒 from Leeds

Table T039-R

Mondays to Saturdays
30 March to 16 May

Newcastle, Middlesborough, Scarborough, York, Hull, Leeds and Wakefield - Huddersfield - Manchester, Manchester Airport and Liverpool

			NT	TP	GC SO	NT	NT	TP	TP	NT	TP	TP	GC SX	NT	TP	TP	NT	NT	NT	NT	TP	TP	TP	TP	NT
			◇	◇1 🛒	■ 1 ☕		◇	◇1 🛒	◇1	◇	◇1 🛒	◇1	■ 1 ☕		◇1 🛒	◇1 A 🛒			◇	◇	◇1 🛒	◇1	◇1 🛒	◇1	
Edinburgh	26	d																							
Morpeth	26	d																							
Newcastle 8	26 ⛴	a																							
		d		08 43				09 06													10 06				
Chester-le-Street	26	d		08 52																					
Durham	26	d		08 59				09 18													10 18				
Darlington 5	26	a		09 16				09 35													10 35				
		d		09 17				09 36													10 36				
Redcar Central	44	d									09 07												10 07		
Middlesbrough	44	d									09 21												10 21		
Thornaby	44	d									09 27												10 27		
Yarm		d									09 35												10 35		
Northallerton	26	d			09 33						09 50		09 59										10 50		
Thirsk	26	d			09 42						09 59		10 08										10 59		
Scarborough	43	d													09 34										
Seamer	43	d													09 40										
Malton		d													09 59										
York 8	26	a		09 48	09 59			10 02			10 17		10 24		10 24						11 02		11 17		
		d		09 49				10 05			10 20				10 29						11 05		11 20		
Hull	29	d														10 08									
Brough	29	d														10 20									
Howden	29	d																							
Selby	29,40	d														10 40									
South Milford	40	d																							
Garforth	40	d													10 46										
Cross Gates	40	d																							
Leeds 10		a		10 12				10 27			10 42				10 56	11 03					11 27		11 42		
		d	10 12	10 15			10 17	10 30		10 42	10 45	10 47			11 00	11 07			11 12	11 17	11 30		11 45	11 47	
Cottingley		d										10 52												11 52	
Morley		d					10 26					10 56								11 26				11 56	
Batley		d					10 31					11 01								11 31				12 01	
Dewsbury		a		10 26			10 34				10 55	11 03								11 34			11 55	12 03	
		d		10 27			10 35				10 57	11 04								11 35			11 57	12 04	
Ravensthorpe		d										11 07												12 07	
Castleford		d																10 58							
Normanton		d																11 04							
Wakefield Kirkgate		d																11 10							
Mirfield		d					10 42					11 11						11 24		11 42				12 11	
Deighton		d										11 17						11 30						12 17	
Huddersfield		a		10 37				10 47			11 05	11 22			11 17	11 24		11 35			11 47		12 05	12 22	
		d		10 38				10 48	10 53		11 08				11 18	11 25					11 48	11 53	12 08		
Slaithwaite		d							11 00													12 00			
Marsden		d							11 05													12 05			
Greenfield		d							11 14													12 14			
Mossley (Grtr Manchester)		d							11 18													12 18			
Stalybridge		a							11 22						11 36	11 43						12 22			
		d				11 00			11 22					11 30	11 39	11 43	12 00					12 22			12 31
Ashton-under-Lyne	⛴	d				11 04								11 34			12 04								12 35
Manchester Victoria	⛴	a	11 29	11 08		11 15	11 53	11 21		12 05	11 38			11 44	11 54		12 15		12 42	12 53	12 20		12 38		12 45
		d		11 09				11 24			11 40				11 56						12 24		12 39		
Manchester Oxford Road		a		11 15							11 45												12 45		
Manchester Piccadilly		a		11 19					11 39		11 49					12 04						12 39	12 49		
		d		11 20							11 51												12 51		
Gatley		a									12 01												13 01		
Manchester Airport	⛴✈	a		11 41							12 13												13 13		
Newton-le-Willows	90	a						11 40													12 40				
Lea Green	90	a													12 16										
Liverpool Lime Street 10	90	a						12 02							12 32						12 59				

A 🛒 from Leeds

Table T039-R

Mondays to Saturdays

30 March to 16 May

Newcastle, Middlesborough, Scarborough, York, Hull, Leeds and Wakefield - Huddersfield - Manchester, Manchester Airport and Liverpool

Station			TP	TP	NT	NT	TP SX	TP SO	NT		NT SX	NT SO	TP SX	TP SO	TP	TP	TP	NT	TP SX	TP SO	TP	NT	NT	TP	NT
			◇1 ⌶	◇1 A ⌶		◇	◇1 ⌶	◇1 ⌶			◇	◇	◇1 ⌶	◇1 ⌶	◇1	◇1 ⌶	◇1		◇1 ⌶	◇1 ⌶	◇1 A ⌶		◇	◇1 ⌶	
Edinburgh	26	d											09 33	09 33											
Morpeth	26	d											10 48	10 48											
Newcastle 8	26 ⇌	a											11 02	11 02											
		d					10 47	10 47					11 05	11 05										11 43	
Chester-le-Street	26	d																						11 52	
Durham	26	d					10 59	10 59					11 17	11 17										11 59	
Darlington 5	26	a					11 16	11 16					11 33	11 33										12 16	
		d					11 17	11 17					11 34	11 34										12 17	
Redcar Central	44	d														11 07									
Middlesbrough	44	d														11 21									
Thornaby	44	d														11 27									
Yarm		d														11 35									
Northallerton	26	d					11 28	11 28								11 50								12 28	
Thirsk	26	d														11 59									
Scarborough	43	d	10 34																11 34	11 34					
Seamer	43	d	10 40																11 40	11 40					
Malton		d	10 59																11 58	11 58					
York 8	26	a	11 24				11 47	11 47					12 01	12 01		12 17			12 24	12 24				12 47	
		d	11 28				11 49	11 50					12 04	12 04		12 20			12 28	12 28				12 49	
Hull	29	d		11 06																	12 08				
Brough	29	d		11 18																	12 20				
Howden	29	d																							
Selby	29,40	d		11 38																	12 41				
South Milford	40	d																							
Garforth	40	d	11 46																12 46	12 46					
Cross Gates	40	d																							
Leeds 10		a	11 56	12 03			12 12	12 12					12 27	12 27		12 42			12 56	12 58	13 05			13 12	
		d	12 00	12 07		12 12	12 15	12 15			12 17	12 17	12 30	12 30		12 45	12 47		13 00	13 00	13 07		13 12	13 15	
Cottingley		d															12 52								
Morley		d									12 25	12 26					12 56								
Batley		d									12 30	12 31					13 01								
Dewsbury		a					12 26	12 26			12 33	12 34				12 55	13 03							13 26	
		d					12 27	12 27			12 33	12 35				12 57	13 04							13 27	
Ravensthorpe		d															13 07								
Castleford		d			11 58																	12 58			
Normanton		d			12 04																	13 04			
Wakefield Kirkgate		d			12 10																	13 10			
Mirfield		d			12 24						12 40	12 45					13 11					13 24			
Deighton		d			12 30												13 17					13 30			
Huddersfield		a	12 17	12 24	12 35		12 37	12 37					12 47	12 47		13 05	13 22		13 17	13 17	13 24	13 35		13 37	
		d	12 18	12 25			12 38	12 38					12 48	12 49	12 53	13 08			13 18	13 18	13 25			13 38	
Slaithwaite		d													13 00										
Marsden		d													13 05										
Greenfield		d													13 14										
Mossley (Grtr Manchester)		d													13 18										
Stalybridge		a	12 36	12 43											13 22				13 36	13 36	13 43				
		d	12 37	12 43					13 00						13 22			13 30	13 37	13 37	13 43				14 00
Ashton-under-Lyne	⇌	d							13 04									13 34							14 04
Manchester Victoria	⇌	a	12 50			13 46	13 08	13 08	13 15		13 54	13 54	13 21	13 21		13 38		13 44	13 50	13 50			14 29	14 08	14 16
		d	12 54				13 10	13 10					13 24	13 24		13 39			13 54	13 54				14 10	
Manchester Oxford Road		a					13 15	13 15								13 45								14 15	
Manchester Piccadilly		a		13 04			13 20	13 20							13 39	13 49					14 04			14 19	
		d					13 20	13 20								13 51								14 20	
Gatley		a														14 01									
Manchester Airport	⇌✈	a					13 41	13 41								14 13								14 41	
Newton-le-Willows	90	a											13 40	13 40											
Lea Green	90	a	13 15																14 16	14 16					
Liverpool Lime Street 10	90	a	13 32										13 59	13 59					14 32	14 32					

A ⌶ from Leeds

Table T039-R

Mondays to Saturdays

30 March to 16 May

Newcastle, Middlesborough, Scarborough, York, Hull, Leeds and Wakefield - Huddersfield - Manchester, Manchester Airport and Liverpool

Station			NT	TP SX	TP SO	TP	NT	TP	TP	NT	TP	TP	GC SO	NT	NT	TP	GC SX		NT	NT	TP	TP	TP	TP	NT	TP
			◇	◇1 ⌶	◇1 ⌶	◇1	◇	◇1 ⌶	◇1		◇1 ⌶	◇1 A ⌶	■ 1 ⊏		◇	◇1 ⌶	■ 1 ⊏			◇	◇1 ⌶	◇1	◇1 ⌶	◇1		◇1 ⌶
Edinburgh	26	d		10 21	10 16																11 33					
Morpeth	26	d		11 33	11 48																12 46					
Newcastle 8	26 ⇌	a		11 53	12 02																13 00					
		d		12 06	12 06											12 45					13 06					
Chester-le-Street	26	d																								
Durham	26	d		12 18	12 18											12 59					13 18					
Darlington 5	26	a		12 35	12 35											13 16					13 35					
		d		12 36	12 36											13 17					13 36					
Redcar Central	44	d						12 07															13 07			
Middlesbrough	44	d						12 21															13 21			
Thornaby	44	d						12 27															13 27			
Yarm		d						12 35															13 35			
Northallerton	26	d						12 50					13 20			13 28	13 33						13 50			
Thirsk	26	d						12 59					13 29				13 43						13 59			
Scarborough	43	d									12 34															13 34
Seamer	43	d									12 40															13 40
Malton		d									12 58															13 58
York 8	26	a		13 02	13 02			13 17			13 24		13 46			13 48	13 59				14 02		14 17			14 24
		d		13 04	13 05			13 20			13 28					13 50					14 05		14 20			14 28
Hull	29	d										13 08														
Brough	29	d										13 20														
Howden	29	d																								
Selby	29,40	d										13 40														
South Milford	40	d																								
Garforth	40	d									13 46															14 46
Cross Gates	40	d																								
Leeds 10		a		13 27	13 27			13 43			13 56	14 03				14 13					14 27		14 42			14 56
		d	13 17	13 30	13 30		13 42	13 45	13 47		14 00	14 07			14 12	14 15				14 17	14 30		14 45	14 47		15 00
Cottingley		d							13 52															14 52		
Morley		d	13 26						13 56											14 26				14 56		
Batley		d	13 31						14 01											14 31				15 01		
Dewsbury		a	13 34					13 55	14 03							14 26				14 34			14 55	15 03		
		d	13 35					13 57	14 04							14 27				14 35			14 57	15 04		
Ravensthorpe		d							14 07															15 07		
Castleford		d												13 58												
Normanton		d												14 04												
Wakefield Kirkgate		d												14 10												
Mirfield		d	13 42						14 11					14 24						14 42				15 11		
Deighton		d							14 17					14 30										15 17		
Huddersfield		a		13 47	13 47			14 05	14 22		14 17	14 24		14 35		14 37					14 47		15 05	15 22		15 17
		d		13 48	13 48	13 53		14 08			14 18	14 24				14 38					14 48	14 53	15 08			15 18
Slaithwaite		d				14 00																15 00				
Marsden		d				14 05																15 05				
Greenfield		d				14 14																15 14				
Mossley (Grtr Manchester)		d				14 18																15 18				
Stalybridge		a				14 22					14 36	14 42										15 22				15 36
		d				14 22				14 30	14 37	14 43							15 01			15 22			15 30	15 37
Ashton-under-Lyne	⇌	d								14 34									15 05						15 34	
Manchester Victoria	⇌	a	14 53	14 20	14 20		15 06	14 38		14 44	14 50				15 29	15 08			15 16	15 53	15 21		15 38		15 44	15 51
		d		14 24	14 24			14 40			14 54					15 10					15 24		15 40			15 54
Manchester Oxford Road		a						14 45								15 15							15 45			
Manchester Piccadilly		a				14 39		14 49				15 04				15 19						15 39	15 49			
		d						14 51								15 20							15 51			
Gatley		a						15 01															16 01			
Manchester Airport	⇌✈	a						15 13								15 41							16 13			
Newton-le-Willows	90	a		14 40	14 40																15 40					
Lea Green	90	a									15 16															16 15
Liverpool Lime Street 10	90	a		14 59	14 59						15 32										16 00					16 32

A ⌶ from Leeds

Table T039-R

Mondays to Saturdays

30 March to 16 May

Newcastle, Middlesborough, Scarborough, York, Hull, Leeds and Wakefield - Huddersfield - Manchester, Manchester Airport and Liverpool

	TP	TP	NT	NT	TP	TP	NT		NT	TP	TP	TP	NT	TP	TP	TP	NT	TP	TP	TP	NT	NT	TP
	SO	SX			SX	SO				SO	SX			SO	SX				SX	SO			SO
	◇1	◇1		◇	◇1	◇1			◇	◇1	◇1	◇1	◇	◇1	◇1	◇1		◇1	◇1	◇1		◇	◇1
	A	A																	A	A			
	🛒	🛒			🛒	🛒				🛒	🛒			🛒	🛒			🛒	🛒	🛒			🛒
Edinburgh 26 d										12 33	12 33												
Morpeth 26 d										13 49	13 49												
Newcastle 8 26 ⛴ a										14 03	14 03												
d					13 43	13 43				14 06	14 06												14 47
Chester-le-Street 26 d					13 51	13 51																	
Durham 26 d					13 58	13 58				14 18	14 18												14 59
Darlington 5 26 a					14 16	14 16				14 35	14 35												15 16
d					14 17	14 17				14 36	14 36												15 17
Redcar Central 44 d														14 07	14 07								
Middlesbrough 44 d														14 21	14 21								
Thornaby 44 d														14 27	14 27								
Yarm d														14 35	14 35								
Northallerton 26 d					14 28	14 28								14 50	14 50								15 28
Thirsk 26 d														14 59	14 59								
Scarborough 43 d																		14 34					
Seamer 43 d																		14 40					
Malton d																		14 58					
York 8 26 a					14 47	14 47				15 02	15 02			15 17	15 17			15 24					15 47
d					14 49	14 49				15 04	15 05			15 20	15 20			15 28					15 49
Hull 29 d	14 07	14 07																	15 03	15 08			
Brough 29 d	14 20	14 20																	15 15	15 20			
Howden 29 d																							
Selby 29,40 d	14 40	14 40																	15 36	15 40			
South Milford 40 d																							
Garforth 40 d																		15 46					
Cross Gates 40 d																							
Leeds 10 a	15 03	15 03			15 12	15 12				15 27	15 27			15 42	15 42			15 56	16 03	16 03			16 12
d	15 07	15 07		15 12	15 15	15 15			15 17	15 30	15 30		15 42	15 45	15 45	15 47		16 00	16 07	16 07		16 12	16 15
Cottingley d																15 52							
Morley d									15 26							15 56							
Batley d									15 31							16 01							
Dewsbury a					15 26	15 26			15 34					15 55	15 55	16 03							16 26
d					15 27	15 27			15 35					15 57	15 57	16 04							16 27
Ravensthorpe d																16 07							
Castleford d			14 58																		15 58		
Normanton d			15 04																		16 04		
Wakefield Kirkgate d			15 10																		16 10		
Mirfield d			15 24						15 42							16 11					16 24		
Deighton d			15 30													16 17					16 30		
Huddersfield a	15 24	15 24	15 35		15 37	15 37				15 47	15 47			16 05	16 05	16 22		16 17	16 24	16 24	16 35		16 37
d	15 25	15 25			15 38	15 38				15 48	15 48	15 53		16 08	16 08			16 18	16 25	16 25			16 38
Slaithwaite d												16 00							16 32	16 32			
Marsden d												16 05							16 37	16 37			
Greenfield d												16 14							16 45	16 45			
Mossley (Grtr Manchester) d												16 18							16 49	16 49			
Stalybridge a	15 43	15 43										16 22						16 36	16 53	16 53			
d	15 43	15 50					16 00					16 22					16 29	16 37	16 54	16 54			
Ashton-under-Lyne ⛴ d							16 04										16 33						
Manchester Victoria ⛴ a				16 29	16 08	16 08	16 15		16 54	16 20	16 20		17 05	16 38	16 38		16 44	16 51				17 34	17 08
d					16 10	16 10				16 24	16 24			16 39	16 39			16 54					17 10
Manchester Oxford Road a					16 15	16 15								16 45	16 45								17 15
Manchester Piccadilly a	16 04	16 14			16 19	16 19						16 41		16 49	16 49				17 14	17 16			17 19
d					16 20	16 20								16 51	16 51								17 20
Gatley a														17 01	17 01								
Manchester Airport ⛴✈ a					16 40	16 41								17 13	17 16								17 40
Newton-le-Willows 90 a										16 41	16 40							17 16					
Lea Green 90 a																							
Liverpool Lime Street 10 90 a										17 01	16 59							17 32					

A 🛒 from Leeds

NRT DECEMBER 19 EDITION

Table T039-R

Mondays to Saturdays

30 March to 16 May

Newcastle, Middlesborough, Scarborough, York, Hull, Leeds and Wakefield - Huddersfield - Manchester, Manchester Airport and Liverpool

	TP	NT	NT	TP	TP	TP	TP	TP	NT	TP	TP	NT	NT	TP	GC		GC	NT	NT	TP	TP	TP	TP	TP
	SX			SO	SX										SO		SX			SO	SX			
															R		R							
	◇1		◇	◇1	◇1	◇1	◇1	◇1		◇1	◇1		◇	◇1	1		1		◇	◇1	◇1	◇1	◇1	◇1
											A													
	🛒			🛒	🛒		🛒			🛒	🛒			🛒	⊏		⊏			🛒	🛒		🛒	
Edinburgh 26 d				13 19	13 19															14 33	14 33			
Morpeth 26 d				14 37	14 32															15 47	15 47			
Newcastle 8 26 ⛴ a				14 52	14 50															16 01	16 02			
d	14 47			15 03	15 03									15 43						16 06	16 06			
Chester-le-Street 26 d														15 52										
Durham 26 d	14 59			15 15	15 15									15 59						16 18	16 18			
Darlington 5 26 a	15 16			15 32	15 32									16 16						16 35	16 35			
d	15 17			15 33	15 33									16 17						16 36	16 36			
Redcar Central 44 d							15 07																16 07	
Middlesbrough 44 d							15 21																16 21	
Thornaby 44 d							15 27																16 27	
Yarm d							15 35																16 35	
Northallerton 26 d	15 28						15 50								16 33		16 33						16 50	
Thirsk 26 d							15 59								16 43		16 43						16 59	
Scarborough 43 d										15 34														
Seamer 43 d										15 40														
Malton d										15 58														
York 8 26 a	15 47			15 59	15 59		16 17			16 24				16 48	16 59		17 00			17 02	17 02		17 17	
d	15 50			16 01	16 01		16 20			16 28				16 49						17 04	17 04		17 20	
Hull 29 d											16 08													
Brough 29 d											16 20													
Howden 29 d																								
Selby 29,40 d											16 40													
South Milford 40 d																								
Garforth 40 d										16 46														
Cross Gates 40 d																								
Leeds 10 a	16 12			16 27	16 27		16 42			16 57	17 03			17 12						17 27	17 27		17 42	
d	16 15		16 17	16 30	16 30		16 45	16 47		17 00	17 07		17 12	17 15					17 17	17 30	17 30		17 45	17 47
Cottingley d								16 52											17 23					17 52
Morley d			16 25					16 56											17 27					17 56
Batley d			16 30					17 01											17 32					18 01
Dewsbury a	16 26		16 33				16 55	17 03						17 26					17 35				17 55	18 03
d	16 27		16 34				16 57	17 04						17 27					17 36				17 57	18 04
Ravensthorpe d			16 37					17 07																18 07
Castleford d												16 58												
Normanton d												17 04												
Wakefield Kirkgate d												17 10												
Mirfield d			16 42					17 11				17 24							17 43					18 11
Deighton d								17 17				17 30												18 17
Huddersfield a	16 37			16 47	16 47		17 05	17 22		17 17	17 24	17 35		17 37						17 47	17 47		18 05	18 22
d	16 38			16 48	16 48	16 53	17 08			17 21	17 25			17 38						17 48	17 48	17 54	18 08	
Slaithwaite d						17 00					17 32											18 01		
Marsden d						17 05					17 37											18 06		
Greenfield d						17 14					17 45											18 15		
Mossley (Grtr Manchester) d						17 18					17 49											18 19		
Stalybridge a						17 22				17 40	17 53											18 23		
d		17 00				17 22			17 31	17 41	17 54							18 00				18 23		
Ashton-under-Lyne ⛴ d		17 04							17 35									18 04						
Manchester Victoria ⛴ a	17 08	17 15	17 53	17 20	17 20		17 38		17 45	17 54			18 44	18 08				18 15	18 53	18 22	18 22		18 38	
d	17 10			17 24	17 24		17 39			17 56				18 10						18 24	18 24		18 39	
Manchester Oxford Road a	17 15						17 45							18 15									18 45	
Manchester Piccadilly a	17 19					17 39	17 49				18 11			18 19								18 39	18 49	
d	17 20						17 51							18 20									18 51	
Gatley a							18 01																19 01	
Manchester Airport ⛴✈ a	17 40						18 14							18 41									19 16	
Newton-le-Willows 90 a				17 40	17 40															18 40	18 40			
Lea Green 90 a										18 16														
Liverpool Lime Street 10 90 a				17 59	18 02					18 33										19 01	19 01			

A 🛒 from Leeds

Table T039-R

Mondays to Saturdays

30 March to 16 May

Newcastle, Middlesborough, Scarborough, York, Hull, Leeds and Wakefield - Huddersfield - Manchester, Manchester Airport and Liverpool

	NT	TP	TP	TP	TP	NT	NT	TP	NT	NT	TP	TP	TP	TP	TP	NT	TP	TP	NT	NT	TP	GC
		SO	SX	SX	SO						SX	SO										SO
		◇1 ╤	◇1 ╤	◇1 A ╤	◇1 A ╤		◇	◇1 ╤		◇	◇1 ╤	◇1 ╤	◇1	◇1 ╤	◇1		◇1	◇1 A ╤		◇	◇1 ╤	■ 1 ℞
Edinburgh 26 d											15 33	15 33										
Morpeth 26 d											16 48	16 48										
Newcastle 8 26 ⛴ a											17 03	17 03										
d								16 43			17 06	17 06									17 43	
Chester-le-Street 26 d								16 52													17 52	
Durham 26 d								16 59			17 18	17 18									17 59	
Darlington 5 26 a								17 15			17 35	17 35									18 16	
d								17 17			17 36	17 36									18 17	
Redcar Central 44 d														17 07								
Middlesbrough 44 d														17 21								
Thornaby 44 d														17 27								
Yarm d														17 35								
Northallerton 26 d								17 28						17 50							18 28	18 32
Thirsk 26 d														17 59								18 43
Scarborough 43 d		16 34	16 34														17 34					
Seamer 43 d		16 40	16 40														17 40					
Malton d		16 58	16 58														17 58					
York 8 26 a		17 24	17 25					17 47			18 02	18 02		18 17			18 24				18 47	18 59
d		17 28	17 28					17 49			18 05	18 05		18 18			18 28				18 49	
Hull 29 d				17 03	17 08													18 08				
Brough 29 d				17 15	17 20													18 20				
Howden 29 d																						
Selby 29,40 d				17 37	17 40													18 40				
South Milford 40 d																						
Garforth 40 d		17 46	17 46														18 45					
Cross Gates 40 d																						
Leeds 10 a		17 56	17 56	18 03	18 03			18 12			18 27	18 27		18 42			18 55	19 04			19 12	
d		18 00	18 00	18 07	18 07		18 12	18 15		18 17	18 29	18 29		18 45	18 47		19 00	19 07		19 12	19 15	
Cottingley d															18 52							
Morley d										18 25					18 56							
Batley d										18 30					19 01							
Dewsbury a								18 26		18 33				18 55	19 03						19 26	
d								18 27		18 33				18 57	19 04						19 27	
Ravensthorpe d															19 07							
Castleford d						17 58													18 58			
Normanton d						18 04													19 04			
Wakefield Kirkgate d						18 10													19 10			
Mirfield d						18 24				18 40					19 11				19 24			
Deighton d						18 30									19 17				19 30			
Huddersfield a		18 17	18 17	18 24	18 24	18 35		18 37			18 46	18 46		19 05	19 22		19 17	19 24	19 35		19 37	
d		18 18	18 18	18 25	18 25			18 38			18 48	18 48	18 53	19 08			19 18	19 25			19 38	
Slaithwaite d				18 32	18 32								19 00									
Marsden d				18 37	18 37								19 05									
Greenfield d				18 45	18 45								19 14									
Mossley (Grtr Manchester) d				18 49	18 49								19 18									
Stalybridge a		18 36	18 36	18 53	18 53								19 22				19 36	19 43				
d	18 31	18 37	18 37	18 54	18 54				19 00				19 22			19 31	19 37	19 43				
Ashton-under-Lyne ⛴ d	18 35								19 04							19 35						
Manchester Victoria ⛴ a	18 47	18 52	18 52				19 29	19 08	19 15	19 53	19 20	19 20		19 38		19 46	19 50			20 29	20 09	
d		18 54	18 54					19 10			19 24	19 24		19 39			19 54				20 10	
Manchester Oxford Road a								19 15						19 45							20 15	
Manchester Piccadilly a				19 14	19 11			19 19					19 39	19 49				20 04			20 19	
d								19 20						19 51							20 20	
Gatley a														20 01								
Manchester Airport ⛴✈ a								19 42						20 13							20 40	
Newton-le-Willows 90 a											19 40	19 40					20 12					
Lea Green 90 a		19 17	19 17								19 47	19 47					20 19					
Liverpool Lime Street 10 90 a		19 33	19 33								20 03	20 05					20 35					

A ╤ from Leeds

Table T039-R

Mondays to Saturdays

30 March to 16 May

Newcastle, Middlesborough, Scarborough, York, Hull, Leeds and Wakefield - Huddersfield - Manchester, Manchester Airport and Liverpool

	NT	NT	TP	TP	TP	GC	TP	TP	NT	TP	TP	TP	TP	TP	TP	NT	NT	TP	NT	NT	TP	TP	TP
			SO	SX		SX				SO	SX	SX	SO	SX	SX						SO	SX	
		◇	◇1 ╤	◇1 ╤	◇1	■ 1 ℞	◇1	◇1		◇1	◇1	◇1	◇1 A ╤	◇1	◇1 ╤		◇	◇1 ╤		◇	◇1 ╤	◇1 ╤	◇1
Edinburgh 26 d			16 21	16 33																	17 32	17 32	
Morpeth 26 d			17 48	17 48																	18 52	18 52	
Newcastle 8 26 ⛴ a			18 04	18 04																	19 06	19 06	
d			18 07	18 07														18 43			19 09	19 09	
Chester-le-Street 26 d																		18 52					
Durham 26 d			18 19	18 19														19 00			19 21	19 21	
Darlington 5 26 a			18 36	18 36														19 16					
d			18 37	18 37														19 17					
Redcar Central 44 d							18 07																
Middlesbrough 44 d							18 21																
Thornaby 44 d							18 27																
Yarm d							18 35																
Northallerton 26 d						18 41	18 50											19 28					
Thirsk 26 d						18 51	18 59																
Scarborough 43 d										18 34	18 34												
Seamer 43 d										18 40	18 40												
Malton d										18 58	18 58												
York 8 26 a			19 03	19 03		19 09	19 17			19 24	19 24							19 47			20 02	20 02	
d			19 06	19 06			19 20			19 28	19 28							19 49			20 05	20 05	
Hull 29 d												19 03	19 08										
Brough 29 d												19 15	19 20										
Howden 29 d																							
Selby 29,40 d												19 38	19 40										
South Milford 40 d																							
Garforth 40 d										19 46	19 46												
Cross Gates 40 d															←								
Leeds 10 a			19 28	19 28			19 42			19 56	19 56	20 03	20 03		20 03			20 12			20 27	20 27	
d		19 17	19 30	19 30			19 45	19 47		20 00	20 00	20 07	20 07		20 07		20 12	20 15		20 18	20 30	20 30	
Cottingley d								19 52				→											
Morley d		19 25						19 56												20 26			
Batley d		19 30						20 01												20 31			
Dewsbury a		19 33					19 55	20 03										20 26		20 34			
d		19 34					19 57	20 04										20 27		20 35			
Ravensthorpe d								20 07															
Castleford d																19 58							
Normanton d																20 04							
Wakefield Kirkgate d																20 10							
Mirfield d		19 41						20 11								20 24				20 42			
Deighton d								20 17								20 30							
Huddersfield a			19 47	19 47			20 05	20 22		20 17	20 17		20 24		20 24	20 35		20 37			20 47	20 47	
d			19 48	19 48	19 53		20 08			20 18	20 18		20 25		20 25			20 38			20 48	20 48	20 53
Slaithwaite d					20 00																		21 00
Marsden d					20 05																		21 05
Greenfield d					20 14																		21 14
Mossley (Grtr Manchester) d					20 18									←									21 18
Stalybridge a					20 22					20 36	20 45		20 43	20 45	20 48								21 22
d	20 00				20 22				20 31	20 37	20 46		20 46	20 46	20 53				21 00				21 22
Ashton-under-Lyne ⛴ d	20 04								20 35		→								21 04				
Manchester Victoria ⛴ a	20 15	20 53	20 21	20 21			20 38		20 46	20 52				21 01			21 46	21 11	21 14	21 54	21 19	21 22	
d			20 24	20 24			20 39														21 24	21 24	
Manchester Oxford Road a							20 45																
Manchester Piccadilly a					20 39		20 49						21 04		21 15								21 39
d							20 51																
Gatley a							21 01																
Manchester Airport ⛴✈ a							21 11																
Newton-le-Willows 90 a																					21 40	21 40	
Lea Green 90 a																					21 47	21 46	
Liverpool Lime Street 10 90 a			20 56	20 56																	22 05	22 05	

A ╤ from Leeds

Table T039-R

Mondays to Saturdays
30 March to 16 May

Newcastle, Middlesborough, Scarborough, York, Hull, Leeds and Wakefield - Huddersfield - Manchester, Manchester Airport and Liverpool

	NT ◇	TP ◇1	TP ◇1	NT	TP SX ◇1	TP SO ◇1	TP ◇1 A ✠		NT SX	NT	NT SO	NT ◇	NT ◇	TP SO ◇1 B ✠	TP SX ◇1 B ✠	TP ◇1	NT	NT ◇	TP ◇1	TP SO ◇1	TP SX ◇1	TP ◇1	TP ◇1 A ✠
Edinburgh 26 d														18 33	18 11								
Morpeth 26 d														19 47	19 33								
Newcastle 8 26 ⇌ a														20 01	19 47								
d														20 06	20 06								
Chester-le-Street 26 d																							
Durham 26 d														20 18	20 18								
Darlington 5 26 a														20 35	20 35								
d														20 36	20 36								
Redcar Central 44 d		19 07																				20 07	
Middlesbrough 44 d		19 21																				20 21	
Thornaby 44 d		19 27																				20 27	
Yarm d		19 35																				20 39	
Northallerton 26 d		19 50																				20 54	
Thirsk 26 d		19 59																				21 05	
Scarborough 43 d					19 34	19 34														20 34	20 34		
Seamer 43 d					19 40	19 40														20 40	20 40		
Malton d					19 58	19 58														20 58	20 58		
York 8 26 a		20 17			20 24	20 25								21 02	21 02					21 24	21 24	21 25	
d		20 20			20 28	20 28								21 05	21 05					21 28	21 28		
Hull 29 d							20 08																21 08
Brough 29 d							20 20																21 20
Howden 29 d																							
Selby 29,40 d							20 41																21 40
South Milford 40 d																							
Garforth 40 d					20 46	20 46														21 46	21 46		
Cross Gates 40 d																							
Leeds 10 a		20 43			20 56	20 56	21 03							21 27	21 27					21 56	21 56		22 03
d	20 42	20 45	20 47		21 00	21 00	21 07					21 12	21 17	21 30	21 30			21 42	21 47	22 00	22 00		22 07
Cottingley d			20 52																21 52				
Morley d			20 56										21 25						21 56				
Batley d			21 01										21 30						22 01				
Dewsbury a		20 55	21 03				21 17						21 33	21 41	21 41				22 03				22 17
d		20 57	21 04				21 18						21 34	21 42	21 42				22 04				22 18
Ravensthorpe d			21 07																22 07				
Castleford d										20 58													
Normanton d										21 04													
Wakefield Kirkgate d										21 10													
Mirfield d			21 11							21 24			21 41						22 11				
Deighton d			21 17							21 30									22 17				
Huddersfield a		21 05	21 22		21 17	21 17	21 26			21 35				21 50	21 50				22 22	22 17	22 17		22 26
d		21 08			21 18	21 18	21 31							21 51	21 51	21 56				22 18	22 18		22 27
Slaithwaite d																22 03							
Marsden d																22 08							
Greenfield d																22 17							
Mossley (Grtr Manchester) d																22 21							
Stalybridge a					21 39	21 39	21 51									22 25				22 39	22 39		22 45
d				21 29	21 40	21 40	21 51		22 02		22 03					22 25	22 31			22 40	22 40		22 46
Ashton-under-Lyne ⇌ d				21 33					22 05		22 06						22 35						
Manchester Victoria ⇌ a	22 06	21 40		21 44	21 54	21 54			22 17		22 18	22 35	22 55	22 23	22 25		22 46	23 08		22 53	22 53		23 00
d					21 56	21 56								22 24	22 26					22 55	22 55		23 02
Manchester Oxford Road a					22 02	22 02														23 00	23 01		
Manchester Piccadilly a					22 06	22 06	22 10									22 44				23 04	23 05		
d					22 07	22 07														23 05	23 12		
Gatley a																							
Manchester Airport ⇌✈ a					22 22	22 22														23 20	23 28		
Newton-le-Willows 90 a														22 40	22 46								
Lea Green 90 a														22 47	22 54								23 23
Liverpool Lime Street 10 90 a														23 06	23 14								23 43

A ✠ from Leeds

B ✠ from York

NRT DECEMBER 19 EDITION

Table T039-R

Mondays to Saturdays
30 March to 16 May

Newcastle, Middlesborough, Scarborough, York, Hull, Leeds and Wakefield - Huddersfield - Manchester, Manchester Airport and Liverpool

	NT SO	NT	NT SX	NT ◇	NT	TP ◇1	TP SX ◇1 A ✠	TP SO ◇1 A ✠	TP SX ◇1 ✠	TP ◇1	NT ◇	TP SX ◇1	TP SO ◇1	TP ◇1	TP SO ◇1		TP SX ◇1 B ✠	TP SO ◇1 B ✠	TP SX ◇1 ✠	NT	TP SO ◇1 ✠	TP ◇1	TP SX ◇1	TP ◇1 ✠
Edinburgh 26 d							19 30	19 30																
Morpeth 26 d							20 45	20 45																
Newcastle 8 26 ⇌ a							20 59	20 59																
d							21 02	21 02							22 00						22 00			
Chester-le-Street 26 d							21 11	21 11																
Durham 26 d							21 18	21 18							22 15						22 15			
Darlington 5 26 a							21 35	21 35							22 32						22 32			
d							21 36	21 36							22 33						22 33			
Redcar Central 44 d										21 07														22 07
Middlesbrough 44 d										21 21														22 21
Thornaby 44 d										21 27														22 27
Yarm d										21 35														22 35
Northallerton 26 d										21 50					22 44						22 44			22 50
Thirsk 26 d										21 59														22 59
Scarborough 43 d														21 34									22 15	
Seamer 43 d														21 40									22 20	
Malton d														21 58									22 39	
York 8 26 a							22 02	22 02		22 19				22 24	23 03						23 03		23 04	23 19
d							22 05	22 05						22 28							23 05			
Hull 29 d																	22 08	22 08						
Brough 29 d																	22 20	22 20						
Howden 29 d																								
Selby 29,40 d																	22 40	22 40						
South Milford 40 d																								
Garforth 40 d														22 47										
Cross Gates 40 d									←															
Leeds 10 a							22 26	22 27	22 26					22 58			23 03	23 03			23 27			
d				22 12	22 21		22 28	22 28	22 28		22 42	22 46	22 47	23 00			23 05	23 07			23 30	23 47		
Cottingley d							→					22 52	22 52									23 52		
Morley d					22 29							22 56	22 56									23 56		
Batley d					22 34							23 01	23 01						←			00 02		
Dewsbury a					22 37			22 41	22 41			23 03	23 03				23 15		23 15		23 40	00 03		
d					22 38			22 42	22 42			23 04	23 04				23 18		23 18		23 41	00 04		
Ravensthorpe d												23 07	23 07				→					00 07		
Castleford d		21 58																		22 58				
Normanton d		22 04																		23 04				
Wakefield Kirkgate d		22 10																		23 11				
Mirfield d		22 24			22a44							23 11	23 11							23 25		00 11		
Deighton d		22 30										23 18	23 18							23 31		00 17		
Huddersfield a		22 35						22 50	22 50			23 22	23 22	23 17				23 24	23 26	23 36	23 50	00 22		
d						22 46		22 51	22 51					23 18				23 25	23 27		23 51			
Slaithwaite d						22 52												23 32	23 33					
Marsden d						23 04												23 37	23 37					
Greenfield d						23 13												23 46	23 46					
Mossley (Grtr Manchester) d						23 17												23 50	23 50					
Stalybridge a						23 21								23 36				23 54	23 54					
d	23 00		23 03			23 24								23 37				23 54	23 54					
Ashton-under-Lyne ⇌ d	23 03		23 06																					
Manchester Victoria ⇌ a	23 14		23 16	23 37				23 23	23 23		00 11			23 50										
d								23 24	23 25					23 52										
Manchester Oxford Road a														23 57										
Manchester Piccadilly a						23 41								00 01				00 14	00 11		00 23			
d														00 03							00 33			
Gatley a																								
Manchester Airport ⇌✈ a														00 19							00 49			
Newton-le-Willows 90 a								23 40	23 41															
Lea Green 90 a								23 47	23 47															
Liverpool Lime Street 10 90 a								00 05	00 05															

A ✠ from York

B ✠ from Leeds

Table T039-R

Mondays to Saturdays
30 March to 16 May

Newcastle, Middlesborough, Scarborough, York, Hull, Leeds and Wakefield - Huddersfield - Manchester, Manchester Airport and Liverpool

	TP SO 1	TP SO ◇1	TP ◇1	TP SX ◇1	TP WO ◇1 🍴	TP SX ◇1 🍴
Edinburgh 26 d					22 12	
Morpeth 26 d						
Newcastle 8 26 ⇌ a						
d	22 30					
Chester-le-Street 26 d	22 40					
Durham 26 d	22a46					
Darlington 5 26 a						
d						
Redcar Central 44 d						23 07
Middlesbrough 44 d						23 22
Thornaby 44 d						23 28
Yarm d						23 37
Northallerton 26 d						23 54
Thirsk 26 d						00 03
Scarborough 43 d		22 42		22 45		
Seamer 43 d		22 48		22 51		
Malton d		23 06		23 11		
York 8 26 a		23 33		23 35		00 29
d		23 37		23 39		
Hull 29 d			23 08			
Brough 29 d			23 20			
Howden 29 d						
Selby 29,40 d			23 40			
South Milford 40 d						
Garforth 40 d						
Cross Gates 40 d						
Leeds 10 a		00 02	00 04	00 06		
d		00 07		00 07		
Cottingley d						
Morley d						
Batley d						
Dewsbury a						
d						
Ravensthorpe d						
Castleford d						
Normanton d						
Wakefield Kirkgate d						
Mirfield d						
Deighton d						
Huddersfield a						
d						
Slaithwaite d						
Marsden d						
Greenfield d						
Mossley (Grtr Manchester) d						
Stalybridge a						
d						
Ashton-under-Lyne ⇌ d						
Manchester Victoria ⇌ a						
d						
Manchester Oxford Road a						
Manchester Piccadilly a		00 56		01 06	01 42	
d						
Gatley a						
Manchester Airport ⇌✈ a						
Newton-le-Willows 90 a						
Lea Green 90 a						
Liverpool Lime Street 10 90 a						

Table T039-R

Sundays
15 December to 5 January

Newcastle, Middlesborough, Scarborough, York, Hull, Leeds and Wakefield - Huddersfield - Manchester, Manchester Airport and Liverpool

	TP	TP	TP	TP	TP	TP	TP	TP	TP	TP	TP	NT	TP	TP	NT		TP	TP	TP	TP	NT	TP	NT	TP
	◇1 A	◇1 A	◇1	◇1	◇1	◇1	◇1	◇1 🍴	◇1	◇1 🍴	◇1 🍴		◇1 🍴	◇1	◇		◇1 🍴	◇1	◇1 🍴	◇1 B 🍴		◇1 🍴	◇	◇1 🍴
Edinburgh 26 d																								
Morpeth 26 d																								
Newcastle 8 26 ⇌ a																								
d																						07 49		08 06
Chester-le-Street 26 d																								
Durham 26 d																						08 01		08 18
Darlington 5 26 a																						08 18		08 35
d																						08 19		08 36
Redcar Central 44 d																								
Middlesbrough 44 d																								
Thornaby 44 d																								
Yarm d																								
Northallerton 26 d																								
Thirsk 26 d																								
Scarborough 43 d																								
Seamer 43 d																								
Malton d																								
York 8 26 a																						08 45		09 02
d			02 08	03 45	04 51	05 51		07 00			07 31						08 18		08 26			08 48		09 05
Hull 29 d																				08 08				
Brough 29 d																				08 20				
Howden 29 d																								
Selby 29,40 d																				08 41				
South Milford 40 d																								
Garforth 40 d																			08 43					
Cross Gates 40 d																								
Leeds 10 a			02 48	04 23	05 31	06 31		07 40			08 10						08 43		08 53	09 05		09 12		09 27
d		00 07	02 53	04 28	05 43	06 36		07 45	07 47		08 15				08 18		08 45	08 47	09 00	09 07		09 15	09 19	09 30
Cottingley d									07 52									08 52						
Morley d									07 56									08 56						
Batley d	00 02								08 01									09 01						
Dewsbury a	00 03				05 53	06 46		07 56	08 03		08 26						08 55	09 03				09 26		
d	00 04				05 54	06 47		07 57	08 04		08 27						08 56	09 04				09 27		
Ravensthorpe d	00 07								08 07									09 07						
Castleford d																								
Normanton d																								
Wakefield Kirkgate d																								
Mirfield d	00 11								08 11									09 11						
Deighton d	00 17								08 17									09 17						
Huddersfield a	00 22		03 10	04 45	06 02	06 56		08 05	08 22		08 35						09 05	09 22	09 17	09 24		09 36		09 47
d			03 11	04 46	06 03	06 57	07 53	08 06			08 36			08 53			09 09		09 18	09 25		09 37		09 48
Slaithwaite d							08 00							08 59						09 32				
Marsden d							08 05							09 05						09 37				
Greenfield d							08 14							09 13						09 45				
Mossley (Grtr Manchester) d							08 17							09 17						09 49				
Stalybridge a						07 15	08 21	08 25						09 21					09 36	09 53				
d						07 16	08 22	08 26				09 04		09 21					09 37	09 53	10 03			
Ashton-under-Lyne ⇌ d												09 07									10 06			
Manchester Victoria ⇌ a							08 36	08 39			09 08	09 18		09 34	09 46		09 41		09 50		10 17		10 43	10 22
d								08 44		08 52			09 22						09 52					10 24
Manchester Oxford Road a								08 49																
Manchester Piccadilly a		00 56	03 42	05 16	06 33	07 31		08 53												10 12		10 20		
d			03 47	05 21	06 44	07 42		08 56																
Gatley a																								
Manchester Airport ⇌✈ a			04 02	05 37	07 00	08 03		09 12																
Newton-le-Willows 90 a										09 08			09 38											10 40
Lea Green 90 a										09 14									10 17					
Liverpool Lime Street 10 90 a										09 34			09 59						10 33					10 59

A not 15 December

B 🍴 from Leeds

Table T039-R

Sundays
15 December to 5 January

Newcastle, Middlesborough, Scarborough, York, Hull, Leeds and Wakefield - Huddersfield - Manchester, Manchester Airport and Liverpool

Station		TP	TP	TP	TP	TP	TP	NT	NT	TP	TP	TP	TP	TP	TP	TP	GC	NT	NT	TP	TP	TP	TP
		◇1	◇1 ⌶	◇1	◇1 ⌶	◇1 A ⌶	◇1 ⌶		◇	◇1 ⌶	◇1	◇1 ⌶	◇1	◇1 ⌶	◇1 A ⌶	◇1 ⌶	1 ⊡		◇	◇1 ⌶	◇1	◇1 ⌶	◇1
Edinburgh 26	d																						
Morpeth 26	d																						
Newcastle [8] 26	a																						
	d						08 47			09 03						09 43				10 06			
Chester-le-Street 26	d															09 52							
Durham 26	d						08 59			09 15						09 59				10 18			
Darlington [5] 26	a						09 16			09 32						10 16				10 35			
	d						09 17			09 33						10 17				10 36			
Redcar Central 44	d																					10 05	
Middlesbrough 44	d											09 29										10 18	
Thornaby 44	d											09 35										10 24	
Yarm	d											09 43										10 33	
Northallerton 26	d						09 28										10 25					10 48	
Thirsk 26	d																10 34					10 56	
Scarborough 43	d				08 35									09 32									
Seamer 43	d				08 41									09 38									
Malton	d				08 59									09 59									
York [8] 26	a				09 24		09 47			10 01		10 17		10 24		10 48	10 51			11 02		11 14	
	d		09 18		09 27		09 49			10 04		10 20		10 27		10 49				11 05		11 16	
Hull 29	d					09 08									10 08								
Brough 29	d					09 20									10 20								
Howden 29	d																						
Selby 29,40	d					09 40									10 40								
South Milford 40	d																						
Garforth 40	d				09 45									10 43									
Cross Gates 40	d																						
Leeds [10]	a		09 42		09 56	10 03	10 12			10 27		10 43		10 56	11 03	11 12				11 27		11 42	
	d		09 45	09 47	10 00	10 07	10 15		10 15	10 30		10 45	10 47	11 00	11 07	11 15			11 18	11 30		11 45	11 47
Cottingley	d			09 52									10 52										11 52
Morley	d			09 56									10 56										11 56
Batley	d			10 01									11 01										12 01
Dewsbury	a		09 55	10 03			10 26					10 55	11 03			11 26						11 55	12 03
	d		09 57	10 04			10 27					10 57	11 04			11 27						11 56	12 04
Ravensthorpe	d			10 07									11 07										12 07
Castleford	d																						
Normanton	d																						
Wakefield Kirkgate	d																						
Mirfield	d			10 11									11 11										12 11
Deighton	d			10 17									11 17										12 17
Huddersfield	a		10 05	10 22	10 17	10 24	10 38			10 47		11 05	11 22	11 17	11 24	11 37				11 47		12 05	12 22
	d	09 53	10 08		10 18	10 25	10 39			10 48	10 53	11 08		11 18	11 25	11 37				11 48	11 53	12 08	
Slaithwaite	d	10 00									11 00										12 00		
Marsden	d	10 05									11 05										12 05		
Greenfield	d	10 14									11 14										12 13		
Mossley (Grtr Manchester)	d	10 18									11 18										12 17		
Stalybridge	a	10 22			10 36	10 43					11 22			11 36	11 43						12 21		
	d	10 22			10 37	10 43		11 03			11 22			11 37	11 43			12 03			12 21		
Ashton-under-Lyne	d							11 06										12 06					
Manchester Victoria	a		10 40		10 51		11 09	11 17	11 44	11 22		11 38		11 51		12 09		12 17	12 43	12 22		12 38	
	d				10 53		11 10			11 24		11 40		11 54		12 10				12 23		12 39	
Manchester Oxford Road	a						11 16					11 45				12 16						12 45	
Manchester Piccadilly	a	10 41				11 09	11 20				11 41	11 49			12 12	12 20					12 41	12 49	
	d						11 21					11 52				12 21						12 53	
Gatley	a											12 02										13 03	
Manchester Airport	a						11 38					12 14				12 39						13 16	
Newton-le-Willows 90	a									11 40										12 39			
Lea Green 90	a				11 12									12 18									
Liverpool Lime Street [10] 90	a				11 28					11 59				12 34						12 59			

A ⌶ from Leeds

NRT DECEMBER 19 EDITION

Table T039-R

Sundays
15 December to 5 January

Newcastle, Middlesborough, Scarborough, York, Hull, Leeds and Wakefield - Huddersfield - Manchester, Manchester Airport and Liverpool

Station		TP	TP	TP	NT	NT	TP	TP	TP	TP	TP	TP	TP	NT	NT	TP	TP	TP	TP	TP	TP	GC	TP	NT
		◇1 ⌶	◇1 A ⌶	◇1 ⌶		◇	◇1 ⌶	◇1	◇1 ⌶	◇1	◇1 ⌶	◇1 A ⌶	◇1 ⌶		◇	◇1 ⌶	◇1	◇1 ⌶	◇1	◇1 ⌶	◇1 A ⌶	1 ⊡	◇1 ⌶	
Edinburgh 26	d						09 20									10 20								
Morpeth 26	d						10 30									11 33								
Newcastle [8] 26	a						10 44									11 47								
	d			10 47			11 06						11 43			12 05							12 46	
Chester-le-Street 26	d												11 53											
Durham 26	d			10 59			11 18						12 00			12 17							12 59	
Darlington [5] 26	a			11 16			11 35						12 16			12 34							13 16	
	d			11 17			11 36						12 18			12 35							13 17	
Redcar Central 44	d								11 05									12 05						
Middlesbrough 44	d								11 18									12 18						
Thornaby 44	d								11 24									12 24						
Yarm	d								11 33									12 33						
Northallerton 26	d			11 28					11 48				12 29					12 48				13 15	13 28	
Thirsk 26	d								11 56									12 56				13 27		
Scarborough 43	d	10 32									11 32									12 32				
Seamer 43	d	10 38									11 38									12 38				
Malton	d	10 57									11 57									12 57				
York [8] 26	a	11 23		11 47			12 02		12 14		12 23		12 48			13 01		13 14		13 23		13 44	13 47	
	d	11 27		11 49			12 05		12 16		12 27		12 50			13 05		13 16		13 27			13 49	
Hull 29	d		11 04									12 06									13 04			
Brough 29	d		11 16									12 18									13 16			
Howden 29	d																							
Selby 29,40	d		11 36									12 40									13 38			
South Milford 40	d																							
Garforth 40	d	11 46	11 51								12 47									13 46				
Cross Gates 40	d		11 56																					
Leeds [10]	a	11 56	12 03	12 12			12 27		12 43		12 56	13 03	13 13			13 28		13 43		13 56	14 03		14 12	
	d	12 00	12 07	12 15		12 18	12 30		12 45	12 47	13 00	13 07	13 14		13 18	13 30		13 45	13 47	14 00	14 07		14 15	
Cottingley	d									12 52									13 52					
Morley	d									12 56									13 56					
Batley	d									13 01									14 01					
Dewsbury	a			12 26					12 55	13 03			13 25					13 55	14 03				14 26	
	d			12 27					12 56	13 04			13 26					13 56	14 04				14 27	
Ravensthorpe	d									13 07									14 07					
Castleford	d																							
Normanton	d																							
Wakefield Kirkgate	d																							
Mirfield	d									13 11									14 11					
Deighton	d									13 17									14 17					
Huddersfield	a	12 17	12 24	12 36			12 47		13 06	13 22	13 17	13 24	13 36			13 47		14 06	14 22	14 17	14 24		14 36	
	d	12 18	12 25	12 38			12 48	12 53	13 08		13 18	13 25	13 38			13 48	13 53	14 08		14 18	14 25		14 38	
Slaithwaite	d							13 00									14 00							
Marsden	d							13 05									14 05							
Greenfield	d							13 14									14 14							
Mossley (Grtr Manchester)	d							13 18									14 18							
Stalybridge	a	12 36	12 43					13 22			13 36	13 43					14 22			14 36	14 43			
	d	12 37	12 43		13 03			13 22			13 37	13 43		14 03			14 22			14 37	14 43			15 03
Ashton-under-Lyne	d				13 06									14 06										15 06
Manchester Victoria	a	12 50		13 09	13 17	13 43	13 21		13 38		13 50		14 09	14 18	14 46	14 22		14 38		14 50			15 09	15 18
	d	12 52		13 10			13 23		13 39		13 54		14 10			14 24		14 39		14 54			15 10	
Manchester Oxford Road	a			13 16					13 45				14 16					14 45					15 16	
Manchester Piccadilly	a		13 10	13 20				13 41	13 50			14 09	14 20				14 41	14 50			15 09		15 20	
	d			13 21					13 51				14 20					14 51					15 20	
Gatley	a								14 00									15 00						
Manchester Airport	a			13 37					14 16				14 36					15 16					15 36	
Newton-le-Willows 90	a						13 39									14 40								
Lea Green 90	a	13 11									14 18									15 18				
Liverpool Lime Street [10] 90	a	13 29					13 58				14 34					14 59				15 34				

A ⌶ from Leeds

Table T039-R

Sundays 15 December to 5 January

Newcastle, Middlesborough, Scarborough, York, Hull, Leeds and Wakefield - Huddersfield - Manchester, Manchester Airport and Liverpool

	NT ◇	TP ◇1 🛒	TP ◇1	TP ◇1 🛒	TP ◇1	TP ◇1 🛒	TP ◇1 A 🛒	TP ◇1 🛒	NT	NT ◇	TP ◇1 🛒	TP ◇1	TP ◇1 🛒	TP ◇1	TP ◇1 🛒	TP ◇1 A 🛒	GC 1 🍴	TP ◇1 🛒	NT	NT ◇	TP ◇1 🛒	TP ◇1
Edinburgh 26 d		11 33									12 24										13 33	
Morpeth 26 d		12 48									13 38										14 49	
Newcastle 8 26 ⛴ a		13 02									13 53										15 03	
d		13 05						13 43			13 56							14 47			15 05	
Chester-le-Street 26 d								13 52														
Durham 26 d		13 17						13 59			14 08							14 59			15 18	
Darlington 8 26 a		13 34						14 15			14 25							15 16			15 34	
d		13 35						14 16			14 26							15 17			15 36	
Redcar Central 44 d				13 05									14 03									
Middlesbrough 44 d				13 18									14 15									
Thornaby 44 d				13 24									14 21									
Yarm d				13 33									14 32									
Northallerton 26 d				13 48									14 47				15 18	15 29				
Thirsk 26 d				13 56									14 55				15 27					
Scarborough 43 d						13 32									14 32							
Seamer 43 d						13 38									14 38							
Malton d						13 57									14 57							
York 8 26 a		14 02		14 14		14 24		14 43			14 53		15 13		15 23		15 44	15 48			16 02	
d		14 04		14 16		14 27		14 48			15 05		15 15		15 27			15 50			16 05	
Hull 29 d							14 06									15 06						
Brough 29 d							14 18									15 18						
Howden 29 d																						
Selby 29,40 d							14 38									15 38						
South Milford 40 d																						
Garforth 40 d						14 47									15 46							
Cross Gates 40 d																						
Leeds 10 a		14 27		14 43		14 56	15 03	15 11			15 27		15 43		15 56	16 03		16 12			16 28	
d	14 19	14 30		14 45	14 47	15 00	15 07	15 15		15 18	15 30		15 45	15 47	16 00	16 07		16 15		16 19	16 30	
Cottingley d					14 52									15 52								
Morley d					14 56									15 56								
Batley d					15 01									16 01								
Dewsbury a				14 55	15 03			15 25					15 55	16 03				16 26				
d				14 57	15 04			15 26					15 57	16 04				16 27				
Ravensthorpe d					15 07									16 07								
Castleford d																						
Normanton d																						
Wakefield Kirkgate d																						
Mirfield d					15 11									16 11								
Deighton d					15 17									16 17								
Huddersfield a		14 47		15 05	15 22	15 17	15 24	15 36			15 47		16 05	16 22	16 17	16 24		16 35			16 47	
d		14 48	14 53	15 08		15 18	15 24	15 38			15 48	15 53	16 08		16 18	16 25		16 37			16 48	16 53
Slaithwaite d			15 00									16 00										17 00
Marsden d			15 05									16 05										17 05
Greenfield d			15 14									16 14										17 14
Mossley (Grtr Manchester) d			15 18									16 18										17 18
Stalybridge a			15 22			15 36	15 42					16 22			16 36	16 43						17 22
d			15 22			15 37	15 43		16 03			16 22			16 37	16 43			17 03			17 22
Ashton-under-Lyne ⛴ d									16 06										17 06			
Manchester Victoria ⛴ a	15 44	15 20		15 38		15 50		16 10	16 18	16 44	16 21		16 38		16 50			17 09	17 18	17 44	17 21	
d		15 23		15 40		15 54		16 11			16 23		16 39		16 54			17 10			17 23	
Manchester Oxford Road a				15 45				16 17					16 45					17 16				
Manchester Piccadilly a			15 41	15 50			16 09	16 20				16 41	16 49			17 09		17 20				17 41
d				15 51				16 21					16 51					17 20				
Gatley a				16 00									16 59									
Manchester Airport ⛴✈ a				16 16				16 37					17 16					17 36				
Newton-le-Willows 90 a		15 39									16 39										17 39	
Lea Green 90 a						16 18									17 18							
Liverpool Lime Street 10 90 a		15 58				16 34					16 58				17 34						17 58	

A 🛒 from Leeds

Table T039-R

Sundays 15 December to 5 January

Newcastle, Middlesborough, Scarborough, York, Hull, Leeds and Wakefield - Huddersfield - Manchester, Manchester Airport and Liverpool

	TP ◇1 🛒	TP ◇1	TP ◇1 🛒	TP ◇1 A 🛒	TP ◇1 🛒	NT	NT ◇	TP ◇1 🛒	TP ◇1	TP ◇1 🛒	TP ◇1	TP ◇1 🛒	TP ◇1 A 🛒	TP ◇1 🛒	NT	NT ◇	TP ◇1 🛒	TP ◇1	TP ◇1 🛒	TP ◇1	TP ◇1 🛒	TP ◇1 A 🛒	TP ◇1 🛒
Edinburgh 26 d								14 21									15 20						
Morpeth 26 d								15 31									16 30						
Newcastle 8 26 ⛴ a								15 44									16 44						
d					15 43			16 00						16 43			17 06						17 43
Chester-le-Street 26 d					15 52									16 52									17 52
Durham 26 d					15 59			16 15						16 59			17 18						17 59
Darlington 8 26 a					16 16			16 31						17 16			17 35						18 15
d					16 17			16 33						17 17			17 36						18 17
Redcar Central 44 d	15 05									16 05									17 05				
Middlesbrough 44 d	15 18									16 18									17 18				
Thornaby 44 d	15 24									16 24									17 24				
Yarm d	15 33									16 33									17 33				
Northallerton 26 d	15 48				16 28														17 48				18 28
Thirsk 26 d	15 56									16 55									17 56				
Scarborough 43 d			15 32									16 32									17 32		
Seamer 43 d			15 38									16 38									17 38		
Malton d			15 57									16 57									17 57		
York 8 26 a	16 14		16 23		16 47			16 59		17 16		17 23		17 48			18 02		18 14		18 23		18 47
d	16 16		16 27		16 49			17 05		17 18		17 27		17 49			18 05		18 18		18 27		18 49
Hull 29 d				16 06									17 06									18 06	
Brough 29 d				16 18									17 18									18 18	
Howden 29 d																							
Selby 29,40 d				16 39									17 38									18 38	
South Milford 40 d																							
Garforth 40 d												17 46									18 47		
Cross Gates 40 d																							
Leeds 10 a	16 43		16 56	17 03	17 12			17 28		17 44		17 56	18 03	18 12			18 27		18 43		18 56	19 03	19 13
d	16 45	16 47	17 00	17 07	17 15		17 18	17 30		17 45	17 48	18 00	18 07	18 15		18 18	18 30		18 45	18 47	19 00	19 07	19 15
Cottingley d		16 52									17 53									18 52			
Morley d		16 56									17 56									18 56			
Batley d		17 01									18 01									19 01			
Dewsbury a	16 55	17 03			17 25					17 55	18 04			18 26					18 56	19 03			19 26
d	16 57	17 04			17 26					17 57	18 04			18 27					18 58	19 04			19 27
Ravensthorpe d		17 07									18 07									19 07			
Castleford d																							
Normanton d																							
Wakefield Kirkgate d																							
Mirfield d		17 11									18 11									19 11			
Deighton d		17 17									18 17									19 17			
Huddersfield a	17 05	17 22	17 17	17 24	17 37			17 47		18 06	18 22	18 17	18 24	18 35			18 47		19 06	19 22	19 17	19 24	19 37
d	17 08		17 18	17 25	17 39			17 49	17 53	18 08		18 18	18 25	18 37			18 48	18 53	19 08		19 18	19 25	19 38
Slaithwaite d									18 00									19 00					
Marsden d									18 05									19 05					
Greenfield d									18 14									19 14					
Mossley (Grtr Manchester) d									18 18									19 18					
Stalybridge a			17 36	17 43					18 22			18 36	18 43					19 22			19 36	19 43	
d			17 37	17 43		18 03			18 22			18 37	18 43		19 03			19 22			19 37	19 43	
Ashton-under-Lyne ⛴ d						18 06									19 06								
Manchester Victoria ⛴ a	17 38		17 54		18 09	18 18	18 43	18 21		18 38		18 50		19 09	19 18	19 43	19 21		19 38		19 50		20 09
d	17 39		17 55		18 10			18 23		18 39		18 54		19 10			19 23		19 39		19 54		20 10
Manchester Oxford Road a	17 45				18 16					18 45				19 16					19 45				20 16
Manchester Piccadilly a	17 50			18 09	18 20				18 41	18 50			19 09	19 20				19 41	19 50			20 09	20 20
d	17 51				18 20					18 51				19 20					19 51				20 20
Gatley a	18 00									19 00									20 00				
Manchester Airport ⛴✈ a	18 16				18 36					19 16				19 36					20 16				20 37
Newton-le-Willows 90 a								18 39									19 39				20 13		
Lea Green 90 a			18 18									19 18									20 19		
Liverpool Lime Street 10 90 a			18 34					18 58				19 34					20 00				20 35		

A 🛒 from Leeds

Table T039-R

Sundays

15 December to 5 January

Newcastle, Middlesborough, Scarborough, York, Hull, Leeds and Wakefield - Huddersfield - Manchester, Manchester Airport and Liverpool

		NT	NT	TP	TP	TP	TP	TP		TP	GC	TP	NT	NT	TP	TP	TP	TP	TP	TP	NT	NT	TP	TP
			◇	◇1 🛒	◇1	◇1	◇1	◇1		◇1 A 🛒	■ 1	◇1 🛒		◇	◇1 🛒	◇1	◇1	◇1	◇1	◇1 A 🛒		◇	◇1 B 🛒	◇1
Edinburgh	26 d			16 34											17 19								18 20	
Morpeth	26 d			17 48											18 30								19 30	
Newcastle 8	26 a			18 02											18 44								19 44	
	d			18 04								18 43			19 06								20 06	
Chester-le-Street	26 d											18 52												
Durham	26 d			18 17								18 59			19 18								20 18	
Darlington 5	26 a			18 33								19 16			19 35								20 35	
	d			18 35								19 17			19 36								20 36	
Redcar Central	44 d					18 02											19 05							
Middlesbrough	44 d					18 15											19 19							
Thornaby	44 d					18 21											19 25							
Yarm	d					18 29											19 33							
Northallerton	26 d					18 44					19 20	19 28					19 50							
Thirsk	26 d					18 53					19 29						19 58							
Scarborough	43 d							18 32											19 32					
Seamer	43 d							18 38											19 38					
Malton	d							18 57											19 57					
York 8	26 a			19 02		19 11		19 23			19 46	19 50			20 02		20 16		20 23				21 02	
	d			19 05		19 16		19 27				19 51			20 05		20 18		20 27				21 05	
Hull	29 d									19 04										20 06				
Brough	29 d									19 16										20 18				
Howden	29 d																							
Selby	29,40 d									19 38										20 39				
South Milford	40 d																							
Garforth	40 d							19 46											20 46					
Cross Gates	40 d																							
Leeds 10	a			19 27		19 43		19 56		20 03		20 14			20 27		20 43		20 56	21 03			21 27	
	d		19 19	19 30		19 45	19 47	20 00		20 07		20 15		20 18	20 30		20 45	20 47	21 00	21 07		21 18	21 30	
Cottingley	d						19 52											20 52						
Morley	d						19 56											20 56						
Batley	d						20 01											21 01						
Dewsbury	a					19 55	20 03					20 26					20 55	21 03		21 17			21 41	
	d					19 57	20 04					20 27					20 57	21 04		21 18			21 42	
Ravensthorpe	d						20 07											21 07						
Castleford	d																							
Normanton	d																							
Wakefield Kirkgate	d																							
Mirfield	d						20 11											21 10						
Deighton	d						20 17											21 17						
Huddersfield	a			19 47		20 05	20 22	20 17		20 24		20 37			20 47		21 05	21 22	21 17	21 26			21 50	
	d			19 48	19 53	20 08		20 18		20 25		20 39			20 48	20 53	21 08		21 21	21 27			21 51	21 53
Slaithwaite	d				20 00											21 00								22 00
Marsden	d				20 05											21 05								22 05
Greenfield	d				20 14											21 14								22 14
Mossley (Grtr Manchester)	d				20 18											21 18								22 18
Stalybridge	a				20 22			20 36		20 43						21 22			21 39	21 45				22 22
	d	20 03			20 22			20 37		20 43			21 03			21 22			21 40	21 46	22 03			22 22
Ashton-under-Lyne	d	20 06											21 06								22 06			
Manchester Victoria	a	20 18	20 44	20 21		20 38		20 55				21 11	21 17	21 45	21 22		21 40		21 53		22 17	22 45	22 23	
	d			20 23		20 39									21 24				21 54				22 24	
Manchester Oxford Road	a					20 45													22 00					
Manchester Piccadilly	a				20 41	20 50				21 09						21 41			22 04	22 07				22 41
	d					20 51													22 05					
Gatley	a					21 00																		
Manchester Airport	a					21 16													22 22					
Newton-le-Willows	90 a														21 40								22 40	
Lea Green	90 a														21 46								22 48	
Liverpool Lime Street 10	90 a			20 55											22 02								23 05	

A 🛒 from Leeds B 🛒 from York

Table T039-R

Sundays

15 December to 5 January

Newcastle, Middlesborough, Scarborough, York, Hull, Leeds and Wakefield - Huddersfield - Manchester, Manchester Airport and Liverpool

		TP	TP	TP	TP	NT	NT	TP	TP	TP	TP	TP	TP	TP	NT	TP		TP	TP	TP
		◇1	◇1	◇1	◇1 A 🛒		◇	◇1 B 🛒	◇1	◇1	◇1	◇1	◇1 🛒	◇1 A 🛒	◇	◇1		◇1	◇1	◇1 🛒
Edinburgh	26 d							19 30												
Morpeth	26 d							20 40												
Newcastle 8	26 a							20 55												
	d							21 02												
Chester-le-Street	26 d							21 11												
Durham	26 d							21 18												
Darlington 5	26 a							21 35												
	d							21 36												
Redcar Central	44 d	20 08								21 05			22 05							23 05
Middlesbrough	44 d	20 22								21 19			22 19							23 19
Thornaby	44 d	20 28								21 25			22 25							23 25
Yarm	d	20 36								21 33			22 33							23 33
Northallerton	26 d	20 53								21 50			22 50							
Thirsk	26 d	21 01								21 58			22 58							
Scarborough	43 d			20 32								21 32						22 42		
Seamer	43 d			20 38								21 38						22 48		
Malton	d			20 57								21 57						23 06		
York 8	26 a	21 21		21 23				22 02		22 18		22 23	23 18					23 33		00 18
	d			21 27				22 05				22 27						23 37		
Hull	29 d				21 06									22 06					23 04	
Brough	29 d				21 18									22 18					23 16	
Howden	29 d																			
Selby	29,40 d				21 38									22 38					23 36	
South Milford	40 d																			
Garforth	40 d			21 46								22 44								
Cross Gates	40 d																			
Leeds 10	a			21 55	22 03			22 27				22 53		23 03				00 02	00 02	
	d		21 47	22 00	22 07		22 11	22 29			22 47	22 57		23 07	23 19	23 47		00 05		
Cottingley	d		21 52								22 52					23 52				
Morley	d		21 56								22 56					23 56				
Batley	d		22 01								23 01					00 02				
Dewsbury	a		22 03		22 17			22 39			23 03	23 07				00 03				
	d		22 04		22 18			22 40			23 04	23 08				00 04				
Ravensthorpe	d		22 07								23 07					00 07				
Castleford	d																			
Normanton	d																			
Wakefield Kirkgate	d																			
Mirfield	d		22 11								23 11					00 11				
Deighton	d		22 17								23 17					00 17				
Huddersfield	a		22 22	22 17	22 26			22 49			23 22	23 17		23 24		00 22				
	d			22 21	22 27			22 50	22 54			23 18		23 25						
Slaithwaite	d								23 00					23 32						
Marsden	d								23 05					23 37						
Greenfield	d								23 14					23 46						
Mossley (Grtr Manchester)	d								23 18					23 50						
Stalybridge	a			22 39	22 45				23 22			23 36		23 54						
	d			22 40	22 46	23 03			23 22			23 37		23 54						
Ashton-under-Lyne	d					23 06														
Manchester Victoria	a			22 53	22 59	23 17	23 38	23 22				23 50			00 42					
	d			22 56	23 00			23 23				23 54								
Manchester Oxford Road	a			23 04								23 59								
Manchester Piccadilly	a			23 09					23 42			00 04		00 11				01 23		
	d			23 11								00 05								
Gatley	a																			
Manchester Airport	a			23 26								00 20								
Newton-le-Willows	90 a				23 16			23 39												
Lea Green	90 a				23 22			23 45												
Liverpool Lime Street 10	90 a				23 41			00 03												

A 🛒 from Leeds B 🛒 from York

Table T039-R

Sundays

12 January to 29 March

Newcastle, Middlesborough, Scarborough, York, Hull, Leeds and Wakefield - Huddersfield - Manchester, Manchester Airport and Liverpool

	TP ◇■ A	TP ◇■ A	TP B 🚌	TP ◇■ A	TP B 🚌	TP ◇■ A	TP ◇■ A	TP B 🚌	TP ◇■ A	TP B 🚌	TP B 🚌	TP ◇■ A	TP B 🚌	TP ◇■ ⊼	TP B 🚌		TP B 🚌	TP ◇■ A ⊼	TP B 🚌	TP B 🚌	TP ◇■ A	NT	TP B 🚌	TP ◇■ A ⊼
Edinburgh 26 d																								
Morpeth 26 d																								
Newcastle ■ 26 ⇌ a																								
d																								
Chester-le-Street 26 d																								
Durham 26 d																								
Darlington ■ 26 a																								
d																								
Redcar Central 44 d																								
Middlesbrough 44 d																								
Thornaby 44 d																								
Yarm d																								
Northallerton 26 d																								
Thirsk 26 d																								
Scarborough 43 d																								
Seamer 43 d																								
Malton d																								
York ■ 26 a																								
d			01 30	02 08		03 45	04 51	04 55	05 51		05 55				06 55			07 00						07 31
Hull 29 d																								
Brough 29 d																								
Howden 29 d																								
Selby 29,40 d																								
South Milford 40 d																								
Garforth 40 d																								
Cross Gates 40 d																				←				
Leeds ■10 a			02 20	02 48		04 23	05 31	05 45	06 31		06 45				07 45			07 40		07 45				08 10
d		00 07	02 20	02 53		04 28	05 43	05 45	06 36		06 45				07 45			07 45		07 45	07 47			08 15
Cottingley d															→						07 52			
Morley d																					07 56			
Batley d	00 02																				08 01		←	
Dewsbury a	00 03						05 53	06 10	06 46		07 10							07 56		08 10	08 03		08 10	08 26
d	00 04						05 54	06 10	06 47		07 10							07 57		08 10	08 04		08 10	08 27
Ravensthorpe d	00 07																			→	08 07			
Castleford d																								
Normanton d																								
Wakefield Kirkgate d																								
Mirfield d	00 11																				08 11			
Deighton d	00 17																				08 17			
Huddersfield a	00 22		02 55	03 10		04 45	06 02	06 35	06 56		07 35							08 05			08 22		08 35	08 35
d			02 55	03 11		04 46	06 03	06 35	06 57		07 35	07 53					08 00	08 06					08 35	08 36
Slaithwaite d												08 00					08 20							
Marsden d												08 05					08 30							
Greenfield d												08 14					08 57							
Mossley (Grtr Manchester) d										←		08 17	←				09 13							
Stalybridge a								07 25	07 15	07 25	08 25	08 21	08 25				09 30	08 25					09 20	
d								07 25	07 16	07 25	08 25	08 22	08 25				09 30	08 26				09 04	09 20	
Ashton-under-Lyne ⇌ d								→			→						→					09 07		
Manchester Victoria ⇌ a												08 36										09 18		09 08
d														08 52										
Manchester Oxford Road a					←														←					
Manchester Piccadilly a		00 56	03 55	03 42	03 55	05 16	06 33		07 31	07 45			08s45					08 41	08s45				09 45	
d			03 55	03 47	03 55	05 21	06 44		07 42	07 45								08 56						
Gatley a			→										→											
Manchester Airport ⇌✈ a				04 02	04 20	05 37	07 00		08 03	08 10								09 12	09 10					
Newton-le-Willows 90 a														09 08										
Lea Green 90 a														09 14										
Liverpool Lime Street ■10 90 a														09 34										

A until 16 February

B from 23 February

Table T039-R

Sundays

12 January to 29 March

Newcastle, Middlesborough, Scarborough, York, Hull, Leeds and Wakefield - Huddersfield - Manchester, Manchester Airport and Liverpool

	TP ◇■ ⊼	TP ◇■ A	TP B 🚌	NT ◇	TP B 🚌	TP ◇■ B ⊼	TP ◇■ A ⊼		TP ◇■ B ⊼	TP ◇■ A	TP ◇■ A ⊼	TP ◇■ C ⊼	TP B 🚌	TP ◇■ ⊼	NT	NT ◇	TP ◇■ ⊼	TP ◇■	TP ◇■ ⊼	TP ◇■	TP ◇■ ⊼	TP ◇■ C ⊼	TP ◇■ ⊼
Edinburgh 26 d																							
Morpeth 26 d																							
Newcastle ■ 26 ⇌ a																							
d														07 49			08 06						08 47
Chester-le-Street 26 d																							
Durham 26 d														08 01			08 18						08 59
Darlington ■ 26 a														08 18			08 35						09 16
d														08 19			08 36						09 17
Redcar Central 44 d																							
Middlesbrough 44 d																							
Thornaby 44 d																							
Yarm d																							
Northallerton 26 d																							09 28
Thirsk 26 d																							
Scarborough 43 d																					08 35		
Seamer 43 d																					08 41		
Malton d																					08 59		
York ■ 26 a														08 45			09 02				09 24		09 47
d						08 18	08 18				08 26			08 48			09 05		09 18		09 27		09 49
Hull 29 d												08 08										09 08	
Brough 29 d												08 20										09 20	
Howden 29 d																							
Selby 29,40 d												08 41										09 40	
South Milford 40 d																							
Garforth 40 d											08 43										09 45		
Cross Gates 40 d																							
Leeds ■10 a						08 41	08 43				08 53	09 05		09 12			09 27		09 42		09 56	10 03	10 12
d				08 18	08 25		08 45			08 47	09 00	09 07		09 15		09 19	09 30		09 45	09 47	10 00	10 07	10 15
Cottingley d					08 40					08 52										09 52			
Morley d					08 50					08 56										09 56			
Batley d					09 00					09 01			←							10 01			
Dewsbury a					09 08		08 55			09 03			09 08	09 26					09 55	10 03			10 26
d					09 08		08 56			09 04			09 08	09 27					09 57	10 04			10 27
Ravensthorpe d					→					09 07			09 15							10 07			
Castleford d																							
Normanton d																							
Wakefield Kirkgate d																							
Mirfield d										09 11			09 20							10 11			
Deighton d										09 17			09 30							10 17			
Huddersfield a							09 05			09 22	09 17	09 24	09 39	09 36			09 47		10 05	10 22	10 17	10 24	10 38
d		08 53					09 09				09 18	09 25		09 37			09 48	09 53	10 08		10 18	10 25	10 39
Slaithwaite d		08 59										09 32						10 00					
Marsden d		09 05										09 37						10 05					
Greenfield d		09 13										09 45						10 14					
Mossley (Grtr Manchester) d		09 17	←									09 49						10 18					
Stalybridge a		09 21	09 30								09 36	09 53						10 22			10 36	10 43	
d		09 21	09 30								09 37	09 53			10 03			10 22			10 37	10 43	
Ashton-under-Lyne ⇌ d															10 06								
Manchester Victoria ⇌ a		09 34		09 46			09 41				09 50				10 17	10 43	10 22		10 40		10 51		11 09
d	09 22								09 52		09 52						10 24				10 53		11 10
Manchester Oxford Road a																							11 16
Manchester Piccadilly a			09 55									10 12		10 20				10 41				11 09	11 20
d																							11 21
Gatley a																							
Manchester Airport ⇌✈ a																							11 38
Newton-le-Willows 90 a	09 38																10 40						
Lea Green 90 a									10 17		10 17										11 12		
Liverpool Lime Street ■10 90 a	09 59								10 33		10 33						10 59				11 28		

A until 16 February

B from 23 February

C ⊼ from Leeds

Table T039-R

Sundays
12 January to 29 March

Newcastle, Middlesborough, Scarborough, York, Hull, Leeds and Wakefield - Huddersfield - Manchester, Manchester Airport and Liverpool

	NT	NT	TP	TP	TP	TP	TP	TP	TP	GC	NT	NT	TP	TP	TP		TP	TP	TP	TP	NT	NT	TP	TP
		◇	◇■ 🛒	◇■	◇■ 🛒	◇■	◇■ 🛒	◇■ A 🛒	◇■ 🛒	■ ■		◇	◇■ 🛒	◇■	◇■ 🛒		◇■	◇■ 🛒	◇■ A 🛒	◇■ 🛒		◇	◇■ 🛒	◇■
Edinburgh 26 d																							09 20	
Morpeth 26 d																							10 30	
Newcastle ■ 26 a																							10 44	
d			09 03						09 43				10 06							10 47			11 06	
Chester-le-Street 26 d									09 52															
Durham 26 d			09 15						09 59				10 18							10 59			11 18	
Darlington ■ 26 a			09 32						10 16				10 35							11 16			11 35	
d			09 33						10 17				10 36							11 17			11 36	
Redcar Central 44 d															10 05									
Middlesbrough 44 d					09 29										10 18									
Thornaby 44 d					09 35										10 24									
Yarm d					09 43										10 33									
Northallerton 26 d										10 25					10 48					11 28				
Thirsk 26 d										10 34					10 56									
Scarborough 43 d							09 32											10 32						
Seamer 43 d							09 38											10 38						
Malton d							09 59											10 57						
York ■ 26 a			10 01		10 17		10 24		10 48	10 51			11 02		11 14			11 23		11 47			12 02	
d			10 04		10 20		10 27		10 49				11 05		11 16			11 27		11 49			12 05	
Hull 29 d								10 08											11 04					
Brough 29 d								10 20											11 16					
Howden 29 d																								
Selby 29,40 d								10 40											11 36					
South Milford 40 d																								
Garforth 40 d							10 43											11 46	11 51					
Cross Gates 40 d																			11 56					
Leeds ■ a			10 27		10 43		10 56	11 03	11 12				11 27		11 42			11 56	12 03	12 12			12 27	
d		10 15	10 30		10 45	10 47	11 00	11 07	11 15			11 18	11 30		11 45		11 47	12 00	12 07	12 15		12 18	12 30	
Cottingley d						10 52											11 52							
Morley d						10 56											11 56							
Batley d						11 01											12 01							
Dewsbury a					10 55	11 03			11 26						11 55		12 03			12 26				
d					10 57	11 04			11 27						11 56		12 04			12 27				
Ravensthorpe d						11 07											12 07							
Castleford d																								
Normanton d																								
Wakefield Kirkgate d																								
Mirfield d						11 11											12 11							
Deighton d						11 17											12 17							
Huddersfield a			10 47		11 05	11 22	11 17	11 24	11 37				11 47		12 05		12 22	12 17	12 24	12 36			12 47	
d			10 48	10 53	11 08		11 18	11 25	11 37				11 48	11 53	12 08			12 18	12 25	12 38			12 48	12 53
Slaithwaite d				11 00										12 00										13 00
Marsden d				11 05										12 05										13 05
Greenfield d				11 14										12 13										13 14
Mossley (Grtr Manchester) d				11 18										12 17										13 18
Stalybridge a				11 22			11 36	11 43						12 21				12 36	12 43					13 22
d	11 03			11 22			11 37	11 43			12 03			12 21				12 37	12 43		13 03			13 22
Ashton-under-Lyne d	11 06										12 06										13 06			
Manchester Victoria a	11 17	11 44	11 22		11 38		11 51		12 09		12 17	12 43	12 22		12 38			12 50		13 09	13 17	13 43	13 21	
d			11 24		11 40		11 54		12 10				12 23		12 39			12 52		13 10			13 23	
Manchester Oxford Road a					11 45				12 16						12 45					13 16				
Manchester Piccadilly a				11 41	11 49			12 12	12 20					12 41	12 49				13 10	13 20				13 41
d					11 52				12 21						12 53					13 21				
Gatley a					12 02										13 03									
Manchester Airport a					12 14				12 39						13 16					13 37				
Newton-le-Willows 90 a			11 40										12 39										13 39	
Lea Green 90 a							12 18											13 11						
Liverpool Lime Street ■ 90 a			11 59				12 34						12 59					13 29					13 58	

A 🛒 from Leeds

Table T039-R

Sundays
12 January to 29 March

Newcastle, Middlesborough, Scarborough, York, Hull, Leeds and Wakefield - Huddersfield - Manchester, Manchester Airport and Liverpool

	TP	TP	TP	TP	TP	NT	NT		TP	TP	TP	TP	TP	TP	GC	TP	NT	NT	TP	TP	TP	TP	TP
	◇■ 🛒	◇■	◇■ 🛒	◇■ A 🛒	◇■ 🛒		◇		◇■ 🛒	◇■	◇■ 🛒	◇■	◇■ 🛒	◇■ A 🛒	■ ■	◇■ 🛒		◇	◇■ 🛒	◇■	◇■ 🛒	◇■	◇■ 🛒
Edinburgh 26 d									10 20										11 33				
Morpeth 26 d									11 33										12 48				
Newcastle ■ 26 a									11 47										13 02				
d					11 43				12 05							12 46			13 05				
Chester-le-Street 26 d					11 53																		
Durham 26 d					12 00				12 17							12 59			13 17				
Darlington ■ 26 a					12 16				12 34							13 16			13 34				
d					12 18				12 35							13 17			13 35				
Redcar Central 44 d	11 05										12 05										13 05		
Middlesbrough 44 d	11 18										12 18										13 18		
Thornaby 44 d	11 24										12 24										13 24		
Yarm d	11 33										12 33										13 33		
Northallerton 26 d	11 48				12 29						12 48				13 15	13 28					13 48		
Thirsk 26 d	11 56										12 56				13 27						13 56		
Scarborough 43 d			11 32										12 32										13 32
Seamer 43 d			11 38										12 38										13 38
Malton d			11 57										12 57										13 57
York ■ 26 a	12 14		12 23		12 48				13 01		13 14		13 23		13 44	13 47			14 02		14 14		14 24
d	12 16		12 27		12 50				13 05		13 16		13 27			13 49			14 04		14 16		14 27
Hull 29 d				12 06										13 04									
Brough 29 d				12 18										13 16									
Howden 29 d																							
Selby 29,40 d				12 40										13 38									
South Milford 40 d																							
Garforth 40 d			12 47										13 46										14 47
Cross Gates 40 d																							
Leeds ■ a	12 43		12 56	13 03	13 13				13 28		13 43		13 56	14 03		14 12			14 27		14 43		14 56
d	12 45	12 47	13 00	13 07	13 14		13 18		13 30		13 45	13 47	14 00	14 07		14 15		14 19	14 30		14 45	14 47	15 00
Cottingley d		12 52										13 52										14 52	
Morley d		12 56										13 56										14 56	
Batley d		13 01										14 01										15 01	
Dewsbury a	12 55	13 03			13 25						13 55	14 03				14 26					14 55	15 03	
d	12 56	13 04			13 26						13 56	14 04				14 27					14 57	15 04	
Ravensthorpe d		13 07										14 07										15 07	
Castleford d																							
Normanton d																							
Wakefield Kirkgate d																							
Mirfield d		13 11										14 11										15 11	
Deighton d		13 17										14 17										15 17	
Huddersfield a	13 06	13 22	13 17	13 24	13 36				13 47		14 06	14 22	14 17	14 24		14 36			14 47		15 05	15 22	15 17
d	13 08		13 18	13 25	13 38				13 48	13 53	14 08		14 18	14 25		14 38			14 48	14 53	15 08		15 18
Slaithwaite d										14 00										15 00			
Marsden d										14 05										15 05			
Greenfield d										14 14										15 14			
Mossley (Grtr Manchester) d										14 18										15 18			
Stalybridge a			13 36	13 43						14 22			14 36	14 43						15 22			15 36
d			13 37	13 43		14 03				14 22			14 37	14 43			15 03			15 22			15 37
Ashton-under-Lyne d						14 06											15 06						
Manchester Victoria a	13 38		13 50		14 09	14 18	14 46		14 22		14 38		14 50			15 09	15 18	15 44	15 20		15 38		15 50
d	13 39		13 54		14 10				14 24		14 39		14 54			15 10			15 23		15 40		15 54
Manchester Oxford Road a	13 45				14 16						14 45					15 16					15 45		
Manchester Piccadilly a	13 50			14 09	14 20					14 41	14 50			15 09		15 20				15 41	15 50		
d	13 51				14 20						14 51					15 20					15 51		
Gatley a	14 00										15 00										16 00		
Manchester Airport a	14 16				14 36						15 16					15 36					16 16		
Newton-le-Willows 90 a									14 40										15 39				
Lea Green 90 a			14 18										15 18										16 18
Liverpool Lime Street ■ 90 a			14 34						14 59				15 34						15 58				16 34

A 🛒 from Leeds

Table T039-R

Sundays

12 January to 29 March

Newcastle, Middlesborough, Scarborough, York, Hull, Leeds and Wakefield - Huddersfield - Manchester, Manchester Airport and Liverpool

		TP	TP	NT	NT	TP	TP	TP	TP	TP	TP	GC	TP	NT	NT	TP	TP	TP	TP	TP	TP	TP	NT	NT
		◇■	◇■		◇	◇■	◇■	◇■	◇■	◇■	◇■	■ ■	◇■		◇	◇■	◇■	◇■	◇■	◇■	◇■	◇■		◇
		A									A										A			
		✠	✠			✠		✠		✠	✠	⊓	✠			✠		✠		✠	✠	✠		
Edinburgh	26 d					12 24										13 33								
Morpeth	26 d					13 38										14 49								
Newcastle ■	26 ⇌ a					13 53										15 03								
	d		13 43			13 56							14 47			15 05						15 43		
Chester-le-Street	26 d		13 52																			15 52		
Durham	26 d		13 59			14 08							14 59			15 18						15 59		
Darlington ■	26 a		14 15			14 25							15 16			15 34						16 16		
	d		14 16			14 26							15 17			15 36						16 17		
Redcar Central	44 d							14 03										15 05						
Middlesbrough	44 d							14 15										15 18						
Thornaby	44 d							14 21										15 24						
Yarm	d							14 32										15 33						
Northallerton	26 d							14 47				15 18	15 29					15 48				16 28		
Thirsk	26 d							14 55				15 27						15 56						
Scarborough	43 d									14 32										15 32				
Seamer	43 d									14 38										15 38				
Malton	d									14 57										15 57				
York ■	26 a		14 43			14 53		15 13		15 23		15 44	15 48			16 02		16 14		16 23		16 47		
	d		14 48			15 05		15 15		15 27			15 50			16 05		16 16		16 27		16 49		
Hull	29 d	14 06									15 06										16 06			
Brough	29 d	14 18									15 18										16 18			
Howden	29 d																							
Selby	29,40 d	14 38									15 38										16 39			
South Milford	40 d																							
Garforth	40 d									15 46														
Cross Gates	40 d																							
Leeds ■	a	15 03	15 11			15 27		15 43		15 56	16 03		16 12			16 28		16 43		16 56	17 03	17 12		
	d	15 07	15 15		15 18	15 30		15 45	15 47	16 00	16 07		16 15		16 19	16 30		16 45	16 47	17 00	17 07	17 15		17 18
Cottingley	d								15 52										16 52					
Morley	d								15 56										16 56					
Batley	d								16 01										17 01					
Dewsbury	a		15 25					15 55	16 03				16 26					16 55	17 03			17 25		
	d		15 26					15 57	16 04				16 27					16 57	17 04			17 26		
Ravensthorpe	d								16 07										17 07					
Castleford	d																							
Normanton	d																							
Wakefield Kirkgate	d																							
Mirfield	d								16 11										17 11					
Deighton	d								16 17										17 17					
Huddersfield	a	15 24	15 36			15 47		16 05	16 22	16 17	16 24		16 35			16 47		17 05	17 22	17 17	17 24	17 37		
	d	15 24	15 38			15 48	15 53	16 08		16 18	16 25		16 37			16 48	16 53	17 08		17 18	17 25	17 39		
Slaithwaite	d						16 00										17 00							
Marsden	d						16 05										17 05							
Greenfield	d						16 14										17 14							
Mossley (Grtr Manchester)	d						16 18										17 18							
Stalybridge	a	15 42					16 22			16 36	16 43						17 22			17 36	17 43			
	d	15 43		16 03			16 22			16 37	16 43			17 03			17 22			17 37	17 43		18 03	
Ashton-under-Lyne	⇌ d			16 06										17 06									18 06	
Manchester Victoria	⇌ a		16 10	16 18	16 44	16 21		16 38		16 50			17 09	17 18	17 44	17 21		17 38		17 54		18 09	18 18	18 43
	d		16 11			16 23		16 39		16 54			17 10			17 23		17 39		17 55		18 10		
Manchester Oxford Road	a		16 17					16 45					17 16					17 45				18 16		
Manchester Piccadilly	a	16 09	16 20				16 41	16 49			17 09		17 20				17 41	17 50			18 09	18 20		
	d		16 21					16 51					17 20					17 51				18 20		
Gatley	a							16 59										18 00						
Manchester Airport	⇌✈ a		16 37					17 16					17 36					18 16				18 36		
Newton-le-Willows	90 a					16 39										17 39								
Lea Green	90 a									17 18										18 18				
Liverpool Lime Street ■	90 a					16 58				17 34						17 58				18 34				

A ✠ from Leeds

Table T039-R

Sundays

12 January to 29 March

Newcastle, Middlesborough, Scarborough, York, Hull, Leeds and Wakefield - Huddersfield - Manchester, Manchester Airport and Liverpool

		TP	TP	TP	TP	TP	TP	TP	NT	NT	TP	TP	TP	TP	TP	TP	TP	NT	NT	TP	TP	TP	TP
		◇■	◇■	◇■	◇■	◇■	◇■	◇■		◇	◇■	◇■	◇■	◇■	◇■	◇■	◇■		◇	◇■	◇■	◇■	◇■
							A									A							
		✠		✠		✠	✠	✠			✠		✠		✠	✠	✠			✠			
Edinburgh	26 d	14 21									15 20									16 34			
Morpeth	26 d	15 31									16 30									17 48			
Newcastle ■	26 ⇌ a	15 44									16 44									18 02			
	d	16 00						16 43			17 06						17 43			18 04			
Chester-le-Street	26 d							16 52									17 52						
Durham	26 d	16 15						16 59			17 18						17 59			18 17			
Darlington ■	26 a	16 31						17 16			17 35						18 15			18 33			
	d	16 33						17 17			17 36						18 17			18 35			
Redcar Central	44 d			16 05									17 05									18 02	
Middlesbrough	44 d			16 18									17 18									18 15	
Thornaby	44 d			16 24									17 24									18 21	
Yarm	d			16 33									17 33									18 29	
Northallerton	26 d												17 48				18 28					18 44	
Thirsk	26 d			16 55									17 56									18 53	
Scarborough	43 d					16 32									17 32								
Seamer	43 d					16 38									17 38								
Malton	d					16 57									17 57								
York ■	26 a	16 59		17 16		17 23		17 48			18 02		18 14		18 23		18 47			19 02		19 11	
	d	17 05		17 18		17 27		17 49			18 05		18 18		18 27		18 49			19 05		19 16	
Hull	29 d						17 06									18 06							
Brough	29 d						17 18									18 18							
Howden	29 d																						
Selby	29,40 d						17 38									18 38							
South Milford	40 d																						
Garforth	40 d					17 46									18 47								
Cross Gates	40 d																						
Leeds ■	a	17 28		17 44		17 56	18 03	18 12			18 27		18 43		18 56	19 03	19 13			19 27		19 43	
	d	17 30		17 45	17 48	18 00	18 07	18 15		18 18	18 30		18 45	18 47	19 00	19 07	19 15		19 19	19 30		19 45	19 47
Cottingley	d				17 53									18 52									19 52
Morley	d				17 56									18 56									19 56
Batley	d				18 01									19 01									20 01
Dewsbury	a			17 55	18 04			18 26					18 56	19 03			19 26					19 55	20 03
	d			17 57	18 04			18 27					18 58	19 04			19 27					19 57	20 04
Ravensthorpe	d				18 07									19 07									20 07
Castleford	d																						
Normanton	d																						
Wakefield Kirkgate	d																						
Mirfield	d				18 11									19 11									20 11
Deighton	d				18 17									19 17									20 17
Huddersfield	a	17 47		18 06	18 22	18 17	18 24	18 35			18 47		19 06	19 22	19 17	19 24	19 37			19 47		20 05	20 22
	d	17 49	17 53	18 08		18 18	18 25	18 37			18 48	18 53	19 08		19 18	19 25	19 38			19 48	19 53	20 08	
Slaithwaite	d		18 00									19 00									20 00		
Marsden	d		18 05									19 05									20 05		
Greenfield	d		18 14									19 14									20 14		
Mossley (Grtr Manchester)	d		18 18									19 18									20 18		
Stalybridge	a		18 22			18 36	18 43					19 22			19 36	19 43					20 22		
	d		18 22			18 37	18 43		19 03			19 22			19 37	19 43		20 03			20 22		
Ashton-under-Lyne	⇌ d								19 06									20 06					
Manchester Victoria	⇌ a	18 21		18 38		18 50		19 09	19 18	19 43	19 21		19 38		19 50		20 09	20 18	20 44	20 21		20 38	
	d	18 23		18 39		18 54		19 10			19 23		19 39		19 54		20 10			20 23		20 39	
Manchester Oxford Road	a			18 45				19 16					19 45				20 16					20 45	
Manchester Piccadilly	a		18 41	18 50			19 09	19 20				19 41	19 50			20 09	20 20				20 41	20 50	
	d			18 51				19 20					19 51				20 20					20 51	
Gatley	a			19 00									20 00									21 00	
Manchester Airport	⇌✈ a			19 16				19 36					20 16				20 37					21 16	
Newton-le-Willows	90 a	18 39									19 39				20 13								
Lea Green	90 a					19 18									20 19								
Liverpool Lime Street ■	90 a	18 58				19 34					20 00				20 35					20 55			

A ✠ from Leeds

Table T039-R

Sundays
12 January to 29 March

Newcastle, Middlesborough, Scarborough, York, Hull, Leeds and Wakefield - Huddersfield - Manchester, Manchester Airport and Liverpool

		TP	TP	GC	TP	NT	NT	TP	TP	TP	TP	TP	TP	NT	NT	TP	TP	TP	TP	TP	TP	NT	NT	TP
		◇1	◇1	■1	◇1		◇	◇1	◇1	◇1	◇1	◇1	◇1		◇	◇1	◇1	◇1	◇1	◇1	◇1		◇	◇1
			A										A			B					A			B
			🛒	🍽	🛒			🛒					🛒			🛒					🛒			🛒
Edinburgh 26	d							17 19								18 20								19 30
Morpeth 26	d							18 30								19 30								20 40
Newcastle 8 26 ⛴	a							18 44								19 44								20 55
	d				18 43			19 06								20 06								21 02
Chester-le-Street 26	d				18 52																			21 11
Durham 26	d				18 59			19 18								20 18								21 18
Darlington 5 26	a				19 16			19 35								20 35								21 35
	d				19 17			19 36								20 36								21 36
Redcar Central 44	d									19 05								20 08						
Middlesbrough 44	d									19 19								20 22						
Thornaby 44	d									19 25								20 28						
Yarm	d									19 33								20 36						
Northallerton 26	d			19 20	19 28					19 50								20 53						
Thirsk 26	d			19 29						19 58								21 01						
Scarborough 43	d	18 32										19 32								20 32				
Seamer 43	d	18 38										19 38								20 38				
Malton	d	18 57										19 57								20 57				
York 8 26	a	19 23		19 46	19 50			20 02		20 16		20 23				21 02		21 21		21 23				22 02
	d	19 27			19 51			20 05		20 18		20 27				21 05				21 27				22 05
Hull 29	d		19 04										20 06								21 06			
Brough 29	d		19 16										20 18								21 18			
Howden 29	d																							
Selby 29,40	d		19 38										20 39								21 38			
South Milford 40	d																							
Garforth 40	d	19 46										20 46								21 46				
Cross Gates 40	d																							
Leeds 10	a	19 56	20 03		20 14			20 27		20 43		20 56	21 03			21 27				21 55	22 03			22 27
	d	20 00	20 07		20 15		20 18	20 30		20 45	20 47	21 00	21 07		21 18	21 30			21 47	22 00	22 07		22 11	22 29
Cottingley	d										20 52								21 52					
Morley	d										20 56								21 56					
Batley	d										21 01								22 01					
Dewsbury	a				20 26					20 55	21 03		21 17			21 41			22 03		22 17			22 39
	d				20 27					20 57	21 04		21 18			21 42			22 04		22 18			22 40
Ravensthorpe	d										21 07								22 07					
Castleford	d																							
Normanton	d																							
Wakefield Kirkgate	d																							
Mirfield	d										21 10								22 11					
Deighton	d										21 17								22 17					
Huddersfield	a	20 17	20 24		20 37			20 47		21 05	21 22	21 17	21 26			21 50			22 22	22 17	22 26			22 49
	d	20 18	20 25		20 39			20 48	20 53	21 08		21 21	21 27			21 51	21 53			22 21	22 27			22 50
Slaithwaite	d								21 00								22 00							
Marsden	d								21 05								22 05							
Greenfield	d								21 14								22 14							
Mossley (Grtr Manchester)	d								21 18								22 18							
Stalybridge	a	20 36	20 43						21 22			21 39	21 45				22 22			22 39	22 45			
	d	20 37	20 43			21 03			21 22			21 40	21 46	22 03			22 22			22 40	22 46	23 03		
Ashton-under-Lyne ⛴	d					21 06								22 06								23 06		
Manchester Victoria ⛴	a	20 55			21 11	21 17	21 45	21 22		21 40		21 53		22 17	22 45	22 23				22 53	22 59	23 17	23 38	23 22
	d							21 24				21 54				22 24				22 56	23 00			23 23
Manchester Oxford Road	a											22 00								23 04				
Manchester Piccadilly	a		21 09						21 41			22 04	22 07				22 41			23 09				
	d											22 05								23 11				
Gatley	a																							
Manchester Airport ⛴✈	a											22 22								23 26				
Newton-le-Willows 90	a							21 40								22 40					23 16			23 39
Lea Green 90	a							21 46								22 48					23 22			23 45
Liverpool Lime Street 10 90	a							22 02								23 05					23 41			00 03

A 🛒 from Leeds
B 🛒 from York

Table T039-R

Sundays
12 January to 29 March

Newcastle, Middlesborough, Scarborough, York, Hull, Leeds and Wakefield - Huddersfield - Manchester, Manchester Airport and Liverpool

		TP	TP	TP	TP	TP	TP	NT	TP	TP	TP	TP
		◇1	◇1	◇1	◇1	◇1	◇1	◇	◇1	◇1	◇1	◇1
							A					
						🛒	🛒					🛒
Edinburgh 26	d											
Morpeth 26	d											
Newcastle 8 26 ⛴	a											
	d											
Chester-le-Street 26	d											
Durham 26	d											
Darlington 5 26	a											
	d											
Redcar Central 44	d		21 05			22 05						23 05
Middlesbrough 44	d		21 19			22 19						23 19
Thornaby 44	d		21 25			22 25						23 25
Yarm	d		21 33			22 33						23 33
Northallerton 26	d		21 50			22 50						
Thirsk 26	d		21 58			22 58						
Scarborough 43	d				21 32					22 42		
Seamer 43	d				21 38					22 48		
Malton	d				21 57					23 06		
York 8 26	a		22 18		22 23	23 18				23 33		00 18
	d				22 27					23 37		
Hull 29	d						22 06				23 04	
Brough 29	d						22 18				23 16	
Howden 29	d											
Selby 29,40	d						22 38				23 36	
South Milford 40	d											
Garforth 40	d				22 44							
Cross Gates 40	d											
Leeds 10	a				22 53		23 03			00 02	00 02	
	d			22 47	22 57		23 07	23 19	23 47	00 05		
Cottingley	d			22 52					23 52			
Morley	d			22 56					23 56			
Batley	d			23 01					00 02			
Dewsbury	a			23 03	23 07				00 03			
	d			23 04	23 08				00 04			
Ravensthorpe	d			23 07					00 07			
Castleford	d											
Normanton	d											
Wakefield Kirkgate	d											
Mirfield	d			23 11					00 11			
Deighton	d			23 17					00 17			
Huddersfield	a			23 22	23 17		23 24		00 22			
	d	22 54			23 18		23 25					
Slaithwaite	d	23 00					23 32					
Marsden	d	23 05					23 37					
Greenfield	d	23 14					23 46					
Mossley (Grtr Manchester)	d	23 18					23 50					
Stalybridge	a	23 22			23 36		23 54					
	d	23 22			23 37		23 54					
Ashton-under-Lyne ⛴	d											
Manchester Victoria ⛴	a				23 50			00 42				
	d				23 54							
Manchester Oxford Road	a				23 59							
Manchester Piccadilly	a	23 42			00 04		00 11			01 23		
	d				00 05							
Gatley	a											
Manchester Airport ⛴✈	a				00 20							
Newton-le-Willows 90	a											
Lea Green 90	a											
Liverpool Lime Street 10 90	a											

A 🛒 from Leeds

Table T039-R

Sundays

5 April to 10 May

Newcastle, Middlesborough, Scarborough, York, Hull, Leeds and Wakefield - Huddersfield - Manchester, Manchester Airport and Liverpool

	TP	TP	TP	TP	TP	TP	TP	TP	TP	TP	TP	NT	TP	TP	NT		TP	TP	TP	TP	NT	TP	NT	TP
	◇1	◇1	◇1	◇1	◇1	◇1	◇1	◇1	◇1	◇1	◇1		◇1	◇1	◇		◇1	◇1	◇1	◇1		◇1	◇	◇1
								ℍ		ℍ	ℍ		ℍ				ℍ		ℍ	A ℍ		ℍ		ℍ
Edinburgh 26 d																								
Morpeth 26 d																								
Newcastle 8 26 a																								
d																						07 49		08 06
Chester-le-Street 26 d																								
Durham 26 d																						08 01		08 18
Darlington 8 26 a																						08 18		08 35
d																						08 19		08 36
Redcar Central 44 d																								
Middlesbrough 44 d																								
Thornaby 44 d																								
Yarm d																								
Northallerton 26 d																								
Thirsk 26 d																								
Scarborough 43 d																								
Seamer 43 d																								
Malton d																								
York 8 26 a																						08 45		09 02
d			02 25	04 00	05 15	06 08		07 17			07 44						08 18		08 26			08 48		09 05
Hull 29 d																				08 08				
Brough 29 d																				08 20				
Howden 29 d																								
Selby 29,40 d																				08 41				
South Milford 40 d																								
Garforth 40 d																			08 43					
Cross Gates 40 d																								
Leeds 10 a			02 50	04 25	05 40	06 33		07 42			08 13						08 43		08 53	09 05		09 12		09 27
d		00 07	02 53	04 28	05 43	06 36		07 45	07 47		08 15				08 18		08 45	08 47	09 00	09 07		09 15	09 19	09 30
Cottingley d									07 52									08 52						
Morley d									07 56									08 56						
Batley d	00 02								08 01									09 01						
Dewsbury a	00 03				05 53	06 46		07 55	08 03		08 26						08 55	09 03				09 26		
d	00 04				05 54	06 47		07 56	08 04		08 27						08 56	09 04				09 27		
Ravensthorpe d	00 07								08 07									09 07						
Castleford d																								
Normanton d																								
Wakefield Kirkgate d																								
Mirfield d	00 11								08 11									09 11						
Deighton d	00 17								08 17									09 17						
Huddersfield a	00 22		03 10	04 45	06 02	06 56		08 05	08 22		08 35						09 05	09 22	09 17	09 24		09 36		09 47
d			03 11	04 46	06 03	06 57	07 53	08 06			08 36			08 53			09 07		09 18	09 25		09 37		09 48
Slaithwaite d							08 00							08 59						09 32				
Marsden d							08 05							09 05						09 37				
Greenfield d							08 14							09 13						09 45				
Mossley (Grtr Manchester) d							08 17							09 17						09 49				
Stalybridge a						07 15	08 21	08 25						09 21					09 36	09 53				
d						07 16	08 22	08 26				09 04		09 21					09 37	09 53	10 03			
Ashton-under-Lyne ⇌ d												09 07									10 06			
Manchester Victoria ⇌ a							08 36	08 39			09 08	09 18		09 34	09 46		09 41		09 50		10 17		10 43	10 22
d								08 44		08 52			09 22						09 52					10 24
Manchester Oxford Road a								08 49																
Manchester Piccadilly a		00 56	03 42	05 16	06 33	07 31		08 53												10 12		10 20		
d			03 47	05 21	06 44	07 42		08 56																
Gatley a																								
Manchester Airport ⇌✈ a			04 02	05 37	07 00	08 07		09 12																
Newton-le-Willows 90 a										09 08			09 38											10 40
Lea Green 90 a										09 14									10 17					
Liverpool Lime Street 10 90 a										09 34			09 59						10 33					10 59

A ℍ from Leeds

Table T039-R

Sundays

5 April to 10 May

Newcastle, Middlesborough, Scarborough, York, Hull, Leeds and Wakefield - Huddersfield - Manchester, Manchester Airport and Liverpool

	TP	TP	TP	TP	TP	TP	NT		NT	TP	TP	TP	TP	TP	TP	TP	GC	NT	NT	TP	TP	TP	TP
	◇1	◇1	◇1	◇1	◇1	◇1			◇	◇1	◇1	◇1	◇1	◇1	◇1	◇1	■ 1		◇	◇1	◇1	◇1	◇1
		ℍ		ℍ	A ℍ	ℍ				ℍ		ℍ		ℍ	A ℍ	ℍ	⊏			ℍ		ℍ	
Edinburgh 26 d																							
Morpeth 26 d																							
Newcastle 8 26 a																							
d						08 47				09 03						09 43				10 06			
Chester-le-Street 26 d																09 52							
Durham 26 d						08 59				09 15						09 59				10 18			
Darlington 8 26 a						09 16				09 32						10 16				10 35			
d						09 17				09 33						10 17				10 36			
Redcar Central 44 d																						10 05	
Middlesbrough 44 d												09 29										10 18	
Thornaby 44 d												09 35										10 24	
Yarm d												09 43										10 33	
Northallerton 26 d						09 28											10 25					10 48	
Thirsk 26 d																	10 34					10 56	
Scarborough 43 d				08 35										09 32									
Seamer 43 d				08 41										09 38									
Malton d				08 59										09 59									
York 8 26 a				09 24		09 47				10 01		10 17		10 24		10 48	10 51			11 02		11 14	
d		09 18		09 27		09 49				10 04		10 20		10 27		10 49				11 05		11 16	
Hull 29 d					09 08										10 08								
Brough 29 d					09 20										10 20								
Howden 29 d																							
Selby 29,40 d					09 40										10 40								
South Milford 40 d																							
Garforth 40 d				09 45										10 43									
Cross Gates 40 d																							
Leeds 10 a		09 42		09 56	10 03	10 12				10 27		10 43		10 56	11 03	11 12				11 27		11 42	
d		09 45	09 47	10 00	10 07	10 15			10 15	10 30		10 45	10 47	11 00	11 07	11 15			11 18	11 30		11 45	11 47
Cottingley d			09 52										10 52										11 52
Morley d			09 56										10 56										11 56
Batley d			10 01										11 01										12 01
Dewsbury a		09 55	10 03			10 26						10 55	11 03			11 26						11 55	12 03
d		09 57	10 04			10 27						10 57	11 04			11 27						11 56	12 04
Ravensthorpe d			10 07										11 07										12 07
Castleford d																							
Normanton d																							
Wakefield Kirkgate d																							
Mirfield d			10 11										11 11										12 11
Deighton d			10 17										11 17										12 17
Huddersfield a		10 05	10 22	10 17	10 24	10 38				10 47		11 05	11 22	11 17	11 24	11 37				11 47		12 05	12 22
d	09 53	10 08		10 18	10 25	10 39				10 48	10 53	11 08		11 18	11 25	11 37				11 48	11 53	12 08	
Slaithwaite d	10 00										11 00										12 00		
Marsden d	10 05										11 05										12 05		
Greenfield d	10 14										11 14										12 13		
Mossley (Grtr Manchester) d	10 18										11 18										12 17		
Stalybridge a	10 22			10 36	10 43						11 22			11 36	11 43						12 21		
d	10 22			10 37	10 43		11 03				11 22			11 37	11 43			12 03			12 21		
Ashton-under-Lyne ⇌ d							11 06											12 06					
Manchester Victoria ⇌ a		10 40		10 51		11 09	11 17		11 44	11 22		11 38		11 51		12 09		12 17	12 43	12 22		12 38	
d				10 53		11 10				11 24		11 40		11 54		12 10				12 23		12 39	
Manchester Oxford Road a						11 16						11 45				12 16						12 45	
Manchester Piccadilly a	10 41				11 05	11 20					11 42	11 49			12 09	12 20					12 41	12 49	
d						11 21						11 52				12 20						12 53	
Gatley a												12 02										13 03	
Manchester Airport ⇌✈ a						11 38						12 14				12 39						13 16	
Newton-le-Willows 90 a										11 40										12 39			
Lea Green 90 a				11 12										12 18									
Liverpool Lime Street 10 90 a				11 28						11 59				12 34						12 59			

A ℍ from Leeds

Table T039-R

Sundays
5 April to 10 May

Newcastle, Middlesborough, Scarborough, York, Hull, Leeds and Wakefield - Huddersfield - Manchester, Manchester Airport and Liverpool

	TP	TP	TP	NT	NT	TP	TP	TP	TP	TP	TP	TP	NT	NT	TP		TP	TP	TP	TP	TP	GC	TP	NT
	◇1 🚲	◇1 A 🚲	◇1 🚲		◇	◇1 🚲	◇1	◇1 🚲	◇1	◇1 🚲	◇1 A 🚲	◇1 🚲		◇	◇1 🚲		◇1	◇1 🚲	◇1	◇1 🚲	◇1 A 🚲	R 1	◇1 🚲	
Edinburgh 26 d						09 20									10 20									
Morpeth 26 d						10 30									11 33									
Newcastle 8 26 a						10 44									11 47									
d			10 47			11 06						11 43			12 05								12 46	
Chester-le-Street 26 d												11 53												
Durham 26 d			10 59			11 18						12 00			12 17								12 59	
Darlington 5 26 a			11 16			11 35						12 16			12 34								13 16	
d			11 17			11 36						12 18			12 35								13 17	
Redcar Central 44 d								11 05										12 05						
Middlesbrough 44 d								11 18										12 18						
Thornaby 44 d								11 24										12 24						
Yarm d								11 33										12 33						
Northallerton 26 d			11 28					11 48				12 29						12 48				13 15	13 28	
Thirsk 26 d								11 56										12 56				13 27		
Scarborough 43 d	10 32									11 32										12 32				
Seamer 43 d	10 38									11 38										12 38				
Malton d	10 57									11 57										12 57				
York 8 26 a	11 23		11 47			12 02		12 14		12 23		12 48			13 01			13 14		13 23		13 44	13 47	
d	11 27		11 49			12 05		12 16		12 27		12 50			13 05			13 16		13 27			13 49	
Hull 29 d		11 04									12 06										13 04			
Brough 29 d		11 16									12 18										13 16			
Howden 29 d																								
Selby 29,40 d		11 36									12 40										13 38			
South Milford 40 d																								
Garforth 40 d	11 46	11 51								12 47										13 46				
Cross Gates 40 d		11 56																						
Leeds 10 a	11 56	12 03	12 12			12 27		12 43		12 56	13 03	13 13			13 28			13 43		13 56	14 03		14 12	
d	12 00	12 07	12 15		12 18	12 30		12 45	12 47	13 00	13 07	13 14		13 18	13 30			13 45	13 47	14 00	14 07		14 15	
Cottingley d									12 52										13 52					
Morley d									12 56										13 56					
Batley d									13 01										14 01					
Dewsbury a			12 26					12 55	13 03			13 25						13 55	14 03				14 26	
d			12 27					12 56	13 04			13 26						13 56	14 04				14 27	
Ravensthorpe d									13 07										14 07					
Castleford d																								
Normanton d																								
Wakefield Kirkgate d																								
Mirfield d									13 11										14 11					
Deighton d									13 17										14 17					
Huddersfield a	12 17	12 24	12 36			12 47		13 06	13 22	13 17	13 24	13 36			13 47			14 06	14 22	14 17	14 24		14 36	
d	12 18	12 25	12 38			12 48	12 53	13 08		13 18	13 25	13 38			13 48		13 53	14 08		14 18	14 25		14 38	
Slaithwaite d							13 00										14 00							
Marsden d							13 05										14 05							
Greenfield d							13 14										14 14							
Mossley (Grtr Manchester) d							13 18										14 18							
Stalybridge a	12 36	12 43					13 22			13 36	13 43						14 22			14 36	14 43			
d	12 37	12 43		13 03			13 22			13 37	13 43		14 03				14 22			14 37	14 43			15 03
Ashton-under-Lyne 🚊 d				13 06									14 06											15 06
Manchester Victoria 🚊 a	12 50		13 09	13 17	13 43	13 21		13 38		13 50		14 09	14 18	14 46	14 22			14 38		14 50			15 09	15 18
d	12 52		13 10			13 23		13 39		13 54		14 10			14 24			14 39		14 54			15 10	
Manchester Oxford Road a			13 16					13 45				14 16						14 45					15 16	
Manchester Piccadilly a		13 10	13 20				13 41	13 50			14 09	14 20					14 41	14 50			15 09		15 20	
d			13 20					13 51				14 20						14 51					15 20	
Gatley a								14 00										15 00						
Manchester Airport 🚊✈ a			13 36					14 16				14 36						15 16					15 36	
Newton-le-Willows 90 a						13 39									14 40									
Lea Green 90 a	13 11									14 18										15 18				
Liverpool Lime Street 10 90 a	13 29					13 58				14 34					14 59					15 34				

A 🚲 from Leeds

NRT DECEMBER 19 EDITION

Table T039-R

Sundays
5 April to 10 May

Newcastle, Middlesborough, Scarborough, York, Hull, Leeds and Wakefield - Huddersfield - Manchester, Manchester Airport and Liverpool

	NT	TP	TP	TP	TP	TP	TP		TP	NT	NT	TP	TP	TP	TP	TP	TP	GC	TP	NT	NT	TP	TP
	◇	◇1 🚲	◇1	◇1 🚲	◇1	◇1 🚲	◇1 A 🚲		◇1 🚲		◇	◇1 🚲	◇1	◇1 🚲	◇1	◇1 🚲	◇1 A 🚲	R 1	◇1 🚲		◇	◇1 🚲	◇1
Edinburgh 26 d		11 33										12 24										13 33	
Morpeth 26 d		12 48										13 38										14 49	
Newcastle 8 26 a		13 02										13 53										15 03	
d		13 05							13 43			13 56							14 47			15 05	
Chester-le-Street 26 d									13 52														
Durham 26 d		13 17							13 59			14 08							14 59			15 18	
Darlington 5 26 a		13 34							14 15			14 25							15 16			15 34	
d		13 35							14 16			14 26							15 17			15 36	
Redcar Central 44 d				13 05										14 03									
Middlesbrough 44 d				13 18										14 15									
Thornaby 44 d				13 24										14 21									
Yarm d				13 33										14 32									
Northallerton 26 d				13 48										14 47				15 18	15 29				
Thirsk 26 d				13 56										14 55				15 27					
Scarborough 43 d						13 32										14 32							
Seamer 43 d						13 38										14 38							
Malton d						13 57										14 57							
York 8 26 a		14 02		14 14		14 24			14 43			14 53		15 13		15 23		15 44	15 48			16 02	
d		14 04		14 16		14 27			14 48			15 05		15 15		15 27			15 50			16 05	
Hull 29 d							14 06										15 06						
Brough 29 d							14 18										15 18						
Howden 29 d																							
Selby 29,40 d							14 38										15 38						
South Milford 40 d																							
Garforth 40 d						14 47										15 46							
Cross Gates 40 d																							
Leeds 10 a		14 27		14 43		14 56	15 03		15 11			15 27		15 43		15 56	16 03		16 12			16 28	
d	14 19	14 30		14 45	14 47	15 00	15 07		15 15		15 18	15 30		15 45	15 47	16 00	16 07		16 15		16 19	16 30	
Cottingley d					14 52										15 52								
Morley d					14 56										15 56								
Batley d					15 01										16 01								
Dewsbury a				14 55	15 03				15 25					15 55	16 03				16 26				
d				14 57	15 04				15 26					15 57	16 04				16 27				
Ravensthorpe d					15 07										16 07								
Castleford d																							
Normanton d																							
Wakefield Kirkgate d																							
Mirfield d					15 11										16 11								
Deighton d					15 17										16 17								
Huddersfield a		14 47		15 05	15 22	15 17	15 24		15 36			15 47		16 05	16 22	16 17	16 24		16 35			16 47	
d		14 48	14 53	15 08		15 18	15 24		15 38			15 48	15 53	16 08		16 18	16 25		16 37			16 48	16 53
Slaithwaite d			15 00										16 00										17 00
Marsden d			15 05										16 05										17 05
Greenfield d			15 14										16 14										17 14
Mossley (Grtr Manchester) d			15 18										16 18										17 18
Stalybridge a			15 22			15 36	15 42						16 22			16 36	16 43						17 22
d			15 22			15 37	15 43			16 03			16 22			16 37	16 43			17 03			17 22
Ashton-under-Lyne 🚊 d										16 06										17 06			
Manchester Victoria 🚊 a	15 44	15 20		15 38		15 50			16 10	16 18	16 44	16 21		16 38		16 50			17 09	17 18	17 44	17 21	
d		15 23		15 40		15 54			16 11			16 23		16 39		16 54			17 10			17 23	
Manchester Oxford Road a				15 45					16 17					16 45					17 16				
Manchester Piccadilly a			15 41	15 50			16 09		16 20				16 41	16 49			17 09		17 20				17 41
d				15 51					16 21					16 51					17 20				
Gatley a				16 00										16 59									
Manchester Airport 🚊✈ a				16 16					16 37					17 16					17 36				
Newton-le-Willows 90 a		15 39										16 39										17 39	
Lea Green 90 a						16 18										17 18							
Liverpool Lime Street 10 90 a		15 58				16 34						16 58				17 34						17 58	

A 🚲 from Leeds

Table T039-R

Sundays
5 April to 10 May

Newcastle, Middlesborough, Scarborough, York, Hull, Leeds and Wakefield - Huddersfield - Manchester, Manchester Airport and Liverpool

		TP	TP	TP	TP	TP	NT	NT	TP	TP	TP	TP	TP	TP	TP	NT		NT	TP	TP	TP	TP	TP	TP	TP
		◇1	◇1	◇1	◇1	◇1		◇	◇1	◇1	◇1	◇1	◇1	◇1	◇1			◇	◇1	◇1	◇1	◇1	◇1	◇1	◇1
					A									A										A	
		⊼		⊼	⊼	⊼			⊼		⊼		⊼	⊼	⊼				⊼		⊼		⊼	⊼	⊼
Edinburgh	26 d								14 21										15 20						
Morpeth	26 d								15 31										16 30						
Newcastle 8	26 ⛴ a								15 44										16 44						
	d					15 43			16 00						16 43				17 06						17 43
Chester-le-Street	26 d					15 52									16 52										17 52
Durham	26 d					15 59			16 15						16 59				17 18						17 59
Darlington 5	26 a					16 16			16 31						17 16				17 35						18 15
	d					16 17			16 33						17 17				17 36						18 17
Redcar Central	44 d	15 05									16 05										17 05				
Middlesbrough	44 d	15 18									16 18										17 18				
Thornaby	44 d	15 24									16 24										17 24				
Yarm	d	15 33									16 33										17 33				
Northallerton	26 d	15 48				16 28															17 48				18 28
Thirsk	26 d	15 56									16 55										17 56				
Scarborough	43 d			15 32									16 32										17 32		
Seamer	43 d			15 38									16 38										17 38		
Malton	d			15 57									16 57										17 57		
York 8	26 a	16 14		16 23		16 47			16 59		17 16		17 23		17 48				18 02		18 14		18 23		18 47
	d	16 16		16 27		16 49			17 05		17 18		17 27		17 49				18 05		18 18		18 27		18 49
Hull	29 d				16 06									17 06										18 06	
Brough	29 d				16 18									17 18										18 18	
Howden	29 d																								
Selby	29,40 d				16 39									17 38										18 38	
South Milford	40 d																								
Garforth	40 d												17 46										18 47		
Cross Gates	40 d																								
Leeds 10	a	16 43		16 56	17 03	17 12			17 28		17 44		17 56	18 03	18 12				18 27		18 43		18 56	19 03	19 13
	d	16 45	16 47	17 00	17 07	17 15		17 18	17 30		17 45	17 48	18 00	18 07	18 15			18 18	18 30		18 45	18 47	19 00	19 07	19 15
Cottingley	d		16 52									17 53										18 52			
Morley	d		16 56									17 56										18 56			
Batley	d		17 01									18 01										19 01			
Dewsbury	a	16 55	17 03			17 25					17 55	18 04			18 26						18 56	19 03			19 26
	d	16 57	17 04			17 26					17 57	18 04			18 27						18 58	19 04			19 27
Ravensthorpe	d		17 07									18 07										19 07			
Castleford	d																								
Normanton	d																								
Wakefield Kirkgate	d																								
Mirfield	d		17 11									18 11										19 11			
Deighton	d		17 17									18 17										19 17			
Huddersfield	a	17 05	17 22	17 17	17 24	17 37			17 47		18 06	18 22	18 17	18 24	18 35				18 47		19 06	19 22	19 17	19 24	19 37
	d	17 08		17 18	17 25	17 39			17 49	17 53	18 08		18 18	18 25	18 37				18 48	18 53	19 08		19 18	19 25	19 38
Slaithwaite	d									18 00										19 00					
Marsden	d									18 05										19 05					
Greenfield	d									18 14										19 14					
Mossley (Grtr Manchester)	d									18 18										19 18					
Stalybridge	a			17 36	17 43					18 22			18 36	18 43						19 22			19 36	19 43	
	d			17 37	17 43		18 03			18 22			18 37	18 43		19 03				19 22			19 37	19 43	
Ashton-under-Lyne	⛴ d						18 06									19 06									
Manchester Victoria	⛴ a	17 38		17 54		18 09	18 18	18 43	18 21		18 38		18 50		19 09	19 18		19 43	19 21		19 38		19 50		20 09
	d	17 39		17 55		18 10			18 23		18 39		18 54		19 10				19 23		19 39		19 54		20 10
Manchester Oxford Road	a	17 45				18 16					18 45				19 16						19 45				20 16
Manchester Piccadilly	a	17 50			18 09	18 20				18 41	18 50			19 09	19 20					19 41	19 50			20 09	20 20
	d	17 51				18 20					18 51				19 20						19 51				20 20
Gatley	a	18 00									19 00										20 00				
Manchester Airport	⛴✈ a	18 16				18 36					19 16				19 36						20 16				20 37
Newton-le-Willows	90 a								18 39										19 39				20 13		
Lea Green	90 a			18 18									19 18										20 19		
Liverpool Lime Street 10	90 a			18 34					18 58				19 34						20 00				20 35		

A ⊼ from Leeds

Table T039-R

Sundays
5 April to 10 May

Newcastle, Middlesborough, Scarborough, York, Hull, Leeds and Wakefield - Huddersfield - Manchester, Manchester Airport and Liverpool

		NT	NT	TP	TP	TP	TP	TP		TP	GC	TP	NT	NT	TP	TP	TP	TP	TP	TP	NT	NT	TP	TP	
			◇	◇1	◇1	◇1	◇1	◇1		◇1	▪ 1	◇1		◇	◇1	◇1	◇1	◇1	◇1	◇1		◇	◇1	◇1	
										A										A			B		
				⊼						⊼	⊏	⊼			⊼					⊼			⊼		
Edinburgh	26 d			16 34											17 19								18 20		
Morpeth	26 d			17 48											18 30								19 30		
Newcastle 8	26 ⛴ a			18 02											18 44								19 44		
	d			18 04								18 43			19 06								20 06		
Chester-le-Street	26 d											18 52													
Durham	26 d			18 17								18 59			19 18								20 18		
Darlington 5	26 a			18 33								19 16			19 35								20 35		
	d			18 35								19 17			19 36								20 36		
Redcar Central	44 d					18 02											19 05								
Middlesbrough	44 d					18 15											19 19								
Thornaby	44 d					18 21											19 25								
Yarm	d					18 29											19 33								
Northallerton	26 d					18 44					19 20	19 28					19 50								
Thirsk	26 d					18 53					19 29						19 58								
Scarborough	43 d							18 32											19 32						
Seamer	43 d							18 38											19 38						
Malton	d							18 57											19 57						
York 8	26 a			19 02		19 11		19 23			19 46	19 50			20 02		20 16		20 23				21 02		
	d			19 05		19 16		19 27				19 51			20 05		20 18		20 27				21 05		
Hull	29 d									19 04										20 06					
Brough	29 d									19 16										20 18					
Howden	29 d																								
Selby	29,40 d									19 38										20 39					
South Milford	40 d																								
Garforth	40 d							19 46											20 46						
Cross Gates	40 d																								
Leeds 10	a			19 27		19 43		19 56		20 03		20 14			20 27		20 43		20 56	21 03			21 27		
	d		19 19	19 30		19 45	19 47	20 00		20 07		20 15		20 18	20 30		20 45	20 47	21 00	21 07		21 18	21 30		
Cottingley	d						19 52											20 52							
Morley	d						19 56											20 56							
Batley	d						20 01											21 01							
Dewsbury	a					19 55	20 03					20 26					20 55	21 03		21 17			21 41		
	d					19 57	20 04					20 27					20 57	21 04		21 18			21 42		
Ravensthorpe	d						20 07											21 07							
Castleford	d																								
Normanton	d																								
Wakefield Kirkgate	d																								
Mirfield	d						20 11											21 10							
Deighton	d						20 17											21 17							
Huddersfield	a			19 47		20 05	20 22	20 17		20 24		20 37			20 47		21 05	21 22	21 17	21 26			21 50		
	d			19 48	19 53	20 08		20 18		20 25		20 39			20 48	20 53	21 08		21 21	21 27			21 51	21 53	
Slaithwaite	d				20 00											21 00								22 00	
Marsden	d				20 05											21 05								22 05	
Greenfield	d				20 14											21 14								22 14	
Mossley (Grtr Manchester)	d				20 18											21 18								22 18	
Stalybridge	a				20 22			20 36		20 43						21 22			21 39	21 45				22 22	
	d	20 03			20 22			20 37		20 43			21 03			21 22			21 40	21 46	22 03			22 22	
Ashton-under-Lyne	⛴ d	20 06											21 06								22 06				
Manchester Victoria	⛴ a	20 18	20 44	20 21		20 38		20 55				21 11	21 17	21 45	21 22		21 40		21 53		22 17	22 45	22 23		
	d			20 23		20 39									21 24				21 54				22 24		
Manchester Oxford Road	a					20 45													22 00						
Manchester Piccadilly	a				20 41	20 50				21 09						21 41			22 04	22 07				22 41	
	d					20 51													22 05						
Gatley	a					21 00																			
Manchester Airport	⛴✈ a					21 16													22 22						
Newton-le-Willows	90 a														21 40								22 40		
Lea Green	90 a														21 46								22 48		
Liverpool Lime Street 10	90 a			20 55											22 02								23 05		

A ⊼ from Leeds

B ⊼ from York

Table T039-R

Sundays
5 April to 10 May

Newcastle, Middlesborough, Scarborough, York, Hull, Leeds and Wakefield - Huddersfield - Manchester, Manchester Airport and Liverpool

			TP	TP	TP	TP	NT	NT	TP	TP	TP	TP	TP	TP	TP	NT	TP	TP	TP	TP
			◇1	◇1	◇1	◇1		◇	◇1	◇1	◇1	◇1	◇1	◇1	◇1	◇	◇1	◇1	◇1	◇1
						A ⌶			B ⌶					⌶	A ⌶					⌶
Edinburgh	26	d							19 30											
Morpeth	26	d							20 40											
Newcastle 8	26	a							20 55											
		d							21 02											
Chester-le-Street	26	d							21 11											
Durham	26	d							21 18											
Darlington 8	26	a							21 35											
		d							21 36											
Redcar Central	44	d	20 08								21 05			22 05						23 05
Middlesbrough	44	d	20 22								21 19			22 19						23 19
Thornaby	44	d	20 28								21 25			22 25						23 25
Yarm		d	20 36								21 33			22 33						23 33
Northallerton	26	d	20 53								21 50			22 50						
Thirsk	26	d	21 01								21 58			22 58						
Scarborough	43	d			20 32								21 32					22 42		
Seamer	43	d			20 38								21 38					22 48		
Malton		d			20 57								21 57					23 06		
York 8	26	a	21 21		21 23				22 02		22 18		22 23	23 18				23 33		00 18
		d			21 27				22 05				22 27					23 37		
Hull	29	d				21 06									22 06				23 04	
Brough	29	d				21 18									22 18				23 16	
Howden	29	d																		
Selby	29,40	d				21 38									22 38				23 36	
South Milford	40	d																		
Garforth	40	d			21 46								22 44							
Cross Gates	40	d																		
Leeds 10		a			21 55	22 03			22 27				22 53		23 03			00 02	00 02	
		d		21 47	22 00	22 07		22 11	22 29			22 47	22 57		23 07	23 19	23 47	00 05		
Cottingley		d		21 52								22 52					23 52			
Morley		d		21 56								22 56					23 56			
Batley		d		22 01								23 01					00 02			
Dewsbury		a		22 03		22 17			22 39			23 03	23 07				00 03			
		d		22 04		22 18			22 40			23 04	23 08				00 04			
Ravensthorpe		d		22 07								23 07					00 07			
Castleford		d																		
Normanton		d																		
Wakefield Kirkgate		d																		
Mirfield		d		22 11								23 11					00 11			
Deighton		d		22 17								23 17					00 17			
Huddersfield		a		22 22	22 17	22 26			22 49			23 22	23 17		23 24		00 22			
		d			22 21	22 27			22 50	22 54			23 18		23 25					
Slaithwaite		d								23 00					23 32					
Marsden		d								23 05					23 37					
Greenfield		d								23 14					23 46					
Mossley (Grtr Manchester)		d								23 18					23 50					
Stalybridge		a			22 39	22 45				23 22			23 36		23 54					
		d			22 40	22 46	23 03			23 22			23 37		23 54					
Ashton-under-Lyne	⇌	d					23 06													
Manchester Victoria	⇌	a			22 53	22 59	23 17	23 38	23 22				23 50			00 42				
		d			22 56	23 00			23 23				23 54							
Manchester Oxford Road		a			23 04								23 59							
Manchester Piccadilly		a			23 09					23 42			00 04		00 11			01 23		
		d			23 11								00 05							
Gatley		a																		
Manchester Airport	⇌✈	a			23 26								00 20							
Newton-le-Willows	90	a				23 16			23 39											
Lea Green	90	a				23 22			23 45											
Liverpool Lime Street 10	90	a				23 41			00 03											

A ⌶ from Leeds
B ⌶ from York

NRT DECEMBER 19 EDITION

Table T040-F

Mondays to Fridays
16 December to 15 May

York and Selby - Leeds

Miles	Miles				GR MX	TP MO	TP MX	TP MX	TP MO	TP	TP	TP	NT	TP	TP	TP	NT	TP	NT	TP	TP	TP	XC	TP	NT
					1 ⊏	◇1	◇1	◇1	◇1	◇1	◇1	◇1	◇	◇1	◇1	◇1		◇1 ⌶	◇	◇1	◇1 ⌶	◇1	◇1	◇1 ⌶	◇
0	—	**York** 8	33	d	00 16	01 38	01 38	02 47	02 52	03 40	04 27	05 15	05 19	05 28		05 49		06 05	06 12	06 18	06 28		06 45	06 49	
8¼	—	Ulleskelf	33	d																					
10½	—	Church Fenton	33	d									05 30						06 29						
—	0	**Selby**		d											05 42		05 47					06 37			06 45
—	7¾	South Milford		d													05 58								06 58
15¾	11	Micklefield		d									05 36				06 04		06 35						07 04
17½	12¾	East Garforth		d									05 40				06 09		06 39						07 09
18	13¼	Garforth		d									05 42	05 48			06 11		06 41		06 47	06 52			07 11
21	16¼	Cross Gates		d									05 47				06 16		06 46			06 57			07 16
25½	20¾	**Leeds** 10		a	00 45	02 05	02 18	03 27	03 19	04 05	04 53	05 42	05 54	05 58	06 04	06 12	06 25	06 28	06 53	06 42	06 57	07 04	07 08	07 13	07 25
—	—	Bradford Interchange	37	a									06 14				06 48		07 15						07 48

			TP	NT	NT	TP	TP	NT	TP	XC	NT	TP	NT	TP	NT	TP	NT	TP	NT	TP	XC	TP	NT	TP
			◇1 ⌶		◇	◇1 ⌶	◇1 ⌶		◇1 ⌶	◇1 ⌶		◇1 ⌶	◇	◇1 ⌶		◇1 ⌶	◇	◇1 ⌶		◇1	◇1 ⌶	◇1 ⌶	◇	◇1 ⌶
York 8	33	d	07 05	07 07	07 13	07 19	07 27			07 44	07 47	07 50		08 04	08 07	08 20	08 23	08 28			08 44	08 49		09 05
Ulleskelf	33	d			07 21						07 57													
Church Fenton	33	d			07 30						08 01						08 34							
Selby		d						07 27	07 40				07 49						08 25	08 40			08 48	
South Milford		d						07 38					08 04						08 37				08 59	
Micklefield		d		07 22				07 44					08 09		08 21				08 44				09 05	
East Garforth		d		07 26				07 48							08 25				08 49				09 09	
Garforth		d		07 28			07 43		07 55				08 14		08 27			08 45		08 55			09 12	
Cross Gates		d			07 41		07 48	07 53			08 12				08 32		08 45	08 50	08 54				09 16	
Leeds 10		a	07 28	07 39	07 48	07 42	07 56	08 02	08 04	08 08	08 22	08 12	08 25	08 28	08 39	08 42	08 52	08 57	09 01	09 04	09 08	09 12	09 24	09 27
Bradford Interchange	37	a			08 12								08 48				09 14						09 48	

			NT	TP	NT	TP	TP	XC	TP	NT	TP	NT	TP	NT	TP	TP	XC	TP	NT	TP	NT	TP	NT	TP
				◇1 ⌶	◇	◇1 ⌶	◇1	◇1 ⌶	◇1 ⌶	◇	◇1 ⌶		◇1 ⌶	◇	◇1 ⌶	◇1	◇1 ⌶	◇1 ⌶	◇	◇1 ⌶		◇1 ⌶	◇	◇1 ⌶
York 8	33	d	09 08	09 20	09 23	09 28		09 44	09 49		10 05	10 09	10 20	10 23	10 29		10 44	10 49		11 05	11 07	11 20	11 23	11 28
Ulleskelf	33	d																						
Church Fenton	33	d			09 34									10 34									11 34	
Selby		d					09 40			09 48						10 40			10 48					
South Milford		d								09 59									10 59					
Micklefield		d	09 22							10 05		10 22							11 05		11 21			
East Garforth		d	09 26							10 09		10 26							11 09		11 25			
Garforth		d	09 28			09 46				10 12		10 28			10 46				11 12		11 27			11 46
Cross Gates		d	09 33							10 16		10 33							11 16		11 32			
Leeds 10		a	09 41	09 43	09 50	09 56	10 03	10 07	10 12	10 24	10 27	10 40	10 42	10 50	10 56	11 03	11 07	11 12	11 24	11 27	11 40	11 42	11 50	11 56
Bradford Interchange	37	a			10 15					10 48				11 14					11 48				12 14	

			TP	XC	TP	NT	TP	NT	TP	NT	TP	TP	XC	TP	NT	TP	NT	TP	NT	TP	TP	XC	TP	NT
			◇1	◇1 ⌶	◇1 ⌶	◇	◇1 ⌶		◇1 ⌶	◇	◇1 ⌶	◇1	◇1 ⌶	◇1 ⌶	◇	◇1 ⌶		◇1 ⌶	◇	◇1 ⌶	◇1	◇1 ⌶	◇1 ⌶	◇
York 8	33	d		11 44	11 49		12 04	12 07	12 20	12 23	12 28		12 44	12 49		13 04	13 08	13 20	13 23	13 28		13 44	13 50	
Ulleskelf	33	d																						
Church Fenton	33	d								12 34									13 34					
Selby		d	11 38			11 48						12 41			12 48						13 40			13 48
South Milford		d				11 59									12 59									13 59
Micklefield		d				12 05		12 21							13 05		13 22							14 05
East Garforth		d				12 09		12 24							13 09		13 26							14 09
Garforth		d				12 12		12 27			12 46				13 12		13 28			13 46				14 12
Cross Gates		d				12 16		12 31							13 16		13 33							14 16
Leeds 10		a	12 03	12 09	12 12	12 24	12 27	12 39	12 42	12 50	12 56	13 05	13 08	13 12	13 24	13 27	13 41	13 43	13 50	13 56	14 03	14 07	14 13	14 24
Bradford Interchange	37	a				12 48				13 15					13 48				14 15					14 48

			TP	NT	TP	NT	TP	TP	XC	TP	NT	TP	NT	TP	NT	TP	TP	XC	TP	NT	TP	NT	XC	TP
			◇1 ⌶		◇1 ⌶	◇	◇1 ⌶	◇1	◇1 ⌶	◇1 ⌶	◇	◇1 ⌶		◇1 ⌶	◇	◇1 ⌶	◇1	◇1 ⌶	◇1 ⌶	◇	◇1 ⌶		◇1 ⌶	◇1 ⌶
York 8	33	d	14 05	14 08	14 20	14 23	14 28		14 44	14 49		15 05	15 07	15 20	15 23	15 28		15 44	15 50		16 01	16 04	16 13	16 20
Ulleskelf	33	d																						
Church Fenton	33	d				14 34									15 34									
Selby		d						14 40			14 49						15 36			15 48				
South Milford		d									15 00									15 59				
Micklefield		d		14 21							15 05		15 21							16 05		16 18		
East Garforth		d		14 25							15 09		15 25							16 09		16 22		
Garforth		d		14 27			14 46				15 12		15 27			15 46				16 11		16 24		
Cross Gates		d		14 32							15 16		15 32							16 16		16 29		
Leeds 10		a	14 27	14 40	14 42	14 50	14 56	15 03	15 07	15 12	15 24	15 27	15 39	15 42	15 50	15 56	16 03	16 07	16 12	16 24	16 27	16 35	16 38	16 42
Bradford Interchange	37	a				15 15					15 48				16 15					16 48				

			NT	TP	TP	XC	TP	NT	TP	NT	TP	NT	TP	TP	XC	TP	NT	TP	NT	TP	NT	TP	NT	TP	XC
			◇	◇1 ⌶	◇1	◇1 ⌶	◇1 ⌶	◇	◇1 ⌶		◇1 ⌶	◇	◇1 ⌶	◇1	◇1 ⌶	◇1 ⌶	◇	◇1 ⌶		◇1 ⌶	◇	◇1		◇1	◇1 ⌶
York 8	33	d	16 23	16 28		16 44	16 49		17 04	17 07	17 20	17 23	17 28		17 44	17 49		18 05	18 08	18 18	18 22	18 28			18 44
Ulleskelf	33	d																	18 17						
Church Fenton	33	d	16 34									17 34									18 33				
Selby		d			16 40			16 48						17 37			17 48						18 25	18 40	
South Milford		d						16 59									17 58						18 37		
Micklefield		d						17 05		17 21							18 05		18 26				18 45		
East Garforth		d						17 09		17 25							18 09						18 49		
Garforth		d		16 46				17 12		17 27			17 46				18 12		18 30			18 45			
Cross Gates		d						17 16		17 32							18 16				18 44		18 53		
Leeds 10		a	16 54	16 57	17 03	17 07	17 12	17 24	17 27	17 39	17 42	17 51	17 56	18 03	18 07	18 12	18 24	18 27	18 39	18 42	18 51	18 55	19 01	19 04	19 07
Bradford Interchange	37	a	17 15					17 48				18 15					18 48				19 15				

Table T040-F

York and Selby - Leeds

Mondays to Fridays

16 December to 15 May

		TP	NT	TP	NT	TP	NT	TP	TP	XC	TP	NT	TP	NT	TP	NT	TP	TP	XC	NT	TP	NT	NT
		◇1 ⊼	◇	◇1 ⊼		◇1	◇	◇1	◇1	◇1 ⊼	◇1 ⊼	◇	◇1 ⊼		◇1	◇	◇1	◇1	◇1 ⊼	◇	◇1 ⊼		◇
York 8	33 d	18 49		19 06	19 08	19 20	19 23	19 28		19 44	19 49		20 05	20 08	20 20	20 23	20 28		20 44		21 05	21 08	21 23
Ulleskelf	33 d																						
Church Fenton	33 d						19 34									20 34						21 19	21 34
Selby	d		18 48						19 38			19 50						20 41		20 48			
South Milford	d		18 59									19 59								20 59			
Micklefield	d		19 05		19 22							20 05		20 22						21 05		21 26	
East Garforth	d		19 09		19 26							20 09		20 26						21 09		21 30	
Garforth	d		19 12		19 28			19 46				20 12		20 28			20 46			21 12		21 32	
Cross Gates	d		19 16		19 33							20 16		20 33						21 16		21 37	
Leeds 10	a	19 12	19 24	19 28	19 42	19 42	19 50	19 56	20 03	20 07	20 12	20 24	20 27	20 40	20 43	20 50	20 56	21 03	21 07	21 24	21 27	21 47	21 50
Bradford Interchange	37 a		19 48				20 15					20 48				21 15				21 48			22 15

		TP	TP	NT	TP	NT	TP	TP	NT	TP	NT	NT	TP	TP
		◇1	◇1	◇	◇1 ⊼	◇	◇1	◇1	◇	◇1 ⊼	◇		◇1	◇1
York 8	33 d	21 28			22 05	22 19	22 28			23 05		23 13		23 39
Ulleskelf	33 d													
Church Fenton	33 d					22 30						23 29		
Selby	d		21 40	21 48				22 40	22 48		23 05		23 40	
South Milford	d			21 59					22 59		23 15			
Micklefield	d			22 05		22 36			23 05		23 23	23 37		
East Garforth	d			22 09		22 40			23 09		23 27	23 41		
Garforth	d	21 46		22 12		22 42	22 47		23 12		23 29	23 43		
Cross Gates	d			22 16		22 47			23 16		23 34	23 48		
Leeds 10	a	21 56	22 03	22 24	22 26	22 55	22 58	23 03	23 24	23 28	23 42	23 56	00 04	00 06
Bradford Interchange	37 a			22 49		23 15			23 48					

Saturdays

21 December to 16 May

		GR	TP	TP	TP	TP	TP	NT	TP	TP	TP	NT	TP	NT	XC	TP	TP	TP	TP	NT	TP	NT	NT	TP
		1	◇1	◇1	◇1	◇1	◇1	◇	◇1	◇1	◇1		◇1 ⊼	◇	◇1	◇1	◇1 ⊼	◇1	◇1 ⊼	◇	◇1 ⊼		◇	◇1 ⊼
York 8	33 d	00 16	01 38	02 52	03 40	04 27	05 15	05 19	05 28		05 49		06 05	06 12	06 12	06 18	06 28		06 49		07 05	07 07	07 13	07 19
Ulleskelf	33 d																						07 21	
Church Fenton	33 d							05 30						06 29									07 30	
Selby	d									05 42		05 47						06 37		06 45				
South Milford	d											05 58								06 58				
Micklefield	d							05 36				06 04		06 35						07 04		07 22		
East Garforth	d							05 40				06 09		06 39						07 09		07 26		
Garforth	d							05 42	05 48			06 11		06 41			06 47	06 52		07 11		07 28		
Cross Gates	d							05 47				06 16		06 46				06 57		07 16			07 41	
Leeds 10	a	00 45	02 18	03 18	04 19	04 53	05 42	05 54	05 58	06 04	06 12	06 25	06 28	06 53	06 56	06 42	06 57	07 04	07 13	07 25	07 28	07 39	07 48	07 42
Bradford Interchange	37 a							06 14				06 48		07 15						07 48			08 12	

		TP	NT	TP	XC	NT	TP	NT	TP	NT	TP	NT	TP	NT	TP	XC	TP	NT	TP	NT	TP	NT	TP
		◇1 ⊼		◇1 ⊼	◇1		◇1 ⊼	◇	◇1 ⊼		◇1 ⊼	◇	◇1 ⊼		◇1	◇1 ⊼	◇1 ⊼	◇	◇1 ⊼		◇1 ⊼	◇	◇1 ⊼
York 8	33 d	07 27			07 44	07 47	07 50		08 04	08 07	08 20	08 23	08 28			08 44	08 49		09 05	09 08	09 20	09 23	09 28
Ulleskelf	33 d					07 57																	
Church Fenton	33 d					08 01						08 34										09 34	
Selby	d		07 27	07 40				07 49						08 25	08 40			08 48					
South Milford	d		07 39					08 04						08 37				08 59					
Micklefield	d		07 44					08 09		08 21				08 44				09 05		09 22			
East Garforth	d		07 48							08 25				08 49				09 09		09 26			
Garforth	d	07 43		07 55				08 14		08 27			08 45		08 55			09 12		09 28			09 46
Cross Gates	d	07 48	07 53			08 12				08 32		08 45	08 50	08 54				09 16		09 33			
Leeds 10	a	07 56	08 02	08 04	08 07	08 22	08 12	08 25	08 28	08 39	08 42	08 52	08 57	09 01	09 04	09 08	09 12	09 24	09 27	09 41	09 43	09 50	09 56
Bradford Interchange	37 a							08 48				09 14						09 48				10 15	

		TP	XC	TP	NT	TP	NT	TP	NT	TP	TP	XC	TP	NT	TP	NT	TP	NT	TP	TP	XC	TP	NT
		◇1	◇1 ⊼	◇1 ⊼	◇	◇1 ⊼		◇1 ⊼	◇	◇1 ⊼	◇1	◇1 ⊼	◇1 ⊼	◇	◇1 ⊼		◇1 ⊼	◇	◇1 ⊼	◇1	◇1 ⊼	◇1 ⊼	◇
York 8	33 d		09 44	09 49		10 05	10 09	10 20	10 23	10 29		10 43	10 49		11 05	11 07	11 20	11 23	11 28		11 44	11 50	
Ulleskelf	33 d																						
Church Fenton	33 d								10 34									11 34					
Selby	d	09 40			09 48						10 40			10 48						11 38			11 48
South Milford	d				09 59									10 59									11 59
Micklefield	d				10 05		10 22							11 05		11 21							12 05
East Garforth	d				10 09		10 26							11 09		11 25							12 09
Garforth	d				10 12		10 28			10 46				11 12		11 27			11 46				12 12
Cross Gates	d				10 16		10 33							11 16		11 32							12 16
Leeds 10	a	10 03	10 07	10 12	10 24	10 27	10 40	10 42	10 50	10 56	11 03	11 07	11 12	11 24	11 27	11 40	11 42	11 50	11 56	12 03	12 07	12 12	12 24
Bradford Interchange	37 a				10 48				11 14					11 48				12 14					12 48

		TP	NT	TP	NT	TP	TP	XC	TP	NT	TP	NT	TP	NT	TP	TP	XC	TP	NT	TP	NT	TP	NT
		◇1 ⊼		◇1 ⊼	◇	◇1 ⊼	◇1	◇1 ⊼	◇1 ⊼	◇	◇1 ⊼		◇1 ⊼	◇	◇1 ⊼	◇1	◇1 ⊼	◇1 ⊼	◇	◇1 ⊼		◇1 ⊼	◇
York 8	33 d	12 04	12 07	12 20	12 23	12 28		12 44	12 49		13 05	13 08	13 20	13 23	13 28		13 44	13 50		14 05	14 08	14 20	14 23
Ulleskelf	33 d																						
Church Fenton	33 d				12 34									13 34									14 34
Selby	d						12 41			12 48						13 40			13 48				
South Milford	d									12 59									13 59				
Micklefield	d		12 22							13 05		13 22							14 05		14 21		
East Garforth	d		12 25							13 09		13 26							14 09		14 25		
Garforth	d		12 28			12 46				13 12		13 28			13 46				14 12		14 27		
Cross Gates	d		12 32							13 16		13 33							14 16		14 32		
Leeds 10	a	12 27	12 40	12 42	12 55	12 58	13 05	13 08	13 12	13 24	13 27	13 41	13 43	13 50	13 56	14 03	14 07	14 13	14 24	14 27	14 40	14 42	14 50
Bradford Interchange	37 a				13 15					13 48				14 15					14 48				15 15

Table T040-F

York and Selby - Leeds

Saturdays

21 December to 16 May

		TP	TP	XC	TP	NT	TP	NT	TP	NT	TP	TP	XC	TP	NT	TP	NT	XC	TP	NT	TP	TP	XC
		◇1 ⊼	◇1	◇1 ⊼	◇1 ⊼	◇	◇1 ⊼		◇1 ⊼	◇	◇1 ⊼	◇1	◇1 ⊼	◇1 ⊼	◇	◇1 ⊼		◇1 ⊼	◇1 ⊼	◇	◇1 ⊼	◇1	◇1 ⊼
York 8	33 d	14 28		14 44	14 49		15 04	15 07	15 20	15 23	15 28		15 44	15 49		16 01	16 04	16 13	16 20	16 23	16 28		16 44
Ulleskelf	33 d																						
Church Fenton	33 d									15 34										16 34			
Selby	d		14 40			14 49						15 40			15 47							16 40	
South Milford	d					15 00									15 58								
Micklefield	d					15 05		15 21							16 05		16 18						
East Garforth	d					15 09		15 25							16 09		16 22						
Garforth	d	14 46				15 12		15 27			15 46				16 12		16 24				16 46		
Cross Gates	d					15 16		15 32							16 16		16 29						
Leeds 10	a	14 56	15 03	15 07	15 12	15 24	15 27	15 39	15 42	15 50	15 56	16 03	16 07	16 12	16 24	16 27	16 35	16 38	16 42	16 54	16 57	17 03	17 07
Bradford Interchange	37 a					15 48				16 15					16 48					17 15			

		TP	NT	TP	NT	TP	NT	TP	TP	XC	TP	NT	TP	NT	TP	NT	TP	NT	TP	XC	TP	NT	TP	NT
		◇1 ⊼	◇	◇1 ⊼		◇1 ⊼	◇	◇1 ⊼	◇1	◇1 ⊼	◇1 ⊼	◇	◇1 ⊼		◇1 ⊼	◇	◇1		◇1	◇1 ⊼	◇1 ⊼	◇	◇1 ⊼	
York 8	33 d	16 49		17 04	17 07	17 20	17 23	17 28		17 44	17 49		18 05	18 08	18 18	18 22	18 28			18 44	18 49		19 06	19 08
Ulleskelf	33 d													18 17										
Church Fenton	33 d						17 34									18 33								
Selby	d		16 48						17 40			17 48						18 25	18 40			18 48		
South Milford	d		16 59									17 58						18 37				18 59		
Micklefield	d		17 05		17 21							18 05		18 26				18 45				19 05		19 22
East Garforth	d		17 09		17 25							18 09						18 49				19 09		19 26
Garforth	d		17 12		17 27			17 46				18 12		18 30			18 45					19 12		19 28
Cross Gates	d		17 16		17 32							18 16						18 53				19 16		19 33
Leeds 10	a	17 12	17 24	17 27	17 39	17 42	17 51	17 56	18 03	18 07	18 12	18 24	18 27	18 39	18 42	18 49	18 55	19 01	19 04	19 07	19 12	19 24	19 28	19 42
Bradford Interchange	37 a		17 48				18 15					18 48				19 15						19 48		

		TP	NT	TP	TP	XC	TP	NT	TP	NT	TP	NT	TP	TP	XC	NT	TP	NT	NT	TP	TP	NT	TP
		◇1	◇	◇1	◇1	◇1 ⊼	◇1 ⊼	◇	◇1 ⊼		◇1	◇	◇1	◇1	◇1 ⊼	◇	◇1 ⊼		◇	◇1	◇1	◇	◇1 ⊼
York 8	33 d	19 20	19 23	19 28		19 44	19 49		20 05	20 08	20 20	20 23	20 28		20 45		21 05	21 08	21 23	21 28			22 05
Ulleskelf	33 d																						
Church Fenton	33 d		19 34									20 34						21 19	21 34				
Selby	d				19 40			19 50						20 41		20 48					21 40	21 47	
South Milford	d							19 59								20 59						21 58	
Micklefield	d							20 05		20 22						21 05		21 26				22 03	
East Garforth	d							20 09		20 26						21 09		21 30				22 08	
Garforth	d			19 46				20 12		20 28			20 46			21 12		21 32		21 46		22 10	
Cross Gates	d							20 16		20 33						21 16		21 37				22 15	
Leeds 10	a	19 42	19 50	19 56	20 03	20 07	20 12	20 24	20 27	20 40	20 43	20 50	20 56	21 03	21 08	21 24	21 27	21 47	21 50	21 56	22 03	22 23	22 27
Bradford Interchange	37 a		20 15					20 48				21 15				21 48			22 15			22 49	

		NT	TP	TP	NT	TP	NT	NT	TP	TP
		◇	◇1	◇1	◇	◇1 ⊼	◇		◇1 A	◇1
York 8	33 d	22 19	22 28			23 05		23 13	23 37	
Ulleskelf	33 d									
Church Fenton	33 d	22 30						23 29		
Selby	d			22 40	22 48		23 05			23 40
South Milford	d				22 59		23 15			
Micklefield	d	22 36			23 05		23 23	23 37		
East Garforth	d	22 40			23 09		23 27	23 41		
Garforth	d	22 42	22 47		23 12		23 29	23 43		
Cross Gates	d	22 47			23 16		23 34	23 48		
Leeds 10	a	22 55	22 58	23 03	23 24	23 27	23 42	23 56	00 02	00 04
Bradford Interchange	37 a	23 15			23 49					

Sundays

15 December to 16 February

		TP	TP	TP	TP	TP	TP	TP	TP	NT	TP	TP	NT	TP	NT	TP	NT	TP	XC	TP	TP	NT	TP	NT
		◇1	◇1	◇1	◇1	◇1 ⊼	◇1 ⊼	◇1 ⊼	◇1 ⊼		◇1	◇1 ⊼		◇1 ⊼		◇1 ⊼	◇	◇1 ⊼	◇1 ⊼	◇1	◇1 ⊼		◇1 ⊼	◇
York 8	33 d	02 08	03 45	04 51	05 51	07 00	07 31	08 18	08 26	08 29		08 48		09 05	09 07	09 18	09 21	09 27	09 36		09 49		10 04	10 08
Ulleskelf	33 d																							
Church Fenton	33 d																09 33							10 20
Selby	d										08 41		08 45							09 40		09 48		
South Milford	d												08 56									09 59		
Micklefield	d									08 44			09 02		09 22							10 05		
East Garforth	d									08 47			09 06		09 25							10 09		
Garforth	d								08 43	08 50			09 08		09 28			09 45				10 11		
Cross Gates	d									08 55			09 13									10 16		
Leeds 10	a	02 48	04 23	05 31	06 31	07 40	08 10	08 43	08 53	09 02	09 05	09 12	09 21	09 27	09 39	09 42	09 52	09 56	09 59	10 03	10 12	10 24	10 27	10 39
Bradford Interchange	37 a																10 10							11 07

A until 15 February, from 4 April

Table T040-F

Sundays

15 December to 16 February

York and Selby - Leeds

	TP	NT	TP	XC	TP	TP	NT	TP	NT	TP	NT	TP	TP	XC	TP	NT	TP	NT	TP	NT	TP	TP
	◇1 🍴		◇1 🍴	◇1 🍴	◇1	◇1 🍴		◇1 🍴		◇1 🍴	◇	◇1 🍴	◇1	◇1 🍴	◇1 🍴		◇1 🍴		◇1 🍴	◇	◇1 🍴	◇1
York 8 33 d	10 20	10 21	10 27	10 34		10 49		11 05	11 07	11 16	11 21	11 27		11 41	11 49		12 05	12 07	12 16	12 21	12 27	
Ulleskelf 33 d																						
Church Fenton 33 d											11 33									12 33		
Selby d					10 40		10 47						11 36			11 49						12 40
South Milford d							10 59									11 59						
Micklefield d		10 36					11 05		11 22							12 05		12 22				
East Garforth d							11 09		11 25							12 09		12 25				
Garforth d		10 40	10 43				11 11		11 28			11 46	11 51			12 11		12 28			12 47	
Cross Gates d		10 45					11 16		11 32				11 56			12 16		12 32				
Leeds 10 a	10 43	10 53	10 56	10 58	11 03	11 12	11 24	11 27	11 40	11 42	11 53	11 56	12 03	12 08	12 12	12 24	12 27	12 40	12 43	12 53	12 56	13 03
Bradford Interchange 37 a											12 15									13 15		

	XC	TP	NT	TP	NT	TP	NT	TP	TP	XC	TP	NT	TP	NT	TP	NT	TP	TP	XC	TP	NT	TP
	◇1 🍴	◇1 🍴		◇1 🍴		◇1 🍴	◇	◇1 🍴	◇1	◇1 🍴	◇1 🍴		◇1 🍴		◇1 🍴	◇	◇1 🍴	◇1	◇1 🍴	◇1 🍴		◇1 🍴
York 8 33 d	12 45	12 50		13 05	13 07	13 16	13 21	13 27		13 45	13 49		14 04	14 07	14 16	14 21	14 27		14 44	14 48		15 05
Ulleskelf 33 d																						
Church Fenton 33 d							13 33									14 33						
Selby d			12 47						13 38			13 47						14 38			14 47	
South Milford d			12 59									13 59									14 59	
Micklefield d			13 06		13 22							14 04		14 22							15 04	
East Garforth d			13 10		13 25							14 08		14 25							15 08	
Garforth d			13 12		13 28			13 46				14 11		14 28			14 47				15 11	
Cross Gates d			13 17		13 32							14 15		14 32							15 15	
Leeds 10 a	13 08	13 13	13 25	13 28	13 40	13 43	13 52	13 56	14 03	14 08	14 12	14 24	14 27	14 40	14 43	14 52	14 56	15 03	15 07	15 11	15 23	15 27
Bradford Interchange 37 a							14 17									15 14						

	NT	TP	NT	TP	TP	XC	TP	NT	TP	NT	TP	NT	TP	TP	XC	TP	NT	TP	NT	TP	NT	TP
		◇1 🍴	◇	◇1 🍴	◇1	◇1 🍴	◇1 🍴		◇1 🍴		◇1 🍴	◇	◇1 🍴	◇1	◇1 🍴	◇1 🍴		◇1 🍴		◇1 🍴	◇	◇1 🍴
York 8 33 d	15 07	15 15	15 21	15 27		15 44	15 50		16 05	16 07	16 16	16 21	16 27		16 44	16 49		17 05	17 07	17 18	17 21	17 27
Ulleskelf 33 d																						
Church Fenton 33 d			15 33									16 33									17 33	
Selby d					15 38			15 47						16 39			16 47					
South Milford d								15 59									16 59					
Micklefield d	15 22							16 05		16 22							17 05		17 22			
East Garforth d	15 25							16 09		16 25							17 09		17 27			
Garforth d	15 28			15 46				16 12		16 28							17 12		17 29			17 46
Cross Gates d	15 32							16 16		16 32							17 16		17 34			
Leeds 10 a	15 40	15 43	15 52	15 56	16 03	16 07	16 12	16 25	16 28	16 40	16 43	16 52	16 56	17 03	17 09	17 12	17 25	17 28	17 42	17 44	17 53	17 56
Bradford Interchange 37 a			16 15									17 14									18 15	

	TP	XC	TP	NT	TP	NT	TP	NT	TP	TP	XC	TP	NT	TP	NT	TP	NT	TP	TP	XC	TP	NT
	◇1	◇1 🍴	◇1 🍴		◇1 🍴		◇1 🍴	◇	◇1 🍴	◇1	◇1 🍴	◇1 🍴		◇1 🍴		◇1	◇	◇1	◇1	◇1 🍴	◇1 🍴	
York 8 33 d		17 44	17 49		18 05	18 07	18 18	18 21	18 27		18 45	18 49		19 05	19 07	19 16	19 21	19 27		19 45	19 51	
Ulleskelf 33 d																						
Church Fenton 33 d								18 33									19 33					
Selby d	17 38			17 47						18 38			18 47						19 38			19 47
South Milford d				17 59									18 59									19 59
Micklefield d				18 05		18 22							19 05		19 23							20 06
East Garforth d				18 09		18 25									19 26							20 10
Garforth d				18 11		18 28			18 47				19 10		19 29			19 46				20 13
Cross Gates d				18 16		18 32							19 15		19 33							20 17
Leeds 10 a	18 03	18 10	18 12	18 24	18 27	18 40	18 43	18 52	18 56	19 03	19 08	19 13	19 23	19 27	19 41	19 43	19 52	19 56	20 03	20 08	20 14	20 25
Bradford Interchange 37 a								19 15									20 14					

	TP	NT	TP	NT	TP	TP	XC	NT	TP	NT	NT	TP	TP	NT	TP	NT	TP	TP	NT	TP	GR	TP	TP
	◇1 🍴		◇1	◇	◇1	◇1	◇1 🍴		◇1 🍴		◇	◇1	◇1		◇1 🍴	◇	◇1	◇1		◇1 🍴	R 1 🍴	◇1	◇1
York 8 33 d	20 05	20 07	20 18	20 21	20 27		20 45		21 05	21 07	21 21	21 27			22 05	22 07	22 27			23 05	23 08		23 37
Ulleskelf 33 d																							
Church Fenton 33 d				20 32							21 33												
Selby d						20 39		20 47					21 38	21 47				22 38	22 51			23 36	
South Milford d								20 59						21 59					23 02				
Micklefield d		20 22						21 04		21 23				22 04		22 23							
East Garforth d		20 25						21 08		21 27				22 08		22 27							
Garforth d		20 28			20 46			21 11		21 30		21 46		22 11		22 30	22 44						
Cross Gates d		20 32						21 15		21 34				22 15		22 34							
Leeds 10 a	20 27	20 40	20 43	20 53	20 56	21 03	21 08	21 24	21 27	21 43	21 53	21 55	22 03	22 23	22 27	22 43	22 53	23 03	23 19	23 27	23 35	00 02	00 02
Bradford Interchange 37 a				21 14							22 15												

NRT DECEMBER 19 EDITION

Table T040-F

Sundays

23 February to 29 March

York and Selby - Leeds

	TP	TP	TP	TP	TP	NT	TP	TP	NT	TP	NT	TP	NT	TP	XC	TP	TP	NT	TP	NT	TP	NT
	🚌	🚌	🚌	🚌	◇1 🍴		◇1	◇1 🍴		◇1 🍴		◇1 🍴	◇	◇1 🍴	◇1 🍴	◇1	◇1 🍴		◇1 🍴	◇	◇1 🍴	
York 8 33 d	01 30	04 55	05 55	06 55	08 18	08 29		08 48		09 05	09 07	09 18	09 21	09 27	09 36		09 49		10 04	10 08	10 20	10 21
Ulleskelf 33 d																						
Church Fenton 33 d													09 33							10 20		
Selby d							08 41		08 45							09 40		09 48				
South Milford d									08 56									09 59				
Micklefield d						08 44			09 02		09 22							10 05				10 36
East Garforth d						08 47			09 06		09 25							10 09				
Garforth d						08 50			09 08		09 28			09 45				10 11				10 40
Cross Gates d						08 55			09 13									10 16				10 45
Leeds 10 a	02 20	05 45	06 45	07 45	08 41	09 02	09 05	09 12	09 21	09 27	09 39	09 42	09 52	09 56	09 59	10 03	10 12	10 24	10 27	10 39	10 43	10 53
Bradford Interchange 37 a													10 10							11 07		

	TP	XC	TP	TP	NT	TP	NT	TP	NT	TP	TP	XC	TP	NT	TP	NT	TP	NT	TP	TP	XC	TP
	◇1 🍴	◇1 🍴	◇1	◇1 🍴		◇1 🍴		◇1 🍴	◇	◇1 🍴	◇1	◇1 🍴	◇1 🍴		◇1 🍴		◇1 🍴	◇	◇1 🍴	◇1	◇1 🍴	◇1 🍴
York 8 33 d	10 27	10 34		10 49		11 05	11 07	11 16	11 21	11 27		11 41	11 49		12 05	12 07	12 16	12 21	12 27		12 45	12 50
Ulleskelf 33 d																						
Church Fenton 33 d									11 33									12 33				
Selby d			10 40		10 47						11 36			11 49						12 40		
South Milford d					10 59									11 59								
Micklefield d					11 05		11 22							12 05		12 22						
East Garforth d					11 09		11 25							12 09		12 25						
Garforth d	10 43				11 11		11 28			11 46	11 51			12 11		12 28			12 47			
Cross Gates d					11 16		11 32				11 56			12 16		12 32						
Leeds 10 a	10 56	10 58	11 03	11 12	11 24	11 27	11 40	11 42	11 53	11 56	12 03	12 08	12 12	12 24	12 27	12 40	12 43	12 53	12 56	13 03	13 08	13 13
Bradford Interchange 37 a									12 15									13 15				

	NT	TP	NT	TP	NT	TP	TP	XC	TP	NT	TP	NT	TP	NT	TP	TP	XC	TP	NT	TP	NT	TP
		◇1 🍴		◇1 🍴	◇	◇1 🍴	◇1	◇1 🍴	◇1 🍴		◇1 🍴		◇1 🍴	◇	◇1 🍴	◇1	◇1 🍴	◇1 🍴		◇1 🍴		◇1 🍴
York 8 33 d		13 05	13 07	13 16	13 21	13 27		13 45	13 49		14 04	14 07	14 16	14 21	14 27		14 44	14 48		15 05	15 07	15 15
Ulleskelf 33 d																						
Church Fenton 33 d					13 33									14 33								
Selby d	12 47						13 38			13 47						14 38			14 47			
South Milford d	12 59									13 59									14 59			
Micklefield d	13 06		13 22							14 04		14 22							15 04		15 22	
East Garforth d	13 10		13 25							14 08		14 25							15 08		15 25	
Garforth d	13 12		13 28			13 46				14 11		14 28			14 47				15 11		15 28	
Cross Gates d	13 17		13 32							14 15		14 32							15 15		15 32	
Leeds 10 a	13 25	13 28	13 40	13 43	13 52	13 56	14 03	14 08	14 12	14 24	14 27	14 40	14 43	14 52	14 56	15 03	15 07	15 11	15 23	15 27	15 40	15 43
Bradford Interchange 37 a					14 17									15 14								

	NT	TP	TP	XC	TP	NT	TP	NT	TP	NT	TP	TP	XC	TP	NT	TP	NT	TP	NT	TP	TP	XC
	◇	◇1 🍴	◇1	◇1 🍴	◇1 🍴		◇1 🍴		◇1 🍴	◇	◇1 🍴	◇1	◇1 🍴	◇1 🍴		◇1 🍴		◇1 🍴	◇	◇1 🍴	◇1	◇1 🍴
York 8 33 d	15 21	15 27		15 44	15 50		16 05	16 07	16 16	16 21	16 27		16 44	16 49		17 05	17 07	17 18	17 21	17 27		17 44
Ulleskelf 33 d																						
Church Fenton 33 d	15 33									16 33									17 33			
Selby d			15 38			15 47						16 39			16 47						17 38	
South Milford d						15 59									16 59							
Micklefield d						16 05		16 22							17 05		17 22					
East Garforth d						16 09		16 25							17 09		17 27					
Garforth d		15 46				16 12		16 28							17 12		17 29			17 46		
Cross Gates d						16 16		16 32							17 16		17 34					
Leeds 10 a	15 52	15 56	16 03	16 07	16 12	16 25	16 28	16 40	16 43	16 52	16 56	17 03	17 09	17 12	17 25	17 28	17 42	17 44	17 53	17 56	18 03	18 10
Bradford Interchange 37 a	16 15									17 14									18 15			

	TP	NT	TP	NT	TP	NT	TP	TP	XC	TP	NT	TP	NT	TP	NT	TP	TP	XC	TP	NT	TP	NT
	◇1 🍴		◇1 🍴		◇1 🍴	◇	◇1 🍴	◇1	◇1 🍴	◇1 🍴		◇1 🍴		◇1	◇	◇1	◇1	◇1 🍴	◇1 🍴		◇1 🍴	
York 8 33 d	17 49		18 05	18 07	18 18	18 21	18 27		18 45	18 49		19 05	19 07	19 16	19 21	19 27		19 45	19 51		20 05	20 07
Ulleskelf 33 d																						
Church Fenton 33 d						18 33									19 33							
Selby d		17 47						18 38			18 47						19 38			19 47		
South Milford d		17 59									18 59									19 59		
Micklefield d		18 05		18 22							19 05		19 23							20 06		20 22
East Garforth d		18 09		18 25									19 26							20 10		20 25
Garforth d		18 11		18 28			18 47				19 10		19 29			19 46				20 13		20 28
Cross Gates d		18 16		18 32							19 15		19 33							20 17		20 32
Leeds 10 a	18 12	18 24	18 27	18 40	18 43	18 52	18 56	19 03	19 08	19 13	19 23	19 27	19 41	19 43	19 52	19 56	20 03	20 08	20 14	20 25	20 27	20 40
Bradford Interchange 37 a						19 15									20 14							

	TP	NT	TP	TP	XC	NT	TP	NT	NT	TP	TP	NT	TP	NT	TP	TP	NT	TP	GR	TP	TP
	◇1	◇	◇1	◇1	◇1 🍴		◇1 🍴		◇	◇1	◇1		◇1 🍴	◇	◇1	◇1		◇1 🍴	R 1 🍴	◇1	◇1
York 8 33 d	20 18	20 21	20 27		20 45		21 05	21 07	21 21	21 27			22 05	22 07	22 27			23 05	23 08		23 37
Ulleskelf 33 d																					
Church Fenton 33 d		20 32							21 33												
Selby d				20 39		20 47					21 38	21 47				22 38	22 51			23 36	
South Milford d						20 59						21 59					23 02				
Micklefield d						21 04		21 23				22 04		22 23							
East Garforth d						21 08		21 27				22 08		22 27							
Garforth d			20 46			21 11		21 30		21 46		22 11		22 30	22 44						
Cross Gates d						21 15		21 34				22 15		22 34							
Leeds 10 a	20 43	20 53	20 56	21 03	21 08	21 24	21 27	21 43	21 53	21 55	22 03	22 23	22 27	22 43	22 53	23 03	23 19	23 27	23 35	00 02	00 02
Bradford Interchange 37 a		21 14							22 15												

Table T040-F

Sundays
5 April to 10 May

York and Selby - Leeds

	TP ◇1		TP ◇1	TP ◇1	TP ◇1	TP ◇1 ⊼	TP ◇1 ⊼	TP ◇1 ⊼	TP ◇1 ⊼	NT	TP ◇1	TP ◇1 ⊼	NT	TP ◇1 ⊼		NT	TP ◇1	NT ◇	TP ◇1 ⊼	XC ◇1 ⊼	TP ◇1	TP ◇1 ⊼	NT	TP ◇1 ⊼
York 8 ... 33 d	02 25		04 00	05 15	06 08	07 17	07 44	08 18	08 26	08 29		08 48		09 05		09 07	09 18	09 21	09 27	09 36		09 49		10 04
Ulleskelf ... 33 d																								
Church Fenton ... 33 d																		09 33						
Selby ... d											08 41		08 45								09 40		09 48	
South Milford ... d													08 56										09 59	
Micklefield ... d										08 44			09 02			09 22							10 05	
East Garforth ... d										08 47			09 06			09 25							10 09	
Garforth ... d									08 43	08 50			09 08			09 28			09 45				10 11	
Cross Gates ... d										08 55			09 13										10 16	
Leeds 10 ... a	02 50		04 25	05 40	06 33	07 42	08 13	08 43	08 53	09 02	09 05	09 12	09 21	09 27		09 39	09 42	09 52	09 56	09 59	10 03	10 12	10 24	10 27
Bradford Interchange ... 37 a																		10 10						

	NT ◇	TP ◇1 ⊼	NT		TP ◇1 ⊼	XC ◇1 ⊼	TP ◇1	TP ◇1 ⊼	NT	TP ◇1 ⊼	NT	TP ◇1 ⊼	NT ◇	TP ◇1 ⊼	TP ◇1	XC ◇1 ⊼		TP ◇1	NT	TP ◇1 ⊼	NT	TP ◇1 ⊼	NT ◇	TP ◇1 ⊼
York 8 ... 33 d	10 08	10 20	10 21		10 27	10 34		10 49		11 05	11 07	11 16	11 21	11 27		11 41		11 49		12 05	12 07	12 16	12 21	12 27
Ulleskelf ... 33 d																								
Church Fenton ... 33 d	10 20												11 33										12 33	
Selby ... d							10 40		10 47						11 36				11 49					
South Milford ... d									10 59										11 59					
Micklefield ... d			10 36						11 05		11 22								12 05		12 22			
East Garforth ... d									11 09		11 25								12 09		12 25			
Garforth ... d			10 40		10 43				11 11		11 28			11 46	11 51				12 11		12 28			12 47
Cross Gates ... d			10 45						11 16		11 32				11 56				12 16		12 32			
Leeds 10 ... a	10 39	10 43	10 53		10 56	10 58	11 03	11 12	11 24	11 27	11 40	11 42	11 53	11 56	12 03	12 08		12 12	12 24	12 27	12 40	12 43	12 53	12 56
Bradford Interchange ... 37 a	11 07												12 15										13 15	

	TP ◇1	XC ◇1 ⊼	TP ◇1 ⊼	NT	TP ◇1 ⊼		NT	TP ◇1 ⊼	NT ◇	TP ◇1 ⊼	TP ◇1	XC ◇1 ⊼	TP ◇1 ⊼	NT	TP ◇1 ⊼	NT	TP ◇1 ⊼	NT ◇		TP ◇1 ⊼	TP ◇1	XC ◇1 ⊼	TP ◇1 ⊼	NT
York 8 ... 33 d		12 45	12 50		13 05		13 07	13 16	13 21	13 27		13 45	13 49		14 04	14 07	14 16	14 21		14 27		14 44	14 48	
Ulleskelf ... 33 d																								
Church Fenton ... 33 d									13 33									14 33						
Selby ... d	12 40			12 47							13 38			13 47							14 38			14 47
South Milford ... d				12 59										13 59										14 59
Micklefield ... d				13 06			13 22							14 04		14 22								15 04
East Garforth ... d				13 10			13 25							14 08		14 25								15 08
Garforth ... d				13 12			13 28			13 46				14 11		14 28				14 47				15 11
Cross Gates ... d				13 17			13 32							14 15		14 32								15 15
Leeds 10 ... a	13 03	13 08	13 13	13 25	13 28		13 40	13 43	13 52	13 56	14 03	14 08	14 12	14 24	14 27	14 40	14 43	14 52		14 56	15 03	15 07	15 11	15 23
Bradford Interchange ... 37 a									14 17									15 14						

	TP ◇1 ⊼	NT	TP ◇1 ⊼	NT ◇	TP ◇1 ⊼	TP ◇1	XC ◇1 ⊼		TP ◇1 ⊼	NT	TP ◇1 ⊼	NT	TP ◇1 ⊼	NT ◇	TP ◇1 ⊼	TP ◇1	XC ◇1 ⊼	TP ◇1 ⊼	NT	TP ◇1 ⊼		NT	TP ◇1 ⊼	NT ◇
York 8 ... 33 d	15 05	15 07	15 15	15 21	15 27		15 44		15 50		16 05	16 07	16 16	16 21	16 27		16 44	16 49		17 05		17 07	17 18	17 21
Ulleskelf ... 33 d																								
Church Fenton ... 33 d				15 33										16 33										17 33
Selby ... d						15 38				15 47						16 39			16 47					
South Milford ... d										15 59									16 59					
Micklefield ... d		15 22								16 05		16 22							17 05			17 22		
East Garforth ... d		15 25								16 09		16 25							17 09			17 27		
Garforth ... d		15 28			15 46					16 12		16 28							17 12			17 29		
Cross Gates ... d		15 32								16 16		16 32							17 16			17 34		
Leeds 10 ... a	15 27	15 40	15 43	15 52	15 56	16 03	16 07		16 12	16 25	16 28	16 40	16 43	16 52	16 56	17 03	17 09	17 12	17 25	17 28		17 42	17 44	17 53
Bradford Interchange ... 37 a				16 15										17 14										18 15

	TP ◇1 ⊼	TP ◇1	XC ◇1 ⊼	TP ◇1 ⊼	NT	TP ◇1 ⊼	NT	TP ◇1 ⊼	NT ◇		TP ◇1 ⊼	TP ◇1	XC ◇1 ⊼	TP ◇1 ⊼	NT	TP ◇1 ⊼	NT	TP ◇1	NT ◇	TP ◇1	TP ◇1	XC ◇1 ⊼		TP ◇1 ⊼
York 8 ... 33 d	17 27		17 44	17 49		18 05	18 07	18 18	18 21		18 27		18 45	18 49		19 05	19 07	19 16	19 21	19 27		19 45		19 51
Ulleskelf ... 33 d																								
Church Fenton ... 33 d									18 33										19 33					
Selby ... d		17 38			17 47							18 38			18 47						19 38			
South Milford ... d					17 59										18 59									
Micklefield ... d					18 05		18 22								19 05		19 23							
East Garforth ... d					18 09		18 25										19 26							
Garforth ... d	17 46				18 11		18 28				18 47				19 10		19 29			19 46				
Cross Gates ... d					18 16		18 32								19 15		19 33							
Leeds 10 ... a	17 56	18 03	18 10	18 12	18 24	18 27	18 40	18 43	18 52		18 56	19 03	19 08	19 13	19 23	19 27	19 41	19 43	19 52	19 56	20 03	20 08		20 14
Bradford Interchange ... 37 a									19 15										20 14					

	NT	TP ◇1 ⊼	NT	TP ◇1	NT ◇	TP ◇1	TP ◇1	XC ◇1 ⊼	NT	TP ◇1 ⊼	NT		NT ◇	TP ◇1	TP ◇1	NT	TP ◇1 ⊼	NT ◇	TP ◇1	TP ◇1	NT	TP ◇1 ⊼	GR ■ 1	TP ◇1	TP ◇1	
York 8 ... 33 d		20 05	20 07	20 18	20 21	20 27		20 45		21 05	21 07		21 21	21 27			22 05	22 07	22 27			23 05	23 08		23 37	
Ulleskelf ... 33 d																										
Church Fenton ... 33 d					20 32								21 33													
Selby ... d	19 47						20 39		20 47						21 38	21 47				22 38	22 51			23 36		
South Milford ... d	19 59								20 59							21 59					23 02					
Micklefield ... d	20 06		20 22						21 04		21 23					22 04		22 23								
East Garforth ... d	20 10		20 25						21 08		21 27					22 08		22 27								
Garforth ... d	20 13		20 28			20 46			21 11		21 30			21 46		22 11		22 30	22 44							
Cross Gates ... d	20 17		20 32						21 15		21 34					22 15		22 34								
Leeds 10 ... a	20 25	20 27	20 40	20 43	20 53	20 56	21 03	21 08	21 24	21 27	21 43		21 53	21 55	22 03	22 23	22 27	22 43	22 53	23 03	23 19	23 27	23 35	00 02	00 02	
Bradford Interchange ... 37 a					21 14								22 15													

Table T040-R

Mondays to Fridays
16 December to 15 May

Leeds - Selby and York

Miles	Miles		TP MO ◇1	TP MX ◇1 ⊼	TP MO ◇1		TP MX ◇1	TP MO ◇1	TP MX ◇1	TP MO ◇1	TP MX ◇1	TP MO ◇1	TP MX ◇1	NT	TP ◇1	XC ◇1 ⊼	TP ◇1 ⊼	NT ◇		TP ◇1 ⊼	NT	NT	TP ◇1	TP ◇1 ⊼
—	—	Bradford Interchange ... 37 d																						
0	0	**Leeds 10** ... d	00 22	00 29	00 46		00 53	01 06	01 43	02 11	02 19	04 20	04 20	05 20	05 35	05 43	05 52	05 55		06 15	06 19	06 25	06 36	06 42
4¼	4¼	Cross Gates ... d												05 26				06 02			06 25	06 31		
7¼	7¼	Garforth ... d												05 32				06 07			06 31	06 36		
8	8	East Garforth ... d												05 34				06 09			06 33	06 39		
9	9	Micklefield ... d												05 38				06 12			06 37	06 43		
—	12¾	South Milford ... d																06 17			06 42			
—	20¾	**Selby** ... a													05 54			06 27			06 54		07 07	
14¾	—	Church Fenton ... 33 a																				06 49		
16½	—	Ulleskelf ... 33 a																						
25½	—	**York 8** ... 33 a	01 02	01 10	01 26		01 29	01 32	02 27	02 39	02 58	04 45	05 00	05 55		06 05	06 15			06 37		07 02		07 05

	TP ◇1 ⊼	NT ◇	GR ■ 1	TP ◇1	NT	TP ◇1	TP ◇1		NT ◇	TP ◇1	NT	TP ◇1 ⊼	NT ◇	XC ◇1 ⊼	TP ◇1 ⊼	NT	TP ◇1 ⊼	NT ◇	TP ◇1 ⊼	TP ◇1 ⊼		TP ◇1 ⊼	NT ◇	XC ◇1 ⊼
Bradford Interchange ... 37 d		06 31							07 07		07 21		07 29					08 07					08 30	
Leeds 10 ... d	06 51	06 54	07 08	07 14	07 18	07 27	07 34		07 37	07 42	07 46	07 51	07 54	08 08	08 14	08 18	08 27	08 30	08 34	08 42		08 51	08 54	09 08
Cross Gates ... d		07 01			07 24								08 01			08 24							09 01	
Garforth ... d		07 06			07 30	07 36					07 55		08 06			08 30	08 36						09 06	
East Garforth ... d		07 08			07 32								08 08			08 32							09 08	
Micklefield ... d		07 11			07 36						08 00		08 11			08 35							09 11	
South Milford ... d		07 16											08 16										09 16	
Selby ... a		07 26					07 53						08 26						08 55				09 28	
Church Fenton ... 33 a																		08 48						
Ulleskelf ... 33 a											08 08													
York 8 ... 33 a	07 14		07 31	07 36	07 54	07 58			08 01	08 05	08 19	08 18		08 30	08 36	08 52	08 54	09 01		09 05		09 14		09 30

	TP ◇1 ⊼	NT	TP ◇1 ⊼	NT ◇	TP ◇1 ⊼	TP ◇1 ⊼	TP ◇1 ⊼	NT ◇	XC ◇1 ⊼		TP ◇1 ⊼	NT	TP ◇1 ⊼	NT ◇	TP ◇1 ⊼	TP ◇1 ⊼	TP ◇1 ⊼	NT ◇	XC ◇1 ⊼	TP ◇1 ⊼	NT	TP ◇1 ⊼		NT ◇
Bradford Interchange ... 37 d				09 07				09 30						10 07				10 30						11 07
Leeds 10 ... d	09 14	09 18	09 27	09 30	09 34	09 42	09 51	09 54	10 08		10 14	10 18	10 27	10 30	10 34	10 42	10 51	10 54	11 08	11 14	11 18	11 27		11 30
Cross Gates ... d		09 24						10 01				10 24						11 01			11 24			
Garforth ... d		09 30	09 36					10 06				10 30	10 36					11 06			11 30	11 36		
East Garforth ... d		09 32						10 08				10 32						11 08			11 32			
Micklefield ... d		09 36						10 11				10 36						11 11			11 36			
South Milford ... d								10 16										11 16						
Selby ... a					09 57			10 26							10 56			11 26						
Church Fenton ... 33 a				09 48										10 48										11 48
Ulleskelf ... 33 a																								
York 8 ... 33 a	09 36	09 54	09 55	09 59		10 04	10 14		10 30		10 36	10 51	10 55	10 59		11 05	11 15		11 30	11 36	11 53	11 57		12 00

	TP ◇1 ⊼	TP ◇1 ⊼	TP ◇1 ⊼	NT ◇	XC ◇1 ⊼	TP ◇1 ⊼	NT	TP ◇1 ⊼	NT ◇	TP ◇1 ⊼	TP ◇1 ⊼		TP ◇1 ⊼	NT ◇	XC ◇1 ⊼	TP ◇1 ⊼	NT	TP ◇1 ⊼	NT ◇	TP ◇1 ⊼	TP ◇1 ⊼	TP ◇1 ⊼	NT ◇	XC ◇1 ⊼
Bradford Interchange ... 37 d				11 31					12 07					12 31					13 07				13 31	
Leeds 10 ... d	11 34	11 42	11 51	11 54	12 08	12 14	12 18	12 27	12 30	12 34	12 42		12 51	12 54	13 08	13 14	13 18	13 27	13 30	13 34	13 42	13 51	13 54	14 08
Cross Gates ... d				12 01			12 24							13 01			13 24						14 01	
Garforth ... d				12 06			12 30	12 36						13 06			13 30	13 36					14 06	
East Garforth ... d				12 08			12 32							13 08			13 32						14 08	
Micklefield ... d				12 11			12 36							13 11			13 36						14 11	
South Milford ... d				12 16										13 16									14 16	
Selby ... a	11 56			12 26						12 56				13 26						13 56			14 26	
Church Fenton ... 33 a									12 48										13 48					
Ulleskelf ... 33 a																								
York 8 ... 33 a		12 05	12 14		12 31	12 36	12 53	12 55	13 01		13 05		13 14		13 30	13 36	13 53	13 55	14 00		14 05	14 14		14 30

		TP ◇1 ⊼	NT	TP ◇1 ⊼	NT ◇	TP ◇1 ⊼	TP ◇1 ⊼	TP ◇1 ⊼	NT ◇	XC ◇1 ⊼	TP ◇1 ⊼	NT	TP ◇1 ⊼		NT ◇	TP ◇1 ⊼	TP ◇1 ⊼	TP ◇1 ⊼	NT ◇	XC ◇1 ⊼	TP ◇1 ⊼	NT	TP ◇1 ⊼	NT ◇
Bradford Interchange ... 37 d					14 08				14 30						15 07				15 30					16 07
Leeds 10 ... d		14 14	14 18	14 27	14 30	14 34	14 42	14 51	14 54	15 08	15 14	15 18	15 27		15 30	15 33	15 42	15 51	15 54	16 08	16 14	16 18	16 27	16 30
Cross Gates ... d			14 24						15 01			15 24							16 01			16 24		
Garforth ... d			14 30	14 36					15 06			15 30	15 36						16 06			16 30	16 36	
East Garforth ... d			14 32						15 08			15 32							16 08			16 32		
Micklefield ... d			14 36						15 11			15 36							16 11			16 36		
South Milford ... d									15 16										16 16					
Selby ... a						14 56			15 26							15 55			16 27					
Church Fenton ... 33 a					14 48										15 48									16 48
Ulleskelf ... 33 a																								
York 8 ... 33 a		14 36	14 53	14 55	15 00		15 05	15 14		15 30	15 36	15 53	15 55		15 59		16 05	16 14		16 30	16 36	16 53	16 55	17 00

	TP ◇1 ⊼	TP ◇1 ⊼		TP ◇1 ⊼	NT ◇	XC ◇1 ⊼	TP ◇1 ⊼	NT	NT	TP ◇1 ⊼	NT ◇	TP ◇1 ⊼	TP ◇1 ⊼	NT	TP ◇1 ⊼		NT ◇	XC ◇1 ⊼	TP ◇1 ⊼	NT	TP ◇1 ⊼	NT ◇	TP ◇1 ⊼	XC ◇1 ⊼
Bradford Interchange ... 37 d					16 30						17 07						17 30					18 07		
Leeds 10 ... d	16 34	16 42		16 51	16 54	17 07	17 13	17 16	17 19	17 27	17 30	17 34	17 42	17 46	17 51		17 54	18 08	18 14	18 18	18 27	18 30	18 34	18 38
Cross Gates ... d	16 40				17 01				17 26			17 41		17 53			18 01			18 24			18 40	
Garforth ... d	16 45				17 06			17 25	17 31	17 36		17 45		17 58			18 06			18 30	18 36		18 45	
East Garforth ... d					17 08			17 28	17 34		17 41						18 08			18 32				
Micklefield ... d					17 11			17 32			17 45						18 11			18 36				
South Milford ... d					17 16				17 41								18 16							
Selby ... a	16 59				17 26				17 55			17 59					18 26						18 58	
Church Fenton ... 33 a											17 51											18 48		
Ulleskelf ... 33 a														18 07										
York 8 ... 33 a		17 05		17 14		17 30	17 35	17 51		17 55	18 02		18 05	18 19	18 18			18 31	18 36	18 52	18 55	19 00		19 04

Table T040-R

Leeds - Selby and York

Mondays to Fridays
16 December to 15 May

	TP	TP	NT	XC	TP	NT	TP	NT	TP	TP	TP	NT	XC	TP	NT	TP	NT	TP	TP	TP	NT	TP
	◇1 ⊼	◇1 ⊼	◇	◇1 ⊼	◇1 ⊼		◇1	◇	◇1 ⊼	◇1 ⊼	◇1 ⊼	◇	◇1 ⊼	◇1		◇1	◇	◇1	◇1	◇1	◇	◇1
Bradford Interchange 37 d			18 31					19 07				19 31					20 07				20 30	
Leeds 10 d	18 42	18 51	18 54	19 07	19 14	19 18	19 27	19 30	19 34	19 42	19 51	19 54	20 08	20 14	20 18	20 27	20 30	20 33	20 42	20 51	20 54	21 14
Cross Gates d			19 01			19 24						20 01			20 24						21 01	
Garforth d			19 06			19 30	19 36					20 06			20 29	20 36					21 06	
East Garforth d			19 08			19 32						20 08			20 31						21 08	
Micklefield d			19 11			19 36						20 11			20 35						21 11	
South Milford d			19 16									20 16									21 16	
Selby a			19 31						19 56			20 26						20 56			21 26	
Church Fenton 33 a								19 48									20 48					
Ulleskelf 33 a																						
York 8 33 a	19 05	19 14		19 30	19 36	19 53	19 55	20 00		20 05	20 14		20 30	20 36	20 51	20 57	21 00		21 06	21 14		21 36

	NT	TP	NT	TP	TP	TP	NT	TP	NT	TP	TP	NT	TP	NT	TP	TP
		◇1	◇	◇1	◇1	◇1	◇	◇1	◇	◇1	◇1	◇	◇1	◇	◇1	◇1
Bradford Interchange 37 d			21 07				21 31		22 07			22 35		23 07		
Leeds 10 d	21 17	21 27	21 30	21 34	21 42	21 51	21 55	22 14	22 28	22 37	22 42	22 59	23 13	23 27	23 33	23 42
Cross Gates d	21 24						22 01		22 34			23 05		23 33		
Garforth d	21 30	21 36					22 06		22 39			23 10		23 37		
East Garforth d	21 32						22 08		22 41			23 12		23 39		
Micklefield d	21 36						22 12		22 45			23 16		23 43		
South Milford d							22 16			22 53		23 20				
Selby a				21 56			22 28			23 02		23 31			23 51	
Church Fenton 33 a			21 48						22 50					23 48		
Ulleskelf 33 a	21 43															
York 8 33 a	21 56	21 55	22 00		22 07	22 13		22 36	23 02		23 07		23 40	00 01		00 10

Saturdays
21 December to 16 May

	TP	TP	TP	TP	TP	NT	TP	TP	NT	TP	NT	TP	TP	TP	NT	GR	TP	NT	TP	TP	NT	TP	NT
	◇1	◇1	◇1	◇1	◇1		◇1	◇1 ⊼	◇	◇1 ⊼		◇1	◇1 ⊼	◇1 ⊼	◇	■ 1 ⊏	◇1		◇1	◇1	◇	◇1	
Bradford Interchange 37 d															06 31						07 07		07 21
Leeds 10 d	00 29	00 53	01 13	02 19	04 32	05 20	05 35	05 52	05 55	06 15	06 25	06 36	06 42	06 51	06 54	07 08	07 14	07 18	07 27	07 34	07 37	07 42	07 46
Cross Gates d						05 26			06 02		06 31				07 01			07 24					
Garforth d						05 32			06 07		06 36				07 06			07 30	07 36				07 55
East Garforth d						05 34			06 09		06 39				07 08			07 32					
Micklefield d						05 38			06 12		06 43				07 11			07 36					08 00
South Milford d									06 17						07 16								
Selby a							05 54		06 27			07 07			07 26					07 53			
Church Fenton 33 a											06 49												
Ulleskelf 33 a																							08 08
York 8 33 a	01 10	01 29	01 39	02 58	04 57	05 55		06 15		06 37	07 02		07 05	07 17		07 31	07 36	07 54	07 58		08 01	08 05	08 19

	TP	NT	XC	TP	NT	TP	NT	TP	TP	TP	NT	XC	TP	NT	TP	NT	TP	TP	TP	NT	XC	TP
	◇1 ⊼	◇	◇1 ⊼	◇1 ⊼		◇1 ⊼	◇	◇1 ⊼	◇1 ⊼	◇1 ⊼	◇	◇1 ⊼	◇1 ⊼		◇1 ⊼	◇	◇1 ⊼	◇1 ⊼	◇1 ⊼	◇	◇1 ⊼	◇1 ⊼
Bradford Interchange 37 d		07 29					08 07				08 30					09 07				09 30		
Leeds 10 d	07 51	07 54	08 08	08 14	08 18	08 27	08 30	08 34	08 42	08 51	08 54	09 08	09 14	09 18	09 27	09 30	09 34	09 42	09 51	09 54	10 08	10 14
Cross Gates d		08 01			08 24						09 01			09 24						10 01		
Garforth d		08 06			08 30	08 36					09 06			09 30	09 36					10 06		
East Garforth d		08 08			08 32						09 08			09 32						10 08		
Micklefield d		08 11			08 35						09 11			09 36						10 11		
South Milford d		08 16									09 16									10 16		
Selby a		08 26						08 55			09 28						09 57			10 26		
Church Fenton 33 a							08 48									09 48						
Ulleskelf 33 a																						
York 8 33 a	08 18		08 29	08 36	08 52	08 54	09 01		09 05	09 14		09 30	09 36	09 54	09 55	09 59		10 04	10 14		10 30	10 36

	NT	TP	NT	TP	TP	TP	NT	XC	TP	NT	TP	NT	TP	TP	TP	NT	XC	TP	NT	TP	NT	TP
		◇1 ⊼	◇	◇1 ⊼	◇1 ⊼	◇1 ⊼	◇	◇1 ⊼	◇1 ⊼		◇1 ⊼	◇	◇1 ⊼	◇1 ⊼	◇1 ⊼	◇	◇1 ⊼	◇1 ⊼		◇1 ⊼	◇	◇1 ⊼
Bradford Interchange 37 d			10 07				10 30					11 07				11 31					12 07	
Leeds 10 d	10 18	10 27	10 30	10 34	10 42	10 51	10 54	11 08	11 14	11 18	11 27	11 30	11 34	11 42	11 51	11 54	12 08	12 14	12 18	12 27	12 30	12 34
Cross Gates d	10 24						11 01			11 24						12 01			12 24			
Garforth d	10 30	10 36					11 06			11 30	11 36					12 06			12 30	12 36		
East Garforth d	10 32						11 08			11 32						12 08			12 32			
Micklefield d	10 36						11 11			11 36						12 11			12 36			
South Milford d							11 16									12 16						
Selby a				10 56			11 26						11 56			12 26						12 56
Church Fenton 33 a			10 48									11 48									12 48	
Ulleskelf 33 a																						
York 8 33 a	10 51	10 55	10 59		11 05	11 15		11 30	11 36	11 53	11 57	12 00		12 05	12 14		12 30	12 36	12 53	12 55	13 01	

	TP	TP	NT	XC	TP	NT	TP	NT	TP	TP	TP	NT	XC	TP	NT	TP	NT	TP	TP	TP	NT	XC
	◇1 ⊼	◇1 ⊼	◇	◇1 ⊼	◇1 ⊼		◇1 ⊼	◇	◇1 ⊼	◇1 ⊼	◇1 ⊼	◇	◇1 ⊼	◇1 ⊼		◇1 ⊼	◇	◇1 ⊼	◇1 ⊼	◇1 ⊼	◇	◇1 ⊼
Bradford Interchange 37 d			12 31					13 07				13 31					14 07				14 30	
Leeds 10 d	12 42	12 51	12 54	13 08	13 14	13 18	13 27	13 30	13 34	13 42	13 51	13 54	14 08	14 14	14 18	14 27	14 30	14 34	14 42	14 51	14 54	15 08
Cross Gates d			13 01			13 24						14 01			14 24						15 01	
Garforth d			13 06			13 30	13 36					14 06			14 30	14 36					15 06	
East Garforth d			13 08			13 32						14 08			14 32						15 08	
Micklefield d			13 11			13 36						14 11			14 36						15 11	
South Milford d			13 16									14 16									15 16	
Selby a			13 26						13 56			14 26						14 56			15 26	
Church Fenton 33 a								13 48									14 48					
Ulleskelf 33 a																						
York 8 33 a	13 05	13 14		13 30	13 36	13 53	13 55	14 00		14 05	14 14		14 30	14 36	14 53	14 55	14 59		15 05	15 14		15 30

Table T040-R

Saturdays
21 December to 16 May

Leeds - Selby and York

	TP	NT	TP	NT	TP	TP	TP	NT	XC	TP	NT	TP	NT	TP	TP	TP	NT	XC	TP	NT	NT	TP
	◇1 ⊼		◇1 ⊼	◇	◇1 ⊼	◇1 ⊼	◇1 ⊼	◇	◇1 ⊼	◇1 ⊼		◇1 ⊼	◇	◇1 ⊼	◇1 ⊼	◇1 ⊼	◇	◇1 ⊼	◇1 ⊼			◇1 ⊼
Bradford Interchange 37 d				15 07				15 30					16 07				16 30					
Leeds 10 d	15 14	15 18	15 27	15 30	15 33	15 42	15 51	15 54	16 08	16 14	16 18	16 27	16 30	16 34	16 42	16 51	16 54	17 08	17 13	17 16	17 19	17 27
Cross Gates d		15 24						16 01			16 24			16 40			17 01				17 26	
Garforth d		15 30	15 36					16 06			16 30	16 36		16 45			17 06			17 25	17 31	17 36
East Garforth d		15 32						16 08			16 32						17 08			17 28	17 34	
Micklefield d		15 36						16 11			16 36						17 11			17 32		
South Milford d								16 16									17 16				17 41	
Selby a					15 55			16 27						16 59			17 26				17 55	
Church Fenton 33 a				15 48									16 48									
Ulleskelf 33 a																						
York 8 33 a	15 36	15 53	15 55	15 59		16 05	16 14		16 30	16 36	16 53	16 55	17 00		17 05	17 14		17 30	17 35	17 51		17 55

	NT	TP	TP	NT	TP	NT	XC	TP	NT	TP	NT	TP	XC	TP	TP	NT	XC	TP	NT	TP	NT	TP	TP
	◇	◇1 ⊼	◇1 ⊼		◇1 ⊼	◇	◇1 ⊼	◇1 ⊼		◇1 ⊼	◇	◇1 ⊼	◇1 ⊼	◇1 ⊼	◇1 ⊼	◇	◇1 ⊼	◇1 ⊼		◇1 ⊼	◇	◇1 ⊼	◇1 ⊼
Bradford Interchange 37 d	17 07					17 30					18 07					18 31					19 07		
Leeds 10 d	17 30	17 34	17 42	17 46	17 51	17 54	18 08	18 14	18 18	18 27	18 30	18 34	18 38	18 42	18 51	18 54	19 07	19 14	19 18	19 27	19 30	19 34	19 42
Cross Gates d		17 41		17 53		18 01			18 24			18 40				19 01			19 24				
Garforth d		17 45		17 58		18 06			18 30	18 36		18 45				19 06			19 30	19 36			
East Garforth d	17 41					18 08			18 32							19 08			19 32				
Micklefield d	17 45					18 11			18 36							19 11			19 36				
South Milford d						18 16										19 16							
Selby a		17 59				18 26						18 58				19 31						19 56	
Church Fenton 33 a	17 51										18 48										19 48		
Ulleskelf 33 a				18 07																			
York 8 33 a	18 02		18 05	18 19	18 18		18 30	18 36	18 52	18 55	19 00		19 04	19 05	19 14		19 30	19 36	19 53	19 55	20 00		20 05

	TP	NT	XC	TP	NT	TP	NT	TP	TP	TP	NT	XC	TP	NT	TP	NT	TP	TP	TP	NT	TP	NT
	◇1 ⊼	◇	◇1 ⊼	◇1		◇1	◇	◇1	◇1	◇1	◇	◇1	◇1		◇1	◇	◇1	◇1	◇1	◇	◇1	◇
Bradford Interchange 37 d		19 31					20 07				20 30					21 07				21 31		22 07
Leeds 10 d	19 51	19 54	20 08	20 14	20 18	20 27	20 30	20 33	20 42	20 51	20 54	21 09	21 14	21 17	21 27	21 30	21 34	21 42	21 51	21 55	22 14	22 28
Cross Gates d		20 01			20 24						21 01			21 24						22 01		22 34
Garforth d		20 06			20 29	20 36					21 06			21 30	21 36					22 06		22 39
East Garforth d		20 08			20 31						21 08			21 32						22 08		22 41
Micklefield d		20 11			20 35						21 11			21 36						22 12		22 45
South Milford d		20 16									21 16									22 16		
Selby a		20 26						20 56			21 26						21 56			22 28		
Church Fenton 33 a							20 48									21 48						22 50
Ulleskelf 33 a														21 43								
York 8 33 a	20 14		20 30	20 36	20 51	20 57	21 02		21 06	21 14		21 46	21 36	21 56	21 55	22 00		22 07	22 14		22 36	23 02

	TP	TP	NT	TP	NT	TP	TP
	◇1	◇1	◇	◇1	◇	◇1	◇1
Bradford Interchange 37 d			22 30		23 04		
Leeds 10 d	22 37	22 42	22 54	23 13	23 24	23 34	23 42
Cross Gates d			23 01		23 30		
Garforth d			23 06		23 34		
East Garforth d			23 08		23 36		
Micklefield d			23 11		23 40		
South Milford d	22 53		23 16				
Selby a	23 02		23 26			23 52	
Church Fenton 33 a					23 45		
Ulleskelf 33 a							
York 8 33 a		23 07		23 40	23 57		00 10

Sundays
15 December to 16 February

	TP	TP	TP	TP	TP	TP	TP	NT	GR	TP	TP	NT	XC	TP	NT	NT	TP	NT	XC	TP	TP	NT	TP
	◇1 A	◇1 A	◇1 A	◇1	◇1	◇1	◇1 ⊼		■ 1 ⊏	◇1 ⊼	◇1 ⊼		◇1 ⊼	◇1 ⊼		◇	◇1 ⊼		◇1 ⊼	◇1 ⊼	◇1 ⊼		◇1 ⊼
Bradford Interchange 37 d																09 14							
Leeds 10 d	00 22	00 48	01 05	02 03	05 33	06 38	07 42	08 14	08 30	08 35	08 41	08 54	09 18	09 22	09 25	09 42	09 51	09 55	10 09	10 14	10 22	10 26	10 34
Cross Gates d								08 20				09 00			09 31			10 01				10 32	
Garforth d								08 26				09 06		09 31	09 37			10 07			10 31	10 38	
East Garforth d								08 28				09 08			09 39			10 09				10 40	
Micklefield d								08 32				09 12			09 43			10 13				10 44	
South Milford d												09 17						10 20					
Selby a										09 00		09 30						10 32					11 00
Church Fenton 33 a								08 38								09 57							
Ulleskelf 33 a																							
York 8 33 a	01 02	01 25	01 44	02 44	06 14	07 19	08 04	08 51	08 55		09 04		09 40	09 55	09 59	10 11	10 14		10 31	10 36	10 54	11 00	

A not 15 December

Table T040-R

Sundays

15 December to 16 February

Leeds - Selby and York

	TP	NT	TP		NT	XC	TP	TP	NT	TP	TP	NT	TP	NT	XC	TP		TP	NT	TP	TP	NT	TP	NT
	◇1 ⌶	◇	◇1 ⌶			◇1 ⌶	◇1 ⌶	◇1 ⌶		◇1 ⌶	◇1 ⌶	◇	◇1 ⌶		◇1 ⌶	◇1 ⌶		◇1 ⌶		◇1 ⌶	◇1 ⌶	◇	◇1 ⌶	
Bradford Interchange 37 d		10 13										11 18										12 16		
Leeds 10 d	10 42	10 45	10 51		10 55	11 07	11 14	11 23	11 26	11 34	11 42	11 45	11 51	11 55	12 08	12 14		12 22	12 26	12 34	12 41	12 44	12 51	12 59
Cross Gates d					11 01				11 32					12 01					12 32					
Garforth d					11 07			11 32	11 38					12 07				12 31	12 38					
East Garforth d					11 09				11 40					12 09					12 40					
Micklefield d					11 13				11 44					12 13					12 44					
South Milford d					11 18									12 18										13 13
Selby a					11 30					11 59				12 30						13 00				13 26
Church Fenton 33 a		11 01										12 00										12 59		
Ulleskelf 33 a																								
York 8 33 a	11 05	11 13	11 15			11 29	11 36	11 48	12 00		12 04	12 14	12 14		12 30	12 36		12 52	13 00		13 05	13 12	13 15	

	XC	TP	TP	NT	TP		NT	TP	TP	NT	XC	TP	TP	NT	TP	NT	TP	TP		NT	XC	TP	TP	NT
	◇1 ⌶	◇1 ⌶	◇1 ⌶		◇1 ⌶		◇	◇1 ⌶	◇1 ⌶		◇1 ⌶	◇1 ⌶	◇1 ⌶		◇1 ⌶	◇	◇1 ⌶	◇1 ⌶			◇1 ⌶	◇1 ⌶	◇1 ⌶	
Bradford Interchange 37 d							13 13									14 11								
Leeds 10 d	13 06	13 14	13 22	13 26	13 34		13 42	13 45	13 51	13 55	14 07	14 12	14 21	14 25	14 34	14 41	14 44	14 51		14 55	15 07	15 13	15 22	15 26
Cross Gates d				13 32						14 01				14 31						15 01				15 32
Garforth d			13 31	13 38						14 06			14 30	14 37						15 07			15 31	15 38
East Garforth d				13 40						14 08				14 39						15 09				15 40
Micklefield d				13 44						14 12				14 43						15 13				15 44
South Milford d										14 17										15 18				
Selby a					14 00					14 30					15 00					15 30				
Church Fenton 33 a							13 56									14 55								
Ulleskelf 33 a																								
York 8 33 a	13 28	13 36	13 52	14 00			14 10	14 10	14 14		14 29	14 34	14 51	14 59		15 09	15 06	15 14			15 29	15 35	15 56	16 00

	TP	TP	NT	TP	NT	XC	TP		TP	NT	TP	TP	NT	TP	NT	XC	TP	TP	NT	TP		TP	NT	TP
	◇1 ⌶	◇1 ⌶	◇	◇1 ⌶		◇1 ⌶	◇1 ⌶		◇1 ⌶		◇1 ⌶	◇1 ⌶	◇	◇1 ⌶		◇1 ⌶	◇1 ⌶	◇1 ⌶		◇1 ⌶		◇1 ⌶	◇	◇1 ⌶
Bradford Interchange 37 d			15 14										16 13										17 13	
Leeds 10 d	15 34	15 42	15 45	15 51	15 54	16 07	16 13		16 23	16 26	16 34	16 42	16 45	16 52	16 55	17 07	17 14	17 23	17 26	17 34		17 42	17 45	17 51
Cross Gates d					16 00					16 33	16 40				17 01				17 33	17 40				
Garforth d					16 06				16 32	16 38	16 45				17 07			17 32	17 38	17 45				
East Garforth d					16 08					16 40					17 09				17 40					
Micklefield d					16 12					16 44					17 13				17 44					
South Milford d					16 17										17 18									
Selby a	16 00				16 29						17 00				17 30					18 00				
Church Fenton 33 a			15 59										16 59										17 59	
Ulleskelf 33 a																								
York 8 33 a		16 05	16 13	16 14		16 29	16 35		16 53	17 01		17 05	17 13	17 15		17 29	17 36	17 53	18 01			18 05	18 14	18 15

	NT	XC	TP	TP	NT	TP	TP	NT	TP		XC	NT	XC	TP	TP	NT	TP	TP	NT	TP	NT	XC		TP
		◇1 ⌶	◇1 ⌶	◇1 ⌶		◇1 ⌶	◇1 ⌶	◇	◇1 ⌶		◇1 ⌶		◇1 ⌶	◇1 ⌶	◇1 ⌶		◇1 ⌶	◇1 ⌶	◇	◇1 ⌶		◇1 ⌶		◇1
Bradford Interchange 37 d								18 14											19 14					
Leeds 10 d	17 55	18 07	18 14	18 23	18 26	18 34	18 42	18 45	18 52		18 56	18 59	19 08	19 14	19 25	19 28	19 34	19 42	19 45	19 51	19 55	20 09		20 14
Cross Gates d	18 01				18 33	18 40						19 06				19 34					20 01			
Garforth d	18 07			18 32	18 38	18 45						19 11			19 34	19 40					20 07			
East Garforth d	18 09				18 40											19 42					20 09			
Micklefield d	18 13				18 44											19 46					20 13			
South Milford d	18 18											19 18									20 18			
Selby a	18 30					19 00						19 30					20 00				20 33			
Church Fenton 33 a								18 59											19 59					
Ulleskelf 33 a																								
York 8 33 a		18 29	18 36	18 53	19 01		19 05	19 13	19 14		19 18		19 30	19 36	19 55	20 02		20 05	20 13	20 17		20 30		20 36

	TP	NT	TP	TP	NT	TP	NT	XC	TP	TP	NT		TP	TP	NT	TP	NT	TP	NT	TP	TP	NT	NT	TP
	◇1		◇1	◇1	◇	◇1		◇1	◇1	◇1			◇1	◇1	◇	◇1		◇1 ⌶		◇1	◇1	◇		◇1
Bradford Interchange 37 d					20 13										21 13							22 20		
Leeds 10 d	20 23	20 26	20 34	20 42	20 45	20 52	20 55	21 08	21 14	21 23	21 26		21 34	21 42	21 45	21 51	21 55	22 14	22 24	22 34	22 43	22 46	22 54	23 14
Cross Gates d		20 33					21 01				21 33						22 01		22 30				23 00	
Garforth d	20 32	20 38					21 07			21 32	21 38						22 07		22 36				23 06	
East Garforth d		20 40					21 09				21 40						22 09		22 38				23 08	
Micklefield d		20 44					21 13				21 44						22 13		22 42				23 12	
South Milford d							21 18										22 18			22 53			23 17	
Selby a			21 00				21 30						22 00				22 30			23 02			23 29	
Church Fenton 33 a					20 59										21 59							23 00		
Ulleskelf 33 a																								
York 8 33 a	20 53	21 01		21 07	21 11	21 14		21 31	21 36	21 53	22 01			22 07	22 12	22 14		22 36	22 58		23 08	23 14		23 41

	TP	TP	NT
	◇1	◇1	◇
Bradford Interchange 37 d			23 14
Leeds 10 d	23 33	23 42	23 45
Cross Gates d			
Garforth d			
East Garforth d			
Micklefield d			
South Milford d			
Selby a	23 51		
Church Fenton 33 a			00 01
Ulleskelf 33 a			
York 8 33 a		00 10	00 16

Table T040-R

Sundays

23 February to 29 March

Leeds - Selby and York

	TP		TP	TP	TP	TP	NT	GR	TP	TP	NT	XC	TP	NT		NT	TP	NT	XC	TP	TP	NT	TP	NT
	🚌		🚌	🚌	🚌	🚌		■1 ⊏	◇1 ⌶	◇		◇1 ⌶	◇1 ⌶			◇	◇1 ⌶		◇1 ⌶	◇1 ⌶	◇1 ⌶		◇1 ⌶	◇
Bradford Interchange 37 d																09 14								10 13
Leeds 10 d	00 50		01 35	03 00	05 30	07 35	08 14	08 30	08 35	08 45	08 54	09 18	09 22	09 25		09 42	09 51	09 55	10 09	10 14	10 22	10 26	10 34	10 45
Cross Gates d							08 20				09 00			09 31				10 01				10 32		
Garforth d							08 26				09 06		09 31	09 37				10 07			10 31	10 38		
East Garforth d							08 28				09 08			09 39				10 09				10 40		
Micklefield d							08 32				09 12			09 43				10 13				10 44		
South Milford d											09 17							10 20						
Selby a									09 00		09 30							10 32					11 00	
Church Fenton 33 a							08 38									09 57								11 01
Ulleskelf 33 a																								
York 8 33 a	01 40		02 25	03 50	06 20	08 25	08 51	08 55		09 07		09 40	09 55	09 59		10 11	10 14		10 31	10 36	10 54	11 00		11 13

	TP	NT	XC		TP	TP	NT	TP	TP	NT	TP	NT	XC	TP	TP	NT		TP	TP	NT	TP	NT	XC	TP
	◇1 ⌶		◇1 ⌶		◇1 ⌶	◇1 ⌶		◇1 ⌶	◇1 ⌶	◇	◇1 ⌶		◇1 ⌶	◇1 ⌶	◇1 ⌶			◇1 ⌶	◇1 ⌶	◇	◇1 ⌶		◇1 ⌶	◇1 ⌶
Bradford Interchange 37 d										11 18										12 16				
Leeds 10 d	10 51	10 55	11 07		11 14	11 23	11 26	11 34	11 42	11 45	11 51	11 55	12 08	12 14	12 22	12 26		12 34	12 41	12 44	12 51	12 59	13 06	13 14
Cross Gates d		11 01					11 32					12 01				12 32								
Garforth d		11 07				11 32	11 38					12 07			12 31	12 38								
East Garforth d		11 09					11 40					12 09				12 40								
Micklefield d		11 13					11 44					12 13				12 44								
South Milford d		11 18										12 18										13 13		
Selby a		11 30						11 59				12 30						13 00				13 26		
Church Fenton 33 a										12 00										12 59				
Ulleskelf 33 a																								
York 8 33 a	11 15		11 29		11 36	11 48	12 00		12 04	12 14	12 14		12 30	12 36	12 52	13 00			13 05	13 12	13 15		13 28	13 36

	TP	NT	TP	NT	TP		TP	NT	XC	TP	TP	NT	TP	NT	TP	TP	NT	XC		TP	TP	NT	TP	TP
	◇1 ⌶		◇1 ⌶	◇	◇1 ⌶		◇1 ⌶		◇1 ⌶	◇1 ⌶	◇1 ⌶		◇1 ⌶	◇	◇1 ⌶	◇1 ⌶		◇1 ⌶		◇1 ⌶	◇1 ⌶		◇1 ⌶	◇1 ⌶
Bradford Interchange 37 d				13 13										14 11										
Leeds 10 d	13 22	13 26	13 34	13 42	13 45		13 51	13 55	14 07	14 12	14 21	14 25	14 34	14 41	14 44	14 51	14 55	15 07		15 13	15 22	15 26	15 34	15 42
Cross Gates d		13 32						14 01				14 31					15 01					15 32		
Garforth d	13 31	13 38						14 06			14 30	14 37					15 07				15 31	15 38		
East Garforth d		13 40						14 08				14 39					15 09					15 40		
Micklefield d		13 44						14 12				14 43					15 13					15 44		
South Milford d								14 17									15 18							
Selby a			14 00					14 30					15 00				15 30						16 00	
Church Fenton 33 a				13 56										14 55										
Ulleskelf 33 a																								
York 8 33 a	13 52	14 00		14 10	14 10		14 14		14 29	14 34	14 51	14 59		15 09	15 06	15 14		15 29		15 35	15 56	16 00		16 05

	NT	TP	NT	XC	TP	TP	NT		TP	TP	NT	TP	NT	XC	TP	TP	NT	TP	TP	NT		TP	NT	XC
	◇	◇1 ⌶		◇1 ⌶	◇1 ⌶	◇1 ⌶			◇1 ⌶	◇1 ⌶	◇	◇1 ⌶		◇1 ⌶	◇1 ⌶	◇1 ⌶		◇1 ⌶	◇1 ⌶	◇		◇1 ⌶		◇1 ⌶
Bradford Interchange 37 d	15 14										16 13									17 13				
Leeds 10 d	15 45	15 51	15 54	16 07	16 13	16 23	16 26		16 34	16 42	16 45	16 52	16 55	17 07	17 14	17 23	17 26	17 34	17 42	17 45		17 51	17 55	18 07
Cross Gates d			16 00				16 33		16 40				17 01				17 33	17 40					18 01	
Garforth d			16 06			16 32	16 38		16 45				17 07			17 32	17 38	17 45					18 07	
East Garforth d			16 08				16 40						17 09				17 40						18 09	
Micklefield d			16 12				16 44						17 13				17 44						18 13	
South Milford d			16 17										17 18										18 18	
Selby a			16 29						17 00				17 30					18 00					18 30	
Church Fenton 33 a	15 59										16 59									17 59				
Ulleskelf 33 a																								
York 8 33 a	16 13	16 14		16 29	16 35	16 53	17 01			17 05	17 13	17 15		17 29	17 36	17 53	18 01		18 05	18 14		18 15		18 29

	TP	TP	NT	TP	TP	NT	TP	XC	NT		XC	TP	TP	NT	TP	TP	NT	TP	NT	XC	TP	TP		NT
	◇1 ⌶	◇1 ⌶		◇1 ⌶	◇1 ⌶	◇	◇1 ⌶	◇1 ⌶			◇1 ⌶	◇1 ⌶	◇1 ⌶		◇1 ⌶	◇1 ⌶	◇	◇1 ⌶		◇1 ⌶	◇1	◇1		
Bradford Interchange 37 d						18 14											19 14							
Leeds 10 d	18 14	18 23	18 26	18 34	18 42	18 45	18 52	18 56	18 59		19 08	19 14	19 25	19 28	19 34	19 42	19 45	19 51	19 55	20 09	20 14	20 23		20 26
Cross Gates d			18 33	18 40					19 06					19 34					20 01					20 33
Garforth d		18 32	18 38	18 45					19 11				19 34	19 40					20 07			20 32		20 38
East Garforth d			18 40											19 42					20 09					20 40
Micklefield d			18 44											19 46					20 13					20 44
South Milford d									19 18										20 18					
Selby a				19 00					19 30						20 00				20 33					
Church Fenton 33 a						18 59											19 59							
Ulleskelf 33 a																								
York 8 33 a	18 36	18 53	19 01		19 05	19 13	19 14	19 18			19 30	19 36	19 55	20 02		20 05	20 13	20 17		20 30	20 36	20 53		21 01

	TP	TP	NT	TP	NT	XC	TP	TP	NT	TP	TP		NT	TP	NT	TP	NT	TP	TP	NT	NT	TP	TP	TP
	◇1	◇1	◇	◇1		◇1	◇1	◇1		◇1	◇1		◇	◇1		◇1 ⌶		◇1	◇1	◇		◇1	◇1	◇1
Bradford Interchange 37 d			20 13										21 13							22 20				
Leeds 10 d	20 34	20 42	20 45	20 52	20 55	21 08	21 14	21 23	21 26	21 34	21 42		21 45	21 51	21 55	22 14	22 24	22 34	22 43	22 46	22 54	23 14	23 33	23 42
Cross Gates d					21 01				21 33						22 01		22 30				23 00			
Garforth d					21 07			21 32	21 38						22 07		22 36				23 06			
East Garforth d					21 09				21 40						22 09		22 38				23 08			
Micklefield d					21 13				21 44						22 13		22 42				23 12			
South Milford d					21 18										22 18			22 53			23 17			
Selby a	21 00				21 30					22 00					22 30			23 02			23 29		23 51	
Church Fenton 33 a			20 59										21 59							23 00				
Ulleskelf 33 a																								
York 8 33 a		21 07	21 11	21 14		21 31	21 36	21 53	22 01		22 07		22 12	22 14		22 36	22 58		23 08	23 14		23 41		00 10

Table T040-R

Sundays

23 February to 29 March

Leeds - Selby and York

		NT
		◇
Bradford Interchange	37 d	23 14
Leeds 10	d	23 45
Cross Gates	d	
Garforth	d	
East Garforth	d	
Micklefield	d	
South Milford	d	
Selby	a	
Church Fenton	33 a	00 01
Ulleskelf	33 a	
York 8	33 a	00 16

Sundays

5 April to 10 May

		TP	TP	TP	TP	TP	TP	TP	NT	GR	TP	TP	NT		XC	TP	NT	NT	TP	NT	XC	TP	TP	NT	TP
		◇1	◇1	◇1	◇1	◇1	◇1	◇1 ⊼		1 ⊡	◇1 ⊼	◇1 ⊼			◇1 ⊼	◇1 ⊼		◇	◇1 ⊼		◇1 ⊼	◇1 ⊼	◇1 ⊼		◇1 ⊼
Bradford Interchange	37 d																	09 14							
Leeds 10	d	00 22	00 48	00 56	01 54	05 31	06 36	07 42	08 14	08 30	08 35	08 41	08 54		09 18	09 22	09 25	09 42	09 51	09 55	10 09	10 14	10 22	10 26	10 34
Cross Gates	d								08 20				09 00				09 31			10 01				10 32	
Garforth	d								08 26				09 06			09 31	09 37			10 07			10 31	10 38	
East Garforth	d								08 28				09 08				09 39			10 09				10 40	
Micklefield	d								08 32				09 12				09 43			10 13				10 44	
South Milford	d												09 17							10 20					
Selby	a										09 00		09 30							10 32					11 00
Church Fenton	33 a								08 38									09 57							
Ulleskelf	33 a																								
York 8	33 a	01 02	01 15	01 23	02 21	05 58	07 03	08 04	08 51	08 55		09 04			09 40	09 55	09 59	10 11	10 14		10 31	10 36	10 54	11 00	

		TP		NT	TP	NT	XC	TP	TP	NT	TP	TP	NT	TP	NT		XC	TP	TP	NT	TP	TP	NT	TP	NT
		◇1 ⊼		◇	◇1 ⊼		◇1 ⊼	◇1 ⊼	◇1 ⊼		◇1 ⊼	◇1 ⊼	◇	◇1 ⊼			◇1 ⊼	◇1 ⊼	◇1 ⊼		◇1 ⊼	◇1 ⊼	◇	◇1 ⊼	
Bradford Interchange	37 d			10 13									11 18										12 16		
Leeds 10	d	10 42		10 45	10 51	10 55	11 07	11 14	11 23	11 26	11 34	11 42	11 45	11 51	11 55		12 08	12 14	12 22	12 26	12 34	12 41	12 44	12 51	12 59
Cross Gates	d					11 01				11 32					12 01					12 32					
Garforth	d					11 07			11 32	11 38					12 07				12 31	12 38					
East Garforth	d					11 09				11 40					12 09					12 40					
Micklefield	d					11 13				11 44					12 13					12 44					
South Milford	d					11 18									12 18										13 13
Selby	a					11 30					11 59				12 30						13 00				13 26
Church Fenton	33 a			11 01									12 00										12 59		
Ulleskelf	33 a																								
York 8	33 a	11 05		11 13	11 15		11 29	11 36	11 48	12 00		12 04	12 14	12 14			12 30	12 36	12 52	13 00		13 05	13 12	13 15	

		XC	TP	TP		NT	TP	NT	TP	TP	NT	XC	TP	TP	NT	TP	NT		TP	TP	NT	XC	TP	TP	NT
		◇1 ⊼	◇1 ⊼	◇1 ⊼			◇1 ⊼	◇	◇1 ⊼	◇1 ⊼		◇1 ⊼	◇1 ⊼	◇1 ⊼		◇1 ⊼	◇		◇1 ⊼	◇1 ⊼		◇1 ⊼	◇1 ⊼	◇1 ⊼	
Bradford Interchange	37 d							13 13									14 11								
Leeds 10	d	13 06	13 14	13 22		13 26	13 34	13 42	13 45	13 51	13 55	14 07	14 12	14 21	14 25	14 34	14 41		14 44	14 51	14 55	15 07	15 13	15 22	15 26
Cross Gates	d					13 32					14 01				14 31						15 01				15 32
Garforth	d			13 31		13 38					14 06			14 30	14 37						15 07			15 31	15 38
East Garforth	d					13 40					14 08				14 39						15 09				15 40
Micklefield	d					13 44					14 12				14 43						15 13				15 44
South Milford	d										14 17										15 18				
Selby	a						14 00				14 30					15 00					15 30				
Church Fenton	33 a							13 56									14 55								
Ulleskelf	33 a																								
York 8	33 a	13 28	13 36	13 52		14 00		14 10	14 10	14 14		14 29	14 34	14 51	14 59		15 09		15 06	15 14		15 29	15 35	15 56	16 00

		TP	TP	NT	TP	NT		XC	TP	TP	NT	TP	TP	NT	TP	NT	XC	TP	TP		NT	TP	TP	NT	TP
		◇1 ⊼	◇1 ⊼	◇	◇1 ⊼			◇1 ⊼	◇1 ⊼	◇1 ⊼		◇1 ⊼	◇1 ⊼	◇	◇1 ⊼		◇1 ⊼	◇1 ⊼	◇1 ⊼			◇1 ⊼	◇1 ⊼	◇	◇1 ⊼
Bradford Interchange	37 d			15 14										16 13										17 13	
Leeds 10	d	15 34	15 42	15 45	15 51	15 54		16 07	16 13	16 23	16 26	16 34	16 42	16 45	16 52	16 55	17 07	17 14	17 23		17 26	17 34	17 42	17 45	17 51
Cross Gates	d					16 00					16 33	16 40				17 01					17 33	17 40			
Garforth	d					16 06				16 32	16 38	16 45				17 07			17 32		17 38	17 45			
East Garforth	d					16 08					16 40					17 09					17 40				
Micklefield	d					16 12					16 44					17 13					17 44				
South Milford	d					16 17										17 18									
Selby	a	16 00				16 29						17 00				17 30						18 00			
Church Fenton	33 a			15 59										16 59										17 59	
Ulleskelf	33 a																								
York 8	33 a		16 05	16 13	16 14			16 29	16 35	16 53	17 01		17 05	17 13	17 15		17 29	17 36	17 53		18 01		18 05	18 14	18 15

		NT	XC	TP	TP	NT	TP	TP		NT	TP	XC	NT	XC	TP	TP	NT	TP	TP	NT	TP		NT	XC	TP
			◇1 ⊼	◇1 ⊼	◇1 ⊼		◇1 ⊼	◇1 ⊼		◇	◇1 ⊼	◇1 ⊼		◇1 ⊼	◇1 ⊼	◇1 ⊼		◇1 ⊼	◇1 ⊼	◇	◇1 ⊼			◇1 ⊼	◇1
Bradford Interchange	37 d									18 14										19 14					
Leeds 10	d	17 55	18 07	18 14	18 23	18 26	18 34	18 42		18 45	18 52	18 56	18 59	19 08	19 14	19 25	19 28	19 34	19 42	19 45	19 51		19 55	20 09	20 14
Cross Gates	d	18 01				18 33	18 40						19 06				19 34						20 01		
Garforth	d	18 07			18 32	18 38	18 45						19 11			19 34	19 40						20 07		
East Garforth	d	18 09				18 40											19 42						20 09		
Micklefield	d	18 13				18 44											19 46						20 13		
South Milford	d	18 18											19 18										20 18		
Selby	a	18 30					19 00						19 30					20 00					20 33		
Church Fenton	33 a									18 59										19 59					
Ulleskelf	33 a																								
York 8	33 a		18 29	18 36	18 53	19 01		19 05		19 13	19 14	19 18		19 30	19 36	19 55	20 02		20 05	20 13	20 17			20 30	20 36

Table T040-R

Sundays

5 April to 10 May

Leeds - Selby and York

		TP	NT	TP	TP	NT	TP	NT	XC	TP	TP	NT		TP	TP	NT	TP	NT	TP	NT	TP	TP	NT	NT	TP
		◇1		◇1	◇1	◇	◇1		◇1	◇1	◇1			◇1	◇1	◇	◇1		◇1 ⊼		◇1	◇1	◇		◇1
Bradford Interchange	37 d					20 13										21 13							22 20		
Leeds 10	d	20 23	20 26	20 34	20 42	20 45	20 52	20 55	21 08	21 14	21 23	21 26		21 34	21 42	21 45	21 51	21 55	22 14	22 24	22 34	22 43	22 46	22 54	23 14
Cross Gates	d		20 33					21 01				21 33						22 01		22 30				23 00	
Garforth	d	20 32	20 38					21 07			21 32	21 38						22 07		22 36				23 06	
East Garforth	d		20 40					21 09				21 40						22 09		22 38				23 08	
Micklefield	d		20 44					21 13				21 44						22 13		22 42				23 12	
South Milford	d							21 18										22 18			22 53			23 17	
Selby	a			21 00				21 30						22 00				22 30			23 02			23 29	
Church Fenton	33 a					20 59										21 59							23 00		
Ulleskelf	33 a																								
York 8	33 a	20 53	21 01		21 07	21 11	21 14		21 31	21 36	21 53	22 01			22 07	22 12	22 14		22 36	22 58		23 08	23 14		23 41

			TP	TP	NT
			◇1	◇1	◇
Bradford Interchange	37 d				23 14
Leeds 10	d		23 33	23 42	23 45
Cross Gates	d				
Garforth	d				
East Garforth	d				
Micklefield	d				
South Milford	d				
Selby	a		23 51		
Church Fenton	33 a				00 01
Ulleskelf	33 a				
York 8	33 a			00 10	00 16

AVAILABLE FROM MP Middleton Press

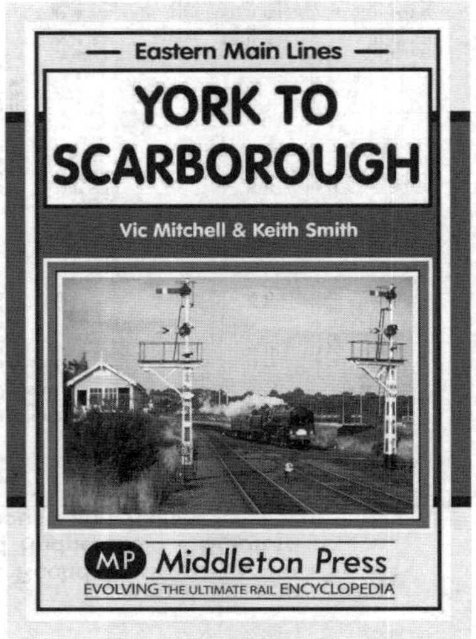

Table T041-F

Mondays to Fridays

16 December to 15 May

Manchester Victoria, Rochdale, Blackpool North and Huddersfield - Bradford and Leeds via Brighouse and Halifax

Miles	Miles	Miles	Miles		NT MO	NT MX	NT	NT	NT	NT	NT	NT	NT	NT	NT	NT	NT	NT	NT	NT	NT	NT
					◇ A	◇ A		◇ B	◇	◇	C				◇ B	◇		◇ D	◇	◇		C
0	—	—	—	Manchester Victoria d					05 45		06 00	06 10				06 32		06 37	06 42		06 55	07 04
4	—	—	—	Moston d					05 52			06 17							06 50			
6	—	—	—	Mills Hill d					05 57			06 21							06 54			
8¾	—	—	—	Castleton d					06 02			06 27							07 00			
10½	—	—	—	Rochdale a					06 06		06 13	06 31				06 44		06 50	07 04		07 09	07 17
—	—	—	—	d					06 06		06 14					06 45		06 51	07 05			07 18
12¾	—	—	—	Smithy Bridge d					06 10		06 18							06 55				07 22
13¾	—	—	—	Littleborough d					06 14		06 21							06 58	07 10			07 25
17¼	—	—	—	Walsden d					06 20									07 04				07 31
19¼	—	—	—	Todmorden d					06 23		06 29					06 58		07 08	07 17			07 35
—	0	—	—	Blackpool North 97 d						05 19										06 20		
—	3	—	—	Poulton-le-Fylde 97 d						05 25										06 26		
—	17½	—	—	Preston ■ 97 d						05 46										06 46		
—	29½	—	—	Blackburn 97 d						06 03										07 03		
—	35¾	—	—	Accrington 97 d						06 11										07 11		
—	42	—	—	Burnley Manchester Road 97 a						06 20	06 45									07 19		07 51
—	—	—	—	d						06 20										07 20		
23½	54¾	—	0	Hebden Bridge a					06 30	06 41						07 04		07 14	07 23	07 41		
—	—	—	—	d			05 43		06 31	06 42				06 49		07 04	07 09	07 15	07 24	07 42		
24¾	56	—	1¼	Mytholmroyd d			05 46							06 52		07 07	07 12	07 18				
28½	60	—	5½	Sowerby Bridge d		00 04	05 51		06 38					06 57		07 12	07 19	07 24	07 31			
—	—	0	—	Huddersfield 39 d									06 35									
—	—	—	—	London Kings Cross 15 ⊖26 d																		
—	—	5¾	11	Brighouse d									06 45					07 33				
—	—	—	15	Mirfield 39 a														07 40				
—	—	—	—	d														07 40				
—	—	—	18	Dewsbury 39 a														07 45				
32¼	63½	10½	—	Halifax a		00 11	05 59		06 45	06 52			06 56	07 03		07 18	07 25		07 38	07 52		
—	—	—	—	d		00 11	06 00	06 17	06 46	06 53			06 57	07 07	07 14	07 19	07 26		07 39	07 53		
—	—	—	—	Low Moor d			06 07						07 04			07 27						
40¾	71½	—	—	Bradford Interchange a		00 25	06 15	06 28	06 59	07 05			07 11	07 19	07 27	07 34	07 40		07 51	08 05		
—	—	—	—	d	00 01	00 27	06 18	06 31	07 01	07 07				07 21	07 29	07 37	07 43		07 53	08 07		
43¾	75	—	—	New Pudsey 37 a	00 09		06 26	06 39	07 09	07 15				07 30	07 37	07 45	07 52		08 01	08 15		
45¾	77	—	—	Bramley 37 a	00 13		06 30	06 43	07 13						07 41	07 49	07 58		08 05			
49¾	81	—	27¼	Leeds ■ 37,39 a	00 21	00 46	06 39	06 52	07 23	07 31				07 41	07 49	08 00	08 07	08 06	08 14	08 26		
—	—	—	—	Selby 40 a				07 26							08 26							
—	—	—	—	York ■ 40 a						08 01				08 19						09 01		

	NT	NT	NT	NT	NT	NT	NT	NT	NT	NT	NT	NT	NT	NT	NT	NT	NT	NT	NT	NT	NT	NT
	E		◇ F	◇ B	◇ D	G	◇	◇	H	G		◇ I	◇ B	◇ J	G	◇	◇	K	E		◇ F	◇ B
Manchester Victoria d	07 11		07 19		07 36	07 42	07 57		08 04	08 10		08 20		08 37	08 42	08 56		09 04	09 09		09 20	
Moston d	07 18					07 50				08 17					08 50				09 16			
Mills Hill d	07 22					07 54				08 21					08 54				09 20			
Castleton d	07 27					08 00				08 26					09 00				09 25			
Rochdale a	07 31		07 32		07 49	08 04	08 11		08 17	08 30		08 33		08 51	09 04	09 09		09 17	09 29		09 33	
d			07 33		07 50		08 12		08 18			08 34		08 51		09 10		09 18			09 33	
Smithy Bridge d					07 54		08 16		08 22					08 55				09 22				
Littleborough d					07 57		08 19		08 25					08 58				09 25				
Walsden d					08 03				08 31					09 04				09 31				
Todmorden d			07 43		08 06		08 26		08 35			08 44		09 08		09 21		09 35			09 44	
Blackpool North 97 d								07 20									08 20					
Poulton-le-Fylde 97 d								07 26									08 26					
Preston ■ 97 d								07 46									08 45					
Blackburn 97 d								08 03									09 03					
Accrington 97 d								08 11									09 11					
Burnley Manchester Road 97 a								08 20	08 51								09 20	09 50				
d								08 20									09 20					
Hebden Bridge a			07 49		08 13		08 32	08 41				08 51		09 14		09 27	09 41				09 50	
d			07 50		08 13		08 33	08 42				08 51		09 15		09 27	09 42				09 50	
Mytholmroyd d			07 53		08 16							08 54		09 18							09 53	
Sowerby Bridge d			07 58		08 22		08 40					08 59		09 23							09 58	
Huddersfield 39 d		07 35									08 35									09 35		
London Kings Cross 15 ⊖26 d																						
Brighouse d		07 45			08 31						08 45			09 32						09 45		
Mirfield 39 a					08 39									09 39								
d					08 39									09 39								
Dewsbury 39 a					08 45									09 44								
Halifax a		07 56	08 04				08 47	08 52			08 56	09 05				09 38	09 52			09 56	10 05	
d		07 57	08 05	08 17			08 47	08 53			08 57	09 06	09 17			09 38	09 53			09 57	10 05	10 17
Low Moor d		08 04	08 11								09 04	09 12								10 04	10 12	
Bradford Interchange a		08 11	08 18	08 28			08 59	09 05			09 11	09 19	09 28			09 50	10 05			10 11	10 20	10 28
d			08 20	08 30			09 02	09 07				09 21	09 30			09 53	10 07				10 23	10 30
New Pudsey 37 a			08 28	08 38			09 10	09 15				09 29	09 38			10 01	10 15				10 31	10 38
Bramley 37 a			08 32	08 42			09 13					09 33	09 42			10 04					10 34	10 42
Leeds ■ 37,39 a			08 41	08 53	09 04		09 22	09 27				09 43	09 52	10 04		10 13	10 27				10 43	10 52
Selby 40 a				09 28									10 26									11 26
York ■ 40 a								09 59									10 59					

A From Manchester Victoria
B To Hull
C To Blackburn
D From Wigan North Western
E From Blackburn
F From Chester
G From Clitheroe
H From Southport to Blackburn
I From Ellesmere Port
J From Wigan Wallgate
K From Wigan Wallgate to Blackburn

For connections from Liverpool Lime Street refer to Table T090

Table T041-F

Mondays to Fridays

16 December to 15 May

Manchester Victoria, Rochdale, Blackpool North and Huddersfield - Bradford and Leeds via Brighouse and Halifax

	NT MX	NT MO	NT	NT	NT	NT	NT	NT	NT	NT	NT	NT	NT	NT	NT	NT	NT	NT	NT	NT	NT	NT
	◇ A	◇ A	B	◇	◇	C	D		◇ E	◇ F	◇ G	B	◇	◇	H	D		◇ E	◇ F	◇ A	B	◇
Manchester Victoria d	09 37	09 37	09 42	09 56		10 04	10 09		10 20		10 37	10 42	10 55		11 04	11 09		11 20		11 34	11 41	11 55
Moston d			09 50				10 16					10 50				11 16					11 48	
Mills Hill d			09 54				10 20					10 54				11 20					11 52	
Castleton d			10 00				10 25					11 00				11 25					11 58	
Rochdale a	09 50	09 50	10 04	10 09		10 17	10 29		10 32		10 50	11 04	11 08		11 17	11 29		11 32		11 49	12 01	12 10
d	09 51	09 51		10 10		10 18			10 33		10 51		11 09		11 18			11 33		11 50		12 11
Smithy Bridge d	09 55	09 55				10 22					10 55				11 22					11 54		
Littleborough d	09 58	09 58				10 25					10 58				11 25					11 57		
Walsden d	10 04	10 04									11 04									12 03		
Todmorden d	10 07	10 07		10 21		10 33			10 43		11 07		11 23		11 33			11 43		12 06		12 22
Blackpool North 97 d					09 20									10 20								
Poulton-le-Fylde 97 d					09 26									10 26								
Preston ■ 97 d					09 46									10 46								
Blackburn 97 d					10 03									11 03								
Accrington 97 d					10 11									11 11								
Burnley Manchester Road 97 a					10 20	10 48								11 19	11 49							
d					10 20									11 20								
Hebden Bridge a	10 13	10 13		10 27	10 41				10 49		11 14		11 30	11 41				11 49		12 13		12 28
d	10 14	10 14		10 27	10 42				10 50		11 14		11 31	11 42				11 50		12 14		12 29
Mytholmroyd d	10 16	10 17							10 53		11 17							11 53		12 17		
Sowerby Bridge d	10 22	10 23							10 58		11 23							11 58		12 22		
Huddersfield 39 d								10 35									11 35					
London Kings Cross 15 ⊖26 d																						
Brighouse d	10 32	10 32						10 45			11 32						11 45			12 31		
Mirfield 39 a	10 39	10 39									11 38									12 39		
d	10 39	10 39									11 39									12 39		
Dewsbury 39 a	10 44	10 44									11 44									12 44		
Halifax a				10 38	10 52			10 56	11 04				11 41	11 52			11 56	12 04				12 39
d				10 38	10 53			10 57	11 05	11 17			11 42	11 53			11 57	12 05	12 17			12 40
Low Moor d								11 04	11 11								12 04	12 11				
Bradford Interchange a				10 50	11 05			11 11	11 19	11 28			11 54	12 05			12 11	12 19	12 28			12 52
d				10 53	11 07				11 21	11 31			11 56	12 07				12 21	12 31			12 57
New Pudsey 37 a				11 01	11 15				11 29	11 39			12 04	12 15				12 29	12 39			13 05
Bramley 37 a				11 04					11 33	11 43			12 08					12 33	12 43			13 09
Leeds ■ 37,39 a	11 03	11 03		11 13	11 27				11 42	11 52	12 03		12 18	12 27				12 42	12 52	13 03		13 18
Selby 40 a										12 26									13 26			
York ■ 40 a					12 00									13 01								

	NT	NT	NT	NT	NT	NT	NT	NT	NT	GC	NT	NT	NT	NT	NT	NT	NT	NT	NT	NT	NT
	◇	H	D		◇ E	◇ F	◇ A	B	◇	■ 1	◇	H	D		◇ E	◇ F	◇ A	B	◇	◇	C
Manchester Victoria d		12 04	12 09		12 20		12 37	12 42	12 56			13 04	13 09		13 20		13 37	13 42	13 55		14 04
Moston d			12 16					12 50					13 16					13 50			
Mills Hill d			12 20					12 54					13 20					13 54			
Castleton d			12 26					13 00					13 25					14 00			
Rochdale a		12 17	12 29		12 32		12 50	13 04	13 09			13 17	13 29		13 32		13 50	14 04	14 08		14 17
d		12 18			12 33		12 51		13 10			13 18			13 33		13 51		14 09		14 18
Smithy Bridge d		12 22					12 55					13 22					13 55				14 22
Littleborough d		12 25					12 58					13 25					13 58				14 25
Walsden d							13 04										14 04				
Todmorden d		12 33			12 43		13 07		13 21			13 33			13 43		14 07		14 20		14 33
Blackpool North 97 d	11 20										12 20									13 21	
Poulton-le-Fylde 97 d	11 26										12 26									13 27	
Preston ■ 97 d	11 46										12 46									13 46	
Blackburn 97 d	12 03										13 03									14 03	
Accrington 97 d	12 11										13 11									14 11	
Burnley Manchester Road 97 a	12 20	12 49									13 20	13 49								14 19	14 49
d	12 20										13 20									14 20	
Hebden Bridge a	12 41				12 49		13 14		13 27		13 41				13 49		14 14		14 26	14 41	
d	12 42				12 50		13 14		13 27		13 42				13 50		14 14		14 26	14 42	
Mytholmroyd d					12 53		13 17								13 53		14 17				
Sowerby Bridge d					12 58		13 23								13 58		14 23				
Huddersfield 39 d				12 35										13 35							
London Kings Cross 15 ⊖26 d										10 57											
Brighouse d				12 45			13 32			13 36				13 45			14 32				
Mirfield 39 a							13 39										14 39				
d							13 39										14 39				
Dewsbury 39 a							13 44										14 44				
Halifax a	12 52			12 56	13 04				13 38	13 47	13 52			13 56	14 04				14 37	14 52	
d	12 53			12 57	13 05	13 17			13 38	13 48	13 53			13 57	14 05	14 17			14 37	14 53	
Low Moor d				13 04	13 11					13 55				14 04	14 11						
Bradford Interchange a	13 05			13 11	13 19	13 28			13 50	14 03	14 06			14 11	14 19	14 28			14 49	15 05	
d	13 07				13 22	13 31			13 56		14 08				14 21	14 30			14 52	15 07	
New Pudsey 37 a	13 15				13 30	13 39			14 04		14 16				14 29	14 38			15 00	15 15	
Bramley 37 a					13 33	13 43			14 07						14 33	14 42			15 03		
Leeds ■ 37,39 a	13 27				13 43	13 52	14 03		14 18		14 27				14 42	14 52	15 03		15 13	15 27	
Selby 40 a						14 26										15 26					
York ■ 40 a	14 00										15 00									15 59	

A From Wigan Wallgate
B From Clitheroe
C From Wigan North Western to Blackburn
D From Blackburn
E From Chester
F To Hull
G From Wigan North Western
H From Wigan Wallgate to Blackburn

For connections from Liverpool Lime Street refer to Table T090

Table T041-F

Mondays to Fridays

16 December to 15 May

Manchester Victoria, Rochdale, Blackpool North and Huddersfield - Bradford and Leeds via Brighouse and Halifax

	NT A	NT	NT ◇ B	NT ◇ C	NT ◇ D	NT E	NT ◇		NT ◇	NT F	NT A	NT	NT ◇ B	NT ◇ C	NT ◇ G	NT E	NT ◇		NT ◇	NT F	NT A	NT	NT ◇ B	NT ◇ C
Manchester Victoria d	14 09		14 20		14 36	14 43	14 56			15 04	15 09		15 20		15 36	15 42	15 56			16 04	16 09		16 20	
Moston d	14 16					14 53					15 16					15 49					16 16			
Mills Hill d	14 20					14 57					15 20					15 53					16 20		16 28	
Castleton d	14 25					15 05					15 25					15 58					16 25			
Rochdale a	14 29		14 32		14 49	15 09	15 13			15 17	15 29		15 32		15 49	16 02	16 10			16 17	16 29		16 35	
d			14 33		14 50		15 14			15 18			15 33		15 49		16 11			16 18			16 35	
Smithy Bridge d					14 54					15 22					15 53					16 22				
Littleborough d					14 57					15 25					15 56					16 25				
Walsden d					15 03										16 02					16 31				
Todmorden d			14 43		15 06		15 25			15 33			15 43		16 06		16 23			16 35			16 45	
Blackpool North 97 d									14 20										15 20					
Poulton-le-Fylde 97 d									14 26										15 26					
Preston 97 d									14 46										15 46					
Blackburn 97 d									15 03										16 03					
Accrington 97 d									15 11										16 11					
Burnley Manchester Road 97 a									15 20	15 48									16 19	16 50				
d									15 20										16 20					
Hebden Bridge a			14 49		15 13		15 31		15 41				15 49		16 13		16 29		16 41				16 51	
d			14 50		15 13		15 31		15 42				15 50		16 14		16 30		16 42				16 52	
Mytholmroyd d			14 53		15 16								15 53		16 17								16 54	
Sowerby Bridge d			14 58		15 22								15 58		16 23								16 59	
Huddersfield 39 d		14 35										15 35										16 35		
London Kings Cross ⊖26 d																								
Brighouse d		14 45			15 31							15 45			16 32							16 45		
Mirfield 39 a					15 38										16 38									
d					15 38										16 38									
Dewsbury 39 a					15 43										16 43									
Halifax a		14 56	15 04				15 42		15 52			15 56	16 04				16 40		16 52			16 56	17 06	
d		14 57	15 05	15 17			15 42		15 53			15 57	16 05	16 17			16 41		16 53			16 57	17 06	17 17
Low Moor d		15 04	15 11									16 04	16 11									17 04	17 12	
Bradford Interchange a		15 11	15 19	15 28			15 54		16 05			16 11	16 19	16 28			16 53		17 05			17 11	17 20	17 28
d			15 21	15 30			15 57		16 07				16 21	16 30			16 55		17 07				17 22	17 30
New Pudsey 37 a			15 29	15 38			16 05		16 15				16 29	16 38			17 03		17 15				17 30	17 38
Bramley 37 a			15 34	15 42			16 08						16 33	16 42			17 07						17 34	17 42
Leeds 37,39 a			15 43	15 52	16 02		16 18		16 27				16 42	16 52	17 04		17 19		17 29				17 43	17 52
Selby 40 a				16 27										17 26										18 26
York 40 a									17 00										18 02					

	NT ◇ D	NT E	NT ◇		GC	NT ◇	NT F	NT A	NT	NT ◇ B	NT ◇ C	NT ◇ D	NT E		NT ◇	NT ◇	NT H	NT A	NT	GC	NT ◇ B	NT ◇ C	NT ◇ D	
Manchester Victoria d	16 37	16 42	16 56				17 04	17 09		17 20		17 37	17 42		17 56		18 04	18 09			18 20		18 37	
Moston d		16 50						17 16					17 50					18 16						
Mills Hill d		16 54						17 20		17 28			17 54					18 20						
Castleton d		17 00						17 25		17 34			18 00					18 25						
Rochdale a	16 50	17 04	17 10				17 17	17 29		17 37		17 50	18 04		18 09		18 17	18 29			18 32		18 50	
d	16 51		17 10				17 18			17 37		17 50			18 10		18 18				18 33		18 51	
Smithy Bridge d	16 55		17 14				17 22					17 54			18 14		18 22				18 37		18 55	
Littleborough d	16 58		17 18				17 25					17 58			18 17		18 25				18 40		18 58	
Walsden d	17 04						17 31					18 04					18 31						19 04	
Todmorden d	17 07		17 25				17 35			17 48		18 07			18 24		18 35				18 48		19 08	
Blackpool North 97 d						16 20										17 20								
Poulton-le-Fylde 97 d						16 26										17 26								
Preston 97 d						16 46										17 46								
Blackburn 97 d						17 03										18 03								
Accrington 97 d						17 11										18 11								
Burnley Manchester Road 97 a						17 20	17 51									18 20	18 51							
d						17 20										18 20								
Hebden Bridge a	17 14		17 31			17 41				17 54		18 14			18 30	18 41					18 54		19 14	
d	17 14		17 31			17 42				17 54		18 14			18 31	18 42					18 54		19 15	
Mytholmroyd d	17 17									17 57		18 17									18 57		19 17	
Sowerby Bridge d	17 22									18 02		18 22									19 02		19 23	
Huddersfield 39 d									17 35										18 35					
London Kings Cross ⊖26 d					14 48															16 27				
Brighouse d	17 32				17 35				17 45			18 31							18 45	18 54			19 32	
Mirfield 39 a	17 39											18 38											19 39	
d	17 39											18 38											19 39	
Dewsbury 39 a	17 44											18 43											19 44	
Halifax a			17 42		17 46	17 52			17 56	18 08					18 41	18 52			18 56	19 05	19 10			
d			17 42		17 47	17 53			17 57	18 09	18 17				18 42	18 53			18 57	19 06	19 10	19 17		
Low Moor d					17 54				18 04	18 15									19 04	19 14	19 16			
Bradford Interchange a			17 54		18 01	18 05			18 13	18 22	18 28				18 54	19 05			19 11	19 21	19 24	19 28		
d			17 59			18 07				18 25	18 31				18 58	19 07					19 26	19 31		
New Pudsey 37 a			18 07			18 15				18 33	18 39				19 06	19 15					19 34	19 39		
Bramley 37 a			18 10							18 36	18 43				19 10						19 38	19 43		
Leeds 37,39 a	18 03		18 21			18 27				18 43	18 52	19 02			19 19	19 27					19 47	19 53	20 03	
Selby 40 a											19 31											20 26		
York 40 a						19 00										20 00								

A From Blackburn
B From Chester
C To Hull
D From Wigan Wallgate
E From Clitheroe
F From Wigan Wallgate to Blackburn
G From Wigan North Western
H From Wigan North Western to Blackburn

For connections from Liverpool Lime Street refer to Table T090

NRT DECEMBER 19 EDITION

Table T041-F

Mondays to Fridays

16 December to 15 May

Manchester Victoria, Rochdale, Blackpool North and Huddersfield - Bradford and Leeds via Brighouse and Halifax

	NT A	NT ◇	NT ◇	NT B	NT A	NT	NT ◇	NT ◇ C	NT ◇ D		NT A	NT ◇	NT ◇	NT B	NT E	NT	NT ◇ F	NT ◇ C	NT ◇ G		NT A	NT ◇	NT ◇	NT H
Manchester Victoria d	18 42	18 56		19 04	19 09		19 21		19 36		19 41	19 56		20 04	20 10		20 19		20 37		20 42	20 56		21 04
Moston d	18 50				19 16						19 49				20 17						20 50			
Mills Hill d	18 54				19 20						19 53				20 21						20 54			
Castleton d	19 00				19 26						19 59				20 26						21 00			
Rochdale a	19 04	19 09		19 17	19 29		19 33		19 49		20 03	20 09		20 17	20 30		20 33		20 50		21 04	21 09		21 17
d		19 10		19 18			19 34		19 50			20 10		20 18			20 34		20 51			21 10		21 18
Smithy Bridge d		19 14		19 22					19 54					20 22					20 55					21 22
Littleborough d		19 17		19 25					19 57					20 25					20 58					21 25
Walsden d									20 03										21 04					21 31
Todmorden d		19 24		19 33			19 44		20 07			20 21		20 33			20 44		21 07			21 21		21 36
Blackpool North 97 d			18 19										19 20										20 20	
Poulton-le-Fylde 97 d			18 25										19 26										20 26	
Preston 97 d			18 46										19 46										20 46	
Blackburn 97 d			19 03										20 03										21 03	
Accrington 97 d			19 11										20 11										21 11	
Burnley Manchester Road 97 a			19 20	19 48									20 20	20 48									21 20	21 51
d			19 20										20 20										21 20	
Hebden Bridge a		19 30	19 41				19 50		20 14			20 27	20 41				20 50		21 14			21 27	21 41	
d		19 31	19 42				19 50		20 15			20 27	20 42				20 50		21 14			21 27	21 42	
Mytholmroyd d							19 53		20 17								20 53		21 17					
Sowerby Bridge d							19 59		20 23								20 58		21 23					
Huddersfield 39 d						19 35										20 35								
London Kings Cross ⊖26 d																								
Brighouse d						19 45			20 32							20 45			21 32					
Mirfield 39 a									20 39										21 39					
d									20 39										21 39					
Dewsbury 39 a									20 44										21 44					
Halifax a		19 41	19 52			19 56	20 05					20 38	20 52			20 56	21 05					21 38	21 52	
d		19 42	19 53			19 57	20 05	20 17				20 38	20 53			20 57	21 05	21 17				21 38	21 53	
Low Moor d						20 04										21 04	21 12							
Bradford Interchange a		19 54	20 05			20 11	20 18	20 28				20 50	21 05			21 11	21 19	21 28				21 50	22 05	
d		19 58	20 07				20 21	20 30				20 53	21 07				21 22	21 31				21 53	22 07	
New Pudsey 37 a		20 06	20 15				20 29	20 38				21 01	21 15				21 30	21 39				22 01	22 15	
Bramley 37 a		20 10					20 33	20 42				21 04					21 33	21 43				22 04		
Leeds 37,39 a		20 19	20 26				20 43	20 52	21 04			21 14	21 28				21 43	21 53	22 05			22 13	22 27	
Selby 40 a								21 26										22 28						
York 40 a			21 00										22 00										23 02	

	NT	NT ◇ F	NT A	NT ◇ C	GC		NT ◇	NT ◇	NT I	NT	NT	NT	NT	NT ◇	NT ◇		NT I	NT ◇	NT
Manchester Victoria d		21 19	21 38				21 56		22 04	22 42					22 56		23 04	23 19	23 32
Moston d			21 46							22 50									23 40
Mills Hill d			21 50							22 54									23 44
Castleton d			21 56							23 00									23 50
Rochdale a		21 31	22 00				22 09		22 17	23 04					23 09		23 17	23 32	23 54
d		21 32					22 10		22 18						23 10		23 18	23 33	
Smithy Bridge d									22 22								23 22	23 37	
Littleborough d									22 25								23 25	23 40	
Walsden d									22 31									23 46	
Todmorden d		21 43					22 21		22 35						23 21		23 33	23 50	
Blackpool North 97 d								21 17						22 02					
Poulton-le-Fylde 97 d								21 23											
Preston 97 d								21 44						22 25					
Blackburn 97 d								22 01						22 42					
Accrington 97 d								22 09						22 50					
Burnley Manchester Road 97 a								22 18	22 51					22 58			23 49		
d								22 18						22 59					
Hebden Bridge a		21 49					22 27	22 39						23 23	23 27			23 56	
d		21 50					22 27	22 40						23 23	23 27			23 56	
Mytholmroyd d		21 53						22 42										23 59	
Sowerby Bridge d		21 58						22 47										00 04	
Huddersfield 39 d	21 35										22 49		23 00						
London Kings Cross ⊖26 d					19 54														
Brighouse d	21 45				22 11						23 00		23 12						
Mirfield 39 a																			
d																			
Dewsbury 39 a																			
Halifax a	21 56	22 04			22 25		22 38	22 53			23 10		23 23		23 38			00 11	
d	21 57	22 05		22 21	22 26		22 38	22 54			23 11	23 17	23 23		23 38			00 11	
Low Moor d	22 04	22 11			22 34						23 18								
Bradford Interchange a	22 11	22 20		22 32	22 41		22 50	23 05			23 25	23 30	23 36	23 47	23 50			00 25	
d		22 22		22 35			22 53	23 07			23 27	23 34			23 53			00 27	
New Pudsey 37 a		22 30		22 43			23 01	23 15			23 37	23 42			00 01				
Bramley 37 a		22 34		22 47			23 04				23 41	23 45			00 05				
Leeds 37,39 a		22 45		22 57			23 13	23 26			23 50	23 55			00 14			00 46	
Selby 40 a				23 31															
York 40 a								00 01											

A From Clitheroe
B From Wigan Wallgate to Blackburn
C To Hull
D From Wigan Wallgate
E From Blackburn
F From Chester
G From Wigan North Western
H From Kirkby to Blackburn
I To Blackburn

For connections from Liverpool Lime Street refer to Table T090

Table T041-F

Saturdays
21 December to 16 May

Manchester Victoria, Rochdale, Blackpool North and Huddersfield - Bradford and Leeds via Brighouse and Halifax

Station		NT ◇ A	NT	NT ◇ B	NT ◇	NT ◇	NT C	NT	NT	NT	NT ◇ B	NT ◇	NT ◇ D	NT ◇	NT ◇	NT	NT C	NT E	NT	NT ◇ F	NT ◇ B	NT ◇ D	NT G
Manchester Victoria ⇌	d				05 45		06 00	06 10				06 31	06 37	06 42		06 55	07 04	07 09		07 19		07 36	07 42
Moston	d				05 52			06 17						06 50				07 16					07 50
Mills Hill	d				05 57			06 21						06 54				07 20					07 54
Castleton	d				06 02			06 27						07 00				07 25					08 00
Rochdale ⇌	a				06 06		06 13	06 31				06 43	06 50	07 04		07 09	07 17	07 29		07 32		07 49	08 04
	d				06 06		06 14					06 44	06 51	07 05			07 18			07 33		07 50	
Smithy Bridge	d				06 10		06 18						06 55				07 22					07 54	
Littleborough	d				06 14		06 21						06 58	07 10			07 25					07 57	
Walsden	d				06 20								07 04				07 31					08 03	
Todmorden	d				06 23		06 29					06 58	07 08	07 17			07 35			07 43		08 06	
Blackpool North 97	d					05 19									06 20								
Poulton-le-Fylde 97	d					05 25									06 26								
Preston 8 97	d					05 46									06 46								
Blackburn 97	d					06 03									07 03								
Accrington 97	d					06 11									07 11								
Burnley Manchester Road 97	a					06 20	06 45								07 19		07 51						
	d					06 20									07 20								
Hebden Bridge	a				06 30	06 41						07 04	07 14	07 23	07 41					07 49		08 13	
	d		05 43		06 31	06 42				06 49		07 04	07 15	07 24	07 42					07 50		08 13	
Mytholmroyd	d		05 46							06 52		07 07	07 18							07 53		08 16	
Sowerby Bridge	d	00 04	05 51		06 38					06 57		07 12	07 24	07 31						07 58		08 22	
Huddersfield 39	d								06 35										07 35				
London Kings Cross 15 ⊖26	d																						
Brighouse	d								06 45				07 33						07 45			08 31	
Mirfield 39	a												07 40									08 39	
	d												07 40									08 39	
Dewsbury 39	a												07 45									08 45	
Halifax	a	00 11	05 59		06 45	06 52			06 56	07 03		07 18		07 38	07 52				07 56	08 04			
	d	00 11	06 00	06 17	06 46	06 53			06 57	07 07	07 14	07 19		07 39	07 53				07 57	08 05	08 17		
Low Moor	d		06 07						07 04			07 27							08 04	08 11			
Bradford Interchange	a	00 25	06 15	06 28	06 59	07 05			07 11	07 19	07 27	07 34		07 51	08 05				08 11	08 18	08 28		
	d	00 27	06 18	06 31	07 01	07 07				07 21	07 29	07 37		07 53	08 07					08 20	08 30		
New Pudsey 37	a		06 26	06 39	07 09	07 15				07 30	07 37	07 45		08 01	08 15					08 28	08 38		
Bramley 37	a		06 30	06 43	07 13						07 41	07 49		08 05						08 32	08 42		
Leeds 10 37,39	a	00 46	06 39	06 52	07 23	07 31				07 41	07 49	08 00	08 06	08 14	08 26					08 41	08 53	09 04	
Selby 40	a			07 26							08 26										09 28		
York 8 40	a					08 01				08 19					09 01								

Station		NT ◇	NT ◇	NT H	NT G	NT	NT ◇ F	NT ◇ B	NT ◇ I	NT G	NT ◇	NT ◇	NT J	NT E	NT	NT ◇ F	NT ◇ B	NT ◇ I	NT G	NT ◇	NT ◇	NT K	NT E
Manchester Victoria ⇌	d	07 57		08 04	08 10		08 20		08 37	08 42	08 56		09 04	09 09		09 20		09 37	09 42	09 56		10 04	10 09
Moston	d				08 17					08 50				09 16					09 50				10 16
Mills Hill	d				08 21					08 54				09 20					09 54				10 20
Castleton	d				08 26					09 00				09 25					10 00				10 25
Rochdale ⇌	a	08 11		08 17	08 30		08 33		08 51	09 04	09 09		09 17	09 29		09 33		09 50	10 04	10 09		10 17	10 29
	d	08 12		08 18			08 34		08 51		09 10		09 18			09 33		09 51		10 09		10 18	
Smithy Bridge	d	08 16		08 22					08 55				09 22					09 55				10 22	
Littleborough	d	08 19		08 25					08 58				09 25					09 58				10 25	
Walsden	d			08 31					09 04				09 31					10 04					
Todmorden	d	08 26		08 35			08 44		09 08		09 21		09 35			09 44		10 07		10 20		10 33	
Blackpool North 97	d		07 20									08 20									09 20		
Poulton-le-Fylde 97	d		07 26									08 26									09 26		
Preston 8 97	d		07 46									08 45									09 46		
Blackburn 97	d		08 03									09 03									10 03		
Accrington 97	d		08 11									09 11									10 11		
Burnley Manchester Road 97	a		08 20	08 51								09 20	09 50								10 20	10 48	
	d		08 20									09 20									10 20		
Hebden Bridge	a	08 32	08 41				08 50		09 14		09 27	09 41				09 50		10 13		10 26	10 41		
	d	08 33	08 42				08 51		09 15		09 27	09 42				09 50		10 14		10 27	10 42		
Mytholmroyd	d						08 54		09 18							09 53		10 16					
Sowerby Bridge	d	08 40					08 59		09 23							09 58		10 22					
Huddersfield 39	d					08 35									09 35								
London Kings Cross 15 ⊖26	d																						
Brighouse	d					08 45			09 32						09 45			10 32					
Mirfield 39	a								09 39									10 39					
	d								09 39									10 39					
Dewsbury 39	a								09 44									10 44					
Halifax	a	08 47	08 52			08 56	09 05				09 38	09 52			09 56	10 05				10 37	10 52		
	d	08 47	08 53			08 57	09 06	09 17			09 38	09 53			09 57	10 05	10 17			10 38	10 53		
Low Moor	d					09 04	09 12								10 04	10 12							
Bradford Interchange	a	08 59	09 05			09 11	09 20	09 28			09 50	10 05			10 11	10 19	10 28			10 50	11 05		
	d	09 02	09 07				09 22	09 30			09 53	10 07				10 22	10 30			10 53	11 07		
New Pudsey 37	a	09 10	09 15				09 30	09 38			10 01	10 15				10 30	10 38			11 01	11 15		
Bramley 37	a	09 13					09 34	09 42			10 04					10 33	10 42			11 04			
Leeds 10 37,39	a	09 22	09 27				09 43	09 52	10 04		10 13	10 27				10 43	10 52	11 03		11 13	11 27		
Selby 40	a							10 26									11 26						
York 8 40	a		09 59									10 59									12 00		

A From Manchester Victoria
B To Hull
C To Blackburn
D From Wigan North Western
E From Blackburn
F From Chester
G From Clitheroe
H From Southport to Blackburn
I From Wigan Wallgate
J From Wigan Wallgate to Blackburn
K From Wigan North Western to Blackburn

For connections from Liverpool Lime Street refer to Table T090

Table T041-F

Saturdays
21 December to 16 May

Manchester Victoria, Rochdale, Blackpool North and Huddersfield - Bradford and Leeds via Brighouse and Halifax

Station		NT	NT ◇ A	NT ◇ B	NT ◇ C	NT D	NT ◇	NT ◇	NT E	NT F	NT	NT ◇ A	NT ◇ B	NT ◇ G	NT D	NT ◇	NT ◇	NT E	NT F	NT	NT ◇ A	NT ◇ B
Manchester Victoria ⇌	d		10 20		10 37	10 42	10 55		11 04	11 09		11 20		11 34	11 41	11 55		12 04	12 09		12 20	
Moston	d					10 50				11 16					11 48				12 16			
Mills Hill	d					10 54				11 20					11 52				12 20			
Castleton	d					11 00				11 25					11 58				12 26			
Rochdale ⇌	a		10 32		10 50	11 04	11 08		11 17	11 29		11 32		11 49	12 01	12 10		12 17	12 29		12 32	
	d		10 33		10 51		11 09		11 18			11 33		11 50		12 11		12 18			12 33	
Smithy Bridge	d				10 55				11 22					11 54				12 22				
Littleborough	d				10 58				11 25					11 57				12 25				
Walsden	d				11 04									12 03								
Todmorden	d		10 43		11 07		11 23		11 33			11 43		12 06		12 22		12 33			12 43	
Blackpool North 97	d							10 20									11 20					
Poulton-le-Fylde 97	d							10 26									11 26					
Preston 8 97	d							10 46									11 46					
Blackburn 97	d							11 03									12 03					
Accrington 97	d							11 11									12 11					
Burnley Manchester Road 97	a							11 19	11 49								12 20	12 49				
	d							11 20									12 20					
Hebden Bridge	a		10 49		11 14		11 30	11 41				11 49		12 13		12 28	12 41				12 49	
	d		10 50		11 14		11 31	11 42				11 50		12 14		12 29	12 42				12 50	
Mytholmroyd	d		10 53		11 17							11 53		12 17							12 53	
Sowerby Bridge	d		10 58		11 23							11 58		12 22							12 58	
Huddersfield 39	d	10 35									11 35									12 35		
London Kings Cross 15 ⊖26	d																					
Brighouse	d	10 45			11 32						11 45			12 31						12 45		
Mirfield 39	a				11 38									12 39								
	d				11 39									12 39								
Dewsbury 39	a				11 44									12 44								
Halifax	a	10 56	11 04				11 41	11 52			11 56	12 04				12 39	12 52			12 56	13 04	
	d	10 57	11 05	11 17			11 42	11 53			11 57	12 05	12 17			12 40	12 53			12 57	13 05	13 17
Low Moor	d	11 04	11 11								12 04	12 11								13 04	13 11	
Bradford Interchange	a	11 11	11 19	11 28			11 54	12 05			12 11	12 19	12 28			12 52	13 05			13 11	13 19	13 28
	d		11 21	11 31			11 56	12 07				12 21	12 31			12 57	13 07				13 21	13 31
New Pudsey 37	a		11 29	11 39			12 04	12 15				12 29	12 39			13 05	13 15				13 29	13 39
Bramley 37	a		11 33	11 43			12 08					12 33	12 43			13 09					13 33	13 43
Leeds 10 37,39	a		11 42	11 52	12 03		12 18	12 27				12 42	12 52	13 03		13 18	13 27				13 42	13 52
Selby 40	a			12 26									13 26									14 26
York 8 40	a							13 01									14 00					

Station		GC 8 1	NT ◇ G	NT D	NT ◇	NT ◇	NT E	NT F	NT	NT ◇ A	NT ◇ B	NT ◇ G	NT D	NT ◇	NT ◇	NT H	NT F	NT	NT ◇ A	NT ◇ B	NT ◇ G	NT D	NT ◇
Manchester Victoria ⇌	d		12 37	12 42	12 56		13 04	13 09		13 20		13 37	13 42	13 55		14 04	14 09		14 20		14 36	14 43	14 56
Moston	d			12 50				13 16					13 50				14 16					14 53	
Mills Hill	d			12 54				13 20					13 54				14 20					14 57	
Castleton	d			13 00				13 25					14 00				14 25					15 05	
Rochdale ⇌	a		12 50	13 04	13 09		13 17	13 29		13 32		13 50	14 04	14 08		14 17	14 29		14 32		14 49	15 09	15 13
	d		12 51		13 10		13 18			13 33		13 51		14 09		14 18			14 33		14 50		15 14
Smithy Bridge	d		12 55				13 22					13 55				14 22					14 54		
Littleborough	d		12 58				13 25					13 58				14 25					14 57		
Walsden	d		13 04									14 04									15 03		
Todmorden	d		13 07		13 21		13 33			13 43		14 07		14 20		14 33			14 43		15 06		15 25
Blackpool North 97	d					12 20									13 21								
Poulton-le-Fylde 97	d					12 26									13 27								
Preston 8 97	d					12 46									13 46								
Blackburn 97	d					13 03									14 03								
Accrington 97	d					13 11									14 11								
Burnley Manchester Road 97	a					13 20	13 49								14 19	14 49							
	d					13 20									14 20								
Hebden Bridge	a		13 14		13 27	13 41				13 49		14 14		14 26	14 41				14 49		15 13		15 31
	d		13 14		13 27	13 42				13 50		14 14		14 26	14 42				14 50		15 13		15 31
Mytholmroyd	d		13 17							13 53		14 17							14 53		15 16		
Sowerby Bridge	d		13 23							13 58		14 23							14 58		15 22		
Huddersfield 39	d								13 35									14 35					
London Kings Cross 15 ⊖26	d	10 48																					
Brighouse	d	13 10	13 32						13 45			14 32						14 45			15 31		
Mirfield 39	a		13 39									14 39									15 38		
	d		13 39									14 39									15 38		
Dewsbury 39	a		13 44									14 44									15 43		
Halifax	a	13 20			13 38	13 52			13 56	14 04				14 37	14 52			14 56	15 04				15 42
	d	13 22			13 38	13 53			13 57	14 05	14 17			14 37	14 53			14 57	15 05	15 17			15 42
Low Moor	d	13 29							14 04	14 11								15 04	15 11				
Bradford Interchange	a	13 37			13 50	14 05			14 11	14 19	14 28			14 49	15 05			15 11	15 20	15 28			15 54
	d				13 56	14 07				14 21	14 30			14 52	15 07				15 24	15 30			15 57
New Pudsey 37	a				14 04	14 15				14 29	14 38			15 00	15 15				15 32	15 38			16 05
Bramley 37	a				14 07					14 33	14 42			15 03					15 35	15 42			16 08
Leeds 10 37,39	a		14 03		14 18	14 27				14 42	14 52	15 03		15 13	15 27				15 45	15 52	16 02		16 18
Selby 40	a										15 26									16 27			
York 8 40	a					14 59									15 59								

A From Chester
B To Hull
C From Wigan North Western
D From Clitheroe
E From Wigan Wallgate to Blackburn
F From Blackburn
G From Wigan Wallgate
H From Wigan North Western to Blackburn

For connections from Liverpool Lime Street refer to Table T090

Table T041-F

Saturdays
21 December to 16 May

Manchester Victoria, Rochdale, Blackpool North and Huddersfield - Bradford and Leeds via Brighouse and Halifax

	NT	NT	NT	NT	NT	NT	NT	NT	NT	NT	NT	NT	NT	NT	NT	NT	NT	NT	NT	NT	NT
	◇				◇	◇	◇		◇	◇				◇	◇	◇		◇	◇		
		A	B		C	D	E	F			A	B		C	D	G	F			A	B
Manchester Victoria d		15 04	15 09		15 20		15 36	15 42	15 54		16 04	16 09		16 20		16 37	16 42	16 56		17 04	17 09
Moston d			15 16					15 49				16 16					16 54				17 16
Mills Hill d			15 20					15 53				16 20		16 28			16 58				17 20
Castleton d			15 25					15 58				16 25					17 07				17 25
Rochdale a		15 17	15 29		15 32		15 49	16 02	16 10		16 17	16 29		16 35		16 50	17 10	17 12		17 17	17 29
d		15 18			15 33		15 49		16 11		16 18			16 35		16 51		17 13		17 18	
Smithy Bridge d		15 22					15 53				16 22					16 55		17 17		17 22	
Littleborough d		15 25					15 56				16 25					16 58		17 20		17 25	
Walsden d							16 02				16 31					17 04				17 31	
Todmorden d		15 33			15 43		16 06		16 23		16 35			16 45		17 07		17 27		17 35	
Blackpool North 97 d	14 20									15 20									16 20		
Poulton-le-Fylde 97 d	14 26									15 26									16 26		
Preston 8 97 d	14 46									15 46									16 46		
Blackburn 97 d	15 03									16 03									17 03		
Accrington 97 d	15 11									16 11									17 11		
Burnley Manchester Road 97 a	15 20	15 48								16 19	16 50								17 20	17 51	
d	15 20									16 20									17 20		
Hebden Bridge a	15 41				15 49		16 13		16 29	16 41				16 51		17 14		17 33	17 41		
d	15 42				15 50		16 14		16 30	16 42				16 52		17 14		17 33	17 42		
Mytholmroyd d					15 53		16 17							16 54		17 17					
Sowerby Bridge d					15 58		16 23							16 59		17 22					
Huddersfield 39 d				15 35									16 35								
London Kings Cross 15 ⊖26 d																					
Brighouse d				15 45			16 32						16 45			17 32					
Mirfield 39 a							16 38									17 39					
d							16 38									17 39					
Dewsbury 39 a							16 43									17 44					
Halifax a	15 52			15 56	16 04				16 40	16 52			16 56	17 06				17 44	17 52		
d	15 53			15 57	16 05	16 17			16 41	16 53			16 57	17 06	17 17			17 44	17 53		
Low Moor d				16 04	16 11								17 04	17 12							
Bradford Interchange a	16 05			16 11	16 19	16 28			16 53	17 05			17 11	17 20	17 28			17 56	18 05		
d	16 07				16 21	16 30			16 55	17 07				17 22	17 30			17 59	18 07		
New Pudsey 37 a	16 15				16 29	16 38			17 03	17 15				17 30	17 38			18 07	18 15		
Bramley 37 a					16 33	16 42			17 07					17 34	17 42			18 10			
Leeds 10 37,39 a	16 27				16 43	16 52	17 04		17 19	17 28				17 43	17 52	18 03		18 21	18 27		
Selby 40 a						17 26									18 26						
York 8 40 a	17 00									18 02									19 00		

	NT	NT	NT	GC	NT	NT	NT	NT	NT	NT	NT	GC	NT	NT	NT	NT	NT	NT	NT	NT	NT	NT
		◇	◇	■ 1	◇		◇	◇				■ 1	◇	◇	◇		◇	◇				◇
		C	D		G	F			H	B			C	D	G	F			A	F		C
Manchester Victoria d		17 20			17 37	17 42	17 56		18 04	18 09			18 20		18 37	18 42	18 56		19 04	19 09		19 19
Moston d						17 50				18 16						18 50				19 16		
Mills Hill d		17 28				17 54				18 20						18 54				19 20		
Castleton d		17 34				18 00				18 25						19 00				19 26		
Rochdale a		17 37			17 50	18 04	18 09		18 17	18 29			18 32		18 50	19 04	19 09		19 17	19 29		19 31
d		17 37			17 50		18 10		18 18				18 33		18 51		19 10		19 18			19 32
Smithy Bridge d					17 54		18 14		18 22				18 37		18 55		19 14		19 22			
Littleborough d					17 58		18 17		18 25				18 40		18 58		19 17		19 25			
Walsden d					18 04				18 31						19 04							
Todmorden d		17 48			18 07		18 24		18 35				18 48		19 08		19 24		19 33			19 43
Blackpool North 97 d								17 20										18 21				
Poulton-le-Fylde 97 d								17 26										18 27				
Preston 8 97 d								17 46										18 46				
Blackburn 97 d								18 03										19 03				
Accrington 97 d								18 11										19 11				
Burnley Manchester Road 97 a								18 20	18 51									19 20	19 48			
d								18 20										19 20				
Hebden Bridge a		17 54			18 13		18 30	18 41					18 54		19 14		19 30	19 41				19 49
d		17 54			18 14		18 31	18 42					18 54		19 15		19 31	19 42				19 50
Mytholmroyd d		17 57			18 17								18 57		19 17							19 53
Sowerby Bridge d		18 02			18 22								19 02		19 23							19 58
Huddersfield 39 d	17 35										18 35										19 35	
London Kings Cross 15 ⊖26 d				15 48								16 27										
Brighouse d	17 45			18 10	18 31						18 45	18 54			19 32						19 45	
Mirfield 39 a					18 38										19 39							
d					18 38										19 39							
Dewsbury 39 a					18 43										19 44							
Halifax a	17 56	18 08		18 21			18 41	18 52			18 56	19 05	19 10				19 41	19 52			19 56	20 04
d	17 57	18 09	18 17	18 22			18 42	18 53			18 57	19 06	19 10	19 17			19 42	19 53			19 57	20 05
Low Moor d	18 04	18 15		18 30							19 04	19 14	19 16								20 04	20 11
Bradford Interchange a	18 13	18 22	18 28	18 40			18 54	19 05			19 11	19 21	19 24	19 28			19 54	20 05			20 11	20 19
d		18 25	18 31				18 58	19 07					19 26	19 31			19 58	20 07				20 21
New Pudsey 37 a		18 33	18 39				19 06	19 15					19 34	19 39			20 06	20 15				20 29
Bramley 37 a		18 36	18 43				19 10						19 38	19 43			20 10					20 33
Leeds 10 37,39 a		18 45	18 52		19 02		19 19	19 27					19 47	19 53	20 03		20 19	20 26				20 43
Selby 40 a			19 31											20 26								
York 8 40 a								20 00										21 02				

A From Wigan Wallgate to Blackburn
B From Blackburn
C From Chester
D To Hull
E From Wigan North Western
F From Clitheroe
G From Wigan Wallgate
H From Wigan North Western to Blackburn

For connections from Liverpool Lime Street refer to Table T090

NRT DECEMBER 19 EDITION

Table T041-F

Saturdays
21 December to 16 May

Manchester Victoria, Rochdale, Blackpool North and Huddersfield - Bradford and Leeds via Brighouse and Halifax

	NT	NT	NT	NT	NT	NT	NT	NT	NT	NT	NT	NT	NT	NT	NT	NT	NT	NT	NT	NT	NT	GC
	◇	◇		◇	◇				◇	◇	◇		◇	◇			◇		◇	◇	◇	■ 1
	A	B	C			D	E		F	A	G	C			H		F	C	A			
Manchester Victoria d		19 36	19 41	19 56		20 04	20 10		20 19		20 37	20 42	20 56		21 04		21 19	21 38		21 56		
Moston d			19 49				20 17					20 50						21 46				
Mills Hill d			19 53				20 21					20 54						21 50				
Castleton d			19 59				20 26					21 00						21 56				
Rochdale a		19 49	20 03	20 09		20 17	20 30		20 33		20 50	21 04	21 09		21 17		21 31	22 00		22 09		
d		19 50		20 10		20 18			20 34		20 51		21 10		21 18		21 32			22 10		
Smithy Bridge d		19 54				20 22					20 55				21 22							
Littleborough d		19 57				20 25					20 58				21 25							
Walsden d		20 03									21 04				21 31							
Todmorden d		20 07		20 21		20 33			20 44		21 07		21 21		21 36		21 43			22 21		
Blackpool North 97 d					19 20									20 20							21 18	
Poulton-le-Fylde 97 d					19 26									20 26							21 24	
Preston 8 97 d					19 46									20 46							21 43	
Blackburn 97 d					20 03									21 03							22 00	
Accrington 97 d					20 11									21 11							22 08	
Burnley Manchester Road 97 a					20 20	20 48								21 20	21 51						22 17	
d					20 20									21 20							22 17	
Hebden Bridge a		20 14		20 27	20 41				20 50		21 14		21 27	21 41			21 49			22 27	22 38	
d		20 15		20 27	20 42				20 50		21 14		21 27	21 42			21 50			22 27	22 39	
Mytholmroyd d		20 17							20 53		21 17						21 53					
Sowerby Bridge d		20 23							20 58		21 23						21 58					
Huddersfield 39 d								20 35								21 35						
London Kings Cross 15 ⊖26 d																						19 57
Brighouse d		20 32						20 45			21 32					21 45						22 41
Mirfield 39 a		20 39									21 39											
d		20 39									21 39											
Dewsbury 39 a		20 44									21 44											
Halifax a				20 38	20 52			20 56	21 05				21 38	21 52		21 56	22 04			22 38	22 49	22 53
d	20 17			20 38	20 53			20 57	21 05	21 17			21 38	21 53		21 57	22 05		22 17	22 38	22 50	22 54
Low Moor d								21 04	21 12							22 04	22 11					23 01
Bradford Interchange a	20 28			20 50	21 05			21 11	21 19	21 28			21 50	22 05		22 11	22 19		22 28	22 50	23 02	23 09
d	20 30			20 53	21 07				21 22	21 31			21 53	22 07			22 21		22 30	22 53	23 04	
New Pudsey 37 a	20 38			21 01	21 15				21 30	21 39			22 01	22 15			22 29		22 38	23 01	23 12	
Bramley 37 a	20 42			21 04					21 33	21 43			22 04				22 33		22 42	23 04		
Leeds 10 37,39 a	20 52	21 04		21 14	21 28				21 43	21 53	22 05		22 13	22 26			22 42		22 52	23 13	23 23	
Selby 40 a	21 26									22 28									23 26			
York 8 40 a					22 00									23 02							23 57	

	NT	NT	NT	NT	NT	NT	NT	NT
						◇		
	I	I	J				I	
Manchester Victoria d	22 04	22 42				22 56	23 04	23 32
Moston d		22 49						23 40
Mills Hill d		22 53						23 44
Castleton d		22 59						23 50
Rochdale a	22 17	23 02				23 09	23 17	23 54
d	22 18	23 03				23 10	23 18	
Smithy Bridge d	22 22						23 22	
Littleborough d	22 25						23 25	
Walsden d	22 31							
Todmorden d	22 35	23 15				23 21	23 33	
Blackpool North 97 d								
Poulton-le-Fylde 97 d								
Preston 8 97 d								
Blackburn 97 d								
Accrington 97 d								
Burnley Manchester Road 97 a	22 51	23 30					23 49	
d								
Hebden Bridge a						23 27		
d						23 27		
Mytholmroyd d								
Sowerby Bridge d								
Huddersfield 39 d			22 49		23 00			
London Kings Cross 15 ⊖26 d								
Brighouse d			23 00		23 12			
Mirfield 39 a								
d								
Dewsbury 39 a								
Halifax a			23 10		23 23	23 38		
d			23 11	23 17	23 23	23 38		
Low Moor d			23 18					
Bradford Interchange a			23 25	23 30	23 36	23 50		
d			23 27	23 34		23 53		
New Pudsey 37 a			23 37	23 42		00 01		
Bramley 37 a			23 41	23 45		00 05		
Leeds 10 37,39 a			23 50	23 55		00 14		
Selby 40 a								
York 8 40 a								

A To Hull
B From Wigan Wallgate
C From Clitheroe
D From Wigan Wallgate to Blackburn
E From Blackburn
F From Chester
G From Wigan North Western
H From Kirkby to Blackburn
I To Blackburn
J from 22 February

For connections from Liverpool Lime Street refer to Table T090

Table T041-F

Sundays

15 December to 10 May

Manchester Victoria, Rochdale, Blackpool North and Huddersfield - Bradford and Leeds via Brighouse and Halifax

	GC	NT	NT	NT	NT	NT	NT	NT	NT	NT	NT	NT	NT	NT	NT	NT	NT	NT	NT	NT	NT	NT
		A	◇		◇	◇	B		◇	◇	C		◇	◇	C		◇	◇	C		◇	◇
Manchester Victoria d		08 33			08 54		08 59		09 56		10 00		10 56		11 01		11 56		12 01		12 57	
Moston d		08 40					09 06				10 07				11 08				12 08			
Mills Hill d		08 44					09 10				10 11				11 12				12 12			
Castleton d		08 50					09 16				10 17				11 17				12 18			
Rochdale a		08 53			09 07		09 19		10 09		10 20		11 09		11 21		12 09		12 21		13 10	
d		08 54			09 08		09 20		10 09		10 21		11 10		11 21		12 10		12 21		13 10	
Smithy Bridge d		08 58					09 24				10 25				11 25				12 25			
Littleborough d		09 01			09 14		09 27		10 15		10 28		11 15		11 28		12 15		12 28		13 15	
Walsden d					09 20				10 21				11 21				12 21				13 21	
Todmorden d		09 09			09 24		09 35		10 25		10 36		11 25		11 36		12 25		12 36		13 25	
Blackpool North 97 d										09 18				10 20				11 17				12 17
Poulton-le-Fylde 97 d										09 24				10 27				11 23				12 23
Preston 97 d										09 47				10 47				11 43				12 42
Blackburn 97 d						09 04				10 07				11 07				12 04				13 02
Accrington 97 d						09 12				10 15				11 15				12 12				13 10
Burnley Manchester Road 97 a		09 25				09 20	09 51			10 23	10 52			11 23	11 52			12 20	12 52			13 18
d						09 21				10 24				11 24				12 21				13 19
Hebden Bridge a					09 32	09 42			10 31	10 46			11 31	11 45			12 31	12 42			13 31	13 40
d					09 32	09 43			10 31	10 46			11 32	11 45			12 31	12 43			13 31	13 41
Mytholmroyd d						09 46				10 49				11 48				12 46				13 44
Sowerby Bridge d						09 51				10 55				11 54				12 51				13 49
Huddersfield 39 d				09 04				10 04				11 04				12 04				13 04		
London Kings Cross ⊖26 d																						
Brighouse d				09 14				10 14				11 14				12 14				13 14		
Mirfield 39 a																						
d																						
Dewsbury 39 a																						
Halifax a				09 24	09 43	09 57		10 24	10 42	11 01		11 24	11 43	12 00		12 24	12 42	12 57		13 24	13 42	13 55
d			08 58	09 24	09 44	09 58		10 24	10 43	11 01		11 25	11 43	12 00		12 25	12 43	12 58		13 24	13 43	13 56
Low Moor d	07 50			09 32				10 32				11 33				12 33				13 32		
Bradford Interchange a	08 00		09 11	09 40	09 58	10 11		10 40	10 56	11 14		11 41	11 57	12 13		12 41	12 56	13 11		13 40	13 56	14 09
d			09 14	09 44	10 00	10 13		10 44	10 59	11 18		11 44	11 59	12 16		12 44	12 59	13 13		13 44	13 59	14 11
New Pudsey 37 a			09 22	09 52	10 09	10 21		10 52	11 07	11 26		11 52	12 08	12 26		12 52	13 07	13 21		13 52	14 07	14 19
Bramley 37 a				09 56	10 13			10 56	11 11			11 56	12 12			12 56	13 11			13 58	14 11	
Leeds 37,39 a			09 35	10 04	10 21	10 32		11 04	11 19	11 38		12 04	12 20	12 36		13 04	13 19	13 33		14 06	14 20	14 31
Selby 40 a																						
York 40 a			10 11			11 13				12 14				13 12				14 10				15 09

	GC	NT	NT	NT	NT	NT	NT	NT	NT	NT	NT	NT	NT	NT	NT	NT	NT	GC	NT	NT	NT	NT
		C		◇	◇	C		◇	◇	C		◇	◇	C		◇	◇		C		◇	◇
Manchester Victoria d		13 02		13 57		14 02		14 57		15 02		15 57		16 02		16 57			17 02		17 57	
Moston d		13 09				14 09				15 09				16 09					17 09			
Mills Hill d		13 13				14 13				15 13				16 13					17 13			
Castleton d		13 18				14 18				15 18				16 18					17 18			
Rochdale a		13 22		14 10		14 22		15 10		15 22		16 10		16 22		17 10			17 22		18 10	
d		13 22		14 10		14 22		15 10		15 22		16 10		16 22		17 10			17 22		18 10	
Smithy Bridge d		13 26				14 26				15 26				16 26					17 26			
Littleborough d		13 29		14 15		14 29		15 15		15 29		16 15		16 29		17 15			17 29		18 15	
Walsden d				14 21				15 21				16 21				17 21					18 21	
Todmorden d		13 37		14 25		14 37		15 25		15 37		16 25		16 37		17 25			17 37		18 25	
Blackpool North 97 d					13 17				14 16				15 17				16 16					17 17
Poulton-le-Fylde 97 d					13 23				14 22				15 23				16 22					17 23
Preston 97 d					13 42				14 41				15 44				16 41					17 42
Blackburn 97 d					14 04				15 04				16 04				17 04					18 04
Accrington 97 d					14 12				15 12				16 12				17 12					18 12
Burnley Manchester Road 97 a		13 52			14 20	14 52			15 20	15 52			16 20	16 52			17 20		17 52			18 20
d					14 21				15 21				16 21				17 21					18 21
Hebden Bridge a				14 31	14 42			15 31	15 42			16 31	16 42			17 31	17 43				18 31	18 43
d				14 32	14 43			15 31	15 43			16 31	16 43			17 31	17 43				18 31	18 43
Mytholmroyd d				14 34	14 46				15 46				16 46				17 46					18 46
Sowerby Bridge d				14 40	14 51				15 51				16 51				17 52					18 52
Huddersfield 39 d			14 04				15 04				16 04				17 04					18 04		
London Kings Cross ⊖26 d	11 50																	15 50				
Brighouse d	14 06		14 14				15 14				16 14				17 14			18 11		18 15		
Mirfield 39 a																						
d																						
Dewsbury 39 a																						
Halifax a	14 20		14 25	14 46	14 57		15 24	15 42	15 57		16 24	16 42	16 57		17 24	17 42	17 58	18 22		18 26	18 42	18 58
d	14 21		14 25	14 47	14 58		15 24	15 43	15 58		16 24	16 43	16 58		17 24	17 43	17 58	18 22		18 26	18 43	18 58
Low Moor d	14 29		14 33				15 32				16 32				17 32			18 30		18 34		
Bradford Interchange a	14 37		14 41	15 00	15 11		15 40	15 56	16 11		16 40	16 56	17 11		17 40	17 56	18 12	18 37		18 42	18 56	19 11
d			14 44	15 02	15 14		15 44	15 59	16 13		16 44	16 59	17 13		17 44	17 59	18 14			18 45	18 59	19 14
New Pudsey 37 a			14 52	15 11	15 22		15 52	16 07	16 21		16 52	17 07	17 21		17 52	18 07	18 22			18 53	19 07	19 22
Bramley 37 a			14 56	15 15			15 56	16 13			16 56	17 11			17 56	18 11				18 57	19 12	
Leeds 37,39 a			15 04	15 23	15 35		16 04	16 25	16 33		17 04	17 19	17 33		18 06	18 19	18 35			19 05	19 23	19 32
Selby 40 a																						
York 40 a					16 13				17 13				18 14				19 13					20 13

A To Blackburn

B From Wigan Wallgate to Blackburn

C From Southport to Blackburn

For connections from Liverpool Lime Street refer to Table T090

Table T041-F

Sundays

15 December to 10 May

Manchester Victoria, Rochdale, Blackpool North and Huddersfield - Bradford and Leeds via Brighouse and Halifax

	NT	NT	NT	NT	NT	NT	NT	NT	NT	NT	GC	NT	GC	NT	NT	NT	NT	NT	NT	NT	NT
	A		◇	◇	A		◇	◇	A			◇		◇	A		◇	◇	A		◇
Manchester Victoria d	18 02		18 57		19 02		19 57		20 02			20 57			21 02		21 57		22 02		22 57
Moston d	18 09				19 09				20 09						21 09				22 09		
Mills Hill d	18 13				19 13				20 13						21 13				22 13		
Castleton d	18 18				19 18				20 18						21 18				22 18		
Rochdale a	18 22		19 10		19 22		20 10		20 22			21 10			21 22		22 10		22 22		23 12
d	18 22		19 10		19 22		20 10		20 22			21 10			21 22		22 10		22 22		23 12
Smithy Bridge d	18 26				19 26				20 26						21 26				22 26		
Littleborough d	18 29		19 15		19 29		20 15		20 29			21 16			21 29		22 15		22 29		23 18
Walsden d			19 21				20 21					21 22					22 21				23 24
Todmorden d	18 37		19 25		19 37		20 25		20 37			21 26			21 37		22 25		22 37		23 27
Blackpool North 97 d				18 17				19 17						20 17				21 17			
Poulton-le-Fylde 97 d				18 23				19 23						20 23				21 23			
Preston 97 d				18 44				19 42						20 44				21 44			
Blackburn 97 d				19 04				20 04						21 04				22 01			
Accrington 97 d				19 12				20 12						21 12				22 11			
Burnley Manchester Road 97 a	18 52			19 20	19 52			20 20	20 52					21 20	21 52			22 21	22 52		
d				19 21				20 21						21 21				22 21			
Hebden Bridge a			19 31	19 42			20 31	20 42				21 32		21 42			22 31	22 43			23 33
d			19 31	19 43			20 31	20 43				21 32		21 43			22 31	22 43			23 33
Mytholmroyd d				19 46				20 46						21 46				22 46			
Sowerby Bridge d				19 51				20 51						21 55				22 52			
Huddersfield 39 d		19 04				20 04				21 04						22 04				23 04	
London Kings Cross ⊖26 d											18 53		19 22								
Brighouse d		19 14				20 14				21 14	21 22		21 46			22 14				23 14	
Mirfield 39 a																					
d																					
Dewsbury 39 a																					
Halifax a		19 24	19 42	19 57		20 24	20 42	20 57		21 24	21 33	21 43	21 57	22 03		22 28	22 42	22 58		23 24	23 44
d		19 24	19 43	19 58		20 24	20 43	20 58		21 24	21 33	21 44	21 58	22 03		22 28	22 43	22 58		23 24	23 45
Low Moor d		19 32				20 32				21 32	21 40		22 06			22 35				23 32	
Bradford Interchange a		19 40	19 56	20 11		20 40	20 55	21 11		21 40	21 48	21 57	22 13	22 16		22 44	22 56	23 11		23 40	23 58
d		19 44	19 59	20 13		20 44	21 00	21 13		21 44		22 00		22 20		22 46	22 59	23 14		23 44	00 01
New Pudsey 37 a		19 52	20 07	20 21		20 52	21 08	21 21		21 52		22 08		22 28		22 57	23 07	23 22		23 52	00 09
Bramley 37 a		19 56	20 13			20 56	21 13			21 56		22 12				23 01	23 11			23 56	00 13
Leeds 37,39 a		20 03	20 21	20 33		21 04	21 24	21 33		22 04		22 24		22 41		23 10	23 22	23 34		00 04	00 21
Selby 40 a																					
York 40 a				21 11				22 12						23 14				00 16			

	NT
	B
Manchester Victoria d	23 02
Moston d	23 09
Mills Hill d	23 13
Castleton d	23 19
Rochdale a	23 23
d	
Smithy Bridge d	
Littleborough d	
Walsden d	
Todmorden d	
Blackpool North 97 d	
Poulton-le-Fylde 97 d	
Preston 97 d	
Blackburn 97 d	
Accrington 97 d	
Burnley Manchester Road 97 a	
d	
Hebden Bridge a	
d	
Mytholmroyd d	
Sowerby Bridge d	
Huddersfield 39 d	
London Kings Cross ⊖26 d	
Brighouse d	
Mirfield 39 a	
d	
Dewsbury 39 a	
Halifax a	
d	
Low Moor d	
Bradford Interchange a	
d	
New Pudsey 37 a	
Bramley 37 a	
Leeds 37,39 a	
Selby 40 a	
York 40 a	

A From Southport to Blackburn

B From Southport

For connections from Liverpool Lime Street refer to Table T090

Table T041-R

Mondays to Fridays
16 December to 15 May

Leeds and Bradford - Huddersfield, Blackpool North, Rochdale and Manchester Victoria via Halifax and Brighouse

Miles	Miles	Miles	Miles				NT MO A	NT MX ◇ B	NT MX A	NT MX C	NT MO ◇ D	NT	NT E	NT ◇	NT ◇ F	NT G	NT	NT ◇ H	NT I	NT ◇	NT ◇	NT J	NT ◇ F	NT G
—	—	—	—	York 8	40	d														05 19				
—	—	—	—	Selby	40	d																		
0	0	—	0	**Leeds 10**	37,39	d						05 01		05 12	05 19		05 22	05 42		05 57	06 12		06 17	
4	4	—	—	Bramley	37	d						05 09		05 18			05 30	05 49			06 18			
5¾	5¾	—	—	New Pudsey	37	d						05 14		05 22			05 35	05 53		06 06	06 22			
9½	9½	—	—	**Bradford Interchange**	37	a						05 22		05 30			05 43	06 01		06 14	06 30			
—	—	—	—			d						05 25		05 33			05 47	06 03		06 16	06 33			
—	—	—	—	Low Moor		d						05 31						06 10						
17½	17½	0	—	**Halifax**		a						05 38		05 43			05 59	06 16		06 27	06 43			
—	—	—	—			d						05 39		05 44				06 17		06 27	06 44			
—	—	—	9¼	Dewsbury	39	d									05 38								06 34	
—	—	—	12¼	Mirfield	39	a									05 44								06 40	
—	—	—	—			d									05 45								06 40	
—	—	5¼	16¼	Brighouse		d				00 03		05 50			05 55								06 54	
—	—	—	—	London Kings Cross 15 ⊖26		a																		
—	—	10½	—	**Huddersfield**	39	a				00 16		06 02												
21	21	—	22	Sowerby Bridge		d									06 06			06 23					07 04	
25	25	—	26	Mytholmroyd		d									06 11			06 28					07 09	
26¼	26¼	—	27¼	**Hebden Bridge**		a								05 54	06 14			06 31		06 37	06 54		07 12	
—	—	—	—			d					00 05			05 54	06 15			06 32		06 38	06 54		07 13	
—	39	—	—	Burnley Manchester Road	97	a														07 01				
—	—	—	—			d		00 02											06 38	07 03				
—	45¾	—	—	Accrington	97	a		00 10												07 12				
—	51½	—	—	Blackburn	97	a		00 20												07 21				
—	63½	—	—	**Preston 8**	97	a														07 45				
—	78	—	—	Poulton-le-Fylde	97	a														08 05				
—	81	—	—	**Blackpool North**	97	a														08 12				
30½	—	—	—	Todmorden		d					00 12			06 01	06 22			06 39	06 55		07 01		07 20	
32	—	—	—	Walsden		d					00 15				06 25								07 23	
36	—	—	—	Littleborough		d			00 02		00 21			06 08	06 32				07 02		07 08		07 30	
37	—	—	—	Smithy Bridge		d			00 05						06 34				07 04				07 32	
39¼	—	—	—	**Rochdale**		a			00 09		00 26			06 14	06 38			06 50	07 08		07 14		07 36	
—	—	—	—			d			00 09		00 27		05 53	06 14	06 39	06 42		06 50	07 09		07 14	07 18	07 37	07 42
41	—	—	—	Castleton		d							05 56			06 45						07 21		07 45
43¾	—	—	—	Mills Hill		d							06 01			06 50						07 26		07 50
45¾	—	—	—	Moston		d	00 01						06 05			06 54						07 30		07 53
49¾	—	—	—	**Manchester Victoria**		a	00 11		00 23		00 42		06 13	06 31	06 53	07 03		07 06	07 24		07 30	07 39	07 52	08 02

			NT	NT	GC ■ 1	NT ◇ H	NT K	NT J	NT ◇	NT	NT ◇	NT ◇ L	NT G	NT ◇ M	GC ■ 1	NT ◇ H	NT I	NT J	NT ◇	NT ◇	NT ◇ F	NT G	NT	NT ◇ M
York 8	40	d							06 12										07 13					
Selby	40	d		05 47										06 45										07 49
Leeds 10	37,39	d		06 27		06 42			06 57		07 12	07 17		07 27		07 42			07 55	08 12	08 17			08 27
Bramley	37	d		06 35		06 49					07 18			07 35		07 49				08 18				08 35
New Pudsey	37	d		06 40		06 53			07 07		07 22			07 40		07 53			08 04	08 22				08 40
Bradford Interchange	37	a		06 48		07 01			07 15		07 30			07 48		08 01			08 12	08 30				08 48
		d	06 36	06 51	06 55	07 03			07 17	07 36	07 41			07 52	07 56	08 03			08 14	08 33			08 36	08 51
Low Moor		d	06 42		07 02	07 10				07 42					08 02	08 10							08 42	
Halifax		a	06 49	07 03	07 09	07 16			07 28	07 49	07 53			08 04	08 09	08 16			08 25	08 43			08 49	09 03
		d	06 50		07 10	07 17			07 28	07 50	07 55				08 10	08 17			08 25	08 44			08 50	
Dewsbury	39	d										07 34									08 34			
Mirfield	39	a										07 40									08 40			
		d										07 40									08 41			
Brighouse		d	07 00		07 20					08 00		07 54			08 24						08 56		09 00	
London Kings Cross 15 ⊖26		a			10 09										11 17									
Huddersfield	39	a	07 13							08 13													09 13	
Sowerby Bridge		d				07 23						08 06				08 23					09 06			
Mytholmroyd		d				07 28						08 12				08 28					09 12			
Hebden Bridge		a				07 31			07 38		08 05	08 15				08 31			08 38	08 54	09 15			
		d				07 32			07 39		08 05	08 15				08 32			08 38	08 54	09 15			
Burnley Manchester Road	97	a							08 02										08 58					
		d					07 32		08 04								08 38		09 03					
Accrington	97	a							08 12										09 11					
Blackburn	97	a							08 21										09 20					
Preston 8	97	a							08 44										09 38					
Poulton-le-Fylde	97	a							09 01										09 55					
Blackpool North	97	a							09 08										10 02					
Todmorden		d				07 39	07 50				08 12	08 23				08 39	08 55			09 07	09 23			
Walsden		d					07 53					08 26									09 26			
Littleborough		d					08 00				08 19	08 32					09 02				09 32			
Smithy Bridge		d					08 02					08 34					09 05				09 34			
Rochdale		a				07 50	08 06				08 24	08 38				08 50	09 09			09 24	09 38			
		d				07 50	08 07	08 14			08 25	08 39	08 42			08 50	09 09	09 14		09 24	09 39	09 42		
Castleton		d						08 17					08 45					09 17				09 45		
Mills Hill		d						08 22			08 31		08 50					09 22				09 50		
Moston		d						08 26					08 53					09 26				09 54		
Manchester Victoria		a				08 05	08 24	08 35			08 42	08 53	09 03			09 05	09 24	09 35		09 40	09 54	10 03		

A From Blackburn
B From York
C From Bradford Interchange
D From Leeds
E To Kirkby
F To Wigan Wallgate
G To Blackburn
H To Chester
I From Blackburn to Wigan Wallgate
J To Clitheroe
K From Blackburn to Wigan North Western
L To Wigan North Western
M From Hull

For connections to Liverpool Lime Street refer to Table T090

NRT DECEMBER 19 EDITION

Table T041-R

Mondays to Fridays
16 December to 15 May

Leeds and Bradford - Huddersfield, Blackpool North, Rochdale and Manchester Victoria via Halifax and Brighouse

			NT ◇ A	NT B	NT ◇	NT ◇	NT C	NT ◇ D	NT E	NT	NT ◇ F	NT ◇ A	NT B	NT ◇	GC ■ 1	NT ◇	NT C	NT ◇ D	NT E	NT	NT ◇ F	NT ◇ A	NT G	NT C
York 8	40	d			08 23									09 23										
Selby	40	d									08 48										09 48			
Leeds 10	37,39	d	08 42		08 57	09 12		09 17			09 27	09 42		09 57		10 12		10 17			10 27	10 42		
Bramley	37	d	08 49			09 18					09 35	09 49				10 18					10 35	10 49		
New Pudsey	37	d	08 53		09 06	09 22					09 40	09 53		10 06		10 22					10 40	10 53		
Bradford Interchange	37	a	09 01		09 14	09 30					09 48	10 01		10 15		10 30					10 48	11 01		
		d	09 03		09 16	09 33				09 36	09 51	10 03		10 17	10 22	10 33				10 36	10 51	11 03		
Low Moor		d	09 10							09 42		10 10			10 28					10 42		11 10		
Halifax		a	09 16		09 27	09 43				09 49	10 02	10 16		10 28	10 35	10 43				10 49	11 03	11 16		
		d	09 17		09 27	09 44				09 50		10 17		10 28	10 36	10 44				10 50		11 17		
Dewsbury	39	d						09 35										10 35						
Mirfield	39	a						09 41										10 41						
		d						09 42										10 42						
Brighouse		d						09 54		10 00					10 47			10 55		11 00				
London Kings Cross 15 ⊖26		a													13 44									
Huddersfield	39	a								10 13										11 13				
Sowerby Bridge		d	09 23					10 05				10 23						11 06				11 23		
Mytholmroyd		d	09 28					10 11				10 28						11 11				11 28		
Hebden Bridge		a	09 31		09 37	09 54		10 14				10 31		10 38		10 54		11 14				11 31		
		d	09 32		09 38	09 54		10 15				10 32		10 39		10 54		11 15				11 32		
Burnley Manchester Road	97	a			10 01									11 01										
		d		09 38	10 03								10 38	11 03									11 38	
Accrington	97	a			10 11									11 11										
Blackburn	97	a			10 20									11 20										
Preston 8	97	a			10 38									11 38										
Poulton-le-Fylde	97	a			10 55									11 55										
Blackpool North	97	a			11 02									12 02										
Todmorden		d	09 39	09 55		10 01		10 22				10 39	10 55			11 01		11 22				11 39	11 55	
Walsden		d						10 25										11 25						
Littleborough		d		10 02				10 32					11 02					11 32					12 02	
Smithy Bridge		d		10 05				10 34					11 05					11 34					12 05	
Rochdale		a	09 50	10 09		10 13		10 38				10 50	11 09			11 13		11 38				11 50	12 09	
		d	09 50	10 09		10 14	10 18	10 39	10 42			10 50	11 09			11 14	11 18	11 39	11 42			11 50	12 09	12 18
Castleton		d					10 21		10 45								11 21		11 45					12 21
Mills Hill		d					10 26		10 50								11 26		11 50					12 26
Moston		d					10 30		10 54								11 30		11 54					12 30
Manchester Victoria		a	10 05	10 24		10 29	10 39	10 53	11 03			11 06	11 24			11 29	11 39	11 53	12 03			12 05	12 24	12 39

			NT ◇	NT ◇	NT ◇ D	NT E	NT	NT ◇ F	NT ◇ A	NT B	NT C	NT ◇	NT ◇	NT E	NT ◇ H	NT	NT ◇ F	NT ◇ A	NT B	NT ◇	NT ◇	NT C	NT ◇ D
York 8	40	d	10 23									11 23								12 23			
Selby	40	d						10 48									11 48						
Leeds 10	37,39	d	10 57	11 12	11 17			11 27	11 42			11 57	12 12		12 17		12 27	12 42		12 57	13 12		13 17
Bramley	37	d		11 18				11 35	11 49				12 18				12 35	12 49			13 18		
New Pudsey	37	d	11 06	11 22				11 40	11 53			12 06	12 22				12 40	12 53		13 07	13 22		
Bradford Interchange	37	a	11 14	11 30				11 48	12 01			12 14	12 30				12 48	13 01		13 15	13 30		
		d	11 18	11 33			11 36	11 51	12 03			12 17	12 33			12 36	12 51	13 03		13 17	13 33		
Low Moor		d					11 42		12 10							12 42		13 10					
Halifax		a	11 29	11 43			11 49	12 03	12 16			12 27	12 43			12 49	13 03	13 16		13 28	13 43		
		d	11 29	11 44			11 50		12 17			12 28	12 44			12 50		13 17		13 28	13 44		
Dewsbury	39	d			11 35										12 33								13 35
Mirfield	39	a			11 41										12 40								13 41
		d			11 42										12 40								13 42
Brighouse		d			11 57		12 00								12 54	13 00							13 54
London Kings Cross 15 ⊖26		a																					
Huddersfield	39	a					12 13									13 13							
Sowerby Bridge		d			12 06				12 23						13 06			13 23					14 06
Mytholmroyd		d			12 11				12 28						13 12			13 28					14 11
Hebden Bridge		a	11 39	11 54	12 14				12 31			12 38	12 57		13 15			13 31		13 38	13 54		14 14
		d	11 40	11 54	12 15				12 32			12 38	12 58		13 15			13 32		13 39	13 54		14 15
Burnley Manchester Road	97	a	12 01									13 01								14 01			
		d	12 03							12 38		13 03							13 38	14 03			
Accrington	97	a	12 11									13 11								14 11			
Blackburn	97	a	12 20									13 20								14 20			
Preston 8	97	a	12 38									13 38								14 38			
Poulton-le-Fylde	97	a	12 55									13 55								14 55			
Blackpool North	97	a	13 02									14 02								15 02			
Todmorden		d		12 01	12 22				12 39	12 55			13 08		13 23			13 39	13 55		14 01		14 22
Walsden		d			12 25										13 26								14 25
Littleborough		d			12 32					13 02					13 32				14 02				14 32
Smithy Bridge		d			12 34					13 05					13 35				14 05				14 34
Rochdale		a		12 19	12 38				12 49	13 09			13 19		13 39			13 50	14 09		14 13		14 38
		d		12 25	12 39	12 42			12 50	13 09	13 18		13 25	13 34	13 39			13 50	14 09		14 14	14 18	14 39
Castleton		d				12 45					13 21		13 28									14 21	
Mills Hill		d				12 50					13 26		13 33	13 40								14 26	
Moston		d				12 54					13 30		13 36									14 30	
Manchester Victoria		a		12 42	12 53	13 03			13 05	13 24	13 39		13 46	14 02	13 54			14 05	14 24		14 29	14 39	14 53

A To Chester
B From Blackburn to Wigan Wallgate
C To Clitheroe
D To Wigan Wallgate
E To Blackburn
F From Hull
G From Blackburn to Wigan North Western
H To Wigan North Western

For connections to Liverpool Lime Street refer to Table T090

Table T041-R

Mondays to Fridays
16 December to 15 May

Leeds and Bradford - Huddersfield, Blackpool North, Rochdale and Manchester Victoria via Halifax and Brighouse

Station			NT	NT	NT	NT	NT	NT	NT		NT	NT	NT	NT	GC	NT	NT	NT	NT		NT	NT	NT	NT	NT	NT
					◇	◇		◇	◇			◇			■	◇	◇		◇		◇			◇		◇
			A		B	C	D				E	F	E			B	C	G				E	A	F		B
York 8	40	d						13 23											14 23							
Selby	40	d			12 48											13 48										14 49
Leeds 10	37,39	d			13 27	13 42		13 57	14 12			14 17				14 27	14 42		14 57		15 12			15 17		15 27
Bramley	37	d			13 35	13 49			14 18							14 35	14 49				15 18					15 35
New Pudsey	37	d			13 40	13 53		14 06	14 22							14 40	14 53		15 06		15 22					15 40
Bradford Interchange	37	a			13 48	14 01		14 15	14 30							14 48	15 01		15 15		15 30					15 48
		d		13 36	13 51	14 03		14 17	14 33					14 36	14 50	14 54	15 03		15 17		15 33				15 36	15 51
Low Moor		d		13 42		14 10								14 42	14 56		15 10								15 42	
Halifax		a		13 49	14 04	14 16		14 28	14 43					14 49	15 02	15 06	15 16		15 28		15 43				15 49	16 03
		d		13 50		14 17		14 28	14 44					14 50	15 03		15 17		15 28		15 44				15 50	
Dewsbury	39	d										14 35												15 35		
Mirfield	39	a										14 41												15 41		
		d										14 42												15 42		
Brighouse		d		14 00								14 54		15 00	15 17									15 54	16 00	
London Kings Cross 15 ⊖26		a													18 07											
Huddersfield	39	a		14 13										15 13											16 13	
Sowerby Bridge		d				14 23						15 06					15 23							16 06		
Mytholmroyd		d				14 28						15 11					15 28							16 11		
Hebden Bridge		a				14 31		14 38	14 54			15 14					15 31		15 38		15 54			16 14		
		d				14 32		14 39	14 54			15 15					15 32		15 39		15 54			16 15		
Burnley Manchester Road	97	a						15 01											16 01							
		d					14 38	15 03										15 38	16 03							
Accrington	97	a						15 11											16 11							
Blackburn	97	a						15 20											16 20							
Preston 8	97	a						15 38											16 39							
Poulton-le-Fylde	97	a						15 55											16 56							
Blackpool North	97	a						16 02											17 03							
Todmorden		d				14 39	14 55		15 01			15 22					15 39	15 55			16 01			16 22		
Walsden		d										15 25												16 25		
Littleborough		d					15 02					15 32						16 02						16 32		
Smithy Bridge		d					15 05					15 34						16 05						16 34		
Rochdale		a				14 50	15 09		15 13			15 38					15 50	16 09			16 13			16 38		
		d	14 42			14 50	15 09		15 14		15 18	15 39	15 42				15 50	16 09			16 13	16 18	16 33	16 39		
Castleton		d	14 45								15 21		15 45									16 21	16 36			
Mills Hill		d	14 50								15 26		15 50									16 26	16 41			
Moston		d	14 54								15 30		15 54									16 30				
Manchester Victoria		a	15 03			15 06	15 24		15 29		15 39	15 53	16 03				16 05	16 24			16 29	16 39	17 02	16 54		

Station			NT	NT	NT		NT	NT	NT	NT	NT	NT	NT	NT	NT		NT	NT	NT	NT	NT	NT	NT	NT	NT	
			◇		◇		◇		◇		◇	◇					◇	◇	◇			◇	◇		◇	
			H	D				E	F		B	C	A	I	E				J	E		B	C	D		
York 8	40	d			15 23												16 23								17 23	
Selby	40	d									15 48											16 48				
Leeds 10	37,39	d	15 42		15 57		16 12		16 17		16 27	16 42					16 57	17 12	17 17			17 27	17 42		17 57	
Bramley	37	d	15 49				16 18				16 35	16 49						17 18				17 35	17 49			
New Pudsey	37	d	15 53		16 06		16 22				16 40	16 53					17 06	17 22				17 40	17 53		18 06	
Bradford Interchange	37	a	16 01		16 15		16 30				16 48	17 01					17 15	17 30				17 48	18 01		18 15	
		d	16 03		16 17		16 33			16 36	16 51	17 03					17 17	17 33			17 36	17 51	18 03		18 17	
Low Moor		d	16 10							16 42		17 10									17 42		18 10			
Halifax		a	16 16		16 28		16 43			16 49	17 03	17 16					17 28	17 44			17 49	18 03	18 16		18 28	
		d	16 17		16 28		16 44			16 50		17 17					17 28	17 44			17 50		18 17		18 28	
Dewsbury	39	d							16 34										17 36							
Mirfield	39	a							16 41										17 42							
		d							16 42										17 43							
Brighouse		d							16 54	17 00									17 55		18 00					
London Kings Cross 15 ⊖26		a																								
Huddersfield	39	a								17 11											18 13					
Sowerby Bridge		d	16 23						17 07			17 23					17 34		18 06				18 23		18 34	
Mytholmroyd		d	16 28						17 12			17 28							18 11				18 28			
Hebden Bridge		a	16 31		16 38		16 54		17 15			17 31					17 41	18 00	18 14				18 31		18 41	
		d	16 32		16 39		16 54		17 16			17 32					17 41	18 00	18 15				18 32		18 41	
Burnley Manchester Road	97	a			16 58												18 00								19 01	
		d		16 36	17 03									17 38			18 03							18 38	19 03	
Accrington	97	a			17 11												18 11								19 11	
Blackburn	97	a			17 20												18 20								19 20	
Preston 8	97	a			17 40												18 40								19 38	
Poulton-le-Fylde	97	a			17 58												18 58								19 55	
Blackpool North	97	a			18 06												19 05								20 02	
Todmorden		d	16 39	16 53			17 01		17 23			17 39		17 55				18 07	18 22				18 39	18 55		
Walsden		d		16 56					17 26										18 25							
Littleborough		d		17 02			17 08		17 32					18 02					18 32					19 02		
Smithy Bridge		d		17 05			17 11		17 34					18 05					18 34					19 05		
Rochdale		a	16 50	17 09			17 15		17 38			17 50		18 09				18 21	18 38				18 50	19 09		
		d	16 50	17 09			17 15	17 19	17 39			17 50	17 54	18 09	18 18			18 22	18 39	18 42			18 50	19 09		
Castleton		d						17 22					17 57		18 21					18 45						
Mills Hill		d						17 27					18 02					18 30		18 50						
Moston		d					17 24						18 06					18 33		18 54						
Manchester Victoria		a	17 05	17 24			17 34	17 39	17 53			18 05	18 15	18 24	18 36			18 44	18 53	19 03			19 05	19 24		

A To Blackburn
B From Hull
C To Chester
D From Blackburn to Wigan Wallgate
E To Clitheroe
F To Wigan Wallgate
G From Blackburn to Wigan North Western
H To Ellesmere Port
I From Blackburn to Kirkby
J To Wigan North Western

For connections to Liverpool Lime Street refer to Table T090

Table T041-R

Mondays to Fridays
16 December to 15 May

Leeds and Bradford - Huddersfield, Blackpool North, Rochdale and Manchester Victoria via Halifax and Brighouse

Station			NT	NT	NT	NT	NT	NT	NT	NT	NT		NT	NT	NT	NT	NT	NT	NT	NT	NT		NT	NT	NT	NT
			◇		◇			◇	◇		◇		◇		◇			◇	◇				◇	◇	◇	
				A	B	C		D	E	F				A	G	C		D	E	H	A				G	A
York 8	40	d									18 22												19 23			
Selby	40	d						17 48										18 48								
Leeds 10	37,39	d	18 12		18 17			18 27	18 42		18 57		19 12		19 17			19 27	19 40				19 57	20 12	20 18	
Bramley	37	d	18 18					18 35	18 49				19 18					19 35	19 47					20 18		
New Pudsey	37	d	18 22					18 40	18 53		19 06		19 22					19 40	19 51				20 07	20 22		
Bradford Interchange	37	a	18 30					18 48	19 01		19 15		19 30					19 48	19 59				20 15	20 30		
		d	18 33				18 36	18 51	19 03		19 17		19 33				19 36	19 51	20 03				20 17	20 33		
Low Moor		d					18 42		19 10								19 42		20 10							
Halifax		a	18 43				18 49	19 03	19 16		19 28		19 43				19 49	20 03	20 16				20 28	20 43		
		d	18 44				18 50		19 17		19 28		19 44				19 50		20 17				20 28	20 44		
Dewsbury	39	d			18 33										19 34										20 35	
Mirfield	39	a			18 40										19 40										20 41	
		d			18 40										19 41										20 42	
Brighouse		d			18 49		19 00								19 55		20 00								20 54	
London Kings Cross 15 ⊖26		a																								
Huddersfield	39	a					19 13										20 13									
Sowerby Bridge		d			19 01				19 23		19 34				20 06				20 23						21 06	
Mytholmroyd		d			19 09				19 28						20 12				20 28						21 12	
Hebden Bridge		a	18 54		19 12				19 31		19 41		19 54		20 15				20 31				20 38	20 54	21 15	
		d	18 54		19 15				19 32		19 41		19 54		20 15				20 32				20 39	20 54	21 15	
Burnley Manchester Road	97	a									20 01												21 01			
		d								19 38	20 03									20 36			21 03			
Accrington	97	a									20 11												21 11			
Blackburn	97	a									20 20												21 20			
Preston 8	97	a									20 38												21 41			
Poulton-le-Fylde	97	a									20 55												21 58			
Blackpool North	97	a									21 04												22 05			
Todmorden		d	19 01		19 22				19 39	19 55			20 01		20 23				20 39	20 53				21 03	21 23	
Walsden		d			19 25										20 26					20 56					21 26	
Littleborough		d			19 32					20 02					20 32					21 02					21 32	
Smithy Bridge		d			19 34					20 05					20 35					21 04					21 35	
Rochdale		a	19 13		19 38				19 49	20 09			20 13		20 39				20 50	21 08				21 20	21 39	
		d	19 14	19 18	19 39	19 42			19 50	20 09			20 13	20 18	20 39	20 42			20 50	21 09	21 18			21 30	21 39	21 42
Castleton		d		19 21		19 45								20 21		20 45					21 21					21 45
Mills Hill		d		19 26		19 50								20 26		20 50					21 26					21 50
Moston		d		19 30		19 54								20 30		20 53					21 29					21 54
Manchester Victoria		a	19 29	19 39	19 53	20 02			20 05	20 24			20 29	20 39	20 53	21 02			21 06	21 23	21 38			21 46	21 54	22 07

Station			NT	NT	NT	NT	NT		NT	NT	NT	NT	NT	NT	NT	NT	NT		NT	NT	NT	NT	NT	NT	NT	NT
				◇	◇		◇		◇	◇			◇	◇		◇			◇		◇	◇		◇		◇
				D		I					C		D		H						D		J			D
York 8	40	d					20 23									21 23								22 19		
Selby	40	d		19 50									20 48								21 48					22 48
Leeds 10	37,39	d		20 27	20 42		20 57		21 12	21 17			21 27	21 42		21 57			22 12	22 21	22 27	22 42		22 57		23 27
Bramley	37	d		20 35	20 49				21 18				21 35	21 49					22 18		22 36	22 49				23 35
New Pudsey	37	d		20 40	20 53		21 07		21 22				21 40	21 53		22 06			22 22		22 40	22 53		23 06		23 40
Bradford Interchange	37	a		20 48	21 01		21 15		21 30				21 48	22 01		22 15			22 30		22 49	23 01		23 15		23 48
		d	20 36	20 51	21 03		21 17		21 33			21 36	21 51	22 03		22 16	22 20		22 33		22 51	23 03		23 17	23 40	23 51
Low Moor		d	20 42		21 10							21 42		22 10			22 26					23 10			23 46	
Halifax		a	20 49	21 03	21 16		21 28		21 43			21 49	22 03	22 16		22 27	22 33		22 43		23 04	23 16		23 28	23 53	00 05
		d	20 50		21 17		21 28		21 44			21 50		22 17		22 27	22 34		22 44			23 17		23 28	23 53	
Dewsbury	39	d								21 34										22 38						
Mirfield	39	a								21 40										22 44						
		d								21 41										22 44						
Brighouse		d	21 00							21 57		22 00					22 45			22 55					00 03	
London Kings Cross 15 ⊖26		a																								
Huddersfield	39	a	21 13									22 13					22 56								00 16	
Sowerby Bridge		d			21 23					22 06				22 23						23 04		23 23		23 34		
Mytholmroyd		d			21 28					22 12				22 28						23 09		23 28		23 39		
Hebden Bridge		a			21 31		21 40		21 54	22 15				22 31		22 37			22 54	23 12		23 31		23 42		
		d			21 32		21 41		21 54	22 15				22 32		22 38			22 54			23 32		23 42		
Burnley Manchester Road	97	a					22 01									22 58								00 01		
		d				21 41	22 03								22 38	23 03							23 38	00 02		
Accrington	97	a					22 11									23 11								00 10		
Blackburn	97	a					22 20									23 20								00 20		
Preston 8	97	a					22 38									23 38										
Poulton-le-Fylde	97	a					22 56									23 57										
Blackpool North	97	a					23 07									00 04										
Todmorden		d			21 39	21 58			22 03	22 23				22 39	22 55				23 01			23 39	23 55			
Walsden		d				22 01				22 26					22 58							23 42				
Littleborough		d				22 07				22 32					23 04							23 49	00 02			
Smithy Bridge		d				22 10				22 35					23 07							23 51	00 05			
Rochdale		a			21 50	22 14			22 18	22 39				22 50	23 11				23 16			23 55	00 09			
		d			21 50	22 14			22 19	22 39	22 43			22 50	23 11				23 16			23 56	00 09			
Castleton		d									22 46				23 14											
Mills Hill		d									22 51				23 20											
Moston		d									22 55				23 24											
Manchester Victoria		a			22 06	22 29			22 35	22 55	23 05			23 08	23 33				23 37			00 11	00 23			

A To Clitheroe
B To Wigan Wallgate
C To Blackburn
D From Hull
E To Chester
F From Blackburn to Wigan North Western
G To Wigan North Western
H From Blackburn to Wigan Wallgate
I From Blackburn to Southport
J From Blackburn

For connections to Liverpool Lime Street refer to Table T090

Table T041-R

Saturdays
21 December to 16 May

Leeds and Bradford - Huddersfield, Blackpool North, Rochdale and Manchester Victoria via Halifax and Brighouse

Station			NT	NT	NT	NT	NT	NT	NT	NT	NT
			◇ A	B	C		D	◇	◇ E	F	
York 8	40	d									
Selby	40	d									
Leeds 10	37,39	d				05 01		05 12	05 19		05 22
Bramley	37	d				05 09		05 18			05 30
New Pudsey	37	d				05 14		05 22			05 35
Bradford Interchange	37	a				05 22		05 30			05 43
		d				05 25		05 33			05 47
Low Moor		d				05 31					
Halifax		a				05 38		05 43			05 59
		d				05 39		05 44			
Dewsbury	39	d							05 38		
Mirfield	39	a							05 44		
		d							05 45		
Brighouse		d			00 03	05 50			05 55		
London Kings Cross 15 ⊖26		a									
Huddersfield	39	a			00 16	06 02					
Sowerby Bridge		d							06 06		
Mytholmroyd		d							06 11		
Hebden Bridge		a						05 54	06 14		
		d						05 54	06 15		
Burnley Manchester Road	97	a									
		d	00 02								
Accrington	97	a	00 10								
Blackburn	97	a	00 20								
Preston 8	97	a									
Poulton-le-Fylde	97	a									
Blackpool North	97	a									
Todmorden		d						06 01	06 22		
Walsden		d							06 25		
Littleborough		d		00 02				06 08	06 32		
Smithy Bridge		d		00 05					06 34		
Rochdale		a		00 09				06 14	06 38		
		d		00 09			05 53	06 14	06 39	06 42	
Castleton		d					05 56			06 45	
Mills Hill		d					06 01			06 50	
Moston		d					06 05			06 54	
Manchester Victoria		a		00 23			06 13	06 30	06 53	07 03	

Station			NT	NT	NT	NT	NT	NT	NT	NT	NT	GC	NT	NT	NT
			◇ G	H	◇	◇	I	◇ E	F			1	◇ G	J	I
York 8	40	d			05 19										
Selby	40	d									05 47				
Leeds 10	37,39	d	05 42		05 57	06 12		06 17			06 27		06 42		
Bramley	37	d	05 49			06 18					06 35		06 49		
New Pudsey	37	d	05 53		06 06	06 22					06 40		06 53		
Bradford Interchange	37	a	06 01		06 14	06 30					06 48		07 01		
		d	06 03		06 16	06 33				06 36	06 51	06 55	07 03		
Low Moor		d	06 10							06 42		07 02	07 10		
Halifax		a	06 16		06 27	06 43				06 49	07 03	07 09	07 16		
		d	06 17		06 27	06 44				06 50		07 10	07 17		
Dewsbury	39	d						06 34							
Mirfield	39	a						06 40							
		d						06 40							
Brighouse		d						06 54		07 00		07 20			
London Kings Cross 15 ⊖26		a										10 11			
Huddersfield	39	a								07 13					
Sowerby Bridge		d	06 23					07 04					07 23		
Mytholmroyd		d	06 28					07 09					07 28		
Hebden Bridge		a	06 31		06 37	06 54		07 12					07 31		
		d	06 32		06 38	06 54		07 13					07 32		
Burnley Manchester Road	97	a			07 01										
		d		06 38	07 03									07 32	
Accrington	97	a			07 12										
Blackburn	97	a			07 21										
Preston 8	97	a			07 45										
Poulton-le-Fylde	97	a			08 05										
Blackpool North	97	a			08 12										
Todmorden		d	06 39	06 55		07 01		07 20					07 39	07 50	
Walsden		d						07 23						07 53	
Littleborough		d		07 02		07 08		07 30						08 00	
Smithy Bridge		d		07 04				07 32						08 02	
Rochdale		a	06 50	07 08		07 14		07 36					07 50	08 06	
		d	06 50	07 09		07 14	07 18	07 37	07 42				07 50	08 07	08 14
Castleton		d					07 21		07 45						08 17
Mills Hill		d					07 26		07 50						08 22
Moston		d					07 30		07 53						08 26
Manchester Victoria		a	07 06	07 24		07 30	07 39	07 52	08 02				08 05	08 24	08 35

Station			NT	NT	NT	NT	NT	NT	NT	NT	NT
			◇		◇	◇ K	F	◇ L	◇ G	H	I
York 8	40	d	06 12								
Selby	40	d						06 45			
Leeds 10	37,39	d	06 57		07 12	07 17		07 27	07 42		
Bramley	37	d			07 18			07 35	07 49		
New Pudsey	37	d	07 07		07 22			07 40	07 53		
Bradford Interchange	37	a	07 15		07 30			07 48	08 01		
		d	07 17	07 36	07 42			07 52	08 03		
Low Moor		d		07 42					08 10		
Halifax		a	07 28	07 49	07 53			08 04	08 16		
		d	07 28	07 50	07 55				08 17		
Dewsbury	39	d				07 34					
Mirfield	39	a				07 40					
		d				07 40					
Brighouse		d		08 00		07 54					
London Kings Cross 15 ⊖26		a									
Huddersfield	39	a		08 13							
Sowerby Bridge		d				08 06			08 23		
Mytholmroyd		d				08 12			08 28		
Hebden Bridge		a	07 38		08 05	08 15			08 31		
		d	07 39		08 05	08 15			08 32		
Burnley Manchester Road	97	a	08 02								
		d	08 04							08 38	
Accrington	97	a	08 12								
Blackburn	97	a	08 21								
Preston 8	97	a	08 44								
Poulton-le-Fylde	97	a	09 01								
Blackpool North	97	a	09 08								
Todmorden		d			08 12	08 23			08 39	08 55	
Walsden		d				08 26					
Littleborough		d			08 19	08 32				09 02	
Smithy Bridge		d				08 34				09 05	
Rochdale		a			08 24	08 38			08 50	09 09	
		d			08 25	08 39	08 42		08 50	09 09	09 14
Castleton		d					08 45				09 17
Mills Hill		d			08 31		08 50				09 22
Moston		d					08 53				09 26
Manchester Victoria		a			08 42	08 53	09 03		09 05	09 24	09 35

Station			NT	NT	NT	NT	NT	GC	NT	NT	NT	NT	NT	NT	NT
			◇	◇	◇ E	F		1	◇ L	◇ G	H	◇	◇	I	◇ E
York 8	40	d	07 13									08 23			
Selby	40	d							07 49						
Leeds 10	37,39	d	07 55	08 12	08 17				08 27	08 42		08 57	09 12		09 17
Bramley	37	d		08 18					08 35	08 49			09 18		
New Pudsey	37	d	08 04	08 22					08 40	08 53		09 06	09 22		
Bradford Interchange	37	a	08 12	08 30					08 48	09 01		09 14	09 30		
		d	08 14	08 33			08 36	08 44	08 51	09 03		09 16	09 33		
Low Moor		d					08 42	08 50		09 10					
Halifax		a	08 25	08 43			08 49	08 56	09 03	09 16		09 27	09 43		
		d	08 25	08 44			08 50	08 57		09 17		09 27	09 44		
Dewsbury	39	d			08 34										09 35
Mirfield	39	a			08 40										09 41
		d			08 41										09 42
Brighouse		d			08 56		09 00	09 13							09 54
London Kings Cross 15 ⊖26		a						11 58							
Huddersfield	39	a					09 13								
Sowerby Bridge		d			09 06					09 23					10 05
Mytholmroyd		d			09 12					09 28					10 11
Hebden Bridge		a	08 38	08 54	09 15					09 31		09 37	09 54		10 14
		d	08 38	08 54	09 15					09 32		09 38	09 54		10 15
Burnley Manchester Road	97	a	08 58									10 01			
		d	09 03								09 38	10 03			
Accrington	97	a	09 11									10 11			
Blackburn	97	a	09 20									10 20			
Preston 8	97	a	09 38									10 38			
Poulton-le-Fylde	97	a	09 55									10 55			
Blackpool North	97	a	10 02									11 02			
Todmorden		d		09 07	09 23					09 39	09 55		10 01		10 22
Walsden		d			09 26										10 25
Littleborough		d			09 32						10 02				10 32
Smithy Bridge		d			09 34						10 05				10 34
Rochdale		a		09 24	09 38					09 50	10 09		10 13		10 38
		d		09 24	09 39	09 42				09 50	10 09		10 14	10 18	10 39
Castleton		d				09 45								10 21	
Mills Hill		d				09 50								10 26	
Moston		d				09 54								10 30	
Manchester Victoria		a		09 45	09 54	10 03				10 05	10 24		10 29	10 39	10 53

A From York
B From Blackburn
C From Bradford Interchange
D To Kirkby
E To Wigan Wallgate
F To Blackburn
G To Chester
H From Blackburn to Wigan Wallgate
I To Clitheroe
J From Blackburn to Wigan North Western
K To Wigan North Western
L From Hull

For connections to Liverpool Lime Street refer to Table T090

Table T041-R

Saturdays
21 December to 16 May

Leeds and Bradford - Huddersfield, Blackpool North, Rochdale and Manchester Victoria via Halifax and Brighouse

Station			NT	NT	NT	NT	NT	NT	GC	NT	NT	NT
			A		◇ B	◇ C	D	◇	1	◇	E	◇ F
York 8	40	d						09 23				
Selby	40	d			08 48							
Leeds 10	37,39	d			09 27	09 42		09 57		10 12		10 17
Bramley	37	d			09 35	09 49				10 18		
New Pudsey	37	d			09 40	09 53		10 06		10 22		
Bradford Interchange	37	a			09 48	10 01		10 15		10 30		
		d		09 36	09 51	10 03		10 17	10 22	10 33		
Low Moor		d		09 42		10 10			10 28			
Halifax		a		09 49	10 02	10 16		10 28	10 35	10 43		
		d		09 50		10 17		10 28	10 36	10 44		
Dewsbury	39	d										10 35
Mirfield	39	a										10 41
		d										10 42
Brighouse		d		10 00					10 47			10 55
London Kings Cross 15 ⊖26		a							13 44			
Huddersfield	39	a		10 13								
Sowerby Bridge		d				10 23						11 06
Mytholmroyd		d				10 28						11 11
Hebden Bridge		a				10 31		10 38		10 54		11 14
		d				10 32		10 39		10 54		11 15
Burnley Manchester Road	97	a						11 01				
		d					10 38	11 03				
Accrington	97	a						11 11				
Blackburn	97	a						11 20				
Preston 8	97	a						11 38				
Poulton-le-Fylde	97	a						11 55				
Blackpool North	97	a						12 02				
Todmorden		d				10 39	10 55			11 01		11 22
Walsden		d										11 25
Littleborough		d					11 02					11 32
Smithy Bridge		d					11 05					11 34
Rochdale		a				10 50	11 09			11 13		11 38
		d	10 42			10 50	11 09			11 14	11 22	11 39
Castleton		d	10 45								11 25	
Mills Hill		d	10 50								11 30	
Moston		d	10 54								11 34	
Manchester Victoria		a	11 03			11 06	11 24			11 29	11 43	11 53

Station			NT	NT	NT	NT	NT	NT	NT	NT	NT	NT	NT
			A		◇ B	◇ C	G	E	◇	◇	◇ F	A	
York 8	40	d							10 23				
Selby	40	d			09 48								
Leeds 10	37,39	d			10 27	10 42			10 57	11 12	11 17		
Bramley	37	d			10 35	10 49				11 18			
New Pudsey	37	d			10 40	10 53			11 06	11 22			
Bradford Interchange	37	a			10 48	11 01			11 14	11 30			
		d		10 36	10 51	11 03			11 18	11 33			11 36
Low Moor		d		10 42		11 10							11 42
Halifax		a		10 49	11 03	11 16			11 29	11 43			11 49
		d		10 50		11 17			11 29	11 44			11 50
Dewsbury	39	d									11 35		
Mirfield	39	a									11 41		
		d									11 42		
Brighouse		d		11 00							11 57		12 00
London Kings Cross 15 ⊖26		a											
Huddersfield	39	a		11 13									12 13
Sowerby Bridge		d				11 23					12 06		
Mytholmroyd		d				11 28					12 11		
Hebden Bridge		a				11 31			11 39	11 54	12 14		
		d				11 32			11 40	11 54	12 15		
Burnley Manchester Road	97	a							12 01				
		d					11 38		12 03				
Accrington	97	a							12 11				
Blackburn	97	a							12 20				
Preston 8	97	a							12 38				
Poulton-le-Fylde	97	a							12 55				
Blackpool North	97	a							13 02				
Todmorden		d				11 39	11 55			12 01	12 22		
Walsden		d									12 25		
Littleborough		d					12 02				12 32		
Smithy Bridge		d					12 05				12 34		
Rochdale		a				11 50	12 09			12 19	12 38		
		d	11 42			11 50	12 09	12 18		12 25	12 39	12 42	
Castleton		d	11 45					12 21				12 45	
Mills Hill		d	11 50					12 26				12 50	
Moston		d	11 54					12 30				12 54	
Manchester Victoria		a	12 03			12 05	12 24	12 39		12 42	12 53	13 03	

Station			NT	NT	NT	NT	NT	NT	NT	NT	NT	NT
			◇ B	◇ C	D	E	◇	◇	A	◇ H		◇ B
York 8	40	d					11 23					
Selby	40	d	10 48									11 48
Leeds 10	37,39	d	11 27	11 42			11 57	12 12		12 17		12 27
Bramley	37	d	11 35	11 49				12 18				12 35
New Pudsey	37	d	11 40	11 53			12 06	12 22				12 40
Bradford Interchange	37	a	11 48	12 01			12 14	12 30				12 48
		d	11 51	12 03			12 17	12 33			12 36	12 51
Low Moor		d		12 10							12 42	
Halifax		a	12 03	12 16			12 27	12 43			12 49	13 03
		d		12 17			12 28	12 44			12 50	
Dewsbury	39	d								12 35		
Mirfield	39	a								12 41		
		d								12 45		
Brighouse		d								12 54	13 00	
London Kings Cross 15 ⊖26		a										
Huddersfield	39	a									13 13	
Sowerby Bridge		d		12 23						13 06		
Mytholmroyd		d		12 28						13 12		
Hebden Bridge		a		12 31			12 38	12 57		13 15		
		d		12 32			12 38	12 58		13 15		
Burnley Manchester Road	97	a					13 01					
		d			12 38		13 03					
Accrington	97	a					13 11					
Blackburn	97	a					13 20					
Preston 8	97	a					13 38					
Poulton-le-Fylde	97	a					13 55					
Blackpool North	97	a					14 02					
Todmorden		d		12 39	12 55			13 08		13 23		
Walsden		d								13 26		
Littleborough		d			13 02					13 32		
Smithy Bridge		d			13 05					13 35		
Rochdale		a		12 50	13 09			13 19		13 39		
		d		12 50	13 09	13 18		13 25	13 34	13 39		
Castleton		d				13 21		13 28				
Mills Hill		d				13 26		13 33	13 40			
Moston		d				13 30		13 36				
Manchester Victoria		a		13 05	13 24	13 39		13 46	14 02	13 54		

Station			NT	NT	NT	NT	NT	NT	NT	NT	NT	NT	NT	NT
			◇ C	D	◇	◇	E	◇ F	A		◇ B	◇ C	D	◇
York 8	40	d			12 23									13 23
Selby	40	d									12 48			
Leeds 10	37,39	d	12 42		12 57	13 12		13 17			13 27	13 42		13 57
Bramley	37	d	12 49			13 18					13 35	13 49		
New Pudsey	37	d	12 53		13 06	13 22					13 40	13 53		14 06
Bradford Interchange	37	a	13 01		13 15	13 30					13 48	14 01		14 15
		d	13 03		13 17	13 33				13 36	13 51	14 03		14 17
Low Moor		d	13 10							13 42		14 10		
Halifax		a	13 16		13 28	13 43				13 49	14 04	14 16		14 28
		d	13 17		13 28	13 44				13 50		14 17		14 28
Dewsbury	39	d						13 35						
Mirfield	39	a						13 41						
		d						13 42						
Brighouse		d						13 54		14 00				
London Kings Cross 15 ⊖26		a												
Huddersfield	39	a								14 13				
Sowerby Bridge		d	13 23					14 06				14 23		
Mytholmroyd		d	13 28					14 11				14 28		
Hebden Bridge		a	13 31		13 38	13 54		14 14				14 31		14 38
		d	13 32		13 39	13 54		14 15				14 32		14 39
Burnley Manchester Road	97	a			14 01									15 01
		d		13 38	14 03								14 38	15 03
Accrington	97	a			14 11									15 11
Blackburn	97	a			14 20									15 20
Preston 8	97	a			14 38									15 38
Poulton-le-Fylde	97	a			14 57									15 55
Blackpool North	97	a			15 04									16 02
Todmorden		d	13 39	13 55		14 01		14 22				14 39	14 55	
Walsden		d						14 25						
Littleborough		d		14 02				14 32					15 02	
Smithy Bridge		d		14 05				14 34					15 05	
Rochdale		a	13 50	14 09		14 13		14 38				14 50	15 09	
		d	13 50	14 09		14 14	14 18	14 39	14 42			14 50	15 09	
Castleton		d					14 21		14 45					
Mills Hill		d					14 26		14 50					
Moston		d					14 30		14 54					
Manchester Victoria		a	14 05	14 24		14 29	14 39	14 53	15 03			15 06	15 24	

A To Blackburn
B From Hull
C To Chester
D From Blackburn to Wigan Wallgate
E To Clitheroe
F To Wigan Wallgate
G From Blackburn to Wigan North Western
H To Wigan North Western

For connections to Liverpool Lime Street refer to Table T090

Table T041-R

Saturdays
21 December to 16 May

Leeds and Bradford - Huddersfield, Blackpool North, Rochdale and Manchester Victoria via Halifax and Brighouse

Station			NT ◇	NT A	NT ◇ B	NT A	NT	NT ◇ C	NT ◇ D	NT E	NT ◇	GC	NT ◇	NT A	NT ◇ B	NT F	NT	NT ◇ C	NT ◇ D	NT G	NT ◇	NT ◇	NT A
York	40	d									14 23										15 23		
Selby	40	d						13 48										14 49					
Leeds	37,39	d	14 12		14 17			14 27	14 42		14 57		15 12		15 17			15 27	15 42		15 57	16 12	
Bramley	37	d	14 18					14 35	14 49				15 18					15 35	15 49			16 18	
New Pudsey	37	d	14 22					14 40	14 53		15 06		15 22					15 40	15 53		16 07	16 22	
Bradford Interchange	37	a	14 30					14 48	15 01		15 15		15 30					15 48	16 01		16 15	16 30	
		d	14 33				14 36	14 54	15 03		15 17	15 22	15 33				15 36	15 51	16 03		16 17	16 33	
Low Moor		d					14 42		15 10			15 28					15 42		16 10				
Halifax		a	14 43				14 49	15 06	15 16		15 28	15 34	15 43				15 49	16 03	16 16		16 28	16 43	
		d	14 44				14 50		15 17		15 28	15 35	15 44				15 50		16 17		16 28	16 44	
Dewsbury	39	d			14 35										15 35								
Mirfield	39	a			14 41										15 41								
		d			14 42										15 42								
Brighouse		d			14 54		15 00					15 48			15 54		16 00						
London Kings Cross ⊖26		a										18 47											
Huddersfield	39	a					15 13										16 13						
Sowerby Bridge		d			15 06				15 23						16 06				16 23				
Mytholmroyd		d			15 11				15 28						16 11				16 28				
Hebden Bridge		a	14 54		15 14				15 31		15 38		15 54		16 14				16 31		16 38	16 54	
		d	14 54		15 15				15 32		15 39		15 54		16 15				16 32		16 39	16 54	
Burnley Manchester Road	97	a									16 01										16 58		
		d								15 38	16 03									16 36	17 03		
Accrington	97	a									16 11										17 11		
Blackburn	97	a									16 20										17 20		
Preston	97	a									16 39										17 40		
Poulton-le-Fylde	97	a									16 56										17 58		
Blackpool North	97	a									17 03										18 06		
Todmorden		d	15 01		15 22				15 39	15 55			16 01		16 22				16 39	16 53		17 01	
Walsden		d			15 25										16 25					16 56			
Littleborough		d			15 32					16 02					16 32					17 02		17 08	
Smithy Bridge		d			15 34					16 05					16 34					17 05		17 11	
Rochdale		a	15 13		15 38				15 50	16 09			16 13		16 38				16 50	17 09		17 15	
		d	15 14	15 18	15 39	15 42			15 50	16 09			16 13	16 18	16 39	16 42			16 50	17 09		17 15	17 19
Castleton		d		15 21		15 45								16 21		16 45							17 22
Mills Hill		d		15 26		15 50								16 26		16 50							17 27
Moston		d		15 30		15 54								16 30		16 54						17 24	
Manchester Victoria		a	15 29	15 39	15 53	16 03			16 05	16 24			16 29	16 39	16 54	17 03			17 05	17 24		17 34	17 39

Station			NT ◇ B	NT	NT ◇ C	NT ◇ D	NT F	NT H	NT A	NT ◇	NT ◇	NT ◇ I	NT A	NT	NT ◇ C	NT ◇ D	NT G	NT ◇	NT ◇	NT A	NT ◇ B	NT F	NT	NT ◇ C
York	40	d								16 23								17 23						
Selby	40	d			15 47										16 48									17 48
Leeds	37,39	d	16 17		16 27	16 42				16 57	17 12	17 17			17 27	17 42		17 57	18 12		18 17			18 27
Bramley	37	d			16 35	16 49					17 18				17 35	17 49			18 18					18 35
New Pudsey	37	d			16 40	16 53				17 06	17 22				17 40	17 53		18 06	18 22					18 40
Bradford Interchange	37	a			16 48	17 01				17 15	17 30				17 48	18 01		18 15	18 30					18 48
		d		16 36	16 52	17 03				17 17	17 33			17 36	17 53	18 03		18 17	18 33				18 36	18 51
Low Moor		d		16 42		17 10								17 42		18 10							18 42	
Halifax		a		16 49	17 04	17 16				17 28	17 44			17 49	18 05	18 16		18 28	18 43				18 49	19 03
		d		16 50		17 17				17 28	17 44			17 50		18 17		18 28	18 44				18 50	
Dewsbury	39	d	16 34									17 36									18 33			
Mirfield	39	a	16 41									17 42									18 40			
		d	16 42									17 43									18 40			
Brighouse		d	16 54	17 00								17 55		18 00							18 49		19 00	
London Kings Cross ⊖26		a																						
Huddersfield	39	a		17 11										18 13									19 13	
Sowerby Bridge		d	17 07			17 23				17 34		18 06				18 23		18 34			19 01			
Mytholmroyd		d	17 12			17 28						18 11				18 28					19 09			
Hebden Bridge		a	17 15			17 31				17 41	18 00	18 14				18 31		18 41	18 54		19 12			
		d	17 16			17 32				17 41	18 00	18 15				18 32		18 41	18 54		19 15			
Burnley Manchester Road	97	a								18 00								19 01						
		d						17 38		18 03							18 38	19 03						
Accrington	97	a								18 11								19 11						
Blackburn	97	a								18 20								19 20						
Preston	97	a								18 40								19 38						
Poulton-le-Fylde	97	a								18 58								19 55						
Blackpool North	97	a								19 05								20 02						
Todmorden		d	17 23			17 39		17 55			18 07	18 22				18 39	18 55		19 01		19 22			
Walsden		d	17 26									18 25									19 25			
Littleborough		d	17 32					18 02				18 32					19 02				19 32			
Smithy Bridge		d	17 34					18 05				18 34					19 05				19 34			
Rochdale		a	17 38			17 50		18 09			18 21	18 38				18 50	19 09		19 13		19 38			
		d	17 39			17 50	17 54	18 09	18 18		18 22	18 39	18 42			18 50	19 09		19 14	19 18	19 39	19 42		
Castleton		d					17 57		18 21				18 45							19 21		19 45		
Mills Hill		d					18 02				18 30		18 50							19 26		19 50		
Moston		d					18 06				18 33		18 54							19 30		19 54		
Manchester Victoria		a	17 53			18 05	18 15	18 24	18 36		18 44	18 53	19 03			19 05	19 24		19 29	19 39	19 53	20 02		

A To Clitheroe
B To Wigan Wallgate
C From Hull
D To Chester
E From Blackburn to Wigan North Western
F To Blackburn
G From Blackburn to Wigan Wallgate
H From Blackburn to Kirkby
I To Wigan North Western

For connections to Liverpool Lime Street refer to Table T090

Table T041-R

Saturdays
21 December to 16 May

Leeds and Bradford - Huddersfield, Blackpool North, Rochdale and Manchester Victoria via Halifax and Brighouse

Station			NT ◇ A	NT B	NT ◇	NT ◇	NT C	NT ◇ D	NT E	NT	NT ◇ F	NT ◇ A	NT G	NT C	NT ◇	NT ◇	NT ◇ D	NT C	NT	NT ◇ F	NT ◇	NT H	NT ◇	NT ◇
York	40	d			18 22										19 23								20 23	
Selby	40	d									18 48									19 50				
Leeds	37,39	d	18 42		18 57	19 12		19 17			19 27	19 40			19 57	20 12	20 18			20 27	20 42		20 57	21 12
Bramley	37	d	18 49			19 18					19 35	19 47				20 18				20 35	20 49			21 18
New Pudsey	37	d	18 53		19 06	19 22					19 40	19 51			20 07	20 22				20 40	20 53		21 06	21 22
Bradford Interchange	37	a	19 01		19 15	19 30					19 48	19 59			20 15	20 30				20 48	21 01		21 15	21 30
		d	19 03		19 17	19 33				19 36	19 51	20 03			20 17	20 33			20 36	20 51	21 03		21 17	21 33
Low Moor		d	19 10							19 42		20 10							20 42		21 10			
Halifax		a	19 16		19 28	19 43				19 49	20 03	20 16			20 28	20 43			20 49	21 03	21 16		21 28	21 43
		d	19 17		19 28	19 44				19 50		20 17			20 28	20 44			20 50		21 17		21 28	21 44
Dewsbury	39	d						19 34									20 35							
Mirfield	39	a						19 40									20 41							
		d						19 41									20 42							
Brighouse		d						19 55		20 00							20 54		21 00					
London Kings Cross ⊖26		a																						
Huddersfield	39	a								20 13									21 13					
Sowerby Bridge		d	19 23		19 34			20 06				20 23					21 06				21 23			
Mytholmroyd		d	19 28					20 12				20 28					21 12				21 28			
Hebden Bridge		a	19 31		19 41	19 54		20 15				20 31			20 38	20 54	21 15				21 31		21 40	21 54
		d	19 32		19 41	19 54		20 15				20 32			20 39	20 54	21 15				21 32		21 41	21 54
Burnley Manchester Road	97	a			20 01										21 01								22 01	
		d		19 38	20 03								20 36		21 03							21 41	22 03	
Accrington	97	a			20 11										21 11								22 11	
Blackburn	97	a			20 20										21 20								22 20	
Preston	97	a			20 38										21 39								22 38	
Poulton-le-Fylde	97	a			20 55										21 56								22 56	
Blackpool North	97	a			21 04										22 03								23 06	
Todmorden		d	19 39	19 55		20 01		20 23				20 39	20 53			21 03	21 23				21 39	21 58		22 03
Walsden		d						20 26					20 56				21 26					22 01		
Littleborough		d		20 02				20 32					21 02				21 32					22 07		
Smithy Bridge		d		20 05				20 35					21 04				21 35					22 10		
Rochdale		a	19 50	20 09		20 13		20 39				20 50	21 08			21 20	21 39				21 50	22 14		22 18
		d	19 50	20 09		20 13	20 18	20 39	20 42			20 50	21 09	21 18		21 30	21 39	21 42			21 50	22 14		22 19
Castleton		d					20 21		20 45					21 21				21 45						
Mills Hill		d					20 26		20 50					21 26				21 50						
Moston		d					20 30		20 53					21 29				21 54						
Manchester Victoria		a	20 05	20 24		20 29	20 39	20 53	21 02			21 06	21 23	21 38		21 46	21 54	22 07			22 06	22 29		22 35

Station			NT ◇	NT E	NT	NT ◇ F	NT ◇	NT I	NT ◇	NT	NT ◇	NT	NT ◇ F	NT ◇	NT I	NT ◇	NT	NT ◇ F
York	40	d							21 23							22 19		
Selby	40	d				20 48							21 47					22 48
Leeds	37,39	d	21 17			21 27	21 42		21 57		22 12	22 21	22 27	22 42		22 57		23 27
Bramley	37	d				21 35	21 49				22 18		22 36	22 49				23 35
New Pudsey	37	d				21 40	21 53		22 06		22 22		22 40	22 53		23 07		23 40
Bradford Interchange	37	a				21 48	22 01		22 15		22 30		22 49	23 01		23 15		23 49
		d			21 36	21 51	22 03		22 16	22 20	22 33		22 51	23 03		23 17	23 40	
Low Moor		d			21 42		22 10			22 26				23 10			23 46	
Halifax		a			21 49	22 03	22 16		22 27	22 33	22 43		23 04	23 16		23 28	23 53	
		d			21 50		22 17		22 27	22 34	22 44			23 17		23 28	23 53	
Dewsbury	39	d	21 34									22 38						
Mirfield	39	a	21 40									22 44						
		d	21 41									22 44						
Brighouse		d	21 57		22 00					22 45		22 55					00 03	
London Kings Cross ⊖26		a																
Huddersfield	39	a			22 13					22 56							00 16	
Sowerby Bridge		d	22 06				22 23					23 04		23 23		23 34		
Mytholmroyd		d	22 12				22 28					23 09		23 28		23 39		
Hebden Bridge		a	22 15				22 31		22 37		22 54	23 12		23 31		23 42		
		d	22 15				22 32		22 38		22 54			23 32		23 42		
Burnley Manchester Road	97	a							22 58							00 01		
		d						22 38	23 03						23 38	00 02		
Accrington	97	a							23 11							00 11		
Blackburn	97	a							23 20							00 22		
Preston	97	a							23 38									
Poulton-le-Fylde	97	a							23 57									
Blackpool North	97	a							00 04									
Todmorden		d	22 23				22 39	22 55			23 01			23 39	23 55			
Walsden		d	22 26					22 58						23 42				
Littleborough		d	22 32					23 04						23 49	00 02			
Smithy Bridge		d	22 35					23 07						23 51	00 05			
Rochdale		a	22 39				22 50	23 11			23 16			23 55	00 09			
		d	22 39	22 43			22 50	23 11			23 16			23 56	00 09			
Castleton		d		22 46				23 14										
Mills Hill		d		22 51				23 20										
Moston		d		22 55				23 24										
Manchester Victoria		a	22 55	23 05			23 08	23 33			23 37			00 11	00 23			

A To Chester
B From Blackburn to Wigan North Western
C To Clitheroe
D To Wigan North Western
E To Blackburn
F From Hull
G From Blackburn to Wigan Wallgate
H From Blackburn to Southport
I From Blackburn

For connections to Liverpool Lime Street refer to Table T090

Table T041-R

Sundays
15 December to 10 May

Leeds and Bradford - Huddersfield, Blackpool North, Rochdale and Manchester Victoria via Halifax and Brighouse

	NT ◇ A	NT B	NT C	GC D	GC ■ 1 E	NT	NT F	NT G	NT ◇	NT	NT G	NT ◇	NT	NT G	NT ◇	NT ◇	NT	NT G	NT ◇	NT ◇	NT	GC ■ 1
York ■ 40 d															09 21				10 08			
Selby 40 d																						
Leeds 37,39 d						07 58			08 18	08 29		09 19	09 29		09 52	10 15	10 29		10 49	11 18	11 29	
Bramley 37 d						08 06			08 26	08 41		09 27	09 37			10 25	10 37			11 26	11 37	
New Pudsey 37 d						08 10			08 30	08 45		09 31	09 41		10 02	10 31	10 41		10 59	11 30	11 41	
Bradford Interchange 37 a						08 19			08 38	08 54		09 39	09 50		10 10	10 39	10 50		11 07	11 38	11 50	
d					07 57	08 21			08 41	08 56		09 42	09 52		10 16	10 42	10 52		11 10	11 42	11 52	12 05
Low Moor d					08 04	08 28				09 03			09 59				10 59				11 59	12 11
Halifax a					08 10	08 36			08 52	09 10		09 53	10 06		10 27	10 54	11 06		11 21	11 53	12 06	12 18
d				07 34	08 11				08 53	09 11		09 54	10 06		10 27	10 54	11 06		11 21	11 54	12 06	12 19
Dewsbury 39 d																						
Mirfield 39 a																						
d																						
Brighouse d			00 03	07a54	08 21					09 21			10 16				11 16				12 16	12 30
London Kings Cross 15 ⊖26 a					10 40																	14 54
Huddersfield 39 a			00 16							09 33			10 35				11 34				12 33	
Sowerby Bridge d															10 33				11 27			
Mytholmroyd d															10 39				11 33			
Hebden Bridge a									09 03			10 04			10 42	11 05			11 36	12 04		
d									09 04			10 05			10 42	11 06			11 36	12 05		
Burnley Manchester Road 97 a															11 03				11 58			
d	00 02						08 07	08 32			09 32			10 32	11 03			11 32	12 00			
Accrington 97 a	00 11														11 12				12 09			
Blackburn 97 a	00 22														11 21				12 20			
Preston ■ 97 a															11 40				12 39			
Poulton-le-Fylde 97 a															11 57				12 58			
Blackpool North 97 a															12 04				13 05			
Todmorden d							08 24	08 49	09 11		09 49	10 12		10 49		11 13		11 49		12 12		
Walsden d									09 14			10 15				11 16				12 15		
Littleborough d		00 02					08 31	08 56	09 20		09 56	10 21		10 56		11 22		11 56		12 21		
Smithy Bridge d		00 05					08 34	08 58			09 58			10 58				11 58				
Rochdale a		00 09					08 38	09 02	09 25		10 02	10 26		11 02		11 27		12 02		12 26		
d		00 09					08 38	09 03	09 26		10 03	10 27		11 03		11 28		12 03		12 27		
Castleton d							08 41	09 06			10 06			11 06				12 06				
Mills Hill d							08 47	09 11			10 11			11 11				12 11				
Moston d							08 50	09 15			10 15			11 15				12 15				
Manchester Victoria a		00 23					08 59	09 24	09 46		10 24	10 43		11 24		11 44		12 24		12 43		

	NT G	NT ◇	NT ◇	NT	NT G	NT ◇	NT ◇	NT	NT G	NT ◇	NT ◇	NT	GC ■ 1	NT G	NT ◇	NT ◇	NT	GC ■ 1	NT G	NT ◇	NT ◇	NT
York ■ 40 d		11 21				12 21				13 21					14 21					15 21		
Selby 40 d																						
Leeds 37,39 d		11 57	12 18	12 29		12 57	13 18	13 29		13 57	14 19	14 29			14 56	15 18	15 29			15 57	16 19	16 31
Bramley 37 d			12 27	12 37			13 27	13 37			14 27	14 37				15 26	15 37				16 27	16 39
New Pudsey 37 d		12 06	12 31	12 41		13 06	13 31	13 41		14 06	14 31	14 41			15 05	15 30	15 41			16 07	16 31	16 43
Bradford Interchange 37 a		12 15	12 39	12 50		13 15	13 39	13 50		14 17	14 39	14 50			15 14	15 38	15 50			16 15	16 39	16 52
d		12 17	12 42	12 52		13 18	13 42	13 52		14 21	14 42	14 52	15 08		15 19	15 42	15 52	15 59		16 19	16 42	16 54
Low Moor d				12 59				13 59				14 59	15 14				15 59	16 05				17 01
Halifax a		12 29	12 54	13 06		13 29	13 54	14 06		14 32	14 54	15 06	15 20		15 32	15 54	16 06	16 11		16 30	16 54	17 08
d		12 29	12 54	13 06		13 30	13 54	14 06		14 32	14 54	15 06	15 21		15 33	15 54	16 06	16 12		16 31	16 54	17 08
Dewsbury 39 d																						
Mirfield 39 a																						
d																						
Brighouse d				13 16				14 16				15 16	15 36				16 16	16 22				17 18
London Kings Cross 15 ⊖26 a													17 56					18 44				
Huddersfield 39 a				13 31				14 32				15 32					16 32					17 34
Sowerby Bridge d		12 35				13 36				14 38					15 39					16 37		
Mytholmroyd d		12 41				13 41				14 44					15 44					16 42		
Hebden Bridge a		12 44	13 05			13 44	14 07			14 47	15 05				15 47	16 05				16 45	17 06	
d		12 44	13 05			13 45	14 08			14 47	15 06				15 48	16 06				16 46	17 07	
Burnley Manchester Road 97 a		13 04				14 05				15 07					16 07					17 05		
d	12 32	13 04			13 32	14 05			14 32	15 08				15 32	16 08				16 32	17 06		
Accrington 97 a		13 13				14 14				15 16					16 16					17 14		
Blackburn 97 a		13 21				14 22				15 25					16 25					17 23		
Preston ■ 97 a		13 40				14 41				15 42					16 43					17 41		
Poulton-le-Fylde 97 a		13 59				14 58				15 59					17 00					17 58		
Blackpool North 97 a		14 06				15 05				16 06					17 07					18 05		
Todmorden d	12 49		13 13		13 49		14 15		14 49		15 13			15 49		16 13			16 49		17 14	
Walsden d			13 16				14 18				15 16					16 16					17 17	
Littleborough d	12 56		13 22		13 56		14 24		14 56		15 22			15 56		16 22			16 56		17 23	
Smithy Bridge d	12 58				13 58				14 58					15 58					16 58			
Rochdale a	13 02		13 27		14 02		14 29		15 02		15 27			16 02		16 27			17 02		17 28	
d	13 03		13 27		14 03		14 30		15 03		15 28			16 03		16 28			17 03		17 29	
Castleton d	13 06				14 06				15 06					16 06					17 06			
Mills Hill d	13 11				14 11				15 11					16 11					17 11			
Moston d	13 15				14 15				15 15					16 15					17 15			
Manchester Victoria a	13 24		13 43		14 24		14 46		15 24		15 44			16 24		16 44			17 24		17 44	

A not 15 December. From York
B not 15 December. From Blackburn
C not 15 December. From Bradford Interchange
D To Wakefield Kirkgate
E until 16 February, from 5 April
F From Blackburn
G From Blackburn to Southport

For connections to Liverpool Lime Street refer to Table T090

Table T041-R

Sundays
15 December to 10 May

Leeds and Bradford - Huddersfield, Blackpool North, Rochdale and Manchester Victoria via Halifax and Brighouse

	NT A	NT ◇	NT ◇	NT	NT A	NT ◇	NT ◇	NT	NT A	NT ◇	NT ◇	NT	NT A	NT ◇	NT ◇	NT	NT B	NT ◇	NT ◇	NT	NT B
York ■ 40 d		16 21				17 21				18 21				19 21				20 21			
Selby 40 d																					
Leeds 37,39 d		16 56	17 18	17 29		17 56	18 18	18 29		18 56	19 19	19 29		19 56	20 18	20 29		20 56	21 18	21 32	
Bramley 37 d			17 27	17 37			18 27	18 37			19 27	19 37			20 27	20 37			21 27	21 40	
New Pudsey 37 d		17 05	17 31	17 41		18 05	18 31	18 41		19 05	19 31	19 41		20 05	20 31	20 41		21 06	21 31	21 44	
Bradford Interchange 37 a		17 14	17 39	17 50		18 15	18 39	18 50		19 15	19 39	19 50		20 14	20 39	20 50		21 14	21 39	21 53	
d		17 18	17 42	17 52		18 17	18 42	18 52		19 17	19 42	19 52		20 18	20 42	20 52		21 18	21 42	21 55	
Low Moor d				17 59				18 59				19 59				20 59				22 02	
Halifax a		17 29	17 54	18 06		18 29	18 54	19 06		19 29	19 53	20 06		20 29	20 53	21 06		21 29	21 53	22 09	
d		17 29	17 54	18 06		18 29	18 54	19 06		19 29	19 54	20 06		20 29	20 54	21 06		21 30	21 54	22 09	
Dewsbury 39 d																					
Mirfield 39 a																					
d																					
Brighouse d				18 16				19 16				20 16				21 16				22 19	
London Kings Cross 15 ⊖26 a																					
Huddersfield 39 a				18 31				19 34				20 34				21 32				22 30	
Sowerby Bridge d		17 35				18 36				19 36				20 35				21 36			
Mytholmroyd d		17 41				18 41				19 41				20 41				21 41			
Hebden Bridge a		17 44	18 05			18 44	19 05			19 44	20 04			20 44	21 04			21 44	22 04		
d		17 44	18 05			18 45	19 06			19 45	20 05			20 44	21 05			21 45	22 05		
Burnley Manchester Road 97 a		18 04				19 04				20 04				21 04				22 04			
d	17 32	18 04			18 32	19 05			19 32	20 05			20 36	21 04			21 33	22 05			22 33
Accrington 97 a		18 13				19 13				20 13				21 13				22 13			
Blackburn 97 a		18 21				19 22				20 22				21 21				22 22			
Preston ■ 97 a		18 40				19 41				20 41				21 40				22 41			
Poulton-le-Fylde 97 a		18 57				19 58				20 58				21 57				22 58			
Blackpool North 97 a		19 04				20 05				21 05				22 04				23 05			
Todmorden d	17 49		18 13		18 49		19 13		19 49		20 13		20 55		21 14		21 50		22 13		22 50
Walsden d			18 16				19 16				20 16				21 17				22 16		
Littleborough d	17 56		18 22		18 56		19 22		19 56		20 22		21 02		21 23		21 57		22 22		22 57
Smithy Bridge d	17 58				18 58				19 58				21 05				21 59				22 59
Rochdale a	18 02		18 27		19 02		19 27		20 02		20 27		21 09		21 28		22 03		22 27		23 03
d	18 03		18 27		19 03		19 28		20 03		20 28		21 09		21 29		22 04		22 28		23 04
Castleton d	18 06				19 06				20 06				21 12				22 07				23 07
Mills Hill d	18 11				19 11				20 11				21 18				22 12				23 12
Moston d	18 15				19 15				20 15				21 21				22 16				23 16
Manchester Victoria a	18 24		18 43		19 24		19 43		20 24		20 44		21 30		21 45		22 25		22 45		23 25

	NT ◇	NT ◇	NT	NT B	NT ◇
York ■ 40 d	21 21				
Selby 40 d					
Leeds 37,39 d	21 56	22 11	22 31		23 19
Bramley 37 d		22 20	22 39		23 27
New Pudsey 37 d	22 05	22 25	22 43		23 31
Bradford Interchange 37 a	22 15	22 34	22 52		23 39
d	22 17	22 38	22 54		23 42
Low Moor d			23 01		
Halifax a	22 29	22 49	23 08		23 53
d	22 29	22 50	23 08		23 54
Dewsbury 39 d					
Mirfield 39 a					
d					
Brighouse d			23 19		
London Kings Cross 15 ⊖26 a					
Huddersfield 39 a			23 37		
Sowerby Bridge d	22 37				
Mytholmroyd d	22 43				
Hebden Bridge a	22 46	23 00			00 04
d	22 46	23 01			00 05
Burnley Manchester Road 97 a	23 09				
d	23 10			23 19	
Accrington 97 a	23 18				
Blackburn 97 a	23 27				
Preston ■ 97 a	23 46				
Poulton-le-Fylde 97 a	00 06				
Blackpool North 97 a	00 13				
Todmorden d		23 08		23 35	00 12
Walsden d		23 11			00 15
Littleborough d		23 17		23 42	00 21
Smithy Bridge d				23 45	
Rochdale a		23 22		23 49	00 26
d		23 23		23 49	00 27
Castleton d				23 52	
Mills Hill d				23 57	
Moston d				00 01	
Manchester Victoria a		23 38		00 11	00 42

A From Blackburn to Southport
B From Blackburn

For connections to Liverpool Lime Street refer to Table T090

Table T042-F

Mondays to Fridays

16 December to 15 May

Leeds - Morecambe and Carlisle

Miles	Miles	Miles			NT	NT	NT	NT	NT	NT	NT	NT	NT	NT	NT	NT	NT	NT	NT	NT	NT
						◇ ⊼	◇	◇ ⊼	◇	◇ ⊼	◇	◇ ⊼	◇	◇ ⊼	◇	◇ ⊼	◇ ⊼	◇	◇ ⊼	◇	⊼
0	0	—	**Leeds ■10**	36,37 d		05 17	07 20	07 48	08 18	09 19	10 18	10 49	12 18	13 18	14 18	15 18	16 48	17 26	18 18	19 18	19 49
10¾	10¾	—	Shipley	36,37 d		05 30	07 33	08 01	08 32	09 32	10 33	11 03	12 33	13 33	14 33	15 33	17 02	17 40	18 32	19 32	20 02
13¾	13¾	—	Bingley	36 d		05 37	07 38	08 06	08 37	09 37	10 37	11 07	12 37	13 37	14 38	15 37	17 07	17 45	18 37	19 37	20 07
17	17	—	Keighley	36 d		05 44	07 43	08 11	08 42	09 42	10 43	11 13	12 43	13 43	14 43	15 43	17 13	17 52	18 42	19 43	20 12
26¼	26¼	—	**Skipton**	36 a		06 00	07 58	08 24	08 55	09 57	10 55	11 25	12 56	13 55	14 57	15 55	17 25	18 08	18 55	19 57	20 26
—	—	—	Skipton	d	05 22	06 02	07 59	08 26	08 56	09 59	10 57	11 27	12 58	13 57	14 58	15 59	17 27	18 10	18 56	20 00	20 27
30	30	—	Gargrave	a	05 27		08 05	08 31	09 02	10 04	11 02	11 32	13 03		15 04	16 04	17 32	18 15	19 02	20 05	20 33
—	—	0	Blackpool North	97 d																	
—	—	17½	Preston ■8	97 d																	
—	—	29¾	Blackburn	94,97 d																	
—	—	39½	Clitheroe	94 d																	
36	36	53	Hellifield	d	05 37	06 14	08 15	08 40	09 10	10 13	11 11	11 41	13 12	14 09	15 13	16 13	17 41	18 24	19 10	20 14	20 42
37¼	37¼	—	Long Preston	d	05 40		08 18		09 13	10 15	11 14	11 44	13 15		15 15		17 43	18 26	19 13	20 17	20 44
—	41	—	Giggleswick	d	05 48		08 27		09 21		11 22		13 23		15 23			18 34		20 25	
—	47¾	—	Clapham (Nth Yorkshire)	d	05 56		08 35		09 29		11 30		13 31		15 31			18 43		20 34	
—	51	—	Bentham	d	06 03		08 42		09 35		11 36		13 37		15 38			18 49		20 40	
—	54¾	—	Wennington	d	06 08		08 48		09 40		11 42		13 43		15 43			18 55		20 46	
—	64	—	Carnforth	82 d	06 22		09 04		09 57		12 01		14 01		15 59			19 15		21 05	
—	70	—	**Lancaster ■6**	65,82,98 a	06 31		09 13		10 06		12 10		14 09		16 08			19 24		21 14	
—	72½	—	Bare Lane	98 d					10 23		12 20		14 20		16 28			19 47			
—	74	—	**Morecambe**	98 a					10 27		12 24		14 24		16 32			19 51			
—	78¾	—	Heysham Port	⛴ a																	
41	—	—	Settle	d		06 22		08 50		10 22		11 51		14 17		16 20	17 49		19 19		20 50
47¼	—	—	Horton-in-Ribblesdale	d		06 30		08 58		10 31		11 59		14 25		16 29	17 58		19 27		20 59
52	—	—	Ribblehead	d		06 38		09 06		10 39		12 07		14 33		16 37	18 06		19 35		21a08
58	—	—	Dent	d		06 48		09 16		10 48		12 17		14 43		16 46	18 15		19 44		
61½	—	—	Garsdale	d		06 53		09 21		10 54		12 22		14 48		16 52	18 21		19 50		
71¼	—	—	Kirkby Stephen	d		07 06		09 34		11 06		12 35		15 01		17 04	18 33		20 02		
82	—	—	Appleby	d		07 18		09 48		11 19		12 48		15 14		17 17	18 46		20 15		
93	—	—	Langwathby	d		07 32		10 01		11 32		13 02		15 28		17 31	19 00		20 28		
97¼	—	—	Lazonby & Kirkoswald	d		07 38		10 07		11 38		13 08		15 33		17 36	19 05		20 34		
102¾	—	—	Armathwaite	d		07 46		10 15		11 46		13 16		15 41		17 44	19 13		20 42		
112¾	—	—	**Carlisle ■8**	65 a		08 03		10 31		12 01		13 31		16 01		18 00	19 28		20 57		

Saturdays

21 December to 16 May

		NT	NT	NT	NT	NT	NT	NT	NT	NT	NT	NT	NT	NT	NT	NT	NT	NT
			◇ ⊼	◇	◇ ⊼	◇	◇ ⊼	◇	◇ ⊼	◇	◇ ⊼	◇	◇ ⊼	◇ ⊼	◇	◇ ⊼	◇	⊼
Leeds ■10	36,37 d		06 20	07 20	07 48	08 18	09 19	10 18	10 49	12 18	13 18	14 18	15 18	16 48	17 26	18 18	19 18	19 49
Shipley	36,37 d		06 33	07 33	08 01	08 32	09 32	10 33	11 03	12 33	13 33	14 33	15 33	17 02	17 40	18 32	19 32	20 02
Bingley	36 d		06 40	07 38	08 06	08 37	09 37	10 37	11 07	12 37	13 37	14 38	15 37	17 07	17 45	18 37	19 37	20 07
Keighley	36 d		06 47	07 43	08 11	08 42	09 42	10 43	11 13	12 43	13 43	14 43	15 43	17 13	17 52	18 42	19 43	20 12
Skipton	36 a		07 03	07 58	08 24	08 55	09 57	10 55	11 25	12 56	13 55	14 57	15 55	17 25	18 07	18 55	19 57	20 26
Skipton	d	05 19	07 05	07 59	08 26	08 56	09 59	10 57	11 27	12 58	13 57	14 58	15 59	17 27	18 08	18 56	20 00	20 27
Gargrave	a	05 24		08 05	08 31	09 02	10 04	11 02	11 32	13 03		15 04	16 04	17 32	18 14	19 02	20 05	20 33
Blackpool North	97 d																	
Preston ■8	97 d																	
Blackburn	94,97 d																	
Clitheroe	94 d																	
Hellifield	d	05 34	07 18	08 15	08 40	09 10	10 13	11 11	11 41	13 12	14 09	15 13	16 13	17 41	18 22	19 10	20 14	20 42
Long Preston	d	05 37		08 18		09 13	10 15	11 14	11 44	13 15		15 15		17 43	18 25	19 13	20 17	20 44
Giggleswick	d	05 45		08 27		09 21		11 22		13 23		15 23			18 33		20 25	
Clapham (Nth Yorkshire)	d	05 54		08 35		09 29		11 30		13 31		15 31			18 41		20 34	
Bentham	d	06 01		08 42		09 35		11 36		13 37		15 38			18 48		20 40	
Wennington	d	06 06		08 48		09 40		11 42		13 43		15 43			18 53		20 46	
Carnforth	82 d	06 21		09 04		09 57		12 01		14 01		15 59			19 10		21 09	
Lancaster ■6	65,82,98 a	06 32		09 13		10 06		12 10		14 09		16 08			19 19		21 17	
Bare Lane	98 d					10 23		12 20		14 20		16 28			19 41			
Morecambe	98 a					10 27		12 24		14 24		16 32			19 45			
Heysham Port	⛴ a																	
Settle	d		07 26		08 50		10 22		11 51		14 17		16 20	17 49		19 19		20 50
Horton-in-Ribblesdale	d		07 34		08 58		10 31		11 59		14 25		16 29	17 58		19 27		20 59
Ribblehead	d		07 42		09 06		10 39		12 07		14 33		16 37	18 06		19 35		21a08
Dent	d		07 52		09 16		10 48		12 17		14 43		16 46	18 15		19 44		
Garsdale	d		07 57		09 21		10 54		12 22		14 48		16 52	18 21		19 50		
Kirkby Stephen	d		08 10		09 34		11 06		12 35		15 01		17 04	18 33		20 02		
Appleby	d		08 22		09 48		11 19		12 48		15 14		17 17	18 46		20 15		
Langwathby	d		08 36		10 01		11 32		13 02		15 28		17 31	19 00		20 28		
Lazonby & Kirkoswald	d		08 42		10 07		11 38		13 08		15 33		17 36	19 05		20 34		
Armathwaite	d		08 50		10 15		11 46		13 16		15 41		17 44	19 13		20 42		
Carlisle ■8	65 a		09 05		10 30		12 01		13 31		16 01		18 00	19 28		20 57		

Table T042-F

Sundays

15 December to 10 May

Leeds - Morecambe and Carlisle

		NT	NT	NT	NT	NT	NT	NT	NT	NT	NT	NT	NT	NT
		◇		◇	◇	◇ A	◇	◇	◇	◇		◇	◇	◇
Leeds ■10	36,37 d	08 32		08 59	10 32	11 16	12 28	13 32	14 24	15 32		16 23	17 32	18 52
Shipley	36,37 d	08 45		09 13	10 45	11 29	12 41	13 45	14 37	15 45		16 37	17 45	19 05
Bingley	36 d	08 52		09 20	10 50	11 34	12 45	13 49	14 42	15 49		16 41	17 49	19 09
Keighley	36 d	08 59		09 27	10 55	11 39	12 51	13 55	14 47	15 55		16 47	17 55	19 16
Skipton	36 a	09 15		09 43	11 08	11 52	13 03	14 07	15 02	16 08		17 01	18 08	19 33
Skipton	d	09 17		09 45	11 10	11 52	13 05	14 09	15 03	16 09		17 01	18 09	19 33
Gargrave	a	09 22		09 50	11 15		13 11	14 14	15 09	16 15			18 15	
Blackpool North	97 d		08 12											
Preston ■8	97 d		08 39								15 29			
Blackburn	94,97 d		09 00								15 51			
Clitheroe	94 d		09 24								16 12			
Hellifield	d	09 31	09a47	09 59	11 24	12 04	13 19	14 23	15 17	16 23	16a35	17 13	18 23	19 45
Long Preston	d	09 34			11 26		13 22	14 26	15 20	16 26			18 26	
Giggleswick	d	09 41			11 34			14 34		16 34			18 34	
Clapham (Nth Yorkshire)	d	09 49			11 42			14 42		16 42			18 42	
Bentham	d	09 56			11 48			14 48		16 48			18 48	
Wennington	d	10 01			11 53			14 53		16 53			18 53	
Carnforth	82 d	10 16			12 10			15 10		17 10			19 08	
Lancaster ■6	65,82,98 a	10 27			12 19			15 21		17 21			19 21	
Bare Lane	98 d	10 35			12 35			15 28		17 30			19 34	
Morecambe	98 a	10 39			12 39			15 33		17 34			19 38	
Heysham Port	⛴ a				12 58									
Settle	d			10 07		12 13	13 28		15 26			17 21		19 53
Horton-in-Ribblesdale	d			10 16			13 37		15 35			17 30		20 02
Ribblehead	d			10 24			13 45		15 43			17 38		20 10
Dent	d			10 34			13 55		15 53			17 48		20 20
Garsdale	d			10 40			14 01		15 59			17 53		20 25
Kirkby Stephen	d			10 53		12 51	14 14		16 12			18 06		20 38
Appleby	d			11 06		13 05	14 26		16 24			18 19		20 51
Langwathby	d			11 20			14 40		16 38			18 33		21 05
Lazonby & Kirkoswald	d			11 26			14 46		16 44			18 39		21 11
Armathwaite	d			11 34			14 54		16 52			18 47		21 19
Carlisle ■8	65 a			11 52		13 44	15 11		17 08			19 03		21 39

A From Nottingham

SUNDAY RETURN TIMES

Table T042-R

Sundays

15 December to 10 May

Carlisle and Morecambe - Leeds

		NT	NT	NT	NT	NT	NT	NT	NT	NT	NT	NT	NT	NT
			◇	◇	◇	◇	◇	◇ A		◇	◇	◇	◇	◇
Carlisle ■8	65 d		09 25		12 25			15 20		16 07		17 25	19 11	
Armathwaite	d		09 39		12 39			15 34				17 39	19 25	
Lazonby & Kirkoswald	d		09 46		12 46			15 41				17 46	19 32	
Langwathby	d		09 53		12 53			15 48				17 53	19 39	
Appleby	d		10 07		13 07			16 02		16 44		18 08	19 53	
Kirkby Stephen	d		10 21		13 21			16 15		16 57		18 22	20 07	
Garsdale	d		10 34		13 34			16 28				18 35	20 20	
Dent	d		10 40		13 40			16 33				18 41	20 26	
Ribblehead	d		10 49		13 49			16 43				18 50	20 35	
Horton-in-Ribblesdale	d		10 56		13 56			16 50				18 57	20 42	
Settle	d		11 04		14 04			16 58		17 34		19 06	20 51	
Heysham Port	⛴ d					13 05								
Morecambe	98 d			10 49		13 23	15 40				17 38			20 04
Bare Lane	98 d			10 53		13 27	15 44				17 42			20 08
Lancaster ■6	65,82,98 d			11 02		13 44	15 52				17 51			20 18
Carnforth	82 d			11 13		13 54	16 02				18 01			20 29
Wennington	d			11 27		14 08	16 15				18 14			20 43
Bentham	d			11 33		14 14	16 21				18 20			20 48
Clapham (Nth Yorkshire)	d			11 39		14 20	16 27				18 26			20 55
Giggleswick	d			11 48		14 29	16 36				18 35			21 03
Long Preston	d		11 10	11 57	14 10	14 37	16 45	17 04			18 44		20 56	21 12
Hellifield	d	10 30	11 13	12 00	14 13	14 40	16 48	17 07	17 15	17 42	18 47	19 13	20 59	21 15
Clitheroe	94 a	10 53							17 36					
Blackburn	94,97 a	11 25							18 00					
Preston ■8	97 a	11 57							18 21					
Blackpool North	97 a								18 47					
Gargrave	d		11 21	12 08	14 21	14 48	16 56				18 55		21 07	21 23
Skipton	a		11 30	12 17	14 30	14 56	17 04	17 20		17 57	19 03	19 28	21 16	21 32
Skipton	36 d		11 30	12 22	14 30	14 58	17 06	17 23		17 58	19 05	19 30	21 17	21 33
Keighley	36 d		11 40	12 32	14 40	15 08	17 16	17 33		18 08	19 15	19 40	21 27	21 43
Bingley	36 d		11 44	12 38	14 44	15 12	17 21	17 40		18 13	19 20	19 45	21 32	21 48
Shipley	36,37 d		11 49	12 48	14 49	15 17	17 26	17 47		18 18	19 25	19 50	21 38	21 54
Leeds ■10	36,37 a		12 06	13 07	15 09	15 37	17 45	18 05		18 32	19 45	20 08	21 55	22 10

A To Nottingham

Table T042-R

Mondays to Fridays

16 December to 15 May

Carlisle and Morecambe - Leeds

Miles	Miles	Miles				NT ◊ 🛒	NT ◊	NT ◊ 🛒	NT ◊	NT ◊	NT ◊ 🛒	NT ◊	NT	NT ◊ 🛒	NT ◊	NT ◊ 🛒	NT ◊ 🛒	NT ◊	NT ◊ 🛒	NT ◊	NT ◊ 🛒	NT 🛒	NT	NT
0	—	—	**Carlisle** ■8	65	d	05 51		08 24			10 49			13 40		14 50	16 18		18 24		20 13			
10	—	—	Armathwaite		d	06 05		08 38			11 04					15 04	16 32		18 38		20 27			
15½	—	—	Lazonby & Kirkoswald		d	06 12		08 45			11 12					15 11	16 39		18 45		20 34			
19¾	—	—	Langwathby		d	06 19		08 52			11 18					15 18	16 46		18 52		20 41			
30¾	—	—	Appleby		d	06 33		09 06			11 33			14 17		15 32	17 00		19 06		20 55			
41½	—	—	Kirkby Stephen		d	06 46		09 20			11 46			14 31		15 46	17 14		19 20		21 08			
51¼	—	—	Garsdale		d	07 00		09 33			12 05					15 59	17 27		19 33		21 21			
54¾	—	—	Dent		d	07 05		09 38			12 10					16 04	17 32		19 38					
60¾	—	—	Ribblehead		d	07 14		09 48			12 19					16 14	17 42		19 48			21 45		
65½	—	—	Horton-in-Ribblesdale		d	07 21		09 54			12 26					16 20	17 48		19 54			21 51		
71¾	—	—	Settle		d	07 29		10 02			12 34			15 07		16 28	17 56		20 02		21 49	21 59		
—	0	—	Heysham Port	⛴	d								13 20											
—	4¼	—	**Morecambe**	98	d					10 33		12 32	13 39		14 32			17 31		20 07				22 52
—	5¾	—	Bare Lane	98	d					10 37		12 36	13 43		14 37			17 35		20 11				22 56
—	8¼	—	**Lancaster** ■6	65,82,98	d		06 48		09 41	10 46		12 45	13a48		14 48			17 45		20 30			21 30	23 03
—	14¼	—	Carnforth	82	d		06 59		09 50	10 55		12 55			14 57			17 55		20 40			21 43	
—	24	—	Wennington		d		07 13		10 04	11 09		13 08			15 11			18 09		20 54			21 57	
—	27¼	—	Bentham		d		07 19		10 10	11 15		13 14			15 17			18 15		21 00			22 02	
—	30½	—	Clapham (Nth Yorkshire)		d		07 26		10 16	11 21		13 20			15 23			18 21		21 06			22 09	
—	37¼	—	Giggleswick		d		07 35		10 27	11 32		13 31			15 34			18 32		21 17			22 19	
75½	41	—	Long Preston		d	07 34	07 43		10 33	11 38		13 37			15 40	16 34	18 02	18 39	20 08	21 23		22 05	22 26	
76¾	42¼	0	Hellifield		d	07 37	07 46	10 10	10 37	11 41	12 41	13 40		15 14	15 43	16 37	18 05	18 42	20 11	21 26		22 08	22 28	
—	—	13½	Clitheroe	94	a																			
—	—	23¼	Blackburn	94,97	a																			
—	—	35½	Preston ■8	97	a																			23 24
—	—	53	Blackpool North	97	a																			
82¾	48¼	—	Gargrave		d	07 45	07 55		10 45	11 50		13 49		15 22	15 51	16 45	18 13	18 50	20 19	21 34		22 16	22 37	
86½	52	—	Skipton		a	07 53	08 03	10 24	10 53	11 57	12 55	13 56		15 28	15 58	16 54	18 21	18 58	20 27	21 41	22 10	22 25	22 44	
—	—	—	**Skipton**	36	d	07 55	08 05	10 25	10 59	11 59	12 56	13 59		15 29	16 00	16 59	18 29	18 59	20 29	21 43	22 11	22 26		
95¾	61¼	—	Keighley	36	d	08 05	08 17	10 38	11 09	12 09	13 09	14 09		15 41	16 10	17 09	18 39	19 09	20 39	21 55	22 21	22 41		
99	67½	—	Bingley	36	d	08 10	08 22	10 45	11 14	12 14	13 14	14 14		15 46	16 15	17 14	18 44	19 14	20 44	22 00	22 26	22 47		
102	67½	—	Shipley	36,37	d	08 15	08 27	10 50	11 19	12 19	13 20	14 20		15 51	16 20	17 20	18 50	19 20	20 51	22 06	22 31	22 55		
112¾	78¼	—	**Leeds** ■10	36,37	a	08 33	08 41	11 08	11 38	12 38	13 38	14 37		16 05	16 39	17 39	19 08	19 38	21 06	22 22	22 48	23 12		

Saturdays

21 December to 16 May

			NT	NT ◊	NT ◊ 🛒	NT ◊	NT ◊ 🛒	NT ◊	NT ◊ 🛒	NT ◊	NT	NT ◊ 🛒	NT ◊	NT ◊ 🛒	NT ◊ 🛒	NT ◊	NT ◊ 🛒	NT ◊	NT ◊ 🛒	NT 🛒	NT
Carlisle ■8	65	d			07 54		09 27		10 49			13 40		14 50	16 18		18 24		20 15		
Armathwaite		d			08 08		09 41		11 04					15 04	16 32		18 38		20 29		
Lazonby & Kirkoswald		d			08 15		09 48		11 12					15 11	16 39		18 45		20 36		
Langwathby		d			08 21		09 55		11 18					15 18	16 46		18 52		20 43		
Appleby		d			08 36		10 09		11 33			14 16		15 32	17 00		19 06		20 57		
Kirkby Stephen		d			08 49		10 23		11 46			14 29		15 46	17 14		19 20		21 11		
Garsdale		d			09 03		10 36		12 05					15 59	17 27		19 33		21 24		
Dent		d			09 08		10 41		12 10					16 04	17 32		19 38				
Ribblehead		d	07 14		09 17		10 51		12 19					16 14	17 42		19 48			21 45	
Horton-in-Ribblesdale		d	07 20		09 24		10 57		12 26					16 20	17 48		19 54			21 53	
Settle		d	07 28		09 32		11 05		12 34			15 06		16 28	17 56		20 02		21 48	22 01	
Heysham Port	⛴	d									13 20										
Morecambe	98	d						10 33		12 32	13 39		14 32			17 31		20 07			
Bare Lane	98	d						10 37		12 36	13 43		14 37			17 35		20 11			
Lancaster ■6	65,82,98	d		06 48		09 41		10 46		12 45	13a48		14 47			17 45		20 30			21 30
Carnforth	82	d		06 59		09 50		10 55		12 55			14 56			17 55		20 40			21 43
Wennington		d		07 13		10 04		11 09		13 08			15 10			18 09		20 54			21 57
Bentham		d		07 19		10 10		11 15		13 14			15 16			18 15		21 00			22 02
Clapham (Nth Yorkshire)		d		07 26		10 16		11 21		13 20			15 22			18 21		21 06			22 09
Giggleswick		d		07 35		10 27		11 32		13 31			15 33			18 32		21 17			22 19
Long Preston		d	07 34	07 43		10 33		11 38		13 37			15 39	16 34	18 02	18 39	20 08	21 23		22 07	22 26
Hellifield		d	07 37	07 46	09 39	10 37	11 13	11 41	12 41	13 40		15 14	15 42	16 37	18 05	18 42	20 11	21 26		22 10	22 28
Clitheroe	94	a																			
Blackburn	94,97	a																			
Preston ■8	97	a																			
Blackpool North	97	a																			
Gargrave		d	07 45	07 55		10 45		11 50		13 49		15 22	15 50	16 45	18 13	18 50	20 19	21 34		22 18	22 37
Skipton		a	07 53	08 03	09 54	10 53	11 27	11 57	12 55	13 56		15 27	15 57	16 54	18 21	18 58	20 27	21 41	22 09	22 26	22 44
Skipton	36	d	07 55	08 05	09 56	10 59	11 28	11 59	12 56	13 59		15 29	15 59	16 59	18 29	18 59	20 29	21 43	22 11	22 26	
Keighley	36	d	08 08	08 17	10 09	11 09	11 38	12 09	13 09	14 09		15 41	16 09	17 09	18 39	19 09	20 39	21 55	22 21	22 41	
Bingley	36	d	08 13	08 22	10 13	11 14	11 45	12 14	13 14	14 14		15 46	16 14	17 14	18 44	19 14	20 44	22 00	22 26	22 47	
Shipley	36,37	d	08 19	08 27	10 19	11 19	11 50	12 19	13 20	14 20		15 51	16 20	17 20	18 50	19 20	20 51	22 06	22 31	22 54	
Leeds ■10	36,37	a	08 35	08 41	10 37	11 38	12 04	12 38	13 38	14 37		16 05	16 39	17 39	19 08	19 38	21 09	22 22	22 48	23 11	

See opposite page for Sunday times.

Table T043-F

Mondays to Fridays

16 December to 15 May

Hull - Beverley, Bridlington and Scarborough

Miles				NT	NT	NT	NT	NT	NT ■ A	NT	NT	NT ◊ A	NT	NT ◊ A	NT	NT ◊ A	NT ◊ B	NT ◊ A	NT ◊ B	NT ◊ A	NT ◊ B	NT ◊ A	NT ◊ B	NT ◊ A
0	**Hull**		d	05 31	05 57	06 13	06 39	06 45	07 22	07 47	08 01	08 21	09 00	09 21	10 00	10 21	11 00	11 21	12 00	12 21	13 00	13 21	14 00	14 21
4	Cottingham		d		06 04	06 20	06 46	06 52	07 29	07 54	08 09	08 28	09 08	09 28	10 08	10 28	11 08	11 28	12 08	12 29	13 08	13 28	14 08	14 29
8¼	**Beverley**		d		06 11	06 28	06 53	06a58	07 36	08 00	08 16	08 35	09 14	09 35	10 15	10 35	11 14	11 35	12 14	12 35	13 14	13 35	14 14	14 35
11¼	Arram		d			06 32					08 21								12 19				14 19	
16¼	Hutton Cranswick		d		06 20	06 39	07 02		07 45	08 09	08 28		09 23		10 24		11 23		12 25		13 23		14 25	
19½	Driffield		d		06 25	06 44	07 07		07 50	08 15	08 33	08 47	09 29	09 47	10 29	10 47	11 29	11 47	12 31	12 47	13 29	13 47	14 31	14 47
21½	Nafferton		d		06 29	06 48	07 11		07 54	08 18	08 38		09 33		10 33		11 33		12 35		13 33		14 35	
31	**Bridlington**		a	06 08	06 43	07 00	07 25		08 07	08 28	08 52	09 02	09 46	10 02	10 47	11 02	11 45	12 02	12 47	13 03	13 45	14 02	14 47	15 03
—			d	06 09			07 31		08 10			09 03		10 03		11 03		12 03		13 03		14 03		15 03
34½	Bempton		d				07 38		08 16			09 09		10 09		11 09		12 09		13 10		14 09		15 10
41¾	Hunmanby		d	06 24			07 48		08 26			09 20		10 20		11 20		12 20		13 20		14 20		15 20
44½	Filey		d	06 29			07 53		08 31			09 24		10 24		11 24		12 24		13 25		14 24		15 25
51	Seamer	39	d	06 38			08 05		08 42			09 34		10 34		11 34		12 34		13 34		14 34		15 34
53¾	**Scarborough**	39	a	06 46			08 12		08 48			09 40		10 40		11 40		12 40		13 40		14 40		15 40

			NT ◊ B	NT ◊ A	NT ◊ B	NT ◊ A	NT ◊ B	NT ◊ A	NT	NT ◊ B	NT ◊ A	HT ◊■1 C ⊠	NT ◊ B	NT ◊ A	NT ◊ B	NT ◊ A	NT ◊ B	HT ◊■1 C ⊠	NT ◊ A	NT
Hull		d	15 00	15 21	16 00	16 21	17 02	17 21	17 33	18 02	18 22	18 28	19 01	19 21	20 00	20 21	21 00	21 33	22 17	23 16
Cottingham		d	15 08	15 28	16 08	16 28	17 10	17 28	17 40	18 10	18 29	18 35	19 09	19 28	20 08	20 29	21 08	21 40	22 24	23 23
Beverley		d	15 14	15 35	16 14	16 35	17 16	17 35	17 47	18 17	18 36	18a41	19 16	19 35	20 14	20 36	21 14	21a46	22 31	23a29
Arram		d					17 21								20 19					
Hutton Cranswick		d	15 23		16 23		17 27		17 56	18 26			19 25		20 25		21 23		22 40	
Driffield		d	15 29	15 47	16 29	16 47	17 33	17 47	18 01	18 31	18 48		19 31	19 47	20 31	20 48	21 29		22 45	
Nafferton		d	15 33		16 33		17 37		18 05	18 35			19 35		20 35		21 33		22 49	
Bridlington		a	15 45	16 02	16 45	17 02	17 49	18 02	18 18	18 48	19 03		19 48	20 02	20 47	21 03	21 45		23 02	
		d		16 03		17 03		18 03			19 04			20 03						
Bempton		d		16 09		17 09		18 09			19 10			20 09						
Hunmanby		d		16 20		17 20		18 20			19 21			20 20						
Filey		d		16 24		17 24		18 24			19 25			20 24						
Seamer	39	d		16 34		17 34		18 34			19 35			20 34						
Scarborough	39	a		16 39		17 40		18 40			19 40			20 40						

Saturdays

21 December to 16 May

			NT	NT	NT	NT	NT	NT ■ A	NT	NT	NT ◊ A	NT	NT ◊ A	NT	NT ◊ A	NT ◊ B	NT ◊ A	NT ◊ B	NT ◊ A	NT ◊ B	NT ◊ A	NT ◊ B	NT ◊ A	NT ◊ B
Hull		d	05 31	05 57	06 13	06 39	06 45	07 22	07 47	08 01	08 21	09 00	09 21	10 00	10 21	11 00	11 21	12 00	12 21	13 00	13 21	14 00	14 21	15 00
Cottingham		d		06 04	06 20	06 46	06 52	07 29	07 54	08 09	08 28	09 08	09 28	10 08	10 28	11 08	11 28	12 08	12 29	13 08	13 28	14 08	14 29	15 08
Beverley		d		06 11	06 28	06 53	06a58	07 36	08 00	08 16	08 35	09 14	09 35	10 15	10 35	11 14	11 35	12 14	12 35	13 14	13 35	14 14	14 35	15 14
Arram		d			06 32					08 21								12 19				14 19		
Hutton Cranswick		d		06 20	06 39	07 02		07 45	08 09	08 28		09 23		10 24		11 23		12 25		13 23		14 25		15 23
Driffield		d		06 25	06 44	07 07		07 50	08 15	08 33	08 47	09 29	09 47	10 29	10 47	11 29	11 47	12 31	12 47	13 29	13 47	14 31	14 47	15 29
Nafferton		d		06 29	06 48	07 11		07 54	08 18	08 38		09 33		10 33		11 33		12 35		13 33		14 35		15 33
Bridlington		a	06 08	06 43	07 00	07 25		08 07	08 28	08 52	09 02	09 46	10 02	10 47	11 02	11 45	12 02	12 47	13 03	13 45	14 02	14 47	15 03	15 45
		d	06 09			07 31		08 10			09 03		10 03		11 03		12 03		13 03		14 03		15 03	
Bempton		d				07 38		08 16			09 09		10 09		11 09		12 09		13 10		14 09		15 10	
Hunmanby		d	06 24			07 48		08 26			09 20		10 20		11 20		12 20		13 20		14 20		15 20	
Filey		d	06 29			07 53		08 31			09 24		10 24		11 24		12 24		13 25		14 24		15 25	
Seamer	39	d	06 38			08 05		08 42			09 34		10 34		11 34		12 34		13 34		14 34		15 34	
Scarborough	39	a	06 46			08 12		08 48			09 40		10 40		11 40		12 40		13 40		14 40		15 40	

			NT ◊ A	NT ◊ B	NT ◊ A	NT ◊ B	NT ◊ A	NT	NT ◊ B	NT ◊ A	NT ◊ B	NT ◊ A	NT ◊ B	NT ◊ A	HT ◊■1 C ⊠	NT ◊ B	NT ◊ A	NT
Hull		d	15 21	16 00	16 21	17 02	17 21	17 33	18 02	18 22	19 01	19 21	20 00	20 21	20 28	21 00	22 17	23 16
Cottingham		d	15 28	16 08	16 28	17 10	17 28	17 40	18 10	18 29	19 09	19 28	20 08	20 29	20 37	21 08	22 24	23 23
Beverley		d	15 35	16 14	16 35	17 16	17 35	17 47	18 17	18 36	19 16	19 35	20 14	20 36	20a44	21 14	22 31	23a29
Arram		d				17 21							20 19					
Hutton Cranswick		d		16 23		17 27		17 56	18 26		19 25		20 25			21 23	22 40	
Driffield		d	15 47	16 29	16 47	17 33	17 47	18 01	18 31	18 48	19 31	19 47	20 31	20 48		21 29	22 45	
Nafferton		d		16 33		17 37		18 05	18 35		19 35		20 35			21 33	22 49	
Bridlington		a	16 02	16 45	17 02	17 49	18 02	18 18	18 48	19 03	19 48	20 02	20 47	21 03		21 45	23 02	
		d	16 03		17 03		18 03			19 04		20 03						
Bempton		d	16 09		17 09		18 09			19 10		20 09						
Hunmanby		d	16 20		17 20		18 20			19 21		20 20						
Filey		d	16 24		17 24		18 24			19 25		20 24						
Seamer	39	d	16 34		17 34		18 34			19 35		20 34						
Scarborough	39	a	16 39		17 40		18 40			19 40		20 40						

A From Sheffield   B From York   C From London Kings Cross

Table T043-F

Hull - Beverley, Bridlington and Scarborough

Sundays

15 December to 10 May

		NT	NT ◇ A	NT ◇ A	NT ◇ A	NT ◇ A	NT ◇ A	NT ◇ A	NT ◇ A	NT ◇ A	NT	NT ◇ A	NT ◇ A	NT ◇ A	HT ◇1 B ⊠	NT ◇ A
Hull	d	08 35	10 03	10 48	11 57	13 07	14 00	15 00	16 00	16 59	17 26	17 59	19 07	19 55	20 26	20 54
Cottingham	d	08 43	10 11	10 56	12 05	13 15	14 08	15 08	16 08	17 07	17 34	18 07	19 15	20 03	20 33	21 02
Beverley	d	08 49	10 19	11 02	12 13	13 21	14 16	15 16	16 16	17 16	17 40	18 15	19 21	20 09	20a39	21 09
Arram	d	08 54									17 45					
Hutton Cranswick	d	09 00	10 28	11 12	12 23	13 30	14 26	15 26	16 26	17 26	17 51	18 25	19 30	20 18		21 18
Driffield	d	09 06	10 34	11 17	12 28	13 36	14 31	15 31	16 31	17 31	17 57	18 30	19 36	20 24		21 23
Nafferton	d	09 10	10 38	11 22	12 33	13 40	14 36	15 36	16 36	17 36	18 01	18 35	19 40	20 28		21 27
Bridlington	a	09 24	10 51	11 34	12 46	13 53	14 49	15 49	16 49	17 49	18 17	18 48	19 53	20 42		21 40
	d	09 24	10 53	11 34	12 53	13 53	14 53	15 53	16 53	17 53		18 52	19 53			
Bempton	d	09 30	11 00	11 40	13 00	14 00	15 00	16 00	17 00	18 00		18 59	20 00			
Hunmanby	d	09 41	11 10	11 51	13 10	14 10	15 10	16 10	17 10	18 10		19 09	20 10			
Filey	d	09 46	11 17	11 56	13 17	14 17	15 17	16 17	17 17	18 17		19 16	20 17			
Seamer 39	d	09 58	11 27	12 07	13 27	14 27	15 27	16 27	17 27	18 27		19 26	20 27			
Scarborough 39	a	10 05	11 34	12 15	13 34	14 34	15 34	16 34	17 34	18 34		19 33	20 34			

A From Sheffield

B From London Kings Cross

SUNDAY RETURN TIMES

NRT DECEMBER 19 EDITION

Table T043-R

Scarborough, Bridlington and Beverley - Hull

Sundays

15 December to 10 May

		NT ◇ A	HT ◇1 B ⊠	NT	NT	NT ◇ A		NT ◇ A	NT	NT ◇ A	NT ◇ A	NT ◇ A	NT	NT	NT
Scarborough 39	d			10 13	10 54	12 01	and hourly until	17 01		18 01	19 01	20 01			21 26
Seamer 39	d			10 18	10 59	12 06		17 06		18 06	19 06	20 06			21 31
Filey	d			10 28	11 09	12 16		17 16		18 16	19 16	20 16			21 41
Hunmanby	d			10 33	11 14	12 21		17 21		18 21	19 21	20 21			21 46
Bempton	d			10 43	11 24	12 31		17 31		18 31	19 31	20 31			21 55
Bridlington	a			10 51	11 32	12 39		17 39		18 39	19 39	20 39			22 04
	d	09 41		10 52	11 34	12 40		17 40	18 23	18 40	19 40	20 40	21 27	21 50	22 05
Nafferton	d	09 52		11 04	11 45	12 51		17 51	18 34	18 51	19 51	20 51	21 38		22 16
Driffield	d	09 56		11 08	11 50	12 55		17 55	18 38	18 55	19 55	20 55	21 43		22 20
Hutton Cranswick	d	10 01		11 14	11 55	13 00		18 00	18 43	19 00	20 00	21 00	21 48		22 25
Arram	d	10 08							18 50						
Beverley	d	10 13	10 52	11 23	12 05	13 10		18 10	18 55	19 10	20 10	21 10	21 58		22 34
Cottingham	d	10 19	10 58	11 30	12 11	13 16		18 16	19 01	19 16	20 16	21 16	22 04		22 41
Hull	a	10 26	11 05	11 39	12 20	13 25		18 25	19 12	19 25	20 25	21 25	22 13	22 25	22 51

A To Sheffield

B To London Kings Cross

Table T043-R

Scarborough, Bridlington and Beverley - Hull

Mondays to Fridays

16 December to 15 May

Miles			HT ◇1 A ⊠	NT	NT ◇ B	NT	NT	HT ◇1 A ⊠	NT ◇ B	NT ◇ C	NT ◇ B	NT C	NT ◇ B	NT ◇ C	NT ◇ B	NT ◇ C	NT ◇ B	NT ◇ C	NT ◇ B	NT ◇ B	NT ◇ C	NT ◇ B	NT ◇ C
0	**Scarborough** 39	d							06 53			08 15	09 00		10 00		11 00		12 00	13 00		14 00	
2¾	Seamer 39	d							06 58			08 20	09 05		10 05		11 05		12 05	13 05		14 05	
9¼	Filey	d							07 08			08 30	09 15		10 15		11 15		12 15	13 15		14 15	
12	Hunmanby	d							07 13			08 35	09 20		10 20		11 20		12 20	13 20		14 20	
19¾	Bempton	d							07 22			08 44	09 30		10 30		11 30		12 30	13 30		14 30	
22¾	**Bridlington**	a							07 30			08 51	09 38		10 38		11 38		12 38	13 38		14 38	
—		d				06 45	07 03		07 34	07 59	08 35	08 55	09 39	10 00	10 39	11 00	11 39	12 00	12 39	13 39	14 00	14 39	15 00
32¼	Nafferton	d				06 56	07 14		07 45	08 10	08 46	09 06		10 11		11 11		12 11			14 11		15 11
34¾	Driffield	d				07 00	07 18		07 50	08 14	08 50	09 10	09 52	10 15	10 52	11 15	11 52	12 15	12 52	13 52	14 15	14 52	15 15
37½	Hutton Cranswick	d				07 05	07 23		07 55	08 19	08 55	09 15		10 20		11 20		12 20			14 20		15 20
42½	Arram	d					07 30			08 26													
45½	**Beverley**	d	06 04	06 23	07 03	07 15	07 35	07 53	08 05	08 31	09 05	09 25	10 05	10 30	11 05	11 30	12 05	12 30	13 05	14 05	14 30	15 05	15 30
49¾	Cottingham	d	06 10	06 29	07 09	07 21	07 41	07 59	08 11	08 37	09 11	09 31	10 11	10 36	11 11	11 36	12 11	12 36	13 11	14 11	14 36	15 11	15 36
53¾	**Hull**	a	06 18	06 38	07 16	07 32	07 53	08 06	08 20	08 46	09 20	09 40	10 20	10 45	11 20	11 45	12 21	12 45	13 20	14 21	14 45	15 20	15 45

		NT ◇ B	NT ◇ C	NT ◇ B	NT ◇ C	NT ◇ B	NT ◇ C	NT	NT ◇ B	NT ◇ C	NT ◇ B	NT ◇ C	NT ◇ B	NT ◇ C	NT	NT	NT	NT
Scarborough 39	d	15 00		16 00		17 00			18 00		19 00		20 00				21 14	
Seamer 39	d	15 05		16 05		17 05			18 05		19 05		20 05				21 20	
Filey	d	15 15		16 15		17 15			18 15		19 15		20 15				21 31	
Hunmanby	d	15 20		16 20		17 20			18 20		19 20		20 21				21 36	
Bempton	d	15 30		16 30		17 30			18 30		19 30		20 31				21 46	
Bridlington	a	15 38		16 38		17 38			18 38		19 38		20 39				21 53	
	d	15 39	16 00	16 39	17 00	17 39	18 00	18 24	18 39	19 00	19 39	19 56	20 40	21 00	21 37	21 58	22 33	23 06
Nafferton	d		16 11		17 11		18 11			19 11		20 07		21 11	21 48		22 44	23 17
Driffield	d	15 52	16 15	16 52	17 15	17 52	18 15	18 37	18 52	19 15	19 53	20 12	20 53	21 15	21 53	22 11	22 49	23 21
Hutton Cranswick	d		16 20		17 20		18 20			19 20		20 17		21 20	21 58	22 16	22 54	23 26
Arram	d				17 27													
Beverley	d	16 05	16 30	17 05	17 32	18 05	18 30	18 52	19 05	19 30	20 05	20 29	21 06	21 30	22 08	22 25	23 04	23 36
Cottingham	d	16 11	16 36	17 11	17 38	18 11	18 36	18 58	19 11	19 36	20 12	20 35	21 12	21 36	22 14	22 31	23 10	23 42
Hull	a	16 20	16 45	17 20	17 47	18 20	18 45	19 07	19 20	19 45	20 21	20 46	21 20	21 45	22 23	22 41	23 20	23 51

Saturdays

21 December to 16 May

		HT ◇1 A ⊠	NT	NT ◇ B	NT	NT	NT ◇ B	NT ◇ C	NT ◇ B	NT C	NT ◇ B	NT ◇ C	NT ◇ B	NT ◇ C	NT ◇ B	NT ◇ C	NT ◇ B	NT ◇ B	NT ◇ C	NT ◇ B	NT ◇ C	NT ◇ B	NT ◇ C
Scarborough 39	d						06 53			08 15	09 00		10 00		11 00		12 00	13 00		14 00		15 00	
Seamer 39	d						06 58			08 20	09 05		10 05		11 05		12 05	13 05		14 05		15 05	
Filey	d						07 08			08 30	09 15		10 15		11 15		12 15	13 15		14 15		15 15	
Hunmanby	d						07 13			08 35	09 20		10 20		11 20		12 20	13 20		14 20		15 20	
Bempton	d						07 22			08 44	09 30		10 30		11 30		12 30	13 30		14 30		15 30	
Bridlington	a						07 30			08 51	09 38		10 38		11 38		12 38	13 38		14 38		15 38	
	d				06 45	07 03	07 34	07 59	08 35	08 55	09 39	10 00	10 39	10 58	11 39	12 00	12 39	13 39	14 00	14 39	15 00	15 39	16 00
Nafferton	d				06 56	07 14	07 45	08 10	08 46	09 06		10 11		11 09		12 11			14 11		15 11		16 11
Driffield	d				07 00	07 18	07 50	08 14	08 50	09 10	09 52	10 15	10 52	11 13	11 52	12 15	12 52	13 52	14 15	14 52	15 15	15 52	16 15
Hutton Cranswick	d				07 05	07 23	07 55	08 19	08 55	09 15		10 20		11 18		12 20			14 20		15 20		16 20
Arram	d					07 30		08 26						11 25									
Beverley	d	05 57	06 23	07 03	07 15	07 35	08 05	08 31	09 05	09 25	10 05	10 30	11 05	11 30	12 05	12 30	13 05	14 05	14 30	15 05	15 30	16 05	16 30
Cottingham	d	06 03	06 29	07 09	07 21	07 41	08 11	08 37	09 11	09 31	10 11	10 36	11 11	11 36	12 11	12 36	13 11	14 11	14 36	15 11	15 36	16 11	16 36
Hull	a	06 12	06 38	07 16	07 32	07 53	08 20	08 46	09 20	09 40	10 20	10 45	11 20	11 45	12 21	12 45	13 20	14 21	14 45	15 20	15 45	16 20	16 45

		NT ◇ B	NT ◇ C	NT ◇ B	NT ◇ C	NT	NT ◇ B	NT ◇ C	NT ◇ B	NT ◇ C	NT ◇ B	NT ◇ C	NT	NT	NT	NT
Scarborough 39	d	16 00		17 00			18 00		19 00		20 00			21 14		
Seamer 39	d	16 05		17 05			18 05		19 05		20 05			21 20		
Filey	d	16 15		17 15			18 15		19 15		20 15			21 31		
Hunmanby	d	16 20		17 20			18 20		19 20		20 21			21 36		
Bempton	d	16 30		17 30			18 30		19 30		20 31			21 46		
Bridlington	a	16 38		17 38			18 38		19 38		20 39			21 53		
	d	16 39	17 00	17 39	18 00	18 24	18 39	19 00	19 39	19 56	20 40	21 00	21 37	21 58	22 33	23 06
Nafferton	d		17 11		18 11			19 11		20 07		21 11	21 48		22 44	23 17
Driffield	d	16 52	17 15	17 52	18 15	18 37	18 52	19 15	19 53	20 12	20 53	21 15	21 53	22 11	22 49	23 21
Hutton Cranswick	d		17 20		18 20			19 20		20 17		21 20	21 58	22 16	22 54	23 26
Arram	d		17 27													
Beverley	d	17 05	17 32	18 05	18 30	18 52	19 05	19 30	20 05	20 29	21 06	21 30	22 08	22 25	23 04	23 36
Cottingham	d	17 11	17 38	18 11	18 36	18 58	19 11	19 36	20 12	20 35	21 12	21 36	22 14	22 31	23 10	23 42
Hull	a	17 20	17 47	18 20	18 45	19 07	19 20	19 45	20 21	20 46	21 20	21 45	22 23	22 41	23 20	23 51

A To London Kings Cross

B To Sheffield

C To York

← See Sunday times, left.

Table T044-F

Mondays to Fridays

16 December to 15 May

Saltburn and Middlesbrough - Darlington, Bishop Auckland, Sunderland and Newcastle

Miles	Miles			TP	GR	NT	TP	NT	NT	NT	NT	TP	NT	NT	NT	NT	TP	NT	NT	NT	TP	NT	NT
				◇1 A	B	◇ C	◇1 A			◇ C	D	◇1 A					◇1 A		D		◇1 A		E
0	—	**Saltburn**	d							06 18				06 59		07 18		07 59		08 22		08 59	09 07
2	—	Marske	d							06 23				07 04		07 23		08 04		08 27		09 04	09 12
2¾	—	Longbeck	d							06 25				07 06		07 25		08 06		08 29		09 06	09 14
4	—	Redcar East	d							06 28				07 09		07 28		08 09		08 32		09 09	09 17
5	—	**Redcar Central**	d				06 07			06 31		07 06		07 12		07 31	08 07	08 12		08 35	09 07	09 12	09 20
6¾	—	British Steel Redcar §	d																				
10	—	South Bank	d							06 38				07 19		07 38		08 19				09 19	
12½	0	**Middlesbrough**	a				06 19			06 44		07 18		07 25		07 44	08 19	08 25		08 47	09 19	09 25	09 31
—	—		d	05 12		05 46	06 21			06 45	06 59	07 20		07 25	07 35	07 45	08 20	08 25	08 35	08 47	09 21	09 25	
15¾	3¼	Thornaby	d	05a17		05 52	06a26			06 50	07 04	07a25		07 31	07 40	07 50	08a25	08 31	08 40	08 53	09a26	09 31	
—	—	London Kings Cross 15 ⊖26	d																				
18¾	—	Eaglescliffe	a			05 57				06 55				07 38		07 56		08 36		08 58		09 36	
—	—		d			05 57				06 56				07 38		07 58		08 36		08 58		09 36	
19½	—	Allens West	d			06 00				06 58				07 41		08 01		08 39		09 01		09 39	
22	—	Tees-side Airport	d																				
23¾	—	Dinsdale	d			06 06				07 05				07 47		08 07		08 45		09 07		09 45	
27½	—	**Darlington** 7 26	a			06 15				07 17				07 55		08 17		08 53		09 16		09 53	
—	—		d			06 20		06 35		07 21			07 25			08 22		08 55				09 55	
—	—	Durham	d			06 41				07 42						08 42							
—	—	Chester-le-Street	d			06 48				07 50						08 49							
28¾	—	North Road	d					06 38					07 28					08 59				09 58	
33¼	—	Heighington	d					06 47					07 37					09 07				10 06	
34½	—	Newton Aycliffe	d					06 50					07 40					09 10				10 09	
36¾	—	Shildon	d					06 54					07 44					09 15				10 14	
39½	—	**Bishop Auckland**	a					07 01					07 51					09 21				10 20	
—	5½	Stockton	d								07 10				07 46				08 46				
—	10	Billingham	d								07 18				07 53				08 53				
—	15	Seaton Carew	d								07 24				07 59				08 59				
—	17¾	**Hartlepool**	d						06 53		07 30				08 05				09 05				
—	30	Seaham	d						07 09		07 46				08 20				09 20				
—	35¼	**Sunderland** ⛴	a						07 18		07 55				08 30				09 30				
—	—		d		05 40				07 19		07 56				08 30				09 30				
—	44½	Heworth ⛴	d						07 33		08 10				08 45				09 45				
—	47¼	**Newcastle** 8 26,45 ⛴	a		05 56	06 59			07 42	08 00	08 19				08 53	08 59			09 53				
—	—	Metrocentre 48	a			07 09			07 51	08 14					09 03				10 03				
—	—	Hexham 48	a			07 44			08 20	08 38					09 38				10 38				

		NT	NT	TP	NT	NT	NT	GC	TP	NT	NT	NT	TP	NT	NT	NT	TP	NT	NT	NT	GC	TP	NT
		D		◇1 A				■ 1	◇1 A		D		◇1 A		D		◇1 A				■ 1	◇1 A	
Saltburn	d		09 22		09 59		10 22			10 59		11 22		11 59		12 22		12 59		13 22			13 59
Marske	d		09 27		10 04		10 27			11 04		11 27		12 04		12 27		13 04		13 27			14 04
Longbeck	d		09 29		10 06		10 29			11 06		11 29		12 06		12 29		13 06		13 29			14 06
Redcar East	d		09 32		10 09		10 32			11 09		11 32		12 09		12 32		13 09		13 32			14 09
Redcar Central	d		09 35	10 07	10 12		10 35		11 07	11 12		11 35	12 07	12 12		12 35	13 07	13 12		13 35		14 07	14 12
British Steel Redcar §	d																						
South Bank	d				10 19					11 19				12 19				13 19					14 19
Middlesbrough	a		09 47	10 19	10 25		10 47		11 19	11 25		11 47	12 19	12 25		12 47	13 19	13 25		13 47		14 19	14 25
	d	09 35	09 47	10 21	10 25	10 35	10 47		11 21	11 25	11 35	11 47	12 21	12 25	12 35	12 47	13 21	13 25	13 35	13 47		14 21	14 25
Thornaby	d	09 40	09 52	10a26	10 31	10 40	10 52		11a26	11 31	11 40	11 53	12a26	12 31	12 40	12 52	13a26	13 31	13 40	13 52		14a26	14 31
London Kings Cross 15 ⊖26	d							08 27													11 27		
Eaglescliffe	a		09 57		10 36		10 57	11 15		11 36		11 58		12 36		12 57		13 36		13 57	14 04		14 36
	d		09 57		10 36		10 57	11 16		11 36		11 58		12 36		12 57		13 36		13 57	14 04		14 36
Allens West	d		10 00		10 39		11 00			11 39		12 01		12 39		13 00		13 39		14 00			14 39
Tees-side Airport	d																						
Dinsdale	d		10 06		10 45		11 06			11 45		12 07		12 45		13 06		13 45		14 06			14 45
Darlington 7 26	a		10 16		10 54		11 16			11 54		12 16		12 54		13 16		13 53		14 16			14 54
	d				10 55					11 55				12 55				13 55					14 55
Durham	d																						
Chester-le-Street	d																						
North Road	d				10 59					11 59				12 59				13 58					14 59
Heighington	d				11 07					12 07				13 07				14 06					15 07
Newton Aycliffe	d				11 10					12 10				13 10				14 09					15 10
Shildon	d				11 15					12 15				13 15				14 14					15 15
Bishop Auckland	a				11 21					12 21				13 21				14 20					15 21
Stockton	d	09 46				10 46					11 46				12 46				13 46				
Billingham	d	09 53				10 53					11 53				12 53				13 53				
Seaton Carew	d	09 59				10 59					11 59				12 59				13 59				
Hartlepool	d	10 05				11 05		11 38			12 05				13 05				14 05		14 24		
Seaham	d	10 20				11 20					12 20				13 20				14 20				
Sunderland ⛴	a	10 30				11 30		12 02			12 30				13 30				14 30		14 51		
	d	10 30				11 30					12 30				13 30				14 30				
Heworth ⛴	d	10 45				11 45					12 45				13 45				14 45				
Newcastle 8 26,45 ⛴	a	10 53				11 53					12 53				13 53				14 53				
Metrocentre 48	a	11 03				12 08					13 03				14 03				15 03				
Hexham 48	a	11 38				12 43					13 38				14 38				15 38				

§ For authorised access only to BSC Redcar
A To Manchester Airport
B To London Kings Cross
C To Carlisle
D From Nunthorpe
E To Nunthorpe

For services between Middlesbrough and Nunthorpe, refer to Table T045

NRT DECEMBER 19 EDITION

Table T044-F

Mondays to Fridays

16 December to 15 May

Saltburn and Middlesbrough - Darlington, Bishop Auckland, Sunderland and Newcastle

		NT	NT	TP	NT	NT	GC	NT	TP	NT	NT	NT	TP	NT	NT	NT	TP	NT	NT	NT	GC	TP
		A		◇1 B		C	■ 1		◇1 B		C		◇1 B		D		◇1 B		E		■ 1	◇1 F
Saltburn	d		14 22		14 59			15 22		15 59		16 22		16 59		17 22		17 59		18 22		
Marske	d		14 27		15 04			15 27		16 04		16 27		17 04		17 27		18 04		18 27		
Longbeck	d		14 29		15 06			15 29		16 06		16 29		17 06		17 29		18 06		18 29		
Redcar East	d		14 32		15 09			15 32		16 09		16 32		17 09		17 32		18 09		18 32		
Redcar Central	d		14 35	15 07	15 12			15 35	16 07	16 12		16 35	17 07	17 12		17 35	18 07	18 12		18 35		19 07
British Steel Redcar §	d																					
South Bank	d				15 19					16 19				17 19				18 19				
Middlesbrough	a		14 47	15 19	15 25			15 47	16 19	16 25		16 47	17 19	17 25		17 47	18 19	18 25		18 47		19 19
	d	14 35	14 47	15 21	15 25	15 35		15 47	16 21	16 25	16 35	16 47	17 21	17 25	17 35	17 47	18 21	18 25	18 35	18 47		19 21
Thornaby	d	14 40	14 52	15a26	15 31	15 40		15 52	16a26	16 31	16 40	16 52	17a26	17 31	17 40	17 52	18a26	18 31	18 40	18 52		19a26
London Kings Cross 15 ⊖26	d						12 57														16 48	
Eaglescliffe	a		14 57		15 36		15 43	15 57		16 36		16 57		17 36		17 57		18 36		18 57	19 27	
	d		14 57		15 36		15 46	15 57		16 36		16 57		17 36		17 57		18 36		18 57	19 28	
Allens West	d		15 00		15 39			16 00		16 39		17 00		17 39		18 00		18 39		19 00		
Tees-side Airport	d																					
Dinsdale	d		15 06		15 45			16 06		16 45		17 06		17 45		18 06		18 45		19 06		
Darlington 7 26	a		15 16		15 53			16 16		16 53		17 16		17 53		18 16		18 54		19 16		
	d				15 55					16 55				17 55				18 55				
Durham	d																					
Chester-le-Street	d																					
North Road	d				15 58					16 58				17 59				18 59				
Heighington	d				16 06					17 06				18 07				19 07				
Newton Aycliffe	d				16 09					17 09				18 10				19 10				
Shildon	d				16 14					17 14				18 15				19 15				
Bishop Auckland	a				16 20					17 20				18 21				19 21				
Stockton	d	14 46				15 46					16 46				17 46				18 46			
Billingham	d	14 53				15 53					16 53				17 53				18 53			
Seaton Carew	d	14 59				15 59					16 59				17 59				18 59			
Hartlepool	d	15 05				16 05	16 13				17 05				18 05				19 05		19 53	
Seaham	d	15 20				16 20					17 20				18 20				19 20			
Sunderland ⛴	a	15 30				16 30	16 38				17 30				18 30				19 29		20 21	
	d	15 30				16 30					17 30				18 30				19 30			
Heworth ⛴	d	15 45				16 45					17 45				18 42				19 41			
Newcastle 8 26,45 ⛴	a	15 53				16 53					17 53				18 50				19 49			
Metrocentre 48	a	16 03				17 03					18 03				19 03				19 59			
Hexham 48	a	16 38									18 38				19 38							

		NT	NT	NT	TP	NT	NT	NT	TP	NT	NT	NT	GC	GR	TP	NT	NT	TP	NT
			C		◇1 G		C		◇1 G				■ 1	■ 1	◇1 G			◇1 G	
Saltburn	d	18 59		19 22		19 59		20 24		20 59		21 22				21 59			22 56
Marske	d	19 04		19 27		20 04		20 29		21 04		21 27				22 04			23 01
Longbeck	d	19 06		19 29		20 06		20 31		21 06		21 29				22 06			23 05
Redcar East	d	19 09		19 32		20 09		20 34		21 09		21 32				22 09			23 08
Redcar Central	d	19 12		19 35	20 07	20 12		20 37	21 07	21 12		21 35			22 07	22 12		23 07	23 13
British Steel Redcar §	d																		
South Bank	d	19 19				20 19				21 19						22 19			23 21
Middlesbrough	a	19 25		19 47	20 19	20 25		20 49	21 19	21 25		21 46			22 19	22 25		23 20	23 27
	d	19 25	19 35	19 47	20 21	20 25	20 35	20 49	21 21	21 25	21 34	21 47			22 21		22 31	23 22	23 27
Thornaby	d	19 31	19 40	19 52	20a26	20 31	20 40	20 54	21a26	21 31	21 39	21 52			22a26		22 36	23a27	23 35
London Kings Cross 15 ⊖26	d												19 27	20 00					
Eaglescliffe	a	19 36		19 57		20 36		20 59		21 36		21 57	22 02				22 41		23 43
	d	19 36		19 57		20 36		20 59		21 36		21 57	22 03				22 42		23 43
Allens West	d	19 39		20 00		20 39		21 02		21 39		22 00					22 44		23 46
Tees-side Airport	d																		
Dinsdale	d	19 45		20 06		20 45		21 08		21 45		22 06					22 50		23 52
Darlington 7 26	a	19 53		20 16		20 54		21 16		21 54		22 18		22 21			22 59		00 01
	d	19 55				20 55								22 23					
Durham	d													22 41					
Chester-le-Street	d																		
North Road	d	19 58				20 59													
Heighington	d	20 07				21 07													
Newton Aycliffe	d	20 10				21 10													
Shildon	d	20 14				21 15													
Bishop Auckland	a	20 21				21 21													
Stockton	d		19 46				20 46				21 45								
Billingham	d		19 53				20 53				21 52								
Seaton Carew	d		19 59				20 59				21 58								
Hartlepool	d		20 05				21 05				22 04		22 24						
Seaham	d		20 20				21 20				22 19								
Sunderland ⛴	a		20 29				21 29				22 29		22 52	23 23					
	d		20 30				21 30				22 29								
Heworth ⛴	d		20 44				21 47				22 41								
Newcastle 8 26,45 ⛴	a		20 51				21 55				22 49								
Metrocentre 48	a		21 01				22 05				23 01								
Hexham 48	a										23 36								

§ For authorised access only to BSC Redcar
A From Castleton Moor
B To Manchester Airport
C From Nunthorpe
D From Whitby
E From Battersby
F To Manchester Victoria
G To York

For services between Middlesbrough and Nunthorpe, refer to Table T045

Table T044-F

Saturdays

21 December to 16 May

Saltburn and Middlesbrough - Darlington, Bishop Auckland, Sunderland and Newcastle

		TP ◇1 A ⊼	NT ◇ B	TP ◇1 A ⊼	NT	NT	NT ◇ B	NT C	TP ◇1 A ⊼	NT	NT	NT	NT	TP ◇1 A ⊼	NT	NT C	NT	TP ◇1 A ⊼	NT	NT D	NT C	NT	TP ◇1 A ⊼
Saltburn	d						06 18				06 59		07 18		07 59		08 22		08 59	09 07		09 22	
Marske	d						06 23				07 04		07 23		08 04		08 27		09 04	09 12		09 27	
Longbeck	d						06 25				07 06		07 25		08 06		08 29		09 06	09 14		09 29	
Redcar East	d						06 28				07 09		07 28		08 09		08 32		09 09	09 17		09 32	
Redcar Central	d			06 07			06 31		07 06		07 12		07 31	08 07	08 12		08 35	09 07	09 12	09 20		09 35	10 07
British Steel Redcar §	d																						
South Bank	d						06 38				07 19		07 38		08 19				09 19				
Middlesbrough	a			06 19			06 44		07 18		07 25		07 44	08 19	08 25		08 47	09 19	09 25	09 31		09 47	10 19
	d	05 19	05 46	06 21			06 45	06 59	07 20		07 25	07 35	07 45	08 20	08 25	08 35	08 47	09 21	09 25		09 35	09 47	10 21
Thornaby	d	05a24	05 52	06a26			06 50	07 04	07a25		07 31	07 40	07 50	08a25	08 31	08 40	08 53	09a26	09 31		09 40	09 52	10a26
London Kings Cross 15 ⊖26	d																						
Eaglescliffe	a		05 57				06 55				07 38		07 56		08 36		08 58		09 36			09 57	
	d		05 57				06 56				07 38		08 00		08 36		08 58		09 36			09 57	
Allens West	d		06 00				06 58				07 41		08 03		08 39		09 01		09 39			10 00	
Tees-side Airport	d																						
Dinsdale	d		06 06				07 05				07 47		08 09		08 45		09 07		09 45			10 06	
Darlington 7 26	a		06 15				07 17				07 55		08 20		08 53		09 16		09 53			10 16	
	d		06 20		06 35		07 21			07 28			08 22		08 55				09 55				
Durham	d		06 41				07 42						08 42										
Chester-le-Street	d		06 48				07 50						08 49										
North Road	d				06 38					07 31					08 59				09 58				
Heighington	d				06 47					07 40					09 07				10 06				
Newton Aycliffe	d				06 50					07 43					09 10				10 09				
Shildon	d				06 54					07 47					09 15				10 14				
Bishop Auckland	a				07 01					07 54					09 21				10 20				
Stockton	d							07 10				07 46				08 46					09 46		
Billingham	d							07 18				07 53				08 53					09 53		
Seaton Carew	d							07 24				07 59				08 59					09 59		
Hartlepool	d					06 50		07 30				08 05				09 05					10 05		
Seaham	d					07 06		07 46				08 20				09 20					10 20		
Sunderland ⛴	a					07 15		07 55				08 30				09 30					10 30		
	d					07 16		07 56				08 30				09 30					10 30		
Heworth ⛴	d					07 33		08 10				08 45				09 45					10 45		
Newcastle 8 26,45 ⛴	a		06 59			07 42	08 00	08 19				08 53	09 01			09 53					10 53		
Metrocentre 48	a		07 09			07 51	08 14					09 03				10 03					11 03		
Hexham 48	a		07 44			08 20	08 38					09 38				10 38					11 38		

		NT	GC 1	NT	NT	TP ◇1 A ⊼	NT	NT C	NT	TP ◇1 A ⊼	NT	NT C	NT	TP ◇1 A ⊼	NT	NT	NT	GC 1	TP ◇1 A ⊼	NT	NT E	NT	TP ◇1 A ⊼
Saltburn	d	09 59			10 22		10 59		11 22		11 59		12 22		12 59		13 22			13 59		14 22	
Marske	d	10 04			10 27		11 04		11 27		12 04		12 27		13 04		13 27			14 04		14 27	
Longbeck	d	10 06			10 29		11 06		11 29		12 06		12 29		13 06		13 29			14 06		14 29	
Redcar East	d	10 09			10 32		11 09		11 32		12 09		12 32		13 09		13 32			14 09		14 32	
Redcar Central	d	10 12			10 35	11 07	11 12		11 35	12 07	12 12		12 35	13 07	13 12		13 35		14 07	14 12		14 35	15 07
British Steel Redcar §	d																						
South Bank	d	10 19					11 19				12 19				13 19					14 19			
Middlesbrough	a	10 25			10 47	11 19	11 25		11 47	12 19	12 25		12 47	13 19	13 25		13 47		14 19	14 25		14 47	15 19
	d	10 25		10 35	10 47	11 21	11 25	11 35	11 47	12 21	12 25	12 35	12 47	13 21	13 25	13 35	13 47		14 21	14 25	14 35	14 47	15 21
Thornaby	d	10 31		10 40	10 52	11a26	11 31	11 40	11 53	12a26	12 31	12 40	12 52	13a26	13 31	13 40	13 52		14a26	14 31	14 40	14 52	15a26
London Kings Cross 15 ⊖26	d		07 48															11 27					
Eaglescliffe	a	10 36	10 36		10 57		11 36		11 58		12 36		12 57		13 36		13 57	14 04		14 36		14 57	
	d	10 36	10 37		10 57		11 36		11 58		12 36		12 57		13 36		13 57	14 04		14 36		14 57	
Allens West	d	10 39			11 00		11 39		12 01		12 39		13 00		13 39		14 00			14 39		15 00	
Tees-side Airport	d																						
Dinsdale	d	10 45			11 06		11 45		12 07		12 45		13 06		13 45		14 06			14 45		15 06	
Darlington 7 26	a	10 54			11 16		11 54		12 16		12 54		13 16		13 53		14 16			14 54		15 16	
	d	10 55					11 55				12 55				13 55					14 55			
Durham	d																						
Chester-le-Street	d																						
North Road	d	10 59					11 59				12 59				13 58					14 59			
Heighington	d	11 07					12 07				13 07				14 06					15 07			
Newton Aycliffe	d	11 10					12 10				13 10				14 09					15 10			
Shildon	d	11 15					12 15				13 15				14 14					15 15			
Bishop Auckland	a	11 21					12 21				13 21				14 20					15 21			
Stockton	d			10 46				11 46				12 46				13 46					14 46		
Billingham	d			10 53				11 53				12 53				13 53					14 53		
Seaton Carew	d			10 59				11 59				12 59				13 59					14 59		
Hartlepool	d		10 59	11 05				12 05				13 05				14 05		14 24			15 05		
Seaham	d			11 20				12 20				13 20				14 20					15 20		
Sunderland ⛴	a		11 26	11 30				12 30				13 30				14 30		14 51			15 30		
	d			11 30				12 30				13 30				14 30					15 30		
Heworth ⛴	d			11 45				12 45				13 45				14 45					15 45		
Newcastle 8 26,45 ⛴	a			11 53				12 53				13 53				14 53					15 53		
Metrocentre 48	a			12 08				13 03				14 03				15 03					16 03		
Hexham 48	a			12 43				13 38				14 38				15 38					16 38		

§ For authorised access only to BSC Redcar
A To Manchester Airport
B To Carlisle
C From Nunthorpe
D To Nunthorpe
E From Castleton Moor

For services between Middlesbrough and Nunthorpe, refer to Table T045

Table T044-F

Saturdays

21 December to 16 May

Saltburn and Middlesbrough - Darlington, Bishop Auckland, Sunderland and Newcastle

		NT	NT A	NT	GC 1	TP ◇1 B ⊼	NT	NT A	NT	TP ◇1 B ⊼	NT	NT C	NT	TP ◇1 B	NT	NT D	NT	GC 1	TP ◇1 E	NT	NT A	NT
Saltburn	d	14 59		15 22			15 59		16 22		16 59		17 22		17 59		18 22			18 59		19 22
Marske	d	15 04		15 27			16 04		16 27		17 04		17 27		18 04		18 27			19 04		19 27
Longbeck	d	15 06		15 29			16 06		16 29		17 06		17 29		18 06		18 29			19 06		19 29
Redcar East	d	15 09		15 32			16 09		16 32		17 09		17 32		18 09		18 32			19 09		19 32
Redcar Central	d	15 12		15 35		16 07	16 12		16 35	17 07	17 12		17 35	18 07	18 12		18 35		19 07	19 12		19 35
British Steel Redcar §	d																					
South Bank	d	15 19					16 19				17 19				18 19					19 19		
Middlesbrough	a	15 25		15 47		16 19	16 25		16 47	17 19	17 25		17 47	18 19	18 25		18 47		19 19	19 25		19 47
	d	15 25	15 35	15 47		16 21	16 25	16 35	16 47	17 21	17 25	17 35	17 47	18 21	18 25	18 35	18 47		19 21	19 25	19 35	19 47
Thornaby	d	15 31	15 40	15 52		16a26	16 31	16 40	16 52	17a26	17 31	17 40	17 52	18a26	18 31	18 40	18 52		19a26	19 31	19 40	19 52
London Kings Cross 15 ⊖26	d				13 18													16 48				
Eaglescliffe	a	15 36		15 57	16 01		16 36		16 57		17 36		17 57		18 36		18 57	19 27		19 36		19 57
	d	15 36		15 57	16 02		16 36		16 57		17 36		17 57		18 36		18 57	19 28		19 36		19 57
Allens West	d	15 39		16 00			16 39		17 00		17 39		18 00		18 39		19 00			19 39		20 00
Tees-side Airport	d																					
Dinsdale	d	15 45		16 06			16 45		17 06		17 45		18 06		18 45		19 06			19 45		20 06
Darlington 7 26	a	15 53		16 16			16 53		17 16		17 53		18 16		18 54		19 16			19 53		20 16
	d	15 55					16 55				17 55				18 55					19 55		
Durham	d																					
Chester-le-Street	d																					
North Road	d	15 58					16 58				17 59				18 59					19 58		
Heighington	d	16 06					17 06				18 07				19 07					20 07		
Newton Aycliffe	d	16 09					17 09				18 10				19 10					20 10		
Shildon	d	16 14					17 14				18 15				19 15					20 14		
Bishop Auckland	a	16 20					17 20				18 21				19 21					20 21		
Stockton	d		15 46					16 46				17 46				18 46					19 46	
Billingham	d		15 53					16 53				17 53				18 53					19 53	
Seaton Carew	d		15 59					16 59				17 59				18 59					19 59	
Hartlepool	d		16 05		16 23			17 05				18 05				19 05		19 53			20 05	
Seaham	d		16 20					17 20				18 20				19 20					20 20	
Sunderland ⛴	a		16 30		16 51			17 30				18 30				19 29		20 21			20 29	
	d		16 30					17 30				18 30				19 30					20 30	
Heworth ⛴	d		16 45					17 45				18 42				19 41					20 44	
Newcastle 8 26,45 ⛴	a		16 53					17 53				18 50				19 49					20 51	
Metrocentre 48	a		17 03					18 03				19 03				20 03					21 01	
Hexham 48	a							18 38				19 38										

		TP ◇1 F	NT	NT A	NT	TP ◇1 F	NT	NT	NT	GC 1	TP ◇1 F ⊼	NT	NT
Saltburn	d		19 59		20 24		20 59		21 22			21 59	22 56
Marske	d		20 04		20 29		21 04		21 27			22 04	23 01
Longbeck	d		20 06		20 31		21 06		21 29			22 06	23 05
Redcar East	d		20 09		20 34		21 09		21 32			22 09	23 08
Redcar Central	d	20 07	20 12		20 37	21 07	21 12		21 35		22 07	22 12	23 13
British Steel Redcar §	d												
South Bank	d		20 19				21 19					22 19	23 21
Middlesbrough	a	20 19	20 25		20 49	21 19	21 25		21 46		22 19	22 25	23 27
	d	20 21	20 25	20 35	20 49	21 21	21 25	21 35	21 47		22 21	22 25	23 27
Thornaby	d	20a26	20 31	20 40	20 54	21a26	21 31	21 40	21 52		22a26	22 31	23 35
London Kings Cross 15 ⊖26	d									19 27			
Eaglescliffe	a		20 36		20 59		21 36		21 57	22 02		22 36	23 43
	d		20 36		20 59		21 36		21 57	22 03		22 36	23 43
Allens West	d		20 39		21 02		21 39		22 00			22 39	23 46
Tees-side Airport	d												
Dinsdale	d		20 45		21 08		21 45		22 06			22 45	23 52
Darlington 7 26	a		20 54		21 16		21 54		22 13			22 55	00 01
	d		20 55										
Durham	d												
Chester-le-Street	d												
North Road	d		20 59										
Heighington	d		21 07										
Newton Aycliffe	d		21 10										
Shildon	d		21 15										
Bishop Auckland	a		21 21										
Stockton	d			20 46				21 46					
Billingham	d			20 53				21 53					
Seaton Carew	d			20 59				21 59					
Hartlepool	d			21 05				22 05		22 24			
Seaham	d			21 20				22 20					
Sunderland ⛴	a			21 29				22 30		22 52			
	d			21 30				22 30					
Heworth ⛴	d			21 47				22 42					
Newcastle 8 26,45 ⛴	a			21 55				22 50					
Metrocentre 48	a			22 05									
Hexham 48	a												

§ For authorised access only to BSC Redcar
A From Nunthorpe
B To Manchester Airport
C From Whitby
D From Battersby to Prudhoe
E To Manchester Victoria
F To York

For services between Middlesbrough and Nunthorpe, refer to Table T045

Table T044-F

Sundays
15 December to 10 May

Saltburn and Middlesbrough - Darlington, Bishop Auckland, Sunderland and Newcastle

	NT	NT	NT	NT	NT	NT	TP	NT	NT	TP	NT	NT	TP	NT	NT	NT	GC	TP	NT	NT	TP	NT
		◇ A			◇ A		◇■1 B	◇ A		◇■1 B		◇ C	◇■1 B		◇ A	D	■ 1	◇■1 B		◇ C	◇■1 B	E
Saltburn d									09 20		09 57			10 57					11 57			
Marske d									09 25		10 02			11 02					12 02			
Longbeck d									09 27		10 04			11 04					12 04			
Redcar East d									09 30		10 07			11 07					12 07			
Redcar Central d									09 33	10 05	10 10		11 05	11 10				12 05	12 10		13 05	
British Steel Redcar § d																						
South Bank d									09 40		10 17			11 17					12 17			
Middlesbrough a									09 47	10 17	10 23		11 17	11 23				12 17	12 23		13 17	
d				08 24	08 32	09 23	09 29	09 34		10 18	10 24	10 34	11 18	11 24	11 34	11 49		12 18	12 23	12 34	13 18	
Thornaby d				08 30	08 37	09 29	09a34	09 39		10a23	10 29	10 40	11a23	11 29	11 39	11 55		12a23	12 28	12 39	13a23	
London Kings Cross ⊖26 d																	09 50					
Eaglescliffe a				08 35		09 34					10 34			11 34		12 00	12 24		12 33			
d				08 35		09 34					10 34			11 34		12 00	12 25		12 33			13 29
Allens West d				08 38		09 37					10 37			11 37		12 03			12 36			
Tees-side Airport d																						
Dinsdale d				08 44		09 43					10 43			11 43		12 09			12 42			
Darlington 26 a				08 53		09 51					10 52			11 51		12 17			12 51			
d	07 35	08 02	08 40			09 53					10 53			11 53					12 52			
Durham d		08 22																				
Chester-le-Street d		08 29																				
North Road d	07 38		08 43			09 56					10 57			11 56					12 56			
Heighington d	07 47		08 52			10 05					11 05			12 05					13 04			
Newton Aycliffe d	07 50		08 55			10 08					11 08			12 08					13 07			
Shildon d	07 54		08 59			10 12					11 13			12 12					13 12			
Bishop Auckland a	08 01		09 06			10 19					11 19			12 19					13 18			
Stockton d					08 44			09 45				10 45			11 45					12 45		13 35
Billingham d					08 52			09 52				10 53			11 52					12 52		13 42
Seaton Carew d					08 58			09 58				10 59			11 58					12 58		13 48
Hartlepool d					09 04			10 04				11 04			12 04		12 45			13 04		13a55
Seaham d					09 19			10 19				11 20			12 19					13 19		
Sunderland a					09 29			10 29				11 29			12 29		13 09			13 29		
d					09 30			10 30				11 30			12 30					13 30		
Heworth d					09 42			10 42				11 42			12 42					13 42		
Newcastle 26,45 a		08 40			09 50			10 50				11 50			12 51					13 50		
Metrocentre 48 a		08 52			10 02			11 02				12 02			13 02					14 02		
Hexham 48 a		09 27			10 36			11 34				12 37			13 34					14 37		

	NT	NT	TP	NT	NT	NT	TP	NT	NT	GC	TP	NT	NT	TP	NT	NT	NT	TP	NT	NT	NT	GC
		◇ C	◇■1 B		◇ F	G	◇■1 B		◇ C	■ 1	◇■1 B		◇ C	◇■1 B	E		◇ F	◇■1 B		◇ C	G	■ 1
Saltburn d	12 57			13 58				14 56				15 58				16 57			17 57			
Marske d	13 02			14 03				15 01				16 03				17 02			18 02			
Longbeck d	13 04			14 05				15 03				16 05				17 04			18 04			
Redcar East d	13 07			14 08				15 06				16 08				17 07			18 07			
Redcar Central d	13 10		14 03	14 11			15 05	15 09			16 05	16 11		17 05		17 10		18 02	18 10			
British Steel Redcar § d																						
South Bank d	13 17			14 18				15 16				16 18				17 17			18 17			
Middlesbrough a	13 23		14 14	14 24			15 17	15 22			16 17	16 24		17 17		17 23		18 14	18 23			
d	13 24	13 34	14 15	14 24	14 32		15 18	15 22	15 35		16 18	16 25	16 34	17 18		17 23	17 34	18 15	18 23	18 34		
Thornaby d	13 29	13 39	14a20	14 30	14 37		15a23	15 28	15 40		16a23	16 30	16 39	17a23		17 29	17 39	18a20	18 29	18 39		
London Kings Cross ⊖26 d										13 48												16 53
Eaglescliffe a	13 34			14 35				15 33		16 23		16 35				17 34			18 34			19 30
d	13 34			14 35		14 47		15 33		16 24		16 36			17 31	17 34			18 34		18 45	19 32
Allens West d	13 37			14 38		14 50		15 36				16 38				17 37			18 37		18 48	
Tees-side Airport d						14 54																
Dinsdale d	13 43			14 45		14 58		15 42				16 44				17 43			18 43		18 54	
Darlington 26 a	13 52			14 53		15 07		15 50				16 53				17 51			18 50		19 03	
d	13 53			14 55				15 52				16 54				17 53			18 52			
Durham d																						
Chester-le-Street d																						
North Road d	13 57			14 58				15 55				16 58				17 56			18 55			
Heighington d	14 05			15 07				16 04				17 06				18 05			19 04			
Newton Aycliffe d	14 08			15 10				16 07				17 09				18 08			19 07			
Shildon d	14 13			15 14				16 11				17 14				18 12			19 11			
Bishop Auckland a	14 19			15 21				16 18				17 20				18 19			19 18			
Stockton d		13 45			14 43				15 46				16 45		17 36		17 45			18 45		
Billingham d		13 52			14 50				15 53				16 52		17 43		17 52			18 52		
Seaton Carew d		13 58			14 56				15 59				16 58		17 50		17 58			18 58		
Hartlepool d		14 04			15 02				16 05	16 46			17 04		17a57		18 04			19 04		19 55
Seaham d		14 19			15 17				16 20				17 19				18 19			19 19		
Sunderland a		14 29			15 29				16 29	17 10			17 29				18 29			19 29		20 21
d		14 30			15 30				16 30				17 30				18 30			19 30		
Heworth d		14 42			15 42				16 42				17 42				18 42			19 42		
Newcastle 26,45 a		14 50			15 52				16 50				17 50				18 50			19 50		
Metrocentre 48 a		15 02			16 02				17 02				18 02				19 02			20 02		
Hexham 48 a		15 34			16 37				17 34				18 37				19 34			20 37		

§ For authorised access only to BSC Redcar
A To Carlisle
B To Manchester Airport
C From Nunthorpe to Carlisle
D From Whitby
E From Darlington
F From Whitby to Carlisle
G From Hartlepool

For services between Middlesbrough and Nunthorpe, refer to Table T045

Table T044-F

Sundays
15 December to 10 May

Saltburn and Middlesbrough - Darlington, Bishop Auckland, Sunderland and Newcastle

	TP	NT	NT	NT	NT	TP	NT	GC	TP	NT	NT	TP	NT	TP	NT
	◇■1 A		◇ B	C		◇■1 D		■ 1	◇■1 D			◇■1 D		◇■1 D	
Saltburn d		18 57			19 51					20 57			21 57		22 57
Marske d		19 02			19 56					21 02			22 02		23 02
Longbeck d		19 04			19 58					21 04			22 04		23 04
Redcar East d		19 07			20 01					21 07			22 07		23 07
Redcar Central d	19 05	19 10			20 04	20 08			21 05	21 10		22 05	22 10	23 05	23 10
British Steel Redcar § d															
South Bank d		19 17			20 11					21 17			22 17		23 17
Middlesbrough a	19 16	19 23			20 17	20 21			21 16	21 23		22 16	22 23	23 16	23 23
d	19 19	19 23	19 34	20 01	20 17	20 22	20 33		21 19	21 24	21 33	22 19	22 31	23 19	23 23
Thornaby d	19a24	19 29	19 39	20 06	20 23	20a27	20 38		21a24	21 29	21 39	22a24	22 36	23a24	23 29
London Kings Cross ⊖26 d								18 22							
Eaglescliffe a		19 34		20 11	20 28			21 00		21 34			22 41		23 34
d		19 34		20 11	20 28			21 01		21 34			22 41		23 34
Allens West d		19 37		20 14	20 31					21 37			22 44		23 37
Tees-side Airport d															
Dinsdale d		19 43		20 20	20 37					21 43			22 50		23 43
Darlington 26 a		19 51		20 28	20 47					21 54			22 59		23 52
d		19 53													
Durham d															
Chester-le-Street d															
North Road d		19 56													
Heighington d		20 05													
Newton Aycliffe d		20 08													
Shildon d		20 12													
Bishop Auckland a		20 19													
Stockton d			19 45				20 44				21 44				
Billingham d			19 52				20 53				21 53				
Seaton Carew d			19 58				20 59				21 59				
Hartlepool d			20 04				21 04	21 26			22 04				
Seaham d			20 19				21 20				22 20				
Sunderland a			20 29				21 29	21 51			22 29				
d			20 30				21 30				22 30				
Heworth d			20 42				21 42				22 42				
Newcastle 26,45 a			20 50				21 50				22 50				
Metrocentre 48 a			21 08												
Hexham 48 a			21 43												

§ For authorised access only to BSC Redcar
A To Manchester Victoria
B To Carlisle
C From Whitby
D To York

For services between Middlesbrough and Nunthorpe, refer to Table T045

Table T044-R

Mondays to Fridays

16 December to 15 May

Newcastle, Sunderland, Bishop Auckland and Darlington - Middlesbrough and Saltburn

Miles	Miles		NT MX	NT	TP	NT	NT	GR	NT	TP	NT	GC	NT	NT	TP	NT	NT	NT	TP	NT	GC	NT
			A		◇1 B			■ 1 ⊡		◇1 C ✕	D	■ 1 ⊡			◇1 E		F		◇1 E ✕		■ 1 ⊡	
—	—	Hexham 48 d											06 09				06 46					
—	—	Metrocentre 48 d	00 13										06 42				07 22					
—	0	**Newcastle** 26,45 ⛴ d	00a23						06 00				06 54				07 41					08 40
—	2¾	Heworth ⛴ d							06 08				07 01				07 48					08 47
—	12	**Sunderland** ⛴ a							06 25				07 13				08 01					09 01
—		d						05 40	06 25			06 43	07 14				08 02				08 44	09 02
—	17¼	Seaham d							06 33				07 21				08 09					09 09
—	30	**Hartlepool** d										07 05	07 37				08 25				09 08	09 25
—	32¼	Seaton Carew d							06 59				07 42				08 29					09 29
—	37¾	Billingham d							07 06				07 49				08 36					09 36
—	41¾	Stockton d							07 14				07 56				08 43					09 44
0	—	**Bishop Auckland** d												07 26				08 25				
2¾	—	Shildon d												07 31				08 30				
5	—	Newton Aycliffe d												07 36				08 35				
6¾	—	Heighington d												07 40				08 39				
10¾	—	North Road d												07 48				08 47				
—	—	Chester-le-Street 26 d																				
—	—	Durham 26 d						06 12														
12	—	**Darlington** 7 26 a						06 30						07 53				08 52				
—	—	d			06 09	06 15	06 28	06 32			07 13			07 55		08 21		08 54		09 21		
15¾	—	Dinsdale d				06 21	06 35				07 19			08 01		08 27		09 00		09 27		
20	—	Allens West d				06 27	06 42				07 26			08 08		08 34		09 07		09 34		
20¾	—	Eaglescliffe a				06 29	06 45				07 28	07 34		08 10		08 36		09 09		09 36	09 39	
—	—	d				06 30	06 46				07 28	07 35		08 10		08 36		09 09		09 36	09 39	
—	—	London Kings Cross 15 ⊖26 a						09 09				10 14									12 32	
23¾	44	Thornaby d			06 28	06 36	06 51		07 19	07 28	07 39		08 03	08 16	08 29	08 42	08 49	09 15	09 29	09 42		09 50
27	47¾	**Middlesbrough** a			06 34		06 58		07 25	07 35	07 45		08 11	08 22	08 35	08 48	08 55	09 21	09 36	09 48		09 57
—	—	d		06 25	06 35		07 09		07 29	07 36			08 15	08 23	08 36	08 48		09 22	09 37	09 48		
29½	—	South Bank d		06 29			07 13		07 33				08 20	08 27				09 26				
32¼	—	British Steel Redcar § d																				
34½	—	**Redcar Central** d		06 37	06a47	06 57	07 21		07 41	07a50			08 29	08 35	08a48	08 59		09 34	09a49	09 59		
35½	—	Redcar East d		06 39		06 59	07 23		07 43				08 32	08 37		09 01		09 36		10 01		
37	—	Longbeck d		06 43		07 03	07 27		07 47				08 36	08 41		09 05		09 40		10 05		
37¾	—	Marske d		06 45		07 05	07 29		07 49				08 38	08 43		09 07		09 42		10 07		
39½	—	**Saltburn** a		06 51		07 11	07 35		07 55				08 44	08 49		09 13		09 48		10 13		

	NT	TP	NT	NT	NT	TP	NT	NT	NT	TP	NT	NT	NT	GC	TP	NT	NT	NT	TP	NT	NT	NT
		◇1 E ✕		D		◇1 E ✕		D		◇1 E ✕		G		■ 1 ⊡	◇1 E ✕		H		◇1 E ✕		D	
Hexham 48 d								09 56				10 56					11 56				12 56	
Metrocentre 48 d								10 29				11 29					12 29				13 29	
Newcastle 26,45 ⛴ d				09 41				10 41				11 40					12 41				13 41	
Heworth ⛴ d				09 48				10 48				11 47					12 48				13 48	
Sunderland ⛴ a				10 02				11 01				12 01					13 01				14 01	
d				10 03				11 02				12 02		12 30			13 02				14 02	
Seaham d				10 10				11 09				12 09					13 09				14 09	
Hartlepool d				10 26				11 25				12 25		12 55			13 25				14 29	
Seaton Carew d				10 30				11 29				12 29					13 29				14 33	
Billingham d				10 37				11 36				12 36					13 36				14 40	
Stockton d				10 44				11 43				12 43					13 43				14 47	
Bishop Auckland d	09 26				10 25				11 26				12 26					13 26				14 25
Shildon d	09 31				10 30				11 31				12 31					13 31				14 30
Newton Aycliffe d	09 36				10 35				11 36				12 36					13 36				14 35
Heighington d	09 40				10 39				11 40				12 40					13 40				14 39
North Road d	09 48				10 47				11 48				12 48					13 48				14 47
Chester-le-Street 26 d																						
Durham 26 d																						
Darlington 7 26 a	09 52				10 52				11 53				12 53					13 53				14 52
d	09 55		10 21		10 54		11 21		11 55		12 21		12 55			13 21		13 55		14 21		14 54
Dinsdale d	10 01		10 27		11 00		11 27		12 01		12 27		13 01			13 27		14 01		14 27		15 00
Allens West d	10 08		10 33		11 07		11 34		12 08		12 34		13 08			13 34		14 08		14 34		15 07
Eaglescliffe a	10 10		10 35		11 09		11 36		12 10		12 36		13 10	13 13		13 36		14 10		14 36		15 09
d	10 10		10 36		11 09		11 36		12 10		12 36		13 10	13 14		13 36		14 10		14 36		15 09
London Kings Cross 15 ⊖26 a														16 08								
Thornaby d	10 16	10 31	10 42	10 50	11 15	11 31	11 42	11 49	12 16	12 28	12 42	12 49	13 16		13 29	13 42	13 49	14 16	14 31	14 42	14 53	15 15
Middlesbrough a	10 23	10 37	10 48	10 56	11 21	11 37	11 48	11 55	12 22	12 35	12 48	12 55	13 22		13 35	13 48	13 55	14 22	14 37	14 48	14 59	15 21
d	10 24	10 38	10 48		11 22	11 38	11 48		12 23	12 36	12 48		13 23		13 37	13 48		14 23	14 38	14 48		15 22
South Bank d	10 29				11 26				12 27				13 27					14 27				15 26
British Steel Redcar § d																						
Redcar Central d	10 36	10a50	10 59		11 34	11a50	11 59		12 35	12a48	12 59		13 35		13a49	13 59		14 35	14a50	14 59		15 34
Redcar East d	10 39		11 01		11 36		12 01		12 37		13 01		13 37			14 01		14 37		15 01		15 36
Longbeck d	10 43		11 05		11 40		12 05		12 41		13 05		13 41			14 05		14 41		15 05		15 40
Marske d	10 45		11 07		11 42		12 07		12 43		13 07		13 43			14 07		14 43		15 07		15 42
Saltburn a	10 51		11 13		11 48		12 13		12 49		13 13		13 49			14 13		14 49		15 13		15 48

§ For authorised access only to BSC Redcar
A From Hexham
B From York
C From Manchester Victoria
D To Nunthorpe
E From Manchester Airport
F From Carlisle to Nunthorpe
G To Castleton Moor
H To Whitby

For services between Nunthorpe and Middlesbrough, refer to Table T045

Table T044-R

Mondays to Fridays

16 December to 15 May

Newcastle, Sunderland, Bishop Auckland and Darlington - Middlesbrough and Saltburn

	TP	NT	NT	NT	GC	TP	NT	NT	NT	TP	NT	NT	NT	GC	NT	TP	NT	NT	NT	TP	NT
	◇1 A ✕		B		■ 1 ⊡	◇1 A ✕		C		◇1 A ✕		D		■ 1 ⊡		◇1 A ✕		B		◇1 A ✕	
Hexham 48 d			13 56					14 56				15 56						16 54			
Metrocentre 48 d			14 29					15 29				16 29			17 13			17 27			
Newcastle 8 26,45 ⛴ d			14 41					15 41				16 41			17 25			17 41			
Heworth ⛴ d			14 48					15 48				16 48			17 32			17 48			
Sunderland ⛴ a			15 01					16 01				17 01			17 49			18 01			
d			15 02		15 30			16 02				17 02		17 30	17 49			18 02			
Seaham d			15 09					16 09				17 09			17 57			18 09			
Hartlepool d			15 25		15 54			16 25				17 25		17 56	18 13			18 25			
Seaton Carew d			15 29					16 29				17 29			18 17			18 29			
Billingham d			15 36					16 36				17 36			18 24			18 36			
Stockton d			15 43					16 43				17 43			18a33			18 43			
Bishop Auckland d				15 26					16 25				17 25						18 26		
Shildon d				15 31					16 30				17 30						18 31		
Newton Aycliffe d				15 36					16 35				17 35						18 36		
Heighington d				15 40					16 39				17 39						18 40		
North Road d				15 48					16 47				17 47						18 48		
Chester-le-Street 26 d																					
Durham 26 d																					
Darlington 7 26 a				15 53					16 52				17 52						18 53		
d		15 21		15 55			16 21		16 54		17 21		17 54				18 21		18 55		19 21
Dinsdale d		15 27		16 01			16 27		17 00		17 27		18 00				18 27		19 01		19 27
Allens West d		15 34		16 08			16 34		17 07		17 34		18 07				18 34		19 08		19 34
Eaglescliffe a		15 36		16 10	16 13		16 36		17 09		17 36		18 09	18 16			18 36		19 10		19 36
d		15 36		16 10	16 15		16 36		17 09		17 36		18 09	18 17			18 36		19 10		19 36
London Kings Cross 15 ⊖26 a					19 07									21 07							
Thornaby d	15 31	15 42	15 49	16 16		16 31	16 42	16 49	17 15	17 31	17 42	17 49	18 15			18 28	18 42	18 49	19 16	19 28	19 42
Middlesbrough a	15 37	15 48	15 55	16 22		16 37	16 48	16 55	17 21	17 37	17 48	17 55	18 21			18 35	18 48	18 55	19 22	19 35	19 48
d	15 38	15 48		16 23		16 38	16 48		17 22	17 38	17 48		18 22			18 36	18 48		19 23	19 36	19 48
South Bank d				16 27					17 26				18 27						19 27		
British Steel Redcar § d																					
Redcar Central d	15a50	15 59		16 35		16a50	16 59		17 34	17a50	17 59		18 36			18a48	18 59		19 35	19a48	19 59
Redcar East d		16 01		16 37			17 01		17 36		18 01		18 38				19 01		19 37		20 01
Longbeck d		16 05		16 41			17 05		17 40		18 05		18 42				19 05		19 41		20 05
Marske d		16 07		16 43			17 07		17 42		18 07		18 44				19 07		19 43		20 07
Saltburn a		16 13		16 49			17 13		17 48		18 13		18 50				19 13		19 49		20 13

	NT	NT	TP	NT	NT	NT	TP	NT	NT	TP	NT	NT	NT	GR
	B		◇1 A ✕				◇1 A			◇1 A	◇ E	◇ E		■ 1 F ⊡
Hexham 48 d	17 59				18 56			20 00			21 01	22 00		
Metrocentre 48 d	18 32				19 29			20 33			21 34	22 33		
Newcastle 8 26,45 ⛴ d	18 45				19 45			20 45			21 45	22 49		23 00
Heworth ⛴ d	18 52				19 52			20 52			21 52	22 56		
Sunderland ⛴ a	19 08				20 07			21 06			22 05	23 08		23 23
d	19 08				20 08			21 06			22 06	23 09		
Seaham d	19 15				20 15			21 13			22 13	23 16		
Hartlepool d	19 31				20 31			21 29			22 29	23a32		
Seaton Carew d	19 36				20 35			21 34			22 33			
Billingham d	19 42				20 42			21 41			22 40			
Stockton d	19 49				20 49			21 48			22 47			
Bishop Auckland d		19 26				20 26			21 26					
Shildon d		19 31				20 31			21 31					
Newton Aycliffe d		19 36				20 36			21 36					
Heighington d		19 40				20 40			21 40					
North Road d		19 48				20 48			21 48					
Chester-le-Street 26 d														
Durham 26 d														
Darlington 7 26 a		19 53				20 53			21 53					
d		19 55		20 21		20 55			21 55				22 40	
Dinsdale d		20 01		20 27		21 01			22 01				22 46	
Allens West d		20 08		20 34		21 08			22 08				22 53	
Eaglescliffe a		20 10		20 36		21 10			22 10				22 55	
d		20 10		20 36		21 10			22 10				22 55	
London Kings Cross 15 ⊖26 a														
Thornaby d	19 56	20 16	20 31	20 42	20 55	21 16	21 29	21 55	22 16	22 28	22 53		23 01	
Middlesbrough a	20 01	20 22	20 37	20 48	21 02	21 22	21 35	22 01	22 22	22 35	23 00		23 07	
d		20 23	20 39	20 48		21 23	21 36		22 23	22 36				
South Bank d		20 27				21 27			22 27					
British Steel Redcar § d														
Redcar Central d		20 35	20a51	20 59		21 35	21a48		22 35	22a48				
Redcar East d		20 37		21 01		21 37			22 37					
Longbeck d		20 41		21 05		21 41			22 41					
Marske d		20 43		21 07		21 43			22 43					
Saltburn a		20 49		21 13		21 49			22 49					

§ For authorised access only to BSC Redcar
A From Manchester Airport
B To Nunthorpe
C To Battersby
D To Whitby
E From Carlisle
F From London Kings Cross

For services between Nunthorpe and Middlesbrough, refer to Table T045

Table T044-R

Saturdays

21 December to 16 May

Newcastle, Sunderland, Bishop Auckland and Darlington - Middlesbrough and Saltburn

	NT A	NT	TP ◇1 B	NT	NT	NT	TP ◇1 C	NT D	GC ■1	NT	NT	TP ◇1 E	NT	NT F	NT	GC ■1	TP ◇1 E	NT	NT	NT	TP ◇1 E	NT
Hexham 48 d										06 09				06 46								
Metrocentre 48 d	00 13									06 42				07 22								
Newcastle 8 26,45 d	00a23					06 00				06 54				07 35					08 33			
Heworth d						06 08				07 01				07 42					08 40			
Sunderland a						06 21				07 20				07 55					08 52			
d						06 22			06 43	07 21				08 02		08 28			08 54			
Seaham d						06 29				07 28				08 09					09 01			
Hartlepool d									07 08	07 44				08 25		08 53			09 25			
Seaton Carew d						07 00				07 49				08 29					09 30			
Billingham d						07 07				07 56				08 36					09 37			
Stockton d						07 15				08 03				08 44					09 44			
Bishop Auckland d											07 26				08 25					09 26		
Shildon d											07 31				08 30					09 31		
Newton Aycliffe d											07 36				08 35					09 36		
Heighington d											07 40				08 39					09 40		
North Road d											07 48				08 47					09 48		
Chester-le-Street 26 d																						
Durham 26 d																						
Darlington 7 26 a											07 53				08 52					09 53		
d			06 09	06 18	06 28			07 13			07 55		08 21		08 54			09 21		09 55		10 21
Dinsdale d				06 24	06 35			07 19			08 01		08 27		09 00			09 27		10 01		10 27
Allens West d				06 30	06 42			07 26			08 08		08 33		09 07			09 34		10 08		10 33
Eaglescliffe a				06 32	06 45			07 28	07 34		08 10		08 35		09 09	09 11		09 36		10 10		10 35
d				06 33	06 46			07 28	07 35		08 10		08 36		09 09	09 15		09 36		10 10		10 36
London Kings Cross 15 ⊖26 a									10 18							12 08						
Thornaby d			06 28	06 38	06 51	07 20	07 28	07 39		08 09	08 16	08 29	08 42	08 49	09 15		09 29	09 42	09 50	10 16	10 31	10 42
Middlesbrough a			06 34		06 58	07 26	07 35	07 45		08 14	08 22	08 35	08 48	08 55	09 21		09 36	09 48	09 57	10 22	10 37	10 48
d		06 25	06 35		07 09	07 29	07 36			08 15	08 23	08 36	08 48		09 22		09 37	09 48		10 23	10 38	10 48
South Bank d		06 29			07 13	07 33				08 20	08 27				09 26					10 27		
British Steel Redcar § d																						
Redcar Central d		06 37	06a47	06 59	07 21	07 41	07a50			08 29	08 35	08a48	08 59		09 34		09a49	09 59		10 35	10a50	10 59
Redcar East d		06 39		07 02	07 23	07 43				08 32	08 37		09 01		09 36			10 01		10 37		11 01
Longbeck d		06 43		07 05	07 27	07 47				08 36	08 41		09 05		09 40			10 05		10 41		11 05
Marske d		06 45		07 07	07 29	07 49				08 38	08 43		09 07		09 42			10 07		10 43		11 07
Saltburn a		06 51		07 13	07 35	07 55				08 44	08 49		09 13		09 48			10 13		10 49		11 13

	NT D	NT	TP ◇1 E	NT	NT D	NT	TP ◇1 E	NT	NT G	GC ■1	NT	TP ◇1 E	NT	NT H	NT	TP ◇1 E	NT	NT D	NT	TP ◇1 E	NT	NT D
Hexham 48 d					09 56				10 56					11 56				12 56				13 56
Metrocentre 48 d					10 29				11 29					12 29				13 29				14 29
Newcastle 8 26,45 d	09 41				10 41				11 40					12 41				13 41				14 41
Heworth d	09 48				10 48				11 47					12 48				13 48				14 48
Sunderland a	10 02				11 01				12 01					13 01				14 01				15 01
d	10 03				11 02				12 02	12 18				13 02				14 02				15 02
Seaham d	10 10				11 09				12 09					13 09				14 09				15 09
Hartlepool d	10 26				11 25				12 25	12 42				13 25				14 29				15 25
Seaton Carew d	10 30				11 29				12 29					13 29				14 33				15 29
Billingham d	10 37				11 36				12 36					13 36				14 40				15 36
Stockton d	10 44				11 43				12 43					13 43				14 47				15 43
Bishop Auckland d		10 25				11 26					12 26				13 26				14 25			
Shildon d		10 30				11 31					12 31				13 31				14 30			
Newton Aycliffe d		10 35				11 36					12 36				13 36				14 35			
Heighington d		10 39				11 40					12 40				13 40				14 39			
North Road d		10 47				11 48					12 48				13 48				14 47			
Chester-le-Street 26 d																						
Durham 26 d																						
Darlington 7 26 a		10 52				11 53					12 53				13 53				14 52			
d		10 54		11 21		11 55		12 21			12 55		13 21		13 55		14 21		14 54		15 21	
Dinsdale d		11 00		11 27		12 01		12 27			13 01		13 27		14 01		14 27		15 00		15 27	
Allens West d		11 07		11 34		12 08		12 34			13 08		13 34		14 08		14 34		15 07		15 34	
Eaglescliffe a		11 09		11 36		12 10		12 36		13 01	13 10		13 36		14 10		14 36		15 09		15 36	
d		11 09		11 36		12 10		12 36		13 02	13 10		13 36		14 10		14 36		15 09		15 36	
London Kings Cross 15 ⊖26 a										15 44												
Thornaby d	10 50	11 15	11 31	11 42	11 49	12 16	12 31	12 42	12 49		13 16	13 29	13 42	13 49	14 16	14 28	14 42	14 53	15 15	15 28	15 42	15 49
Middlesbrough a	10 56	11 21	11 37	11 48	11 55	12 22	12 37	12 48	12 55		13 22	13 35	13 48	13 55	14 22	14 35	14 48	14 59	15 21	15 35	15 48	15 55
d		11 22	11 39	11 48		12 23	12 38	12 48			13 23	13 37	13 48		14 23	14 36	14 48		15 22	15 36	15 48	
South Bank d		11 26				12 27					13 27				14 27				15 26			
British Steel Redcar § d																						
Redcar Central d		11 34	11a50	11 59		12 35	12a50	12 59			13 35	13a49	13 59		14 35	14a48	14 59		15 34	15a48	15 59	
Redcar East d		11 36		12 01		12 37		13 01			13 37		14 01		14 37		15 01		15 36		16 01	
Longbeck d		11 40		12 05		12 41		13 05			13 41		14 05		14 41		15 05		15 40		16 05	
Marske d		11 42		12 07		12 43		13 07			13 43		14 07		14 43		15 07		15 42		16 07	
Saltburn a		11 48		12 13		12 49		13 13			13 49		14 13		14 49		15 13		15 48		16 13	

§ For authorised access only to BSC Redcar
A From Hexham
B From York
C From Manchester Victoria
D To Nunthorpe
E From Manchester Airport
F From Carlisle to Nunthorpe
G To Castleton Moor
H To Whitby

For services between Nunthorpe and Middlesbrough, refer to Table T045

Table T044-R

Saturdays

21 December to 16 May

Newcastle, Sunderland, Bishop Auckland and Darlington - Middlesbrough and Saltburn

	NT	GC ■1	TP ◇1 A	NT	NT B	NT	TP ◇1 A	NT	NT C	NT	GC ■1	NT	TP ◇1 A	NT	NT D	NT	TP ◇1 A	NT	NT D	NT	TP ◇1 A
Hexham 48 d					14 56				15 53						16 54				17 59		
Metrocentre 48 d					15 29				16 26			17 13			17 27				18 32		
Newcastle 8 26,45 d					15 41				16 41			17 25			17 41				18 45		
Heworth d					15 48				16 48			17 32			17 48				18 52		
Sunderland a					16 01				17 01			17 49			18 01				19 08		
d		15 29			16 02				17 02		17 29	17 49			18 02				19 08		
Seaham d					16 09				17 09			17 57			18 09				19 15		
Hartlepool d		15 53			16 28				17 25		17 54	18 13			18 25				19 31		
Seaton Carew d					16 32				17 29			18 17			18 29				19 36		
Billingham d					16 39				17 36			18 24			18 36				19 42		
Stockton d					16 46				17 43			18a33			18 43				19 49		
Bishop Auckland d	15 26					16 25				17 25						18 26				19 26	
Shildon d	15 31					16 30				17 30						18 31				19 31	
Newton Aycliffe d	15 36					16 35				17 35						18 36				19 36	
Heighington d	15 40					16 39				17 39						18 40				19 40	
North Road d	15 48					16 47				17 47						18 48				19 48	
Chester-le-Street 26 d																					
Durham 26 d																					
Darlington 7 26 a	15 53					16 52				17 52						18 53				19 53	
d	15 55			16 21		16 54		17 21		17 54				18 21		18 55		19 21		19 55	
Dinsdale d	16 01			16 27		17 00		17 27		18 00				18 27		19 01		19 27		20 01	
Allens West d	16 08			16 34		17 07		17 34		18 07				18 34		19 08		19 34		20 08	
Eaglescliffe a	16 10	16 12		16 36		17 09		17 36		18 09	18 13			18 36		19 10		19 36		20 10	
d	16 10	16 13		16 36		17 09		17 36		18 09	18 14			18 36		19 10		19 36		20 10	
London Kings Cross 15 ⊖26 a		19 09									20 59										
Thornaby d	16 16		16 28	16 42	16 52	17 15	17 31	17 42	17 49	18 17			18 28	18 42	18 49	19 16	19 28	19 42	19 56	20 16	20 31
Middlesbrough a	16 22		16 35	16 48	16 58	17 21	17 37	17 48	17 55	18 23			18 35	18 48	18 55	19 22	19 35	19 48	20 01	20 22	20 37
d	16 23		16 36	16 48		17 22	17 38	17 48		18 24			18 36	18 48		19 23	19 36	19 48		20 23	20 39
South Bank d	16 27					17 26				18 29						19 27				20 27	
British Steel Redcar § d																					
Redcar Central d	16 35		16a48	16 59		17 34	17a50	17 59		18 38			18a48	18 59		19 35	19a48	19 59		20 35	20a51
Redcar East d	16 37			17 01		17 36		18 01		18 40				19 01		19 37		20 01		20 37	
Longbeck d	16 41			17 05		17 40		18 05		18 44				19 05		19 41		20 05		20 41	
Marske d	16 43			17 07		17 42		18 07		18 46				19 07		19 43		20 07		20 43	
Saltburn a	16 49			17 13		17 48		18 13		18 52				19 13		19 49		20 13		20 49	

	NT	NT	NT	TP ◇1 A	NT	NT	TP ◇1 A	NT ◇ E	NT	NT ◇ E	NT
Hexham 48 d		18 56			20 00			21 01		22 00	
Metrocentre 48 d		19 29			20 33			21 34		22 33	
Newcastle 8 26,45 d		19 45			20 45			21 45	22 33	22 45	
Heworth d		19 52			20 52			21 52	22 40	22 52	
Sunderland a		20 07			21 06			22 05	22 52	23 05	
d		20 08			21 06			22 06	22 53		
Seaham d		20 15			21 13			22 13	23 00		
Hartlepool d		20 31			21 29			22 29	23a17		
Seaton Carew d		20 35			21 34			22 33			
Billingham d		20 42			21 41			22 40			
Stockton d		20 49			21 48			22 47			
Bishop Auckland d			20 26			21 26					
Shildon d			20 31			21 31					
Newton Aycliffe d			20 36			21 36					
Heighington d			20 40			21 40					
North Road d			20 48			21 48					
Chester-le-Street 26 d											
Durham 26 d											
Darlington 7 26 a			20 53			21 53					
d	20 21		20 55			21 55					22 40
Dinsdale d	20 27		21 01			22 01					22 46
Allens West d	20 34		21 08			22 08					22 53
Eaglescliffe a	20 36		21 10			22 10					22 55
d	20 36		21 10			22 10					22 55
London Kings Cross 15 ⊖26 a											
Thornaby d	20 42	20 55	21 16	21 29	21 55	22 16	22 31	22 53			23 01
Middlesbrough a	20 48	21 01	21 22	21 35	22 01	22 22	22 40	22 59			23 08
d	20 48		21 23	21 36		22 23					
South Bank d			21 27			22 27					
British Steel Redcar § d											
Redcar Central d	20 59		21 35	21a48		22 35					
Redcar East d	21 01		21 37			22 37					
Longbeck d	21 05		21 41			22 41					
Marske d	21 07		21 43			22 43					
Saltburn a	21 13		21 49			22 49					

§ For authorised access only to BSC Redcar
A From Manchester Airport
B To Battersby
C To Whitby
D To Nunthorpe
E From Carlisle

For services between Nunthorpe and Middlesbrough, refer to Table T045

Table T044-R

Sundays

15 December to 10 May

Newcastle, Sunderland, Bishop Auckland and Darlington - Middlesbrough and Saltburn

		NT	NT	NT	TP	NT	GC	NT	TP	NT		NT	TP	NT	NT	TP	NT	GC	NT	NT		TP	NT	NT	TP
		A			◇1 B	C	R 1		◇1 B	A			◇1 D	◇ C		◇1 D	◇ E	R 1		F		◇1 D	◇ G		◇1 H
Hexham	48 d																10 46						11 45		
Metrocentre	48 d																11 17						12 18		
Newcastle 8	26,45 d					08 30				09 32				10 30			11 30						12 30		
Heworth	d					08 37				09 39				10 37			11 37						12 37		
Sunderland	a					08 49				09 52				10 50			11 50						12 50		
	d					08 50	09 23			09 52				10 51			11 51	12 12					12 51		
Seaham	d					08 57				10 00				10 58			11 58						12 58		
Hartlepool	d					09 13	09 47			10 16				11 14			12 14	12 36					13 14		
Seaton Carew	d					09 18				10 20				11 18			12 19						13 18		
Billingham	d					09 25				10 27				11 25			12 26						13 25		
Stockton	d					09 32				10 34				11 32			12 33						13 32		
Bishop Auckland	d			08 12				09 23				10 23			11 23				12 23					13 24	
Shildon	d			08 18				09 29				10 29			11 29				12 29					13 30	
Newton Aycliffe	d			08 22				09 33				10 33			11 33				12 33					13 34	
Heighington	d			08 26				09 37				10 37			11 37				12 37					13 38	
North Road	d			08 34				09 45				10 45			11 45				12 47					13 46	
Chester-le-Street	26 d																								
Durham	26 d																								
Darlington 7	26 a			08 40				09 50				10 50			11 50				12 52					13 52	
	d	08 09		08 41				09 52				10 52			11 51				12 53	13 13				13 53	
Dinsdale	d	08 15		08 47				09 58				10 58			11 57				12 59	13 19				13 59	
Allens West	d	08 22		08 54				10 05				11 05			12 04				13 06	13 27				14 06	
Eaglescliffe	a	08 24		08 56			10 06	10 07				11 07			12 06			12 56	13 08	13 29				14 08	
	d	08 24		08 56			10 07	10 07				11 07			12 06			12 57	13 08					14 08	
London Kings Cross 15 ⊖26	a						12 42											15 41							
Thornaby	d	08a29		09 02	09 31	09 37		10 13	10 31	10 40		11 15	11 35	11 40	12 12	12 25	12 38		13 14			13 28	13 38	14 14	14 28
Middlesbrough	a			09 08	09 37	09 43		10 19	10 37	10 46		11 21	11 41	11 46	12 18	12 31	12 44		13 20			13 35	13 44	14 20	14 35
	d		08 45	09 09	09 38			10 19	10 40			11 21	11 42		12 19	12 34			13 21			13 37		14 21	14 37
South Bank	d		08 49	09 13				10 24				11 26			12 23				13 25					14 25	
British Steel Redcar §	d																								
Redcar Central	d		08 57	09 21	09a50			10 31	10a52			11 33	11a54		12 31	12a46			13 33			13a49		14 33	14a49
Redcar East	d		08 59	09 23				10 34				11 36			12 33				13 35					14 35	
Longbeck	d		09 03	09 27				10 38				11 40			12 37				13 39					14 39	
Marske	d		09 05	09 29				10 40				11 42			12 39				13 41					14 41	
Saltburn	a		09 11	09 35				10 46				11 48			12 45				13 47					14 47	

		NT	NT	GC	NT	TP		NT	NT	TP	NT	NT	NT	TP	NT	NT		TP	NT	NT	GC	NT	TP	NT	NT
		◇ E	I	R 1		◇1 H		◇ E		◇1 H	◇ G		F	◇1 H	◇ E			◇1 H	◇ J	I	R 1		◇1 H	◇ J	
Hexham	48 d	12 46						13 45			14 46				15 45				16 46					17 45	
Metrocentre	48 d	13 17						14 18			15 17				16 18				17 17					18 17	
Newcastle 8	26,45 d	13 30						14 30			15 30				16 30				17 30					18 30	
Heworth	d	13 37						14 37			15 37				16 37				17 37					18 37	
Sunderland	a	13 50						14 50			15 50				16 50				17 50					18 50	
	d	13 51		14 12				14 51			15 51				16 51				17 51		18 12			18 51	
Seaham	d	13 58						14 58			15 58				16 58				17 58					18 58	
Hartlepool	d	14 14	14 24	14 39				15 14			16 14				17 14				18 14	18 19	18 36			19 14	
Seaton Carew	d	14 18	14 28					15 18			16 18				17 18				18 18	18 24				19 18	
Billingham	d	14 25	14 35					15 25			16 25				17 25				18 25	18 30				19 25	
Stockton	d	14 32	14 42					15 32			16 32				17 32				18 32	18 38				19 32	
Bishop Auckland	d				14 26				15 24			16 25				17 23						18 23			19 22
Shildon	d				14 32				15 30			16 31				17 29						18 29			19 28
Newton Aycliffe	d				14 36				15 35			16 35				17 34						18 33			19 33
Heighington	d				14 40				15 39			16 39				17 38						18 37			19 37
North Road	d				14 48				15 47			16 47				17 46						18 45			19 45
Chester-le-Street	26 d																								
Durham	26 d																								
Darlington 7	26 a				14 54				15 51			16 53				17 50						18 50			19 49
	d				14 55				15 53			16 54	17 16			17 52						18 51			19 52
Dinsdale	d				15 01				15 59			17 00	17 22			17 58						18 57			19 58
Allens West	d				15 08				16 06			17 07	17 29			18 05						19 04			20 05
Eaglescliffe	a		14 47	14 57	15 10				16 08			17 09	17 31			18 07				18 45	18 55	19 06			20 07
	d			14 58	15 10				16 08			17 09				18 07					18 57	19 06			20 07
London Kings Cross 15 ⊖26	a			17 42																	21 43				
Thornaby	d	14 38			15 16	15 28		15 38	16 14	16 35	16 38	17 15		17 31	17 38	18 13		18 28	18 38			19 12	19 31	19 38	20 13
Middlesbrough	a	14 44			15 22	15 35		15 44	16 20	16 40	16 46	17 21		17 37	17 44	18 19		18 35	18 45			19 18	19 37	19 45	20 19
	d				15 23	15 37			16 20	16 42		17 22		17 40		18 19		18 37				19 19	19 40		20 19
South Bank	d				15 27				16 25			17 26				18 24						19 23			20 24
British Steel Redcar §	d																								
Redcar Central	d				15 35	15a49			16 32	16a55		17 34		17a52		18 31		18a49				19 31	19a52		20 31
Redcar East	d				15 37				16 35			17 36				18 34						19 33			20 34
Longbeck	d				15 41				16 39			17 40				18 38						19 37			20 38
Marske	d				15 43				16 41			17 42				18 40						19 39			20 40
Saltburn	a				15 49				16 47			17 48				18 46						19 45			20 46

§ For authorised access only to BSC Redcar
A To Whitby
B From York
C To Nunthorpe
D From Manchester Victoria
E From Carlisle to Nunthorpe
F To Hartlepool
G From Carlisle to Whitby
H From Manchester Airport
I To Darlington
J From Carlisle

For services between Nunthorpe and Middlesbrough, refer to Table T045

Table T044-R

Sundays

15 December to 10 May

Newcastle, Sunderland, Bishop Auckland and Darlington - Middlesbrough and Saltburn

		TP		NT	NT	TP	NT	NT	NT	TP	NT	NT
		◇1 A		◇ B		◇1 A	◇ B			◇1 A	◇ B	
Hexham	48 d			18 46			19 45				20 45	
Metrocentre	48 d			19 17			20 18		20 58		21 18	
Newcastle 8	26,45 d			19 30			20 30		21 15		21 30	
Heworth	d			19 37			20 37				21 37	
Sunderland	a			19 50			20 50				21 50	
	d			19 51			20 51				21 51	
Seaham	d			19 58			20 58				21 58	
Hartlepool	d			20 14			21 14				22 14	
Seaton Carew	d			20 18			21 18				22 18	
Billingham	d			20 25			21 25				22 25	
Stockton	d			20 32			21 32				22 32	
Bishop Auckland	d				20 22							
Shildon	d				20 28							
Newton Aycliffe	d				20 33							
Heighington	d				20 37							
North Road	d				20 45							
Chester-le-Street	26 d								21 25			
Durham	26 d								21 33			
Darlington 7	26 a				20 49				21 54			
	d				20 51			21 27	21 57			22 52
Dinsdale	d				20 57			21 33	22 03			22 58
Allens West	d				21 04			21 40	22 10			23 05
Eaglescliffe	a				21 06			21 42	22 12			23 07
	d				21 06			21 42	22 12			23 07
London Kings Cross 15 ⊖26	a											
Thornaby	d	20 31		20 38	21 12	21 30	21 38	21 49	22 18	22 31	22 38	23 13
Middlesbrough	a	20 37		20 45	21 18	21 36	21 45	21 56	22 24	22 37	22 45	23 19
	d	20 39			21 18	21 39			22 24	22 40		
South Bank	d				21 23				22 29			
British Steel Redcar §	d											
Redcar Central	d	20a51			21 30	21a51			22 36	22a52		
Redcar East	d				21 33				22 39			
Longbeck	d				21 37				22 43			
Marske	d				21 39				22 45			
Saltburn	a				21 45				22 51			

§ For authorised access only to BSC Redcar A From Manchester Airport B From Carlisle

For services between Nunthorpe and Middlesbrough, refer to Table T045

Table T045-F

Mondays to Fridays
16 December to 15 May

Middlesbrough and Pickering - Whitby

Miles	Miles			NT	NT	NT	NT	NT	NY 1 A	NY 1 A	NT	NT	NT	NT	NT	NY 1 A	NT	NT	NT	NY 1 A	NT	NT	NT
—	—	Newcastle 44	d					07 41					09 41	10 41	11 40		12 41	13 41	14 41		15 41	16 41	17 41
0	—	**Middlesbrough**	d	04 58	06 20	06 55	07 57	08 56			09 34	10 20	10 56	11 57	12 56		14 02	14 59	15 58		17 00	17 55	18 56
2½	—	James Cook	d	05 02	06 24		08 02	09 00			09 38	10 24	11 00	12 02	13 00		14 06	15 04	16 02		17 04	17 59	19 00
3	—	Marton	d		06 27		08 04	09 03			09 41	10 27	11 03	12 04	13 03		14 09	15 06	16 05		17 07	18 02	19 03
4	—	Gypsy Lane	d					09 06				10 30	11 06	12 07			14 12	15 09	16 08		17 10	18 05	19 06
4½	—	Nunthorpe	d	05 10	06a33		08a11	09a09			09a48	10 34	11a09	12a11	13 14		14 21	15a13	16a11		17 18	18 09	19a09
8½	—	Great Ayton	d									10 41			13 21		14 28				17 25	18 16	
11	—	Battersby	a	05 22		07 22						10 47			13 27		14 34				17 31	18 22	
—	—		d	05 25		07 25						10 50			13 30		14 37					18 25	
12¾	—	Kildale	d									10 55					14 42					18 30	
16¾	—	Commondale	d									11 03			13 41		14 50					18 37	
18½	—	Castleton Moor	d	05 39								11 06			13a45		14 53					18 41	
20	—	Danby	d									11 10					14 57					18 44	
23½	—	Lealholm	d	05 48								11 16					15 04					18 51	
25½	—	Glaisdale	a	05 53		08 06						11 21					15 09					18 56	
—	—		d	05 56		08 09						11 24					15 11					18 58	
27¼	—	Egton	d	06 00								11 28					15 15					19 02	
—	0	**Pickering** §	d							09 25						12 00				15 00			
—	6	Levisham §	d							09 44						12 20				15 20			
—	14½	Goathland §	d							10 10						12 50				15 50			
28¾	18	Grosmont	d						09 19	10 40		11 32				13 15	15 19			16 27		19 06	
32	21¼	Sleights	d									11 40					15 28					19 15	
33½	22¾	Ruswarp	d									11 45					15 32					19 19	
35	24¼	**Whitby**	a	06 19		08 37			09 45	11 10		11 51				13 45	15 38			16 57		19 25	

		NT	NT	NT
Newcastle 44	d	18 45		
Middlesbrough	d	20 01	20 43	21 20
James Cook	d	20 06	20 47	21 24
Marton	d	20 08	20 50	21 27
Gypsy Lane	d	20 11	20 53	21 30
Nunthorpe	d	20a15	21 00	21a33
Great Ayton	d		21 07	
Battersby	a		21 13	
	d		21 16	
Kildale	d			
Commondale	d			
Castleton Moor	d		21 30	
Danby	d		21 33	
Lealholm	d		21 40	
Glaisdale	a		21 45	
	d		21 47	
Egton	d		21 51	
Pickering §	d			
Levisham §	d			
Goathland §	d			
Grosmont	d		21 55	
Sleights	d		22 03	
Ruswarp	d		22 08	
Whitby	a		22 13	

Saturdays
21 December to 16 May

		NT	NT	NT	NT	NT	NY 1 B	NY 1 B	NT	NT	NT	NT	NT	NY 1 B	NT	NT	NT	NY 1 B	NT	NT	NT	NT	NT
Newcastle 44	d					07 35					09 41	10 41	11 40		12 41	13 41	14 41		15 41	16 41	17 41	18 45	
Middlesbrough	d	04 58	06 20	06 55	07 57	08 56			09 34	10 20	10 56	11 58	12 56		14 02	14 59	15 58		17 00	17 55	18 56	20 01	20 43
James Cook	d	05 02	06 24		08 02	09 00			09 38	10 24	11 00	12 02	13 00		14 06	15 04	16 02		17 04	17 59	19 00	20 06	20 47
Marton	d		06 27		08 04	09 03			09 41	10 27	11 03	12 05	13 03		14 09	15 06	16 05		17 07	18 02	19 03	20 08	20 50
Gypsy Lane	d					09 06				10 30	11 06	12 08			14 12	15 09	16 08		17 10	18 05	19 06	20 11	20 53
Nunthorpe	d	05 10	06a33		08a11	09a09			09a48	10 34	11a09	12a11	13 14		14 21	15a13	16a11		17 18	18 09	19a09	20a15	21 00
Great Ayton	d									10 41			13 21		14 28				17 25	18 16			21 07
Battersby	a	05 22								10 47			13 27		14 34				17 31	18 22			21 13
	d	05 25								10 50			13 30		14 37					18 25			21 16
Kildale	d									10 55					14 42					18 30			
Commondale	d									11 03			13 41		14 50					18 37			
Castleton Moor	d	05 39								11 06			13a45		14 53					18 41			21 30
Danby	d									11 10					14 57					18 44			21 33
Lealholm	d	05 48								11 16					15 04					18 51			21 40
Glaisdale	a	05 53								11 21					15 09					18 56			21 45
	d	05 56								11 24					15 11					18 58			21 47
Egton	d	06 00								11 28					15 15					19 02			21 51
Pickering §	d							09 25						12 00				15 00					
Levisham §	d							09 44						12 20				15 20					
Goathland §	d							10 10						12 50				15 50					
Grosmont	d						09 19	10 40		11 32				13 15	15 19			16 27		19 06			21 55
Sleights	d									11 40					15 28					19 15			22 03
Ruswarp	d									11 45					15 32					19 19			22 08
Whitby	a	06 19		08 37			09 45	11 10		11 51				13 45	15 38			16 57		19 25			22 13

§ North Yorkshire Moors Railway. For full service between Grosmont and Pickering please see separate publicity

A from 30 March
B from 28 March

For connections to Darlington refer to Table T044

Table T045-F

Saturdays
21 December to 16 May

Middlesbrough and Pickering - Whitby

		NT
Newcastle 44	d	
Middlesbrough	d	21 20
James Cook	d	21 24
Marton	d	21 27
Gypsy Lane	d	21 30
Nunthorpe	d	21a33
Great Ayton	d	
Battersby	a	
	d	
Kildale	d	
Commondale	d	
Castleton Moor	d	
Danby	d	
Lealholm	d	
Glaisdale	a	
	d	
Egton	d	
Pickering §	d	
Levisham §	d	
Goathland §	d	
Grosmont	d	
Sleights	d	
Ruswarp	d	
Whitby	a	

Sundays
15 December to 10 May

		NY 1 A	NT	NT	NY 1 A	NT	NT ◇	NT ◇	NY 1 A	NT ◇	NT ◇	NT ◇	NY 1 A	NT ◇	NT ◇
Newcastle 44	d			08 30		09 32	10 30	11 30		12 30	13 30	14 30		15 30	16 30
Middlesbrough	d		08 41	09 45		10 46	11 49	12 46		13 45	14 45	15 44		16 52	17 50
James Cook	d		08 45	09 49		10 51	11 53	12 50		13 49	14 49	15 49		16 56	17 54
Marton	d		08 48	09 52		10 54	11 56	12 53		13 52	14 52	15 51		16 59	17 57
Gypsy Lane	d		08 51	09 55		10 57	11 59	12 56		13 55	14 55	15 54		17 02	18 00
Nunthorpe	d		08 55	09a58		11 00	12a02	12a59		14 02	14a58	15a58		17 06	18a03
Great Ayton	d		09 02			11 07				14 09				17 13	
Battersby	a		09 08			11 13				14 15				17 19	
	d		09 11			11 26				14 18				17 22	
Kildale	d		09 16			11 31				14 23				17 27	
Commondale	d		09 23			11 39				14 31				17 35	
Castleton Moor	d		09 27			11 42				14 34				17 38	
Danby	d		09 30			11 46				14 38				17 42	
Lealholm	d		09 37			11 52				14 44				17 48	
Glaisdale	a		09 42			11 57				14 49				17 53	
	d		09 44			12 00				14 52				17 56	
Egton	d		09 48			12 04				14 56				18 00	
Pickering §	d				09 30				11 55						
Levisham §	d				09 50				12 15						
Goathland §	d				10 25				12 50						
Grosmont	d	08 34	09 52		10 50	12 08			13 19	15 00			16 15	18 04	
Sleights	d		10 01			12 16				15 08				18 12	
Ruswarp	d		10 05			12 21				15 13				18 17	
Whitby	a	08 59	10 12		11 18	12 26			13 44	15 18			16 40	18 23	

§ North Yorkshire Moors Railway. For full service between Grosmont and Pickering please see separate publicity

A from 29 March

For connections to Darlington refer to Table T044

Table T045-R

Mondays to Fridays

16 December to 15 May

Whitby - Pickering and Middlesbrough

Miles	Miles			NT	NT	NT	NT	NT	NY 1 A	NT	NT	NT	NY 1 A	NT	NY 1 A	NT	NT	NT	NY 1 A	NT	NT	NT	NT
0	0	**Whitby**	d		06 33			08 45	10 00			11 58	12 45		14 00			16 00	17 10				19 44
1¼	1¼	Ruswarp	d					08 49				12 02						16 04					19 48
3	3	Sleights	d					08 54				12 07						16 09					19 53
6¼	6¼	Grosmont	d					09 02	10 30			12 15	13 30		14 30			16 18	17 45				20 01
—	9¾	Goathland §	a						10 50				13 45		14 45				17 59				
—	18¾	Levisham §	a						11 16				14 16		15 16				18 24				
—	24¼	**Pickering** §	a						11 38				14 38		15 38				18 43				
7¾	—	Egton	d		06 51			09 06				12 19						16 22					20 05
9½	—	Glaisdale	a		06 55			09 10				12 23						16 26					20 09
—	—		d		06 58			09 13				12 26						16 29					20 12
11½	—	Lealholm	d		07 03			09 18				12 31						16 34					20 17
15	—	Danby	d					09 25				12 38						16 41					20 24
16½	—	Castleton Moor	d		07 12			09 28				12 41		13 50				16 45					20 27
18¼	—	Commondale	d					09 32				12 45						16 48					20 31
22¼	—	Kildale	d					09 39				12 52						16 56					20 38
24	—	Battersby	a		07 27			09 44				12 57		14 05				17 02					20 43
—	—		d		07 30			09 47				13 00		14 07				17 05		17 42			20 46
26½	—	Great Ayton	d		07 35			09 53				13 06		14 12				17 10		17 47			20 52
30½	—	Nunthorpe	d	06 41	07 42	08 20	09 15	10 01		11 20	12 20	13 15		14 20		15 20	16 20	17 17		18 20	19 20	20 20	21 00
31	—	Gypsy Lane	d	06 43	07 45	08 22	09 18	10 03		11 23	12 23	13 17		14 23		15 23	16 22	17 20		18 22	19 22	20 22	21 02
32	—	Marton	d	06 46	07 47	08 25	09 20	10 06		11 25	12 25	13 21		14 26		15 25	16 25	17 23		18 25	19 25	20 25	21 05
32½	—	James Cook	d	06 49	07 50	08 28	09 23	10 09		11 28	12 28	13 24		14 28		15 28	16 28	17 25		18 28	19 28	20 28	21 08
35	—	**Middlesbrough**	a	06 54	07 56	08 33	09 29	10 15		11 34	12 34	13 30		14 34		15 34	16 33	17 32		18 34	19 33	20 33	21 14
—	—	Newcastle 44	a	08 19		09 53	10 53			12 53	13 53			15 53		16 53	17 53	18 50		19 49	20 51	21 55	

		NT	NT
Whitby	d		22 21
Ruswarp	d		
Sleights	d		
Grosmont	d		22 36
Goathland §	a		
Levisham §	a		
Pickering §	a		
Egton	d		22 40
Glaisdale	a		22 44
	d		22 47
Lealholm	d		22 52
Danby	d		
Castleton Moor	d		23 01
Commondale	d		
Kildale	d		
Battersby	a		23 15
	d		23 18
Great Ayton	d		
Nunthorpe	d	21 40	23 31
Gypsy Lane	d	21 42	23 33
Marton	d	21 45	23 36
James Cook	d	21 48	23 38
Middlesbrough	a	21 53	23 45
Newcastle 44	a		

Saturdays

21 December to 16 May

		NT	NT	NT	NT	NT	NY 1 B	NT	NT	NT	NY 1 B	NT	NY 1 B	NT	NT	NT	NY 1 B	NT	NT	NT	NT	NT	NT
Whitby	d		06 33			08 45	10 00			11 58	12 45		14 00			16 00	17 10				19 44		22 21
Ruswarp	d					08 49				12 02						16 04					19 48		
Sleights	d					08 54				12 07						16 09					19 53		
Grosmont	d					09 02	10 30			12 15	13 30		14 30			16 18	17 45				20 01		22 36
Goathland §	a						10 48				13 45		14 45				17 59						
Levisham §	a						11 16				14 16		15 16				18 24						
Pickering §	a						11 38				14 38		15 38				18 43						
Egton	d		06 51			09 06				12 19						16 22					20 05		22 40
Glaisdale	a		06 55			09 10				12 23						16 26					20 09		22 44
	d		06 58			09 13				12 26						16 29					20 12		22 47
Lealholm	d		07 03			09 18				12 31						16 34					20 17		22 52
Danby	d					09 25				12 38						16 41					20 24		
Castleton Moor	d		07 12			09 28				12 41		13 50				16 45					20 27		23 01
Commondale	d					09 32				12 45						16 48					20 31		
Kildale	d					09 39				12 52						16 56					20 38		
Battersby	a		07 27			09 44				12 57		14 05				17 02					20 43		23 15
	d		07 30			09 47				13 00		14 07				17 05		17 42			20 46		23 18
Great Ayton	d		07 35			09 53				13 06		14 12				17 10		17 47			20 52		
Nunthorpe	d	06 41	07 42	08 20	09 15	10 01		11 20	12 20	13 15		14 20		15 20	16 20	17 17		18 20	19 20	20 20	20 59	21 40	23 31
Gypsy Lane	d	06 43	07 45	08 23	09 18	10 03		11 23	12 22	13 17		14 23		15 23	16 22	17 20		18 22	19 22	20 22	21 01	21 42	23 33
Marton	d	06 46	07 47	08 25	09 20	10 06		11 25	12 25	13 21		14 26		15 25	16 25	17 23		18 25	19 25	20 25	21 05	21 45	23 36
James Cook	d	06 49	07 50	08 28	09 23	10 09		11 28	12 28	13 24		14 28		15 28	16 28	17 25		18 28	19 28	20 28	21 08	21 48	23 38
Middlesbrough	a	06 54	07 56	08 34	09 29	10 15		11 34	12 33	13 30		14 34		15 34	16 33	17 32		18 34	19 33	20 33	21 14	21 53	23 45
Newcastle 44	a	08 19		09 53	10 53			12 53	13 53			15 53		16 53	17 53	18 50		19 49	20 51	21 55			

§ North Yorkshire Moors Railway. For full service between Grosmont and Pickering please see separate publicity

A from 30 March
B from 28 March

For connections to Darlington refer to Table T044

Table T045-R

Sundays

15 December to 10 May

Whitby - Pickering and Middlesbrough

		NY 1 A	NT ◇	NT	NY 1 A	NT ◇	NT ◇	NT ◇	NY 1 A	NT ◇	NT ◇	NT ◇	NY 1 A	NT ◇	NT
Whitby	d	09 14		10 19	11 32			12 46	13 57			15 46	16 55		18 30
Ruswarp	d			10 23				12 50				15 50	17 09		18 34
Sleights	d			10 28				12 55				15 55			18 39
Grosmont	d	09 55		10 36	12 20			13 03	14 30			16 03	17 30		18 47
Goathland §	a	10 10			12 35				14 45				17 45		
Levisham §	a	10 46			13 11				15 16				18 08		
Pickering §	a	11 10			13 35				15 40				18 30		
Egton	d			10 40				13 07				16 07			18 51
Glaisdale	a			10 44				13 11				16 11			18 55
	d			10 47				13 14				16 14			18 58
Lealholm	d			10 52				13 19				16 19			19 03
Danby	d			10 59				13 26				16 26			19 10
Castleton Moor	d			11 02				13 30				16 30			19 13
Commondale	d			11 06				13 33				16 33			19 17
Kildale	d			11 13				13 41				16 41			19 24
Battersby	a			11 18				13 46				16 46			19 29
	d			11 21				13 49				16 49			19 32
Great Ayton	d			11 27				13 54				16 54			19 38
Nunthorpe	d		10 20	11 34		12 17	13 17	14 13		15 20	16 19	17 15		18 17	19 46
Gypsy Lane	d		10 22	11 37		12 19	13 19	14 15		15 22	16 21	17 17		18 19	19 48
Marton	d		10 25	11 40		12 22	13 22	14 18		15 25	16 24	17 20		18 22	19 51
James Cook	d		10 28	11 43		12 25	13 25	14 21		15 28	16 27	17 23		18 25	19 54
Middlesbrough	a		10 33	11 48		12 31	13 31	14 28		15 33	16 32	17 28		18 32	20 00
Newcastle 44	a		11 50			13 50	14 50	15 52		16 50	17 50	18 50		19 50	

§ North Yorkshire Moors Railway. For full service between Grosmont and Pickering please see separate publicity

A from 29 March

For connections to Darlington refer to Table T044

Table T047-F

Stansted Airport - Leicester - Birmingham New Street

Mondays to Fridays
16 December to 15 May

Miles	Miles			XC 1	XC 1	XC ◇1	XC 1	XC ◇1	XC 1 A	XC 1	XC ◇1	XC 1	XC ◇1	XC 1	EM ◇ B 🚲	XC ◇1	XC 1	XC ◇1	XC 1	XC ◇1 🚲	XC 1	LE C	XC ◇1 🚲
0	—	**Stansted Airport** ✈	d					05 27			06 12		07 21			08 21		09 21		10 27		10 48	11 27
10½	—	Audley End	d					05 41			06 27		07 41			08 41		09 41		10 41		11 02	11 41
24½	—	Cambridge	d			05 15		05 57			06 57		08 01			09 01		10 00		11 01		11 20	12 01
39¾	—	Ely 6	d			05 30		06 12			07 12		08 16			09 16		10 16		11 16		11a36	12 16
54¾	—	March	d			05 46		06 30			07 28		08 32			09 32		10 32		11 32			12 32
69¾	—	Peterborough 8	d			06 10		06 54			07 54		08 54			09 54		10 54		11 54			12 54
81¾	—	Stamford	d			06 23		07 07			08 07		09 07			10 07		11 07		12 07			13 07
95½	—	Oakham	d			06 37		07 21			08 21		09 21		09 48	10 21		11 21		12 21			13 21
106¾	—	Melton Mowbray	d			06 48		07 32			08 32		09 32		09a59	10 32		11 32		12 32			13 32
121½	0	**Leicester**	a			07 09		07 49			08 49		09 49			10 49		11 49		12 49			13 49
—	—		d	06 18	06 48	07 10	07 22	07 50		08 18	08 50	09 15	09 50	10 18		10 50	11 18	11 50	12 18	12 50	13 18		13 50
—	4	South Wigston	d	06 24	06 54		07 28	07 56						10 24					12 24				
—	7	Narborough	d	06 29	06 59		07 33	08 01		08 28		09 25		10 29			11 28		12 29		13 28		
—	15	Hinckley	d	06 38	07 08		07 42	08 09		08 36		09 33		10 38			11 36		12 38		13 36		
140	18½	Nuneaton	d	06 45	07 15	07 29	07 48	08 16		08 45	09 09	09 43	10 09	10 45		11 09	11 43	12 09	12 45	13 09	13 43		14 09
151½	30	Coleshill Parkway	d	07 00	07 30	07 45	08 04	08 31		09 00	09 25	10 00	10 25	11 00		11 25	11 58	12 25	13 00	13 25	13 58		14 25
—	32¼	Water Orton	d		07 34		08 08		08 43			10 03					12 02				14 02		
161¼	39¾	**Birmingham New Street** 12	a	07 14	07 45	07 58	08 19	08 44	08 55	09 15	09 38	10 15	10 38	11 14		11 38	12 14	12 38	13 14	13 38	14 14		14 38

		XC 1	LE C	XC ◇1 🚲	XC 1	LE C	XC ◇1 🚲	XC 1 🚲	LE C	XC ◇1 🚲	XC 1	LE C	XC ◇1 🚲	LE C	XC 1	XC ◇1 🚲	XC 1	LE C	XC ◇1 🚲	XC 1 D	LE C	EM ◇ E 🚲	XC ◇1
Stansted Airport ✈	d		11 48	12 27		12 48	13 27		13 48	14 27		14 48	15 27	15 37		16 27		16 48	17 27		17 56		18 21
Audley End	d		12 02	12 41		13 02	13 41		14 02	14 41		15 02	15 41	15 56		16 41		17 05	17 41		18 11		18 41
Cambridge	d		12 20	13 01		13 20	14 01		14 20	15 01		15 20	16 01	16 16		17 01		17 29	18 01		18 30		19 01
Ely 6	d		12a36	13 16		13a36	14 16		14a36	15 16		15a36	16 16	16a32		17 16		17a47	18 16		18a48		19 16
March	d			13 32			14 32			15 32			16 32			17 32			18 34				19 32
Peterborough 8	d			13 54			14 54			15 54			16 54			17 54			18 54				19 54
Stamford	d			14 07			15 07			16 07			17 07			18 07			19 07				20 07
Oakham	d			14 21			15 21			16 21			17 21			18 21			19 21			19 29	20 21
Melton Mowbray	d			14 32			15 32			16 32			17 32			18 32			19 32			19a39	20 32
Leicester	a			14 49			15 49			16 49			17 49			18 49			19 49				20 49
	d	14 18		14 50	15 18		15 50	16 18		16 50	17 18		17 50		18 18	18 50	19 18		19 50	20 18			20 50
South Wigston	d	14 24						16 24			17 24		17 56		18 24		19 24			20 24			
Narborough	d	14 29			15 28			16 29			17 29		18 01		18 29		19 29			20 29			
Hinckley	d	14 38			15 36			16 38			17 38		18 09		18 38		19 38			20 38			
Nuneaton	d	14 45		15 09	15 43		16 09	16 45		17 09	17 45		18 16		18 45	19 09	19 45		20 09	20 45			21 09
Coleshill Parkway	d	15 00		15 25	15 58		16 25	17 00		17 25	18 00		18 31		19 00	19 25	20 00		20 25	21 00			21 25
Water Orton	d				16 02																		
Birmingham New Street 12	a	15 15		15 38	16 14		16 38	17 14		17 38	18 14		18 44		19 15	19 38	20 14		20 38	21 15			21 38

		XC 1	XC ◇1	XC 1	EM F	XC ◇1	LE C
Stansted Airport ✈	d		19 21			20 21	22 10
Audley End	d		19 41			20 41	22 23
Cambridge	d		20 01			21 02	22 57
Ely 6	d		20 16			21 17	23a13
March	d		20 32			21 33	
Peterborough 8	d		20 52		21 31	22 00	
Stamford	d		21 05		21 45	22 13	
Oakham	d		21 19		22 01	22 27	
Melton Mowbray	d		21 30		22a12	22 38	
Leicester	a		21 47			22 55	
	d	21 16	21 48	22 27		22 56	
South Wigston	d	21 22		22 33			
Narborough	d	21 27		22 38			
Hinckley	d	21 36		22 47			
Nuneaton	d	21 45	22 07	22 53		23 15	
Coleshill Parkway	d	22 00	22 23	23 09		23 31	
Water Orton	d						
Birmingham New Street 12	a	22 14	22 36	23 22		23 44	

Saturdays
21 December to 16 May

		XC 1	XC 1	XC ◇1	XC ◇1	XC 1 A	XC 1	XC ◇1	XC 1	LE C	XC ◇1	XC 1	LE C	XC ◇1	XC 1	LE C	XC ◇1	XC 1	LE C	XC ◇1 🚲	XC 1	LE C	XC ◇1 🚲
Stansted Airport ✈	d				05 27			06 27		06 48	07 27		07 48	08 27		08 48	09 27		09 48	10 27		10 48	11 27
Audley End	d				05 41			06 41		07 02	07 41		08 02	08 41		09 02	09 41		10 02	10 41		11 02	11 41
Cambridge	d			05 15	05 57			06 58		07 20	08 01		08 20	09 01		09 30	10 01		10 26	11 01		11 20	12 01
Ely 6	d			05 30	06 12			07 13		07a37	08 16		08a36	09 16		09a47	10 16		10a42	11 16		11a36	12 16
March	d			05 46	06 30			07 29			08 32			09 32			10 32			11 32			12 32
Peterborough 8	d			06 10	06 54			07 54			08 54			09 54			10 54			11 54			12 54
Stamford	d			06 23	07 07			08 07			09 07			10 07			11 07			12 07			13 07
Oakham	d			06 37	07 21			08 21			09 21			10 21			11 21			12 21			13 21
Melton Mowbray	d			06 48	07 32			08 32			09 32			10 32			11 32			12 32			13 32
Leicester	a			07 05	07 49			08 49			09 49			10 49			11 49			12 49			13 49
	d	05 48	06 48	07 08	07 50		08 18	08 50	09 18		09 50	10 18		10 50	11 18		11 50	12 18		12 50	13 18		13 50
South Wigston	d	05 54	06 54				08 25					10 24						12 24					
Narborough	d	05 59	06 59				08 30		09 28			10 29			11 28			12 29			13 28		
Hinckley	d	06 08	07 08				08 38		09 36			10 38			11 36			12 38			13 36		
Nuneaton	d	06 15	07 15	07 30	08 09		08 45	09 09	09 43		10 09	10 45		11 09	11 43		12 09	12 45		13 09	13 43		14 09
Coleshill Parkway	d	06 30	07 30	07 47	08 25		09 00	09 25	09 58		10 25	11 00		11 25	11 58		12 25	13 00		13 25	13 58		14 25
Water Orton	d		07 36			08 43			10 02						12 02						14 02		
Birmingham New Street 12	a	06 44	07 47	08 03	08 38	08 55	09 14	09 38	10 15		10 38	11 15		11 38	12 15		12 38	13 15		13 38	14 14		14 38

A From Nottingham
B From Corby to Derby
C To Norwich
D To Gloucester
E From St Pancras International
F From Spalding to Nottingham

Table T047-F

Stansted Airport - Leicester - Birmingham New Street

Saturdays
21 December to 16 May

		XC 1	LE A	XC ◇1 🚲	XC 1	LE A	XC ◇1 🚲	XC 1 🚲	LE A	XC ◇1 🚲	XC 1	LE A	XC ◇1 🚲	XC 1	LE A	XC ◇1 🚲	XC 1	LE A	XC ◇1 🚲	XC 1	LE A	XC ◇1
Stansted Airport ✈	d		11 48	12 27		12 48	13 27		13 48	14 27		14 48	15 27		15 48	16 27		16 48	17 27		17 48	18 27
Audley End	d		12 02	12 41		13 02	13 41		14 02	14 41		15 02	15 41		16 02	16 41		17 02	17 41		18 02	18 41
Cambridge	d		12 20	13 01		13 20	14 01		14 20	15 01		15 20	16 01		16 20	17 01		17 20	18 01		18 20	19 01
Ely 6	d		12a36	13 16		13a36	14 16		14a36	15 16		15a36	16 16		16a35	17 16		17a36	18 16		18a36	19 16
March	d			13 32			14 32			15 32			16 32			17 32			18 34			19 32
Peterborough 8	d			13 54			14 54			15 54			16 54			17 54			18 54			19 54
Stamford	d			14 07			15 07			16 07			17 07			18 07			19 07			20 07
Oakham	d			14 21			15 21			16 21			17 21			18 21			19 21			20 21
Melton Mowbray	d			14 32			15 32			16 32			17 32			18 32			19 32			20 32
Leicester	a			14 49			15 49			16 49			17 49			18 49			19 49			20 49
	d	14 18		14 50	15 18		15 50	16 18		16 50	17 18		17 50	18 18		18 50	19 18		19 50	20 18		20 50
South Wigston	d	14 24						16 24			17 24			18 24			19 24			20 24		
Narborough	d	14 29			15 28			16 29			17 29			18 29			19 29			20 29		
Hinckley	d	14 38			15 36			16 38			17 38			18 38			19 38			20 38		
Nuneaton	d	14 45		15 09	15 43		16 09	16 45		17 09	17 45		18 09	18 45		19 09	19 45		20 09	20 45		21 09
Coleshill Parkway	d	15 00		15 25	15 58		16 25	17 00		17 25	18 00		18 25	19 00		19 25	20 00		20 25	21 00		21 25
Water Orton	d				16 02																	
Birmingham New Street 12	a	15 14		15 38	16 14		16 38	17 14		17 38	18 15		18 38	19 14		19 38	20 14		20 38	21 14		21 38

		XC 1	LE A	XC ◇1	XC 1	LE A	LE A	LE A
Stansted Airport ✈	d		18 48	19 27		19 48	20 48	22 10
Audley End	d		19 02	19 41		20 02	21 02	22 25
Cambridge	d		19 20	20 01		20 20	21 20	22 55
Ely 6	d		19a37	20 16		20a36	21a35	23a11
March	d			20 32				
Peterborough 8	d			20 54				
Stamford	d			21 07				
Oakham	d			21 21				
Melton Mowbray	d			21 32				
Leicester	a			21 48				
	d	21 18		21 49	22 20			
South Wigston	d	21 24			22 26			
Narborough	d	21 29			22 31			
Hinckley	d	21 38			22 40			
Nuneaton	d	21 45		22 09	22 46			
Coleshill Parkway	d	22 00		22 25	23 02			
Water Orton	d							
Birmingham New Street 12	a	22 14		22 38	23 15			

Sundays
15 December to 10 May

		LE ◇ A	LE A	XC 1	XC 1	XC 1	XC ◇1	XC 1	LE A	XC ◇1	XC 1	LE A	XC ◇1 B 🚲	XC 1	LE A	XC ◇1	XC 1	LE A	XC ◇1	XC 1	LE A	XC ◇1 🚲	XC 1
Stansted Airport ✈	d	08 18	10 09				10 27		11 09	11 27		12 09	12 27		13 09	13 27		14 09	14 27		15 09	15 27	
Audley End	d	08 33	10 26				10 41		11 26	11 41		12 26	12 41		13 26	13 41		14 26	14 41		15 26	15 41	
Cambridge	d	08 50	10 50				11 01		11 50	12 01		12 50	13 01		13 50	14 01		14 50	15 01		15 50	16 01	
Ely 6	d	09a07	11a07				11 16		12a07	12 16		13a07	13 16		14a07	14 16		15a07	15 16		16a07	16 16	
March	d						11 32			12 32			13 32			14 32			15 32			16 32	
Peterborough 8	d						11 54			12 54			13 54			14 54			15 54			16 54	
Stamford	d						12 07			13 07			14 07			15 07			16 07			17 07	
Oakham	d						12 21			13 21			14 21			15 21			16 21			17 21	
Melton Mowbray	d						12 32			13 32			14 32			15 32			16 32			17 32	
Leicester	a						12 49			13 49			14 49			15 49			16 49			17 49	
	d			10 20	11 20	12 20	12 50	13 20		13 50	14 20		14 50	15 20		15 50	16 20		16 50	17 20		17 50	18 20
South Wigston	d					12 26					14 26						16 26			17 26			
Narborough	d			10 30	11 30	12 31		13 30			14 31			15 30			16 31			17 31			18 30
Hinckley	d			10 38	11 38	12 40		13 38			14 40			15 38			16 40			17 40			18 38
Nuneaton	d			10 46	11 46	12 46	13 09	13 46		14 09	14 46		15 09	15 46		16 09	16 46		17 09	17 46		18 09	18 46
Coleshill Parkway	d			11 02	12 02	13 02	13 25	14 02		14 25	15 02		15 25	16 02		16 25	17 02		17 25	18 02		18 25	19 02
Water Orton	d																						
Birmingham New Street 12	a			11 15	12 15	13 15	13 38	14 15		14 38	15 15		15 38	16 15		16 38	17 15		17 38	18 15		18 38	19 15

		LE A	XC ◇1 🚲	XC 1	LE A	XC ◇1 🚲	XC 1	LE A	XC ◇1	LE A	XC ◇1	XC 1	LE A	LE A
Stansted Airport ✈	d	16 09	16 27		17 09	17 27		18 09	18 27	19 09	19 27		20 09	21 11
Audley End	d	16 26	16 41		17 26	17 41		18 26	18 41	19 26	19 41		20 26	21 33
Cambridge	d	16 50	17 01		17 50	18 01		18 50	19 01	19 50	20 01		20 50	21 50
Ely 6	d	17a07	17 16		18a07	18 16		19a07	19 16	20a07	20 16		21a07	22a07
March	d		17 32			18 32			19 32		20 32			
Peterborough 8	d		17 54			18 54			19 54		20 54			
Stamford	d		18 07			19 07			20 07		21 07			
Oakham	d		18 21			19 21			20 21		21 21			
Melton Mowbray	d		18 32			19 32			20 32		21 32			
Leicester	a		18 49			19 49			20 49		21 49			
	d		18 50	19 20		19 50	20 20		20 50		21 50	22 20		
South Wigston	d			19 26			20 26					22 26		
Narborough	d			19 31			20 31					22 31		
Hinckley	d			19 40			20 40					22 40		
Nuneaton	d		19 09	19 46		20 09	20 46		21 09		22 09	22 46		
Coleshill Parkway	d		19 25	20 02		20 25	21 02		21 25		22 25	23 02		
Water Orton	d													
Birmingham New Street 12	a		19 38	20 15		20 38	21 15		21 38		22 38	23 15		

A To Norwich
B 🚲 from Peterborough

Table T047-R

Birmingham New Street - Leicester - Stansted Airport

Mondays to Fridays
16 December to 15 May

Miles	Miles			EM	EM	XC	XC	EM	XC	XC	LE	XC	XC	LE	XC	XC	LE	XC	XC	LE	XC	XC	LE
				◇ A	◇1 B 🛒	◇1	1	◇ A	◇1 🛒	1	C	◇1 🛒	1 D	C	◇1 E 🛒	1	C	◇1 🛒	1	C	◇1 🛒	1	C
0	0	**Birmingham New Street** 12	d			05 19	05 52		06 22	06 52		07 22	07 52		08 22	08 52		09 22	09 52		10 22	10 52	
—	7½	Water Orton	d													09 04						11 04	
9¾	9¾	Coleshill Parkway	d			05 33	06 06		06 36	07 06		07 35	08 06		08 36	09 08		09 36	10 09		10 37	11 08	
21¼	21¼	Nuneaton	d			05 48	06 21		06 51	07 24		07 50	08 24		08 51	09 24		09 51	10 24		10 52	11 24	
—	24¾	Hinckley	d			05 54	06 27			07 30		07 57	08 30			09 30			10 31			11 30	
—	32¾	Narborough	d			06 03	06 36			07 39		08 05	08 39			09 39			10 39			11 39	
—	35¾	South Wigston	d				06 41			07 44		08 10	08 44						10 44				
39¾	39¾	**Leicester**	a			06 13	06 47		07 15	07 50		08 17	08 50		09 11	09 50		10 10	10 51		11 11	11 49	
—	—		d			06 15			07 18			08 18			09 18			10 18			11 18		
54½	—	Melton Mowbray	d	05 36	05 58	06 31		06 53	07 34			08 34			09 34			10 34			11 34		
65¾	—	Oakham	d	05 49	06a09	06 43		07 06	07 46			08 46			09 46			10 46			11 46		
79½	—	Stamford	d	06 05		06 57		07 20	08 00			09 00			10 00			11 00			12 00		
91¾	—	Peterborough 8	d	06 28		07 13		07 38	08 19			09 19			10 19			11 19			12 19		
106½	—	March	d	06 44		07 32		07 54	08 34			09 34			10 34			11 34			12 34		
122	—	Ely 6	d	07a02		07 53		08a12	08 54		09 31	09 53		10 27	10 53		11 31	11 54		12 27	12 53		13 31
136¾	—	Cambridge	d			08 11			09 14		09 50	10 11		10 48	11 11		11 50	12 11		12 48	13 11		13 50
150¾	—	Audley End	d			08 26			09 29		10 07	10 26		11 06	11 26		12 07	12 26		13 06	13 26		14 07
161¼	—	**Stansted Airport** ✈	a			08 41			09 44		10 24	10 41		11 24	11 41		12 24	12 41		13 24	13 41		14 24

		XC	XC	LE	XC	XC	LE	XC	XC	LE	XC	XC	XC	XC	XC	EM	XC	XC	XC	XC	XC	XC	LE
		◇1 🛒	1	C	◇1 🛒	1	C	◇1 🛒	1	C	◇1 F 🛒	1	◇1	1	1	◇1 G 🛒	◇1	◇1	1	◇1	1 H	1	C
Birmingham New Street 12	d	11 22	11 52		12 22	12 52		13 22	13 52		14 22	14 52	15 22	15 52	16 09		16 22	16 52	17 09	17 22	17 39	17 52	
Water Orton	d					13 04						15 04			16 20				17 20		17a49	18 04	
Coleshill Parkway	d	11 36	12 07		12 36	13 08		13 36	14 09		14 36	15 08	15 37	16 09	16 24		16 36	17 06	17 24	17 36		18 08	
Nuneaton	d	11 51	12 24		12 51	13 24		13 51	14 24		14 51	15 24	15 52	16 24	16 40		16 52	17 21	17 40	17 51		18 24	
Hinckley	d		12 30			13 30			14 30			15 30		16 30	16 47			17 28	17 47	17 57		18 30	
Narborough	d		12 39			13 39			14 39			15 39		16 39	16 55			17 36		18 06		18 39	
South Wigston	d		12 44						14 44					16 44					18 03			18 44	
Leicester	a	12 12	12 50		13 15	13 51		14 11	14 50		15 11	15 49	16 11	16 50	17 08		17 16	17 51	18 11	18 16		18 50	
	d	12 18			13 18			14 18			15 18		16 18				17 18	17 58		18 18			
Melton Mowbray	d	12 34			13 34			14 34			15 34		16 34			17 11	17 34	18 15		18 34			
Oakham	d	12 46			13 46			14 46			15 46		16 46			17a22	17 46	18 27		18 46			
Stamford	d	13 00			14 00			15 00			16 00		17 00				18 00	18 41		19 00			
Peterborough 8	d	13 19			14 19			15 19			16 19		17 19				18 18	19 00		19 19			
March	d	13 34			14 34			15 34			16 34		17 38				18 33	19 15		19 34			
Ely 6	d	13 53		14 26	14 53		15 27	15 53		16 27	16 54		18 00				18 52	19 34		19 53			20 27
Cambridge	d	14 11		14 48	15 11		15 47	16 11		16 47	17 11		18 17				19 11	19a50		20 11			20 48
Audley End	d	14 26		15 06	15 26		16 05	16 26		17 05	17 26		18 35				19 26			20 26			21 06
Stansted Airport ✈	a	14 41		15 31	15 41		16 24	16 41		17 24	17 41		18 54				19 41			20 41			21 24

		XC	XC	XC	XC	XC	XC	XC
		◇1	1	◇1	1	◇1	1	1
Birmingham New Street 12	d	18 22	18 52	19 22	19 52	20 24	20 52	22 22
Water Orton	d				20 04			
Coleshill Parkway	d	18 36	19 06	19 36	20 08	20 38	21 06	22 36
Nuneaton	d	18 51	19 21	19 51	20 23	20 54	21 24	22 51
Hinckley	d		19 28		20 29		21 30	22 59
Narborough	d		19 36		20 38		21 39	23 08
South Wigston	d		19 41		20 43		21 44	23 13
Leicester	a	19 11	19 48	20 13	20 49	21 15	21 51	23 19
	d	19 18		20 18		21 17		
Melton Mowbray	d	19 34		20 34		21 34		
Oakham	d	19 46		20 46		21 46		
Stamford	d	20 00		21 00		22 00		
Peterborough 8	d	20 19		21 19		22 19		
March	d	20 34		21 34		22 34		
Ely 6	d	20 53		21 53		22 53		
Cambridge	d	21 11		22 11		23a09		
Audley End	d	21 26		22 26				
Stansted Airport ✈	a	21 41		22 41				

Saturdays
21 December to 16 May

		LE	EM	LE	XC	XC	EM	LE	XC	XC	LE	XC	XC	LE	XC	XC	LE	XC	XC	LE	XC	XC	LE
		C	◇ A	C	◇1	1	◇ A	C	◇1 🛒	1	C	◇1 🛒	1	C	◇1 I 🛒	1	C	◇1 🛒	1	C	◇1 🛒	1	C
Birmingham New Street 12	d				05 22	05 52			06 22	06 52		07 22	07 52		08 22	08 52		09 22	09 52		10 22	10 52	
Water Orton	d									07 04						09 04						11 04	
Coleshill Parkway	d				05 36	06 06			06 36	07 08		07 36	08 06		08 36	09 08		09 36	10 09		10 36	11 08	
Nuneaton	d				05 51	06 23			06 51	07 24		07 51	08 24		08 51	09 24		09 51	10 24		10 51	11 24	
Hinckley	d					06 29				07 30			08 30			09 30			10 30			11 30	
Narborough	d					06 38				07 39			08 39			09 39			10 39			11 39	
South Wigston	d					06 43				07 44			08 44						10 44				
Leicester	a				06 10	06 49			07 15	07 50		08 11	08 49		09 11	09 49		10 11	10 50		11 10	11 49	
	d				06 15				07 18			08 18			09 18			10 18			11 18		
Melton Mowbray	d		05 40		06 31		06 53		07 34			08 36			09 34			10 34			11 34		
Oakham	d		05 52		06 43		07 05		07 46			08 47			09 46			10 46			11 46		
Stamford	d		06 08		06 57		07 19		08 00			09 01			10 00			11 00			12 00		
Peterborough 8	d		06 27		07 13		07 35		08 19			09 19			10 19			11 19			12 19		
March	d		06 43		07 32		07 53		08 34			09 34			10 34			11 34			12 34		
Ely 6	d	06 27	07a03	07 26	07 53		08a13	08 27	08 53		09 27	09 53		10 27	10 53		11 27	11 53		12 27	12 53		13 31
Cambridge	d	06 51		07 48	08 11			08 48	09 11		09 48	10 11		10 48	11 11		11 48	12 11		12 48	13 11		13 51
Audley End	d	07 08		08 07	08 26			09 07	09 26		10 07	10 26		11 07	11 26		12 07	12 26		13 07	13 26		14 08
Stansted Airport ✈	a	07 24		08 24	08 41			09 24	09 41		10 24	10 41		11 24	11 41		12 24	12 41		13 24	13 41		14 24

A From Nottingham to Norwich
B To St Pancras International
C From Norwich
D Extra dwell to provide robust connection out of LM's 1U20
E From Bristol Temple Meads
F 🛒 to Leicester
G From Derby to Kettering
H To Derby
I From Gloucester

Table T047-R

Birmingham New Street - Leicester - Stansted Airport

Saturdays
21 December to 16 May

		XC	XC	LE	XC	XC	LE	XC	XC	LE	XC	XC	LE	XC	XC	LE	XC	XC	LE	XC	XC	LE
		◇1 🛒	1	A	◇1 🛒	1	A	◇1 🛒	1	A	◇1 B 🛒	1	A	◇1	1	A	◇1	1	A	◇1	1	A
Birmingham New Street 12	d	11 22	11 52		12 22	12 52		13 22	13 52		14 22	14 52		15 22	15 52		16 22	16 52		17 22	17 52	
Water Orton	d					13 04						15 04						17 04				
Coleshill Parkway	d	11 36	12 09		12 36	13 08		13 36	14 09		14 36	15 08		15 36	16 09		16 36	17 08		17 36	18 07	
Nuneaton	d	11 51	12 24		12 51	13 24		13 51	14 24		14 51	15 24		15 51	16 24		16 51	17 24		17 51	18 24	
Hinckley	d		12 30			13 30			14 30			15 30			16 30			17 30			18 30	
Narborough	d		12 39			13 39			14 39			15 39			16 39			17 39			18 39	
South Wigston	d		12 44						14 44						16 44						18 44	
Leicester	a	12 10	12 50		13 10	13 49		14 10	14 50		15 11	15 49		16 11	16 51		17 14	17 49		18 10	18 51	
	d	12 18			13 18			14 18			15 18			16 18			17 18			18 18		
Melton Mowbray	d	12 34			13 34			14 34			15 34			16 34			17 34			18 34		
Oakham	d	12 46			13 46			14 46			15 46			16 46			17 46			18 46		
Stamford	d	13 00			14 00			15 00			16 00			17 00			18 00			19 00		
Peterborough 8	d	13 19			14 19			15 19			16 19			17 19			18 19			19 19		
March	d	13 34			14 34			15 34			16 34			17 38			18 34			19 34		
Ely 6	d	13 53		14 27	14 53		15 28	15 53		16 26	16 53		17 27	18 00		18 27	18 53		19 27	19 53		20 27
Cambridge	d	14 11		14 48	15 11		15 48	16 11		16 48	17 11		17 48	18 17		18 48	19 11		19 48	20 11		20 48
Audley End	d	14 26		15 07	15 26		16 07	16 26		17 07	17 26		18 07	18 32		19 07	19 26		20 07	20 26		21 07
Stansted Airport ✈	a	14 41		15 24	15 41		16 24	16 41		17 24	17 41		18 24	18 52		19 24	19 41		20 24	20 41		21 24

		XC	XC	XC	XC	XC	XC	XC
		◇1	1	◇1	1	◇1	1	1
Birmingham New Street 12	d	18 22	18 52	19 22	19 52	20 22	20 52	22 22
Water Orton	d				20 04			
Coleshill Parkway	d	18 36	19 06	19 36	20 08	20 36	21 06	22 36
Nuneaton	d	18 51	19 24	19 51	20 24	20 51	21 24	22 51
Hinckley	d		19 30		20 30		21 30	22 57
Narborough	d		19 39		20 39		21 39	23 06
South Wigston	d		19 44		20 44		21 44	23 11
Leicester	a	19 10	19 50	20 10	20 50	21 13	21 50	23 17
	d	19 18		20 18		21 18		
Melton Mowbray	d	19 34		20 34		21 34		
Oakham	d	19 46		20 46		21 46		
Stamford	d	20 00		21 00		22 00		
Peterborough 8	d	20 19		21 19		22 14		
March	d	20 34		21 34		22 30		
Ely 6	d	20 53		21 53		22 48		
Cambridge	d	21 11		22 11		23a03		
Audley End	d	21 26		22 26				
Stansted Airport ✈	a	21 41		22 41				

Sundays
15 December to 10 May

		XC	LE	XC	LE	LE	LE	XC	XC	LE	XC	XC	LE	XC	XC	LE	XC	XC	LE	XC	XC	LE	XC
		1	A	1	A	A	A	◇1 🛒	1	A	◇1 🛒	1	A	◇1 🛒	1	A	◇1	1	A	◇1	1	A	◇1
Birmingham New Street 12	d	09 52		10 52				11 22	11 52		12 22	12 52		13 22	13 52		14 22	14 52		15 22	15 52		16 22
Water Orton	d																						
Coleshill Parkway	d	10 06		11 06				11 36	12 06		12 36	13 06		13 36	14 06		14 36	15 06		15 36	16 06		16 36
Nuneaton	d	10 21		11 21				11 51	12 21		12 51	13 21		13 51	14 21		14 51	15 21		15 51	16 21		16 51
Hinckley	d	10 27		11 27					12 28			13 28			14 28			15 28			16 28		
Narborough	d	10 36		11 36					12 36			13 36			14 36			15 36			16 36		
South Wigston	d	10 41							12 41						14 41						16 41		
Leicester	a	10 47		11 48				12 15	12 48		13 10	13 46		14 12	14 48		15 12	15 46		16 11	16 48		17 12
	d							12 18			13 18			14 18			15 18			16 18			17 18
Melton Mowbray	d							12 34			13 34			14 34			15 34			16 34			17 34
Oakham	d							12 46			13 46			14 46			15 46			16 46			17 46
Stamford	d							13 00			14 00			15 00			16 00			17 00			18 00
Peterborough 8	d							13 19			14 19			15 19			16 19			17 19			18 19
March	d							13 34			14 34			15 34			16 34			17 34			18 34
Ely 6	d		10 03		11 03	12 03	13 03	13 53		14 03	14 53		15 03	15 53		16 03	16 53		17 03	17 53		18 03	18 53
Cambridge	d		10 25		11 25	12 25	13 25	14 15		14 25	15 15		15 25	16 15		16 25	17 15		17 25	18 15		18 25	19 15
Audley End	d		10 43		11 43	12 43	13 43	14 30		14 43	15 30		15 43	16 30		16 43	17 30		17 43	18 30		18 43	19 30
Stansted Airport ✈	a		11 05		12 05	13 05	14 05	14 45		15 05	15 45		16 05	16 45		17 05	17 45		18 05	18 45		19 05	19 45

		XC	LE	XC	XC	LE	XC	XC	LE	XC	XC	XC	XC	XC
		1	A	◇1	1	A	◇1	1	A	◇1	1	◇1	1	◇1 C
Birmingham New Street 12	d	16 52		17 22	17 52		18 22	18 52		19 22	19 52	20 22	20 52	21 52
Water Orton	d													
Coleshill Parkway	d	17 06		17 36	18 06		18 36	19 06		19 36	20 06	20 36	21 06	22 07
Nuneaton	d	17 21		17 51	18 21		18 51	19 21		19 51	20 21	20 51	21 21	22 22
Hinckley	d	17 28			18 28			19 28			20 28		21 28	22 28
Narborough	d	17 36			18 36			19 36			20 36		21 36	22 37
South Wigston	d	17 41			18 41			19 41			20 41		21 41	22 42
Leicester	a	17 48		18 16	18 48		19 14	19 48		20 10	20 48	21 13	21 48	22 48
	d			18 18			19 18			20 18		21 18		
Melton Mowbray	d			18 34			19 34			20 34		21 34		
Oakham	d			18 46			19 46			20 46		21 46		
Stamford	d			19 00			20 00			21 00		22 00		
Peterborough 8	d			19 19			20 19			21 19		22 17		
March	d			19 34			20 34			21 34		22 32		
Ely 6	d		19 03	19 53		20 03	20 53		21 03	21 53		22 51		
Cambridge	d		19 25	20 15		20 25	21 13		21 25	22 15		23a06		
Audley End	d		19 43	20 30		20 43	21 30		21 43	22 30				
Stansted Airport ✈	a		20 05	20 45		21 05	21 45		22 05	22 45				

A From Norwich
B 🛒 to Leicester
C From Cardiff Central

Table T048-F

Mondays to Fridays
16 December to 15 May

Chathill and Morpeth - Newcastle - Metrocentre, Hexham and Carlisle

Miles	Miles			TP MX	NT	NT	GR	TP	NT	NT	GR	XC		NT	TP	NT	NT	XC	NT	NT	GR	XC		TP	NT
				◇1		◇	1	◇1	◇		1	◇1			◇1	◇	◇	◇1			1	◇1		◇1	◇
0	—	**Chathill**	d														07 10								
11¼	—	Alnmouth for Alnwick 26	d				06 21				06 56	07 11					07 22	08 03			09 00				
17½	—	Acklington	d														07 43								
22¾	—	Widdrington	d														07 50								
27½	—	Pegswood	d														07 56								
39½	—	**Morpeth** 26	d	00 01			06 38	06 43			07 12				07 44		08 00	08 18		08 55		09 24		09 29	
36¼	—	Cramlington	d														08 09			09 04					
45½	—	Manors	d														08 19			09 14					
46	—	**Newcastle** 8 26 ⛴	a	00 27			06 52	06 57			07 26	07 38			07 58		08 22	08 32		09 17	09 27	09 39		09 44	
—	—	Sunderland 26,44 ⛴	d											07 19					08 30						
—	0	**Newcastle** 8 ⛴	d		05 42	06 20			07 02	07 25				07 44		08 05	08 23		08 55	09 23					09 46
48¼	2¼	Dunston	d			06 25				07 30									09 00						
49½	3½	**Metrocentre**	a		05 49	06 28			07 09	07 33				07 51		08 14	08 30		09 03	09 30					09 53
—	—		d		05 49	06 29			07 10	07 34				07 52		08 14	08 31		09 04	09 31					09 54
—	5½	Blaydon	d		05 54	06 33			07 14	07 38							08 35		09 08						
—	9¾	Wylam	d		06 00	06 39			07 20	07 44							08 41		09 14						
—	12	Prudhoe	d		06 04	06 44			07 25	07 49				08 02		08 25	08 46		09 19	09 42					10 07
—	14½	Stocksfield	d		06 09	06 48			07 29					08 07			08 50		09 23						
—	16¾	Riding Mill	d		06 13				07 34					08 11			08 55		09 28						
—	19¼	Corbridge	d		06 17				07 38								08 59		09 32						
—	22¼	**Hexham**	a		06 23	06 58			07 44	08 01				08 20		08 38	09 05		09 38	09 54					10 21
—	—		d		06 24	06 59			07 44	08 02						08 38	09 05			09 55					10 22
—	30	Haydon Bridge	d			07 08				08 11							09 15								10 31
—	33¾	Bardon Mill	d			07 14				08 17							09 21								
—	38½	Haltwhistle	d		06 43	07 22			08 03	08 25						08 57	09 28			10 14					10 42
—	50¾	Brampton (Cumbria)	d			07 37				08 40															10 57
—	57½	Wetheral	d			07 46			08 26	08 49						09 20	09 51								11 07
—	61¾	**Carlisle** 8	a		07 13	07 59			08 36	08 59						09 29	10 01			10 44					11 17

		NT	NT	XC	NT	NT	TP	NT		GR	XC	NT	TP	NT	NT	XC	NT	NT		TP	NT	GR	XC	NT	NT
				◇1	◇		◇1			1	◇1	◇	◇1			◇1	◇			◇1		1	◇1	◇	
Chathill	d																								
Alnmouth for Alnwick 26	d			10 12						11 00						12 12						13 00			
Acklington	d																								
Widdrington	d																								
Pegswood	d																								
Morpeth 26	d		09 55				10 48	10 55			11 22		11 33		11 55					12 46	12 55		13 21		
Cramlington	d		10 04					11 04							12 04						13 04				
Manors	d		10 14					11 14							12 14						13 14				
Newcastle 8 26 ⛴	a		10 16	10 39			11 02	11 16		11 27	11 36		11 53		12 16	12 38				13 00	13 16	13 27	13 35		
Sunderland 26,44 ⛴	d	09 30				10 30								11 30				12 30							13 30
Newcastle 8 ⛴	d	09 55	10 23		10 46	10 55		11 23				11 51		12 00	12 23		12 39	12 55			13 23			13 39	13 55
Dunston	d	10 00				11 00								12 05				13 00							14 00
Metrocentre	a	10 03	10 30		10 53	11 03		11 30				12 00		12 08	12 30		12 46	13 03			13 30			13 46	14 03
	d	10 04	10 31		10 54	11 04		11 31				12 01		12 09	12 31		12 47	13 04			13 31			13 47	14 04
Blaydon	d	10 08				11 08								12 13				13 08							14 08
Wylam	d	10 14				11 14								12 19				13 14							14 14
Prudhoe	d	10 19	10 42		11 05	11 19		11 42				12 12		12 24	12 42		12 59	13 19			13 42			13 58	14 19
Stocksfield	d	10 23				11 23								12 28				13 23							14 23
Riding Mill	d	10 28				11 28								12 33				13 28							14 28
Corbridge	d	10 32				11 32								12 37				13 32							14 32
Hexham	a	10 38	10 54		11 17	11 38		11 54				12 30		12 43	12 54		13 10	13 38			13 54			14 10	14 38
	d		10 55		11 18			11 55				12 32			12 55		13 11				13 55			14 11	
Haydon Bridge	d				11 29							12 41					13 20							14 20	
Bardon Mill	d				11 35												13 26								
Haltwhistle	d		11 14		11 42			12 14				12 53			13 14		13 34				14 14			14 31	
Brampton (Cumbria)	d											13 08												14 46	
Wetheral	d				12 05							13 17					13 56							14 56	
Carlisle 8	a		11 44		12 15			12 44				13 27			13 46		14 06				14 44			15 06	

For connections to and from London Kings Cross refer to Table T026

Table T048-F

Mondays to Fridays
16 December to 15 May

Chathill and Morpeth - Newcastle - Metrocentre, Hexham and Carlisle

		TP	NT	NT	XC	TP	NT	NT	GR	NT		NT	TP	NT	NT	NT	TP	NT	NT	XC		NT	TP	NT	NT
		◇1		◇	◇1	◇1			1	◇			◇1		◇		◇1		◇	◇1			◇1		◇
Chathill	d																								
Alnmouth for Alnwick 26	d				14 13				15 00											17 07					
Acklington	d																								
Widdrington	d																								
Pegswood	d																								
Morpeth 26	d	13 49	13 55			14 32		14 55	15 15				15 47	15 55			16 48		16 55	17 21			17 48		17 55
Cramlington	d		14 04					15 04						16 04					17 04						18 04
Manors	d		14 14					15 14						16 14					17 14						18 14
Newcastle 8 26 ⛴	a	14 03	14 18		14 40	14 50		15 18	15 30				16 02	16 18			17 03		17 17	17 36			18 04		
Sunderland 26,44 ⛴	d						14 30					15 30				16 30						17 30			
Newcastle 8 ⛴	d		14 23	14 33			14 55	15 23		15 40		15 55		16 23	16 40	16 55		17 05	17 23			17 55		18 08	
Dunston	d						15 00					16 00				17 00						18 00			
Metrocentre	a		14 30	14 40			15 03	15 30		15 47		16 03		16 30	16 47	17 03		17 12	17 30			18 03		18 17	18 30
	d		14 31	14 41			15 04	15 31		15 48		16 04		16 31	16 48			17 13	17 31			18 04		18 17	18 31
Blaydon	d						15 08					16 08			16 52			17 17	17 35			18 08		18 22	18 35
Wylam	d						15 14					16 14			16 58			17 23	17 41			18 15		18 28	18 42
Prudhoe	d		14 42	14 52			15 19	15 42		15 59		16 19		16 42	17 03			17 28	17 46			18 19		18a33	18 46
Stocksfield	d						15 23					16 23			17 07			17 32	17 50			18 24			18 50
Riding Mill	d						15 28					16 28			17 12			17 37	17 55			18 28			18 55
Corbridge	d						15 32					16 32			17 16			17 41	17 59			18 32			18 59
Hexham	a		14 54	15 04			15 38	15 54		16 11		16 38		16 54	17 22			17 47	18 05			18 38			19 05
	d		14 55	15 05				15 55		16 12				16 55	17 22				18 05						19 05
Haydon Bridge	d			15 14						16 21					17 32				18 15						19 15
Bardon Mill	d			15 20											17 38				18 21						19 21
Haltwhistle	d		15 14	15 28				16 14		16 32				17 14	17 45				18 28						19 28
Brampton (Cumbria)	d									16 47									18 43						19 43
Wetheral	d			15 50						16 57					18 07				18 52						19 52
Carlisle 8	a		15 44	15 59				16 44		17 07				17 44	18 17				19 02						20 02

		GR	XC	NT	TP	NT		XC	TP	NT	NT	GR	NT	TP	GR	NT		XC	NT	TP	NT	GR	NT	NT	GR FO
		1	◇1		◇1	◇		◇1	◇1		◇	1		◇1	1	◇		◇1		◇1		1			1
Chathill	d										19 15														
Alnmouth for Alnwick 26	d	18 00						19 14			19 27	19 43		20 31	20 40			21 09				22 11			23 09
Acklington	d										19 35														
Widdrington	d										19 42														
Pegswood	d										19 48														
Morpeth 26	d		18 24		18 52	18 57			19 33		19 52	20 00		20 45	20 57	21 02				21 45	21 57	22 28	22 55		23 26
Cramlington	d					19 06					20 01					21 11					22 06		23 04		
Manors	d					19 16					20 11					21 21					22 16		23 14		
Newcastle 8 26 ⛴	a	18 27	18 38		19 06	19 18		19 40	19 47			20 14		20 59	21 12	21 23		21 35		21 59	22 18	22 42	23 17		23 54
Sunderland 26,44 ⛴	d			18 30						19 30			20 30						21 30					22 29	
Newcastle 8 ⛴	d			18 55		19 23				19 51			20 53			21 25			21 56		22 23			22 53	
Dunston	d			19 00						19 56			20 58						22 02		22 28			22 58	
Metrocentre	a			19 03		19 30				19 59	20 30		21 01			21 32			22 05		22 32			23 01	
	d			19 04		19 31					20 31					21 33								23 02	
Blaydon	d			19 08		19 35					20 35					21 37								23 06	
Wylam	d			19 14		19 41					20 41					21 43								23 12	
Prudhoe	d			19 19		19 46					20 46					21 48								23 17	
Stocksfield	d			19 23		19 50					20 50					21 52								23 21	
Riding Mill	d			19 28		19 55					20 55					21 57								23 26	
Corbridge	d			19 32		19 59					20 59					22 01								23 30	
Hexham	a			19 38		20 05					21 05					22 07								23 36	
	d					20 05					21 05					22 07									
Haydon Bridge	d					20 15					21 14					22 17									
Bardon Mill	d					20 21										22 23									
Haltwhistle	d					20 28					21 26					22 30									
Brampton (Cumbria)	d					20 43										22 45									
Wetheral	d					20 52										22 54									
Carlisle 8	a					21 02					21 56					23 04									

For connections to and from London Kings Cross refer to Table T026

Table T048-F

Mondays to Fridays
16 December to 15 May

Chathill and Morpeth - Newcastle - Metrocentre, Hexham and Carlisle

Station		TP
		◇1
Chathill	d	
Alnmouth for Alnwick 26	d	23 35
Acklington	d	
Widdrington	d	
Pegswood	d	
Morpeth 26	d	00 01
Cramlington	d	
Manors	d	
Newcastle 26	a	00 27
Sunderland 26,44	d	
Newcastle	d	
Dunston	d	
Metrocentre	a	
	d	
Blaydon	d	
Wylam	d	
Prudhoe	d	
Stocksfield	d	
Riding Mill	d	
Corbridge	d	
Hexham	a	
	d	
Haydon Bridge	d	
Bardon Mill	d	
Haltwhistle	d	
Brampton (Cumbria)	d	
Wetheral	d	
Carlisle	a	

Saturdays
21 December to 16 May

Station		TP	NT	NT	TP	NT	NT	GR	XC	NT	TP	NT	NT	XC	NT	NT	GR	XC	TP	NT	NT	NT	NT
		◇1		◇	◇1	◇		1	◇1		◇1	◇	◇	◇1			1	◇1	◇1	◇			◇
Chathill	d												07 10										
Alnmouth for Alnwick 26	d							06 56	07 10				07 22	08 03			09 01	09 12					
Acklington	d												07 43										
Widdrington	d												07 50										
Pegswood	d												07 56										
Morpeth 26	d	00 01			06 43			07 12			07 44		08 00	08 18		08 55			09 29			09 55	
Cramlington	d												08 09			09 04						10 04	
Manors	d												08 19			09 14						10 14	
Newcastle 26	a	00 27			06 57			07 26	07 37		08 02		08 22	08 32		09 17	09 27	09 39	09 45			10 16	
Sunderland 26,44	d									07 16					08 30						09 30		
Newcastle	d		05 42	06 20		07 02	07 25			07 44		08 05	08 23		08 55	09 23				09 46	09 55	10 23	10 31
Dunston	d			06 25			07 30								09 00						10 00		
Metrocentre	a		05 49	06 28		07 09	07 33			07 51		08 14	08 30		09 03	09 30				09 53	10 03	10 30	10 38
	d		05 49	06 29		07 10	07 34			07 52		08 14	08 31		09 04	09 31				09 54	10 04	10 31	10 43
Blaydon	d		05 54	06 33		07 14	07 38						08 35		09 08						10 08		
Wylam	d		06 00	06 39		07 20	07 44						08 41		09 14						10 14		
Prudhoe	d		06 04	06 44		07 25	07 49			08 02		08 25	08 46		09 19	09 42				10 07	10 19	10 42	10 54
Stocksfield	d		06 09	06 48		07 29				08 07			08 50		09 23						10 23		
Riding Mill	d		06 13			07 34				08 11			08 55		09 28						10 28		
Corbridge	d		06 17			07 38							08 59		09 32						10 32		
Hexham	a		06 23	06 58		07 44	08 01			08 20		08 38	09 05		09 38	09 54				10 21	10 38	10 54	11 08
	d		06 24	06 59		07 44	08 02					08 38	09 05			09 55				10 22		10 55	11 09
Haydon Bridge	d			07 08			08 11					08 47	09 15							10 31			11 18
Bardon Mill	d			07 14			08 17						09 21										11 24
Haltwhistle	d		06 43	07 22		08 03	08 25					08 59	09 28			10 14				10 42		11 14	11 32
Brampton (Cumbria)	d			07 37			08 40													10 57			
Wetheral	d			07 46		08 26	08 49					09 21	09 51							11 07			11 55
Carlisle	a		07 13	07 59		08 36	08 59					09 32	10 01			10 44				11 17		11 44	12 05

For connections to and from London Kings Cross refer to Table T026

Table T048-F

Saturdays
21 December to 16 May

Chathill and Morpeth - Newcastle - Metrocentre, Hexham and Carlisle

Station		NT	TP	NT	GR	XC	NT	NT	TP	NT	NT	XC	NT	TP	NT	GR	XC	NT	NT	TP	NT	XC
			◇1		1	◇1	◇		◇1		◇	◇1		◇1		1	◇1	◇		◇1		◇1
Chathill	d																					
Alnmouth for Alnwick 26	d				11 00							12 13				13 00						14 12
Acklington	d																					
Widdrington	d																					
Pegswood	d																					
Morpeth 26	d		10 48	10 55		11 22			11 48	11 55				12 46	12 55		13 20			13 49	13 55	
Cramlington	d			11 04						12 04					13 04						14 04	
Manors	d			11 14						12 14					13 14						14 14	
Newcastle 26	a		11 02	11 16	11 27	11 36			12 02	12 16		12 40		13 00	13 16	13 27	13 34			14 03	14 18	14 39
Sunderland 26,44	d	10 30						11 30					12 30						13 30			
Newcastle	d	10 55		11 23			11 51	12 00		12 23	12 39		12 55		13 23			13 39	13 55		14 23	
Dunston	d	11 00						12 05					13 00						14 00			
Metrocentre	a	11 03		11 30			12 00	12 08		12 30	12 46		13 03		13 30			13 46	14 03		14 30	
	d	11 04		11 31			12 01	12 09		12 31	12 47		13 04		13 31			13 47	14 04		14 31	
Blaydon	d	11 08						12 13					13 08						14 08			
Wylam	d	11 14						12 19					13 14						14 14			
Prudhoe	d	11 19		11 42			12 12	12 24		12 42	12 59		13 19		13 42			13 58	14 19		14 42	
Stocksfield	d	11 23						12 28					13 23						14 23			
Riding Mill	d	11 28						12 33					13 28						14 28			
Corbridge	d	11 32						12 37					13 32						14 32			
Hexham	a	11 38		11 54			12 30	12 43		12 54	13 10		13 38		13 54			14 10	14 38		14 54	
	d			11 55			12 32			12 55	13 11				13 55			14 11			14 55	
Haydon Bridge	d						12 41				13 20							14 20				
Bardon Mill	d										13 26											
Haltwhistle	d			12 14			12 53			13 14	13 34				14 14			14 31			15 14	
Brampton (Cumbria)	d						13 08											14 46				
Wetheral	d						13 17				13 56							14 56				
Carlisle	a			12 44			13 27			13 46	14 06				14 44			15 06			15 44	

Station		NT	TP	NT	NT	GR	XC	NT	NT	TP	NT	NT	NT	TP	NT	NT	XC	NT	TP	NT	NT	GR	NT
		◇	◇1			1	◇1	◇		◇1		◇		◇1		◇	◇1		◇1		◇	1	
Chathill	d																						
Alnmouth for Alnwick 26	d					15 00											17 06					18 00	
Acklington	d																						
Widdrington	d																						
Pegswood	d																						
Morpeth 26	d		14 37		14 55	15 15	15 22			15 47	15 55			16 48		16 55	17 20		17 48		17 55		
Cramlington	d				15 04						16 04					17 04					18 04		
Manors	d				15 14						16 14					17 14					18 14		
Newcastle 26	a		14 52		15 18	15 30	15 36			16 01	16 18			17 03		17 17	17 34		18 04			18 26	
Sunderland 26,44	d			14 30					15 30				16 30					17 30					18 30
Newcastle	d	14 40		14 55	15 23			15 40	15 55		16 23	16 40	16 55		17 05	17 23		17 55		18 08			18 55
Dunston	d			15 00					16 00				17 00					18 00					19 00
Metrocentre	a	14 47		15 03	15 30			15 47	16 03		16 30	16 47	17 03		17 12	17 30		18 03		18 17	18 30		19 03
	d	14 48		15 04	15 31			15 48	16 04		16 31	16 48			17 13	17 31		18 04		18 17	18 31		19 04
Blaydon	d			15 08					16 08			16 52			17 17	17 35		18 08		18 22	18 35		19 08
Wylam	d			15 14					16 14			16 58			17 23	17 41		18 15		18 28	18 42		19 14
Prudhoe	d	14 59		15 19	15 42			15 59	16 19		16 42	17 03			17 28	17 46		18 19		18a33	18 46		19 19
Stocksfield	d			15 23					16 23			17 07			17 32	17 50		18 24			18 50		19 23
Riding Mill	d			15 28					16 28			17 12			17 37	17 55		18 28			18 55		19 28
Corbridge	d			15 32					16 32			17 16			17 41	17 59		18 32			18 59		19 32
Hexham	a	15 11		15 38	15 54			16 11	16 38		16 54	17 22			17 47	18 05		18 38			19 05		19 38
	d	15 12			15 55			16 12			16 55	17 22				18 05					19 05		
Haydon Bridge	d	15 21						16 21				17 32				18 15					19 15		
Bardon Mill	d	15 27										17 38				18 21					19 21		
Haltwhistle	d	15 35			16 14			16 32			17 14	17 45				18 28					19 28		
Brampton (Cumbria)	d							16 47								18 43					19 43		
Wetheral	d	15 57						16 57				18 07				18 52					19 52		
Carlisle	a	16 07			16 44			17 07			17 44	18 17				19 02					20 02		

For connections to and from London Kings Cross refer to Table T026

Table T048-F

Saturdays
21 December to 16 May

Chathill and Morpeth - Newcastle - Metrocentre, Hexham and Carlisle

	TP	NT	XC	NT	TP		NT	NT	GR	NT	TP	NT	NT	GR	NT		NT	NT
	◇1 ✠	◇	◇1 ✠		◇1		◇		■ 1 ⊏		◇1		◇	■ 1 ⊏				
Chathill d								19 34										
Alnmouth for Alnwick 26 d			19 14					19 46	20 08		20 31			21 09				
Acklington d								19 54										
Widdrington d								20 01										
Pegswood d								20 07										
Morpeth 26 d	18 52	18 57			19 47			20 11	20 25		20 45	20 54		21 26			22 11	22 55
Cramlington d		19 06						20 19				21 03					22 20	23 04
Manors d		19 16						20 29				21 13					22 30	23 14
Newcastle 8 26 ⛴ a	19 06	19 18	19 40		20 01			20 34	20 41		20 59	21 16		21 43			22 32	23 17
Sunderland 26,44 ⛴ d				19 30						20 30					21 30			
Newcastle 8 ⛴ d		19 23		19 55			20 33			20 53			21 25		21 56		22 36	
Dunston d				20 00						20 58					22 02		22 41	
Metrocentre a		19 30		20 03			20 40			21 01			21 32		22 05		22 44	
d		19 31		20 04			20 41						21 33				22 45	
Blaydon d		19 35		20 08			20 45						21 37				22 49	
Wylam d		19 41		20 14			20 51						21 43				22 55	
Prudhoe d		19 46		20a19			20 56						21 48				23 00	
Stocksfield d		19 50					21 00						21 52				23 04	
Riding Mill d		19 55					21 05						21 57				23 09	
Corbridge d		19 59					21 09						22 01				23 13	
Hexham a		20 05					21 15						22 07				23 19	
d		20 05					21 15						22 07					
Haydon Bridge d		20 15					21 24						22 17					
Bardon Mill d		20 21											22 23					
Haltwhistle d		20 28					21 36						22 30					
Brampton (Cumbria) d		20 43					21 51						22 45					
Wetheral d		20 52					22 00						22 54					
Carlisle 8 a		21 02					22 11						23 04					

Sundays
15 December to 10 May

	NT	NT	NT	NT	NT	TP	NT	NT	GR		NT	XC	TP	NT	NT	NT	XC	GR	NT		NT	TP	GR	NT
	◇		◇			◇1 ✠	◇		■ 1 ⊏			◇1 ✠	◇1 ✠	◇			◇1 ✠	■ 1 ⊏	◇			◇1 ✠	■ 1 ⊏	
Chathill d																								
Alnmouth for Alnwick 26 d									11 00			11 07					12 10						13 00	
Acklington d																								
Widdrington d																								
Pegswood d																								
Morpeth 26 d		09 05		09 54		10 30						11 22	11 33		11 50			12 34				12 48		
Cramlington d		09 14		10 03											11 59									
Manors d		09 24		10 13											12 09									
Newcastle 8 26 ⛴ a		09 26		10 15		10 44			11 27			11 36	11 47		12 11		12 36	12 48				13 02	13 27	
Sunderland 26,44 ⛴ d			09 30				10 30							11 30					12 30					
Newcastle 8 ⛴ d	08 45	09 30	09 55	10 16	10 35		10 55	11 15			11 35			11 55	12 15	12 35			12 55		13 15			13 35
Dunston d		09 35		10 21				11 21							12 20						13 21			
Metrocentre a	08 52	09 39	10 02	10 25	10 43		11 02	11 24			11 43			12 02	12 24	12 43			13 02		13 24			13 43
d	08 53		10 03				11 03							12 03					13 03					
Blaydon d	08 57		10 07											12 07										
Wylam d	09 03		10 13				11 11							12 13					13 11					
Prudhoe d	09 08		10 17				11 15							12 18					13 15					
Stocksfield d	09 12		10 22				11 20							12 22					13 20					
Riding Mill d	09 17		10 26				11 24							12 27					13 24					
Corbridge d	09 21		10 30				11 28							12 31					13 28					
Hexham a	09 27		10 36				11 34							12 37					13 34					
d	09 27		10 37				11 35							12 37					13 35					
Haydon Bridge d	09 37		10 46				11 44												13 44					
Bardon Mill d	09 43		10 52				11 50												13 50					
Haltwhistle d	09 50		11 00				11 58							12 56					13 58					
Brampton (Cumbria) d	10 05		11 15											13 11										
Wetheral d	10 14		11 24											13 20										
Carlisle 8 a	10 24		11 34				12 32							13 30					14 28					

For connections to and from London Kings Cross refer to Table T026

Table T048-F

Sundays
15 December to 10 May

Chathill and Morpeth - Newcastle - Metrocentre, Hexham and Carlisle

	GR		TP	NT	NT	NT	XC	NT	NT	TP	GR		XC	NT	TP	NT	NT	NT	XC	TP	NT		NT	GR
	■ 1 ⊏		◇1 ✠	◇			◇1 ✠	◇		◇1 ✠	■ 1 ⊏		◇1 ✠		◇1 ✠	◇			◇1 ✠	◇1 ✠	◇			■ 1 ⊏
Chathill d																								
Alnmouth for Alnwick 26 d							14 11				15 00													17 00
Acklington d																								
Widdrington d																								
Pegswood d																								
Morpeth 26 d	13 33		13 38		13 50					14 49			15 20		15 31		15 50		16 22	16 30				
Cramlington d					13 59												15 59							
Manors d					14 09												16 09							
Newcastle 8 26 ⛴ a	13 47		13 53		14 11		14 37			15 03	15 28		15 35		15 44		16 11		16 36	16 44				17 27
Sunderland 26,44 ⛴ d				13 30				14 30								15 30					16 30			
Newcastle 8 ⛴ d				13 55	14 15	14 28		14 55	15 15					15 35		15 55	16 15	16 35			16 55		17 15	
Dunston d					14 20				15 21								16 20						17 21	
Metrocentre a				14 02	14 24	14 36		15 02	15 24					15 43		16 02	16 24	16 43			17 02		17 24	
d				14 03				15 03								16 03					17 03			
Blaydon d				14 07												16 07								
Wylam d				14 13				15 11								16 13					17 11			
Prudhoe d				14 18				15 15								16 18					17 15			
Stocksfield d				14 22				15 20								16 22					17 20			
Riding Mill d				14 27				15 24								16 27					17 24			
Corbridge d				14 31				15 28								16 31					17 28			
Hexham a				14 37				15 34								16 37					17 34			
d				14 37				15 35								16 37					17 35			
Haydon Bridge d								15 44								16 46					17 44			
Bardon Mill d								15 50													17 50			
Haltwhistle d				14 56				15 58								16 58					17 58			
Brampton (Cumbria) d				15 11												17 13								
Wetheral d				15 20												17 22								
Carlisle 8 a				15 30				16 28								17 33					18 29			

	NT	XC	GR	NT	TP	NT	NT		TP	NT	NT	GR	XC	TP	NT	NT	NT		TP	NT	GR	TP	NT	GR
		◇1 ✠	■ 1 ⊏	◇	◇1 ✠				◇1 ✠	◇		■ 1 ⊏	◇1 ✠	◇1	◇				◇1	◇	■ 1 ⊏	◇1		■ 1 ⊏
Chathill d																								
Alnmouth for Alnwick 26 d		17 08										19 01									21 10			22 10
Acklington d																								
Widdrington d																								
Pegswood d																								
Morpeth 26 d		17 22	17 33		17 48	17 55			18 30				19 23	19 30		19 50			20 40		21 27	21 40	21 45	
Cramlington d						18 04										19 59							21 54	
Manors d						18 14										20 09							22 04	
Newcastle 8 26 ⛴ a		17 36	17 47		18 02	18 16			18 44			19 28	19 38	19 44		20 11			20 55		21 41	21 55	22 06	22 38
Sunderland 26,44 ⛴ d				17 30						18 30					19 30					20 30				
Newcastle 8 ⛴ d	17 32			17 55		18 17	18 35			18 55	19 15				19 55	20 15	20 35			21 00				
Dunston d						18 22					19 20					20 20				21 05				
Metrocentre a	17 40			18 02		18 26	18 43			19 02	19 24				20 02	20 24	20 43			21 08				
d				18 03						19 03					20 03					21 09				
Blaydon d				18 07											20 07					21 13				
Wylam d				18 13						19 11					20 13					21 19				
Prudhoe d				18 18						19 15					20 18					21 24				
Stocksfield d				18 22						19 20					20 22					21 28				
Riding Mill d				18 27						19 24					20 27					21 33				
Corbridge d				18 31						19 28					20 31					21 37				
Hexham a				18 37						19 34					20 37					21 43				
d				18 37						19 35					20 37					21 43				
Haydon Bridge d				18 46						19 44					20 47					21 53				
Bardon Mill d										19 50					20 53					21 59				
Haltwhistle d				18 58						19 58					21 00					22 06				
Brampton (Cumbria) d				19 13											21 15					22 21				
Wetheral d				19 22											21 24					22 30				
Carlisle 8 a				19 36						20 28					21 34					22 40				

For connections to and from London Kings Cross refer to Table T026

Table T048-R

Mondays to Fridays
16 December to 15 May

Carlisle, Hexham and Metrocentre - Newcastle - Morpeth and Chathill

Miles	Miles			NT MX	TP	NT	GR	NT	NT	TP	NT	XC	GR	NT	TP	SR	GR	NT	NT	TP	XC	NT	SR
0	—	**Carlisle**	d								05 44			06 32		06 57		07 26				08 03	08 20
4¼	—	Wetheral	d								05 51			06 39		07 04						08 10	08 27
11	—	Brampton (Cumbria)	d								06 05					07 14							08 37
23¼	—	Haltwhistle	d								06 20			07 06		07 29		07 54				08 33	08 52
28	—	Bardon Mill	d								06 27			07 13		07 36						08 40	08 59
31½	—	Haydon Bridge	d								06 33			07 19		07 42						08 46	09 05
39½	—	**Hexham**	a								06 43			07 30		07 52		08 13				08 56	09 15
—	—		d					06 09	06 37		06 46			07 31		07 52		08 14	08 26			08 57	09 18
42½	—	Corbridge	d					06 14	06 42		06 51			07 35		07 57			08 31			09 01	
45	—	Riding Mill	d					06 18	06 46		06 55			07 40		08 01			08 35			09 06	
47½	—	Stocksfield	d					06 22	06 50		06 59			07 44		08 05			08 39			09 10	
49½	—	Prudhoe	d					06 27	06 55		07 04			07 48		08 10		08 26	08 44			09 14	09 30
52	—	Wylam	d	00 04				06 31	06 59		07 09			07 53		08 14		08 31				09 19	
56¼	—	Blaydon	d					06 37	07 05		07 15			07 59		08 20		08 41				09 25	
58¼	—	**Metrocentre**	a	00 13				06 42	07 10		07 19			08 04		08 25		08 45	08 55			09 29	09 42
—	—		d	00 13				06 42	07 10		07 22			08 04		08 25		08 46	08 56			09 30	09 44
59½	1¼	Dunston	d					06 45	07 13		07 25			08 07		08 28						09 33	
61½	3½	**Newcastle**	a	00 23				06 52	07 20		07 32			08 14		08 35		08 54	09 06			09 45	09 54
—	—	Sunderland 26,44	a					07 13			08 01												
—	—	**Newcastle** 26	d		05 53	05 57	06 22			07 21		07 35	07 42	08 16	08 21		08 42	08 59		09 21	09 33	09 57	
—	4	Manors	d			06 00								08 19				09 01				09 59	
—	13¼	Cramlington	d			06 10								08 30				09 11				10 09	
—	20	**Morpeth** 26	d		06 08	06 19	06 38			07a34		07a47		08a38	08a34		08a55	09a18		09a33		10a17	
—	22	Pegswood	d																				
—	26½	Widdrington	d																				
—	32	Acklington	d																				
—	38½	Alnmouth for Alnwick 26	d		06a21	06 35	06a53						08a08								09a57		
—	49½	**Chathill**	a			06 48																	

		NT	NT	TP	GR	NT	NT	NT	TP	XC	NT	NT	NT	TP	GR	NT	NT	NT	TP	XC	NT	NT	NT
Carlisle	d	08 50				09 22	09 52				10 23	10 54				11 25	11 52				12 25	12 53	
Wetheral	d	08 57				09 32					10 30					11 32					12 32		
Brampton (Cumbria)	d					09 42										11 42							
Haltwhistle	d	09 20				09 57	10 20				10 53	11 22				11 57	12 20				12 55	13 21	
Bardon Mill	d										11 00										13 02		
Haydon Bridge	d	09 31				10 07					11 06					12 07					13 08		
Hexham	a	09 41				10 17	10 39				11 16	11 41				12 17	12 39				13 18	13 40	
	d	09 42	09 56			10 18	10 40	10 56			11 18	11 42	11 56			12 18	12 40	12 56			13 19	13 41	13 56
Corbridge	d		10 00					11 00					12 00					13 00					14 00
Riding Mill	d		10 05					11 05					12 05					13 05					14 05
Stocksfield	d		10 09					11 09					12 09					13 09					14 09
Prudhoe	d	09 54	10 13			10 30	10 52	11 13			11 30	11 54	12 13			12 30	12 52	13 13			13 31	13 53	14 13
Wylam	d		10 18					11 18					12 18					13 18					14 18
Blaydon	d		10 24					11 24					12 24					13 24					14 24
Metrocentre	a	10 05	10 28			10 41	11 03	11 28			11 42	12 05	12 28			12 41	13 03	13 28			13 42	14 04	14 28
	d	10 06	10 29			10 44	11 04	11 29			11 44	12 06	12 29			12 44	13 04	13 29			13 44	14 05	14 29
Dunston	d		10 32					11 32					12 32					13 32					14 32
Newcastle	a	10 14	10 39			10 53	11 12	11 39			11 53	12 16	12 39			12 52	13 13	13 39			13 52	14 13	14 39
Sunderland 26,44	a		11 01					12 01					13 01					14 01					15 01
Newcastle 26	d			10 21	10 42	10 57			11 21	11 32	11 57			12 21	12 39	12 57			13 21	13 35	13 57		
Manors	d					10 59					11 59					12 59					13 59		
Cramlington	d					11 09					12 09					13 09					14 09		
Morpeth 26	d			10a34		11a18			11a34	11a45	12a18			12a34	12 55	13a18			13a34		14a18		
Pegswood	d																						
Widdrington	d																						
Acklington	d																						
Alnmouth for Alnwick 26	d				11a07										13a09					13a59			
Chathill	a																						

For connections to and from London Kings Cross refer to Table T026

Table T048-R

Mondays to Fridays
16 December to 15 May

Carlisle, Hexham and Metrocentre - Newcastle - Morpeth and Chathill

		TP	XC	GR	NT	NT	NT	TP	XC	NT	NT	NT	TP	XC	GR	NT	NT A	NT	NT	TP	NT	XC	NT
Carlisle	d				13 32	13 55				14 31	14 54					15 21		15 52					16 22
Wetheral	d				13 39					14 38						15 28							16 29
Brampton (Cumbria)	d				13 49											15 38							
Haltwhistle	d				14 04	14 23				15 04	15 22					15 53		16 20					16 52
Bardon Mill	d									15 11													16 59
Haydon Bridge	d				14 14					15 17						16 03							17 05
Hexham	a				14 24	14 42				15 27	15 41					16 13		16 39					17 15
	d				14 25	14 43	14 56			15 29	15 42	15 56				16 14		16 40			16 54		17 16
Corbridge	d						15 00					16 00									16 58		
Riding Mill	d						15 05					16 05									17 03		
Stocksfield	d						15 09					16 09									17 07		
Prudhoe	d				14 37	14 55	15 13			15 41	15 54	16 13				16 26		16 52			17 11		17 28
Wylam	d						15 18					16 18									17 16		
Blaydon	d						15 24					16 24									17 22		
Metrocentre	a				14 48	15 06	15 28			15 52	16 05	16 28				16 37		17 03			17 26		17 39
	d				14 49	15 07	15 29			15 54	16 06	16 29				16 38		17 04	17 13		17 27		17 40
Dunston	d						15 32					16 32							17 16		17 30		17 43
Newcastle	a				14 57	15 15	15 39			16 03	16 15	16 39				16 49		17 14	17 22		17 36		17 50
Sunderland 26,44	a						16 01					17 01							17 49		18 01		
Newcastle 26	d	14 21	14 35	14 43	14 59			15 21	15 37	16 05			16 21	16 35	16 42		17 10			17 20		17 37	17 55
Manors	d				15 01					16 07							17 12						17 58
Cramlington	d				15 11					16 17							17 22						18 09
Morpeth 26	d	14a34	14a47		15a19			15a33		16a26			16a34	16 49	16 57		17a30			17a33			18 17
Pegswood	d																						18 21
Widdrington	d																						18 27
Acklington	d																						18 34
Alnmouth for Alnwick 26	d			15a08					16a01					17a03	17a10							18a01	18 41
Chathill	a																						18 54

		NT	NT	TP	XC	GR	NT	NT	NT	NT	TP	XC	GR	XC	SR	TP	NT	GR	XC	NT	TP	NT
Carlisle	d	16 54					17 24		17 53						18 39							
Wetheral	d						17 31								18 46							
Brampton (Cumbria)	d						17 41								18 56							
Haltwhistle	d	17 22					17 56		18 21						19 11							
Bardon Mill	d						18 03								19 18							
Haydon Bridge	d						18 09								19 24							
Hexham	a	17 41					18 19		18 40						19 34							
	d	17 42	17 59				18 20		18 41	18 56					19 34					20 00		
Corbridge	d		18 04							19 00										20 05		
Riding Mill	d		18 08							19 05										20 09		
Stocksfield	d		18 12							19 09										20 13		
Prudhoe	d	17 54	18 17				18 32	18 39	18 53	19 13					19 46					20 18		
Wylam	d		18 21					18 44		19 18										20 22		
Blaydon	d		18 27					18 50		19 24										20 28		
Metrocentre	a	18 05	18 32				18 43	18 54	19 04	19 28					19 58					20 33		
	d	18 06	18 32				18 44	18 55	19 05	19 29					19 58		20 08			20 33		21 11
Dunston	d	18 09	18 35					18 58		19 32							20 11					21 14
Newcastle	a	18 15	18 42				18 53	19 05	19 14	19 39					20 07		20 17			20 43		21 20
Sunderland 26,44	a		19 08							20 07										21 06		
Newcastle 26	d	18 17		18 21	18 35	18 44		19 08			19 21	19 35	19 44	20 03		20 16	20 19	20 33	20 39		21 16	21 21
Manors	d	18 20						19 11									20 22					21 24
Cramlington	d	18 30						19 21									20 32					21 34
Morpeth 26	d	18a38		18a34	18a49			19a29			19a34		19a57			20a29	20a40		20a52		21a31	21a42
Pegswood	d																					
Widdrington	d																					
Acklington	d																					
Alnmouth for Alnwick 26	d					19a09						20a01		20a28				20a58				
Chathill	a																					

A not 25 December, 26 December, 1 January

For connections to and from London Kings Cross refer to Table T026

Table T048-R

Mondays to Fridays
16 December to 15 May

Carlisle, Hexham and Metrocentre - Newcastle - Morpeth and Chathill

		XC	GR	NT	NT	GR FO	NT	NT	NT	NT
		◇1	1	◇		1	◇		◇	
Carlisle	d			20 09			21 07		22 04	
Wetheral	d						21 14		22 11	
Brampton (Cumbria)	d						21 24		22 21	
Haltwhistle	d			20 37			21 39		22 36	
Bardon Mill	d			20 44					22 43	
Haydon Bridge	d			20 50			21 49		22 49	
Hexham	a			21 00			21 59		22 59	
	d			21 01			22 00		22 59	23 41
Corbridge	d			21 05			22 04		23 04	23 46
Riding Mill	d			21 10			22 09		23 08	23 50
Stocksfield	d			21 14			22 13		23 12	23 54
Prudhoe	d			21 18			22 17		23 17	23 59
Wylam	d			21 23			22 22		23 21	00 04
Blaydon	d			21 29			22 28		23 27	
Metrocentre	a			21 33			22 32		23 32	00 13
	d			21 34	22 13		22 33	23 00	23 32	00 13
Dunston	d				22 16			23 03		
Newcastle	a			21 43	22 22		22 42	23 09	23 41	00 23
Sunderland 26,44	a			22 05			23 08			
Newcastle 26	d	21 35	21 38		22 23	22 40				
Manors	d				22 26					
Cramlington	d				22 37					
Morpeth 26	d		21 54		22a45	22 56				
Pegswood	d									
Widdrington	d									
Acklington	d									
Alnmouth for Alnwick 26	d	22a00	22a07			23a09				
Chathill	a									

Saturdays
21 December to 16 May

		NT	TP	NT	GR	NT	NT	TP	NT	XC	GR	NT	TP	SR	GR	NT	NT	TP	XC	NT	NT	NT	NT
			◇1	◇	1			◇1		◇1	1		◇1		1	◇		◇1	◇1	◇	◇		
Carlisle	d								05 44			06 32		06 57		07 26				08 03	08 20	08 50	
Wetheral	d								05 51			06 39		07 04						08 10	08 27	08 57	
Brampton (Cumbria)	d								06 05					07 14							08 37		
Haltwhistle	d								06 20			07 06		07 29		07 54				08 33	08 52	09 20	
Bardon Mill	d								06 27			07 13		07 36						08 40			
Haydon Bridge	d								06 33			07 19		07 42						08 46	09 02	09 31	
Hexham	a								06 43			07 30		07 52		08 13				08 56	09 15	09 41	
	d					06 09	06 37		06 46			07 31		07 52		08 14	08 26			08 57	09 16	09 42	09 56
Corbridge	d					06 14	06 42		06 51			07 35		07 57			08 31			09 01			10 00
Riding Mill	d					06 18	06 46		06 55			07 40		08 01			08 35			09 06			10 05
Stocksfield	d					06 22	06 50		06 59			07 44		08 05			08 39			09 10			10 09
Prudhoe	d					06 27	06 55		07 04			07 48		08 10		08 26	08 44			09 14	09 28	09 54	10 13
Wylam	d	00 04				06 31	06 59		07 09			07 53		08 14		08 31				09 19			10 18
Blaydon	d					06 37	07 05		07 15			07 59		08 20		08 41				09 25			10 24
Metrocentre	a	00 13				06 42	07 10		07 19			08 04		08 25		08 45	08 55			09 29	09 39	10 05	10 28
	d	00 13				06 42	07 10		07 22			08 04		08 25		08 46	08 56			09 30	09 40	10 06	10 29
Dunston	d					06 45	07 13		07 25			08 07		08 28						09 33			10 32
Newcastle	a	00 23				06 52	07 20		07 32			08 14		08 35		08 54	09 06			09 40	09 50	10 15	10 39
Sunderland 26,44	a					07 20			07 55														11 01
Newcastle 26	d		05 53	05 57	06 20			07 21		07 38	07 42	08 16	08 21		08 42	08 59		09 21	09 33	09 57			
Manors	d			06 00								08 19				09 01				09 59			
Cramlington	d			06 10								08 30				09 11				10 10			
Morpeth 26	d		06 08	06 19	06 36			07a34		07a50		08a38	08a34		08a55	09a18		09a33		10a18			
Pegswood	d																						
Widdrington	d																						
Acklington	d																						
Alnmouth for Alnwick 26	d		06a21	06 35	06a50						08a08								09a57				
Chathill	a			06 48																			

For connections to and from London Kings Cross refer to Table T026

NRT DECEMBER 19 EDITION

Table T048-R

Saturdays
21 December to 16 May

Carlisle, Hexham and Metrocentre - Newcastle - Morpeth and Chathill

		TP	GR	NT	NT	NT	TP	XC	NT	NT	NT	TP	GR	NT	NT	NT	TP	XC	NT	NT	NT	TP
		◇1	1	◇			◇1	◇1	◇	◇		◇1	1	◇			◇1	◇1	◇			◇1
Carlisle	d			09 22	09 52				10 23	10 54				11 25	11 52				12 25	12 53		
Wetheral	d			09 32					10 30					11 32					12 32			
Brampton (Cumbria)	d			09 42										11 42								
Haltwhistle	d			09 57	10 20				10 53	11 22				11 57	12 20				12 55	13 21		
Bardon Mill	d								11 00										13 02			
Haydon Bridge	d			10 07					11 06					12 07					13 08			
Hexham	a			10 17	10 39				11 16	11 41				12 17	12 39				13 18	13 40		
	d			10 18	10 40	10 56			11 18	11 42	11 56			12 18	12 40	12 56			13 19	13 41	13 56	
Corbridge	d					11 00					12 00					13 00					14 00	
Riding Mill	d					11 05					12 05					13 05					14 05	
Stocksfield	d					11 09					12 09					13 09					14 09	
Prudhoe	d			10 30	10 52	11 13			11 30	11 54	12 13			12 30	12 52	13 13			13 31	13 53	14 13	
Wylam	d					11 18					12 18					13 18					14 18	
Blaydon	d					11 24					12 24					13 24					14 24	
Metrocentre	a			10 41	11 03	11 28			11 42	12 05	12 28			12 41	13 03	13 28			13 42	14 04	14 28	
	d			10 44	11 04	11 29			11 44	12 06	12 29			12 44	13 04	13 29			13 44	14 05	14 29	
Dunston	d					11 32					12 32					13 32					14 32	
Newcastle	a			10 53	11 12	11 39			11 53	12 16	12 39			12 52	13 13	13 39			13 52	14 13	14 39	
Sunderland 26,44	a					12 01					13 01					14 01					15 01	
Newcastle 26	d	10 21	10 41	10 57			11 21	11 33	11 57			12 21	12 39	12 57			13 21	13 35	13 57			14 21
Manors	d			10 59					11 59					12 59					13 59			
Cramlington	d			11 09					12 09					13 09					14 09			
Morpeth 26	d	10a34		11a18			11a34	11a45	12a18			12a34	12 54	13a18			13a34		14a18			14a34
Pegswood	d																					
Widdrington	d																					
Acklington	d																					
Alnmouth for Alnwick 26	d		11a06										13a07					13a59				
Chathill	a																					

		XC	GR	NT	NT	NT	TP	XC	NT	NT	NT	TP	XC	GR	NT	NT	NT	NT	TP	XC	NT	NT	NT
		◇1	1	◇			◇1	◇1	◇			◇1	◇1	1	◇	◇ A			◇1	◇1		◇	
Carlisle	d			13 32	13 55				14 31	14 54					15 25		15 52					16 22	16 54
Wetheral	d			13 39					14 38						15 32							16 29	
Brampton (Cumbria)	d			13 49											15 42								
Haltwhistle	d			14 04	14 23				15 04	15 22					15 57		16 20					16 52	17 22
Bardon Mill	d								15 11													16 59	
Haydon Bridge	d			14 14					15 17						16 07							17 05	
Hexham	a			14 24	14 42				15 27	15 41					16 17		16 39					17 15	17 41
	d			14 25	14 43	14 56			15 29	15 42	15 53				16 18		16 40				16 54	17 16	17 42
Corbridge	d					15 00					15 57										16 58		
Riding Mill	d					15 05					16 02										17 03		
Stocksfield	d					15 09					16 06										17 07		
Prudhoe	d			14 37	14 55	15 13			15 41	15 54	16 10				16 30		16 52				17 11	17 28	17 54
Wylam	d					15 18					16 15										17 16		
Blaydon	d					15 24					16 21										17 22		
Metrocentre	a			14 48	15 06	15 28			15 52	16 05	16 25				16 42		17 03				17 26	17 39	18 05
	d			14 49	15 07	15 29			15 54	16 06	16 26				16 43		17 04	17 13			17 27	17 40	18 06
Dunston	d					15 32					16 29							17 16			17 30	17 43	18 09
Newcastle	a			14 57	15 15	15 39			16 03	16 15	16 36				16 52		17 14	17 22			17 36	17 50	18 15
Sunderland 26,44	a					16 01					17 01							17 49			18 01		
Newcastle 26	d	14 35	14 42	14 59			15 21	15 35	16 05			16 21	16 35	16 42		17 10			17 20	17 35		17 55	18 17
Manors	d			15 01					16 07							17 12						17 58	18 20
Cramlington	d			15 11					16 17							17 22						18 09	18 30
Morpeth 26	d	14a47		15a19			15a33		16a26			16a34	16 49	16 57		17a30			17a33			18 17	18a38
Pegswood	d																					18 21	
Widdrington	d																					18 27	
Acklington	d																					18 34	
Alnmouth for Alnwick 26	d		15a07					15a59					17a03	17a10						17a59		18 41	
Chathill	a																					18 54	

A not 16 May

For connections to and from London Kings Cross refer to Table T026

Table T048-R

Saturdays

21 December to 16 May

Carlisle, Hexham and Metrocentre - Newcastle - Morpeth and Chathill

		NT	TP	GR	NT	NT	NT	NT	TP	XC		GR	SR	NT	NT	XC	GR	NT	XC	NT		NT	NT	NT	NT
			◇1	1	◇		◇		◇1	◇1		1				◇1	1		◇1			◇		◇	◇
Carlisle	d				17 24		17 53															20 09		21 07	22 04
Wetheral	d				17 31								18 56											21 14	22 11
Brampton (Cumbria)	d				17 41								19 06											21 24	22 21
Haltwhistle	d				17 56		18 21						19 21									20 37		21 39	22 36
Bardon Mill	d				18 03								19 28									20 44			22 43
Haydon Bridge	d				18 09								19 33									20 50		21 49	22 49
Hexham	a				18 19		18 40						19 43									21 00		21 59	22 59
	d	17 59			18 20		18 41	18 56					19 44	20 00								21 01		22 00	22 59
Corbridge	d	18 04						19 00						20 05								21 05		22 04	23 04
Riding Mill	d	18 08						19 05						20 09								21 10		22 09	23 08
Stocksfield	d	18 12						19 09						20 13								21 14		22 13	23 12
Prudhoe	d	18 17			18 32	18 39	18 53	19 13					19 55	20 18				20 40				21 18		22 17	23 17
Wylam	d	18 21				18 44		19 18						20 22				20 45				21 23		22 22	23 21
Blaydon	d	18 27				18 50		19 24						20 28				20 50				21 29		22 28	23 27
Metrocentre	a	18 32			18 43	18 54	19 04	19 28					20 07	20 33				20 55				21 33		22 32	23 32
	d	18 32			18 44	18 55	19 05	19 29					20 07	20 33				20 58		21 21		21 34	22 13	22 33	23 32
Dunston	d	18 35				18 58		19 32										21 01		21 24			22 16		
Newcastle	a	18 42			18 53	19 05	19 14	19 39					20 16	20 43				21 08		21 30		21 43	22 21	22 42	23 41
Sunderland 26,44	a	19 08						20 07						21 06								22 05		23 05	
Newcastle 26	d		18 21	18 44		19 08			19 21	19 35		19 44			20 21	20 38	20 52		21 34	21 36			22 23		
Manors	d					19 11									20 23					21 39			22 26		
Cramlington	d					19 21									20 34					21 49			22 37		
Morpeth 26	d		18a34			19a29			19a34			19a57			20a42	20a50	21 08			21a57			22a45		
Pegswood	d																								
Widdrington	d																								
Acklington	d																								
Alnmouth for Alnwick 26	d			19a09						20a01							21a23		21a59						
Chathill	a																								

		NT
Carlisle	d	
Wetheral	d	
Brampton (Cumbria)	d	
Haltwhistle	d	
Bardon Mill	d	
Haydon Bridge	d	
Hexham	a	
	d	23 25
Corbridge	d	23 30
Riding Mill	d	23 34
Stocksfield	d	23 38
Prudhoe	d	23 43
Wylam	d	
Blaydon	d	
Metrocentre	a	23 54
	d	23 55
Dunston	d	
Newcastle	a	00 05
Sunderland 26,44	a	
Newcastle 26	d	
Manors	d	
Cramlington	d	
Morpeth 26	d	
Pegswood	d	
Widdrington	d	
Acklington	d	
Alnmouth for Alnwick 26	d	
Chathill	a	

For connections to and from London Kings Cross refer to Table T026

Table T048-R

Sundays

15 December to 10 May

Carlisle, Hexham and Metrocentre - Newcastle - Morpeth and Chathill

		NT	GR	TP	NT	XC		NT	GR	TP	NT	NT	NT	TP	NT	NT		XC	GR	NT	TP	NT	GR	NT	NT
			1	◇1		◇1			1	◇1	◇			◇1	◇			◇1	1		◇1	◇	1		
Carlisle	d										08 44				09 54							10 54			
Wetheral	d										08 51											11 01			
Brampton (Cumbria)	d										09 01											11 11			
Haltwhistle	d										09 16				10 22							11 26			
Bardon Mill	d										09 23				10 29										
Haydon Bridge	d										09 29				10 35										
Hexham	a										09 39				10 45							11 45			
	d										09 39				10 46							11 45			
Corbridge	d										09 44				10 50							11 50			
Riding Mill	d										09 48				10 55							11 54			
Stocksfield	d										09 52				10 59							11 58			
Prudhoe	d										09 57				11 03							12 03			
Wylam	d										10 01				11 08							12 07			
Blaydon	d										10 07											12 13			
Metrocentre	a										10 12				11 16							12 18			
	d							09 50			10 13	10 38	10 58		11 17	11 38				11 58		12 18		12 38	12 58
Dunston	d							09 53				10 41				11 41								12 41	
Newcastle	a							09 59			10 23	10 53	11 06		11 26	11 48				12 07		12 27		12 48	13 06
Sunderland 26,44	a														11 50							12 50			
Newcastle 26	d	08 30	08 45	09 20	09 23	09 45			10 12	10 21		11 05		11 21				11 31	11 40		12 14		12 38	12 56	
Manors	d	08 32			09 26							11 07												12 59	
Cramlington	d	08 43			09 36							11 18												13 10	
Morpeth 26	d	08a51	09 01	09a33	09a44	09 58			10 28	10a34		11a26		11a34				11a43	11a53		12a27			13a18	
Pegswood	d																								
Widdrington	d																								
Acklington	d																								
Alnmouth for Alnwick 26	d		09a14			10a12			10a42														13a03		
Chathill	a																								

		TP		NT	NT	XC	NT	GR	NT	XC	GR	TP		NT	NT	TP	NT	NT	XC	NT	TP	NT		XC	GR
		◇1		◇		◇1		1	◇	◇1	1	◇1				◇1	◇		◇1		◇1	◇		◇1	1
Carlisle	d			11 54					12 54								13 54					14 52			
Wetheral	d								13 01													14 59			
Brampton (Cumbria)	d								13 11													15 09			
Haltwhistle	d			12 22					13 26								14 22					15 24			
Bardon Mill	d			12 29													14 29								
Haydon Bridge	d			12 35													14 35					15 34			
Hexham	a			12 45					13 45								14 45					15 44			
	d			12 46					13 45								14 46					15 45			
Corbridge	d			12 50					13 50								14 50					15 49			
Riding Mill	d			12 55					13 54								14 55					15 54			
Stocksfield	d			12 59					13 58								14 59					15 58			
Prudhoe	d			13 03					14 03								15 03					16 02			
Wylam	d			13 08					14 07								15 08					16 07			
Blaydon	d								14 13													16 13			
Metrocentre	a			13 16					14 18								15 16					16 17			
	d			13 17	13 38		13 58		14 18					14 38	14 58		15 17	15 40		15 58		16 18			
Dunston	d				13 41									14 41				15 43							
Newcastle	a			13 27	13 49		14 06		14 27					14 48	15 06		15 26	15 49		16 08		16 27			
Sunderland 26,44	a			13 50					14 50								15 50					16 50			
Newcastle 26	d	13 24				13 31		14 23		14 29	14 37	14 41		14 56		15 21			15 29		16 21			16 29	16 38
Manors	d													14 59											
Cramlington	d													15 09											
Morpeth 26	d	13a36						14a36		14a43		14a54		15a17		15a34					16a34				
Pegswood	d																								
Widdrington	d																								
Acklington	d																								
Alnmouth for Alnwick 26	d					13a55					15a02								15a53					16a55	17a03
Chathill	a																								

For connections to and from London Kings Cross refer to Table T026

Table T048-R

Sundays
15 December to 10 May

Carlisle, Hexham and Metrocentre - Newcastle - Morpeth and Chathill

		NT	NT	TP	NT	NT	XC	NT	TP	NT	GR	NT	NT	TP	NT	NT	XC	GR	TP	NT	XC	GR
				◇[1]	◇		◇[1]		◇[1]	◇	[1]			◇[1]	◇		◇[1]	[1]	◇[1]	◇	◇[1]	[1]
Carlisle	d				15 54					16 52					17 54					18 48		
Wetheral	d									16 59										18 56		
Brampton (Cumbria)	d									17 09										19 05		
Haltwhistle	d				16 22					17 24					18 22					19 20		
Bardon Mill	d				16 29										18 29					19 27		
Haydon Bridge	d				16 35					17 34					18 35					19 33		
Hexham	a				16 45					17 44					18 45					19 43		
	d				16 46					17 45					18 46					19 45		
Corbridge	d				16 50					17 49					18 50					19 49		
Riding Mill	d				16 55					17 54					18 55					19 54		
Stocksfield	d				16 59					17 58					18 59					19 58		
Prudhoe	d				17 03					18 02					19 03					20 02		
Wylam	d				17 08					18 07					19 08					20 07		
Blaydon	d									18 12										20 13		
Metrocentre	a				17 16					18 17					19 16					20 17		
	d	16 38	16 58		17 17	17 38		17 58		18 17		18 38	18 58		19 17	19 48				20 18		
Dunston	d	16 41				17 41						18 41				19 51						
Newcastle	a	16 48	17 06		17 26	17 47		18 08		18 26		18 48	19 06		19 26	19 57				20 27		
Sunderland 26,44	a				17 50					18 50					19 50					20 50		
Newcastle 26	d	16 56		17 21			17 28		18 18		18 38	19 00		19 21			19 32	19 42	20 16		20 37	20 41
Manors	d	16 59										19 03										
Cramlington	d	17 09										19 13										
Morpeth 26	d	17a17		17a34			17 42		18a31			19a21		19a34				19a55	20a29		20a49	20 57
Pegswood	d																					
Widdrington	d																					
Acklington	d																					
Alnmouth for Alnwick 26	d						17a55				19a04						19a57					21a10
Chathill	a																					

		NT	NT	NT	XC	GR	NT
				◇	◇[1]	[1]	◇
Carlisle	d			19 50			20 38
Wetheral	d			19 57			20 45
Brampton (Cumbria)	d			20 07			20 55
Haltwhistle	d			20 22			21 10
Bardon Mill	d			20 29			21 17
Haydon Bridge	d			20 35			21 23
Hexham	a			20 45			21 33
	d			20 45			21 33
Corbridge	d			20 50			21 38
Riding Mill	d			20 54			21 42
Stocksfield	d			20 58			21 46
Prudhoe	d			21 03			21 51
Wylam	d			21 07			21 55
Blaydon	d			21 13			22 01
Metrocentre	a			21 18			22 05
	d	20 38	20 58	21 18			22 06
Dunston	d	20 41					22 09
Newcastle	a	20 48	21 06	21 27			22 16
Sunderland 26,44	a			21 50			
Newcastle 26	d	21 04			21 34	21 52	
Manors	d	21 07					
Cramlington	d	21 17					
Morpeth 26	d	21a25				22 08	
Pegswood	d						
Widdrington	d						
Acklington	d						
Alnmouth for Alnwick 26	d				21a59	22a23	
Chathill	a						

For connections to and from London Kings Cross refer to Table T026

NRT DECEMBER 19 EDITION

Table T049-F

Mondays to Fridays
16 December to 15 May

East Anglia - East Midlands - North West England

Miles			EM	EM	EM	EM MO	EM MX	EM	EM	EM	EM	EM	EM	EM	EM	EM	EM	EM	EM	EM	EM
			◇	◇	◇	◇	◇	◇	◇	◇	◇	◇	◇	◇	◇	◇	◇	◇	◇	◇	A
0	**Norwich**	d				05 50	05 50	06 51	07 57	08 56	09 57	10 57	11 57	12 57	13 57	14 57	15 48	16 56	17 54	18 57	
30¾	Thetford	d				06 24	06 24	07 19	08 24	09 24	10 24	11 24	12 24	13 24	14 24	15 24	16 23	17 27	18 27	19 24	
53¾	Ely [6]	d				06 51	06 51	07 44	08 51	09 51	10 50	11 51	12 49	13 51	14 49	15 48	16 50	17 52	18 52	19 52	
69	March	d				07 07	07 07	08 00	09 07			12 08							19 08		
83¾	**Peterborough** [8]	a				07 25	07 25	08 22	09 25	10 26	11 27	12 24	13 23	14 25	15 30	16 25	17 24	18 25	19 26	20 25	
—		d				07 29	07 29	08 25	09 27	10 28	11 28	12 26	13 26	14 26	15 30	16 27	17 26	18 26	19 26	20 27	21 31
113	Grantham [7]	a				07 57	07 57	08 55	09 55	10 58	12 01	12 58	13 56	14 57	16 00	16 57	17 58	18 54	19 58	20 58	
—	East Midlands Parkway	a																			
134¾	**Nottingham** [8]	a				08 40	08 40	09 27	10 35	11 34	12 35	13 36	14 35	15 34	16 35	17 35	18 31	19 35	20 31	21 36	23 00
—		d	05 23	06 35	07 45	08 47	08 47	09 47	10 51	11 47	12 47	13 47	14 47	15 47	16 47	17 47	18 47	19 40			
141	Ilkeston	d			07 59						13 00			16 00							
146¾	Langley Mill	a														18 02					
154	Alfreton	a		06 55	08 10	09 08	09 08	10 08	11 11	12 08	13 10	14 09	15 08	16 10	17 08	18 10	19 08	20 05			
163¾	Chesterfield	a	05 51	07 06	08 20	09 20	09 20	10 21	11 22	12 21	13 20	14 20	15 20	16 20	17 20	18 21	19 20	20 20			
176¾	**Sheffield** [7]	a	06 15	07 24	08 39	09 37	09 38	10 37	11 37	12 37	13 37	14 37	15 37	16 37	17 38	18 37	19 37	20 35			
—		d	06 18	07 32	08 42	09 42	09 42	10 42	11 42	12 42	13 42	14 42	15 42	16 42	17 39	18 42	19 42	20 39			
212	Stockport	a	07 25	08 25	09 25	10 26	10 25	11 25	12 25	13 25	14 25	15 25	16 25	17 25	18 25	19 25	20 25	21 25			
218	**Manchester Piccadilly** [10]	a	07 38	08 37	09 37	10 37	10 37	11 37	12 37	13 37	14 37	15 37	16 37	17 37	18 37	19 37	20 38	21 36			
219	Manchester Oxford Road	a	07 42	08 41	09 41	10 41	10 41	11 41	12 41	13 41	14 41	15 41	16 41	17 41	18 41	19 41	20 41				
235	Warrington Central	a	07 58	08 58	09 58	10 58	10 58	11 58	12 58	13 58	14 58	15 58	16 58	18 03	18 58	19 58	20 58				
241	Widnes	a	08 06	09 06	10 06	11 06	11 06	12 06	13 06	14 06	15 06	16 06	17 06	18 11	19 06	20 06	21 06				
248	Liverpool South Parkway [7]	a	08 20	09 15	10 15	11 15	11 15	12 15	13 15	14 15	15 15	16 15	17 15	18 22	19 20	20 16	21 20				
254	**Liverpool Lime Street** [10]	a	08 34	09 28	10 31	11 32	11 32	12 32	13 32	14 32	15 32	16 32	17 32	18 36	19 35	20 34	21 36				

Saturdays
21 December to 16 May

		EM	EM	EM	EM	EM	EM	EM	EM	EM	EM	EM	EM	EM	EM	EM	EM	EM	EM
		◇	◇	◇	◇	◇	◇	◇	◇	◇	◇	◇	◇	◇	◇	◇	◇	◇	A
Norwich	d				05 50	06 53	07 57	08 56	09 57	10 57	11 57	12 57	13 57	14 57	15 52	16 54	17 50	18 57	
Thetford	d				06 23	07 20	08 24	09 24	10 24	11 24	12 24	13 24	14 24	15 24	16 23	17 24	18 23	19 24	
Ely [6]	d				06 51	07 48	08 48	09 46	10 48	11 48	12 51	13 48	14 50	15 47	16 47	17 47	18 48	19 48	
March	d				07 07	08 04	09 05			12 05							19 05		
Peterborough [8]	a				07 25	08 27	09 22	10 21	11 20	12 21	13 26	14 25	15 23	16 25	17 23	18 23	19 24	20 23	
	d				07 27	08 29	09 28	10 22	11 23	12 24	13 28	14 26	15 24	16 27	17 25	18 26	19 30	20 26	21 27
Grantham [7]	a				07 55	08 59	09 56	10 54	11 55	12 57	13 56	14 55	15 55	16 57	17 57	18 55	19 57	20 58	22 00
East Midlands Parkway	a																		
Nottingham [8]	a				08 39	09 37	10 35	11 36	12 36	13 35	14 33	15 35	16 35	17 35	18 30	19 31	20 36	21 32	22 32
	d	05 20	06 40	07 46	08 48	09 47	10 47	11 47	12 47	13 47	14 47	15 47	16 44	17 44	18 47	19 39			
Ilkeston	d			07 59					13 00			16 00							
Langley Mill	a													17 59					
Alfreton	a		07 00	08 09	09 09	10 08	11 08	12 08	13 10	14 08	15 08	16 10	17 05	18 08	19 08	20 01			
Chesterfield	a	05 49	07 11	08 19	09 20	10 20	11 20	12 20	13 22	14 20	15 20	16 20	17 15	18 18	19 20	20 11			
Sheffield [7]	a	06 15	07 28	08 37	09 37	10 37	11 37	12 37	13 37	14 37	15 37	16 37	17 34	18 34	19 37	20 29			
	d	06 20	07 32	08 42	09 42	10 42	11 42	12 42	13 42	14 42	15 42	16 42	17 38	18 37	19 42	20 34			
Stockport	a	07 26	08 25	09 25	10 26	11 25	12 25	13 25	14 25	15 25	16 25	17 25	18 25	19 25	20 25	21 19			
Manchester Piccadilly [10]	a	07 39	08 37	09 37	10 37	11 37	12 37	13 37	14 37	15 37	16 37	17 37	18 37	19 37	20 37	21 29			
Manchester Oxford Road	a	07 42	08 41	09 41	10 41	11 41	12 41	13 41	14 41	15 41	16 41	17 41	18 41	19 41	20 41				
Warrington Central	a	07 58	08 58	09 58	10 58	11 58	12 58	13 58	14 58	15 58	16 58	18 03	18 58	19 58	20 58				
Widnes	a	08 06	09 06	10 06	11 06	12 06	13 06	14 06	15 06	16 06	17 06	18 11	19 06	20 06	21 06				
Liverpool South Parkway [7]	a	08 20	09 15	10 15	11 15	12 15	13 15	14 15	15 15	16 15	17 15	18 22	19 19	20 18	21 19				
Liverpool Lime Street [10]	a	08 33	09 30	10 30	11 32	12 32	13 32	14 32	15 30	16 32	17 32	18 36	19 35	20 33	21 32				

Sundays
15 December to 10 May

		EM	EM	EM	EM	EM	EM	EM	EM	EM	EM	EM	EM	EM	EM
		◇	◇	◇	◇	◇	◇	◇	◇	◇	◇	◇	◇	◇	◇
Norwich	d					10 47			13 47	14 53	15 54	16 54	17 54	18 56	20 52
Thetford	d					11 14			14 14	15 20	16 21	17 21	18 21	19 23	21 19
Ely [6]	d					11 39			14 40	15 46		17 49	18 47	19 49	21 44
March	d									16 03					
Peterborough [8]	a					12 11			15 13	16 20	17 12	18 20	19 20	20 23	22 16
	d					12 16		14 31	15 23	16 24	17 19	18 26	19 22	20 30	22 23
Grantham [7]	a					12 46		15 07	15 53	16 56	17 49	18 57	19 52	21 00	22 53
East Midlands Parkway	a														
Nottingham [8]	a					13 30		15 39	16 24	17 31	18 27	19 33	20 31	21 34	23 28
	d	09 47	10 48	11 44	12 40	13 42	14 47	15 47	16 42	17 39	18 40	19 42			
Ilkeston	d			11 56					16 57						
Langley Mill	a				12 56	13 57	15 02		17 03	17 56	18 55				
Alfreton	a	10 04	11 08	12 07	13 04	14 05	15 10	16 07	17 11	18 04	19 03	20 03			
Chesterfield	a	10 18	11 19	12 18	13 17	14 16	15 21	16 18	17 21	18 15	19 14	20 12			
Sheffield [7]	a	10 37	11 35	12 35	13 33	14 34	15 39	16 35	17 39	18 33	19 31	20 30			
	d	10 41	11 39	12 39	13 38	14 37	15 43	16 39	17 44	18 37	19 35	20 35			
Stockport	a	11 26	12 25	13 25	14 26	15 25	16 25	17 28	18 25	19 25	20 26	21 25			
Manchester Piccadilly [10]	a	11 38	12 37	13 37	14 37	15 37	16 37	17 38	18 37	19 37	20 38	21 36			
Manchester Oxford Road	a	11 41	12 41	13 41	14 41	15 41	16 41	17 41	18 41	19 42					
Warrington Central	a	11 58	12 58	13 58	14 58	15 58	16 58	17 58	18 58	19 59					
Widnes	a	12 06	13 06	14 06	15 06	16 06	17 06	18 06	19 06	20 07					
Liverpool South Parkway [7]	a	12 16	13 16	14 16	15 16	16 16	17 16	18 16	19 16	20 17					
Liverpool Lime Street [10]	a	12 30	13 31	14 32	15 30	16 28	17 32	18 30	19 30	20 31					

A From Spalding

Table T049-R

Mondays to Fridays
16 December to 15 May

North West England - East Midlands - East Anglia

Miles			EM MO ◇ A	EM MX ◇ A	EM ◇	EM B	EM MO C	EM ◇	EM	EM ◇ D	EM ◇	EM ◇	EM ◇	EM ◇	EM ◇	EM ◇	EM ◇	EM ◇	EM ◇	EM ◇	EM ◇	EM ◇	EM ◇
0	**Liverpool Lime Street**	d										06 47	07 42	08 52	09 51	10 51	11 51	12 51	13 51	14 51	15 51	16 50	17 51
6	Liverpool South Parkway	d										06 58	07 53	09 03	10 02	11 02	12 02	13 02	14 02	15 02	16 02	17 01	18 02
12	Widnes	d										07 07	08 05	09 11	10 10	11 10	12 10	13 10	14 10	15 10	16 10	17 09	18 10
18	Warrington Central	d										07 15	08 13	09 19	10 18	11 18	12 18	13 18	14 18	15 18	16 18	17 17	18 18
34	Manchester Oxford Road	d										07 38	08 38	09 39	10 38	11 38	12 38	13 38	14 38	15 38	16 38	17 38	18 39
35	**Manchester Piccadilly**	d										07 42	08 43	09 43	10 42	11 42	12 42	13 42	14 42	15 42	16 42	17 42	18 43
41	Stockport	d										07 54	08 54	09 54	10 54	11 54	12 55	13 54	14 54	15 54	16 54	17 55	18 54
77	**Sheffield**	a										08 36	09 35	10 34	11 35	12 35	13 34	14 35	15 34	16 34	17 39	18 47	19 35
—		d										08 38	09 38	10 37	11 38	12 38	13 37	14 38	15 37	16 37	17 43	18 51	19 37
89	Chesterfield	d		00 02								08 54	09 52	10 54	11 54	12 52	13 52	14 52	15 53	16 53	18 01	19 07	19 52
100	Alfreton	d										09 05	10 02	11 05	12 05	13 03	14 03	15 03	16 05	17 04	18 11	19 19	20 03
—	Langley Mill	d	00 02																				
113	Ilkeston	d											10 12					15 13					
118	**Nottingham**	a	00 23	00 45								09 27	10 27	11 26	12 29	13 27	14 27	15 28	16 27	17 27	18 31	19 40	20 27
—		d			04 56	05 07	05 07	06 07	06 53	07 52	08 35	09 34	10 34	11 34	12 34	13 34	14 34	15 34	16 35	17 34	18 37		20 34
—	East Midlands Parkway	d						06 21															
141	Grantham	d				05 51	05 56			08 27	09 10	10 11	11 10	12 12	13 09	14 11	15 11	16 11	17 11	18 11	19 10		21 10
170	**Peterborough**	a			06 21	06 22	06 26	07 34	09 23	08 58	09 36	10 42	11 39	12 40	13 39	14 39	15 38	16 39	17 42	18 38	19 40		21 37
—		d			06 28			07 38		09 03	09 40	10 45	11 41	12 42	13 41	14 41	15 40	16 41	17 44	18 45	19 42		21 39
—	March	a			06 43			07 53												18 59			
200	Ely	a			07 02			08 12		09 41	10 13	11 19	12 13	13 14	14 13	15 14	16 13	17 13	18 19	19 19	20 15		22 13
—	Ipswich	a																					
223	Thetford	a			07 33			08 38		10 09	10 39	11 43	12 38	13 40	14 38	15 39	16 39	17 40	18 43	19 44	20 38		22 38
254	**Norwich**	a			08 13			09 15		10 45	11 12	12 15	13 13	14 13	15 11	16 15	17 14	18 13	19 16	20 19	21 13		23 18

		EM ◇	EM ◇	EM ◇
Liverpool Lime Street	d	18 51	19 51	21 37
Liverpool South Parkway	d	19 02	20 02	21 47
Widnes	d	19 10	20 10	21 56
Warrington Central	d	19 18	20 18	22 04
Manchester Oxford Road	d	19 38	20 38	22 24
Manchester Piccadilly	d	19 42	20 42	22 28
Stockport	d	19 54	20 53	22 39
Sheffield	a	20 37	21 35	23 36
	d	20 41	21 37	23 38
Chesterfield	d	20 56	21 55	00 02
Alfreton	d	21 08	22 05	
Langley Mill	d		22 13	
Ilkeston	d		22 18	
Nottingham	a	21 34	22 31	00 45
	d			
East Midlands Parkway	d			
Grantham	d			
Peterborough	a			
	d			
March	a			
Ely	a			
Ipswich	d			
Thetford	a			
Norwich	a			

Saturdays
21 December to 16 May

		EM ◇ A	EM ◇	EM E	EM ◇	EM	EM ◇	EM ◇	EM ◇	EM ◇	EM ◇	EM ◇	EM ◇	EM ◇	EM ◇	EM ◇	EM ◇	EM ◇	EM ◇	EM ◇	EM ◇	EM ◇	EM ◇
Liverpool Lime Street	d								06 47	07 42	08 52	09 51	10 51	11 51	12 51	13 51	14 51	15 51	16 51	17 51	18 51	19 52	20 49
Liverpool South Parkway	d								06 58	07 52	09 02	10 02	11 02	12 02	13 02	14 02	15 02	16 02	17 02	18 02	19 02	20 02	21 00
Widnes	d								07 07	08 05	09 10	10 10	11 10	12 10	13 10	14 10	15 10	16 10	17 10	18 10	19 10	20 10	21 08
Warrington Central	d								07 15	08 13	09 18	10 18	11 18	12 18	13 18	14 18	15 18	16 18	17 18	18 18	19 18	20 18	21 16
Manchester Oxford Road	d								07 38	08 38	09 38	10 38	11 38	12 38	13 38	14 38	15 38	16 38	17 38	18 38	19 38	20 38	21 37
Manchester Piccadilly	d								07 42	08 43	09 42	10 42	11 42	12 42	13 42	14 42	15 42	16 42	17 42	18 42	19 42	20 42	21 41
Stockport	d								07 56	08 55	09 54	10 55	11 54	12 55	13 55	14 55	15 55	16 55	17 55	18 55	19 55	20 55	21 52
Sheffield	a								08 35	09 34	10 34	11 36	12 35	13 36	14 36	15 36	16 35	17 37	18 37	19 35	20 35	21 34	22 31
	d								08 37	09 37	10 37	11 38	12 38	13 38	14 38	15 38	16 38	17 41	18 40	19 37	20 39	21 38	22 42
Chesterfield	d	00 02							08 52	09 52	10 52	11 52	12 52	13 54	14 54	15 53	16 54	17 57	18 58	19 53	20 54	21 54	22 56
Alfreton	d								09 03	10 03	11 02	12 03	13 02	14 04	15 04	16 04	17 05	18 08	19 09	20 04	21 05	22 05	23 07
Langley Mill	d																					22 13	
Ilkeston	d											12 13	13 12									22 18	
Nottingham	a	00 45							09 27	10 27	11 27	12 27	13 27	14 27	15 27	16 27	17 27	18 29	19 29	20 28	21 33	22 34	23 28
	d		05 05	05 07	06 07	06 53	07 45	08 35	09 34	10 34	11 34	12 34	13 34	14 34	15 34	16 34	17 34	18 37		20 35			
East Midlands Parkway	d				06 20																		
Grantham	d			05 51			08 20	09 10	10 11	11 05	12 13	13 11	14 11	15 06	16 08	17 06	18 11	19 10		21 08			
Peterborough	a		06 24	06 25	07 33	09 24	08 55	09 36	10 38	11 36	12 40	13 38	14 40	15 41	16 39	17 36	18 38	19 39		21 39			
	d		06 27		07 35		09 00	09 45	10 40	11 41	12 44	13 40	14 41	15 45	16 39	17 40	18 44	19 41		21 40			
March	a		06 42		07 52												19 00						
Ely	a		07 03		08 13		09 35	10 19	11 13	12 13	13 19	14 13	15 14	16 19	17 13	18 13	19 19	20 14		22 13			
Ipswich	d																						
Thetford	a		07 30		08 37		10 06	10 43	11 37	12 38	13 43	14 37	15 40	16 43	17 37	18 37	19 43	20 38		22 37			
Norwich	a		08 13		09 15		10 43	11 15	12 13	13 13	14 12	15 13	16 12	17 12	18 14	19 13	20 16	21 13		23 19			

A From Liverpool Lime Street
B until 3 April, MX from 7 April. To Spalding
C from 6 April. To Spalding
D From Mansfield Woodhouse
E To Spalding

Table T049-R

Saturdays
21 December to 16 May

North West England - East Midlands - East Anglia

		EM ◇
Liverpool Lime Street	d	21 37
Liverpool South Parkway	d	21 47
Widnes	d	21 56
Warrington Central	d	22 04
Manchester Oxford Road	d	22 25
Manchester Piccadilly	d	22 29
Stockport	d	22 38
Sheffield	a	23 35
	d	23 38
Chesterfield	d	23 53
Alfreton	d	
Langley Mill	d	
Ilkeston	d	
Nottingham	a	00 29
	d	
East Midlands Parkway	d	
Grantham	d	
Peterborough	a	
	d	
March	a	
Ely	a	
Ipswich	a	
Thetford	a	
Norwich	a	

Sundays
15 December to 10 May

		EM ◇	EM ◇	EM ◇	EM ◇	EM ◇	EM ◇	EM ◇	EM ◇	EM ◇	EM ◇	EM ◇	EM ◇
Liverpool Lime Street	d				12 52	13 52	14 52	15 52	16 52	17 52	18 52	19 52	21 16
Liverpool South Parkway	d				13 03	14 03	15 03	16 03	17 03	18 03	19 03	20 03	21 26
Widnes	d				13 11	14 11	15 11	16 11	17 11	18 11	19 11	20 11	21 35
Warrington Central	d				13 19	14 19	15 19	16 19	17 19	18 19	19 19	20 19	21 43
Manchester Oxford Road	d				13 39	14 39	15 39	16 39	17 39	18 39	19 39	20 39	22 08
Manchester Piccadilly	d			12 43	13 43	14 43	15 43	16 43	17 43	18 43	19 43	20 43	22 13
Stockport	d			12 55	13 51	14 54	15 54	16 54	17 54	18 53	19 54	20 53	22 30
Sheffield	a			13 37	14 37	15 34	16 38	17 35	18 36	19 35	20 35	21 34	23 26
	d		12 43	13 48	14 41	15 39	16 43	17 40	18 40	19 40	20 40	21 38	23 30
Chesterfield	d		12 57	14 02	14 55	15 53	16 57	17 54	18 54	19 54	20 54	21 56	23 44
Alfreton	d		13 08	14 12	15 08	16 04	17 07	18 05	19 05	20 05	21 05	22 06	23 55
Langley Mill	d				15 15	16 11	17 15	18 12	19 12	20 12	21 12	22 14	00 02
Ilkeston	d			14 22				18 17					
Nottingham	a		13 34	14 35	15 32	16 28	17 30	18 34	19 33	20 30	21 33	22 36	00 23
	d	12 40	13 47	14 45	15 50	16 45	17 36	18 46		20 45			
East Midlands Parkway	d												
Grantham	d	13 15	14 22	15 20	16 22	17 21	18 17	19 23		21 20			
Peterborough	a	13 41	14 51	15 51	16 52	17 50	18 46	19 56		21 52			
	d	13 43	14 58	15 58	16 59	17 57	18 49	19 57		21 54			
March	a					18 12							
Ely	a	14 16	15 31	16 31	17 32	18 31	19 22	20 32		22 27			
Ipswich	d												
Thetford	a	14 43	16 01	16 55	17 56	18 55	19 51	20 56		22 51			
Norwich	a	15 23	16 35	17 26	18 30	19 28	20 26	21 37		23 25			

Table T050-F

Derby - Stoke-on-Trent and Crewe

Mondays to Fridays
16 December to 15 May

Miles	Station		NT ◇ A	NT ◇ B	LM ■1 C	NT ◇ B	EM	NT ◇ B	LM ■1 D	EM	NT ◇ B	LM ■1 C	EM	NT ◇ B	LM ■1 E	EM	NT ◇ B	LM ■1 E	EM	NT ◇ B	LM ■1 E	EM	NT ◇ B
0	**Derby** 6	d					06 40			07 40			08 42			09 42			10 42			11 42	
1¼	Peartree	d								07 44													
11¼	Tutbury & Hatton	d					06 55			07 56			08 56			09 56			10 56			11 57	
19	Uttoxeter	d					07 06			08 07			09 07			10 07			11 07			12 07	
30	Blythe Bridge	d					07 20			08 21			09 21			10 21			11 21			12 22	
33½	Longton	d					07 26			08 27			09 27			10 27			11 27			12 28	
36	**Stoke-on-Trent**	a					07 32			08 32			09 33			10 33			11 33			12 36	
—		d	06 29	06 58	07 14	07 25	07 33	07 56	08 12	08 34	08 56	09 13	09 34	09 56	10 12	10 34	10 56	11 13	11 34	11 56	12 14	12 37	12 57
38¾	Longport	d	06 33				07 38	08 00		08 39			09 39			10 39			11 39			12 42	
42¼	Kidsgrove	d	06a37	07a05	07 27	07a34	07 44	08a04	08 20	08 45	09a03	09 21	09 45	10a03	10 19	10 45	11a03	11 21	11 45	12a03	12 25	12 49	13a04
44½	Alsager	d			07 32		07 48		08 24	08 49		09 25	09 49		10 23	10 49		11 25	11 49		12 29	12 53	
51	**Crewe** 10	a			07 43		07 59		08 33	08 59		09 34	10 01		10 32	11 01		11 34	12 01		12 38	13 03	

Station		LM ■1 E	EM	NT ◇ B	LM ■1 E	EM	NT ◇ B	LM ■1 E	EM	NT ◇ B	LM ■1 E	EM	NT ◇ B	LM ■1 E	EM	NT ◇ B	LM ■1 E	EM	NT ◇ B	LM ■1 E	EM	NT ◇ B	LM ■1 C
Derby 6	d		12 42			13 42			14 42			15 42			16 42			17 42			18 44		
Peartree	d														16 44			17 44					
Tutbury & Hatton	d		12 56			13 56			14 56			15 56			16 55			17 56			18 59		
Uttoxeter	d		13 07			14 07			15 07			16 07			17 06			18 07			19 09		
Blythe Bridge	d		13 21			14 21			15 21			16 21			17 21			18 22			19 24		
Longton	d		13 27			14 27			15 27			16 27			17 27			18 27			19 30		
Stoke-on-Trent	a		13 33			14 33			15 33			16 33			17 33			18 33			19 35		
	d	13 13	13 34	13 56	14 12	14 34	14 56	15 11	15 34	15 56	16 14	16 34	16 57	17 12	17 34	17 56	18 14	18 34	18 58	19 11	19 36	19 58	20 15
Longport	d		13 39			14 39			15 39			16 39			17 39			18 39			19 41		
Kidsgrove	d	13 23	13 45	14a03	14 21	14 45	15a03	15 20	15 45	16a03	16 21	16 45	17a04	17 21	17 46	18a03	18 22	18 46	19a05	19 20	19 47	20a05	20 23
Alsager	d	13 27	13 49		14 25	14 49		15 24	15 49		16 25	16 49		17 25	17 50		18 27	18 50		19 24	19 51		20 27
Crewe 10	a	13 36	14 01		14 34	15 01		15 33	16 01		16 34	17 01		17 36	18 01		18 36	19 01		19 37	20 03		20 36

Station		EM	NT ◇ B	LM ■1 E	EM	VT ◇■1 E	LM ■1 E	NT ◇ F	LM ■1 E
Derby 6	d	19 43			20 42				
Peartree	d								
Tutbury & Hatton	d	19 56			20 56				
Uttoxeter	d	20 07			21 07				
Blythe Bridge	d	20 22			21 21				
Longton	d	20 27			21 27				
Stoke-on-Trent	a	20 34			21 33				
	d	20 34	20 58	21 12	21 34	22 11	22 16	22 20	23 16
Longport	d	20 39			21 39				
Kidsgrove	d	20 46	21a05	21 20	21 45		22 24	22a27	23 25
Alsager	d	20 50		21 24	21 49		22 28		23 29
Crewe 10	a	21 01		21 33	21 59	22 30	22 37		23 38

Saturdays
21 December to 16 May

Station		NT ◇ A	NT ◇ B	LM ■1 C	EM	NT ◇ B	LM ■1 D	EM	NT ◇ B	LM ■1 D	EM	NT ◇ B	LM ■1 D	EM	NT ◇ B	LM ■1 E	EM	NT ◇ B	LM ■1 E	EM	NT ◇ B	LM ■1 E	EM
Derby 6	d				06 40			07 40			08 42			09 42			10 42			11 42			12 42
Peartree	d							07 44															
Tutbury & Hatton	d				06 55			07 55			08 56			09 56			10 56			11 56			12 56
Uttoxeter	d				07 06			08 07			09 07			10 07			11 07			12 07			13 07
Blythe Bridge	d				07 20			08 21			09 21			10 21			11 21			12 21			13 21
Longton	d				07 26			08 27			09 27			10 27			11 27			12 27			13 27
Stoke-on-Trent	a				07 32			08 32			09 33			10 33			11 33			12 33			13 33
	d	06 29	06 58	07 04	07 33	07 56	08 10	08 34	08 56	09 14	09 34	09 56	10 14	10 34	10 56	11 14	11 34	11 56	12 13	12 34	12 56	13 13	13 34
Longport	d	06 33			07 38	08 00		08 39			09 39			10 39			11 39			12 39			13 39
Kidsgrove	d	06a37	07a05	07 13	07 43	08a04	08 18	08 45	09a03	09 22	09 45	10a03	10 23	10 45	11a03	11 22	11 45	12a03	12 22	12 45	13a03	13 21	13 45
Alsager	d			07 17	07 47		08 22	08 49		09 26	09 49		10 27	10 49		11 26	11 49		12 26	12 49		13 25	13 49
Crewe 10	a			07 26	07 59		08 31	08 59		09 35	10 01		10 36	11 01		11 35	12 01		12 35	13 01		13 34	14 01

Station		NT ◇ B	LM ■1 E	EM	NT ◇ B	LM ■1 E	EM	NT ◇ B	LM ■1 E	EM	NT ◇ B	LM ■1 E	EM	NT ◇ B	LM ■1 E	EM	NT ◇ B	LM ■1 E	EM	NT ◇ B	LM ■1 E	EM	NT ◇ B
Derby 6	d			13 42			14 42			15 42			16 42			17 42			18 42			19 42	
Peartree	d															17 45							
Tutbury & Hatton	d			13 56			14 56			15 56			16 55			17 57			18 56			19 56	
Uttoxeter	d			14 07			15 07			16 07			17 07			18 06			19 07			20 07	
Blythe Bridge	d			14 21			15 21			16 21			17 21			18 20			19 21			20 21	
Longton	d			14 27			15 27			16 27			17 27			18 27			19 27			20 27	
Stoke-on-Trent	a			14 33			15 33			16 33			17 32			18 32			19 33			20 33	
	d	13 56	14 12	14 34	14 56	15 14	15 34	15 58	16 11	16 34	16 56	17 12	17 34	17 56	18 14	18 34	18 58	19 12	19 34	19 58	20 12	20 34	20 58
Longport	d			14 39			15 39			16 39			17 39			18 39			19 39			20 39	
Kidsgrove	d	14a03	14 20	14 45	15a03	15 23	15 45	16a05	16 20	16 45	17a03	17 21	17 45	18a03	18 23	18 45	19a05	19 21	19 45	20a05	20 21	20 45	21a05
Alsager	d		14 24	14 49		15 27	15 49		16 24	16 49		17 25	17 49		18 27	18 49		19 25	19 49		20 25	20 49	
Crewe 10	a		14 33	15 01		15 36	16 01		16 33	17 01		17 34	18 01		18 37	19 01		19 34	20 01		20 34	21 01	

A To Blackpool North
B To Manchester Piccadilly
C From Birmingham New Street
D From Northampton
E From London Euston
F To Stockport

NRT DECEMBER 19 EDITION

Table T050-F

Derby - Stoke-on-Trent and Crewe

Saturdays
21 December to 16 May

Station		EM	LM ■1 A	NT ◇ B
Derby 6	d	20 42		
Peartree	d			
Tutbury & Hatton	d	20 56		
Uttoxeter	d	21 07		
Blythe Bridge	d	21 21		
Longton	d	21 27		
Stoke-on-Trent	a	21 33		
	d	21 34	22 04	22 29
Longport	d	21 39		
Kidsgrove	d	21 45	22 12	22a36
Alsager	d	21 49	22 16	
Crewe 10	a	22 01	22 25	

Sundays
15 December to 10 May

Station		NT ◇ B	LM ■1 C	NT ◇ D	LM ■1 E	LM ■1 F	LM ■1 F	NT ◇ B	LM ■1 F	LM ■1 F	EM	LM ■1 F	NT ◇ B	EM	LM ■1 F	EM	LM ■1 F	EM	LM ■1 F	EM	LM ■1 F	NT ◇ B	EM
Derby 6	d										14 40			15 42		16 41		17 41		18 41			19 41
Peartree	d																						
Tutbury & Hatton	d										14 54			15 56		16 55		17 55		18 55			19 55
Uttoxeter	d										15 05			16 07		17 06		18 06		19 05			20 06
Blythe Bridge	d										15 19			16 21		17 20		18 20		19 19			20 20
Longton	d										15 25			16 27		17 26		18 26		19 26			20 26
Stoke-on-Trent	a										15 33			16 33		17 33		18 33		19 33			20 34
	d	09 30	09 33	10 30	10 40	11 45	12 38	13 25	13 35	14 33	15 33	15 42	16 30	16 33	16 43	17 33	17 43	18 34	18 38	19 33	19 42	20 30	20 34
Longport	d										15 38			16 38		17 38		18 39		19 38			20 39
Kidsgrove	d	09a37	09 41	10a37	10 48	11 53	12 46	13a32	13 43	14 41	15 45	15 52	16a37	16 45	16 51	17 45	17 51	18 45	18 51	19 45	19 52	20a37	20 46
Alsager	d		09 45		10 52	11 57	12 50		13 47	14 45	15 49	15 56		16 49	16 56	17 49	17 56	18 49	18 56	19 49	19 56		20 50
Crewe 10	a		09 54		11 01	12 06	12 59		13 56	14 54	16 03	16 05		17 02	17 05	18 05	18 05	19 01	19 05	20 02	20 08		21 00

Station		LM ■1 F	EM	LM ■1 F	LM ■1 A	LM ■1 F	NT ◇ B
Derby 6	d		20 40				
Peartree	d						
Tutbury & Hatton	d		20 54				
Uttoxeter	d		21 05				
Blythe Bridge	d		21 19				
Longton	d		21 25				
Stoke-on-Trent	a		21 34				
	d	20 41	21 34	21 40	22 17	22 54	23 00
Longport	d		21 39				
Kidsgrove	d	20 52	21 46	21 52	22 26	23 02	23a07
Alsager	d	20 56	21 50	21 56	22 30	23 06	
Crewe 10	a	21 06	22 01	22 05	22 39	23 15	

A From London Euston
B To Manchester Piccadilly
C From Birmingham New Street
D To Manchester Oxford Road
E From Birmingham International
F From Coventry

Table T050-R

Crewe and Stoke-on-Trent - Derby

Mondays to Fridays
16 December to 15 May

Miles			LM	EM	NT	LM	LM	EM	NT	LM	EM	NT	LM	EM	NT	LM	EM	NT	LM	EM	NT	LM	EM
			1 A		◇ B	1 C	1 A		◇ B	1 C		◇ B	1 C		◇ B	1 C		◇ B	1 C		◇ B	1 C	
0	Crewe 10	d	06 01	06 07		06 35	06 52	06 58		08 01	08 07		09 01	09 07		10 01	10 07		11 01	11 07		12 01	12 07
6¼	Alsager	d	06 10	06 16		06 43	07 01	07 07		08 09	08 16		09 09	09 16		10 09	10 16		11 09	11 16		12 09	12 16
8½	Kidsgrove	d	06 16	06 21	06 25	06 48	07 08	07 12	07 21	08 14	08 21	08 30	09 14	09 21	09 31	10 14	10 21	10 31	11 14	11 21	11 31	12 14	12 21
12	Longport	d		06 27				07 18			08 27			09 27			10 27			11 27			12 27
15	Stoke-on-Trent	a	06 24	06 31	06 35	06 56	07 17	07 23	07 30	08 23	08 31	08 38	09 23	09 31	09 39	10 23	10 31	10 39	11 23	11 31	11 39	12 23	12 31
—		d		06 33				07 24			08 33			09 33			10 33			11 33			12 33
17½	Longton	d		06 40				07 30			08 39			09 39			10 39			11 39			12 39
20¾	Blythe Bridge	d		06 46				07 36			08 45			09 45			10 45			11 45			12 45
31¾	Uttoxeter	d		06 58				07 49			08 58			09 58			10 58			11 58			12 58
39½	Tutbury & Hatton	d		07 07				07 58			09 07			10 07			11 07			12 07			13 07
49½	Peartree	d		07 20																			
51	Derby 6	a		07 25				08 15			09 24			10 21			11 22			12 21			13 26

		NT	LM	EM	NT	LM	EM	NT	LM	EM	NT	LM	EM	NT	LM	EM	NT	LM	EM	NT	LM	EM
		◇ B	1 C		◇ B	1 C		◇ B	1 C		◇ B	1 C		◇ B	1 C		◇ B	1 C		◇ B	1 C	
Crewe 10	d		13 03	13 07		14 01	14 07		15 01	15 07		16 01	16 07		17 01	17 07		18 01	18 07		19 01	19 07
Alsager	d		13 11	13 17		14 09	14 16		15 09	15 16		16 09	16 16		17 09	17 16		18 09	18 16		19 09	19 16
Kidsgrove	d	12 31	13 16	13 23	13 31	14 14	14 21	14 31	15 14	15 21	15 31	16 14	16 21	16 31	17 14	17 21	17 31	18 14	18 21	18 31	19 14	19 21
Longport	d			13 29			14 27			15 27			16 27			17 27			18 27			19 27
Stoke-on-Trent	a	12 39	13 25	13 33	13 39	14 23	14 31	14 39	15 23	15 31	15 39	16 23	16 31	16 39	17 23	17 31	17 39	18 23	18 31	18 39	19 23	19 31
	d			13 34			14 33			15 33			16 33			17 33			18 33			19 33
Longton	d			13 40			14 39			15 39			16 39			17 39			18 39			19 39
Blythe Bridge	d			13 46			14 45			15 45			16 45			17 45			18 45			19 45
Uttoxeter	d			13 59			14 58			15 58			16 58			17 58			18 58			19 58
Tutbury & Hatton	d			14 08			15 07			16 07			17 07			18 07			19 07			20 07
Peartree	d									16 19												
Derby 6	a			14 22			15 26			16 23			17 22			18 21			19 24			20 25

		NT	LM	NT	EM	LM	NT	NT	NT
		◇ B	1 D	◇ B		1 A	◇ B	◇ B	◇ B
Crewe 10	d		20 01		20 45	21 14			
Alsager	d		20 10		20 58	21 23			
Kidsgrove	d	19 31	20 14	20 31	21 07	21 27	21 31	22 31	23 06
Longport	d				21 12				
Stoke-on-Trent	a	19 39	20 23	20 39	21 16	21 36	21 40	22 40	23 15
	d				21 18				
Longton	d				21 24				
Blythe Bridge	d				21 30				
Uttoxeter	d				21 42				
Tutbury & Hatton	d				21 51				
Peartree	d								
Derby 6	a				22 07				

Saturdays
21 December to 16 May

		LM	EM	NT	LM	EM	NT	LM	EM	NT	LM	EM	NT	LM	EM	NT	LM	EM	NT	LM	EM	NT	LM
		1 C		◇ B	1 C		◇ B	1 C		◇ B	1 C		◇ B	1 C		◇ B	1 C		◇ B	1 C		◇ B	1 C
Crewe 10	d	06 01	06 07		07 01	07 07		08 01	08 07		09 01	09 07		10 01	10 07		11 01	11 07		12 01	12 07		13 01
Alsager	d	06 10	06 16		07 09	07 16		08 09	08 16		09 09	09 16		10 09	10 16		11 09	11 16		12 09	12 16		13 09
Kidsgrove	d	06 16	06 21	06 25	07 14	07 21	07 32	08 15	08 21	08 30	09 14	09 21	09 31	10 14	10 21	10 31	11 14	11 21	11 31	12 14	12 21	12 31	13 14
Longport	d		06 27			07 27			08 27			09 27			10 27			11 27			12 27		
Stoke-on-Trent	a	06 24	06 31	06 35	07 23	07 31	07 40	08 24	08 31	08 38	09 23	09 31	09 39	10 23	10 31	10 39	11 23	11 31	11 39	12 23	12 31	12 39	13 23
	d		06 33			07 33			08 33			09 33			10 33			11 33			12 33		
Longton	d		06 39			07 39			08 39			09 39			10 39			11 39			12 39		
Blythe Bridge	d		06 45			07 45			08 45			09 45			10 45			11 45			12 45		
Uttoxeter	d		06 58			07 58			08 58			09 58			10 58			11 58			12 58		
Tutbury & Hatton	d		07 07			08 07			09 07			10 07			11 07			12 07			13 07		
Peartree	d		07 20																				
Derby 6	a		07 23			08 26			09 25			10 23			11 25			12 23			13 23		

		EM	NT	LM	EM	NT	LM	EM	NT	LM	EM	NT	LM	EM	NT	LM	EM	NT	LM	EM	NT	LM	NT
			◇ B	1 C		◇ B	1 C		◇ B	1 C		◇ B	1 E		◇ B	1 C		◇ B	1 C		◇ B	1 C	◇ B
Crewe 10	d	13 07		14 01	14 07		15 01	15 07		16 01	16 07		17 02	17 07		18 01	18 07		19 01	19 07		20 02	
Alsager	d	13 16		14 09	14 16		15 09	15 16		16 09	16 16		17 11	17 16		18 10	18 16		19 10	19 16		20 11	
Kidsgrove	d	13 21	13 31	14 14	14 21	14 31	15 14	15 21	15 31	16 14	16 21	16 31	17 15	17 21	17 31	18 15	18 21	18 31	19 14	19 21	19 31	20 16	20 31
Longport	d	13 27			14 27			15 27			16 27			17 27			18 27			19 27			
Stoke-on-Trent	a	13 31	13 39	14 23	14 32	14 39	15 23	15 31	15 39	16 23	16 31	16 39	17 23	17 31	17 39	18 23	18 31	18 39	19 23	19 31	19 39	20 24	20 39
	d	13 33			14 33			15 33			16 33			17 33			18 33			19 33			
Longton	d	13 39			14 39			15 39			16 39			17 39			18 39			19 39			
Blythe Bridge	d	13 45			14 45			15 45			16 45			17 45			18 45			19 45			
Uttoxeter	d	13 58			14 58			15 58			16 58			17 58			18 58			19 58			
Tutbury & Hatton	d	14 07			15 07			16 07			17 07			18 07			19 07			20 07			
Peartree	d							16 20															
Derby 6	a	14 23			15 23			16 23			17 23			18 23			19 23			20 21			

A To Walsall
B From Manchester Piccadilly
C To London Euston
D To Northampton
E To Milton Keynes Central

Table T050-R

Crewe and Stoke-on-Trent - Derby

Saturdays
21 December to 16 May

		EM	LM	NT	NT
			1 A	◇ B	◇ B
Crewe 10	d	20 45	21 02		
Alsager	d	20 54	21 11		
Kidsgrove	d	21 08	21 15	21 31	22 31
Longport	d	21 14			
Stoke-on-Trent	a	21 18	21 23	21 40	22 40
	d	21 19			
Longton	d	21 25			
Blythe Bridge	d	21 31			
Uttoxeter	d	21 44			
Tutbury & Hatton	d	21 53			
Peartree	d				
Derby 6	a	22 08			

Sundays
15 December to 10 May

		LM	NT	LM	LM	LM	NT	LM	EM	LM	EM	LM	NT	EM	LM	EM	LM	EM	LM	EM	LM	NT	LM
		1 C	◇ B	1 C	1 C	1 C	◇ D	1 C		1 C		1 C	◇ B		1 C		1 C		1 C		1 C	◇ B	1 C
Crewe 10	d	09 12		10 10	11 12	12 12		13 12	14 04	14 12	15 05	15 15		16 07	16 15	17 08	17 15	18 08	18 16	19 08	19 15		20 04
Alsager	d	09 21		10 19	11 20	12 20		13 20	14 13	14 20	15 14	15 24		16 16	16 24	17 17	17 23	18 17	18 24	19 16	19 24		20 13
Kidsgrove	d	09 25	09 36	10 24	11 25	12 25	12 31	13 25	14 18	14 25	15 21	15 28	15 32	16 21	16 28	17 22	17 28	18 22	18 29	19 21	19 29	19 33	20 17
Longport	d								14 24		15 26			16 27		17 28		18 29		19 29			
Stoke-on-Trent	a	09 34	09 45	10 33	11 34	12 34	12 40	13 33	14 29	14 34	15 30	15 36	15 40	16 33	16 37	17 32	17 37	18 34	18 38	19 33	19 38	19 41	20 24
	d								14 29		15 32			16 34		17 34		18 34		19 35			
Longton	d								14 35		15 38			16 40		17 41		18 41		19 41			
Blythe Bridge	d								14 41		15 44			16 46		17 47		18 47		19 47			
Uttoxeter	d								14 54		15 57			16 58		17 59		18 59		19 59			
Tutbury & Hatton	d								15 03		16 06			17 07		18 08		19 08		20 08			
Peartree	d																						
Derby 6	a								15 19		16 23			17 26		18 28		19 28		20 27			

		EM	NT	LM	EM	LM	NT
			◇ B	1 C		1 A	◇ B
Crewe 10	d	20 15		21 08	21 16	22 11	
Alsager	d	20 24		21 17	21 25	22 19	
Kidsgrove	d	20 30	21 08	21 21	21 31	22 24	22 43
Longport	d	20 35			21 36		
Stoke-on-Trent	a	20 40	21 17	21 29	21 40	22 32	22 51
	d	20 40			21 42		
Longton	d	20 46			21 48		
Blythe Bridge	d	20 52			21 54		
Uttoxeter	d	21 05			22 06		
Tutbury & Hatton	d	21 14			22 15		
Peartree	d						
Derby 6	a	21 33			22 32		

A To Birmingham New Street
B From Manchester Piccadilly
C To Coventry
D From Manchester Oxford Road

Table T051-F

Mondays to Fridays

16 December to 15 May

Scotland, The North East, North West England - The South West and South Coast

Station		XC	XC	XC	XC	XC	XC	XC	XC	XC		XC	XC	XC	VT	VT	XC	XC	XC	XC		XC	XC	VT	XC
		◇■	◇■	◇■ 🍴	◇■ A 🍴	◇■ 🍴	◇■	◇■ B 🍴	◇■ 🍴	◇■ B 🍴		◇■ B 🍴	◇■ 🍴	◇■ B 🍴	◇■ ⊠	◇■ ⊠	◇■ 🍴	◇■	◇■ 🍴	◇■ 🍴		■	■ ■ 🍴	◇■ ⊠	◇■ C 🍴
Aberdeen	d																								
Stonehaven	d																								
Montrose	d																								
Arbroath	d																								
Dundee	d																								
Leuchars	d																								
Cupar	d																								
Ladybank	d																								
Markinch	d																								
Kirkcaldy	d																								
Inverkeithing	d																								
Glasgow Central	d																								
Motherwell	d																								
Haymarket	d																								
Edinburgh	d																								
Haymarket	d																								
Lockerbie	d																								
Carlisle	d																								
Penrith North Lakes	d																								
Oxenholme Lake District	d																								
Lancaster	d																							06 58	
Preston	d														06 17									07 18	
Wigan North Western	d														06 29									07 29	
Warrington Bank Quay	d														06 40									07 41	
M'chester Piccadilly	d							05 11					06 00			06 27				07 05			07 27		
Stockport	d												06 08			06 36				07 13			07 36		
Wilmslow	d												06 16												
Crewe	d							05 46					06 39		07 01									08 01	
Macclesfield	d															06 48				07 26			07 49		
Congleton	d																								
Stoke-on-Trent	d							06 06								07 06				07 44			08 07		
Stafford	d							06 25					07 01			07 24				08 03			08 26		
Wolverhampton	d							06 39					07 16		07 37	07 45				08 17			08 40	08 45	
Dunbar	d																								
Berwick-upon-Tweed	d																								
Alnmouth for Alnwick	d																								
Morpeth	d																								
Newcastle	d																								
Chester-le-Street	d																								
Durham	d																								
Darlington	d																								
York	d																		06 24						06 45
Leeds	d																06 11								07 10
Wakefield Westgate	d																06 23								07 23
Doncaster	d																		06 47						
Sheffield	d											05 59					06 53		07 18						07 53
Chesterfield	d											06 26					07 06		07 30						08 06
Nottingham	d									06 00				06 43				07 05				07 37			
Derby	d						06 10			06 36		06 50		07 13			07 27	07 36	07 49			08 06			08 28
Burton-on-Trent	d						06 20			06 48		07 00		07 23			07 38	07 50	08 00			08 18			08 39
Tamworth	d						06 31		←	07 01		07 10		07 34			07 50	08 03	08 10			08 30			08 50
Birmingham New Street	a						06 52	06 55	06 52	07 25		07 28	07 33	07 54	07 56	08 07	08 08	08 25	08 28	08 33		08 55	08 57	09 05	09 08
Birmingham New Street	d	05 00	05 37	06 04	06 33	06 42	07 12	07 04	07 12	07 30		07 33	07 42	08 04		08 10	08 12	08 30	08 33	08 42			09 04	09 10	09 12
Cheltenham Spa	a	06 04	06 39			07 20	→		07 50	08 14			08 24				08 50	09 14		09 28					09 50
Gloucester	a	06 13	06 49							08 25								09 26							
Bristol Parkway	a					07 54			08 25				08 54				09 20			09 59					10 20
Bristol Temple Meads	a					08 05			08 38				09 05				09 40			10 09					10 31
Newport (South Wales)	a	07 09	07 42							09 10								10 11							
Cardiff Central	a	07 22	08 00							09 27								10 25							
Weston-super-Mare	a																								
Taunton	a					08 42			09 16								10 17								11 17
Tiverton Parkway	a					08 54			09 28								10 30								11 30
Exeter St Davids	a					09 09			09 44								10 45								11 45
Dawlish	a																								
Teignmouth	a																								
Newton Abbot	a					09 30			10 06								11 08								12 07
Torquay	a					09 44																			
Paignton	a					09 54																			
Totnes	a								10 18								11 20								12 20
Plymouth	a								10 45								11 48								12 47
Liskeard	a																								
Bodmin Parkway	a																								
Lostwithiel	a																								
Par	a																								
St Austell	a																								
Truro	a																								
Redruth	a																								
Camborne	a																								
Hayle	a																								
St Erth	a																								
Penzance	a																								
Birmingham International	d			06 14				07 14						08 14		08 20							09 14	09 20	
Coventry	d			06 25				07 25						08 25		08a30							09 25	09a30	
Leamington Spa	d			06 37	07 00			07 37				08 00		08 37					09 00				09 37		
Banbury	a			06 53	07 16			07 53				08 16		08 53					09 16				09 53		
Oxford	a			07 14	07 35			08 14				08 39		09 14					09 40				10 12		
Reading	a			07 41	08 03			08 42				09 11		09 40					10 06				10 40		
Guildford	a																								
Basingstoke	a			08 11	08 41			09 10						10 09					10 42				11 09		
Winchester	a			08 26	08 57			09 26						10 26					10 58				11 26		
Southampton Airport Pkway	a			08 35	09 09			09 35						10 35					11 08				11 35		
Southampton Central	a			08 42	09 17			09 43						10 43					11 17				11 43		
Brockenhurst	a			09 00				09 58						10 58									11 58		
Bournemouth	a			09 16				10 13						11 13									12 13		

A 🍴 from Reading B 🍴 from Birmingham New Street C 🍴 from Leeds

Table T051-F

Mondays to Fridays

16 December to 15 May

Scotland, The North East, North West England - The South West and South Coast

Station		XC	XC	XC	XC	XC		VT	XC	XC	XC	XC	XC	XC	VT	XC		XC	XC	XC	XC	XC	VT	XC	XC
		◇■ A 🍴	■ ◇■ B 🍴	◇■ 🍴	■	◇■ 🍴		◇■ ⊠	◇■ 🍴	◇■ 🍴	◇■ 🍴	◇■ 🍴	■	◇■ 🍴	◇■ ⊠	◇■ 🍴		◇■ 🍴	◇■ 🍴	◇■ 🍴	■	◇■ 🍴	◇■ ⊠	◇■ C 🍴	◇■ 🍴
Aberdeen	d																								
Stonehaven	d																								
Montrose	d																								
Arbroath	d																								
Dundee	d																								
Leuchars	d																								
Cupar	d																								
Ladybank	d																								
Markinch	d																								
Kirkcaldy	d																								
Inverkeithing	d																								
Glasgow Central	d							05 49															08 00	06 01	
Motherwell	d							06 04																06 16	
Haymarket	d																							06 57	
Edinburgh	d														06 52	06 06			07 00					07 10	
Haymarket	d														06 57										
Lockerbie	d																								
Carlisle	d							07 02							08 08								09 10		
Penrith North Lakes	d							07 17							08 22										
Oxenholme Lake District	d							07 41																	
Lancaster	d							07 56							08 57								09 57		
Preston	d							08 17							09 18								10 17		
Wigan North Western	d							08 29							09 29								10 29		
Warrington Bank Quay	d							08 40							09 40								10 40		
M'chester Piccadilly	d			08 05		08 27						09 05		09 27						10 05		10 27			
Stockport	d			08 13		08 36						09 13		09 36						10 13		10 36			
Wilmslow	d																								
Crewe	d							09 01							10 01								11 01		
Macclesfield	d			08 26		08 49						09 26		09 49						10 26		10 49			
Congleton	d																								
Stoke-on-Trent	d			08 44		09 07						09 44		10 07						10 44		11 07			
Stafford	d			09 02		09 26						10 03		10 24						11 03		11 28			
Wolverhampton	d			09 17		09 40		09 45				10 17		10 42	10 45					11 17		11 42	11 45		
Dunbar	d																							07 32	
Berwick-upon-Tweed	d															06 50			07 43						
Alnmouth for Alnwick	d															07 11			08 03						
Morpeth	d																		08 18						
Newcastle	d		06 24						06 40		07 35					07 40			08 35					08 40	
Chester-le-Street	d																								
Durham	d		06 37						06 52		07 47					07 53			08 48					08 54	
Darlington	d		06 55						07 10		08 06					08 12			09 06					09 12	
York	d		07 28						07 44		08 35					08 44			09 37					09 44	
Leeds	d								08 11							09 11								10 11	
Wakefield Westgate	d								08 23							09 23								10 23	
Doncaster	d		07 52								08 57								10 00						
Sheffield	d		08 18						08 55		09 24					09 56			10 24					10 56	
Chesterfield	d		08 30						09 08							10 09								11 08	
Nottingham	d	08 09			08 39					09 07			09 41					10 07			10 41				11 07
Derby	d	08 38	08 53		09 10				09 29	09 38	09 53		10 10			10 30		10 38	10 53		11 10			11 32	11 38
Burton-on-Trent	d	08 50			09 22				09 40	09 52			10 21					10 50			11 21				11 49
Tamworth	d	09 02			09 34					10 03			10 33			10 50		11 02			11 33				12 02
Birmingham New Street	a	09 24	09 27	09 33	09 55	09 58		10 05	10 06	10 24	10 27	10 33	10 55	10 58	11 05	11 08		11 24	11 27	11 33	11 55	11 59	12 05	12 06	12 24
Birmingham New Street	d	09 30	09 33	09 42		10 04		10 10	10 12	10 30	10 33	10 42		11 04	11 10	11 12		11 30	11 33	11 42		12 04	12 10	12 12	12 30
Cheltenham Spa	a	10 16		10 24					10 50	11 14		11 27				11 50		12 14		12 25				12 50	13 14
Gloucester	a	10 25								11 23								12 23							13 25
Bristol Parkway	a			10 58					11 20			11 58				12 20				12 54				13 20	
Bristol Temple Meads	a			11 08					11 31			12 08				12 32				13 04				13 32	
Newport (South Wales)	a	11 11								12 09								13 10							14 11
Cardiff Central	a	11 25								12 22								13 26							14 25
Weston-super-Mare	a			11 33																					
Taunton	a			11 59					12 17							13 17				13 41				14 17	
Tiverton Parkway	a			12 11					12 29							13 30				13 53				14 29	
Exeter St Davids	a			12 26					12 44							13 45				14 08				14 45	
Dawlish	a			12 39																					
Teignmouth	a			12 44																					
Newton Abbot	a			12 51					13 06							14 08								15 07	
Torquay	a			13 01																					
Paignton	a			13 08																					
Totnes	a								13 19							14 20								15 19	
Plymouth	a								13 46							14 48								15 47	
Liskeard	a																								
Bodmin Parkway	a																								
Lostwithiel	a																								
Par	a																								
St Austell	a																								
Truro	a																								
Redruth	a																								
Camborne	a																								
Hayle	a																								
St Erth	a																								
Penzance	a																								
Birmingham International	d					10 14		10 20						11 14	11 20							12 14	12 20		
Coventry	d					10 25		10a30						11 25	11a30							12 25	12a30		
Leamington Spa	d		10 04			10 37					11 00			11 37					12 03			12 37			
Banbury	a		10 20			10 53					11 17			11 53					12 19			12 53			
Oxford	a		10 40			11 12					11 40			12 12					12 41			13 12			
Reading	a		11 10			11 39					12 07			12 42					13 06			13 40			
Guildford	a																								
Basingstoke	a					12 10					12 42			13 09								14 10			
Winchester	a					12 26					12 58			13 26								14 26			
Southampton Airport Pkway	a					12 35					13 09			13 35								14 34			
Southampton Central	a					12 43					13 18			13 42								14 42			
Brockenhurst	a					12 58								13 58								14 57			
Bournemouth	a					13 13								14 13								15 12			

A 🍴 from Birmingham New Street B◇ from Birmingham New St ■to Birmingham NewSt C 🍴 from Edinburgh

Table T051-F

Mondays to Fridays

16 December to 15 May

Scotland, The North East, North West England - The South West and South Coast

	XC	XC	XC	XC	VT	XC	XC	XC	XC	XC	XC	VT	XC	XC	XC	XC	XC	XC	VT	XC	XC
	◇1 ⊤	◇1 ⊤	1	◇1 ⊤	◇1 ⊠	◇1 A ⊤	◇1 ⊤	◇1 ⊤	◇1 ⊤	1	◇1 ⊤	◇1 ⊠	◇1 A ⊤	◇1 ⊤	◇1 ⊤	◇1 ⊤	1 ⊤	◇1 ⊤	◇1 ⊏	◇1 B ⊤	◇1 ⊤
Aberdeen d																					
Stonehaven d																					
Montrose d																					
Arbroath d																					
Dundee d						06 33															
Leuchars [3] d						06 46															
Cupar d						06 55															
Ladybank d						07 03															
Markinch d						07 11															
Kirkcaldy d						07 22															
Inverkeithing d						07 40															
Glasgow Central [15] d												10 00	07 48							09 00	
Motherwell d													08 08							09 15	
Haymarket d						08 00							08 51							09 54	
Edinburgh [10] d					08 52	08 08							09 07						10 52	10 10	
Haymarket d					08 57														10 57		
Lockerbie d																					
Carlisle [8] d					10 08							11 13							12 08		
Penrith North Lakes d												11 28									
Oxenholme Lake District d					10 43														12 43		
Lancaster [6] d					10 57														12 57		
Preston [8] d					11 17							12 17							13 17		
Wigan North Western d					11 29							12 29							13 29		
Warrington Bank Quay d					11 40							12 40							13 40		
M'chester Piccadilly [10] d		11 05		11 27					12 05		12 27					13 05		13 27			
Stockport d		11 13		11 36					12 13		12 36					13 13		13 36			
Wilmslow d																					
Crewe [10] d					12 01							13 01							14 01		
Macclesfield d		11 26		11 49					12 26		12 49					13 26		13 49			
Congleton d																					
Stoke-on-Trent d		11 44		12 07					12 44		13 07					13 44		14 07			
Stafford d		12 03		12 28					13 01		13 28					14 03		14 25			
Wolverhampton [7] d		12 17		12 42	12 45				13 17		13 42	13 45				14 17		14 39	14 45		
Dunbar d													09 28								
Berwick-upon-Tweed d						08 51							09 52							10 51	
Alnmouth for Alnwick d													10 12								
Morpeth d						09 24														11 22	
Newcastle [8] d	09 35					09 41		10 35					10 42		11 35					11 39	
Chester-le-Street d																					
Durham d	09 49					09 55		10 47					10 54		11 49					11 53	
Darlington [7] d	10 07					10 12		11 06					11 12		12 07					12 12	
York [8] d	10 35					10 44		11 36					11 44		12 35					12 44	
Leeds [10] d						11 11							12 11							13 11	
Wakefield Westgate [7] d						11 23							12 23							13 23	
Doncaster [7] d	10 59							11 59							12 59						
Sheffield [7] d	11 24					11 56		12 24					12 56		13 24					13 56	
Chesterfield d						12 09							13 08							14 08	
Nottingham [8] d			11 41				12 07			12 41				13 07			13 41				14 07
Derby [6] d	11 53		12 10			12 30	12 38	12 53		13 10			13 30	13 38	13 53		14 10			14 30	14 38
Burton-on-Trent d			12 21				12 49			13 24			13 41	13 49			14 21				14 50
Tamworth d			12 33			12 50	13 02			13 35				14 03			14 33			14 48	15 04
Birmingham New Street [12] a	12 27	12 33	12 55	12 59	13 05	13 08	13 24	13 27	13 33	13 55	13 59	14 05	14 05	14 24	14 27	14 33	14 55	14 59	15 05	15 05	15 24
Birmingham New Street [12] d	12 33	12 42		13 04	13 10	13 12	13 30	13 33	13 42		14 04	14 10	14 12	14 30	14 33	14 42		15 04	15 10	15 12	15 30
Cheltenham Spa [5] a		13 27				13 50	14 14		14 24				14 50	15 14		15 26				15 50	16 14
Gloucester [7] a							14 23							15 25							16 24
Bristol Parkway [7] a		13 58				14 21			14 54				15 20			15 55				16 21	
Bristol Temple Meads [10] a		14 08				14 32			15 04				15 34			16 06				16 32	
Newport (South Wales) a							15 10							16 10							17 12
Cardiff Central [7] a							15 23							16 29							17 25
Weston-super-Mare a																					
Taunton a						15 17			15 40				16 17			16 42				17 17	
Tiverton Parkway a						15 30			15 52				16 29			16 54				17 29	
Exeter St Davids [6] a						15 45			16 07				16 45			17 09				17 44	
Dawlish a																					
Teignmouth a																					
Newton Abbot a						16 07							17 05							18 04	
Torquay a																					
Paignton a																					
Totnes a						16 20							17 18							18 17	
Plymouth a						16 47							17 45							18 44	
Liskeard [6] a																				19 16	
Bodmin Parkway a																				19 29	
Lostwithiel a																					
Par a																				19 40	
St Austell a																				19 47	
Truro a																				20 04	
Redruth a																				20 19	
Camborne a																				20 25	
Hayle a																					
St Erth a																				20 35	
Penzance a																				20 45	
Birmingham International d				13 14	13 20						14 14	14 20						15 14	15 20		
Coventry d				13 25	13a30						14 25	14a30						15 25	15a30		
Leamington Spa [8] d	13 00			13 37				14 03			14 37				15 00			15 37			
Banbury a	13 19			13 53				14 19			14 53				15 16			15 53			
Oxford a	13 40			14 12				14 40			15 12				15 40			16 12			
Reading [7] a	14 09			14 40				15 05			15 39				16 07			16 41			
Guildford a																					
Basingstoke a	14 41			15 10							16 10				16 42			17 10			
Winchester a	14 58			15 26							16 26				16 58			17 26			
Southampton Airport Pkway a	15 08			15 35							16 35				17 08			17 35			
Southampton Central a	15 17			15 42							16 43				17 17			17 42			
Brockenhurst [3] a				15 58							16 58							17 58			
Bournemouth a				16 13							17 14							18 14			

A ⊤ from Edinburgh

B ⊤ from Edinburgh to Plymouth

Table T051-F

Mondays to Fridays

16 December to 15 May

Scotland, The North East, North West England - The South West and South Coast

	XC	XC	XC	XC	VT	XC	XC	XC	XC	XC	XC	VT	XC	XC	XC	XC	XC	XC	VT	XC	XC	XC
	◇1 ⊤	◇1 A ⊤	1	◇1 ⊤	◇1 ⊏	■ ◇1 B ⊤	◇1	◇1 C ⊤	◇1 ⊤	1 ⊤	◇1 ⊤	◇1 ⊏	◇1 D ⊤	◇1	◇1 ⊤	◇1 ⊤	1 ⊤	◇1 ⊤	◇1 ⊏	◇1 ⊤	◇1	◇1 ⊤
Aberdeen d						08 20																
Stonehaven d						08 37																
Montrose d						08 59																
Arbroath d						09 14																
Dundee d						09 33																
Leuchars [3] d						09 46																
Cupar d						09 53																
Ladybank d						10 01																
Markinch d						10 08																
Kirkcaldy d						10 18																
Inverkeithing d						10 34																
Glasgow Central [15] d					12 00								11 00						14 00			
Motherwell d													11 15									
Haymarket d						10 50							11 57									
Edinburgh [10] d						11 06						12 52	12 08							13 08		
Haymarket d												12 58										
Lockerbie d																						
Carlisle [8] d					13 12							14 08							15 11			
Penrith North Lakes d												14 22										
Oxenholme Lake District d																			15 45			
Lancaster [6] d					13 57							14 57										
Preston [8] d					14 17							15 17							16 17			
Wigan North Western d					14 29							15 29							16 29			
Warrington Bank Quay d					14 40							15 40							16 40			
M'chester Piccadilly [10] d		14 05		14 27					15 05		15 27					16 05		16 27				
Stockport d		14 13		14 36					15 13		15 36					16 13		16 36				
Wilmslow d																						
Crewe [10] d					15 01							16 01							17 01			
Macclesfield d		14 26		14 49					15 26		15 49					16 26		16 49				
Congleton d																						
Stoke-on-Trent d		14 44		15 07					15 44		16 07					16 44		17 07				
Stafford d		15 03		15 28					16 03		16 25					17 03		17 25				
Wolverhampton [7] d		15 17		15 42	15 45				16 17		16 39	16 45				17 17		17 39	17 45			
Dunbar d						11 28														13 30		
Berwick-upon-Tweed d						11 51							12 50									
Alnmouth for Alnwick d						12 12														14 13		
Morpeth d													13 21									
Newcastle [8] d	12 35					12 42		13 35					13 39		14 36					14 42		15 15
Chester-le-Street d																						
Durham d	12 48					12 54		13 48					13 53		14 48					14 55		15 28
Darlington [7] d	13 06					13 12		14 06					14 11		15 06					15 13		15 45
York [8] d	13 35					13 44		14 35					14 44		15 36					15 44		16 13
Leeds [10] d						14 11							15 11							16 11		16 41
Wakefield Westgate [7] d						14 23							15 23							16 23		16 53
Doncaster [7] d	14 00							14 59							16 00							
Sheffield [7] d	14 24					14 56		15 24					15 56		16 24					16 56		17 24
Chesterfield d						15 08							16 08							17 09		
Nottingham [8] d			14 41				15 07			15 41				16 07			16 41				17 07	
Derby [6] d	14 53		15 10			15 28	15 38	15 52		16 10			16 30	16 38	16 53		17 10			17 30	17 38	17 53
Burton-on-Trent d			15 24			15 38	15 49			16 21				16 49			17 24			17 41	17 49	
Tamworth d			15 35				16 02			16 33			16 49	17 02			17 35				18 00	
Birmingham New Street [12] a	15 27	15 33	15 55	15 58	16 04	16 04	16 24	16 27	16 33	16 55	16 58	17 05	17 06	17 24	17 27	17 33	17 55	17 59	18 05	18 05	18 24	18 27
Birmingham New Street [12] d	15 33	15 42		16 04	16 10	16 12	16 30	16 33	16 42		17 04	17 10	17 12	17 30	17 33	17 42		18 04	18 10	18 12	18 30	18 33
Cheltenham Spa [5] a		16 24				16 50	17 18		17 28				17 50	18 18		18 24				18 50	19 14	
Gloucester [7] a							17 28							18 27						19 01	19 23	
Bristol Parkway [7] a		16 58				17 20			17 58				18 20			18 55				19 34		
Bristol Temple Meads [10] a		17 08				17 32			18 08				18 33			19 05				19 45		
Newport (South Wales) a							18 15							19 14							20 12	
Cardiff Central [7] a							18 29							19 28							20 27	
Weston-super-Mare a																						
Taunton a		17 42				18 17			18 44				19 18							20 18		
Tiverton Parkway a		17 54				18 29			18 58				19 31							20 31		
Exeter St Davids [6] a		18 09				18 44			19 13				19 46							20 47		
Dawlish a		18 22																				
Teignmouth a		18 27																				
Newton Abbot a		18 34				19 05							20 06							21 09		
Torquay a		18 44																				
Paignton a		18 51																				
Totnes a						19 18							20 19							21 21		
Plymouth a						19 45							20 46							21 51		
Liskeard [6] a						20 13							21 14									
Bodmin Parkway a						20 25							21 26									
Lostwithiel a													21 31									
Par a						20 35							21 37									
St Austell a						20 41							21 44									
Truro a						20 57							22 00									
Redruth a						21 09							22 11									
Camborne a						21 15							22 18									
Hayle a													22 26									
St Erth a						21 25							22 30									
Penzance a						21 35							22 39									
Birmingham International d				16 14	16 20						17 14	17 20						18 14	18 20			
Coventry d				16 25	16a30						17 25	17a30						18 25	18a30			
Leamington Spa [8] d	16 03			16 37				17 00			17 37				18 01			18 37				19 01
Banbury a	16 20			16 53				17 16			17 54				18 17			18 54				19 17
Oxford a	16 40			17 14				17 39			18 13				18 40			19 14				19 40
Reading [7] a	17 09			17 39				18 11			18 42				19 10			19 39				20 10
Guildford a								18 51														
Basingstoke a				18 09							19 09							20 09				
Winchester a				18 25							19 25							20 26				
Southampton Airport Pkway a				18 34							19 33							20 35				
Southampton Central a				18 43							19 41							20 43				
Brockenhurst [3] a				18 58							19 57							21 00				
Bournemouth a				19 13							20 12							21 15				

A ⊤ to Bristol Temple Meads

B ⊤ to Plymouth ◇ from Edinburgh ■ to Edinburgh

C ⊤ to Reading

D ⊤ to Plymouth

Table T051-F

Scotland, The North East, North West England - The South West and South Coast

Mondays to Fridays
16 December to 15 May

		XC	XC	XC	VT	XC	XC	XC	XC	XC	XC	VT	XC	XC	XC	XC	XC	XC	XC	VT	XC	XC
														FO	FX							
		◇1	◇1	1	1	◇1	◇1	◇1	◇1	1	◇1	◇1	◇1	◇1	◇1	◇1	◇1	1	◇1	1	◇1	◇1
		A	B			A			A		B		A			C	C		C		C	
Aberdeen	d																					
Stonehaven	d																					
Montrose	d																					
Arbroath	d																					
Dundee	d																					
Leuchars 3	d																					
Cupar	d																					
Ladybank	d																					
Markinch	d																					
Kirkcaldy	d																					
Inverkeithing	d																					
Glasgow Central 15	d					13 00						16 00									15 00	
Motherwell	d					13 16															15 16	
Haymarket	d					13 55															15 57	
Edinburgh 10	d				14 52	14 09							15 08							16 52	16 08	
Haymarket	d				14 58															16 57		
Lockerbie	d																					
Carlisle 8	d				16 08							17 11								18 10		
Penrith North Lakes	d				16 21																	
Oxenholme Lake District	d											17 45								18 44		
Lancaster 6	d				16 58															18 59		
Preston 8	d				17 17							18 17								19 18		
Wigan North Western	d				17 29							18 29								19 32		
Warrington Bank Quay	d				17 40							18 40								19 42		
M'chester Piccadilly 10	d	17 05	17 27						18 05		18 27						19 05		19 27			
Stockport	d	17 13	17 36						18 13		18 36						19 13		19 36			
Wilmslow	d		17 44																			
Crewe 10	d		18 07		18 01							19 01								20 03		
Macclesfield	d	17 26							18 26								19 26		19 49			
Congleton	d										18 54											
Stoke-on-Trent	d	17 44							18 44		19 07						19 44		20 07			
Stafford	d	18 03	18 27						19 01		19 27						20 03		20 26			
Wolverhampton 7	d	18 17	18 41		18 45				19 17		19 41	19 45					20 17		20 42	20 46		
Dunbar	d												15 29									
Berwick-upon-Tweed	d					14 50																
Alnmouth for Alnwick	d																				17 07	
Morpeth	d																				17 21	
Newcastle 8	d					15 39		16 35					16 39			17 32					17 39	18 35
Chester-le-Street	d															17 41						
Durham	d					15 51		16 48					16 53			17 48					17 54	18 48
Darlington 7	d					16 09		17 06					17 12			18 06					18 12	19 07
York 8	d					16 44		17 36					17 44			18 36					18 44	19 36
Leeds 10	d					17 11							18 11								19 11	
Wakefield Westgate 7	d					17 23							18 23								19 23	
Doncaster 7	d							18 00								19 00						19 59
Sheffield 7	d					17 56		18 24					18 56			19 24					19 56	20 24
Chesterfield	d					18 08							19 11								20 10	
Nottingham 8	d			17 41			18 07			18 41				19 07	19 07			19 36				
Derby 6	d			18 13		18 29	18 40	18 53		19 10			19 31	19 38	19 38	19 53		20 10			20 31	20 53
Burton-on-Trent	d			18 27			18 51			19 21			19 41	19 49	19 49			20 22				
Tamworth	d			18 38		18 50	19 03			19 33				20 03	20 03			20 33			20 50	
Birmingham New Street 12	a	18 33	18 57	18 57	19 05	19 08	19 24	19 27	19 33	19 55	19 57	20 05	20 07	20 24	20 24	20 27	20 33	20 55	20 58	21 04	21 06	21 29
Birmingham New Street 12	d	18 42	19 04		19 10	19 12	19 30	19 33	19 42		20 04	20 10	20 12	20 30	20 30	20 33	20 42		21 04	21 10	21 12	
Cheltenham Spa 5	a	19 26				19 50	20 14		20 24				20 51	21 14	21 14		21 24				21 50	
Gloucester 7	a						20 23							21 23	21 23						22 01	
Bristol Parkway 7	a	19 56				20 20			20 54				21 21				21 55				22 31	
Bristol Temple Meads 10	a	20 07				20 31			21 04				21 36				22 05				22 44	
Newport (South Wales)	a	20 46					21 10							22 16	22 17							
Cardiff Central 7	a	21 02					21 27							22 30	22 36							
Weston-super-Mare	a																					
Taunton	a					21 07			21 44				22 14									
Tiverton Parkway	a					21 19			21 56				22 26									
Exeter St Davids 6	a					21 34			22 11				22 41									
Dawlish	a																					
Teignmouth	a																					
Newton Abbot	a					21 54			22 31				23 01									
Torquay	a																					
Paignton	a																					
Totnes	a					22 06			22 43				23 13									
Plymouth	a					22 35			23 10				23 40									
Liskeard 6	a																					
Bodmin Parkway	a																					
Lostwithiel	a																					
Par	a																					
St Austell	a																					
Truro	a																					
Redruth	a																					
Camborne	a																					
Hayle	a																					
St Erth	a																					
Penzance	a																					
Birmingham International	d		19 14		19 20						20 14	20 20							21 14	21 20		
Coventry	d		19 25		19a30						20 25	20a30							21 25	21a30		
Leamington Spa 8	d		19 37					20 02			20 37					21 00			21 37			
Banbury	a		19 53					20 18			20 53					21 16			21 53			
Oxford	a		20 13					20 40			21 12					21 39			22 13			
Reading 7	a		20 43					21 06			21 40					22 07			22 40			
Guildford	a																					
Basingstoke	a		21 09								22 09					22 41			23 07			
Winchester	a		21 25								22 24					22 58			23 25			
Southampton Airport Pkway	a		21 34								22 33					23 11			23 36			
Southampton Central	a		21 41								22 41					23 20			23 43			
Brockenhurst 3	a		21 57								22 58											
Bournemouth	a		22 15								23 17											

A to Bristol Temple Meads
B to Reading
C to Birmingham New Street

Table T051-F

Scotland, The North East, North West England - The South West and South Coast

Mondays to Fridays
16 December to 15 May

		XC	XC	VT	XC	XC	XC	XC	XC	VT	XC	XC	XC	XC
										FX				
		1	◇1	◇1	1	◇1	◇1	◇1	◇1	◇1	◇1	1	◇1	◇1
								A					A	
Aberdeen	d													
Stonehaven	d													
Montrose	d													
Arbroath	d													
Dundee	d													
Leuchars 3	d													
Cupar	d													
Ladybank	d													
Markinch	d													
Kirkcaldy	d													
Inverkeithing	d													
Glasgow Central 15	d			17 40									17 00	
Motherwell	d												17 16	
Haymarket	d												17 58	
Edinburgh 10	d							17 07		18 52			18 08	
Haymarket	d									18 56				
Lockerbie	d			18 35										
Carlisle 8	d			18 57						20 07				
Penrith North Lakes	d													
Oxenholme Lake District	d			19 33						20 42				
Lancaster 6	d			19 47						20 56				
Preston 8	d			20 08						21 17				
Wigan North Western	d			20 20						21 29				
Warrington Bank Quay	d			20 32						21 40				
M'chester Piccadilly 10	d		20 05			20 27					21 27			22 07
Stockport	d		20 13			20 36					21 36			22 17
Wilmslow	d													
Crewe 10	d			20 54						22 01				
Macclesfield	d		20 26			20 49					21 49			22 29
Congleton	d													
Stoke-on-Trent	d		20 44			21 07					22 07			22 47
Stafford	d		21 03	21 15		21 29					22 28			23 06
Wolverhampton 7	d		21 17	21 33		21 43				22 33	22 42			23 20
Dunbar	d							17 29					18 30	
Berwick-upon-Tweed	d							17 52					18 54	
Alnmouth for Alnwick	d												19 14	
Morpeth	d							18 24						
Newcastle 8	d							18 40	19 35				19 42	
Chester-le-Street	d													
Durham	d							18 54	19 49				19 55	
Darlington 7	d							19 12	20 07				20 13	
York 8	d							19 44	20 36				20 44	
Leeds 10	d							20 10					21 11	
Wakefield Westgate 7	d							20 23					21 23	
Doncaster 7	d								21 01					
Sheffield 7	d							20 58	21 29				22 01	
Chesterfield	d							21 10	21 41				22 25	
Nottingham 8	d				20 40							21 38		
Derby 6	d				21 10			21 31	22 02			22 12	22 46	
Burton-on-Trent	d				21 24			21 41				22 23	22 56	
Tamworth	d				21 35			21 51				22 34	23 07	
Birmingham New Street 12	a		21 33	21 54	21 58	22 00		22 09	22 51	22 52	22 59	23 02	23 26	23 37
Birmingham New Street 12	d	21 30					22 04	22 12						
Cheltenham Spa 5	a	22 21						22 50						
Gloucester 7	a	22 32												
Bristol Parkway 7	a							23 20						
Bristol Temple Meads 10	a							23 30						
Newport (South Wales)	a													
Cardiff Central 7	a													
Weston-super-Mare	a													
Taunton	a													
Tiverton Parkway	a													
Exeter St Davids 6	a													
Dawlish	a													
Teignmouth	a													
Newton Abbot	a													
Torquay	a													
Paignton	a													
Totnes	a													
Plymouth	a													
Liskeard 6	a													
Bodmin Parkway	a													
Lostwithiel	a													
Par	a													
St Austell	a													
Truro	a													
Redruth	a													
Camborne	a													
Hayle	a													
St Erth	a													
Penzance	a													
Birmingham International	d						22 14							
Coventry	d						22 25							
Leamington Spa 8	d						22 37							
Banbury	a						22 53							
Oxford	a						23 12							
Reading 7	a						23 50							
Guildford	a													
Basingstoke	a													
Winchester	a													
Southampton Airport Pkway	a													
Southampton Central	a													
Brockenhurst 3	a													
Bournemouth	a													

A to Leeds

Table T051-F

Saturdays

21 December to 16 May

Scotland, The North East, North West England - The South West and South Coast

	XC ◇1	XC ◇1	XC ◇1 ✠	XC ◇1 A ✠	XC ◇1 ✠	XC ◇1	XC ◇1 B ✠	XC ◇1 ✠	XC ◇1 B ✠	XC ◇1 B ✠	XC ◇1 ✠	XC ◇1 B ✠	VT ◇1 ⊡	XC ◇1 ✠	XC ◇1	XC ◇1 ✠	XC ◇1 ✠	XC 1	XC ◇1 ✠	VT ◇1 ⊡	XC ◇1 C ✠	XC ◇1 B ✠
Aberdeen d																						
Stonehaven d																						
Montrose d																						
Arbroath d																						
Dundee d																						
Leuchars d																						
Cupar d																						
Ladybank d																						
Markinch d																						
Kirkcaldy d																						
Inverkeithing d																						
Glasgow Central d																						
Motherwell d																						
Haymarket d																						
Edinburgh d																						
Haymarket d																						
Lockerbie d																						
Carlisle d																						
Penrith North Lakes d																						
Oxenholme Lake District d																						
Lancaster d																				06 58		
Preston d													06 17							07 17		
Wigan North Western d													06 29							07 29		
Warrington Bank Quay d													06 40							07 41		
M'chester Piccadilly d							05 11				06 00						07 05		07 27			
Stockport d											06 08						07 13		07 36			
Wilmslow d																						
Crewe d							05 46						07 01							08 03		
Macclesfield d											06 21						07 26		07 49			
Congleton d																						
Stoke-on-Trent d							06 06				06 39						07 44		08 07			
Stafford d							06 28				07 03						08 03		08 28			
Wolverhampton d							06 42				07 17		07 45				08 17		08 42	08 45		
Dunbar d																						
Berwick-upon-Tweed d																						
Alnmouth for Alnwick d																						
Morpeth d																						
Newcastle d																						
Chester-le-Street d																						
Durham d																						
Darlington d																						
York d																06 24					06 12	
Leeds d														06 11							07 11	
Wakefield Westgate d														06 23							07 23	
Doncaster d																06 47						
Sheffield d														06 53		07 18					07 56	
Chesterfield d														07 06		07 30					08 08	
Nottingham d									06 00			06 44			07 00			07 37				08 06
Derby d						06 10			06 36	06 49		07 12		07 27	07 36	07 49		08 06			08 28	08 38
Burton-on-Trent d						06 20			06 48	06 59		07 22		07 38	07 50	07 59		08 18			08 38	08 49
Tamworth d						06 31		←	07 01	07 09		07 33		07 49	08 02	08 10		08 30			08 49	09 03
Birmingham New Street a						06 50	06 58	06 50	07 25	07 28	07 34	07 52	08 05	08 08	08 25	08 28	08 33	08 55	08 58	09 06	09 08	09 25
Birmingham New Street d	05 00	05 42	06 04	06 33	06 42	07 12	07 04	07 12	07 30	07 33	07 42	08 04	08 10	08 12	08 30	08 33	08 42		09 04		09 12	09 30
Cheltenham Spa a	06 00	06 41			07 24	→		07 50	08 14		08 24			08 50	09 14		09 28				09 50	10 14
Gloucester a	06 11	06 52							08 23						09 23							10 23
Bristol Parkway a					07 54			08 20			08 54			09 21			09 57				10 20	
Bristol Temple Meads a					08 04			08 36			09 05			09 34			10 08				10 36	
Newport (South Wales) a	07 06	07 49							09 09						10 14							11 10
Cardiff Central a	07 20	08 06							09 23						10 29							11 25
Weston-super-Mare a																						
Taunton a					08 41			09 18						10 17							11 17	
Tiverton Parkway a					08 53			09 30						10 30							11 29	
Exeter St Davids a					09 08			09 47						10 45							11 45	
Dawlish a																						
Teignmouth a																						
Newton Abbot a					09 31			10 08						11 08							12 06	
Torquay a					09 45																	
Paignton a					09 54																	
Totnes a								10 20						11 20							12 18	
Plymouth a								10 48						11 48							12 45	
Liskeard a																						
Bodmin Parkway a																						
Lostwithiel a																						
Par a																						
St Austell a																						
Truro a																						
Redruth a																						
Camborne a																						
Hayle a																						
St Erth a																						
Penzance a																						
Birmingham International d			06 14				07 14					08 14	08 20						09 14			
Coventry d			06 25				07 25					08 25	08a30						09 25			
Leamington Spa d			06 37	07 00			07 37			08 01		08 37				09 00			09 37			
Banbury a			06 55	07 16			07 53			08 19		08 53				09 16			09 54			
Oxford a			07 14	07 40			08 12			08 42		09 12				09 40			10 13			
Reading a			07 41	08 06			08 37			09 09		09 40				10 06			10 39			
Guildford a																						
Basingstoke a			08 08	08 40			09 11					10 09				10 40			11 10			
Winchester a			08 26	08 58			09 26					10 25				10 56			11 28			
Southampton Airport Pkway a			08 35	09 08			09 35					10 35				11 09			11 37			
Southampton Central a			08 43	09 17			09 42					10 43				11 17			11 44			
Brockenhurst a			08 58				09 58					10 58							11 59			
Bournemouth a			09 13				10 13					11 13							12 14			

A ✠ from Reading B ✠ from Birmingham New Street C ✠ from Leeds

Table T051-F

Saturdays

21 December to 16 May

Scotland, The North East, North West England - The South West and South Coast

	XC ◇1 A ✠	XC ◇1 ✠	XC 1	XC ◇1 ✠	VT ◇1 ⊡	XC ◇1 B ✠	XC ◇1 ✠	XC ◇1 ✠	XC ◇1 ✠	XC 1	XC ◇1 ✠	VT ◇1 ⊡	XC ◇1 ✠	XC ◇1 ✠	XC ◇1 ✠	XC ◇1 ✠	XC 1	XC ◇1 ✠	VT ◇1 ⊡	XC ◇1 C ✠	XC ◇1 ✠	XC ◇1 ✠
Aberdeen d																						
Stonehaven d																						
Montrose d																						
Arbroath d																						
Dundee d																						
Leuchars d																						
Cupar d																						
Ladybank d																						
Markinch d																						
Kirkcaldy d																						
Inverkeithing d																						
Glasgow Central d					05 50														08 00	06 01		
Motherwell d					06 05															06 16		
Haymarket d																				06 57		
Edinburgh d												06 52	06 06		07 00					07 07		
Haymarket d												06 56										
Lockerbie d																						
Carlisle d					07 02							08 07							09 12			
Penrith North Lakes d					07 17							08 22										
Oxenholme Lake District d					07 41																	
Lancaster d					07 56							08 57							09 58			
Preston d					08 17							09 17							10 17			
Wigan North Western d					08 29							09 29							10 29			
Warrington Bank Quay d					08 40							09 40							10 40			
M'chester Piccadilly d		08 05		08 27					09 05		09 27					10 05		10 27				
Stockport d		08 13		08 36					09 13		09 36					10 13		10 36				
Wilmslow d																						
Crewe d					09 01							10 01							11 01			
Macclesfield d		08 26		08 49					09 26		09 49					10 26		10 49				
Congleton d																						
Stoke-on-Trent d		08 44		09 07					09 44		10 07					10 44		11 07				
Stafford d		09 03		09 28					10 03		10 28					11 03		11 28				
Wolverhampton d		09 17		09 42	09 45				10 17		10 42	10 45				11 17		11 42	11 45			
Dunbar d																				07 29		
Berwick-upon-Tweed d													06 49		07 43							
Alnmouth for Alnwick d													07 10		08 03							
Morpeth d															08 18							
Newcastle d	06 23					06 40		07 35					07 39		08 35					08 40		09 35
Chester-le-Street d																						
Durham d	06 36					06 52		07 47					07 53		08 48					08 54		09 49
Darlington d	06 54					07 10		08 06					08 11		09 06					09 12		10 07
York d	07 28					07 44		08 35					08 44		09 37					09 44		10 35
Leeds d						08 11							09 11							10 11		
Wakefield Westgate d						08 23							09 23							10 23		
Doncaster d	07 52							08 58							10 00							10 59
Sheffield d	08 18					08 54		09 24					09 56		10 24					10 56		11 24
Chesterfield d	08 31					09 07							10 09							11 09		
Nottingham d			08 41				09 06			09 41				10 06			10 41				11 06	
Derby d	08 53		09 10			09 31	09 38	09 53		10 10			10 30	10 38	10 52		11 10			11 31	11 38	11 53
Burton-on-Trent d			09 22			09 42	09 51			10 21				10 49			11 21			11 42	11 49	
Tamworth d			09 34				10 03			10 33			10 50	11 02			11 33				12 02	
Birmingham New Street a	09 28	09 33	09 55	09 58	10 05	10 05	10 24	10 27	10 33	10 55	10 58	11 05	11 08	11 25	11 28	11 33	11 55	11 58	12 05	12 08	12 24	12 27
Birmingham New Street d	09 33	09 42		10 04	10 10	10 12	10 30	10 33	10 42		11 04	11 10	11 12	11 30	11 33	11 42		12 04	12 10	12 12	12 30	12 33
Cheltenham Spa a		10 24				10 50	11 14		11 24				11 50	12 14		12 24				12 50	13 14	
Gloucester a							11 23							12 23							13 23	
Bristol Parkway a		10 54				11 21			11 54				12 25			12 54				13 21		
Bristol Temple Meads a		11 09				11 36			12 05				12 38			13 05				13 34		
Newport (South Wales) a							12 12							13 14							14 12	
Cardiff Central a							12 26							13 27							14 25	
Weston-super-Mare a		11 30																				
Taunton a		12 00				12 17							13 17							14 17		
Tiverton Parkway a		12 12				12 29							13 30							14 30		
Exeter St Davids a		12 31				12 45							13 45							14 45		
Dawlish a		12 44																				
Teignmouth a		12 49																				
Newton Abbot a		12 56				13 07							14 08							15 08		
Torquay a		13 06																				
Paignton a		13 14																				
Totnes a						13 20							14 20							15 21		
Plymouth a						13 47							14 48							15 48		
Liskeard a																						
Bodmin Parkway a																						
Lostwithiel a																						
Par a																						
St Austell a																						
Truro a																						
Redruth a																						
Camborne a																						
Hayle a																						
St Erth a																						
Penzance a																						
Birmingham International d				10 14	10 20						11 14	11 20						12 14	12 20			
Coventry d				10 25	10a30						11 25	11a30						12 25	12a30			
Leamington Spa d	10 03			10 37				11 00			11 37				12 03			12 37				13 00
Banbury a	10 19			10 53				11 16			11 53				12 19			12 53				13 16
Oxford a	10 42			11 12				11 40			12 13				12 41			13 12				13 40
Reading a	11 07			11 39				12 07			12 39				13 07			13 39				14 06
Guildford a																						
Basingstoke a				12 09				12 40			13 09							14 09				14 40
Winchester a				12 25				12 56			13 25							14 25				14 58
Southampton Airport Pkway a				12 33				13 08			13 33							14 33				15 08
Southampton Central a				12 41				13 16			13 41							14 43				15 17
Brockenhurst a				12 58							13 57							14 58				
Bournemouth a				13 13							14 12							15 13				

A 1 ✠ from Birmingham New Street B ✠ from Leeds C ✠ from Edinburgh

Table T051-F

Saturdays

21 December to 16 May

Scotland, The North East, North West England - The South West and South Coast

		XC	XC	XC	VT	XC	XC	XC	XC	XC	XC	XC	VT	XC	XC	XC	XC	XC	XC	VT	XC	XC
		◇1	1	◇1	◇1	◇1	◇1	◇1	◇1	1	◇1	◇1	◇1	◇1	◇1	◇1	◇1	1	◇1	◇1	◇1	◇1
						A						A									B	
		🛒		🛒	☕	🛒	🛒	🛒	🛒		🛒	🛒	☕	🛒	🛒	🛒	🛒	🛒	🛒	☕	🛒	🛒
Aberdeen	d																					
Stonehaven	d																					
Montrose	d																					
Arbroath	d																					
Dundee	d					06 33																
Leuchars	d					06 46																
Cupar	d					06 55																
Ladybank	d					07 03																
Markinch	d					07 11																
Kirkcaldy	d					07 22																
Inverkeithing	d					07 39																
Glasgow Central	d											07 48	10 00								09 00	
Motherwell	d											08 08									09 15	
Haymarket	d					07 59						08 52									09 58	
Edinburgh	d				08 53	08 08						09 08								10 52	10 06	
Haymarket	d				08 59															10 57		
Lockerbie	d																					
Carlisle	d				10 08								11 11							12 07		
Penrith North Lakes	d												11 25									
Oxenholme Lake District	d				10 42															12 43		
Lancaster	d				10 57															12 57		
Preston	d				11 17								12 17							13 17		
Wigan North Western	d				11 29								12 29							13 29		
Warrington Bank Quay	d				11 40								12 40							13 40		
M'chester Piccadilly	d	11 05		11 27					12 05		12 27						13 05		13 27			
Stockport	d	11 13		11 36					12 13		12 36						13 13		13 36			
Wilmslow	d																					
Crewe	d				12 01								13 03							14 01		
Macclesfield	d	11 26		11 49					12 26		12 49						13 26		13 49			
Congleton	d																					
Stoke-on-Trent	d	11 44		12 07					12 44		13 07						13 44		14 07			
Stafford	d	12 03		12 28					13 03		13 28						14 03		14 28			
Wolverhampton	d	12 17		12 42	12 45				13 17		13 42		13 45				14 17		14 42	14 45		
Dunbar	d											09 29										
Berwick-upon-Tweed	d					08 51						09 53									10 48	
Alnmouth for Alnwick	d					09 12																
Morpeth	d																				11 22	
Newcastle	d					09 41		10 35				10 41				11 35					11 39	
Chester-le-Street	d																					
Durham	d					09 54		10 47				10 54				11 49					11 54	
Darlington	d					10 12		11 06				11 11				12 07					12 12	
York	d					10 43		11 36				11 44				12 35					12 44	
Leeds	d					11 11						12 11									13 11	
Wakefield Westgate	d					11 23						12 23									13 23	
Doncaster	d							11 59								12 59						
Sheffield	d					11 56		12 24				12 56				13 24					13 56	
Chesterfield	d					12 09						13 08									14 09	
Nottingham	d		11 41				12 06			12 41					13 06			13 41				14 06
Derby	d		12 10			12 30	12 38	12 57		13 10		13 28			13 38	13 52		14 10			14 30	14 38
Burton-on-Trent	d		12 21				12 49			13 24		13 38			13 49			14 21				14 49
Tamworth	d		12 33			12 49	13 02			13 35				←	14 02			14 33			14 50	15 02
Birmingham New Street	a	12 33	12 55	12 58	13 05	13 08	13 24	13 28	13 33	13 55	13 58	14 03	14 05	14 03	14 24	14 27	14 34	14 55	14 58	15 05	15 08	15 24
Birmingham New Street	d	12 42		13 04	13 10	13 12	13 30	13 33	13 42		14 04	14 12	14 10	14 12	14 30	14 33	14 42		15 04	15 10	15 12	15 30
Cheltenham Spa	a	13 29				13 50	14 14		14 24			→		14 50	15 14		15 29				15 50	16 14
Gloucester	a						14 23								15 23							16 23
Bristol Parkway	a	13 59				14 21			14 57					15 21			15 59				16 21	
Bristol Temple Meads	a	14 09				14 36			15 07					15 36			16 09				16 34	
Newport (South Wales)	a						15 10								16 11							17 12
Cardiff Central	a						15 27								16 25							17 26
Weston-super-Mare	a																					
Taunton	a					15 17			15 41					16 15							17 17	
Tiverton Parkway	a					15 30			15 53					16 27							17 30	
Exeter St Davids	a					15 45			16 08					16 43							17 45	
Dawlish	a																					
Teignmouth	a																					
Newton Abbot	a					16 14								17 04							18 06	
Torquay	a																					
Paignton	a																					
Totnes	a					16 27								17 17							18 19	
Plymouth	a					16 54								17 44							18 46	
Liskeard	a																				19 24	
Bodmin Parkway	a																				19 37	
Lostwithiel	a																					
Par	a																				19 47	
St Austell	a																				19 55	
Truro	a																				20 12	
Redruth	a																				20 26	
Camborne	a																				20 32	
Hayle	a																					
St Erth	a																				20 42	
Penzance	a																				20 53	
Birmingham International	d			13 14	13 20						14 14		14 20						15 14	15 20		
Coventry	d			13 25	13a30						14 25		14a30						15 25	15a30		
Leamington Spa	d			13 37				14 03			14 37					15 00			15 37			
Banbury	a			13 53				14 19			14 55					15 20			15 53			
Oxford	a			14 12				14 40			15 14					15 40			16 12			
Reading	a			14 40				15 06			15 39					16 06			16 39			
Guildford	a																					
Basingstoke	a			15 09							16 09					16 40			17 09			
Winchester	a			15 26							16 26					16 58			17 26			
Southampton Airport Pkway	a			15 35							16 35					17 08			17 35			
Southampton Central	a			15 42							16 42					17 17			17 42			
Brockenhurst	a			15 58							16 58								17 58			
Bournemouth	a			16 13							17 13								18 13			

A 🛒 from Edinburgh
B 🛒 to Plymouth

Table T051-F

Saturdays

21 December to 16 May

Scotland, The North East, North West England - The South West and South Coast

		XC	XC	XC	XC	XC	VT	XC	XC	XC	XC	XC	XC	VT	XC	XC	XC	XC	XC	XC	VT	XC	XC
		◇1	◇1	1	◇1	◇1	◇1	◇1	◇1	◇1	◇1	1	◇1	◇1	◇1	◇1	◇1	◇1	1	◇1	◇1	◇1	◇1
								A		B					A								
		🛒	🛒		🛒	🛒	☕	🛒		🛒	🛒	🛒	🛒	☕	🛒		🛒	🛒	🛒	🛒	☕	🛒	
Aberdeen	d					08 20																	
Stonehaven	d					08 37																	
Montrose	d					08 59																	
Arbroath	d					09 14																	
Dundee	d					09 33																	
Leuchars	d					09 46																	
Cupar	d					09 53																	
Ladybank	d					10 01																	
Markinch	d					10 08																	
Kirkcaldy	d					10 18																	
Inverkeithing	d					10 34																	
Glasgow Central	d						12 00								11 00						14 00		
Motherwell	d														11 15								
Haymarket	d					10 50									11 54								
Edinburgh	d					11 08								12 52	12 06							13 09	
Haymarket	d													12 57									
Lockerbie	d																						
Carlisle	d						13 13							14 08							15 11		
Penrith North Lakes	d													14 22									
Oxenholme Lake District	d																				15 45		
Lancaster	d						14 00							14 57									
Preston	d						14 20							15 17							16 17		
Wigan North Western	d						14 32							15 29							16 29		
Warrington Bank Quay	d						14 43							15 40							16 40		
M'chester Piccadilly	d		14 05		14 27						15 05		15 27					16 05		16 27			
Stockport	d		14 13		14 36						15 13		15 36					16 13		16 36			
Wilmslow	d																						
Crewe	d						15 02							16 01							17 01		
Macclesfield	d		14 26		14 49						15 26		15 49					16 26		16 49			
Congleton	d																						
Stoke-on-Trent	d		14 44		15 07						15 44		16 07					16 44		17 07			
Stafford	d		15 03		15 28						16 03		16 28					17 03		17 25			
Wolverhampton	d		15 17		15 42		15 45				16 17		16 42	16 45				17 17		17 42	17 45		
Dunbar	d					11 29																13 30	
Berwick-upon-Tweed	d					11 53									12 47								
Alnmouth for Alnwick	d					12 13																14 12	
Morpeth	d														13 20								
Newcastle	d	12 35				12 42				13 35					13 39		14 36					14 42	
Chester-le-Street	d																						
Durham	d	12 48				12 54				13 48					13 54		14 48					14 54	
Darlington	d	13 06				13 12				14 06					14 11		15 06					15 12	
York	d	13 35				13 44				14 35					14 44		15 36					15 44	
Leeds	d					14 11									15 11							16 11	
Wakefield Westgate	d					14 23									15 23							16 23	
Doncaster	d	14 00								14 59							16 00						
Sheffield	d	14 24				14 56				15 24					15 56		16 24					16 56	
Chesterfield	d					15 08									16 08							17 08	
Nottingham	d			14 41					15 06			15 41				16 06			16 41				17 06
Derby	d	14 53		15 10		15 28			15 38	15 52		16 10			16 31	16 38	16 52		17 10			17 28	17 38
Burton-on-Trent	d			15 24		15 38			15 49			16 21				16 49			17 24			17 41	17 49
Tamworth	d			15 35				←	16 02			16 33			16 50	17 02			17 35				18 01
Birmingham New Street	a	15 27	15 33	15 55	15 58	16 03	16 05	16 03	16 24	16 27	16 33	16 55	16 58	17 05	17 06	17 25	17 28	17 33	17 55	17 58	18 05	18 05	18 24
Birmingham New Street	d	15 33	15 42		16 04	16 12	16 10	16 12	16 30	16 33	16 42		17 04	17 10	17 12	17 30	17 33	17 42		18 04	18 10	18 12	18 30
Cheltenham Spa	a		16 24			→		16 50	17 14		17 24				17 50	18 18		18 24				18 50	19 14
Gloucester	a								17 23							18 27							19 23
Bristol Parkway	a		16 54					17 21			17 54				18 29			18 54				19 21	
Bristol Temple Meads	a		17 04					17 35			18 04				18 42			19 05				19 36	
Newport (South Wales)	a								18 11							19 11							20 07
Cardiff Central	a								18 26							19 24							20 20
Weston-super-Mare	a																						
Taunton	a		17 39					18 17							19 17							20 16	
Tiverton Parkway	a		17 51					18 29							19 29							20 28	
Exeter St Davids	a		18 07					18 45							19 45							20 44	
Dawlish	a		18 27																				
Teignmouth	a		18 32																				
Newton Abbot	a		18 39					19 05							20 04							21 04	
Torquay	a		18 49																				
Paignton	a		18 56																				
Totnes	a							19 18							20 17							21 17	
Plymouth	a							19 45							20 44							21 44	
Liskeard	a							20 13							21 13								
Bodmin Parkway	a							20 25							21 25								
Lostwithiel	a							20 30															
Par	a							20 36							21 35								
St Austell	a							20 43							21 41								
Truro	a							20 59							21 57								
Redruth	a							21 10							22 09								
Camborne	a							21 17							22 15								
Hayle	a							21 25															
St Erth	a							21 29							22 26								
Penzance	a							21 39							22 39								
Birmingham International	d				16 14		16 20						17 14	17 20						18 14	18 20		
Coventry	d				16 25		16a30						17 25	17a30						18 25	18a30		
Leamington Spa	d	16 03			16 37					17 00			17 37				18 02			18 37			
Banbury	a	16 19			16 53					17 16			17 53				18 18			18 53			
Oxford	a	16 40			17 12					17 41			18 12				18 40			19 12			
Reading	a	17 06			17 39					18 06			18 39				19 06			19 39			
Guildford	a									19 01													
Basingstoke	a				18 09								19 09							20 09			
Winchester	a				18 25								19 26							20 26			
Southampton Airport Pkway	a				18 33								19 35							20 35			
Southampton Central	a				18 41								19 42							20 42			
Brockenhurst	a				18 57								19 57							20 58			
Bournemouth	a				19 13								20 12							21 13			

A 🛒 to Plymouth
B 🛒 to Reading

Scotland, The North East, North West England - The South West and South Coast

		XC	XC	XC	XC	XC	XC	XC	XC	XC	XC	XC	XC	XC	XC	XC	XC	XC	XC	XC	VT	XC
		◇1	◇1	1	◇1	◇1	◇1	◇1	◇1	1	◇1	◇1	◇1	◇1	◇1	1	◇1	◇1	◇1	◇1	◇1	1
			A		B				A		B	A		C	C		C					
		🍴	🍴	🍴	🍴	🍴		🍴	🍴		🍴	🍴		🍴	🍴		🍴	🍴	🍴		☕	
Aberdeen	d																					
Stonehaven	d																					
Montrose	d																					
Arbroath	d																					
Dundee	d																					
Leuchars 3	d																					
Cupar	d																					
Ladybank	d																					
Markinch	d																					
Kirkcaldy	d																					
Inverkeithing	d																					
Glasgow Central 15	d					13 00												15 00			18 00	
Motherwell	d					13 16												15 16				
Haymarket	d					13 58												15 57				
Edinburgh 10	d					14 07						15 08						16 06				
Haymarket	d																					
Lockerbie	d																					
Carlisle 8	d																				19 11	
Penrith North Lakes	d																					
Oxenholme Lake District	d																					
Lancaster 6	d																				19 58	
Preston 8	d																				20 18	
Wigan North Western	d																				20 30	
Warrington Bank Quay	d																				20 41	
M'chester Piccadilly 10	d		17 05		17 27				18 05		18 27				19 05		19 27			20 05		
Stockport	d		17 13		17 36				18 13		18 36				19 13		19 36			20 13		
Wilmslow	d																					
Crewe 10	d																				21 02	
Macclesfield	d		17 26						18 26						19 26		19 49			20 26		
Congleton	d				17 54						18 54											
Stoke-on-Trent	d		17 44		18 07				18 44		19 07				19 44		20 07			20 44		
Stafford	d		18 03		18 28				19 03		19 28				20 03		20 28			21 03		
Wolverhampton 7	d		18 17		18 42				19 17		19 42				20 17		20 42			21 17	21 35	
Dunbar	d											15 29										
Berwick-upon-Tweed	d					14 48																
Alnmouth for Alnwick	d																	17 06				
Morpeth	d					15 22												17 20				
Newcastle 8	d	15 11				15 39		16 35				16 39		17 32				17 39	18 36			
Chester-le-Street	d													17 41								
Durham	d	15 24				15 51		16 48				16 53		17 48				17 54	18 49			
Darlington 7	d	15 41				16 09		17 06				17 12		18 06				18 12	19 07			
York 8	d	16 13				16 44		17 36				17 44		18 36				18 44	19 36			
Leeds 10	d	16 41				17 11						18 11						19 11				
Wakefield Westgate 7	d	16 53				17 23						18 23						19 23				
Doncaster 7	d							18 00						19 00					19 59			
Sheffield 7	d	17 24				17 56		18 24				18 56		19 24				19 56	20 24			
Chesterfield	d					18 08						19 08						20 08				
Nottingham 8	d			17 41			18 06			18 41			19 06			19 29						20 37
Derby 6	d	17 52		18 10		18 28	18 38	18 52		19 10		19 31	19 38	19 53		20 11		20 28	20 53			21 10
Burton-on-Trent	d			18 24			18 49			19 21		19 41	19 50			20 22						21 23
Tamworth	d			18 35		18 47	19 02			19 33			20 02			20 34		20 46				21 35
Birmingham New Street 12	a	18 27	18 33	18 55	18 58	19 06	19 24	19 27	19 33	19 55	19 58	20 05	20 24	20 27	20 33	20 55	20 58	21 03	21 23	21 33	21 53	21 56
Birmingham New Street 12	d	18 33	18 42		19 04	19 12	19 30	19 33	19 42		20 04	20 12	20 30	20 33	20 42		21 04	21 12				
Cheltenham Spa 5	a		19 29			19 50	20 14		20 24			20 50	21 14		21 24			21 50				
Gloucester 7	a						20 23						21 24					22 01				
Bristol Parkway 7	a		19 59			20 22			20 54			21 20			21 57			22 31				
Bristol Temple Meads 10	a		20 09			20 34			21 04			21 34			22 12			22 41				
Newport (South Wales)	a		20 46				21 09						22 23									
Cardiff Central 7	a		21 00				21 22						22 43									
Weston-super-Mare	a																					
Taunton	a					21 16			21 37			22 16										
Tiverton Parkway	a					21 28			21 49			22 28										
Exeter St Davids 6	a					21 44			22 04			22 44										
Dawlish	a																					
Teignmouth	a																					
Newton Abbot	a					22 04			22 24			23 07										
Torquay	a																					
Paignton	a																					
Totnes	a					22 17			22 36			23 20										
Plymouth	a					22 44			23 03			23 47										
Liskeard 6	a																					
Bodmin Parkway	a																					
Lostwithiel	a																					
Par	a																					
St Austell	a																					
Truro	a																					
Redruth	a																					
Camborne	a																					
Hayle	a																					
St Erth	a																					
Penzance	a																					
Birmingham International ✈	d				19 14						20 14						21 14					
Coventry	d				19 25						20 25						21 25					
Leamington Spa 8	d	19 00			19 37			20 02			20 37			21 00			21 37					
Banbury	a	19 16			19 53			20 18			20 54			21 16			21 53					
Oxford	a	19 40			20 12			20 40			21 13			21 40			22 13					
Reading 7	a	20 06			20 39			21 06			21 39			22 07			22 41					
Guildford	a																					
Basingstoke	a				21 09						22 10			22 41			23 09					
Winchester	a				21 26						22 26			22 58			23 26					
Southampton Airport Pkway ✈	a				21 35						22 35			23 11			23 35					
Southampton Central ⛴	a				21 43						22 42			23 20			23 43					
Brockenhurst 3	a				21 58						22 58											
Bournemouth	a				22 15						23 19											

A 🍴 to Bristol Temple Meads B 🍴 to Reading C 🍴 to Birmingham New Street

Table T051-F

Saturdays
21 December to 16 May

Scotland, The North East, North West England - The South West and South Coast

		XC	XC	XC	XC	VT	VT	XC	XC	XC
		◇1	◇1	◇1	◇1	◇1	◇1	◇1	1	◇1
			A							A
			🍴			☕	☕			🍴
Aberdeen	d									
Stonehaven	d									
Montrose	d									
Arbroath	d									
Dundee	d									
Leuchars 3	d									
Cupar	d									
Ladybank	d									
Markinch	d									
Kirkcaldy	d									
Inverkeithing	d									
Glasgow Central 15	d					18 40				17 00
Motherwell	d									17 15
Haymarket	d									17 58
Edinburgh 10	d		17 08				18 52			18 07
Haymarket	d						18 56			
Lockerbie	d									
Carlisle 8	d					19 49	20 09			
Penrith North Lakes	d					20 03	20 23			
Oxenholme Lake District	d					20 26	20 47			
Lancaster 6	d					20 41	21 02			
Preston 8	d					21 02	21 22			
Wigan North Western	d					21 14	21 33			
Warrington Bank Quay	d					21 25	21 44			
M'chester Piccadilly 10	d	20 27		21 05				21 27		
Stockport	d	20 36		21 13				21 36		
Wilmslow	d									
Crewe 10	d					21 45	22 06			
Macclesfield	d	20 49		21 26				21 49		
Congleton	d									
Stoke-on-Trent	d	21 07		21 44				22 07		
Stafford	d	21 28		22 03		22 08	22 25	22 30		
Wolverhampton 7	d	21 42		22 17		22 26	22 39	22 44		
Dunbar	d		17 31							18 30
Berwick-upon-Tweed	d		17 54							18 53
Alnmouth for Alnwick	d									19 14
Morpeth	d									
Newcastle 8	d		18 40		19 35					19 45
Chester-le-Street	d									
Durham	d		18 54		19 49					19 57
Darlington 7	d		19 12		20 07					20 15
York 8	d		19 44		20 35					20 45
Leeds 10	d		20 10							21 11
Wakefield Westgate 7	d		20 23							21 23
Doncaster 7	d				20 59					
Sheffield 7	d		20 56		21 25					21 55
Chesterfield	d		21 08		21 37					22 07
Nottingham 8	d								21 39	
Derby 6	d		21 28		21 56				22 12	22 26
Burton-on-Trent	d		21 38						22 23	22 37
Tamworth	d		21 49						22 35	22 47
Birmingham New Street 12	a	22 00	22 05	22 33	22 44	22 49	22 57	23 00	23 02	23 05
Birmingham New Street 12	d									
Cheltenham Spa 5	a									
Gloucester 7	a									
Bristol Parkway 7	a									
Bristol Temple Meads 10	a									
Newport (South Wales)	a									
Cardiff Central 7	a									
Weston-super-Mare	a									
Taunton	a									
Tiverton Parkway	a									
Exeter St Davids 6	a									
Dawlish	a									
Teignmouth	a									
Newton Abbot	a									
Torquay	a									
Paignton	a									
Totnes	a									
Plymouth	a									
Liskeard 6	a									
Bodmin Parkway	a									
Lostwithiel	a									
Par	a									
St Austell	a									
Truro	a									
Redruth	a									
Camborne	a									
Hayle	a									
St Erth	a									
Penzance	a									
Birmingham International ✈	d									
Coventry	d									
Leamington Spa 8	d									
Banbury	a									
Oxford	a									
Reading 7	a									
Guildford	a									
Basingstoke	a									
Winchester	a									
Southampton Airport Pkway ✈	a									
Southampton Central ⛴	a									
Brockenhurst 3	a									
Bournemouth	a									

A 🍴 to Leeds

Table T051-F

Sundays

15 December to 10 May

Scotland, The North East, North West England - The South West and South Coast

Station		XC	XC A	XC	XC	XC	XC	XC B	XC	VT	XC	XC	XC B	XC	VT	XC	XC	XC B	XC	XC	XC	VT	XC
Aberdeen	d																						
Stonehaven	d																						
Montrose	d																						
Arbroath	d																						
Dundee	d																						
Leuchars 3	d																						
Cupar	d																						
Ladybank	d																						
Markinch	d																						
Kirkcaldy	d																						
Inverkeithing	d																						
Glasgow Central 15	d																						
Motherwell	d																						
Haymarket	d																						
Edinburgh 10	d																						09 08
Haymarket	d																						
Lockerbie	d																						
Carlisle 8	d																						
Penrith North Lakes	d																						
Oxenholme Lake District	d																						
Lancaster 6	d																					11 58	
Preston 8	d									10 17					11 17							12 17	
Wigan North Western	d									10 28					11 28							12 29	
Warrington Bank Quay	d									10 39					11 40							12 40	
M'chester Piccadilly 10	d			08 27			09 27				10 27					11 27					12 27		
Stockport	d			08 35			09 35				10 35					11 35					12 35		
Wilmslow	d			08 43																			
Crewe 10	d			09 05						11 02					12 02							13 02	
Macclesfield	d						09 48				10 48					11 48					12 48		
Congleton	d																						
Stoke-on-Trent	d						10 06				11 06					12 06					13 06		
Stafford	d			09 28			10 28				11 28					12 28					13 28		
Wolverhampton 7	d			09 42			10 42			11 36	11 43				12 33	12 42					13 42	13 45	
Dunbar	d																						
Berwick-upon-Tweed	d																						09 51
Alnmouth for Alnwick	d																						
Morpeth	d																						
Newcastle 8	d																09 35						10 39
Chester-le-Street	d																						
Durham	d																09 47						10 53
Darlington 7	d																10 05						11 10
York 8	d											09 36					10 34						11 41
Leeds 10	d					08 10			09 00			10 01					11 00						12 11
Wakefield Westgate 7	d					08 23			09 12			10 14					11 12						12 24
Doncaster 7	d								09 31			10 32					11 30						
Sheffield 7	d					08 55			09 58			10 55					11 57						12 57
Chesterfield	d					09 08			10 11			11 09					12 09						13 10
Nottingham 8	d							09 55					11 10					12 10					
Derby 6	d					09 30		10 20	10 33			11 29	11 36				12 29	12 36					13 31
Burton-on-Trent	d							10 31				11 40	11 47					12 47					13 42
Tamworth	d							10 43	10 52				11 59				12 47	12 59					
Birmingham New Street 12	a			09 58		10 18	10 59	11 02	11 20	11 55	12 00	12 06	12 19		12 50	12 58	13 04	13 23			13 58	14 05	14 07
Birmingham New Street 12	d	09 04	09 30	10 04	10 12	10 30	11 04	11 12	11 30		12 04	12 12	12 30	12 33		13 04	13 12	13 30	13 33	13 43	14 04	14 10	14 12
Cheltenham Spa 5	a		10 08		10 58	11 08		11 59	12 08			12 50	13 14				13 50	14 14		14 26			14 50
Gloucester 7	a				11 10			12 09					13 27					14 23					
Bristol Parkway 7	a		10 38			11 40			12 42			13 20					14 20			14 55			15 22
Bristol Temple Meads 10	a		10 49			11 50			12 52			13 34					14 34			15 06			15 36
Newport (South Wales)	a				11 53			12 53					14 11					15 07					
Cardiff Central 7	a				12 06			13 06					14 24					15 21					
Weston-super-Mare	a																						
Taunton	a		11 29			12 26			13 26			14 17					15 15						16 16
Tiverton Parkway	a		11 43			12 38			13 38			14 30					15 27						16 28
Exeter St Davids 6	a		11 59			12 54			13 54			14 45					15 43						16 44
Dawlish	a																						
Teignmouth	a																						
Newton Abbot	a		12 19			13 15			14 14			15 06					16 03						17 04
Torquay	a																						
Paignton	a																						
Totnes	a		12 32			13 28			14 27			15 18					16 17						17 17
Plymouth	a		12 59			13 55			14 54			15 46					16 44						17 44
Liskeard 6	a		13 30																				
Bodmin Parkway	a		13 42																				
Lostwithiel	a																						
Par	a		13 52																				
St Austell	a		13 58																				
Truro	a		14 14																				
Redruth	a		14 26																				
Camborne	a		14 32																				
Hayle	a																						
St Erth	a		14 42																				
Penzance	a		14 52																				
Birmingham International ✈	d	09 14		10 14			11 14				12 14			12 43		13 14					14 14	14 20	
Coventry	d	09 25		10 25			11 25				12 25			12 55		13 25					14 25	14a30	
Leamington Spa 8	d	09 37		10 37			11 37				12 37			13 09		13 37			14 00		14 37		
Banbury	a	09 53		10 53			11 53				12 53			13 25		13 53			14 16		14 53		
Oxford	a	10 12		11 12			12 12				13 12			13 44		14 12			14 35		15 12		
Reading 7	a	10 39		11 39			12 39				13 39			14 09		14 39			15 00		15 39		
Guildford	a																						
Basingstoke	a	11 09		12 09			13 09				14 09					15 09					16 09		
Winchester	a	11 25		12 26			13 26				14 26					15 26					16 26		
Southampton Airport Pkway ✈	a	11 33		12 34			13 34				14 34					15 34					16 35		
Southampton Central ⛴	a	11 43		12 43			13 43				14 43					15 43					16 42		
Brockenhurst 3	a	12 07		13 07			14 07				15 07					16 07					17 06		
Bournemouth	a	12 26		13 26			14 26				15 26					16 26					17 26		

A ✠ to Plymouth   B ✠ from Birmingham New Street

Table T051-F

Sundays

15 December to 10 May

Scotland, The North East, North West England - The South West and South Coast

Station		XC	XC	XC	XC	XC	VT	XC A	XC	XC	XC	XC	XC	VT	XC	XC	XC	XC	XC	XC B	VT	XC A	XC C
Aberdeen	d																						
Stonehaven	d																						
Montrose	d																						
Arbroath	d																						
Dundee	d																						
Leuchars 3	d																						
Cupar	d																						
Ladybank	d																						
Markinch	d																						
Kirkcaldy	d																						
Inverkeithing	d																						
Glasgow Central 15	d													11 55						10 55			
Motherwell	d																			11 14			
Haymarket	d																			11 53			
Edinburgh 10	d					10 08	10 51						11 05							12 08	12 51		
Haymarket	d						10 55														12 55		
Lockerbie	d																						
Carlisle 8	d						12 07							13 07							14 07		
Penrith North Lakes	d																				14 22		
Oxenholme Lake District	d						12 43																
Lancaster 6	d						12 57							13 57							14 57		
Preston 8	d						13 17							14 17							15 17		
Wigan North Western	d						13 29							14 29							15 28		
Warrington Bank Quay	d						13 40							14 41							15 39		
M'chester Piccadilly 10	d			13 05	13 27						14 05	14 27						15 05	15 27				
Stockport	d			13 13	13 37						14 13	14 35						15 13	15 36				
Wilmslow	d																						
Crewe 10	d						14 02							15 02							16 01		
Macclesfield	d			13 26	13 50						14 26	14 48						15 26	15 49				
Congleton	d																						
Stoke-on-Trent	d			13 45	14 08						14 45	15 06						15 45	16 07				
Stafford	d			14 03	14 28						15 03	15 28						16 03	16 28				
Wolverhampton 7	d			14 17	14 42		14 45				15 17	15 42		15 45				16 17	16 42		16 45		
Dunbar	d												11 26										
Berwick-upon-Tweed	d												11 50							12 49			
Alnmouth for Alnwick	d					11 07							12 10										
Morpeth	d					11 22																	
Newcastle 8	d					11 40							12 40				13 36			13 40			
Chester-le-Street	d																						
Durham	d					11 52							12 53				13 48			13 53			
Darlington 7	d					12 10							13 10				14 06			14 10			
York 8	d					12 45							13 45				14 35			14 44			
Leeds 10	d					13 11							14 11							15 11			
Wakefield Westgate 7	d					13 24							14 23							15 23			
Doncaster 7	d																15 00						
Sheffield 7	d					13 57				14 22			14 55				15 24			15 55			
Chesterfield	d					14 09				14 34			15 07							16 07			
Nottingham 8	d	13 10							14 10							15 10							16 10
Derby 6	d	13 36	13 53			14 29			14 36	14 53			15 27			15 36	15 53			16 27			16 36
Burton-on-Trent	d	13 47							14 47				15 37			15 47							16 47
Tamworth	d	13 59				14 47		←	14 59						←	15 59				16 45		←	16 59
Birmingham New Street 12	a	14 21	14 27	14 33	14 58	15 04	15 05	15 04	15 19	15 27	15 33	15 58	16 00	16 05	16 00	16 20	16 25	16 34	16 58	17 02	17 05	17 02	17 19
Birmingham New Street 12	d	14 30	14 33	14 42	15 04	15 12	15 10	15 12	15 30	15 33	15 42	16 04	16 12	16 10	16 12	16 30	16 33	16 42	17 04	17 12	17 10	17 12	17 30
Cheltenham Spa 5	a	15 14		15 24		→		15 50	16 14		16 27		→		16 50	17 14		17 24		→		17 50	18 14
Gloucester 7	a	15 27							16 23							17 23							18 23
Bristol Parkway 7	a			15 55				16 20			16 56				17 20			17 54				18 20	
Bristol Temple Meads 10	a			16 09				16 34			17 07				17 34			18 08				18 34	
Newport (South Wales)	a	16 11							17 07							18 07							19 07
Cardiff Central 7	a	16 25							17 20							18 20							19 21
Weston-super-Mare	a																						
Taunton	a			16 47				17 16							18 17							19 16	
Tiverton Parkway	a			17 00				17 28							18 30							19 28	
Exeter St Davids 6	a			17 15				17 44							18 45							19 44	
Dawlish	a			17 28																			
Teignmouth	a			17 33																			
Newton Abbot	a			17 40				18 05							19 06							20 07	
Torquay	a			17 50																			
Paignton	a			17 57																			
Totnes	a							18 18							19 19							20 20	
Plymouth	a							18 45							19 46							20 47	
Liskeard 6	a							19 13														21 13	
Bodmin Parkway	a							19 25														21 25	
Lostwithiel	a																						
Par	a							19 35														21 35	
St Austell	a							19 41														21 41	
Truro	a							19 57														21 57	
Redruth	a							20 09														22 09	
Camborne	a							20 15														22 15	
Hayle	a																						
St Erth	a							20 25														22 25	
Penzance	a							20 35														22 35	
Birmingham International ✈	d		14 43		15 14		15 20					16 14		16 20			16 44		17 14		17 20		
Coventry	d		14 55		15 25		15a30					16 25		16a30			16 55		17 25		17a30		
Leamington Spa 8	d		15 09		15 37					16 00		16 37					17 09		17 37				
Banbury	a		15 25		15 53					16 16		16 53					17 25		17 53				
Oxford	a		15 44		16 12					16 35		17 12					17 44		18 12				
Reading 7	a		16 09		16 39					17 02		17 39					18 09		18 39				
Guildford	a																						
Basingstoke	a				17 09							18 09							19 09				
Winchester	a				17 24							18 24							19 24				
Southampton Airport Pkway ✈	a				17 33							18 33							19 33				
Southampton Central ⛴	a				17 42							18 42							19 42				
Brockenhurst 3	a				18 06							19 06							20 06				
Bournemouth	a				18 26							19 26							20 26				

A ✠ to Plymouth   B ✠ from Edinburgh   C ✠ to Birmingham New Street

Table T051-F

Sundays

15 December to 10 May

Scotland, The North East, North West England - The South West and South Coast

		XC ◇1 ⊥	XC ◇1 ⊥	XC ◇1 ⊥	XC ◇1 ⊥	VT ◇1 ⊡	XC ◇1 ⊥	XC ◇1 A ⊥	XC ◇1 ⊥	XC ◇1 B ⊥	XC ◇1 C ⊥	XC ◇1 D ⊥	VT ◇1 ⊡	XC ◇1 B ⊥	XC ◇1 A ⊥	XC ◇1 ⊥	XC ◇1 A ⊥	XC ◇1 C ⊥	XC ◇1 D ⊥	VT ◇1 ⊡	XC ◇1 B ⊥	XC ◇1
Aberdeen	d											11 10										
Stonehaven	d											11 27										
Montrose	d											11 49										
Arbroath	d											12 04										
Dundee	d											12 22										
Leuchars	d											12 35										
Cupar	d											12 43										
Ladybank	d											12 50										
Markinch	d											12 58										
Kirkcaldy	d											13 08										
Inverkeithing	d											13 24										
Glasgow Central	d				12 02	13 55													13 48	15 57		
Motherwell	d				12 18														14 03			
Haymarket	d				12 56							13 39							14 42			
Edinburgh	d				13 08				13 55			14 08	14 51						15 08			
Haymarket	d												14 56									
Lockerbie	d																					
Carlisle	d					15 11							16 07							17 10		
Penrith North Lakes	d												16 22									
Oxenholme Lake District	d					15 45														17 44		
Lancaster	d												16 57									
Preston	d					16 17							17 17							18 17		
Wigan North Western	d					16 30							17 30							18 28		
Warrington Bank Quay	d					16 41							17 41							18 40		
M'chester Piccadilly	d		16 05	16 27						17 05	17 27						18 05	18 27				
Stockport	d		16 13	16 36						17 13	17 35						18 13	18 35				
Wilmslow	d																					
Crewe	d					17 02							18 03							19 01		
Macclesfield	d		16 26	16 50						17 26	17 48						18 26	18 48				
Congleton	d																					
Stoke-on-Trent	d		16 45	17 08						17 45	18 06						18 46	19 06				
Stafford	d		17 03	17 25						18 03	18 28						19 03	19 28				
Wolverhampton	d		17 17	17 41		17 45				18 17	18 42		18 45				19 17	19 42		19 45		
Dunbar	d				13 29														15 29			
Berwick-upon-Tweed	d								14 36			14 49										
Alnmouth for Alnwick	d				14 11																	
Morpeth	d											15 20							16 22			
Newcastle	d	14 36			14 41				15 25			15 40				16 35			16 40			
Chester-le-Street	d																					
Durham	d	14 48			14 53				15 38			15 52				16 47			16 52			
Darlington	d	15 06			15 10				15 57			16 10				17 05			17 10			
York	d	15 35			15 44				16 25			16 44				17 35			17 44			
Leeds	d				16 11							17 12							18 11			
Wakefield Westgate	d				16 23							17 24							18 23			
Doncaster	d	15 58							16 51							17 58						
Sheffield	d	16 24			16 55				17 24			17 55				18 24			18 55			
Chesterfield	d				17 07							18 07							19 07			
Nottingham	d							17 10							18 10							19 10
Derby	d	16 53			17 26			17 36	17 53			18 27			18 36	18 53			19 27			19 36
Burton-on-Trent	d				17 36			17 47							18 47				19 37			19 47
Tamworth	d						←	17 59				18 45		←	18 59						←	19 59
Birmingham New Street	a	17 27	17 34	17 59	17 59	18 05	17 59	18 19	18 27	18 33	18 59	19 03	19 05	19 03	19 19	19 27	19 33	19 58	20 00	20 05	20 00	20 20
Birmingham New Street	d	17 33	17 42	18 04	18 12	18 10	18 12	18 30	18 33	18 42	19 04	19 12	19 10	19 12	19 30	19 33	19 42	20 04	20 12	20 10	20 12	
Cheltenham Spa	a		18 28		→		18 50	19 14		19 24		→		19 50	20 14		20 27		→		20 50	
Gloucester	a							19 23							20 24							
Bristol Parkway	a		19 02				19 22			19 53				20 20			20 56				21 20	
Bristol Temple Meads	a		19 12				19 36			20 05				20 35			21 06				21 35	
Newport (South Wales)	a							20 07							21 07							
Cardiff Central	a							20 21							21 21							
Weston-super-Mare	a									20 37												
Taunton	a						20 15			20 58				21 16							22 16	
Tiverton Parkway	a						20 28			21 11				21 28							22 28	
Exeter St Davids	a						20 44			21 27				21 44							22 44	
Dawlish	a									21 40												
Teignmouth	a									21 45												
Newton Abbot	a						21 08			21 52				22 04							23 04	
Torquay	a																					
Paignton	a																					
Totnes	a						21 20							22 17							23 17	
Plymouth	a						21 48			22 36				22 44							23 44	
Liskeard	a																					
Bodmin Parkway	a																					
Lostwithiel	a																					
Par	a																					
St Austell	a																					
Truro	a																					
Redruth	a																					
Camborne	a																					
Hayle	a																					
St Erth	a																					
Penzance	a																					
Birmingham International	d			18 14		18 20			18 43		19 14		19 20			19 44		20 14		20 20		
Coventry	d			18 25		18a30			18 55		19 25		19a30			19 55		20 25		20a30		
Leamington Spa	d	18 00		18 37					19 09		19 37					20 10		20 37				
Banbury	a	18 16		18 53					19 25		19 53					20 26		20 53				
Oxford	a	18 35		19 12					19 44		20 12					20 46		21 12				
Reading	a	19 06		19 39					20 09		20 39					21 11		21 39				
Guildford	a																					
Basingstoke	a			20 09							21 09							22 09				
Winchester	a			20 24							21 26							22 25				
Southampton Airport Pkwy	a			20 33							21 34							22 33				
Southampton Central	a			20 42							21 43							22 43				
Brockenhurst	a			21 06							22 07											
Bournemouth	a			21 26							22 26											

A ⊥ to Birmingham New Street
B ⊥ to Bristol Temple Meads
C ⊥ to Reading
D ⊥ from Edinburgh

Table T051-F

Sundays

15 December to 10 May

Scotland, The North East, North West England - The South West and South Coast

		XC ◇1 A ⊥	XC ◇1 A ⊥	VT ◇1 ⊡	XC ◇1 A ⊥	XC ◇1 B ⊥	XC ◇1	XC ◇1 ⊥	XC ◇1	XC ◇1 C ⊥	XC ◇1	XC ◇1	VT ◇1 ⊡	XC ◇1	VT ◇1 ⊡	XC ◇1 D ⊥	XC ◇1
Aberdeen	d																
Stonehaven	d																
Montrose	d																
Arbroath	d																
Dundee	d																
Leuchars	d																
Cupar	d																
Ladybank	d																
Markinch	d																
Kirkcaldy	d																
Inverkeithing	d																
Glasgow Central	d					14 55							18 37			16 55	
Motherwell	d					15 13										17 13	
Haymarket	d					15 52										17 51	
Edinburgh	d			16 51		16 08				17 08					18 51	18 06	
Haymarket	d			16 55											18 56		
Lockerbie	d																
Carlisle	d			18 07									19 48		20 07		
Penrith North Lakes	d														20 22		
Oxenholme Lake District	d			18 42									20 23				
Lancaster	d			18 57									20 37		20 57		
Preston	d			19 17									20 57		21 17		
Wigan North Western	d			19 29									21 08		21 30		
Warrington Bank Quay	d			19 40									21 19		21 41		
M'chester Piccadilly	d		19 05		19 27				20 05					21 05			22 05
Stockport	d		19 13		19 35				20 13					21 13			22 13
Wilmslow	d																
Crewe	d			20 02									21 41		22 03		
Macclesfield	d		19 26		19 48				20 26					21 26			22 26
Congleton	d																
Stoke-on-Trent	d		19 46		20 06				20 44					21 46			22 44
Stafford	d		20 03		20 28				21 03				22 01	22 05			23 04
Wolverhampton	d		20 17	20 34	20 42				21 17				22 14	22 20	22 33		23 18
Dunbar	d									17 29						18 28	
Berwick-upon-Tweed	d									17 53						18 52	
Alnmouth for Alnwick	d					17 08											
Morpeth	d					17 22										19 23	
Newcastle	d	17 35				17 40		18 25		18 39		19 26				19 41	
Chester-le-Street	d																
Durham	d	17 48				17 53		18 37		18 52		19 39				19 53	
Darlington	d	18 06				18 11		18 56		19 09		19 56				20 10	
York	d	18 35				18 45		19 24		19 45		20 26				20 45	
Leeds	d					19 12				20 11						21 11	
Wakefield Westgate	d					19 24				20 23						21 23	
Doncaster	d	18 58						19 54				20 51					
Sheffield	d	19 24				19 56		20 21		20 54		21 20				21 54	
Chesterfield	d					20 08				21 06		21 32				22 06	
Nottingham	d						20 10				21 10						
Derby	d	19 53				20 27	20 36	20 53		21 26	21 36	21 53				22 27	
Burton-on-Trent	d						20 47			21 36	21 47	22 03				22 37	
Tamworth	d					20 45	20 59			21 47	21 59	22 13				22 47	
Birmingham New Street	a	20 23	20 33	20 51	20 58	21 02	21 19	21 23	21 33	22 03	22 20	22 30	22 32	22 36	22 52	23 04	23 35
Birmingham New Street	d	20 33	20 42		21 04	21 12			21 42	22 12							
Cheltenham Spa	a		21 24			21 50			22 24	22 50							
Gloucester	a					22 01											
Bristol Parkway	a		22 00			22 31			22 54	23 20							
Bristol Temple Meads	a		22 11			22 41			23 04	23 30							
Newport (South Wales)	a																
Cardiff Central	a																
Weston-super-Mare	a																
Taunton	a																
Tiverton Parkway	a																
Exeter St Davids	a																
Dawlish	a																
Teignmouth	a																
Newton Abbot	a																
Torquay	a																
Paignton	a																
Totnes	a																
Plymouth	a																
Liskeard	a																
Bodmin Parkway	a																
Lostwithiel	a																
Par	a																
St Austell	a																
Truro	a																
Redruth	a																
Camborne	a																
Hayle	a																
St Erth	a																
Penzance	a																
Birmingham International	d				21 14												
Coventry	d				21 25												
Leamington Spa	d	21 00			21 37												
Banbury	a	21 17			21 53												
Oxford	a	21 37			22 12												
Reading	a	22 02			22 39												
Guildford	a	22 41															
Basingstoke	a																
Winchester	a																
Southampton Airport Pkwy	a																
Southampton Central	a																
Brockenhurst	a																
Bournemouth	a																

A ⊥ to Birmingham New Street
B ⊥ from Edinburgh to Birmingham New Street
C ⊥ to Leeds
D ⊥ from Edinburgh to Leeds

Table T051-R

Mondays to Fridays
16 December to 15 May

South Coast and the South West - North West England, The North East and Scotland

Station		XC ◇1	XC ◇1 🍴	VT ◇1 ⊠	XC 1	XC ◇1 🍴	XC ◇1 🍴	XC 1	XC ◇1 🍴	XC ◇1 🍴		VT ◇1 ⊠	XC 1 🍴	XC ◇1 🍴	XC ◇1 🍴	XC 1	XC ◇1 A 🍴	XC ◇1	XC ◇1 🍴	VT ◇1 ⊠		XC 1 🍴	XC ◇1 A 🍴	XC ◇1 🍴	XC ◇1
Bournemouth	d																								
Brockenhurst	d																								
Southampton Central	d																05 15								
Southampton Airport Pkwy	d																05 22								
Winchester	d																05 31								
Basingstoke	d																05 49								
Guildford	d																						06 01		
Reading	d																06 15						06 45		
Oxford	d																06 39						07 08		
Banbury	d																06 57						07 26		
Leamington Spa	d																07 15						07 45		
Coventry	d																07 27			07 42					
Birmingham International	d																07 38			07 53					
Penzance	d																								
St Erth	d																								
Hayle	d																								
Camborne	d																								
Redruth	d																								
Truro	d																								
St Austell	d																								
Par	d																								
Lostwithiel	d																								
Bodmin Parkway	d																								
Liskeard	d																								
Plymouth	d																								
Totnes	d																								
Paignton	d																								
Torquay	d																								
Newton Abbot	d																								
Teignmouth	d																								
Dawlish	d																								
Exeter St Davids	d																								
Tiverton Parkway	d																								
Taunton	d																								
Weston-super-Mare	d																								
Cardiff Central	d																								06 38
Newport (South Wales)	d																								06 54
Bristol Temple Meads	d																	06 24	06 32					07 00	
Bristol Parkway	d																	06 34	06 41					07 09	
Gloucester	d																	07 07							07 45
Cheltenham Spa	d																	07 17	07 11					07 41	07 56
Birmingham New Street	a																07 48	08 15	07 56	08 09			08 12	08 26	08 45
Birmingham New Street	d	05 57	06 03	06 15	06 19	06 30	06 30	06 49	06 53	07 03		07 15	07 19	07 30	07 31	07 49	07 57		08 03	08 15		08 19	08 30	08 31	08 49
Tamworth	d				06 39			07 07		07 20			07 40			08 09			08 19			08 36			09 09
Burton-on-Trent	d				06 50			07 20		07 30			07 51			08 21			08 29			08 47			09 21
Derby	a		06 33		07 03		07 10	07 35		07 41			08 04	08 08		08 36			08 41			08 59	09 04		09 32
Nottingham	a				07 37			08 13					08 33			09 09						09 31			10 03
Chesterfield	a		07 00				07 30			07 59				08 33					09 02						
Sheffield	a		07 14				07 46			08 20				08 48					09 18				09 48		
Doncaster	a						08 14							09 15									10 15		
Wakefield Westgate	a		07 46							08 48									09 46						
Leeds	a		08 03							09 02									10 00						
York	a		08 30				08 40			09 30				09 40					10 30				10 40		
Darlington	a		08 58				09 14			09 58				10 12					10 59				11 14		
Durham	a		09 16				09 31			10 15				10 29					11 15				11 31		
Chester-le-Street	a																								
Newcastle	a		09 29				09 45			10 29				10 43					11 29				11 46		
Morpeth	a																		11 45						
Alnmouth for Alnwick	a		09 57																						
Berwick-upon-Tweed	a		10 19																12 18						
Dunbar	a									11 38															
Wolverhampton	d	06 14		06 37		06 48			07 10			07 37			07 49		08 14			08 37				08 48	
Stafford	a	06 27				07 01			07 23						08 02		08 27							09 01	
Stoke-on-Trent	a	06 43				07 17									08 18		08 43							09 17	
Congleton	a	06 57																							
Macclesfield	a	07 05				07 37									08 36		09 01							09 36	
Crewe	a			07 08					07 43			08 08								09 07					
Wilmslow	a								08 00																
Stockport	a	07 19				07 49			08 13						08 49		09 13							09 49	
M'chester Piccadilly	a	07 30				08 00			08 23						09 00		09 24							10 00	
Warrington Bank Quay	a			07 26								08 26								09 26					
Wigan North Western	a			07 37								08 37								09 37					
Preston	a			07 51								08 51								09 51					
Lancaster	a			08 07								09 07								10 08					
Oxenholme Lake District	a			08 21																10 21					
Penrith North Lakes	a											09 43													
Carlisle	a			09 00								09 59								10 59					
Lockerbie	a																								
Haymarket	a			10 12																12 16					
Edinburgh	a		11 06	10 18						12 04									13 02	12 22					
Haymarket	a		11 14																13 15						
Motherwell	a		11 54																13 54						
Glasgow Central	a		12 11									11 15							14 12						
Inverkeithing	a																								
Kirkcaldy	a																								
Markinch	a																								
Ladybank	a																								
Cupar	a																								
Leuchars	a																								
Dundee	a																								
Arbroath	a																								
Montrose	a																								
Stonehaven	a																								
Aberdeen	a																								

A 🍴 from Reading

NRT DECEMBER 19 EDITION

Table T051-R

Mondays to Fridays
16 December to 15 May

South Coast and the South West - North West England, The North East and Scotland

Station		XC ◇1 A 🍴	XC ◇1 🍴	XC 1 🍴	VT ◇1 ⊠	XC ◇1 🍴		XC ◇1 B 🍴	XC ◇1	XC ◇1 🍴	XC ◇1 🍴	XC ◇1 🍴	VT ◇1 ⊠	XC ◇1 A 🍴	XC ◇1 C 🍴	XC ◇1		XC ◇1 🍴	XC ◇1 🍴	VT ◇1 ⊠	XC ◇1 🍴	XC ◇1 🍴	XC ◇1 🍴	XC ◇1 🍴	XC ■ 1 🍴
Bournemouth	d									06 30								07 30							08 45
Brockenhurst	d									06 46								07 48							09 00
Southampton Central	d	06 16								07 14				07 56				08 12							09 17
Southampton Airport Pkwy	d	06 23								07 22				08 03				08 19							09 24
Winchester	d	06 32								07 31				08 12				08 31							09 33
Basingstoke	d	06 49								07 51				08 28				08 49							09 49
Guildford	d																								
Reading	d	07 14				07 45				08 15				08 50				09 12				09 45			10 15
Oxford	d	07 39				08 08				08 39				09 14				09 39				10 10			10 39
Banbury	d	07 57				08 28				08 57				09 33				09 57				10 28			10 57
Leamington Spa	d	08 15				08 50				09 15				09 51				10 15				10 50			11 15
Coventry	d	08 27			08 42					09 27			09 42					10 27		10 42					11 27
Birmingham International	d	08 38			08 53					09 38			09 53					10 38		10 53					11 38
Penzance	d																								
St Erth	d																								
Hayle	d																								
Camborne	d																								
Redruth	d																								
Truro	d																								
St Austell	d																								
Par	d																								
Lostwithiel	d																								
Bodmin Parkway	d																								
Liskeard	d																								
Plymouth	d		05 25								06 27								07 27						
Totnes	d		05 51								06 53								07 53						
Paignton	d														07 01										
Torquay	d														07 07										
Newton Abbot	d		06 04								07 06				07 17				08 06						
Teignmouth	d														07 24										
Dawlish	d														07 29										
Exeter St Davids	d		06 25								07 27				07 42				08 27						
Tiverton Parkway	d		06 38								07 41				07 56				08 41						
Taunton	d		06 51								07 53				08 08				08 53						
Weston-super-Mare	d														08 38										
Cardiff Central	d							06 57	07 45							08 45								09 45	
Newport (South Wales)	d							07 11	08 01							09 00								09 59	
Bristol Temple Meads	d		07 34					08 00			08 34				09 00				09 34				10 00		
Bristol Parkway	d		07 44					08 09			08 44				09 09				09 44				10 09		
Gloucester	d								08 49							09 49								10 48	
Cheltenham Spa	d		08 16					08 40	08 59		09 16				09 40	10 00			10 16				10 40	10 59	
Birmingham New Street	a	08 48	08 56		09 05	09 18		09 25	09 45	09 49	09 58		10 04	10 18	10 23	10 45		10 48	10 56	11 05		11 18	11 25	11 45	11 48
Birmingham New Street	d	08 57	09 03	09 12	09 15	09 28		09 31	09 49	09 57	10 03	10 12	10 15	10 28	10 31	10 49		10 57	11 03	11 15	11 19	11 30	11 31	11 49	11 57
Tamworth	d			09 29					10 08		10 19	10 29				11 09					11 36			12 07	
Burton-on-Trent	d		09 27	09 40					10 19			10 40				11 21			11 26		11 48			12 19	
Derby	a		09 37	09 52		09 58			10 34		10 42	10 52		10 58		11 35			11 40		12 00	12 04		12 35	
Nottingham	a			10 24					11 03			11 24				12 07					12 28			13 03	
Chesterfield	a		10 01								11 02								12 02						
Sheffield	a		10 18			10 27					11 18			11 27					12 18			12 47			
Doncaster	a					10 52								11 53								13 16			
Wakefield Westgate	a		10 45								11 45								12 45						
Leeds	a		11 01								12 01								13 00						
York	a		11 30			11 15					12 31			12 15					13 30			13 40			
Darlington	a		11 59			11 43					12 59			12 43					14 02			14 12			
Durham	a		12 16			12 00					13 15			13 00					14 19			14 29			
Chester-le-Street	a																								
Newcastle	a		12 29			12 14					13 29			13 16					14 32			14 43			
Morpeth	a																		14 47						
Alnmouth for Alnwick	a										13 59														
Berwick-upon-Tweed	a										14 21														
Dunbar	a		13 41																15 40						
Wolverhampton	d	09 14			09 37			09 48		10 14			10 37		10 48			11 14		11 37			11 48		12 14
Stafford	a	09 27						10 01		10 27					11 01			11 27					12 01		12 27
Stoke-on-Trent	a	09 43						10 17		10 43					11 17			11 43					12 17		12 43
Congleton	a																								
Macclesfield	a	10 01						10 36		11 01					11 36			12 01					12 36		13 01
Crewe	a				10 07								11 07							12 07					
Wilmslow	a																								
Stockport	a	10 13						10 49		11 13					11 49			12 13					12 49		13 13
M'chester Piccadilly	a	10 24						11 00		11 24					12 00			12 24					13 00		13 24
Warrington Bank Quay	a				10 26								11 26							12 26					
Wigan North Western	a				10 37								11 37							12 37					
Preston	a				10 51								11 51							12 51					
Lancaster	a				11 08								12 08							13 08					
Oxenholme Lake District	a												12 20							13 21					
Penrith North Lakes	a				11 45																				
Carlisle	a				12 01								13 00							14 00					
Lockerbie	a																								
Haymarket	a												14 10												
Edinburgh	a		14 07								15 08		14 17						16 06						
Haymarket	a										15 16														
Motherwell	a										15 54									14 58					
Glasgow Central	a				13 15						16 12									15 15					
Inverkeithing	a																								
Kirkcaldy	a																								
Markinch	a																								
Ladybank	a																								
Cupar	a																								
Leuchars	a																								
Dundee	a																								
Arbroath	a																								
Montrose	a																								
Stonehaven	a																								
Aberdeen	a																								

A 🍴 from Reading B 🍴 from Bristol Temple Meads C 🍴 from Newton Abbot

16 December to 15 May

South Coast and the South West - North West England, The North East and Scotland

		XC	VT	XC	XC	XC	XC	XC	XC	VT	XC	XC	XC	XC	XC	XC	VT	XC	XC	XC	XC	XC
																■			■			
		◇1	◇1	◇1	◇1	◇1	◇1	◇1	◇1	◇1	1	◇1	◇1	◇1	◇1	◇1	◇1	1	1	◇1	◇1	◇1
		A							B							C						
		⊼	☕	⊼	⊼	⊼		⊼	⊼	⊠		⊼	⊼	⊼	⊼	⊼	⊠		⊼	⊼	⊼	⊼
Bournemouth	d							09 45							10 45							11 45
Brockenhurst [3]	d							10 00							11 00							12 00
Southampton Central	d				09 47			10 17							11 17				11 47			12 17
Southampton Airport Pkway	d				09 54			10 24							11 24				11 54			12 24
Winchester	d				10 03			10 33							11 33				12 03			12 33
Basingstoke	d				10 20			10 49							11 49				12 19			12 49
Guildford	d																					
Reading [7]	d				10 45			11 15				11 45			12 13				12 45			13 15
Oxford	d				11 10			11 39				12 10			12 39				13 10			13 39
Banbury	d				11 31			11 57				12 28			12 57				13 31			13 57
Leamington Spa [8]	d				11 48			12 15				12 50			13 15				13 50			14 15
Coventry	d		11 42					12 27		12 42					13 27		13 42					14 27
Birmingham International	d		11 53					12 38		12 53					13 38		13 53					14 38
Penzance	d	06 30														08 37						
St Erth	d	06 38														08 45						
Hayle	d																					
Camborne	d	06 48														08 55						
Redruth	d	06 54														09 01						
Truro	d	07 06														09 13						
St Austell	d	07 22														09 29						
Par	d	07 28														09 35						
Lostwithiel	d																					
Bodmin Parkway	d	07 39														09 46						
Liskeard [6]	d	07 51														09 58						
Plymouth	d	08 25							09 27							10 27						
Totnes	d	08 51							09 53							10 53						
Paignton	d												10 14									
Torquay	d												10 20									
Newton Abbot	d	09 03							10 06				10 29			11 06						
Teignmouth	d												10 36									
Dawlish	d												10 41									
Exeter St Davids [6]	d	09 27							10 27				10 54			11 27						
Tiverton Parkway	d	09 41							10 41				11 08			11 41						
Taunton	d	09 53							10 53				11 21			11 53						
Weston-super-Mare	d																					
Cardiff Central [7]	d						10 45							11 45							12 45	
Newport (South Wales)	d						11 00							11 58							12 59	
Bristol Temple Meads [10]	d	10 34				11 00			11 34				12 00			12 35				13 00		
Bristol Parkway [7]	d	10 44				11 09			11 44				12 09			12 45				13 09		
Gloucester [7]	d						11 48							12 44							13 48	
Cheltenham Spa	d	11 16				11 40	11 59		12 16				12 40	12 55		13 16				13 40	13 59	
Birmingham New Street [12]	a	11 58	12 04		12 18	12 25	12 45	12 48	12 56	13 04		13 18	13 25	13 45	13 48	13 56	14 04		14 18	14 23	14 45	14 48
Birmingham New Street [12]	d	12 03	12 15	12 19	12 30	12 31	12 49	12 57	13 03	13 15	13 19	13 30	13 31	13 49	13 57	14 03	14 15	14 19	14 30	14 31	14 49	14 57
Tamworth	d	12 20		12 36			13 09				13 36			14 09		14 19		14 36			15 09	
Burton-on-Trent	d			12 48			13 20		13 26		13 48			14 20				14 48			15 20	
Derby [6]	a	12 40		13 00	13 04		13 32		13 39		14 00	14 04		14 32		14 37		15 00	15 04		15 36	
Nottingham [8]	a			13 28			14 03				14 28			15 03				15 28			16 03	
Chesterfield	a	13 02							14 02							15 02						
Sheffield [7]	a	13 18			13 44				14 18			14 47				15 18			15 47			
Doncaster [7]	a				14 14							15 15							16 15			
Wakefield Westgate [7]	a	13 46							14 46							15 46						
Leeds [10]	a	14 00							15 00							16 00						
York [8]	a	14 30			14 39				15 30			15 40				16 30			16 40			
Darlington [7]	a	14 59			15 13				15 59			16 13				16 58			17 13			
Durham	a	15 15			15 30				16 17			16 30				17 15			17 30			
Chester-le-Street	a																					
Newcastle [8]	a	15 29			15 45				16 32			16 44				17 29			17 43			
Morpeth	a								16 48													
Alnmouth for Alnwick	a	16 01							17 03							18 01						
Berwick-upon-Tweed	a	16 23														18 23						
Dunbar	a								17 44													
Wolverhampton [7]	d		12 37			12 48		13 14		13 37			13 48		14 14		14 36			14 48		15 14
Stafford	a					13 01		13 27					14 01		14 27					15 01		15 27
Stoke-on-Trent	a					13 18		13 43					14 17		14 43					15 17		15 43
Congleton	a																					
Macclesfield	a					13 36		14 01					14 36		15 01					15 36		16 01
Crewe [10]	a		13 07							14 07							15 05					
Wilmslow	a																					
Stockport	a					13 49		14 13					14 49		15 13					15 49		16 13
M'chester Piccadilly [10]	a					14 00		14 24					15 00		15 24					16 00		16 24
Warrington Bank Quay	a		13 26							14 26							15 24					
Wigan North Western	a		13 37							14 37							15 34					
Preston [8]	a		13 51							14 51							15 51					
Lancaster [6]	a		14 08							15 08							16 07					
Oxenholme Lake District	a									15 22												
Penrith North Lakes	a		14 42														16 44					
Carlisle [8]	a		15 00							16 01							17 00					
Lockerbie	a																					
Haymarket	a		16 12														18 15					
Edinburgh [10]	a	17 05	16 18						18 07							19 07	18 21					
Haymarket	a	17 16							18 15							19 15						
Motherwell	a	17 55														19 54						
Glasgow Central [15]	a	18 11								17 15						20 15						
Inverkeithing	a								18 29													
Kirkcaldy	a								18 45													
Markinch	a								18 54													
Ladybank	a								19 02													
Cupar	a								19 09													
Leuchars [3]	a								19 19													
Dundee	a								19 33													
Arbroath	a								19 51													
Montrose	a								20 05													
Stonehaven	a								20 26													
Aberdeen	a								20 44													

A ⊼ from Plymouth
B ⊼ to Edinburgh
C ⊼ from Plymouth to Edinburgh ◇ from Plymouth ■ to Plymouth

16 December to 15 May

South Coast and the South West - North West England, The North East and Scotland

		XC	XC	VT	XC	XC	XC	XC	XC	VT	XC	XC	XC	XC	XC	XC	VT	XC	XC	XC	XC	XC	XC
										■							■						
		◇1	1	◇1	◇1	◇1	◇1	◇1	◇1	1	◇1	◇1	◇1	◇1	◇1	◇1	1	1	◇1	◇1	1	◇1	◇1
		A							A			B		C		B						C	
		⊼		☕	⊼	⊼	⊼	⊼	⊼	☕		⊼	⊼	⊼	⊼	⊼	☕		⊼	⊼		⊼	⊼
Bournemouth	d							12 45							13 45								14 45
Brockenhurst [3]	d							13 00							14 00								15 00
Southampton Central	d							13 16				13 47			14 15								15 17
Southampton Airport Pkway	d							13 23				13 54			14 22								15 24
Winchester	d							13 32				14 03			14 31								15 33
Basingstoke	d							13 49				14 19			14 49								15 49
Guildford	d																						
Reading [7]	d				13 45			14 15				14 45			15 15				15 45				16 15
Oxford	d				14 10			14 39				15 10			15 39				16 10				16 39
Banbury	d				14 31			14 57				15 28			15 57				16 28				16 58
Leamington Spa [8]	d				14 50			15 15				15 50			16 15				16 50				17 15
Coventry	d			14 42				15 27		15 42					16 27		16 42						17 27
Birmingham International	d			14 53				15 38		15 53					16 38		16 53						17 38
Penzance	d	09 25																					
St Erth	d	09 34																					
Hayle	d	09 38																					
Camborne	d	09 48																					
Redruth	d	09 54																					
Truro	d	10 07																					
St Austell	d	10 24																					
Par	d	10 31																					
Lostwithiel	d	10 38																					
Bodmin Parkway	d	10 44																					
Liskeard [6]	d	10 56																					
Plymouth	d	11 27				11 50			12 27							13 27							
Totnes	d	11 53				12 16			12 53							13 53							
Paignton	d																						
Torquay	d																						
Newton Abbot	d	12 06				12 28			13 06							14 06							
Teignmouth	d																						
Dawlish	d																						
Exeter St Davids [6]	d	12 27				12 52			13 27							14 27				14 45			
Tiverton Parkway	d	12 41				13 06			13 41							14 41				14 58			
Taunton	d	12 53				13 21			13 53							14 53				15 11			
Weston-super-Mare	d																			15 34			
Cardiff Central [7]	d						13 45							14 45								15 45	
Newport (South Wales)	d						13 58							14 59								15 59	
Bristol Temple Meads [10]	d	13 34				14 00			14 30				15 00			15 32				16 00			
Bristol Parkway [7]	d	13 44				14 09			14 41				15 09			15 45				16 10			
Gloucester [7]	d						14 48							15 48								16 46	
Cheltenham Spa	d	14 16				14 40	14 59		15 11				15 40	15 59		16 16				16 40		16 57	
Birmingham New Street [12]	a	14 56		15 04	15 18	15 23	15 44	15 48	15 56	16 04		16 17	16 23	16 45	16 48	16 56	17 05		17 18	17 24		17 45	17 48
Birmingham New Street [12]	d	15 03	15 12	15 15	15 28	15 31	15 49	15 57	16 03	16 15	16 19	16 30	16 31	16 49	16 57	17 03	17 15	17 19	17 30	17 31	17 39	17 49	17 57
Tamworth	d		15 29				16 09		16 20		16 36			17 09				17 36			18 03	18 09	
Burton-on-Trent	d	15 26	15 40				16 21				16 48			17 21		17 26		17 47			18 14	18 21	
Derby [6]	a	15 40	15 52		15 58		16 32		16 39		17 00	17 05		17 32		17 40		18 00	18 05		18 28	18 33	
Nottingham [8]	a		16 24				17 03				17 31			18 03				18 31				19 05	
Chesterfield	a	16 02							17 03							18 02							
Sheffield [7]	a	16 18			16 27				17 18			17 48				18 18			18 48				
Doncaster [7]	a				16 53														19 17				
Wakefield Westgate [7]	a	16 46							17 46			18 18				18 48							
Leeds [10]	a	17 01							18 00			18 36				19 05							
York [8]	a	17 30			17 14				18 31			19 04				19 30			19 41				
Darlington [7]	a	17 59			17 42				19 00			19 32				20 04			20 13				
Durham	a	18 16			17 59				19 18			19 48				20 22			20 30				
Chester-le-Street	a																						
Newcastle [8]	a	18 32			18 13				19 33			20 02				20 36			20 44				
Morpeth	a	18 49														20 52							
Alnmouth for Alnwick	a								20 01			20 28											
Berwick-upon-Tweed	a	19 22							20 25							21 26							
Dunbar	a	19 45														21 49							
Wolverhampton [7]	d			15 37		15 48		16 14		16 37			16 48		17 14		17 37			17 48			18 14
Stafford	a					16 01		16 27					17 02		17 27					18 01			18 27
Stoke-on-Trent	a					16 17		16 43					17 19		17 43					18 17			18 43
Congleton	a																						
Macclesfield	a					16 36		17 01					17 36		18 01					18 36			19 01
Crewe [10]	a			16 07						17 07							18 07						
Wilmslow	a																						
Stockport	a					16 49		17 13					17 49		18 13					18 49			19 13
M'chester Piccadilly [10]	a					17 00		17 24					18 00		18 24					19 00			19 24
Warrington Bank Quay	a			16 26						17 26							18 26						
Wigan North Western	a			16 37						17 37							18 37						
Preston [8]	a			16 51						17 51							18 51						
Lancaster [6]	a			17 08						18 09							19 08						
Oxenholme Lake District	a			17 22						18 22							19 22						
Penrith North Lakes	a			17 47						18 48													
Carlisle [8]	a			18 04						19 05							20 02						
Lockerbie	a																						
Haymarket	a									20 17													
Edinburgh [10]	a	20 10							21 09	20 25		21 29				22 14							
Haymarket	a	20 17							21 17														
Motherwell	a								21 59														
Glasgow Central [15]	a			19 23					22 21								21 15						
Inverkeithing	a	20 32																					
Kirkcaldy	a																						
Markinch	a	21 04																					
Ladybank	a	21 12																					
Cupar	a	21 20																					
Leuchars [3]	a	21 28																					
Dundee	a	21 43																					
Arbroath	a																						
Montrose	a																						
Stonehaven	a																						
Aberdeen	a																						

A ⊼ to Edinburgh
B ⊼ to Newcastle
C ⊼ to Birmingham New Street

Table T051-R

Mondays to Fridays
16 December to 15 May

South Coast and the South West - North West England, The North East and Scotland

		XC	VT	VT	XC	XC	XC	XC	XC	XC	XC	VT	XC	XC	XC	XC	XC	VT	XC	XC	XC	XC
		◇1	◇1	◇1	1	◇1	◇1	◇1	◇1	◇1	1	◇1	◇1	◇1	◇1	◇1	◇1	◇1	◇1	◇1	◇1	◇1
		A						B							B		B		B			B
		🛒	☕	☕		🛒	🛒	🛒	🛒	🛒		☕	🛒	🛒	🛒	🛒	🛒	⊠	🛒	🛒		🛒
Bournemouth	d								15 45							16 45						17 45
Brockenhurst [3]	d								16 00							17 00						18 00
Southampton Central	d					15 46			16 17							17 17			17 47			18 15
Southampton Airport Pkway	d					15 53			16 24							17 24			17 54			18 22
Winchester	d					16 02			16 33							17 33			18 03			18 31
Basingstoke	d					16 19			16 49							17 49			18 19			18 49
Guildford	d																					
Reading [7]	d					16 45			17 15				17 43			18 15			18 45			19 15
Oxford	d					17 10			17 39				18 10			18 40			19 10			19 39
Banbury	d					17 32			17 57				18 28			18 58			19 29			19 57
Leamington Spa [8]	d					17 51			18 15				18 50			19 16			19 50			20 15
Coventry	d		17 42	17 42					18 27			18 42				19 28		19 42				20 27
Birmingham International	d		17 53	17 53					18 38			18 53				19 38		19 53				20 38
Penzance	d																					
St Erth	d																					
Hayle	d																					
Camborne	d																					
Redruth	d																					
Truro	d																					
St Austell	d																					
Par	d																					
Lostwithiel	d																					
Bodmin Parkway	d																					
Liskeard [6]	d																					
Plymouth	d	14 27								15 27							16 27					
Totnes	d	14 53								15 53							16 53					
Paignton	d						15 15															
Torquay	d						15 21															
Newton Abbot	d	15 06					15 34			16 06							17 05					
Teignmouth	d						15 41															
Dawlish	d						15 46															
Exeter St Davids [6]	d	15 27					15 59			16 27				16 56			17 27			17 59		
Tiverton Parkway	d	15 41					16 13			16 41				17 10			17 40			18 13		
Taunton	d	15 53					16 25			16 53				17 22			17 53			18 25		
Weston-super-Mare	d																					
Cardiff Central [7]	d							16 45							17 45						18 45	
Newport (South Wales)	d							16 59							17 59						18 58	
Bristol Temple Meads [10]	d	16 34					17 00			17 34				18 00			18 34			19 00		
Bristol Parkway [7]	d	16 44					17 09			17 44				18 09			18 44			19 09		
Gloucester [7]	d							17 48							18 44						19 47	
Cheltenham Spa	d	17 16					17 40	17 59		18 16				18 40	18 55		19 16			19 40	19 58	
Birmingham New Street [12]	a	17 56	18 04	18 05		18 18	18 23	18 45	18 48	18 56		19 05	19 18	19 23	19 45	19 48	19 56	20 08	20 18	20 23	20 45	20 48
Birmingham New Street [12]	d	18 03	18 15	18 15	18 19	18 30	18 31	18 49	18 57	19 03	19 12	19 15	19 28	19 31	19 49	19 57	20 03	20 15	20 30	20 31	20 49	20 57
Tamworth	d	18 19			18 36			19 09			19 29				20 09		20 19				21 09	
Burton-on-Trent	d				18 48			19 21		19 29	19 40				20 21						21 21	
Derby [6]	a	18 39			19 00	19 05		19 32		19 40	19 53		19 58		20 33		20 37		21 09		21 32	
Nottingham [8]	a				19 31			20 03			20 21				21 04						22 13	
Chesterfield	a	19 02				19 27				20 03							21 05		21 37			
Sheffield [7]	a	19 18				19 43				20 18			20 27				21 20		21 50			
Doncaster [7]	a					20 13							20 53						22 28			
Wakefield Westgate [7]	a	19 46								20 47							21 46					
Leeds [10]	a	20 05								21 02							22 02					
York [8]	a	20 30				20 41							21 15						22 51			
Darlington [7]	a	20 58				21 12							21 43									
Durham	a	21 15				21 29							22 00									
Chester-le-Street	a																					
Newcastle [8]	a	21 29				21 44							22 14									
Morpeth	a																					
Alnmouth for Alnwick	a	22 00																				
Berwick-upon-Tweed	a																					
Dunbar	a																					
Wolverhampton [7]	d		18 37	18 37			18 48		19 14			19 37		19 50		20 14		20 37		20 48		21 14
Stafford	a						19 01		19 27					20 03		20 27		20 50		21 01		21 27
Stoke-on-Trent	a						19 17		19 43					20 19		20 43				21 17		21 44
Congleton	a																					
Macclesfield	a						19 36		20 01					20 36		21 01				21 36		22 01
Crewe [10]	a		19 05	19 05								20 07						21 15				
Wilmslow	a																					
Stockport	a						19 49		20 13					20 49		21 13				21 49		22 15
M'chester Piccadilly [10]	a						20 00		20 24					20 59		21 24				22 00		22 25
Warrington Bank Quay	a			19 28								20 26										
Wigan North Western	a			19 39								20 37										
Preston [8]	a			19 54								20 51										
Lancaster [6]	a			20 10								21 08										
Oxenholme Lake District	a											21 23										
Penrith North Lakes	a			20 48																		
Carlisle [8]	a			21 04								22 01										
Lockerbie	a																					
Haymarket	a			22 16																		
Edinburgh [10]	a	23 03		22 22																		
Haymarket	a																					
Motherwell	a																					
Glasgow Central [15]	a											23 17										
Inverkeithing	a																					
Kirkcaldy	a																					
Markinch	a																					
Ladybank	a																					
Cupar	a																					
Leuchars [3]	a																					
Dundee	a																					
Arbroath	a																					
Montrose	a																					
Stonehaven	a																					
Aberdeen	a																					

A 🛒 to Newcastle

B 🛒 to Birmingham New Street

Table T051-R

Mondays to Fridays
16 December to 15 May

South Coast and the South West - North West England, The North East and Scotland

		XC	VT	XC	XC	XC	XC	XC	XC	XC	XC	XC	XC	XC	XC	XC	XC	XC
		◇1	◇1	◇1	◇1	◇1	◇1	◇1	1	◇1	◇1	◇1	◇1	◇1	1	◇1	◇1	◇1
		A				A		B										
		🛒	☕			🛒		🛒										
Bournemouth	d					18 45							19 45					
Brockenhurst [3]	d					19 00							20 00					
Southampton Central	d					19 17							20 17					
Southampton Airport Pkway	d					19 24							20 24					
Winchester	d					19 33							20 33					
Basingstoke	d					19 49							20 49					
Guildford	d																	
Reading [7]	d			19 45		20 15				20 45			21 13				22 02	
Oxford	d			20 10		20 39				21 10			21 37				22 30	
Banbury	d			20 28		20 57				21 30			21 57				22 48	
Leamington Spa [8]	d			20 50		21 15				21 50			22 15				23 09	
Coventry	d		20 42			21 27							22 27				23 20	
Birmingham International	d		20 53			21 38							22 38				23 31	
Penzance	d																	
St Erth	d																	
Hayle	d																	
Camborne	d																	
Redruth	d																	
Truro	d																	
St Austell	d																	
Par	d																	
Lostwithiel	d																	
Bodmin Parkway	d																	
Liskeard [6]	d																	
Plymouth	d	17 27						18 27										
Totnes	d	17 53						18 53										
Paignton	d															20 18		
Torquay	d															20 24		
Newton Abbot	d	18 06						19 05								20 33		
Teignmouth	d																	
Dawlish	d																	
Exeter St Davids [6]	d	18 27						19 27			20 00					20 56		
Tiverton Parkway	d	18 41						19 41			20 15					21 09		
Taunton	d	18 53						19 53			20 27					21 22		
Weston-super-Mare	d																	
Cardiff Central [7]	d						19 49							21 05				21 45
Newport (South Wales)	d						20 02							21 18				21 58
Bristol Temple Meads [10]	d	19 34			20 00			20 34			21 01					22 00		
Bristol Parkway [7]	d	19 44			20 10			20 43			21 10					22 09		
Gloucester [7]	d				20 45		20 55							22 02				22 48
Cheltenham Spa	d	20 16			20 55		21 06	21 16			21 41			22 13		22 42		22 59
Birmingham New Street [12]	a	20 56	21 05	21 23	21 37	21 48	21 54	22 01		22 18	22 25		22 48	23 05		23 41	23 56	23 59
Birmingham New Street [12]	d	21 03	21 15			21 57			22 03			22 30			23 09			
Tamworth	d	21 20							22 27						23 28			
Burton-on-Trent	d	21 31							22 39						23 40			
Derby [6]	a	21 42							22 53						23 53			
Nottingham [8]	a								23 26						00 16			
Chesterfield	a	22 06																
Sheffield [7]	a	22 23																
Doncaster [7]	a																	
Wakefield Westgate [7]	a	22 53																
Leeds [10]	a	23 08																
York [8]	a																	
Darlington [7]	a																	
Durham	a																	
Chester-le-Street	a																	
Newcastle [8]	a																	
Morpeth	a																	
Alnmouth for Alnwick	a																	
Berwick-upon-Tweed	a																	
Dunbar	a																	
Wolverhampton [7]	d		21 37			22 14						22 48						
Stafford	a		21 53			22 27						23 01						
Stoke-on-Trent	a		22 10			22 43						23 20						
Congleton	a																	
Macclesfield	a					23 01												
Crewe [10]	a		22 30															
Wilmslow	a																	
Stockport	a					23 13												
M'chester Piccadilly [10]	a					23 24						00 15						
Warrington Bank Quay	a																	
Wigan North Western	a																	
Preston [8]	a																	
Lancaster [6]	a																	
Oxenholme Lake District	a																	
Penrith North Lakes	a																	
Carlisle [8]	a																	
Lockerbie	a																	
Haymarket	a																	
Edinburgh [10]	a																	
Haymarket	a																	
Motherwell	a																	
Glasgow Central [15]	a																	
Inverkeithing	a																	
Kirkcaldy	a																	
Markinch	a																	
Ladybank	a																	
Cupar	a																	
Leuchars [3]	a																	
Dundee	a																	
Arbroath	a																	
Montrose	a																	
Stonehaven	a																	
Aberdeen	a																	

A 🛒 to Birmingham New Street

B 🛒 to Bristol Temple Meads

Table T051-R

Saturdays 21 December to 16 May

South Coast and the South West - North West England, The North East and Scotland

		XC	XC	VT	XC	XC	XC	XC	XC	XC		VT	XC	VT	XC	XC	XC	XC	XC	XC		VT	XC	XC	XC
		◇1	◇1	◇1	1	◇1	◇1	1	◇1	◇1		◇1	1	◇1	◇1	◇1	1	◇1	◇1	◇1		◇1	1	◇1	◇1
																		A						A	
			🛒	☕		🛒	🛒		🛒	🛒		☕	🛒	☕	🛒	🛒		🛒	🛒			☕	🛒	🛒	🛒
Bournemouth	d																								
Brockenhurst	d																								
Southampton Central	d																	05 09							
Southampton Airport Pkway ✈	d																	05 16							
Winchester	d																	05 25							
Basingstoke	d																	05 40							
Guildford	d																							06 09	
Reading	d																	06 15						06 47	
Oxford	d																	06 39						07 12	
Banbury	d																	06 57						07 32	
Leamington Spa	d																	07 15						07 50	
Coventry	d																	07 27							
Birmingham International ✈	d																	07 38							
Penzance	d																								
St Erth	d																								
Hayle	d																								
Camborne	d																								
Redruth	d																								
Truro	d																								
St Austell	d																								
Par	d																								
Lostwithiel	d																								
Bodmin Parkway	d																								
Liskeard	d																								
Plymouth	d																								
Totnes	d																								
Paignton	d																								
Torquay	d																								
Newton Abbot	d																								
Teignmouth	d																								
Dawlish	d																								
Exeter St Davids	d																								
Tiverton Parkway	d																								
Taunton	d																								
Weston-super-Mare	d																								
Cardiff Central	d																								
Newport (South Wales)	d																								
Bristol Temple Meads	d																		06 15						07 00
Bristol Parkway	d																		06 25						07 09
Gloucester	d																		06 57	07 02					
Cheltenham Spa	d																		07 08	07 14					07 40
Birmingham New Street	a																	07 48	07 56	08 06				08 18	08 25
Birmingham New Street	d	05 57	06 01	06 15	06 19	06 30	06 31	06 49	06 57	07 03		07 15	07 19	07 21	07 30	07 31	07 49	07 57	08 03			08 15	08 19	08 30	08 31
Tamworth	d		06 19		06 39	06 46		07 07		07 19			07 39		07 46		08 07		08 19				08 36		
Burton-on-Trent	d		06 30		06 51	06 56		07 19		07 29			07 50		07 56		08 19		08 29				08 48		
Derby	a		06 40		07 03	07 07		07 35		07 40			08 05		08 08		08 36		08 40				08 59	09 05	
Nottingham	a				07 36			08 09					08 31				09 05						09 30		
Chesterfield	a		07 01			07 32				08 02					08 33				09 02						
Sheffield	a		07 15			07 46				08 20					08 48				09 18					09 47	
Doncaster	a					08 14									09 17									10 15	
Wakefield Westgate	a		07 46							08 48									09 46						
Leeds	a		08 01							09 02									10 00						
York	a		08 29			08 40				09 30					09 40				10 30					10 40	
Darlington	a		08 59			09 14				09 58					10 12				10 59					11 14	
Durham	a		09 16			09 31				10 15					10 29				11 15					11 31	
Chester-le-Street	a																								
Newcastle	a		09 29			09 45				10 29					10 43				11 29					11 46	
Morpeth	a																		11 45						
Alnmouth for Alnwick	a		09 57																						
Berwick-upon-Tweed	a		10 19																12 18						
Dunbar	a									11 38															
Wolverhampton	d	06 14		06 37			06 48		07 14			07 37		07 40		07 50		08 14				08 37			08 48
Stafford	a	06 27					07 01		07 29					07 58		08 03		08 27							09 01
Stoke-on-Trent	a	06 43					07 17									08 19		08 43							09 17
Congleton	a	06 56																							
Macclesfield	a	07 04					07 36									08 36		09 01							09 36
Crewe	a			07 08					07 50			08 04		08 18								09 07			
Wilmslow	a								08 07																
Stockport	a	07 19					07 49		08 16							08 49		09 13							09 49
M'chester Piccadilly	a	07 31					07 59		08 29							08 59		09 24							10 00
Warrington Bank Quay	a			07 26								08 26		08 40								09 26			
Wigan North Western	a			07 37								08 37		08 51								09 37			
Preston	a			07 51								08 51		09 09								09 51			
Lancaster	a			08 07								09 10										10 08			
Oxenholme Lake District	a			08 21																		10 21			
Penrith North Lakes	a											09 46													
Carlisle	a			09 00								10 02										10 59			
Lockerbie	a																								
Haymarket	a			10 13																		12 12			
Edinburgh	a		11 03	10 18						12 05									13 05			12 19			
Haymarket	a		11 15																13 14						
Motherwell	a		11 54																13 54						
Glasgow Central	a		12 12									11 15							14 12						
Inverkeithing	a																								
Kirkcaldy	a																								
Markinch	a																								
Ladybank	a																								
Cupar	a																								
Leuchars	a																								
Dundee	a																								
Arbroath	a																								
Montrose	a																								
Stonehaven	a																								
Aberdeen	a																								

A 🛒 from Reading

Table T051-R

Saturdays 21 December to 16 May

South Coast and the South West - North West England, The North East and Scotland

		XC	XC	XC	VT	XC		XC	XC	XC	XC	XC	XC	VT	XC	XC		XC	XC	XC	XC	VT	XC	XC	XC
		◇1	◇1	◇1	◇1	1		◇1	◇1	◇1	◇1	◇1	1	◇1	◇1	◇1		◇1	◇1	◇1	1	◇1	◇1	◇1	◇1
			A					A	B						A	C									
			🛒	🛒	☕	🛒		🛒	🛒		🛒	🛒	🛒	☕	🛒	🛒			🛒	🛒	🛒	☕	🛒	🛒	🛒
Bournemouth	d							06 25			06 38								07 47						
Brockenhurst	d							06 40			06 53								08 02						
Southampton Central	d		06 20					06 54			07 11				07 49				08 20						
Southampton Airport Pkway ✈	d		06 27					07 01			07 18				07 56				08 27						
Winchester	d		06 36					07 10			07 29				08 05				08 36						
Basingstoke	d		06 51					07 26			07 51				08 20				08 51						
Guildford	d																								
Reading	d		07 15					07 46			08 15				08 45				09 15				09 45		
Oxford	d		07 39					08 11			08 40				09 10				09 39				10 10		
Banbury	d		07 57					08 30			08 57				09 28				09 57				10 28		
Leamington Spa	d		08 15					08 50			09 15				09 50				10 15				10 50		
Coventry	d		08 27		08 42						09 27			09 42					10 27			10 42			
Birmingham International ✈	d		08 38		08 53						09 38			09 53					10 38			10 53			
Penzance	d																								
St Erth	d																								
Hayle	d																								
Camborne	d																								
Redruth	d																								
Truro	d																								
St Austell	d																								
Par	d																								
Lostwithiel	d																								
Bodmin Parkway	d																								
Liskeard	d																								
Plymouth	d			05 27								06 23								07 24					
Totnes	d			05 53								06 49								07 50					
Paignton	d															07 00									
Torquay	d															07 06									
Newton Abbot	d			06 06								07 02				07 19				08 03					
Teignmouth	d															07 26									
Dawlish	d															07 31									
Exeter St Davids	d			06 27								07 26				07 45				08 27					
Tiverton Parkway	d			06 40								07 40				07 58				08 41					
Taunton	d			06 53								07 53				08 10				08 53					
Weston-super-Mare	d																								
Cardiff Central	d	06 38							07 00	07 45								08 45							09 45
Newport (South Wales)	d	06 53							07 14	08 02								08 59							09 58
Bristol Temple Meads	d			07 34					08 00			08 34				09 00				09 34				10 00	
Bristol Parkway	d			07 44					08 09			08 44				09 10				09 44				10 09	
Gloucester	d	07 44								08 48								09 48							10 48
Cheltenham Spa	d	07 55		08 16					08 41	08 59		09 16				09 40		09 59		10 16				10 40	10 59
Birmingham New Street	a	08 45	08 48	08 56	09 04			09 18	09 25	09 45	09 48	09 56		10 04	10 18	10 25		10 45	10 48	10 56		11 05	11 18	11 25	11 45
Birmingham New Street	d	08 49	08 57	09 03	09 15	09 19		09 30	09 31	09 49	09 57	10 03	10 12	10 15	10 28	10 31		10 49	10 57	11 03	11 12	11 15	11 28	11 31	11 49
Tamworth	d	09 09				09 36				10 06		10 19	10 29					11 09			11 29				12 06
Burton-on-Trent	d	09 21		09 28		09 48				10 17			10 40					11 21		11 28	11 40				12 17
Derby	a	09 36		09 38		10 00		10 05		10 31		10 37	10 52		10 58			11 36		11 38	11 53		11 58		12 31
Nottingham	a	10 03				10 28				11 03			11 22					12 03			12 22				13 03
Chesterfield	a			10 02								11 02								12 02					
Sheffield	a			10 18				10 48				11 18			11 27					12 18			12 27		
Doncaster	a							11 14							11 52								12 53		
Wakefield Westgate	a			10 45								11 45								12 46					
Leeds	a			11 00								12 00								13 00					
York	a			11 30				11 40				12 30			12 15					13 30			13 15		
Darlington	a			11 59				12 11				12 59			12 43					14 02			13 43		
Durham	a			12 16				12 28				13 15			13 00					14 19			14 00		
Chester-le-Street	a																								
Newcastle	a			12 30				12 42				13 29			13 16					14 32			14 14		
Morpeth	a																			14 47					
Alnmouth for Alnwick	a											13 59													
Berwick-upon-Tweed	a											14 21													
Dunbar	a			13 38																15 40					
Wolverhampton	d		09 14		09 37				09 48		10 14			10 37		10 48			11 14			11 37		11 48	
Stafford	a		09 27						10 03		10 27					11 01			11 27					12 01	
Stoke-on-Trent	a		09 43						10 19		10 43					11 17			11 43					12 17	
Congleton	a																								
Macclesfield	a		10 01						10 36		11 01					11 36			12 01					12 36	
Crewe	a				10 07									11 07								12 07			
Wilmslow	a																								
Stockport	a		10 13						10 49		11 13					11 49			12 13					12 49	
M'chester Piccadilly	a		10 24						11 00		11 24					12 00			12 24					13 00	
Warrington Bank Quay	a				10 26									11 26								12 26			
Wigan North Western	a				10 37									11 37								12 37			
Preston	a				10 51									11 51								12 51			
Lancaster	a				11 10									12 07								13 08			
Oxenholme Lake District	a													12 21								13 21			
Penrith North Lakes	a				11 45																				
Carlisle	a				12 01									13 00								14 00			
Lockerbie	a																								
Haymarket	a													14 11											
Edinburgh	a			14 05								15 03		14 17						16 06					
Haymarket	a											15 15													
Motherwell	a											15 54										14 58			
Glasgow Central	a				13 15							16 12										15 15			
Inverkeithing	a																								
Kirkcaldy	a																								
Markinch	a																								
Ladybank	a																								
Cupar	a																								
Leuchars	a																								
Dundee	a																								
Arbroath	a																								
Montrose	a																								
Stonehaven	a																								
Aberdeen	a																								

A 🛒 from Reading B 🛒 from Bristol Temple Meads C 🛒 from Newton Abbot

Table T051-R

Saturdays
21 December to 16 May

South Coast and the South West - North West England, The North East and Scotland

		XC	XC	XC	VT	XC	XC	XC	XC	XC	XC	VT	XC	XC	XC	XC	XC	VT	XC	XC	XC	XC
		◇1 ✠	◇1 A ✠	1 ✠	◇1 ⊐	◇1 ✠	◇1 ✠	◇1	◇1 ✠	◇1 A ✠	1	◇1 ⊐	◇1 ✠	◇1 ✠	◇1 ✠	◇1 ✠	◇1 B ✠	◇1 ⊐	1	◇1 ✠	◇1 ✠	◇1 ✠
Bournemouth	d	08 47							09 47							10 47						
Brockenhurst	d	09 02							10 02							11 02						
Southampton Central	d	09 18				09 47			10 17							11 20				11 47		
Southampton Airport Pkway	d	09 25				09 54			10 24							11 27				11 54		
Winchester	d	09 34				10 03			10 33							11 36				12 03		
Basingstoke	d	09 51				10 20			10 51							11 51				12 20		
Guildford	d																						
Reading	d	10 15				10 45			11 15				11 45			12 15				12 45		
Oxford	d	10 39				11 10			11 39				12 10			12 39				13 10		
Banbury	d	10 57				11 28			11 57				12 28			12 57				13 28		
Leamington Spa	d	11 15				11 50			12 15				12 50			13 15				13 50		
Coventry	d	11 27			11 42				12 27			12 42				13 27		13 42				
Birmingham International	d	11 38			11 53				12 38			12 53				13 38		13 53				
Penzance	d		06 30														08 33					
St Erth	d		06 38														08 43					
Hayle	d		06 42																			
Camborne	d		06 50														08 53					
Redruth	d		06 57														08 59					
Truro	d		07 08														09 11					
St Austell	d		07 24														09 27					
Par	d		07 31														09 33					
Lostwithiel	d		07 37																			
Bodmin Parkway	d		07 44														09 44					
Liskeard	d		07 56														09 56					
Plymouth	d		08 27							09 27							10 27					
Totnes	d		08 53							09 53							10 53					
Paignton	d													10 12								
Torquay	d													10 18								
Newton Abbot	d		09 06							10 06				10 27			11 06					
Teignmouth	d													10 34								
Dawlish	d													10 39								
Exeter St Davids	d		09 27							10 27				10 53			11 27					
Tiverton Parkway	d		09 41							10 41				11 07			11 41					
Taunton	d		09 53							10 53				11 19			11 53					
Weston-super-Mare	d																						
Cardiff Central	d							10 45							11 45							12 45
Newport (South Wales)	d							11 01							11 58							13 00
Bristol Temple Meads	d		10 34				11 00			11 34				12 00			12 35				13 00	
Bristol Parkway	d		10 44				11 09			11 44				12 09			12 45				13 09	
Gloucester	d							11 48							12 44							13 48
Cheltenham Spa	d		11 16				11 40	11 59		12 16				12 40	12 55		13 16				13 40	13 59
Birmingham New Street	a	11 48	11 56		12 04	12 18	12 25	12 45	12 48	12 56		13 04	13 18	13 25	13 45	13 48	13 56	14 04		14 18	14 25	14 45
Birmingham New Street	d	11 57	12 03	12 12	12 15	12 28	12 31	12 49	12 57	13 03	13 12	13 15	13 28	13 31	13 49	13 57	14 03	14 15	14 19	14 30	14 31	14 49
Tamworth	d		12 19	12 29				13 09			13 29				14 09		14 19		14 36			15 09
Burton-on-Trent	d			12 40				13 21		13 27	13 40				14 20				14 48			15 21
Derby	a		12 37	12 52		12 58		13 35		13 40	13 52		13 58		14 32		14 37		15 00	15 04		15 35
Nottingham	a			13 22				14 03			14 22				15 03				15 28			16 03
Chesterfield	a		13 02							14 02							15 02					
Sheffield	a		13 18			13 27				14 18			14 27				15 18			15 47		
Doncaster	a					13 53							14 53							16 17		
Wakefield Westgate	a		13 45							14 46							15 45					
Leeds	a		14 02							15 00							16 01					
York	a		14 30			14 14				15 30			15 15				16 30			16 40		
Darlington	a		14 59			14 42				15 59			15 43				16 58			17 13		
Durham	a		15 17			14 59				16 17			16 00				17 15			17 30		
Chester-le-Street	a																						
Newcastle	a		15 31			15 15				16 30			16 14				17 29			17 44		
Morpeth	a									16 48												
Alnmouth for Alnwick	a		15 59							17 03							17 59					
Berwick-upon-Tweed	a		16 21														18 20					
Dunbar	a									17 44												
Wolverhampton	d	12 14			12 37		12 48		13 14			13 37		13 48		14 14		14 37			14 48	
Stafford	a	12 27					13 01		13 27					14 01		14 27					15 01	
Stoke-on-Trent	a	12 43					13 17		13 43					14 17		14 43					15 17	
Congleton	a																						
Macclesfield	a	13 01					13 36		14 01					14 36		15 01					15 36	
Crewe	a				13 07							14 07						15 06				
Wilmslow	a																						
Stockport	a	13 13					13 49		14 13					14 49		15 13					15 49	
M'chester Piccadilly	a	13 24					14 00		14 24					15 00		15 24					16 00	
Warrington Bank Quay	a				13 26							14 26						15 26				
Wigan North Western	a				13 37							14 37						15 37				
Preston	a				13 51							14 51						15 51				
Lancaster	a				14 08							15 07						16 08				
Oxenholme Lake District	a											15 21										
Penrith North Lakes	a				14 42													16 44				
Carlisle	a				14 59							16 02						17 00				
Lockerbie	a																						
Haymarket	a				16 15													18 14				
Edinburgh	a		17 05		16 23					18 06							19 02	18 22				
Haymarket	a		17 15							18 15							19 14					
Motherwell	a		17 54														19 53					
Glasgow Central	a		18 11									17 15					20 15					
Inverkeithing	a									18 29												
Kirkcaldy	a									18 43												
Markinch	a									18 53												
Ladybank	a									19 00												
Cupar	a									19 07												
Leuchars	a									19 14												
Dundee	a									19 28												
Arbroath	a									19 48												
Montrose	a									20 02												
Stonehaven	a									20 23												
Aberdeen	a									20 42												

A ✠ to Edinburgh
B ✠ from Plymouth to Edinburgh

NRT DECEMBER 19 EDITION

Table T051-R

Saturdays
21 December to 16 May

South Coast and the South West - North West England, The North East and Scotland

		XC	XC	VT	XC	XC	XC	XC	XC	XC	VT	XC	XC	XC	XC	XC	XC	VT	XC	XC	XC	XC	XC
		◇1 ✠	◇1 A ✠	◇1 ⊐	1	◇1 ✠	◇1 ✠	◇1 ✠	◇1 ✠	◇1 A ✠	■ 1 ⊐	1	◇1 ✠	◇1 ✠	◇1 B ✠	◇1 ✠	◇1 C ✠	■ 1 ⊐	1	◇1 ✠	◇1 ✠	◇1 B ✠	◇1 ✠
Bournemouth	d	11 47							12 47							13 47							14 47
Brockenhurst	d	12 02							13 02							14 02							15 02
Southampton Central	d	12 20							13 20				13 47			14 20							15 20
Southampton Airport Pkway	d	12 27							13 27				13 54			14 27							15 27
Winchester	d	12 36							13 36				14 03			14 36							15 36
Basingstoke	d	12 51							13 51				14 20			14 51							15 51
Guildford	d																							
Reading	d	13 15				13 45			14 15				14 45			15 15				15 45			16 15
Oxford	d	13 39				14 10			14 39				15 10			15 39				16 10			16 39
Banbury	d	13 57				14 28			14 57				15 28			15 57				16 28			16 57
Leamington Spa	d	14 15				14 50			15 15				15 50			16 15				16 50			17 15
Coventry	d	14 27		14 42					15 27		15 42					16 27		16 42					17 27
Birmingham International	d	14 38		14 53					15 38		15 53					16 38		16 53					17 38
Penzance	d						09 43																
St Erth	d						09 51																
Hayle	d																							
Camborne	d						10 01																
Redruth	d						10 08																
Truro	d						10 19																
St Austell	d						10 35																
Par	d						10 42																
Lostwithiel	d						10 48																
Bodmin Parkway	d						10 55																
Liskeard	d						11 14																
Plymouth	d		11 27				11 50			12 27							13 27						
Totnes	d		11 53				12 16			12 53							13 53						
Paignton	d																				13 57		
Torquay	d																				14 03		
Newton Abbot	d		12 06				12 28			13 06							14 06				14 13		
Teignmouth	d																				14 20		
Dawlish	d																				14 26		
Exeter St Davids	d		12 27				12 53			13 27							14 27				14 40		
Tiverton Parkway	d		12 41				13 07			13 41							14 41				14 53		
Taunton	d		12 53				13 20			13 53							14 53				15 06		
Weston-super-Mare	d																				15 27		
Cardiff Central	d							13 45							14 45							15 45	
Newport (South Wales)	d							13 59							14 59							15 59	
Bristol Temple Meads	d		13 35				14 00			14 34				15 00			15 34				16 00		
Bristol Parkway	d		13 45				14 09			14 44				15 09			15 44				16 10		
Gloucester	d							14 48							15 48							16 48	
Cheltenham Spa	d		14 16				14 40	14 59		15 16				15 40	15 59		16 16				16 41	16 59	
Birmingham New Street	a	14 48	14 56	15 04		15 18	15 25	15 45	15 48	15 56	16 05		16 18	16 25	16 45	16 48	16 56	17 05		17 18	17 25	17 45	17 48
Birmingham New Street	d	14 57	15 03	15 15	15 19	15 30	15 31	15 49	15 57	16 03	16 15	16 19	16 30	16 31	16 49	16 57	17 03	17 15	17 19	17 30	17 31	17 49	17 57
Tamworth	d				15 36			16 09		16 19		16 36			17 09				17 36			18 09	
Burton-on-Trent	d		15 27		15 48			16 21				16 48	16 54		17 21		17 27		17 47			18 21	
Derby	a		15 40		16 00	16 05		16 36		16 39		17 00	17 05		17 35		17 40		17 59	18 05		18 35	
Nottingham	a				16 28			17 03				17 31			18 03				18 31			19 03	
Chesterfield	a		16 02							17 03							18 02						
Sheffield	a		16 18			16 47				17 18			17 47				18 18			18 46			
Doncaster	a					17 13														19 13			
Wakefield Westgate	a		16 45							17 47			18 18				18 49						
Leeds	a		17 00							18 01			18 36				19 03						
York	a		17 30			17 42				18 30			19 04				19 30			19 41			
Darlington	a		17 59			18 17				19 00			19 32				20 04			20 13			
Durham	a		18 15			18 34				19 18			19 48				20 21			20 30			
Chester-le-Street	a																							
Newcastle	a		18 33			18 47				19 33			20 02				20 35			20 44			
Morpeth	a																20 50						
Alnmouth for Alnwick	a									20 01													
Berwick-upon-Tweed	a		19 22							20 25							21 23						
Dunbar	a		19 45														21 45						
Wolverhampton	d	15 14		15 36			15 48		16 14		16 37			16 48		17 14		17 37			17 48		18 14
Stafford	a	15 27					16 01		16 27					17 01		17 27					18 01		18 27
Stoke-on-Trent	a	15 43					16 17		16 43					17 17		17 43					18 17		18 43
Congleton	a																							
Macclesfield	a	16 01					16 36		17 01					17 36		18 01					18 36		19 01
Crewe	a			16 06							17 07							18 07					
Wilmslow	a																							
Stockport	a	16 13					16 49		17 13					17 49		18 13					18 49		19 13
M'chester Piccadilly	a	16 24					17 00		17 24					18 00		18 24					19 01		19 24
Warrington Bank Quay	a			16 26							17 26							18 25					
Wigan North Western	a			16 37							17 37							18 37					
Preston	a			16 51							17 51							18 51					
Lancaster	a			17 08							18 08							19 08					
Oxenholme Lake District	a			17 22							18 21							19 23					
Penrith North Lakes	a										18 48												
Carlisle	a			18 01							19 04							20 02					
Lockerbie	a																							
Haymarket	a										20 17												
Edinburgh	a		20 08							21 09	20 22						22 08						
Haymarket	a		20 16							21 15													
Motherwell	a									21 56													
Glasgow Central	a			19 15						22 20								21 15					
Inverkeithing	a		20 31																				
Kirkcaldy	a		20 51																				
Markinch	a		21 03																				
Ladybank	a		21 11																				
Cupar	a		21 18																				
Leuchars	a		21 26																				
Dundee	a		21 43																				
Arbroath	a																							
Montrose	a																							
Stonehaven	a																							
Aberdeen	a																							

A ✠ to Edinburgh
B ✠ to Birmingham New Street
C ✠ to Newcastle

South Coast and the South West - North West England, The North East and Scotland

	XC ◇1 A ⌶	XC 1	VT ◇1	XC ◇1 ⌶	XC ◇1 ⌶	XC ◇1 B ⌶	XC ◇1 ⌶	XC ◇1 C ⌶	VT ◇1	XC 1	XC ◇1 ⌶	XC ◇1 ⌶	XC ◇1 B ⌶	XC ◇1 B ⌶	XC ◇1 B ⌶	VT ◇1	XC ◇1 B ⌶	XC ◇1 B ⌶	XC ◇1	XC ◇1 B ⌶	XC ◇1 B ⌶
Bournemouth d							15 47							16 47						17 47	
Brockenhurst 3 d							16 02							17 02						18 02	
Southampton Central d				15 47			16 20							17 20			17 47			18 20	
Southampton Airport Pkway d				15 54			16 27							17 27			17 54			18 27	
Winchester d				16 03			16 36							17 36			18 03			18 36	
Basingstoke d				16 20			16 51							17 51			18 20			18 51	
Guildford d																					
Reading 7 d				16 45			17 15				17 45			18 15			18 45			19 15	
Oxford d				17 10			17 39				18 10			18 39			19 10			19 39	
Banbury d				17 28			17 57				18 28			18 57			19 28			19 57	
Leamington Spa 8 d				17 50			18 15				18 50			19 15			19 50			20 15	
Coventry d			17 42				18 27		18 42					19 27		19 42				20 27	
Birmingham International d			17 53				18 38		18 53					19 38		19 53				20 38	
Penzance d																					
St Erth d																					
Hayle d																					
Camborne d																					
Redruth d																					
Truro d																					
St Austell d																					
Par d																					
Lostwithiel d																					
Bodmin Parkway d																					
Liskeard 6 d																					
Plymouth d	14 27							15 27							16 27						17 27
Totnes d	14 53							15 53							16 53						17 53
Paignton d																					
Torquay d																					
Newton Abbot d	15 06							16 06							17 06						18 06
Teignmouth d																					
Dawlish d																					
Exeter St Davids 6 d	15 27							16 27				16 45			17 27						18 27
Tiverton Parkway d	15 41							16 41				16 59			17 41						18 41
Taunton d	15 53							16 53				17 12			17 53						18 53
Weston-super-Mare d																					
Cardiff Central 7 d						16 45							17 45						18 45		
Newport (South Wales) d						16 58							17 58						18 58		
Bristol Temple Meads 10 d	16 34				17 00			17 34				18 00			18 34			19 00			19 32
Bristol Parkway 7 d	16 44				17 09			17 44				18 09			18 44			19 09			19 42
Gloucester 7 d						17 48							18 44						19 48		
Cheltenham Spa d	17 16				17 40	17 59		18 16				18 40	18 55		19 16			19 40	19 59		20 12
Birmingham New Street 12 a	17 56		18 04	18 18	18 25	18 45	18 48	18 56	19 05		19 18	19 25	19 45	19 48	19 56	20 06	20 18	20 25	20 45	20 48	20 52
Birmingham New Street 12 d	18 03	18 12	18 15	18 28	18 31	18 49	18 57	19 03	19 15	19 19	19 30	19 31	19 49	19 57	20 03	20 15	20 30	20 31	20 49	20 57	21 03
Tamworth d	18 19	18 29				19 09				19 36			20 09		20 19				21 09		21 19
Burton-on-Trent d		18 40				19 21		19 27		19 47			20 21						21 21		21 30
Derby 6 a	18 40	18 52		18 58		19 32		19 39		20 00	20 03		20 35		20 40		21 23		21 35		21 41
Nottingham 8 a		19 22				20 03				20 28			21 03						22 13		
Chesterfield a	19 02							20 03			20 33				21 04		21 46				22 07
Sheffield 7 a	19 18			19 27				20 18			20 47				21 19		21 59				22 23
Doncaster 7 a				19 53							21 17						22 26				22 50
Wakefield Westgate 7 a	19 46							20 47							21 47						23 12
Leeds 10 a	20 05							21 02							22 02						23 26
York 8 a	20 30			20 15				21 46			21 41						22 47				
Darlington 7 a	20 59			20 43							22 13										
Durham a	21 16			21 00							22 32										
Chester-le-Street a																					
Newcastle 8 a	21 29			21 16							22 46										
Morpeth a																					
Alnmouth for Alnwick a	21 59																				
Berwick-upon-Tweed a																					
Dunbar a																					
Wolverhampton 7 d			18 37		18 48		19 14		19 37			19 48		20 14		20 37		20 48		21 18	
Stafford a					19 01		19 27					20 01		20 27		20 51		21 01		21 31	
Stoke-on-Trent a					19 17		19 43					20 17		20 43				21 17		21 47	
Congleton a																					
Macclesfield a					19 36		20 01					20 36		21 01				21 36		22 05	
Crewe 10 a			19 07						20 07							21 09					
Wilmslow a																					
Stockport a					19 49		20 13					20 49		21 13				21 49		22 17	
M'chester Piccadilly 10 a					20 00		20 24					20 59		21 24				22 00		22 33	
Warrington Bank Quay a			19 26						20 26												
Wigan North Western a			19 37						20 37												
Preston 8 a			19 52						20 52												
Lancaster 6 a																					
Oxenholme Lake District a																					
Penrith North Lakes a																					
Carlisle 8 a																					
Lockerbie a																					
Haymarket a																					
Edinburgh 10 a	23 00																				
Haymarket a																					
Motherwell a																					
Glasgow Central 15 a																					
Inverkeithing a																					
Kirkcaldy a																					
Markinch a																					
Ladybank a																					
Cupar a																					
Leuchars 3 a																					
Dundee a																					
Arbroath a																					
Montrose a																					
Stonehaven a																					
Aberdeen a																					

A ⌶ to Newcastle B ⌶ to Birmingham New Street C ⌶ to Leeds

South Coast and the South West - North West England, The North East and Scotland

	XC ◇1	XC ◇1	XC ◇1 A ⌶	XC ◇1 B ⌶	XC ◇1	XC ◇1	XC ◇1	XC ◇1	XC ◇1	XC 1	XC ◇1
Bournemouth d			18 47						19 47		
Brockenhurst 3 d			19 02						20 02		
Southampton Central d			19 20						20 20		
Southampton Airport Pkway d			19 27						20 27		
Winchester d			19 36						20 36		
Basingstoke d			19 51						20 51		
Guildford d											
Reading 7 d	19 45		20 15			20 45			21 15		21 45
Oxford d	20 11		20 39			21 10			21 39		22 10
Banbury d	20 29		20 57			21 28			21 57		22 28
Leamington Spa 8 d	20 50		21 15			21 50			22 15		22 50
Coventry d			21 27			22 02			22 27		
Birmingham International d			21 38			22 12			22 38		
Penzance d											
St Erth d											
Hayle d											
Camborne d											
Redruth d											
Truro d											
St Austell d											
Par d											
Lostwithiel d											
Bodmin Parkway d											
Liskeard 6 d											
Plymouth d				18 27							
Totnes d				18 53							
Paignton d											
Torquay d											
Newton Abbot d				19 06							
Teignmouth d											
Dawlish d											
Exeter St Davids 6 d				19 27							
Tiverton Parkway d				19 41							
Taunton d				19 53							
Weston-super-Mare d											
Cardiff Central 7 d					20 00			20 48			
Newport (South Wales) d					20 13			21 01			
Bristol Temple Meads 10 d		20 00		20 30							
Bristol Parkway 7 d		20 09		20 41							
Gloucester 7 d					21 06			21 48			
Cheltenham Spa d		20 40		21 11	21 17			21 59			
Birmingham New Street 12 a	21 18	21 36	21 48	21 51	22 07	22 22		22 45	22 48		23 18
Birmingham New Street 12 d			21 57		22 10		22 31			22 49	
Tamworth d					22 27					23 08	
Burton-on-Trent d					22 39					23 20	
Derby 6 a					22 53					23 33	
Nottingham 8 a					23 27						
Chesterfield a											
Sheffield 7 a											
Doncaster 7 a											
Wakefield Westgate 7 a											
Leeds 10 a											
York 8 a											
Darlington 7 a											
Durham a											
Chester-le-Street a											
Newcastle 8 a											
Morpeth a											
Alnmouth for Alnwick a											
Berwick-upon-Tweed a											
Dunbar a											
Wolverhampton 7 d			22 14				22 48				
Stafford a			22 27				23 01				
Stoke-on-Trent a			22 43				23 17				
Congleton a											
Macclesfield a			23 01				23 38				
Crewe 10 a											
Wilmslow a											
Stockport a			23 13				23 53				
M'chester Piccadilly 10 a			23 29				00 10				
Warrington Bank Quay a											
Wigan North Western a											
Preston 8 a											
Lancaster 6 a											
Oxenholme Lake District a											
Penrith North Lakes a											
Carlisle 8 a											
Lockerbie a											
Haymarket a											
Edinburgh 10 a											
Haymarket a											
Motherwell a											
Glasgow Central 15 a											
Inverkeithing a											
Kirkcaldy a											
Markinch a											
Ladybank a											
Cupar a											
Leuchars 3 a											
Dundee a											
Arbroath a											
Montrose a											
Stonehaven a											
Aberdeen a											

A ⌶ to Birmingham New Street B ⌶ to Bristol Temple Meads

Table T051-R

Sundays

15 December to 10 May

South Coast and the South West - North West England, The North East and Scotland

		VT	XC	XC	VT	XC	XC	VT	XC	XC	XC	VT	XC	XC	XC	VT	XC	XC	XC	XC	VT	XC	XC
							A		B	C								D		A			
Bournemouth	d																		09 40				
Brockenhurst 3	d																		09 55				
Southampton Central	d													09 20					10 20				
Southampton Airport Pkway	d													09 27					10 27				
Winchester	d													09 36					10 36				
Basingstoke	d													09 51					10 51				
Guildford	d																						
Reading 7	d								09 15	09 15				10 15					11 15				
Oxford	d								09 39	09 39				10 39					11 39				
Banbury	d								09 57	09 57				10 57					11 57				
Leamington Spa 8	d								10 15	10 15				11 15					12 15				
Coventry	d								10 27	10 27				11 27					12 27				
Birmingham International	d								10 38	10 38				11 38					12 38				
Penzance	d																						
St Erth	d																						
Hayle	d																						
Camborne	d																						
Redruth	d																						
Truro	d																						
St Austell	d																						
Par	d																						
Lostwithiel	d																						
Bodmin Parkway	d																						
Liskeard 6	d																						
Plymouth	d																			09 25			
Totnes	d																			09 51			
Paignton	d																						
Torquay	d																						
Newton Abbot	d																			10 04			
Teignmouth	d																						
Dawlish	d																						
Exeter St Davids 6	d																			10 27			
Tiverton Parkway	d																			10 41			
Taunton	d																			10 53			
Weston-super-Mare	d																						
Cardiff Central 7	d																	10 45					
Newport (South Wales)	d																	10 58					
Bristol Temple Meads 10	d										09 15				10 29					11 29			
Bristol Parkway 7	d										09 24				10 39					11 39			
Gloucester 7	d										10 01							11 48					
Cheltenham Spa	d										10 11				11 11			11 59		12 11			
Birmingham New Street 12	a								10 49	10 49	10 49			11 49	11 50			12 45	12 49	12 49			
Birmingham New Street 12	d	08 45	09 01	09 03	09 20	10 01	10 03	10 20	11 01	11 01	11 03	11 20	11 49	11 57	12 03	12 20	12 30	12 49	12 57	13 03	13 20	13 30	13 31
Tamworth	d			09 19			10 19						12 07		12 19			13 07					
Burton-on-Trent	d			09 28			10 29				11 26		12 19					13 19		13 26			
Derby 6	a			09 40			10 40				11 36		12 32		12 37		13 00	13 33		13 36		14 00	
Nottingham 8	a												13 00					13 58					
Chesterfield	a			10 02			11 02				12 03				13 02		13 28			14 02		14 28	
Sheffield 7	a			10 18			11 18				12 18				13 18		13 44			14 17		14 43	
Doncaster 7	a																14 14					15 18	
Wakefield Westgate 7	a			10 45			11 45				12 45				13 45					14 45			
Leeds 10	a			10 59			11 59				13 00				14 00					15 00			
York 8	a			11 29			12 30				13 28				14 29		14 40			15 29		15 41	
Darlington 7	a			11 57			12 58				13 57				14 57		15 16			15 57		16 11	
Durham	a			12 14			13 15				14 13				15 14		15 33			16 14		16 28	
Chester-le-Street	a																						
Newcastle 8	a			12 27			13 28				14 27				15 27		15 46			16 27		16 42	
Morpeth	a										14 43												
Alnmouth for Alnwick	a						13 55								15 53					16 55			
Berwick-upon-Tweed	a						14 16								16 14								
Dunbar	a			13 35							15 36									17 37			
Wolverhampton 7	d	09 04	09 18		09 37	10 18		10 37	11 18	11 18		11 37		12 15		12 37			13 14		13 37		13 48
Stafford	a	09 18	09 31			10 31			11 31	11 31				12 29					13 27				14 01
Stoke-on-Trent	a		09 51			10 48			11 48	11 48				12 45					13 43				14 17
Congleton	a																						
Macclesfield	a		10 09			11 08			12 08	12 08				13 04					14 04				14 36
Crewe 10	a	09 36			10 07			11 10				12 07				13 07					14 06		
Wilmslow	a																						
Stockport	a		10 22			11 22			12 24	12 24				13 16					14 16				14 50
M'chester Piccadilly 10	a		10 38			11 33			12 40	12 42				13 28					14 29				14 59
Warrington Bank Quay	a	09 54			10 26			11 28				12 26				13 26					14 25		
Wigan North Western	a	10 05			10 37			11 39				12 37				13 37					14 37		
Preston 8	a	10 21			10 52			11 53				12 51				13 52					14 51		
Lancaster 6	a				11 16			12 09				13 07				14 09					15 09		
Oxenholme Lake District	a				11 32			12 23				13 21									15 23		
Penrith North Lakes	a															14 45							
Carlisle 8	a				12 10			13 02				14 00				15 01					16 01		
Lockerbie	a																						
Haymarket	a							14 16								16 13							
Edinburgh 10	a			13 58			15 00	14 21			15 59				16 57	16 20				17 59			
Haymarket	a						15 13								17 14					18 16			
Motherwell	a						15 55								17 52								
Glasgow Central 15	a				13 27		16 12					15 15			18 13						17 15		
Inverkeithing	a																			18 30			
Kirkcaldy	a																			18 45			
Markinch	a																			18 55			
Ladybank	a																			19 02			
Cupar	a																			19 09			
Leuchars 3	a																			19 16			
Dundee	a																			19 30			
Arbroath	a																			19 50			
Montrose	a																			20 04			
Stonehaven	a																			20 25			
Aberdeen	a																			20 43			

A to Edinburgh
B from 5 April
C until 29 March
D from Birmingham New Street

NRT DECEMBER 19 EDITION

Table T051-R

Sundays

15 December to 10 May

South Coast and the South West - North West England, The North East and Scotland

		XC	XC	XC	VT	XC	XC	XC	XC	XC	VT	XC	XC	XC	XC	XC	VT	XC	XC	XC	XC	XC	VT
		A		B		C				D						B							
Bournemouth	d		10 40						11 40						12 40						13 40		
Brockenhurst 3	d		10 55						11 55						12 55						13 55		
Southampton Central	d		11 20						12 20						13 20						14 20		
Southampton Airport Pkway	d		11 27						12 27						13 27						14 27		
Winchester	d		11 36						12 36						13 36						14 36		
Basingstoke	d		11 51						12 51						13 51						14 51		
Guildford	d					12 14																	
Reading 7	d		12 15			12 52			13 15			13 42			14 15			14 42			15 15		
Oxford	d		12 40			13 16			13 39			14 06			14 39			15 06			15 39		
Banbury	d		12 58			13 34			13 57			14 24			14 57			15 24			15 57		
Leamington Spa 8	d		13 16			13 52			14 15			14 42			15 15			15 42			16 15		
Coventry	d		13 28		13 42				14 27		14 43	14 54			15 27		15 42	15 54			16 27		16 42
Birmingham International	d		13 38		13 53				14 38		14 54	15 04			15 38		15 53	16 04			16 38		16 53
Penzance	d									09 30													
St Erth	d									09 38													
Hayle	d																						
Camborne	d									09 48													
Redruth	d									09 55													
Truro	d									10 08													
St Austell	d									10 24													
Par	d									10 30													
Lostwithiel	d																						
Bodmin Parkway	d									10 41													
Liskeard 6	d									10 55													
Plymouth	d			10 25						11 27			12 00			12 27			12 53			13 25	
Totnes	d			10 51						11 53						12 53						13 51	
Paignton	d						10 50																
Torquay	d						10 56																
Newton Abbot	d			11 04			11 08			12 06			12 38			13 06			13 30			14 04	
Teignmouth	d						11 15																
Dawlish	d						11 20																
Exeter St Davids 6	d			11 27			11 34			12 27			13 00			13 27			13 54			14 27	
Tiverton Parkway	d			11 41			11 48			12 41			13 13			13 41						14 41	
Taunton	d			11 53			12 00			12 53			13 26			13 53						14 53	
Weston-super-Mare	d						12 22																
Cardiff Central 7	d	11 45						12 45						13 45						14 45			
Newport (South Wales)	d	11 58						12 58						14 00						14 58			
Bristol Temple Meads 10	d			12 29			13 00			13 29			14 00			14 29			15 00			15 29	
Bristol Parkway 7	d			12 39			13 09			13 39			14 09			14 39			15 09			15 39	
Gloucester 7	d	12 48						13 48						14 48						15 48			
Cheltenham Spa	d	12 59		13 11			13 40	13 59		14 11			14 40	14 59		15 11			15 40	15 59		16 11	
Birmingham New Street 12	a	13 45	13 48	13 49	14 05	14 18	14 18	14 45	14 48	14 49	15 05	15 14	15 18	15 45	15 48	15 52	16 05	16 14	16 18	16 45	16 48	16 49	17 04
Birmingham New Street 12	d	13 49	13 57	14 03	14 15	14 30	14 31	14 49	14 57	15 03	15 15	15 30	15 31	15 49	15 57	16 03	16 15	16 30	16 31	16 49	16 57	17 03	17 15
Tamworth	d	14 07		14 20				15 09						16 07		16 19				17 07			
Burton-on-Trent	d	14 19						15 21		15 25				16 19						17 20		17 25	
Derby 6	a	14 32		14 38		15 00		15 34		15 39		16 00		16 34		16 39		17 00		17 33		17 37	
Nottingham 8	a	15 00						16 00						16 59						17 59			
Chesterfield	a			15 00						16 01						17 03						18 05	
Sheffield 7	a			15 18		15 45				16 18		16 41				17 19		17 43				18 18	
Doncaster 7	a					16 12						17 14						18 14					
Wakefield Westgate 7	a			15 45						16 45						17 46		18 32				18 45	
Leeds 10	a			16 00						16 59						18 01		18 47				19 01	
York 8	a			16 29		16 37				17 29		17 40				18 29		19 18				19 30	
Darlington 7	a			16 57		17 10				17 57		18 09				18 59		19 48				19 59	
Durham	a			17 13		17 27				18 14		18 26				19 16		20 05				20 16	
Chester-le-Street	a																						
Newcastle 8	a			17 27		17 41				18 27		18 41				19 30		20 20				20 29	
Morpeth	a			17 41																		20 49	
Alnmouth for Alnwick	a			17 55												19 57							
Berwick-upon-Tweed	a			18 17						19 11						20 20						21 22	
Dunbar	a									19 34												21 44	
Wolverhampton 7	d		14 14		14 37		14 48		15 14		15 37		15 48		16 14		16 37		16 48		17 14		17 37
Stafford	a		14 27				15 01		15 27				16 01		16 27				17 01		17 27		
Stoke-on-Trent	a		14 43				15 17		15 45				16 17		16 46				17 17		17 46		
Congleton	a																						
Macclesfield	a		15 01				15 36		16 04				16 36		17 04				17 36		18 04		
Crewe 10	a				15 07						16 08						17 07						18 07
Wilmslow	a																						
Stockport	a		15 14				15 50		16 16				16 50		17 16				17 50		18 16		
M'chester Piccadilly 10	a		15 24				15 59		16 29				16 59		17 29				17 59		18 29		
Warrington Bank Quay	a				15 26						16 26						17 26						18 26
Wigan North Western	a				15 37						16 37						17 37						18 37
Preston 8	a				15 52						16 51						17 52						18 52
Lancaster 6	a				16 08						17 07						18 08						19 08
Oxenholme Lake District	a										17 21						18 22						19 21
Penrith North Lakes	a				16 44												18 48						
Carlisle 8	a				17 00						18 01						19 04						20 00
Lockerbie	a																						
Haymarket	a				18 11												20 16						
Edinburgh 10	a			18 59	18 20					19 59						21 03	20 22					22 06	
Haymarket	a			19 22												21 16							
Motherwell	a			20 01												21 55							
Glasgow Central 15	a			20 20							19 13					22 12							21 12
Inverkeithing	a																						
Kirkcaldy	a																						
Markinch	a																						
Ladybank	a																						
Cupar	a																						
Leuchars 3	a																						
Dundee	a																						
Arbroath	a																						
Montrose	a																						
Stonehaven	a																						
Aberdeen	a																						

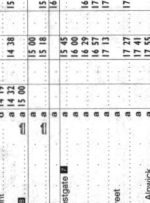

A from Birmingham New Street
B to Edinburgh
C from Reading
D from Plymouth

Table T051-R

Sundays

15 December to 10 May

South Coast and the South West - North West England, The North East and Scotland

		XC	XC	XC	XC	XC	VT	XC	XC	XC	XC	XC	VT	XC	XC	XC	XC	XC	VT	XC	XC	XC
		◇■	◇■	◇■	◇■	◇■	◇■	◇■	◇■	◇■	◇■	◇■	■ ■	◇■	◇■	◇■	◇■	◇■	◇■	◇■	◇■	◇■
		A		B		A		C	D	B		E		B		B	B	B				B
		⊼	⊼	⊼	⊼	⊼	⊡	⊼	⊼	⊼	⊼	⊼	⊡	⊼	⊼	⊼	⊼	⊼	⊡	⊼	⊼	⊼
Bournemouth	d				14 40						15 40						16 40					
Brockenhurst	d				14 55						15 55						16 55					
Southampton Central	d				15 20						16 20						17 20					
Southampton Airport Pkway	d				15 27						16 27						17 27					
Winchester	d				15 36						16 36						17 36					
Basingstoke	d				15 51						16 51						17 51					
Guildford	d																					
Reading	d	15 42			16 15			16 42			17 15			17 42			18 15			18 42		
Oxford	d	16 06			16 39			17 06			17 39			18 06			18 39			19 06		
Banbury	d	16 24			16 57			17 24			17 57			18 24			18 57			19 24		
Leamington Spa	d	16 42			17 15			17 42			18 15			18 42			19 15			19 42		
Coventry	d	16 54			17 27		17 42	17 54			18 27		18 42	18 54			19 27		19 42	19 54		
Birmingham International	d	17 04			17 38		17 53	18 04			18 38		18 53	19 04			19 38		19 53	20 04		
Penzance	d								12 35													
St Erth	d								12 43													
Hayle	d								12 47													
Camborne	d								12 55													
Redruth	d								13 02													
Truro	d								13 13													
St Austell	d								13 30													
Par	d								13 36													
Lostwithiel	d								13 43													
Bodmin Parkway	d								13 50													
Liskeard	d								14 02													
Plymouth	d					14 25			14 34			15 27						16 25				
Totnes	d					14 51			15 00			15 53						16 51				
Paignton	d																					
Torquay	d																					
Newton Abbot	d					15 04			15 13			16 06						17 04				
Teignmouth	d																					
Dawlish	d																					
Exeter St Davids	d					15 27			15 34			16 27						17 27				
Tiverton Parkway	d					15 41			15 47			16 41						17 41				
Taunton	d					15 53			16 00			16 53						17 53				
Weston-super-Mare	d								16 30													
Cardiff Central	d			15 45						16 45						17 45						18 45
Newport (South Wales)	d			15 58						16 59						17 58						18 59
Bristol Temple Meads	d		16 00			16 29			17 00			17 29			18 00			18 29			19 00	
Bristol Parkway	d		16 09			16 39			17 09			17 39			18 09			18 39			19 09	
Gloucester	d			16 48						17 48						18 48						19 48
Cheltenham Spa	d		16 40	16 59		17 11			17 40	17 59		18 11			18 40	18 59		19 11			19 40	19 59
Birmingham New Street	a	17 14	17 18	17 45	17 48	17 50	18 05	18 14	18 18	18 45	18 48	18 50	19 04	19 14	19 19	19 45	19 48	19 50	20 05	20 14	20 27	20 45
Birmingham New Street	d	17 30	17 31	17 49	17 57	18 03	18 15	18 30	18 31	18 49	18 57	19 03	19 15	19 30	19 31	19 49	19 57	20 03	20 15		20 31	20 49
Tamworth	d			18 07		18 19				19 09						20 07		20 19				21 06
Burton-on-Trent	d			18 20						19 21		19 26				20 19						21 19
Derby	a	18 00		18 34		18 39		19 00		19 34		19 39		20 00		20 34		20 39				21 34
Nottingham	a			19 00						20 00						21 00						22 00
Chesterfield	a					19 04						20 02						21 03				
Sheffield	a	18 40				19 20		19 41				20 18		20 41				21 18				
Doncaster	a	19 14						20 14						21 20								
Wakefield Westgate	a					19 49						20 47						21 48				
Leeds	a					20 07						21 02						22 02				
York	a	19 43				20 30		20 42				21 31		21 44								
Darlington	a	20 20				21 00		21 13						22 24								
Durham	a	20 37				21 17		21 31						22 41								
Chester-le-Street	a																					
Newcastle	a	20 50				21 31		21 45						23 10								
Morpeth	a																					
Alnmouth for Alnwick	a					21 59																
Berwick-upon-Tweed	a																					
Dunbar	a																					
Wolverhampton	d		17 48		18 14		18 37		18 48		19 14		19 37		19 48		20 14		20 37		20 52	
Stafford	a		18 01		18 27				19 01		19 27				20 01		20 28		20 51		21 05	
Stoke-on-Trent	a		18 17		18 44				19 17		19 45				20 19		20 44				21 21	
Congleton	a																					
Macclesfield	a		18 36		19 04				19 36		20 04				20 36		21 03				21 39	
Crewe	a						19 07						20 07						21 10			
Wilmslow	a																					
Stockport	a		18 50		19 17				19 50		20 16				20 50		21 15				21 52	
M'chester Piccadilly	a		18 59		19 29				19 59		20 28				21 00		21 29				22 02	
Warrington Bank Quay	a						19 26						20 26									
Wigan North Western	a						19 37						20 37									
Preston	a						19 52						20 52									
Lancaster	a						20 08						21 09									
Oxenholme Lake District	a												21 23									
Penrith North Lakes	a						20 45															
Carlisle	a						20 59						22 01									
Lockerbie	a												22 20									
Haymarket	a						22 14															
Edinburgh	a	22 18				23 03	22 19															
Haymarket	a																					
Motherwell	a												23 04									
Glasgow Central	a												23 21									
Inverkeithing	a																					
Kirkcaldy	a																					
Markinch	a																					
Ladybank	a																					
Cupar	a																					
Leuchars	a																					
Dundee	a																					
Arbroath	a																					
Montrose	a																					
Stonehaven	a																					
Aberdeen	a																					

A ⊼ to Newcastle
B ⊼ to Birmingham New Street
C ⊼ to Sheffield
D ⊼ from Plymouth
E ⊼ to Leeds

Sundays

15 December to 10 May

South Coast and the South West - North West England, The North East and Scotland

		XC	XC	VT	XC	XC	XC	XC	XC	XC	XC	XC	XC	XC
		◇■	◇■	◇■	◇■	◇■	◇■	◇■	◇■	◇■	◇■	◇■	◇■	◇■
		A	B			C		D	C					
		⊼	⊼	⊡		⊼		⊼	⊼					
Bournemouth	d	17 40						18 40			19 40			
Brockenhurst	d	17 55						18 55			19 55			
Southampton Central	d	18 20						19 20			20 20			
Southampton Airport Pkway	d	18 27						19 27			20 27			
Winchester	d	18 36						19 36			20 36			
Basingstoke	d	18 51						19 51			20 51			
Guildford	d													
Reading	d	19 15			19 39			20 15		20 42	21 12		21 42	
Oxford	d	19 39			20 06			20 39		21 06	21 36		22 06	
Banbury	d	19 57			20 24			20 57		21 24	21 54		22 24	
Leamington Spa	d	20 15			20 42			21 15		21 42	22 12		22 42	
Coventry	d	20 27		20 42	20 54			21 27		21 54	22 24		22 54	
Birmingham International	d	20 38		20 53	21 04			21 38		22 04	22 34		23 04	
Penzance	d		15 35											
St Erth	d		15 43											
Hayle	d													
Camborne	d		15 53											
Redruth	d		15 59											
Truro	d		16 11											
St Austell	d		16 27											
Par	d		16 33											
Lostwithiel	d													
Bodmin Parkway	d		16 44											
Liskeard	d		16 56											
Plymouth	d		17 27						18 27					
Totnes	d		17 53						18 53					
Paignton	d					18 20								
Torquay	d					18 26								
Newton Abbot	d		18 06			18 35			19 06					
Teignmouth	d													
Dawlish	d													
Exeter St Davids	d		18 27			18 58			19 27					
Tiverton Parkway	d		18 41			19 11			19 41					
Taunton	d		18 53			19 24			19 53					
Weston-super-Mare	d													
Cardiff Central	d						19 45					20 45		
Newport (South Wales)	d						20 01					20 59		
Bristol Temple Meads	d		19 31			20 00			20 29					22 10
Bristol Parkway	d		19 40			20 09			20 39					22 19
Gloucester	d						20 48					21 48		
Cheltenham Spa	d		20 11			20 40	20 59		21 11			21 59		22 50
Birmingham New Street	a	20 48	20 54	21 05	21 15	21 18	21 45	21 48	21 50	22 14	22 44	22 45	23 14	23 39
Birmingham New Street	d	20 57	21 03	21 15				21 57	22 03					
Tamworth	d		21 19						22 19					
Burton-on-Trent	d		21 29											
Derby	a		21 40						22 39					
Nottingham	a													
Chesterfield	a		22 02						23 02					
Sheffield	a		22 18						23 18					
Doncaster	a													
Wakefield Westgate	a		22 48											
Leeds	a		23 02						00 09					
York	a													
Darlington	a													
Durham	a													
Chester-le-Street	a													
Newcastle	a													
Morpeth	a													
Alnmouth for Alnwick	a													
Berwick-upon-Tweed	a													
Dunbar	a													
Wolverhampton	d	21 14		21 37				22 14						
Stafford	a	21 27		21 55				22 27						
Stoke-on-Trent	a	21 44						22 43						
Congleton	a													
Macclesfield	a	22 03						23 01						
Crewe	a			22 16										
Wilmslow	a													
Stockport	a	22 15						23 14						
M'chester Piccadilly	a	22 26						23 24						
Warrington Bank Quay	a			22 36										
Wigan North Western	a			22 47										
Preston	a			23 02										
Lancaster	a													
Oxenholme Lake District	a													
Penrith North Lakes	a													
Carlisle	a													
Lockerbie	a													
Haymarket	a													
Edinburgh	a													
Haymarket	a													
Motherwell	a													
Glasgow Central	a													
Inverkeithing	a													
Kirkcaldy	a													
Markinch	a													
Ladybank	a													
Cupar	a													
Leuchars	a													
Dundee	a													
Arbroath	a													
Montrose	a													
Stonehaven	a													
Aberdeen	a													

A ⊼ to Birmingham New Street
B ⊼ from Plymouth to Birmingham New Street
C ⊼ to Bristol Temple Meads
D ⊼ to Reading

Table T052-F

Mondays to Fridays
16 December to 15 May

Brighton, Gatwick Airport, Kent & South London - Luton, Bedford, Cambridge and Peterborough (via London)

Miles	Station		TL MX A	TL MO 1 B	TL MX A	TL MX 1 B	TL MX C	TL MO 1 B	TL MX 1 D	TL MX 1 B	TL 1 B	TL 1	TL 1 E	TL 1 E	TL 1 E	TL 1 E	TL 1 E	TL 1 E	TL	TL 1	TL	TL 1 E	TL F
0	Brighton 10	d										00 04								04 12			
—	Horsham	d																					
24¼	Gatwick Airport 10 ✈	d								00 04	00 21	00 42	01 46	02 21	02 46	03 21	03 46	04 21		04 41		05 19	
40½	East Croydon	d						00 10	00 09	00 23	00 40	01 10	02 10	02 40	03 10	03 40	04 10	04 40		05 10		05 40	
—	Rainham (Kent)	d																					
—	Dartford	d																					05 15
—	Abbey Wood	d																					05 28
—	Woolwich Arsenal	d																					05 34
—	Greenwich	d																					05 47
—	Maidstone East	d																					
—	Sevenoaks	d																					
—	Swanley	d																					
—	St Mary Cray	d																					
—	Orpington	d																	04 33		05 03		
—	Bromley South	d																	04 43		05 13		
—	Catford	d					00 06												04 55		05 25		
—	Peckham Rye 4 195	d					00 14												05 04		05 34		
—	Denmark Hill 4 195	d					00 17												05 07		05 37		
—	Sutton 4 179	d																					
—	Wimbledon ⊖	d																					
—	Streatham 4	d																					
—	Tulse Hill 3	d																					
—	Herne Hill 4 173,179	d																					
—	Loughborough Jn 173,179	d																					
—	Elephant & Castle ⊖ 173,179	d			00 04		00 24												05 14		05 44		
50½	London Bridge ⊖	d																		05 25		05 55	05 58
—	**London Blackfriars** ⊖	a			00 08		00 29	00 36	00 36	00 49	01 06	01 36	02 36	03 06	03 36	04 06	04 36	05 06	05 19	05 31	05 49	06 01	06 04
—	**London Blackfriars 3** ⊖	d	00 02	00 06	00 09	00 22		00 36	00 37	00 50	01 06	01 36	02 36	03 06	03 36	04 06	04 36	05 06	05 19	05 31	05 49	06 01	06 04
—	**City Thameslink 3**	d																05 08	05 21	05 33	05 51	06 03	06 06
—	**Farringdon 3** ⊖	d	00 06	00 11	00 13	00 26			00 41									05 11	05 24	05 36	05 54	06 06	06 09
52¾	St Pancras International ⊖	d	00 11	00 16	00 18	00 31		00 46	00 46	01 01	01 16	01 44	02 44	03 14	03 44	04 14	04 44	05 16	05 28	05 40	05 58	06 10	06 13
—	Finsbury Park ⊖	a							00 52														
—	Welwyn Garden City	a							01 14														
—	Stevenage	a							01 23														
—	Hitchin	a							01 32														
—	Letchworth Garden City	a																					
—	Royston	a																					
—	Cambridge	a																					
—	Huntingdon	a							02 01														
—	Peterborough	a							02 19														
—	Kentish Town ⊖	a		00 20	00 22			00 50		01 05		01 48	02 48		03 48		04 48		05 33		06 03		06 18
—	West Hampstead Thameslink ⊖	a	00 19	00 24	00 26	00 39		00 54		01 09	01 24	01 52	02 52	03 22	03 52	04 22	04 52	05 24	05 37	05 48	06 07	06 18	06 22
—	Elstree & Borehamwood	a		00 39	00 40			01 09		01 24		02 07	03 07		04 07		05 07		05 50		06 21		06 36
72	St Albans City	a	00 35	00 49	00 51	00 56		01 19		01 34	01 40	02 17	03 17	03 40	04 17	04 40	05 17	05 40	06 00	06 04	06 31	06 30	06 46
76¾	Harpenden	a	00 42	00 57	00 58	01 02		01 27		01 40	01 47	02 25	03 25	03 47	04 25	04 47	05 25	05 47	06 06	06 10	06 41	06 36	06 56
81½	Luton Airport Parkway 7 ✈	a	00 47	01 02	01 03	01 07		01 32		01 45	01 52	02 30	03 30	03 52	04 30	04 52	05 30	05 52	06 11	06 16	06 46	06 42	07 01
82½	Luton 10	a	00 51	01 06	01 07	01 11		01 36		01 49	01 56	02 34	03 34	03 56	04 34	04 56	05 34	05 56	06 16	06 20	06 51	06 46	07 06
101¾	Bedford	a	01 18	01 31	01 32	01 36		02 01		02 14	02 21	02 59	03 59	04 21	04 59	05 21	05 59	06 21		06 45		07 11	

A From Sutton (Surrey)
B From Brighton
C From Sevenoaks
D From Horsham
E From Three Bridges
F From Gillingham (Kent)

Table T052-F

Mondays to Fridays
16 December to 15 May

Brighton, Gatwick Airport, Kent & South London - Luton, Bedford, Cambridge and Peterborough (via London)

Station		TL	TL 1	TL	TL 1 A	TL	TL B	TL 1	TL	TL ◇1	TL 1 C	TL	TL 1	TL	TL 1 A	TL	TL 1	TL	TL 1 A	TL	TL 1 C	TL	TL 1
Brighton 10	d		05 06							05 28			05 38				05 52						06 05
Horsham	d							05 25															
Gatwick Airport 10 ✈	d		05 46		05 32			05 49		06 06			06 16		05 56		06 25		06 13				06 46
East Croydon	d		06 01		06 03			06 16		06 21	06 25		06 31		06 31		06 41		06 46		06 51		07 01
Rainham (Kent)	d																	05 30					
Dartford	d						05 45											06 15					
Abbey Wood	d						05 58											06 28					
Woolwich Arsenal	d						06 04											06 34					
Greenwich	d						06 17											06 47					
Maidstone East	d																						
Sevenoaks	d					05 22										05 52							
Swanley	d					05 41										06 11							
St Mary Cray	d					05 45										06 15							
Orpington	d	05 33										06 03										06 30	
Bromley South	d	05 43				05 53						06 13				06 23						06 43	
Catford	d	05 55				06 05						06 25				06 35						06 55	
Peckham Rye 4 195	d	06 04				06 14						06 34				06 44						07 04	
Denmark Hill 4 195	d	06 07				06 17						06 37				06 47						07 07	
Sutton 4 179	d			05 46					05 49					06 16						06 19			
Wimbledon ⊖	d								06 07											06 37			
Streatham 4	d			06 03					06 18					06 33						06 48			
Tulse Hill 3	d			06 08					06 23					06 38						06 53			
Herne Hill 4 173,179	d			06 12					06 27					06 42						06 57			
Loughborough Jn 173,179	d			06 15					06 30					06 45						07 00			
Elephant & Castle ⊖ 173,179	d	06 14		06 19		06 24			06 34			06 44		06 49		06 54				07 04		07 14	
London Bridge ⊖	d		06 16		06 21		06 28	06 31		06 35	06 41		06 46		06 51		06 54	06 58	07 01		07 06		07 16
London Blackfriars ⊖	a	06 19	06 21	06 24	06 26	06 29	06 34	06 36	06 39	06 41	06 46	06 49	06 51	06 54	06 56	06 59	07 01	07 04	07 06	07 09	07 11	07 19	07 21
London Blackfriars 3 ⊖	d	06 19	06 22	06 24	06 27		06 34	06 37	06 39	06 42	06 47	06 49	06 52	06 54	06 57		07 02	07 04	07 07	07 09	07 12	07 19	07 22
City Thameslink 3	d	06 21	06 24	06 26	06 29		06 36	06 39	06 41	06 44	06 49	06 51	06 54	06 56	06 59		07 04	07 06	07 09	07 11	07 14	07 21	07 24
Farringdon 3 ⊖	d	06 24	06 26	06 29	06 31		06 39	06 41	06 44	06 46	06 51	06 54	06 56	06 59	07 01		07 06	07 09	07 11	07 14	07 16	07 24	07 26
St Pancras International ⊖	d	06 28	06 31	06 33	06 36		06 43	06 46	06 48	06 51	06 56	06 58	07 01	07 03	07 06		07 11	07 13	07 16	07 18	07 21	07 28	07 31
Finsbury Park ⊖	a		06 40					06 52					07 07						07 22				07 37
Welwyn Garden City	a																						
Stevenage	a		07 01					07 13					07 31						07 43				08 01
Hitchin	a		07 08					07 19					07 38						07 49				08 07
Letchworth Garden City	a		07 13										07 43										08 12
Royston	a		07 24										07 56										08 24
Cambridge	a		07 43										08 12										
Huntingdon	a							07 48											08 18				
Peterborough	a							08 06											08 40				
Kentish Town ⊖	a			06 38					06 53					07 08						07 23		07 33	
West Hampstead Thameslink ⊖	a	06 36		06 43	06 44		06 51		06 57			07 06		07 13				07 21		07 27	07 29	07 37	
Elstree & Borehamwood	a	06 50		06 57			07 05		07 11			07 20		07 27				07 36		07 40		07 51	
St Albans City	a	07 00		07 07	06 56		07 15		07 21	07 09	07 14	07 30		07 37	07 24		07 28	07 46		07 51	07 41	08 01	
Harpenden	a	07 09			07 03		07 26				07 20	07 39					07 34	07 56			07 47	08 11	
Luton Airport Parkway 7 ✈	a	07 14			07 08		07 31			07 18	07 26	07 44			07 33		07 39	08 01			07 53	08 17	
Luton 10	a	07 20			07 12		07 36			07 22	07 30	07 50			07 37		07 43	08 06			07 57	08 20	
Bedford	a				07 37					07 42	07 54				07 58		08 11				08 21		

A From Three Bridges
B From Gillingham (Kent)
C From East Grinstead

Table T052-F

Mondays to Fridays
16 December to 15 May

Brighton, Gatwick Airport, Kent & South London - Luton, Bedford, Cambridge and Peterborough (via London)

		TL	TL [1]	TL	TL [1]	TL	TL [1]	TL	TL [1] A	TL [1] B	TL	TL [1]	TL	TL [1]	TL	TL [1]	TL	TL [1]	TL	TL [1] B	TL	TL [1]	TL
Brighton [10]	d				06 22							06 37				06 48						07 07	
Horsham	d		06 04				06 24							06 34									
Gatwick Airport [10] ✈	d		06 29		06 55		06 43					07 16		06 59		07 25		07 13				07 46	
East Croydon	d		07 01		07 10		07 16		07 21	07 25		07 31		07 31		07 40		07 46		07 55		08 01	
Rainham (Kent)	d					06 00											06 30						
Dartford	d					06 46											07 15						
Abbey Wood	d					06 58											07 28						
Woolwich Arsenal	d					07 04											07 34						
Greenwich	d					07 17											07 47						
Maidstone East	d																						
Sevenoaks	d			06 22											06 45								
Swanley	d			06 41											07 04								
St Mary Cray	d			06 45											07 08								
Orpington	d										06 59										07 30		
Bromley South	d			06 53							07 13				07 23						07 43		
Catford	d			07 05							07 25				07 35						07 55		
Peckham Rye [4] 195	d			07 14							07 34				07 44						08 04		
Denmark Hill [4] 195	d			07 17							07 37				07 47						08 07		
Sutton [4] 179	d	06 46						06 49					07 16						07 19				07 46
Wimbledon ⊖	d							07 07											07 37				
Streatham [4]	d	07 03						07 18					07 33						07 48				08 03
Tulse Hill [3]	d	07 08						07 23					07 38						07 53				08 08
Herne Hill [4] 173,179	d	07 12						07 27					07 42						07 57				08 12
Loughborough Jn 173,179	d	07 15						07 30					07 45						08 00				08 15
Elephant & Castle ⊖173,179	d	07 19		07 24				07 34			07 44		07 49		07 54				08 04		08 14		08 19
London Bridge ⊖	d		07 21		07 24	07 28	07 31		07 35	07 41		07 46		07 51		07 54	07 58	08 01		08 11		08 16	
London Blackfriars ⊖	a	07 24	07 26	07 29	07 31	07 34	07 36	07 39	07 41	07 46	07 49	07 51	07 54	07 56	07 59	08 01	08 04	08 06	08 09	08 16	08 19	08 21	08 24
London Blackfriars [3] ⊖	d	07 24	07 27		07 32	07 34	07 37	07 39	07 42	07 47	07 49	07 52	07 54	07 57		08 02	08 04	08 07	08 09	08 17	08 19	08 22	08 24
City Thameslink [3]	d	07 26	07 29		07 34	07 36	07 39	07 41	07 44	07 49	07 51	07 54	07 56	07 59		08 04	08 06	08 09	08 11	08 19	08 21	08 24	08 26
Farringdon [3] ⊖	d	07 29	07 31		07 36	07 39	07 41	07 44	07 46	07 51	07 54	07 56	07 59	08 01		08 06	08 09	08 11	08 14	08 21	08 24	08 26	08 29
St Pancras International ⊖	d	07 33	07 36		07 41	07 43	07 46	07 48	07 51	07 56	07 58	08 01	08 03	08 06		08 11	08 13	08 16	08 18	08 26	08 28	08 31	08 33
Finsbury Park ⊖	a						07 52					08 07						08 22				08 37	
Welwyn Garden City	a																						
Stevenage	a						08 13					08 31						08 43				09 01	
Hitchin	a						08 19					08 38						08 49				09 08	
Letchworth Garden City	a											08 43										09 13	
Royston	a											08 56										09 25	
Cambridge	a											09 11										09 42	
Huntingdon	a						08 48											09 18					
Peterborough	a						09 05											09 35					
Kentish Town ⊖	a					07 48					08 03		08 08				08 18		08 23		08 33		
West Hampstead Thameslink ⊖	a	07 43				07 52		07 58			08 07		08 13				08 22		08 29		08 37		08 43
Elstree & Borehamwood	a	07 56				08 06		08 11			08 21		08 26				08 36		08 41		08 51		08 56
St Albans City	a	08 06	07 54		07 58	08 16		08 21		08 13	08 31		08 36	08 25		08 29	08 46		08 51	08 43	09 01		09 06
Harpenden	a				08 07	08 24				08 20	08 39					08 35	08 55			08 51	09 10		
Luton Airport Parkway [7] ✈	a				08 12	08 29				08 25	08 44			08 33		08 40	09 01			08 56	09 15		
Luton [10]	a		08 04		08 15	08 34			08 17	08 29	08 50			08 37		08 44	09 04			09 00	09 20		
Bedford	a		08 30		08 35				08 45	08 54				09 00		09 09				09 24			

A From Littlehampton
B From East Grinstead

Table T052-F

Mondays to Fridays
16 December to 15 May

Brighton, Gatwick Airport, Kent & South London - Luton, Bedford, Cambridge and Peterborough (via London)

		TL [1]	TL	TL [1]	TL	TL [1]	TL	TL [1] A	TL [1] B	TL	TL [1]	TL	TL [1]	TL	TL	TL [1]	TL	TL [1]	TL [1] B	TL	TL [1]	TL	TL [1]
Brighton [10]	d			07 18							07 37							08 00			08 07		
Horsham	d	07 04											07 34										08 04
Gatwick Airport [10] ✈	d	07 29		07 55		07 43					08 16		07 59			08 13		08 36			08 46		08 29
East Croydon	d	08 01		08 10		08 16		08 21	08 25		08 31		08 31			08 46		08 51	08 55		09 01		09 01
Rainham (Kent)	d				06 56										07 30								
Dartford	d				07 45										08 15								
Abbey Wood	d				07 57										08 28								
Woolwich Arsenal	d				08 04										08 34								
Greenwich	d				08 17										08 47								
Maidstone East	d																						
Sevenoaks	d		07 18											07 45									
Swanley	d		07 37											08 04									
St Mary Cray	d		07 41											08 08									
Orpington	d									08 03										08 29			
Bromley South	d		07 53							08 13				08 23						08 43			
Catford	d		08 05							08 25				08 35						08 55			
Peckham Rye [4] 195	d		08 14							08 34				08 44						09 04			
Denmark Hill [4] 195	d		08 17							08 37				08 47						09 07			
Sutton [4] 179	d						07 49					08 16					08 19					08 46	
Wimbledon ⊖	d						08 07										08 37						
Streatham [4]	d						08 18					08 33					08 48					09 03	
Tulse Hill [3]	d						08 23					08 38					08 53					09 08	
Herne Hill [4] 173,179	d						08 27					08 42					08 57					09 12	
Loughborough Jn 173,179	d						08 30					08 45					09 00					09 15	
Elephant & Castle ⊖173,179	d		08 24				08 34			08 44		08 49		08 54			09 04			09 14		09 19	
London Bridge ⊖	d	08 21		08 24	08 28	08 31		08 35	08 41		08 46		08 51		08 58	09 01		09 05	09 11		09 16		09 21
London Blackfriars ⊖	a	08 26	08 29	08 31	08 34	08 36	08 39	08 41	08 46	08 49	08 51	08 54	08 56	08 59	09 04	09 06	09 09	09 11	09 16	09 19	09 21	09 24	09 26
London Blackfriars [3] ⊖	d	08 27		08 32	08 34	08 37	08 39	08 42	08 47	08 49	08 52	08 54	08 57		09 04	09 07	09 09	09 12	09 17	09 19	09 22	09 24	09 27
City Thameslink [3]	d	08 29		08 34	08 36	08 39	08 41	08 44	08 49	08 51	08 54	08 56	08 59		09 06	09 09	09 11	09 14	09 19	09 21	09 24	09 26	09 29
Farringdon [3] ⊖	d	08 31		08 36	08 39	08 41	08 44	08 46	08 51	08 54	08 56	08 59	09 01		09 09	09 11	09 14	09 16	09 21	09 24	09 26	09 29	09 31
St Pancras International ⊖	d	08 36		08 41	08 43	08 46	08 48	08 51	08 56	08 58	09 01	09 03	09 06		09 13	09 16	09 18	09 21	09 26	09 28	09 31	09 33	09 36
Finsbury Park ⊖	a					08 52					09 07					09 22					09 41		
Welwyn Garden City	a																						
Stevenage	a					09 13					09 31					09 43					10 01		
Hitchin	a					09 19					09 38					09 49					10 08		
Letchworth Garden City	a										09 43										10 13		
Royston	a										09 56										10 24		
Cambridge	a										10 12										10 40		
Huntingdon	a					09 48										10 18							
Peterborough	a					10 05										10 40							
Kentish Town ⊖	a				08 48					09 03					09 18					09 33			
West Hampstead Thameslink ⊖	a				08 52		08 58			09 07		09 14			09 22		09 28			09 37		09 44	09 44
Elstree & Borehamwood	a						09 11			09 21		09 26					09 41			09 51		09 55	
St Albans City	a	08 54		08 59			09 21		09 15	09 31		09 36	09 24				09 51		09 45	10 01		10 06	09 56
Harpenden	a			09 05					09 21	09 37			09 31					09 43	09 51	10 07			10 02
Luton Airport Parkway [7] ✈	a	09 02		09 11					09 26	09 42			09 36					09 48	09 56	10 12			10 07
Luton [10]	a	09 06		09 15				09 17	09 30	09 49			09 40					09 52	10 00	10 19			10 11
Bedford	a	09 28		09 38				09 42	09 54				10 05					10 16	10 26				10 36

A From Littlehampton
B From East Grinstead

Table T052-F

Mondays to Fridays

16 December to 15 May

Brighton, Gatwick Airport, Kent & South London - Luton, Bedford, Cambridge and Peterborough (via London)

		TL	TL	TL	TL	TL	TL	TL	TL	TL	TL	TL	TL	TL	TL	TL	TL	TL	TL	TL	TL	TL	TL
				1		1	1		1		1			1		1		1		1			1
							A																
Brighton 10	d					08 30			08 37							09 02		09 08					
Horsham	d										08 34			08 55									09 25
Gatwick Airport 10 ✈	d			08 43		09 06			09 16		08 59			09 19		09 36		09 46		09 33			09 49
East Croydon	d			09 16		09 21	09 25		09 31		09 31			09 45		09 51		10 01		10 03			10 15
Rainham (Kent)	d		08 01										08 30									09 00	
Dartford	d		08 46										09 15									09 45	
Abbey Wood	d		08 58										09 28									09 58	
Woolwich Arsenal	d		09 04										09 34									10 04	
Greenwich	d		09 17										09 47									10 17	
Maidstone East	d																						
Sevenoaks	d	08 22										08 52									09 22		
Swanley	d	08 41										09 11									09 41		
St Mary Cray	d	08 45										09 15									09 45		
Orpington	d							09 03									09 33						
Bromley South	d	08 53						09 13				09 23					09 43				09 53		
Catford	d	09 05						09 25				09 35					09 55				10 05		
Peckham Rye 4 195	d	09 14						09 34				09 44					10 04				10 14		
Denmark Hill 4 195	d	09 17						09 37				09 47					10 07				10 17		
Sutton 4 179	d				08 49					09 16					09 19				09 46				
Wimbledon ⊖	d				09 07										09 37								
Streatham 4	d				09 18					09 33					09 48				10 03				
Tulse Hill 3	d				09 23					09 38					09 53				10 08				
Herne Hill 4 173,179	d				09 27					09 42					09 57				10 12				
Loughborough Jn 173,179	d				09 30					09 45					10 00				10 15				
Elephant & Castle ⊖173,179	d	09 24			09 34			09 44		09 49		09 54			10 04		10 14		10 19		10 24		
London Bridge ⊖	d		09 28	09 31		09 35	09 41		09 46		09 51		09 58	10 01		10 05		10 16		10 21		10 28	10 31
London Blackfriars ⊖	a	09 29	09 34	09 36	09 39	09 41	09 46	09 49	09 51	09 54	09 56	09 59	10 04	10 06	10 09	10 11	10 19	10 21	10 24	10 26	10 29	10 34	10 36
London Blackfriars 3 ⊖	d		09 34	09 37	09 39	09 42	09 47	09 49	09 52	09 54	09 57		10 04	10 07	10 09	10 12	10 19	10 22	10 24	10 27		10 34	10 37
City Thameslink 3	d		09 36	09 39	09 41	09 44	09 49	09 51	09 54	09 56	09 59		10 06	10 09	10 11	10 14	10 21	10 24	10 26	10 29		10 36	10 39
Farringdon 3 ⊖	d		09 39	09 41	09 44	09 46	09 51	09 54	09 56	09 59	10 01		10 09	10 11	10 14	10 16	10 24	10 26	10 29	10 31		10 39	10 41
St Pancras International ⊖	d		09 43	09 46	09 48	09 51	09 56	09 58	10 01	10 03	10 06		10 13	10 16	10 18	10 21	10 28	10 31	10 33	10 36		10 43	10 46
Finsbury Park ⊖	a			09 52					10 07					10 22				10 37					10 52
Welwyn Garden City	a																						
Stevenage	a			10 13					10 31					10 43				11 01					11 13
Hitchin	a			10 20					10 38					10 49				11 08					11 20
Letchworth Garden City	a								10 43									11 13					
Royston	a								10 56									11 24					
Cambridge	a								11 11									11 40					
Huntingdon	a			10 49										11 18									11 48
Peterborough	a			11 05										11 39									12 05
Kentish Town ⊖	a		09 48		09 53			10 03		10 08					10 23		10 33		10 38				
West Hampstead Thameslink ⊖	a		09 52		09 58					10 14			10 21		10 29	10 29			10 44			10 51	
Elstree & Borehamwood	a		10 06		10 12					10 27			10 35		10 42				10 57			11 05	
St Albans City	a		10 19		10 23		10 15			10 37	10 25		10 45		10 52	10 41			11 07	10 54		11 15	
Harpenden	a		10 27			10 13	10 21				10 31		10 51			10 47				11 02		11 21	
Luton Airport Parkway 7 ✈	a		10 32			10 18	10 26				10 37		10 56			10 52				11 07		11 26	
Luton 10	a		10 36			10 22	10 30				10 40		11 01			10 56				11 11		11 31	
Bedford	a					10 44	10 55				11 05					11 21				11 36			

A From East Grinstead

Table T052-F

Mondays to Fridays

16 December to 15 May

Brighton, Gatwick Airport, Kent & South London - Luton, Bedford, Cambridge and Peterborough (via London)

		TL	TL	TL	TL	TL	TL	TL	TL	TL	TL	TL	TL	TL	TL	TL	TL	TL	TL	TL	TL	TL
			1		1		1			1		1		1		1			1		1	
Brighton 10	d		09 28		09 38							09 58		10 08							10 28	
Horsham	d									09 55									10 25			
Gatwick Airport 10 ✈	d		10 06		10 17		10 03			10 19		10 36		10 46		10 33			10 49		11 06	
East Croydon	d		10 21		10 32		10 33			10 45		10 51		11 01		11 03			11 15		11 21	
Rainham (Kent)	d								09 28									09 58				
Dartford	d								10 15									10 45				
Abbey Wood	d								10 28									10 58				
Woolwich Arsenal	d								10 34									11 04				
Greenwich	d								10 47									11 17				
Maidstone East	d																					
Sevenoaks	d							09 52									10 22					
Swanley	d							10 11									10 41					
St Mary Cray	d							10 15									10 45					
Orpington	d			10 03									10 33									11 03
Bromley South	d			10 13				10 23					10 43				10 53					11 13
Catford	d			10 25				10 35					10 55				11 05					11 25
Peckham Rye 4 195	d			10 34				10 44					11 04				11 14					11 34
Denmark Hill 4 195	d			10 37				10 47					11 07				11 17					11 37
Sutton 4 179	d	09 49				10 16					10 19				10 46					10 49		
Wimbledon ⊖	d	10 07									10 37									11 07		
Streatham 4	d	10 18				10 33					10 48				11 03					11 18		
Tulse Hill 3	d	10 23				10 38					10 53				11 08					11 23		
Herne Hill 4 173,179	d	10 27				10 42					10 57				11 12					11 27		
Loughborough Jn 173,179	d	10 30				10 45					11 00				11 15					11 30		
Elephant & Castle ⊖173,179	d	10 34		10 44		10 49		10 54			11 04		11 14		11 19		11 24			11 34		11 44
London Bridge ⊖	d		10 35		10 46		10 51		10 58	11 01		11 05		11 16		11 21		11 28	11 31		11 35	
London Blackfriars ⊖	a	10 39	10 41	10 49	10 51	10 54	10 56	10 59	11 04	11 06	11 09	11 11	11 19	11 21	11 24	11 26	11 29	11 34	11 36	11 39	11 41	11 49
London Blackfriars 3 ⊖	d	10 39	10 42	10 49	10 52	10 54	10 57		11 04	11 07	11 09	11 12	11 19	11 22	11 24	11 27		11 34	11 37	11 39	11 42	11 49
City Thameslink 3	d	10 41	10 44	10 51	10 54	10 56	10 59		11 06	11 09	11 11	11 14	11 21	11 24	11 26	11 29		11 36	11 39	11 41	11 44	11 51
Farringdon 3 ⊖	d	10 44	10 46	10 54	10 56	10 59	11 01		11 09	11 11	11 14	11 16	11 24	11 26	11 29	11 31		11 39	11 41	11 44	11 46	11 54
St Pancras International ⊖	d	10 48	10 51	10 58	11 01	11 03	11 06		11 13	11 16	11 18	11 21	11 28	11 31	11 33	11 36		11 43	11 46	11 48	11 51	11 58
Finsbury Park ⊖	a				11 07					11 22				11 37					11 52			
Welwyn Garden City	a																					
Stevenage	a				11 31					11 43				12 01					12 13			
Hitchin	a				11 38					11 49				12 08					12 19			
Letchworth Garden City	a				11 43									12 13								
Royston	a				11 56									12 24								
Cambridge	a				12 11									12 40								
Huntingdon	a									12 18									12 48			
Peterborough	a									12 39									13 05			
Kentish Town ⊖	a	10 53		11 03		11 08					11 23		11 33		11 38					11 53		12 03
West Hampstead Thameslink ⊖	a	10 59	10 59			11 14			11 21		11 29	11 29			11 44			11 51		11 59	11 59	
Elstree & Borehamwood	a	11 12				11 28			11 35		11 42				11 57			12 05		12 12		
St Albans City	a	11 22	11 11			11 38	11 24		11 45		11 52	11 41			12 07	11 54		12 15		12 22	12 11	
Harpenden	a		11 17				11 31		11 51			11 47				12 01		12 21			12 17	
Luton Airport Parkway 7 ✈	a		11 22				11 36		11 56			11 52				12 06		12 26			12 22	
Luton 10	a		11 26				11 40		12 01			11 56				12 10		12 31			12 26	
Bedford	a		11 51				12 05					12 21				12 35					12 51	

Table T052-F

Mondays to Fridays

16 December to 15 May

Brighton, Gatwick Airport, Kent & South London - Luton, Bedford, Cambridge and Peterborough (via London)

Station			TL [1]	TL	TL [1]	TL	TL	TL [1]	TL	TL [1]	TL	TL [1]		TL	TL [1]	TL	TL	TL [1]	TL	TL [1]	TL	TL [1]	TL		TL [1]	TL
Brighton [10]		d	10 38							10 58		11 08								11 28		11 38				
Horsham		d						10 55										11 25								
Gatwick Airport [10]	✈	d	11 16		11 03			11 19		11 36		11 46			11 33			11 49		12 06		12 16			12 03	
East Croydon		d	11 31		11 33			11 45		11 51		12 01			12 03			12 15		12 21		12 31			12 33	
Rainham (Kent)		d					10 28										10 58									
Dartford		d					11 15										11 45									
Abbey Wood		d					11 28										11 58									
Woolwich Arsenal		d					11 34										12 04									
Greenwich		d					11 47										12 17									
Maidstone East		d																								
Sevenoaks		d				10 52										11 22										11 52
Swanley		d				11 11										11 41										12 11
St Mary Cray		d				11 15										11 45										12 15
Orpington		d									11 33										12 03					
Bromley South		d				11 23					11 43					11 53					12 13					12 23
Catford		d				11 35					11 55					12 05					12 25					12 35
Peckham Rye [4]	195	d				11 44					12 04					12 14					12 34					12 44
Denmark Hill [4]	195	d				11 47					12 07					12 17					12 37					12 47
Sutton [4]	179	d		11 16					11 19					11 46					11 49				12 16			
Wimbledon	⊖	d							11 37										12 07							
Streatham [4]		d		11 33					11 48					12 03					12 18				12 33			
Tulse Hill [3]		d		11 38					11 53					12 08					12 23				12 38			
Herne Hill [4]	173,179	d		11 42					11 57					12 12					12 27				12 42			
Loughborough Jn	173,179	d		11 45					12 00					12 15					12 30				12 45			
Elephant & Castle	⊖173,179	d		11 49		11 54			12 04		12 14			12 19		12 24			12 34		12 44		12 49			12 54
London Bridge	⊖	d	11 46		11 51		11 58	12 01		12 05		12 16			12 21		12 28	12 31		12 35		12 46			12 51	
London Blackfriars	⊖	a	11 51	11 54	11 56	11 59	12 04	12 06	12 09	12 11	12 19	12 21		12 24	12 26	12 29	12 34	12 36	12 39	12 41	12 49	12 51	12 54		12 56	12 59
London Blackfriars [3]	⊖	d	11 52	11 54	11 57		12 04	12 07	12 09	12 12	12 19	12 22		12 24	12 27		12 34	12 37	12 39	12 42	12 49	12 52	12 54		12 57	
City Thameslink [3]		d	11 54	11 56	11 59		12 06	12 09	12 11	12 14	12 21	12 24		12 26	12 29		12 36	12 39	12 41	12 44	12 51	12 54	12 56		12 59	
Farringdon [3]	⊖	d	11 56	11 59	12 01		12 09	12 11	12 14	12 16	12 24	12 26		12 29	12 31		12 39	12 41	12 44	12 46	12 54	12 56	12 59		13 01	
St Pancras International	⊖	d	12 01	12 03	12 06		12 13	12 16	12 18	12 21	12 28	12 31		12 33	12 36		12 43	12 46	12 48	12 51	12 58	13 01	13 03		13 06	
Finsbury Park	⊖	a	12 07					12 22				12 37						12 52				13 07				
Welwyn Garden City		a																								
Stevenage		a	12 31					12 43				13 01						13 13				13 31				
Hitchin		a	12 38					12 49				13 08						13 19				13 38				
Letchworth Garden City		a	12 43									13 13										13 43				
Royston		a	12 56									13 24										13 56				
Cambridge		a	13 11									13 40										14 11				
Huntingdon		a						13 18										13 48								
Peterborough		a						13 39										14 05								
Kentish Town	⊖	a		12 08					12 23		12 33			12 38					12 53		13 03		13 08			
West Hampstead Thameslink	⊖	a		12 14			12 21		12 29	12 29				12 44			12 51		12 59	12 59			13 14			
Elstree & Borehamwood		a		12 27			12 35		12 42					12 57			13 05		13 12				13 27			
St Albans City		a		12 37	12 24		12 45		12 52	12 41				13 07	12 54		13 15		13 22	13 11			13 37		13 24	
Harpenden		a			12 31		12 51			12 47					13 01		13 21			13 17					13 31	
Luton Airport Parkway [7]	✈	a			12 36		12 56			12 52					13 06		13 26			13 22					13 36	
Luton [10]		a			12 40		13 01			12 56					13 10		13 31			13 26					13 40	
Bedford		a			13 05					13 21					13 35					13 51					14 05	

Table T052-F

Mondays to Fridays

16 December to 15 May

Brighton, Gatwick Airport, Kent & South London - Luton, Bedford, Cambridge and Peterborough (via London)

Station			TL	TL [1]	TL	TL [1]	TL	TL [1]	TL	TL [1]		TL	TL	TL [1]	TL	TL [1]	TL	TL [1]	TL	TL [1]	TL		TL	TL [1]	TL	TL [1]
Brighton [10]		d				11 58		12 08								12 28		12 38								12 58
Horsham		d		11 55										12 23										12 55		
Gatwick Airport [10]	✈	d		12 19		12 36		12 46		12 32				12 49		13 06		13 16		13 03				13 19		13 36
East Croydon		d		12 45		12 51		13 01		13 03				13 15		13 21		13 31		13 33				13 45		13 51
Rainham (Kent)		d	11 28										11 58										12 28			
Dartford		d	12 15										12 45										13 15			
Abbey Wood		d	12 28										12 58										13 28			
Woolwich Arsenal		d	12 34										13 04										13 34			
Greenwich		d	12 47										13 17										13 47			
Maidstone East		d																								
Sevenoaks		d										12 22									12 52					
Swanley		d										12 41									13 11					
St Mary Cray		d										12 45									13 15					
Orpington		d					12 33										13 03									
Bromley South		d					12 43					12 53					13 13				13 23					
Catford		d					12 55					13 05					13 25				13 35					
Peckham Rye [4]	195	d					13 04					13 14					13 34				13 44					
Denmark Hill [4]	195	d					13 07					13 17					13 37				13 47					
Sutton [4]	179	d			12 19				12 46						12 49				13 16						13 19	
Wimbledon	⊖	d			12 37										13 07										13 37	
Streatham [4]		d			12 48				13 03						13 18				13 33						13 48	
Tulse Hill [3]		d			12 53				13 08						13 23				13 38						13 53	
Herne Hill [4]	173,179	d			12 57				13 12						13 27				13 42						13 57	
Loughborough Jn	173,179	d			13 00				13 15						13 30				13 45						14 00	
Elephant & Castle	⊖173,179	d			13 04		13 14		13 19			13 24			13 34		13 44		13 49		13 54				14 04	
London Bridge	⊖	d	12 58	13 01		13 05		13 16		13 21			13 28	13 31		13 35		13 46		13 51			13 58	14 01		14 05
London Blackfriars	⊖	a	13 04	13 06	13 09	13 11	13 19	13 21	13 24	13 26		13 29	13 34	13 36	13 39	13 41	13 49	13 51	13 54	13 56	13 59		14 04	14 06	14 09	14 11
London Blackfriars [3]	⊖	d	13 04	13 07	13 09	13 12	13 19	13 22	13 24	13 27			13 34	13 37	13 39	13 42	13 49	13 52	13 54	13 57			14 04	14 07	14 09	14 12
City Thameslink [3]		d	13 06	13 09	13 11	13 14	13 21	13 24	13 26	13 29			13 36	13 39	13 41	13 44	13 51	13 54	13 56	13 59			14 06	14 09	14 11	14 14
Farringdon [3]	⊖	d	13 09	13 11	13 14	13 16	13 24	13 26	13 29	13 31			13 39	13 41	13 44	13 46	13 54	13 56	13 59	14 01			14 09	14 11	14 14	14 16
St Pancras International	⊖	d	13 13	13 16	13 18	13 21	13 28	13 31	13 33	13 36			13 43	13 46	13 48	13 51	13 58	14 01	14 03	14 06			14 13	14 16	14 18	14 21
Finsbury Park	⊖	a		13 22				13 37						13 52				14 07						14 22		
Welwyn Garden City		a																								
Stevenage		a		13 43				14 01						14 13				14 31						14 43		
Hitchin		a		13 49				14 08						14 19				14 38						14 49		
Letchworth Garden City		a						14 13										14 43								
Royston		a						14 24										14 56								
Cambridge		a						14 40										15 11								
Huntingdon		a		14 18										14 48										15 18		
Peterborough		a		14 39										15 07										15 39		
Kentish Town	⊖	a			13 23		13 33		13 38						13 53		14 03		14 08						14 23	
West Hampstead Thameslink	⊖	a	13 21		13 29	13 29			13 44				13 51		13 59	13 59			14 14				14 21		14 29	14 29
Elstree & Borehamwood		a	13 35		13 42				13 57				14 05		14 12				14 27				14 35		14 42	
St Albans City		a	13 45		13 52	13 41			14 07	13 54			14 15		14 22	14 11			14 37	14 24			14 45		14 52	14 41
Harpenden		a	13 51			13 47				14 01			14 21			14 17				14 31			14 51			14 47
Luton Airport Parkway [7]	✈	a	13 56			13 52				14 06			14 26			14 22				14 36			14 56			14 52
Luton [10]		a	14 01			13 56				14 10			14 31			14 26				14 40			15 01			14 56
Bedford		a				14 21				14 35						14 51				15 05						15 21

Table T052-F

Mondays to Fridays
16 December to 15 May

Brighton, Gatwick Airport, Kent & South London - Luton, Bedford, Cambridge and Peterborough (via London)

Station		TL	TL 1	TL	TL 1	TL	TL	TL 1	TL	TL 1	TL	TL 1	TL	TL 1	TL	TL	TL 1	TL	TL 1	TL	TL 1	TL	TL 1
Brighton 10	d		13 08							13 28		13 38							13 58		14 08		
Horsham	d							13 25									13 55						
Gatwick Airport 10 ✈	d		13 46		13 32			13 49		14 06		14 16		14 03			14 19		14 36		14 46		14 32
East Croydon	d		14 01		14 03			14 15		14 21		14 31		14 33			14 45		14 51		15 01		15 03
Rainham (Kent)	d						12 58									13 28							
Dartford	d						13 45									14 15							
Abbey Wood	d						13 58									14 28							
Woolwich Arsenal	d						14 04									14 34							
Greenwich	d						14 17									14 47							
Maidstone East	d																						
Sevenoaks	d					13 22									13 52								
Swanley	d					13 41									14 11								
St Mary Cray	d					13 45									14 15								
Orpington	d	13 33									14 03									14 33			
Bromley South	d	13 43				13 53					14 13				14 23					14 43			
Catford	d	13 55				14 05					14 25				14 35					14 55			
Peckham Rye 4	195 d	14 04				14 14					14 34				14 44					15 04			
Denmark Hill 4	195 d	14 07				14 17					14 37				14 47					15 07			
Sutton 4	179 d			13 46					13 49				14 16					14 18				14 46	
Wimbledon ⊖	d								14 07									14 36					
Streatham 4	d			14 03					14 18				14 33					14 46				15 03	
Tulse Hill 3	d			14 08					14 23				14 38					14 53				15 08	
Herne Hill 4	173,179 d			14 12					14 27				14 42					14 57				15 12	
Loughborough Jn	173,179 d			14 15					14 30				14 45					15 00				15 15	
Elephant & Castle ⊖	173,179 d	14 14		14 19		14 24			14 34		14 44		14 49		14 54			15 04		15 14		15 19	
London Bridge ⊖	d		14 16		14 21		14 28	14 31		14 35		14 46		14 51		14 58	15 01		15 05		15 16		15 21
London Blackfriars ⊖	a	14 19	14 21	14 24	14 26	14 29	14 34	14 36	14 39	14 41	14 49	14 51	14 54	14 56	14 59	15 04	15 06	15 09	15 11	15 19	15 21	15 24	15 26
London Blackfriars 3 ⊖	d	14 19	14 22	14 24	14 27		14 34	14 37	14 39	14 42	14 49	14 52	14 54	14 57		15 04	15 07	15 09	15 12	15 19	15 22	15 24	15 27
City Thameslink 3	d	14 21	14 24	14 26	14 29		14 36	14 39	14 41	14 44	14 51	14 54	14 56	14 59		15 06	15 09	15 11	15 14	15 21	15 24	15 26	15 29
Farringdon 3 ⊖	d	14 24	14 26	14 29	14 31		14 39	14 41	14 44	14 46	14 54	14 56	14 59	15 01		15 09	15 11	15 14	15 16	15 24	15 26	15 29	15 31
St Pancras International ⊖	d	14 28	14 31	14 33	14 36		14 43	14 46	14 48	14 51	14 58	15 01	15 03	15 06		15 13	15 16	15 18	15 21	15 28	15 31	15 33	15 36
Finsbury Park ⊖	a		14 37					14 52				15 07					15 22				15 37		
Welwyn Garden City	a																						
Stevenage	a		15 01					15 13				15 31					15 43				16 01		
Hitchin	a		15 08					15 20				15 38					15 49				16 08		
Letchworth Garden City	a		15 13									15 43									16 13		
Royston	a		15 24									15 56									16 24		
Cambridge	a		15 40									16 11									16 40		
Huntingdon	a							15 48									16 18						
Peterborough	a							16 05									16 39						
Kentish Town ⊖	a	14 33		14 38					14 53		15 03		15 08					15 23		15 33		15 38	
West Hampstead Thameslink ⊖	a			14 44			14 51		14 59	14 59			15 14			15 21		15 29	15 29			15 44	
Elstree & Borehamwood	a			14 57			15 05		15 12				15 27			15 35		15 42				15 57	
St Albans City	a			15 07	14 54		15 15		15 22	15 11			15 37	15 24		15 45		15 52	15 41			16 07	15 54
Harpenden	a				15 01		15 21			15 17				15 31		15 51			15 47				16 01
Luton Airport Parkway 7 ✈	a				15 06		15 26			15 22				15 36		15 56			15 52				16 06
Luton 10	a				15 10		15 31			15 26				15 40		16 01			15 56				16 10
Bedford	a				15 35					15 51				16 05					16 21				16 35

NRT DECEMBER 19 EDITION

Table T052-F

Mondays to Fridays
16 December to 15 May

Brighton, Gatwick Airport, Kent & South London - Luton, Bedford, Cambridge and Peterborough (via London)

Station		TL	TL	TL 1	TL	TL 1	TL	TL 1	TL	TL 1	TL	TL	TL 1	TL	TL 1	TL 1	TL	TL 1	TL	TL 1	TL	TL	TL 1
Brighton 10	d					14 28		14 38							14 56			15 08					
Horsham	d			14 25									14 55										15 25
Gatwick Airport 10 ✈	d			14 49		15 06		15 16		15 03			15 19		15 36	15 27		15 46		15 32			15 49
East Croydon	d			15 15		15 21		15 31		15 33			15 45		15 51	15 54		16 01		16 03			16 15
Rainham (Kent)	d		13 58									14 28										14 58	
Dartford	d		14 45									15 15										15 45	
Abbey Wood	d		14 58									15 28										15 58	
Woolwich Arsenal	d		15 04									15 34										16 04	
Greenwich	d		15 17									15 47										16 17	
Maidstone East	d																						
Sevenoaks	d	14 22									14 52										15 22		
Swanley	d	14 41									15 11										15 41		
St Mary Cray	d	14 45									15 15										15 45		
Orpington	d						15 03										15 33						
Bromley South	d	14 53					15 13				15 23						15 43				15 53		
Catford	d	15 05					15 25				15 35						15 55				16 05		
Peckham Rye 4	195 d	15 14					15 34				15 44						16 04				16 14		
Denmark Hill 4	195 d	15 17					15 37				15 47						16 07				16 17		
Sutton 4	179 d				14 49				15 16					15 19					15 46				
Wimbledon ⊖	d				15 07									15 37									
Streatham 4	d				15 18				15 33					15 48					16 03				
Tulse Hill 3	d				15 23				15 38					15 53					16 08				
Herne Hill 4	173,179 d				15 27				15 42					15 57					16 12				
Loughborough Jn	173,179 d				15 30				15 45					16 00					16 15				
Elephant & Castle ⊖	173,179 d	15 24			15 34		15 44		15 49		15 54			16 04			16 14		16 19		16 24		
London Bridge ⊖	d		15 28	15 31		15 35		15 46		15 51		15 58	16 01		16 05	16 11		16 16		16 21		16 28	16 31
London Blackfriars ⊖	a	15 29	15 34	15 36	15 39	15 41	15 49	15 51	15 54	15 56	15 59	16 04	16 06	16 09	16 11	16 16	16 19	16 21	16 24	16 26	16 29	16 34	16 36
London Blackfriars 3 ⊖	d		15 34	15 37	15 39	15 42	15 49	15 52	15 54	15 57		16 04	16 07	16 09	16 12	16 17	16 19	16 22	16 24	16 27		16 34	16 37
City Thameslink 3	d		15 36	15 39	15 41	15 44	15 51	15 54	15 56	15 59		16 06	16 09	16 11	16 14	16 19	16 21	16 24	16 26	16 29		16 36	16 39
Farringdon 3 ⊖	d		15 39	15 41	15 44	15 46	15 54	15 56	15 59	16 01		16 09	16 11	16 14	16 16	16 21	16 24	16 26	16 29	16 31		16 39	16 41
St Pancras International ⊖	d		15 43	15 46	15 48	15 51	15 58	16 01	16 03	16 06		16 13	16 16	16 18	16 21	16 26	16 28	16 31	16 33	16 36		16 43	16 46
Finsbury Park ⊖	a			15 52				16 07					16 22					16 37					16 52
Welwyn Garden City	a																						
Stevenage	a			16 13				16 31					16 43					16 58					17 13
Hitchin	a			16 19				16 38					16 49					17 05					17 19
Letchworth Garden City	a							16 43										17 11					
Royston	a							16 56										17 24					
Cambridge	a							17 11										17 40					
Huntingdon	a			16 48									17 18										17 48
Peterborough	a			17 05									17 35										18 05
Kentish Town ⊖	a				15 53		16 03		16 08			16 18					16 33					16 48	
West Hampstead Thameslink ⊖	a		15 51		15 59	15 59			16 14			16 22		16 29			16 37		16 44	16 44		16 52	
Elstree & Borehamwood	a		16 05		16 12				16 27			16 37		16 41			16 52		16 56			17 07	
St Albans City	a		16 19		16 23	16 14			16 37	16 24		16 46		16 51	16 39	16 44	17 01		17 06	16 56		17 16	
Harpenden	a		16 27			16 20				16 30		16 54				16 50	17 07			17 02		17 26	
Luton Airport Parkway 7 ✈	a		16 32			16 25				16 36		17 00				16 56	17 13			17 07		17 31	
Luton 10	a		16 36			16 29				16 40		17 05			16 49	17 00	17 20			17 11		17 36	
Bedford	a					16 53				17 09					17 06	17 26				17 35			

Table T052-F

Mondays to Fridays

16 December to 15 May

Brighton, Gatwick Airport, Kent & South London - Luton, Bedford, Cambridge and Peterborough (via London)

	TL	TL ■	TL ■	TL	TL ■	TL	TL ■	TL	TL ■ A	TL	TL ■	TL	TL ■	TL ■	TL	TL ■	TL	TL ■	TL	TL ■ A	TL	TL ■
Brighton [10] d		15 26			15 38								15 58			16 08						
Horsham d											15 55											16 25
Gatwick Airport [10] ✈ d		16 06	15 57		16 16		16 03		16 24		16 19		16 36	16 27		16 46		16 33		16 54		16 49
East Croydon d		16 21	16 24		16 31		16 33		16 40		16 45		16 51	16 54		17 01		17 03		17 10		17 15
Rainham (Kent) d										15 28											16 00	
Dartford d										16 15											16 45	
Abbey Wood d										16 28											16 58	
Woolwich Arsenal d										16 34											17 04	
Greenwich d										16 47											17 17	
Maidstone East d																						
Sevenoaks d								15 52											16 22			
Swanley d								16 11											16 41			
St Mary Cray d								16 15											16 45			
Orpington d				16 03											16 33							
Bromley South d				16 13				16 23							16 43				16 53			
Catford d				16 25				16 35							16 55				17 05			
Peckham Rye [4] 195 d				16 34				16 44							17 04				17 14			
Denmark Hill [4] 195 d				16 37				16 47							17 07				17 17			
Sutton [4] 179 d	15 49					16 16						16 19					16 46					
Wimbledon ⊖ d	16 07											16 37										
Streatham [4] d	16 18					16 33						16 48					17 03					
Tulse Hill [3] d	16 23					16 38						16 53					17 08					
Herne Hill [4] 173,179 d	16 27					16 42						16 57					17 12					
Loughborough Jn 173,179 d	16 30					16 45						17 00					17 15					
Elephant & Castle ⊖173,179 d	16 34			16 44		16 49		16 54				17 04			17 14		17 19		17 24			
London Bridge ⊖ d		16 35	16 41		16 46		16 51		16 55	16 58	17 01		17 05	17 11		17 16		17 21		17 24	17 28	17 31
London Blackfriars ⊖ a	16 39	16 41	16 46	16 49	16 51	16 54	16 56	16 59	17 01	17 04	17 06	17 09	17 11	17 16	17 19	17 21	17 24	17 26	17 29	17 31	17 34	17 36
London Blackfriars [3] ⊖ d	16 39	16 42	16 47	16 49	16 52	16 54	16 57		17 02	17 04	17 07	17 09	17 12	17 17	17 19	17 22	17 24	17 27		17 32	17 34	17 37
City Thameslink [3] d	16 41	16 44	16 49	16 51	16 54	16 56	16 59		17 04	17 06	17 09	17 11	17 14	17 19	17 21	17 24	17 26	17 29		17 34	17 36	17 39
Farringdon [3] ⊖ d	16 44	16 46	16 51	16 54	16 56	16 59	17 01		17 06	17 09	17 11	17 14	17 16	17 21	17 24	17 26	17 29	17 31		17 36	17 39	17 41
St Pancras International ⊖ d	16 48	16 51	16 56	16 58	17 01	17 03	17 06		17 11	17 13	17 16	17 18	17 21	17 26	17 28	17 31	17 33	17 36		17 41	17 43	17 46
Finsbury Park ⊖ a					17 07						17 22					17 37						17 52
Welwyn Garden City a																						
Stevenage a					17 28						17 43					17 58						18 13
Hitchin a					17 35						17 49					18 05						18 19
Letchworth Garden City a					17 41											18 11						
Royston a					17 54											18 24						
Cambridge a					18 12											18 43						
Huntingdon a											18 18											18 48
Peterborough a											18 34											19 05
Kentish Town ⊖ a				17 03						17 18					17 33						17 48	
West Hampstead Thameslink ⊖ a	16 58			17 07		17 14				17 22		17 29			17 37		17 43				17 52	
Elstree & Borehamwood a	17 11			17 22		17 26				17 37		17 41			17 52		17 56				18 07	
St Albans City a	17 21	17 09	17 14	17 31		17 36	17 24		17 28	17 46		17 51	17 39	17 44	18 01		18 06	17 54		17 58	18 19	
Harpenden a			17 20	17 41			17 30		17 35	17 54				17 50	18 09			18 00		18 05	18 25	
Luton Airport Parkway [7] ✈ a			17 26	17 46					17 41	18 00				17 56	18 15					18 10	18 31	
Luton [10] a		17 19	17 30	17 50			17 36		17 45	18 05			17 49	18 00	18 21			18 06		18 14	18 35	
Bedford a		17 40	17 55				17 58		18 09				18 06	18 25				18 28		18 41		

A From Three Bridges

Table T052-F

Mondays to Fridays

16 December to 15 May

Brighton, Gatwick Airport, Kent & South London - Luton, Bedford, Cambridge and Peterborough (via London)

	TL	TL ■	TL ■	TL	TL ■	TL	TL ■	TL	TL ■ A	TL	TL ■	TL	TL ■	TL ■	TL	TL ■	TL	TL ■	TL	TL	TL ■
Brighton [10] d		16 28			16 38								16 58			17 08					
Horsham d											16 55										17 25
Gatwick Airport [10] ✈ d		17 06	16 57		17 16		17 03		17 24		17 19		17 36	17 27		17 46		17 33			17 49
East Croydon d		17 21	17 25		17 31		17 33		17 40		17 45		17 51	17 55		18 01		18 03			18 15
Rainham (Kent) d										16 30										17 00	
Dartford d										17 15										17 45	
Abbey Wood d										17 28										17 58	
Woolwich Arsenal d										17 34										18 04	
Greenwich d										17 47										18 17	
Maidstone East d																					
Sevenoaks d								16 52											17 22		
Swanley d								17 11											17 41		
St Mary Cray d								17 15											17 45		
Orpington d				17 03											17 33						
Bromley South d				17 13				17 23							17 43				17 53		
Catford d				17 25				17 35							17 55				18 05		
Peckham Rye [4] 195 d				17 34				17 44							18 04				18 14		
Denmark Hill [4] 195 d				17 37				17 47							18 07				18 17		
Sutton [4] 179 d	16 49					17 16						17 19					17 46				
Wimbledon ⊖ d	17 07											17 37									
Streatham [4] d	17 18					17 33						17 48					18 03				
Tulse Hill [3] d	17 23					17 38						17 53					18 08				
Herne Hill [4] 173,179 d	17 27					17 42						17 57					18 12				
Loughborough Jn 173,179 d	17 30					17 45						18 00					18 15				
Elephant & Castle ⊖173,179 d	17 34			17 44		17 49		17 54				18 04			18 14		18 19		18 24		
London Bridge ⊖ d		17 35	17 41		17 46		17 51		17 54	17 58	18 01		18 05	18 11		18 16		18 21		18 28	18 31
London Blackfriars ⊖ a	17 39	17 41	17 46	17 49	17 51	17 54	17 56	17 59	18 01	18 04	18 06	18 09	18 11	18 16	18 19	18 21	18 24	18 26	18 29	18 34	18 36
London Blackfriars [3] ⊖ d	17 39	17 42	17 47	17 49	17 52	17 54	17 57		18 02	18 04	18 07	18 09	18 12	18 17	18 19	18 22	18 24	18 27		18 34	18 37
City Thameslink [3] d	17 41	17 44	17 49	17 51	17 54	17 56	17 59		18 04	18 06	18 09	18 11	18 14	18 19	18 21	18 24	18 26	18 29		18 36	18 39
Farringdon [3] ⊖ d	17 44	17 46	17 51	17 54	17 56	17 59	18 01		18 06	18 09	18 11	18 14	18 16	18 21	18 24	18 26	18 29	18 31		18 39	18 41
St Pancras International ⊖ d	17 48	17 51	17 56	17 58	18 01	18 03	18 06		18 11	18 13	18 16	18 18	18 21	18 26	18 28	18 31	18 33	18 36		18 43	18 46
Finsbury Park ⊖ a					18 07						18 22					18 37					18 52
Welwyn Garden City a																					
Stevenage a					18 28						18 43					18 58					19 13
Hitchin a					18 35						18 49					19 05					19 19
Letchworth Garden City a					18 41											19 11					
Royston a					18 54											19 24					
Cambridge a					19 10											19 42					
Huntingdon a											19 18										19 48
Peterborough a											19 41										20 05
Kentish Town ⊖ a				18 03						18 18					18 33					18 48	
West Hampstead Thameslink ⊖ a	17 58			18 07		18 14				18 22		18 28			18 37		18 44			18 52	
Elstree & Borehamwood a	18 11			18 22		18 26				18 37		18 41			18 52		18 56			19 07	
St Albans City a	18 23	18 09	18 15	18 31		18 36	18 24		18 28	18 46		18 51	18 39	18 44	19 01		19 06	18 54		19 16	
Harpenden a			18 21	18 41			18 30		18 36	18 54				18 50	19 09			19 01		19 26	
Luton Airport Parkway [7] ✈ a			18 27	18 46					18 41	19 00				18 56	19 15			19 07		19 31	
Luton [10] a		18 18	18 31	18 51			18 36		18 45	19 05			18 49	19 00	19 21			19 11		19 36	
Bedford a		18 36	18 55				18 59		19 15				19 06	19 25				19 36			

A From Three Bridges

Table T052-F

Mondays to Fridays

16 December to 15 May

Brighton, Gatwick Airport, Kent & South London - Luton, Bedford, Cambridge and Peterborough (via London)

	TL	TL ■	TL ■	TL	TL ■	TL	TL ■	TL	TL		TL ■	TL	TL ■	TL ■	TL	TL ■	TL	TL ■	TL	TL		TL ■	TL	TL ■
			A											A										
Brighton [10] d		17 28			17 38								17 58			18 08								18 28
Horsham d											17 55											18 25		
Gatwick Airport [10] ✈ d		18 06			18 16		18 03				18 19		18 36			18 46		18 33				18 49		19 06
East Croydon d		18 21	18 25		18 31		18 33				18 45		18 51	18 55		19 01		19 03				19 15		19 21
Rainham (Kent) d									17 28											18 00				
Dartford d									18 15											18 46				
Abbey Wood d									18 28											18 59				
Woolwich Arsenal d									18 34											19 05				
Greenwich d									18 47											19 18				
Maidstone East d																								
Sevenoaks d								17 52											18 22					
Swanley d								18 11											18 41					
St Mary Cray d								18 15											18 45					
Orpington d				18 02											18 33									
Bromley South d				18 13				18 23							18 43				18 53					
Catford d				18 25				18 35							18 55				19 05					
Peckham Rye [4] 195 d				18 34				18 44							19 04				19 14					
Denmark Hill [4] 195 d				18 37				18 47							19 07				19 17					
Sutton [4] 179 d	17 49					18 16						18 19					18 46						18 49	
Wimbledon ⊖ d	18 07											18 37											19 07	
Streatham [4] d	18 18					18 33						18 48					19 03						19 18	
Tulse Hill [3] d	18 23					18 38						18 53					19 08						19 23	
Herne Hill [4] 173,179 d	18 27					18 42						18 57					19 12						19 27	
Loughborough Jn 173,179 d	18 30					18 45						19 00					19 15						19 30	
Elephant & Castle ⊖173,179 d	18 34			18 44		18 49		18 54				19 04			19 14		19 19		19 24				19 34	
London Bridge ⊖ d		18 35	18 41		18 46		18 51		18 58		19 01		19 05	19 11		19 16		19 21		19 28		19 31		19 35
London Blackfriars ⊖ a	18 39	18 41	18 46	18 49	18 51	18 54	18 56	18 59	19 04		19 06	19 09	19 11	19 16	19 19	19 21	19 24	19 26	19 29	19 34		19 36	19 39	19 41
London Blackfriars [3] ⊖ d	18 39	18 42	18 47	18 49	18 52	18 54	18 57		19 04		19 07	19 09	19 12	19 17	19 19	19 22	19 24	19 27		19 34		19 37	19 39	19 42
City Thameslink [3] d	18 41	18 44	18 49	18 51	18 54	18 56	18 59		19 06		19 09	19 11	19 14	19 19	19 21	19 24	19 26	19 29		19 36		19 39	19 41	19 44
Farringdon [3] ⊖ d	18 44	18 46	18 51	18 54	18 56	18 59	19 01		19 09		19 11	19 14	19 16	19 21	19 24	19 26	19 29	19 31		19 39		19 41	19 44	19 46
St Pancras International ⊖ d	18 48	18 51	18 56	18 58	19 01	19 03	19 06		19 13		19 16	19 18	19 21	19 26	19 28	19 31	19 33	19 36		19 43		19 46	19 48	19 51
Finsbury Park ⊖ a					19 07						19 22					19 37						19 52		
Welwyn Garden City a																								
Stevenage a					19 31						19 43					19 58						20 12		
Hitchin a					19 38						19 49					20 05						20 19		
Letchworth Garden City a					19 44											20 11								
Royston a					19 56											20 23								
Cambridge a					20 11											20 43								
Huntingdon a											20 18											20 48		
Peterborough a											20 35											21 05		
Kentish Town ⊖ a				19 03					19 18								19 38						19 53	
West Hampstead Thameslink ⊖ a	18 58			19 07		19 14			19 22			19 29			19 36		19 44	19 44		19 51			19 59	
Elstree & Borehamwood a	19 11			19 22		19 26			19 37			19 41					19 57			20 05			20 12	
St Albans City a	19 21	19 09	19 14	19 31		19 36	19 24		19 49			19 53	19 39	19 45			20 07	19 56		20 15			20 22	20 09
Harpenden a		19 15	19 20	19 41			19 31		19 57				19 45	19 51				20 02		20 27				20 15
Luton Airport Parkway [7] ✈ a			19 26	19 46			19 36		20 02					19 57				20 07		20 32				
Luton [10] a		19 22	19 30	19 51			19 40		20 06				19 52	20 01				20 11		20 36				20 22
Bedford a		19 44	19 55				20 05						20 14	20 26				20 36						20 44

A From East Grinstead

Table T052-F

Mondays to Fridays

16 December to 15 May

Brighton, Gatwick Airport, Kent & South London - Luton, Bedford, Cambridge and Peterborough (via London)

	TL ■	TL	TL ■	TL	TL ■	TL	TL		TL ■	TL	TL ■	TL	TL ■	TL	TL ■	TL	TL	TL ■		TL	TL ■	TL	TL	TL ■
	A																							
Brighton [10] d			18 38								18 58		19 08								19 26			
Horsham d									18 55									19 25						
Gatwick Airport [10] ✈ d			19 16		19 03				19 19		19 36		19 46		19 33			19 49			20 06			20 03
East Croydon d	19 25		19 31		19 33				19 45		19 51		20 01		20 03			20 15			20 21			20 33
Rainham (Kent) d							18 30										18 58							
Dartford d							19 15										19 45							
Abbey Wood d							19 28										19 58							
Woolwich Arsenal d							19 34										20 04							
Greenwich d							19 47										20 17							
Maidstone East d																								
Sevenoaks d						18 52										19 22								
Swanley d						19 11										19 41								
St Mary Cray d						19 15										19 45								
Orpington d		19 03										19 33										20 03		
Bromley South d		19 13				19 23						19 43				19 53						20 13		
Catford d		19 25				19 35						19 55				20 05						20 25		
Peckham Rye [4] 195 d		19 34				19 44						20 04				20 14						20 34		
Denmark Hill [4] 195 d		19 37				19 47						20 07				20 17						20 37		
Sutton [4] 179 d				19 16						19 19				19 46						19 49			20 16	
Wimbledon ⊖ d										19 37										20 07				
Streatham [4] d				19 33						19 48				20 03						20 18			20 33	
Tulse Hill [3] d				19 38						19 53				20 08						20 23			20 38	
Herne Hill [4] 173,179 d				19 42						19 57				20 12						20 27			20 42	
Loughborough Jn 173,179 d				19 45						20 00				20 15						20 30			20 45	
Elephant & Castle ⊖173,179 d		19 44		19 49		19 54				20 04		20 14		20 19		20 24				20 34		20 44	20 49	
London Bridge ⊖ d	19 41		19 46		19 51		19 58		20 01		20 05		20 16		20 21		20 28	20 31			20 35			20 51
London Blackfriars ⊖ a	19 46	19 49	19 51	19 54	19 56	19 59	20 04		20 06	20 09	20 11	20 19	20 21	20 24	20 26	20 29	20 34	20 36		20 39	20 41	20 49	20 54	20 56
London Blackfriars [3] ⊖ d	19 47	19 49	19 52	19 54	19 57		20 04		20 07	20 09	20 12	20 19	20 22	20 24	20 27		20 34	20 37		20 39	20 42	20 49	20 54	20 57
City Thameslink [3] d	19 49	19 51	19 54	19 56	19 59		20 06		20 09	20 11	20 14	20 21	20 24	20 26	20 29		20 36	20 39		20 41	20 44	20 51	20 56	20 59
Farringdon [3] ⊖ d	19 51	19 54	19 56	19 59	20 01		20 09		20 11	20 14	20 16	20 24	20 26	20 29	20 31		20 39	20 41		20 44	20 46	20 54	20 59	21 01
St Pancras International ⊖ d	19 56	19 58	20 01	20 03	20 06		20 13		20 16	20 18	20 21	20 28	20 31	20 33	20 36		20 43	20 46		20 48	20 51	20 58	21 03	21 06
Finsbury Park ⊖ a			20 07						20 22				20 37					20 52						
Welwyn Garden City a																								
Stevenage a			20 28						20 43				20 58					21 13						
Hitchin a			20 35						20 49				21 05					21 19						
Letchworth Garden City a			20 41										21 11											
Royston a			20 54										21 24											
Cambridge a			21 14										21 40											
Huntingdon a									21 18									21 48						
Peterborough a									21 35									22 05						
Kentish Town ⊖ a				20 08						20 23		20 33		20 38						20 53		21 03	21 08	
West Hampstead Thameslink ⊖ a		20 06		20 14			20 21			20 29	20 29			20 44			20 51			20 59	20 59		21 14	
Elstree & Borehamwood a				20 27			20 35			20 42				20 57			21 05			21 12			21 27	
St Albans City a	20 14			20 37	20 24		20 45			20 52	20 41			21 08	20 54		21 15			21 22	21 11		21 37	21 24
Harpenden a	20 20				20 31		20 51				20 47				21 01		21 21				21 17			21 31
Luton Airport Parkway [7] ✈ a	20 26				20 36		20 56				20 52				21 06		21 26				21 22			21 36
Luton [10] a	20 30				20 40		21 01				20 56				21 10		21 31				21 26			21 40
Bedford a	20 56				21 05						21 21				21 35						21 51			22 05

A From East Grinstead

Table T052-F

Mondays to Fridays

16 December to 15 May

Brighton, Gatwick Airport, Kent & South London - Luton, Bedford, Cambridge and Peterborough (via London)

		TL	TL	TL 1	TL 1	TL		TL	TL 1	TL	TL 1	TL	TL	TL 1	TL	TL 1	TL		TL	TL 1	TL	TL	TL 1	TL	TL 1
Brighton 10	d				19 58				20 08							20 26									20 58
Horsham	d			19 55										20 25									20 55		
Gatwick Airport 10 ✈	d			20 19	20 36				20 46		20 32			20 49		21 06				21 03			21 19		21 36
East Croydon	d			20 45	20 51				21 01		21 03			21 15		21 21				21 33			21 45		21 51
Rainham (Kent)	d		19 28										19 58									20 28			
Dartford	d		20 15										20 45									21 15			
Abbey Wood	d		20 28										20 58									21 28			
Woolwich Arsenal	d		20 34										21 04									21 34			
Greenwich	d		20 47										21 17									21 47			
Maidstone East	d																								
Sevenoaks	d	19 52										20 22									20 52				
Swanley	d	20 11										20 41									21 11				
St Mary Cray	d	20 15										20 45									21 15				
Orpington	d							20 33									21 03								
Bromley South	d	20 23						20 43				20 53					21 13				21 23				
Catford	d	20 35						20 55				21 05					21 25				21 35				
Peckham Rye 4 195	d	20 44						21 04				21 14					21 34				21 44				
Denmark Hill 4 195	d	20 47						21 07				21 17					21 37				21 47				
Sutton 4 179	d					20 21				20 46					20 49				21 16					21 19	
Wimbledon ⊖	d					20 43									21 07									21 37	
Streatham 4	d					20 54				21 03					21 18				21 33					21 48	
Tulse Hill 3	d					20 59				21 08					21 23				21 38					21 53	
Herne Hill 4 173,179	d					21 04				21 12					21 27				21 42					21 57	
Loughborough Jn 173,179	d					21 07				21 15					21 30				21 45					22 00	
Elephant & Castle ⊖173,179	d	20 54				21 11		21 14		21 19		21 24			21 34		21 44		21 49		21 54			22 04	
London Bridge ⊖	d		20 58	21 01	21 05				21 16		21 21		21 28	21 31		21 35				21 51		21 58	22 01		22 05
London Blackfriars ⊖	a	20 59	21 04	21 06	21 11	21 16		21 19	21 21	21 24	21 26	21 29	21 34	21 36	21 39	21 41	21 49		21 54	21 56	21 59	22 04	22 06	22 09	22 11
London Blackfriars 3 ⊖	d		21 04	21 07	21 12	21 17		21 19	21 22	21 24	21 27		21 34	21 37	21 39	21 42	21 49		21 54	21 57		22 04	22 07	22 09	22 12
City Thameslink 3	d		21 06	21 09	21 14	21 19		21 21	21 24	21 26	21 29		21 36	21 39	21 41	21 44	21 51		21 56	21 59		22 06	22 09	22 11	22 14
Farringdon 3 ⊖	d		21 09	21 11	21 16	21 21		21 24	21 26	21 29	21 31		21 39	21 41	21 44	21 46	21 54		21 59	22 01		22 09	22 11	22 14	22 16
St Pancras International ⊖	d		21 13	21 16	21 21	21 26		21 28	21 31	21 33	21 36		21 43	21 46	21 48	21 51	21 58		22 03	22 06		22 13	22 16	22 18	22 21
Finsbury Park ⊖	a			21 22					21 37					21 52									22 22		
Welwyn Garden City	a																								
Stevenage	a			21 43					21 58					22 13									22 43		
Hitchin	a			21 49					22 05					22 19									22 49		
Letchworth Garden City	a								22 11																
Royston	a								22 24																
Cambridge	a								22 40																
Huntingdon	a			22 18										22 48									23 18		
Peterborough	a			22 35										23 05									23 37		
Kentish Town ⊖	a		21 18					21 33		21 38					21 53		22 03		22 08					22 23	
West Hampstead Thameslink ⊖	a		21 22		21 29	21 34				21 44			21 51		21 59	21 59			22 14			22 21		22 29	22 29
Elstree & Borehamwood	a		21 38			21 44				21 57			22 05		22 13				22 27					22 41	
St Albans City	a		21 48		21 41	21 54				22 07	21 54		22 15		22 23	22 11			22 37	22 24				22 51	22 41
Harpenden	a		21 57		21 47						22 01		22 21			22 17				22 31				22 58	22 47
Luton Airport Parkway 7 ✈	a		22 02		21 52						22 06		22 26			22 22				22 36				23 05	22 52
Luton 10	a		22 06		21 56						22 10		22 31			22 26				22 40				23 09	22 56
Bedford	a				22 21						22 35					22 51				23 05				23 30	23 21

Table T052-F

Mondays to Fridays

16 December to 15 May

Brighton, Gatwick Airport, Kent & South London - Luton, Bedford, Cambridge and Peterborough (via London)

		TL	TL 1	TL		TL 1	TL	TL	TL 1	TL	TL 1	TL	TL	TL	TL		TL 1	TL 1	TL	TL	TL 1	TL	TL	TL	TL 1
Brighton 10	d		21 08								21 26							21 58			22 08				
Horsham	d								21 26								21 55								22 25
Gatwick Airport 10 ✈	d		21 46			21 32			21 49		22 06						22 19	22 36			22 46				22 49
East Croydon	d		22 01			22 03			22 15		22 21						22 45	22 51			23 01				23 15
Rainham (Kent)	d							20 58							21 28									22 00	
Dartford	d							21 45							22 15									22 45	
Abbey Wood	d							21 58							22 28									22 58	
Woolwich Arsenal	d							22 04							22 34									23 04	
Greenwich	d							22 17							22 47									23 17	
Maidstone East	d																								
Sevenoaks	d						21 22							21 52									22 22		
Swanley	d						21 41							22 11									22 41		
St Mary Cray	d						21 45							22 15									22 45		
Orpington	d	21 33										22 03								22 33					
Bromley South	d	21 43					21 53					22 13		22 23						22 43			22 53		
Catford	d	21 55					22 05					22 25		22 35						22 55			23 05		
Peckham Rye 4 195	d	22 04					22 14					22 34		22 44						23 04			23 14		
Denmark Hill 4 195	d	22 07					22 17					22 37		22 47						23 07			23 17		
Sutton 4 179	d			21 46						21 49			22 18						22 19			22 48			
Wimbledon ⊖	d									22 07									22 41						
Streatham 4	d			22 03						22 18			22 35						22 52			23 05			
Tulse Hill 3	d			22 08						22 23			22 40						22 57			23 10			
Herne Hill 4 173,179	d			22 12						22 27			22 44						23 04			23 14			
Loughborough Jn 173,179	d			22 15						22 30			22 47						23 07			23 17			
Elephant & Castle ⊖173,179	d	22 14		22 19			22 24			22 34		22 44	22 51	22 54					23 11	23 14		23 21	23 24		
London Bridge ⊖	d		22 16			22 21		22 28	22 31		22 35				22 58		23 01	23 05			23 16			23 28	23 31
London Blackfriars ⊖	a	22 19	22 21	22 24		22 26	22 29	22 34	22 36	22 39	22 41	22 49	22 56	22 59	23 04		23 06	23 11	23 16	23 19	23 21	23 26	23 29	23 34	23 36
London Blackfriars 3 ⊖	d	22 19	22 22	22 24		22 27		22 34	22 37	22 39	22 42	22 49	22 59		23 04		23 07	23 12	23 17		23 22	23 29		23 34	23 37
City Thameslink 3	d	22 21	22 24	22 26		22 29		22 36	22 39	22 41	22 44	22 51													
Farringdon 3 ⊖	d	22 24	22 26	22 29		22 31		22 39	22 41	22 44	22 46	22 54	23 04		23 09		23 11	23 16	23 21		23 26	23 33		23 39	23 41
St Pancras International ⊖	d	22 28	22 31	22 33		22 36		22 43	22 46	22 48	22 51	22 58	23 08		23 13		23 16	23 21	23 26		23 31	23 38		23 43	23 46
Finsbury Park ⊖	a		22 40						22 52								23 22				23 40				23 52
Welwyn Garden City	a																								
Stevenage	a		23 00						23 14								23 44				00 01				00 13
Hitchin	a		23 06						23 20								23 50				00 08				00 22
Letchworth Garden City	a		23 12																		00 13				
Royston	a		23 25																		00 24				
Cambridge	a		23 41																		00 41				
Huntingdon	a								23 48								00 19								00 50
Peterborough	a								00 07								00 37								01 09
Kentish Town ⊖	a	22 33		22 38						22 53			23 13						23 30			23 42			
West Hampstead Thameslink ⊖	a			22 44				22 51		23 02	22 59	23 06	23 18		23 21			23 29	23 35			23 46		23 51	
Elstree & Borehamwood	a			22 57						23 16			23 31						23 49			00 01			
St Albans City	a			23 08		22 56				23 26	23 15		23 41					23 46	23 58			00 11			
Harpenden	a			23 15		23 04				23 33	23 22		23 48					23 52	00 06			00 18			
Luton Airport Parkway 7 ✈	a			23 20		23 09				23 38	23 27		23 53					23 57	00 11			00 23			
Luton 10	a			23 24		23 13				23 42	23 31		23 57					00 01	00 15			00 27			
Bedford	a			23 49		23 38				00 03	23 55		00 18					00 26	00 40			00 48			

Table T052-F

Mondays to Fridays

16 December to 15 May

Brighton, Gatwick Airport, Kent & South London - Luton, Bedford, Cambridge and Peterborough (via London)

		TL 1	TL	TL	TL	TL	TL	TL 1	TL	TL 1	TL 1	TL 1
Brighton 10	d	22 26						22 56			23 24	23 42
Horsham	d									23 11		
Gatwick Airport 10 ✈	d	23 06						23 34		23 35	00 04	00 21
East Croydon	d	23 21						23 53		00 09	00 23	00 40
Rainham (Kent)	d											
Dartford	d											
Abbey Wood	d											
Woolwich Arsenal	d											
Greenwich	d											
Maidstone East	d											
Sevenoaks	d				22 52				23 22			
Swanley	d				23 11				23 41			
St Mary Cray	d				23 15				23 45			
Orpington	d			23 03								
Bromley South	d			23 13	23 23				23 53			
Catford	d			23 25	23 35				00 06			
Peckham Rye 4 195	d			23 34	23 44				00 14			
Denmark Hill 4 195	d			23 37	23 47				00 17			
Sutton 4 179	d		22 49			23 18	23 19					
Wimbledon ⊖	d		23 11				23 37					
Streatham 4	d		23 22			23 35	23 48					
Tulse Hill 3	d		23 27			23 40	23 53					
Herne Hill 4 173,179	d		23 34			23 44	23 57					
Loughborough Jn 173,179	d		23 37			23 47						
Elephant & Castle ⊖173,179	d		23 41	23 44	23 54	23 54	00 04		00 24			
London Bridge ⊖	d	23 35										
London Blackfriars ⊖	a	23 41	23 46	23 49	23 59	00 01	00 08	00 18	00 29	00 36	00 49	01 06
London Blackfriars 3 ⊖	d	23 42	23 49			00 02	00 09	00 22		00 37	00 50	01 06
City Thameslink 3	d											
Farringdon 3 ⊖	d	23 46	23 53			00 06	00 13	00 26		00 41		
St Pancras International ⊖	d	23 51	23 58			00 11	00 18	00 31		00 46	01 01	01 16
Finsbury Park ⊖	a									00 52		
Welwyn Garden City	a									01 14		
Stevenage	a									01 23		
Hitchin	a									01 32		
Letchworth Garden City	a											
Royston	a											
Cambridge	a											
Huntingdon	a									02 01		
Peterborough	a									02 19		
Kentish Town ⊖	a		00 01				00 22				01 05	
West Hampstead Thameslink ⊖	a	23 59	00 06			00 19	00 26	00 39			01 09	01 24
Elstree & Borehamwood	a		00 20				00 40				01 24	
St Albans City	a	00 16	00 31			00 35	00 51	00 56			01 34	01 40
Harpenden	a	00 22	00 38			00 42	00 58	01 02			01 40	01 47
Luton Airport Parkway 7 ✈	a	00 27	00 43			00 47	01 03	01 07			01 45	01 52
Luton 10	a	00 31	00 47			00 51	01 07	01 11			01 49	01 56
Bedford	a	00 58	01 08			01 18	01 32	01 36			02 14	02 21

NRT DECEMBER 19 EDITION

Table T052-F

Saturdays

21 December to 16 May

Brighton, Gatwick Airport, Kent & South London - Luton, Bedford, Cambridge and Peterborough (via London)

		TL A	TL A	TL 1 B	TL C	TL 1 D	TL 1 B	TL 1 B	TL 1	TL 1 E	TL 1 E	TL 1 E	TL 1 E	TL 1 E	TL 1 E	TL	TL 1	TL 1 E	TL F	TL 1	TL	TL 1 E	TL
Brighton 10	d								00 04								04 12			05 06			
Horsham	d																						
Gatwick Airport 10 ✈	d						00 04	00 21	00 42	01 46	02 21	02 46	03 21	03 46	04 21		04 41	05 20		05 46		05 33	
East Croydon	d					00 09	00 23	00 40	01 10	02 10	02 40	03 10	03 40	04 10	04 40		05 10	05 39		06 01		06 03	
Rainham (Kent)	d																						
Dartford	d																		05 15				
Abbey Wood	d																		05 28				
Woolwich Arsenal	d																		05 34				
Greenwich	d																		05 47				
Maidstone East	d																						
Sevenoaks	d																						05 22
Swanley	d																						05 41
St Mary Cray	d																						05 45
Orpington	d																						
Bromley South	d																						05 53
Catford	d				00 06																		06 05
Peckham Rye 4 195	d				00 14																		06 14
Denmark Hill 4 195	d				00 17																		06 17
Sutton 4 179	d																				05 46		
Wimbledon ⊖	d																						
Streatham 4	d																				06 03		
Tulse Hill 3	d																				06 08		
Herne Hill 4 173,179	d																				06 12		
Loughborough Jn 173,179	d																				06 15		
Elephant & Castle ⊖173,179	d		00 04		00 24																06 19		06 24
London Bridge ⊖	d																05 26	05 55	05 58	06 16		06 21	
London Blackfriars ⊖	a		00 08		00 29	00 36	00 49	01 06	01 36	02 36	03 06	03 36	04 06	04 36	05 06		05 31	06 01	06 04	06 21	06 24	06 26	06 29
London Blackfriars 3 ⊖	d	00 02	00 09	00 22		00 37	00 50	01 06	01 36	02 36	03 06	03 36	04 06	04 36	05 06	05 27	05 32	06 02	06 04	06 22	06 24	06 27	
City Thameslink 3	d																						
Farringdon 3 ⊖	d	00 06	00 13	00 26		00 41									05 11	05 31	05 36	06 06	06 09	06 26	06 29	06 31	
St Pancras International ⊖	d	00 11	00 18	00 31		00 46	01 01	01 16	01 44	02 44	03 14	03 44	04 14	04 44	05 16	05 36	05 41	06 11	06 13	06 31	06 33	06 36	
Finsbury Park ⊖	a					00 52														06 41			
Welwyn Garden City	a					01 14																	
Stevenage	a					01 23														07 01			
Hitchin	a					01 32														07 08			
Letchworth Garden City	a																			07 13			
Royston	a																			07 24			
Cambridge	a																			07 40			
Huntingdon	a					02 01																	
Peterborough	a					02 19																	
Kentish Town ⊖	a		00 22				01 05		01 48	02 48		03 48	04 18	04 48		05 40			06 18		06 38		
West Hampstead Thameslink ⊖	a	00 19	00 26	00 39			01 09	01 24	01 52	02 52	03 22	03 52	04 22	04 52	05 24	05 44	05 48	06 19	06 22		06 44	06 44	
Elstree & Borehamwood	a		00 40				01 24		02 07	03 07		04 07	04 37	05 07		05 58			06 36		06 57		
St Albans City	a	00 35	00 51	00 56			01 34	01 40	02 17	03 17	03 40	04 17	04 47	05 17	05 40	06 08	06 00	06 31	06 46		07 07	06 56	
Harpenden	a	00 42	00 58	01 02			01 40	01 47	02 25	03 25	03 47	04 25	04 55	05 25	05 47		06 06	06 37				07 03	
Luton Airport Parkway 7 ✈	a	00 47	01 03	01 07			01 45	01 52	02 30	03 30	03 52	04 30	05 00	05 30	05 52		06 11	06 42				07 08	
Luton 10	a	00 51	01 07	01 11			01 49	01 56	02 34	03 34	03 56	04 34	05 04	05 34	05 56		06 15	06 46				07 12	
Bedford	a	01 18	01 32	01 36			02 14	02 21	02 59	03 59	04 21	05 01	05 33	05 59	06 21		06 41	07 11				07 37	

A From Sutton (Surrey)
B From Brighton
C From Sevenoaks
D From Horsham
E From Three Bridges
F From Gillingham (Kent)

Table T052-F

Saturdays

21 December to 16 May

Brighton, Gatwick Airport, Kent & South London - Luton, Bedford, Cambridge and Peterborough (via London)

			TL	TL 1	TL	TL 1	TL	TL 1	TL	TL	TL 1	TL	TL 1	TL 1	TL	TL 1	TL	TL	TL 1	TL	TL 1	TL	TL 1	TL
			A																					
Brighton 10		d				05 26							05 58	06 08							06 26			
Horsham		d		05 25							05 55								06 25					
Gatwick Airport 10 ✈		d		05 49		06 06		06 03			06 19		06 36	06 46		06 33			06 49		07 06		07 03	
East Croydon 🚊		d		06 15		06 21		06 33			06 45		06 51	07 01		07 03			07 15		07 21		07 33	
Rainham (Kent)		d								05 28								05 58						
Dartford		d	05 45							06 15								06 45						
Abbey Wood		d	05 58							06 28								06 58						
Woolwich Arsenal		d	06 04							06 34								07 04						
Greenwich		d	06 17							06 47								07 17						
Maidstone East		d																						
Sevenoaks		d							05 52								06 22							06 52
Swanley		d							06 11								06 41							07 11
St Mary Cray		d							06 15								06 45							07 15
Orpington		d																						
Bromley South		d							06 23								06 53							07 23
Catford		d							06 35								07 05							07 35
Peckham Rye 4	195	d							06 44								07 14							07 44
Denmark Hill 4	195	d							06 47								07 17							07 47
Sutton 4	179	d			05 49		06 16					06 19			06 46					06 49		07 16		
Wimbledon ⊖		d			06 07							06 37								07 07				
Streatham 4		d			06 18		06 33					06 48			07 03					07 18		07 33		
Tulse Hill 3		d			06 23		06 38					06 53			07 08					07 23		07 38		
Herne Hill 4	173,179	d			06 27		06 42					06 57			07 12					07 27		07 42		
Loughborough Jn	173,179	d			06 30		06 45					07 00			07 15					07 30		07 45		
Elephant & Castle ⊖	173,179	d			06 34		06 49		06 54			07 04			07 19		07 24			07 34		07 49		07 54
London Bridge ⊖		d	06 28	06 31		06 35		06 51		06 58	07 01		07 05	07 16		07 21		07 28	07 31		07 35		07 51	
London Blackfriars ⊖		a	06 34	06 36	06 39	06 41	06 54	06 56	06 59	07 04	07 06	07 09	07 11	07 21	07 24	07 26	07 29	07 34	07 36	07 39	07 41	07 54	07 56	07 59
London Blackfriars 3 ⊖		d	06 34	06 37	06 39	06 42	06 54	06 57		07 04	07 07	07 09	07 12	07 22	07 24	07 27		07 34	07 37	07 39	07 42	07 54	07 57	
City Thameslink 3		d																						
Farringdon 3 ⊖		d	06 39	06 41	06 44	06 46	06 59	07 01		07 09	07 11	07 14	07 16	07 26	07 29	07 31		07 39	07 41	07 44	07 46	07 59	08 01	
St Pancras International ⊖		d	06 43	06 46	06 48	06 51	07 03	07 06		07 13	07 16	07 18	07 21	07 31	07 33	07 36		07 43	07 46	07 48	07 51	08 03	08 06	
Finsbury Park ⊖		a		06 52							07 22			07 41					07 52					
Welwyn Garden City		a																						
Stevenage		a		07 13							07 43			08 01					08 13					
Hitchin		a		07 19							07 49			08 08					08 19					
Letchworth Garden City		a												08 13										
Royston		a												08 24										
Cambridge		a												08 40										
Huntingdon		a		07 48							08 18								08 48					
Peterborough		a		08 05							08 39								09 08					
Kentish Town ⊖		a	06 48		06 53		07 08			07 18		07 23			07 38			07 48		07 53		08 08		
West Hampstead Thameslink ⊖		a			06 59	06 59	07 14					07 29	07 29		07 44					07 59	07 59	08 14		
Elstree & Borehamwood		a			07 12		07 27					07 42			07 57					08 12		08 27		
St Albans City		a			07 22	07 11	07 37	07 24				07 52	07 41		08 07	07 54				08 22	08 11	08 37	08 24	
Harpenden		a				07 17		07 31					07 47			08 01					08 17		08 31	
Luton Airport Parkway 7 ✈		a				07 22		07 36					07 52			08 06					08 22		08 36	
Luton 10		a				07 26		07 40					07 56			08 10					08 26		08 40	
Bedford		a				07 51		08 05					08 21			08 35					08 51		09 05	

A From Gillingham (Kent)

Table T052-F

Saturdays

21 December to 16 May

Brighton, Gatwick Airport, Kent & South London - Luton, Bedford, Cambridge and Peterborough (via London)

			TL	TL 1	TL	TL 1	TL 1	TL	TL 1	TL	TL	TL 1	TL	TL 1	TL	TL 1	TL	TL	TL 1	TL	TL 1	TL 1	TL	TL 1
Brighton 10		d				06 58	07 08							07 26							07 58	08 08		
Horsham		d		06 55								07 25							07 55					
Gatwick Airport 10 ✈		d		07 19		07 36	07 46		07 33			07 49		08 06		08 03			08 19		08 36	08 46		08 33
East Croydon 🚊		d		07 45		07 51	08 01		08 03			08 15		08 21		08 33			08 45		08 51	09 01		09 03
Rainham (Kent)		d	06 28								06 58							07 28						
Dartford		d	07 15								07 45							08 15						
Abbey Wood		d	07 28								07 58							08 28						
Woolwich Arsenal		d	07 34								08 04							08 34						
Greenwich		d	07 47								08 17							08 47						
Maidstone East		d																						
Sevenoaks		d								07 22							07 52							
Swanley		d								07 41							08 11							
St Mary Cray		d								07 45							08 15							
Orpington		d																						
Bromley South		d								07 53							08 23							
Catford		d								08 05							08 35							
Peckham Rye 4	195	d								08 14							08 44							
Denmark Hill 4	195	d								08 17							08 47							
Sutton 4	179	d			07 19			07 46					07 49		08 16					08 19			08 46	
Wimbledon ⊖		d			07 37								08 07							08 37				
Streatham 4		d			07 48			08 03					08 18		08 33					08 48			09 03	
Tulse Hill 3		d			07 53			08 08					08 23		08 38					08 53			09 08	
Herne Hill 4	173,179	d			07 57			08 12					08 27		08 42					08 57			09 12	
Loughborough Jn	173,179	d			08 00			08 15					08 30		08 45					09 00			09 15	
Elephant & Castle ⊖	173,179	d			08 04			08 19		08 24			08 34		08 49		08 54			09 04			09 19	
London Bridge ⊖		d	07 58	08 01		08 05	08 16		08 21		08 28	08 31		08 35		08 51		08 58	09 01		09 05	09 16		09 21
London Blackfriars ⊖		a	08 04	08 06	08 09	08 11	08 21	08 24	08 26	08 29	08 34	08 36	08 39	08 41	08 54	08 56	08 59	09 04	09 06	09 09	09 11	09 21	09 24	09 26
London Blackfriars 3 ⊖		d	08 04	08 07	08 09	08 12	08 22	08 24	08 27		08 34	08 37	08 39	08 42	08 54	08 57		09 04	09 07	09 09	09 12	09 22	09 24	09 27
City Thameslink 3		d																09 06	09 09	09 11	09 14	09 24	09 26	09 29
Farringdon 3 ⊖		d	08 09	08 11	08 14	08 16	08 26	08 29	08 31		08 39	08 41	08 44	08 46	08 59	09 01		09 09	09 11	09 14	09 16	09 26	09 29	09 31
St Pancras International ⊖		d	08 13	08 16	08 18	08 21	08 31	08 33	08 36		08 43	08 46	08 48	08 51	09 03	09 06		09 13	09 16	09 18	09 21	09 31	09 33	09 36
Finsbury Park ⊖		a		08 22			08 41					08 52							09 22			09 41		
Welwyn Garden City		a																						
Stevenage		a		08 43			09 01					09 13							09 43			10 01		
Hitchin		a		08 49			09 08					09 19							09 49			10 08		
Letchworth Garden City		a					09 13															10 13		
Royston		a					09 24															10 24		
Cambridge		a					09 40															10 40		
Huntingdon		a		09 18								09 48							10 18					
Peterborough		a		09 36								10 05							10 40					
Kentish Town ⊖		a	08 18		08 23			08 38			08 48		08 53		09 08			09 18		09 23			09 38	
West Hampstead Thameslink ⊖		a			08 29	08 29		08 44					08 59	08 59	09 14					09 29	09 29		09 44	
Elstree & Borehamwood		a			08 42			08 57					09 12		09 27					09 42			09 57	
St Albans City		a			08 52	08 41		09 07	08 54				09 22	09 11	09 37	09 24				09 52	09 41		10 07	09 54
Harpenden		a				08 47			09 01					09 17		09 31					09 47			10 01
Luton Airport Parkway 7 ✈		a				08 52			09 06					09 22		09 36					09 52			10 06
Luton 10		a				08 56			09 10					09 26		09 40					09 56			10 10
Bedford		a				09 21			09 35					09 51		10 05					10 21			10 35

Table T052-F

Saturdays

21 December to 16 May

Brighton, Gatwick Airport, Kent & South London - Luton, Bedford, Cambridge and Peterborough (via London)

Station		TL	TL	TL 1	TL	TL 1	TL	TL 1	TL	TL	TL 1	TL	TL 1	TL 1	TL	TL 1	TL	TL	TL 1	TL	TL 1	TL	TL 1
Brighton 10	d					08 26							08 58	09 08							09 26		
Horsham	d			08 25							08 55								09 25				
Gatwick Airport 10 ✈	d			08 49		09 06		09 03			09 19		09 36	09 46		09 33			09 49		10 06		10 03
East Croydon	d			09 15		09 21		09 33			09 45		09 51	10 01		10 03			10 15		10 21		10 33
Rainham (Kent)	d		07 58							08 28								08 58					
Dartford	d		08 45							09 15								09 45					
Abbey Wood	d		08 58							09 28								09 58					
Woolwich Arsenal	d		09 04							09 34								10 04					
Greenwich	d		09 17							09 47								10 17					
Maidstone East	d																						
Sevenoaks	d	08 22							08 52								09 22						
Swanley	d	08 41							09 11								09 41						
St Mary Cray	d	08 45							09 15								09 45						
Orpington	d																						
Bromley South	d	08 53							09 23								09 53						
Catford	d	09 05							09 35								10 05						
Peckham Rye 4 (195)	d	09 14							09 44								10 14						
Denmark Hill 4 (195)	d	09 17							09 47								10 17						
Sutton 4 (179)	d				08 49		09 16					09 19			09 46					09 49		10 16	
Wimbledon ⊖	d				09 07							09 37								10 07			
Streatham 4	d				09 18		09 33					09 48			10 03					10 18		10 33	
Tulse Hill 3	d				09 23		09 38					09 53			10 08					10 23		10 38	
Herne Hill 4 (173,179)	d				09 27		09 42					09 57			10 12					10 27		10 42	
Loughborough Jn (173,179)	d				09 30		09 45					10 00			10 15					10 30		10 45	
Elephant & Castle ⊖ (173,179)	d	09 24			09 34		09 49		09 54			10 04			10 19		10 24			10 34		10 49	
London Bridge ⊖	d		09 28	09 31		09 35		09 51		09 58	10 01		10 05	10 16		10 21		10 28	10 31		10 35		10 51
London Blackfriars ⊖	a	09 29	09 34	09 36	09 39	09 41	09 54	09 56	09 59	10 04	10 06	10 09	10 11	10 21	10 24	10 26	10 29	10 34	10 36	10 39	10 41	10 54	10 56
London Blackfriars 3 ⊖	d		09 34	09 37	09 39	09 42	09 54	09 57		10 04	10 07	10 09	10 12	10 22	10 24	10 27		10 34	10 37	10 39	10 42	10 54	10 57
City Thameslink 3	d		09 36	09 39	09 41	09 44	09 56	09 59		10 06	10 09	10 11	10 14	10 24	10 26	10 29		10 36	10 39	10 41	10 44	10 56	10 59
Farringdon 3 ⊖	d		09 39	09 41	09 44	09 46	09 59	10 01		10 09	10 11	10 14	10 16	10 26	10 29	10 31		10 39	10 41	10 44	10 46	10 59	11 01
St Pancras International ⊖	d		09 43	09 46	09 48	09 51	10 03	10 06		10 13	10 16	10 18	10 21	10 31	10 33	10 36		10 43	10 46	10 48	10 51	11 03	11 06
Finsbury Park ⊖	a			09 52							10 22			10 41					10 52				
Welwyn Garden City	a																						
Stevenage	a			10 13							10 43			11 01					11 13				
Hitchin	a			10 19							10 49			11 08					11 18				
Letchworth Garden City	a													11 13									
Royston	a													11 24									
Cambridge	a													11 40									
Huntingdon	a			10 48							11 18								11 48				
Peterborough	a			11 05							11 39								12 05				
Kentish Town ⊖	a		09 48		09 53		10 08			10 18		10 23			10 38			10 48		10 53		11 08	
West Hampstead Thameslink ⊖	a				09 59	09 59	10 14					10 29	10 29		10 44					10 59	10 59	11 14	
Elstree & Borehamwood	a				10 12		10 27					10 42			10 57					11 12		11 27	
St Albans City	a				10 22	10 11	10 37	10 24				10 52	10 41		11 07	10 54				11 22	11 11	11 37	11 24
Harpenden	a					10 17		10 31					10 47			11 01					11 17		11 31
Luton Airport Parkway 7 ✈	a					10 22		10 36					10 52			11 06					11 22		11 36
Luton 10	a					10 26		10 40					10 56			11 10					11 26		11 40
Bedford	a					10 51		11 05					11 21			11 35					11 51		12 05

Table T052-F

Saturdays

21 December to 16 May

Brighton, Gatwick Airport, Kent & South London - Luton, Bedford, Cambridge and Peterborough (via London)

Station		TL	TL	TL 1	TL	TL 1	TL 1	TL	TL 1	TL	TL	TL 1	TL	TL 1	TL	TL 1	TL	TL	TL 1	TL	TL 1	TL 1	TL
Brighton 10	d					09 58	10 08							10 26							10 58	11 08	
Horsham	d			09 55								10 25							10 55				
Gatwick Airport 10 ✈	d			10 19		10 36	10 46		10 33			10 49		11 06		11 03			11 19		11 36	11 46	
East Croydon	d			10 45		10 51	11 01		11 03			11 15		11 21		11 33			11 45		11 51	12 01	
Rainham (Kent)	d		09 28								09 58							10 28					
Dartford	d		10 15								10 45							11 15					
Abbey Wood	d		10 28								10 58							11 28					
Woolwich Arsenal	d		10 34								11 04							11 34					
Greenwich	d		10 47								11 17							11 47					
Maidstone East	d																						
Sevenoaks	d	09 52								10 22							10 52						
Swanley	d	10 11								10 41							11 11						
St Mary Cray	d	10 15								10 45							11 15						
Orpington	d																						
Bromley South	d	10 23								10 53							11 23						
Catford	d	10 35								11 05							11 35						
Peckham Rye 4 (195)	d	10 44								11 14							11 44						
Denmark Hill 4 (195)	d	10 47								11 17							11 47						
Sutton 4 (179)	d				10 19			10 46					10 49		11 16					11 19			11 46
Wimbledon ⊖	d				10 37								11 07							11 37			
Streatham 4	d				10 48			11 03					11 18		11 33					11 48			12 03
Tulse Hill 3	d				10 53			11 08					11 23		11 38					11 53			12 08
Herne Hill 4 (173,179)	d				10 57			11 12					11 27		11 42					11 57			12 12
Loughborough Jn (173,179)	d				11 00			11 15					11 30		11 45					12 00			12 15
Elephant & Castle ⊖ (173,179)	d	10 54			11 04			11 19		11 24			11 34		11 49		11 54			12 04			12 19
London Bridge ⊖	d		10 58	11 01		11 05	11 16		11 21		11 28	11 31		11 35		11 51		11 58	12 01		12 05	12 16	
London Blackfriars ⊖	a	10 59	11 04	11 06	11 09	11 11	11 21	11 24	11 26	11 29	11 34	11 36	11 39	11 41	11 54	11 56	11 59	12 04	12 06	12 09	12 11	12 21	12 24
London Blackfriars 3 ⊖	d		11 04	11 07	11 09	11 12	11 22	11 24	11 27		11 34	11 37	11 39	11 42	11 54	11 57		12 04	12 07	12 09	12 12	12 22	12 24
City Thameslink 3	d		11 06	11 09	11 11	11 14	11 24	11 26	11 29		11 36	11 39	11 41	11 44	11 56	11 59		12 06	12 09	12 11	12 14	12 24	12 26
Farringdon 3 ⊖	d		11 09	11 11	11 14	11 16	11 26	11 29	11 31		11 39	11 41	11 44	11 46	11 59	12 01		12 09	12 11	12 14	12 16	12 26	12 29
St Pancras International ⊖	d		11 13	11 16	11 18	11 21	11 31	11 33	11 36		11 43	11 46	11 48	11 51	12 03	12 06		12 13	12 16	12 18	12 21	12 31	12 33
Finsbury Park ⊖	a			11 22			11 41					11 53							12 22			12 41	
Welwyn Garden City	a																						
Stevenage	a			11 43			12 01					12 13							12 43			13 01	
Hitchin	a			11 49			12 08					12 19							12 49			13 08	
Letchworth Garden City	a						12 13															13 13	
Royston	a						12 24															13 24	
Cambridge	a						12 40															13 40	
Huntingdon	a			12 18								12 48							13 18				
Peterborough	a			12 39								13 05							13 39				
Kentish Town ⊖	a		11 18		11 23			11 38			11 48		11 53		12 08			12 18		12 23			12 38
West Hampstead Thameslink ⊖	a				11 29	11 29		11 44					11 59	11 59	12 14					12 29	12 29		12 44
Elstree & Borehamwood	a				11 42			11 57					12 12		12 27					12 42			12 57
St Albans City	a				11 52	11 41		12 07	11 54				12 22	12 11	12 37	12 24				12 52	12 41		13 07
Harpenden	a					11 47			12 01					12 17		12 31					12 47		
Luton Airport Parkway 7 ✈	a					11 52			12 06					12 22		12 36					12 52		
Luton 10	a					11 56			12 10					12 26		12 40					12 56		
Bedford	a					12 21			12 35					12 51		13 05					13 21		

Table T052-F

Saturdays
21 December to 16 May

Brighton, Gatwick Airport, Kent & South London - Luton, Bedford, Cambridge and Peterborough (via London)

		TL ■	TL	TL	TL ■	TL	TL ■	TL	TL ■	TL	TL	TL ■	TL	TL ■	TL ■	TL	TL ■	TL	TL	TL ■	TL	TL ■
Brighton ■	d						11 26							11 58	12 08							12 26
Horsham	d				11 25							11 55								12 25		
Gatwick Airport ■ ✈	d	11 33			11 49		12 06		12 03			12 19		12 36	12 46		12 33			12 49		13 06
East Croydon	d	12 03			12 15		12 21		12 33			12 45		12 51	13 01		13 03			13 15		13 21
Rainham (Kent)	d			10 58							11 28								11 58			
Dartford	d			11 45							12 15								12 45			
Abbey Wood	d			11 58							12 28								12 58			
Woolwich Arsenal	d			12 04							12 34								13 04			
Greenwich	d			12 17							12 47								13 17			
Maidstone East	d																					
Sevenoaks	d		11 22							11 52								12 22				
Swanley	d		11 41							12 11								12 41				
St Mary Cray	d		11 45							12 15								12 45				
Orpington	d																					
Bromley South	d		11 53							12 23								12 53				
Catford	d		12 05							12 35								13 05				
Peckham Rye ■ 195	d		12 14							12 44								13 14				
Denmark Hill ■ 195	d		12 17							12 47								13 17				
Sutton ■ 179	d					11 49		12 16					12 19			12 46					12 49	
Wimbledon ⊖	d					12 07							12 37								13 07	
Streatham ■	d					12 18		12 33					12 48			13 03					13 18	
Tulse Hill ■	d					12 23		12 38					12 53			13 08					13 23	
Herne Hill ■ 173,179	d					12 27		12 42					12 57			13 12					13 27	
Loughborough Jn 173,179	d					12 30		12 45					13 00			13 15					13 30	
Elephant & Castle ⊖ 173,179	d		12 24			12 34		12 49		12 54			13 04			13 19		13 24			13 34	
London Bridge ⊖	d	12 21		12 28	12 31		12 35		12 51		12 58	13 01		13 05	13 16		13 21		13 28	13 31		13 35
London Blackfriars ⊖	a	12 26	12 29	12 34	12 36	12 39	12 41	12 54	12 56	12 59	13 04	13 06	13 09	13 11	13 21	13 24	13 26	13 29	13 34	13 36	13 39	13 41
London Blackfriars ■ ⊖	d	12 27		12 34	12 37	12 39	12 42	12 54	12 57		13 04	13 07	13 09	13 12	13 22	13 24	13 27		13 34	13 37	13 39	13 42
City Thameslink ■	d	12 29		12 36	12 39	12 41	12 44	12 56	12 59		13 06	13 09	13 11	13 14	13 24	13 26	13 29		13 36	13 39	13 41	13 44
Farringdon ■ ⊖	d	12 31		12 39	12 41	12 44	12 46	12 59	13 01		13 09	13 11	13 14	13 16	13 26	13 29	13 31		13 39	13 41	13 44	13 46
St Pancras International ⊖	d	12 36		12 43	12 46	12 48	12 51	13 03	13 06		13 13	13 16	13 18	13 21	13 31	13 33	13 36		13 43	13 46	13 48	13 51
Finsbury Park ⊖	a				12 52							13 22			13 41					13 52		
Welwyn Garden City	a																					
Stevenage	a				13 13							13 43			14 01					14 13		
Hitchin	a				13 19							13 49			14 08					14 19		
Letchworth Garden City	a														14 13							
Royston	a														14 24							
Cambridge	a														14 40							
Huntingdon	a				13 48							14 18								14 48		
Peterborough	a				14 05							14 40								15 05		
Kentish Town ⊖	a			12 48		12 53		13 08			13 18		13 23			13 38			13 48		13 53	
West Hampstead Thameslink ⊖	a					12 59	12 59	13 14					13 29	13 29		13 44					13 59	13 59
Elstree & Borehamwood	a					13 12		13 27					13 42			13 57					14 12	
St Albans City	a	12 54				13 22	13 11	13 37	13 24				13 52	13 41		14 07	13 54				14 22	14 11
Harpenden	a	13 01					13 17		13 31					13 47			14 01					14 17
Luton Airport Parkway ■ ✈	a	13 06					13 22		13 36					13 52			14 06					14 22
Luton ■	a	13 10					13 26		13 40					13 56			14 10					14 26
Bedford	a	13 35					13 51		14 05					14 21			14 35					14 51

Table T052-F

Saturdays
21 December to 16 May

Brighton, Gatwick Airport, Kent & South London - Luton, Bedford, Cambridge and Peterborough (via London)

		TL	TL ■	TL	TL	TL ■	TL	TL ■	TL ■	TL	TL ■	TL	TL	TL ■	TL	TL ■	TL	TL ■	TL	TL	TL ■	TL	TL ■
Brighton ■	d							12 58	13 08							13 26							13 58
Horsham	d					12 55								13 25							13 55		
Gatwick Airport ■ ✈	d		13 03			13 19		13 36	13 46		13 33			13 49		14 06		14 03			14 19		14 36
East Croydon	d		13 33			13 45		13 51	14 01		14 03			14 15		14 21		14 33			14 45		14 51
Rainham (Kent)	d				12 28								12 58							13 28			
Dartford	d				13 15								13 45							14 15			
Abbey Wood	d				13 28								13 58							14 28			
Woolwich Arsenal	d				13 34								14 04							14 34			
Greenwich	d				13 47								14 17							14 47			
Maidstone East	d																						
Sevenoaks	d			12 52								13 22							13 52				
Swanley	d			13 11								13 41							14 11				
St Mary Cray	d			13 15								13 45							14 15				
Orpington	d																						
Bromley South	d			13 23								13 53							14 23				
Catford	d			13 35								14 05							14 35				
Peckham Rye ■ 195	d			13 44								14 14							14 44				
Denmark Hill ■ 195	d			13 47								14 17							14 47				
Sutton ■ 179	d	13 16					13 19			13 46					13 49		14 16					14 19	
Wimbledon ⊖	d						13 37								14 07							14 37	
Streatham ■	d	13 33					13 48			14 03					14 18		14 33					14 48	
Tulse Hill ■	d	13 38					13 53			14 08					14 23		14 38					14 53	
Herne Hill ■ 173,179	d	13 42					13 57			14 12					14 27		14 42					14 57	
Loughborough Jn 173,179	d	13 45					14 00			14 15					14 30		14 45					15 00	
Elephant & Castle ⊖ 173,179	d	13 49		13 54			14 04			14 19		14 24			14 34		14 49		14 54			15 04	
London Bridge ⊖	d		13 51		13 58	14 01		14 05	14 16		14 21		14 28	14 31		14 35		14 51		14 58	15 01		15 05
London Blackfriars ⊖	a	13 54	13 56	13 59	14 04	14 06	14 09	14 11	14 21	14 24	14 26	14 29	14 34	14 36	14 39	14 41	14 54	14 56	14 59	15 04	15 06	15 09	15 11
London Blackfriars ■ ⊖	d	13 54	13 57		14 04	14 07	14 09	14 12	14 22	14 24	14 27		14 34	14 37	14 39	14 42	14 54	14 57		15 04	15 07	15 09	15 12
City Thameslink ■	d	13 56	13 59		14 06	14 09	14 11	14 14	14 24	14 26	14 29		14 36	14 39	14 41	14 44	14 56	14 59		15 06	15 09	15 11	15 14
Farringdon ■ ⊖	d	13 59	14 01		14 09	14 11	14 14	14 16	14 26	14 29	14 31		14 39	14 41	14 44	14 46	14 59	15 01		15 09	15 11	15 14	15 16
St Pancras International ⊖	d	14 03	14 06		14 13	14 16	14 18	14 21	14 31	14 33	14 36		14 43	14 46	14 48	14 51	15 03	15 06		15 13	15 16	15 18	15 21
Finsbury Park ⊖	a					14 22			14 41					14 52							15 22		
Welwyn Garden City	a																						
Stevenage	a					14 43			15 01					15 13							15 43		
Hitchin	a					14 49			15 08					15 19							15 49		
Letchworth Garden City	a								15 13														
Royston	a								15 24														
Cambridge	a								15 40														
Huntingdon	a					15 18								15 48							16 18		
Peterborough	a					15 39								16 07							16 40		
Kentish Town ⊖	a	14 08			14 18		14 23			14 38			14 48		14 53		15 08			15 18		15 23	
West Hampstead Thameslink ⊖	a	14 14					14 29	14 29		14 44					14 59	14 59	15 14					15 29	15 29
Elstree & Borehamwood	a	14 27					14 42			14 57					15 12		15 27					15 42	
St Albans City	a	14 37	14 24				14 52	14 41		15 07	14 54				15 22	15 11	15 37	15 24				15 52	15 41
Harpenden	a		14 31					14 47			15 01					15 17		15 31					15 47
Luton Airport Parkway ■ ✈	a		14 36					14 52			15 06					15 22		15 36					15 52
Luton ■	a		14 40					14 56			15 10					15 26		15 40					15 56
Bedford	a		15 05					15 21			15 35					15 51		16 05					16 21

Table T052-F

Saturdays

21 December to 16 May

Brighton, Gatwick Airport, Kent & South London - Luton, Bedford, Cambridge and Peterborough (via London)

		TL 1	TL	TL 1	TL	TL	TL 1	TL		TL 1	TL	TL 1	TL	TL	TL 1	TL	TL 1	TL 1	TL		TL 1	TL	TL	TL 1	TL
Brighton 10	d	14 08								14 26							14 58	15 08							
Horsham	d						14 25								14 55									15 25	
Gatwick Airport 10 ✈	d	14 46		14 33			14 49			15 06		15 03			15 19		15 36	15 46			15 32			15 49	
East Croydon	d	15 01		15 03			15 15			15 21		15 33			15 45		15 51	16 01			16 03			16 15	
Rainham (Kent)	d					13 58								14 28									14 58		
Dartford	d					14 45								15 15									15 45		
Abbey Wood	d					14 58								15 28									15 58		
Woolwich Arsenal	d					15 04								15 34									16 04		
Greenwich	d					15 17								15 47									16 17		
Maidstone East	d																								
Sevenoaks	d				14 22								14 52									15 22			
Swanley	d				14 41								15 11									15 41			
St Mary Cray	d				14 45								15 15									15 45			
Orpington	d																								
Bromley South	d				14 53								15 23									15 53			
Catford	d				15 05								15 35									16 05			
Peckham Rye 4 195	d				15 14								15 44									16 14			
Denmark Hill 4 195	d				15 17								15 47									16 17			
Sutton 4 179	d		14 46					14 49			15 16					15 19			15 46						15 49
Wimbledon ⊖	d							15 07								15 37									16 07
Streatham 4	d		15 03					15 18			15 33					15 48			16 03						16 18
Tulse Hill 3	d		15 08					15 23			15 38					15 53			16 08						16 23
Herne Hill 4 173,179	d		15 12					15 27			15 42					15 57			16 12						16 27
Loughborough Jn 173,179	d		15 15					15 30			15 45					16 00			16 15						16 30
Elephant & Castle ⊖173,179	d		15 19		15 24			15 34			15 49		15 54			16 04			16 19			16 24			16 34
London Bridge ⊖	d	15 16		15 21		15 28	15 31			15 35		15 51		15 58	16 01		16 05	16 16			16 21		16 28	16 31	
London Blackfriars ⊖	a	15 21	15 24	15 26	15 29	15 34	15 36	15 39		15 41	15 54	15 56	15 59	16 04	16 06	16 09	16 11	16 21	16 24		16 26	16 29	16 34	16 36	16 39
London Blackfriars 3 ⊖	d	15 22	15 24	15 27		15 34	15 37	15 39		15 42	15 54	15 57		16 04	16 07	16 09	16 12	16 22	16 24		16 27		16 34	16 37	16 39
City Thameslink 3	d	15 24	15 26	15 29		15 36	15 39	15 41		15 44	15 56	15 59		16 06	16 09	16 11	16 14	16 24	16 26		16 29		16 36	16 39	16 41
Farringdon 3 ⊖	d	15 26	15 29	15 31		15 39	15 41	15 44		15 46	15 59	16 01		16 09	16 11	16 14	16 16	16 26	16 29		16 31		16 39	16 41	16 44
St Pancras International ⊖	d	15 31	15 33	15 36		15 43	15 46	15 48		15 51	16 03	16 06		16 13	16 16	16 18	16 21	16 31	16 33		16 36		16 43	16 46	16 48
Finsbury Park ⊖	a	15 41					15 52								16 22			16 41						16 52	
Welwyn Garden City	a																								
Stevenage	a	16 01					16 13								16 43			17 01						17 13	
Hitchin	a	16 08					16 19								16 49			17 08						17 19	
Letchworth Garden City	a	16 13																17 13							
Royston	a	16 24																17 24							
Cambridge	a	16 40																17 40							
Huntingdon	a						16 48								17 18									17 48	
Peterborough	a						17 05								17 34									18 04	
Kentish Town ⊖	a		15 38			15 48		15 53			16 08			16 18		16 23			16 38				16 48		16 53
West Hampstead Thameslink ⊖	a		15 44					15 59		15 59	16 14					16 29	16 29		16 44						16 59
Elstree & Borehamwood	a		15 57					16 12			16 27					16 42			16 57						17 12
St Albans City	a		16 07	15 54				16 22		16 11	16 37	16 24				16 52	16 41		17 07		16 54				17 22
Harpenden	a			16 01						16 17		16 31					16 47				17 01				
Luton Airport Parkway 7 ✈	a			16 06						16 22		16 36					16 52				17 06				
Luton 10	a			16 10						16 26		16 40					16 56				17 10				
Bedford	a			16 35						16 51		17 05					17 21				17 35				

Table T052-F

Saturdays

21 December to 16 May

Brighton, Gatwick Airport, Kent & South London - Luton, Bedford, Cambridge and Peterborough (via London)

		TL 1	TL	TL 1	TL	TL		TL 1	TL	TL 1	TL 1	TL	TL 1	TL	TL	TL 1	TL		TL 1	TL	TL 1	TL	TL	TL 1	TL
Brighton 10	d	15 26								15 58	16 08								16 26						
Horsham	d							15 55								16 25								16 55	
Gatwick Airport 10 ✈	d	16 06		16 03				16 19		16 36	16 46		16 33			16 49			17 06		17 03			17 19	
East Croydon	d	16 21		16 33				16 45		16 51	17 01		17 03			17 15			17 21		17 33			17 45	
Rainham (Kent)	d					15 28									15 58								16 28		
Dartford	d					16 15									16 45								17 15		
Abbey Wood	d					16 28									16 58								17 28		
Woolwich Arsenal	d					16 34									17 04								17 34		
Greenwich	d					16 47									17 17								17 47		
Maidstone East	d																								
Sevenoaks	d				15 52									16 22								16 52			
Swanley	d				16 11									16 41								17 11			
St Mary Cray	d				16 15									16 45								17 15			
Orpington	d																								
Bromley South	d				16 23									16 53								17 23			
Catford	d				16 35									17 05								17 35			
Peckham Rye 4 195	d				16 44									17 14								17 44			
Denmark Hill 4 195	d				16 47									17 17								17 47			
Sutton 4 179	d		16 16						16 19			16 46					16 49			17 16					17 19
Wimbledon ⊖	d								16 37								17 07								17 37
Streatham 4	d		16 33						16 48			17 03					17 18			17 33					17 48
Tulse Hill 3	d		16 38						16 53			17 08					17 23			17 38					17 53
Herne Hill 4 173,179	d		16 42						16 57			17 12					17 27			17 42					17 57
Loughborough Jn 173,179	d		16 45						17 00			17 15					17 30			17 45					18 00
Elephant & Castle ⊖173,179	d		16 49		16 54				17 04			17 19		17 24			17 34			17 49		17 54			18 04
London Bridge ⊖	d	16 35		16 51		16 58		17 01		17 05	17 16		17 21		17 28	17 31			17 35		17 51		17 58	18 01	
London Blackfriars ⊖	a	16 41	16 54	16 56	16 59	17 04		17 06	17 09	17 11	17 21	17 24	17 26	17 29	17 34	17 36	17 39		17 41	17 54	17 56	17 59	18 04	18 06	18 09
London Blackfriars 3 ⊖	d	16 42	16 54	16 57		17 04		17 07	17 09	17 12	17 22	17 24	17 27		17 34	17 37	17 39		17 42	17 54	17 57		18 04	18 07	18 09
City Thameslink 3	d	16 44	16 56	16 59		17 06		17 09	17 11	17 14	17 24	17 26	17 29		17 36	17 39	17 41		17 44	17 56	17 59		18 06	18 09	18 11
Farringdon 3 ⊖	d	16 46	16 59	17 01		17 09		17 11	17 14	17 16	17 26	17 29	17 31		17 39	17 41	17 44		17 46	17 59	18 01		18 09	18 11	18 14
St Pancras International ⊖	d	16 51	17 03	17 06		17 13		17 16	17 18	17 21	17 31	17 33	17 36		17 43	17 46	17 48		17 51	18 03	18 06		18 13	18 16	18 18
Finsbury Park ⊖	a							17 22			17 41					17 52								18 22	
Welwyn Garden City	a																								
Stevenage	a							17 43			18 01					18 13								18 43	
Hitchin	a							17 49			18 08					18 19								18 49	
Letchworth Garden City	a										18 13														
Royston	a										18 24														
Cambridge	a										18 40														
Huntingdon	a							18 18								18 48								19 18	
Peterborough	a							18 37								19 05								19 34	
Kentish Town ⊖	a		17 08			17 18			17 23			17 38			17 48		17 53			18 08			18 18		18 23
West Hampstead Thameslink ⊖	a	16 59	17 14						17 29	17 29		17 44					17 59		17 59	18 14					18 29
Elstree & Borehamwood	a		17 27						17 42			17 57					18 12			18 27					18 42
St Albans City	a	17 11	17 37	17 24					17 52	17 41		18 07	17 54				18 22		18 11	18 37	18 24				18 52
Harpenden	a	17 17		17 31						17 47			18 01						18 17		18 31				
Luton Airport Parkway 7 ✈	a	17 22		17 36						17 52			18 06						18 22		18 36				
Luton 10	a	17 26		17 40						17 56			18 10						18 26		18 40				
Bedford	a	17 51		18 05						18 21			18 35						18 51		19 05				

Table T052-F

Saturdays
21 December to 16 May

Brighton, Gatwick Airport, Kent & South London - Luton, Bedford, Cambridge and Peterborough (via London)

		TL 1	TL 1	TL	TL 1	TL	TL	TL 1	TL	TL 1	TL	TL 1	TL	TL	TL 1	TL	TL 1	TL 1	TL	TL 1	TL	TL	TL 1
Brighton 10	d	16 58	17 08							17 26							17 58	18 08					
Horsham	d							17 25							17 55								18 25
Gatwick Airport 10 ✈	d	17 36	17 46		17 33			17 49		18 06		18 03			18 19		18 36	18 46		18 33			18 49
East Croydon	d	17 51	18 01		18 03			18 15		18 21		18 33			18 45		18 51	19 01		19 03			19 15
Rainham (Kent)	d						16 58							17 28								17 58	
Dartford	d						17 45							18 15								18 45	
Abbey Wood	d						17 58							18 28								18 58	
Woolwich Arsenal	d						18 04							18 34								19 04	
Greenwich	d						18 17							18 47								19 17	
Maidstone East	d																						
Sevenoaks	d					17 22							17 52								18 22		
Swanley	d					17 41							18 11								18 41		
St Mary Cray	d					17 45							18 15								18 45		
Orpington	d																						
Bromley South	d					17 53							18 23								18 53		
Catford	d					18 05							18 35								19 05		
Peckham Rye 4 195	d					18 14							18 44								19 14		
Denmark Hill 4 195	d					18 17							18 47								19 17		
Sutton 4 179	d			17 46					17 49		18 16					18 19			18 46				
Wimbledon ⊖	d								18 07							18 37							
Streatham 4	d			18 03					18 18		18 33					18 48			19 03				
Tulse Hill 3	d			18 08					18 23		18 38					18 53			19 08				
Herne Hill 4 173,179	d			18 12					18 27		18 42					18 57			19 12				
Loughborough Jn 173,179	d			18 15					18 30		18 45					19 00			19 15				
Elephant & Castle ⊖173,179	d			18 19		18 24			18 34		18 49		18 54			19 04			19 19		19 24		
London Bridge ⊖	d	18 05	18 16		18 21		18 28	18 31		18 35		18 51		18 58	19 01		19 05	19 16		19 21		19 28	19 31
London Blackfriars ⊖	a	18 11	18 21	18 24	18 26	18 29	18 34	18 36	18 39	18 41	18 54	18 56	18 59	19 04	19 06	19 09	19 11	19 21	19 24	19 26	19 29	19 34	19 36
London Blackfriars 3 ⊖	d	18 12	18 22	18 24	18 27		18 34	18 37	18 39	18 42	18 54	18 57		19 04	19 07	19 09	19 12	19 22	19 24	19 27		19 34	19 37
City Thameslink 3	d	18 14	18 24	18 26	18 29		18 36	18 39	18 41	18 44	18 56	18 59		19 06	19 09	19 11	19 14	19 24	19 26	19 29		19 36	19 39
Farringdon 3 ⊖	d	18 16	18 26	18 29	18 31		18 39	18 41	18 44	18 46	18 59	19 01		19 09	19 11	19 14	19 16	19 26	19 29	19 31		19 39	19 41
St Pancras International ⊖	d	18 21	18 31	18 33	18 36		18 43	18 46	18 48	18 51	19 03	19 06		19 13	19 16	19 18	19 21	19 31	19 33	19 36		19 43	19 46
Finsbury Park ⊖	a		18 41					18 52							19 22			19 41					19 52
Welwyn Garden City	a																						
Stevenage	a		19 01					19 13							19 43			20 01					20 13
Hitchin	a		19 08					19 19							19 49			20 08					20 19
Letchworth Garden City	a		19 13															20 13					
Royston	a		19 24															20 24					
Cambridge	a		19 40															20 40					
Huntingdon	a							19 48							20 18								20 48
Peterborough	a							20 04							20 40								21 04
Kentish Town ⊖	a			18 38			18 48		18 53		19 08			19 18		19 23			19 38			19 48	
West Hampstead Thameslink ⊖	a	18 29		18 44					18 59	18 59	19 14					19 29	19 29		19 44				
Elstree & Borehamwood	a			18 57					19 12		19 27					19 42			19 57				
St Albans City	a	18 41		19 07	18 54				19 22	19 11	19 37	19 24				19 52	19 41		20 07	19 54			
Harpenden	a	18 47			19 01					19 17		19 31					19 47			20 01			
Luton Airport Parkway 7 ✈	a	18 52			19 06					19 22		19 36					19 52			20 06			
Luton 10	a	18 56			19 10					19 26		19 40					19 56			20 10			
Bedford	a	19 21			19 35					19 51		20 05					20 21			20 35			

Table T052-F

Saturdays
21 December to 16 May

Brighton, Gatwick Airport, Kent & South London - Luton, Bedford, Cambridge and Peterborough (via London)

		TL	TL 1	TL	TL 1	TL	TL	TL 1	TL	TL 1	TL 1	TL	TL 1	TL	TL	TL 1	TL	TL 1	TL	TL 1	TL	TL
Brighton 10	d		18 26							18 58	19 08							19 26				
Horsham	d							18 55								19 25						
Gatwick Airport 10 ✈	d		19 06		19 03			19 19		19 36	19 46		19 33			19 49		20 06		20 03		
East Croydon	d		19 21		19 33			19 45		19 51	20 01		20 03			20 15		20 21		20 33		
Rainham (Kent)	d						18 28								18 58							19 28
Dartford	d						19 15								19 45							20 15
Abbey Wood	d						19 28								19 58							20 28
Woolwich Arsenal	d						19 34								20 04							20 34
Greenwich	d						19 47								20 17							20 47
Maidstone East	d																					
Sevenoaks	d					18 52								19 22							19 52	
Swanley	d					19 11								19 41							20 11	
St Mary Cray	d					19 15								19 45							20 15	
Orpington	d																					
Bromley South	d					19 23								19 53							20 23	
Catford	d					19 35								20 05							20 35	
Peckham Rye 4 195	d					19 44								20 14							20 44	
Denmark Hill 4 195	d					19 47								20 17							20 47	
Sutton 4 179	d	18 49		19 16					19 19			19 46					19 49		20 16			
Wimbledon ⊖	d	19 07							19 37								20 07					
Streatham 4	d	19 18		19 33					19 48			20 03					20 18		20 33			
Tulse Hill 3	d	19 23		19 38					19 53			20 08					20 23		20 38			
Herne Hill 4 173,179	d	19 27		19 42					19 57			20 12					20 27		20 42			
Loughborough Jn 173,179	d	19 30		19 45					20 00			20 15					20 30		20 45			
Elephant & Castle ⊖173,179	d	19 34		19 49		19 54			20 04			20 19		20 24			20 34		20 49		20 54	
London Bridge ⊖	d		19 35		19 51		19 58	20 01		20 05	20 16		20 21		20 28	20 31		20 35		20 51		20 58
London Blackfriars ⊖	a	19 39	19 41	19 54	19 56	19 59	20 04	20 06	20 09	20 11	20 21	20 24	20 26	20 29	20 34	20 36	20 39	20 41	20 54	20 56	20 59	21 04
London Blackfriars 3 ⊖	d	19 39	19 42	19 54	19 57		20 04	20 07	20 09	20 12	20 22	20 24	20 27		20 34	20 37	20 39	20 42	20 54	20 57		21 04
City Thameslink 3	d	19 41	19 44	19 56	19 59		20 06	20 09	20 11	20 14	20 24	20 26	20 29		20 36	20 39	20 41	20 44	20 56	20 59		
Farringdon 3 ⊖	d	19 44	19 46	19 59	20 01		20 09	20 11	20 14	20 16	20 26	20 29	20 31		20 39	20 41	20 44	20 46	20 59	21 01		21 09
St Pancras International ⊖	d	19 48	19 51	20 03	20 06		20 13	20 16	20 18	20 21	20 31	20 33	20 36		20 43	20 46	20 48	20 51	21 03	21 06		21 13
Finsbury Park ⊖	a							20 22			20 41					20 52						
Welwyn Garden City	a																					
Stevenage	a							20 43			21 01					21 13						
Hitchin	a							20 49			21 08					21 19						
Letchworth Garden City	a										21 13											
Royston	a										21 24											
Cambridge	a										21 40											
Huntingdon	a							21 18								21 48						
Peterborough	a							21 34								22 05						
Kentish Town ⊖	a	19 53		20 08			20 18		20 23			20 38			20 48		20 53		21 08			21 18
West Hampstead Thameslink ⊖	a	19 59	19 59	20 14					20 29	20 29		20 44					20 59	20 59	21 14			
Elstree & Borehamwood	a	20 12		20 27					20 42			20 57					21 12		21 27			
St Albans City	a	20 22	20 11	20 37	20 25				20 52	20 41		21 07	20 54				21 22	21 11	21 37	21 24		
Harpenden	a		20 17		20 32					20 47			21 01					21 17		21 31		
Luton Airport Parkway 7 ✈	a		20 22		20 37					20 52			21 06					21 22		21 36		
Luton 10	a		20 26		20 41					20 56			21 10					21 26		21 40		
Bedford	a		20 51		21 06					21 21			21 35					21 51		22 05		

Table T052-F

Saturdays

21 December to 16 May

Brighton, Gatwick Airport, Kent & South London - Luton, Bedford, Cambridge and Peterborough (via London)

Station			TL 1	TL	TL 1	TL 1	TL	TL 1	TL	TL	TL 1	TL		TL 1	TL	TL 1	TL	TL	TL 1	TL	TL 1	TL 1	TL		TL 1	TL
Brighton 10		d			19 58	20 08								20 26							20 58	21 08				
Horsham		d	19 55								20 25								20 55							
Gatwick Airport 10	✈	d	20 19		20 36	20 46		20 33			20 49			21 06		21 03			21 19		21 36	21 46			21 33	
East Croydon		d	20 45		20 51	21 01		21 03			21 15			21 21		21 33			21 45		21 51	22 01			22 03	
Rainham (Kent)		d								19 58								20 28								
Dartford		d								20 45								21 15								
Abbey Wood		d								20 58								21 28								
Woolwich Arsenal		d								21 04								21 34								
Greenwich		d								21 17								21 47								
Maidstone East		d																								
Sevenoaks		d							20 22								20 52									21 22
Swanley		d							20 41								21 11									21 41
St Mary Cray		d							20 45								21 15									21 45
Orpington		d																								
Bromley South		d							20 53								21 23									21 53
Catford		d							21 05								21 35									22 05
Peckham Rye 4	195	d							21 14								21 44									22 14
Denmark Hill 4	195	d							21 17								21 47									22 17
Sutton 4	179	d		20 19			20 46					20 49			21 16					21 19			21 46			
Wimbledon	⊖	d		20 37								21 07								21 37						
Streatham 4		d		20 48			21 03					21 18			21 33					21 48			22 03			
Tulse Hill 3		d		20 53			21 08					21 23			21 38					21 53			22 08			
Herne Hill 4	173,179	d		20 57			21 12					21 27			21 42					21 57			22 12			
Loughborough Jn	173,179	d		21 00			21 15					21 30			21 45					22 00			22 15			
Elephant & Castle	⊖ 173,179	d		21 04			21 19		21 24			21 34			21 49		21 54			22 04			22 19			22 24
London Bridge	⊖	d	21 01		21 05	21 16		21 21		21 28	21 31			21 35		21 51		21 58	22 01		22 05	22 16			22 21	
London Blackfriars	⊖	a	21 06	21 09	21 11	21 21	21 24	21 26	21 29	21 34	21 36	21 39		21 41	21 54	21 56	21 59	22 04	22 06	22 09	22 11	22 21	22 24		22 26	22 29
London Blackfriars 3	⊖	d	21 07	21 09	21 12	21 22	21 24	21 27		21 34	21 37	21 39		21 42	21 54	21 57		22 04	22 07	22 09	22 12	22 22	22 24		22 27	
City Thameslink 3		d																								
Farringdon 3	⊖	d	21 11	21 14	21 16	21 26	21 29	21 31		21 39	21 41	21 44		21 46	21 59	22 01		22 09	22 11	22 14	22 16	22 26	22 29		22 31	
St Pancras International	⊖	d	21 16	21 18	21 21	21 31	21 33	21 36		21 43	21 46	21 48		21 51	22 03	22 06		22 13	22 16	22 18	22 21	22 31	22 33		22 36	
Finsbury Park	⊖	a	21 22			21 41					21 52								22 22			22 41				
Welwyn Garden City		a																								
Stevenage		a	21 43			22 01					22 13								22 43			23 01				
Hitchin		a	21 49			22 08					22 19								22 49			23 08				
Letchworth Garden City		a				22 13																23 13				
Royston		a				22 24																23 24				
Cambridge		a				22 40																23 40				
Huntingdon		a	22 18								22 48								23 18							
Peterborough		a	22 39								23 05								23 37							
Kentish Town	⊖	a		21 23			21 38			21 48		21 53			22 08			22 18		22 23			22 38			
West Hampstead Thameslink	⊖	a		21 29	21 29		21 44					21 59		21 59	22 14					22 29	22 29		22 44			
Elstree & Borehamwood		a		21 42			21 57					22 12			22 27					22 41			22 57			
St Albans City		a		21 52	21 41		22 07	21 54				22 22		22 11	22 37	22 24				22 51	22 41		23 08		22 56	
Harpenden		a			21 47			22 01						22 17		22 31				22 58	22 48		23 15		23 04	
Luton Airport Parkway 7	✈	a			21 52			22 06						22 22		22 36				23 03	22 53		23 20		23 09	
Luton 10		a			21 56			22 10						22 26		22 40				23 07	22 57		23 24		23 13	
Bedford		a			22 21			22 35						22 51		23 05				23 28	23 22		23 46		23 39	

Table T052-F

Saturdays

21 December to 16 May

Brighton, Gatwick Airport, Kent & South London - Luton, Bedford, Cambridge and Peterborough (via London)

Station			TL	TL 1	TL	TL 1	TL	TL	TL	TL 1		TL 1	TL	TL 1	TL	TL	TL	TL 1	TL 1	TL	TL		TL	TL	TL 1	TL
Brighton 10		d				21 26						21 58		22 08					22 26						22 56	
Horsham		d		21 25						21 55								22 25								
Gatwick Airport 10	✈	d		21 49		22 06				22 19		22 36		22 46				22 49	23 06						23 34	
East Croydon		d		22 16		22 21				22 46		22 51		23 01				23 15	23 21						23 53	
Rainham (Kent)		d	20 58						21 28								21 58									
Dartford		d	21 45						22 15								22 45									
Abbey Wood		d	21 58						22 28								22 58									
Woolwich Arsenal		d	22 04						22 34								23 04									
Greenwich		d	22 17						22 47								23 17									
Maidstone East		d																								
Sevenoaks		d						21 52								22 22					22 52					23 22
Swanley		d						22 11								22 41					23 11					23 41
St Mary Cray		d						22 15								22 45					23 15					23 45
Orpington		d																								
Bromley South		d						22 23								22 53					23 23					23 53
Catford		d						22 35								23 05					23 35					00 06
Peckham Rye 4	195	d						22 44								23 14					23 44					00 14
Denmark Hill 4	195	d						22 47								23 17					23 47					00 17
Sutton 4	179	d			21 49		22 18						22 19		22 48					22 49			23 18	23 19		
Wimbledon	⊖	d			22 07								22 41							23 11				23 37		
Streatham 4		d			22 18		22 35						22 52		23 05					23 22			23 35	23 48		
Tulse Hill 3		d			22 23		22 40						22 57		23 10					23 27			23 40	23 53		
Herne Hill 4	173,179	d			22 27		22 44						23 04		23 14					23 34			23 44	23 57		
Loughborough Jn	173,179	d			22 30		22 47						23 07		23 17					23 37			23 47			
Elephant & Castle	⊖ 173,179	d			22 34		22 51	22 54					23 11		23 21	23 24				23 41	23 55		23 54	00 04		00 24
London Bridge	⊖	d	22 28	22 31		22 35			22 58	23 01		23 05		23 16			23 28	23 31	23 35							
London Blackfriars	⊖	a	22 34	22 36	22 39	22 41	22 59	22 59	23 04	23 06		23 11	23 16	23 21	23 26	23 29	23 34	23 36	23 41	23 46	23 59		00 01	00 08	00 19	00 29
London Blackfriars 3	⊖	d	22 34	22 37	22 39	22 42	22 59		23 04	23 07		23 12	23 17	23 22	23 27		23 34	23 37	23 42	23 49			00 02	00 09	00 22	
City Thameslink 3		d																								
Farringdon 3	⊖	d	22 39	22 41	22 44	22 46	23 04		23 09	23 11		23 16	23 21	23 26	23 31		23 39	23 41	23 46	23 53			00 06	00 13	00 26	
St Pancras International	⊖	d	22 43	22 46	22 48	22 51	23 08		23 13	23 16		23 21	23 26	23 31	23 36		23 43	23 46	23 51	23 58			00 11	00 18	00 31	
Finsbury Park	⊖	a		22 52						23 22				23 41				23 52								
Welwyn Garden City		a																								
Stevenage		a		23 13						23 43				00 01				00 13								
Hitchin		a		23 19						23 49				00 08				00 22								
Letchworth Garden City		a												00 13												
Royston		a												00 24												
Cambridge		a												00 41												
Huntingdon		a		23 48						00 19								00 50								
Peterborough		a		00 07						00 39								01 09								
Kentish Town	⊖	a			22 53		23 13						23 30		23 40					00 01				00 22		
West Hampstead Thameslink	⊖	a	22 51		23 02	22 59	23 17		23 21			23 29	23 34		23 44		23 51		23 59	00 06			00 19	00 26	00 39	
Elstree & Borehamwood		a			23 15		23 30						23 48		23 58					00 20				00 40		
St Albans City		a			23 26	23 15	23 41					23 46	23 58		00 09				00 16	00 31			00 35	00 51	00 56	
Harpenden		a			23 33	23 22	23 48					23 52	00 06		00 16				00 22	00 38			00 42	00 58	01 02	
Luton Airport Parkway 7	✈	a			23 38	23 27	23 53					23 57	00 11		00 21				00 27	00 43			00 47	01 03	01 07	
Luton 10		a			23 42	23 31	23 57					00 01	00 15		00 25				00 31	00 47			00 51	01 07	01 11	
Bedford		a			00 03	23 55	00 18					00 26	00 40		00 50				00 56	01 08			01 18	01 32	01 36	

Table T052-F

Saturdays

21 December to 16 May

Brighton, Gatwick Airport, Kent & South London - Luton, Bedford, Cambridge and Peterborough (via London)

		TL ■ A	TL ■ B	TL ■	TL ■
Brighton ■	d			23 24	23 42
Horsham	d	23 11	23 11		
Gatwick Airport ■ ✈	d	23 34	23 34	00 04	00 21
East Croydon ⇌	d	00 10	00 10	00 23	00 40
Rainham (Kent)	d				
Dartford	d				
Abbey Wood	d				
Woolwich Arsenal	d				
Greenwich	d				
Maidstone East	d				
Sevenoaks	d				
Swanley	d				
St Mary Cray	d				
Orpington	d				
Bromley South	d				
Catford	d				
Peckham Rye ■ 195	d				
Denmark Hill ■ 195	d				
Sutton ■ 179	d				
Wimbledon ⊖	d				
Streatham ■	d				
Tulse Hill ■	d				
Herne Hill ■ 173,179	d				
Loughborough Jn 173,179	d				
Elephant & Castle ⊖173,179	d				
London Bridge ⊖	d				
London Blackfriars ⊖	a	00 36	00 36	00 49	01 06
London Blackfriars ■ ⊖	d	00 37	00 37	00 50	01 06
City Thameslink ■	d				
Farringdon ■ ⊖	d	00 41	00 41		
St Pancras International ⊖	d	00 46	00 46	01 01	01 16
Finsbury Park ⊖	a	00 52	00 52		
Welwyn Garden City	a	01 14	01 14		
Stevenage	a	01 23	01 23		
Hitchin	a	01 32	01 32		
Letchworth Garden City	a				
Royston	a				
Cambridge	a				
Huntingdon	a		02 00		
Peterborough	a		02 21		
Kentish Town ⊖	a			01 05	
West Hampstead Thameslink ⊖	a			01 09	01 24
Elstree & Borehamwood	a			01 24	
St Albans City	a			01 34	01 40
Harpenden	a			01 40	01 47
Luton Airport Parkway ■ ✈	a			01 45	01 52
Luton ■	a			01 49	01 56
Bedford	a			02 14	02 21

A from 22 February until 28 March
B until 15 February, from 4 April

Table T052-F

Sundays

15 December to 10 May

Brighton, Gatwick Airport, Kent & South London - Luton, Bedford, Cambridge and Peterborough (via London)

		TL A	TL A	TL ■ B	TL C	TL ■ D	TL ■ E	TL ■ B	TL ■ B	TL ■	TL ■		TL	TL ■ F	TL ■	TL	TL	TL	TL ■ F	TL ■	TL	TL ■		TL	TL
Brighton ■	d									00 04					08 42					09 08					
Horsham	d																								
Gatwick Airport ■ ✈	d							00 04	00 21	00 42	08 46			08 49	09 19				09 19	09 49		09 46			
East Croydon ⇌	d					00 10	00 10	00 23	00 40	01 10	09 07			09 18	09 34				09 48	10 04		10 07			
Rainham (Kent)	d																08 30							09 00	
Dartford	d																09 15							09 45	
Abbey Wood	d																09 28							09 58	
Woolwich Arsenal	d																09 34							10 04	
Greenwich	d																09 47							10 17	
Maidstone East	d																								
Sevenoaks	d												08 28					08 58							09 28
Swanley	d												08 47					09 17							09 47
St Mary Cray	d												08 51					09 21							09 51
Orpington	d																								
Bromley South	d												08 59					09 29							09 59
Catford	d				00 06								09 11					09 41							10 11
Peckham Rye ■ 195	d				00 14								09 20					09 50							10 20
Denmark Hill ■ 195	d				00 17								09 23					09 53							10 23
Sutton ■ 179	d															09 09					09 39				
Wimbledon ⊖	d															09 27					09 57				
Streatham ■	d															09 37					10 07				
Tulse Hill ■	d															09 41					10 11				
Herne Hill ■ 173,179	d															09 45					10 15				
Loughborough Jn 173,179	d															09 48					10 18				
Elephant & Castle ⊖173,179	d		00 04		00 24								09 30			09 53		10 00			10 23				10 30
London Bridge ⊖	d										09 25			09 33	09 49		09 58		10 03	10 19		10 25		10 28	
London Blackfriars ⊖	a		00 08		00 29	00 36	00 36	00 49	01 06	01 36	09 30		09 34	09 38	09 54	09 57	10 04	10 04	10 08	10 24	10 27	10 30		10 34	10 34
London Blackfriars ■ ⊖	d	00 02	00 09	00 22		00 37	00 37	00 50	01 06	01 36	09 31			09 39	09 55	09 58	10 05		10 09	10 25	10 28	10 31		10 35	
City Thameslink ■	d																								
Farringdon ■ ⊖	d	00 06	00 13	00 26		00 41	00 41				09 35			09 43	09 59	10 02	10 09		10 13	10 29	10 32	10 35		10 39	
St Pancras International ⊖	d	00 11	00 18	00 31		00 46	00 46	01 01	01 16	01 44	09 40			09 48	10 04	10 07	10 14		10 18	10 34	10 37	10 40		10 44	
Finsbury Park ⊖	a					00 52	00 52				09 46											10 46			
Welwyn Garden City	a					01 14	01 14																		
Stevenage	a					01 23	01 23				10 06											11 06			
Hitchin	a					01 32	01 32				10 12											11 12			
Letchworth Garden City	a										10 18											11 18			
Royston	a										10 29											11 29			
Cambridge	a										10 48											11 48			
Huntingdon	a						02 00																		
Peterborough	a						02 21																		
Kentish Town ⊖	a		00 22					01 05		01 48						10 11	10 18				10 41			10 48	
West Hampstead Thameslink ⊖	a	00 19	00 26	00 39				01 09	01 24	01 52					10 12	10 15			10 26	10 42	10 45				
Elstree & Borehamwood	a		00 40					01 24		02 07						10 28					10 58				
St Albans City	a	00 35	00 51	00 56				01 34	01 40	02 17				10 10	10 28	10 38			10 42	10 58	11 08				
Harpenden	a	00 42	00 58	01 02				01 40	01 47	02 25				10 17	10 35	10 45			10 49	11 05	11 15				
Luton Airport Parkway ■ ✈	a	00 47	01 03	01 07				01 45	01 52	02 30				10 22	10 40	10 50			10 54	11 10	11 20				
Luton ■	a	00 51	01 07	01 11				01 49	01 56	02 34				10 26	10 44	10 54			10 58	11 14	11 24				
Bedford	a	01 18	01 32	01 36				02 14	02 21	02 59				10 52	11 09				11 24	11 40					

A not 15 December. From Sutton (Surrey)
B not 15 December. From Brighton
C not 15 December. From Sevenoaks
D from 23 February until 29 March. From Horsham
E from 22 December until 16 February, from 5 April. From Horsham
F From Three Bridges

Table T052-F

Sundays

15 December to 10 May

Brighton, Gatwick Airport, Kent & South London - Luton, Bedford, Cambridge and Peterborough (via London)

		TL 1 A	TL 1	TL	TL	TL	TL 1	TL	TL 1		TL	TL 1	TL	TL	TL 1 A	TL	TL 1	TL	TL	TL		TL 1	TL	TL 1	TL
Brighton 10	d		09 42						10 08								10 42							11 08	
Horsham	d																								
Gatwick Airport 10	d	09 49	10 19				10 19		10 49			10 46			10 49		11 19					11 19		11 49	
East Croydon	d	10 18	10 34				10 48		11 04			11 07			11 18		11 34					11 48		12 04	
Rainham (Kent)	d				09 30								10 00						10 30						
Dartford	d				10 15								10 46						11 15						
Abbey Wood	d				10 28								10 58						11 28						
Woolwich Arsenal	d				10 34								11 04						11 34						
Greenwich	d				10 47								11 17						11 47						
Maidstone East	d																								
Sevenoaks	d					09 58								10 28						10 58					
Swanley	d					10 17								10 47						11 17					
St Mary Cray	d					10 21								10 51						11 21					
Orpington	d																								
Bromley South	d					10 29								10 59						11 29					
Catford	d					10 41								11 11						11 41					
Peckham Rye 4 195	d					10 50								11 20						11 50					
Denmark Hill 4 195	d					10 53								11 23						11 53					
Sutton 4 179	d			10 09				10 40			10 39					11 10		11 09					11 40		11 39
Wimbledon	d			10 27							10 57							11 27							11 57
Streatham 4	d			10 37				10 55			11 07					11 25		11 37					11 55		12 07
Tulse Hill 3	d			10 41				10 59			11 11					11 29		11 41					11 59		12 11
Herne Hill 4 173,179	d			10 45				11 03			11 15					11 33		11 45					12 03		12 15
Loughborough Jn 173,179	d			10 48				11 06			11 18					11 36		11 48					12 06		12 18
Elephant & Castle 173,179	d			10 53		11 00		11 11			11 23			11 30		11 41		11 53		12 00			12 11		12 23
London Bridge	d	10 33	10 49		10 58		11 03		11 19			11 25	11 28		11 33		11 49		11 58			12 03		12 19	
London Blackfriars	a	10 38	10 54	10 57	11 04	11 04	11 08	11 15	11 24		11 27	11 30	11 34	11 34	11 38	11 45	11 54	11 57	12 04	12 04		12 08	12 15	12 24	12 27
London Blackfriars 3	d	10 39	10 55	10 58	11 05		11 09		11 25		11 28	11 31	11 35		11 39		11 55	11 58	12 05			12 09	12 16	12 25	12 28
City Thameslink 3	d																								
Farringdon 3	d	10 43	10 59	11 02	11 09		11 13		11 29		11 32	11 35	11 39		11 43		11 59	12 02	12 09			12 13	12 20	12 29	12 32
St Pancras International	d	10 48	11 04	11 07	11 14		11 18		11 34		11 37	11 40	11 44		11 48		12 04	12 07	12 14			12 18	12 25	12 34	12 37
Finsbury Park	a											11 46													
Welwyn Garden City	a																								
Stevenage	a											12 06													
Hitchin	a											12 12													
Letchworth Garden City	a											12 18													
Royston	a											12 29													
Cambridge	a											12 48													
Huntingdon	a																								
Peterborough	a																								
Kentish Town	a			11 11	11 18						11 41		11 48					12 11	12 18						12 41
West Hampstead Thameslink	a	10 56	11 12	11 15			11 26		11 42		11 45				11 56		12 12	12 16				12 26	12 34	12 42	12 46
Elstree & Borehamwood	a			11 28							12 00							12 31					12 44		13 01
St Albans City	a	11 12	11 28	11 38			11 42		11 58		12 10				12 14		12 28	12 42				12 38	12 54	12 58	13 12
Harpenden	a	11 19	11 35	11 45			11 49		12 05		12 17				12 21		12 34					12 45	13 00	13 04	
Luton Airport Parkway 7	a	11 24	11 40	11 50			11 54		12 10		12 22				12 26		12 39					12 51	13 05	13 09	
Luton 10	a	11 28	11 44	11 54			11 58		12 14		12 26				12 30		12 43					12 55	13 10	13 13	
Bedford	a	11 54	12 09				12 24		12 39						12 55		13 10					13 20		13 39	

A From Three Bridges

NRT DECEMBER 19 EDITION

Table T052-F

Sundays

15 December to 10 May

Brighton, Gatwick Airport, Kent & South London - Luton, Bedford, Cambridge and Peterborough (via London)

		TL 1	TL	TL	TL 1 A	TL	TL 1		TL	TL	TL	TL 1	TL	TL 1	TL	TL 1	TL	TL		TL 1 A	TL	TL 1	TL	TL	TL
Brighton 10	d						11 42							12 08								12 42			
Horsham	d																								
Gatwick Airport 10	d	11 46			11 49		12 19					12 19		12 49		12 46				12 49		13 19			
East Croydon	d	12 07			12 18		12 34					12 48		13 04		13 07				13 18		13 34			
Rainham (Kent)	d		11 00							11 30							12 00							12 30	
Dartford	d		11 45							12 15							12 45							13 15	
Abbey Wood	d		11 58							12 28							12 58							13 28	
Woolwich Arsenal	d		12 04							12 34							13 04							13 34	
Greenwich	d		12 17							12 47							13 17							13 47	
Maidstone East	d																								
Sevenoaks	d			11 28							11 58							12 28							12 58
Swanley	d			11 47							12 17							12 47							13 17
St Mary Cray	d			11 51							12 21							12 51							13 21
Orpington	d																								
Bromley South	d			11 59							12 29							12 59							13 29
Catford	d			12 11							12 41							13 11							13 41
Peckham Rye 4 195	d			12 20							12 50							13 20							13 50
Denmark Hill 4 195	d			12 23							12 53							13 23							13 53
Sutton 4 179	d					12 10			12 09				12 40		12 39						13 10		13 09		
Wimbledon	d								12 27						12 57								13 27		
Streatham 4	d					12 25			12 37				12 55		13 07						13 25		13 37		
Tulse Hill 3	d					12 29			12 41				12 59		13 11						13 29		13 41		
Herne Hill 4 173,179	d					12 33			12 45				13 03		13 15						13 33		13 45		
Loughborough Jn 173,179	d					12 36			12 48				13 06		13 18						13 36		13 48		
Elephant & Castle 173,179	d			12 30		12 41			12 53		13 00		13 11		13 23			13 30			13 41		13 53		14 00
London Bridge	d	12 25	12 28		12 33		12 49			12 58		13 03		13 19		13 25	13 28			13 33		13 49		13 58	
London Blackfriars	a	12 30	12 34	12 34	12 38	12 45	12 54		12 57	13 04	13 04	13 08	13 15	13 24	13 27	13 30	13 34	13 34		13 38	13 45	13 54	13 57	14 04	14 04
London Blackfriars 3	d	12 31	12 35		12 41	12 46	12 55		12 58	13 05		13 09	13 16	13 25	13 28	13 31	13 35			13 39	13 46	13 55	13 58	14 05	
City Thameslink 3	d																								
Farringdon 3	d	12 35	12 39		12 45	12 50	12 59		13 02	13 09		13 13	13 20	13 29	13 32	13 35	13 39			13 43	13 50	13 59	14 02	14 09	
St Pancras International	d	12 40	12 44		12 50	12 55	13 04		13 07	13 14		13 18	13 25	13 34	13 37	13 40	13 44			13 48	13 55	14 04	14 07	14 14	
Finsbury Park	a	12 45														13 46									
Welwyn Garden City	a																								
Stevenage	a	13 06														14 06									
Hitchin	a	13 12														14 12									
Letchworth Garden City	a	13 18														14 18									
Royston	a	13 29														14 29									
Cambridge	a	13 48														14 48									
Huntingdon	a																								
Peterborough	a																								
Kentish Town	a		12 48						13 11	13 18					13 41		13 48						14 11	14 18	
West Hampstead Thameslink	a				12 59	13 04	13 12		13 15			13 26	13 34	13 42	13 46					13 56	14 03	14 12	14 16		
Elstree & Borehamwood	a					13 14			13 31				13 44		14 01						14 14		14 31		
St Albans City	a				13 12	13 24	13 28		13 42			13 38	13 54	13 58	14 14					14 10	14 24	14 28	14 44		
Harpenden	a				13 18	13 30	13 34					13 45	14 00	14 04						14 16	14 30	14 34			
Luton Airport Parkway 7	a				13 23	13 35	13 39					13 51	14 05	14 09						14 21	14 35	14 39			
Luton 10	a				13 27	13 40	13 43					13 55	14 10	14 13						14 25	14 40	14 43			
Bedford	a				13 52		14 08					14 20		14 38						14 50		15 08			

A From Three Bridges

Table T052-F

Sundays
15 December to 10 May

Brighton, Gatwick Airport, Kent & South London - Luton, Bedford, Cambridge and Peterborough (via London)

Station		TL [1]	TL	TL [1]	TL		TL [1]	TL	TL	TL [1] A	TL	TL [1]	TL	TL	TL	TL [1]		TL	TL [1]	TL	TL [1]	TL	TL	TL [1] A	TL
Brighton [10]	d			13 08								13 42							14 08						
Horsham	d																								
Gatwick Airport [10] ✈	d	13 19		13 49			13 46			13 49		14 19				14 19			14 49		14 46			14 49	
East Croydon	d	13 48		14 04			14 07			14 18		14 34				14 48			15 04		15 07			15 18	
Rainham (Kent)	d							13 00						13 30								14 00			
Dartford	d							13 45						14 15								14 45			
Abbey Wood	d							13 58						14 28								14 58			
Woolwich Arsenal	d							14 04						14 34								15 04			
Greenwich	d							14 17						14 47								15 17			
Maidstone East	d																								
Sevenoaks	d								13 28						13 58								14 28		
Swanley	d								13 47						14 17								14 47		
St Mary Cray	d								13 51						14 21								14 51		
Orpington	d																								
Bromley South	d								13 59						14 29								14 59		
Catford	d								14 11						14 41								15 11		
Peckham Rye [4] 195	d								14 20						14 50								15 20		
Denmark Hill [4] 195	d								14 23						14 53								15 23		
Sutton [4] 179	d		13 40		13 39						14 10		14 09					14 40		14 39					15 10
Wimbledon ⊖	d				13 57								14 27							14 57					
Streatham [4]	d		13 55		14 07						14 25		14 37					14 55		15 07					15 25
Tulse Hill [3]	d		13 59		14 11						14 29		14 41					14 59		15 11					15 29
Herne Hill [4] 173,179	d		14 03		14 15						14 33		14 45					15 03		15 15					15 33
Loughborough Jn 173,179	d		14 06		14 18						14 36		14 48					15 06		15 18					15 36
Elephant & Castle ⊖173,179	d		14 11		14 23				14 30		14 41		14 53		15 00			15 11		15 23			15 30		15 41
London Bridge ⊖	d	14 03		14 19			14 25	14 28		14 33		14 49		14 58		15 03			15 19		15 25	15 28		15 33	
London Blackfriars ⊖	a	14 08	14 15	14 24	14 27		14 30	14 34	14 34	14 38	14 45	14 54	14 57	15 04	15 04	15 08		15 15	15 24	15 27	15 30	15 34	15 34	15 38	15 45
London Blackfriars [3] ⊖	d	14 09	14 16	14 25	14 28		14 31	14 35		14 39	14 46	14 55	14 58	15 05		15 09		15 16	15 25	15 28	15 31	15 35		15 39	15 46
City Thameslink [3]	d																								
Farringdon [3] ⊖	d	14 13	14 20	14 29	14 32		14 35	14 39		14 43	14 50	14 59	15 02	15 09		15 13		15 20	15 29	15 32	15 35	15 39		15 43	15 50
St Pancras International ⊖	d	14 18	14 25	14 34	14 37		14 40	14 44		14 48	14 55	15 04	15 07	15 14		15 18		15 25	15 34	15 37	15 40	15 44		15 48	15 55
Finsbury Park ⊖	a						14 46														15 46				
Welwyn Garden City	a																								
Stevenage	a						15 06														16 06				
Hitchin	a						15 12														16 12				
Letchworth Garden City	a						15 18														16 18				
Royston	a						15 29														16 29				
Cambridge	a						15 48														16 48				
Huntingdon	a																								
Peterborough	a																								
Kentish Town ⊖	a				14 41			14 48					15 11	15 18						15 41		15 48			
West Hampstead Thameslink ⊖	a	14 26	14 34	14 42	14 46					14 56	15 03	15 12	15 16			15 26		15 34	15 42	15 46				15 56	16 03
Elstree & Borehamwood	a		14 44		15 01						15 14		15 31					15 44		16 01					16 14
St Albans City	a	14 40	14 54	14 58	15 14					15 10	15 24	15 28	15 42			15 38		15 54	15 58	16 14				16 10	16 24
Harpenden	a	14 46	15 00	15 04						15 16	15 30	15 34				15 45		16 00	16 04					16 16	16 30
Luton Airport Parkway [7] ✈	a	14 51	15 05	15 09						15 21	15 35	15 39				15 51		16 05	16 09					16 21	16 35
Luton [10]	a	14 55	15 10	15 13						15 25	15 40	15 43				15 55		16 10	16 13					16 25	16 40
Bedford	a	15 20		15 38						15 50		16 08				16 20			16 38					16 50	

A From Three Bridges

Table T052-F

Sundays
15 December to 10 May

Brighton, Gatwick Airport, Kent & South London - Luton, Bedford, Cambridge and Peterborough (via London)

Station		TL [1]	TL		TL	TL	TL [1]	TL	TL [1]	TL	TL [1]	TL	TL	TL [1] A		TL	TL [1]	TL	TL	TL	TL [1]	TL	TL [1]	TL	TL [1]
Brighton [10]	d	14 42							15 08								15 42						16 08		
Horsham	d																								
Gatwick Airport [10] ✈	d	15 19					15 19		15 49		15 46			15 49			16 19				16 19		16 49		16 46
East Croydon	d	15 34					15 48		16 04		16 07			16 18			16 34				16 48		17 04		17 07
Rainham (Kent)	d				14 30							15 00							15 30						
Dartford	d				15 15							15 45							16 15						
Abbey Wood	d				15 28							15 58							16 28						
Woolwich Arsenal	d				15 34							16 04							16 34						
Greenwich	d				15 47							16 17							16 47						
Maidstone East	d																								
Sevenoaks	d					14 58							15 28							15 58					
Swanley	d					15 17							15 47							16 17					
St Mary Cray	d					15 21							15 51							16 21					
Orpington	d																								
Bromley South	d					15 29							15 59							16 29					
Catford	d					15 41							16 11							16 41					
Peckham Rye [4] 195	d					15 50							16 20							16 50					
Denmark Hill [4] 195	d					15 53							16 23							16 53					
Sutton [4] 179	d		15 09					15 40		15 39						16 10		16 09				16 40		16 39	
Wimbledon ⊖	d		15 27							15 57								16 27						16 57	
Streatham [4]	d		15 37					15 55		16 07						16 25		16 37				16 55		17 07	
Tulse Hill [3]	d		15 41					15 59		16 11						16 29		16 41				16 59		17 11	
Herne Hill [4] 173,179	d		15 45					16 03		16 15						16 33		16 45				17 03		17 15	
Loughborough Jn 173,179	d		15 48					16 06		16 18						16 36		16 48				17 06		17 18	
Elephant & Castle ⊖173,179	d		15 53			16 00		16 11		16 23			16 30			16 41		16 53		17 00		17 11		17 23	
London Bridge ⊖	d	15 49			15 58		16 03		16 19		16 25	16 28		16 33			16 49		16 58		17 03		17 19		17 25
London Blackfriars ⊖	a	15 54	15 57		16 04	16 04	16 08	16 15	16 24	16 27	16 30	16 34	16 34	16 38		16 45	16 54	16 57	17 04	17 04	17 08	17 15	17 24	17 27	17 30
London Blackfriars [3] ⊖	d	15 55	15 58		16 05		16 09	16 16	16 25	16 28	16 31	16 35		16 39		16 46	16 55	16 58	17 05		17 09	17 16	17 25	17 28	17 31
City Thameslink [3]	d																								
Farringdon [3] ⊖	d	15 59	16 02		16 09		16 13	16 20	16 29	16 32	16 35	16 39		16 43		16 50	16 59	17 02	17 09		17 13	17 20	17 29	17 32	17 35
St Pancras International ⊖	d	16 04	16 07		16 14		16 18	16 25	16 34	16 37	16 40	16 44		16 48		16 55	17 04	17 07	17 14		17 18	17 25	17 34	17 37	17 40
Finsbury Park ⊖	a										16 46														17 45
Welwyn Garden City	a																								
Stevenage	a										17 06														18 06
Hitchin	a										17 12														18 12
Letchworth Garden City	a										17 18														18 18
Royston	a										17 29														18 29
Cambridge	a										17 48														18 48
Huntingdon	a																								
Peterborough	a																								
Kentish Town ⊖	a		16 11		16 18					16 41		16 48						17 11	17 18					17 41	
West Hampstead Thameslink ⊖	a	16 12	16 16				16 26	16 34	16 42	16 46				16 56		17 03	17 12	17 16			17 26	17 34	17 42	17 46	
Elstree & Borehamwood	a		16 31					16 44		17 01						17 14		17 31				17 44		18 01	
St Albans City	a	16 28	16 42				16 38	16 54	16 58	17 12				17 08		17 24	17 28	17 44			17 40	17 54	17 58	18 12	
Harpenden	a	16 34					16 45	17 00	17 04					17 15		17 30	17 34				17 46	18 00	18 04		
Luton Airport Parkway [7] ✈	a	16 39					16 51	17 05	17 09					17 21		17 35	17 39				17 51	18 05	18 09		
Luton [10]	a	16 43					16 55	17 10	17 13					17 25		17 40	17 43				17 55	18 10	18 13		
Bedford	a	17 08					17 20		17 38					17 50			18 08				18 20		18 38		

A From Three Bridges

Table T052-F

Sundays
15 December to 10 May

Brighton, Gatwick Airport, Kent & South London - Luton, Bedford, Cambridge and Peterborough (via London)

Station		TL	TL	TL 1 A	TL	TL 1	TL	TL	TL	TL 1	TL	TL 1	TL	TL 1	TL	TL	TL 1 A	TL	TL 1	TL	TL	TL
Brighton 10	d					16 42						17 08							17 42			
Horsham	d																					
Gatwick Airport 10 ✈	d			16 49		17 19				17 19		17 49		17 46			17 49		18 19			
East Croydon	d			17 18		17 34				17 48		18 04		18 07			18 18		18 34			
Rainham (Kent)	d	16 00						16 30							17 00						17 30	
Dartford	d	16 45						17 15							17 45						18 15	
Abbey Wood	d	16 58						17 28							17 58						18 28	
Woolwich Arsenal	d	17 04						17 34							18 04						18 34	
Greenwich	d	17 17						17 47							18 17						18 47	
Maidstone East	d																					
Sevenoaks	d		16 28						16 58							17 28						17 58
Swanley	d		16 47						17 17							17 47						18 17
St Mary Cray	d		16 51						17 21							17 51						18 21
Orpington	d																					
Bromley South	d		16 59						17 29							17 59						18 29
Catford	d		17 11						17 41							18 11						18 41
Peckham Rye 4	195 d		17 20						17 50							18 20						18 50
Denmark Hill 4	195 d		17 23						17 53							18 23						18 53
Sutton 4	179 d				17 10		17 09				17 40		17 39					18 10		18 09		
Wimbledon ⊖	d						17 27						17 57							18 27		
Streatham 4	d				17 25		17 37				17 55		18 07					18 25		18 37		
Tulse Hill 3	d				17 29		17 41				17 59		18 11					18 29		18 41		
Herne Hill 4	173,179 d				17 33		17 45				18 03		18 15					18 33		18 45		
Loughborough Jn	173,179 d				17 36		17 48				18 06		18 18					18 36		18 48		
Elephant & Castle ⊖	173,179 d		17 30		17 41		17 53		18 00		18 11		18 23			18 30		18 41		18 53		19 00
London Bridge ⊖	d	17 28		17 33		17 49		17 58		18 03		18 19		18 25	18 28		18 33		18 49		18 58	
London Blackfriars ⊖	a	17 34	17 34	17 38	17 45	17 54	17 57	18 04	18 04	18 08	18 15	18 24	18 27	18 30	18 34	18 34	18 38	18 45	18 54	18 57	19 04	19 04
London Blackfriars 3 ⊖	d	17 35		17 39	17 46	17 55	17 58	18 05		18 09	18 16	18 25	18 28	18 31	18 35		18 39	18 46	18 55	18 58	19 05	
City Thameslink 3	d																					
Farringdon 3 ⊖	d	17 39		17 43	17 50	17 59	18 02	18 09		18 13	18 20	18 29	18 32	18 35	18 39		18 43	18 50	18 59	19 02	19 09	
St Pancras International ⊖	d	17 44		17 48	17 55	18 04	18 07	18 14		18 18	18 25	18 34	18 37	18 40	18 44		18 48	18 55	19 04	19 07	19 14	
Finsbury Park ⊖	a													18 46								
Welwyn Garden City	a																					
Stevenage	a													19 06								
Hitchin	a													19 12								
Letchworth Garden City	a													19 18								
Royston	a													19 29								
Cambridge	a													19 48								
Huntingdon	a																					
Peterborough	a																					
Kentish Town ⊖	a	17 48					18 11	18 18					18 41		18 48					19 11	19 18	
West Hampstead Thameslink ⊖	a			17 56	18 03	18 12	18 16			18 26	18 34	18 42	18 46				18 56	19 04	19 12	19 16		
Elstree & Borehamwood	a				18 14		18 31				18 44		19 01					19 14		19 31		
St Albans City	a			18 08	18 24	18 28	18 42			18 38	18 54	18 58	19 12				19 08	19 24	19 28	19 44		
Harpenden	a			18 15	18 30	18 34				18 45	19 00	19 04					19 15	19 30	19 34			
Luton Airport Parkway 7 ✈	a			18 21	18 35	18 39				18 51	19 05	19 09					19 21	19 35	19 39			
Luton 10	a			18 25	18 40	18 43				18 55	19 10	19 13					19 25	19 40	19 43			
Bedford	a			18 50		19 08				19 20		19 38					19 51		20 09			

A From Three Bridges

NRT DECEMBER 19 EDITION

Table T052-F

Sundays
15 December to 10 May

Brighton, Gatwick Airport, Kent & South London - Luton, Bedford, Cambridge and Peterborough (via London)

Station		TL 1	TL	TL 1	TL	TL 1	TL	TL	TL 1 A	TL	TL 1	TL	TL	TL	TL 1	TL	TL 1	TL	TL 1	TL	TL	TL 1 A	TL
Brighton 10	d			18 08							18 42						19 08						
Horsham	d																						
Gatwick Airport 10 ✈	d	18 19		18 49		18 46			18 49		19 19				19 19		19 49		19 46			19 49	
East Croydon	d	18 48		19 04		19 07			19 18		19 34				19 48		20 04		20 07			20 18	
Rainham (Kent)	d						18 00						18 30							19 00			
Dartford	d						18 45						19 15							19 45			
Abbey Wood	d						18 58						19 28							19 58			
Woolwich Arsenal	d						19 04						19 34							20 04			
Greenwich	d						19 17						19 47							20 17			
Maidstone East	d																						
Sevenoaks	d							18 28						18 58							19 28		
Swanley	d							18 47						19 17							19 47		
St Mary Cray	d							18 51						19 21							19 51		
Orpington	d																						
Bromley South	d							18 59						19 29							19 59		
Catford	d							19 11						19 41							20 11		
Peckham Rye 4	195 d							19 20						19 50							20 20		
Denmark Hill 4	195 d							19 23						19 53							20 23		
Sutton 4	179 d		18 40		18 39					19 10		19 09				19 40		19 39					20 10
Wimbledon ⊖	d				18 57							19 27						19 57					
Streatham 4	d		18 55		19 07					19 25		19 37				19 55		20 07					20 25
Tulse Hill 3	d		18 59		19 11					19 29		19 41				19 59		20 11					20 29
Herne Hill 4	173,179 d		19 03		19 15					19 33		19 45				20 03		20 15					20 33
Loughborough Jn	173,179 d		19 06		19 18					19 36		19 48				20 06		20 18					20 36
Elephant & Castle ⊖	173,179 d		19 11		19 23			19 30		19 41		19 53		20 00		20 11		20 23			20 30		20 41
London Bridge ⊖	d	19 03		19 19		19 25	19 28		19 33		19 49		19 58		20 03		20 19		20 25	20 28		20 33	
London Blackfriars ⊖	a	19 08	19 15	19 24	19 27	19 30	19 34	19 34	19 38	19 45	19 54	19 57	20 04	20 04	20 08	20 15	20 24	20 27	20 30	20 34	20 34	20 38	20 45
London Blackfriars 3 ⊖	d	19 09	19 16	19 25	19 28	19 31	19 35		19 39	19 46	19 55	19 58	20 05		20 09	20 16	20 25	20 28	20 31	20 35		20 39	20 46
City Thameslink 3	d																						
Farringdon 3 ⊖	d	19 13	19 20	19 29	19 32	19 35	19 39		19 43	19 50	19 59	20 02	20 09		20 13	20 20	20 29	20 32	20 35	20 39		20 43	20 50
St Pancras International ⊖	d	19 18	19 25	19 34	19 37	19 40	19 44		19 48	19 55	20 04	20 07	20 14		20 18	20 25	20 34	20 37	20 40	20 44		20 48	20 55
Finsbury Park ⊖	a					19 46													20 46				
Welwyn Garden City	a																						
Stevenage	a					20 06													21 06				
Hitchin	a					20 12													21 12				
Letchworth Garden City	a					20 18													21 18				
Royston	a					20 29													21 29				
Cambridge	a					20 48													21 45				
Huntingdon	a																						
Peterborough	a																						
Kentish Town ⊖	a				19 41		19 48					20 11	20 18					20 41		20 48			
West Hampstead Thameslink ⊖	a	19 26	19 34	19 42	19 46				19 56	20 03	20 12	20 16			20 26	20 33	20 42	20 46				20 56	21 04
Elstree & Borehamwood	a		19 44		20 01					20 14		20 31				20 44		21 01					21 14
St Albans City	a	19 40	19 54	19 58	20 12				20 08	20 24	20 28	20 42			20 38	20 54	20 58	21 12				21 08	21 24
Harpenden	a	19 46	20 00	20 04					20 15	20 30	20 34				20 45	21 00	21 04					21 15	21 30
Luton Airport Parkway 7 ✈	a	19 51	20 05	20 09					20 21	20 35	20 39				20 51	21 05	21 09					21 21	21 35
Luton 10	a	19 55	20 10	20 13					20 25	20 40	20 43				20 55	21 10	21 13					21 25	21 40
Bedford	a	20 20		20 38					20 50		21 08				21 20		21 38					21 50	

A From Three Bridges

Table T052-F

Sundays

15 December to 10 May

Brighton, Gatwick Airport, Kent & South London - Luton, Bedford, Cambridge and Peterborough (via London)

Station		TL ■	TL	TL	TL	TL ■	TL	TL ■	TL	TL ■	TL	TL
Brighton ■	d	19 42						20 08				
Horsham	d											
Gatwick Airport ■ ✈	d	20 19				20 19		20 49		20 46		
East Croydon	d	20 34				20 48		21 04		21 07		
Rainham (Kent)	d			19 30							20 00	
Dartford	d			20 15							20 45	
Abbey Wood	d			20 28							20 58	
Woolwich Arsenal	d			20 34							21 04	
Greenwich	d			20 47							21 17	
Maidstone East	d											
Sevenoaks	d				19 58							20 28
Swanley	d				20 17							20 47
St Mary Cray	d				20 21							20 51
Orpington	d											
Bromley South	d				20 29							20 59
Catford	d				20 41							21 11
Peckham Rye ■ 195	d				20 50							21 20
Denmark Hill ■ 195	d				20 53							21 23
Sutton ■ 179	d		20 09				20 40		20 39			
Wimbledon ⊖	d		20 27						20 57			
Streatham ■	d		20 37				20 55		21 07			
Tulse Hill ■	d		20 41				20 59		21 11			
Herne Hill ■ 173,179	d		20 45				21 03		21 15			
Loughborough Jn 173,179	d		20 48				21 06		21 18			
Elephant & Castle ⊖173,179	d		20 53		21 00		21 11		21 23			21 30
London Bridge ⊖	d	20 49		20 58		21 03		21 19		21 25	21 28	
London Blackfriars ⊖	a	20 54	20 57	21 04	21 04	21 08	21 15	21 24	21 27	21 30	21 34	21 34
London Blackfriars ■ ⊖	d	20 55	20 58	21 05		21 09	21 16	21 25	21 28	21 31	21 35	
City Thameslink ■	d											
Farringdon ■ ⊖	d	20 59	21 02	21 09		21 13	21 20	21 29	21 32	21 35	21 39	
St Pancras International ⊖	d	21 04	21 07	21 14		21 18	21 25	21 34	21 37	21 40	21 44	
Finsbury Park ⊖	a									21 46		
Welwyn Garden City	a											
Stevenage	a									22 07		
Hitchin	a									22 13		
Letchworth Garden City	a									22 18		
Royston	a									22 30		
Cambridge	a									22 48		
Huntingdon	a											
Peterborough	a											
Kentish Town ⊖	a		21 11	21 18					21 41		21 48	
West Hampstead Thameslink ⊖	a	21 12	21 16			21 26	21 34	21 42	21 46			
Elstree & Borehamwood	a		21 31				21 44		22 01			
St Albans City	a	21 28	21 42			21 38	21 54	21 58	22 12			
Harpenden	a	21 34				21 46	22 00	22 04				
Luton Airport Parkway ■ ✈	a	21 39				21 51	22 05	22 09				
Luton ■	a	21 43				21 55	22 10	22 13				
Bedford	a	22 08				22 20		22 38				

Station		TL ■ A	TL	TL ■	TL	TL	TL	TL ■	TL	TL ■	TL	TL ■
Brighton ■	d			20 42						21 08		
Horsham	d											
Gatwick Airport ■ ✈	d	20 49		21 19				21 19		21 49		21 46
East Croydon	d	21 18		21 34				21 48		22 04		22 07
Rainham (Kent)	d					20 30						
Dartford	d					21 15						
Abbey Wood	d					21 28						
Woolwich Arsenal	d					21 34						
Greenwich	d					21 47						
Maidstone East	d											
Sevenoaks	d						20 58					
Swanley	d						21 17					
St Mary Cray	d						21 21					
Orpington	d											
Bromley South	d						21 29					
Catford	d						21 41					
Peckham Rye ■ 195	d						21 50					
Denmark Hill ■ 195	d						21 53					
Sutton ■ 179	d		21 10		21 09				21 40		21 39	
Wimbledon ⊖	d				21 27						21 57	
Streatham ■	d		21 25		21 37				21 55		22 07	
Tulse Hill ■	d		21 29		21 41				21 59		22 11	
Herne Hill ■ 173,179	d		21 33		21 45				22 03		22 15	
Loughborough Jn 173,179	d		21 36		21 48				22 06		22 18	
Elephant & Castle ⊖173,179	d		21 41		21 53		22 00		22 11		22 23	
London Bridge ⊖	d	21 33		21 49		21 58		22 03		22 19		22 25
London Blackfriars ⊖	a	21 38	21 45	21 54	21 57	22 04	22 04	22 08	22 15	22 24	22 27	22 30
London Blackfriars ■ ⊖	d	21 39	21 46	21 55	21 58	22 05		22 09	22 16	22 25	22 28	22 31
City Thameslink ■	d											
Farringdon ■ ⊖	d	21 43	21 50	21 59	22 02	22 09		22 13	22 20	22 29	22 32	22 35
St Pancras International ⊖	d	21 48	21 55	22 04	22 07	22 14		22 18	22 25	22 34	22 37	22 40
Finsbury Park ⊖	a											22 46
Welwyn Garden City	a											
Stevenage	a											23 07
Hitchin	a											23 13
Letchworth Garden City	a											23 18
Royston	a											23 29
Cambridge	a											23 45
Huntingdon	a											
Peterborough	a											
Kentish Town ⊖	a				22 11	22 18					22 41	
West Hampstead Thameslink ⊖	a	21 56	22 04	22 12	22 15			22 26	22 33	22 42	22 45	
Elstree & Borehamwood	a		22 14		22 30						23 00	
St Albans City	a	22 08	22 24	22 28	22 40			22 38		22 58	23 10	
Harpenden	a	22 15	22 30	22 34	22 49			22 45		23 04	23 17	
Luton Airport Parkway ■ ✈	a	22 21	22 35	22 39	22 55			22 51		23 09	23 22	
Luton ■	a	22 25	22 40	22 43	22 59			22 55		23 13	23 26	
Bedford	a	22 50		23 08	23 24			23 20		23 38		

A From Three Bridges

Table T052-F

Sundays

15 December to 10 May

Brighton, Gatwick Airport, Kent & South London - Luton, Bedford, Cambridge and Peterborough (via London)

Station		TL	TL	TL	TL ■	TL	TL	TL	TL	TL ■	TL	TL	TL ■	TL ■	TL ■
Brighton ■	d				21 42					22 08			22 42	23 08	23 42
Horsham	d														
Gatwick Airport ■ ✈	d				22 19					22 49			23 21	23 50	00 21
East Croydon	d				22 34					23 04			23 40	00 10	00 40
Rainham (Kent)	d	21 00					21 30				22 00				
Dartford	d	21 45					22 15				22 45				
Abbey Wood	d	21 58					22 28				22 58				
Woolwich Arsenal	d	22 04					22 34				23 04				
Greenwich	d	22 17					22 47				23 17				
Maidstone East	d														
Sevenoaks	d		21 28					21 58				22 28			
Swanley	d		21 47					22 17				22 47			
St Mary Cray	d		21 51					22 21				22 51			
Orpington	d														
Bromley South	d		21 59					22 29				22 59			
Catford	d		22 11					22 41				23 11			
Peckham Rye ■ 195	d		22 20					22 50				23 20			
Denmark Hill ■ 195	d		22 23					22 53				23 23			
Sutton ■ 179	d			22 10		22 09			22 40						
Wimbledon ⊖	d					22 27									
Streatham ■	d			22 25		22 37			22 55						
Tulse Hill ■	d			22 29		22 41			22 59						
Herne Hill ■ 173,179	d			22 33		22 45			23 03						
Loughborough Jn 173,179	d			22 36		22 48			23 06						
Elephant & Castle ⊖173,179	d		22 30	22 41		22 53		23 00	23 11			23 30			
London Bridge ⊖	d	22 28			22 49		22 58			23 19	23 28				
London Blackfriars ⊖	a	22 34	22 34	22 45	22 54	22 57	23 04	23 04	23 15	23 24	23 34	23 34	00 06	00 36	01 06
London Blackfriars ■ ⊖	d	22 35			22 55	22 58	23 05		23 16	23 27	23 37		00 06	00 36	01 06
City Thameslink ■	d														
Farringdon ■ ⊖	d	22 39			22 59	23 02	23 09		23 20	23 31	23 41		00 11		
St Pancras International ⊖	d	22 44			23 04	23 07	23 14		23 25	23 36	23 46		00 16	00 46	01 16
Finsbury Park ⊖	a														
Welwyn Garden City	a														
Stevenage	a														
Hitchin	a														
Letchworth Garden City	a														
Royston	a														
Cambridge	a														
Huntingdon	a														
Peterborough	a														
Kentish Town ⊖	a	22 48				23 11	23 18		23 29		23 50		00 20	00 50	
West Hampstead Thameslink ⊖	a				23 12	23 15	23 22		23 33	23 44	23 54		00 24	00 54	01 24
Elstree & Borehamwood	a					23 30			23 48		00 09		00 39	01 09	
St Albans City	a				23 28	23 40			23 58	00 02	00 19		00 49	01 19	01 40
Harpenden	a				23 35	23 47			00 05	00 09	00 27		00 57	01 27	01 47
Luton Airport Parkway ■ ✈	a				23 40	23 52			00 10	00 14	00 32		01 02	01 32	01 52
Luton ■	a				23 44	23 56			00 14	00 18	00 36		01 06	01 36	01 56
Bedford	a				00 09	00 21			00 35	00 43	01 01		01 31	02 01	02 21

Table T052-R

Mondays to Fridays
16 December to 15 May

Cambridge and Peterborough (via London), Bedford, Luton - South London & Kent, Gatwick Airport, Brighton

Miles	Station		TL MO 1 A	TL MX 1 A	TL 1 B	TL MO 1 A	TL MX 1 A	TL 1 C	TL 1 C	TL 1 C	TL 1 C	TL 1	TL 1	TL	TL 1	TL	TL	TL	TL 1	TL	TL 1 D	TL	TL
0	Bedford	d						00 15	01 15	01 53	02 15	02 53	03 10		03 45				04 13				
19½	Luton 10	d				00 10	00 10	00 40	01 40	02 18	02 41	03 18	03 35		04 10		04 20		04 38				
20½	Luton Airport Parkway 7 ✈	d				00 13	00 13	00 43	01 43	02 21	02 44	03 21	03 38		04 13		04 23		04 41				
25¼	Harpenden	d				00 18	00 18	00 48	01 48	02 26	02 50	03 26	03 43		04 18		04 28		04 46				
29¾	St Albans City	d				00 25	00 25	00 55	01 55	02 33	02 56	03 33	03 50		04 25		04 35		04 53				
—	Elstree & Borehamwood	d						01 04	02 04		03 05		03 59				04 44						
—	West Hampstead Thameslink ⊖	d			00 09	00 41	00 42	01 20	02 20	02 50	03 21	03 50	04 15		04 41		04 59		05 09	05 16		05 20	
—	Kentish Town ⊖	d			00 13			01 24	02 24		03 25		04 19				05 04			05 21			
—	Peterborough	d																					
—	Huntingdon	d																					
—	Cambridge	d																					
—	Royston	d																					
—	Letchworth Garden City	d																					
—	Hitchin	d																					
—	Stevenage	d																					
—	Welwyn Garden City	d																					
—	Finsbury Park ⊖	d																					
49¾	St Pancras International ⊖	d			00 21	00 51	00 52	01 32	02 32	03 02	03 32	04 02	04 32		04 52		05 12		05 20	05 27		05 30	
—	**Farringdon 3** ⊖	d			00 26										04 56		05 17		05 24	05 32		05 35	
—	**City Thameslink 3**	d													04 58		05 19		05 26	05 34		05 37	
—	**London Blackfriars** ⊖	a			00 30	01 00	01 01	01 39	02 39	03 09	03 39	04 09	04 39		05 00		05 21		05 28	05 36		05 39	
—	**London Blackfriars 3** ⊖	d	00 01	00 02	00 31	01 01	01 02	01 40	02 40	03 10	03 40	04 10	04 40	04 56	05 01	05 16	05 21	05 26	05 29	05 36		05 39	05 46
52¾	London Bridge ⊖	d																	05 35		05 37	05 46	
—	Elephant & Castle ⊖ 173,179	a												04 59		05 19	05 25	05 29		05 40			05 49
—	Loughborough Jn 173,179	a															05 30			05 45			
—	Herne Hill 4 173,179	a															05 34			05 49			
—	Tulse Hill 3	a															05 39			05 54			
—	Streatham 4	a															05 44			05 59			
—	Wimbledon ⊖	a															05 54						
—	Sutton 4 179	a															06 14			06 17			
—	Denmark Hill 4 195	a												05 07		05 27		05 37					05 57
—	Peckham Rye 4 195	a												05 10		05 30		05 41					06 00
—	Catford	a												05 19		05 39		05 50					06 09
—	Bromley South	a												05 32		05 52		06 03					06 22
—	Orpington	a												05 44				06 14					
—	St Mary Cray	a														06 01							06 31
—	Swanley	a														06 05							06 35
—	Sevenoaks	a														06 25							06 55
—	Maidstone East	a																					
—	Greenwich	a																				05 55	
—	Woolwich Arsenal	a																				06 08	
—	Abbey Wood	a																				06 14	
—	Dartford	a																				06 25	
—	Rainham (Kent)	a																				07 09	
61¾	East Croydon	a	00 27	00 27	00 57	01 27	01 28	02 06	03 06	03 36	04 06	04 36	05 06		05 27				05 48		05 54		
77¾	Gatwick Airport 10 ✈	a	00 47	00 47	01 20	01 56	01 56	02 30	03 30	03 56	04 30	04 57	05 31		05 47				06 04				
—	Horsham	a																					
101¾	Brighton 10	a	01 24	01 24		02 28	02 28					05 32	06 10		06 26				06 42				

A From Bedford
B From Bedford to Three Bridges
C To Three Bridges
D To East Grinstead

NRT DECEMBER 19 EDITION

Table T052-R

Mondays to Fridays
16 December to 15 May

Cambridge and Peterborough (via London), Bedford, Luton - South London & Kent, Gatwick Airport, Brighton

Station		TL	TL 1	TL	TL 1	TL 1 A	TL	TL 1	TL	TL	TL	TL 1	TL	TL 1	TL 1 A	TL	TL 1	TL	TL 1	TL	TL	TL 1	TL
Bedford	d				04 43									05 15	05 25				05 44				
Luton 10	d	04 50			05 08						05 20			05 40	05 48	05 36			06 02				06 00
Luton Airport Parkway 7 ✈	d	04 53			05 11						05 23			05 43	05 51	05 39							06 03
Harpenden	d	04 58			05 16						05 28			05 48	05 56	05 44			06 08				06 09
St Albans City	d	05 05			05 23						05 35			05 55	06 01	05 51			06 13		06 07		06 15
Elstree & Borehamwood	d	05 14									05 44					06 00					06 16		06 24
West Hampstead Thameslink ⊖	d	05 31		05 36	05 39	05 43			05 52		05 59		06 06	06 09		06 17		06 21			06 32		06 36
Kentish Town ⊖	d	05 36		05 41			05 51				06 04		06 11			06 21					06 36		
Peterborough	d		04 20									04 54										05 24	
Huntingdon	d		04 35									05 11										05 41	
Cambridge	d							04 54									05 24						
Royston	d							05 09									05 38						
Letchworth Garden City	d							05 21									05 51						
Hitchin	d		05 07					05 26				05 41					05 56					06 11	
Stevenage	d		05 13					05 32				05 47					06 02					06 17	
Welwyn Garden City	d		05 22																				
Finsbury Park ⊖	d		05 37					05 52				06 08					06 22					06 38	
St Pancras International ⊖	d	05 42	05 45	05 47	05 50	05 55	05 57	06 00	06 02		06 12	06 15	06 17	06 20	06 25	06 27	06 30	06 32	06 35		06 42	06 45	06 47
Farringdon 3 ⊖	d	05 47	05 49	05 52	05 54	05 59	06 02	06 04	06 07		06 17	06 19	06 22	06 24	06 29	06 32	06 34	06 37	06 39		06 47	06 49	06 52
City Thameslink 3	d	05 49	05 51	05 54	05 56	06 01	06 04	06 06	06 09		06 19	06 21	06 24	06 26	06 31	06 34	06 36	06 39	06 41		06 49	06 51	06 54
London Blackfriars ⊖	a	05 51	05 53	05 56	05 58	06 03	06 06	06 08	06 11		06 21	06 23	06 26	06 28	06 33	06 36	06 38	06 41	06 43		06 51	06 53	06 56
London Blackfriars 3 ⊖	d	05 51	05 54	05 56	05 59	06 04	06 06	06 09	06 11	06 16	06 21	06 24	06 26	06 29	06 34	06 36	06 39	06 41	06 44	06 46	06 51	06 54	06 56
London Bridge ⊖	d		06 00		06 05	06 11		06 15	06 18			06 30		06 35	06 41		06 45	06 48	06 51			07 00	
Elephant & Castle ⊖ 173,179	a	05 55		06 00			06 10			06 19	06 25		06 30			06 40				06 49	06 55		07 00
Loughborough Jn 173,179	a	06 00					06 15				06 30					06 45					07 00		
Herne Hill 4 173,179	a	06 04					06 19				06 34					06 49					07 04		
Tulse Hill 3	a	06 09					06 24				06 39					06 54					07 09		
Streatham 4	a	06 14					06 29				06 44					06 59					07 14		
Wimbledon ⊖	a	06 24									06 54										07 24		
Sutton 4 179	a	06 44					06 47				07 14					07 17					07 44		
Denmark Hill 4 195	a			06 07						06 27			06 37							06 57			07 07
Peckham Rye 4 195	a			06 10						06 30			06 40							07 00			07 10
Catford	a			06 19						06 39			06 49							07 09			07 19
Bromley South	a			06 32						06 52			07 02							07 22			07 32
Orpington	a			06 44									07 14										07 45
St Mary Cray	a									07 01										07 32			
Swanley	a									07 05										07 36			
Sevenoaks	a									07 27										07 56			
Maidstone East	a																						
Greenwich	a								06 27									06 57					
Woolwich Arsenal	a								06 40									07 10					
Abbey Wood	a								06 46									07 16					
Dartford	a								06 57									07 29					
Rainham (Kent)	a								07 44									08 21					
East Croydon	a		06 16		06 18	06 24		06 28				06 46		06 48	06 54		06 59		07 06			07 16	
Gatwick Airport 10 ✈	a		06 50		06 34			06 44				07 19		07 04			07 14		07 28			07 46	
Horsham	a		07 13									07 45										08 11	
Brighton 10	a				07 14			07 22						07 42			07 49						

A To East Grinstead

Table T052-R

Mondays to Fridays

16 December to 15 May

Cambridge and Peterborough (via London), Bedford, Luton - South London & Kent, Gatwick Airport, Brighton

	TL 1	TL 1 A	TL	TL 1	TL	TL	TL 1	TL	TL 1	TL	TL 1	TL 1 A	TL	TL 1	TL	TL	TL 1	TL	TL 1	TL	TL 1	TL 1 A
Bedford d	05 48	06 04			06 01		06 22				06 18	06 34			06 31		06 52				06 48	07 04
Luton 10 d	06 12	06 22			06 25		06 39			06 30	06 42	06 52			06 55		07 09			07 00	07 12	07 22
Luton Airport Parkway 7 ✈ d	06 15				06 28					06 33	06 45				06 58					07 03	07 15	
Harpenden d	06 21	06 28			06 33					06 39	06 51	06 58			07 04					07 09	07 21	07 28
St Albans City d	06 27	06 33	06 22		06 38		06 48	06 34		06 45	06 57	07 03	06 52		07 10		07 18	07 07		07 15	07 27	07 33
Elstree & Borehamwood d			06 31					06 43		06 54			07 01					07 16		07 24		
West Hampstead Thameslink ⊖ d	06 39		06 47					07 02		07 06	07 09		07 17					07 32		07 36		
Kentish Town ⊖ d			06 51					07 06					07 21					07 36				
Peterborough d									05 54										06 24			
Huntingdon d									06 11										06 41			
Cambridge d				05 54										06 24								
Royston d				06 08										06 38								
Letchworth Garden City d				06 21										06 51								
Hitchin d				06 26					06 41					06 56					07 11			
Stevenage d				06 32					06 47					07 02					07 17			
Welwyn Garden City d																						
Finsbury Park ⊖ d				06 52					07 08					07 22					07 38			
St Pancras International ⊖ d	06 50	06 55	06 57	07 00	07 02		07 10	07 12	07 15	07 17	07 20	07 25	07 27	07 30	07 32		07 40	07 42	07 45	07 47	07 50	07 55
Farringdon 3 ⊖ d	06 54	06 59	07 02	07 04	07 07		07 14	07 17	07 19	07 22	07 24	07 29	07 32	07 34	07 37		07 44	07 47	07 49	07 52	07 54	07 59
City Thameslink 3 d	06 56	07 01	07 04	07 06	07 09		07 16	07 19	07 21	07 24	07 26	07 31	07 34	07 36	07 39		07 46	07 49	07 51	07 54	07 56	08 01
London Blackfriars ⊖ a	06 58	07 03	07 06	07 08	07 11		07 18	07 21	07 23	07 26	07 28	07 33	07 36	07 38	07 41		07 48	07 51	07 53	07 56	07 58	08 03
London Blackfriars 3 ⊖ d	06 59	07 04	07 06	07 09	07 11	07 16	07 19	07 21	07 24	07 26	07 29	07 34	07 36	07 39	07 41	07 46	07 49	07 51	07 54	07 56	07 59	08 04
London Bridge ⊖ d	07 05	07 11		07 15	07 18		07 25		07 30		07 35	07 41		07 45	07 48		07 55		08 00		08 05	08 11
Elephant & Castle ⊖173,179 a			07 10			07 19		07 25		07 30			07 40			07 49		07 55		08 00		
Loughborough Jn. 173,179 a			07 15					07 30					07 45					08 00				
Herne Hill 4 173,179 a			07 19					07 34					07 49					08 04				
Tulse Hill 3 a			07 24					07 39					07 54					08 09				
Streatham 4 a			07 29					07 44					07 59					08 14				
Wimbledon ⊖ a								07 54										08 24				
Sutton 4 179 a			07 47					08 14					08 17					08 44				
Denmark Hill 4 195 a						07 27				07 38						07 57				08 07		
Peckham Rye 4 195 a						07 30				07 41						08 00				08 10		
Catford a						07 39				07 50						08 09				08 19		
Bromley South a						07 52				08 03						08 22				08 32		
Orpington a										08 18										08 47		
St Mary Cray a						08 02										08 31						
Swanley a						08 07										08 36						
Sevenoaks a						08 26										08 55						
Maidstone East a																						
Greenwich a					07 27										07 57							
Woolwich Arsenal a					07 40										08 10							
Abbey Wood a					07 46										08 16							
Dartford a					07 57										08 27							
Rainham (Kent) a					08 49										09 11							
East Croydon ⇌ a	07 18	07 24		07 29			07 38		07 46		07 48	07 54		08 00			08 08		08 16		08 18	08 24
Gatwick Airport 10 ✈ a	07 34			07 44			07 53		08 16		08 04			08 15			08 23		08 45		08 34	
Horsham a									08 42										09 11			
Brighton 10 a	08 12			08 19							08 42			08 50							09 12	

A To East Grinstead

Table T052-R

Mondays to Fridays

16 December to 15 May

Cambridge and Peterborough (via London), Bedford, Luton - South London & Kent, Gatwick Airport, Brighton

	TL	TL 1	TL	TL 1 A	TL	TL 1 B	TL	TL 1	TL	TL 1	TL 1	TL	TL 1	TL	TL 1 C	TL	TL 1 A	TL	TL 1	TL	TL 1	TL 1
Bedford d				07 01		07 22				07 18	07 34						07 52				07 48	08 04
Luton 10 d			07 16	07 26		07 39			07 30	07 42	07 52			07 46	07 58		08 09			08 02	08 12	08 22
Luton Airport Parkway 7 ✈ d			07 19	07 29					07 33	07 45				07 49	08 01					08 05	08 15	
Harpenden d			07 25	07 34					07 39	07 50	07 58			07 55	08 06					08 10	08 20	08 28
St Albans City d	07 22		07 30	07 41		07 48	07 36		07 45	07 56	08 03	07 52		08 00	08 12		08 18	08 07		08 16	08 26	08 33
Elstree & Borehamwood d	07 31		07 39				07 46		07 54			08 01		08 09				08 16		08 24		
West Hampstead Thameslink ⊖ d	07 47		07 51				08 02		08 06			08 17		08 21				08 32		08 36		
Kentish Town ⊖ d	07 51						08 06					08 21						08 36				
Peterborough d								06 54											07 24			
Huntingdon d								07 11											07 41			
Cambridge d		06 54											07 24									
Royston d		07 08											07 38									
Letchworth Garden City d		07 21											07 51									
Hitchin d		07 26						07 41					07 56						08 11			
Stevenage d		07 32						07 47					08 02						08 17			
Welwyn Garden City d																						
Finsbury Park ⊖ d		07 52						08 08					08 22						08 38			
St Pancras International ⊖ d	07 57	08 00	08 02	08 05		08 10	08 12	08 15	08 17	08 20	08 25	08 27	08 30	08 32	08 35		08 40	08 42	08 45	08 47	08 50	08 55
Farringdon 3 ⊖ d	08 02	08 04	08 07	08 09		08 14	08 17	08 19	08 22	08 24	08 29	08 32	08 34	08 37	08 39		08 44	08 47	08 49	08 52	08 54	08 59
City Thameslink 3 d	08 04	08 06	08 09	08 11		08 16	08 19	08 21	08 24	08 26	08 31	08 34	08 36	08 39	08 41		08 46	08 49	08 51	08 54	08 56	09 01
London Blackfriars ⊖ a	08 06	08 08	08 11	08 13		08 18	08 21	08 23	08 26	08 28	08 33	08 36	08 38	08 41	08 43		08 48	08 51	08 53	08 56	08 58	09 03
London Blackfriars 3 ⊖ d	08 06	08 09	08 11	08 14	08 16	08 19	08 21	08 24	08 26	08 29	08 34	08 36	08 39	08 41	08 44	08 46	08 49	08 51	08 54	08 56	08 59	09 04
London Bridge ⊖ d		08 15	08 18	08 21		08 25		08 30		08 35	08 41		08 45	08 48	08 51		08 55		09 00		09 05	09 11
Elephant & Castle ⊖173,179 a	08 10				08 19		08 25		08 30			08 40				08 49		08 55		09 00		
Loughborough Jn. 173,179 a	08 15						08 30					08 45						09 00				
Herne Hill 4 173,179 a	08 19						08 34					08 49						09 04				
Tulse Hill 3 a	08 24						08 39					08 54						09 09				
Streatham 4 a	08 30						08 44					09 00						09 14				
Wimbledon ⊖ a							08 54											09 24				
Sutton 4 179 a	08 47						09 14					09 17						09 44				
Denmark Hill 4 195 a					08 27				08 37							08 57				09 07		
Peckham Rye 4 195 a					08 30				08 40							09 00				09 11		
Catford a					08 39				08 49							09 09				09 20		
Bromley South a					08 52				09 02							09 22				09 33		
Orpington a									09 16											09 46		
St Mary Cray a					09 01											09 32						
Swanley a					09 05											09 36						
Sevenoaks a					09 25											09 56						
Maidstone East a																						
Greenwich a			08 27											08 57								
Woolwich Arsenal a			08 40											09 10								
Abbey Wood a			08 46											09 16								
Dartford a			08 57											09 27								
Rainham (Kent) a			09 41											10 11								
East Croydon ⇌ a		08 29		08 36		08 38		08 46		08 48	08 54		08 58		09 06		09 08		09 14		09 18	09 24
Gatwick Airport 10 ✈ a		08 44		09 05				09 15		09 04	09 19		09 14		09 35		09 23		09 43		09 34	09 47
Horsham a								09 39											10 08			
Brighton 10 a		09 20								09 42			09 49								10 12	

A To Three Bridges

B To Littlehampton

C From Flitwick to Three Bridges

Table T052-R

Mondays to Fridays

16 December to 15 May

Cambridge and Peterborough (via London), Bedford, Luton - South London & Kent, Gatwick Airport, Brighton

		TL	TL [1]	TL		TL [1]	TL	TL [1] A	TL	TL [1]	TL	TL [1]	TL	TL [1]	TL		TL [1]	TL	TL [1] A	TL	TL [1]	TL	TL [1]	TL	TL [1]
Bedford	d					08 01		08 22				08 18					08 32		08 46				08 50		
Luton [10]	d			08 16		08 26		08 39			08 30	08 42			08 46		08 56		09 07			09 00	09 13		
Luton Airport Parkway [7] ✈	d			08 19		08 29					08 33	08 45			08 49		08 59					09 03	09 16		
Harpenden	d			08 24		08 34					08 39	08 50			08 54		09 04		09 13			09 09	09 21		
St Albans City	d	08 22		08 30		08 41		08 48	08 37		08 45	08 56	08 52		09 00		09 11		09 18	09 07		09 15	09 26	09 22	
Elstree & Borehamwood	d	08 31		08 39					08 46		08 54		09 01		09 09					09 16		09 24		09 31	
West Hampstead Thameslink ⊖	d	08 47		08 51					09 02		09 06		09 17		09 21					09 32		09 36		09 47	
Kentish Town ⊖	d	08 51							09 06				09 21							09 36				09 51	
Peterborough	d									07 54											08 23				
Huntingdon	d									08 11											08 38				
Cambridge	d		07 54																						08 54
Royston	d		08 08											08 38											09 09
Letchworth Garden City	d		08 21											08 51											09 20
Hitchin	d		08 26							08 41				08 56							09 07				09 24
Stevenage	d		08 32							08 47				09 02							09 13				09 30
Welwyn Garden City	d																								
Finsbury Park ⊖	d		08 52							09 08				09 22							09 38				09 52
St Pancras International ⊖	d	08 57	09 00	09 02		09 05		09 10	09 12	09 15	09 17	09 20	09 27	09 30	09 32		09 35		09 40	09 42	09 45	09 47	09 50	09 57	10 00
Farringdon [3] ⊖	d	09 02	09 04	09 07		09 09		09 14	09 17	09 19	09 22	09 24	09 32	09 34	09 37		09 39		09 44	09 47	09 49	09 52	09 54	10 02	10 04
City Thameslink [3]	d	09 04	09 06	09 09		09 11		09 16	09 19	09 21	09 24	09 26	09 34	09 36	09 39		09 41		09 46	09 49	09 51	09 54	09 56	10 04	10 06
London Blackfriars ⊖	a	09 06	09 08	09 11		09 13		09 18	09 21	09 23	09 26	09 28	09 36	09 38	09 41		09 43		09 48	09 51	09 53	09 56	09 58	10 06	10 08
London Blackfriars [3] ⊖	d	09 06	09 09	09 11		09 14	09 16	09 19	09 21	09 24	09 26	09 29	09 36	09 39	09 41		09 44	09 46	09 49	09 51	09 54	09 56	09 59	10 06	10 09
London Bridge ⊖	d		09 15	09 18		09 21		09 25		09 30		09 35		09 45	09 48		09 51		09 55		10 00		10 05		10 15
Elephant & Castle ⊖173,179	a	09 10					09 19		09 25		09 30		09 40					09 49		09 55		10 00		10 10	
Loughborough Jn. 173,179	a	09 15							09 30				09 45							10 00				10 15	
Herne Hill [4] 173,179	a	09 19							09 34				09 49							10 04				10 19	
Tulse Hill [3]	a	09 24							09 39				09 54							10 09				10 24	
Streatham [4]	a	09 30							09 44				09 59							10 14				10 29	
Wimbledon ⊖	a								09 54											10 24					
Sutton [4] 179	a	09 47							10 14				10 17							10 44				10 47	
Denmark Hill [4] 195	a						09 27				09 37							09 57				10 07			
Peckham Rye [4] 195	a						09 30				09 40							10 00				10 10			
Catford	a						09 39				09 49							10 09				10 19			
Bromley South	a						09 52				10 02							10 22				10 32			
Orpington	a										10 14											10 45			
St Mary Cray	a						10 01											10 31							
Swanley	a						10 05											10 35							
Sevenoaks	a						10 25											10 55							
Maidstone East	a																								
Greenwich	a			09 27											09 57										
Woolwich Arsenal	a			09 40											10 10										
Abbey Wood	a			09 46											10 16										
Dartford	a			09 57											10 27										
Rainham (Kent)	a			10 41											11 11										
East Croydon 🚌	a		09 28			09 36		09 38		09 44		09 48		09 58			10 06		10 08		10 14		10 18		10 28
Gatwick Airport [10] ✈	a		09 44			10 08		09 53		10 13		10 04		10 14			10 38		10 23		10 43		10 34		10 44
Horsham	a									10 38											11 08				
Brighton [10]	a		10 19									10 42		10 49									11 12		11 19

A To Three Bridges

NRT DECEMBER 19 EDITION

Table T052-R

Mondays to Fridays

16 December to 15 May

Cambridge and Peterborough (via London), Bedford, Luton - South London & Kent, Gatwick Airport, Brighton

		TL		TL [1]	TL	TL	TL [1]	TL [1]	TL	TL [1]	TL	TL [1]	TL		TL [1]	TL	TL	TL [1]	TL	TL [1]	TL	TL [1]	TL	TL [1]	
Bedford	d			09 02						09 16					09 34					09 48				10 04	
Luton [10]	d	09 17		09 26						09 41			09 46		09 59					10 12			10 16	10 28	
Luton Airport Parkway [7] ✈	d	09 20		09 29						09 44			09 51		10 02					10 15			10 21	10 31	
Harpenden	d	09 25		09 34						09 49			09 56		10 08					10 22			10 26	10 38	
St Albans City	d	09 30		09 41		09 37				09 55	09 51		10 01		10 13		10 07			10 27	10 22		10 31	10 43	
Elstree & Borehamwood	d	09 39				09 46					10 01		10 10				10 16				10 31		10 40		
West Hampstead Thameslink ⊖	d	09 51				10 01				10 09	10 16		10 21				10 31			10 39	10 46		10 51		
Kentish Town ⊖	d					10 06			10 11		10 21						10 36		10 41		10 51				
Peterborough	d							08 56										09 26							
Huntingdon	d							09 12										09 41							
Cambridge	d											09 24										09 54			
Royston	d											09 38										10 09			
Letchworth Garden City	d											09 51										10 21			
Hitchin	d							09 41				09 56						10 11				10 26			
Stevenage	d							09 47				10 02						10 17				10 32			
Welwyn Garden City	d																								
Finsbury Park ⊖	d							10 08				10 22						10 38				10 52			
St Pancras International ⊖	d	10 02		10 05		10 12		10 15	10 17	10 20	10 27	10 30	10 32		10 35		10 42	10 45	10 47	10 50	10 57	11 00	11 02	11 05	
Farringdon [3] ⊖	d	10 07		10 09		10 17		10 19	10 22	10 24	10 32	10 34	10 37		10 39		10 47	10 49	10 52	10 54	11 02	11 04	11 07	11 09	
City Thameslink [3]	d	10 09		10 11		10 19		10 21	10 24	10 26	10 34	10 36	10 39		10 41		10 49	10 51	10 54	10 56	11 04	11 06	11 09	11 11	
London Blackfriars ⊖	a	10 11		10 13		10 21		10 23	10 26	10 28	10 36	10 38	10 41		10 43		10 51	10 53	10 56	10 58	11 06	11 08	11 11	11 13	
London Blackfriars [3] ⊖	d	10 11		10 14	10 16	10 21		10 24	10 26	10 29	10 36	10 39	10 41		10 44	10 46	10 51	10 54	10 56	10 59	11 06	11 09	11 11	11 14	
London Bridge ⊖	d	10 18		10 21			10 22	10 30		10 35		10 45	10 48		10 51			11 00		11 05		11 15	11 18	11 21	
Elephant & Castle ⊖173,179	a				10 19	10 25			10 30		10 40					10 49	10 55		11 00		11 10				
Loughborough Jn. 173,179	a					10 30					10 45						11 00				11 15				
Herne Hill [4] 173,179	a					10 34					10 49						11 04				11 19				
Tulse Hill [3]	a					10 39					10 54						11 09				11 24				
Streatham [4]	a					10 44					10 59						11 14				11 29				
Wimbledon ⊖	a					10 54											11 24								
Sutton [4] 179	a					11 14					11 17						11 44				11 47				
Denmark Hill [4] 195	a				10 27				10 37							10 57			11 07						
Peckham Rye [4] 195	a				10 30				10 40							11 00			11 10						
Catford	a				10 39				10 49							11 09			11 19						
Bromley South	a				10 52				11 02							11 22			11 32						
Orpington	a								11 14										11 44						
St Mary Cray	a				11 01											11 31									
Swanley	a				11 05											11 35									
Sevenoaks	a				11 25											11 55									
Maidstone East	a																								
Greenwich	a	10 27											10 57										11 27		
Woolwich Arsenal	a	10 40											11 10										11 40		
Abbey Wood	a	10 46											11 16										11 46		
Dartford	a	10 57											11 27										11 57		
Rainham (Kent)	a	11 41											12 11										12 41		
East Croydon 🚌	a			10 36			10 38	10 44		10 48		10 58			11 06			11 14		11 18		11 28		11 36	
Gatwick Airport [10] ✈	a			11 08			10 53	11 12		11 04		11 14			11 38			11 43		11 34		11 44		12 08	
Horsham	a							11 38										12 08							
Brighton [10]	a									11 42		11 49								12 12		12 19			

Table T052-R

Cambridge and Peterborough (via London), Bedford, Luton - South London & Kent, Gatwick Airport, Brighton

Mondays to Fridays

16 December to 15 May

	TL	TL	TL ■	TL	TL ■	TL	TL ■	TL	TL ■	TL		TL	TL ■	TL	TL ■	TL	TL ■	TL	TL ■	TL	TL		TL ■	TL
Bedford d					10 19				10 35						10 49				11 05					
Luton ■ d					10 43			10 48	10 59						11 13			11 18	11 29					
Luton Airport Parkway ■ ✈ d					10 46			10 51	11 02						11 16			11 21	11 32					
Harpenden d					10 52			10 56	11 08						11 22			11 26	11 38					
St Albans City d		10 38			10 57	10 52		11 01	11 13			11 07			11 27	11 22		11 31	11 43		11 37			
Elstree & Borehamwood d		10 47				11 01		11 10				11 16				11 31		11 40			11 46			
West Hampstead Thameslink ⊖ d		11 01			11 09	11 16		11 21				11 32			11 39	11 46		11 51			12 01			
Kentish Town ⊖ d		11 06		11 12		11 21						11 36		11 41		11 51					12 06			12 11
Peterborough d			09 54										10 24										10 54	
Huntingdon d			10 11										10 41										11 11	
Cambridge d							10 24										10 54							
Royston d							10 38										11 09							
Letchworth Garden City d							10 51										11 21							
Hitchin d			10 41				10 56						11 11				11 26						11 41	
Stevenage d			10 47				11 02						11 17				11 32						11 47	
Welwyn Garden City d																								
Finsbury Park ⊖ d			11 08				11 22						11 38				11 52						12 08	
St Pancras International ⊖ d		11 12	11 15	11 17	11 20	11 27	11 30	11 32	11 35			11 42	11 45	11 47	11 50	11 57	12 00	12 02	12 05		12 12		12 15	12 17
Farringdon ■ ⊖ d		11 17	11 19	11 22	11 24	11 32	11 34	11 37	11 39			11 47	11 49	11 52	11 54	12 02	12 04	12 07	12 09		12 17		12 19	12 22
City Thameslink ■ d		11 19	11 21	11 24	11 26	11 34	11 36	11 39	11 41			11 49	11 51	11 54	11 56	12 04	12 06	12 09	12 11		12 19		12 21	12 24
London Blackfriars ⊖ a		11 21	11 23	11 26	11 28	11 36	11 38	11 41	11 43			11 51	11 53	11 56	11 58	12 06	12 08	12 11	12 13		12 21		12 23	12 26
London Blackfriars ■ ⊖ d	11 16	11 21	11 24	11 26	11 29	11 36	11 39	11 41	11 44	11 46		11 51	11 54	11 56	11 59	12 06	12 09	12 11	12 14	12 16	12 21		12 24	12 26
London Bridge ⊖ d			11 30		11 35		11 45	11 48	11 51				12 00		12 05		12 15	12 18	12 21				12 30	
Elephant & Castle ⊖173,179 a	11 19	11 25		11 30		11 40				11 49		11 55		12 00		12 10				12 19	12 25			12 30
Loughborough Jn. 173,179 a		11 30				11 45						12 00				12 15					12 30			
Herne Hill ■ 173,179 a		11 34				11 49						12 04				12 19					12 34			
Tulse Hill ■ a		11 39				11 54						12 09				12 24					12 39			
Streatham ■ a		11 44				11 59						12 14				12 29					12 44			
Wimbledon ⊖ a		11 54										12 24									12 54			
Sutton ■ 179 a		12 14				12 17						12 44				12 47					13 14			
Denmark Hill ■ 195 a	11 27			11 37						11 57				12 07						12 27				12 37
Peckham Rye ■ 195 a	11 30			11 40						12 00				12 10						12 30				12 40
Catford a	11 39			11 49						12 09				12 19						12 39				12 49
Bromley South a	11 52			12 02						12 22				12 32						12 52				13 02
Orpington a				12 14										12 44										13 14
St Mary Cray a	12 01									12 31										13 01				
Swanley a	12 05									12 35										13 05				
Sevenoaks a	12 25									12 55										13 25				
Maidstone East a																								
Greenwich a								11 57										12 27						
Woolwich Arsenal a								12 10										12 40						
Abbey Wood a								12 16										12 46						
Dartford a								12 27										12 57						
Rainham (Kent) a								13 11										13 41						
East Croydon ⇌ a			11 44		11 48		11 58		12 06				12 14		12 18		12 28		12 36				12 44	
Gatwick Airport ■ ✈ a			12 13		12 04		12 14		12 38				12 43		12 34		12 44		13 08				13 13	
Horsham a			12 38										13 08										13 38	
Brighton ■ a					12 42		12 49								13 12		13 19							

Table T052-R

Cambridge and Peterborough (via London), Bedford, Luton - South London & Kent, Gatwick Airport, Brighton

Mondays to Fridays

16 December to 15 May

	TL ■	TL	TL ■	TL	TL ■	TL	TL	TL ■		TL	TL ■	TL	TL ■	TL	TL ■	TL	TL	TL ■	TL		TL ■	TL	TL ■	TL
Bedford d	11 19				11 35						11 49				12 05						12 19			
Luton ■ d	11 43			11 48	11 59						12 13			12 18	12 29						12 43			12 48
Luton Airport Parkway ■ ✈ d	11 46			11 51	12 02						12 16			12 21	12 32						12 46			12 51
Harpenden d	11 52			11 56	12 08						12 22			12 26	12 38						12 52			12 56
St Albans City d	11 57	11 53		12 01	12 13		12 07				12 27	12 22		12 31	12 43		12 37				12 57	12 52		13 01
Elstree & Borehamwood d		12 02		12 10			12 16					12 31		12 40			12 46					13 01		13 10
West Hampstead Thameslink ⊖ d	12 09	12 16		12 21			12 31				12 39	12 46		12 51			13 01				13 09	13 16		13 21
Kentish Town ⊖ d		12 21					12 36			12 41		12 51					13 06		13 11			13 21		
Peterborough d								11 23										11 54						
Huntingdon d								11 41										12 11						
Cambridge d			11 24										11 54										12 24	
Royston d			11 38										12 09										12 38	
Letchworth Garden City d			11 51										12 21										12 51	
Hitchin d			11 55					12 11					12 26					12 41					12 56	
Stevenage d			12 01					12 17					12 32					12 47					13 02	
Welwyn Garden City d																								
Finsbury Park ⊖ d			12 22					12 38					12 52					13 08					13 22	
St Pancras International ⊖ d	12 20	12 27	12 30	12 32	12 35		12 42	12 45		12 47	12 50	12 57	13 00	13 02	13 05		13 12	13 15	13 17		13 20	13 27	13 30	13 32
Farringdon ■ ⊖ d	12 24	12 32	12 34	12 37	12 39		12 47	12 49		12 52	12 54	13 02	13 04	13 07	13 09		13 17	13 19	13 22		13 24	13 32	13 34	13 37
City Thameslink ■ d	12 26	12 34	12 36	12 39	12 41		12 49	12 51		12 54	12 56	13 04	13 06	13 09	13 11		13 19	13 21	13 24		13 26	13 34	13 36	13 39
London Blackfriars ⊖ a	12 28	12 36	12 38	12 41	12 43		12 51	12 53		12 56	12 58	13 06	13 08	13 11	13 13		13 21	13 23	13 26		13 28	13 36	13 38	13 41
London Blackfriars ■ ⊖ d	12 29	12 36	12 39	12 41	12 44	12 46	12 51	12 54		12 56	12 59	13 06	13 09	13 11	13 14	13 16	13 21	13 24	13 26		13 29	13 36	13 39	13 41
London Bridge ⊖ d	12 35		12 45	12 48	12 51			13 00			13 05		13 15	13 18	13 21			13 30			13 35		13 45	13 48
Elephant & Castle ⊖173,179 a		12 40				12 49	12 55			13 00		13 10				13 19	13 25		13 30			13 40		
Loughborough Jn. 173,179 a		12 45					13 00					13 15					13 30					13 45		
Herne Hill ■ 173,179 a		12 49					13 04					13 19					13 34					13 49		
Tulse Hill ■ a		12 54					13 09					13 24					13 39					13 54		
Streatham ■ a		12 59					13 14					13 29					13 44					13 59		
Wimbledon ⊖ a							13 24										13 54							
Sutton ■ 179 a		13 17					13 44					13 47					14 14					14 17		
Denmark Hill ■ 195 a						12 57				13 07						13 27			13 37					
Peckham Rye ■ 195 a						13 00				13 10						13 30			13 40					
Catford a						13 09				13 19						13 39			13 49					
Bromley South a						13 22				13 32						13 52			14 02					
Orpington a										13 44									14 14					
St Mary Cray a						13 31										14 01								
Swanley a						13 35										14 05								
Sevenoaks a						13 55										14 25								
Maidstone East a																								
Greenwich a				12 57										13 27										13 57
Woolwich Arsenal a				13 10										13 40										14 10
Abbey Wood a				13 16										13 46										14 16
Dartford a				13 27										13 57										14 27
Rainham (Kent) a				14 11										14 41										15 11
East Croydon ⇌ a	12 48		12 58		13 06			13 14			13 18		13 28		13 36			13 44			13 48		13 58	
Gatwick Airport ■ ✈ a	13 04		13 14		13 38			13 43			13 34		13 44		14 08			14 13			14 04		14 14	
Horsham a								14 08										14 38						
Brighton ■ a	13 42		13 49								14 12		14 19								14 42		14 49	

Table T052-R

Mondays to Fridays
16 December to 15 May

Cambridge and Peterborough (via London), Bedford, Luton - South London & Kent, Gatwick Airport, Brighton

Station		TL 1	TL	TL	TL 1	TL	TL 1		TL	TL 1	TL	TL 1	TL	TL	TL 1	TL	TL 1	TL		TL 1	TL	TL 1	TL	TL	TL 1
Bedford	d	12 35					12 49					13 05					13 19					13 35			
Luton 10	d	12 59					13 13				13 18	13 29					13 43				13 48	13 59			
Luton Airport Parkway 7 ✈	d	13 02					13 16				13 21	13 32					13 46				13 51	14 02			
Harpenden	d	13 08					13 22				13 26	13 38					13 52				13 56	14 08			
St Albans City	d	13 13		13 07			13 27		13 22		13 31	13 43		13 37			13 57	13 52			14 01	14 13		14 07	
Elstree & Borehamwood	d			13 16					13 31		13 40			13 46				14 01			14 10			14 16	
West Hampstead Thameslink ⊖	d			13 31			13 39		13 46		13 51			14 01			14 09	14 16			14 21			14 31	
Kentish Town ⊖	d			13 36		13 41			13 51					14 06		14 11		14 21						14 36	
Peterborough	d				12 24										12 54										13 24
Huntingdon	d				12 41										13 11										13 41
Cambridge	d									12 54										13 24					
Royston	d									13 09										13 38					
Letchworth Garden City	d									13 21										13 51					
Hitchin	d				13 11					13 26					13 41					13 56					14 11
Stevenage	d				13 17					13 32					13 47					14 02					14 17
Welwyn Garden City	d																								
Finsbury Park ⊖	d				13 38					13 52					14 08					14 22					14 38
St Pancras International ⊖	d	13 35		13 42	13 45	13 47	13 50		13 57	14 00	14 02	14 05		14 12	14 15	14 17	14 20	14 27		14 30	14 32	14 35		14 42	14 45
Farringdon 3 ⊖	d	13 39		13 47	13 49	13 52	13 54		14 02	14 04	14 07	14 09		14 17	14 19	14 22	14 24	14 32		14 34	14 37	14 39		14 47	14 49
City Thameslink 3	d	13 41		13 49	13 51	13 54	13 56		14 04	14 06	14 09	14 11		14 19	14 21	14 24	14 26	14 34		14 36	14 39	14 41		14 49	14 51
London Blackfriars ⊖	a	13 43		13 51	13 53	13 56	13 58		14 06	14 08	14 11	14 13		14 21	14 23	14 26	14 28	14 36		14 38	14 41	14 43		14 51	14 53
London Blackfriars 3 ⊖	d	13 44	13 46	13 51	13 54	13 56	13 59		14 06	14 09	14 11	14 14	14 16	14 21	14 24	14 26	14 29	14 36		14 39	14 41	14 44	14 46	14 51	14 54
London Bridge ⊖	d	13 51			14 00		14 05			14 15	14 18	14 21			14 30		14 35			14 45	14 48	14 51			15 00
Elephant & Castle ⊖173,179	a		13 49	13 55		14 00			14 10				14 19	14 25		14 30		14 40					14 49	14 55	
Loughborough Jn. 173,179	a			14 00					14 15					14 30				14 45						15 00	
Herne Hill 4 173,179	a			14 04					14 19					14 34				14 49						15 04	
Tulse Hill 3	a			14 09					14 24					14 39				14 54						15 09	
Streatham 4	a			14 14					14 29					14 42				14 59						15 14	
Wimbledon ⊖	a			14 24										14 52										15 24	
Sutton 4 179	a			14 44					14 47					15 14				15 17						15 44	
Denmark Hill 4 195	a		13 57			14 07							14 27			14 37							14 57		
Peckham Rye 4 195	a		14 00			14 10							14 30			14 40							15 00		
Catford	a		14 09			14 19							14 39			14 49							15 09		
Bromley South	a		14 22			14 32							14 52			15 02							15 22		
Orpington	a					14 44										15 14									
St Mary Cray	a		14 31										15 01										15 31		
Swanley	a		14 35										15 05										15 35		
Sevenoaks	a		14 55										15 25										15 55		
Maidstone East	a																								
Greenwich	a										14 27										14 57				
Woolwich Arsenal	a										14 40										15 10				
Abbey Wood	a										14 46										15 16				
Dartford	a										14 57										15 27				
Rainham (Kent)	a										15 41										16 11				
East Croydon	a	14 06			14 14		14 18			14 28		14 36			14 44		14 48			14 58		15 06			15 14
Gatwick Airport 10 ✈	a	14 38			14 43		14 34			14 44		15 08			15 13		15 04			15 14		15 38			15 43
Horsham	a				15 08										15 38										16 08
Brighton 10	a						15 12			15 19							15 42			15 49					

NRT DECEMBER 19 EDITION

Table T052-R

Mondays to Fridays
16 December to 15 May

Cambridge and Peterborough (via London), Bedford, Luton - South London & Kent, Gatwick Airport, Brighton

Station		TL	TL 1	TL	TL 1		TL	TL 1	TL	TL	TL 1	TL	TL 1	TL	TL 1	TL		TL 1	TL	TL	TL 1	TL	TL 1	TL	TL 1
Bedford	d		13 49					14 05					14 19					14 35					14 49		
Luton 10	d		14 13				14 18	14 29					14 43			14 48		14 59					15 13		
Luton Airport Parkway 7 ✈	d		14 16				14 21	14 32					14 46			14 51		15 02					15 16		
Harpenden	d		14 22				14 26	14 38					14 52			14 56		15 08					15 22		
St Albans City	d		14 27	14 22			14 31	14 43		14 37			14 57	14 52		15 01		15 13		15 07			15 27	15 22	
Elstree & Borehamwood	d			14 31			14 40			14 46				15 01		15 10				15 16				15 31	
West Hampstead Thameslink ⊖	d		14 39	14 46			14 51			15 01			15 09	15 16		15 21				15 31			15 39	15 46	
Kentish Town ⊖	d	14 41		14 51						15 06		15 11		15 21						15 36		15 41		15 51	
Peterborough	d										13 54										14 24				
Huntingdon	d										14 11										14 41				
Cambridge	d				13 54										14 24										14 54
Royston	d				14 09										14 38										15 09
Letchworth Garden City	d				14 21										14 51										15 21
Hitchin	d				14 26						14 41				14 56						15 11				15 26
Stevenage	d				14 32						14 47				15 02						15 17				15 32
Welwyn Garden City	d																								
Finsbury Park ⊖	d				14 52						15 08				15 22						15 38				15 52
St Pancras International ⊖	d	14 47	14 50	14 57	15 00		15 02	15 05		15 12	15 15	15 17	15 20	15 27	15 30	15 32		15 35		15 42	15 45	15 47	15 50	15 57	16 00
Farringdon 3 ⊖	d	14 52	14 54	15 02	15 04		15 07	15 09		15 17	15 19	15 22	15 24	15 32	15 34	15 37		15 39		15 47	15 49	15 52	15 54	16 02	16 04
City Thameslink 3	d	14 54	14 56	15 04	15 06		15 09	15 11		15 19	15 21	15 24	15 26	15 34	15 36	15 39		15 41		15 49	15 51	15 54	15 56	16 04	16 06
London Blackfriars ⊖	a	14 56	14 58	15 06	15 08		15 11	15 13		15 21	15 23	15 26	15 28	15 36	15 38	15 41		15 43		15 51	15 53	15 56	15 58	16 06	16 08
London Blackfriars 3 ⊖	d	14 56	14 59	15 06	15 09		15 11	15 14	15 16	15 21	15 24	15 26	15 29	15 36	15 39	15 41		15 44	15 46	15 51	15 54	15 56	15 59	16 06	16 09
London Bridge ⊖	d		15 05		15 15		15 18	15 21			15 30		15 35		15 45	15 48		15 51			16 00		16 05		16 15
Elephant & Castle ⊖173,179	a	15 00		15 10					15 19	15 25		15 30		15 40					15 49	15 55		16 00		16 10	
Loughborough Jn. 173,179	a			15 15						15 30				15 45						16 00				16 15	
Herne Hill 4 173,179	a			15 19						15 34				15 49						16 04				16 19	
Tulse Hill 3	a			15 24						15 39				15 54						16 09				16 24	
Streatham 4	a			15 29						15 44				15 59						16 14				16 29	
Wimbledon ⊖	a									15 54										16 24					
Sutton 4 179	a			15 47						16 14				16 17						16 44				16 47	
Denmark Hill 4 195	a	15 07							15 27			15 37							15 57			16 07			
Peckham Rye 4 195	a	15 10							15 30			15 41							16 00			16 10			
Catford	a	15 19							15 39			15 50							16 09			16 19			
Bromley South	a	15 32							15 52			16 03							16 22			16 32			
Orpington	a	15 44										16 14										16 44			
St Mary Cray	a								16 01										16 31						
Swanley	a								16 05										16 35						
Sevenoaks	a								16 25										16 55						
Maidstone East	a																								
Greenwich	a						15 27									15 57									
Woolwich Arsenal	a						15 40									16 10									
Abbey Wood	a						15 46									16 16									
Dartford	a						15 57									16 27									
Rainham (Kent)	a						16 41									17 11									
East Croydon	a		15 18		15 28			15 36			15 44		15 48		15 58			16 06			16 14		16 19		16 29
Gatwick Airport 10 ✈	a		15 34		15 44			16 08			16 13		16 04		16 14			16 38			16 43		16 35		16 44
Horsham	a										16 38										17 10				
Brighton 10	a		16 12		16 19								16 42		16 49								17 13		17 21

Table T052-R

Mondays to Fridays

16 December to 15 May

Cambridge and Peterborough (via London), Bedford, Luton - South London & Kent, Gatwick Airport, Brighton

		TL	TL 1		TL	TL	TL 1	TL	TL 1	TL 1 A	TL	TL 1	TL	TL 1		TL	TL 1 B	TL	TL 1	TL	TL 1	TL 1 A	TL	TL 1	TL
Bedford	d		15 05						15 19					15 35			15 44				15 48	16 06			
Luton 10	d	15 18	15 29						15 43	15 49			15 48	15 59			16 06				16 13	16 23			16 18
Luton Airport Parkway 7 ✈	d	15 21	15 32						15 46	15 52			15 51	16 02			16 09				16 16				16 21
Harpenden	d	15 26	15 38						15 52				15 56	16 08							16 22				16 26
St Albans City	d	15 31	15 43			15 37			15 57	16 01	15 52		16 01	16 13			16 18	16 07			16 27	16 33	16 22		16 31
Elstree & Borehamwood	d	15 40				15 46					16 01		16 10					16 16					16 31		16 40
West Hampstead Thameslink ⊖	d	15 51				16 01			16 09		16 17		16 21					16 32		16 36	16 39		16 47		16 51
Kentish Town ⊖	d					16 06		16 11			16 22							16 37		16 41			16 52		
Peterborough	d						14 54												15 24						
Huntingdon	d						15 11												15 41						
Cambridge	d											15 24												15 54	
Royston	d											15 38												16 09	
Letchworth Garden City	d											15 51												16 21	
Hitchin	d						15 41					15 56							16 11					16 26	
Stevenage	d						15 47					16 02							16 17					16 32	
Welwyn Garden City	d																								
Finsbury Park ⊖	d						16 08					16 22							16 38					16 52	
St Pancras International ⊖	d	16 02	16 05			16 12	16 15	16 17	16 20	16 25	16 27	16 30	16 32	16 35			16 40	16 42	16 45	16 47	16 50	16 55	16 57	17 00	17 02
Farringdon 3 ⊖	d	16 07	16 09			16 17	16 19	16 22	16 24	16 29	16 32	16 34	16 37	16 39			16 44	16 47	16 49	16 52	16 54	16 59	17 02	17 04	17 07
City Thameslink 3	d	16 09	16 11			16 19	16 21	16 24	16 26	16 31	16 34	16 36	16 39	16 41			16 46	16 49	16 51	16 54	16 56	17 01	17 04	17 06	17 09
London Blackfriars ⊖	a	16 11	16 13			16 21	16 23	16 26	16 28	16 33	16 36	16 38	16 41	16 43			16 48	16 51	16 53	16 56	16 58	17 03	17 06	17 08	17 11
London Blackfriars 3 ⊖	d	16 11	16 14		16 16	16 21	16 24	16 26	16 29	16 34	16 36	16 39	16 41	16 44		16 46	16 49	16 51	16 54	16 56	16 59	17 04	17 06	17 09	17 11
London Bridge ⊖	d	16 18	16 21				16 30		16 35	16 41		16 45	16 48	16 51			16 55		17 00		17 05	17 11		17 15	17 18
Elephant & Castle ⊖173,179	a				16 19	16 25		16 30			16 40					16 49		16 55		17 00			17 10		
Loughborough Jn. 173,179	a					16 30					16 45							17 00					17 15		
Herne Hill 4 173,179	a					16 34					16 49							17 04					17 19		
Tulse Hill 3	a					16 39					16 54							17 09					17 24		
Streatham 4	a					16 44					16 59							17 14					17 29		
Wimbledon ⊖	a					16 54												17 24							
Sutton 4 179	a					17 14					17 17							17 44					17 47		
Denmark Hill 4 195	a				16 27			16 37								16 57				17 07					
Peckham Rye 4 195	a				16 30			16 40								17 00				17 10					
Catford	a				16 39			16 49								17 09				17 19					
Bromley South	a				16 52			17 02								17 22				17 32					
Orpington	a							17 14												17 45					
St Mary Cray	a				17 01											17 31									
Swanley	a				17 05											17 35									
Sevenoaks	a				17 25											17 55									
Maidstone East	a																								
Greenwich	a	16 27											16 57												17 27
Woolwich Arsenal	a	16 40											17 10												17 40
Abbey Wood	a	16 46											17 16												17 46
Dartford	a	16 57											17 27												17 57
Rainham (Kent)	a	17 42											18 19												18 42
East Croydon	a		16 36				16 44		16 49	16 54		16 59		17 06			17 08		17 14		17 19	17 24		17 29	
Gatwick Airport 10 ✈	a		17 11				17 15		17 04			17 14		17 41					17 45		17 35			17 44	
Horsham	a						17 45												18 12						
Brighton 10	a								17 46			17 51									18 15			18 21	

A To East Grinstead
B To Littlehampton

Table T052-R

Mondays to Fridays

16 December to 15 May

Cambridge and Peterborough (via London), Bedford, Luton - South London & Kent, Gatwick Airport, Brighton

			TL 1	TL	TL	TL 1	TL	TL 1	TL 1 A	TL	TL 1	TL		TL 1	TL	TL 1 B	TL	TL 1	TL	TL 1	TL 1 A	TL	TL 1		TL
Bedford	d		16 02					16 18	16 32					16 35		16 45				16 49					
Luton 10	d		16 27					16 42	16 51			16 46		16 59		17 04				17 13	17 21				17 17
Luton Airport Parkway 7 ✈	d		16 30					16 45	16 54			16 49		17 02		17 07				17 16	17 24				17 20
Harpenden	d		16 35					16 50				16 54		17 08		17 12				17 21					17 25
St Albans City	d		16 41		16 38			16 56	17 03	16 52		17 00		17 13		17 18	17 07			17 27	17 33	17 22			17 30
Elstree & Borehamwood	d				16 47					17 01		17 09					17 16					17 31			17 39
West Hampstead Thameslink ⊖	d		16 54		17 02		17 06			17 17		17 21					17 32		17 36	17 39		17 47			17 51
Kentish Town ⊖	d				17 07		17 11			17 22							17 37		17 41			17 52			
Peterborough	d					15 54												16 24							
Huntingdon	d					16 11												16 41							
Cambridge	d										16 24												16 54		
Royston	d										16 38												17 09		
Letchworth Garden City	d										16 51												17 21		
Hitchin	d					16 41					16 56							17 11					17 26		
Stevenage	d					16 47					17 02							17 17					17 32		
Welwyn Garden City	d																								
Finsbury Park ⊖	d					17 08					17 22							17 38					17 52		
St Pancras International ⊖	d		17 05		17 12	17 15	17 17	17 20	17 25	17 27	17 30	17 32		17 35		17 40	17 42	17 45	17 47	17 50	17 55	17 57	18 00		18 02
Farringdon 3 ⊖	d		17 09		17 17	17 19	17 22	17 24	17 29	17 32	17 34	17 37		17 39		17 44	17 47	17 49	17 52	17 54	17 59	18 02	18 04		18 07
City Thameslink 3	d		17 11		17 19	17 21	17 24	17 26	17 31	17 34	17 36	17 39		17 41		17 46	17 49	17 51	17 54	17 56	18 01	18 04	18 06		18 09
London Blackfriars ⊖	a		17 13		17 21	17 23	17 26	17 28	17 33	17 36	17 38	17 41		17 43		17 48	17 51	17 53	17 56	17 58	18 03	18 06	18 08		18 11
London Blackfriars 3 ⊖	d		17 14	17 16	17 21	17 24	17 26	17 29	17 34	17 36	17 39	17 41		17 44	17 46	17 49	17 51	17 54	17 56	17 59	18 04	18 06	18 09		18 11
London Bridge ⊖	d		17 21			17 30		17 35	17 41		17 45	17 48		17 51		17 55		18 00		18 05	18 11		18 15		18 18
Elephant & Castle ⊖173,179	a			17 19	17 25		17 30			17 40					17 50		17 55		18 00			18 10			
Loughborough Jn. 173,179	a				17 30					17 45							18 00					18 15			
Herne Hill 4 173,179	a				17 34					17 49							18 04					18 19			
Tulse Hill 3	a				17 39					17 54							18 09					18 24			
Streatham 4	a				17 44					17 59							18 14					18 29			
Wimbledon ⊖	a				17 54												18 24								
Sutton 4 179	a				18 14					18 17							18 44					18 47			
Denmark Hill 4 195	a			17 27			17 37								17 57				18 07						
Peckham Rye 4 195	a			17 30			17 40								18 00				18 10						
Catford	a			17 39			17 49								18 09				18 19						
Bromley South	a			17 52			18 02								18 22				18 32						
Orpington	a						18 16												18 48						
St Mary Cray	a			18 01											18 30										
Swanley	a			18 05											18 34										
Sevenoaks	a			18 25											18 55										
Maidstone East	a																								
Greenwich	a											17 57													18 27
Woolwich Arsenal	a											18 10													18 40
Abbey Wood	a											18 16													18 46
Dartford	a											18 29													18 57
Rainham (Kent)	a											19 19													19 44
East Croydon	a		17 36			17 45		17 49	17 54		17 59			18 06		18 08		18 14		18 19	18 24		18 29		
Gatwick Airport 10 ✈	a		18 11			18 15		18 05			18 14			18 41				18 45		18 35			18 44		
Horsham	a					18 42												19 12							
Brighton 10	a							18 46			18 51									19 15			19 21		

A To East Grinstead
B To Littlehampton

Table T052-R

Mondays to Fridays
16 December to 15 May

Cambridge and Peterborough (via London), Bedford, Luton - South London & Kent, Gatwick Airport, Brighton

	TL 1	TL	TL	TL 1	TL	TL 1	TL 1 A	TL	TL 1	TL	TL 1	TL	TL	TL 1	TL	TL 1	TL 1 A	TL	TL 1	TL	TL 1	TL
Bedford d	17 04					17 18	17 28				17 40					17 46	17 56				18 06	
Luton 10 d	17 28				17 32	17 42	17 53			17 46	17 57				18 02	18 12	18 20			18 16	18 27	
Luton Airport Parkway 7 ✈ d	17 31				17 35	17 45				17 49	18 00				18 05	18 15	18 22			18 19	18 30	
Harpenden d	17 36				17 40	17 50				17 54	18 06				18 10	18 20	18 27			18 24	18 36	
St Albans City d	17 42		17 37		17 46	17 56	18 03	17 52		18 00	18 12		18 07		18 16	18 26	18 33	18 22		18 30	18 42	
Elstree & Borehamwood d			17 46		17 54			18 01		18 09			18 16		18 24			18 31		18 39		
West Hampstead Thameslink ⊖ d	17 54		18 01		18 06			18 17		18 21	18 24		18 31		18 36			18 47		18 51	18 54	
Kentish Town ⊖ d			18 06		18 11			18 22					18 36		18 41			18 52				
Peterborough d				16 53										17 24								
Huntingdon d				17 11										17 41								
Cambridge d									17 25										17 54			
Royston d									17 39										18 09			
Letchworth Garden City d									17 52										18 21			
Hitchin d				17 41					17 56					18 11					18 26			
Stevenage d				17 47					18 02					18 17					18 32			
Welwyn Garden City d																						
Finsbury Park ⊖ d				18 08					18 22					18 37					18 52			
St Pancras International ⊖ d	18 05		18 12	18 15	18 17	18 20	18 25	18 27	18 30	18 32	18 35		18 42	18 45	18 47	18 50	18 55	18 57	19 00	19 02	19 05	
Farringdon 3 ⊖ d	18 09		18 17	18 19	18 22	18 24	18 29	18 32	18 34	18 37	18 39		18 47	18 49	18 52	18 54	18 59	19 02	19 04	19 07	19 09	
City Thameslink 3 d	18 11		18 19	18 21	18 24	18 26	18 31	18 34	18 36	18 39	18 41		18 49	18 51	18 54	18 56	19 01	19 04	19 06	19 09	19 11	
London Blackfriars ⊖ a	18 13		18 21	18 23	18 26	18 28	18 33	18 36	18 38	18 41	18 43		18 51	18 53	18 56	18 58	19 03	19 06	19 08	19 11	19 13	
London Blackfriars 3 ⊖ d	18 14	18 16	18 21	18 24	18 26	18 29	18 34	18 36	18 39	18 41	18 44	18 46	18 51	18 54	18 56	18 59	19 04	19 06	19 09	19 11	19 14	19 16
London Bridge ⊖ d	18 21			18 30		18 35	18 41		18 45	18 48	18 51			19 00		19 05	19 11		19 15	19 18	19 21	
Elephant & Castle ⊖173,179 a		18 19	18 25		18 30			18 40				18 49	18 55		19 00			19 10				19 19
Loughborough Jn. 173,179 a			18 30					18 45					19 00					19 15				
Herne Hill 4 173,179 a			18 34					18 49					19 04					19 19				
Tulse Hill 3 a			18 39					18 54					19 09					19 24				
Streatham 4 a			18 44					18 59					19 14					19 29				
Wimbledon ⊖ a			18 54										19 24									
Sutton 4 179 a			19 14					19 17					19 44					19 47				
Denmark Hill 4 195 a		18 27			18 37							18 57			19 07							19 27
Peckham Rye 4 195 a		18 30			18 40							19 00			19 10							19 30
Catford a		18 39			18 49							19 09			19 19							19 39
Bromley South a		18 52			19 02							19 22			19 32							19 52
Orpington a					19 14										19 44							
St Mary Cray a		19 01										19 31										20 01
Swanley a		19 06										19 35										20 05
Sevenoaks a		19 25										19 55										20 25
Maidstone East a																						
Greenwich a										18 57										19 27		
Woolwich Arsenal a										19 10										19 40		
Abbey Wood a										19 16										19 46		
Dartford a										19 27										19 57		
Rainham (Kent) a										20 12										20 41		
East Croydon a	18 36			18 44		18 49	18 54		18 59		19 06			19 14		19 19	19 24		19 29		19 36	
Gatwick Airport 10 ✈ a	19 11			19 15		19 05			19 14		19 41			19 45		19 35			19 44		20 11	
Horsham a				19 42										20 12								
Brighton 10 a						19 46			19 51							20 13			20 19			

A To East Grinstead

NRT DECEMBER 19 EDITION

Table T052-R

Mondays to Fridays
16 December to 15 May

Cambridge and Peterborough (via London), Bedford, Luton - South London & Kent, Gatwick Airport, Brighton

	TL	TL 1	TL	TL 1	TL	TL 1	TL	TL 1	TL	TL	TL 1	TL	TL 1	TL	TL 1	TL	TL 1	TL	TL	TL 1	TL 1	TL
Bedford d				18 16				18 32					18 46				19 02					
Luton 10 d			18 32	18 42			18 46	18 57				19 02	19 12			19 18	19 27					19 32
Luton Airport Parkway 7 ✈ d			18 35	18 45			18 49	19 00				19 05	19 15			19 21	19 30					19 35
Harpenden d			18 40	18 50			18 54	19 06				19 10	19 21			19 26	19 36					19 40
St Albans City d	18 37		18 46	18 56	18 52		19 00	19 11		19 07		19 16	19 27	19 22		19 31	19 42		19 37			19 46
Elstree & Borehamwood d	18 46		18 54		19 01		19 09			19 16		19 24		19 31		19 40			19 46			19 54
West Hampstead Thameslink ⊖ d	19 00		19 07		19 16		19 21			19 31		19 36	19 39	19 46		19 51			20 01			20 06
Kentish Town ⊖ d	19 05		19 11		19 21					19 36		19 41		19 51					20 06			20 11
Peterborough d		17 54									18 24										18 52	
Huntingdon d		18 11									18 41										19 11	
Cambridge d						18 23									18 53							
Royston d						18 38									19 09							
Letchworth Garden City d						18 51									19 21							
Hitchin d		18 41				18 56					19 11				19 26						19 41	
Stevenage d		18 47				19 02					19 17				19 32						19 47	
Welwyn Garden City d																						
Finsbury Park ⊖ d		19 08				19 22					19 38				19 52						20 08	
St Pancras International ⊖ d	19 12	19 15	19 17	19 20	19 27	19 30	19 32	19 35		19 42	19 45	19 47	19 50	19 57	20 00	20 02	20 05		20 12		20 15	20 17
Farringdon 3 ⊖ d	19 17	19 19	19 22	19 24	19 32	19 34	19 37	19 39		19 47	19 49	19 52	19 54	20 02	20 04	20 07	20 09		20 17		20 19	20 22
City Thameslink 3 d	19 19	19 21	19 24	19 26	19 34	19 36	19 39	19 41		19 49	19 51	19 54	19 56	20 04	20 06	20 09	20 11		20 19		20 21	20 24
London Blackfriars ⊖ a	19 21	19 23	19 26	19 28	19 36	19 38	19 41	19 43		19 51	19 53	19 56	19 58	20 06	20 08	20 11	20 13		20 21		20 23	20 26
London Blackfriars 3 ⊖ d	19 21	19 24	19 26	19 29	19 36	19 39	19 41	19 44	19 46	19 51	19 54	19 56	19 59	20 06	20 09	20 11	20 14	20 16	20 21		20 24	20 26
London Bridge ⊖ d		19 30		19 35		19 45	19 48	19 51			20 00		20 05		20 15	20 18	20 21			20 22	20 30	
Elephant & Castle ⊖173,179 a	19 25		19 30		19 40				19 49	19 55		20 00		20 10				20 19	20 25			20 30
Loughborough Jn. 173,179 a	19 30				19 45					20 00				20 15					20 30			
Herne Hill 4 173,179 a	19 34				19 49					20 04				20 19					20 34			
Tulse Hill 3 a	19 39				19 54					20 09				20 24					20 39			
Streatham 4 a	19 44				19 59					20 14				20 30					20 44			
Wimbledon ⊖ a	19 54									20 24									20 54			
Sutton 4 179 a	20 14				20 17					20 44				20 47					21 14			
Denmark Hill 4 195 a			19 37						19 57			20 08						20 27				20 37
Peckham Rye 4 195 a			19 40						20 00			20 11						20 30				20 40
Catford a			19 49						20 09			20 19						20 39				20 49
Bromley South a			20 03						20 22			20 32						20 52				21 02
Orpington a			20 14									20 44										21 14
St Mary Cray a									20 31									21 01				
Swanley a									20 35									21 05				
Sevenoaks a									20 55									21 25				
Maidstone East a																						
Greenwich a							19 57									20 27						
Woolwich Arsenal a							20 10									20 40						
Abbey Wood a							20 16									20 46						
Dartford a							20 27									20 57						
Rainham (Kent) a							21 11									21 41						
East Croydon a		19 44		19 48		19 58		20 06			20 14		20 18		20 28		20 36			20 38	20 44	
Gatwick Airport 10 ✈ a		20 14		20 04		20 14		20 38			20 43		20 34		20 44		21 08			20 53	21 13	
Horsham a		20 39									21 08									21 13	21 38	
Brighton 10 a				20 42		20 49							21 12		21 19							

Table T052-R

Mondays to Fridays
16 December to 15 May

Cambridge and Peterborough (via London), Bedford, Luton - South London & Kent, Gatwick Airport, Brighton

		TL 1	TL	TL	TL 1	TL		TL	TL 1 A	TL 1	TL	TL 1	TL	TL 1	TL	TL 1	TL		TL	TL 1	TL 1	TL	TL 1	TL	TL
Bedford	d	19 16			19 32							19 48				20 04							20 18		
Luton 10	d	19 43		19 48	19 57							20 14			20 18	20 29							20 43		20 48
Luton Airport Parkway 7 ✈	d	19 46		19 51	20 00							20 16			20 21	20 32							20 46		20 51
Harpenden	d	19 52		19 56	20 08							20 22			20 26	20 38							20 52		20 56
St Albans City	d	19 57	19 52	20 01	20 13			20 08				20 27	20 22		20 31	20 43			20 37				20 57	20 52	21 01
Elstree & Borehamwood	d		20 01	20 10				20 17					20 31		20 40				20 46					21 01	21 10
West Hampstead Thameslink ⊖	d	20 09	20 16	20 21				20 31				20 39	20 46		20 51				21 01				21 09	21 16	21 21
Kentish Town ⊖	d		20 21					20 36			20 41		20 51						21 06			21 11		21 21	
Peterborough	d									19 24											19 54				
Huntingdon	d									19 41											20 11				
Cambridge	d													19 54											
Royston	d													20 09											
Letchworth Garden City	d													20 21											
Hitchin	d									20 11				20 26							20 41				
Stevenage	d									20 17				20 32							20 47				
Welwyn Garden City	d																								
Finsbury Park ⊖	d									20 38				20 52							21 08				
St Pancras International ⊖	d	20 20	20 27	20 32	20 35			20 42		20 45	20 47	20 50	20 57	21 00	21 02	21 05			21 12		21 15	21 17	21 20	21 27	21 32
Farringdon 3 ⊖	d	20 24	20 32	20 37	20 39			20 47		20 49	20 52	20 54	21 02	21 04	21 07	21 09			21 17		21 19	21 22	21 24	21 32	21 37
City Thameslink 3	d	20 26	20 34	20 39	20 41			20 49		20 51	20 54	20 56	21 04	21 06	21 09	21 11			21 19		21 21	21 24	21 26	21 34	21 39
London Blackfriars ⊖	a	20 28	20 36	20 41	20 43			20 51		20 53	20 56	20 58	21 06	21 08	21 11	21 13			21 21		21 23	21 26	21 28	21 36	21 41
London Blackfriars 3 ⊖	d	20 29	20 36	20 41	20 44	20 46		20 51		20 54	20 56	20 59	21 06	21 09	21 11	21 14	21 16		21 21		21 24	21 26	21 29	21 36	21 41
London Bridge ⊖	d	20 35		20 48	20 51				20 52	21 00		21 05		21 15	21 18	21 21				21 22	21 30		21 35		21 48
Elephant & Castle ⊖ 173,179	a		20 40			20 49		20 55			21 00		21 10				21 19		21 25			21 30		21 40	
Loughborough Jn. 173,179	a		20 45					21 00					21 15						21 30					21 45	
Herne Hill 4 173,179	a		20 49					21 04					21 19						21 34					21 49	
Tulse Hill 3	a		20 54					21 09					21 24						21 41					21 54	
Streatham 4	a		21 00					21 14					21 29						21 44					21 59	
Wimbledon ⊖	a							21 24											21 54						
Sutton 4 179	a		21 17					21 44					21 47						22 14					22 17	
Denmark Hill 4 195	a					20 57					21 07						21 27					21 37			
Peckham Rye 4 195	a					21 00					21 10						21 30					21 40			
Catford	a					21 09					21 19						21 39					21 49			
Bromley South	a					21 22					21 32						21 52					22 02			
Orpington	a										21 44											22 14			
St Mary Cray	a					21 31											22 01								
Swanley	a					21 35											22 05								
Sevenoaks	a					21 55											22 25								
Maidstone East	a																								
Greenwich	a			20 57											21 27										21 57
Woolwich Arsenal	a			21 10											21 40										22 10
Abbey Wood	a			21 16											21 46										22 16
Dartford	a			21 27											21 57										22 27
Rainham (Kent)	a			22 12											22 41										23 11
East Croydon	a	20 48			21 06				21 08	21 14		21 21		21 28		21 36				21 38	21 44		21 48		
Gatwick Airport 10 ✈	a	21 04			21 38				21 23	21 43		21 36		21 44		22 08				21 53	22 13		22 04		
Horsham	a									22 08											22 38				
Brighton 10	a	21 45										22 13		22 20									22 45		

A To Three Bridges

Table T052-R

Mondays to Fridays
16 December to 15 May

Cambridge and Peterborough (via London), Bedford, Luton - South London & Kent, Gatwick Airport, Brighton

		TL 1	TL	TL		TL 1	TL	TL 1	TL	TL 1	TL	TL 1	TL	TL	TL 1		TL	TL 1	TL	TL A	TL 1 B	TL	TL	TL 1	TL
Bedford	d	20 32						20 49				21 02						21 19			21 35				
Luton 10	d	20 59						21 13			21 18	21 29						21 43		21 48	21 59				
Luton Airport Parkway 7 ✈	d	21 02						21 16			21 21	21 32						21 46		21 51	22 02				
Harpenden	d	21 08						21 22			21 26	21 38						21 52		21 56	22 08				
St Albans City	d	21 13		21 07				21 27	21 22		21 31	21 43		21 37				21 57	21 52	22 01	22 13		22 08		
Elstree & Borehamwood	d			21 16					21 31		21 40			21 46					22 01	22 10			22 17		
West Hampstead Thameslink ⊖	d			21 31				21 39	21 46		21 51			22 01				22 09	22 16	22 21			22 31		
Kentish Town ⊖	d			21 36			21 41		21 51					22 06			22 11		22 21				22 36		22 41
Peterborough	d					20 24									20 54									21 24	
Huntingdon	d					20 41									21 11									21 41	
Cambridge	d									20 54															
Royston	d									21 08															
Letchworth Garden City	d									21 19															
Hitchin	d					21 11				21 24					21 41									22 10	
Stevenage	d					21 17				21 30					21 47									22 16	
Welwyn Garden City	d																								
Finsbury Park ⊖	d					21 37				21 52					22 07									22 37	
St Pancras International ⊖	d	21 35		21 42		21 45	21 47	21 50	21 57	22 00	22 02	22 05		22 12	22 15		22 17	22 20	22 27	22 32	22 35		22 42	22 45	22 47
Farringdon 3 ⊖	d	21 39		21 47		21 49	21 52	21 54	22 02	22 04	22 07	22 09		22 17	22 19		22 22	22 24	22 32	22 37	22 39		22 47	22 49	22 52
City Thameslink 3	d	21 41		21 49		21 51	21 54	21 56	22 04	22 06	22 09	22 11		22 19	22 21		22 24	22 26	22 34	22 39	22 41		22 49	22 51	22 54
London Blackfriars ⊖	a	21 43		21 51		21 53	21 56	21 58	22 06	22 08	22 11	22 13		22 21	22 23		22 26	22 28	22 36	22 41	22 43		22 51	22 53	22 56
London Blackfriars 3 ⊖	d	21 44	21 46	21 51		21 54	21 56	21 59	22 06	22 09	22 11	22 14	22 16	22 21	22 24		22 26	22 29	22 36	22 41	22 44	22 46	22 51	22 54	22 56
London Bridge ⊖	d	21 51				22 00		22 05		22 15	22 18	22 21			22 30			22 35		22 48	22 51			23 00	
Elephant & Castle ⊖ 173,179	a		21 49	21 55			22 00		22 10				22 19	22 25			22 30		22 40			22 49	22 55		23 00
Loughborough Jn. 173,179	a			22 00					22 15					22 30					22 45				23 00		
Herne Hill 4 173,179	a			22 04					22 19					22 34					22 49				23 04		
Tulse Hill 3	a			22 09					22 24					22 39					22 54				23 09		
Streatham 4	a			22 14					22 29					22 44					22 59				23 14		
Wimbledon ⊖	a			22 24										22 54									23 24		
Sutton 4 179	a			22 44					22 47					23 14					23 17				23 44		
Denmark Hill 4 195	a		21 57				22 07						22 27				22 37					22 57			23 07
Peckham Rye 4 195	a		22 00				22 10						22 30				22 40					23 00			23 10
Catford	a		22 09				22 19						22 39				22 49					23 09			23 19
Bromley South	a		22 22				22 32						22 52				23 02					23 22			23 32
Orpington	a						22 44										23 14								23 44
St Mary Cray	a		22 31										23 01									23 31			
Swanley	a		22 35										23 05									23 35			
Sevenoaks	a		22 55										23 25									23 55			
Maidstone East	a																								
Greenwich	a										22 27									22 57					
Woolwich Arsenal	a										22 40									23 10					
Abbey Wood	a										22 46									23 16					
Dartford	a										22 57									23 27					
Rainham (Kent)	a										23 41														
East Croydon	a	22 06				22 14		22 18		22 28		22 36			22 44			22 48			23 06			23 15	
Gatwick Airport 10 ✈	a	22 38				22 43		22 34		22 44		23 08			23 12			23 04			23 37			23 41	
Horsham	a					23 08									23 38									00 06	
Brighton 10	a							23 12		23 19								23 45							

A To Gillingham (Kent)

B To Three Bridges

Table T052-R

Mondays to Fridays

16 December to 15 May

Cambridge and Peterborough (via London), Bedford, Luton - South London & Kent, Gatwick Airport, Brighton

	TL ■		TL	TL ■	TL	TL ■	TL	TL	TL ■	TL ■	TL	TL		TL ■	TL ■	TL ■
					A										B	
Bedford d	21 49					22 05				22 17				22 45	23 05	23 45
Luton ■ d	22 13				22 18	22 28				22 41		22 54		23 10	23 30	00 10
Luton Airport Parkway ■ ✈ d	22 16				22 21	22 31				22 44		22 57		23 13	23 33	00 13
Harpenden d	22 22				22 26	22 36				22 49		23 03		23 18	23 38	00 18
St Albans City d	22 27		22 22		22 31	22 41		22 37		22 55		23 09		23 25	23 45	00 25
Elstree & Borehamwood d			22 31		22 40			22 46				23 18			23 54	
West Hampstead Thameslink ⊖ d	22 39		22 46		22 51			23 01		23 11		23 33		23 41	00 09	00 42
Kentish Town ⊖ d			22 51					23 06				23 38			00 13	
Peterborough d									21 54							
Huntingdon d									22 11							
Cambridge d				21 54												
Royston d				22 09												
Letchworth Garden City d				22 21												
Hitchin d				22 26					22 41							
Stevenage d				22 32					22 47							
Welwyn Garden City d																
Finsbury Park ⊖ d				22 52					23 07							
St Pancras International ⊖ d	22 50		22 57	23 00	23 02	23 05		23 12	23 15	23 22		23 44		23 51	00 21	00 52
Farringdon ■ ⊖ d	22 54		23 02	23 04	23 07	23 10		23 17	23 19	23 27		23 49		23 56	00 26	
City Thameslink ■ d	22 56															
London Blackfriars ⊖ a	22 58		23 06	23 08	23 11	23 13		23 21	23 23	23 30		23 53		23 59	00 30	01 01
London Blackfriars ■ ⊖ d	22 59		23 06	23 09	23 11	23 14	23 16	23 21	23 24	23 31	23 46	23 53		00 02	00 31	01 02
London Bridge ⊖ d	23 05			23 15	23 18	23 21			23 30	23 37						
Elephant & Castle ⊖ 173,179 a			23 10				23 19	23 25			23 49	23 57				
Loughborough Jn. 173,179 a			23 15					23 30				00 02				
Herne Hill ■ 173,179 a			23 19					23 34				00 06				
Tulse Hill ■ a			23 24					23 39				00 10				
Streatham ■ a			23 29					23 44				00 14				
Wimbledon ⊖ a								23 54				00 24				
Sutton ■ 179 a			23 47					00 14				00 44				
Denmark Hill ■ 195 a							23 27				23 57					
Peckham Rye ■ 195 a							23 30				00 01					
Catford a							23 39				00 10					
Bromley South a							23 52				00 23					
Orpington a																
St Mary Cray a							00 01				00 31					
Swanley a							00 06				00 35					
Sevenoaks a							00 25				00 55					
Maidstone East a																
Greenwich a					23 27											
Woolwich Arsenal a					23 40											
Abbey Wood a					23 46											
Dartford a					23 57											
Rainham (Kent) a																
East Croydon 🚋 a	23 18			23 28		23 36			23 44	23 50				00 27	00 57	01 28
Gatwick Airport ■ ✈ a	23 34			23 47		00 01			00 12	00 18				00 47	01 20	01 56
Horsham a									00 36							
Brighton ■ a	00 12			00 23						00 57				01 24		02 28

A To Gillingham (Kent)

B To Three Bridges

NRT DECEMBER 19 EDITION

Table T052-R

Saturdays

21 December to 16 May

Cambridge and Peterborough (via London), Bedford, Luton - South London & Kent, Gatwick Airport, Brighton

	TL ■	TL ■	TL ■	TL ■	TL ■	TL ■	TL ■	TL ■	TL ■	TL ■		TL	TL	TL ■	TL	TL	TL	TL	TL ■	TL ■	TL		TL ■	TL
	A	B	A	C	C	C	C																	
Bedford d				00 15	01 15	01 53	02 15	02 53	03 10	03 45				04 13						04 43				
Luton ■ d			00 10	00 40	01 40	02 18	02 40	03 18	03 35	04 10			04 20	04 38				04 50		05 08				
Luton Airport Parkway ■ ✈ d			00 13	00 43	01 43	02 21	02 43	03 21	03 38	04 13			04 23	04 41				04 53		05 11				
Harpenden d			00 18	00 48	01 48	02 26	02 48	03 26	03 43	04 18			04 28	04 46				04 58		05 16				
St Albans City d			00 25	00 55	01 55	02 33	02 55	03 33	03 50	04 25			04 35	04 53				05 05		05 23				
Elstree & Borehamwood d				01 04	02 04		03 04		03 59				04 44					05 14						
West Hampstead Thameslink ⊖ d		00 09	00 42	01 20	02 20	02 50	03 20	03 50	04 15	04 41			04 59	05 09	05 16	05 22		05 29		05 39	05 46			05 52
Kentish Town ⊖ d		00 13		01 24	02 24		03 24		04 19				05 04		05 21			05 34			05 51			
Peterborough d																			04 18					
Huntingdon d																			04 33					
Cambridge d																							04 54	
Royston d																							05 09	
Letchworth Garden City d																							05 21	
Hitchin d																			05 05				05 26	
Stevenage d																			05 11				05 32	
Welwyn Garden City d																			05 20					
Finsbury Park ⊖ d																			05 35				05 52	
St Pancras International ⊖ d		00 21	00 52	01 32	02 32	03 02	03 32	04 02	04 32	04 51			05 12	05 20	05 27	05 32		05 42	05 45	05 50	05 57		06 00	06 02
Farringdon ■ ⊖ d		00 26								04 56			05 17	05 24	05 32	05 37		05 47	05 49	05 54	06 02		06 04	06 07
City Thameslink ■ d																								
London Blackfriars ⊖ a		00 30	01 01	01 39	02 39	03 09	03 39	04 09	04 39	05 00			05 21	05 28	05 36	05 41		05 51	05 53	05 58	06 06		06 08	06 11
London Blackfriars ■ ⊖ d	00 02	00 31	01 02	01 40	02 40	03 10	03 40	04 10	04 40	05 01		05 16	05 21	05 29	05 36	05 41	05 46	05 51	05 54	05 59	06 06		06 09	06 11
London Bridge ⊖ d														05 35		05 48			06 00	06 05			06 15	06 18
Elephant & Castle ⊖ 173,179 a												05 19	05 25		05 40		05 49	05 55			06 10			
Loughborough Jn. 173,179 a													05 30		05 45			06 00			06 15			
Herne Hill ■ 173,179 a													05 34		05 49			06 04			06 19			
Tulse Hill ■ a													05 39		05 54			06 09			06 24			
Streatham ■ a													05 44		05 59			06 14			06 29			
Wimbledon ⊖ a													05 54					06 24						
Sutton ■ 179 a													06 14		06 17			06 44			06 47			
Denmark Hill ■ 195 a												05 27					05 57							
Peckham Rye ■ 195 a												05 30					06 00							
Catford a												05 39					06 09							
Bromley South a												05 52					06 22							
Orpington a																								
St Mary Cray a												06 01					06 31							
Swanley a												06 05					06 35							
Sevenoaks a												06 25					06 55							
Maidstone East a																								
Greenwich a																05 57								06 27
Woolwich Arsenal a																06 10								06 40
Abbey Wood a																06 16								06 46
Dartford a																06 27								06 57
Rainham (Kent) a																07 11								07 41
East Croydon 🚋 a	00 27	00 57	01 28	02 06	03 06	03 36	04 06	04 36	05 06	05 27				05 48					06 14	06 18			06 28	
Gatwick Airport ■ ✈ a	00 47	01 20	01 56	02 30	03 30	03 58	04 30	05 02	05 31	05 47				06 04					06 50	06 34			06 44	
Horsham a																			07 14					
Brighton ■ a	01 24		02 28					05 38	06 07	06 26				06 46						07 06			07 22	

A From Bedford

B From Bedford to Three Bridges

C To Three Bridges

Table T052-R

Saturdays
21 December to 16 May

Cambridge and Peterborough (via London), Bedford, Luton - South London & Kent, Gatwick Airport, Brighton

Station		TL	TL	TL 1	TL 1	TL	TL	TL	TL		TL 1	TL 1	TL	TL 1	TL	TL 1	TL	TL	TL 1	TL 1		TL	TL	TL 1	TL
Bedford	d				05 15							05 49				06 05		06 02		06 19				06 35	
Luton 10	d		05 20		05 40	05 36						06 13				06 29		06 22		06 43				06 59	
Luton Airport Parkway 7 ✈	d		05 23		05 43	05 39						06 16				06 32		06 25		06 46				07 02	
Harpenden	d		05 28		05 48	05 44						06 22				06 38		06 30		06 52				07 08	
St Albans City	d		05 35		05 55	05 51			06 07			06 27	06 23			06 43		06 37		06 57		06 52		07 13	
Elstree & Borehamwood	d		05 44			06 00			06 16				06 32					06 46				07 01			
West Hampstead Thameslink ⊖	d		05 59		06 09	06 17	06 22		06 31			06 39	06 46					07 01		07 09		07 16			
Kentish Town ⊖	d		06 04			06 21			06 36				06 51		06 56			07 06				07 21	07 26		
Peterborough	d			04 54							05 24								05 54						
Huntingdon	d			05 11							05 41								06 11						
Cambridge	d													05 54											
Royston	d													06 09											
Letchworth Garden City	d													06 21											
Hitchin	d			05 41							06 11			06 26					06 41						
Stevenage	d			05 47							06 17			06 32					06 47						
Welwyn Garden City	d																								
Finsbury Park ⊖	d			06 08							06 38			06 52					07 08						
St Pancras International ⊖	d		06 12	06 15	06 20	06 27	06 32		06 42		06 45	06 50	06 57	07 00	07 02	07 05		07 12	07 15	07 20		07 27	07 32	07 35	
Farringdon 3 ⊖	d		06 17	06 19	06 24	06 32	06 37		06 47		06 49	06 54	07 02	07 04	07 07	07 09		07 17	07 19	07 24		07 32	07 37	07 39	
City Thameslink 3	d																								
London Blackfriars ⊖	a		06 21	06 23	06 28	06 36	06 41		06 51		06 53	06 58	07 06	07 08	07 11	07 13		07 21	07 23	07 28		07 36	07 41	07 43	
London Blackfriars 3 ⊖	d	06 16	06 21	06 24	06 29	06 36	06 41	06 46	06 51		06 54	06 59	07 06	07 09	07 11	07 14	07 16	07 21	07 24	07 29		07 36	07 41	07 44	07 46
London Bridge ⊖	d			06 30	06 35		06 48				07 00	07 05		07 15	07 18	07 21			07 30	07 35			07 48	07 51	
Elephant & Castle ⊖173,179	a	06 19	06 25			06 40		06 49	06 55				07 10				07 19	07 25				07 40			07 49
Loughborough Jn. 173,179	a		06 30			06 45			07 00				07 15					07 30				07 45			
Herne Hill 4 173,179	a		06 34			06 49			07 04				07 19					07 34				07 49			
Tulse Hill 3	a		06 39			06 54			07 09				07 24					07 39				07 54			
Streatham 4	a		06 44			06 59			07 14				07 29					07 44				07 59			
Wimbledon ⊖	a		06 54						07 24									07 54							
Sutton 4 179	a		07 14			07 17			07 44				07 47					08 14				08 17			
Denmark Hill 4 195	a	06 27						06 57									07 27								07 57
Peckham Rye 4 195	a	06 30						07 00									07 30								08 00
Catford	a	06 39						07 09									07 39								08 09
Bromley South	a	06 52						07 22									07 52								08 22
Orpington	a																								
St Mary Cray	a	07 01						07 31									08 01								08 31
Swanley	a	07 05						07 35									08 05								08 35
Sevenoaks	a	07 25						07 55									08 25								08 55
Maidstone East	a																								
Greenwich	a						06 57								07 27								07 57		
Woolwich Arsenal	a						07 10								07 40								08 10		
Abbey Wood	a						07 16								07 46								08 16		
Dartford	a						07 27								07 57								08 27		
Rainham (Kent)	a						08 11								08 41								09 11		
East Croydon 🚌	a			06 44	06 48						07 14	07 18		07 28		07 36			07 44	07 48				08 06	
Gatwick Airport 10 ✈	a			07 12	07 04						07 42	07 34		07 44		08 08			08 12	08 04				08 38	
Horsham	a			07 38							08 08								08 38						
Brighton 10	a				07 44							08 12		08 19						08 46					

Table T052-R

Saturdays
21 December to 16 May

Cambridge and Peterborough (via London), Bedford, Luton - South London & Kent, Gatwick Airport, Brighton

Station		TL	TL 1	TL 1	TL	TL 1	TL		TL 1	TL	TL	TL 1	TL 1	TL	TL	TL 1	TL	TL		TL 1	TL 1	TL	TL 1	TL	TL 1
Bedford	d			06 49					07 05				07 19			07 35					07 49				08 05
Luton 10	d			07 13					07 29				07 43			07 59					08 13				08 29
Luton Airport Parkway 7 ✈	d			07 16					07 32				07 46			08 02					08 16				08 32
Harpenden	d			07 22					07 38				07 52			08 08					08 22				08 38
St Albans City	d	07 07		07 27	07 22				07 43		07 37		07 57	07 52		08 13		08 07			08 27	08 22			08 43
Elstree & Borehamwood	d	07 16			07 31						07 46			08 01				08 16				08 31			
West Hampstead Thameslink ⊖	d	07 31		07 39	07 46						08 01		08 09	08 16				08 31			08 39	08 46			
Kentish Town ⊖	d	07 36			07 51		07 56				08 06			08 21	08 26			08 36				08 51		08 56	
Peterborough	d		06 24									06 54								07 24					
Huntingdon	d		06 41									07 11								07 41					
Cambridge	d					06 54																	07 54		
Royston	d					07 09																	08 09		
Letchworth Garden City	d					07 21																	08 21		
Hitchin	d		07 11			07 26						07 41								08 11			08 26		
Stevenage	d		07 17			07 32						07 47								08 17			08 32		
Welwyn Garden City	d																								
Finsbury Park ⊖	d		07 38			07 52						08 08								08 38			08 52		
St Pancras International ⊖	d	07 42	07 45	07 50	07 57	08 00	08 02		08 05		08 12	08 15	08 20	08 27	08 32	08 35		08 42		08 45	08 50	08 57	09 00	09 02	09 05
Farringdon 3 ⊖	d	07 47	07 49	07 54	08 02	08 04	08 07		08 09		08 17	08 19	08 24	08 32	08 37	08 39		08 47		08 49	08 54	09 02	09 04	09 07	09 09
City Thameslink 3	d																					09 04	09 06	09 09	09 11
London Blackfriars ⊖	a	07 51	07 53	07 58	08 06	08 08	08 11		08 13		08 21	08 23	08 28	08 36	08 41	08 43		08 51		08 53	08 58	09 06	09 08	09 11	09 13
London Blackfriars 3 ⊖	d	07 51	07 54	07 59	08 06	08 09	08 11		08 14	08 16	08 21	08 24	08 29	08 36	08 41	08 44	08 46	08 51		08 54	08 59	09 06	09 09	09 11	09 14
London Bridge ⊖	d		08 00	08 05		08 15	08 18		08 21			08 30	08 35		08 48	08 51				09 00	09 05		09 15	09 18	09 21
Elephant & Castle ⊖173,179	a	07 55			08 10					08 19	08 25			08 40			08 49	08 55				09 10			
Loughborough Jn. 173,179	a	08 00			08 15						08 30			08 45				09 00				09 15			
Herne Hill 4 173,179	a	08 04			08 19						08 34			08 49				09 04				09 19			
Tulse Hill 3	a	08 09			08 24						08 39			08 54				09 09				09 24			
Streatham 4	a	08 14			08 29						08 44			08 59				09 14				09 29			
Wimbledon ⊖	a	08 24									08 54							09 24							
Sutton 4 179	a	08 44			08 47						09 14			09 17				09 44				09 47			
Denmark Hill 4 195	a									08 27							08 57								
Peckham Rye 4 195	a									08 30							09 00								
Catford	a									08 39							09 09								
Bromley South	a									08 52							09 22								
Orpington	a																								
St Mary Cray	a									09 01							09 31								
Swanley	a									09 05							09 35								
Sevenoaks	a									09 25							09 55								
Maidstone East	a																								
Greenwich	a						08 27								08 57									09 27	
Woolwich Arsenal	a						08 40								09 10									09 40	
Abbey Wood	a						08 46								09 16									09 46	
Dartford	a						08 57								09 27									09 57	
Rainham (Kent)	a						09 41								10 11									10 41	
East Croydon 🚌	a		08 14	08 18		08 28			08 36			08 44	08 48			09 06				09 14	09 18		09 28		09 36
Gatwick Airport 10 ✈	a		08 42	08 34		08 44			09 08			09 12	09 04			09 38				09 42	09 34		09 44		10 08
Horsham	a		09 08									09 38								10 08					
Brighton 10	a			09 12		09 19							09 44								10 12		10 19		

Table T052-R

Saturdays

21 December to 16 May

Cambridge and Peterborough (via London), Bedford, Luton - South London & Kent, Gatwick Airport, Brighton

		TL	TL	TL 1	TL 1		TL	TL	TL 1	TL	TL	TL 1	TL 1	TL	TL 1	TL		TL 1	TL	TL	TL 1	TL 1	TL	TL	TL 1
Bedford	d				08 19				08 35				08 49					09 05				09 19			09 35
Luton 10	d				08 43				08 59				09 13					09 29				09 43			09 59
Luton Airport Parkway 7 ✈	d				08 46				09 02				09 16					09 32				09 46			10 02
Harpenden	d				08 52				09 08				09 22					09 38				09 52			10 08
St Albans City	d		08 37		08 57		08 52		09 13		09 07		09 27	09 22				09 43		09 37		09 57	09 52		10 13
Elstree & Borehamwood	d		08 46				09 01				09 16			09 31						09 46			10 01		
West Hampstead Thameslink ⊖	d		09 01		09 09		09 16				09 31		09 39	09 46						10 01		10 09	10 16		
Kentish Town ⊖	d		09 06				09 21	09 26			09 36			09 51		09 56				10 06			10 21	10 26	
Peterborough	d			07 54								08 24									08 54				
Huntingdon	d			08 11								08 41									09 11				
Cambridge	d														08 54										
Royston	d														09 09										
Letchworth Garden City	d														09 21										
Hitchin	d			08 41								09 11			09 26						09 41				
Stevenage	d			08 47								09 17			09 32						09 47				
Welwyn Garden City	d																								
Finsbury Park ⊖	d			09 08								09 38			09 52						10 08				
St Pancras International ⊖	d		09 12	09 15	09 20		09 27	09 32	09 35		09 42	09 45	09 50	09 57	10 00	10 02		10 05		10 12	10 15	10 20	10 27	10 32	10 35
Farringdon 3 ⊖	d		09 17	09 19	09 24		09 32	09 37	09 39		09 47	09 49	09 54	10 02	10 04	10 07		10 09		10 17	10 19	10 24	10 32	10 37	10 39
City Thameslink 3	d		09 19	09 21	09 26		09 34	09 39	09 41		09 49	09 51	09 56	10 04	10 06	10 09		10 11		10 19	10 21	10 26	10 34	10 39	10 41
London Blackfriars ⊖	a		09 21	09 23	09 28		09 36	09 41	09 43		09 51	09 53	09 58	10 06	10 08	10 11		10 13		10 21	10 23	10 28	10 36	10 41	10 43
London Blackfriars 3 ⊖	d	09 16	09 21	09 24	09 29		09 36	09 41	09 44	09 46	09 51	09 54	09 59	10 06	10 09	10 11		10 14	10 16	10 21	10 24	10 29	10 36	10 41	10 44
London Bridge ⊖	d			09 30	09 35			09 48	09 51			10 00	10 05		10 15	10 18		10 21			10 30	10 35		10 48	10 51
Elephant & Castle ⊖173,179	a	09 19	09 25				09 40			09 49	09 55			10 10					10 19	10 25			10 40		
Loughborough Jn. 173,179	a		09 30				09 45				10 00			10 15						10 30			10 45		
Herne Hill 4 173,179	a		09 34				09 49				10 04			10 19						10 34			10 49		
Tulse Hill 3	a		09 39				09 54				10 09			10 24						10 39			10 54		
Streatham 4	a		09 44				09 59				10 14			10 29						10 44			10 59		
Wimbledon ⊖	a		09 54								10 24									10 54					
Sutton 4 179	a		10 14				10 17				10 44			10 47						11 14			11 17		
Denmark Hill 4 195	a	09 27								09 57									10 27						
Peckham Rye 4 195	a	09 30								10 00									10 30						
Catford	a	09 39								10 09									10 39						
Bromley South	a	09 52								10 22									10 52						
Orpington	a																								
St Mary Cray	a	10 01								10 31									11 01						
Swanley	a	10 05								10 35									11 05						
Sevenoaks	a	10 25								10 55									11 25						
Maidstone East	a																								
Greenwich	a							09 57								10 27								10 57	
Woolwich Arsenal	a							10 10								10 40								11 10	
Abbey Wood	a							10 16								10 46								11 16	
Dartford	a							10 27								10 57								11 27	
Rainham (Kent)	a							11 11								11 41								12 11	
East Croydon 🚌	a			09 44	09 48				10 06			10 14	10 18		10 28			10 36			10 44	10 48			11 06
Gatwick Airport 10 ✈	a			10 12	10 04				10 38			10 42	10 34		10 44			11 08			11 12	11 04			11 38
Horsham	a			10 38								11 08									11 38				
Brighton 10	a				10 44								11 12		11 19							11 44			

Table T052-R

Saturdays

21 December to 16 May

Cambridge and Peterborough (via London), Bedford, Luton - South London & Kent, Gatwick Airport, Brighton

		TL	TL		TL 1	TL 1	TL	TL 1	TL	TL 1	TL	TL	TL 1	TL 1		TL	TL	TL 1	TL	TL	TL 1	TL 1	TL	TL 1	TL
Bedford	d					09 49				10 05				10 19				10 35				10 49			
Luton 10	d					10 13				10 29				10 43				10 59				11 13			
Luton Airport Parkway 7 ✈	d					10 16				10 32				10 46				11 02				11 16			
Harpenden	d					10 22				10 38				10 52				11 08				11 22			
St Albans City	d		10 07			10 27	10 22			10 43		10 37		10 57		10 52		11 13		11 07		11 27	11 22		
Elstree & Borehamwood	d		10 16				10 31					10 46				11 01				11 16			11 31		
West Hampstead Thameslink ⊖	d		10 31			10 39	10 46					11 01		11 09		11 16				11 31		11 39	11 46		
Kentish Town ⊖	d		10 36				10 51		10 56			11 06				11 21	11 26			11 36			11 51		11 56
Peterborough	d				09 24								09 54								10 24				
Huntingdon	d				09 41								10 11								10 41				
Cambridge	d							09 54																10 54	
Royston	d							10 09																11 09	
Letchworth Garden City	d							10 21																11 21	
Hitchin	d				10 11			10 26					10 41								11 11			11 25	
Stevenage	d				10 17			10 32					10 47								11 17			11 31	
Welwyn Garden City	d																								
Finsbury Park ⊖	d				10 38			10 52					11 08								11 38			11 52	
St Pancras International ⊖	d		10 42		10 45	10 50	10 57	11 00	11 02	11 05		11 12	11 15	11 20		11 27	11 32	11 35		11 42	11 45	11 50	11 57	12 00	12 02
Farringdon 3 ⊖	d		10 47		10 49	10 54	11 02	11 04	11 07	11 09		11 17	11 19	11 24		11 32	11 37	11 39		11 47	11 49	11 54	12 02	12 04	12 07
City Thameslink 3	d		10 49		10 51	10 56	11 04	11 06	11 09	11 11		11 19	11 21	11 26		11 34	11 39	11 41		11 49	11 51	11 56	12 04	12 06	12 09
London Blackfriars ⊖	a		10 51		10 53	10 58	11 06	11 08	11 11	11 13		11 21	11 23	11 28		11 36	11 41	11 43		11 51	11 53	11 58	12 06	12 08	12 11
London Blackfriars 3 ⊖	d	10 46	10 51		10 54	10 59	11 06	11 09	11 11	11 14	11 16	11 21	11 24	11 29		11 36	11 41	11 44	11 46	11 51	11 54	11 59	12 06	12 09	12 11
London Bridge ⊖	d				11 00	11 05		11 15	11 18	11 21			11 30	11 35			11 48	11 51			12 00	12 05		12 15	12 18
Elephant & Castle ⊖173,179	a	10 49	10 55				11 10				11 19	11 25				11 40			11 49	11 55			12 10		
Loughborough Jn. 173,179	a		11 00				11 15					11 30				11 45				12 00			12 15		
Herne Hill 4 173,179	a		11 04				11 19					11 34				11 49				12 04			12 19		
Tulse Hill 3	a		11 09				11 24					11 39				11 54				12 09			12 24		
Streatham 4	a		11 14				11 29					11 44				11 59				12 14			12 29		
Wimbledon ⊖	a		11 24									11 54								12 24					
Sutton 4 179	a		11 44				11 47					12 14				12 17				12 44			12 47		
Denmark Hill 4 195	a	10 57									11 27								11 57						
Peckham Rye 4 195	a	11 00									11 30								12 00						
Catford	a	11 09									11 39								12 09						
Bromley South	a	11 22									11 52								12 22						
Orpington	a																								
St Mary Cray	a	11 31									12 01								12 31						
Swanley	a	11 35									12 05								12 35						
Sevenoaks	a	11 55									12 25								12 55						
Maidstone East	a																								
Greenwich	a								11 27								11 57								12 27
Woolwich Arsenal	a								11 40								12 10								12 40
Abbey Wood	a								11 46								12 16								12 46
Dartford	a								11 57								12 27								12 57
Rainham (Kent)	a								12 41								13 11								13 41
East Croydon 🚌	a				11 14	11 18		11 28		11 36			11 44	11 48				12 06			12 14	12 18		12 28	
Gatwick Airport 10 ✈	a				11 42	11 34		11 44		12 08			12 12	12 04				12 38			12 42	12 34		12 44	
Horsham	a				12 08								12 38								13 08				
Brighton 10	a					12 12		12 19						12 44								13 12		13 19	

Table T052-R

Saturdays

21 December to 16 May

Cambridge and Peterborough (via London), Bedford, Luton - South London & Kent, Gatwick Airport, Brighton

		TL ■	TL	TL	TL ■	TL ■	TL	TL	TL ■	TL	TL	TL ■	TL ■	TL	TL ■	TL	TL ■	TL	TL	TL ■	TL ■	TL
Bedford	d	11 05				11 19			11 35				11 49				12 05				12 19	
Luton ■	d	11 29				11 43			11 59				12 13				12 29				12 43	
Luton Airport Parkway ■ ✈	d	11 32				11 46			12 02				12 16				12 32				12 46	
Harpenden	d	11 38				11 52			12 08				12 22				12 38				12 52	
St Albans City	d	11 43		11 37		11 57	11 52		12 13		12 07		12 27	12 22			12 43		12 37		12 57	12 52
Elstree & Borehamwood	d			11 46			12 01				12 16			12 31					12 46			13 01
West Hampstead Thameslink ⊖	d			12 01		12 09	12 16				12 31		12 39	12 46					13 01		13 09	13 16
Kentish Town ⊖	d			12 06			12 21	12 26			12 36			12 51		12 56			13 06			13 21
Peterborough	d				10 53							11 24								11 54		
Huntingdon	d				11 11							11 41								12 11		
Cambridge	d														11 54							
Royston	d														12 09							
Letchworth Garden City	d														12 21							
Hitchin	d				11 41							12 11			12 26					12 41		
Stevenage	d				11 47							12 17			12 32					12 47		
Welwyn Garden City	d																					
Finsbury Park ⊖	d				12 08							12 38			12 52					13 08		
St Pancras International ⊖	d	12 05		12 12	12 15	12 20	12 27	12 32	12 35		12 42	12 45	12 50	12 57	13 00	13 02	13 05		13 12	13 15	13 20	13 27
Farringdon ■ ⊖	d	12 09		12 17	12 19	12 24	12 32	12 37	12 39		12 47	12 49	12 54	13 02	13 04	13 07	13 09		13 17	13 19	13 24	13 32
City Thameslink ■	d	12 11		12 19	12 21	12 26	12 34	12 39	12 41		12 49	12 51	12 56	13 04	13 06	13 09	13 11		13 19	13 21	13 26	13 34
London Blackfriars ⊖	a	12 13		12 21	12 23	12 28	12 36	12 41	12 43		12 51	12 53	12 58	13 06	13 08	13 11	13 13		13 21	13 23	13 28	13 36
London Blackfriars ■ ⊖	d	12 14	12 16	12 21	12 24	12 29	12 36	12 41	12 44	12 46	12 51	12 54	12 59	13 06	13 09	13 11	13 14	13 16	13 21	13 24	13 29	13 36
London Bridge ⊖	d	12 21			12 30	12 35		12 48	12 51			13 00	13 05		13 15	13 18	13 21			13 30	13 35	
Elephant & Castle ⊖173,179	a		12 19	12 25			12 40			12 49	12 55			13 10				13 19	13 25			13 40
Loughborough Jn. 173,179	a			12 30			12 45				13 00			13 15					13 30			13 45
Herne Hill ■ 173,179	a			12 34			12 49				13 04			13 19					13 34			13 49
Tulse Hill ■	a			12 39			12 54				13 09			13 24					13 39			13 54
Streatham ■	a			12 44			12 59				13 14			13 29					13 44			13 59
Wimbledon ⊖	a			12 54							13 24								13 54			
Sutton ■ 179	a			13 14			13 17				13 44			13 47					14 14			14 17
Denmark Hill ■ 195	a		12 27							12 57								13 27				
Peckham Rye ■ 195	a		12 30							13 00								13 30				
Catford	a		12 39							13 09								13 39				
Bromley South	a		12 52							13 22								13 52				
Orpington	a																					
St Mary Cray	a		13 01							13 31								14 01				
Swanley	a		13 05							13 35								14 05				
Sevenoaks	a		13 25							13 55								14 25				
Maidstone East	a																					
Greenwich	a							12 57								13 27						
Woolwich Arsenal	a							13 10								13 40						
Abbey Wood	a							13 16								13 46						
Dartford	a							13 27								13 57						
Rainham (Kent)	a							14 11								14 41						
East Croydon	a	12 36			12 44	12 48			13 06			13 14	13 18		13 28		13 36			13 44	13 48	
Gatwick Airport ■ ✈	a	13 08			13 12	13 04			13 38			13 42	13 34		13 44		14 08			14 12	14 04	
Horsham	a				13 38							14 08								14 38		
Brighton ■	a					13 44							14 12		14 19						14 44	

Table T052-R

Saturdays

21 December to 16 May

Cambridge and Peterborough (via London), Bedford, Luton - South London & Kent, Gatwick Airport, Brighton

		TL	TL ■	TL	TL	TL ■	TL ■	TL	TL ■	TL	TL ■	TL	TL	TL ■	TL ■	TL	TL	TL ■	TL	TL	TL ■	TL ■	TL
Bedford	d		12 35				12 49				13 05				13 19			13 35				13 49	
Luton ■	d		12 59				13 13				13 29				13 43			13 59				14 13	
Luton Airport Parkway ■ ✈	d		13 02				13 16				13 32				13 46			14 02				14 16	
Harpenden	d		13 08				13 22				13 38				13 52			14 08				14 22	
St Albans City	d		13 13		13 07		13 27	13 22			13 43		13 37		13 57	13 52		14 13		14 07		14 27	14 22
Elstree & Borehamwood	d				13 16			13 31					13 46			14 01				14 16			14 31
West Hampstead Thameslink ⊖	d				13 31		13 39	13 46					14 01		14 09	14 16				14 31		14 39	14 46
Kentish Town ⊖	d	13 26			13 36			13 51		13 56			14 06			14 21	14 26			14 36			14 51
Peterborough	d					12 24								12 54							13 24		
Huntingdon	d					12 41								13 11							13 41		
Cambridge	d								12 54														
Royston	d								13 09														
Letchworth Garden City	d								13 21														
Hitchin	d					13 11			13 26					13 41							14 11		
Stevenage	d					13 17			13 32					13 47							14 17		
Welwyn Garden City	d																						
Finsbury Park ⊖	d					13 38			13 52					14 08							14 38		
St Pancras International ⊖	d	13 32	13 35		13 42	13 45	13 50	13 57	14 00	14 02	14 05		14 12	14 15	14 20	14 27	14 32	14 35		14 42	14 45	14 50	14 57
Farringdon ■ ⊖	d	13 37	13 39		13 47	13 49	13 54	14 02	14 04	14 07	14 09		14 17	14 19	14 24	14 32	14 37	14 39		14 47	14 49	14 54	15 02
City Thameslink ■	d	13 39	13 41		13 49	13 51	13 56	14 04	14 06	14 09	14 11		14 19	14 21	14 26	14 34	14 39	14 41		14 49	14 51	14 56	15 04
London Blackfriars ⊖	a	13 41	13 43		13 51	13 53	13 58	14 06	14 08	14 11	14 13		14 21	14 23	14 28	14 36	14 41	14 43		14 51	14 53	14 58	15 06
London Blackfriars ■ ⊖	d	13 41	13 44	13 46	13 51	13 54	13 59	14 06	14 09	14 11	14 14	14 16	14 21	14 24	14 29	14 36	14 41	14 44	14 46	14 51	14 54	14 59	15 06
London Bridge ⊖	d	13 48	13 51			14 00	14 05		14 15	14 18	14 21			14 30	14 35		14 48	14 51			15 00	15 05	
Elephant & Castle ⊖173,179	a			13 49	13 55			14 10				14 19	14 25			14 40			14 49	14 55			15 10
Loughborough Jn. 173,179	a				14 00			14 15					14 30			14 45				15 00			15 15
Herne Hill ■ 173,179	a				14 04			14 19					14 34			14 49				15 04			15 19
Tulse Hill ■	a				14 09			14 24					14 39			14 54				15 09			15 24
Streatham ■	a				14 14			14 29					14 44			14 59				15 14			15 29
Wimbledon ⊖	a				14 24								14 54							15 24			
Sutton ■ 179	a				14 44			14 47					15 14			15 17				15 44			15 47
Denmark Hill ■ 195	a			13 57								14 27							14 57				
Peckham Rye ■ 195	a			14 00								14 30							15 00				
Catford	a			14 09								14 39							15 09				
Bromley South	a			14 22								14 52							15 22				
Orpington	a																						
St Mary Cray	a			14 31								15 01							15 31				
Swanley	a			14 35								15 05							15 35				
Sevenoaks	a			14 55								15 25							15 55				
Maidstone East	a																						
Greenwich	a	13 57								14 27							14 57						
Woolwich Arsenal	a	14 10								14 40							15 10						
Abbey Wood	a	14 16								14 46							15 16						
Dartford	a	14 27								14 57							15 27						
Rainham (Kent)	a	15 11								15 41							16 11						
East Croydon	a		14 06			14 14	14 18		14 28		14 36			14 44	14 48			15 06			15 14	15 18	
Gatwick Airport ■ ✈	a		14 38			14 42	14 34		14 44		15 08			15 12	15 04			15 38			15 42	15 34	
Horsham	a					15 08								15 38							16 08		
Brighton ■	a						15 12		15 19						15 44							16 12	

Table T052-R

Saturdays

21 December to 16 May

Cambridge and Peterborough (via London), Bedford, Luton - South London & Kent, Gatwick Airport, Brighton

Station		TL 1	TL	TL 1	TL	TL	TL 1	TL 1	TL	TL	TL 1	TL	TL	TL 1	TL 1	TL	TL 1	TL	TL 1	TL	TL	TL 1	TL 1
Bedford	d			14 05				14 19			14 35				14 49				15 05				15 19
Luton 10	d			14 29				14 43			14 59				15 13				15 29				15 43
Luton Airport Parkway 7 ✈	d			14 32				14 46			15 02				15 16				15 32				15 46
Harpenden	d			14 38				14 52			15 08				15 22				15 38				15 52
St Albans City	d			14 43		14 37		14 57	14 52		15 13		15 07		15 27	15 22			15 43		15 37		15 57
Elstree & Borehamwood	d					14 46			15 01				15 16			15 31					15 46		
West Hampstead Thameslink ⊖	d					15 01		15 09	15 16				15 31		15 39	15 46					16 01		16 09
Kentish Town ⊖	d		14 56			15 06			15 21	15 26			15 36			15 51		15 56			16 06		
Peterborough	d						13 54							14 24								14 54	
Huntingdon	d						14 11							14 41								15 11	
Cambridge	d	13 54															14 54						
Royston	d	14 09															15 09						
Letchworth Garden City	d	14 21															15 21						
Hitchin	d	14 26					14 41							15 11			15 26					15 41	
Stevenage	d	14 32					14 47							15 17			15 31					15 47	
Welwyn Garden City	d																						
Finsbury Park ⊖	d	14 52					15 08							15 38			15 52					16 08	
St Pancras International ⊖	d	15 00	15 02	15 05		15 12	15 15	15 20	15 27	15 32	15 35		15 42	15 45	15 50	15 57	16 00	16 02	16 05		16 12	16 15	16 20
Farringdon 3 ⊖	d	15 04	15 07	15 09		15 17	15 19	15 24	15 32	15 37	15 39		15 47	15 49	15 54	16 02	16 04	16 07	16 09		16 17	16 19	16 24
City Thameslink 3	d	15 06	15 09	15 11		15 19	15 21	15 26	15 34	15 39	15 41		15 49	15 51	15 56	16 04	16 06	16 09	16 11		16 19	16 21	16 26
London Blackfriars ⊖	a	15 08	15 11	15 13		15 21	15 23	15 28	15 36	15 41	15 43		15 51	15 53	15 58	16 06	16 08	16 11	16 13		16 21	16 23	16 28
London Blackfriars 3 ⊖	d	15 09	15 11	15 14	15 16	15 21	15 24	15 29	15 36	15 41	15 44	15 46	15 51	15 54	15 59	16 06	16 09	16 11	16 14	16 16	16 21	16 24	16 29
London Bridge ⊖	d	15 15	15 18	15 21			15 30	15 35		15 48	15 51			16 00	16 05		16 15	16 18	16 21			16 30	16 35
Elephant & Castle ⊖173,179	a				15 19	15 25			15 40			15 49	15 55			16 10				16 19	16 25		
Loughborough Jn. 173,179	a					15 30			15 45				16 00			16 15					16 30		
Herne Hill 4 173,179	a					15 34			15 49				16 04			16 19					16 34		
Tulse Hill 3	a					15 39			15 54				16 09			16 24					16 39		
Streatham 4	a					15 44			15 59				16 14			16 29					16 44		
Wimbledon ⊖	a					15 54							16 24								16 54		
Sutton 4 179	a					16 14			16 17				16 44			16 47					17 14		
Denmark Hill 4 195	a				15 27							15 57								16 27			
Peckham Rye 4 195	a				15 30							16 00								16 30			
Catford	a				15 39							16 09								16 39			
Bromley South	a				15 52							16 22								16 52			
Orpington	a																						
St Mary Cray	a				16 01							16 31								17 01			
Swanley	a				16 05							16 35								17 05			
Sevenoaks	a				16 25							16 55								17 25			
Maidstone East	a																						
Greenwich	a		15 27							15 57								16 27					
Woolwich Arsenal	a		15 40							16 10								16 40					
Abbey Wood	a		15 46							16 16								16 46					
Dartford	a		15 57							16 27								16 57					
Rainham (Kent)	a		16 41							17 11								17 41					
East Croydon 🚌	a	15 28		15 36			15 44	15 48			16 06			16 14	16 18		16 28		16 36			16 44	16 48
Gatwick Airport 10 ✈	a	15 44		16 08			16 12	16 04			16 38			16 42	16 34		16 44		17 08			17 12	17 04
Horsham	a						16 38							17 08								17 38	
Brighton 10	a	16 19						16 44							17 12		17 19						17 44

Table T052-R

Saturdays

21 December to 16 May

Cambridge and Peterborough (via London), Bedford, Luton - South London & Kent, Gatwick Airport, Brighton

Station		TL	TL	TL 1	TL	TL	TL 1	TL 1	TL	TL 1	TL	TL 1	TL	TL	TL 1	TL 1	TL	TL	TL 1	TL	TL	TL 1	TL 1
Bedford	d			15 35				15 49				16 05				16 19			16 35				16 49
Luton 10	d			15 59				16 13				16 29				16 43			16 59				17 13
Luton Airport Parkway 7 ✈	d			16 02				16 16				16 32				16 46			17 02				17 16
Harpenden	d			16 08				16 22				16 38				16 52			17 08				17 22
St Albans City	d	15 52		16 13		16 07		16 27	16 22			16 43		16 37		16 57	16 52		17 13		17 07		17 27
Elstree & Borehamwood	d	16 01				16 16			16 31					16 46			17 01				17 16		
West Hampstead Thameslink ⊖	d	16 16				16 31		16 39	16 46					17 01		17 09	17 16				17 31		17 39
Kentish Town ⊖	d	16 21	16 26			16 36			16 51		16 56			17 06			17 21	17 26			17 36		
Peterborough	d						15 24								15 54							16 24	
Huntingdon	d						15 41								16 11							16 41	
Cambridge	d									15 54													
Royston	d									16 09													
Letchworth Garden City	d									16 21													
Hitchin	d						16 11			16 26					16 41							17 11	
Stevenage	d						16 17			16 32					16 47							17 17	
Welwyn Garden City	d																						
Finsbury Park ⊖	d						16 38			16 52					17 08							17 38	
St Pancras International ⊖	d	16 27	16 32	16 35		16 42	16 45	16 50	16 57	17 00	17 02	17 05		17 12	17 15	17 20	17 27	17 32	17 35		17 42	17 45	17 50
Farringdon 3 ⊖	d	16 32	16 37	16 39		16 47	16 49	16 54	17 02	17 04	17 07	17 09		17 17	17 19	17 24	17 32	17 37	17 39		17 47	17 49	17 54
City Thameslink 3	d	16 34	16 39	16 41		16 49	16 51	16 56	17 04	17 06	17 09	17 11		17 19	17 21	17 26	17 34	17 39	17 41		17 49	17 51	17 56
London Blackfriars ⊖	a	16 36	16 41	16 43		16 51	16 53	16 58	17 06	17 08	17 11	17 13		17 21	17 23	17 28	17 36	17 41	17 43		17 51	17 53	17 58
London Blackfriars 3 ⊖	d	16 36	16 41	16 44	16 46	16 51	16 54	16 59	17 06	17 09	17 11	17 14	17 16	17 21	17 24	17 29	17 36	17 41	17 44	17 46	17 51	17 54	17 59
London Bridge ⊖	d		16 48	16 51			17 00	17 05		17 15	17 18	17 21			17 30	17 35		17 48	17 51			18 00	18 05
Elephant & Castle ⊖173,179	a	16 40			16 49	16 55			17 10				17 19	17 25			17 40			17 49	17 55		
Loughborough Jn. 173,179	a	16 45				17 00			17 15					17 30			17 45				18 00		
Herne Hill 4 173,179	a	16 49				17 04			17 19					17 34			17 49				18 04		
Tulse Hill 3	a	16 54				17 09			17 24					17 39			17 54				18 09		
Streatham 4	a	16 59				17 14			17 29					17 44			17 59				18 14		
Wimbledon ⊖	a					17 24								17 54							18 24		
Sutton 4 179	a	17 17				17 44			17 47					18 14			18 17				18 44		
Denmark Hill 4 195	a				16 57								17 27							17 57			
Peckham Rye 4 195	a				17 00								17 30							18 00			
Catford	a				17 09								17 39							18 09			
Bromley South	a				17 22								17 52							18 22			
Orpington	a																						
St Mary Cray	a				17 31								18 01							18 31			
Swanley	a				17 35								18 05							18 35			
Sevenoaks	a				17 55								18 25							18 55			
Maidstone East	a																						
Greenwich	a		16 57								17 27							17 57					
Woolwich Arsenal	a		17 10								17 40							18 10					
Abbey Wood	a		17 16								17 46							18 16					
Dartford	a		17 27								17 57							18 27					
Rainham (Kent)	a		18 11								18 41							19 11					
East Croydon 🚌	a			17 06			17 14	17 18		17 28		17 36			17 44	17 48			18 06			18 14	18 18
Gatwick Airport 10 ✈	a			17 38			17 42	17 34		17 44		18 08			18 12	18 04			18 38			18 42	18 34
Horsham	a						18 08								18 38							19 08	
Brighton 10	a							18 12		18 19						18 44							19 12

Table T052-R

Saturdays

21 December to 16 May

Cambridge and Peterborough (via London), Bedford, Luton - South London & Kent, Gatwick Airport, Brighton

	TL	TL 1	TL		TL 1	TL	TL	TL 1	TL 1	TL	TL	TL 1	TL	TL		TL 1	TL 1	TL	TL 1	TL	TL 1	TL	TL	TL 1
Bedford d					17 05				17 19			17 35					17 49				18 05			
Luton 10 d					17 29				17 43			17 59					18 13				18 29			
Luton Airport Parkway 7 ✈ d					17 32				17 46			18 02					18 16				18 32			
Harpenden d					17 38				17 52			18 08					18 22				18 38			
St Albans City d	17 22				17 43		17 37		17 57	17 52		18 13		18 07			18 27	18 22			18 43		18 37	
Elstree & Borehamwood d	17 31						17 46			18 01				18 16				18 31					18 46	
West Hampstead Thameslink ⊖ d	17 46						18 01		18 09	18 16				18 31			18 39	18 46					19 01	
Kentish Town ⊖ d	17 51		17 56				18 06			18 21	18 26			18 36				18 51		18 56			19 06	
Peterborough d								16 54								17 24								17 56
Huntingdon d								17 11								17 41								18 12
Cambridge d		16 54																	17 54					
Royston d		17 09																	18 09					
Letchworth Garden City d		17 21																	18 21					
Hitchin d		17 26						17 41								18 11			18 26					18 41
Stevenage d		17 32						17 47								18 17			18 32					18 47
Welwyn Garden City d																								
Finsbury Park ⊖ d		17 52						18 08								18 38			18 52					19 08
St Pancras International ⊖ d	17 57	18 00	18 02		18 05		18 12	18 15	18 20	18 27	18 32	18 35		18 42		18 45	18 50	18 57	19 00	19 02	19 05		19 12	19 15
Farringdon 3 ⊖ d	18 02	18 04	18 07		18 09		18 17	18 19	18 24	18 32	18 37	18 39		18 47		18 49	18 54	19 02	19 04	19 07	19 09		19 17	19 19
City Thameslink 3 d	18 04	18 06	18 09		18 11		18 19	18 21	18 26	18 34	18 39	18 41		18 49		18 51	18 56	19 04	19 06	19 09	19 11		19 19	19 21
London Blackfriars ⊖ a	18 06	18 08	18 11		18 13		18 21	18 23	18 28	18 36	18 41	18 43		18 51		18 53	18 58	19 06	19 08	19 11	19 13		19 21	19 23
London Blackfriars 3 ⊖ d	18 06	18 09	18 11		18 14	18 16	18 21	18 24	18 29	18 36	18 41	18 44	18 46	18 51		18 54	18 59	19 06	19 09	19 11	19 14	19 16	19 21	19 24
London Bridge ⊖ d		18 15	18 18		18 21			18 30	18 35		18 48	18 51				19 00	19 05		19 15	19 18	19 21			19 30
Elephant & Castle ⊖173,179 a	18 10					18 19	18 25			18 40			18 49	18 55				19 10				19 19	19 25	
Loughborough Jn. 173,179 a	18 15						18 30			18 45				19 00				19 15					19 30	
Herne Hill 4 173,179 a	18 19						18 34			18 49				19 04				19 19					19 34	
Tulse Hill 3 a	18 24						18 39			18 54				19 09				19 24					19 39	
Streatham 4 a	18 29						18 44			18 59				19 14				19 29					19 44	
Wimbledon ⊖ a							18 54							19 24									19 54	
Sutton 4 179 a	18 47						19 14			19 17				19 44				19 47					20 14	
Denmark Hill 4 195 a						18 27							18 57									19 27		
Peckham Rye 4 195 a						18 30							19 00									19 30		
Catford a						18 39							19 09									19 39		
Bromley South a						18 52							19 22									19 52		
Orpington a																								
St Mary Cray a						19 01							19 31									20 01		
Swanley a						19 05							19 35									20 05		
Sevenoaks a						19 25							19 55									20 25		
Maidstone East a																								
Greenwich a			18 27								18 57									19 27				
Woolwich Arsenal a			18 40								19 10									19 40				
Abbey Wood a			18 46								19 16									19 46				
Dartford a			18 57								19 27									19 57				
Rainham (Kent) a			19 41								20 11									20 41				
East Croydon 🚌 a		18 28			18 36			18 44	18 48			19 06				19 14	19 18		19 28		19 36			19 44
Gatwick Airport 10 ✈ a		18 44			19 08			19 12	19 04			19 38				19 42	19 34		19 44		20 08			20 12
Horsham a								19 38								20 08								20 38
Brighton 10 a		19 19							19 44								20 12		20 19					

Table T052-R

Saturdays

21 December to 16 May

Cambridge and Peterborough (via London), Bedford, Luton - South London & Kent, Gatwick Airport, Brighton

	TL 1		TL	TL	TL 1	TL	TL	TL 1	TL 1	TL	TL 1	TL		TL 1	TL	TL	TL 1	TL 1	TL	TL	TL 1	TL	TL	
Bedford d	18 19				18 35				18 49					19 05				19 19			19 35			
Luton 10 d	18 43				18 59				19 13					19 29				19 43			19 59			
Luton Airport Parkway 7 ✈ d	18 46				19 02				19 16					19 32				19 46			20 02			
Harpenden d	18 52				19 08				19 22					19 38				19 52			20 08			
St Albans City d	18 57		18 52		19 13		19 07		19 27	19 22				19 43		19 37		19 57	19 52		20 13		20 07	
Elstree & Borehamwood d			19 01				19 16			19 31						19 46			20 01				20 16	
West Hampstead Thameslink ⊖ d	19 09		19 16				19 31		19 39	19 46						20 01		20 09	20 16				20 31	
Kentish Town ⊖ d			19 21	19 26			19 36			19 51		19 56				20 06			20 21	20 26			20 36	
Peterborough d								18 24									18 54							
Huntingdon d								18 41									19 11							
Cambridge d											18 54													
Royston d											19 09													
Letchworth Garden City d											19 21													
Hitchin d								19 11			19 26						19 41							
Stevenage d								19 17			19 32						19 47							
Welwyn Garden City d																								
Finsbury Park ⊖ d								19 38			19 52						20 08							
St Pancras International ⊖ d	19 20		19 27	19 32	19 35		19 42	19 45	19 50	19 57	20 00	20 02		20 05		20 12	20 15	20 20	20 27	20 32	20 35		20 42	
Farringdon 3 ⊖ d	19 24		19 32	19 37	19 39		19 47	19 49	19 54	20 02	20 04	20 07		20 09		20 17	20 19	20 24	20 32	20 37	20 39		20 47	
City Thameslink 3 d	19 26		19 34	19 39	19 41		19 49	19 51	19 56	20 04	20 06	20 09		20 11		20 19	20 21	20 26	20 34	20 39	20 41		20 49	
London Blackfriars ⊖ a	19 28		19 36	19 41	19 43		19 51	19 53	19 58	20 06	20 08	20 11		20 13		20 21	20 23	20 28	20 36	20 41	20 43		20 51	
London Blackfriars 3 ⊖ d	19 29		19 36	19 41	19 44	19 46	19 51	19 54	19 59	20 06	20 09	20 11		20 14	20 16	20 21	20 24	20 29	20 36	20 41	20 44	20 46	20 51	
London Bridge ⊖ d	19 35			19 48	19 51			20 00	20 05		20 15	20 18		20 21			20 30	20 35		20 48	20 51			
Elephant & Castle ⊖173,179 a			19 40			19 49	19 55			20 10					20 19	20 25			20 40			20 49	20 55	
Loughborough Jn. 173,179 a			19 45				20 00			20 15						20 30			20 45				21 00	
Herne Hill 4 173,179 a			19 49				20 04			20 19						20 34			20 49				21 04	
Tulse Hill 3 a			19 54				20 09			20 24						20 39			20 54				21 09	
Streatham 4 a			19 59				20 14			20 29						20 44			20 59				21 14	
Wimbledon ⊖ a							20 24									20 54							21 24	
Sutton 4 179 a			20 17				20 44			20 47						21 14			21 17				21 44	
Denmark Hill 4 195 a						19 57									20 27							20 57		
Peckham Rye 4 195 a						20 00									20 30							21 00		
Catford a						20 09									20 39							21 09		
Bromley South a						20 22									20 52							21 22		
Orpington a																								
St Mary Cray a						20 31									21 01							21 31		
Swanley a						20 35									21 05							21 35		
Sevenoaks a						20 55									21 25							21 55		
Maidstone East a																								
Greenwich a				19 57								20 27								20 57				
Woolwich Arsenal a				20 10								20 40								21 10				
Abbey Wood a				20 16								20 46								21 16				
Dartford a				20 27								20 57								21 27				
Rainham (Kent) a				21 11								21 41								22 11				
East Croydon 🚌 a	19 48				20 06			20 14	20 18		20 28			20 36			20 44	20 48			21 06			
Gatwick Airport 10 ✈ a	20 04				20 38			20 42	20 34		20 44			21 08			21 12	21 04			21 38			
Horsham a								21 08									21 38							
Brighton 10 a	20 44								21 12		21 19							21 44						

Table T052-R

Saturdays

21 December to 16 May

Cambridge and Peterborough (via London), Bedford, Luton - South London & Kent, Gatwick Airport, Brighton

		TL 1	TL 1	TL	TL 1	TL	TL 1	TL	TL	TL 1	TL 1	TL	TL	TL 1	TL	TL	TL 1	TL 1	TL	TL 1	TL	TL 1	TL
Bedford	d		19 49				20 05				20 19			20 34				20 49				21 05	
Luton 10	d		20 13				20 29				20 43			20 59				21 13				21 29	
Luton Airport Parkway 7 ✈	d		20 16				20 32				20 46			21 02				21 16				21 32	
Harpenden	d		20 22				20 38				20 52			21 08				21 22				21 38	
St Albans City	d		20 27	20 22			20 43		20 37		20 57	20 52		21 13		21 07		21 27	21 22			21 43	
Elstree & Borehamwood	d			20 31					20 46			21 01				21 16			21 31				
West Hampstead Thameslink ⊖	d		20 39	20 46					21 01		21 09	21 16				21 31		21 39	21 46				
Kentish Town ⊖	d			20 51		20 56			21 06			21 21	21 26			21 36			21 51		21 56		
Peterborough	d	19 24								19 54							20 24						
Huntingdon	d	19 41								20 11							20 41						
Cambridge	d				19 54															20 54			
Royston	d				20 09															21 09			
Letchworth Garden City	d				20 21															21 21			
Hitchin	d	20 11			20 26					20 41							21 11			21 26			
Stevenage	d	20 17			20 32					20 47							21 17			21 32			
Welwyn Garden City	d																						
Finsbury Park ⊖	d	20 38			20 52					21 08							21 37			21 52			
St Pancras International ⊖	d	20 45	20 50	20 57	21 00	21 02	21 05		21 12	21 15	21 20	21 27	21 32	21 35		21 42	21 45	21 50	21 57	22 00	22 02	22 05	
Farringdon 3 ⊖	d	20 49	20 54	21 02	21 04	21 07	21 09		21 17	21 19	21 24	21 32	21 37	21 39		21 47	21 49	21 54	22 02	22 04	22 07	22 09	
City Thameslink 3	d	20 51	20 56																				
London Blackfriars ⊖	a	20 53	20 58	21 06	21 08	21 11	21 13		21 21	21 23	21 28	21 36	21 41	21 43		21 51	21 53	21 58	22 06	22 08	22 11	22 13	
London Blackfriars 3 ⊖	d	20 54	20 59	21 06	21 09	21 11	21 14	21 16	21 21	21 24	21 29	21 36	21 41	21 44	21 46	21 51	21 54	21 59	22 06	22 09	22 11	22 14	22 16
London Bridge ⊖	d	21 00	21 05		21 15	21 18	21 21			21 30	21 35		21 48	21 51			22 00	22 05		22 15	22 18	22 21	
Elephant & Castle ⊖ 173,179	a			21 10				21 19	21 25			21 40			21 49	21 55			22 10				22 19
Loughborough Jn. 173,179	a			21 15					21 30			21 45				22 00			22 15				
Herne Hill 4 173,179	a			21 19					21 34			21 49				22 04			22 19				
Tulse Hill 3	a			21 24					21 39			21 54				22 09			22 24				
Streatham 4	a			21 29					21 44			21 59				22 14			22 29				
Wimbledon ⊖	a								21 54							22 24							
Sutton 4 179	a			21 47					22 14			22 17				22 44			22 47				
Denmark Hill 4 195	a							21 27							21 57								22 27
Peckham Rye 4 195	a							21 30							22 00								22 30
Catford	a							21 39							22 09								22 39
Bromley South	a							21 52							22 22								22 52
Orpington	a																						
St Mary Cray	a							22 01							22 31								23 01
Swanley	a							22 05							22 35								23 05
Sevenoaks	a							22 25							22 55								23 25
Maidstone East	a																						
Greenwich	a					21 27							21 57								22 27		
Woolwich Arsenal	a					21 40							22 10								22 40		
Abbey Wood	a					21 46							22 16								22 46		
Dartford	a					21 57							22 27								22 57		
Rainham (Kent)	a					22 41							23 11								23 41		
East Croydon 🚋	a	21 14	21 18		21 28		21 36			21 44	21 48			22 06			22 14	22 18		22 28		22 36	
Gatwick Airport 10 ✈	a	21 42	21 34		21 44		22 08			22 12	22 04			22 38			22 42	22 34		22 44		23 08	
Horsham	a	22 08								22 38							23 08						
Brighton 10	a		22 12		22 19						22 44							23 12		23 19			

NRT DECEMBER 19 EDITION

Table T052-R

Saturdays

21 December to 16 May

Cambridge and Peterborough (via London), Bedford, Luton - South London & Kent, Gatwick Airport, Brighton

		TL	TL 1	TL 1	TL	TL A	TL 1 B	TL	TL	TL 1	TL 1	TL	TL 1	TL A	TL 1	TL	TL	TL 1	TL 1	TL	TL	TL 1	TL 1 C
Bedford	d			21 19			21 35				21 49				22 05				22 17			22 45	23 05
Luton 10	d			21 43			21 59				22 13				22 28				22 41		22 54	23 10	23 30
Luton Airport Parkway 7 ✈	d			21 46			22 02				22 16				22 31				22 44		22 57	23 13	23 33
Harpenden	d			21 52			22 08				22 22				22 36				22 49		23 03	23 18	23 38
St Albans City	d	21 37		21 57	21 52		22 13		22 07		22 27	22 22			22 42		22 37		22 55		23 09	23 25	23 45
Elstree & Borehamwood	d	21 46			22 01				22 16			22 31					22 46				23 18		23 54
West Hampstead Thameslink ⊖	d	22 01		22 09	22 16				22 31		22 39	22 46					23 01		23 11		23 33	23 41	00 09
Kentish Town ⊖	d	22 06			22 21	22 26			22 36			22 51		22 56			23 06				23 38		00 13
Peterborough	d		20 54							21 24								21 54					
Huntingdon	d		21 11							21 41								22 11					
Cambridge	d												21 54										
Royston	d												22 09										
Letchworth Garden City	d												22 22										
Hitchin	d		21 41							22 11			22 26					22 41					
Stevenage	d		21 47							22 17			22 32					22 47					
Welwyn Garden City	d																						
Finsbury Park ⊖	d		22 07							22 37			22 53					23 07					
St Pancras International ⊖	d	22 12	22 15	22 20	22 27	22 32	22 35		22 42	22 45	22 50	22 57	23 00	23 02	23 05		23 12	23 15	23 22		23 44	23 51	00 21
Farringdon 3 ⊖	d	22 17	22 19	22 24	22 32	22 37	22 39		22 47	22 49	22 54	23 02	23 04	23 07	23 10		23 17	23 19	23 27		23 49	23 56	00 26
City Thameslink 3	d																						
London Blackfriars ⊖	a	22 21	22 23	22 28	22 36	22 41	22 43		22 51	22 53	22 58	23 06	23 08	23 11	23 13		23 21	23 23	23 30		23 53	23 59	00 30
London Blackfriars 3 ⊖	d	22 21	22 24	22 29	22 36	22 41	22 44	22 46	22 51	22 54	22 59	23 06	23 09	23 11	23 14	23 16	23 21	23 24	23 31	23 46	23 53	00 01	00 31
London Bridge ⊖	d		22 30	22 35		22 48	22 51			23 00	23 05		23 15	23 18	23 21			23 30	23 37				
Elephant & Castle ⊖ 173,179	a	22 25			22 40			22 49	22 55			23 10				23 19	23 25			23 50	23 57		
Loughborough Jn. 173,179	a	22 30			22 45				23 00			23 15					23 30				00 02		
Herne Hill 4 173,179	a	22 34			22 49				23 04			23 19					23 34				00 06		
Tulse Hill 3	a	22 39			22 54				23 09			23 24					23 39				00 10		
Streatham 4	a	22 44			22 59				23 14			23 29					23 44				00 14		
Wimbledon ⊖	a	22 54							23 24								23 54				00 24		
Sutton 4 179	a	23 14			23 17				23 44			23 47					00 14				00 44		
Denmark Hill 4 195	a							22 57								23 27				23 57			
Peckham Rye 4 195	a							23 00								23 30				00 01			
Catford	a							23 09								23 39				00 10			
Bromley South	a							23 22								23 52				00 22			
Orpington	a																						
St Mary Cray	a							23 31								00 01				00 31			
Swanley	a							23 35								00 06				00 35			
Sevenoaks	a							23 55								00 25				00 55			
Maidstone East	a																						
Greenwich	a					22 57								23 27									
Woolwich Arsenal	a					23 10								23 40									
Abbey Wood	a					23 16								23 46									
Dartford	a					23 27								23 57									
Rainham (Kent)	a																						
East Croydon 🚋	a		22 44	22 48			23 06			23 14	23 18		23 28		23 36			23 44	23 50			00 27	00 57
Gatwick Airport 10 ✈	a		23 12	23 04			23 37			23 42	23 34		23 47		00 01			00 12	00 17			00 47	01 20
Horsham	a		23 38							00 06								00 36					
Brighton 10	a			23 45							00 12		00 23						00 56			01 24	

A To Gillingham (Kent)

B To Three Bridges

C not 4 January. To Three Bridges

Table T052-R

Saturdays

21 December to 16 May

Cambridge and Peterborough (via London), Bedford, Luton - South London & Kent, Gatwick Airport, Brighton

		TL 1 A	TL 1
Bedford	d	23 05	23 35
Luton 10	d	23 30	23 59
Luton Airport Parkway 7 ✈	d	23 33	00 03
Harpenden	d	23 38	00 08
St Albans City	d	23 45	00 15
Elstree & Borehamwood	d	23 54	00 24
West Hampstead Thameslink ⊖	d	00 09	00 39
Kentish Town ⊖	d	00 13	00 43
Peterborough	d		
Huntingdon	d		
Cambridge	d		
Royston	d		
Letchworth Garden City	d		
Hitchin	d		
Stevenage	d		
Welwyn Garden City	d		
Finsbury Park ⊖	d		
St Pancras International ⊖	d	00 21	00 51
Farringdon 3 ⊖	d	00 26	
City Thameslink 3	d		
London Blackfriars ⊖	a	00 30	01 00
London Blackfriars 3 ⊖	d	00 31	01 01
London Bridge ⊖	d		
Elephant & Castle ⊖ 173,179	a		
Loughborough Jn. 173,179	a		
Herne Hill 4 173,179	a		
Tulse Hill 3	a		
Streatham 4	a		
Wimbledon ⊖	a		
Sutton 4 179	a		
Denmark Hill 4 195	a		
Peckham Rye 4 195	a		
Catford	a		
Bromley South	a		
Orpington	a		
St Mary Cray	a		
Swanley	a		
Sevenoaks	a		
Maidstone East	a		
Greenwich	a		
Woolwich Arsenal	a		
Abbey Wood	a		
Dartford	a		
Rainham (Kent)	a		
East Croydon	a	00 57	01 27
Gatwick Airport 10 ✈	a	01 28	01 56
Horsham	a		
Brighton 10	a		02 28

A 4 January. To Three Bridges

Table T052-R

Sundays

15 December to 10 May

Cambridge and Peterborough (via London), Bedford, Luton - South London & Kent, Gatwick Airport, Brighton

		TL 1 A	TL 1 B	TL 1 C	TL 1 A	TL 1	TL 1	TL 1	TL 1	TL	TL 1		TL	TL 1	TL	TL	TL 1	TL	TL 1	TL 1	TL	TL 1		TL	TL
Bedford	d																					08 19			
Luton 10	d																					08 44			
Luton Airport Parkway 7 ✈	d				00 03																	08 47			
Harpenden	d				00 08																	08 52			
St Albans City	d				00 15																	08 59			
Elstree & Borehamwood	d				00 24																				
West Hampstead Thameslink ⊖	d		00 09	00 09	00 39																	09 15		09 20	
Kentish Town ⊖	d		00 13	00 13	00 43																			09 26	
Peterborough	d																								
Huntingdon	d																								
Cambridge	d																								
Royston	d																								
Letchworth Garden City	d																								
Hitchin	d																								
Stevenage	d																								
Welwyn Garden City	d																								
Finsbury Park ⊖	d																								
St Pancras International ⊖	d		00 21	00 21	00 51																	09 26		09 32	
Farringdon 3 ⊖	d		00 26	00 26																		09 30		09 36	
City Thameslink 3	d																								
London Blackfriars ⊖	a		00 30	00 30	01 00																	09 34		09 40	
London Blackfriars 3 ⊖	d	00 01	00 31	00 31	01 01																09 30	09 35		09 41	09 42
London Bridge ⊖	d					07 11	07 19	07 41	08 11	08 18	08 19		08 30	08 41	08 48	09 00	09 11	09 18	09 19	09 27		09 41		09 48	
Elephant & Castle ⊖ 173,179	a																				09 33				09 45
Loughborough Jn. 173,179	a																				09 39				
Herne Hill 4 173,179	a																				09 42				
Tulse Hill 3	a												08 43			09 13					09 48				
Streatham 4	a												08 50			09 20					09 52				
Wimbledon ⊖	a																								
Sutton 4 179	a												09 05			09 35					10 07				
Denmark Hill 4 195	a																								09 53
Peckham Rye 4 195	a																								09 56
Catford	a																								10 05
Bromley South	a																								10 18
Orpington	a																								
St Mary Cray	a																								10 25
Swanley	a																								10 30
Sevenoaks	a																								10 49
Maidstone East	a																								
Greenwich	a									08 27					08 57			09 27						09 57	
Woolwich Arsenal	a									08 40					09 10			09 40						10 10	
Abbey Wood	a									08 46					09 16			09 46						10 16	
Dartford	a									08 57					09 27			09 57						10 27	
Rainham (Kent)	a									09 41					10 11			10 41						11 11	
East Croydon	a	00 27	00 57	00 57	01 27	07 24	07 35	07 54	08 24		08 35			08 54			09 24		09 37	09 41		09 54			
Gatwick Airport 10 ✈	a	00 47	01 20	01 28	01 56	07 43	08 06	08 14	08 43		09 07			09 09			09 39		10 02	10 09		10 09			
Horsham	a						08 31				09 31								10 25						
Brighton 10	a	01 24			02 28	08 21		08 52	09 21					09 47			10 15					10 47			

A not 15 December. From Bedford

B not 15 December, 5 January. From Bedford to Three Bridges

C 5 January. From Bedford to Three Bridges

Table T052-R

Sundays
15 December to 10 May

Cambridge and Peterborough (via London), Bedford, Luton - South London & Kent, Gatwick Airport, Brighton

	TL ■	TL	TL ■ A	TL	TL ■	TL	TL	TL	TL ■	TL ■	TL	TL ■	TL	TL	TL ■	TL	TL ■ A	TL	TL ■	TL	TL	TL
Bedford d			08 35		08 49					09 05		09 19					09 35		09 49			
Luton d		08 48	09 00		09 14			09 18		09 30		09 44				09 48	10 00		10 14			10 18
Luton Airport Parkway ✈ d		08 51	09 03		09 17			09 21		09 33		09 47				09 51	10 03		10 17			10 21
Harpenden d		08 56	09 08		09 22			09 26		09 38		09 52				09 56	10 08		10 22			10 26
St Albans City d		09 03	09 15		09 29			09 33		09 45		09 59				10 03	10 15		10 29			10 33
Elstree & Borehamwood d		09 12						09 42								10 12						10 42
West Hampstead Thameslink ⊖ d		09 26	09 30		09 45	09 50		09 56		10 00		10 15				10 26	10 30		10 45			10 56
Kentish Town ⊖ d		09 31				09 56		10 01					10 26			10 31				10 56		11 01
Peterborough d																						
Huntingdon d																						
Cambridge d	08 28														09 28							
Royston d	08 43														09 43							
Letchworth Garden City d	08 54														09 54							
Hitchin d	08 59														09 59							
Stevenage d	09 05														10 05							
Welwyn Garden City d																						
Finsbury Park ⊖ d	09 28														10 28							
St Pancras International ⊖ d	09 35	09 38	09 41		09 56	10 02		10 08		10 11		10 26	10 32		10 35	10 38	10 41		10 56	11 02		11 08
Farringdon ⊖ d	09 39	09 42	09 45		10 00	10 06		10 12		10 15		10 30	10 36		10 39	10 42	10 45		11 00	11 06		11 12
City Thameslink d																						
London Blackfriars ⊖ a	09 43	09 46	09 49		10 04	10 10		10 16		10 19		10 34	10 40		10 43	10 46	10 49		11 04	11 10		11 16
London Blackfriars ⊖ d	09 44	09 47	09 50	10 00	10 05	10 11	10 12	10 17		10 20	10 30	10 35	10 41	10 42	10 44	10 47	10 50	11 00	11 05	11 11	11 12	11 17
London Bridge ⊖ d	09 51		09 56		10 11	10 18			10 21	10 26		10 41	10 48		10 51		10 56		11 11	11 18		
Elephant & Castle ⊖173,179 a		09 50		10 03			10 15	10 20			10 33			10 45		10 50		11 03			11 15	11 20
Loughborough Jn. 173,179 a		09 56		10 09				10 26			10 39					10 56		11 09				11 26
Herne Hill 173,179 a		09 59		10 12				10 29			10 42					10 59		11 12				11 29
Tulse Hill a		10 04		10 18				10 34			10 48					11 04		11 18				11 34
Streatham a		10 08		10 22				10 38			10 52					11 08		11 22				11 38
Wimbledon ⊖ a		10 18						10 48								11 18						11 48
Sutton 179 a		10 38		10 37				11 08			11 07					11 38		11 37				12 08
Denmark Hill 195 a							10 23							10 53							11 23	
Peckham Rye 195 a							10 26							10 56							11 26	
Catford a							10 35							11 05							11 35	
Bromley South a							10 48							11 18							11 48	
Orpington a																						
St Mary Cray a							10 55							11 25							11 55	
Swanley a							11 00							11 30							12 00	
Sevenoaks a							11 19							11 49							12 19	
Maidstone East a																						
Greenwich a						10 27							10 57							11 27		
Woolwich Arsenal a						10 40							11 10							11 40		
Abbey Wood a						10 46							11 16							11 46		
Dartford a						10 57							11 27							11 57		
Rainham (Kent) a						11 41							12 11							12 41		
East Croydon a	10 07		10 10		10 24				10 37	10 40		10 54			11 07		11 10		11 24			
Gatwick Airport ✈ a	10 27		10 42		10 39				11 02	11 09		11 09			11 27		11 42		11 39			
Horsham a									11 25													
Brighton a					11 15							11 47							12 15			

A To Three Bridges

NRT DECEMBER 19 EDITION

Table T052-R

Sundays
15 December to 10 May

Cambridge and Peterborough (via London), Bedford, Luton - South London & Kent, Gatwick Airport, Brighton

	TL ■	TL ■	TL	TL ■	TL	TL	TL ■	TL	TL ■ A	TL	TL ■	TL	TL	TL	TL ■	TL ■	TL	TL ■	TL	TL	TL ■	TL
Bedford d		10 05		10 19					10 35		10 49					11 05		11 19				
Luton d		10 30		10 44				10 48	11 00		11 14			11 18		11 30		11 44				11 48
Luton Airport Parkway ✈ d		10 33		10 47				10 51	11 03		11 17			11 21		11 33		11 47				11 51
Harpenden d		10 38		10 52				10 56	11 08		11 22			11 26		11 38		11 52				11 56
St Albans City d		10 45		10 59				11 03	11 15		11 29			11 33		11 45		11 59				12 03
Elstree & Borehamwood d								11 12						11 42								12 12
West Hampstead Thameslink ⊖ d		11 00		11 15				11 26	11 30		11 45			11 56		12 00		12 15				12 26
Kentish Town ⊖ d					11 26			11 31				11 56		12 01					12 26			12 31
Peterborough d																						
Huntingdon d																						
Cambridge d							10 28														11 28	
Royston d							10 43														11 43	
Letchworth Garden City d							10 54														11 54	
Hitchin d							10 59														11 59	
Stevenage d							11 05														12 05	
Welwyn Garden City d																						
Finsbury Park ⊖ d							11 28														12 28	
St Pancras International ⊖ d		11 11		11 26	11 32		11 35	11 38	11 41		11 56	12 02		12 08		12 11	12 21	12 26	12 32		12 35	12 38
Farringdon ⊖ d		11 15		11 30	11 36		11 39	11 42	11 45		12 00	12 06		12 12		12 15	12 25	12 30	12 36		12 39	12 42
City Thameslink d																						
London Blackfriars ⊖ a		11 19		11 34	11 40		11 43	11 46	11 49		12 04	12 10		12 16		12 19	12 29	12 34	12 40		12 43	12 46
London Blackfriars ⊖ d		11 20	11 30	11 35	11 41	11 42	11 44	11 47	11 50	12 00	12 05	12 11	12 12	12 17		12 20	12 30	12 35	12 41	12 42	12 44	12 47
London Bridge ⊖ d	11 21	11 26		11 41	11 48		11 51		11 56		12 11	12 18			12 21	12 26		12 41	12 48		12 51	
Elephant & Castle ⊖173,179 a			11 33			11 45		11 50		12 03			12 15	12 20			12 33			12 45		12 50
Loughborough Jn. 173,179 a			11 39					11 56		12 09				12 26			12 39					12 56
Herne Hill 173,179 a			11 42					11 59		12 12				12 29			12 42					12 59
Tulse Hill a			11 48					12 04		12 18				12 34			12 48					13 04
Streatham a			11 52					12 08		12 22				12 38			12 52					13 08
Wimbledon ⊖ a								12 18						12 48								13 18
Sutton 179 a			12 07					12 38		12 37				13 08			13 07					13 38
Denmark Hill 195 a						11 53							12 23							12 53		
Peckham Rye 195 a						11 56							12 26							12 56		
Catford a						12 05							12 35							13 05		
Bromley South a						12 18							12 48							13 18		
Orpington a																						
St Mary Cray a						12 25							12 55							13 25		
Swanley a						12 30							13 00							13 30		
Sevenoaks a						12 49							13 19							13 49		
Maidstone East a																						
Greenwich a					11 57							12 27							12 57			
Woolwich Arsenal a					12 10							12 40							13 10			
Abbey Wood a					12 16							12 46							13 16			
Dartford a					12 27							12 57							13 27			
Rainham (Kent) a					13 11							13 41							14 11			
East Croydon a	11 37	11 40		11 54			12 07		12 10		12 24				12 37	12 40		12 54			13 07	
Gatwick Airport ✈ a	12 02	12 09		12 09			12 27		12 42		12 39				13 02	13 09		13 09			13 27	
Horsham a	12 25														13 25							
Brighton a				12 47							13 15							13 47				

A To Three Bridges

Table T052-R

Sundays
15 December to 10 May

Cambridge and Peterborough (via London), Bedford, Luton - South London & Kent, Gatwick Airport, Brighton

Station		TL ■ A	TL	TL ■	TL	TL	TL	TL ■	TL ■	TL	TL ■	TL	TL	TL ■	TL	TL ■ A	TL	TL ■	TL	TL	TL	TL ■	TL ■
Bedford	d	11 37		11 51					12 07		12 21					12 37		12 51					13 05
Luton	d	12 02	11 58	12 16			12 22		12 32		12 46				12 52	13 02		13 16			13 22		13 29
Luton Airport Parkway ✈	d	12 05	12 01	12 19			12 25		12 35		12 49				12 55	13 05		13 19			13 25		13 32
Harpenden	d	12 10	12 06	12 24			12 30		12 40		12 54				13 00	13 10		13 24			13 30		13 37
St Albans City	d	12 17	12 16	12 30			12 37		12 47	12 46	13 00				13 07	13 17	13 16	13 30			13 37		13 43
Elstree & Borehamwood	d		12 25				12 46			12 55					13 16		13 25				13 46		
West Hampstead Thameslink ⊖	d	12 30	12 39	12 45			12 56		13 00	13 09	13 15				13 26	13 30	13 39	13 45			13 56		14 00
Kentish Town ⊖	d		12 44		12 56					13 14		13 26					13 44		13 56				
Peterborough	d																						
Huntingdon	d																						
Cambridge	d													12 28									
Royston	d													12 43									
Letchworth Garden City	d													12 54									
Hitchin	d													12 59									
Stevenage	d													13 05									
Welwyn Garden City	d																						
Finsbury Park ⊖	d													13 28									
St Pancras International ⊖	d	12 41	12 51	12 56	13 02		13 08		13 11	13 21	13 26	13 32		13 35	13 38	13 41	13 51	13 56	14 02		14 08		14 11
Farringdon ⊖	d	12 45	12 55	13 00	13 06		13 12		13 15	13 25	13 30	13 36		13 39	13 42	13 45	13 55	14 00	14 06		14 12		14 15
City Thameslink	d																						
London Blackfriars ⊖	a	12 49	12 59	13 04	13 10		13 16		13 19	13 29	13 34	13 40		13 43	13 46	13 49	13 59	14 04	14 10		14 16		14 19
London Blackfriars ⊖	d	12 50	13 00	13 05	13 11	13 12	13 17		13 20	13 30	13 35	13 41	13 42	13 44	13 47	13 50	14 00	14 05	14 11	14 12	14 17		14 20
London Bridge ⊖	d	12 56		13 11	13 18			13 21	13 26		13 41	13 48		13 51		13 56		14 11	14 18			14 21	14 26
Elephant & Castle ⊖173,179	a		13 03			13 15	13 20			13 33			13 45		13 50		14 03			14 15	14 20		
Loughborough Jn. 173,179	a		13 09				13 26			13 39					13 56		14 09				14 26		
Herne Hill 173,179	a		13 12				13 29			13 42					13 59		14 12				14 29		
Tulse Hill	a		13 18				13 34			13 48					14 04		14 18				14 34		
Streatham	a		13 22				13 38			13 52					14 08		14 22				14 38		
Wimbledon ⊖	a						13 48								14 18						14 48		
Sutton 179	a		13 37				14 08			14 07					14 38		14 37				15 08		
Denmark Hill 195	a					13 23							13 53							14 23			
Peckham Rye 195	a					13 26							13 56							14 26			
Catford	a					13 35							14 05							14 35			
Bromley South	a					13 48							14 18							14 48			
Orpington	a																						
St Mary Cray	a					13 55							14 25							14 55			
Swanley	a					14 00							14 30							15 00			
Sevenoaks	a					14 19							14 49							15 19			
Maidstone East	a																						
Greenwich	a				13 27							13 57							14 27				
Woolwich Arsenal	a				13 40							14 10							14 40				
Abbey Wood	a				13 46							14 16							14 46				
Dartford	a				13 57							14 27							14 57				
Rainham (Kent)	a				14 41							15 11							15 41				
East Croydon	a	13 10		13 24				13 37	13 40		13 54			14 07		14 10		14 24				14 37	14 40
Gatwick Airport ✈	a	13 42		13 39				14 02	14 09		14 09			14 27		14 42		14 39				15 02	15 09
Horsham	a							14 25														15 25	
Brighton	a			14 15							14 47							15 15					

A To Three Bridges

Table T052-R

Sundays
15 December to 10 May

Cambridge and Peterborough (via London), Bedford, Luton - South London & Kent, Gatwick Airport, Brighton

Station		TL	TL ■	TL	TL	TL ■	TL	TL ■ A	TL	TL ■	TL	TL	TL	TL ■	TL ■	TL	TL ■	TL	TL	TL ■	TL	TL ■ A	TL
Bedford	d		13 21					13 37		13 51					14 05		14 21					14 37	
Luton	d		13 46				13 52	14 02		14 16			14 22		14 29		14 46				14 52	15 02	
Luton Airport Parkway ✈	d		13 49				13 55	14 05		14 19			14 25		14 32		14 49				14 55	15 05	
Harpenden	d		13 54				14 00	14 10		14 24			14 30		14 37		14 54				15 00	15 10	
St Albans City	d	13 47	14 00				14 07	14 17	14 16	14 30			14 37		14 43	14 47	15 00				15 07	15 17	15 16
Elstree & Borehamwood	d	13 56					14 16		14 25				14 46			14 56					15 16		15 25
West Hampstead Thameslink ⊖	d	14 09	14 15				14 26	14 30	14 39	14 45			14 56		15 00	15 09	15 15				15 26	15 30	15 39
Kentish Town ⊖	d	14 14		14 26					14 44		14 56					15 14		15 26					15 44
Peterborough	d																						
Huntingdon	d																						
Cambridge	d					13 28														14 28			
Royston	d					13 43														14 43			
Letchworth Garden City	d					13 54														14 54			
Hitchin	d					13 59														14 59			
Stevenage	d					14 05														15 05			
Welwyn Garden City	d																						
Finsbury Park ⊖	d					14 28														15 27			
St Pancras International ⊖	d	14 21	14 26	14 32		14 35	14 38	14 41	14 51	14 56	15 02		15 08		15 11	15 21	15 26	15 32		15 35	15 38	15 41	15 51
Farringdon ⊖	d	14 25	14 30	14 36		14 39	14 42	14 45	14 55	15 00	15 06		15 12		15 15	15 25	15 30	15 36		15 39	15 42	15 45	15 55
City Thameslink	d																						
London Blackfriars ⊖	a	14 29	14 34	14 40		14 43	14 46	14 49	14 59	15 04	15 10		15 16		15 19	15 29	15 34	15 40		15 43	15 46	15 49	15 59
London Blackfriars ⊖	d	14 30	14 35	14 41	14 42	14 44	14 47	14 50	15 00	15 05	15 11	15 12	15 17		15 20	15 30	15 35	15 41	15 42	15 44	15 47	15 50	16 00
London Bridge ⊖	d		14 41	14 48		14 51		14 56		15 11	15 18			15 21	15 26		15 41	15 48		15 51		15 56	
Elephant & Castle ⊖173,179	a	14 33			14 45		14 50		15 03			15 15	15 20			15 33			15 45		15 50		16 03
Loughborough Jn. 173,179	a	14 39					14 56		15 09				15 26			15 39					15 56		16 09
Herne Hill 173,179	a	14 42					14 59		15 12				15 29			15 42					15 59		16 12
Tulse Hill	a	14 48					15 04		15 18				15 34			15 48					16 04		16 18
Streatham	a	14 52					15 08		15 22				15 38			15 52					16 08		16 22
Wimbledon ⊖	a						15 18						15 48								16 18		
Sutton 179	a	15 07					15 38		15 37				16 08			16 07					16 38		16 37
Denmark Hill 195	a				14 53							15 23							15 53				
Peckham Rye 195	a				14 56							15 26							15 56				
Catford	a				15 05							15 35							16 05				
Bromley South	a				15 18							15 48							16 18				
Orpington	a																						
St Mary Cray	a				15 25							15 55							16 25				
Swanley	a				15 30							16 00							16 30				
Sevenoaks	a				15 49							16 19							16 49				
Maidstone East	a																						
Greenwich	a			14 57							15 27							15 57					
Woolwich Arsenal	a			15 10							15 40							16 10					
Abbey Wood	a			15 16							15 46							16 16					
Dartford	a			15 27							15 57							16 27					
Rainham (Kent)	a			16 11							16 41							17 11					
East Croydon	a		14 54			15 07		15 10		15 24				15 37	15 40		15 54			16 07		16 10	
Gatwick Airport ✈	a		15 09			15 27		15 42		15 39				16 02	16 09		16 09			16 27		16 42	
Horsham	a													16 25									
Brighton	a		15 47							16 15							16 47						

A To Three Bridges

Table T052-R

Sundays
15 December to 10 May

Cambridge and Peterborough (via London), Bedford, Luton - South London & Kent, Gatwick Airport, Brighton

		TL 1	TL	TL	TL	TL 1	TL 1	TL	TL 1	TL	TL	TL 1	TL	TL 1 A	TL	TL 1	TL	TL	TL	TL 1	TL 1	TL
Bedford	d	14 51					15 05		15 21					15 37		15 51					16 05	
Luton 10	d	15 16			15 22		15 29		15 46				15 52	16 02		16 16			16 22		16 29	
Luton Airport Parkway 7 ✈	d	15 19			15 25		15 32		15 49				15 55	16 05		16 19			16 25		16 32	
Harpenden	d	15 24			15 30		15 37		15 54				16 00	16 10		16 24			16 30		16 37	
St Albans City	d	15 30			15 37		15 43	15 47	16 00				16 07	16 17	16 16	16 30			16 37		16 43	16 47
Elstree & Borehamwood	d				15 46			15 56					16 16		16 25				16 46			16 56
West Hampstead Thameslink ⊖	d	15 45			15 56		16 00	16 09	16 15				16 26	16 30	16 39	16 45			16 56		17 00	17 09
Kentish Town ⊖	d		15 56					16 14		16 26					16 44		16 56					17 14
Peterborough	d																					
Huntingdon	d																					
Cambridge	d											15 28										
Royston	d											15 43										
Letchworth Garden City	d											15 54										
Hitchin	d											15 59										
Stevenage	d											16 05										
Welwyn Garden City	d																					
Finsbury Park ⊖	d											16 27										
St Pancras International ⊖	d	15 56	16 02		16 08		16 11	16 21	16 26	16 32		16 35	16 38	16 41	16 51	16 56	17 02		17 08		17 11	17 21
Farringdon 3 ⊖	d	16 00	16 06		16 12		16 15	16 25	16 30	16 36		16 39	16 42	16 45	16 55	17 00	17 06		17 12		17 15	17 25
City Thameslink 3	d																					
London Blackfriars ⊖	a	16 04	16 10		16 16		16 19	16 29	16 34	16 40		16 43	16 46	16 49	16 59	17 04	17 10		17 16		17 19	17 29
London Blackfriars 3 ⊖	d	16 05	16 11	16 12	16 17		16 20	16 30	16 35	16 41	16 42	16 44	16 47	16 50	17 00	17 05	17 11	17 12	17 17		17 20	17 30
London Bridge ⊖	d	16 11	16 18			16 21	16 26		16 41	16 48		16 51		16 56		17 11	17 18			17 21	17 26	
Elephant & Castle ⊖ 173,179	a			16 15	16 20			16 33			16 45		16 50		17 03			17 15	17 20			17 33
Loughborough Jn. 173,179	a				16 26			16 39					16 56		17 09				17 26			17 39
Herne Hill 4 173,179	a				16 29			16 42					16 59		17 12				17 29			17 42
Tulse Hill 3	a				16 34			16 48					17 04		17 18				17 34			17 48
Streatham 4	a				16 38			16 52					17 08		17 22				17 38			17 52
Wimbledon ⊖	a				16 48								17 18						17 48			
Sutton 4 179	a				17 08			17 07					17 38		17 37				18 08			18 07
Denmark Hill 4 195	a			16 23							16 53							17 23				
Peckham Rye 4 195	a			16 26							16 56							17 26				
Catford	a			16 35							17 05							17 35				
Bromley South	a			16 48							17 18							17 48				
Orpington	a																					
St Mary Cray	a			16 55							17 25							17 55				
Swanley	a			17 00							17 30							18 00				
Sevenoaks	a			17 19							17 49							18 19				
Maidstone East	a																					
Greenwich	a		16 27							16 57							17 27					
Woolwich Arsenal	a		16 40							17 10							17 40					
Abbey Wood	a		16 46							17 16							17 46					
Dartford	a		16 57							17 27							17 57					
Rainham (Kent)	a		17 41							18 11							18 41					
East Croydon 🚌	a	16 24				16 37	16 40		16 54			17 07		17 10		17 24				17 37	17 40	
Gatwick Airport 10 ✈	a	16 39				17 02	17 09		17 09			17 27		17 42		17 39				18 02	18 09	
Horsham	a					17 25														18 25		
Brighton 10	a	17 15							17 47							18 15						

A To Three Bridges

AVAILABLE FROM
MP Middleton Press

NRT DECEMBER 19 EDITION

Table T052-R

Sundays
15 December to 10 May

Cambridge and Peterborough (via London), Bedford, Luton - South London & Kent, Gatwick Airport, Brighton

		TL 1	TL	TL	TL 1	TL	TL 1 A	TL	TL 1	TL	TL	TL	TL 1	TL 1	TL	TL 1	TL	TL	TL 1	TL	TL 1 A	TL	TL 1
Bedford	d	16 21					16 37		16 51					17 05		17 21					17 37		17 51
Luton 10	d	16 46				16 52	17 02		17 16			17 22		17 29		17 46				17 52	18 02		18 16
Luton Airport Parkway 7 ✈	d	16 49				16 55	17 05		17 19			17 25		17 32		17 49				17 55	18 05		18 19
Harpenden	d	16 54				17 00	17 10		17 24			17 30		17 37		17 54				18 00	18 10		18 24
St Albans City	d	17 00				17 07	17 17	17 16	17 30			17 37		17 43	17 47	18 00				18 07	18 17	18 16	18 30
Elstree & Borehamwood	d					17 16		17 25				17 46			17 56					18 16		18 25	
West Hampstead Thameslink ⊖	d	17 15				17 26	17 30	17 39	17 45			17 56		18 00	18 09	18 15				18 26	18 30	18 39	18 45
Kentish Town ⊖	d		17 26					17 44		17 56					18 14		18 26					18 44	
Peterborough	d																						
Huntingdon	d																						
Cambridge	d				16 28														17 28				
Royston	d				16 43														17 43				
Letchworth Garden City	d				16 54														17 54				
Hitchin	d				16 59														17 59				
Stevenage	d				17 05														18 05				
Welwyn Garden City	d																						
Finsbury Park ⊖	d				17 27														18 28				
St Pancras International ⊖	d	17 26	17 32		17 35	17 38	17 41	17 51	17 56	18 02		18 08		18 11	18 21	18 26	18 32		18 35	18 38	18 41	18 51	18 56
Farringdon 3 ⊖	d	17 30	17 36		17 39	17 42	17 45	17 55	18 00	18 06		18 12		18 15	18 25	18 30	18 36		18 39	18 42	18 45	18 55	19 00
City Thameslink 3	d																						
London Blackfriars ⊖	a	17 34	17 40		17 43	17 46	17 49	17 59	18 04	18 10		18 16		18 19	18 29	18 34	18 40		18 43	18 46	18 49	18 59	19 04
London Blackfriars 3 ⊖	d	17 35	17 41	17 42	17 44	17 47	17 50	18 00	18 05	18 11	18 12	18 17		18 20	18 30	18 35	18 41	18 42	18 44	18 47	18 50	19 00	19 05
London Bridge ⊖	d	17 41	17 48		17 51		17 56		18 11	18 18			18 21	18 26		18 41	18 48		18 51		18 56		19 11
Elephant & Castle ⊖ 173,179	a			17 45		17 50		18 03			18 15	18 20			18 33			18 45		18 50		19 03	
Loughborough Jn. 173,179	a					17 56		18 09				18 26			18 39					18 56		19 09	
Herne Hill 4 173,179	a					17 59		18 12				18 29			18 42					18 59		19 12	
Tulse Hill 3	a					18 04		18 18				18 34			18 48					19 04		19 18	
Streatham 4	a					18 08		18 22				18 38			18 52					19 08		19 22	
Wimbledon ⊖	a					18 18						18 48								19 18			
Sutton 4 179	a					18 38		18 37				19 08			19 07					19 38		19 37	
Denmark Hill 4 195	a			17 53							18 23							18 53					
Peckham Rye 4 195	a			17 56							18 26							18 56					
Catford	a			18 05							18 35							19 05					
Bromley South	a			18 18							18 48							19 18					
Orpington	a																						
St Mary Cray	a			18 25							18 55							19 25					
Swanley	a			18 30							19 00							19 30					
Sevenoaks	a			18 49							19 19							19 49					
Maidstone East	a																						
Greenwich	a		17 57							18 27							18 57						
Woolwich Arsenal	a		18 10							18 40							19 10						
Abbey Wood	a		18 16							18 46							19 16						
Dartford	a		18 27							18 57							19 27						
Rainham (Kent)	a		19 11							19 41							20 11						
East Croydon 🚌	a	17 54			18 07		18 10		18 24				18 37	18 40		18 54			19 07		19 10		19 24
Gatwick Airport 10 ✈	a	18 09			18 27		18 42		18 39				19 02	19 09		19 09			19 27		19 42		19 39
Horsham	a												19 25										
Brighton 10	a	18 47							19 15							19 47							20 15

A To Three Bridges

Table T052-R

Sundays
15 December to 10 May

Cambridge and Peterborough (via London), Bedford, Luton - South London & Kent, Gatwick Airport, Brighton

		TL	TL	TL	TL 1	TL 1	TL	TL 1	TL	TL	TL 1	TL	TL 1 A	TL	TL 1	TL	TL	TL	TL 1	TL 1	TL	TL 1	TL
Bedford	d					18 07		18 21					18 37		18 51					19 05		19 21	
Luton 10	d			18 22		18 32		18 46				18 52	19 02		19 16			19 22		19 29		19 46	
Luton Airport Parkway 7 ✈	d			18 25		18 35		18 49				18 55	19 05		19 19			19 25		19 32		19 49	
Harpenden	d			18 30		18 40		18 54				19 00	19 10		19 24			19 30		19 37		19 54	
St Albans City	d			18 37		18 47	18 46	19 00				19 07	19 17	19 16	19 30			19 37		19 43	19 47	20 00	
Elstree & Borehamwood	d			18 46			18 55					19 16		19 25				19 46			19 56		
West Hampstead Thameslink ⊖	d			18 57		19 00	19 09	19 15				19 26	19 30	19 39	19 45			19 56		20 00	20 09	20 15	
Kentish Town ⊖	d	18 56					19 14		19 26					19 44		19 56					20 14		20 26
Peterborough	d																						
Huntingdon	d																						
Cambridge	d										18 28												
Royston	d										18 43												
Letchworth Garden City	d										18 54												
Hitchin	d										18 59												
Stevenage	d										19 05												
Welwyn Garden City	d																						
Finsbury Park ⊖	d										19 28												
St Pancras International ⊖	d	19 02		19 08		19 11	19 21	19 26	19 32		19 35	19 38	19 41	19 51	19 56	20 02		20 08		20 11	20 21	20 26	20 32
Farringdon 3 ⊖	d	19 06		19 12		19 15	19 25	19 30	19 36		19 39	19 42	19 45	19 55	20 00	20 06		20 12		20 15	20 25	20 30	20 36
City Thameslink 3	d																						
London Blackfriars ⊖	a	19 10		19 16		19 19	19 29	19 34	19 40		19 43	19 46	19 49	19 59	20 04	20 10		20 16		20 19	20 29	20 34	20 40
London Blackfriars 3 ⊖	d	19 11	19 12	19 17		19 20	19 30	19 35	19 41	19 42	19 44	19 47	19 50	20 00	20 05	20 11	20 12	20 17		20 20	20 30	20 35	20 41
London Bridge ⊖	d	19 18			19 21	19 26		19 41	19 48		19 51		19 56		20 11	20 18			20 21	20 26		20 41	20 48
Elephant & Castle ⊖ 173,179	a		19 15	19 20			19 33			19 45		19 50		20 03			20 15	20 20			20 33		
Loughborough Jn. 173,179	a			19 26			19 39					19 56		20 09				20 26			20 39		
Herne Hill 4 173,179	a			19 29			19 42					19 59		20 12				20 29			20 42		
Tulse Hill 3	a			19 34			19 48					20 04		20 18				20 34			20 48		
Streatham 4	a			19 38			19 52					20 08		20 22				20 38			20 52		
Wimbledon ⊖	a			19 48								20 18						20 48					
Sutton 4 179	a			20 08			20 07					20 38		20 37				21 08			21 07		
Denmark Hill 4 195	a		19 23							19 53							20 23						
Peckham Rye 4 195	a		19 26							19 56							20 26						
Catford	a		19 35							20 05							20 35						
Bromley South	a		19 48							20 18							20 48						
Orpington	a																						
St Mary Cray	a		19 55							20 25							20 55						
Swanley	a		20 00							20 30							21 00						
Sevenoaks	a		20 19							20 49							21 20						
Maidstone East	a																						
Greenwich	a	19 27							19 57							20 27							20 57
Woolwich Arsenal	a	19 40							20 10							20 40							21 10
Abbey Wood	a	19 46							20 16							20 46							21 16
Dartford	a	19 57							20 27							20 57							21 27
Rainham (Kent)	a	20 41							21 11							21 41							22 11
East Croydon	a				19 37	19 40		19 54			20 07		20 10		20 24				20 37	20 40		20 54	
Gatwick Airport 10 ✈	a				20 02	20 09		20 09			20 27		20 42		20 39				21 02	21 09		21 09	
Horsham	a				20 25														21 25				
Brighton 10	a							20 47							21 15							21 47	

A To Three Bridges

Table T052-R

Sundays
15 December to 10 May

Cambridge and Peterborough (via London), Bedford, Luton - South London & Kent, Gatwick Airport, Brighton

		TL	TL 1	TL	TL 1	TL	TL 1	TL	TL	TL	TL 1	TL 1 A	TL	TL 1	TL	TL	TL 1 A	TL	TL 1 A	TL 1	TL	TL	TL 1
Bedford	d				19 35		19 51					20 07		20 21					20 37	20 51			
Luton 10	d			19 52	19 59		20 16			20 22		20 32		20 46				20 52	21 02	21 16			
Luton Airport Parkway 7 ✈	d			19 55	20 02		20 19			20 25		20 35		20 49				20 55	21 05	21 19			
Harpenden	d			20 00	20 07		20 24			20 30		20 40		20 54				21 00	21 10	21 24			
St Albans City	d			20 07	20 13	20 17	20 30			20 37		20 47	20 46	21 00				21 07	21 17	21 31	21 27		
Elstree & Borehamwood	d			20 16		20 26				20 46			20 55					21 16			21 36		
West Hampstead Thameslink ⊖	d			20 26	20 30	20 39	20 45			20 57		21 00	21 09	21 15				21 26	21 30	21 45	21 50		
Kentish Town ⊖	d					20 44		20 56					21 14		21 26						21 55		
Peterborough	d																						
Huntingdon	d																						
Cambridge	d		19 28														20 28						
Royston	d		19 43														20 43						
Letchworth Garden City	d		19 54														20 54						
Hitchin	d		19 59														20 59						
Stevenage	d		20 05														21 05						
Welwyn Garden City	d																						
Finsbury Park ⊖	d		20 28														21 28						
St Pancras International ⊖	d		20 35	20 38	20 41	20 51	20 56	21 02		21 08		21 11	21 21	21 26	21 32		21 35	21 38	21 41	21 56	22 02		
Farringdon 3 ⊖	d		20 39	20 42	20 45	20 55	21 00	21 06		21 12		21 15	21 25	21 30	21 36		21 39	21 42	21 45	22 00	22 06		
City Thameslink 3	d																						
London Blackfriars ⊖	a		20 43	20 46	20 49	20 59	21 04	21 10		21 16		21 19	21 29	21 34	21 40		21 43	21 46	21 49	22 04	22 10		
London Blackfriars 3 ⊖	d	20 42	20 44	20 47	20 50	21 00	21 05	21 11	21 12	21 17		21 20	21 30	21 35	21 41	21 42	21 44	21 47	21 50	22 05	22 11	22 12	
London Bridge ⊖	d		20 51		20 56		21 11	21 18			21 21	21 26		21 41	21 48		21 51		21 56	22 11	22 18		22 21
Elephant & Castle ⊖ 173,179	a	20 45		20 50		21 03			21 15	21 20			21 33			21 45		21 50				22 15	
Loughborough Jn. 173,179	a			20 56		21 09				21 26			21 39					21 56					
Herne Hill 4 173,179	a			20 59		21 12				21 29			21 42					21 59					
Tulse Hill 3	a			21 04		21 18				21 34			21 48					22 04					
Streatham 4	a			21 08		21 22				21 38			21 52					22 08					
Wimbledon ⊖	a			21 18						21 48								22 18					
Sutton 4 179	a			21 38		21 37				22 08			22 07					22 38					
Denmark Hill 4 195	a	20 53							21 23							21 53						22 23	
Peckham Rye 4 195	a	20 56							21 26							21 56						22 26	
Catford	a	21 05							21 35							22 05						22 35	
Bromley South	a	21 18							21 48							22 18						22 48	
Orpington	a																						
St Mary Cray	a	21 25							21 55							22 25						22 55	
Swanley	a	21 30							22 00							22 30						23 00	
Sevenoaks	a	21 49							22 19							22 49						23 19	
Maidstone East	a																						
Greenwich	a							21 27							21 57						22 27		
Woolwich Arsenal	a							21 40							22 10						22 40		
Abbey Wood	a							21 46							22 16						22 46		
Dartford	a							21 57							22 27						22 57		
Rainham (Kent)	a							22 41							23 11						23 41		
East Croydon	a		21 07		21 10		21 24				21 37	21 40		21 54			22 07		22 10	22 24			22 37
Gatwick Airport 10 ✈	a		21 27		21 39		21 39				22 02	22 09		22 09			22 26		22 39	22 39			23 02
Horsham	a										22 25												23 25
Brighton 10	a						22 15							22 47						23 15			

A To Three Bridges

Table T052-R

Sundays
15 December to 10 May

Cambridge and Peterborough (via London), Bedford, Luton - South London & Kent, Gatwick Airport, Brighton

		TL ■	TL ■	TL A	TL	TL ■ B	TL ■	TL A	TL	TL ■	TL	TL ■ B	TL ■	TL ■ B	TL ■
Bedford	d	21 09	21 21				21 51			22 11			22 45	23 05	23 45
Luton ■10	d	21 33	21 46				22 16			22 36			23 10	23 30	00 10
Luton Airport Parkway ■ ✈	d	21 36	21 49				22 19			22 39			23 13	23 33	00 13
Harpenden	d	21 41	21 54				22 24			22 44			23 18	23 38	00 18
St Albans City	d	21 48	22 01	21 57			22 31	22 27		22 51			23 25	23 45	00 25
Elstree & Borehamwood	d			22 06				22 36		23 00				23 54	
West Hampstead Thameslink ⊖	d	22 00	22 15	22 20			22 45	22 50		23 14			23 41	00 09	00 41
Kentish Town ⊖	d			22 25				22 55		23 19				00 13	
Peterborough	d														
Huntingdon	d														
Cambridge	d					21 28									
Royston	d					21 43									
Letchworth Garden City	d					21 54									
Hitchin	d					21 59									
Stevenage	d					22 05									
Welwyn Garden City	d														
Finsbury Park ⊖	d					22 28									
St Pancras International ⊖	d	22 11	22 26	22 32		22 35	22 56	23 02		23 26			23 51	00 21	00 51
Farringdon ■ ⊖	d	22 15	22 30	22 36		22 39	23 00	23 06		23 30			23 56	00 26	
City Thameslink ■	d														
London Blackfriars ⊖	a	22 19	22 34	22 40		22 43	23 04	23 10		23 34			23 59	00 30	01 00
London Blackfriars ■ ⊖	d	22 20	22 35	22 41	22 42	22 44	23 05	23 11	23 12	23 35	23 42		00 01	00 31	01 01
London Bridge ⊖	d	22 26	22 41	22 48		22 51	23 11	23 18		23 41		23 45			
Elephant & Castle ⊖173,179	a				22 45				23 15		23 45				
Loughborough Jn. 173,179	a														
Herne Hill ■ 173,179	a														
Tulse Hill ■	a														
Streatham ■	a														
Wimbledon ⊖	a														
Sutton ■ 179	a														
Denmark Hill ■ 195	a				22 53				23 23		23 53				
Peckham Rye ■ 195	a				22 56				23 26		23 56				
Catford	a				23 05				23 35		00 05				
Bromley South	a				23 18				23 48		00 18				
Orpington	a														
St Mary Cray	a				23 25				23 55		00 25				
Swanley	a				23 30				23 59		00 30				
Sevenoaks	a				23 49				00 19		00 49				
Maidstone East	a														
Greenwich	a			22 57				23 27							
Woolwich Arsenal	a			23 10				23 40							
Abbey Wood	a			23 16				23 46							
Dartford	a			23 27				23 57							
Rainham (Kent)	a														
East Croydon	a	22 40	22 54			23 07	23 24			23 54		23 59	00 27	00 57	01 27
Gatwick Airport ■10 ✈	a	23 09	23 09			23 35	23 42			00 17		00 29	00 47	01 20	01 56
Horsham	a														
Brighton ■10	a		23 47				00 19			00 54			01 24		02 28

A To Gillingham (Kent)
B To Three Bridges

Table T052MML-F

Mondays to Fridays
16 December to 15 May

Gatwick Airport and London - St Albans, Luton and Bedford

Miles	Miles	Miles			TL MO A	TL MX ■ B	TL MO A	TL MX A	TL MO ■ B	TL MX A	TL MX ■ B	TL MO C	TL MX A	TL MX A	EM MX ◇■ D 🛒	TL MO ■ B	TL MX A	TL MX ■ B	TL MO ■ B	TL MX ■ B	TL ■ B	TL ■ B	TL ■ E	TL ■ E
0	—	—	Gatwick Airport ✈	d																00 04	00 21	00 42	01 46	02 21
—	0	—	Elephant & Castle ⊖173,179	d													00 04							
—	—	0	London Bridge ⊖	d																				
27	1	1	London Blackfriars ⊖	d										00 02		00 06	00 09	00 22	00 36	00 50	01 06	01 36	02 36	03 06
—	—	—	City Thameslink ■	d																				
—	—	—	Farringdon ■ ⊖	d										00 06		00 11	00 13	00 26						
29	—	—	St Pancras International ⊖	d										00 11	00 15	00 16	00 18	00 31	00 46	01 01	01 16	01 44	02 44	03 14
—	—	—	**Kentish Town** ⊖	d									00 01			00 20	00 22		00 50	01 05		01 48	02 48	
33	—	—	**WestHampsteadThameslink** ⊖	d									00 06	00 20		00 24	00 26	00 39	00 54	01 09	01 24	01 52	02 52	03 22
—	—	—	**Cricklewood**	d									00 10			00 28	00 30		00 58	01 13		01 56	02 56	
—	—	—	**Hendon**	d								00 02	00 13			00 32	00 33		01 02	01 17		02 00	03 00	
—	—	—	**Mill Hill Broadway**	d								00 05	00 16			00 35	00 36		01 05	01 20		02 03	03 03	
—	—	—	**Elstree & Borehamwood**	d						00 01		00 09	00 20			00 39	00 40		01 09	01 24		02 07	03 07	
—	—	—	**Radlett**	d						00 05		00 13	00 24			00 43	00 44		01 13	01 28		02 11	03 11	
49	—	—	**St Albans City**	d					00 03	00 12	00 16	00 21	00 32	00 36		00 51	00 52	00 56	01 21	01 34	01 41	02 19	03 19	03 41
54	—	—	**Harpenden**	d			00 05	00 06	00 09	00 18	00 22	00 27	00 38	00 42		00 57	00 58	01 02	01 27	01 40	01 47	02 25	03 25	03 47
58	—	—	**Luton Airport Parkway** ■ ✈	d			00 10	00 11	00 14	00 23	00 28	00 32	00 43	00 48	00 55	01 02	01 03	01 08	01 32	01 46	01 52	02 30	03 30	03 52
59	—	—	**Luton** ■10	d		00 02	00 15	00 16	00 19	00 28	00 32	00 37	00 48	00 52	00 58	01 07	01 08	01 12	01 37	01 50	01 57	02 35	03 35	03 57
61	—	—	**Leagrave**	d	00 01	00 06		00 20	00 23		00 36	00 41		00 56		01 11	01 12	01 16	01 41	01 54	02 01	02 39	03 39	04 01
65	—	—	**Harlington**	d	00 05	00 11		00 24	00 27		00 41	00 45		01 01		01 15	01 16	01 21	01 45	01 59	02 05	02 43	03 43	04 05
68	—	—	**Flitwick**	d	00 09	00 15		00 28	00 31		00 45	00 49		01 05		01 19	01 20	01 25	01 49	02 03	02 09	02 47	03 47	04 09
78	—	—	**Bedford** ■	a	00 21	00 26	00 35	00 40	00 43	00 48	00 58	01 01	01 08	01 18	01 26	01 31	01 32	01 36	02 01	02 14	02 21	02 59	03 59	04 21

		TL ■ E	TL ■ E	TL ■ E	TL ■ E	EM ◇■ F 🛒	TL G	TL ■ B	EM ◇■ F 🛒	TL H	TL ■ E	TL G	TL I	TL H	TL A	TL ■ E	TL G	TL J	TL A	TL ◇■ B	EM ◇■ K 🛒	TL ■ L
Gatwick Airport ✈	d	02 46	03 21	03 46	04 21			04 41			05 19					05 32				06 06		
Elephant & Castle ⊖173,179	d						05 14			05 44				06 14	06 19				06 34			
London Bridge ⊖	d							05 25			05 55		05 58			06 21		06 28		06 35		06 41
London Blackfriars ⊖	d	03 36	04 06	04 36	05 06		05 19	05 31		05 49	06 01		06 04	06 19	06 24	06 27		06 34	06 39	06 42		06 47
City Thameslink ■	d				05 08		05 21	05 33		05 51	06 03		06 06	06 21	06 26	06 29		06 36	06 41	06 44		06 49
Farringdon ■ ⊖	d				05 11		05 24	05 36		05 54	06 06		06 09	06 24	06 29	06 31		06 39	06 44	06 46		06 51
St Pancras International ⊖	d	03 44	04 14	04 44	05 16	05 52	05 28	05 40	06 23	05 58	06 10		06 13	06 28	06 33	06 36		06 43	06 48	06 51	07 04	06 56
Kentish Town ⊖	d	03 48		04 48			05 33			06 03			06 18		06 38				06 53			
WestHampsteadThameslink ⊖	d	03 52	04 22	04 52	05 24		05 37	05 48		06 07	06 18		06 22	06 37	06 44	06 44		06 52	06 58			
Cricklewood	d	03 56		04 56			05 40			06 10			06 25		06 47				07 01			
Hendon	d	04 00		05 00			05 43			06 14			06 29		06 50				07 04			
Mill Hill Broadway	d	04 03		05 03			05 46			06 17			06 32	06 46	06 53			07 01	07 07			
Elstree & Borehamwood	d	04 07		05 07			05 50			06 21		←	06 36	06 50	06 57		←	07 05	07 11			
Radlett	d	04 11		05 11			05 54			06 25		06 25	06 40	06 54	07 01		06 54	07 09	07 15			
St Albans City	d	04 19	04 41	05 19	05 41		06 01	06 05		→	06 30	06 32	06 49	→	07a07	06 57	07 02	→	07a21	07 10		07 14
Harpenden	d	04 25	04 47	05 25	05 47		06 06	06 11			06 37	06 41	06 56			07 03	07 09					07 21
Luton Airport Parkway ■ ✈	d	04 30	04 52	05 30	05 52		06 12	06 16			06 42	06 47	07 02			07 08	07 16			07 18		07 26
Luton ■10	d	04 35	04 57	05 35	05 57	06 15	06a16	06 21	06 46		06 47	06a51	07a06			07 13	07a20			07 22	07 27	07 31
Leagrave	d	04 39	05 01	05 39	06 01			06 25			06 51					07 16						07 34
Harlington	d	04 43	05 05	05 43	06 05			06 29			06 55					07 21						07 39
Flitwick	d	04 47	05 09	05 47	06 09			06 33			06 59					07 25						07 43
Bedford ■	a	04 59	05 21	05 59	06 21	06 28		06 45	06 59		07 11					07 37				07 42	07 41	07 54

		TL I	TL H	TL A	TL ■ E	TL ■ B	TL G	TL M	TL A	TL ■ L	EM ◇■ K 🛒	TL C	EM ◇■ N 🛒	TL H	TL A	TL ■ O	TL ■ B	TL G	TL M	TL A	TL ■ P	TL ■ L	EM ◇■ K 🛒
Gatwick Airport ✈	d				05 56	06 25										06 29	06 55						
Elephant & Castle ⊖173,179	d		06 44	06 49					07 04					07 14	07 19					07 34			
London Bridge ⊖	d				06 51	06 54		06 58		07 06						07 21	07 24		07 28		07 35	07 41	
London Blackfriars ⊖	d		06 49	06 54	06 57	07 02		07 04	07 09	07 12				07 19	07 24	07 27	07 32		07 34	07 39	07 42	07 47	
City Thameslink ■	d		06 51	06 56	06 59	07 04		07 06	07 11	07 14				07 21	07 26	07 29	07 34		07 36	07 41	07 44	07 49	
Farringdon ■ ⊖	d		06 54	06 59	07 01	07 06		07 09	07 14	07 16				07 24	07 29	07 31	07 36		07 39	07 44	07 46	07 51	
St Pancras International ⊖	d		06 58	07 03	07 06	07 11		07 13	07 18	07 21	07 35		07 49	07 28	07 33	07 36	07 41		07 43	07 48	07 51	07 56	08 05
Kentish Town ⊖	d			07 08					07 23					07 33					07 48				
WestHampsteadThameslink ⊖	d		07 07	07 14				07 22	07 28	07 29				07 37	07 43				07 52	07 58			
Cricklewood	d			07 17				07 25						07 40					07 55				
Hendon	d			07 20				07 29						07 44					07 59				
Mill Hill Broadway	d		07 16	07 23				07 32	07 36					07 47	07 52				08 02	08 07			
Elstree & Borehamwood	d	←	07 20	07 27			←	07 36	07 40			←		07 51	07 56			←	08 06	08 11			
Radlett	d	07 09	07 24	07 31			07 24	07 40	07 44			07 40		07 55	07 59			07 55	08 10	08 14			
St Albans City	d	07 17	→	07a37	07 25	07 29	07 32	→	07a51	07 41		07 47		→	08a06	07 54	07 59	08 02	→	08a21		08 14	
Harpenden	d	07 26				07 34	07 39			07 48		07 56					08 07	08 11				08 20	
Luton Airport Parkway ■ ✈	d	07 32			07 34	07 40	07 46			07 53	07 56	08 02					08 12	08 17				08 25	08 28
Luton ■10	d	07a36			07 38	07 44	07a50			07 58		08a06				08 05	08 15	08a20			08 18	08 30	
Leagrave	d					07 48				08 01						08 10	08 19				08 23	08 34	
Harlington	d					07 52				08 06						08 14					08 27	08 38	
Flitwick	d				07 47	07 56				08 10						08 18					08 31	08 42	
Bedford ■	a				07 58	08 11				08 21	08 10		08 24			08 30	08 35				08 45	08 54	08 42

A From Sutton (Surrey)
B From Brighton
C From Rainham (Kent)
D To Leicester
E From Three Bridges
F To Sheffield
G From Orpington
H From Orpington to Luton
I From Gillingham (Kent)
J From Gillingham (Kent) to Luton
K To Nottingham
L From East Grinstead
M From Rainham (Kent) to Luton
N To Corby
O From Horsham
P From Littlehampton

Table T052MML-F

Mondays to Fridays

16 December to 15 May

Gatwick Airport and London - St Albans, Luton and Bedford

Station		TL	TL	TL	TL ■1	TL ■1	TL	TL	TL	TL ■1	TL	TL	TL	TL ■1	EM ◇■1	TL ■1	TL	TL	TL	EM ◇■1	TL ■1	TL ■1	TL
		A	B	C	D	E	F	G	C	H	A	B	C	D	I 🍴	E	F	A	C	J 🍴	K	H	B
Gatwick Airport ✈	d				06 59	07 25								07 29		07 55							
Elephant & Castle ⊖173,179	d		07 44	07 49					08 04			08 14	08 19						08 34				08 44
London Bridge ⊖	d				07 51	07 54		07 58		08 11				08 21		08 24		08 28			08 35	08 41	
London Blackfriars ⊖	d		07 49	07 54	07 57	08 02		08 04	08 09	08 17		08 19	08 24	08 27		08 32		08 34	08 39		08 42	08 47	08 49
City Thameslink ■3	d		07 51	07 56	07 59	08 04		08 06	08 11	08 19		08 21	08 26	08 29		08 34		08 36	08 41		08 44	08 49	08 51
Farringdon ■3 ⊖	d		07 54	07 59	08 01	08 06		08 09	08 14	08 21		08 24	08 29	08 31		08 36		08 39	08 44		08 46	08 51	08 54
St Pancras International ⊖	d		07 58	08 03	08 06	08 11		08 13	08 18	08 26		08 28	08 33	08 36	08 47	08 41		08 43	08 48	09 05	08 51	08 56	08 58
Kentish Town ⊖	d		08 03	08 08				08 18	08 23			08 33						08 48					09 03
WestHampsteadThameslink ⊖	d		08 07	08 13				08 22	08 29			08 37	08 43					08a52	08 58				09 07
Cricklewood	d		08 10					08 25				08 40											09 10
Hendon	d		08 14					08 29				08 44											09 14
Mill Hill Broadway	d		08 17	08 22				08 32	08 37			08 47	08 52						09 07				09 17
Elstree & Borehamwood	d	←	08 21	08 26			←	08 36	08 41		←	08 51	08 56				←		09 11				09 21
Radlett	d	08 10	08 25	08 29			08 25	08 40	08 44		08 40	08 55	08 59				08 55		09 14				09 25
St Albans City	d	08 17	→	08a36	08 25	08 29	08 32	→	08a51	08 44	08 47	→	09a06	08 54		08 59	09 02		09a21			09 15	→
Harpenden	d	08 24				08 35	08 39			08 51	08 55					09 06	09 10					09 21	
Luton Airport Parkway ■7 ✈	d	08 30			08 34	08 40	08 46			08 57	09 01			09 03		09 11	09 16			09 26		09 26	
Luton ■10	d	08a34			08 38	08 45	08a50			09 01	09a04			09 07	09 12	09 16	09a20				09 18	09 31	
Leagrave	d					08 49				09 04											09 22	09 34	
Harlington	d					08 53				09 09											09 26	09 39	
Flitwick	d				08 47	08 57				09 13				09 16							09 30	09 43	
Bedford ■7	a				09 00	09 09				09 24				09 28	09 26	09 38				09 40	09 42	09 54	

Station		TL	TL ■1	TL	TL	TL	TL ■1	TL ■1	EM ◇■1	TL	TL	TL ■1	TL	TL	TL	TL ■1	TL ■1	EM ◇■1	TL	TL	TL ■1	TL	TL
		C	D	F	A	C	E	H	I 🍴	B	C	D	F	G	C	E	H	J 🍴	A	C	D	G	C
Gatwick Airport ✈	d		07 59				08 36					08 29				09 06					08 59		
Elephant & Castle ⊖173,179	d	08 49				09 04				09 14	09 19				09 34					09 49			10 04
London Bridge ⊖	d		08 51		08 58		09 05	09 11				09 21		09 28		09 35	09 41				09 51	09 58	
London Blackfriars ⊖	d	08 54	08 57		09 04	09 09	09 12	09 17		09 19	09 24	09 27		09 34	09 39	09 42	09 47			09 54	09 57	10 04	10 09
City Thameslink ■3	d	08 56	08 59		09 06	09 11	09 14	09 19		09 21	09 26	09 29		09 36	09 41	09 44	09 49			09 56	09 59	10 06	10 11
Farringdon ■3 ⊖	d	08 59	09 01		09 09	09 14	09 16	09 21		09 24	09 29	09 31		09 39	09 44	09 46	09 51			09 59	10 01	10 09	10 14
St Pancras International ⊖	d	09 03	09 06		09 13	09 18	09 21	09 26	09 47	09 28	09 33	09 36		09 43	09 48	09 51	09 56	10 05		10 03	10 06	10 13	10 18
Kentish Town ⊖	d				09 18					09 33				09 48	09 53					10 08			10 23
WestHampsteadThameslink ⊖	d	09 14			09a22	09 28				09 37	09 44	09 44		09 52	09 59					10 14		10 22	10 29
Cricklewood	d									09 40				09 55	10 02					10 17			10 32
Hendon	d									09 44				09 59	10 05					10 20			10 35
Mill Hill Broadway	d	09 22				09 37				09 47	09 51			10 02	10 08					10 23		10 31	10 38
Elstree & Borehamwood	d	09 26		←		09 41				09 51	09 55		←	10 06	10 12				←	10 27		10 35	10 42
Radlett	d	09 29		09 25		09 44				09 55	09 59		09 55	10 14	10 18				10 14	10 31		10 39	10 46
St Albans City	d	09a36	09 25	09 32		09a51		09 45		→	10a06	09 56	10 02	→	10a23		10 16		10 20	10a37	10 25	→	10a52
Harpenden	d		09 31	09 37			09 43	09 51				10 02	10 07			10 13	10 21		10 27		10 31		
Luton Airport Parkway ■7 ✈	d		09 36	09 45			09 49	09 56				10 08	10 15			10 19	10 27	10 28	10 32		10 37		
Luton ■10	d		09 40	09a49			09 53	10 01	10 09			10 12	10a19			10 23	10 31		10a36		10 41		
Leagrave	d		09 44					10 04				10 16					10 35				10 44		
Harlington	d		09 48					10 09				10 20					10 39				10 49		
Flitwick	d		09 52				10 02	10 13				10 24				10 32	10 43				10 53		
Bedford ■7	a		10 05				10 16	10 26	10 23			10 36				10 44	10 55	10 42			11 05		

Station		TL ■1	TL	TL	EM ◇■1	TL ■1	TL	TL	TL ■1	EM ◇■1	TL	TL	TL ■1	TL	TL	TL ■1	TL	TL	EM ◇■1	TL ■1	TL	TL
		E	A	C	I 🍴		G	C	E	J 🍴	A	C		G	C	E	A	C	I 🍴		G	C
Gatwick Airport ✈	d	09 36				09 33			10 06				10 03			10 36				10 33		
Elephant & Castle ⊖173,179	d			10 19				10 34				10 49			11 04			11 19				11 34
London Bridge ⊖	d	10 05				10 21	10 28		10 35				10 51	10 58		11 05				11 21	11 28	
London Blackfriars ⊖	d	10 12		10 24		10 27	10 34	10 39	10 42			10 54	10 57	11 04	11 09	11 12		11 24		11 27	11 34	11 39
City Thameslink ■3	d	10 14		10 26		10 29	10 36	10 41	10 44			10 56	10 59	11 06	11 11	11 14		11 26		11 29	11 36	11 41
Farringdon ■3 ⊖	d	10 16		10 29		10 31	10 39	10 44	10 46			10 59	11 01	11 09	11 14	11 16		11 29		11 31	11 39	11 44
St Pancras International ⊖	d	10 21		10 33	10 47	10 36	10 43	10 48	10 51	11 05		11 03	11 06	11 13	11 18	11 21		11 33	11 47	11 36	11 43	11 48
Kentish Town ⊖	d			10 38				10 53				11 08			11 23			11 38				11 53
WestHampsteadThameslink ⊖	d	10 29		10 44			10 52	10 59	10 59			11 14		11 22	11 29	11 29		11 44			11 52	11 59
Cricklewood	d			10 47				11 02				11 17			11 32			11 47				12 02
Hendon	d			10 50				11 05				11 21			11 35			11 50				12 05
Mill Hill Broadway	d			10 53			11 01	11 08				11 24		11 31	11 38			11 53			12 01	12 08
Elstree & Borehamwood	d		←	10 57			11 05	11 12			←	11 28		11 35	11 42		←	11 57			12 05	12 12
Radlett	d		10 39	11 01			11 09	11 16			11 09	11 32		11 39	11 46		11 39	12 01			12 09	12 16
St Albans City	d	10 41	10 45	11a07		10 55	→	11a22	11 11		11 15	11a38	11 25	→	11a52	11 41	11 45	12a07		11 55	→	12a22
Harpenden	d	10 47	10 51			11 02			11 17		11 21		11 31			11 47	11 51			12 01		
Luton Airport Parkway ■7 ✈	d	10 53	10 57			11 07			11 23	11 26	11 27		11 36			11 53	11 57			12 06		
Luton ■10	d	10 57	11a01		11 09	11 12			11 27		11a31		11 41			11 57	12a01		12 09	12 11		
Leagrave	d	11 01				11 16			11 31				11 45			12 01				12 15		
Harlington	d	11 05				11 20			11 35				11 49			12 05				12 19		
Flitwick	d	11 09				11 24			11 39				11 53			12 09				12 23		
Bedford ■7	a	11 21			11 23	11 36			11 51	11 40			12 05			12 21			12 23	12 35		

A From Rainham (Kent)
B From Orpington to Luton
C From Sutton (Surrey)
D From Horsham
E From Brighton
F From Orpington
G From Rainham (Kent) to Luton
H From East Grinstead
I To Corby
J To Nottingham
K From Littlehampton

Table T052MML-F

Mondays to Fridays

16 December to 15 May

Gatwick Airport and London - St Albans, Luton and Bedford

Station		TL ■1	EM ◇■1	TL	TL	TL ■1	TL	TL	TL ■1	TL	TL	EM ◇■1	TL ■1	TL	TL	TL ■1	EM ◇■1	TL	TL	TL ■1	TL	TL	TL ■1
		A	B 🍴	C	D		E	D	A	C	D	F 🍴		E	D	A	B 🍴	C	D		E	D	A
Gatwick Airport ✈	d	11 06				11 03			11 36				11 33			12 06				12 03			12 36
Elephant & Castle ⊖173,179	d				11 49			12 04			12 19				12 34				12 49			13 04	
London Bridge ⊖	d	11 35				11 51	11 58		12 05				12 21	12 28		12 35				12 51	12 58		13 05
London Blackfriars ⊖	d	11 42			11 54	11 57	12 04	12 09	12 12		12 24		12 27	12 34	12 39	12 42			12 54	12 57	13 04	13 09	13 12
City Thameslink ■3	d	11 44			11 56	11 59	12 06	12 11	12 14		12 26		12 29	12 36	12 41	12 44			12 56	12 59	13 06	13 11	13 14
Farringdon ■3 ⊖	d	11 46			11 59	12 01	12 09	12 14	12 16		12 29		12 31	12 39	12 44	12 46			12 59	13 01	13 09	13 14	13 16
St Pancras International ⊖	d	11 51	12 05		12 03	12 06	12 13	12 18	12 21		12 33	12 47	12 36	12 43	12 48	12 51	13 05		13 03	13 06	13 13	13 18	13 21
Kentish Town ⊖	d				12 08			12 23			12 38				12 53				13 08			13 23	
WestHampsteadThameslink ⊖	d	11 59			12 14		12 22	12 29	12 29		12 44			12 52	12 59	12 59			13 14		13 22	13 29	13 29
Cricklewood	d				12 17			12 32			12 47				13 02				13 17			13 32	
Hendon	d				12 20			12 35			12 50				13 05				13 20			13 35	
Mill Hill Broadway	d				12 23		12 31	12 38			12 53			13 01	13 08				13 23		13 31	13 38	
Elstree & Borehamwood	d			←	12 27		12 35	12 42		←	12 57			13 05	13 12			←	13 27		13 35	13 42	
Radlett	d			12 09	12 31		12 39	12 46		12 39	13 01			13 09	13 16			13 09	13 31		13 39	13 46	
St Albans City	d	12 11		12 15	12a37	12 25	→	12a52	12 41	12 45	13a07		12 55	→	13a22	13 11		13 15	13a37	13 25	→	13a52	13 41
Harpenden	d	12 17		12 21		12 31			12 47	12 51			13 01			13 17		13 21		13 31			13 47
Luton Airport Parkway ■7 ✈	d	12 23	12 26	12 27		12 36			12 53	12 57			13 06			13 23	13 26	13 27		13 36			13 53
Luton ■10	d	12 27		12a31		12 41			12 57	13a01		13 09	13 11			13 27		13a31		13 41			13 57
Leagrave	d	12 31				12 45			13 01				13 15			13 31				13 45			14 01
Harlington	d	12 35				12 49			13 05				13 19			13 35				13 49			14 05
Flitwick	d	12 39				12 53			13 09				13 23			13 39				13 53			14 09
Bedford ■7	a	12 51	12 40			13 05			13 21			13 23	13 35			13 51	13 40			14 05			14 21

Station		TL	TL	EM ◇■1	TL ■1	TL	TL	TL ■1	EM ◇■1	TL	TL	TL ■1	TL	TL	TL ■1	TL	TL	EM ◇■1	TL ■1	TL	TL	TL ■1	EM ◇■1
		C	D	F 🍴		E	D	A	B 🍴	C	D		E	D	A	C	D	F 🍴		E	D	A	B 🍴
Gatwick Airport ✈	d				12 32			13 06				13 03			13 36				13 32			14 06	
Elephant & Castle ⊖173,179	d		13 19				13 34				13 49			14 04			14 19				14 34		
London Bridge ⊖	d				13 21	13 28		13 35				13 51	13 58		14 05				14 21	14 28		14 35	
London Blackfriars ⊖	d		13 24		13 27	13 34	13 39	13 42			13 54	13 57	14 04	14 09	14 12		14 24		14 27	14 34	14 39	14 42	
City Thameslink ■3	d		13 26		13 29	13 36	13 41	13 44			13 56	13 59	14 06	14 11	14 14		14 26		14 29	14 36	14 41	14 44	
Farringdon ■3 ⊖	d		13 29		13 31	13 39	13 44	13 46			13 59	14 01	14 09	14 14	14 16		14 29		14 31	14 39	14 44	14 46	
St Pancras International ⊖	d		13 33	13 47	13 36	13 43	13 48	13 51	14 05		14 03	14 06	14 13	14 18	14 21		14 33	14 47	14 36	14 43	14 48	14 51	15 05
Kentish Town ⊖	d		13 38				13 53				14 08			14 23			14 38				14 53		
WestHampsteadThameslink ⊖	d		13 44			13 52	13 59	13 59			14 15		14 22	14 29	14 29		14 44			14 52	14 59	14 59	
Cricklewood	d		13 47				14 02				14 17			14 32			14 47				15 02		
Hendon	d		13 50				14 05				14 20			14 35			14 50				15 05		
Mill Hill Broadway	d		13 53			14 01	14 08				14 23		14 31	14 38			14 53			15 01	15 08		
Elstree & Borehamwood	d	←	13 57			14 05	14 12			←	14 27		14 35	14 42		←	14 57			15 05	15 12		
Radlett	d	13 39	14 01			14 09	14 16			14 09	14 31		14 39	14 46		14 39	15 01			15 09	15 16		
St Albans City	d	13 45	14a07		13 55	→	14a22	14 11		14 15	14a37	14 25	→	14a52	14 41	14 45	15a07		14 55	→	15a22	15 11	
Harpenden	d	13 51			14 01			14 17		14 21		14 31			14 47	14 51			15 01			15 17	
Luton Airport Parkway ■7 ✈	d	13 57			14 06			14 23	14 26	14 27		14 36			14 53	14 57			15 06			15 23	15 26
Luton ■10	d	14a01		14 09	14 11			14 27		14a31		14 41			14 57	15a01		15 09	15 11			15 27	
Leagrave	d				14 15			14 31				14 45			15 01				15 15			15 31	
Harlington	d				14 19			14 35				14 49			15 05				15 19			15 35	
Flitwick	d				14 23			14 39				14 53			15 09				15 23			15 39	
Bedford ■7	a			14 23	14 35			14 51	14 40			15 05			15 21			15 23	15 35			15 51	15 40

Station		TL	TL	TL ■1	TL	TL	TL ■1	TL	TL	EM ◇■1	TL ■1	TL	TL	TL ■1	TL	TL	TL ■1	TL	TL	TL ■1	TL ■1	TL	TL
		C	D		E	D	A	C	D	F 🍴		E	D	A	C	D		E	D	A		C	G
Gatwick Airport ✈	d			14 03			14 36				14 32			15 06			15 03			15 36	15 27		
Elephant & Castle ⊖173,179	d		14 49			15 04			15 19				15 34			15 49			16 04				16 14
London Bridge ⊖	d			14 51	14 58		15 05				15 21	15 28		15 35			15 51	15 58		16 05	16 11		
London Blackfriars ⊖	d		14 54	14 57	15 04	15 09	15 12		15 24		15 27	15 34	15 39	15 42		15 54	15 57	16 04	16 09	16 12	16 17		16 19
City Thameslink ■3	d		14 56	14 59	15 06	15 11	15 14		15 26		15 29	15 36	15 41	15 44		15 56	15 59	16 06	16 11	16 14	16 19		16 21
Farringdon ■3 ⊖	d		14 59	15 01	15 09	15 14	15 16		15 29		15 31	15 39	15 44	15 46		15 59	16 01	16 09	16 14	16 16	16 21		16 24
St Pancras International ⊖	d		15 03	15 06	15 13	15 18	15 21		15 33	15 47	15 36	15 43	15 48	15 51		16 03	16 06	16 13	16 18	16 21	16 26		16 28
Kentish Town ⊖	d		15 08			15 23			15 38				15 53			16 08		16 18					16 33
WestHampsteadThameslink ⊖	d		15 14		15 22	15 29	15 29		15 44			15 52	15 59	15 59		16 14		16 22	16 29				16 37
Cricklewood	d		15 17			15 32			15 47				16 02			16 17		16 26					16 41
Hendon	d		15 20			15 35			15 50				16 05			16 20		16 29					16 44
Mill Hill Broadway	d		15 23		15 31	15 38			15 53			16 01	16 08			16 23		16 33	16 37				16 48
Elstree & Borehamwood	d	←	15 27		15 35	15 42		←	15 57			16 05	16 12		←	16 27		16 37	16 41			←	16 52
Radlett	d	15 09	15 31		15 39	15 46		15 39	16 01			16 13	16 17		16 13	16 31		16 40	16 45			16 40	16 56
St Albans City	d	15 15	15a37	15 25	→	15a52	15 41	15 45	16a07		15 55	→	16a23	16 14	16 19	16a37	16 25	→	16a51	16 39	16 44	16 47	→
Harpenden	d	15 21		15 31			15 47	15 51			16 01			16 20	16 27		16 31				16 51	16 55	
Luton Airport Parkway ■7 ✈	d	15 27		15 36			15 53	15 57			16 06			16 25	16 32		16 36				16 56	17 01	
Luton ■10	d	15a31		15 41			15 57	16a01		16 09	16 11			16 29	16a36		16 41			16 50	17 01	17a05	
Leagrave	d			15 45			16 01				16 15			16 33			16 46				17 05		
Harlington	d			15 49			16 05				16 19			16 37			16 51				17 09		
Flitwick	d			15 53			16 09				16 23			16 41			16 55				17 13		
Bedford ■7	a			16 05			16 21			16 23	16 35			16 53			17 09			17 06	17 26		

A From Brighton
B To Nottingham
C From Rainham (Kent)
D From Sutton (Surrey)
E From Rainham (Kent) to Luton
F To Corby
G From Orpington to Luton

Table T052MML-F

Mondays to Fridays

16 December to 15 May

Gatwick Airport and London - St Albans, Luton and Bedford

Station		TL A	TL 1	TL B	TL C	TL A	TL 1 D	TL 1	TL E	TL F	TL A	TL 1	TL 1 G	TL B	TL C	TL A	TL 1 D	TL 1	TL E	TL F	TL A	TL 1
Gatwick Airport	d		15 32				16 06	15 57				16 03	16 24				16 36	16 27				16 33
Elephant & Castle ⊖173,179	d	16 19				16 34				16 44	16 49					17 04				17 14	17 19	
London Bridge ⊖	d		16 21		16 28		16 35	16 41				16 51	16 55		16 58		17 05	17 11				17 21
London Blackfriars ⊖	d	16 24	16 27		16 34	16 39	16 42	16 47		16 49	16 54	16 57	17 02		17 04	17 09	17 12	17 17		17 19	17 24	17 27
City Thameslink 3	d	16 26	16 29		16 36	16 41	16 44	16 49		16 51	16 56	16 59	17 04		17 06	17 11	17 14	17 19		17 21	17 26	17 29
Farringdon 3 ⊖	d	16 29	16 31		16 39	16 44	16 46	16 51		16 54	16 59	17 01	17 06		17 09	17 14	17 16	17 21		17 24	17 29	17 31
St Pancras International ⊖	d	16 33	16 36		16 43	16 48	16 51	16 56		16 58	17 03	17 06	17 11		17 13	17 18	17 21	17 26		17 28	17 33	17 36
Kentish Town ⊖	d				16 48					17 03					17 18					17 33		
WestHampsteadThameslink ⊖	d	16 44	16 44		16 52	16 59				17 07	17 14				17 22	17 29				17 37	17 44	
Cricklewood	d				16 56					17 11					17 26					17 41		
Hendon	d				16 59					17 14					17 29					17 44		
Mill Hill Broadway	d	16 52			17 03	17 07				17 18	17 22				17 33	17 37				17 48	17 52	
Elstree & Borehamwood	d	16 56		←	17 07	17 11			←	17 22	17 26			←	17 37	17 41			←	17 52	17 56	
Radlett	d	17 00		16 56	17 10	17 15			17 10	17 25	17 30			17 25	17 40	17 45			17 40	17 55	18 00	
St Albans City	d	17a06	16 56	17 02	→	17a21	17 09	17 14	17 17	→	17a36	17 24	17 29	17 32	→	17a51	17 39	17 44	17 47	→	18a06	17 54
Harpenden	d		17 02	17 08				17 21	17 26			17 30	17 36	17 41				17 51	17 55			18 00
Luton Airport Parkway 7 ✈	d		17 08	17 14				17 26	17 32				17 41	17 47				17 56	18 01			
Luton 10	d		17 12	17a20			17 20	17 31	17a36			17 37	17 45	17a50			17 50	18 01	18a05			18 07
Leagrave	d		17 15					17 35					17 49					18 05				
Harlington	d		17 20					17 39					17 53					18 09				
Flitwick	d		17 24					17 43				17 47	17 57					18 13				18 17
Bedford 7	a		17 35				17 40	17 55				17 58	18 09				18 06	18 25				18 28

Station		TL 1 G	TL B	TL C	TL A	TL 1 D	TL 1	TL E	TL F	TL A	TL 1	TL 1 G	TL B	TL C	TL A	TL 1 D	TL 1	TL E	TL F	TL A	TL 1	TL B	TL C
Gatwick Airport	d	16 54				17 06	16 57				17 03	17 24				17 36	17 27				17 33		
Elephant & Castle ⊖173,179	d				17 34				17 44	17 49					18 04				18 14	18 19			
London Bridge ⊖	d	17 24		17 28		17 35	17 41				17 51	17 54		17 58		18 05	18 11				18 21		18 28
London Blackfriars ⊖	d	17 32		17 34	17 39	17 42	17 47		17 49	17 54	17 57	18 02		18 04	18 09	18 12	18 17		18 19	18 24	18 27		18 34
City Thameslink 3	d	17 34		17 36	17 41	17 44	17 49		17 51	17 56	17 59	18 04		18 06	18 11	18 14	18 19		18 21	18 26	18 29		18 36
Farringdon 3 ⊖	d	17 36		17 39	17 44	17 46	17 51		17 54	17 59	18 01	18 06		18 09	18 14	18 16	18 21		18 24	18 29	18 31		18 39
St Pancras International ⊖	d	17 41		17 43	17 48	17 51	17 56		17 58	18 03	18 06	18 11		18 13	18 18	18 21	18 26		18 28	18 33	18 36		18 43
Kentish Town ⊖	d			17 48					18 03					18 18					18 33				18 48
WestHampsteadThameslink ⊖	d			17 52	17 59				18 07	18 14				18 22	18 29				18 37	18 44			18 52
Cricklewood	d			17 56					18 11					18 26					18 41				18 56
Hendon	d			17 59					18 14					18 29					18 44				18 59
Mill Hill Broadway	d			18 03	18 07				18 18	18 22				18 33	18 37				18 48	18 52			19 03
Elstree & Borehamwood	d		←	18 07	18 11			←	18 22	18 26			←	18 37	18 41			←	18 52	18 56		←	19 07
Radlett	d		17 55	18 14	18 18			18 14	18 25	18 30			18 25	18 40	18 45			18 40	18 55	19 00		18 55	19 10
St Albans City	d	17 59	18 02	→	18a23	18 09	18 16	18 20	→	18a36	18 24	18 29	18 32	→	18a51	18 39	18 44	18 47	→	19a06	18 55	19 02	→
Harpenden	d	18 05	18 10				18 22	18 26			18 30	18 36	18 41				18 51	18 55			19 02	19 10	
Luton Airport Parkway 7 ✈	d	18 11	18 16				18 27	18 31				18 42	18 47				18 56	19 01			19 07	19 16	
Luton 10	d	18 15	18a21			18 19	18 32	18a35			18 37	18 46	18a51			18 50	19 01	19a05			19 12	19a21	
Leagrave	d	18 19					18 35					18 50					19 05				19 16		
Harlington	d	18 24					18 40					18 55					19 09				19 20		
Flitwick	d	18 28					18 44				18 47	18 59					19 13				19 24		
Bedford 7	a	18 41				18 36	18 55				18 59	19 15				19 06	19 25				19 36		

Station		TL A	TL 1 D	TL 1 H	EM ◇1 I	TL E	TL F	TL A	TL 1	TL B	TL C	TL A	TL 1 D	TL 1 H	TL E	TL A	EM ◇1 J	TL 1	TL C	TL A	TL 1 D	TL 1 H	EM ◇1 K
Gatwick Airport	d		18 06						18 03				18 36					18 33			19 06		
Elephant & Castle ⊖173,179	d	18 34					18 44	18 49				19 04				19 19				19 34			
London Bridge ⊖	d		18 35	18 41					18 51		18 58		19 05	19 11				19 21	19 28		19 35	19 41	
London Blackfriars ⊖	d	18 39	18 42	18 47			18 49	18 54	18 57		19 04	19 09	19 12	19 17		19 24		19 27	19 34	19 39	19 42	19 47	
City Thameslink 3	d	18 41	18 44	18 49			18 51	18 56	18 59		19 06	19 11	19 14	19 19		19 26		19 29	19 36	19 41	19 44	19 49	
Farringdon 3 ⊖	d	18 44	18 46	18 51			18 54	18 59	19 01		19 09	19 14	19 16	19 21		19 29		19 31	19 39	19 44	19 46	19 51	
St Pancras International ⊖	d	18 48	18 51	18 56	19 04		18 58	19 03	19 06		19 13	19 18	19 21	19 26		19 33	19 47	19 36	19 43	19 48	19 51	19 56	20 05
Kentish Town ⊖	d						19 03				19 18					19 38				19 53			
WestHampsteadThameslink ⊖	d	18 59					19 07	19 14			19 22	19 29				19 44		19 44	19 52	19 59			
Cricklewood	d						19 11				19 26					19 47				20 02			
Hendon	d						19 14				19 29					19 50				20 05			
Mill Hill Broadway	d	19 07					19 18	19 22			19 33	19 37				19 53			20 01	20 08			
Elstree & Borehamwood	d	19 11				←	19 22	19 26		←	19 37	19 41			←	19 57			20 05	20 12			
Radlett	d	19 15				19 10	19 25	19 30		19 25	19 44	19 48			19 44	20 01			20 09	20 16			
St Albans City	d	19a21	19 10	19 14		19 17	→	19a36	19 25	19 32	→	19a53	19 40	19 46	19 50	20a07		19 56	→	20a22	20 10	20 14	
Harpenden	d		19 16	19 21		19 26			19 31	19 41			19 46	19 52	19 57			20 02			20 16	20 21	
Luton Airport Parkway 7 ✈	d			19 26	19 28	19 32			19 36	19 47				19 57	20 02			20 08				20 26	20 29
Luton 10	d		19 22	19 31		19a36			19 41	19a51			19 52	20 02	20a06		20 10	20 12			20 22	20 31	
Leagrave	d			19 35					19 45					20 05				20 16				20 35	
Harlington	d			19 39					19 49					20 10				20 21				20 39	
Flitwick	d		19 33	19 43					19 53				20 03	20 14				20 25			20 33	20 43	
Bedford 7	a		19 44	19 55	19 43				20 05				20 14	20 26			20 23	20 36			20 44	20 56	20 42

A From Sutton (Surrey)
B From Orpington
C From Rainham (Kent) to Luton
D From Brighton
E From Rainham (Kent)
F From Orpington to Luton
G From Three Bridges
H From East Grinstead
I To Leeds
J To Corby
K To Nottingham

Table T052MML-F

Mondays to Fridays

16 December to 15 May

Gatwick Airport and London - St Albans, Luton and Bedford

Station		TL A	TL B	TL 1	TL C	TL B	TL 1 D	TL A	TL B	TL 1	TL C	TL B	TL 1 D	TL A	TL B	EM ◇1 E	TL 1	EM ◇1 F	TL C	TL 1 D	TL A	TL B	TL B
Gatwick Airport	d			19 03			19 36			19 33			20 06				20 03			20 36			
Elephant & Castle ⊖173,179	d		19 49			20 04			20 19			20 34			20 49							21 11	21 19
London Bridge ⊖	d			19 51	19 58		20 05			20 21	20 28		20 35				20 51		20 58	21 05			
London Blackfriars ⊖	d		19 54	19 57	20 04	20 09	20 12		20 24	20 27	20 34	20 39	20 42		20 54		20 57		21 04	21 12		21 17	21 24
City Thameslink 3	d		19 56	19 59	20 06	20 11	20 14		20 26	20 29	20 36	20 41	20 44		20 56		20 59		21 06	21 14		21 19	21 26
Farringdon 3 ⊖	d		19 59	20 01	20 09	20 14	20 16		20 29	20 31	20 39	20 44	20 46		20 59		21 01		21 09	21 16		21 21	21 29
St Pancras International ⊖	d		20 03	20 06	20 13	20 18	20 21		20 33	20 36	20 43	20 48	20 51		21 03	21 05	21 06	21 30	21 13	21 21		21 26	21 33
Kentish Town ⊖	d		20 08			20 23			20 38			20 53			21 08				21 18				21 38
WestHampsteadThameslink ⊖	d		20 14		20 22	20 29	20 29		20 44		20 52	20 59	20 59		21 14				21 24	21 29		21 34	21 44
Cricklewood	d		20 17			20 32			20 47			21 02			21 17				21 27				21 47
Hendon	d		20 20			20 35			20 50			21 05			21 20				21 31				21 50
Mill Hill Broadway	d		20 23		20 31	20 38			20 53		21 01	21 08			21 23				21 34			21 40	21 53
Elstree & Borehamwood	d	←	20 27		20 35	20 42		←	20 57		21 05	21 12		←	21 27				21 38		←	21 44	21 57
Radlett	d	20 09	20 31		20 39	20 46		20 39	21 01		21 09	21 16		21 09	21 31				21 42		21 42	21 48	22 01
St Albans City	d	20 17	20a37	20 25	→	20a52	20 41	20 45	21a08	20 55	→	21a22	21 11	21 15	21a37		21 25		→	21 41	21 48	21a54	22a07
Harpenden	d	20 27		20 31			20 47	20 51		21 01			21 17	21 21			21 31			21 47	21 57		
Luton Airport Parkway 7 ✈	d	20 32		20 36			20 53	20 57		21 06			21 23	21 27		21 27	21 36			21 53	22 02		
Luton 10	d	20a36		20 41			20 57	21a01		21 11			21 27	21a31			21 41	21 55		21 57	22a06		
Leagrave	d			20 45			21 01			21 15			21 31				21 45			22 01			
Harlington	d			20 49			21 05			21 19			21 35				21 49			22 05			
Flitwick	d			20 53			21 09			21 23			21 39				21 53			22 09			
Bedford 7	a			21 05			21 21			21 35			21 51			21 40	22 05	22 08		22 21			

Station		TL 1	EM ◇1 F	EM ◇1 E	TL C	TL B	TL 1 D	TL A	TL B	TL 1	TL A	EM ◇1 G	TL H	TL 1 D	TL B	TL H	TL 1	TL B	TL A	TL H	TL 1 D	TL B
Gatwick Airport	d	20 32					21 06			21 03				21 36			21 32				22 06	
Elephant & Castle ⊖173,179	d					21 34			21 49				22 04			22 19				22 34		
London Bridge ⊖	d	21 21			21 28		21 35			21 51	21 58			22 05			22 21		22 28		22 35	
London Blackfriars ⊖	d	21 27			21 34	21 39	21 42		21 54	21 57	22 04		22 09	22 12		22 24	22 27		22 34	22 39	22 42	
City Thameslink 3	d	21 29			21 36	21 41	21 44		21 56	21 59	22 06		22 11	22 14		22 26	22 29		22 36	22 41	22 44	
Farringdon 3 ⊖	d	21 31			21 39	21 44	21 46		21 59	22 01	22 09		22 14	22 16		22 29	22 31		22 39	22 44	22 46	
St Pancras International ⊖	d	21 36	21 50	22 00	21 43	21 48	21 51		22 03	22 06	22 13	22 20	22 18	22 21		22 33	22 36		22 43	22 48	22 51	←
Kentish Town ⊖	d					21 53			22 08				22 23			22 38				22 58		22 58
WestHampsteadThameslink ⊖	d				21 52	21 59	21 59		22 14		22a21		22 29	22 29		22 44			22a51	→	22 59	23 02
Cricklewood	d					22 02			22 17				22 31			22 47						23 06
Hendon	d					22 06			22 20				22 34			22 50						23 09
Mill Hill Broadway	d				22 01	22 09			22 23				22 37			22 53						23 12
Elstree & Borehamwood	d				22 05	22 13		←	22 27				22 41		←	22 57		←				23 16
Radlett	d				22 09	22 17		22 09	22 31				22 45		22 45	23 01		23 01				23 20
St Albans City	d	21 55			→	22a23	22 11	22 15	22a37	22 25			→	22 41	22 53	→	22 57	23 09			23 16	23 27
Harpenden	d	22 01					22 17	22 21		22 31				22 47	22 58		23 04	23 15			23 22	23 33
Luton Airport Parkway 7 ✈	d	22 06	22 13				22 23	22 27		22 36		22 42		22 53	23 05		23 10	23 20			23 27	23 38
Luton 10	d	22 11		22 25			22 27	22a31		22 41				22 57	23 09		23 14	23 25			23 31	23 43
Leagrave	d	22 15					22 31			22 45				23 01			23 18				23 35	
Harlington	d	22 19					22 35			22 49				23 05			23 23				23 40	
Flitwick	d	22 23					22 39			22 53				23 09			23 27				23 44	
Bedford 7	a	22 35	22 26	22 39			22 51			23 05		22 57		23 21	23 30		23 38	23 49			23 55	00 03

Station		EM ◇1 F	TL B	TL A	TL 1 D	TL B	TL B	TL A	TL 1 D	TL B	TL B	TL 1 D
Gatwick Airport	d				22 36				23 06			23 34
Elephant & Castle ⊖173,179	d		22 51			23 11	23 21			23 41	23 54	
London Bridge ⊖	d			22 58	23 05			23 28	23 35			
London Blackfriars ⊖	d		22 59	23 04	23 12	23 17	23 29	23 34	23 42	23 49	00 02	00 22
City Thameslink 3	d											
Farringdon 3 ⊖	d		23 04	23 09	23 16	23 21	23 33	23 39	23 46	23 53	00 06	00 26
St Pancras International ⊖	d	23 08	23 08	23 13	23 21	23 26	23 38	23 43	23 51	23 58	00 11	00 31
Kentish Town ⊖	d		23 14			23 31	23 42			00 01		
WestHampsteadThameslink ⊖	d		23 18	23a21	23 29	23 35	23 46	23a51	23 59	00 06	00 20	00 39
Cricklewood	d		23 21			23 39	23 50			00 10		
Hendon	d		23 24			23 42	23 54			00 13		
Mill Hill Broadway	d		23 27			23 45	23 57			00 16		
Elstree & Borehamwood	d		23 31			23 49	00 01			00 20		
Radlett	d		23 35			23 53	00 05			00 24		
St Albans City	d		23 42		23 46	23 59	00 12		00 16	00 32	00 36	00 56
Harpenden	d		23 48		23 52	00 06	00 18		00 22	00 38	00 42	01 02
Luton Airport Parkway 7 ✈	d		23 54		23 58	00 11	00 23		00 28	00 43	00 48	01 08
Luton 10	d	23 47	23 58		00 02	00 16	00 28		00 32	00 48	00 52	01 12
Leagrave	d				00 06	00 20			00 36		00 56	01 16
Harlington	d				00 11	00 24			00 41		01 01	01 21
Flitwick	d				00 15	00 28			00 45		01 05	01 25
Bedford 7	a	00 08	00 18		00 26	00 40	00 48		00 58	01 08	01 18	01 36

A From Rainham (Kent)
B From Sutton (Surrey)
C From Rainham (Kent) to Luton
D From Brighton
E To Nottingham
F To Derby
G To Sheffield
H From Sutton (Surrey) to Bedford

Table T052MML-F

Saturdays

21 December to 16 May

Gatwick Airport and London - St Albans, Luton and Bedford

Station		TL ■ A	TL B	TL B	TL ■ A	TL B	TL B	EM ◇■ C	TL B	TL ■ A	TL ■ A	TL ■ A	TL ■ A	TL ■ D	TL ■ D	TL ■ D	TL ■ D	TL ■ D	TL ■ D	TL	EM ◇■ E	TL ■ A	TL ■ D
Gatwick Airport ✈	d										00 04	00 21	00 42	01 46	02 21	02 46	03 21	03 46	04 21			04 41	05 20
Elephant & Castle ⊖173,179	d								00 04														
London Bridge ⊖	d																					05 26	05 55
London Blackfriars ⊖	d						00 02		00 09	00 22	00 50	01 06	01 36	02 36	03 06	03 36	04 06	04 36	05 06	05 27		05 32	06 02
City Thameslink ■	d																						
Farringdon ■ ⊖	d						00 06		00 13	00 26									05 11	05 31		05 36	06 06
St Pancras International ⊖	d						00 11	00 15	00 18	00 31	01 01	01 16	01 44	02 44	03 14	03 44	04 14	04 44	05 16	05 36	05 48	05 41	06 11
Kentish Town ⊖	d					00 01			00 22		01 05		01 48	02 48		03 48	04 18	04 48		05 40			
WestHampsteadThameslink ⊖	d					00 06	00 20		00 26	00 39	01 09	01 24	01 52	02 52	03 22	03 52	04 22	04 52	05 24	05 44		05 48	06 19
Cricklewood	d					00 10			00 30		01 13		01 56	02 56		03 56	04 26	04 56		05 48			
Hendon	d					00 13			00 33		01 17		02 00	03 00		04 00	04 30	05 00		05 51			
Mill Hill Broadway	d					00 16			00 36		01 20		02 03	03 03		04 03	04 33	05 03		05 54			
Elstree & Borehamwood	d			00 01		00 20			00 40		01 24		02 07	03 07		04 07	04 37	05 07		05 58			
Radlett	d			00 05		00 24			00 44		01 28		02 11	03 11		04 11	04 41	05 11		06 02			
St Albans City	d			00 12	00 16	00 32	00 36		00 52	00 56	01 34	01 41	02 19	03 19	03 41	04 19	04 49	05 19	05 41	06a08		06 00	06 31
Harpenden	d		00 06	00 18	00 22	00 38	00 42		00 58	01 02	01 40	01 47	02 25	03 25	03 47	04 25	04 55	05 25	05 47			06 06	06 37
Luton Airport Parkway ■ ✈	d		00 11	00 23	00 28	00 43	00 48	00 53	01 03	01 08	01 46	01 52	02 30	03 30	03 52	04 30	05 00	05 30	05 52			06 12	06 43
Luton ■	d	00 02	00 16	00 28	00 32	00 48	00 52	00 57	01 08	01 12	01 50	01 57	02 35	03 35	03 57	04 35	05 05	05 35	05 57		06 14	06 16	06 47
Leagrave	d	00 06	00 20		00 36		00 56		01 12	01 16	01 54	02 01	02 39	03 39	04 01	04 39	05 09	05 39	06 01			06 20	06 51
Harlington	d	00 11	00 24		00 41		01 01		01 16	01 21	01 59	02 05	02 43	03 43	04 05	04 43	05 13	05 43	06 05			06 24	06 55
Flitwick	d	00 15	00 28		00 45		01 05		01 20	01 25	02 03	02 09	02 47	03 47	04 09	04 47	05 17	05 47	06 09			06 28	06 59
Bedford ■	a	00 26	00 40	00 48	00 58	01 08	01 18	01 25	01 32	01 36	02 14	02 21	02 59	03 59	04 21	05 01	05 33	05 59	06 21		06 27	06 41	07 11

Station		TL F	TL B	TL ■ D	TL F	TL B	EM ◇■ G	TL ■ A	TL B	TL ■	TL H	TL B	TL ■ A	TL B	EM ◇■ G	EM ◇■ I	TL ■	TL H	TL B	TL ■ A	TL B	EM ◇■ G	TL ■
Gatwick Airport ✈	d			05 33				06 06		06 03			06 36				06 33			07 06			07 03
Elephant & Castle ⊖173,179	d		06 19			06 34			06 49			07 04		07 19					07 34		07 49		
London Bridge ⊖	d	05 58		06 21	06 28			06 35		06 51	06 58		07 05				07 21	07 28		07 35			07 51
London Blackfriars ⊖	d	06 04	06 24	06 27	06 34	06 39		06 42	06 54	06 57	07 04	07 09	07 12	07 24			07 27	07 34	07 39	07 42	07 54		07 57
City Thameslink ■	d																						
Farringdon ■ ⊖	d	06 09	06 29	06 31	06 39	06 44		06 46	06 59	07 01	07 09	07 14	07 16	07 29			07 31	07 39	07 44	07 46	07 59		08 01
St Pancras International ⊖	d	06 13	06 33	06 36	06 43	06 48	07 05	06 51	07 03	07 06	07 13	07 18	07 21	07 33	07 35	07 47	07 36	07 43	07 48	07 51	08 03	08 05	08 06
Kentish Town ⊖	d	06 18	06 38		06a48	06 53			07 08		07a18	07 23		07 38				07a48	07 53		08 08		
WestHampsteadThameslink ⊖	d	06 22	06 44	06 44		06 59		06 59	07 14			07 29	07 29	07 44					07 59	07 59	08 14		
Cricklewood	d	06 25	06 47			07 02			07 17			07 32		07 47					08 02		08 17		
Hendon	d	06 29	06 50			07 05			07 20			07 35		07 50					08 05		08 20		
Mill Hill Broadway	d	06 32	06 53			07 08			07 23			07 38		07 53					08 08		08 23		
Elstree & Borehamwood	d	06 36	06 57			07 12			07 27			07 42		07 57					08 12		08 27		
Radlett	d	06 39	07 01			07 16			07 31			07 46		08 01					08 16		08 31		
St Albans City	d	06a46	07a07	06 57		07a22		07 11	07a37	07 25		07a52	07 41	08a07			07 55		08a22	08 11	08a37		08 25
Harpenden	d			07 03				07 17		07 31			07 47				08 01			08 17			08 31
Luton Airport Parkway ■ ✈	d			07 08				07 23		07 36			07 53		07 56		08 06			08 23		08 26	08 36
Luton ■	d			07 13			07 27	07 27		07 41			07 57			08 09	08 11			08 27			08 41
Leagrave	d			07 17				07 31		07 45			08 01				08 15			08 31			08 45
Harlington	d			07 21				07 35		07 49			08 05				08 19			08 35			08 49
Flitwick	d			07 25				07 39		07 53			08 09				08 23			08 39			08 53
Bedford ■	a			07 37			07 40	07 51		08 05			08 21		08 10	08 23	08 35			08 51		08 39	09 05

Station		TL H	TL B	TL ■ A	TL B	EM ◇■ I	TL ■	TL H	TL B	TL ■ A	TL B	EM ◇■ G	TL ■	TL H	TL B	TL ■ A	TL B	EM ◇■ I	TL ■	TL H	TL B	TL ■ A	TL B
Gatwick Airport ✈	d			07 36			07 33			08 06			08 03			08 36			08 33			09 06	
Elephant & Castle ⊖173,179	d		08 04		08 19				08 34		08 49				09 04		09 19				09 34		09 49
London Bridge ⊖	d	07 58		08 05			08 21	08 28		08 35			08 51	08 58		09 05			09 21	09 28		09 35	
London Blackfriars ⊖	d	08 04	08 09	08 12	08 24		08 27	08 34	08 39	08 42	08 54		08 57	09 04	09 09	09 12	09 24		09 27	09 34	09 39	09 42	09 54
City Thameslink ■	d													09 06	09 11	09 14	09 26		09 29	09 36	09 41	09 44	09 56
Farringdon ■ ⊖	d	08 09	08 14	08 16	08 29		08 31	08 39	08 44	08 46	08 59		09 01	09 09	09 14	09 16	09 29		09 31	09 39	09 44	09 46	09 59
St Pancras International ⊖	d	08 13	08 18	08 21	08 33	08 47	08 36	08 43	08 48	08 51	09 03	09 05	09 06	09 13	09 18	09 21	09 33	09 47	09 36	09 43	09 48	09 51	10 03
Kentish Town ⊖	d	08a18	08 23		08 38			08a48	08 53		09 08			09a18	09 23		09 38			09a48	09 53		10 08
WestHampsteadThameslink ⊖	d		08 29	08 29	08 44				08 59	08 59	09 14				09 29	09 29	09 44				09 59	09 59	10 14
Cricklewood	d		08 32		08 47				09 02		09 17				09 32		09 47				10 02		10 17
Hendon	d		08 35		08 50				09 05		09 20				09 35		09 50				10 05		10 20
Mill Hill Broadway	d		08 38		08 53				09 08		09 23				09 38		09 53				10 08		10 23
Elstree & Borehamwood	d		08 42		08 57				09 12		09 27				09 42		09 57				10 12		10 27
Radlett	d		08 46		09 01				09 16		09 31				09 46		10 01				10 16		10 31
St Albans City	d		08a52	08 41	09a07		08 55		09a22	09 11	09a37		09 25		09a52	09 41	10a07		09 55		10a22	10 11	10a37
Harpenden	d			08 47			09 01			09 17			09 31			09 47			10 01			10 17	
Luton Airport Parkway ■ ✈	d			08 53			09 06			09 23		09 26	09 36			09 53			10 06			10 23	
Luton ■	d			08 57		09 09	09 11			09 27			09 41			09 57		10 09	10 11			10 27	
Leagrave	d			09 01			09 15			09 31			09 45			10 01			10 15			10 31	
Harlington	d			09 05			09 19			09 35			09 49			10 05			10 19			10 35	
Flitwick	d			09 09			09 23			09 39			09 53			10 09			10 23			10 39	
Bedford ■	a			09 21		09 23	09 35			09 51		09 40	10 05			10 21		10 23	10 35			10 51	

A From Brighton
B From Sutton (Surrey)
C To Leicester
D From Three Bridges
E To Sheffield
F From Gillingham (Kent)
G To Nottingham
H From Rainham (Kent)
I To Corby

Table T052MML-F

Saturdays

21 December to 16 May

Gatwick Airport and London - St Albans, Luton and Bedford

Station		EM ◇■ A	TL ■	TL B	TL C	TL ■ D	TL C	EM ◇■ E	TL ■	TL B	TL C	TL ■ D	TL C	EM ◇■ A	TL ■	TL B	TL C	TL ■ D	TL C	EM ◇■ E	TL ■	TL B
Gatwick Airport ✈	d		09 03			09 36			09 33			10 06			10 03			10 36			10 33	
Elephant & Castle ⊖173,179	d				10 04		10 19				10 34		10 49				11 04		11 19			
London Bridge ⊖	d		09 51	09 58		10 05			10 21	10 28		10 35			10 51	10 58		11 05			11 21	11 28
London Blackfriars ⊖	d		09 57	10 04	10 09	10 12	10 24		10 27	10 34	10 39	10 42	10 54		10 57	11 04	11 09	11 12	11 24		11 27	11 34
City Thameslink ■	d		09 59	10 06	10 11	10 14	10 26		10 29	10 36	10 41	10 44	10 56		10 59	11 06	11 11	11 14	11 26		11 29	11 36
Farringdon ■ ⊖	d		10 01	10 09	10 14	10 16	10 29		10 31	10 39	10 44	10 46	10 59		11 01	11 09	11 14	11 16	11 29		11 31	11 39
St Pancras International ⊖	d	10 05	10 06	10 13	10 18	10 21	10 33	10 47	10 36	10 43	10 48	10 51	11 03	11 05	11 06	11 13	11 18	11 21	11 33	11 47	11 36	11 43
Kentish Town ⊖	d			10a18	10 23		10 38			10a48	10 53		11 08			11a18	11 23		11 38			11a48
WestHampsteadThameslink ⊖	d				10 29	10 29	10 44				10 59	10 59	11 14				11 29	11 29	11 44			
Cricklewood	d				10 32		10 47				11 02		11 17				11 32		11 47			
Hendon	d				10 35		10 50				11 05		11 20				11 35		11 50			
Mill Hill Broadway	d				10 38		10 53				11 08		11 23				11 38		11 53			
Elstree & Borehamwood	d				10 42		10 57				11 12		11 27				11 42		11 57			
Radlett	d				10 46		11 01				11 16		11 31				11 46		12 01			
St Albans City	d		10 25		10a52	10 41	11a07		10 55		11a22	11 11	11a37		11 25		11a52	11 41	12a07		11 55	
Harpenden	d		10 31			10 47			11 01			11 17			11 31			11 47			12 01	
Luton Airport Parkway ■ ✈	d	10 26	10 36			10 53			11 06			11 23		11 26	11 36			11 53			12 06	
Luton ■	d		10 41			10 57		11 09	11 11			11 27			11 41			11 57		12 10	12 11	
Leagrave	d		10 45			11 01			11 15			11 31			11 45			12 01			12 15	
Harlington	d		10 49			11 05			11 19			11 35			11 49			12 05			12 19	
Flitwick	d		10 53			11 09			11 23			11 39			11 53			12 09			12 23	
Bedford ■	a	10 40	11 05			11 21		11 23	11 35			11 51		11 40	12 05			12 21		12 24	12 35	

Station		TL C	TL ■ D	TL C	EM ◇■ A	TL ■	TL B	TL C	TL ■ D	TL C	EM ◇■ E	TL ■	TL B	TL C	TL ■ D	TL C	EM ◇■ A	TL ■	TL B	TL C	TL ■ D	TL C	EM ◇■ E
Gatwick Airport ✈	d		11 06			11 03			11 36			11 33			12 06			12 03			12 36		
Elephant & Castle ⊖173,179	d	11 34		11 49				12 04		12 19				12 34		12 49				13 04		13 19	
London Bridge ⊖	d		11 35			11 51	11 58		12 05			12 21	12 28		12 35			12 51	12 58		13 05		
London Blackfriars ⊖	d	11 39	11 42	11 54		11 57	12 04	12 09	12 12	12 24		12 27	12 34	12 39	12 42	12 54		12 57	13 04	13 09	13 12	13 24	
City Thameslink ■	d	11 41	11 44	11 56		11 59	12 06	12 11	12 14	12 26		12 29	12 36	12 41	12 44	12 56		12 59	13 06	13 11	13 14	13 26	
Farringdon ■ ⊖	d	11 44	11 46	11 59		12 01	12 09	12 14	12 16	12 29		12 31	12 39	12 44	12 46	12 59		13 01	13 09	13 14	13 16	13 29	
St Pancras International ⊖	d	11 48	11 51	12 03	12 05	12 06	12 13	12 18	12 21	12 33	12 47	12 36	12 43	12 48	12 51	13 03	13 05	13 06	13 13	13 18	13 21	13 33	13 47
Kentish Town ⊖	d	11 53		12 08			12a18	12 23		12 38			12a48	12 53		13 08			13a18	13 23		13 38	
WestHampsteadThameslink ⊖	d	11 59	11 59	12 14				12 29	12 29	12 44				12 59	12 59	13 14				13 29	13 29	13 44	
Cricklewood	d	12 02		12 17				12 32		12 47				13 02		13 17				13 32		13 47	
Hendon	d	12 05		12 20				12 35		12 50				13 05		13 20				13 35		13 50	
Mill Hill Broadway	d	12 08		12 23				12 38		12 53				13 08		13 23				13 38		13 53	
Elstree & Borehamwood	d	12 12		12 27				12 42		12 57				13 12		13 27				13 42		13 57	
Radlett	d	12 16		12 31				12 46		13 01				13 16		13 31				13 46		14 01	
St Albans City	d	12a22	12 11	12a37		12 25		12a52	12 41	13a07		12 55		13a22	13 11	13a37		13 25		13a52	13 41	14a07	
Harpenden	d		12 17			12 31			12 47			13 01			13 17			13 31			13 47		
Luton Airport Parkway ■ ✈	d		12 23		12 26	12 36			12 53			13 06			13 23		13 26	13 36			13 53		
Luton ■	d		12 27			12 41			12 57		13 09	13 11			13 27			13 41			13 57		14 09
Leagrave	d		12 31			12 45			13 01			13 15			13 31			13 45			14 01		
Harlington	d		12 35			12 49			13 05			13 19			13 35			13 49			14 05		
Flitwick	d		12 39			12 53			13 09			13 23			13 39			13 53			14 09		
Bedford ■	a		12 51		12 40	13 05			13 21		13 23	13 35			13 51		13 40	14 05			14 21		14 23

Station		TL ■	TL B	TL C	TL ■ D	TL C	EM ◇■ A	TL ■	TL B	TL C	TL ■ D	TL C	EM ◇■ E	TL ■	TL B	TL C	TL ■ D	TL C	EM ◇■ A	TL ■	TL B	TL C	TL ■ D
Gatwick Airport ✈	d	12 33			13 06			13 03			13 36			13 33			14 06			14 03			14 36
Elephant & Castle ⊖173,179	d			13 34		13 49				14 04		14 19				14 34		14 49				15 04	
London Bridge ⊖	d	13 21	13 28		13 35			13 51	13 58		14 05			14 21	14 28		14 35			14 51	14 58		15 05
London Blackfriars ⊖	d	13 27	13 34	13 39	13 42	13 54		13 57	14 04	14 09	14 12	14 24		14 27	14 34	14 39	14 42	14 54		14 57	15 04	15 09	15 12
City Thameslink ■	d	13 29	13 36	13 41	13 44	13 56		13 59	14 06	14 11	14 14	14 26		14 29	14 36	14 41	14 44	14 56		14 59	15 06	15 11	15 14
Farringdon ■ ⊖	d	13 31	13 39	13 44	13 46	13 59		14 01	14 09	14 14	14 16	14 29		14 31	14 39	14 44	14 46	14 59		15 01	15 09	15 14	15 16
St Pancras International ⊖	d	13 36	13 43	13 48	13 51	14 03	14 05	14 06	14 13	14 18	14 21	14 33	14 47	14 36	14 43	14 48	14 51	15 03	15 05	15 06	15 13	15 18	15 21
Kentish Town ⊖	d		13a48	13 53		14 08			14a18	14 23		14 38			14a48	14 53		15 08			15a18	15 23	
WestHampsteadThameslink ⊖	d			13 59	13 59	14 14				14 29	14 29	14 44				14 59	14 59	15 14				15 29	15 29
Cricklewood	d			14 02		14 17				14 32		14 47				15 02		15 17				15 32	
Hendon	d			14 05		14 20				14 35		14 50				15 05		15 20				15 35	
Mill Hill Broadway	d			14 08		14 23				14 38		14 53				15 08		15 23				15 38	
Elstree & Borehamwood	d			14 12		14 27				14 42		14 57				15 12		15 27				15 42	
Radlett	d			14 16		14 31				14 46		15 01				15 16		15 31				15 46	
St Albans City	d	13 55		14a22	14 11	14a37		14 25		14a52	14 41	15a07		14 55		15a22	15 11	15a37		15 25		15a52	15 41
Harpenden	d	14 01			14 17			14 31			14 47			15 01			15 17			15 31			15 47
Luton Airport Parkway ■ ✈	d	14 06			14 23		14 26	14 36			14 53			15 06			15 23		15 26	15 36			15 53
Luton ■	d	14 11			14 27			14 41			14 57		15 09	15 11			15 27			15 41			15 57
Leagrave	d	14 15			14 31			14 45			15 01			15 15			15 31			15 45			16 01
Harlington	d	14 19			14 35			14 49			15 05			15 19			15 35			15 49			16 05
Flitwick	d	14 23			14 39			14 53			15 09			15 23			15 39			15 53			16 09
Bedford ■	a	14 35			14 51		14 40	15 05			15 21		15 23	15 35			15 51		15 40	16 05			16 21

A To Nottingham
B From Rainham (Kent)
C From Sutton (Surrey)
D From Brighton
E To Corby

Table T052MML-F

Saturdays

21 December to 16 May

Gatwick Airport and London - St Albans, Luton and Bedford

		TL	EM	TL	TL	TL	TL	TL	EM	TL	TL	TL	TL	TL	EM	TL	TL	TL	TL	TL	EM	TL	TL
			◇■	■			■		◇■	■			■		◇■	■			■		◇■	■	
		A	B		C	A	D	A	E		C	A	D	A	B		C	A	D	A	F		C
Gatwick Airport	d			14 33			15 06			15 03			15 36			15 32			16 06			16 03	
Elephant & Castle ⊖173,179	d	15 19				15 34		15 49				16 04		16 19				16 34		16 49			
London Bridge ⊖	d			15 21	15 28		15 35			15 51	15 58		16 05			16 21	16 28		16 35			16 51	16 58
London Blackfriars ⊖	d	15 24		15 27	15 34	15 39	15 42	15 54		15 57	16 04	16 09	16 12	16 24		16 27	16 34	16 39	16 42	16 54		16 57	17 04
City Thameslink ■	d	15 26		15 29	15 36	15 41	15 44	15 56		15 59	16 06	16 11	16 14	16 26		16 29	16 36	16 41	16 44	16 56		16 59	17 06
Farringdon ■ ⊖	d	15 29		15 31	15 39	15 44	15 46	15 59		16 01	16 09	16 14	16 16	16 29		16 31	16 39	16 44	16 46	16 59		17 01	17 09
St Pancras International ⊖	d	15 33	15 47	15 36	15 43	15 48	15 51	16 03	16 05	16 06	16 13	16 18	16 21	16 33	16 47	16 36	16 43	16 48	16 51	17 03	17 05	17 06	17 13
Kentish Town ⊖	d	15 38			15a48	15 53		16 08			16a18	16 23		16 38			16a48	16 53		17 08			17a18
WestHampsteadThameslink ⊖	d	15 44				15 59	15 59	16 14				16 29	16 29	16 44				16 59	16 59	17 14			
Cricklewood	d	15 47				16 02		16 17				16 32		16 47				17 02		17 17			
Hendon	d	15 50				16 05		16 20				16 35		16 50				17 05		17 20			
Mill Hill Broadway	d	15 53				16 08		16 23				16 38		16 53				17 08		17 23			
Elstree & Borehamwood	d	15 57				16 12		16 27				16 42		16 57				17 12		17 27			
Radlett	d	16 01				16 16		16 31				16 46		17 01				17 16		17 31			
St Albans City	d	16a07		15 55		16a22	16 11	16a37		16 25		16a52	16 41	17a07		16 55		17a22	17 11	17a37		17 25	
Harpenden	d			16 01			16 17			16 31			16 47			17 01			17 17			17 31	
Luton Airport Parkway ■ ✈	d			16 06			16 23		16 26	16 36			16 53			17 06			17 23		17 26	17 36	
Luton ■	d		16 09	16 11			16 27			16 41			16 57		17 10	17 11			17 27			17 41	
Leagrave	d			16 15			16 31			16 45			17 01			17 15			17 31			17 45	
Harlington	d			16 19			16 35			16 49			17 05			17 19			17 35			17 49	
Flitwick	d			16 23			16 39			16 53			17 09			17 23			17 39			17 53	
Bedford ■	a		16 23	16 35			16 51		16 40	17 05			17 21		17 23	17 35			17 51		17 40	18 05	

		TL	TL	TL	EM	TL	TL	TL	TL	TL	EM	TL	TL	TL	TL	TL	EM	TL	TL	TL	TL	TL
			■		◇■	■			■		◇■	■			■		◇■	■			■	
		A	D	A	B		C	A	D	A	E		C	A	D	A	B		C	A	D	A
Gatwick Airport	d		16 36			16 33			17 06			17 03			17 36			17 33			18 06	
Elephant & Castle ⊖173,179	d	17 04		17 19				17 34		17 49				18 04		18 19				18 34		18 49
London Bridge ⊖	d		17 05			17 21	17 28		17 35			17 51	17 58		18 05			18 21	18 28		18 35	
London Blackfriars ⊖	d	17 09	17 12	17 24		17 27	17 34	17 39	17 42	17 54		17 57	18 04	18 09	18 12	18 24		18 27	18 34	18 39	18 42	18 54
City Thameslink ■	d	17 11	17 14	17 26		17 29	17 36	17 41	17 44	17 56		17 59	18 06	18 11	18 14	18 26		18 29	18 36	18 41	18 44	18 56
Farringdon ■ ⊖	d	17 14	17 16	17 29		17 31	17 39	17 44	17 46	17 59		18 01	18 09	18 14	18 16	18 29		18 31	18 39	18 44	18 46	18 59
St Pancras International ⊖	d	17 18	17 21	17 33	17 47	17 36	17 43	17 48	17 51	18 03	18 05	18 06	18 13	18 18	18 21	18 33	18 47	18 36	18 43	18 48	18 51	19 03
Kentish Town ⊖	d	17 23		17 38			17a48	17 53		18 08			18a18	18 23		18 38			18a48	18 53		19 08
WestHampsteadThameslink ⊖	d	17 29	17 29	17 44				17 59	17 59	18 14				18 29	18 29	18 44				18 59	18 59	19 14
Cricklewood	d	17 32		17 47				18 02		18 17				18 32		18 47				19 02		19 17
Hendon	d	17 35		17 50				18 05		18 20				18 35		18 50				19 05		19 20
Mill Hill Broadway	d	17 38		17 53				18 08		18 23				18 38		18 53				19 08		19 23
Elstree & Borehamwood	d	17 42		17 57				18 12		18 27				18 42		18 57				19 12		19 27
Radlett	d	17 46		18 01				18 16		18 31				18 46		19 01				19 16		19 31
St Albans City	d	17a52	17 41	18a07		17 55		18a22	18 11	18a37		18 25		18a52	18 41	19a07		18 55		19a22	19 11	19a37
Harpenden	d		17 47			18 01			18 17			18 31			18 47			19 01			19 17	
Luton Airport Parkway ■ ✈	d		17 53			18 06			18 23		18 26	18 36			18 53			19 06			19 23	
Luton ■	d		17 57		18 09	18 11			18 27			18 41			18 57		19 09	19 11			19 27	
Leagrave	d		18 01			18 15			18 31			18 45			19 01			19 15			19 31	
Harlington	d		18 05			18 19			18 35			18 49			19 05			19 19			19 35	
Flitwick	d		18 09			18 23			18 39			18 53			19 09			19 23			19 39	
Bedford ■	a		18 21		18 23	18 35			18 51		18 40	19 05			19 21		19 23	19 35			19 51	

		EM	TL	TL	TL	TL	TL	EM	TL	TL	TL	TL	TL	EM	TL	TL	TL	TL	TL	TL	TL	TL	TL
		◇■	■			■		◇■	■			■		◇■	■			■		■			■
		E		C	A	D	A	B		C	A	D	A	E		C	A	D	A		C	A	D
Gatwick Airport	d		18 03			18 36			18 33			19 06			19 03			19 36		19 33			20 06
Elephant & Castle ⊖173,179	d				19 04		19 19				19 34		19 49				20 04		20 19			20 34	
London Bridge ⊖	d		18 51	18 58		19 05			19 21	19 28		19 35			19 51	19 58		20 05		20 21	20 28		20 35
London Blackfriars ⊖	d		18 57	19 04	19 09	19 12	19 24		19 27	19 34	19 39	19 42	19 54		19 57	20 04	20 09	20 12	20 24	20 27	20 34	20 39	20 42
City Thameslink ■	d		18 59	19 06	19 11	19 14	19 26		19 29	19 36	19 41	19 44	19 56		19 59	20 06	20 11	20 14	20 26	20 29	20 36	20 41	20 44
Farringdon ■ ⊖	d		19 01	19 09	19 14	19 16	19 29		19 31	19 39	19 44	19 46	19 59		20 01	20 09	20 14	20 16	20 29	20 31	20 39	20 44	20 46
St Pancras International ⊖	d	19 05	19 06	19 13	19 18	19 21	19 33	19 47	19 36	19 43	19 48	19 51	20 03	20 05	20 06	20 13	20 18	20 21	20 33	20 36	20 43	20 48	20 51
Kentish Town ⊖	d			19a18	19 23		19 38			19a48	19 53		20 08			20a18	20 23		20 38		20a48	20 53	
WestHampsteadThameslink ⊖	d				19 29	19 29	19 44				19 59	19 59	20 14				20 29	20 29	20 44			20 59	20 59
Cricklewood	d				19 32		19 47				20 02		20 17				20 32		20 47			21 02	
Hendon	d				19 35		19 50				20 05		20 20				20 35		20 50			21 05	
Mill Hill Broadway	d				19 38		19 53				20 08		20 23				20 38		20 53			21 08	
Elstree & Borehamwood	d				19 42		19 57				20 12		20 27				20 42		20 57			21 12	
Radlett	d				19 46		20 01				20 16		20 31				20 46		21 01			21 16	
St Albans City	d		19 25		19a52	19 41	20a07		19 55		20a22	20 11	20a37		20 26		20a52	20 41	21a07	20 55		21a22	21 11
Harpenden	d		19 31			19 47			20 01			20 17			20 32			20 47		21 01			21 17
Luton Airport Parkway ■ ✈	d	19 26	19 36			19 53			20 06			20 23		20 27	20 37			20 53		21 06			21 23
Luton ■	d		19 41			19 57		20 10	20 11			20 27			20 42			20 57		21 11			21 27
Leagrave	d		19 45			20 01			20 15			20 31			20 46			21 01		21 15			21 31
Harlington	d		19 49			20 05			20 19			20 35			20 50			21 05		21 19			21 35
Flitwick	d		19 53			20 09			20 23			20 39			20 54			21 09		21 23			21 39
Bedford ■	a	19 40	20 05			20 21		20 23	20 35			20 51		20 40	21 06			21 21		21 35			21 51

A From Sutton (Surrey)
B To Corby
C From Rainham (Kent)
D From Brighton
E To Nottingham
F To Lincoln

Table T052MML-F

Saturdays

21 December to 16 May

Gatwick Airport and London - St Albans, Luton and Bedford

		TL	TL	TL	TL	EM	TL	TL	TL	TL	TL	EM	EM	TL	TL	TL	TL	EM	TL	TL	TL	TL	TL
			■			◇■	■		■			◇■	◇■	■		■		◇■		■			■
		A		B	A	C	D	A		B	A	C	E	D	A		B	C	F	D	A	F	
Gatwick Airport	d		20 03				20 36		20 33					21 06		21 03				21 36			21 33
Elephant & Castle ⊖173,179	d	20 49			21 04			21 19			21 34				21 49				22 04			22 19	
London Bridge ⊖	d		20 51	20 58			21 05		21 21	21 28				21 35		21 51	21 58			22 05			22 21
London Blackfriars ⊖	d	20 54	20 57	21 04	21 09		21 12	21 24	21 27	21 34	21 39			21 42	21 54	21 57	22 04		22 09	22 12		22 24	22 27
City Thameslink ■	d	20 56	20 59																				
Farringdon ■ ⊖	d	20 59	21 01	21 09	21 14		21 16	21 29	21 31	21 39	21 44			21 46	21 59	22 01	22 09		22 14	22 16		22 29	22 31
St Pancras International ⊖	d	21 03	21 06	21 13	21 18	21 30	21 21	21 33	21 36	21 43	21 48	21 50	22 00	21 51	22 03	22 06	22 13	22 20	22 18	22 21		22 33	22 36
Kentish Town ⊖	d	21 08		21a18	21 23			21 38		21a48	21 53				22 08		22a18		22 23			22 38	
WestHampsteadThameslink ⊖	d	21 14			21 29		21 29	21 44			21 59			21 59	22 14				22 29	22 29		22 44	
Cricklewood	d	21 17			21 32			21 47			22 02				22 17				22 31			22 47	
Hendon	d	21 20			21 35			21 50			22 05				22 20				22 34			22 50	
Mill Hill Broadway	d	21 23			21 38			21 53			22 08				22 23				22 37			22 53	
Elstree & Borehamwood	d	21 27			21 42			21 57			22 12				22 27				22 41		←	22 57	
Radlett	d	21 31			21 46			22 01			22 16				22 31				22 45		22 45	23 01	
St Albans City	d	21a37	21 25		21a52		21 41	22a07	21 55		22a22			22 11	22a37	22 25			→	22 41	22 53	→	22 57
Harpenden	d		21 31				21 47		22 01					22 17		22 31				22 48	22 58		23 04
Luton Airport Parkway ■ ✈	d		21 36				21 53		22 06			22 13		22 23		22 36		22 42		22 54	23 04		23 10
Luton ■	d		21 41			21 54	21 57		22 11				22 25	22 27		22 41				22 58	23 08		23 14
Leagrave	d		21 45				22 01		22 15					22 31		22 45				23 02			23 18
Harlington	d		21 49				22 05		22 19					22 35		22 49				23 07			23 23
Flitwick	d		21 53				22 09		22 23					22 39		22 53				23 11			23 27
Bedford ■	a		22 05			22 10	22 21		22 35			22 28	22 41	22 51		23 05		22 57		23 22	23 28		23 39

		TL	TL	TL	TL	TL	TL	TL	TL	TL	TL	TL	TL	TL	TL	TL
					■				■				■			■
		A	B	F	D	A	A	B	D	A	A	B	D	A	A	D
Gatwick Airport	d				22 06				22 36				23 06			23 34
Elephant & Castle ⊖173,179	d			22 34			22 51			23 11	23 21			23 41	23 54	
London Bridge ⊖	d		22 28		22 35			22 58	23 05			23 28	23 35			
London Blackfriars ⊖	d		22 34	22 39	22 42		22 59	23 04	23 12	23 17	23 27	23 34	23 42	23 49	00 02	00 22
City Thameslink ■	d															
Farringdon ■ ⊖	d		22 39	22 44	22 46		23 04	23 09	23 16	23 21	23 31	23 39	23 46	23 53	00 06	00 26
St Pancras International ⊖	d		22 43	22 48	22 51	←	23 08	23 13	23 21	23 26	23 36	23 43	23 51	23 58	00 11	00 31
Kentish Town ⊖	d			22 58		22 58	23 13			23 30	23 40			00 01		
WestHampsteadThameslink ⊖	d		22a51	→	22 59	23 02	23 17	23a21	23 29	23 34	23 44	23a51	23 59	00 06	00 19	00 39
Cricklewood	d					23 05	23 20			23 38	23 48			00 10		
Hendon	d					23 08	23 23			23 41	23 51			00 13		
Mill Hill Broadway	d					23 11	23 26			23 44	23 54			00 16		
Elstree & Borehamwood	d	←				23 15	23 30			23 48	23 58			00 20		
Radlett	d	23 01				23 19	23 34			23 52	00 02			00 24		
St Albans City	d	23 09			23 16	23 27	23 42		23 46	23 59	00 10		00 16	00 32	00 36	00 56
Harpenden	d	23 15			23 22	23 33	23 48		23 52	00 06	00 16		00 22	00 38	00 42	01 02
Luton Airport Parkway ■ ✈	d	23 20			23 27	23 38	23 53		23 58	00 11	00 22		00 28	00 43	00 48	01 08
Luton ■	d	23 25			23 31	23 43	23 58		00 02	00 16	00 26		00 32	00 48	00 52	01 12
Leagrave	d				23 35				00 06	00 20	00 30		00 36		00 56	01 16
Harlington	d				23 40				00 11	00 24	00 35		00 41		01 01	01 21
Flitwick	d				23 44				00 15	00 28	00 39		00 45		01 05	01 25
Bedford ■	a	23 46			23 55	00 03	00 18		00 26	00 40	00 50		00 56	01 08	01 18	01 36

Sundays

15 December to 10 May

		TL	TL	TL	TL	TL	TL	TL	TL	TL	TL	TL	TL	TL	TL	TL	TL	TL	EM	TL	TL	EM	TL	TL
		■			■				■	■	■	■	■	■	■	■	■	■	◇■	■	■	◇■	■	■
		G	H	H	G	H	H	H	G	G	G	D							E			I		J
Gatwick Airport	d									00 04	00 21	00 42												08 49
Elephant & Castle ⊖173,179	d							00 04																
London Bridge ⊖	d																							09 33
London Blackfriars ⊖	d						00 02	00 09	00 22	00 50	01 06	01 36												09 39
City Thameslink ■	d																							
Farringdon ■ ⊖	d						00 06	00 13	00 26															09 43
St Pancras International ⊖	d						00 11	00 18	00 31	01 01	01 16	01 44	06 18	07 18	07 48	08 18	08 48	09 00	09 03	09 18	09 30		09 33	09 48
Kentish Town ⊖	d					00 01		00 22		01 05		01 48	06 23	07 23	07 53	08 23			09 11				09 38	
WestHampsteadThameslink ⊖	d					00 06	00 19	00 26	00 39	01 09	01 24	01 52	06 27	07 27	07 57	08 27	08 56		09 15	09 25			09 42	
Cricklewood	d					00 10		00 30		01 13		01 55	06 31	07 31	08 01	08 31			09 17				09 46	
Hendon	d					00 13		00 33		01 17		02 00	06 35	07 35	08 05	08 35			09 20				09 49	
Mill Hill Broadway	d					00 16		00 36		01 20		02 03	06 38	07 38	08 08	08 38			09 23				09 52	
Elstree & Borehamwood	d					00 20		00 40		01 24		02 07	06 42	07 42	08 12	08 42			09 27				09 56	
Radlett	d			00 02		00 24		00 44		01 28		02 11	06 46	07 46	08 16	08 46			09 31				10 00	
St Albans City	d			00 10	00 16	00 32	00 36	00 52	00 56	01 34	01 41	02 19	06 54	07 54	08 24	08 54	09 13		09 38	09 42			10 07	10 11
Harpenden	d		00 06	00 16	00 22	00 38	00 42	00 58	01 02	01 40	01 47	02 25	07 00	08 00	08 30	09 00	09 19		09 44	09 48			10 13	10 17
Luton Airport Parkway ■ ✈	d		00 11	00 22	00 28	00 43	00 48	01 03	01 08	01 46	01 52	02 30	07 05	08 05	08 35	09 05	09 24	09 29	09 49	09 53			10 18	10 22
Luton ■	d	00 02	00 16	00 26	00 32	00 48	00 52	01 08	01 12	01 50	01 57	02 35	07 10	08 10	08 40	09 10	09 29		09a53	09 57	10 02		10a22	10 27
Leagrave	d	00 06	00 20	00 30	00 36		00 56	01 12	01 16	01 54	02 01	02 39	07 14	08 14	08 44	09 14	09 33			10 01				10 31
Harlington	d	00 11	00 24	00 35	00 41		01 01	01 16	01 21	01 59	02 05	02 43	07 18	08 18	08 48	09 18	09 37			10 06				10 35
Flitwick	d	00 15	00 28	00 39	00 45		01 05	01 20	01 25	02 03	02 09	02 47	07 22	08 22	08 52	09 22	09 41			10 10				10 39
Bedford ■	a	00 26	00 40	00 50	00 56	01 08	01 18	01 32	01 36	02 14	02 21	02 59	07 34	08 34	09 04	09 34	09 53	09 55		10 22	10 22			10 52

A From Sutton (Surrey)
B From Rainham (Kent)
C To Derby
D From Brighton
E To Nottingham
F From Sutton (Surrey) to Bedford
G not 15 December. From Brighton
H not 15 December. From Sutton (Surrey)
I To Sheffield
J From Three Bridges

Table T052MML-F

Sundays

15 December to 10 May

Gatwick Airport and London - St Albans, Luton and Bedford

	EM ◇1 A	TL 1 B	TL C	TL D	TL 1 E	EM ◇1 F	TL 1 B	TL C	TL D	TL 1 E	EM ◇1 A	TL 1 B	TL C	TL D	TL 1	EM ◇1 F	TL 1 B	TL C	TL D	TL 1 E	EM ◇1 A	TL 1 B
Gatwick Airport ✈ d		09 19			09 19		09 49			09 49		10 19			10 19		10 49			10 49		11 19
Elephant & Castle ⊖173,179 d			09 53					10 23					10 53					11 23				
London Bridge ⊖ d		09 49		09 58	10 03		10 19		10 28	10 33		10 49		10 58	11 03		11 19		11 28	11 33		11 49
London Blackfriars ⊖ d		09 55	09 58	10 05	10 09		10 25	10 28	10 35	10 39		10 55	10 58	11 05	11 09		11 25	11 28	11 35	11 39		11 55
City Thameslink 3 d																						
Farringdon 3 ⊖ d		09 59	10 02	10 09	10 13		10 29	10 32	10 39	10 43		10 59	11 02	11 09	11 13		11 29	11 32	11 39	11 43		11 59
St Pancras International ⊖ d	10 00	10 04	10 07	10 14	10 18	10 30	10 34	10 37	10 44	10 48	11 00	11 04	11 07	11 14	11 18	11 30	11 34	11 37	11 44	11 48	12 10	12 04
Kentish Town ⊖ d			10 11	10a18				10 41	10a48				11 11	11a18				11 41	11a48			
WestHampsteadThameslink ⊖ d		10 12	10 15		10 26		10 42	10 45		10 56		11 12	11 15		11 26		11 42	11 45		11 56		12 12
Cricklewood d			10 18					10 48					11 18					11 49				
Hendon d			10 21					10 51					11 21					11 53				
Mill Hill Broadway d			10 24					10 54					11 24					11 56				
Elstree & Borehamwood d			10 28					10 58					11 28					12 00				
Radlett d			10 32					11 02					11 32					12 04				
St Albans City d		10 29	10 39		10 43		10 59	11 09		11 13		11 29	11 39		11 43		11 59	12 11		12 15		12 29
Harpenden d		10 35	10 45		10 49		11 05	11 15		11 19		11 35	11 45		11 49		12 05	12 17		12 21		12 34
Luton Airport Parkway 7 ✈ d	10 29	10 40	10 50		10 54		11 10	11 20		11 24	11 29	11 40	11 50		11 54	11 59	12 10	12 22		12 26	12 32	12 40
Luton 10 d		10 45	10a54		10 59	11 02	11 15	11a24		11 29	11 33	11 45	11a54		11 59	12 03	12 15	12a26		12 31	12 35	12 44
Leagrave d		10 49			11 03		11 19			11 33		11 49			12 03		12 19			12 35		12 48
Harlington d		10 53			11 07		11 23			11 37		11 53			12 07		12 23			12 39		12 52
Flitwick d		10 57			11 11		11 27			11 42		11 57			12 11		12 27			12 43		12 56
Bedford 7 a	10 54	11 09			11 24	11 26	11 40			11 54	11 55	12 09			12 24	12 19	12 39			12 55	12 49	13 10

	TL C	TL D	TL 1 G	EM ◇1 H	TL 1 I	TL C	TL 1 B	TL C	TL D	TL 1 E	EM ◇1 A	TL C	TL 1 B	TL C	TL D	TL 1 G	EM ◇1 H	TL 1 I	TL C	TL 1 B	TL C	TL D
Gatwick Airport ✈ d			11 19				11 49			11 49			12 19			12 19				12 49		
Elephant & Castle ⊖173,179 d	11 53					12 11		12 23				12 41		12 53					13 11		13 23	
London Bridge ⊖ d		11 58	12 03				12 19		12 28	12 33			12 49		12 58	13 03				13 19		13 28
London Blackfriars ⊖ d	11 58	12 05	12 09			12 16	12 25	12 28	12 35	12 41		12 46	12 55	12 58	13 05	13 09			13 16	13 25	13 28	13 35
City Thameslink 3 d																						
Farringdon 3 ⊖ d	12 02	12 09	12 13			12 20	12 29	12 32	12 39	12 45		12 50	12 59	13 02	13 09	13 13			13 20	13 29	13 32	13 39
St Pancras International ⊖ d	12 07	12 14	12 18	12 30		12 25	12 34	12 37	12 44	12 50	13 10	12 55	13 04	13 07	13 14	13 18	13 30		13 25	13 34	13 37	13 44
Kentish Town ⊖ d	12 11	12a18						12 41	12a48					13 11	13a18						13 41	13a48
WestHampsteadThameslink ⊖ d	12 16		12 26			12 34	12 42	12 46		12 59		13 04	13 12	13 16		13 26			13 34	13 42	13 46	
Cricklewood d	12 20							12 50						13 20							13 50	
Hendon d	12 24							12 54						13 24							13 54	
Mill Hill Broadway d	12 27					12 40		12 57				13 10		13 27					13 40		13 57	
Elstree & Borehamwood d	12 31					12 44		13 01				13 14		13 31					13 44		14 01	
Radlett d	12 35					12 48		13 05				13 18		13 35					13 48		14 08	
St Albans City d	12a42		12 39			12 55	12 59	13a12		13 13		13 25	13 29	13a42		13 39			13 55	13 59	14a14	
Harpenden d			12 46			13 00	13 04			13 18		13 30	13 34			13 46			14 00	14 04		
Luton Airport Parkway 7 ✈ d			12 51	12 52	←	13 06	13 10			13 24	13 32	13 36	13 40			13 51	13 52	←	14 06	14 10		
Luton 10 d			12 56	12 54	12 56	13a10	13 14			13 28	13 35	13a40	13 44			13 56	13 54	13 56	14a10	14 14		
Leagrave d			→		13 00		13 18			13 32			13 48			→		14 00		14 18		
Harlington d					13 04		13 22			13 36			13 52					14 04		14 22		
Flitwick d					13 08		13 26			13 40			13 56					14 08		14 26		
Bedford 7 a				13 08	13 20		13 39			13 52	13 49		14 08				14 08	14 20		14 38		

	TL 1 E	EM ◇1 A	TL C	TL 1 B	TL C	TL D	EM ◇1 H	TL 1	TL C	TL 1 B	TL C	TL D	TL 1 E	EM ◇1 A	TL C	TL 1 B	TL C	TL D	TL 1	EM ◇1 J	TL C	TL 1 B
Gatwick Airport ✈ d	12 49			13 19				13 19		13 49			13 49			14 19			14 19			14 49
Elephant & Castle ⊖173,179 d			13 41		13 53				14 11		14 23				14 41		14 53				15 11	
London Bridge ⊖ d	13 33			13 49		13 58		14 03		14 19		14 28	14 33			14 49		14 58	15 03			15 19
London Blackfriars ⊖ d	13 39		13 46	13 55	13 58	14 05		14 09	14 16	14 25	14 28	14 35	14 39		14 46	14 55	14 58	15 05	15 09		15 16	15 25
City Thameslink 3 d																						
Farringdon 3 ⊖ d	13 43		13 50	13 59	14 02	14 09		14 13	14 20	14 29	14 32	14 39	14 43		14 50	14 59	15 02	15 09	15 13		15 20	15 29
St Pancras International ⊖ d	13 48	14 10	13 55	14 04	14 07	14 14	14 30	14 18	14 25	14 34	14 37	14 44	14 48	15 10	14 55	15 04	15 07	15 14	15 18	15 40	15 25	15 34
Kentish Town ⊖ d					14 11	14a18					14 41	14a48					15 11	15a18				
WestHampsteadThameslink ⊖ d	13 56		14 04	14 12	14 16			14 26	14 34	14 42	14 46		14 56		15 04	15 12	15 16		15 26		15 34	15 42
Cricklewood d					14 20						14 50						15 20					
Hendon d					14 24						14 54						15 24					
Mill Hill Broadway d			14 10		14 27				14 40		14 57				15 10		15 27				15 40	
Elstree & Borehamwood d			14 14		14 31				14 44		15 01				15 14		15 31				15 44	
Radlett d			14 18		14 38				14 48		15 08				15 18		15 35				15 48	
St Albans City d	14 10		14 25	14 29	14a44			14 40	14 55	14 59	15a14		15 11		15 25	15 29	15a42		15 39		15 55	15 59
Harpenden d	14 16		14 30	14 34				14 46	15 00	15 04			15 16		15 30	15 34			15 46		16 00	16 04
Luton Airport Parkway 7 ✈ d	14 21	14 32	14 36	14 40				14 51	15 06	15 10			15 22	15 33	15 36	15 40			15 51		16 06	16 10
Luton 10 d	14 26		14a40	14 44			14 53	14 56	15a10	15 14			15 26		15a40	15 44			15 56	16 03	16a10	16 14
Leagrave d	14 30			14 48				15 00		15 18			15 30			15 48			16 00			16 18
Harlington d	14 34			14 52				15 04		15 22			15 34			15 52			16 04			16 22
Flitwick d	14 38			14 56				15 09		15 26			15 38			15 56			16 08			16 26
Bedford 7 a	14 50	14 46		15 08			15 06	15 20		15 38			15 50	15 48		16 08			16 20	16 17		16 38

A To Nottingham
B From Brighton
C From Sutton (Surrey)
D From Rainham (Kent)
E From Three Bridges
F To Sheffield
G To Bedford
H To Corby
I From Gatwick Airport
J To Derby

Table T052MML-F

Sundays

15 December to 10 May

Gatwick Airport and London - St Albans, Luton and Bedford

	TL A	TL B	TL 1 C	EM ◇1 D	TL A	TL 1 E	TL A	TL B	TL 1	EM ◇1 F	TL A	TL 1 E	TL A	TL B	TL 1 C	EM ◇1 D	TL A	TL 1 E	TL A	TL B	TL 1	EM ◇1 F
Gatwick Airport ✈ d			14 49			15 19			15 19			15 49			15 49			16 19			16 19	
Elephant & Castle ⊖173,179 d	15 23				15 41		15 53				16 11		16 23				16 41		16 53			
London Bridge ⊖ d		15 28	15 33			15 49		15 58	16 03			16 19		16 28	16 33			16 49		16 58	17 03	
London Blackfriars ⊖ d	15 28	15 35	15 39		15 46	15 55	15 58	16 05	16 09		16 16	16 25	16 28	16 35	16 39		16 46	16 55	16 58	17 05	17 09	
City Thameslink 3 d																						
Farringdon 3 ⊖ d	15 32	15 39	15 43		15 50	15 59	16 02	16 09	16 13		16 20	16 29	16 32	16 39	16 43		16 50	16 59	17 02	17 09	17 13	
St Pancras International ⊖ d	15 37	15 44	15 48	16 10	15 55	16 04	16 07	16 14	16 18	16 40	16 25	16 34	16 37	16 44	16 48	17 10	16 55	17 04	17 07	17 14	17 18	17 40
Kentish Town ⊖ d	15 41	15a48					16 11	16a18					16 41	16a48					17 11	17a18		
WestHampsteadThameslink ⊖ d	15 46		15 56		16 04	16 12	16 16		16 26		16 34	16 42	16 46		16 56		17 04	17 12	17 16		17 26	
Cricklewood d	15 50						16 20						16 50						17 20			
Hendon d	15 54						16 24						16 54						17 24			
Mill Hill Broadway d	15 57				16 10		16 27				16 40		16 57				17 10		17 27			
Elstree & Borehamwood d	16 01				16 14		16 31				16 44		17 01				17 14		17 31			
Radlett d	16 08				16 18		16 35				16 48		17 05				17 18		17 38			
St Albans City d	16a14		16 11		16 25	16 29	16a42		16 39		16 55	16 59	17a12		17 09		17 25	17 29	17a44		17 40	
Harpenden d			16 16		16 30	16 34			16 46		17 00	17 04			17 16		17 30	17 34			17 46	
Luton Airport Parkway 7 ✈ d			16 22	16 32	16 36	16 40			16 51		17 06	17 10			17 21	17 32	17 36	17 40			17 51	
Luton 10 d			16 26		16a40	16 44			16 56	17 03	17a10	17 14			17 26		17a40	17 44			17 56	18 03
Leagrave d			16 30			16 48			17 00			17 18			17 30			17 48			18 00	
Harlington d			16 34			16 52			17 04			17 22			17 34			17 52			18 04	
Flitwick d			16 38			16 56			17 08			17 26			17 38			17 56			18 08	
Bedford 7 a			16 50	16 46		17 08			17 20	17 17		17 38			17 50	17 46		18 08			18 20	18 17

	TL A	TL 1 E	TL A	TL B	TL 1 C	EM ◇1 D	TL A	TL 1 E	TL A	TL B	TL 1	EM ◇1 F	TL A	TL 1 E	TL A	TL B	TL 1 C	EM ◇1 D	TL A	TL 1 E	TL A	TL B
Gatwick Airport ✈ d		16 49			16 49			17 19			17 19			17 49			17 49			18 19		
Elephant & Castle ⊖173,179 d	17 11		17 23				17 41		17 53				18 11		18 23				18 41		18 53	
London Bridge ⊖ d		17 19		17 28	17 33			17 49		17 58	18 03			18 19		18 28	18 33			18 49		18 58
London Blackfriars ⊖ d	17 16	17 25	17 28	17 35	17 39		17 46	17 55	17 58	18 05	18 09		18 16	18 25	18 28	18 35	18 39		18 46	18 55	18 58	19 05
City Thameslink 3 d																						
Farringdon 3 ⊖ d	17 20	17 29	17 32	17 39	17 43		17 50	17 59	18 02	18 09	18 13		18 20	18 29	18 32	18 39	18 43		18 50	18 59	19 02	19 09
St Pancras International ⊖ d	17 25	17 34	17 37	17 44	17 48	18 10	17 55	18 04	18 07	18 14	18 18	18 40	18 25	18 34	18 37	18 44	18 48	19 10	18 55	19 04	19 07	19 14
Kentish Town ⊖ d			17 41	17a48					18 11	18a18					18 41	18a48					19 11	19a18
WestHampsteadThameslink ⊖ d	17 34	17 42	17 46		17 56		18 04	18 12	18 16		18 26		18 34	18 42	18 46		18 56		19 04	19 12	19 16	
Cricklewood d			17 50						18 20						18 50						19 20	
Hendon d			17 54						18 24						18 54						19 24	
Mill Hill Broadway d	17 40		17 57				18 10		18 27				18 40		18 57				19 10		19 27	
Elstree & Borehamwood d	17 44		18 01				18 14		18 31				18 44		19 01				19 14		19 31	
Radlett d	17 48		18 05				18 18		18 35				18 48		19 05				19 18		19 38	
St Albans City d	17 55	17 59	18a12		18 09		18 25	18 29	18a42		18 39		18 55	18 59	19a12		19 09		19 25	19 29	19a44	
Harpenden d	18 00	18 04			18 16		18 30	18 34			18 46		19 00	19 04			19 16		19 30	19 34		
Luton Airport Parkway 7 ✈ d	18 06	18 10			18 21	18 32	18 36	18 40			18 51		19 06	19 10			19 21	19 32	19 36	19 40		
Luton 10 d	18a10	18 14			18 26		18a40	18 44			18 56	19 03	19a10	19 14			19 26		19a40	19 44		
Leagrave d		18 18			18 30			18 48			19 00			19 18			19 30			19 48		
Harlington d		18 22			18 34			18 52			19 04			19 22			19 34			19 52		
Flitwick d		18 26			18 38			18 56			19 08			19 26			19 38			19 56		
Bedford 7 a		18 38			18 50	18 46		19 08			19 20	19 17		19 38			19 51	19 46		20 09		

	TL 1	EM ◇1 F	TL A	TL 1 E	TL A	TL B	TL 1 C	EM ◇1 D	TL A	TL 1 E	TL A	TL B	TL 1	EM ◇1 G	TL A	TL 1 E	TL A	TL B	TL 1 C	EM ◇1 D	TL A	TL 1 E
Gatwick Airport ✈ d	18 19			18 49			18 49			19 19			19 19			19 49			19 49			20 19
Elephant & Castle ⊖173,179 d			19 11		19 23				19 41		19 53				20 11		20 23				20 41	
London Bridge ⊖ d	19 03			19 19		19 28	19 33			19 49		19 58	20 03			20 19		20 28	20 33			20 49
London Blackfriars ⊖ d	19 09		19 16	19 25	19 28	19 35	19 39		19 46	19 55	19 58	20 05	20 09		20 16	20 25	20 28	20 35	20 39		20 46	20 55
City Thameslink 3 d																						
Farringdon 3 ⊖ d	19 13		19 20	19 29	19 32	19 39	19 43		19 50	19 59	20 02	20 09	20 13		20 20	20 29	20 32	20 39	20 43		20 50	20 59
St Pancras International ⊖ d	19 18	19 40	19 25	19 34	19 37	19 44	19 48	20 10	19 55	20 04	20 07	20 14	20 18	20 40	20 25	20 34	20 37	20 44	20 48	21 10	20 55	21 04
Kentish Town ⊖ d					19 41	19a48					20 11	20a18					20 41	20a48				
WestHampsteadThameslink ⊖ d	19 26		19 34	19 42	19 46		19 56		20 04	20 12	20 16		20 26		20 34	20 42	20 46		20 56		21 04	21 12
Cricklewood d					19 50						20 20						20 50					
Hendon d					19 54						20 24						20 54					
Mill Hill Broadway d			19 40		19 57				20 10		20 27				20 40		20 57				21 10	
Elstree & Borehamwood d			19 44		20 01				20 14		20 31				20 44		21 01				21 14	
Radlett d			19 48		20 05				20 18		20 35				20 48		21 05				21 18	
St Albans City d	19 40		19 55	19 59	20a12		20 09		20 25	20 29	20a42		20 39		20 55	20 59	21a12		21 09		21 25	21 29
Harpenden d	19 46		20 00	20 04			20 16		20 30	20 34			20 46		21 00	21 04			21 16		21 30	21 34
Luton Airport Parkway 7 ✈ d	19 51		20 06	20 10			20 21	20 32	20 36	20 40			20 51		21 06	21 10			21 21	21 32	21 36	21 40
Luton 10 d	19 56	20 03	20a10	20 14			20 26		20a40	20 44			20 56	21 04	21a10	21 14			21 26		21a40	21 44
Leagrave d	20 00			20 18			20 30			20 48			21 00			21 18			21 30			21 48
Harlington d	20 04			20 22			20 34			20 52			21 04			21 22			21 34			21 52
Flitwick d	20 08			20 26			20 38			20 56			21 08			21 26			21 38			21 56
Bedford 7 a	20 20	20 17		20 38			20 50	20 46		21 08			21 20	21 19		21 38			21 50	21 46		22 08

A From Sutton (Surrey)
B From Rainham (Kent)
C From Three Bridges
D To Nottingham
E From Brighton
F To Derby
G To Leeds

Table T052MML-F

Sundays
15 December to 10 May

Gatwick Airport and London - St Albans, Luton and Bedford

Station		TL A	TL B	EM ◇1 C	TL ■1	TL A	TL ■1 D	TL A	TL B	TL ■1 E	TL A	TL ■1 D	TL F	TL B	TL ■1	EM ◇1 G	TL A	TL ■1 D	TL A	TL B	EM ◇1 H	TL ■1 D
Gatwick Airport ✈	d				20 19		20 49			20 49		21 19			21 19			21 49				22 19
Elephant & Castle ⊖173,179	d	20 53				21 11		21 23			21 41		21 53						22 23			
London Bridge ⊖	d		20 58		21 03		21 19		21 28	21 33		21 49		21 58	22 03			22 19		22 28		22 49
London Blackfriars ⊖	d	20 58	21 05		21 09	21 16	21 25	21 28	21 35	21 39	21 46	21 55	21 58	22 05	22 09			22 25	22 28	22 35		22 55
City Thameslink 3	d																					
Farringdon 3 ⊖	d	21 02	21 09		21 13	21 20	21 29	21 32	21 39	21 43	21 50	21 59	22 02	22 09	22 13			22 29	22 32	22 39		22 59
St Pancras International ⊖	d	21 07	21 14	21 30	21 18	21 25	21 34	21 37	21 44	21 48	21 55	22 04	22 07	22 14	22 18	22 30		22 34	22 37	22 44	23 00	23 04
Kentish Town ⊖	d	21 11	21a18					21 41	21a48				22 11	22a18					22 41	22a48		
WestHampsteadThameslink ⊖	d	21 16			21 26	21 34	21 42	21 46		21 56	22 04	22 12	22 15		22 26			22 42	22 45			23 12
Cricklewood	d	21 20						21 50					22 19						22 49			
Hendon	d	21 24						21 54					22 23						22 53			
Mill Hill Broadway	d	21 27				21 40		21 57			22 10		22 26						22 56			
Elstree & Borehamwood	d	21 31				21 44		22 01			22 14		22 30				←		23 00			
Radlett	d	21 35				21 48		22 05			22 18		22 34				22 34		23 04			
St Albans City	d	21a42			21 39	21 55	21 59	22a12		22 09	22 25	22 29	→		22 39		22 41	22 59	23 11			23 29
Harpenden	d				21 46	22 00	22 04			22 16	22 30	22 34			22 46		22 50	23 04	23 17			23 35
Luton Airport Parkway 7 ✈	d				21 52	22 06	22 10			22 21	22 36	22 40			22 51	22 52	22 55	23 10	23 22		23 28	23 40
Luton 10	d			21 54	21 56	22a10	22 14			22 26	22a40	22 44			22 56		23 00	23 14	23a26			23 45
Leagrave	d				22 00		22 18			22 30		22 48			23 00		23 04	23 18				23 49
Harlington	d				22 04		22 22			22 34		22 52			23 04		23 08	23 22				23 53
Flitwick	d				22 08		22 26			22 38		22 56			23 08		23 13	23 26				23 57
Bedford 7	a			22 07	22 20		22 38			22 50		23 08			23 20	23 11	23 24	23 38			23 53	00 09

Station		TL A	TL B	TL A	TL ■1 D	TL B	TL ■1 D	TL ■1 D
Gatwick Airport ✈	d				22 49		23 21	23 50
Elephant & Castle ⊖173,179	d	22 53		23 11				
London Bridge ⊖	d		22 58		23 19	23 28		
London Blackfriars ⊖	d	22 58	23 05	23 16	23 27	23 37	00 06	00 36
City Thameslink 3	d							
Farringdon 3 ⊖	d	23 02	23 09	23 20	23 31	23 41	00 11	
St Pancras International ⊖	d	23 07	23 14	23 25	23 36	23 46	00 16	00 46
Kentish Town ⊖	d	23 11	23 18	23 29		23 50	00 20	00 50
WestHampsteadThameslink ⊖	d	23 15	23a22	23 33	23 44	23 54	00 24	00 54
Cricklewood	d	23 19		23 37		23 58	00 28	00 58
Hendon	d	23 23		23 41		00 02	00 32	01 02
Mill Hill Broadway	d	23 26		23 44		00 05	00 35	01 05
Elstree & Borehamwood	d	23 30		23 48		00 09	00 39	01 09
Radlett	d	23 34		23 52		00 13	00 43	01 13
St Albans City	d	23 41		23 59	00 03	00 21	00 51	01 21
Harpenden	d	23 47		00 05	00 09	00 27	00 57	01 27
Luton Airport Parkway 7 ✈	d	23 52		00 10	00 14	00 32	01 02	01 32
Luton 10	d	23 57		00 15	00 19	00 37	01 07	01 37
Leagrave	d	00 01			00 23	00 41	01 11	01 41
Harlington	d	00 05			00 27	00 45	01 15	01 45
Flitwick	d	00 09			00 31	00 49	01 19	01 49
Bedford 7	a	00 21		00 35	00 43	01 01	01 31	02 01

A From Sutton (Surrey)
B From Rainham (Kent)
C To Sheffield
D From Brighton
E From Three Bridges
F From Sutton (Surrey) to Bedford
G To Nottingham
H To Derby

NRT DECEMBER 19 EDITION

Table T052MML-R

Mondays to Fridays
16 December to 15 May

Bedford, Luton and St Albans - London and Gatwick Airport

Miles	Miles	Miles	Station		TL ■1 A	TL MO ■1 B	TL MX ■1 B	TL ■1 C	TL ■1 C	TL ■1 C	TL ■1 C	TL ■1 D	TL ■1 D	TL ■1 D	TL E	TL ■1 D	TL E	TL F	TL E	TL G	TL ■1 D	TL ■1 H	TL E
0	—	—	Bedford 7	d				00 15	01 15	01 53	02 15	02 53	03 10	03 45		04 13					04 43		
10	—	—	Flitwick	d				00 26	01 26	02 04	02 26	03 04	03 21	03 56		04 24					04 54		
13	—	—	Harlington	d		00 01	00 01	00 30	01 30	02 08	02 31	03 08	03 25	04 00		04 28					04 58		
17	—	—	Leagrave	d		00 06	00 06	00 35	01 35	02 13	02 37	03 13	03 30	04 05		04 33					05 03		
19	—	—	Luton 10	d		00 10	00 10	00 40	01 40	02 18	02 41	03 18	03 35	04 10	04 20	04 38			04 50		05 08		
20	—	—	Luton Airport Parkway 7 ✈	d		00 13	00 13	00 43	01 43	02 21	02 44	03 21	03 38	04 13	04 23	04 41			04 53		05 11		
24	—	—	Harpenden	d		00 18	00 18	00 48	01 48	02 26	02 50	03 26	03 43	04 18	04 28	04 46			04 58		05 16		
29	—	—	St Albans City	d		00 25	00 25	00 55	01 55	02 33	02 56	03 33	03 50	04 25	04 35	04 53			05 05		05 23		
—	—	—	Radlett	d					01 00	02 00		03 02		03 55	04 41				05 11				
—	—	—	Elstree & Borehamwood	d					01 04	02 04		03 05		03 59	04 44				05 14				
—	—	—	Mill Hill Broadway	d					01 08	02 08		03 09		04 03	04 48				05 18				
—	—	—	Hendon	d	00 01				01 11	02 11		03 13		04 06	04 52				05 22				
—	—	—	Cricklewood	d	00 06				01 16	02 16		03 17		04 11	04 56				05 28				
45	—	—	WestHampsteadThameslink ⊖	d	00 09	00 41	00 42	01 20	02 20	02 50	03 21	03 50	04 15	04 41	04 59	05 09	05 16	05 20	05 31	05 36	05 39	05 43	
—	—	—	Kentish Town ⊖	d	00 13				01 24	02 24		03 25		04 19	05 04		05 21		05 36	05 41			
49	—	—	St Pancras International ⊖	a	00 19	00 51	00 52	01 30	02 31	03 01	03 31	04 01	04 25	04 51	05 10	05 19	05 27	05 30	05 42	05 47	05 49	05 53	05 57
—	—	—	Farringdon 3 ⊖	a	00 25									04 56	05 16	05 24	05 31	05 34	05 46	05 51	05 54	05 59	06 01
—	—	—	City Thameslink 3	a										04 58	05 18	05 26	05 33	05 36	05 48	05 53	05 56	06 01	06 03
51	0	—	London Blackfriars ⊖	a	00 30	01 00	01 01	01 39	02 39	03 09	03 39	04 09	04 39	05 00	05 21	05 28	05 36	05 39	05 51	05 56	05 58	06 03	06 06
—	—	0	London Bridge ⊖	a												05 34		05 45			06 04	06 10	
—	1	1	Elephant & Castle ⊖173,179	a											05 25		05 40		05 55	06 00			06 10
78	—	—	Gatwick Airport ✈	a	01 20	01 56	01 56	02 30	03 30	03 56	04 30	04 57	05 31	05 47		06 04					06 34		

Station		TL F	TL E	TL G	TL E	TL ■1 D	TL ■1 H	TL I	EM ◇1 J	TL F	TL G	TL E	TL ■1	TL K	TL L	TL E	TL ■1 D	TL F	TL ■1 H	TL K	TL E	TL M
Bedford 7	d					05 15	05 25		05 38				05 44				05 48	06 01	06 04			
Flitwick	d					05 26	05 35						05 53				05 59	06 12	06 13			←
Harlington	d					05 30	05 39										06 03	06 16				06 16
Leagrave	d					05 35	05 44										06 08	→				06 21
Luton 10	d		05 20		05 36	05 40	05 48			06 00			06 02		←		06 12		06 22			06 25
Luton Airport Parkway 7 ✈	d		05 23		05 39	05 43	05 51		05 58	06 03					06 03		06 15					06 28
Harpenden	d		05 28		05 44	05 48	05 56			→			06 08		06 09		06 21		06 28			06 33
St Albans City	d		05 35		05 51	05 55	06 01	←			06 07		06 13	←	06 15	06 22	06 27		06 33	←	06 34	06 38
Radlett	d		05 41		05 57			05 57			06 12			06 12	06 20	06 27				06 27	06 39	
Elstree & Borehamwood	d		05 44		→			06 00			→			06 16	06 24	→				06 31	06 43	
Mill Hill Broadway	d		05 48					06 04						06 20	06 28					06 35	→	
Hendon	d		05 52					06 08						06 23						06 38		
Cricklewood	d		05 56					06 13						06 28						06 43		
WestHampsteadThameslink ⊖	d	05 52	05 59	06 06		06 09		06 17		06 21				06 32	06 36		06 39			06 47		
Kentish Town ⊖	d		06 04	06 11				06 21						06 36						06 51		
St Pancras International ⊖	a	06 02	06 10	06 17		06 19	06 24	06 27	06 24	06 32			06 34		06 47		06 49		06 54	06 57		07 02
Farringdon 3 ⊖	a	06 06	06 16	06 21		06 24	06 29	06 31		06 36			06 39	06 46	06 51		06 54		06 59	07 01		07 06
City Thameslink 3	a	06 08	06 18	06 23		06 26	06 31	06 33		06 38			06 41	06 48	06 53		06 56		07 01	07 03		07 08
London Blackfriars ⊖	a	06 11	06 21	06 26		06 28	06 33	06 36		06 41			06 43	06 51	06 56		06 58		07 03	07 06		07 11
London Bridge ⊖	a	06 17				06 34	06 40			06 47			06 50				07 04		07 10			07 17
Elephant & Castle ⊖173,179	a		06 25	06 30				06 40						06 55	07 00					07 10		
Gatwick Airport ✈	a					07 04							07 28				07 34					

Station		EM ◇1 N	TL G	TL ■1 D	TL ■1	TL K	TL L	TL E	TL ■1 B	TL F	TL ■1 H	TL K	TL E	TL M	TL G	EM ◇1 O	TL ■1 D	TL ■1	TL K	TL L	TL E	TL ■1 B	TL F
Bedford 7	d			06 18	06 22				←	06 31	06 34						06 48	06 52				←	
Flitwick	d			06 29					06 29	06 42	06 43			←			06 59					06 59	
Harlington	d			→					06 33	06 46				06 46			→					07 03	
Leagrave	d								06 38	→				06 51								07 08	
Luton 10	d	06 27	06 30		06 39				06 42		06 52			06 55	07 00			07 09				07 12	07 16
Luton Airport Parkway 7 ✈	d		06 33						06 45					06 58	07 03	07 05						07 15	07 19
Harpenden	d		06 39						06 51		06 58			07 04	07 09							07 21	07 25
St Albans City	d		06 45		06 48		←	06 52	06 57		07 03	←	07 07	07 10	07 15			07 18		←	07 22	07 27	07 30
Radlett	d		06 50			←	06 50	06 57				06 57	07 12		07 20				←	07 20	07 27		07 35
Elstree & Borehamwood	d		→			06 43	06 54	→				07 01	07 16		→				07 16	07 24	07 31		→
Mill Hill Broadway	d					06 47	06 58					07 05	→						07 20	07 28	→		
Hendon	d					06 51						07 08							07 23				
Cricklewood	d					06 56						07 13							07 28				
WestHampsteadThameslink ⊖	d					07 02	07 06		07 09			07 17							07 32	07 36			
Kentish Town ⊖	d					07 06						07 21							07 36				
St Pancras International ⊖	a	06 54			07 09				07 19		07 24	07 27		07 32		07 36		07 39				07 49	
Farringdon 3 ⊖	a				07 14	07 16	07 21		07 24		07 29	07 31		07 36				07 44	07 46	07 51		07 54	
City Thameslink 3	a				07 16	07 18	07 23		07 26		07 31	07 33		07 38				07 46	07 48	07 53		07 56	
London Blackfriars ⊖	a				07 18	07 21	07 26		07 28		07 33	07 36		07 41				07 48	07 51	07 56		07 58	
London Bridge ⊖	a				07 24				07 34		07 40			07 47				07 54				08 04	
Elephant & Castle ⊖173,179	a					07 25	07 30					07 40							07 55	08 00			
Gatwick Airport ✈	a				07 53				08 04									08 23				08 34	

A From Bedford to Three Bridges
B From Bedford to Brighton
C To Three Bridges
D To Brighton
E To Sutton (Surrey)
F To Rainham (Kent)
G To Orpington
H To East Grinstead
I From Luton to Sutton (Surrey)
J From Leicester
K From St Albans City to Sutton (Surrey)
L From Luton to Orpington
M From Bedford to Rainham (Kent)
N From Derby
O From Nottingham

Table T052MML-R

Mondays to Fridays

16 December to 15 May

Bedford, Luton and St Albans - London and Gatwick Airport

Station	TL ■ A	TL ■ B	TL C	TL D	TL E	TL ■ F		TL G	EM ◇■ H ⊠	TL ■ I	TL ■ J	TL C	TL K	TL E	TL ■ L	TL M	TL ■		TL C	TL D	TL E	TL ■ A	EM ◇■ N ⊠	TL G
Bedford ■ d	07 01	07 04								07 18	07 22				←		07 34							
Flitwick d	07 12	07 13				←				07 29					07 29		07 43					07 44		
Harlington d	07 16					07 16				→					07 33							07 48		
Leagrave d	→					07 21									07 38							07 53		
Luton ■ d		07 22				07 26		07 30			07 39				07 42	07 46	07 52					07 58		08 02
Luton Airport Parkway ■ ✈ d						07 29		07 33	07 44						07 45	07 49						08 01	08 03	08 05
Harpenden d		07 28				07 34		07 39							07 50	07 55	07 58					08 06		08 10
St Albans City d		07 33		←	07 36	07 41		07 45			07 48		←	07 52	07 56	08 00	08 03			←	08 07	08 12		08 16
Radlett d			←	07 35	07 41			07 50				←	07 50	07 57		08 05			←	08 05	08 12			08 21
Elstree & Borehamwood d			07 31	07 39	07 46			→				07 46	07 54	08 01		→			08 01	08 09	08 16			→
Mill Hill Broadway d			07 35	07 43	→							07 50	07 58	→					08 05	08 13	→			
Hendon d			07 38									07 53							08 08					
Cricklewood d			07 43									07 58							08 13					
WestHampsteadThameslink ⊖ d			07 47	07 51								08 02	08 06						08 17	08 21				
Kentish Town ⊖ d			07 51									08 06							08 21					
St Pancras International ⊖ a		07 54				08 04			08 09		08 09				08 19		08 24					08 34	08 27	
Farringdon ■ ⊖ a		07 59	08 01	08 06		08 09					08 14	08 16	08 21		08 24		08 29		08 31	08 36		08 39		
City Thameslink ■ a		08 01	08 03	08 08		08 11					08 16	08 18	08 23		08 26		08 31		08 33	08 38		08 41		
London Blackfriars ⊖ a		08 03	08 06	08 11		08 13					08 18	08 21	08 26		08 28		08 33		08 36	08 41		08 43		
London Bridge ⊖ a		08 10		08 17		08 20					08 24				08 34		08 40			08 47		08 50		
Elephant & Castle ⊖173,179 a			08 10									08 25	08 30						08 40					
Gatwick Airport ✈ a						09 05									09 04		09 19					09 35		

Station	TL ■ I	TL ■ A	TL C	TL K		TL E	TL ■ L	TL M	TL ■ O	TL ■	TL C	TL D	TL E	TL ■ P	TL G		TL ■ I	TL ■ A	TL C	TL K	TL E	TL ■ L	TL C	TL M
Bedford ■ d	07 48	07 52					←		08 01	08 04							08 18	08 22				←		
Flitwick d	07 59						07 59		08 12	08 13				←			08 29					08 29		
Harlington d	→						08 03		08 16					08 16			→					08 33		
Leagrave d							08 08		→					08 21								08 38		
Luton ■ d		08 09					08 12	08 16		08 22				08 26	08 30			08 39				08 42		08 46
Luton Airport Parkway ■ ✈ d							08 15	08 19						08 29	08 33							08 45		08 49
Harpenden d							08 20	08 24		08 28				08 34	08 39							08 50		08 54
St Albans City d		08 18		←		08 22	08 26	08 30		08 33		←	08 37	08 41	08 45			08 48		←	08 52	08 56	←	09 00
Radlett d			←	08 21		08 27		08 35			←	08 35	08 42		08 50				←	08 50	08 57		08 57	09 05
Elstree & Borehamwood d			08 16	08 24		08 31		→			08 31	08 39	08 46		→				08 46	08 54	→		09 01	09 09
Mill Hill Broadway d			08 20	08 28		→					08 35	08 43	→						08 50	08 58			09 05	09 13
Hendon d			08 23								08 38								08 53				09 08	
Cricklewood d			08 28								08 43								08 58				09 13	
WestHampsteadThameslink ⊖ d			08 32	08 36							08 47	08 51							09 02	09 06			09 17	09 21
Kentish Town ⊖ d			08 36								08 51								09 06				09 21	
St Pancras International ⊖ a		08 39					08 49			08 54				09 04				09 09				09 19		09 32
Farringdon ■ ⊖ a		08 44	08 46	08 51			08 54			08 59	09 01	09 06		09 09				09 14	09 16	09 21		09 24	09 31	09 36
City Thameslink ■ a		08 46	08 48	08 53			08 56			09 01	09 03	09 08		09 11				09 16	09 18	09 23		09 26	09 33	09 38
London Blackfriars ⊖ a		08 48	08 51	08 56			08 58			09 03	09 06	09 11		09 13				09 18	09 21	09 26		09 28	09 36	09 41
London Bridge ⊖ a		08 54					09 04			09 10		09 17		09 20				09 24				09 34		09 47
Elephant & Castle ⊖173,179 a			08 55	09 00							09 10								09 25	09 30			09 40	
Gatwick Airport ✈ a		09 23					09 34			09 47				10 08				09 53				10 04		

Station	TL E	TL ■		TL G	TL ■ A	TL C	TL K	TL E	TL ■ I	TL C	TL M	TL E	TL ■		TL C	EM ◇■ Q ⊠	TL G	TL E	TL ■ I	TL C	TL M	TL E	TL ■	TL C
Bedford ■ d		08 32			08 46				08 50				09 02						09 16				09 34	
Flitwick d		08 43			08 56				09 00				09 13						09 27				09 45	
Harlington d		08 47							09 04				09 17						09 31				09 49	
Leagrave d		08 52							09 09				09 22						09 36				09 54	
Luton ■ d		08 56		09 00	09 07				09 13		09 17		09 26						09 41		09 46		09 59	
Luton Airport Parkway ■ ✈ d		08 59		09 03					09 16		09 20		09 29			09 31			09 44		09 51		10 02	
Harpenden d		09 04		09 09	09 13				09 21		09 25		09 34						09 49		09 56		10 08	
St Albans City d	09 07	09 11		09 15	09 18		←	09 22	09 26	←	09 30	09 37	09 41		←			09 51	09 55	←	10 01	10 07	10 13	←
Radlett d	09 12			09 20		←	09 20	09 27		09 27	09 35	09 42			09 42			09 56		09 56	10 06	10 12		10 12
Elstree & Borehamwood d	09 16			→		09 16	09 24	→		09 31	09 39	→			09 46			→		10 01	10 10	→		10 16
Mill Hill Broadway d	→					09 20	09 28			09 35	09 43				09 50					10 05	10 14			10 20
Hendon d						09 23				09 38					09 53					10 08				10 23
Cricklewood d						09 28				09 43					09 58					10 13				10 28
WestHampsteadThameslink ⊖ d						09 32	09 36			09 47	09 51				10 01				10 09	10 16	10 21			10 31
Kentish Town ⊖ d						09 36				09 51					10 06		10 11			10 21				10 36
St Pancras International ⊖ a		09 34			09 39				09 49		10 02		10 04			09 55	10 17		10 19	10 27	10 32		10 34	
Farringdon ■ ⊖ a		09 39			09 44	09 46	09 51		09 54	10 01	10 06		10 09		10 16		10 21		10 24	10 31	10 36		10 39	10 46
City Thameslink ■ a		09 41			09 46	09 48	09 53		09 56	10 03	10 08		10 11		10 18		10 23		10 26	10 33	10 38		10 41	10 48
London Blackfriars ⊖ a		09 43			09 48	09 51	09 56		09 58	10 06	10 11		10 13		10 21		10 26		10 28	10 36	10 41		10 43	10 51
London Bridge ⊖ a		09 50			09 54				10 04		10 17		10 20						10 34		10 47		10 50	
Elephant & Castle ⊖173,179 a						09 55	10 00			10 10					10 25		10 30			10 40				10 55
Gatwick Airport ✈ a		10 38			10 23				10 34				11 08						11 04				11 38	

A To Three Bridges
B To East Grinstead
C From St Albans City to Sutton (Surrey)
D From Luton to Rainham (Kent)
E To Sutton (Surrey)
F From Bedford to Three Bridges
G To Orpington
H From Sheffield
I To Brighton
J To Littlehampton
K From Luton to Orpington
L From Bedford to Brighton
M To Rainham (Kent)
N From Sheffield. The Sheffield Continental
O To Gatwick Airport
P From Bedford
Q From Lincoln

Table T052MML-R

Mondays to Fridays

16 December to 15 May

Bedford, Luton and St Albans - London and Gatwick Airport

Station	TL A	TL B	TL ■ C	TL D	TL E	TL B	TL ■	TL D	EM ◇■ F ⊠		TL A	TL ■ C	EM ◇■ G ⊠	TL B	TL ■ H	TL D	TL E	TL B	TL ■	TL D		TL A	TL B	TL ■ C
Bedford ■ d			09 48				10 04		10 13			10 19	10 23		←				10 35					10 49
Flitwick d			09 59				10 15					10 30			10 30				10 46					11 00
Harlington d			10 03				10 19					→			10 34				10 50					11 04
Leagrave d			10 08				10 24								10 39				10 55					11 09
Luton ■ d			10 12		10 16		10 28		10 28						10 43		10 48		10 59					11 13
Luton Airport Parkway ■ ✈ d			10 15		10 21		10 31						10 39		10 46		10 51		11 02					11 16
Harpenden d			10 22		10 26		10 38								10 52		10 56		11 08					11 22
St Albans City d		10 22	10 27	←	10 31	10 38	10 43	←						10 52	10 57	←	11 01	11 07	11 13	←			11 22	11 27
Radlett d		10 27		10 27	10 36	10 43		10 43						10 57		10 57	11 06	11 12		11 12			11 27	
Elstree & Borehamwood d		→		10 31	10 40	→		10 47						→		11 01	11 10	→		11 16			→	
Mill Hill Broadway d				10 35	10 44			10 50								11 05	11 14			11 20				
Hendon d				10 38				10 54								11 08				11 23				
Cricklewood d				10 43				10 58								11 13				11 28				
WestHampsteadThameslink ⊖ d			10 39	10 46	10 51			11 01							11 09	11 16	11 21			11 32				11 39
Kentish Town ⊖ d	10 41			10 51				11 06			11 12					11 21				11 36		11 41		
St Pancras International ⊖ a	10 47		10 49	10 57	11 02		11 04		10 51		11 17		11 05		11 19	11 27	11 32		11 34			11 47		11 49
Farringdon ■ ⊖ a	10 51		10 54	11 01	11 06		11 09	11 16			11 21				11 24	11 31	11 36		11 39	11 46		11 51		11 54
City Thameslink ■ a	10 53		10 56	11 03	11 08		11 11	11 18			11 23				11 26	11 33	11 38		11 41	11 48		11 53		11 56
London Blackfriars ⊖ a	10 56		10 58	11 06	11 11		11 13	11 21			11 26				11 28	11 36	11 41		11 43	11 51		11 56		11 58
London Bridge ⊖ a			11 04		11 17		11 20								11 34		11 47		11 50					12 04
Elephant & Castle ⊖173,179 a	11 00			11 10				11 25			11 30					11 40				11 55		12 00		
Gatwick Airport ✈ a			11 34				12 08								12 04				12 38					12 34

Station	TL D	TL E	TL ■ I	EM ◇■ F ⊠	TL B	TL ■ J	TL D		TL A	TL ■ C	EM ◇■ G ⊠	TL B	TL ■ H	TL D	TL E	TL B	TL ■	TL D		TL A	TL B	TL ■ C	TL D	TL E
Bedford ■ d			11 05	11 13		←				11 19	11 23		←				11 35					11 49		
Flitwick d			11 16			11 16				11 30			11 30				11 46					12 00		
Harlington d			→			11 20				→			11 34				11 50					12 04		
Leagrave d						11 25							11 39				11 55					12 09		
Luton ■ d		11 18		11 28		11 29							11 43		11 48		11 59					12 13		12 18
Luton Airport Parkway ■ ✈ d		11 21				11 32					11 39		11 46		11 51		12 02					12 16		12 21
Harpenden d		11 26				11 38							11 52		11 56		12 08					12 22		12 26
St Albans City d	←	11 31			11 37	11 43	←					11 53	11 57	←	12 01	12 07	12 13	←			12 22	12 27	←	12 31
Radlett d	11 27	11 36			11 42		11 42					11 58		11 58	12 06	12 12		12 12			12 27		12 27	12 36
Elstree & Borehamwood d	11 31	11 40			→		11 46					→		12 02	12 10	→		12 16			→		12 31	12 40
Mill Hill Broadway d	11 35	11 44					11 50							12 05	12 14			12 20					12 35	12 44
Hendon d	11 38						11 53							12 09				12 23					12 38	
Cricklewood d	11 43						11 58							12 13				12 28					12 43	
WestHampsteadThameslink ⊖ d	11 46	11 51					12 01						12 09	12 16	12 21			12 31				12 39	12 46	12 51
Kentish Town ⊖ d	11 51						12 06		12 11					12 21				12 36		12 41			12 51	
St Pancras International ⊖ a	11 57	12 02		11 52		12 04			12 17		12 07		12 19	12 27	12 32		12 34			12 47		12 49	12 57	13 02
Farringdon ■ ⊖ a	12 01	12 06				12 09	12 16		12 21				12 24	12 31	12 36		12 39	12 46		12 51		12 54	13 01	13 06
City Thameslink ■ a	12 03	12 08				12 11	12 18		12 23				12 26	12 33	12 38		12 41	12 48		12 53		12 56	13 03	13 08
London Blackfriars ⊖ a	12 06	12 11				12 13	12 21		12 26				12 28	12 36	12 41		12 43	12 51		12 56		12 58	13 06	13 11
London Bridge ⊖ a		12 17				12 20							12 34		12 47		12 50					13 04		13 17
Elephant & Castle ⊖173,179 a	12 10						12 25		12 30					12 40				12 55		13 00			13 10	
Gatwick Airport ✈ a						13 08							13 04				13 38					13 34		

Station	TL ■ I	EM ◇■ F ⊠	TL B	TL ■ J	TL D		TL A	TL ■ C	EM ◇■ G ⊠	TL B	TL ■ H	TL D	TL E	TL B	TL ■	TL D		TL A	TL B	TL ■ C	TL D	TL E	TL ■ I	EM ◇■ F ⊠
Bedford ■ d	12 05	12 13		←				12 19	12 23		←				12 35					12 49			13 05	13 13
Flitwick d	12 16			12 16				12 30			12 30				12 46					13 00			13 16	
Harlington d	→			12 20				→			12 34				12 50					13 04			→	
Leagrave d				12 25							12 39				12 55					13 09				
Luton ■ d		12 28		12 29							12 43		12 48		12 59					13 13		13 18		13 28
Luton Airport Parkway ■ ✈ d				12 32					12 39		12 46		12 51		13 02					13 16		13 21		
Harpenden d				12 38							12 52		12 56		13 08					13 22		13 26		
St Albans City d			12 37	12 43	←					12 52	12 57	←	13 01	13 07	13 13	←			13 22	13 27	←	13 31		
Radlett d			12 42		12 42					12 57		12 57	13 06	13 12		13 12			13 27		13 27	13 36		
Elstree & Borehamwood d			→		12 46					→		13 01	13 10	→		13 16			→		13 31	13 40		
Mill Hill Broadway d					12 50							13 05	13 14			13 20					13 35	13 44		
Hendon d					12 53							13 08				13 23					13 38			
Cricklewood d					12 58							13 13				13 28					13 43			
WestHampsteadThameslink ⊖ d					13 01						13 09	13 16	13 21			13 31				13 39	13 46	13 51		
Kentish Town ⊖ d					13 06		13 11					13 21				13 36		13 41			13 51			
St Pancras International ⊖ a		12 51		13 04			13 17		13 06		13 19	13 27	13 32		13 34			13 47		13 49	13 57	14 02		13 51
Farringdon ■ ⊖ a				13 09	13 16		13 21				13 24	13 31	13 36		13 39	13 46		13 51		13 54	14 01	14 06		
City Thameslink ■ a				13 11	13 18		13 23				13 26	13 33	13 38		13 41	13 48		13 53		13 56	14 03	14 08		
London Blackfriars ⊖ a				13 13	13 21		13 26				13 28	13 36	13 41		13 43	13 51		13 56		13 58	14 06	14 11		
London Bridge ⊖ a				13 20							13 34		13 47		13 50					14 04		14 17		
Elephant & Castle ⊖173,179 a					13 25		13 30					13 40				13 55		14 00			14 10			
Gatwick Airport ✈ a				14 08							14 04				14 38					14 34				

A To Orpington
B To Sutton (Surrey)
C To Brighton
D From St Albans City to Sutton (Surrey)
E To Rainham (Kent)
F From Corby
G From Nottingham
H From Bedford to Brighton
I To Gatwick Airport
J From Bedford

Table T052MML-R

Mondays to Fridays

16 December to 15 May

Bedford, Luton and St Albans - London and Gatwick Airport

		TL	TL	TL	TL	TL	EM	TL	TL	TL	TL	TL	TL	TL	TL	TL	TL	TL	TL	TL	EM	TL
		A	B	C	D	E	F	A	G	C	H	A		C	D	A	E	C	H	I	J	A
Bedford	d		←			13 19	13 23		←				13 35				13 49			14 05	14 13	
Flitwick	d		13 16			13 30			13 30				13 46				14 00			14 16		
Harlington	d		13 20			→			13 34				13 50				14 04			→		
Leagrave	d		13 25						13 39				13 55				14 09					
Luton	d		13 29						13 43		13 48		13 59				14 13		14 18		14 28	
Luton Airport Parkway ✈	d		13 32				13 39		13 46		13 51		14 02				14 16		14 21			
Harpenden	d		13 38						13 52		13 56		14 08				14 22		14 26			
St Albans City	d	13 37	13 43	←				13 52	13 57	←	14 01	14 07	14 13	←		14 22	14 27	←	14 31			14 37
Radlett	d	13 42		13 42				13 57		13 57	14 06	14 12		14 12		14 27		14 27	14 36			14 42
Elstree & Borehamwood	d	→		13 46				→		14 01	14 10	→		14 16		→		14 31	14 40			→
Mill Hill Broadway	d			13 50						14 05	14 14			14 20				14 35	14 44			
Hendon	d			13 53						14 08				14 23				14 38				
Cricklewood	d			13 58						14 13				14 28				14 43				
WestHampsteadThameslink ⊖	d			14 01					14 09	14 16	14 21			14 31			14 39	14 46	14 51			
Kentish Town ⊖	d			14 06	14 11					14 21				14 36	14 41			14 51				
St Pancras International ⊖	a		14 04		14 17		14 07		14 19	14 27	14 32		14 34		14 47		14 49	14 57	15 02		14 51	
Farringdon ⊖	a		14 09	14 16	14 21				14 24	14 31	14 36		14 39	14 46	14 51		14 54	15 01	15 06			
City Thameslink	a		14 11	14 18	14 23				14 26	14 33	14 38		14 41	14 48	14 53		14 56	15 03	15 08			
London Blackfriars ⊖	a		14 13	14 21	14 26				14 28	14 36	14 41		14 43	14 51	14 56		14 58	15 06	15 11			
London Bridge ⊖	a		14 20						14 34		14 47		14 50				15 04		15 17			
Elephant & Castle ⊖173,179	a			14 25	14 30					14 40				14 55	15 00			15 10				
Gatwick Airport ✈	a		15 08						15 04				15 38				15 34					

		TL	TL	TL	TL	EM	TL	TL	TL	TL	TL	TL	TL	TL	TL	TL	TL	TL	TL	EM	TL	TL	TL
		B	C	D	E	F	A	G	C	H	A		C	D	A	E	C	H	I	J	A	B	C
Bedford	d	←			14 19	14 23		←				14 35				14 49			15 05	15 13		←	
Flitwick	d	14 16			14 30			14 30				14 46				15 00			15 16			15 16	
Harlington	d	14 20			→			14 34				14 50				15 04			→			15 20	
Leagrave	d	14 25						14 39				14 55				15 09						15 25	
Luton	d	14 29						14 43		14 48		14 59				15 13		15 18		15 28		15 29	
Luton Airport Parkway ✈	d	14 32				14 39		14 46		14 51		15 02				15 16		15 21				15 32	
Harpenden	d	14 38						14 52		14 56		15 08				15 22		15 26				15 38	
St Albans City	d	14 43	←				14 52	14 57	←	15 01	15 07	15 13	←		15 22	15 27	←	15 31			15 37	15 43	←
Radlett	d		14 42				14 57		14 57	15 06	15 12		15 12		15 27		15 27	15 36			15 42		15 42
Elstree & Borehamwood	d		14 46				→		15 01	15 10	→		15 16		→		15 31	15 40			→		15 46
Mill Hill Broadway	d		14 50						15 05	15 14			15 20				15 35	15 44					15 50
Hendon	d		14 53						15 08				15 23				15 38						15 53
Cricklewood	d		14 58						15 13				15 28				15 43						15 58
WestHampsteadThameslink ⊖	d		15 01					15 09	15 16	15 21			15 31			15 39	15 46	15 51					16 01
Kentish Town ⊖	d		15 06	15 11					15 21				15 36	15 41			15 51						16 06
St Pancras International ⊖	a	15 04		15 17		15 05		15 19	15 27	15 32		15 34		15 47		15 49	15 57	16 02		15 51		16 04	
Farringdon ⊖	a	15 09	15 16	15 21				15 24	15 31	15 36		15 39	15 46	15 51		15 54	16 01	16 06				16 09	16 16
City Thameslink	a	15 11	15 18	15 23				15 26	15 33	15 38		15 41	15 48	15 53		15 56	16 03	16 08				16 11	16 18
London Blackfriars ⊖	a	15 13	15 21	15 26				15 28	15 36	15 41		15 43	15 51	15 56		15 58	16 06	16 11				16 13	16 21
London Bridge ⊖	a	15 20						15 34		15 47		15 50				16 04		16 17				16 20	
Elephant & Castle ⊖173,179	a		15 25	15 30					15 40				15 55	16 00			16 10						16 25
Gatwick Airport ✈	a	16 08						16 04				16 38				16 35						17 11	

		TL	TL	EM	TL	TL	TL	TL	TL	TL	TL	TL	TL	TL	TL	TL	TL	TL	TL	TL	TL	TL	TL
		D	E	F	A	G	H	K	C	L	A		M	C	D	A	E	C	H	I	K	C	L
Bedford	d		15 19	15 23		←						15 35	15 44				15 48			16 02	16 06		
Flitwick	d		15 30			15 30						15 46					15 59			16 13			
Harlington	d		→			15 34						15 50					16 03			→			
Leagrave	d					15 39						15 55	16 00				16 08						
Luton	d					15 43	15 48	15 49				15 59	16 06				16 13		16 18		16 23		
Luton Airport Parkway ✈	d			15 39		15 46	15 51	15 52		←		16 02	16 09				16 16		16 21				
Harpenden	d					15 52	15 56			15 56		16 08					16 22		16 26				
St Albans City	d				15 52	15 57	→	16 01	←	16 01	16 07	16 13	16 18	←		16 22	16 27	←	16 31		16 33		←
Radlett	d				15 57				15 57	16 06	16 12			16 12		16 27		16 27	16 36			←	16 36
Elstree & Borehamwood	d				→				16 01	16 10	→			16 16		→		16 31	→			16 31	16 40
Mill Hill Broadway	d								16 05	16 14				16 20				→				16 35	16 43
Hendon	d								16 08					16 23								16 38	
Cricklewood	d								16 13					16 28								16 43	
WestHampsteadThameslink ⊖	d					16 09			16 17	16 21				16 32	16 36		16 39					16 47	16 51
Kentish Town ⊖	d	16 11							16 22					16 37	16 41							16 52	
St Pancras International ⊖	a	16 17		16 11		16 19		16 24				16 34	16 39		16 47		16 49				16 54		
Farringdon ⊖	a	16 21				16 24		16 29	16 31	16 36		16 39	16 44	16 46	16 51		16 54				16 59	17 01	17 06
City Thameslink	a	16 23				16 26		16 31	16 33	16 38		16 41	16 46	16 48	16 53		16 56				17 01	17 03	17 08
London Blackfriars ⊖	a	16 26				16 28		16 33	16 36	16 41		16 43	16 48	16 51	16 56		16 58				17 03	17 06	17 11
London Bridge ⊖	a					16 34		16 40		16 47		16 50	16 54				17 04				17 10		17 17
Elephant & Castle ⊖173,179	a	16 30							16 40					16 55	17 00							17 10	
Gatwick Airport ✈	a					17 04						17 41					17 35						

A To Sutton (Surrey)
B From Bedford
C From St Albans City to Sutton (Surrey)
D To Orpington
E To Brighton
F From Nottingham
G From Bedford to Brighton
H To Rainham (Kent)
I To Gatwick Airport
J From Corby
K To East Grinstead
L From Luton to Rainham (Kent)
M To Littlehampton

Table T052MML-R

Mondays to Fridays

16 December to 15 May

Bedford, Luton and St Albans - London and Gatwick Airport

		EM	TL	TL	TL	TL	TL	EM	TL	TL	TL	TL	TL	TL	TL	TL	TL	TL	TL	TL	TL	TL	TL
		A	B	C	D	E	F	G	B	H	I	J	D	K	B		L	D	E	B	F	D	I
Bedford	d	16 12		←			16 18	16 22		←		16 32				16 35	16 45				16 49		
Flitwick	d			16 13			16 29			16 29						16 46					17 00		
Harlington	d			16 17			→			16 33						16 50					17 04		
Leagrave	d			16 22						16 38						16 55	17 00				17 09		
Luton	d	16 27		16 27						16 42	16 46	16 51				16 59	17 04				17 13		17 17
Luton Airport Parkway ✈	d			16 30				16 38		16 45	16 49	16 54				17 02	17 07				17 16		17 20
Harpenden	d			16 35						16 50	16 54					17 08	17 12				17 21		17 25
St Albans City	d		16 38	16 41	←				16 52	16 56	17 00	17 03		←	17 07	17 13	17 18	←		17 22	17 27	←	17 30
Radlett	d		16 43		16 43				16 57		17 05		←	17 05	17 12			17 12		17 27		17 27	17 35
Elstree & Borehamwood	d		→		16 47				17 01		→		17 01	17 09	→			17 16		→		17 31	→
Mill Hill Broadway	d				16 50				→				17 05	17 13				17 20				→	
Hendon	d				16 54								17 08					17 23					
Cricklewood	d				16 58								17 13					17 28					
WestHampsteadThameslink ⊖	d			16 54	17 02	17 06							17 17	17 21				17 32	17 36		17 39		
Kentish Town ⊖	d				17 07	17 11							17 22					17 37	17 41				
St Pancras International ⊖	a	16 55		17 04	17 12	17 17		17 12		17 19		17 24				17 34	17 39		17 47		17 49		
Farringdon ⊖	a			17 09	17 16	17 21				17 24		17 29	17 31	17 36		17 39	17 44	17 46	17 51		17 54		
City Thameslink	a			17 11	17 18	17 23				17 26		17 31	17 33	17 38		17 41	17 46	17 48	17 53		17 56		
London Blackfriars ⊖	a			17 13	17 21	17 26				17 28		17 33	17 36	17 41		17 43	17 48	17 51	17 56		17 58		
London Bridge ⊖	a			17 20						17 34		17 40		17 47		17 50	17 54				18 04		
Elephant & Castle ⊖173,179	a				17 25	17 30							17 40					17 55	18 00				
Gatwick Airport ✈	a			18 11						18 05						18 41					18 35		

		TL	TL	TL	TL	TL	TL	EM	TL	TL	EM	TL	TL	TL	TL	TL	TL	TL	TL	TL	TL	EM	TL
		J	D	K	B		D	A	E	F	G	B	H	I	J	D	K	B		D	E	G	B
Bedford	d					17 04		17 14		17 18	17 23		←		17 28				17 40				
Flitwick	d					17 15				17 29			17 29		17 39								
Harlington	d					17 19				→			17 33		17 43								
Leagrave	d					17 24							17 38		17 48								
Luton	d	17 21				17 28		17 30	17 32				17 42	17 46	17 53				17 57		18 02	18 05	
Luton Airport Parkway ✈	d	17 24				17 31			17 35		17 38		17 45	17 49					18 00		18 05		
Harpenden	d					17 36			17 40				17 50	17 54					18 06		18 10		
St Albans City	d	17 33		←	17 37	17 42	←		17 46			17 52	17 56	18 00	18 03		←	18 07	18 12	←	18 16		18 22
Radlett	d		←	17 35	17 42		17 42		17 51			17 57		18 05		←	18 05	18 12		18 12	18 21		18 27
Elstree & Borehamwood	d		17 31	17 39	→		17 46		17 54			18 01		→		18 01	18 09	→		18 16	18 24		18 31
Mill Hill Broadway	d		17 35	17 43			17 50		17 58			→				18 05	18 13			18 20	18 28		→
Hendon	d		17 38				17 53									18 08				18 23			
Cricklewood	d		17 43				17 58									18 13				18 28			
WestHampsteadThameslink ⊖	d		17 47	17 51		17 54	18 01		18 06							18 17	18 21		18 24	18 31	18 36		
Kentish Town ⊖	d		17 52				18 06		18 11							18 22				18 36	18 41		
St Pancras International ⊖	a	17 54				18 04	18 12	17 55	18 17		18 06		18 19		18 24				18 34	18 42	18 47	18 35	
Farringdon ⊖	a	17 59	18 01	18 06		18 09	18 16		18 21				18 24		18 29	18 31	18 36		18 39	18 46	18 51		
City Thameslink	a	18 01	18 03	18 08		18 11	18 18		18 23				18 26		18 31	18 33	18 38		18 41	18 48	18 53		
London Blackfriars ⊖	a	18 03	18 06	18 11		18 13	18 21		18 26				18 28		18 33	18 36	18 41		18 43	18 51	18 56		
London Bridge ⊖	a	18 10		18 17		18 20							18 34		18 40		18 47		18 50				
Elephant & Castle ⊖173,179	a		18 10				18 25		18 30							18 40				18 55	19 00		
Gatwick Airport ✈	a					19 11							19 05						19 41				

		TL	TL	TL	TL	TL	TL	EM	TL	TL	TL	TL	TL	EM	TL	TL	TL	TL	TL	TL	TL	TL
		F	I	J	D	K	M	A	B	C	D	E	F	G	B	H	D	I	B		D	E
Bedford	d	17 46		17 56			18 06	18 10					18 16	18 24		←				18 32		
Flitwick	d	17 57		18 06									18 27			18 27				18 43		
Harlington	d	18 01		18 10						←			→			18 31				18 47		
Leagrave	d	18 06		18 15			18 23			18 23						18 36				18 52		
Luton	d	18 12	18 16	18 20			→	18 26		18 27		18 32				18 42		18 46		18 57		19 02
Luton Airport Parkway ✈	d	18 15	18 19	18 22						18 30		18 35		18 41		18 45		18 49		19 00		19 05
Harpenden	d	18 20	18 24	18 27						18 36		18 40				18 50		18 54		19 06		19 10
St Albans City	d	18 26	18 30	18 33		←			18 37	18 42	←	18 46			18 52	18 56	←	19 00	19 07	19 11	←	19 16
Radlett	d		18 35		←	18 35			18 42		18 42	18 51			18 57		18 57	19 05	19 12		19 12	19 21
Elstree & Borehamwood	d		→		18 31	18 39			→		18 46	18 54			→		19 01	19 09	→		19 16	19 24
Mill Hill Broadway	d				18 35	18 43					18 49	18 58					19 05	19 13			19 20	19 28
Hendon	d				18 38						18 53						19 08				19 23	
Cricklewood	d				18 43						18 57						19 13				19 28	
WestHampsteadThameslink ⊖	d				18 47	18 51				18 54	19 00	19 07					19 16	19 21			19 31	19 36
Kentish Town ⊖	d				18 52						19 05	19 11					19 21				19 36	19 41
St Pancras International ⊖	a	18 49		18 54				18 54		19 04	19 12	19 17		19 06		19 19		19 32		19 34		19 47
Farringdon ⊖	a	18 54		18 59	19 01	19 06				19 09	19 16	19 21				19 24	19 31	19 36		19 39	19 46	19 51
City Thameslink	a	18 56		19 01	19 03	19 08				19 11	19 18	19 23				19 26	19 33	19 38		19 41	19 48	19 53
London Blackfriars ⊖	a	18 58		19 03	19 06	19 11				19 13	19 21	19 26				19 28	19 36	19 41		19 43	19 51	19 56
London Bridge ⊖	a	19 04		19 10		19 17				19 20						19 34		19 47		19 50		
Elephant & Castle ⊖173,179	a				19 10						19 25	19 30					19 40				19 55	20 00
Gatwick Airport ✈	a	19 35								20 11						20 04				20 38		

A From Corby
B To Sutton (Surrey)
C From Bedford
D From St Albans City to Sutton (Surrey)
E To Orpington
F To Brighton
G From Nottingham
H From Bedford to Brighton
I To Rainham (Kent)
J To East Grinstead
K From Luton to Rainham (Kent)
L To Littlehampton
M To Gatwick Airport

Table T052MML-R

Bedford, Luton and St Albans - London and Gatwick Airport

Mondays to Fridays
16 December to 15 May

		TL	TL	TL	TL	TL	TL	TL	EM	TL	TL	EM	TL	TL	TL	TL	TL	TL	TL	TL	TL	TL	TL
			1				1		◇1		1	◇1		1				1				1	
		A	B	C	D	A		C	E	F	B	G	A	H	C	D	A		C	F	A	B	C
Bedford 7	d		18 46				19 02		19 12		19 16	19 25		←				19 32				19 48	
Flitwick	d		18 57				19 13				19 27			19 27				19 43				19 59	
Harlington	d		19 01				19 17				→			19 31				19 47				20 03	
Leagrave	d		19 06				19 22							19 36				19 52				20 08	
Luton 10	d		19 12		19 18		19 27		19 28	19 32				19 43		19 48		19 57				20 14	
Luton Airport Parkway 7	d		19 15		19 21		19 30			19 35		19 41		19 46		19 51		20 00				20 16	
Harpenden	d		19 21		19 26		19 36			19 40				19 52		19 56		20 08				20 22	
St Albans City	d	19 22	19 27	←	19 31	19 37	19 42	←		19 46			19 52	19 57	←	20 01	20 08	20 13	←		20 22	20 27	←
Radlett	d	19 27		19 27	19 36	19 42		19 42		19 51			19 57		19 57	20 06	20 13		20 13		20 27		20 27
Elstree & Borehamwood	d	→		19 31	19 40	→		19 46		19 54			→		20 01	20 10	→		20 17		→		20 31
Mill Hill Broadway	d			19 35	19 44			19 50		19 58					20 05	20 14			20 20				20 35
Hendon	d			19 38				19 53							20 08				20 24				20 38
Cricklewood	d			19 43				19 58							20 13				20 28				20 43
WestHampsteadThameslink ⊖	d		19 39	19 46	19 51			20 01		20 06				20 09	20 16	20 21			20 31			20 39	20 46
Kentish Town ⊖	d			19 51				20 06		20 11					20 21				20 36	20 41			20 51
St Pancras International ⊖	a		19 49	19 57	20 02		20 04		19 57	20 17		20 07		20 19	20 27	20 32		20 34		20 47		20 49	20 57
Farringdon 3 ⊖	a		19 54	20 01	20 06		20 09	20 16		20 21				20 24	20 31	20 36		20 39	20 46	20 51		20 54	21 01
City Thameslink 3	a		19 56	20 03	20 08		20 11	20 18		20 23				20 26	20 33	20 38		20 41	20 48	20 53		20 56	21 03
London Blackfriars ⊖	a		19 58	20 06	20 11		20 13	20 21		20 26				20 28	20 36	20 41		20 43	20 51	20 56		20 58	21 06
London Bridge ⊖	a		20 04		20 17		20 20							20 34		20 47		20 50				21 04	
Elephant & Castle ⊖173,179	a			20 10				20 25		20 30					20 40				20 55	21 00			21 10
Gatwick Airport ✈	a		20 34				21 08							21 04				21 38				21 36	

		TL	TL	EM	TL	TL	TL	TL	TL	EM	TL	TL	TL	TL	TL	TL	TL	TL	TL	TL	TL	TL	TL
			1	◇1		1			1	◇1		1				1				1			1
		D	I	E	A	J	C	F	B	G	A	H	C	D	A		C	F	A	B	C	D	I
Bedford 7	d		20 04	20 09		←			20 18	20 23		←				20 32				20 49			21 02
Flitwick	d		20 15			20 15			20 29			20 29				20 43				21 00			21 13
Harlington	d		→			20 19			→			20 33				20 47				21 04			→
Leagrave	d					20 24						20 38				20 52				21 09			
Luton 10	d	20 18		20 25		20 29						20 43		20 48		20 59				21 13		21 18	
Luton Airport Parkway 7	d	20 21				20 32				20 38		20 46		20 51		21 02				21 16		21 21	
Harpenden	d	20 26				20 38						20 52		20 56		21 08				21 22		21 26	
St Albans City	d	20 31			20 37	20 43	←				20 52	20 57	←	21 01	21 07	21 13	←		21 22	21 27	←	21 31	
Radlett	d	20 36			20 42		20 42				20 57		20 57	21 06	21 12		21 12		21 27		21 27	21 36	
Elstree & Borehamwood	d	20 40			→		20 46				→		21 01	21 10	→		21 16		→		21 31	21 40	
Mill Hill Broadway	d	20 44					20 50						21 05	21 14			21 20				21 35	21 44	
Hendon	d						20 53						21 08				21 23				21 38		
Cricklewood	d						20 58						21 13				21 28				21 43		
WestHampsteadThameslink ⊖	d	20 51					21 01					21 09	21 16	21 21			21 31			21 39	21 46	21 51	
Kentish Town ⊖	d						21 06	21 11					21 21				21 36	21 41			21 51		
St Pancras International ⊖	a	21 02		20 51		21 04		21 17		21 06		21 19	21 27	21 32		21 34		21 47		21 49	21 57	22 02	
Farringdon 3 ⊖	a	21 06				21 09	21 16	21 21				21 24	21 31	21 36		21 39	21 46	21 51		21 54	22 01	22 06	
City Thameslink 3	a	21 08				21 11	21 18	21 23				21 26	21 33	21 38		21 41	21 48	21 53		21 56	22 03	22 08	
London Blackfriars ⊖	a	21 11				21 13	21 21	21 26				21 28	21 36	21 41		21 43	21 51	21 56		21 58	22 06	22 11	
London Bridge ⊖	a	21 17				21 20						21 34		21 47		21 50				22 04		22 17	
Elephant & Castle ⊖173,179	a						21 25	21 30					21 40				21 55	22 00			22 10		
Gatwick Airport ✈	a					22 08						22 04				22 38				22 34			

		EM	TL	TL	TL	TL	TL	EM	TL	TL	TL	TL	TL	TL	TL	TL	TL	TL	TL	TL	TL	TL	TL
		◇1		1			1	◇1		1				1				1				1	
		E	A	J	C	F	B	G	A	H	C	K	A	L	C	F	A	B	C	K	A		C
Bedford 7	d	21 13		←			21 19	21 26		←				21 35				21 49				22 05	
Flitwick	d			21 13			21 30			21 30				21 46				22 00				22 15	
Harlington	d			21 17			→			21 34				21 50				22 04				22 19	
Leagrave	d			21 22						21 39				21 55				22 09				22 24	
Luton 10	d	21 28		21 29						21 43		21 48		21 59				22 13		22 18		22 28	
Luton Airport Parkway 7	d			21 32				21 43		21 46		21 51		22 02				22 16		22 21		22 31	
Harpenden	d			21 38						21 52		21 56		22 08				22 22		22 26		22 36	
St Albans City	d		21 37	21 43	←				21 52	21 57	←	22 01	22 08	22 13	←		22 22	22 27	←	22 31	22 37	22 41	←
Radlett	d		21 42		21 42				21 57		21 57	22 06	22 13		22 13		22 27		22 27	22 36	22 42		22 42
Elstree & Borehamwood	d		→		21 46				→		22 01	22 10	→		22 17		→		22 31	22 40	→		22 46
Mill Hill Broadway	d				21 50						22 05	22 14			22 20				22 35	22 44			22 50
Hendon	d				21 53						22 08				22 24				22 38				22 53
Cricklewood	d				21 58						22 13				22 28				22 43				22 58
WestHampsteadThameslink ⊖	d				22 01					22 09	22 16	22 21			22 31			22 39	22 46	22 51			23 01
Kentish Town ⊖	d				22 06	22 11					22 21				22 36	22 41			22 51				23 06
St Pancras International ⊖	a	21 55		22 04		22 17		22 07		22 19	22 27	22 32		22 34		22 47		22 49	22 57	23 02		23 05	
Farringdon 3 ⊖	a			22 09	22 16	22 21				22 24	22 31	22 36		22 39	22 46	22 51		22 54	23 01	23 06		23 09	23 16
City Thameslink 3	a			22 11	22 18	22 23				22 26	22 33	22 38		22 41	22 48	22 53		22 56					
London Blackfriars ⊖	a			22 13	22 21	22 26				22 28	22 36	22 41		22 43	22 51	22 56		22 58	23 06	23 11		23 13	23 21
London Bridge ⊖	a			22 20						22 34		22 47		22 50				23 04		23 17		23 20	
Elephant & Castle ⊖173,179	a				22 25	22 30					22 40				22 55	23 00			23 10				23 25
Gatwick Airport ✈	a			23 08						23 04				23 37				23 34				00 01	

A To Sutton (Surrey)
B To Brighton
C From St Albans City to Sutton (Surrey)
D To Rainham (Kent)
E From Corby
F To Orpington
G From Nottingham
H From Bedford to Brighton
I To Gatwick Airport
J From Bedford
K To Gillingham (Kent)
L To Three Bridges

Table T052MML-R

Bedford, Luton and St Albans - London and Gatwick Airport

Mondays to Fridays
16 December to 15 May

		EM	TL	TL	EM	TL	TL	TL
		◇1	1		◇1	1	1	1
		A	B	C	A	B	D	B
Bedford 7	d	22 13	22 17		22 40	22 45	23 05	23 45
Flitwick	d		22 28			22 56	23 16	23 56
Harlington	d		22 32			23 00	23 20	00 01
Leagrave	d		22 37			23 05	23 25	00 06
Luton 10	d	22 28	22 41	22 54	22 55	23 10	23 30	00 10
Luton Airport Parkway 7	d	22 31	22 44	22 57		23 13	23 33	00 13
Harpenden	d		22 49	23 03		23 18	23 38	00 18
St Albans City	d		22 55	23 09		23 25	23 45	00 25
Radlett	d			23 14			23 50	
Elstree & Borehamwood	d			23 18			23 54	
Mill Hill Broadway	d			23 22			23 58	
Hendon	d			23 25			00 01	
Cricklewood	d			23 30			00 06	
WestHampsteadThameslink ⊖	d		23 11	23 33		23 41	00 09	00 42
Kentish Town ⊖	d			23 38			00 13	
St Pancras International ⊖	a	22 57	23 22	23 44	23 24	23 51	00 19	00 52
Farringdon 3 ⊖	a		23 26	23 48		23 55	00 25	
City Thameslink 3	a							
London Blackfriars ⊖	a		23 30	23 53		23 59	00 30	01 01
London Bridge ⊖	a		23 36					
Elephant & Castle ⊖173,179	a			23 57				
Gatwick Airport ✈	a		00 18			00 47	01 20	01 56

Saturdays
21 December to 16 May

		TL	TL	TL	TL	TL	TL	TL	TL	TL	TL	TL	TL	TL	TL	TL	TL	TL	TL	TL	TL	TL	EM
		1	1	1	1	1	1	1	1	1		1				1					1		◇1
		E	F	D	D	D	D	B	B	B	C	B	C	G	C	B	C	G	C	C	B	H	I
Bedford 7	d			00 15	01 15	01 53	02 15	02 53	03 10	03 45		04 13				04 43					05 15		05 34
Flitwick	d			00 26	01 26	02 04	02 26	03 04	03 21	03 56		04 24				04 54					05 26		
Harlington	d		00 01	00 30	01 30	02 08	02 30	03 08	03 25	04 00		04 28				04 58					05 30		
Leagrave	d		00 06	00 35	01 35	02 13	02 35	03 13	03 30	04 05		04 33				05 03					05 35		
Luton 10	d		00 10	00 40	01 40	02 18	02 40	03 18	03 35	04 10	04 20	04 38			04 50	05 08			05 20	05 36	05 40		
Luton Airport Parkway 7	d		00 13	00 43	01 43	02 21	02 43	03 21	03 38	04 13	04 23	04 41			04 53	05 11			05 23	05 39	05 43		05 52
Harpenden	d		00 18	00 48	01 48	02 26	02 48	03 26	03 43	04 18	04 28	04 46			04 58	05 16			05 28	05 44	05 48		
St Albans City	d		00 25	00 55	01 55	02 33	02 55	03 33	03 50	04 25	04 35	04 53			05 05	05 23			05 35	05 51	05 55	←	
Radlett	d			01 00	02 00		03 00		03 55		04 41				05 11				05 41	05 57		05 57	
Elstree & Borehamwood	d			01 04	02 04		03 04		03 59		04 44				05 14				05 44	→		06 00	
Mill Hill Broadway	d			01 08	02 08		03 08		04 03		04 48				05 18				05 48			06 04	
Hendon	d	00 01		01 11	02 11		03 11		04 06		04 52				05 22				05 52			06 08	
Cricklewood	d	00 06		01 16	02 16		03 16		04 11		04 56				05 26				05 56			06 13	
WestHampsteadThameslink ⊖	d	00 09	00 42	01 20	02 20	02 50	03 20	03 50	04 15	04 41	04 59	05 09	05 16	05 22	05 29	05 39	05 46	05 52	05 59		06 09	06 17	
Kentish Town ⊖	d	00 13		01 24	02 24		03 24		04 19		05 04		05 21		05 34		05 51		06 04			06 21	
St Pancras International ⊖	a	00 19	00 52	01 30	02 31	03 01	03 31	04 01	04 25	04 51	05 10	05 19	05 27	05 32	05 40	05 49	05 57	06 02	06 10		06 19	06 27	06 21
Farringdon 3 ⊖	a	00 25								04 55	05 16	05 24	05 31	05 36	05 46	05 54	06 01	06 06	06 16		06 24	06 31	
City Thameslink 3	a																						
London Blackfriars ⊖	a	00 30	01 01	01 39	02 39	03 09	03 39	04 09	04 39	05 00	05 21	05 28	05 36	05 41	05 51	05 58	06 06	06 11	06 21		06 28	06 36	
London Bridge ⊖	a											05 34		05 47		06 04		06 17			06 34		
Elephant & Castle ⊖173,179	a										05 25		05 40		05 55		06 10		06 25			06 40	
Gatwick Airport ✈	a	01 20	01 56	02 30	03 30	03 58	04 30	05 02	05 31	05 47		06 04				06 34					07 04		

		TL	TL	TL	TL	TL	TL	TL	TL	TL	TL	TL	TL	TL	TL	EM	TL	TL	TL	TL	TL	TL	TL
					1				1			1			1	◇1		1			1		
		G	C	C	B	J	G	C		K	C	B	J	G	L	M	C	N	J	C	B	J	G
Bedford 7	d				05 49			06 02	06 05			06 19			06 35	06 38		←			06 49		
Flitwick	d				06 00				06 16			06 30			06 46			06 46			07 00		
Harlington	d				06 04				06 20			06 34			→			06 50			07 04		
Leagrave	d				06 09				06 25			06 39						06 55			07 09		
Luton 10	d				06 13			06 22	06 29			06 43				06 53		06 59			07 13		
Luton Airport Parkway 7	d				06 16			06 25	06 32			06 46						07 02			07 16		
Harpenden	d				06 22			06 30	06 38			06 52						07 08			07 22		
St Albans City	d		06 07	06 23	06 27	←		06 37	06 43	←	06 52	06 57	←				07 07	07 13	←	07 22	07 27	←	
Radlett	d		06 12	06 28		06 28		06 42		06 42	06 57		06 57				07 12		07 12	07 27		07 27	
Elstree & Borehamwood	d		06 16	→		06 32		→		06 46	→		07 01				→		07 16	→		07 31	
Mill Hill Broadway	d		06 20			06 35				06 50			07 05						07 20			07 35	
Hendon	d		06 23			06 39				06 53			07 08						07 23			07 38	
Cricklewood	d		06 28			06 43				06 58			07 13						07 28			07 43	
WestHampsteadThameslink ⊖	d	06 22	06 31		06 39	06 46				07 01		07 09	07 16						07 31		07 39	07 46	
Kentish Town ⊖	d		06 36			06 51	06 56			07 06			07 21	07 26					07 36			07 51	07 56
St Pancras International ⊖	a	06 32	06 42		06 49	06 57	07 02		07 04			07 19	07 27	07 32		07 21		07 34			07 49	07 57	08 02
Farringdon 3 ⊖	a	06 36	06 46		06 54	07 01	07 06		07 09	07 16		07 24	07 31	07 36				07 39	07 46		07 54	08 01	08 06
City Thameslink 3	a																						
London Blackfriars ⊖	a	06 41	06 51		06 58	07 06	07 11		07 13	07 21		07 28	07 36	07 41				07 43	07 51		07 58	08 06	08 11
London Bridge ⊖	a	06 47			07 04		07 17		07 20			07 34		07 47				07 50			08 04		08 17
Elephant & Castle ⊖173,179	a		06 55			07 10				07 25			07 40						07 55			08 10	
Gatwick Airport ✈	a				07 34				08 08			08 04						08 38			08 34		

A From Nottingham
B To Brighton
C To Sutton (Surrey)
D To Three Bridges
E From Bedford to Three Bridges
F From Bedford to Brighton
G To Rainham (Kent)
H From Luton to Sutton (Surrey)
I From Leicester
J From St Albans City to Sutton (Surrey)
K From Bedford to Sutton (Surrey)
L To Gatwick Airport
M From Derby
N From Bedford

Table T052MML-R

Saturdays
21 December to 16 May

Bedford, Luton and St Albans - London and Gatwick Airport

		TL	TL ■	TL	TL ■	EM ◇■	TL ■	EM ◇■	TL	TL ■	TL	TL	TL	TL ■	TL	TL	TL ■	TL	TL	TL	TL ■	TL	TL ■
		A		B	C	D	E	F	A	G	B	H	A	I	B	A	C	B	H	A		B	C
Bedford ■	d		07 05		07 19	07 23	07 35	07 42						←			07 49				08 05		08 19
Flitwick	d		07 16		07 30		07 46							07 46			08 00				08 16		08 30
Harlington	d		07 20		07 34		→							07 50			08 04				08 20		→
Leagrave	d		07 25		07 39									07 55			08 09				08 25		
Luton ■	d		07 29		07 43			07 57		←				07 59			08 13				08 29		
Luton Airport Parkway ■ ✈	d		07 32		07 46	07 39				07 46				08 02			08 16				08 32		
Harpenden	d		07 38		→					07 52				08 08			08 22				08 38		
St Albans City	d	07 37	07 43	←					07 52	07 57	←		08 07	08 13	←	08 22	08 27	←		08 37	08 43	←	
Radlett	d	07 42		07 42					07 57		07 57		08 12		08 12	08 27		08 27		08 42		08 42	
Elstree & Borehamwood	d	→		07 46					→		08 01		→		08 16	→		08 31		→		08 46	
Mill Hill Broadway	d			07 50							08 05				08 20			08 35				08 50	
Hendon	d			07 53							08 08				08 23			08 38				08 53	
Cricklewood	d			07 58							08 13				08 28			08 43				08 58	
WestHampsteadThameslink ⊖	d			08 01						08 09	08 16				08 31		08 39	08 46				09 01	
Kentish Town ⊖	d			08 06							08 21	08 26			08 36			08 51	08 56			09 06	
St Pancras International ⊖	a		08 04			08 05		08 22		08 19	08 27	08 32		08 34			08 49	08 57	09 02		09 04		
Farringdon ■ ⊖	a		08 09	08 16						08 24	08 31	08 36		08 39	08 46		08 54	09 01	09 06		09 09	09 16	
City Thameslink ■	a																	09 03	09 08		09 11	09 18	
London Blackfriars ⊖	a		08 13	08 21						08 28	08 36	08 41		08 43	08 51		08 58	09 06	09 11		09 13	09 21	
London Bridge ⊖	a		08 20							08 34		08 47		08 50			09 04		09 17		09 20		
Elephant & Castle ⊖173,179	a			08 25							08 40				08 55			09 10				09 25	
Gatwick Airport ✈	a		09 08							09 04				09 38			09 34				10 08		

		EM ◇■	TL	TL ■	TL	TL	TL	TL ■	TL	TL	TL ■	TL	TL	TL ■	EM ◇■	TL	TL ■	TL	TL ■	EM ◇■	TL	TL ■	TL
		D	A	G	B	H	A		B	A	C	B	H	E	J	A	I	B	C	K	A	G	B
Bedford ■	d	08 24		←				08 35			08 49			09 05	09 12		←		09 19	09 23		←	
Flitwick	d			08 30				08 46			09 00			09 16			09 16		09 30			09 30	
Harlington	d			08 34				08 50			09 04			→			09 20		→			09 34	
Leagrave	d			08 39				08 55			09 09						09 25					09 39	
Luton ■	d			08 43				08 59			09 13				09 28		09 29					09 43	
Luton Airport Parkway ■ ✈	d	08 39		08 46				09 02			09 16						09 32			09 38		09 46	
Harpenden	d			08 52				09 08			09 22						09 38					09 52	
St Albans City	d		08 52	08 57	←		09 07	09 13	←	09 22	09 27	←				09 37	09 43	←			09 52	09 57	←
Radlett	d		08 57		08 57		09 12		09 12	09 27		09 27				09 42		09 42			09 57		09 57
Elstree & Borehamwood	d		→		09 01		→		09 16	→		09 31				→		09 46			→		10 01
Mill Hill Broadway	d				09 05				09 20			09 35						09 50					10 05
Hendon	d				09 08				09 23			09 38						09 53					10 08
Cricklewood	d				09 13				09 28			09 43						09 58					10 13
WestHampsteadThameslink ⊖	d			09 09	09 16				09 31		09 39	09 46						10 01				10 09	10 16
Kentish Town ⊖	d				09 21	09 26			09 36			09 51	09 56					10 06					10 21
St Pancras International ⊖	a	09 07		09 19	09 27	09 32		09 34			09 49	09 57	10 02		09 51		10 04			10 07		10 19	10 27
Farringdon ■ ⊖	a			09 24	09 31	09 36		09 39	09 46		09 54	10 01	10 06				10 09	10 16				10 24	10 31
City Thameslink ■	a			09 26	09 33	09 38		09 41	09 48		09 56	10 03	10 08				10 11	10 18				10 26	10 33
London Blackfriars ⊖	a			09 28	09 36	09 41		09 43	09 51		09 58	10 06	10 11				10 13	10 21				10 28	10 36
London Bridge ⊖	a			09 34		09 47		09 50			10 04		10 17				10 20					10 34	
Elephant & Castle ⊖173,179	a				09 40				09 55			10 10						10 25					10 40
Gatwick Airport ✈	a			10 04				10 38			10 34						11 08					11 04	

		TL	TL	TL ■	TL	TL	TL ■	TL	TL	TL ■	EM ◇■	TL	TL ■	TL	TL ■	EM ◇■	TL	TL ■	TL	TL	TL	TL ■
		H	A		B	A	C	B	H	E	J	A	I	B	C	D	A	G	B	H	A	
Bedford ■	d			09 35			09 49			10 05	10 12		←		10 19	10 23		←				10 35
Flitwick	d			09 46			10 00			10 16			10 16		10 30			10 30				10 46
Harlington	d			09 50			10 04			→			10 20		→			10 34				10 50
Leagrave	d			09 55			10 09						10 25					10 39				10 55
Luton ■	d			09 59			10 13				10 28		10 29					10 43				10 59
Luton Airport Parkway ■ ✈	d			10 02			10 16						10 32			10 39		10 46				11 02
Harpenden	d			10 08			10 22						10 38					10 52				11 08
St Albans City	d		10 07	10 13	←	10 22	10 27	←				10 37	10 43	←			10 52	10 57	←		11 07	11 13
Radlett	d		10 12		10 12	10 27		10 27				10 42		10 42			10 57		10 57		11 12	
Elstree & Borehamwood	d		→		10 16	→		10 31				→		10 46			→		11 01		→	
Mill Hill Broadway	d				10 20			10 35						10 50					11 05			
Hendon	d				10 23			10 38						10 53					11 08			
Cricklewood	d				10 28			10 43						10 58					11 13			
WestHampsteadThameslink ⊖	d				10 31		10 39	10 46						11 01				11 09	11 16			
Kentish Town ⊖	d	10 26			10 36			10 51	10 56					11 06					11 21	11 26		
St Pancras International ⊖	a	10 32		10 34			10 49	10 57	11 02		10 51		11 04			11 08		11 19	11 27	11 32		11 34
Farringdon ■ ⊖	a	10 36		10 39	10 46		10 54	11 01	11 06				11 09	11 16				11 24	11 31	11 36		11 39
City Thameslink ■	a	10 38		10 41	10 48		10 56	11 03	11 08				11 11	11 18				11 26	11 33	11 38		11 41
London Blackfriars ⊖	a	10 41		10 43	10 51		10 58	11 06	11 11				11 13	11 21				11 28	11 36	11 41		11 43
London Bridge ⊖	a	10 47		10 50			11 04		11 17				11 20					11 34		11 47		11 50
Elephant & Castle ⊖173,179	a				10 55			11 10						11 25					11 40			
Gatwick Airport ✈	a			11 38			11 34						12 08					12 04				12 38

A To Sutton (Surrey)
B From St Albans City to Sutton (Surrey)
C To Brighton
D From Nottingham
E To Gatwick Airport
F From Derby
G From Bedford to Brighton
H To Rainham (Kent)
I From Bedford
J From Corby
K From Lincoln

Table T052MML-R

Saturdays
21 December to 16 May

Bedford, Luton and St Albans - London and Gatwick Airport

		TL	TL	TL ■	TL	TL	TL ■	EM ◇■	TL	TL ■	TL	TL ■	EM ◇■	TL	TL ■	TL	TL	TL	TL ■	TL	TL	TL ■	TL
		A	B	C	A	D	E	F	B	G	A	C	H	B	I	A	D	B		A	B	C	A
Bedford ■	d			10 49			11 05	11 12		←		11 19	11 22		←				11 35			11 49	
Flitwick	d			11 00			11 16			11 16		11 30			11 30				11 46			12 00	
Harlington	d			11 04			→			11 20		→			11 34				11 50			12 04	
Leagrave	d			11 09						11 25					11 39				11 55			12 09	
Luton ■	d			11 13				11 28		11 29					11 43				11 59			12 13	
Luton Airport Parkway ■ ✈	d			11 16						11 32			11 38		11 46				12 02			12 16	
Harpenden	d			11 22						11 38					11 52				12 08			12 22	
St Albans City	d	←	11 22	11 27	←				11 37	11 43	←			11 52	11 57	←		12 07	12 13	←	12 22	12 27	←
Radlett	d	11 12	11 27		11 27				11 42		11 42			11 57		11 57		12 12		12 12	12 27		12 27
Elstree & Borehamwood	d	11 16	→		11 31				→		11 46			→		12 01		→		12 16	→		12 31
Mill Hill Broadway	d	11 20			11 35						11 50					12 05				12 20			12 35
Hendon	d	11 23			11 38						11 53					12 08				12 23			12 38
Cricklewood	d	11 28			11 43						11 58					12 13				12 28			12 43
WestHampsteadThameslink ⊖	d	11 31		11 39	11 46						12 01				12 09	12 16				12 31		12 39	12 46
Kentish Town ⊖	d	11 36			11 51	11 56					12 06					12 21	12 26			12 36			12 51
St Pancras International ⊖	a			11 49	11 57	12 02		11 50		12 04			12 07		12 19	12 27	12 32		12 34			12 49	12 57
Farringdon ■ ⊖	a	11 46		11 54	12 01	12 06				12 09	12 16				12 24	12 31	12 36		12 39	12 46		12 54	13 01
City Thameslink ■	a	11 48		11 56	12 03	12 08				12 11	12 18				12 26	12 33	12 38		12 41	12 48		12 56	13 03
London Blackfriars ⊖	a	11 51		11 58	12 06	12 11				12 13	12 21				12 28	12 36	12 41		12 43	12 51		12 58	13 06
London Bridge ⊖	a			12 04		12 17				12 20					12 34		12 47		12 50			13 04	
Elephant & Castle ⊖173,179	a	11 55			12 10						12 25					12 40				12 55			13 10
Gatwick Airport ✈	a			12 34						13 08					13 04				13 38			13 34	

		TL	TL ■	EM ◇■	TL	TL ■	TL	TL ■	EM ◇■	TL	TL ■	TL	TL	TL	TL ■	TL	TL	TL ■	TL	TL	TL ■	EM ◇■	TL
		D	E	F	B	G	A	C	H	B	I	A	D	B		A	B	C	A	D	E	F	B
Bedford ■	d		12 05	12 12		←		12 19	12 23		←				12 35			12 49			13 05	13 11	
Flitwick	d		12 16			12 16		12 30			12 30				12 46			13 00			13 16		
Harlington	d		→			12 20		→			12 34				12 50			13 04			→		
Leagrave	d					12 25					12 39				12 55			13 09					
Luton ■	d			12 27		12 29					12 43				12 59			13 13				13 28	
Luton Airport Parkway ■ ✈	d					12 32			12 39		12 46				13 02			13 16					
Harpenden	d					12 38					12 52				13 08			13 22					
St Albans City	d				12 37	12 43	←			12 52	12 57	←		13 07	13 13	←	13 22	13 27	←				13 37
Radlett	d				12 42		12 42			12 57		12 57		13 12		13 12	13 27		13 27				13 42
Elstree & Borehamwood	d				→		12 46			→		13 01		→		13 16	→		13 31				→
Mill Hill Broadway	d						12 50					13 05				13 20			13 35				
Hendon	d						12 53					13 08				13 23			13 38				
Cricklewood	d						12 58					13 13				13 28			13 43				
WestHampsteadThameslink ⊖	d						13 01				13 09	13 16				13 31		13 39	13 46				
Kentish Town ⊖	d	12 56					13 06					13 21	13 26			13 36			13 51	13 56			
St Pancras International ⊖	a	13 02		12 51		13 04			13 08		13 19	13 27	13 32		13 34			13 49	13 57	14 02		13 51	
Farringdon ■ ⊖	a	13 06				13 09	13 16				13 24	13 31	13 36		13 39	13 46		13 54	14 01	14 06			
City Thameslink ■	a	13 08				13 11	13 18				13 26	13 33	13 38		13 41	13 48		13 56	14 03	14 08			
London Blackfriars ⊖	a	13 11				13 13	13 21				13 28	13 36	13 41		13 43	13 51		13 58	14 06	14 11			
London Bridge ⊖	a	13 17				13 20					13 34		13 47		13 50			14 04		14 17			
Elephant & Castle ⊖173,179	a						13 25					13 40				13 55			14 10				
Gatwick Airport ✈	a					14 08					14 04				14 38			14 34					

		TL ■	TL	TL ■	EM ◇■	TL	TL ■	TL	TL	TL	TL ■	TL	TL	TL ■	TL	TL	TL ■	EM ◇■	TL	TL ■	TL	TL ■	EM ◇■
		G	A	C	H	B	I	A	D	B		A	B	C	A	D	E	F	B	G	A	C	H
Bedford ■	d	←		13 19	13 23		←				13 35			13 49			14 05	14 12		←		14 19	14 23
Flitwick	d	13 16		13 30			13 30				13 46			14 00			14 16			14 16		14 30	
Harlington	d	13 20		→			13 34				13 50			14 04			→			14 20		→	
Leagrave	d	13 25					13 39				13 55			14 09						14 25			
Luton ■	d	13 29					13 43				13 59			14 13				14 28		14 29			
Luton Airport Parkway ■ ✈	d	13 32			13 39		13 46				14 02			14 16						14 32			14 39
Harpenden	d	13 38					13 52				14 08			14 22						14 38			
St Albans City	d	13 43	←			13 52	13 57	←		14 07	14 13	←	14 22	14 27	←				14 37	14 43	←		
Radlett	d		13 42			13 57		13 57		14 12		14 12	14 27		14 27				14 42		14 42		
Elstree & Borehamwood	d		13 46			→		14 01		→		14 16	→		14 31				→		14 46		
Mill Hill Broadway	d		13 50					14 05				14 20			14 35						14 50		
Hendon	d		13 53					14 08				14 23			14 38						14 53		
Cricklewood	d		13 58					14 13				14 28			14 43						14 58		
WestHampsteadThameslink ⊖	d		14 01				14 09	14 16				14 31		14 39	14 46						15 01		
Kentish Town ⊖	d		14 06					14 21	14 26			14 36			14 51	14 56					15 06		
St Pancras International ⊖	a	14 04			14 08		14 19	14 27	14 32		14 34			14 49	14 57	15 02		14 50		15 04			15 07
Farringdon ■ ⊖	a	14 09	14 16				14 24	14 31	14 36		14 39	14 46		14 54	15 01	15 06				15 09	15 16		
City Thameslink ■	a	14 11	14 18				14 26	14 33	14 38		14 41	14 48		14 56	15 03	15 08				15 11	15 18		
London Blackfriars ⊖	a	14 13	14 21				14 28	14 36	14 41		14 43	14 51		14 58	15 06	15 11				15 13	15 21		
London Bridge ⊖	a	14 20					14 34		14 47		14 50			15 04		15 17				15 20			
Elephant & Castle ⊖173,179	a		14 25					14 40				14 55			15 10						15 25		
Gatwick Airport ✈	a	15 08					15 04				15 38			15 34						16 08			

A From St Albans City to Sutton (Surrey)
B To Sutton (Surrey)
C To Brighton
D To Rainham (Kent)
E To Gatwick Airport
F From Corby
G From Bedford
H From Nottingham
I From Bedford to Brighton

Table T052MML-R

Saturdays

21 December to 16 May

Bedford, Luton and St Albans - London and Gatwick Airport

Station		TL A	TL [1] B	TL C	TL D	TL A	TL [1]	TL C	TL A	TL [1] E	TL C	TL D	TL [1] F	EM ◇[1] G	TL A	TL [1] H	TL C	TL [1] E	EM ◇[1] I	TL A	TL [1] B	TL C	TL D
Bedford [7]	d		←				14 35			14 49			15 05	15 11		←		15 19	15 23		←		
Flitwick	d		14 30				14 46			15 00			15 16			15 16		15 30			15 30		
Harlington	d		14 34				14 50			15 04			→			15 20		→			15 34		
Leagrave	d		14 39				14 55			15 09						15 25					15 39		
Luton [10]	d		14 43				14 59			15 13				15 28		15 29					15 43		
Luton Airport Parkway [7] ✈	d		14 46				15 02			15 16						15 32			15 38		15 46		
Harpenden	d		14 52				15 08			15 22						15 38					15 52		
St Albans City	d	14 52	14 57	←		15 07	15 13	←	15 22	15 27	←				15 37	15 43	←			15 52	15 57	←	
Radlett	d	14 57		14 57		15 12		15 12	15 27		15 27				15 42		15 42			15 57		15 57	
Elstree & Borehamwood	d	→		15 01		→		15 16	→		15 31				→		15 46			→		16 01	
Mill Hill Broadway	d			15 05				15 20			15 35						15 50					16 05	
Hendon	d			15 08				15 23			15 38						15 53					16 08	
Cricklewood	d			15 13				15 28			15 43						15 58					16 13	
WestHampsteadThameslink ⊖	d		15 09	15 16				15 31		15 39	15 46						16 01				16 09	16 16	
Kentish Town ⊖	d			15 21	15 26			15 36			15 51	15 56					16 06					16 21	16 26
St Pancras International ⊖	a		15 19	15 27	15 32		15 34			15 49	15 57	16 02		15 51		16 04			16 06		16 19	16 27	16 32
Farringdon [3] ⊖	a		15 24	15 31	15 36		15 39	15 46		15 54	16 01	16 06				16 09	16 16				16 24	16 31	16 36
City Thameslink [3]	a		15 26	15 33	15 38		15 41	15 48		15 56	16 03	16 08				16 11	16 18				16 26	16 33	16 38
London Blackfriars ⊖	a		15 28	15 36	15 41		15 43	15 51		15 58	16 06	16 11				16 13	16 21				16 28	16 36	16 41
London Bridge ⊖	a		15 34		15 47		15 50			16 04		16 17				16 20					16 34		16 47
Elephant & Castle ⊖173,179	a			15 40				15 55			16 10						16 25					16 40	
Gatwick Airport ✈	a		16 04				16 38			16 34						17 08					17 04		

Station		TL A	TL [1]	TL C	TL A	TL [1] E	TL C	TL D	TL [1] F	EM ◇[1] G	TL A	TL [1] H	TL C	TL [1] E	EM ◇[1] I	TL A	TL [1] B	TL C	TL D	TL A	TL [1]	TL C	TL A
Bedford [7]	d		15 35			15 49			16 05	16 12		←		16 19	16 23		←				16 35		
Flitwick	d		15 46			16 00			16 16			16 16		16 30			16 30				16 46		
Harlington	d		15 50			16 04			→			16 20		→			16 34				16 50		
Leagrave	d		15 55			16 09						16 25					16 39				16 55		
Luton [10]	d		15 59			16 13				16 28		16 29					16 43				16 59		
Luton Airport Parkway [7] ✈	d		16 02			16 16						16 32			16 39		16 46				17 02		
Harpenden	d		16 08			16 22						16 38					16 52				17 08		
St Albans City	d	16 07	16 13	←	16 22	16 27	←				16 37	16 43	←			16 52	16 57	←		17 07	17 13	←	17 22
Radlett	d	16 12		16 12	16 27		16 27				16 42		16 42			16 57		16 57		17 12		17 12	17 27
Elstree & Borehamwood	d	→		16 16	→		16 31				→		16 46			→		17 01		→		17 16	→
Mill Hill Broadway	d			16 20			16 35						16 50					17 05				17 20	
Hendon	d			16 23			16 38						16 53					17 08				17 23	
Cricklewood	d			16 28			16 43						16 58					17 13				17 28	
WestHampsteadThameslink ⊖	d			16 31		16 39	16 46						17 01				17 09	17 16				17 31	
Kentish Town ⊖	d			16 36			16 51	16 56					17 06					17 21	17 26			17 36	
St Pancras International ⊖	a		16 34			16 49	16 57	17 02		16 50		17 04			17 08		17 19	17 27	17 32		17 34		
Farringdon [3] ⊖	a		16 39	16 46		16 54	17 01	17 06				17 09	17 16				17 24	17 31	17 36		17 39	17 46	
City Thameslink [3]	a		16 41	16 48		16 56	17 03	17 08				17 11	17 18				17 26	17 33	17 38		17 41	17 48	
London Blackfriars ⊖	a		16 43	16 51		16 58	17 06	17 11				17 13	17 21				17 28	17 36	17 41		17 43	17 51	
London Bridge ⊖	a		16 50			17 04		17 17				17 20					17 34		17 47		17 50		
Elephant & Castle ⊖173,179	a			16 55			17 10						17 25					17 40				17 55	
Gatwick Airport ✈	a		17 38			17 34						18 08					18 04				18 38		

Station		TL [1] E	TL C	TL D	TL [1] F	EM ◇[1] G	TL A	TL [1] H	TL C	TL [1] E	EM ◇[1] I	TL A	TL [1] B	TL C	TL D	TL A	TL [1]	TL C	TL A	TL [1] E	TL C	TL D	TL [1] F
Bedford [7]	d	16 49			17 05	17 12		←		17 19	17 23		←				17 35			17 49			18 05
Flitwick	d	17 00			17 16			17 16		17 30			17 30				17 46			18 00			18 16
Harlington	d	17 04			→			17 20		→			17 34				17 50			18 04			→
Leagrave	d	17 09						17 25					17 39				17 55			18 09			
Luton [10]	d	17 13				17 28		17 29					17 43				17 59			18 13			
Luton Airport Parkway [7] ✈	d	17 16						17 32			17 39		17 46				18 02			18 16			
Harpenden	d	17 22						17 38					17 52				18 08			18 22			
St Albans City	d	17 27	←				17 37	17 43	←			17 52	17 57	←		18 07	18 13	←	18 22	18 27	←		
Radlett	d		17 27				17 42		17 42			17 57		17 57		18 12		18 12	18 27		18 27		
Elstree & Borehamwood	d		17 31				→		17 46			→		18 01		→		18 16	→		18 31		
Mill Hill Broadway	d		17 35						17 50					18 05				18 20			18 35		
Hendon	d		17 38						17 53					18 08				18 23			18 38		
Cricklewood	d		17 43						17 58					18 13				18 28			18 43		
WestHampsteadThameslink ⊖	d	17 39	17 46						18 01				18 09	18 16				18 31		18 39	18 46		
Kentish Town ⊖	d		17 51	17 56					18 06					18 21	18 26			18 36			18 51	18 56	
St Pancras International ⊖	a	17 49	17 57	18 02		17 51		18 04			18 08		18 19	18 27	18 32		18 34			18 49	18 57	19 02	
Farringdon [3] ⊖	a	17 54	18 01	18 06				18 09	18 16				18 24	18 31	18 36		18 39	18 46		18 54	19 01	19 06	
City Thameslink [3]	a	17 56	18 03	18 08				18 11	18 18				18 26	18 33	18 38		18 41	18 48		18 56	19 03	19 08	
London Blackfriars ⊖	a	17 58	18 06	18 11				18 13	18 21				18 28	18 36	18 41		18 43	18 51		18 58	19 06	19 11	
London Bridge ⊖	a	18 04		18 17				18 20					18 34		18 47		18 50			19 04		19 17	
Elephant & Castle ⊖173,179	a		18 10						18 25					18 40				18 55			19 10		
Gatwick Airport ✈	a	18 34						19 08					19 04				19 38			19 34			

A To Sutton (Surrey)
B From Bedford to Brighton
C From St Albans City to Sutton (Surrey)
D To Rainham (Kent)
E To Brighton
F To Gatwick Airport
G From Corby
H From Bedford
I From Nottingham

Table T052MML-R

Saturdays

21 December to 16 May

Bedford, Luton and St Albans - London and Gatwick Airport

Station		EM ◇[1] A	TL B	TL [1] C	TL D	TL [1] E	EM ◇[1] F	TL B	TL [1] G	TL D	TL H	TL B	TL [1]	TL D	TL B	TL [1] E	TL D	TL H	TL [1] I	EM ◇[1] A	TL B	TL [1] C	TL D
Bedford [7]	d	18 12		←		18 19	18 23		←				18 35			18 49			19 05	19 12		←	
Flitwick	d			18 16		18 30			18 30				18 46			19 00			19 16			19 16	
Harlington	d			18 20		→			18 34				18 50			19 04			→			19 20	
Leagrave	d			18 25					18 39				18 55			19 09						19 25	
Luton [10]	d	18 27		18 29					18 43				18 59			19 13				19 27		19 29	
Luton Airport Parkway [7] ✈	d			18 32			18 39		18 46				19 02			19 16						19 32	
Harpenden	d			18 38					18 52				19 08			19 22						19 38	
St Albans City	d		18 37	18 43	←			18 52	18 57	←		19 07	19 13	←	19 22	19 27	←				19 37	19 43	←
Radlett	d		18 42		18 42			18 57		18 57		19 12		19 12	19 27		19 27				19 42		19 42
Elstree & Borehamwood	d		→		18 46			→		19 01		→		19 16	→		19 31				→		19 46
Mill Hill Broadway	d				18 50					19 05				19 20			19 35						19 50
Hendon	d				18 53					19 08				19 23			19 38						19 53
Cricklewood	d				18 58					19 13				19 28			19 43						19 58
WestHampsteadThameslink ⊖	d				19 01				19 09	19 16				19 31		19 39	19 46						20 01
Kentish Town ⊖	d				19 06					19 21	19 26			19 36			19 51	19 56					20 06
St Pancras International ⊖	a	18 50		19 04			19 08		19 19	19 27	19 32		19 34			19 49	19 57	20 02		19 51		20 04	
Farringdon [3] ⊖	a			19 09	19 16				19 24	19 31	19 36		19 39	19 46		19 54	20 01	20 06				20 09	20 16
City Thameslink [3]	a			19 11	19 18				19 26	19 33	19 38		19 41	19 48		19 56	20 03	20 08				20 11	20 18
London Blackfriars ⊖	a			19 13	19 21				19 28	19 36	19 41		19 43	19 51		19 58	20 06	20 11				20 13	20 21
London Bridge ⊖	a			19 20					19 34		19 47		19 50			20 04		20 17				20 20	
Elephant & Castle ⊖173,179	a				19 25					19 40				19 55			20 10						20 25
Gatwick Airport ✈	a			20 08					20 04				20 38			20 34						21 08	

Station		TL [1] E	EM ◇[1] F	TL B	TL [1] G	TL D	TL H	TL B	TL [1]	TL D	TL B	TL [1] E	TL D	TL H	TL [1] I	EM ◇[1] A	TL B	TL [1] C	TL D	TL [1] E	EM ◇[1] F	TL B
Bedford [7]	d	19 19	19 23		←				19 35			19 49			20 05	20 12		←		20 19	20 23	
Flitwick	d	19 30			19 30				19 46			20 00			20 16			20 16		20 30		
Harlington	d	→			19 34				19 50			20 04			→			20 20		→		
Leagrave	d				19 39				19 55			20 09						20 25				
Luton [10]	d				19 43				19 59			20 13				20 28		20 29				
Luton Airport Parkway [7] ✈	d		19 39		19 46				20 02			20 16						20 32			20 39	
Harpenden	d				19 52				20 08			20 22						20 38				
St Albans City	d			19 52	19 57	←		20 07	20 13	←	20 22	20 27	←				20 37	20 43	←			20 52
Radlett	d			19 57		19 57		20 12		20 12	20 27		20 27				20 42		20 42			20 57
Elstree & Borehamwood	d			→		20 01		→		20 16	→		20 31				→		20 46			→
Mill Hill Broadway	d					20 05				20 20			20 35						20 50			
Hendon	d					20 08				20 23			20 38						20 53			
Cricklewood	d					20 13				20 28			20 43						20 58			
WestHampsteadThameslink ⊖	d				20 09	20 16				20 31		20 39	20 46						21 01			
Kentish Town ⊖	d					20 21	20 26			20 36			20 51	20 56					21 06			
St Pancras International ⊖	a		20 08		20 19	20 27	20 32		20 34			20 49	20 57	21 02		20 52		21 04			21 08	
Farringdon [3] ⊖	a				20 24	20 31	20 36		20 39	20 46		20 54	21 01	21 06				21 09	21 16			
City Thameslink [3]	a				20 26	20 33	20 38		20 41	20 48		20 56										
London Blackfriars ⊖	a				20 28	20 36	20 41		20 43	20 51		20 58	21 06	21 11				21 13	21 21			
London Bridge ⊖	a				20 34		20 47		20 50			21 04		21 17				21 20				
Elephant & Castle ⊖173,179	a					20 40				20 55			21 10						21 25			
Gatwick Airport ✈	a				21 04				21 38			21 34						22 08				

Station		TL [1] G	TL D	TL H	TL B	TL [1]	TL D	TL B	TL [1] E	TL D	TL H	TL [1] I	EM ◇[1] A	TL B	TL [1] C	TL D	TL [1] E	EM ◇[1] F	TL B	TL [1] G	TL D	TL J	TL B
Bedford [7]	d	←				20 34			20 49			21 05	21 12		←		21 19	21 26		←			
Flitwick	d	20 30				20 45			21 00			21 16			21 16		21 30			21 30			
Harlington	d	20 34				20 49			21 04			→			21 20		→			21 34			
Leagrave	d	20 39				20 54			21 09						21 25					21 39			
Luton [10]	d	20 43				20 59			21 13				21 27		21 29					21 43			
Luton Airport Parkway [7] ✈	d	20 46				21 02			21 16						21 32			21 42		21 46			
Harpenden	d	20 52				21 08			21 22						21 38					21 52			
St Albans City	d	20 57	←		21 07	21 13	←	21 22	21 27	←				21 37	21 43	←			21 52	21 57	←		22 07
Radlett	d		20 57		21 12		21 12	21 27		21 27				21 42		21 42			21 57		21 57		22 12
Elstree & Borehamwood	d		21 01		→		21 16	→		21 31				→		21 46			→		22 01		→
Mill Hill Broadway	d		21 05				21 20			21 35						21 50					22 05		
Hendon	d		21 08				21 23			21 38						21 53					22 08		
Cricklewood	d		21 13				21 28			21 43						21 58					22 13		
WestHampsteadThameslink ⊖	d	21 09	21 16				21 31		21 39	21 46						22 01				22 09	22 16		
Kentish Town ⊖	d		21 21	21 26			21 36			21 51	21 56					22 06					22 21	22 26	
St Pancras International ⊖	a	21 19	21 27	21 32		21 34			21 49	21 57	22 02		21 51		22 04			22 09		22 19	22 27	22 32	
Farringdon [3] ⊖	a	21 24	21 31	21 36		21 39	21 46		21 54	22 01	22 06				22 09	22 16				22 24	22 31	22 36	
City Thameslink [3]	a																						
London Blackfriars ⊖	a	21 28	21 36	21 41		21 43	21 51		21 58	22 06	22 11				22 13	22 21				22 28	22 36	22 41	
London Bridge ⊖	a	21 34		21 47		21 50			22 04		22 17				22 20					22 34		22 47	
Elephant & Castle ⊖173,179	a		21 40				21 55			22 10						22 25					22 40		
Gatwick Airport ✈	a	22 04				22 38			22 34						23 08					23 04			

A From Corby
B To Sutton (Surrey)
C From Bedford
D From St Albans City to Sutton (Surrey)
E To Brighton
F From Nottingham
G From Bedford to Brighton
H To Rainham (Kent)
I To Gatwick Airport
J To Gillingham (Kent)

Table T052MML-R

Bedford, Luton and St Albans - London and Gatwick Airport

Saturdays

21 December to 16 May

	TL■ A	TL B	TL C	TL■ D	TL B	TL E	TL C	TL■	TL B	TL■ D	EM◇■ F	TL■ G	EM◇■ F	TL C	TL■ D	TL■ H	TL■ I	TL■ D
Bedford ■ d	21 35			21 49				22 05		22 17	22 20	←	22 39		22 45	23 05	23 05	23 35
Flitwick d	21 46			22 00				22 15		22 28		22 28			22 56	23 16	23 16	23 46
Harlington d	21 50			22 04				22 19		→		22 32			23 00	23 20	23 20	23 50
Leagrave d	21 55			22 09				22 24				22 37			23 05	23 25	23 25	23 55
Luton ■ d	21 59			22 13				22 28			22 35	22 41	22 54	22 54	23 10	23 30	23 30	23 59
Luton Airport Parkway ■ ✈ d	22 02			22 16				22 31			22 39	22 44		22 57	23 13	23 33	23 33	00 03
Harpenden d	22 08			22 22				22 36				22 49		23 03	23 18	23 38	23 38	00 08
St Albans City d	22 13	←	22 22	22 27	←		22 37	22 42	←			22 55		23 09	23 25	23 45	23 45	00 15
Radlett d		22 12	22 27		22 27		22 42		22 42					23 14		23 50	23 50	00 20
Elstree & Borehamwood d		22 16	→		22 31		→		22 46					23 18		23 54	23 54	00 24
Mill Hill Broadway d		22 20			22 35				22 50					23 22		23 58	23 58	00 28
Hendon d		22 23			22 38				22 53					23 25		00 01	00 01	00 31
Cricklewood d		22 28			22 43				22 58					23 30		00 06	00 06	00 36
WestHampsteadThameslink ⊖ d		22 31		22 39	22 46				23 01			23 11		23 33	23 41	00 09	00 09	00 39
Kentish Town ⊖ d		22 36			22 51	22 56			23 06					23 38		00 13	00 13	00 43
St Pancras International ⊖ a	22 34			22 49	22 57	23 02		23 05			23 11	23 22	23 29	23 44	23 51	00 19	00 19	00 49
Farringdon ■ ⊖ a	22 39	22 46		22 54	23 01	23 06		23 09	23 16			23 26		23 48	23 55	00 25	00 25	
City Thameslink ■ a																		
London Blackfriars ⊖ a	22 43	22 51		22 58	23 06	23 11		23 13	23 21			23 30		23 53	23 59	00 30	00 30	01 00
London Bridge ⊖ a	22 50			23 04		23 17		23 20				23 36						
Elephant & Castle ⊖173,179 a		22 55			23 10				23 25					23 57				
Gatwick Airport ✈ a	23 37			23 34				00 01				00 17			00 47	01 20	01 28	01 56

Sundays

15 December to 10 May

	TL■ J	TL■ K	TL■ L	TL■	TL■	TL■	TL■	TL■	TL■	EM◇■ M	TL■ D	TL N	TL C	TL■ A	EM◇■ F	TL■ D	TL N	TL C	TL■	EM◇■ M	TL■ D	TL N
Bedford ■ d				05 55	06 25	06 55	07 35		08 05	08 15	08 19			08 35	08 45	08 49			09 05	09 15	09 19	
Flitwick d				06 06	06 36	07 06	07 46		08 16		08 30			08 46		09 00			09 16		09 30	
Harlington d				06 10	06 40	07 10	07 50		08 20		08 34			08 50		09 04			09 20		09 34	
Leagrave d				06 15	06 45	07 15	07 55		08 25		08 39			08 55		09 09			09 25		09 39	
Luton ■ d				06 20	06 50	07 20	08 00	08 04	08 30	08 35	08 44		08 48	09 00		09 14		09 18	09 30	09 35	09 44	
Luton Airport Parkway ■ ✈ d			00 03	06 23	06 53	07 23	08 03	08 07	08 33		08 47		08 51	09 03	09 06	09 17		09 21	09 33		09 47	
Harpenden d			00 08	06 28	06 58	07 28	08 08	08 12	08 38		08 52		08 56	09 08		09 22		09 26	09 38		09 52	
St Albans City d			00 15	06 35	07 05	07 35	08 15	08 19	08 45		08 59		09 03	09 15		09 29		09 33	09 45		09 59	
Radlett d			00 20	06 40	07 10	07 40		08 24					09 09					09 39				
Elstree & Borehamwood d			00 24	06 44	07 14	07 44		08 28					09 12					09 42				
Mill Hill Broadway d			00 28	06 48	07 18	07 48		08 32					09 16					09 46				
Hendon d	00 01	00 01	00 31	06 51	07 21	07 51		08 35					09 19					09 49				
Cricklewood d	00 06	00 06	00 36	06 56	07 26	07 56		08 40					09 24					09 54				
WestHampsteadThameslink ⊖ d	00 09	00 09	00 39	06 59	07 29	07 59	08 31	08 43	09 01		09 15	09 20	09 26	09 30		09 45	09 50	09 56	10 00		10 15	
Kentish Town ⊖ d	00 13	00 13	00 43	07 05	07 35	08 05		08 49				09 26	09 31				09 56	10 01				10 26
St Pancras International ⊖ a	00 19	00 19	00 49	07 10	07 40	08 10	08 40	08 55	09 10	09 13	09 25	09 31	09 37	09 40	09 42	09 55	10 01	10 07	10 10	10 11	10 25	10 31
Farringdon ■ ⊖ a	00 25	00 25									09 30	09 36	09 42	09 45		10 00	10 06	10 12	10 15		10 30	10 36
City Thameslink ■ a																						
London Blackfriars ⊖ a	00 30	00 30	01 00								09 34	09 40	09 46	09 49		10 04	10 10	10 16	10 19		10 34	10 40
London Bridge ⊖ a											09 40	09 46		09 55		10 10	10 16		10 25		10 40	10 46
Elephant & Castle ⊖173,179 a													09 50					10 20				
Gatwick Airport ✈ a	01 20	01 28	01 56								10 09			10 42		10 39			11 09		11 09	

	TL C	TL■ A	EM◇■ F	TL■ D	TL N	TL C	TL■	EM◇■ O	TL■ D	TL N	TL C	TL■ A	EM◇■ F	TL■ D	TL N	TL C	TL■	EM◇■ O	TL■ D	TL N	TL C	TL C
Bedford ■ d		09 35	09 45	09 49			10 05	10 15	10 19			10 35	10 45	10 49			11 05	11 15	11 19			
Flitwick d		09 46		10 00			10 16		10 30			10 46		11 00			11 16		11 30			
Harlington d		09 50		10 04			10 20		10 34			10 50		11 04			11 20		11 34			
Leagrave d		09 55		10 09			10 25		10 39			10 55		11 09			11 25		11 39			
Luton ■ d	09 48	10 00		10 14		10 18	10 30	10 34	10 44		10 48	11 00		11 14		11 18	11 30	11 36	11 44		11 48	11 58
Luton Airport Parkway ■ ✈ d	09 51	10 03	10 06	10 17		10 21	10 33		10 47		10 51	11 03	11 06	11 17		11 21	11 33		11 47		11 51	12 01
Harpenden d	09 56	10 08		10 22		10 26	10 38		10 52		10 56	11 08		11 22		11 26	11 38		11 52		11 56	12 06
St Albans City d	10 03	10 15		10 29		10 33	10 45		10 59		11 03	11 15		11 29		11 33	11 45		11 59		12 03	12 16
Radlett d	10 09					10 39					11 09					11 39					12 08	12 21
Elstree & Borehamwood d	10 12					10 42					11 12					11 42					12 12	→
Mill Hill Broadway d	10 16					10 46					11 16					11 46					12 16	
Hendon d	10 19					10 49					11 19					11 49					12 19	
Cricklewood d	10 24					10 54					11 24					11 54					12 24	
WestHampsteadThameslink ⊖ d	10 26	10 30		10 45		10 56	11 00		11 15		11 26	11 30		11 45		11 56	12 00		12 15		12 26	
Kentish Town ⊖ d	10 31				10 56	11 01				11 26	11 31				11 56	12 01				12 26	12 31	
St Pancras International ⊖ a	10 37	10 40	10 42	10 55	11 01	11 07	11 10	11 11	11 25	11 31	11 37	11 40	11 42	11 55	12 01	12 07	12 10	12 13	12 25	12 31	12 37	
Farringdon ■ ⊖ a	10 42	10 45		11 00	11 06	11 12	11 15		11 30	11 36	11 42	11 45		12 00	12 06	12 12	12 15		12 30	12 36	12 42	
City Thameslink ■ a																						
London Blackfriars ⊖ a	10 46	10 49		11 04	11 10	11 16	11 19		11 34	11 40	11 46	11 49		12 04	12 10	12 16	12 19		12 34	12 40	12 46	
London Bridge ⊖ a		10 55		11 10	11 16		11 25		11 40	11 46		11 55		12 10	12 16		12 25		12 40	12 46		
Elephant & Castle ⊖173,179 a	10 50					11 20					11 50					12 20					12 50	
Gatwick Airport ✈ a		11 42		11 39			12 09		12 09			12 42		12 39			13 09		13 09			

A To Three Bridges
B From St Albans City to Sutton (Surrey)
C To Sutton (Surrey)
D To Brighton
E To Gillingham (Kent)
F From Nottingham
G From Bedford to Brighton
H not 4 January. To Three Bridges
I 4 January. To Three Bridges
J not 15 December, 5 January. From Bedford to Three Bridges
K 5 January. From Bedford to Three Bridges
L not 15 December. From Bedford to Brighton
M From Derby
N To Rainham (Kent)
O From Sheffield

NRT DECEMBER 19 EDITION

Table T052MML-R

Bedford, Luton and St Albans - London and Gatwick Airport

Sundays

15 December to 10 May

	TL■ A	TL B	TL■ C	EM◇■ D	TL■ E	TL F	TL G	TL■ H	EM◇■ I	TL G	TL■ J	TL K	TL■ C	TL F	TL G	TL G	TL■ A	TL K	TL■ C	EM◇■ L	TL■ E	TL F
Bedford ■ d	11 37		11 51	11 57	←			12 07	12 15		←		12 21				12 37		12 51	13 02	←	
Flitwick d	11 48		12 02		12 02			12 18			12 18		12 32				12 48		13 02		13 02	
Harlington d	11 52		→		12 06			→			12 22		12 36				12 52		→		13 06	
Leagrave d	11 57				12 11						12 27		12 41				12 57				13 11	
Luton ■ d	12 02				12 16		12 22		12 30		12 32		12 46		12 52		13 02				13 16	
Luton Airport Parkway ■ ✈ d	12 05			12 14	12 19		12 25				12 35		12 49		12 55		13 05			13 18	13 19	
Harpenden d	12 10				12 24		12 30				12 40		12 54		13 00		13 10				13 24	
St Albans City d	12 17	←			12 30		12 37			12 46	12 47	←	13 00		13 07	13 16	13 17	←			13 30	
Radlett d		12 21					12 42			12 51		12 51			13 12	13 21		13 21				
Elstree & Borehamwood d		12 25					12 46			→		12 55			13 16	→		13 25				
Mill Hill Broadway d		12 29					12 50					12 59			13 20			13 29				
Hendon d		12 32										13 02						13 32				
Cricklewood d		12 37										13 07						13 37				
WestHampsteadThameslink ⊖ d	12 30	12 39			12 45		12 56				13 00	13 09	13 15		13 26		13 30	13 39			13 45	
Kentish Town ⊖ d		12 44				12 56						13 14		13 26				13 44				13 56
St Pancras International ⊖ a	12 40	12 50		12 41	12 55	13 01	13 07		12 54		13 10	13 20	13 25	13 31	13 37		13 40	13 50		13 45	13 55	14 01
Farringdon ■ ⊖ a	12 45	12 55			13 00	13 06	13 12				13 15	13 25	13 30	13 36	13 42		13 45	13 55			14 00	14 06
City Thameslink ■ a																						
London Blackfriars ⊖ a	12 49	12 59			13 04	13 10	13 16				13 19	13 29	13 34	13 40	13 46		13 49	13 59			14 04	14 10
London Bridge ⊖ a	12 55				13 10	13 16					13 25		13 40	13 46			13 55				14 10	14 16
Elephant & Castle ⊖173,179 a		13 03					13 20					13 33			13 50			14 03				
Gatwick Airport ✈ a	13 42				13 39						14 09		14 09				14 42				14 39	

	TL G	TL■	TL G	TL■ C	TL F	TL G	TL■ A	EM◇■ M	TL G	TL■ N	TL K	TL■ C	TL F	TL G	TL■ H	EM◇■ D	TL■ J	TL G	TL■ C	TL F	TL G	TL■ A
Bedford ■ d		13 05		13 21			13 37	13 43		←		13 51			14 05	14 15	←		14 21			14 37
Flitwick d		13 16		13 32			13 47			13 47		14 02			14 16		14 16		14 32			14 48
Harlington d		13 20		13 36			→			13 52		14 06			→		14 20		14 36			→
Leagrave d		13 25		13 41						13 57		14 11					14 25		14 41			
Luton ■ d	13 22	13 29		13 46		13 52		14 00		14 02		14 16		14 22			14 29		14 46		14 52	
Luton Airport Parkway ■ ✈ d	13 25	13 32		13 49		13 55				14 05		14 19		14 25		14 31	14 32		14 49		14 55	
Harpenden d	13 30	13 37		13 54		14 00				14 10		14 24		14 30			14 37		14 54		15 00	
St Albans City d	13 37	13 43	13 47	14 00		14 07			14 16	14 17	←	14 30		14 37			14 43	14 47	15 00		15 07	
Radlett d	13 42		13 52			14 12			14 21		14 21			14 42				14 52			15 12	
Elstree & Borehamwood d	13 46		13 56			14 16			→		14 25			14 46				14 56			15 16	
Mill Hill Broadway d	13 50		13 59			14 20					14 29			14 50				14 59			15 20	
Hendon d			14 03								14 32							15 03				
Cricklewood d			14 07								14 37							15 07				
WestHampsteadThameslink ⊖ d	13 56	14 00	14 09	14 15		14 26				14 30	14 39	14 45		14 56			15 00	15 09	15 15		15 26	
Kentish Town ⊖ d			14 14		14 26						14 44		14 56					15 14		15 26		
St Pancras International ⊖ a	14 07	14 10	14 20	14 25	14 31	14 37		14 24		14 40	14 50	14 55	15 01	15 07		14 59	15 10	15 20	15 25	15 31	15 37	
Farringdon ■ ⊖ a	14 12	14 15	14 25	14 30	14 36	14 42				14 45	14 55	15 00	15 06	15 12			15 15	15 25	15 30	15 36	15 42	
City Thameslink ■ a																						
London Blackfriars ⊖ a	14 16	14 19	14 29	14 34	14 40	14 46				14 49	14 59	15 04	15 10	15 16			15 19	15 29	15 34	15 40	15 46	
London Bridge ⊖ a		14 25		14 40	14 46					14 55		15 10	15 16				15 25		15 40	15 46		
Elephant & Castle ⊖173,179 a	14 20		14 33			14 50					15 03			15 20				15 33			15 50	
Gatwick Airport ✈ a		15 09		15 09						15 42		15 39					16 09		16 09			

	EM◇■ M	TL G	TL■ N	TL K	TL■ C	TL F	TL G	TL■ H	EM◇■ D	TL■ J	TL G	TL■ C	TL F	TL G	TL■ A	EM◇■ M	TL G	TL■ N	TL K	TL■ C	TL F
Bedford ■ d	14 45		←		14 51			15 05	15 15	←		15 21			15 37	15 45		←		15 51	
Flitwick d			14 48		15 02			15 16		15 16		15 32			15 48			15 48		16 02	
Harlington d			14 52		15 06			→		15 20		15 36			→			15 52		16 06	
Leagrave d			14 57		15 11					15 25		15 41						15 57		16 11	
Luton ■ d	15 00		15 02		15 16		15 22			15 29		15 46		15 52		16 00		16 02		16 16	
Luton Airport Parkway ■ ✈ d			15 05		15 19		15 25		15 31	15 32		15 49		15 55				16 05		16 19	
Harpenden d			15 10		15 24		15 30			15 37		15 54		16 00				16 10		16 24	
St Albans City d		15 16	15 17	←	15 30		15 37			15 43	15 47	16 00		16 07			16 16	16 17	←	16 30	
Radlett d		15 21		15 21			15 42				15 52			16 12			16 21		16 21		
Elstree & Borehamwood d		→		15 25			15 46				15 56			16 16			→		16 25		
Mill Hill Broadway d				15 29			15 50				15 59			16 20					16 29		
Hendon d				15 32							16 03								16 32		
Cricklewood d				15 37							16 07								16 37		
WestHampsteadThameslink ⊖ d			15 30	15 39	15 45		15 56			16 00	16 09	16 15		16 26				16 30	16 39	16 45	
Kentish Town ⊖ d				15 44		15 56					16 14		16 26						16 44		16 56
St Pancras International ⊖ a	15 24		15 40	15 50	15 55	16 01	16 07		15 59	16 10	16 20	16 25	16 31	16 37		16 24		16 40	16 50	16 55	17 01
Farringdon ■ ⊖ a			15 45	15 55	16 00	16 06	16 12			16 15	16 25	16 30	16 36	16 42				16 45	16 55	17 00	17 06
City Thameslink ■ a																					
London Blackfriars ⊖ a			15 49	15 59	16 04	16 10	16 16			16 19	16 29	16 34	16 40	16 46				16 49	16 59	17 04	17 10
London Bridge ⊖ a			15 55		16 10	16 16				16 25		16 40	16 46					16 55		17 10	17 16
Elephant & Castle ⊖173,179 a				16 03			16 20				16 33			16 50					17 03		
Gatwick Airport ✈ a			16 42		16 39					17 09		17 09						17 42		17 39	

A To Three Bridges
B From Luton to Sutton (Surrey)
C To Brighton
D From Nottingham
E From Bedford to Brighton
F To Rainham (Kent)
G To Sutton (Surrey)
H To Gatwick Airport
I From Sheffield
J From Bedford
K From St Albans City to Sutton (Surrey)
L From Leeds
M From Corby
N From Bedford to Three Bridges

Table T052MML-R

Sundays

15 December to 10 May

Bedford, Luton and St Albans - London and Gatwick Airport

		TL A	TL ■ B	EM ◇■ C ☕	TL ■ D	TL A	EM ◇■ E ☕	TL ■ F	TL G	TL A	TL A	TL ■ H	TL I	TL ■ F	TL G	TL A	TL ■ B	EM ◇■ C ☕	TL ■ D	TL A	TL ■ F	EM ◇■ J ☕	TL G
Bedford 7	d		16 05	16 09	←			16 21				16 37		16 51			17 05	17 09	←		17 21	17 28	
Flitwick	d		16 16		16 16			16 32				16 48		17 02			17 16		17 16		17 32		
Harlington	d		→		16 20			16 36				16 52		17 06			→		17 20		17 36		
Leagrave	d				16 25			16 41				16 57		17 11					17 25		17 41		
Luton 10	d	16 22			16 29		16 41	16 46		16 52		17 02		17 16		17 22			17 29		17 46	17 47	
Luton Airport Parkway 7 ✈	d	16 25		16 25	16 32			16 49		16 55		17 05		17 19		17 25		17 26	17 32		17 49		
Harpenden	d	16 30			16 37			16 54		17 00		17 10		17 24		17 30			17 37		17 54		
St Albans City	d	16 37			16 43	16 47		17 00		17 07	17 16	17 17	←	17 30		17 37			17 43	17 47	18 00		
Radlett	d	16 42				16 52				17 12	17 21		17 21			17 42				17 52			
Elstree & Borehamwood	d	16 46				16 56				17 16	→		17 25			17 46				17 56			
Mill Hill Broadway	d	16 50				16 59				17 20			17 29			17 50				17 59			
Hendon	d					17 03							17 32							18 03			
Cricklewood	d					17 07							17 37							18 07			
WestHampsteadThameslink ⊖	d	16 56			17 00	17 09		17 15		17 26		17 30	17 39	17 45		17 56			18 00	18 09	18 15		
Kentish Town ⊖	d					17 14			17 26				17 44		17 56					18 14			18 26
St Pancras International ⊖	a	17 07		16 48	17 10	17 20	17 05	17 25	17 31	17 37		17 40	17 50	17 55	18 01	18 07		17 50	18 10	18 20	18 25	18 12	18 31
Farringdon 3 ⊖	a	17 12			17 15	17 25		17 30	17 36	17 42		17 45	17 55	18 00	18 06	18 12			18 15	18 25	18 30		18 36
City Thameslink 3	a																						
London Blackfriars ⊖	a	17 16			17 19	17 29		17 34	17 40	17 46		17 49	17 59	18 04	18 10	18 16			18 19	18 29	18 34		18 40
London Bridge ⊖	a				17 25			17 40	17 46			17 55		18 10	18 16				18 25		18 40		18 46
Elephant & Castle ⊖173,179	a	17 20				17 33				17 50			18 03			18 20				18 33			
Gatwick Airport ✈	a				18 09			18 09				18 42		18 39					19 09		19 09		

		TL A	TL A	TL ■ H	TL I	TL ■ F	TL G	TL A	TL ■ B	EM ◇■ C ☕	EM ◇■ K ☕	TL A	TL ■ D	TL I	TL ■ F	TL G	TL A	TL A	TL ■ H	TL I	TL ■ F	TL G	TL A
Bedford 7	d			17 37		17 51			18 07	18 08	18 17		←		18 21				18 37		18 51		
Flitwick	d			17 48		18 02			18 18				18 18		18 32				18 48		19 02		
Harlington	d			17 52		18 06			→				18 22		18 36				18 52		19 06		
Leagrave	d			17 57		18 11							18 27		18 41				18 57		19 11		
Luton 10	d	17 52		18 02		18 16		18 22			18 32		18 32		18 46		18 52		19 02		19 16		19 22
Luton Airport Parkway 7 ✈	d	17 55		18 05		18 19		18 25		18 25			18 35		18 49		18 55		19 05		19 19		19 25
Harpenden	d	18 00		18 10		18 24		18 30					18 40		18 54		19 00		19 10		19 24		19 30
St Albans City	d	18 07	18 16	18 17	←	18 30		18 37				18 46	18 47	←	19 00		19 07	19 16	19 17	←	19 30		19 37
Radlett	d	18 12	18 21		18 21			18 42				18 51		18 51			19 12	19 21		19 21			19 42
Elstree & Borehamwood	d	18 16	→		18 25			18 46				→		18 55			19 16	→		19 25			19 46
Mill Hill Broadway	d	18 20			18 29			18 50						18 59			19 20			19 29			19 50
Hendon	d				18 32									19 02						19 32			
Cricklewood	d				18 37									19 07						19 37			
WestHampsteadThameslink ⊖	d	18 26		18 30	18 39	18 45		18 57					19 00	19 09	19 15		19 26		19 30	19 39	19 45		19 56
Kentish Town ⊖	d				18 44		18 56							19 14		19 26				19 44		19 56	
St Pancras International ⊖	a	18 37		18 40	18 50	18 55	19 01	19 07		18 47	18 55		19 10	19 20	19 25	19 31	19 37		19 40	19 50	19 55	20 01	20 07
Farringdon 3 ⊖	a	18 42		18 45	18 55	19 00	19 06	19 12					19 15	19 25	19 30	19 36	19 42		19 45	19 55	20 00	20 06	20 12
City Thameslink 3	a																						
London Blackfriars ⊖	a	18 46		18 49	18 59	19 04	19 10	19 16					19 19	19 29	19 34	19 40	19 46		19 49	19 59	20 04	20 10	20 16
London Bridge ⊖	a			18 55		19 10	19 16						19 25		19 40	19 46			19 55		20 10	20 16	
Elephant & Castle ⊖173,179	a	18 50			19 03			19 20						19 33			19 50			20 03			20 20
Gatwick Airport ✈	a			19 42		19 39							20 09		20 09				20 42		20 39		

		TL ■ B	EM ◇■ C ☕	TL ■ D	TL A	TL ■ F	EM ◇■ K ☕	TL ■ L	TL G	TL A	TL ■	TL A	TL ■ F	EM ◇■ C ☕	TL ■ L	TL G	TL A	TL ■ H	EM ◇■ C ☕	TL A	TL ■ M	TL I	TL ■ F
Bedford 7	d	19 05	19 09	←		19 21	19 28	←			19 35		19 51	19 59	←			20 07	20 10		←		20 21
Flitwick	d	19 16		19 16		19 32		19 32			19 46		20 02		20 02			20 18			20 18		20 32
Harlington	d	→		19 20		→		19 36			19 50		→		20 06			→			20 22		20 36
Leagrave	d			19 25				19 41			19 55				20 11						20 27		20 41
Luton 10	d			19 29			19 45	19 46		19 52	19 59			20 15	20 16		20 22				20 32		20 46
Luton Airport Parkway 7 ✈	d		19 26	19 32				19 49		19 55	20 02				20 19		20 25		20 26		20 35		20 49
Harpenden	d			19 37				19 54		20 00	20 07				20 24		20 30				20 40		20 54
St Albans City	d			19 43	19 47			20 00		20 07	20 13	20 17			20 30		20 37			20 46	20 47	←	21 00
Radlett	d				19 52					20 12		20 22					20 42			20 51		20 51	
Elstree & Borehamwood	d				19 56					20 16		20 26					20 46			→		20 55	
Mill Hill Broadway	d				19 59					20 20		20 29					20 50					20 59	
Hendon	d				20 03							20 33										21 02	
Cricklewood	d				20 07							20 37										21 07	
WestHampsteadThameslink ⊖	d			20 00	20 09			20 15		20 26	20 30	20 39			20 45		20 57				21 00	21 09	21 15
Kentish Town ⊖	d				20 14				20 26			20 44				20 56						21 14	
St Pancras International ⊖	a		19 50	20 10	20 20		20 08	20 25	20 31	20 37	20 40	20 50		20 39	20 55	21 01	21 07		20 50		21 10	21 20	21 25
Farringdon 3 ⊖	a			20 15	20 25			20 30	20 36	20 42	20 45	20 55			21 00	21 06	21 12				21 15	21 25	21 30
City Thameslink 3	a																						
London Blackfriars ⊖	a			20 19	20 29			20 34	20 40	20 46	20 49	20 59			21 04	21 10	21 16				21 19	21 29	21 34
London Bridge ⊖	a			20 25				20 40	20 46		20 55				21 10	21 16					21 25		21 40
Elephant & Castle ⊖173,179	a				20 33					20 50		21 03					21 20					21 33	
Gatwick Airport ✈	a			21 09				21 09			21 39				21 39						22 09		22 09

A To Sutton (Surrey)
B To Gatwick Airport
C From Nottingham
D From Bedford
E From Sheffield
F To Brighton
G To Rainham (Kent)
H To Three Bridges
I From St Albans City to Sutton (Surrey)
J From Leeds
K From Derby
L From Bedford to Brighton
M From Bedford to Three Bridges

Table T052MML-R

Sundays

15 December to 10 May

Bedford, Luton and St Albans - London and Gatwick Airport

		TL A	TL B	TL ■ C	EM ◇■ D ☕	TL ■ E	TL A	TL ■ F	TL G	EM ◇■ H ☕	TL ■	TL I	TL ■ F	EM ◇■ J ☕	TL ■ K	TL L	TL I	TL ■ F	TL L	TL ■ F	EM ◇■ J ☕	EM ◇■ H ☕	TL ■ F
Bedford 7	d			20 37	20 41	←		20 51		21 09	21 09		21 21	21 29	←			21 51		22 11	22 20	22 39	22 45
Flitwick	d			20 48		20 48		21 02			21 20		21 32		21 32			22 02		22 22			22 56
Harlington	d			→		20 52		21 06			21 24		→		21 36			22 06		22 26			23 00
Leagrave	d					20 57		21 11			21 29				21 41			22 11		22 31			23 05
Luton 10	d		20 52		20 56	21 02		21 16		21 24	21 33			21 45	21 46			22 16		22 36	22 36	22 54	23 10
Luton Airport Parkway 7 ✈	d		20 55		20 59	21 05		21 19			21 36				21 49			22 19		22 39			23 13
Harpenden	d		21 00			21 10		21 24			21 41				21 54			22 24		22 44			23 18
St Albans City	d		21 07			21 17	21 27	21 31	←		21 48	21 57			22 01	←	22 27	22 31	←	22 51			23 25
Radlett	d		21 12				21 32		21 32			22 02				22 02	22 32		22 32	22 56			
Elstree & Borehamwood	d		21 16				→		21 36			→				22 06	→		22 36	23 00			
Mill Hill Broadway	d		21 20						21 40							22 10			22 40	23 04			
Hendon	d								21 43							22 13			22 43	23 07			
Cricklewood	d								21 48							22 18			22 48	23 12			
WestHampsteadThameslink ⊖	d		21 26			21 30		21 45	21 50		22 00				22 15	22 20		22 45	22 50	23 14			23 41
Kentish Town ⊖	d	21 26							21 55							22 25			22 55	23 19			
St Pancras International ⊖	a	21 31	21 37		21 22	21 40		21 55	22 01	21 48	22 10			22 11	22 25	22 31		22 55	23 01	23 25	23 00	23 24	23 51
Farringdon 3 ⊖	a	21 36	21 42			21 45		22 00	22 06		22 15				22 30	22 36		23 00	23 06	23 30			23 55
City Thameslink 3	a																						
London Blackfriars ⊖	a	21 40	21 46			21 49		22 04	22 10		22 19				22 34	22 40		23 04	23 10	23 34			23 59
London Bridge ⊖	a	21 46				21 55		22 10	22 16		22 25				22 40	22 46		23 10	23 16	23 40			
Elephant & Castle ⊖173,179	a		21 50																				
Gatwick Airport ✈	a					22 39		22 39			23 09				23 09			23 42		00 17			00 47

		TL ■ C	TL ■ F
Bedford 7	d	23 05	23 45
Flitwick	d	23 16	23 56
Harlington	d	23 20	00 01
Leagrave	d	23 25	00 06
Luton 10	d	23 30	00 10
Luton Airport Parkway 7 ✈	d	23 33	00 13
Harpenden	d	23 38	00 18
St Albans City	d	23 45	00 25
Radlett	d	23 50	
Elstree & Borehamwood	d	23 54	
Mill Hill Broadway	d	23 58	
Hendon	d	00 01	
Cricklewood	d	00 06	
WestHampsteadThameslink ⊖	d	00 09	00 41
Kentish Town ⊖	d	00 13	
St Pancras International ⊖	a	00 19	00 51
Farringdon 3 ⊖	a	00 25	
City Thameslink 3	a		
London Blackfriars ⊖	a	00 30	01 00
London Bridge ⊖	a		
Elephant & Castle ⊖173,179	a		
Gatwick Airport ✈	a	01 20	01 56

A To Rainham (Kent)
B To Sutton (Surrey)
C To Three Bridges
D From York
E From Bedford to Three Bridges
F To Brighton
G From St Albans City to Rainham (Kent)
H From Nottingham
I To Gillingham (Kent)
J From Sheffield
K From Bedford to Brighton
L From St Albans City to Gillingham (Kent)

Table T053-F

Mondays to Fridays
16 December to 15 May

London - East Midlands - Sheffield

Miles	Miles	Miles	Miles	Station	EM MX ◇■ A	EM MO ◇■ A	EM MO ◇■ A	EM MX ◇■ A	EM MX ◇■	TP MX ◇■ B	TP MO ◇■ B	TP ◇■ B	NT	TP ◇■ C	NT	NT	EM D	NT ◇ E	NT	NT	NT F	TP ◇■ G
0	0	—	—	St Pancras International ⊖52 d					00 15													
29¼	29¼	—	—	Luton Airport Parkway 52 ✈ d					00 55													
30¼	30¼	—	—	Luton 52 d					00 58													
49¾	49¾	—	—	Bedford 52 d				00 09	01 26													
65¼	65¼	—	—	Wellingborough d			00 15	00 22	01 36													
72	72	0	—	Kettering a			00 25	00 38	01 46													
				d			00 26	00 39	01 46													
—	—	7½	—	Corby a																		
—	—	21¾	—	Oakham 47 a																		
—	—	33¼	0	Melton Mowbray 47 a																		
83	83	—	—	Market Harborough d			00 36	00 49	01 58													
99¼	99¼	48½	—	**Leicester** a			00 51	01 07	02 13													
				d		00 11	00 52	01 08														
103	103	—	—	Syston d																		
105¾	105¾	—	12¼	Sileby d																		
107¾	107¾	—	—	Barrow Upon Soar d																		
111¾	111¾	—	—	Loughborough d		00 21	01 02	01 18														
117½	117½	—	—	East Midlands Parkway ✈ d	00 02	00 29	01 10	01 26														
123¼	—	—	—	Beeston a		00 34		01 32														
126½	—	—	—	**Nottingham** a		00 41		01 39														
				d				01 46														
—	—	—	—	Newark Castle 27 a																		
—	—	—	—	Lincoln 27 a																		
138½	—	—	—	Langley Mill d																		
144¾	—	—	—	Alfreton d																		
—	120½	—	—	Long Eaton a																		
—	128½	—	—	**Derby** a	00 14		01 21	02 04														
				d	00 17												05 42					
—	—	—	—	Belper a													05 54					
				d																		
155	152¾	—	—	Chesterfield a	00 34																	
—	—	—	—	Dronfield a																		
167¾	165	—	—	**Sheffield** a	00 51																	
				d						03 24	03 45	05 09	05 15	05 21	05 25	05 28		05 42	05 48	06 02	06 05	06 09
—	—	—	—	Manchester Piccadilly 78 a						04 52	04 37	06 03										07 02
—	—	—	—	Doncaster 29 a										05 51	06 02			06 11	06 25		06 42	
—	—	—	—	Wakefield Kirkgate 31,34 a												06 15				06 48		
—	—	—	—	Wakefield Westgate 31 a									06 12									
—	—	—	—	Leeds 31,34 a									06 31			06 44				07 25		
—	—	—	—	York 29 a																		

Station	NT	EM ◇ H	NT ◇	NT	XC ◇■ I	NT ◇ J	NT ◇ E	NT F	NT	TP ◇■ K	TP ◇■ L	EM ◇■	NT ◇	NT	NT ◇	XC ◇■ M	EM D	NT ◇	NT F	EM ◇ H	EM	NT ◇ N
St Pancras International ⊖52 d																						
Luton Airport Parkway 52 ✈ d																						
Luton 52 d																						
Bedford 52 d																						
Wellingborough d																						
Kettering a																						
d																						
Corby a																						
Oakham 47 a																						
Melton Mowbray 47 a																						
Market Harborough d																						
Leicester a																						
d																					06 26	
Syston d																					06 33	
Sileby d																					06 38	
Barrow Upon Soar d																					06 43	
Loughborough d																					06 48	
East Midlands Parkway ✈ d																					06 56	
Beeston a																					07 06	
Nottingham a																					07 16	
d		05 23													06 16		06 17			06 35		
Newark Castle 27 a																						
Lincoln 27 a																						
Langley Mill d															06 35							
Alfreton d															06 43					06 56		
Long Eaton a																	06 35					
Derby a																	06 49					
d					05 59							06 27				06 43	06 51					
Belper a																	07 03					
d																						
Chesterfield a		05 51			06 16							06 44			06 53	07 00				07 06		
Dronfield a															07 00					07 14		
Sheffield a		06 15			06 31							07 09			07 10	07 14				07 24		
d	06 16	06 18	06 19	06 27	06 33	06 44	06 55	07 01	07 04	07 07	07 08		07 10	07 12	07 18	07 21		07 24	07 31	07 32		07 47
Manchester Piccadilly 78 a		07 38								08 02			08 34							08 37		
Doncaster 29 a				07 05	06 59		07 22	07 46			07 32								08 09			
Wakefield Kirkgate 31,34 a			06 54			07 22			07 50						07 57							08 23
Wakefield Westgate 31 a	07 12													08 16		07 46						
Leeds 31,34 a	07 31		07 16			07 43			08 26					08 34	08 17	08 03						08 44
York 29 a					07 24											08 30		08 48				

A From St Pancras International
B To Manchester Airport
C To Cleethorpes
D To Matlock
E To Scarborough
F To Adwick
G From Doncaster to Manchester Airport
H To Liverpool Lime Street
I To Newcastle
J From Chesterfield
K From Cleethorpes to Manchester Airport
L From Manchester Airport to Cleethorpes
M From Birmingham New Street to Glasgow Central
N From Retford

For connections from Gatwick Airport refer to Table T052

NRT DECEMBER 19 EDITION

Table T053-F

Mondays to Fridays
16 December to 15 May

London - East Midlands - Sheffield

Station	XC ◇■ A	NT ◇ B	EM ◇■	NT	NT	TP ◇■ C	TP ◇■ D	NT	NT ◇	XC ◇■ E	EM ◇■	NT	EM F	NT ◇	EM ◇ G	EM	NT ◇ H	EM ◇■	EM ◇■	XC ◇■ A	NT ◇ B	NT
St Pancras International ⊖52 d											05 52							06 23				
Luton Airport Parkway 52 ✈ d																						
Luton 52 d											06 15							06 46				
Bedford 52 d											06 29							07 00				
Wellingborough d											06 41							07 12				
Kettering a											06 47							07 18				
d											06 48							07 19	07 38			
Corby a																			07 47			
Oakham 47 a																						
Melton Mowbray 47 a																						
Market Harborough d											06 58							07 29				
Leicester a											07 10							07 41				
d											07 12					07 28		07 42				
Syston d																07 35						
Sileby d																07 40						
Barrow Upon Soar d																07 45						
Loughborough d											07 22					07 50		07 52				
East Midlands Parkway ✈ d											07 29					08 00						
Beeston a																08 09						
Nottingham a																08 16						
d									07 18				07 20		07 45							
Newark Castle 27 a																						
Lincoln 27 a																						
Langley Mill d									07 37													
Alfreton d									07 45						08 10							
Long Eaton a											07 33		07 37									
Derby a											07 44		07 51					08 06				
d	07 13		07 17							07 42	07 44		07 53					08 09		08 14		
Belper a			07 28										08 05									
d			07 29																			
Chesterfield a	07 30		07 41						07 56	07 59	08 03				08 20			08 27		08 33		
Dronfield a			07 48						08 04						08 27							
Sheffield a	07 46		08 00						08 15	08 20	08 24				08 39			08 46		08 48		
d	07 50	07 57		08 04	08 07	08 08	08 11	08 16	08 19	08 22		08 32		08 33	08 42		08 45			08 50	08 56	09 03
Manchester Piccadilly 78 a						09 02								09 41	09 37							
Doncaster 29 a	08 14	08 22			08 46		08 36					09 08								09 15	09 22	
Wakefield Kirkgate 31,34 a				08 49					08 55								09 24					09 49
Wakefield Westgate 31 a								09 12		08 48												
Leeds 31,34 a				09 24				09 31	09 14	09 02							09 44					10 25
York 29 a	08 40									09 30										09 40		

Station	NT I	TP ◇■ C	TP ◇■ D	NT ◇	NT	NT ◇	XC ◇■ J	NT	EM F	EM ◇■	EM MO ◇ K	EM MX ◇ K	NT ◇ H	EM L	EM ◇■	EM ◇■	EM M	EM ◇■	EM ◇■	EM ◇■	XC ◇■ N
St Pancras International ⊖52 d										06 48					07 04	07 32		07 35		07 49	
Luton Airport Parkway 52 ✈ d										07 10								07 56			
Luton 52 d															07 27						
Bedford 52 d															07 41			08 10		08 25	
Wellingborough d															07 54			08 23		08 37	
Kettering a															08 03			08 30		08 45	
d															08 04			08 30	08 32	08 46	
Corby a																			08 41	08 56	
Oakham 47 a																					
Melton Mowbray 47 a																					
Market Harborough d															08 15	08 27		08 41			
Leicester a										07 54					08 31	08 39		08 54			
d										07 56				08 26	08 32	08 40		08 55			
Syston d														08 34							
Sileby d														08 40							
Barrow Upon Soar d														08 46			←				
Loughborough d										08 06				08 51	08 43	08 50	08 51	09 04			
East Midlands Parkway ✈ d										08 13				→	08 51	08 58	08 59				
Beeston a										08 20							09 10	09 15			
Nottingham a										08 27					09 02		09 17	09 23			
d						08 17			08 20		08 47	08 47					09 28				
Newark Castle 27 a																	09 50				
Lincoln 27 a																	10 17				
Langley Mill d						08 36															
Alfreton d						08 44					09 08	09 08									
Long Eaton a									08 37							09 01					
Derby a									08 50							09 14					
d							08 45		08 52							09 15					09 21
Belper a									09 04												
d																					
Chesterfield a						08 55	09 02				09 20	09 20				09 32					
Dronfield a						09 02															
Sheffield a						09 13	09 18				09 37	09 38				09 47					09 48
d	09 06	09 11	09 11	09 14	09 15	09 18	09 21	09 32			09 42	09 42	09 45								09 51
Manchester Piccadilly 78 a		10 02		10 34							10 37	10 37									
Doncaster 29 a	09 45		09 37					10 10													10 15
Wakefield Kirkgate 31,34 a						09 55							10 24								
Wakefield Westgate 31 a					10 12		09 46														
Leeds 31,34 a					10 31	10 14	10 00						10 44								
York 29 a							10 30														10 40

A From Birmingham New Street to Newcastle
B To Scarborough
C From Cleethorpes to Manchester Airport
D From Manchester Airport to Cleethorpes
E From Birmingham New Street to Edinburgh
F From Newark Castle to Matlock
G To Liverpool Lime Street
H From Lincoln
I To Adwick
J From Bath Spa to Glasgow Central
K From Norwich to Liverpool Lime Street
L To Lincoln
M From Leicester
N From Guildford to Newcastle

For connections from Gatwick Airport refer to Table T052

Table T053-F

London - East Midlands - Sheffield

Mondays to Fridays

16 December to 15 May

Station		NT ◇ A	NT	EM ◇■ ⌶	NT B	TP ◇■ C ⌶	TP ◇■ D	NT ◇		NT	NT ◇	XC ◇■ E ⌶	EM F	XC ◇■ G ⌶	NT	EM ◇ H	EM ◇■ ⌶	EM I		EM ◇■ ⌶	NT ◇ J	EM ◇■ ⌶	EM ◇■ ⌶	EM ◇■ ⌶	NT ◇ A
St Pancras International ⊖52	d			08 02													08 05			08 31		08 34		08 47	
Luton Airport Parkway 52 ✈	d																08 28								
Luton 52	d																							09 12	
Bedford 52	d																08 42							09 27	
Wellingborough	d																08 55							09 39	
Kettering	a																09 02							09 50	
	d																09 02						09 04	09 51	
Corby	a																						09 13	10 00	
Oakham 47	a																								
Melton Mowbray 47	a																								
Market Harborough	d																09 13					09 32			
Leicester	a			09 06													09 25			09 37		09 46			
	d			09 07													09 26	09 30		09 38		09 46			
Syston	d																	09 37							
Sileby	d																	09 42							
Barrow Upon Soar	d																	09 48							
Loughborough	d																09 35	09 53		09 48					
East Midlands Parkway ✈	d																	→		09 56		10 03			
Beeston	a																09 47								
Nottingham	a																09 57					10 15			
	d										09 17		09 18			09 47									
Newark Castle 27	a																								
Lincoln 27	a																								
Langley Mill	d										09 36														
Alfreton	d										09 44					10 08									
Long Eaton	a												09 35							09 59					
Derby	a			09 28									09 47							10 10					
	d			09 30								09 44	09 48	10 00						10 11					
Belper	a												10 00												
	d																								
Chesterfield	a			09 47							09 55	10 01				10 21				10 28					
Dronfield	a										10 02														
Sheffield	a			10 03							10 13	10 18		10 27		10 37				10 42					
	d	09 57	10 02		10 05	10 11	10 11	10 14		10 15	10 18	10 21		10 29	10 32	10 42					10 45				10 57
Manchester Piccadilly 78	a					11 02		11 32								11 37									
Doncaster 29	a	10 22			10 45		10 35							10 52	11 09										11 22
Wakefield Kirkgate 31,34	a		10 48								10 55										11 24				
Wakefield Westgate 31	a									11 12		10 45													
Leeds 31,34	a		11 25							11 31	11 14	11 01									11 44				
York 29	a											11 30		11 15											

Station		EM ◇■ ⌶	NT	NT B		TP ◇■ D	TP ◇■ C ⌶	NT ◇	NT	NT ◇	XC ◇■ K ⌶	EM F	EM L	XC ◇■ M ⌶		NT	NT ◇	EM ◇ H	EM ◇■ ⌶	EM I	EM ◇■ ⌶	NT ◇ J	EM ◇■ ⌶	EM ◇■ ⌶	
St Pancras International ⊖52	d	09 02																	09 05		09 31		09 34		
Luton Airport Parkway 52 ✈	d																		09 26						
Luton 52	d																								
Bedford 52	d																		09 40						
Wellingborough	d																		09 53						
Kettering	a																		10 00						
	d																		10 00					10 26	
Corby	a																							10 34	
Oakham 47	a																								
Melton Mowbray 47	a																								
Market Harborough	d																		10 11				10 31		
Leicester	a	10 06																	10 23		10 34		10 44		
	d	10 06																	10 24	10 30	10 35		10 45		
Syston	d																			10 36					
Sileby	d																			10 42					
Barrow Upon Soar	d																			10 48					
Loughborough	d												← 09 53						10 33	10 53	10 45				
East Midlands Parkway ✈	d												10 05							→	10 53		11 02		
Beeston	a												10 12						10 43						
Nottingham	a												10 20						10 52				11 14		
	d									10 17		10 16	10 29					10 51							
Newark Castle 27	a												10 51												
Lincoln 27	a												11 26												
Langley Mill	d									10 36															
Alfreton	d									10 44								11 12							
Long Eaton	a											10 33									10 56				
Derby	a	10 27										10 46									11 06				
	d	10 29									10 44	10 48		11 00							11 09				
Belper	a											11 00													
	d																								
Chesterfield	a	10 47								10 55	11 02							11 22			11 27				
Dronfield	a									11 02															
Sheffield	a	11 01								11 13	11 18			11 27				11 37			11 41				
	d		11 02	11 05		11 10	11 11	11 14	11 15	11 18	11 21			11 29		11 32	11 41	11 42				11 45			
Manchester Piccadilly 78	a						12 02	12 32										12 37							
Doncaster 29	a			11 45		11 35								11 53		12 09									
Wakefield Kirkgate 31,34	a		11 48							11 55												12 24			
Wakefield Westgate 31	a								12 12		11 45														
Leeds 31,34	a		12 25						12 31	12 14	12 01											12 44			
York 29	a										12 31			12 15			13 05								

A To Scarborough
B To Adwick
C From Cleethorpes to Manchester Airport
D From Manchester Airport to Cleethorpes
E From Plymouth to Edinburgh
F From Newark Castle to Matlock
G From Reading to Newcastle
H From Norwich to Liverpool Lime Street
I To Lincoln
J From Lincoln
K From Plymouth to Glasgow Central
L From Leicester
M From Southampton Central to Newcastle

For connections from Gatwick Airport refer to Table T052

Table T053-F

London - East Midlands - Sheffield

Mondays to Fridays

16 December to 15 May

Station		EM ◇■ ⌶	NT ◇ A	EM ◇■ ⌶	NT	NT B	TP ◇■ C ⌶	TP ◇■ D	NT ◇	NT		NT ◇	XC ◇■ E ⌶	NT	EM F	EM G	EM ◇ H	EM ◇■ ⌶	EM I	EM ◇■ ⌶		NT ◇ J	EM ◇■ ⌶	EM ◇■ ⌶	EM ◇■ ⌶
St Pancras International ⊖52	d	09 47		10 02														10 05		10 31			10 34		10 47
Luton Airport Parkway 52 ✈	d																	10 28							
Luton 52	d	10 09																							11 09
Bedford 52	d	10 24																10 42							11 24
Wellingborough	d	10 36																10 56							11 35
Kettering	a	10 45																11 03							11 46
	d	10 46																11 03						11 24	11 47
Corby	a	10 55																						11 33	11 56
Oakham 47	a																								
Melton Mowbray 47	a																								
Market Harborough	d																	11 15					11 29		
Leicester	a			11 04														11 29		11 34			11 43		
	d			11 04														11 30	11 30	11 35			11 44		
Syston	d																		11 37						
Sileby	d																		11 42						
Barrow Upon Soar	d																		11 48						
Loughborough	d															← 10 53		11 40	11 53	11 46					
East Midlands Parkway ✈	d															11 05			→	11 53			12 01		
Beeston	a															11 12		11 56							
Nottingham	a															11 20		12 05					12 13		
	d											11 17			11 20	11 29	11 47								
Newark Castle 27	a															11 51									
Lincoln 27	a															12 21									
Langley Mill	d											11 36													
Alfreton	d											11 44					12 08								
Long Eaton	a														11 37					11 57					
Derby	a			11 25											11 50					12 08					
	d			11 30									11 45		11 52					12 08					
Belper	a														12 04										
	d																								
Chesterfield	a			11 47								11 55	12 02				12 21			12 26					
Dronfield	a											12 02													
Sheffield	a			12 01								12 13	12 18				12 37			12 41					
	d		11 57		12 02	12 05	12 11	12 11	12 14	12 15		12 18	12 21	12 32			12 42					12 45			
Manchester Piccadilly 78	a						13 02		13 32								13 37								
Doncaster 29	a		12 22			12 45		12 35						13 09											
Wakefield Kirkgate 31,34	a				12 48							12 55										13 24			
Wakefield Westgate 31	a									13 12			12 45												
Leeds 31,34	a				13 25					13 31		13 14	13 00									13 44			
York 29	a												13 30												

Station		XC ◇■ K ⌶	NT ◇ A	EM ◇■ ⌶	NT	NT B		TP ◇■ C ⌶	TP ◇■ D	NT ◇	NT	NT ◇	XC ◇■ L ⌶	NT	EM F	EM G		EM ◇ H	EM ◇■ ⌶	EM I	EM ◇■ ⌶	NT ◇ J	EM ◇■ ⌶	EM ◇■ ⌶	XC ◇■ M ⌶
St Pancras International ⊖52	d			11 02															11 05		11 31		11 34	11 47	
Luton Airport Parkway 52 ✈	d																		11 26						
Luton 52	d																							12 09	
Bedford 52	d																		11 40					12 24	
Wellingborough	d																		11 53					12 36	
Kettering	a																		12 00					12 44	
	d																		12 00					12 45	
Corby	a																							12 54	
Oakham 47	a																								
Melton Mowbray 47	a																								
Market Harborough	d																		12 11				12 29		
Leicester	a			12 05															12 23		12 34		12 42		
	d			12 05															12 24	12 30	12 35		12 43		
Syston	d																			12 37					
Sileby	d																			12 42					
Barrow Upon Soar	d																			12 48					
Loughborough	d															← 11 53			12 33	12 53	12 45				
East Midlands Parkway ✈	d															12 03				→	12 52		13 00		
Beeston	a															12 11			12 43						
Nottingham	a															12 20			12 52				13 13		
	d											12 17			12 20	12 29		12 47							
Newark Castle 27	a															12 51									
Lincoln 27	a															13 23									
Langley Mill	d											12 36													
Alfreton	d											12 44						13 10							
Long Eaton	a														12 37						12 57				
Derby	a			12 25											12 51						13 08				
	d	12 16		12 28									12 45		12 52						13 10				13 16
Belper	a														13 04										
	d																								
Chesterfield	a			12 47								12 55	13 02					13 20			13 27				
Dronfield	a											13 02													
Sheffield	a	12 47		13 01								13 13	13 18					13 37			13 41				13 44
	d	12 51	12 57		13 02	13 05		13 11	13 11	13 14	13 15	13 18	13 21	13 32				13 42				13 43			13 46
Manchester Piccadilly 78	a							14 02		14 31								14 37							
Doncaster 29	a	13 16	13 22			13 45			13 35					14 10											14 14
Wakefield Kirkgate 31,34	a				13 50							13 55										14 24			
Wakefield Westgate 31	a										14 12		13 46												
Leeds 31,34	a				14 25						14 31	14 14	14 00									14 44			
York 29	a	13 40											14 30												14 39

A To Scarborough
B To Adwick
C From Cleethorpes to Manchester Airport
D From Manchester Airport to Cleethorpes
E From Plymouth to Edinburgh
F From Newark Castle to Matlock
G From Leicester
H From Norwich to Liverpool Lime Street
I To Lincoln
J From Lincoln
K From Reading to Newcastle
L From Penzance to Glasgow Central
M From Southampton Central to Newcastle

For connections from Gatwick Airport refer to Table T052

Table T053-F

Mondays to Fridays

16 December to 15 May

London - East Midlands - Sheffield

Station		NT	EM	NT	NT	TP	TP	NT	NT	NT	XC	NT	EM	EM	EM	EM	EM	EM	NT	EM	EM	XC
		◇	◇■			◇■	◇■	◇		◇	◇■				◇	◇■		◇■	◇	◇■	◇■	◇■
		A			B	C	D				E		F	G	H		I		J			K
			⊼			⊼					⊼					⊼		⊼		⊼	⊼	⊼
St Pancras International ⊖52	d		12 02													12 05		12 31		12 34	12 47	
Luton Airport Parkway ■ 52 ✈	d															12 26						
Luton ■ 52	d																				13 09	
Bedford ■ 52	d															12 40					13 24	
Wellingborough	d															12 53					13 36	
Kettering ■	a															13 00					13 44	
	d															13 00					13 45	
Corby	a																				13 54	
Oakham 47	a																					
Melton Mowbray 47	a																					
Market Harborough	d															13 11				13 29		
Leicester	a		13 04													13 24		13 34		13 42		
	d		13 04													13 25	13 30	13 35		13 43		
Syston	d																13 37					
Sileby	d																13 42					
Barrow Upon Soar	d													←			13 48					
Loughborough	d													12 53		13 34	13 53	13 46				
East Midlands Parkway ✈	d													13 04			→	13 53		14 00		
Beeston	a													13 11		13 44						
Nottingham ■	a													13 20		13 53				14 12		
	d									13 17			13 20	13 29	13 47							
Newark Castle 27	a													13 51								
Lincoln 27	a													14 23								
Langley Mill	d									13 36												
Alfreton	d									13 44					14 10							
Long Eaton	a												13 37					13 57				
Derby ■	a		13 26										13 50					14 08				
	d		13 28								13 45		13 52					14 09				14 16
Belper	a												14 04									
	d																					
Chesterfield	a		13 47							13 55	14 02				14 20			14 27				
Dronfield	a									14 02												
Sheffield ■	a		14 02							14 13	14 18				14 37			14 41				14 47
	d	13 57		14 02	14 05	14 11	14 11	14 14	14 15	14 18	14 21	14 32			14 42				14 45			14 51
Manchester Piccadilly 78	a					15 02		15 34							15 37							
Doncaster ■ 29	a	14 22			14 45		14 35					15 10										15 15
Wakefield Kirkgate ■ 31,34	a			14 48						14 55									15 24			
Wakefield Westgate ■ 31	a								15 12		14 46											
Leeds ■ 31,34	a			15 25					15 31	15 14	15 00								15 44			
York ■ 29	a										15 30											15 40

Station		NT	EM	NT	NT	TP	TP	NT	NT	XC	NT	EM	EM	NT	EM	EM	EM	EM	NT	EM	EM	NT	XC
		◇	◇■			◇■	◇■		◇	◇■				◇	◇	◇■		◇■	◇	◇■	◇■	◇	■
		A			B	C	D			L		F	G		H		I		J				M
			⊼			⊼				⊼						⊼		⊼		⊼	⊼		⊼
St Pancras International ⊖52	d		13 02													13 05		13 31		13 34	13 47		
Luton Airport Parkway ■ 52 ✈	d															13 26							
Luton ■ 52	d																				14 09		
Bedford ■ 52	d															13 40					14 24		
Wellingborough	d															13 53					14 36		
Kettering ■	a															14 00					14 44		
	d															14 00					14 45		
Corby	a																				14 54		
Oakham 47	a																						
Melton Mowbray 47	a																						
Market Harborough	d															14 11				14 29			
Leicester	a		14 04													14 23		14 34		14 42			
	d		14 04													14 24	14 30	14 35		14 43			
Syston	d																14 37						
Sileby	d																14 42						
Barrow Upon Soar	d												←				14 48						
Loughborough	d												13 53			14 33	14 53	14 45					
East Midlands Parkway ✈	d												14 03				→	14 52		15 00			
Beeston	a												14 10			14 43							
Nottingham ■	a												14 19			14 52				15 12			
	d								14 17			14 20	14 29		14 47								
Newark Castle 27	a												14 52										
Lincoln 27	a												15 22										
Langley Mill	d								14 36														
Alfreton	d								14 44						15 08								
Long Eaton	a											14 37						14 57					
Derby ■	a		14 25									14 50						15 08					
	d		14 28							14 45		14 52						15 09					15 16
Belper	a											15 04											
	d																						
Chesterfield	a		14 47						14 55	15 02					15 20			15 27					
Dronfield	a								15 02														
Sheffield ■	a		15 01						15 13	15 18					15 37			15 41					15 47
	d	14 57		15 02	15 05	15 11	15 11	15 15	15 18	15 21	15 32			15 40	15 42				15 45			15 45	15 51
Manchester Piccadilly 78	a					16 02									16 37							17 02	
Doncaster ■ 29	a	15 22			15 45		15 35				16 10												16 15
Wakefield Kirkgate ■ 31,34	a			15 48					15 55										16 23				
Wakefield Westgate ■ 31	a							16 12		15 46													
Leeds ■ 31,34	a			16 25				16 31	16 14	16 00									16 44				
York ■ 29	a									16 30				17 00									16 40

A To Scarborough
B To Adwick
C From Cleethorpes to Manchester Airport
D From Manchester Airport to Cleethorpes
E From Plymouth to Aberdeen
F From Newark Castle to Matlock
G From Leicester
H From Norwich to Liverpool Lime Street
I To Lincoln
J From Lincoln
K From Reading to Newcastle
L From Penzance to Glasgow Central
M From Southampton Central to Newcastle

For connections from Gatwick Airport refer to Table T052

Table T053-F

Mondays to Fridays

16 December to 15 May

London - East Midlands - Sheffield

Station		NT	EM	NT	NT	TP	TP	NT	NT	NT	XC	EM	EM	XC	NT	EM	EM	EM	EM	NT	EM	EM
		◇	◇■			◇■	◇■	◇		◇	◇■			◇■		◇	◇■		◇■	◇	◇■	◇■
		A			B	C	D				E	F	G	H		I		J		K		
			⊼			⊼					⊼			⊼			⊼		⊼		⊼	⊼
St Pancras International ⊖52	d		14 02														14 05		14 31		14 34	
Luton Airport Parkway ■ 52 ✈	d																14 26					
Luton ■ 52	d																					
Bedford ■ 52	d																14 40					
Wellingborough	d																14 53					
Kettering ■	a																15 00					
	d																15 00					15 26
Corby	a																					15 34
Oakham 47	a																					
Melton Mowbray 47	a																					
Market Harborough	d																15 11				15 29	
Leicester	a		15 04														15 23		15 34		15 42	
	d		15 04														15 24	15 30	15 35		15 43	
Syston	d																	15 36				
Sileby	d																	15 41				
Barrow Upon Soar	d												←					15 48				
Loughborough	d												14 53				15 33	15 53	15 45			
East Midlands Parkway ✈	d												15 04					→	15 52		16 00	
Beeston	a												15 11				15 43					
Nottingham ■	a												15 20				15 52				16 12	
	d									15 17		15 18	15 29			15 47						
Newark Castle 27	a												15 51									
Lincoln 27	a												16 23									
Langley Mill	d									15 36												
Alfreton	d									15 44						16 10						
Long Eaton	a											15 35							15 57			
Derby ■	a		15 25									15 46							16 08			
	d		15 28								15 43	15 48		16 00					16 09			
Belper	a											16 00										
	d																					
Chesterfield	a		15 47							15 55	16 02					16 20			16 27			
Dronfield	a									16 02												
Sheffield ■	a		16 01							16 13	16 18			16 27		16 37			16 41			
	d	15 57		16 02	16 05	16 11	16 11	16 14	16 15	16 18	16 21			16 29	16 32	16 42				16 45		
Manchester Piccadilly 78	a					17 02		17 34								17 37						
Doncaster ■ 29	a	16 22			16 45		16 35							16 53	17 10							
Wakefield Kirkgate ■ 31,34	a			16 48						16 55										17 24		
Wakefield Westgate ■ 31	a								17 12		16 46											
Leeds ■ 31,34	a			17 25					17 31	17 14	17 01									17 44		
York ■ 29	a										17 30			17 14								

Station		EM	NT	EM	NT	NT	TP	TP	NT	NT	NT	XC	NT	EM	EM	EM	EM	EM	EM	NT	EM	EM	EM
		◇■	◇	◇■			◇■	◇■	◇		◇	◇■				◇	◇■		◇■	◇	◇■	◇■	◇■
			A			B	C	D				L		F	M	I		N		K			
		⊼		⊼			⊼					⊼					⊼		⊼		⊼	⊼	⊼
St Pancras International ⊖52	d	14 47		15 02													15 05		15 31		15 34		15 47
Luton Airport Parkway ■ 52 ✈	d																15 26						
Luton ■ 52	d	15 09																					16 09
Bedford ■ 52	d	15 24															15 40						16 24
Wellingborough	d	15 36															15 53						16 35
Kettering ■	a	15 44															16 00						16 44
	d	15 45															16 00					16 26	16 45
Corby	a	15 54																				16 36	16 54
Oakham 47	a																						
Melton Mowbray 47	a																						
Market Harborough	d																16 11				16 29		
Leicester	a			16 04													16 23		16 34		16 42		
	d			16 05													16 24	16 30	16 35		16 43		
Syston	d																	16 35					
Sileby	d																	16 41					
Barrow Upon Soar	d														←			16 48					
Loughborough	d														15 53		16 33	16 53	16 45				
East Midlands Parkway ✈	d														16 02			→	16 52		17 00		
Beeston	a														16 10		16 44						
Nottingham ■	a														16 20		16 54				17 12		
	d										16 17			16 20	16 27	16 47							
Newark Castle 27	a														16 51								
Lincoln 27	a														17 18								
Langley Mill	d										16 36												
Alfreton	d										16 44					17 08							
Long Eaton	a													16 37					16 57				
Derby ■	a			16 26										16 51					17 08				
	d			16 29								16 44		16 52					17 09				
Belper	a													17 04									
	d																						
Chesterfield	a			16 47							16 55	17 03				17 20			17 27				
Dronfield	a										17 02												
Sheffield ■	a			17 02							17 13	17 18				17 38			17 44				
	d		16 57		17 02	17 05	17 11	17 11	17 14	17 15	17 18	17 21	17 32			17 39				17 45			
Manchester Piccadilly 78	a						18 02		18 31							18 37							
Doncaster ■ 29	a		17 24			17 45		17 35					18 10										
Wakefield Kirkgate ■ 31,34	a				17 48						17 55									18 24			
Wakefield Westgate ■ 31	a									18 12		17 46											
Leeds ■ 31,34	a				18 25					18 31	18 14	18 00								18 44			
York ■ 29	a											18 31											

A To Scarborough
B To Adwick
C From Cleethorpes to Manchester Airport
D From Manchester Airport to Cleethorpes
E From Penzance to Dundee
F From Newark Castle to Matlock
G From Leicester
H From Reading to Newcastle
I From Norwich to Liverpool Lime Street
J To Sleaford
K From Lincoln
L From Plymouth to Glasgow Central
M From Leicester to Sleaford
N To Lincoln

For connections from Gatwick Airport refer to Table T052

Table T053-F

London - East Midlands - Sheffield

Mondays to Fridays

16 December to 15 May

	XC ◇■ A ⌶	NT ◇ B	EM ◇■ ⌶	NT	NT C		TP ◇■ D ⌶	TP ◇■ E	NT ◇	NT	NT ◇	XC ◇■ F ⌶	NT	EM G	EM H		EM ◇ I	EM ◇■ ⌶	EM	EM ◇■ ⌶	NT ◇ J	XC ◇■ K ⌶	EM ◇■ ⌶	NT ◇ L
St Pancras International ⊖52 d			16 02															16 05					16 31	
Luton Airport Parkway [7] 52 ✈ d																		16 26						
Luton [10] 52 d																								
Bedford [7] 52 d																								
Wellingborough d																		16 50						
Kettering [5] a																		16 57						
d																		16 58		17 23				
Corby a																				17 32				
Oakham 47 a																								
Melton Mowbray 47 a																								
Market Harborough d																		17 08						
Leicester a			17 04															17 21					17 39	
d			17 05															17 22	17 27				17 40	
Syston d																			17 35					
Sileby d																			17 40					
Barrow Upon Soar d															←				17 45					
Loughborough d															16 53			17 32	17 51				17 50	
East Midlands Parkway ✈ d															17 02				17 59				17 59	
Beeston a															17 10			17 43	18 07					
Nottingham [8] a															17 19			17 53	18 15					
d											17 17			17 20	17 26		17 47		18 17					
Newark Castle 27 a															17 56				18 51					
Lincoln 27 a															18 28				19 22					
Langley Mill d											17 36						18 03							
Alfreton d											17 44						18 11							
Long Eaton a														17 38									18 03	
Derby [6] a			17 26											17 51									18 14	
d	17 18		17 28									17 42		17 53								18 16	18 20	
Belper a														18 05										
d																								
Chesterfield a			17 46								17 55	18 02					18 21						18 38	
Dronfield a											18 02													
Sheffield [7] a	17 48		18 02								18 13	18 18					18 37					18 48	18 55	
d	17 51	17 57		18 02	18 05		18 11	18 11	18 14	18 15	18 18	18 21	18 30				18 42				18 45	18 51		18 57
Manchester Piccadilly 78 a							19 03		19 34								19 37							
Doncaster [7] 29 a		18 23			18 46			18 35					19 09									19 17		19 22
Wakefield Kirkgate [4] 31,34 a				18 48							18 55										19 24			
Wakefield Westgate [7] 31 a	18 18									19 12		18 48												
Leeds [10] 31,34 a	18 36			19 24						19 31	19 14	19 05									19 44			
York [8] 29 a	19 04											19 30										19 41		

	EM ◇■ ⌶		EM ◇■ ⌶	NT	EM ◇■ M ⌶	NT C	TP ◇■ D	TP ◇■ E	NT ◇	NT	NT ◇		XC ◇■ F ⌶	NT	EM G	EM ◇ I	EM ◇■ ⌶	EM N	NT ◇ J	XC ◇■ O ⌶	EM ◇■ ⌶		EM H	EM ◇■ ⌶
St Pancras International ⊖52 d	16 34		16 50		17 02												17 05							17 19
Luton Airport Parkway [7] 52 ✈ d																								17 42
Luton [10] 52 d																								
Bedford [7] 52 d																								
Wellingborough d			17 33														17 50							18 06
Kettering [5] a			17 44														17 57							18 14
d			17 46														17 57				18 10			18 15
Corby a			17 55																					
Oakham 47 a																								
Melton Mowbray 47 a																								
Market Harborough d	17 34																18 09							18 26
Leicester a	17 47				18 07												18 21				18 34			18 40
d	17 48				18 08												18 23	18 26			18 36			18 41
Syston d																		18 33						
Sileby d																		18 38						
Barrow Upon Soar d																		18 43					←	
Loughborough d																	18 35	18 48			18 45		18 48	18 52
East Midlands Parkway ✈ d	18 06																18 43	→			18 53		18 56	19 01
Beeston a																	18 48						19 04	
Nottingham [8] a	18 19																18 57						19 13	19 16
d											18 17				18 20	18 47							19 19	19 24
Newark Castle 27 a																							19 54	
Lincoln 27 a																							20 21	
Langley Mill d											18 36													
Alfreton d											18 44					19 08								
Long Eaton a															18 37						18 59			19 43
Derby [6] a					18 29										18 50						19 13			19 55
d					18 29								18 45		18 52					19 09	19 15			
Belper a															19 04									
d																								
Chesterfield a					18 47						18 55		19 02			19 20				19 27	19 32			
Dronfield a											19 02													
Sheffield [7] a					19 05						19 13		19 18			19 37				19 43	19 50			
d				19 02		19 05	19 11	19 11	19 14	19 15	19 18		19 21	19 32		19 42			19 45	19 51				
Manchester Piccadilly 78 a							20 02		20 31							20 38								
Doncaster [7] 29 a						19 45		19 37						20 10						20 13				
Wakefield Kirkgate [4] 31,34 a				19 48							19 55								20 24					
Wakefield Westgate [7] 31 a										20 18			19 46											
Leeds [10] 31,34 a				20 25						20 36	20 15		20 05						20 44					
York [8] 29 a													20 30							20 41				

A From Southampton Central to Edinburgh
B To Scarborough
C To Adwick
D From Cleethorpes to Manchester Airport
E From Manchester Airport to Cleethorpes
F From Plymouth to Edinburgh
G From Newark Castle to Matlock
H From Leicester
I From Norwich to Liverpool Lime Street
J From Lincoln
K From Reading to Newcastle
L To Bridlington
M The Master Cutler
N To Lincoln
O From Southampton Central to Newcastle

For connections from Gatwick Airport refer to Table T052

Table T053-F

London - East Midlands - Sheffield

Mondays to Fridays

16 December to 15 May

	EM ◇■ ⌶	EM ◇■ ⌶	NT ◇ A	EM ◇■ B ⌶	NT FX	NT FO	NT C		TP ◇■ D	TP ◇■ E	NT ◇	NT	NT ◇	XC ◇■ F ⌶	EM G	XC ◇■ H ⌶	NT		EM ◇ I	EM ◇■ ⌶	EM	NT ◇ J	EM ◇■ ⌶	NT ◇ K
St Pancras International ⊖52 d	17 34	17 50		18 02																18 05			18 19	
Luton Airport Parkway [7] 52 ✈ d		18 15																					18 42	
Luton [10] 52 d																								
Bedford [7] 52 d																								
Wellingborough d		18 36																		18 49				
Kettering [5] a		18 48																		18 55				
d		18 54																		18 56				
Corby a		19 03																						
Oakham 47 a		19 28																						
Melton Mowbray 47 a		19 39																						
Market Harborough d	18 32																						19 18	
Leicester a	18 45			19 05																19 17			19 31	
d	18 47			19 06																19 21	19 31		19 33	
Syston d																					19 38			
Sileby d																					19 44			
Barrow Upon Soar d																					19 49			
Loughborough d																					19 54		19 44	
East Midlands Parkway ✈ d	19 05																			19 37	20 03			
Beeston a	19 12																			19 45	20 10			
Nottingham [8] a	19 22																			19 53	20 19			
d													19 17		19 17				19 40	20 00				
Newark Castle 27 a																				20 24				
Lincoln 27 a																				20 52				
Langley Mill d													19 36											
Alfreton d													19 44						20 09					
Long Eaton a															19 34								19 57	
Derby [6] a				19 27											19 46								20 07	
d				19 29										19 43	19 48	20 00							20 12	
Belper a															20 00									
d																								
Chesterfield a				19 46									19 55	20 03					20 20				20 32	
Dronfield a													20 02											
Sheffield [7] a				20 02									20 13	20 18		20 27			20 35				20 47	
d			19 57		20 02	20 02	20 05		20 11	20 11	20 14	20 15	20 18	20 21		20 29	20 32		20 39			20 45		20 57
Manchester Piccadilly 78 a									21 02		21 28								21 36					
Doncaster [7] 29 a			20 22				20 44			20 35						20 53	21 09							21 22
Wakefield Kirkgate [4] 31,34 a					20 48	20 48							20 55									21 24		
Wakefield Westgate [7] 31 a												21 12		20 47										
Leeds [10] 31,34 a					21 25	21 26						21 30	21 14	21 02								21 44		
York [8] 29 a																21 15								

	NT	NT C	TP ◇■ L		TP ◇■ E	NT ◇	NT	NT ◇	EM ◇■ M ⌶	EM ◇■ ⌶	EM ◇■ ⌶	XC ◇■ F	EM ◇■ N ⌶		EM O	XC ◇■ P	NT ◇ A	EM ◇■ ⌶	NT C	TP ◇■ D	TP ◇■ E	NT	EM Q	
St Pancras International ⊖52 d									18 34	18 47	19 01							19 04						
Luton Airport Parkway [7] 52 ✈ d																		19 28						
Luton [10] 52 d																								
Bedford [7] 52 d																								
Wellingborough d									19 20	19 29								19 43						
Kettering [5] a									19 28	19 37								19 56						
d									19 29	19 39														
Corby a										19 48														
Oakham 47 a																								
Melton Mowbray 47 a																								
Market Harborough d									19 40									20 12						
Leicester a									19 54		20 09							20 28						
d									19 54		20 09							20 28					20 30	
Syston d																							20 36	
Sileby d																							20 42	
Barrow Upon Soar d																							20 48	
Loughborough d									20 06		20 20							20 38					20 53	
East Midlands Parkway ✈ d									20 15		20 27												→	
Beeston a													←					20 53						
Nottingham [8] a									20 28				20 28					21 02						
d								20 17	20 33				20 33		20 20			21 08						
Newark Castle 27 a									→															
Lincoln 27 a																								
Langley Mill d								20 36					20 49					21 25						
Alfreton d								20 44					20 57					21 33						
Long Eaton a															20 38									
Derby [6] a											20 37				20 50									
d											20 38	20 48			20 52	21 19								
Belper a															21 04									
d																								
Chesterfield a								20 55			21 00	21 05	21 09			21 37		21 43						
Dronfield a								21 02																
Sheffield [7] a								21 13			21 19	21 20	21 24			21 50		21 59						
d	21 02	21 05	21 11		21 11	21 14	21 15	21 18				21 23	21 26			21 52	21 57	22 04	22 07	22 10	22 11	22 15		
Manchester Piccadilly 78 a			22 08			22 32														23 02				
Doncaster [7] 29 a		21 52			21 47											22 28	22 22		22 46		22 35			
Wakefield Kirkgate [4] 31,34 a	21 48							21 55																
Wakefield Westgate [7] 31 a							22 12					21 46	21 57					22 33				23 15		
Leeds [10] 31,34 a	22 25						22 29	22 14				22 02	22 20					22 49				23 34		
York [8] 29 a																22 51								

A To Hull
B The South Yorkshireman
C To Adwick
D From Cleethorpes to Manchester Airport
E From Manchester Airport to Cleethorpes
F From Plymouth
G To Matlock
H From Reading to Newcastle
I From Norwich
J From Lincoln
K To Bridlington
L From Cleethorpes
M To Leeds
N From St Pancras International
O From Newark Castle to Matlock
P From Southampton Central
Q To Lincoln

For connections from Gatwick Airport refer to Table T052

Table T053-F

Mondays to Fridays

16 December to 15 May

London - East Midlands - Sheffield

	EM ◇1 ⛾	NT ◇	EM A	EM ◇1 ⛾	EM ◇1 ⛾	EM ◇1 ⛾	EM ◇1 ⛾	EM B	XC ◇1 C	NT	EM ◇1 ⛾	EM D	EM ◇1 ⛾	NT FO ◇	NT FX ◇	NT ◇ E	EM ◇1 ⛾	NT	TP ◇1 F	NT FO	NT FX	NT
St Pancras International ⊖52 d	19 32			19 35	19 47	20 01	20 05				20 31		20 34				21 01					
Luton Airport Parkway 7 52 ✈ d							20 29															
Luton 10 52 d					20 10																	
Bedford 7 52 d					20 24		20 42															
Wellingborough d					20 35		20 55						21 18									
Kettering 5 a				20 26	20 44		21 02						21 24									
d				20 27	20 45		21 03						21 25									
Corby a					20 54																	
Oakham 47 a																						
Melton Mowbray 47 a																						
Market Harborough d	20 29			20 39			21 13						21 35									
Leicester a	20 42			20 53		21 10	21 26				21 35		21 47				22 06					
d	20 43			20 54		21 11	21 27	21 30			21 37		21 48				22 07					
Syston d								21 37														
Sileby d								21 42														
Barrow Upon Soar d			←					21 48														
Loughborough d			20 53	21 05			21 36	21 53			21 48											
East Midlands Parkway ✈ d	20 56		21 02	21 14				→			21 56		22 01									
Beeston a			21 09				21 47															
Nottingham 8 ⇌ a	21 09		21 19				21 54						22 19									
d		21 12	21 20																			
Newark Castle 27 a			21 50																			
Lincoln 27 a			22 20																			
Langley Mill d		21 36																				
Alfreton d		21 44																				
Long Eaton a				21 17							22 00											
Derby 6 a				21 30		21 35					22 13						22 30					
d						21 37			21 46			22 19					22 30					
Belper a												22 31										
d																						
Chesterfield a		21 55				21 57			22 06								22 51					
Dronfield a		22 02																				
Sheffield 7 ⇌ a		22 14				22 17			22 23								23 04					
d		22 18				22 21			22 24	22 31				22 47	22 47	22 59		23 05	23 12	23 15	23 15	23 18
Manchester Piccadilly 78 a														00 18	00 20							
Doncaster 7 29 a																23 25		23 43	23 53			
Wakefield Kirkgate 4 31,34 a		22 55								23 17												00 04
Wakefield Westgate 7 31 a						22 48			22 53												00 12	
Leeds 10 31,34 a		23 14				23 06			23 08	23 58										00 30	00 30	
York 8 29 a																						

	NT ◇	EM A	EM ◇1 ⛾	EM ◇1 ⛾	EM ◇1 ⛾	EM ◇1 ⛾	NT	NT ◇	NT ◇	EM ◇1 ⛾	EM ◇1 ⛾	EM ◇1 ⛾	EM ◇1 ⛾
St Pancras International ⊖52 d			21 05		21 30	21 50				22 00		22 20	23 08
Luton Airport Parkway 7 52 ✈ d			21 27			22 13						22 42	
Luton 10 52 d					21 55					22 25			23 47
Bedford 7 52 d			21 43		22 09	22 26				22 40		22 58	00 09
Wellingborough d			21 55		22 21	22 39				22 53		23 11	00 22
Kettering 5 a			22 02		22 27	22 46				23 01		23 18	00 38
d			22 03	22 11	22 28	22 47				23 02	23 11	23 19	00 39
Corby a				22 25							23 20		
Oakham 47 a													
Melton Mowbray 47 a													
Market Harborough d			22 13		22 38	22 57				23 13		23 29	00 49
Leicester a			22 25		22 50	23 08				23 28		23 44	01 07
d			22 26		22 52	23 09				23 30		23 44	01 08
Syston d													
Sileby d													
Barrow Upon Soar d		←											
Loughborough d		21 53	22 36		23 02	23 19				23 42		23 54	01 18
East Midlands Parkway ✈ d		22 03	22 44		23 09	23 28				23 50		00 02	01 26
Beeston a		22 14								23 58			01 32
Nottingham 8 ⇌ a		22 24	22 54							00 06			01 39
d	22 15								23 18				01 46
Newark Castle 27 a													
Lincoln 27 a													
Langley Mill d									23 36				
Alfreton d									23 44				
Long Eaton a						23 31							
Derby 6 a	22 37				23 19	23 43						00 14	02 04
d	22 39											00 17	
Belper a													
d													
Chesterfield a	23 03								23 54			00 34	
Dronfield a									00 01				
Sheffield 7 ⇌ a	23 25								00 15			00 51	
d							23 27	23 27					
Manchester Piccadilly 78 a								00 36					
Doncaster 7 29 a							00 04						
Wakefield Kirkgate 4 31,34 a													
Wakefield Westgate 7 31 a													
Leeds 10 31,34 a													
York 8 29 a													

A From Leicester
B To Nottingham
C From Plymouth
D To Matlock
E To Hull
F From Manchester Airport

For connections from Gatwick Airport refer to Table T052

NRT DECEMBER 19 EDITION

Table T053-F

Saturdays

21 December to 16 May

London - East Midlands - Sheffield

	EM ◇1 A ⛾	EM ◇1 A ⛾	EM ◇1 ⛾	TP ◇1 B	TP ◇1 B	NT	TP ◇1 C	NT	NT	EM D	NT ◇ E	NT	NT	NT F	TP ◇1 G	NT	NT ◇	EM ◇ H	NT	NT ◇ I	XC ◇1 J	NT ◇ E
St Pancras International ⊖52 d			00 15																			
Luton Airport Parkway 7 52 ✈ d			00 53																			
Luton 10 52 d			00 57																			
Bedford 7 52 d		00 09	01 25																			
Wellingborough d		00 22	01 36																			
Kettering 5 a		00 38	01 46																			
d		00 39	01 46																			
Corby a																						
Oakham 47 a																						
Melton Mowbray 47 a																						
Market Harborough d		00 49	01 58																			
Leicester a		01 07	02 13																			
d		01 08																				
Syston d																						
Sileby d																						
Barrow Upon Soar d																						
Loughborough d		01 18																				
East Midlands Parkway ✈ d	00 02	01 26																				
Beeston a		01 32																				
Nottingham 8 ⇌ a		01 39																				
d		01 46																05 20				
Newark Castle 27 a																						
Lincoln 27 a																						
Langley Mill d																						
Alfreton d																						
Long Eaton a																						
Derby 6 a	00 14	02 04																				
d	00 17									05 42											05 57	
Belper a										05 54												
d																						
Chesterfield a	00 34																	05 49			06 29	
Dronfield a																						
Sheffield 7 ⇌ a	00 51																	06 15			06 46	
d				03 24	05 09	05 15	05 21	05 25	05 28		05 42	05 48	06 04	06 07	06 09	06 16	06 19	06 20	06 27	06 44	06 52	06 55
Manchester Piccadilly 78 a				04 52	06 03										07 02			07 39				
Doncaster 7 29 a							05 51	06 02			06 11	06 25		06 44					07 05		07 15	07 22
Wakefield Kirkgate 4 31,34 a									06 15				06 49				06 54			07 22		
Wakefield Westgate 7 31 a						06 12										07 12						
Leeds 10 31,34 a						06 31			06 44				07 25			07 31	07 16			07 43		
York 8 29 a																					07 41	

	NT F	NT	TP ◇1 K ⛾	EM ◇1 ⛾	TP ◇1 L	NT ◇	NT	NT ◇	XC ◇1 M ⛾	EM D	NT ◇	NT F	EM ◇ H	EM	NT ◇ N	XC ◇1 O ⛾	NT ◇ E	NT	EM ◇1 ⛾	NT	TP ◇1 K	TP ◇1 L
St Pancras International ⊖52 d																						
Luton Airport Parkway 7 52 ✈ d																						
Luton 10 52 d																						
Bedford 7 52 d																						
Wellingborough d																						
Kettering 5 a																						
d																						
Corby a																						
Oakham 47 a																						
Melton Mowbray 47 a																						
Market Harborough d																						
Leicester a																						
d														06 26								
Syston d														06 33								
Sileby d														06 38								
Barrow Upon Soar d														06 43								
Loughborough d														06 48								
East Midlands Parkway ✈ d														06 56								
Beeston a														07 06								
Nottingham 8 ⇌ a														07 15								
d								06 17		06 20			06 40									
Newark Castle 27 a																						
Lincoln 27 a																						
Langley Mill d								06 36														
Alfreton d								06 44					07 01									
Long Eaton a										06 37												
Derby 6 a										06 50												
d				06 27					06 44	06 52						07 13			07 26			
Belper a										07 04									07 33			
d																			07 34			
Chesterfield a				06 45				06 54	07 01				07 11			07 32			07 46			
Dronfield a								07 01					07 18						07 55			
Sheffield 7 ⇌ a				07 08				07 11	07 15				07 28			07 46			08 07			
d	07 01	07 04	07 07		07 08	07 14	07 15	07 18	07 21		07 25	07 31	07 32		07 47	07 52	07 57	08 04		08 07	08 08	08 11
Manchester Piccadilly 78 a			08 02			08 34							08 37								09 02	
Doncaster 7 29 a	07 46				07 32							08 09				08 14	08 22			08 46		08 36
Wakefield Kirkgate 4 31,34 a		07 50						07 57							08 23			08 49				
Wakefield Westgate 7 31 a							08 18		07 46													
Leeds 10 31,34 a		08 26					08 36	08 17	08 01						08 44			09 24				
York 8 29 a									08 29		08 49					08 40						

A From St Pancras International
B To Manchester Airport
C To Cleethorpes
D To Matlock
E To Scarborough
F To Adwick
G From Doncaster to Manchester Airport
H To Liverpool Lime Street
I From Chesterfield
J To Newcastle
K From Cleethorpes to Manchester Airport
L From Manchester Airport to Cleethorpes
M From Birmingham New Street to Glasgow Central
N From Retford
O From Birmingham New Street to Newcastle

For connections from Gatwick Airport refer to Table T052

Table T053-F

Saturdays

21 December to 16 May

London - East Midlands - Sheffield

	NT		NT	NT	XC	EM	NT	EM	EM	EM	NT		XC	NT	NT	NT	TP	TP	NT	NT	EM		EM	NT
	◇			◇	◇■ A ✠	◇■ ✠		B	◇ C		◇ D		◇■ E ✠	◇ F		G	◇■ H ✠	◇■ I ✠	◇		◇■ J ✠		◇■ ✠	◇
St Pancras International ⊖52 d						05 48															06 33			
Luton Airport Parkway ■ 52 ✈ d																								
Luton ■ 52 d						06 14															06 56			
Bedford ■ 52 d						06 28																		
Wellingborough d						06 40																		
Kettering ■ a						06 47															07 22			
d						06 48															07 23		07 38	
Corby a																							07 47	
Oakham 47 a																								
Melton Mowbray 47 a																								
Market Harborough d						06 58															07 33			
Leicester a						07 10															07 45			
d						07 12				07 28											07 48			
Syston d										07 35														
Sileby d										07 40														
Barrow Upon Soar d										07 45														
Loughborough d						07 23				07 50											07 58			
East Midlands Parkway ✈ d										07 58											08 05			
Beeston a										08 06														
Nottingham ■ a										08 15														
d				07 18				07 20	07 46															08 17
Newark Castle 27 a																								
Lincoln 27 a																								
Langley Mill d				07 37																				08 36
Alfreton d				07 45					08 09															08 44
Long Eaton a						07 31		07 37																
Derby ■ a						07 42		07 50													08 18			
d					07 45	07 48		07 52					08 15								08 24			
Belper a								08 04																
d																								
Chesterfield a				07 57	08 02	08 10			08 19				08 33								08 41			08 55
Dronfield a				08 04					08 26															09 02
Sheffield ■ a				08 15	08 20	08 28			08 37				08 48								08 56			09 13
d	08 13		08 16	08 19	08 22		08 32		08 42		08 45		08 50	08 56	09 03	09 06	09 11	09 11	09 14	09 15	09 29			09 18
Manchester Piccadilly 78 a	09 34								09 37								10 02		10 32		→			
Doncaster ■ 29 a							09 08						09 17	09 22		09 45		09 37						
Wakefield Kirkgate ■ 31,34 a				08 56							09 23				09 49									
Wakefield Westgate ■ 31 a			09 12		08 48															10 12				09 55
Leeds ■ 31,34 a			09 31	09 14	09 02						09 44				10 24					10 31				10 14
York ■ 29 a					09 30								09 40											

	XC	EM	EM	EM	NT	EM	EM		EM	EM	EM	EM	EM	NT	XC	NT	EM		NT	NT	TP	TP	NT	NT
	◇■ K ✠	◇■ L ✠	M	◇■ ✠		◇ N	◇■ ✠		O	◇■ ✠	P	◇■ ✠	◇■ ✠	◇ D	◇■ Q ✠	◇ F	◇■ ✠			G	◇■ H ✠	◇■ I	◇	
St Pancras International ⊖52 d				06 48			07 05					07 35	07 47				08 02							
Luton Airport Parkway ■ 52 ✈ d				07 10								07 56												
Luton ■ 52 d							07 27						08 09											
Bedford ■ 52 d							07 40					08 10	08 24											
Wellingborough d							07 52					08 23	08 36											
Kettering ■ a							08 00					08 30	08 44											
d							08 01					08 30	08 45											
Corby a													08 53											
Oakham 47 a																								
Melton Mowbray 47 a																								
Market Harborough d							08 11					08 41												
Leicester a				07 54			08 23					08 53					09 04							
d				07 56			08 25		08 26	08 35		08 54					09 05							
Syston d									08 33															
Sileby d									08 38															
Barrow Upon Soar d									08 43		←													
Loughborough d				08 05			08 35		08 48	08 45	08 48	09 03												
East Midlands Parkway ✈ d				08 13			08 42		→	08 52	08 56													
Beeston a				08 20							09 04	09 13												
Nottingham ■ a				08 28			08 54				09 11	09 22												
d			08 20			08 48					09 22													
Newark Castle 27 a											09 49													
Lincoln 27 a											10 19													
Langley Mill d																								
Alfreton d						09 09																		
Long Eaton a			08 37							08 56														
Derby ■ a			08 50							09 08							09 26							
d	08 45		08 52							09 09					09 15		09 28							
Belper a			09 04																					
d																								
Chesterfield a	09 02					09 20				09 27							09 45							
Dronfield a		←																						
Sheffield ■ a	09 18	08 56				09 37				09 44					09 47		10 00							
d	09 21	09 29			09 29	09 42								09 45	09 51	09 59			10 02	10 05	10 11	10 11	10 14	10 15
Manchester Piccadilly 78 a						10 37															11 02		11 32	
Doncaster ■ 29 a		09 58			10 10										10 15	10 26				10 45		10 35		
Wakefield Kirkgate ■ 31,34 a														10 24					10 48					
Wakefield Westgate ■ 31 a	09 46																							11 12
Leeds ■ 31,34 a	10 00													10 44					11 25					11 31
York ■ 29 a	10 30	10 23													10 40									

A From Birmingham New Street to Edinburgh
B To Matlock
C To Liverpool Lime Street
D From Lincoln
E From Birmingham New Street to Newcastle
F To Scarborough
G To Adwick
H From Cleethorpes to Manchester Airport
I From Manchester Airport to Cleethorpes
J To York
K From Bristol Temple Meads to Glasgow Central
L From St Pancras International
M From Newark Castle to Matlock
N From Norwich to Liverpool Lime Street
O To Lincoln
P From Leicester
Q From Guildford to Newcastle

For connections from Gatwick Airport refer to Table T052

Table T053-F

Saturdays

21 December to 16 May

London - East Midlands - Sheffield

	NT	XC	NT		EM	EM	EM	EM	EM	EM	EM	EM	NT		XC	NT	EM	NT	NT	TP	TP	NT	NT
	◇	◇■ A ✠			B	◇ C	◇■ ✠	D	◇■ ✠	E	◇■ ✠	◇■ ✠	◇ F		◇■ G ✠	◇ H	◇■ ✠		I	◇■ J	◇■ K ✠	◇	
St Pancras International ⊖52 d							08 05		08 31		08 34	08 47					09 02						
Luton Airport Parkway ■ 52 ✈ d							08 26																
Luton ■ 52 d												09 09											
Bedford ■ 52 d							08 40					09 24											
Wellingborough d							08 53					09 36											
Kettering ■ a							09 00					09 44											
d							09 00					09 45											
Corby a												09 53											
Oakham 47 a																							
Melton Mowbray 47 a																							
Market Harborough d							09 11				09 29												
Leicester a							09 23		09 34		09 42						10 04						
d							09 24	09 26	09 35		09 43						10 05						
Syston d								09 33															
Sileby d								09 38															
Barrow Upon Soar d								09 43		←													
Loughborough d							09 33	09 48	09 45	09 48													
East Midlands Parkway ✈ d								→	09 52	09 56	10 02												
Beeston a							09 44			10 04													
Nottingham ■ a							09 53			10 14	10 15												
d	09 17				09 20	09 47				10 29													
Newark Castle 27 a										10 51													
Lincoln 27 a										11 25													
Langley Mill d	09 36																						
Alfreton d	09 44					10 08																	
Long Eaton a					09 37				09 56														
Derby ■ a					09 49				10 09								10 26						
d		09 45			09 52				10 09						10 16		10 28						
Belper a					10 04																		
d																							
Chesterfield a	09 55	10 02				10 20			10 26								10 45						
Dronfield a	10 02																						
Sheffield ■ a	10 13	10 18				10 37			10 40						10 48		11 00						
d	10 18	10 21	10 32			10 42							10 45		10 51	10 57		11 02	11 05	11 10	11 11	11 14	11 15
Manchester Piccadilly 78 a						11 37															12 02	12 32	
Doncaster ■ 29 a			11 09												11 14	11 22			11 45	11 35			
Wakefield Kirkgate ■ 31,34 a	10 55												11 24					11 48					
Wakefield Westgate ■ 31 a		10 45																					12 12
Leeds ■ 31,34 a	11 14	11 00											11 44					12 25					12 31
York ■ 29 a		11 30													11 40								

	NT	XC	EM	XC	NT	NT	EM	EM	EM		EM	EM	EM	EM	NT	NT	EM	NT	NT		TP	TP	NT	NT
	◇	◇■ L ✠	B	◇■ M ✠		◇	◇ C	◇■ ✠	D		◇■ ✠	E	◇■ ✠	◇■ ✠	◇ F	◇ H	◇■ ✠		I		◇■ K ✠	◇■ J	◇	
St Pancras International ⊖52 d								09 05			09 31		09 34	09 47			10 02							
Luton Airport Parkway ■ 52 ✈ d								09 26																
Luton ■ 52 d														10 09										
Bedford ■ 52 d								09 40						10 24										
Wellingborough d								09 53						10 36										
Kettering ■ a								10 00						10 44										
d								10 00						10 45										
Corby a														10 53										
Oakham 47 a																								
Melton Mowbray 47 a																								
Market Harborough d								10 11					10 29											
Leicester a								10 23			10 34		10 42				11 04							
d								10 24	10 26		10 35		10 43				11 05							
Syston d									10 33															
Sileby d									10 38															
Barrow Upon Soar d									10 43			←												
Loughborough d								10 33	10 48		10 45	10 48												
East Midlands Parkway ✈ d									→		10 52	10 56	11 00											
Beeston a								10 43				11 04												
Nottingham ■ a								10 54				11 14	11 16											
d	10 17		10 18				10 47					11 29												
Newark Castle 27 a												11 51												
Lincoln 27 a												12 26												
Langley Mill d	10 36																							
Alfreton d	10 44						11 08																	
Long Eaton a			10 33								10 56													
Derby ■ a			10 46								11 09						11 26							
d		10 45	10 49	11 00							11 09						11 28							
Belper a			11 01																					
d																								
Chesterfield a	10 55	11 02					11 20				11 26						11 46							
Dronfield a	11 02																							
Sheffield ■ a	11 13	11 18		11 27			11 37				11 41						12 00							
d	11 18	11 21		11 29	11 32	11 41	11 42								11 45	11 57		12 02	12 05		12 11	12 11	12 14	12 15
Manchester Piccadilly 78 a							12 37														13 02		13 32	
Doncaster ■ 29 a				11 52	12 09											12 22			12 45			12 35		
Wakefield Kirkgate ■ 31,34 a	11 55														12 24			12 48						
Wakefield Westgate ■ 31 a		11 45																						13 12
Leeds ■ 31,34 a	12 14	12 00													12 44			13 25						13 31
York ■ 29 a		12 30		12 15		12 56																		

A From Plymouth to Edinburgh
B From Newark Castle to Matlock
C From Norwich to Liverpool Lime Street
D To Lincoln
E From Leicester
F From Lincoln
G From Bournemouth to Newcastle
H To Scarborough
I To Adwick
J From Manchester Airport to Cleethorpes
K From Cleethorpes to Manchester Airport
L From Plymouth to Glasgow Central
M From Southampton Central to Newcastle

For connections from Gatwick Airport refer to Table T052

Table T053-F

Saturdays

21 December to 16 May

London - East Midlands - Sheffield

		NT ◇	XC ◇1 A 🍴	EM B	XC ◇1 C 🍴	NT		EM ◇ D	EM ◇1 🍴	EM E	EM ◇1 🍴	EM F	EM ◇1 🍴	EM ◇1 🍴	NT ◇ G	NT ◇ H		EM ◇1 🍴	NT	NT I	TP ◇1 J 🍴	TP ◇1 K	NT ◇	NT	NT ◇
St Pancras International ⊖52	d								10 05		10 31		10 34	10 47				11 02							
Luton Airport Parkway 7 52 ✈	d								10 26																
Luton 10 52	d													11 09											
Bedford 7 52	d								10 40					11 24											
Wellingborough	d								10 53					11 36											
Kettering 5	a								11 00					11 44											
	d								11 00					11 45											
Corby	a													11 53											
Oakham 47	a																								
Melton Mowbray 47	a																								
Market Harborough	d								11 11				11 29												
Leicester	a								11 23		11 34		11 42					12 04							
	d								11 24	11 26	11 35		11 43					12 05							
Syston	d									11 33															
Sileby	d									11 38															
Barrow Upon Soar	d									11 43		←													
Loughborough	d								11 33	11 48	11 45	11 48													
East Midlands Parkway ✈	d									→	11 52	11 56	12 00												
Beeston	a								11 43			12 04													
Nottingham 8	a								11 52			12 14	12 16												
	d	11 17		11 20				11 47				12 29													12 17
Newark Castle 27	a											12 51													
Lincoln 27	a											13 22													
Langley Mill	d	11 36																							12 36
Alfreton	d	11 44						12 08																	12 44
Long Eaton	a			11 36							11 56														
Derby 6	a			11 47							12 09							12 26							
	d		11 45	11 48	12 00						12 09							12 28							
Belper	a			12 00																					
	d																								
Chesterfield	a	11 55	12 02					12 20			12 27							12 45							12 55
Dronfield	a	12 02																							13 02
Sheffield 7	a	12 13	12 18		12 27			12 37			12 42							13 00							13 13
	d	12 18	12 21		12 29	12 32		12 42							12 45	12 57			13 02	13 05	13 11	13 11	13 14	13 15	13 18
Manchester Piccadilly 78	a							13 37													14 02		14 32		
Doncaster 7 29	a				12 53	13 09										13 22				13 45		13 35			
Wakefield Kirkgate 4 31,34	a	12 55													13 24				13 50						13 55
Wakefield Westgate 7 31	a		12 46																					14 12	
Leeds 10 31,34	a	13 14	13 00												13 44				14 25					14 31	14 14
York 8 29	a		13 30		13 15																				

		XC ◇1 L 🍴		EM B	XC ◇1 M 🍴	NT	EM ◇ D	EM ◇1 🍴	EM E	EM ◇1 🍴	EM F	EM ◇1 🍴		EM ◇1 🍴	NT ◇ G	NT ◇ H	EM ◇1 🍴	NT	NT I	TP ◇1 J 🍴	TP ◇1 K	NT ◇		NT	NT ◇
St Pancras International ⊖52	d							11 05		11 31		11 34		11 47			12 02								
Luton Airport Parkway 7 52 ✈	d							11 26																	
Luton 10 52	d													12 10											
Bedford 7 52	d							11 40						12 25											
Wellingborough	d							11 53						12 37											
Kettering 5	a							12 00						12 46											
	d							12 00						12 47											
Corby	a													12 56											
Oakham 47	a																								
Melton Mowbray 47	a																								
Market Harborough	d							12 11				12 29													
Leicester	a							12 23		12 34		12 42					13 04								
	d							12 24	12 26	12 35		12 43					13 05								
Syston	d								12 33																
Sileby	d								12 38																
Barrow Upon Soar	d								12 43		←														
Loughborough	d							12 33	12 48	12 45	12 48														
East Midlands Parkway ✈	d								→	12 52	12 56	13 00													
Beeston	a							12 43			13 04														
Nottingham 8	a							12 52			13 14	13 16													
	d			12 18			12 47				13 29														13 17
Newark Castle 27	a										13 50														
Lincoln 27	a										14 24														
Langley Mill	d																								13 36
Alfreton	d						13 10																		13 44
Long Eaton	a			12 34						12 56															
Derby 6	a			12 48						13 09							13 26								
	d	12 44		12 48	13 00					13 09							13 28								
Belper	a			13 00																					
	d																								
Chesterfield	a	13 02					13 22			13 26							13 45								13 55
Dronfield	a																								14 02
Sheffield 7	a	13 18			13 27		13 37			13 41							14 00								14 13
	d	13 21			13 29	13 32	13 42								13 43	13 57		14 02	14 05	14 11	14 11	14 14		14 15	14 18
Manchester Piccadilly 78	a						14 37													15 02		15 34			
Doncaster 7 29	a				13 53	14 10										14 22			14 45		14 35				
Wakefield Kirkgate 4 31,34	a														14 24			14 48							14 55
Wakefield Westgate 7 31	a	13 45																						15 12	
Leeds 10 31,34	a	14 02													14 44			15 25						15 31	15 14
York 8 29	a	14 30			14 14																				

A From Plymouth to Edinburgh
B From Newark Castle to Matlock
C From Reading to Newcastle
D From Norwich to Liverpool Lime Street
E To Lincoln
F From Leicester
G From Lincoln
H To Scarborough
I To Adwick
J From Cleethorpes to Manchester Airport
K From Manchester Airport to Cleethorpes
L From Penzance to Glasgow Central
M From Southampton Central to Newcastle

For connections from Gatwick Airport refer to Table T052

NRT DECEMBER 19 EDITION

Table T053-F

Saturdays

21 December to 16 May

London - East Midlands - Sheffield

		XC ◇1 A 🍴	EM B	XC ◇1 C 🍴	NT	EM ◇ D	EM ◇1 🍴	EM E		EM ◇1 🍴	EM F	EM ◇1 🍴	EM ◇1 🍴	NT ◇ G	NT ◇ H	EM ◇1 🍴	NT	NT I		TP ◇1 J 🍴	TP ◇1 K	NT ◇	NT	NT ◇	XC ◇1 L 🍴
St Pancras International ⊖52	d						12 05			12 31		12 34	12 47			13 02									
Luton Airport Parkway 7 52 ✈	d						12 26																		
Luton 10 52	d												13 09												
Bedford 7 52	d						12 40						13 24												
Wellingborough	d						12 53						13 36												
Kettering 5	a						13 00						13 44												
	d						13 00						13 45												
Corby	a												13 53												
Oakham 47	a																								
Melton Mowbray 47	a																								
Market Harborough	d						13 11					13 29													
Leicester	a						13 23			13 34		13 42				14 04									
	d						13 24	13 26		13 35		13 43				14 05									
Syston	d							13 33																	
Sileby	d							13 38																	
Barrow Upon Soar	d							13 43			←														
Loughborough	d						13 33	13 48		13 45	13 48														
East Midlands Parkway ✈	d							→		13 52	13 56	14 00													
Beeston	a						13 43				14 04														
Nottingham 8	a						13 52				14 14	14 16													
	d		13 17			13 47					14 19													14 17	
Newark Castle 27	a										14 42														
Lincoln 27	a										15 11														
Langley Mill	d																							14 36	
Alfreton	d					14 08																		14 44	
Long Eaton	a		13 34							13 56															
Derby 6	a		13 47							14 09						14 26									
	d	13 45	13 48	14 00						14 09						14 28									14 45
Belper	a		14 00																						
	d																								
Chesterfield	a	14 02				14 20				14 26						14 45								14 55	15 02
Dronfield	a																							15 02	
Sheffield 7	a	14 18		14 27		14 37				14 42						15 00								15 13	15 18
	d	14 21		14 29	14 32	14 42								14 45	14 57		15 02	15 05		15 11	15 11	15 14	15 15	15 18	15 21
Manchester Piccadilly 78	a					15 37														16 02		16 31			
Doncaster 7 29	a			14 53	15 10										15 22			15 45			15 35				
Wakefield Kirkgate 4 31,34	a													15 24			15 48							15 55	
Wakefield Westgate 7 31	a	14 46																					16 12		15 45
Leeds 10 31,34	a	15 00												15 44			16 25						16 31	16 14	16 01
York 8 29	a	15 30		15 15																					16 30

		NT	EM B	NT ◇		EM ◇ D	EM ◇1 🍴	EM E	EM ◇1 🍴	EM F	EM ◇1 🍴	EM ◇1 🍴	NT ◇ G	XC ◇1 M 🍴		NT ◇ H	EM ◇1 🍴	NT	NT I	TP ◇1 J 🍴	TP ◇1 K	NT ◇	NT	NT ◇	
St Pancras International ⊖52	d						13 05		13 31		13 34	13 47					14 02								
Luton Airport Parkway 7 52 ✈	d						13 26																		
Luton 10 52	d											14 09													
Bedford 7 52	d						13 40					14 24													
Wellingborough	d						13 53					14 36													
Kettering 5	a						14 00					14 44													
	d						14 00					14 45													
Corby	a											14 53													
Oakham 47	a																								
Melton Mowbray 47	a																								
Market Harborough	d						14 11				14 29														
Leicester	a						14 23		14 34		14 42						15 04								
	d						14 24	14 26	14 35		14 43						15 05								
Syston	d							14 33																	
Sileby	d							14 38																	
Barrow Upon Soar	d							14 43		←															
Loughborough	d						14 33	14 48	14 45	14 48															
East Midlands Parkway ✈	d							→	14 52	14 56	15 00														
Beeston	a						14 43			15 04															
Nottingham 8	a						14 52			15 14	15 16														
	d		14 20			14 47				15 28														15 17	
Newark Castle 27	a									15 49															
Lincoln 27	a									16 25															
Langley Mill	d																							15 36	
Alfreton	d					15 08																		15 44	
Long Eaton	a		14 37						14 56																
Derby 6	a		14 50						15 09								15 26								
	d		14 52						15 09					15 16			15 28								
Belper	a		15 04																						
	d																								
Chesterfield	a					15 20			15 26								15 45							15 55	
Dronfield	a																							16 02	
Sheffield 7	a					15 37			15 41					15 47			16 00							16 13	
	d	15 32		15 41		15 42							15 45	15 51		15 57		16 02	16 05	16 11	16 11	16 14	16 15	16 18	
Manchester Piccadilly 78	a					16 37														17 02		17 31			
Doncaster 7 29	a	16 10												16 17		16 22			16 45		16 35				
Wakefield Kirkgate 4 31,34	a												16 24					16 48						16 55	
Wakefield Westgate 7 31	a																						17 12		
Leeds 10 31,34	a												16 44					17 25					17 31	17 14	
York 8 29	a			16 58										16 40											

A From Plymouth to Aberdeen
B From Newark Castle to Matlock
C From Reading to Newcastle
D From Norwich to Liverpool Lime Street
E To Lincoln
F From Leicester
G From Lincoln
H To Scarborough
I To Adwick
J From Cleethorpes to Manchester Airport
K From Manchester Airport to Cleethorpes
L From Penzance to Glasgow Central
M From Southampton Central to Newcastle

For connections from Gatwick Airport refer to Table T052

Table T053-F

Saturdays

21 December to 16 May

London - East Midlands - Sheffield

		XC	NT	EM	EM	EM	EM	EM	EM	EM		EM	NT	XC	NT	EM	NT	NT	TP	TP		NT	NT	NT	XC
		◇■			◇	◇■		◇■		◇■		◇■	◇	◇■	◇	◇■			◇■	◇■		◇		◇	◇■
		A		B	C		D		E				F	G	H			I	J	K					L
		🛒				🛒		🛒		🛒		🛒		🛒		🛒			🛒						🛒
St Pancras International ⊖52	d					14 05		14 31		14 34		14 47				15 02									
Luton Airport Parkway [7] 52 ✈	d					14 26																			
Luton [10] 52	d											15 09													
Bedford [7] 52	d					14 40						15 24													
Wellingborough	d					14 53						15 36													
Kettering [5]	a					15 00						15 44													
	d					15 00						15 45													
Corby	a											15 53													
Oakham 47	a																								
Melton Mowbray 47	a																								
Market Harborough	d					15 11				15 29															
Leicester	a					15 23		15 34		15 42						16 04									
	d					15 24	15 26	15 35		15 43						16 05									
Syston	d						15 33																		
Sileby	d						15 38																		
Barrow Upon Soar	d						15 43		←																
Loughborough	d					15 33	15 48	15 45	15 48																
East Midlands Parkway ✈	d						→	15 52	15 56	16 00															
Beeston	a					15 43			16 04																
Nottingham [8] 🚊	a					15 52			16 14	16 16															
	d			15 20	15 47				16 21															16 17	
Newark Castle 27	a								16 42																
Lincoln 27	a								17 08																
Langley Mill	d																							16 36	
Alfreton	d				16 10																			16 44	
Long Eaton	a			15 37				15 56																	
Derby [6]	a			15 50				16 09								16 26									
	d	15 45		15 52				16 09						16 16		16 28									16 44
Belper	a			16 04																					
	d																								
Chesterfield	a	16 02			16 20			16 26								16 45								16 55	17 03
Dronfield	a																							17 02	
Sheffield [7] 🚊	a	16 18			16 37			16 41						16 47		17 00								17 13	17 18
	d	16 21	16 32		16 42								16 45	16 51	16 57		17 02	17 05	17 11	17 11		17 14	17 15	17 18	17 21
Manchester Piccadilly 78	a				17 37														18 02			18 31			
Doncaster [7] 29	a		17 10											17 13	17 24			17 45		17 35					
Wakefield Kirkgate [4] 31,34	a												17 24				17 48							17 55	
Wakefield Westgate [7] 31	a	16 45																					18 12		17 47
Leeds [10] 31,34	a	17 00											17 44				18 25						18 31	18 14	18 01
York [8] 29	a	17 30												17 42											18 30

		NT	EM	EM	EM	EM		EM	EM	EM	EM	NT	XC	NT	EM	NT		NT	TP	TP	NT	NT	NT	XC	NT
				◇	◇■			◇■		◇■	◇■	◇	◇■	◇	◇■				◇■	◇■	◇		◇	◇■	
			B	C		D			E			F	M	H				I	J	K		N		O	
					🛒			🛒		🛒	🛒		🛒		🛒				🛒					🛒	
St Pancras International ⊖52	d				15 05			15 31		15 34	15 47				16 02										
Luton Airport Parkway [7] 52 ✈	d				15 26																				
Luton [10] 52	d										16 09														
Bedford [7] 52	d				15 40						16 24														
Wellingborough	d				15 53						16 35														
Kettering [5]	a				16 00						16 44														
	d				16 00						16 45														
Corby	a										16 53														
Oakham 47	a																								
Melton Mowbray 47	a																								
Market Harborough	d				16 11					16 29															
Leicester	a				16 23			16 34		16 42					17 04										
	d				16 24	16 26		16 35		16 43					17 05										
Syston	d					16 33																			
Sileby	d					16 38																			
Barrow Upon Soar	d					16 43			←																
Loughborough	d				16 33	16 48		16 45	16 48																
East Midlands Parkway ✈	d					→		16 52	16 56	17 00															
Beeston	a				16 43				17 04																
Nottingham [8] 🚊	a				16 52				17 14	17 16															
	d		16 20	16 44					17 31														17 17		
Newark Castle 27	a								17 52																
Lincoln 27	a								18 24																
Langley Mill	d																						17 36		
Alfreton	d			17 05																			17 44		
Long Eaton	a		16 37					16 56																	
Derby [6]	a		16 49					17 09							17 26										
	d		16 52					17 09					17 16		17 28									17 45	
Belper	a		17 04																						
	d																								
Chesterfield	a			17 15				17 26							17 45								17 55	18 02	
Dronfield	a																						18 02		
Sheffield [7] 🚊	a			17 34				17 41					17 47		18 00								18 13	18 18	
	d	17 32		17 38								17 45	17 51	17 57		18 02		18 05	18 11	18 11	18 14	18 15	18 18	18 21	18 30
Manchester Piccadilly 78	a			18 37															19 03		19 31				
Doncaster [7] 29	a	18 10												18 23				18 46		18 35					19 09
Wakefield Kirkgate [4] 31,34	a											18 24				18 48							18 55		
Wakefield Westgate [7] 31	a												18 18									19 12		18 49	
Leeds [10] 31,34	a											18 44	18 36			19 24						19 31	19 14	19 03	
York [8] 29	a												19 04											19 30	

A From Plymouth to Dundee
B From Newark Castle to Matlock
C From Norwich to Liverpool Lime Street
D To Lincoln
E From Leicester
F From Lincoln
G From Reading to Newcastle
H To Scarborough
I To Adwick
J From Cleethorpes to Manchester Airport
K From Manchester Airport to Cleethorpes
L From Plymouth to Glasgow Central
M From Southampton Central to Newcastle
N from 22 February
O From Plymouth to Edinburgh

For connections from Gatwick Airport refer to Table T052

Table T053-F

Saturdays

21 December to 16 May

London - East Midlands - Sheffield

		EM		EM	EM	EM	EM	EM	EM	EM	NT	XC		NT	EM	NT	NT	TP	TP	NT	NT	NT		XC	EM
				◇	◇■		◇■		◇■	◇■	◇	◇■		◇	◇■			◇■	◇■	◇		◇		◇■	
		A		B		C		D			E	F		G			H	I	J					K	A
					🛒		🛒		🛒	🛒		🛒			🛒									🛒	
St Pancras International ⊖52	d				16 05		16 31		16 34	16 47					17 02										
Luton Airport Parkway [7] 52 ✈	d				16 26																				
Luton [10] 52	d									17 10															
Bedford [7] 52	d				16 40					17 24															
Wellingborough	d				16 53					17 36															
Kettering [5]	a				17 00					17 43															
	d				17 00					17 45															
Corby	a									17 53															
Oakham 47	a																								
Melton Mowbray 47	a																								
Market Harborough	d				17 11				17 29																
Leicester	a				17 23		17 34		17 42						18 04										
	d				17 24	17 26	17 35		17 43						18 05										
Syston	d					17 33																			
Sileby	d					17 38																			
Barrow Upon Soar	d					17 43		←																	
Loughborough	d				17 33	17 48	17 45	17 48																	
East Midlands Parkway ✈	d					→	17 52	17 56	18 00																
Beeston	a				17 43			18 04																	
Nottingham [8] 🚊	a				17 55			18 14	18 16																
	d	17 20		17 44				18 17														18 17			18 18
Newark Castle 27	a							18 43																	
Lincoln 27	a							19 23																	
Langley Mill	d			18 00																		18 36			
Alfreton	d			18 08																		18 44			
Long Eaton	a	17 38					17 56																		18 34
Derby [6]	a	17 51					18 09								18 26										18 47
	d	17 53					18 09					18 16			18 28									18 45	18 48
Belper	a	18 05																							19 00
	d																								
Chesterfield	a			18 18			18 27								18 45							18 55		19 02	
Dronfield	a																					19 02			
Sheffield [7] 🚊	a			18 34			18 40					18 46			19 00							19 13		19 18	
	d			18 37							18 45	18 51		18 57		19 02	19 05	19 11	19 11	19 14	19 15	19 18		19 21	
Manchester Piccadilly 78	a			19 37														20 02		20 31					
Doncaster [7] 29	a											19 13		19 22			19 45		19 37						
Wakefield Kirkgate [4] 31,34	a										19 24					19 48						19 55			
Wakefield Westgate [7] 31	a																				20 18			19 46	
Leeds [10] 31,34	a										19 44					20 25					20 36	20 15		20 05	
York [8] 29	a											19 41												20 30	

		XC	NT	EM	EM	EM	EM	EM		EM	EM	NT	NT	EM	NT	NT	TP	TP		NT	NT	NT	XC	NT	EM
		◇■		◇	◇■		◇■			◇■	◇■	◇	◇	◇■			◇■	◇■		◇		◇	◇■		
		L		B		M		D				E	N			H	I	J					O		A
		🛒			🛒		🛒			🛒	🛒			🛒									🛒		
St Pancras International ⊖52	d				17 05		17 31			17 34	17 47			18 02											
Luton Airport Parkway [7] 52 ✈	d				17 26																				
Luton [10] 52	d										18 09														
Bedford [7] 52	d				17 40						18 24														
Wellingborough	d				17 53						18 35														
Kettering [5]	a				18 00						18 44														
	d				18 00						18 45														
Corby	a										18 53														
Oakham 47	a																								
Melton Mowbray 47	a																								
Market Harborough	d				18 11					18 29															
Leicester	a				18 23		18 34			18 42				19 04											
	d				18 24	18 26	18 35			18 43				19 05											
Syston	d					18 33																			
Sileby	d					18 38																			
Barrow Upon Soar	d					18 43		←																	
Loughborough	d				18 33	18 48	18 45	18 48																	
East Midlands Parkway ✈	d					→	18 52	18 56		19 00															
Beeston	a				18 43			19 04																	
Nottingham [8] 🚊	a				18 54			19 15		19 18															
	d			18 47	19 29																	19 17			19 20
Newark Castle 27	a				19 52																				
Lincoln 27	a				20 26																				
Langley Mill	d																					19 36			
Alfreton	d			19 08																		19 44			
Long Eaton	a						18 56																		19 36
Derby [6]	a						19 09							19 26											19 51
	d	19 00					19 09							19 28									19 43		19 52
Belper	a																								20 04
	d																								
Chesterfield	a			19 20			19 26							19 45								19 55	20 03		
Dronfield	a																					20 02			
Sheffield [7] 🚊	a	19 27		19 37			19 43							20 02								20 13	20 18		
	d	19 29	19 32	19 42								19 45	19 57		20 02	20 05	20 11	20 11		20 14	20 15	20 18	20 21	20 32	
Manchester Piccadilly 78	a			20 37													21 02			21 28					
Doncaster [7] 29	a	19 53	20 10										20 22			20 44		20 35						21 09	
Wakefield Kirkgate [4] 31,34	a											20 24			20 48							20 55			
Wakefield Westgate [7] 31	a																				21 12		20 47		
Leeds [10] 31,34	a											20 44			21 25						21 30	21 14	21 02		
York [8] 29	a	20 15																					21 46		

A From Newark Castle to Matlock
B From Norwich to Liverpool Lime Street
C To Lincoln
D From Leicester
E From Lincoln
F From Reading to Newcastle
G To Bridlington
H To Adwick
I From Cleethorpes to Manchester Airport
J From Manchester Airport to Cleethorpes
K From Plymouth to Edinburgh
L From Southampton Central to Newcastle
M To Nottingham
N To Hull
O From Plymouth. 🛒 to Leeds

For connections from Gatwick Airport refer to Table T052

Table T053-F

Saturdays

21 December to 16 May

London - East Midlands - Sheffield

Station		EM	EM	EM	EM	EM	NT	XC	NT	EM	EM	EM	NT	NT	TP	TP	NT	NT	NT	XC	EM	EM
		◇	◇1		◇1		◇	◇1	◇	◇1	◇1	◇1			◇1	◇1	◇		◇	◇1	◇1	
		A		B		C	D	E	F	G				H	I	J				K	L	M
St Pancras International ⊖52	d		18 05		18 31					18 34	18 47	19 02										
Luton Airport Parkway 7 52 ✈	d		18 26																			
Luton 10 52	d										19 09											
Bedford 7 52	d		18 40								19 24											
Wellingborough	d		18 53								19 36											
Kettering 5	a		19 00								19 44											
	d		19 00								19 45											
Corby	a										19 56											
Oakham 47	a																					
Melton Mowbray 47	a																					
Market Harborough	d		19 11							19 29											←	
Leicester	a		19 23		19 34					19 42		20 04									19 42	
	d		19 24	19 26	19 35					19 43		20 05									19 43	
Syston	d			19 33						→												
Sileby	d			19 38																		
Barrow Upon Soar	d			19 43		←																
Loughborough	d		19 33	19 48	19 45	19 48																
East Midlands Parkway ✈	d			→	19 52	19 56															20 00	
Beeston	a		19 43			20 04																
Nottingham 8	a		19 52			20 13															20 17	
	d	19 39				20 30													20 17		20 24	20 20
Newark Castle 27	a					20 58																
Lincoln 27	a					21 32																
Langley Mill	d																		20 36		20 43	
Alfreton	d	20 01																	20 44		20 51	
Long Eaton	a				19 56																	20 37
Derby 6	a				20 09							20 26										20 50
	d				20 09			20 16				20 28								20 44		20 52
Belper	a																					21 04
	d																					
Chesterfield	a	20 11			20 27			20 33				20 45							20 55	21 04	21 08	
Dronfield	a																		21 02			
Sheffield 7	a	20 29			20 40			20 47				21 00							21 13	21 19	21 24	
	d	20 34					20 45	20 50	20 57				21 02	21 05	21 11	21 11	21 14	21 15	21 18	21 21	21 26	
Manchester Piccadilly 78	a	21 29													22 04		22 32					
Doncaster 7 29	a							21 17	21 22					21 52		21 47						
Wakefield Kirkgate 4 31,34	a						21 24						21 48						21 55			
Wakefield Westgate 7 31	a																	22 12		21 47	21 57	
Leeds 10 31,34	a						21 44						22 25					22 29	22 14	22 02	22 14	
York 8 29	a							21 41														

Station		EM	EM	EM	NT	XC	NT	TP	TP	NT	NT	EM	EM	EM	EM	NT	EM	EM	XC	EM	EM	EM	EM
		◇1		◇1	◇	◇1		◇1	◇1	◇			◇1	◇1	◇1	◇	◇1		◇1	◇1		◇1	◇1
			B		N	O	H	P	J	Q		C						R	K		C		
St Pancras International ⊖52	d	19 05		19 31									19 34	19 47	20 02		20 05			20 31		20 34	
Luton Airport Parkway 7 52 ✈	d	19 26															20 27						
Luton 10 52	d													20 10									
Bedford 7 52	d	19 40												20 24			20 40						
Wellingborough	d	19 53												20 36			20 52						
Kettering 5	a	20 00												20 44			20 59					21 21	
	d	20 00												20 45			21 00					21 22	22 06
Corby	a													20 53									22 20
Oakham 47	a																						
Melton Mowbray 47	a																						
Market Harborough	d	20 11											20 29				21 10					21 32	
Leicester	a	20 23		20 34									20 42		21 08		21 22			21 34		21 45	
	d	20 24	20 26	20 35									20 43		21 09		21 23	21 26		21 35		21 45	
Syston	d		20 33															21 33					
Sileby	d		20 38															21 38					
Barrow Upon Soar	d		20 43									←						21 43			←		
Loughborough	d	20 33	20 48	20 45								20 48					21 32	21 48		21 45	21 48		
East Midlands Parkway ✈	d		→	20 52								20 56	21 00				21 42	→		21 52	21 57	22 02	
Beeston	a	20 43										21 04					21 47				22 10		
Nottingham 8	a	20 52										21 14	21 16				21 54				22 17	22 22	
	d										21 12	21 24											
Newark Castle 27	a											21 55											
Lincoln 27	a											22 40											
Langley Mill	d										21 36												
Alfreton	d										21 44												
Long Eaton	a			20 56																22 00			
Derby 6	a			21 10											21 32					22 12			
	d					21 27									21 42				21 46				
Belper	a																						
	d																						
Chesterfield	a					21 46					21 55				22 01				22 07				
Dronfield	a										22 02												
Sheffield 7	a					21 59					22 13				22 18				22 23				
	d				21 57	22 03	22 07	22 10	22 11	22 15	22 18				22 21	22 24			22 25				
Manchester Piccadilly 78	a							23 02								23 41							
Doncaster 7 29	a				22 22	22 26	22 46		22 35										22 50				
Wakefield Kirkgate 4 31,34	a										22 55												
Wakefield Westgate 7 31	a									23 23					22 48				23 12				
Leeds 10 31,34	a									23 41	23 14				23 07				23 26				
York 8 29	a					22 47																	

A From Norwich
B To Lincoln
C From Leicester
D From Lincoln
E From Reading to Newcastle
F To Bridlington
G To Leeds
H To Adwick
I From Cleethorpes
J From Manchester Airport to Cleethorpes
K From Plymouth
L From St Pancras International
M From Newark Castle to Matlock
N To Hull
O From Southampton Central
P From Cleethorpes to Manchester Airport
Q from 22 February
R To Nottingham

For connections from Gatwick Airport refer to Table T052

Table T053-F

Saturdays

21 December to 16 May

London - East Midlands - Sheffield

Station		EM	NT	NT	EM	NT	TP	NT	NT	EM	NT	EM	EM	EM	EM	EM
				◇	◇1		◇1	◇		◇1	◇	◇1	◇1	◇1	◇1	◇1
		A		B			C									
St Pancras International ⊖52	d				21 00					21 20		21 30	21 50	22 00		22 20
Luton Airport Parkway 7 52 ✈	d												22 13			22 42
Luton 10 52	d											21 54		22 25		
Bedford 7 52	d											22 10	22 29	22 42		22 58
Wellingborough	d											22 23	22 41	22 55		23 10
Kettering 5	a											22 32	22 48	23 02		23 17
	d											22 33	22 49	23 03	23 10	23 18
Corby	a														23 24	
Oakham 47	a															
Melton Mowbray 47	a															
Market Harborough	d									22 13		22 44	22 59	23 14		23 28
Leicester	a				22 04					22 25		22 58	23 11	23 29		23 40
	d				22 05					22 27		22 59	23 12	23 30		23 41
Syston	d															
Sileby	d															
Barrow Upon Soar	d															
Loughborough	d									22 37			23 22	23 41		23 52
East Midlands Parkway ✈	d									22 44		23 15	23 30	23 50		23 59
Beeston	a													23 58		
Nottingham 8	a									22 56				00 07		
	d							22 15			23 18					
Newark Castle 27	a															
Lincoln 27	a															
Langley Mill	d										23 36					
Alfreton	d										23 44					
Long Eaton	a												23 33			00 03
Derby 6	a				22 26			22 37				23 29	23 45			00 14
	d	22 16			22 28			22 39								
Belper	a	22 28														
	d															
Chesterfield	a				22 47			23 01			23 54					
Dronfield	a										00 01					
Sheffield 7	a				23 00			23 18			00 15					
	d		22 31	22 59		23 05	23 09		23 27							
Manchester Piccadilly 78	a															
Doncaster 7 29	a			23 25		23 43	23 35		00 04							
Wakefield Kirkgate 4 31,34	a		23 17													
Wakefield Westgate 7 31	a															
Leeds 10 31,34	a		23 59													
York 8 29	a															

Sundays

15 December to 10 May

Station		TP	EM	NT	NT	NT	NT	NT	NT	NT	TP	TP	NT	NT	XC	NT	NT	EM	NT	TP	TP	NT	NT
		◇1			◇	◇		◇			◇1	◇1	◇	◇	◇1	◇		◇1		◇1	◇1	◇	◇
		D	A	B	E	F		G			H	D			I	G				H	J	K	
St Pancras International ⊖52	d																						
Luton Airport Parkway 7 52 ✈	d																						
Luton 10 52	d																						
Bedford 7 52	d																						
Wellingborough	d																						
Kettering 5	a																						
	d																	09 55					
Corby	a																	10 04					
Oakham 47	a																						
Melton Mowbray 47	a																						
Market Harborough	d																						
Leicester	a																						
	d																						
Syston	d																						
Sileby	d																						
Barrow Upon Soar	d																						
Loughborough	d																						
East Midlands Parkway ✈	d																						
Beeston	a																						
Nottingham 8	a																						
	d																					09 18	
Newark Castle 27	a																						
Lincoln 27	a																						
Langley Mill	d																					09 38	
Alfreton	d																					09 46	
Long Eaton	a																						
Derby 6	a																						
	d		07 56																				
Belper	a		08 08																				
	d																						
Chesterfield	a																					09 56	
Dronfield	a																					10 03	
Sheffield 7	a																					10 16	
	d	07 51		08 06	08 14	08 14	08 27	08 36	08 39	09 06	09 10	09 11	09 14	09 17	09 21	09 25	09 35		10 06	10 10	10 14	10 17	10 17
Manchester Piccadilly 78	a	08 43			09 33	09 35						10 03	10 33								11 06		11 34
Doncaster 7 29	a			08 43				09 03		09 45	09 36					09 50			10 45	10 36			
Wakefield Kirkgate 4 31,34	a								09 22					09 57								10 53	
Wakefield Westgate 7 31	a						09 19								09 45		10 27						
Leeds 10 31,34	a						09 39		09 56					10 24	10 02		10 44					11 13	
York 8 29	a														10 31								

A To Matlock
B To Hull
C From Manchester Airport
D To Manchester Airport
E from 5 April
F until 29 March
G To Scarborough
H From Manchester Airport to Cleethorpes
I To Glasgow Central
J From Doncaster to Manchester Airport
K To Carlisle

For connections from Gatwick Airport refer to Table T052

Table T053-F

London - East Midlands - Sheffield

Sundays
15 December to 10 May

Station	XC ◇■ A	NT ◇ B	EM C	NT	EM ◇ D	NT	NT	TP ◇■ E	TP ◇■ F	NT ◇ G	NT ◇ H	NT ◇	XC ◇■ I	NT	EM ◇■	NT ◇ B	EM ◇ D	EM ◇■	NT	TP ◇■ E	TP ◇■ F	NT ◇
St Pancras International ⊖52 d																		09 00				
Luton Airport Parkway 52 ✈ d																		09 29				
Luton 52 d																						
Bedford 52 d																		09 55				
Wellingborough d																		10 08				
Kettering a																		10 15				
Kettering d																		10 16				
Corby a																						
Oakham 47 a																						
Melton Mowbray 47 a																						
Market Harborough d																		10 26				
Leicester a																		10 40				
Leicester d															10 20			10 41				
Syston d																						
Sileby d																						
Barrow Upon Soar d																						
Loughborough d															10 30			10 51				
East Midlands Parkway ✈ d															10 37			10 59				
Beeston a																		11 04				
Nottingham a																		11 12				
Nottingham d			09 26		09 47							10 17					10 48					
Newark Castle 27 a																						
Lincoln 27 a																						
Langley Mill d												10 35										
Alfreton d					10 05							10 43					11 09					
Long Eaton a			09 43												10 41							
Derby a			09 54												10 53							
Derby d	09 45		09 56										10 45		10 54							
Belper a			10 08																			
Belper d																						
Chesterfield a	10 02				10 18							10 53	11 02		11 13		11 19					
Dronfield a					10 25							11 00										
Sheffield a	10 18				10 37							11 13	11 18		11 28		11 35					
Sheffield d	10 21	10 25		10 30	10 41	10 51	11 06	11 10	11 11	11 15	11 15	11 16	11 21	11 24	11 31	11 34	11 39		12 06	12 10	12 11	12 14
Manchester Piccadilly 78 a					11 38				12 10	12 34	12 43						12 37				13 04	13 34
Doncaster 29 a		10 50					11 44	11 36							11 54	12 00			12 45	12 34		
Wakefield Kirkgate 31,34 a						11 29						11 51										
Wakefield Westgate 31 a	10 45			11 22									11 45	12 24								
Leeds 31,34 a	10 59			11 42		12 06						12 11	11 59	12 42								
York 29 a	11 29												12 30		12 19							

Station	NT ◇	XC ◇■ J	EM ◇■	NT ◇ B	EM ◇■	EM K	NT	EM ◇ D	EM ◇■	NT	NT	TP ◇■ F	TP ◇■ E	NT ◇	NT ◇	XC ◇■ L	NT ◇ B	EM ◇■	NT	EM ◇■	EM ◇ D
St Pancras International ⊖52 d			09 30						10 00									10 30			
Luton Airport Parkway 52 ✈ d									10 29												
Luton 52 d			10 02															11 02			
Bedford 52 d			10 23						10 54									11 27			
Wellingborough d			10 36						11 08									11 38			
Kettering a			10 42						11 15									11 45			
Kettering d			10 42		10 55				11 16									11 45		11 55	
Corby a					11 04															12 04	
Oakham 47 a																					
Melton Mowbray 47 a																					
Market Harborough d			10 53						11 27									11 55			
Leicester a			11 08						11 44									12 10			
Leicester d			11 10						11 45									12 12			
Syston d																					
Sileby d																					
Barrow Upon Soar d																					
Loughborough d			11 20						11 56									12 22			
East Midlands Parkway ✈ d			11 27						12 05									12 29			
Beeston a																					
Nottingham a									12 16												
Nottingham d	11 18					11 27		11 44							12 19						12 40
Newark Castle 27 a																					
Lincoln 27 a																					
Langley Mill d	11 36														12 37						12 56
Alfreton d	11 44							12 08							12 45						13 04
Long Eaton a			11 31			11 43												12 33			
Derby a			11 43															12 45			
Derby d		11 46	11 50													12 45		12 48			
Belper a						12 08															
Belper d																					
Chesterfield a	11 54	12 03	12 09					12 18							12 55	13 02		13 10			13 17
Dronfield a	12 01														13 02						
Sheffield a	12 14	12 18	12 23					12 35							13 15	13 18		13 27			13 33
Sheffield d	12 16	12 21		12 25			12 31	12 39		12 44	13 06	13 10	13 10	13 14	13 17	13 21	13 24		13 31		13 38
Manchester Piccadilly 78 a								13 37				14 03		14 33							14 37
Doncaster 29 a				12 50							13 44		13 34				13 50				
Wakefield Kirkgate 31,34 a	13 02									13 29					13 55						
Wakefield Westgate 31 a		12 45					13 22									13 45			14 23		
Leeds 31,34 a	13 22	13 00					13 42			14 04					14 18	14 00			14 43		
York 29 a		13 28														14 29					

A From Birmingham New Street to Edinburgh
B To Scarborough
C To Matlock
D To Liverpool Lime Street
E From Manchester Airport to Cleethorpes
F From Cleethorpes to Manchester Airport
G from 5 April
H until 29 March
I From Birmingham New Street to Glasgow Central
J From Bristol Temple Meads to Edinburgh
K From Grantham to Matlock
L From Bristol Temple Meads to Glasgow Central

For connections from Gatwick Airport refer to Table T052

Table T053-F

London - East Midlands - Sheffield

Sundays
15 December to 10 May

Station	EM ◇■	XC ◇■ A	NT	TP ◇■ B	TP ◇■ C	NT ◇	NT ◇	XC ◇■ D	NT ◇ E	EM ◇■	NT	EM ◇■	EM F	EM ◇ G	EM ◇■	EM ◇■	NT	XC ◇■ A	NT	TP ◇■ B	TP ◇■ C	NT ◇
St Pancras International ⊖52 d	11 00									11 30					12 10	12 30						
Luton Airport Parkway 52 ✈ d	11 29									11 59					12 32	12 52						
Luton 52 d	11 33									12 03					12 35	12 54						
Bedford 52 d	11 55									12 20					12 49	13 09						
Wellingborough d	12 08									12 32					13 02	13 21						
Kettering a	12 15									12 39					13 08	13 32						
Kettering d	12 16									12 40		12 50			13 09	13 34						
Corby a												12 59				13 44						
Oakham 47 a																						
Melton Mowbray 47 a																						
Market Harborough d	12 26									12 50					13 19							
Leicester a	12 41									13 05					13 34							
Leicester d	12 42									13 06					13 36							
Syston d																						
Sileby d																						
Barrow Upon Soar d																						
Loughborough d	12 52									13 16					13 46							
East Midlands Parkway ✈ d	13 00									13 24					13 53							
Beeston a	13 05														13 59							
Nottingham a	13 13														14 07							
Nottingham d							13 19						13 23	13 42								
Newark Castle 27 a																						
Lincoln 27 a																						
Langley Mill d							13 37							13 58								
Alfreton d							13 45							14 06								
Long Eaton a										13 27			13 40									
Derby a										13 44			13 51									
Derby d		13 11						13 45		13 50			13 56					14 11				
Belper a													14 08									
Belper d																						
Chesterfield a		13 28					13 55	14 02		14 10				14 16				14 28				
Dronfield a							14 02															
Sheffield a		13 44					14 15	14 17		14 26				14 34				14 43				
Sheffield d		13 52	14 06	14 10	14 11	14 14	14 17	14 21	14 25		14 31			14 37			14 44	14 52	15 06	15 10	15 11	15 14
Manchester Piccadilly 78 a					15 03	15 34								15 37							16 02	16 33
Doncaster 29 a		14 14	14 44	14 34					14 51									15 18	15 44	15 35		
Wakefield Kirkgate 31,34 a							14 55										15 28					
Wakefield Westgate 31 a								14 45			15 23											
Leeds 31,34 a							15 17	15 00			15 44						16 04					
York 29 a		14 40						15 29										15 41				

Station	NT ◇	XC ◇■ H	NT ◇ E	EM ◇■	NT	EM ◇ I	EM ◇■	EM ◇■	XC ◇■ J	NT	TP ◇■ C	TP ◇■ B	NT ◇ K	NT ◇	NT ◇	XC ◇■ L	NT ◇ E	EM ◇■	NT	EM F	EM ◇ M
St Pancras International ⊖52 d				12 50			13 10	13 30										13 55			
Luton Airport Parkway 52 ✈ d							13 32	13 52													
Luton 52 d							13 35	13 54													
Bedford 52 d							13 49	14 09													
Wellingborough d							14 02	14 21													
Kettering a				13 38			14 08	14 31													
Kettering d				13 39			14 09	14 32													
Corby a								14 42													
Oakham 47 a																					
Melton Mowbray 47 a																					
Market Harborough d				13 50			14 19											14 51			
Leicester a				14 07			14 34											15 07			
Leicester d				14 08			14 36											15 09			
Syston d																					
Sileby d																					
Barrow Upon Soar d																					
Loughborough d				14 19			14 46											15 20			
East Midlands Parkway ✈ d				14 28			14 53											15 28			
Beeston a							14 59														
Nottingham a							15 07														
Nottingham d	14 19					14 47									15 20					15 28	15 47
Newark Castle 27 a																					
Lincoln 27 a																					
Langley Mill d	14 37					15 03									15 38						
Alfreton d	14 45					15 11									15 46						16 08
Long Eaton a				14 31														15 32		15 45	
Derby a				14 45														15 44		15 56	
Derby d		14 42		14 49					15 11							15 44		15 48		15 58	
Belper a																				16 10	
Belper d																					
Chesterfield a	14 55	15 00		15 08		15 21									15 56	16 01		16 08			16 18
Dronfield a	15 02														16 03						
Sheffield a	15 15	15 18		15 29		15 39			15 45						16 14	16 18		16 29			16 35
Sheffield d	15 17	15 21	15 25		15 31	15 43			15 50	16 06	16 10	16 10	16 13	16 14	16 17	16 21	16 25		16 31		16 39
Manchester Piccadilly 78 a						16 37					17 02			17 33							17 38
Doncaster 29 a			15 50						16 12	16 45		16 34					16 54				
Wakefield Kirkgate 31,34 a	15 52														16 56						
Wakefield Westgate 31 a		15 45			16 25											16 45			17 24		
Leeds 31,34 a	16 15	16 00			16 44										17 17	16 59			17 43		
York 29 a		16 29							16 37				17 36			17 29					

A From Birmingham New Street to Newcastle
B From Manchester Airport to Cleethorpes
C From Cleethorpes to Manchester Airport
D From Plymouth to Aberdeen
E To Scarborough
F To Matlock
G From Norwich to Liverpool Lime Street
H From Plymouth to Glasgow Central
I To Liverpool Lime Street
J From Guildford to Newcastle
K via Pontefract Baghill
L From Penzance to Edinburgh
M From Peterborough to Liverpool Lime Street

For connections from Gatwick Airport refer to Table T052

Table T053-F

Sundays

15 December to 10 May

London - East Midlands - Sheffield

	EM ◇■	EM ◇■	NT	XC ◇■ A	NT	TP ◇■ B	TP ◇■ C	NT ◇	NT ◇		XC ◇■ D	NT ◇ E	NT	EM ◇■	EM F	EM ◇ G	EM ◇■	XC ◇■ A	EM ◇■		EM ◇■	NT	TP ◇■ B	TP ◇■ C
St Pancras International ⊖52 d	14 10	14 30												14 55			15 10		15 40					
Luton Airport Parkway 7 52 ✈ d	14 32																15 33							
Luton 10 52 d		14 53																	16 03					
Bedford 7 52 d	14 46	15 07															15 48		16 17					
Wellingborough d	14 59	15 19															16 02		16 30					
Kettering 5 a	15 05	15 31															16 10		16 36					
d	15 06	15 33															16 11		16 37		16 50			
Corby a		15 43																			16 59			
Oakham 47 a																								
Melton Mowbray 47 a																								
Market Harborough d	15 16													15 51			16 22							
Leicester a	15 31													16 06			16 38		17 01					
d	15 33													16 08			16 38		17 02					
Syston d																								
Sileby d																								
Barrow Upon Soar d																								
Loughborough d	15 43													16 19			16 51		17 12					
East Midlands Parkway ✈ d	15 50													16 27			16 59		17 20					
Beeston a	15 59																17 05							
Nottingham 8 a	16 06																17 14							
d									16 19						16 23	16 42								
Newark Castle 27 a																								
Lincoln 27 a																								
Langley Mill d									16 37							17 03								
Alfreton d									16 45							17 11								
Long Eaton a														16 32	16 40									
Derby 6 a														16 45	16 51				17 37					
d				16 11							16 44			16 49	16 56			17 12						
Belper a															17 09									
d																								
Chesterfield a									16 55		17 03			17 12		17 21								
Dronfield a									17 02															
Sheffield 7 a				16 41					17 15		17 19			17 28		17 39		17 43						
d			16 44	16 52	17 06	17 10	17 10	17 14	17 17		17 21	17 25	17 30	17 34		17 44		17 52				18 06	18 11	18 11
Manchester Piccadilly 78 a						18 03		18 33								18 37							19 03	
Doncaster 7 29 a				17 14	17 44		17 34					17 50						18 14				18 45		18 35
Wakefield Kirkgate 4 31,34 a			17 28						17 52															
Wakefield Westgate 7 31 a											17 46		18 24	18 00				18 32						
Leeds 10 31,34 a			18 04						18 17		18 01		18 43	18 16				18 47						
York 8 29 a				17 40							18 29							19 18						

	NT ◇	NT ◇	XC ◇■ H	NT ◇ I	EM ◇■		NT	EM F	EM ◇ G	EM ◇■	NT	XC ◇■ J	EM ◇■	NT ◇ K	EM ◇■		EM ◇■	NT	TP ◇■ B	TP ◇■ C	NT ◇	NT ◇	EM ◇■	XC ◇■ H
St Pancras International ⊖52 d					15 55					16 10			16 35		16 40								17 06	
Luton Airport Parkway 7 52 ✈ d										16 32														
Luton 10 52 d															17 03									
Bedford 7 52 d										16 46					17 17									
Wellingborough d										16 59					17 30									
Kettering 5 a										17 05					17 36									
d										17 06					17 37		17 50							
Corby a																	17 59							
Oakham 47 a																								
Melton Mowbray 47 a																								
Market Harborough d					16 51					17 16					17 47									
Leicester a					17 07					17 31			17 43		18 02								18 11	
d					17 09					17 33			17 44		18 04								18 12	
Syston d																								
Sileby d																								
Barrow Upon Soar d																								
Loughborough d										17 43					18 14									
East Midlands Parkway ✈ d					17 25					17 50			18 00		18 21								18 26	
Beeston a										17 58														
Nottingham 8 a										18 05													18 36	
d		17 19						17 22	17 39													18 19		
Newark Castle 27 a																								
Lincoln 27 a																								
Langley Mill d		17 37							17 57													18 37		
Alfreton d		17 45							18 05													18 45		
Long Eaton a					17 29			17 40							18 26									
Derby 6 a					17 44			17 51					18 12		18 36									
d			17 48		17 51			17 56				18 10	18 12											18 45
Belper a								18 08																
d																								
Chesterfield a		17 55	18 05		18 10				18 15				18 33									18 55		19 04
Dronfield a		18 02																				19 02		
Sheffield 7 a		18 15	18 18		18 27				18 33			18 40	18 50									19 14		19 20
d	18 14	18 17	18 21	18 25			18 31		18 37		18 45	18 52		19 00				19 06	19 11	19 11	19 14	19 16		19 21
Manchester Piccadilly 78 a	19 33								19 37										20 03		20 32			
Doncaster 7 29 a				18 50								19 14						19 45		19 35				
Wakefield Kirkgate 4 31,34 a		18 52									19 28											19 52		
Wakefield Westgate 7 31 a			18 45				19 23																	19 49
Leeds 10 31,34 a		19 15	19 01				19 43				20 04											20 15		20 07
York 8 29 a			19 30									19 43		20 16										20 30

A From Reading to Newcastle
B From Cleethorpes to Manchester Airport
C From Manchester Airport to Cleethorpes
D From Plymouth to Glasgow Central
E To Scarborough
F To Matlock
G From Norwich to Liverpool Lime Street
H From Plymouth to Edinburgh
I To Bridlington
J From Reading to Edinburgh
K via Pontefract Baghill

For connections from Gatwick Airport refer to Table T052

Table T053-F

Sundays

15 December to 10 May

London - East Midlands - Sheffield

	NT ◇ A		NT	EM ◇ B	EM ◇■	XC ◇■ C	EM ◇■	NT	EM ◇■	EM ◇■	TP ◇■ D		TP ◇■ E	NT ◇	NT ◇	XC ◇■ F	NT ◇ G	EM H	EM ◇■	NT	EM ◇ B		EM ◇■	NT
St Pancras International ⊖52 d					17 10		17 35		17 40										18 05				18 10	
Luton Airport Parkway 7 52 ✈ d					17 32																		18 32	
Luton 10 52 d									18 03															
Bedford 7 52 d					17 46				18 17														18 46	
Wellingborough d					17 58				18 30														18 58	
Kettering 5 a					18 05				18 36														19 05	
d					18 06				18 37	18 55													19 06	
Corby a										19 04														
Oakham 47 a																								
Melton Mowbray 47 a																								
Market Harborough d					18 15				18 47														19 16	
Leicester a					18 31		18 41		19 02										19 09				19 31	
d					18 33		18 42		19 04										19 10				19 33	
Syston d																								
Sileby d																								
Barrow Upon Soar d																								
Loughborough d					18 43				19 14														19 43	
East Midlands Parkway ✈ d					18 50		18 56		19 21										19 26				19 50	
Beeston a					18 58																		19 58	
Nottingham 8 a					19 05														19 37				20 05	
d				18 40											19 19			19 22			19 42			
Newark Castle 27 a																								
Lincoln 27 a																								
Langley Mill d				18 56											19 37									
Alfreton d				19 04											19 45						20 03			
Long Eaton a									19 25									19 39						
Derby 6 a							19 08		19 37									19 50						
d						19 07	19 16									19 42		19 52						
Belper a																		20 04						
d																								
Chesterfield a				19 14			19 34								19 55	20 02					20 12			
Dronfield a															20 02									
Sheffield 7 a				19 31		19 41	19 50								20 15	20 18					20 30			
d	19 25		19 31	19 35		19 52		20 06			20 11		20 11	20 14	20 17	20 22	20 25			20 31	20 35			20 48
Manchester Piccadilly 78 a				20 38							21 04			21 35							21 36			
Doncaster 7 29 a	19 50					20 14		20 46					20 35				20 50							
Wakefield Kirkgate 4 31,34 a															20 52									
Wakefield Westgate 7 31 a			20 23													20 47				21 28				
Leeds 10 31,34 a			20 44												21 14	21 02				21 45				22 07
York 8 29 a						20 42										21 31								

	XC ◇■ I	EM ◇■	NT	EM ◇■	EM ◇■	TP ◇■ D	TP ◇■ E		NT ◇	EM ◇■	EM ◇■	XC ◇■ J	NT ◇ G	NT	NT ◇	EM ◇■	NT		EM ◇■	EM ◇■	TP ◇■ E	TP ◇■ K	NT ◇	XC ◇■ L
St Pancras International ⊖52 d		18 35		18 40						19 05	19 10					19 35			19 40					
Luton Airport Parkway 7 52 ✈ d											19 32													
Luton 10 52 d				19 03															20 03					
Bedford 7 52 d				19 17							19 46								20 17					
Wellingborough d				19 30							19 58								20 30					
Kettering 5 a				19 36							20 05								20 36					
d				19 37	19 50						20 05								20 37	20 50				
Corby a					19 59															20 59				
Oakham 47 a																								
Melton Mowbray 47 a																								
Market Harborough d				19 47							20 15								20 47					
Leicester a		19 43		20 02						20 18	20 31					20 41			21 02					
d		19 45		20 04						20 22	20 33					20 42			21 04					
Syston d																								
Sileby d																								
Barrow Upon Soar d																								
Loughborough d				20 14							20 43								21 14					
East Midlands Parkway ✈ d		20 01		20 21						20 39	20 50					20 56			21 21					
Beeston a											20 58													
Nottingham 8 a										20 51	21 05													
d									20 11															
Newark Castle 27 a																								
Lincoln 27 a																								
Langley Mill d									20 29															
Alfreton d									20 37															
Long Eaton a				20 25															21 25					
Derby 6 a		20 11		20 37												21 07			21 36					
d	20 09	20 14										20 43				21 09								21 45
Belper a																								
d																								
Chesterfield a		20 35							20 47			21 03				21 26								22 02
Dronfield a									20 54															
Sheffield 7 a	20 41	20 51							21 07			21 18				21 43								22 18
d	20 54	21 03	21 06			21 11	21 11		21 17			21 21	21 25	21 31	21 32		22 08				22 12	22 13	22 16	22 21
Manchester Piccadilly 78 a						22 05									22 34							23 19	23 37	
Doncaster 7 29 a	21 20		21 45				21 35						21 50				22 47				22 36			
Wakefield Kirkgate 4 31,34 a									21 52															
Wakefield Westgate 7 31 a		21 32										21 48		22 23										22 48
Leeds 10 31,34 a		21 49							22 15			22 02		22 45										23 02
York 8 29 a	21 44																							

A To Bridlington
B From Norwich
C From Reading to Newcastle. ⚯ to Sheffield
D From Cleethorpes to Manchester Airport
E From Manchester Airport to Cleethorpes
F From Plymouth. ⚯ to Leeds
G To Hull
H To Matlock
I From Reading to Newcastle
J From Plymouth
K From Cleethorpes
L From Penzance

For connections from Gatwick Airport refer to Table T052

Table T053-F

London - East Midlands - Sheffield

Sundays

15 December to 10 May

Station		NT	EM	NT	NT	TP	EM	EM	EM	XC	EM	NT	EM	NT	EM	EM	EM	EM
		◇			◇	◇1	◇1	◇1	◇1	◇1	◇1		◇1	◇	◇1	◇1	◇1	◇1
		A	B			C				D								
							☕	☕	☕		☕		☕		☕	☕	☕	☕
St Pancras International ⊖52	d						20 00	20 10	20 35		20 40				21 10	21 30	22 30	23 00
Luton Airport Parkway [7] 52 ✈	d							20 32							21 32		22 52	23 28
Luton [10] 52	d										21 04					21 54		
Bedford [7] 52	d							20 47			21 20				21 46	22 07	23 11	23 53
Wellingborough	d							20 58			21 33				21 59	22 20	23 34	00 15
Kettering [5]	a							21 05			21 40				22 05	22 27	23 44	00 25
	d							21 06			21 41		21 55		22 06	22 28	23 45	00 26
Corby	a												22 04					
Oakham 47	a																	
Melton Mowbray 47	a																	
Market Harborough	d							21 16			21 52				22 16	22 38	23 55	00 36
Leicester	a						21 08	21 31	21 41		22 09				22 31	22 52	00 09	00 51
	d						21 10	21 33	21 42		22 10				22 33	22 54	00 11	00 52
Syston	d																	
Sileby	d																	
Barrow Upon Soar	d																	
Loughborough	d						21 21	21 43	21 52						22 47	23 04	00 21	01 02
East Midlands Parkway ✈	d						21 29	21 50	22 00		22 26				22 58	23 16	00 29	01 10
Beeston	a							21 58							23 04		00 34	
Nottingham [8]	a						21 45	22 05							23 11		00 41	
	d		21 24		21 33									22 33				
Newark Castle 27	a																	
Lincoln 27	a																	
Langley Mill	d				21 57									22 57				
Alfreton	d				22 05									23 05				
Long Eaton	a		21 41													23 23		
Derby [6]	a		21 52						22 11		22 40					23 35		01 21
	d		21 55							22 43	22 48					23 36		
Belper	a		22 07															
	d																	
Chesterfield	a				22 15					23 02	23 07			23 15		23 54		
Dronfield	a				22 22									23 22				
Sheffield [7]	a				22 34					23 18	23 23			23 35		00 12		
	d	22 25		22 32	22 44	23 11				23 19	23 26	23 30						
Manchester Piccadilly 78	a																	
Doncaster [7] 29	a	22 50				23 42						00 06						
Wakefield Kirkgate [4] 31,34	a				23 31													
Wakefield Westgate [7] 31	a			23 24							23 52							
Leeds [10] 31,34	a			23 45	00 07					00 09	00 08							
York [8] 29	a																	

A To Hull
B To Matlock
C From Manchester Airport
D From Plymouth

For connections from Gatwick Airport refer to Table T052

Table T053-R

Sheffield - East Midlands - London

Mondays to Fridays

16 December to 15 May

Miles	Miles	Miles	Miles	Station		EM MO	EM MX	EM MO	EM MX	EM	EM	EM	EM	EM	EM	NT	EM	EM	EM	NT	XC	EM	EM
						◇	◇	◇1	◇1	◇1	◇1		◇1			◇	◇1	◇1			◇1	◇1	◇1
						A	A														B		
								⌶	⌶	⌶	⌶	🚌	⌶	🚌			⌶	⊠	🚌			⌶	⌶
—	—	—	—	York [8] 29	d																		
—	—	—	—	Leeds [10] 31,34	d																		
—	—	—	—	Wakefield Westgate [7] 31	d																		
—	—	—	—	Wakefield Kirkgate [4] 31,34	d																		
—	—	—	—	Doncaster [7] 29	d																		
—	—	—	—	Manchester Piccadilly 78	d																		
0	0	—	—	**Sheffield** [7]	a																		
—	—	—	—		d											05 15		05 31		05 45	05 59		
—	—	—	—	Dronfield	d											05 24							
12¼	12¼	—	—	Chesterfield	d		00 02									05 30		05 44			06 26		
—	—	—	—	Belper	a																		
—	—	—	—		d																		
—	36½	—	—	**Derby** [6]	a													06 03			06 43		
—	—	—	—		d					05 02	05 19							06 05					
—	44	—	—	Long Eaton	d						05 28												
22½	—	—	—	Alfreton	d											05 46							
34½	—	—	—	Langley Mill	d	00 02										05 53							
—	—	—	—	Lincoln 27	d															07a07			
—	—	—	—	Newark Castle 27	d																		
40¾	—	—	—	**Nottingham** [8]	a	00 23	00 45									06 11							
—	—	—	—		d								05 32		05 38								06 31
44	—	—	—	Beeston	d																		06 37
—	—	—	—	East Midlands Parkway ✈	d					05 13			05 43					06 17					06 43
55½	53¼	—	—	Loughborough	d					05 20			05 51		05 58			06 26					
59½	57¼	—	—	Barrow Upon Soar	d										06 02								
61½	59¾	—	0	Sileby	d										06 07								
64¼	62	—	—	Syston	d										06 12								
68	65¾	0	—	**Leicester**	a					05 29	05 42		06 03		06 20			06 37					06 56
—	—	—	—		d			04 42	04 52	05 31	05 44		06 04					06 39					06 59
84¼	82	—	—	Market Harborough	d					05 44	05 57		06 19					06 54					07 12
—	—	15¼	12¼	Melton Mowbray 47	d												05 58						
—	—	26¾	—	Oakham 47	d												06 10						
—	—	41	—	Corby	d												06 33					07 08	
95¼	93	48½	—	Kettering [5]	a			05 03	05 12	05 53	06 06		06 29				06 41	07 04				07 17	07 21
—	—	—	—		d			05 04	05 13	05 55	06 08		06 31				06 43	07 05					07 23
102¼	100	—	—	Wellingborough	d			05 14	05 23	06 03	06 16	06 26	06 39	06 50			06 52	07 14	07 24				07 31
117½	115¼	—	—	Bedford [7] 52	d			05 38	05 38			07a11		07a35					08a14				
137	134¾	—	—	Luton [10] 52	d					06 27													
138	135¾	—	—	Luton Airport Parkway [7] 52 ✈	d			05 58	05 58				07 05					07 44					
167¼	165	—	—	**St Pancras International** ⊖52	a			06 24	06 24	06 54	07 08		07 36				07 39	08 09					08 24

Station		EM	EM	EM	EM	NT	TP	EM	EM	EM	NT	NT	NT	EM	EM	EM	EM	XC	EM	EM	NT	NT	NT
		◇1			◇1	◇	◇1		◇1		◇	◇			◇1	◇1	◇1	◇1	◇1		◇		◇
		C		D			E					F		G			C	H					I
		⊠	🚌		⌶				⊠	🚌					⊠	⌶	⊠	⌶	⌶	🚌			
York [8] 29	d																						
Leeds [10] 31,34	d								05 19									06 11				05 34	
Wakefield Westgate [7] 31	d								05 32									06 23				05 50	
Wakefield Kirkgate [4] 31,34	d																						
Doncaster [7] 29	d						05 36		05 59		06 03	06 12	06 06										
Manchester Piccadilly 78	d																				05 46		
Sheffield [7]	a						06 08		06 23		06 32	06 44	06 46					06 51			06 56	07 00	
	d	06 00				06 03			06 25		06 35						06 49	06 53					07 02
Dronfield	d					06 13																	07 11
Chesterfield	d	06 13				06 19			06 39								07 01	07 06					07 17
Belper	a																						
	d			06 42										07 03									
Derby [6]	a	06 33		06 55					07 03					07 16			07 21	07 25					
	d	06 34							07 05								07 23		07 30				
Long Eaton	d	06 44																	07 41				
Alfreton	d					06 29																	07 28
Langley Mill	d					06 36																	07 35
Lincoln 27	d										07a57												
Newark Castle 27	d																						
Nottingham [8]	a					07 00																	07 53
	d				06 52										07 11								
Beeston	d				06 58										07 18								
East Midlands Parkway ✈	d				07 04										07 26		07 34						
Loughborough	d	06 54						06 59	07 22								07 42		07 51				
Barrow Upon Soar	d							07 04															
Sileby	d							07 08															
Syston	d							07 14															
Leicester	a	07 05			07 17			07 22	07 33						07 41		07 53		08 02				
	d	07 06			07 19				07 36						07 43		07 55		08 03				
Market Harborough	d				07 33										07 58				08 18				
Melton Mowbray 47	d																						
Oakham 47	d																						
Corby	d															08 02							
Kettering [5]	a	07 27			07 42				07 57						08 08	08 11	08 15		08 28				
	d	07 29			07 43				07 59						08 09		08 17		08 30				
Wellingborough	d	07 37	07 48		07 51				08 07	08 14							08 25		08 41	08 48			
Bedford [7] 52	d		08a43							09a09										09a38			
Luton [10] 52	d																						
Luton Airport Parkway [7] 52 ✈	d	08 03																					
St Pancras International ⊖52	a	08 27			08 41				08 55						09 09		09 12		09 42				

A From Liverpool Lime Street
B To Reading
C The Sheffield Continental
D From Matlock
E To Manchester Airport
F From Hull
G From Ambergate
H To Plymouth
I From Retford

For connections to Gatwick Airport refer to Table T052

Table T053-R

Mondays to Fridays

16 December to 15 May

Sheffield - East Midlands - London

Station	TP A	TP B	XC C	NT	NT	EM D	EM	EM	EM	EM E	EM	EM F	NT	NT G	EM H	EM I	NT J	XC K	NT	NT	NT	NT
York 29 d			06 24															06 45				
Leeds 31,34 d				05 54								06 34	06 38					07 10	06 32	06 47	07 03	
Wakefield Westgate 31 d												06 47						07 23		07 02		
Wakefield Kirkgate 31,34 d				06 27									06 56						07 03		07 23	
Doncaster 29 d	06 25		06 47		06 34									06 55			07 20					
Manchester Piccadilly 78 d		06 15																				06 38
Sheffield a	07 05	07 06	07 12	07 15	07 18							07 22	07 34	07 39			07 47	07 51	07 54	07 57	08 00	08 04
Sheffield d			07 18			07 25						07 28	07 37		07 46			07 53			08 03	
Dronfield d																					08 13	
Chesterfield d			07 30			07 37						07 42			07 59			08 06			08 20	
Belper a																						
Belper d										07 59												
Derby a			07 47			07 54				08 10					08 17			08 25				
Derby d						07 56				08 12					08 19							
Long Eaton d										08 23					08 29							
Alfreton d												07 53									08 33	
Langley Mill d												08 01									08 41	
Lincoln 27 d									07 04				08a47									
Newark Castle 27 d									07 30													
Nottingham a									07 56			08 24									08 59	
Nottingham d							07 30	08 00	08 05			08 32										
Beeston d							07 36		08 11	08a33						←						
East Midlands Parkway d							07 44	08 09				08 43			08 34	08 43						
Loughborough d							07 56		08 21			→			08 42							
Barrow Upon Soar d							08 01															
Sileby d							08 05															
Syston d							08 10															
Leicester a						08 14	08 18	08 21	08 31						08 53	08 58						
Leicester d						08 16		08 24	08 32						08 55	08 59						
Market Harborough d									08 46							09 13						
Melton Mowbray 47 d																						
Oakham 47 d																						
Corby d											08 48											
Kettering a									08 55		08 57											
Kettering d									08 56													
Wellingborough d									09 03													
Bedford 52 d																						
Luton 52 d																						
Luton Airport Parkway 52 d									09 31													
St Pancras International 52 a						09 27		09 38	09 55						10 04	10 11						

Station	TP A	TP B	NT G	XC L	EM	NT	EM M	NT	EM	EM	EM N	NT G	NT O	NT	EM E	XC P	EM	NT	EM	EM	NT
York 29 d				07 28												07 44					
Leeds 31,34 d								07 38						07 32		08 11		07 48			08 04
Wakefield Westgate 31 d																08 23		08 03			
Wakefield Kirkgate 31,34 d								07 55						08 03							08 22
Doncaster 29 d	07 42		07 26	07 52								08 00	08 22								
Manchester Piccadilly 78 d		07 18				07 11					07 42										
Sheffield a	08 06	08 10	08 10	08 15		08 32		08 34			08 36	08 44	08 48	08 51		08 55		09 01			09 04
Sheffield d				08 18	08 26			08 37			08 38					08 55	09 00				09 06
Dronfield d																					09 16
Chesterfield d				08 30	08 38						08 54					09 08	09 12				09 22
Belper a																					
Belper d															08 59						
Derby a				08 47	08 57										09 10	09 25	09 30				
Derby d					08 58										09 13		09 31				
Long Eaton d															09 24		09 38				
Alfreton d											09 05										09 33
Langley Mill d																					09 40
Lincoln 27 d							07 35	09a48											08 36		
Newark Castle 27 d							08 06												09 07		
Nottingham a							08 32				09 27								09 30		09 59
Nottingham d							08 34			09 12									09 33	09 45	
Beeston d							08 40			09 18					09a35				09 39		
East Midlands Parkway d							08 49										09 44		09 47	09 56	
Loughborough d							08 58			09 26							09 50		09 56		
Barrow Upon Soar d							09 02												10 00		
Sileby d							09 06												10 05		
Syston d							09 11												10 10		
Leicester a					09 18		09 23			09 36							10 00		10 22	10 12	
Leicester d					09 18					09 38							10 02			10 13	
Market Harborough d										09 51										10 26	
Melton Mowbray 47 d																					
Oakham 47 d																					
Corby d									09 32												
Kettering a									09 40	10 00											
Kettering d									09 41	10 01											
Wellingborough d									09 50	10 08											
Bedford 52 d									10 13	10 23											
Luton 52 d									10 28												
Luton Airport Parkway 52 d										10 39											
St Pancras International 52 a					10 25				10 51	11 05							11 08			11 25	

A From Cleethorpes to Manchester Airport
B From Manchester Airport to Cleethorpes
C To Southampton Central
D The Master Cutler
E From Matlock to Newark Castle
F To St Pancras International
G From Adwick
H The South Yorkshireman
I From Leeds
J From Hull
K To Plymouth. ⌶ from Leeds
L From Newcastle to Reading
M From Sleaford
N From Liverpool Lime Street to Norwich
O From Beverley
P From Newcastle to Plymouth

For connections to Gatwick Airport refer to Table T052

Table T053-R

Mondays to Fridays

16 December to 15 May

Sheffield - East Midlands - London

Station	TP A	TP B	NT C	XC D	EM	NT	EM	EM	EM	EM E	NT C	NT F	NT	EM G	XC H	EM	NT	EM	EM	NT	NT	TP A
York 29 d				08 35											08 44							
Leeds 31,34 d						08 38							08 32		09 11		08 48			09 09		
Wakefield Westgate 31 d															09 23		09 04					
Wakefield Kirkgate 31,34 d						08 55							09 03							09 26		
Doncaster 29 d		08 42	08 32	08 57							09 03	09 20										
Manchester Piccadilly 78 d	08 19									08 43											08 49	09 18
Sheffield a	09 09	09 09	09 14	09 22		09 34				09 35	09 44	09 49	09 51		09 54		10 01			10 04	10 05	10 09
Sheffield d				09 24	09 29	09 37				09 38					09 56	10 00				10 06		
Dronfield d																				10 16		
Chesterfield d					09 41					09 52					10 09	10 13				10 22		
Belper a																						
Belper d														09 59								
Derby a				09 51	10 00									10 10	10 28	10 32						
Derby d					10 04									10 13		10 33						
Long Eaton d														10 22		10 40						
Alfreton d										10 02										10 32		
Langley Mill d																				10 40		
Lincoln 27 d						10a55												09 37				
Newark Castle 27 d																		10 07				
Nottingham a										10 27								10 30		10 58		
Nottingham d									10 12									10 35	10 45			
Beeston d									10 18					10a33				10 41				
East Midlands Parkway d																10 46		10 50	10 56			
Loughborough d									10 27							10 52		10 58				
Barrow Upon Soar d																		11 03				
Sileby d																		11 07				
Syston d																		11 12				
Leicester a					10 25				10 37							11 02		11 23	11 12			
Leicester d					10 26				10 38							11 03			11 13			
Market Harborough d									10 51										11 26			
Melton Mowbray 47 d																						
Oakham 47 d																						
Corby d							10 10	10 41														
Kettering a							10 18	10 49	11 00													
Kettering d								10 50	11 01													
Wellingborough d								10 59	11 08													
Bedford 52 d								11 13	11 23													
Luton 52 d								11 28														
Luton Airport Parkway 52 d									11 39													
St Pancras International 52 a					11 36			11 52	12 07							12 09			12 24			

Station	TP B	NT C	XC I	EM	NT	NT	EM	EM	EM	EM E	NT	NT J	NT	EM G	XC K	EM	NT	NT	EM	EM	NT
York 29 d			09 37		09 15										09 44						
Leeds 31,34 d						09 38							09 32		10 11		09 48				10 09
Wakefield Westgate 31 d															10 23		10 03				
Wakefield Kirkgate 31,34 d						09 55							10 03								10 26
Doncaster 29 d	09 42	09 35	10 00								10 04	10 21									
Manchester Piccadilly 78 d										09 43								09 42			
Sheffield a	10 09	10 14	10 22		10 33	10 34				10 34	10 44	10 50	10 52		10 55		11 01	11 04			11 04
Sheffield d			10 24	10 29		10 37				10 37					10 56	11 00					11 06
Dronfield d																					11 16
Chesterfield d				10 41						10 54					11 08	11 13					11 22
Belper a																					
Belper d														10 59							
Derby a			10 51	11 00										11 10	11 26	11 31					
Derby d				11 02										11 12		11 32					
Long Eaton d														11 22		11 40					
Alfreton d										11 05											11 32
Langley Mill d																					11 40
Lincoln 27 d						11a49													10 36		
Newark Castle 27 d																			11 06		
Nottingham a										11 26									11 30		11 58
Nottingham d									11 12										11 36	11 45	
Beeston d									11 18					11a32					11 42		
East Midlands Parkway d																11 45			11 50	11 56	
Loughborough d									11 27							11 52			11 58		
Barrow Upon Soar d																			12 03		
Sileby d																			12 07		
Syston d																			12 12		
Leicester a				11 22					11 37							12 02			12 23	12 13	
Leicester d				11 24					11 38							12 03				12 13	
Market Harborough d									11 51											12 26	
Melton Mowbray 47 d																					
Oakham 47 d																					
Corby d							11 05	11 41													
Kettering a							11 13	11 49	12 00												
Kettering d								11 51	12 01												
Wellingborough d								11 59	12 08												
Bedford 52 d								12 13	12 23												
Luton 52 d								12 28													
Luton Airport Parkway 52 d									12 39												
St Pancras International 52 a				12 36				12 51	13 06							13 08				13 25	

A From Manchester Airport to Cleethorpes
B From Cleethorpes to Manchester Airport
C From Adwick
D From Newcastle to Southampton Central
E From Liverpool Lime Street to Norwich
F From Scarborough
G From Matlock to Newark Castle
H From Edinburgh to Plymouth
I From Edinburgh to Reading
J From Bridlington
K From Glasgow Central to Plymouth

For connections to Gatwick Airport refer to Table T052

Table T053-R

Mondays to Fridays

16 December to 15 May

Sheffield - East Midlands - London

		TP ◇■ A 🍴	TP ◇■ B	NT C	XC ◇■ D 🍴	EM ◇■ 🍴	NT ◇	EM ◇■ 🍴	EM ◇■ 🍴	EM ◇ E		NT	NT ◇ F	NT	EM G	XC ◇■ H 🍴	EM ◇■ 🍴	NT	NT ◇	EM		EM ◇■ 🍴	NT ◇	TP ◇■ A 🍴	TP ◇■ B
York ■ 29	d				10 35											10 44									
Leeds ■ 31,34	d						10 38							10 32		11 11		10 48					11 09		
Wakefield Westgate ■ 31	d															11 23		11 03							
Wakefield Kirkgate ■ 31,34	d						10 55							11 03									11 26		
Doncaster ■ 29	d		10 42	10 35	10 59							11 04	11 21												11 42
Manchester Piccadilly 78	d	10 18								10 42									10 49					11 18	
Sheffield ■	a	11 08	11 09	11 14	11 21		11 34			11 35		11 44	11 49	11 51		11 54		12 01	12 04				12 04	12 08	12 08
	d				11 24	11 29	11 37			11 38						11 56	12 00						12 06		
Dronfield	d																						12 16		
Chesterfield	d					11 41				11 54						12 09	12 13						12 22		
Belper	a																								
	d														11 59										
Derby ■	a				11 51	12 00									12 10	12 28	12 32								
	d					12 04									12 12		12 32								
Long Eaton	d														12 21		12 42								
Alfreton	d									12 05													12 32		
Langley Mill	d																						12 40		
Lincoln 27	d						12a48													11 40					
Newark Castle 27	d																			12 06					
Nottingham ■	a									12 29										12 30			12 58		
	d								12 12											12 35		12 45			
Beeston	d								12 18						12a33					12 41					
East Midlands Parkway	d																12 47			12 49		12 56			
Loughborough	d								12 27								12 54			12 57					
Barrow Upon Soar	d																			13 02					
Sileby	d																			13 06					
Syston	d																			13 11					
Leicester	a					12 25			12 37								13 04			13 22		13 13			
	d					12 26			12 38								13 05					13 13			
Market Harborough	d								12 51													13 26			
Melton Mowbray 47	d																								
Oakham 47	d																								
Corby	d							12 41																	
Kettering ■	a							12 49	13 00																
	d							12 51	13 01																
Wellingborough	d							12 59	13 08																
Bedford ■ 52	d							13 13	13 23																
Luton ■ 52	d							13 28																	
Luton Airport Parkway ■ 52	d								13 39																
St Pancras International ⊖52	a					13 36		13 51	14 07								14 12					14 25			

		NT C	XC ◇■ I 🍴	EM ◇■ 🍴	NT ◇	EM ◇■ 🍴		EM ◇■ 🍴	EM ◇ E	NT	NT ◇ F	NT	EM G	XC ◇■ J 🍴	EM ◇■ 🍴	NT		NT ◇	EM	EM ◇■ 🍴	NT ◇	TP ◇■ A 🍴	TP ◇■ B	NT C	XC ◇■ D 🍴
York ■ 29	d		11 36											11 44											12 35
Leeds ■ 31,34	d				11 38							11 32		12 11		11 48					12 09				
Wakefield Westgate ■ 31	d													12 23		12 03									
Wakefield Kirkgate ■ 31,34	d				11 55							12 03									12 26				
Doncaster ■ 29	d	11 35	11 59							12 03	12 21												12 42	12 35	12 59
Manchester Piccadilly 78	d								11 42									11 49				12 18			
Sheffield ■	a	12 14	12 21		12 34				12 35	12 44	12 50	12 52		12 55		13 01		13 04			13 04	13 08	13 08	13 14	13 21
	d		12 24	12 29	12 37				12 38					12 56	13 00						13 06				13 24
Dronfield	d																				13 16				
Chesterfield	d			12 41					12 52					13 08	13 13						13 22				
Belper	a																								
	d												12 59												
Derby ■	a		12 51	13 00									13 10	13 27	13 31										13 51
	d			13 04									13 13		13 32										
Long Eaton	d												13 24		13 40										
Alfreton	d								13 03												13 32				
Langley Mill	d																				13 40				
Lincoln 27	d				13a49														12 34						
Newark Castle 27	d																		13 05						
Nottingham ■	a								13 27										13 30		13 58				
	d							13 12											13 36	13 45					
Beeston	d							13 18					13a35						13 42						
East Midlands Parkway	d														13 46				13 50	13 56					
Loughborough	d							13 27							13 52				13 58						
Barrow Upon Soar	d																		14 03						
Sileby	d																		14 07						
Syston	d																		14 12						
Leicester	a			13 25				13 37							14 02				14 23	14 13					
	d			13 26				13 38							14 03					14 13					
Market Harborough	d							13 51												14 26					
Melton Mowbray 47	d																								
Oakham 47	d																								
Corby	d					13 41																			
Kettering ■	a					13 49		14 00																	
	d					13 51		14 01																	
Wellingborough	d					13 59		14 09																	
Bedford ■ 52	d					14 13		14 23																	
Luton ■ 52	d					14 28																			
Luton Airport Parkway ■ 52	d							14 39																	
St Pancras International ⊖52	a			14 38		14 51		15 05							15 08					15 25					

A From Manchester Airport to Cleethorpes
B From Cleethorpes to Manchester Airport
C From Adwick
D From Newcastle to Southampton Central
E From Liverpool Lime Street to Norwich
F From Scarborough
G From Matlock to Newark Castle
H From Dundee to Plymouth
I From Newcastle to Reading
J From Glasgow Central to Plymouth

For connections to Gatwick Airport refer to Table T052

Table T053-R

Mondays to Fridays

16 December to 15 May

Sheffield - East Midlands - London

		EM ◇■ 🍴		NT ◇	EM ◇■ 🍴	EM ◇■ 🍴	EM ◇ A	NT	NT ◇ B	NT	EM C	XC ◇■ D 🍴		EM ◇■ 🍴	NT	NT ◇	EM	EM ◇■ 🍴	NT ◇	TP ◇■ E 🍴	TP ◇■ F	NT G		XC ◇■ H 🍴	EM ◇■ 🍴
York ■ 29	d											12 44												13 35	
Leeds ■ 31,34	d			12 38						12 32		13 11			12 48				13 09						
Wakefield Westgate ■ 31	d											13 23			13 03										
Wakefield Kirkgate ■ 31,34	d			12 55						13 03									13 26						
Doncaster ■ 29	d							13 04	13 21												13 42	13 35		14 00	
Manchester Piccadilly 78	d						12 42									12 49				13 18					
Sheffield ■	a			13 34			13 34	13 44	13 49	13 51		13 54			14 01	14 04			14 04	14 08	14 08	14 14		14 22	
	d	13 29		13 37			13 37					13 56		14 00					14 06					14 24	14 29
Dronfield	d																		14 16						
Chesterfield	d	13 41					13 52					14 08		14 13					14 22						14 41
Belper	a																								
	d										13 59														
Derby ■	a	14 00									14 10	14 25		14 32										14 51	15 00
	d	14 04									14 12			14 33											15 04
Long Eaton	d										14 21			14 42											
Alfreton	d						14 03												14 32						
Langley Mill	d																		14 40						
Lincoln 27	d			14a48													13 37								
Newark Castle 27	d																14 07								
Nottingham ■	a						14 27										14 30		14 58						
	d					14 12											14 35	14 45							
Beeston	d					14 18					14a32						14 41								
East Midlands Parkway	d													14 47			14 50	14 56							
Loughborough	d					14 27								14 55			14 58								
Barrow Upon Soar	d																15 03								
Sileby	d																15 07								
Syston	d																15 12								
Leicester	a	14 25				14 37								15 07			15 23	15 13							15 25
	d	14 26				14 38								15 08				15 13							15 26
Market Harborough	d					14 51												15 26							
Melton Mowbray 47	d																								
Oakham 47	d																								
Corby	d				14 41																				
Kettering ■	a				14 49	15 00																			
	d				14 51	15 01																			
Wellingborough	d				14 59	15 08																			
Bedford ■ 52	d				15 13	15 23																			
Luton ■ 52	d				15 28																				
Luton Airport Parkway ■ 52	d					15 39																			
St Pancras International ⊖52	a	15 39			15 51	16 11								16 25				16 28							16 41

		NT ◇	NT ◇	EM ◇■ 🍴	EM ◇■ 🍴	EM ◇■ 🍴	EM ◇ A	NT		NT ◇ B	NT	EM C	XC ◇■ I 🍴	EM ◇■ 🍴	NT	NT ◇	EM	EM ◇■ 🍴		NT ◇	TP ◇■ E 🍴	TP ◇■ F	NT G	XC ◇■ J 🍴	EM ◇■ 🍴
York ■ 29	d	13 15											13 44											14 35	
Leeds ■ 31,34	d		13 38								13 32		14 11		13 48					14 09					
Wakefield Westgate ■ 31	d												14 23		14 03										
Wakefield Kirkgate ■ 31,34	d		13 55								14 03									14 26					
Doncaster ■ 29	d							14 05		14 21												14 42	14 35	14 59	
Manchester Piccadilly 78	d						13 42									13 49					14 18				
Sheffield ■	a	14 32	14 34				14 35	14 44		14 49	14 51		14 55		15 01	15 04				15 04	15 08	15 08	15 14	15 21	
	d		14 37				14 38						14 56	15 00						15 06				15 24	15 29
Dronfield	d																			15 16					
Chesterfield	d						14 52						15 08	15 12						15 22					15 41
Belper	a																								
	d											14 59													
Derby ■	a											15 10	15 25	15 31										15 51	16 00
	d											15 12		15 31											16 04
Long Eaton	d											15 23		15 40											
Alfreton	d						15 03													15 32					
Langley Mill	d																			15 40					
Lincoln 27	d		15a48														14 36								
Newark Castle 27	d																15 06								
Nottingham ■	a						15 28										15 30			15 58					
	d					15 12											15 36	15 45							
Beeston	d					15 18						15a34					15 42								
East Midlands Parkway	d													15 44			15 50	15 56							
Loughborough	d					15 27								15 52			15 59								
Barrow Upon Soar	d																16 03								
Sileby	d																16 07								
Syston	d																16 12								
Leicester	a					15 37								16 01			16 23	16 13							16 25
	d					15 38								16 02				16 13							16 26
Market Harborough	d					15 51												16 26							
Melton Mowbray 47	d																								
Oakham 47	d																								
Corby	d			15 05	15 41																				
Kettering ■	a			15 14	15 49	16 00																			
	d				15 50	16 01																			
Wellingborough	d				15 59	16 08																			
Bedford ■ 52	d				16 12	16 22																			
Luton ■ 52	d				16 27																				
Luton Airport Parkway ■ 52	d					16 38																			
St Pancras International ⊖52	a				16 55	17 12								17 12				17 25							17 39

A From Liverpool Lime Street to Norwich
B From Scarborough
C From Matlock to Newark Castle
D From Glasgow Central to Penzance
E From Manchester Airport to Cleethorpes
F From Cleethorpes to Manchester Airport
G From Adwick
H From Newcastle to Reading
I From Aberdeen to Penzance
J From Newcastle to Guildford

For connections to Gatwick Airport refer to Table T052

Table T053-R

Mondays to Fridays

16 December to 15 May

Sheffield - East Midlands - London

	NT ◇	EM ◇1 ⊼	EM ◇1 ⊼	EM ◇1 ⊼	EM ◇ A	NT	NT ◇ B	NT	EM C	XC ◇1 D ⊼	EM ◇1 ⊼	EM ◇1 ⊼	EM ◇1 ⊼	NT	NT ◇	EM	EM ◇1 ⊼	NT ◇	TP ◇1 E ⊼	TP ◇1 F	NT G
York 29 d										14 44											
Leeds 31,34 d	14 38							14 32		15 11				14 48				15 09			
Wakefield Westgate 31 d										15 23				15 03							
Wakefield Kirkgate 31,34 d	14 55							15 03										15 26			
Doncaster 29 d						15 04	15 21													15 42	15 35
Manchester Piccadilly 78 d					14 42										14 49				15 18		
Sheffield a	15 34				15 34	15 44	15 50	15 52		15 55				16 01	16 04			16 04	16 08	16 08	16 14
Sheffield d	15 37				15 37					15 56			16 00					16 06			
Dronfield d																		16 16			
Chesterfield d					15 53					16 08			16 13					16 22			
Belper a																					
Belper d									15 59												
Derby a									16 11	16 26			16 31								
Derby d									16 11			16 27	16 32								
Long Eaton d									16 21				16 40								
Alfreton d					16 05													16 32			
Langley Mill d																		16 40			
Lincoln 27 d	16a49															15 36					
Newark Castle 27 d																16 07					
Nottingham a					16 27											16 30		16 58			
Nottingham d				16 12												16 32	16 45				
Beeston d				16 18					16a32							16 38					
East Midlands Parkway d												16 40	16 45			16 48	16 56				
Loughborough d				16 27									16 52			16 57					
Barrow Upon Soar d																17 01					
Sileby d																17 05					
Syston d																17 10					
Leicester a				16 37									17 02			17 22	17 13				
Leicester d				16 38									17 03				17 13				
Market Harborough d				16 51													17 26				
Melton Mowbray 47 d												17 11									
Oakham 47 d												17 23									
Corby d		16 05	16 43								17 05	17 49									
Kettering a		16 14	16 51	17 00							17 14	17 58	17 23								
Kettering d			16 52	17 01									17 24								
Wellingborough d			17 01	17 08																	
Bedford 52 d			17 14	17 23																	
Luton 52 d			17 30														18 05				
Luton Airport Parkway 52 d				17 38																	
St Pancras International 52 a			17 55	18 06									18 14				18 35				

	XC ◇1 H ⊼	EM ◇1 ⊼	NT ◇	EM ◇1 ⊼	EM ◇1 ⊼	EM ◇ A	NT	NT ◇ B	NT	EM I	XC ◇1 J ⊼	EM ◇1 ⊼	NT	NT ◇	EM	EM ◇1 ⊼	NT ◇	TP ◇1 F	TP ◇1 E ⊼	NT G	XC ◇1 H ⊼	EM ◇1 ⊼
York 29 d	15 36										15 44										16 13	
Leeds 31,34 d			15 38						15 32		16 11		15 48				16 09				16 41	
Wakefield Westgate 31 d											16 23		16 03								16 53	
Wakefield Kirkgate 31,34 d			15 55						16 03								16 26					
Doncaster 29 d	16 00						16 04	16 21										16 42		16 35		
Manchester Piccadilly 78 d						15 42								15 49					16 18			
Sheffield a	16 22		16 34			16 34	16 44	16 49	16 51		16 54		17 01	17 04			17 04	17 08	17 09	17 14	17 21	
Sheffield d	16 24	16 29	16 37			16 37					16 56	17 00					17 06				17 24	17 29
Dronfield d						16 48											17 16					
Chesterfield d		16 41				16 53					17 09	17 13					17 22					17 41
Belper a																						17 53
Belper d										16 59												17 54
Derby a	16 51	17 00								17 10	17 28	17 32									17 51	18 03
Derby d		17 02								17 12		17 32										18 04
Long Eaton d										17 23		17 41										
Alfreton d						17 04											17 32					
Langley Mill d																	17 40					
Lincoln 27 d			17a56												16 34							
Newark Castle 27 d															17 04							
Nottingham a						17 27									17 29		17 58					
Nottingham d					17 12										17 33	17 45						
Beeston d					17 18					17a34					17 39							
East Midlands Parkway d												17 46			17 49	17 57						
Loughborough d					17 26							17 53			17 58							
Barrow Upon Soar d															18 02							
Sileby d															18 06							
Syston d															18 11							
Leicester a		17 22			17 36							18 04			18 23	18 13						18 25
Leicester d		17 23			17 37							18 04				18 14						18 26
Market Harborough d					17 50											18 27						
Melton Mowbray 47 d																						
Oakham 47 d																						
Corby d				17 39																		
Kettering a				17 47	17 59											18 38						
Kettering d				17 48	18 00											18 39						
Wellingborough d				17 57	18 08																	
Bedford 52 d				18 10	18 24																	
Luton 52 d				18 26																		
Luton Airport Parkway 52 d					18 41																	
St Pancras International 52 a		18 39		18 54	19 06							19 11				19 36						19 39

A From Liverpool Lime Street to Norwich
B From Scarborough
C From Matlock to Newark Castle
D From Glasgow Central to Penzance
E From Manchester Airport to Cleethorpes
F From Cleethorpes to Manchester Airport
G From Adwick
H From Newcastle to Reading
I From Matlock to Nottingham
J From Edinburgh to Plymouth

For connections to Gatwick Airport refer to Table T052

Table T053-R

Mondays to Fridays

16 December to 15 May

Sheffield - East Midlands - London

	NT ◇	EM ◇1 ⊼	EM ◇1 ⊼	EM ◇ A	NT	NT ◇ B	NT	EM C	XC ◇1 D ⊼	EM ◇1 ⊼	NT	EM	EM ◇1 ⊼	NT ◇	TP ◇1 E	NT ◇	TP ◇1 F ⊼	NT G	XC ◇1 H ⊼	EM ◇1 ⊼	NT ◇	EM ◇1 ⊼
York 29 d									16 44										17 36		17 15	
Leeds 31,34 d	16 38						16 32		17 11		16 48			17 09								
Wakefield Westgate 31 d									17 23		17 04											
Wakefield Kirkgate 31,34 d	16 55						17 03							17 27								
Doncaster 29 d					17 04	17 21									17 42			17 35	18 00			
Manchester Piccadilly 78 d				16 42												16 49	17 18					
Sheffield a	17 34			17 39	17 44	17 49	17 51		17 54		18 01			18 04	18 08	18 10	18 10	18 14	18 22		18 32	
Sheffield d	17 37			17 43					17 56	18 00				18 06					18 24	18 29		
Dronfield d				17 54										18 16								
Chesterfield d				18 01					18 08	18 13				18 22						18 41		
Belper a																						
Belper d								17 59														
Derby a								18 10	18 27	18 32									18 51	19 00		
Derby d								18 11		18 32										19 04		
Long Eaton d								18 25		18 41												
Alfreton d				18 11										18 32								
Langley Mill d														18 40								
Lincoln 27 d	18a57											17 30										
Newark Castle 27 d												17 59										
Nottingham a				18 31								18 34		18 58								
Nottingham d			18 12									18 36	18 45									
Beeston d			18 18					18a37				18 42										
East Midlands Parkway d										18 45		18 52	18 56									
Loughborough d			18 27							18 53		19 00										
Barrow Upon Soar d												19 05										
Sileby d												19 09										
Syston d												19 14										
Leicester a			18 37							19 03		19 23	19 13							19 25		
Leicester d			18 38							19 03			19 13							19 26		
Market Harborough d			18 51										19 26									
Melton Mowbray 47 d																						
Oakham 47 d																						
Corby d		18 37																				19 39
Kettering a		18 46	19 00																			19 47
Kettering d		18 47	19 01																			19 48
Wellingborough d		18 56	19 08																			19 57
Bedford 52 d		19 12	19 25																			20 09
Luton 52 d		19 28																				20 25
Luton Airport Parkway 52 d			19 41																			
St Pancras International 52 a		19 57	20 07							20 11			20 25							20 40		20 51

	EM ◇1 ⊼	EM I	EM	NT ◇	NT	EM ◇ J	NT ◇ B	NT	XC ◇1 K ⊼	NT	EM ◇1 ⊼	EM ◇1 ⊼	NT ◇	NT ◇	TP ◇1 F ⊼	TP ◇1 E	NT G	XC ◇1 L ⊼	EM ◇1 ⊼	EM ◇1 ⊼	EM ◇1 ⊼
York 29 d									17 44									18 36			
Leeds 31,34 d				17 38				17 32	18 11	17 48			18 03								
Wakefield Westgate 31 d									18 23	18 03											
Wakefield Kirkgate 31,34 d				17 55				18 03					18 22								
Doncaster 29 d					18 04		18 21									18 42	18 35	19 00			
Manchester Piccadilly 78 d						17 42								17 49	18 18						
Sheffield a				18 34	18 44	18 47	18 49	18 51	18 54	19 01			19 04	19 05	19 08	19 09	19 14	19 22			
Sheffield d				18 37		18 51			18 56		19 02		19 06					19 24	19 29		
Dronfield d													19 16								
Chesterfield d						19 07			19 11		19 16		19 22						19 42		
Belper a																					
Belper d		18 59																			
Derby a		19 10							19 29		19 35							19 51	20 02		
Derby d		19 13									19 35								20 02		
Long Eaton d		19 22									19 44										
Alfreton d						19 19							19 32								
Langley Mill d													19 40								
Lincoln 27 d			18 35	20a06																	
Newark Castle 27 d			19 03																		
Nottingham a			19 30			19 40							19 58								
Nottingham d	19 12		19 32									19 45									20 12
Beeston d	19 18	19a34	19 39																		20 18
East Midlands Parkway d			19 48								19 50	19 56									20 25
Loughborough d	19 27		19 57								19 57										20 32
Barrow Upon Soar d			20 01																		
Sileby d			20 05																		
Syston d			20 11																		
Leicester a	19 37		20 22								20 08	20 12							20 27		20 43
Leicester d	19 38										20 08	20 13							20 27		20 43
Market Harborough d	19 51											20 27									20 56
Melton Mowbray 47 d																					
Oakham 47 d																					
Corby d																				20 41	
Kettering a	20 00																			20 49	21 05
Kettering d	20 01																			20 51	21 06
Wellingborough d	20 08																			20 59	21 14
Bedford 52 d	20 23																			21 13	21 26
Luton 52 d																				21 28	
Luton Airport Parkway 52 d	20 38																				21 43
St Pancras International 52 a	21 06										21 21	21 25							21 38	21 55	22 07

A From Liverpool Lime Street to Norwich
B From Scarborough
C From Matlock to Newark Castle
D From Glasgow Central to Plymouth
E From Cleethorpes to Manchester Airport
F From Manchester Airport to Cleethorpes
G From Adwick
H From Newcastle to Reading
I From Matlock to Nottingham
J From Liverpool Lime Street
K From Edinburgh to Plymouth
L From Newcastle to Southampton Central

For connections to Gatwick Airport refer to Table T052

Table T053-R

Mondays to Fridays

16 December to 15 May

Sheffield - East Midlands - London

	EM ◇ A	NT ◇	NT	NT ◇ B	NT	EM C	XC ◇1 D ⌶	NT	EM	EM ◇1 ⌶	NT ◇	NT ◇	TP ◇1 E	TP ◇1 F	NT G	XC ◇1 H ⌶	EM ◇ I	NT	NT ◇ B	EM C	EM ◇1 ⌶	NT
York 29 d							18 44									19 36						
Leeds 31,34 d		18 38			18 32		19 11	18 48			19 03											19 32
Wakefield Westgate 31 d							19 23	19 03														
Wakefield Kirkgate 31,34 d		18 57			19 03						19 21											20 03
Doncaster 29 d			19 04	19 20										19 42	19 35	19 59		20 06	20 21			
Manchester Piccadilly 78 d	18 43											18 49	19 18				19 42					
Sheffield a	19 35	19 35	19 44	19 49	19 51		19 55	20 01			20 04	20 05	20 08	20 09	20 14	20 21	20 37	20 44	20 49			20 51
d	19 37	19 38					19 56				20 06					20 24	20 41				20 49	
Dronfield d											20 16											
Chesterfield d	19 52						20 10				20 22						20 56				21 02	
Belper a																						
d						19 59														20 59		
Derby a						20 10	20 27									20 51				21 10	21 21	
d						20 15														21 13	21 22	
Long Eaton d						20 24														21 24		
Alfreton d	20 03										20 32						21 08					
Langley Mill d											20 40											
Lincoln 27 d		20a58																				
Newark Castle 27 d																						
Nottingham a	20 27										20 59						21 34					
d									20 35	20 55												
Beeston d						20a36			20 42	21 01										21a35		
East Midlands Parkway d									20 50	21 07											21 33	
Loughborough d									20 58	21 15											21 39	
Barrow Upon Soar d									21 03													
Sileby d									21 07													
Syston d									21 12													
Leicester a									21 23	21 27											21 51	
d										21 29											21 52	
Market Harborough d										21 42												
Melton Mowbray 47 d																						
Oakham 47 d																						
Corby d																						
Kettering a										21 51												
d										21 52												
Wellingborough d										21 59												
Bedford 52 d										22 13												
Luton 52 d										22 28												
Luton Airport Parkway 52 d										22 31												
St Pancras International 52 a										22 57											23 01	

	NT	XC ◇1 J ⌶	NT ◇	EM ⌶	EM ◇1 ⌶	NT ◇	EM	NT	TP ◇1 E	TP ◇1 K	NT G	XC ◇1 H	EM ◇ I	NT	NT ◇ B	NT	EM L	XC ◇1 M ⌶	NT	EM ◇1 ⌶	NT ◇
York 29 d		19 44										20 36						20 44			
Leeds 31,34 d		20 10				20 04		19 48								20 32		21 11	20 48		21 04
Wakefield Westgate 31 d		20 23						20 03										21 23	21 03		
Wakefield Kirkgate 31,34 d						20 22										21 03					21 21
Doncaster 29 d										20 42	20 35	21 01		21 04	21 21						
Manchester Piccadilly 78 d			19 49						20 18				20 42								
Sheffield a		20 54	20 57			21 01		21 04	21 08	21 09	21 17	21 25	21 35	21 45	21 49	21 51		21 54	21 59		22 02
d	20 53	20 58				21 04						21 29	21 37					22 01		22 01	22 04
Dronfield d						21 14							21 49								22 14
Chesterfield d		21 10				21 20						21 41	21 55					22 25		22 13	22 20
Belper a																					
d																	22 03				
Derby a		21 27				21 41						21 58					22 14	22 42		22 34	
d						21 42															
Long Eaton d																					
Alfreton d													22 05								22 31
Langley Mill d													22 13								22 38
Lincoln 27 d	22a11																				
Newark Castle 27 d																					
Nottingham a						22 00							22 31								22 57
d					21 29		22 01														
Beeston d							22 07														
East Midlands Parkway d							22 16														
Loughborough d					21 46		22 24														
Barrow Upon Soar d							22 29														
Sileby d							22 33														
Syston d							22 38														
Leicester a					21 56		22 50														
d					21 57																
Market Harborough d					22 10																
Melton Mowbray 47 d																					
Oakham 47 d																					
Corby d				21 43																	
Kettering a				21 52	22 19																
d					22 20																
Wellingborough d					22 27																
Bedford 52 d					22 40																
Luton 52 d					22 55																
Luton Airport Parkway 52 d																					
St Pancras International 52 a					23 24																

A From Liverpool Lime Street to Norwich
B From Scarborough
C From Matlock to Nottingham
D From Glasgow Central to Bristol Temple Meads
E From Manchester Airport to Cleethorpes
F From Cleethorpes to Manchester Airport
G From Adwick
H From Newcastle to Birmingham New Street
I From Liverpool Lime Street
J From Edinburgh to Bristol Temple Meads. ⌶ to Leeds
K From Cleethorpes to Manchester Piccadilly
L From Matlock
M From Glasgow Central to Birmingham New Street. ⌶ to Leeds

For connections to Gatwick Airport refer to Table T052

Table T053-R

Mondays to Fridays

16 December to 15 May

Sheffield - East Midlands - London

	EM	TP ◇1 A	TP ◇1 B	NT ◇	NT C	NT ◇	NT ◇	NT ◇ D	NT	NT ◇	NT	TP ◇1 E	NT C	EM ◇1 ⌶	TP ◇1 F	EM G	EM ◇1 ⌶	EM ◇ H	NT	NT	NT	NT ◇ I
York 29 d																						
Leeds 31,34 d							21 37		21 32		21 48								22 30	22 32		
Wakefield Westgate 31 d											22 03								22 45			
Wakefield Kirkgate 31,34 d							21 53		22 03											23 03		
Doncaster 29 d			21 43		21 35	21 51		22 17					22 37		22 44						23 35	23 43
Manchester Piccadilly 78 d		21 18		20 49						21 19		22 20						22 28				
Sheffield a		22 08	22 08	22 09	22 14	22 19	22 40	22 45	22 51	22 52	23 04	23 09	23 14		23 18			23 36	23 41	23 51	00 13	00 17
d																	23 21	23 38				
Dronfield d																						
Chesterfield d																	23 45	00 02				
Belper a																						
d																23 17						
Derby a																23 28	00 04					
d																23 29						
Long Eaton d																23 38						
Alfreton d																						
Langley Mill d																						
Lincoln 27 d																						
Newark Castle 27 d																						
Nottingham a																		00 45				
d	23 10																					
Beeston d	23 15															23a51						
East Midlands Parkway d	23 23																					
Loughborough d	23 31																					
Barrow Upon Soar d																						
Sileby d																						
Syston d																						
Leicester a	23 47																					
d																						
Market Harborough d																						
Melton Mowbray 47 d																						
Oakham 47 d																						
Corby d														22 43								
Kettering a														22 52								
d																						
Wellingborough d																						
Bedford 52 d																						
Luton 52 d																						
Luton Airport Parkway 52 d																						
St Pancras International 52 a																						

	NT	NT	NT	TP ◇1 J
York 29 d				
Leeds 31,34 d		23 02	23 11	
Wakefield Westgate 31 d			23 26	
Wakefield Kirkgate 31,34 d		23 34		
Doncaster 29 d	23 49			
Manchester Piccadilly 78 d				23 50
Sheffield a	00 21	00 24	00 28	01 20
d				
Dronfield d				
Chesterfield d				
Belper a				
d				
Derby a				
d				
Long Eaton d				
Alfreton d				
Langley Mill d				
Lincoln 27 d				
Newark Castle 27 d				
Nottingham a				
d				
Beeston d				
East Midlands Parkway d				
Loughborough d				
Barrow Upon Soar d				
Sileby d				
Syston d				
Leicester a				
d				
Market Harborough d				
Melton Mowbray 47 d				
Oakham 47 d				
Corby d				
Kettering a				
d				
Wellingborough d				
Bedford 52 d				
Luton 52 d				
Luton Airport Parkway 52 d				
St Pancras International 52 a				

A From Manchester Airport to Cleethorpes
B From Cleethorpes to Manchester Airport
C From Adwick
D From Scarborough
E From Manchester Airport to Doncaster
F From Cleethorpes
G From Matlock to Nottingham
H From Liverpool Lime Street
I From Hull
J From Manchester Airport

For connections to Gatwick Airport refer to Table T052

Table T053-R

Saturdays

21 December to 16 May

Sheffield - East Midlands - London

Station			EM ◇ A	EM ◇1 ⌶	NT ◇	EM ◇1 ⌶	EM ◇1 ⌶	NT	EM ◇1 ⌶	EM ◇1 ⌶	EM ◇1 ⌶		EM ◇1 ⌶	NT ◇	TP ◇1 B	EM C	EM	EM ◇1 ⌶	NT ◇	NT ◇ D	NT		XC ◇1 E ⌶	NT ◇	NT	EM ◇1 ⌶
York 8	29	d																								
Leeds 10	31,34	d																					06 11		05 34	
Wakefield Westgate 7	31	d																					06 23		05 50	
Wakefield Kirkgate 4	31,34	d																								
Doncaster 7	29	d													05 36				06 00	06 12	06 06					
Manchester Piccadilly	78	d																						05 46		
Sheffield 7	⇌	a													06 08				06 26	06 44	06 46		06 51	06 56	07 00	
		d			05 15		05 29	05 45						06 01				06 27	06 35				06 53			
Dronfield		d			05 24									06 13												
Chesterfield		d	00 02		05 30		05 41							06 19				06 39					07 06			
Belper		a																								
		d														06 43										
Derby 6		a					06 00									06 55		07 00					07 25			
		d				05 21	06 01				06 30							07 04								
Long Eaton		d				05 30					06 38															
Alfreton		d			05 45									06 29												
Langley Mill		d			05 53									06 36												
Lincoln	27	d						07a07											08a01							
Newark Castle	27	d																								
Nottingham 8	⇌	a	00 45		06 11									07 00												
		d							06 12				06 40													07 12
Beeston		d							06 18																	07 18
East Midlands Parkway	✈	d				05 35					06 43		06 51													
Loughborough		d				05 42			06 27		06 50						06 59									07 29
Barrow Upon Soar		d															07 04									
Sileby		d															07 08									
Syston		d															07 14									
Leicester		a				05 52	06 22		06 37		06 59		07 11				07 22	07 25								07 38
		d		04 45		05 53	06 24		06 38		07 01		07 12					07 25								07 40
Market Harborough		d				06 07			06 52				07 26													07 53
Melton Mowbray	47	d																								
Oakham	47	d																								
Corby		d								07 06																
Kettering 5		a		05 04		06 16			07 01	07 15	07 20															08 02
		d		05 05		06 17			07 02		07 22															08 03
Wellingborough		d		05 17		06 24			07 09		07 29															08 10
Bedford 7	52	d		05 34		06 38			07 23		07 42															08 24
Luton 10	52	d				06 53					07 57															
Luton Airport Parkway 7	52 ✈	d		05 52					07 39																	08 39
St Pancras International	⊖52	a		06 21		07 21	07 33		08 05		08 22		08 26					08 38								09 07

Station			EM ◇1 ⌶	EM	EM ◇1 ⌶	NT ◇ F	TP ◇1 G		TP ◇1 H	XC ◇1 I ⌶	NT	NT	EM ◇1 ⊠	EM ◇1 ⌶	EM ◇1 ⌶	EM J	EM ◇1 ⌶		EM K	EM ◇1 ⊠	NT ◇	NT L	NT ◇ D	XC ◇1 M ⌶	NT	NT
York 8	29	d								06 24														06 12		
Leeds 10	31,34	d									05 54									06 34	06 38			07 11	06 32	06 47
Wakefield Westgate 7	31	d																		06 46				07 23		07 02
Wakefield Kirkgate 4	31,34	d									06 27										06 56				07 03	
Doncaster 7	29	d					06 25			06 47		06 34										06 55	07 20			
Manchester Piccadilly	78	d							06 15																	
Sheffield 7	⇌	a					07 05		07 06	07 12	07 15	07 18								07 24	07 34	07 39	07 47	07 51	07 55	07 57
		d				07 02				07 18			07 29							07 37	07 37			07 56		
Dronfield		d				07 11																				
Chesterfield		d				07 17				07 30			07 41							07 50				08 08		
Belper		a																								
		d														07 59										
Derby 6		a								07 48			07 59			08 10								08 25		
		d	07 31										08 04			08 13	08 31									
Long Eaton		d	07 41													08 25	08 41									
Alfreton		d				07 28														08 01						
Langley Mill		d				07 35														08 09						
Lincoln	27	d													07 04				07 35		08a47					
Newark Castle	27	d													07 29				08 05							
Nottingham 8	⇌	a				07 53									07 57				08 28	08 25						
		d		07 33	07 45										08 12				08 36	08 45						
Beeston		d		07 39											08 18	08a33			08 42							
East Midlands Parkway	✈	d	07 45	07 50	07 56												08 45		08 50	08 56						
Loughborough		d	07 53	07 58											08 28		08 53		08 58							
Barrow Upon Soar		d		08 03															09 03							
Sileby		d		08 07															09 07							
Syston		d		08 12															09 12							
Leicester		a	08 02	08 23	08 11								08 25		08 37		09 02		09 25	09 11						
		d	08 03		08 13								08 25		08 39		09 03			09 13						
Market Harborough		d			08 27										08 52					09 26						
Melton Mowbray	47	d																								
Oakham	47	d																								
Corby		d												08 41												
Kettering 5		a												08 49	09 01											
		d												08 51	09 02											
Wellingborough		d												08 59	09 09											
Bedford 7	52	d												09 12	09 23											
Luton 10	52	d												09 28												
Luton Airport Parkway 7	52 ✈	d													09 38											
St Pancras International	⊖52	a	09 11		09 25								09 36	09 51	10 07		10 10			10 25						

A From Liverpool Lime Street
B To Manchester Airport
C From Matlock
D From Hull
E To Plymouth
F From Retford
G From Cleethorpes to Manchester Airport
H From Manchester Airport to Cleethorpes
I To Southampton Central
J From Matlock to Newark Castle
K From Sleaford
L From Adwick
M To Plymouth. ⌶ from Leeds

For connections to Gatwick Airport refer to Table T052

Table T053-R

Saturdays

21 December to 16 May

Sheffield - East Midlands - London

Station			NT ◇		NT ◇	TP ◇1 A	TP ◇1 B ⌶	NT C	XC ◇ D	EM ◇1 ⌶	EM ◇1 ⌶	EM ◇1 ⌶	EM E		EM ◇1 F ⌶	NT ◇	EM ◇ G	NT C	NT ◇ H	NT	XC ◇1 I ⌶	NT	EM ◇1 ⌶		EM	EM ◇1 J ⌶
York 8	29	d							07 28												07 44					
Leeds 10	31,34	d	07 03												07 40	07 38				07 32	08 11	07 48				
Wakefield Westgate 7	31	d													07 53						08 23	08 03				
Wakefield Kirkgate 4	31,34	d	07 22													07 55				08 03						
Doncaster 7	29	d				07 42		07 26	07 52									08 00	08 22							
Manchester Piccadilly	78	d			06 39		07 18										07 42									
Sheffield 7	⇌	a	08 00		08 04	08 06	08 10	08 10	08 15						08 25	08 34	08 35	08 44	08 48	08 50	08 54	09 00				
		d	08 03						08 18	08 29					08 34	08 37	08 37				08 54		09 00			
Dronfield		d	08 13																							
Chesterfield		d	08 19						08 31	08 41					08 47		08 52				09 07		09 13			
Belper		a																								
		d											08 59													
Derby 6		a							08 48	08 59			09 10								09 27		09 31			
		d								09 04			09 11										09 32			
Long Eaton		d											09 21										09 41			
Alfreton		d	08 29												08 57		09 03									
Langley Mill		d	08 37																							
Lincoln	27	d														09a48									08 37	
Newark Castle	27	d																							09 06	
Nottingham 8	⇌	a	08 55												09 19		09 27								09 32	
		d										09 12			09 45										09 36	
Beeston		d										09 18	09a32												09 42	←
East Midlands Parkway	✈	d													09 56								09 45		09 50	09 56
Loughborough		d										09 28			↦								09 53		09 58	
Barrow Upon Soar		d																							10 03	
Sileby		d																							10 07	
Syston		d																							10 12	
Leicester		a								09 24		09 37											10 02		10 23	10 11
		d								09 25		09 39											10 03			10 13
Market Harborough		d										09 52														10 26
Melton Mowbray	47	d																								
Oakham	47	d																								
Corby		d									09 41															
Kettering 5		a									09 49	10 01														
		d									09 51	10 02														
Wellingborough		d									09 59	10 09														
Bedford 7	52	d									10 12	10 23														
Luton 10	52	d									10 28															
Luton Airport Parkway 7	52 ✈	d										10 39														
St Pancras International	⊖52	a								10 35	10 51	11 08											11 11			11 25

Station			NT ◇	NT ◇	TP ◇1 B ⌶	TP ◇1 A	NT C	XC ◇1 K ⌶	EM ◇1 ⌶		NT ◇	EM ◇1 ⌶	EM ◇1 ⌶	EM ◇ G	NT C	NT ◇ L	NT	EM E	XC ◇1 M ⌶		EM ◇1 ⌶	NT	EM	EM ◇1 ⌶	NT ◇	NT ◇
York 8	29	d						08 35											08 44							
Leeds 10	31,34	d	08 04								08 38						08 32		09 11			08 48			09 09	
Wakefield Westgate 7	31	d																	09 23			09 04				
Wakefield Kirkgate 4	31,34	d	08 22								08 55						09 03								09 26	
Doncaster 7	29	d				08 42	08 32	08 58							09 03	09 20										
Manchester Piccadilly	78	d		07 49	08 19									08 43												08 49
Sheffield 7	⇌	a	09 04	09 05	09 09	09 09	09 14	09 22			09 34			09 34	09 44	09 49	09 51		09 54			10 01			10 04	10 05
		d	09 06					09 24	09 29		09 37			09 37					09 56		10 00				10 06	
Dronfield		d	09 16																						10 16	
Chesterfield		d	09 22						09 41					09 52					10 09		10 13				10 22	
Belper		a																								
		d																09 59								
Derby 6		a						09 51	09 59									10 10	10 28		10 31					
		d							10 04									10 12			10 32					
Long Eaton		d																10 24			10 40					
Alfreton		d	09 33											10 03											10 32	
Langley Mill		d	09 40																						10 40	
Lincoln	27	d									10a55												09 36			
Newark Castle	27	d																					10 06			
Nottingham 8	⇌	a	09 59											10 27									10 30		10 58	
		d											10 12										10 35	10 45		
Beeston		d											10 18					10a35					10 41			
East Midlands Parkway	✈	d																			10 45		10 50	10 56		
Loughborough		d											10 28								10 53		10 58			
Barrow Upon Soar		d																					11 03			
Sileby		d																					11 07			
Syston		d																					11 12			
Leicester		a							10 24				10 37								11 02		11 23	11 11		
		d							10 25				10 39								11 03			11 13		
Market Harborough		d											10 52											11 26		
Melton Mowbray	47	d																								
Oakham	47	d																								
Corby		d										10 41														
Kettering 5		a										10 49	11 01													
		d										10 51	11 02													
Wellingborough		d										10 59	11 09													
Bedford 7	52	d										11 12	11 22													
Luton 10	52	d										11 28														
Luton Airport Parkway 7	52 ✈	d											11 38													
St Pancras International	⊖52	a							11 36			11 50	12 07								12 11			12 25		

A From Cleethorpes to Manchester Airport
B From Manchester Airport to Cleethorpes
C From Adwick
D From Newcastle to Reading
E From Matlock to Newark Castle
F To St Pancras International
G From Liverpool Lime Street to Norwich
H From Beverley
I From Newcastle to Plymouth. ⌶ from Leeds
J From Leeds
K From Newcastle to Southampton Central
L From Scarborough
M From Edinburgh to Plymouth

For connections to Gatwick Airport refer to Table T052

Table T053-R

Sheffield - East Midlands - London

Saturdays

21 December to 16 May

Station			TP ◇1 A	TP ◇1 B	NT C	XC ◇1 D	EM ◇1	NT ◇	NT ◇	EM ◇1	EM ◇1	EM ◇ E	NT	NT ◇ F	NT	EM G	XC ◇1 H	EM ◇1	NT	EM	EM ◇1	NT ◇	NT ◇
York	29	d				09 37		09 15									09 44						
Leeds	31,34	d							09 38						09 32		10 11		09 48			10 09	
Wakefield Westgate	31	d															10 23		10 03				
Wakefield Kirkgate	31,34	d							09 55						10 03							10 26	
Doncaster	29	d		09 42	09 35	10 00							10 04	10 21									
Manchester Piccadilly	78	d	09 18									09 42											09 49
Sheffield		a	10 09	10 09	10 14	10 22		10 33	10 34			10 34	10 44	10 50	10 52		10 54		11 01			11 04	11 05
		d				10 24	10 29		10 37			10 37					10 56	11 00				11 06	
Dronfield		d																				11 16	
Chesterfield		d					10 41					10 52					11 09	11 13				11 22	
Belper		a																					
		d														10 59							
Derby		a				10 51	10 59									11 10	11 28	11 31					
		d					11 04									11 12		11 32					
Long Eaton		d														11 22		11 40					
Alfreton		d										11 02										11 32	
Langley Mill		d																				11 40	
Lincoln	27	d							11a49											10 36			
Newark Castle	27	d																		11 04			
Nottingham		a										11 27								11 31		11 58	
		d									11 12									11 35	11 45		
Beeston		d									11 18					11a32				11 41			
East Midlands Parkway		d																11 46		11 49	11 56		
Loughborough		d									11 28							11 52		11 58			
Barrow Upon Soar		d																		12 02			
Sileby		d																		12 06			
Syston		d																		12 11			
Leicester		a					11 24				11 37							12 02		12 23	12 11		
		d					11 25				11 39							12 03			12 12		
Market Harborough		d									11 52										12 26		
Melton Mowbray	47	d																					
Oakham	47	d																					
Corby		d								11 41													
Kettering		a								11 49	12 01												
		d								11 51	12 02												
Wellingborough		d								11 59	12 09												
Bedford	52	d								12 12	12 23												
Luton	52	d								12 27													
Luton Airport Parkway	52	d									12 39												
St Pancras International	52	a					12 35			12 51	13 08							13 11			13 25		

Station			TP ◇1 A	TP ◇1 B	NT C	XC ◇1 I	EM ◇1	NT ◇	EM ◇1	EM ◇1	EM ◇ E	NT	NT ◇ J	NT	EM G	XC ◇1 K	EM ◇1	NT	NT ◇	EM	EM ◇1	NT ◇	TP ◇1 A	TP ◇1 B
York	29	d				10 35										10 43								
Leeds	31,34	d						10 38						10 32		11 11		10 48				11 09		
Wakefield Westgate	31	d														11 23		11 03						
Wakefield Kirkgate	31,34	d						10 55						11 03								11 26		
Doncaster	29	d		10 42	10 35	10 59						11 04	11 21											11 42
Manchester Piccadilly	78	d	10 18								10 42								10 49				11 18	
Sheffield		a	11 08	11 09	11 14	11 21		11 34			11 36	11 44	11 49	11 51		11 54		12 01	12 04			12 04	12 08	12 08
		d				11 24	11 29	11 37			11 38					11 56	12 00					12 06		
Dronfield		d																				12 16		
Chesterfield		d					11 42				11 52					12 09	12 13					12 22		
Belper		a																						
		d													11 59									
Derby		a				11 51	12 00								12 10	12 28	12 31							
		d					12 04								12 12		12 32							
Long Eaton		d													12 21		12 40							
Alfreton		d									12 03											12 32		
Langley Mill		d																				12 40		
Lincoln	27	d						12a48												11 40				
Newark Castle	27	d																		12 04				
Nottingham		a									12 27									12 27		12 58		
		d								12 12										12 35	12 45			
Beeston		d								12 18					12a32					12 41				
East Midlands Parkway		d															12 45			12 49	12 56			
Loughborough		d								12 28							12 52			12 57				
Barrow Upon Soar		d																		13 02				
Sileby		d																		13 06				
Syston		d																		13 11				
Leicester		a					12 24			12 37							13 02			13 23	13 11			
		d					12 25			12 39							13 03				13 12			
Market Harborough		d								12 52											13 26			
Melton Mowbray	47	d																						
Oakham	47	d																						
Corby		d							12 41															
Kettering		a							12 49	13 01														
		d							12 51	13 02														
Wellingborough		d							12 59	13 09														
Bedford	52	d							13 11	13 23														
Luton	52	d							13 28															
Luton Airport Parkway	52	d								13 39														
St Pancras International	52	a					13 36		13 51	14 08							14 11				14 25			

A From Manchester Airport to Cleethorpes
B From Cleethorpes to Manchester Airport
C From Adwick
D From Edinburgh to Reading
E From Liverpool Lime Street to Norwich
F From Bridlington
G From Matlock to Newark Castle
H From Glasgow Central to Plymouth
I From Newcastle to Southampton Central
J From Scarborough
K From Dundee to Plymouth

For connections to Gatwick Airport refer to Table T052

Table T053-R

Sheffield - East Midlands - London

Saturdays

21 December to 16 May

Station			NT A	XC ◇1 B	EM ◇1	NT ◇	EM ◇1	EM ◇1	EM ◇ C	NT	NT ◇ D	NT	EM E	XC ◇1 F	EM ◇1	NT	EM	EM ◇1	NT ◇	NT ◇	TP ◇1 G	TP ◇1 H	NT A	XC ◇1 I
York	29	d		11 36										11 44										12 35
Leeds	31,34	d				11 38						11 32		12 11		11 48			12 09					
Wakefield Westgate	31	d												12 23		12 03								
Wakefield Kirkgate	31,34	d				11 55						12 03							12 26					
Doncaster	29	d	11 35	11 59						12 03	12 21											12 42	12 35	12 59
Manchester Piccadilly	78	d							11 42											11 49	12 18			
Sheffield		a	12 14	12 21		12 34			12 35	12 44	12 50	12 52		12 55		13 01			13 04	13 05	13 08	13 08	13 14	13 21
		d		12 24	12 29	12 37			12 38					12 56	13 00				13 06					13 24
Dronfield		d																	13 16					
Chesterfield		d			12 41				12 52					13 08	13 13				13 22					
Belper		a																						
		d											12 59											
Derby		a		12 56	13 00								13 10	13 26	13 31									13 51
		d			13 04								13 12		13 32									
Long Eaton		d											13 23		13 40									
Alfreton		d							13 02										13 32					
Langley Mill		d																	13 40					
Lincoln	27	d				13a49											12 36							
Newark Castle	27	d															13 05							
Nottingham		a							13 27								13 29		13 58					
		d						13 12									13 35	13 45						
Beeston		d						13 18					13a33				13 41							
East Midlands Parkway		d													13 45		13 49	13 56						
Loughborough		d						13 28							13 52		13 57							
Barrow Upon Soar		d															14 02							
Sileby		d															14 06							
Syston		d															14 11							
Leicester		a			13 24			13 37							14 02		14 23	14 11						
		d			13 25			13 39							14 03			14 13						
Market Harborough		d						13 52										14 26						
Melton Mowbray	47	d																						
Oakham	47	d																						
Corby		d					13 41																	
Kettering		a					13 49	14 01																
		d					13 51	14 02																
Wellingborough		d					13 59	14 09																
Bedford	52	d					14 12	14 23																
Luton	52	d					14 28																	
Luton Airport Parkway	52	d						14 39																
St Pancras International	52	a			14 35		14 50	15 07							15 10			15 25						

Station			EM ◇1	NT ◇	EM ◇1	EM ◇1	EM ◇ C	NT	NT ◇ D	NT	EM E	XC ◇1 J	EM ◇1	NT	NT ◇	EM	EM ◇1	NT ◇	TP ◇1 G	TP ◇1 H	NT A	XC ◇1 B	EM ◇1
York	29	d										12 44										13 35	
Leeds	31,34	d		12 38						12 32		13 11		12 48				13 09					
Wakefield Westgate	31	d										13 23		13 03									
Wakefield Kirkgate	31,34	d		12 55						13 03								13 26					
Doncaster	29	d						13 04	13 21											13 42	13 35	14 00	
Manchester Piccadilly	78	d					12 42								12 49				13 18				
Sheffield		a		13 34			13 36	13 44	13 49	13 51		13 54		14 01	14 04			14 04	14 08	14 08	14 14	14 22	
		d	13 29	13 37			13 38					13 56	14 00					14 06				14 24	14 29
Dronfield		d																14 16					
Chesterfield		d	13 42				13 54					14 09	14 13					14 22					14 41
Belper		a																					
		d									13 59												
Derby		a	14 00								14 10	14 28	14 31									14 51	14 59
		d	14 04								14 12		14 32										15 04
Long Eaton		d									14 21		14 40										
Alfreton		d					14 04											14 32					
Langley Mill		d																14 40					
Lincoln	27	d		14a48												13 37							
Newark Castle	27	d														14 05							
Nottingham		a					14 27									14 28		14 58					
		d				14 12										14 35	14 45						
Beeston		d				14 18					14a32					14 41							
East Midlands Parkway		d											14 45			14 50	14 56						
Loughborough		d				14 28							14 52			14 58							
Barrow Upon Soar		d														15 03							
Sileby		d														15 07							
Syston		d														15 12							
Leicester		a	14 24			14 37							15 02			15 23	15 11						15 24
		d	14 25			14 39							15 03				15 13						15 25
Market Harborough		d				14 52											15 26						
Melton Mowbray	47	d																					
Oakham	47	d																					
Corby		d			14 41																		
Kettering		a			14 49	15 01																	
		d			14 51	15 02																	
Wellingborough		d			14 59	15 09																	
Bedford	52	d			15 11	15 23																	
Luton	52	d			15 28																		
Luton Airport Parkway	52	d				15 38																	
St Pancras International	52	a	15 36		15 51	16 06							16 10				16 25						16 36

A From Adwick
B From Newcastle to Reading
C From Liverpool Lime Street to Norwich
D From Scarborough
E From Matlock to Newark Castle
F From Glasgow Central to Plymouth
G From Manchester Airport to Cleethorpes
H From Cleethorpes to Manchester Airport
I From Newcastle to Southampton Central
J From Glasgow Central to Penzance

For connections to Gatwick Airport refer to Table T052

Table T053-R

Saturdays

21 December to 16 May

Sheffield - East Midlands - London

			NT ◇	NT ◇	EM ◇■	EM ◇■	EM ◇ A	NT	NT ◇ B	NT	EM C	XC ◇■ D	EM ◇■	NT	EM	EM ◇■	NT ◇	NT ◇	TP ◇■ E	TP ◇■ F	NT G	XC ◇■ H	EM ◇■	NT ◇
York 8	29	d	13 15									13 44										14 35		
Leeds 10	31,34	d		13 38						13 32		14 11		13 48			14 09							14 38
Wakefield Westgate 7	31	d										14 23		14 03										
Wakefield Kirkgate 4	31,34	d		13 55						14 03							14 26							14 55
Doncaster 7	29	d						14 05	14 21											14 42	14 35	14 59		
Manchester Piccadilly	78	d					13 42											13 49	14 18					
Sheffield 7		a	14 32	14 34			14 36	14 44	14 49	14 51		14 54		15 01			15 04	15 05	15 08	15 08	15 14	15 21		15 34
		d		14 37			14 38					14 56	15 00				15 06					15 24	15 29	15 37
Dronfield		d															15 16							
Chesterfield		d					14 54					15 08	15 13				15 22						15 41	
Belper		a																						
		d									14 59													
Derby 6		a									15 10	15 25	15 30									15 51	15 59	
		d									15 12		15 32										16 04	
Long Eaton		d									15 24		15 40											
Alfreton		d					15 04										15 32							
Langley Mill		d															15 40							
Lincoln	27	d		15a48											14 33									16a49
Newark Castle	27	d													15 04									
Nottingham 8		a					15 27								15 30		15 58							
		d				15 12									15 34	15 45								
Beeston		d				15 18					15a35				15 40									
East Midlands Parkway ✈		d											15 45		15 49	15 56								
Loughborough		d				15 28							15 52		15 58									
Barrow Upon Soar		d													16 02									
Sileby		d													16 06									
Syston		d													16 11									
Leicester		a				15 37							16 02		16 23	16 11							16 24	
		d				15 39							16 03			16 13							16 25	
Market Harborough		d				15 52										16 26								
Melton Mowbray	47	d																						
Oakham	47	d																						
Corby		d			15 41																			
Kettering 5		a			15 49	16 01																		
		d			15 51	16 02																		
Wellingborough		d			15 59	16 09																		
Bedford 7	52	d			16 12	16 23																		
Luton 10	52	d			16 28																			
Luton Airport Parkway 7	52 ✈	d				16 39																		
St Pancras International	⊖52	a			16 50	17 08							17 11			17 25							17 36	

			EM ◇■	EM ◇■	EM ◇ A	NT	NT ◇ B	NT	EM C	XC ◇■ I	NT	EM ◇■	NT ◇	EM	EM ◇■	NT ◇	TP ◇■ E	TP ◇■ F	NT G	XC ◇■ J	EM ◇■	NT ◇	EM ◇■
York 8	29	d								14 44										15 36			
Leeds 10	31,34	d						14 32		15 11	14 48					15 09						15 38	
Wakefield Westgate 7	31	d								15 23	15 03												
Wakefield Kirkgate 4	31,34	d						15 03								15 26						15 55	
Doncaster 7	29	d				15 04	15 21											15 42	15 35	16 00			
Manchester Piccadilly	78	d			14 42								14 49				15 18						
Sheffield 7		a			15 36	15 44	15 50	15 52		15 55	16 01		16 04			16 04	16 08	16 08	16 14	16 22		16 34	
		d			15 38					15 56		16 01				16 06				16 24	16 29	16 37	
Dronfield		d														16 16							
Chesterfield		d			15 53					16 08		16 13				16 22					16 41		
Belper		a																					
		d							15 59														
Derby 6		a							16 10	16 26		16 31								16 51	16 59		
		d							16 11			16 32									17 04		
Long Eaton		d							16 21			16 40											
Alfreton		d			16 04											16 32							
Langley Mill		d														16 40							
Lincoln	27	d												15 27								17a56	
Newark Castle	27	d												15 59									
Nottingham 8		a			16 27									16 27		16 58							
		d		16 12										16 33	16 45								
Beeston		d		16 18					16a32					16 39									
East Midlands Parkway ✈		d										16 45		16 49	16 56								
Loughborough		d		16 28								16 52		16 58									
Barrow Upon Soar		d												17 02									
Sileby		d												17 06									
Syston		d												17 11									
Leicester		a		16 37								17 02		17 23	17 11						17 24		
		d		16 39								17 03			17 13						17 25		
Market Harborough		d		16 52											17 26								
Melton Mowbray	47	d																					
Oakham	47	d																					
Corby		d	16 41																				17 41
Kettering 5		a	16 49	17 01																			17 49
		d	16 51	17 02																			17 51
Wellingborough		d	16 59	17 09																			17 59
Bedford 7	52	d	17 12	17 23																			18 12
Luton 10	52	d	17 28																				18 27
Luton Airport Parkway 7	52 ✈	d		17 39																			
St Pancras International	⊖52	a	17 51	18 08								18 11			18 25						18 34		18 50

A From Liverpool Lime Street to Norwich
B From Scarborough
C From Matlock to Newark Castle
D From Aberdeen to Penzance
E From Manchester Airport to Cleethorpes
F From Cleethorpes to Manchester Airport
G From Adwick
H From Newcastle to Guildford
I From Glasgow Central to Penzance
J From Newcastle to Reading

For connections to Gatwick Airport refer to Table T052

Table T053-R

Saturdays

21 December to 16 May

Sheffield - East Midlands - London

			EM ◇■	EM ◇ A	NT	NT ◇ B	NT	EM C	XC ◇■ D	EM ◇■	NT	NT ◇	EM	EM ◇■	NT ◇	TP ◇■ E	TP ◇■ F	NT G	XC ◇■ H	EM ◇■	NT ◇	EM ◇■	EM ◇■	EM ◇ A
York 8	29	d							15 44										16 13					
Leeds 10	31,34	d					15 32		16 11		15 48				16 09				16 41		16 38			
Wakefield Westgate 7	31	d							16 23		16 03								16 53					
Wakefield Kirkgate 4	31,34	d					16 03								16 26						16 55			
Doncaster 7	29	d			16 04	16 21										16 42		16 35						
Manchester Piccadilly	78	d		15 42								15 49					16 18							16 42
Sheffield 7		a		16 35	16 44	16 49	16 51		16 54		17 01	17 04			17 04	17 08	17 09	17 14	17 21		17 34			17 37
		d		16 38					16 56	17 00					17 06				17 24	17 29	17 37			17 41
Dronfield		d		16 48											17 16									17 51
Chesterfield		d		16 54					17 08	17 11					17 22					17 41				17 57
Belper		a																						
		d						16 59																
Derby 6		a						17 10	17 25	17 30									17 51	17 59				
		d						17 10		17 31										18 04				
Long Eaton		d						17 22		17 40														
Alfreton		d		17 05											17 32									18 08
Langley Mill		d													17 40									
Lincoln	27	d											16 35								18a57			
Newark Castle	27	d											17 04											
Nottingham 8		a		17 27									17 30		17 58									18 29
		d	17 12										17 33	17 45									18 12	
Beeston		d	17 18					17a33					17 38										18 18	
East Midlands Parkway ✈		d								17 45			17 48	17 56										
Loughborough		d	17 28							17 52			17 57										18 28	
Barrow Upon Soar		d											18 01											
Sileby		d											18 05											
Syston		d											18 10											
Leicester		a	17 37							18 02			18 23	18 11						18 24			18 37	
		d	17 39							18 03				18 13						18 25			18 39	
Market Harborough		d	17 52											18 26									18 52	
Melton Mowbray	47	d																						
Oakham	47	d																						
Corby		d																				18 41		
Kettering 5		a	18 01																			18 49	19 01	
		d	18 02																			18 51	19 02	
Wellingborough		d	18 09																			18 59	19 09	
Bedford 7	52	d	18 23																			19 12	19 23	
Luton 10	52	d																				19 27		
Luton Airport Parkway 7	52 ✈	d	18 39																				19 39	
St Pancras International	⊖52	a	19 08							19 11				19 25						19 36		19 51	20 08	

			NT	NT ◇ B	NT	EM C	XC ◇■ I	EM ◇■	NT	EM	EM ◇■	NT ◇	NT ◇	TP ◇■ E	TP ◇■ F	NT G	XC ◇■ H	EM ◇■	NT ◇	NT ◇	EM ◇■	EM ◇■	EM ◇ J	EM K
York 8	29	d					16 44										17 36		17 15					
Leeds 10	31,34	d			16 32		17 11		16 48			17 09								17 38				
Wakefield Westgate 7	31	d					17 23		17 04															
Wakefield Kirkgate 4	31,34	d			17 03							17 27								17 55				
Doncaster 7	29	d	17 04	17 21										17 42		17 35	18 00							
Manchester Piccadilly	78	d											16 49		17 18								17 42	
Sheffield 7		a	17 44	17 49	17 51		17 54		18 01			18 04	18 06	18 08	18 10	18 14	18 22		18 32	18 34			18 37	
		d					17 56	18 00				18 06					18 24	18 29		18 37			18 40	
Dronfield		d										18 16												
Chesterfield		d					18 08	18 12				18 22						18 41					18 58	
Belper		a																						
		d				17 59																		18 59
Derby 6		a				18 10	18 25	18 30									18 51	18 59						19 10
		d				18 11		18 31										19 04						19 12
Long Eaton		d				18 25		18 40																19 21
Alfreton		d										18 32											19 09	
Langley Mill		d										18 40												
Lincoln	27	d								17 30										20a06				
Newark Castle	27	d								17 58														
Nottingham 8		a								18 33		18 58											19 29	
		d								18 35	18 45											19 12		
Beeston		d				18a35				18 40												19 18		19a32
East Midlands Parkway ✈		d						18 45		18 49	18 56													
Loughborough		d						18 52		18 58												19 28		
Barrow Upon Soar		d								19 02														
Sileby		d								19 06														
Syston		d								19 11														
Leicester		a						19 02		19 23	19 11							19 23				19 37		
		d						19 02			19 13							19 25				19 39		
Market Harborough		d									19 26											19 52		
Melton Mowbray	47	d																						
Oakham	47	d																						
Corby		d																			19 41			
Kettering 5		a																19 46			19 49	20 01		
		d																19 47			19 51	20 02		
Wellingborough		d																			19 59	20 09		
Bedford 7	52	d																			20 12	20 23		
Luton 10	52	d																			20 28			
Luton Airport Parkway 7	52 ✈	d																				20 39		
St Pancras International	⊖52	a						20 11			20 25							20 38			20 52	21 08		

A From Liverpool Lime Street to Norwich
B From Scarborough
C From Matlock to Newark Castle
D From Edinburgh to Plymouth
E From Cleethorpes to Manchester Airport
F From Manchester Airport to Cleethorpes
G From Adwick
H From Newcastle to Reading
I From Glasgow Central to Plymouth
J From Liverpool Lime Street
K From Matlock to Nottingham

For connections to Gatwick Airport refer to Table T052

Table T053-R

Sheffield - East Midlands - London

Station		EM	NT	NT	NT	XC	EM	NT	NT	EM	EM	NT	TP	TP	NT	XC	EM	EM	EM	EM	NT	NT
		◇1 A		◇ B		◇1 C	◇1 D		◇		◇1	◇	◇1 E	◇1 F	G	◇1 H	◇1	◇1	◇1	◇ I	◇	
York 8	29 d	17 50				17 44										18 36						
Leeds 10	31,34 d				17 32	18 11		17 48				18 03									18 38	
Wakefield Westgate 7	31 d					18 23		18 03														
Wakefield Kirkgate 4	31,34 d				18 03							18 22									18 57	
Doncaster 7	29 d	18 13	18 04	18 21										18 42	18 35	19 00						19 04
Manchester Piccadilly	78 d						←		17 49				18 18							18 42		
Sheffield 7	a	18 38	18 44	18 49	18 51	18 54	18 38	19 01	19 04			19 04	19 08	19 09	19 14	19 22				19 35	19 35	19 44
	d	19 00				18 56	19 00					19 06				19 24	19 29			19 37	19 38	
Dronfield	d	→										19 16										
Chesterfield	d					19 08	19 12					19 22					19 41			19 53		
Belper	a																					
	d																					
Derby 6	a					19 25	19 29									19 51	19 59					
	d						19 31										20 04					
Long Eaton	d						19 40															
Alfreton	d											19 32								20 04		
Langley Mill	d											19 40										
Lincoln	27 d									18 31											20a58	
Newark Castle	27 d									19 00												
Nottingham 8	a									19 24		19 58								20 28		
	d									19 36	19 45								20 12			
Beeston	d									19 42									20 18			
East Midlands Parkway	d						19 45			19 50	19 56								20 24			
Loughborough	d						19 52			19 58									20 32			
Barrow Upon Soar	d									20 03												
Sileby	d									20 07												
Syston	d									20 12												
Leicester	a						20 02			20 23	20 11						20 24		20 41			
	d						20 03				20 13						20 25		20 42			
Market Harborough	d										20 26								20 55			
Melton Mowbray	47 d																					
Oakham	47 d																					
Corby	d																	20 41				
Kettering 5	a																	20 49	21 04			
	d																	20 51	21 04			
Wellingborough	d																	20 59	21 13			
Bedford 7	52 d																	21 12	21 26			
Luton 10	52 d																	21 27				
Luton Airport Parkway 7	52 d																		21 42			
St Pancras International	52 a						21 10				21 25						21 35	21 51	22 09			

Station		NT	NT	EM	XC	NT	EM	NT	NT	TP	TP	NT	XC	EM	EM	EM	EM	EM	EM	EM	NT	NT	NT
		◇ B		J	◇1 K			◇	◇	◇1 E	◇1 F	G	◇1 L	◇1	◇1	◇1	J	◇1	◇ M			◇ B	
York 8	29 d				18 44								19 36										
Leeds 10	31,34 d		18 32		19 11	18 48		19 03															19 32
Wakefield Westgate 7	31 d				19 23	19 03																	
Wakefield Kirkgate 4	31,34 d		19 03					19 21															20 03
Doncaster 7	29 d	19 20									19 42	19 35	19 59								20 06	20 21	
Manchester Piccadilly	78 d								18 49	19 18									19 42				
Sheffield 7	a	19 49	19 51		19 54	20 01		20 04	20 05	20 08	20 09	20 14	20 21						20 35		20 44	20 49	20 51
	d				19 56			20 06					20 24	20 29					20 39				
Dronfield	d							20 16															
Chesterfield	d				20 08			20 22						20 41					20 54				
Belper	a																						
	d			19 59													20 59						
Derby 6	a			20 10	20 25								20 51	21 00			21 10						
	d			20 12										21 01			21 12						
Long Eaton	d			20 21													21 21						
Alfreton	d							20 32											21 05				
Langley Mill	d							20 40															
Lincoln	27 d																						
Newark Castle	27 d																						
Nottingham 8	a							20 59											21 33				
	d						20 33									21 05		21 30		21 34			
Beeston	d			20a33			20 39									21 11	21a33			21 40			
East Midlands Parkway	d						20 50							21 13		21 17				21 49			
Loughborough	d						20 58							21 20		21 25		21 46		21 58			
Barrow Upon Soar	d						21 03													22 03			
Sileby	d						21 07													22 07			
Syston	d						21 12													22 12			
Leicester	a						21 23							21 31		21 34		21 55		22 22			
	d															21 36		21 56					
Market Harborough	d															21 49		22 09					
Melton Mowbray	47 d																						
Oakham	47 d																						
Corby	d														21 43								
Kettering 5	a														21 52	21 57		22 18					
	d															21 57		22 19					
Wellingborough	d															22 06		22 26					
Bedford 7	52 d															22 20		22 39					
Luton 10	52 d															22 35		22 54					
Luton Airport Parkway 7	52 d															22 39							
St Pancras International	52 a															23 11		23 29					

A To St Pancras International
B From Scarborough
C From Edinburgh to Plymouth
D From York
E From Manchester Airport to Cleethorpes
F From Cleethorpes to Manchester Airport
G From Adwick
H From Newcastle to Southampton Central
I From Liverpool Lime Street to Norwich
J From Matlock to Nottingham
K From Glasgow Central to Bristol Temple Meads
L From Newcastle to Birmingham New Street
M From Liverpool Lime Street

For connections to Gatwick Airport refer to Table T052

Table T053-R

Sheffield - East Midlands - London

Station		NT	XC	NT	NT	NT	TP	TP	NT	XC	EM	NT	NT	NT	EM	XC	NT	NT	EM	TP	TP	NT
			◇1 A	◇		◇	◇1 B	◇1 C	D	◇1 E	◇ F		◇ G		H	◇1 I		◇		◇1 B	◇1 J	◇
York 8	29 d		19 44							20 35						20 45						
Leeds 10	31,34 d		20 10	20 04	19 48									20 32		21 11	20 48	21 04				
Wakefield Westgate 7	31 d		20 23		20 03											21 23	21 03					
Wakefield Kirkgate 4	31,34 d			20 22										21 03				21 21				
Doncaster 7	29 d							20 42	20 35	20 59		21 04	21 21								21 43	
Manchester Piccadilly	78 d					19 49	20 18				20 42									21 18		20 49
Sheffield 7	a		20 54	21 01	21 04	21 05	21 08	21 09	21 17	21 21	21 34	21 45	21 49	21 51		21 53	21 59	22 02		22 08	22 08	22 09
	d	20 53	20 56	21 04						21 25	21 38					21 55		22 04				
Dronfield	d			21 14							21 49							22 14				
Chesterfield	d		21 08	21 20						21 37	21 54					22 07		22 20				
Belper	a																					
	d														22 03							
Derby 6	a		21 25	21 41						21 54					22 14	22 24						
	d			21 42																		
Long Eaton	d																					
Alfreton	d										22 05							22 31				
Langley Mill	d										22 13							22 38				
Lincoln	27 d	22a11																				
Newark Castle	27 d																					
Nottingham 8	a			22 00							22 34							22 57				
	d																		23 05			
Beeston	d																		23 10			
East Midlands Parkway	d																		23 18			
Loughborough	d																		23 26			
Barrow Upon Soar	d																					
Sileby	d																					
Syston	d																					
Leicester	a																		23 45			
	d																					
Market Harborough	d																					
Melton Mowbray	47 d																					
Oakham	47 d																					
Corby	d																					
Kettering 5	a																					
	d																					
Wellingborough	d																					
Bedford 7	52 d																					
Luton 10	52 d																					
Luton Airport Parkway 7	52 d																					
St Pancras International	52 a																					

Station		NT	NT	NT	EM	NT	NT	NT	NT	TP	NT	EM	EM	EM	NT	EM	NT	NT	NT	NT	NT
		D	◇	◇	◇ F	◇	◇ G			◇1 K	D	◇1	L	◇1		◇ F				◇ M	
York 8	29 d																				
Leeds 10	31,34 d					21 37		21 32	21 48						22 15		22 32	22 44			
Wakefield Westgate 7	31 d								22 03						22 30			22 59			
Wakefield Kirkgate 4	31,34 d					21 53		22 03									23 03				
Doncaster 7	29 d	21 35	21 51				22 17				22 37								23 35	23 43	23 49
Manchester Piccadilly	78 d			21 19	21 41					22 17						22 29					
Sheffield 7	a	22 14	22 19	22 28	22 31	22 40	22 44	22 51	23 04	23 07	23 14				23 25	23 35	23 51	23 55	00 13	00 17	00 21
	d				22 42									23 20		23 38					
Dronfield	d																				
Chesterfield	d				22 56									23 32		23 53					
Belper	a																				
	d												23 17								
Derby 6	a												23 28	00 05							
	d												23 29								
Long Eaton	d												23 38								
Alfreton	d				23 07																
Langley Mill	d																				
Lincoln	27 d																				
Newark Castle	27 d																				
Nottingham 8	a				23 28											00 29					
	d																				
Beeston	d												23a49								
East Midlands Parkway	d																				
Loughborough	d																				
Barrow Upon Soar	d																				
Sileby	d																				
Syston	d																				
Leicester	a																				
	d																				
Market Harborough	d																				
Melton Mowbray	47 d																				
Oakham	47 d																				
Corby	d											22 43									
Kettering 5	a											22 52									
	d																				
Wellingborough	d																				
Bedford 7	52 d																				
Luton 10	52 d																				
Luton Airport Parkway 7	52 d																				
St Pancras International	52 a																				

A From Edinburgh to Birmingham New Street. to Leeds
B From Manchester Airport to Cleethorpes
C From Cleethorpes to Manchester Piccadilly
D From Adwick
E From Newcastle to Birmingham New Street
F From Liverpool Lime Street
G From Scarborough
H From Matlock
I From Glasgow Central to Birmingham New Street. to Leeds
J From Cleethorpes to Manchester Airport
K From Manchester Airport to Doncaster
L From Matlock to Nottingham
M From Hull

For connections to Gatwick Airport refer to Table T052

Table T053-R

Sundays

15 December to 10 May

Sheffield - East Midlands - London

Station	Table	a/d	EM	EM	EM	EM	EM	EM	NT	NT	EM		XC	NT	NT	EM	NT	TP	EM	EM	NT		NT	NT	NT	NT
			◇1	◇1	◇1	◇1	◇1	◇1		◇			◇1	◇	◇	◇1	◇	◇1	◇1	◇1				◇		
											A		B	C	D			E						C		
			☕	☕	☕	☕	☕	☕					🛒			☕		🛒	☕	☕						
York 8	29	d																								
Leeds 10	31,34	d											08 10												08 33	08 46
Wakefield Westgate 7	31	d											08 23													09 01
Wakefield Kirkgate 4	31,34	d																							09 03	
Doncaster 7	29	d							08 07												09 03					
Manchester Piccadilly	78	d												07 42	07 43			08 13						08 29		
Sheffield 7		a							08 45				08 52	09 04	09 04			09 08			09 41			09 48	09 50	09 53
		d						08 18		08 45			08 55				09 05			09 25			09 41			
Dronfield		d															09 15									
Chesterfield		d						08 31					09 08				09 21			09 37						
Belper		a																								
		d									09 01															
Derby 6		a						08 49			09 12		09 27							09 56						
		d	06 50		07 51			08 51			09 14									09 58						
Long Eaton		d			08 01			09 00			09 24									10 07						
Alfreton		d															09 32									
Langley Mill		d															09 39									
Lincoln	27	d								09a57													11a00			
Newark Castle	27	d																								
Nottingham 8		a															10 00									
		d		07 29		08 22										09 20										
Beeston		d				08 28					09a34															
East Midlands Parkway		d	07 02	07 39	08 05	08 35		09 05								09 31				10 12						
Loughborough		d			08 13	08 43		09 12								09 40				10 19						
Barrow Upon Soar		d																								
Sileby		d																								
Syston		d																								
Leicester		a	07 19	07 53	08 23	08 53		09 23								09 52				10 29						
		d	07 20	07 55	08 25	08 55		09 24								09 54				10 31						
Market Harborough		d	07 38	08 11	08 41	09 11		09 40								10 11				10 44						
Melton Mowbray	47	d																								
Oakham	47	d																								
Corby		d					09 30												10 25							
Kettering 5		a	07 48	08 20	08 50	09 20	09 39	09 49								10 21			10 34	10 53						
		d	07 49	08 21	08 51	09 21		09 50								10 22				10 54						
Wellingborough		d	07 57	08 28	08 58	09 28		10 02								10 30				11 01						
Bedford 7	52	d	08 15	08 45	09 15	09 45		10 15								10 45				11 15						
Luton 10	52	d	08 35		09 35			10 34												11 36						
Luton Airport Parkway 7	52 ✈	d		09 06		10 06										11 06										
St Pancras International	⊖52	a	09 13	09 42	10 11	10 42		11 11								11 42				12 13						

Station	Table	a/d	XC	NT	EM	NT	TP		TP	NT	EM	EM	EM	EM	EM	NT	NT		NT	NT	XC	NT	NT	TP	TP	NT
			◇1		◇1	◇	◇1		◇1		◇1	◇1		◇1	◇1		◇		◇	◇	◇1	◇	◇	◇1	◇1	
			B	D			E		F	G			A						D	H	B	C		E	I	
			🛒		☕		🛒				☕	☕		☕	☕						🛒			🛒		
York 8	29	d																			09 36					
Leeds 10	31,34	d	09 00			09 09									09 50	09 25					10 01		10 09			
Wakefield Westgate 7	31	d	09 12												10 02	09 39					10 14					
Wakefield Kirkgate 4	31,34	d				09 25																	10 25			
Doncaster 7	29	d	09 31						09 45	09 37										10 21	10 32				10 43	10 35
Manchester Piccadilly	78	d		08 45			09 10												09 31			09 45		10 14		
Sheffield 7		a	09 56	10 02		10 03	10 08		10 12	10 18					10 30	10 36			10 48	10 49	10 54	11 02	11 03	11 05	11 10	11 15
		d	09 58			10 06						10 25			10 35		10 41				10 55		11 06			
Dronfield		d				10 16																	11 16			
Chesterfield		d	10 11			10 22						10 37			10 48						11 09		11 22			
Belper		a																								
		d											11 00													
Derby 6		a	10 30									10 56	11 11								11 28					
		d										10 57	11 13													
Long Eaton		d										11 07	11 24													
Alfreton		d				10 32																	11 32			
Langley Mill		d				10 40																	11 40			
Lincoln	27	d															11a56									
Newark Castle	27	d																								
Nottingham 8		a				11 00									11 21								12 00			
		d			10 30										11 39											
Beeston		d			10 37								11a34													
East Midlands Parkway		d			10 45							11 11			11 50											
Loughborough		d			10 53							11 19			11 59											
Barrow Upon Soar		d																								
Sileby		d																								
Syston		d																								
Leicester		a			11 06							11 29			12 11											
		d			11 08							11 30			12 13											
Market Harborough		d			11 22							11 43			12 27											
Melton Mowbray	47	d																								
Oakham	47	d																								
Corby		d									11 25			12 20												
Kettering 5		a			11 32						11 34	11 52		12 29	12 37											
		d			11 33							11 53			12 38											
Wellingborough		d			11 41							12 01			12 46											
Bedford 7	52	d			11 57							12 15			13 02											
Luton 10	52	d										12 30														
Luton Airport Parkway 7	52 ✈	d			12 14										13 18											
St Pancras International	⊖52	a			12 41							12 54			13 45											

A From Matlock to Nottingham
B To Plymouth
C from 5 April
D until 29 March
E From Manchester Airport to Cleethorpes
F To Manchester Airport
G From Goole
H From Hull
I From Cleethorpes to Manchester Airport

For connections to Gatwick Airport refer to Table T052

NRT DECEMBER 19 EDITION

Table T053-R

Sundays

15 December to 10 May

Sheffield - East Midlands - London

Station	Table	a/d	NT		NT	EM	NT	NT	XC	NT	EM	EM	NT		TP	TP	NT	NT	EM	NT	EM	EM	XC		NT	NT
						◇1		◇	◇1	◇	◇1	◇1	◇		◇1	◇1		◇	◇	◇		◇1	◇1			◇
								A	B						C	D		E	F	G	H		I			
						☕			🛒		☕	☕				🛒						☕	🛒			
York 8	29	d							10 34														11 41			
Leeds 10	31,34	d	10 18			10 50	10 31		11 00				11 09										12 11		11 48	
Wakefield Westgate 7	31	d				11 03	10 47		11 12														12 24		12 03	
Wakefield Kirkgate 4	31,34	d	10 47										11 25													
Doncaster 7	29	d						11 22	11 30						11 43		11 34			12 19						
Manchester Piccadilly	78	d								10 45						11 19										11 45
Sheffield 7		a	11 38			11 41	11 45	11 51	11 54	12 02			12 03		12 08	12 09	12 13			12 46			12 53		12 58	13 02
		d			11 41	11 43			11 57				12 06					12 41	12 43			12 49	12 57			
Dronfield		d											12 16													
Chesterfield		d				11 55			12 09				12 22						12 57			13 02	13 10			
Belper		a																								
		d																			13 00					
Derby 6		a				12 17			12 26												13 11	13 21	13 29			
		d				12 17															13 13	13 22				
Long Eaton		d				12 29															13 23	13 31				
Alfreton		d											12 32						13 08							
Langley Mill		d											12 40													
Lincoln	27	d			13a00													13a56								
Newark Castle	27	d																								
Nottingham 8		a											13 00						13 34							
		d										12 49														
Beeston		d										12 56									13a34					
East Midlands Parkway		d				12 34						13 03										13 35				
Loughborough		d				12 42						13 12										13 43				
Barrow Upon Soar		d																								
Sileby		d																								
Syston		d																								
Leicester		a				12 54						13 24										13 53				
		d				12 56						13 26										13 54				
Market Harborough		d				13 10						13 40										14 07				
Melton Mowbray	47	d																								
Oakham	47	d																								
Corby		d									13 13															
Kettering 5		a									13 21	13 50														
		d									13 22	13 51														
Wellingborough		d									13 32	13 59														
Bedford 7	52	d									13 43	14 15														
Luton 10	52	d									14 00															
Luton Airport Parkway 7	52 ✈	d										14 31														
St Pancras International	⊖52	a				14 09					14 24	14 59										15 02				

Station	Table	a/d	EM	EM	NT	TP	TP	NT	NT		EM	NT	EM	EM	NT	XC	NT	NT	NT		EM	EM	NT	TP	TP	NT
			◇1	◇1	◇	◇1	◇1		◇		◇		◇1	◇	◇	◇1		◇	◇		◇1	◇1	◇	◇1	◇1	
						D	C		E		F			J	G	K		L	M					D	C	
			☕	☕		🛒							☕			🛒					☕	☕		🛒		
York 8	29	d														12 45										
Leeds 10	31,34	d			12 09							12 17				13 11	12 48						13 09			
Wakefield Westgate 7	31	d														13 24	13 03									
Wakefield Kirkgate 4	31,34	d			12 25							12 46											13 25			
Doncaster 7	29	d					12 43	12 33							13 23										13 44	13 33
Manchester Piccadilly	78	d				12 19					12 43			←				12 45	12 52					13 20		
Sheffield 7		a			13 03	13 08	13 08	13 12			13 37	13 38		13 37	13 49	13 54	13 59	14 02	14 02				14 03	14 09	14 09	14 13
		d			13 06				13 36		13 48		13 43	13 48		13 57							14 06			
Dronfield		d			13 16						→												14 16			
Chesterfield		d			13 22								13 56	14 02		14 09							14 22			
Belper		a																								
		d																								
Derby 6		a											14 15			14 26										
		d											14 16													
Long Eaton		d											14 26													
Alfreton		d			13 32									14 12									14 32			
Langley Mill		d			13 40																		14 40			
Lincoln	27	d							14a55																	
Newark Castle	27	d																								
Nottingham 8		a			14 00									14 35									15 00			
		d		13 49																		14 52				
Beeston		d		13 56																		14 58				
East Midlands Parkway		d		14 03									14 30									15 04				
Loughborough		d		14 12									14 38									15 12				
Barrow Upon Soar		d																								
Sileby		d																								
Syston		d																								
Leicester		a		14 24									14 53									15 22				
		d		14 26									14 55									15 24				
Market Harborough		d		14 40									15 08									15 37				
Melton Mowbray	47	d																								
Oakham	47	d																								
Corby		d	14 13																		15 13					
Kettering 5		a	14 21	14 50																	15 21	15 46				
		d	14 22	14 51																	15 22	15 47				
Wellingborough		d	14 31	14 59																	15 31	15 54				
Bedford 7	52	d	14 45	15 15																	15 45	16 09				
Luton 10	52	d	15 00																		16 00					
Luton Airport Parkway 7	52 ✈	d		15 31																		16 25				
St Pancras International	⊖52	a	15 24	15 59									16 04								16 24	16 48				

A From Bridlington
B From Newcastle to Plymouth
C From Cleethorpes to Manchester Airport
D From Manchester Airport to Cleethorpes
E From Huddersfield
F To Norwich
G From Hull
H From Matlock to Nottingham
I From Edinburgh to Plymouth
J From Manchester Piccadilly to Norwich
K From Edinburgh to Penzance
L from 5 April
M until 29 March

For connections to Gatwick Airport refer to Table T052

Table T053-R

Sundays

15 December to 10 May

Sheffield - East Midlands - London

			XC	EM	NT	NT	EM	EM	XC	NT	NT	EM	EM	EM	NT	TP	TP	NT	EM	XC	EM	EM	NT
			◇■	◇	◇	◇		◇■	◇■		◇	◇■	◇■	◇■	◇	◇■	◇■		◇■	◇■	◇■	◇	
			A	B	C	D	E		F							G	H		I	J	K	B	
York 8	29	d							13 45											14 35			
Leeds 10	31,34	d							14 11	13 48					14 09				14 34				14 17
Wakefield Westgate 7	31	d							14 23	14 03									14 47				
Wakefield Kirkgate 4	31,34	d													14 25								14 46
Doncaster 7	29	d				14 21											14 44	14 33		15 00			
Manchester Piccadilly	78	d		13 43							13 43					14 19					←	14 43	
Sheffield 7		a		14 37		14 48			14 51	14 57	15 01				15 03	15 08	15 09	15 14	15 18	15 22	15 18	15 34	15 39
		d	14 22	14 41	14 41			14 49	14 55						15 06				15 28	15 24	15 28	15 39	
Dronfield		d													15 16				→				
Chesterfield		d	14 34	14 55				15 01	15 07						15 22						15 42	15 53	
Belper		a																					
		d					15 03																
Derby 6		a	14 51				15 14	15 19	15 24											15 51	16 02		
		d					15 15	15 21													16 02		
Long Eaton		d					15 24	15 30															
Alfreton		d		15 08											15 32							16 04	
Langley Mill		d		15 15											15 40							16 11	
Lincoln	27	d			15a57																		
Newark Castle	27	d																					
Nottingham 8		a		15 32											16 00							16 28	
		d										15 43		15 52									
Beeston		d					15a35							15 58									
East Midlands Parkway		d						15 35				15 53		16 05							16 16		
Loughborough		d						15 42						16 12							16 25		
Barrow Upon Soar		d																					
Sileby		d																					
Syston		d																					
Leicester		a						15 53				16 11		16 23							16 37		
		d						15 55				16 12		16 24							16 39		
Market Harborough		d												16 37							16 53		
Melton Mowbray	47	d																					
Oakham	47	d																					
Corby		d											16 20										
Kettering 5		a											16 29	16 46							17 03		
		d												16 47							17 03		
Wellingborough		d												16 55							17 12		
Bedford 7	52	d												17 09							17 28		
Luton 10	52	d						16 41													17 47		
Luton Airport Parkway 7	52	d												17 26									
St Pancras International	⊖52	a						17 05				17 23		17 50							18 12		

			NT	NT	EM	XC	NT	NT	EM	EM	EM	NT	TP	TP	NT	XC	EM	NT	EM	NT	EM	EM	XC	NT
			◇	◇	◇■	◇■		◇	◇■	◇■	◇■	◇	◇■	◇■		◇■	◇■	◇	◇	◇		◇■	◇■	
			C	D		L							G	H		J		C	B	D	E		M	
York 8	29	d				14 44										15 35							15 44	
Leeds 10	31,34	d				15 11	14 46					15 09											16 11	15 42
Wakefield Westgate 7	31	d				15 23	15 03																16 23	15 57
Wakefield Kirkgate 4	31,34	d										15 25												
Doncaster 7	29	d		15 21										15 43	15 30	15 58				16 22				
Manchester Piccadilly	78	d						14 45					15 18						15 43					
Sheffield 7		a		15 48		15 53	15 58	16 02				16 03	16 08	16 08	16 13	16 20			16 38	16 49			16 52	16 56
		d	15 42		15 50	15 55						16 06				16 24		16 37	16 43			16 49	16 55	
Dronfield		d										16 16												
Chesterfield		d			16 02	16 07						16 22							16 57			17 00	17 07	
Belper		a																						
		d																			17 01			
Derby 6		a			16 21	16 24										16 51					17 12	17 19	17 24	
		d			16 26												16 57				17 14	17 23		
Long Eaton		d															17 07				17 24			
Alfreton		d										16 32							17 07					
Langley Mill		d										16 40							17 15					
Lincoln	27	d	16a57															17a58						
Newark Castle	27	d																						
Nottingham 8		a										17 00							17 30					
		d							16 45		16 50													
Beeston		d									16 57										17a34			
East Midlands Parkway		d			16 37				16 55		17 03						17 11					17 35		
Loughborough		d									17 11						17 19							
Barrow Upon Soar		d																						
Sileby		d																						
Syston		d																						
Leicester		a			16 53				17 09		17 21						17 29					17 53		
		d			16 55				17 10		17 23						17 31					17 54		
Market Harborough		d									17 36						17 44							
Melton Mowbray	47	d																						
Oakham	47	d																						
Corby		d								17 20														
Kettering 5		a								17 29	17 45						17 54							
		d									17 46						17 55							
Wellingborough		d									17 54						18 02							
Bedford 7	52	d									18 08						18 17							
Luton 10	52	d															18 32							
Luton Airport Parkway 7	52	d									18 25													
St Pancras International	⊖52	a			18 02				18 17		18 47						18 55					19 10		

A To Reading
B From Liverpool Lime Street to Norwich
C From Huddersfield
D From Scarborough
E From Matlock to Nottingham
F From Edinburgh to Plymouth
G From Manchester Airport to Cleethorpes
H From Cleethorpes to Manchester Airport
I To St Pancras International
J From Newcastle to Reading
K From Leeds
L From Glasgow Central to Penzance
M From Glasgow Central to Plymouth

For connections to Gatwick Airport refer to Table T052

Table T053-R

Sundays

15 December to 10 May

Sheffield - East Midlands - London

			NT	EM	EM	EM	NT	TP	TP	NT	XC	EM	NT	EM	NT	NT	EM	EM	XC	NT	NT	EM	EM	EM
			◇	◇■	◇■	◇■	◇	◇■	◇■		◇■	◇■	◇	◇		◇		◇■	◇■		◇	◇■	◇■	◇■
								A	B		C		D	E		F	G		H					
York 8	29	d									16 25								16 44					
Leeds 10	31,34	d					16 09								16 17				17 12	16 48				
Wakefield Westgate 7	31	d																	17 24	17 03				
Wakefield Kirkgate 4	31,34	d					16 25								16 48									
Doncaster 7	29	d							16 44	16 35	16 51					17 21								
Manchester Piccadilly	78	d	15 45					16 19						16 43							16 45			
Sheffield 7		a	17 02				17 05	17 08	17 09	17 14	17 19			17 35	17 40	17 48			17 53	17 58	18 03			
		d					17 06				17 24		17 38	17 40				17 50	17 55					
Dronfield		d					17 16																	
Chesterfield		d					17 22							17 54				18 02	18 07					
Belper		a																						
		d															18 05							
Derby 6		a									17 51						18 16	18 21	18 24					
		d										18 06					18 17	18 26						
Long Eaton		d										18 15					18 27							
Alfreton		d					17 32							18 05										
Langley Mill		d					17 40							18 12										
Lincoln	27	d											18a54											
Newark Castle	27	d																						
Nottingham 8		a					18 00							18 34										
		d		17 45		17 52																	18 45	18 52
Beeston		d				17 58											18a38							18 58
East Midlands Parkway		d		17 55		18 04						18 20						18 37					18 55	19 05
Loughborough		d				18 12						18 28											19 02	19 12
Barrow Upon Soar		d																						
Sileby		d																						
Syston		d																						
Leicester		a		18 13		18 22						18 38						18 53					19 13	19 23
		d		18 14		18 25						18 40						18 54					19 14	19 25
Market Harborough		d				18 38						18 53											19 27	19 38
Melton Mowbray	47	d																						
Oakham	47	d																						
Corby		d			18 20																	19 20		
Kettering 5		a			18 29	18 47						19 02										19 29	19 36	19 47
		d				18 48						19 05											19 37	19 48
Wellingborough		d				18 56						19 12											19 45	19 55
Bedford 7	52	d				19 09						19 28											19 59	20 10
Luton 10	52	d										19 45											20 15	
Luton Airport Parkway 7	52	d				19 26																		20 26
St Pancras International	⊖52	a		19 25		19 50						20 08						20 03					20 39	20 50

			NT	TP	TP	NT	XC	EM	NT	EM	EM	NT	XC	NT	NT	EM	EM	NT	TP	TP	NT	NT	XC
			◇	◇■	◇■		◇■	◇			◇■	◇	◇■		◇	◇■	◇■	◇	◇■	◇■		◇	◇■
				B	A		I	J		G		F	K					L	A	B			M
York 8	29	d					17 35				17 48		17 44									18 02	18 35
Leeds 10	31,34	d	17 09										18 11	17 49				18 09					
Wakefield Westgate 7	31	d											18 23	18 06									
Wakefield Kirkgate 4	31,34	d	17 26															18 26					
Doncaster 7	29	d		17 43		17 33	17 58				18 13	18 22								18 44	18 29		18 58
Manchester Piccadilly	78	d			17 19			17 43							17 45				18 19				
Sheffield 7		a	18 03	18 07	18 09	18 11	18 20	18 36			18 40	18 49	18 53	18 59	19 02			19 03	19 09	19 09	19 12	19 19	19 20
		d	18 06				18 24	18 40	18 42		18 47		18 55					19 06					19 24
Dronfield		d	18 16															19 16					
Chesterfield		d	18 22					18 54			19 00		19 07					19 22					
Belper		a																					
		d								19 00													
Derby 6		a					18 51			19 11	19 19		19 24										19 51
		d								19 14	19 19												
Long Eaton		d								19 23	19 30												
Alfreton		d	18 32					19 05										19 32					
Langley Mill		d	18 40					19 12										19 40					
Lincoln	27	d							20a04														
Newark Castle	27	d																					
Nottingham 8		a	19 00					19 33										20 00					
		d															19 52						
Beeston		d								19a38							19 58						
East Midlands Parkway		d									19 34						20 05						
Loughborough		d									19 42						20 12						
Barrow Upon Soar		d																					
Sileby		d																					
Syston		d																					
Leicester		a									19 53						20 22						
		d									19 55						20 24						
Market Harborough		d									20 08						20 37						
Melton Mowbray	47	d																					
Oakham	47	d																					
Corby		d														20 20							
Kettering 5		a									20 15					20 29	20 46						
		d									20 15						20 47						
Wellingborough		d									20 25						20 54						
Bedford 7	52	d									20 41						21 09						
Luton 10	52	d									20 56						21 24						
Luton Airport Parkway 7	52	d									20 59												
St Pancras International	⊖52	a									21 22						21 48						

A From Manchester Airport to Cleethorpes
B From Cleethorpes to Manchester Airport
C From Edinburgh to Reading
D From Huddersfield
E From Liverpool Lime Street to Norwich
F From Scarborough
G From Matlock to Nottingham
H From Aberdeen to Plymouth
I From Newcastle to Reading
J From Liverpool Lime Street
K From Glasgow Central to Plymouth
L From Carlisle
M From Newcastle to Guildford

For connections to Gatwick Airport refer to Table T052

Table T053-R

Sundays
15 December to 10 May

Sheffield - East Midlands - London

Station		EM ◇1 ꝑ	NT ◇	EM ◇ A	NT	NT ◇ B	XC ◇1 C ✠	NT	NT ◇	NT ◇	TP ◇1 D	TP ◇1 E	NT	NT	XC ◇1 F ✠	EM ◇1 ꝑ	EM ◇1 ꝑ	EM G	EM ◇1 ꝑ	EM ◇ H	NT ◇ B	XC ◇1 I ✠	NT
York 29	d						18 45								19 24							19 45	
Leeds 31,34	d				18 14		19 12	18 48		19 09												20 11	19 48
Wakefield Westgate 31	d						19 24	19 03														20 23	20 03
Wakefield Kirkgate 31,34	d				18 48					19 25													
Doncaster 29	d					19 21					19 42		19 33		19 54						20 21		
Manchester Piccadilly 78	d			18 43					18 45			19 19								19 43			
Sheffield	a			19 35	19 43	19 48	19 53	19 59	20 02	20 03	20 08	20 09	20 11		20 16					20 35	20 47	20 52	20 59
	d	19 28	19 34	19 40			19 56			20 06				20 20	20 21		20 26			20 40		20 54	
Dronfield	d									20 16													
Chesterfield	d	19 41		19 54			20 08			20 22							20 39			20 54		21 06	
Belper	a																						
	d																	21 00					
Derby	a	20 00					20 25								20 48		20 59	21 12				21 23	
	d	20 02															21 01	21 13					
Long Eaton	d	20 12																21 22					
Alfreton	d			20 05						20 32										21 05			
Langley Mill	d			20 12						20 40										21 12			
Lincoln 27	d		20a49											21a41									
Newark Castle 27	d																						
Nottingham	a			20 30						21 00										21 33			
	d																		21 21				
Beeston	d																	21a33					
East Midlands Parkway	d	20 18															21 13		21 31				
Loughborough	d	20 26																	21 39				
Barrow Upon Soar	d																						
Sileby	d																						
Syston	d																						
Leicester	a	20 39															21 30		21 53				
	d	20 40															21 32		21 54				
Market Harborough	d	20 54															21 46		22 08				
Melton Mowbray 47	d																						
Oakham 47	d																						
Corby	d															21 25							
Kettering	a	21 04														21 34	21 56		22 17				
	d	21 05															21 57		22 18				
Wellingborough	d	21 13															22 05		22 25				
Bedford 52	d	21 29															22 20		22 39				
Luton 52	d	21 45															22 36		22 54				
Luton Airport Parkway 52	d																						
St Pancras International ⊖52	a	22 11															23 00		23 24				

Station		NT ◇	NT ◇	NT	TP ◇1 D	TP ◇1 E	XC ◇1 F	NT ◇	EM ◇ H	NT	NT ◇ B	XC ◇1 J ✠	NT	NT ◇	NT ◇ K	NT ◇	TP ◇1 L	TP ◇1 E	NT	EM M	EM ◇1 ꝑ	NT ◇ B
York 29	d						20 26					20 45			20 48							
Leeds 31,34	d		20 09							20 17		21 11	20 48			21 09						
Wakefield Westgate 31	d											21 23	21 03									
Wakefield Kirkgate 31,34	d		20 25							20 46						21 30						
Doncaster 29	d			20 28	20 43		20 51				21 21						21 44		21 33			22 21
Manchester Piccadilly 78	d	19 45				20 18			20 43					20 42				21 19				
Sheffield	a	21 02	21 03	21 05	21 08	21 09	21 13		21 34	21 38	21 49	21 52	21 59	22 00	22 03	22 07	22 10	22 11	22 13			22 50
	d		21 06				21 20	21 23	21 38			21 54				22 08					22 36	
Dronfield	d		21 16						21 50							22 18						
Chesterfield	d		21 22				21 32		21 56			22 06				22 24					22 48	
Belper	a																					
	d																			23 07		
Derby	a						21 50					22 24								23 18	23 23	
	d																					
Long Eaton	d																					
Alfreton	d		21 32						22 06							22 35						
Langley Mill	d		21 40						22 14							22 42						
Lincoln 27	d							22a45														
Newark Castle 27	d																					
Nottingham	a		22 00						22 36							23 05						
	d																					
Beeston	d																					
East Midlands Parkway	d																					
Loughborough	d																					
Barrow Upon Soar	d																					
Sileby	d																					
Syston	d																					
Leicester	a																					
	d																					
Market Harborough	d																					
Melton Mowbray 47	d																					
Oakham 47	d																					
Corby	d																					
Kettering	a																					
	d																					
Wellingborough	d																					
Bedford 52	d																					
Luton 52	d																					
Luton Airport Parkway 52	d																					
St Pancras International ⊖52	a																					

A From Liverpool Lime Street to Norwich
B From Scarborough
C From Glasgow Central to Bristol Temple Meads
D From Cleethorpes to Manchester Airport
E From Manchester Airport to Cleethorpes
F From Newcastle to Birmingham New Street
G From Matlock to Nottingham
H From Liverpool Lime Street
I From Edinburgh to Bristol Temple Meads. ✠ to Leeds
J From Glasgow Central to Birmingham New Street. ✠ to Leeds
K via Pontefract Baghill
L From Cleethorpes to Manchester Piccadilly
M From Matlock

For connections to Gatwick Airport refer to Table T052

Table T053-R

Sundays
15 December to 10 May

Sheffield - East Midlands - London

Station		NT	TP ◇1 A	NT ◇	NT ◇	TP ◇1 B	NT	EM ◇ C	NT	NT	TP ◇1 D
York 29	d										
Leeds 31,34	d	21 46			22 09				22 18	22 37	
Wakefield Westgate 31	d	22 03								22 52	
Wakefield Kirkgate 31,34	d				22 25				22 47		
Doncaster 29	d		22 29				22 40				
Manchester Piccadilly 78	d			21 45		22 19		22 13			23 20
Sheffield	a	22 56	23 00	23 02	23 03	23 09	23 20	23 26	23 35	23 45	00 10
	d							23 30			
Dronfield	d										
Chesterfield	d							23 44			
Belper	a										
	d										
Derby	a										
	d										
Long Eaton	d										
Alfreton	d							23 55			
Langley Mill	d							00 02			
Lincoln 27	d										
Newark Castle 27	d										
Nottingham	a							00 23			
	d										
Beeston	d										
East Midlands Parkway	d										
Loughborough	d										
Barrow Upon Soar	d										
Sileby	d										
Syston	d										
Leicester	a										
	d										
Market Harborough	d										
Melton Mowbray 47	d										
Oakham 47	d										
Corby	d										
Kettering	a										
	d										
Wellingborough	d										
Bedford 52	d										
Luton 52	d										
Luton Airport Parkway 52	d										
St Pancras International ⊖52	a										

A From Cleethorpes
B From Manchester Airport to Doncaster
C From Liverpool Lime Street
D From Manchester Airport

For connections to Gatwick Airport refer to Table T052

Table T055-F

Nottingham - Mansfield - Worksop

Mondays to Fridays
16 December to 15 May

Miles			EM	EM	EM	EM	EM	EM	EM	EM	EM	EM	EM	EM	EM	EM	EM	EM	EM	EM	EM	EM	EM
0	**Nottingham 8**	d	05 40	06 05	07 01	08 26	08 54	09 26	09 55	10 27	10 55	11 26	11 55	12 26	12 55	13 26	13 55	14 26	14 55	15 26	15 55	16 26	16 55
5¼	Bulwell	d	05 49	06 14	07 10	08 36	09 03		10 05		11 05		12 05		13 05		14 05		15 05		16 05		17 06
8¼	Hucknall	d	05 54	06 19	07 16	08 41	09 08	09 39	10 10	10 39	11 10	11 39	12 10	12 39	13 10	13 39	14 10	14 39	15 10	15 39	16 10	16 39	17 11
10¾	Newstead	d	05 59	06 24	07 21	08 46	09 13	09 44		10 45		11 44		12 44		13 44		14 44		15 44		16 44	17 17
13¾	Kirkby In Ashfield	d	06 05	06 30	07 31	08 52	09 19	09 49	10 19	10 50	11 19	11 49	12 19	12 49	13 19	13 49	14 19	14 49	15 19	15 49	16 19	16 49	17 23
14½	Sutton Parkway	d	06 08	06 33	07 34	08 55	09 22	09 52	10 22	10 54	11 22	11 52	12 22	12 52	13 22	13 52	14 22	14 52	15 22	15 52	16 22	16 52	17 26
17¼	**Mansfield**	d	06 13	06 38	07 40	09 00	09 27	09 57	10 27	10 59	11 27	11 57	12 27	12 57	13 27	13 57	14 27	14 57	15 27	15 57	16 27	16 57	17 32
18¾	Mansfield Woodhouse	d	06 18	06 47	07 45	09 04	09a34	10 02	10a34	11 04	11a34	12 02	12a34	13 02	13a34	14 02	14a34	15 02	15a34	16 02	16a34	17 02	17a39
21½	Shirebrook	d	06 24	06 54	07 51	09 11		10 08		11 10		12 08		13 08		14 08		15 08		16 08		17 08	
22¾	Langwith - Whaley Thorns	d	06 28	06 58	07 55	09 15		10 12		11 14		12 12		13 12		14 12		15 12		16 12		17 12	
25½	Creswell (Derbys)	d	06 32	07 02	07 59	09 19		10 16		11 19		12 16		13 16		14 16		15 16		16 16		17 16	
26¾	Whitwell	d	06 36	07 09	08 03	09 22		10 20		11 22		12 20		13 20		14 20		15 20		16 20		17 20	
31½	**Worksop**	a	06 49	07 20	08 18	09 33		10 33		11 34		12 33		13 33		14 33		15 33		16 33		17 33	

		EM	EM	EM	EM	EM	EM
Nottingham 8	d	17 26	17 55	18 56	19 56	20 55	22 05
Bulwell	d	17 38	18 12	19 05	20 05	21 05	22 19
Hucknall	d	17 44	18 17	19 10	20 17	21 17	22 25
Newstead	d	17 49	18 22	19 15	20 22	21 22	22 30
Kirkby In Ashfield	d	17 55	18 28	19 21	20 28	21 28	22 36
Sutton Parkway	d	17 58	18 31	19 24	20 31	21 31	22 40
Mansfield	d	18 03	18 36	19 29	20 36	21 36	22 45
Mansfield Woodhouse	d	18 08	18 41	19 35	20 41	21 41	22 50
Shirebrook	d	18 14	18 47	19 41	20 47	21 47	22 57
Langwith - Whaley Thorns	d	18 18	18 51	19 45	20 51	21 51	23 01
Creswell (Derbys)	d	18 22	18 55	19 49	20 55	21 55	23 06
Whitwell	d	18 26	18 58	19 52	20 58	21 58	23 09
Worksop	a	18 36	19 08	20 02	21 09	22 08	23 19

Saturdays
21 December to 16 May

		EM	EM	EM	EM	EM	EM	EM	EM	EM	EM	EM	EM	EM	EM	EM	EM	EM	EM	EM	EM	EM	EM
Nottingham 8	d	05 40	06 05	07 03	08 26	08 54	09 26	09 55	10 26	10 55	11 26	11 55	12 26	12 55	13 26	13 55	14 26	14 55	15 26	15 55	16 26	16 55	17 26
Bulwell	d	05 49	06 14	07 12	08 36	09 03		10 05		11 05		12 05		13 05		14 05		15 05		16 05		17 06	17 38
Hucknall	d	05 54	06 19	07 18	08 41	09 08	09 39	10 10	10 39	11 10	11 39	12 10	12 38	13 10	13 39	14 10	14 39	15 10	15 39	16 10	16 39	17 11	17 44
Newstead	d	05 59	06 24	07 23	08 46	09 13	09 44		10 44		11 44		12 43		13 44		14 44		15 44		16 44	17 17	17 49
Kirkby In Ashfield	d	06 05	06 30	07 31	08 52	09 19	09 49	10 19	10 49	11 19	11 49	12 19	12 49	13 19	13 49	14 19	14 49	15 19	15 49	16 19	16 49	17 23	17 55
Sutton Parkway	d	06 08	06 33	07 34	08 55	09 22	09 52	10 22	10 52	11 22	11 52	12 22	12 52	13 22	13 52	14 22	14 52	15 22	15 52	16 22	16 52	17 26	17 58
Mansfield	d	06 13	06 38	07 40	09 00	09 27	09 57	10 27	10 57	11 27	11 57	12 27	12 57	13 27	13 57	14 27	14 57	15 27	15 57	16 27	16 57	17 32	18 03
Mansfield Woodhouse	d	06 18	06 47	07 45	09 04	09a34	10 02	10a34	11 02	11a34	12 02	12a34	13 01	13a34	14 02	14a34	15 02	15a34	16 02	16a34	17 02	17a39	18 08
Shirebrook	d	06 24	06 54	07 51	09 11		10 08		11 08		12 08		13 08		14 08		15 08		16 08		17 08		18 14
Langwith - Whaley Thorns	d	06 28	06 58	07 55	09 15		10 12		11 12		12 12		13 12		14 12		15 12		16 12		17 12		18 18
Creswell (Derbys)	d	06 32	07 02	07 59	09 19		10 16		11 16		12 16		13 16		14 16		15 16		16 16		17 16		18 22
Whitwell	d	06 36	07 05	08 03	09 22		10 20		11 20		12 20		13 19		14 20		15 20		16 20		17 20		18 26
Worksop	a	06 48	07 18	08 14	09 33		10 33		11 33		12 33		13 33		14 33		15 33		16 31		17 31		18 36

		EM	EM	EM	EM	EM		EM
Nottingham 8	d	17 55	18 55	19 55	20 55	22 05		23 05
Bulwell	d	18 12	19 05	20 05	21 05	22 19		23 19
Hucknall	d	18 17	19 10	20 17	21 17	22 25		23 24
Newstead	d	18 22	19 15	20 22	21 22	22 30		23 29
Kirkby In Ashfield	d	18 28	19 21	20 28	21 28	22 36		23 34
Sutton Parkway	d	18 31	19 24	20 31	21 31	22 40		23 38
Mansfield	d	18 36	19 29	20 36	21 36	22 45		23 43
Mansfield Woodhouse	d	18 41	19 35	20 41	21 41	22 50		23a48
Shirebrook	d	18 47	19 41	20 47	21 47	22 57		
Langwith - Whaley Thorns	d	18 51	19 45	20 51	21 51	23 01		
Creswell (Derbys)	d	18 55	19 49	20 55	21 55	23 06		
Whitwell	d	18 58	19 52	20 58	21 58	23 09		
Worksop	a	19 07	20 03	21 09	22 08	23 19		

Sundays
15 December to 10 May

		EM	EM	EM	EM	EM	EM	EM	EM
Nottingham 8	d	08 07	09 42	11 28	13 28	15 25	16 53	18 29	20 25
Bulwell	d	08 16	09 51	11 40	13 38	15 35	17 03	18 39	20 35
Hucknall	d	08 21	09 57	11 46	13 43	15 40	17 08	18 44	20 40
Newstead	d	08 26	10 02	11 51	13 48	15 45	17 13	18 49	20 45
Kirkby In Ashfield	d	08 32	10 07	11 56	13 53	15 50	17 18	18 54	20 50
Sutton Parkway	d	08 35	10 10	11 59	13 56	15 53	17 21	18 57	20 53
Mansfield	d	08 40	10 16	12 05	14 01	15 58	17 26	19 02	20 58
Mansfield Woodhouse	d	08a47	10a22	12a10	14a08	16a05	17a33	19a09	21a05
Shirebrook	d								
Langwith - Whaley Thorns	d								
Creswell (Derbys)	d								
Whitwell	d								
Worksop	a								

Table T055-R

Worksop - Mansfield - Nottingham

Mondays to Fridays
16 December to 15 May

Miles			EM	EM ◇	EM	EM	EM	EM	EM	EM	EM	EM	EM	EM	EM	EM	EM	EM	EM	EM	EM	EM	EM
0	**Worksop**	d	05 49		06 56		07 38	08 38		09 38		10 38		11 38		12 38		13 38		14 38		15 38	
4¾	Whitwell	d	05 58		07 05		07 47	08 47		09 47		10 47		11 47		12 47		13 47		14 47		15 47	
6	Creswell (Derbys)	d	06 02		07 08		07 50	08 50		09 50		10 50		11 50		12 50		13 50		14 50		15 50	
9¼	Langwith - Whaley Thorns	d	06 06		07 12		07 53	08 53		09 53		10 53		11 53		12 53		13 53		14 53		15 53	
10	Shirebrook	d	06 10		07 16		07 58	08 58		09 58		10 58		11 58		12 58		13 58		14 58		15 58	
12¾	Mansfield Woodhouse	d	06 17	07 07	07 24	07 39	08 06	09 06	09 37	10 06	10 37	11 06	11 37	12 06	12 37	13 06	13 37	14 06	14 37	15 06	15 37	16 06	16 37
14¾	**Mansfield**	d	06 21	07 11	07 29	07 43	08 10	09 10	09 40	10 10	10 40	11 10	11 40	12 10	12 40	13 10	13 40	14 10	14 40	15 10	15 40	16 10	16 40
17	Sutton Parkway	d	06 27	07 17	07 35	07 48	08 15	09 15	09 46	10 16	10 46	11 16	11 46	12 16	12 46	13 16	13 46	14 16	14 46	15 16	15 46	16 16	16 46
17¾	Kirkby In Ashfield	d	06 30	07 20	07 38	07 52	08 18	09 18	09 49	10 19	10 49	11 19	11 49	12 19	12 49	13 19	13 49	14 19	14 49	15 19	15 49	16 19	16 49
20¾	Newstead	d	06 35	07 26	07 43	07 57	08 23	09 23	09 53		10 53		11 53		12 53		13 53		14 53		15 53		16 53
23¾	Hucknall	d	06 40	07 30	07 48	08 02	08 28	09 27	09 58	10 26	10 58	11 26	11 58	12 26	12 58	13 26	13 58	14 26	14 58	15 26	15 58	16 26	16 58
26	Bulwell	d	06 44	07 35	07 53	08 06	08 32	09 31		10 30		11 30		12 30		13 30		14 30		15 30		16 30	
31½	**Nottingham 8**	a	06 56	07 48	08 04	08 22	08 44	09 44	10 16	10 43	11 15	11 43	12 15	12 43	13 15	13 43	14 15	14 43	15 15	15 43	16 15	16 43	17 15

		EM	EM	EM		EM	EM	EM	EM	EM
Worksop	d	16 38		17 46		18 41	19 22	20 22	21 22	22 22
Whitwell	d	16 47		17 54		18 50	19 30	20 30	21 30	22 30
Creswell (Derbys)	d	16 50		17 58		18 53	19 34	20 34	21 34	22 34
Langwith - Whaley Thorns	d	16 53		18 01		18 56	19 37	20 37	21 37	22 37
Shirebrook	d	16 58		18 06		19 01	19 41	20 41	21 41	22 41
Mansfield Woodhouse	d	17 06	17 42	18 14		19 09	19 49	20 49	21 49	22 49
Mansfield	d	17 10	17 46	18 18		19 13	19 53	20 53	21 53	22 53
Sutton Parkway	d	17 16	17 52	18 24		19 18	19 58	20 58	21 58	22 58
Kirkby In Ashfield	d	17 22	17 55	18 27		19 21	20 01	21 01	22 01	23 01
Newstead	d		17 59	18 32		19 26	20 06	21 06	22 06	23 06
Hucknall	d	17 29	18 04	18 36		19 30	20 10	21 10	22 10	23 10
Bulwell	d	17 33		18 40		19 34	20 14	21 14	22 14	23 14
Nottingham 8	a	17 47	18 19	18 52		19 47	20 32	21 25	22 25	23 26

Saturdays
21 December to 16 May

		EM	EM	EM	EM	EM	EM	EM	EM	EM	EM	EM	EM	EM	EM	EM	EM	EM	EM	EM	EM	EM	EM
Worksop	d	05 49	06 56	07 38	08 38		09 38		10 38		11 38		12 38		13 38		14 38		15 38		16 38		17 46
Whitwell	d	05 59	07 05	07 47	08 47		09 47		10 47		11 47		12 47		13 47		14 47		15 47		16 50		17 54
Creswell (Derbys)	d	06 02	07 08	07 50	08 50		09 50		10 50		11 50		12 50		13 50		14 50		15 50		16 53		17 58
Langwith - Whaley Thorns	d	06 06	07 11	07 53	08 53		09 53		10 53		11 53		12 53		13 53		14 53		15 53		16 56		18 01
Shirebrook	d	06 10	07 16	07 58	08 58		09 58		10 58		11 58		12 58		13 58		14 58		15 58		17 01		18 06
Mansfield Woodhouse	d	06 17	07 24	08 06	09 06	09 37	10 06	10 37	11 06	11 37	12 06	12 37	13 06	13 37	14 06	14 37	15 06	15 37	16 06	16 37	17 09	17 42	18 14
Mansfield	d	06 22	07 29	08 10	09 10	09 40	10 10	10 40	11 10	11 40	12 10	12 40	13 10	13 40	14 10	14 40	15 10	15 40	16 10	16 40	17 13	17 46	18 18
Sutton Parkway	d	06 27	07 35	08 15	09 15	09 46	10 16	10 46	11 16	11 46	12 16	12 46	13 16	13 46	14 16	14 46	15 16	15 46	16 16	16 46	17 18	17 52	18 24
Kirkby In Ashfield	d	06 30	07 38	08 18	09 18	09 49	10 19	10 49	11 19	11 49	12 19	12 49	13 19	13 49	14 19	14 49	15 19	15 49	16 19	16 49	17 21	17 55	18 27
Newstead	d	06 35	07 43	08 23	09 23	09 53		10 53		11 53		12 53		13 53		14 53		15 53		16 53		17 59	18 32
Hucknall	d	06 40	07 48	08 28	09 27	09 58	10 26	10 58	11 26	11 58	12 26	12 58	13 26	13 58	14 26	14 58	15 26	15 58	16 26	16 58	17 28	18 04	18 36
Bulwell	d	06 44	07 53	08 32	09 31		10 30		11 30		12 30		13 30		14 30		15 30		16 30		17 32		18 40
Nottingham 8	a	06 55	08 05	08 46	09 44	10 15	10 43	11 15	11 43	12 15	12 43	13 15	13 43	14 15	14 43	15 14	15 43	16 15	16 43	17 15	17 45	18 19	18 52

		EM	EM	EM	EM	EM
Worksop	d	18 41	19 22	20 22	21 22	22 22
Whitwell	d	18 50	19 30	20 30	21 30	22 30
Creswell (Derbys)	d	18 53	19 34	20 34	21 34	22 34
Langwith - Whaley Thorns	d	18 56	19 37	20 37	21 37	22 37
Shirebrook	d	19 01	19 41	20 41	21 41	22 41
Mansfield Woodhouse	d	19 09	19 49	20 49	21 49	22 49
Mansfield	d	19 13	19 53	20 53	21 53	22 53
Sutton Parkway	d	19 18	19 58	20 58	21 58	22 58
Kirkby In Ashfield	d	19 21	20 01	21 01	22 01	23 01
Newstead	d	19 26	20 06	21 06	22 06	23 06
Hucknall	d	19 30	20 10	21 10	22 10	23 10
Bulwell	d	19 34	20 14	21 14	22 14	23 14
Nottingham 8	a	19 48	20 30	21 25	22 26	23 26

Sundays
15 December to 10 May

		EM	EM	EM	EM	EM	EM	EM	EM
Worksop	d								
Whitwell	d								
Creswell (Derbys)	d								
Langwith - Whaley Thorns	d								
Shirebrook	d								
Mansfield Woodhouse	d	08 52	10 29	12 14	14 11	16 09	17 36	19 18	21 07
Mansfield	d	08 55	10 33	12 17	14 15	16 12	17 39	19 21	21 10
Sutton Parkway	d	09 01	10 38	12 23	14 20	16 18	17 45	19 27	21 16
Kirkby In Ashfield	d	09 04	10 41	12 26	14 23	16 21	17 48	19 30	21 19
Newstead	d	09 08	10 46	12 30	14 28	16 25	17 52	19 34	21 23
Hucknall	d	09 13	10 51	12 35	14 33	16 30	17 57	19 39	21 28
Bulwell	d	09 17	10 55	12 39	14 37	16 34	18 01	19 43	21 32
Nottingham 8	a	09 31	11 07	12 51	14 50	16 46	18 13	19 55	21 44

Table T056-F

Mondays to Fridays
16 December to 15 May

Nottingham - Derby - Matlock

Miles			EM MX ◇1 A ⊥	EM	XC ◇1 B	EM	XC ◇1 C	EM G	XC ◇1 B	EM D	XC 1 E	XC ◇1 B	EM D	XC 1 E	XC ◇1 B ⊥	EM D	XC 1 E	XC ◇1 B ⊥	EM D	XC 1 E	XC ◇1 B ⊥	EM D	XC 1 E	XC ◇1 B ⊥
0	**Nottingham 8** ⇐	d	01 46		06 00	06 17	06 43		07 05	07 20	07 37	08 09	08 20	08 39	09 07	09 18	09 41	10 07	10 16	10 41	11 07	11 20	11 41	12 07
3¼	Beeston	d			06 06	06 24	06 49		07 11	07 25	07 42	08 15	08 25	08 44	09 12	09 23		10 12	10 22		11 12	11 25		12 12
4¾	Attenborough	d			06 09	06 27			07 14	07 29			08 29			09 27			10 25			11 29		
7¾	Long Eaton	d			06 18	06 36			07 22	07 38	07 52	08 24	08 37	08 54	09 24	09 35		10 24	10 33		11 22	11 37		12 22
13½	Spondon	d			06 25	06 43				07 44			08 44	09 01										
16	**Derby 6**	a	02 04		06 31	06 49	07 05	07 17	07 32	07 51	08 02	08 34	08 50	09 07	09 34	09 47	10 01	10 34	10 46	11 01	11 33	11 50	12 02	12 33
—		d		05 42		06 51				07 53			08 52			09 48			10 48			11 52		
21¼	Duffield	d		05 49		06 58				08 00			08 59			09 55			10 55			11 59		
23¾	Belper	d		05 54		07 03		07 28		08 05			09 04			10 00			11 00			12 04		
26½	Ambergate	d		06 00		07 09				08 11			09 10			10 06			11 06			12 10		
28½	Whatstandwell	d		06 04		07 13				08 15			09 14			10 10			11 10			12 14		
31½	Cromford	d		06 09		07 18				08 20			09 19			10 15			11 15			12 19		
32¼	Matlock Bath	d		06 12		07 21				08 23			09 22			10 18			11 18			12 22		
33¾	**Matlock**	a		06 15		07 25				08 27			09 26			10 22			11 22			12 26		

		EM D	XC 1 E	XC ◇1 B ⊥	EM D	XC 1 E ⊥	XC ◇1 B ⊥	EM D	XC 1 E	XC ◇1 B	EM D	XC 1 E ⊥	XC ◇1 B	EM D	XC 1 E ⊥	EM	XC ◇1 B	EM D	XC 1 E ⊥	XC ◇1 B	EM D	XC 1 E	XC ◇1 B
Nottingham 8 ⇐	d	12 20	12 41	13 07	13 20	13 41	14 07	14 20	14 41	15 07	15 18	15 41	16 07	16 20	16 41	16 49	17 07	17 20	17 41	18 07	18 20	18 41	19 07
Beeston	d	12 25		13 12	13 25		14 12	14 25		15 12	15 23		16 12	16 25		16 54	17 12	17 25		18 12	18 25		19 12
Attenborough	d	12 29			13 29			14 29			15 27			16 29		16 57		17 29			18 29		
Long Eaton	d	12 37		13 22	13 37		14 22	14 37		15 22	15 35		16 22	16 37		17 06	17 23	17 38	17 53	18 26	18 37		19 24
Spondon	d				13 44													17 46	18 00				
Derby 6	a	12 51	13 02	13 34	13 50	14 02	14 34	14 50	15 02	15 33	15 46	16 01	16 34	16 51	17 02	17 17	17 34	17 51	18 06	18 36	18 50	19 02	19 34
	d	12 52			13 52			14 52			15 48			16 52				17 53			18 52		
Duffield	d	12 59			13 59			14 59			15 55			16 59				18 00			18 59		
Belper	d	13 04			14 04			15 04			16 00			17 04				18 05			19 04		
Ambergate	d	13 10			14 10			15 10			16 06			17 10				18 11			19 10		
Whatstandwell	d	13 14			14 14			15 14			16 10			17 14				18 15			19 14		
Cromford	d	13 19			14 19			15 19			16 15			17 19				18 20			19 19		
Matlock Bath	d	13 22			14 22			15 22			16 18			17 22				18 23			19 22		
Matlock	a	13 26			14 26			15 26			16 22			17 26				18 27			19 26		

		EM	EM ◇1 A ⊥	XC 1 E	EM D	XC 1 E	EM	XC 1 E	EM	NT ◇ F	EM	EM
Nottingham 8 ⇐	d	19 17	19 24	19 36	20 20	20 40	21 20	21 38		22 15	22 19	23 20
Beeston	d	19 22		19 43	20 25	20 46	21 25	21 43			22 25	23 25
Attenborough	d	19 26		19 46	20 29		21 29	21 46			22 29	23 29
Long Eaton	d	19 34	19 44	19 54	20 38	20 55	21 37	21 55			22 37	23 36
Spondon	d	19 41						22 02				
Derby 6	a	19 46	19 55	20 05	20 50	21 05	21 49	22 08		22 37	22 48	23 50
	d	19 48			20 52				22 19			
Duffield	d	19 55			21 00				22 26			
Belper	d	20 00			21 05				22 31			
Ambergate	d	20 06			21 10				22 37			
Whatstandwell	d	20 10			21 14				22 41			
Cromford	d	20 15			21 20				22 46			
Matlock Bath	d	20 18			21 22				22 49			
Matlock	a	20 22			21 26				22 53			

Saturdays
21 December to 16 May

		EM ◇1 A ⊥	EM	XC ◇1 B	EM	XC ◇1 C	XC ◇1 B	EM	XC 1 E	XC ◇1 B	EM D	XC 1 E	XC ◇1 B ⊥	EM D	XC 1 E	XC ◇1 B ⊥	EM D	XC 1 E	XC ◇1 B ⊥	EM D	XC 1 E	XC ◇1 B ⊥	EM D
Nottingham 8 ⇐	d	01 46		06 00	06 20	06 44	07 00	07 20	07 37	08 06	08 20	08 41	09 06	09 20	09 41	10 06	10 18	10 41	11 06	11 20	11 41	12 06	12 18
Beeston	d			06 06	06 25	06 50	07 06	07 25	07 43	08 12	08 25		09 12	09 25		10 12	10 24		11 12	11 25		12 12	12 23
Attenborough	d			06 09	06 29		07 09	07 29			08 29			09 29			10 27			11 29			12 27
Long Eaton	d			06 17	06 37		07 17	07 37	07 52	08 22	08 37		09 22	09 37		10 22	10 33		11 22	11 36		12 22	12 34
Spondon	d			06 24	06 45						08 44	08 58											
Derby 6	a	02 04		06 30	06 50	07 06	07 27	07 50	08 02	08 33	08 50	09 04	09 33	09 49	10 01	10 33	10 46	11 01	11 33	11 47	12 01	12 33	12 48
	d		05 42		06 52			07 52			08 52			09 52			10 49			11 48			12 48
Duffield	d		05 49		06 59			07 59			08 59			09 59			10 56			11 56			12 55
Belper	d		05 54		07 04			08 04			09 04			10 04			11 01			12 01			13 00
Ambergate	d		06 00		07 10			08 10			09 10			10 10			11 07			12 06			13 06
Whatstandwell	d		06 04		07 14			08 14			09 14			10 14			11 11			12 10			13 10
Cromford	d		06 09		07 19			08 19			09 19			10 19			11 16			12 16			13 15
Matlock Bath	d		06 12		07 22			08 22			09 22			10 22			11 19			12 18			13 18
Matlock	a		06 15		07 25			08 26			09 26			10 26			11 23			12 22			13 22

A From St Pancras International
B To Cardiff Central
C To Bournemouth
D From Newark Castle
E To Birmingham New Street
F To Sheffield
G To Sheffield

For connections from St Pancras International refer to Table T053

NRT DECEMBER 19 EDITION

Table T056-F

Saturdays
21 December to 16 May

Nottingham - Derby - Matlock

		XC 1 A	XC ◇1 B ⊥	EM C	XC 1 A ⊥	XC ◇1 B ⊥	EM C	XC 1 A	XC ◇1 B	EM C	XC 1 A ⊥	XC ◇1 B	EM C	XC 1 A ⊥	XC ◇1 B	EM C	XC 1 A ⊥	XC ◇1 B	EM C	XC 1 A	XC ◇1 B	EM C
Nottingham 8 ⇐	d	12 41	13 06	13 17	13 41	14 06	14 20	14 41	15 06	15 20	15 41	16 06	16 20	16 41	17 06	17 20	17 41	18 06	18 18	18 41	19 06	19 20
Beeston	d		13 12	13 23		14 12	14 25		15 12	15 25		16 12	16 25		17 12	17 25		18 12	18 23		19 12	19 25
Attenborough	d			13 26			14 29			15 29			16 29			17 29			18 27			19 29
Long Eaton	d		13 22	13 34		14 22	14 37		15 22	15 37		16 22	16 37		17 22	17 38		18 22	18 34		19 22	19 37
Spondon	d			13 41												17 46					19 29	19 44
Derby 6	a	13 01	13 33	13 47	14 01	14 34	14 50	15 01	15 33	15 50	16 04	16 33	16 49	17 04	17 33	17 51	18 01	18 33	18 47	19 01	19 35	19 51
	d			13 48			14 52			15 52			16 52			17 53			18 48			19 52
Duffield	d			13 56			14 59			15 59			16 59			18 00			18 56			19 59
Belper	d			14 01			15 04			16 04			17 04			18 05			19 01			20 04
Ambergate	d			14 06			15 10			16 10			17 10			18 11			19 06			20 10
Whatstandwell	d			14 10			15 14			16 14			17 14			18 15			19 10			20 14
Cromford	d			14 16			15 19			16 19			17 19			18 20			19 16			20 19
Matlock Bath	d			14 18			15 22			16 22			17 22			18 23			19 18			20 22
Matlock	a			14 22			15 26			16 26			17 26			18 27			19 22			20 26

		XC 1 A	EM C	XC 1 A	EM	XC 1 A	EM	NT ◇ D	EM	EM
Nottingham 8 ⇐	d	19 29	20 20	20 37	21 20	21 39		22 15	22 20	23 20
Beeston	d	19 35	20 25	20 43	21 25	21 45			22 25	23 25
Attenborough	d	19 38	20 29		21 29	21 48			22 29	23 29
Long Eaton	d	19 47	20 37	20 52	21 37	21 56			22 38	23 37
Spondon	d					22 03				
Derby 6	a	19 58	20 50	21 02	21 50	22 09		22 37	22 52	23 50
	d		20 52				22 16			
Duffield	d		20 59				22 23			
Belper	d		21 04				22 28			
Ambergate	d		21 10				22 34			
Whatstandwell	d		21 14				22 38			
Cromford	d		21 19				22 43			
Matlock Bath	d		21 22				22 46			
Matlock	a		21 26				22 49			

Sundays
15 December to 10 May

		EM	EM	XC ◇1 B	XC ◇1 B	EM E	XC ◇1 B	XC ◇1 B ⊥	EM	XC ◇1 B ⊥	EM	XC ◇1 B ⊥	EM	XC ◇1 B ⊥	EM	XC ◇1 B ⊥	EM	XC ◇1 B ⊥	EM	XC ◇1 A	EM	XC ◇1 A	EM
Nottingham 8 ⇐	d		09 26	09 55	11 10	11 27	12 10	13 10	13 23	14 10	14 22	15 10	15 28	16 10	16 23	17 10	17 22	18 10	18 22	19 10	19 22	20 10	20 20
Beeston	d		09 32			11 32			13 29		14 28		15 34		16 29		17 28		18 28		19 28		20 26
Attenborough	d		09 35			11 36			13 32		14 31		15 37		16 32		17 31		18 31		19 31		20 29
Long Eaton	d		09 43			11 43			13 40		14 39		15 45		16 40		17 40		18 39		19 39		20 37
Spondon	d																						
Derby 6	a		09 54	10 15	11 30		12 30	13 30	13 51	14 30	14 50	15 30	15 56	16 30	16 51	17 30	17 51	18 30	18 51	19 30	19 50	20 30	20 49
	d	07 56	09 56						13 56				15 58		16 56		17 56				19 52		
Duffield	d	08 03	10 03			12 04			14 03				16 05		17 04		18 03				19 59		
Belper	d	08 08	10 08			12 09			14 08				16 10		17 09		18 08				20 04		
Ambergate	d	08 14	10 14			12 14			14 14				16 16		17 14		18 14				20 10		
Whatstandwell	d	08 18	10 18			12 18			14 18				16 20		17 18		18 18				20 14		
Cromford	d	08 23	10 23			12 24			14 23				16 25		17 24		18 23				20 19		
Matlock Bath	d	08 26	10 26			12 26			14 26				16 28		17 26		18 26				20 22		
Matlock	a	08 30	10 30			12 30			14 30				16 32		17 30		18 30				20 26		

		XC ◇1 A	EM
Nottingham 8 ⇐	d	21 10	21 24
Beeston	d		21 30
Attenborough	d		21 33
Long Eaton	d		21 41
Spondon	d		
Derby 6	a	21 30	21 52
	d		21 55
Duffield	d		22 02
Belper	d		22 07
Ambergate	d		22 13
Whatstandwell	d		22 17
Cromford	d		22 23
Matlock Bath	d		22 25
Matlock	a		22 29

A To Birmingham New Street
B To Cardiff Central
C From Newark Castle
D To Sheffield
E From Grantham

For connections from St Pancras International refer to Table T053

Table T056-R

Mondays to Fridays
16 December to 15 May

Matlock - Derby - Nottingham

Miles			XC	EM	EM	EM	EM	XC	EM	EM	XC	XC	EM	EM	XC	XC	EM	XC	XC	EM	XC	XC	EM
			◇				◇1	1			1	1	◇		1	1		◇1	1		◇1	◇1	
						A		B			B	B	C		B	B	C	D	B	C	D	B	C
							🍴					🍴				🍴			🍴			🍴	
0	**Matlock**	d			06 21								07 37				08 37			09 37			10 37
1	Matlock Bath	d			06 23								07 39				08 39			09 39			10 39
1¾	Cromford	d			06 26								07 42				08 42			09 42			10 42
4¼	Whatstandwell	d			06 31								07 47				08 47			09 47			10 47
6¾	Ambergate	d			06 36				06 57				07 52				08 52			09 52			10 52
9½	Belper	d			06 42				07 03				07 59				08 59			09 59			10 59
12	Duffield	d			06 46				07 07				08 03				09 03			10 03			11 03
17¼	**Derby** 6	a			06 55				07 16				08 10				09 10			10 10			11 10
—		d	06 00	06 27			07 00	07 09		07 36	07 44	08 08	08 12	08 27	08 40	09 08	09 13	09 40	09 58	10 13	10 40	10 56	11 12
19¾	Spondon	d		06 32				07 13			07 48		08 16										
25¾	Long Eaton	d		06 39				07 20		07 46	07 55	08 17	08 23	08 37	08 49		09 24	09 49		10 22	10 49		11 22
28¾	Attenborough	d		06 47		07 03		07 27		07 54			08 30	08 44	08 59		09 32			10 30			11 29
30	Beeston	d	06 14	06 50		07 06		07 31		07 57	08 04	08 26	08 34	08 47	09 03		09 35	09 57		10 33	10 57		11 32
33¼	**Nottingham** 8	a	06 20	06 59		07 16	07 19	07 37		08 06	08 13	08 33	08 44	08 56	09 09	09 31	09 41	10 03	10 24	10 40	11 03	11 24	11 39

		XC	XC	EM	XC	XC	EM	XC	XC	EM	XC	XC	EM	XC	XC	EM	XC	XC	EM	XC	EM	EM	XC
		◇1	◇1		◇1	◇1		◇1	1		◇1	1		◇1	1		◇1	◇1		◇1			1
		D	B	C	D	B	C	D	B	C	D	B	C	D	B	C	D	B		D		F	B
			🍴		🍴	🍴					🍴			🍴			🍴						
Matlock	d			11 37			12 37			13 37			14 37			15 37			16 37				
Matlock Bath	d			11 39			12 39			13 39			14 39			15 39			16 39				
Cromford	d			11 42			12 42			13 42			14 42			15 42			16 42				
Whatstandwell	d			11 47			12 47			13 47			14 47			15 47			16 47				
Ambergate	d			11 52			12 52			13 52			14 52			15 53			16 52				
Belper	d			11 59			12 59			13 59			14 59			15 59			16 59			17 54	
Duffield	d			12 03			13 03			14 03			15 03			16 04			17 03				
Derby 6	a			12 10			13 10			14 10			15 10			16 11			17 10				
	d	11 40	12 08	12 12	12 40	13 08	13 13	13 40	14 08	14 12	14 40	15 08	15 12	15 40	15 59	16 11	16 40	17 08	17 12	17 40	17 54	18 03	18 08
Spondon	d						13 17												17 16		17 59		
Long Eaton	d	11 49		12 21	12 49		13 24	13 49		14 21	14 49		15 23	15 49		16 21	16 49	17 17	17 23	17 49	18 06		18 17
Attenborough	d			12 30			13 32			14 29			15 31			16 29			17 31		18 17		
Beeston	d	12 01		12 33	12 57		13 35	13 57		14 32	14 57		15 34	15 57		16 32	16 57	17 25	17 34	17 57	18 20		18 25
Nottingham 8	a	12 07	12 28	12 40	13 03	13 28	13 41	14 03	14 28	14 39	15 03	15 28	15 40	16 03	16 24	16 39	17 03	17 31	17 40	18 03	18 26		18 31

		EM	XC	XC	EM	XC	XC	EM	XC	EM	NT	XC	EM	XC	EM	XC
			◇1	1		◇1	1		◇1		◇	◇1		1		1
		C	D	B		D	B		D		E	D		B		B
Matlock	d	17 37			18 37			19 37		20 37			21 41		22 56	
Matlock Bath	d	17 39			18 39			19 39		20 39			21 43		22 58	
Cromford	d	17 42			18 42			19 42		20 42			21 46		23 01	
Whatstandwell	d	17 47			18 47			19 47		20 47			21 51		23 06	
Ambergate	d	17 52			18 52			19 52		20 52			21 56		23 10	
Belper	d	17 59			18 59			19 59		20 59			22 03		23 17	
Duffield	d	18 03			19 03			20 03		21 03			22 07		23 21	
Derby 6	a	18 10			19 10			20 10		21 10			22 14		23 28	
	d	18 11	18 40	19 08	19 13	19 40	19 58	20 15	20 41	21 13	21 42	21 46		22 59	23 29	23 57
Spondon	d	18 18										21 50		23 03		
Long Eaton	d	18 25	18 49	19 17	19 22	19 49		20 24	20 50	21 24		21 57		23 10	23 38	
Attenborough	d	18 34			19 31			20 33		21 32		22 04		23 17	23 48	
Beeston	d	18 37	18 57	19 25	19 34	19 57		20 36	20 58	21 35		22 07		23 20	23 51	
Nottingham 8	a	18 46	19 05	19 31	19 44	20 03	20 21	20 43	21 04	21 41	22 00	22 13		23 26	00 01	00 16

Saturdays
21 December to 16 May

		EM	EM	EM	XC	EM	XC	XC	EM	XC	XC	EM	XC	XC	EM	XC	XC	EM	XC	XC	EM	XC	XC
					1		1	1		1	1		◇1	1		◇1	1		◇1	1		◇1	1
				A	B		B	B	C	B	B	C	D	B	C	D	B	C	D	B	C	D	B
								🍴			🍴			🍴			🍴			🍴		🍴	🍴
Matlock	d		06 21						07 37			08 37			09 37			10 37			11 37		
Matlock Bath	d		06 23						07 39			08 39			09 39			10 39			11 39		
Cromford	d		06 26						07 42			08 42			09 42			10 42			11 42		
Whatstandwell	d		06 31						07 47			08 47			09 47			10 47			11 47		
Ambergate	d		06 36						07 52			08 52			09 52			10 52			11 52		
Belper	d		06 43						07 59			08 59			09 59			10 59			11 59		
Duffield	d		06 47						08 03			09 03			10 03			11 03			12 03		
Derby 6	a		06 55						08 10			09 10			10 10			11 10			12 10		
	d	06 12			07 08	07 13	07 43	08 08	08 13	08 40	09 08	09 11	09 40	10 08	10 12	10 40	10 58	11 12	11 40	11 59	12 12	12 40	12 58
Spondon	d	06 16			07 12		07 47		08 18														
Long Eaton	d	06 22			07 19	07 23	07 54	08 17	08 25	08 49		09 21	09 49		10 24	10 49		11 22	11 49		12 21	12 49	
Attenborough	d	06 31		07 03	07 26	07 31			08 30	08 55		09 29			10 32			11 29			12 29		
Beeston	d	06 34		07 06	07 29	07 34	08 02	08 25	08 33	08 59		09 32	09 57		10 35	10 57		11 32	11 57		12 32	12 57	
Nottingham 8	a	06 43		07 15	07 36	07 44	08 09	08 31	08 46	09 05	09 30	09 39	10 03	10 28	10 41	11 03	11 22	11 39	12 03	12 22	12 39	13 03	13 22

A From Leicester
B From Birmingham New Street
C To Newark Castle
D From Cardiff Central
E From Leeds
F From Sheffield to St Pancras

For connections to St Pancras International refer to Table T053

Table T056-R

Saturdays
21 December to 16 May

Matlock - Derby - Nottingham

		EM	XC	XC	EM	XC	XC	EM	XC	XC	EM	XC	XC	EM	XC	XC	EM	XC	XC	EM	XC	XC
			◇1	1		◇1	1		◇1	1		◇1	1		◇1	1		◇1	1		◇1	1
		A	B	C	A	B	C	A	B	C	A	B	C	A	B	C	A	B	C		B	C
						🍴			🍴			🍴										
Matlock	d	12 37			13 37			14 37			15 37			16 37			17 37			18 37		
Matlock Bath	d	12 39			13 39			14 39			15 39			16 39			17 39			18 39		
Cromford	d	12 42			13 42			14 42			15 42			16 42			17 42			18 42		
Whatstandwell	d	12 47			13 47			14 47			15 47			16 47			17 47			18 47		
Ambergate	d	12 52			13 52			14 52			15 52			16 52			17 52			18 52		
Belper	d	12 59			13 59			14 59			15 59			16 59			17 59			18 59		
Duffield	d	13 03			14 03			15 03			16 03			17 03			18 03			19 03		
Derby 6	a	13 10			14 10			15 10			16 10			17 10			18 10			19 10		
	d	13 12	13 40	13 58	14 12	14 40	15 08	15 12	15 40	16 08	16 11	16 40	17 08	17 10	17 40	18 08	18 11	18 40	18 56	19 12	19 40	20 08
Spondon	d	13 16												17 15			18 18					
Long Eaton	d	13 23	13 49		14 21	14 49		15 24	15 49		16 21	16 49	17 17	17 22	17 49	18 17	18 25	18 49	19 05	19 21	19 49	
Attenborough	d	13 30			14 29			15 32			16 29			17 30			18 32			19 29		
Beeston	d	13 33	13 57		14 32	14 57		15 35	15 57		16 32	16 57	17 25	17 33	17 57	18 25	18 36	18 57	19 13	19 32	19 57	
Nottingham 8	a	13 40	14 03	14 22	14 39	15 03	15 28	15 41	16 03	16 28	16 39	17 03	17 31	17 39	18 03	18 31	18 45	19 03	19 22	19 39	20 03	20 28

		EM	XC	EM	NT	XC	EM	XC	EM
			◇1		◇	◇1		◇1	
			B		D	B		B	
Matlock	d	19 37		20 37			21 41		22 55
Matlock Bath	d	19 39		20 39			21 43		22 57
Cromford	d	19 42		20 42			21 46		23 00
Whatstandwell	d	19 47		20 47			21 51		23 05
Ambergate	d	19 52		20 52			21 56		23 10
Belper	d	19 59		20 59			22 03		23 17
Duffield	d	20 03		21 03			22 07		23 21
Derby 6	a	20 10		21 10			22 14		23 28
	d	20 12	20 40	21 12	21 42	21 46		22 59	23 29
Spondon	d					21 50		23 03	
Long Eaton	d	20 21	20 49	21 21		21 57		23 10	23 38
Attenborough	d	20 30		21 30		22 04		23 17	23 46
Beeston	d	20 33	20 57	21 33		22 07		23 20	23 49
Nottingham 8	a	20 39	21 03	21 39	22 00	22 13		23 27	23 58

Sundays
15 December to 10 May

		EM	EM	XC	EM	XC	XC	EM	XC	EM	XC	EM	XC	EM	XC	EM	XC	EM	XC	EM	XC	EM	EM
				◇1		◇1	◇1		◇1		◇1		◇1		◇1		◇1		◇1		◇1		
				C		B	B		B		B		B		B		B		B		B		
				🍴		🍴	🍴		🍴		🍴		🍴										
Matlock	d	08 38	10 38		12 38			14 41				16 38		17 42		18 38				20 38			22 44
Matlock Bath	d	08 40	10 40		12 40			14 43				16 40		17 44		18 40				20 40			22 46
Cromford	d	08 43	10 43		12 43			14 46				16 43		17 47		18 43				20 43			22 49
Whatstandwell	d	08 48	10 48		12 48			14 51				16 48		17 52		18 48				20 48			22 54
Ambergate	d	08 54	10 54		12 54			14 56				16 54		17 58		18 54				20 55			23 00
Belper	d	09 01	11 00		13 00			15 03				17 01		18 05		19 00				21 00			23 07
Duffield	d	09 05	11 04		13 04			15 07				17 05		18 09		19 04				21 04			23 11
Derby 6	a	09 12	11 11		13 11			15 14				17 12		18 16		19 11				21 12			23 18
	d	09 14	11 13	12 40	13 13	13 38	14 40	15 15	15 40	16 14	16 39	17 14	17 39	18 17	18 40	19 14	19 39	20 14	20 38	21 13	21 40	22 21	
Spondon	d																						
Long Eaton	d	09 24	11 24		13 23			15 24		16 23		17 24		18 27		19 23		20 23		21 22		22 31	
Attenborough	d	09 31	11 31		13 31			15 32		16 31		17 31		18 35		19 35		20 31		21 30		22 38	
Beeston	d	09 34	11 34		13 34			15 35		16 34		17 34		18 38		19 38		20 34		21 33		22 41	
Nottingham 8	a	09 41	11 41	13 00	13 41	13 58	15 00	15 41	16 00	16 43	16 59	17 44	17 59	18 45	19 00	19 44	20 00	20 41	21 00	21 39	22 00	22 48	

A To Newark Castle
B From Cardiff Central
C From Birmingham New Street
D From Leeds

For connections to St Pancras International refer to Table T053

Table T057-F

Mondays to Fridays

16 December to 15 May

Nottingham and Derby - Birmingham - Bristol and Cardiff

Miles	Miles				AW	XC	XC	XC	AW	XC	XC	XC	XC	AW	XC	XC	XC	XC	XC	XC	XC	XC	XC	XC
					◇	◇■1	◇■1	◇■1	◇	◇■1	◇■1	◇■1	◇■1	◇	◇■1	◇■1	◇■1	◇■1	◇■1	■1	◇■1	◇■1	■1	◇■1
					A			B	A	C	D	E	F	A	G	H		I	F		J	D	K	L
								⚒		⚒	⚒		⚒			⚒	⚒	⚒	⚒		⚒	⚒	⚒	⚒
0	—	**Nottingham** 8	56 ⇌	d							06 00				06 43		07 05			07 37		08 09		
3¼	—	Beeston	56	d							06 06				06 49		07 11			07 42		08 15		
4¾	—	Attenborough	56	d							06 09						07 14							
8	—	Long Eaton	56	d							06 18						07 22			07 52		08 24		
16	—	**Derby** 6	56	d						06 10	06 36	06 50			07 13	07 27	07 36	07 49		08 06	08 28	08 38	08 53	
22¼	—	Willington		d													07 44							
27	—	Burton-on-Trent		d						06 20	06 48	07 00			07 23	07 38	07 50	08 00		08 18	08 39	08 50		
40	—	Tamworth		d						06 31	07 01	07 10			07 34	07 50	08 03	08 10		08 30	08 50	09 02		
41¾	—	Wilnecote		d							07 05						08 07			08 34				
49½	—	Water Orton		d																08 43				
57¼	0	**Birmingham New Street** 12		a						06 52	07 25	07 28			07 54	08 08	08 25	08 28		08 55	09 08	09 24	09 27	
—	—			d		05 00	05 37	06 42		07 12	07 30		07 42			08 12	08 30		08 42		09 12	09 30		09 42
58¾	2½	University		a							07 36						08 36					09 36		
—	—	Worcestershire Parkway		d							07 58						08 58					10 00		
95½	40¾	Ashchurch for Tewkesbury		d			06 30																	
102¾	48	Cheltenham Spa 4		d	05 37	06 05	06 39	07 26	07 46	07 52	08 15		08 26	08 46		08 52	09 15		09 29		09 52	10 16		10 28
109¼	—	Gloucester 7	134	a	05 49	06 13	06 49		07 57		08 25			08 57			09 26					10 25		
—	—			d	05 49	06 15	06 51		07 58		08 26			08 57			09 27					10 26		
—	87½	Bristol Parkway 7	134	a				07 54		08 25			08 54			09 20			09 59		10 20			10 58
—	93¾	**Bristol Temple Meads** 10	134	a				08 05		08 38			09 05			09 40			10 09		10 31			11 08
128¾	—	Lydney		a	06 08	06 34	07 10		08 16					09 16								10 45		
136½	—	Chepstow		a	06 18	06 43	07 19		08 26		08 52			09 25			09 53							
143¼	—	Caldicot		a	06 26	06 52	07 28		08 34					09 34										
144	—	Severn Tunnel Jn	132	a	06 29	06 57	07 31		08 37					09 38										
154	—	Newport (South Wales)	132	a	06 42	07 09	07 42		08 50		09 10			09 50			10 11					11 11		
165¾	—	**Cardiff Central** 7	132	a	06 57	07 22	08 00		09 07		09 27			10 06			10 25					11 25		

			AW	XC	XC	XC	XC	XC	AW	XC	XC	XC	XC	XC	XC	XC	XC	XC	XC	AW	XC	XC	XC	AW
			◇	■1	◇■1	◇■1	◇■1	◇■1	◇	■1	◇■1	◇■1	◇■1	◇■1	■1	◇■1	◇■1	◇■1	◇■1	◇	■1	◇■1	◇■1	◇
			A		M		N	F			O		P	Q		R		N	F	A		S		
					⚒	⚒	⚒	⚒			⚒	⚒	⚒	⚒		⚒	⚒	⚒	⚒			⚒	⚒	
Nottingham 8	56 ⇌	d		08 39		09 07				09 41		10 07			10 41		11 07				11 41		12 07	
Beeston	56	d		08 44		09 12						10 12					11 12						12 12	
Attenborough	56	d																						
Long Eaton	56	d		08 54		09 24						10 24					11 22						12 22	
Derby 6	56	d		09 10	09 29	09 38	09 53			10 10	10 30	10 38	10 53		11 10	11 32	11 38	11 53			12 10	12 30	12 38	
Willington		d				09 46																		
Burton-on-Trent		d		09 22	09 40	09 52				10 21		10 50			11 21		11 49				12 21		12 49	
Tamworth		d		09 34		10 03				10 33	10 50	11 02			11 33		12 02				12 33	12 50	13 02	
Wilnecote		d		09 38						10 37					11 37						12 37			
Water Orton		d																						
Birmingham New Street 12		a		09 55	10 06	10 24	10 27			10 55	11 08	11 24	11 27		11 55	12 06	12 24	12 27			12 55	13 08	13 24	
		d			10 12	10 30		10 42			11 12	11 30		11 42		12 12	12 30		12 42			13 12	13 30	
University		a				10 36						11 36					12 36						13 36	
Worcestershire Parkway		d				10 58						11 58					12 58						13 58	
Ashchurch for Tewkesbury		d																						
Cheltenham Spa 4		d	10 40		10 52	11 15		11 28	11 46		11 52	12 14		12 26		12 52	13 15		13 30	13 45		13 52	14 15	
Gloucester 7	134	a	10 51			11 23			11 58			12 23					13 25			13 56			14 23	
		d	10 53			11 25			11 59			12 25					13 27			13 59			14 25	14 48
Bristol Parkway 7	134	a			11 20			11 58			12 20			12 54		13 20			13 58			14 21		
Bristol Temple Meads 10	134	a			11 31			12 08			12 32			13 04		13 32			14 08			14 32		
Lydney		a	11 12						12 18								13 46			14 17				15 07
Chepstow		a	11 21			11 51			12 27			12 51								14 27			14 51	15 16
Caldicot		a	11 30						12 36											14 35				15 25
Severn Tunnel Jn	132	a	11 33						12 39											14 38				15 28
Newport (South Wales)	132	a	11 46			12 09			12 52			13 10					14 11			14 51			15 10	15 41
Cardiff Central 7	132	a	12 15			12 22			13 07			13 26					14 25			15 07			15 23	15 55

- **A** To Maesteg
- **B** To Paignton
- **C** To Plymouth. ⚒ from Birmingham New Street
- **D** ⚒ from Birmingham New Street
- **E** From Sheffield to Reading
- **F** From Manchester Piccadilly
- **G** To Bournemouth
- **H** From Leeds to Plymouth
- **I** From York to Southampton Central
- **J** From York to Plymouth
- **K** From Newcastle to Reading
- **L** From Manchester Piccadilly to Paignton
- **M** From Newcastle to Plymouth
- **N** From Newcastle to Southampton Central
- **O** From Edinburgh to Plymouth
- **P** From Edinburgh to Reading
- **Q** From Manchester Piccadilly to Exeter St Davids
- **R** From Glasgow Central to Plymouth
- **S** From Dundee to Plymouth

Trains between Gloucester & Cheltenham are shown on Table T058

Trains between Birmingham & Bromsgrove are shown on Table T069

Table T057-F

Mondays to Fridays

16 December to 15 May

Nottingham and Derby - Birmingham - Bristol and Cardiff

			XC	XC	XC	XC	XC	XC	XC	XC	XC	XC	XC	XC	AW	XC	XC	XC	XC	XC	AW	XC	XC	XC
			◇■1	◇■1	■1	◇■1	◇■1	◇■1	◇■1	■1	◇■1	◇■1	◇■1	◇■1	◇	■1	◇■1	◇■1	◇■1	◇■1	◇	■1	◇■1	◇■1
			A	B		C		D	B		E		A	F	G		H		I	B	G		E	
			⚒	⚒		⚒	⚒	⚒	⚒	⚒	⚒	⚒	⚒	⚒			⚒		⚒	⚒		⚒	⚒	
Nottingham 8	56 ⇌	d			12 41		13 07			13 41		14 07				14 41		15 07				15 41		16 07
Beeston	56	d					13 12					14 12						15 12						16 12
Attenborough	56	d																						
Long Eaton	56	d					13 22					14 22						15 22						16 22
Derby 6	56	d	12 53		13 10	13 30	13 38	13 53		14 10	14 30	14 38	14 53			15 10	15 28	15 38	15 52			16 10	16 30	16 38
Willington		d			13 17											15 17								
Burton-on-Trent		d			13 24	13 41	13 49			14 21		14 50				15 24	15 38	15 49				16 21		16 49
Tamworth		d			13 35		14 03			14 33	14 48	15 04				15 35		16 02				16 33	16 49	17 02
Wilnecote		d								14 37												16 37		
Water Orton		d																						
Birmingham New Street 12		a	13 27		13 55	14 05	14 24	14 27		14 55	15 05	15 24	15 27			15 55	16 04	16 24	16 27			16 55	17 06	17 24
		d		13 42		14 12	14 30		14 42		15 12	15 30		15 42			16 12	16 30		16 42			17 12	17 30
University		a					14 36					15 36						16 36						17 36
Worcestershire Parkway		d					14 58					15 58						16 58						17 58
Ashchurch for Tewkesbury		d																17 09						18 09
Cheltenham Spa 4		d		14 26		14 52	15 15		15 28		15 52	16 15		16 28	16 45		16 52	17 18		17 30	17 45		17 52	18 18
Gloucester 7	134	a					15 25					16 24			16 59			17 28			17 59			18 27
		d					15 26					16 25			17 00			17 30			18 00			18 31
Bristol Parkway 7	134	a		14 54		15 20			15 55		16 21			16 58			17 20			17 58			18 20	
Bristol Temple Meads 10	134	a		15 04		15 34			16 06		16 32			17 08			17 32			18 08			18 33	
Lydney		a										16 44			17 19			17 49			18 19			
Chepstow		a					15 52					16 54			17 28						18 28			
Caldicot		a													17 37						18 37			
Severn Tunnel Jn	132	a													17 40						18 40			
Newport (South Wales)	132	a					16 10					17 12			17 53			18 15			18 53			19 14
Cardiff Central 7	132	a					16 29					17 25			18 11			18 29			19 08			19 28

			XC	XC	AW	XC	XC	XC	XC	XC	AW	XC	XC	XC	XC	XC	XC	XC	XC FO	XC FX	XC	XC	XC	XC
			◇■1	◇■1	◇	■1	◇■1	◇■1	◇■1	◇■1	◇	■1	◇■1	◇■1	◇■1	◇■1	■1	◇■1	◇■1	◇■1	◇■1	◇■1	■1	◇■1
			A	J	G		K		A	L	G		C		A	M		K			D	J		N
			⚒	⚒		⚒	⚒		⚒	⚒		⚒	⚒		⚒	⚒		⚒			⚒			⚒
Nottingham 8	56 ⇌	d				16 41		17 07				17 41		18 07			18 41		19 07	19 07			19 36	
Beeston	56	d						17 12						18 12					19 12	19 12			19 43	
Attenborough	56	d																					19 46	
Long Eaton	56	d						17 23				17 53		18 26					19 24	19 24			19 54	
Derby 6	56	d	16 53			17 10	17 30	17 38	17 53			18 13	18 29	18 40	18 53		19 10	19 31	19 38	19 38	19 53		20 10	20 31
Willington		d				17 17						18 20												
Burton-on-Trent		d				17 24	17 41	17 49				18 27		18 51			19 21	19 41	19 49	19 49			20 22	
Tamworth		d				17 35		18 00				18 38	18 50	19 03			19 33		20 03	20 03			20 33	20 50
Wilnecote		d						18 04									19 37						20 37	
Water Orton		d																						
Birmingham New Street 12		a	17 27			17 55	18 05	18 24	18 27			18 57	19 08	19 24	19 27		19 55	20 07	20 24	20 24	20 27		20 55	21 06
		d		17 42			18 12	18 30		18 42			19 12	19 30		19 42		20 12	20 30	20 30		20 42		21 12
University		a						18 36						19 36					20 36	20 36				
Worcestershire Parkway		d						18 58						19 58					20 58	20 58				
Ashchurch for Tewkesbury		d																						
Cheltenham Spa 4		d		18 26	18 45		18 52	19 15		19 28	19 46		19 52	20 15		20 26		20 53	21 15	21 15		21 26		21 52
Gloucester 7	134	a			18 58		19 01	19 23			19 58			20 23					21 23	21 23				22 01
		d			19 00		19 08	19 30			20 00			20 25					21 25	21 25				22 05
Bristol Parkway 7	134	a		18 55			19 34			19 56			20 20			20 54		21 21				21 55		22 31
Bristol Temple Meads 10	134	a		19 05			19 45			20 07			20 31			21 04		21 36				22 05		22 44
Lydney		a			19 19						20 19								21 44	21 44				
Chepstow		a			19 29						20 28								21 53	21 53				
Caldicot		a			19 37						20 37								22 02	22 02				
Severn Tunnel Jn	132	a			19 40					20 35	20 40								22 05	22 05				
Newport (South Wales)	132	a			19 54			20 12		20 46	20 54			21 10					22 16	22 17				
Cardiff Central 7	132	a			20 10			20 27		21 02	21 09			21 27					22 30	22 36				

- **A** From Newcastle to Reading
- **B** From Manchester Piccadilly to Exeter St Davids
- **C** From Glasgow Central to Plymouth
- **D** From Newcastle to Southampton Central
- **E** From Glasgow Central to Penzance
- **F** From Manchester Piccadilly to Paignton
- **G** To Maesteg
- **H** From Aberdeen to Penzance
- **I** From Newcastle to Guildford
- **J** From Manchester Piccadilly
- **K** From Edinburgh to Plymouth
- **L** From Manchester Piccadilly. ⚒ to Bristol Temple Meads
- **M** From Manchester Piccadilly to Plymouth
- **N** From Glasgow Central. ⚒ to Birmingham New Street

Trains between Gloucester & Cheltenham are shown on Table T058

Trains between Birmingham & Bromsgrove are shown on Table T069

Table T057-F

Mondays to Fridays

16 December to 15 May

Nottingham and Derby - Birmingham - Bristol and Cardiff

		XC ◇1 A ⊥	XC 1 B	XC 1	XC ◇1 C	AW FO ◇	XC ◇1 A	XC 1	XC ◇1 D	AW FX ◇
Nottingham 8	56 ⛴ d			20 40				21 38		
Beeston	56 d			20 46				21 43		
Attenborough	56 d							21 46		
Long Eaton	56 d			20 55				21 55		
Derby 6	56 d	20 53		21 10	21 31		22 02	22 12	22 46	
Willington	d			21 17						
Burton-on-Trent	d			21 24	21 41			22 23	22 56	
Tamworth	d			21 35	21 51			22 34	23 07	
Wilnecote	d			21 39				22 38		
Water Orton	d									
Birmingham New Street 12	a	21 29		21 58	22 09		22 51	23 02	23 26	
	d		21 30		22 12					
University	a		21 36							
Worcestershire Parkway	d		21 58							
Ashchurch for Tewkesbury	d		22 11							
Cheltenham Spa 4	d		22 22		22 52	22 58				22 58
Gloucester 7	134 a		22 32			23 10				23 10
	d					23 10				23 10
Bristol Parkway 7	134 a				23 20					
Bristol Temple Meads 10	134 a				23 30					
Lydney	a					23 29				23 29
Chepstow	a					23 39				23 39
Caldicot	a					23 47				23 47
Severn Tunnel Jn	132 a					23 50				23 50
Newport (South Wales)	132 a					00 07				00 13
Cardiff Central 7	132 a					00 22				00 34

Saturdays

21 December to 16 May

		AW ◇ E	XC ◇1	XC ◇1	XC ◇1 F ⊥	AW ◇	XC ◇1 G ⊥	XC ◇1 H ⊥	XC ◇1 I	XC ◇1 J ⊥	AW ◇ E	XC ◇1 K	XC ◇1 L ⊥	XC ◇1	XC ◇1 M ⊥	XC ◇1 J ⊥	XC 1	XC ◇1 N ⊥	XC ◇1 H ⊥	XC ◇ O	XC ◇1 P ⊥	AW ◇ E	XC 1
Nottingham 8	56 ⛴ d							06 00				06 44		07 00			07 37		08 06				08 41
Beeston	56 d							06 06				06 50		07 06			07 43		08 12				
Attenborough	56 d							06 09						07 09									
Long Eaton	56 d							06 17						07 17			07 52		08 22				
Derby 6	56 d						06 10	06 36	06 49			07 12	07 27	07 36	07 49		08 06	08 28	08 38	08 53			09 10
Willington	d													07 43									
Burton-on-Trent	d						06 20	06 48	06 59			07 22	07 38	07 50	07 59		08 18	08 38	08 49				09 22
Tamworth	d						06 31	07 01	07 09			07 33	07 49	08 02	08 10		08 30	08 49	09 03				09 34
Wilnecote	d							07 05						08 05			08 34						09 38
Water Orton	d																08 43						
Birmingham New Street 12	a						06 50	07 25	07 28			07 52	08 08	08 25	08 28		08 55	09 08	09 25	09 28			09 55
	d		05 00	05 42	06 42		07 12	07 30		07 42			08 12	08 30		08 42		09 12	09 30		09 42		
University	a							07 36						08 36					09 36				
Worcestershire Parkway	d							07 58						08 58					09 58				
Ashchurch for Tewkesbury	d			06 33																			
Cheltenham Spa 4	d		06 03	06 42	07 26	07 45	07 52	08 15		08 26	08 45		08 52	09 15		09 29		09 52	10 15		10 26	10 40	
Gloucester 7	134 a		06 11	06 52		07 57		08 23			08 59			09 23					10 23			10 52	
	d	05 50	06 15	06 54		07 57		08 25			08 59			09 25					10 25			10 53	
Bristol Parkway 7	134 a				07 54		08 20			08 54			09 21			09 57		10 20			10 54		
Bristol Temple Meads 10	134 a				08 04		08 36			09 05			09 34			10 08		10 36			11 09		
Lydney	a	06 09	06 34	07 13		08 16					09 18								10 44			11 12	
Chepstow	a	06 18	06 43	07 22		08 26		08 51			09 28			09 51								11 21	
Caldicot	a	06 27	06 52	07 31		08 34					09 36											11 30	
Severn Tunnel Jn	132 a	06 30	06 55	07 34		08 37					09 39											11 33	
Newport (South Wales)	132 a	06 43	07 06	07 49		08 51		09 09			09 53			10 14					11 10			11 47	
Cardiff Central 7	132 a	07 01	07 20	08 06		09 07		09 23			10 14			10 29					11 25			12 01	

A From Newcastle
B From Leicester
C From Edinburgh
D From Glasgow Central
E To Maesteg
F To Paignton
G To Plymouth. ⊥ from Birmingham New Street
H ⊥ from Birmingham New Street
I To Reading
J From Manchester Piccadilly
K To Bournemouth
L From Leeds to Plymouth
M From York to Southampton Central
N From York to Plymouth
O From Newcastle to Reading
P From Manchester Piccadilly to Paignton

Trains between Gloucester & Cheltenham are shown on Table T058

Trains between Birmingham & Bromsgrove are shown on Table T069

Table T057-F

Saturdays

21 December to 16 May

Nottingham and Derby - Birmingham - Bristol and Cardiff

		XC ◇1 A ⊥	XC ◇1 ⊥	XC ◇1 B ⊥	XC ◇1 C ⊥	AW ◇	XC 1	XC ◇1 D ⊥	XC ◇1 ⊥	XC ◇1 E ⊥	XC ◇1 C ⊥	XC 1	XC ◇1 F ⊥	XC ◇1 ⊥	XC ◇1 B ⊥	XC ◇1 C ⊥	AW ◇ G	XC 1	XC ◇1 H ⊥	XC ◇1 ⊥	AW ◇ I ⊥	XC ◇1 J ⊥
Nottingham 8	56 ⛴ d		09 06				09 41		10 06			10 41		11 06				11 41		12 06		
Beeston	56 d		09 12						10 12					11 12						12 12		
Attenborough	56 d																					
Long Eaton	56 d		09 22						10 22					11 22						12 22		
Derby 6	56 d	09 31	09 38	09 53			10 10	10 30	10 38	10 52		11 10	11 31	11 38	11 53			12 10	12 30	12 38		12 57
Willington	d		09 45																			
Burton-on-Trent	d	09 42	09 51				10 21		10 49			11 21	11 42	11 49				12 21		12 49		
Tamworth	d		10 03				10 33	10 50	11 02			11 33		12 02				12 33	12 49	13 02		
Wilnecote	d						10 37					11 37						12 37				
Water Orton	d																					
Birmingham New Street 12	a	10 05	10 24	10 27			10 55	11 08	11 25	11 28		11 55	12 08	12 24	12 27			12 55	13 08	13 24		13 28
	d	10 12	10 30		10 42			11 12	11 30		11 42		12 12	12 30		12 42			13 12	13 30		
University	a		10 36						11 36					12 36						13 36		
Worcestershire Parkway	d		10 58						11 58					12 58						13 58		
Ashchurch for Tewkesbury	d																					
Cheltenham Spa 4	d	10 52	11 15		11 26	11 46		11 52	12 15		12 26		12 52	13 15		13 30	13 45		13 52	14 15		
Gloucester 7	134 a		11 23			11 57			12 23					13 23			13 57			14 23		
	d		11 25			11 58			12 25					13 25			13 58			14 25	14 42	
Bristol Parkway 7	134 a	11 21			11 54			12 25			12 54		13 21			13 59			14 21			
Bristol Temple Meads 10	134 a	11 36			12 05			12 38			13 05		13 34			14 09			14 36			
Lydney	a					12 17								13 44			14 17				15 01	
Chepstow	a		11 51			12 26			12 51								14 26			14 51	15 10	
Caldicot	a					12 35											14 35				15 19	
Severn Tunnel Jn	132 a					12 38											14 38				15 23	
Newport (South Wales)	132 a		12 12			12 52			13 14					14 12			14 51			15 10	15 37	
Cardiff Central 7	132 a		12 26			13 06			13 27					14 25			15 09			15 27	15 51	

		XC ◇1 K ⊥	XC 1	XC ◇1 F ⊥	XC ◇1 ⊥	XC ◇1 B ⊥	XC ◇1 C ⊥	XC 1 ⊥	XC ◇1 L ⊥	XC ◇1 ⊥	XC ◇1 J ⊥	XC ◇1 M ⊥	AW ◇ G	XC 1	XC ◇1 N ⊥	XC ◇1	XC ◇1 O ⊥	XC ◇1 C ⊥	AW ◇ G	XC 1 ⊥	XC ◇1 L ⊥	XC ◇1	XC ◇1 J ⊥
Nottingham 8	56 ⛴ d		12 41		13 06			13 41		14 06				14 41		15 06				15 41		16 06	
Beeston	56 d				13 12					14 12						15 12						16 12	
Attenborough	56 d																						
Long Eaton	56 d				13 22					14 22						15 22						16 22	
Derby 6	56 d		13 10	13 28	13 38	13 52		14 10	14 30	14 38	14 53			15 10	15 28	15 38	15 52			16 10	16 31	16 38	16 52
Willington	d		13 17											15 17									
Burton-on-Trent	d		13 24	13 38	13 49			14 21		14 49				15 24	15 38	15 49				16 21		16 49	
Tamworth	d		13 35		14 02			14 33	14 50	15 02				15 35		16 02				16 33	16 50	17 02	
Wilnecote	d							14 37												16 37			
Water Orton	d																						
Birmingham New Street 12	a		13 55	14 03	14 24	14 27		14 55	15 08	15 24	15 27			15 55	16 03	16 24	16 27			16 55	17 06	17 25	17 28
	d	13 42		14 12	14 30		14 42		15 12	15 30		15 42			16 12	16 30		16 42			17 12	17 30	
University	a				14 36					15 36						16 36						17 36	
Worcestershire Parkway	d				14 58					15 58						16 58						17 58	
Ashchurch for Tewkesbury	d																					18 09	
Cheltenham Spa 4	d	14 26		14 52	15 15		15 31		15 52	16 15		16 26	16 45		16 52	17 15		17 26	17 35		17 52	18 18	
Gloucester 7	134 a				15 23					16 23			16 57			17 23			17 46			18 27	
	d				15 25					16 25			16 58			17 25			17 46			18 28	
Bristol Parkway 7	134 a	14 57		15 21			15 59		16 21			16 54			17 21			17 54			18 29		
Bristol Temple Meads 10	134 a	15 07		15 36			16 09		16 34			17 04			17 35			18 04			18 42		
Lydney	a									16 44			17 17			17 44			18 05				
Chepstow	a				15 51					16 53			17 26						18 14				
Caldicot	a												17 35						18 23				
Severn Tunnel Jn	132 a												17 38						18 26				
Newport (South Wales)	132 a				16 11					17 12			17 51			18 11			18 38			19 11	
Cardiff Central 7	132 a				16 25					17 26			18 09			18 26			18 52			19 24	

A From Newcastle to Plymouth
B From Newcastle to Southampton Central
C From Manchester Piccadilly
D From Edinburgh to Plymouth
E From Edinburgh to Reading
F From Glasgow Central to Plymouth
G To Maesteg
H From Dundee to Plymouth
I To Fishguard Harbour
J From Newcastle to Reading
K From Manchester Piccadilly to Exeter St Davids
L From Glasgow Central to Penzance
M From Manchester Piccadilly to Paignton
N From Aberdeen to Penzance
O From Newcastle to Guildford

Trains between Gloucester & Cheltenham are shown on Table T058

Trains between Birmingham & Bromsgrove are shown on Table T069

Table T057-F

Saturdays

21 December to 16 May

Nottingham and Derby - Birmingham - Bristol and Cardiff

			XC	AW	XC	XC	XC	XC	XC	AW	XC	XC	XC	XC	XC	XC	XC	XC	XC	XC	XC	XC	XC	XC
			◇1	◇	1	◇1	◇1	◇1	◇1	◇	1	◇1	◇1	◇1	◇1	1	◇1	◇1	◇1	◇1	1	◇1	◇1	1
			A	B		C		D	E			F		D	G		C		H	A		I	J	
			✠		✠	✠		✠	✠		✠	✠		✠	✠		✠		✠			✠	✠	
Nottingham 8	56	d			16 41		17 06				17 41		18 06			18 41		19 06			19 29			20 37
Beeston	56	d					17 12						18 12					19 12			19 35			20 43
Attenborough	56	d																			19 38			
Long Eaton	56	d					17 22						18 22					19 22			19 47			20 52
Derby 6	56	d			17 10	17 28	17 38	17 52			18 10	18 28	18 38	18 52		19 10	19 31	19 38	19 53		20 11	20 28	20 53	21 10
Willington		d			17 17						18 17													21 17
Burton-on-Trent		d			17 24	17 41	17 49				18 24		18 49			19 21	19 41	19 50			20 22			21 23
Tamworth		d			17 35		18 01				18 35	18 47	19 02			19 33		20 02			20 34	20 46		21 35
Wilnecote		d					18 05									19 37					20 38			21 39
Water Orton		d																						
Birmingham New Street 12		a			17 55	18 05	18 24	18 27			18 55	19 06	19 24	19 27		19 55	20 05	20 24	20 27		20 55	21 03	21 23	21 56
		d	17 42			18 12	18 30		18 42			19 12	19 30		19 42		20 12	20 30		20 42		21 12		
University		a					18 36						19 36					20 36						
Worcestershire Parkway		d					18 58						19 58					20 58						
Ashchurch for Tewkesbury		d																						
Cheltenham Spa 4		d	18 26	18 45		18 52	19 15		19 31	19 45		19 52	20 15		20 26		20 52	21 15		21 26		21 52		
Gloucester 7	134	a		18 57			19 23			19 57			20 23					21 24				22 01		
		d		18 58			19 25			19 58			20 25					21 26				22 05		
Bristol Parkway 7	134	a	18 54			19 21			19 59			20 22			20 54		21 20			21 57		22 31		
Bristol Temple Meads 10	134	a	19 05			19 36			20 09			20 34			21 04		21 34			22 12		22 41		
Lydney		a		19 17						20 17								21 45						
Chepstow		a		19 26						20 26								21 54						
Caldicot		a		19 35						20 35								22 03						
Severn Tunnel Jn	132	a		19 38					20 35	20 39								22 06						
Newport (South Wales)	132	a		19 51			20 07		20 46	20 52			21 09					22 23						
Cardiff Central 7	132	a		20 08			20 20		21 00	21 07			21 22					22 43						

			XC	XC	XC	XC	AW
			◇1	◇1	1	◇1	◇
			K	J		I	
			✠				
Nottingham 8	56	d			21 39		
Beeston	56	d			21 45		
Attenborough	56	d			21 48		
Long Eaton	56	d			21 56		
Derby 6	56	d	21 28	21 56	22 12	22 26	
Willington		d					
Burton-on-Trent		d	21 38		22 23	22 37	
Tamworth		d	21 49		22 35	22 47	
Wilnecote		d			22 38		
Water Orton		d					
Birmingham New Street 12		a	22 05	22 44	23 02	23 05	
		d					
University		a					
Worcestershire Parkway		d					
Ashchurch for Tewkesbury		d					
Cheltenham Spa 4		d					
Gloucester 7	134	a					
		d					23 09
Bristol Parkway 7	134	a					
Bristol Temple Meads 10	134	a					
Lydney		a					23 28
Chepstow		a					23 37
Caldicot		a					23 46
Severn Tunnel Jn	132	a					23 49
Newport (South Wales)	132	a					00 12
Cardiff Central 7	132	a					00 36

A From Manchester Piccadilly
B To Maesteg
C From Edinburgh to Plymouth
D From Newcastle to Reading
E From Manchester Piccadilly. ✠ to Bristol Temple Meads
F From Glasgow Central to Plymouth
G From Manchester Piccadilly to Plymouth
H From Newcastle to Southampton Central
I From Glasgow Central
J From Newcastle
K From Edinburgh

Trains between Gloucester & Cheltenham are shown on Table T058

Trains between Birmingham & Bromsgrove are shown on Table T069

Table T057-F

Sundays

15 December to 10 May

Nottingham and Derby - Birmingham - Bristol and Cardiff

			AW	XC	AW	XC	XC	XC	XC	AW	XC	XC	EM	XC	AW	XC	XC	XC	XC	XC	XC	XC	AW	XC
			◇	◇1	◇	◇1	◇1	◇1	◇1	◇	◇1	◇1		◇1	◇	◇1	◇1	◇1	◇1	◇1	◇1	◇1	◇	◇1
				A			B	C	B		D	C	E	F		C		G		H	I	J		
				✠		✠	✠	✠	✠		✠	✠		✠		✠	✠	✠	✠	✠	✠	✠		✠
Nottingham 8	56	d						09 55				11 10	11 27			12 10			13 10					14 10
Beeston	56	d											11 32											
Attenborough	56	d											11 36											
Long Eaton	56	d											11a43											
Derby 6	56	d					09 30	10 20	10 33		11 29	11 36		12 29		12 36		13 31	13 36	13 53		14 29		14 36
Willington		d																						
Burton-on-Trent		d						10 31			11 40	11 47				12 47		13 42	13 47					14 47
Tamworth		d						10 43	10 52			11 59		12 47		12 59			13 59			14 47		14 59
Wilnecote		d																						
Water Orton		d																						
Birmingham New Street 12		a					10 18	11 02	11 20		12 06	12 19		13 04		13 23		14 07	14 21	14 27		15 04		15 19
		d		09 30		10 12	10 30	11 12	11 30		12 12	12 30		13 12		13 30	13 43	14 12	14 30		14 42	15 12		15 30
University		a				10 18		11 18				12 36				13 36			14 36					15 36
Worcestershire Parkway		d				10 40		11 40				12 58				13 58			14 58					15 58
Ashchurch for Tewkesbury		d																						
Cheltenham Spa 4		d		10 10	10 37	11 01	11 10	12 01	12 10	12 21	12 52	13 19		13 52	14 10	14 15	14 27	14 52	15 15		15 26	15 52	16 10	16 15
Gloucester 7	134	a			10 47	11 10		12 09		12 32		13 27			14 22	14 23			15 27				16 20	16 23
		d	08 45		10 48	11 11		12 11		12 36		13 29			14 29	14 25			15 29				16 29	16 25
Bristol Parkway 7	134	a		10 38			11 40		12 42		13 20			14 20			14 55	15 22			15 55	16 20		
Bristol Temple Meads 10	134	a		10 49			11 50		12 52		13 34			14 34			15 06	15 36			16 09	16 34		
Lydney		a	09 04		11 07					12 55					14 48								16 48	
Chepstow		a	09 13		11 16					13 04					15 02								16 57	
Caldicot		a	09 22		11 25					13 15					15 13								17 06	
Severn Tunnel Jn	132	a	09 25		11 28					13 20					15 20								17 09	
Newport (South Wales)	132	a	09 44		11 41	11 53		12 53		13 33		14 11			15 35	15 07			16 11				17 22	17 07
Cardiff Central 7	132	a	10 03		11 55	12 06		13 06		13 47		14 24			15 49	15 21			16 25				17 37	17 20

			XC	XC	XC	XC	XC	XC	XC	XC	XC	XC	AW	XC	XC	XC	XC	XC	AW	XC	XC	XC	XC
			◇1	◇1	◇1	◇1	◇1	◇1	◇1	◇1	◇1	◇1	◇	◇1	◇1	◇1	◇1	◇1	◇	◇1	◇1	◇1	◇1
			K	L	G		M	L	N	O	M	L		P	O	Q	R	S		O	M	L	P
			✠	✠	✠	✠	✠	✠	✠	✠	✠	✠		✠	✠	✠	✠	✠		✠	✠		✠
Nottingham 8	56	d				15 10				16 10					17 10					18 10			
Beeston	56	d																					
Attenborough	56	d																					
Long Eaton	56	d																					
Derby 6	56	d	14 53		15 27	15 36	15 53		16 27	16 36	16 53			17 26	17 36	17 53		18 27		18 36	18 53		19 27
Willington		d																					
Burton-on-Trent		d			15 37	15 47				16 47				17 36	17 47					18 47			19 37
Tamworth		d				15 59			16 45	16 59					17 59			18 45		18 59			
Wilnecote		d				16 03																	
Water Orton		d																					
Birmingham New Street 12		a	15 27		16 00	16 20	16 25		17 02	17 19	17 27			17 59	18 19	18 27		19 03		19 19	19 27		20 00
		d		15 42	16 12	16 30		16 42	17 12	17 30		17 42		18 12	18 30		18 42	19 12		19 30		19 42	20 12
University		a				16 36				17 36					18 36					19 36			
Worcestershire Parkway		d				16 58				17 58					18 58					19 58			
Ashchurch for Tewkesbury		d																					
Cheltenham Spa 4		d		16 28	16 52	17 15		17 26	17 52	18 15		18 29	18 35	18 52	19 15		19 26	19 52	20 10	20 15		20 28	20 52
Gloucester 7	134	a				17 23				18 23			18 47		19 23				20 22	20 24			
		d				17 25				18 25			18 48		19 25				20 33	20 26			
Bristol Parkway 7	134	a		16 56	17 20			17 54	18 20			19 02		19 22			19 53	20 20				20 56	21 20
Bristol Temple Meads 10	134	a		17 07	17 34			18 08	18 34			19 12		19 36			20 05	20 35				21 06	21 35
Lydney		a											19 07						20 51				
Chepstow		a											19 16						21 01				
Caldicot		a											19 25						21 10				
Severn Tunnel Jn	132	a											19 31						21 16				
Newport (South Wales)	132	a				18 07				19 07			19 51		20 07				21 33	21 07			
Cardiff Central 7	132	a				18 20				19 21			20 09		20 21				21 48	21 21			

A To Penzance
B From Leeds to Plymouth
C ✠ from Birmingham New Street
D From York to Plymouth
E From Grantham to Matlock
F From Newcastle to Reading
G From Edinburgh to Plymouth
H To Reading
I From Manchester Piccadilly to Paignton
J From Edinburgh to Penzance
K From Sheffield to Reading
L From Manchester Piccadilly
M From Newcastle to Reading
N From Glasgow Central to Penzance
O ✠ to Birmingham New Street
P From Glasgow Central to Plymouth
Q From Edinburgh to Reading
R From Manchester Piccadilly to Plymouth
S From Aberdeen to Plymouth

Trains between Gloucester & Cheltenham are shown on Table T058

Trains between Birmingham & Bromsgrove are shown on Table T069

Table T057-F

Sundays
15 December to 10 May

Nottingham and Derby - Birmingham - Bristol and Cardiff

			XC ◇1	XC ◇1 A ✠	XC ◇1 B	XC ◇1 C ✠	XC ◇1	XC ◇1 D ✠	XC ◇1 B	XC ◇1 E	XC ◇1	XC ◇1 D	XC ◇1 F	AW ◇
Nottingham [8]	56 ⇌	d	19 10				20 10				21 10			
Beeston	56	d												
Attenborough	56	d												
Long Eaton	56	d												
Derby [6]	56	d	19 36	19 53		20 27	20 36	20 53		21 26	21 36	21 53	22 27	
Willington		d												
Burton-on-Trent		d	19 47				20 47			21 36	21 47	22 03	22 37	
Tamworth		d	19 59			20 45	20 59			21 47	21 59	22 13	22 47	
Wilnecote		d	20 03								22 03			
Water Orton		d												
Birmingham New Street [12]		a	20 20	20 23		21 02	21 19	21 23		22 03	22 20	22 30	23 04	
		d			20 42	21 12			21 42	22 12				
University		a												
Worcestershire Parkway		d												
Ashchurch for Tewkesbury		d												
Cheltenham Spa [4]		d			21 26	21 52			22 26	22 52				
Gloucester [7]	134	a				22 01								
		d				22 05								22 33
Bristol Parkway [7]	134	a			22 00	22 31			22 54	23 20				
Bristol Temple Meads [10]	134	a			22 11	22 41			23 04	23 30				
Lydney		a												22 52
Chepstow		a												23 01
Caldicot		a												23 10
Severn Tunnel Jn	132	a												23 14
Newport (South Wales)	132	a												23 33
Cardiff Central [7]	132	a												23 52

A From Newcastle to Guildford
B From Manchester Piccadilly
C From Glasgow Central. ✠ to Birmingham New Street
D From Newcastle
E From Edinburgh
F From Glasgow Central

Trains between Gloucester & Cheltenham are shown on Table T058

Trains between Birmingham & Bromsgrove are shown on Table T069

Table T057-R

Mondays to Fridays
16 December to 15 May

Cardiff and Bristol - Birmingham - Derby and Nottingham

Miles	Miles				XC ◇1 A ✠	XC 1	XC ◇1 B ✠	XC 1	XC ◇1 C ✠	XC 1 ✠	XC ◇1 B ✠	XC 1	XC ◇1 D ✠	XC ◇1 E	XC 1 ✠	AW ◇	XC ◇1 F ✠	XC ◇1 G ✠	XC ◇1	XC ◇1 H ✠	XC 1 ✠	AW ◇	XC ◇1 I ✠	XC ◇1 J ✠
0	—	**Cardiff Central** [7]	132	d												06 10			06 38			07 06	06 57	
11¾	—	Newport (South Wales)	132	d												06 24			06 54			07 20	07 11	
21½	—	Severn Tunnel Jn	132	d												06 34			07 04			07 30	07 21	
22¼	—	Caldicot		d												06 37			07 07			07 33		
29	—	Chepstow		d												06 45			07 15			07 41		
37	—	Lydney		d												06 54			07 24			07 50		
—	0	**Bristol Temple Meads** [10]	134	d									06 32	06 24			07 00			07 34			08 00	
—	5¾	Bristol Parkway [7]	134	d									06 41	06 34			07 09			07 44			08 09	
56½	—	Gloucester [7]	134	a										07 04		07 16			07 43			08 10		
—	—			d										07 07		07 17			07 45			08 11		
63	45¼	Cheltenham Spa [4]		a									07 10	07 16		07 27	07 39		07 54	08 13		08 21	08 38	
—	—			d									07 11	07 17			07 41		07 56	08 16			08 40	
70¼	52½	Ashchurch for Tewkesbury		d										07 25					08 03					
—	—	Worcestershire Parkway		d										07 36					08 14					
109¾	90¾	University		d										08 09					08 39					
111	93¼	**Birmingham New Street** [12]		a									07 56	08 15			08 26		08 45	08 56			09 25	
—	—			d	06 03	06 19	06 30	06 49	07 03	07 19	07 30	07 49	08 03		08 19			08 30	08 49	09 03	09 12			09 28
116	—	Water Orton		d																				
124	—	Wilnecote		d		06 35				07 36									09 05					
125¾	—	Tamworth		d		06 39		07 07	07 20	07 40		08 09	08 19		08 36				09 09		09 29			
138¾	—	Burton-on-Trent		d		06 50		07 20	07 30	07 51		08 21	08 29		08 47				09 21	09 27	09 40			
143½	—	Willington		d				07 26				08 27												
149¾	—	**Derby** [6]	56	d	06a33	07 09	07a10	07 44	07a41	08 08	08a08	08 40	08a41		09 08			09a04	09 40	09a37	09 58			09a58
157¾	—	Long Eaton	56	d		07 20		07 55		08 17		08 49							09 49					
160	—	Attenborough	56	d		07 27						08 59												
162¼	—	Beeston	56	d		07 31		08 04		08 26		09 03							09 57					
165¾	—	**Nottingham** [8]	56 ⇌	a		07 37		08 13		08 33		09 09			09 31				10 03		10 24			

			XC ◇1	XC ◇1 K ✠	XC ◇1 ✠	XC ◇1 L ✠	XC ◇1 M ✠	XC ◇1	XC ◇1 H ✠	XC ◇1 ✠	AW ◇ N	XC ◇1 F ✠	XC ◇1 J ✠	XC ◇1 ✠	XC ◇1 O ✠	AW ◇ N	XC ◇1 ✠	XC ◇1 F ✠	XC ◇1 M ✠	XC ◇1	XC ◇1 P ✠	XC 1	XC ◇1 L ✠	XC ◇1 J ✠
Cardiff Central [7]	132	d	07 45					08 45			09 07			09 45		10 09				10 45				
Newport (South Wales)	132	d	08 01					09 00			09 22			09 59		10 23				11 00				
Severn Tunnel Jn	132	d									09 33					10 33								
Caldicot		d									09 36					10 36								
Chepstow		d						09 19			09 45			10 17		10 44								
Lydney		d	08 27								09 54					10 53				11 25				
Bristol Temple Meads [10]	134	d		08 34		09 00			09 34			10 00			10 34			11 00			11 34		12 00	
Bristol Parkway [7]	134	d		08 44		09 09			09 44			10 09			10 44			11 09			11 44		12 09	
Gloucester [7]	134	a	08 46					09 45			10 15			10 43		11 13				11 44				
		d	08 49					09 49			10 16			10 48		11 14				11 48				
Cheltenham Spa [4]		a	08 58	09 14		09 38		09 58	10 14		10 26	10 38		10 58	11 13	11 25		11 38		11 58	12 13		12 38	
		d	08 59	09 16		09 40		10 00	10 16			10 40		10 59	11 16			11 40		11 59	12 16		12 40	
Ashchurch for Tewkesbury		d																						
Worcestershire Parkway		d	09 14					10 14						11 14						12 14				
University		d	09 39					10 39						11 39						12 39				
Birmingham New Street [12]		a	09 45	09 58		10 23		10 45	10 56			11 25		11 45	11 58			12 25		12 45	12 56		13 25	
		d	09 49	10 03	10 12		10 28	10 49	11 03	11 19			11 30	11 49	12 03		12 19		12 30	12 49	13 03	13 19		13 30
Water Orton		d																						
Wilnecote		d						11 05												13 05				
Tamworth		d	10 08	10 19	10 29			11 09		11 36				12 07	12 20		12 36			13 09		13 36		
Burton-on-Trent		d	10 19		10 40			11 21	11 26	11 48				12 19			12 48			13 20	13 26	13 48		
Willington		d	10 25											12 25										
Derby [6]	56	d	10 40	10a42	10 56		10a58	11 40	11a40	12 08			12a04	12 40	12a40		13 08		13a04	13 40	13a39	14 08		14a04
Long Eaton	56	d	10 49					11 49						12 49						13 49				
Attenborough	56	d																						
Beeston	56	d	10 57					12 01						12 57						13 57				
Nottingham [8]	56 ⇌	a	11 03		11 24			12 07		12 28				13 03			13 28			14 03		14 28		

A To Glasgow Central
B To Newcastle
C To Edinburgh
D From Bath Spa to Glasgow Central
E To Stansted Airport
F To Manchester Piccadilly
G From Guildford to Newcastle
H From Plymouth to Edinburgh
I To Manchester Piccadilly. ✠ from Bristol Temple Meads
J From Reading to Newcastle
K From Plymouth to Glasgow Central
L From Paignton to Manchester Piccadilly
M From Southampton Central to Newcastle
N From Maesteg
O From Penzance to Glasgow Central
P From Plymouth to Aberdeen

Trains between Gloucester & Cheltenham are shown on Table T058

Trains between Birmingham & Bromsgrove are shown on Table T069

Table T057-R

Mondays to Fridays
16 December to 15 May

Cardiff and Bristol - Birmingham - Derby and Nottingham

	XC ◇1 ⛾	XC ◇1 A ⛾	AW ◇ B	XC 1	XC ◇1 C ⛾	XC 1 D ⛾	XC ◇1 ⛾	AW ◇ B	XC ◇1 E ⛾	XC 1	XC ◇1 F ⛾	XC ◇1 G ⛾	XC ◇1 ⛾	XC ◇1 H ⛾	XC ◇1	XC ◇1 C ⛾	XC ◇1 I ⛾	XC ◇1 J ⛾	XC ◇1 K ⛾	XC 1	AW ◇ B	XC ◇1 L ⛾
Cardiff Central 7 132 d	11 45		12 10				12 45	13 10					13 45					14 45			15 09	
Newport (South Wales) 132 d	11 58		12 24				12 59	13 25					13 58					14 59			15 23	
Severn Tunnel Jn 132 d			12 36					13 35													15 33	
Caldicot d			12 38					13 38													15 36	
Chepstow d	12 16		12 47				13 17	13 46										15 17			15 44	
Lydney d			12 55					13 55					14 23								15 53	
Bristol Temple Meads 10 134 d		12 35			13 00				13 34		14 00			14 30		15 00			15 32			16 00
Bristol Parkway 7 134 d		12 45			13 09				13 44		14 09			14 41		15 09			15 45			16 10
Gloucester 7 134 a	12 42		13 16				13 43	14 15					14 43					15 45			16 13	
d	12 44		13 16				13 48						14 48					15 48			16 14	
Cheltenham Spa 4 a	12 54	13 14	13 27		13 38		13 58		14 14		14 38		14 57	15 10		15 38		15 58	16 14		16 24	16 39
d	12 55	13 16			13 40		13 59		14 16		14 40		14 59	15 11		15 40		15 59	16 16			16 40
Ashchurch for Tewkesbury d	13 03																					
Worcestershire Parkway d	13 14						14 14						15 13					16 14				
University d	13 39						14 39						15 38					16 39				
Birmingham New Street 12 a	13 45	13 56			14 23		14 45		14 56		15 23		15 44	15 56		16 23		16 45	16 56			17 24
d	13 49	14 03		14 19		14 30	14 49		15 03	15 12		15 28	15 49	16 03	16 19		16 30	16 49	17 03	17 19		
Water Orton d																						
Wilnecote d	14 05						15 05						16 05					17 05				
Tamworth d	14 09	14 19		14 36			15 09			15 29			16 09	16 20	16 36			17 09		17 36		
Burton-on-Trent d	14 20			14 48			15 20		15 26	15 40			16 21		16 48			17 21	17 26	17 47		
Willington d							15 26															
Derby 6 56 d	14 40	14a37		15 08		15a04	15 40		15a40	15 59		15a58	16 40	16a39	17 08		17a05	17 40	17a40	18 08		
Long Eaton 56 d	14 49						15 49						16 49		17 17			17 49		18 17		
Attenborough 56 d																						
Beeston 56 d	14 57						15 57						16 57		17 25			17 57		18 25		
Nottingham 8 56 a	15 03			15 28			16 03			16 24			17 03		17 31			18 03		18 31		

	XC ◇1 G ⛾	XC 1	XC ◇1 J ⛾	XC ◇1 K ⛾	AW ◇ B	XC 1	XC ◇1 M ⛾	XC ◇1 D ⛾	XC ◇1 J ⛾	XC ◇1 N ⛾	XC 1	AW ◇ B	XC ◇1 L ⛾	XC ◇1 G ⛾	XC ◇1 J ⛾	XC ◇1 O ⛾	AW ◇ B	XC ◇1 L ⛾	XC ◇1 P	XC 1	XC ◇1 O ⛾
Cardiff Central 7 132 d			15 45		16 08				16 45			17 07			17 45		18 07			18 45	
Newport (South Wales) 132 d			15 59		16 24				16 59			17 22			17 59		18 21			18 58	
Severn Tunnel Jn 132 d					16 35							17 33					18 31				
Caldicot d					16 37							17 35					18 34				
Chepstow d			16 17		16 46							17 44			18 17		18 42			19 16	
Lydney d					16 55				17 25			17 52					18 51				
Bristol Temple Meads 10 134 d				16 34			17 00			17 34			18 00			18 34		19 00			19 34
Bristol Parkway 7 134 d				16 44			17 09			17 44			18 09			18 44		19 09			19 44
Gloucester 7 134 a			16 43		17 17				17 44			18 13			18 43		19 11			19 42	
d			16 46		17 17				17 48			18 14			18 44		19 12			19 47	
Cheltenham Spa 4 a			16 56	17 13	17 27		17 38		17 58	18 13		18 24	18 38		18 54	19 13	19 22	19 38		19 57	20 13
d			16 57	17 16			17 40		17 59	18 16			18 40		18 55	19 16		19 40		19 58	20 16
Ashchurch for Tewkesbury d															19 03						
Worcestershire Parkway d			17 12						18 14						19 14					20 14	
University d			17 39						18 39						19 39					20 39	
Birmingham New Street 12 a			17 45	17 56			18 23		18 45	18 56			19 23		19 45	19 56		20 23		20 45	20 56
d	17 30	17 39	17 49	18 03		18 19		18 30	18 49	19 03	19 12			19 28	19 49	20 03			20 30	20 49	21 03
Water Orton d		17 50																			
Wilnecote d		17 59	18 05						19 05						20 05					21 05	
Tamworth d		18 03	18 09	18 19		18 36			19 09		19 29				20 09	20 19				21 09	21 20
Burton-on-Trent d		18 14	18 21			18 48			19 21	19 29	19 40				20 21					21 21	21 31
Willington d		18 20																			
Derby 6 56 d	18a05	18a28	18 40	18a39		19 08		19a05	19 40	19a40	19 58			19a58	20 41	20a37			21a09	21 46	21a42
Long Eaton 56 d			18 49			19 17			19 49						20 50					21 57	
Attenborough 56 d																				22 04	
Beeston 56 d			18 57			19 25			19 57						20 58					22 07	
Nottingham 8 56 a			19 05			19 31			20 03		20 21				21 04					22 13	

A From Penzance to Glasgow Central
B From Maesteg
C To Manchester Piccadilly
D From Southampton Central to Newcastle
E From Penzance to Dundee
F From Plymouth to Manchester Piccadilly
G From Reading to Newcastle
H From Plymouth to Glasgow Central
I From Southampton Central to Edinburgh
J ⛾ to Birmingham New Street
K From Plymouth to Edinburgh
L From Exeter St Davids to Manchester Piccadilly
M From Paignton to Manchester Piccadilly
N From Plymouth to Leeds
O From Plymouth to Leeds. ⛾ to Birmingham New Street
P From Southampton Central to York

Trains between Gloucester & Cheltenham are shown on Table T058

Trains between Birmingham & Bromsgrove are shown on Table T069

Table T057-R

Mondays to Fridays
16 December to 15 May

Cardiff and Bristol - Birmingham - Derby and Nottingham

	XC ◇1	XC ◇1	XC ◇1 A	XC 1	XC ◇1 B	XC ◇1	XC 1	AW ◇ C	XC ◇1 D	XC ◇1	AW FO ◇ C	AW FX ◇ C
Cardiff Central 7 132 d		19 49				21 05		21 09		21 45	23 20	23 20
Newport (South Wales) 132 d		20 02				21 18		21 24		21 58	23 35	23 40
Severn Tunnel Jn 132 d		20 14						21 35			23 49	23 58
Caldicot d		20 16						21 38			23 52	00 01
Chepstow d		20 25						21 47			00 02	00 10
Lydney d		20 33						21 56			00 11	00 19
Bristol Temple Meads 10 134 d	20 00		20 34		21 01				22 00			
Bristol Parkway 7 134 d	20 10		20 43		21 10				22 09			
Gloucester 7 134 a	20 38	20 53				22 00		22 17		22 44	00 32	00 40
d	20 45	20 55				22 02		22 18		22 48		
Cheltenham Spa 4 a	20 53	21 04	21 12		21 39	22 12		22 28	22 40	22 57		
d	20 55	21 06	21 16		21 41	22 13			22 42	22 59		
Ashchurch for Tewkesbury d						22 21						
Worcestershire Parkway d		21 20				22 32						
University d		21 46										
Birmingham New Street 12 a	21 37	21 54	22 01		22 25	23 05			23 41	23 59		
d				22 03			23 09					
Water Orton d												
Wilnecote d							23 24					
Tamworth d				22 27			23 28					
Burton-on-Trent d				22 39			23 40					
Willington d							23 45					
Derby 6 56 d				22 59			23 57					
Long Eaton 56 d				23 10								
Attenborough 56 d				23 17								
Beeston 56 d				23 20								
Nottingham 8 56 a				23 26			00 16					

Saturdays
21 December to 16 May

	XC ◇1 E ⛾	XC 1	XC ◇1 F ⛾	XC 1	XC ◇1 G ⛾	XC 1 ⛾	XC ◇1 F ⛾	XC 1	XC ◇1 E ⛾	XC ◇1 H	XC 1 ⛾	AW ◇	XC ◇1 I ⛾	XC ◇1 J ⛾	XC ◇1	XC ◇1 K ⛾	XC 1 ⛾	AW ◇	XC ◇1 L ⛾	XC ◇1 M ⛾	XC ◇1	XC ◇1 N ⛾
Cardiff Central 7 132 d												06 10			06 38			07 06	07 00		07 45	
Newport (South Wales) 132 d												06 26			06 53			07 22	07 14		08 02	
Severn Tunnel Jn 132 d												06 37			07 03			07 34	07 25			
Caldicot d												06 39			07 06			07 36				
Chepstow d												06 48			07 14			07 45				
Lydney d												06 57			07 23			07 54			08 27	
Bristol Temple Meads 10 134 d									06 15				07 00			07 34			08 00			08 34
Bristol Parkway 7 134 d									06 25				07 09			07 44			08 09			08 44
Gloucester 7 134 a									06 53			07 19			07 42			08 19			08 46	
d									06 57	07 02		07 21			07 44			08 22			08 48	
Cheltenham Spa 4 a									07 05	07 13		07 34	07 38		07 54	08 13		08 33	08 39		08 58	09 13
d									07 08	07 14			07 40		07 55	08 16			08 41		08 59	09 16
Ashchurch for Tewkesbury d										07 22					08 03							
Worcestershire Parkway d										07 33					08 14						09 14	
University d										08 00					08 39						09 39	
Birmingham New Street 12 a									07 56	08 06			08 25		08 45	08 56			09 25		09 45	09 56
d	06 01	06 19	06 30	06 49	07 03	07 19	07 30	07 49	08 03		08 19			08 30	08 49	09 03	09 19			09 30	09 49	10 03
Water Orton d																						
Wilnecote d		06 35				07 35									09 05							
Tamworth d	06 19	06 39	06 46	07 07	07 19	07 39	07 46	08 07	08 19		08 36				09 09		09 36				10 06	10 19
Burton-on-Trent d	06 30	06 51	06 56	07 19	07 29	07 50	07 56	08 19	08 29		08 48				09 21	09 28	09 48				10 17	
Willington d				07 25				08 25													10 23	
Derby 6 56 d	06a40	07 08	07a07	07 43	07a40	08 08	08a08	08 40	08a40		09 08			09a05	09 40	09a38	10 08			10a05	10 40	10a37
Long Eaton 56 d		07 19		07 54		08 17		08 49							09 49						10 49	
Attenborough 56 d		07 26						08 55														
Beeston 56 d		07 29		08 02		08 25		08 59							09 57						10 57	
Nottingham 8 56 a		07 36		08 09		08 31		09 05			09 30				10 03		10 28				11 03	

A From Plymouth
B From Exeter St Davids
C From Maesteg
D From Paignton
E To Glasgow Central
F To Newcastle
G To Edinburgh
H To Stansted Airport
I To Manchester Piccadilly
J From Guildford to Newcastle
K From Plymouth to Edinburgh
L To Manchester Piccadilly. ⛾ from Bristol Temple Meads
M From Bournemouth to Newcastle
N From Plymouth to Glasgow Central

Trains between Gloucester & Cheltenham are shown on Table T058

Trains between Birmingham & Bromsgrove are shown on Table T069

Table T057-R

Saturdays

21 December to 16 May

Cardiff and Bristol - Birmingham - Derby and Nottingham

		XC 1 ᛏ		XC ◇1 A ᛏ	XC ◇1 B ᛏ	XC ◇1 ᛏ	XC ◇1 C ᛏ	XC 1 ᛏ	AW ◇ D	XC ◇1 E ᛏ	XC ◇1 F ᛏ	XC ◇1 ᛏ		XC ◇1 G ᛏ	AW ◇ D	XC 1 ᛏ	XC ◇1 E ᛏ	XC ◇1 B ᛏ	XC ◇1 ᛏ	XC ◇1 H ᛏ	XC 1 ᛏ	XC ◇1 A ᛏ		XC ◇1 F ᛏ	XC ◇1 ᛏ
Cardiff Central 7	132 d					08 45			09 04			09 45			10 07				10 45						11 45
Newport (South Wales)	132 d					08 59			09 20			09 58			10 22				11 01						11 58
Severn Tunnel Jn	132 d								09 31						10 32										
Caldicot	d								09 33						10 35										
Chepstow	d					09 17			09 42			10 16			10 43										12 17
Lydney	d								09 51						10 52				11 26						
Bristol Temple Meads 10	134 d			09 00			09 34			10 00				10 34			11 00			11 34		12 00			
Bristol Parkway 7	134 d			09 10			09 44			10 09				10 44			11 09			11 44		12 09			
Gloucester 7	134 a					09 43			10 13			10 42			11 12				11 45						12 43
	d					09 48			10 13			10 48			11 13				11 48						12 44
Cheltenham Spa 4	a			09 38		09 58	10 14		10 24	10 38		10 58		11 14	11 23		11 38		11 58	12 13		12 38			12 54
	d			09 40		09 59	10 16			10 40		10 59		11 16			11 40		11 59	12 16		12 40			12 55
Ashchurch for Tewkesbury	d																								13 03
Worcestershire Parkway	d					10 14						11 14							12 14						13 14
University	d					10 39						11 39							12 39						13 39
Birmingham New Street 12	a			10 25		10 45	10 56			11 25		11 45		11 56			12 25		12 45	12 56		13 25			13 45
	d	10 12			10 28	10 49	11 03	11 12			11 28	11 49		12 03		12 12		12 28	12 49	13 03	13 12			13 28	13 49
Water Orton	d																								
Wilnecote	d					11 05													13 05						14 05
Tamworth	d	10 29				11 09		11 29				12 06		12 19		12 29			13 09		13 29				14 09
Burton-on-Trent	d	10 40				11 21	11 28	11 40				12 17				12 40			13 21	13 27	13 40				14 20
Willington	d											12 23													
Derby 6	56 d	10 58			10a58	11 40	11a38	11 59			11a58	12 40		12a37		12 58		12a58	13 40	13a40	13 58			13a58	14 40
Long Eaton	56 d					11 49						12 49							13 49						14 49
Attenborough	56 d																								
Beeston	56 d					11 57						12 57							13 57						14 57
Nottingham 8	56 ⛴ a	11 22				12 03		12 22				13 03				13 22			14 03		14 22				15 03

		XC ◇1 G ᛏ	AW ◇ D	XC 1	XC ◇1 E ᛏ	XC ◇1 B ᛏ	XC ◇1 ᛏ	AW ◇		XC ◇1 I ᛏ	XC 1	XC ◇1 J ᛏ	XC ◇1 F ᛏ	XC ◇1 ᛏ	XC ◇1 K ᛏ	XC 1	XC ◇1 E ᛏ	XC ◇1 B ᛏ		XC ◇1 L ᛏ	XC ◇1 C ᛏ	XC 1	AW ◇	XC ◇1 A ᛏ	XC ◇1 F ᛏ
Cardiff Central 7	132 d		12 07				12 45	13 12						13 45						14 45			15 07		
Newport (South Wales)	132 d		12 21				13 00	13 27						13 59						14 59			15 22		
Severn Tunnel Jn	132 d		12 32					13 38															15 32		
Caldicot	d		12 34					13 41															15 35		
Chepstow	d		12 43				13 18	13 50												15 17			15 43		
Lydney	d		12 51					13 59						14 24									15 52		
Bristol Temple Meads 10	134 d	12 35			13 00					13 35		14 00			14 34		15 00				15 34			16 00	
Bristol Parkway 7	134 d	12 45			13 09					13 45		14 09			14 44		15 09				15 44			16 10	
Gloucester 7	134 a		13 11				13 44	14 21						14 43						15 43			16 11		
	d		13 12				13 48							14 48						15 48			16 16		
Cheltenham Spa 4	a	13 14	13 22		13 38		13 58			14 14		14 38		14 58	15 13		15 38			15 58	16 13		16 27	16 40	
	d	13 16			13 40		13 59			14 16		14 40		14 59	15 16		15 40			15 59	16 16			16 41	
Ashchurch for Tewkesbury	d																								
Worcestershire Parkway	d						14 14							15 14						16 14					
University	d						14 39							15 39						16 39					
Birmingham New Street 12	a	13 56			14 25		14 45			14 56		15 25		15 45	15 56		16 25			16 45	16 56			17 25	
	d	14 03		14 19		14 30	14 49			15 03	15 19		15 30	15 49	16 03	16 19		16 30		16 49	17 03	17 19			17 30
Water Orton	d																								
Wilnecote	d						15 05							16 05						17 05					
Tamworth	d	14 19		14 36			15 09				15 36			16 09	16 19	16 36				17 09		17 36			
Burton-on-Trent	d			14 48			15 21			15 27	15 48			16 21		16 48		16 54		17 21	17 27	17 47			
Willington	d						15 27																		
Derby 6	56 d	14a37		15 08		15a04	15 40			15a40	16 08		16a05	16 40	16a39	17 08		17a05		17 40	17a40	18 08			18a05
Long Eaton	56 d						15 49							16 49		17 17				17 49		18 17			
Attenborough	56 d																								
Beeston	56 d						15 57							16 57		17 25				17 57		18 25			
Nottingham 8	56 ⛴ a			15 28			16 03				16 28			17 03		17 31				18 03		18 31			

A From Paignton to Manchester Piccadilly
B From Southampton Central to Newcastle
C From Plymouth to Edinburgh
D From Maesteg
E To Manchester Piccadilly
F From Reading to Newcastle
G From Penzance to Glasgow Central
H From Plymouth to Aberdeen
I From Plymouth to Dundee
J From Penzance to Manchester Piccadilly
K From Plymouth to Glasgow Central
L ᛏ to Birmingham New Street

Trains between Gloucester & Cheltenham are shown on Table T058

Trains between Birmingham & Bromsgrove are shown on Table T069

Table T057-R

Saturdays

21 December to 16 May

Cardiff and Bristol - Birmingham - Derby and Nottingham

		XC ◇1 A ᛏ	XC ◇1 B ᛏ	AW ◇ C	XC 1	XC ◇1 D ᛏ	XC ◇1 E ᛏ	XC ◇1 A ᛏ	XC ◇1 F ᛏ	XC 1		AW ◇ C	XC ◇1 G ᛏ	XC ◇1 H ᛏ	XC ◇1 A ᛏ	XC ◇1 I ᛏ	AW ◇ C	XC ◇1 D ᛏ	XC ◇1 J	XC ◇1		XC ◇1 I ᛏ	XC ◇1	XC ◇1 K	XC ◇1
Cardiff Central 7	132 d	15 45		16 06				16 45				17 07			17 45		18 06			18 45					20 00
Newport (South Wales)	132 d	15 59		16 21				16 58				17 21			17 58		18 21			18 58					20 13
Severn Tunnel Jn	132 d			16 31								17 32					18 32								20 25
Caldicot	d			16 34								17 34					18 35								20 27
Chepstow	d	16 17		16 42								17 43			18 16		18 44			19 16					20 36
Lydney	d			16 51				17 23				17 51					18 53								20 44
Bristol Temple Meads 10	134 d		16 34			17 00			17 34				18 00			18 34		19 00				19 32	20 00	20 30	
Bristol Parkway 7	134 d		16 44			17 09			17 44				18 09			18 44		19 09				19 42	20 09	20 41	
Gloucester 7	134 a	16 43		17 12				17 43				18 13			18 42		19 14			19 42					21 04
	d	16 48		17 12				17 48				18 14			18 44		19 15			19 48					21 06
Cheltenham Spa 4	a	16 58	17 13	17 22		17 38		17 58	18 13			18 23	18 38		18 54	19 14	19 26	19 38		19 58		20 11	20 38	21 10	21 16
	d	16 59	17 16			17 40		17 59	18 16				18 40		18 55	19 16		19 40		19 59		20 12	20 40	21 11	21 17
Ashchurch for Tewkesbury	d														19 03										21 25
Worcestershire Parkway	d	17 14						18 14							19 14					20 14					
University	d	17 39						18 39							19 39					20 39					22 00
Birmingham New Street 12	a	17 45	17 56			18 25		18 45	18 56				19 25		19 45	19 56		20 25		20 45		20 52	21 36	21 51	22 07
	d	17 49	18 03		18 12		18 28	18 49	19 03	19 19				19 30	19 49	20 03			20 30	20 49		21 03			22 10
Water Orton	d																								
Wilnecote	d	18 05						19 05							20 05					21 05					
Tamworth	d	18 09	18 19		18 29			19 09		19 36					20 09	20 19				21 09		21 19			22 27
Burton-on-Trent	d	18 21			18 40			19 21	19 27	19 47					20 21					21 21		21 30			22 39
Willington	d	18 27																							22 45
Derby 6	56 d	18 40	18a40		18 56		18a58	19 40	19a39	20 08				20a03	20 40	20a40			21a23	21 46		21a41			22 59
Long Eaton	56 d	18 49			19 05			19 49							20 49					21 57					23 10
Attenborough	56 d																			22 04					23 17
Beeston	56 d	18 57			19 13			19 57							20 57					22 07					23 20
Nottingham 8	56 ⛴ a	19 03			19 22			20 03		20 28					21 03					22 13					23 27

		XC ◇1	XC 1	AW ◇ C	AW ◇ C
Cardiff Central 7	132 d	20 48		21 11	23 18
Newport (South Wales)	132 d	21 01		21 27	23 37
Severn Tunnel Jn	132 d			21 38	23 56
Caldicot	d			21 40	23 59
Chepstow	d			21 49	00 08
Lydney	d			21 58	00 17
Bristol Temple Meads 10	134 d				
Bristol Parkway 7	134 d				
Gloucester 7	134 a	21 43		22 20	00 40
	d	21 48			
Cheltenham Spa 4	a	21 58			
	d	21 59			
Ashchurch for Tewkesbury	d				
Worcestershire Parkway	d	22 14			
University	d	22 39			
Birmingham New Street 12	a	22 45			
	d		22 49		
Water Orton	d				
Wilnecote	d		23 04		
Tamworth	d		23 08		
Burton-on-Trent	d		23 20		
Willington	d				
Derby 6	56 d		23a33		
Long Eaton	56 d				
Attenborough	56 d				
Beeston	56 d				
Nottingham 8	56 ⛴ a				

A ᛏ to Birmingham New Street
B From Plymouth to Edinburgh
C From Maesteg
D To Manchester Piccadilly
E From Southampton Central to Newcastle
F From Plymouth to York
G From Exeter St Davids to Manchester Piccadilly
H From Reading to Newcastle
I From Plymouth to Leeds. ᛏ to Birmingham New Street
J From Southampton Central to York
K From Plymouth

Trains between Gloucester & Cheltenham are shown on Table T058

Trains between Birmingham & Bromsgrove are shown on Table T069

Table T057-R

Sundays
15 December to 10 May

Cardiff and Bristol - Birmingham - Derby and Nottingham

	AW	XC	GW	GW	XC	XC	XC	XC	AW	XC	XC	XC	XC	XC	XC	XC	XC	AW	XC	XC	XC	XC
	◇	◇1	◇	◇	◇1	◇1	◇1	◇1	◇	◇1	◇1	◇1	◇1	◇1	◇1	◇1	◇1	◇	◇1	◇1	◇1	◇1
		A	B	C	D	A		D		E	F	G	E	F	H	I	J			K	L	M
		🍴			🍴	🍴	🍴	🍴		🍴	🍴	🍴	🍴	🍴	🍴	🍴	🍴		🍴	🍴	🍴	🍴
Cardiff Central [7] 132 d	08 23		09 13	09 20					10 30		10 45			11 45				12 24	12 45			
Newport (South Wales) 132 d	08 41		09 31	09 38					10 45		10 58			11 58				12 39	12 58			
Severn Tunnel Jn 132 d	09 03		09a48	09a48					10 58									12 52				
Caldicot d	09 05								11 01									12 55				
Chepstow d	09 14								11 10									13 04				
Lydney d	09 23								11 19									13 13				
Bristol Temple Meads [10] 134 d						09 15		10 29				11 29			12 29	13 00				13 29	14 00	
Bristol Parkway [7] 134 d						09 24		10 39				11 39			12 39	13 09				13 39	14 09	
Gloucester [7] 134 a	09 45					09 52			11 41		11 46			12 40				13 34	13 40			
d	09 46					10 01			11 42		11 48			12 48				13 35	13 48			
Cheltenham Spa [4] a	09 56					10 10		11 08	11 52		11 58	12 08		12 58	13 08	13 38		13 44	13 57	14 08	14 38	
d						10 11		11 11			11 59	12 11		12 59	13 11	13 40			13 59	14 11	14 40	
Ashchurch for Tewkesbury d																						
Worcestershire Parkway d											12 14			13 14					14 13			
University d											12 39			13 39					14 39			
Birmingham New Street [12] a						10 49		11 50			12 45	12 49		13 45	13 49	14 18			14 45	14 49	15 18	
d		09 03			10 03	11 03	11 49	12 03		12 30	12 49	13 03	13 30	13 49	14 03		14 30		14 49	15 03		15 30
Water Orton d																						
Wilnecote d																			15 04			
Tamworth d		09 19			10 19		12 07	12 19			13 07			14 07	14 20				15 09			
Burton-on-Trent d		09 28			10 29	11 26	12 19				13 19	13 26		14 19					15 21	15 25		
Willington d																						
Derby [6] 56 d		09a40			10a40	11a36	12 40	12a37		13a00	13 38	13a36	14a00	14 40	14a38		15a00		15 40	15a39		16a00
Long Eaton 56 d																						
Attenborough 56 d																						
Beeston 56 d																						
Nottingham [8] 56 ⛴ a							13 00				13 58			15 00					16 00			

	XC	XC	XC	XC	AW	XC	XC	XC	XC	XC	XC	XC	XC	AW	XC	XC	XC	XC	XC	XC	XC
	◇1	◇1	◇1	◇1	◇	◇1	◇1	◇1	◇1	◇1	◇1	◇1	◇1	◇	◇1	◇1	◇1	◇1	◇1	◇1	◇1
		H	L	M			N	O	P	Q	N	R	M		Q	S	O	M	Q	T	O
	🍴	🍴	🍴	🍴		🍴	🍴	🍴	🍴	🍴	🍴	🍴	🍴		🍴	🍴	🍴		🍴	🍴	🍴
Cardiff Central [7] 132 d	13 45				14 25	14 45				15 45				16 25	16 45				17 45		
Newport (South Wales) 132 d	14 00				14 40	14 58				15 58				16 40	16 59				17 58		
Severn Tunnel Jn 132 d					14 53									16 53							
Caldicot d					14 55									16 56							
Chepstow d					15 04									17 05							
Lydney d					15 13									17 14							
Bristol Temple Meads [10] 134 d		14 29	15 00				15 29	16 00			16 29	17 00				17 29	18 00			18 29	19 00
Bristol Parkway [7] 134 d		14 39	15 09				15 39	16 09			16 39	17 09				17 39	18 09			18 39	19 09
Gloucester [7] 134 a	14 44				15 35	15 41				16 40				17 35	17 41				18 40		
d	14 48				15 35	15 48				16 48				17 36	17 48				18 48		
Cheltenham Spa [4] a	14 58	15 08	15 38		15 46	15 57	16 08	16 38		16 58	17 08	17 38		17 46	17 58	18 08	18 38		18 58	19 08	19 38
d	14 59	15 11	15 40			15 59	16 11	16 40		16 59	17 11	17 40			17 59	18 11	18 40		18 59	19 11	19 40
Ashchurch for Tewkesbury d																					
Worcestershire Parkway d	15 14					16 13				17 14					18 14				19 14		
University d	15 39					16 39				17 39					18 39				19 39		
Birmingham New Street [12] a	15 45	15 52	16 18			16 45	16 49	17 18		17 45	17 50	18 18			18 45	18 50	19 19		19 45	19 50	20 27
d	15 49	16 03		16 30		16 49	17 03		17 30	17 49	18 03		18 30		18 49	19 03		19 30	19 49	20 03	
Water Orton d																					
Wilnecote d															19 05						
Tamworth d	16 07	16 19				17 07				18 07	18 19				19 09				20 07	20 19	
Burton-on-Trent d	16 19					17 20	17 25			18 20					19 21	19 26			20 19		
Willington d																					
Derby [6] 56 d	16 39	16a39		17a00		17 39	17a37		18a00	18 40	18a39		19a00		19 39	19a39		20a00	20 38	20a39	
Long Eaton 56 d																					
Attenborough 56 d																					
Beeston 56 d																					
Nottingham [8] 56 ⛴ a	16 59					17 59				19 00					20 00				21 00		

A To Edinburgh
B until 29 March. To Portsmouth Harbour
C from 5 April. To Portsmouth Harbour
D To Glasgow Central
E To Newcastle
F 🍴 from Birmingham New Street
G From Plymouth to Aberdeen
H From Plymouth to Glasgow Central
I From Paignton to Manchester Piccadilly
J From Guildford to Newcastle
K From Penzance to Edinburgh
L From Plymouth to Manchester Piccadilly
M From Reading to Newcastle
N From Plymouth to Edinburgh
O To Manchester Piccadilly
P From Reading to Edinburgh
Q 🍴 to Birmingham New Street
R From Penzance to Manchester Piccadilly
S From Plymouth to York
T From Plymouth to Leeds. 🍴 to Birmingham New Street

Trains between Gloucester & Cheltenham are shown on Table T058

Trains between Birmingham & Bromsgrove are shown on Table T069

Table T057-R

Sundays
15 December to 10 May

Cardiff and Bristol - Birmingham - Derby and Nottingham

	AW	XC	XC	XC	XC	AW	XC	XC	XC	AW
	◇	◇1	◇1	◇1	◇1	◇	◇1	◇1	◇1	◇
		A	B	C	D		E			
		🍴	🍴							
Cardiff Central [7] 132 d	18 24	18 45			19 45	20 24		20 45		22 26
Newport (South Wales) 132 d	18 39	18 59			20 01	20 39		20 59		22 41
Severn Tunnel Jn 132 d	18 53					20 50				22 57
Caldicot d	18 55					20 53				22 59
Chepstow d	19 04					21 02				23 08
Lydney d	19 13					21 11				23 17
Bristol Temple Meads [10] 134 d			19 31	20 00			20 29		22 10	
Bristol Parkway [7] 134 d			19 40	20 09			20 39		22 19	
Gloucester [7] 134 a	19 35	19 41			20 43	21 35		21 41		23 41
d	19 35	19 48			20 48			21 48		
Cheltenham Spa [4] a	19 45	19 58	20 09	20 38	20 57		21 08	21 58	22 48	
d		19 59	20 11	20 40	20 59		21 11	21 59	22 50	
Ashchurch for Tewkesbury d										
Worcestershire Parkway d		20 14			21 13			22 14		
University d		20 39			21 39			22 39		
Birmingham New Street [12] a		20 45	20 54	21 18	21 45		21 50	22 45	23 39	
d		20 49	21 03				22 03			
Water Orton d										
Wilnecote d										
Tamworth d		21 06	21 19				22 19			
Burton-on-Trent d		21 19	21 29							
Willington d										
Derby [6] 56 d		21 40	21a40				22a39			
Long Eaton 56 d										
Attenborough 56 d										
Beeston 56 d										
Nottingham [8] 56 ⛴ a		22 00								

A 🍴 to Birmingham New Street
B From Penzance to Leeds. 🍴 to Birmingham New Street
C From Paignton
D To Leicester
E From Plymouth to Leeds

Trains between Gloucester & Cheltenham are shown on Table T058

Trains between Birmingham & Bromsgrove are shown on Table T069

COMING SOON from MP Middleton Press

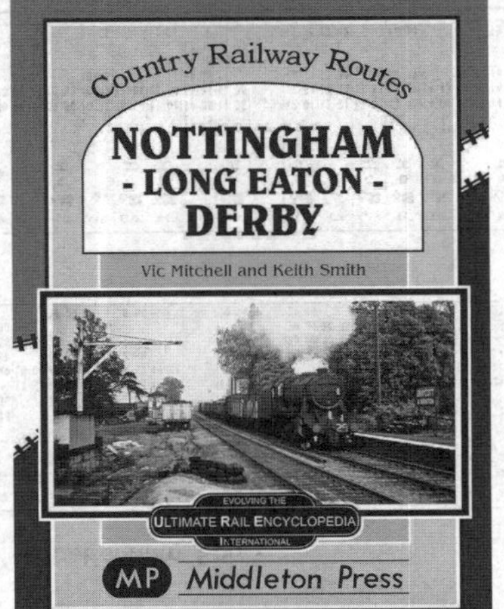

Country Railway Routes
NOTTINGHAM
- LONG EATON -
DERBY
Vic Mitchell and Keith Smith
EVOLVING THE
ULTIMATE RAIL ENCYCLOPEDIA
INTERNATIONAL
MP Middleton Press

Table T058-F

Worcester Shrub Hill - Cheltenham Spa - Gloucester

Mondays to Fridays
16 December to 15 May

Miles	Station		GW ◇1 A	AW ◇ B	GW C	GW ◇1 A	XC ◇1 D	GW E	XC ◇1 D	GW ◇1 A	GW ◇ C	GW ◇ F	AW ◇ B	GW ◇1 A	XC ◇1 G	GW ◇ F	AW ◇ B	GW ◇1 A	XC ◇1 G	GW H	GW ◇1 A	XC ◇1 G	GW ◇ F
0	Worcester Shrub Hill	d			05 20							07 08		07 25						08 58			
12	Ashchurch for Tewkesbury	d			05 36				06 30			07 24								09 14			
19¼	**Cheltenham Spa**	d	04 56	05 37	05 46	05 53	06 05	06 14	06 39	06 48		07 34	07 46	07 58	08 15		08 46	08 58	09 15	09 23	09 58	10 16	
25¾	**Gloucester**	a	05 04	05 49	05 55	06 01	06 13	06 23	06 49	06 58		07 44	07 57	08 06	08 25		08 57	09 06	09 26	09 35	10 07	10 25	
—		d		05 49	06 04		06 15	06 26	06 51		07 00	07 46	07 58		08 26	08 42	08 57		09 27	09 41		10 26	10 42
—	Bristol Parkway	d			06 43			07 02			07 40	08 22				09 19				10 16			11 16
—	Bristol Temple Meads	a			06 55			07 17			07 51	08 34				09 33				10 29			11 27
—	Cardiff Central	a		06 57			07 22		08 00				09 07		09 27		10 06		10 25			11 25	

Station		AW ◇ B	GW ◇1 A	XC ◇1 G	GW ◇ I	AW ◇	GW ◇1 A	XC ◇1 G	GW J	GW ◇1 A	XC ◇1 G	GW ◇ K	AW ◇ B	GW ◇1 A	XC ◇1 G	GW L	AW ◇	GW ◇1 M	XC ◇1 G	GW ◇ K	GW ◇1 A	XC ◇1 G	GW ◇ F
Worcester Shrub Hill	d				10 56							12 57								14 56			
Ashchurch for Tewkesbury	d				11 13							13 13								15 13			
Cheltenham Spa	d	10 40	10 58	11 15	11 22	11 46	11 58	12 14		12 58	13 15	13 22	13 45	13 58	14 15			14 58	15 15	15 22	15 58	16 15	
Gloucester	a	10 51	11 06	11 23	11 32	11 58	12 07	12 23		13 07	13 25	13 34	13 56	14 07	14 23			15 07	15 25	15 33	16 06	16 24	
	d	10 53		11 25	11 40	11 59		12 25	12 42		13 27	13 37	13 59		14 25	14 41	14 48		15 26	15 38		16 25	16 42
Bristol Parkway	d				12 16				13 16			14 13				15 16				16 14			17 16
Bristol Temple Meads	a				12 29				13 28			14 29				15 29				16 28			17 27
Cardiff Central	a	12 15		12 22		13 07		13 26			14 25		15 07		15 23		15 55		16 29			17 25	

Station		AW ◇ B	GW ◇1 A	XC ◇1 G	GW N	AW ◇ B	GW ◇1 A	XC ◇1 G	GW J	AW ◇ B	GW ◇1 A	XC ◇1 G	GW O	XC ◇1 P	GW Q	AW ◇ B	GW ◇1 A	XC ◇1 G	GW	GW ◇1 A	XC FO ◇1 G	XC FX ◇1 G
Worcester Shrub Hill	d				16 59								18 56									
Ashchurch for Tewkesbury	d			17 09	17 15			18 09					19 13									
Cheltenham Spa	d	16 45	16 58	17 18	17 24	17 45	17 58	18 18		18 45	18 58	19 15	19 22	19 28	←	19 46	19 58	20 15		20 58	21 15	21 15
Gloucester	a	16 59	17 07	17 28	17 37	17 59	18 06	18 27		18 58	19 06	19 23	19 33		19 33	19 58	20 07	20 23		21 06	21 23	21 23
	d	17 00		17 30	17 42	18 00		18 31	18 42	19 00		19 30	19 42		19 42	20 00		20 25	20 42		21 25	21 25
Bristol Parkway	d				18 16				19 16				→	19 57	20 16				21 16			
Bristol Temple Meads	a				18 29				19 29					20 07	20 28				21 28			
Cardiff Central	a	18 11		18 29		19 08		19 28		20 10		20 27		21 02		21 09		21 27			22 30	22 36

Station		GW R	GW S	XC 1 T	AW FO ◇	AW FX ◇	GW
Worcester Shrub Hill	d	21 33					22 37
Ashchurch for Tewkesbury	d	21 50		22 11			22 53
Cheltenham Spa	d	22 00	22 16	22 22	22 58	22 58	23 03
Gloucester	a	22 08	22 25	22 32	23 10	23 10	23 13
	d	22 11			23 10	23 10	23 17
Bristol Parkway	d	22 45					23 47
Bristol Temple Meads	a	22 57					23 58
Cardiff Central	a				00 22	00 34	

Saturdays
21 December to 16 May

Station		GW ◇1 A	AW ◇ B	XC ◇1 D	GW	XC ◇1 D	GW ◇1 A	GW E	GW ◇ F	AW ◇	GW ◇1 A	XC ◇1 G	GW ◇ F	AW ◇ B	GW ◇1 A	XC ◇1 G	GW L	GW ◇1 A	XC ◇1 G	GW ◇ F	AW ◇ B	GW ◇1 A	XC ◇1 G
Worcester Shrub Hill	d								06 52								08 58						
Ashchurch for Tewkesbury	d					06 33			07 08								09 14						
Cheltenham Spa	d	05 40		06 03		06 42	06 49	06 54	07 18	07 45	07 58	08 15		08 45	08 58	09 15	09 23	09 58	10 15		10 40	10 58	11 15
Gloucester	a	05 49		06 11		06 52	06 58	07 04	07 27	07 57	08 07	08 23		08 59	09 07	09 23	09 32	10 06	10 23		10 52	11 06	11 23
	d		05 50	06 15	06 18	06 54		07 06	07 40	07 57		08 25	08 42	08 59		09 25	09 41		10 25	10 42	10 53		11 25
Bristol Parkway	d				06 55			07 42	08 15				09 18				10 17			11 18			
Bristol Temple Meads	a				07 10			07 53	08 28				09 30				10 32			11 32			
Cardiff Central	a		07 01	07 20		08 06				09 07		09 23		10 14		10 29			11 25		12 01		12 26

Station		GW ◇ I	AW ◇	GW ◇1 A	XC ◇1 G	GW J	GW ◇1 A	XC ◇1 G	GW ◇ K	AW ◇ B	GW ◇1 A	XC ◇1 G	GW L	AW ◇ U	GW ◇1 A	XC ◇1 G	GW ◇ K	GW ◇1 A	XC ◇1 G	GW ◇ F	AW ◇ B	GW ◇1 A	XC ◇1 G
Worcester Shrub Hill	d	11 09							12 59								14 59						
Ashchurch for Tewkesbury	d	11 25							13 15								15 15						
Cheltenham Spa	d	11 34	11 46	11 58	12 15		12 58	13 15	13 24	13 45	13 58	14 15			14 58	15 15	15 24	15 58	16 15		16 45	16 58	17 15
Gloucester	a	11 43	11 57	12 07	12 23		13 06	13 23	13 33	13 57	14 07	14 23			15 07	15 23	15 33	16 06	16 23		16 57	17 07	17 23
	d	11 46	11 58		12 25	12 42		13 25	13 42	13 58		14 25	14 42	14 42		15 25	15 42		16 25	16 42	16 58		17 25
Bristol Parkway	d	12 22				13 18			14 18				15 18				16 18			17 18			
Bristol Temple Meads	a	12 33				13 30			14 31				15 32				16 30			17 32			
Cardiff Central	a		13 06		13 27			14 25		15 09		15 27		15 51		16 25			17 26		18 09		18 26

A To London Paddington
B To Maesteg
C To Taunton
D From Birmingham New Street
E To Weston-super-Mare
F To Weymouth
G From Nottingham
H From Worcester Foregate Street to Westbury
I From Great Malvern to Brighton
J To Frome
K From Great Malvern to Weymouth
L To Westbury
M To London Paddington. The Cheltenham Spa Express
N From Great Malvern to Westbury
O From Worcester Foregate Street to Bristol Temple Meads
P From Manchester Piccadilly. ⚯ to Bristol Temple Meads
Q From Worcester Foregate Street
R From Great Malvern
S To Swindon
T From Leicester
U To Fishguard Harbour

Table T058-F

Worcester Shrub Hill - Cheltenham Spa - Gloucester

Saturdays
21 December to 16 May

Station		AW ◇ A	GW B	GW ◇1 C	XC ◇1 D	GW E	AW ◇ A	GW ◇1 C	XC ◇1 D	GW F	XC ◇1 G	GW H	AW ◇	GW ◇1 C	XC ◇1 D	GW ◇1 C	XC ◇1 D	GW	GW I	GW H	GW	AW ◇
Worcester Shrub Hill	d		17 14							18 59										21 41	22 28	
Ashchurch for Tewkesbury	d		17 30		18 09					19 15										21 57	22 44	
Cheltenham Spa	d	17 35	17 40	17 58	18 18		18 45	19 00	19 15	19 24	19 31	←	19 45	19 58	20 15	21 00	21 15	21 20	21 31	22 06	22 53	
Gloucester	a	17 46	17 49	18 06	18 27		18 57	19 11	19 23	19 34		19 34	19 57	20 07	20 23	21 12	21 24	21 30	21 40	22 19	23 02	
	d	17 46	17 50		18 28	18 42	18 58		19 25	19 42		19 42	19 58		20 25		21 26	21 33				23 09
Bristol Parkway	d		18 26			19 18				→	20 00	20 19						22 08				
Bristol Temple Meads	a		18 38			19 35					20 09	20 31						22 22				
Cardiff Central	a	18 52			19 24		20 08		20 20		21 00		21 07		21 22		22 43					00 36

Sundays
15 December to 10 May

Station		AW ◇	GW ◇1 C	GW J	GW ◇1 C	AW ◇	GW ◇1 C	XC ◇1 K	GW	GW ◇1 C	XC ◇1 D	AW ◇	GW ◇1 C	XC ◇1 D	GW ◇1 C	AW ◇ L	XC ◇1 D	AW ◇ M	GW J	GW ◇1 C	XC ◇1 D	GW ◇1 C	AW ◇ L
Worcester Shrub Hill	d								11 00										13 55				
Ashchurch for Tewkesbury	d								11 15										14 12				
Cheltenham Spa	d		08 58	09 19	09 50	10 37	10 54	11 01	11 25	11 55	12 01	12 21	13 01	13 19	14 01	14 10	14 15	←	14 21	14 58	15 15	15 58	16 10
Gloucester	a		09 10	09 29	10 02	10 47	11 06	11 10	11 35	12 06	12 09	12 32	13 13	13 27	14 13	14 22	14 23	14 22	14 32	15 11	15 27	16 10	16 20
	d	08 45		09 30		10 48		11 11	11 38		12 11	12 36		13 29		14 29	14 25	14 29	14 43		15 29		16 29
Bristol Parkway	d			10 07					12 15							→			15 19				→
Bristol Temple Meads	a			10 20					12 27										15 30				
Cardiff Central	a	10 03				11 55		12 06			13 06	13 47		14 24			15 21	15 49			16 25		

Station		XC ◇1 D	AW ◇ M	GW	GW ◇1 C	XC ◇1 D	GW ◇1 C	XC ◇1 D	GW	AW ◇	GW ◇1 C	XC ◇1 D	GW ◇1 C	AW ◇ L	XC ◇1 D	AW ◇ M	GW	GW ◇1 C	GW 1 I	GW	AW ◇
Worcester Shrub Hill	d			15 57					17 56								19 56				
Ashchurch for Tewkesbury	d			16 13					18 14								20 14				
Cheltenham Spa	d	16 15	←	16 22	17 00	17 15	18 00	18 15	18 22	18 35	19 00	19 15	19 58	20 10	20 15	←	20 22	20 58	21 58	22 05	
Gloucester	a	16 23	16 20	16 32	17 12	17 23	18 12	18 23	18 32	18 47	19 12	19 23	20 11	20 22	20 24	20 22	20 32	21 10	22 07	22 15	
	d	16 25	16 29	16 39		17 25		18 25	18 36	18 48		19 25		20 33	20 26	20 33	20 39				22 33
Bristol Parkway	d			17 14					19 11					→			21 16				
Bristol Temple Meads	a			17 29					19 24								21 30				
Cardiff Central	a	17 20	17 37			18 20		19 21		20 09		20 21			21 21	21 48					23 52

A To Maesteg
B From Great Malvern to Southampton Central
C To London Paddington
D From Nottingham
E To Frome
F From Great Malvern to Bristol Temple Meads
G From Manchester Piccadilly. ⚯ to Bristol Temple Meads
H From Great Malvern
I To Swindon
J To Taunton
K From Birmingham New Street
L To Cardiff Central
M From Cheltenham Spa

Table T058-R

Gloucester - Cheltenham Spa - Worcester Shrub Hill

Mondays to Fridays
16 December to 15 May

Miles			GW MO	GW MX	GW	GW	GW	XC		GW	AW	GW	XC	GW	GW	XC	AW	GW		XC	GW	GW	GW	XC	AW
			◇1					◇1			◇	◇1	◇1	◇1		◇1	◇	◇1		◇1		◇1		◇1	◇
			A	A			B	C		D		E	F	G	H	I		E		F	J	E	K	F	L
			⚲									⚲		⚲		⚲		⚲				⚲			
—	Cardiff Central 7	d									06 10		06 38			06 57	07 06			07 45				08 45	09 07
—	Bristol Temple Meads 10	d					06 10	06 24							07 38	08 00							08 37		
—	Bristol Parkway 10	d					06 22	06 34		←					07 54	08 09		←					08 51		
0	Gloucester 7	a					07 00	07 04		07 00	07 16		07 43		08 31		08 10			08 46			09 31	09 45	10 15
—		d	00 03	00 34	04 37	06 00	07 11	07 07		07 11	07 17	07 24	07 45	08 22			08 11	08 22		08 49	08 56	09 17	09 35	09 49	10 16
6½	Cheltenham Spa 4	a	00 12	00 43	04 46	06 09	→	07 16		07 21	07 27	07 32	07 54	→		08 38	08 21	08 31		08 58	09 05	09 25	09 44	09 58	10 26
13¾	Ashchurch for Tewkesbury	a			04 55	06 18		07 24		07 31			08 03										09 53		
25¾	Worcester Shrub Hill 7	a			05 13	06 36				07 48		07 58											10 11		

		GW	GW	XC		AW	GW	GW	XC	GW	GW	XC	AW	GW		GW	XC	AW	GW	GW	XC	GW	GW	XC
		◇1		◇1		◇	◇1	◇	◇1	◇1	◇	◇1	◇	◇1		◇	◇1	◇	◇1	◇	◇1	◇1	◇	◇1
		M	J	F		L	E	N	F	E	O	F	L	E		P	F	L	E	O	F	E	N	F
		⚲		⚲			⚲			⚲		⚲		⚲			⚲		⚲		⚲	⚲		⚲
Cardiff Central 7	d			09 45		10 09			10 45			11 45	12 10				12 45	13 10			13 45			14 45
Bristol Temple Meads 10	d		09 38					10 37			11 37					12 38				13 38			14 38	
Bristol Parkway 10	d		09 50					10 50			11 50					12 50				13 50			14 51	
Gloucester 7	a		10 29	10 43		11 13		11 29	11 44		12 27	12 42	13 16			13 29	13 43	14 15		14 27	14 43		15 30	15 45
	d	10 21		10 48		11 14	11 20	11 37	11 48	12 19		12 44	13 16	13 21		13 36	13 48		14 19		14 48	15 20	15 36	15 48
Cheltenham Spa 4	a	10 30		10 58		11 25	11 30	11 46	11 58	12 27		12 54	13 27	13 31		13 45	13 58		14 27		14 57	15 28	15 45	15 58
Ashchurch for Tewkesbury	a							11 55				13 02				13 55							15 54	
Worcester Shrub Hill 7	a							12 13								14 12							16 12	

		AW	GW	GW	XC	AW	GW	GW	XC	AW		GW	GW	XC	AW	GW	GW	XC	GW	GW		XC	GW	GW	GW
		◇	◇1	◇	◇1	◇	◇1		◇1	◇		◇1	◇	◇1	◇	◇1		◇1	◇1			◇1	◇1		
		L	E	O	F	L	E	Q	F	L		E	O	F	L	E	K	F	E	R		S	E	R	J
			⚲		⚲		⚲		⚲			⚲		⚲		⚲		⚲	⚲				⚲		
Cardiff Central 7	d	15 09			15 45	16 08			16 45	17 07				17 45	18 07			18 45				19 49			
Bristol Temple Meads 10	d			15 38				16 38					17 38				18 41			19 46				20 45	
Bristol Parkway 10	d			15 51				16 51					17 51				18 56			19 58				21 01	
Gloucester 7	a	16 13		16 29	16 43	17 17		17 33	17 44	18 13			18 30	18 43	19 11		19 33	19 42		20 34		20 53		21 47	
	d	16 14	16 24		16 46	17 17	17 22	17 39	17 48	18 14		18 22		18 44	19 12	19 24	19 39	19 47	20 22			20 55	21 23	21 50	21 56
Cheltenham Spa 4	a	16 24	16 32		16 56	17 27	17 31	17 48	17 58	18 24		18 30		18 54	19 22	19 32	19 48	19 57	20 31			21 04	21 32	22 00	22 05
Ashchurch for Tewkesbury	a							17 57						19 02			19 57						21 40	22 09	
Worcester Shrub Hill 7	a							18 20									20 15						22 09	22 27	

		XC	AW	GW	GW	XC		GW	GW FX	GW FO	AW FO	AW FX
		◇1	◇	◇1		◇1		◇1	◇		◇	◇
		S	L	E		S		E	O		L	L
				⚲				⚲				
Cardiff Central 7	d	21 05	21 09			21 45					23 20	23 20
Bristol Temple Meads 10	d				21 45				22 45	22 46		
Bristol Parkway 10	d				21 58				23 00	23 00		
Gloucester 7	a	22 00	22 17		22 34	22 44			23 38	23 40	00 32	00 40
	d	22 02	22 18	22 25		22 48		23 23				
Cheltenham Spa 4	a	22 12	22 28	22 34		22 57		23 32				
Ashchurch for Tewkesbury	a	22 20										
Worcester Shrub Hill 7	a											

Saturdays
21 December to 16 May

		GW	GW	XC	GW	AW	XC	GW	GW	XC		AW	XC	GW	GW	XC	AW	GW	GW	XC		AW	GW	GW	XC
				◇1		◇	◇1	◇1		◇1		◇	◇1	◇1		◇1	◇	◇1		◇1		◇	◇1	◇	◇1
		A		C			F	A	H	I			F	E	K	F	L	E	J	F		L	E	N	F
								⚲		⚲				⚲				⚲		⚲			⚲		
Cardiff Central 7	d					06 10	06 38			07 00		07 06	07 45			08 45	09 04			09 45		10 07			10 45
Bristol Temple Meads 10	d				06 20				07 39	08 00					08 39				09 39					10 39	
Bristol Parkway 10	d				06 33				07 51	08 09					08 51				09 51					10 51	
Gloucester 7	a				07 12	07 19	07 42		08 28			08 19	08 46		09 28	09 43	10 13		10 30	10 42		11 12		11 28	11 45
	d	00 34	06 00	07 02	07 17	07 21	07 44	08 19				08 22	08 48	09 19	09 37	09 48	10 13	10 20		10 48		11 13	11 20	11 38	11 48
Cheltenham Spa 4	a	00 43	06 09	07 13	07 27	07 34	07 54	08 28		08 39		08 33	08 58	09 28	09 46	09 58	10 24	10 29		10 58		11 23	11 31	11 47	11 58
Ashchurch for Tewkesbury	a		06 18	07 21	07 36		08 02								09 55									11 56	
Worcester Shrub Hill 7	a		06 37		07 54										10 13									12 14	

		GW	GW	XC	AW	GW		GW	XC	GW	AW	GW	XC	GW	GW	XC		AW	GW	GW	XC	AW	GW	GW	XC
		◇1	◇	◇1	◇	◇1		◇	◇1	◇1	◇	◇	◇1	◇1		◇1		◇	◇1	◇	◇1	◇	◇1		◇1
		E	O	F	L	E		P	F	E		O	F	E	N	F			E	O	F	L	E	Q	F
		⚲				⚲			⚲	⚲			⚲	⚲		⚲			⚲				⚲		⚲
Cardiff Central 7	d			11 45	12 07				12 45		13 12		13 45			14 45		15 07			15 45	16 06			16 45
Bristol Temple Meads 10	d		11 39					12 39				13 39			14 39					15 39				16 39	
Bristol Parkway 10	d		11 51					12 51				13 51			14 51					15 51				16 51	
Gloucester 7	a		12 29	12 43	13 11			13 28	13 44		14 21	14 30	14 43		15 28	15 43		16 11		16 28	16 43	17 12		17 28	17 43
	d	12 20		12 44	13 12	13 20		13 38	13 48	14 20			14 48	15 19	15 37	15 48		16 16	16 20		16 48	17 12	17 19	17 38	17 48
Cheltenham Spa 4	a	12 29		12 54	13 22	13 31		13 47	13 58	14 28			14 58	15 27	15 46	15 58		16 27	16 31		16 58	17 22	17 27	17 47	17 58
Ashchurch for Tewkesbury	a			13 02				13 56							15 55									17 56	
Worcester Shrub Hill 7	a							14 13							16 13									18 14	

A From Swindon
B To Worcester Foregate Street
C To Stansted Airport
D From Bristol Temple Meads to Worcester Foregate Street
E From London Paddington
F To Nottingham
G From London Paddington to Cheltenham Spa
H From Salisbury
I To Manchester Piccadilly. ⚲ from Bristol Temple Meads
J From Westbury
K From Warminster to Great Malvern
L From Maesteg
M From London Paddington. The Cheltenham Spa Express
N From Southampton Central to Great Malvern
O From Weymouth
P From Brighton to Great Malvern
Q From Warminster to Worcester Foregate Street
R From Weston-super-Mare
S To Birmingham New Street

Table T058-R

Gloucester - Cheltenham Spa - Worcester Shrub Hill

Saturdays
21 December to 16 May

		AW		GW	GW	XC	AW	GW	GW	XC	GW	GW		XC	GW	GW	XC	GW	AW	GW	AW
		◇		◇1	◇	◇1	◇	◇1		◇1	◇1			◇1	◇1		◇1	◇1	◇		◇
		A		B	C	D	A	B	E	D	B	F		D	B		G	B	A		A
				⚲		⚲		⚲			⚲				⚲			⚲			
Cardiff Central 7	d	17 07				17 45	18 06			18 45				20 00			20 48		21 11		23 18
Bristol Temple Meads 10	d				17 39				18 39			19 39				20 39				22 06	
Bristol Parkway 10	d				17 51				18 51			19 51				20 51				22 19	
Gloucester 7	a	18 13			18 30	18 42	19 14		19 28	19 42		20 29		21 04		21 32	21 43		22 20	22 55	00 40
	d	18 14		18 21		18 44	19 15	19 23	19 38	19 48	20 22	20 36		21 06	21 19	21 37	21 48	22 19			
Cheltenham Spa 4	a	18 23		18 31		18 54	19 26	19 32	19 48	19 58	20 32	20 46		21 16	21 28	21 46	21 58	22 28			
Ashchurch for Tewkesbury	a					19 02			19 57					21 24		21 55					
Worcester Shrub Hill 7	a								20 15							22 14					

Sundays
15 December to 10 May

		AW	GW	GW	GW	AW	XC	GW	GW	XC		GW	AW	XC	GW	GW	XC	GW	AW	XC		GW	GW	XC	GW
		◇		◇1	◇1	◇	◇1	◇1		◇1		◇1	◇	◇1	◇1		◇1	◇1	◇	◇1		◇1		◇1	◇1
				B	B		D	B		D		B		D	B		D	B		D		B		D	B
				⚲	⚲			⚲				⚲		⚲	⚲		⚲	⚲		⚲		⚲		⚲	⚲
Cardiff Central 7	d	08 23				10 30	10 45			11 45			12 24	12 45			13 45		14 25	14 45				15 45	
Bristol Temple Meads 10	d		09 20						11 38							13 38							15 38		
Bristol Parkway 10	d		09 29						11 48							13 48							15 48		
Gloucester 7	a	09 45	10 09			11 41	11 46		12 28	12 40			13 34	13 40		14 28	14 44		15 35	15 41			16 29	16 40	
	d	09 46	10 13	10 21	11 25	11 42	11 48	12 23	12 39	12 48		13 21	13 35	13 48	14 22	14 38	14 48	15 21	15 35	15 48		16 21	16 37	16 48	17 22
Cheltenham Spa 4	a	09 56	10 22	10 30	11 34	11 52	11 58	12 32	12 49	12 58		13 31	13 44	13 57	14 31	14 48	14 58	15 31	15 46	15 57		16 32	16 46	16 58	17 32
Ashchurch for Tewkesbury	a		10 30						12 57							14 57							16 57		
Worcester Shrub Hill 7	a		10 48						13 20							15 22							17 22		

		AW	XC	GW	GW	XC		GW	AW	XC	GW	XC	GW	GW	AW	XC		GW	GW	AW
		◇	◇1	◇1		◇1		◇1	◇	◇1	◇1	◇1	◇1		◇	◇1		◇1		◇
			D	B		D		B		D	B	H	B			G		B		
			⚲	⚲		⚲		⚲		⚲	⚲		⚲					⚲		
Cardiff Central 7	d	16 25	16 45			17 45			18 24	18 45		19 45			20 24	20 45				22 26
Bristol Temple Meads 10	d				17 38									20 37					22 30	
Bristol Parkway 10	d				17 47									20 46					22 39	
Gloucester 7	a	17 35	17 41		18 27	18 40			19 35	19 41		20 43		21 28	21 35	21 41			23 19	23 41
	d	17 36	17 48	18 22	18 39	18 48		19 21	19 35	19 48	20 21	20 48	21 24	21 32		21 48		22 24		
Cheltenham Spa 4	a	17 46	17 58	18 32	18 48	18 58		19 31	19 45	19 58	20 32	20 57	21 33	21 41		21 58		22 33		
Ashchurch for Tewkesbury	a				18 57															
Worcester Shrub Hill 7	a				19 22															

A From Maesteg
B From London Paddington
C From Weymouth
D To Nottingham
E From Warminster to Great Malvern
F From Westbury
G To Birmingham New Street
H To Leicester

Table T059-F

Mondays to Fridays
16 December to 15 May

Stratford - Highbury & Islington, West Hampstead, Willesden Junction, Clapham Junction and Richmond

Miles	Miles			LO MX	LO MO	LO MX	LO MX	LO MX	LO MX	LO MX	LO	LO	LO	LO	LO	LO	LO	LO	LO	LO	LO	LO	LO	LO
0	—	**Stratford** 7 ⊖ ⇌	d							00 15						05 47		05 58	06 07	06 10	06 17	06 22	06 28	06 35
1	—	Hackney Wick	d						00 03	00 18						05 50		06 01	06 10	06 14	06 20	06 27	06 31	06 39
1¾	—	Homerton	d						00 05	00 21						05 53		06 04	06 13	06 17	06 23	06 30	06 34	06 42
2½	—	Hackney Central	d						00 07	00 23						05 55		06 06	06 15	06 19	06 25	06 32	06 36	06 44
3¼	—	Dalston Kingsland	d						00 09	00 25						05 57		06 08	06 17	06 21	06 27	06 34	06 38	06 46
4¼	—	Canonbury 178	d						00 11	00 27						05 59		06 10	06 19	06 23	06 29	06 36	06 40	06 48
4¾	—	**Highbury & Islington** ⊖178	d						00 14	00 29						06 01		06 12	06 21	06 25	06 31	06 38	06 42	06 50
5¼	—	Caledonian Rd & Barnsbury	d					00 01	00 16	00 31						06 03		06 14	06 24	06 27	06 33	06 40	06 44	06 52
6¼	—	Camden Road	d					00 03	00 19	00 34						06 06		06 17	06 27	06 30	06 36	06 43	06 47	06 55
6¾	—	Kentish Town West	d					00 06	00 21	00 37						06 09		06 20	06 29	06 33	06 39	06 46	06 50	06 58
7½	—	**Gospel Oak**	d					00 08	00 23	00 40						06 11		06 22	06 31	06 37	06 43	06 48	06 52	07 02
8	—	Hampstead Heath	d					00 10	00 25	00 42						06 13		06 24	06 33	06 39	06 45	06 50	06 54	07 04
9	—	Finchley Road & Frognal	d					00 12	00 27	00 44						06 15		06 26	06 35	06 41	06 47	06 52	06 56	07 06
9½	—	West Hampstead ⊖	d					00 14	00 29	00 46						06 17		06 28	06 37	06 43	06 49	06 54	06 58	07 08
10	—	Brondesbury	d				00 01	00 16	00 31	00 47						06 18		06 29	06 39	06 45	06 50	06 55	06 59	07 09
10¼	—	Brondesbury Park	d				00 02	00 17	00 32	00 49						06 20		06 31	06 40	06 46	06 52	06 57	07 01	07 11
11	—	Kensal Rise	d				00 04	00 19	00 34	00 51						06 22		06 33	06 42	06 48	06 54	06 59	07 03	07 13
12	0	**Willesden Jn. High Level** ⊖	a				00 10	00 25	00 40	00 57						06 26		06 38	06 46	06 53	06 58	07 02	07 07	07 16
—	—		d			00 01					05 58	06 02	06 10	06 14	06 23	06 27	06 35	06 40	06 47	06 54	06 59	07 03	07 08	07 17
12	—	**Willesden Jn Low Level** ⊖	a																					
—	2	**Shepherd's Bush** ⊖66,176	d		00 05	00 09					06 05		06 16		06 30		06 41		06 53		07 05		07 17	
—	2¾	**Kensington (Olympia)** ⊖176	d		00 07	00 11					06 07		06 18		06 32		06 43		06 55		07 07		07 19	
—	3½	West Brompton ⊖176	d		00 10	00 14					06 10		06 21		06 35		06 46		06 58		07 10		07 22	
—	4½	Imperial Wharf 176	d		00a13	00 17					06 13		06 24		06 38		06 49		07 01		07 13		07 25	
—	6	**Clapham Junction** 10 66,176	a			00 22					06 19		06 31		06 44		06 56		07 09		07 19		07 30	
13¾	—	Acton Central	d	00 02								06 07		06 19		06 37		06 46		06 59		07 10		07 24
14¼	—	South Acton	d	00 04								06 09		06 21		06 40		06 49		07 02		07 13		07 26
15¼	—	Gunnersbury ⊖	d	00 08								06 13		06 24		06 44		06 52		07 05		07 19		07 29
16¼	—	Kew Gardens ⊖	d	00 11								06 16		06 27		06 47		06 55		07 08		07 22		07 32
17¾	—	**Richmond** ⊖	a	00 15								06 23		06 35		06 51		07 00		07 13		07 26		07 38

		LO	LO	LO	LO	LO	LO	LO	LO	LO	LO	LO	LO	LO	LO	LO	LO	LO	LO	LO	LO	LO	LO
Stratford 7 ⊖ ⇌	d	06 39	06 47	06 53	06 59	07 05	07 11	07 18	07 23	07 30	07 35	07 41	07 47	07 54	07 59	08 06	08 11	08 17	08 21	08 28	08 37	08 42	08 47
Hackney Wick	d	06 43	06 50	06 56	07 02	07 08	07 14	07 21	07 26	07 33	07 38	07 44	07 50	07 57	08 02	08 09	08 14	08 20	08 24	08 31	08 40	08 45	08 50
Homerton	d	06 46	06 53	06 59	07 05	07 11	07 17	07 24	07 29	07 36	07 41	07 47	07 53	08 00	08 05	08 12	08 17	08 23	08 27	08 34	08 43	08 48	08 53
Hackney Central	d	06 48	06 55	07 01	07 07	07 13	07 19	07 26	07 31	07 38	07 43	07 49	07 55	08 02	08 07	08 14	08 19	08 25	08 29	08 36	08 45	08 50	08 55
Dalston Kingsland	d	06 50	06 57	07 03	07 09	07 15	07 21	07 28	07 33	07 40	07 45	07 51	07 57	08 04	08 09	08 16	08 21	08 27	08 31	08 38	08 47	08 52	08 57
Canonbury 178	d	06 52	06 59	07 05	07 11	07 17	07 23	07 30	07 35	07 42	07 47	07 53	07 59	08 06	08 11	08 18	08 23	08 29	08 33	08 40	08 49	08 54	08 59
Highbury & Islington ⊖178	d	06 54	07 02	07 08	07 14	07 20	07 26	07 33	07 38	07 45	07 50	07 56	08 02	08 09	08 14	08 21	08 26	08 32	08 36	08 43	08 52	08 57	09 01
Caledonian Rd & Barnsbury	d	06 56	07 04	07 10	07 16	07 22	07 28	07 35	07 40	07 47	07 52	07 58	08 04	08 11	08 16	08 23	08 28	08 34	08 38	08 45	08 54	08 59	09 03
Camden Road	d	06 59	07 09	07 13	07 20	07 25	07 31	07 38	07 43	07 50	07 55	08 01	08 10	08 14	08 19	08 26	08 31	08 37	08 41	08 48	08 57	09 02	09 06
Kentish Town West	d	07 02	07 11	07 15	07 22	07 27	07 33	07 41	07 45	07 52	07 57	08 03	08 12	08 16	08 21	08 28	08 33	08 39	08 43	08 50	08 59	09 04	09 09
Gospel Oak	d	07 06	07 13	07 19	07 25	07 31	07 37	07 43	07 51	07 55	08 01	08 07	08 14	08 19	08 25	08 31	08 37	08 43	08 47	08 53	09 01	09 06	09 15
Hampstead Heath	d	07 08	07 15	07 21	07 27	07 33	07 39	07 45	07 54	07 58	08 03	08 09	08 16	08 21	08 27	08 33	08 39	08 45	08 49	08 55	09 03	09 08	09 17
Finchley Road & Frognal	d	07 10	07 17	07 23	07 29	07 35	07 41	07 47	07 56	08 00	08 05	08 11	08 18	08 23	08 29	08 35	08 41	08 47	08 51	08 57	09 05	09 10	09 19
West Hampstead ⊖	d	07 12	07 19	07 25	07 31	07 37	07 43	07 49	07 58	08 02	08 07	08 13	08 20	08 25	08 31	08 37	08 43	08 49	08 53	08 59	09 07	09 12	09 21
Brondesbury	d	07 13	07 21	07 27	07 33	07 39	07 45	07 51	07 59	08 03	08 09	08 15	08 22	08 27	08 33	08 39	08 45	08 51	08 55	09 00	09 09	09 14	09 23
Brondesbury Park	d	07 15	07 22	07 28	07 34	07 40	07 46	07 52	08 01	08 05	08 10	08 16	08 23	08 28	08 34	08 40	08 46	08 52	08 56	09 02	09 10	09 15	09 24
Kensal Rise	d	07 17	07 24	07 30	07 36	07 42	07 48	07 54	08 03	08 07	08 12	08 18	08 25	08 30	08 36	08 42	08 48	08 54	08 58	09 04	09 12	09 17	09 26
Willesden Jn. High Level ⊖	a	07 21	07 29	07 34	07 41	07 46	07 53	07 58	08 06	08 10	08 17	08 22	08 29	08 34	08 41	08 46	08 52	08 58	09 03	09 08	09 17	09 21	09 29
	d	07 22	07 30	07 35	07 42	07 47	07 54	07 59	08 07	08 11	08 18	08 23	08 30	08 35	08 42	08 47	08 53	08 59	09 04	09 09	09 18	09 22	09 30
Willesden Jn Low Level ⊖	a																						
Shepherd's Bush ⊖66,176	d	07 29		07 42		07 54		08 06		08 17		08 30		08 43		08 54		09 06		09 17		09 29	
Kensington (Olympia) ⊖176	d	07 31		07 44		07 56		08 09		08 19		08 32		08 45		08 56		09 08		09 19		09 31	
West Brompton ⊖176	d	07 34		07 46		07 59		08 11		08 22		08 34		08 47		08 58		09 10		09 22		09 33	
Imperial Wharf 176	d	07 37		07a49		08 02		08 14		08 25		08 37		08 50		09 01		09 13		09 25		09 36	
Clapham Junction 10 66,176	a	07 44				08 10		08 23		08 32		08 46		08 56		09 08		09 19		09 33		09 44	
Acton Central	d		07 35		07 47		07 59		08 12		08 23		08 35		08 47		08 58		09 11		09 24		09 35
South Acton	d		07 38		07 50		08 02		08 14		08 26		08 38		08 50		09 00		09 14		09 27		09 38
Gunnersbury ⊖	d		07 41		07 55		08 05		08 19		08 29		08 41		08 53		09 03		09 18		09 30		09 42
Kew Gardens ⊖	d		07 44		07 58		08 08		08 22		08 32		08 44		08 56		09 06		09 21		09 33		09 45
Richmond ⊖	a		07 49		08 03		08 13		08 27		08 37		08 49		09 01		09 13		09 25		09 39		09 50

For services between Shepherds Bush and Clapham Junction refer to Table T066 and T176

Table T059-F

Mondays to Fridays
16 December to 15 May

Stratford - Highbury & Islington, West Hampstead, Willesden Junction, Clapham Junction and Richmond

		LO	LO	LO	LO	LO	LO	LO	LO	LO	LO	LO	LO	LO	LO	LO	LO	LO	LO	LO	LO	LO	LO
Stratford 7 ⊖ ⇌	d	08 53	08 57	09 06	09 12	09 15	09 24	09 28	09 35	09 41	09 45	09 53	09 57	10 08	10 15	10 23	10 30	10 39	10 46	10 53	11 00	11 08	11 15
Hackney Wick	d	08 56	09 00	09 08	09 16	09 20	09 28	09 31	09 38	09 45	09 49	09 56	10 00	10 13	10 18	10 26	10 33	10 43	10 49	10 56	11 03	11 11	11 18
Homerton	d	08 59	09 03	09 11	09 18	09 23	09 30	09 34	09 41	09 47	09 52	09 59	10 03	10 15	10 21	10 29	10 36	10 45	10 52	10 59	11 06	11 14	11 21
Hackney Central	d	09 01	09 05	09 13	09 20	09 25	09 32	09 36	09 43	09 49	09 54	10 01	10 05	10 17	10 23	10 31	10 38	10 47	10 54	11 01	11 08	11 16	11 23
Dalston Kingsland	d	09 03	09 07	09 15	09 22	09 27	09 35	09 38	09 45	09 51	09 56	10 03	10 07	10 19	10 25	10 33	10 40	10 49	10 56	11 03	11 10	11 18	11 25
Canonbury 178	d	09 05	09 09	09 17	09 24	09 29	09 37	09 40	09 47	09 53	09 58	10 05	10 09	10 21	10 27	10 35	10 42	10 51	10 58	11 05	11 12	11 20	11 27
Highbury & Islington ⊖178	d	09 07	09 11	09 19	09 27	09 31	09 39	09 44	09 49	09 56	10 00	10 07	10 11	10 24	10 29	10 37	10 44	10 54	11 01	11 07	11 14	11 22	11 29
Caledonian Rd & Barnsbury	d	09 09	09 13	09 21	09 29	09 33	09 41	09 46	09 51	09 58	10 02	10 09	10 13	10 26	10 31	10 39	10 46	10 56	11 03	11 09	11 16	11 24	11 31
Camden Road	d	09 12	09 16	09 24	09 32	09 36	09 45	09 49	09 54	10 01	10 05	10 12	10 16	10 29	10 34	10 43	10 49	10 59	11 07	11 14	11 19	11 27	11 34
Kentish Town West	d	09 15	09 19	09 27	09 34	09 39	09 48	09 52	09 57	10 03	10 08	10 15	10 19	10 31	10 37	10 46	10 52	11 01	11 09	11 17	11 22	11 30	11 37
Gospel Oak	d	09 20	09 24	09 33	09 37	09 41	09 50	09 54	09 59	10 05	10 10	10 17	10 21	10 35	10 40	10 49	10 54	11 03	11 11	11 19	11 24	11 34	11 40
Hampstead Heath	d	09 22	09 26	09 35	09 39	09 44	09 52	09 57	10 01	10 07	10 12	10 19	10 24	10 37	10 42	10 52	10 56	11 05	11 14	11 22	11 26	11 36	11 42
Finchley Road & Frognal	d	09 24	09 28	09 37	09 41	09 46	09 54	09 59	10 03	10 09	10 14	10 21	10 26	10 39	10 44	10 54	10 58	11 07	11 16	11 24	11 28	11 38	11 44
West Hampstead ⊖	d	09 26	09 30	09 39	09 43	09 48	09 56	10 01	10 05	10 11	10 16	10 23	10 28	10 41	10 46	10 56	11 00	11 09	11 18	11 26	11 30	11 40	11 46
Brondesbury	d	09 27	09 32	09 40	09 45	09 49	09 58	10 02	10 07	10 13	10 17	10 25	10 29	10 42	10 48	10 57	11 02	11 11	11 19	11 27	11 32	11 41	11 48
Brondesbury Park	d	09 29	09 33	09 42	09 46	09 51	09 59	10 04	10 08	10 14	10 19	10 26	10 31	10 44	10 49	10 59	11 03	11 12	11 21	11 29	11 33	11 43	11 49
Kensal Rise	d	09 31	09 35	09 44	09 48	09 53	10 01	10 06	10 10	10 16	10 21	10 28	10 33	10 46	10 51	11 01	11 05	11 14	11 23	11 31	11 35	11 45	11 51
Willesden Jn. High Level ⊖	a	09 34	09 38	09 47	09 51	09 56	10 05	10 10	10 14	10 19	10 24	10 32	10 37	10 49	10 54	11 04	11 08	11 18	11 26	11 34	11 38	11 49	11 54
	d	09 35	09 39	09 48	09 52	09 57	10 06	10 11	10 15	10 20	10 26	10 33	10 38	10 50	10 55	11 05	11 09	11 19	11 27	11 35	11 39	11 50	11 56
Willesden Jn Low Level ⊖	a																						
Shepherd's Bush ⊖66,176	d	09 41		09 56		10 05		10 18		10 27		10 42		10 56		11 11		11 26		11 41		11 56	
Kensington (Olympia) ⊖176	d	09 43		09 58		10 07		10 20		10 29		10 44		10 58		11 13		11 29		11 43		11 58	
West Brompton ⊖176	d	09 46		10 01		10 10		10 22		10 32		10 47		11 01		11 16		11 32		11 46		12 01	
Imperial Wharf 176	d	09 49		10 04		10 13		10 25		10 35		10 50		11 04		11 19		11 35		11 49		12 04	
Clapham Junction 10 66,176	a	09 55		10 11		10 20		10 33		10 43		10 58		11 10		11 25		11 41		11 55		12 10	
Acton Central	d		09 45		09 58		10 11		10 20		10 32		10 45		11 04		11 14		11 32		11 44		12 03
South Acton	d		09 47		10 01		10 14		10 23		10 37		10 47		11 06		11 17		11 35		11 47		12 06
Gunnersbury ⊖	d		09 55		10 06		10 17		10 26		10 42		10 53		11 09		11 20		11 38		11 50		12 09
Kew Gardens ⊖	d		09 58		10 09		10 20		10 29		10 45		10 56		11 12		11 23		11 41		11 53		12 12
Richmond ⊖	a		10 02		10 15		10 26		10 37		10 49		11 01		11 18		11 32		11 48		12 02		12 17

		LO	LO	LO	LO	LO	LO	LO	LO	LO	LO	LO	LO	LO	LO	LO	LO	LO	LO	LO	LO	LO	LO
Stratford 7 ⊖ ⇌	d	11 23	11 28	11 38	11 45	11 53	12 00	12 08	12 15	12 23	12 30	12 38	12 45	12 53	13 00	13 08	13 15	13 23	13 30	13 39	13 45	13 53	13 59
Hackney Wick	d	11 26	11 31	11 41	11 48	11 56	12 03	12 11	12 18	12 26	12 33	12 41	12 48	12 56	13 03	13 11	13 18	13 26	13 33	13 42	13 48	13 56	14 02
Homerton	d	11 29	11 34	11 44	11 51	11 59	12 06	12 14	12 21	12 29	12 36	12 44	12 51	12 59	13 06	13 14	13 21	13 29	13 36	13 45	13 51	13 59	14 05
Hackney Central	d	11 31	11 36	11 46	11 53	12 01	12 08	12 16	12 23	12 31	12 38	12 46	12 53	13 01	13 08	13 16	13 23	13 31	13 38	13 48	13 53	14 01	14 07
Dalston Kingsland	d	11 33	11 38	11 48	11 55	12 03	12 10	12 18	12 25	12 33	12 40	12 48	12 55	13 03	13 10	13 18	13 25	13 33	13 40	13 51	13 55	14 03	14 09
Canonbury 178	d	11 35	11 40	11 50	11 57	12 05	12 12	12 20	12 27	12 35	12 42	12 50	12 57	13 05	13 12	13 20	13 27	13 35	13 42	13 53	13 57	14 05	14 11
Highbury & Islington ⊖178	d	11 37	11 42	11 52	11 59	12 07	12 15	12 22	12 29	12 37	12 44	12 52	12 59	13 07	13 14	13 22	13 29	13 37	13 44	13 55	13 59	14 07	14 13
Caledonian Rd & Barnsbury	d	11 39	11 45	11 54	12 01	12 09	12 17	12 24	12 31	12 39	12 46	12 54	13 01	13 09	13 16	13 24	13 31	13 39	13 46	13 57	14 01	14 09	14 15
Camden Road	d	11 42	11 49	11 57	12 04	12 12	12 20	12 27	12 34	12 42	12 49	12 57	13 06	13 12	13 19	13 27	13 34	13 42	13 49	14 00	14 04	14 12	14 18
Kentish Town West	d	11 45	11 52	12 00	12 07	12 15	12 23	12 30	12 37	12 45	12 52	13 00	13 08	13 15	13 22	13 30	13 37	13 45	13 52	14 03	14 07	14 15	14 21
Gospel Oak	d	11 49	11 56	12 02	12 10	12 17	12 26	12 34	12 39	12 49	12 56	13 05	13 11	13 19	13 24	13 34	13 41	13 49	13 56	14 05	14 11	14 19	14 24
Hampstead Heath	d	11 51	11 59	12 04	12 12	12 19	12 28	12 36	12 41	12 51	12 59	13 08	13 13	13 21	13 26	13 36	13 43	13 51	13 58	14 07	14 13	14 22	14 26
Finchley Road & Frognal	d	11 53	12 01	12 06	12 14	12 21	12 30	12 38	12 43	12 53	13 01	13 10	13 15	13 23	13 28	13 38	13 45	13 53	14 00	14 09	14 15	14 24	14 28
West Hampstead ⊖	d	11 55	12 03	12 08	12 16	12 23	12 32	12 40	12 45	12 55	13 03	13 12	13 17	13 25	13 30	13 40	13 47	13 55	14 02	14 11	14 17	14 26	14 30
Brondesbury	d	11 56	12 05	12 09	12 18	12 24	12 34	12 41	12 47	12 56	13 05	13 13	13 18	13 27	13 31	13 41	13 49	13 56	14 04	14 12	14 19	14 27	14 32
Brondesbury Park	d	11 58	12 06	12 11	12 19	12 26	12 35	12 43	12 48	12 58	13 06	13 15	13 20	13 28	13 33	13 43	13 50	13 58	14 05	14 14	14 20	14 29	14 33
Kensal Rise	d	12 00	12 08	12 13	12 21	12 28	12 37	12 45	12 50	13 00	13 08	13 17	13 22	13 30	13 35	13 45	13 52	14 00	14 07	14 16	14 22	14 31	14 35
Willesden Jn. High Level ⊖	a	12 04	12 11	12 16	12 24	12 31	12 42	12 48	12 53	13 04	13 12	13 20	13 25	13 33	13 38	13 49	13 57	14 03	14 12	14 20	14 26	14 34	14 38
	d	12 05	12 12	12 17	12 25	12 32	12 43	12 49	12 55	13 05	13 13	13 21	13 26	13 34	13 39	13 50	13 58	14 04	14 13	14 21	14 28	14 35	14 39
Willesden Jn Low Level ⊖	a																						
Shepherd's Bush ⊖66,176	d	12 11		12 27		12 41		12 55		13 11		13 27		13 41		13 56		14 11		14 28		14 41	
Kensington (Olympia) ⊖176	d	12 13		12 29		12 43		12 57		13 13		13 29		13 43		13 58		14 13		14 30		14 43	
West Brompton ⊖176	d	12 16		12 32		12 46		13 00		13 16		13 32		13 46		14 01		14 16		14 32		14 46	
Imperial Wharf 176	d	12 19		12 35		12 49		13 03		13 19		13 35		13 49		14 04		14 19		14 35		14 49	
Clapham Junction 10 66,176	a	12 25		12 40		12 55		13 10		13 25		13 40		13 55		14 10		14 25		14 41		14 55	
Acton Central	d		12 17		12 30		12 48		13 00		13 20		13 31		13 44		14 03		14 18		14 33		14 46
South Acton	d		12 20		12 33		12 51		13 02		13 22		13 33		13 46		14 06		14 21		14 36		14 49
Gunnersbury ⊖	d		12 23		12 38		12 54		13 08		13 25		13 38		13 49		14 09		14 24		14 39		14 52
Kew Gardens ⊖	d		12 26		12 41		12 57		13 11		13 28		13 41		13 52		14 12		14 27		14 42		14 55
Richmond ⊖	a		12 31		12 47		13 02		13 17		13 33		13 47		14 02		14 17		14 32		14 48		15 01

For services between Shepherds Bush and Clapham Junction refer to Table T066 and T176

Table T059-F

Mondays to Fridays
16 December to 15 May

Stratford - Highbury & Islington, West Hampstead, Willesden Junction, Clapham Junction and Richmond

Station	LO	LO	LO	LO	LO	LO	LO	LO	LO	LO	LO	LO	LO	LO	LO	LO	LO	LO	LO	LO	LO	LO
Stratford 7 ⊖ d	14 07	14 15	14 23	14 30	14 38	14 45	14 53	14 59	15 05	15 12	15 20	15 24	15 29	15 36	15 42	15 48	15 55	15 59	16 05	16 09	16 19	16 23
Hackney Wick d	14 10	14 18	14 26	14 33	14 41	14 48	14 56	15 02	15 08	15 15	15 23	15 27	15 32	15 39	15 45	15 51	15 58	16 02	16 08	16 12	16 22	16 26
Homerton d	14 13	14 21	14 29	14 36	14 44	14 51	14 59	15 05	15 11	15 18	15 26	15 30	15 35	15 42	15 48	15 54	16 01	16 05	16 11	16 15	16 25	16 29
Hackney Central d	14 15	14 23	14 31	14 38	14 46	14 53	15 01	15 07	15 13	15 20	15 28	15 32	15 37	15 44	15 50	15 56	16 03	16 07	16 13	16 17	16 27	16 31
Dalston Kingsland d	14 17	14 25	14 33	14 40	14 48	14 55	15 03	15 09	15 15	15 22	15 30	15 34	15 39	15 46	15 52	15 58	16 05	16 10	16 15	16 19	16 29	16 33
Canonbury 178 d	14 19	14 27	14 35	14 42	14 50	14 57	15 05	15 11	15 17	15 24	15 32	15 36	15 41	15 48	15 54	16 00	16 07	16 12	16 17	16 21	16 31	16 35
Highbury & Islington ⊖178 d	14 21	14 29	14 37	14 44	14 52	14 59	15 07	15 13	15 19	15 26	15 34	15 38	15 43	15 50	15 56	16 02	16 10	16 15	16 19	16 23	16 34	16 38
Caledonian Rd & Barnsbury d	14 23	14 31	14 39	14 46	14 54	15 01	15 09	15 15	15 21	15 28	15 36	15 40	15 45	15 52	15 58	16 06	16 12	16 17	16 21	16 25	16 36	16 40
Camden Road d	14 26	14 34	14 43	14 49	14 57	15 04	15 12	15 18	15 24	15 31	15 39	15 43	15 48	15 55	16 01	16 09	16 15	16 20	16 24	16 28	16 39	16 43
Kentish Town West d	14 29	14 37	14 46	14 52	15 00	15 07	15 15	15 21	15 27	15 34	15 42	15 46	15 51	15 58	16 04	16 11	16 17	16 23	16 27	16 32	16 41	16 45
Gospel Oak d	14 33	14 41	14 50	14 56	15 04	15 11	15 20	15 24	15 32	15 36	15 45	15 49	15 54	16 02	16 07	16 13	16 19	16 25	16 30	16 37	16 43	16 49
Hampstead Heath d	14 35	14 44	14 52	14 58	15 07	15 13	15 22	15 26	15 35	15 39	15 48	15 52	15 57	16 05	16 10	16 15	16 21	16 27	16 32	16 39	16 45	16 51
Finchley Road & Frognal d	14 37	14 46	14 54	15 00	15 09	15 15	15 24	15 28	15 37	15 41	15 50	15 54	15 59	16 07	16 12	16 17	16 23	16 29	16 34	16 41	16 47	16 53
West Hampstead ⊖ d	14 39	14 48	14 56	15 02	15 11	15 17	15 26	15 30	15 39	15 43	15 52	15 56	16 01	16 09	16 14	16 19	16 25	16 31	16 36	16 43	16 49	16 55
Brondesbury d	14 40	14 49	14 58	15 04	15 12	15 18	15 27	15 32	15 40	15 45	15 53	15 58	16 02	16 11	16 15	16 21	16 27	16 33	16 37	16 44	16 51	16 57
Brondesbury Park d	14 42	14 51	14 59	15 05	15 14	15 20	15 29	15 33	15 42	15 46	15 55	15 59	16 04	16 12	16 17	16 22	16 28	16 34	16 39	16 46	16 52	16 58
Kensal Rise d	14 44	14 53	15 01	15 07	15 16	15 22	15 31	15 35	15 44	15 48	15 57	16 01	16 06	16 14	16 19	16 24	16 30	16 36	16 41	16 48	16 54	17 00
Willesden Jn. High Level ⊖ a	14 48	14 57	15 04	15 10	15 20	15 25	15 34	15 38	15 47	15 51	16 00	16 04	16 09	16 17	16 22	16 27	16 33	16 41	16 46	16 52	16 58	17 04
d	14 49	14 58	15 05	15 11	15 21	15 26	15 35	15 39	15 48	15 52	16 01	16 05	16 10	16 18	16 23	16 28	16 35	16 42	16 47	16 53	16 59	17 05
Willesden Jn Low Level ⊖ a																						
Shepherd's Bush ⊖66,176 d	14 56		15 12		15 27		15 43		15 54		16 07		16 17		16 29		16 41		16 54		17 06	
Kensington (Olympia) ⊖176 d	14 58		15 14		15 30		15 45		15 56		16 09		16 19		16 31		16 43		16 56		17 08	
West Brompton ⊖176 d	15 01		15 16		15 33		15 47		15 59		16 12		16 22		16 34		16 46		16 59		17 10	
Imperial Wharf 176 d	15 04		15 19		15 36		15 50		16 02		16 15		16 25		16 37		16 49		17 02		17 13	
Clapham Junction 10 66,176 a	15 09		15 28		15 43		15 58		16 07		16 22		16 31		16 44		16 57		17 10		17 21	
Acton Central d		15 03		15 16		15 31		15 46		15 57		16 10		16 24		16 34		16 47		16 58		17 10
South Acton d		15 06		15 19		15 33		15 49		16 00		16 13		16 27		16 37		16 49		17 00		17 13
Gunnersbury ⊖ d		15 09		15 22		15 39		15 52		16 04		16 16		16 30		16 40		16 52		17 03		17 18
Kew Gardens ⊖ d		15 12		15 25		15 42		15 55		16 07		16 19		16 33		16 43		16 55		17 06		17 21
Richmond ⊖ a		15 17		15 32		15 48		16 01		16 14		16 26		16 38		16 50		17 01		17 13		17 25

Station	LO	LO	LO	LO	LO	LO	LO	LO	LO	LO	LO	LO	LO	LO	LO	LO	LO	LO	LO	LO	LO	LO
Stratford 7 ⊖ d	16 29	16 35	16 41	16 47	16 53	16 59	17 06	17 11	17 17	17 23	17 31	17 35	17 41	17 47	17 53	17 59	18 08	18 14	18 19	18 23	18 29	18 36
Hackney Wick d	16 32	16 39	16 44	16 50	16 56	17 02	17 09	17 14	17 20	17 26	17 34	17 39	17 44	17 51	17 56	18 03	18 11	18 17	18 22	18 26	18 32	18 39
Homerton d	16 35	16 41	16 47	16 53	16 59	17 05	17 12	17 17	17 23	17 29	17 37	17 41	17 47	17 53	17 59	18 06	18 14	18 20	18 25	18 29	18 35	18 42
Hackney Central d	16 37	16 43	16 49	16 55	17 01	17 07	17 14	17 19	17 25	17 31	17 39	17 44	17 49	17 55	18 01	18 08	18 16	18 22	18 27	18 31	18 37	18 44
Dalston Kingsland d	16 39	16 46	16 51	16 57	17 03	17 09	17 16	17 21	17 27	17 33	17 41	17 46	17 51	17 57	18 03	18 11	18 18	18 24	18 29	18 33	18 39	18 46
Canonbury 178 d	16 41	16 48	16 53	16 59	17 05	17 11	17 18	17 23	17 29	17 35	17 43	17 48	17 53	17 59	18 05	18 13	18 20	18 26	18 31	18 35	18 41	18 48
Highbury & Islington ⊖178 d	16 44	16 51	16 56	17 02	17 08	17 14	17 21	17 26	17 32	17 38	17 46	17 52	17 56	18 02	18 08	18 17	18 23	18 29	18 34	18 38	18 44	18 51
Caledonian Rd & Barnsbury d	16 46	16 53	16 58	17 04	17 10	17 16	17 23	17 28	17 34	17 40	17 48	17 54	17 58	18 05	18 10	18 19	18 25	18 31	18 36	18 40	18 46	18 53
Camden Road d	16 49	16 56	17 01	17 07	17 13	17 19	17 26	17 31	17 37	17 43	17 51	17 57	18 01	18 08	18 13	18 22	18 28	18 34	18 39	18 43	18 49	18 56
Kentish Town West d	16 51	16 59	17 03	17 09	17 15	17 21	17 28	17 33	17 39	17 45	17 53	17 59	18 03	18 11	18 15	18 24	18 30	18 36	18 41	18 45	18 51	18 58
Gospel Oak d	16 55	17 01	17 07	17 13	17 19	17 25	17 31	17 37	17 41	17 49	17 55	18 03	18 07	18 14	18 19	18 26	18 33	18 38	18 43	18 50	18 55	19 02
Hampstead Heath d	16 57	17 03	17 09	17 15	17 21	17 27	17 33	17 39	17 43	17 52	17 57	18 05	18 09	18 16	18 21	18 29	18 35	18 40	18 45	18 53	18 57	19 06
Finchley Road & Frognal d	16 59	17 05	17 11	17 17	17 23	17 29	17 35	17 41	17 45	17 54	17 59	18 07	18 11	18 18	18 23	18 31	18 37	18 42	18 47	18 55	18 59	19 08
West Hampstead ⊖ d	17 01	17 07	17 13	17 19	17 25	17 31	17 37	17 43	17 47	17 56	18 01	18 09	18 13	18 20	18 25	18 33	18 39	18 44	18 49	18 57	19 01	19 10
Brondesbury d	17 03	17 09	17 15	17 21	17 27	17 33	17 39	17 45	17 49	17 57	18 03	18 10	18 15	18 22	18 27	18 35	18 40	18 46	18 51	18 59	19 03	19 11
Brondesbury Park d	17 04	17 10	17 16	17 22	17 28	17 34	17 40	17 46	17 50	17 59	18 04	18 12	18 16	18 23	18 28	18 36	18 42	18 47	18 52	19 00	19 04	19 13
Kensal Rise d	17 06	17 12	17 18	17 24	17 30	17 36	17 42	17 48	17 52	18 01	18 06	18 14	18 18	18 25	18 30	18 38	18 44	18 49	18 54	19 02	19 06	19 15
Willesden Jn. High Level ⊖ a	17 10	17 17	17 22	17 29	17 34	17 41	17 46	17 53	17 58	18 05	18 10	18 18	18 22	18 28	18 33	18 42	18 47	18 52	18 57	19 05	19 10	19 18
d	17 11	17 18	17 23	17 30	17 35	17 42	17 47	17 54	17 59	18 06	18 11	18 19	18 23	18 29	18 34	18 43	18 48	18 53	18 58	19 06	19 11	19 19
Willesden Jn Low Level ⊖ a																						
Shepherd's Bush ⊖66,176 d	17 17		17 30		17 42		17 54		18 06		18 17		18 30		18 42		18 55		19 06		19 17	
Kensington (Olympia) ⊖176 d	17 19		17 32		17 44		17 56		18 08		18 19		18 32		18 44		18 57		19 08		19 19	
West Brompton ⊖176 d	17 22		17 34		17 46		17 59		18 10		18 22		18 34		18 46		18 59		19 10		19 22	
Imperial Wharf 176 d	17 25		17 37		17 49		18 02		18 13		18 25		18 37		18 49		19 02		19 13		19 25	
Clapham Junction 10 66,176 a	17 31		17 43		17 58		18 11		18 22		18 33		18 46		18 58		19 10		19 21		19 34	
Acton Central d		17 23		17 35		17 47		17 59		18 11		18 24		18 35		18 48		18 59		19 11		19 25
South Acton d		17 26		17 38		17 50		18 02		18 14		18 26		18 38		18 50		19 02		19 14		19 28
Gunnersbury ⊖ d		17 29		17 41		17 53		18 06		18 18		18 30		18 41		18 53		19 07		19 17		19 31
Kew Gardens ⊖ d		17 32		17 44		17 56		18 09		18 21		18 33		18 44		18 56		19 10		19 20		19 34
Richmond ⊖ a		17 37		17 49		18 01		18 14		18 26		18 37		18 50		19 01		19 16		19 25		19 38

For services between Shepherds Bush and Clapham Junction refer to Table T066 and T176

Table T059-F

Mondays to Fridays
16 December to 15 May

Stratford - Highbury & Islington, West Hampstead, Willesden Junction, Clapham Junction and Richmond

Station	LO	LO	LO	LO	LO	LO	LO	LO	LO	LO	LO	LO	LO	LO	LO	LO	LO	LO	LO	LO	LO	LO
Stratford 7 ⊖ d	18 41	18 47	18 53	18 57	19 05	19 12	19 17	19 22	19 29	19 35	19 42	19 45	19 53	19 59	20 05	20 13	20 20	20 25	20 35	20 42	20 46	20 58
Hackney Wick d	18 44	18 50	18 56	19 00	19 08	19 16	19 20	19 25	19 32	19 38	19 45	19 49	19 56	20 03	20 08	20 16	20 24	20 28	20 39	20 46	20 49	21 01
Homerton d	18 47	18 53	18 59	19 03	19 11	19 19	19 23	19 28	19 35	19 41	19 48	19 51	19 59	20 05	20 11	20 19	20 27	20 31	20 41	20 48	20 52	21 04
Hackney Central d	18 49	18 55	19 01	19 05	19 13	19 21	19 25	19 30	19 37	19 43	19 50	19 53	20 01	20 07	20 13	20 21	20 29	20 33	20 43	20 50	20 54	21 06
Dalston Kingsland d	18 51	18 57	19 03	19 07	19 15	19 23	19 27	19 32	19 39	19 45	19 52	19 55	20 03	20 10	20 15	20 23	20 31	20 35	20 45	20 52	20 56	21 08
Canonbury 178 d	18 53	18 59	19 05	19 09	19 17	19 25	19 29	19 34	19 41	19 47	19 54	19 57	20 05	20 12	20 17	20 25	20 33	20 37	20 47	20 54	20 58	21 10
Highbury & Islington ⊖178 d	18 56	19 01	19 07	19 11	19 19	19 27	19 31	19 36	19 43	19 49	19 56	20 00	20 07	20 14	20 19	20 27	20 35	20 39	20 50	20 57	21 00	21 12
Caledonian Rd & Barnsbury d	18 58	19 03	19 09	19 13	19 21	19 29	19 33	19 38	19 45	19 51	19 58	20 02	20 09	20 17	20 21	20 29	20 37	20 41	20 52	20 59	21 02	21 14
Camden Road d	19 01	19 06	19 12	19 17	19 24	19 33	19 36	19 41	19 48	19 54	20 01	20 05	20 12	20 20	20 24	20 32	20 40	20 44	20 55	21 02	21 05	21 17
Kentish Town West d	19 03	19 09	19 15	19 20	19 27	19 35	19 39	19 44	19 51	19 57	20 04	20 08	20 15	20 22	20 27	20 35	20 43	20 47	20 57	21 04	21 08	21 20
Gospel Oak d	19 07	19 13	19 17	19 25	19 30	19 38	19 43	19 49	19 55	20 00	20 07	20 11	20 19	20 25	20 30	20 38	20 45	20 49	21 00	21 06	21 12	21 23
Hampstead Heath d	19 09	19 15	19 19	19 28	19 32	19 40	19 46	19 51	19 57	20 02	20 09	20 13	20 22	20 27	20 32	20 41	20 47	20 51	21 02	21 08	21 14	21 26
Finchley Road & Frognal d	19 11	19 17	19 21	19 30	19 34	19 42	19 48	19 53	19 59	20 04	20 11	20 15	20 24	20 29	20 34	20 43	20 49	20 53	21 04	21 10	21 16	21 28
West Hampstead ⊖ d	19 13	19 19	19 23	19 32	19 36	19 44	19 50	19 55	20 01	20 06	20 13	20 17	20 26	20 31	20 36	20 45	20 51	20 55	21 06	21 12	21 18	21 30
Brondesbury d	19 15	19 20	19 25	19 33	19 38	19 46	19 51	19 57	20 02	20 08	20 14	20 19	20 27	20 33	20 37	20 46	20 52	20 57	21 08	21 14	21 20	21 32
Brondesbury Park d	19 16	19 22	19 26	19 35	19 39	19 47	19 53	19 58	20 04	20 09	20 16	20 20	20 29	20 34	20 39	20 48	20 54	20 58	21 09	21 15	21 21	21 34
Kensal Rise d	19 18	19 24	19 28	19 37	19 41	19 49	19 55	20 00	20 06	20 11	20 18	20 22	20 31	20 36	20 41	20 50	20 56	21 00	21 11	21 17	21 23	21 36
Willesden Jn. High Level ⊖ a	19 22	19 27	19 31	19 40	19 44	19 53	19 58	20 05	20 10	20 14	20 21	20 26	20 34	20 39	20 44	20 53	21 00	21 05	21 15	21 20	21 26	21 39
d	19 23	19 28	19 32	19 41	19 47	19 54	19 59	20 06	20 11	20 15	20 22	20 27	20 35	20 40	20 45	20 54	21 01	21 06	21 16	21 21	21 27	21 40
Willesden Jn Low Level ⊖ a																						
Shepherd's Bush ⊖66,176 d	19 30		19 41		19 53		20 05		20 17		20 29		20 41		20 53		21 07		21 23		21 36	
Kensington (Olympia) ⊖176 d	19 32		19 43		19 55		20 07		20 19		20 31		20 43		20 55		21 09		21 26		21 38	
West Brompton ⊖176 d	19 34		19 46		19 58		20 10		20 22		20 34		20 46		20 57		21 12		21 29		21 41	
Imperial Wharf 176 d	19 37		19 50		20 01		20 13		20 25		20a37		20 49		21 01		21 15		21 32		21 45	
Clapham Junction 10 66,176 a	19 43		19 58		20 07		20 19		20 31				20 55		21 07		21 22		21 37		21 51	
Acton Central d		19 34		19 47		20 00		20 13		20 22		20 32		20 45		21 00		21 11		21 26		21 45
South Acton d		19 37		19 49		20 03		20 16		20 24		20 35		20 48		21 03		21 14		21 29		21 48
Gunnersbury ⊖ d		19 43		19 54		20 06		20 20		20 28		20 39		20 53		21 07		21 18		21 32		21 53
Kew Gardens ⊖ d		19 46		19 57		20 09		20 23		20 31		20 43		20 56		21 10		21 21		21 35		21 56
Richmond ⊖ a		19 50		20 02		20 14		20 27		20 37		20 49		21 01		21 15		21 27		21 44		22 00

Station	LO	LO	LO	LO	LO	LO	LO	LO	LO	LO	LO	LO	LO	LO	LO	LO	LO	LO	LO	LO	LO
Stratford 7 ⊖ d	21 07	21 14	21 19	21 26	21 34	21 41	21 49	21 57	22 04	22 10	22 14	22 27	22 36	22 45		22 59		23 12	23 27	23 44	23 59
Hackney Wick d	21 10	21 17	21 22	21 29	21 37	21 44	21 52	22 00	22 07	22 13	22 17	22 30	22 39	22 48		23 02		23 16	23 30	23 47	00 03
Homerton d	21 13	21 20	21 25	21 32	21 40	21 47	21 55	22 03	22 10	22 16	22 20	22 33	22 42	22 51		23 05		23 18	23 33	23 50	00 05
Hackney Central d	21 15	21 22	21 27	21 34	21 42	21 49	21 57	22 05	22 12	22 18	22 22	22 35	22 44	22 53		23 07		23 20	23 35	23 52	00 07
Dalston Kingsland d	21 17	21 24	21 29	21 36	21 44	21 51	21 59	22 07	22 14	22 20	22 24	22 37	22 46	22 55		23 09		23 22	23 37	23 54	00 09
Canonbury 178 d	21 19	21 26	21 31	21 38	21 46	21 53	22 01	22 09	22 16	22 22	22 26	22 39	22 48	22 57		23 11		23 24	23 39	23 56	00 11
Highbury & Islington ⊖178 d	21 21	21 28	21 33	21 40	21 48	21 55	22 03	22 11	22 18	22 24	22 28	22 41	22 50	22 59		23 13		23 27	23 41	23 58	00 14
Caledonian Rd & Barnsbury d	21 23	21 30	21 35	21 42	21 50	21 57	22 05	22 13	22 20	22 26	22 30	22 43	22 52	23 01		23 15		23 29	23 43	00 01	00 16
Camden Road d	21 26	21 34	21 38	21 45	21 53	22 00	22 08	22 16	22 23	22 29	22 33	22 47	22 55	23 04		23 18		23 32	23 47	00 03	00 19
Kentish Town West d	21 29	21 37	21 41	21 48	21 56	22 03	22 11	22 19	22 26	22 32	22 36	22 49	22 58	23 07		23 21		23 34	23 50	00 06	00 21
Gospel Oak d	21 31	21 39	21 43	21 50	22 00	22 08	22 15	22 23	22 30	22 36	22 40	22 54	23 04	23 11		23 23		23 37	23 53	00 08	00 23
Hampstead Heath d	21 34	21 42	21 47	21 52	22 02	22 10	22 17	22 25	22 32	22 38	22 42	22 57	23 06	23 13		23 25		23 39	23 55	00 10	00 25
Finchley Road & Frognal d	21 36	21 44	21 49	21 54	22 04	22 12	22 19	22 27	22 34	22 40	22 44	22 59	23 08	23 15		23 27		23 41	23 57	00 12	00 27
West Hampstead ⊖ d	21 38	21 46	21 51	21 56	22 06	22 14	22 21	22 29	22 36	22 42	22 46	23 01	23 10	23 17		23 29		23 43	23 59	00 14	00 29
Brondesbury d	21 39	21 48	21 52	21 57	22 07	22 16	22 22	22 31	22 37	22 43	22 48	23 02	23 11	23 18		23 31		23 45	00 01	00 16	00 31
Brondesbury Park d	21 41	21 49	21 54	21 59	22 09	22 17	22 24	22 32	22 39	22 45	22 49	23 04	23 13	23 20		23 32		23 46	00 02	00 17	00 32
Kensal Rise d	21 43	21 51	21 56	22 01	22 11	22 19	22 26	22 34	22 41	22 47	22 51	23 07	23 15	23 22		23 34		23 48	00 04	00 19	00 34
Willesden Jn. High Level ⊖ a	21 47	21 55	22 00	22 05	22 15	22 24	22 30	22 39	22 45	22 51	22 57	23 10	23 18	23 25		23 39		23 52	00 10	00 25	00 40
d	21 48	21 56	22 01	22 07	22 16	22 25	22 31	22 40	22 46	22 53	23 00	23 11	23 19	23 26	23 30	23 40	23 44	23 53			
Willesden Jn Low Level ⊖ a																					
Shepherd's Bush ⊖66,176 d	21 55		22 07		22 23		22 37		22 52		23 07		23 26		23 36		23 52				
Kensington (Olympia) ⊖176 d	21 57		22 09		22 25		22 39		22 54		23 09		23 28		23 38		23 54				
West Brompton ⊖176 d	21 59		22 12		22 28		22 42		22 57		23 12		23 31		23 41		23 56				
Imperial Wharf 176 d	22 02		22 15		22 31		22 45		23 00		23 15		23a34		23 44		23 59				
Clapham Junction 10 66,176 a	22 09		22 21		22 36		22 51		23 06		23 21				23 51		00 05				
Acton Central d		22 01		22 13		22 30		22 45		23 01		23 16		23 32		23 45		00 02			
South Acton d		22 04		22 16		22 33		22 48		23 04		23 19		23 35		23 48		00 04			
Gunnersbury ⊖ d		22 07		22 21		22 37		22 52		23 08		23 22		23 39		23 51		00 08			
Kew Gardens ⊖ d		22 10		22 24		22 40		22 55		23 11		23 25		23 42		23 54		00 11			
Richmond ⊖ a		22 16		22 29		22 45		22 59		23 15		23 29		23 47		00 01		00 15			

For services between Shepherds Bush and Clapham Junction refer to Table T066 and T176

Table T059-F

Saturdays
21 December to 16 May

Stratford - Highbury & Islington, West Hampstead, Willesden Junction, Clapham Junction and Richmond

Station		LO	LO	LO	LO	LO	LO	LO	LO	LO	LO	LO	LO	LO	LO	LO	LO	LO	LO	LO	LO	LO	LO
Stratford [7] ⊖	d						00 15				05 43	05 55	06 01	06 08	06 14	06 23	06 30	06 38	06 47	06 53	07 00	07 08	07 15
Hackney Wick	d					00 03	00 18				05 46	05 58	06 04	06 11	06 17	06 27	06 33	06 42	06 50	06 56	07 03	07 11	07 18
Homerton	d					00 05	00 21				05 49	06 01	06 07	06 14	06 20	06 30	06 36	06 45	06 53	06 59	07 06	07 14	07 21
Hackney Central	d					00 07	00 23				05 51	06 03	06 09	06 16	06 22	06 32	06 38	06 47	06 55	07 01	07 08	07 16	07 23
Dalston Kingsland	d					00 09	00 25				05 53	06 05	06 11	06 18	06 24	06 34	06 40	06 49	06 57	07 03	07 10	07 18	07 25
Canonbury 178	d					00 11	00 27				05 55	06 07	06 13	06 20	06 26	06 36	06 42	06 51	06 59	07 05	07 12	07 20	07 27
Highbury & Islington ⊖178	d					00 14	00 29				05 57	06 09	06 15	06 22	06 28	06 38	06 44	06 53	07 01	07 07	07 14	07 22	07 29
Caledonian Rd & Barnsbury	d			00 01		00 16	00 31				05 59	06 11	06 17	06 24	06 30	06 40	06 46	06 55	07 03	07 10	07 16	07 24	07 31
Camden Road	d			00 03		00 19	00 34				06 02	06 14	06 20	06 27	06 33	06 43	06 49	06 58	07 06	07 13	07 19	07 27	07 34
Kentish Town West	d			00 06		00 21	00 37				06 05	06 17	06 23	06 30	06 36	06 46	06 52	07 01	07 09	07 15	07 22	07 30	07 37
Gospel Oak	d			00 08		00 23	00 39				06 07	06 21	06 27	06 34	06 40	06 49	06 56	07 04	07 11	07 19	07 26	07 34	07 41
Hampstead Heath	d			00 10		00 25	00 41				06 09	06 23	06 29	06 36	06 42	06 51	06 58	07 06	07 13	07 21	07 28	07 36	07 43
Finchley Road & Frognal	d			00 12		00 27	00 43				06 11	06 25	06 31	06 38	06 44	06 53	07 00	07 08	07 15	07 23	07 30	07 38	07 45
West Hampstead ⊖	d			00 14		00 29	00 45				06 13	06 27	06 33	06 40	06 46	06 55	07 02	07 10	07 17	07 25	07 32	07 40	07 47
Brondesbury	d		00 01	00 16		00 31	00 47				06 15	06 28	06 35	06 41	06 48	06 56	07 04	07 11	07 19	07 26	07 34	07 41	07 49
Brondesbury Park	d		00 02	00 17		00 32	00 48				06 16	06 30	06 36	06 43	06 49	06 58	07 05	07 13	07 20	07 28	07 35	07 43	07 50
Kensal Rise	d		00 04	00 19		00 34	00 50				06 18	06 32	06 38	06 45	06 51	07 00	07 07	07 15	07 22	07 30	07 37	07 45	07 52
Willesden Jn. High Level ⊖	a		00 10	00 25		00 40	00 56				06 23	06 36	06 42	06 49	06 56	07 04	07 12	07 19	07 27	07 34	07 42	07 49	07 57
	d	00 01						06 05	06 10	06 20	06 24	06 37	06 43	06 50	06 57	07 05	07 13	07 20	07 28	07 35	07 43	07 50	07 58
Willesden Jn Low Level ⊖	a																						
Shepherd's Bush ⊖66,176	d	00 09						06 11		06 26		06 43		06 56		07 11		07 26		07 41		07 56	
Kensington (Olympia) ⊖176	d	00 11						06 13		06 28		06 45		06 58		07 13		07 28		07 43		07 58	
West Brompton ⊖176	d	00 14						06 16		06 31		06 48		07 01		07 16		07 31		07 46		08 01	
Imperial Wharf 176	d	00 17						06 19		06 34		06 51		07 04		07 19		07 34		07 49		08 04	
Clapham Junction [10] 66,176	a	00 22						06 26		06 41		06 57		07 10		07 25		07 40		07 55		08 10	
Acton Central	d				00 02				06 15		06 29		06 48		07 02		07 18		07 33		07 48		08 03
South Acton	d				00 04				06 17		06 32		06 50		07 05		07 21		07 36		07 51		08 06
Gunnersbury ⊖	d				00 08				06 20		06 35		06 53		07 09		07 24		07 39		07 54		08 09
Kew Gardens ⊖	d				00 11				06 23		06 38		06 56		07 12		07 27		07 42		07 57		08 12
Richmond ⊖	a				00 15				06 32		06 45		07 03		07 16		07 32		07 49		08 02		08 17

Station		LO	LO	LO	LO	LO	LO	LO	LO	LO	LO	LO	LO	LO	LO	LO	LO	LO	LO	LO	LO	LO	LO
Stratford [7] ⊖	d	07 23	07 30	07 38	07 45	07 53	08 00	08 08	08 15	08 23	08 30	08 38	08 45	08 53	09 00	09 08	09 15	09 23	09 30	09 38	09 45	09 53	10 00
Hackney Wick	d	07 26	07 33	07 42	07 48	07 56	08 03	08 11	08 18	08 27	08 33	08 41	08 48	08 56	09 03	09 11	09 18	09 26	09 34	09 41	09 48	09 57	10 03
Homerton	d	07 29	07 36	07 44	07 51	07 59	08 06	08 14	08 21	08 30	08 36	08 44	08 51	08 59	09 06	09 14	09 21	09 29	09 37	09 44	09 51	10 00	10 06
Hackney Central	d	07 31	07 38	07 46	07 53	08 01	08 08	08 16	08 23	08 32	08 38	08 46	08 53	09 01	09 08	09 16	09 23	09 31	09 39	09 46	09 53	10 02	10 08
Dalston Kingsland	d	07 33	07 40	07 48	07 55	08 03	08 10	08 18	08 25	08 34	08 40	08 48	08 55	09 03	09 10	09 18	09 25	09 33	09 41	09 48	09 55	10 04	10 10
Canonbury 178	d	07 35	07 42	07 50	07 57	08 05	08 12	08 20	08 27	08 36	08 42	08 50	08 57	09 05	09 12	09 20	09 27	09 35	09 43	09 50	09 57	10 06	10 12
Highbury & Islington ⊖178	d	07 37	07 44	07 53	07 59	08 07	08 14	08 22	08 29	08 38	08 44	08 52	08 59	09 07	09 14	09 22	09 29	09 37	09 45	09 52	09 59	10 08	10 14
Caledonian Rd & Barnsbury	d	07 39	07 46	07 55	08 02	08 09	08 16	08 24	08 31	08 40	08 46	08 54	09 01	09 09	09 16	09 24	09 31	09 39	09 47	09 54	10 01	10 10	10 16
Camden Road	d	07 42	07 49	07 58	08 05	08 12	08 19	08 27	08 34	08 43	08 49	08 57	09 04	09 12	09 19	09 27	09 34	09 42	09 52	09 57	10 04	10 13	10 19
Kentish Town West	d	07 45	07 52	08 00	08 09	08 15	08 22	08 30	08 37	08 46	08 52	09 00	09 07	09 15	09 22	09 30	09 37	09 45	09 54	10 00	10 07	10 16	10 22
Gospel Oak	d	07 49	07 56	08 03	08 12	08 19	08 26	08 34	08 41	08 49	08 56	09 04	09 11	09 19	09 26	09 34	09 41	09 49	09 58	10 04	10 11	10 21	10 26
Hampstead Heath	d	07 51	07 58	08 05	08 14	08 21	08 28	08 36	08 43	08 51	08 58	09 06	09 13	09 21	09 28	09 36	09 43	09 51	10 00	10 06	10 13	10 23	10 28
Finchley Road & Frognal	d	07 53	08 00	08 07	08 16	08 23	08 30	08 38	08 45	08 53	09 00	09 08	09 15	09 23	09 30	09 38	09 45	09 53	10 02	10 08	10 15	10 25	10 30
West Hampstead ⊖	d	07 55	08 02	08 09	08 18	08 25	08 32	08 40	08 47	08 55	09 02	09 10	09 17	09 25	09 32	09 40	09 47	09 55	10 04	10 10	10 17	10 27	10 32
Brondesbury	d	07 56	08 04	08 11	08 20	08 26	08 34	08 41	08 49	08 56	09 04	09 11	09 19	09 26	09 34	09 41	09 49	09 56	10 05	10 11	10 19	10 28	10 34
Brondesbury Park	d	07 58	08 05	08 12	08 21	08 28	08 35	08 43	08 50	08 58	09 05	09 13	09 20	09 28	09 35	09 43	09 50	09 58	10 07	10 13	10 20	10 30	10 35
Kensal Rise	d	08 00	08 07	08 14	08 23	08 30	08 37	08 45	08 52	09 00	09 07	09 15	09 22	09 30	09 37	09 45	09 52	10 00	10 09	10 15	10 22	10 32	10 37
Willesden Jn. High Level ⊖	a	08 04	08 12	08 19	08 27	08 34	08 42	08 49	08 57	09 04	09 12	09 19	09 27	09 34	09 42	09 49	09 57	10 03	10 12	10 19	10 25	10 35	10 42
	d	08 05	08 13	08 20	08 28	08 35	08 43	08 50	08 58	09 05	09 13	09 20	09 28	09 35	09 43	09 50	09 58	10 04	10 13	10 20	10 26	10 36	10 43
Willesden Jn Low Level ⊖	a																						
Shepherd's Bush ⊖66,176	d	08 11		08 27		08 41		08 56		09 11		09 26		09 41		09 56		10 11		10 26		10 42	
Kensington (Olympia) ⊖176	d	08 13		08 29		08 43		08 58		09 13		09 28		09 43		09 58		10 13		10 28		10 44	
West Brompton ⊖176	d	08 16		08 31		08 46		09 01		09 16		09 31		09 46		10 01		10 16		10 31		10 47	
Imperial Wharf 176	d	08 19		08 34		08 49		09 04		09 19		09 34		09 49		10 04		10 19		10 34		10 50	
Clapham Junction [10] 66,176	a	08 25		08 40		08 55		09 10		09 25		09 40		09 55		10 10		10 25		10 40		10 55	
Acton Central	d		08 18		08 33		08 48		09 03		09 18		09 33		09 48		10 03		10 18		10 33		10 48
South Acton	d		08 21		08 36		08 51		09 06		09 21		09 36		09 51		10 06		10 21		10 36		10 51
Gunnersbury ⊖	d		08 24		08 39		08 54		09 09		09 24		09 39		09 54		10 09		10 24		10 39		10 54
Kew Gardens ⊖	d		08 27		08 42		08 57		09 12		09 27		09 42		09 57		10 12		10 27		10 42		10 57
Richmond ⊖	a		08 32		08 47		09 02		09 17		09 32		09 47		10 02		10 17		10 32		10 47		11 02

For services between Shepherds Bush and Clapham Junction refer to Table T066 and T176

Table T059-F

Saturdays
21 December to 16 May

Stratford - Highbury & Islington, West Hampstead, Willesden Junction, Clapham Junction and Richmond

Station		LO	LO	LO	LO	LO	LO	LO	LO	LO	LO	LO	LO	LO	LO	LO	LO	LO	LO	LO	LO	LO	LO
Stratford [7] ⊖	d	10 08	10 15	10 23	10 30	10 38	10 45	10 53	11 00	11 08	11 15	11 23	11 30	11 38	11 45	11 53	12 00	12 08	12 15	12 23	12 30	12 38	12 45
Hackney Wick	d	10 11	10 18	10 26	10 33	10 42	10 48	10 56	11 03	11 11	11 19	11 26	11 33	11 41	11 48	11 56	12 03	12 12	12 18	12 26	12 33	12 41	12 48
Homerton	d	10 14	10 21	10 29	10 36	10 44	10 51	10 59	11 06	11 14	11 22	11 29	11 36	11 44	11 51	11 59	12 06	12 15	12 21	12 29	12 36	12 44	12 51
Hackney Central	d	10 16	10 23	10 31	10 38	10 46	10 53	11 01	11 08	11 16	11 24	11 31	11 38	11 46	11 53	12 01	12 08	12 17	12 23	12 31	12 38	12 46	12 53
Dalston Kingsland	d	10 18	10 25	10 33	10 40	10 48	10 55	11 03	11 10	11 18	11 26	11 33	11 40	11 48	11 55	12 03	12 10	12 19	12 25	12 33	12 40	12 48	12 55
Canonbury 178	d	10 20	10 27	10 35	10 42	10 50	10 57	11 05	11 12	11 20	11 28	11 35	11 42	11 50	11 57	12 05	12 12	12 21	12 27	12 35	12 42	12 50	12 57
Highbury & Islington ⊖178	d	10 22	10 29	10 37	10 44	10 53	10 59	11 07	11 14	11 22	11 30	11 37	11 44	11 52	11 59	12 07	12 14	12 23	12 29	12 37	12 44	12 53	12 59
Caledonian Rd & Barnsbury	d	10 24	10 31	10 39	10 46	10 55	11 01	11 09	11 16	11 24	11 32	11 39	11 46	11 54	12 01	12 09	12 16	12 25	12 31	12 39	12 46	12 55	13 01
Camden Road	d	10 27	10 34	10 42	10 49	10 58	11 04	11 12	11 19	11 27	11 36	11 42	11 49	11 58	12 06	12 12	12 19	12 28	12 34	12 42	12 49	12 58	13 04
Kentish Town West	d	10 30	10 37	10 45	10 52	11 00	11 07	11 15	11 22	11 30	11 39	11 45	11 52	12 01	12 09	12 15	12 22	12 31	12 37	12 45	12 52	13 01	13 07
Gospel Oak	d	10 34	10 41	10 49	10 56	11 04	11 11	11 19	11 25	11 34	11 43	11 49	11 56	12 04	12 11	12 19	12 25	12 35	12 41	12 49	12 55	13 04	13 11
Hampstead Heath	d	10 36	10 43	10 51	10 58	11 06	11 13	11 22	11 27	11 36	11 45	11 51	11 58	12 06	12 13	12 21	12 27	12 37	12 43	12 51	12 57	13 06	13 13
Finchley Road & Frognal	d	10 38	10 45	10 53	11 00	11 08	11 15	11 24	11 29	11 38	11 47	11 53	12 00	12 08	12 15	12 23	12 29	12 39	12 45	12 53	12 59	13 08	13 15
West Hampstead ⊖	d	10 40	10 47	10 55	11 02	11 10	11 17	11 26	11 31	11 40	11 49	11 55	12 02	12 10	12 17	12 25	12 31	12 41	12 47	12 55	13 01	13 10	13 17
Brondesbury	d	10 41	10 49	10 56	11 04	11 11	11 19	11 27	11 32	11 41	11 51	11 56	12 04	12 11	12 19	12 26	12 33	12 42	12 49	12 56	13 03	13 11	13 19
Brondesbury Park	d	10 43	10 50	10 58	11 05	11 13	11 20	11 29	11 34	11 43	11 52	11 58	12 05	12 13	12 20	12 28	12 34	12 44	12 50	12 58	13 04	13 13	13 20
Kensal Rise	d	10 45	10 52	11 00	11 07	11 15	11 22	11 31	11 36	11 45	11 54	12 00	12 07	12 15	12 22	12 30	12 36	12 46	12 52	13 00	13 06	13 15	13 22
Willesden Jn. High Level ⊖	a	10 49	10 57	11 04	11 12	11 19	11 25	11 34	11 40	11 49	11 57	12 04	12 12	12 19	12 27	12 34	12 41	12 50	12 57	13 04	13 11	13 19	13 27
	d	10 50	10 58	11 05	11 13	11 20	11 26	11 35	11 41	11 50	11 58	12 05	12 13	12 20	12 28	12 35	12 42	12 51	12 58	13 05	13 12	13 20	13 28
Willesden Jn Low Level ⊖	a																						
Shepherd's Bush ⊖66,176	d	10 56		11 11		11 26		11 41		11 56		12 11		12 26		12 41		12 57		13 11		13 26	
Kensington (Olympia) ⊖176	d	10 58		11 13		11 28		11 43		11 58		12 13		12 28		12 43		12 59		13 13		13 28	
West Brompton ⊖176	d	11 01		11 16		11 31		11 46		12 01		12 16		12 31		12 46		13 02		13 16		13 31	
Imperial Wharf 176	d	11 04		11 19		11 34		11 49		12 04		12 19		12 34		12 49		13 05		13 19		13 34	
Clapham Junction [10] 66,176	a	11 10		11 25		11 40		11 55		12 10		12 25		12 40		12 55		13 13		13 25		13 40	
Acton Central	d		11 03		11 18		11 33		11 47		12 03		12 18		12 33		12 47		13 03		13 18		13 33
South Acton	d		11 06		11 21		11 36		11 50		12 06		12 21		12 36		12 50		13 06		13 21		13 36
Gunnersbury ⊖	d		11 09		11 24		11 39		11 53		12 09		12 24		12 39		12 53		13 09		13 24		13 39
Kew Gardens ⊖	d		11 12		11 27		11 42		11 56		12 12		12 27		12 42		12 56		13 12		13 27		13 42
Richmond ⊖	a		11 17		11 32		11 47		12 02		12 17		12 32		12 47		13 02		13 17		13 32		13 47

Station		LO	LO	LO	LO	LO	LO	LO	LO	LO	LO	LO	LO	LO	LO	LO	LO	LO	LO	LO	LO	LO	LO
Stratford [7] ⊖	d	12 53	13 00	13 07	13 15	13 23	13 30	13 38	13 45	13 53	14 00	14 08	14 15	14 23	14 33	14 38	14 45	14 53	15 00	15 08	15 15	15 23	15 30
Hackney Wick	d	12 56	13 03	13 10	13 18	13 26	13 33	13 41	13 48	13 56	14 03	14 11	14 18	14 26	14 36	14 41	14 48	14 56	15 03	15 11	15 18	15 26	15 33
Homerton	d	12 59	13 06	13 13	13 21	13 29	13 36	13 44	13 51	13 59	14 06	14 14	14 21	14 29	14 39	14 44	14 51	14 59	15 06	15 14	15 21	15 29	15 36
Hackney Central	d	13 01	13 08	13 15	13 23	13 31	13 38	13 46	13 53	14 01	14 08	14 16	14 23	14 31	14 41	14 46	14 53	15 01	15 08	15 16	15 23	15 31	15 38
Dalston Kingsland	d	13 03	13 10	13 17	13 25	13 33	13 40	13 48	13 55	14 03	14 10	14 18	14 25	14 33	14 43	14 48	14 55	15 03	15 10	15 18	15 25	15 33	15 40
Canonbury 178	d	13 05	13 12	13 19	13 27	13 35	13 42	13 50	13 57	14 05	14 12	14 20	14 27	14 35	14 45	14 50	14 57	15 05	15 12	15 20	15 27	15 35	15 42
Highbury & Islington ⊖178	d	13 07	13 14	13 21	13 29	13 37	13 44	13 52	13 59	14 07	14 14	14 22	14 29	14 37	14 47	14 52	14 59	15 07	15 14	15 22	15 29	15 37	15 44
Caledonian Rd & Barnsbury	d	13 09	13 16	13 23	13 31	13 39	13 46	13 54	14 01	14 09	14 16	14 24	14 31	14 39	14 49	14 54	15 01	15 09	15 16	15 24	15 31	15 39	15 46
Camden Road	d	13 12	13 19	13 26	13 34	13 42	13 49	13 57	14 04	14 12	14 19	14 27	14 34	14 42	14 52	14 57	15 04	15 12	15 19	15 27	15 34	15 42	15 49
Kentish Town West	d	13 15	13 22	13 29	13 37	13 45	13 52	14 00	14 07	14 15	14 22	14 30	14 37	14 45	14 55	15 00	15 07	15 15	15 22	15 30	15 37	15 45	15 52
Gospel Oak	d	13 19	13 26	13 33	13 41	13 49	13 55	14 04	14 11	14 19	14 26	14 34	14 41	14 49	14 57	15 04	15 11	15 19	15 26	15 34	15 41	15 49	15 56
Hampstead Heath	d	13 21	13 28	13 35	13 44	13 51	13 57	14 06	14 13	14 21	14 28	14 36	14 43	14 51	14 59	15 06	15 13	15 21	15 28	15 36	15 43	15 51	15 58
Finchley Road & Frognal	d	13 23	13 30	13 37	13 46	13 53	13 59	14 08	14 15	14 23	14 30	14 38	14 45	14 53	15 01	15 08	15 15	15 23	15 30	15 38	15 45	15 53	16 00
West Hampstead ⊖	d	13 25	13 32	13 39	13 48	13 55	14 01	14 10	14 17	14 25	14 32	14 40	14 47	14 55	15 03	15 10	15 17	15 25	15 32	15 40	15 47	15 55	16 02
Brondesbury	d	13 26	13 34	13 40	13 49	13 56	14 03	14 11	14 19	14 26	14 34	14 41	14 49	14 56	15 04	15 11	15 19	15 26	15 34	15 41	15 49	15 56	16 04
Brondesbury Park	d	13 28	13 35	13 42	13 51	13 58	14 04	14 13	14 20	14 28	14 35	14 43	14 50	14 58	15 06	15 13	15 20	15 28	15 35	15 43	15 50	15 58	16 05
Kensal Rise	d	13 30	13 37	13 44	13 53	14 00	14 06	14 15	14 22	14 30	14 37	14 45	14 52	15 00	15 08	15 15	15 22	15 30	15 37	15 45	15 52	16 00	16 07
Willesden Jn. High Level ⊖	a	13 34	13 42	13 48	13 57	14 04	14 11	14 19	14 27	14 34	14 42	14 49	14 57	15 04	15 12	15 19	15 27	15 34	15 42	15 49	15 57	16 04	16 12
	d	13 35	13 43	13 49	13 58	14 05	14 12	14 20	14 28	14 35	14 43	14 50	14 58	15 05	15 13	15 20	15 28	15 35	15 43	15 50	15 58	16 05	16 13
Willesden Jn Low Level ⊖	a																						
Shepherd's Bush ⊖66,176	d	13 41		13 56		14 11		14 26		14 41		14 56		15 11		15 26		15 41		15 56		16 11	
Kensington (Olympia) ⊖176	d	13 43		13 58		14 13		14 28		14 43		14 58		15 13		15 28		15 43		15 58		16 13	
West Brompton ⊖176	d	13 46		14 01		14 16		14 31		14 46		15 01		15 16		15 31		15 46		16 01		16 16	
Imperial Wharf 176	d	13 49		14 04		14 19		14 34		14 49		15 04		15 19		15 34		15 49		16 04		16 19	
Clapham Junction [10] 66,176	a	13 55		14 12		14 25		14 40		14 55		15 10		15 25		15 40		15 55		16 10		16 25	
Acton Central	d		13 48		14 03		14 18		14 33		14 48		15 03		15 18		15 33		15 48		16 03		16 18
South Acton	d		13 51		14 06		14 21		14 36		14 51		15 06		15 21		15 36		15 51		16 06		16 21
Gunnersbury ⊖	d		13 54		14 09		14 24		14 39		14 54		15 09		15 24		15 39		15 54		16 09		16 24
Kew Gardens ⊖	d		13 57		14 12		14 27		14 42		14 57		15 12		15 27		15 42		15 57		16 12		16 27
Richmond ⊖	a		14 02		14 17		14 32		14 47		15 02		15 17		15 35		15 47		16 02		16 17		16 32

For services between Shepherds Bush and Clapham Junction refer to Table T066 and T176

Table T059-F

Saturdays
21 December to 16 May

Stratford - Highbury & Islington, West Hampstead, Willesden Junction, Clapham Junction and Richmond

		LO	LO	LO	LO	LO	LO	LO	LO	LO	LO	LO	LO	LO	LO	LO	LO	LO	LO	LO	LO	LO	LO
Stratford 7 ⊖ ⇌	d	15 38	15 45	15 53	16 00	16 08	16 15	16 23	16 30	16 38	16 45	16 53	17 00	17 08	17 15	17 23	17 30	17 38	17 45	17 53	18 00	18 08	18 15
Hackney Wick	d	15 41	15 48	15 56	16 03	16 11	16 18	16 26	16 33	16 41	16 48	16 56	17 03	17 11	17 18	17 26	17 33	17 41	17 48	17 56	18 03	18 11	18 18
Homerton	d	15 44	15 51	15 59	16 06	16 14	16 21	16 29	16 36	16 44	16 51	16 59	17 06	17 14	17 21	17 29	17 36	17 44	17 51	17 59	18 06	18 14	18 21
Hackney Central	d	15 46	15 53	16 01	16 08	16 16	16 23	16 31	16 38	16 46	16 53	17 01	17 08	17 16	17 23	17 31	17 38	17 46	17 53	18 01	18 08	18 16	18 23
Dalston Kingsland	d	15 48	15 55	16 03	16 10	16 18	16 25	16 33	16 40	16 48	16 55	17 03	17 10	17 18	17 25	17 33	17 40	17 48	17 55	18 03	18 10	18 18	18 25
Canonbury 178	d	15 50	15 57	16 05	16 12	16 20	16 27	16 35	16 42	16 50	16 57	17 05	17 12	17 20	17 27	17 35	17 42	17 50	17 57	18 05	18 12	18 20	18 27
Highbury & Islington ⊖178	d	15 52	15 59	16 07	16 14	16 22	16 29	16 37	16 44	16 52	16 59	17 07	17 14	17 22	17 29	17 37	17 44	17 52	17 59	18 07	18 14	18 22	18 29
Caledonian Rd & Barnsbury	d	15 54	16 01	16 09	16 16	16 24	16 31	16 39	16 46	16 54	17 01	17 09	17 16	17 24	17 31	17 39	17 46	17 54	18 01	18 09	18 16	18 24	18 31
Camden Road	d	15 57	16 04	16 12	16 19	16 27	16 34	16 42	16 49	16 57	17 04	17 12	17 19	17 27	17 34	17 42	17 49	17 57	18 04	18 12	18 19	18 27	18 34
Kentish Town West	d	16 00	16 07	16 15	16 22	16 30	16 37	16 45	16 52	17 00	17 07	17 15	17 22	17 30	17 37	17 45	17 52	18 00	18 07	18 15	18 22	18 30	18 37
Gospel Oak	d	16 04	16 11	16 19	16 26	16 34	16 41	16 49	16 56	17 04	17 11	17 19	17 26	17 34	17 41	17 49	17 56	18 04	18 11	18 19	18 26	18 34	18 41
Hampstead Heath	d	16 06	16 13	16 21	16 28	16 36	16 43	16 51	16 58	17 06	17 13	17 21	17 28	17 36	17 43	17 51	17 58	18 06	18 13	18 21	18 28	18 36	18 43
Finchley Road & Frognal	d	16 08	16 15	16 23	16 30	16 38	16 45	16 53	17 00	17 08	17 15	17 23	17 30	17 38	17 45	17 53	18 00	18 08	18 15	18 23	18 30	18 38	18 45
West Hampstead ⊖	d	16 10	16 17	16 25	16 32	16 40	16 47	16 55	17 02	17 10	17 17	17 25	17 32	17 40	17 47	17 55	18 02	18 10	18 17	18 25	18 32	18 40	18 47
Brondesbury	d	16 11	16 19	16 27	16 34	16 41	16 49	16 56	17 04	17 11	17 19	17 26	17 34	17 41	17 49	17 56	18 04	18 11	18 19	18 26	18 34	18 41	18 49
Brondesbury Park	d	16 13	16 20	16 28	16 35	16 43	16 50	16 58	17 05	17 13	17 20	17 28	17 35	17 43	17 50	17 58	18 05	18 13	18 20	18 28	18 35	18 43	18 50
Kensal Rise	d	16 15	16 22	16 30	16 37	16 45	16 52	17 00	17 07	17 15	17 22	17 30	17 37	17 45	17 52	18 00	18 07	18 15	18 22	18 30	18 37	18 45	18 52
Willesden Jn. High Level ⊖	a	16 19	16 25	16 34	16 42	16 49	16 57	17 04	17 12	17 19	17 27	17 34	17 42	17 49	17 57	18 04	18 12	18 19	18 27	18 34	18 42	18 49	18 57
	d	16 20	16 26	16 35	16 43	16 50	16 58	17 05	17 13	17 20	17 28	17 35	17 43	17 50	17 58	18 05	18 13	18 20	18 28	18 35	18 43	18 50	18 58
Willesden Jn Low Level ⊖	a																						
Shepherd's Bush ⊖66,176	d	16 26		16 41		16 56		17 11		17 26		17 41		17 56		18 11		18 26		18 41		18 56	
Kensington (Olympia) ⊖176	d	16 28		16 43		16 58		17 13		17 28		17 43		17 58		18 13		18 28		18 43		18 58	
West Brompton ⊖176	d	16 31		16 46		17 01		17 16		17 31		17 46		18 01		18 16		18 31		18 46		19 01	
Imperial Wharf 176	d	16 34		16 49		17 04		17 19		17 34		17 49		18 04		18 19		18 34		18 49		19 04	
Clapham Junction 10 66,176	a	16 40		16 55		17 10		17 25		17 40		17 55		18 13		18 28		18 43		18 58		19 10	
Acton Central	d		16 33		16 48		17 03		17 18		17 33		17 48		18 03		18 18		18 33		18 48		19 03
South Acton	d		16 36		16 51		17 06		17 21		17 36		17 51		18 06		18 21		18 36		18 51		19 06
Gunnersbury ⊖	d		16 39		16 54		17 09		17 24		17 39		17 54		18 09		18 24		18 39		18 54		19 09
Kew Gardens ⊖	d		16 42		16 57		17 12		17 27		17 42		17 57		18 12		18 27		18 42		18 57		19 12
Richmond ⊖	a		16 47		17 02		17 17		17 32		17 47		18 02		18 17		18 32		18 47		19 02		19 17

		LO	LO	LO	LO	LO	LO	LO	LO	LO	LO	LO	LO	LO	LO	LO	LO	LO	LO	LO	LO	LO	LO
Stratford 7 ⊖ ⇌	d	18 23	18 30	18 38	18 45	18 53	19 00	19 08	19 15	19 23	19 30	19 38	19 45	19 53	20 00	20 08	20 15	20 23	20 30	20 38	20 45	20 53	21 00
Hackney Wick	d	18 26	18 33	18 41	18 48	18 56	19 03	19 11	19 18	19 26	19 33	19 41	19 48	19 56	20 03	20 11	20 18	20 26	20 33	20 41	20 48	20 56	21 03
Homerton	d	18 29	18 36	18 44	18 51	18 59	19 06	19 14	19 21	19 29	19 36	19 44	19 51	19 59	20 06	20 14	20 21	20 29	20 36	20 44	20 51	20 59	21 06
Hackney Central	d	18 31	18 38	18 46	18 53	19 01	19 08	19 16	19 23	19 31	19 38	19 46	19 53	20 01	20 08	20 16	20 23	20 31	20 38	20 46	20 53	21 01	21 08
Dalston Kingsland	d	18 33	18 40	18 48	18 55	19 03	19 10	19 18	19 25	19 33	19 40	19 48	19 55	20 03	20 10	20 18	20 25	20 33	20 40	20 48	20 55	21 03	21 10
Canonbury 178	d	18 35	18 42	18 50	18 57	19 05	19 12	19 20	19 27	19 35	19 42	19 50	19 57	20 05	20 12	20 20	20 27	20 35	20 42	20 50	20 57	21 05	21 12
Highbury & Islington ⊖178	d	18 37	18 44	18 52	18 59	19 07	19 14	19 22	19 29	19 37	19 44	19 52	19 59	20 07	20 14	20 22	20 29	20 37	20 44	20 52	20 59	21 07	21 14
Caledonian Rd & Barnsbury	d	18 39	18 46	18 54	19 01	19 09	19 16	19 24	19 31	19 39	19 46	19 54	20 01	20 09	20 16	20 24	20 31	20 39	20 46	20 54	21 01	21 09	21 16
Camden Road	d	18 42	18 49	18 57	19 04	19 12	19 19	19 27	19 34	19 42	19 49	19 57	20 04	20 12	20 19	20 27	20 34	20 42	20 49	20 57	21 04	21 12	21 22
Kentish Town West	d	18 45	18 52	19 00	19 07	19 15	19 22	19 30	19 37	19 45	19 52	20 00	20 07	20 15	20 22	20 30	20 37	20 45	20 52	21 00	21 07	21 15	21 25
Gospel Oak	d	18 49	18 56	19 04	19 11	19 19	19 26	19 32	19 41	19 49	19 56	20 04	20 11	20 19	20 26	20 34	20 41	20 49	20 56	21 04	21 11	21 18	21 27
Hampstead Heath	d	18 51	18 58	19 06	19 13	19 21	19 28	19 34	19 43	19 51	19 58	20 06	20 13	20 21	20 28	20 36	20 43	20 51	20 58	21 06	21 13	21 20	21 29
Finchley Road & Frognal	d	18 53	19 00	19 08	19 15	19 23	19 30	19 36	19 45	19 53	20 00	20 08	20 15	20 23	20 30	20 38	20 45	20 53	21 00	21 08	21 15	21 22	21 31
West Hampstead ⊖	d	18 55	19 02	19 10	19 17	19 25	19 32	19 38	19 47	19 55	20 02	20 10	20 17	20 25	20 32	20 40	20 47	20 55	21 02	21 10	21 17	21 24	21 33
Brondesbury	d	18 56	19 04	19 11	19 19	19 26	19 34	19 39	19 49	19 56	20 04	20 11	20 19	20 26	20 34	20 41	20 49	20 56	21 04	21 11	21 19	21 25	21 35
Brondesbury Park	d	18 58	19 05	19 13	19 20	19 28	19 35	19 41	19 50	19 58	20 05	20 13	20 20	20 28	20 35	20 43	20 50	20 58	21 05	21 13	21 20	21 27	21 36
Kensal Rise	d	19 00	19 07	19 15	19 22	19 30	19 37	19 43	19 52	20 00	20 07	20 15	20 22	20 30	20 37	20 45	20 52	21 00	21 07	21 15	21 22	21 29	21 38
Willesden Jn. High Level ⊖	a	19 04	19 12	19 19	19 27	19 34	19 42	19 47	19 57	20 04	20 12	20 19	20 27	20 34	20 42	20 49	20 57	21 04	21 12	21 19	21 27	21 34	21 44
	d	19 05	19 13	19 20	19 28	19 35	19 43	19 50	19 58	20 05	20 13	20 20	20 28	20 35	20 43	20 50	20 58	21 05	21 13	21 20	21 28	21 35	21 45
Willesden Jn Low Level ⊖	a																						
Shepherd's Bush ⊖66,176	d	19 11		19 26		19 41		19 56		20 11		20 26		20 41		20 56		21 11		21 26		21 41	
Kensington (Olympia) ⊖176	d	19 13		19 28		19 43		19 58		20 13		20 28		20 43		20 58		21 13		21 28		21 43	
West Brompton ⊖176	d	19 16		19 31		19 46		20 01		20 16		20 31		20 46		21 01		21 16		21 31		21 46	
Imperial Wharf 176	d	19 19		19 34		19 49		20 04		20 19		20 34		20 49		21 04		21 19		21a34		21 49	
Clapham Junction 10 66,176	a	19 25		19 40		19 55		20 10		20 25		20 40		20 55		21 10		21 25				21 55	
Acton Central	d		19 18		19 33		19 48		20 03		20 18		20 33		20 48		21 03		21 18		21 33		21 52
South Acton	d		19 21		19 36		19 51		20 06		20 21		20 36		20 51		21 06		21 21		21 36		21 55
Gunnersbury ⊖	d		19 24		19 39		19 54		20 09		20 24		20 39		20 54		21 09		21 24		21 39		22 00
Kew Gardens ⊖	d		19 27		19 42		19 57		20 12		20 27		20 42		20 57		21 12		21 27		21 42		22 03
Richmond ⊖	a		19 32		19 47		20 02		20 17		20 32		20 47		21 02		21 17		21 32		21 47		22 07

For services between Shepherds Bush and Clapham Junction refer to Table T066 and T176

NRT DECEMBER 19 EDITION

Table T059-F

Saturdays
21 December to 16 May

Stratford - Highbury & Islington, West Hampstead, Willesden Junction, Clapham Junction and Richmond

		LO	LO	LO	LO	LO	LO	LO	LO	LO	LO	LO	LO	LO	LO	LO	LO	LO	LO	LO	LO	LO
Stratford 7 ⊖ ⇌	d	21 08	21 15	21 23	21 30	21 38	21 45	21 53	22 00	22 08	22 15		22 30	22 38	22 45		23 00	23 08	23 15	23 30	23 45	23 59
Hackney Wick	d	21 11	21 18	21 26	21 33	21 41	21 48	21 56	22 03	22 11	22 18		22 33	22 41	22 48		23 03	23 11	23 18	23 33	23 48	00 02
Homerton	d	21 14	21 21	21 29	21 36	21 44	21 51	21 59	22 06	22 14	22 21		22 36	22 44	22 51		23 06	23 14	23 21	23 36	23 51	00 05
Hackney Central	d	21 16	21 23	21 31	21 38	21 46	21 53	22 01	22 08	22 16	22 23		22 38	22 46	22 53		23 08	23 16	23 23	23 38	23 53	00 07
Dalston Kingsland	d	21 18	21 25	21 33	21 40	21 48	21 55	22 03	22 10	22 18	22 25		22 40	22 48	22 55		23 10	23 18	23 25	23 40	23 55	00 09
Canonbury 178	d	21 20	21 27	21 35	21 42	21 50	21 57	22 05	22 12	22 20	22 27		22 42	22 50	22 57		23 12	23 20	23 27	23 42	23 57	00 11
Highbury & Islington ⊖178	d	21 22	21 29	21 37	21 44	21 52	21 59	22 07	22 14	22 22	22 29		22 44	22 52	22 59		23 14	23 22	23 29	23 44	23 59	00 13
Caledonian Rd & Barnsbury	d	21 24	21 31	21 39	21 46	21 54	22 01	22 09	22 16	22 24	22 31		22 46	22 54	23 01		23 16	23 24	23 31	23 46	00 02	00 15
Camden Road	d	21 27	21 34	21 42	21 50	21 57	22 04	22 12	22 19	22 27	22 34		22 49	22 57	23 04		23 19	23 27	23 34	23 49	00 04	00 18
Kentish Town West	d	21 30	21 37	21 45	21 53	22 00	22 07	22 15	22 22	22 30	22 37		22 52	23 00	23 07		23 22	23 30	23 37	23 52	00 07	00 21
Gospel Oak	d	21 34	21 41	21 49	21 57	22 04	22 11	22 19	22 26	22 34	22 41		22 56	23 04	23 11		23 25	23 34	23 41	23 56	00 11	00 25
Hampstead Heath	d	21 36	21 43	21 51	22 01	22 06	22 13	22 21	22 28	22 36	22 43		22 58	23 07	23 13		23 27	23 36	23 43	23 58	00 13	00 27
Finchley Road & Frognal	d	21 38	21 45	21 53	22 03	22 08	22 15	22 23	22 30	22 38	22 45		23 00	23 09	23 15		23 29	23 38	23 45	00 01	00 15	00 29
West Hampstead ⊖	d	21 40	21 47	21 55	22 05	22 10	22 17	22 25	22 32	22 40	22 47		23 02	23 11	23 17		23 31	23 40	23 47	00 02	00 17	00 31
Brondesbury	d	21 41	21 49	21 56	22 06	22 11	22 19	22 26	22 34	22 41	22 49		23 04	23 12	23 19		23 33	23 41	23 49	00 04	00 19	00 33
Brondesbury Park	d	21 43	21 50	21 58	22 08	22 13	22 20	22 28	22 35	22 43	22 50		23 05	23 14	23 20		23 34	23 43	23 50	00 05	00 20	00 34
Kensal Rise	d	21 45	21 52	22 00	22 10	22 15	22 22	22 30	22 37	22 45	22 52		23 07	23 16	23 22		23 36	23 45	23 52	00 07	00 22	00 36
Willesden Jn. High Level ⊖	a	21 49	21 57	22 04	22 13	22 19	22 27	22 34	22 42	22 49	22 57		23 11	23 19	23 27		23 39	23 49	23 57	00 13		00 40
	d	21 50	21 58	22 05	22 14	22 20	22 28	22 35	22 43	22 50	22 58	23 05	23 13	23 20	23 28	23 35	23 40	23 50	23 58			
Willesden Jn Low Level ⊖	a																				00 32	
Shepherd's Bush ⊖66,176	d	21 57		22 11		22 26		22 41		22 56		23 11		23 26		23 41		23 56				
Kensington (Olympia) ⊖176	d	21 59		22 13		22 28		22 43		22 58		23 13		23 28		23 43		23 58				
West Brompton ⊖176	d	22 01		22 16		22 31		22 46		23 01		23 16		23 31		23 46		00 02				
Imperial Wharf 176	d	22 04		22 19		22 34		22 49		23 04		23 19		23 34		23 49		00 05				
Clapham Junction 10 66,176	a	22 10		22 25		22 40		22 55		23 10		23 26		23 40		23 56		00 10				
Acton Central	d		22 03		22 19		22 33		22 48		23 03		23 18		23 33		23 45		00 03			
South Acton	d		22 06		22 22		22 36		22 51		23 06		23 21		23 36		23 48		00 06			
Gunnersbury ⊖	d		22 09		22 25		22 39		22 54		23 09		23 24		23 39		23 51		00 09			
Kew Gardens ⊖	d		22 12		22 28		22 42		22 57		23 12		23 27		23 42		23 54		00 12			
Richmond ⊖	a		22 17		22 32		22 47		23 02		23 17		23 32		23 47		00 02		00 17			

Sundays
15 December to 10 May

		LO A	LO A	LO	LO A	LO A	LO A	LO	LO	LO	LO	LO	LO	LO	LO	LO	LO	LO	LO	LO	LO	LO	LO	LO
Stratford 7 ⊖ ⇌	d							00 15									09 05	09 13		09 28	09 35	09 43	09 50	09 58
Hackney Wick	d						00 02	00 18									09 08	09 16		09 31	09 38	09 46	09 53	10 01
Homerton	d						00 05	00 21									09 11	09 19		09 34	09 41	09 49	09 56	10 04
Hackney Central	d						00 07	00 23									09 13	09 21		09 36	09 43	09 51	09 58	10 06
Dalston Kingsland	d						00 09	00 25									09 15	09 23		09 38	09 45	09 53	10 00	10 08
Canonbury 178	d						00 11	00 27									09 17	09 25		09 40	09 47	09 55	10 02	10 10
Highbury & Islington ⊖178	d						00 13	00 29									09 19	09 27		09 42	09 49	09 57	10 04	10 12
Caledonian Rd & Barnsbury	d					00 02	00 15	00 31									09 21	09 29		09 44	09 51	09 59	10 06	10 14
Camden Road	d					00 04	00 18	00 34									09 24	09 32		09 47	09 54	10 02	10 09	10 17
Kentish Town West	d					00 07	00 21	00 37									09 27	09 35		09 50	09 57	10 05	10 12	10 20
Gospel Oak	d					00 11	00 25	00 40									09 31	09 39		09 54	10 01	10 09	10 16	10 24
Hampstead Heath	d					00 13	00 27	00 42									09 33	09 41		09 56	10 03	10 11	10 18	10 26
Finchley Road & Frognal	d				00 01	00 15	00 29	00 44									09 35	09 43		09 58	10 05	10 13	10 20	10 28
West Hampstead ⊖	d				00 02	00 17	00 31	00 46									09 37	09 45		10 00	10 07	10 15	10 22	10 30
Brondesbury	d				00 04	00 19	00 33	00 48									09 38	09 46		10 01	10 08	10 16	10 23	10 31
Brondesbury Park	d				00 05	00 20	00 34	00 49									09 40	09 48		10 03	10 10	10 18	10 25	10 33
Kensal Rise	d				00 07	00 22	00 36	00 51									09 42	09 50		10 05	10 12	10 20	10 27	10 35
Willesden Jn. High Level ⊖	a				00 13		00 40										09 47	09 55		10 10	10 16	10 25	10 31	10 40
	d			00 05					08 35	08 47	08 56	09 05	09 20	09 26	09 32	09 43	09 48	09 56	10 02	10 11	10 17	10 26	10 32	10 41
Willesden Jn Low Level ⊖	a					00 32		01 01																
Shepherd's Bush ⊖66,176	d			00 11					08 41	08 53		09 11	09 26		09 38		09 54		10 08		10 23		10 38	
Kensington (Olympia) ⊖176	d			00 13					08 43	08 55		09 13	09 28		09 40		09 56		10 10		10 25		10 40	
West Brompton ⊖176	d	00 02		00 16					08 46	08 58		09 16	09 31		09 43		09 59		10 13		10 28		10 43	
Imperial Wharf 176	d	00 05		00 19					08 49	09 01		09 19	09 34		09 46		10 02		10 16		10 31		10 46	
Clapham Junction 10 66,176	a	00 10		00 26					08 56	09 08		09 26	09 41		09 53		10 09		10 24		10 39		10 54	
Acton Central	d		00 03								09 01			09 31		09 48		10 01		10 16		10 31		10 46
South Acton	d		00 06								09 05			09 35		09 50		10 05		10 19		10 35		10 49
Gunnersbury ⊖	d		00 09								09 08			09 38		09 53		10 08		10 22		10 38		10 52
Kew Gardens ⊖	d		00 12								09 11			09 41		09 56		10 11		10 25		10 41		10 55
Richmond ⊖	a		00 17								09 20			09 50		10 05		10 16		10 30		10 46		11 00

A not 15 December

For services between Shepherds Bush and Clapham Junction refer to Table T066 and T176

Table T059-F

Sundays

15 December to 10 May

Stratford - Highbury & Islington, West Hampstead, Willesden Junction, Clapham Junction and Richmond

	LO	LO	LO		LO	LO	LO	LO	LO	LO	LO	LO	LO	LO	LO	LO	LO	LO	LO	LO	LO	LO
Stratford 7 ⊖ d	10 05	10 13	10 20		12 28	12 35	12 43	12 50	12 58	13 05	13 13	13 20	13 28	13 35	13 43	13 50	13 58	14 05	14 13	14 20	14 28	14 35
Hackney Wick d	10 08	10 16	10 23		12 31	12 38	12 46	12 53	13 01	13 08	13 16	13 23	13 31	13 38	13 46	13 53	14 01	14 08	14 16	14 23	14 31	14 38
Homerton d	10 11	10 19	10 26		12 34	12 41	12 49	12 56	13 04	13 11	13 19	13 26	13 34	13 41	13 49	13 56	14 04	14 11	14 19	14 26	14 34	14 41
Hackney Central d	10 13	10 21	10 28		12 36	12 43	12 51	12 58	13 06	13 13	13 21	13 28	13 36	13 43	13 51	13 58	14 06	14 13	14 21	14 28	14 36	14 43
Dalston Kingsland d	10 15	10 23	10 30		12 38	12 45	12 53	13 00	13 08	13 15	13 23	13 30	13 38	13 45	13 53	14 00	14 08	14 15	14 23	14 30	14 38	14 45
Canonbury 178 d	10 17	10 25	10 32		12 40	12 47	12 55	13 02	13 10	13 17	13 25	13 32	13 40	13 47	13 55	14 02	14 10	14 17	14 26	14 32	14 40	14 47
Highbury & Islington ⊖178 d	10 19	10 27	10 34		12 42	12 49	12 57	13 04	13 12	13 19	13 27	13 34	13 42	13 49	13 57	14 04	14 12	14 19	14 29	14 34	14 42	14 49
Caledonian Rd & Barnsbury d	10 21	10 29	10 36		12 44	12 51	12 59	13 06	13 14	13 21	13 29	13 36	13 44	13 51	13 59	14 06	14 14	14 21	14 31	14 36	14 44	14 51
Camden Road d	10 24	10 32	10 39		12 47	12 54	13 02	13 09	13 17	13 24	13 32	13 39	13 47	13 54	14 02	14 09	14 17	14 24	14 34	14 39	14 47	14 54
Kentish Town West d	10 27	10 35	10 42		12 50	12 57	13 05	13 12	13 20	13 27	13 35	13 42	13 50	13 57	14 05	14 12	14 20	14 27	14 36	14 42	14 50	14 57
Gospel Oak d	10 31	10 39	10 46		12 54	13 01	13 09	13 16	13 24	13 31	13 39	13 46	13 54	14 01	14 09	14 16	14 24	14 31	14 39	14 46	14 54	15 01
Hampstead Heath d	10 33	10 41	10 48	and at the same minutes past each hour until	12 56	13 03	13 11	13 18	13 26	13 33	13 41	13 48	13 56	14 03	14 11	14 18	14 26	14 33	14 41	14 48	14 56	15 03
Finchley Road & Frognal d	10 35	10 43	10 50		12 58	13 05	13 13	13 20	13 28	13 35	13 43	13 50	13 58	14 05	14 13	14 20	14 28	14 35	14 43	14 50	14 58	15 05
West Hampstead ⊖ d	10 37	10 45	10 52		13 00	13 07	13 15	13 22	13 30	13 37	13 45	13 52	14 00	14 07	14 15	14 22	14 30	14 37	14 45	14 52	15 00	15 07
Brondesbury d	10 38	10 46	10 53		13 01	13 08	13 16	13 23	13 31	13 38	13 46	13 53	14 01	14 08	14 16	14 23	14 31	14 38	14 46	14 53	15 01	15 08
Brondesbury Park d	10 40	10 48	10 55		13 03	13 10	13 18	13 25	13 33	13 40	13 48	13 55	14 03	14 10	14 18	14 25	14 33	14 40	14 48	14 55	15 03	15 10
Kensal Rise d	10 42	10 50	10 57		13 05	13 12	13 20	13 27	13 35	13 42	13 50	13 57	14 05	14 12	14 20	14 27	14 35	14 42	14 50	14 57	15 05	15 12
Willesden Jn. High Level ⊖ a	10 46	10 55	11 01		13 10	13 16	13 25	13 31	13 40	13 46	13 55	14 01	14 10	14 16	14 25	14 31	14 40	14 46	14 55	15 01	15 10	15 16
d	10 47	10 56	11 02		13 11	13 17	13 26	13 32	13 41	13 47	13 56	14 02	14 11	14 17	14 26	14 32	14 41	14 47	14 56	15 02	15 11	15 17
Willesden Jn Low Level ⊖ a																						
Shepherd's Bush ⊖66,176 d	10 53		11 08			13 23		13 38		13 53		14 08		14 23		14 38		14 53		15 08		15 23
Kensington (Olympia) ⊖176 d	10 55		11 10			13 25		13 40		13 55		14 10		14 25		14 40		14 55		15 10		15 25
West Brompton ⊖176 d	10 58		11 13			13 28		13 43		13 58		14 13		14 28		14 43		14 58		15 13		15 28
Imperial Wharf 176 d	11 01		11 16			13 31		13 46		14 01		14 16		14 31		14 46		15 01		15 16		15 31
Clapham Junction 10 66,176 a	11 09		11 24			13 39		13 54		14 09		14 24		14 39		14 54		15 09		15 24		15 39
Acton Central d		11 01			13 16		13 31		13 46		14 01		14 16		14 31		14 46		15 01		15 16	
South Acton d		11 05			13 19		13 35		13 49		14 05		14 19		14 35		14 49		15 05		15 19	
Gunnersbury ⊖ d		11 08			13 22		13 38		13 52		14 08		14 22		14 38		14 52		15 08		15 22	
Kew Gardens ⊖ d		11 11			13 25		13 41		13 55		14 11		14 25		14 41		14 55		15 11		15 25	
Richmond ⊖ a		11 16			13 30		13 46		14 00		14 16		14 30		14 46		15 00		15 16		15 30	

	LO	LO	LO	LO	LO	LO	LO	LO	LO	LO	LO	LO	LO	LO	LO	LO	LO	LO	LO	LO	LO	LO
Stratford 7 ⊖ d	14 43	14 50	14 58	15 05	15 13	15 20	15 28	15 35	15 43	15 50	15 58	16 05	16 13	16 20	16 28	16 35	16 43	16 50	16 58	17 05	17 13	17 20
Hackney Wick d	14 46	14 53	15 01	15 08	15 16	15 23	15 31	15 38	15 46	15 53	16 01	16 08	16 16	16 23	16 31	16 38	16 46	16 53	17 01	17 08	17 16	17 23
Homerton d	14 49	14 56	15 04	15 11	15 19	15 26	15 34	15 41	15 49	15 56	16 04	16 11	16 19	16 26	16 34	16 41	16 49	16 56	17 04	17 11	17 19	17 26
Hackney Central d	14 51	14 58	15 06	15 13	15 21	15 28	15 36	15 43	15 51	15 58	16 06	16 13	16 21	16 28	16 36	16 43	16 51	16 58	17 06	17 13	17 21	17 28
Dalston Kingsland d	14 53	15 00	15 08	15 15	15 23	15 30	15 38	15 45	15 53	16 00	16 08	16 15	16 23	16 30	16 38	16 45	16 53	17 00	17 08	17 15	17 23	17 30
Canonbury 178 d	14 55	15 02	15 10	15 17	15 25	15 32	15 40	15 47	15 55	16 02	16 10	16 17	16 25	16 32	16 40	16 47	16 55	17 02	17 10	17 17	17 25	17 32
Highbury & Islington ⊖178 d	14 57	15 04	15 12	15 19	15 27	15 34	15 42	15 49	15 57	16 04	16 12	16 19	16 27	16 34	16 42	16 49	16 57	17 04	17 12	17 19	17 27	17 34
Caledonian Rd & Barnsbury d	14 59	15 06	15 14	15 21	15 29	15 36	15 44	15 51	15 59	16 06	16 14	16 21	16 29	16 36	16 44	16 51	16 59	17 06	17 14	17 21	17 29	17 36
Camden Road d	15 02	15 09	15 17	15 24	15 32	15 39	15 47	15 54	16 02	16 09	16 17	16 24	16 32	16 39	16 47	16 54	17 02	17 09	17 17	17 24	17 32	17 39
Kentish Town West d	15 05	15 12	15 20	15 27	15 35	15 42	15 50	15 57	16 05	16 12	16 20	16 27	16 35	16 42	16 50	16 57	17 05	17 12	17 20	17 27	17 35	17 42
Gospel Oak d	15 09	15 16	15 24	15 31	15 39	15 46	15 54	16 01	16 09	16 16	16 24	16 31	16 39	16 46	16 54	17 01	17 09	17 16	17 24	17 31	17 39	17 46
Hampstead Heath d	15 11	15 18	15 26	15 33	15 41	15 48	15 56	16 03	16 11	16 18	16 26	16 33	16 41	16 48	16 56	17 03	17 11	17 18	17 26	17 33	17 41	17 48
Finchley Road & Frognal d	15 13	15 20	15 28	15 35	15 43	15 50	15 58	16 05	16 13	16 20	16 28	16 35	16 43	16 50	16 58	17 05	17 13	17 20	17 28	17 35	17 43	17 50
West Hampstead ⊖ d	15 15	15 22	15 30	15 37	15 45	15 52	16 00	16 07	16 15	16 22	16 30	16 37	16 45	16 52	17 00	17 07	17 15	17 22	17 30	17 37	17 45	17 52
Brondesbury d	15 16	15 23	15 31	15 38	15 46	15 53	16 01	16 08	16 16	16 23	16 31	16 38	16 46	16 53	17 01	17 08	17 16	17 23	17 31	17 38	17 46	17 53
Brondesbury Park d	15 18	15 25	15 33	15 40	15 48	15 55	16 03	16 10	16 18	16 25	16 33	16 40	16 48	16 55	17 03	17 10	17 18	17 25	17 33	17 40	17 48	17 55
Kensal Rise d	15 20	15 27	15 35	15 42	15 50	15 57	16 05	16 12	16 20	16 27	16 35	16 42	16 50	16 57	17 05	17 12	17 20	17 27	17 35	17 42	17 50	17 57
Willesden Jn. High Level ⊖ a	15 25	15 31	15 40	15 46	15 55	16 01	16 10	16 16	16 25	16 31	16 40	16 46	16 55	17 01	17 10	17 16	17 25	17 31	17 40	17 46	17 55	18 01
d	15 26	15 32	15 41	15 47	15 56	16 02	16 11	16 17	16 26	16 32	16 41	16 47	16 56	17 02	17 11	17 17	17 26	17 32	17 41	17 47	17 56	18 02
Willesden Jn Low Level ⊖ a																						
Shepherd's Bush ⊖66,176 d		15 38		15 53		16 08		16 23		16 38		16 53		17 08		17 23		17 38		17 53		18 08
Kensington (Olympia) ⊖176 d		15 40		15 55		16 10		16 25		16 40		16 55		17 10		17 25		17 40		17 55		18 10
West Brompton ⊖176 d		15 43		15 58		16 13		16 28		16 43		16 58		17 13		17 28		17 43		17 58		18 13
Imperial Wharf 176 d		15 46		16 01		16 16		16 31		16 46		17 01		17 16		17 31		17 46		18 01		18 16
Clapham Junction 10 66,176 a		15 54		16 09		16 24		16 39		16 54		17 10		17 25		17 40		17 55		18 10		18 24
Acton Central d	15 31		15 46		16 01		16 16		16 31		16 46		17 01		17 16		17 31		17 46		18 01	
South Acton d	15 35		15 49		16 05		16 19		16 35		16 49		17 05		17 19		17 35		17 49		18 05	
Gunnersbury ⊖ d	15 38		15 52		16 08		16 22		16 38		16 52		17 08		17 22		17 38		17 52		18 08	
Kew Gardens ⊖ d	15 41		15 55		16 11		16 25		16 41		16 55		17 11		17 25		17 41		17 55		18 11	
Richmond ⊖ a	15 46		16 00		16 16		16 30		16 46		17 00		17 16		17 30		17 46		18 00		18 16	

For services between Shepherds Bush and Clapham Junction refer to Table T066 and T176

Table T059-F

Sundays

15 December to 10 May

Stratford - Highbury & Islington, West Hampstead, Willesden Junction, Clapham Junction and Richmond

	LO	LO	LO	LO	LO	LO	LO	LO	LO	LO	LO	LO	LO	LO	LO	LO	LO	LO	LO	LO	LO	LO
Stratford 7 ⊖ d	17 28	17 35	17 43	17 50	17 58	18 05	18 13	18 20	18 28	18 35	18 43	18 50	18 58	19 05	19 13	19 20	19 28	19 35	19 43	19 50	19 58	20 05
Hackney Wick d	17 31	17 38	17 46	17 53	18 01	18 08	18 16	18 23	18 31	18 38	18 46	18 53	19 01	19 08	19 16	19 23	19 31	19 38	19 46	19 53	20 01	20 08
Homerton d	17 34	17 41	17 49	17 56	18 04	18 11	18 19	18 26	18 34	18 41	18 49	18 56	19 04	19 11	19 19	19 26	19 34	19 41	19 49	19 56	20 04	20 11
Hackney Central d	17 36	17 43	17 51	17 58	18 06	18 13	18 21	18 28	18 36	18 43	18 51	18 58	19 06	19 13	19 21	19 28	19 36	19 43	19 51	19 58	20 06	20 13
Dalston Kingsland d	17 38	17 45	17 53	18 00	18 08	18 15	18 23	18 30	18 38	18 45	18 53	19 00	19 08	19 15	19 23	19 30	19 38	19 45	19 53	20 00	20 08	20 15
Canonbury 178 d	17 40	17 47	17 55	18 02	18 10	18 17	18 25	18 32	18 40	18 47	18 55	19 02	19 10	19 17	19 25	19 32	19 40	19 47	19 55	20 02	20 10	20 17
Highbury & Islington ⊖178 d	17 42	17 49	17 57	18 04	18 12	18 19	18 27	18 34	18 42	18 49	18 57	19 04	19 12	19 19	19 27	19 34	19 42	19 49	19 57	20 04	20 12	20 19
Caledonian Rd & Barnsbury d	17 44	17 51	17 59	18 06	18 14	18 21	18 29	18 36	18 44	18 51	18 59	19 06	19 14	19 21	19 29	19 36	19 44	19 51	19 59	20 06	20 14	20 21
Camden Road d	17 47	17 54	18 02	18 09	18 17	18 24	18 32	18 39	18 47	18 54	19 02	19 09	19 17	19 24	19 32	19 39	19 49	19 54	20 02	20 09	20 17	20 24
Kentish Town West d	17 50	17 57	18 05	18 12	18 20	18 27	18 35	18 42	18 50	18 57	19 05	19 12	19 20	19 27	19 35	19 42	19 51	19 57	20 05	20 12	20 20	20 27
Gospel Oak d	17 54	18 01	18 09	18 16	18 24	18 31	18 39	18 46	18 54	19 01	19 09	19 16	19 24	19 31	19 39	19 45	19 55	20 01	20 09	20 16	20 24	20 31
Hampstead Heath d	17 56	18 03	18 11	18 18	18 26	18 33	18 41	18 48	18 56	19 03	19 11	19 18	19 26	19 33	19 41	19 47	19 57	20 03	20 11	20 18	20 26	20 33
Finchley Road & Frognal d	17 58	18 05	18 13	18 20	18 28	18 35	18 43	18 50	18 58	19 05	19 13	19 20	19 28	19 35	19 43	19 49	19 59	20 05	20 13	20 20	20 28	20 35
West Hampstead ⊖ d	18 00	18 07	18 15	18 22	18 30	18 37	18 45	18 52	19 00	19 07	19 15	19 22	19 30	19 37	19 45	19 51	20 01	20 07	20 15	20 22	20 30	20 37
Brondesbury d	18 01	18 08	18 16	18 23	18 31	18 38	18 46	18 53	19 01	19 08	19 16	19 23	19 31	19 38	19 46	19 52	20 02	20 08	20 16	20 23	20 31	20 38
Brondesbury Park d	18 03	18 10	18 18	18 25	18 33	18 40	18 48	18 55	19 03	19 10	19 18	19 25	19 33	19 40	19 48	19 54	20 04	20 10	20 18	20 25	20 33	20 40
Kensal Rise d	18 05	18 12	18 20	18 27	18 35	18 42	18 50	18 57	19 05	19 12	19 20	19 27	19 35	19 42	19 50	19 56	20 06	20 12	20 20	20 27	20 35	20 42
Willesden Jn. High Level ⊖ a	18 10	18 16	18 25	18 31	18 40	18 46	18 55	19 01	19 10	19 16	19 25	19 31	19 40	19 46	19 55	20 00	20 10	20 16	20 25	20 31	20 40	20 46
d	18 11	18 17	18 26	18 32	18 41	18 47	18 56	19 02	19 11	19 17	19 26	19 32	19 41	19 47	19 56	20 01	20 11	20 17	20 26	20 32	20 41	20 47
Willesden Jn Low Level ⊖ a																						
Shepherd's Bush ⊖66,176 d		18 23		18 38		18 53		19 08		19 23		19 38		19 53		20 08		20 24		20 38		20 53
Kensington (Olympia) ⊖176 d		18 25		18 40		18 55		19 10		19 25		19 40		19 55		20 10		20 26		20 40		20 55
West Brompton ⊖176 d		18 28		18 43		18 58		19 13		19 28		19 43		19 58		20 13		20 29		20 43		20 58
Imperial Wharf 176 d		18 31		18 46		19 01		19 16		19 31		19 46		20 01		20 16		20 32		20 46		21 01
Clapham Junction 10 66,176 a		18 39		18 54		19 09		19 24		19 39		19 54		20 09		20 24		20 39		20 54		21 09
Acton Central d	18 16		18 31		18 46		19 01		19 16		19 31		19 46		20 01		20 16		20 31		20 46	
South Acton d	18 19		18 35		18 49		19 05		19 19		19 35		19 49		20 05		20 19		20 35		20 49	
Gunnersbury ⊖ d	18 22		18 38		18 52		19 08		19 22		19 38		19 52		20 08		20 22		20 38		20 52	
Kew Gardens ⊖ d	18 25		18 41		18 55		19 11		19 25		19 41		19 55		20 11		20 25		20 41		20 55	
Richmond ⊖ a	18 30		18 46		19 00		19 16		19 30		19 46		20 00		20 16		20 30		20 46		21 00	

	LO	LO	LO	LO	LO	LO	LO	LO	LO	LO	LO	LO	LO	LO	LO	LO	LO	LO	LO	LO	LO	LO	LO	LO	LO
Stratford 7 ⊖ d	20 13	20 20	20 28	20 35	20 43	20 50	20 58	21 05	21 13		21 28	21 35	21 44		21 58	22 05	22 15		22 30		22 45	23 00			
Hackney Wick d	20 16	20 23	20 31	20 38	20 46	20 53	21 01	21 08	21 16		21 31	21 38	21 47		22 01	22 08	22 18		22 33		22 48	23 03			
Homerton d	20 19	20 26	20 34	20 41	20 49	20 56	21 04	21 11	21 19		21 34	21 41	21 50		22 04	22 11	22 21		22 36		22 51	23 06			
Hackney Central d	20 21	20 28	20 36	20 43	20 51	20 58	21 06	21 13	21 21		21 36	21 43	21 52		22 06	22 13	22 23		22 38		22 53	23 08			
Dalston Kingsland d	20 23	20 30	20 38	20 45	20 53	21 00	21 08	21 15	21 23		21 38	21 45	21 54		22 08	22 15	22 25		22 40		22 55	23 10			
Canonbury 178 d	20 25	20 32	20 40	20 47	20 55	21 02	21 10	21 17	21 25		21 40	21 47	21 56		22 10	22 17	22 27		22 42		22 57	23 12			
Highbury & Islington ⊖178 d	20 27	20 34	20 42	20 49	20 57	21 04	21 12	21 19	21 27		21 42	21 49	21 58		22 12	22 19	22 31		22 44		22 59	23 14			
Caledonian Rd & Barnsbury d	20 29	20 36	20 44	20 51	20 59	21 06	21 14	21 21	21 29		21 44	21 51	22 00		22 14	22 21	22 33		22 46		23 01	23 16			
Camden Road d	20 32	20 39	20 47	20 54	21 02	21 09	21 17	21 24	21 32		21 47	21 54	22 03		22 17	22 24	22 36		22 49		23a07	23 19			
Kentish Town West d	20 35	20 42	20 50	20 57	21 05	21 12	21 20	21 27	21 35		21 50	21 57	22 06		22 20	22 27	22 39		22 52			23 22			
Gospel Oak d	20 39	20 46	20 54	21 01	21 09	21 16	21 24	21 30	21 39		21 54	22 01	22 10		22 24	22 31	22 41		22 56			23 26			
Hampstead Heath d	20 41	20 48	20 56	21 03	21 11	21 18	21 26	21 32	21 41		21 56	22 03	22 12		22 26	22 33	22 43		22 58			23 28			
Finchley Road & Frognal d	20 43	20 50	20 58	21 05	21 13	21 20	21 28	21 34	21 43		21 58	22 05	22 14		22 28	22 35	22 45		23 00			23 30			
West Hampstead ⊖ d	20 45	20 52	21 00	21 07	21 15	21 22	21 30	21 36	21 45		22 00	22 07	22 16		22 30	22 37	22 47		23 02			23 32			
Brondesbury d	20 46	20 53	21 01	21 08	21 16	21 23	21 31	21 37	21 46		22 01	22 08	22 17		22 31	22 38	22 48		23 03			23 34			
Brondesbury Park d	20 48	20 55	21 03	21 10	21 18	21 25	21 33	21 39	21 48		22 03	22 10	22 19		22 33	22 40	22 50		23 05			23 35			
Kensal Rise d	20 50	20 57	21 05	21 12	21 20	21 27	21 35	21 41	21 50		22 05	22 12	22 21		22 35	22 42	22 52		23 07			23 37			
Willesden Jn. High Level ⊖ a	20 55	21 01	21 10	21 16	21 25	21 31	21 40	21 45	21 55		22 10	22 16	22 26		22 40	22 46	22 57		23 11						
d	20 56	21 02	21 11	21 17	21 26	21 32	21 41	21 46	21 56	22 02	22 11	22 17	22 27	22 32	22 41	22 47	22 58	23 02	23 12	23 17			23 32	23 47	23 59
Willesden Jn Low Level ⊖ a																						23 50			
Shepherd's Bush ⊖66,176 d		21 08		21 23		21 38		21 53		22 08		22 24		22 38		22 53		23 08		23 23			23 38	23 53	00 05
Kensington (Olympia) ⊖176 d		21 10		21 25		21 40		21 55		22 10		22 26		22 40		22 55		23 10		23 25			23 40	23 55	00 07
West Brompton ⊖176 d		21 13		21 28		21 43		21 58		22 13		22 29		22 43		22 58		23 13		23 28			23 43	23 58	00 10
Imperial Wharf 176 d		21 16		21 31		21 46		22 01		22 16		22 32		22 46		23 01		23 16		23 31			23 46	00a01	00a13
Clapham Junction 10 66,176 a		21 24		21 39		21 54		22 09		22 23		22 39		22 53		23 09		23 23		23 38			23 53		
Acton Central d	21 01		21 16		21 31		21 46		22 01		22 16		22 32		22 46		23 03		23 18						
South Acton d	21 05		21 19		21 35		21 49		22 05		22 19		22 35		22 49		23 06		23 21						
Gunnersbury ⊖ d	21 08		21 22		21 38		21 52		22 08		22 22		22 38		22 52		23 09		23 24						
Kew Gardens ⊖ d	21 11		21 25		21 41		21 55		22 11		22 25		22 41		22 55		23 12		23 27						
Richmond ⊖ a	21 16		21 30		21 46		22 00		22 16		22 30		22 46		23 00		23 17		23 32						

For services between Shepherds Bush and Clapham Junction refer to Table T066 and T176

Table T059-R

Mondays to Fridays
16 December to 15 May

Richmond and Clapham Junction - Willesden Junction, West Hampstead, Highbury & Islington and Stratford

Miles	Miles		LO MX	LO	LO	LO	LO	LO	LO	LO	LO	LO	LO	LO	LO	LO	LO	LO	LO	LO	LO	LO
0	—	**Richmond** ⊖ d				05 54		06 08		06 21		06 34		06 45		06 57		07 09		07 21		07 34
1¼	—	Kew Gardens ⊖ d				05 57		06 11		06 25		06 37		06 48		07 00		07 13		07 25		07 37
2½	—	Gunnersbury ⊖ d				06 00		06 14		06 28		06 40		06 51		07 03		07 16		07 28		07 40
3	—	South Acton d				06 03		06 17		06 30		06 43		06 54		07 06		07 19		07 31		07 43
3¾	—	Acton Central d				06 06		06 20		06 33		06 46		06 57		07 09		07 22		07 34		07 46
—	0	**Clapham Junction** [10] 66,176 d							06 12		06 26		06 36		06 50		07 02		07 14		07 26	
—	1½	Imperial Wharf 176 d					06 04		06 16		06 30		06 40		06 54		07 06		07 18		07 30	
—	2½	West Brompton ⊖176 d					06 07		06 19		06 33		06 43		06 57		07 09		07 21		07 33	
—	3¼	**Kensington (Olympia)** ⊖176 d					06 10		06 22		06 36		06 46		07 00		07 12		07 24		07 36	
—	4	**Shepherd's Bush** ⊖66,176 d					06 12		06 24		06 38		06 49		07 02		07 14		07 26		07 38	
5½	—	**Willesden Jn Low Level** ⊖ d			05 52																	
5½	6	**Willesden Jn. High Level** ⊖ a				06 13	06 21	06 25	06 34	06 38	06 46	06 53	06 58	07 03	07 10	07 16	07 22	07 27	07 34	07 39	07 46	07 51
—	—	d				06 15	06 22	06 26	06 35	06 39	06 47	06 54	06 59	07 04	07 12	07 17	07 23	07 28	07 35	07 40	07 47	07 52
6½	—	Kensal Rise d			06 00	06 17	06 24	06 29	06 37	06 42	06 49	06 57	07 01	07 06	07 15	07 19	07 27	07 32	07 37	07 42	07 49	07 54
7¼	—	Brondesbury Park d			06 02	06 19	06 26	06 31	06 39	06 44	06 51	06 59	07 03	07 08	07 17	07 21	07 29	07 34	07 39	07 44	07 51	07 56
7½	—	Brondesbury d			06 04	06 21	06 28	06 32	06 41	06 45	06 53	07 00	07 05	07 10	07 18	07 23	07 30	07 35	07 41	07 46	07 53	07 58
8	—	West Hampstead ⊖ d			06 06	06 23	06 30	06 34	06 43	06 47	06 55	07 02	07 07	07 12	07 20	07 25	07 33	07 37	07 43	07 48	07 55	08 00
8½	—	Finchley Road & Frognal d			06 07	06 24	06 32	06 36	06 44	06 49	06 56	07 04	07 08	07 13	07 22	07 26	07 35	07 39	07 44	07 49	07 56	08 01
9¼	—	Hampstead Heath d			06 10	06 27	06 34	06 38	06 47	06 51	06 59	07 06	07 11	07 16	07 24	07 29	07 37	07 41	07 47	07 52	07 59	08 04
10	—	**Gospel Oak** d			06 14	06 29	06 37	06 41	06 49	06 54	07 01	07 10	07 14	07 18	07 27	07 31	07 40	07 44	07 49	07 54	08 01	08 06
10¾	—	Kentish Town West d			06 16	06 31	06 39	06 43	06 51	06 56	07 03	07 12	07 16	07 20	07 29	07 33	07 42	07 46	07 51	07 56	08 03	08 08
11¼	—	Camden Road d		06 02	06 20	06 34	06 42	06 46	06 56	07 01	07 08	07 15	07 18	07 25	07 31	07 36	07 44	07 49	07 54	07 59	08 08	08 13
12¼	—	Caledonian Rd & Barnsbury d		06 05	06 23	06 37	06 45	06 49	06 59	07 04	07 12	07 18	07 21	07 28	07 34	07 39	07 47	07 52	07 57	08 02	08 11	08 16
12¾	—	**Highbury & Islington** ⊖178 d		06 07	06 25	06 39	06 47	06 52	07 02	07 07	07 15	07 21	07 24	07 31	07 37	07 42	07 50	07 55	08 00	08 05	08 14	08 19
13¼	—	Canonbury ⊖178 d		06 09	06 27	06 42	06 49	06 54	07 04	07 09	07 17	07 23	07 26	07 33	07 39	07 44	07 52	07 57	08 02	08 07	08 16	08 21
14¼	—	Dalston Kingsland d		06 11	06 29	06 44	06 51	06 56	07 06	07 11	07 19	07 25	07 28	07 35	07 41	07 46	07 54	07 59	08 04	08 09	08 18	08 23
15	—	Hackney Central d	00 01	06 13	06 31	06 46	06 53	06 58	07 08	07 13	07 21	07 27	07 30	07 37	07 43	07 48	07 56	08 01	08 06	08 11	08 20	08 25
15¾	—	Homerton d	00 03	06 15	06 33	06 48	06 55	07 00	07 10	07 15	07 23	07 29	07 32	07 39	07 45	07 50	07 58	08 03	08 08	08 13	08 22	08 27
16½	—	Hackney Wick d	00 05	06 18	06 36	06 50	06 58	07 02	07 12	07 17	07 25	07 31	07 35	07 41	07 48	07 53	08 00	08 05	08 10	08 16	08 25	08 29
17½	—	**Stratford** [7] ⊖ a	00 09	06 28	06 44	06 56	07 04	07 10	07 17	07 23	07 30	07 36	07 40	07 47	07 54	07 59	08 06	08 11	08 19	08 23	08 31	08 36

	LO	LO	LO	LO	LO	LO	LO	LO	LO	LO	LO	LO	LO	LO	LO	LO	LO	LO	LO	LO	LO	LO
Richmond ⊖ d		07 45		07 56		08 09		08 21		08 34		08 45		08 57		09 09		09 26		09 41		09 57
Kew Gardens ⊖ d		07 48		07 59		08 12		08 25		08 37		08 48		09 00		09 13		09 29		09 45		10 00
Gunnersbury ⊖ d		07 51		08 02		08 15		08 28		08 40		08 51		09 03		09 16		09 32		09 48		10 03
South Acton d		07 54		08 05		08 18		08 31		08 43		08 54		09 06		09 19		09 35		09 51		10 06
Acton Central d		07 57		08 08		08 21		08 34		08 46		08 57		09 09		09 22		09 38		09 54		10 09
Clapham Junction [10] 66,176 d	07 36		07 48				08 14		08 27		08 36		08 50		09 02		09 14		09 29		09 48	
Imperial Wharf 176 d	07 40		07 53		08 05		08 18		08 31		08 40		08 54		09 06		09 18		09 33		09 52	
West Brompton ⊖176 d	07 43		07 56		08 09		08 21		08 34		08 43		08 57		09 09		09 21		09 36		09 55	
Kensington (Olympia) ⊖176 d	07 46		08 00		08 12		08 24		08 37		08 46		09 00		09 12		09 24		09 39		09 58	
Shepherd's Bush ⊖66,176 d	07 48		08 02		08 14		08 26		08 40		08 48		09 02		09 14		09 26		09 41		10 00	
Willesden Jn Low Level ⊖ d																						
Willesden Jn. High Level ⊖ a	07 56	08 03	08 10	08 15	08 22	08 26	08 34	08 39	08 46	08 51	08 56	09 03	09 10	09 16	09 22	09 29	09 34	09 43	09 49	09 59	10 07	10 15
d	07 59	08 04	08 11	08 16	08 23	08 27	08 35	08 40	08 47	08 52	08 59	09 04	09 12	09 17	09 25	09 30	09 35	09 44	09 50	10 00	10 08	10 16
Kensal Rise d	08 01	08 06	08 13	08 18	08 25	08 30	08 38	08 42	08 50	08 54	09 01	09 06	09 15	09 20	09 28	09 32	09 37	09 46	09 52	10 02	10 10	10 18
Brondesbury Park d	08 03	08 08	08 15	08 20	08 27	08 32	08 40	08 44	08 52	08 56	09 03	09 08	09 17	09 22	09 30	09 34	09 39	09 48	09 54	10 04	10 12	10 20
Brondesbury d	08 05	08 10	08 17	08 22	08 29	08 33	08 41	08 46	08 53	08 58	09 05	09 10	09 18	09 23	09 31	09 36	09 41	09 50	09 56	10 06	10 14	10 22
West Hampstead ⊖ d	08 07	08 12	08 19	08 24	08 31	08 35	08 43	08 48	08 55	09 00	09 07	09 12	09 20	09 25	09 33	09 38	09 43	09 52	09 58	10 08	10 16	10 24
Finchley Road & Frognal d	08 08	08 13	08 20	08 25	08 32	08 37	08 45	08 49	08 57	09 01	09 09	09 13	09 22	09 27	09 35	09 39	09 44	09 53	09 59	10 09	10 17	10 25
Hampstead Heath d	08 11	08 16	08 23	08 28	08 35	08 39	08 47	08 52	08 59	09 04	09 11	09 16	09 24	09 29	09 37	09 42	09 47	09 56	10 02	10 12	10 20	10 28
Gospel Oak d	08 14	08 19	08 25	08 30	08 37	08 42	08 50	08 54	09 02	09 06	09 14	09 18	09 27	09 32	09 40	09 44	09 49	09 58	10 06	10 14	10 22	10 30
Kentish Town West d	08 16	08 21	08 27	08 32	08 39	08 44	08 52	08 56	09 04	09 08	09 16	09 22	09 29	09 34	09 42	09 46	09 51	10 00	10 08	10 16	10 24	10 32
Camden Road d	08 19	08 25	08 30	08 36	08 42	08 49	08 56	09 01	09 06	09 11	09 18	09 27	09 31	09 37	09 44	09 51	09 55	10 05	10 11	10 21	10 28	10 35
Caledonian Rd & Barnsbury d	08 22	08 28	08 34	08 39	08 45	08 52	08 59	09 04	09 09	09 14	09 21	09 30	09 34	09 40	09 47	09 55	09 58	10 08	10 14	10 24	10 31	10 38
Highbury & Islington ⊖178 d	08 25	08 31	08 37	08 42	08 48	08 55	09 03	09 06	09 12	09 16	09 24	09 33	09 37	09 42	09 50	09 58	10 01	10 10	10 16	10 26	10 35	10 40
Canonbury ⊖178 d	08 27	08 33	08 39	08 44	08 50	08 57	09 05	09 08	09 14	09 18	09 26	09 35	09 39	09 44	09 52	10 00	10 03	10 12	10 18	10 28	10 37	10 42
Dalston Kingsland d	08 29	08 35	08 41	08 46	08 52	08 59	09 07	09 10	09 16	09 20	09 28	09 37	09 41	09 46	09 54	10 02	10 05	10 14	10 20	10 30	10 39	10 44
Hackney Central d	08 31	08 37	08 43	08 48	08 54	09 01	09 09	09 12	09 18	09 22	09 30	09 39	09 43	09 48	09 56	10 04	10 07	10 16	10 22	10 32	10 41	10 46
Homerton d	08 33	08 39	08 45	08 50	08 56	09 03	09 11	09 14	09 20	09 24	09 32	09 41	09 45	09 50	09 58	10 06	10 09	10 18	10 24	10 34	10 43	10 48
Hackney Wick d	08 35	08 41	08 47	08 52	08 58	09 05	09 13	09 17	09 22	09 27	09 35	09 43	09 47	09 53	10 00	10 09	10 13	10 21	10 27	10 37	10 46	10 51
Stratford [7] ⊖ a	08 41	08 47	08 53	08 58	09 06	09 11	09 19	09 23	09 31	09 36	09 41	09 48	09 55	09 59	10 07	10 14	10 18	10 28	10 33	10 43	10 52	10 59

For services between Shepherds Bush and Clapham Junction refer to Table T066 and T176

Table T059-R

Mondays to Fridays
16 December to 15 May

Richmond and Clapham Junction - Willesden Junction, West Hampstead, Highbury & Islington and Stratford

	LO	LO	LO	LO	LO	LO	LO	LO	LO	LO	LO	LO	LO	LO	LO	LO	LO	LO	LO	LO	LO	LO
Richmond ⊖ d		10 08		10 26		10 40		10 56		11 08		11 26		11 40		11 56		12 10		12 28		12 40
Kew Gardens ⊖ d		10 11		10 30		10 43		11 00		11 11		11 30		11 43		12 00		12 13		12 31		12 43
Gunnersbury ⊖ d		10 14		10 33		10 46		11 03		11 14		11 33		11 46		12 03		12 16		12 35		12 46
South Acton d		10 17		10 36		10 49		11 06		11 17		11 36		11 49		12 06		12 19		12 38		12 49
Acton Central d		10 20		10 39		10 53		11 09		11 20		11 39		11 53		12 09		12 23		12 41		12 52
Clapham Junction [10] 66,176 d	10 01		10 17		10 30		10 48		11 02		11 17		11 32		11 47		12 02		12 17		12 32	
Imperial Wharf 176 d	10 05		10 21		10 34		10 52		11 06		11 21		11 36		11 51		12 06		12 21		12 36	
West Brompton ⊖176 d	10 08		10 24		10 37		10 55		11 09		11 24		11 39		11 54		12 09		12 24		12 39	
Kensington (Olympia) ⊖176 d	10 11		10 27		10 42		10 58		11 12		11 27		11 42		11 57		12 12		12 27		12 42	
Shepherd's Bush ⊖66,176 d	10 13		10 29		10 44		11 00		11 14		11 29		11 44		11 59		12 14		12 29		12 44	
Willesden Jn Low Level ⊖ d																						
Willesden Jn. High Level ⊖ a	10 23	10 28	10 38	10 46	10 52	10 59	11 08	11 16	11 21	11 25	11 39	11 44	11 52	11 59	12 07	12 14	12 23	12 28	12 36	12 46	12 52	12 57
d	10 24	10 29	10 39	10 48	10 53	11 00	11 09	11 17	11 22	11 26	11 40	11 45	11 53	12 00	12 08	12 15	12 24	12 29	12 37	12 47	12 53	12 58
Kensal Rise d	10 27	10 31	10 42	10 50	10 55	11 03	11 11	11 20	11 24	11 29	11 42	11 47	11 55	12 03	12 10	12 18	12 26	12 32	12 39	12 50	12 56	13 01
Brondesbury Park d	10 29	10 33	10 44	10 52	10 57	11 05	11 13	11 22	11 26	11 31	11 44	11 49	11 57	12 05	12 12	12 20	12 28	12 34	12 41	12 52	12 58	13 03
Brondesbury d	10 30	10 35	10 45	10 54	10 59	11 06	11 15	11 23	11 28	11 32	11 46	11 51	11 59	12 06	12 14	12 21	12 30	12 35	12 43	12 53	12 59	13 04
West Hampstead ⊖ d	10 32	10 37	10 47	10 56	11 01	11 08	11 17	11 25	11 31	11 35	11 48	11 53	12 01	12 08	12 16	12 24	12 32	12 37	12 45	12 55	13 01	13 06
Finchley Road & Frognal d	10 34	10 38	10 49	10 57	11 02	11 10	11 18	11 27	11 32	11 37	11 49	11 54	12 02	12 10	12 17	12 25	12 33	12 39	12 46	12 57	13 03	13 08
Hampstead Heath d	10 37	10 42	10 51	11 00	11 05	11 12	11 21	11 29	11 35	11 39	11 52	11 57	12 05	12 12	12 20	12 28	12 36	12 41	12 49	12 59	13 05	13 10
Gospel Oak d	10 41	10 44	10 54	11 03	11 07	11 15	11 23	11 32	11 37	11 42	11 57	12 01	12 07	12 15	12 22	12 31	12 39	12 44	12 51	13 02	13 08	13 14
Kentish Town West d	10 43	10 47	10 56	11 05	11 09	11 17	11 25	11 34	11 39	11 44	11 59	12 03	12 09	12 17	12 24	12 33	12 41	12 46	12 53	13 04	13 10	13 16
Camden Road d	10 46	10 50	10 58	11 08	11 14	11 21	11 30	11 36	11 44	11 48	12 01	12 07	12 14	12 20	12 28	12 35	12 45	12 51	12 58	13 06	13 14	13 20
Caledonian Rd & Barnsbury d	10 49	10 53	11 01	11 11	11 17	11 24	11 33	11 39	11 47	11 51	12 04	12 10	12 17	12 23	12 31	12 39	12 48	12 54	13 01	13 09	13 17	13 23
Highbury & Islington ⊖178 d	10 52	10 56	11 04	11 13	11 19	11 26	11 35	11 42	11 49	11 54	12 07	12 13	12 19	12 26	12 34	12 42	12 50	12 59	13 03	13 12	13 20	13 26
Canonbury ⊖178 d	10 54	10 58	11 07	11 15	11 21	11 29	11 37	11 44	11 51	11 56	12 09	12 15	12 21	12 28	12 36	12 44	12 52	13 01	13 05	13 14	13 22	13 28
Dalston Kingsland d	10 56	11 00	11 09	11 17	11 23	11 31	11 39	11 46	11 53	11 58	12 11	12 17	12 23	12 30	12 38	12 46	12 54	13 03	13 07	13 16	13 24	13 30
Hackney Central d	10 58	11 02	11 11	11 19	11 25	11 33	11 41	11 48	11 55	12 00	12 13	12 19	12 25	12 32	12 40	12 48	12 56	13 05	13 09	13 18	13 26	13 32
Homerton d	11 00	11 04	11 13	11 21	11 27	11 35	11 43	11 50	11 57	12 02	12 15	12 21	12 27	12 34	12 42	12 50	12 58	13 07	13 11	13 20	13 28	13 34
Hackney Wick d	11 02	11 08	11 15	11 24	11 30	11 38	11 46	11 53	12 00	12 04	12 17	12 23	12 30	12 36	12 45	12 52	13 01	13 09	13 14	13 22	13 30	13 37
Stratford [7] ⊖ a	11 07	11 14	11 21	11 30	11 34	11 42	11 52	11 58	12 06	12 11	12 22	12 28	12 36	12 42	12 51	12 58	13 06	13 14	13 21	13 30	13 36	13 42

	LO	LO	LO	LO	LO	LO	LO	LO	LO	LO	LO	LO	LO	LO	LO	LO	LO	LO	LO	LO	LO	LO
Richmond ⊖ d		12 56		13 10		13 26		13 40		13 56		14 10		14 21		14 32		14 45		14 57		15 09
Kew Gardens ⊖ d		13 00		13 13		13 30		13 43		13 59		14 13		14 24		14 35		14 49		15 00		15 12
Gunnersbury ⊖ d		13 03		13 16		13 33		13 46		14 02		14 16		14 27		14 38		14 52		15 03		15 15
South Acton d		13 06		13 19		13 36		13 49		14 05		14 19		14 30		14 41		14 55		15 06		15 18
Acton Central d		13 09		13 23		13 39		13 52		14 08		14 24		14 33		14 45		14 59		15 10		15 21
Clapham Junction [10] 66,176 d	12 47		13 02		13 17		13 32		13 47		14 02		14 15				14 36		14 50		15 02	
Imperial Wharf 176 d	12 51		13 06		13 21		13 36		13 51		14 06		14 19		14 30		14 40		14 54		15 06	
West Brompton ⊖176 d	12 54		13 09		13 24		13 39		13 54		14 09		14 22		14 33		14 43		14 57		15 09	
Kensington (Olympia) ⊖176 d	12 57		13 12		13 27		13 42		13 57		14 12		14 25		14 36		14 46		15 00		15 12	
Shepherd's Bush ⊖66,176 d	12 59		13 14		13 29		13 44		13 59		14 14		14 27		14 38		14 48		15 02		15 14	
Willesden Jn Low Level ⊖ d																						
Willesden Jn. High Level ⊖ a	13 06	13 14	13 21	13 29	13 37	13 44	13 52	13 58	14 06	14 16	14 21	14 30	14 35	14 39	14 45	14 51	14 56	15 05	15 09	15 16	15 22	15 27
d	13 07	13 16	13 22	13 31	13 38	13 45	13 53	14 00	14 07	14 18	14 22	14 31	14 36	14 40	14 46	14 52	14 57	15 06	15 11	15 17	15 23	15 28
Kensal Rise d	13 09	13 19	13 24	13 34	13 40	13 47	13 55	14 02	14 10	14 20	14 25	14 34	14 38	14 43	14 48	14 55	14 59	15 08	15 13	15 20	15 25	15 30
Brondesbury Park d	13 11	13 21	13 26	13 36	13 42	13 49	13 57	14 04	14 12	14 22	14 27	14 36	14 40	14 45	14 50	14 58	15 02	15 10	15 15	15 22	15 27	15 32
Brondesbury d	13 13	13 22	13 28	13 37	13 44	13 51	13 59	14 06	14 13	14 24	14 28	14 37	14 42	14 46	14 52	15 00	15 05	15 12	15 17	15 23	15 29	15 34
West Hampstead ⊖ d	13 15	13 24	13 30	13 39	13 46	13 53	14 01	14 08	14 15	14 26	14 30	14 39	14 44	14 48	14 54	15 02	15 07	15 14	15 19	15 25	15 31	15 36
Finchley Road & Frognal d	13 16	13 26	13 31	13 41	13 47	13 54	14 02	14 09	14 17	14 27	14 32	14 41	14 45	14 50	14 55	15 04	15 08	15 16	15 20	15 27	15 32	15 37
Hampstead Heath d	13 19	13 28	13 34	13 43	13 50	13 57	14 05	14 12	14 19	14 30	14 34	14 43	14 48	14 52	14 58	15 06	15 11	15 18	15 23	15 29	15 35	15 40
Gospel Oak d	13 22	13 31	13 36	13 46	13 52	13 59	14 07	14 14	14 22	14 32	14 37	14 46	14 50	14 55	15 00	15 09	15 13	15 21	15 25	15 32	15 37	15 42
Kentish Town West d	13 24	13 33	13 38	13 48	13 54	14 01	14 09	14 16	14 24	14 34	14 39	14 48	14 52	14 57	15 02	15 11	15 15	15 23	15 27	15 34	15 39	15 44
Camden Road d	13 29	13 36	13 43	13 50	13 59	14 06	14 14	14 21	14 26	14 37	14 42	14 50	14 55	15 00	15 05	15 13	15 18	15 26	15 31	15 39	15 43	15 47
Caledonian Rd & Barnsbury d	13 32	13 39	13 46	13 53	14 02	14 09	14 17	14 24	14 30	14 40	14 45	14 53	14 58	15 03	15 08	15 16	15 21	15 29	15 34	15 42	15 46	15 50
Highbury & Islington ⊖178 d	13 34	13 41	13 48	13 56	14 04	14 11	14 19	14 26	14 33	14 42	14 48	14 56	15 00	15 05	15 11	15 19	15 23	15 31	15 36	15 45	15 48	15 52
Canonbury ⊖178 d	13 36	13 43	13 50	13 58	14 06	14 13	14 21	14 28	14 35	14 44	14 50	14 58	15 02	15 07	15 13	15 21	15 25	15 33	15 38	15 47	15 50	15 54
Dalston Kingsland d	13 38	13 45	13 52	14 00	14 08	14 15	14 23	14 30	14 38	14 46	14 52	15 00	15 04	15 09	15 15	15 23	15 27	15 35	15 40	15 49	15 52	15 56
Hackney Central d	13 40	13 47	13 54	14 02	14 10	14 17	14 25	14 32	14 40	14 48	14 54	15 02	15 06	15 11	15 17	15 25	15 29	15 37	15 42	15 51	15 55	15 58
Homerton d	13 42	13 49	13 56	14 04	14 12	14 19	14 27	14 34	14 43	14 50	14 56	15 04	15 08	15 13	15 19	15 27	15 31	15 39	15 44	15 53	15 57	16 00
Hackney Wick d	13 45	13 52	13 59	14 06	14 15	14 22	14 30	14 37	14 45	14 53	14 58	15 06	15 11	15 16	15 21	15 29	15 34	15 42	15 47	15 55	15 59	16 03
Stratford [7] ⊖ a	13 51	13 58	14 06	14 12	14 21	14 28	14 36	14 42	14 51	14 58	15 06	15 12	15 19	15 23	15 30	15 34	15 40	15 47	15 56	16 00	16 06	16 11

For services between Shepherds Bush and Clapham Junction refer to Table T066 and T176

Table T059-R

Mondays to Fridays
16 December to 15 May

Richmond and Clapham Junction - Willesden Junction, West Hampstead, Highbury & Islington and Stratford

Station		LO	LO	LO	LO	LO	LO	LO	LO	LO	LO	LO	LO	LO	LO	LO	LO	LO	LO	LO	LO	LO	LO
Richmond ⊖	d		15 20		15 32		15 45		15 57		16 09		16 20		16 33		16 45		17 03		17 10		17 20
Kew Gardens ⊖	d		15 23		15 35		15 49		16 00		16 13		16 24		16 36		16 48		17 06		17 14		17 24
Gunnersbury ⊖	d		15 26		15 38		15 52		16 03		16 16		16 27		16 39		16 51		17 09		17 17		17 27
South Acton	d		15 29		15 41		15 55		16 06		16 19		16 30		16 42		16 54		17 12		17 20		17 30
Acton Central	d		15 33		15 45		15 59		16 10		16 22		16 33		16 45		16 57		17 15		17 23		17 33
Clapham Junction 10 66,176	d	15 15				15 36		15 50		16 02		16 14		16 26		16 36		16 50		17 03		17 14	
Imperial Wharf 176	d	15 19		15 30		15 40		15 54		16 06		16 18		16 30		16 40		16 54		17 07		17 18	
West Brompton ⊖176	d	15 22		15 33		15 43		15 57		16 09		16 21		16 33		16 43		16 57		17 11		17 21	
Kensington (Olympia) ⊖176	d	15 25		15 36		15 46		16 00		16 12		16 24		16 36		16 46		17 00		17 14		17 24	
Shepherd's Bush ⊖66,176	d	15 28		15 38		15 48		16 02		16 15		16 26		16 38		16 48		17 02		17 17		17 27	
Willesden Jn Low Level ⊖	d																						
Willesden Jn. High Level ⊖	a	15 34	15 40	15 46	15 51	15 56	16 04	16 09	16 18	16 23	16 27	16 34	16 39	16 46	16 51	16 56	17 03	17 10	17 20	17 24	17 29	17 34	17 39
	d	15 35	15 43	15 47	15 52	15 57	16 05	16 11	16 19	16 24	16 28	16 36	16 40	16 47	16 52	16 57	17 04	17 11	17 21	17 25	17 30	17 35	17 40
Kensal Rise	d	15 38	15 45	15 50	15 55	15 59	16 08	16 13	16 22	16 26	16 31	16 38	16 43	16 49	16 54	16 59	17 08	17 13	17 23	17 28	17 32	17 37	17 42
Brondesbury Park	d	15 40	15 47	15 52	15 57	16 01	16 10	16 15	16 24	16 28	16 33	16 40	16 45	16 51	16 56	17 01	17 10	17 15	17 25	17 30	17 34	17 39	17 44
Brondesbury	d	15 41	15 49	15 53	15 58	16 03	16 11	16 17	16 25	16 30	16 34	16 42	16 46	16 53	16 58	17 03	17 12	17 17	17 27	17 31	17 36	17 41	17 46
West Hampstead ⊖	d	15 43	15 52	15 55	16 00	16 05	16 13	16 19	16 27	16 32	16 36	16 44	16 48	16 55	17 00	17 05	17 14	17 19	17 29	17 33	17 38	17 43	17 48
Finchley Road & Frognal	d	15 45	15 53	15 57	16 02	16 06	16 15	16 20	16 29	16 33	16 38	16 45	16 50	16 56	17 01	17 06	17 15	17 20	17 30	17 35	17 39	17 44	17 49
Hampstead Heath	d	15 47	15 56	15 59	16 04	16 09	16 17	16 23	16 31	16 36	16 40	16 48	16 52	16 59	17 04	17 09	17 18	17 23	17 33	17 37	17 42	17 47	17 52
Gospel Oak	d	15 51	15 58	16 02	16 07	16 11	16 20	16 25	16 34	16 38	16 43	16 50	16 55	17 01	17 06	17 11	17 20	17 25	17 35	17 40	17 44	17 49	17 54
Kentish Town West	d	15 53	16 00	16 04	16 09	16 13	16 22	16 27	16 36	16 40	16 45	16 52	16 57	17 03	17 08	17 13	17 22	17 27	17 37	17 42	17 46	17 51	17 56
Camden Road	d	15 57	16 03	16 07	16 13	16 17	16 25	16 31	16 38	16 44	16 49	16 55	17 01	17 07	17 13	17 16	17 25	17 30	17 40	17 45	17 50	17 55	18 01
Caledonian Rd & Barnsbury	d	16 00	16 06	16 10	16 16	16 20	16 28	16 34	16 41	16 47	16 52	16 58	17 04	17 10	17 16	17 19	17 28	17 33	17 43	17 48	17 53	17 58	18 04
Highbury & Islington ⊖178	d	16 03	16 08	16 12	16 18	16 22	16 31	16 37	16 44	16 50	16 55	17 01	17 07	17 13	17 20	17 23	17 31	17 36	17 46	17 51	17 56	18 01	18 07
Canonbury ⊖178	d	16 05	16 11	16 14	16 20	16 24	16 33	16 39	16 46	16 52	16 57	17 03	17 09	17 15	17 22	17 25	17 33	17 38	17 48	17 53	17 58	18 03	18 09
Dalston Kingsland	d	16 07	16 13	16 16	16 22	16 26	16 35	16 41	16 48	16 54	16 59	17 05	17 11	17 17	17 24	17 27	17 35	17 40	17 50	17 55	18 00	18 05	18 11
Hackney Central	d	16 09	16 15	16 18	16 24	16 28	16 37	16 43	16 50	16 56	17 01	17 07	17 13	17 19	17 26	17 29	17 37	17 42	17 52	17 58	18 02	18 07	18 13
Homerton	d	16 11	16 17	16 20	16 26	16 30	16 39	16 45	16 52	16 58	17 03	17 09	17 15	17 21	17 28	17 31	17 39	17 44	17 54	18 00	18 04	18 09	18 15
Hackney Wick	d	16 13	16 19	16 23	16 29	16 33	16 41	16 47	16 55	17 00	17 06	17 11	17 17	17 23	17 30	17 34	17 41	17 46	17 56	18 03	18 07	18 11	18 17
Stratford 7 ⊖	a	16 19	16 26	16 30	16 34	16 40	16 47	16 56	16 59	17 06	17 11	17 18	17 26	17 30	17 35	17 40	17 47	17 56	18 05	18 08	18 12	18 19	18 26

Station		LO	LO	LO	LO	LO	LO	LO	LO	LO	LO	LO	LO	LO	LO	LO	LO	LO	LO	LO	LO	LO	LO
Richmond ⊖	d		17 33		17 45		17 57		18 07		18 20		18 32		18 45		18 56		19 09		19 22		19 32
Kew Gardens ⊖	d		17 36		17 48		18 00		18 10		18 23		18 35		18 48		18 59		19 13		19 25		19 35
Gunnersbury ⊖	d		17 39		17 51		18 03		18 13		18 26		18 38		18 51		19 02		19 16		19 28		19 38
South Acton	d		17 42		17 54		18 06		18 16		18 29		18 41		18 54		19 05		19 19		19 31		19 41
Acton Central	d		17 45		17 57		18 09		18 21		18 33		18 45		18 57		19 09		19 22		19 36		19 44
Clapham Junction 10 66,176	d	17 26		17 36		17 50		18 02		18 14		18 26		18 36		18 50		19 02		19 14		19 27	
Imperial Wharf 176	d	17 30		17 40		17 54		18 06		18 18		18 31		18 40		18 54		19 06		19 18		19 31	
West Brompton ⊖176	d	17 33		17 43		17 57		18 09		18 21		18 34		18 43		18 57		19 09		19 21		19 34	
Kensington (Olympia) ⊖176	d	17 36		17 46		18 00		18 12		18 24		18 37		18 46		19 00		19 12		19 24		19 37	
Shepherd's Bush ⊖66,176	d	17 38		17 48		18 02		18 14		18 26		18 40		18 48		19 02		19 15		19 26		19 39	
Willesden Jn Low Level ⊖	d																						
Willesden Jn. High Level ⊖	a	17 46	17 51	17 56	18 03	18 10	18 15	18 22	18 27	18 34	18 39	18 47	18 51	18 56	19 03	19 10	19 15	19 22	19 27	19 34	19 43	19 47	19 53
	d	17 47	17 52	17 58	18 04	18 11	18 16	18 23	18 28	18 35	18 40	18 48	18 52	18 57	19 04	19 11	19 16	19 23	19 28	19 35	19 44	19 48	19 54
Kensal Rise	d	17 49	17 54	18 00	18 06	18 13	18 18	18 25	18 30	18 37	18 42	18 51	18 55	19 00	19 06	19 13	19 18	19 25	19 30	19 37	19 46	19 51	19 56
Brondesbury Park	d	17 51	17 56	18 02	18 08	18 15	18 20	18 27	18 32	18 39	18 44	18 53	18 57	19 02	19 08	19 15	19 20	19 27	19 32	19 39	19 48	19 53	19 58
Brondesbury	d	17 53	17 58	18 04	18 10	18 17	18 22	18 29	18 34	18 41	18 46	18 54	18 58	19 03	19 10	19 17	19 22	19 29	19 34	19 41	19 50	19 54	20 00
West Hampstead ⊖	d	17 55	18 00	18 06	18 12	18 19	18 24	18 31	18 36	18 43	18 48	18 56	19 00	19 05	19 12	19 19	19 24	19 31	19 36	19 44	19 52	19 56	20 02
Finchley Road & Frognal	d	17 57	18 01	18 07	18 13	18 20	18 25	18 32	18 37	18 44	18 49	18 58	19 02	19 07	19 13	19 20	19 25	19 32	19 37	19 45	19 53	19 58	20 03
Hampstead Heath	d	17 59	18 04	18 10	18 16	18 23	18 28	18 35	18 40	18 47	18 52	19 00	19 04	19 09	19 16	19 23	19 28	19 35	19 40	19 48	19 56	20 00	20 06
Gospel Oak	d	18 02	18 06	18 12	18 18	18 25	18 30	18 37	18 42	18 49	18 54	19 03	19 07	19 12	19 18	19 25	19 30	19 37	19 42	19 50	19 58	20 03	20 08
Kentish Town West	d	18 04	18 08	18 14	18 20	18 27	18 32	18 39	18 44	18 51	18 56	19 05	19 09	19 14	19 20	19 27	19 32	19 39	19 44	19 52	20 00	20 05	20 10
Camden Road	d	18 07	18 13	18 18	18 25	18 31	18 37	18 43	18 47	18 55	19 01	19 07	19 13	19 16	19 25	19 31	19 37	19 42	19 49	19 55	20 03	20 08	20 13
Caledonian Rd & Barnsbury	d	18 10	18 16	18 21	18 28	18 34	18 40	18 46	18 50	18 58	19 04	19 10	19 16	19 19	19 28	19 34	19 40	19 45	19 52	19 58	20 06	20 11	20 16
Highbury & Islington ⊖178	d	18 13	18 19	18 24	18 31	18 37	18 43	18 49	18 53	19 01	19 06	19 13	19 18	19 22	19 30	19 36	19 43	19 47	19 55	20 01	20 08	20 14	20 18
Canonbury ⊖178	d	18 15	18 21	18 26	18 33	18 39	18 45	18 51	18 55	19 03	19 08	19 16	19 20	19 24	19 32	19 38	19 45	19 49	19 57	20 03	20 10	20 16	20 20
Dalston Kingsland	d	18 17	18 23	18 28	18 35	18 41	18 47	18 53	18 57	19 05	19 10	19 18	19 22	19 26	19 34	19 40	19 47	19 51	19 59	20 05	20 12	20 18	20 22
Hackney Central	d	18 19	18 25	18 30	18 37	18 43	18 49	18 55	18 59	19 07	19 12	19 20	19 24	19 28	19 36	19 42	19 49	19 53	20 01	20 07	20 14	20 20	20 24
Homerton	d	18 21	18 27	18 32	18 39	18 45	18 51	18 57	19 01	19 09	19 14	19 22	19 26	19 30	19 38	19 44	19 51	19 55	20 03	20 09	20 16	20 22	20 26
Hackney Wick	d	18 23	18 29	18 34	18 41	18 47	18 53	18 59	19 04	19 11	19 17	19 24	19 29	19 32	19 41	19 47	19 53	19 58	20 06	20 11	20 19	20 24	20 29
Stratford 7 ⊖	a	18 31	18 35	18 41	18 47	18 56	18 59	19 07	19 09	19 19	19 22	19 31	19 34	19 41	19 47	19 56	19 58	20 06	20 11	20 18	20 24	20 31	20 34

For services between Shepherds Bush and Clapham Junction refer to Table T066 and T176

Table T059-R

Mondays to Fridays
16 December to 15 May

Richmond and Clapham Junction - Willesden Junction, West Hampstead, Highbury & Islington and Stratford

Station		LO	LO	LO	LO	LO	LO	LO	LO	LO	LO	LO	LO	LO	LO	LO	LO	LO	LO	LO	LO	LO	LO
Richmond ⊖	d		19 46		19 59		20 09		20 22		20 38		20 52		21 07		21 29		21 38		21 50		22 09
Kew Gardens ⊖	d		19 49		20 02		20 12		20 25		20 41		20 55		21 10		21 32		21 41		21 53		22 12
Gunnersbury ⊖	d		19 52		20 05		20 15		20 28		20 44		20 58		21 13		21 35		21 44		21 57		22 15
South Acton	d		19 55		20 08		20 18		20 31		20 47		21 01		21 16		21 39		21 47		22 00		22 18
Acton Central	d		19 58		20 12		20 21		20 34		20 50		21 04		21 19		21 42		21 50		22 07		22 22
Clapham Junction 10 66,176	d	19 36		19 50		20 02		20 14		20 28		20 44		21 00		21 17		21 30		21 44		21 59	
Imperial Wharf 176	d	19 40		19 54		20 06		20 18		20 32		20 48		21 04		21 22		21 35		21 48		22 03	
West Brompton ⊖176	d	19 43		19 57		20 09		20 21		20 35		20 51		21 07		21 26		21 38		21 51		22 06	
Kensington (Olympia) ⊖176	d	19 46		20 00		20 12		20 24		20 38		20 54		21 10		21 29		21 42		21 54		22 10	
Shepherd's Bush ⊖66,176	d	19 48		20 02		20 14		20 26		20 40		20 56		21 12		21 31		21 44		21 56		22 12	
Willesden Jn Low Level ⊖	d																						
Willesden Jn. High Level ⊖	a	19 57	20 05	20 11	20 19	20 23	20 28	20 34	20 40	20 48	20 56	21 04	21 09	21 19	21 24	21 38	21 47	21 51	21 56	22 05	22 13	22 24	22 28
	d	19 58	20 07	20 12	20 20	20 24	20 29	20 35	20 42	20 49	20 57	21 05	21 10	21 20	21 25	21 39	21 48	21 52	21 57	22 08	22 15	22 25	22 29
Kensal Rise	d	20 01	20 09	20 14	20 22	20 27	20 31	20 37	20 44	20 51	20 59	21 07	21 12	21 22	21 27	21 42	21 50	21 55	21 59	22 10	22 18	22 27	22 32
Brondesbury Park	d	20 03	20 11	20 16	20 24	20 29	20 33	20 39	20 46	20 53	21 01	21 09	21 14	21 24	21 29	21 44	21 52	21 57	22 01	22 12	22 20	22 29	22 34
Brondesbury	d	20 04	20 13	20 18	20 26	20 30	20 35	20 41	20 48	20 55	21 03	21 11	21 16	21 26	21 31	21 45	21 54	21 58	22 03	22 14	22 21	22 31	22 35
West Hampstead ⊖	d	20 06	20 15	20 20	20 28	20 32	20 37	20 44	20 50	20 57	21 05	21 13	21 18	21 28	21 33	21 47	21 56	22 00	22 05	22 16	22 25	22 33	22 37
Finchley Road & Frognal	d	20 08	20 16	20 21	20 29	20 34	20 38	20 46	20 51	20 58	21 06	21 14	21 19	21 29	21 34	21 49	21 57	22 02	22 06	22 18	22 26	22 34	22 39
Hampstead Heath	d	20 10	20 19	20 24	20 32	20 36	20 41	20 48	20 54	21 01	21 09	21 17	21 22	21 32	21 37	21 51	22 00	22 04	22 09	22 20	22 29	22 37	22 41
Gospel Oak	d	20 13	20 21	20 26	20 34	20 39	20 43	20 51	20 56	21 03	21 11	21 19	21 25	21 34	21 39	21 54	22 02	22 07	22 11	22 23	22 31	22 39	22 44
Kentish Town West	d	20 15	20 23	20 28	20 36	20 41	20 45	20 54	20 58	21 05	21 13	21 21	21 27	21 36	21 41	21 56	22 04	22 09	22 13	22 25	22 33	22 41	22 46
Camden Road	d	20 17	20 26	20 31	20 40	20 44	20 49	20 57	21 03	21 10	21 18	21 26	21 32	21 39	21 45	21 58	22 09	22 13	22 18	22 28	22 36	22 44	22 48
Caledonian Rd & Barnsbury	d	20 20	20 29	20 34	20 44	20 48	20 52	21 00	21 06	21 13	21 21	21 29	21 36	21 42	21 48	22 01	22 12	22 16	22 21	22 31	22 39	22 47	22 51
Highbury & Islington ⊖178	d	20 23	20 31	20 36	20 47	20 50	20 54	21 03	21 08	21 15	21 23	21 31	21 38	21 44	21 50	22 04	22 15	22 19	22 23	22 34	22 41	22 49	22 54
Canonbury ⊖178	d	20 25	20 34	20 38	20 49	20 53	20 57	21 05	21 10	21 17	21 25	21 33	21 40	21 46	21 52	22 06	22 17	22 21	22 25	22 36	22 43	22 51	22 56
Dalston Kingsland	d	20 27	20 36	20 40	20 51	20 55	20 59	21 07	21 12	21 19	21 27	21 35	21 42	21 48	21 54	22 08	22 19	22 23	22 27	22 38	22 45	22 53	22 58
Hackney Central	d	20 29	20 38	20 42	20 53	20 57	21 01	21 09	21 14	21 21	21 29	21 37	21 44	21 50	21 56	22 10	22 21	22 25	22 29	22 40	22 47	22 55	23 00
Homerton	d	20 31	20 40	20 44	20 55	20 59	21 03	21 11	21 16	21 23	21 31	21 39	21 46	21 52	21 58	22 12	22 23	22 27	22 31	22 42	22 49	22 57	23 02
Hackney Wick	d	20 33	20 43	20 47	20 57	21 01	21 05	21 13	21 19	21 26	21 34	21 42	21 49	21 55	22 01	22 14	22 25	22 29	22 34	22 44	22 52	23 00	23 04
Stratford 7 ⊖	a	20 40	20 48	20 54	21 02	21 06	21 11	21 18	21 24	21 32	21 40	21 48	21 54	22 04	22 09	22 21	22 31	22 34	22 40	22 49	22 56	23 05	23 11

Station		LO	LO	LO	LO	LO	LO	LO	LO	LO	LO	LO	LO
Richmond ⊖	d		22 22		22 38		22 52		23 07		23 25		
Kew Gardens ⊖	d		22 25		22 41		22 55		23 10		23 29		
Gunnersbury ⊖	d		22 28		22 44		22 58		23 13		23 32		
South Acton	d		22 31		22 47		23 01		23 16		23 35		
Acton Central	d		22 35		22 50		23 05		23 19		23 38		
Clapham Junction 10 66,176	d	22 14		22 29		22 44		23 00		23 15		23 30	
Imperial Wharf 176	d	22 18		22 33		22 48		23 04		23 19		23 34	23 51
West Brompton ⊖176	d	22 21		22 36		22 51		23 07		23 22		23 37	23 54
Kensington (Olympia) ⊖176	d	22 24		22 39		22 54		23 10		23 25		23 40	23 57
Shepherd's Bush ⊖66,176	d	22 26		22 41		22 56		23 13		23 27		23 42	23 59
Willesden Jn Low Level ⊖	d												
Willesden Jn. High Level ⊖	a	22 34	22 41	22 49	22 57	23 03	23 10	23 21	23 24	23 36	23 44	23 51	00 06
	d	22 35	22 42	22 50	22 58	23 04	23 11		23 25				
Kensal Rise	d	22 38	22 45	22 52	23 01	23 06	23 13		23 27				
Brondesbury Park	d	22 40	22 47	22 54	23 03	23 08	23 15		23 29				
Brondesbury	d	22 41	22 48	22 56	23 04	23 10	23 17		23 31				
West Hampstead ⊖	d	22 43	22 50	22 58	23 06	23 12	23 19		23 33				
Finchley Road & Frognal	d	22 45	22 52	22 59	23 08	23 13	23 20		23 34				
Hampstead Heath	d	22 47	22 54	23 02	23 10	23 16	23 23		23 37				
Gospel Oak	d	22 50	22 57	23 04	23 13	23 22	23 26		23 40				
Kentish Town West	d	22 52	22 59	23 06	23 15	23 24	23 28		23 42				
Camden Road	d	22 56	23 04	23 11	23 19	23 29	23 33		23 47				
Caledonian Rd & Barnsbury	d	22 59	23 07	23 14	23 22	23 32	23 36		23 50				
Highbury & Islington ⊖178	d	23 01	23 09	23 16	23 25	23 34	23 38		23 52				
Canonbury ⊖178	d	23 03	23 11	23 18	23 27	23 38	23 42		23 56				
Dalston Kingsland	d	23 05	23 13	23 20	23 29	23 40	23 44		23 58				
Hackney Central	d	23 07	23 15	23 22	23 31	23 42	23 46		00 01				
Homerton	d	23 09	23 17	23 24	23 33	23 44	23 48		00 03				
Hackney Wick	d	23 12	23 20	23 27	23 35	23 46	23 50		00 05				
Stratford 7 ⊖	a	23 18	23 24	23 33	23 40	23 50	23 54		00 09				

For services between Shepherds Bush and Clapham Junction refer to Table T066 and T176

Table T059-R

Saturdays

21 December to 16 May

Richmond and Clapham Junction - Willesden Junction, West Hampstead, Highbury & Islington and Stratford

		LO	LO	LO	LO	LO	LO	LO	LO	LO	LO	LO
Richmond	⊖ d				05 56		06 10		06 27		06 40	
Kew Gardens	⊖ d				05 59		06 13		06 30		06 43	
Gunnersbury	⊖ d				06 02		06 16		06 33		06 46	
South Acton	d				06 05		06 19		06 36		06 49	
Acton Central	d				06 08		06 23		06 39		06 53	
Clapham Junction [10] 66,176	d							06 17		06 32		06 47
Imperial Wharf 176	d		05 54			06 06		06 21		06 36		06 51
West Brompton ⊖176	d		05 57			06 09		06 24		06 39		06 54
Kensington (Olympia) ⊖176	d		06 00			06 12		06 27		06 42		06 57
Shepherd's Bush ⊖66,176	d		06 02			06 14		06 29		06 44		06 59
Willesden Jn Low Level	⊖ d			06 00								
Willesden Jn. High Level	⊖ a		06 11		06 14	06 22	06 29	06 37	06 44	06 52	06 59	07 07
	d				06 15	06 23	06 30	06 38	06 45	06 53	07 00	07 08
Kensal Rise	d			06 07	06 17	06 25	06 33	06 40	06 47	06 55	07 02	07 10
Brondesbury Park	d			06 09	06 19	06 27	06 35	06 42	06 49	06 57	07 04	07 12
Brondesbury	d			06 10	06 21	06 29	06 37	06 44	06 51	06 59	07 06	07 14
West Hampstead	⊖ d			06 12	06 23	06 31	06 39	06 46	06 53	07 01	07 08	07 16
Finchley Road & Frognal	d			06 14	06 24	06 32	06 40	06 47	06 54	07 02	07 09	07 17
Hampstead Heath	d			06 16	06 27	06 35	06 43	06 50	06 57	07 05	07 12	07 20
Gospel Oak	d			06 19	06 29	06 37	06 45	06 52	06 59	07 07	07 14	07 22
Kentish Town West	d			06 21	06 31	06 39	06 47	06 54	07 01	07 09	07 16	07 24
Camden Road	d			06 23	06 36	06 44	06 51	06 59	07 06	07 13	07 21	07 29
Caledonian Rd & Barnsbury	d			06 26	06 39	06 47	06 54	07 02	07 09	07 16	07 25	07 32
Highbury & Islington ⊖178	d			06 29	06 43	06 49	06 56	07 04	07 11	07 19	07 28	07 34
Canonbury ⊖178	d			06 31	06 45	06 51	06 58	07 06	07 13	07 21	07 30	07 36
Dalston Kingsland	d			06 33	06 47	06 53	07 00	07 08	07 15	07 23	07 32	07 38
Hackney Central	d	00 01		06 35	06 49	06 55	07 02	07 10	07 17	07 25	07 34	07 40
Homerton	d	00 03		06 37	06 51	06 57	07 04	07 12	07 19	07 27	07 36	07 42
Hackney Wick	d	00 05		06 39	06 54	07 00	07 07	07 15	07 22	07 30	07 38	07 45
Stratford [7]	⊖ ⛴ a	00 09		06 47	06 58	07 06	07 12	07 21	07 29	07 36	07 42	07 51

		LO	LO	LO	LO	LO	LO	LO	LO	LO	LO	LO
Richmond	⊖ d	06 56		07 10		07 27		07 40		07 57		08 10
Kew Gardens	⊖ d	07 00		07 13		07 30		07 43		08 00		08 13
Gunnersbury	⊖ d	07 03		07 16		07 33		07 46		08 03		08 16
South Acton	d	07 06		07 19		07 36		07 49		08 06		08 19
Acton Central	d	07 09		07 23		07 39		07 53		08 09		08 23
Clapham Junction [10] 66,176	d		07 02		07 17		07 32		07 47		08 02	
Imperial Wharf 176	d		07 06		07 21		07 36		07 51		08 06	
West Brompton ⊖176	d		07 09		07 24		07 39		07 54		08 09	
Kensington (Olympia) ⊖176	d		07 12		07 27		07 42		07 57		08 12	
Shepherd's Bush ⊖66,176	d		07 14		07 29		07 44		07 59		08 14	
Willesden Jn Low Level	⊖ d											
Willesden Jn. High Level	⊖ a	07 14	07 22	07 29	07 37	07 44	07 52	07 59	08 07	08 14	08 22	08 29
	d	07 15	07 23	07 30	07 38	07 45	07 53	08 00	08 08	08 15	08 23	08 30
Kensal Rise	d	07 18	07 25	07 32	07 40	07 47	07 55	08 02	08 10	08 17	08 25	08 32
Brondesbury Park	d	07 20	07 27	07 34	07 42	07 49	07 57	08 04	08 12	08 19	08 27	08 34
Brondesbury	d	07 21	07 29	07 36	07 44	07 51	07 59	08 06	08 14	08 21	08 29	08 36
West Hampstead	⊖ d	07 23	07 31	07 38	07 46	07 53	08 01	08 08	08 16	08 23	08 31	08 38
Finchley Road & Frognal	d	07 25	07 32	07 39	07 47	07 54	08 02	08 09	08 17	08 24	08 32	08 39
Hampstead Heath	d	07 27	07 35	07 42	07 50	07 57	08 05	08 12	08 20	08 27	08 35	08 42
Gospel Oak	d	07 30	07 37	07 44	07 52	07 59	08 07	08 14	08 22	08 29	08 37	08 44
Kentish Town West	d	07 32	07 39	07 46	07 54	08 01	08 09	08 16	08 24	08 31	08 39	08 46
Camden Road	d	07 36	07 44	07 50	07 59	08 06	08 14	08 21	08 29	08 36	08 43	08 51
Caledonian Rd & Barnsbury	d	07 39	07 47	07 53	08 03	08 09	08 17	08 24	08 32	08 39	08 46	08 54
Highbury & Islington ⊖178	d	07 41	07 49	07 56	08 05	08 11	08 19	08 26	08 34	08 41	08 48	08 57
Canonbury ⊖178	d	07 43	07 51	07 58	08 07	08 13	08 21	08 28	08 36	08 43	08 50	08 59
Dalston Kingsland	d	07 45	07 53	08 00	08 09	08 15	08 23	08 30	08 38	08 45	08 52	09 01
Hackney Central	d	07 47	07 55	08 02	08 11	08 17	08 25	08 32	08 40	08 47	08 54	09 03
Homerton	d	07 49	07 57	08 04	08 13	08 19	08 27	08 34	08 42	08 49	08 56	09 05
Hackney Wick	d	07 52	08 00	08 06	08 16	08 22	08 30	08 37	08 45	08 52	08 59	09 08
Stratford [7]	⊖ ⛴ a	07 58	08 06	08 12	08 21	08 29	08 36	08 42	08 51	08 59	09 06	09 12

		LO	LO	LO	LO	LO	LO	LO	LO	LO	LO	LO
Richmond	⊖ d		08 27		08 40		08 56		09 10		09 27	
Kew Gardens	⊖ d		08 30		08 43		09 00		09 13		09 30	
Gunnersbury	⊖ d		08 33		08 46		09 03		09 16		09 33	
South Acton	d		08 36		08 49		09 06		09 19		09 36	
Acton Central	d		08 39		08 53		09 09		09 23		09 39	
Clapham Junction [10] 66,176	d	08 17		08 32		08 47		09 02		09 17		09 32
Imperial Wharf 176	d	08 21		08 36		08 51		09 06		09 21		09 36
West Brompton ⊖176	d	08 24		08 39		08 54		09 09		09 24		09 39
Kensington (Olympia) ⊖176	d	08 27		08 42		08 57		09 12		09 27		09 42
Shepherd's Bush ⊖66,176	d	08 29		08 44		08 59		09 14		09 29		09 44
Willesden Jn Low Level	⊖ d											
Willesden Jn. High Level	⊖ a	08 37	08 44	08 52	08 59	09 07	09 14	09 22	09 29	09 37	09 44	09 52
	d	08 38	08 45	08 53	09 00	09 08	09 15	09 23	09 30	09 38	09 45	09 53
Kensal Rise	d	08 40	08 47	08 55	09 02	09 10	09 17	09 25	09 33	09 40	09 47	09 55
Brondesbury Park	d	08 42	08 49	08 57	09 04	09 12	09 19	09 27	09 35	09 42	09 49	09 57
Brondesbury	d	08 44	08 51	08 59	09 06	09 14	09 21	09 29	09 37	09 44	09 51	09 59
West Hampstead	⊖ d	08 46	08 53	09 01	09 08	09 16	09 23	09 31	09 39	09 46	09 53	10 01
Finchley Road & Frognal	d	08 47	08 54	09 02	09 09	09 17	09 24	09 32	09 41	09 47	09 54	10 02
Hampstead Heath	d	08 50	08 57	09 05	09 12	09 20	09 27	09 35	09 43	09 50	09 57	10 05
Gospel Oak	d	08 52	08 59	09 07	09 14	09 22	09 29	09 37	09 46	09 52	09 59	10 07
Kentish Town West	d	08 54	09 01	09 09	09 16	09 24	09 31	09 39	09 48	09 54	10 01	10 09
Camden Road	d	08 59	09 06	09 14	09 21	09 29	09 36	09 44	09 51	09 59	10 06	10 14
Caledonian Rd & Barnsbury	d	09 02	09 09	09 17	09 24	09 32	09 39	09 47	09 54	10 02	10 09	10 17
Highbury & Islington ⊖178	d	09 04	09 11	09 19	09 26	09 34	09 41	09 50	09 57	10 04	10 12	10 19
Canonbury ⊖178	d	09 06	09 13	09 21	09 28	09 36	09 43	09 52	09 59	10 06	10 14	10 21
Dalston Kingsland	d	09 08	09 15	09 23	09 30	09 38	09 45	09 54	10 01	10 08	10 16	10 23
Hackney Central	d	09 10	09 17	09 25	09 32	09 40	09 47	09 56	10 03	10 10	10 18	10 25
Homerton	d	09 12	09 19	09 27	09 34	09 42	09 49	09 58	10 05	10 12	10 20	10 27
Hackney Wick	d	09 15	09 22	09 30	09 37	09 45	09 52	10 01	10 07	10 15	10 23	10 30
Stratford [7]	⊖ ⛴ a	09 21	09 29	09 36	09 42	09 51	09 58	10 06	10 12	10 21	10 29	10 36

		LO	LO	LO	LO	LO	LO	LO	LO	LO	LO	LO
Richmond	⊖ d	09 40		09 57		10 10		10 26		10 40		10 57
Kew Gardens	⊖ d	09 43		10 00		10 13		10 30		10 43		11 00
Gunnersbury	⊖ d	09 46		10 03		10 16		10 33		10 46		11 03
South Acton	d	09 49		10 06		10 19		10 36		10 49		11 06
Acton Central	d	09 53		10 10		10 22		10 39		10 53		11 09
Clapham Junction [10] 66,176	d		09 47		10 02		10 17		10 32		10 47	
Imperial Wharf 176	d		09 51		10 06		10 21		10 36		10 51	
West Brompton ⊖176	d		09 54		10 09		10 24		10 39		10 54	
Kensington (Olympia) ⊖176	d		09 57		10 12		10 27		10 42		10 57	
Shepherd's Bush ⊖66,176	d		09 59		10 14		10 29		10 44		10 59	
Willesden Jn Low Level	⊖ d											
Willesden Jn. High Level	⊖ a	09 58	10 07	10 16	10 22	10 29	10 37	10 44	10 52	10 59	11 07	11 14
	d	09 59	10 08	10 17	10 23	10 31	10 38	10 45	10 53	11 00	11 08	11 15
Kensal Rise	d	10 01	10 10	10 19	10 25	10 34	10 40	10 47	10 55	11 02	11 10	11 17
Brondesbury Park	d	10 03	10 12	10 21	10 27	10 36	10 42	10 49	10 57	11 04	11 12	11 19
Brondesbury	d	10 05	10 14	10 23	10 29	10 37	10 44	10 51	10 59	11 06	11 14	11 21
West Hampstead	⊖ d	10 07	10 16	10 25	10 31	10 39	10 46	10 53	11 01	11 08	11 16	11 23
Finchley Road & Frognal	d	10 08	10 17	10 26	10 32	10 41	10 47	10 54	11 02	11 09	11 17	11 24
Hampstead Heath	d	10 11	10 20	10 29	10 35	10 43	10 50	10 57	11 05	11 12	11 20	11 27
Gospel Oak	d	10 13	10 22	10 31	10 37	10 46	10 52	10 59	11 07	11 14	11 23	11 29
Kentish Town West	d	10 15	10 24	10 33	10 39	10 48	10 54	11 01	11 09	11 16	11 25	11 31
Camden Road	d	10 20	10 29	10 37	10 44	10 51	10 59	11 06	11 14	11 21	11 30	11 36
Caledonian Rd & Barnsbury	d	10 23	10 32	10 40	10 47	10 54	11 02	11 09	11 17	11 24	11 33	11 39
Highbury & Islington ⊖178	d	10 25	10 34	10 42	10 49	10 56	11 04	11 11	11 19	11 26	11 36	11 41
Canonbury ⊖178	d	10 27	10 36	10 44	10 51	10 58	11 06	11 13	11 21	11 28	11 38	11 43
Dalston Kingsland	d	10 29	10 38	10 46	10 53	11 00	11 08	11 15	11 23	11 30	11 40	11 45
Hackney Central	d	10 31	10 40	10 48	10 55	11 02	11 10	11 17	11 25	11 32	11 42	11 47
Homerton	d	10 33	10 42	10 50	10 57	11 04	11 12	11 19	11 27	11 34	11 44	11 49
Hackney Wick	d	10 36	10 45	10 53	11 00	11 07	11 15	11 22	11 30	11 37	11 46	11 52
Stratford [7]	⊖ ⛴ a	10 42	10 51	10 59	11 06	11 12	11 21	11 28	11 36	11 42	11 51	11 59

For services between Shepherds Bush and Clapham Junction refer to Table T066 and T176

Table T059-R

Saturdays

21 December to 16 May

Richmond and Clapham Junction - Willesden Junction, West Hampstead, Highbury & Islington and Stratford

		LO	LO	LO	LO	LO	LO	LO	LO	LO	LO	LO
Richmond	⊖ d		11 10		11 27		11 40		11 57		12 10	
Kew Gardens	⊖ d		11 13		11 30		11 43		12 00		12 13	
Gunnersbury	⊖ d		11 16		11 33		11 46		12 03		12 16	
South Acton	d		11 19		11 36		11 49		12 06		12 19	
Acton Central	d		11 23		11 39		11 53		12 09		12 23	
Clapham Junction [10] 66,176	d	11 02		11 17		11 32		11 47		12 02		12 17
Imperial Wharf 176	d	11 06		11 21		11 36		11 51		12 06		12 21
West Brompton ⊖176	d	11 09		11 24		11 39		11 54		12 09		12 24
Kensington (Olympia) ⊖176	d	11 12		11 27		11 42		11 57		12 12		12 27
Shepherd's Bush ⊖66,176	d	11 14		11 29		11 44		11 59		12 14		12 29
Willesden Jn Low Level	⊖ d											
Willesden Jn. High Level	⊖ a	11 22	11 29	11 36	11 46	11 53	11 59	12 07	12 16	12 22	12 30	12 37
	d	11 23	11 30	11 37	11 47	11 54	12 00	12 08	12 17	12 23	12 31	12 38
Kensal Rise	d	11 25	11 32	11 39	11 50	11 56	12 02	12 10	12 19	12 25	12 34	12 40
Brondesbury Park	d	11 27	11 34	11 41	11 52	11 58	12 04	12 12	12 21	12 27	12 36	12 42
Brondesbury	d	11 29	11 36	11 43	11 53	12 00	12 06	12 14	12 23	12 29	12 37	12 44
West Hampstead	⊖ d	11 31	11 38	11 45	11 55	12 02	12 08	12 16	12 25	12 31	12 39	12 46
Finchley Road & Frognal	d	11 32	11 39	11 46	11 57	12 03	12 09	12 17	12 26	12 32	12 41	12 47
Hampstead Heath	d	11 35	11 42	11 49	11 59	12 06	12 12	12 20	12 29	12 35	12 43	12 50
Gospel Oak	d	11 37	11 44	11 51	12 02	12 08	12 14	12 22	12 32	12 37	12 46	12 52
Kentish Town West	d	11 39	11 46	11 53	12 04	12 10	12 16	12 24	12 34	12 39	12 48	12 54
Camden Road	d	11 44	11 51	11 58	12 06	12 14	12 21	12 29	12 37	12 44	12 51	12 59
Caledonian Rd & Barnsbury	d	11 47	11 54	12 01	12 09	12 17	12 24	12 32	12 40	12 47	12 54	13 02
Highbury & Islington ⊖178	d	11 49	11 56	12 04	12 12	12 19	12 26	12 34	12 42	12 49	12 56	13 04
Canonbury ⊖178	d	11 51	11 58	12 06	12 14	12 21	12 28	12 36	12 44	12 51	12 58	13 06
Dalston Kingsland	d	11 53	12 00	12 08	12 16	12 23	12 30	12 38	12 46	12 53	13 00	13 08
Hackney Central	d	11 55	12 02	12 10	12 18	12 25	12 32	12 40	12 48	12 55	13 02	13 10
Homerton	d	11 57	12 04	12 12	12 20	12 27	12 34	12 42	12 50	12 57	13 04	13 12
Hackney Wick	d	12 00	12 07	12 15	12 22	12 30	12 37	12 45	12 53	13 00	13 07	13 15
Stratford [7]	⊖ ⛴ a	12 06	12 12	12 21	12 29	12 36	12 42	12 51	12 59	13 06	13 12	13 21

		LO	LO	LO	LO	LO	LO	LO	LO	LO	LO	LO
Richmond	⊖ d	12 27		12 40		12 57		13 10		13 27		13 40
Kew Gardens	⊖ d	12 30		12 43		13 00		13 13		13 30		13 43
Gunnersbury	⊖ d	12 33		12 46		13 03		13 16		13 33		13 46
South Acton	d	12 36		12 49		13 06		13 19		13 36		13 49
Acton Central	d	12 39		12 53		13 09		13 23		13 39		13 53
Clapham Junction [10] 66,176	d		12 32		12 47		13 02		13 17		13 32	
Imperial Wharf 176	d		12 36		12 51		13 06		13 21		13 36	
West Brompton ⊖176	d		12 39		12 54		13 09		13 24		13 39	
Kensington (Olympia) ⊖176	d		12 42		12 57		13 12		13 27		13 42	
Shepherd's Bush ⊖66,176	d		12 44		12 59		13 15		13 29		13 44	
Willesden Jn Low Level	⊖ d											
Willesden Jn. High Level	⊖ a	12 46	12 52	12 59	13 06	13 16	13 22	13 29	13 37	13 44	13 51	13 59
	d	12 47	12 53	13 00	13 07	13 17	13 23	13 30	13 38	13 45	13 53	14 00
Kensal Rise	d	12 49	12 55	13 02	13 09	13 19	13 25	13 32	13 40	13 47	13 55	14 02
Brondesbury Park	d	12 51	12 57	13 04	13 11	13 21	13 27	13 34	13 42	13 49	13 57	14 04
Brondesbury	d	12 53	12 59	13 06	13 13	13 23	13 29	13 36	13 44	13 51	13 59	14 06
West Hampstead	⊖ d	12 55	13 01	13 08	13 15	13 25	13 31	13 38	13 46	13 53	14 01	14 08
Finchley Road & Frognal	d	12 56	13 02	13 09	13 16	13 26	13 32	13 39	13 47	13 54	14 02	14 09
Hampstead Heath	d	12 59	13 05	13 12	13 19	13 29	13 35	13 42	13 50	13 57	14 05	14 12
Gospel Oak	d	13 01	13 07	13 14	13 21	13 31	13 37	13 44	13 52	13 59	14 07	14 14
Kentish Town West	d	13 03	13 09	13 16	13 23	13 33	13 39	13 46	13 54	14 01	14 09	14 16
Camden Road	d	13 06	13 14	13 20	13 28	13 36	13 44	13 51	13 57	14 06	14 14	14 21
Caledonian Rd & Barnsbury	d	13 09	13 17	13 23	13 31	13 39	13 47	13 54	14 00	14 09	14 17	14 24
Highbury & Islington ⊖178	d	13 11	13 19	13 25	13 34	13 41	13 49	13 56	14 02	14 11	14 19	14 26
Canonbury ⊖178	d	13 13	13 21	13 27	13 36	13 43	13 51	13 58	14 04	14 13	14 21	14 28
Dalston Kingsland	d	13 15	13 23	13 29	13 38	13 45	13 53	14 00	14 06	14 15	14 23	14 30
Hackney Central	d	13 17	13 25	13 31	13 40	13 47	13 55	14 02	14 08	14 17	14 25	14 32
Homerton	d	13 19	13 27	13 33	13 42	13 49	13 57	14 04	14 10	14 19	14 27	14 34
Hackney Wick	d	13 22	13 30	13 36	13 45	13 52	14 00	14 07	14 13	14 22	14 30	14 37
Stratford [7]	⊖ ⛴ a	13 29	13 36	13 42	13 51	13 59	14 06	14 12	14 21	14 29	14 36	14 42

		LO	LO	LO	LO	LO	LO	LO	LO	LO	LO	LO
Richmond	⊖ d		13 57		14 10		14 27		14 40		14 57	
Kew Gardens	⊖ d		14 00		14 13		14 30		14 43		15 00	
Gunnersbury	⊖ d		14 03		14 16		14 33		14 46		15 03	
South Acton	d		14 06		14 19		14 36		14 49		15 06	
Acton Central	d		14 09		14 23		14 39		14 53		15 09	
Clapham Junction [10] 66,176	d	13 47		14 03		14 17		14 32		14 47		15 02
Imperial Wharf 176	d	13 51		14 07		14 21		14 36		14 51		15 06
West Brompton ⊖176	d	13 54		14 10		14 24		14 39		14 54		15 09
Kensington (Olympia) ⊖176	d	13 57		14 13		14 27		14 42		14 57		15 12
Shepherd's Bush ⊖66,176	d	13 59		14 16		14 29		14 44		14 59		15 14
Willesden Jn Low Level	⊖ d											
Willesden Jn. High Level	⊖ a	14 06	14 15	14 22	14 28	14 37	14 44	14 52	14 59	15 07	15 14	15 22
	d	14 07	14 16	14 23	14 29	14 38	14 45	14 53	15 00	15 08	15 15	15 23
Kensal Rise	d	14 09	14 19	14 25	14 31	14 40	14 47	14 55	15 02	15 10	15 17	15 25
Brondesbury Park	d	14 11	14 21	14 27	14 33	14 42	14 49	14 57	15 04	15 12	15 19	15 27
Brondesbury	d	14 13	14 22	14 29	14 35	14 44	14 51	14 59	15 06	15 14	15 21	15 29
West Hampstead	⊖ d	14 15	14 24	14 31	14 37	14 46	14 53	15 01	15 08	15 16	15 23	15 31
Finchley Road & Frognal	d	14 16	14 26	14 32	14 38	14 47	14 54	15 02	15 09	15 17	15 24	15 32
Hampstead Heath	d	14 19	14 28	14 35	14 41	14 50	14 57	15 05	15 12	15 20	15 27	15 35
Gospel Oak	d	14 21	14 31	14 37	14 44	14 52	14 59	15 07	15 14	15 22	15 29	15 37
Kentish Town West	d	14 23	14 33	14 39	14 46	14 54	15 01	15 09	15 16	15 24	15 31	15 39
Camden Road	d	14 26	14 36	14 44	14 51	14 59	15 06	15 14	15 21	15 29	15 36	15 44
Caledonian Rd & Barnsbury	d	14 29	14 39	14 47	14 54	15 02	15 09	15 17	15 24	15 32	15 39	15 47
Highbury & Islington ⊖178	d	14 32	14 41	14 49	14 56	15 04	15 11	15 19	15 26	15 34	15 41	15 49
Canonbury ⊖178	d	14 34	14 43	14 51	14 58	15 06	15 13	15 21	15 28	15 36	15 43	15 51
Dalston Kingsland	d	14 37	14 45	14 53	15 00	15 08	15 15	15 23	15 30	15 38	15 45	15 53
Hackney Central	d	14 39	14 47	14 55	15 02	15 10	15 17	15 25	15 32	15 40	15 47	15 55
Homerton	d	14 42	14 49	14 57	15 04	15 12	15 19	15 27	15 34	15 42	15 49	15 57
Hackney Wick	d	14 45	14 52	15 00	15 07	15 15	15 22	15 30	15 37	15 45	15 52	16 00
Stratford [7]	⊖ ⛴ a	14 51	14 59	15 07	15 12	15 21	15 29	15 36	15 42	15 51	15 59	16 06

		LO	LO	LO	LO	LO	LO	LO	LO	LO	LO	LO
Richmond	⊖ d	15 10		15 27		15 40		15 57		16 10		16 27
Kew Gardens	⊖ d	15 13		15 30		15 43		16 00		16 13		16 30
Gunnersbury	⊖ d	15 16		15 33		15 46		16 03		16 16		16 33
South Acton	d	15 19		15 36		15 49		16 06		16 19		16 36
Acton Central	d	15 23		15 39		15 53		16 09		16 23		16 39
Clapham Junction [10] 66,176	d		15 17		15 32		15 47		16 02		16 17	
Imperial Wharf 176	d		15 21		15 36		15 51		16 06		16 21	
West Brompton ⊖176	d		15 24		15 39		15 54		16 09		16 24	
Kensington (Olympia) ⊖176	d		15 27		15 42		15 57		16 12		16 27	
Shepherd's Bush ⊖66,176	d		15 29		15 44		15 59		16 14		16 29	
Willesden Jn Low Level	⊖ d											
Willesden Jn. High Level	⊖ a	15 29	15 37	15 44	15 52	15 58	16 07	16 14	16 22	16 30	16 37	16 44
	d	15 30	15 38	15 45	15 53	15 59	16 08	16 15	16 23	16 31	16 38	16 45
Kensal Rise	d	15 32	15 40	15 47	15 55	16 01	16 10	16 17	16 25	16 33	16 40	16 47
Brondesbury Park	d	15 34	15 42	15 49	15 57	16 03	16 12	16 19	16 27	16 35	16 42	16 49
Brondesbury	d	15 36	15 44	15 51	15 59	16 05	16 14	16 21	16 29	16 37	16 44	16 51
West Hampstead	⊖ d	15 38	15 46	15 53	16 01	16 07	16 16	16 23	16 31	16 39	16 46	16 53
Finchley Road & Frognal	d	15 40	15 47	15 54	16 02	16 08	16 17	16 24	16 32	16 40	16 47	16 54
Hampstead Heath	d	15 42	15 50	15 57	16 05	16 11	16 20	16 27	16 35	16 43	16 50	16 57
Gospel Oak	d	15 45	15 52	15 59	16 07	16 13	16 22	16 29	16 37	16 45	16 52	16 59
Kentish Town West	d	15 47	15 54	16 01	16 09	16 15	16 24	16 31	16 39	16 47	16 54	17 01
Camden Road	d	15 52	15 59	16 06	16 14	16 20	16 27	16 36	16 44	16 51	16 57	17 06
Caledonian Rd & Barnsbury	d	15 55	16 02	16 09	16 17	16 23	16 30	16 39	16 47	16 54	17 00	17 09
Highbury & Islington ⊖178	d	15 57	16 04	16 11	16 19	16 25	16 32	16 41	16 49	16 56	17 02	17 11
Canonbury ⊖178	d	15 59	16 06	16 13	16 21	16 27	16 34	16 43	16 51	16 58	17 04	17 13
Dalston Kingsland	d	16 01	16 08	16 15	16 23	16 29	16 36	16 45	16 53	17 00	17 06	17 15
Hackney Central	d	16 03	16 10	16 17	16 25	16 31	16 38	16 47	16 55	17 02	17 08	17 17
Homerton	d	16 05	16 12	16 19	16 27	16 33	16 40	16 49	16 57	17 04	17 10	17 19
Hackney Wick	d	16 08	16 15	16 22	16 30	16 36	16 43	16 52	17 00	17 07	17 13	17 22
Stratford [7]	⊖ ⛴ a	16 12	16 21	16 29	16 36	16 42	16 51	16 59	17 06	17 12	17 21	17 29

For services between Shepherds Bush and Clapham Junction refer to Table T066 and T176

Table T059-R

Saturdays
21 December to 16 May

Richmond and Clapham Junction - Willesden Junction, West Hampstead, Highbury & Islington and Stratford

Station		LO	LO	LO	LO	LO	LO	LO	LO	LO	LO	LO	LO	LO	LO	LO	LO	LO	LO	LO	LO	LO	LO
Richmond ⊖	d		16 40		16 57		17 10		17 27		17 39		17 57		18 10		18 27		18 40		18 57		19 10
Kew Gardens ⊖	d		16 43		17 00		17 13		17 30		17 42		18 00		18 13		18 30		18 43		19 00		19 13
Gunnersbury ⊖	d		16 46		17 03		17 16		17 33		17 45		18 03		18 16		18 33		18 46		19 03		19 16
South Acton	d		16 49		17 06		17 19		17 36		17 48		18 06		18 19		18 36		18 49		19 06		19 19
Acton Central	d		16 53		17 09		17 23		17 39		17 52		18 09		18 23		18 39		18 53		19 09		19 23
Clapham Junction 10 66,176	d	16 32		16 47		17 02		17 17		17 32		17 47		18 02		18 17		18 32		18 47		19 02	
Imperial Wharf 176	d	16 36		16 51		17 06		17 21		17 36		17 51		18 06		18 21		18 36		18 51		19 06	
West Brompton ⊖176	d	16 39		16 54		17 09		17 24		17 39		17 54		18 09		18 24		18 39		18 54		19 09	
Kensington (Olympia) ⊖176	d	16 42		16 57		17 12		17 27		17 42		17 57		18 12		18 27		18 42		18 57		19 12	
Shepherd's Bush ⊖66,176	d	16 44		16 59		17 14		17 29		17 44		17 59		18 14		18 29		18 44		18 59		19 14	
Willesden Jn Low Level ⊖	d																						
Willesden Jn. High Level ⊖	a	16 52	16 59	17 07	17 14	17 22	17 29	17 37	17 44	17 51	17 57	18 06	18 14	18 22	18 29	18 37	18 44	18 52	18 59	19 07	19 14	19 22	19 29
	d	16 53	17 00	17 08	17 15	17 23	17 30	17 38	17 45	17 52	17 58	18 07	18 15	18 23	18 30	18 38	18 45	18 53	19 00	19 08	19 15	19 23	19 30
Kensal Rise	d	16 55	17 02	17 10	17 17	17 25	17 32	17 40	17 47	17 54	18 00	18 09	18 18	18 26	18 32	18 40	18 47	18 55	19 02	19 10	19 17	19 25	19 32
Brondesbury Park	d	16 57	17 04	17 12	17 19	17 27	17 34	17 42	17 49	17 56	18 02	18 11	18 20	18 28	18 34	18 42	18 49	18 57	19 04	19 12	19 19	19 27	19 34
Brondesbury	d	16 59	17 06	17 14	17 21	17 29	17 36	17 44	17 51	17 58	18 04	18 13	18 21	18 29	18 36	18 44	18 51	18 59	19 06	19 14	19 21	19 29	19 36
West Hampstead ⊖	d	17 01	17 08	17 16	17 23	17 31	17 38	17 46	17 53	18 00	18 06	18 15	18 23	18 31	18 38	18 46	18 53	19 01	19 08	19 16	19 23	19 31	19 38
Finchley Road & Frognal	d	17 02	17 09	17 17	17 24	17 32	17 39	17 47	17 55	18 01	18 07	18 16	18 25	18 33	18 39	18 47	18 54	19 02	19 09	19 17	19 24	19 32	19 39
Hampstead Heath	d	17 05	17 12	17 20	17 27	17 35	17 42	17 50	17 57	18 04	18 10	18 19	18 27	18 35	18 42	18 50	18 57	19 05	19 12	19 20	19 27	19 35	19 42
Gospel Oak	d	17 07	17 14	17 22	17 29	17 37	17 44	17 52	18 00	18 06	18 12	18 21	18 30	18 38	18 44	18 52	18 59	19 07	19 14	19 22	19 29	19 39	19 44
Kentish Town West	d	17 09	17 16	17 24	17 31	17 39	17 46	17 54	18 02	18 08	18 14	18 23	18 32	18 40	18 46	18 54	19 01	19 09	19 16	19 24	19 31	19 41	19 46
Camden Road	d	17 14	17 21	17 29	17 36	17 44	17 51	17 59	18 06	18 11	18 17	18 26	18 36	18 44	18 51	18 59	19 06	19 14	19 21	19 29	19 36	19 44	19 51
Caledonian Rd & Barnsbury	d	17 17	17 24	17 32	17 39	17 47	17 54	18 02	18 09	18 14	18 20	18 29	18 39	18 47	18 54	19 02	19 09	19 17	19 24	19 32	19 39	19 47	19 54
Highbury & Islington ⊖178	d	17 19	17 26	17 34	17 41	17 49	17 56	18 04	18 11	18 17	18 23	18 31	18 41	18 49	18 56	19 04	19 11	19 19	19 26	19 34	19 41	19 49	19 56
Canonbury ⊖178	d	17 21	17 28	17 36	17 43	17 51	17 58	18 06	18 13	18 19	18 25	18 33	18 43	18 51	18 58	19 06	19 13	19 21	19 28	19 36	19 43	19 51	19 58
Dalston Kingsland	d	17 23	17 30	17 38	17 45	17 53	18 00	18 08	18 15	18 22	18 28	18 35	18 45	18 53	19 00	19 08	19 15	19 23	19 30	19 38	19 45	19 53	20 00
Hackney Central	d	17 25	17 32	17 40	17 47	17 55	18 02	18 10	18 17	18 24	18 30	18 37	18 47	18 55	19 02	19 10	19 17	19 25	19 32	19 40	19 47	19 55	20 02
Homerton	d	17 27	17 34	17 42	17 49	17 57	18 04	18 12	18 19	18 27	18 33	18 39	18 49	18 57	19 04	19 12	19 19	19 27	19 34	19 42	19 49	19 57	20 04
Hackney Wick	d	17 30	17 37	17 45	17 52	18 00	18 07	18 15	18 22	18 30	18 36	18 42	18 52	19 00	19 07	19 15	19 22	19 30	19 37	19 45	19 52	20 00	20 07
Stratford 7 ⊖	a	17 36	17 42	17 51	17 59	18 06	18 12	18 22	18 29	18 37	18 41	18 52	18 59	19 07	19 12	19 22	19 29	19 37	19 42	19 51	19 59	20 06	20 12

Station		LO	LO	LO	LO	LO	LO	LO	LO	LO	LO	LO	LO	LO	LO	LO	LO	LO	LO	LO	LO	LO	LO
Richmond ⊖	d		19 27		19 40		19 57		20 10		20 27		20 40		20 57		21 10		21 27		21 40		21 57
Kew Gardens ⊖	d		19 30		19 43		20 00		20 13		20 30		20 43		21 00		21 13		21 30		21 43		22 00
Gunnersbury ⊖	d		19 33		19 46		20 03		20 16		20 33		20 46		21 03		21 16		21 33		21 46		22 03
South Acton	d		19 36		19 49		20 06		20 19		20 36		20 49		21 06		21 19		21 36		21 49		22 06
Acton Central	d		19 39		19 52		20 09		20 23		20 39		20 53		21 09		21 23		21 39		21 53		22 09
Clapham Junction 10 66,176	d	19 17		19 32		19 47		20 02		20 17		20 32		20 47		21 02		21 17		21 33			
Imperial Wharf 176	d	19 21		19 36		19 51		20 06		20 21		20 36		20 51		21 06		21 21		21 37		21 51	
West Brompton ⊖176	d	19 24		19 39		19 54		20 09		20 24		20 39		20 54		21 09		21 24		21 40		21 54	
Kensington (Olympia) ⊖176	d	19 27		19 43		19 57		20 12		20 27		20 42		20 57		21 12		21 27		21 43		21 57	
Shepherd's Bush ⊖66,176	d	19 29		19 45		19 59		20 14		20 29		20 44		20 59		21 14		21 29		21 45		21 59	
Willesden Jn Low Level ⊖	d																						
Willesden Jn. High Level ⊖	a	19 37	19 44	19 52	19 58	20 07	20 14	20 22	20 29	20 37	20 44	20 52	20 59	21 07	21 14	21 22	21 29	21 37	21 44	21 52	21 59	22 07	22 14
	d	19 38	19 45	19 53	20 00	20 08	20 15	20 23	20 31	20 38	20 45	20 53	21 00	21 08	21 15	21 23	21 30	21 38	21 45	21 53	22 00	22 08	22 15
Kensal Rise	d	19 40	19 47	19 55	20 02	20 10	20 17	20 26	20 33	20 40	20 47	20 55	21 02	21 10	21 17	21 25	21 32	21 40	21 47	21 56	22 02	22 10	22 17
Brondesbury Park	d	19 42	19 49	19 57	20 04	20 12	20 19	20 28	20 35	20 42	20 49	20 57	21 04	21 12	21 19	21 27	21 34	21 42	21 49	21 58	22 04	22 12	22 19
Brondesbury	d	19 44	19 51	19 59	20 06	20 14	20 21	20 29	20 37	20 44	20 51	20 59	21 06	21 14	21 21	21 29	21 36	21 44	21 51	22 00	22 06	22 14	22 21
West Hampstead ⊖	d	19 46	19 53	20 01	20 08	20 16	20 23	20 31	20 39	20 46	20 53	21 01	21 08	21 16	21 23	21 31	21 38	21 46	21 53	22 02	22 08	22 16	22 23
Finchley Road & Frognal	d	19 47	19 54	20 02	20 09	20 17	20 24	20 33	20 41	20 47	20 54	21 02	21 09	21 17	21 24	21 32	21 39	21 47	21 54	22 03	22 09	22 17	22 24
Hampstead Heath	d	19 50	19 57	20 05	20 12	20 20	20 27	20 35	20 43	20 50	20 57	21 05	21 12	21 20	21 27	21 35	21 42	21 50	21 57	22 05	22 12	22 20	22 27
Gospel Oak	d	19 52	19 59	20 07	20 14	20 22	20 29	20 38	20 46	20 52	20 59	21 07	21 14	21 22	21 29	21 37	21 44	21 52	21 59	22 08	22 14	22 22	22 29
Kentish Town West	d	19 54	20 01	20 09	20 16	20 24	20 31	20 40	20 48	20 54	21 01	21 09	21 16	21 24	21 31	21 39	21 46	21 54	22 01	22 10	22 16	22 24	22 31
Camden Road	d	19 59	20 06	20 14	20 21	20 29	20 36	20 44	20 52	20 59	21 06	21 14	21 21	21 29	21 36	21 44	21 51	21 59	22 06	22 14	22 21	22 29	22 36
Caledonian Rd & Barnsbury	d	20 02	20 09	20 17	20 24	20 32	20 39	20 47	20 55	21 02	21 09	21 17	21 24	21 32	21 39	21 47	21 54	22 02	22 09	22 17	22 24	22 32	22 39
Highbury & Islington ⊖178	d	20 04	20 11	20 19	20 26	20 34	20 41	20 49	20 57	21 04	21 11	21 19	21 26	21 34	21 41	21 49	21 56	22 04	22 11	22 19	22 26	22 34	22 41
Canonbury ⊖178	d	20 06	20 13	20 21	20 28	20 36	20 43	20 51	20 59	21 06	21 13	21 21	21 28	21 36	21 43	21 51	21 58	22 06	22 13	22 21	22 28	22 36	22 43
Dalston Kingsland	d	20 08	20 15	20 23	20 30	20 38	20 45	20 53	21 01	21 08	21 15	21 23	21 30	21 38	21 45	21 53	22 00	22 08	22 15	22 23	22 30	22 38	22 45
Hackney Central	d	20 10	20 17	20 25	20 32	20 40	20 47	20 55	21 03	21 10	21 17	21 25	21 32	21 40	21 47	21 55	22 02	22 10	22 17	22 25	22 32	22 40	22 47
Homerton	d	20 12	20 19	20 27	20 34	20 42	20 49	20 57	21 05	21 12	21 19	21 27	21 34	21 42	21 49	21 57	22 04	22 12	22 19	22 27	22 34	22 42	22 49
Hackney Wick	d	20 15	20 22	20 30	20 37	20 45	20 52	21 00	21 08	21 15	21 22	21 30	21 37	21 45	21 52	22 00	22 07	22 15	22 22	22 30	22 37	22 45	22 52
Stratford 7 ⊖	a	20 21	20 29	20 36	20 42	20 51	20 59	21 06	21 12	21 21	21 29	21 36	21 42	21 51	21 59	22 06	22 12	22 21	22 29	22 37	22 42	22 51	22 59

For services between Shepherds Bush and Clapham Junction refer to Table T066 and T176

Table T059-R

Saturdays
21 December to 16 May

Richmond and Clapham Junction - Willesden Junction, West Hampstead, Highbury & Islington and Stratford

Station		LO	LO	LO	LO	LO	LO	LO	LO	LO	LO	LO	LO	LO	LO
Richmond ⊖	d		22 18		22 27		22 40		22 57		23 08		23 27		
Kew Gardens ⊖	d		22 21		22 30		22 43		23 00		23 11		23 30		
Gunnersbury ⊖	d		22 24		22 33		22 46		23 03		23 14		23 33		
South Acton	d		22 27		22 36		22 49		23 06		23 17		23 36		
Acton Central	d		22 30		22 39		22 53		23 09		23 20		23 39		
Clapham Junction 10 66,176	d	22 02		22 17		22 32		22 47		23 02		23 17		23 32	23 47
Imperial Wharf 176	d	22 06		22 21		22 36		22 51		23 06		23 21		23 36	23 51
West Brompton ⊖176	d	22 09		22 24		22 39		22 54		23 09		23 24		23 39	23 54
Kensington (Olympia) ⊖176	d	22 12		22 27		22 42		22 57		23 12		23 27		23 42	23 57
Shepherd's Bush ⊖66,176	d	22 14		22 29		22 44		22 59		23 14		23 29		23 44	23 59
Willesden Jn Low Level ⊖	d														
Willesden Jn. High Level ⊖	a	22 22	22 35	22 39	22 44	22 52	22 58	23 08	23 16	23 21	23 25	23 38	23 47	23 55	00 09
	d	22 23	22 36		22 45	22 53	22 59		23 17	23 22	23 26				
Kensal Rise	d	22 25	22 38		22 47	22 55	23 01		23 19	23 24	23 28				
Brondesbury Park	d	22 27	22 40		22 49	22 57	23 03		23 21	23 26	23 30				
Brondesbury	d	22 29	22 42		22 51	22 59	23 05		23 23	23 28	23 32				
West Hampstead ⊖	d	22 31	22 44		22 53	23 01	23 07		23 25	23 30	23 34				
Finchley Road & Frognal	d	22 32	22 45		22 54	23 02	23 08		23 26	23 31	23 35				
Hampstead Heath	d	22 35	22 48		22 57	23 05	23 11		23 29	23 34	23 38				
Gospel Oak	d	22 37	22 50		22 59	23 07	23 14		23 31	23 36	23 40				
Kentish Town West	d	22 39	22 52		23 01	23 09	23 16		23 33	23 38	23 42				
Camden Road	d	22 44	22 55		23 06	23 14	23 21		23 36	23 43	23 47				
Caledonian Rd & Barnsbury	d	22 47	22 58		23 09	23 17	23 24		23 39	23 46	23 50				
Highbury & Islington ⊖178	d	22 49	23 00		23 11	23 19	23 26		23 41	23 48	23 52				
Canonbury ⊖178	d	22 51	23 02		23 13	23 21	23 28		23 43	23 50	23 54				
Dalston Kingsland	d	22 53	23 04		23 15	23 23	23 30		23 45	23 52	23 56				
Hackney Central	d	22 55	23 06		23 17	23 25	23 32		23 47	23 54	23 58				
Homerton	d	22 57	23 08		23 19	23 27	23 34		23 49	23 56	00 01				
Hackney Wick	d	23 00	23 11		23 22	23 30	23 37		23 52	23 59	00 03				
Stratford 7 ⊖	a	23 06	23 20		23 29	23 36	23 42		23 59	00 06	00 10				

Sundays
15 December to 10 May

Station		LO A	LO	LO	LO	LO	LO	LO	LO	LO	LO	LO	LO	LO	LO	LO	LO	LO	LO	LO	LO	LO	LO
Richmond ⊖	d					08 59		09 10		09 27		09 40		09 58		10 10		10 26		10 40		10 56	
Kew Gardens ⊖	d					09 02		09 13		09 30		09 43		10 01		10 13		10 30		10 43		11 00	
Gunnersbury ⊖	d					09 05		09 16		09 33		09 46		10 04		10 16		10 33		10 46		11 03	
South Acton	d					09 08		09 19		09 36		09 49		10 07		10 19		10 36		10 49		11 06	
Acton Central	d					09 11		09 22		09 39		09 52		10 10		10 22		10 39		10 52		11 09	
Clapham Junction 10 66,176	d		08 31		08 51		09 01		09 21		09 31		09 50		10 01		10 13		10 29		10 44		10 59
Imperial Wharf 176	d		08 35		08 55		09 05		09 25		09 35		09 54		10 05		10 17		10 33		10 48		11 03
West Brompton ⊖176	d		08 38		08 58		09 08		09 28		09 38		09 57		10 08		10 20		10 36		10 51		11 06
Kensington (Olympia) ⊖176	d		08 41		09 01		09 11		09 31		09 41		10 00		10 11		10 23		10 39		10 54		11 09
Shepherd's Bush ⊖66,176	d		08 43		09 03		09 13		09 33		09 43		10 02		10 13		10 25		10 41		10 56		11 11
Willesden Jn Low Level ⊖	d			09 01																			
Willesden Jn. High Level ⊖	a		08 52		09 10	09 17	09 22	09 28	09 41	09 46	09 51	09 59	10 10	10 16	10 21	10 28	10 33	10 44	10 50	10 58	11 05	11 15	11 20
	d				09 11	09 18		09 29	09 42	09 47	09 52	10 00	10 11	10 17	10 22	10 29	10 34	10 45	10 51	10 59	11 06	11 16	11 21
Kensal Rise	d			09 05	09 13	09 20		09 31	09 45	09 49	09 55	10 02	10 13	10 19	10 24	10 31	10 36	10 47	10 53	11 01	11 08	11 18	11 23
Brondesbury Park	d			09 07	09 15	09 22		09 33	09 47	09 51	09 57	10 04	10 15	10 21	10 26	10 33	10 38	10 49	10 55	11 03	11 10	11 20	11 25
Brondesbury	d			09 09	09 17	09 24		09 35	09 48	09 53	09 58	10 06	10 17	10 23	10 28	10 35	10 40	10 51	10 57	11 05	11 12	11 22	11 27
West Hampstead ⊖	d			09 11	09 19	09 26		09 37	09 50	09 55	10 00	10 08	10 19	10 25	10 30	10 37	10 42	10 53	10 59	11 07	11 14	11 24	11 29
Finchley Road & Frognal	d			09 12	09 20	09 27		09 38	09 52	09 56	10 02	10 09	10 20	10 26	10 31	10 38	10 43	10 54	11 00	11 08	11 15	11 25	11 30
Hampstead Heath	d			09 15	09 23	09 30		09 41	09 54	09 59	10 04	10 12	10 23	10 29	10 34	10 41	10 46	10 57	11 03	11 11	11 18	11 28	11 33
Gospel Oak	d			09 17	09 25	09 32		09 43	09 57	10 01	10 07	10 14	10 25	10 31	10 36	10 43	10 48	10 59	11 05	11 13	11 20	11 30	11 35
Kentish Town West	d			09 19	09 27	09 34		09 45	09 59	10 03	10 09	10 16	10 27	10 33	10 38	10 45	10 50	11 01	11 07	11 15	11 22	11 32	11 37
Camden Road	d			09 25	09 32	09 39		09 50	10 01	10 07	10 12	10 20	10 31	10 38	10 43	10 50	10 55	11 06	11 12	11 20	11 27	11 36	11 42
Caledonian Rd & Barnsbury	d			09 28	09 35	09 42		09 53	10 04	10 10	10 15	10 23	10 34	10 41	10 46	10 53	10 58	11 09	11 15	11 23	11 30	11 39	11 45
Highbury & Islington ⊖178	d			09 30	09 37	09 44		09 55	10 07	10 12	10 18	10 25	10 36	10 43	10 48	10 55	11 00	11 11	11 17	11 25	11 32	11 41	11 47
Canonbury ⊖178	d			09 32	09 39	09 46		09 57	10 09	10 14	10 20	10 27	10 38	10 45	10 50	10 57	11 02	11 13	11 19	11 27	11 34	11 43	11 49
Dalston Kingsland	d			09 34	09 41	09 48		09 59	10 11	10 16	10 22	10 29	10 40	10 47	10 52	10 59	11 04	11 15	11 21	11 29	11 36	11 45	11 51
Hackney Central	d			09 36	09 43	09 50		10 01	10 13	10 18	10 24	10 31	10 42	10 49	10 54	11 01	11 06	11 17	11 23	11 31	11 38	11 47	11 53
Homerton	d	00 01		09 38	09 45	09 52		10 03	10 15	10 20	10 26	10 33	10 44	10 51	10 56	11 03	11 08	11 19	11 25	11 33	11 40	11 49	11 55
Hackney Wick	d	00 03		09 41	09 48	09 55		10 06	10 17	10 23	10 28	10 36	10 47	10 54	10 59	11 06	11 11	11 22	11 28	11 36	11 43	11 52	11 58
Stratford 7 ⊖	a	00 10		09 49	09 55	10 01		10 12	10 25	10 29	10 35	10 42	10 54	11 00	11 05	11 12	11 17	11 28	11 33	11 42	11 49	11 58	12 04

A not 15 December

For services between Shepherds Bush and Clapham Junction refer to Table T066 and T176

Table T059-R

Sundays
15 December to 10 May

Richmond and Clapham Junction - Willesden Junction, West Hampstead, Highbury & Islington and Stratford

		LO	LO	LO	LO	LO	LO	LO	LO	LO	LO	LO	LO	LO	LO	LO	LO	LO	LO	LO	LO	LO	LO
Richmond ⊖	d	11 10		11 26		11 40		11 56		12 10		12 26		12 40		12 56		13 10		13 26		13 40	
Kew Gardens ⊖	d	11 13		11 30		11 43		12 00		12 13		12 30		12 43		13 00		13 13		13 30		13 43	
Gunnersbury ⊖	d	11 16		11 33		11 46		12 03		12 16		12 33		12 46		13 03		13 16		13 33		13 46	
South Acton	d	11 19		11 36		11 49		12 06		12 19		12 36		12 49		13 06		13 19		13 36		13 49	
Acton Central	d	11 22		11 39		11 52		12 09		12 22		12 39		12 52		13 09		13 22		13 39		13 52	
Clapham Junction 10 66,176	d		11 12		11 29		11 44		11 59		12 14		12 29		12 44		12 59		13 14		13 29		13 43
Imperial Wharf 176	d		11 16		11 33		11 48		12 03		12 18		12 33		12 48		13 03		13 18		13 33		13 47
West Brompton ⊖176	d		11 19		11 36		11 51		12 06		12 21		12 36		12 51		13 06		13 21		13 36		13 50
Kensington (Olympia) ⊖176	d		11 22		11 39		11 54		12 09		12 24		12 39		12 54		13 09		13 24		13 39		13 53
Shepherd's Bush ⊖66,176	d		11 24		11 41		11 56		12 11		12 26		12 41		12 56		13 11		13 26		13 41		13 55
Willesden Jn Low Level ⊖	d																						
Willesden Jn. High Level ⊖	a	11 28	11 33	11 44	11 50	11 58	12 05	12 14	12 20	12 28	12 35	12 44	12 50	12 58	13 05	13 14	13 20	13 28	13 35	13 44	13 50	13 58	14 03
	d	11 29	11 34	11 45	11 51	11 59	12 06	12 15	12 21	12 29	12 36	12 45	12 51	12 59	13 06	13 15	13 21	13 29	13 36	13 45	13 51	13 59	14 04
Kensal Rise	d	11 31	11 36	11 47	11 53	12 01	12 08	12 17	12 23	12 31	12 38	12 47	12 53	13 01	13 08	13 17	13 23	13 31	13 38	13 47	13 53	14 01	14 06
Brondesbury Park	d	11 33	11 38	11 49	11 55	12 03	12 10	12 19	12 25	12 33	12 40	12 49	12 55	13 03	13 10	13 19	13 25	13 33	13 40	13 49	13 55	14 03	14 08
Brondesbury	d	11 35	11 40	11 51	11 57	12 05	12 12	12 21	12 27	12 35	12 42	12 51	12 57	13 05	13 12	13 21	13 27	13 35	13 42	13 51	13 57	14 05	14 10
West Hampstead ⊖	d	11 37	11 42	11 53	11 59	12 07	12 14	12 23	12 29	12 37	12 44	12 53	12 59	13 07	13 14	13 23	13 29	13 37	13 44	13 53	13 59	14 07	14 13
Finchley Road & Frognal	d	11 38	11 43	11 54	12 00	12 08	12 15	12 24	12 30	12 38	12 45	12 54	13 00	13 08	13 15	13 24	13 30	13 38	13 45	13 54	14 00	14 08	14 14
Hampstead Heath	d	11 41	11 46	11 57	12 03	12 11	12 18	12 27	12 33	12 41	12 48	12 57	13 03	13 11	13 18	13 27	13 33	13 41	13 48	13 57	14 03	14 11	14 17
Gospel Oak	d	11 43	11 48	11 59	12 05	12 13	12 20	12 29	12 35	12 43	12 50	12 59	13 05	13 13	13 20	13 29	13 35	13 43	13 50	13 59	14 05	14 13	14 19
Kentish Town West	d	11 45	11 50	12 01	12 07	12 15	12 22	12 31	12 37	12 45	12 52	13 01	13 07	13 15	13 22	13 31	13 37	13 45	13 52	14 01	14 07	14 15	14 21
Camden Road	d	11 50	11 55	12 06	12 12	12 20	12 27	12 36	12 42	12 50	12 57	13 06	13 12	13 20	13 27	13 36	13 42	13 50	13 57	14 06	14 12	14 20	14 25
Caledonian Rd & Barnsbury	d	11 53	11 58	12 09	12 15	12 23	12 30	12 39	12 45	12 53	13 00	13 09	13 15	13 23	13 30	13 39	13 45	13 53	14 00	14 09	14 15	14 23	14 28
Highbury & Islington ⊖178	d	11 55	12 00	12 11	12 17	12 25	12 32	12 41	12 47	12 55	13 02	13 11	13 17	13 25	13 32	13 41	13 47	13 55	14 02	14 11	14 17	14 25	14 31
Canonbury ⊖178	d	11 57	12 02	12 13	12 19	12 27	12 34	12 43	12 49	12 57	13 04	13 13	13 19	13 27	13 34	13 43	13 49	13 57	14 04	14 13	14 19	14 27	14 33
Dalston Kingsland	d	11 59	12 04	12 15	12 21	12 29	12 36	12 45	12 51	12 59	13 06	13 15	13 21	13 29	13 36	13 45	13 51	13 59	14 06	14 15	14 21	14 29	14 35
Hackney Central	d	12 01	12 06	12 17	12 23	12 31	12 38	12 47	12 53	13 01	13 08	13 17	13 23	13 31	13 38	13 47	13 53	14 01	14 08	14 17	14 23	14 31	14 37
Homerton	d	12 03	12 08	12 19	12 25	12 33	12 40	12 49	12 55	13 03	13 10	13 19	13 25	13 33	13 40	13 49	13 55	14 03	14 10	14 19	14 25	14 33	14 39
Hackney Wick	d	12 06	12 11	12 22	12 28	12 36	12 43	12 52	12 58	13 06	13 13	13 22	13 28	13 36	13 43	13 52	13 58	14 06	14 13	14 22	14 28	14 36	14 42
Stratford 7 ⊖	a	12 12	12 17	12 28	12 33	12 42	12 48	12 58	13 03	13 12	13 18	13 28	13 33	13 42	13 48	13 58	14 03	14 12	14 18	14 28	14 33	14 42	14 47

		LO	LO	LO	LO	LO	LO	LO	LO	LO	LO	LO	LO	LO	LO	LO	LO	LO	LO	LO	LO	LO	LO
Richmond ⊖	d	13 56		14 10		14 26		14 40		14 56		15 10		15 26		15 40		15 56		16 09		16 26	
Kew Gardens ⊖	d	14 00		14 13		14 30		14 43		15 00		15 13		15 30		15 43		16 00		16 12		16 30	
Gunnersbury ⊖	d	14 03		14 16		14 33		14 46		15 03		15 16		15 33		15 46		16 03		16 15		16 33	
South Acton	d	14 06		14 19		14 36		14 49		15 06		15 19		15 36		15 49		16 06		16 18		16 36	
Acton Central	d	14 09		14 22		14 39		14 52		15 09		15 22		15 39		15 52		16 09		16 21		16 39	
Clapham Junction 10 66,176	d		13 59		14 14		14 29		14 44		14 59		15 14		15 29		15 44		15 59		16 14		16 29
Imperial Wharf 176	d		14 03		14 18		14 33		14 49		15 03		15 18		15 33		15 48		16 03		16 19		16 33
West Brompton ⊖176	d		14 06		14 21		14 36		14 52		15 06		15 21		15 36		15 51		16 06		16 22		16 36
Kensington (Olympia) ⊖176	d		14 09		14 24		14 39		14 55		15 09		15 24		15 39		15 54		16 09		16 25		16 39
Shepherd's Bush ⊖66,176	d		14 11		14 26		14 41		14 58		15 11		15 26		15 41		15 56		16 11		16 28		16 41
Willesden Jn Low Level ⊖	d																						
Willesden Jn. High Level ⊖	a	14 14	14 20	14 28	14 35	14 44	14 50	14 57	15 07	15 14	15 20	15 28	15 35	15 44	15 50	15 58	16 05	16 14	16 20	16 27	16 37	16 44	16 50
	d	14 15	14 21	14 29	14 36	14 45	14 51	14 58	15 08	15 15	15 21	15 29	15 36	15 45	15 51	15 59	16 06	16 15	16 21	16 28	16 38	16 45	16 51
Kensal Rise	d	14 17	14 23	14 31	14 38	14 47	14 53	15 00	15 10	15 17	15 23	15 31	15 38	15 47	15 53	16 01	16 08	16 17	16 23	16 30	16 40	16 47	16 53
Brondesbury Park	d	14 19	14 25	14 33	14 40	14 49	14 55	15 02	15 12	15 19	15 25	15 33	15 40	15 49	15 55	16 03	16 10	16 19	16 25	16 32	16 42	16 49	16 55
Brondesbury	d	14 21	14 27	14 35	14 42	14 51	14 57	15 04	15 14	15 21	15 27	15 35	15 42	15 51	15 57	16 05	16 12	16 21	16 27	16 34	16 44	16 51	16 57
West Hampstead ⊖	d	14 23	14 29	14 37	14 44	14 53	14 59	15 06	15 16	15 23	15 29	15 37	15 44	15 53	15 59	16 07	16 14	16 23	16 29	16 36	16 46	16 53	16 59
Finchley Road & Frognal	d	14 24	14 30	14 38	14 45	14 54	15 00	15 07	15 17	15 24	15 30	15 38	15 45	15 54	16 00	16 08	16 15	16 24	16 30	16 37	16 47	16 54	17 00
Hampstead Heath	d	14 27	14 33	14 41	14 48	14 57	15 03	15 10	15 20	15 27	15 33	15 41	15 48	15 57	16 03	16 11	16 18	16 27	16 33	16 40	16 50	16 57	17 03
Gospel Oak	d	14 29	14 35	14 43	14 50	14 59	15 05	15 12	15 22	15 29	15 35	15 43	15 50	15 59	16 05	16 13	16 20	16 29	16 35	16 42	16 52	16 59	17 05
Kentish Town West	d	14 31	14 37	14 45	14 52	15 01	15 07	15 14	15 24	15 31	15 37	15 45	15 52	16 01	16 07	16 15	16 22	16 31	16 37	16 44	16 54	17 01	17 07
Camden Road	d	14 36	14 42	14 50	14 57	15 06	15 12	15 19	15 29	15 36	15 42	15 50	15 57	16 06	16 12	16 20	16 27	16 36	16 42	16 49	16 58	17 06	17 12
Caledonian Rd & Barnsbury	d	14 39	14 45	14 53	15 00	15 09	15 15	15 22	15 32	15 39	15 45	15 53	16 00	16 09	16 15	16 23	16 30	16 39	16 45	16 52	17 01	17 09	17 15
Highbury & Islington ⊖178	d	14 41	14 47	14 55	15 02	15 11	15 17	15 24	15 34	15 41	15 47	15 55	16 02	16 11	16 17	16 25	16 32	16 41	16 47	16 54	17 03	17 11	17 17
Canonbury ⊖178	d	14 43	14 49	14 57	15 04	15 13	15 19	15 26	15 36	15 43	15 49	15 57	16 04	16 13	16 19	16 27	16 34	16 43	16 49	16 56	17 05	17 13	17 19
Dalston Kingsland	d	14 45	14 51	14 59	15 06	15 15	15 21	15 28	15 38	15 45	15 51	15 59	16 06	16 15	16 21	16 29	16 36	16 45	16 51	16 58	17 07	17 15	17 21
Hackney Central	d	14 47	14 53	15 01	15 08	15 17	15 23	15 30	15 40	15 47	15 53	16 01	16 08	16 17	16 23	16 31	16 38	16 47	16 53	17 00	17 09	17 17	17 23
Homerton	d	14 49	14 55	15 03	15 10	15 19	15 25	15 32	15 42	15 49	15 55	16 03	16 10	16 19	16 25	16 33	16 40	16 49	16 55	17 02	17 11	17 19	17 25
Hackney Wick	d	14 52	14 58	15 06	15 13	15 22	15 28	15 35	15 45	15 52	15 58	16 06	16 13	16 22	16 28	16 36	16 43	16 52	16 58	17 05	17 14	17 22	17 28
Stratford 7 ⊖	a	14 58	15 03	15 12	15 18	15 28	15 33	15 42	15 49	15 58	16 03	16 12	16 18	16 28	16 33	16 42	16 48	16 58	17 03	17 11	17 18	17 28	17 33

For services between Shepherds Bush and Clapham Junction refer to Table T066 and T176

Table T059-R

Sundays
15 December to 10 May

Richmond and Clapham Junction - Willesden Junction, West Hampstead, Highbury & Islington and Stratford

		LO	LO	LO	LO	LO	LO	LO	LO	LO	LO	LO	LO	LO	LO	LO	LO	LO	LO	LO	LO	LO	LO
Richmond ⊖	d	16 40		16 56		17 10		17 26		17 40		17 56		18 10		18 26		18 40		18 56		19 10	
Kew Gardens ⊖	d	16 43		17 00		17 13		17 30		17 43		18 00		18 13		18 30		18 43		19 00		19 13	
Gunnersbury ⊖	d	16 46		17 03		17 16		17 33		17 46		18 03		18 16		18 33		18 46		19 03		19 16	
South Acton	d	16 49		17 06		17 19		17 36		17 49		18 06		18 19		18 36		18 49		19 06		19 19	
Acton Central	d	16 52		17 09		17 22		17 39		17 52		18 09		18 22		18 39		18 52		19 09		19 22	
Clapham Junction 10 66,176	d		16 44		16 59		17 14		17 29		17 44		17 59		18 14		18 29		18 44		18 59		19 14
Imperial Wharf 176	d		16 48		17 03		17 18		17 33		17 48		18 03		18 18		18 33		18 48		19 03		19 18
West Brompton ⊖176	d		16 51		17 06		17 21		17 36		17 51		18 06		18 21		18 36		18 51		19 06		19 21
Kensington (Olympia) ⊖176	d		16 54		17 09		17 24		17 39		17 54		18 09		18 24		18 39		18 54		19 09		19 24
Shepherd's Bush ⊖66,176	d		16 56		17 11		17 26		17 41		17 56		18 11		18 26		18 41		18 56		19 11		19 26
Willesden Jn Low Level ⊖	d																						
Willesden Jn. High Level ⊖	a	16 58	17 05	17 14	17 20	17 28	17 35	17 44	17 50	17 58	18 05	18 14	18 20	18 28	18 35	18 44	18 50	18 58	19 05	19 14	19 20	19 28	19 35
	d	16 59	17 06	17 15	17 21	17 29	17 36	17 45	17 51	17 59	18 06	18 15	18 21	18 29	18 36	18 45	18 51	18 59	19 06	19 15	19 21	19 29	19 36
Kensal Rise	d	17 01	17 08	17 17	17 23	17 31	17 38	17 47	17 53	18 01	18 08	18 17	18 23	18 31	18 38	18 47	18 53	19 01	19 08	19 17	19 23	19 31	19 38
Brondesbury Park	d	17 03	17 10	17 19	17 25	17 33	17 40	17 49	17 55	18 03	18 10	18 19	18 25	18 33	18 40	18 49	18 55	19 03	19 10	19 19	19 25	19 33	19 40
Brondesbury	d	17 05	17 12	17 21	17 27	17 35	17 42	17 51	17 57	18 05	18 12	18 21	18 27	18 35	18 42	18 51	18 57	19 05	19 12	19 21	19 27	19 35	19 42
West Hampstead ⊖	d	17 07	17 14	17 23	17 29	17 37	17 44	17 53	17 59	18 07	18 14	18 23	18 29	18 37	18 44	18 53	18 59	19 07	19 14	19 23	19 29	19 37	19 44
Finchley Road & Frognal	d	17 08	17 15	17 24	17 30	17 38	17 45	17 54	18 00	18 08	18 15	18 24	18 30	18 38	18 45	18 54	19 00	19 08	19 15	19 24	19 30	19 38	19 45
Hampstead Heath	d	17 11	17 18	17 27	17 33	17 41	17 48	17 57	18 03	18 11	18 18	18 27	18 33	18 41	18 48	18 57	19 03	19 11	19 18	19 27	19 33	19 41	19 48
Gospel Oak	d	17 13	17 20	17 29	17 35	17 43	17 50	17 59	18 05	18 13	18 20	18 29	18 35	18 43	18 50	18 59	19 05	19 13	19 20	19 29	19 35	19 43	19 50
Kentish Town West	d	17 15	17 22	17 31	17 37	17 45	17 52	18 01	18 07	18 15	18 22	18 31	18 37	18 45	18 52	19 01	19 07	19 15	19 22	19 31	19 37	19 45	19 52
Camden Road	d	17 20	17 27	17 36	17 42	17 50	17 57	18 06	18 12	18 20	18 27	18 36	18 42	18 50	18 57	19 06	19 12	19 20	19 27	19 36	19 42	19 50	19 57
Caledonian Rd & Barnsbury	d	17 23	17 30	17 39	17 45	17 53	18 00	18 09	18 15	18 23	18 30	18 39	18 45	18 53	19 00	19 09	19 15	19 23	19 30	19 39	19 45	19 53	20 00
Highbury & Islington ⊖178	d	17 25	17 32	17 41	17 47	17 55	18 02	18 11	18 17	18 25	18 32	18 41	18 47	18 55	19 02	19 11	19 17	19 25	19 32	19 41	19 47	19 55	20 02
Canonbury ⊖178	d	17 27	17 34	17 43	17 49	17 57	18 04	18 13	18 19	18 27	18 34	18 43	18 49	18 57	19 04	19 13	19 19	19 27	19 34	19 43	19 49	19 57	20 04
Dalston Kingsland	d	17 29	17 36	17 45	17 51	17 59	18 06	18 15	18 21	18 29	18 36	18 45	18 51	18 59	19 06	19 15	19 21	19 29	19 36	19 45	19 51	19 59	20 06
Hackney Central	d	17 31	17 38	17 47	17 53	18 01	18 08	18 17	18 23	18 31	18 38	18 47	18 53	19 01	19 08	19 17	19 23	19 31	19 38	19 47	19 53	20 01	20 08
Homerton	d	17 33	17 40	17 49	17 55	18 03	18 10	18 19	18 25	18 33	18 40	18 49	18 55	19 03	19 10	19 19	19 25	19 33	19 40	19 49	19 55	20 03	20 10
Hackney Wick	d	17 36	17 43	17 52	17 58	18 06	18 13	18 22	18 28	18 36	18 43	18 52	18 58	19 06	19 13	19 22	19 28	19 36	19 43	19 52	19 58	20 06	20 13
Stratford 7 ⊖	a	17 42	17 48	17 58	18 03	18 12	18 18	18 28	18 33	18 42	18 48	18 58	19 03	19 12	19 18	19 28	19 33	19 42	19 48	19 58	20 03	20 12	20 18

		LO	LO	LO	LO	LO	LO	LO	LO	LO	LO	LO	LO	LO	LO	LO	LO	LO	LO	LO	LO	LO	LO
Richmond ⊖	d	19 26		19 40		19 56		20 10		20 26		20 40		20 56		21 10		21 26		21 40		21 56	
Kew Gardens ⊖	d	19 30		19 43		20 00		20 13		20 30		20 43		21 00		21 13		21 30		21 43		22 00	
Gunnersbury ⊖	d	19 33		19 46		20 03		20 16		20 33		20 46		21 03		21 16		21 33		21 46		22 03	
South Acton	d	19 36		19 49		20 06		20 19		20 36		20 49		21 06		21 19		21 36		21 49		22 06	
Acton Central	d	19 39		19 52		20 09		20 22		20 39		20 52		21 09		21 22		21 39		21 52		22 09	
Clapham Junction 10 66,176	d		19 29		19 44		19 59		20 14		20 29		20 44		20 59		21 14		21 29		21 44		22 00
Imperial Wharf 176	d		19 33		19 48		20 03		20 18		20 33		20 48		21 03		21 18		21 33		21 48		22 04
West Brompton ⊖176	d		19 36		19 51		20 06		20 21		20 36		20 51		21 06		21 21		21 36		21 51		22 07
Kensington (Olympia) ⊖176	d		19 39		19 54		20 09		20 24		20 39		20 54		21 09		21 24		21 39		21 54		22 10
Shepherd's Bush ⊖66,176	d		19 41		19 56		20 11		20 26		20 41		20 56		21 11		21 26		21 41		21 56		22 12
Willesden Jn Low Level ⊖	d																						
Willesden Jn. High Level ⊖	a	19 44	19 50	19 58	20 05	20 14	20 20	20 28	20 35	20 44	20 50	20 58	21 05	21 14	21 20	21 28	21 35	21 44	21 50	21 58	22 05	22 14	22 21
	d	19 45	19 51	19 59	20 06	20 15	20 21	20 29		20 45	20 51	20 59		21 15	21 21	21 29		21 45	21 51	21 59		22 15	22 22
Kensal Rise	d	19 47	19 53	20 01	20 08	20 17	20 23	20 31		20 47	20 53	21 01		21 17	21 23	21 31		21 47	21 53	22 01		22 17	22 24
Brondesbury Park	d	19 49	19 55	20 03	20 10	20 19	20 25	20 33		20 49	20 55	21 03		21 19	21 25	21 33		21 49	21 55	22 03		22 19	22 26
Brondesbury	d	19 51	19 57	20 05	20 12	20 21	20 27	20 35		20 51	20 57	21 05		21 21	21 27	21 35		21 51	21 57	22 05		22 21	22 28
West Hampstead ⊖	d	19 53	19 59	20 07	20 14	20 23	20 29	20 37		20 53	20 59	21 07		21 23	21 29	21 37		21 53	21 59	22 07		22 23	22 30
Finchley Road & Frognal	d	19 54	20 00	20 08	20 15	20 24	20 30	20 38		20 54	21 00	21 08		21 24	21 30	21 38		21 54	22 00	22 08		22 24	22 31
Hampstead Heath	d	19 57	20 03	20 11	20 18	20 27	20 33	20 41		20 57	21 03	21 11		21 27	21 33	21 41		21 57	22 03	22 11		22 27	22 34
Gospel Oak	d	19 59	20 05	20 13	20 20	20 29	20 35	20 43		20 59	21 05	21 13		21 29	21 37	21 43		21 59	22 05	22 13		22 29	22 36
Kentish Town West	d	20 01	20 07	20 15	20 22	20 31	20 37	20 45		21 01	21 07	21 15		21 31	21 39	21 45		22 01	22 07	22 15		22 32	22 38
Camden Road	d	20 06	20 12	20 20	20 27	20 36	20 42	20 50		21 06	21 12	21 20		21 36	21 42	21 50		22 06	22 12	22 20		22 37	22 43
Caledonian Rd & Barnsbury	d	20 09	20 15	20 23	20 30	20 39	20 45	20 53		21 09	21 15	21 23		21 39	21 45	21 53		22 09	22 15	22 23		22 40	22 46
Highbury & Islington ⊖178	d	20 11	20 17	20 25	20 32	20 41	20 47	20 55		21 11	21 17	21 25		21 41	21 47	21 55		22 11	22 17	22 25		22 42	22 48
Canonbury ⊖178	d	20 13	20 19	20 27	20 34	20 43	20 49	20 57		21 13	21 19	21 27		21 43	21 49	21 57		22 13	22 19	22 27		22 44	22 50
Dalston Kingsland	d	20 15	20 21	20 29	20 36	20 45	20 51	20 59		21 15	21 21	21 29		21 45	21 51	21 59		22 15	22 21	22 29		22 46	22 52
Hackney Central	d	20 17	20 23	20 31	20 38	20 47	20 53	21 01		21 17	21 23	21 31		21 47	21 53	22 01		22 17	22 23	22 31		22 48	22 54
Homerton	d	20 19	20 25	20 33	20 40	20 49	20 55	21 03		21 19	21 25	21 33		21 49	21 55	22 03		22 19	22 25	22 33		22 50	22 56
Hackney Wick	d	20 22	20 28	20 36	20 43	20 52	20 58	21 06		21 22	21 28	21 36		21 52	21 58	22 06		22 22	22 28	22 36		22 53	22 59
Stratford 7 ⊖	a	20 28	20 33	20 42	20 48	20 58	21 03	21 12		21 28	21 33	21 42		21 58	22 03	22 12		22 28	22 33	22 42		22 58	23 04

For services between Shepherds Bush and Clapham Junction refer to Table T066 and T176

Table T059-R

Sundays

15 December to 10 May

Richmond and Clapham Junction - Willesden Junction, West Hampstead, Highbury & Islington and Stratford

		LO	LO	LO	LO	LO	LO	LO	LO	LO	LO	LO
Richmond ⊖	d	22 10		22 26		22 40		23 01				
Kew Gardens ⊖	d	22 13		22 30		22 43		23 04				
Gunnersbury ⊖	d	22 16		22 33		22 46		23 07				
South Acton	d	22 19		22 36		22 49		23 10				
Acton Central	d	22 22		22 39		22 52		23 13				
Clapham Junction 10 66,176	d		22 15		22 31		22 46		23 01	23 16	23 31	23 46
Imperial Wharf 176	d		22 19		22 35		22 50		23 05	23 20	23 35	23 50
West Brompton ⊖176	d		22 22		22 38		22 53		23 08	23 23	23 38	23 53
Kensington (Olympia) ⊖176	d		22 25		22 41		22 56		23 11	23 26	23 41	23 56
Shepherd's Bush ⊖66,176	d		22 27		22 43		22 58		23 13	23 28	23 43	23 58
Willesden Jn Low Level ⊖	d											
Willesden Jn. High Level ⊖	a	22 28	22 37	22 45	22 52	22 58	23 07	23 18	23 22	23 37	23 52	00 05
	d	22 29		22 46		22 59		23 19				
Kensal Rise	d	22 31		22 48		23 01		23 22				
Brondesbury Park	d	22 33		22 50		23 03		23 24				
Brondesbury	d	22 35		22 52		23 05		23 26				
West Hampstead ⊖	d	22 37		22 54		23 07		23 28				
Finchley Road & Frognal	d	22 38		22 55		23 08		23 29				
Hampstead Heath	d	22 41		22 58		23 11		23 32				
Gospel Oak	d	22 43		23 00		23 13		23 34				
Kentish Town West	d	22 45		23 02		23 15		23 36				
Camden Road	d	22 50		23 07		23 20		23 41				
Caledonian Rd & Barnsbury	d	22 53		23 10		23 23		23 44				
Highbury & Islington ⊖178	d	22 55		23 12		23 25		23 46				
Canonbury ⊖178	d	22 57		23 14		23 27		23 48				
Dalston Kingsland	d	22 59		23 16		23 29		23 50				
Hackney Central	d	23 01		23 18		23 31		23 52				
Homerton	d	23 03		23 20		23 33		23 54				
Hackney Wick	d	23 06		23 23		23 36		23 57				
Stratford 7 ⊖ ⛴	a	23 12		23 28		23 42		00 03				

For services between Shepherds Bush and Clapham Junction refer to Table T066 and T176

Table T060-F

Mondays to Fridays

16 December to 15 May

London, Queen's Park and Harrow & Wealdstone - Watford Junction

Miles			LO MX	LO MO	LO MX	LO MO	LO MX	LO MO	LO	LO	LO		LO	LO	LO	LO	LO	LO	LO	LO	LO	LO	LO	
0	**London Euston** 15 ⊖66	d							05 37	06 00	06 15		06 28	06 45	06 58	07 15	07 27	07 45	07 57	08 15	08 28	08 45	08 58	
2½	South Hampstead	d					00 03	00 03	05 42	06 05	06 20		06 33	06 50	07 03	07 20	07 32	07 50	08 02	08 20	08 33	08 50	09 03	
3	Kilburn High Road	d					00 05	00 05	05 44	06 07	06 22		06 35	06 52	07 05	07 22	07 35	07 52	08 05	08 22	08 35	08 52	09 05	
3¾	**Queen's Park (London)** ⊖	d					00 07	00 07	05 46	06 09	06 24		06 37	06 54	07 07	07 24	07 37	07 54	08 07	08 24	08 37	08 54	09 07	
4½	Kensal Green	d					00 09	00 09	05 48	06 11	06 26		06 39	06 56	07 09	07 26	07 39	07 56	08 09	08 26	08 39	08 56	09 09	
5½	**Willesden Jn Low Level**	d					00 12	00 12	05 51	06 14	06 29		06 42	06 59	07 12	07 29	07 42	07 59	08 12	08 29	08 42	08 59	09 12	and at the same minutes past each hour until
6	Harlesden	d			00 01	00 01	00 14	00 14	05 53	06 16	06 31		06 44	07 01	07 14	07 31	07 44	08 01	08 14	08 31	08 44	09 01	09 14	
7	Stonebridge Park	d			00 04	00 04	00 17	00 17	05 56	06 19	06 34		06 47	07 04	07 17	07 34	07 47	08 04	08 17	08 34	08 47	09 04	09 17	
8	Wembley Central 66	d			00 06	00 06	00 19	00 19	05 58	06 21	06 36		06 49	07 06	07 19	07 36	07 49	08 06	08 19	08 36	08 49	09 06	09 19	
9	North Wembley	d			00 08	00 08	00 21	00 21	06 00	06 23	06 38		06 51	07 08	07 21	07 38	07 51	08 08	08 21	08 38	08 51	09 08	09 21	
9½	South Kenton	d			00 10	00 10	00 23	00 23	06 02	06 25	06 40		06 53	07 10	07 23	07 40	07 53	08 10	08 23	08 40	08 53	09 10	09 23	
10¼	Kenton	d			00 12	00 12	00 25	00 25	06 04	06 27	06 42		06 55	07 12	07 25	07 42	07 55	08 12	08 25	08 42	08 55	09 12	09 25	
11¼	**Harrow & Wealdstone** 66	d			00 15	00 15	00 28	00 28	06 07	06 30	06 45		06 58	07 15	07 28	07 45	07 58	08 15	08 28	08 45	08 58	09 15	09 28	
12½	Headstone Lane	d	00 01	00 02	00 18	00 18	00 31	00 31	06 10	06 33	06 48		07 01	07 18	07 31	07 48	08 01	08 18	08 31	08 48	09 01	09 18	09 31	
13¼	Hatch End	d	00 03	00 03	00 20	00 20	00 33	00 33	06 12	06 35	06 50		07 03	07 20	07 33	07 50	08 03	08 20	08 33	08 50	09 03	09 20	09 33	
14¾	Carpenders Park	d	00 06	00 06	00 23	00 23	00 36	00 36	06 15	06 38	06 53		07 06	07 23	07 36	07 53	08 06	08 23	08 36	08 53	09 06	09 23	09 36	
16	Bushey 66	d	00 09	00 09	00 26	00 26	00 39	00 39	06 18	06 41	06 56		07 09	07 26	07 39	07 56	08 09	08 26	08 39	08 56	09 09	09 26	09 39	
16¾	Watford High Street	d	00 11	00 12	00 28	00 29	00 41	00 41	06 20	06 43	06 58		07 12	07 28	07 41	07 59	08 11	08 29	08 41	08 59	09 11	09 29	09 41	
17¾	**Watford Junction** 66	a	00 19	00 19	00 33	00 36	00 46	00 50	06 25	06 48	07 03		07 16	07 33	07 46	08 03	08 19	08 33	08 49	09 03	09 16	09 33	09 46	

		LO	LO	LO	LO		LO	LO	LO	LO	LO	LO	LO	LO		LO	LO	LO	LO		LO	LO	LO	LO
London Euston 15 ⊖66	d	14 15	14 28	14 45	14 58		15 15	15 28	15 44	15 58	16 14	16 27	16 44	16 57		20 14	20 27	20 44	20 57		21 15	21 28	21 44	21 58
South Hampstead	d	14 20	14 33	14 50	15 03		15 20	15 33	15 49	16 03	16 19	16 32	16 49	17 02		20 19	20 32	20 49	21 02		21 19	21 33	21 49	22 03
Kilburn High Road	d	14 22	14 35	14 52	15 05		15 22	15 35	15 51	16 05	16 21	16 34	16 51	17 04		20 21	20 34	20 51	21 04		21 21	21 35	21 51	22 05
Queen's Park (London) ⊖	d	14 24	14 37	14 54	15 07		15 24	15 37	15 54	16 07	16 24	16 37	16 54	17 07		20 24	20 37	20 54	21 07		21 24	21 37	21 54	22 07
Kensal Green	d	14 26	14 39	14 56	15 09		15 26	15 39	15 56	16 09	16 26	16 39	16 56	17 09		20 26	20 39	20 56	21 09		21 26	21 39	21 56	22 09
Willesden Jn Low Level	d	14 29	14 42	14 59	15 12		15 29	15 42	15 59	16 12	16 29	16 42	16 59	17 12	and at the same minutes past each hour until	20 29	20 42	20 59	21 12		21 29	21 42	21 59	22 12
Harlesden	d	14 31	14 44	15 01	15 14		15 31	15 44	16 01	16 14	16 31	16 44	17 01	17 14		20 31	20 44	21 01	21 14		21 31	21 44	22 01	22 14
Stonebridge Park	d	14 34	14 47	15 04	15 17		15 34	15 47	16 04	16 17	16 33	16 46	17 03	17 16		20 33	20 46	21 03	21 16		21 33	21 47	22 04	22 17
Wembley Central 66	d	14 36	14 49	15 06	15 19		15 36	15 49	16 06	16 19	16 36	16 49	17 06	17 19		20 36	20 49	21 06	21 19		21 36	21 49	22 06	22 19
North Wembley	d	14 38	14 51	15 08	15 21		15 38	15 51	16 08	16 21	16 38	16 51	17 08	17 21		20 38	20 51	21 08	21 21		21 38	21 51	22 08	22 21
South Kenton	d	14 40	14 53	15 10	15 23		15 40	15 53	16 10	16 23	16 40	16 53	17 10	17 23		20 40	20 53	21 10	21 23		21 40	21 53	22 10	22 23
Kenton	d	14 42	14 55	15 12	15 25		15 42	15 55	16 12	16 25	16 42	16 55	17 12	17 25		20 42	20 55	21 12	21 25		21 42	21 55	22 12	22 25
Harrow & Wealdstone 66	d	14 45	14 58	15 15	15 28		15 45	15 58	16 15	16 28	16 45	16 58	17 15	17 28		20 45	20 58	21 15	21 28		21 45	21 58	22 15	22 28
Headstone Lane	d	14 48	15 01	15 18	15 31		15 48	16 01	16 18	16 31	16 48	17 01	17 18	17 31		20 48	21 01	21 18	21 31		21 48	22 01	22 18	22 31
Hatch End	d	14 50	15 03	15 20	15 33		15 50	16 03	16 20	16 33	16 50	17 03	17 20	17 33		20 50	21 03	21 20	21 33		21 50	22 03	22 20	22 33
Carpenders Park	d	14 53	15 06	15 23	15 36		15 53	16 06	16 23	16 36	16 53	17 06	17 23	17 36		20 53	21 06	21 23	21 36		21 53	22 06	22 23	22 36
Bushey 66	d	14 56	15 09	15 26	15 39		15 56	16 09	16 26	16 39	16 56	17 09	17 26	17 39		20 56	21 09	21 26	21 39		21 56	22 09	22 26	22 39
Watford High Street	d	14 59	15 11	15 29	15 41		15 59	16 11	16 29	16 41	16 59	17 12	17 29	17 42		20 59	21 12	21 29	21 42		21 59	22 11	22 29	22 41
Watford Junction 66	a	15 03	15 16	15 33	15 46		16 03	16 16	16 36	16 46	17 06	17 19	17 36	17 49		21 06	21 19	21 36	21 49		22 03	22 16	22 36	22 46

		LO	LO	LO	LO	LO		LO	LO	LO
London Euston 15 ⊖66	d	22 15	22 27	22 45	22 57	23 15		23 27	23 45	23 58
South Hampstead	d	22 20	22 33	22 50	23 02	23 20		23 33	23 50	00 03
Kilburn High Road	d	22 22	22 35	22 52	23 04	23 22		23 35	23 52	00 05
Queen's Park (London) ⊖	d	22 24	22 37	22 54	23 07	23 24		23 37	23 54	00 07
Kensal Green	d	22 26	22 39	22 56	23 09	23 26		23 39	23 56	00 09
Willesden Jn Low Level	d	22 29	22 42	22 59	23 12	23 29		23 42	23 59	00 12
Harlesden	d	22 31	22 44	23 01	23 14	23 31		23 44	00 01	00 14
Stonebridge Park	d	22 34	22 47	23 04	23 17	23 34		23 47	00 04	00 17
Wembley Central 66	d	22 36	22 49	23 06	23 19	23 36		23 49	00 06	00 19
North Wembley	d	22 38	22 51	23 08	23 21	23 38		23 51	00 08	00 21
South Kenton	d	22 40	22 53	23 10	23 23	23 40		23 53	00 10	00 23
Kenton	d	22 42	22 55	23 12	23 25	23 42		23 55	00 12	00 25
Harrow & Wealdstone 66	d	22 45	22 58	23 15	23 28	23 45		23 58	00 15	00 28
Headstone Lane	d	22 48	23 01	23 18	23 31	23 48		00 01	00 18	00 31
Hatch End	d	22 50	23 03	23 20	23 33	23 50		00 03	00 20	00 33
Carpenders Park	d	22 53	23 06	23 23	23 36	23 53		00 06	00 23	00 36
Bushey 66	d	22 56	23 09	23 26	23 39	23 56		00 09	00 26	00 39
Watford High Street	d	22 59	23 11	23 29	23 41	23 59		00 11	00 28	00 41
Watford Junction 66	a	23 03	23 19	23 33	23 49	00 07		00 19	00 33	00 46

Saturdays

21 December to 16 May

		LO	LO	LO	LO	LO	LO	LO	LO	LO	LO	LO		LO	LO	LO	LO		LO	LO	LO	LO	LO	LO
London Euston 15 ⊖66	d				05 31	06 00	06 28	06 45	06 58	07 15	07 28	07 45		14 58	15 15	15 28	15 45		15 58	16 15	16 28	16 45	16 58	17 15
South Hampstead	d			00 03	05 36	06 05	06 33	06 50	07 03	07 20	07 33	07 50		15 03	15 20	15 33	15 50		16 03	16 20	16 33	16 50	17 03	17 20
Kilburn High Road	d			00 05	05 38	06 07	06 35	06 52	07 05	07 22	07 35	07 52		15 05	15 22	15 35	15 52		16 05	16 22	16 35	16 52	17 05	17 22
Queen's Park (London) ⊖	d			00 07	05 40	06 09	06 37	06 54	07 07	07 24	07 37	07 54		15 07	15 24	15 37	15 54		16 07	16 24	16 37	16 54	17 07	17 24
Kensal Green	d			00 09	05 42	06 11	06 39	06 56	07 09	07 26	07 39	07 56		15 09	15 26	15 39	15 56		16 09	16 26	16 39	16 56	17 09	17 26
Willesden Jn Low Level	d			00 12	05 45	06 14	06 42	06 59	07 12	07 29	07 42	07 59	and at the same minutes past each hour until	15 12	15 29	15 42	15 59		16 12	16 29	16 42	16 59	17 12	17 29
Harlesden	d		00 01	00 14	05 47	06 16	06 44	07 01	07 14	07 31	07 44	08 01		15 14	15 31	15 44	16 01		16 14	16 31	16 44	17 01	17 14	17 31
Stonebridge Park	d		00 04	00 17	05 50	06 19	06 47	07 04	07 17	07 34	07 47	08 04		15 17	15 34	15 47	16 04		16 17	16 34	16 47	17 04	17 17	17 34
Wembley Central 66	d		00 06	00 19	05 52	06 21	06 49	07 06	07 19	07 36	07 49	08 06		15 19	15 36	15 49	16 06		16 19	16 36	16 49	17 06	17 19	17 36
North Wembley	d		00 08	00 21	05 54	06 23	06 51	07 08	07 21	07 38	07 51	08 08		15 21	15 38	15 51	16 08		16 21	16 38	16 51	17 08	17 21	17 38
South Kenton	d		00 10	00 23	05 56	06 25	06 53	07 10	07 23	07 40	07 53	08 10		15 23	15 40	15 53	16 10		16 23	16 40	16 53	17 10	17 23	17 40
Kenton	d		00 12	00 25	05 58	06 27	06 55	07 12	07 25	07 42	07 55	08 12		15 25	15 42	15 55	16 12		16 25	16 42	16 56	17 12	17 25	17 42
Harrow & Wealdstone 66	d		00 15	00 28	06 01	06 30	06 58	07 15	07 28	07 45	07 58	08 15		15 28	15 45	15 58	16 15		16 28	16 45	16 57	17 15	17 28	17 45
Headstone Lane	d	00 01	00 18	00 31	06 04	06 33	07 01	07 18	07 31	07 48	08 01	08 18		15 31	15 48	16 01	16 18		16 31	16 48	17 00	17 18	17 31	17 48
Hatch End	d	00 03	00 20	00 33	06 06	06 35	07 03	07 20	07 33	07 50	08 03	08 20		15 33	15 50	16 03	16 20		16 33	16 50	17 02	17 20	17 33	17 50
Carpenders Park	d	00 06	00 23	00 36	06 09	06 38	07 06	07 23	07 36	07 53	08 06	08 23		15 36	15 53	16 06	16 23		16 36	16 53	17 05	17 23	17 36	17 53
Bushey 66	d	00 09	00 26	00 39	06 12	06 41	07 09	07 26	07 39	07 56	08 09	08 26		15 39	15 56	16 09	16 26		16 39	16 56	17 08	17 26	17 39	17 56
Watford High Street	d	00 11	00 28	00 41	06 15	06 44	07 11	07 28	07 41	07 59	08 11	08 29		15 41	15 59	16 11	16 29		16 41	16 59	17 11	17 29	17 41	17 59
Watford Junction 66	a	00 19	00 33	00 46	06 19	06 48	07 16	07 33	07 46	08 03	08 16	08 33		15 46	16 03	16 16	16 33		16 46	17 03	17 16	17 33	17 46	18 03

Stations Queen's Park to Harrow & Wealdstone inclusive are also served by London Underground Bakerloo Line Services

Table T060-F

Saturdays

21 December to 16 May

London, Queen's Park and Harrow & Wealdstone - Watford Junction

Station			LO	LO	LO	LO	LO	LO	LO	LO	LO	LO	LO	LO	LO	LO	LO	LO	LO	LO	LO	LO	LO
London Euston 15	⊖66	d	17 28	17 45	17 58	18 15	18 28	18 45	18 58	19 15	19 28	19 44	19 58	20 15	20 28	20 45	20 56	21 14	21 28	21 45	21 58	22 15	22 27
South Hampstead		d	17 33	17 50	18 03	18 20	18 33	18 50	19 03	19 20	19 33	19 49	20 03	20 20	20 33	20 50	21 02	21 19	21 33	21 50	22 03	22 20	22 32
Kilburn High Road		d	17 35	17 52	18 05	18 22	18 35	18 52	19 05	19 22	19 35	19 51	20 05	20 22	20 35	20 52	21 04	21 21	21 35	21 52	22 05	22 22	22 34
Queen's Park (London)	⊖	d	17 37	17 54	18 07	18 24	18 37	18 54	19 07	19 24	19 37	19 54	20 07	20 24	20 37	20 54	21 07	21 24	21 37	21 54	22 07	22 24	22 37
Kensal Green		d	17 39	17 56	18 09	18 26	18 39	18 56	19 09	19 26	19 39	19 56	20 09	20 26	20 39	20 56	21 09	21 26	21 39	21 56	22 09	22 26	22 39
Willesden Jn Low Level		d	17 42	17 59	18 12	18 29	18 42	18 59	19 12	19 29	19 42	19 59	20 12	20 29	20 42	20 59	21 12	21 29	21 42	21 59	22 12	22 29	22 42
Harlesden		d	17 44	18 01	18 14	18 31	18 44	19 01	19 14	19 31	19 44	20 01	20 14	20 31	20 44	21 01	21 14	21 31	21 44	22 01	22 14	22 31	22 44
Stonebridge Park		d	17 47	18 04	18 17	18 34	18 47	19 04	19 17	19 34	19 47	20 04	20 17	20 34	20 47	21 04	21 17	21 34	21 47	22 04	22 17	22 34	22 47
Wembley Central	66	d	17 49	18 06	18 19	18 36	18 49	19 06	19 19	19 36	19 49	20 06	20 19	20 36	20 49	21 06	21 19	21 36	21 49	22 06	22 19	22 36	22 49
North Wembley		d	17 51	18 08	18 21	18 38	18 51	19 08	19 21	19 38	19 51	20 08	20 21	20 38	20 51	21 08	21 21	21 38	21 51	22 08	22 21	22 38	22 51
South Kenton		d	17 53	18 10	18 23	18 40	18 53	19 10	19 23	19 40	19 53	20 10	20 23	20 40	20 53	21 10	21 23	21 40	21 53	22 10	22 23	22 40	22 53
Kenton		d	17 55	18 12	18 25	18 42	18 55	19 12	19 26	19 42	19 55	20 12	20 25	20 42	20 55	21 12	21 25	21 42	21 55	22 12	22 25	22 42	22 55
Harrow & Wealdstone	66	d	17 58	18 15	18 28	18 45	18 58	19 15	19 28	19 45	19 58	20 15	20 28	20 45	20 58	21 15	21 28	21 45	21 58	22 15	22 28	22 45	22 58
Headstone Lane		d	18 01	18 18	18 31	18 48	19 01	19 18	19 31	19 48	20 01	20 18	20 31	20 48	21 01	21 18	21 31	21 48	22 01	22 18	22 31	22 48	23 01
Hatch End		d	18 03	18 20	18 33	18 50	19 03	19 20	19 33	19 50	20 03	20 20	20 33	20 50	21 03	21 20	21 33	21 50	22 03	22 20	22 33	22 50	23 03
Carpenders Park		d	18 06	18 23	18 36	18 53	19 06	19 23	19 36	19 53	20 06	20 23	20 36	20 53	21 06	21 23	21 36	21 53	22 06	22 23	22 36	22 53	23 06
Bushey	66	d	18 09	18 26	18 39	18 56	19 09	19 26	19 39	19 56	20 09	20 26	20 39	20 56	21 09	21 26	21 39	21 56	22 09	22 26	22 39	22 56	23 09
Watford High Street		d	18 11	18 29	18 41	18 59	19 11	19 29	19 42	19 59	20 11	20 29	20 41	20 59	21 11	21 29	21 41	21 59	22 11	22 29	22 41	22 59	23 11
Watford Junction	66	a	18 16	18 33	18 50	19 07	19 20	19 37	19 50	20 07	20 20	20 36	20 50	21 07	21 20	21 37	21 48	22 06	22 20	22 37	22 50	23 07	23 19

Station			LO	LO	LO	LO	LO	LO
London Euston 15	⊖66	d	22 44	22 57	23 15	23 27	23 45	23 58
South Hampstead		d	22 49	23 02	23 20	23 33	23 50	00 03
Kilburn High Road		d	22 51	23 04	23 22	23 35	23 52	00 05
Queen's Park (London)	⊖	d	22 54	23 07	23 24	23 37	23 54	00 07
Kensal Green		d	22 56	23 09	23 26	23 39	23 56	00 09
Willesden Jn Low Level		d	22 59	23 12	23 29	23 42	23 59	00 12
Harlesden		d	23 01	23 14	23 31	23 44	00 01	00 14
Stonebridge Park		d	23 04	23 17	23 34	23 47	00 04	00 17
Wembley Central	66	d	23 06	23 19	23 36	23 49	00 06	00 19
North Wembley		d	23 08	23 21	23 38	23 51	00 08	00 21
South Kenton		d	23 10	23 23	23 40	23 53	00 10	00 23
Kenton		d	23 12	23 25	23 42	23 55	00 12	00 25
Harrow & Wealdstone	66	d	23 15	23 28	23 45	23 58	00 15	00 28
Headstone Lane		d	23 18	23 31	23 48	00 01	00 18	00 31
Hatch End		d	23 20	23 33	23 50	00 03	00 20	00 33
Carpenders Park		d	23 23	23 36	23 53	00 06	00 23	00 36
Bushey	66	d	23 26	23 39	23 56	00 09	00 26	00 39
Watford High Street		d	23 29	23 41	23 59	00 11	00 28	00 41
Watford Junction	66	a	23 36	23 49	00 07	00 19	00 37	00 50

Sundays

15 December to 10 May

Station			LO A	LO A	LO A	LO	LO	LO	LO	LO	LO	LO	LO	LO	LO	LO	LO	LO	LO	LO	LO	LO
London Euston 15	⊖66	d				06 45	07 15	07 45	08 13	08 44	09 13	09 27	09 43	09 58	10 13	10 28	10 43	10 58	11 13	11 28	11 44	11 58
South Hampstead		d			00 03	06 50	07 20	07 50	08 18	08 49	09 18	09 32	09 48	10 03	10 18	10 33	10 48	11 03	11 18	11 33	11 49	12 03
Kilburn High Road		d			00 05	06 52	07 22	07 52	08 20	08 51	09 20	09 34	09 50	10 05	10 20	10 35	10 50	11 05	11 20	11 35	11 51	12 05
Queen's Park (London)	⊖	d			00 07	06 54	07 24	07 54	08 24	08 54	09 24	09 37	09 54	10 07	10 24	10 37	10 54	11 07	11 24	11 37	11 54	12 07
Kensal Green		d			00 09	06 56	07 26	07 56	08 26	08 56	09 26	09 39	09 56	10 09	10 26	10 39	10 56	11 09	11 26	11 39	11 56	12 09
Willesden Jn Low Level		d			00 12	06 59	07 29	07 59	08 29	08 59	09 29	09 42	09 59	10 12	10 29	10 42	10 59	11 12	11 29	11 42	11 59	12 12
Harlesden		d		00 01	00 14	07 01	07 31	08 01	08 31	09 01	09 31	09 44	10 01	10 14	10 31	10 44	11 01	11 14	11 31	11 44	12 01	12 14
Stonebridge Park		d		00 04	00 17	07 04	07 34	08 04	08 34	09 04	09 34	09 47	10 04	10 17	10 34	10 47	11 04	11 17	11 34	11 47	12 04	12 17
Wembley Central	66	d		00 06	00 19	07 06	07 36	08 06	08 36	09 06	09 36	09 49	10 06	10 19	10 36	10 49	11 06	11 19	11 36	11 49	12 06	12 19
North Wembley		d		00 08	00 21	07 08	07 38	08 08	08 38	09 08	09 38	09 51	10 08	10 21	10 38	10 51	11 08	11 21	11 38	11 51	12 08	12 21
South Kenton		d		00 10	00 23	07 10	07 40	08 10	08 40	09 10	09 40	09 53	10 10	10 23	10 40	10 53	11 10	11 23	11 40	11 53	12 10	12 23
Kenton		d		00 12	00 25	07 12	07 42	08 12	08 42	09 12	09 42	09 55	10 12	10 25	10 42	10 55	11 12	11 25	11 42	11 55	12 12	12 25
Harrow & Wealdstone	66	d		00 15	00 28	07 15	07 45	08 15	08 45	09 15	09 45	09 58	10 15	10 28	10 45	10 58	11 15	11 28	11 45	11 58	12 15	12 28
Headstone Lane		d	00 01	00 18	00 31	07 18	07 48	08 18	08 48	09 18	09 48	10 01	10 18	10 31	10 48	11 01	11 18	11 31	11 48	12 01	12 18	12 31
Hatch End		d	00 03	00 20	00 33	07 20	07 50	08 20	08 50	09 20	09 50	10 03	10 20	10 33	10 50	11 03	11 20	11 33	11 50	12 03	12 20	12 33
Carpenders Park		d	00 06	00 23	00 36	07 23	07 53	08 23	08 53	09 23	09 53	10 06	10 23	10 36	10 53	11 06	11 23	11 36	11 53	12 06	12 23	12 36
Bushey	66	d	00 09	00 26	00 39	07 26	07 56	08 26	08 56	09 26	09 56	10 09	10 26	10 39	10 56	11 09	11 26	11 39	11 56	12 09	12 26	12 39
Watford High Street		d	00 11	00 28	00 41	07 28	07 58	08 28	08 58	09 28	09 58	10 11	10 29	10 41	10 59	11 11	11 29	11 41	11 59	12 11	12 29	12 41
Watford Junction	66	a	00 19	00 37	00 50	07 37	08 07	08 37	09 05	09 36	10 05	10 19	10 35	10 50	11 05	11 20	11 35	11 50	12 05	12 20	12 36	12 50

Station			LO	LO	LO	LO		LO	LO	LO	LO	LO	LO	LO	LO	LO	LO	LO	LO	LO	LO	LO	LO
London Euston 15	⊖66	d	12 15	12 28	12 45	12 58	and at the same minutes past each hour until	19 15	19 28	19 45	19 58	20 15	20 28	20 45	20 57	21 15	21 28	21 45	21 58	22 15	22 28	22 45	22 57
South Hampstead		d	12 20	12 33	12 50	13 03		19 20	19 33	19 50	20 03	20 20	20 33	20 50	21 03	21 20	21 33	21 50	22 03	22 20	22 33	22 50	23 02
Kilburn High Road		d	12 22	12 35	12 52	13 05		19 22	19 35	19 52	20 05	20 22	20 35	20 52	21 05	21 22	21 35	21 52	22 05	22 22	22 35	22 52	23 04
Queen's Park (London)	⊖	d	12 24	12 37	12 54	13 07		19 24	19 37	19 54	20 07	20 24	20 37	20 54	21 07	21 24	21 37	21 54	22 07	22 24	22 37	22 54	23 07
Kensal Green		d	12 26	12 39	12 56	13 09		19 26	19 39	19 56	20 09	20 26	20 39	20 56	21 09	21 26	21 39	21 56	22 09	22 26	22 39	22 56	23 09
Willesden Jn Low Level		d	12 29	12 42	12 59	13 12		19 29	19 42	19 59	20 12	20 29	20 42	20 59	21 12	21 29	21 42	21 59	22 12	22 29	22 42	22 59	23 12
Harlesden		d	12 31	12 44	13 01	13 14		19 31	19 44	20 01	20 14	20 31	20 44	21 01	21 14	21 31	21 44	22 01	22 14	22 31	22 44	23 01	23 14
Stonebridge Park		d	12 34	12 47	13 04	13 17		19 34	19 47	20 04	20 17	20 34	20 47	21 04	21 17	21 34	21 47	22 04	22 17	22 34	22 47	23 04	23 17
Wembley Central	66	d	12 36	12 49	13 06	13 19		19 36	19 49	20 06	20 19	20 36	20 49	21 06	21 19	21 36	21 49	22 06	22 19	22 36	22 49	23 06	23 19
North Wembley		d	12 38	12 51	13 08	13 21		19 38	19 51	20 08	20 21	20 38	20 51	21 08	21 21	21 38	21 51	22 08	22 21	22 38	22 51	23 08	23 21
South Kenton		d	12 40	12 53	13 10	13 23		19 40	19 53	20 10	20 23	20 40	20 53	21 10	21 23	21 40	21 53	22 10	22 23	22 40	22 53	23 10	23 23
Kenton		d	12 42	12 55	13 12	13 25		19 42	19 55	20 12	20 25	20 42	20 55	21 12	21 25	21 42	21 55	22 12	22 25	22 42	22 55	23 12	23 25
Harrow & Wealdstone	66	d	12 45	12 58	13 15	13 28		19 45	19 58	20 15	20 28	20 45	20 58	21 15	21 28	21 45	21 58	22 15	22 28	22 45	22 58	23 15	23 28
Headstone Lane		d	12 48	13 01	13 18	13 31		19 48	20 01	20 18	20 31	20 48	21 01	21 18	21 31	21 48	22 01	22 18	22 31	22 48	23 01	23 18	23 31
Hatch End		d	12 50	13 03	13 20	13 33		19 50	20 03	20 20	20 33	20 50	21 03	21 20	21 33	21 50	22 03	22 20	22 33	22 50	23 03	23 20	23 33
Carpenders Park		d	12 53	13 06	13 23	13 36		19 53	20 06	20 23	20 36	20 53	21 06	21 23	21 36	21 53	22 06	22 23	22 36	22 53	23 06	23 23	23 36
Bushey	66	d	12 56	13 09	13 26	13 39		19 56	20 09	20 26	20 39	20 56	21 09	21 26	21 39	21 56	22 09	22 26	22 39	22 56	23 09	23 26	23 39
Watford High Street		d	12 59	13 11	13 29	13 41		19 59	20 11	20 29	20 41	20 59	21 12	21 29	21 41	21 59	22 11	22 29	22 42	22 59	23 11	23 29	23 42
Watford Junction	66	a	13 03	13 16	13 33	13 46		20 03	20 16	20 33	20 46	21 03	21 16	21 33	21 49	22 03	22 16	22 33	22 46	23 03	23 16	23 33	23 49

A not 15 December

Stations Queen's Park to Harrow & Wealdstone inclusive are also served by London Underground Bakerloo Line Services

Table T060-F

Sundays

15 December to 10 May

London, Queen's Park and Harrow & Wealdstone - Watford Junction

Station			LO	LO	LO	LO
London Euston 15	⊖66	d	23 15	23 27	23 44	23 58
South Hampstead		d	23 20	23 33	23 50	00 03
Kilburn High Road		d	23 22	23 35	23 52	00 05
Queen's Park (London)	⊖	d	23 24	23 37	23 54	00 07
Kensal Green		d	23 26	23 39	23 56	00 09
Willesden Jn Low Level		d	23 29	23 42	23 59	00 12
Harlesden		d	23 31	23 44	00 01	00 14
Stonebridge Park		d	23 34	23 47	00 04	00 17
Wembley Central	66	d	23 36	23 49	00 06	00 19
North Wembley		d	23 38	23 51	00 08	00 21
South Kenton		d	23 40	23 53	00 10	00 23
Kenton		d	23 42	23 55	00 12	00 25
Harrow & Wealdstone	66	d	23 45	23 58	00 15	00 28
Headstone Lane		d	23 48	00 02	00 18	00 31
Hatch End		d	23 50	00 03	00 20	00 33
Carpenders Park		d	23 53	00 06	00 23	00 36
Bushey	66	d	23 56	00 09	00 26	00 39
Watford High Street		d	23 58	00 12	00 29	00 41
Watford Junction	66	a	00 03	00 19	00 36	00 50

Stations Queen's Park to Harrow & Wealdstone inclusive are also served by London Underground Bakerloo Line Services

AVAILABLE FROM MP Middleton Press

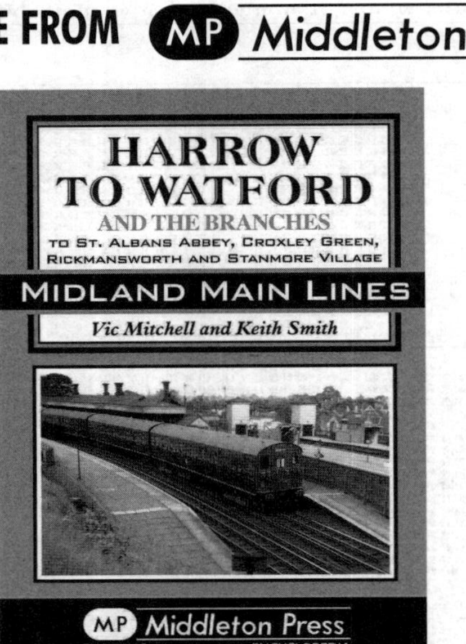

Table T060-R

Watford Junction - Harrow & Wealdstone, Queen's Park and London

Mondays to Fridays
16 December to 15 May

Miles		LO MX	LO MO	LO MX	LO MO	LO	LO	LO	LO	LO	LO	LO	LO	LO	LO	LO	LO	LO	LO	LO	LO
0	**Watford Junction** 66 d					05 13	05 31	05 44	05 59	06 16	06 29	06 46	06 59	07 16	07 29	07 46	07 59	08 16	08 29	08 46	08 59
1	Watford High Street d					05 16	05 34	05 47	06 02	06 19	06 32	06 49	07 02	07 19	07 32	07 49	08 02	08 19	08 32	08 49	09 02
1¾	Bushey 66 d					05 18	05 36	05 49	06 04	06 21	06 34	06 51	07 04	07 21	07 34	07 51	08 04	08 21	08 34	08 51	09 04
3	Carpenders Park d					05 21	05 39	05 52	06 07	06 24	06 37	06 54	07 07	07 24	07 37	07 54	08 07	08 24	08 37	08 54	09 07
4½	Hatch End d					05 24	05 42	05 55	06 10	06 27	06 40	06 57	07 10	07 27	07 40	07 57	08 10	08 27	08 40	08 57	09 10
5¼	Headstone Lane d					05 26	05 44	05 57	06 12	06 29	06 42	06 59	07 12	07 29	07 42	07 59	08 12	08 29	08 42	08 59	09 12
6½	**Harrow & Wealdstone** 66 d					05 29	05 47	06 00	06 16	06 33	06 46	07 03	07 16	07 33	07 46	08 03	08 16	08 33	08 46	09 03	09 16
7½	Kenton d					05 32	05 50	06 03	06 19	06 36	06 49	07 06	07 19	07 36	07 49	08 06	08 19	08 36	08 49	09 06	09 19
8¼	South Kenton d					05 34	05 52	06 05	06 21	06 38	06 51	07 08	07 21	07 38	07 51	08 08	08 21	08 38	08 51	09 08	09 21
8¾	North Wembley d					05 36	05 54	06 07	06 23	06 40	06 53	07 10	07 23	07 40	07 53	08 10	08 23	08 40	08 53	09 10	09 23
9¾	Wembley Central 66 d					05 38	05 56	06 09	06 26	06 43	06 56	07 13	07 26	07 43	07 56	08 13	08 26	08 43	08 56	09 13	09 26
10¾	Stonebridge Park d					05 42	05 59	06 12	06 29	06 46	06 59	07 16	07 29	07 46	07 59	08 16	08 29	08 46	08 59	09 16	09 29
11¾	Harlesden d			00 01	00 02	05 44	06 02	06 15	06 31	06 48	07 01	07 18	07 31	07 48	08 01	08 18	08 31	08 48	09 01	09 18	09 31
12¼	**Willesden Jn Low Level** d			00 03	00 04	05 47	06 04	06 17	06 34	06 51	07 04	07 21	07 34	07 51	08 04	08 21	08 34	08 51	09 04	09 21	09 34
13¼	Kensal Green d			00 06	00 06	05 49	06 07	06 20	06 36	06 53	07 06	07 23	07 36	07 53	08 06	08 23	08 36	08 53	09 06	09 23	09 36
14	**Queen's Park (London)** ⊖ d			00 09	00 09	05 52	06 09	06 22	06 39	06 56	07 09	07 26	07 39	07 56	08 09	08 26	08 39	08 56	09 09	09 26	09 39
14¾	Kilburn High Road d			00 11	00 11	05 54	06 11	06 24	06 41	06 58	07 11	07 28	07 41	07 58	08 11	08 28	08 41	08 58	09 11	09 28	09 41
15¼	South Hampstead d	00 01	00 01	00 13	00 13	05 56	06 13	06 26	06 43	07 00	07 13	07 30	07 43	08 00	08 13	08 30	08 43	09 00	09 13	09 30	09 43
17¾	**London Euston** 15 ⊖66 a	00 09	00 11	00 23	00 24	06 04	06 22	06 35	06 52	07 09	07 22	07 39	07 52	08 09	08 22	08 39	08 52	09 09	09 22	09 39	09 52

	LO	LO	LO	LO		LO	LO	LO	LO	LO	LO	LO	LO	LO	LO	LO	LO	LO	LO	LO
Watford Junction 66 d	09 18	09 31	09 48	10 01	and at the same minutes past each hour until	15 18	15 31	15 48	16 01	16 18	16 31	16 48	17 01	17 18	17 31	17 48	18 01	18 18	18 31	18 48
Watford High Street d	09 21	09 34	09 51	10 04		15 21	15 34	15 51	16 04	16 21	16 34	16 51	17 04	17 21	17 34	17 51	18 04	18 21	18 34	18 51
Bushey 66 d	09 23	09 36	09 53	10 06		15 23	15 36	15 53	16 06	16 23	16 36	16 53	17 06	17 23	17 36	17 53	18 06	18 23	18 36	18 53
Carpenders Park d	09 26	09 39	09 56	10 09		15 26	15 39	15 56	16 09	16 26	16 39	16 56	17 09	17 26	17 39	17 56	18 09	18 26	18 39	18 56
Hatch End d	09 29	09 42	09 59	10 12		15 29	15 42	15 59	16 12	16 29	16 42	16 59	17 12	17 29	17 42	17 59	18 12	18 29	18 42	18 59
Headstone Lane d	09 31	09 44	10 01	10 14		15 31	15 44	16 01	16 14	16 31	16 44	17 01	17 14	17 31	17 44	18 01	18 14	18 31	18 44	19 01
Harrow & Wealdstone 66 d	09 34	09 47	10 04	10 17		15 34	15 47	16 04	16 17	16 34	16 47	17 04	17 17	17 34	17 47	18 04	18 17	18 34	18 47	19 04
Kenton d	09 37	09 50	10 07	10 20		15 37	15 50	16 07	16 20	16 37	16 50	17 07	17 20	17 37	17 50	18 07	18 20	18 37	18 50	19 07
South Kenton d	09 39	09 52	10 09	10 22		15 39	15 52	16 09	16 22	16 39	16 52	17 09	17 22	17 39	17 52	18 09	18 22	18 39	18 52	19 09
North Wembley d	09 41	09 54	10 11	10 24		15 41	15 54	16 11	16 24	16 41	16 54	17 11	17 24	17 41	17 54	18 11	18 24	18 41	18 54	19 11
Wembley Central 66 d	09 43	09 56	10 13	10 26		15 43	15 56	16 13	16 26	16 43	16 56	17 13	17 26	17 43	17 56	18 13	18 26	18 43	18 56	19 13
Stonebridge Park d	09 46	09 59	10 16	10 29		15 46	15 59	16 16	16 29	16 46	16 59	17 16	17 29	17 46	17 59	18 16	18 29	18 46	18 59	19 16
Harlesden d	09 49	10 02	10 19	10 32		15 49	16 02	16 19	16 32	16 49	17 02	17 19	17 32	17 49	18 02	18 19	18 32	18 49	19 02	19 19
Willesden Jn Low Level d	09 51	10 04	10 21	10 34		15 51	16 04	16 21	16 34	16 51	17 04	17 21	17 34	17 51	18 04	18 21	18 34	18 51	19 04	19 21
Kensal Green d	09 54	10 07	10 24	10 37		15 54	16 07	16 24	16 37	16 54	17 07	17 24	17 37	17 54	18 07	18 24	18 37	18 54	19 07	19 24
Queen's Park (London) ⊖ d	09 56	10 09	10 26	10 39		15 56	16 09	16 26	16 39	16 56	17 09	17 26	17 39	17 56	18 09	18 26	18 39	18 56	19 09	19 26
Kilburn High Road d	09 58	10 11	10 28	10 41		15 58	16 11	16 28	16 41	16 58	17 11	17 28	17 41	17 58	18 11	18 28	18 41	18 58	19 11	19 28
South Hampstead d	10 00	10 13	10 30	10 43		16 00	16 13	16 30	16 43	17 00	17 13	17 30	17 43	18 00	18 13	18 30	18 43	19 00	19 13	19 30
London Euston 15 ⊖66 a	10 09	10 22	10 39	10 52		16 09	16 22	16 39	16 52	17 11	17 24	17 41	17 54	18 11	18 24	18 41	18 54	19 09	19 22	19 39

	LO		LO	LO	LO	LO	LO	LO
Watford Junction 66 d	19 01	and at the same minutes past each hour until	22 18	22 31	22 48	23 01	23 18	23 30
Watford High Street d	19 04		22 21	22 34	22 51	23 04	23 22	23 33
Bushey 66 d	19 06		22 23	22 36	22 53	23 06	23 24	23 35
Carpenders Park d	19 09		22 26	22 39	22 56	23 09	23 27	23 38
Hatch End d	19 12		22 29	22 42	22 59	23 12	23 30	23 41
Headstone Lane d	19 14		22 31	22 44	23 01	23 14	23 32	23 43
Harrow & Wealdstone 66 d	19 17		22 34	22 47	23 04	23 17	23 35	23 46
Kenton d	19 20		22 37	22 50	23 07	23 20	23 38	23 49
South Kenton d	19 22		22 39	22 52	23 09	23 22	23 40	23 51
North Wembley d	19 24		22 41	22 54	23 11	23 24	23 42	23 53
Wembley Central 66 d	19 26		22 43	22 56	23 13	23 26	23 44	23 55
Stonebridge Park d	19 29		22 46	22 59	23 16	23 29	23 47	23 58
Harlesden d	19 32		22 49	23 02	23 19	23 32	23 50	00 01
Willesden Jn Low Level d	19 34		22 51	23 04	23 21	23 34	23 52	00 03
Kensal Green d	19 37		22 54	23 07	23 24	23 37	23 54	00 06
Queen's Park (London) ⊖ d	19 39		22 56	23 09	23 26	23 39	23 57	00 09
Kilburn High Road d	19 41		22 58	23 11	23 28	23 41	23 59	00 11
South Hampstead d	19 43		23 00	23 13	23 30	23 43	00 01	00 13
London Euston 15 ⊖66 a	19 52		23 09	23 22	23 39	23 52	00 09	00 23

Saturdays
21 December to 16 May

	LO	LO	LO	LO	LO	LO	LO	LO	LO	LO	LO	LO	LO	LO	LO	LO	LO	LO	LO	LO	LO	
Watford Junction 66 d			05 18	05 48	06 18	06 31	06 48	07 01	07 18	07 31	07 48	08 01	08 18	08 31	08 48	09 01	09 18	09 31	09 48	10 01	10 18	and at the same minutes past each hour until
Watford High Street d			05 21	05 51	06 21	06 34	06 51	07 04	07 21	07 34	07 51	08 04	08 21	08 34	08 51	09 04	09 21	09 34	09 51	10 04	10 21	
Bushey 66 d			05 23	05 53	06 23	06 36	06 53	07 06	07 23	07 36	07 53	08 06	08 23	08 36	08 53	09 06	09 23	09 36	09 53	10 06	10 23	
Carpenders Park d			05 26	05 56	06 26	06 39	06 56	07 09	07 26	07 39	07 56	08 09	08 26	08 39	08 56	09 09	09 26	09 39	09 56	10 09	10 26	
Hatch End d			05 29	05 59	06 29	06 42	06 59	07 12	07 29	07 42	07 59	08 12	08 29	08 42	08 59	09 12	09 29	09 42	09 59	10 12	10 29	
Headstone Lane d			05 31	06 01	06 31	06 44	07 01	07 14	07 31	07 44	08 01	08 14	08 31	08 44	09 01	09 14	09 31	09 44	10 01	10 14	10 31	
Harrow & Wealdstone 66 d			05 34	06 04	06 34	06 47	07 04	07 17	07 34	07 47	08 04	08 17	08 34	08 47	09 04	09 17	09 34	09 47	10 04	10 17	10 34	
Kenton d			05 37	06 07	06 37	06 50	07 07	07 20	07 37	07 50	08 07	08 20	08 37	08 50	09 07	09 20	09 37	09 50	10 07	10 20	10 37	
South Kenton d			05 39	06 09	06 39	06 52	07 09	07 22	07 39	07 52	08 09	08 22	08 39	08 52	09 09	09 22	09 39	09 52	10 09	10 22	10 39	
North Wembley d			05 41	06 11	06 41	06 54	07 11	07 24	07 41	07 54	08 11	08 24	08 41	08 54	09 11	09 24	09 41	09 54	10 11	10 24	10 41	
Wembley Central 66 d			05 43	06 13	06 43	06 56	07 13	07 26	07 43	07 56	08 13	08 26	08 43	08 56	09 13	09 26	09 43	09 56	10 13	10 26	10 43	
Stonebridge Park d			05 46	06 16	06 46	06 59	07 16	07 29	07 46	07 59	08 16	08 29	08 46	08 59	09 16	09 29	09 46	09 59	10 16	10 29	10 46	
Harlesden d		00 01	05 49	06 19	06 49	07 02	07 19	07 32	07 49	08 02	08 19	08 32	08 49	09 02	09 19	09 32	09 49	10 02	10 19	10 32	10 49	
Willesden Jn Low Level d		00 03	05 51	06 21	06 51	07 04	07 21	07 34	07 51	08 04	08 21	08 34	08 51	09 04	09 21	09 34	09 51	10 04	10 21	10 34	10 51	
Kensal Green d		00 06	05 54	06 24	06 54	07 07	07 24	07 37	07 54	08 07	08 24	08 37	08 54	09 07	09 24	09 37	09 54	10 07	10 24	10 37	10 54	
Queen's Park (London) ⊖ d		00 09	05 56	06 26	06 56	07 09	07 26	07 39	07 56	08 09	08 26	08 39	08 56	09 09	09 26	09 39	09 56	10 09	10 26	10 39	10 56	
Kilburn High Road d		00 11	05 58	06 28	06 58	07 11	07 28	07 41	07 58	08 11	08 28	08 41	08 58	09 11	09 28	09 41	09 58	10 11	10 28	10 41	10 58	
South Hampstead d	00 01	00 13	06 00	06 30	07 00	07 13	07 30	07 43	08 00	08 13	08 30	08 43	09 00	09 13	09 30	09 43	10 00	10 13	10 30	10 43	11 00	
London Euston 15 ⊖66 a	00 09	00 23	06 08	06 38	07 08	07 21	07 38	07 51	08 08	08 21	08 38	08 54	09 11	09 24	09 41	09 54	10 11	10 21	10 38	10 51	11 08	

Stations Harrow & Wealdstone to Queen's Park inclusive are also served by London Underground Bakerloo Line Services

Table T060-R

Watford Junction - Harrow & Wealdstone, Queen's Park and London

Saturdays
21 December to 16 May

	LO	LO	LO	LO	LO	LO	LO	LO	LO	LO	LO	LO	LO	LO	LO	LO	LO	LO	LO	LO	LO	LO
Watford Junction 66 d	14 31	14 48	15 01	15 18	15 31	15 48	16 01	16 18	16 31	16 48	17 01	17 18	17 31	17 48	18 01	18 18	18 31	18 48	19 01	19 18	19 31	19 48
Watford High Street d	14 34	14 51	15 04	15 21	15 34	15 51	16 04	16 21	16 34	16 51	17 04	17 21	17 34	17 51	18 04	18 21	18 34	18 51	19 04	19 21	19 34	19 51
Bushey 66 d	14 36	14 53	15 06	15 23	15 36	15 53	16 06	16 23	16 36	16 53	17 06	17 23	17 36	17 53	18 06	18 23	18 36	18 53	19 06	19 23	19 36	19 53
Carpenders Park d	14 39	14 56	15 09	15 26	15 39	15 56	16 09	16 26	16 39	16 56	17 09	17 26	17 39	17 56	18 09	18 26	18 39	18 56	19 09	19 26	19 39	19 56
Hatch End d	14 42	14 59	15 12	15 29	15 42	15 59	16 12	16 29	16 42	16 59	17 12	17 29	17 42	17 59	18 12	18 29	18 42	18 59	19 12	19 29	19 42	19 59
Headstone Lane d	14 44	15 01	15 14	15 31	15 44	16 01	16 14	16 31	16 44	17 01	17 14	17 31	17 44	18 01	18 14	18 31	18 44	19 01	19 14	19 31	19 44	20 01
Harrow & Wealdstone 66 d	14 47	15 04	15 17	15 34	15 47	16 04	16 17	16 34	16 47	17 04	17 17	17 34	17 47	18 04	18 17	18 34	18 47	19 04	19 17	19 34	19 47	20 04
Kenton d	14 50	15 07	15 20	15 37	15 50	16 07	16 20	16 37	16 50	17 07	17 20	17 37	17 50	18 07	18 20	18 37	18 50	19 07	19 20	19 37	19 50	20 07
South Kenton d	14 52	15 09	15 22	15 39	15 52	16 09	16 22	16 39	16 52	17 09	17 22	17 39	17 52	18 09	18 22	18 39	18 52	19 09	19 22	19 39	19 52	20 09
North Wembley d	14 54	15 11	15 24	15 41	15 54	16 11	16 24	16 41	16 54	17 11	17 24	17 41	17 54	18 11	18 24	18 41	18 54	19 11	19 24	19 41	19 54	20 11
Wembley Central 66 d	14 56	15 13	15 26	15 43	15 56	16 13	16 26	16 43	16 56	17 13	17 26	17 43	17 56	18 13	18 26	18 43	18 56	19 13	19 26	19 43	19 56	20 13
Stonebridge Park d	14 59	15 16	15 29	15 46	15 59	16 16	16 29	16 46	16 59	17 16	17 29	17 46	17 59	18 16	18 29	18 46	18 59	19 16	19 29	19 46	19 59	20 16
Harlesden d	15 02	15 19	15 32	15 49	16 02	16 19	16 32	16 49	17 02	17 19	17 32	17 49	18 02	18 19	18 32	18 49	19 02	19 19	19 32	19 49	20 02	20 19
Willesden Jn Low Level d	15 04	15 21	15 34	15 51	16 04	16 21	16 34	16 51	17 04	17 21	17 34	17 51	18 04	18 21	18 34	18 51	19 04	19 21	19 34	19 51	20 04	20 21
Kensal Green d	15 07	15 24	15 37	15 54	16 07	16 24	16 37	16 54	17 07	17 24	17 37	17 54	18 07	18 24	18 37	18 54	19 07	19 24	19 37	19 54	20 07	20 24
Queen's Park (London) ⊖ d	15 09	15 26	15 39	15 56	16 09	16 26	16 39	16 56	17 09	17 26	17 39	17 56	18 09	18 26	18 39	18 56	19 09	19 26	19 39	19 56	20 09	20 26
Kilburn High Road d	15 11	15 28	15 41	15 58	16 11	16 28	16 41	16 58	17 11	17 28	17 41	17 58	18 11	18 28	18 41	18 58	19 11	19 28	19 41	19 58	20 11	20 28
South Hampstead d	15 13	15 30	15 43	16 00	16 13	16 30	16 43	17 00	17 13	17 30	17 43	18 00	18 13	18 30	18 43	19 00	19 13	19 30	19 43	20 00	20 13	20 30
London Euston 15 ⊖66 a	15 21	15 38	15 51	16 08	16 24	16 38	16 51	17 08	17 21	17 38	17 51	18 08	18 21	18 38	18 51	19 08	19 21	19 38	19 51	20 11	20 24	20 41

	LO	LO	LO	LO	LO	LO	LO	LO	LO	LO	LO	LO	LO	LO	LO
Watford Junction 66 d	20 01	20 18	20 31	20 48	21 01	21 18	21 31	21 48	22 01	22 18	22 31	22 48	23 01	23 18	23 31
Watford High Street d	20 04	20 21	20 34	20 51	21 04	21 21	21 34	21 51	22 04	22 21	22 34	22 51	23 04	23 21	23 34
Bushey 66 d	20 06	20 23	20 36	20 53	21 06	21 23	21 36	21 53	22 06	22 23	22 36	22 53	23 06	23 23	23 36
Carpenders Park d	20 09	20 26	20 39	20 56	21 09	21 26	21 39	21 56	22 09	22 26	22 39	22 56	23 09	23 26	23 39
Hatch End d	20 12	20 29	20 42	20 59	21 12	21 29	21 42	21 59	22 12	22 29	22 42	22 59	23 12	23 29	23 42
Headstone Lane d	20 14	20 31	20 44	21 01	21 14	21 31	21 44	22 01	22 14	22 31	22 44	23 01	23 14	23 31	23 44
Harrow & Wealdstone 66 d	20 17	20 34	20 47	21 04	21 17	21 34	21 47	22 04	22 17	22 34	22 47	23 04	23 17	23 34	23 47
Kenton d	20 20	20 37	20 50	21 07	21 20	21 37	21 50	22 07	22 20	22 37	22 50	23 07	23 20	23 37	23 50
South Kenton d	20 22	20 39	20 52	21 09	21 22	21 39	21 52	22 09	22 22	22 39	22 52	23 09	23 22	23 39	23 52
North Wembley d	20 24	20 41	20 54	21 11	21 24	21 41	21 54	22 11	22 24	22 41	22 54	23 11	23 24	23 41	23 54
Wembley Central 66 d	20 26	20 43	20 56	21 13	21 26	21 43	21 56	22 13	22 26	22 43	22 56	23 13	23 26	23 43	23 56
Stonebridge Park d	20 29	20 46	20 59	21 16	21 29	21 46	21 59	22 16	22 29	22 46	22 59	23 16	23 29	23 46	23 59
Harlesden d	20 32	20 49	21 02	21 19	21 32	21 49	22 02	22 19	22 32	22 49	23 02	23 19	23 32	23 49	00 02
Willesden Jn Low Level d	20 34	20 51	21 04	21 21	21 34	21 51	22 04	22 21	22 34	22 51	23 04	23 22	23 34	23 51	00 04
Kensal Green d	20 37	20 54	21 07	21 24	21 37	21 54	22 07	22 24	22 37	22 54	23 07	23 24	23 37	23 54	00 07
Queen's Park (London) ⊖ d	20 39	20 56	21 09	21 26	21 39	21 56	22 09	22 26	22 39	22 56	23 09	23 27	23 39	23 56	00 09
Kilburn High Road d	20 41	20 58	21 11	21 28	21 41	21 58	22 11	22 28	22 41	22 58	23 11	23 29	23 41	23 58	00 11
South Hampstead d	20 43	21 00	21 13	21 30	21 43	22 00	22 13	22 30	22 43	23 00	23 13	23 31	23 43	00 01	00 13
London Euston 15 ⊖66 a	20 54	21 11	21 24	21 41	21 54	22 11	22 24	22 41	22 54	23 11	23 24	23 41	23 54	00 11	00 24

Sundays
15 December to 10 May

	LO A	LO A	LO	LO	LO	LO	LO	LO	LO	LO	LO	LO	LO	LO	LO	LO	LO	LO	LO	LO	LO	
Watford Junction 66 d			06 48	07 18	07 48	08 18	08 48	09 18	09 31	09 48	10 01	10 18	10 31	10 48	11 02	11 18	11 31	11 48	12 02	12 18	12 32	and at the same minutes past each hour until
Watford High Street d			06 51	07 21	07 51	08 21	08 51	09 21	09 34	09 51	10 04	10 21	10 34	10 51	11 05	11 21	11 34	11 51	12 05	12 21	12 35	
Bushey 66 d			06 53	07 23	07 53	08 23	08 53	09 23	09 36	09 53	10 06	10 23	10 36	10 53	11 07	11 23	11 36	11 53	12 07	12 23	12 37	
Carpenders Park d			06 56	07 26	07 56	08 26	08 56	09 26	09 39	09 56	10 09	10 26	10 39	10 56	11 10	11 26	11 39	11 56	12 10	12 26	12 40	
Hatch End d			06 59	07 29	07 59	08 29	08 59	09 29	09 42	09 59	10 12	10 29	10 42	10 59	11 13	11 29	11 42	11 59	12 13	12 29	12 43	
Headstone Lane d			07 01	07 31	08 01	08 31	09 01	09 31	09 44	10 01	10 14	10 31	10 44	11 01	11 15	11 31	11 44	12 01	12 15	12 31	12 45	
Harrow & Wealdstone 66 d			07 04	07 34	08 04	08 34	09 04	09 34	09 47	10 04	10 17	10 34	10 47	11 04	11 18	11 34	11 47	12 04	12 18	12 34	12 48	
Kenton d			07 07	07 37	08 07	08 37	09 07	09 37	09 50	10 07	10 20	10 37	10 50	11 07	11 21	11 37	11 50	12 07	12 21	12 37	12 51	
South Kenton d			07 09	07 39	08 09	08 39	09 09	09 39	09 52	10 09	10 22	10 39	10 52	11 09	11 23	11 39	11 52	12 09	12 23	12 39	12 53	
North Wembley d			07 11	07 41	08 11	08 41	09 11	09 41	09 54	10 11	10 24	10 41	10 54	11 11	11 25	11 41	11 54	12 11	12 25	12 41	12 55	
Wembley Central 66 d			07 13	07 43	08 13	08 43	09 13	09 43	09 56	10 13	10 26	10 43	10 56	11 13	11 27	11 43	11 56	12 13	12 27	12 43	12 57	
Stonebridge Park d			07 16	07 46	08 16	08 46	09 16	09 46	09 59	10 16	10 29	10 46	10 59	11 16	11 30	11 46	11 59	12 16	12 30	12 46	13 00	
Harlesden d		00 02	07 19	07 49	08 19	08 49	09 19	09 49	10 02	10 19	10 32	10 49	11 02	11 19	11 33	11 49	12 02	12 19	12 33	12 49	13 03	
Willesden Jn Low Level d		00 04	07 21	07 51	08 21	08 51	09 21	09 51	10 04	10 21	10 34	10 51	11 04	11 21	11 35	11 51	12 04	12 21	12 35	12 51	13 05	
Kensal Green d		00 07	07 24	07 54	08 24	08 54	09 24	09 54	10 07	10 24	10 37	10 54	11 07	11 24	11 38	11 54	12 07	12 24	12 38	12 54	13 08	
Queen's Park (London) ⊖ d		00 09	07 26	07 56	08 26	08 56	09 26	09 56	10 09	10 26	10 39	10 56	11 09	11 26	11 40	11 56	12 09	12 26	12 40	12 56	13 10	
Kilburn High Road d		00 11	07 28	07 58	08 28	08 58	09 28	09 58	10 11	10 28	10 41	10 58	11 11	11 28	11 42	11 58	12 11	12 28	12 42	12 58	13 12	
South Hampstead d	00 01	00 13	07 30	08 00	08 30	09 00	09 30	10 00	10 13	10 30	10 43	11 00	11 13	11 30	11 44	12 00	12 13	12 30	12 44	13 00	13 14	
London Euston 15 ⊖66 a	00 11	00 24	07 41	08 11	08 41	09 11	09 41	10 11	10 24	10 41	10 54	11 11	11 24	11 41	11 55	12 11	12 21	12 38	12 52	13 08	13 22	

	LO	LO	LO	LO	LO	LO	LO	LO	LO	LO	LO	LO	LO	LO	LO	LO	LO	LO	LO	LO	LO	LO	LO	LO
Watford Junction 66 d	17 48	18 02	18 18	18 32	18 48	19 02	19 18	19 31	19 48	20 01	20 18	20 31	20 48	21 01	21 18	21 31	21 48	22 01	22 18	22 31	22 48	23 01	23 18	23 31
Watford High Street d	17 51	18 05	18 21	18 35	18 51	19 05	19 21	19 34	19 51	20 04	20 21	20 34	20 51	21 04	21 21	21 34	21 51	22 04	22 21	22 34	22 51	23 04	23 21	23 34
Bushey 66 d	17 53	18 07	18 23	18 37	18 53	19 07	19 23	19 36	19 53	20 06	20 23	20 36	20 53	21 06	21 23	21 36	21 53	22 06	22 23	22 36	22 53	23 06	23 23	23 36
Carpenders Park d	17 56	18 10	18 26	18 40	18 56	19 10	19 26	19 39	19 56	20 09	20 26	20 39	20 56	21 09	21 26	21 39	21 56	22 09	22 26	22 39	22 56	23 09	23 26	23 39
Hatch End d	17 59	18 13	18 29	18 43	18 59	19 13	19 29	19 42	19 59	20 12	20 29	20 42	20 59	21 12	21 29	21 42	21 59	22 12	22 29	22 42	22 59	23 12	23 29	23 42
Headstone Lane d	18 01	18 15	18 31	18 45	19 01	19 15	19 31	19 44	20 01	20 14	20 31	20 44	21 01	21 14	21 31	21 44	22 01	22 14	22 31	22 44	23 01	23 14	23 31	23 44
Harrow & Wealdstone 66 d	18 04	18 18	18 34	18 48	19 04	19 18	19 34	19 47	20 04	20 17	20 34	20 47	21 04	21 17	21 34	21 47	22 04	22 17	22 34	22 47	23 04	23 17	23 34	23 47
Kenton d	18 07	18 21	18 37	18 51	19 07	19 21	19 37	19 50	20 07	20 20	20 37	20 50	21 07	21 20	21 37	21 50	22 07	22 20	22 37	22 50	23 07	23 20	23 37	23 50
South Kenton d	18 09	18 23	18 39	18 53	19 09	19 23	19 39	19 52	20 09	20 22	20 39	20 52	21 09	21 22	21 39	21 52	22 09	22 22	22 39	22 52	23 09	23 22	23 39	23 52
North Wembley d	18 11	18 25	18 41	18 55	19 11	19 25	19 41	19 54	20 11	20 24	20 41	20 54	21 11	21 24	21 41	21 54	22 11	22 24	22 41	22 54	23 11	23 24	23 41	23 54
Wembley Central 66 d	18 13	18 27	18 43	18 57	19 13	19 27	19 43	19 56	20 13	20 26	20 43	20 56	21 13	21 26	21 43	21 56	22 13	22 26	22 43	22 56	23 13	23 26	23 43	23 56
Stonebridge Park d	18 16	18 30	18 46	19 00	19 16	19 30	19 46	19 59	20 16	20 29	20 46	20 59	21 16	21 29	21 46	21 59	22 16	22 29	22 46	22 59	23 16	23 29	23 46	23 59
Harlesden d	18 19	18 33	18 49	19 03	19 19	19 33	19 49	20 02	20 19	20 32	20 49	21 02	21 19	21 32	21 49	22 02	22 19	22 32	22 49	23 02	23 18	23 32	23 49	00 02
Willesden Jn Low Level d	18 21	18 35	18 51	19 05	19 21	19 35	19 51	20 04	20 21	20 34	20 51	21 04	21 21	21 34	21 51	22 04	22 21	22 34	22 51	23 04	23 20	23 34	23 51	00 04
Kensal Green d	18 24	18 38	18 54	19 08	19 24	19 38	19 54	20 07	20 24	20 37	20 54	21 07	21 24	21 37	21 54	22 07	22 24	22 37	22 54	23 07	23 23	23 37	23 54	00 06
Queen's Park (London) ⊖ d	18 26	18 40	18 56	19 10	19 26	19 40	19 56	20 09	20 26	20 39	20 56	21 09	21 26	21 39	21 56	22 09	22 26	22 39	22 56	23 09	23 26	23 39	23 56	00 09
Kilburn High Road d	18 28	18 42	18 58	19 12	19 28	19 42	19 58	20 11	20 28	20 41	20 58	21 11	21 28	21 41	21 58	22 11	22 28	22 41	22 58	23 11	23 28	23 41	23 58	00 11
South Hampstead d	18 30	18 44	19 00	19 14	19 30	19 44	20 00	20 13	20 30	20 43	21 00	21 13	21 30	21 43	22 00	22 13	22 30	22 43	23 00	23 13	23 30	23 43	00 01	00 13
London Euston 15 ⊖66 a	18 38	18 52	19 08	19 22	19 38	19 52	20 08	20 24	20 38	20 51	21 08	21 24	21 38	21 51	22 08	22 24	22 38	22 51	23 08	23 24	23 38	23 54	00 11	00 24

A not 15 December

Stations Harrow & Wealdstone to Queen's Park inclusive are also served by London Underground Bakerloo Line Services

Table T061-F

Mondays to Fridays

16 December to 15 May

Watford Junction - St. Albans Abbey

Miles			LM 1	LM 1	LM 1	LM 1	LM 1	LM 1	LM 1	LM 1	LM 1		LM 1	LM 1	LM 1	LM 1	LM 1	LM 1	LM 1	LM 1	LM 1		LM 1	LM 1	LM 1
0	**Watford Junction**	d	05 54	06 38	07 21	08 04	08 54	09 39	10 24	11 09	11 54		12 46	13 33	14 16	15 01	15 46	16 33	17 24	18 11	18 56		19 39	20 33	21 33
0¾	Watford North	d	05 56	06 40	07 23	08 06	08 56	09 41	10 26	11 11	11 56		12 48	13 35	14 18	15 03	15 48	16 35	17 26	18 13	18 58		19 41	20 35	21 35
1¾	Garston (Hertfordshire)	d	05 59	06 43	07 26	08 09	08 59	09 44	10 29	11 14	11 59		12 51	13 38	14 21	15 06	15 51	16 38	17 29	18 16	19 01		19 44	20 38	21 38
3¼	Bricket Wood	d	06 02	06 46	07 29	08 12	09 02	09 47	10 32	11 17	12 02		12 54	13 41	14 24	15 09	15 54	16 41	17 32	18 19	19 04		19 47	20 41	21 41
4½	How Wood	d	06 04	06 48	07 31	08 14	09 04	09 49	10 34	11 19	12 04		12 56	13 43	14 26	15 11	15 56	16 43	17 34	18 21	19 06		19 49	20 43	21 43
5	Park Street	d	06 06	06 50	07 33	08 16	09 06	09 51	10 36	11 21	12 06		12 58	13 45	14 28	15 13	15 58	16 45	17 36	18 23	19 08		19 51	20 45	21 45
6½	**St Albans Abbey**	a	06 10	06 54	07 37	08 20	09 10	09 55	10 40	11 25	12 10		13 02	13 49	14 32	15 17	16 02	16 49	17 40	18 27	19 12		19 55	20 49	21 49

		LM 1
Watford Junction	d	22 21
Watford North	d	22 23
Garston (Hertfordshire)	d	22 26
Bricket Wood	d	22 29
How Wood	d	22 31
Park Street	d	22 33
St Albans Abbey	a	22 37

Saturdays

21 December to 16 May

		LM 1	LM 1	LM 1	LM 1	LM 1	LM 1	LM 1	LM 1	LM 1		LM 1	LM 1	LM 1	LM 1	LM 1	LM 1	LM 1	LM 1	LM 1		LM 1	LM 1	LM 1	LM 1
Watford Junction	d	06 01	06 45	07 33	08 16	09 01	09 46	10 31	11 14	11 56		12 46	13 48	14 33	15 16	15 58	16 46	17 33	18 16	18 59		19 46	20 33	21 33	22 21
Watford North	d	06 03	06 47	07 35	08 18	09 03	09 48	10 33	11 16	11 58		12 48	13 50	14 35	15 18	16 00	16 48	17 35	18 18	19 01		19 48	20 35	21 35	22 23
Garston (Hertfordshire)	d	06 06	06 50	07 38	08 21	09 06	09 51	10 36	11 19	12 01		12 51	13 53	14 38	15 21	16 03	16 51	17 38	18 21	19 04		19 51	20 38	21 38	22 26
Bricket Wood	d	06 09	06 53	07 41	08 24	09 09	09 54	10 39	11 22	12 04		12 54	13 56	14 41	15 24	16 06	16 54	17 41	18 24	19 07		19 54	20 41	21 41	22 29
How Wood	d	06 11	06 55	07 43	08 26	09 11	09 56	10 41	11 24	12 06		12 56	13 58	14 43	15 26	16 08	16 56	17 43	18 26	19 09		19 56	20 43	21 43	22 31
Park Street	d	06 13	06 57	07 45	08 28	09 13	09 58	10 43	11 26	12 08		12 58	14 00	14 45	15 28	16 10	16 58	17 45	18 28	19 11		19 58	20 45	21 45	22 33
St Albans Abbey	a	06 17	07 01	07 49	08 32	09 17	10 02	10 47	11 30	12 12		13 02	14 04	14 49	15 32	16 14	17 02	17 49	18 32	19 15		20 02	20 49	21 49	22 37

Sundays

15 December to 10 May

		LM 1	LM 1	LM 1	LM 1	LM 1		LM 1	LM 1
Watford Junction	d	08 07	09 07	10 20	11 20	12 07	and	22 07	23 04
Watford North	d	08 09	09 09	10 22	11 22	12 09	hourly	22 09	23 06
Garston (Hertfordshire)	d	08 12	09 12	10 25	11 25	12 12	until	22 12	23 09
Bricket Wood	d	08 15	09 15	10 28	11 28	12 15		22 15	23 12
How Wood	d	08 17	09 17	10 30	11 30	12 17		22 17	23 14
Park Street	d	08 19	09 19	10 32	11 32	12 19		22 19	23 16
St Albans Abbey	a	08 23	09 23	10 36	11 36	12 23		22 23	23 20

For connections from London Euston refer to Table T66

NRT DECEMBER 19 EDITION

Table T061-R

Mondays to Fridays

16 December to 15 May

St. Albans Abbey- Watford Junction

Miles			LM 1	LM 1	LM 1	LM 1	LM 1	LM 1		LM 1	LM 1	LM 1	LM 1	LM 1	LM 1	LM 1	LM 1	LM 1		LM 1	LM 1	LM 1	LM 1	LM 1	LM 1
0	**St Albans Abbey**	d	06 14	06 58	07 42	08 25	09 15	10 00		10 45	11 30	12 15	13 07	13 54	14 37	15 22	16 07	16 54		17 45	18 32	19 17	20 00	20 54	21 54
1½	Park Street	d	06 17	07 01	07 45	08 28	09 18	10 03		10 48	11 33	12 18	13 10	13 57	14 40	15 25	16 10	16 57		17 48	18 35	19 20	20 03	20 57	21 57
2¼	How Wood	d	06 19	07 03	07 47	08 30	09 20	10 05		10 50	11 35	12 20	13 12	13 59	14 42	15 27	16 12	16 59		17 50	18 37	19 22	20 05	20 59	21 59
3	Bricket Wood	d	06 22	07 06	07 50	08 33	09 23	10 08		10 53	11 38	12 23	13 15	14 02	14 45	15 30	16 15	17 02		17 53	18 40	19 25	20 08	21 02	22 02
4¾	Garston (Hertfordshire)	d	06 25	07 09	07 53	08 36	09 26	10 11		10 56	11 41	12 26	13 18	14 05	14 48	15 33	16 18	17 05		17 56	18 43	19 28	20 11	21 05	22 05
5½	Watford North	d	06 27	07 11	07 55	08 38	09 28	10 13		10 58	11 43	12 28	13 20	14 07	14 50	15 35	16 20	17 07		17 58	18 45	19 30	20 13	21 07	22 07
6½	**Watford Junction**	a	06 29	07 14	07 58	08 41	09 31	10 16		11 01	11 46	12 31	13 23	14 10	14 53	15 38	16 23	17 10		18 01	18 48	19 33	20 16	21 10	22 10

		LM 1
St Albans Abbey	d	22 44
Park Street	d	22 47
How Wood	d	22 49
Bricket Wood	d	22 52
Garston (Hertfordshire)	d	22 55
Watford North	d	22 57
Watford Junction	a	23 00

Saturdays

21 December to 16 May

		LM 1	LM 1	LM 1	LM 1	LM 1	LM 1	LM 1	LM 1	LM 1		LM 1	LM 1	LM 1	LM 1	LM 1	LM 1	LM 1	LM 1	LM 1		LM 1	LM 1	LM 1	LM 1
St Albans Abbey	d	06 22	07 06	07 54	08 37	09 22	10 07	10 52	11 35	12 17		13 07	14 09	14 54	15 37	16 19	17 07	17 54	18 37	19 20		20 07	20 54	21 54	22 42
Park Street	d	06 25	07 09	07 57	08 40	09 25	10 10	10 55	11 38	12 20		13 10	14 12	14 57	15 40	16 22	17 10	17 57	18 40	19 23		20 10	20 57	21 57	22 45
How Wood	d	06 27	07 11	07 59	08 42	09 27	10 12	10 57	11 40	12 22		13 12	14 14	14 59	15 42	16 24	17 12	17 59	18 42	19 25		20 12	20 59	21 59	22 47
Bricket Wood	d	06 30	07 14	08 02	08 45	09 30	10 15	11 00	11 43	12 25		13 15	14 17	15 02	15 45	16 27	17 15	18 02	18 45	19 28		20 15	21 02	22 02	22 50
Garston (Hertfordshire)	d	06 33	07 17	08 05	08 48	09 33	10 18	11 03	11 46	12 28		13 18	14 20	15 05	15 48	16 30	17 18	18 05	18 48	19 31		20 18	21 05	22 05	22 53
Watford North	d	06 35	07 19	08 07	08 50	09 35	10 20	11 05	11 48	12 30		13 20	14 22	15 07	15 50	16 32	17 20	18 07	18 50	19 33		20 20	21 07	22 07	22 55
Watford Junction	a	06 38	07 22	08 10	08 53	09 38	10 23	11 08	11 51	12 33		13 23	14 25	15 10	15 53	16 35	17 23	18 10	18 53	19 36		20 23	21 10	22 10	22 58

Sundays

15 December to 10 May

		LM 1	LM 1	LM 1	LM 1	LM 1		LM 1	LM 1
St Albans Abbey	d	08 28	09 28	10 42	11 42	12 28	and	22 28	23 26
Park Street	d	08 31	09 31	10 45	11 45	12 31	hourly	22 31	23 29
How Wood	d	08 33	09 33	10 47	11 47	12 33	until	22 33	23 31
Bricket Wood	d	08 36	09 36	10 50	11 50	12 36		22 36	23 34
Garston (Hertfordshire)	d	08 39	09 39	10 53	11 53	12 39		22 39	23 37
Watford North	d	08 41	09 41	10 55	11 55	12 41		22 41	23 39
Watford Junction	a	08 44	09 44	10 58	11 58	12 44		22 44	23 42

For connections to London Euston refer to Table T66

Table T062-F

Mondays to Fridays

16 December to 15 May

Gospel Oak - Barking

Miles			LO MX A	LO	LO	LO	LO		LO	LO	LO	LO	LO	LO	LO	LO	LO	LO	LO	LO	LO	LO
0	**Gospel Oak**	d		06 20	06 35	06 50	07 05	and at the same minutes past each hour until	09 20	09 35	09 50	10 05	10 20	10 34	10 50	11 05	11 20	11 36	11 50	12 05	12 20	12 38
1¼	Upper Holloway	d		06 24	06 39	06 54	07 09		09 24	09 39	09 54	10 09	10 24	10 37	10 54	11 09	11 24	11 39	11 54	12 09	12 24	12 41
2	Crouch Hill	d		06 26	06 41	06 56	07 11		09 26	09 41	09 56	10 11	10 26	10 40	10 56	11 11	11 26	11 41	11 56	12 11	12 26	12 43
3	Harringay Green Lanes	d		06 29	06 44	06 59	07 14		09 29	09 44	09 59	10 14	10 29	10 43	10 59	11 14	11 29	11 44	11 59	12 14	12 29	12 46
4	South Tottenham	d		06 33	06 48	07 03	07 18		09 33	09 48	10 03	10 18	10 33	10 48	11 03	11 18	11 33	11 48	12 03	12 18	12 33	12 50
5½	Blackhorse Road ⊖	d		06 37	06 52	07 07	07 22		09 37	09 52	10 07	10 22	10 37	10 52	11 07	11 22	11 37	11 52	12 07	12 22	12 37	12 54
6¼	Walthamstow Queen's Road	d	00 01	06 39	06 54	07 09	07 24		09 39	09 54	10 09	10 24	10 39	10 54	11 09	11 24	11 39	11 54	12 09	12 24	12 39	12 56
7½	Leyton Midland Road	d	00 02	06 42	06 57	07 12	07 27		09 42	09 57	10 12	10 27	10 42	10 57	11 12	11 27	11 42	11 57	12 12	12 27	12 42	12 59
8¼	Leytonstone High Road	d	00 04	06 44	06 59	07 14	07 29		09 44	09 59	10 14	10 29	10 44	10 59	11 14	11 29	11 44	11 59	12 14	12 29	12 44	13 01
9¼	Wanstead Park	d	00 07	06 46	07 01	07 16	07 31		09 46	10 01	10 16	10 31	10 46	11 01	11 16	11 31	11 46	12 01	12 16	12 31	12 46	13 03
10¼	Woodgrange Park	d	00 09	06 49	07 04	07 19	07 34		09 49	10 04	10 19	10 34	10 49	11 04	11 19	11 34	11 49	12 04	12 19	12 34	12 49	13 06
12	**Barking** ⊖	a	00 16	06 54	07 09	07 24	07 39		09 54	10 09	10 24	10 39	10 54	11 11	11 24	11 39	11 54	12 10	12 24	12 39	12 54	13 12

		LO	LO	LO	LO	LO	LO	LO	LO	LO	LO	LO	LO	LO	LO	LO	LO	LO	LO	LO	LO	LO	LO
Gospel Oak	d	12 50	13 05	13 20	13 35	13 50	14 05	14 20	14 35	14 50	15 05	15 20	15 35	15 50	16 05	16 20	16 35	16 50	17 05	17 20	17 35	17 50	18 05
Upper Holloway	d	12 54	13 09	13 24	13 39	13 54	14 09	14 24	14 39	14 54	15 09	15 24	15 39	15 54	16 09	16 24	16 39	16 54	17 09	17 24	17 39	17 54	18 09
Crouch Hill	d	12 56	13 11	13 26	13 41	13 56	14 11	14 26	14 41	14 56	15 11	15 26	15 41	15 56	16 11	16 26	16 41	16 56	17 11	17 26	17 41	17 56	18 11
Harringay Green Lanes	d	12 59	13 14	13 29	13 44	13 59	14 14	14 29	14 44	14 59	15 14	15 29	15 44	15 59	16 14	16 29	16 44	16 59	17 14	17 29	17 44	17 59	18 14
South Tottenham	d	13 03	13 18	13 33	13 48	14 03	14 18	14 33	14 48	15 03	15 18	15 33	15 48	16 03	16 18	16 33	16 48	17 03	17 18	17 33	17 48	18 03	18 18
Blackhorse Road ⊖	d	13 07	13 22	13 37	13 52	14 07	14 22	14 37	14 52	15 07	15 22	15 37	15 52	16 07	16 22	16 37	16 52	17 07	17 22	17 37	17 52	18 07	18 22
Walthamstow Queen's Road	d	13 09	13 24	13 39	13 54	14 09	14 24	14 39	14 54	15 09	15 24	15 39	15 54	16 09	16 24	16 39	16 54	17 09	17 24	17 39	17 54	18 09	18 24
Leyton Midland Road	d	13 12	13 27	13 42	13 57	14 12	14 27	14 42	14 57	15 12	15 27	15 42	15 57	16 12	16 27	16 42	16 57	17 12	17 27	17 42	17 57	18 12	18 27
Leytonstone High Road	d	13 14	13 29	13 44	13 59	14 14	14 29	14 44	14 59	15 14	15 29	15 44	15 59	16 14	16 29	16 44	16 59	17 14	17 29	17 44	17 59	18 14	18 29
Wanstead Park	d	13 16	13 31	13 46	14 01	14 16	14 31	14 46	15 01	15 16	15 31	15 46	16 01	16 16	16 31	16 46	17 01	17 16	17 31	17 46	18 01	18 16	18 31
Woodgrange Park	d	13 19	13 34	13 49	14 04	14 19	14 34	14 49	15 04	15 19	15 34	15 49	16 04	16 19	16 34	16 49	17 04	17 19	17 34	17 49	18 04	18 19	18 34
Barking ⊖	a	13 24	13 39	13 54	14 09	14 24	14 39	14 54	15 09	15 24	15 39	15 54	16 09	16 24	16 42	16 57	17 12	17 27	17 42	17 57	18 12	18 27	18 42

		LO	LO	LO	LO	LO	LO	LO	LO	LO	LO	LO	LO	LO	LO	LO	LO	LO	LO	LO	LO	LO
Gospel Oak	d	18 20	18 35	18 50	19 05	19 18	19 35	19 50	20 05	20 20	20 38	20 50	21 05	21 20	21 35	21 51	22 06	22 22	22 48	23 05	23 25	23 42
Upper Holloway	d	18 24	18 39	18 54	19 09	19 23	19 39	19 54	20 09	20 24	20 39	20 54	21 09	21 24	21 39	21 54	22 09	22 26	22 51	23 09	23 29	23 45
Crouch Hill	d	18 26	18 41	18 56	19 11	19 26	19 41	19 56	20 11	20 26	20 41	20 56	21 11	21 26	21 41	21 56	22 11	22 28	22 54	23 11	23 31	23 48
Harringay Green Lanes	d	18 29	18 44	18 59	19 14	19 29	19 44	19 59	20 14	20 29	20 44	20 59	21 14	21 29	21 44	21 59	22 14	22 31	22 57	23 14	23 34	23 51
South Tottenham	d	18 33	18 48	19 03	19 18	19 33	19 48	20 03	20 18	20 33	20 48	21 03	21 18	21 33	21 48	22 03	22 18	22 36	23 00	23 18	23 38	23 54
Blackhorse Road ⊖	d	18 37	18 52	19 07	19 22	19 37	19 52	20 07	20 22	20 37	20 52	21 07	21 22	21 37	21 52	22 07	22 22	22 39	23 04	23 22	23 42	23 58
Walthamstow Queen's Road	d	18 39	18 54	19 09	19 24	19 39	19 54	20 09	20 24	20 39	20 54	21 09	21 24	21 39	21 54	22 09	22 24	22 41	23 06	23 24	23 44	00 01
Leyton Midland Road	d	18 42	18 57	19 12	19 27	19 42	19 57	20 12	20 27	20 42	20 57	21 12	21 27	21 42	21 57	22 12	22 27	22 45	23 08	23 27	23 47	00 02
Leytonstone High Road	d	18 44	18 59	19 14	19 29	19 44	19 59	20 14	20 29	20 44	20 59	21 14	21 29	21 44	21 59	22 14	22 29	22 47	23 10	23 29	23 49	00 04
Wanstead Park	d	18 46	19 01	19 16	19 31	19 46	20 01	20 16	20 31	20 46	21 01	21 16	21 31	21 46	22 01	22 16	22 31	22 49	23 13	23 31	23 51	00 07
Woodgrange Park	d	18 49	19 04	19 19	19 34	19 49	20 04	20 19	20 34	20 49	21 04	21 19	21 34	21 49	22 04	22 19	22 34	22 53	23 15	23 34	23 54	00 09
Barking ⊖	a	18 57	19 09	19 24	19 42	19 55	20 09	20 27	20 39	20 54	21 11	21 27	21 39	21 54	22 12	22 28	22 43	22 59	23 22	23 39	23 59	00 16

Saturdays

21 December to 16 May

		LO A	LO	LO	LO	LO		LO	LO	LO	LO	LO	LO	LO	LO	LO	LO	LO	LO	LO	LO	LO
Gospel Oak	d		06 20	06 35	06 50	07 05	and at the same minutes past each hour until	11 20	11 35	11 50	12 05	12 20	12 35	12 50	13 05	13 20	13 35	13 50	14 05	14 20	14 35	14 50
Upper Holloway	d		06 24	06 39	06 54	07 09		11 24	11 39	11 54	12 09	12 24	12 39	12 54	13 09	13 24	13 39	13 54	14 09	14 24	14 39	14 54
Crouch Hill	d		06 26	06 41	06 56	07 11		11 26	11 41	11 56	12 11	12 26	12 41	12 56	13 11	13 26	13 41	13 56	14 11	14 26	14 41	14 56
Harringay Green Lanes	d		06 29	06 44	06 59	07 14		11 29	11 44	11 59	12 14	12 29	12 44	12 59	13 14	13 29	13 44	13 59	14 14	14 29	14 44	14 59
South Tottenham	d		06 33	06 48	07 03	07 18		11 33	11 48	12 03	12 18	12 33	12 48	13 03	13 18	13 33	13 48	14 03	14 18	14 33	14 48	15 03
Blackhorse Road ⊖	d		06 37	06 52	07 07	07 22		11 37	11 52	12 07	12 22	12 37	12 52	13 07	13 22	13 37	13 52	14 07	14 22	14 37	14 52	15 07
Walthamstow Queen's Road	d	00 01	06 39	06 54	07 09	07 24		11 39	11 54	12 09	12 24	12 39	12 54	13 09	13 24	13 39	13 54	14 09	14 24	14 39	14 54	15 09
Leyton Midland Road	d	00 02	06 42	06 57	07 12	07 27		11 42	11 57	12 12	12 27	12 42	12 57	13 12	13 27	13 42	13 57	14 12	14 27	14 42	14 57	15 12
Leytonstone High Road	d	00 04	06 44	06 59	07 14	07 29		11 44	11 59	12 14	12 29	12 44	12 59	13 14	13 29	13 44	13 59	14 14	14 29	14 44	14 59	15 14
Wanstead Park	d	00 07	06 46	07 01	07 16	07 31		11 46	12 01	12 16	12 31	12 46	13 01	13 16	13 31	13 46	14 01	14 16	14 31	14 46	15 01	15 16
Woodgrange Park	d	00 09	06 49	07 04	07 19	07 34		11 49	12 04	12 19	12 34	12 49	13 04	13 19	13 34	13 49	14 04	14 19	14 34	14 49	15 04	15 19
Barking ⊖	a	00 16	06 54	07 09	07 24	07 39		11 54	12 09	12 24	12 39	12 54	13 12	13 24	13 39	13 54	14 09	14 24	14 39	14 54	15 09	15 27

		LO	LO	LO	LO	LO	LO	LO	LO	LO	LO	LO	LO	LO	LO	LO	LO	LO	LO	LO	LO	LO	LO
Gospel Oak	d	15 05	15 20	15 35	15 50	16 05	16 20	16 35	16 50	17 05	17 20	17 35	17 50	18 05	18 20	18 35	18 50	19 05	19 20	19 35	19 50	20 05	20 20
Upper Holloway	d	15 09	15 24	15 39	15 54	16 09	16 24	16 39	16 54	17 09	17 24	17 39	17 54	18 09	18 24	18 39	18 54	19 09	19 24	19 39	19 54	20 09	20 24
Crouch Hill	d	15 11	15 26	15 41	15 56	16 11	16 26	16 41	16 56	17 11	17 26	17 41	17 56	18 11	18 26	18 41	18 56	19 11	19 26	19 41	19 56	20 11	20 26
Harringay Green Lanes	d	15 14	15 29	15 44	15 59	16 14	16 29	16 44	16 59	17 14	17 29	17 44	17 59	18 14	18 29	18 44	18 59	19 14	19 29	19 44	19 59	20 14	20 29
South Tottenham	d	15 18	15 33	15 48	16 03	16 18	16 33	16 48	17 03	17 18	17 33	17 48	18 03	18 18	18 33	18 48	19 03	19 18	19 33	19 48	20 03	20 18	20 33
Blackhorse Road ⊖	d	15 22	15 37	15 52	16 07	16 22	16 37	16 52	17 07	17 22	17 37	17 52	18 07	18 22	18 37	18 52	19 07	19 22	19 37	19 52	20 07	20 22	20 37
Walthamstow Queen's Road	d	15 24	15 39	15 54	16 09	16 24	16 39	16 54	17 09	17 24	17 39	17 54	18 09	18 24	18 39	18 54	19 09	19 24	19 39	19 54	20 09	20 24	20 39
Leyton Midland Road	d	15 27	15 42	15 57	16 12	16 27	16 42	16 57	17 12	17 27	17 42	17 57	18 12	18 27	18 42	18 57	19 12	19 27	19 42	19 57	20 12	20 27	20 42
Leytonstone High Road	d	15 29	15 44	15 59	16 14	16 29	16 44	16 59	17 14	17 29	17 44	17 59	18 14	18 29	18 44	18 59	19 14	19 29	19 44	19 59	20 14	20 29	20 44
Wanstead Park	d	15 31	15 46	16 01	16 16	16 31	16 46	17 01	17 16	17 31	17 46	18 01	18 16	18 31	18 46	19 01	19 16	19 31	19 46	20 01	20 16	20 31	20 46
Woodgrange Park	d	15 34	15 49	16 04	16 19	16 34	16 49	17 04	17 19	17 34	17 49	18 04	18 19	18 34	18 49	19 04	19 19	19 34	19 49	20 04	20 19	20 34	20 49
Barking ⊖	a	15 39	15 54	16 09	16 27	16 39	16 57	17 09	17 24	17 39	17 54	18 09	18 24	18 39	18 54	19 09	19 24	19 39	19 54	20 12	20 24	20 39	20 54

		LO	LO	LO	LO	LO	LO	LO	LO	LO	LO	LO	LO
Gospel Oak	d	20 35	20 50	21 05	21 20	21 35	21 50	22 05	22 22	22 45	23 05	23 25	23 48
Upper Holloway	d	20 39	20 54	21 09	21 24	21 39	21 54	22 09	22 26	22 49	23 09	23 29	23 51
Crouch Hill	d	20 41	20 56	21 11	21 26	21 41	21 56	22 11	22 29	22 51	23 11	23 31	23 54
Harringay Green Lanes	d	20 44	20 59	21 14	21 29	21 44	21 59	22 14	22 32	22 54	23 14	23 34	23 57
South Tottenham	d	20 48	21 03	21 18	21 33	21 48	22 03	22 18	22 36	22 58	23 18	23 38	00 01
Blackhorse Road ⊖	d	20 52	21 07	21 22	21 37	21 52	22 07	22 22	22 40	23 02	23 22	23 42	00 04
Walthamstow Queen's Road	d	20 54	21 09	21 24	21 39	21 54	22 09	22 24	22 42	23 04	23 24	23 44	00 06
Leyton Midland Road	d	20 57	21 12	21 27	21 42	21 57	22 12	22 27	22 45	23 07	23 27	23 47	00 09
Leytonstone High Road	d	20 59	21 14	21 29	21 44	21 59	22 14	22 29	22 47	23 09	23 29	23 49	00 11
Wanstead Park	d	21 01	21 16	21 31	21 46	22 01	22 16	22 31	22 50	23 11	23 31	23 51	00 14
Woodgrange Park	d	21 04	21 19	21 34	21 49	22 04	22 19	22 34	22 53	23 14	23 34	23 54	00 17
Barking ⊖	a	21 09	21 24	21 39	21 54	22 09	22 24	22 39	22 59	23 19	23 39	23 59	00 22

A From Gospel Oak

Table T062-F

Sundays

15 December to 10 May

Gospel Oak - Barking

		LO A	LO	LO	LO	LO	LO		LO	LO	LO	LO	LO	LO	LO	LO
Gospel Oak	d		08 57	09 10	09 25	09 40	09 55	and at the same minutes past each hour until	21 10	21 25	21 40	21 55	22 10	22 30	22 50	23 10
Upper Holloway	d		09 01	09 14	09 29	09 44	09 59		21 14	21 29	21 44	21 59	22 14	22 34	22 54	23 14
Crouch Hill	d		09 04	09 16	09 31	09 46	10 01		21 16	21 31	21 46	22 01	22 16	22 36	22 56	23 16
Harringay Green Lanes	d		09 07	09 19	09 34	09 49	10 04		21 19	21 34	21 49	22 04	22 19	22 39	22 59	23 19
South Tottenham	d	00 01	09 11	09 23	09 38	09 53	10 08		21 23	21 38	21 53	22 08	22 23	22 43	23 03	23 23
Blackhorse Road ⊖	d	00 04	09 14	09 27	09 42	09 57	10 12		21 27	21 42	21 57	22 12	22 27	22 47	23 07	23 26
Walthamstow Queen's Road	d	00 06	09 16	09 29	09 44	09 59	10 14		21 29	21 44	21 59	22 14	22 29	22 49	23 09	23 28
Leyton Midland Road	d	00 09	09 19	09 32	09 47	10 02	10 17		21 32	21 47	22 02	22 17	22 32	22 52	23 12	23 32
Leytonstone High Road	d	00 11	09 21	09 34	09 49	10 04	10 19		21 34	21 49	22 04	22 19	22 34	22 54	23 14	23 34
Wanstead Park	d	00 14	09 24	09 36	09 51	10 06	10 21		21 36	21 51	22 06	22 21	22 36	22 59	23 16	23 36
Woodgrange Park	d	00 17	09 27	09 39	09 54	10 09	10 24		21 39	21 54	22 09	22 24	22 39	23 02	23 19	23 39
Barking ⊖	a	00 22	09 31	09 44	09 59	10 14	10 29		21 44	21 59	22 14	22 29	22 44	23 06	23 24	23 44

A not 15 December. From Gospel Oak

SUNDAY RETURN TIMES

NRT DECEMBER 19 EDITION

Table T062-R

Sundays

15 December to 10 May

Barking - Gospel Oak

		LO A	LO A	LO	LO	LO	LO	LO	LO	LO		LO	LO	LO	LO	LO	LO	LO	LO	LO	LO	LO
Barking ⊖	d			08 53	09 08	09 26	09 38	09 53	10 08	10 23	and at the same minutes past each hour until	20 38	20 53	21 08	21 23	21 38	21 53	22 08	22 23	22 38	22 58	23 18
Woodgrange Park	d			08 57	09 12	09 27	09 42	09 57	10 12	10 27		20 42	20 57	21 12	21 27	21 42	21 57	22 12	22 27	22 42	23 01	23 22
Wanstead Park	d			09 00	09 15	09 30	09 45	10 00	10 15	10 30		20 45	21 00	21 15	21 30	21 45	22 00	22 15	22 30	22 45	23 04	23 25
Leytonstone High Road	d		00 01	09 02	09 17	09 32	09 47	10 02	10 17	10 32		20 47	21 02	21 17	21 32	21 47	22 02	22 17	22 32	22 47	23 06	23 27
Leyton Midland Road	d		00 03	09 05	09 20	09 35	09 50	10 05	10 20	10 35		20 50	21 05	21 20	21 35	21 50	22 05	22 20	22 35	22 50	23 10	23 30
Walthamstow Queen's Road	d		00 06	09 07	09 22	09 37	09 52	10 07	10 22	10 37		20 52	21 07	21 22	21 37	21 52	22 07	22 22	22 37	22 52	23 12	23 32
Blackhorse Road ⊖	d		00 08	09 10	09 25	09 40	09 55	10 10	10 25	10 40		20 55	21 10	21 25	21 40	21 55	22 10	22 25	22 40	22 55	23 15	23 35
South Tottenham	d		00 11	09 14	09 29	09 44	09 59	10 14	10 29	10 44		20 59	21 14	21 29	21 44	21 59	22 14	22 29	22 44	22 59	23 19	23 39
Harringay Green Lanes	d		00 14	09 17	09 32	09 47	10 02	10 17	10 32	10 47		21 02	21 17	21 32	21 47	22 02	22 17	22 32	22 47	23 02	23 22	23 42
Crouch Hill	d	00 01	00 17	09 20	09 35	09 50	10 05	10 20	10 35	10 50		21 05	21 20	21 35	21 50	22 05	22 20	22 35	22 50	23 05	23 25	23 45
Upper Holloway	d	00 04	00 20	09 23	09 38	09 53	10 08	10 23	10 38	10 53		21 08	21 23	21 38	21 53	22 08	22 23	22 38	22 53	23 08	23 28	23 48
Gospel Oak	a	00 08	00 28	09 28	09 43	10 01	10 13	10 28	10 43	10 58		21 13	21 28	21 43	21 58	22 13	22 33	22 43	22 58	23 13	23 33	23 53

		LO
Barking ⊖	d	23 38
Woodgrange Park	d	23 42
Wanstead Park	d	23 45
Leytonstone High Road	d	23 47
Leyton Midland Road	d	23 50
Walthamstow Queen's Road	d	23 52
Blackhorse Road ⊖	d	23 55
South Tottenham	d	23 59
Harringay Green Lanes	d	00 02
Crouch Hill	d	00 05
Upper Holloway	d	00 08
Gospel Oak	a	00 13

A not 15 December. From Barking

Table T062-R

Mondays to Fridays
16 December to 15 May

Barking - Gospel Oak

Miles			LO MX A	LO MO A	LO MX A	LO	LO	LO	LO	LO	LO	LO	LO	LO	LO	LO	LO	LO	LO	LO	LO	LO	LO
0	**Barking** ⊖	d				05 39	05 54	06 06	06 18	06 33	06 48	07 03	07 18	07 33	07 48	08 03	08 18	08 33	08 48	09 03	09 18	09 33	09 48
1¾	Woodgrange Park	d				05 43	05 58	06 10	06 22	06 37	06 52	07 07	07 22	07 37	07 52	08 07	08 22	08 37	08 52	09 07	09 22	09 37	09 52
2¾	Wanstead Park	d				05 46	06 01	06 12	06 25	06 40	06 55	07 10	07 25	07 40	07 55	08 10	08 25	08 40	08 55	09 10	09 25	09 40	09 55
3¼	Leytonstone High Road	d			00 02	05 48	06 03	06 15	06 27	06 42	06 57	07 12	07 27	07 42	07 57	08 12	08 27	08 42	08 57	09 12	09 27	09 42	09 57
4½	Leyton Midland Road	d			00 04	05 51	06 06	06 17	06 30	06 45	07 00	07 15	07 30	07 45	08 00	08 15	08 30	08 45	09 00	09 15	09 30	09 45	10 00
5¾	Walthamstow Queen's Road	d			00 06	05 53	06 08	06 19	06 32	06 47	07 02	07 17	07 32	07 47	08 02	08 17	08 32	08 47	09 02	09 17	09 32	09 47	10 02
6½	Blackhorse Road ⊖	d			00 09	05 56	06 11	06 22	06 35	06 50	07 05	07 20	07 35	07 50	08 05	08 20	08 35	08 50	09 05	09 20	09 35	09 50	10 05
8	South Tottenham	d			00 12	06 00	06 15	06 26	06 39	06 54	07 09	07 24	07 39	07 54	08 09	08 24	08 39	08 54	09 09	09 24	09 39	09 54	10 09
9	Harringay Green Lanes	d		00 02	00 15	06 03	06 18	06 29	06 42	06 57	07 12	07 27	07 42	07 57	08 12	08 27	08 42	08 57	09 12	09 27	09 42	09 57	10 12
10	Crouch Hill	d		00 05	00 18	06 06	06 21	06 32	06 45	07 00	07 15	07 30	07 45	08 00	08 15	08 30	08 45	09 00	09 15	09 30	09 45	10 00	10 15
10¾	Upper Holloway	d	00 01	00 08	00 21	06 09	06 24	06 35	06 48	07 03	07 18	07 33	07 48	08 03	08 18	08 33	08 48	09 03	09 18	09 33	09 48	10 03	10 18
12	**Gospel Oak**	a	00 08	00 13	00 28	06 14	06 29	06 41	06 53	07 11	07 26	07 38	07 53	08 11	08 26	08 41	08 56	09 08	09 23	09 38	09 53	10 08	10 23

		LO	LO	LO	LO	LO	LO	LO	LO	LO	LO	LO	LO	LO	LO	LO	LO	LO	LO	LO	LO	LO
Barking ⊖	d	10 03	10 18	10 33	10 48	11 03	11 18	11 33	11 48	12 03	12 18	12 33	12 48	13 03	13 17	13 33	13 48	14 03	14 18	14 33	14 48	15 03
Woodgrange Park	d	10 07	10 22	10 37	10 52	11 07	11 21	11 37	11 52	12 07	12 22	12 37	12 52	13 07	13 21	13 37	13 52	14 07	14 22	14 37	14 52	15 07
Wanstead Park	d	10 10	10 25	10 40	10 55	11 10	11 24	11 40	11 55	12 10	12 25	12 40	12 55	13 10	13 24	13 40	13 55	14 10	14 25	14 40	14 55	15 10
Leytonstone High Road	d	10 12	10 27	10 42	10 57	11 12	11 26	11 42	11 57	12 12	12 27	12 42	12 57	13 12	13 26	13 42	13 57	14 12	14 27	14 42	14 57	15 12
Leyton Midland Road	d	10 15	10 30	10 45	11 00	11 15	11 29	11 45	12 00	12 15	12 30	12 45	13 00	13 15	13 29	13 45	14 00	14 15	14 30	14 45	15 00	15 15
Walthamstow Queen's Road	d	10 17	10 32	10 47	11 02	11 17	11 31	11 47	12 02	12 17	12 32	12 47	13 02	13 17	13 31	13 47	14 02	14 17	14 32	14 47	15 02	15 17
Blackhorse Road ⊖	d	10 20	10 35	10 50	11 05	11 20	11 34	11 50	12 05	12 20	12 35	12 50	13 05	13 20	13 34	13 50	14 05	14 20	14 35	14 50	15 05	15 20
South Tottenham	d	10 24	10 39	10 54	11 09	11 24	11 38	11 54	12 09	12 24	12 39	12 54	13 09	13 24	13 38	13 54	14 09	14 24	14 39	14 54	15 09	15 24
Harringay Green Lanes	d	10 27	10 42	10 57	11 12	11 27	11 41	11 57	12 12	12 27	12 42	12 57	13 12	13 27	13 41	13 57	14 12	14 27	14 42	14 57	15 12	15 27
Crouch Hill	d	10 30	10 45	11 00	11 15	11 30	11 44	12 00	12 15	12 30	12 45	13 00	13 15	13 30	13 44	14 00	14 15	14 30	14 45	15 00	15 15	15 30
Upper Holloway	d	10 33	10 48	11 03	11 18	11 33	11 48	12 03	12 18	12 33	12 48	13 03	13 18	13 33	13 47	14 03	14 18	14 33	14 48	15 03	15 18	15 33
Gospel Oak	a	10 41	10 53	11 08	11 23	11 41	11 53	12 08	12 23	12 41	12 53	13 08	13 23	13 38	13 55	14 08	14 23	14 38	14 53	15 08	15 23	15 38

		LO	LO	LO	LO	LO	LO	LO	LO	LO	LO	LO	LO	LO	LO	LO	LO	LO	LO	LO	LO	LO	LO
Barking ⊖	d	15 18	15 33	15 48	16 03	16 18	16 33	16 48	17 03	17 18	17 33	17 48	18 03	18 18	18 33	18 48	19 03	19 18	19 33	19 48	20 03	20 18	20 33
Woodgrange Park	d	15 22	15 37	15 52	16 07	16 22	16 37	16 52	17 07	17 22	17 37	17 52	18 07	18 22	18 37	18 52	19 07	19 22	19 37	19 52	20 07	20 22	20 37
Wanstead Park	d	15 25	15 40	15 55	16 10	16 25	16 40	16 55	17 10	17 25	17 40	17 55	18 10	18 25	18 40	18 55	19 10	19 25	19 40	19 55	20 10	20 25	20 40
Leytonstone High Road	d	15 27	15 42	15 57	16 12	16 27	16 42	16 57	17 12	17 27	17 42	17 57	18 12	18 27	18 42	18 57	19 12	19 27	19 42	19 57	20 12	20 27	20 42
Leyton Midland Road	d	15 30	15 45	16 00	16 15	16 30	16 45	17 00	17 15	17 30	17 45	18 00	18 15	18 30	18 45	19 00	19 15	19 30	19 45	20 00	20 15	20 30	20 45
Walthamstow Queen's Road	d	15 32	15 47	16 02	16 17	16 32	16 47	17 02	17 17	17 32	17 47	18 02	18 17	18 32	18 47	19 02	19 17	19 32	19 47	20 02	20 17	20 32	20 47
Blackhorse Road ⊖	d	15 35	15 50	16 05	16 20	16 35	16 50	17 05	17 20	17 35	17 50	18 05	18 20	18 35	18 50	19 05	19 20	19 35	19 50	20 05	20 20	20 35	20 50
South Tottenham	d	15 39	15 54	16 09	16 24	16 39	16 54	17 09	17 24	17 39	17 54	18 09	18 24	18 39	18 54	19 09	19 24	19 39	19 54	20 09	20 24	20 39	20 54
Harringay Green Lanes	d	15 42	15 57	16 12	16 27	16 42	16 57	17 12	17 27	17 42	17 57	18 12	18 27	18 42	18 57	19 12	19 27	19 42	19 57	20 12	20 27	20 42	20 57
Crouch Hill	d	15 45	16 00	16 15	16 30	16 45	17 00	17 15	17 30	17 45	18 00	18 15	18 30	18 45	19 00	19 15	19 30	19 45	20 00	20 15	20 30	20 45	21 00
Upper Holloway	d	15 48	16 03	16 18	16 33	16 48	17 03	17 18	17 33	17 48	18 03	18 18	18 33	18 48	19 03	19 18	19 33	19 48	20 03	20 18	20 33	20 48	21 03
Gospel Oak	a	15 53	16 08	16 23	16 41	16 53	17 08	17 26	17 38	17 53	18 11	18 26	18 41	18 53	19 11	19 26	19 41	19 53	20 08	20 23	20 41	20 53	21 08

		LO	LO	LO	LO	LO	LO	LO	LO	LO	LO	LO	LO
Barking ⊖	d	20 48	21 03	21 20	21 33	21 48	22 03	22 18	22 36	22 53	23 13	23 33	23 53
Woodgrange Park	d	20 52	21 07	21 22	21 37	21 52	22 07	22 22	22 42	22 57	23 17	23 37	23 57
Wanstead Park	d	20 55	21 10	21 25	21 40	21 55	22 10	22 25	22 44	23 00	23 19	23 39	23 59
Leytonstone High Road	d	20 57	21 12	21 27	21 42	21 57	22 12	22 27	22 47	23 02	23 22	23 42	00 02
Leyton Midland Road	d	21 00	21 15	21 30	21 45	22 00	22 14	22 30	22 49	23 05	23 24	23 44	00 04
Walthamstow Queen's Road	d	21 02	21 17	21 32	21 47	22 02	22 17	22 32	22 51	23 07	23 26	23 46	00 06
Blackhorse Road ⊖	d	21 05	21 20	21 35	21 50	22 05	22 19	22 35	22 54	23 10	23 29	23 49	00 09
South Tottenham	d	21 09	21 24	21 39	21 54	22 09	22 23	22 38	22 57	23 14	23 32	23 52	00 12
Harringay Green Lanes	d	21 12	21 27	21 42	21 57	22 12	22 26	22 41	23 00	23 17	23 35	23 55	00 15
Crouch Hill	d	21 15	21 30	21 45	22 00	22 15	22 29	22 44	23 03	23 20	23 38	23 58	00 18
Upper Holloway	d	21 19	21 33	21 48	22 03	22 18	22 31	22 46	23 06	23 23	23 40	00 01	00 21
Gospel Oak	a	21 23	21 38	21 58	22 11	22 26	22 38	22 53	23 11	23 28	23 48	00 08	00 28

Saturdays
21 December to 16 May

		LO A	LO A	LO	LO	LO	LO	LO	LO	LO	LO		LO	LO	LO	LO	LO	LO	LO	LO	LO	LO	LO
Barking ⊖	d			06 20	06 34	06 48	07 03	07 18	07 33	07 48	08 03	and at the same minutes past each hour until	17 18	17 33	17 48	18 03	18 18	18 33	18 48	19 03	19 18	19 33	19 48
Woodgrange Park	d			06 24	06 37	06 52	07 07	07 22	07 37	07 52	08 07		17 22	17 37	17 52	18 07	18 22	18 37	18 52	19 07	19 22	19 37	19 52
Wanstead Park	d			06 27	06 40	06 55	07 10	07 25	07 40	07 55	08 10		17 25	17 40	17 55	18 10	18 25	18 40	18 55	19 10	19 25	19 40	19 55
Leytonstone High Road	d		00 02	06 29	06 42	06 57	07 12	07 27	07 42	07 57	08 12		17 27	17 42	17 57	18 12	18 27	18 42	18 57	19 12	19 27	19 42	19 57
Leyton Midland Road	d		00 04	06 32	06 45	07 00	07 15	07 30	07 45	08 00	08 15		17 30	17 45	18 00	18 15	18 30	18 45	19 00	19 15	19 30	19 45	20 00
Walthamstow Queen's Road	d		00 06	06 34	06 47	07 02	07 17	07 32	07 47	08 02	08 17		17 32	17 47	18 02	18 17	18 32	18 47	19 02	19 17	19 32	19 47	20 02
Blackhorse Road ⊖	d		00 09	06 37	06 50	07 05	07 20	07 35	07 50	08 05	08 20		17 35	17 50	18 05	18 20	18 35	18 50	19 05	19 20	19 35	19 50	20 05
South Tottenham	d		00 12	06 41	06 54	07 09	07 24	07 39	07 54	08 09	08 24		17 39	17 54	18 09	18 24	18 39	18 54	19 09	19 24	19 39	19 54	20 09
Harringay Green Lanes	d		00 15	06 44	06 57	07 12	07 27	07 42	07 57	08 12	08 27		17 42	17 57	18 12	18 27	18 42	18 57	19 12	19 27	19 42	19 57	20 12
Crouch Hill	d		00 18	06 47	07 00	07 15	07 30	07 45	08 00	08 15	08 30		17 45	18 00	18 15	18 30	18 45	19 00	19 15	19 30	19 45	20 00	20 15
Upper Holloway	d	00 01	00 21	06 50	07 03	07 18	07 33	07 48	08 03	08 18	08 33		17 48	18 03	18 18	18 33	18 48	19 03	19 18	19 33	19 48	20 03	20 18
Gospel Oak	a	00 08	00 28	06 55	07 09	07 23	07 41	07 53	08 08	08 23	08 38		17 53	18 08	18 23	18 38	18 53	19 11	19 23	19 41	19 53	20 08	20 26

		LO	LO	LO	LO	LO	LO	LO	LO	LO	LO	LO	LO	LO	LO	LO
Barking ⊖	d	20 03	20 18	20 33	20 48	21 03	21 18	21 33	21 48	22 03	22 18	22 33	22 53	23 13	23 33	23 53
Woodgrange Park	d	20 07	20 22	20 37	20 52	21 07	21 22	21 37	21 52	22 07	22 22	22 37	22 57	23 17	23 37	23 56
Wanstead Park	d	20 10	20 25	20 40	20 55	21 10	21 25	21 40	21 55	22 10	22 25	22 40	23 00	23 19	23 40	23 59
Leytonstone High Road	d	20 12	20 27	20 42	20 57	21 12	21 27	21 42	21 57	22 12	22 27	22 42	23 02	23 22	23 42	00 01
Leyton Midland Road	d	20 15	20 30	20 45	21 00	21 15	21 30	21 45	22 00	22 15	22 30	22 45	23 05	23 25	23 45	00 03
Walthamstow Queen's Road	d	20 17	20 32	20 47	21 02	21 17	21 32	21 47	22 02	22 17	22 32	22 47	23 07	23 27	23 47	00 06
Blackhorse Road ⊖	d	20 20	20 35	20 50	21 05	21 20	21 35	21 50	22 05	22 20	22 35	22 50	23 10	23 30	23 50	00 08
South Tottenham	d	20 24	20 39	20 54	21 09	21 24	21 39	21 54	22 09	22 24	22 39	22 54	23 14	23 34	23 54	00 11
Harringay Green Lanes	d	20 27	20 42	20 57	21 12	21 27	21 42	21 57	22 12	22 27	22 42	22 57	23 17	23 37	23 57	00 14
Crouch Hill	d	20 30	20 45	21 00	21 15	21 30	21 45	22 00	22 15	22 30	22 45	23 00	23 20	23 40	00 01	00 17
Upper Holloway	d	20 33	20 48	21 03	21 18	21 33	21 48	22 03	22 18	22 33	22 48	23 03	23 23	23 44	00 04	00 20
Gospel Oak	a	20 38	20 53	21 11	21 23	21 38	21 53	22 08	22 26	22 38	22 53	23 08	23 28	23 51	00 08	00 28

A From Barking

See opposite page for Sunday times.

NRT DECEMBER 19 EDITION

Table T063-F

Mondays to Fridays
16 December to 15 May

Coventry - Nuneaton

Miles			LM A	LM A	LM A	LM A	LM A		LM A	LM A	LM A	LM A	LM A	LM A	LM A	LM A	LM A	LM A	LM A
0	**Coventry**	d	05 53	06 33	07 15	08 18	09 17	and hourly until	12 17	13 17	14 20	15 16	16 17	17 17	18 17	19 17	20 17	21 17	22 22
4	Coventry Arena	d	06 00	06 41	07 22	08 29	09 24		12 24	13 26	14 30	15 24	16 24	17 25	18 25	19 24	20 25	21 24	22 29
6½	Bedworth	d	06 05	06 46	07 27	08 35	09 29		12 29	13 31	14 37	15 29	16 29	17 30	18 30	19 29	20 30	21 29	22 34
8¼	Bermuda Park	d	06 09	06 49	07 31	08 40	09 33		12 33	13 35	14 43	15 33	16 33	17 33	18 33	19 33	20 34	21 33	22 38
10¼	**Nuneaton**	a	06 14	06 55	07 36	08 45	09 38		12 38	13 41	14 49	15 38	16 40	17 38	18 39	19 38	20 39	21 38	22 43

Saturdays
21 December to 16 May

		LM A	LM A	LM A	LM A	LM A		LM A
Coventry	d	05 50	06 24	07 17	08 21	09 17	and hourly until	21 17
Coventry Arena	d	05 57	06 32	07 24	08 28	09 24		21 24
Bedworth	d	06 02	06 37	07 29	08 33	09 29		21 29
Bermuda Park	d	06 06	06 41	07 33	08 37	09 33		21 33
Nuneaton	a	06 11	06 47	07 38	08 42	09 38		21 38

Sundays
15 December to 10 May

		LM	LM		LM	LM
Coventry	d	11 15	12 39	and hourly until	20 39	21 32
Coventry Arena	d	11 22	12 46		20 46	21 39
Bedworth	d	11 27	12 51		20 51	21 44
Bermuda Park	d	11 31	12 55		20 55	21 48
Nuneaton	a	11 36	13 00		21 00	21 53

A From Leamington Spa

NRT DECEMBER 19 EDITION

Table T063-R

Mondays to Fridays
16 December to 15 May

Nuneaton - Coventry

Miles			LM A	LM A	LM A	LM A	LM A	LM A	LM A	LM A	LM A	LM A	LM A		LM A	LM A	LM A	LM A
0	**Nuneaton**	d	06 20	07 15	08 13	09 16	10 16	11 16	12 17	13 16	14 14	15 14	16 16	and hourly until	20 16	21 14	22 22	23 22
2	Bermuda Park	d	06 24	07 19	08 17	09 20	10 20	11 20	12 21	13 20	14 18	15 18	16 20		20 20	21 18	22 26	23 26
3½	Bedworth	d	06 27	07 22	08 20	09 23	10 23	11 23	12 24	13 23	14 21	15 21	16 23		20 23	21 21	22 29	23 29
6¼	Coventry Arena	d	06 32	07 27	08 25	09 28	10 28	11 28	12 29	13 28	14 26	15 26	16 28		20 28	21 26	22 34	23 34
10¼	**Coventry**	a	06 39	07 35	08 34	09 36	10 36	11 39	12 37	13 36	14 34	15 34	16 36		20 36	21 34	22 42	23 42

Saturdays
21 December to 16 May

		LM A	LM A		LM A	LM A	LM A		LM A	LM A
Nuneaton	d	06 19	07 16	and hourly until	12 16	13 16	14 16	and hourly until	21 16	22 20
Bermuda Park	d	06 23	07 20		12 20	13 20	14 20		21 20	22 24
Bedworth	d	06 26	07 23		12 23	13 23	14 23		21 23	22 27
Coventry Arena	d	06 31	07 28		12 28	13 28	14 28		21 28	22 32
Coventry	a	06 39	07 36		12 36	13 37	14 36		21 36	22 40

Sundays
15 December to 10 May

		LM		LM	LM	LM
Nuneaton	d	12 13	and hourly until	20 13	21 05	22 02
Bermuda Park	d	12 17		20 17	21 09	22 06
Bedworth	d	12 20		20 20	21 12	22 09
Coventry Arena	d	12 25		20 25	21 17	22 14
Coventry	a	12 33		20 33	21 25	22 22

A To Leamington Spa

Table T064-F

Mondays to Saturdays

16 December to 16 May

Bletchley - Bedford

Miles			LM	LM SO	LM SX	LM SO	LM SX	LM SO	LM SX	LM SX	LM SO	LM SO	LM SX	LM	LM	LM	LM	LM	LM	LM SO	LM SX	LM SX	LM SO
0	**Bletchley**	d	05 16	06 16	06 24	07 00	07 32	08 00	08 01	09 06	09 17	10 17	10 18	11 01	12 01	13 01	14 01	15 01	16 01	17 01	17 01	18 01	18 06
1	Fenny Stratford	d	05 19	06 19	06 28	07 03	07 35	08 03	08 04	09 09	09 20	10 20	10 21	11 04	12 04	13 04	14 04	15 04	16 04	17 04	17 04	18 04	18 09
2	Bow Brickhill	d	05 23	06 23	06 32	07 07	07 39	08 07	08 08	09 13	09 24	10 24	10 25	11 08	12 08	13 08	14 08	15 08	16 08	17 08	17 08	18 08	18 13
4	Woburn Sands	d	05 27	06 27	06 36	07 11	07 43	08 11	08 12	09 17	09 28	10 28	10 29	11 12	12 12	13 12	14 12	15 12	16 12	17 12	17 13	18 12	18 17
5	Aspley Guise	d	05 30	06 30	06 39	07 14	07 46	08 14	08 15	09 20	09 31	10 31	10 32	11 15	12 15	13 15	14 15	15 15	16 15	17 15	17 15	18 15	18 20
6¾	Ridgmont	d	05 34	06 34	06 43	07 18	07 50	08 18	08 19	09 24	09 35	10 35	10 36	11 19	12 19	13 19	14 19	15 19	16 19	17 19	17 19	18 19	18 24
8½	Lidlington	d	05 38	06 38	06 47	07 22	07 54	08 22	08 23	09 28	09 39	10 39	10 40	11 23	12 23	13 23	14 23	15 23	16 23	17 23	17 23	18 23	18 28
10	Millbrook (Bedfordshire)	d	05 41	06 41	06 50	07 25	07 57	08 25	08 26	09 31	09 42	10 42	10 43	11 26	12 26	13 26	14 26	15 26	16 26	17 26	17 26	18 26	18 31
11¼	Stewartby	d	05 44	06 44	06 54	07 28	08 00	08 28	08 29	09 34	09 45	10 45	10 46	11 29	12 29	13 29	14 29	15 29	16 29	17 29	17 29	18 29	18 34
13	Kempston Hardwick	d	05 48	06 48	06 57	07 32	08 04	08 32	08 33	09 38	09 49	10 49	10 50	11 33	12 33	13 33	14 33	15 33	16 33	17 33	17 33	18 33	18 38
16	Bedford St Johns	d	05 54	06 54	07 04	07 38	08 10	08 38	08 39	09 44	09 55	10 55	10 56	11 39	12 39	13 39	14 39	15 39	16 39	17 39	17 39	18 39	18 44
16¾	**Bedford** ■7	a	05 58	06 58	07 08	07 42	08 14	08 42	08 43	09 48	09 59	10 59	11 00	11 43	12 43	13 43	14 43	15 43	16 43	17 43	17 43	18 43	18 48

		LM	LM	LM SO	LM SX
Bletchley	d	19 01	20 25	21 26	21 38
Fenny Stratford	d	19 04	20 28	21 29	21 41
Bow Brickhill	d	19 08	20 32	21 33	21 45
Woburn Sands	d	19 12	20 36	21 37	21 49
Aspley Guise	d	19 15	20 39	21 40	21 52
Ridgmont	d	19 19	20 43	21 44	21 56
Lidlington	d	19 23	20 47	21 48	22 00
Millbrook (Bedfordshire)	d	19 26	20 50	21 51	22 03
Stewartby	d	19 29	20 53	21 54	22 06
Kempston Hardwick	d	19 33	20 57	21 58	22 10
Bedford St Johns	d	19 39	21 03	22 04	22 16
Bedford ■7	a	19 43	21 07	22 08	22 20

No Sunday Service

For connections from Milton Keynes Central refer to Table T66

NRT DECEMBER 19 EDITION

Table T064-R

Mondays to Saturdays

16 December to 16 May

Bedford - Bletchley

Miles			LM SX	LM SO	LM SO	LM SX	LM SO	LM SX	LM	LM SX	LM SO	LM SO	LM SX	LM	LM SO	LM SX	LM	LM	LM	LM SX	LM SO	LM	LM
0	**Bedford** ■7	d	06 03	06 04	07 04	07 14	07 47	08 19	08 48	09 55	10 04	11 04	11 05	11 55	12 55	12 58	13 55	14 55	15 55	16 48	16 55	17 55	18 55
0¾	Bedford St Johns	d	06 07	06 07	07 08	07 18	07 51	08 23	08 52	09 59	10 08	11 08	11 09	11 59	12 59	13 02	13 59	14 59	15 59	16 52	16 59	17 59	18 59
3¾	Kempston Hardwick	d	06 13	06 14	07 14	07 24	07 57	08 29	08 58	10 05	10 14	11 14	11 15	12 05	13 05	13 08	14 05	15 05	16 05	16 58	17 05	18 05	19 05
5½	Stewartby	d	06 17	06 17	07 18	07 28	08 01	08 33	09 02	10 09	10 18	11 18	11 19	12 09	13 09	13 12	14 09	15 09	16 09	17 02	17 09	18 09	19 09
6¾	Millbrook (Bedfordshire)	d	06 20	06 21	07 21	07 31	08 04	08 36	09 05	10 12	10 21	11 21	11 22	12 12	13 12	13 15	14 12	15 12	16 12	17 05	17 12	18 12	19 12
8¼	Lidlington	d	06 24	06 24	07 25	07 35	08 08	08 40	09 09	10 16	10 25	11 25	11 26	12 16	13 16	13 19	14 16	15 16	16 16	17 09	17 16	18 16	19 16
10	Ridgmont	d	06 28	06 29	07 29	07 39	08 12	08 44	09 13	10 20	10 29	11 29	11 30	12 20	13 20	13 23	14 20	15 20	16 20	17 13	17 20	18 20	19 20
11¾	Aspley Guise	d	06 32	06 32	07 33	07 43	08 16	08 48	09 17	10 24	10 33	11 33	11 34	12 24	13 24	13 27	14 24	15 24	16 24	17 17	17 24	18 24	19 24
12¾	Woburn Sands	d	06 34	06 35	07 35	07 45	08 18	08 50	09 19	10 26	10 35	11 35	11 36	12 26	13 26	13 29	14 26	15 26	16 26	17 19	17 26	18 26	19 26
14¾	Bow Brickhill	d	06 39	06 40	07 40	07 50	08 23	08 55	09 24	10 31	10 40	11 40	11 41	12 31	13 31	13 34	14 31	15 31	16 31	17 24	17 31	18 31	19 31
15¾	Fenny Stratford	d	06 41	06 42	07 42	07 52	08 25	08 57	09 26	10 33	10 42	11 42	11 43	12 33	13 33	13 36	14 33	15 33	16 33	17 26	17 33	18 33	19 33
16¾	**Bletchley**	a	06 44	06 45	07 45	07 55	08 28	09 00	09 29	10 36	10 45	11 45	11 46	12 36	13 36	13 39	14 36	15 36	16 36	17 29	17 36	18 36	19 36

		LM SX	LM SO	LM	LM SO	LM SX
Bedford ■7	d	19 55	19 56	21 12	22 19	22 38
Bedford St Johns	d	19 59	20 00	21 16	22 23	22 42
Kempston Hardwick	d	20 05	20 06	21 22	22 29	22 48
Stewartby	d	20 09	20 10	21 26	22 33	22 52
Millbrook (Bedfordshire)	d	20 12	20 13	21 29	22 36	22 55
Lidlington	d	20 16	20 17	21 33	22 40	22 59
Ridgmont	d	20 20	20 21	21 37	22 44	23 03
Aspley Guise	d	20 24	20 25	21 41	22 48	23 07
Woburn Sands	d	20 26	20 27	21 43	22 50	23 09
Bow Brickhill	d	20 32	20 33	21 48	22 55	23 14
Fenny Stratford	d	20 34	20 35	21 50	22 57	23 16
Bletchley	a	20 37	20 38	21 53	23 00	23 19

No Sunday Service

For connections to Milton Keynes Central refer to Table T66

Table T065-F

Mondays to Fridays

16 December to 15 May

London & West Midlands to North West England. London, West Midlands & Manchester to Scotland via the West Coast

Miles	Miles	Miles	Miles	Miles				AW MO ◇ A	TP MO ◇■1 B	TP MX ◇■1 C	CS MO D	CS MO D	CS MO D	CS MO E	CS MX F	CS MX F		CS MX F	NT MX ◇ C	CS MX F	TP G	AW MX ◇ H	TP ◇■1	TP MO ◇■1	TP MX ◇■1
0	—	—	—	—	**London Euston** ■15	⊖66	d																		
17½	—	—	—	—	Watford Junction	66	d																		
49¾	—	—	—	—	Milton Keynes Central	66	d													00u10					
82½	0	—	—	—	Rugby	66	d																		
97	—	—	—	—	Nuneaton		d																		
110	—	—	—	—	Tamworth Low Level		d																		
116¼	—	0	—	—	Lichfield Trent Valley		d																		
—	11½	—	—	—	Coventry	68	d																		
—	22	—	—	—	Birmingham International	68	d																		
—	30½	—	—	—	**BirminghamNewSt** ■12	68	d																		
—	43¼	—	—	—	**Wolverhampton** ■7		d																		
—	53¼	—	—	—	Penkridge		d																		
133½	59½	—	—	—	**Stafford**		d																		
—	75¾	30¼	—	—	**Stoke-on-Trent**	84	a																		
—	95¼	50¼	—	—	Macclesfield		a																		
158	—	—	0	—	**Crewe** ■10	81,91	a																		
—	—	—	—	—			d	00 01														00 15			
—	—	—	—	—	**Chester**	81	a	00 23														00 38			
—	—	—	—	—	Wrexham General	75	a																		
—	—	—	—	—	Llandudno Junction	81	a															01 30			
—	—	—	—	—	Bangor (Gwynedd)	81	a															01 47			
—	—	—	—	—	**Holyhead**	81	a															02 15			
—	—	—	—	—	Wilmslow	84	a																		
—	107¼	62¼	—	—	Stockport	84	a																		
—	113	68	—	—	**Manchester Piccadilly** ■10		a																		
—	—	—	22½	—	Runcorn	91	a																		
—	—	—	30	—	Liverpool South Pkwy ■7	91	a																		
—	—	—	35½	—	**Liverpool Lime Street** ■10	91	a																		
—	—	—	—	—			d																		
—	—	—	—	—	Manchester Airport	82	d																04 22		
—	—	—	—	—	**Manchester Picc.** ■10	82	d												00 09				04 36	04 57	04 57
—	—	79¼	—	—	Bolton	82	d																		
182	—	—	—	—	Warrington Bank Quay		d																		
193¾	—	—	—	—	Wigan North Western	90	d																		
209	—	99¼	—	—	**Preston** ■8	90	a												00 59					05 33	05 34
—	—	117½	—	—	**Blackpool North**	97	a												01 27						
—	—	—	—	—	**Preston** ■8	90	d		00 01	00 15	00u33	00u33	00u33		00u56	00u56		00u56						05 36	05 36
230	—	—	—	—	**Lancaster** ■6		d																	05 51	05 51
—	—	—	—	—	Barrow-in-Furness	82	a																		
249	—	—	—	—	Oxenholme Lake District	83	d																	06 05	06 05
—	—	—	—	—	**Windermere**	83	a																		
281¼	—	—	—	—	Penrith North Lakes		d																	06 31	06 31
299	—	—	—	—	**Carlisle** ■8	216	a		01 39	01 25										05s13				06 46	06 46
—	—	—	—	—																					
—	—	—	—	—			d														05 57			06 48	06 48
324¼	—	—	0	—	Lockerbie	225,226	d														06 20			07 07	07 07
372½	—	—	—	0	Carstairs	226,225	a													06s22				07 39	07 39
388½	—	—	—	—	Motherwell	226	a													07s00				07 59	07 59
401¼	—	—	—	—	**GlasgowCentral** ■15	216,226,225	a													07 22				08 20	08 20
—	—	—	75	26¼	Haymarket		a														07s28				
—	—	—	76¼	27½	**Edinburgh** ■10		a						04d50	04d50	04d50					07 23	07 34		08 51		
—	—	—	—	—	**Fort William**	227,400	a						09 57	09 57	09 57										
—	—	—	—	97¼	Perth	229	a					05s41						05s41							
—	—	—	135½	—	Dundee	229	a				06s05					06s05									
—	—	—	206¾	—	**Aberdeen**	229	a				07 40					07 40									
—	—	—	—	215¼	**Inverness**	229	a					08 42						08 42							

A From Birmingham International
B until 6 January, from 24 February until 30 March. From Manchester Airport
C From Manchester Airport
D until 30 March. From London Euston
E from 6 April. From London Euston
F From London Euston
G until 3 April, MX from 7 April
H From Birmingham New Street

Refer to Operator websites for full information about Sleeper Services. Contact details for train operators available at National Rail Enquiries

Table T065-F

Mondays to Fridays

16 December to 15 May

London & West Midlands to North West England. London, West Midlands & Manchester to Scotland via the West Coast

	NT	NT	VT	NT	VT	TP	XC	LM	LM	LM	VT	TP	XC	VT	VT	LM	LM	NT	XC	LM	VT
		◇	◇1	◇	◇1	◇1	◇1	1	1	1	◇1	◇1	◇1	◇1	◇1	1	1	◇	◇1	1	◇1
		A		B				C									C				
			⊠		⊠	⚲					⊠	⚲	⚲	⊠	⊠				⚲		⊠
London Euston 15 ⊖66 d														05 27	05 31						
Watford Junction 66 d														05u45	05u50						
Milton Keynes Central 66 d														06 15	06 23					05 37	
Rugby 66 d								05 42							06 45		06 22			06 19	
Nuneaton d								05 55						06 45			06 39				
Tamworth Low Level d								06 09									06 55				
Lichfield Trent Valley d								06 16									07 02				
Coventry 68 d																				06 30	
Birmingham International 68 ✈ d																05 52				06 46	
BirminghamNewSt 12 68 🚊 d					05 30		05 57		06 02	06 07	06 15		06 30			06 36			06 53	07 04	07 15
Wolverhampton 7 🚊 d					05 48		06 14		06 22	06 32	06 37		06 48			06 56			07 10	07 23	07 37
Penkridge d									06 30							07 05				07 32	
Stafford d					06 01		06 28	06 33	06 38	06 46			07 02	07 08		07 13	07 21		07 24	07 39	
Stoke-on-Trent 84 a							06 43			07 03			07 17								
Macclesfield a							07 05						07 37								
Crewe 10 81,91 a					06 19			06 51	06 57	07 43	07 08			07 27	07 30	07 32	07 40		07 43	07 57	08 08
d			05 57		06 23				06 58		07 09			07 28	07 32	07 33			07 45	07 59	08 09
Chester 81 a					06 43																
Wrexham General 75 a																					
Llandudno Junction 81 a					07 31																
Bangor (Gwynedd) 81 a					07 48																
Holyhead 81 ⛴ a					08 19																
Wilmslow 84 a																			08 00		
Stockport 84 a							07 19						07 49						08 13		
Manchester Piccadilly 10 🚊 a							07 30						08 00						08 23		
Runcorn 91 a									07 23					07 45		07 59				08 24	
Liverpool South Pkwy 7 91 ✈ a									07 32							08 09				08 35	
Liverpool Lime Street 10 91 a									07 42					08 04		08 19				08 44	
d																					
Manchester Airport 82 ✈🚊 d		05 24				06 07						07 07						07 25			
Manchester Picc. 10 82 🚊 d		05 44				06 26						07 26						07 43			
Bolton 82 d						06u42															
Warrington Bank Quay d			06 15								07 27				07 49						08 27
Wigan North Western 90 d		06 15	06 25								07 38				08 00			08 16			08 38
Preston 8 90 a		06 31	06 38			07 02					07 51	08 01			08 14			08 40			08 51
Blackpool North 97 🚊 a				←																	
Preston 8 90 d		06 47	06 41	06 47		07 03					07 53	08 02			08 15			08 42			08 53
Lancaster 6 d	05 59	→	06 55	07 06		07 19					08 08	08 18			08 30			09 00			09 08
Barrow-in-Furness 82 a				08 09														10 03			
Oxenholme Lake District 83 d	06 19		07 11			07 33					08 22				08 43						
Windermere 83 a	06 39																				
Penrith North Lakes d			07 35			07 59						08 54									09 44
Carlisle 8 216 a			07 50			08 14					09 00	09 10			09 21						09 59
d			07 53			08 16					09 01	09 11			09 21						10 02
Lockerbie 225,226 d			08 11			08 35						09 30									
Carstairs 226,225 a																					
Motherwell 226 a												10 14									
GlasgowCentral 15 216,226,225 a			09 16									10 32			10 38						11 15
Haymarket 🚊 a						09s32					10 12										
Edinburgh 10 🚊 a						09 40					10 18										
Fort William 227,400 a																					
Perth 229 a																					
Dundee 229 a																					
Aberdeen 229 a																					
Inverness 229 a																					

A To Barrow-in-Furness
B From Manchester Airport
C From Northampton

Refer to Operator websites for full information about Sleeper Services. Contact details for train operators available at National Rail Enquiries

Table T065-F

Mondays to Fridays

16 December to 15 May

London & West Midlands to North West England. London, West Midlands & Manchester to Scotland via the West Coast

	LM	XC	TP	TP	LM	XC	LM	VT	LM	LM	VT	LM	VT	VT	VT	VT	VT	LM	LM	VT	NT	VT
	1	◇1	◇1	◇1	1	◇1	1	◇1	1	1	◇1	1	◇1	◇1	◇1	◇1	◇1	1	1	◇1	◇	◇1
	A				B	C	B			B		D	E					F	G		H	
		⚲	⚲	⚲		⚲		⊠			⊠		⊠	⊐	⊠	⊠	⊠			⊠		⊠
London Euston 15 ⊖66 d							05 34	06 16	06 28	06 34	06 36		06 43	06 46	06 55	07 07	07 10		07 13	07 20		07 30
Watford Junction 66 d							05 55			06 53	06u51											
Milton Keynes Central 66 d							06 40	06 46	07 01	07 38			07 13		07 27		07 41		07 54	07 50		
Rugby 66 d	06 32						07 19		07 29	08 19				07 40					08 37			
Nuneaton d									07 42													
Tamworth Low Level d									07 55													
Lichfield Trent Valley d									08 02													
Coventry 68 d	06 43					07 27	07 30			08 30			07 42						08 47			
Birmingham International 68 ✈ d	07 01				07 18	07 38	07 42			→			07 53					←	→			
BirminghamNewSt 12 68 🚊 d	07 20	07 31			07 36	07 57	08 04						08 15					08 04				
Wolverhampton 7 🚊 d	07 40	07 49			07 54	08 14	→						→					08 22				
Penkridge d					08 03													08 31				
Stafford d	07 55	08 03			08 11	08 28			08 18							08 24		08 38				
Stoke-on-Trent 84 a	08 11	08 18				08 43		07 45							08 24					08 48		
Macclesfield a		08 36				09 01		08 01				←			08 41							
Crewe 10 81,91 a	08 33				08 30				08 36		08 10	08 30				08 41	08 45	08 56				
d					08 32						08 11	08 32				08 43	08 47	08 58				
Chester 81 a					→												09 08					
Wrexham General 75 a																						
Llandudno Junction 81 a																						
Bangor (Gwynedd) 81 a																						
Holyhead 81 ⛴ a																						
Wilmslow 84 a											08 27											
Stockport 84 a		08 49				09 13		08 17			08 35				08 54					09 16		
Manchester Piccadilly 10 🚊 a		09 00				09 24		08 27			08 46				09 05					09 27		
Runcorn 91 a												08 52				09 00		09 22				
Liverpool South Pkwy 7 91 ✈ a												09 00						09 31				
Liverpool Lime Street 10 91 a												09 11				09 20		09 40				
d			08 12																			
Manchester Airport 82 ✈🚊 d				08 07																	08 27	
Manchester Picc. 10 82 🚊 d				08 27																	08 47	
Bolton 82 d																						
Warrington Bank Quay d														08 45								09 14
Wigan North Western 90 d			08 43											08 57							09 19	09 25
Preston 8 90 a			08 59	09 02										09 14							09 43	09 38
Blackpool North 97 🚊 a														09 37							→	
Preston 8 90 d			09 01	09 04																		09 41
Lancaster 6 d				09 20																		09 55
Barrow-in-Furness 82 a																						
Oxenholme Lake District 83 d				09 34																		
Windermere 83 a																						
Penrith North Lakes d			09 51																			10 32
Carlisle 8 216 a			10 07	10 12																		10 47
d			10 09	10 14																		10 47
Lockerbie 225,226 d																						
Carstairs 226,225 a																						
Motherwell 226 a																						
GlasgowCentral 15 216,226,225 a			11 29																			11 59
Haymarket 🚊 a				11s29																		
Edinburgh 10 🚊 a				11 35																		
Fort William 227,400 a																						
Perth 229 a																						
Dundee 229 a																						
Aberdeen 229 a																						
Inverness 229 a																						

A From Northampton
B To Liverpool Lime Street
C From Southampton Central
D From Birmingham International
E To Edinburgh
F From London Euston
G To Crewe
H To Windermere

Refer to Operator websites for full information about Sleeper Services. Contact details for train operators available at National Rail Enquiries

London & West Midlands to North West England. London, West Midlands & Manchester to Scotland via the West Coast

Station	Table		NT ◇ A	VT ◇[1] B ⊠	NT	TP ◇[1] ✠	VT ◇[1] C ⊠	VT ◇[1] D ⊠	LM [1]	XC ◇[1] E ✠	LM [1]	XC ◇[1] F ✠	LM [1] G	VT ◇[1] H ⊠	LM [1]	LM [1] B	XC ◇[1] I ✠	LM [1] J	XC ◇[1] K ✠	LM [1] J	VT ◇[1] ⊠	VT ◇[1] ⊠	VT ◇[1] ⊠
London Euston [15]	⊖66	d					07 33	07 35						07 43	07 46					07 49	08 00	08 07	08 10
Watford Junction	66	d																		08 04			
Milton Keynes Central	66	d					08 04	08 06						08 13	08 19					08 25		08 38	08 41
Rugby	66	d													08 42					09 18			
Nuneaton		d													08 55								
Tamworth Low Level		d													09 09								
Lichfield Trent Valley		d											←		09 17	←							
Coventry	68	d										08 27	08 30	08 42		08 47			09 27	09 30			
Birmingham International	68 ✈	d		←							08 17	08 38	08 42	08 53		09 05		09 18	09 38	09 42			
BirminghamNewSt [12]	68	d		08 15					08 21	08 31	08 38	08 57	09 04	09 15		09 21	09 31	09 37	09 57	10 04			
Wolverhampton [7]		d		08 37					08 42	08 48	08 58	09 14	09 22	09 37		09 40	09 48	09 57	10 14	10 22			
Penkridge		d									09 07		09 30					10 06		10 30			
Stafford		d							08 56	09 02	09 14	09 28	09 38		09 35	09 54	10 02	10 13	10 28	10 38		09 27	
Stoke-on-Trent	84	a							09 12	09 17		09 43				10 11	10 17		10 43		09 24		
Macclesfield		a								09 36		10 01					10 36		11 01		09 41		
Crewe [10]	81,91	a		09 07			09 10	09 10	09 34		09 32		09 56	10 07	09 53	10 32		10 31		10 56			09 49
		d		09 09			09 11	09 11			09 33		09 58	10 09				10 33		10 59			09 50
Chester	81	a											→	→				→		→			10 10
Wrexham General	75	a																					
Llandudno Junction	81	a																					11 03
Bangor (Gwynedd)	81	a																					11 22
Holyhead	81 ⛴	a																					11 53
Wilmslow	84	a					09 27	09 27															
Stockport	84	a					09 35	09 35		09 49		10 13					10 49		11 13		09 54		
Manchester Piccadilly [10]		a					09 46	09 46		10 00		10 24					11 00		11 24		10 05		
Runcorn	91	a									09 53											10 00	
Liverpool South Pkwy [7]	91 ✈	a									10 02												
Liverpool Lime Street [10]	91	a									10 12											10 20	
		d																					
Manchester Airport	82 ✈	d				09 07																	
Manchester Picc. [10]	82	d				09 26																	
Bolton	82	d				09u44																	
Warrington Bank Quay		d		09 27																			
Wigan North Western	90	d	←	09 38																			
Preston [8]	90	a	09 43	09 51		10 04																	
Blackpool North	97	a																					
Preston [8]	90	d	09 44	09 53		10 06																	
Lancaster [6]		d		10 09	10 13	10 22																	
Barrow-in-Furness	82	a			11 16																		
Oxenholme Lake District	83	d	10 27	10 22		10 36																	
Windermere	83	a	10 49																				
Penrith North Lakes		d				11 01																	
Carlisle [8]	216	a		10 59	13 40	11 17																	
		d		11 02		11 18																	
Lockerbie	225,226	d				11 37																	
Carstairs	226,225	a																					
Motherwell	226	a				12 21																	
GlasgowCentral [15]	216,226,225	a				12 39																	
Haymarket		a		12 16																			
Edinburgh [10]		a		12 22																			
Fort William	227,400	a																					
Perth	229	a																					
Dundee	229	a																					
Aberdeen	229	a																					
Inverness	229	a																					

A From Manchester Airport
B From London Euston
C from 17 February
D until 14 February
E From Bristol Temple Meads
F From Southampton Central
G From London Euston to Liverpool Lime Street
H To Glasgow Central
I From Cardiff Central
J To Liverpool Lime Street
K From Bournemouth

Refer to Operator websites for full information about Sleeper Services. Contact details for train operators available at National Rail Enquiries

Table T065-F

Mondays to Fridays
16 December to 15 May

London & West Midlands to North West England. London, West Midlands & Manchester to Scotland via the West Coast

Station	Table		LM [1] A	LM [1] B	VT ◇[1] ⊠	NT ◇ C	VT ◇[1] ⊠	NT ◇ D	VT ◇[1] A ⊠	TP ◇[1] ✠	VT ◇[1] ⊠	LM [1] E	VT ◇[1] F ⊠	LM [1]	LM [1] A	XC ◇[1] G ✠	LM [1] H	XC ◇[1] I ✠	LM [1] H	VT ◇[1] ⊡	VT ◇[1] ⊠	VT MO ◇[1] ⊠	VT MX ◇[1] ⊠	VT ◇[1] ⊠
London Euston [15]	⊖66	d		08 13	08 20		08 30				08 40		08 43	08 46					08 49	08 54	09 00	09 07	09 07	09 10
Watford Junction	66	d																	09 04					
Milton Keynes Central	66	d		08 53	08 50								09 13	09 19					09 29					09 41
Rugby	66	d		09 36										09 42					10 18	09 46				
Nuneaton		d												09 55										
Tamworth Low Level		d												10 09										
Lichfield Trent Valley		d												10 17	←									
Coventry	68	d		09 47									09 42		09 47			10 27	10 30					
Birmingham International	68 ✈	d		→									09 53		10 05		10 17	10 38	10 42					
BirminghamNewSt [12]	68	d											10 15		10 20	10 31	10 37	10 57	11 04					
Wolverhampton [7]		d											10 37		10 40	10 48	10 57	11 14	11 22					
Penkridge		d															11 06		11 31					
Stafford		d												10 35	10 56	11 02	11 13	11 28	11 38			10 24	10 24	
Stoke-on-Trent	84	a			09 48										11 12	11 17		11 43			10 24			
Macclesfield		a	←						←			←				11 36		12 01			10 41			
Crewe [10]	81,91	a	09 56						10 07		10 10	10 31	11 07	10 53	11 34		11 31		11 56			10 41	10 41	10 45
		d	09 58						10 09		10 11	10 33	11 09				11 33		11 58			10 43	10 43	10 47
Chester	81	a											→				→		→					11 12
Wrexham General	75	a																						
Llandudno Junction	81	a																						11 58
Bangor (Gwynedd)	81	a																						12 19
Holyhead	81 ⛴	a																						12 52
Wilmslow	84	a									10 27													
Stockport	84	a			10 16						10 35					11 49		12 13			10 54			
Manchester Piccadilly [10]		a			10 27						10 46					12 00		12 24			11 05			
Runcorn	91	a	10 25									10 51										11 01	11 01	
Liverpool South Pkwy [7]	91 ✈	a	10 33									11 00												
Liverpool Lime Street [10]	91	a	10 43									11 10										11 19	11 20	
		d																						
Manchester Airport	82 ✈	d				09 28				10 07														
Manchester Picc. [10]	82	d				09 47				10 26														
Bolton	82	d																						
Warrington Bank Quay		d					10 14		10 27											11 00				
Wigan North Western	90	d				10 20	10 25	←	10 38											11 12				
Preston [8]	90	a				10 43	10 38	10 43	10 51	11 02										11 25				
Blackpool North	97	a				→														11 49				
Preston [8]	90	d					10 41	10 44	10 53	11 03														
Lancaster [6]		d					10 56	11 02	11 10															
Barrow-in-Furness	82	a						12 00																
Oxenholme Lake District	83	d					11 09																	
Windermere	83	a																						
Penrith North Lakes		d							11 46															
Carlisle [8]	216	a					11 47		12 01	12 05														
		d					11 47		12 02	12 06														
Lockerbie	225,226	d								12 25														
Carstairs	226,225	a																						
Motherwell	226	a																						
GlasgowCentral [15]	216,226,225	a					12 59		13 15															
Haymarket		a								13s24														
Edinburgh [10]		a								13 29														
Fort William	227,400	a																						
Perth	229	a																						
Dundee	229	a																						
Aberdeen	229	a																						
Inverness	229	a																						

A From London Euston
B To Crewe
C To Barrow-in-Furness
D From Manchester Airport
E From Birmingham International
F To Edinburgh
G From Paignton
H To Liverpool Lime Street
I From Bournemouth

Refer to Operator websites for full information about Sleeper Services. Contact details for train operators available at National Rail Enquiries

Table T065-F

Mondays to Fridays

16 December to 15 May

London & West Midlands to North West England. London, West Midlands & Manchester to Scotland via the West Coast

	LM ■ A	LM ■ B	VT ◇■ ⊠	NT ◇ C	VT ◇■ ⊠	NT ◇ D	VT ◇■ A ⊠	TP ◇■ ✕	VT ◇■ ⊠	LM ■ E	VT ◇■ F ⊠	LM ■	LM ■ A	XC ◇■ G ✕	LM ■ H	XC ■ I ✕	LM ■ H	VT ◇■ ⊠	VT ◇■ ⊠	VT ◇■ ⊠	LM ■ A	LM ■ B
London Euston ■ ⊖66 d		09 13	09 20		09 30				09 40		09 43	09 46					09 49	10 00	10 07	10 10		10 15
Watford Junction 66 d																	10 04					
Milton Keynes Central 66 d		09 55	09 50								10 13	10 19					10 30			10 41		10 55
Rugby 66 d		10 37										10 42					11 18					11 36
Nuneaton d												10 55										
Tamworth Low Level d												11 09										
Lichfield Trent Valley d												11 17	←									
Coventry 68 d		10 48									10 42		10 48			11 27	11 30					11 47
Birmingham International 68 ✈ d		→									10 53		11 06		11 19	11 38	11 42					→
BirminghamNewSt ■ 68 ⇌ d											11 15		11 21	11 31	11 37	11 57	12 04					
Wolverhampton ■ ⇌ d											11 37		11 41	11 48	11 55	12 14	12 22					
Penkridge d															12 04		12 31					
Stafford d												11 35	11 57	12 02	12 11	12 28	12 38		11 24			
Stoke-on-Trent 84 a			10 48										12 13	12 17		12 43		11 24				
Macclesfield a	←						←			←				12 36		13 01		11 41			←	
Crewe ■ 81,91 a	10 56						11 07		11 10	11 31	12 07	11 53	12 38		12 30		12 56		11 41	11 45	11 56	
d	10 59						11 09		11 11	11 33	12 09				12 32		12 59		11 43	11 47	11 58	
Chester 81 a											→				→		→			12 08		
Wrexham General 75 a																						
Llandudno Junction 81 a																						
Bangor (Gwynedd) 81 a																						
Holyhead 81 ⛴ a																						
Wilmslow 84 a									11 27													
Stockport 84 a			11 16						11 35					12 49		13 13		11 54				
Manchester Piccadilly ■ ⇌ a			11 27						11 46					13 00		13 24		12 05				
Runcorn 91 a	11 22									11 53									12 00		12 24	
Liverpool South Pkwy ■ 91 ✈ a	11 31									12 02											12 33	
Liverpool Lime Street ■ 91 a	11 40									12 12									12 21		12 43	
d																						
Manchester Airport 82 ✈⇌ d				10 28				11 07														
Manchester Picc. ■ 82 ⇌ d				10 47				11 26														
Bolton 82 d																						
Warrington Bank Quay d					11 14		11 27															
Wigan North Western 90 d				11 21	11 25	←	11 38															
Preston ■ 90 a				11 42	11 38	11 42	11 51	12 02														
Blackpool North 97 ⇌ a				→																		
Preston ■ 90 d					11 41	11 44	11 53	12 03														
Lancaster ■ d					11 55	12 02	12 08	12 19														
Barrow-in-Furness 82 a						13 05																
Oxenholme Lake District 83 d							12 22	12 33														
Windermere 83 a																						
Penrith North Lakes d					12 31																	
Carlisle ■ 216 a					12 47		13 00	13 12														
d					12 47		13 01	13 12														
Lockerbie 225,226 d								13 33														
Carstairs 226,225 a																						
Motherwell 226 a								14 19														
GlasgowCentral ■ 216,226,225 a					13 59			14 38														
Haymarket ⇌ a							14 10															
Edinburgh ■ ⇌ a							14 17															
Fort William 227,400 a																						
Perth 229 a																						
Dundee 229 a																						
Aberdeen 229 a																						
Inverness 229 a																						

A From London Euston
B To Crewe
C To Barrow-in-Furness
D From Manchester Airport
E From Birmingham International
F To Glasgow Central
G From Bristol Temple Meads
H To Liverpool Lime Street
I From Bournemouth

Refer to Operator websites for full information about Sleeper Services. Contact details for train operators available at National Rail Enquiries

NRT DECEMBER 19 EDITION

Table T065-F

Mondays to Fridays

16 December to 15 May

London & West Midlands to North West England. London, West Midlands & Manchester to Scotland via the West Coast

	VT ◇■ ⊠	NT ◇ A	VT ◇■ ⊠	NT ◇ B	VT ◇■ C ⊠	NT	VT ◇■ ☐P	TP ◇■ ✕	VT ◇■ ⊠	TP ◇■ ✕	LM ■ D	VT ◇■ E ☐P	LM ■	LM ■ C	XC ◇■ F ✕	LM ■ G	XC ◇■ H ✕	LM ■ G	VT ◇■ ⊠	VT ◇■ ⊠	VT ◇■ ⊠
London Euston ■ ⊖66 d	10 20		10 30				10 36		10 40			10 43	10 46					10 49	11 00	11 07	11 10
Watford Junction 66 d																		11 04			
Milton Keynes Central 66 d	10 50											11 13	11 19					11 24			11 41
Rugby 66 d							11 25						11 42					12 18			
Nuneaton d													11 55								
Tamworth Low Level d													12 09								
Lichfield Trent Valley d													12 17	←							
Coventry 68 d												11 42		11 47			12 27	12 30			
Birmingham International 68 ✈ d												11 53		12 05		12 18	12 38	12 42			
BirminghamNewSt ■ 68 ⇌ d												12 15		12 20	12 31	12 37	12 57	13 04			
Wolverhampton ■ ⇌ d												12 37		12 40	12 48	12 57	13 14	13 22			
Penkridge d																13 06		13 30			
Stafford d													12 35	12 56	13 02	13 13	13 28	13 38		12 24	
Stoke-on-Trent 84 a	11 48													13 12	13 18		13 43		12 24		
Macclesfield a					←						←				13 36		14 01		12 41		
Crewe ■ 81,91 a					12 07				12 10		12 30	13 07	12 53	13 36		13 32		13 56		12 41	12 45
d					12 09				12 11		12 32	13 09				13 34		13 57		12 43	12 47
Chester 81 a												→				→		→			13 08
Wrexham General 75 a																					
Llandudno Junction 81 a																					
Bangor (Gwynedd) 81 a																					
Holyhead 81 ⛴ a																					
Wilmslow 84 a									12 27												
Stockport 84 a	12 16								12 35						13 49		14 13		12 54		
Manchester Piccadilly ■ ⇌ a	12 27								12 46						14 00		14 24		13 05		
Runcorn 91 a											12 53									13 00	
Liverpool South Pkwy ■ 91 ✈ a											13 02										
Liverpool Lime Street ■ 91 a											13 11									13 20	
d										12 12											
Manchester Airport 82 ✈⇌ d		11 28						12 07													
Manchester Picc. ■ 82 ⇌ d		11 47						12 26													
Bolton 82 d								12u44													
Warrington Bank Quay d			12 14		12 27		12 34														
Wigan North Western 90 d		12 18	12 25		12 38		12 45			12 50											
Preston ■ 90 a		12 36	12 38		12 51		12 57	13 03		13 06											
Blackpool North 97 ⇌ a				←			13 20														
Preston ■ 90 d		12 46	12 41	12 46	12 53			13 05		13 09											
Lancaster ■ d		→			13 08	13 13		13 21		13 26											
Barrow-in-Furness 82 a						14 16															
Oxenholme Lake District 83 d				13 32	13 23			13 35													
Windermere 83 a				13 53																	
Penrith North Lakes d			13 29							14 05											
Carlisle ■ 216 a			13 45		14 00	16 51		14 13		14 21											
d			13 45		14 00			14 15		14 24											
Lockerbie 225,226 d										14 43											
Carstairs 226,225 a																					
Motherwell 226 a					14 58																
GlasgowCentral ■ 216,226,225 a			14 59		15 15					15 54											
Haymarket ⇌ a								15s31													
Edinburgh ■ ⇌ a								15 36													
Fort William 227,400 a																					
Perth 229 a																					
Dundee 229 a																					
Aberdeen 229 a																					
Inverness 229 a																					

A To Windermere
B From Manchester Airport
C From London Euston
D From Birmingham International
E To Edinburgh
F From Bristol Temple Meads
G To Liverpool Lime Street
H From Bournemouth

Refer to Operator websites for full information about Sleeper Services. Contact details for train operators available at National Rail Enquiries

Table T065-F

Mondays to Fridays

16 December to 15 May

London & West Midlands to North West England. London, West Midlands & Manchester to Scotland via the West Coast

	LM	LM	VT	NT	VT	NT	VT	TP	VT	LM	VT	LM	LM	XC	LM	XC	LM	VT	VT	VT	LM	LM
	■	■	◇■	◇	■	◇	◇■	◇■	◇■	■	◇■	■	■	◇■	■	◇■	■	◇■	◇■	◇■	■	■
	A	B		C		D	A			E	F		A	G	H	I	H				A	B
			⊠		⊠		☕	⌶	⊠		⊠			⌶		⌶		⊠	⊠	⊠		
London Euston ■15 ⊖66 d		11 15	11 20		11 30				11 40		11 43	11 46					11 49	12 00	12 07	12 10		12 15
Watford Junction 66 d																	12 04					
Milton Keynes Central 66 d		11 55	11 50								12 13	12 19					12 25			12 41		12 55
Rugby 66 d		12 37										12 42					13 18			13 03		13 37
Nuneaton d												12 55										
Tamworth Low Level d												13 09										
Lichfield Trent Valley d												13 17	←									
Coventry 68 d		12 47									12 42		12 47			13 27	13 30					13 47
Birmingham International 68 ✈ d		→									12 53		13 05		13 18	13 38	13 42					→
BirminghamNewSt ■12 68 d											13 15		13 21	13 31	13 37	13 57	14 04					
Wolverhampton ■7 d											13 37		13 40	13 48	13 57	14 14	14 22					
Penkridge d															14 06		14 30					
Stafford d												13 41	13 55	14 02	14 13	14 28	14 38		13 24			
Stoke-on-Trent 84 a			12 48										14 12	14 17		14 43		13 24				
Macclesfield a	←						←			←				14 36		15 01		13 41			←	
Crewe ■10 81,91 a	12 56						13 07		13 10	13 32	14 07	14 04	14 34		14 31		14 57		13 41	13 48	13 56	
d	12 59						13 09		13 11	13 34	14 09				14 34		14 58		13 43	13 50	13 57	
Chester 81 a											→				→		→			14 11		
Wrexham General 75 a																						
Llandudno Junction 81 a																						
Bangor (Gwynedd) 81 a																						
Holyhead 81 ⛴ a																						
Wilmslow 84 a									13 27													
Stockport 84 a			13 16						13 35					14 49		15 13		13 54				
Manchester Piccadilly ■10 a			13 27						13 46					15 00		15 24		14 05				
Runcorn 91 a	13 22									13 56									14 00		14 23	
Liverpool South Pkwy ■7 91 ✈ a	13 30									14 04											14 31	
Liverpool Lime Street ■10 91 a	13 40									14 14									14 19		14 42	
d																						
Manchester Airport 82 ✈ d				12 28				13 07														
Manchester Picc. ■10 82 d				12 47				13 26														
Bolton 82 d								13u44														
Warrington Bank Quay d					13 14		13 27															
Wigan North Western 90 d				13 18	13 25	←	13 38															
Preston ■8 90 a				13 43	13 38	13 43	13 51	14 03														
Blackpool North 97 a				→																		
Preston ■8 90 d					13 41	13 44	13 53	14 05														
Lancaster ■6 d					13 55	14 02	14 08	14 21														
Barrow-in-Furness 82 a						15 05																
Oxenholme Lake District 83 d					14 09			14 35														
Windermere 83 a																						
Penrith North Lakes d							14 43	15 00														
Carlisle ■8 216 a					14 47		15 00	15 16														
d					14 47		15 01	15 16														
Lockerbie 225,226 d								15 36														
Carstairs 226,225 a																						
Motherwell 226 a								16s21														
GlasgowCentral ■15 216,226,225 a					15 59			16 39														
Haymarket a							16 12															
Edinburgh ■10 a							16 18															
Fort William 227,400 a																						
Perth 229 a																						
Dundee 229 a																						
Aberdeen 229 a																						
Inverness 229 a																						

A From London Euston
B To Crewe
C To Barrow-in-Furness
D From Manchester Airport
E From Birmingham International
F To Glasgow Central
G From Paignton
H To Liverpool Lime Street
I From Bournemouth

Refer to Operator websites for full information about Sleeper Services. Contact details for train operators available at National Rail Enquiries

Table T065-F

Mondays to Fridays

16 December to 15 May

London & West Midlands to North West England. London, West Midlands & Manchester to Scotland via the West Coast

	VT	NT	VT	NT	VT	TP	VT	LM	NT	VT	LM	LM	XC	LM	XC	LM	VT	VT	VT	LM	LM
	◇■	◇	◇■	◇	◇■	◇■	◇■	■		◇■	■	■	◇■	■	◇■	■	◇■	◇■	◇■	■	■
		A		B	C			D		E		C	F	G	H	G				C	I
	⊠		⊠		⊠	⌶	⊠			⊠			⌶		⌶		☕	☕	☕		
London Euston ■15 ⊖66 d	12 20		12 30				12 40			12 43	12 46					12 49	13 00	13 07	13 10		13 15
Watford Junction 66 d																13 04					
Milton Keynes Central 66 d	12 50									13 13	13 19					13 25			13 41		13 55
Rugby 66 d											13 42					14 18					14 37
Nuneaton d											13 55										
Tamworth Low Level d											14 09										
Lichfield Trent Valley d											14 17	←									
Coventry 68 d										13 42		13 47			14 27	14 30					14 48
Birmingham International 68 ✈ d										13 53		14 05		14 18	14 38	14 42					→
BirminghamNewSt ■12 68 d										14 15		14 21	14 31	14 37	14 57	15 04					
Wolverhampton ■7 d										14 36		14 40	14 48	14 57	15 14	15 22					
Penkridge d														15 06		15 31					
Stafford d											14 35	14 54	15 02	15 13	15 28	15 38		14 24			
Stoke-on-Trent 84 a	13 48											15 11	15 17		15 43		14 24				
Macclesfield a					←			←					15 36		16 01		14 41			←	
Crewe ■10 81,91 a					14 07		14 10	14 31		15 05	14 54	15 33		15 32		15 56		14 41	14 45	14 57	
d					14 09		14 11	14 34		15 07				15 34		15 58		14 43	14 48	14 58	
Chester 81 a										→				→		→			15 08		
Wrexham General 75 a																					
Llandudno Junction 81 a																					
Bangor (Gwynedd) 81 a																					
Holyhead 81 ⛴ a																					
Wilmslow 84 a							14 27														
Stockport 84 a	14 16						14 35						15 49		16 13		14 54				
Manchester Piccadilly ■10 a	14 27						14 46						16 00		16 24		15 05				
Runcorn 91 a								14 54										15 00		15 22	
Liverpool South Pkwy ■7 91 ✈ a								15 04												15 31	
Liverpool Lime Street ■10 91 a								15 14										15 19		15 40	
d																					
Manchester Airport 82 ✈ d		13 28				14 07															
Manchester Picc. ■10 82 d		13 47				14 26															
Bolton 82 d																					
Warrington Bank Quay d			14 14		14 27																
Wigan North Western 90 d		14 18	14 25	←	14 38																
Preston ■8 90 a		14 43	14 38	14 43	14 51	15 02															
Blackpool North 97 a		→																			
Preston ■8 90 d			14 41	14 45	14 53	15 03			15 32												
Lancaster ■6 d			14 56	15 03	15 09	15 19			16 13												
Barrow-in-Furness 82 a				16 05					17 16												
Oxenholme Lake District 83 d					15 23	15 33															
Windermere 83 a																					
Penrith North Lakes d			15 31			15 59															
Carlisle ■8 216 a			15 46		16 01	16 14			19 43												
d			15 46		16 03	16 16															
Lockerbie 225,226 d						16 34															
Carstairs 226,225 a																					
Motherwell 226 a																					
GlasgowCentral ■15 216,226,225 a			16 59		17 15																
Haymarket a						17s32															
Edinburgh ■10 a						17 37															
Fort William 227,400 a																					
Perth 229 a																					
Dundee 229 a																					
Aberdeen 229 a																					
Inverness 229 a																					

A To Barrow-in-Furness
B From Manchester Airport
C From London Euston
D From Birmingham International
E To Edinburgh
F From Bristol Temple Meads
G To Liverpool Lime Street
H From Bournemouth
I To Crewe

Refer to Operator websites for full information about Sleeper Services. Contact details for train operators available at National Rail Enquiries

Table T065-F

Mondays to Fridays
16 December to 15 May

London & West Midlands to North West England. London, West Midlands & Manchester to Scotland via the West Coast

Station	VT	NT	VT	NT	VT	TP	VT	LM	VT	LM	LM	XC	LM	XC	LM	VT	VT	VT	LM	LM	VT	NT
		A		B	C			D	E		C	F	G	H	G				C	I		J
London Euston ⊖66 d	13 20		13 30				13 40		13 43	13 46					13 49	14 00	14 07	14 10		14 15	14 20	
Watford Junction 66 d															14 04							
Milton Keynes Central 66 d	13 50								14 13	14 19					14 26			14 41		14 55	14 50	
Rugby 66 d										14 42					15 18					15 38		
Nuneaton d										14 55												
Tamworth Low Level d										15 09												
Lichfield Trent Valley d										15 17	←											
Coventry 68 d									14 42		14 48			15 27	15 30					15 48		
Birmingham International 68 d									14 53		15 06		15 18	15 38	15 42					→		
BirminghamNewSt 68 d									15 15		15 21	15 31	15 37	15 57	16 04							
Wolverhampton d									15 37		15 40	15 48	15 55	16 14	16 22							
Penkridge d													16 04		16 31							
Stafford d										15 34	15 56	16 02	16 11	16 28	16 38		15 24					
Stoke-on-Trent 84 a	14 48										16 13	16 17		16 43		15 24					15 48	
Macclesfield a					←			←				16 36		17 01		15 41			←			
Crewe 81,91 a					15 05		15 10	15 32	16 07	15 52	16 34		16 30		16 56		15 41	15 45	15 56			
d					15 07		15 11	15 34	16 09				16 32		16 58		15 43	15 47	15 58			
Chester 81 a									→				→		→			16 08				
Wrexham General 75 a																						
Llandudno Junction 81 a																						
Bangor (Gwynedd) 81 a																						
Holyhead 81 a																						
Wilmslow 84 a							15 27															
Stockport 84 a	15 16						15 35					16 49		17 13		15 54					16 16	
Manchester Piccadilly a	15 27						15 46					17 00		17 24		16 05					16 27	
Runcorn 91 a								15 51									16 00		16 25			
Liverpool South Pkwy 91 a								16 00											16 33			
Liverpool Lime Street 91 a								16 10									16 20		16 43			
d																						
Manchester Airport 82 d		14 28				15 07																15 28
Manchester Picc. 82 d		14 47				15 26																15 47
Bolton 82 d																						
Warrington Bank Quay d			15 14		15 25																	
Wigan North Western 90 d		15 20	15 25	←	15 36																	16 18
Preston 90 a		15 43	15 38	15 43	15 51	16 02																16 42
Blackpool North 97 a		→																				→
Preston 90 d			15 41	15 45	15 53	16 03																
Lancaster d					16 08	16 19																
Barrow-in-Furness 82 a																						
Oxenholme Lake District 83 d			16 07	16 31		16 34																
Windermere 83 a				16 53																		
Penrith North Lakes d			16 32		16 45	16 59																
Carlisle 216 a			16 47		17 00	17 15																
d			16 48		17 02	17 16																
Lockerbie 225,226 d						17 35																
Carstairs 226,225 a																						
Motherwell 226 a						18 20																
GlasgowCentral 216,226,225 a			17 59			18 39																
Haymarket a					18 15																	
Edinburgh a					18 21																	
Fort William 227,400 a																						
Perth 229 a																						
Dundee 229 a																						
Aberdeen 229 a																						
Inverness 229 a																						

A To Windermere
B From Manchester Airport
C From London Euston
D From Birmingham International
E To Glasgow Central
F From Plymouth
G To Liverpool Lime Street
H From Bournemouth
I To Crewe
J To Barrow-in-Furness

Refer to Operator websites for full information about Sleeper Services. Contact details for train operators available at National Rail Enquiries

Table T065-F

Mondays to Fridays
16 December to 15 May

London & West Midlands to North West England. London, West Midlands & Manchester to Scotland via the West Coast

Station	VT	NT	VT	VT	TP	LM	TP	VT	LM	LM	XC	LM	XC	LM	VT	VT	VT	LM	LM	VT	VT	NT
		A	B			C		D		B	E	F	G	F				B	H			
London Euston ⊖66 d	14 30			14 40				14 43	14 46					14 49	15 00	15 07	15 10		15 15	15 20	15 30	
Watford Junction 66 d														15 04								
Milton Keynes Central 66 d								15 13	15 19					15 26			15 41		15 55	15 50		
Rugby 66 d									15 42					16 18					16 38			
Nuneaton d									15 55													
Tamworth Low Level d									16 09													
Lichfield Trent Valley d									16 17	←												
Coventry 68 d								15 42		15 48			16 27	16 30					16 49			
Birmingham International 68 d								15 53		16 06		16 18	16 38	16 42					→			
BirminghamNewSt 68 d								16 15		16 22	16 31	16 37	16 57	17 04								
Wolverhampton d								16 37		16 41	16 48	16 57	17 14	17 22								
Penkridge d												17 06		17 31								
Stafford d									16 35	16 55	17 03	17 13	17 28	17 38		16 24						
Stoke-on-Trent 84 a										17 12	17 19		17 43		16 24					16 48		
Macclesfield a			←			←					17 36		18 01		16 41			←		17 05		
Crewe 81,91 a			16 07	16 10		16 30		17 07	16 53	17 36		17 31		17 56		16 41	16 45	16 56				
d			16 09	16 11		16 32		17 09				17 33		17 58		16 43	16 47	16 58				
Chester 81 a								→				→		→			17 08					
Wrexham General 75 a																						
Llandudno Junction 81 a																						
Bangor (Gwynedd) 81 a																						
Holyhead 81 a																						
Wilmslow 84 a				16 27																		
Stockport 84 a				16 35							17 49		18 13		16 54					17 17		
Manchester Piccadilly a				16 46							18 00		18 24		17 05					17 28		
Runcorn 91 a						16 52										17 00		17 24				
Liverpool South Pkwy 91 a						17 01												17 32				
Liverpool Lime Street 91 a						17 11										17 20		17 42				
d					16 12																	
Manchester Airport 82 d							16 07															16 29
Manchester Picc. 82 d							16 26															16 54
Bolton 82 d																						17 17
Warrington Bank Quay d	16 14		16 27																		17 14	
Wigan North Western 90 d	16 25	←	16 38		16 43																17 25	
Preston 90 a	16 38	16 42	16 51		16 59		17 03														17 38	17 43
Blackpool North 97 a																						
Preston 90 d	16 41	16 45	16 53		17 01		17 05														17 41	17 45
Lancaster d	16 56	17 02	17 09		17 17		17 22														17 55	18 03
Barrow-in-Furness 82 a		18 02																				19 05
Oxenholme Lake District 83 d	17 09		17 23				17 36														18 09	
Windermere 83 a																						
Penrith North Lakes d	17 35		17 48		17 55																	
Carlisle 216 a	17 50		18 04		18 10		18 14														18 46	
d	17 51		18 06		18 11		18 16														18 47	
Lockerbie 225,226 d							18 35															
Carstairs 226,225 a																						
Motherwell 226 a																						
GlasgowCentral 216,226,225 a	19 15		19 23		19 38																19 59	
Haymarket a							19s34															
Edinburgh a							19 39															
Fort William 227,400 a																						
Perth 229 a																						
Dundee 229 a																						
Aberdeen 229 a																						
Inverness 229 a																						

A From Manchester Airport
B From London Euston
C From Birmingham International
D To Edinburgh
E From Bristol Temple Meads
F To Liverpool Lime Street
G From Bournemouth
H To Crewe

Refer to Operator websites for full information about Sleeper Services. Contact details for train operators available at National Rail Enquiries

Table T065-F

Mondays to Fridays

16 December to 15 May

London & West Midlands to North West England. London, West Midlands & Manchester to Scotland via the West Coast

	VT	TP	VT	LM	VT	LM	LM	XC	LM	XC	LM	VT	VT	VT	LM	LM	VT	NT	VT	NT	VT
	■ 1	◇1	◇1	1	■ 1	1	1	◇1	1	◇1	1	◇1	◇1	◇1	1	1	◇1	◇	◇1	◇	■ 1
	A			B	C		A	D	E	F	E				A	G		H		I	A
	⊐	⊥	⊐		⊐			⊥		⊥		⊐	⊐	⊐			⊐		⊠		⊐
London Euston 15 ⊖66 d			15 40		15 43	15 46					15 49	16 00	16 07	16 10		16 15	16 20		16 30		
Watford Junction 66 d											16 04										
Milton Keynes Central 66 d					16 13	16 19					16 25			16u41		16 55	16 50				
Rugby 66 d						16 42					17 18					17 36					
Nuneaton d						16 55															
Tamworth Low Level d						17 09															
Lichfield Trent Valley d						17 17	←														
Coventry 68 d					16 42		16 49			17 27	17 30					17 47					
Birmingham International 68 ✈ d					16 53		17 07		17 18	17 38	17 42					→					
BirminghamNewSt 12 68 ⛴ d					17 15		17 22	17 31	17 37	17 57	18 04										
Wolverhampton 7 ⛴ d					17 37		17 40	17 48	17 59	18 14	18 22										
Penkridge d									18 08		18 31										
Stafford d						17 35	17 57	18 02	18 15	18 28	18 38		17 24								
Stoke-on-Trent 84 a							18 13	18 17		18 43		17 24					17 48				
Macclesfield a	←			←				18 36		19 01		17 41			←						←
Crewe 10 81,91 a	17 07		17 10	17 31	18 07	17 53	18 36		18 34		18 57		17 41	17 45	17 56						18 07
d	17 09		17 11	17 33	18 09				18 36		18 59		17 43	17 48	17 58						18 09
Chester 81 a					→				→		→			18 07							
Wrexham General 75 a																					
Llandudno Junction 81 a														18 58							
Bangor (Gwynedd) 81 a														19 18							
Holyhead 81 ⛴ a																					
Wilmslow 84 a			17 27																		
Stockport 84 a			17 35					18 49		19 13		17 54					18 16				
Manchester Piccadilly 10 ⛴ a			17 46					19 00		19 24		18 05					18 27				
Runcorn 91 a				17 52									18 00		18 24						
Liverpool South Pkwy 7 91 ✈ a				18 02											18 32						
Liverpool Lime Street 10 91 a				18 12									18 20		18 44						
d																					
Manchester Airport 82 ✈⛴ d		17 07																17 27			
Manchester Picc. 10 82 ⛴ d		17 27																17 47			
Bolton 82 d																					
Warrington Bank Quay d	17 27																		18 14		18 27
Wigan North Western 90 d	17 38																	18 20	18 25	←	18 38
Preston 8 90 a	17 51	18 02																18 42	18 38	18 42	18 51
Blackpool North 97 ⛴ a																		→			
Preston 8 90 d	17 53	18 04																	18 41	18 45	18 53
Lancaster 6 d	18 09	18 20																	18 58		19 08
Barrow-in-Furness 82 a																					
Oxenholme Lake District 83 d	18 24	18 34																		19 22	19 23
Windermere 83 a																				19 43	
Penrith North Lakes d	18 49	18 59																	19 32		
Carlisle 8 216 a	19 05	19 15																	19 47		20 02
d	19 05	19 15																	19 48		20 02
Lockerbie 225,226 d		19 35																			
Carstairs 226,225 a																					
Motherwell 226 a		20 21																			
GlasgowCentral 15 216,226,225 a		20 39																	20 59		21 15
Haymarket ⛴ a	20 17																				
Edinburgh 10 ⛴ a	20 25																				
Fort William 227,400 a																					
Perth 229 a																					
Dundee 229 a																					
Aberdeen 229 a																					
Inverness 229 a																					

A From London Euston
B From Birmingham International
C To Glasgow Central
D From Exeter St Davids
E To Liverpool Lime Street
F From Bournemouth
G To Crewe
H To Windermere
I From Manchester Airport

Refer to Operator websites for full information about Sleeper Services. Contact details for train operators available at National Rail Enquiries

Table T065-F

Mondays to Fridays

16 December to 15 May

London & West Midlands to North West England. London, West Midlands & Manchester to Scotland via the West Coast

	NT	VT	VT	VT	LM	VT	VT	LM	LM	TP	XC	LM	XC	LM	VT	VT	VT	VT	VT	LM	VT	NT
		◇1	◇1	◇1	1	◇1	◇1	1	1	◇1	◇1	1	◇1	1	◇1	◇1	◇1	◇1	◇1	1	◇1	◇
		A		B	C		D		B		E	F	G							B		H
		⊐	⊐	⊐		⊐	⊐			⊥	⊥		⊥		⊠	⊠	⊠	⊠	⊠		⊠	
London Euston 15 ⊖66 d		16 33	16 40			16 43	16 43	16 46						16 52	16 57	17 00	17 07	17 10	17 10		17 20	
Watford Junction 66 d																						
Milton Keynes Central 66 d				←		17 13	17 13	17 19						17 32				17u41	17u41		17u50	
Rugby 66 d		17 22		17 22				17 47						18 20								
Nuneaton d		→						18 01										18 11	18 11			
Tamworth Low Level d								18 16							18 00							
Lichfield Trent Valley d								18 22	←						18 08							
Coventry 68 d						17 42	17 42		17 47				18 27	18 30								
Birmingham International 68 ✈ d						17 53	17 53		18 06			18 18	18 38	18 42								
BirminghamNewSt 12 68 ⛴ d						18 15	18 15		18 20		18 31	18 37	18 57	19 04								
Wolverhampton 7 ⛴ d						18 37	18 37		18 40		18 48	18 57	19 14	19 22								
Penkridge d												19 06		19 30								
Stafford d				17 58				18 42	18 54		19 02	19 13	19 28	19 38			18 24					
Stoke-on-Trent 84 a									19 11		19 17		19 43			18 24					18 48	
Macclesfield a					←						19 36		20 01			18 41				←		
Crewe 10 81,91 a			18 10	18 17	18 34	19 05	19 05	19 01	19 37			19 31		19 56			18 42	18 53	18 53	18 57		
d			18 11	18 20	18 36		19 11					19 33					18 44	18 56	18 56	18 59		
Chester 81 a							→					→						19 15	19 15			
Wrexham General 75 a																						
Llandudno Junction 81 a																			20 11			
Bangor (Gwynedd) 81 a																			20 27			
Holyhead 81 ⛴ a																			21 00			
Wilmslow 84 a			18 27																			
Stockport 84 a			18 35								19 49		20 13			18 54					19 16	
Manchester Piccadilly 10 ⛴ a			18 46								20 00		20 24			19 05					19 27	
Runcorn 91 a					19 00												19 01			19 23		
Liverpool South Pkwy 7 91 ✈ a					19 09															19 32		
Liverpool Lime Street 10 91 a					19 19												19 22			19 41		
d																						
Manchester Airport 82 ✈⛴ d										18 07												18 28
Manchester Picc. 10 82 ⛴ d										18 26												18 47
Bolton 82 d																						
Warrington Bank Quay d				18 37											18 50							
Wigan North Western 90 d				18 48											19 01							19 20
Preston 8 90 a				19 01						19 04					19 14							19 43
Blackpool North 97 ⛴ a				19 30																		→
Preston 8 90 d										19 05					19 15							
Lancaster 6 d	19 13									19 21					19 30							
Barrow-in-Furness 82 a	20 16																					
Oxenholme Lake District 83 d										19 35					19 45							
Windermere 83 a																						
Penrith North Lakes d										20 01					20 10							
Carlisle 8 216 a	22 42									20 16					20 25							
d										20 18					20 25							
Lockerbie 225,226 d										20 37					20 44							
Carstairs 226,225 a																						
Motherwell 226 a															21 27							
GlasgowCentral 15 216,226,225 a															21 44							
Haymarket ⛴ a										21s34												
Edinburgh 10 ⛴ a										21 40												
Fort William 227,400 a																						
Perth 229 a																						
Dundee 229 a																						
Aberdeen 229 a																						
Inverness 229 a																						

A To Blackpool North
B From London Euston
C From Birmingham International
D To Edinburgh
E From Paignton
F To Liverpool Lime Street
G From Bournemouth
H To Barrow-in-Furness

Refer to Operator websites for full information about Sleeper Services. Contact details for train operators available at National Rail Enquiries

Table T065-F

Mondays to Fridays
16 December to 15 May

London & West Midlands to North West England. London, West Midlands & Manchester to Scotland via the West Coast

	VT	NT		VT	TP	VT	VT	VT	LM	VT	LM	VT		VT	VT	VT	LM	VT	NT	VT	NT	VT		TP
	◇1	◇		◇1	◇1	◇1	◇1	◇1	1	◇1	1	◇1		◇1	◇1	◇1	1	◇1	◇	◇1	◇	◇1		◇1
		A		B		C		B	D	E							F		G		A	B		
	⊠			🍴	☕	⊠	⊠	⊠		🍴		⊠		⊠	⊠	⊠		⊠		⊠		🍴		☕
London Euston 15 ⊖66 d	17 30					17 33	17 40			17 43	17 46	17 57		18 00	18 07	18 10	18 13	18 20		18 30				
Watford Junction 66 d																								
Milton Keynes Central 66 d								←		18u13	18 19					18u41	18 45	18u50						
Rugby 66 d						18 23		18 23			18 48						19 36							
Nuneaton d						→					19 00					19 11								
Tamworth Low Level d											19 15	19 00												
Lichfield Trent Valley d											19 21	19 08												
Coventry 68 d										18 42							19 47							
Birmingham International 68 ✈ d										18 53							→					←		
BirminghamNewSt 12 68 d										19 15												19 15		
Wolverhampton 7 d										→												19 37		
Penkridge d																								
Stafford d								18 56			19 41				19 24									
Stoke-on-Trent 84 a														19 24				19 48						
Macclesfield a				←					←					19 41										
Crewe 10 81,91 a				19 05			19 10	19 14	19 31		20 02				19 41	19 51						20 07		
d				19 11			19 11	19 16	19 33						19 43	19 54						20 09		
Chester 81 a																20 13								
Wrexham General 75 a																20 38								
Llandudno Junction 81 a																								
Bangor (Gwynedd) 81 a																								
Holyhead 81 a																								
Wilmslow 84 a							19 27																	
Stockport 84 a							19 35							19 54				20 16						
Manchester Piccadilly 10 a							19 45							20 05				20 27						
Runcorn 91 a								19 35	19 57						20 00									
Liverpool South Pkwy 7 91 ✈ a									20 06															
Liverpool Lime Street 10 91 a								19 52	20 16						20 20									
d																								20 12
Manchester Airport 82 ✈ d					19 07														19 28					
Manchester Picc. 10 82 d					19 26														19 47					
Bolton 82 d					19u44																			
Warrington Bank Quay d	19 14			19 29								19 50								20 14		20 27		
Wigan North Western 90 d	19 25	←		19 40								20 01							20 18	20 25	←	20 38		20 43
Preston 8 90 a	19 38	19 43		19 54	20 04							20 14							20 42	20 38	20 42	20 51		20 58
Blackpool North 97 a																			→					
Preston 8 90 d	19 41	19 44		19 55	20 06							20 16								20 41	20 44	20 53		20 59
Lancaster 8 d	19 55	20 04		20 11	20 22							20a30								20 55	21 02	21 09		21 15
Barrow-in-Furness 82 a		21 06																			22 01			
Oxenholme Lake District 83 d	20 09				20 36															21 10		21 24		21a30
Windermere 83 a																								
Penrith North Lakes d				20 49	21 01															21 35				
Carlisle 8 216 a	20 47			21 04	21 17															21 50		22 01		
d	20 47			21 06	21 18															21 50		22 03		
Lockerbie 225,226 d					21 37															22 09				
Carstairs 226,225 a																								
Motherwell 226 a	21 45				22 21															22 53				
GlasgowCentral 15 216,226,225 a	22 11				22 40															23 09		23 17		
Haymarket a				22 16																				
Edinburgh 10 a				22 22																				
Fort William 227,400 a																								
Perth 229 a																								
Dundee 229 a																								
Aberdeen 229 a																								
Inverness 229 a																								

A From Manchester Airport
B From London Euston
C To Liverpool Lime Street
D From Birmingham International
E To Glasgow Central
F To Crewe
G To Barrow-in-Furness

Refer to Operator websites for full information about Sleeper Services. Contact details for train operators available at National Rail Enquiries

NRT DECEMBER 19 EDITION

Table T065-F

Mondays to Fridays
16 December to 15 May

London & West Midlands to North West England. London, West Midlands & Manchester to Scotland via the West Coast

	VT	TP	VT	LM	XC	LM	XC	LM		VT	VT FO	LM FX	LM FO	LM	XC	LM	XC	LM		VT ThFO	VT FO	VT	VT	VT
																						2	2	2
	◇1	◇1	◇1	1	◇1	1	◇1	1		◇1	◇1	1	1	1	◇1	1	◇1	1		◇1	◇1	1	1	1
					A		B				C			D	A	E	F				D			
	⊠	☕	⊠		☕		☕			⊠	🍴				☕		☕			🍴	🍴	🍴	🍴	🍴
London Euston 15 ⊖66 d	18 33		18 40							18 43	18 46	18 46	18 49					18 52		18 57		19 00	19 10	19 10
Watford Junction 66 d																								
Milton Keynes Central 66 d										19 13	19 19	19 19	19 24					19 32					19u41	19u41
Rugby 66 d	19 23										19 40	19 46	20 05					20 17						
Nuneaton d												20 02	20 18										20 11	20 11
Tamworth Low Level d			19 44									20 16	20 33											
Lichfield Trent Valley d			19 51									20 23	20 39	←										
Coventry 68 d							19 28			19 42				19 47			20 27	20 30						
Birmingham International 68 ✈ d						19 18	19 38			19 53				20 05		20 18	20 38	20 42						
BirminghamNewSt 12 68 d				19 20	19 31	19 39	19 57	20 00		20 15				20 19	20 31	20 37	20 57	21 04						
Wolverhampton 7 d				19 40	19 50	19 57	20 14	20 21		20 37				20 40	20 48	20 57	21 14	21 23						
Penkridge d						20 06		20 30								21 06		21 32						
Stafford d	19 54			19 57	20 04	20 13	20 28	20 39		20 51	20 24	20 47	20 57	20 54	21 02	21 13	21 28	21 44					20 36	20 36
Stoke-on-Trent 84 a				20 14	20 19		20 43							21 11	21 17		21 44					20 24		
Macclesfield a					20 36		21 01								21 36		22 01				←			
Crewe 10 81,91 a	20 13		20 17	20 36		20 32		20 57		21 15	20 42	21 08	21 18	21 33		21 31		22 04		20s33	20 42		20 51	20 51
d	20 16		20 18			20 35					20 43					21 33					20 43		20 54	20 54
Chester 81 a											→					→							21 19	21 19
Wrexham General 75 a																								
Llandudno Junction 81 a																								22 13
Bangor (Gwynedd) 81 a																								22 30
Holyhead 81 a																								23 01
Wilmslow 84 a			20 33																					
Stockport 84 a			20 42		20 49		21 13								21 49		22 15					20 54		
Manchester Piccadilly 10 a			20 52		20 59		21 24								22 00		22 25			21 09		21 05		
Runcorn 91 a	20 33					20 57																		
Liverpool South Pkwy 7 91 ✈ a						21 06																		
Liverpool Lime Street 10 91 a	20 53					21 17																		
d																								
Manchester Airport 82 ✈ d		20 07																						
Manchester Picc. 10 82 d		20 26																						
Bolton 82 d		20u44																						
Warrington Bank Quay d																					21 03			
Wigan North Western 90 d																					21 14			
Preston 8 90 a		21 03																			21 31			
Blackpool North 97 a																					22 00			
Preston 8 90 d		21 05																						
Lancaster 8 d		21 21																						
Barrow-in-Furness 82 a																								
Oxenholme Lake District 83 d		21 35																						
Windermere 83 a																								
Penrith North Lakes d		22 00																						
Carlisle 8 216 a		22 16																						
d		22 17																						
Lockerbie 225,226 d		22 36																						
Carstairs 226,225 a																								
Motherwell 226 a																								
GlasgowCentral 15 216,226,225 a																								
Haymarket a		23s34																						
Edinburgh 10 a		23 39																						
Fort William 227,400 a																								
Perth 229 a																								
Dundee 229 a																								
Aberdeen 229 a																								
Inverness 229 a																								

A From Exeter St Davids
B From Bournemouth
C To Blackpool North
D From London Euston
E To Liverpool Lime Street
F From Bournemouth. ☕ to BirminghamNewSt

Refer to Operator websites for full information about Sleeper Services. Contact details for train operators available at National Rail Enquiries

Table T065-F

Mondays to Fridays
16 December to 15 May

London & West Midlands to North West England. London, West Midlands & Manchester to Scotland via the West Coast

Station		LM A	VT	VT	TP	VT	LM B	VT	LM	LM C	LM D	XC E	LM	VT	VT	VT	VT F	VT	VT C	LM B	LM	NT	XC
London Euston ⊖66	d	19 15	19 20	19 30		19 40		19 43	19 46				19 53	20 00	20 07	20 10	20 30	20 40			20 46		
Watford Junction 66	d																						
Milton Keynes Central 66	d	19 57	19u50					20 13	20 19				20 31			20 41					21 19		
Rugby 66	d	20 37							20 42				21 20								21 45		
Nuneaton	d								21 00						21 03						22 00		
Tamworth Low Level	d					20 43			21 14								21 35		←		22 15		
Lichfield Trent Valley	d					20 50			21 21	←							21 42		21 42		22 22		
Coventry 68	d	20 47						20 42		20 47		21 27	21 31				→						
Birmingham International 68	d	→						20 53		21 05	21 17	21 38	21 47										
BirminghamNewSt 68	d							21 15		21 21	21 37	21 57	22 12										22 30
Wolverhampton	d							21 37		21 41	21 57	22 14	22 39										22 48
Penkridge	d										22 06		22 49										
Stafford	d					21 04		21 55	21 42	21 59	22 13	22 28	22 58		21 27				22 00		22 44		23 02
Stoke-on-Trent 84	a		20 49					22 10		22 15		22 43	23 16	21 25									23 20
Macclesfield	a		21 06				←					23 01		21 41						←			
Crewe 81,91	a					21 21	21 31	22 30	22 00	22 37	22 35		23 38		21 46	21 46		22 10	22 17	22 35	23 02		
	d					21 23	21 33				22 37				21 48	21 48		22 11	22 19	22 37			
Chester 81	a										→					22 11							
Wrexham General 75	a																						
Llandudno Junction 81	a																						
Bangor (Gwynedd) 81	a																						
Holyhead 81	a																						
Wilmslow 84	a					21 38												22 27					
Stockport 84	a		21 19									23 13		21 54				22 35					
Manchester Piccadilly	a		21 28			21 54						23 24		22 03				22 46					00 15
Runcorn 91	a						21 57								22 06					23 00			
Liverpool South Pkwy 91	a						22 05													23 09			
Liverpool Lime Street 91	a						22 16								22 23					23 20			
	d																						
Manchester Airport 82	d				21 06																	22 10	
Manchester Picc. 82	d				21 22																	22 26	
Bolton 82	d				21u39																		
Warrington Bank Quay	d			21 16															22 36				
Wigan North Western 90	d			21 27															22 47			22 58	
Preston 90	a			21 39	21 59														23 00			23 14	
Blackpool North 97	a																						
Preston 90	d			21 43	22 01																	23 15	
Lancaster	d			21 58	22 20																	23 33	
Barrow-in-Furness 82	a																					00 37	
Oxenholme Lake District 83	d			22 11	22 34																		
Windermere 83	a																						
Penrith North Lakes	d			22 36	23 00																		
Carlisle 216	a			22 51	23 16																		
	d			22 51	23 18																		
Lockerbie 225,226	d				23 37																		
Carstairs 226,225	a																						
Motherwell 226	a																						
GlasgowCentral 216,226,225	a			00 06	00 51																		
Haymarket	a																						
Edinburgh	a																						
Fort William 227,400	a																						
Perth 229	a																						
Dundee 229	a																						
Aberdeen 229	a																						
Inverness 229	a																						

A To Crewe
B From Birmingham International
C From London Euston
D To Liverpool Lime Street
E From Bournemouth. to BirminghamNewSt
F To Preston

Refer to Operator websites for full information about Sleeper Services. Contact details for train operators available at National Rail Enquiries

Table T065-F

Mondays to Fridays
16 December to 15 May

London & West Midlands to North West England. London, West Midlands & Manchester to Scotland via the West Coast

Station		AW A	LM	VT	VT	VT	TP	CS	CS	AW B	VT	LM	VT	VT	CS
London Euston ⊖66	d		20 51	21 00	21 07	21 10		21 15	21 15		21 40	21 49	22 00	23 00	23 50
Watford Junction 66	d					21u25		21u33	21u33					23u19	00u10
Milton Keynes Central 66	d		21 30	21 31	21 39							22 22	22 40		
Rugby 66	d		22 20			22 05						22 46	23 02		
Nuneaton	d				22 08							22 58	23 14		
Tamworth Low Level	d											23 12	23s26		
Lichfield Trent Valley	d											23 18	23s33		
Coventry 68	d		22 31												
Birmingham International 68	d		22 47												
BirminghamNewSt 68	d	22 52	23 09												
Wolverhampton	d	23 27	23 36												
Penkridge	d		23 45												
Stafford	d	23 43	23 52			22 37						23 46	23s48		
Stoke-on-Trent 84	a			22 28							23 07			01s18	
Macclesfield	a			22 44						←	23 24			01s34	
Crewe 81,91	a	00 11	00 19		22 53	22 58				00 11		00 13	00 16		
	d	00 15			22 53	22 59		23u50	23u50	00 15					
Chester 81	a	→								00 38					
Wrexham General 75	a														
Llandudno Junction 81	a									01 30					
Bangor (Gwynedd) 81	a									01 47					
Holyhead 81	a									02 15					
Wilmslow 84	a														
Stockport 84	a			22 58							23 38			01s48	
Manchester Piccadilly	a			23 08							23 50			01 59	
Runcorn 91	a				23 11										
Liverpool South Pkwy 91	a														
Liverpool Lime Street 91	a				23 33										
	d														
Manchester Airport 82	d						23 10								
Manchester Picc. 82	d						23 26								
Bolton 82	d														
Warrington Bank Quay	d					23 21									
Wigan North Western 90	d					23 32									
Preston 90	a					23 50	00 13								
Blackpool North 97	a														
Preston 90	d						00 15	00u56 00u56	00u56						
Lancaster	d														
Barrow-in-Furness 82	a														
Oxenholme Lake District 83	d														
Windermere 83	a														
Penrith North Lakes	d														
Carlisle 216	a						01 25								05s13
	d														
Lockerbie 225,226	d														
Carstairs 226,225	a														06s22
Motherwell 226	a														07s00
GlasgowCentral 216,226,225	a														07 22
Haymarket	a														
Edinburgh	a								04d50						07 23
Fort William 227,400	a								09 57						
Perth 229	a							05s41							
Dundee 229	a							06s05							
Aberdeen 229	a							07 40							
Inverness 229	a							08 42							

A To Holyhead
B From Birmingham New Street

Refer to Operator websites for full information about Sleeper Services. Contact details for train operators available at National Rail Enquiries

Table T065-F

Saturdays

21 December to 16 May

London & West Midlands to North West England. London, West Midlands & Manchester to Scotland via the West Coast

	TP	CS	CS	CS	NT	CS		TP	AW	NT	TP	TP	NT	NT	VT	NT	VT	TP	XC	LM	LM	VT
	A	B	B	B	A	B			C	D				E		A						
London Euston ⊖66 d																						
Watford Junction 66 d						00u10																
Milton Keynes Central 66 d																						
Rugby 66 d																						
Nuneaton d																						
Tamworth Low Level d																						
Lichfield Trent Valley d																						
Coventry 68 d																				05 37		
Birmingham International 68 d																				05 47		
BirminghamNewSt 68 d																	05 30		05 57	06 04	06 07	06 15
Wolverhampton d																	05 48		06 14	06 20	06 33	06 37
Penkridge d																				06 29		
Stafford d																	06 01		06 28	06 37	06 47	
Stoke-on-Trent 84 a																			06 43		07 04	
Macclesfield a																			07 04			
Crewe 81,91 a																	06 20			06 56	07 26	07 08
d									00 15						05 57		06 22			06 58		07 09
Chester 81 a									00 38								06 42					
Wrexham General 75 a																						
Llandudno Junction 81 a									01 30								07 31					
Bangor (Gwynedd) 81 a									01 47								07 48					
Holyhead 81 a									02 15								08 19					
Wilmslow 84 a																						
Stockport 84 a																			07 19			
Manchester Piccadilly a																			07 31			
Runcorn 91 a																				07 24		
Liverpool South Pkwy 91 a																				07 33		
Liverpool Lime Street 91 a																				07 43		
d																						
Manchester Airport 82 d											04 22			05 22				06 07				
Manchester Picc. 82 d					00 09						04 36	05 00		05 42				06 26				
Bolton 82 d										00 39								06u42				
Warrington Bank Quay d															06 15							07 27
Wigan North Western 90 d														06 15	06 25							07 38
Preston 90 a					00 59					01 04		05 33		06 31	06 38			07 02				07 51
Blackpool North 97 a					01 27											←						
Preston 90 d	00 15	00u56	00u56	00u56								05 36		06 47	06 41	06 47		07 03				07 53
Lancaster d												05 51	05 59	→	06 55	07 06		07 19				08 08
Barrow-in-Furness 82 a																08 09						
Oxenholme Lake District 83 d												06 05	06 19		07 09			07 33				08 22
Windermere 83 a													06 39									
Penrith North Lakes d												06 31			07 35			07 59				
Carlisle 216 a	01 25					05s13						06 46			07 50			08 14				09 00
d								06 04				06 49			07 51			08 16				09 01
Lockerbie 225,226 d								06 23				07 07			08 11			08 35				
Carstairs 226,225 a						06s22						07 41										
Motherwell 226 a						07s00						07 59										
GlasgowCentral 216,226,225 a						07 22						08 20			09 12							
Haymarket a								07s27										09s32				10 13
Edinburgh a				04d50			07 23	07 33			08 59							09 39				10 18
Fort William 227,400 a				09 57																		
Perth 229 a			05s41																			
Dundee 229 a		06s05																				
Aberdeen 229 a		07 40																				
Inverness 229 a			08 42																			

A From Manchester Airport
B From London Euston
C From Birmingham New Street
D From Manchester Victoria
E To Barrow-in-Furness

Refer to Operator websites for full information about Sleeper Services. Contact details for train operators available at National Rail Enquiries

Table T065-F

Saturdays

21 December to 16 May

London & West Midlands to North West England. London, West Midlands & Manchester to Scotland via the West Coast

	LM	TP	XC	LM	XC	LM	LM	VT	VT	XC	LM	XC	LM	NT	VT	LM	NT	VT	LM	VT	VT	LM
	A					B	A	C	D		E	F	E	G		H	I	J				A
London Euston ⊖66 d													05 34		06 05				06 29	06 36	06 55	
Watford Junction 66 d													05 53		06u20					06u51		
Milton Keynes Central 66 d						05 39							06 37		06 41				07 02		07 27	
Rugby 66 d	06 02					06 18	06 28						07 18		07 03				07 27			06 57
Nuneaton d	06 21																		07 41			07 11
Tamworth Low Level d	06 35																		07 55			07 28
Lichfield Trent Valley d	06 41																		08 01			07 34
Coventry 68 d						06 30	06 39					07 27	07 30									
Birmingham International 68 d				06 18		06 46	06 54				07 18	07 38	07 46									
BirminghamNewSt 68 d			06 31	06 36	06 57	07 04	07 12	07 15	07 21	07 31	07 36	07 57	08 04									
Wolverhampton d			06 48	06 56	07 14	07 23		07 37	07 40	07 50	07 56	08 14	→									
Penkridge d				07 05		07 31					08 05											
Stafford d	06 58		07 02	07 13	07 31	07 39	07 48		07 59	08 04	08 12	08 28			07 34				08 18			07 54
Stoke-on-Trent 84 a			07 17				08 04			08 19		08 43									08 24	
Macclesfield a			07 36							08 36		09 01				←		←			08 41	
Crewe 81,91 a	07 16			07 31	07 50	07 57	08 31	08 04	08 18		08 31				07 53	07 57		08 04	08 37	08 10		08 14
d				07 33	07 52	07 58		08 08	08 19		08 32				07 55	07 58		08 08		08 11		
Chester 81 a						→		→	→		→											
Wrexham General 75 a																						
Llandudno Junction 81 a																						
Bangor (Gwynedd) 81 a																						
Holyhead 81 a																						
Wilmslow 84 a					08 07															08 27		
Stockport 84 a			07 49		08 16					08 49		09 13								08 35	08 54	
Manchester Piccadilly a			07 59		08 29					08 59		09 24								08 46	09 05	
Runcorn 91 a				07 59												08 23						
Liverpool South Pkwy 91 a				08 10												08 31						
Liverpool Lime Street 91 a				08 19												08 42						
d																						
Manchester Airport 82 d		07 07												07 25								
Manchester Picc. 82 d		07 26												07 43								
Bolton 82 d																						
Warrington Bank Quay d															08 12			08 27				
Wigan North Western 90 d														08 16	08 23		←	08 38				
Preston 90 a		08 01												08 39	08 36		08 39	08 51				
Blackpool North 97 a														→								
Preston 90 d		08 02													08 38		08 42	08 53				
Lancaster d		08 18													08 53		09 00	09 10				
Barrow-in-Furness 82 a																	10 03					
Oxenholme Lake District 83 d															09 06							
Windermere 83 a																						
Penrith North Lakes d		08 54													09 32			09 47				
Carlisle 216 a		09 10													09 47			10 02				
d		09 15													09 49			10 02				
Lockerbie 225,226 d		09 34																				
Carstairs 226,225 a																						
Motherwell 226 a		10 20																				
GlasgowCentral 216,226,225 a		10 38													10 59			11 15				
Haymarket a																						
Edinburgh a																						
Fort William 227,400 a																						
Perth 229 a																						
Dundee 229 a																						
Aberdeen 229 a																						
Inverness 229 a																						

A From Northampton
B From Bletchley to Liverpool Lime Street
C To Glasgow Central
D To Blackpool North
E To Liverpool Lime Street
F From Southampton Central
G To Barrow-in-Furness
H From Bletchley
I From Manchester Airport
J From Birmingham New Street

Refer to Operator websites for full information about Sleeper Services. Contact details for train operators available at National Rail Enquiries

Table T065-F

Saturdays
21 December to 16 May

London & West Midlands to North West England. London, West Midlands & Manchester to Scotland via the West Coast

	TP		TP	VT	LM	VT	LM	VT	NT	VT	NT		VT	NT	TP	VT	VT	LM	XC	LM	XC		LM	VT
	◇■		◇■	◇■	■	◇■	■	◇■	◇	◇■	◇		◇■		◇■	◇■	◇■	■	◇■	■	◇■		■	◇■
				A	B		C		D		E					F	G	H	I		J		K	L
London Euston 15 ⊖66 d						07 07		07 20		07 30						07 33	07 35							07 43
Watford Junction 66 d																								
Milton Keynes Central 66 d								07 50								08 04	08 06							08 13
Rugby 66 d																		07 37					08 18	
Nuneaton d																								
Tamworth Low Level d																								
Lichfield Trent Valley d																								
Coventry 68 d																		07 47			08 27		08 30	08 42
Birmingham International 68 d							←											08 02		08 18	08 38		08 46	08 53
BirminghamNewSt 12 68 d							08 04						08 15					08 21	08 31	08 37	08 57		09 04	09 15
Wolverhampton 7 d							08 22						08 37					08 41	08 48	08 57	09 14		09 22	09 37
Penkridge d							08 31													09 06			09 31	
Stafford d						08 24	08 38											08 57	09 02	09 13	09 28		09 38	
Stoke-on-Trent 84 a								08 48										09 13	09 17		09 43			
Macclesfield a				←	←														09 36		10 01			
Crewe 10 81,91 a				08 18	08 31	08 41	08 56						09 07			09 10	09 10	09 35		09 31			09 58	10 07
d				08 19	08 32	08 43	08 57						09 09			09 11	09 11			09 33			09 59	10 09
Chester 81 a																							→	→
Wrexham General 75 a																								
Llandudno Junction 81 a																								
Bangor (Gwynedd) 81 a																								
Holyhead 81 a																								
Wilmslow 84 a																09 27	09 27							
Stockport 84 a								09 16								09 35	09 35		09 49		10 13			
Manchester Piccadilly 10 a								09 27								09 46	09 46		10 00		10 24			
Runcorn 91 a					08 53	09 00	09 22													09 52				
Liverpool South Pkwy 7 91 a					09 02		09 31													10 00				
Liverpool Lime Street 10 91 a					09 11	09 20	09 40													10 12				
d	08 12																							
Manchester Airport 82 d			08 07						08 27						09 07									
Manchester Picc. 10 82 d			08 27						08 47						09 26									
Bolton 82 d			08u44												09u44									
Warrington Bank Quay d				08 41						09 14			09 27											
Wigan North Western 90 d	08 43			08 52					09 19	09 25	←		09 38											
Preston 8 90 a	08 59		09 03	09 09					09 43	09 38	09 43		09 51		10 04									
Blackpool North 97 a				09 32					→															
Preston 8 90 d	09 01		09 05							09 41	09 44		09 53		10 05									
Lancaster 6 d			09 21							09 55			10 08	10 13	10 21									
Barrow-in-Furness 82 a														11 16										
Oxenholme Lake District 83 d			09 35								10 33		10 22		10 35									
Windermere 83 a											10 52													
Penrith North Lakes d	09 52									10 32					11 01									
Carlisle 8 216 a	10 08		10 13							10 47			10 59	13 40	11 16									
d	10 09		10 15							10 47			11 01		11 17									
Lockerbie 225,226 d															11 37									
Carstairs 226,225 a																								
Motherwell 226 a															12 21									
GlasgowCentral 15 216,226,225 a	11 39									11 59					12 39									
Haymarket a			11s31										12 12											
Edinburgh 10 a			11 36										12 19											
Fort William 227,400 a																								
Perth 229 a																								
Dundee 229 a																								
Aberdeen 229 a																								
Inverness 229 a																								

A From Birmingham New Street
B From Birmingham International
C From London Euston
D To Windermere
E From Manchester Airport
F from 22 February
G until 15 February
H From Northampton
I From Bristol Temple Meads
J From Southampton Central
K From Northampton to Liverpool Lime Street
L To Glasgow Central

Refer to Operator websites for full information about Sleeper Services. Contact details for train operators available at National Rail Enquiries

Table T065-F

Saturdays
21 December to 16 May

London & West Midlands to North West England. London, West Midlands & Manchester to Scotland via the West Coast

	LM	LM	XC	LM	XC	LM	VT		VT	VT	LM	LM	VT	NT	VT	NT	VT		TP	VT	LM	VT	LM	LM
	■	■	◇■	■	◇■	■	◇■		◇■	◇■	■	■	◇■	◇	◇■	◇	◇■		◇■	◇■	■	◇■	■	■
		A	B	C	D	C					A	E		F		G	H				I	J		H
London Euston 15 ⊖66 d	07 46					07 49	08 00		08 07	08 10		08 15	08 20		08 30					08 40		08 43	08 46	
Watford Junction 66 d						08 04																		
Milton Keynes Central 66 d	08 19					08 26				08 41		08 55	08 50									09 13	09 19	
Rugby 66 d	08 42	08 36				09 17						09 36											09 42	
Nuneaton d	08 55																						09 55	
Tamworth Low Level d	09 09																						10 09	
Lichfield Trent Valley d	09 17																						10 17	←
Coventry 68 d		08 47			09 27	09 29						09 47										09 42		09 47
Birmingham International 68 d		09 02		09 18	09 38	09 45						→										09 53		10 02
BirminghamNewSt 12 68 d		09 20	09 31	09 37	09 57	10 03																10 15		10 20
Wolverhampton 7 d		09 41	09 48	09 57	10 14	10 22																10 37		10 41
Penkridge d				10 05		10 31																		
Stafford d	09 35	09 56	10 04	10 13	10 28	10 38			09 24														10 35	10 57
Stoke-on-Trent 84 a		10 14	10 19		10 43		09 24						09 48											11 13
Macclesfield a			10 36		11 01		09 41				←						←				←			
Crewe 10 81,91 a	09 53	10 36		10 31		10 56			09 41	09 46	09 58						10 07			10 10	10 31	11 07	10 53	11 35
d				10 33		10 58			09 43	09 48	09 59						10 09			10 11	10 33	11 09		
Chester 81 a				→		→				10 09												→		
Wrexham General 75 a																								
Llandudno Junction 81 a																								
Bangor (Gwynedd) 81 a																								
Holyhead 81 a																								
Wilmslow 84 a																				10 27				
Stockport 84 a			10 49		11 13		09 54						10 16							10 35				
Manchester Piccadilly 10 a			11 00		11 24		10 05						10 27							10 46				
Runcorn 91 a									10 00		10 25										10 54			
Liverpool South Pkwy 7 91 a											10 33										11 03			
Liverpool Lime Street 10 91 a									10 19		10 44										11 12			
d																								
Manchester Airport 82 d														09 28					10 07					
Manchester Picc. 10 82 d														09 47					10 26					
Bolton 82 d																								
Warrington Bank Quay d															10 14		10 27							
Wigan North Western 90 d														10 20	10 25	←	10 38							
Preston 8 90 a														10 43	10 38	10 43	10 51		11 02					
Blackpool North 97 a														→										
Preston 8 90 d															10 41	10 44	10 53		11 03					
Lancaster 6 d															10 55	11 02	11 12							
Barrow-in-Furness 82 a																12 00								
Oxenholme Lake District 83 d															11 09									
Windermere 83 a																								
Penrith North Lakes d																	11 46							
Carlisle 8 216 a															11 47		12 01		12 05					
d															11 47		12 02		12 06					
Lockerbie 225,226 d																			12 25					
Carstairs 226,225 a																								
Motherwell 226 a																								
GlasgowCentral 15 216,226,225 a															12 59		13 15							
Haymarket a																			13s22					
Edinburgh 10 a																			13 30					
Fort William 227,400 a																								
Perth 229 a																								
Dundee 229 a																								
Aberdeen 229 a																								
Inverness 229 a																								

A From Northampton
B From Cardiff Central
C To Liverpool Lime Street
D From Bournemouth
E To Crewe
F To Barrow-in-Furness
G From Manchester Airport
H From London Euston
I From Birmingham International
J To Edinburgh

Refer to Operator websites for full information about Sleeper Services. Contact details for train operators available at National Rail Enquiries

Table T065-F

Saturdays

21 December to 16 May

London & West Midlands to North West England. London, West Midlands & Manchester to Scotland via the West Coast

		XC	LM	XC	LM	VT	VT	VT	VT	LM	LM	VT	NT	VT	NT	VT	TP	VT	LM	VT	LM	LM
		◇1	1	◇1	1	◇1	◇1	◇1	◇1	1	1	◇1	◇	◇1	◇	◇1	◇1	◇1	1	◇1	1	1
		A	B	C	B					D	E		F		G	D			H	I		D
		🛒		🛒		🍴	🍴	🍴	🍴			🍴		🍴		🍴	🛒	🍴		🍴		
London Euston 15 ⊖66	d				08 49	08 54	09 00	09 07	09 10		09 15	09 20		09 30				09 40		09 43	09 46	
Watford Junction 66	d				09 04																	
Milton Keynes Central 66	d				09 29				09 41		09 55	09 50								10 13	10 19	
Rugby 66	d				10 17	09 46					10 36										10 42	
Nuneaton	d																				10 55	
Tamworth Low Level	d																				11 09	
Lichfield Trent Valley	d																				11 17	←
Coventry 68	d			10 27	10 30						10 47									10 42		10 47
Birmingham International 68 ✈	d		10 18	10 38	10 46						→									10 53		11 02
BirminghamNewSt 12 68 🚊	d	10 31	10 37	10 57	11 04															11 15		11 20
Wolverhampton 7 🚊	d	10 48	10 55	11 14	11 22															11 37		11 41
Penkridge	d		11 03		11 31																	
Stafford	d	11 02	11 11	11 28	11 38			10 24													11 47	11 56
Stoke-on-Trent 84	a	11 17		11 43			10 24					10 48										12 13
Macclesfield	a	11 36		12 01			10 41			←						←			←			
Crewe 10 81,91	a		11 29		11 56			10 43	10 45	10 56						11 07		11 10	11 29	12 07	12 08	12 35
	d		11 31		11 58			10 45	10 48	10 58						11 09		11 11	11 31	12 09		
Chester 81	a		→		→				11 12											→		
Wrexham General 75	a																					
Llandudno Junction 81	a								11 59													
Bangor (Gwynedd) 81	a								12 15													
Holyhead 81 ⛴	a								12 46													
Wilmslow 84	a																	11 27				
Stockport 84	a	11 49		12 13			10 54					11 16						11 35				
Manchester Piccadilly 10 🚊	a	12 00		12 24			11 05					11 27						11 46				
Runcorn 91	a							11 01		11 24									11 52			
Liverpool South Pkwy 7 91 ✈	a									11 32									12 01			
Liverpool Lime Street 10 91	a							11 20		11 43									12 10			
	d																					
Manchester Airport 82 ✈🚊	d												10 28				11 07					
Manchester Picc. 10 82 🚊	d												10 47				11 26					
Bolton 82	d																					
Warrington Bank Quay	d					10 59								11 14		11 27						
Wigan North Western 90	d					11 12							11 21	11 25	←	11 38						
Preston 8 90	a					11 25							11 42	11 38	11 42	11 51	12 02					
Blackpool North 97 🚊	a					11 57							→									
Preston 8 90	d													11 41	11 44	11 53	12 03					
Lancaster 6	d													11 55	12 02	12 09	12 19					
Barrow-in-Furness 82	a														13 05							
Oxenholme Lake District 83	d															12 23	12 33					
Windermere 83	a																					
Penrith North Lakes	d													12 31			12 59					
Carlisle 8 216	a													12 47		13 00	13 14					
	d													12 47		13 01	13 15					
Lockerbie 225,226	d																13 35					
Carstairs 226,225	a																					
Motherwell 226	a																14 20					
GlasgowCentral 15 216,226,225	a													13 59			14 38					
Haymarket 🚊	a															14 11						
Edinburgh 10 🚊	a															14 17						
Fort William 227,400	a																					
Perth 229	a																					
Dundee 229	a																					
Aberdeen 229	a																					
Inverness 229	a																					

A From Paignton
B To Liverpool Lime Street
C From Bournemouth
D From London Euston
E To Crewe
F To Barrow-in-Furness
G From Manchester Airport
H From Birmingham International
I To Glasgow Central

Refer to Operator websites for full information about Sleeper Services. Contact details for train operators available at National Rail Enquiries

Table T065-F

Saturdays

21 December to 16 May

London & West Midlands to North West England. London, West Midlands & Manchester to Scotland via the West Coast

		XC	LM	XC	LM	VT	VT	VT	LM	LM	VT	NT	VT	NT	NT	VT	VT	TP	VT	TP	LM	VT	LM
		◇1	1	◇1	1	◇1	◇1	◇1	1	1	◇1	◇	◇1		◇	◇1	◇1	◇1	◇1	◇1	1	◇1	1
		A	B	C	B				D	E		F			G	D					H	I	
		🛒		🛒		🍴	🍴	🍴			🍴		🍴			🍴	🍴	🛒	🍴	🛒		🍴	
London Euston 15 ⊖66	d				09 49	10 00	10 07	10 10		10 15	10 20		10 30				10 36		10 40			10 43	10 46
Watford Junction 66	d				10 04																		
Milton Keynes Central 66	d				10 31			10 41		10 56	10 50											11 13	11 19
Rugby 66	d				11 18					11 36							11 28						11 42
Nuneaton	d																						11 55
Tamworth Low Level	d																						12 09
Lichfield Trent Valley	d							11 22															12 17
Coventry 68	d			11 27	11 30					11 47												11 42	
Birmingham International 68 ✈	d		11 18	11 38	11 46					→												11 53	
BirminghamNewSt 12 68 🚊	d	11 31	11 37	11 57	12 04																	12 15	
Wolverhampton 7 🚊	d	11 48	11 55	12 14	12 22																	12 37	
Penkridge	d		12 03		12 31																		
Stafford	d	12 02	12 10	12 28	12 38		11 24																12 35
Stoke-on-Trent 84	a	12 17		12 43		11 24					11 48												
Macclesfield	a	12 36		13 01		11 41			←							←					←		
Crewe 10 81,91	a		12 28		12 56		11 41	11 51	11 56							12 07			12 10		12 28	13 07	12 53
	d		12 30		12 59		11 43	11 54	11 58							12 09			12 11		12 30	13 09	
Chester 81	a		→		→			12 15														→	
Wrexham General 75	a																						
Llandudno Junction 81	a																						
Bangor (Gwynedd) 81	a																						
Holyhead 81 ⛴	a																						
Wilmslow 84	a																		12 27				
Stockport 84	a	12 49		13 13		11 54					12 16								12 35				
Manchester Piccadilly 10 🚊	a	13 00		13 24		12 05					12 27								12 46				
Runcorn 91	a						12 00		12 24												12 51		
Liverpool South Pkwy 7 91 ✈	a								12 32												13 00		
Liverpool Lime Street 10 91	a						12 19		12 43												13 09		
	d																			12 11			
Manchester Airport 82 ✈🚊	d											11 28						12 07					
Manchester Picc. 10 82 🚊	d											11 47						12 26					
Bolton 82	d																	12u44					
Warrington Bank Quay	d												12 14			12 27	12 34						
Wigan North Western 90	d											12 18	12 25		←	12 38	12 45			12 50			
Preston 8 90	a											12 42	12 38		12 42	12 51	12 57	13 03		13 06			
Blackpool North 97 🚊	a											→					13 20						
Preston 8 90	d												12 41		12 45	12 53		13 05		13 10			
Lancaster 6	d												12 55	13 01	13 12	13 08		13 21		13 28			
Barrow-in-Furness 82	a													14 04									
Oxenholme Lake District 83	d												13 09		13 32	13 23		13 35					
Windermere 83	a														13 54								
Penrith North Lakes	d																			14 07			
Carlisle 8 216	a												13 47	16 48		14 00		14 13		14 23			
	d												13 47			14 01		14 15		14 24			
Lockerbie 225,226	d																	14 34		14 43			
Carstairs 226,225	a																						
Motherwell 226	a															14 58							
GlasgowCentral 15 216,226,225	a												14 59			15 15				15 45			
Haymarket 🚊	a																	15s33					
Edinburgh 10 🚊	a																	15 39					
Fort William 227,400	a																						
Perth 229	a																						
Dundee 229	a																						
Aberdeen 229	a																						
Inverness 229	a																						

A From Bristol Temple Meads
B To Liverpool Lime Street
C From Bournemouth
D From London Euston
E To Crewe
F To Windermere
G From Manchester Airport
H From Birmingham International
I To Edinburgh

Refer to Operator websites for full information about Sleeper Services. Contact details for train operators available at National Rail Enquiries

Table T065-F

Saturdays

21 December to 16 May

London & West Midlands to North West England. London, West Midlands & Manchester to Scotland via the West Coast

	LM ■ A	XC ◇■ B	LM ■ C	XC ◇■ D	LM ■ C	VT ◇■	VT ◇■	VT ◇■	LM ■ A	LM ■ E	VT ◇■	NT ◇ F	VT ◇■	NT ◇ G	VT ◇■ A	TP ◇■	VT ◇■	LM ■ H	VT ◇■ I	LM ■	LM ■ A	XC ◇■ J
London Euston 15 ⊖66 d					10 49	11 00	11 07	11 10		11 15	11 20		11 30				11 40		11 43	11 46		
Watford Junction 66 d					11 04																	
Milton Keynes Central 66 d					11 24			11 41		11 58	11 50								12 13	12 19		
Rugby 66 d					12 18					12 37										12 42		
Nuneaton d																				12 55		
Tamworth Low Level d																				13 09		
Lichfield Trent Valley d	←																			13 17	←	
Coventry 68 d	11 47			12 27	12 31					12 48									12 42		12 48	
Birmingham International 68 ✈ d	12 02		12 18	12 38	12 47					→									12 53		13 03	
BirminghamNewSt 12 68 d	12 20	12 31	12 37	12 57	13 04														13 15		13 21	13 31
Wolverhampton 7 d	12 41	12 48	12 55	13 14	13 22														13 37		13 40	13 48
Penkridge d			13 03		13 31																	
Stafford d	12 56	13 02	13 11	13 28	13 38		12 24													13 44	13 55	14 02
Stoke-on-Trent 84 a	13 12	13 17		13 43		12 24					12 48										14 11	14 17
Macclesfield a		13 36		14 01		12 41			←						←			←				14 36
Crewe 10 81,91 a	13 34		13 29		13 56		12 42	12 45	12 56						13 07		13 10	13 29	14 07	14 03	14 33	
d			13 30		13 58		12 44	12 47	12 59						13 09		13 11	13 30	14 09			
Chester 81 a			→		→			13 09											→			
Wrexham General 75 a																						
Llandudno Junction 81 a																						
Bangor (Gwynedd) 81 a																						
Holyhead 81 ⛴ a																						
Wilmslow 84 a																	13 27					
Stockport 84 a		13 49		14 13		12 54					13 16						13 35					14 49
Manchester Piccadilly 10 a		14 00		14 24		13 05					13 27						13 46					15 00
Runcorn 91 a							13 00		13 22									13 51				
Liverpool South Pkwy 7 91 ✈ a									13 31									13 59				
Liverpool Lime Street 10 91 a							13 19		13 41									14 09				
d																						
Manchester Airport 82 ✈ d												12 28				13 07						
Manchester Picc. 10 82 d												12 47				13 26						
Bolton 82 d																13u44						
Warrington Bank Quay d													13 14		13 27							
Wigan North Western 90 d												13 19	13 25	←	13 38							
Preston 8 90 a												13 43	13 38	13 43	13 51	14 04						
Blackpool North 97 a												→										
Preston 8 90 d													13 41	13 44	13 53	14 05						
Lancaster 6 d													13 55	14 02	14 08	14 21						
Barrow-in-Furness 82 a														15 05								
Oxenholme Lake District 83 d													14 09			14 35						
Windermere 83 a																						
Penrith North Lakes d															14 43	15 01						
Carlisle 8 216 a													14 46		14 59	15 16						
d													14 47		15 00	15 17						
Lockerbie 225,226 d																15 37						
Carstairs 226,225 a																						
Motherwell 226 a																16s21						
GlasgowCentral 15 216,226,225 a													15 59			16 39						
Haymarket a															16 15							
Edinburgh 10 a															16 23							
Fort William 227,400 a																						
Perth 229 a																						
Dundee 229 a																						
Aberdeen 229 a																						
Inverness 229 a																						

A From London Euston
B From Bristol Temple Meads
C To Liverpool Lime Street
D From Bournemouth
E To Crewe
F To Barrow-in-Furness
G From Manchester Airport
H From Birmingham International
I To Glasgow Central
J From Paignton

Refer to Operator websites for full information about Sleeper Services. Contact details for train operators available at National Rail Enquiries

Table T065-F

Saturdays

21 December to 16 May

London & West Midlands to North West England. London, West Midlands & Manchester to Scotland via the West Coast

	LM ■ A	XC ◇■ B	LM ■ A	VT ◇■	VT ◇■	VT ◇■	LM ■ C	LM ■ D	VT ◇■	NT ◇ E	VT ◇■	NT ◇ F	VT ◇■ C	TP ◇■	VT ◇■	LM ■ G	NT	VT ◇■ H	LM ■	LM ■ C	XC ◇■ I
London Euston 15 ⊖66 d			11 49	12 00	12 07	12 10		12 15	12 20		12 30				12 40			12 43	12 46		
Watford Junction 66 d			12 04																		
Milton Keynes Central 66 d			12 25			12 41		12 56	12 50									13 13	13 19		
Rugby 66 d			13 17			13 04		13 36											13 42		
Nuneaton d																			13 55		
Tamworth Low Level d																			14 09		
Lichfield Trent Valley d																			14 17	←	
Coventry 68 d		13 27	13 30					13 47										13 42		13 47	
Birmingham International 68 ✈ d	13 18	13 38	13 45					→										13 53		14 02	
BirminghamNewSt 12 68 d	13 37	13 57	14 03															14 15		14 20	14 31
Wolverhampton 7 d	13 55	14 14	14 22															14 37		14 40	14 48
Penkridge d	14 04		14 30																		
Stafford d	14 11	14 28	14 38		13 24														14 36	14 57	15 02
Stoke-on-Trent 84 a		14 43		13 24					13 48											15 14	15 17
Macclesfield a		15 01		13 41			←						←			←					15 36
Crewe 10 81,91 a	14 30		14 57		13 41	13 49	13 56						14 07		14 10	14 30		15 06	14 54	15 36	
d	14 31		14 59		13 43	13 51	13 58						14 09		14 11	14 31		15 08			
Chester 81 a	→		→			14 13												→			
Wrexham General 75 a																					
Llandudno Junction 81 a																					
Bangor (Gwynedd) 81 a																					
Holyhead 81 ⛴ a																					
Wilmslow 84 a															14 27						
Stockport 84 a		15 13		13 54					14 16						14 35						15 49
Manchester Piccadilly 10 a		15 24		14 05					14 27						14 46						16 00
Runcorn 91 a					14 00		14 24									14 54					
Liverpool South Pkwy 7 91 ✈ a							14 32									15 03					
Liverpool Lime Street 10 91 a					14 19		14 43									15 14					
d																					
Manchester Airport 82 ✈ d										13 28				14 07							
Manchester Picc. 10 82 d										13 47				14 26							
Bolton 82 d																					
Warrington Bank Quay d											14 14		14 27								
Wigan North Western 90 d										14 18	14 25	←	14 38								
Preston 8 90 a										14 43	14 38	14 43	14 51	15 02							
Blackpool North 97 a										→											
Preston 8 90 d											14 41	14 45	14 53	15 03			15 32				
Lancaster 6 d											14 56	15 03	15 10	15 19			16 13				
Barrow-in-Furness 82 a												16 05					17 16				
Oxenholme Lake District 83 d													15 23	15 33							
Windermere 83 a																					
Penrith North Lakes d											15 31			15 59							
Carlisle 8 216 a											15 46		16 02	16 14			19 43				
d											15 46		16 03	16 16							
Lockerbie 225,226 d														16 34							
Carstairs 226,225 a																					
Motherwell 226 a																					
GlasgowCentral 15 216,226,225 a											16 59		17 15								
Haymarket a														17s32							
Edinburgh 10 a														17 37							
Fort William 227,400 a																					
Perth 229 a																					
Dundee 229 a																					
Aberdeen 229 a																					
Inverness 229 a																					

A To Liverpool Lime Street
B From Bournemouth
C From London Euston
D To Crewe
E To Barrow-in-Furness
F From Manchester Airport
G From Birmingham International
H To Edinburgh
I From Bristol Temple Meads

Refer to Operator websites for full information about Sleeper Services. Contact details for train operators available at National Rail Enquiries

Table T065-F

Saturdays
21 December to 16 May

London & West Midlands to North West England. London, West Midlands & Manchester to Scotland via the West Coast

Station		LM A	XC B	LM A	VT	VT	VT	LM C	LM D	VT	NT E	VT	NT F	VT C	TP	VT	LM G	VT H	LM	LM C	XC I	LM A	XC B
London Euston	⊖66 d			12 49	13 00	13 07	13 10		13 15	13 20		13 30				13 40		13 43	13 46				
Watford Junction	66 d			13 04																			
Milton Keynes Central	66 d			13 25			13 41		13 56	13 50								14 13	14 19				
Rugby	66 d			14 18					14 37										14 42				
Nuneaton	d																		14 55				
Tamworth Low Level	d																		15 09				
Lichfield Trent Valley	d																		15 17	←			
Coventry	68 d		14 27	14 30					14 48									14 42		14 48			15 27
Birmingham International	68 ✈ d	14 18	14 38	14 46					→									14 53		15 03		15 18	15 38
BirminghamNewSt	68 d	14 37	14 57	15 04														15 15		15 21	15 31	15 37	15 57
Wolverhampton	d	14 55	15 14	15 22														15 36		15 39	15 48	15 55	16 14
Penkridge	d	15 03		15 31																		16 03	
Stafford	d	15 11	15 28	15 38		14 24													15 35	15 54	16 02	16 11	16 28
Stoke-on-Trent	84 a		15 43		14 24					14 48										16 11	16 17		16 43
Macclesfield	a		16 01		14 41			←						←			←				16 36		17 01
Crewe	81,91 a	15 29		15 56		14 41	14 45	14 57						15 06		15 10	15 29	16 06	15 53	16 33		16 29	
	d	15 31		15 59		14 43	14 48	14 59						15 08		15 11	15 31	16 09				16 31	
Chester	81 a	→		→			15 07											→				→	
Wrexham General	75 a																						
Llandudno Junction	81 a																						
Bangor (Gwynedd)	81 a																						
Holyhead	81 a																						
Wilmslow	84 a															15 27							
Stockport	84 a		16 13		14 54					15 16						15 35					16 49		17 13
Manchester Piccadilly	a		16 24		15 05					15 27						15 46					17 00		17 24
Runcorn	91 a					15 00		15 23									15 52						
Liverpool South Pkwy	91 ✈ a							15 32									16 01						
Liverpool Lime Street	91 a					15 19		15 42									16 10						
	d																						
Manchester Airport	82 ✈ d										14 28				15 07								
Manchester Picc.	82 d										14 47				15 26								
Bolton	82 d																						
Warrington Bank Quay	d											15 14		15 27									
Wigan North Western	90 d										15 20	15 25	←	15 38									
Preston	90 a										15 43	15 38	15 43	15 51	16 02								
Blackpool North	97 a										→												
Preston	90 d											15 41	15 45	15 53	16 03								
Lancaster	d											15 55		16 10	16 19								
Barrow-in-Furness	82 a																						
Oxenholme Lake District	83 d											16 10	16 31		16 34								
Windermere	83 a												16 53										
Penrith North Lakes	d													16 45	16 59								
Carlisle	216 a											16 48		17 00	17 15								
	d											16 49		17 02	17 16								
Lockerbie	225,226 d														17 35								
Carstairs	226,225 a																						
Motherwell	226 a														18 21								
GlasgowCentral	216,226,225 a											17 59			18 39								
Haymarket	a													18 14									
Edinburgh	a													18 22									
Fort William	227,400 a																						
Perth	229 a																						
Dundee	229 a																						
Aberdeen	229 a																						
Inverness	229 a																						

A To Liverpool Lime Street
B From Bournemouth
C From London Euston
D To Crewe
E To Windermere
F From Manchester Airport
G From Birmingham International
H To Glasgow Central
I From Penzance

Refer to Operator websites for full information about Sleeper Services. Contact details for train operators available at National Rail Enquiries

Table T065-F

Saturdays
21 December to 16 May

London & West Midlands to North West England. London, West Midlands & Manchester to Scotland via the West Coast

Station		LM A	VT	VT	VT	LM B	LM C	VT	NT D	VT	NT E	VT B	VT	TP	LM F	TP	VT G	LM	LM B	XC H	LM A	XC I
London Euston	⊖66 d	13 49	14 00	14 07	14 10		14 15	14 20		14 30			14 40				14 43	14 46				
Watford Junction	66 d	14 04																				
Milton Keynes Central	66 d	14 25			14 41		14 56	14 50									15 13	15 19				
Rugby	66 d	15 19					15 37											15 42				
Nuneaton	d																	15 55				
Tamworth Low Level	d																	16 09				
Lichfield Trent Valley	d																	16 17	←			
Coventry	68 d	15 31					15 48										15 42		15 48			16 27
Birmingham International	68 ✈ d	15 46					→										15 53		16 03		16 18	16 38
BirminghamNewSt	68 d	16 04															16 15		16 21	16 31	16 37	16 57
Wolverhampton	d	16 22															16 37		16 40	16 48	16 55	17 14
Penkridge	d	16 30																			17 03	
Stafford	d	16 38		15 24														16 36	16 55	17 02	17 11	17 28
Stoke-on-Trent	84 a		15 24					15 48											17 12	17 17		17 43
Macclesfield	a		15 41			←						←			←					17 36		18 01
Crewe	81,91 a	16 57		15 41	15 45	15 56						16 06	16 10		16 29		17 07	16 54	17 34		17 29	
	d	16 59		15 43	15 47	15 59						16 09	16 11		16 31		17 08				17 31	
Chester	81 a	→			16 08												→				→	
Wrexham General	75 a																					
Llandudno Junction	81 a				16 59																	
Bangor (Gwynedd)	81 a				17 15																	
Holyhead	81 a				17 46																	
Wilmslow	84 a												16 27									
Stockport	84 a		15 54					16 16					16 35							17 49		18 13
Manchester Piccadilly	a		16 05					16 27					16 46							18 00		18 24
Runcorn	91 a			16 00		16 25									16 51							
Liverpool South Pkwy	91 ✈ a					16 33									17 00							
Liverpool Lime Street	91 a			16 19		16 43									17 10							
	d													16 12								
Manchester Airport	82 ✈ d								15 28							16 07						
Manchester Picc.	82 d								15 47							16 26						
Bolton	82 d															16u44						
Warrington Bank Quay	d									16 14		16 27										
Wigan North Western	90 d								16 18	16 25	←	16 38		16 43								
Preston	90 a								16 42	16 38	16 42	16 51		16 58		17 04						
Blackpool North	97 a								→													
Preston	90 d									16 41	16 45	16 53		16 59		17 05						
Lancaster	d									16 56	17 02	17 09		17 16		17 21						
Barrow-in-Furness	82 a										18 02											
Oxenholme Lake District	83 d											17 23				17 35						
Windermere	83 a																					
Penrith North Lakes	d									17 30				17 54								
Carlisle	216 a									17 46		18 01		18 10		18 14						
	d									17 47		18 03		18 11		18 15						
Lockerbie	225,226 d															18 35						
Carstairs	226,225 a																					
Motherwell	226 a																					
GlasgowCentral	216,226,225 a									18 59		19 15		19 38								
Haymarket	a															19s32						
Edinburgh	a															19 38						
Fort William	227,400 a																					
Perth	229 a																					
Dundee	229 a																					
Aberdeen	229 a																					
Inverness	229 a																					

A To Liverpool Lime Street
B From London Euston
C To Crewe
D To Barrow-in-Furness
E From Manchester Airport
F From Birmingham International
G To Edinburgh
H From Bristol Temple Meads
I From Bournemouth

Refer to Operator websites for full information about Sleeper Services. Contact details for train operators available at National Rail Enquiries

Table T065-F

Saturdays

21 December to 16 May

London & West Midlands to North West England. London, West Midlands & Manchester to Scotland via the West Coast

Station		LM ■ A	VT ◇■ ⊡	VT ◇■ ⊡	VT ◇■ ⊡	LM ■ B	LM ■ C	VT ◇■ ⊡	NT ◇ D	VT ◇■ ⊡	NT ◇ E	VT ■ B ⊡	TP ◇■ ✕	VT ◇■ ⊡	LM ■ F	VT ■ G ⊡	LM ■	LM ■ B	XC ◇■ H ✕	LM ■ A	XC ◇■ I ✕	LM ■ A	VT ◇■ ⊡
London Euston 15 ⊖66	d	14 49	15 00	15 07	15 10		15 15	15 20		15 30				15 40		15 43	15 46					15 49	16 00
Watford Junction 66	d	15 04																				16 04	
Milton Keynes Central 66	d	15 25			15 41		15 56	15 50								16 13	16 19					16 25	
Rugby 66	d	16 18					16 37										16 42					17 17	
Nuneaton	d																16 55						
Tamworth Low Level	d																17 09						
Lichfield Trent Valley	d																17 17	←					
Coventry 68	d	16 30					16 48									16 42		16 48			17 27	17 30	
Birmingham International 68 ✈	d	16 46					→									16 53		17 03		17 18	17 38	17 46	
BirminghamNewSt 12 68 ⛴	d	17 04														17 15		17 21	17 31	17 37	17 57	18 04	
Wolverhampton 7 ⛴	d	17 22														17 37		17 40	17 48	17 55	18 14	18 22	
Penkridge	d	17 30																		18 03		18 31	
Stafford	d	17 38		16 24													17 36	17 57	18 02	18 11	18 28	18 38	
Stoke-on-Trent 84	a		16 24					16 48										18 14	18 17		18 43		17 24
Macclesfield	a		16 41			←						←			←				18 36		19 01		17 41
Crewe 10 81,91	a	17 57		16 41	16 45	16 57						17 07		17 10	17 29	18 07	17 54	18 37		18 29		18 58	
	d	17 59		16 43	16 47	16 59						17 08		17 11	17 31	18 09				18 31		18 59	
Chester 81	a	→			17 08											→				→		→	
Wrexham General 75	a																						
Llandudno Junction 81	a																						
Bangor (Gwynedd) 81	a																						
Holyhead 81 ⛴	a																						
Wilmslow 84	a													17 27									
Stockport 84	a		16 54					17 16						17 35					18 49		19 13		17 54
Manchester Piccadilly 10 ⛴	a		17 05					17 27						17 46					19 01		19 24		18 05
Runcorn 91	a			17 00		17 24									17 52								
Liverpool South Pkwy 7 91 ✈	a					17 33									18 01								
Liverpool Lime Street 10 91	a			17 20		17 43									18 10								
	d																						
Manchester Airport 82 ✈⛴	d								16 28				17 07										
Manchester Picc. 10 82 ⛴	d								16 47				17 27										
Bolton 82	d																						
Warrington Bank Quay	d									17 14		17 27											
Wigan North Western 90	d								17 20	17 25	←	17 38											
Preston 8 90	a								17 43	17 38	17 43	17 51	18 02										
Blackpool North 97 ⛴	a								→														
Preston 8 90	d									17 41	17 45	17 53	18 04										
Lancaster 6	d									17 55	18 03	18 08	18 20										
Barrow-in-Furness 82	a										19 05												
Oxenholme Lake District 83	d									18 09		18 24	18 34										
Windermere 83	a																						
Penrith North Lakes	d											18 49	18 59										
Carlisle 8 216	a									18 47		19 04	19 15										
	d									18 47		19 04	19 15										
Lockerbie 225,226	d												19 35										
Carstairs 226,225	a																						
Motherwell 226	a												20 21										
GlasgowCentral 15 216,226,225	a									19 59			20 40										
Haymarket ⛴	a											20 17											
Edinburgh 10 ⛴	a											20 22											
Fort William 227,400	a																						
Perth 229	a																						
Dundee 229	a																						
Aberdeen 229	a																						
Inverness 229	a																						

A To Liverpool Lime Street
B From London Euston
C To Crewe
D To Barrow-in-Furness
E From Manchester Airport
F From Birmingham International
G To Glasgow Central
H From Paignton
I From Bournemouth

Refer to Operator websites for full information about Sleeper Services. Contact details for train operators available at National Rail Enquiries

Table T065-F

Saturdays

21 December to 16 May

London & West Midlands to North West England. London, West Midlands & Manchester to Scotland via the West Coast

Station		VT ◇■ ⊡	VT ◇■ ⊡	LM ■ A	LM ■ B	VT ◇■ ⊡	NT ◇ C	VT ◇■ ⊡	NT ◇ D	VT ■ A ⊡	VT ◇■ ⊡	TP ◇■ ✕	VT ◇■ ⊡	LM ■ E	VT ◇■ F ⊡	LM ■	LM ■ A	XC ◇■ G ✕	LM ■ H	XC ◇■ I ✕	LM ■ H	VT ◇■ ⊡	VT ◇■ ⊡
London Euston 15 ⊖66	d	16 07	16 10		16 15	16 20		16 30			16 33		16 40		16 43	16 46					16 49	17 00	17 07
Watford Junction 66	d																				17 04		
Milton Keynes Central 66	d		16 41		16 56	16 50									17 13	17 19					17 26		
Rugby 66	d				17 37											17 42					18 19		
Nuneaton	d															17 55							18 03
Tamworth Low Level	d										17 38					18 09							
Lichfield Trent Valley	d										17 45					18 17	←						
Coventry 68	d				17 48										17 42		17 48			18 27	18 30		
Birmingham International 68 ✈	d				→										17 53		18 03		18 18	18 38	18 46		
BirminghamNewSt 12 68 ⛴	d														18 15		18 21	18 31	18 37	18 57	19 04		
Wolverhampton 7 ⛴	d														18 37		18 40	18 48	18 55	19 14	19 22		
Penkridge	d																		19 04		19 31		
Stafford	d	17 24									17 59					18 36	18 55	19 02	19 11	19 28	19 39		18 27
Stoke-on-Trent 84	a					17 48											19 12	19 17		19 43		18 24	
Macclesfield	a			←						←				←				19 36		20 01		18 41	
Crewe 10 81,91	a	17 41	17 45	17 57						18 07			18 10	18 29	19 07	18 54	19 34		19 30		19 58		18 45
	d	17 43	17 48	17 59						18 09			18 11	18 31	19 08				19 32		19 59		18 47
Chester 81	a		18 08												→				→		→		
Wrexham General 75	a																						
Llandudno Junction 81	a		19 03																				
Bangor (Gwynedd) 81	a		19 19																				
Holyhead 81 ⛴	a		19 50																				
Wilmslow 84	a												18 27										
Stockport 84	a					18 16							18 35					19 49		20 13		18 54	
Manchester Piccadilly 10 ⛴	a					18 27							18 46					20 00		20 24		19 05	
Runcorn 91	a	18 00		18 24							18 31			18 51									19 04
Liverpool South Pkwy 7 91 ✈	a			18 32										19 00									
Liverpool Lime Street 10 91	a	18 20		18 42							18 51			19 10									19 22
	d																						
Manchester Airport 82 ✈⛴	d						17 28					18 07											
Manchester Picc. 10 82 ⛴	d						17 47					18 26											
Bolton 82	d											18u44											
Warrington Bank Quay	d							18 14		18 27													
Wigan North Western 90	d						18 20	18 25	←	18 38													
Preston 8 90	a						18 42	18 38	18 42	18 51		19 04											
Blackpool North 97 ⛴	a						→																
Preston 8 90	d							18 41	18 44	18 53		19 05											
Lancaster 6	d							18 55		19 09		19 21											
Barrow-in-Furness 82	a																						
Oxenholme Lake District 83	d							19 09	19 21	19 23		19 35											
Windermere 83	a								19 42														
Penrith North Lakes	d							19 35				20 01											
Carlisle 8 216	a							19 50		20 02		20 16											
	d							19 51		20 02		20 18											
Lockerbie 225,226	d											20 37											
Carstairs 226,225	a																						
Motherwell 226	a																						
GlasgowCentral 15 216,226,225	a							21 02		21 15													
Haymarket ⛴	a											21s34											
Edinburgh 10 ⛴	a											21 40											
Fort William 227,400	a																						
Perth 229	a																						
Dundee 229	a																						
Aberdeen 229	a																						
Inverness 229	a																						

A From London Euston
B To Crewe
C To Windermere
D From Manchester Airport
E From Birmingham International
F To Preston
G From Bristol Temple Meads
H To Liverpool Lime Street
I From Bournemouth

Refer to Operator websites for full information about Sleeper Services. Contact details for train operators available at National Rail Enquiries

Table T065-F

Saturdays

21 December to 16 May

London & West Midlands to North West England. London, West Midlands & Manchester to Scotland via the West Coast

	VT	VT	LM	LM	VT	NT	VT	NT	VT	TP	VT	LM	VT	LM	LM	XC	LM	XC	LM	VT	VT
			A	B		C		D	A			E	F		A	G	H	I	H		
London Euston ⊖66 d	17 10	17 10		17 15	17 20		17 30				17 40		17 43	17 46					17 49	18 00	18 07
Watford Junction 66 d																			18 04		
Milton Keynes Central 66 d	17 41	17 41		17 56	17 50								18 13	18 19					18 25		
Rugby 66 d				18 37										18 42					19 17		
Nuneaton d														18 55							
Tamworth Low Level d														19 09							
Lichfield Trent Valley d														19 17	←						
Coventry 68 d				18 48									18 42		18 48			19 27	19 31		
Birmingham International 68 d				→									18 53		19 03		19 18	19 38	19 47		
BirminghamNewSt 68 d													19 15		19 21	19 31	19 37	19 57	20 04		
Wolverhampton d													19 37		19 40	19 48	19 57	20 14	20 22		
Penkridge d																	20 05		20 30		
Stafford d														19 35	19 55	20 02	20 12	20 28	20 38		19 24
Stoke-on-Trent 84 a					18 48										20 12	20 17		20 43		19 24	
Macclesfield a			←						←			←				20 36		21 01		19 41	
Crewe 81,91 a	18 47	18 47	18 58						19 07		19 10	19 30	20 07	19 53	20 34		20 31		20 57		19 41
d	18 50	18 50	18 59						19 08		19 11	19 32	20 08				20 33		20 58		19 43
Chester 81 a	19 09	19 09											→				→		→		
Wrexham General 75 a																					
Llandudno Junction 81 a		20 05																			
Bangor (Gwynedd) 81 a		20 21																			
Holyhead 81 a		20 52																			
Wilmslow 84 a											19 27										
Stockport 84 a					19 16						19 35					20 49		21 13		19 54	
Manchester Piccadilly a					19 27						19 45					20 59		21 24		20 05	
Runcorn 91 a			19 23									19 53									20 00
Liverpool South Pkwy 91 a			19 32									20 02									
Liverpool Lime Street 91 a			19 42									20 11									20 18
d																					
Manchester Airport 82 d						18 28				19 07											
Manchester Picc. 82 d						18 47				19 26											
Bolton 82 d										19u44											
Warrington Bank Quay d							19 14		19 27												
Wigan North Western 90 d						19 20	19 25	←	19 38												
Preston 90 a						19 43	19 38	19 43	19 52	20 03											
Blackpool North 97 a						→															
Preston 90 d							19 41	19 44		20 05											
Lancaster d							19 55	20 03		20 21											
Barrow-in-Furness 82 a								21 05													
Oxenholme Lake District 83 d							20 09			20 35											
Windermere 83 a																					
Penrith North Lakes d							20 35			21 00											
Carlisle 216 a							20 49			21 16											
d							20 50			21 17											
Lockerbie 225,226 d										21 36											
Carstairs 226,225 a																					
Motherwell 226 a																					
GlasgowCentral 216,226,225 a							22 01														
Haymarket a										22s34											
Edinburgh a										22 39											
Fort William 227,400 a																					
Perth 229 a																					
Dundee 229 a																					
Aberdeen 229 a																					
Inverness 229 a																					

A From London Euston
B To Crewe
C To Barrow-in-Furness
D From Manchester Airport
E From Birmingham International
F To Preston
G From Exeter St Davids
H To Liverpool Lime Street
I From Bournemouth. ✠ to BirminghamNewSt

Refer to Operator websites for full information about Sleeper Services. Contact details for train operators available at National Rail Enquiries

NRT DECEMBER 19 EDITION

Table T065-F

Saturdays

21 December to 16 May

London & West Midlands to North West England. London, West Midlands & Manchester to Scotland via the West Coast

	VT	LM	VT	NT	VT	NT	VT	TP	VT	VT	LM	VT	LM	VT	VT	LM	XC	LM	XC	LM	VT	VT
		A		B		C	A				D					A	E	F	G			
London Euston ⊖66 d	18 10		18 20		18 30				18 33	18 40		18 43	18 46	19 00	19 07					19 10	19 20	19 30
Watford Junction 66 d																						
Milton Keynes Central 66 d	18 41		18 50									19 13	19 19							19 46	19 50	
Rugby 66 d													19 42							20 26		
Nuneaton d													19 55		20 03							
Tamworth Low Level d									19 38				20 09									
Lichfield Trent Valley d									19 45				20 17									
Coventry 68 d												19 42							20 27	20 37		
Birmingham International 68 d												19 53						20 18	20 38	20 55		
BirminghamNewSt 68 d												20 15					20 31	20 37	20 57	21 13		
Wolverhampton d												20 37					20 48	20 55	21 18	21 33		
Penkridge d																		21 04				
Stafford d									19 59			20 52	20 34		20 27		21 02	21 10	21 32	21 47		
Stoke-on-Trent 84 a			19 48											20 24			21 17		21 47	22 03	20 48	
Macclesfield a		←					←				←			20 41		←	21 36		22 05			
Crewe 81,91 a	19 45	19 58					20 07			20 12	20 31	21 09	20 52		20 45	20 57		21 29		22 25		21 02
d	19 47	19 59					20 08			20 12	20 33				20 47	20 58		21 30				21 05
Chester 81 a	20 08																	→				
Wrexham General 75 a																						
Llandudno Junction 81 a																						
Bangor (Gwynedd) 81 a																						
Holyhead 81 a																						
Wilmslow 84 a										20 28												
Stockport 84 a			20 16							20 36				20 54			21 49		22 17		21 21	
Manchester Piccadilly a			20 27							20 45				21 04			22 00		22 33		21 32	
Runcorn 91 a		20 22							20 31		20 58				21 05	21 21						
Liverpool South Pkwy 91 a		20 31									21 08					21 30						
Liverpool Lime Street 91 a		20 41							20 51		21 18				21 27	21 39						
d								20 12														
Manchester Airport 82 d				19 28																		
Manchester Picc. 82 d				19 47																		
Bolton 82 d																						
Warrington Bank Quay d					20 14		20 27															21 23
Wigan North Western 90 d				20 18	20 25	←	20 38	20 43														21 34
Preston 90 a				20 42	20 38	20 42	20 52	21 03														21 47
Blackpool North 97 a				→																		
Preston 90 d					20 41	20 44																
Lancaster d					20 55	21 02																
Barrow-in-Furness 82 a						22 05																
Oxenholme Lake District 83 d					21 10																	
Windermere 83 a																						
Penrith North Lakes d					21 35																	
Carlisle 216 a					21 50																	
d					21 50																	
Lockerbie 225,226 d					22 09																	
Carstairs 226,225 a																						
Motherwell 226 a					22 52																	
GlasgowCentral 216,226,225 a					23 09																	
Haymarket a																						
Edinburgh a																						
Fort William 227,400 a																						
Perth 229 a																						
Dundee 229 a																						
Aberdeen 229 a																						
Inverness 229 a																						

A From London Euston
B To Barrow-in-Furness
C From Manchester Airport
D From Birmingham International
E From Bristol Temple Meads
F To Liverpool Lime Street
G From Bournemouth. ✠ to BirminghamNewSt

Refer to Operator websites for full information about Sleeper Services. Contact details for train operators available at National Rail Enquiries

Table T065-F

Saturdays
21 December to 16 May

London & West Midlands to North West England. London, West Midlands & Manchester to Scotland via the West Coast

		LM	VT	LM	VT	NT	VT	VT	LM	XC	LM	VT	XC	LM
		1	◇1	1	◇1		◇1	◇1	1	◇1	1	◇1	◇1	1
				A		B				C				
London Euston 15	⊖66 d	19 33	19 40		20 11		20 20	20 31			20 34	21 01		
Watford Junction	66 d							20u46			20u51			
Milton Keynes Central	66 d	20 06					21 05				21 22	21 46		
Rugby	66 d	20 30			21 15			21 36			21 48			
Nuneaton	d	20 43					21 33				22 00			
Tamworth Low Level	d	20 58						21 53			22 14			
Lichfield Trent Valley	d	21 04						22 00			22 20			
Coventry	68 d									21 27				
Birmingham International	68 ✈ d								21 18	21 38				22 18
BirminghamNewSt 12	68 ⛴ d								21 36	21 57			22 31	22 38
Wolverhampton 7	⛴ d								21 59	22 14			22 48	22 59
Penkridge	d								22 08					23 08
Stafford	d	21 21			21 46				22 15	22 28	22 43	22 35	23 02	23 15
Stoke-on-Trent	84 a						22 07			22 43			23 17	
Macclesfield	a			←			22 24			23 01			23 38	
Crewe 10	81,91 a	21 39	21 19	21 29	22 05			22 28	22 35		23 01	22 59		23 35
	d		21 20	21 30	22 06			22 30				23 00		
Chester	81 a													
Wrexham General	75 a													
Llandudno Junction	81 a													
Bangor (Gwynedd)	81 a													
Holyhead	81 ⛴ a													
Wilmslow	84 a		21 35									23 15		
Stockport	84 a		21 44				22 37			23 13		23 26	23 53	
Manchester Piccadilly 10	⛴ a		21 53				22 50			23 29		23 39	00 10	
Runcorn	91 a			21 51	22 24									
Liverpool South Pkwy 7	91 ✈ a			22 00										
Liverpool Lime Street 10	91 a			22 09	22 41									
	d													
Manchester Airport	82 ✈⛴ d					22 10								
Manchester Picc. 10	82 ⛴ d					22 26								
Bolton	82 d													
Warrington Bank Quay	d							22 47						
Wigan North Western	90 d							23 01						
Preston 8	90 a					23 09		23 16						
Blackpool North	97 ⛴ a													
Preston 8	90 d					23 10								
Lancaster 6	d					23 28								
Barrow-in-Furness	82 a					00 33								
Oxenholme Lake District	83 d													
Windermere	83 a													
Penrith North Lakes	d													
Carlisle 8	216 a													
	d													
Lockerbie	225,226 d													
Carstairs	226,225 a													
Motherwell	226 a													
GlasgowCentral 15	216,226,225 a													
Haymarket	⛴ a													
Edinburgh 10	⛴ a													
Fort William	227,400 a													
Perth	229 a													
Dundee	229 a													
Aberdeen	229 a													
Inverness	229 a													

A From Birmingham International
B from 22 February until 28 March
C From Bournemouth. to BirminghamNewSt

Refer to Operator websites for full information about Sleeper Services. Contact details for train operators available at National Rail Enquiries

Table T065-F

Sundays
15 December to 10 May

London & West Midlands to North West England. London, West Midlands & Manchester to Scotland via the West Coast

		LM	LM	TP	NT	NT	NT	TP	TP	VT	XC	NT	NT	NT	VT	TP	VT	TP	VT	LM	LM	XC	VT
		1	1	◇1	◇	◇		◇1	◇1	◇1	◇1	◇	◇	◇	◇1	◇1	◇1	◇1	◇1	1	1	◇1	◇1
				A	B	C	A	A	D			D	E	F	G		H			I			J
London Euston 15	⊖66 d																						
Watford Junction	66 d																						
Milton Keynes Central	66 d																						
Rugby	66 d																			08 53			
Nuneaton	d																						
Tamworth Low Level	d																						
Lichfield Trent Valley	d																						
Coventry	68 d																			09 06			
Birmingham International	68 ✈ d																			09 19	09 41		
BirminghamNewSt 12	68 ⛴ d	08 25	08 39							08 45	09 01				09 20					09 42	09 53	10 01	10 20
Wolverhampton 7	⛴ d	08 51	08 59							09 04	09 18				09 37					10 00	10 09	10 18	10 37
Penkridge	d	09 02	09 07																	10 09			
Stafford	d	09 09	09 15							09 18	09 32									10 16	10 23	10 33	
Stoke-on-Trent	84 a		09 32								09 51										10 39	10 48	
Macclesfield	a										10 09											11 08	
Crewe 10	81,91 a	09 29	09 54							09 36					10 07					10 34	11 01		11 10
	d									09 38					10 10				10 27	10 36			11 11
Chester	81 a																			→			→
Wrexham General	75 a																						
Llandudno Junction	81 a																						
Bangor (Gwynedd)	81 a																						
Holyhead	81 ⛴ a																						
Wilmslow	84 a																						
Stockport	84 a										10 22											11 22	
Manchester Piccadilly 10	⛴ a										10 38											11 33	
Runcorn	91 a																						
Liverpool South Pkwy 7	91 ✈ a																						
Liverpool Lime Street 10	91 a																						
	d															10 12							
Manchester Airport	82 ✈⛴ d				08 33			09 05	09 05				09 35	09 35				10 10					
Manchester Picc. 10	82 ⛴ d			08 43	08 53	08 53		09 22	09 22				09 52	09 53				10 26					
Bolton	82 d			09u03				09u44	09u44									10u44					
Warrington Bank Quay	d									09 55					10 28				10 43				
Wigan North Western	90 d				09 22	09 22				10 07			10 28	10 28	10 38	10 44			10 54				
Preston 8	90 a			09 22	09 40	09 40		10 03	10 03	10 21			10 44	10 44	10 52	10 58		11 04	11 13				
Blackpool North	97 ⛴ a																←						
Preston 8	90 d			09 24	09 48	09 48		10 05	10 19			10 30	10 46	10 46	11 02	11 00	11 02	11 09	11 16				
Lancaster 6	d			09 40	10 06	10 06	10 11	10 21	10 35			10 48	11 06	11 06	→		11 18	11 25	11a34				
Barrow-in-Furness	82 a						11 14						12 08	12 08									
Oxenholme Lake District	83 d			09 54	10 30	10 30		10 35				11 07					11 33	11 39					
Windermere	83 a				10 51	10 51						11 28											
Penrith North Lakes	d							11 00															
Carlisle 8	216 a			10 32			13 42	11 16	11 31							12 04	12 10	12 17					
	d			10 34				11 16	11 31							12 05	12 12	12 19					
Lockerbie	225,226 d							11 37															
Carstairs	226,225 a																						
Motherwell	226 a							12 22	12 33														
GlasgowCentral 15	216,226,225 a							12 46	12 55							13 22	13 27						
Haymarket	⛴ a			11s48														13s33					
Edinburgh 10	⛴ a			11 54														13 39					
Fort William	227,400 a																						
Perth	229 a																						
Dundee	229 a																						
Aberdeen	229 a																						
Inverness	229 a																						

A until 5 January, from 23 February until 29 March
B until 5 January
C from 23 February until 29 March
D from 12 January until 16 February, from 5 April
E until 5 January, from 5 April
F from 12 January until 29 March
G To Glasgow Central
H From Birmingham New Street
I To Liverpool Lime Street
J To Edinburgh

Refer to Operator websites for full information about Sleeper Services. Contact details for train operators available at National Rail Enquiries

Table T065-F

Sundays
15 December to 10 May

London & West Midlands to North West England. London, West Midlands & Manchester to Scotland via the West Coast

Station			LM ■ A	VT ◇■	VT ◇■	LM ■ B	VT ◇■	LM ■	XC ◇■ C	XC ◇■ D	LM ■	VT ◇■	LM ■ E	NT ◇	NT ◇ F	VT ◇■ G	LM ■	VT ◇■	LM ■ H	TP ◇■	VT ◇■	VT ◇■ I	LM ■ A	LM ■
London Euston 15	⊖66	d	07 52	08 10	08 16		08 20				08 24	08 47					08 55	09 16			09 20			
Watford Junction	66	d	08 10								08 44						09 14							
Milton Keynes Central	66	d	08 51	08 56			09 06				09 26	09 34					09 57				10 07		10 11	
Rugby	66	d	09 48								10 21	10 10	09 52				10 50						10 56	
Nuneaton		d			09 44								10 05				11 05	10 45						
Tamworth Low Level		d											10 20				11 19							
Lichfield Trent Valley		d											10 26				11 26	11 02						
Coventry	68	d	10 00					10 11	10 27	10 27	10 33												11 07	11 10
Birmingham International	68 ✈	d	10 09					10 29	10 38	10 38	10 51												11 18	11 22
BirminghamNewSt 12	68	d	10 42					10 57	11 01	11 01	11 15											11 20	11 40	11 43
Wolverhampton 7		d	11 02					11 14	11 18	11 18	11 34											11 37	12 00	12 04
Penkridge		d	11 11																				12 10	
Stafford		d	11 19		10 08			11 28	11 33	11 33	11a48		10 47				11 44	11 15					12 17	12 21
Stoke-on-Trent	84	a					10 19	11 44	11 48	11 48											11 21			12 37
Macclesfield		a				←	10 36		12 08	12 08						←			←		11 38			
Crewe 10	81,91	a	11 38	10 17	10 28	10 34		12 06				10 56	11 07			11 10	12 04	11 34	11 38			12 07	12 35	12 59
		d	11 41	10 19	10 30	10 36						10 58				11 11		11 37	11 41			12 09	12 37	
Chester	81	a	→																			→	→	
Wrexham General	75	a																						
Llandudno Junction	81	a																						
Bangor (Gwynedd)	81	a																						
Holyhead	81 ⛴	a																						
Wilmslow	84	a		10 33																				
Stockport	84	a		10 43			10 50		12 24	12 24											11 52			
Manchester Piccadilly 10	⛴	a		10 53			11 00		12 40	12 42											12 04			
Runcorn	91	a			10 48	11 01												11 54	12 03					
Liverpool South Pkwy 7	91 ✈	a				11 10													12 12					
Liverpool Lime Street 10	91	a			11 05	11 20												12 11	12 22					
		d																						
Manchester Airport	82 ✈⛴	d												10 32							11 10			
Manchester Picc. 10	82 ⛴	d												10 54							11 25			
Bolton	82	d													11 19						11u44			
Warrington Bank Quay		d										11 14				11 29								
Wigan North Western	90	d										11 25				11 40								
Preston 8	90	a										11 39		11 43	11 49	11 53					12 04			
Blackpool North	97 ⛴	a													12 15									
Preston 8	90	d										11 41		11 47		11 55					12 05			
Lancaster 6		d										11 56		12 05		12 10					12 21			
Barrow-in-Furness	82	a												13 04										
Oxenholme Lake District	83	d										12 09				12 25					12 35			
Windermere	83	a																						
Penrith North Lakes		d										12 35									13 01			
Carlisle 8	216	a										12 50				13 02					13 16			
		d										12 51				13 03					13 17			
Lockerbie	225,226	d																			13 37			
Carstairs	226,225	a																						
Motherwell	226	a																			14 21			
GlasgowCentral 15	216,226,225	a										14 04									14 42			
Haymarket	⛴	a														14 16								
Edinburgh 10	⛴	a														14 21								
Fort William	227,400	a																						
Perth	229	a																						
Dundee	229	a																						
Aberdeen	229	a																						
Inverness	229	a																						

A To Liverpool Lime Street
B From Rugby
C from 5 April. From Reading
D until 29 March. From Reading
E From Northampton
F From Manchester Oxford Road
G From Birmingham New Street
H From London Euston
I To Glasgow Central

Refer to Operator websites for full information about Sleeper Services. Contact details for train operators available at National Rail Enquiries

Table T065-F

Sundays
15 December to 10 May

London & West Midlands to North West England. London, West Midlands & Manchester to Scotland via the West Coast

Station			XC ◇■ A	LM ■	NT ◇ B	NT ◇ C	VT ◇■	NT ◇ D	NT ◇ E	NT ◇ F	VT ◇■ G	NT	LM ■	VT ◇■	LM ■ H	VT ◇■	TP ◇■ I	VT ◇■ J	LM ■ K	LM ■	XC ◇■ L	LM ■	VT ◇■
London Euston 15	⊖66	d		09 24			09 46						10 01	10 16		10 19						10 31	10 46
Watford Junction	66	d		09 45									10 19									10 47	
Milton Keynes Central	66	d		10 27			10 33						10 58			11 07						11 27	11 33
Rugby	66	d		11 22			11 09						11 52						11 56			12 20	12 09
Nuneaton		d											12 05	11 47									
Tamworth Low Level		d											12 19										
Lichfield Trent Valley		d											12 25										
Coventry	68	d	11 27	11 34															12 07	12 11	12 27	12 32	
Birmingham International	68 ✈	d	11 38	11 52															12 18	12 23	12 38	12 50	
BirminghamNewSt 12	68	d	11 57	12 12														12 20	12 35	12 47	12 57	13 15	
Wolverhampton 7		d	12 15	12 31														12 37	12 55	13 03	13 14	13 33	
Penkridge		d																	13 04				
Stafford		d	12 30	12a45									12 45	12 14					13 10	13 17	13 28	13a47	
Stoke-on-Trent	84	a	12 45													12 24				13 34	13 43		
Macclesfield		a	13 04								←				←	12 40					14 04		
Crewe 10	81,91	a					11 55				12 07		13 03	12 32	12 35			13 07	13 29	13 56			12 56
		d					11 57				12 09			12 34	12 37			13 09	13 31				12 58
Chester	81	a																→	→				
Wrexham General	75	a																					
Llandudno Junction	81	a																					
Bangor (Gwynedd)	81	a																					
Holyhead	81 ⛴	a																					
Wilmslow	84	a																					
Stockport	84	a	13 16													12 55					14 16		
Manchester Piccadilly 10	⛴	a	13 28													13 05					14 29		
Runcorn	91	a												12 51	13 02								
Liverpool South Pkwy 7	91 ✈	a													13 11								
Liverpool Lime Street 10	91	a												13 08	13 21								
		d																					
Manchester Airport	82 ✈⛴	d			11 31																		
Manchester Picc. 10	82 ⛴	d			11 50																		
Bolton	82	d								12 18							12u44						
Warrington Bank Quay		d					12 14				12 27												13 15
Wigan North Western	90	d			12 20	12 20	12 25	←	←		12 38												13 26
Preston 8	90	a			12 42	12 42	12 39	12 42	12 42	12 50	12 51						13 04						13 40
Blackpool North	97 ⛴	a			→	→				13 15													
Preston 8	90	d					12 40	12 44	12 44		12 53						13 05						13 41
Lancaster 6		d					12 55				13 08	13 13					13 21						13 56
Barrow-in-Furness	82	a										14 16											
Oxenholme Lake District	83	d					13 09	13 32	13 32		13 22						13 35						14 10
Windermere	83	a						13 54	13 54														
Penrith North Lakes		d					13 35																14 36
Carlisle 8	216	a					13 50				14 00	16 37					14 14						14 51
		d					13 50				14 01						14 15						14 51
Lockerbie	225,226	d															14 34						
Carstairs	226,225	a																					
Motherwell	226	a																					
GlasgowCentral 15	216,226,225	a					15 04				15 15												16 06
Haymarket	⛴	a															15s33						
Edinburgh 10	⛴	a															15 39						
Fort William	227,400	a																					
Perth	229	a																					
Dundee	229	a																					
Aberdeen	229	a																					
Inverness	229	a																					

A From Southampton Central
B from 5 April. To Windermere
C until 29 March. From Manchester Oxford Road to Windermere
D from 5 April. From Manchester Airport
E until 29 March. From Manchester Oxford Road
F From Manchester Oxford Road
G From Birmingham New Street
H From Milton Keynes Central
I From Manchester Victoria
J To Edinburgh
K From Northampton to Liverpool Lime Street
L From Bournemouth

Refer to Operator websites for full information about Sleeper Services. Contact details for train operators available at National Rail Enquiries

Table T065-F

Sundays
15 December to 10 May

London & West Midlands to North West England. London, West Midlands & Manchester to Scotland via the West Coast

Station		NT	NT	VT	NT	LM	VT	LM	TP	VT	VT	XC	LM	LM	XC	LM	VT	VT	NT	VT	NT	VT	TP
		A	B	C	D			E			F		G		H				B		D	C	
London Euston	⊖66 d					10 53	11 16			11 19						11 24	12 05	12 17		12 28			
Watford Junction	66 d					11 14										11 42							
Milton Keynes Central	66 d					11 58	12 04			12 08						12 28		12 50					
Rugby	66 d					12 39							12 56			13 17							
Nuneaton	d					12 51																	
Tamworth Low Level	d					13 05																	
Lichfield Trent Valley	d					13 11																	
Coventry	68 d												13 08	13 11	13 28	13 31							
Birmingham International	68 ✈ d												13 18	13 23	13 38	13 49							
BirminghamNewSt	68 d										13 20	13 31	13 35	13 44	13 57	14 05							
Wolverhampton	d										13 37	13 48	13 55	14 01	14 14	14 27							
Penkridge	d												14 04										
Stafford	d					13 30	12 53					14 02	14 11	14 15	14 28	14a41	13 25						
Stoke-on-Trent	84 a									13 09		14 17		14 32	14 43			13 50					
Macclesfield	a			←				←		13 26		14 36			15 01							←	
Crewe	81,91 a			13 07		13 48	13 12	13 29			14 06		14 30	14 54			13 43					14 06	
	d			13 09			13 15	13 31			14 09		14 31				13 45					14 09	
Chester	81 a										→		→										
Wrexham General	75 a																						
Llandudno Junction	81 a																						
Bangor (Gwynedd)	81 a																						
Holyhead	81 a																						
Wilmslow	84 a																						
Stockport	84 a									13 41		14 50			15 14			14 22					
Manchester Piccadilly	a									13 50		14 59			15 24			14 32					
Runcorn	91 a						13 32	13 53									14 02						
Liverpool South Pkwy	91 ✈ a							14 02															
Liverpool Lime Street	91 a						13 55	14 12									14 20						
	d																						14 12
Manchester Airport	82 ✈ d		12 41						13 10										13 30				
Manchester Picc.	82 d		13 01						13 26										13 48				
Bolton	82 d	13 20																					
Warrington Bank Quay	d			13 27																14 16		14 27	
Wigan North Western	90 d		13 33	13 38	←														14 21	14 27		14 38	14 43
Preston	90 a	13 51	13 55	13 52	13 55				14 02										14 38	14 41		14 51	14 58
Blackpool North	97 a	14 16	→																		←		
Preston	90 d			13 53	13 59				14 04										14 46	14 42	14 46	14 53	14 59
Lancaster	d			14 09	14 17				14 22										→	14 58	15 04	15 10	15 15
Barrow-in-Furness	82 a				15 20																16 07		
Oxenholme Lake District	83 d								14 36													15 24	
Windermere	83 a																						
Penrith North Lakes	d			14 46					15 02											15 32			
Carlisle	216 a			15 01					15 17											15 47		16 01	16 07
	d			15 03					15 18											15 48		16 03	16 08
Lockerbie	225,226 d								15 38														
Carstairs	226,225 a																						
Motherwell	226 a								16 23														17 09
GlasgowCentral	216,226,225 a								16 43											17 00		17 15	17 28
Haymarket	a			16 13																			
Edinburgh	a			16 20																			
Fort William	227,400 a																						
Perth	229 a																						
Dundee	229 a																						
Aberdeen	229 a																						
Inverness	229 a																						

A From Manchester Oxford Road
B To Barrow-in-Furness
C From Birmingham New Street
D From Manchester Airport
E From Northampton
F To Glasgow Central
G From Northampton to Liverpool Lime Street
H From Bournemouth

Refer to Operator websites for full information about Sleeper Services. Contact details for train operators available at National Rail Enquiries

Table T065-F

Sundays
15 December to 10 May

London & West Midlands to North West England. London, West Midlands & Manchester to Scotland via the West Coast

Station		TP	LM	LM	VT	LM	VT	LM	VT	VT	VT	NT	VT	VT	NT	NT	VT	TP	LM	LM	VT	XC
			A	B		C	D					E	F	G	H		I		A	B		J
London Euston	⊖66 d		12 31	12 34	12 37		12 40	12 43	12 57	13 05	13 17		13 26	13 28					13 32	13 34	13 37	
Watford Junction	66 d			12 50																13 50		
Milton Keynes Central	66 d		13 13	13 28			13 13	13 20			13 50								14 14	14 28		
Rugby	66 d		13 56	14 17				13 47											14 57	15 17		
Nuneaton	d							14 00														
Tamworth Low Level	d							14 15														
Lichfield Trent Valley	d							14 21														
Coventry	68 d		14 08	14 30			13 42												15 09	15 30		
Birmingham International	68 ✈ d		→	→			13 53										←		→	→		
BirminghamNewSt	68 d						14 15										14 15					14 31
Wolverhampton	d						→										14 37					14 48
Penkridge	d																					
Stafford	d							14 40		14 25												15 02
Stoke-on-Trent	84 a								14 24		14 50											15 17
Macclesfield	a					←			14 42													15 36
Crewe	81,91 a				14 12	14 30		14 58		14 43							15 07				15 12	
	d				14 13	14 31				14 45							15 09				15 13	
Chester	81 a																					
Wrexham General	75 a																					
Llandudno Junction	81 a																					
Bangor (Gwynedd)	81 a																					
Holyhead	81 a																					
Wilmslow	84 a				14 28																15 29	
Stockport	84 a				14 38				14 55		15 20										15 38	15 50
Manchester Piccadilly	a				14 48				15 06		15 31										15 48	15 59
Runcorn	91 a					14 57				15 02												
Liverpool South Pkwy	91 ✈ a					15 06																
Liverpool Lime Street	91 a					15 15				15 20												
	d																					
Manchester Airport	82 ✈ d	14 10										14 30						15 10				
Manchester Picc.	82 d	14 26										14 48						15 26				
Bolton	82 d	14u44																15u45				
Warrington Bank Quay	d												15 16	15 16			15 27					
Wigan North Western	90 d											15 18	15 27	15 27			15 38					
Preston	90 a	15 03										15 36	15 41	15 41			15 52	16 04				
Blackpool North	97 a														←							
Preston	90 d	15 05										15 47	15 42	15 42	15 47		15 53	16 06				
Lancaster	d	15 21										→	15 58	15 58		16 03	16 09	16 22				
Barrow-in-Furness	82 a															17 06						
Oxenholme Lake District	83 d												16 12	16 12	16 31			16 36				
Windermere	83 a														16 53							
Penrith North Lakes	d	15 57															16 45	17 02				
Carlisle	216 a	16 13											16 49	16 49		19 47	17 00	17 17				
	d	16 14											16 49	16 49			17 02	17 19				
Lockerbie	225,226 d	16 33																				
Carstairs	226,225 a																	17 38				
Motherwell	226 a																	18 23				
GlasgowCentral	216,226,225 a												18 03	18 03				18 41				
Haymarket	a	17s31															18 11					
Edinburgh	a	17 36															18 20					
Fort William	227,400 a																					
Perth	229 a																					
Dundee	229 a																					
Aberdeen	229 a																					
Inverness	229 a																					

A To Liverpool Lime Street
B To Stafford
C From Northampton
D To Edinburgh
E To Windermere
F from 23 February
G until 16 February
H From Manchester Airport
I From London Euston
J From Paignton

Refer to Operator websites for full information about Sleeper Services. Contact details for train operators available at National Rail Enquiries

Table T065-F

Sundays
15 December to 10 May

London & West Midlands to North West England. London, West Midlands & Manchester to Scotland via the West Coast

		LM	LM	XC	LM	VT	LM	VT	VT	VT	NT	VT	VT	NT	TP	LM	LM	VT	XC	LM	LM	XC	LM
		A		B	A	C					D		A	E		F	G		H	A		B	A
London Euston 15 ⊖66	d					13 40	13 43	13 57	14 05	14 17		14 28				14 31	14 34	14 37					
Watford Junction 66	d																14 50						
Milton Keynes Central 66	d					14 13	14 19			14 50						15 13	15 28						
Rugby 66	d						14 47									15 56	16 17						
Nuneaton	d						15 00																
Tamworth Low Level	d						15 15																
Lichfield Trent Valley	d	←			←		15 21													←			←
Coventry 68	d	14 08	14 11	14 27	14 30	14 43										16 08	16 30			15 09	15 12	15 27	15 30
Birmingham International 68	d	14 18	14 23	14 38	14 48	14 54							←			→	→			15 19	15 24	15 38	15 48
BirminghamNewSt 12 68	d	14 35	14 53	14 57	15 05	15 15							15 15						15 31	15 35	15 53	15 57	16 05
Wolverhampton 7	d	14 55	15 09	15 14	15 27	→							15 37						15 48	15 55	16 09	16 14	16 27
Penkridge	d	15 04																		16 04			
Stafford	d	15 11	15 23	15 28	15a41		15 40		15 25										16 02	16 11	16 23	16 28	16a41
Stoke-on-Trent 84	a		15 42	15 45				15 25		15 50									16 17		16 42	16 46	
Macclesfield	a			16 04				15 42											16 36			17 04	
Crewe 10 81,91	a	15 30	16 05				15 58		15 43				16 08					16 12		16 30	17 05		
	d	15 31							15 45				16 09					16 13		16 31			
Chester 81	a																						
Wrexham General 75	a																						
Llandudno Junction 81	a																						
Bangor (Gwynedd) 81	a																						
Holyhead 81	a																						
Wilmslow 84	a																	16 29					
Stockport 84	a			16 16				15 55		16 23								16 38	16 50			17 16	
Manchester Piccadilly 10	a			16 29				16 05		16 32								16 48	16 59			17 29	
Runcorn 91	a	15 54							16 02											16 57			
Liverpool South Pkwy 7 91	a	16 03																		17 06			
Liverpool Lime Street 10 91	a	16 12							16 23											17 15			
	d																						
Manchester Airport 82	d										15 30				16 10								
Manchester Picc. 10 82	d										15 48				16 26								
Bolton 82	d														16u44								
Warrington Bank Quay	d											16 16	16 27										
Wigan North Western 90	d										16 22	16 27	16 38										
Preston 8 90	a										16 38	16 41	16 51		17 04								
Blackpool North 97	a													←									
Preston 8 90	d										16 57	16 42	16 53	16 57	17 05								
Lancaster 6	d										→	16 57	17 08	17 15	17 21								
Barrow-in-Furness 82	a													18 17									
Oxenholme Lake District 83	d												17 23		17 35								
Windermere 83	a																						
Penrith North Lakes	d											17 32			18 01								
Carlisle 8 216	a											17 47	18 01		18 16								
	d											17 48	18 02		18 18								
Lockerbie 225,226	d														18 37								
Carstairs 226,225	a																						
Motherwell 226	a																						
GlasgowCentral 15 216,226,225	a											19 00	19 13										
Haymarket	a														19s34								
Edinburgh 10	a														19 40								
Fort William 227,400	a																						
Perth 229	a																						
Dundee 229	a																						
Aberdeen 229	a																						
Inverness 229	a																						

A From London Euston
B From Bournemouth
C To Glasgow Central
D To Barrow-in-Furness
E From Manchester Airport
F To Liverpool Lime Street
G To Stafford
H From Plymouth

Refer to Operator websites for full information about Sleeper Services. Contact details for train operators available at National Rail Enquiries

NRT DECEMBER 19 EDITION

Table T065-F

Sundays
15 December to 10 May

London & West Midlands to North West England. London, West Midlands & Manchester to Scotland via the West Coast

		VT	LM	VT	VT	VT	VT	NT	VT	NT	VT	TP	LM	LM	VT	XC	LM	LM	XC	LM	VT	LM	VT
		A						B		C	D		E	F		G	D		H	D	I		
London Euston 15 ⊖66	d	14 40	14 43	14 57	15 05	15 08	15 17		15 28				15 31	15 34	15 37						15 40	15 43	15 57
Watford Junction 66	d													15 50									
Milton Keynes Central 66	d	15 13	15 19			15 42	15 50						16 13	16 28							16 13	16 19	
Rugby 66	d		15 42										16 56	17 17								16 47	
Nuneaton	d		15 57																			17 00	
Tamworth Low Level	d		16 12																			17 15	
Lichfield Trent Valley	d		16 18														←			←		17 21	
Coventry 68	d	15 42											17 08	17 30			16 08	16 11	16 27	16 30	16 42		
Birmingham International 68	d	15 53									←		→	→			16 18	16 23	16 38	16 48	16 53		
BirminghamNewSt 12 68	d	16 15									16 15					16 31	16 35	16 53	16 57	17 05	17 15		
Wolverhampton 7	d	→									16 37					16 48	16 55	17 09	17 14	17 23	→		
Penkridge	d																17 04						
Stafford	d		16 38		16 25											17 02	17 11	17 23	17 28	17a37		17 40	
Stoke-on-Trent 84	a			16 26			16 52									17 17		17 42	17 46				17 25
Macclesfield	a			16 42												17 36			18 04				17 42
Crewe 10 81,91	a		16 57		16 43	16 49					17 07				17 12		17 30	18 05				17 59	
	d				16 45	16 51					17 09				17 13		17 32						
Chester 81	a					17 10																	
Wrexham General 75	a																						
Llandudno Junction 81	a																						
Bangor (Gwynedd) 81	a																						
Holyhead 81	a																						
Wilmslow 84	a														17 29								
Stockport 84	a			16 56			17 23								17 38	17 50			18 16				17 55
Manchester Piccadilly 10	a			17 06			17 32								17 48	17 59			18 29				18 05
Runcorn 91	a				17 02												17 57						
Liverpool South Pkwy 7 91	a																18 06						
Liverpool Lime Street 10 91	a				17 21												18 15						
	d																						
Manchester Airport 82	d							16 30				17 10											
Manchester Picc. 10 82	d							16 48				17 26											
Bolton 82	d											17u45											
Warrington Bank Quay	d								17 16		17 27												
Wigan North Western 90	d							17 19	17 27		17 38												
Preston 8 90	a							17 37	17 41		17 52	18 04											
Blackpool North 97	a									←													
Preston 8 90	d							17 46	17 42	17 46	17 53	18 07											
Lancaster 6	d							→	17 57	18 04	18 09	18 23											
Barrow-in-Furness 82	a									19 07													
Oxenholme Lake District 83	d								18 12		18 24	18 37											
Windermere 83	a																						
Penrith North Lakes	d										18 49	19 02											
Carlisle 8 216	a								18 49		19 04	19 18											
	d								18 49		19 04	19 18											
Lockerbie 225,226	d											19 38											
Carstairs 226,225	a																						
Motherwell 226	a											20 22											
GlasgowCentral 15 216,226,225	a								20 01			20 40											
Haymarket	a										20 16												
Edinburgh 10	a										20 22												
Fort William 227,400	a																						
Perth 229	a																						
Dundee 229	a																						
Aberdeen 229	a																						
Inverness 229	a																						

A To Edinburgh
B To Barrow-in-Furness
C From Manchester Airport
D From London Euston
E To Liverpool Lime Street
F To Stafford
G From Plymouth
H From Bournemouth
I To Glasgow Central

Refer to Operator websites for full information about Sleeper Services. Contact details for train operators available at National Rail Enquiries

Table T065-F

Sundays

15 December to 10 May

London & West Midlands to North West England. London, West Midlands & Manchester to Scotland via the West Coast

	VT	VT	VT	NT A	VT	VT B	TP	TP	NT C	XC D	LM E	LM F	VT	XC G	LM B	LM	XC H	LM B	VT I	LM	VT
London Euston ⊖66 d	16 05	16 08	16 17		16 28						16 32	16 34	16 37						16 40	16 43	16 57
Watford Junction 66 d												16 50									
Milton Keynes Central 66 d		16 42	16 50								17 14	17 28							17 13	17 19	
Rugby 66 d											17 56	18 17								17 46	
Nuneaton d																				17 59	
Tamworth Low Level d																				18 12	
Lichfield Trent Valley d															←			←		18 19	
Coventry 68 d										16 54	18 08	18 30			17 08	17 11	17 27	17 30	17 42		
Birmingham International 68 d						←				17 04	→	→			17 18	17 23	17 38	17 48	17 53		
BirminghamNewSt 68 d						17 15				17 30				17 31	17 35	17 52	17 57	18 06	18 15		
Wolverhampton d						17 37								17 48	17 55	18 08	18 14	18 30	→		
Penkridge d															18 04						
Stafford d	17 26													18 02	18 11	18 21	18 28	18a44		18 35	
Stoke-on-Trent 84 a			17 50											18 17		18 37	18 44				18 25
Macclesfield a														18 36			19 04				18 42
Crewe 81,91 a	17 44	17 48				18 07							18 12		18 30	19 05				18 54	
d	17 46	17 50				18 09							18 13		18 31						
Chester 81 a		18 10																			
Wrexham General 75 a																					
Llandudno Junction 81 a																					
Bangor (Gwynedd) 81 a																					
Holyhead 81 a																					
Wilmslow 84 a													18 29								
Stockport 84 a			18 23										18 38	18 50			19 17				18 56
Manchester Piccadilly a			18 32										18 48	18 59			19 29				19 06
Runcorn 91 a	18 02														18 57						
Liverpool South Pkwy 91 a															19 06						
Liverpool Lime Street 91 a	18 21														19 15						
d							18 12														
Manchester Airport 82 d				17 30				18 10													
Manchester Picc. 82 d				17 48				18 26													
Bolton 82 d								18u43													
Warrington Bank Quay d					18 16	18 27															
Wigan North Western 90 d				18 18	18 27	18 38	18 43														
Preston 90 a				18 36	18 41	18 52	18 58	19 03													
Blackpool North 97 a									←												
Preston 90 d				19 08	18 42	18 53	18 59	19 04	19 08												
Lancaster d				→	18 57	19 08	19 15	19 20													
Barrow-in-Furness 82 a																					
Oxenholme Lake District 83 d					19 12	19 23		19 34	19 41												
Windermere 83 a									20 02												
Penrith North Lakes d					19 37		19 53	20 00													
Carlisle 216 a					19 52	20 00	20 09	20 15													
d					19 53	20 01	20 10	20 17													
Lockerbie 225,226 d							20 29	20 36													
Carstairs 226,225 a																					
Motherwell 226 a							21 15														
GlasgowCentral 216,226,225 a					21 04	21 12	21 32														
Haymarket a								21s33													
Edinburgh a								21 39		22 18											
Fort William 227,400 a																					
Perth 229 a																					
Dundee 229 a																					
Aberdeen 229 a																					
Inverness 229 a																					

A To Windermere
B From London Euston
C From Manchester Airport
D From Reading. to BirminghamNewSt
E To Liverpool Lime Street
F To Crewe
G From Bristol Temple Meads
H From Bournemouth
I To Edinburgh

Refer to Operator websites for full information about Sleeper Services. Contact details for train operators available at National Rail Enquiries

Table T065-F

Sundays

15 December to 10 May

London & West Midlands to North West England. London, West Midlands & Manchester to Scotland via the West Coast

	VT	VT	VT	VT	NT A	VT B	VT C	NT D	VT E	TP	LM F	LM G	VT	XC H	LM E	LM	XC I	LM E	VT J	LM	VT	VT
London Euston ⊖66 d	17 05	17 08	17 08	17 17		17 26	17 28				17 32	17 34	17 37						17 40	17 43	17 57	18 05
Watford Junction 66 d												17 50										
Milton Keynes Central 66 d		17 42	17 42	17 50							18 14	18 28							18 13	18 19		
Rugby 66 d											18 56	19 17								18 47		
Nuneaton d	18 04																			19 00		
Tamworth Low Level d																				19 15		
Lichfield Trent Valley d		18 23	18 23												←			←		19 21		
Coventry 68 d											19 08	19 30			18 08	18 11	18 27	18 30	18 42			
Birmingham International 68 d									←		→	→			18 18	18 23	18 38	18 48	18 53			
BirminghamNewSt 68 d									18 15					18 31	18 35	18 53	18 57	19 05	19 15			
Wolverhampton d									18 37					18 48	18 55	19 09	19 14	19 24	→			
Penkridge d															19 04							
Stafford d		18 40	18 40											19 02	19 11	19 23	19 28	19 39		19 42		19 25
Stoke-on-Trent 84 a				18 50										19 17		19 41	19 45				19 25	
Macclesfield a														19 36			20 04				19 42	
Crewe 81,91 a	18 44	18 57	18 57						19 07				19 12		19 30	20 08		19 57		20 01		19 43
d	18 46	19 00	19 00						19 09				19 13		19 31							19 45
Chester 81 a		19 18	19 19																			
Wrexham General 75 a																						
Llandudno Junction 81 a		20 18																				
Bangor (Gwynedd) 81 a		20 34																				
Holyhead 81 a		21 03																				
Wilmslow 84 a													19 29									
Stockport 84 a				19 23									19 38	19 50			20 16				19 56	
Manchester Piccadilly a				19 32									19 48	19 59			20 28				20 06	
Runcorn 91 a	19 02														19 54							20 02
Liverpool South Pkwy 91 a															20 03							
Liverpool Lime Street 91 a	19 21														20 12							20 20
d																						
Manchester Airport 82 d					18 30					19 10												
Manchester Picc. 82 d					18 48					19 26												
Bolton 82 d										19u44												
Warrington Bank Quay d						19 17	19 17		19 26													
Wigan North Western 90 d					19 18	19 28	19 28		19 38													
Preston 90 a					19 36	19 41	19 41		19 52	20 06												
Blackpool North 97 a								←														
Preston 90 d					19 47	19 43	19 43	19 47	19 53	20 07												
Lancaster d					→	19 58	19 58	20 05	20 09	20 23												
Barrow-in-Furness 82 a								21 08														
Oxenholme Lake District 83 d						20 12	20 12			20 39												
Windermere 83 a																						
Penrith North Lakes d						20 37	20 37		20 46	21 05												
Carlisle 216 a						20 51	20 51		20 59	21 20												
d						20 52	20 52		21 02	21 22												
Lockerbie 225,226 d										21 41												
Carstairs 226,225 a																						
Motherwell 226 a										22 28												
GlasgowCentral 216,226,225 a						22 04	22 04			22 47												
Haymarket a									22 14													
Edinburgh a									22 19													
Fort William 227,400 a																						
Perth 229 a																						
Dundee 229 a																						
Aberdeen 229 a																						
Inverness 229 a																						

A To Barrow-in-Furness
B from 23 February
C until 16 February
D From Manchester Airport
E From London Euston
F To Liverpool Lime Street
G To Crewe
H From Penzance
I From Bournemouth
J To Glasgow Central

Refer to Operator websites for full information about Sleeper Services. Contact details for train operators available at National Rail Enquiries

Table T065-F

Sundays
15 December to 10 May

London & West Midlands to North West England. London, West Midlands & Manchester to Scotland via the West Coast

	VT	VT	VT	NT	VT	NT	VT	TP	LM	LM	VT	XC	LM	LM	XC	LM	VT	LM	VT	VT	VT
	◇1	◇1	◇1	◇	◇1	◇	R 1	◇1	1	1	◇1	◇1	1	1	◇1	1	◇1	1	◇1	◇1	◇1
				A		B	C		D	D		E	C		F	C					
	🍴	🍴	🍴		🍴		🍴	🛒			🍴	🛒			🛒		🍴		🍴	🍴	🍴
London Euston 15 ⊖66 d	18 08	18 08	18 17		18 28				18 31	18 34	18 37						18 40	18 43	18 57	19 05	19 08
Watford Junction 66 d										18 50											
Milton Keynes Central 66 d	18 42	18 42	18 50						19 13	19 28							19 13	19 19			19 42
Rugby 66 d									19 57	20 17								19 47			
Nuneaton d																		20 00		20 04	
Tamworth Low Level d																		20 15			
Lichfield Trent Valley d													←			←		20 21			
Coventry 68 d									20 08	20 30			19 08	19 11	19 27	19 30	19 42				
Birmingham International 68 ✈ d							←		→	→			19 18	19 23	19 38	19 48	19 53				
BirminghamNewSt 12 68 d							19 15					19 31	19 35	19 54	19 57	20 05	20 15				
Wolverhampton 7 d							19 37					19 48	19 55	20 11	20 14	20 26	20 37				
Penkridge d													20 04								
Stafford d												20 02	20 11	20 24	20 29	20 41	20 52	21 00		20 29	
Stoke-on-Trent 84 a			19 50									20 19		20 41	20 44				20 25		
Macclesfield a												20 36			21 03				20 42		
Crewe 10 81,91 a	19 48	19 48					20 07				20 12		20 33	21 06		20 58	21 10	21 19		20 47	20 49
d	19 50	19 50					20 09				20 13		20 35							20 49	20 53
Chester 81 a	20 10	20 12																			21 12
Wrexham General 75 a																					
Llandudno Junction 81 a		21 05																			22 04
Bangor (Gwynedd) 81 a		21 21																			22 20
Holyhead 81 ⛴ a		21 52																			22 51
Wilmslow 84 a											20 29										
Stockport 84 a			20 23								20 38	20 50			21 15				20 56		
Manchester Piccadilly 10 ⛴ a			20 32								20 48	21 00			21 29				21 06		
Runcorn 91 a													21 00							21 06	
Liverpool South Pkwy 7 91 ✈ a													21 09								
Liverpool Lime Street 10 91 a													21 19							21 23	
d																					
Manchester Airport 82 ✈ d				19 30				20 10													
Manchester Picc. 10 82 d				19 48				20 26													
Bolton 82 d																					
Warrington Bank Quay d					20 16		20 27														
Wigan North Western 90 d				20 21	20 27		20 38														
Preston 8 90 a				20 38	20 41		20 52	21 01													
Blackpool North 97 ⛴ a						←															
Preston 8 90 d				20 46	20 42	20 46	20 53	21 03													
Lancaster 6 d				→	20 57	21 13	21 09	21 19													
Barrow-in-Furness 82 a						22 15															
Oxenholme Lake District 83 d					21 12		21 24	21 34													
Windermere 83 a																					
Penrith North Lakes d					21 37			21 59													
Carlisle 8 216 a					21 52		22 01	22 14													
d					21 52		22 02	22 16													
Lockerbie 225,226 d							22 21														
Carstairs 226,225 a																					
Motherwell 226 a					22 50		23 04														
GlasgowCentral 15 216,226,225 a					23 07		23 21														
Haymarket ⛴ a								23s29													
Edinburgh 10 ⛴ a								23 35													
Fort William 227,400 a																					
Perth 229 a																					
Dundee 229 a																					
Aberdeen 229 a																					
Inverness 229 a																					

A To Barrow-in-Furness
B From Manchester Airport
C From London Euston
D To Crewe
E From Bristol Temple Meads
F From Bournemouth. 🛒 to BirminghamNewSt

Refer to Operator websites for full information about Sleeper Services. Contact details for train operators available at National Rail Enquiries

NRT DECEMBER 19 EDITION

Table T065-F

Sundays
15 December to 10 May

London & West Midlands to North West England. London, West Midlands & Manchester to Scotland via the West Coast

	LM	VT	VT	TP	TP	LM	VT	XC	LM	LM	XC	LM	VT	LM	VT	VT	VT	VT	VT	VT	CS	VT
	1	◇1	◇1	◇1	◇1	1	◇1	◇1	1	1	◇1	1	◇1	1	◇1	◇1	◇1	◇1	◇1	◇1	R	◇1
	A			B	C	D		E	F		G	F	H							F	I	
		🍴	🍴	🛒	🛒		🍴	🛒			🛒		🍴		🍴	🍴	🍴	🍴	🍴	🍴	🛏 ✕	🍴
London Euston 15 ⊖66 d	19 11	19 17	19 28			19 31	19 37						19 40	19 47	19 57	20 05	20 08	20 15	20 25		20 27	20 35
Watford Junction 66 d																						
Milton Keynes Central 66 d	19 50	19 50				20 13							20 13				20 41	20 48				
Rugby 66 d	20 37					20 57								20 47								
Nuneaton d														21 00		21 04						
Tamworth Low Level d														21 15					21 32			
Lichfield Trent Valley d									←			←		21 21					21 39			
Coventry 68 d	20 48					21 08			20 08	20 11	20 27	20 30	20 42									
Birmingham International 68 ✈ d	→					→			20 18	20 23	20 38	20 48	20 53							←		
BirminghamNewSt 12 68 d								20 31	20 40	20 43	20 57	21 02	21 15							21 15		
Wolverhampton 7 d								20 52	21 00	21 09	21 14	21 20	→							21 37		
Penkridge d									21 09													
Stafford d								21 06	21 16	21 23	21 28	21 36		21 40			21 33			21 56		22 03
Stoke-on-Trent 84 a		20 50						21 21		21 40	21 44				21 25			21 50				
Macclesfield a								21 39			22 03				21 43							
Crewe 10 81,91 a							21 12		21 35	22 05		21 54		21 58		21 44	21 51		22 10	22 16		22 21
d							21 13									21 46	21 55		22 13	22 17		22 22
Chester 81 a																						
Wrexham General 75 a																						
Llandudno Junction 81 a																						
Bangor (Gwynedd) 81 a																						
Holyhead 81 ⛴ a																						
Wilmslow 84 a							21 28															22 37
Stockport 84 a		21 19					21 38	21 52			22 15				21 59			22 21				22 46
Manchester Piccadilly 10 ⛴ a		21 31					21 49	22 02			22 26				22 09			22 31				22 55
Runcorn 91 a																22 03	22 12					
Liverpool South Pkwy 7 91 ✈ a																						
Liverpool Lime Street 10 91 a																22 20	22 29					
d																						
Manchester Airport 82 ✈ d				21 10	21 10																	
Manchester Picc. 10 82 d				21 26	21 26																	
Bolton 82 d																						
Warrington Bank Quay d			21 16																22 30	22 36		
Wigan North Western 90 d			21 27																22 41	22 47		
Preston 8 90 a			21 41	22 01	22 01														22 55	23 02		
Blackpool North 97 ⛴ a																						
Preston 8 90 d			21 42	22 03	22 03																	
Lancaster 6 d			21 57																			
Barrow-in-Furness 82 a																						
Oxenholme Lake District 83 d			22 12		22 29																	
Windermere 83 a																						
Penrith North Lakes d			22 37																			
Carlisle 8 216 a			22 52	23 06	23 08																	
d			22 52		23 09																	
Lockerbie 225,226 d																						
Carstairs 226,225 a																						
Motherwell 226 a																						
GlasgowCentral 15 216,226,225 a			00 04		00 24																	
Haymarket ⛴ a																						
Edinburgh 10 ⛴ a																					04d50	
Fort William 227,400 a																					09 57	
Perth 229 a																						
Dundee 229 a																						
Aberdeen 229 a																						
Inverness 229 a																						

A To Crewe
B from 12 January until 16 February, from 5 April
C until 5 January, from 23 February until 29 March
D To Liverpool Lime Street
E From Bristol Temple Meads
F From London Euston
G From Bournemouth. 🛒 to BirminghamNewSt
H To Preston
I from 5 April

Refer to Operator websites for full information about Sleeper Services. Contact details for train operators available at National Rail Enquiries

Table T065-F

Sundays

15 December to 10 May

London & West Midlands to North West England. London, West Midlands & Manchester to Scotland via the West Coast

Station	LM	TP	LM	VT	TP	LM	XC	LM	CS	CS	VT	VT	CS	AW	VT	CS
	■	◇■	■	◇■	◇■	■	◇■	■	🅱	🅱	◇■	◇■	🅱	◇	◇■	🅱
	A		A		B	C	D	E	F	F			G			F
London Euston 15 ⊖66 d				20 50					20 59	20 59	21 21	21 25	21 34		21 51	23 30
Watford Junction 66 d									21u20	21u20						23u50
Milton Keynes Central 66 d				21 40								22 17			22 42	
Rugby 66 d				22 01											23 19	
Nuneaton d											22 57				23 30	
Tamworth Low Level d																
Lichfield Trent Valley d	←		←													
Coventry 68 d	20 48		21 08			21 11	21 27									
Birmingham International 68 ✈ d	20 58		21 18			21 23	21 38	←						22 40		
BirminghamNewSt 12 68 d	21 20		21 42			22 00	21 57	22 00						22 55		
Wolverhampton 7 d	21 46		22 02			→	22 14	22 21						23 15		
Penkridge d			22 11					22 29								
Stafford d	22 00		22 19				22 28	22 37			23 23			23 31	23s54	
Stoke-on-Trent 84 a	22 17						22 43	22 53				23 33				
Macclesfield a							23 01					23 49				
Crewe 10 81,91 a	22 39		22 38	22 49				23 15			23 44			23 59	00s16	
d			22 40	22 51					23u40	23u40	23 47			00 01		
Chester 81 a														00 23		
Wrexham General 75 a																
Llandudno Junction 81 a																
Bangor (Gwynedd) 81 a																
Holyhead 81 ⛴ a																
Wilmslow 84 a																
Stockport 84 a							23 14					00 03			00s39	
Manchester Piccadilly 10 a							23 24					00 13			00 48	
Runcorn 91 a			23 05								00 06					
Liverpool South Pkwy 7 91 ✈ a			23 16													
Liverpool Lime Street 10 91 a			23 29								00 29					
d		22 39														
Manchester Airport 82 ✈ d					23 01											
Manchester Picc. 10 82 d					23 15											
Bolton 82 d																
Warrington Bank Quay d				23 08												
Wigan North Western 90 d		23 10		23 19												
Preston 8 90 a		23 33		23 36	23 58											
Blackpool North 97 a																
Preston 8 90 d					00 01				00u33 00u33	00u33						
Lancaster 6 d																
Barrow-in-Furness 82 a																
Oxenholme Lake District 83 d																
Windermere 83 a																
Penrith North Lakes d																
Carlisle 8 216 a					01 39											
d																04s45
Lockerbie 225,226 d																
Carstairs 226,225 a																06s22
Motherwell 226 a																07s00
GlasgowCentral 15 216,226,225 a																07 22
Haymarket a																
Edinburgh 10 a										04d50			05s15			07 23
Fort William 227,400 a										09 57						
Perth 229 a									05s41							
Dundee 229 a									06s05							
Aberdeen 229 a									07 40							
Inverness 229 a									08 42							

A From London Euston
B until 5 January, from 23 February until 29 March
C To Crewe
D From Bournemouth
E From Coventry
F until 29 March
G from 5 April. To Glasgow Central

Refer to Operator websites for full information about Sleeper Services. Contact details for train operators available at National Rail Enquiries

Table T065-R

Mondays to Fridays

16 December to 15 May

Scotland to Manchester, West Midlands & London via the West Coast. North West England to West Midlands & London

Miles	Miles	Miles	Miles	Miles	Station	NT MX	TP TWFO	TP ThO	TP MO	CS MO	CS MO	CS MX	CS MX	AW	VT	XC	LM	LM	VT	XC	VT	LM	LM
										🅱	🅱	🅱	🅱										
							◇■	◇■	◇■						◇■	◇■	■	■	◇■	◇■	◇■	■	■
						A	B	B	C	D	E	F	B			G		H		I			J
—	0	—	—	—	**Inverness** 229 d																		
—	—	0	—	—	**Aberdeen** 229 d																		
—	—	71¼	—	—	Dundee 229 d																		
—	118	—	—	—	Perth 229 d																		
—	—	—	—	—	**Fort William** 227 d																		
—	130¼	187¼	—	—	**Edinburgh** 10 d																		
—	131½	188½	—	—	Haymarket d																		
0	—	—	—	—	**GlasgowCentral** 15 226,216,225 d																		
12¾	—	—	—	—	Motherwell 226 d																		
28¾	158	—	—	—	Carstairs 226,225 d					00 09		00u20											
77	—	263½	—	—	Lockerbie 225,226 d																		
102¼	—	—	—	—	**Carlisle** 8 216 a					01 39													
—	—	—	—	—	d					01 41	01 41	01u44	01u44										
120	—	—	—	—	Penrith North Lakes d																		
—	—	—	—	—	**Windermere** 83 d																		
152¼	—	—	—	—	Oxenholme Lake District 83 d																		
—	—	—	—	—	Barrow-in-Furness 82 d																		
171¼	—	—	—	—	Lancaster 6 d																05 13		
174½	—	—	—	—	**Blackpool North** 97 d																		
192¼	—	—	—	—	**Preston** 8 90 a					03s04	03s04										05 30		
—	—	—	0	—	**Preston** 8 90 d		00 47	00 47	01 06												05 33		
207½	—	—	—	—	Wigan North Western 90 d																05 45		
219¼	—	—	—	—	Warrington Bank Quay d																05 56		
—	—	—	20	—	Bolton 82 a																		
—	—	—	31¼	—	**Manchester Picc.** 10 82 a		01 40	01 42	01 45														
—	—	—	—	—	Manchester Airport ✈ a		01 59		02 02														
—	0	—	—	—	**Liverpool Lime Street** 10 91 a																		
—	—	—	—	—	d														05 26				
—	5½	—	—	—	Liverpool South Pkwy 7 91 ✈ d																		
—	13	—	—	—	Runcorn 91 d														05 43				
—	—	—	—	0	**Manchester Picc.** 10 84 d										05 05	05 11							
—	—	—	37	5¾	Stockport 84 d										05 13								
—	—	—	—	—	Wilmslow 84 d	00 02																	
—	—	—	—	—	**Holyhead** 81 ⛴ d																		
—	—	—	—	—	Bangor (Gwynedd) 81 d																		
—	—	—	—	—	Llandudno Junction 81 d																		
—	—	—	—	—	Wrexham General 75 d																		
—	—	—	—	—	**Chester** 81 d									04 22									
243½	35½	—	—	—	**Crewe** 10 81,91 a	00 32								04 46	05 33	05 43			06 00				
—	—	—	—	—	d									04 59	05 36	05 46	05 47	06 01	06 02			06 05	
—	—	—	49	17¾	Macclesfield d																		
—	—	—	68¾	37¼	**Stoke-on-Trent** 84 d											06 06		06 26		←			←
267¾	—	—	—	53½	**Stafford** a									05 24	05 54	06 22	06 06	06 44	06 20	06 22		06 27	06 44
—	—	—	—	—	d									05 24	05 55	06 25	06 08	06 44	06 21	06 25		06 31	06 44
—	—	—	—	59¼	Penkridge a											→		→				06 37	
—	—	—	—	69¾	**Wolverhampton** 7 a									05 40						06 38		06 48	06 58
—	—	—	—	82½	**BirminghamNewSt** 12 68 a									06 07						06 55		07 10	07 23
—	—	—	—	91	Birmingham International 68 ✈ a															07 13		07 30	
—	—	—	—	101½	Coventry 68 a															07 24		07 43	
285	—	—	99¼	—	Lichfield Trent Valley a												06 25				06 39		
291¼	—	—	—	—	Tamworth Low Level a												06 31				06 46		
304¼	—	—	—	—	Nuneaton a										06 17		06 49						
318¾	—	—	—	113	Rugby 66 a										06 30		07 05		06 52		07 06	07 58	
351½	—	—	—	—	Milton Keynes Central 66 a										06 51				07 12			08 39	
383½	—	—	—	—	Watford Junction 66 a					06 38	06 38	06s39	06s39										
401¼	—	—	—	—	**London Euston** 15 ⊖66 a					07 04	07 04	07 07	07 07		07 25		08 06		07 50		07 56	09 24	

A From Manchester Piccadilly
B From Edinburgh
C until 6 January, from 24 February until 30 March. From Edinburgh
D until 30 March. From Glasgow Central
E until 30 March. From Edinburgh
F From Glasgow Central
G To Bournemouth
H To Walsall
I From Manchester Piccadilly to Bournemouth. Trolley from BirminghamNewSt
J From Crewe to Walsall

Refer to Operator websites for full information about Sleeper Services. Contact details for train operators available at National Rail Enquiries

Table T065-R

Mondays to Fridays

16 December to 15 May

Scotland to Manchester, West Midlands & London via the West Coast. North West England to West Midlands & London

Station	VT	VT	LM	XC	VT	VT	NT	LM	LM	VT	LM	VT	VT	LM	VT	TP	LM	VT	VT	VT	VT
	◇1 ⊠	◇1 ⊠	1 A	◇1 B ᛏ	◇1 ⊠	◇1 ⊠	◇	1	1 C	◇1 ⊠	1 D	◇1 ⊠	◇1 ⊠	1 A	◇1 ⊠	◇1	1 E	◇1 ⊠	◇1 ⊠	◇1 ⊠	◇1 ⊠
Inverness 229 d																					
Aberdeen 229 d																					
Dundee 229 d																					
Perth 229 d																					
Fort William 227 d																					
Edinburgh 10 d																					
Haymarket d																					
GlasgowCentral 15 226,216,225 d																					04 28
Motherwell 226 d																					
Carstairs 226,225 d																					
Lockerbie 225,226 d																					
Carlisle 8 216 a																					05 41
d																					05 43
Penrith North Lakes d																					05 57
Windermere 83 d																					
Oxenholme Lake District 83 d																					06 20
Barrow-in-Furness 82 d							04 53														
Lancaster 6 d							05 46									06 28					06 36
Blackpool North 97 d					05 30																
Preston 8 90 a					05 57		06 06									06 46					06 54
Preston 8 90 d					06 00		06 08						06 17			06 47					06 57
Wigan North Western 90 d					06 11		06 23						06 29								07 10
Warrington Bank Quay d					06 22								06 40								07 20
Bolton 82 a																					
Manchester Picc. 10 82 a							06 57									07 24					
Manchester Airport a							07 18									07 48					
Liverpool Lime Street 10 91 a																					
d		06 05						06 10									06 32			07 00	
Liverpool South Pkwy 7 91 d								06 20									06 42				
Runcorn 91 d		06 21						06 28									06 49			07u15	
Manchester Picc. 10 84 d	05 55			06 00		06 10				06 27					06 35			06 43	07 01		
Stockport 84 d	06 03			06 08		06 18				06 36					06 43			06 51	07u08		
Wilmslow 84 d	06 11			06 16														06 59			
Holyhead 81 d												04 48									
Bangor (Gwynedd) 81 d												05 14									
Llandudno Junction 81 d												05 32									
Wrexham General 75 d																					
Chester 81 d												06 26									
Crewe 10 81,91 a	06 27			06 37	06 42			06 48				06 47	06 59				07 15	07 16			
d	06 28		06 35	06 39				06 50			06 52	06 53	07 01	07 14			07 17	07 18			
Macclesfield d						06 31				06 48					06 56						
Stoke-on-Trent 84 d			06 56			06 48			←	07 06	07 21				07 12						
Stafford a		06 52	07 15	06 58				07 09	07 15	07 22	07 44			07 34			07 37	07 35			
d		06 53	07 15	07 01				07 10	07 15	07 24	07 47			07 39			07 41	07 36			
Penkridge a			→					07 15			→			→			→				
Wolverhampton 7 a				07 14				07 26	07 29	07 40			07 35								
BirminghamNewSt 12 68 a				07 33				07 50	08 04	08 07			07 56								
Birmingham International 68 a								08 05	08 25	08 19											
Coventry 68 a								08 21	08 44	08 30											
Lichfield Trent Valley a		07 07																			
Tamworth Low Level a		07 14																			
Nuneaton a	07 05											07 33									
Rugby 66 a						07 28		08 36	08 58						07 52						
Milton Keynes Central 66 a								09 21	09 40												
Watford Junction 66 a								09 58		09s16											
London Euston 15 ⊖66 a	08 10	08 23				08 20		10 17	10 23	09 33		08 34			08 46			08 53	09 00	09 03	09 06

A To London Euston
B To Bristol Temple Meads
C From Crewe
D To Walsall
E To Rugeley Trent Valley

Refer to Operator websites for full information about Sleeper Services. Contact details for train operators available at National Rail Enquiries

Table T065-R

Mondays to Fridays

16 December to 15 May

Scotland to Manchester, West Midlands & London via the West Coast. North West England to West Midlands & London

Station	LM	LM	LM	XC	VT	LM	TP	XC	NT	VT	VT	VT	TP MX	TP MO	LM	LM	LM	VT	VT	VT	VT	XC
	1 A	1 B	1 C	◇1 D ᛏ	◇1 ⊠	1	◇1 ᛏ	1 E ᛏ	◇	◇1 ⊠	◇1 ⊠	◇1 ⊠	◇1 ᛏ	◇1 ᛏ	1	1	1	◇1 ⊠	◇1 F ⊠	◇1 G ⊠	◇1 ⊠	◇1 H ᛏ
Inverness 229 d																						
Aberdeen 229 d																						
Dundee 229 d																						
Perth 229 d																						
Fort William 227 d																						
Edinburgh 10 d																						
Haymarket d																						
GlasgowCentral 15 226,216,225 d													04 22	04 22					05 40	05 40		
Motherwell 226 d																						
Carstairs 226,225 d																						
Lockerbie 225,226 d													05 50	05 36								
Carlisle 8 216 a													06 14	05 56					06 48	06 48		
d							05 48						06 22	06 22					06 50	06 50		
Penrith North Lakes d							06 03						06 39	06 39								
Windermere 83 d																						
Oxenholme Lake District 83 d							06 27						07 08	07 08					07 25	07 25		
Barrow-in-Furness 82 d									05 48													
Lancaster 6 d							06 45		06 50			06 58	07 23	07 23					07 39	07 39		
Blackpool North 97 d																						
Preston 8 90 a							07 03		07 08			07 15	07 40	07 40					07 57	07 57		
Preston 8 90 d							07 05		07 11			07 18	07 46	07 47					08 00	08 00		
Wigan North Western 90 d							07 17		07 26			07 29							08 11	08 11		
Warrington Bank Quay d												07 41							08 22	08 22		
Bolton 82 a																						
Manchester Picc. 10 82 a									08 00				08 24	08 24								
Manchester Airport a									08 20				08 47	08 47								
Liverpool Lime Street 10 91 a							07 59															
d						07 05											07 35	07 47				
Liverpool South Pkwy 7 91 d						07 15											07 44					
Runcorn 91 d						07 23											07 52	08 03				
Manchester Picc. 10 84 d				07 05	07 15			07 27			07 35										07 55	08 05
Stockport 84 d				07 13	07 23			07 36			07 43										08 04	08 13
Wilmslow 84 d																					08 11	
Holyhead 81 d										05 51												
Bangor (Gwynedd) 81 d										06 18												
Llandudno Junction 81 d										06 36												
Wrexham General 75 d																						
Chester 81 d										07 35												
Crewe 10 81,91 a						07 50				07 54		07 57					08 16	08 21			08 27	
d						07 51				07 57		08 01			08 16	08 01	08 19	08 23			08 29	
Macclesfield d				07 26				07 49			07 56											08 26
Stoke-on-Trent 84 d	←	←	←	07 44	07 50			08 07			08 12					08 26						08 44
Stafford a	07 34	07 37	07 44	08 00		08 09		08 23							08 34	08 45	08 37	08 40				09 00
d	07 39	07 41	07 47	08 03		08 11		08 26							08 36	08 45	08 38	08 42				09 02
Penkridge a		07 47				08 16											08 43					
Wolverhampton 7 a		07 58	08 01	08 16		08 27		08 39				08 33				09 02	08 59					09 15
BirminghamNewSt 12 68 a		08 18	08 21	08 33		08 50		08 57				09 05				09 25	09 21					09 33
Birmingham International 68 a						09 05		09 13				09 19				09 44						
Coventry 68 a						09 20		09 24				09 30				09 59						
Lichfield Trent Valley a	07 56														08 52						08 59	
Tamworth Low Level a	08 03														08 59						09 06	
Nuneaton a	08 18										08 43				09 15							
Rugby 66 a	08 33					09 36				08 45					09 31	10 11						
Milton Keynes Central 66 a	08 55				08 46	10 21						09 57			09 54	10 52						
Watford Junction 66 a						10 58					09s31					11 14						
London Euston 15 ⊖66 a	09 36				09 20	11 18				09 39	09 49	10 33			10 30	11 30		09 59	10 09	10 10	10 16	

A From Crewe
B From Liverpool Lime Street to Rugeley Trent Valley
C From Crewe to Walsall
D To Bristol Temple Meads
E To Bournemouth
F until 14 February
G from 17 February
H To Paignton

Refer to Operator websites for full information about Sleeper Services. Contact details for train operators available at National Rail Enquiries

Table T065-R

Mondays to Fridays
16 December to 15 May

Scotland to Manchester, West Midlands & London via the West Coast. North West England to West Midlands & London

Station			VT ◇1 ⊠	NT WO ◇	NT WX ◇	LM 1	VT ◇1 ⊠	XC ◇1 A 🍴	VT ◇1 ⊠	VT ◇1 B ⊠	VT ◇1 C ⊠	TP ◇1 🍴	LM 1	LM 1	VT ◇1 ⊠	VT ◇1 ⊠	VT ◇1 ⊠	NT ◇	LM 1	XC ◇1 D 🍴	VT ◇1 ⊠	LM 1	XC ◇1 A 🍴
Inverness	229	d																					
Aberdeen	229	d																					
Dundee	229	d																					
Perth	229	d																					
Fort William	227	d																					
Edinburgh		d										06 13											
Haymarket		d										06u17											
GlasgowCentral	226,216,225	d								05 49	05 49						06 30						
Motherwell	226	d								06 04	06 04						06 45						
Carstairs	226,225	d																					
Lockerbie	225,226	d										07 12					07 26						
Carlisle	216	a								07 01	07 01	07 33					07 44						
		d								07 02	07 02	07 34					07 46						
Penrith North Lakes		d								07 17	07 17	07 49					08 00						
Windermere	83	d																					
Oxenholme Lake District	83	d								07 41	07 41	08 13					08 23						
Barrow-in-Furness	82	d		06 47	06 47													07 46					
Lancaster		d		07 46	07 46					07 56	07 56	08 28					08 38	08 46					
Blackpool North	97	d																					
Preston	90	a		08 06	08 06					08 14	08 14	08 46					08 57	09 06					
Preston	90	d		08 08	08 08					08 17	08 17	08 47					08 59	09 08					
Wigan North Western	90	d		08 23	08 23					08 29	08 29						09 11	09 23					
Warrington Bank Quay		d								08 40	08 40						09 22						
Bolton	82	a																					
Manchester Picc.	82	a		08 58	08 59							09 24						09 58					
Manchester Airport		a		09 18	09 18							09 49						10 18					
Liverpool Lime Street	91	a																					
		d				08 05								08 33	08 47							09 05	
Liverpool South Pkwy	91	d				08 15								08 43								09 15	
Runcorn	91	d				08 25								08 50	09 03							09 26	
Manchester Picc.	84	d	08 15					08 27	08 35							08 55				09 05	09 15		09 27
Stockport	84	d	08 23					08 36	08 43							09 04				09 13	09 23		09 36
Wilmslow	84	d														09 11							
Holyhead	81	d					06 55																
Bangor (Gwynedd)	81	d					07 22																
Llandudno Junction	81	d					07 40																
Wrexham General	75	d																					
Chester	81	d					08 35																
Crewe	81,91	a				08 48	08 54			08 57	08 57			09 18	09 22	09 28						09 48	
		d				08 50	08 56			09 01	09 01		09 01	09 20	09 24	09 30			09 33			09 50	
Macclesfield		d						08 49	08 56											09 26			09 49
Stoke-on-Trent	84	d	08 50					09 07	09 12				09 26							09 44	09 50		10 07
Stafford		a				09 09		09 22					09 44	09 39	09 41				09 51	10 00		10 08	10 23
		d				09 10		09 26					09 45	09 39	09 43				09 52	10 03		10 10	10 24
Penkridge		a				09 15								09 45								10 15	
Wolverhampton		a				09 26		09 39		09 33	09 33		10 02	09 58						10 16		10 26	10 37
BirminghamNewSt	68	a				09 50		09 58		10 05	10 05		10 25	10 21						10 33		10 50	10 58
Birmingham International	68	a				10 05		10 13		10 19	10 19		10 44									11 05	11 13
Coventry	68	a				10 20		10 24		10 30	10 30		10 59									11 20	11 24
Lichfield Trent Valley		a																	10 12				
Tamworth Low Level		a																	10 19				
Nuneaton		a							09 44										10 34				
Rugby	66	a				10 32							11 11						10 51			11 32	
Milton Keynes Central	66	a	09 50			11 21	10 02			10 57	10 57		11 50						11 14		10 46	12 21	
Watford Junction	66	a				11 58							12 13									12 58	
London Euston	66	a	10 26			12 16	10 37		10 51	11 34	11 36		12 29		11 00	11 07	11 10		11 51		11 20	13 17	

A To Bournemouth
B until 14 February
C from 17 February
D To Bristol Temple Meads

Refer to Operator websites for full information about Sleeper Services. Contact details for train operators available at National Rail Enquiries

Table T065-R

Mondays to Fridays
16 December to 15 May

Scotland to Manchester, West Midlands & London via the West Coast. North West England to West Midlands & London

Station			VT ◇1 ⊠	VT ◇1 A ⊠	VT ◇1 B ⊠	VT FX ◇1 ⊠	VT FO ◇1 ⊠	TP ◇1 🍴	LM 1	LM 1	VT ◇1 ⊠	VT ◇1 ⊠	LM 1	VT FO ◇1 🛒	VT ◇1 ⊠	XC ◇1 C 🍴	VT ◇1 ⊠	NT ◇	LM 1	VT FX ◇1 D ⊠	VT FX ◇1 B ⊠	VT FO ◇1 ⊠	XC ◇1 E 🍴	VT FX ◇1 D ⊠
Inverness	229	d																						
Aberdeen	229	d																						
Dundee	229	d																						
Perth	229	d																						
Fort William	227	d																						
Edinburgh		d				06 52	06 52																	
Haymarket		d				06 57	06 57																	
GlasgowCentral	226,216,225	d						07 10							07 37									
Motherwell	226	d						07 26							07 53									
Carstairs	226,225	d																						
Lockerbie	225,226	d						08 10																
Carlisle	216	a				08 06	08 06	08 31							08 49									
		d				08 08	08 08	08 32							08 50									
Penrith North Lakes		d				08 22	08 22	08 47																
Windermere	83	d																						
Oxenholme Lake District	83	d						09 11							09 24									
Barrow-in-Furness	82	d																08 46						
Lancaster		d				08 57	08 57	09 26							09 39			09 47						
Blackpool North	97	d																						
Preston	90	a				09 15	09 15	09 44							09 58			10 08						
Preston	90	d				09 18	09 18	09 45						09 51	09 59			10 10						
Wigan North Western	90	d				09 29	09 29							10 04	10 11			10 24						
Warrington Bank Quay		d				09 40	09 40							10 16	10 22									
Bolton	82	a						10s03																
Manchester Picc.	82	a						10 24										10 58						
Manchester Airport		a						10 46										11 18						
Liverpool Lime Street	91	a																						
		d								09 35	09 47								10 05					
Liverpool South Pkwy	91	d								09 45									10 15					
Runcorn	91	d								09 52	10 03								10 26					
Manchester Picc.	84	d		09 35	09 35							09 55				10 05	10 15						10 27	10 35
Stockport	84	d		09 43	09 43							10 04				10 13	10 23						10 36	10 43
Wilmslow	84	d										10 11												
Holyhead	81	d																		08 55	08 55	08 55		
Bangor (Gwynedd)	81	d																		09 22	09 22	09 22		
Llandudno Junction	81	d																		09 40	09 40	09 40		
Wrexham General	75	d																						
Chester	81	d	09 35																	10 35	10 35	10 35		
Crewe	81,91	a	09 54			09 57	09 57			10 16	10 21	10 27		10 38					10 48	10 54	10 54	10 54		
		d	09 56			10 01	10 01		10 01	10 19	10 22	10 29	10 33	10 40					10 50	10 56	10 56	10 56		
Macclesfield		d		09 56	09 56											10 26							10 49	10 56
Stoke-on-Trent	84	d		10 12	10 12				10 26							10 44	10 50						11 07	11 12
Stafford		a							10 46	10 38	10 40		10 51			11 00			11 09				11 24	
		d							10 49	10 40	10 41		10 52			11 03			11 10				11 28	
Penkridge		a								10 45									11 15					
Wolverhampton		a				10 33	10 33		11 05	10 58						11 16			11 26				11 41	
BirminghamNewSt	68	a				11 05	11 05		11 26	11 20						11 33			11 50				11 59	
Birmingham International	68	a				11 19	11 19		11 45										12 05				12 13	
Coventry	68	a				11 30	11 30		12 01										12 21				12 24	
Lichfield Trent Valley		a											11 12											
Tamworth Low Level		a											11 19											
Nuneaton		a											11 34											
Rugby	66	a							12 11				11 52						12 31					
Milton Keynes Central	66	a	11 02			11 57	11 57		12 51				12 14				11 46		13 20	12 02	12 02	12 02		
Watford Junction	66	a							13 14										13 57					
London Euston	66	a	11 37	11 40	11 41	12 33	12 35		13 30		11 59	12 02	12 50	12 32	12 10		12 20		14 17	12 36	12 37	12 38		12 39

A until 14 February
B from 17 February
C To Exeter St Davids
D until 13 February
E To Bournemouth

Refer to Operator websites for full information about Sleeper Services. Contact details for train operators available at National Rail Enquiries

Table T065-R

Mondays to Fridays
16 December to 15 May

Scotland to Manchester, West Midlands & London via the West Coast. North West England to West Midlands & London

	VT FX ◇1 A ⊠	VT FO ◇1 ⊠	VT ◇1 ⊠	LM 1	LM 1	VT ◇1 ⊠	TP ◇1 ⍑	VT ◇1 ⊠	TP ◇1 ⍑	VT ◇1 ⊠	NT ◇	LM 1	XC ◇1 B ⍑	VT ◇1 ⊏	LM 1	XC ◇1 C ⍑	VT ◇1 D ⊏	VT ◇1 A ⊏	VT ◇1 ⊏	VT WX ◇1 ⊠	VT WO ◇1 ⊠	VT ◇1 ⊏
Inverness 229 d																						
Aberdeen 229 d																						
Dundee 229 d																						
Perth 229 d																						
Fort William 227 d																						
Edinburgh 10 d									08 12											08 52	08 52	
Haymarket d									08u16											08 57	08 57	
GlasgowCentral 15 226,216,225 d			08 00				07 45			08 40												
Motherwell 226 d																						
Carstairs 226,225 d																						
Lockerbie 225,226 d							09 02		09 11													
Carlisle 8 216 a			09 09				09 23		09 31	09 48										10 06	10 06	
d			09 10				09 24		09 34	09 49										10 08	10 08	
Penrith North Lakes d							09 39		09 49	10 03												
Windermere 83 d											09 56											
Oxenholme Lake District 83 d							10 03		10 13		10 17									10 43	10 43	
Barrow-in-Furness 82 d																						
Lancaster 6 d			09 57				10 18		10 28	10 38										10 57	10 57	
Blackpool North 97 d																						10 54
Preston 8 90 a			10 15				10 38		10 45	10 56	10 52									11 15	11 15	11 18
Preston 8 90 d			10 17				10 39		10 47	10 59	11 02									11 17	11 17	11 21
Wigan North Western 90 d			10 29				10 52			11 11	11 18									11 29	11 29	11 35
Warrington Bank Quay d			10 40							11 22										11 40	11 40	11 48
Bolton 82 a									11s05													
Manchester Picc. 10 82 a									11 24		11 58											
Manchester Airport a									11 46		12 17											
Liverpool Lime Street 10 91 a							11 24															
d					10 33	10 47									11 05							
Liverpool South Pkwy 7 91 d					10 43										11 15							
Runcorn 91 d					10 50	11 03									11 23							
Manchester Picc. 10 84 d	10 35	10 35						10 55					11 05	11 15		11 27			11 35			
Stockport 84 d	10 43	10 43						11 04					11 13	11 23		11 36			11 43			
Wilmslow 84 d								11 11														
Holyhead 81 d																						
Bangor (Gwynedd) 81 d																						
Llandudno Junction 81 d																						
Wrexham General 75 d																						
Chester 81 d																	11 35	11 35				
Crewe 10 81,91 a			10 57		11 16	11 21		11 27							11 49		11 54	11 54		11 57	11 57	
d			11 01	11 01	11 19	11 22		11 29				11 33			11 51		11 56	11 56		12 01	12 01	
Macclesfield d	10 56	10 56											11 26			11 49			11 56			
Stoke-on-Trent 84 d	11 12	11 12		11 26									11 44	11 50		12 07			12 12			
Stafford a				11 44	11 39	11 40						11 51	12 00		12 09	12 25						
d				11 45	11 40	11 41						11 55	12 03		12 10	12 28						
Penkridge a					11 45										12 15							
Wolverhampton 7 a			11 34	12 02	11 58								12 16		12 26	12 41				12 32	12 32	
BirminghamNewSt 12 68 a			12 05	12 25	12 21								12 33		12 50	12 59				13 05	13 05	
Birmingham International 68 a			12 19	12 44											13 05	13 13				13 19	13 19	
Coventry 68 a			12 30	12 59											13 21	13 24				13 30	13 30	
Lichfield Trent Valley a												12 12										
Tamworth Low Level a												12 19										
Nuneaton a												12 34										
Rugby 66 a				13 11								12 51			13 32							12 59
Milton Keynes Central 66 a			12 57	13 51								13 14		12 46	14 21		13 02	13 02		13 57	13 57	
Watford Junction 66 a				14 14											14 58							
London Euston 15 ⊖66 a	12 40	12 41	13 33	14 30		12 59		13 02		13 08		13 50		13 20	15 17		13 36	13 37	13 40	14 33	14 36	13 53

A from 17 February
B To Bristol Temple Meads
C To Bournemouth
D until 14 February

Refer to Operator websites for full information about Sleeper Services. Contact details for train operators available at National Rail Enquiries

NRT DECEMBER 19 EDITION

Table T065-R

Mondays to Fridays
16 December to 15 May

Scotland to Manchester, West Midlands & London via the West Coast. North West England to West Midlands & London

	TP ◇1 ⍑	LM 1	LM 1	VT ◇1 ⊏	VT ◇1 ⊏	VT ◇1 ⊠	NT ◇	LM 1	XC ◇1 A ⍑	VT ◇1 ⊏	LM 1	XC ◇1 B ⍑	VT WX ◇1 ⊏	VT WO ◇1 ⊏	VT WX ◇1 ⊏	VT WO ◇1 ⊏	VT ◇1 ⊠	TP ◇1 ⍑	LM 1	LM 1	VT ◇1 C ⊏
Inverness 229 d																					
Aberdeen 229 d																					
Dundee 229 d																					
Perth 229 d																					
Fort William 227 d																					
Edinburgh 10 d																		10 12			
Haymarket d																		10u16			
GlasgowCentral 15 226,216,225 d	09 06					09 40											10 00				
Motherwell 226 d	09 23																				
Carstairs 226,225 d																					
Lockerbie 225,226 d	10 10																	11 11			
Carlisle 8 216 a	10 31					10 47											11 11	11 32			
d	10 34					10 49											11 13	11 33			
Penrith North Lakes d	10 49																11 28	11 50			
Windermere 83 d																					
Oxenholme Lake District 83 d	11 13					11 23												12 14			
Barrow-in-Furness 82 d							10 46														
Lancaster 6 d	11 28					11 38	11 46											12 29			
Blackpool North 97 d																					
Preston 8 90 a	11 46					11 56	12 06										12 16	12 46			
Preston 8 90 d	11 47					11 59	12 08										12 17	12 48			
Wigan North Western 90 d						12 11	12 25										12 29				
Warrington Bank Quay d						12 22											12 40				
Bolton 82 a	12s05																				
Manchester Picc. 10 82 a	12 24						12 58											13 24			
Manchester Airport a	12 46						13 18											13 46			
Liverpool Lime Street 10 91 a																					
d			11 33	11 47							12 05									12 33	12 47
Liverpool South Pkwy 7 91 d			11 43								12 16									12 43	
Runcorn 91 d			11 50	12 03							12 23									12 50	13 03
Manchester Picc. 10 84 d					11 55				12 05	12 15		12 27			12 35	12 35					
Stockport 84 d					12 04				12 13	12 23		12 36			12 43	12 43					
Wilmslow 84 d					12 11																
Holyhead 81 d																					
Bangor (Gwynedd) 81 d																					
Llandudno Junction 81 d																					
Wrexham General 75 d																					
Chester 81 d													12 35	12 35							
Crewe 10 81,91 a			12 17	12 21	12 27						12 48		12 54	12 54			12 57			13 17	13 22
d		12 01	12 19	12 22	12 29			12 33			12 51		12 56	12 56			13 01		13 03	13 19	13 24
Macclesfield d									12 26			12 49			12 56	12 56					
Stoke-on-Trent 84 d		12 26							12 44	12 50		13 07			13 12	13 12			13 26		
Stafford a		12 44	12 40	12 40				12 51	13 00		13 10	13 24							13 44	13 38	13 42
d		12 45	12 40	12 41				12 55	13 01		13 11	13 28							13 45	13 41	13 43
Penkridge a			12 46								13 17									13 46	
Wolverhampton 7 a		13 02	12 58						13 16		13 28	13 41					13 33		14 02	13 58	
BirminghamNewSt 12 68 a		13 25	13 20						13 33		13 50	13 59					14 05		14 25	14 20	
Birmingham International 68 a		13 44									14 05	14 13					14 19		14 44		
Coventry 68 a		13 59									14 21	14 24					14 30		14 59		
Lichfield Trent Valley a								13 12													
Tamworth Low Level a								13 19													
Nuneaton a								13 34													
Rugby 66 a		14 11						13 50			14 32								15 11		
Milton Keynes Central 66 a		14 53						14 14		13 46	15 21		14 02	14 02			14 57		15 49		
Watford Junction 66 a		15 15									15 58								16 13		
London Euston 15 ⊖66 a		15 31		14 03	14 06	14 10		14 50		14 20	16 17		14 36	14 39	14 39	14 42	15 34		16 29		15 03

A To Exeter St Davids
B To Bournemouth
C until 14 February

Refer to Operator websites for full information about Sleeper Services. Contact details for train operators available at National Rail Enquiries

Table T065-R

Mondays to Fridays
16 December to 15 May

Scotland to Manchester, West Midlands & London via the West Coast. North West England to West Midlands & London

Station	VT	VT	VT	NT	LM	XC	VT	LM	XC	VT	VT	VT	VT	VT	TP	LM	LM	VT	VT	VT	NT	LM
	A					B			C			D	A									
Inverness 229 d																						
Aberdeen 229 d																						
Dundee 229 d																						
Perth 229 d																						
Fort William 227 d																						
Edinburgh d												10 52	10 52									
Haymarket d												10 57	10 57									
GlasgowCentral 226,216,225 d			10 40												11 08					11 40		
Motherwell 226 d															11 24							
Carstairs 226,225 d																						
Lockerbie 225,226 d															12 09							
Carlisle 216 a			11 47									12 06	12 06		12 29					12 47		
d			11 49									12 08	12 08		12 33					12 49		
Penrith North Lakes d															12 48					13 03		
Windermere 83 d																					13 06	
Oxenholme Lake District 83 d			12 23									12 43	12 43		13 12						13 27	
Barrow-in-Furness 82 d				11 46																		
Lancaster d			12 38	12 46								12 57	12 57		13 28					13 38	13 45	
Blackpool North 97 d														13 03								
Preston 90 a			12 56	13 06								13 16	13 16	13 24	13 46					13 57	14 06	
Preston 90 d			12 59	13 12								13 17	13 17	13 29	13 47					13 59	14 08	
Wigan North Western 90 d			13 11									13 29	13 29	13 41						14 11	14 24	
Warrington Bank Quay d			13 22									13 40	13 40	13 54						14 22		
Bolton 82 a															14s05							
Manchester Picc. 82 a				13 58											14 24						14 58	
Manchester Airport a				14 18											14 46						15 18	
Liverpool Lime Street 91 a																						
d	12 47							13 05									13 33	13 47				
Liverpool South Pkwy 91 d								13 15									13 43					
Runcorn 91 d	13 03							13 23									13 50	14 03				
Manchester Picc. 84 d		12 55				13 05	13 15		13 27		13 35								13 55			
Stockport 84 d		13 04				13 13	13 23		13 36		13 43								14 04			
Wilmslow 84 d		13 11																	14 11			
Holyhead 81 d																						
Bangor (Gwynedd) 81 d																						
Llandudno Junction 81 d																						
Wrexham General 75 d																						
Chester 81 d										13 35												
Crewe 81,91 a	13 22	13 27						13 46		13 54		13 57	13 57				14 17	14 22	14 27			
d	13 24	13 29			13 33			13 49		13 56		14 01	14 01			14 01	14 19	14 24	14 29			14 33
Macclesfield d						13 26			13 49		13 56											
Stoke-on-Trent 84 d						13 44	13 50		14 07		14 12					14 26						
Stafford a	13 42				13 51	14 00		14 09	14 23							14 45	14 38	14 43				14 52
d	13 43				13 55	14 03		14 10	14 25							14 46	14 40	14 44				14 55
Penkridge a								14 15									14 45					
Wolverhampton a						14 16		14 26	14 38			14 34	14 34			15 02	14 58					
BirminghamNewSt 68 a						14 33		14 50	14 59			15 05	15 05			15 25	15 20					
Birmingham International 68 a								15 05	15 13			15 19	15 19			15 44						
Coventry 68 a								15 20	15 24			15 30	15 30			15 59						
Lichfield Trent Valley a					14 12																	15 12
Tamworth Low Level a					14 19																	15 19
Nuneaton a					14 34																	15 34
Rugby 66 a			14 23		14 50			15 31						15 05		16 11						15 50
Milton Keynes Central 66 a					15 14		14 48			15 02		15 57	15 57			16 53						16 15
Watford Junction 66 a																17 15						
London Euston 66 a	15 04	15 07	15 13		15 50		15 25	16 46		15 37	15 40	16 32	16 33	15 59		17 31		16 03	16 06	16 10		16 52

A from 17 February
B To Exeter St Davids
C To Bournemouth
D until 14 February

Refer to Operator websites for full information about Sleeper Services. Contact details for train operators available at National Rail Enquiries

Table T065-R

Mondays to Fridays
16 December to 15 May

Scotland to Manchester, West Midlands & London via the West Coast. North West England to West Midlands & London

Station	XC	VT	LM	VT	VT	XC	VT	VT	LM	LM	VT	TP	TP	VT	TP	VT	NT	LM	XC	VT	LM	VT
	A					B						TO	TX						C			
Inverness 229 d																						
Aberdeen 229 d																						
Dundee 229 d																						
Perth 229 d																						
Fort William 227 d																						
Edinburgh d															12 12							
Haymarket d															12u17							
GlasgowCentral 226,216,225 d								12 00				11 44	12 05			12 40						
Motherwell 226 d																						
Carstairs 226,225 d																						
Lockerbie 225,226 d															13 11							
Carlisle 216 a								13 11				13 25	13 25		13 32	13 47						
d								13 12				13 26	13 26		13 33	13 49						
Penrith North Lakes d												13 42	13 42		13 48							
Windermere 83 d																						
Oxenholme Lake District 83 d												14 06	14 06		14 12	14 24						
Barrow-in-Furness 82 d																	13 53					
Lancaster d								13 57				14 23	14 23		14 28	14 39	14 47					
Blackpool North 97 d																						
Preston 90 a								14 16				14 41	14 41		14 45	14 56	15 07					
Preston 90 d								14 17				14 43	14 43		14 47	14 59	15 09					
Wigan North Western 90 d								14 29				14 57	14 57			15 11	15 24					
Warrington Bank Quay d								14 40								15 22						
Bolton 82 a															15s05							
Manchester Picc. 82 a															15 24		15 58					
Manchester Airport a															15 46		16 17					
Liverpool Lime Street 91 a												15 31	15 31									
d			14 05							14 31	14 47										15 05	
Liverpool South Pkwy 91 d			14 15							14 41											15 15	
Runcorn 91 d			14 25							14 49	15 03										15 24	
Manchester Picc. 84 d	14 05	14 15				14 27	14 35							14 55					15 05	15 15		
Stockport 84 d	14 13	14 23				14 36	14 43							15 04					15 13	15 23		
Wilmslow 84 d														15 11								
Holyhead 81 d				12 53																		13 58
Bangor (Gwynedd) 81 d				13 21																		14 25
Llandudno Junction 81 d				13 39																		14 43
Wrexham General 75 d																						
Chester 81 d					14 35																	15 35
Crewe 81,91 a			14 49	14 54	14 54			14 57		15 17	15 21			15 27							15 51	15 54
d			14 51	14 56	14 56			15 01	15 01	15 21	15 22			15 29				15 33			15 52	15 56
Macclesfield d	14 26					14 49	14 56												15 26			
Stoke-on-Trent 84 d	14 44	14 50				15 07	15 12		15 26										15 44	15 50		
Stafford a	15 00		15 10			15 24			15 44	15 41	15 40							15 51	16 00		16 10	
d	15 03		15 12			15 28			15 45	15 41	15 41							15 55	16 03		16 11	
Penkridge a			15 17							15 47											16 16	
Wolverhampton a	15 16		15 28			15 41		15 35	16 05	15 58									16 16		16 27	
BirminghamNewSt 68 a	15 33		15 50			15 58		16 04	16 24	16 17									16 33		16 50	
Birmingham International 68 a			16 05			16 13		16 19	16 44												17 05	
Coventry 68 a			16 20			16 24		16 30	16 59												17 20	
Lichfield Trent Valley a																		16 12				
Tamworth Low Level a																		16 19				
Nuneaton a																		16 34				
Rugby 66 a			16 31						17 12									16 50			17 32	
Milton Keynes Central 66 a		15 46		16 02	16 02			16 57	17 52									17 15		16 46	18 11	17 02
Watford Junction 66 a									18 14													
London Euston 66 a		16 20	17 46	16 36	16 36		16 40	17 34	18 30		16 59			17 03		17 10		17 51		17 21	18 47	17 37

A To Paignton
B To Bournemouth
C To Exeter St Davids

Refer to Operator websites for full information about Sleeper Services. Contact details for train operators available at National Rail Enquiries

Table T065-R

Mondays to Fridays
16 December to 15 May

Scotland to Manchester, West Midlands & London via the West Coast. North West England to West Midlands & London

	XC	VT	VT	VT	TP	LM	LM	VT	VT	VT	NT	LM	XC	VT	LM	XC	VT	VT	VT	TP
	◇1 A	◇1	◇1	◇1	◇1	1	1	◇1	◇1	◇1 ⊠	◇	1	◇1 B	◇1	1	◇1 A	◇1	◇1	◇1	◇1
Inverness 229 d																				
Aberdeen 229 d																				
Dundee 229 d																				
Perth 229 d																				
Fort William 227 d																				
Edinburgh 10 d			12 52																	14 12
Haymarket d			12 58																	14u17
GlasgowCentral 15 226,216,225 d					13 08					13 40									14 00	
Motherwell 226 d					13 24															
Carstairs 226,225 d																				
Lockerbie 225,226 d					14 08															15 12
Carlisle 8 216 a			14 06		14 29					14 47									15 09	15 32
d			14 08		14 34					14 49									15 11	15 38
Penrith North Lakes d			14 22		14 49															15 54
Windermere 83 d																				
Oxenholme Lake District 83 d					15 13					15 24									15 45	
Barrow-in-Furness 82 d											14 46									
Lancaster 6 d			14 57		15 28					15 39	15 46									16 30
Blackpool North 97 d				15 02																
Preston 8 90 a			15 15	15 24	15 45					15 56	16 06								16 14	16 48
Preston 8 90 d			15 17	15 29	15 47					15 59	16 08								16 17	16 49
Wigan North Western 90 d			15 29	15 45						16 11	16 23								16 29	
Warrington Bank Quay d			15 40	16 00						16 22									16 40	
Bolton 82 a					16s05															
Manchester Picc. 10 82 a					16 24						16 58									17 27
Manchester Airport a					16 48						17 17									17 48
Liverpool Lime Street 10 91 a																				
d							15 33	15 47							16 05					
Liverpool South Pkwy 7 91 d							15 43								16 15					
Runcorn 91 d							15 50	16 03							16 23					
Manchester Picc. 10 84 d	15 27	15 35							15 55				16 05	16 15		16 27		16 35		
Stockport 84 d	15 36	15 43							16 04				16 13	16 23		16 36		16 43		
Wilmslow 84 d									16 11											
Holyhead 81 d																				
Bangor (Gwynedd) 81 d																				
Llandudno Junction 81 d																				
Wrexham General 75 d																				
Chester 81 d																	16 35			
Crewe 10 81,91 a			15 57				16 17	16 22	16 27						16 49		16 54		16 57	
d			16 01			16 01	16 19	16 24	16 29			16 33			16 51		16 56		17 01	
Macclesfield d	15 49	15 56											16 26			16 49		16 56		
Stoke-on-Trent 84 d	16 07	16 12				16 26							16 44	16 50		17 07		17 12		
Stafford a	16 24					16 44	16 39	16 41				16 51	17 00		17 09	17 23				
d	16 25					16 45	16 39	16 44				16 55	17 03		17 10	17 25				
Penkridge a							16 45								17 16					
Wolverhampton 7 a	16 38		16 33			17 02	16 58						17 16		17 26	17 38			17 33	
BirminghamNewSt 12 68 a	16 58		17 05			17 25	17 21						17 33		17 50	17 59			18 05	
Birmingham International 68 a	17 13		17 19			17 44									18 05	18 13			18 19	
Coventry 68 a	17 24		17 30			17 59									18 20	18 24			18 30	
Lichfield Trent Valley a												17 12								
Tamworth Low Level a												17 19								
Nuneaton a												17 34								
Rugby 66 a				17 05		18 12						17 50			18 32					
Milton Keynes Central 66 a			17 57			18 51						18 14		17 46			18 02		18 57	
Watford Junction 66 a						19 14														
London Euston 15 ⊖66 a		17 40	18 33	17 59		19 30		18 03	18 06	18 09		18 50		18 20	19 45		18 36	18 39	19 33	

A To Bournemouth
B To Bristol Temple Meads

Refer to Operator websites for full information about Sleeper Services. Contact details for train operators available at National Rail Enquiries

Table T065-R

Mondays to Fridays
16 December to 15 May

Scotland to Manchester, West Midlands & London via the West Coast. North West England to West Midlands & London

	LM	LM	VT	VT	VT	VT	VT	NT	LM	XC	VT	LM	VT	LM	VT	XC	VT	VT	TP	LM	VT	VT
	1	1	◇1 A	◇1 B	◇1 A	◇1 B	◇1 ⊠	◇	1	◇1 C	◇1 ⊠	1	◇1 ⊠	1 D	1 D	◇1 E	◇1 ⊠	1 F	◇1	1 G	◇1 ⊠	◇1 ⊠
Inverness 229 d																						
Aberdeen 229 d																						
Dundee 229 d																						
Perth 229 d																						
Fort William 227 d																						
Edinburgh 10 d															14 52							
Haymarket d															14 58							
GlasgowCentral 15 226,216,225 d							14 40												15 08			
Motherwell 226 d																			15 24			
Carstairs 226,225 d																						
Lockerbie 225,226 d																			16 08			
Carlisle 8 216 a							15 47								16 06				16 29			
d							15 49								16 08				16 31			
Penrith North Lakes d															16 21				16 46			
Windermere 83 d								16 00														
Oxenholme Lake District 83 d							16 24	16 28											17 10			
Barrow-in-Furness 82 d																						
Lancaster 6 d							16 38								16 58				17 27			
Blackpool North 97 d																						
Preston 8 90 a							16 56	17 02							17 15				17 44			
Preston 8 90 d							16 59	17 08							17 17				17 46			
Wigan North Western 90 d							17 11								17 29							
Warrington Bank Quay d							17 22								17 40							
Bolton 82 a																			18s04			
Manchester Picc. 10 82 a								17 58											18 23			
Manchester Airport a								18 17											18 46			
Liverpool Lime Street 10 91 a																						
d		16 33	16 47	16 47								17 05								17 34	17 47	
Liverpool South Pkwy 7 91 d		16 43										17 15								17 44		
Runcorn 91 d		16 51	17 03	17 03								17 23								17 51	18 03	
Manchester Picc. 10 84 d					16 55	16 55				17 05	17 15					17 27	17 35					17 55
Stockport 84 d					17 04	17 04				17 13	17 23					17 36	17 43					18 04
Wilmslow 84 d					17 11	17 11										17 44						18 11
Holyhead 81 d																						
Bangor (Gwynedd) 81 d																						
Llandudno Junction 81 d																						
Wrexham General 75 d																						
Chester 81 d													17 35									
Crewe 10 81,91 a		17 21			17 27	17 27						17 48	17 54		17 57	18 05				18 16	18 22	18 27
d	17 01	17 23			17 29	17 29			17 33			17 50	17 56	18 01	18 01	18 07				18 17	18 24	18 29
Macclesfield d										17 26							17 56					
Stoke-on-Trent 84 d	17 26									17 44	17 50			18 26			18 12					
Stafford a	17 44	17 41	17 36	17 36					17 51	18 00		18 08		18 45		18 25				18 41	18 41	
d	17 46	17 42	17 37	17 37					17 55	18 03		18 09		18 46		18 27				18 41	18 43	
Penkridge a		17 47										18 14		→						18 47		
Wolverhampton 7 a	18 02	17 58								18 16		18 25			18 32	18 40		←		18 58		
BirminghamNewSt 12 68 a	18 25	18 21								18 33		18 50			19 05	18 57		19 05		19 19		
Birmingham International 68 a		18 45										19 05			→	19 13		19 19				
Coventry 68 a		19 01										19 20				19 24		19 30				
Lichfield Trent Valley a									18 12													
Tamworth Low Level a									18 19													
Nuneaton a									18 34													
Rugby 66 a		19 11							18 50			19 31										
Milton Keynes Central 66 a		19 52	18 23	18 26					19 14		18 46	20 21	19 02					19 58				19 32
Watford Junction 66 a		20 14			18s49	18s50						20 58									19s46	
London Euston 15 ⊖66 a		20 30	18 59	19 02	19 06	19 06	19 09		19 50		19 20	21 17	19 37				19 41	20 33			20 03	20 07

A until 14 February
B from 17 February
C To Cardiff Central
D To London Euston
E To Bournemouth
F From Edinburgh
G To Walsall

Refer to Operator websites for full information about Sleeper Services. Contact details for train operators available at National Rail Enquiries

Table T065-R

Mondays to Fridays
16 December to 15 May

Scotland to Manchester, West Midlands & London via the West Coast. North West England to West Midlands & London

Station		VT	LM A	NT	LM	XC B	VT	LM	XC C	VT D	VT E	VT	TP
Inverness 229	d												
Aberdeen 229	d												
Dundee 229	d												
Perth 229	d												
Fort William 227	d												
Edinburgh	d												16 12
Haymarket	d												16u17
GlasgowCentral 226,216,225	d	15 40										16 00	
Motherwell 226	d												
Carstairs 226,225	d												
Lockerbie 225,226	d												17 11
Carlisle 216	a	16 47										17 10	17 32
	d	16 49										17 11	17 35
Penrith North Lakes	d	17 03											17 50
Windermere 83	d												
Oxenholme Lake District 83	d											17 45	18 14
Barrow-in-Furness 82	d			16 45									
Lancaster	d	17 37		17 46									18 29
Blackpool North 97	d												
Preston 90	a	17 56		18 06								18 14	18 47
Preston 90	d	17 59		18 08								18 17	18 48
Wigan North Western 90	d	18 11		18 23								18 29	
Warrington Bank Quay	d	18 22										18 40	
Bolton 82	a												
Manchester Picc. 82	a			18 58									19 27
Manchester Airport	a			19 17									19 50
Liverpool Lime Street 91	a												
	d							18 05					
Liverpool South Pkwy 91	d							18 15					
Runcorn 91	d							18 23					
Manchester Picc. 84	d					18 05	18 15		18 27	18 35	18 35		
Stockport 84	d					18 13	18 23		18 36	18 43	18 43		
Wilmslow 84	d												
Holyhead 81	d												
Bangor (Gwynedd) 81	d												
Llandudno Junction 81	d												
Wrexham General 75	d												
Chester 81	d												
Crewe 81,91	a							18 48				18 57	
	d				18 33			18 50				19 01	
Macclesfield	d					18 26				18 56	18 56		
Stoke-on-Trent 84	d		←			18 44	18 50		19 07	19 12	19 12		
Stafford	a		18 45		18 51	19 00		19 08	19 23				
	d		18 46		18 55	19 01		19 10	19 27				
Penkridge	a							19 16					
Wolverhampton	a		19 03			19 14		19 27	19 40			19 33	
BirminghamNewSt 68	a		19 26			19 33		19 50	19 57			20 05	
Birmingham International 68	a		19 44					20 05	20 13			20 19	
Coventry 68	a		19 59					20 21	20 24			20 30	
Lichfield Trent Valley	a				19 12								
Tamworth Low Level	a				19 19								
Nuneaton	a				19 34								
Rugby 66	a		20 11		19 55			20 32					
Milton Keynes Central 66	a		20 54		20 16		19 46	21 13				20 58	
Watford Junction 66	a											21s19	
London Euston 66	a	20 12	21 30		20 52		20 21	21 53		20 39	20 41	21 36	

Station		LM	LM	VT	VT	VT	LM	XC F	VT	LM
Inverness 229	d									
Aberdeen 229	d									
Dundee 229	d									
Perth 229	d									
Fort William 227	d									
Edinburgh	d									
Haymarket	d									
GlasgowCentral 226,216,225	d					16 40				
Motherwell 226	d					16 55				
Carstairs 226,225	d									
Lockerbie 225,226	d									
Carlisle 216	a					17 51				
	d					17 52				
Penrith North Lakes	d					18 06				
Windermere 83	d									
Oxenholme Lake District 83	d					18 30				
Barrow-in-Furness 82	d									
Lancaster	d					18 44				
Blackpool North 97	d									
Preston 90	a					19 03				
Preston 90	d					19 05				
Wigan North Western 90	d					19 17				
Warrington Bank Quay	d					19 27				
Bolton 82	a									
Manchester Picc. 82	a									
Manchester Airport	a									
Liverpool Lime Street 91	a									
	d		18 34	18 47						19 11
Liverpool South Pkwy 91	d		18 44							19 21
Runcorn 91	d		18 52	19 03						19 29
Manchester Picc. 84	d				18 55			19 05	19 15	
Stockport 84	d				19 04			19 13	19 23	
Wilmslow 84	d				19 11					
Holyhead 81	d									
Bangor (Gwynedd) 81	d									
Llandudno Junction 81	d									
Wrexham General 75	d									
Chester 81	d									
Crewe 81,91	a		19 17	19 21	19 27					19 53
	d	19 01	19 19	19 22	19 29		19 35			19 55
Macclesfield	d							19 26	19 36	
Stoke-on-Trent 84	d	19 26						19 44	19 53	
Stafford	a	19 44	19 39	19 40			19 52	20 00		20 15
	d	19 45	19 40	19 41			19 52	20 03		20 16
Penkridge	a		19 45							20 21
Wolverhampton	a	20 02	19 58					20 16		20 32
BirminghamNewSt 68	a	20 25	20 20					20 33		20 50
Birmingham International 68	a	20 45								21 05
Coventry 68	a	21 01								21 20
Lichfield Trent Valley	a						20 09			
Tamworth Low Level	a						20 15			
Nuneaton	a						20 31			
Rugby 66	a	21 12					20 47			21 31
Milton Keynes Central 66	a	21 53			20 31	20 45	21 09		20 49	22 20
Watford Junction 66	a	22 34		20s45			21 34			23 00
London Euston 66	a	22 53		21 02	21 05	21 19	21 50		21 23	23 23

A From Crewe
B To Plymouth
C To Bournemouth
D until 14 February
E from 17 February
F To Bristol Temple Meads

Refer to Operator websites for full information about Sleeper Services. Contact details for train operators available at National Rail Enquiries

Table T065-R

Mondays to Fridays
16 December to 15 May

Scotland to Manchester, West Midlands & London via the West Coast. North West England to West Midlands & London

Station		TP	XC A	VT	LM B	VT	TP	LM	LM C	VT
Inverness 229	d									
Aberdeen 229	d									
Dundee 229	d									
Perth 229	d									
Fort William 227	d									
Edinburgh	d					16 52				
Haymarket	d					16 57				
GlasgowCentral 226,216,225	d	16 29					17 08			
Motherwell 226	d						17 25			
Carstairs 226,225	d	17 08								
Lockerbie 225,226	d						18 10			
Carlisle 216	a	18 02				18 08	18 31			
	d	18 04				18 10	18 34			
Penrith North Lakes	d						18 49			
Windermere 83	d									
Oxenholme Lake District 83	d					18 44	19 13			
Barrow-in-Furness 82	d									
Lancaster	d	18 55				18 59	19 29			
Blackpool North 97	d									
Preston 90	a	19 13				19 17	19 46			
Preston 90	d	19 15				19 18	19 48			
Wigan North Western 90	d					19 32				
Warrington Bank Quay	d					19 42				
Bolton 82	a						20s06			
Manchester Picc. 82	a						20 24			
Manchester Airport	a						20 48			
Liverpool Lime Street 91	a	19 59								
	d							19 34		19 47
Liverpool South Pkwy 91	d							19 44		
Runcorn 91	d							19 51		20 03
Manchester Picc. 84	d		19 27							
Stockport 84	d		19 36							
Wilmslow 84	d									
Holyhead 81	d									
Bangor (Gwynedd) 81	d									
Llandudno Junction 81	d									
Wrexham General 75	d									
Chester 81	d			19 35						
Crewe 81,91	a			19 54		20 00		20 16		20 22
	d			19 56	20 01	20 03		20 19		20 24
Macclesfield	d		19 49							
Stoke-on-Trent 84	d		20 07		20 26				←	
Stafford	a		20 24		20 44			20 38	20 44	
	d		20 26		20 48			20 40	20 48	
Penkridge	a				→			20 45		
Wolverhampton	a		20 41			20 37		20 57	21 02	
BirminghamNewSt 68	a		20 58			21 04		21 21	21 25	
Birmingham International 68	a		21 13			21 19			21 45	
Coventry 68	a		21 24			21 30			21 59	
Lichfield Trent Valley	a									
Tamworth Low Level	a									
Nuneaton	a									21 00
Rugby 66	a								22 11	
Milton Keynes Central 66	a			21 03		21 58				
Watford Junction 66	a					22s20				21s47
London Euston 66	a			21 39		22 41				22 04

Station		VT	LM B	XC	NT D	VT	VT	LM	VT	NT E	XC	TP	VT	NT
Inverness 229	d													
Aberdeen 229	d													
Dundee 229	d													
Perth 229	d													
Fort William 227	d													
Edinburgh	d											18 12		
Haymarket	d											18u16		
GlasgowCentral 226,216,225	d					17 30			17 40				18 40	
Motherwell 226	d													
Carstairs 226,225	d													
Lockerbie 225,226	d								18 35			19 12		
Carlisle 216	a					18 45			18 56			19 32	19 47	
	d					18 46			18 57			19 34	19 49	
Penrith North Lakes	d					19 01						19 49		
Windermere 83	d				18 55									
Oxenholme Lake District 83	d				19 16	19 25			19 33			20 13	20 24	
Barrow-in-Furness 82	d													19 43
Lancaster	d				19 33	19 39			19 47			20 29	20 38	20 44
Blackpool North 97	d									←				
Preston 90	a				19 54	19 58			20 06	19 54		20 46	20 56	21 04
Preston 90	d				20 11	20 00			20 08	20 11		20 48	20 59	21 06
Wigan North Western 90	d				→	20 13			20 20	20 27			21 11	
Warrington Bank Quay	d					20 23			20 32				21 21	
Bolton 82	a													
Manchester Picc. 82	a									20 59		21 24		21 47
Manchester Airport	a									21 20		21 41		22 03
Liverpool Lime Street 91	a													
	d							20 06						
Liverpool South Pkwy 91	d							20 16						
Runcorn 91	d							20 24						
Manchester Picc. 84	d	19 55		20 05			20 15				20 27			
Stockport 84	d	20 04		20 13			20 23				20 36			
Wilmslow 84	d	20 11												
Holyhead 81	d													
Bangor (Gwynedd) 81	d													
Llandudno Junction 81	d													
Wrexham General 75	d													
Chester 81	d													
Crewe 81,91	a	20 27				20 42		20 47	20 51					
	d	20 29	20 36			20 44		20 48	20 54					
Macclesfield	d			20 26			20 36				20 49			
Stoke-on-Trent 84	d			20 44			20 52				21 07			
Stafford	a	20 46	20 55	21 00				21 07	21 13		21 23			
	d	20 48	21 03	21 03				21 09	21 15		21 29			
Penkridge	a							21 15						
Wolverhampton	a			21 16				21 26	21 30		21 42			
BirminghamNewSt 68	a			21 33				21 48	21 54		22 00			
Birmingham International 68	a							22 05						
Coventry 68	a							22 20						
Lichfield Trent Valley	a		21 20											
Tamworth Low Level	a		21 26											
Nuneaton	a		21 42											
Rugby 66	a		21 57			21 29		22 32						
Milton Keynes Central 66	a	21 34				21 49	21 52	23 12					22 40	
Watford Junction 66	a						22s13	00 01					23s10	
London Euston 66	a	22 09				22 27	22 30	00 26					23 32	

A To Southampton Central. ⚭ to BirminghamNewSt
B To Northampton
C From Crewe to Northampton
D To Manchester Airport
E From Windermere

Refer to Operator websites for full information about Sleeper Services. Contact details for train operators available at National Rail Enquiries

Table T065-R

Mondays to Fridays
16 December to 15 May

Scotland to Manchester, West Midlands & London via the West Coast. North West England to West Midlands & London

Station		LM	LM	VT	VT	LM	LM	LM	VT	VT FX	XC	VT FO	TP	LM	XC	LM	VT	TP	NT	TP	TP WX	TP WO	LM
		A				B	C																
Inverness	229 d																						
Aberdeen	229 d																						
Dundee	229 d																						
Perth	229 d																						
Fort William	227 d																						
Edinburgh	d									18 52		18 52						20 11			22 12	22 12	
Haymarket	d									18 56		18 56						20u16			22u16	22u16	
GlasgowCentral	226,216,225 d												19 08				20 10			21 01			
Motherwell	226 d																						
Carstairs	226,225 d																						
Lockerbie	225,226 d												20 08				21 04	21 12		22 20	23 16	23 16	
Carlisle	216 a									20 05		20 05	20 28				21 23	21 33		22 41	23 38	23 38	
	d									20 07		20 07	20 30				21 25	21 35		22 42	23 39	23 39	
Penrith North Lakes	d												20 45				21 40			22 57			
Windermere	83 d																		22 45				
Oxenholme Lake District	83 d									20 42		20 42	21 09				22 04	22 11	23 06				
Barrow-in-Furness	82 d																						
Lancaster	d									20 56		20 56	21 24				22 19	22 26	23 24				
Blackpool North	97 d																						
Preston	90 a									21 14		21 14	21 41				22 37	22 44	23 50	00 12	00 46	00 46	
Preston	90 d									21 17		21 17	21 43				22 39	22 45			00 47	00 47	
Wigan North Western	90 d									21 29		21 29					22 53						
Warrington Bank Quay	d									21 40		21 40					23 04						
Bolton	82 a																	23s03					
Manchester Picc.	82 a												22 23					23 24			01 40	01 42	
Manchester Airport	a												22 45					23 46			01 59		
Liverpool Lime Street	91 a																						
	d		20 35	20 48										21 34		22 35							23 35
Liverpool South Pkwy	91 d		20 45											21 44		22 47							23 45
Runcorn	91 d		20 52	21 04										21 51		22 55							23 52
Manchester Picc.	84 d				21 15						21 27				22 07								
Stockport	84 d				21 23						21 36				22 17								
Wilmslow	84 d																						
Holyhead	81 d																						
Bangor (Gwynedd)	81 d								20 20														
Llandudno Junction	81 d								20 38														
Wrexham General	75 d																						
Chester	81 d								21 35														
Crewe	81,91 a		21 17	21 23					21 54	21 59		21 59		22 15		23 25	23 26						00 23
	d	21 14	21 19	21 25		21 29		21 53	21 56	22 01		22 01		22 18									
Macclesfield	d				21 36						21 49				22 29								
Stoke-on-Trent	84 d	21 37			21 53		←				22 07				22 47								
Stafford	a	21 56	21 38	21 42		21 48	21 56	22 11			22 22			22 36	23 03								
	d	21 59	21 40	21 44		21 49	21 59	22 12			22 28			22 37	23 06								
Penkridge	a	→	21 46											22 43									
Wolverhampton	a		21 57				22 14		22 27	22 32	22 41	22 32		22 58	23 19								
BirminghamNewSt	68 a		22 18				22 39		22 48	22 52	22 59	23 06		23 15	23 37								
Birmingham International	68 a											23 19											
Coventry	68 a											23 30											
Lichfield Trent Valley	a			21 57		22 05		22 29															
Tamworth Low Level	a			22 03		22 12		22 35															
Nuneaton	a			22 17		22 27		22 58															
Rugby	66 a			22 30		22 41		23 11				23 43											
Milton Keynes Central	66 a			22 53	23 00			23 44				00 23											
Watford Junction	66 a			23s25	23s30							00s54											
London Euston	66 a			23 44	23 48			00 45				01 13											

A To Walsall **B** To Northampton **C** From Crewe to Walsall

Refer to Operator websites for full information about Sleeper Services. Contact details for train operators available at National Rail Enquiries

Table T065-R

Mondays to Fridays
16 December to 15 May

Scotland to Manchester, West Midlands & London via the West Coast. North West England to West Midlands & London

Station		CS FX	CS FX	CS FO	CS FO	CS	CS	CS
Inverness	229 d						20 45	
Aberdeen	229 d							21 43
Dundee	229 d							23u09
Perth	229 d						23u27	
Fort William	227 d					19 50		
Edinburgh	d		23 40		23 40			
Haymarket	d							
GlasgowCentral	226,216,225 d	23 40		23 40				
Motherwell	226 d	23u59		23u59				
Carstairs	226,225 d	00u20		00u20				
Lockerbie	225,226 d							
Carlisle	216 a							
	d	01u44		01u44				
Penrith North Lakes	d							
Windermere	83 d							
Oxenholme Lake District	83 d							
Barrow-in-Furness	82 d							
Lancaster	d							
Blackpool North	97 d							
Preston	90 a					04s32	04s32	04s32
Preston	90 d							
Wigan North Western	90 d							
Warrington Bank Quay	d							
Bolton	82 a							
Manchester Picc.	82 a							
Manchester Airport	a							
Liverpool Lime Street	91 a							
	d							
Liverpool South Pkwy	91 d							
Runcorn	91 d							
Manchester Picc.	84 d							
Stockport	84 d							
Wilmslow	84 d							
Holyhead	81 d							
Bangor (Gwynedd)	81 d							
Llandudno Junction	81 d							
Wrexham General	75 d							
Chester	81 d							
Crewe	81,91 a					05s37		05s37
	d							
Macclesfield	d							
Stoke-on-Trent	84 d							
Stafford	a							
	d							
Penkridge	a							
Wolverhampton	a							
BirminghamNewSt	68 a							
Birmingham International	68 a							
Coventry	68 a							
Lichfield Trent Valley	a							
Tamworth Low Level	a							
Nuneaton	a							
Rugby	66 a							
Milton Keynes Central	66 a							
Watford Junction	66 a	06s39		06s43				
London Euston	66 a	07 07		07 07		07 49		07 49

Refer to Operator websites for full information about Sleeper Services. Contact details for train operators available at National Rail Enquiries

Table T065-R

Saturdays

21 December to 16 May

Scotland to Manchester, West Midlands & London via the West Coast. North West England to West Midlands & London

	NT	CS	CS	TP	AW	LM	XC	VT	XC	VT	LM	LM	LM	VT	VT	LM	LM	XC	VT	VT	NT	LM
	A	B	C	C			D		E		F		F			G	G	H				
Inverness 229 d																						
Aberdeen 229 d																						
Dundee 229 d																						
Perth 229 d																						
Fort William 227 d																						
Edinburgh d																						
Haymarket d																						
GlasgowCentral 226,216,225 d																						
Motherwell 226 d																						
Carstairs 226,225 d		00u20																				
Lockerbie 225,226 d																						
Carlisle 216 a																						
d		01u44	01u44																			
Penrith North Lakes d																						
Windermere 83 d																						
Oxenholme Lake District 83 d																						
Barrow-in-Furness 82 d																					04 53	
Lancaster d															05 38						05 46	
Blackpool North 97 d																						
Preston 90 a															05 55						06 04	
Preston 90 d				00 47											05 57						06 06	
Wigan North Western 90 d															06 09						06 23	
Warrington Bank Quay d															06 20							
Bolton 82 a																						
Manchester Picc. 82 a				01 40																	06 57	
Manchester Airport a				01 59																	07 18	
Liverpool Lime Street 91 a																						
d										05 46												06 10
Liverpool South Pkwy 91 d																						06 20
Runcorn 91 d										06 03												06 27
Manchester Picc. 84 d							05 11	05 25						05 55				06 00	06 10	06 35		
Stockport 84 d								05 34						06 03				06 08	06 19	06 43		
Wilmslow 84 d	00 02							05 41						06 11								
Holyhead 81 d																						
Bangor (Gwynedd) 81 d																						
Llandudno Junction 81 d																						
Wrexham General 75 d																						
Chester 81 d					04 22																	
Crewe 81,91 a	00 32				04 45		05 42	05 57						06 27								06 47
d					04 59	05 38	05 46	06 00			06 01	06 16	06 24	06 29								06 49
Macclesfield d																		06 21	06 31	06 56		
Stoke-on-Trent 84 d							06 06		←		06 26					←	←	06 39	06 48	07 12		
Stafford a					05 24	05 56	06 22	06 17	06 22	06 34	06 45	06 35	06 42			06 45	06 42	06 55				07 08
d					05 25	05 59	06 28	06 19	06 28	06 35	06 45	06 36	06 47			06 45	06 47	07 03				07 09
Penkridge a							→				→	06 42	→									07 14
Wolverhampton a					05 40				06 41			06 56				07 04		07 16				07 25
BirminghamNewSt 68 a					05 59				06 58			07 22				07 28		07 34				07 50
Birmingham International 68 a									07 13							07 45						08 05
Coventry 68 a									07 24							08 00						08 20
Lichfield Trent Valley a						06 16											07 04		07 11			
Tamworth Low Level a						06 22											07 10		07 17			
Nuneaton a						06 37				06 57							07 25					
Rugby 66 a						06 55		06 49								08 11	07 42			07 52		08 31
Milton Keynes Central 66 a								07 10						07 31	07 38	08 55	08 04					09 22
Watford Junction 66 a		06s43	06s43					07s33		07s45						09 17						09 58
London Euston 66 a		07 07	07 07			07 57		07 50		08 02				08 07	08 13	09 33	08 40		08 23	08 44		10 17

A From Manchester Piccadilly
B From Glasgow Central
C From Edinburgh
D To Bournemouth
E From Manchester Piccadilly to Bournemouth. from BirminghamNewSt
F To London Euston
G From Crewe
H To Bristol Temple Meads

Refer to Operator websites for full information about Sleeper Services. Contact details for train operators available at National Rail Enquiries

Table T065-R

Saturdays

21 December to 16 May

Scotland to Manchester, West Midlands & London via the West Coast. North West England to West Midlands & London

	VT	TP	LM	LM	VT	LM	VT	VT	XC	VT	VT	LM	LM	VT	TP	XC	VT	NT	VT	TP	LM	LM
									A							B						
Inverness 229 d																						
Aberdeen 229 d																						
Dundee 229 d																						
Perth 229 d																						
Fort William 227 d																						
Edinburgh d																						
Haymarket d																						
GlasgowCentral 226,216,225 d								04 26												04 24		
Motherwell 226 d																						
Carstairs 226,225 d																						
Lockerbie 225,226 d																				05 50		
Carlisle 216 a								05 43												06 13		
d								05 44							05 50					06 21		
Penrith North Lakes d								05 58							06 05					06 39		
Windermere 83 d																						
Oxenholme Lake District 83 d								06 21							06 29					07 08		
Barrow-in-Furness 82 d																		05 48				
Lancaster d		06 28						06 36										06 50	06 58	07 23		
Blackpool North 97 d																						
Preston 90 a		06 46						06 54							07 02			07 11	07 15	07 40		
Preston 90 d	06 17	06 47						06 56							07 05			07 12	07 17	07 45		
Wigan North Western 90 d	06 29							07 09										07 26	07 29			
Warrington Bank Quay d	06 40							07 19											07 41			
Bolton 82 a																				08s03		
Manchester Picc. 82 a		07 25																08 01		08 24		
Manchester Airport a		07 49																08 21		08 44		
Liverpool Lime Street 91 a															07 59							
d				06 34	06 44								07 05	07 16								07 35
Liverpool South Pkwy 91 d				06 44									07 15									07 45
Runcorn 91 d				06 51	07 01								07 23	07 33								07 52
Manchester Picc. 84 d							06 55		07 05	07 15						07 27	07 35					
Stockport 84 d							07 04		07 13	07 23						07 36	07 43					
Wilmslow 84 d							07 11															
Holyhead 81 d																						
Bangor (Gwynedd) 81 d																						
Llandudno Junction 81 d																						
Wrexham General 75 d																						
Chester 81 d											07 17											
Crewe 81,91 a	06 57			07 13	07 19		07 27				07 36		07 47	07 54					07 57			08 17
d	07 01		07 01	07 18	07 20	07 25	07 29				07 41	07 44	07 50	07 56					08 03		08 01	08 19
Macclesfield d									07 26							07 49	07 56					
Stoke-on-Trent 84 d			07 29						07 44	07 50						08 07	08 12				08 26	
Stafford a			07 51	07 37	07 38	07 43			08 00			08 02	08 09	08 13		08 24					08 45	08 36
d			07 51	07 38	07 39	07 48			08 03			08 07	08 10	08 15		08 28					08 46	08 38
Penkridge a				07 43									08 15									08 43
Wolverhampton a	07 31		08 06	07 54					08 16				08 26			08 41			08 35		09 03	08 57
BirminghamNewSt 68 a	08 05		08 25	08 21					08 33				08 50			08 58			09 06		09 22	09 16
Birmingham International 68 a	08 19		08 44										09 05			09 13					09 44	
Coventry 68 a	08 30		08 59										09 20			09 24					09 59	
Lichfield Trent Valley a						08 04						08 25		08 29								
Tamworth Low Level a						08 11						08 32		08 36								
Nuneaton a						08 26						08 46										
Rugby 66 a			09 11			08 42						09 03	09 31								10 11	
Milton Keynes Central 66 a	08 58		09 51			09 05				08 46	08 51	09 24	10 21								10 51	
Watford Junction 66 a			10 14										10 58								11 14	
London Euston 66 a	09 36		10 30		08 56	09 50	09 01	09 07		09 21	09 28	10 00	11 17	09 44			09 40				11 30	

A To Bristol Temple Meads
B To Bournemouth

Refer to Operator websites for full information about Sleeper Services. Contact details for train operators available at National Rail Enquiries

Table T065-R

Saturdays

21 December to 16 May

Scotland to Manchester, West Midlands & London via the West Coast. North West England to West Midlands & London

Station	VT	VT	VT	NT	LM	XC A	VT	LM	VT	XC B	VT	VT	TP	LM	LM	VT	VT	VT	NT	LM	XC C
Inverness 229 d																					
Aberdeen 229 d																					
Dundee 229 d																					
Perth 229 d																					
Fort William 227 d																					
Edinburgh d													06 13								
Haymarket d													06u17								
GlasgowCentral 226,216,225 d			05 40									05 50						06 30			
Motherwell 226 d												06 05						06 45			
Carstairs 226,225 d																					
Lockerbie 225,226 d													07 12					07 26			
Carlisle 216 a			06 47									07 01	07 33					07 45			
d			06 49									07 02	07 34					07 47			
Penrith North Lakes d												07 17	07 50					08 01			
Windermere 83 d																					
Oxenholme Lake District 83 d			07 24									07 41	08 14					08 24			
Barrow-in-Furness 82 d				06 47															07 46		
Lancaster d			07 38	07 46								07 56	08 29					08 39	08 46		
Blackpool North 97 d																					
Preston 90 a			07 56	08 06								08 14	08 46					08 57	09 06		
Preston 90 d			07 59	08 08								08 17	08 48					08 59	09 08		
Wigan North Western 90 d			08 11	08 23								08 29						09 11	09 23		
Warrington Bank Quay d			08 22									08 40						09 22			
Bolton 82 a													09s06								
Manchester Picc. 82 a				08 59									09 24						09 58		
Manchester Airport a				09 18									09 46						10 18		
Liverpool Lime Street 91 a																					
d	07 47							08 07							08 34	08 47					
Liverpool South Pkwy 91 d								08 18							08 44						
Runcorn 91 d	08 03							08 25							08 51	09 03					
Manchester Picc. 84 d		07 55				08 05	08 15			08 27	08 35						08 55				09 05
Stockport 84 d		08 04				08 13	08 23			08 36	08 43						09 04				09 13
Wilmslow 84 d		08 11															09 11				
Holyhead 81 d									06 52												
Bangor (Gwynedd) 81 d									07 20												
Llandudno Junction 81 d									07 38												
Wrexham General 75 d																					
Chester 81 d									08 35												
Crewe 81,91 a	08 21	08 27						08 48	08 54			08 57			09 17	09 22	09 28				
d	08 22	08 29			08 33			08 49	08 56			09 01		09 01	09 18	09 24	09 29			09 33	
Macclesfield d						08 26				08 49	08 56										09 26
Stoke-on-Trent 84 d						08 44	08 50			09 07	09 12			09 26							09 44
Stafford a	08 39				08 51	09 00		09 08		09 22				09 44	09 38	09 41				09 51	10 00
d	08 41				08 55	09 03		09 09		09 28				09 45	09 39	09 43				09 55	10 03
Penkridge a								09 15							09 45						
Wolverhampton a						09 16		09 26		09 41		09 32		10 02	09 58						10 16
BirminghamNewSt 68 a						09 33		09 50		09 58		10 05		10 25	10 20						10 33
Birmingham International 68 a								10 05		10 13		10 19		10 44							
Coventry 68 a								10 20		10 24		10 30		10 59							
Lichfield Trent Valley a					09 12															10 12	
Tamworth Low Level a					09 19															10 19	
Nuneaton a	09 03				09 34															10 34	
Rugby 66 a					09 50			10 31						11 11						10 50	
Milton Keynes Central 66 a					10 14		09 46	11 21	10 01			10 57		11 51						11 14	
Watford Junction 66 a								11 58						12 14							
London Euston 66 a	10 03	10 08	10 11		10 52		10 21	12 17	10 36		10 41	11 33		12 30		11 01	11 04	11 09		11 50	

A To Paignton
B To Bournemouth
C To Bristol Temple Meads

Refer to Operator websites for full information about Sleeper Services. Contact details for train operators available at National Rail Enquiries

Table T065-R

Saturdays

21 December to 16 May

Scotland to Manchester, West Midlands & London via the West Coast. North West England to West Midlands & London

Station	VT	LM	VT	XC A	VT	VT	TP	LM	LM	VT	VT	VT	NT	LM	XC B	VT	LM	VT	XC A	VT	VT	TP
Inverness 229 d																						
Aberdeen 229 d																						
Dundee 229 d																						
Perth 229 d																						
Fort William 227 d																						
Edinburgh d						06 52																08 11
Haymarket d						06 56																08u16
GlasgowCentral 226,216,225 d							07 10					07 35									08 00	
Motherwell 226 d							07 26					07 52										
Carstairs 226,225 d																						
Lockerbie 225,226 d							08 10															09 10
Carlisle 216 a						08 06	08 31					08 48									09 10	09 31
d						08 07	08 33					08 49									09 12	09 33
Penrith North Lakes d						08 22	08 48															09 48
Windermere 83 d																						
Oxenholme Lake District 83 d							09 13					09 23										10 12
Barrow-in-Furness 82 d													08 46									
Lancaster d						08 57	09 28					09 38	09 47								09 58	10 27
Blackpool North 97 d																						
Preston 90 a						09 15	09 45					09 57	10 08								10 16	10 45
Preston 90 d						09 17	09 47					09 59	10 10								10 17	10 47
Wigan North Western 90 d						09 29						10 11	10 24								10 29	
Warrington Bank Quay d						09 40						10 22									10 40	
Bolton 82 a							10s05															11s05
Manchester Picc. 82 a							10 24						10 58									11 24
Manchester Airport a							10 46						11 18									11 46
Liverpool Lime Street 91 a																						
d		09 04							09 32	09 47							10 05					
Liverpool South Pkwy 91 d		09 18							09 42								10 18					
Runcorn 91 d		09 27							09 49	10 03							10 26					
Manchester Picc. 84 d	09 15			09 27	09 35						09 55				10 05	10 15			10 27	10 35		
Stockport 84 d	09 23			09 36	09 43						10 04				10 13	10 23			10 36	10 43		
Wilmslow 84 d											10 11											
Holyhead 81 d			07 55															08 55				
Bangor (Gwynedd) 81 d			08 22															09 22				
Llandudno Junction 81 d			08 40															09 40				
Wrexham General 75 d																						
Chester 81 d			09 35															10 35				
Crewe 81,91 a		09 48	09 54			09 57			10 15	10 21	10 27						10 47	10 54			10 57	
d		09 50	09 56			10 01		10 01	10 17	10 22	10 29			10 33			10 49	10 56			11 01	
Macclesfield d				09 49	09 56										10 26				10 49	10 56		
Stoke-on-Trent 84 d	09 50			10 07	10 12			10 26							10 44	10 50			11 07	11 12		
Stafford a		10 10		10 22				10 44	10 38	10 40				10 53	11 00		11 09		11 25			
d		10 10		10 28				10 45	10 38	10 41				10 55	11 03		11 10		11 28			
Penkridge a		10 16							10 46								11 15					
Wolverhampton a		10 27		10 41		10 34		11 03	10 58						11 16		11 26		11 41		11 34	
BirminghamNewSt 68 a		10 50		10 58		11 05		11 25	11 20						11 33		11 50		11 58		12 05	
Birmingham International 68 a		11 05		11 13		11 19		11 44									12 05		12 13		12 19	
Coventry 68 a		11 20		11 24		11 30		11 59									12 20		12 24		12 30	
Lichfield Trent Valley a														11 12								
Tamworth Low Level a														11 19								
Nuneaton a														11 34								
Rugby 66 a		11 31						12 11						11 50			12 31					
Milton Keynes Central 66 a	10 46	12 21	11 01			11 57		12 51						12 15		11 46	13 21	12 01			12 57	
Watford Junction 66 a		12 58						13 14									13 58					
London Euston 66 a	11 20	13 17	11 36		11 39	12 33		13 30		11 58	12 01	12 08		12 51		12 20	14 18	12 36		12 40	13 33	

A To Bournemouth
B To Bristol Temple Meads

Refer to Operator websites for full information about Sleeper Services. Contact details for train operators available at National Rail Enquiries

Table T065-R

Saturdays

21 December to 16 May

Scotland to Manchester, West Midlands & London via the West Coast. North West England to West Midlands & London

Station	LM	LM	VT	TP	VT	VT	NT	LM	XC	VT	LM	XC	VT	VT	VT	VT	TP	LM	LM	VT	VT
									A			B									
Inverness 229 d																					
Aberdeen 229 d																					
Dundee 229 d																					
Perth 229 d																					
Fort William 227 d																					
Edinburgh 10 d															08 53						
Haymarket d															08 59						
GlasgowCentral 15 226,216,225 d				08 05		08 40											09 07				
Motherwell 226 d				08 27													09 23				
Carstairs 226,225 d																					
Lockerbie 225,226 d				09 15													10 14				
Carlisle 8 216 a				09 36		09 48									10 07		10 34				
d				09 38		09 49									10 08		10 36				
Penrith North Lakes d				09 53		10 03											10 51				
Windermere 83 d							10 08														
Oxenholme Lake District 83 d				10 17			10 29								10 42		11 15				
Barrow-in-Furness 82 d																					
Lancaster 6 d				10 32		10 38									10 57		11 30				
Blackpool North 97 d																10 54					
Preston 8 90 a				10 51		10 56	11 04								11 16	11 16	11 47				
Preston 8 90 d				10 53		10 59	11 08								11 17	11 22	11 49				
Wigan North Western 90 d						11 11	11 23								11 29	11 36					
Warrington Bank Quay d						11 22									11 40	11 48					
Bolton 82 a																					
Manchester Picc. 10 82 a							11 58										12 24				
Manchester Airport a							12 18										12 46				
Liverpool Lime Street 10 91 a				11 45																	
d		10 34	10 47								11 05								11 35	11 47	
Liverpool South Pkwy 7 91 d		10 44									11 18								11 45		
Runcorn 91 d		10 51	11 03								11 26								11 52	12 03	
Manchester Picc. 10 84 d					10 55				11 05	11 15		11 27		11 35							11 55
Stockport 84 d					11 04				11 13	11 23		11 36		11 43							12 04
Wilmslow 84 d					11 11																12 11
Holyhead 81 d																					
Bangor (Gwynedd) 81 d																					
Llandudno Junction 81 d																					
Wrexham General 75 d																					
Chester 81 d													11 35								
Crewe 10 81,91 a		11 17	11 21		11 27						11 46		11 54		11 57				12 18	12 21	12 27
d	11 01	11 19	11 22		11 29			11 33			11 50		11 56		12 01			12 01	12 20	12 22	12 29
Macclesfield d									11 26			11 49		11 56							
Stoke-on-Trent 84 d	11 26								11 44	11 50		12 07		12 12				12 26			
Stafford a	11 44	11 39	11 40					11 51	12 00		12 09	12 23						12 44	12 39	12 40	
d	11 45	11 40	11 41					11 55	12 03		12 09	12 28						12 45	12 40	12 41	
Penkridge a		11 45									12 15								12 45		
Wolverhampton 7 a	12 03	11 58							12 16		12 26	12 41			12 33			13 01	12 58		
BirminghamNewSt 12 68 a	12 25	12 20							12 33		12 50	12 58			13 05			13 25	13 20		
Birmingham International 68 a	12 44										13 05	13 13			13 19			13 44			
Coventry 68 a	12 59										13 20	13 24			13 30			13 59			
Lichfield Trent Valley a								12 12													
Tamworth Low Level a								12 19													
Nuneaton a								12 34													
Rugby 66 a	13 11							12 50			13 31					12 55		14 11			
Milton Keynes Central 66 a	13 51							13 14		12 46	14 21		13 02		13 57			14 53			
Watford Junction 66 a	14 14										14 58							15 15			
London Euston 15 ⊖66 a	14 30		13 00		13 03	13 08		13 50		13 21	15 17		13 36	13 39	14 33	13 53		15 31		14 01	14 04

A To Bristol Temple Meads
B To Bournemouth

Refer to Operator websites for full information about Sleeper Services. Contact details for train operators available at National Rail Enquiries

Table T065-R

Saturdays

21 December to 16 May

Scotland to Manchester, West Midlands & London via the West Coast. North West England to West Midlands & London

Station	VT	VT	NT	LM	XC	VT	LM	XC	VT	VT	VT	TP	LM	LM	VT	VT	VT	NT	LM	XC	VT	LM
	A	B			C			D												E		
Inverness 229 d																						
Aberdeen 229 d																						
Dundee 229 d																						
Perth 229 d																						
Fort William 227 d																						
Edinburgh 10 d												10 12										
Haymarket d												10u16										
GlasgowCentral 15 226,216,225 d	09 40	09 40									10 00						10 40					
Motherwell 226 d																						
Carstairs 226,225 d																						
Lockerbie 225,226 d												11 11										
Carlisle 8 216 a	10 48	10 48									11 09	11 31					11 47					
d	10 50	10 50									11 11	11 35					11 49					
Penrith North Lakes d											11 25	11 51										
Windermere 83 d																						
Oxenholme Lake District 83 d	11 24	11 24										12 15					12 23					
Barrow-in-Furness 82 d			10 46															11 46				
Lancaster 6 d	11 39	11 39	11 46									12 30					12 38	12 46				
Blackpool North 97 d																						
Preston 8 90 a	11 57	11 57	12 06								12 15	12 47					12 56	13 06				
Preston 8 90 d	11 59	11 59	12 08								12 17	12 49					12 59	13 12				
Wigan North Western 90 d	12 11	12 11	12 25								12 29						13 11					
Warrington Bank Quay d	12 22	12 22									12 40						13 22					
Bolton 82 a																						
Manchester Picc. 10 82 a			12 58									13 24						13 58				
Manchester Airport a			13 18									13 46						14 18				
Liverpool Lime Street 10 91 a																						
d							12 05							12 35	12 47							13 05
Liverpool South Pkwy 7 91 d							12 18							12 45								13 16
Runcorn 91 d							12 27							12 52	13 03							13 25
Manchester Picc. 10 84 d					12 05	12 15		12 27		12 35						12 55				13 05	13 15	
Stockport 84 d					12 13	12 23		12 36		12 43						13 04				13 13	13 23	
Wilmslow 84 d																13 11						
Holyhead 81 d																						
Bangor (Gwynedd) 81 d																						
Llandudno Junction 81 d																						
Wrexham General 75 d																						
Chester 81 d									12 35													
Crewe 10 81,91 a							12 47		12 54		12 59			13 17	13 22	13 27						13 45
d				12 33			12 50		12 56		13 03		13 01	13 18	13 24	13 29			13 33			13 50
Macclesfield d					12 26			12 49		12 56										13 26		
Stoke-on-Trent 84 d					12 44	12 50		13 07		13 12			13 26							13 44	13 50	
Stafford a				12 51	13 00		13 08	13 22					13 44	13 37	13 41				13 52	14 00		14 09
d				12 55	13 03		13 10	13 28					13 45	13 40	13 42				13 55	14 03		14 09
Penkridge a							13 16							13 46								14 15
Wolverhampton 7 a					13 16		13 27	13 41			13 32		14 02	13 58						14 16		14 26
BirminghamNewSt 12 68 a					13 33		13 51	13 58			14 05		14 25	14 20						14 34		14 50
Birmingham International 68 a							14 05	14 13			14 19		14 44									15 05
Coventry 68 a							14 20	14 24			14 30		14 59									15 20
Lichfield Trent Valley a				13 12															14 12			
Tamworth Low Level a				13 19															14 19			
Nuneaton a				13 34															14 34			
Rugby 66 a				13 50			14 31						15 11				14 22		14 50			15 31
Milton Keynes Central 66 a				14 14		13 46	15 21		14 02		14 57		15 52						15 14			16 21
Watford Junction 66 a							15 58						16 14								14 48	16 58
London Euston 15 ⊖66 a	14 09	14 10		14 50		14 20	16 19		14 36	14 41	15 34		16 30		14 59	15 07	15 13		15 50		15 23	17 17

A until 15 February
B from 22 February
C To Exeter St Davids
D To Bournemouth
E To Bristol Temple Meads

Refer to Operator websites for full information about Sleeper Services. Contact details for train operators available at National Rail Enquiries

Table T065-R

Saturdays
21 December to 16 May

Scotland to Manchester, West Midlands & London via the West Coast. North West England to West Midlands & London

	XC	VT	VT	VT	VT	TP	LM	LM	VT	VT	VT	NT	LM	XC	VT	LM	XC	VT	VT	VT	LM	LM
	◇1	◇1	◇1	◇1	◇1	◇1	1	1	◇1	◇1	◇1	◇	1	◇1	◇1	1	◇1	◇1	◇1	◇1	1	1
	A													B			A					
	🛒	🍴	🍴	🍴	🍴	🛒			🍴	🍴	🍴			🛒	🍴		🛒	🍴	🍴	🍴		
Inverness 229 d																						
Aberdeen 229 d																						
Dundee 229 d																						
Perth 229 d																						
Fort William 227 d																						
Edinburgh 10 d				10 52																		
Haymarket d				10 57																		
GlasgowCentral 15 226,216,225 d						11 08					11 40									12 00		
Motherwell 226 d						11 24																
Carstairs 226,225 d																						
Lockerbie 225,226 d						12 09																
Carlisle 8 216 a				12 04		12 29					12 47									13 11		
d				12 07		12 34					12 49									13 13		
Penrith North Lakes d						12 49					13 03											
Windermere 83 d												13 06										
Oxenholme Lake District 83 d				12 43		13 13						13 28										
Barrow-in-Furness 82 d																						
Lancaster 6 d				12 57		13 28					13 37	13 45								14 00		
Blackpool North 97 d					13 03																	
Preston 8 90 a				13 15	13 24	13 45					13 57	14 05								14 17		
Preston 8 90 d				13 17	13 28	13 47					13 59	14 08								14 20		
Wigan North Western 90 d				13 29	13 41						14 11	14 24								14 32		
Warrington Bank Quay d				13 40	13 52						14 22									14 43		
Bolton 82 a						14s05																
Manchester Picc. 10 82 a						14 24						14 58										
Manchester Airport ✈ a						14 46						15 18										
Liverpool Lime Street 10 91 a																						
d								13 35	13 47							14 05						14 35
Liverpool South Pkwy 7 91 ✈ d								13 45								14 17						14 45
Runcorn 91 d								13 52	14 03							14 25						14 52
Manchester Picc. 10 84 d	13 27		13 35							13 55				14 05	14 15		14 27		14 35			
Stockport 84 d	13 36		13 43							14 04				14 13	14 23		14 36		14 43			
Wilmslow 84 d										14 11												
Holyhead 81 ⛴ d																						
Bangor (Gwynedd) 81 d																						
Llandudno Junction 81 d																						
Wrexham General 75 d																						
Chester 81 d		13 35																14 35				
Crewe 10 81,91 a		13 54		13 57				14 16	14 23	14 27						14 45		14 54		14 58		15 17
d		13 56		14 01			14 01	14 18	14 24	14 29			14 33			14 49		14 56		15 02	15 01	15 19
Macclesfield d	13 49		13 56											14 26			14 49		14 56			
Stoke-on-Trent 84 d	14 07		14 12				14 26							14 44	14 50		15 07		15 12		15 26	
Stafford a	14 24						14 44	14 38	14 42				14 51	15 00		15 08	15 25				15 44	15 38
d	14 28						14 45	14 38	14 43				14 55	15 03		15 08	15 28				15 45	15 39
Penkridge a								14 46								15 14						15 44
Wolverhampton 7 a	14 41			14 33			15 04	15 00						15 16		15 25	15 41			15 34	16 05	15 58
BirminghamNewSt 12 68 a	14 58			15 05			15 25	15 20						15 33		15 50	15 58			16 05	16 24	16 17
Birmingham International 68 ✈ a	15 13			15 19				15 44								16 05	16 13			16 19		16 44
Coventry 68 a	15 24			15 30				15 59								16 20	16 24			16 30		16 59
Lichfield Trent Valley a													15 12									
Tamworth Low Level a													15 19									
Nuneaton a													15 34									
Rugby 66 a					15 03			16 11					15 50			16 31						17 12
Milton Keynes Central 66 a		15 02		15 57				16 52					16 14		15 46	17 21		16 01		16 57		17 52
Watford Junction 66 a								17 14								17 58						18 14
London Euston 15 ⊖66 a		15 37	15 40	16 33	15 58			17 30	16 01	16 04	16 08		16 50		16 21	18 17		16 36	16 40	17 33		18 30

A To Bournemouth
B To Paignton

Refer to Operator websites for full information about Sleeper Services. Contact details for train operators available at National Rail Enquiries

Table T065-R

Saturdays
21 December to 16 May

Scotland to Manchester, West Midlands & London via the West Coast. North West England to West Midlands & London

	VT	TP	VT	TP	VT	NT	LM	XC	VT	LM	VT	XC	VT	VT	TP	LM	LM	VT	VT	VT	NT
	◇1	◇1	◇1	◇1	◇1	◇	1	◇1	◇1	1	◇1	◇1	◇1	◇1	◇1	1	1	◇1	◇1	◇1	◇
								A				B									
	🍴	🛒	🍴	🛒	🍴			🛒	🍴		🍴	🛒	🍴	🍴	🛒			🍴	🍴	🍴	
Inverness 229 d																					
Aberdeen 229 d																					
Dundee 229 d																					
Perth 229 d																					
Fort William 227 d																					
Edinburgh 10 d				12 12										12 52							
Haymarket d				12u16										12 57							
GlasgowCentral 15 226,216,225 d		12 05			12 40										13 08					13 40	
Motherwell 226 d															13 24						
Carstairs 226,225 d																					
Lockerbie 225,226 d		13 07		13 12											14 09						
Carlisle 8 216 a		13 28		13 33	13 47									14 05	14 29					14 47	
d		13 29		13 35	13 49									14 08	14 33					14 49	
Penrith North Lakes d		13 44		13 50										14 22	14 48						
Windermere 83 d																					
Oxenholme Lake District 83 d		14 08		14 14	14 24										15 12					15 23	
Barrow-in-Furness 82 d						13 53															14 46
Lancaster 6 d		14 23		14 29	14 39	14 47								14 57	15 27					15 38	15 46
Blackpool North 97 d																					
Preston 8 90 a		14 42		14 46	14 56	15 08								15 16	15 45					15 56	16 06
Preston 8 90 d		14 43		14 48	14 59	15 10								15 17	15 46					15 59	16 08
Wigan North Western 90 d		14 57			15 11	15 24								15 29						16 11	16 23
Warrington Bank Quay d					15 22									15 40						16 22	
Bolton 82 a				15s06											16s04						
Manchester Picc. 10 82 a				15 24		15 58									16 24						16 58
Manchester Airport ✈ a				15 46		16 18									16 46						17 18
Liverpool Lime Street 10 91 a		15 31																			
d	14 47									15 05							15 33	15 47			
Liverpool South Pkwy 7 91 ✈ d										15 17							15 43				
Runcorn 91 d	15 03									15 26							15 50	16 03			
Manchester Picc. 10 84 d			14 55					15 05	15 15			15 27	15 35						15 55		
Stockport 84 d			15 04					15 13	15 23			15 36	15 43						16 04		
Wilmslow 84 d			15 11																16 11		
Holyhead 81 ⛴ d											13 58										
Bangor (Gwynedd) 81 d											14 25										
Llandudno Junction 81 d											14 43										
Wrexham General 75 d																					
Chester 81 d											15 35										
Crewe 10 81,91 a	15 21		15 27							15 46	15 54			15 58			16 17	16 20	16 27		
d	15 22		15 29				15 33			15 49	15 56			16 01		16 01	16 19	16 22	16 29		
Macclesfield d								15 26				15 49	15 56								
Stoke-on-Trent 84 d								15 44	15 50			16 07	16 12			16 26					
Stafford a	15 40						15 51	16 00		16 08		16 23				16 47	16 38	16 40			
d	15 41						15 55	16 03		16 09		16 28				16 47	16 40	16 41			
Penkridge a										16 15							16 45				
Wolverhampton 7 a								16 16		16 25		16 41		16 33		17 03	16 58				
BirminghamNewSt 12 68 a								16 33		16 50		16 58		17 05		17 26	17 20				
Birmingham International 68 ✈ a										17 05		17 13		17 19			17 45				
Coventry 68 a										17 20		17 24		17 30			18 00				
Lichfield Trent Valley a							16 12														
Tamworth Low Level a							16 19														
Nuneaton a							16 34														
Rugby 66 a							16 50			17 31							18 11				
Milton Keynes Central 66 a							17 14		16 46	18 21	17 01			17 57			18 53				
Watford Junction 66 a										18 58							19 15				
London Euston 15 ⊖66 a	16 59		17 03		17 08		17 50		17 21	19 17	17 36		17 41	18 33			19 31	17 59	18 02	18 08	

A To Bristol Temple Meads
B To Bournemouth

Refer to Operator websites for full information about Sleeper Services. Contact details for train operators available at National Rail Enquiries

Table T065-R

Saturdays
21 December to 16 May

Scotland to Manchester, West Midlands & London via the West Coast. North West England to West Midlands & London

	LM	XC	VT	LM	XC	VT	VT	VT	VT	TP	LM	LM	VT	VT	VT	NT	LM	XC	VT	LM	XC	VT
	1	◇1	◇1	1	◇1	◇1	◇1	◇1	◇1	◇1	1	1	◇1	◇1	◇1	◇	1	◇1	◇1	1	◇1	◇1
		A			B													C			B	
Inverness 229 d																						
Aberdeen 229 d																						
Dundee 229 d																						
Perth 229 d																						
Fort William 227 d																						
Edinburgh [10] d										14 12												
Haymarket d										14u16												
GlasgowCentral [15] 226,216,225 d								14 00							14 40							
Motherwell 226 d																						
Carstairs 226,225 d																						
Lockerbie 225,226 d										15 14												
Carlisle [8] 216 a								15 09		15 34					15 47							
d								15 11		15 36					15 49							
Penrith North Lakes d										15 51												
Windermere 83 d																16 00						
Oxenholme Lake District 83 d								15 45							16 24	16 27						
Barrow-in-Furness 82 d																						
Lancaster [6] d										16 27					16 38	16 45						
Blackpool North 97 d									15 54													
Preston [8] 90 a								16 16	16 17	16 45					16 57	17 06						
Preston [8] 90 d								16 17	16 23	16 46					16 59	17 08						
Wigan North Western 90 d								16 29	16 36						17 11	17 23						
Warrington Bank Quay d								16 40	16 47						17 22							
Bolton 82 a										17s04												
Manchester Picc. [10] 82 a										17 24						17 59						
Manchester Airport a										17 46						18 18						
Liverpool Lime Street [10] 91 a																						
d				16 05								16 35	16 47							17 05		
Liverpool South Pkwy [7] 91 d				16 17								16 45								17 17		
Runcorn 91 d				16 25								16 52	17 03							17 26		
Manchester Picc. [10] 84 d		16 05	16 15		16 27		16 35							16 55				17 05	17 15		17 27	17 35
Stockport 84 d		16 13	16 23		16 36		16 43							17 04				17 13	17 23		17 36	17 43
Wilmslow 84 d														17 11								
Holyhead 81 d																						
Bangor (Gwynedd) 81 d																						
Llandudno Junction 81 d																						
Wrexham General 75 d																						
Chester 81 d						16 35																
Crewe [10] 81,91 a				16 46		16 54		16 57				17 18	17 22	17 27						17 48		
d	16 33			16 49		16 56		17 01			17 02	17 19	17 23	17 29			17 33			17 49		
Macclesfield d		16 26			16 49		16 56											17 26				17 56
Stoke-on-Trent 84 d		16 44	16 50		17 07		17 12				17 26							17 44	17 50		18 07	18 12
Stafford a	16 51	17 00		17 08	17 24						17 44	17 39	17 40				17 51	18 00		18 07	18 23	
d	16 55	17 03		17 08	17 25						17 45	17 39	17 41				17 55	18 03		18 08	18 28	
Penkridge a				17 14								17 46								18 13		
Wolverhampton [7] a		17 16		17 25	17 38			17 33			18 02	17 58						18 16		18 25	18 41	
BirminghamNewSt [12] 68 a		17 33		17 50	17 58			18 05			18 25	18 20						18 33		18 49	18 58	
Birmingham International 68 a				18 05	18 13			18 19			18 44									19 05	19 13	
Coventry 68 a				18 20	18 24			18 30			18 59									19 20	19 24	
Lichfield Trent Valley a	17 12												17 56				18 12					
Tamworth Low Level a	17 19																18 19					
Nuneaton a	17 34																18 34					
Rugby 66 a	17 50			18 31					17 56		19 11						18 50			19 31		
Milton Keynes Central 66 a	18 14		17 46	19 20		18 02		18 57			19 48						19 14		18 48	20 16		
Watford Junction 66 a				19 58																20 47		
London Euston [15] ⊖66 a	18 51		18 20	20 17		18 36	18 41	19 34	18 53				19 07	19 03	19 10		19 50		19 22	21 10		19 38

A To Bristol Temple Meads　B To Bournemouth　C To Cardiff Central

Refer to Operator websites for full information about Sleeper Services. Contact details for train operators available at National Rail Enquiries

Table T065-R

Saturdays
21 December to 16 May

Scotland to Manchester, West Midlands & London via the West Coast. North West England to West Midlands & London

	VT	TP	LM	LM	VT	VT	LM	VT	XC	VT	NT	LM	XC	VT	VT	TP	LM	LM	VT	VT	LM	VT
	◇1	◇1	1	1	◇1	◇1	1	◇1	◇1	◇1	◇	1	◇1	◇1	◇1	◇1	1	1	◇1	◇1	1	◇1
							A		B				C								A	
Inverness 229 d																						
Aberdeen 229 d																						
Dundee 229 d																						
Perth 229 d																						
Fort William 227 d																						
Edinburgh [10] d	14 52															16 11						
Haymarket d	14 57															16u15						
GlasgowCentral [15] 226,216,225 d		15 09						15 40							16 00							16 40
Motherwell 226 d		15 24																				16 55
Carstairs 226,225 d																						
Lockerbie 225,226 d		16 08														17 10						
Carlisle [8] 216 a	16 06	16 29						16 47							17 09	17 30						17 51
d	16 08	16 33						16 49							17 11	17 35						17 52
Penrith North Lakes d	16 22	16 48						17 03								17 50						
Windermere 83 d																						
Oxenholme Lake District 83 d		17 12													17 45	18 14						18 26
Barrow-in-Furness 82 d											16 45											
Lancaster [6] d	16 57	17 27						17 38			17 46					18 29						18 41
Blackpool North 97 d																						
Preston [8] 90 a	17 16	17 44						17 56			18 06				18 15	18 47						19 00
Preston [8] 90 d	17 17	17 46						17 59			18 08				18 17	18 48						19 02
Wigan North Western 90 d	17 29							18 11			18 23				18 29							19 14
Warrington Bank Quay d	17 40							18 22							18 40							19 25
Bolton 82 a		18s04																				
Manchester Picc. [10] 82 a		18 23									18 58					19 24						
Manchester Airport a		18 46									19 17					19 48						
Liverpool Lime Street [10] 91 a																						
d				17 34	17 47							18 06						18 34	18 47			
Liverpool South Pkwy [7] 91 d				17 44								18 16						18 44				
Runcorn 91 d				17 51	18 03							18 23						18 51	19 03			
Manchester Picc. [10] 84 d						17 55			18 05	18 15			18 27	18 35						18 55		
Stockport 84 d						18 03			18 13	18 23			18 36	18 43						19 04		
Wilmslow 84 d						18 11														19 11		
Holyhead 81 d																						
Bangor (Gwynedd) 81 d																						
Llandudno Junction 81 d																						
Wrexham General 75 d																						
Chester 81 d																						
Crewe [10] 81,91 a	17 57			18 18		18 26						18 48			18 57			19 16	19 21	19 27		
d	18 01		18 01	18 20		18 28	18 33					18 49			19 01		19 01	19 19	19 23	19 29	19 33	
Macclesfield d									18 26					18 56								
Stoke-on-Trent 84 d			18 26						18 44	18 50			19 07	19 12			19 26					
Stafford a			18 45	18 38	18 35		18 54		19 00			19 08	19 23				19 45	19 38	19 40		19 51	
d			18 46	18 39	18 36		18 55		19 03			19 09	19 28				19 46	19 41	19 41		19 52	
Penkridge a				18 45								19 15						19 46				
Wolverhampton [7] a	18 33		19 03	18 58					19 16			19 26	19 41		19 34		20 02	19 58				
BirminghamNewSt [12] 68 a	19 05		19 25	19 20					19 33			19 49	19 58		20 05		20 26	20 20				
Birmingham International 68 a	19 19		19 44									20 05	20 13		20 19		20 44					
Coventry 68 a	19 30		19 59									20 20	20 24		20 30		20 59					
Lichfield Trent Valley a							19 12														20 08	
Tamworth Low Level a							19 19														20 15	
Nuneaton a							19 34														20 29	
Rugby 66 a	19 42		20 11				19 50					20 31			20 42		21 11				20 46	
Milton Keynes Central 66 a	20 05		20 50							19 46		21 15			21 04		21 58					20 43
Watford Junction 66 a	20s33		21 29									21 53			21s36		22 30					21s18
London Euston [15] ⊖66 a	20 55		21 54		19 58	20 01		20 13		20 34		22 12		20 59	21 57		22 53		21 13	21 23		21 40

A To Northampton　B To Plymouth　C To Bournemouth

Refer to Operator websites for full information about Sleeper Services. Contact details for train operators available at National Rail Enquiries

Table T065-R

Saturdays
21 December to 16 May

Scotland to Manchester, West Midlands & London via the West Coast. North West England to West Midlands & London

Station	XC	LM	TP	XC	VT	LM	VT	TP	LM	VT	LM	LM	XC	NT	VT	NT	LM	VT	XC	VT	TP
	A			B		C					D			E		F	G				
Inverness 229 d																					
Aberdeen 229 d																					
Dundee 229 d																					
Perth 229 d																					
Fort William 227 d																					
Edinburgh d							16 52														18 12
Haymarket d							16 57														18u16
GlasgowCentral 226,216,225 d			16 29					17 08							17 40			18 00			
Motherwell 226 d								17 23													
Carstairs 226,225 d			17 08																		
Lockerbie 225,226 d								18 08							18 33						19 11
Carlisle 216 a			18 03				18 09	18 28							18 51			19 10			19 31
Carlisle d			18 04				18 09	18 33							18 53			19 11			19 34
Penrith North Lakes d								18 48							19 07						19 49
Windermere 83 d														18 55							
Oxenholme Lake District 83 d							18 45	19 12						19 17	19 30						20 13
Barrow-in-Furness 82 d																					
Lancaster d			18 54				19 00	19 27						19 34	19 44			19 58			20 28
Blackpool North 97 d																←					
Preston 90 a			19 13				19 18	19 45						19 55	20 03	19 55		20 15			20 45
Preston 90 d			19 14				19 20	19 47						20 09	20 05	20 09		20 18			20 47
Wigan North Western 90 d							19 32							→	20 17	20 25		20 30			
Warrington Bank Quay d							19 43								20 28			20 41			
Bolton 82 a								20s05													21s05
Manchester Picc. 82 a								20 24								20 59					21 24
Manchester Airport a								20 48								21 20					21 47
Liverpool Lime Street 91 a			19 59																		
Liverpool Lime Street d		19 11							19 35	19 48							20 04				
Liverpool South Pkwy 91 d		19 21							19 45								20 14				
Runcorn 91 d		19 30							19 52	20 05							20 22				
Manchester Picc. 84 d	19 05			19 27	19 35								20 05						20 27	20 35	
Stockport 84 d	19 13			19 36	19 43								20 13						20 36	20 43	
Wilmslow 84 d																					
Holyhead 81 d																					
Bangor (Gwynedd) 81 d																					
Llandudno Junction 81 d																					
Wrexham General 75 d																					
Chester 81 d																					
Crewe 81,91 a		19 51					20 02		20 17	20 22					20 47		20 51	21 01			
Crewe d		19 53				20 02	20 03		20 19	20 23		20 38			20 49		20 52	21 02			
Macclesfield d	19 26			19 49	19 56								20 26						20 49	20 56	
Stoke-on-Trent 84 d	19 44			20 07	20 12	20 26					←		20 44						21 07	21 12	
Stafford a	20 00	20 11		20 24		20 45			20 40	20 41	20 45	20 56	21 00				21 12		21 22		
Stafford d	20 03	20 11		20 28		20 45			20 40	20 43	20 45	20 58	21 03				21 13		21 28		
Penkridge a		20 17				→			20 46								21 18				
Wolverhampton a	20 16	20 28		20 41			20 34		20 58		21 03		21 16				21 30	21 34	21 41		
BirminghamNewSt 68 a	20 33	20 50		20 58			21 05		21 20		21 24		21 33				21 50	21 53	22 00		
Birmingham International 68 a		21 05		21 13			21 19				21 45						22 05				
Coventry 68 a		21 20		21 24			21 30				22 00						22 20				
Lichfield Trent Valley a												21 15									
Tamworth Low Level a												21 21									
Nuneaton a												21 36									
Rugby 66 a		21 31					21 42				22 11	21 52					22 31				
Milton Keynes Central 66 a		22 21			21 10		22 04				22 58	22 15			21 51					22 10	
Watford Junction 66 a		23 06					22s34				23 44									22s39	
London Euston 66 a		23 31			22 01		22 56			22 18	00 05	23 03			22 47					23 00	

A To Bristol Temple Meads
B To Southampton Central. ✠ to BirminghamNewSt
C To London Euston
D From Crewe
E To Manchester Airport
F From Windermere
G To Northampton

Refer to Operator websites for full information about Sleeper Services. Contact details for train operators available at National Rail Enquiries

Table T065-R

Saturdays
21 December to 16 May

Scotland to Manchester, West Midlands & London via the West Coast. North West England to West Midlands & London

Station	NT	LM	LM	LM	XC	VT	NT	LM	XC	VT	XC	TP	NT	LM	LM	NT	NT
	A	B		C			D		B		E		F			G	
Inverness 229 d																	
Aberdeen 229 d																	
Dundee 229 d																	
Perth 229 d																	
Fort William 227 d																	
Edinburgh d										18 52							
Haymarket d										18 56							
GlasgowCentral 226,216,225 d						18 40						18 47					
Motherwell 226 d																	
Carstairs 226,225 d																	
Lockerbie 225,226 d												19 55					
Carlisle 216 a						19 47				20 03		20 16					
Carlisle d						19 49				20 09		20 17					
Penrith North Lakes d						20 03				20 23		20 32					
Windermere 83 d													20 43			22 26	22 25
Oxenholme Lake District 83 d						20 26				20 47		20 56	21 02			22 47	23 10
Barrow-in-Furness 82 d	19 34																
Lancaster d	20 35					20 41				21 02		21 11	21a26			23 06	23 55
Blackpool North 97 d							←										
Preston 90 a	20 56					20 59	20 56			21 19		21 29				23 29	00 35
Preston 90 d	21 05					21 02	21 05			21 22		21 36					
Wigan North Western 90 d	→					21 14				21 33							
Warrington Bank Quay d						21 25				21 44							
Bolton 82 a																	
Manchester Picc. 82 a							21 48					22 19					
Manchester Airport a							22 04					22 39					
Liverpool Lime Street 91 a																	
Liverpool Lime Street d			20 35					21 15						21 34	22 03		
Liverpool South Pkwy 91 d			20 45					21 26						21 44	22 14		
Runcorn 91 d			20 52					21 34						21 51	22 21		
Manchester Picc. 84 d					21 05				21 27								
Stockport 84 d					21 13				21 36								
Wilmslow 84 d																	
Holyhead 81 d																	
Bangor (Gwynedd) 81 d																	
Llandudno Junction 81 d																	
Wrexham General 75 d																	
Chester 81 d																	
Crewe 81,91 a			21 16			21 44		22 00		22 04				22 20	22 44		
Crewe d		21 02	21 19			21 45				22 06				22 21			
Macclesfield d					21 26				21 49								
Stoke-on-Trent 84 d		21 26		←	21 44				22 07		←						
Stafford a		21 44	21 38	21 44	22 00	22 07			22 22	22 24	22 22			22 40			
Stafford d		21 45	21 38	21 45	22 03	22 08			22 30	22 25	22 30			22 41			
Penkridge a		→	21 44						→					22 46			
Wolverhampton a			21 55	21 59	22 16	22 22				22 38	22 43			22 57			
BirminghamNewSt 68 a			22 17	22 25	22 33	22 49				22 57	23 00			23 18			
Birmingham International 68 a																	
Coventry 68 a																	
Lichfield Trent Valley a																	
Tamworth Low Level a																	
Nuneaton a																	
Rugby 66 a																	
Milton Keynes Central 66 a																	
Watford Junction 66 a																	
London Euston 66 a																	

A To Manchester Airport
B To Birmingham New Street
C From Crewe
D From Barrow-in-Furness
E From Manchester Piccadilly
F from 11 January until 15 February, from 4 April
G from 22 February until 28 March

Refer to Operator websites for full information about Sleeper Services. Contact details for train operators available at National Rail Enquiries

Table T065-R

Sundays

15 December to 10 May

Scotland to Manchester, West Midlands & London via the West Coast. North West England to West Midlands & London

	NT	VT	VT	LM	VT	XC	LM	VT	LM	VT	VT	LM	LM	XC	LM	LM	VT	LM	VT	VT	LM	NT
	A					B	C		D					B		C		D	E	F		G
Inverness 229 d																						
Aberdeen 229 d																						
Dundee 229 d																						
Perth 229 d																						
Fort William 227 d																						
Edinburgh 10 d																						
Haymarket d																						
GlasgowCentral 15 226,216,225 d																						
Motherwell 226 d																						
Carstairs 226,225 d																						
Lockerbie 225,226 d																						
Carlisle 8 216 a																						
d																						
Penrith North Lakes d																						
Windermere 83 d																						
Oxenholme Lake District 83 d																						
Barrow-in-Furness 82 d																						08 40
Lancaster 6 d																						09 40
Blackpool North 97 d																						
Preston 8 90 a																						10 02
Preston 8 90 d										09 00									10 00	10 00		10 08
Wigan North Western 90 d										09 11									10 12	10 12		10a24
Warrington Bank Quay d										09 22									10 22	10 22		
Bolton 82 a																						
Manchester Picc. 10 82 a																						
Manchester Airport a																						
Liverpool Lime Street 10 91 a																						
d					08 18			08 38									09 38					
Liverpool South Pkwy 7 91 d																						
Runcorn 91 d					08 35			08 54									09 54					
Manchester Picc. 10 84 d		08 05	08 20			08 27					09 20			09 27								
Stockport 84 d		08 14	08 28			08 35					09 28			09 35								
Wilmslow 84 d	00 02	08 22				08 43																
Holyhead 81 d																						
Bangor (Gwynedd) 81 d																						
Llandudno Junction 81 d																						
Wrexham General 75 d																						
Chester 81 d																						
Crewe 10 81,91 a	00 32	08 39			08 52	09 01		09 11		09 41							10 12		10 41	10 41		
d		08 43		08 48	08 53	09 05	09 12	09 13		09 43		09 49	09 52		10 10	10 10	10 14		10 44	10 44	10 51	
Macclesfield d			08 41								09 40			09 48								
Stoke-on-Trent 84 d			08 57				09 35		←		10 00			10 06		10 33		←				
Stafford a		09 01		09 06		09 24	09 55	09 31	09 55			10 06	10 10	10 22	10 29	10 52	10 32	10 52			11 08	
d		09 02		09 11		09 28	09 56	09 32	09 56			10 15	10 20	10 28	10 31	10 58	10 33	10 58			11 12	
Penkridge a				09 17			→		10 01						10 36	→						
Wolverhampton 7 a				09 28		09 41			10 12			10 29		10 41	10 48			11 12			11 26	
BirminghamNewSt 12 68 a				09 50		09 58			10 28			10 51		10 59	11 09			11 29			11 49	
Birmingham International 68 a				10 03		10 13			10 51			11 03		11 13	11 23			11 52			12 04	
Coventry 68 a				10 15		10 24			11 05			11 14		11 24	11 35			12 06			12 15	
Lichfield Trent Valley a					09 23								10 36									
Tamworth Low Level a													10 43									
Nuneaton a								09 54					10 58				10 55					
Rugby 66 a				10 26						10 31		11 26	11 19		11 47				11 31	11 31	12 26	
Milton Keynes Central 66 a				11 22	10 19					11 06	11 16	12 04	11 58		12 26		11 45		12 05	12 05	13 04	
Watford Junction 66 a		10s33	10s39	11 53				11s15		11s42		12 38	12 31		13 00						13 38	
London Euston 15 66 a		10 56	11 01	12 16	11 04			11 34		12 02	12 06	12 59	12 49		13 18		12 29		12 42	12 43	14 01	

A not 15 December. From Manchester Piccadilly
B To Bournemouth
C To Coventry
D From Crewe
E until 16 February
F from 23 February
G until 5 January, from 23 February until 29 March. To Manchester Oxford Road

Refer to Operator websites for full information about Sleeper Services. Contact details for train operators available at National Rail Enquiries

Table T065-R

Sundays

15 December to 10 May

Scotland to Manchester, West Midlands & London via the West Coast. North West England to West Midlands & London

	VT	VT	XC	VT	LM	LM	VT	LM	LM	VT	VT	NT	VT	LM	VT	XC	VT	TP	TP	LM	LM	LM
			A			B			C							A		D	E	B		
Inverness 229 d																						
Aberdeen 229 d																						
Dundee 229 d																						
Perth 229 d																						
Fort William 227 d																						
Edinburgh 10 d																		09 13	09 15			
Haymarket d																		09 18	09 20			
GlasgowCentral 15 226,216,225 d																						
Motherwell 226 d																						
Carstairs 226,225 d																						
Lockerbie 225,226 d																		10 12	10 23			
Carlisle 8 216 a																		10 33	10 43			
d																		10 34	10 45			
Penrith North Lakes d																		10 49	11 00			
Windermere 83 d																						
Oxenholme Lake District 83 d																		11 13	11 23			
Barrow-in-Furness 82 d												09 47										
Lancaster 6 d												10 47						11 28	11 38			
Blackpool North 97 d																						
Preston 8 90 a												11 08						11 46	11 56			
Preston 8 90 d		10 17								10 58		11 09			11 17			11 57	11 57			
Wigan North Western 90 d		10 28								11 09		11 24			11 28							
Warrington Bank Quay d		10 39								11 20					11 40							
Bolton 82 a																						
Manchester Picc. 10 82 a												12 01						12 40	12 40			
Manchester Airport a												12 20						13 00	13 00			
Liverpool Lime Street 10 91 a																						
d					10 12		10 38															11 35
Liverpool South Pkwy 7 91 d					10 22																	11 45
Runcorn 91 d					10 29		10 54															11 52
Manchester Picc. 10 84 d	10 20		10 27	10 35							11 15					11 27	11 35					
Stockport 84 d	10 29		10 35	10 46							11 24					11 35	11 44					
Wilmslow 84 d	10 37																					
Holyhead 81 d																						
Bangor (Gwynedd) 81 d																						
Llandudno Junction 81 d																						
Wrexham General 75 d																						
Chester 81 d													11 28									
Crewe 10 81,91 a	10 53	10 59			10 55		11 12			11 39			11 47		11 59							12 17
d	10 55	11 02			11 05	11 12	11 14	11 23		11 42			11 49		12 02					12 12	12 16	12 19
Macclesfield d			10 48	10 57												11 48	11 57					
Stoke-on-Trent 84 d			11 06	11 15		11 34			←		11 52					12 06	12 14			12 34		
Stafford a			11 23		11 24	11 53	11 34	11 41	11 53							12 24				12 53	12 34	12 37
d			11 28		11 30	11 53	11 36	11 41	11 53					12 12		12 28				12 53	12 37	12 38
Penkridge a					11 36	→														→		12 44
Wolverhampton 7 a		11 34	11 42		11 47				12 07					12 26	12 33	12 41						12 55
BirminghamNewSt 12 68 a		11 55	12 00		12 11				12 27					12 46	12 50	12 58						13 14
Birmingham International 68 a			12 13		12 23				12 53					13 04		13 13						13 28
Coventry 68 a			12 24		12 36				13 06					13 17		13 24						13 47
Lichfield Trent Valley a								11 58													12 53	
Tamworth Low Level a								12 04													13 00	
Nuneaton a							11 58	12 19					12 31								13 15	
Rugby 66 a					12 47			12 35						13 27							13 30	13 57
Milton Keynes Central 66 a				12 21	13 27			12 58			12 50		13 03	14 04							13 54	14 41
Watford Junction 66 a	12s36				14 04		12s51							14 38								15 18
London Euston 15 66 a	12 53			12 57	14 24		13 09	13 49		13 20	13 28		13 42	15 01			13 45				14 33	15 40

A To Bournemouth
B To Coventry
C From Crewe
D until 5 January, from 23 February until 29 March
E from 12 January until 16 February, from 5 April

Refer to Operator websites for full information about Sleeper Services. Contact details for train operators available at National Rail Enquiries

Table T065-R

Sundays

15 December to 10 May

Scotland to Manchester, West Midlands & London via the West Coast. North West England to West Midlands & London

	VT		LM	VT	VT	VT	NT	VT	LM	XC	VT		VT	LM	TP	LM	LM	VT	LM	TP	VT		XC	NT
	◇1		1	◇1	◇1	◇1	◇	◇1	1	◇1	◇1		◇1	1	◇1	1	1	◇1	1	◇1	◇1		◇1	◇
			A							B				C					A				D	E
Inverness 229 d																								
Aberdeen 229 d																								
Dundee 229 d																								
Perth 229 d																								
Fort William 227 d																								
Edinburgh 10 d															10 13									
Haymarket d															10u17									
GlasgowCentral 15 226,216,225 d					09 38															10 13				
Motherwell 226 d																				10 30				
Carstairs 226,225 d																								
Lockerbie 225,226 d															11 12					11 17				
Carlisle 8 216 a					10 49										11 32					11 38				
d					10 51										11 34					11 40				
Penrith North Lakes d					11 05										11 49									
Windermere 83 d																								
Oxenholme Lake District 83 d					11 28										12 13					12 18				
Barrow-in-Furness 82 d							10 47																	11 37
Lancaster 6 d					11 43		11 49						11 58		12 28					12 33				12 39
Blackpool North 97 d																								
Preston 8 90 a					12 01		12 09						12 15		12 45					12 52				13 00
Preston 8 90 d					12 04		12 11						12 17		12 47					12 54				13 09
Wigan North Western 90 d					12 15								12 29							13 08				→
Warrington Bank Quay d					12 26								12 40											
Bolton 82 a							12 34								13s05									
Manchester Picc. 10 82 a							12 56								13 25									
Manchester Airport a							13 17								13 42									
Liverpool Lime Street 10 91 a																				13 43				
d	11 47																12 33	12 47						
Liverpool South Pkwy 7 91 d																	12 43							
Runcorn 91 d	12 05																12 50	13 05						
Manchester Picc. 10 84 d				11 55		12 15				12 27	12 35										12 55		13 05	
Stockport 84 d				12 05		12 21				12 35	12 43										13 05		13 13	
Wilmslow 84 d				12 13																	13 13			
Holyhead 81 d								10 55																
Bangor (Gwynedd) 81 d								11 22																
Llandudno Junction 81 d								11 40																
Wrexham General 75 d																								
Chester 81 d								12 33																
Crewe 10 81,91 a	12 21			12 29				12 53					12 59				13 17	13 21			13 29			
d	12 23			12 30				12 56					13 02	13 12		13 16	13 19	13 23			13 30			
Macclesfield d										12 48	12 57												13 26	
Stoke-on-Trent 84 d			←			12 49				13 06	13 14			13 33					←				13 45	
Stafford a	12 42		12 53							13 24				13 53		13 34	13 38	13 42	13 53				14 00	
d	12 43		12 53						13 13	13 28				13 53		13 37	13 38	13 43	13 53				14 03	
Penkridge a														→			13 44							
Wolverhampton 7 a			13 07						13 27	13 41			13 32				13 55		14 10				14 16	
BirminghamNewSt 12 68 a			13 24						13 50	13 58			14 05				14 14		14 27				14 33	
Birmingham International 68 a			13 52						14 04	14 13			14 19				14 28		14 52					
Coventry 68 a			14 05						14 17	14 24			14 30				14 47		15 07					
Lichfield Trent Valley a																13 53								
Tamworth Low Level a																14 00								
Nuneaton a																14 15								
Rugby 66 a									14 27							14 30	14 57							
Milton Keynes Central 66 a						13 45		14 03	15 04				14 58			14 54	15 41							
Watford Junction 66 a									15 38								16 18							
London Euston 15 ⊖66 a	14 03			14 09	14 15	14 26		14 40	16 01		14 46		15 37			15 33	16 40	15 03			15 06			

A From Crewe
B To Bournemouth
C To Coventry
D To Paignton
E To Manchester Airport

Refer to Operator websites for full information about Sleeper Services. Contact details for train operators available at National Rail Enquiries

Table T065-R

Sundays

15 December to 10 May

Scotland to Manchester, West Midlands & London via the West Coast. North West England to West Midlands & London

	VT	NT	VT	VT	VT	LM	XC		VT	VT	LM	TP	LM	LM	VT	LM	VT		VT	XC	VT	VT	VT	NT
	◇1	◇	◇1	◇1	◇1	1	◇1		◇1	◇1	1	◇1	1	1	◇1	1	◇1		◇1	◇1	◇1	◇1	◇1	◇
		A					B				C					D				E				
Inverness 229 d																								
Aberdeen 229 d																								
Dundee 229 d																								
Perth 229 d																								
Fort William 227 d																								
Edinburgh 10 d										10 51														
Haymarket d										10 55														
GlasgowCentral 15 226,216,225 d	10 38											11 05							11 38					
Motherwell 226 d	10 54											11 25												
Carstairs 226,225 d																								
Lockerbie 225,226 d												12 09												
Carlisle 8 216 a	11 51									12 05		12 30							12 47					
d	11 53									12 07		12 33							12 49					
Penrith North Lakes d	12 07											12 48												
Windermere 83 d																								13 08
Oxenholme Lake District 83 d	12 31									12 43		13 12							13 23					13 28
Barrow-in-Furness 82 d																								
Lancaster 6 d	12 45									12 57		13 27							13 38					13 46
Blackpool North 97 d		←																						
Preston 8 90 a	13 03	13 00								13 15		13 44							13 56					14 07
Preston 8 90 d	13 06	13 09								13 17		13 46							13 59					14 10
Wigan North Western 90 d	13 17	13 23								13 29									14 11					14 24
Warrington Bank Quay d	13 29									13 40									14 22					
Bolton 82 a												14s05												
Manchester Picc. 10 82 a		14 00										14 26												15 01
Manchester Airport a		14 18										14 42												15 19
Liverpool Lime Street 10 91 a																								
d														13 35	13 47									
Liverpool South Pkwy 7 91 d														13 45										
Runcorn 91 d														13 52	14 05									
Manchester Picc. 10 84 d			13 15				13 27		13 35								13 55			14 05	14 15			
Stockport 84 d			13 23				13 37		13 42								14 05			14 13	14 22			
Wilmslow 84 d																	14 12							
Holyhead 81 d					11 50																	12 50		
Bangor (Gwynedd) 81 d					12 17																	13 18		
Llandudno Junction 81 d					12 35																	13 36		
Wrexham General 75 d																								
Chester 81 d				13 30	13 30																	14 33	14 33	
Crewe 10 81,91 a				13 50	13 50					13 59				14 17	14 21		14 28					14 54	14 54	
d				13 52	13 53					14 02	14 12		14 16	14 19	14 23		14 30					14 55	14 56	
Macclesfield d							13 50		13 55											14 26				
Stoke-on-Trent 84 d			13 51				14 08		14 12		14 34					←				14 45	14 50			
Stafford a							14 24				14 53		14 34	14 38	14 43	14 53				15 00				
d						14 12	14 28				14 53		14 37	14 40	14 43	14 53				15 03				
Penkridge a											→			14 45										
Wolverhampton 7 a						14 26	14 41			14 33				14 56		15 11				15 16				
BirminghamNewSt 12 68 a						14 50	14 58			15 05				15 14		15 27				15 33				
Birmingham International 68 a						15 04	15 13			15 19				15 28		15 52								
Coventry 68 a						15 17	15 24			15 30				15 47		16 06								
Lichfield Trent Valley a													14 53											
Tamworth Low Level a													15 00											
Nuneaton a				14 31	14 31								15 15											
Rugby 66 a						15 27							15 30	15 57										
Milton Keynes Central 66 a			14 48	15 03	15 03	16 04				15 58			15 54	16 41							15 48	16 03	16 03	
Watford Junction 66 a						16 38								17 18										
London Euston 15 ⊖66 a	15 18		15 25	15 41	15 41	17 01			15 46	16 37			16 33	17 40	16 03		16 06		16 11		16 26	16 40	16 40	

A From Barrow-in-Furness
B To Bournemouth
C To Coventry
D From Crewe
E To Bristol Temple Meads

Refer to Operator websites for full information about Sleeper Services. Contact details for train operators available at National Rail Enquiries

Table T065-R

Sundays

15 December to 10 May

Scotland to Manchester, West Midlands & London via the West Coast. North West England to West Midlands & London

			LM	XC	VT	VT	LM	TP	LM	LM	VT	LM	VT	VT	XC	VT	NT	VT	LM	XC	VT	VT	LM
			■	◇■	◇■	◇■	■	◇■	■	■	◇■	■	◇■	◇■	◇■	◇■	◇	◇■	■	◇■	◇■	◇■	■
				A			B					C			D					A			B
Inverness	229	d																					
Aberdeen	229	d																					
Dundee	229	d																					
Perth	229	d																					
Fort William	227	d																					
Edinburgh		d						12 12														12 51	
Haymarket		d						12u16														12 55	
Glasgow Central	226,216,225	d				11 55								12 38									
Motherwell	226	d																					
Carstairs	226,225	d																					
Lockerbie	225,226	d						13 11															
Carlisle	216	a				13 06		13 31						13 47								14 04	
		d				13 07		13 33						13 49								14 07	
Penrith North Lakes		d						13 48														14 22	
Windermere	83	d																					
Oxenholme Lake District	83	d						14 12						14 23									
Barrow-in-Furness	82	d															13 47						
Lancaster		d				13 57		14 27						14 38			14 47					14 57	
Blackpool North	97	d																					
Preston	90	a				14 15		14 45						14 56			15 08					15 15	
Preston	90	d				14 17		14 46						14 59			15 09					15 17	
Wigan North Western	90	d				14 29								15 11			15 23					15 28	
Warrington Bank Quay		d				14 41								15 22								15 39	
Bolton	82	a						15s04															
Manchester Picc.	82	a						15 24									16 01						
Manchester Airport		a						15 42									16 19						
Liverpool Lime Street	91	a																					
		d								14 32	14 47												
Liverpool South Pkwy	91	d								14 43													
Runcorn	91	d								14 50	15 05												
Manchester Picc.	84	d		14 27	14 35								14 55		15 05	15 15				15 27	15 35		
Stockport	84	d		14 35	14 42								15 04		15 13	15 22				15 36	15 42		
Wilmslow	84	d											15 12										
Holyhead	81	d																13 55					
Bangor (Gwynedd)	81	d																14 22					
Llandudno Junction	81	d																14 40					
Wrexham General	75	d																					
Chester	81	d																15 32					
Crewe	81,91	a				15 00				15 17	15 21		15 28					15 52				15 59	
		d				15 02	15 15		15 16	15 19	15 23		15 30					15 54				16 01	16 15
Macclesfield		d		14 48	14 55										15 26					15 49	15 55		
Stoke-on-Trent	84	d		15 06	15 12		15 37					←			15 45	15 50				16 07	16 12		16 37
Stafford		a		15 23			15 57		15 34	15 39	15 42	15 57			16 00					16 23			16 56
		d	15 12	15 28			15 57		15 37	15 40	15 43	15 57			16 03				16 12	16 28			16 57
Penkridge		a					↦			15 45													↦
Wolverhampton		a	15 26	15 41		15 34				15 56		16 11			16 16				16 26	16 41		16 32	
Birmingham New St	68	a	15 50	15 58		16 05				16 14		16 28			16 34				16 50	16 58		17 05	
Birmingham International	68	a	16 04	16 13		16 19				16 28		16 53							17 04	17 13		17 19	
Coventry	68	a	16 17	16 24		16 30				16 47		17 06							17 17	17 24		17 30	
Lichfield Trent Valley		a							15 53														
Tamworth Low Level		a							16 00														
Nuneaton		a							16 15														
Rugby	66	a	16 27						16 30	16 57									17 27				
Milton Keynes Central	66	a	17 04			16 58			16 53	17 41						16 47		17 03	18 04			17 57	
Watford Junction	66	a	17 38							18 18									18 38				
London Euston	66	a	18 01		16 45	17 36			17 32	18 40	17 04		17 07	17 11		17 27		17 40	19 01		17 45	18 35	

A To Bournemouth
B To Coventry
C From Crewe
D To Bristol Temple Meads

Refer to Operator websites for full information about Sleeper Services. Contact details for train operators available at National Rail Enquiries

Table T065-R

Sundays

15 December to 10 May

Scotland to Manchester, West Midlands & London via the West Coast. North West England to West Midlands & London

			TP	LM	LM	VT	LM	VT	VT	XC	VT	NT	VT	LM	XC	VT	VT	VT	LM	LM	LM	VT	LM	TP
			◇■	■	■	◇■	■	◇■	◇■	◇■	◇■	◇	◇■	■	◇■	◇■	◇■	◇■	■	■	■	◇■	■	◇■
							A			B					C		D	E	F				A	
Inverness	229	d																						
Aberdeen	229	d																						
Dundee	229	d																						
Perth	229	d																						
Fort William	227	d																						
Edinburgh		d																						
Haymarket		d																						
Glasgow Central	226,216,225	d	13 06						13 38								13 55	13 55						14 05
Motherwell	226	d	13 25																					
Carstairs	226,225	d																						
Lockerbie	225,226	d	14 09																					
Carlisle	216	a	14 30						14 47								15 09	15 09						15 21
		d	14 33						14 49								15 11	15 11						15 23
Penrith North Lakes		d	14 48																					15 38
Windermere	83	d																						
Oxenholme Lake District	83	d	15 14						15 23								15 45	15 45						16 02
Barrow-in-Furness	82	d										14 44												
Lancaster		d	15 29						15 38			15 47												16 17
Blackpool North	97	d																						
Preston	90	a	15 46						15 56			16 08					16 14	16 14						16 36
Preston	90	d	15 48						15 59			16 09					16 17	16 17						16 38
Wigan North Western	90	d							16 11			16 23					16 30	16 30						16 50
Warrington Bank Quay		d							16 22								16 41	16 41						
Bolton	82	a	16s06																					
Manchester Picc.	82	a	16 24									17 01												
Manchester Airport		a	16 42									17 19												
Liverpool Lime Street	91	a																						17 28
		d			15 35	15 47							16 19								16 32	16 47		
Liverpool South Pkwy	91	d			15 45																16 43			
Runcorn	91	d			15 52	16 05							16 35								16 50	17 05		
Manchester Picc.	84	d						15 55		16 05	16 15				16 27	16 35								
Stockport	84	d						16 03		16 13	16 23				16 36	16 42								
Wilmslow	84	d						16 11																
Holyhead	81	d																						
Bangor (Gwynedd)	81	d																						
Llandudno Junction	81	d																						
Wrexham General	75	d																						
Chester	81	d																						
Crewe	81,91	a			16 17	16 21		16 27					16 51				16 59	16 59			17 17	17 21		
		d		16 16	16 19	16 23		16 30					16 54				17 02	17 02	17 15	17 16	17 19	17 23		
Macclesfield		d								16 26					16 50	16 55								
Stoke-on-Trent	84	d					←			16 45	16 50				17 08	17 12			17 37				←	
Stafford		a		16 34	16 37	16 42	16 56			17 00					17 24				17 57	17 34	17 38	17 41	17 57	
		d		16 37	16 38	16 43	16 57			17 03				17 12	17 25				17 58	17 37	17 38	17 42	17 58	
Penkridge		a			16 43														↦		17 44			
Wolverhampton		a			16 54		17 11			17 16				17 26	17 39		17 33	17 33			17 55		18 13	
Birmingham New St	68	a			17 14		17 27			17 34				17 51	17 59		18 05	18 05			18 14		18 30	
Birmingham International	68	a			17 28		17 52							18 04	18 13		18 19	18 19			18 28		18 52	
Coventry	68	a			17 47		18 06							18 15	18 24		18 30	18 30			18 47		19 06	
Lichfield Trent Valley		a		16 53									17 24							17 53				
Tamworth Low Level		a		17 00																18 00				
Nuneaton		a		17 15																18 15				
Rugby	66	a		17 30	17 57									18 25						18 30	18 57			
Milton Keynes Central	66	a		17 53	18 41						17 47		18 02	19 04			18 59	19 00		18 53	19 41			
Watford Junction	66	a			19 18									19 38							20 18			
London Euston	66	a		18 32	19 40	18 03		18 06	18 11		18 27		18 39	20 01		18 46	19 36	19 39		19 32	20 40	19 02		

A From Crewe
B To Bristol Temple Meads
C To Bournemouth
D until 16 February
E from 23 February
F To Coventry

Refer to Operator websites for full information about Sleeper Services. Contact details for train operators available at National Rail Enquiries

Table T065-R

Sundays

15 December to 10 May

Scotland to Manchester, West Midlands & London via the West Coast. North West England to West Midlands & London

Station	VT	XC	TP	VT	VT	NT	VT	VT	LM	XC	VT	VT	LM	TP	LM	LM	VT	LM	VT	VT	XC	VT
		A					B	C		D					E			F			G	
Inverness 229 d																						
Aberdeen 229 d																						
Dundee 229 d																						
Perth 229 d																						
Fort William 227 d																						
Edinburgh d			14 12									14 51										
Haymarket d			14u16									14 56										
GlasgowCentral 226,216,225 d				14 38										15 05						15 38		
Motherwell 226 d														15 25								
Carstairs 226,225 d																						
Lockerbie 225,226 d			15 11											16 13								
Carlisle 216 a			15 31	15 47								16 02		16 34						16 47		
d			15 33	15 49								16 07		16 35						16 49		
Penrith North Lakes d			15 48									16 22		16 50						17 03		
Windermere 83 d						15 53																
Oxenholme Lake District 83 d			16 12	16 23		16 15								17 14								
Barrow-in-Furness 82 d																						
Lancaster d			16 27	16 38		16 46						16 57		17 29						17 38		
Blackpool North 97 d																						
Preston 90 a			16 44	16 56		17 06						17 16		17 47						17 56		
Preston 90 d			16 46	16 59		17 09						17 17		17 48						17 59		
Wigan North Western 90 d				17 10		17 23						17 30								18 11		
Warrington Bank Quay d				17 21								17 41								18 22		
Bolton 82 a			17s04											18s06								
Manchester Picc. 82 a			17 24			18 01								18 25								
Manchester Airport a			17 42			18 19								18 42								
Liverpool Lime Street 91 a																						
d																17 35	17 47					
Liverpool South Pkwy 91 d																17 45						
Runcorn 91 d																17 52	18 05					
Manchester Picc. 84 d	16 55	17 05			17 15					17 27	17 35								17 55		18 05	18 15
Stockport 84 d	17 03	17 13			17 22					17 35	17 42								18 03		18 13	18 22
Wilmslow 84 d	17 11																		18 11			
Holyhead 81 d																						
Bangor (Gwynedd) 81 d																						
Llandudno Junction 81 d																						
Wrexham General 75 d																						
Chester 81 d							17 35	17 35														
Crewe 81,91 a	17 27						17 53	17 53				18 00				18 17	18 21		18 27			
d	17 30						17 55	17 55				18 03	18 16		18 16	18 19	18 23		18 29			
Macclesfield d		17 26								17 48	17 55										18 26	
Stoke-on-Trent 84 d		17 45			17 50					18 06	18 12				18 38			←			18 46	18 51
Stafford a		18 00								18 25			18 34		18 58	18 38	18 42	18 58			19 01	
d		18 03							18 12	18 28			18 37		18 58	18 38	18 43	18 58			19 03	
Penkridge a															→	18 44						
Wolverhampton a		18 16							18 26	18 41		18 34				18 55		19 13			19 16	
BirminghamNewSt 68 a		18 33							18 51	18 59		19 05				19 14		19 30			19 33	
Birmingham International 68 a									19 04	19 13		19 19				19 28		19 52				
Coventry 68 a									19 17	19 24		19 30				19 47		20 06				
Lichfield Trent Valley a													18 53									
Tamworth Low Level a													19 00									
Nuneaton a													19 15									
Rugby 66 a									19 28				19 30			19 57						
Milton Keynes Central 66 a					18 47		19 03	19 03	20 09			19 58	19 53			20 40						19 47
Watford Junction 66 a									20 51							21 23						
London Euston 66 a	19 05			19 10	19 26		19 41	19 42	21 14		19 46	20 37	20 32			21 43	20 03		20 06	20 11		20 26

A To Plymouth
B until 16 February
C from 23 February
D To Bournemouth
E To Coventry
F From Crewe
G To Bristol Temple Meads

Refer to Operator websites for full information about Sleeper Services. Contact details for train operators available at National Rail Enquiries

NRT DECEMBER 19 EDITION

Table T065-R

Sundays

15 December to 10 May

Scotland to Manchester, West Midlands & London via the West Coast. North West England to West Midlands & London

Station	NT	VT	LM	XC	VT	VT	LM	TP	LM	VT	VT	VT	LM	LM	XC	VT	VT	LM	VT	XC	VT
			A	B			C		A					D	E	F	G	A		H	
Inverness 229 d																					
Aberdeen 229 d																					
Dundee 229 d																					
Perth 229 d																					
Fort William 227 d																					
Edinburgh d								16 14											16 51		
Haymarket d								16u18											16 55		
GlasgowCentral 226,216,225 d						15 57						16 38									
Motherwell 226 d												16 53									
Carstairs 226,225 d																					
Lockerbie 225,226 d								17 13													
Carlisle 216 a						17 08		17 33				17 49							18 05		
d						17 10		17 35				17 51							18 07		
Penrith North Lakes d								17 50				18 05									
Windermere 83 d																					
Oxenholme Lake District 83 d						17 44		18 14				18 28							18 42		
Barrow-in-Furness 82 d	16 44																				
Lancaster d	17 47							18 29				18 43							18 57		
Blackpool North 97 d																					
Preston 90 a	18 08					18 13		18 46				19 01							19 15		
Preston 90 d	18 09					18 17		18 48				19 04							19 17		
Wigan North Western 90 d	18 23					18 28						19 15							19 29		
Warrington Bank Quay d						18 40						19 27							19 40		
Bolton 82 a								19s06													
Manchester Picc. 82 a	19 01							19 25													
Manchester Airport a	19 19							19 42													
Liverpool Lime Street 91 a																					
d									18 32	18 47											
Liverpool South Pkwy 91 d									18 42												
Runcorn 91 d									18 50	19 05											
Manchester Picc. 84 d				18 27	18 35						18 55				19 05	19 15	19 15			19 27	19 35
Stockport 84 d				18 35	18 42						19 03				19 13	19 22	19 22			19 35	19 41
Wilmslow 84 d											19 11										
Holyhead 81 d																					
Bangor (Gwynedd) 81 d																					
Llandudno Junction 81 d																					
Wrexham General 75 d																					
Chester 81 d		18 35																			
Crewe 81,91 a		18 53				18 59			19 17	19 21	19 27								19 59		
d		18 55				19 01	19 15		19 18	19 23	19 29		19 33					19 50	20 02		
Macclesfield d				18 48	18 55										19 26					19 48	19 54
Stoke-on-Trent 84 d				19 06	19 12		19 38							←	19 46	19 50	19 50			20 06	20 11
Stafford a				19 22			19 58		19 37	19 41			19 51	19 58	20 01			20 09		20 22	
d			19 12	19 28			19 58		19 37	19 43			19 51	19 58	20 03			20 12		20 28	
Penkridge a							→		19 43												
Wolverhampton a			19 26	19 41		19 33			19 54					20 12	20 16			20 26	20 33	20 41	
BirminghamNewSt 68 a			19 50	19 58		20 05			20 11					20 30	20 33			20 48	20 51	20 58	
Birmingham International 68 a			20 04	20 13		20 19			20 23					20 52				21 03		21 13	
Coventry 68 a			20 17	20 24		20 30			20 37					21 06				21 16		21 24	
Lichfield Trent Valley a					19 34								20 07								
Tamworth Low Level a													20 14								
Nuneaton a													20 28								
Rugby 66 a			20 28						20 47				20 44					21 27			
Milton Keynes Central 66 a		20 03				20 59							21 06			20 47	20 47				
Watford Junction 66 a													21 38								
London Euston 66 a		20 41			20 45	21 47				21 02	21 10	21 19	21 58			21 31	21 32				22 01

A To Northampton
B To Southampton Central
C To Coventry
D From Crewe
E To Bristol Temple Meads
F until 16 February
G from 23 February
H To Reading. Catering to BirminghamNewSt

Refer to Operator websites for full information about Sleeper Services. Contact details for train operators available at National Rail Enquiries

Table T065-R

Sundays
15 December to 10 May

Scotland to Manchester, West Midlands & London via the West Coast. North West England to West Midlands & London

	TP	LM	LM	LM	VT	LM	VT	XC	AW	VT	NT	TP	LM	VT	LM	VT	LM	LM	VT	XC	NT	VT
	◇1	1	1	1	◇1	1	◇1	◇1	◇	◇1	◇	◇1	1	◇1	1	◇1	1	1	◇1	◇1	◇	◇1
		A				B		C					A				D	B				
	🛒				⊡		⊡		🛒	⊡		🛒		⊡		⊡			⊡			⊡
Inverness 229 d																						
Aberdeen 229 d																						
Dundee 229 d																						
Perth 229 d																						
Fort William 227 d																						
Edinburgh [10] 🚋 d												18 14										18 51
Haymarket 🚋 d												18u18										18 56
GlasgowCentral [15] 226,216,225 d	17 04						17 38												18 37			
Motherwell 226 d	17 20																					
Carstairs 226,225 d																						
Lockerbie 225,226 d	18 05						18 32					19 13										
Carlisle [8] 216 a	18 29						18 50					19 33							19 46			20 02
d	18 34						18 52					19 35							19 48			20 07
Penrith North Lakes d	18 49						19 06					19 50										20 22
Windermere 83 d											19 01											
Oxenholme Lake District 83 d	19 13						19 29				19 23	20 14							20 23			
Barrow-in-Furness 82 d																					19 47	
Lancaster [6] d	19 28						19 44					20 29							20 37		20 47	20 57
Blackpool North 97 🚋 d																						
Preston [8] 90 a	19 46						20 02				19 59	20 46							20 55		21 08	21 15
Preston [8] 90 d	19 47						20 05				20 09	20 48							20 57		21 09	21 17
Wigan North Western 90 d							20 17				20 23								21 08		21 23	21 30
Warrington Bank Quay d							20 28												21 19			21 41
Bolton 82 a	20s05											21s06										
Manchester Picc. [10] 82 🚋 a	20 24										20 59	21 23									21 55	
Manchester Airport ✈🚋 a	20 44										21 17	21 42									22 13	
Liverpool Lime Street [10] 91 a																						
d				19 32	19 47										20 35	20 47						
Liverpool South Pkwy [7] 91 ✈ d				19 42											20 45							
Runcorn 91 d				19 50	20 04										20 52	21 03						
Manchester Picc. [10] 84 🚋 d								20 05		20 21				20 55						21 05		
Stockport 84 d								20 13		20 27				21 03						21 13		
Wilmslow 84 d																						
Holyhead 81 ⛴ d									18 26													
Bangor (Gwynedd) 81 d									19 05													
Llandudno Junction 81 d									19 24													
Wrexham General 75 d																						
Chester 81 d									20 27													
Crewe [10] 81,91 a				20 17	20 22		20 47		20 49						21 15	21 22			21 39			22 00
d		20 04	20 16	20 19	20 24		20 49		20 52				21 08		21 19	21 24	21 33		21 41			22 03
Macclesfield d								20 26		20 40				21 16						21 26		
Stoke-on-Trent 84 d		20 25				←		20 44		20 58			21 30	21 34				←		21 46		
Stafford a		20 44	20 34	20 37	20 41	20 44		21 00	21 13				21 51		21 38	21 42	21 50	21 51	22 00	22 04		
d		20 45	20 34	20 39	20 43	20 45		21 03	21 13				21 52		21 38	21 43	21 51	21 52	22 01	22 05		
Penkridge a		→		20 44									→		21 44							
Wolverhampton [7] 🚋 a				20 55		21 00		21 16	21 32						21 55			22 06	22 13	22 18		22 32
BirminghamNewSt [12] 68 🚋 a				21 14		21 18		21 33	21 53						22 12			22 30	22 32	22 36		22 52
Birmingham International 68 ✈ a				21 28		21 50			22 07						22 26			22 53				
Coventry 68 a				21 47		22 01									22 44			23 04				
Lichfield Trent Valley a			20 51													21 59	22 07					
Tamworth Low Level a			20 57													22 06	22 14					
Nuneaton a			21 12													22 17	22 29					
Rugby 66 a			21 31	21 57											22 55	22 31	22 45					
Milton Keynes Central 66 a			22 11	22 41	21 37		21 52			21 58				22 49	23 41	23 04						
Watford Junction 66 a			22 54	23 22			22s31							23s28	00 22	23s34						
London Euston [15] ⊖66 a			23 17	23 43	22 27		22 53			22 56				23 47	00 43	23 53						

A To Coventry
B From Crewe
C To Bristol Temple Meads
D To Northampton

Refer to Operator websites for full information about Sleeper Services. Contact details for train operators available at National Rail Enquiries

Table T065-R

Sundays
15 December to 10 May

Scotland to Manchester, West Midlands & London via the West Coast. North West England to West Midlands & London

	LM	LM	LM	TP	XC	TP	NT	VT	TP	TP	NT	TP	CS	CS	CS	LM	CS	CS	CS	CS	CS	CS
	1	1	1	◇1	◇1	◇1		◇1	◇1	1		◇1	R	R	R	1	R	R	R	R	R	R
	A		B				C			D	D	E	D	D	F		D	D	D	C	C	C
				🛒		🛒		⊡	🛒	🛒		🛒	🛏 ✕	🛏 ✕	🛏 ✕		🛏 ✕	🛏 ✕	🛏 ✕	🛏 ✕	🛏 ✕	🛏 ✕
Inverness 229 d																		20 26			20 26	
Aberdeen 229 d																			21 43			21 43
Dundee 229 d																			23u09			23u09
Perth 229 d																		23u07			23u07	
Fort William 227 d																	19 00			19 00		
Edinburgh [10] 🚋 d									20 15			22 10		23 15	23u18							
Haymarket 🚋 d									20u20			22u14										
GlasgowCentral [15] 226,216,225 d				18 47		19 15		20 08		21 08			23 15									
Motherwell 226 d				19 04		19 32							23 31									
Carstairs 226,225 d													00 09									
Lockerbie 225,226 d						20 16		21 04	21 14	22 08		23 09										
Carlisle [8] 216 a				20 13		20 37		21 23	21 35	22 29		23 30	01 39	01 39								
d				20 14		20 38		21 25	21 36			23 31	01 41									
Penrith North Lakes d				20 29		20 53		21 40														
Windermere 83 d							21 38				21 44											
Oxenholme Lake District 83 d				20 53		21 17	21 57	22 04	22 12		22 16											
Barrow-in-Furness 82 d																						
Lancaster [6] d				21 12		21 32		22 20	22 27		22 35											
Blackpool North 97 🚋 d																						
Preston [8] 90 a				21 30		21 50	22 35	22 38	22 45		22 57	01 04	03s04				04s29	04s29	04s29			
Preston [8] 90 d				21 32		21 51		22 41	22 46			01 06										
Wigan North Western 90 d				21 45				22 53														
Warrington Bank Quay d								23 04														
Bolton 82 a									23s04													
Manchester Picc. [10] 82 🚋 a						22 27			23 23			01 45										
Manchester Airport ✈🚋 a						22 43			23 40			02 02										
Liverpool Lime Street [10] 91 a				22 20																		
d		21 34														23 39						
Liverpool South Pkwy [7] 91 ✈ d		21 44														23 49						
Runcorn 91 d		21 51														23 59						
Manchester Picc. [10] 84 🚋 d					22 05																	
Stockport 84 d					22 13																	
Wilmslow 84 d																						
Holyhead 81 ⛴ d																						
Bangor (Gwynedd) 81 d																						
Llandudno Junction 81 d																						
Wrexham General 75 d																						
Chester 81 d																						
Crewe [10] 81,91 a		22 20						23 22								00 30	05s37		05s37			
d	22 11	22 21																				
Macclesfield d					22 26																	
Stoke-on-Trent 84 d	22 32		←		22 44																	
Stafford a	22 51	22 41	22 51		23 00																	
d	22 51	22 42	22 51		23 04																	
Penkridge a	→	22 47																				
Wolverhampton [7] 🚋 a		22 58	23 05		23 17																	
BirminghamNewSt [12] 68 🚋 a		23 16	23 32		23 35																	
Birmingham International 68 ✈ a																						
Coventry 68 a																						
Lichfield Trent Valley a																						
Tamworth Low Level a																						
Nuneaton a																						
Rugby 66 a																						
Milton Keynes Central 66 a																						
Watford Junction 66 a													06 38									
London Euston [15] ⊖66 a													07 04		07 07		07 49		07 49	09 05	09 05	09 05

A To Birmingham New Street
B From Crewe
C from 5 April
D until 29 March
E until 5 January, from 23 February until 29 March
F from 5 April. From Glasgow Central

Refer to Operator websites for full information about Sleeper Services. Contact details for train operators available at National Rail Enquiries

Table T066-F

Mondays to Fridays
16 December to 15 May

London - Watford Junction, Milton Keynes, Northampton and West Midlands

Miles	Miles	Miles		LM MO A	VT MO ◇ A	LM MX A	LM MX A	VT MX ◇ A	LM MO A	LM MX A	LM MO	LM MX	LM MO	LM MX	LM	SN	LM B	VT ◇ B ⊠	VT ◇ C ⊠	LM B	VT ◇ D ⊠	SN E
0	0	—	**London Euston** ⊖60 d								00 05	00 05	00 35	00 35	01 34			05 27	05 31	05 34	06 16	
—	—	0	East Croydon 176 d																			
—	—	7¼	Clapham Junction 176 d													05 03						05 32
—	—	8¾	Imperial Wharf 176 d													05 07						05 37
—	—	9¼	West Brompton ⊖176 d													05 10						05 40
—	—	11¼	Kensington (Olympia) ⊖176 d													05 14						05 44
—	—	12½	Shepherd's Bush ⊖176 d													05 17						05 47
8	—	16¾	Wembley Central ⊖60,176 d										00 45	00 46	01 45							06 02
11½	—	—	Harrow & Wealdstone ⊖60 d								00 17	00 17	00 50	00 51	01 50	05 33				05 46		06 06
16	—	—	Bushey 60 d								00s22	00 22	00s55	00 56								
17½	17½	—	**Watford Junction** 60 a								00 25	00 25	00 58	00 58	01 56	05 40				05 54		06 13
—	—	—	d						00 01	00 04	00 25	00 25	00 58	00 59	01 57			05u45	05u50	05 55		06 14
21	—	—	Kings Langley d						00 05	00 09			01 03	01 04						05 59		
23	—	—	Apsley d						00 09	00 12			01 06	01 07						06 03		
24½	—	—	Hemel Hempstead d						00 12	00 15	00 32	00 32	01 09	01 10	02 04					06 06		06 21
28	—	—	Berkhamsted d						00 17	00 20	00 37	00 37	01 14	01 15	02 09					06 10		06 26
31¾	—	—	Tring d						00 22	00 25	00 42	00 42	01 19	01 20	02 13					06 18		06 33
36	—	—	Cheddington d						00 27		00 47	00 47	01 25	01 26						06 23		
40¼	—	—	Leighton Buzzard d			00 01	00 07		00 34	00 35	00 54	00 54	01 31	01 32	02 22					06 28		06 42
46¾	—	—	Bletchley d			00 08	00 14		00 41	00 42	01 01	01 01	01 38	01 39	02 29					06 35		06 49
49¾	49¾	—	**Milton Keynes Central** a			00 16	00 22		00 49	00 50	01 09	01 09	01 47	01 47	02 37			06 13	06 22	06 40	06 46	06 55
—	—	—	d	00 07	00 12	00 17	00 22	00 28	00 49		01 09	01 09	01 47	01 48			05 37	06 15	06 23	06 40		
52½	52½	—	Wolverton d	00 11		00 21	00 26		00 53		01 13	01 13	01 50	01 51			05 41			06 44		
65¾	—	—	**Northampton** 68 a	00 25		00 34	00 44		01 07		01 26	01 28	02 04	02 05			05 53			06 56		
—	—	—	d														05 56			06 57		
75¼	—	—	Long Buckby 68 a														06 07			→		
84½	82½	—	**Rugby** 68 a		00s47			01 00									06 18		06 45			
96	—	—	Coventry 68 a		00s59			01 13									06 29					
—	—	—	Nuneaton 65 a															06 44				
106¾	—	—	Birmingham International 68 a		01s09			01 23									06 41					
115¾	—	—	**Birmingham New Street** 68 a		01s22			01 35									07 01					
120½	—	—	Sandwell & Dudley 68 a																			
128	—	—	Wolverhampton 68 a		01 42			02 04									07 22					

	LM	VT ◇ ⊠	LM F	LM G	VT ◇ H ⊠	VT ◇ I	VT ◇ ⊠	LM J	SN	VT ◇ D ⊠	LM B	SN	VT ◇ K ⊠	LM	VT ◇ D ⊠	LM G	SN L	LM	VT ◇ ⊠	VT ◇ M ⊠	VT ◇ N ⊠	VT ◇ C ⊠
London Euston ⊖60 d	06 03	06 20		06 28	06 43	06 46	07 03	06 12		06 55	06 34		07 10	06 54	07 20	07 13		07 12	07 23	07 33	07 35	07 43
East Croydon 176 d																						
Clapham Junction 176 d									05 53			06 20					06 40					
Imperial Wharf 176 d									05 58			06 24					06 45					
West Brompton ⊖176 d									06 01			06 27					06 47					
Kensington (Olympia) ⊖176 d									06 05			06 31					06 51					
Shepherd's Bush ⊖176 d									06 08			06 34					06 54					
Wembley Central ⊖60,176 d									06 26			06 47					07 07					
Harrow & Wealdstone ⊖60 d	06 15							06 26	06 31		06 46						07 12					
Bushey 60 d								06 31														
Watford Junction 60 a	06 22							06 34	06 38		06 53	06 57		07 09			07 18	07 28				
d	06 22	06u34						06 34			06 53			07 11			07 19	07 29	07u37			
Kings Langley d	06 27										06 58							07 33				
Apsley d	06 31										07 02							07 37				
Hemel Hempstead d	06 34							06 42			07 05			07 18			07 26	07 40				
Berkhamsted d	06 39							06 48			07 10			07 23			07 31	07 45				
Tring d	06a45							06 54			07 16						07 38	07a51				
Cheddington d								06 59			07 21											
Leighton Buzzard d								07 04			07 26			07 36		07 41	07 47					
Bletchley d								07 11			07 32			07 43		07 49	07 54					
Milton Keynes Central a				07 00	07 13			07 16		07 25	07 37		07 40	07 48	07 50	07 53	08 02			08 03	08 05	08 13
d				07 01	07 13			07 16			07 38					07 54						08 13
Wolverton d			←					07 20			07 42					07 58						
Northampton 68 a			06 56					07 37			07 54					08 10						
d			06 57					07 38			07 56					08 14						
Long Buckby 68 a			07 08					07 48			08 07					08 25						
Rugby 68 a		07 12	07 18	07 24		07 39	07 51	07 59			08 18					08 36						
Coventry 68 a		07 22	07 29		07 42		08 02	08 10			08 29					08 47			08 22			08 42
Nuneaton 65 a				07 41																		
Birmingham International 68 a		07 33	07 41		07 53		08 13	08 28			08 41					09 05			08 33			08 53
Birmingham New Street 68 a		07 45	07 51		08 09		08 25	08 42			08 54					09 18			08 45			09 05
Sandwell & Dudley 68 a					08 24																	09 24
Wolverhampton 68 a			08 21		08 37						09 21					09 39						09 37

A From London Euston
B To Liverpool Lime Street
C To Glasgow Central
D To Manchester Piccadilly
E From Balham
F From London Euston to Liverpool Lime Street
G To Crewe
H To Edinburgh
I To Blackpool North
J To Rugeley Trent Valley
K To Chester
L From Selhurst
M from 17 February. To Manchester Piccadilly
N until 14 February. To Manchester Piccadilly

NRT DECEMBER 19 EDITION

Table T066-F

Mondays to Fridays
16 December to 15 May

London - Watford Junction, Milton Keynes, Northampton and West Midlands

	LM A	VT ◇ ⊠	LM B	LM	LM C	LM D	VT ◇ D ⊠	VT ◇ E ⊠	LM	VT ◇ F ⊠	LM G	LM A	SN	LM	LM	VT ◇ ⊠	VT ◇ H ⊠	LM A	VT ◇ I	VT ◇ ⊠	LM B	LM
London Euston ⊖60 d	07 46	08 03	07 23	07 34	07 42	07 49	08 07	08 10	07 52	08 20	08 13	08 13		08 07	08 12	08 23	08 43	08 46	08 54	09 03	08 22	08 34
East Croydon 176 d													07 10									
Clapham Junction 176 d													07 39									
Imperial Wharf 176 d													07 44									
West Brompton ⊖176 d													07 47									
Kensington (Olympia) ⊖176 d													07 51									
Shepherd's Bush ⊖176 d													07 53									
Wembley Central ⊖60,176 d													08 08									
Harrow & Wealdstone ⊖60 d			07 34	07 46									08 12	08 21	08 25						08 34	08 46
Bushey 60 d				07 52										08 26	08 30							08 52
Watford Junction 60 a			07 41	07 54	08 03	08 03			08 11				08 19	08 29	08 33						08 40	08 54
d			07 41	07 55		08 04			08 11				08 19	08 29		08u37					08 40	08 55
Kings Langley d				07 59										08 34								08 59
Apsley d				08 03										08 37								09 03
Hemel Hempstead d			07 49	08 06					08 18				08 27	08 40							08 47	09 06
Berkhamsted d			07 54	08 11					08 23				08 31	08 45							08 52	09 10
Tring d			08 00	08a17									08 37	08a52							08 58	09a17
Cheddington d			08 05																		09 03	
Leighton Buzzard d			08 10						08 36		08 40	08 40	08 47								09 08	
Bletchley d			08 18						08 43		08 47	08 47	08 54								09 15	
Milton Keynes Central a	08 18		08 22			08 25	08 37	08 40	08 48	08 50	08 52	08 52	09 00				09 13	09 18			09 20	
d	08 19		08 22			08 25					08 53	08 53					09 13	09 19			09 21	
Wolverton d			08 26								08 57	08 57									09 25	
Northampton 68 a			08 38			08 43					09 09	09 09									09 37	
d			08 39			08 56					09 14	09 14									09 38	
Long Buckby 68 a			08 49			09 07					09 25	09 25									09 49	
Rugby 68 a	08 42	08 51	09 00			09 18					09 36	09 36						09 42	09 44	09 51	10 00	
Coventry 68 a		09 02	09 12			09 29					09 46	09 46				09 22	09 42			10 02	10 10	
Nuneaton 65 a	08 53																	09 53				
Birmingham International 68 a		09 13	09 29			09 41					10 04	10 04				09 33	09 53			10 13	10 28	
Birmingham New Street 68 a		09 24	09 41			09 54					10 15	10 15				09 45	10 04			10 26	10 41	
Sandwell & Dudley 68 a																	10 24					
Wolverhampton 68 a						10 21						10 39					10 37					

	SN	LM D	VT ◇ E ⊠	LM	VT ◇ F ⊠	LM G	LM A	SN	LM	VT ◇ ⊠	VT ◇ J ⊠	LM A	VT ◇ ⊠	LM B	LM	LM D	VT ◇ K ⊠	LM	VT ◇ F ⊠	VT ◇ I	LM G
London Euston ⊖60 d		08 49	09 10	08 51	09 20	09 13	09 13		09 04	09 23	09 43	09 46	10 03	09 24	09 34	09 49	10 10	09 54	10 20	10 36	10 15
East Croydon 176 d	07 40							08 11													
Clapham Junction 176 d	08 18							08 40													
Imperial Wharf 176 d	08 22							08 44													
West Brompton ⊖176 d	08 25							08 47													
Kensington (Olympia) ⊖176 d	08 29							08 51													
Shepherd's Bush ⊖176 d	08 31							08 53													
Wembley Central ⊖60,176 d	08 47							09 08							09 44						
Harrow & Wealdstone ⊖60 d	08 52							09 13	09 17						09 49						
Bushey 60 d									09 22						09 54						
Watford Junction 60 a	09 00	09 03		09 07				09 20	09 25					09 39	09 57	10 03		10 09			
d		09 04		09 07				09 21	09 26	09u37				09 40	09 57	10 04		10 11			
Kings Langley d									09 30						10 02						
Apsley d									09 34						10 05						
Hemel Hempstead d				09 15				09 28	09 37					09 47	10 08			10 18			
Berkhamsted d				09 20				09 33	09 42					09 52	10 12			10 23			
Tring d								09 40	09a49					09 58	10a20						
Cheddington d														10 03							
Leighton Buzzard d				09 32		09 43	09 43	09 48						10 08				10 36			10 43
Bletchley d		09 24		09 39		09 50	09 50	09 56						10 15		10 25		10 43			10 50
Milton Keynes Central a		09 29	09 40	09 44	09 50	09 55	09 55	10 01			10 13	10 18		10 20		10 30	10 40	10 47	10 50		10 55
d		09 29				09 55	09 55				10 13	10 19		10 21		10 30		10 49			10 55
Wolverton d						09 59	09 59							10 25				10 53			10 59
Northampton 68 a		09 44				10 14	10 14							10 37		10 45		11 05			11 12
d		09 54				10 15	10 15							10 38		10 56					11 14
Long Buckby 68 a		10 05				10 26	10 26							10 49		11 07					11 25
Rugby 68 a		10 16				10 37	10 37					10 42	10 51	11 00		11 18				11 24	11 36
Coventry 68 a		10 29				10 47	10 47			10 22	10 42		11 02	11 11		11 29					11 46
Nuneaton 65 a												10 53									
Birmingham International 68 a		10 41				11 05	11 05			10 33	10 53		11 13	11 29		11 41					12 04
Birmingham New Street 68 a		10 54				11 16	11 16			10 44	11 05		11 24	11 41		11 54					12 15
Sandwell & Dudley 68 a											11 24										
Wolverhampton 68 a		11 21					11 40				11 37					12 21					

A To Crewe
B To Rugeley Trent Valley
C not from 25 December until 1 January
D To Liverpool Lime Street
E To Holyhead
F To Manchester Piccadilly
G To Walsall
H To Edinburgh
I To Blackpool North
J To Glasgow Central
K To Chester

Table T066-F

London - Watford Junction, Milton Keynes, Northampton and West Midlands

	LM	SN	LM	VT	VT	VT	LM	VT	LM	LM	LM	VT	LM	VT	LM	LM	SN	LM	VT	VT	LM	VT
	■	■	■	◇■	◇■	◇■	■	◇■	■	■	■	◇■	■	◇■	■	■	■	■	◇■	◇■	■	◇■
	A				B	C	A		D		E	F		G	H	A				I	A	
				⊠	⊠	⊡		⊠				⊠		⊠					⊠	⊠		⊠
London Euston ⊖60 d	10 15		10 04	10 23	10 23	10 43	10 46	11 03	10 24	10 33	10 49	11 10	10 54	11 20	11 15	11 15		11 03	11 23	11 43	11 46	12 03
East Croydon 176 d		09 10															10 10					
Clapham Junction 176 d		09 39															10 41					
Imperial Wharf 176 d		09 44															10 45					
West Brompton ⊖176 d		09 47															10 48					
Kensington (Olympia) ⊖176 d		09 50															10 51					
Shepherd's Bush ⊖176 d		09 53															10 54					
Wembley Central ⊖60,176 d		10 08								10 43							11 09	11 13				
Harrow & Wealdstone ⊖60 d		10 12	10 16							10 48							11 13	11 18				
Bushey 60 d			10 22							10 53								11 23				
Watford Junction 60 a		10 19	10 24						10 39	10 56	11 03		11 09				11 20	11 26				
d		10 19	10 25	10u37	10u37				10 39	10 56	11 04		11 11				11 20	11 26	11u37			
Kings Langley d			10 29							11 01								11 31				
Apsley d			10 33							11 04								11 34				
Hemel Hempstead d		10 27	10 36						10 47	11 07			11 18				11 28	11 37				
Berkhamsted d		10 31	10 41						10 52	11 11			11 23				11 32	11 42				
Tring d		10 38	10a48						10 58	11a19							11 38	11a49				
Cheddington d									11 03													
Leighton Buzzard d	10 43	10 47							11 08				11 36		11 43	11 43	11 47					
Bletchley d	10 50	10 56							11 15				11 43		11 50	11 50	11 54					
Milton Keynes Central a	10 55	11 01				11 13	11 18		11 20		11 24	11 40	11 48	11 50	11 55	11 55	11 59			12 13	12 18	
d	10 55					11 13	11 19		11 20		11 24				11 55	11 55				12 13	12 19	
Wolverton d	10 59								11 24						11 59	11 59						
Northampton 68 a	11 12								11 37		11 42				12 12	12 12						
d	11 14								11 38		11 56				12 14	12 14						
Long Buckby 68 a	11 25								11 48		12 07				12 25	12 25						
Rugby 68 a	11 36						11 42	11 51	11 59		12 18				12 36	12 36					12 42	12 51
Coventry 68 a	11 46			11 22	11 22	11 42		12 02	12 10		12 29				12 47	12 47			12 22	12 42		13 02
Nuneaton 65 a							11 54														12 53	
Birmingham International 68 ✈ a	12 04			11 33	11 33	11 53		12 13	12 28		12 41				13 05	13 05			12 33	12 53		13 13
Birmingham New Street 68 a	12 15			11 45	11 45	12 04		12 25	12 40		12 54				13 16	13 16			12 44	13 04		13 24
Sandwell & Dudley 68 a						12 24														13 24		
Wolverhampton 68 a	12 38				12 10	12 37					13 21					13 39				13 37		

	LM	LM	LM	VT	LM	VT	LM	LM	SN	LM	VT	VT	LM	VT	LM	LM	LM	VT	LM	VT	LM
	■	■	■	◇■	■	◇■	■	■	■	■	◇■	◇■	■	◇■	■	■	■	◇■	■	◇■	■
	D		E	F		G	H	A				C	A		D		E	F		G	H
				⊠		⊠					⊠	⊠		⊡				⊡		⊡	
London Euston ⊖60 d	11 24	11 34	11 49	12 10	11 54	12 20	12 15	12 15		12 03	12 23	12 43	12 46	13 03	12 24	12 34	12 49	13 10	12 53	13 20	13 15
East Croydon 176 d									11 10												
Clapham Junction 176 d									11 39												
Imperial Wharf 176 d									11 44												
West Brompton ⊖176 d									11 47												
Kensington (Olympia) ⊖176 d									11 50												
Shepherd's Bush ⊖176 d									11 53												
Wembley Central ⊖60,176 d									12 09	12 13											
Harrow & Wealdstone ⊖60 d		11 46							12 13	12 18						12 46					
Bushey 60 d		11 52								12 23						12 52					
Watford Junction 60 a	11 39	11 54	12 03		12 09				12 20	12 26					12 39	12 54	13 03		13 08		
d	11 40	11 55	12 04		12 10				12 20	12 26	12u37				12 40	12 55	13 04		13 09		
Kings Langley d		11 59								12 31						12 59					
Apsley d		12 03								12 34						13 03					
Hemel Hempstead d	11 47	12 06			12 17				12 28	12 37					12 47	13 06			13 16		
Berkhamsted d	11 52	12 10			12 22				12 32	12 42					12 52	13 10			13 21		
Tring d	11 58	12a17							12 38	12a49					12 58	13a17					
Cheddington d	12 03														13 03						
Leighton Buzzard d	12 08				12 34		12 43	12 43	12 47						13 08				13 34		13 43
Bletchley d	12 15				12 41		12 50	12 50	12 54						13 15				13 41		13 50
Milton Keynes Central a	12 20		12 24	12 40	12 46	12 50	12 55	12 55	13 00			13 13	13 18		13 20		13 24	13 40	13 46	13 50	13 55
d	12 21		12 25	12 41			12 55	12 55				13 13	13 19		13 20		13 25				13 55
Wolverton d	12 25						12 59	12 59							13 24						13 59
Northampton 68 a	12 37		12 43				13 12	13 12							13 37		13 42				14 12
d	12 38		12 56				13 14	13 14							13 38		13 54				14 14
Long Buckby 68 a	12 49		13 07				13 25	13 25							13 49		14 05				14 25
Rugby 68 a	13 00		13 18	13 02			13 36	13 36					13 42	13 51	14 00		14 16				14 37
Coventry 68 a	13 10		13 29				13 47	13 47			13 22	13 42		14 02	14 11		14 29				14 47
Nuneaton 65 a													13 55								
Birmingham International 68 ✈ a	13 28		13 41				14 05	14 05			13 33	13 53		14 13	14 29		14 41				15 05
Birmingham New Street 68 a	13 40		13 51				14 16	14 16			13 44	14 04		14 26	14 40		14 51				15 16
Sandwell & Dudley 68 a												14 24									
Wolverhampton 68 a			14 21					14 39				14 36					15 21				

A To Crewe
B To Shrewsbury
C To Edinburgh
D To Rugeley Trent Valley
E To Liverpool Lime Street
F To Chester
G To Manchester Piccadilly
H To Walsall
I To Glasgow Central

Table T066-F

London - Watford Junction, Milton Keynes, Northampton and West Midlands

	LM	SN	LM	VT	VT	LM	VT	LM	LM	LM	VT	LM	VT	LM	LM	SN	SN	LM	VT	VT	LM	VT
																MWFO	TThO					
	■	■	■	◇■	◇■	■	◇■	■	■	■	◇■	■	◇■	■	■	■	■	■	◇■	◇■	■	◇■
	A				B	A		C		D	E		F	G	A		H			I	A	
				⊡	⊡		⊡				⊡		⊡						⊡	⊡		⊡
London Euston ⊖60 d	13 15		13 03	13 23	13 43	13 46	14 03	13 24	13 34	13 49	14 10	13 54	14 20	14 15	14 15			14 04	14 23	14 43	14 46	15 03
East Croydon 176 d		12 10														13 10						
Clapham Junction 176 d		12 39														13 39	13 39					
Imperial Wharf 176 d		12 45														13 44	13 44					
West Brompton ⊖176 d		12 48														13 47	13 47					
Kensington (Olympia) ⊖176 d		12 51														13 50	13 50					
Shepherd's Bush ⊖176 d		12 53														13 53	13 53					
Wembley Central ⊖60,176 d		13 09	13 13													14 09	14 09					
Harrow & Wealdstone ⊖60 d		13 14	13 18						13 47							14 13	14 13	14 17				
Bushey 60 d			13 23						13 52									14 23				
Watford Junction 60 a		13 20	13 26					13 39	13 55	14 03		14 09				14 20	14 20	14 25				
d		13 21	13 26	13u37				13 39	13 55	14 04		14 11				14 20	14 20	14 26	14u37			
Kings Langley d			13 31						14 00									14 30				
Apsley d			13 34						14 03									14 34				
Hemel Hempstead d		13 28	13 37					13 47	14 06			14 18				14 28	14 28	14 37				
Berkhamsted d		13 33	13 42					13 52	14 11			14 23				14 32	14 32	14 42				
Tring d		13 39	13a49					13 58	14a18							14 38	14 38	14a47				
Cheddington d								14 03														
Leighton Buzzard d	13 43	13 47						14 09				14 36		14 42	14 42	14 47	14 47					
Bletchley d	13 50	13 54						14 16				14 43		14 49	14 49	14 54	14 54					
Milton Keynes Central a	13 55	14 00			14 13	14 18		14 21		14 25	14 40	14 48	14 50	14 54	14 54	14 59	14 59			15 13	15 18	
d	13 55				14 13	14 19		14 22		14 26				14 55	14 55					15 13	15 19	
Wolverton d	13 59							14 25						14 59	14 59							
Northampton 68 a	14 12							14 38		14 43				15 12	15 12							
d	14 14							14 39		14 56				15 14	15 14							
Long Buckby 68 a	14 25							14 50		15 07				15 26	15 26							
Rugby 68 a	14 37					14 42	14 51	15 01		15 18				15 37	15 37						15 42	15 51
Coventry 68 a	14 47			14 22	14 42		15 02	15 11		15 29				15 48	15 48				15 22	15 42		16 02
Nuneaton 65 a						14 53															15 55	
Birmingham International 68 ✈ a	15 05			14 33	14 53		15 13	15 28		15 41				16 05	16 05				15 33	15 53		16 13
Birmingham New Street 68 a	15 16			14 45	15 04		15 25	15 40		15 51				16 17	16 17				15 43	16 04		16 25
Sandwell & Dudley 68 a					15 24															16 24		
Wolverhampton 68 a	15 39				15 37					16 21					16 40					16 37		

	LM	LM	LM	VT	LM	VT	LM	SN	LM	VT	VT	LM	VT	LM	LM	LM	SN	LM	VT	VT	LM	LM
	■	■	■	◇■	■	◇■	■	■	■	◇■	■	■	◇■	■	■	■	■	■	◇■	◇■	■	■
	C		D	E		F	A				B	A		C		D			F	J	G	A
				⊡		⊡				⊡	⊡		⊡						⊡	⊡		
London Euston ⊖60 d	14 24	14 34	14 49	15 10	14 52	15 20	15 15		15 03	15 23	15 43	15 46	16 03	15 24	15 34	15 49		15 53	16 20	16 33	16 15	16 15
East Croydon 176 d								14 10														
Clapham Junction 176 d								14 40									15 22					
Imperial Wharf 176 d								14 45									15 26					
West Brompton ⊖176 d								14 48									15 29					
Kensington (Olympia) ⊖176 d								14 51									15 32					
Shepherd's Bush ⊖176 d								14 54									15 34					
Wembley Central ⊖60,176 d		14 44						15 09	15 13								15 52					
Harrow & Wealdstone ⊖60 d		14 49						15 13	15 18						15 46		15 57					
Bushey 60 d		14 54							15 23						15 52							
Watford Junction 60 a	14 39	14 57	15 03		15 07			15 20	15 26					15 39	15 54	16 03	16 04	16 08				
d	14 40	14 57	15 04		15 08			15 20	15 26	15u37				15 39	15 55	16 04		16 09				
Kings Langley d		15 02							15 31						15 59							
Apsley d		15 05							15 34						16 03							
Hemel Hempstead d	14 47	15 08			15 15			15 28	15 37					15 47	16 06			16 16				
Berkhamsted d	14 53	15 12			15 21			15 32	15 42					15 52	16 10			16 21				
Tring d	14 59	15a19						15 38	15a49					15 58	16a17							
Cheddington d	15 04													16 03								
Leighton Buzzard d	15 09				15 35		15 42	15 47						16 09				16 34			16 42	16 42
Bletchley d	15 16				15 41		15 49	15 54						16 15				16 41			16 49	16 49
Milton Keynes Central a	15 21		15 24	15 40	15 46	15 50	15 54	16 00			16 13	16 18		16 20		16 24		16 46	16 50		16 54	16 54
d	15 21		15 26				15 55				16 13	16 19		16 21		16 25					16 55	16 55
Wolverton d	15 25						15 59							16 25							16 59	16 59
Northampton 68 a	15 37		15 42				16 12							16 37		16 43					17 11	17 11
d	15 38		15 56				16 14							16 38		16 55					17 13	17 13
Long Buckby 68 a	15 48		16 07				16 25							16 49		17 06					17 24	17 24
Rugby 68 a	15 59		16 18				16 36					16 42	16 51	17 01		17 17				17 21	17 35	17 35
Coventry 68 a	16 10		16 29				16 48			16 22	16 42		17 02	17 11		17 29					17 47	17 47
Nuneaton 65 a												16 53										
Birmingham International 68 ✈ a	16 28		16 41				17 06			16 33	16 53		17 13	17 28		17 42					18 05	18 05
Birmingham New Street 68 a	16 40		16 52				17 17			16 44	17 05		17 27	17 40		17 52					18 16	18 16
Sandwell & Dudley 68 a											17 24											
Wolverhampton 68 a			17 21				17 39				17 37					18 21						18 38

A To Crewe
B To Glasgow Central
C To Rugeley Trent Valley
D To Liverpool Lime Street
E To Chester
F To Manchester Piccadilly
G To Walsall
H From Selhurst
I To Edinburgh
J To Blackpool North

Table T066-F

Mondays to Fridays
16 December to 15 May

London - Watford Junction, Milton Keynes, Northampton and West Midlands

		SN ■	LM ■	LM ■	VT ◇■ ⊏	VT ◇■ A ⊏	VT ◇■ B ⊏	LM ■ A	VT ◇■ ⊠	LM ■ C	LM ■	LM ■ A	VT FX ◇■ D ⊠	VT FO ◇■ D ⊠	VT ◇■ E ⊠	LM ■	LM ■	LM ■	LM ■	SN ■	LM ■	LM ■
London Euston ⊖60	d		16 03	16 08	16 23	16 43	16 43	16 46	17 03	16 30	16 33	16 52	17 10	17 10	17 33	17 13	16 49	16 54	17 16		17 04	17 11
East Croydon 176	d	15 10																		16 10		
Clapham Junction 176	d	15 39																		16 39		
Imperial Wharf 176	d	15 44																		16 44		
West Brompton ⊖176	d	15 47																		16 47		
Kensington (Olympia) ⊖176	d	15 51																		16 51		
Shepherd's Bush ⊖176	d	15 53																		16 53		
Wembley Central ⊖60,176	d	16 08		16 18							16 43									17 07		
Harrow & Wealdstone ⊖60	d	16 12	16 16	16 23													17 02	17 06		17 12	17 17	17 23
Bushey 60	d		16 21	16 29							16 52						17 07	17 12			17 22	
Watford Junction 60	a	16 19	16 24	16 32							16 54						17 09	17 14		17 18	17 26	17 30
	d	16 19	16 25		16u37						16 55						17 10	17 15		17 19		17 30
Kings Langley	d		16 29								17 00						17 15					17 35
Apsley	d		16 33								17 04							17 21				
Hemel Hempstead	d	16 27	16 36								17 07						17 20	17 24		17 28		17 39
Berkhamsted	d	16 31	16 41								17 12						17 25	17 29		17 33		17 44
Tring	d	16 37	16a48							16 59	17a18						17 30	17a35		17 39		17a51
Cheddington	d									17 04							17 35					
Leighton Buzzard	d	16 47								17 09		17 20							17 43	17 48		
Bletchley	d	16 54								17 16		17 27					17 45			17 55		
Milton Keynes Central	a	17 00				17 13	17 13	17 18		17 21		17 32		17 40		17 46	17 50		17 54	18 01		
	d					17 13	17 13	17 19		17 22		17 32	17u41	17 41		17 49			17 55			
Wolverton	d									17 26		17 36							17 59			
Northampton 68	a									17 38		17 49				18 11			18 15			
	d									17 39		17 58				18 20						
Long Buckby 68	a									17 49		18 08				18 31						
Rugby 68	a							17 42	17 51	18 00		18 19			18 21	18 41						
Coventry 68	a				17 22	17 42	17 42		18 02	18 11		18 30				18 52						
Nuneaton 65	a							17 59					18 10	18 10								
Birmingham International 68 ✈	a				17 33	17 53	17 53		18 13	18 29		18 42				19 10						
Birmingham New Street 68	a				17 44	18 04	18 05		18 25	18 40		18 52				19 20						
Sandwell & Dudley 68	a					18 24	18 24															
Wolverhampton 68	a					18 36	18 37					19 21										

		VT ◇■ ⊠	VT ◇■ F ⊏	LM ■ A	VT ◇■ ⊠	LM ■ C	LM ■	LM ■	LM ■	LM ■	VT FX ◇■ G ⊠	VT FO ◇■ G ⊠	VT ◇■ E ⊠	LM ■ A	LM ■	LM ■	SN ■	LM ■	LM ■	VT ◇■ ⊠	VT ◇■ A ⊠	VT FO ◇■ H ⊏	LM FX ■ A
London Euston ⊖60	d	17 23	17 43	17 46	18 03	17 23	17 30	17 34	17 38	17 52	18 10	18 10	18 33	18 13	17 53	18 16		18 05	18 11	18 23	18 43	18 46	18 46
East Croydon 176	d																17 10						
Clapham Junction 176	d																17 39						
Imperial Wharf 176	d																17 44						
West Brompton ⊖176	d																17 47						
Kensington (Olympia) ⊖176	d																17 51						
Shepherd's Bush ⊖176	d																17 53						
Wembley Central ⊖60,176	d					17 33											18 09						
Harrow & Wealdstone ⊖60	d								17 51								18 13	18 17					
Bushey 60	d							17 50	17 55										18 27				
Watford Junction 60	a					17 42	17 47	17 53	18 00						18 09		18 20	18 24	18 30				
	d	17u37				17 42	17 47	17 53							18 10		18 20	18 24	18 30	18u37			
Kings Langley	d							17 58										18 29					
Apsley	d					17 49		18 01										18 33					
Hemel Hempstead	d					17 52	17 55	18 05							18 17		18 28		18 38				
Berkhamsted	d					17 57	18 00	18 09							18 22		18 32		18 42				
Tring	d						18 06	18a16							18 27		18 38	18 43	18a51				
Cheddington	d						18 11											18 49					
Leighton Buzzard	d					18 09				18 21						18 43	18 47	18 54					
Bletchley	d					18 16	18 21								18 41		18 54	19 00					
Milton Keynes Central	a			18 18		18 21	18 27			18 30		18 40		18 45	18 46	18 55	19 00	19 05			19 13	19 17	19 18
	d		18u13	18 19		18 22				18 31	18u41	18 41		18 45	18 47	18 56		19 05			19 13	19 19	19 19
Wolverton	d					18 25				18 35					18 51	19 00		19 09					
Northampton 68	a					18 38				18 47				19 00	19 05	19 18		19 25					
	d					18 39				18 56				19 09									
Long Buckby 68	a					18 49				19 07				19 21									
Rugby 68	a			18 42	18 51	19 00				19 19			19 22	19 35								19 39	19 42
Coventry 68	a	18 22	18 42		19 02	19 11				19 30				19 46						19 22	19 42		
Nuneaton 65	a			19 00							19 10	19 10											20 01
Birmingham International 68 ✈	a	18 33	18 53		19 13	19 29				19 42				20 04						19 33	19 53		
Birmingham New Street 68	a	18 45	19 05		19 24	19 41				19 52				20 15						19 44	20 08		
Sandwell & Dudley 68	a		19 24																	19 58	20 24		
Wolverhampton 68	a		19 37		20 00									20 39						20 11	20 37		

A To Crewe
B To Edinburgh
C To Rugeley Trent Valley
D To Chester
E To Liverpool Lime Street
F To Glasgow Central
G To Wrexham General
H To Blackpool North

Table T066-F

Mondays to Fridays
16 December to 15 May

London - Watford Junction, Milton Keynes, Northampton and West Midlands

		VT ■ ⊏	LM ■ A	LM FO ■ B	LM ■	LM ■	LM ■	LM ■ B	VT ThO ■ C ⊏	VT ThX ■ C ⊏	VT ThX ■ D ⊏	LM ■	LM ■ E	LM ■ B	SN ■	LM ■	VT ■ ⊏	VT ◇■ B ⊏	LM ■ B	LM ■	LM ■	VT ◇■ ⊏
London Euston ⊖60	d	19 03	18 21	18 49	18 30	18 34	18 41	18 52	19 10	19 10	19 20	18 54	19 15	19 15		19 05	19 23	19 43	19 46	19 30	19 34	20 03
East Croydon 176	d														18 10							
Clapham Junction 176	d														18 39							
Imperial Wharf 176	d														18 44							
West Brompton ⊖176	d														18 47							
Kensington (Olympia) ⊖176	d														18 51							
Shepherd's Bush ⊖176	d														18 53							
Wembley Central ⊖60,176	d														19 09						19 44	
Harrow & Wealdstone ⊖60	d		18 33			18 46						19 06			19 13	19 18					19 49	
Bushey 60	d					18 52	18 58									19 23					19 54	
Watford Junction 60	a		18 39		18 46	18 54	19 01					19 13			19 20	19 26				19 45	19 57	
	d		18 41		18 47	18 55	19 01					19 13			19 20	19 26	19u37			19 46	19 57	
Kings Langley	d		18 46			19 00	19 06									19 31					20 02	
Apsley	d				18 53		19 10									19 35					20 05	
Hemel Hempstead	d		18 52			19 05	19 13					19 21			19 28	19 37				19 53	20 08	
Berkhamsted	d				19 01	19 10						19 26			19 32	19 42				19 58	20 13	
Tring	d		19 00			19a16						19 32			19 38	19a49				20 04	20a19	
Cheddington	d				19 10		19 24													20 09		
Leighton Buzzard	d		19 10				19 29	19 20				19 39	19 42	19 42	19 47					20 14		
Bletchley	d				19 19		19a38	19 27				19 46			19 55					20 21		
Milton Keynes Central	a		19 19	19 22	19 25			19 32		19 40	19 50	19 53	19 56	19 56	20 04			20 13	20 18	20 26		
	d		19 20	19 24				19 32	19u41	19 41			19 57	19 57				20 13	20 19			
Wolverton	d		19 24					19 36					20 01	20 01								
Northampton 68	a		19 36	19 42				19 53					20 13	20 13								
	d		19 38	19 45				19 55					20 14	20 14								
Long Buckby 68	a		19 48					20 06					20 25	20 25								
Rugby 68	a	19 51	19 59	20 04				20 17					20 36	20 36					20 42			20 51
Coventry 68	a	20 02	20 10					20 29					20 47	20 47			20 22	20 42				21 02
Nuneaton 65	a			20 17					20 10	20 10									20 53			
Birmingham International 68 ✈	a	20 13	20 28					20 41					21 04	21 04			20 33	20 53				21 13
Birmingham New Street 68	a	20 25	20 40					20 51					21 16	21 16			20 45	21 05				21 26
Sandwell & Dudley 68	a																20 58	21 24				
Wolverhampton 68	a							21 22						21 40			21 10	21 37				21 57

		LM ■ B	VT ◇■ C ⊏	LM ■	LM ■	SN ■	LM ■	VT ◇■ F ⊏	VT ◇■ ⊏	VT ◇■ ⊏	LM ■ B	LM ■	LM ■	LM ■ B	VT ◇■ D ⊏	VT ◇■ ⊏	VT ◇■ F ⊏	LM ■	LM ■	SN ■	LM ■	VT ◇■ G ⊏	LM ■ H
London Euston ⊖60	d	19 53	20 10	19 54	20 16		20 04	20 07	20 23	20 43	20 46	20 24	20 34	20 51	21 00	21 03	21 07	20 54	21 13		21 04	21 10	
East Croydon 176	d					19 10														20 10			
Clapham Junction 176	d					19 40														20 36			
Imperial Wharf 176	d					19 45														20 41			
West Brompton ⊖176	d					19 48														20 44			
Kensington (Olympia) ⊖176	d					19 51														20 47			
Shepherd's Bush ⊖176	d					19 54														20 50			
Wembley Central ⊖60,176	d					20 08							20 44					21 03		21 08			
Harrow & Wealdstone ⊖60	d					20 12	20 17						20 49							21 12	21 17		
Bushey 60	d						20 22						20 55								21 22		
Watford Junction 60	a			20 09		20 19	20 24					20 42	20 57					21 12		21 19	21 25		
	d			20 11		20 19	20 25		20u37			20 43	20 58					21 13		21 19	21 25	21u25	
Kings Langley	d						20 30						21 02								21 30		
Apsley	d						20 34						21 06								21 33		
Hemel Hempstead	d			20 18		20 27	20 36					20 51	21 09					21 20		21 27	21 36		
Berkhamsted	d			20 23		20 32	20 41					20 56	21 14					21 25		21 31	21 41		
Tring	d					20 38	20a48					21 02	21a20							21 38	21 47		
Cheddington	d											21 07									21 52		
Leighton Buzzard	d	20 21		20 36	20 43	20 47						21 12		21 19				21 38	21 44	21 48	21 57		
Bletchley	d			20 43	20 50	20 54						21 19						21 45	21 52	21 56	22a05		
Milton Keynes Central	a	20 30	20 40	20 48	20 56	21 00				21 13	21 18	21 24		21 30	21 30	21 34	21 38	21 50	21 56	22 02			
	d	20 31		20 49	20 56					21 13	21 19			21 30		21 35	21 39	21 50	21 56				
Wolverton	d	20 35		20 53	21 00									21 34				21 54	22 00				
Northampton 68	a	20 48		21 09	21 13									21 48				22 08	22 13				
	d	20 57			21 15									21 57					22 20				
Long Buckby 68	a	21 08			21 26									22 08					22 30				←
Rugby 68	a	21 19			21 37						21 42			22 19		21 56			22 41			22 03	22 19
Coventry 68	a	21 30			21 48				21 22	21 42				→		22 07			22 52				22 30
Nuneaton 65	a							21 02			21 57						22 07						
Birmingham International 68 ✈	a	21 46			22 03				21 33	21 53						22 17			23 10				22 46
Birmingham New Street 68	a	22 02			22 18				21 44	22 05						22 30			23 22				23 03
Sandwell & Dudley 68	a	22 21							21 58	22 16						22 41							23 20
Wolverhampton 68	a	22 33							22 09	22 28						22 53							23 35

A To Rugeley Trent Valley
B To Crewe
C To Chester
D To Manchester Piccadilly
E To Walsall
F To Liverpool Lime Street
G To Preston
H From London Euston to Crewe

Table T066-F

London - Watford Junction, Milton Keynes, Northampton and West Midlands

Mondays to Fridays
16 December to 15 May

Station	LM 1	LM 1	VT ◇1 ⊒	LM 1 A	LM 1 B	VT ◇1 A ⊒	LM 1 C	LM 1	SN 1	LM 1	LM 1	VT ◇1 ⊒	LM 1	LM 1	SN 1 D	LM 1	VT FX ◇1 ⊒	VT FO ◇1 ⊒	LM 1
London Euston [15] ⊖60 d	21 24	21 34	21 43	21 49	21 53	22 00		21 54		22 06	22 24	22 30	22 42	23 04		23 22	23 30	23 30	23 42
East Croydon 176 ⇌ d									21 10										
Clapham Junction 176 d									21 36						22 36				
Imperial Wharf 176 d									21 41						22 41				
West Brompton ⊖176 d									21 44						22 44				
Kensington (Olympia) ⊖176 d									21 47						22 48				
Shepherd's Bush ⊖176 d									21 50						22 51				
Wembley Central ⊖60,176 d														23 14		23 31			
Harrow & Wealdstone ⊖60 d		21 47						22 06	22 16	22 20			22 57	23 19	23 24				23 58
Bushey 60 d		21 52						22 12		22 25			23 03	23 24					
Watford Junction 60 a	21 40	21 55						22 14	22 23	22 28	22 39		23 05	23 27	23 34	23 40			00 04
d	21 41	21 55	21u58					22 15		22 28	22 41	22u45	23 06	23 28		23 41			00 04
Kings Langley d		22 00								22 33			23 10	23 32					00 09
Apsley d		22 03								22 37			23 14	23 36					00 12
Hemel Hempstead d	21 48	22 06						22 22		22 39	22 48		23 17	23 39		23 48			00 15
Berkhamsted d	21 53	22 11						22 28		22 44	22 53		23 22	23 44		23 53			00 20
Tring d		22 17						22 34		22 49			23 26	23 49					00 25
Cheddington d								22 39		22 54				23 54					
Leighton Buzzard d	22 06	22 24			22 20			22 45		23 00	23 07		23 35	00 01		00 07			00 35
Bletchley d	22 14	22a31						22 52		23 07	23 14		23 42	00 08		00 14			00 42
Milton Keynes Central [10] a	22 19		22 17	22 21	22 33	22 38		23 00		23 15	23 22	23 28	23 50	00 16		00 22	00 27	00 27	00 50
d			22 17	22 22	22 34	22 40		23 00		23 17	23 23	23 29		00 17		00 22	00 28	00 28	
Wolverton d					22 38		←	23 04			23 27			00 21		00 26			
Northampton 68 a					22 51		22 51	23 19		23 30	23 41			00 34		00 44			
d					22 56		22 56	23 19											
Long Buckby 68 a					→		23 07	23 30											
Rugby 68 a				22 45		23 01	23 17	23 41				23 58					01 00	01 07	
Coventry 68 a			22 45				23 29	23 51				00 10					01 13	01 17	
Nuneaton 65 a				22 57		23 12													
Birmingham International 68 ✈ a			22 59				23 47	00 10				00 20					01 23	01 27	
Birmingham New Street [12] 68 ⇌ a			23 11				00 04	00 28				00 32					01 35	01 39	
Sandwell & Dudley 68 a			23 31																
Wolverhampton [7] 68 ⇌ a			23 44									01 00					02 04	02 08	

Saturdays
21 December to 16 May

Station	LM 1 C	LM 1 C	VT ◇1 C ⊒	LM 1 C	LM 1	LM 1	LM 1	SN 1	LM 1 E	LM 1 E	SN 1 F	VT ◇1 G ⊒	VT ◇1 ⊒	LM 1 A	VT ◇1 ⊒	LM 1 H	SN 1	VT ◇1 I ⊒	VT ◇1 I ⊒	SN 1	LM 1	VT ◇1 ⊒
London Euston [15] ⊖60 d					00 05	00 35	01 34			05 34		06 05	06 23	06 29	07 03	06 24		06 55	07 20		07 03	07 23
East Croydon 176 ⇌ d																				06 10		
Clapham Junction 176 d								05 09			05 39						06 09			06 40		
Imperial Wharf 176 d								05 13			05 43						06 14			06 45		
West Brompton ⊖176 d								05 16			05 46						06 17			06 48		
Kensington (Olympia) ⊖176 d								05 20			05 50						06 20			06 51		
Shepherd's Bush ⊖176 d								05 23			05 53						06 23			06 54		
Wembley Central ⊖60,176 d						00 46	01 45				06 07						06 38			07 09	07 13	
Harrow & Wealdstone ⊖60 d					00 17	00 51	01 50	05 41		05 46	06 12						06 43			07 13	07 18	
Bushey 60 d						00 56															07 23	
Watford Junction 60 a					00 23	00 58	01 56	05 47		05 52	06 18					06 39	06 50			07 20	07 26	
d				00 04	00 25	00 59	01 57			05 53	06 19	06u20	06u37			06 39				07 20	07 26	07u37
Kings Langley d				00 09		01 04				05 57											07 31	
Apsley d				00 12		01 07				06 01											07 34	
Hemel Hempstead d				00 15	00 32	01 10	02 04			06 04	06 26					06 47				07 28	07 37	
Berkhamsted d				00 20	00 37	01 15	02 09			06 09	06 31					06 52				07 32	07 42	
Tring d				00 25	00 42	01 20	02 13			06 15	06 37					06 58				07 38	07a49	
Cheddington d					00 47	01 26				06 20						07 03						
Leighton Buzzard d	00 01	00 07		00 35	00 54	01 32	02 22			06 25	06 46					07 08				07 47		
Bletchley d	00 08	00 14		00 42	01 01	01 39	02 29		05 32	06 31	06 53					07 15				07 54		
Milton Keynes Central [10] a	00 16	00 22		00 50	01 09	01 47	02 37		05 38	06 36	06 59	06 39		07 01		07 20		07 25	07 50	07 59		
d	00 17	00 22	00 28		01 09	01 48			05 39	06 37		06 41		07 02		07 20						
Wolverton d	00 21	00 26			01 13	01 51			05 42	06 40						07 24						
Northampton 68 a	00 34	00 44			01 28	02 05			05 55	06 53						07 37						
d									05 56	06 53						07 37						
Long Buckby 68 a									06 07	07 04						07 47						
Rugby 68 a			01 07						06 18	07 15		07 02		07 25	07 51	07 59						
Coventry 68 a			01 17						06 29	07 29			07 22		08 02	08 09						08 22
Nuneaton 65 a														07 40								
Birmingham International 68 ✈ a			01 27						06 45	07 45			07 33		08 13	08 27						08 33
Birmingham New Street [12] 68 ⇌ a			01 39						07 00	08 01			07 45		08 24	08 39						08 45
Sandwell & Dudley 68 a																						
Wolverhampton [7] 68 ⇌ a			02 08						07 22	08 21												

A To Crewe
B To Birmingham New Street
C From London Euston
D From Selhurst
E To Liverpool Lime Street
F From Balham
G To Glasgow Central
H To Rugeley Trent Valley
I To Manchester Piccadilly

Table T066-F

London - Watford Junction, Milton Keynes, Northampton and West Midlands

Saturdays
21 December to 16 May

Station	VT ◇1 A ⊒	VT ◇1 B ⊒	VT ◇1 C ⊒	LM 1 D	VT ◇1 ⊒	LM 1 E	LM 1	LM 1 F	VT ◇1 G ⊒	LM 1	VT ◇1 H ⊒	LM 1 E	LM 1 D	SN 1	LM 1	VT ◇1 ⊒	VT ◇1 I ⊒	LM 1 D	VT ◇1 J ⊒	VT ◇1 ⊒	LM 1 E	LM 1
London Euston [15] ⊖60 d	07 33	07 35	07 43	07 46	08 03	07 24	07 34	07 49	08 10	07 52	08 20	08 15	08 15		08 03	08 23	08 43	08 46	08 54	09 03	08 24	08 34
East Croydon 176 ⇌ d														07 10								
Clapham Junction 176 d														07 40								
Imperial Wharf 176 d														07 45								
West Brompton ⊖176 d														07 48								
Kensington (Olympia) ⊖176 d														07 51								
Shepherd's Bush ⊖176 d														07 54								
Wembley Central ⊖60,176 d														08 09	08 13							
Harrow & Wealdstone ⊖60 d							07 46							08 13	08 18							08 46
Bushey 60 d							07 52								08 23							08 52
Watford Junction 60 a						07 39	07 54	08 03		08 07				08 20	08 26						08 39	08 54
d						07 39	07 55	08 04		08 09				08 20	08 26	08u37					08 39	08 55
Kings Langley d							07 59								08 31							08 59
Apsley d							08 03								08 34							09 03
Hemel Hempstead d						07 47	08 06			08 16				08 28	08 37						08 47	09 06
Berkhamsted d						07 52	08 11			08 21				08 32	08 42						08 52	09 10
Tring d						07 58	08a17							08 38	08a49						08 58	09a17
Cheddington d						08 03				08 30											09 03	
Leighton Buzzard d						08 08				08 35		08 42	08 42	08 47							09 08	
Bletchley d						08 15				08 42		08 49	08 49	08 54							09 15	
Milton Keynes Central [10] a	08 03	08 05	08 13	08 18		08 20		08 25	08 40	08 47	08 50	08 54	08 54	08 59			09 13	09 18			09 20	
d			08 13	08 19		08 20		08 26				08 55	08 55				09 13	09 19			09 20	
Wolverton d						08 24						08 59	08 59								09 24	
Northampton 68 a						08 37		08 41				09 12	09 12								09 37	
d						08 37		08 55				09 14	09 14								09 37	
Long Buckby 68 a						08 48		09 06				09 25	09 25								09 48	
Rugby 68 a				08 42	08 51	08 59		09 17				09 36	09 36					09 42	09 45	09 51	09 59	
Coventry 68 a			08 42		09 02	09 09		09 28				09 46	09 46			09 22	09 42			10 02	10 09	
Nuneaton 65 a				08 55														09 54				
Birmingham International 68 ✈ a			08 53		09 13	09 27		09 45				10 01	10 01			09 33	09 53			10 13	10 27	
Birmingham New Street [12] 68 ⇌ a			09 04		09 23	09 39		10 00				10 13	10 13			09 45	10 04			10 24	10 39	
Sandwell & Dudley 68 a			09 24														10 24					
Wolverhampton [7] 68 ⇌ a			09 37					10 21					10 40				10 37					

Station	LM 1 F	VT ◇1 K ⊒	LM 1	VT ◇1 H ⊒	LM 1 L	LM 1 D	SN 1	LM 1	VT ◇1 ⊒	VT ◇1 C ⊒	LM 1 D	VT ◇1 ⊒	LM 1 E	LM 1	LM 1 F	VT ◇1 G ⊒	LM 1	VT ◇1 H ⊒	VT ◇1 J ⊒	LM 1 L	LM 1 D
London Euston [15] ⊖60 d	08 49	09 10	08 54	09 20	09 15	09 15		09 03	09 23	09 43	09 46	10 03	09 24	09 34	09 49	10 10	09 54	10 20	10 36	10 15	10 15
East Croydon 176 ⇌ d							08 10														
Clapham Junction 176 d							08 40														
Imperial Wharf 176 d							08 45														
West Brompton ⊖176 d							08 48														
Kensington (Olympia) ⊖176 d							08 51														
Shepherd's Bush ⊖176 d							08 54														
Wembley Central ⊖60,176 d							09 09	09 13													
Harrow & Wealdstone ⊖60 d							09 13	09 18						09 46							
Bushey 60 d								09 23						09 52							
Watford Junction 60 a	09 03		09 09				09 20	09 26					09 39	09 54	10 03		10 09				
d	09 04		09 11				09 20	09 26	09u37				09 39	09 55	10 04		10 11				
Kings Langley d								09 31						09 59							
Apsley d								09 34						10 03							
Hemel Hempstead d			09 18				09 28	09 37					09 47	10 06			10 18				
Berkhamsted d			09 23				09 32	09 42					09 52	10 10			10 23				
Tring d							09 38	09a49					09 58	10a17							
Cheddington d													10 03								
Leighton Buzzard d			09 36		09 43	09 43	09 49						10 08				10 36			10 43	10 43
Bletchley d	09 24		09 43		09 51	09 51	09 56						10 15		10 25		10 43			10 51	10 51
Milton Keynes Central [10] a	09 29	09 40	09 48	09 50	09 55	09 55	10 01			10 13	10 18		10 20		10 30	10 40	10 48	10 50		10 55	10 55
d	09 29				09 55	09 55				10 13	10 19		10 20		10 31					10 56	10 56
Wolverton d					09 59	09 59							10 24							11 00	11 00
Northampton 68 a	09 44				10 12	10 12							10 37		10 47					11 12	11 12
d	09 55				10 13	10 13							10 37		10 56					11 14	11 14
Long Buckby 68 a	10 06				10 24	10 24							10 48		11 07					11 25	11 25
Rugby 68 a	10 17				10 35	10 35					10 42	10 51	10 59		11 18				11 24	11 35	11 35
Coventry 68 a	10 29				10 46	10 46			10 22	10 42		11 02	11 09		11 29					11 46	11 46
Nuneaton 65 a											10 54										
Birmingham International 68 ✈ a	10 45				11 01	11 01			10 33	10 53		11 13	11 27		11 45					12 01	12 01
Birmingham New Street [12] 68 ⇌ a	11 01				11 13	11 13			10 45	11 05		11 24	11 39		12 01					12 13	12 13
Sandwell & Dudley 68 a										11 24											
Wolverhampton [7] 68 ⇌ a	11 21					11 40				11 37					12 21						12 40

A from 22 February. To Manchester Piccadilly
B until 15 February. To Manchester Piccadilly
C To Glasgow Central
D To Crewe
E To Rugeley Trent Valley
F To Liverpool Lime Street
G To Chester
H To Manchester Piccadilly
I To Edinburgh
J To Blackpool North
K To Holyhead
L To Walsall

Table T066-F

Saturdays

21 December to 16 May

London - Watford Junction, Milton Keynes, Northampton and West Midlands

	SN	LM	VT	VT	LM	VT	LM	LM	LM	VT	LM	VT	LM	LM	SN	LM	VT	VT	VT	LM	VT	LM
	1	1	◇1	◇1	1	◇1	1	1	1	◇1	1	◇1	1	1	1	1	◇1	◇1	◇1	1	◇1	1
				A	B		C		D	E		F	C	B				G	H	B		C
			⊡	⊡		⊡				⊡		⊡					⊡	⊡	⊡		⊡	
London Euston 15 ⊖60 d		10 03	10 23	10 43	10 46	11 03	10 24	10 34	10 49	11 10	10 54	11 20	11 15	11 15		11 03	11 23	11 23	11 43	11 46	12 03	11 24
East Croydon 176 d	09 10														10 10							
Clapham Junction 176 d	09 40														10 40							
Imperial Wharf 176 d	09 45														10 45							
West Brompton ⊖176 d	09 48														10 48							
Kensington (Olympia) ⊖176 d	09 51														10 51							
Shepherd's Bush ⊖176 d	09 54														10 54							
Wembley Central ⊖60,176 d	10 09	10 13													11 09	11 13						
Harrow & Wealdstone ⊖60 d	10 13	10 18						10 46							11 13	11 18						
Bushey 60 d		10 23						10 52								11 23						
Watford Junction 60 a	10 20	10 26					10 39	10 54	11 03		11 09				11 20	11 26						11 39
d	10 20	10 26	10u37				10 39	10 55	11 04		11 11				11 20	11 26	11u37	11u37				11 39
Kings Langley d		10 31						10 59								11 31						
Apsley d		10 34						11 03								11 34						
Hemel Hempstead d	10 28	10 37					10 47	11 06			11 18				11 28	11 37						11 47
Berkhamsted d	10 32	10 42					10 52	11 10			11 23				11 32	11 42						11 52
Tring d	10 38	10a49					10 58	11a17							11 38	11a49						11 58
Cheddington d							11 03															12 03
Leighton Buzzard d	10 47						11 08				11 36		11 43	11 43	11 47							12 09
Bletchley d	10 55						11 15				11 43		11 51	11 51	11 55							12 16
Milton Keynes Central 10 a	11 00			11 13	11 18		11 20		11 24	11 40	11 48	11 50	11 55	11 55	12 00				12 13	12 18		12 21
d				11 13	11 19		11 20		11 24				11 58	11 58					12 13	12 19		12 21
Wolverton d							11 24						12 02	12 02								12 25
Northampton 68 a							11 37		11 42				12 15	12 15								12 38
d							11 37		11 56				12 15	12 15								12 38
Long Buckby 68 a							11 48		12 07				12 26	12 26								12 49
Rugby 68 a					11 42	11 51	11 59		12 18				12 35	12 35						12 42	12 51	12 59
Coventry 68 a			11 22	11 42		12 02	12 09		12 29				12 47	12 47			12 22	12 22	12 42		13 02	13 09
Nuneaton 65 a					11 54															12 54		
Birmingham International 68 ✈ a			11 33	11 53		12 13	12 27		12 46				13 02	13 02			12 33	12 33	12 53		13 13	13 27
Birmingham New Street 12 68 a			11 45	12 04		12 24	12 39		13 02				13 14	13 14			12 44	12 44	13 04		13 24	13 39
Sandwell & Dudley 68 a				12 24															13 24			
Wolverhampton 7 68 a				12 37					13 22					13 39				13 09	13 37			

	LM	LM	VT	LM	VT	LM	LM	SN	LM	VT	VT	LM	VT	LM	LM	LM	VT	LM	VT	LM	LM
	1	1	◇1	1	◇1	1	1	1	1	◇1	◇1	1	◇1	1	1	1	◇1	1	◇1	1	1
		D	E		F	I	B				A	B		C		D	E		F	C	B
			⊡		⊡					⊡	⊡		⊡				⊡		⊡		
London Euston 15 ⊖60 d	11 34	11 49	12 10	11 54	12 20	12 15	12 15		12 03	12 23	12 43	12 46	13 03	12 24	12 34	12 49	13 10	12 54	13 20	13 15	13 15
East Croydon 176 d								11 10													
Clapham Junction 176 d								11 40													
Imperial Wharf 176 d								11 45													
West Brompton ⊖176 d								11 48													
Kensington (Olympia) ⊖176 d								11 51													
Shepherd's Bush ⊖176 d								11 54													
Wembley Central ⊖60,176 d								12 09	12 13												
Harrow & Wealdstone ⊖60 d	11 46							12 13	12 18						12 46						
Bushey 60 d	11 52								12 23						12 52						
Watford Junction 60 a	11 54	12 03		12 09				12 20	12 26					12 39	12 54	13 03		13 09			
d	11 55	12 04		12 11				12 20	12 26	12u37				12 39	12 55	13 04		13 11			
Kings Langley d	11 59								12 31						12 59						
Apsley d	12 03								12 34						13 03						
Hemel Hempstead d	12 06			12 18				12 28	12 37					12 47	13 06			13 18			
Berkhamsted d	12 10			12 23				12 32	12 42					12 52	13 10			13 23			
Tring d	12a17							12 38	12a49					12 58	13a17						
Cheddington d														13 03							
Leighton Buzzard d				12 36		12 43	12 43	12 47						13 08				13 36		13 43	13 43
Bletchley d				12 43		12 51	12 51	12 55						13 15				13 43		13 51	13 51
Milton Keynes Central 10 a		12 24	12 40	12 48	12 50	12 55	12 55	13 00			13 13	13 18		13 20		13 24	13 40	13 48	13 50	13 55	13 55
d		12 25	12 41			12 56	12 56				13 13	13 19		13 20		13 25				13 56	13 56
Wolverton d						13 00	13 00							13 24						14 00	14 00
Northampton 68 a		12 42				13 12	13 12							13 37		13 42				14 12	14 12
d		12 51				13 14	13 14							13 37		13 55				14 14	14 14
Long Buckby 68 a		13 02				13 25	13 25							13 48		14 06				14 25	14 25
Rugby 68 a		13 17	13 03			13 35	13 35					13 42	13 51	13 59		14 17				14 35	14 35
Coventry 68 a		13 28				13 46	13 46			13 22	13 42		14 02	14 09		14 29				14 47	14 47
Nuneaton 65 a												13 54									
Birmingham International 68 ✈ a		13 45				14 01	14 01			13 33	13 53		14 13	14 27		14 45				15 02	15 02
Birmingham New Street 12 68 a		14 00				14 13	14 13			13 45	14 04		14 24	14 39		15 01				15 14	15 14
Sandwell & Dudley 68 a											14 24										
Wolverhampton 7 68 a		14 21					14 39				14 37					15 21					15 39

A To Edinburgh
B To Crewe
C To Rugeley Trent Valley
D To Liverpool Lime Street
E To Chester
F To Manchester Piccadilly
G To Shrewsbury
H To Glasgow Central
I To Walsall

Table T066-F

Saturdays

21 December to 16 May

London - Watford Junction, Milton Keynes, Northampton and West Midlands

	SN	LM	VT	VT	LM	VT	LM	LM	LM	VT	LM	VT	LM	LM	SN	LM	VT	VT	LM	VT	LM	LM
	1	1	◇1	◇1	1	◇1	1	1	1	◇1	1	◇1	1	1	1	1	◇1	1	1	◇1	1	1
				A	B		C		D	E		F	C	B				G	B		C	
			⊡	⊡		⊡				⊡		⊡					⊡	⊡		⊡		
London Euston 15 ⊖60 d		13 03	13 23	13 43	13 46	14 03	13 24	13 34	13 49	14 10	13 54	14 20	14 15	14 15		14 03	14 23	14 43	14 46	15 03	14 24	14 34
East Croydon 176 d	12 10														13 10							
Clapham Junction 176 d	12 40														13 40							
Imperial Wharf 176 d	12 45														13 45							
West Brompton ⊖176 d	12 48														13 48							
Kensington (Olympia) ⊖176 d	12 51														13 51							
Shepherd's Bush ⊖176 d	12 54														13 54							
Wembley Central ⊖60,176 d	13 09	13 13													14 09	14 13						
Harrow & Wealdstone ⊖60 d	13 13	13 18						13 46							14 13	14 18						14 46
Bushey 60 d		13 23						13 52								14 23						14 52
Watford Junction 60 a	13 20	13 26					13 39	13 54	14 03		14 09				14 20	14 26					14 39	14 54
d	13 20	13 26	13u37				13 40	13 55	14 04		14 11				14 20	14 26	14u37				14 39	14 55
Kings Langley d		13 31						13 59								14 31						14 59
Apsley d		13 34						14 03								14 34						15 03
Hemel Hempstead d	13 28	13 37					13 48	14 06			14 18				14 28	14 37					14 47	15 06
Berkhamsted d	13 33	13 42					13 53	14 10			14 23				14 32	14 42					14 52	15 10
Tring d	13 39	13a49					13 59	14a17							14 38	14a49					14 58	15a17
Cheddington d							14 04														15 03	
Leighton Buzzard d	13 47						14 09				14 36		14 42	14 42	14 47						15 08	
Bletchley d	13 55						14 16				14 43		14 50	14 50	14 54						15 15	
Milton Keynes Central 10 a	14 00			14 13	14 18		14 21		14 24	14 40	14 48	14 50	14 54	14 54	15 00			15 13	15 18		15 20	
d				14 13	14 19		14 21		14 25				14 56	14 56				15 13	15 19		15 20	
Wolverton d							14 25						15 00	15 00							15 24	
Northampton 68 a							14 38		14 43				15 14	15 14							15 37	
d							14 38		14 55				15 15	15 15							15 38	
Long Buckby 68 a							14 49		15 06				15 25	15 25							15 50	
Rugby 68 a					14 42	14 51	15 00		15 19				15 35	15 35					15 42	15 51	16 01	
Coventry 68 a			14 22	14 42		15 02	15 10		15 30				15 47	15 47			15 22	15 42		16 02	16 12	
Nuneaton 65 a					14 54														15 54			
Birmingham International 68 ✈ a			14 33	14 53		15 13	15 28		15 46				16 02	16 02			15 33	15 53		16 13	16 29	
Birmingham New Street 12 68 a			14 45	15 04		15 24	15 40		16 01				16 14	16 14			15 44	16 05		16 24	16 41	
Sandwell & Dudley 68 a				15 24														16 24				
Wolverhampton 7 68 a				15 36					16 21					16 39				16 37				

	LM	VT	LM	VT	LM	LM	SN	LM	VT	VT	LM	VT	LM	LM	LM	VT	LM	VT	LM	LM	SN	LM
	1	◇1	1	◇1	1	1	1	1	◇1	1	1	◇1	1	1	1	◇1	1	◇1	1	1	1	1
	D	H		F	C	B				A	B		C		D	E		F	C	B		
		⊡		⊡					⊡	⊡		⊡				⊡		⊡				
London Euston 15 ⊖60 d	14 49	15 10	14 54	15 20	15 15	15 15		15 03	15 23	15 43	15 46	16 03	15 24	15 34	15 49	16 10	15 54	16 20	16 15	16 15		16 03
East Croydon 176 d							14 10														15 10	
Clapham Junction 176 d							14 40														15 40	
Imperial Wharf 176 d							14 45														15 45	
West Brompton ⊖176 d							14 48														15 48	
Kensington (Olympia) ⊖176 d							14 51														15 51	
Shepherd's Bush ⊖176 d							14 54														15 54	
Wembley Central ⊖60,176 d							15 09	15 13													16 09	16 13
Harrow & Wealdstone ⊖60 d							15 13	15 18						15 46							16 13	16 18
Bushey 60 d								15 23						15 52								16 23
Watford Junction 60 a	15 03		15 11				15 20	15 26					15 39	15 54	16 03		16 09				16 20	16 26
d	15 04		15 11				15 20	15 26	15u37				15 39	15 55	16 04		16 11				16 20	16 26
Kings Langley d								15 31						15 59								16 31
Apsley d								15 34						16 03								16 34
Hemel Hempstead d			15 19				15 28	15 37					15 47	16 06			16 18				16 28	16 37
Berkhamsted d			15 24				15 32	15 42					15 52	16 10			16 23				16 32	16 42
Tring d							15 38	15a49					15 58	16a17							16 38	16a49
Cheddington d													16 03									
Leighton Buzzard d			15 36		15 43	15 43	15 47						16 08				16 36		16 43	16 43	16 47	
Bletchley d			15 43		15 51	15 51	15 55						16 15				16 43		16 51	16 51	16 55	
Milton Keynes Central 10 a	15 25	15 40	15 48	15 50	15 55	15 55	16 01			16 13	16 18		16 20		16 24	16 40	16 48	16 50	16 55	16 55	17 00	
d	15 25				15 56	15 56				16 13	16 19		16 20		16 25				16 56	16 56		
Wolverton d					16 00	16 00							16 24						17 00	17 00		
Northampton 68 a	15 43				16 12	16 12							16 37		16 42				17 12	17 12		
d	15 56				16 14	16 14							16 37		16 55				17 14	17 14		
Long Buckby 68 a	16 07				16 25	16 25							16 48		17 06				17 25	17 25		
Rugby 68 a	16 18				16 35	16 35					16 42	16 51	16 59		17 17				17 35	17 35		
Coventry 68 a	16 29				16 47	16 47			16 22	16 42		17 02	17 09		17 28				17 47	17 47		
Nuneaton 65 a											16 54											
Birmingham International 68 ✈ a	16 45				17 02	17 02			16 33	16 53		17 13	17 27		17 46				18 02	18 02		
Birmingham New Street 12 68 a	17 01				17 14	17 14			16 45	17 05		17 24	17 39		18 01				18 14	18 14		
Sandwell & Dudley 68 a										17 24												
Wolverhampton 7 68 a	17 21					17 39				17 37					18 21					18 39		

A To Glasgow Central
B To Crewe
C To Rugeley Trent Valley
D To Liverpool Lime Street
E To Holyhead
F To Manchester Piccadilly
G To Edinburgh
H To Chester

Table T066-F

Saturdays

21 December to 16 May

London - Watford Junction, Milton Keynes, Northampton and West Midlands

	VT ◇■	VT ◇■ A	LM ■ B	VT ◇■	LM ■ C	LM ■	LM ■ D	VT ◇■ E	LM ■	VT ◇■ F	LM ■ C	LM ■ B	SN ■	LM ■	VT ◇■ D	VT ◇■	VT ◇■ A	LM ■ B	VT ◇■	LM ■ C	LM ■
London Euston ⊖60 d	16 23	16 43	16 46	17 03	16 24	16 34	16 49	17 10	16 54	17 20	17 15	17 15		17 03	17 07	17 23	17 43	17 46	18 03	17 24	17 34
East Croydon 176 d													16 10								
Clapham Junction 176 d													16 40								
Imperial Wharf 176 d													16 45								
West Brompton ⊖176 d													16 48								
Kensington (Olympia) ⊖176 d													16 51								
Shepherd's Bush ⊖176 d													16 54								
Wembley Central ⊖60,176 d													17 09	17 13							
Harrow & Wealdstone ⊖60 d						16 46							17 13	17 18							17 46
Bushey 60 d						16 52								17 23							17 52
Watford Junction 60 a					16 39	16 54	17 03		17 09				17 20	17 26						17 39	17 54
d	16u37				16 39	16 55	17 04		17 11				17 20	17 26		17u37				17 39	17 55
Kings Langley d						16 59								17 31							17 59
Apsley d						17 03								17 34							18 03
Hemel Hempstead d					16 47	17 06			17 18				17 28	17 37						17 47	18 06
Berkhamsted d					16 52	17 10			17 23				17 32	17 42						17 52	18 10
Tring d					16 58	17a17							17 38	17a49						17 58	18a17
Cheddington d					17 03															18 03	
Leighton Buzzard d					17 08				17 36		17 42	17 42	17 47							18 08	
Bletchley d					17 15				17 43		17 49	17 49	17 54							18 15	
Milton Keynes Central a		17 13	17 18		17 20		17 26	17 40	17 48	17 50	17 54	17 54	17 59				18 13	18 18		18 20	
d		17 13	17 19		17 20		17 26				17 56	17 56					18 13	18 19		18 20	
Wolverton d					17 24						18 00	18 00								18 24	
Northampton 68 a					17 37		17 42				18 12	18 12								18 37	
d					17 37		17 56				18 14	18 14								18 37	
Long Buckby 68 a					17 48		18 07				18 25	18 25								18 48	
Rugby 68 a			17 42	17 51	17 59		18 18				18 35	18 35						18 42	18 51	18 59	
Coventry 68 a	17 22	17 42		18 02	18 09		18 29				18 47	18 47				18 22	18 42		19 02	19 09	
Nuneaton 65 a			17 54												18 02			18 54			
Birmingham International 68 ✈ a	17 33	17 53		18 13	18 27		18 45				19 02	19 02				18 33	18 53		19 13	19 27	
Birmingham New Street 68 a	17 45	18 04		18 24	18 39		19 01				19 14	19 14				18 45	19 05		19 24	19 39	
Sandwell & Dudley 68 a		18 24														18 58	19 24		19 48		
Wolverhampton 68 a		18 37					19 22					19 38				19 10	19 37		19 59		

	LM ■ D	VT ◇■ E	LM ■	VT ◇■ F	LM ■	SN ■	LM ■	VT ◇■	VT ◇■ B	LM ■ B	VT ◇■	LM ■ C	LM ■	LM ■	LM ■	SN ■	LM ■	VT ◇■ D	LM ■ B	VT ◇■ F	LM ■ B	LM ■
London Euston ⊖60 d	17 49	18 10	17 54	18 20	18 15		18 03	18 23	18 43	18 46	19 03	18 24	18 34	18 49	18 51		19 03	19 07	19 10	19 20	19 33	19 20
East Croydon 176 d						17 10										18 09						
Clapham Junction 176 d						17 40										18 40						
Imperial Wharf 176 d						17 45										18 45						
West Brompton ⊖176 d						17 48										18 48						
Kensington (Olympia) ⊖176 d						17 51										18 51						
Shepherd's Bush ⊖176 d						17 54										18 54						
Wembley Central ⊖60,176 d						18 09	18 13									19 08	19 13					
Harrow & Wealdstone ⊖60 d						18 13	18 18						18 46			19 13	19 18					
Bushey 60 d							18 23						18 52				19 23					
Watford Junction 60 a	18 03		18 09			18 20	18 26					18 39	18 54	19 03	19 06	19 20	19 26					19 35
d	18 04		18 11			18 20	18 26	18u37				18 39	18 55	19 04	19 07		19 26					19 36
Kings Langley d							18 31						18 59				19 31					
Apsley d							18 34						19 03				19 34					
Hemel Hempstead d			18 18			18 28	18 37					18 46	19 06		19 14		19 37					19 44
Berkhamsted d			18 23			18 32	18 42					18 51	19 10		19 19		19 42					19 49
Tring d						18 38	18a49					18 57	19a17		19 25		19a49					
Cheddington d												19 03			19 30							
Leighton Buzzard d			18 36		18 43	18 47						19 08			19 35							20 01
Bletchley d			18 43		18 51	18 55						19 15			19a42							
Milton Keynes Central a	18 25	18 40	18 48	18 50	18 55	19 01			19 13	19 18		19 20		19 25					19 42	19 50	20 05	20 10
d	18 25				18 56				19 13	19 19		19 20		19 25					19 46		20 06	20 10
Wolverton d					19 00							19 24							19 50			
Northampton 68 a	18 42				19 12							19 37		19 45					20 04			20 25
d	18 55				19 14							19 37		19 56					20 04			20 30
Long Buckby 68 a	19 06				19 25							19 48		20 07					20 15			20 42
Rugby 68 a	19 17				19 35					19 42	19 51	19 59		20 19					20 25		20 30	20 53
Coventry 68 a	19 28				19 47			19 22	19 42		20 02	20 09		20 30					20 36			21 05
Nuneaton 65 a										19 54								20 02			20 41	
Birmingham International 68 ✈ a	19 46				20 02			19 33	19 53		20 13	20 27		20 46					20 54			21 23
Birmingham New Street 68 a	20 01				20 14			19 44	20 06		20 24	20 39		21 02					21 06			21 41
Sandwell & Dudley 68 a								19 58	20 24		20 54											
Wolverhampton 68 a	20 21							20 11	20 37		21 09								21 32			

A To Preston
B To Crewe
C To Rugeley Trent Valley
D To Liverpool Lime Street
E To Chester
F To Manchester Piccadilly

Table T066-F

Saturdays

21 December to 16 May

London - Watford Junction, Milton Keynes, Northampton and West Midlands

	VT ◇■	VT ◇■	VT ◇■ A	LM ■	LM ■	LM ■	SN ■	LM ■	VT ◇■ B	VT ◇■	VT ◇■ C	LM ■ D	LM ■ E	LM ■	VT ◇■ B	VT ◇■	LM ■ F	LM ■ E	SN ■	LM ■ E	VT ◇■
London Euston ⊖60 d	19 23	19 43	20 11	19 30	19 41	19 47		20 02	20 20	20 25	20 31	20 34	20 39	20 42	21 01	21 03		21 09		21 31	21 42
East Croydon 176 d							19 10												20 10		
Clapham Junction 176 d							19 36												20 51		
Imperial Wharf 176 d							19 41												20 56		
West Brompton ⊖176 d							19 44												20 59		
Kensington (Olympia) ⊖176 d							19 47												21 03		
Shepherd's Bush ⊖176 d							19 50												21 06		
Wembley Central ⊖60,176 d																			21 21		
Harrow & Wealdstone ⊖60 d				19 42	19 53		20 07											21 21	21 26		
Bushey 60 d				19 48		20s02												21s26			
Watford Junction 60 a				19 50	19 59	20 05	20 14	20 18					20 54	20 59				21 29	21 33		
d	19u37			19 51	20 01	20 06		20 19		20u40	20u46	20u51	20 55	21 00		21u19		21 29			21u58
Kings Langley d				19 55		20 10								21 04							
Apsley d				19 59		20 14								21 08							
Hemel Hempstead d				20 02	20 08	20 17							21 02					21 37		21 53	
Berkhamsted d				20 08	20 13	20 22							21 07					21 42		21 58	
Tring d				20 13	20 18									21 16				21 47			
Cheddington d					20 23									21 21				21 52			
Leighton Buzzard d				20 22	20 30	20 36		20 40					21 20					21 59		22 09	
Bletchley d				20 29	20 37	20 43		20 47					21 27	21 31				22 06		22 16	
Milton Keynes Central a		20 20		20 37	20 45	20 49		20 53	21 03			21 21	21 34	21 39	21 44	21 51		22 14		22 24	22 29
d		20 20		20 37	20 46	20 50			21 05			21 22	21 35	21 42		21 51		22 14		22 25	22 30
Wolverton d				20 41	20 49	20 54							21 38				←	22 18		22 29	
Northampton 68 a				20 55	21 03	21 09							21 53	21 57			21 53	22 31		22 44	
d				20 57		21 18							21 56				21 56	22 40		22 53	
Long Buckby 68 a				21 07		21 28							→				22 07	→		→	
Rugby 68 a			21 15	21 18		21 39					21 34	21 46				22 12	22 18				22 52
Coventry 68 a	20 22	20 49		21 29		21 49				21 36						22 23	22 29				23 02
Nuneaton 65 a									21 32			21 59									
Birmingham International 68 ✈ a	20 33	21 00		21 45		22 04				21 49						22 33	22 45				23 13
Birmingham New Street 68 a	20 45	21 11		22 01		22 18				22 05						22 45	22 59				23 24
Sandwell & Dudley 68 a	20 58									22 24						22 56					23 35
Wolverhampton 68 a	21 12	21 35								22 37						23 09					23 47

	LM ■ F	LM ■ F	LM ■	SN ■	LM ■	LM ■	SN ■	LM ■	LM ■	LM ■
London Euston ⊖60 d			21 54		22 12	22 34		23 05	23 21	23 40
East Croydon 176 d				21 10			22 10			
Clapham Junction 176 d				21 39			22 39			
Imperial Wharf 176 d				21 44			22 44			
West Brompton ⊖176 d				21 47			22 47			
Kensington (Olympia) ⊖176 d				21 50			22 50			
Shepherd's Bush ⊖176 d				21 53			22 53			
Wembley Central ⊖60,176 d				22 11	22 23		23 07	23 15		
Harrow & Wealdstone ⊖60 d			22 06	22 16	22 27		23 11	23 19	23 34	23 52
Bushey 60 d			22s11		22s32					23s57
Watford Junction 60 a			22 14	22 24	22 35	22 52	23 18	23 25	23 40	00 01
d			22 15		22 36	22 53		23 26	23 41	00 02
Kings Langley d			22 19					23 30	23 45	00 06
Apsley d			22 23					23 34	23 49	00 10
Hemel Hempstead d			22 26		22 43	23 00		23 37	23 52	00 13
Berkhamsted d			22 31		22 48	23 05		23 42	23 57	00 18
Tring d			22 36			23 10		23 47	00 03	00 23
Cheddington d			22 41					23 52	00 08	00 28
Leighton Buzzard d			22 48		23 02	23 20		23 59	00 14	00 35
Bletchley d			22 55		23 09	23 27		00 06	00 21	00 42
Milton Keynes Central a			23 03		23 17	23 35		00 14	00 29	00 47
d			23 04		23 17	23 35		00 15	00 30	00 47
Wolverton d	←	←	23 08		23 21	23 39		00 19	00 34	00 51
Northampton 68 a	22 31	22 44	23 21		23 35	23 53		00 33	00 48	01 08
d	22 40	22 53								
Long Buckby 68 a	22 51	23 03								
Rugby 68 a	23 02	23 14								
Coventry 68 a	23 13	23 25								
Nuneaton 65 a										
Birmingham International 68 ✈ a	23 28	23 43								
Birmingham New Street 68 a	23 43	00 02								
Sandwell & Dudley 68 a										
Wolverhampton 68 a										

A To Liverpool Lime Street
B To Manchester Piccadilly
C To Preston
D To Crewe
E To Birmingham New Street
F From London Euston

Table T066-F

Sundays
15 December to 10 May

London - Watford Junction, Milton Keynes, Northampton and West Midlands

	LM	LM	LM	LM	LM	LM	LM	LM	LM	LM	LM	LM	VT	VT	VT	LM	SN	VT	VT	LM	LM	VT
	A	A	A		Bus	Bus	Bus	Bus	Bus			B	C	B	C	D		E		F	G	B
London Euston ⊖60 d				00 15	02 00	02 00	02 00	02 00	02 00	06 51	07 18	07 52	08 10	08 16	08 20	08 24		08 47	08 50		08 55	09 16
East Croydon 176 d																						
Clapham Junction 176 d																	08 15					
Imperial Wharf 176 d																	08 19					
West Brompton ⊖176 d																	08 22					
Kensington (Olympia) ⊖176 d																	08 26					
Shepherd's Bush ⊖176 d																	08 29					
Wembley Central ⊖60,176 d									02 30													
Harrow & Wealdstone ⊖60 d				00 29				02 35	02 45	07 03	07 30	08 04				08 36	08 47				09 07	
Bushey 60 d											07s35					08s41						
Watford Junction 60 a				00 35	02 50		02 50	02 55	03 05	07 09	07 38	08 10				08 44	08 55				09 13	
d			00 02	00 35	02 50		02 50	02 55	03 05	07 10	07 39	08 10				08 44			09u07		09 14	
Kings Langley d			00 06	00 40					03 20		07 43					08 49						
Apsley d			00 10	00 44					03 30		07 47					08 52						
Hemel Hempstead d			00 13	00 46		03 00	03 15		03 35	07 17	07 50	08 17				08 55					09 21	
Berkhamsted d			00 18	00 51				03 20	03 45	07 22	07 55	08 22				09 00					09 26	
Tring d		00 03	00 23	00 56					04 00	07 26		08 27									09 29	
Cheddington d		00 08	00 28	01 01					04 20	07 32		08 32									09 35	
Leighton Buzzard d		00 14	00 35	01 06			03 51		04 40	07 38	08 08	08 39				09 14					09 41	
Bletchley d	00 06	00 21	00 42	01 13			04 16		05 05	07 45	08 15	08 45				09 21					09 48	
Milton Keynes Central 10 a	00 14	00 29	00 47	01 19	04 00	04 00	04 31	04 10	05 20	07 54	08 23	08 50	08 55		09 05	09 26		09 33	09 37		09 57	
d	00 15	00 30	00 47	01 19						07 55	08 24	08 51				09 26		09 34	09 39		09 57	
Wolverton d	00 19	00 34	00 51	01 23						07 59	08 28	08 55				09 30				←	10 01	
Northampton 68 a	00 33	00 48	01 08	01 37						08 12	08 41	09 08				09 45				09 45	10 14	
d												09 26				09 59				09 59	10 28	
Long Buckby 68 a												09 37				→				10 10	10 38	
Rugby 68 a												09 48						10 08	10 13	10 21	10 49	
Coventry 68 a												09 59							10 23	10 32		
Nuneaton 65 a														09 43							11 02	10 44
Birmingham International 68 ✈ a												10 09							10 34	10 50		
Birmingham New Street 12 68 ⇌ a												10 26							10 45	11 02		
Sandwell & Dudley 68 a																			10 58			
Wolverhampton 7 68 ⇌ a												11 01							11 10	11 33		

	VT	LM	LM	SN	VT	VT	LM	LM	LM	VT	VT	LM	LM	SN	VT	VT	LM	LM	VT	VT	LM	SN
	C	B	D		E		F		G	B	C		D		E		F	G	B	C	D	
London Euston ⊖60 d	09 20		09 24		09 46	09 50		09 55	10 01	10 16	10 19	10 22	10 31		10 46	10 49		10 53	11 16	11 19	11 24	
East Croydon 176 d																						
Clapham Junction 176 d				09 13										10 17								11 16
Imperial Wharf 176 d				09 17										10 21								11 20
West Brompton ⊖176 d				09 20										10 24								11 23
Kensington (Olympia) ⊖176 d				09 24										10 28								11 27
Shepherd's Bush ⊖176 d				09 27										10 31								11 30
Wembley Central ⊖60,176 d																						
Harrow & Wealdstone ⊖60 d			09 36	09 47					10 13			10 35		10 47				11 06			11 36	11 48
Bushey 60 d			09s41															11s11				
Watford Junction 60 a			09 44	09 55				10 10	10 19			10 41	10 46	10 59				11 13			11 42	11 57
d			09 45			10u06		10 11	10 19			10 41	10 47			11u07		11 14			11 42	
Kings Langley d			09 49																		11 47	
Apsley d			09 53										10 53								11 51	
Hemel Hempstead d			09 56					10 18	10 26			10 48	10 56					11 21			11 53	
Berkhamsted d			10 01					10 23	10 31			10 53	11 00					11 26			11 58	
Tring d									10 36									11 30				
Cheddington d									10 41									11 36				
Leighton Buzzard d			10 14					10 36	10 47			11 06	11 13					11 42			12 12	
Bletchley d			10 21					10 43				11 13						11 49			12 19	
Milton Keynes Central 10 a	10 06		10 26		10 32	10 37		10 51	10 58		11 06	11 21	11 26		11 32	11 37		11 57	12 02	12 08	12 27	
d		10 11	10 27		10 33	10 38		10 51	10 58				11 27		11 33	11 38		11 58			12 28	
Wolverton d		10 15	10 31				←		11 02				11 31				←	12 01			12 32	
Northampton 68 a		10 32	10 44				10 44	11 05	11 16				11 45				11 45	12 16			12 44	
d		10 37	11 00				11 00	11 11	11 30				11 58				11 58	12 17			12 55	
Long Buckby 68 a			→				11 11	11 22	11 40				→				12 09	12 28			→	
Rugby 68 a		10 56			11 07	11 13	11 22	11 33	11 51						12 07	12 13	12 20	12 39				
Coventry 68 a		11 06				11 22	11 33	11 45								12 23	12 31					
Nuneaton 65 a									12 03	11 46								12 50				
Birmingham International 68 ✈ a		11 16				11 33	11 51	11 55								12 34	12 49					
Birmingham New Street 12 68 ⇌ a		11 27				11 46	12 03	12 06								12 45	13 01					
Sandwell & Dudley 68 a						11 57										12 58						
Wolverhampton 7 68 ⇌ a		11 59				12 11	12 30									13 10	13 33					

A not 15 December. From London Euston
B To Liverpool Lime Street
C To Manchester Piccadilly
D To Stafford
E To Glasgow Central
F From London Euston to Stafford
G To Crewe

NRT DECEMBER 19 EDITION

Table T066-F

Sundays
15 December to 10 May

London - Watford Junction, Milton Keynes, Northampton and West Midlands

	VT	LM	LM	LM	LM	VT	VT	SN	LM	VT	LM	VT	LM	LM	LM	LM	LM	VT	VT	SN	VT
		A				B			C	D	E		F	G				B			H
London Euston ⊖60 d	11 49		11 54	12 08	12 12	12 17	12 20		12 31	12 40	12 43	13 00		12 34	12 54	13 08	13 12	13 17	13 20		13 40
East Croydon 176 d																					
Clapham Junction 176 d								12 05												13 05	
Imperial Wharf 176 d								12 09												13 09	
West Brompton ⊖176 d								12 12												13 12	
Kensington (Olympia) ⊖176 d								12 16												13 16	
Shepherd's Bush ⊖176 d								12 19												13 19	
Wembley Central ⊖60,176 d																					
Harrow & Wealdstone ⊖60 d			12 06		12 24			12 35							13 06		13 24			13 35	
Bushey 60 d			12s11		12 30												13 30				
Watford Junction 60 a			12 14	12 22	12 32			12 43						12 49	13 12	13 22	13 32			13 43	
d	12u04		12 14	12 23	12 33		12u34							12 50	13 13	13 23	13 33		13u34		
Kings Langley d			12 19		12 37												13 37				
Apsley d					12 41												13 41				
Hemel Hempstead d			12 24		12 44									12 57	13 20		13 44				
Berkhamsted d			12 29		12 49									13 02	13 25		13 49				
Tring d			12 34		12a55										13 32		13a55				
Cheddington d			12 39												13 37						
Leighton Buzzard d			12 46						12 59					13 15	13 42						
Bletchley d			12 53						13 06					13 22	13 49						
Milton Keynes Central 10 a	12 29		12 59	12 46		12 50			13 13	13 13	13 18			13 27	13 54	13 46		13 50			14 13
d	12 30			12 52					13 13	13 13	13 20			13 28		13 50					14 13
Wolverton d		←		12 56					13 17				←	13 32		13 54					
Northampton 68 a		12 44		13 08					13 30				13 30	13 44		14 06					
d		12 55		13 15					13 34				13 34	13 55		14 15					
Long Buckby 68 a		13 06		13 25					→				13 44	14 06		14 25					
Rugby 68 a	12 49	13 17		13 36							13 43	13 51	13 56	14 17		14 36					
Coventry 68 a	13 00	13 29		13 47			13 22			13 42		14 02	14 07	14 29		14 47			14 22		14 43
Nuneaton 65 a											13 59										
Birmingham International 68 ✈ a	13 10	13 48		13 56			13 33			13 53		14 13	14 17	14 47		14 56			14 33		14 53
Birmingham New Street 12 68 ⇌ a	13 22	14 00		14 07			13 44			14 05		14 23	14 30	15 00		15 07			14 44		15 05
Sandwell & Dudley 68 a							13 55			14 24											15 25
Wolverhampton 7 68 ⇌ a		14 24					14 07			14 37			14 54	15 26							15 36

	LM	LM	VT	LM	LM	LM	LM	VT	LM	SN	VT	LM	VT	LM	VT	LM	LM	VT	LM	LM	LM	VT
	C	E		F	G						B	C	D	E		F	G	I				B
London Euston ⊖60 d	13 32	13 43	14 00		13 34	13 54	14 08	14 20	14 12		14 17	14 31	14 40	14 43	15 00		14 34	15 08	14 54	15 06	15 12	15 17
East Croydon 176 d																						
Clapham Junction 176 d										14 05												
Imperial Wharf 176 d										14 09												
West Brompton ⊖176 d										14 12												
Kensington (Olympia) ⊖176 d										14 16												
Shepherd's Bush ⊖176 d										14 19												
Wembley Central ⊖60,176 d																						
Harrow & Wealdstone ⊖60 d						14 06			14 26	14 35									15 06		15 24	
Bushey 60 d									14 32												15 30	
Watford Junction 60 a					13 49	14 12	14 22		14 34	14 43							14 49		15 12	15 21	15 32	
d					13 50	14 13	14 23	14u34	14 35								14 50		15 13	15 21	15 33	
Kings Langley d									14 39												15 37	
Apsley d									14 43												15 41	
Hemel Hempstead d					13 57	14 20			14 46								14 57		15 20		15 44	
Berkhamsted d					14 02	14 25			14 51								15 02		15 25		15 49	
Tring d						14 32			14a57										15 32		15a55	
Cheddington d						14 37													15 37			
Leighton Buzzard d	14 00				14 15	14 42						14 58					15 15		15 42			
Bletchley d	14 07				14 22	14 49						15 05					15 22		15 49			
Milton Keynes Central 10 a	14 14	14 18			14 27	14 54	14 46				14 50	15 12	15 13	15 18			15 27	15 41	15 54	15 46		15 50
d	14 14	14 19			14 28		14 50					15 13	15 13	15 19			15 28			15 50		
Wolverton d	14 18			←	14 32		14 54					15 17				←	15 32			15 54		
Northampton 68 a	14 31			14 31	14 44		15 07					15 30				15 30	15 44			16 07		
d	14 35			14 35	14 55		15 15					15 34				15 34	15 55			16 15		
Long Buckby 68 a	→			14 45	15 06		15 25					→				15 44	16 06			16 25		
Rugby 68 a		14 42	14 51	14 57	15 17		15 36							15 42	15 51	15 56	16 17			16 36		
Coventry 68 a			15 02	15 08	15 29		15 47	15 22					15 42		16 02	16 07	16 29			16 47		
Nuneaton 65 a		14 59												15 54								
Birmingham International 68 ✈ a			15 13	15 18	15 47		15 56	15 32					15 53		16 12	16 17	16 47			16 56		
Birmingham New Street 12 68 ⇌ a			15 23	15 31	16 00		16 07	15 45					16 05		16 22	16 29	17 00			17 07		
Sandwell & Dudley 68 a													16 24									
Wolverhampton 7 68 ⇌ a				15 54	16 26								16 37			16 54	17 22					

A From London Euston to Stafford
B To Manchester Piccadilly
C To Liverpool Lime Street
D To Edinburgh
E To Crewe
F From London Euston to Liverpool Lime Street
G To Stafford
H To Glasgow Central
I To Chester

London - Watford Junction, Milton Keynes, Northampton and West Midlands

Sundays
15 December to 10 May

Station		VT	SN	LM A	VT B	LM C	VT	LM D	LM E	VT F	LM	LM	LM	VT G	VT	SN	VT H	LM A	LM C	VT	LM D	LM C
London Euston ⊖60	d	15 20		15 31	15 40	15 43	16 00		15 34	16 08	15 54	16 06	16 12	16 17	16 20		16 40	16 32	16 43	17 00		16 34
East Croydon 176	d																					
Clapham Junction 176	d		15 05													16 05						
Imperial Wharf 176	d		15 09													16 09						
West Brompton ⊖176	d		15 12													16 12						
Kensington (Olympia) ⊖176	d		15 16													16 16						
Shepherd's Bush ⊖176	d		15 19													16 19						
Wembley Central ⊖60,176	d																					
Harrow & Wealdstone ⊖60	d		15 35								16 06		16 24			16 35						
Bushey 60	d												16 30									
Watford Junction 60	a		15 43						15 49		16 12	16 21	16 32			16 43						16 49
	d	15u34							15 50		16 13	16 21	16 33		16u34							16 50
Kings Langley	d												16 37									
Apsley	d												16 41									
Hemel Hempstead	d								15 57		16 20		16 44									16 57
Berkhamsted	d								16 02		16 25		16 49									17 02
Tring	d										16 32		16a55									
Cheddington	d										16 37											
Leighton Buzzard	d			15 58					16 15		16 42							16 59				17 15
Bletchley	d			16 05					16 22		16 49							17 06				17 22
Milton Keynes Central	a			16 12	16 13	16 18			16 27	16 41	16 54	16 46		16 50			17 13	17 13	17 18			17 27
	d			16 13	16 13	16 19			16 28			16 49					17 13	17 14	17 19			17 28
Wolverton	d			16 17				←	16 32			16 53						17 18			←	17 32
Northampton 68	a			16 30				16 30	16 44			17 06						17 31			17 31	17 44
	d			16 34				16 34	16 55			17 15						17 34			17 34	17 55
Long Buckby 68	a			→				16 44	17 06			17 25						→			17 44	18 06
Rugby 68	a					16 42	16 51	16 56	17 17			17 36							17 42	17 51	17 56	18 17
Coventry 68	a	16 22			16 42		17 02	17 07	17 29			17 47			17 22		17 42			18 02	18 07	18 29
Nuneaton 65	a					16 59													17 58			
Birmingham International 68	a	16 33			16 52		17 13	17 17	17 47			17 56			17 33		17 53			18 13	18 17	18 47
Birmingham New Street 68	a	16 45			17 04		17 23	17 30	18 00			18 06			17 45		18 05			18 23	18 30	19 00
Sandwell & Dudley 68	a				17 25												18 24					
Wolverhampton 68	a				17 37			17 54	18 28								18 37				18 54	19 23

Station		VT F	LM	VT A	LM	VT	LM	SN	VT G	VT B	LM A	LM C	VT	LM D	LM C	VT F	LM	LM	LM	VT G	VT	SN	LM C
London Euston ⊖60	d	17 08	16 54	17 05	17 06	17 20	17 12		17 17	17 40	17 32	17 43	18 00		17 34	18 08	17 54	18 06	18 12	18 17	18 20		18 31
East Croydon 176	d																						
Clapham Junction 176	d							17 05														18 05	
Imperial Wharf 176	d							17 09														18 09	
West Brompton ⊖176	d							17 12														18 12	
Kensington (Olympia) ⊖176	d							17 16														18 16	
Shepherd's Bush ⊖176	d							17 19														18 19	
Wembley Central ⊖60,176	d																						
Harrow & Wealdstone ⊖60	d		17 06				17 26	17 35									18 06		18 24			18 35	
Bushey 60	d						17 32												18 30				
Watford Junction 60	a		17 12		17 21		17 34	17 43							17 49		18 12	18 21	18 32			18 43	
	d		17 13		17 21	17u34	17 35								17 50		18 13	18 21	18 33		18u34		
Kings Langley	d						17 39												18 37				
Apsley	d						17 43												18 41				
Hemel Hempstead	d		17 20				17 46								17 57		18 20		18 44				
Berkhamsted	d		17 25				17 51								18 02		18 25		18 49				
Tring	d		17 32				17a57										18 32		18a55				
Cheddington	d		17 37														18 37						
Leighton Buzzard	d		17 42								18 00				18 15		18 42						18 58
Bletchley	d		17 49								18 07				18 22		18 49						
Milton Keynes Central	a	17 41	17 54		17 46				17 50	18 13	18 14	18 18			18 27	18 41	18 54	18 46		18 50			19 10
	d				17 49					18 13	18 14	18 19			18 28			18 47					19 13
Wolverton	d				17 53						18 18			←	18 32			18 51					19 17
Northampton 68	a				18 06						18 31			18 31	18 44			19 04					19 30
	d				18 16						18 34			18 34	18 55			19 07					19 34
Long Buckby 68	a				18 26						→			18 44	19 06			19 18					→
Rugby 68	a				18 37							18 42	18 51	18 56	19 17			19 29					
Coventry 68	a				18 48	18 22				18 42			19 02	19 07	19 29			19 47			19 22		
Nuneaton 65	a			18 03								18 59											
Birmingham International 68	a				18 57	18 33				18 53			19 13	19 17	19 47			19 56			19 33		
Birmingham New Street 68	a				19 07	18 45				19 04			19 23	19 30	20 01			20 09			19 44		
Sandwell & Dudley 68	a									19 24			19 47										
Wolverhampton 68	a									19 37			19 59	19 54	20 25								

A To Liverpool Lime Street
B To Glasgow Central
C To Crewe
D From London Euston to Liverpool Lime Street
E To Stafford
F To Chester
G To Manchester Piccadilly
H To Edinburgh

London - Watford Junction, Milton Keynes, Northampton and West Midlands

Sundays
15 December to 10 May

Station		VT A	LM A	VT	LM B	LM A	VT C	LM A	VT D	LM	VT E	LM	VT	SN	LM A	VT	LM E	VT F	LM	VT E	VT D	LM	VT E
London Euston ⊖60	d	18 40	18 43	19 00		18 34	19 08	19 11	19 17	18 54	19 05	19 12	19 20		19 47	20 00	19 31	19 40	19 34	20 08	20 15	19 50	20 05
East Croydon 176	d																						
Clapham Junction 176	d													19 05									
Imperial Wharf 176	d													19 09									
West Brompton ⊖176	d													19 12									
Kensington (Olympia) ⊖176	d													19 16									
Shepherd's Bush ⊖176	d													19 19									
Wembley Central ⊖60,176	d																						
Harrow & Wealdstone ⊖60	d									19 06		19 24		19 35								20 02	
Bushey 60	d											19 30											
Watford Junction 60	a					18 49				19 12		19 32		19 43					19 49			20 08	
	d					18 50				19 13		19 33	19u34						19 50			20 09	
Kings Langley	d											19 37											
Apsley	d											19 41											
Hemel Hempstead	d					18 57				19 20		19 44							19 57			20 16	
Berkhamsted	d					19 02				19 25		19 49							20 02			20 21	
Tring	d									19 32		19a55										20 28	
Cheddington	d									19 37												20 33	
Leighton Buzzard	d					19 15				19 42							19 58		20 15			20 38	
Bletchley	d					19 22				19 49							20 05		20 22			20 45	
Milton Keynes Central	a	19 13	19 18			19 27	19 41	19 46	19 50	19 54							20 12	20 13	20 27	20 41	20 48	20 50	
	d	19 13	19 19			19 28		19 50									20 13	20 13	20 28			20 51	
Wolverton	d				←	19 32		19 54									20 17		20 32				
Northampton 68	a				19 30	19 44		20 06									20 30		20 44			21 05	
	d				19 34	19 55		20 09									20 34		20 55				
Long Buckby 68	a				19 44	20 06		20 19									20 44		21 06				
Rugby 68	a		19 42	19 51	19 56	20 17		20 30							20 44	20 51	20 56		21 17				
Coventry 68	a	19 42		20 02	20 07	20 29		20 47					20 22			21 02	21 07	20 42	21 29				
Nuneaton 65	a		19 59								20 03				20 59								21 03
Birmingham International 68	a	19 53		20 13	20 17	20 47		20 58					20 33			21 13	21 17	20 53	21 47				
Birmingham New Street 68	a	20 05		20 23	20 30	20 59		21 08					20 45			21 23	21 32	21 05	21 59				
Sandwell & Dudley 68	a	20 24		20 36									20 57					21 24					
Wolverhampton 68	a	20 37		20 48	20 59	21 19		21 40					21 10				22 01	21 37					

Station		LM	LM	VT	SN	VT	LM G	LM	VT F	VT	LM H	LM	VT E	VT D	LM	SN	LM	VT D	VT	LM I	VT	LM H
London Euston ⊖60	d	20 07	20 11	20 18		20 38	20 34	20 42	20 50	20 54		21 06	21 21	21 25	21 31		21 40	21 51	21 55	22 01	22 25	
East Croydon 176	d																					
Clapham Junction 176	d				20 05											21 19						
Imperial Wharf 176	d				20 09											21 23						
West Brompton ⊖176	d				20 12											21 26						
Kensington (Olympia) ⊖176	d				20 16											21 30						
Shepherd's Bush ⊖176	d				20 19											21 33						
Wembley Central ⊖60,176	d																					
Harrow & Wealdstone ⊖60	d	20 19	20 23		20 35											21 50	21 55			22 14		
Bushey 60	d		20 29														22s00					
Watford Junction 60	a	20 25	20 31		20 43		20 49	20 57				21 25			21 46	22 00	22 03			22 20		
	d	20 26	20 32	20u32			20 50	20 58		21u11		21 25			21 47		22 04		22u13	22 21	22u41	
Kings Langley	d		20 36												21 51							
Apsley	d		20 40												21 55							
Hemel Hempstead	d	20 33	20 43				20 57					21 32			21 57					22 28		
Berkhamsted	d	20 38	20 48				21 01					21 37			22 02					22 33		
Tring	d		20 53									21 41			22 07					22 38		
Cheddington	d											21 46								22 43		
Leighton Buzzard	d	20 50					21 14	21 20				21 53			22 17		22 24			22 50		
Bletchley	d						21 21					22 00			22 24					22 57		
Milton Keynes Central	a	21 02	21 09			21 17	21 30	21 35	21 38	21 43		22 08		22 17	22 32		22 36	22 40	22 45	23 05	23 13	
	d	21 02				21 17	21 31		21 40	21 45		22 08			22 32		22 37	22 42	22 47	23 06	23 14	
Wolverton	d						21 35				←	22 12					22 40			23 10		←
Northampton 68	a	21 20					21 48				21 48	22 25			22 48		22 55			23 24		23 24
	d						21 57				21 57	22 37			22 51					23 33		23 33
Long Buckby 68	a						→				22 08	22 47			23 02					→		23 43
Rugby 68	a								22 00	22 05	22 19	22 58			23 13			23 17	23 22		23 46	23 54
Coventry 68	a			21 20		21 46				22 16	22 31	23 08			23 23				23 33		23 57	00 04
Nuneaton 65	a												22 56					23 29				
Birmingham International 68	a			21 30		21 56				22 26	22 49	23 18			23 54				23 43		00 07	
Birmingham New Street 68	a			21 44		22 09				22 39	23 02	23 36			00 07				23 56		00 19	
Sandwell & Dudley 68	a			21 55		22 24				22 50		23 50										
Wolverhampton 68	a			22 08		22 36				23 02		00 04							00 15		00 39	

A To Crewe
B From London Euston to Crewe
C To Holyhead
D To Manchester Piccadilly
E To Liverpool Lime Street
F To Preston
G To Birmingham New Street
H From London Euston
I To Coventry

Table T066-F

Sundays
15 December to 10 May

London - Watford Junction, Milton Keynes, Northampton and West Midlands

	LM	SN	LM	LM	VT	LM
London Euston ⊖60 d	22 31		22 40	22 59	23 24	23 39
East Croydon 176 d						
Clapham Junction 176 d		22 19				
Imperial Wharf 176 d		22 23				
West Brompton ⊖176 d		22 26				
Kensington (Olympia) ⊖176 d		22 30				
Shepherd's Bush ⊖176 d		22 33				
Wembley Central ⊖60,176 d						
Harrow & Wealdstone ⊖60 d	22 43	22 49	22 54	23 12		23 51
Bushey 60 d	22s48					23s56
Watford Junction 60 a	22 51	22 58	23 01	23 18		23 59
d	22 52		23 02	23 19	23u39	00 01
Kings Langley d	22 56			23 23		00 05
Apsley d	23 00			23 27		00 09
Hemel Hempstead d	23 03		23 10	23 30		00 12
Berkhamsted d	23 08		23 15	23 35		00 17
Tring d			23 20	23 40		00 22
Cheddington d			23 25	23 45		00 27
Leighton Buzzard d	23 21		23 32	23 52		00 34
Bletchley d	23 28		23 39	23 59		00 41
Milton Keynes Central a	23 36		23 47	00 07	00 11	00 49
d	23 36		23 48	00 07	00 12	00 49
Wolverton d	23 40			00 11		00 53
Northampton 68 a	23 53		00 04	00 25		01 07
d						
Long Buckby 68 a						
Rugby 68 a					00s47	
Coventry 68 a					00s59	
Nuneaton 65 a						
Birmingham International 68 a					01s09	
Birmingham New Street 68 a					01s22	
Sandwell & Dudley 68 a						
Wolverhampton 68 a					01 42	

Table T066-R

Mondays to Fridays
16 December to 15 May

West Midlands, Northampton, Milton Keynes and Watford Junction - London

Miles	Miles	Miles		LM MO A	LM MX B	LM MO B	LM MX C	LM MX D	VT MX E	LM	LM		LM	SN	LM	LM	LM	LM	LM	CS MO F	LM		LM G	VT
0	—	—	Wolverhampton 68 d																					05 00
7½	—	—	Sandwell & Dudley 68 d																					
12¾	—	—	**Birmingham New Street** 68 d																					05 29
21¼	—	—	Birmingham International 68 d																					05 40
—	—	—	Nuneaton 65 d																					
32	—	—	Coventry 68 d																					05 51
43½	0	—	**Rugby** 68 d															05 15						06 03
53	—	—	Long Buckby 68 d															05 24						
62¼	—	—	**Northampton** 68 a															05 36						
—	—	—	d								04 14		04 48		05 05			05 45						
75½	30	—	Wolverton d								04 27		05 00		05 17			05 56						
78¼	32¼	—	**Milton Keynes Central** a								04 30		05 03		05 21			06 00						06 24
—	—	—	d						00 24	03 30	04 30		05 04		05 21		05 53	06 01					06 19	06 26
81¼	—	—	Bletchley d							03 35	04 35		05 09		05 26	05 38	05 58	06 06					→	
87¾	—	—	Leighton Buzzard d					00 02		03 42	04 42		05 15		05 33	05 45	06 05	06 13						
92	—	—	Cheddington d					00 12					05 24			05 50								
96¼	—	—	Tring d					00 17		03 54	04 55		05 30			05 57					06 26			
100	—	—	Berkhamsted d			00 07		00 22		03 59	05 01		05 35		05 50	06 02	06 17				06 31			
103½	—	—	Hemel Hempstead d			00 12		00 27		04 03	05 05		05 39		05 54	06 06	06 21				06 36			
105	—	—	Apsley d			00 15							05 42			06 09					06 39			
107	—	—	Kings Langley d			00 18							05 45			06 12					06 43			
110½	65	—	**Watford Junction** 60 a			00 22		00 34	00s54	04 10	05 13		05 49		06 01	06 17	06 29	06 29			06 47			06s47
—	—	—	d		00 01	00 23		00 34		04 11	05 13		05 50	05 54	06 02	06 17	06 30	06 30	06 34	06 40	06 48			
112	—	—	Bushey 60 d	00 02	00 03											06 20			06 37		06 51			
116½	—	—	Harrow & Wealdstone ⊖60 d	00 08	00 09	00 29	00 26			04 17	05 20		05 56	06 00		06 26			06 43		06 56			
119¾	—	0	Wembley Central ⊖60,176 d		00 13		00 31			04 21	05 24			06 05					06 48					
—	—	4¼	Shepherd's Bush ⊖176 a											06 21										
—	—	5½	Kensington (Olympia) ⊖176 a											06 23										
—	—	7½	West Brompton ⊖176 a											06 26										
—	—	8	Imperial Wharf 176 a											06 29										
—	—	9	Clapham Junction 176 a											06 34										
—	—	16¾	East Croydon 176 a											06 59										
128	82½	—	**London Euston** ⊖60 a	00 23	00 26	00 43	00 45	00 54	01 13	04 34	05 38		06 10		06 22	06 40	06 54	06 45	07 01	07 04	07 10			07 05

	SN	LM	LM	LM G	VT	VT	LM		LM	SN	LM	VT H	LM D	VT	SN I	LM G	VT B		LM	LM G	LM	LM G	VT	SN J
Wolverhampton 68 d						05 24								05 45								05 53	06 04	
Sandwell & Dudley 68 d						05 34								05 55								06 02	06 15	
Birmingham New Street 68 d				05 33	05 45	05 50								06 10								06 13	06 30	
Birmingham International 68 d				05 44	05 55	06 00								06 20								06 30	06 40	
Nuneaton 65 d												06 18												
Coventry 68 d			05 38	06 02	06 06	06 11								06 31					06 22			06 48	06 51	
Rugby 68 d			05 49	06 13	06 20							06 32					06 53		06 33			06 59		
Long Buckby 68 d			05 59	06 22															06 43			07 11		
Northampton 68 a			06 13	06 34	06 39														06 54			07 24		
d			06 22	06 35	06 41											06 50			07 04	07 10	07 15	07 38		
Wolverton d		←	06 34	06 47									←			07 02			07 16		07 27	07 50		
Milton Keynes Central a			06 38	06 51		06 38						06 51	06 51	06 59		07 06	07 12		07 20	07 24	07 31	07 54		
d		06 19	06 38	06 53		06 38					06 47	06 52	06 53	06 59	07 01	07 06	07 14		07 21	07 25	07 32	07 55		
Bletchley d		06 24	06 43	→			06 34				06 52		06 58		07 06	07 11				07 30		→		
Leighton Buzzard d		06 31	06 50				06 41				06 59		07 06		07 13				07 30	07 37	07 41			
Cheddington d		06 37									07 04									07 41				
Tring d		06 42					06 50		07 00		07 10				07 21	07 27				→				←
Berkhamsted d		06 46					06 56		07 05		07 15				07 26	→								07 26
Hemel Hempstead d		06 52					07 01		07 10		07 19				→									07 30
Apsley d							07 04				07 23													
Kings Langley d							07 08				07 26													
Watford Junction 60 a		07 00	07 06				07 12		07 17		07 31												07s37	07 38
d	06 53	07 01	07 07				07 13		07 19	07 24	07 32													07 38
Bushey 60 d									07 22		07 35													
Harrow & Wealdstone ⊖60 d	07 00						07 19			07 31	07 40													07 45
Wembley Central ⊖60,176 d	07 05								07 31	07 36														07 50
Shepherd's Bush ⊖176 a	07 22									07 50														08 11
Kensington (Olympia) ⊖176 a	07 24									07 52														08 13
West Brompton ⊖176 a	07 27									07 55														08 16
Imperial Wharf 176 a	07 30									07 57														08 19
Clapham Junction 176 a	07 35									08 04														08 25
East Croydon 176 a	08 01									08 31														09 01
London Euston ⊖60 a		07 19	07 22		07 28	07 13	07 33		07 41		07 55	07 25	07 38	07 33			07 50		08 01		08 13		07 53	

A From Northampton
B From Liverpool Lime Street
C From Crewe
D From Birmingham New Street
E From Wolverhampton
F until 30 March. From Edinburgh
G To London Euston
H From Manchester Piccadilly
I To East Croydon
J From Milton Keynes Central

Table T066-R

Mondays to Fridays
16 December to 15 May

West Midlands, Northampton, Milton Keynes and Watford Junction - London

Station	VT ◇■ A ⊠	LM ■ B	LM ■ C	VT ◇■ D ⊠	LM ■ E	VT ◇■ ⊠	LM ■	VT ◇■ D ⊠	LM ■ B	LM ■	LM ■ F	LM ■	LM ■	LM ■	LM ■	LM ■	SN ■	LM ■	VT ◇■ ⊠	VT ◇■ G ⊠	LM ■ C
Wolverhampton 68 d						06 27													06 45		06 48
Sandwell & Dudley 68 d						06 38													06 56		
Birmingham New Street 68 d					06 33	06 50												06 54	07 10		07 16
Birmingham International 68 d					06 45	07 00												07 05	07 20		07 31
Nuneaton 65 d			06 50	07 07																07 34	
Coventry 68 d					07 02	07 11												07 22	07 31		07 48
Rugby 68 d	07 07		07 11		07 12			07 30										07 32			07 59
Long Buckby 68 d					07 22													07 41			08 09
Northampton 68 a					07 33													07 54			08 21
d					07 42													08 04			08 23
Wolverton d											←							08 16			08 35
Milton Keynes Central a						07s40					07 54							08 20			08 39
d											07 55				07 59		08 12	08 21			08 41
Bletchley d										07 39	08 00			07 53	08 05		08 17	08 26			08 46
Leighton Buzzard d									←	07 47	08 07			08 00	08 12		08 24	08 32			08 53
Cheddington d		←							07 41					08 05							
Tring d		07 27							07 47				08 05	08 11		08 26	08 34				
Berkhamsted d		07 32							07 52	07 59				08 16		08 31	08 38				
Hemel Hempstead d		07 37							07 56	08 04				08 20	08 28	08 36	08 43				
Apsley d		07 40							08 00				08 13			08 39					
Kings Langley d									08 03				08 17			08 43					
Watford Junction 60 a		07 47							08 07	08 12			08 21	08 27	08 36	08 47	08 51				
d		07 47					07 55		08 08	08 13		08 17	08 22	08 28	08 37	08 48	08 52				
Bushey 60 d							07 59					08 20									
Harrow & Wealdstone 60 d							08 04			08 19		08 26	08 30	08 34		08 54	08 59				
Wembley Central 60,176 d																	09 04				
Shepherd's Bush 176 a																	09 22				
Kensington (Olympia) 176 a																	09 24				
West Brompton 176 a																	09 27				
Imperial Wharf 176 a																	09 30				
Clapham Junction 176 a																	09 35				
East Croydon 176 a																	10 00				
London Euston 60 a	07 56	08 05	08 06	08 10	08 28	08 16	08 18	08 20	08 26	08 32	08 38	08 42	08 44	08 48	08 57	09 10	.	09 11	08 31	08 34	09 24

Station	VT ◇■ ⊠	VT ◇■ D ⊠	VT ◇■ ⊠	LM ■	VT ◇■ D ⊠	LM ■	LM ■ H	SN ■	VT ◇■ I ⊠	LM ■ J	LM ■ C	SN ■ K	LM ■ L	VT ◇■ D ⊠	VT ◇■ G ⊠	LM ■	LM ■	VT ◇■ D ⊠	LM ■ M	LM ■ N	VT ◇■ ⊠	LM ■
Wolverhampton 68 d	07 05								07 24				07 28	07 45					07 40			
Sandwell & Dudley 68 d	07 15												07 40	07 57					}			
Birmingham New Street 68 d	07 30						07 33		07 50				07 54	08 10					08 14		08 30	
Birmingham International 68 d			07 42				07 45		08 00				08 05	08 20					08 25		08 40	
Nuneaton 65 d											08 18							08 45				
Coventry 68 d			07 53				08 04		08 11				08 21	08 31					08 48		08 51	
Rugby 68 d		07 55					08 14		08 22		08 34		08 39		08 46				08 58			
Long Buckby 68 d							08 24						08 48						09 08			
Northampton 68 a							08 36						09 00						09 20			
d							08 37						09 05						09 24			
Wolverton d													09 17						09 36			←
Milton Keynes Central a							08 50				08 55		09 21						09 40		09 18	
d					08 47		08 51			08 57	09 00	09 12	09 22						09 41		09 20	08 57
Bletchley d										→		→	→						→			09 02
Leighton Buzzard d																						09 09
Cheddington d																						09 14
Tring d						08 48										09 01						09 20
Berkhamsted d						08 53										09 06						09 25
Hemel Hempstead d						08 57										09 10						09 29
Apsley d																09 13						
Kings Langley d																09 17						
Watford Junction 60 a						09 04	09 13							09s16		09 21		09s31				09 36
d				08 56		09 05	09 13	09 14								09 22	09 26					09 37
Bushey 60 d				08 59		09 08										09 25	09 29					
Harrow & Wealdstone 60 d				09 05		09 13		09 23								09 30	09 34					09 44
Wembley Central 60,176 d						09 18		09 28														
Shepherd's Bush 176 a								09 46														
Kensington (Olympia) 176 a								09 48														
West Brompton 176 a								09 51														
Imperial Wharf 176 a								09 54														
Clapham Junction 176 a								10 00														
East Croydon 176 a																						
London Euston 60 a	08 43	08 46	08 50	09 19	09 20	09 30	09 29	.	09 15	.	09 36	.	.	09 33	09 39	09 44	09 48	09 49	.	.	09 53	09 59

A From Lancaster
B From Northampton
C From Crewe
D From Manchester Piccadilly
E From Walsall
F From Wolverhampton
G From Holyhead
H From Rugeley Trent Valley
I From Shrewsbury
J To London Euston
K To East Croydon
L From Liverpool Lime Street to London Euston
M From Crewe to London Euston
N From Rugeley Trent Valley to London Euston

Table T066-R

Mondays to Fridays
16 December to 15 May

West Midlands, Northampton, Milton Keynes and Watford Junction - London

Station	LM ■	SN ■	LM ■ A	LM ■ B	LM ■ C	VT ◇■ D ⊠	LM ■ B	LM ■	LM ■ E	LM ■ E	VT ◇■ ⊠	LM ■ F	VT ◇■ G ⊠	VT ◇■ H ⊠	LM ■ I	VT ◇■ D ⊠	LM ■	SN ■ J	LM ■ F	LM ■ C	VT ◇■ ⊠	LM ■
Wolverhampton 68 d												08 30	08 45									
Sandwell & Dudley 68 d													08 55									
Birmingham New Street 68 d										08 33	08 50	08 54	09 10							09 13	09 30	
Birmingham International 68 d										08 45	09 00	09 05	09 20							09 28	09 40	
Nuneaton 65 d							09 16									09 45						
Coventry 68 d										09 00	09 11	09 25	09 31							09 47	09 51	
Rugby 68 d							09 32			09 11	09 23	09 36								09 58		
Long Buckby 68 d										09 21		09 46								10 09		
Northampton 68 a										09 33		09 59								10 21		
d										09 52		10 05								10 26		
Wolverton d		←	←	←	←							10 17			←		←		←	10 38		
Milton Keynes Central a			09 21	09 40	09 40		09 54			10 05		10 21	09 57		10 05				10 21	10 42		
d		09 12	09 22	09 41	09 41	09 50	09 55		09 55	10 06		10 22	09 59	10 03	10 06		09 55	10 12	10 22	10 43		
Bletchley d		09 17	09 27	09 46	09 46				→	→		→					10 00	10 17	10 27	10 48		
Leighton Buzzard d		09 24	09 34	09 53	09 53												10 07	10 24	10 34	10 55		
Cheddington d																	10 12					
Tring d	09 26	09 34						09 57									10 18	10 34				10 26
Berkhamsted d	09 31	09 38	09 47					10 02									10 23	10 38	10 46			10 31
Hemel Hempstead d	09 36	09 43	09 51					10 06									10 27	10 43	→			10 35
Apsley d	09 39							10 09										→				10 38
Kings Langley d	09 42							10 13														10 41
Watford Junction 60 a	09 46	09 51	09 58					10 17							10 28		10 34				10s39	10 46
d	09 47	09 52	09 59					10 18							10 28		10 35					10 46
Bushey 60 d	09 50							10 21														10 49
Harrow & Wealdstone 60 d	09 55	09 59						10 26														10 55
Wembley Central 60,176 d		10 04																				
Shepherd's Bush 176 a		10 22																				
Kensington (Olympia) 176 a		10 24																				
West Brompton 176 a		10 27																				
Imperial Wharf 176 a		10 30																				
Clapham Junction 176 a		10 35																				
East Croydon 176 a		10 59																				
London Euston 60 a	10 10	.	10 17	10 23	10 23	10 26	10 30	10 40	.	.	10 13	.	10 33	10 37	10 44	10 51	10 53	.	.	11 25	10 56	11 10

Station	SN ■ K	LM ■ A	VT ◇■ D ⊠	LM ■ E	LM ■ A	LM ■ B	VT ◇■ ⊠	LM ■ F	VT ◇■ L ⊠	VT ◇■ M ⊠	VT ◇■ N ⊠	LM ■	LM ■	SN TThO ■ O	SN MWFO ■ J	LM ■ B	LM ■ F	LM ■ C	VT ◇■ ⊠	LM ■	SN TThO ■ K
Wolverhampton 68 d					09 02	09 06		09 31	09 45	09 45											
Sandwell & Dudley 68 d					}				09 55	09 55											
Birmingham New Street 68 d					09 33		09 50	09 54	10 10	10 10								10 14	10 30		
Birmingham International 68 d					09 45		10 00	10 05	10 20	10 20								10 28	10 40		
Nuneaton 65 d																10 35					
Coventry 68 d					10 01		10 11	10 22	10 31	10 31								10 49	10 51		
Rugby 68 d					10 12		10 23	10 32								10 53		10 59			
Long Buckby 68 d					10 23			10 42										11 09			
Northampton 68 a					10 35			10 54										11 21			
d					10 39			11 05										11 25			
Wolverton d								11 17					←				←	11 37			
Milton Keynes Central a					10 52			11 21	10 57	10 57						11 14	11 21	11 41			
d			10 47	10 48	10 53			11 22	10 59	10 59	11 03		10 48	11 12	11 12	11 15	11 22	11 41			
Bletchley d				→				→					10 53	11 17	11 17		11 27	11 46			
Leighton Buzzard d													11 00	11 24	11 24		11 34	11 53			
Cheddington d													11 05								
Tring d		←										10 58	11 11	11 34	11 34					11 25	
Berkhamsted d	←	10 46										11 03	11 16	11 38	11 38		11 46			11 30	←
Hemel Hempstead d	10 43	10 51										11 07	11 20	11 43	11 43		→			11 35	11 43
Apsley d												11 10		→	→					11 38	
Kings Langley d												11 13								11 41	
Watford Junction 60 a	10 51	10 58			11 14							11 18	11 27						11s40	11 45	11 51
d	10 52	10 59			11 15							11 19	11 28							11 46	11 52
Bushey 60 d												11 22								11 49	
Harrow & Wealdstone 60 d	10 59											11 27								11 54	11 59
Wembley Central 60,176 d	11 04																			11 59	12 03
Shepherd's Bush 176 a	11 22																				12 22
Kensington (Olympia) 176 a	11 24																				12 24
West Brompton 176 a	11 27																				12 27
Imperial Wharf 176 a	11 30																				12 30
Clapham Junction 176 a	11 35																				12 35
East Croydon 176 a	11 59																				
London Euston 60 a	.	11 18	11 20	.	11 30		11 14	.	11 34	11 36	11 37	11 41	11 46	.	.	11 51	.	12 24	11 56	12 11	.

A From Liverpool Lime Street
B From Crewe
C From Rugeley Trent Valley
D From Manchester Piccadilly
E To London Euston
F From Liverpool Lime Street to London Euston
G From Lancaster
H From Holyhead
I From Birmingham New Street
J To East Croydon
K From Milton Keynes Central
L until 14 February. From Glasgow Central
M from 17 February. From Glasgow Central
N From Chester
O To Clapham Junction

Table T066-R

Mondays to Fridays
16 December to 15 May

West Midlands, Northampton, Milton Keynes and Watford Junction - London

	SN	LM	VT	LM	LM	VT	LM		LM	LM	VT	VT	VT	VT	VT	SN	LM		LM	LM	VT	LM	SN	LM
	MW FO										FX	FO	FX	FX	FO									
	■	■	◇■	■	■	◇■	■		■	■	◇■	◇■	◇■	◇■	◇■	■	■		■	■	◇■	■	■	■
	A	B	C	B	D					E	F	F	G	H	I	J	D		E	K			A	B
			⊠			⊠					⊠	⊠	⊠	⊠	⊠						☕			
Wolverhampton 7 68 d				09 59	10 06					10 31	10 45	10 45												
Sandwell & Dudley 68 d											10 55	10 55												
Birmingham New Street 12 68 d				10 33		10 50				10 54	11 10	11 10								11 14	11 30			
Birmingham International 68 d				10 45		11 00				11 05	11 20	11 20								11 27	11 40			
Nuneaton 65 d																	11 35							
Coventry 68 d				11 01		11 11				11 22	11 31	11 31								11 49	11 51			
Rugby 68 d				11 12		11 23				11 32							11 53			12 00				
Long Buckby 68 d				11 21						11 42										12 10				
Northampton 68 a				11 33						11 54										12 22				
d				11 37						12 05										12 25				
Wolverton d										12 17									←	12 37				
Milton Keynes Central 10 a				11 50						12 21	11 57	11 57					12 14		12 21	12 41				
d			11 47	11 51					11 55	12 22	11 59	11 59	12 03	12 03	12 03	12 12	12 15		12 22	12 42				
Bletchley d									12 00	→						12 17			12 27	12 47				
Leighton Buzzard d									12 07							12 24			12 34	12 54				
Cheddington d									12 12															
Tring d		←					11 57		12 18							12 34						12 26		←
Berkhamsted d	←	11 46					12 02		12 23							12 38			12 46			12 31	←	12 46
Hemel Hempstead d	11 43	11 51					12 07		12 27							12 43			→			12 36	12 43	12 51
Apsley d							12 10									→						12 39		
Kings Langley d							12 13															12 42		
Watford Junction 60 a	11 51	11 58		12 13			12 17		12 34												12s39	12 46	12 51	12 58
d	11 52	11 58		12 14			12 18		12 35													12 47	12 52	12 59
Bushey 60 d							12 21															12 50		
Harrow & Wealdstone ⊖60 d	11 59						12 26															12 55	12 59	
Wembley Central ⊖60,176 d	12 03						12 31																13 04	
Shepherd's Bush ⊖176 a	12 22																						13 22	
Kensington (Olympia) ⊖176 a	12 24																						13 24	
West Brompton ⊖176 a	12 27																						13 27	
Imperial Wharf 176 a	12 30																						13 30	
Clapham Junction 176 a	12 35																						13 35	
East Croydon 176 a	12 59																						13 59	
London Euston 15 ⊖60 a		12 16	12 20	12 29		12 14	12 43		12 53		12 33	12 35	12 36	12 37	12 38		12 50			13 24	12 55	13 10		13 17

	VT	LM	LM		VT	LM	LM	LM	VT	VT	VT	SN	LM		LM	VT	LM	VT	LM	SN	LM	VT	LM	
	◇■	■	■		◇■	■	■	■	◇■	◇■	◇■	■	■		■	◇■	■	◇■	■	■	■	◇■	■	
	C	B	D					E	L	M	N	J	D		E	O	K			A	B	C	P	
	☕				☕				⊠	☕	☕					☕		☕				☕		
Wolverhampton 7 68 d		10 59	11 07					11 31	11 45															
Sandwell & Dudley 68 d									11 55															
Birmingham New Street 12 68 d		11 33			11 50			11 54	12 10								12 14	12 30						
Birmingham International 68 d		11 45			12 00			12 05	12 20								12 29	12 40						
Nuneaton 65 d													12 35											
Coventry 68 d		12 01			12 11			12 21	12 31								12 49	12 51						
Rugby 68 d		12 12			12 23			12 32					12 53			13 00	13 00							
Long Buckby 68 d		12 21						12 41									13 10							
Northampton 68 a		12 33						12 54									13 21							
d		12 38						13 04									13 24							
Wolverton d								13 16							←		13 36							
Milton Keynes Central 10 a		12 51						13 20	12 57				13 14		13 20		13 40							
d	12 47	12 53					12 55	13 21	12 59	13 03	13 03	13 12	13 15		13 21		13 41					13 47	13 52	
Bletchley d							13 00	→				13 17			13 26		13 46						→	
Leighton Buzzard d							13 07					13 24			13 33		13 53							
Cheddington d							13 12																	
Tring d						12 56	13 18					13 34							13 26		←			
Berkhamsted d						13 01	13 23					13 38			13 46				13 31	←	13 46			
Hemel Hempstead d						13 06	13 27					13 43			→				13 36	13 43	13 50			
Apsley d						13 09						→							13 39					
Kings Langley d						13 12													13 42					
Watford Junction 60 a		13 14				13 16	13 34											13s42	13 46	13 51	13 57			
d		13 15				13 17	13 35												13 47	13 52	13 58			
Bushey 60 d						13 20													13 50					
Harrow & Wealdstone ⊖60 d						13 25													13 55	13 59				
Wembley Central ⊖60,176 d						13 30														14 04				
Shepherd's Bush ⊖176 a																				14 22				
Kensington (Olympia) ⊖176 a																				14 24				
West Brompton ⊖176 a																				14 27				
Imperial Wharf 176 a																				14 30				
Clapham Junction 176 a																				14 35				
East Croydon 176 a																				14 59				
London Euston 15 ⊖60 a	13 20	13 30			13 14	13 42	13 53		13 33	13 36	13 37		13 50			13 53	14 24	13 58	14 10		14 17	14 20		

A From Milton Keynes Central
B From Liverpool Lime Street
C From Manchester Piccadilly
D From Crewe
E From Liverpool Lime Street to London Euston
F From Edinburgh
G until 13 February. From Holyhead
H from 17 February. From Holyhead
I From Holyhead
J To East Croydon
K From Rugeley Trent Valley
L From Glasgow Central
M until 14 February. From Chester
N from 17 February. From Chester
O From Blackpool North
P To London Euston

NRT DECEMBER 19 EDITION

Table T066-R

Mondays to Fridays
16 December to 15 May

West Midlands, Northampton, Milton Keynes and Watford Junction - London

	LM	LM	VT	LM	VT	VT	VT	VT	LM		LM	SN	LM	LM	LM	VT	LM	SN	VT		LM	VT	LM	LM
					WX	WO	WX	WO																
	■	■	◇■	■	◇■	◇■	◇■	◇■	■		■	■	■	■	■	◇■	■	■	◇■		■	◇■	■	■
	A	B		C	D	D	E	E				F	B	C	G			H	I		A	J	A	B
			☕		⊠	⊠	☕	☕								☕			⊠			☕		
Wolverhampton 7 68 d	12 01	12 07		12 30	12 45	12 45																	12 59	13 07
Sandwell & Dudley 68 d					12 55	12 55																		
Birmingham New Street 12 68 d		12 33	12 50	12 54	13 10	13 10									13 14	13 30								13 33
Birmingham International 68 d		12 44	13 00	13 05	13 20	13 20									13 25	13 40								13 45
Nuneaton 65 d													13 35											
Coventry 68 d		13 01	13 11	13 22	13 31	13 31									13 49	13 51								14 01
Rugby 68 d		13 12	13 23	13 32									13 53		13 59				14 24					14 12
Long Buckby 68 d		13 21		13 42											14 09									14 21
Northampton 68 a		13 34		13 54											14 21									14 33
d		13 38		14 05											14 23									14 38
Wolverton d				14 17							←			←	14 35									
Milton Keynes Central 10 a		13 51		14 21	13 57	13 57							14 14	14 21	14 39									14 53
d		13 53		14 22	13 59	13 59	14 03	14 03			13 52	14 12	14 15	14 22	14 40							14 50		14 54
Bletchley d				→							13 57	14 17		14 27	14 45									
Leighton Buzzard d											14 04	14 24		14 34	14 52									
Cheddington d											14 09													
Tring d									13 56		14 15	14 34					14 25				←			
Berkhamsted d									14 01		14 20	14 39		14 46			14 30	←			14 46			
Hemel Hempstead d									14 06		14 24	14 44		→			14 35	14 44			14 51			
Apsley d									14 09			→					14 38							
Kings Langley d									14 12								14 41							
Watford Junction 60 a		14 14							14 16		14 31					14s39	14 45	14 52			14 58			15 15
d		14 15							14 17		14 32						14 46	14 52			14 59			15 16
Bushey 60 d									14 20								14 49							
Harrow & Wealdstone ⊖60 d									14 25								14 54	15 00						
Wembley Central ⊖60,176 d									14 30								14 59	15 04						
Shepherd's Bush ⊖176 a																		15 22						
Kensington (Olympia) ⊖176 a																		15 24						
West Brompton ⊖176 a																		15 27						
Imperial Wharf 176 a																		15 30						
Clapham Junction 176 a																		15 35						
East Croydon 176 a																		16 00						
London Euston 15 ⊖60 a		14 30	14 14		14 33	14 36	14 36	14 39	14 42		14 53		14 50		15 22	14 55	15 11		15 13		15 17	15 25		15 31

	VT	LM	LM	LM	VT		VT	SN	LM	LM	LM	VT	VT	LM	SN		LM	VT	SN	LM	LM	VT	LM	LM
	◇■	■	■	■	◇■		◇■	■	■	■	■	◇■	◇■	■	■		■	◇■	■	■	■	◇■	■	■
				C	I		E	F	B	C	G		K		H		A	J		A	B			A
	☕				⊠		☕					☕	☕					☕				☕		
Wolverhampton 7 68 d				13 32	13 45															13 59	14 07			14 31
Sandwell & Dudley 68 d					13 55																			
Birmingham New Street 12 68 d	13 50			13 54	14 10						14 14	14 30									14 33	14 50		14 54
Birmingham International 68 d	14 00			14 06	14 20						14 25	14 40									14 44	15 00		15 05
Nuneaton 65 d									14 35															
Coventry 68 d	14 11			14 22	14 31						14 48	14 51									15 01	15 11		15 21
Rugby 68 d	14 26			14 32					14 53		14 59		15 07								15 12	15 23		15 31
Long Buckby 68 d				14 42							15 09										15 21			15 41
Northampton 68 a				14 54							15 21										15 33			15 51
d				15 05							15 25										15 36			15 58
Wolverton d				15 17						←	15 37													
Milton Keynes Central 10 a				15 21	14 57				15 14	15 21	15 41										15 49			
d			14 55	15 22	14 59		15 03	15 12	15 15	15 22	15 42							15 47			15 51			
Bletchley d			15 00	→				15 17		15 27	15 47													
Leighton Buzzard d			15 07					15 24		15 34	15 54													
Cheddington d			15 12																					
Tring d		14 56	15 18					15 34						15 26			←						15 56	
Berkhamsted d		15 01	15 23					15 38		15 46				15 31	←		15 46						16 01	
Hemel Hempstead d		15 06	15 27					15 43		→				15 36	15 43		15 51						16 06	
Apsley d		15 09						→						15 39									16 09	
Kings Langley d		15 12												15 42									16 12	
Watford Junction 60 a		15 16	15 34									15s39		15 46	15 51		15 58				16 13		16 16	
d		15 17	15 35											15 47	15 52		15 59		16 12		16 14		16 17	
Bushey 60 d		15 20												15 50									16 20	
Harrow & Wealdstone ⊖60 d		15 25												15 55	15 59				16 20				16 25	
Wembley Central ⊖60,176 d															16 04				16 25				16 30	
Shepherd's Bush ⊖176 a															16 22				16 46					
Kensington (Olympia) ⊖176 a															16 24				16 48					
West Brompton ⊖176 a															16 27				16 51					
Imperial Wharf 176 a															16 30				16 54					
Clapham Junction 176 a															16 35				17 01					
East Croydon 176 a															17 00				17 30					
London Euston 15 ⊖60 a	15 16	15 40	15 56		15 34		15 37		15 50		16 25	15 56	15 59	16 11			16 17	16 20			16 29	16 13	16 42	16 46

A From Liverpool Lime Street
B From Crewe
C From Liverpool Lime Street to London Euston
D From Edinburgh
E From Chester
F To East Croydon
G From Rugeley Trent Valley
H From Milton Keynes Central
I From Glasgow Central
J From Manchester Piccadilly
K From Blackpool North

West Midlands, Northampton, Milton Keynes and Watford Junction - London

	LM 1	VT ◇1 A ☕	VT ◇1 B ☕	VT ◇1 C ☕	SN 1 D	LM 1 E	LM 1 F	LM 1 G	VT ◇1 ☕	LM 1	LM 1	SN 1 H	LM 1 I	VT ◇1 J ☕	LM 1 K	LM 1 E	VT ◇1 ☕	LM 1	LM 1 K	LM 1	VT ◇1 L ☕
Wolverhampton 7 68 d		14 45	14 45												14 59	15 07			15 31		15 45
Sandwell & Dudley 68 d		14 55	14 55																		15 55
Birmingham New Street 12 68 d		15 10	15 10					15 14	15 30						15 33		15 50		15 54		16 10
Birmingham International 68 ✈ d		15 20	15 20					15 29	15 40						15 44		16 00		16 05		16 20
Nuneaton 65 d						15 35															
Coventry 68 d		15 31	15 31					15 49	15 51						16 01		16 11		16 21		16 31
Rugby 68 d						15 53		15 59							16 11		16 23		16 32		
Long Buckby 68 d								16 09							16 21				16 42		
Northampton 68 a								16 23							16 33				16 56		
d							16 05	16 24							16 38				16 58		
Wolverton d							16 17	16 38													
Milton Keynes Central 10 a		15 57	15 57			16 15	16 21	16 42							16 53						16 57
d	15 53	15 59	15 59	16 03	16 12	16 16	16 22	16 42						16 47	16 53					16 55	16 59
Bletchley d	15 57				16 17		16 27	16 47												17 00	
Leighton Buzzard d	16 04				16 24		16 34	16 54												17 07	
Cheddington d	16 10																			17 12	
Tring d	16 15				16 34						16 26		←					16 57		17 18	
Berkhamsted d	16 20				16 38		16 46				16 31	←	16 46					17 02		17 23	
Hemel Hempstead d	16 25				16 43		→				16 36	16 43	16 51					17 07		17 27	
Apsley d					→						16 39							17 10			
Kings Langley d											16 42							17 13			
Watford Junction 60 a	16 32								16s39		16 47	16 51	16 58		17 15			17 18		17 34	
d	16 33									16 44	16 48	16 52	16 59		17 15			17 18		17 35	
Bushey 60 d										16 47	16 51							17 22			
Harrow & Wealdstone ⊖60 d										16 52	16 56	17 00						17 27			
Wembley Central ⊖60,176 d												17 05									
Shepherd's Bush ⊖176 a												17 22									
Kensington (Olympia) ⊖176 a												17 24									
West Brompton ⊖176 a												17 27									
Imperial Wharf 176 a												17 30									
Clapham Junction 176 a												17 35									
East Croydon 176 a												18 00									
London Euston 15 ⊖60 a	16 53	16 32	16 33	16 36		16 52		17 25	16 56	17 05	17 11		17 18	17 21	17 31		17 14	17 41	17 46	17 56	17 34

	VT ◇1 C ☕	SN 1 D	LM 1 E	LM 1 F	LM 1 G	VT ◇1 M ☕	VT ◇1 ☕	VT ◇1 N ☕	LM 1	LM 1	SN 1 H	LM 1 I	VT ◇1 J ☕	LM 1	LM 1 K	LM 1 E	VT ◇1 ☕	LM 1	LM 1	LM 1 O	VT ◇1 P ☕	VT ◇1 Q ☕
Wolverhampton 7 68 d						16 03									15 58	16 07				16 31	16 45	
Sandwell & Dudley 68 d																					16 55	
Birmingham New Street 12 68 d					16 14	16 30	16 30								16 33		16 50			16 54	17 10	
Birmingham International 68 ✈ d					16 29	16 40	16 40								16 44		17 00			17 05	17 20	
Nuneaton 65 d			16 35																			
Coventry 68 d					16 48	16 51	16 51								17 01		17 11			17 22	17 31	
Rugby 68 d			16 53		16 58			17 06							17 15		17 23			17 32		
Long Buckby 68 d					17 08										17 26					17 42		
Northampton 68 a					17 20										17 38					17 55		
d				17 06	17 24										17 39					17 56		
Wolverton d				17 17	17 37																	
Milton Keynes Central 10 a			17 15	17 21	17 41										17 52					18 11	17 57	
d	17 03	17 12	17 15	17 22	17 42								17 47		17 53				17 57	18 12	17 59	18 03
Bletchley d		17 17		17 27	17 47														18 03	→		
Leighton Buzzard d		17 24		17 34	17 55														18 09			
Cheddington d																			18 15			
Tring d		17 34								17 27		←						17 59	18 21			
Berkhamsted d		17 38		17 46						17 32	←	17 46						18 04	18 26			
Hemel Hempstead d		17 43		→						17 37	17 43	17 51						18 09	18 31			
Apsley d		→								17 40								18 12				
Kings Langley d										17 43								18 15				
Watford Junction 60 a						17s39	17s39			17 47	17 51	17 58			18 14			18 20	18 38			
d									17 43	17 48	17 52	18 00		18 10	18 15			18 20	18 38			
Bushey 60 d										17 51				18 13				18 23				
Harrow & Wealdstone ⊖60 d									17 50	17 56	18 00			18 18				18 28				
Wembley Central ⊖60,176 d											18 05											
Shepherd's Bush ⊖176 a											18 22											
Kensington (Olympia) ⊖176 a											18 24											
West Brompton ⊖176 a											18 27											
Imperial Wharf 176 a											18 30											
Clapham Junction 176 a											18 35											
East Croydon 176 a											19 01											
London Euston 15 ⊖60 a	17 37		17 51		18 25	17 56	17 56	17 59	18 05	18 11		18 18	18 20	18 31	18 30		18 14	18 42	18 57		18 33	18 36

A until 14 February. From Edinburgh
B from 17 February. From Edinburgh
C From Holyhead
D To East Croydon
E From Crewe
F To London Euston
G From Rugeley Trent Valley
H From Milton Keynes Central
I From Northampton
J From Manchester Piccadilly
K From Liverpool Lime Street
L From Glasgow Central
M From Shrewsbury
N From Blackpool North
O From Liverpool Lime Street to London Euston
P From Edinburgh
Q From Chester

Table T066-R

Mondays to Fridays

16 December to 15 May

West Midlands, Northampton, Milton Keynes and Watford Junction - London

	LM 1 A	SN 1 B	LM 1 C	LM 1 D	VT ◇1 E ☕	VT ◇1 F ☕	LM 1 G	VT ◇1 ⊠	LM 1	SN 1 H	LM 1 I	VT ◇1 J ⊠	LM 1 D	LM 1 A	LM 1 C	VT ◇1 ⊠	LM 1 A	VT ◇1 K ☕	VT ◇1 L ⊠	LM 1	LM 1
Wolverhampton 7 68 d														17 00	17 07		17 30	17 45			
Sandwell & Dudley 68 d																		17 55			
Birmingham New Street 12 68 d							17 14	17 30						17 33		17 50	17 54	18 10			
Birmingham International 68 ✈ d							17 27	17 40						17 44		18 00	18 05	18 20			
Nuneaton 65 d			17 35																		
Coventry 68 d							17 48	17 51						18 01		18 11	18 22	18 31			
Rugby 68 d			17 53				17 58							18 13		18 23	18 32				
Long Buckby 68 d							18 08							18 22			18 42				
Northampton 68 a							18 23							18 34			18 54				
d				18 05			18 25							18 37			18 55				
Wolverton d	←			18 17			18 37														←
Milton Keynes Central 10 a	18 11		18 14	18 21			18 41							18 51				18 57			
d	18 12	18 12	18 15	18 22	18 25	18 27	18 42					18 47	18 47	18 52				18 59	19 03		18 47
Bletchley d		18 18		18 27			18 47						→								18 52
Leighton Buzzard d		18 25		18 34			18 55														18 59
Cheddington d																					19 04
Tring d		18 35							18 25		←									18 59	19 10
Berkhamsted d		18 39		18 46					18 30	←	18 46									19 04	19 15
Hemel Hempstead d		18 44		→					18 35	18 44	18 51									19 08	19 19
Apsley d		→							18 38											19 11	
Kings Langley d									18 41											19 15	
Watford Junction 60 a								18s38	18 46	18 51	18 58			19 14						19 19	19 26
d									18 46	18 52	18 59			19 14						19 20	19 27
Bushey 60 d									18 49											19 23	
Harrow & Wealdstone ⊖60 d									18 54	18 59										19 28	
Wembley Central ⊖60,176 d										19 05											
Shepherd's Bush ⊖176 a										19 22											
Kensington (Olympia) ⊖176 a										19 24											
West Brompton ⊖176 a										19 27											
Imperial Wharf 176 a										19 30											
Clapham Junction 176 a										19 35											
East Croydon 176 a										19 59											
London Euston 15 ⊖60 a	18 47		18 50		18 59	19 02	19 25	18 56	19 10		19 18	19 20		19 30		19 13	19 45	19 33	19 37	19 41	19 45

	LM 1 C	SN MO 1 B	SN MX 1 B	LM 1 D	VT ◇1 J ⊠	LM 1 G	VT ◇1 ⊠	LM 1	SN MO 1 H	SN MX 1 H	LM 1 I	VT ◇1 J ⊠	LM 1 D	LM 1 A	LM 1 C	VT ◇1 ⊠	LM 1 M	VT 1 N ☕	LM 1	LM 1	SN 1 O	LM 1 C
Wolverhampton 7 68 d														18 01	18 06		18 30	18 45				
Sandwell & Dudley 68 d																		18 55				
Birmingham New Street 12 68 d						18 14	18 30							18 33		18 50	18 54	19 10				
Birmingham International 68 ✈ d						18 29	18 40							18 46		19 00	19 05	19 20				
Nuneaton 65 d	18 35																					19 39
Coventry 68 d						18 48	18 51							19 01		19 11	19 21	19 31				
Rugby 68 d	18 53					18 58								19 12		19 23	19 32					19 55
Long Buckby 68 d						19 08								19 22			19 42					
Northampton 68 a						19 20								19 37			19 55					
d				19 06		19 25								19 38			20 05					
Wolverton d				19 18		19 37											20 17			←		
Milton Keynes Central 10 a	19 14			19 22		19 41								19 52			20 21	19 58				20 16
d	19 15	19 16	19 16	19 23	19 34	19 42						19 47	19 47	19 52			20 22	20 00		19 47	20 12	20 17
Bletchley d		19 21	19 21	19 28		19 47							→				→			19 52	20 19	
Leighton Buzzard d		19 28	19 28	19 35		19 54														19 59	20 26	
Cheddington d																				20 04		
Tring d		19 36	19 37					19 29			←								19 56	20 10	20 35	
Berkhamsted d		19 41	19 41	19 47				19 34		←	19 47								20 01	20 15	20 40	
Hemel Hempstead d		19 45	19 46	→				19 39		19 46	19 52								20 06	20 19	20 44	
Apsley d			→					19 42											20 09		→	
Kings Langley d								19 45	←										20 12			
Watford Junction 60 a		19 53					19s39	19 49	19 53	19 53	19 59			20 14					20 16	20 26		
d		19 54						19 50	19 54	19 54	19 59			20 15					20 17	20 27		
Bushey 60 d		→						19 53											20 20			
Harrow & Wealdstone ⊖60 d								19 58	20 02	20 02									20 25			
Wembley Central ⊖60,176 d									20 06	20 06									20 30			
Shepherd's Bush ⊖176 a									20 22	20 22												
Kensington (Olympia) ⊖176 a									20 24	20 24												
West Brompton ⊖176 a									20 27	20 27												
Imperial Wharf 176 a									20 30	20 30												
Clapham Junction 176 a									20 35	20 35												
East Croydon 176 a									20 59	20 59												
London Euston 15 ⊖60 a	19 50				20 07	20 25	19 55	20 12			20 18	20 21		20 30		20 15		20 33	20 42	20 46		20 52

A From Liverpool Lime Street
B To East Croydon
C From Crewe
D To London Euston
E until 14 February. From Liverpool Lime Street
F from 17 February. From Liverpool Lime Street
G From Rugeley Trent Valley
H From Milton Keynes Central
I From Northampton
J From Manchester Piccadilly
K From Glasgow Central
L From Chester
M From Liverpool Lime Street to London Euston
N From Edinburgh
O To Clapham Junction

Table T066-R

Mondays to Fridays

16 December to 15 May

West Midlands, Northampton, Milton Keynes and Watford Junction - London

	LM	VT	LM	VT	LM		SN	LM	VT	VT	LM	LM	LM	LM	VT		VT	LM	LM	VT	LM	SN	LM	LM
	1 A	◇1 B ⊠	1 C	◇1	1		1 D	1 E	◇1 F ⊠	◇1 B	1	1 G	1 H	1 A	◇1 F ⊠		◇1 I	1	1 H	◇1 E	1	1	1 E	1
Wolverhampton 7 68 d													19 07	19 30	19 45									
Sandwell & Dudley 68 d															19 55									
Birmingham New Street 12 68 d			19 13	19 30									19 33	19 54	20 10									
Birmingham International 68 d			19 29	19 40									19 44	20 06	20 20									
Nuneaton 65 d																			20 32	21 01				
Coventry 68 d			19 48	19 51									20 01	20 22	20 31									
Rugby 68 d			19 58	20 04									20 12	20 33					20 48					
Long Buckby 68 d			20 08										20 24	20 43										
Northampton 68 a			20 20										20 37	20 55										
d			20 22										20 38	20 59										21 04
Wolverton d	←		20 37															←					←	21 16
Milton Keynes Central 10 a	20 21		20 41										20 54	21 13	20 58				21 09				21 13	21 20
d	20 22	20 32	20 44						20 46	20 50		20 50	20 55	21 14	21 00		21 04	20 50	21 10			21 12	21 14	21 22
Bletchley d	20 27		20 50									→		→				20 55				21 17		21 27
Leighton Buzzard d	20 34		20 57															21 02				21 24		21 34
Cheddington d																		21 07						
Tring d					20 26			←			20 58							21 13			21 27	21 34		
Berkhamsted d	20 46				20 31		←	20 46			21 03							21 18			21 32	21 38		21 47
Hemel Hempstead d	→				20 36		20 44	20 51			21 08							21 22			21 37	21 43		21 51
Apsley d					20 39						21 11										21 40			
Kings Langley d					20 42						21 14										21 43			
Watford Junction 60 a				20s41	20 46		20 52	20 58			21 18				21s19			21 29	21 34	21s47	21 47	21 51		21 58
d					20 47		20 52	20 59			21 19							21 30	21 34		21 48	21 52		21 59
Bushey 60 d					20 50						21 22										21 51			
Harrow & Wealdstone ⊖60 d					20 55		20 59				21 27										21 56	22 00		
Wembley Central ⊖60,176 d							21 04				21 32										22 01			
Shepherd's Bush ⊖176 a							21 18															22 18		
Kensington (Olympia) ⊖176 a							21 21															22 21		
West Brompton ⊖176 a							21 24															22 24		
Imperial Wharf 176 a							21 27															22 27		
Clapham Junction 176 a							21 32															22 31		
East Croydon 176 a																						22 59		
London Euston 15 ⊖60 a		21 05	21 27	20 57	21 10			21 17	21 19	21 23	21 43		21 30		21 36		21 39	21 47	21 50	22 04	22 13		21 53	22 24

	VT		VT	LM	LM	VT	VT	LM	VT	SN	LM		SN	LM	VT	VT	VT	LM	VT	SN	LM		LM	LM
	◇1 B		◇1 F	1 E	1 H	◇1	◇1 B	1 A	1 J ⊠	1	1		1	1 E	◇1 F ⊠	◇1 E	◇1 B	1 A	◇1	1	1 E		1 H	1
Wolverhampton 7 68 d				19 59	20 07			20 33	20 46									21 29	21 46					
Sandwell & Dudley 68 d									20 56										21 55					
Birmingham New Street 12 68 d				20 33		20 50		20 54	21 10									21 54	22 10					22 14
Birmingham International 68 d				20 45		21 00		21 05	21 20									22 05	22 20					22 30
Nuneaton 65 d																22 18							22 58	
Coventry 68 d				21 02		21 11		21 21	21 31									22 22	22 31					22 48
Rugby 68 d			21 30	21 14		21 23		21 31								22 31		22 32	22 45				23 12	23 00
Long Buckby 68 d				21 24				21 41										22 42						23 10
Northampton 68 a				21 35				21 54										22 54						23 21
d				21 37				22 04										22 55						23 34
Wolverton d				21 49				22 16						←				23 08			←			23 46
Milton Keynes Central 10 a			21 49	21 53				22 20	21 58					22 20		22 53		23 12	23 06		23 12		23 44	23 50
d	21 36		21 51	21 53			21 54	22 21	21 59		22 05		22 10	22 21	22 42	22 54	23 01	23 13	23 08		23 13		23 45	23 50
Bletchley d				21 58				→			22 10		22 15	22 26				→			23 18		23 50	23 55
Leighton Buzzard d				22 05							22 17		22 22	22 35							23 25		23 57	00 02
Cheddington d				22 11							22 22										23 29			00 12
Tring d				22 17							22 28		22 34								23 40			00 17
Berkhamsted d				22 22							22 33		22 38	22 48							23 45			00 22
Hemel Hempstead d				22 27							22 37		22 43	22 53							23 49			00 27
Apsley d											22 40										23 52			
Kings Langley d											22 43										23 55			
Watford Junction 60 a				22 34			22s13		22s20		22 48		22 52	23 00	23s10	23s25	23s30		23s37		00 01			00 34
d				22 34						22 28	22 48		22 53	23 01						23 42	00 01			00 34
Bushey 60 d											22 51										00 03			
Harrow & Wealdstone ⊖60 d										22 34	22 57		23 00							23 48	00 09		00 26	
Wembley Central ⊖60,176 d											23 01										00 13		00 31	
Shepherd's Bush ⊖176 a										22 57			23 22							00 06				
Kensington (Olympia) ⊖176 a										22 59			23 24							00 08				
West Brompton ⊖176 a										23 02			23 27							00 10				
Imperial Wharf 176 a										23 05			23 29							00 13				
Clapham Junction 176 a										23 10			23 34							00 17				
East Croydon 176 a																								
London Euston 15 ⊖60 a	22 09		22 27	22 53		22 12	22 30		22 41		23 13			23 23	23 32	23 44	23 48		00 01		00 26		00 45	00 54

A From Liverpool Lime Street to London Euston
B From Manchester Piccadilly
C From Rugeley Trent Valley
D From Milton Keynes Central
E From Liverpool Lime Street
F From Glasgow Central
G To London Euston
H From Crewe
I From Chester
J From Edinburgh

NRT DECEMBER 19 EDITION

Table T066-R

Mondays to Fridays

16 December to 15 May

West Midlands, Northampton, Milton Keynes and Watford Junction - London

	VT
	◇1 A ⊠
Wolverhampton 7 68 d	22 45
Sandwell & Dudley 68 d	22 55
Birmingham New Street 12 68 d	23 10
Birmingham International 68 d	23 20
Nuneaton 65 d	
Coventry 68 d	23 31
Rugby 68 d	23 44
Long Buckby 68 d	
Northampton 68 a	00s05
d	
Wolverton d	
Milton Keynes Central 10 a	00 23
d	00 24
Bletchley d	
Leighton Buzzard d	
Cheddington d	
Tring d	
Berkhamsted d	
Hemel Hempstead d	
Apsley d	
Kings Langley d	
Watford Junction 60 a	00s54
d	
Bushey 60 d	
Harrow & Wealdstone ⊖60 d	
Wembley Central ⊖60,176 d	
Shepherd's Bush ⊖176 a	
Kensington (Olympia) ⊖176 a	
West Brompton ⊖176 a	
Imperial Wharf 176 a	
Clapham Junction 176 a	
East Croydon 176 a	
London Euston 15 ⊖60 a	01 13

Saturdays

21 December to 16 May

	LM	LM	LM	VT	LM	LM	SN	LM	LM		SN	LM	LM	LM	LM	LM	VT	VT	LM		VT	SN	LM	VT
	1 B	1 C	1 D	◇1 A ⊠	1	1	1	1	1		1	1	1	1	1 E	1	◇1	◇1	1 F		◇1 G	1 H	1 E	◇1 G
Wolverhampton 7 68 d																		05 45						
Sandwell & Dudley 68 d																		05 55						
Birmingham New Street 12 68 d																05 33	05 50	06 10						
Birmingham International 68 d																05 44	06 00	06 20						
Nuneaton 65 d																								
Coventry 68 d																06 02	06 11	06 31						
Rugby 68 d																06 13	06 23				06 51			
Long Buckby 68 d																06 22								
Northampton 68 a																06 34								
d								05 15				06 04	06 14			06 38							07 05	
Wolverton d								05 27				06 16				06 50							07 17	
Milton Keynes Central 10 a								05 31				06 20	06 28			06 54		06 59			07 10		07 21	
d				00 24	03 40	04 35		05 32				06 20	06 28		06 47	06 55		06 59			07 12	07 13	07 22	07 32
Bletchley d					03 45	04 40		05 37	06 10			06 25		06 40	06 52	07 00						07 18	07 27	
Leighton Buzzard d			00 02		03 52	04 47		05 44	06 16			06 32	06 37	06 47	06 59	07 07			←			07 25	07 33	
Cheddington d			00 12					05 51							07 04				07 04					
Tring d			00 17		04 04	04 59		05 56	06 26			06 42		06 56	→				07 10			07 34		
Berkhamsted d			00 22		04 09	05 04		06 01	06 31			06 47		07 01					07 15			07 38	07 46	
Hemel Hempstead d			00 27		04 13	05 08		06 06	06 36			06 52		07 05					07 19			07 43	→	
Apsley d								06 09	06 39					07 08								→		
Kings Langley d								06 12	06 42					07 12										
Watford Junction 60 a			00 34	00s54	04 20	05 15		06 16	06 46			06 59		07 16				07s19	07 26		07s33			
d	00 01		00 34		04 21	05 16	05 52	06 17	06 47		06 55	07 05		07 17					07 27					
Bushey 60 d	00 03							06 20	06 50					07 20										
Harrow & Wealdstone ⊖60 d	00 09	00 26			04 27	05 22	05 58	06 25	06 55		07 01			07 25										
Wembley Central ⊖60,176 d	00 13	00 31			04 32	05 27	06 03				07 06			07 29										
Shepherd's Bush ⊖176 a							06 19				07 21													
Kensington (Olympia) ⊖176 a							06 21				07 23													
West Brompton ⊖176 a							06 24				07 26													
Imperial Wharf 176 a							06 27				07 29													
Clapham Junction 176 a							06 32				07 34													
East Croydon 176 a							06 59				07 59													
London Euston 15 ⊖60 a	00 26	00 45	00 54	01 13	04 45	05 40		06 40	07 10			07 22	07 07	07 41		07 39	07 13	07 36	07 45		07 50			08 07

A From Edinburgh
B From Liverpool Lime Street
C From Crewe
D From Birmingham New Street
E To London Euston
F From Milton Keynes Central
G From Manchester Piccadilly
H To East Croydon

Table T066-R

Saturdays

21 December to 16 May

West Midlands, Northampton, Milton Keynes and Watford Junction - London

	LM	VT	LM	VT	LM	SN	VT	LM	LM	LM	VT	LM	VT	LM	LM	VT	LM	SN	LM	LM	VT	LM
	1	◇1	1	◇1	1	1	◇1	1	1	1	◇1	1	◇1	1	1	◇1	1	1	1	1	◇1	1
			A	B		C	D	E	F			F		A		G	E	H	I	J		
Wolverhampton 7 68 d		06 06									06 27		06 45								07 05	
Sandwell & Dudley 68 d		06 17									06 37		06 56								07 15	
Birmingham New Street 12 68 d	06 14	06 30								06 33	06 50	06 54	07 10							07 16	07 30	
Birmingham International 68 d	06 30	06 40								06 45	07 00	07 05	07 20							07 31	07 40	
Nuneaton 65 d			06 39	06 59										07 26								
Coventry 68 d	06 48	06 51								07 01	07 11	07 21	07 31							07 48	07 51	
Rugby 68 d	06 59		07 02							07 12	07 23	07 31		07 43		07 54				08 00		
Long Buckby 68 d	07 08									07 22		07 41								08 10		
Northampton 68 a	07 20									07 34		07 53								08 22		
d	07 22								07 30	07 38		08 05								08 24		
Wolverton d	07 34								07 42			08 17					←		←	08 36		
Milton Keynes Central 10 a	07 38								07 46	07 53		08 21	07 58	08 04			07 46		08 21	08 40		
d	07 38						07 39		07 47	07 54		08 22	07 59	08 05			07 47	08 13	08 22	08 41		
Bletchley d	07 43				07 09				→			→					07 52	08 18	08 27	08 46		
Leighton Buzzard d	07 50				07 15												07 59	08 25	08 33	08 53		
Cheddington d																	08 03					
Tring d					07 25			←							07 56		08 10	08 34				08 25
Berkhamsted d					07 30	←		07 46							08 01		08 15	08 38	08 46			08 30
Hemel Hempstead d					07 35	07 43		07 51							08 06		08 19	08 43	→			08 35
Apsley d					07 38										08 09			→				08 38
Kings Langley d					07 41										08 12							08 41
Watford Junction 60 a		07s37		07s45	07 45	07 51		07 58		08 15					08 16		08 26				08s37	08 45
d					07 46	07 52		07 59		08 16					08 17		08 27					08 46
Bushey 60 d					07 49										08 20							08 49
Harrow & Wealdstone ⊖60 d					07 54	07 59									08 25							08 54
Wembley Central ⊖60,176 d						08 04									08 30							
Shepherd's Bush ⊖176 a						08 19																
Kensington (Olympia) ⊖176 a						08 21																
West Brompton ⊖176 a						08 24																
Imperial Wharf 176 a						08 27																
Clapham Junction 176 a						08 32																
East Croydon 176 a						08 59																
London Euston 15 ⊖60 a	08 20	07 53	07 57	08 02	08 10		08 13	08 18		08 31	08 17		08 34	08 40	08 42	08 44	08 46			09 24	08 53	09 10

	SN	LM	VT	VT	LM	LM	LM	VT	LM	VT	LM	SN	LM	LM	LM	LM	VT	VT	LM	SN	LM
	1	1	◇1	◇1	1	1	1	◇1	1	◇1	1	1	1	1	1	1	◇1	◇1	1	1	1
	C	K	G	L		F	A		M	N		H	A	M	A	J		B		C	B
Wolverhampton 7 68 d							07 09	07 25	07 31	07 45											
Sandwell & Dudley 68 d										07 55											
Birmingham New Street 12 68 d							07 34	07 50	07 54	08 10						08 14	08 30				
Birmingham International 68 d							07 45	08 00	08 05	08 20						08 30	08 40				
Nuneaton 65 d													08 27		08 47			09 04			
Coventry 68 d							08 01	08 11	08 21	08 31						08 48	08 51				
Rugby 68 d							08 12	08 23	08 32				08 43		09 03	08 59					
Long Buckby 68 d							08 21		08 41							09 08					
Northampton 68 a							08 33		08 57							09 20					
d							08 41		09 05							09 25					
Wolverton d									09 17		←			←		09 37					
Milton Keynes Central 10 a							08 55		09 22	08 58			09 05	09 22	09 24	09 41					
d			08 47	08 52		08 55	08 56		09 22	08 59	08 55	09 12	09 14	09 22	09 25	09 42					
Bletchley d						→			→		09 00	09 17		09 27		09 47					
Leighton Buzzard d											09 07	09 24		09 34		09 54					
Cheddington d											09 12										
Tring d		←			08 56						09 18	09 34							09 25		←
Berkhamsted d	←	08 46			09 01						09 23	09 38		09 46					09 30	←	09 46
Hemel Hempstead d	08 43	08 51			09 06						09 27	09 43		→					09 35	09 43	09 51
Apsley d					09 09							→							09 38		
Kings Langley d					09 12														09 41		
Watford Junction 60 a	08 51	08 58			09 16		09 17				09 34						09s39		09 45	09 51	09 58
d	08 52	08 59			09 17		09 18				09 35								09 46	09 52	09 59
Bushey 60 d					09 20														09 49		
Harrow & Wealdstone ⊖60 d	08 59				09 25														09 54	09 59	
Wembley Central ⊖60,176 d	09 04				09 30															10 04	
Shepherd's Bush ⊖176 a	09 19																			10 19	
Kensington (Olympia) ⊖176 a	09 21																			10 21	
West Brompton ⊖176 a	09 24																			10 24	
Imperial Wharf 176 a	09 27																			10 27	
Clapham Junction 176 a	09 32																			10 32	
East Croydon 176 a	09 59																			10 59	
London Euston 15 ⊖60 a		09 17	09 21	09 28	09 42		09 33	09 13		09 36	09 53		09 50		10 00	10 25	09 57	10 03	10 10		10 17

A From Crewe
B From Liverpool Lime Street
C From Milton Keynes Central
D From Lancaster
E From Northampton
F To London Euston
G From Manchester Piccadilly
H To East Croydon
I From Birmingham New Street to London Euston
J From Rugeley Trent Valley
K From Birmingham New Street
L From Chester
M From Liverpool Lime Street to London Euston
N From Preston

Table T066-R

Saturdays

21 December to 16 May

West Midlands, Northampton, Milton Keynes and Watford Junction - London

	VT	LM	LM	VT	LM	LM	LM	VT	VT	SN	LM	LM	LM	VT	VT	LM	SN	LM	VT	LM	LM	VT
	◇1	1	1	◇1	1	1	1	◇1	◇1	1	1	1	1	◇1	◇1	1	1	1	◇1	1	1	◇1
	A	B	C				D		E	F	C	D	G	H			I	B	A	B	C	
Wolverhampton 7 68 d		08 00	08 07				08 30							09 03						08 57	09 06	
Sandwell & Dudley 68 d																						
Birmingham New Street 12 68 d		08 33		08 50			08 54	09 10					09 14	09 30	09 30					09 33		09 50
Birmingham International 68 d		08 45		09 00			09 05	09 20					09 30	09 40	09 40					09 44		10 00
Nuneaton 65 d											09 35											
Coventry 68 d		09 01		09 11			09 21	09 31					09 48	09 51	09 51					10 01		10 11
Rugby 68 d		09 12		09 23			09 32				09 53		09 59							10 12		10 23
Long Buckby 68 d		09 21					09 41						10 08							10 21		
Northampton 68 a		09 33					09 53						10 20							10 33		
d		09 38					10 05						10 25							10 38		
Wolverton d							10 17					←	10 37									
Milton Keynes Central 10 a		09 51					10 21	09 57			10 14	10 21	10 41							10 51		
d	09 47	09 53				09 55	10 22	09 59	10 02	10 12	10 16	10 22	10 42						10 47	10 53		
Bletchley d						10 00	→			10 17		10 27	10 47									
Leighton Buzzard d						10 07				10 24		10 34	10 54									
Cheddington d						10 12																
Tring d					09 56	10 18				10 34						10 26		←				
Berkhamsted d					10 01	10 23				10 38		10 46				10 31	←	10 46				
Hemel Hempstead d					10 06	10 27				10 43		→				10 36	10 43	10 51				
Apsley d					10 09					→						10 39						
Kings Langley d					10 12											10 42						
Watford Junction 60 a		10 14			10 16	10 34								10s41	10s41	10 46	10 51	10 58		11 14		
d		10 15			10 17	10 35										10 47	10 52	10 59		11 15		
Bushey 60 d					10 20											10 50						
Harrow & Wealdstone ⊖60 d					10 25											10 55	10 59					
Wembley Central ⊖60,176 d					10 30												11 04					
Shepherd's Bush ⊖176 a																	11 19					
Kensington (Olympia) ⊖176 a																	11 21					
West Brompton ⊖176 a																	11 24					
Imperial Wharf 176 a																	11 27					
Clapham Junction 176 a																	11 32					
East Croydon 176 a																	11 59					
London Euston 15 ⊖60 a	10 21	10 30		10 15	10 42	10 53		10 33	10 36		10 52		11 25	10 57	10 57	11 10		11 17	11 20	11 30		11 13

	LM	LM	LM	VT	VT	SN	LM	LM	LM	VT	LM	SN	LM	VT	LM	LM	VT	LM	LM	LM	VT
	1	1	1	◇1	◇1	1	1	1	1	◇1	1	1	1	◇1	1	1	◇1	1	1	1	◇1
			D	J	E	F	C	D	G			I	B	A	B	C				D	K
Wolverhampton 7 68 d			09 29	09 45											10 00	10 06				10 32	10 45
Sandwell & Dudley 68 d				09 55																	10 55
Birmingham New Street 12 68 d			09 54	10 10					10 14	10 30					10 33		10 50			10 54	11 10
Birmingham International 68 d			10 05	10 20					10 30	10 40					10 45		11 00			11 05	11 20
Nuneaton 65 d							10 35														
Coventry 68 d			10 21	10 31					10 48	10 51					11 01		11 11			11 21	11 31
Rugby 68 d			10 32				10 53		10 59						11 12		11 22			11 32	
Long Buckby 68 d			10 41						11 08						11 21					11 41	
Northampton 68 a			10 53						11 20						11 33					11 55	
d			11 05						11 25						11 37					12 05	
Wolverton d			11 17					←	11 37											12 17	
Milton Keynes Central 10 a			11 21	10 57			11 14	11 21	11 41						11 51					12 21	11 57
d		10 55	11 22	10 59	11 02	11 12	11 15	11 22	11 41					11 47	11 52				11 55	12 22	11 59
Bletchley d		11 00	→			11 17		11 27	11 46										12 00	→	
Leighton Buzzard d		11 07				11 24		11 34	11 53										12 07		
Cheddington d		11 12																	12 12		
Tring d	10 56	11 18				11 34					11 25		←					11 56	12 18		
Berkhamsted d	11 01	11 23				11 38		11 46			11 30	←	11 46					12 01	12 23		
Hemel Hempstead d	11 06	11 27				11 43		→			11 35	11 43	11 51					12 06	12 27		
Apsley d	11 09					→					11 38							12 09			
Kings Langley d	11 12										11 41							12 12			
Watford Junction 60 a	11 16	11 34								11s39	11 45	11 51	11 58		12 14			12 16	12 34		
d	11 17	11 35									11 46	11 52	11 59		12 14			12 17	12 35		
Bushey 60 d	11 20										11 49							12 20			
Harrow & Wealdstone ⊖60 d	11 25										11 54	11 59						12 25			
Wembley Central ⊖60,176 d	11 30											12 04						12 30			
Shepherd's Bush ⊖176 a												12 19									
Kensington (Olympia) ⊖176 a												12 21									
West Brompton ⊖176 a												12 24									
Imperial Wharf 176 a												12 27									
Clapham Junction 176 a												12 32									
East Croydon 176 a												12 59									
London Euston 15 ⊖60 a	11 42	11 53		11 33	11 36		11 50		12 24	11 55	12 10		12 17	12 20	12 30		12 12	12 42	12 53		12 33

A From Manchester Piccadilly
B From Liverpool Lime Street
C From Crewe
D From Liverpool Lime Street to London Euston
E From Holyhead
F To East Croydon
G From Rugeley Trent Valley
H From Shrewsbury
I From Milton Keynes Central
J From Glasgow Central
K From Edinburgh

Table T066-R

Saturdays

21 December to 16 May

West Midlands, Northampton, Milton Keynes and Watford Junction - London

	VT	SN	LM	LM	LM	VT	LM	SN	LM		VT	LM	LM	VT	LM	LM	LM	VT	VT		SN	LM	LM	VT
	A	B	C	D	E			F	G		H	G	C				D	I	J		B	C	D	K
Wolverhampton 68 d												11 00	11 06				11 32	11 45						
Sandwell & Dudley 68 d																		11 55						
Birmingham New Street 68 d					11 14	11 30						11 33		11 50			11 54	12 10						
Birmingham International 68 d					11 30	11 40						11 45		12 00			12 05	12 20						
Nuneaton 65 d			11 35																			12 35		
Coventry 68 d					11 48	11 51						12 01		12 11			12 21	12 31						
Rugby 68 d			11 54		11 59							12 12		12 23			12 32					12 53		12 57
Long Buckby 68 d					12 08							12 21					12 41							
Northampton 68 a					12 20							12 33					12 53							
d					12 25							12 38					13 05							
Wolverton d				←	12 37												13 17						←	
Milton Keynes Central a			12 15	12 21	12 41							12 51					13 21	12 57				13 14	13 21	
d	12 02	12 12	12 15	12 22	12 42						12 47	12 53				12 55	13 22	12 58	13 03		13 12	13 15	13 22	
Bletchley d		12 17		12 27	12 47											13 00	→				13 17		13 27	
Leighton Buzzard d		12 24		12 34	12 54											13 07					13 24		13 34	
Cheddington d																13 12								
Tring d		12 34					12 25		←						12 56	13 18					13 34			
Berkhamsted d		12 38		12 46			12 30	←	12 46						13 01	13 23					13 38		13 46	
Hemel Hempstead d		12 43		→			12 35	12 43	12 51						13 06	13 27					13 43		→	
Apsley d		→					12 38								13 09						→			
Kings Langley d							12 41								13 12									
Watford Junction 60 a						12s40	12 45	12 51	12 58			13 14			13 16	13 34								
d							12 46	12 52	12 59			13 15			13 17	13 35								
Bushey 60 d							12 49								13 20									
Harrow & Wealdstone ⊖60 d							12 54	12 59							13 25									
Wembley Central ⊖60,176 d								13 04							13 30									
Shepherd's Bush ⊖176 a								13 19																
Kensington (Olympia) ⊖176 a								13 21																
West Brompton ⊖176 a								13 24																
Imperial Wharf 176 a								13 27																
Clapham Junction 176 a								13 32																
East Croydon 176 a								13 59																
London Euston ⊖60 a	12 36		12 51		13 24	12 56	13 10		13 17		13 21	13 30		13 14	13 42	13 53		13 33	13 36			13 50		13 53

	LM	VT	LM	SN	LM		VT	LM	LM	VT	LM	LM	LM	VT	VT		SN	LM	LM	LM	VT	LM	SN	VT
	E			F	G		H	G	C				D	L	J		B	C	D	E			F	I
Wolverhampton 68 d								12 00	12 06				12 31	12 45										
Sandwell & Dudley 68 d														12 55										
Birmingham New Street 68 d	12 14	12 30						12 33		12 50			12 54	13 10						13 14	13 30			
Birmingham International 68 d	12 30	12 40						12 45		13 00			13 05	13 20						13 30	13 40			
Nuneaton 65 d																		13 35						
Coventry 68 d	12 48	12 51						13 01		13 11			13 21	13 31						13 48	13 51			
Rugby 68 d	12 59							13 12		13 23			13 32					13 53		13 59				14 24
Long Buckby 68 d	13 08							13 21					13 41							14 08				
Northampton 68 a	13 20							13 33					13 53							14 20				
d	13 25							13 38					14 05							14 22				
Wolverton d	13 37												14 17						←	14 34				
Milton Keynes Central a	13 41							13 51					14 21	13 57				14 14	14 21	14 38				
d	13 41						13 47	13 53				13 55	14 22	13 59	14 03		14 12	14 15	14 22	14 38				
Bletchley d	13 46											14 00	→				14 17		14 27	14 43				
Leighton Buzzard d	13 53											14 07					14 24		14 34	14 50				
Cheddington d												14 12												
Tring d			13 26		←						13 56	14 18					14 34					14 25		
Berkhamsted d			13 31	←	13 46						14 01	14 23					14 38		14 46			14 30	←	
Hemel Hempstead d			13 36	13 43	13 51						14 06	14 27					14 43		→			14 35	14 43	
Apsley d			13 39								14 09						→					14 38		
Kings Langley d			13 42								14 12											14 41		
Watford Junction 60 a		13s42	13 46	13 51	13 58			14 14			14 16	14 34									14s39	14 45	14 51	
d			13 47	13 52	13 59			14 15			14 17	14 35										14 46	14 52	
Bushey 60 d			13 50								14 20											14 49		
Harrow & Wealdstone ⊖60 d			13 55	13 59							14 25											14 54	14 59	
Wembley Central ⊖60,176 d				14 04							14 30												15 04	
Shepherd's Bush ⊖176 a				14 19																			15 19	
Kensington (Olympia) ⊖176 a				14 21																			15 21	
West Brompton ⊖176 a				14 24																			15 24	
Imperial Wharf 176 a				14 27																			15 27	
Clapham Junction 176 a				14 32																			15 32	
East Croydon 176 a				14 59																			15 59	
London Euston ⊖60 a	14 24	13 58	14 10		14 18		14 20	14 30		14 13	14 42	14 53		14 33	14 36			14 50		15 20	14 55	15 10		15 13

A From Holyhead
B To East Croydon
C From Crewe
D From Liverpool Lime Street to London Euston
E From Rugeley Trent Valley
F From Milton Keynes Central
G From Liverpool Lime Street
H From Manchester Piccadilly
I From Glasgow Central
J From Chester
K From Blackpool North
L From Edinburgh

NRT DECEMBER 19 EDITION

Table T066-R

Saturdays

21 December to 16 May

West Midlands, Northampton, Milton Keynes and Watford Junction - London

	LM		VT	LM	LM	VT	LM	LM	LM	VT	VT		SN	LM	LM	LM	VT	VT	LM	SN	LM		VT
	A		B	A	C				D	E	F		G	C	D	H		I		J	A		B
Wolverhampton 68 d				13 00	13 06				13 31	13 45													
Sandwell & Dudley 68 d										13 55													
Birmingham New Street 68 d				13 33		13 50			13 54	14 10						14 14	14 30						
Birmingham International 68 d				13 44		14 00			14 05	14 20						14 30	14 40						
Nuneaton 65 d														14 35									
Coventry 68 d				14 01		14 11			14 21	14 31						14 48	14 51						
Rugby 68 d				14 12		14 26			14 32					14 53		15 01		15 04					
Long Buckby 68 d				14 22					14 41							15 10							
Northampton 68 a				14 34					14 53							15 22							
d				14 39					15 01							15 24							
Wolverton d									15 17						←	15 36							
Milton Keynes Central a				14 53					15 21	14 57				15 14	15 21	15 40							
d			14 50	14 53				14 55	15 22	14 59	15 03		15 12	15 15	15 22	15 41							15 47
Bletchley d								15 00	→				15 17		15 27	15 46							
Leighton Buzzard d								15 07					15 24		15 34	15 53							
Cheddington d								15 12															
Tring d	←						14 56	15 18					15 34						15 25		←		
Berkhamsted d	14 46						15 01	15 23					15 38		15 46				15 30	←	15 46		
Hemel Hempstead d	14 51						15 06	15 27					15 43		→				15 35	15 43	15 51		
Apsley d							15 09						→						15 38				
Kings Langley d							15 12												15 41				
Watford Junction 60 a	14 58			15 15			15 16	15 34									15s39		15 45	15 51	15 58		
d	14 59			15 15			15 17	15 35											15 46	15 52	15 59		
Bushey 60 d							15 20												15 49				
Harrow & Wealdstone ⊖60 d							15 25												15 54	15 59			
Wembley Central ⊖60,176 d							15 30													16 04			
Shepherd's Bush ⊖176 a																				16 19			
Kensington (Olympia) ⊖176 a																				16 21			
West Brompton ⊖176 a																				16 24			
Imperial Wharf 176 a																				16 27			
Clapham Junction 176 a																				16 32			
East Croydon 176 a																				16 59			
London Euston ⊖60 a	15 17		15 23	15 31		15 16	15 42	15 55		15 34	15 37			15 50		16 24	15 55	15 58	16 10		16 19		16 21

	LM	LM	VT	LM	LM	LM	VT	VT		SN	LM	LM	LM	VT	LM	SN	LM	VT		LM	LM	VT	LM	LM
	A	C				D	K	F		G	C	D	H			J	A	B		A	C			
Wolverhampton 68 d	14 00	14 06				14 31	14 45													15 01	15 06			
Sandwell & Dudley 68 d							14 55																	
Birmingham New Street 68 d	14 33		14 50			14 54	15 10						15 14	15 30						15 33		15 50		
Birmingham International 68 d	14 45		15 00			15 05	15 20						15 30	15 40						15 44		16 00		
Nuneaton 65 d											15 35													
Coventry 68 d	15 01		15 11			15 21	15 31						15 48	15 51						16 01		16 11		
Rugby 68 d	15 12		15 22			15 32					15 53		15 59							16 12		16 23		
Long Buckby 68 d	15 21					15 41							16 08							16 21				
Northampton 68 a	15 33					15 53							16 20							16 33				
d	15 38					16 04							16 25							16 38				
Wolverton d						16 17						←	16 37											
Milton Keynes Central a	15 52					16 21	15 57				16 14	16 21	16 41							16 52				
d	15 53				15 58	16 22	15 59	16 02		16 12	16 15	16 22	16 42					16 47		16 53				16 55
Bletchley d					16 03	→				16 17		16 27	16 47											17 00
Leighton Buzzard d					16 10					16 24		16 34	16 54											17 07
Cheddington d					16 15																			17 12
Tring d				15 56	16 21					16 34					16 25		←						16 56	17 18
Berkhamsted d				16 01	16 26					16 38		16 46			16 30	←	16 46						17 01	17 23
Hemel Hempstead d				16 06	16 30					16 43		→			16 35	16 43	16 51						17 06	17 27
Apsley d				16 09						→					16 38								17 09	
Kings Langley d				16 12											16 41								17 12	
Watford Junction 60 a	16 14			16 16	16 37									16s39	16 45	16 51	16 58			17 14			17 16	17 34
d	16 15			16 17	16 38										16 46	16 52	16 59			17 15			17 17	17 35
Bushey 60 d				16 20											16 49								17 20	
Harrow & Wealdstone ⊖60 d				16 25											16 54	16 59							17 25	
Wembley Central ⊖60,176 d				16 30												17 04							17 30	
Shepherd's Bush ⊖176 a																17 19								
Kensington (Olympia) ⊖176 a																17 21								
West Brompton ⊖176 a																17 24								
Imperial Wharf 176 a																17 27								
Clapham Junction 176 a																17 32								
East Croydon 176 a																17 59								
London Euston ⊖60 a	16 30		16 13	16 42	16 56		16 33	16 36			16 50		17 24	16 55	17 10		17 17	17 21		17 30		17 13	17 42	17 53

A From Liverpool Lime Street
B From Manchester Piccadilly
C From Crewe
D From Liverpool Lime Street to London Euston
E From Glasgow Central
F From Chester
G To East Croydon
H From Rugeley Trent Valley
I From Blackpool North
J From Milton Keynes Central
K From Edinburgh

Table T066-R

Saturdays

21 December to 16 May

West Midlands, Northampton, Milton Keynes and Watford Junction - London

	LM A	VT ◇1 B ☕	VT ◇1 C ☕	SN D	LM E	LM A	LM F	VT ◇1 G ☕	VT ◇1 ☕	LM	SN H	LM I	VT ◇1 J ☕	LM I	LM E	VT ◇1 ☕	LM	LM	LM A	VT ◇1 K ☕	VT ◇1 L ☕	SN D
Wolverhampton 68 d	15 30	15 45						16 03						15 58	16 07				16 31	16 45		
Sandwell & Dudley 68 d		15 55																		16 55		
Birmingham New Street 68 d	15 54	16 10					16 14	16 30	16 30					16 33		16 50			16 54	17 10		
Birmingham International 68 d	16 05	16 20					16 30	16 40	16 40					16 44		17 00			17 05	17 20		
Nuneaton 65 d					16 35																	
Coventry 68 d	16 21	16 31					16 48	16 51	16 51					17 01		17 11			17 21	17 31		
Rugby 68 d	16 32				16 53		16 59							17 15		17 23			17 32			
Long Buckby 68 d	16 43						17 08							17 26					17 41			
Northampton 68 a	16 57						17 20							17 38					17 53			
d	17 05						17 25							17 39					18 05			
Wolverton d	17 17					←	17 37												18 17			
Milton Keynes Central a	17 21	16 57			17 14	17 21	17 41							17 52					18 21	17 57		
d	17 22	16 59	17 02	17 12	17 15	17 22	17 42						17 47	17 53				17 55	18 22	17 59	18 03	18 12
Bletchley d	→			17 17		17 27	17 47											18 00	→			18 17
Leighton Buzzard d				17 24		17 34	17 54											18 07				18 24
Cheddington d																		18 12				
Tring d				17 34						17 25		←					17 56	18 18				18 34
Berkhamsted d				17 38		17 46				17 30	←	17 46					18 01	18 23				18 38
Hemel Hempstead d				17 43		→				17 35	17 43	17 51					18 05	18 27				18 43
Apsley d				→						17 38							18 08					→
Kings Langley d										17 41							18 12					
Watford Junction 60 a								17s39	17s39	17 45	17 51	17 58		18 14			18 16	18 34				
d										17 46	17 52	17 59		18 15			18 17	18 35				
Bushey 60 d										17 49							18 20					
Harrow & Wealdstone ⊖60 d										17 54	17 59						18 25					
Wembley Central ⊖60,176 d											18 04						18 30					
Shepherd's Bush ⊖176 a											18 19											
Kensington (Olympia) ⊖176 a											18 21											
West Brompton ⊖176 a											18 24											
Imperial Wharf 176 a											18 27											
Clapham Junction 176 a											18 32											
East Croydon 176 a											18 59											
London Euston ⊖60 a		17 33	17 36		17 50		18 24	17 55	17 55	18 10		18 17	18 20	18 30		18 13	18 42	18 53		18 33	18 36	

	LM E	LM A	VT ◇1 M ☕	LM F	VT ◇1 ☕	LM	SN H	LM I	VT ◇1 J ☕	LM I	LM E	VT ◇1 ☕	LM	SN	LM	LM A	VT ◇1 B ☕	SN D	LM E	LM N	VT ◇1 ☕
Wolverhampton 68 d										17 00	17 06					17 30	17 45				
Sandwell & Dudley 68 d																	17 55				
Birmingham New Street 68 d				17 14	17 30					17 33		17 50				17 54	18 10			18 14	18 30
Birmingham International 68 d				17 31	17 40					17 45		18 00				18 05	18 20			18 30	18 40
Nuneaton 65 d	17 35																		18 35		
Coventry 68 d				17 49	17 51					18 01		18 11				18 21	18 31			18 48	18 51
Rugby 68 d	17 53		17 58	17 59						18 12		18 23				18 32			18 53	18 59	
Long Buckby 68 d				18 08						18 22						18 41				19 08	
Northampton 68 a				18 21						18 37						18 53				19 20	
d				18 25						18 39						19 04				19 27	
Wolverton d		←		18 37												19 16				19 39	
Milton Keynes Central a	18 14	18 21		18 41						18 53						19 20	18 57		19 14	19 43	
d	18 15	18 22		18 42					18 49	18 53					18 55	19 21	18 59	19 13	19 15	19 44	
Bletchley d		18 27		18 47											19 00	→		→		→	
Leighton Buzzard d		18 34		18 54											19 07						
Cheddington d															19 12						
Tring d						18 25		←					18 56		19 18						
Berkhamsted d		18 46				18 30	←	18 46					19 01		19 23						
Hemel Hempstead d		→				18 35	18 43	18 51					19 06		19 27						
Apsley d						18 38							19 09								
Kings Langley d						18 41							19 12								
Watford Junction 60 a					18s42	18 45	18 51	18 58		19 15			19 16		19 34						19s39
d						18 46	18 51	18 59		19 16			19 17	19 31	19 35						
Bushey 60 d						18 49							19 20								
Harrow & Wealdstone ⊖60 d						18 54	18 59						19 26	19 37							
Wembley Central ⊖60,176 d							19 03							19 42	19 46						
Shepherd's Bush ⊖176 a							19 19							20 00							
Kensington (Olympia) ⊖176 a							19 21							20 03							
West Brompton ⊖176 a							19 24							20 06							
Imperial Wharf 176 a							19 27							20 09							
Clapham Junction 176 a							19 32							20 13							
East Croydon 176 a							19 59														
London Euston ⊖60 a	18 51		18 53	19 26	18 59	19 10		19 17	19 22	19 31		19 14	19 40		19 58		19 34		19 50		19 55

A From Liverpool Lime Street to London Euston
B From Glasgow Central
C From Holyhead
D To East Croydon
E From Crewe
F From Rugeley Trent Valley
G From Shrewsbury
H From Milton Keynes Central
I From Liverpool Lime Street
J From Manchester Piccadilly
K From Edinburgh
L From Chester
M From Blackpool North
N From Rugeley Trent Valley to London Euston

Table T066-R

Saturdays

21 December to 16 May

West Midlands, Northampton, Milton Keynes and Watford Junction - London

	LM	SN	LM A	VT ◇1 B ☕	LM A	LM C	VT ◇1 ☕	LM	LM D	LM E	VT ◇1 F ☕	SN	LM A	LM D	VT ◇1 G ☕	LM A	LM C	LM E	VT ◇1 G ☕	SN	VT ◇1 B ☕	LM A
Wolverhampton 68 d					18 00	18 06				18 29	18 45					19 00	19 06	19 29	19 45			
Sandwell & Dudley 68 d											18 55								19 55			
Birmingham New Street 68 d					18 33		18 50			18 54	19 10			19 14		19 33		19 54	20 10			
Birmingham International 68 d					18 44		19 00			19 05	19 20			19 30		19 44		20 05	20 20			
Nuneaton 65 d																						
Coventry 68 d					19 01		19 11			19 21	19 31			19 48		20 01		20 21	20 31			
Rugby 68 d					19 12		19 23			19 32	19 43			19 59		20 12		20 32	20 43			
Long Buckby 68 d					19 21					19 41				20 08		20 21		20 41				
Northampton 68 a					19 33					19 53				20 20		20 35		20 53				
d					19 33					20 00				20 23		20 36		21 00				
Wolverton d		←	←						←	20 12			←					21 11				←
Milton Keynes Central a			19 20		19 48				19 43	20 16	20 05		20 16	20 37		20 50		21 15	21 04			21 15
d		19 13	19 21	19 47					19 44	20 16	20 07		20 16	20 37	20 45	20 51		21 16	21 05		21 11	21 16
Bletchley d		19 18	19 26						19 49	→			20 21			20 56		→				21 20
Leighton Buzzard d		19 25	19 33						19 56				20 28	20 46								21 27
Cheddington d									20 01					20 53								
Tring d	19 25	19 34	19 42					19 57	20 07							21 13						
Berkhamsted d	19 30	19 38	19 47					20 02	20 12							21 18						21 42
Hemel Hempstead d	19 35	19 43	19 51					20 07	20 16					21 04		21 22						21 46
Apsley d	19 38							20 10						21 07								
Kings Langley d	19 41							20 13						21 10								
Watford Junction 60 a	19 45	19 50	19 58					20 17	20 23		20s33		20 47	21 14	21s18	21 29			21s36			21 53
d	19 46	19 51	19 59					20 18	20 23			20 43	20 48	21 15		21 30				21 46		21 54
Bushey 60 d	19 49															21 33						
Harrow & Wealdstone ⊖60 d	19 54	20 00						20 24	20 30			20 49				21 38				21 52		
Wembley Central ⊖60,176 d		20 04						20 29				20 54								21 57		
Shepherd's Bush ⊖176 a		20 19										21 15								22 15		
Kensington (Olympia) ⊖176 a		20 22										21 18								22 17		
West Brompton ⊖176 a		20 25										21 23								22 26		
Imperial Wharf 176 a		20 28										21 26								22 29		
Clapham Junction 176 a		20 33										21 30								22 33		
East Croydon 176 a		20 59										21 59								22 59		
London Euston ⊖60 a	20 10		20 17	20 34			20 23	20 41	20 45		20 55		21 10	21 34	21 40	21 54			21 57		22 01	22 12

	LM D	VT ◇1 G ☕	LM A	LM C	LM E	VT ◇1 F ☕	VT ◇1 B ☕	SN	LM C	LM A	VT ◇1 H ☕	VT ◇1 I ☕	SN	LM C	LM
Wolverhampton 68 d			20 00	20 08	20 31	20 45					21 09	21 09		21 04	
Sandwell & Dudley 68 d						20 55					21 19	21 19			
Birmingham New Street 68 d	20 14		20 33		20 54	21 10					21 30	21 30		21 34	22 14
Birmingham International 68 d	20 30		20 44		21 05	21 20					21 40	21 40		21 46	22 30
Nuneaton 65 d									21 37						
Coventry 68 d	20 48		21 01		21 21	21 31					21 51	21 51		22 01	22 48
Rugby 68 d	20 58		21 12		21 32	21 44			21 53		22 03	22 03		22 12	22 59
Long Buckby 68 d	21 08		21 24		21 41									22 21	23 08
Northampton 68 a	21 23		21 34		21 53									22 33	23 21
d	21 24		21 43		22 05									22 42	23 30
Wolverton d			21 54		22 17					←				22 54	23 42
Milton Keynes Central a	21 39		21 58		22 21	22 04			22 15	22 21	22 24	22 24		22 58	23 46
d	21 40	21 55	21 59		22 21	22 06	22 11		22 15	22 21	22 26	22 26		22 58	23 46
Bletchley d			22 04		→					22 26				23 03	23 51
Leighton Buzzard d	21 49									22 33				23 10	23 58
Cheddington d	21 53									22 38				23 15	
Tring d	22 00									22 44				23 22	
Berkhamsted d	22 05									22 49				23 29	
Hemel Hempstead d	22 10									22 54				23 34	
Apsley d	22 13									22 57				23 37	
Kings Langley d	22 16									23 00				23 40	
Watford Junction 60 a	22 20		22 30			22s34	22s39			23 06	23s11	23s11		23 44	00 19
d	22 21		22 31					22 53		23 07			23 26	23 45	00 20
Bushey 60 d															
Harrow & Wealdstone ⊖60 d								22 59		23 14			23 32	23 51	
Wembley Central ⊖60,176 d								23 04					23 37		
Shepherd's Bush ⊖176 a								23 22					23 52		
Kensington (Olympia) ⊖176 a								23 24					23 54		
West Brompton ⊖176 a								23 27					23 57		
Imperial Wharf 176 a								23 29					00 01		
Clapham Junction 176 a								23 34					00 06		
East Croydon 176 a															
London Euston ⊖60 a	22 41	22 47	22 53			22 56	23 00		23 03	23 31	23 34	23 35		00 05	00 40

A From Liverpool Lime Street
B From Manchester Piccadilly
C From Crewe
D From Rugeley Trent Valley
E From Liverpool Lime Street to London Euston
F From Edinburgh
G From Glasgow Central
H until 15 February
I from 22 February

Table T066-R

Sundays

15 December to 10 May

West Midlands, Northampton, Milton Keynes and Watford Junction - London

	LM	LM	LM	LM	LM	LM	LM	LM	SN	LM	LM	LM	VT	SN	LM	VT	LM	LM	LM	VT	VT	SN
	1		1		1	1	1	1		1	1	1	◇1		1	◇1	1	1	1	◇1	◇1	
	A															B			C		B	
		🚌		🚌									🍴			🍴				🍴	🍴	
Wolverhampton 7 68 🚌 d													08 05							09 05		
Sandwell & Dudley 68 d													08 15							09 15		
Birmingham New Street 12 68 🚌 d													08 30						09 14	09 30		
Birmingham International 68 ✈ d													08 40						09 25	09 40		
Nuneaton 65 d																					09 55	
Coventry 68 d													08 51						09 44	09 51		
Rugby 68 d													09 04						09 55	10 04		
Long Buckby 68 d																			10 04			
Northampton 68 a																			10 16			
d				06 15			07 52	08 15		08 21	08 45	08 50			09 25		09 59	10 08	10 30			
Wolverton d				06 47			08 04	08 27		08 33	08 57	09 02			09 38		10 11	10 20	10 44			
Milton Keynes Central 10 a				07 00			08 08	08 31		08 37	09 01	09 06	09 36		09 41		10 15	10 25	10 48	10 37		
d			06 42		07 10	07 38	08 08	08 31		08 37	09 01	09 06	09 38		09 42	10 20	10 24	10 28	10 48	10 39		
Bletchley d			06 47		07 15	07 43	08 13	08 36		08 42	09 06	09 11			09 47			10 33	→			
Leighton Buzzard d			06 53		07 22	07 50	08 20	08 43		08 49	09 13	09 18			09 54		10 33	10 40				
Cheddington d					07 26		08 25					09 23						10 45				
Tring d					07 36		08 34					09 32					10 43					
Berkhamsted d			07 09		07 41	08 05	08 39			09 04		09 36			10 09			10 54				
Hemel Hempstead d			07 14		07 45	08 10	08 44			09 09		09 40			10 14			10 59				
Apsley d			07 17			08 13				09 12					10 17							
Kings Langley d			07 20			08 16				09 16					10 20							
Watford Junction 60 a			07 24		07 52	08 20	08 51	09 06		09 20	09 36	09 48	10s07		10 24		10 55	11 06		11s11	11s15	
d	00 20	00 40	07 25		07 53	08 21	08 52	09 08	09 17	09 22	09 38	09 49		10 17	10 25		10 55	11 06				11 22
Bushey 60 d						08 24				09 25					10 27							
Harrow & Wealdstone ⊖60 d		01 00	07 31		07 59	08 29	08 58		09 23	09 29		09 55		10 23				11 13				11 28
Wembley Central ⊖60,176 d		01 15																				
Shepherd's Bush ⊖176 a									09 44					10 44								11 47
Kensington (Olympia) ⊖176 a									09 46					10 46								11 49
West Brompton ⊖176 a									09 49					10 49								11 52
Imperial Wharf 176 a									09 52					10 52								11 55
Clapham Junction 176 a									09 57					10 57								12 00
East Croydon 176 🚌 a																						
London Euston 15 ⊖60 a	00 40	01 45	07 45		08 13	08 43	09 12	09 27		09 44	09 58	10 10	10 25		10 44	11 04	11 15	11 28		11 31	11 34	

	LM	LM	VT	VT	LM	LM	LM	VT	LM	VT	SN	LM	LM	LM	LM	VT	VT	VT	VT	LM	LM	LM
	1	1	◇1	◇1	1	1	1	◇1	1	◇1		1	1	1	1	◇1	◇1	◇1	◇1	1	1	1
	D		E	F	G		C		H	B		C	G	I	G	J	K	F	B		G	C
			🍴	🍴				🍴		🍴						🍴	🍴	🍴	🍴			
Wolverhampton 7 68 🚌 d					09 30		09 51	10 05							10 31						10 52	
Sandwell & Dudley 68 d					09 40		10 01	10 15														
Birmingham New Street 12 68 🚌 d					09 54		10 14	10 30							10 54						11 14	11 17
Birmingham International 68 ✈ d					10 04		10 25	10 40							11 05						11 24	11 28
Nuneaton 65 d										10 56			11 00						11 59			
Coventry 68 d					10 16		10 44	10 51							11 15						11 36	11 47
Rugby 68 d			10 32		10 26		10 55	11 04					11 20		11 27	11 31	11 31				11 47	11 58
Long Buckby 68 d					10 36		11 04						11 29		11 36						11 57	12 08
Northampton 68 a					10 46		11 16						11 41		11 48						12 09	12 19
d		10 38			11 04	11 12	11 25						11 44		11 48						12 10	12 25
Wolverton d	←				11 18				←						12 00						12 22	12 37
Milton Keynes Central 10 a	10 48	10 53	11 06		11 22	11 26	11 40	11 35	11 40	11 45			11 58		12 04	12 05	12 05				12 26	12 41
d	10 48	10 53	11 08	11 17	11 22	11 26	11 41	11 37	11 41	11 46		11 51	12 00		12 05	12 07	12 07	12 22			12 27	12 41
Bletchley d	10 53	10 58				11 31	→		11 46			11 56	12 05		12 10					12 16	12 32	→
Leighton Buzzard d	11 00	11 05				11 38			11 53			12 01	12 12	←	12 17					12 23	12 39	
Cheddington d						11 43						12 07		12 07						12 28		
Tring d						11 50						→		12 13						12 35		
Berkhamsted d	11 16	11 20				11 55			12 06					12 18						12 40		
Hemel Hempstead d	11 20	11 24				12 00			12 11					12 22						12 44		
Apsley d		11 28												12 25								
Kings Langley d		11 31												12 28								
Watford Junction 60 a	11 27	11 35	11s42		11 53	12 08		12s08	12 18				12 31	12 33	12 38				12s51	12 51	13 00	
d	11 28	11 35			11 54	12 09			12 18		12 23		12 32	12 33	12 38					12 52	13 00	
Bushey 60 d		11 39												12 36								
Harrow & Wealdstone ⊖60 d		11 44			12 00	12 15			12 25		12 29			12 41						12 58		
Wembley Central ⊖60,176 d																						
Shepherd's Bush ⊖176 a											12 48											
Kensington (Olympia) ⊖176 a											12 50											
West Brompton ⊖176 a											12 53											
Imperial Wharf 176 a											12 56											
Clapham Junction 176 a											13 00											
East Croydon 176 🚌 a																						
London Euston 15 ⊖60 a	11 47	11 59	12 02	12 06	12 16	12 29		12 25	12 40	12 29			12 49	12 55	12 59	12 42	12 43	12 57	13 09	13 12	13 18	

A not 15 December. From Birmingham New Street
B From Liverpool Lime Street
C To London Euston
D From Birmingham New Street
E From Preston
F From Manchester Piccadilly
G From Crewe
H From Wolverhampton
I From Milton Keynes Central
J until 16 February. From Preston
K from 23 February. From Preston

Table T066-R

Sundays

15 December to 10 May

West Midlands, Northampton, Milton Keynes and Watford Junction - London

	VT	VT	LM	VT	LM	SN	LM	VT	VT	LM	LM	LM	LM	LM	VT	LM	VT	LM	VT	LM	LM
	◇1	◇1	1	◇1	1		1	◇1	◇1	1	1	1	1	1	◇1	1	◇1	1	◇1	1	1
			A	B	C		D		E		C	F	G	F				H	B	C	I
	🍴	🍴		🍴				🍴	🍴						🍴		🍴		🍴		
Wolverhampton 7 68 🚌 d	11 05						11 28	11 45					11 48								12 29
Sandwell & Dudley 68 d	11 14							11 55													
Birmingham New Street 12 68 🚌 d	11 30	11 50					11 54	12 10					12 14	12 17	12 30		12 50				12 54
Birmingham International 68 ✈ d	11 40	12 00					12 05	12 20					12 25	12 29	12 40		13 00				13 05
Nuneaton 65 d					12 20				12 32											13 15	
Coventry 68 d	11 51	12 11					12 15	12 31					12 37	12 48	12 51		13 11				13 17
Rugby 68 d	12 05	12 25			12 36		12 27						12 47	12 58			13 27			13 33	13 28
Long Buckby 68 d							12 36						12 57	13 08							13 37
Northampton 68 a							12 48						13 09	13 20							13 48
d							12 48						13 11	13 25							13 48
Wolverton d			←				13 00				←		13 23	13 37		←		←			14 00
Milton Keynes Central 10 a	12 26		12 41		12 58		13 04	13 00	13 03		13 04		13 27	13 41				13 27		13 54	14 04
d	12 27		12 41	12 52	13 01		13 05	13 01	13 04		13 05	13 11	13 28	13 41		13 11		13 28	13 46	13 55	14 05
Bletchley d			12 46				→				13 10	→	→	→		13 16		13 33			→
Leighton Buzzard d			12 53								13 17					13 23		13 40			
Cheddington d																13 29					
Tring d										13 14						13 35					
Berkhamsted d			13 07							13 19						13 40					
Hemel Hempstead d			13 11							13 24						13 45		13 56			
Apsley d										13 27											
Kings Langley d										13 30											
Watford Junction 60 a			13 18							13 34	13 38				13s38	13 52		14 04			
d			13 19			13 23				13 35	13 39					13 52		14 05			
Bushey 60 d										13 38											
Harrow & Wealdstone ⊖60 d			13 25			13 29				13 43						13 59					
Wembley Central ⊖60,176 d																					
Shepherd's Bush ⊖176 a						13 48															
Kensington (Olympia) ⊖176 a						13 50															
West Brompton ⊖176 a						13 53															
Imperial Wharf 176 a						13 56															
Clapham Junction 176 a						14 00															
East Croydon 176 🚌 a																					
London Euston 15 ⊖60 a	13 04	13 17	13 40	13 28	13 49			13 38	13 42	13 57	14 01				13 57	14 13	14 19	14 24	14 26	14 33	

	VT	LM	VT	SN	LM	LM	LM	LM	LM	VT	LM	VT	LM	VT	LM	LM	VT	LM	VT	SN	LM	LM
	◇1	1	◇1		1	1	1	1	1	◇1	1	◇1	1	◇1	1	1	◇1	1	◇1		1	1
		A	J			K	F	F	G				A	B	C	I	L	H	J			K
	🍴		🍴							🍴		🍴		🍴			🍴		🍴			
Wolverhampton 7 68 🚌 d	12 45								12 57							13 34	13 45					
Sandwell & Dudley 68 d	12 55																13 55					
Birmingham New Street 12 68 🚌 d	13 10							13 14	13 17	13 30		13 50				13 54	14 10					
Birmingham International 68 ✈ d	13 20							13 24	13 28	13 40		14 00				14 05	14 20					
Nuneaton 65 d															14 15				14 32			
Coventry 68 d	13 31							13 37	13 47	13 51		14 11				14 17	14 31					
Rugby 68 d								13 47	13 58			14 22			14 33	14 28						
Long Buckby 68 d								13 57	14 07							14 37						
Northampton 68 a								14 09	14 19							14 48						
d								14 10	14 25							14 48						
Wolverton d		←				←		14 22	14 37		←		←			15 00		←				←
Milton Keynes Central 10 a	13 58	13 41				14 04		14 26	14 41				14 26		14 54	15 04	14 58	14 41	15 03			15 04
d	13 59	13 41	14 04			14 05	14 11	14 27	14 41		14 11		14 27	14 50	14 55	15 05	14 59	14 41	15 04			15 05
Bletchley d		13 46				14 10	→	→	→		14 16		14 32			→		14 46				15 10
Leighton Buzzard d		13 53				14 17					14 23		14 39					14 53				15 17
Cheddington d											14 28											
Tring d					14 14						14 35										15 14	
Berkhamsted d		14 07			14 19						14 40							15 07			15 19	
Hemel Hempstead d		14 11			14 24						14 44							15 11			15 24	
Apsley d					14 27																15 27	
Kings Langley d					14 30																15 30	
Watford Junction 60 a		14 18			14 34	14 38				14s38	14 51		15 00					15 18			15 34	15 38
d		14 19		14 23	14 35	14 39					14 52		15 00					15 19		15 23	15 35	15 39
Bushey 60 d					14 38																15 38	
Harrow & Wealdstone ⊖60 d		14 25		14 29	14 43						14 58							15 25		15 29	15 43	
Wembley Central ⊖60,176 d																						
Shepherd's Bush ⊖176 a				14 48																15 48		
Kensington (Olympia) ⊖176 a				14 50																15 50		
West Brompton ⊖176 a				14 53																15 53		
Imperial Wharf 176 a				14 56																15 56		
Clapham Junction 176 a				15 00																16 00		
East Croydon 176 🚌 a																						
London Euston 15 ⊖60 a	14 36	14 40	14 40		14 57	15 01				14 57	15 12	15 15	15 18	15 25	15 33		15 37	15 40	15 41		15 57	16 01

A From Birmingham New Street
B From Manchester Piccadilly
C From Crewe
D From Crewe to London Euston
E From Chester
F To London Euston
G From Liverpool Lime Street to London Euston
H From Liverpool Lime Street
I From Stafford to London Euston
J From Holyhead
K From Stafford
L From Lancaster

Table T066-R

Sundays

15 December to 10 May

West Midlands, Northampton, Milton Keynes and Watford Junction - London

	LM	LM	LM	VT	LM	LM	VT	VT	VT	LM	LM	VT	LM	VT	SN	LM	LM	LM	LM	LM	VT
	A	A	B			C	D	E	F	G	H	I	J	K			L	A	A	B	
Wolverhampton 68 d			13 57								14 32	14 45								14 57	
Sandwell & Dudley 68 d												14 55									
Birmingham New Street 68 d		14 14	14 17	14 30			14 50	14 50			14 54	15 10							15 14	15 17	15 30
Birmingham International 68 d		14 24	14 28	14 40			15 00	15 00			15 05	15 20							15 24	15 28	15 40
Nuneaton 65 d										15 15											
Coventry 68 d		14 37	14 47	14 51			15 11	15 11			15 17	15 31							15 37	15 47	15 51
Rugby 68 d		14 47	14 58				15 25	15 25		15 33	15 28								15 47	15 58	
Long Buckby 68 d		14 57	15 07								15 37								15 57	16 07	
Northampton 68 a		15 09	15 19								15 48								16 09	16 19	
d		15 10	15 25								15 48								16 10	16 25	
Wolverton d		15 22	15 37		←	←					16 00		←				←		16 22	16 37	
Milton Keynes Central a		15 26	15 41			15 26				15 54	16 04	15 58	15 41				16 04		16 26	16 41	
d	15 11	15 27	15 41		15 11	15 27			15 49	15 55	16 05	15 59	15 41	16 04			16 05	16 11	16 27	16 41	
Bletchley d	→	→	→		15 16	15 32					→		15 46				16 10	→	→	→	
Leighton Buzzard d					15 23	15 39							15 53				16 17				
Cheddington d					15 28																
Tring d					15 35											16 14					
Berkhamsted d					15 40								16 07			16 19					
Hemel Hempstead d					15 44								16 11			16 24					
Apsley d																16 27					
Kings Langley d																16 30					
Watford Junction 60 a				15s39	15 51	16 00							16 18			16 34	16 38				16s38
d					15 52	16 00							16 19		16 23	16 35	16 39				
Bushey 60 d																16 38					
Harrow & Wealdstone ⊖60 d					15 58								16 25		16 29	16 43					
Wembley Central ⊖60,176 d																					
Shepherd's Bush ⊖176 a															16 48						
Kensington (Olympia) ⊖176 a															16 50						
West Brompton ⊖176 a															16 53						
Imperial Wharf 176 a															16 56						
Clapham Junction 176 a															17 00						
East Croydon 176 a																					
London Euston ⊖60 a				15 57	16 12	16 18	16 18	16 20	16 26	16 33		16 37	16 40	16 40		16 57	17 01				16 57

	LM	VT	LM	VT	LM	LM	VT	LM	VT	SN	LM	LM	LM	LM	LM	VT	VT	LM	LM	VT	VT	LM
			C	F	G	H	M	J	K			L	A	A	B	N			C		F	G
Wolverhampton 68 d						15 32	15 45								15 57	16 04						
Sandwell & Dudley 68 d							15 55															
Birmingham New Street 68 d		15 50				15 54	16 10							16 14	16 17	16 30	16 30			16 50		
Birmingham International 68 d		16 00				16 05	16 20							16 24	16 28	16 40	16 40			17 00		
Nuneaton 65 d					16 15																	17 15
Coventry 68 d		16 11				16 17	16 31							16 37	16 47	16 51	16 51			17 11		
Rugby 68 d		16 24			16 32	16 28								16 47	16 58					17 25		17 32
Long Buckby 68 d						16 37								16 57	17 07							
Northampton 68 a						16 48								17 09	17 19							
d						16 48								17 10	17 25							
Wolverton d	←		←			17 00		←				←		17 22	17 37			←	←			
Milton Keynes Central a			16 26		16 53	17 04	16 58	16 41				17 04		17 26	17 41				17 26			17 53
d	16 11		16 27	16 49	16 54	17 05	16 59	16 41	17 04			17 05	17 11	17 27	17 41			17 11	17 27		17 49	17 54
Bletchley d	16 16		16 32			→		16 46				17 10	→	→	→			17 16	17 32			
Leighton Buzzard d	16 23		16 39					16 53				17 17						17 23	17 39			
Cheddington d	16 28																	17 28				
Tring d	16 35										17 14							17 35				
Berkhamsted d	16 40							17 07			17 19							17 40				
Hemel Hempstead d	16 44							17 11			17 24							17 44				
Apsley d											17 27											
Kings Langley d											17 30											
Watford Junction 60 a	16 51		17 00					17 18			17 34	17 38				17s38	17s38	17 51	18 00			
d	16 52		17 00					17 19		17 23	17 35	17 39						17 52	18 00			
Bushey 60 d											17 38											
Harrow & Wealdstone ⊖60 d	16 58							17 25		17 29	17 43							17 58				
Wembley Central ⊖60,176 d																						
Shepherd's Bush ⊖176 a										17 48												
Kensington (Olympia) ⊖176 a										17 50												
West Brompton ⊖176 a										17 53												
Imperial Wharf 176 a										17 56												
Clapham Junction 176 a										18 00												
East Croydon 176 a																						
London Euston ⊖60 a	17 12	17 17	17 18	17 27	17 32		17 36	17 40	17 40		17 57	18 01				17 57	17 57	18 12	18 18	18 18	18 27	18 32

A To London Euston
B From Liverpool Lime Street to London Euston
C From Birmingham New Street
D until 16 February
E from 23 February
F From Manchester Piccadilly
G From Crewe
H From Stafford to London Euston
I From Edinburgh
J From Liverpool Lime Street
K From Holyhead
L From Stafford
M From Glasgow Central
N From Shrewsbury

Table T066-R

Sundays

15 December to 10 May

West Midlands, Northampton, Milton Keynes and Watford Junction - London

	LM	VT	VT	LM	SN	LM	LM	LM	LM	VT	LM	LM	VT	LM	VT	LM	LM	VT	VT	LM	VT	VT
	A	B	C	C			D	D	E		F			G	H	I	A	J	K	C	L	M
Wolverhampton 68 d	16 31	16 45							16 57								17 31	17 45	17 45			
Sandwell & Dudley 68 d		16 55																17 55	17 55			
Birmingham New Street 68 d	16 54	17 10						17 14	17 17	17 30			17 50				17 54	18 10	18 10			
Birmingham International 68 d	17 05	17 20						17 24	17 28	17 40			18 00				18 05	18 20	18 20			
Nuneaton 65 d																18 15						
Coventry 68 d	17 17	17 31						17 37	17 47	17 51			18 11				18 15	18 31	18 31			
Rugby 68 d	17 28							17 50	17 58				18 25			18 32	18 26					
Long Buckby 68 d	17 37							18 00	18 07								18 35					
Northampton 68 a	17 48							18 12	18 19								18 46					
d	17 48							18 13	18 25								18 48					
Wolverton d	18 00			←				18 25	18 37		←	←		←			19 00			←		
Milton Keynes Central a	18 04	17 57		17 41				18 29	18 41		18 04			18 29		18 53	19 04	18 59	19 00	18 41		
d	18 05	17 58	18 03	17 41			18 11	18 30	18 41		18 05	18 11		18 30	18 48	18 54	19 05	19 00	19 01	18 41	19 04	19 04
Bletchley d	→			17 46			→	→	→		18 10	18 16		18 35			→			18 46		
Leighton Buzzard d				17 53							18 17	18 23		18 42						18 53		
Cheddington d												18 28										
Tring d						18 14						18 35										
Berkhamsted d				18 07		18 19						18 40								19 07		
Hemel Hempstead d				18 11		18 24						18 44								19 11		
Apsley d						18 27																
Kings Langley d						18 30																
Watford Junction 60 a				18 18		18 34				18s36	18 38	18 51		19 03						19 18		
d				18 19	18 23	18 35					18 39	18 52		19 03						19 19		
Bushey 60 d						18 38																
Harrow & Wealdstone ⊖60 d				18 25	18 29	18 43						18 58								19 25		
Wembley Central ⊖60,176 d																						
Shepherd's Bush ⊖176 a					18 48																	
Kensington (Olympia) ⊖176 a					18 50																	
West Brompton ⊖176 a					18 53																	
Imperial Wharf 176 a					18 56																	
Clapham Junction 176 a					19 00																	
East Croydon 176 a																						
London Euston ⊖60 a		18 35	18 39	18 40		18 57				18 55	19 01	19 12	19 17	19 24	19 26	19 32		19 36	19 39	19 40	19 41	19 42

	SN	LM	LM	LM	LM	LM	VT	LM	VT	LM	VT	LM	LM	VT	LM	VT	SN	LM	LM	LM	VT
			F	D	D	E				G	H	I	A	B	C	N				E	
Wolverhampton 68 d						17 57							18 30	18 45						18 57	
Sandwell & Dudley 68 d														18 55							
Birmingham New Street 68 d					18 14	18 17	18 30		18 50				18 54	19 10					19 14	19 17	19 30
Birmingham International 68 d					18 24	18 28	18 40		19 00				19 05	19 20					19 24	19 28	19 40
Nuneaton 65 d												19 15									
Coventry 68 d					18 37	18 47	18 51		19 11				19 18	19 31					19 37	19 47	19 51
Rugby 68 d					18 47	19 00			19 26			19 32	19 28						19 47	19 58	
Long Buckby 68 d					18 57	19 09							19 38						19 57	20 07	
Northampton 68 a					19 08	19 21							19 48						20 09	20 19	
d					19 09	19 25							19 53						20 11	20 25	
Wolverton d			←			19 37		←		←			20 05		←				20 23	20 36	
Milton Keynes Central a			19 04		19 23	19 41				19 23		19 53	20 09	19 58	19 41				20 27	20 40	
d			19 05	19 11	19 24	19 41		19 11		19 24	19 49	19 54	20 11	20 00	19 41	20 04				20 41	
Bletchley d			19 10	→	→	→		19 16		19 29			→		19 46					→	
Leighton Buzzard d			19 17					19 23		19 36					19 53						
Cheddington d								19 28													
Tring d		19 14						19 35		19 45								20 14			
Berkhamsted d		19 19						19 40		19 50					20 07			20 19			
Hemel Hempstead d		19 24						19 44		19 54					20 11			20 24			
Apsley d		19 27																20 27			
Kings Langley d		19 30																20 30			
Watford Junction 60 a		19 34	19 38				19s38	19 51		20 01					20 18			20 34			20s39
d	19 23	19 35	19 39					19 52		20 02					20 19		20 23	20 35			
Bushey 60 d		19 38						19 55										20 38			
Harrow & Wealdstone ⊖60 d	19 29	19 43						20 00							20 25		20 29	20 43			
Wembley Central ⊖60,176 d																					
Shepherd's Bush ⊖176 a	19 48																20 48				
Kensington (Olympia) ⊖176 a	19 50																20 50				
West Brompton ⊖176 a	19 53																20 53				
Imperial Wharf 176 a	19 56																20 56				
Clapham Junction 176 a	20 00																21 00				
East Croydon 176 a																					
London Euston ⊖60 a		19 57	20 01				19 57	20 14	20 18	20 19	20 26	20 32		20 37	20 40	20 41		20 57			20 57

A From Stafford to London Euston
B From Edinburgh
C From Liverpool Lime Street
D To London Euston
E From Liverpool Lime Street to London Euston
F From Stafford
G From Birmingham New Street
H From Manchester Piccadilly
I From Crewe
J until 16 February. From Glasgow Central
K from 23 February. From Glasgow Central
L until 16 February. From Chester
M from 23 February. From Chester
N From Chester

NRT DECEMBER 19 EDITION

Table T066-R

Sundays
15 December to 10 May

West Midlands, Northampton, Milton Keynes and Watford Junction - London

	LM A	VT B	VT C	SN	LM D	VT E	LM F	LM	LM G	VT	SN	VT D	LM H	VT E	VT I	LM F	LM J	VT	SN	LM D	VT I	VT D
Wolverhampton 68 d						19 45											20 57	21 06				
Sandwell & Dudley 68 d						19 55												21 17				
Birmingham New Street 68 d						20 10			20 17	20 30							21 17	21 30				
Birmingham International 68 d						20 20			20 28	20 40							21 28	21 40				
Nuneaton 65 d							20 29									21 15						22 18
Coventry 68 d						20 31			20 44	20 51							21 47	21 51				
Rugby 68 d							20 44		20 55	21 05						21 31	21 58	22 04				22 32
Long Buckby 68 d									21 04							21 41	22 07					
Northampton 68 a									21 17							21 53	22 18					
d									21 29							21 55	22 25					
Wolverton d	←				←				21 41				←			22 07	22 37			←		
Milton Keynes Central a	20 09				20 40	20 59	21 06		21 45	21 26			21 45			22 11	22 41	22 35		22 41		23 04
d	20 11	20 49	20 49		20 41	21 01	21 07	21 17	21 45	21 28		21 38	21 45	21 54	22 00	22 11	22 41	22 37		22 41	22 51	23 05
Bletchley d	20 16				20 46				→				21 50			22 16	→			22 46		
Leighton Buzzard d	20 23				20 52		21 15	21 26					21 57			22 23				22 52		
Cheddington d	20 28							21 34								22 32						
Tring d	20 35							21 39								22 37						
Berkhamsted d	20 40				21 07			21 44					22 12			22 42				23 07		
Hemel Hempstead d	20 44				21 12			21 49					22 16			22 47				23 12		
Apsley d					21 15								22 19							23 15		
Kings Langley d					21 18								22 22							23 18		
Watford Junction 60 a	20 51				21 23		21 38	21 56		22s03			22 27	22s31		22 54		23s05		23 22	23s28	23s34
d	20 52			21 17	21 23		21 39	21 56			22 18		22 27			22 54			23 17	23 23		
Bushey 60 d								21 59								22 57						
Harrow & Wealdstone ⊖60 d	20 58			21 24	21 29			22 04			22 24		22 33			23 03			23 23	23 29		
Wembley Central ⊖60,176 d																						
Shepherd's Bush ⊖176 a				21 43							22 44								23 44			
Kensington (Olympia) ⊖176 a				21 45							22 47								23 47			
West Brompton ⊖176 a				21 47							22 50								23 50			
Imperial Wharf 176 a				21 50							22 53								23 53			
Clapham Junction 176 a				21 54							22 57								23 57			
East Croydon 176 a																						
London Euston ⊖60 a	21 14	21 31	21 32		21 43	21 47	21 58	22 18		22 24		22 27	22 47	22 53	22 56	23 17		23 23		23 43	23 47	23 53

	LM	LM J	VT	LM D	VT
Wolverhampton 68 d		21 55	22 05		22 37
Sandwell & Dudley 68 d			22 16		22 48
Birmingham New Street 68 d		22 15	22 30		23 00
Birmingham International 68 d		22 26	22 40		23 10
Nuneaton 65 d					
Coventry 68 d		22 45	22 51		23 21
Rugby 68 d		22 55	23 04		23 35
Long Buckby 68 d		23 05			
Northampton 68 a		23 16			23s54
d	23 00	23 25			
Wolverton d	23 12	23 37		←	
Milton Keynes Central a	23 16	23 41	23 35	23 41	00s13
d	23 16	23 41	23 37	23 41	
Bletchley d	23 21	→		23 46	
Leighton Buzzard d	23 28			23 52	
Cheddington d	23 36				
Tring d	23 42				
Berkhamsted d	23 47			00 07	
Hemel Hempstead d	23 52			00 12	
Apsley d				00 15	
Kings Langley d				00 18	
Watford Junction 60 a	23 59		00s05	00 22	00s43
d	23 59			00 23	
Bushey 60 d	00 02				
Harrow & Wealdstone ⊖60 d	00 08			00 29	
Wembley Central ⊖60,176 d					
Shepherd's Bush ⊖176 a					
Kensington (Olympia) ⊖176 a					
West Brompton ⊖176 a					
Imperial Wharf 176 a					
Clapham Junction 176 a					
East Croydon 176 a					
London Euston ⊖60 a	00 23		00 26	00 43	01 03

A From Stafford
B until 16 February. From Manchester Piccadilly
C from 23 February. From Manchester Piccadilly
D From Liverpool Lime Street
E From Glasgow Central
F From Crewe
G To London Euston
H From Birmingham New Street
I From Manchester Piccadilly
J From Liverpool Lime Street to London Euston

NRT DECEMBER 19 EDITION

Table T067-F

Mondays to Fridays
16 December to 15 May

London - Stoke-on-Trent and Crewe

Miles	Miles		VT	XC	LM	LM	LM	XC	LM	LM	VT	VT	LM	LM	XC	LM	LM	XC	LM	LM	LM	LM
			⊠	⌶				⌶	🚌		⊠	⊠			⌶			⌶				
0	—	London Euston ⊖66 d									05 27	05 31								05 34	06 28	06 34
17¾	—	Watford Junction 66 d									05u45	05u50								05 55		06 53
49¾	—	Milton Keynes Central 66 d									06 15	06 23				05 37				06 40	07 01	07 38
65¾	—	Northampton 68 d			05 20					06 00						05 56	06 04			06 57		07 56
84½	—	Rugby d			05 42					06 22		06 45				06 19	06 32			07 19	07 29	08 19
99	—	Nuneaton a			05 53					06 34	06 44										07 41	
—	—	d			05 55					06 39	06 45										07 42	
104	—	Atherstone d			06 01					06 45											07 47	
108	—	Polesworth d								06 50												
111½	—	Tamworth d			06 09					06 55											07 55	
117¾	—	Lichfield Trent Valley d			06 16					07 02											08 02	
125¾	—	Rugeley Trent Valley d			06 24					07 09				←							08 09	
135½	0	Stafford d	06 01	06 28	06 33	06 38	06 46	07 02		07 21	07 08		07 13	07 21	07 24	07 39	07 55	08 03	08 11	08 38	08 18	09 38
—	—	Norton Bridge Station Drv d								→										→		→
144½	—	Stone d					06 55										08 04					
—	—	Stone Crown Street d							07 14													
—	—	Stone Granville Square a																				
—	—	Barlaston Orchard Place d							07 23													
—	—	Wedgwood Old Road Bridge d																				
151¾	—	Stoke-on-Trent 50 d		06a43			07 14	07a17	07 47								08 12	08a18				
—	—	Hanley Bus Station a							07 57													
159	—	Kidsgrove 50 d					07 27										08 20					
161¼	—	Alsager 50 d					07 32										08 24					
167¾	24½	Crewe 65,50 a	06 19		06 51	06 57	07 43				07 27	07 30	07 32	07 40	07 43	07 57	08 33		08 30		08 36	

	VT	VT	VT	XC	VT	LM	LM	LM	XC	LM	LM	VT A	VT B	VT	LM	LM	VT	XC	VT	LM	LM	LM
	⊠	⊠	⊠	⌶	⊠		🚌		⌶			⊠	⊠	⊠			⊠	⌶	⊠			
London Euston ⊖66 d	06 36	06 43	07 07		07 10						07 13	07 33	07 35	07 43	07 46	07 49	08 07		08 10			08 13
Watford Junction 66 d	06u51															08 04						
Milton Keynes Central 66 d		07 13			07 41						07 54	08 04	08 06	08 13	08 19	08 25	08 38		08 41			08 53
Northampton 68 d											08 14					08 56						09 14
Rugby d											08 37				08 42	09 18						09 36
Nuneaton a															08 53							
d															08 55							
Atherstone d															09 01							
Polesworth d																						
Tamworth d															09 09							
Lichfield Trent Valley d															09 17							
Rugeley Trent Valley d						←									09 24					←	←	
Stafford d			08 24	08 28		08 38		08 56	09 02	09 14	09 54				09 35	10 38	09a27	09 28		09 35	09 38	10 56
Norton Bridge Station Drv d											→				→	→						→
Stone d								09 05														
Stone Crown Street d							08 39															
Stone Granville Square a																						
Barlaston Orchard Place d							08 48															
Wedgwood Old Road Bridge d																						
Stoke-on-Trent 50 d				08a43			09 12	09 13	09a17									09a43				
Hanley Bus Station a							09 19															
Kidsgrove 50 d								09 21														
Alsager 50 d								09 25														
Crewe 65,50 a	08 10	09 07	08 41		08 45	08 56		09 34		09 32		09 10	09 10	10 07					09 49	09 53	09 56	

	VT	LM	XC	LM	LM	VT	LM	LM	VT	XC	VT	LM	LM	LM	VT	LM	XC	LM	LM	VT	LM
	⊠		⌶	🚌		⊠			⊠	⌶	⊠				⊠		⌶	🚌		⊠	
London Euston ⊖66 d	08 40					08 43	08 46	08 49	09 07		09 10			09 13	09 40					09 43	09 46
Watford Junction 66 d								09 04													
Milton Keynes Central 66 d						09 13	09 19	09 29			09 41			09 55						10 13	10 19
Northampton 68 d								09 54						10 15							
Rugby d							09 42	10 18						10 37							10 42
Nuneaton a							09 53														10 53
d							09 55														10 55
Atherstone d							10 01														11 01
Polesworth d																					
Tamworth d							10 09														11 09
Lichfield Trent Valley d							10 17														11 17
Rugeley Trent Valley d		←					10 24					←	←			←					11 24
Stafford d		09 54	10 02		10 13		10 35	11 38	10 24	10 28		10 35	10 38	11 57		10 56	11 02		11 13		11 35
Norton Bridge Station Drv d							→	→						→							→
Stone d		10 04														11 05					
Stone Crown Street d				09 49														10 49			
Stone Granville Square a																					
Barlaston Orchard Place d				09 58														10 58			
Wedgwood Old Road Bridge d																					
Stoke-on-Trent 50 d		10 12	10a17	10 22						10a43						11 13	11a17	11 22			
Hanley Bus Station a				10 29														11 29			
Kidsgrove 50 d		10 19														11 21					
Alsager 50 d		10 23														11 25					
Crewe 65,50 a	10 10	10 32			10 31	11 07			10 41		10 45	10 53	10 56		11 10	11 34			11 31	12 07	

A from 17 February
B until 14 February

Table T067-F

Mondays to Fridays

16 December to 15 May

London - Stoke-on-Trent and Crewe

	LM	VT	XC	VT	LM	LM	LM	VT	LM	XC	LM	LM	VT	LM	LM	VT	XC	VT	LM	LM	LM	VT
London Euston ⊖66 d	09 49	10 07		10 10			10 15	10 40					10 43	10 46	10 49	11 07		11 10			11 15	11 40
Watford Junction 66 d	10 04														11 04							
Milton Keynes Central 66 d	10 30			10 41			10 55						11 13	11 19	11 24			11 41			11 55	
Northampton 68 d	10 56						11 14								11 56						12 14	
Rugby d	11 18						11 36							11 42	12 18						12 37	
Nuneaton a														11 54								
d														11 55								
Atherstone d														12 01								
Polesworth d																						
Tamworth d														12 09								
Lichfield Trent Valley d														12 17								
Rugeley Trent Valley d					←	←			←					12 24					←	←		
Stafford d	12 38	11 24	11 28		11 35	11 38	12 56		11 57	12 02		12 11		12 35	13 38	12 24	12 28		12 35	12 38	13 55	
Norton Bridge Station Drv d	→						→							→	→						→	
Stone d									12 06													
Stone Crown Street d											11 49											
Stone Granville Square a																						
Barlaston Orchard Place d											11 58											
Wedgwood Old Road Bridge d																						
Stoke-on-Trent 50 d			11a43						12 14	12a17	12 22						12a43					
Hanley Bus Station a											12 29											
Kidsgrove 50 d									12 25													
Alsager 50 d									12 29													
Crewe 65,50 a		11 41		11 45	11 53	11 56		12 10	12 38			12 30	13 07			12 41		12 45	12 53	12 56		13 10

	LM	XC	LM	LM	VT	LM	LM	VT	XC	VT	LM	LM	LM	VT	LM	XC	LM	LM	VT	LM	LM	VT
London Euston ⊖66 d					11 43	11 46	11 49	12 07		12 10			12 15	12 40					12 43	12 46	12 49	13 07
Watford Junction 66 d							12 04														13 04	
Milton Keynes Central 66 d					12 13	12 19	12 25			12 41			12 55						13 13	13 19	13 25	
Northampton 68 d							12 56						13 14								13 54	
Rugby d						12 42	13 18			13 03			13 37							13 42	14 18	
Nuneaton a						12 53														13 55		
d						12 55														13 55		
Atherstone d						13 01														14 01		
Polesworth d																						
Tamworth d						13 09														14 09		
Lichfield Trent Valley d						13 17														14 17		
Rugeley Trent Valley d	←					13 24					←	←			←					14 24		
Stafford d	12 56	13 02		13 13		13 41	14 38	13 24	13 28		13 38	13 41	14 54		13 55	14 02		14 13		14 35	15 38	14 24
Norton Bridge Station Drv d						→	→						→							→	→	
Stone d	13 05														14 04							
Stone Crown Street d			12 49														13 49					
Stone Granville Square a																						
Barlaston Orchard Place d			12 58														13 58					
Wedgwood Old Road Bridge d																						
Stoke-on-Trent 50 d	13 13	13a18	13 22						13a43						14 12	14a17	14 22					
Hanley Bus Station a			13 29														14 29					
Kidsgrove 50 d	13 23														14 21							
Alsager 50 d	13 27														14 25							
Crewe 65,50 a	13 36			13 32	14 07			13 41		13 48	13 56	14 04		14 10	14 34			14 31	15 05			14 41

	XC	VT	LM	LM	LM	VT	LM	XC	LM	VT	LM	LM	VT	XC	VT	LM	LM	LM	VT	LM	XC
London Euston ⊖66 d		13 10			13 15	13 40				13 43	13 46	13 49	14 07		14 10			14 15	14 40		
Watford Junction 66 d												14 04									
Milton Keynes Central 66 d		13 41			13 55					14 13	14 19	14 26			14 41			14 55			
Northampton 68 d					14 14							14 56						15 14			
Rugby d					14 37						14 42	15 18						15 38			
Nuneaton a											14 53										
d											14 55										
Atherstone d											15 01										
Polesworth d																					
Tamworth d											15 09										
Lichfield Trent Valley d											15 17										
Rugeley Trent Valley d			←	←			←				15 24					←	←			←	
Stafford d	14 28		14 35	14 38	15 56		14 54	15 02	15 13		15 34	16 38	15 24	15 28		15 34	15 38	16 55		15 56	16 02
Norton Bridge Station Drv d					→						→	→						→			
Stone d							15 03													16 06	
Stone Crown Street d																					
Stone Granville Square a																					
Barlaston Orchard Place d																					
Wedgwood Old Road Bridge d																					
Stoke-on-Trent 50 d	14a43						15 11	15a17						15a43						16 14	16a17
Hanley Bus Station a																					
Kidsgrove 50 d							15 20													16 21	
Alsager 50 d							15 24													16 25	
Crewe 65,50 a		14 45	14 54	14 57		15 10	15 33		15 32	16 07			15 41		15 45	15 52	15 56		16 10	16 34	

Table T067-F

Mondays to Fridays

16 December to 15 May

London - Stoke-on-Trent and Crewe

	LM	LM	VT	LM	LM	VT	XC	VT	LM	LM	LM	VT	LM	XC	LM	VT	LM	LM	VT	XC	VT	LM
London Euston ⊖66 d			14 43	14 46	14 49	15 07		15 10			15 15	15 40				15 43	15 46	15 49	16 07		16 10	
Watford Junction 66 d					15 04													16 04				
Milton Keynes Central 66 d			15 13	15 19	15 26			15 41			15 55					16 13	16 19	16 25			16u41	
Northampton 68 d					15 56						16 14							16 55				
Rugby d				15 42	16 18						16 38						16 42	17 18				
Nuneaton a				15 55													16 53					
d				15 55													16 55					
Atherstone d				16 01													17 01					
Polesworth d																						
Tamworth d				16 09													17 09					
Lichfield Trent Valley d				16 17													17 17					
Rugeley Trent Valley d				16 24					←	←			←				17 24					←
Stafford d		16 11		16 35	17 38	16 24	16 28		16 35	16 38	17 57		16 55	17 03	17 13		17 35	18 38	17 24	17 28		17 35
Norton Bridge Station Drv d				→	→						→						→	→				
Stone d													17 04									
Stone Crown Street d	15 53																					
Stone Granville Square a																						
Barlaston Orchard Place d	16 03																					
Wedgwood Old Road Bridge d	16 11																					
Stoke-on-Trent 50 d	16 36						16a43						17 12	17a19						17a43		
Hanley Bus Station a	16 46																					
Kidsgrove 50 d													17 21									
Alsager 50 d													17 25									
Crewe 65,50 a		16 30	17 07			16 41		16 45	16 53	16 56		17 10	17 36		17 31	18 07			17 41		17 45	17 53

	LM	LM	LM	VT	XC	VT	LM	LM	VT	LM	LM	LM	VT	XC	VT	LM	LM	LM	VT	XC	VT
London Euston ⊖66 d			16 15	16 33		16 40			16 43		16 46	16 52	17 07		17 10				17 33		17 40
Watford Junction 66 d																					
Milton Keynes Central 66 d			16 55						17 13		17 19	17 32			17u41						
Northampton 68 d			17 13									17 58									
Rugby d			17 36	17 22							17 47	18 20							18 23		
Nuneaton a											17 59				18 10						
d											18 01				18 11						
Atherstone d											18 07										
Polesworth d																					
Tamworth d											18 16										
Lichfield Trent Valley d											18 22										
Rugeley Trent Valley d	←	←									18 30					←	←	←			
Stafford d	17 38	17 57	18 54	17 58	18 02			18 15			18 42	19 38	18 24	18 28		18 38	18 42	18 54	18 56	19 02	
Norton Bridge Station Drv d			→								→	→									
Stone d		18 06																19 03			
Stone Crown Street d							17 54			18 49											
Stone Granville Square a																					
Barlaston Orchard Place d							18 03			18a58											
Wedgwood Old Road Bridge d																					
Stoke-on-Trent 50 d		18 14			18a17		18 27							18a43				19 11		19a17	
Hanley Bus Station a							18 34														
Kidsgrove 50 d		18 22																19 20			
Alsager 50 d		18 27																19 24			
Crewe 65,50 a	17 56	18 36		18 17		18 10		18 34	19 05				18 42		18 53	18 57	19 01	19 37	19 14		19 10

	LM	VT	LM	VT	XC	VT	LM	LM	LM	VT	VT	LM	XC	LM	VT	VT FO	XC	LM FX	LM FO	LM	VT ThFO	VT
London Euston ⊖66 d		17 43	17 46	18 07		18 10			18 13	18 33	18 40				18 43	18 46		18 46	18 49	18 52	18 57	19 10
Watford Junction 66 d																						
Milton Keynes Central 66 d		18u13	18 19			18u41			18 45						19 13	19 19		19 19	19 24	19 32		19u41
Northampton 68 d									19 09										19 45	19 55		
Rugby d			18 48						19 36	19 23						19 40		19 46	20 05	20 17		
Nuneaton a			19 00			19 10												20 01	20 17			20 10
d			19 00			19 11												20 02	20 18			20 11
Atherstone d			19 06															20 08				
Polesworth d																			→			
Tamworth d			19 15								19 44							20 16				
Lichfield Trent Valley d			19 21								19 51							20 23				
Rugeley Trent Valley d			19 29				←	←										20 30				
Stafford d	19 13		19 41	19 24	19 28		19 38	19 41	20 54	19 54		19 57	20 04	20 13	20 51	20 24	20 28	20 47		21 44		20 36
Norton Bridge Station Drv d			→						→						→			→		→		
Stone d												20 06										
Stone Crown Street d																						
Stone Granville Square a																						
Barlaston Orchard Place d																						
Wedgwood Old Road Bridge d																						
Stoke-on-Trent 50 d					19a43							20 15	20a19				20a43					
Hanley Bus Station a																						
Kidsgrove 50 d												20 23										
Alsager 50 d												20 27										
Crewe 65,50 a	19 31	20 07		19 41		19 51	19 56	20 02		20 13	20 17	20 36		20 32		20 42					20s33	20 51

Table T067-F

London - Stoke-on-Trent and Crewe

Mondays to Fridays
16 December to 15 May

	LM	LM FX	VT	LM	LM FO	XC	LM	VT	LM	VT	LM	LM	VT	XC	VT	LM	LM	VT	LM	VT	VT	LM
	1	1	◇1 ⊠	1	1	◇1 🛒	1	◇1 ☕	1	◇1 ☕	1	1	◇1 ☕	◇1	◇1 ☕	1	1	◇1 ☕	1	◇1 ☕	◇1 ☕	1
London Euston 15 ⊖66 d							19 15	19 40		19 43	19 46	19 53	20 07		20 10					20 30	20 40	
Watford Junction 66 d																						
Milton Keynes Central 66 d							19 57			20 13	20 19	20 31			20 41							
Northampton 68 d							20 14					20 57										
Rugby d					←		20 37				20 42	21 20										
Nuneaton a					20 17						20 53		21 02									
d					20 18						21 00		21 03									
Atherstone d					20 24						21 06											
Polesworth d																						
Tamworth d					20 33			20 43			21 14									21 35		
Lichfield Trent Valley d					20 39			20 50			21 21									21 42		
Rugeley Trent Valley d		←	←	←	20 47						21 28					←	←	←	←			
Stafford d	20 39	20 47	20 51	20 54	20 57	21 02	21 59	21 04	21 13	21 55	21 42	22 58	21 27	21 28		21 42	21 44	21 55	21 59	22 00		22 13
Norton Bridge Station Drv d							→			→	→	→										
Stone d				21 04															22 08			
Stone Crown Street d																						
Stone Granville Square a																						
Barlaston Orchard Place d																						
Wedgwood Old Road Bridge d																						
Stoke-on-Trent 50 d				21 12		21a17								21a44				22 11	22 16			
Hanley Bus Station a																						
Kidsgrove 50 d				21 20															22 24			
Alsager 50 d				21 24															22 28			
Crewe 65,50 a	20 57	21 08	21 15	21 33	21 18			21 21	21 31				21 46		21 46	22 00	22 04	22 30	22 37	22 17	22 10	22 35

	XC	LM	LM	VT	VT	LM	LM	XC	AW	LM	VT	LM
	◇1	1	1	◇1 ☕	◇1 ☕	1	1	◇1	◇	1	◇1 ☕	1
London Euston 15 ⊖66 d		20 46	20 51	21 07	21 10					21 49	22 00	
Watford Junction 66 d					21u25							
Milton Keynes Central 66 d		21 19	21 30	21 39						22 22	22 40	
Northampton 68 d			21 57									
Rugby d		21 45	22 20		22 05					22 46	23 02	
Nuneaton a		21 57		22 07						22 57	23 12	
d		22 00		22 08						22 58	23 14	
Atherstone d		22 06								23 04		
Polesworth d												
Tamworth d		22 15								23 12	23s26	
Lichfield Trent Valley d		22 22								23 18	23s33	
Rugeley Trent Valley d		22 29				←	←			23 25		←
Stafford d	22 28	22 44	23 52		22 37	22 44	22 58	23 02	23 43	23 46	23s48	23 52
Norton Bridge Station Drv d		→	→									
Stone d							23 08					
Stone Crown Street d												
Stone Granville Square a												
Barlaston Orchard Place d												
Wedgwood Old Road Bridge d												
Stoke-on-Trent 50 d	22a43						23 16	23a20				
Hanley Bus Station a												
Kidsgrove 50 d							23 25					
Alsager 50 d							23 29					
Crewe 65,50 a				22 53	22 58	23 02	23 38		00 11	00 13	00 16	00 19

Saturdays
21 December to 16 May

	VT	XC	LM	LM	LM	XC	LM	LM	XC	LM	VT	LM	LM	LM	VT	XC	LM	LM	VT	VT	XC	LM
	◇1 ☕	◇1	1	1	1	◇1 🛒	1	🚌	◇1 🛒	1	◇1 ☕	1	1	1	◇1 ☕	◇1 🛒	1	1	◇1 ☕	◇1 ☕	◇1 🛒	1
London Euston 15 ⊖66 d										05 34	06 05							06 29	06 36	07 07		
Watford Junction 66 d										05 53	06u20								06u51			
Milton Keynes Central 66 d										06 37	06 41	05 39						07 02				
Northampton 68 d					05 41					06 53		05 56	06 04	06 37								
Rugby d					06 02					07 18	07 03	06 18	06 28	06 57				07 27				
Nuneaton a					06 14									07 09				07 40				
d					06 21									07 11				07 41				
Atherstone d					06 26									07 16				07 47				
Polesworth d														07 22								
Tamworth d					06 35									07 28				07 55				
Lichfield Trent Valley d					06 41									07 34				08 01				
Rugeley Trent Valley d					06 48									07 42				08 09				←
Stafford d	06 01	06 28	06 37	06 47	06 58	07 02	07 13		07 31	08 38	07 34	07 39	07 48	07 54	07 59	08 04	08 12	08 18		08 24	08 28	08 38
Norton Bridge Station Drv d										→												
Stone d				06 56									07 57									
Stone Crown Street d								07 14														
Stone Granville Square a																						
Barlaston Orchard Place d								07 23														
Wedgwood Old Road Bridge d																						
Stoke-on-Trent 50 d		06a43		07 04		07a17		07 47					08 10			08a19					08a43	
Hanley Bus Station a								07 57														
Kidsgrove 50 d				07 13									08 18									
Alsager 50 d				07 17									08 22									
Crewe 65,50 a	06 20		06 56	07 26	07 16		07 31		07 50		07 53	07 57	08 31	08 14	08 18		08 31	08 37	08 10	08 41		08 56

Table T067-F

London - Stoke-on-Trent and Crewe

Saturdays
21 December to 16 May

	VT	VT	LM	LM	XC	LM	VT	LM	LM	VT	XC	VT	LM	LM	LM	VT	LM	XC	LM	VT	LM	LM
	◇1 A ☕	◇1 B ☕	🚌	1	◇1 🛒	1	◇1 ☕	1	1	◇1 ☕	◇1 🛒	◇1 ☕	1	1	1	◇1 ☕	1	◇1 🛒	1	◇1 ☕	1	1
London Euston 15 ⊖66 d	07 33	07 35					07 43	07 46	07 49	08 07		08 10			08 15	08 40				08 43	08 46	08 49
Watford Junction 66 d									08 04													09 04
Milton Keynes Central 66 d	08 04	08 06					08 13	08 19	08 26			08 41			08 55					09 13	09 19	09 29
Northampton 68 d				07 14					08 55					07 56	09 14		08 14					09 55
Rugby d				07 37				08 42	09 17					08 18	09 36		08 36				09 42	10 17
Nuneaton a								08 55													09 54	
d								08 55													09 55	
Atherstone d								09 01													10 01	
Polesworth d																						
Tamworth d								09 09													10 09	
Lichfield Trent Valley d								09 17													10 17	
Rugeley Trent Valley d								09 24					←								10 24	
Stafford d				08 57	09 02	09 13		09 35	10 38	09 24	09 28		09 35	09 38	10 57		09 56	10 04	10 13		10 35	11 38
Norton Bridge Station Drv d								→	→						→						→	→
Stone d				09 06													10 06					
Stone Crown Street d			08 39																			
Stone Granville Square a																						
Barlaston Orchard Place d			08 48																			
Wedgwood Old Road Bridge d																						
Stoke-on-Trent 50 d			09 12	09 14	09a17						09a43						10 14	10a19				
Hanley Bus Station a			09 19																			
Kidsgrove 50 d				09 22													10 23					
Alsager 50 d				09 26													10 27					
Crewe 65,50 a	09 10	09 10		09 35		09 31	10 07			09 41		09 46	09 53	09 58		10 10	10 36		10 31	11 07		

	VT	XC	VT	LM	LM	LM	VT	LM	XC	LM	LM	VT	LM	LM	VT	XC	VT	LM	LM	LM	VT
	◇1 ☕	◇1 🛒	◇1 ☕	1	1	1	◇1 ☕	1	◇1 🛒	🚌	1	◇1 ☕	1	1	◇1 ☕	◇1 🛒	◇1 ☕	1	1	1	◇1 ☕
London Euston 15 ⊖66 d	09 07		09 10			09 15	09 40					09 43	09 46	09 49	10 07		10 10			10 15	10 40
Watford Junction 66 d														10 04							
Milton Keynes Central 66 d			09 41			09 55						10 13	10 19	10 31			10 41			10 56	
Northampton 68 d						10 13								10 56						11 14	
Rugby d						10 36							10 42	11 18						11 36	
Nuneaton a													10 54								
d													10 55								
Atherstone d													11 01								
Polesworth d																					
Tamworth d													11 09								
Lichfield Trent Valley d													11 17				11 22				
Rugeley Trent Valley d				←	←			←					11 24					←	←		
Stafford d	10 24	10 28		10 35	10 38	11 56		10 57	11 02		11 11		11 47	12 38	11 24	11 28		11 38	11 47	12 56	
Norton Bridge Station Drv d						→							→	→						→	
Stone d								11 06													
Stone Crown Street d										10 49											
Stone Granville Square a																					
Barlaston Orchard Place d										10 58											
Wedgwood Old Road Bridge d																					
Stoke-on-Trent 50 d		10a43						11 14	11a17	11 22						11a43					
Hanley Bus Station a										11 29											
Kidsgrove 50 d								11 22													
Alsager 50 d								11 26													
Crewe 65,50 a	10 43		10 45	10 53	10 56		11 10	11 35			11 29	12 07			11 41		11 51	11 56	12 08		12 10

	LM	XC	LM	LM	VT	LM	LM	VT	XC	VT	LM	LM	LM	VT	LM	XC	LM	VT	LM	LM	VT	XC
	1	◇1 🛒	🚌	1	◇1 ☕	1	1	◇1 ☕	◇1 🛒	◇1 ☕	1	1	1	◇1 ☕	1	◇1 🛒	1	◇1 ☕	1	1	◇1 ☕	◇1 🛒
London Euston 15 ⊖66 d					10 43	10 46	10 49	11 07		11 10			11 15	11 40				11 43	11 46	11 49	12 07	
Watford Junction 66 d							11 04													12 04		
Milton Keynes Central 66 d					11 13	11 19	11 24			11 41			11 58					12 13	12 19	12 25		
Northampton 68 d							11 56						12 15							12 51		
Rugby d						11 42	12 18						12 37						12 42	13 17		
Nuneaton a						11 54													12 54			
d						11 55													12 55			
Atherstone d						12 01													13 01			
Polesworth d																						
Tamworth d						12 09													13 09			
Lichfield Trent Valley d						12 17													13 17			
Rugeley Trent Valley d	←					12 24					←	←			←				13 24			
Stafford d	11 56	12 02		12 10		12 35	13 38	12 24	12 28		12 35	12 38	13 55		12 56	13 02	13 11		13 44	14 38	13 24	13 28
Norton Bridge Station Drv d						→	→						→						→	→		
Stone d	12 05														13 05							
Stone Crown Street d			11 49																			
Stone Granville Square a																						
Barlaston Orchard Place d			11 58																			
Wedgwood Old Road Bridge d																						
Stoke-on-Trent 50 d	12 13	12a17	12 22						12a43						13 13	13a17						13a43
Hanley Bus Station a			12 29																			
Kidsgrove 50 d	12 22														13 21							
Alsager 50 d	12 26														13 25							
Crewe 65,50 a	12 35			12 28	13 07			12 42		12 45	12 53	12 56		13 10	13 34		13 29	14 07			13 41	

A from 22 February
B until 15 February

Table T067-F

Saturdays

21 December to 16 May

London - Stoke-on-Trent and Crewe

Station			VT	LM	LM	LM	VT	LM	XC	LM	LM	VT	LM	LM	VT	XC	VT	LM	LM	LM	VT	LM	XC
			◇1 🍴	1	1	1	◇1 🍴	1	◇1 🍴	🚌	1	◇1 🍴	1	1	◇1 🍴	◇1 🍴	◇1 🍴	1	1	1	◇1 🍴	1	◇1 🍴
London Euston 15	⊖66	d	12 10			12 15	12 40					12 43	12 46	12 49	13 07		13 10			13 15	13 40		
Watford Junction	66	d												13 04									
Milton Keynes Central	66	d	12 41			12 56						13 13	13 19	13 25			13 41			13 56			
Northampton	68	d				13 14								13 55						14 14			
Rugby		d	13 04			13 36							13 42	14 18						14 37			
Nuneaton		a											13 54										
		d											13 55										
Atherstone		d											14 01										
Polesworth		d																					
Tamworth		d											14 09										
Lichfield Trent Valley		d											14 17										
Rugeley Trent Valley		d		←	←			←					14 24					←	←			←	
Stafford		d		13 38	13 44	14 57		13 55	14 02		14 11		14 36	15 38	14 24	14 28		14 36	14 38	15 54		14 57	15 02
Norton Bridge Station Drv		d				→							→	→						→			
Stone		d						14 04														15 06	
Stone Crown Street		d								13 49													
Stone Granville Square		a																					
Barlaston Orchard Place		d								13 58													
Wedgwood Old Road Bridge		d																					
Stoke-on-Trent	50	d						14 12	14a17	14 22						14a43						15 14	15a17
Hanley Bus Station		a								14 29													
Kidsgrove	50	d						14 20														15 23	
Alsager	50	d						14 24														15 27	
Crewe	65,50	a	13 49	13 56	14 03		14 10	14 33			14 30	15 06			14 41		14 45	14 54	14 57		15 10	15 36	

Station			LM	VT	LM	LM	VT	XC	VT	LM	LM	LM	VT	LM	XC	LM	LM	VT	LM	LM	VT	XC	VT	LM
			1	◇1 🍴	1	1	◇1 🍴	◇1 🍴	◇1 🍴	1	1	1	◇1 🍴	1	◇1	🚌	1	1 🍴	1	1	◇1 🍴	◇1 🍴	◇1 🍴	1
London Euston 15	⊖66	d		13 43	13 46	13 49	14 07		14 10			14 15	14 40					14 43	14 46	14 49	15 07		15 10	
Watford Junction	66	d				14 04														15 04				
Milton Keynes Central	66	d		14 13	14 19	14 25			14 41			14 56						15 13	15 19	15 25			15 41	
Northampton	68	d				14 55						15 15								15 56				
Rugby		d			14 42	15 19						15 37							15 42	16 18				
Nuneaton		a			14 54														15 54					
		d			14 55														15 55					
Atherstone		d			15 01														16 01					
Polesworth		d																						
Tamworth		d			15 09														16 09					
Lichfield Trent Valley		d			15 17														16 17					
Rugeley Trent Valley		d			15 24					←	←			←					16 24					←
Stafford		d	15 11		15 35	16 38	15 24	15 28		15 35	15 38	16 55		15 54	16 02		16 11		16 36	17 38	16 24	16 28		16 36
Norton Bridge Station Drv		d			→	→						→							→	→				
Stone		d												16 03										
Stone Crown Street		d														15 49								
Stone Granville Square		a																						
Barlaston Orchard Place		d														15 58								
Wedgwood Old Road Bridge		d																						
Stoke-on-Trent	50	d						15a43						16 11	16a17	16 22						16a43		
Hanley Bus Station		a														16 32								
Kidsgrove	50	d												16 20										
Alsager	50	d												16 24										
Crewe	65,50	a	15 29	16 06			15 41		15 45	15 53	15 56		16 10	16 33			16 29	17 07			16 41		16 45	16 54

Station			LM	LM	VT	LM	XC	LM	VT	LM	LM	VT	XC	VT	LM	LM	LM	LM	VT	XC	VT	LM	LM	VT
			1	1	◇1 🍴	1	◇1 🍴	1	1 🍴	1	1	◇1 🍴	◇1 🍴	◇1 🍴	1	1	1	1	◇1 🍴	◇1 🍴	◇1 🍴	🚌	1	◇1 🍴
London Euston 15	⊖66	d		15 15	15 40				15 43	15 46	15 49	16 07		16 10				16 15	16 33		16 40			16 43
Watford Junction	66	d									16 04													
Milton Keynes Central	66	d		15 56					16 13	16 19	16 25			16 41				16 56						17 13
Northampton	68	d		16 14							16 55							17 14						
Rugby		d		16 37						16 42	17 17							17 37						
Nuneaton		a								16 54														
		d								16 55														
Atherstone		d								17 01														
Polesworth		d																						
Tamworth		d								17 09									17 38					
Lichfield Trent Valley		d								17 17									17 45					
Rugeley Trent Valley		d	←			←				17 24					←		←							
Stafford		d	16 38	17 57		16 55	17 02	17 11		17 36	18 38	17 24	17 28		17 36	17 38	17 57	18 55	17a58	18 02			18 11	
Norton Bridge Station Drv		d		→						→	→							→						
Stone		d				17 04											18 06							
Stone Crown Street		d																				17 49		
Stone Granville Square		a																						
Barlaston Orchard Place		d																				17 58		
Wedgwood Old Road Bridge		d																						
Stoke-on-Trent	50	d				17 12	17a17						17a43				18 14			18a17		18 22		
Hanley Bus Station		a																				18 29		
Kidsgrove	50	d				17 21											18 23							
Alsager	50	d				17 25											18 27							
Crewe	65,50	a	16 57		17 10	17 34		17 29	18 07			17 41		17 45	17 54	17 57	18 37				18 10		18 29	19 07

Table T067-F

Saturdays

21 December to 16 May

London - Stoke-on-Trent and Crewe

Station			LM	LM	VT	XC	VT	LM	LM	LM	VT	LM	XC	LM	VT	LM	LM	VT	XC	VT	LM	LM	LM
			1	1	◇1 🍴	◇1 🍴	◇1 🍴	1	1	1	◇1 🍴	1	◇1 🍴	1	◇1 🍴	1	1	◇1 🍴	◇1 🍴	◇1 🍴	1	1	1
London Euston 15	⊖66	d	16 46	16 49	17 07		17 10			17 15	17 40				17 43	17 46	17 49	18 07		18 10			
Watford Junction	66	d		17 04													18 04						
Milton Keynes Central	66	d	17 19	17 26			17 41			17 56					18 13	18 19	18 25			18 41			
Northampton	68	d		17 56						18 14							18 55						
Rugby		d	17 42	18 19						18 37						18 42	19 17						
Nuneaton		a	17 54		18 02											18 54							
		d	17 55		18 03											18 55							
Atherstone		d	18 01													19 01							
Polesworth		d																					
Tamworth		d	18 09													19 09							
Lichfield Trent Valley		d	18 17													19 17							
Rugeley Trent Valley		d	18 24					←	←			←				19 24					←	←	←
Stafford		d	18 36	19 39	18 27	18 28		18 36	18 38	19 55		18 55	19 02	19 11		19 35	20 38	19 24	19 28		19 35	19 39	19 55
Norton Bridge Station Drv		d	→	→						→						→	→						
Stone		d										19 04											20 04
Stone Crown Street		d																					
Stone Granville Square		a																					
Barlaston Orchard Place		d																					
Wedgwood Old Road Bridge		d																					
Stoke-on-Trent	50	d				18a43						19 12	19a17						19a43				20 12
Hanley Bus Station		a																					
Kidsgrove	50	d										19 21											20 21
Alsager	50	d										19 25											20 25
Crewe	65,50	a			18 45		18 47	18 54	18 58		19 10	19 34		19 30	20 07			19 41		19 45	19 53	19 58	20 34

Station			VT	XC	VT	LM	VT	LM	VT	XC	LM	LM	LM	VT	VT	XC	LM	LM	XC	VT	VT	LM	VT	VT
			◇1 🍴	◇1 🍴	◇1 🍴	1	◇1 🍴	1	◇1 🍴	◇1	1	1	1	◇1 🍴	◇1 🍴	◇1	1	1	◇1	◇1 🍴	◇1 🍴	1	◇1 🍴	◇1 🍴
London Euston 15	⊖66	d	18 33		18 40		18 43	18 46	19 07				19 10	19 30				19 33		19 40	20 11		20 20	20 31
Watford Junction	66	d																						20u46
Milton Keynes Central	66	d					19 13	19 19					19 46					20 06					21 05	
Northampton	68	d											20 04											
Rugby		d						19 42					20 26					20 30			21 15			21 36
Nuneaton		a						19 54	20 02									20 41					21 32	
		d						19 55	20 03									20 43					21 33	
Atherstone		d						20 01										20 49						
Polesworth		d																						
Tamworth		d	19 38					20 09										20 58						21 53
Lichfield Trent Valley		d	19 45					20 17										21 04						22 00
Rugeley Trent Valley		d						20 24			←	←			←			21 12				←		
Stafford		d	19a58	20 02		20 12	20 52	20 34	20 27	20 28	20 34	20 38	21 47		20 52	21 02	21 10	21 21	21 32		21 46	21 47		
Norton Bridge Station Drv		d					→	→					→											
Stone		d																				21 56		
Stone Crown Street		d																						
Stone Granville Square		a																						
Barlaston Orchard Place		d																						
Wedgwood Old Road Bridge		d																						
Stoke-on-Trent	50	d		20a17						20a43						21a17			21a47			22 04	22a07	
Hanley Bus Station		a																						
Kidsgrove	50	d																				22 12		
Alsager	50	d																				22 16		
Crewe	65,50	a			20 12	20 31			20 45		20 52	20 57		21 02	21 09		21 29	21 39		21 19	22 05	22 25		22 28

Station			LM	XC	LM	VT	LM	XC	LM
			1	◇1	1	◇1 🍴	1	◇1	1
London Euston 15	⊖66	d			20 34	21 01			
Watford Junction	66	d			20u51				
Milton Keynes Central	66	d			21 22	21 46			
Northampton	68	d							
Rugby		d			21 48				
Nuneaton		a			21 59				
		d			22 00				
Atherstone		d			22 06				
Polesworth		d							
Tamworth		d			22 14				
Lichfield Trent Valley		d			22 20				
Rugeley Trent Valley		d			22 27		←		
Stafford		d	22 15	22 28	22 43	22 35	22 43	23 02	23 15
Norton Bridge Station Drv		d			→				
Stone		d							
Stone Crown Street		d							
Stone Granville Square		a							
Barlaston Orchard Place		d							
Wedgwood Old Road Bridge		d							
Stoke-on-Trent	50	d		22a43				23a17	
Hanley Bus Station		a							
Kidsgrove	50	d							
Alsager	50	d							
Crewe	65,50	a	22 35			22 59	23 01		23 35

Table T067-F

Sundays
15 December to 10 May

London - Stoke-on-Trent and Crewe

	LM 1	LM 1	VT ◇1	XC ◇1	LM 1	VT ◇1	VT ◇1	LM 1	LM 1		XC ◇1	LM 1	LM 1	XC ◇1	LM 1	VT ◇1	LM 1	VT ◇1	LM 1		LM 1	XC ◇1	LM 1	LM 1
London Euston 15 ⊖66 d					07 52	08 10	08 16								08 24	08 47	08 55	09 16					←	
Watford Junction 66 d					08 10										08 44		09 14						09 14	
Milton Keynes Central 66 d					08 51	08 56									09 26	09 34	→						09 57	10 11
Northampton 68 d					09 26							09 30			09 59								10 28	10 37
Rugby d					09 48			08 53				09 52			10 21	10 10							10 50	10 56
Nuneaton a							09 43					10 05						10 44					11 02	
d							09 44					10 05						10 45					11 05	
Atherstone d												10 11											11 11	
Polesworth d																								
Tamworth d												10 20											11 19	
Lichfield Trent Valley d												10 26						11 02					11 26	
Rugeley Trent Valley d												10 34							←		←	←	11 34	
Stafford d	09 09	09 15	09 18	09 32	11 19		10 08	10 16	10 23		10 33	10 47	11 28	11 33	11a48			11 15	11 19		11 28	11 33	11 44	12 17
Norton Bridge Station Drv d					→								→	→										→
Stone d		09 25							10 32												11 37			
Stone Crown Street d																								
Stone Granville Square a																								
Barlaston Orchard Place d																								
Wedgwood Old Road Bridge d																								
Stoke-on-Trent 50 d		09 33		09a51					10 40		10a48										11 45	11a48		
Hanley Bus Station a																								
Kidsgrove 50 d		09 41							10 48												11 53			
Alsager 50 d		09 45							10 52												11 57			
Crewe 65,50 a	09 29	09 54	09 36			10 17	10 28	10 34	11 01			11 07				10 56		11 34	11 38		12 06		12 04	

	LM 1	XC ◇1	LM 1	VT ◇1	LM 1		VT ◇1	LM 1	LM 1	XC ◇1	LM 1	LM 1	LM 1	XC ◇1	LM 1		VT ◇1	LM 1	VT ◇1	LM 1	LM 1	LM 1	VT ◇1	XC ◇1
London Euston 15 ⊖66 d			09 24	09 46	10 01		10 16				←				10 31		10 46	10 53	11 16			11 24	12 05	
Watford Junction 66 d			09 45		10 19						10 19				10 47			11 14				11 42		
Milton Keynes Central 66 d			10 27	10 33	→						10 58				11 27		11 33	11 58	12 04			12 28		
Northampton 68 d			11 00								11 30	11 34			11 58			12 17				12 55		
Rugby d			11 22	11 09							11 52	11 56			12 20		12 09	12 39				13 17		
Nuneaton a							11 46				12 03							12 50						
d							11 47				12 05							12 51						
Atherstone d											12 11							12 57						
Polesworth d																								
Tamworth d											12 19							13 05						
Lichfield Trent Valley d											12 25							13 11						
Rugeley Trent Valley d								←	←	←	12 33							13 19		←	←			←
Stafford d	12 21	12 30	12a45				12 14	12 17	12 21	12 30	12 45	13 10	13 17	13 28	13a47			13 30	12 53	13 10	13 17	14a41	13 25	13 28
Norton Bridge Station Drv d	→	→										→	→	→				→						
Stone d									12 30												13 26			
Stone Crown Street d																								
Stone Granville Square a																								
Barlaston Orchard Place d																								
Wedgwood Old Road Bridge d																								
Stoke-on-Trent 50 d									12 38	12a45											13 35			13a43
Hanley Bus Station a																								
Kidsgrove 50 d									12 46												13 43			
Alsager 50 d									12 50												13 47			
Crewe 65,50 a				11 55			12 32	12 35	12 59		13 03						12 56		13 12	13 29	13 56		13 43	

	LM 1		XC ◇1	LM 1	LM 1	LM 1	XC ◇1	LM 1	VT ◇1	VT ◇1	LM 1		VT ◇1	XC ◇1	LM 1	XC ◇1	LM 1	LM 1	LM 1	XC ◇1	LM 1		VT ◇1	VT ◇1
London Euston 15 ⊖66 d						12 31		12 34	12 37	12 40	12 43		13 05						13 32		13 34		13 37	13 40
Watford Junction 66 d								12 50													13 50			
Milton Keynes Central 66 d						13 13		13 28		13 13	13 20								14 14		14 28			14 13
Northampton 68 d				12 34		13 34		13 55											14 35		14 55			
Rugby d				12 56		13 56		14 17			13 47								14 57		15 17			
Nuneaton a											13 59													
d											14 00													
Atherstone d											14 06													
Polesworth d																								
Tamworth d											14 15													
Lichfield Trent Valley d											14 21													
Rugeley Trent Valley d	←										14 29			←	←		←							
Stafford d	13 30		14 02	14 11	14 15	15 11	14 28	15a41			14 40		14 25	14 28	14 40	15 02	15 11	15 23	16 11	15 28	16a41			
Norton Bridge Station Drv d						→	→				→								→	→				
Stone d					14 24													15 32						
Stone Crown Street d																								
Stone Granville Square a																								
Barlaston Orchard Place d																								
Wedgwood Old Road Bridge d																								
Stoke-on-Trent 50 d			14a17		14 33									14a43		15a17		15 42						
Hanley Bus Station a																								
Kidsgrove 50 d					14 41													15 52						
Alsager 50 d					14 45													15 56						
Crewe 65,50 a	13 48			14 30	14 54				14 12	15 07			14 43		14 58		15 30	16 05					15 12	16 08

Table T067-F

Sundays
15 December to 10 May

London - Stoke-on-Trent and Crewe

	LM 1	VT ◇1	XC ◇1	LM 1	XC ◇1	LM 1	LM 1		LM 1	XC ◇1	LM 1	VT ◇1	VT ◇1	LM 1	VT ◇1	XC ◇1	VT ◇1		LM 1	XC ◇1	LM 1	LM 1	LM 1	XC ◇1
London Euston 15 ⊖66 d	13 43	14 05							14 31		14 34	14 37	14 40	14 43	15 05		15 08						15 31	
Watford Junction 66 d											14 50													
Milton Keynes Central 66 d	14 19								15 13		15 28		15 13	15 19			15 42						16 13	
Northampton 68 d									15 34		15 55												16 34	
Rugby d	14 47								15 56		16 17			15 42									16 56	
Nuneaton a	14 59													15 54										
d	15 00													15 57										
Atherstone d	15 06													16 03										
Polesworth d																								
Tamworth d	15 15													16 12										
Lichfield Trent Valley d	15 21													16 18										
Rugeley Trent Valley d	15 29		←	←		←								16 26		←			←		←			
Stafford d	15 40	15 25	15 28	15 40	16 02	16 11	16 23		17 11	16 28	17a37			16 38	16 25	16 28			16 38	17 02	17 11	17 23	18 11	17 28
Norton Bridge Station Drv d	→								→	→				→									→	→
Stone d							16 32															17 32		
Stone Crown Street d																								
Stone Granville Square a																								
Barlaston Orchard Place d																								
Wedgwood Old Road Bridge d																								
Stoke-on-Trent 50 d			15a45		16a17		16 43									16a46				17a17		17 43		
Hanley Bus Station a																								
Kidsgrove 50 d							16 51															17 51		
Alsager 50 d							16 56															17 56		
Crewe 65,50 a		15 43		15 58		16 30	17 05					16 12	17 07		16 43		16 49		16 57		17 30	18 05		

	LM 1	VT ◇1	VT ◇1		LM 1	VT ◇1	XC ◇1	VT ◇1	LM 1	XC ◇1	LM 1	LM 1	XC ◇1		LM 1	LM 1	VT ◇1	VT ◇1	LM 1	VT ◇1	VT ◇1	XC ◇1	LM 1	
London Euston 15 ⊖66 d	15 34	15 37	15 40		15 43	16 05		16 08							16 32	16 34	16 37	16 40	16 43	17 05	17 08		17 32	
Watford Junction 66 d	15 50															16 50								
Milton Keynes Central 66 d	16 28		16 13		16 19			16 42							17 14	17 28		17 13	17 19		17 42		18 14	
Northampton 68 d	16 55														17 34	17 55							18 34	
Rugby d	17 17				16 47										17 56	18 17			17 46				18 56	
Nuneaton a					16 59														17 58	18 03				
d					17 00														17 59	18 04				
Atherstone d					17 06														18 04					
Polesworth d																								
Tamworth d					17 15														18 12					
Lichfield Trent Valley d					17 21														18 19		18 23			
Rugeley Trent Valley d					17 29		←		←		←								18 26					
Stafford d	18a44				17 40	17 26	17 28		17 40	18 02	18 11	18 21	18 28		19 11	19 39			18 35		18 40	19 02	20 11	
Norton Bridge Station Drv d					→										→	→							→	
Stone d												18 30												
Stone Crown Street d																								
Stone Granville Square a																								
Barlaston Orchard Place d																								
Wedgwood Old Road Bridge d																								
Stoke-on-Trent 50 d							17a46			18a17		18 38	18a44									19a17		
Hanley Bus Station a																								
Kidsgrove 50 d												18 51												
Alsager 50 d												18 56												
Crewe 65,50 a		17 12	18 07			17 44		17 48	17 59		18 30	19 05					18 12	19 07	18 54	18 44	18 57			

	LM 1	VT ◇1	LM 1	VT 1	LM 1	LM 1	VT ◇1	XC ◇1	VT ◇1		LM 1	LM 1	XC ◇1	LM 1	LM 1	VT ◇1	LM 1	LM 1	XC ◇1		VT ◇1	LM 1	VT ◇1	VT ◇1
London Euston 15 ⊖66 d	17 34	17 37		17 40		17 43	18 05		18 08					18 31	18 34	18 37					18 40	18 43	19 05	19 08
Watford Junction 66 d	17 50														18 50									
Milton Keynes Central 66 d	18 28			18 13		18 19			18 42					19 13	19 28						19 13	19 19		19 42
Northampton 68 d	18 55													19 34	19 55									
Rugby d	19 17					18 47								19 57	20 17							19 47		
Nuneaton a						18 59																19 59	20 03	
d						19 00																20 00	20 04	
Atherstone d						19 06																20 06		
Polesworth d																								
Tamworth d						19 15																20 15		
Lichfield Trent Valley d						19 21																20 21		
Rugeley Trent Valley d			←			19 29					←	←					←					20 29		
Stafford d	20 41		19 11		19 23	19 42	19 25	19 28			19 39	19 42	20 02	21 16	21 36		20 11	20 24	20 29		20 52	21 00	20 29	
Norton Bridge Station Drv d	→					→								→	→						→	→		
Stone d					19 32													20 33						
Stone Crown Street d																								
Stone Granville Square a																								
Barlaston Orchard Place d																								
Wedgwood Old Road Bridge d																								
Stoke-on-Trent 50 d					19 42			19a45					20a19					20 41	20a44					
Hanley Bus Station a																								
Kidsgrove 50 d					19 52													20 52						
Alsager 50 d					19 56													20 56						
Crewe 65,50 a		19 12	19 30	20 07	20 08		19 43		19 48		19 57	20 01				20 12	20 33	21 06					20 47	20 49

Table T067-F

Sundays
15 December to 10 May

London - Stoke-on-Trent and Crewe

	LM	VT	LM	LM	VT	LM	XC	LM	VT	LM	VT	LM	XC	VT	LM	LM	VT	VT	LM	VT	LM	VT
	1	◇1	1	1	◇1	1	◇1	1	◇1	1	◇1	1	◇1	◇1	1	1	◇1	◇1	1	◇1	1	◇1
London Euston 15 ⊖66 d			19 11	19 31	19 37				19 40	19 47	20 05			20 08			20 25			20 35		20 50
Watford Junction 66 d																						
Milton Keynes Central 66 d			19 50	20 13					20 13					20 41								21 40
Northampton 68 d			20 09	20 34																		
Rugby d			20 37	20 57						20 47												22 01
Nuneaton a										20 59	21 03											
d										21 00	21 04											
Atherstone d										21 06												
Polesworth d																						
Tamworth d										21 15							21 32					
Lichfield Trent Valley d										21 21							21 39					
Rugeley Trent Valley d	←	←				←		←		21 29					←	←		←	←		←	
Stafford d	20 41	20 52	22 00	22 19		21 00	21 06	21 16	21 56	21 40		21 23	21 28	21 33	21 36	21 40		21 56	22 00	22 03	22 19	
Norton Bridge Station Drv d			→	→					→	→												
Stone d												21 32							22 09			
Stone Crown Street d																						
Stone Granville Square a																						
Barlaston Orchard Place d																						
Wedgwood Old Road Bridge d																						
Stoke-on-Trent 50 d							21a21					21 40	21a44						22 17			
Hanley Bus Station a																						
Kidsgrove 50 d												21 52							22 26			
Alsager 50 d												21 56							22 30			
Crewe 65,50 a	20 58	21 10			21 12	21 19		21 35			21 44	22 05		21 51	21 54	21 58	22 10	22 16	22 39	22 21	22 38	22 49

	XC	LM	VT	AW	VT
	◇1	1	◇1	◇	◇1
London Euston 15 ⊖66 d			21 21		21 51
Watford Junction 66 d					
Milton Keynes Central 66 d					22 42
Northampton 68 d					
Rugby d					23 19
Nuneaton a			22 56		23 29
d			22 57		23 30
Atherstone d					
Polesworth d					
Tamworth d					
Lichfield Trent Valley d					
Rugeley Trent Valley d					
Stafford d	22 28	22 37	23 23	23 31	23s54
Norton Bridge Station Drv d					
Stone d		22 46			
Stone Crown Street d					
Stone Granville Square a					
Barlaston Orchard Place d					
Wedgwood Old Road Bridge d					
Stoke-on-Trent 50 d	22a43	22 54			
Hanley Bus Station a					
Kidsgrove 50 d		23 02			
Alsager 50 d		23 06			
Crewe 65,50 a		23 15	23 44	23 59	00s16

Table T067-R

Mondays to Fridays
16 December to 15 May

Crewe and Stoke-on-Trent - London

Miles	Miles		AW	VT	LM	XC	LM	LM	VT	LM	VT	VT	LM	XC	LM	LM	VT	LM	VT	LM	LM	LM
				◇1 ⊠	🚌	◇1 ⌶	1	1	◇1 ⊠	1	◇1 ⊠	◇1 ⊠	1	◇1 ⌶	1	1	◇1 ⊠	1	◇1 ⊠	🚌	1	1
0	0	**Crewe** 65,50 d	04 59	05 36		05 46	05 47	06 01	06 02	06 05	06 28		06 35	06 39	06 50			06 52	06 53		07 14	07 17
6¼	—	Alsager 50 d						06 10					06 43					07 01				
8½	—	Kidsgrove 50 d						06 16					06 48					07 08				
—	—	Hanley Bus Station d			05 55															07 30		
15	—	**Stoke-on-Trent** 50 d			06 02	06 06		06 26					06 56				07 06	07 21		07 37		
—	—	Wedgwood Old Road Bridge d																		07 56		
—	—	Barlaston Orchard Place d			06 23															08 04		
—	—	Stone Granville Square d			06a33															08a19		
—	—	Stone Crown Street d																				
23¾	—	Stone d						06 34					07 05					07 30				
—	—	Norton Bridge Station Drv d														←						
32¼	24½	**Stafford** d	05a24	05 55		06a22	06 08	06a44	06 21	06 31		06 53	07 15	06a58	07 10	07 15	07 24	07a44			07 39	07 41
42	—	Rugeley Trent Valley d					06 18						→								→	→
50	—	Lichfield Trent Valley d					06 25					07 08										
56¼	—	Tamworth d					06 34					07 15										
59¾	—	Polesworth d																				
63¾	—	Atherstone d					06 43															
68¾	—	Nuneaton a		06 17			06 49				07 05								07 33			
—	—	d		06 18			06 50				07 07								07 34			
83¼	—	Rugby a		06 30			07 05		06 52	07 58					08 36	08 58						
102	—	Northampton 68 a								08 21					09 00	09 20						
118	—	Milton Keynes Central 66 a		06 51					07 12	08 39					09 21	09 40						
150¼	—	Watford Junction 66 a													→	→	09s16					
167¾	—	**London Euston** 15 ⊖66 a		07 25			08 06		07 50	09 24	08 10	08 23					09 33		08 34			

	VT	LM	LM	XC	LM	VT	XC	VT	LM	LM	LM	VT	LM	VT	LM	LM	VT	VT	XC	LM	VT	XC
	◇1 ⊠	1	1	◇1 ⌶	1	◇1 ⊠	R 1 ⌶	◇1 ⊠	1	1	🚌	◇1 ⊠	1	◇1 ⊠	1	1	◇1 ⊠	◇1 ⊠	◇1 ⌶	1	◇1 ⊠	◇1 ⌶
Crewe 65,50 d	07 18				07 51	07 57						08 01	08 16		08 01	08 19	08 23	08 29		08 50	08 56	
Alsager 50 d															08 09							
Kidsgrove 50 d															08 14							
Hanley Bus Station d											08 25											
Stoke-on-Trent 50 d				07 44			08 07	08 12			08 32				08 26				08 44			09 07
Wedgwood Old Road Bridge d																						
Barlaston Orchard Place d											08 53											
Stone Granville Square d											09a03											
Stone Crown Street d																						
Stone d															08 34							
Norton Bridge Station Drv d		←	←																			
Stafford d	07 36	07 39	07 41	08a00	08 11		08a23						08 36		08 45	08 38	08 42		09a00	09 10		09a22
Rugeley Trent Valley d		07 49	09a07										08 45									
Lichfield Trent Valley d		07 57											08 53					09 00				
Tamworth d		08 04											09 01					09 07				
Polesworth d																						
Atherstone d		08 12											09 09									
Nuneaton a		08 18						08 43					09 15									
d		08 18						08 45					09 16									
Rugby a		08 33			09 36	08 45							09 31		10 11	10 11				10 32		
Northampton 68 a					09 59				←	←				←	10 35					10 54		
Milton Keynes Central 66 a		08 55			10 21				09 21	09 40		09 57	09 54	09 57	10 52					11 21	10 02	
Watford Junction 66 a					→			09s31	09 58			→			11 14					→		
London Euston 15 ⊖66 a	08 53	09 36				09 39		09 49	10 17	10 23			10 30	10 33	11 30		09 59	10 16			10 37	

	VT	LM	VT	VT	LM	LM	VT	LM	VT	LM	XC	LM	VT	LM	LM	VT FX	VT FO	XC	LM	LM	VT
	◇1 ⊠	1	◇1 A ⊠	◇1 B ⊠	1	1	◇1 ⊠	🚌	◇1 ⊠	1	◇1 ⌶	1	◇1 ⊠	1	1	◇1 ⊠	◇1 ⊠	◇1 ⌶	1	1	◇1 ⊠
Crewe 65,50 d			09 01	09 01	09 01	09 20	09 24		09 30	09 33		09 50	09 56			10 01	10 01		10 01	10 19	10 22
Alsager 50 d					09 09														10 09		
Kidsgrove 50 d					09 14														10 14		
Hanley Bus Station d								09 25													
Stoke-on-Trent 50 d	09 12				09 26			09 32			09 44							10 07	10 26		
Wedgwood Old Road Bridge d																					
Barlaston Orchard Place d								09 53													
Stone Granville Square d								10a03													
Stone Crown Street d																					
Stone d					09 34														10 34		
Norton Bridge Station Drv d																					
Stafford d					09 45	09 39	09 43			09 52	10a00	10 10						10a23	10 49	10 40	10 41
Rugeley Trent Valley d										10 05											
Lichfield Trent Valley d										10 13											
Tamworth d										10 20											
Polesworth d																					
Atherstone d										10 28											
Nuneaton a	09 44									10 34											
d	09 45									10 35											
Rugby a					11 11	11 11				10 51		11 32							12 11	12 11	
Northampton 68 a		←			11 33							11 54		←	←				12 33		
Milton Keynes Central 66 a		10 21	10 57	10 57	11 50					11 14		12 21	11 02	11 14	11 21	11 57	11 57		12 51		
Watford Junction 66 a		10 58			12 13					→		→			11 58				13 14		
London Euston 15 ⊖66 a	10 51	11 18	11 34	11 36	12 29		11 00		11 07				11 37	11 51	12 16	12 33	12 35		13 30		11 59

A until 14 February

B from 17 February

Table T067-R

Mondays to Fridays
16 December to 15 May

Crewe and Stoke-on-Trent - London

Station		LM	VT	LM	VT FO	XC	LM	VT FX A	VT FX B	VT FO	LM	LM	VT	XC	LM	LM	VT	LM	VT	LM	XC	LM	VT C
Crewe 65,50	d		10 29	10 33	10 40		10 50	10 56	10 56	10 56			11 01		11 01	11 19	11 22		11 29	11 33		11 51	11 56
Alsager 50	d														11 09								
Kidsgrove 50	d														11 14								
Hanley Bus Station	d	10 25																11 25					
Stoke-on-Trent 50	d	10 32				10 44								11 07	11 26			11 32			11 44		
Wedgwood Old Road Bridge	d																						
Barlaston Orchard Place	d	10 53																11 53					
Stone Granville Square	d	11a03																12a03					
Stone Crown Street	d																						
Stone	d														11 34								
Norton Bridge Station Drv	d																						
Stafford	d			10 52		11a00	11 10							11a24	11 45	11 40	11 41			11 55	12a00	12 10	
Rugeley Trent Valley	d			11 05																12 05			
Lichfield Trent Valley	d			11 13																12 13			
Tamworth	d			11 20																12 20			
Polesworth	d																						
Atherstone	d			11 28																12 28			
Nuneaton	a			11 34																12 34			
	d			11 35																12 35			
Rugby	a			11 52			12 31								13 11	13 11				12 51		13 32	
Northampton 68	a						12 54				←	←			13 34							13 54	
Milton Keynes Central 66	a			12 14			13 20	12 02	12 02	12 02	12 14	12 21	12 57		13 51					13 14		14 21	13 02
Watford Junction 66	a			→			→					12 58			14 14					→		→	
London Euston ⊖66	a		12 02		12 32			12 36	12 37	12 38	12 50	13 17	13 33		14 30		12 59		13 02				13 36

Station		VT B	LM	LM	VT WX	VT WO	XC	LM	LM	VT	VT	LM	XC	LM	VT WX	VT WO	LM	LM	VT	XC	LM	LM	VT C
Crewe 65,50	d	11 56			12 01	12 01		12 01	12 19	12 22	12 29	12 33		12 51	12 56	12 56			13 01		13 03	13 19	13 24
Alsager 50	d							12 09													13 11		
Kidsgrove 50	d							12 14													13 16		
Hanley Bus Station	d																						
Stoke-on-Trent 50	d						12 07	12 26					12 44							13 07	13 26		
Wedgwood Old Road Bridge	d																						
Barlaston Orchard Place	d																						
Stone Granville Square	d																						
Stone Crown Street	d																						
Stone	d							12 34													13 34		
Norton Bridge Station Drv	d																						
Stafford	d						12a25	12 45	12 40	12 41		12 55	13a00	13 11						13a24	13 45	13 41	13 43
Rugeley Trent Valley	d											13 05											
Lichfield Trent Valley	d											13 13											
Tamworth	d											13 20											
Polesworth	d																						
Atherstone	d											13 28											
Nuneaton	a											13 34											
	d											13 35											
Rugby	a							14 11	14 11			13 50		14 32							15 11	15 11	
Northampton 68	a		←	←				14 33						14 54			←	←			15 33		
Milton Keynes Central 66	a	13 02	13 14	13 20	13 57	13 57		14 53				14 14		15 21	14 02	14 02	14 14	14 21	14 57		15 49		
Watford Junction 66	a			13 57				15 15				→		→				14 58			16 13		
London Euston ⊖66	a	13 37	13 50	14 17	14 33	14 36		15 31		14 03	14 06				14 36	14 39	14 50	15 17	15 34		16 29		15 03

Station		VT B	LM	VT	LM	XC	LM	VT	LM	LM	VT C	VT B	XC	LM	LM	VT	VT	LM	XC	LM	LM	VT
Crewe 65,50	d	13 24		13 29	13 33		13 49	13 56			14 01	14 01		14 01	14 19	14 24	14 29	14 33			14 51	14 56
Alsager 50	d													14 09								
Kidsgrove 50	d													14 14								
Hanley Bus Station	d		13 25																	14 50		
Stoke-on-Trent 50	d		13 32			13 44							14 07	14 26					14 44	14 57		
Wedgwood Old Road Bridge	d																					
Barlaston Orchard Place	d		13 53																	15 18		
Stone Granville Square	d		14a03																	15a28		
Stone Crown Street	d																					
Stone	d													14 34								
Norton Bridge Station Drv	d																					
Stafford	d	13 43			13 55	14a00	14 10						14a23	14 46	14 40	14 44		14 55	15a00		15 12	
Rugeley Trent Valley	d				14 05													15 05				
Lichfield Trent Valley	d				14 13													15 13				
Tamworth	d				14 20													15 20				
Polesworth	d																					
Atherstone	d				14 28													15 28				
Nuneaton	a				14 34													15 34				
	d				14 35													15 35				
Rugby	a				14 50		15 31							16 11	16 11			15 50			16 31	
Northampton 68	a						15 51		←	←				16 33							16 56	
Milton Keynes Central 66	a				15 14			15 02	15 14	15 21	15 57	15 57		16 53				16 15				16 02
Watford Junction 66	a				→					15 58				17 15				→				
London Euston ⊖66	a	15 04		15 07			16 46	15 37	15 50	16 17	16 32	16 33		17 31		16 03	16 06				17 46	16 36

A until 13 February **B** from 17 February **C** until 14 February

Table T067-R

Mondays to Fridays
16 December to 15 May

Crewe and Stoke-on-Trent - London

Station		LM	VT	XC	LM	LM	VT	VT	LM	XC	LM	LM	VT	LM	VT	XC	LM	LM	VT	VT	LM	XC	LM
Crewe 65,50	d		15 01		15 01	15 21	15 22	15 29	15 33			15 52	15 56		16 01		16 01	16 19	16 24	16 29	16 33		16 51
Alsager 50	d				15 09												16 09						
Kidsgrove 50	d				15 14												16 14						
Hanley Bus Station	d										15 50												
Stoke-on-Trent 50	d			15 07	15 26					15 44	15 57					16 07	16 26					16 44	
Wedgwood Old Road Bridge	d																						
Barlaston Orchard Place	d										16 18												
Stone Granville Square	d										16a28												
Stone Crown Street	d																						
Stone	d				15 34												16 34						
Norton Bridge Station Drv	d																						
Stafford	d			15a24	15 45	15 41	15 41		15 55	16a00		16 11				16a24	16 45	16 39	16 44		16 55	17a00	17 10
Rugeley Trent Valley	d								16 05												17 05		
Lichfield Trent Valley	d								16 13												17 13		
Tamworth	d								16 20												17 20		
Polesworth	d																						
Atherstone	d								16 28												17 28		
Nuneaton	a								16 34												17 34		
	d								16 35												17 35		
Rugby	a				17 12	17 12			16 50			17 32					18 12	18 12			17 50		18 32
Northampton 68	a	←			17 38							17 55		←			18 34						18 54
Milton Keynes Central 66	a	16 15	16 57		17 52				17 15			18 11	17 02	17 15	17 57		18 51				18 14		
Watford Junction 66	a				18 14				→			→					19 14				→		
London Euston ⊖66	a	16 52	17 34		18 30		16 59	17 03					17 37	17 51	18 33		19 30		18 03	18 06			19 45

Station		VT	LM	LM	XC	VT A	VT B	VT	LM	LM	VT A	VT B	LM	LM	XC	LM	VT	LM	VT	LM	XC	LM
Crewe 65,50	d	16 56						17 01	17 01	17 23	17 29	17 29		17 33		17 50	17 56		18 01	18 01	18 07	18 17
Alsager 50	d								17 09											18 09		
Kidsgrove 50	d								17 14											18 14		
Hanley Bus Station	d												17 30									
Stoke-on-Trent 50	d				17 07				17 26				17 37		17 44					18 26		
Wedgwood Old Road Bridge	d																					
Barlaston Orchard Place	d												17 58									
Stone Granville Square	d												18a08									
Stone Crown Street	d																					
Stone	d								17 34											18 34		
Norton Bridge Station Drv	d																					
Stafford	d				17a23	17 37	17 37		17 46	17 42				17 55	18a00	18 09				18 46	18a25	18a41
Rugeley Trent Valley	d													18 05						→		
Lichfield Trent Valley	d													18 13								
Tamworth	d													18 20								
Polesworth	d																					
Atherstone	d													18 28								
Nuneaton	a													18 34								
	d													18 35								
Rugby	a								19 11	19 11				18 50		19 31						
Northampton 68	a		←	←					19 37							19 55		←				
Milton Keynes Central 66	a	18 02	18 11	18 14		18 23	18 26	18 57	19 52					19 14		20 21	19 02	19 14	19 58			
Watford Junction 66	a								20 14		18s49	18s50		→		→			→			
London Euston ⊖66	a	18 36	18 47	18 50		18 59	19 02	19 33	20 30		19 06	19 06					19 37	19 50				

Station		VT	LM	VT	VT	LM	LM	XC	LM	XC	VT	LM	LM	VT	VT	LM	VT	LM	XC	LM	VT	LM	LM
Crewe 65,50	d	18 24		18 29		18 33			18 50		19 01	19 01	19 19	19 22	19 29			19 35		19 55	19 56		
Alsager 50	d											19 09											
Kidsgrove 50	d											19 14											
Hanley Bus Station	d																						
Stoke-on-Trent 50	d							18 44		19 07		19 26							19 44				
Wedgwood Old Road Bridge	d																						
Barlaston Orchard Place	d																						
Stone Granville Square	d																						
Stone Crown Street	d																						
Stone	d											19 34											
Norton Bridge Station Drv	d		←																				
Stafford	d	18 43	18 46			18 55		19a00	19 10	19a23		19 45	19 40	19 41				19 52	20a00	20 16			
Rugeley Trent Valley	d					19 05												20 02					
Lichfield Trent Valley	d					19 13												20 09					
Tamworth	d					19 20												20 16					
Polesworth	d																						
Atherstone	d					19 28												20 25					
Nuneaton	a					19 34												20 31					
	d					19 39												20 32					
Rugby	a		20 11			19 55			20 32			21 12	21 12					20 47		21 31			
Northampton 68	a		20 37		←		←		20 55			21 35				←	←			21 54		←	←
Milton Keynes Central 66	a		20 54	19 32	19 58	20 16	20 21		21 13		20 58	21 53			20 31	20 54	20 58	21 09		22 20	21 03	21 09	21 13
Watford Junction 66	a	19s46	→				20 58		→		→	22 34		20s45			21s19	→		→		21 34	
London Euston ⊖66	a	20 03		20 07	20 33	20 52	21 17					22 53		21 02	21 05	21 30	21 36				21 39	21 50	21 53

A until 14 February **B** from 17 February

Table T067-R

Crewe and Stoke-on-Trent - London

Mondays to Fridays

16 December to 15 May

	XC	LM	VT	LM	VT	VT	XC	LM	VT	VT	LM	LM	VT	XC	LM	LM	VT	LM	LM	LM	VT	XC
																					FO	
	◇1	1	1 ⊠	1	◇1	◇1	◇1	1	◇1	1 ⊠	1	1	◇1 ⊠	◇1	1	1	◇1	1	1	1	◇1 ⊠	◇1
Crewe 65,50 d		20 01	20 03	20 19	20 24	20 29		20 36	20 44			20 48	20 54		21 14	21 19	21 25		21 29	21 53	22 01	
Alsager 50 d		20 10													21 23							
Kidsgrove 50 d		20 14													21 27							
Hanley Bus Station d																						
Stoke-on-Trent 50 d	20 07	20 26					20 44							21 07	21 37							22 07
Wedgwood Old Road Bridge d																						
Barlaston Orchard Place d																						
Stone Granville Square d																						
Stone Crown Street d																						
Stone d		20 34													21 45							
Norton Bridge Station Drv d																						
Stafford d	20a24	20 48		20a38		20 48	21a00	21 03				21 09	21a13	21a23	21a56	21a38	21 44		21 49	22 12		22a22
Rugeley Trent Valley d								21 13											21 58	22 22		
Lichfield Trent Valley d								21 20									21 58		22 06	22 29		
Tamworth d								21 27									22 05		22 13	22 36		
Polesworth d																						
Atherstone d								21 36											22 21	22 48		
Nuneaton a					21 00			21 42									22 17		22 27	22 58		
d					21 01			21 42									22 18		22 28	22 58		
Rugby a		22 11						21 57	21 29			22 32					22 30		22 41	23 11	23 43	
Northampton 68 a		22 35						22 21		←	←	22 54						←	23 03		00s05	
Milton Keynes Central 66 a			21 58			21 34			21 49	21 58	22 20	23 12					22 53	23 12		23 44	00 23	
Watford Junction 66 a			→		21s47					22s20	23 00	→					23s25	00 01			00s54	
London Euston 15 ⊖66 a					22 04	22 09			22 27	22 41	23 23						23 44	00 26		00 45	01 13	

	LM	XC
	1	◇1
Crewe 65,50 d	22 18	
Alsager 50 d		
Kidsgrove 50 d		
Hanley Bus Station d		
Stoke-on-Trent 50 d		22 47
Wedgwood Old Road Bridge d		
Barlaston Orchard Place d		
Stone Granville Square d		
Stone Crown Street d		
Stone d		
Norton Bridge Station Drv d		
Stafford d	22a36	23a03
Rugeley Trent Valley d		
Lichfield Trent Valley d		
Tamworth d		
Polesworth d		
Atherstone d		
Nuneaton a		
d		
Rugby a		
Northampton 68 a		
Milton Keynes Central 66 a		
Watford Junction 66 a		
London Euston 15 ⊖66 a		

Saturdays

21 December to 16 May

	AW	LM	XC	VT	VT	LM	LM	LM	VT	LM	XC	LM	VT	LM	LM	VT	LM	VT	VT	LM	VT	LM
		1	◇1	◇1	◇1	1	1	1	◇1	1	◇1	1	◇1	1	1	◇1	1	◇1	◇1	1	◇1	1
Crewe 65,50 d	04 59	05 38	05 46	06 00		06 01	06 16	06 24	06 29			06 49	07 01	07 01	07 18	07 20	07 25	07 29	07 41			
Alsager 50 d						06 10								07 09								
Kidsgrove 50 d						06 16								07 14								
Hanley Bus Station d																						
Stoke-on-Trent 50 d			06 06			06 26					06 39			07 29								
Wedgwood Old Road Bridge d																						
Barlaston Orchard Place d																						
Stone Granville Square d																						
Stone Crown Street d																						
Stone d						06 34								07 40								
Norton Bridge Station Drv d																						
Stafford d	05a24	05 59	06a22	06 19	06 35	06 45	06a35	06 47			06a55	07 09		07 51	07 38	07 39	07 48					
Rugeley Trent Valley d		06 09						06 57									07 57					
Lichfield Trent Valley d		06 16						07 04									08 05					
Tamworth d		06 23						07 11									08 12					
Polesworth d																						
Atherstone d		06 31						07 19									08 20					
Nuneaton a		06 37			06 57			07 25									08 26					
d		06 39			06 59			07 26									08 27					
Rugby a		06 55		06 49		08 11		07 42				08 31		09 11	09 11		08 42					
Northampton 68 a						08 33				←		08 57		09 33						←	←	←
Milton Keynes Central 66 a				07 10		08 55		08 04	07 31	08 04		09 22	08 58	09 51			09 05		08 51	08 55	08 58	09 05
Watford Junction 66 a				07s33	07s45	→		→				→	→	10 14			→			09 17		
London Euston 15 ⊖66 a		07 57		07 50	08 02				08 07	08 40				10 30		08 56		09 01	09 28	09 33	09 36	09 50

Table T067-R

Crewe and Stoke-on-Trent - London

Saturdays

21 December to 16 May

	LM	XC	LM	LM	VT	XC	LM	LM	VT	LM	VT	LM	XC	LM	VT	LM	LM	VT	XC	LM	LM	VT
	1	◇1	1	1	◇1	◇1	1	1	◇1		◇1	1	◇1	1	◇1	1	1	◇1	◇1	1	1	◇1
Crewe 65,50 d			07 44	07 50	07 56		08 01	08 19	08 22		08 29	08 33		08 49	08 56			09 01		09 01	09 18	09 24
Alsager 50 d							08 09													09 09		
Kidsgrove 50 d							08 15													09 14		
Hanley Bus Station d										08 25												
Stoke-on-Trent 50 d		07 44				08 07	08 26			08 32			08 44						09 07	09 26		
Wedgwood Old Road Bridge d																						
Barlaston Orchard Place d										08 53												
Stone Granville Square d										09a03												
Stone Crown Street d																						
Stone d							08 35													09 34		
Norton Bridge Station Drv d																						
Stafford d		08a00	08 07	08 10	08 15	08a24	08 46	08 38	08 41			08 55	09a00	09 09					09a22	09 45	09 39	09 43
Rugeley Trent Valley d			08 18									09 05										
Lichfield Trent Valley d			08 26		08 30							09 13										
Tamworth d			08 32		08 37							09 20										
Polesworth d																						
Atherstone d			08 40									09 28										
Nuneaton a			08 46						09 03			09 34										
d			08 47						09 04			09 35										
Rugby a			09 03	09 31			10 11	10 11				09 50		10 31						11 11	11 11	
Northampton 68 a	←			09 53			10 33							10 53		←	←			11 33		
Milton Keynes Central 66 a	09 22		09 24	10 21			10 51					10 14		11 21	10 01	10 14	10 21	10 57		11 51		
Watford Junction 66 a	09 58			→			11 14					→		→			10 58			12 14		
London Euston 15 ⊖66 a	10 17		10 00		09 44		11 30		10 03		10 08				10 36	10 52	11 17	11 33		12 30		11 01

	LM	VT	LM	XC	LM	VT	LM	LM	VT	XC	LM	LM	VT	VT	LM	XC	LM	VT	LM	LM	VT
		◇1	1	◇1	1	◇1	1	1	◇1	◇1	1	1	◇1	◇1	1	◇1	1	◇1	1	1	◇1
Crewe 65,50 d		09 29	09 33		09 50	09 56			10 01		10 01	10 17	10 22	10 29	10 33		10 49	10 56			11 01
Alsager 50 d											10 09										
Kidsgrove 50 d											10 14										
Hanley Bus Station d	09 25																				
Stoke-on-Trent 50 d	09 32			09 44						10 07	10 26					10 44					
Wedgwood Old Road Bridge d																					
Barlaston Orchard Place d	09 53																				
Stone Granville Square d	10a03																				
Stone Crown Street d																					
Stone d											10 34										
Norton Bridge Station Drv d																					
Stafford d			09 55	10a00	10 10					10a22	10 45	10 38	10 41		10 55	11a00	11 10				
Rugeley Trent Valley d			10 05												11 05						
Lichfield Trent Valley d			10 13												11 13						
Tamworth d			10 20												11 20						
Polesworth d																					
Atherstone d			10 28												11 28						
Nuneaton a			10 34												11 34						
d			10 35												11 35						
Rugby a			10 50		11 31						12 11	12 11			11 50		12 31				
Northampton 68 a					11 55		←	←			12 33						12 53		←	←	
Milton Keynes Central 66 a			11 14		12 21	11 01	11 14	11 21	11 57		12 51				12 15		13 21	12 01	12 15	12 21	12 57
Watford Junction 66 a			→		→			11 58			13 14				→		→			12 58	
London Euston 15 ⊖66 a		11 04				11 36	11 50	12 17	12 33		13 30		11 58	12 01				12 36	12 51	13 17	13 33

	XC	LM	LM	VT	LM	VT	LM	XC	LM	VT	LM	LM	VT	XC	LM	LM	VT	VT	LM	XC	LM	VT
	◇1	1	1	◇1		◇1	1	◇1	1	◇1	1	1	◇1	◇1	1	1	◇1	◇1	1	◇1	1	◇1
Crewe 65,50 d		11 01	11 19	11 22		11 29	11 33		11 50	11 56			12 01		12 01	12 20	12 22	12 29	12 33		12 50	12 56
Alsager 50 d		11 09													12 09							
Kidsgrove 50 d		11 14													12 14							
Hanley Bus Station d					11 25																	
Stoke-on-Trent 50 d	11 07	11 26			11 32			11 44						12 07	12 26					12 44		
Wedgwood Old Road Bridge d																						
Barlaston Orchard Place d					11 53																	
Stone Granville Square d					12a03																	
Stone Crown Street d																						
Stone d		11 34													12 34							
Norton Bridge Station Drv d																						
Stafford d	11a25	11 45	11 40	11 41			11 55	12a00	12 09					12a23	12 45	12 40	12 41		12 55	13a00	13 10	
Rugeley Trent Valley d							12 05												13 05			
Lichfield Trent Valley d							12 13												13 13			
Tamworth d							12 20												13 20			
Polesworth d																						
Atherstone d							12 28												13 28			
Nuneaton a							12 34												13 34			
d							12 35												13 35			
Rugby a		13 11	13 11				12 50		13 31						14 11	14 11			13 50		14 31	
Northampton 68 a		13 33							13 53		←	←			14 34						14 53	
Milton Keynes Central 66 a		13 51					13 14		14 21	13 02	13 14	13 21	13 57		14 53				14 14		15 21	14 02
Watford Junction 66 a		14 14					→		→			13 58			15 15				→		→	
London Euston 15 ⊖66 a		14 30		13 00		13 03				13 36	13 50	14 18	14 33		15 31		14 01	14 04				14 36

Table T067-R

Crewe and Stoke-on-Trent - London

Saturdays

21 December to 16 May

Station			LM	LM	XC	VT	LM	LM	VT	LM (bus)	VT	LM	XC	LM	VT	LM	LM	VT	XC	LM	LM	VT	VT
Crewe	65,50	d				13 03	13 01	13 18	13 24		13 29	13 33		13 50	13 56			14 01		14 01	14 18	14 24	14 29
Alsager	50	d					13 09													14 09			
Kidsgrove	50	d					13 14													14 14			
Hanley Bus Station		d								13 25													
Stoke-on-Trent	50	d			13 07		13 26			13 32			13 44						14 07	14 26			
Wedgwood Old Road Bridge		d																					
Barlaston Orchard Place		d								13 53													
Stone Granville Square		d								14a03													
Stone Crown Street		d																					
Stone		d					13 34													14 34			
Norton Bridge Station Drv.		d																					
Stafford		d			13a22		13 45	13 40	13 42			13 55	14a00	14 09					14a24	14 45	14 38	14 43	
Rugeley Trent Valley		d										14 05											
Lichfield Trent Valley		d										14 13											
Tamworth		d										14 20											
Polesworth		d																					
Atherstone		d										14 28											
Nuneaton		a										14 34											
		d										14 35											
Rugby		a					15 11	15 11				14 50		15 31						16 11	16 11		
Northampton	68	a	←	←			15 33							15 53		←	←			16 33			
Milton Keynes Central	66	a	14 14	14 21		14 57	15 52					15 14		16 21	15 02	15 14	15 21	15 57		16 52			
Watford Junction	66	a		14 58			16 14					→		→			15 58			17 14			
London Euston 15	⊖66	a	14 50	15 17		15 34	16 30		14 59		15 07				15 37	15 50	16 19	16 33		17 30		16 01	16 04

Station			LM	XC	LM	VT	LM	LM	XC	VT	LM	LM	VT	LM (bus)	VT	LM	XC	LM	VT	LM	LM	VT	XC
Crewe	65,50	d	14 33		14 49	14 56				15 02	15 01	15 19	15 22		15 29	15 33		15 49	15 56			16 01	
Alsager	50	d									15 09												
Kidsgrove	50	d									15 14												
Hanley Bus Station		d												15 25									
Stoke-on-Trent	50	d		14 44					15 07		15 26			15 32			15 44						16 07
Wedgwood Old Road Bridge		d																					
Barlaston Orchard Place		d												15 53									
Stone Granville Square		d												16a03									
Stone Crown Street		d																					
Stone		d									15 34												
Norton Bridge Station Drv.		d																					
Stafford		d	14 55	15a00	15 08				15a25		15 45	15 39	15 41			15 55	16a00	16 09					16a23
Rugeley Trent Valley		d	15 05													16 05							
Lichfield Trent Valley		d	15 13													16 13							
Tamworth		d	15 20													16 20							
Polesworth		d																					
Atherstone		d	15 28													16 28							
Nuneaton		a	15 34													16 34							
		d	15 35													16 35							
Rugby		a	15 50		16 31						17 12	17 12				16 50		17 31					
Northampton	68	a			16 57		←	←			17 38							17 53		←	←		
Milton Keynes Central	66	a	16 14		17 21	16 01	16 14	16 21		16 57	17 52					17 14		18 21	17 01	17 14	17 21	17 57	
Watford Junction	66	a	→		→			16 58			18 14					→		→			17 58		
London Euston 15	⊖66	a				16 36	16 50	17 17		17 33	18 30		16 59		17 03				17 36	17 50	18 17	18 33	

Station			LM	LM	VT	VT	LM	XC	LM	VT	LM	LM	VT	XC	LM	LM	VT	VT	LM (bus)	LM	XC	LM	XC	VT
Crewe	65,50	d	16 01	16 19	16 22	16 29	16 33		16 49	16 56			17 01		17 02	17 19	17 23	17 29		17 33		17 49		
Alsager	50	d	16 09												17 11									
Kidsgrove	50	d	16 14												17 15									
Hanley Bus Station		d																	17 30					
Stoke-on-Trent	50	d	16 26					16 44						17 07	17 26				17 37		17 44		18 07	
Wedgwood Old Road Bridge		d																						
Barlaston Orchard Place		d																	17 58					
Stone Granville Square		d																	18a08					
Stone Crown Street		d																						
Stone		d	16 34												17 34									
Norton Bridge Station Drv.		d																						
Stafford		d	16 47	16 40	16 41		16 55	17a00	17 08					17a24	17 45	17 39	17 41			17 55	18a00	18 08	18a23	18 36
Rugeley Trent Valley		d					17 05													18 05				
Lichfield Trent Valley		d					17 13										17 57			18 13				
Tamworth		d					17 20													18 20				
Polesworth		d																						
Atherstone		d					17 28													18 28				
Nuneaton		a					17 34													18 34				
		d					17 35													18 35				
Rugby		a	18 11	18 11			17 50		18 31						19 11	19 11				18 50		19 31		
Northampton	68	a	18 37						18 53		←	←			19 33							19 53		
Milton Keynes Central	66	a	18 53				18 14		19 20	18 02	18 14	18 21	18 57		19 48					19 14		20 16		
Watford Junction	66	a	19 15				→		→			18 58										→		
London Euston 15	⊖66	a	19 31		17 59	18 02				18 36	18 51	19 17	19 34				19 07	19 03		19 50				19 58

NRT DECEMBER 19 EDITION

Table T067-R

Crewe and Stoke-on-Trent - London

Saturdays

21 December to 16 May

Station			LM	VT	LM	LM	LM	VT	LM	XC	LM	VT	LM	XC	LM	LM	VT	VT	LM	XC	LM	XC	LM
Crewe	65,50	d		18 01		18 01	18 20	18 28	18 33		18 49	19 01			19 01	19 19	19 23	19 29	19 33		19 53		20 02
Alsager	50	d				18 10									19 10								20 11
Kidsgrove	50	d				18 15									19 14								20 16
Hanley Bus Station		d																					
Stoke-on-Trent	50	d				18 26				18 44				19 07	19 26					19 44		20 07	20 26
Wedgwood Old Road Bridge		d																					
Barlaston Orchard Place		d																					
Stone Granville Square		d																					
Stone Crown Street		d																					
Stone		d				18 34									19 34								20 35
Norton Bridge Station Drv.		d																					
Stafford		d				18 46	18 39		18 55	19a00	19 09			19a23	19 46	19 41	19 41		19 52	20a00	20 11	20a24	20 45
Rugeley Trent Valley		d							19 05										20 01				→
Lichfield Trent Valley		d							19 13										20 09				
Tamworth		d							19 20										20 15				
Polesworth		d																					
Atherstone		d							19 28										20 23				
Nuneaton		a							19 34										20 29				
		d							19 35										20 30				
Rugby		a		19 42		20 11	20 11		19 50		20 31	20 42			21 11	21 11			20 46		21 31		
Northampton	68	a	←		←	20 35			20 11		20 53		←		21 34				21 07		21 53		
Milton Keynes Central	66	a	19 20	20 05	20 16	20 50					21 15	21 04	21 15		21 58						22 21		
Watford Junction	66	a	19 58	20s33	20 47	21 29					→	21s36	21 53		22 30						→		
London Euston 15	⊖66	a	20 17	20 55	21 10	21 54		20 01				21 57	22 12		22 53		21 13	21 23					

Station			VT	LM	VT	LM	LM	XC	VT	VT	LM	LM	LM	LM	XC	LM	LM	XC	VT	XC	VT	LM
Crewe	65,50	d	20 03	20 19	20 23		20 38		20 49					20 52		21 02	21 19		21 45		22 06	22 21
Alsager	50	d														21 11						
Kidsgrove	50	d														21 15						
Hanley Bus Station		d																				
Stoke-on-Trent	50	d						20 44							21 07	21 26		21 44		22 07		
Wedgwood Old Road Bridge		d																				
Barlaston Orchard Place		d																				
Stone Granville Square		d																				
Stone Crown Street		d																				
Stone		d														21 34						
Norton Bridge Station Drv.		d				←																
Stafford		d		20a40	20 43	20 45	20 58	21a00						21 13	21a22	21a44	21a38	22a00	22a07	22a22	22a24	22a40
Rugeley Trent Valley		d					21 08															
Lichfield Trent Valley		d					21 15															
Tamworth		d					21 22															
Polesworth		d																				
Atherstone		d					21 30															
Nuneaton		a					21 36															
		d					21 37															
Rugby		a	21 42			22 11	21 52							22 31								
Northampton	68	a				22 33				←	←	←	←	22 53								
Milton Keynes Central	66	a	22 04			22 58	22 15		21 51	22 04	22 15	22 21	22 58									
Watford Junction	66	a	→			→	→			22s34		23 06	23 44									
London Euston 15	⊖66	a			22 18				22 47	22 56	23 03	23 31	00 05									

Sundays

15 December to 10 May

Station			VT	LM	VT	XC	LM	VT	VT	LM	LM	LM	XC	LM	LM	VT	LM	LM	VT A	VT B	LM	VT	XC	LM
Crewe	65,50	d	08 43	08 48	08 53	09 05	09 12	09 13	09 43		09 49	09 52		10 10	10 10	10 14			10 44	10 44	10 51	10 55		11 05
Alsager	50	d					09 21								10 19									
Kidsgrove	50	d					09 25								10 24									
Hanley Bus Station		d																						
Stoke-on-Trent	50	d					09 35						10 06		10 33								11 06	
Wedgwood Old Road Bridge		d																						
Barlaston Orchard Place		d																						
Stone Granville Square		d																						
Stone Crown Street		d																						
Stone		d					09 43								10 42									
Norton Bridge Station Drv.		d																						
Stafford		d	09 02	09 11		09a24	09a55	09 32			10 15	10 20	10a22	10 31	10a52	10 33					11 12		11a23	11 30
Rugeley Trent Valley		d										10 29												
Lichfield Trent Valley		d			09 24							10 37					←							
Tamworth		d										10 44					10 44							
Polesworth		d										→												
Atherstone		d															10 52							
Nuneaton		a						09 54								10 55	10 58							
		d						09 55								10 56	11 00							
Rugby		a		10 26					10 31		11 26			11 47			11 19		11 31	11 31	12 26			12 47
Northampton	68	a		10 46						←	11 48			12 09			11 41	←			12 48			13 09
Milton Keynes Central	66	a		11 22	10 19				11 06	11 22	12 04			12 26		11 45	11 58	12 04	12 05	12 05	13 04			13 27
Watford Junction	66	a	10s33	→				11s15	11s42	11 53	→			→			12 31	12 38			→	12s36		→
London Euston 15	⊖66	a	10 56		11 04			11 34	12 02	12 16						12 29	12 49	12 59	12 42	12 43		12 53		

A until 16 February

B from 23 February

Crewe and Stoke-on-Trent - London

	LM	VT	LM	LM	VT	VT	LM	LM	LM	XC	LM	LM	LM	VT	LM	VT	VT	LM	LM	XC	VT	LM
	1	◇1	1	1	◇1	◇1	1	1	1	◇1	1	1	1	◇1	1	◇1	◇1	1	1	◇1	◇1	1
		⊡			⊡	⊡				⊼				⊡		⊡	⊡			⊼	⊡	
Crewe 65,50 d	11 12	11 14		11 23	11 42	11 49					12 12	12 16	12 19	12 23		12 30	12 56				13 02	13 12
Alsager 50 d	11 20										12 20											13 20
Kidsgrove 50 d	11 25										12 25											13 25
Hanley Bus Station d																						
Stoke-on-Trent 50 d	11 34									12 06	12 34									13 06		13 33
Wedgwood Old Road Bridge d																						
Barlaston Orchard Place d																						
Stone Granville Square d																						
Stone Crown Street d																						
Stone d	11 43										12 43											13 42
Norton Bridge Station Drv d																						
Stafford d	11a53	11 36		11 41					12 12	12a24	12a53	12 37	12 38	12 43	13 13					13a24		13a53
Rugeley Trent Valley d				11 51								12 46										
Lichfield Trent Valley d				11 58								12 54										
Tamworth d				12 05								13 00										
Polesworth d																						
Atherstone d				12 13								13 09										
Nuneaton a		11 58		12 19		12 31						13 15										
d		11 59		12 20		12 32						13 15										
Rugby a				12 35					13 27			13 30	13 57		14 27							
Northampton 68 a			←				←	←	13 48				14 19		14 48			←	←			
Milton Keynes Central 66 a			12 26	12 58		13 03	13 04	13 27	14 04			13 54	14 41		15 04		14 03	14 04	14 41		14 58	
Watford Junction 66 a		12s51	13 00				13 38	14 04	→				→		→			14 38	15 18		→	
London Euston 15 ⊖66 a		13 09	13 18	13 49	13 20	13 42	14 01	14 24				14 33		14 03		14 09	14 40	15 01	15 40			

	LM	LM	VT	VT	VT	XC	LM	VT	VT	LM	LM	XC	VT	LM	LM	LM	VT	VT	VT	XC	LM
	1	1	◇1	◇1	◇1	◇1	1	◇1	◇1	1	1	◇1	◇1	1	1	1	◇1	◇1	◇1	◇1	1
			⊡	⊡	⊡	⊼		⊡	⊡			⊼	⊡				⊡	⊡	⊡	⊼	
Crewe 65,50 d	13 16	13 19	13 23	13 30				13 52	13 53				14 02	14 12	14 16	14 19	14 23	14 30			
Alsager 50 d														14 20							
Kidsgrove 50 d														14 25							
Hanley Bus Station d																					
Stoke-on-Trent 50 d						13 45						14 08		14 34						14 45	
Wedgwood Old Road Bridge d																					
Barlaston Orchard Place d																					
Stone Granville Square d																					
Stone Crown Street d																					
Stone d														14 43							
Norton Bridge Station Drv d																					
Stafford d	13 37	13 38	13 43			14a00	14 12					14a24		14a53	14 37	14 40	14 43			15a00	15 12
Rugeley Trent Valley d	13 46														14 46						
Lichfield Trent Valley d	13 54														14 54						
Tamworth d	14 00														15 00						
Polesworth d																					
Atherstone d	14 09														15 09						
Nuneaton a	14 15							14 31	14 31						15 15						
d	14 15							14 32	14 32						15 15						
Rugby a	14 30	14 57					15 27								15 30	15 57					16 27
Northampton 68 a		15 19			←		15 48			←	←					16 19			←		16 48
Milton Keynes Central 66 a	14 54	15 41			14 58		16 04	15 03	15 03	15 04	15 41		15 58		15 54	16 41			15 58		17 04
Watford Junction 66 a		→					→			15 38	16 18		→			→					→
London Euston 15 ⊖66 a	15 33		15 03	15 06	15 37			15 41	15 41	16 01	16 40				16 33		16 03	16 06	16 37		

	VT	VT	LM	LM	XC	VT	LM	LM	LM	VT	VT	VT	XC	LM	VT	LM	LM	XC	VT	LM	LM	LM
	◇1	◇1	1	1	◇1	◇1	1	1	1	◇1	◇1	◇1	◇1	1	◇1	1	1	◇1	◇1	1	1	1
	⊡	⊡			⊼	⊡				⊡	⊡	⊡	⊼		⊡			⊼	⊡			
Crewe 65,50 d	14 55	14 56				15 02	15 15	15 16	15 19	15 23	15 30				15 54				16 01	16 15	16 16	16 19
Alsager 50 d							15 24													16 24		
Kidsgrove 50 d							15 28													16 28		
Hanley Bus Station d																						
Stoke-on-Trent 50 d					15 06		15 37						15 45					16 07		16 37		
Wedgwood Old Road Bridge d																						
Barlaston Orchard Place d																						
Stone Granville Square d																						
Stone Crown Street d																						
Stone d							15 47													16 46		
Norton Bridge Station Drv d																						
Stafford d					15a23		15a57	15 37	15 40	15 43			16a00	16 12				16a23		16a56	16 37	16 38
Rugeley Trent Valley d								15 46													16 46	
Lichfield Trent Valley d								15 54													16 54	
Tamworth d								16 00													17 00	
Polesworth d																						
Atherstone d								16 09													17 09	
Nuneaton a								16 15													17 15	
d								16 15													17 15	
Rugby a								16 30	16 57					17 27							17 30	17 57
Northampton 68 a			←	←					17 19			←		17 48		←	←					18 19
Milton Keynes Central 66 a	16 03	16 03	16 04	16 41		16 58		16 53	17 41			16 58		18 04	17 03	17 04	17 41		17 57		17 53	18 41
Watford Junction 66 a			16 38	17 18		→			→					→		17 38	18 18		→			→
London Euston 15 ⊖66 a	16 40	16 40	17 01	17 40				17 32		17 04	17 07	17 36			17 40	18 01	18 40				18 32	

Table T067-R

Sundays

15 December to 10 May

Crewe and Stoke-on-Trent - London

	VT	VT	VT	XC	LM	VT	LM	LM	XC	VT	VT	LM	LM	LM	VT	VT	VT	VT	XC	LM	VT
	◇1	◇1	◇1	◇1	1	◇1	1	1	◇1	◇1	◇1	1	1	1	◇1	◇1	◇1	◇1	◇1	1	◇1
										A	B						A	B			A
	⊡	⊡	⊡	⊼		⊡			⊼	⊡	⊡				⊡	⊡	⊡	⊡	⊼		⊡
Crewe 65,50 d	16 23	16 30				16 54				17 02	17 02	17 15	17 16	17 19	17 23	17 30					17 55
Alsager 50 d												17 23									
Kidsgrove 50 d												17 28									
Hanley Bus Station d																					
Stoke-on-Trent 50 d				16 45					17 08			17 37							17 45		
Wedgwood Old Road Bridge d																					
Barlaston Orchard Place d																					
Stone Granville Square d																					
Stone Crown Street d																					
Stone d												17 47									
Norton Bridge Station Drv d																					
Stafford d	16 43			17a00	17 12				17a24			17a57	17 37	17 38	17 42				18a00	18 12	
Rugeley Trent Valley d													17 46								
Lichfield Trent Valley d						17 25							17 54								
Tamworth d													18 00								
Polesworth d																					
Atherstone d													18 09								
Nuneaton a													18 15								
d													18 15								
Rugby a					18 25								18 30	18 57						19 28	
Northampton 68 a			←		18 46		←	←						19 21			←	←		19 48	
Milton Keynes Central 66 a			17 57		19 04	18 02	18 04	18 41		18 59	19 00		18 53	19 41			18 59	19 00		20 09	19 03
Watford Junction 66 a					→		18 38	19 18		→	→			→						→	
London Euston 15 ⊖66 a	18 03	18 06	18 35			18 39	19 01	19 40					19 32		19 02	19 05	19 36	19 39			19 41

	VT	LM	LM	XC	VT	LM	LM	LM	VT	VT	VT	XC	LM	VT	LM	LM	VT	XC	LM	LM	VT	VT
	◇1	1	1	◇1	◇1	1	1	1	◇1	◇1	◇1	◇1	1	◇1	1	1	◇1	◇1	1	1	◇1	◇1
	B																					
	⊡			⊼	⊡				⊡	⊡	⊡	⊼		⊡			⊡	⊼			⊡	⊡
Crewe 65,50 d	17 55				18 03	18 16	18 16	18 19	18 23	18 29				18 55			19 01		19 15	19 18	19 23	19 29
Alsager 50 d							18 24												19 24			
Kidsgrove 50 d							18 29												19 29			
Hanley Bus Station d																						
Stoke-on-Trent 50 d				18 06			18 38					18 46						19 06	19 38			
Wedgwood Old Road Bridge d																						
Barlaston Orchard Place d																						
Stone Granville Square d																						
Stone Crown Street d																						
Stone d							18 48												19 48			
Norton Bridge Station Drv d																						
Stafford d				18a25		18 37	18a58	18 38	18 43			19a01	19 12					19a22	19a58	19 37	19 43	
Rugeley Trent Valley d						18 46																
Lichfield Trent Valley d						18 54																
Tamworth d						19 00																
Polesworth d																						
Atherstone d						19 09																
Nuneaton a						19 15																
d						19 15																
Rugby a						19 30		19 57					20 28							20 47		
Northampton 68 a		←	←					20 19			←		20 48		←	←				21 09		
Milton Keynes Central 66 a	19 03	19 04	19 41		19 58	19 53		20 40			19 58			20 03	20 09	20 40	20 59					
Watford Junction 66 a		19 38	20 18		→			→							20 51	21 23						
London Euston 15 ⊖66 a	19 42	20 01	20 40			20 32			20 03	20 06	20 37			20 41	21 14	21 43	21 47				21 02	21 10

	LM	XC	LM	XC	LM	LM	LM	VT	XC	VT	LM	LM	AW	LM	LM	VT	LM	LM	VT	XC	LM	LM	XC
	1	◇1	1	◇1	1	1	1	◇1	◇1	◇1	1	1	◇	1	1	◇1	1	1	◇1	◇1	1	1	◇1
		⊼		⊼				⊡		⊡			⊼			⊡			⊡				
Crewe 65,50 d	19 33		19 50		20 04	20 16	20 19	20 24		20 49			20 52	21 08	21 19	21 24		21 33	21 41		22 11	22 21	
Alsager 50 d					20 13									21 17							22 19		
Kidsgrove 50 d					20 17									21 21							22 24		
Hanley Bus Station d																							
Stoke-on-Trent 50 d		19 46		20 06	20 25				20 44					21 30						21 46	22 32		22 44
Wedgwood Old Road Bridge d																							
Barlaston Orchard Place d																							
Stone Granville Square d																							
Stone Crown Street d																							
Stone d					20 33									21 39							22 41		
Norton Bridge Station Drv d																							
Stafford d	19 51	20a01	20 12	20a22	20a44	20 34	20 39	20 43	21a00				21a13	21a51	21 38	21 43		21 51	22a00	22a04	22a51	22a41	23a00
Rugeley Trent Valley d	20 00					20 44												22 00					
Lichfield Trent Valley d	20 08					20 51										22 00		22 08					
Tamworth d	20 14					20 58										22 07		22 15					
Polesworth d																							
Atherstone d	20 22					21 06												22 23					
Nuneaton a	20 28					21 12										22 17		22 29					
d	20 29					21 15										22 18		22 30					
Rugby a	20 44		21 27			21 31	21 57								22 55	22 31		22 45					
Northampton 68 a			21 49			21 53	22 18				←	←			23 16		←	23 08					
Milton Keynes Central 66 a	21 06					22 11	22 41	21 37		21 52	22 11	22 41			23 41	23 04	23 41						
Watford Junction 66 a	21 38					→	→			22s31	22 54	23 22			→	23s34	00 22						
London Euston 15 ⊖66 a	21 58							22 27		22 53	23 17	23 43				23 53	00 43						

A until 16 February

B from 23 February

Table T068-F

Mondays to Fridays

16 December to 15 May

Northampton - Coventry - Birmingham - Wolverhampton - Stafford

Miles			LM MX A	VT MO B	LM MX B	VT MX B	VT MX B	VT C	XC D	LM E	LM F		LM E	LM	VT G	LM H	AW I	LM F	XC D	LM J	LM K		LM	LM	XC D
—	London Euston ⊖66	d																							
0	**Northampton** 66	d														05 16		05 20							
9½	Long Buckby	d														05 26		05 31							
18¾	Rugby	d				00 01	01 00									05 38		05 42							
32¼	**Coventry**	a				00 10	01 13									05 48									
—		d				00 10	01 13							05 45		05 49								06 11	
34	Canley	d												05 48										06 14	
36	Tile Hill	d												05 52		05 56								06 18	
38	Berkswell	d			00 02									05 55										06 21	
41¼	Hampton-in-Arden	d			00 07									05 59		06 03								06 25	
43	**Birmingham International** ✈	a			00 10	00 20	01 23							06 02		06 06								06 28	
—		d		00 08	00 10	00 20	01 23						05 52	06 03		06 06								06 29	
45	Marston Green	d			00 13								05 55			06 09								06 32	
46½	Lea Hall	d			00 17								05 58			06 13									
47¾	Stechford	d			00 19								06 01			06 15									
49½	Adderley Park	d			00 23								06 04								←			06 36	
51½	**BirminghamNewStreet**	a		00 19	00 28	00 32	01 35						06 09	06 12		06 22					06 09			06 42	
—		d		00 22		00 34	01 37	05 30	05 57	06 02	06 07		06 36		06 15		06 25		06 30	06 33	06 36		06 39		06 53
54¾	Smethwick Rolfe Street	d	00 01								06 12		→										06 45		
55½	Smethwick Galton Bridge	d	00 03							06 08	06 15						06 31				06 43		06 47		
56¾	Sandwell & Dudley	d	00 06								06 18				06 24								06 50		
57¾	Dudley Port	d	00 10								06 22												06 54		
58½	Tipton	d	00 12								06 24												06 56		
60	Coseley	d	00 15							06 15	06 27										06 51		06 59		
64¼	**Wolverhampton**	a	00 21	00 39		01 00	02 04	05 47	06 13	06 21	06 32				06 37		06 43		06 47	06 51	06 56		07 04		07 09
—		d						05 48	06 14	06 22	06 32								06 48		06 56				07 10
74¼	Penkridge	d								06 30											07 05				
79½	**Stafford**	a						06 00	06 27	06 37	06 46							06 33	07 01		07 12				07 23

		LM J	LM L	LM A	LM F	LM	LM M		VT N	LM F	AW O	LM J	XC D	LM E	LM	LM M	VT		XC P	LM J	LM E	LM	LM Q	VT G	LM
London Euston ⊖66	d																06 20				05 34			06 43	
Northampton 66	d		05 56		06 00		06 04			06 04					06 14						06 57				07 15
Long Buckby	d		06 07		06 11		06 15			06 15					06 29						07 08				07 26
Rugby	d		06 19		06 22		06 32			06 32					06 50		07 13				07 19				07 37
Coventry	a		06 29				06 42			06 42					07 01		07 22				07 29			07 42	07 48
	d		06 30				06 43			06 43					07 06	07 18	07 22		07 27		07 30			07 42	07 49
Canley	d						06 46			06 46					07 09	07 21									
Tile Hill	d		06 35				06 50			06 50					07 13						07 35				07 54
Berkswell	d						06 53			06 53					07 16										07 57
Hampton-in-Arden	d						06 57			06 57					07 21										08 01
Birmingham International ✈	a		06 41				07 00			07 00					07 24	07 29	07 33		07 36		07 41			07 53	08 04
	d		06 46			06 52	07 01			07 01	07 09			07 18	07 24	07 30	07 33		07 38		07 42	07 46		07 53	08 05
Marston Green	d					06 55	07 04			07 04					07 27							07 49			08 08
Lea Hall	d					06 58								07 23								07 52			
Stechford	d					07 01								07 26								07 55			
Adderley Park	d													07 29											08 13
BirminghamNewStreet	a		07 01			07 08	07 13			07 13	07 21			07 33	07 36	07 40	07 45		07 48		07 51	08 01		08 09	08 17
	d	07 00	07 04	07 07					07 15	07 20	07 23	07 26	07 31	07 36	07 39				07 57	08 00	08 04		08 07	08 15	
Smethwick Rolfe Street	d			07 12											07 45								08 13		
Smethwick Galton Bridge	d		07 10	07 15						07 26	07 29	07 33			07 47						08 10		08 15		
Sandwell & Dudley	d	07 08		07 18					07 24						07 50					08 08			08 18	08 24	
Dudley Port	d			07 22											07 53								08 22		
Tipton	d			07 24											07 56								08 24		
Coseley	d			07 27										07 47	07 59								08 27		
Wolverhampton	a	07 18	07 22	07 33					07 37	07 38	07 42	07 45	07 48	07 53	08 04				08 13	08 18	08 21		08 33	08 37	
	d		07 23							07 40			07 49	07 54					08 14		08 22				
Penkridge	d		07 32											08 03							08 31				
Stafford	a		07 39		07 18					07 54			08 02	08 10					08 27		08 38				

A From Rugeley Trent Valley
B From London Euston
C To Holyhead
D To Manchester Piccadilly
E To Liverpool Lime Street
F To Crewe
G To Edinburgh
H To Walsall
I To Aberystwyth
J To Shrewsbury
K From Birmingham International to Liverpool Lime Street
L From Milton Keynes Central to Liverpool Lime Street
M To Rugeley Trent Valley
N To Glasgow Central
O To Llandudno
P From Southampton Central to Manchester Piccadilly
Q From Walsall

NRT DECEMBER 19 EDITION

Table T068-F

Mondays to Fridays

16 December to 15 May

Northampton - Coventry - Birmingham - Wolverhampton - Stafford

		LM A	AW B	VT	XC C	LM D	LM E	LM F	LM G		VT	XC H	LM D	LM E	LM	LM	VT I	LM A	AW B		VT	XC J	LM D	LM E	LM F
London Euston ⊖66	d			07 03					06 12		07 23			06 34			07 43	07 13			08 03				
Northampton 66	d								07 38					07 56				08 14							
Long Buckby	d								07 48					08 07				08 25							
Rugby	d			07 51					08 00					08 19				08 37			08 51				
Coventry	a			08 02					08 10		08 22			08 29			08 42	08 47			09 02				
	d			08 02					08 11		08 22	08 27		08 30			08 42	08 47			09 02				
Canley	d								08 14									08 50							
Tile Hill	d								08 18					08 35				08 54							
Berkswell	d								08 21									08 57							
Hampton-in-Arden	d								08 25									09 02							
Birmingham International ✈	a			08 13					08 28		08 33	08 36		08 41			08 53	09 05			09 13				
	d		08 08	08 13			08 17		08 29		08 33	08 38		08 42	08 46		08 53	09 05	09 10		09 13			09 18	
Marston Green	d						08 20		08 32						08 49			09 08							
Lea Hall	d						08 23								08 52									09 23	
Stechford	d						08 26							08 47										09 26	
Adderley Park	d						08 29																	09 29	
BirminghamNewStreet	a		08 21	08 25			08 34		08 42		08 45	08 48		08 54	09 00		09 05	09 18	09 22		09 24			09 34	
	d	08 21	08 25		08 31	08 35	08 38	08 41				08 57	09 00	09 04		09 07	09 15	09 21	09 25			09 31	09 34	09 37	09 40
Smethwick Rolfe Street	d							08 47								09 13									09 46
Smethwick Galton Bridge	d	08 28	08 31				08 45	08 49						09 10		09 15		09 28	09 31						09 48
Sandwell & Dudley	d							08 52					09 08			09 17	09 24								09 51
Dudley Port	d							08 56								09 21									09 55
Tipton	d							08 58								09 23									09 57
Coseley	d						08 52	09 01								09 27								09 50	10 00
Wolverhampton	a	08 40	08 44		08 47	08 52	08 58	09 07				09 13	09 18	09 21		09 33	09 37	09 39	09 43			09 47	09 51	09 56	10 05
	d	08 42			08 48		08 58					09 14		09 22				09 40				09 48		09 57	
Penkridge	d						09 07							09 30										10 06	
Stafford	a	08 55			09 01		09 13					09 27		09 38				09 54				10 01		10 12	

		LM G	VT	XC K	LM D		LM E	LM	LM F	VT L	LM M	LM A	AW B	VT	XC N		LM D	LM E	LM F	LM G	VT	XC K	LM D	LM E	LM
London Euston ⊖66	d	07 23	08 23				07 49			08 43	08 13	08 13		09 03						08 22	09 23			08 49	
Northampton 66	d	08 39					08 56				09 14	09 14								09 38				09 54	
Long Buckby	d	08 50					09 07				09 25	09 25								09 49				10 06	
Rugby	d	09 01					09 18				09 36	09 36		09 51						10 00				10 18	
Coventry	a	09 12	09 22				09 29			09 42	09 46	09 46		10 02						10 10	10 22			10 29	
	d	09 12	09 22	09 27			09 30			09 42	09 47	09 47		10 02						10 11	10 22	10 27		10 30	
Canley	d	09 15									09 50	09 50								10 14					
Tile Hill	d	09 19					09 35				09 54	09 54								10 18				10 35	
Berkswell	d	09 22									09 57	09 57								10 21					
Hampton-in-Arden	d	09 26									10 01	10 01								10 25					
Birmingham International ✈	a	09 29	09 33	09 36			09 41			09 53	10 04	10 04		10 13						10 28	10 33	10 36		10 41	
	d	09 30	09 33	09 38			09 42	09 46		09 53	10 05	10 05	10 09	10 13				10 17		10 29	10 34	10 38		10 42	10 46
Marston Green	d	09 33						09 49			10 08	10 08								10 32					10 49
Lea Hall	d							09 52										10 22							10 52
Stechford	d							09 55										10 25							10 55
Adderley Park	d																	10 28							
BirminghamNewStreet	a	09 41	09 45	09 49			09 54	10 01		10 04	10 15	10 15	10 20	10 26				10 34		10 41	10 44	10 48		10 54	11 01
	d			09 57	10 00		10 04		10 07	10 15		10 20	10 25		10 31		10 34	10 37	10 40			10 57	11 00	11 04	
Smethwick Rolfe Street	d								10 13										10 49						
Smethwick Galton Bridge	d						10 10		10 15			10 27	10 31						10 51					11 10	
Sandwell & Dudley	d				10 08				10 17	10 24									10 54				11 08		
Dudley Port	d								10 21										10 58						
Tipton	d								10 23										11 00						
Coseley	d								10 27									10 50	11 04						
Wolverhampton	a			10 13	10 18		10 21		10 33	10 37		10 39	10 43		10 47		10 51	10 56	11 09			11 13	11 18	11 21	
	d			10 14			10 22					10 40			10 48			10 57				11 14		11 22	
Penkridge	d						10 30											11 06						11 31	
Stafford	a			10 27			10 37					10 55			11 01			11 12				11 27		11 38	

A To Crewe
B To Aberystwyth
C From Bristol Temple Meads to Manchester Piccadilly
D To Shrewsbury
E To Liverpool Lime Street
F From Walsall
G To Rugeley Trent Valley
H From Southampton Central to Manchester Piccadilly
I To Glasgow Central
J From Cardiff Central to Manchester Piccadilly
K From Bournemouth to Manchester Piccadilly
L To Edinburgh
M To Walsall
N From Paignton to Manchester Piccadilly

Table T068-F

Northampton - Coventry - Birmingham - Wolverhampton - Stafford

Mondays to Fridays
16 December to 15 May

		LM	VT	LM	LM	AW	VT	XC	LM	LM	LM	LM	VT	VT	XC	LM	LM	LM	LM	VT	LM	LM	AW
		A	◇■ B ⊠	■ C	■ D	◇ E ⊥	◇■ ⊠	◇■ F ⊥	G	■ H	A	■ I	◇■ ⊠	◇■ G ⊠	■ ◇■ J ⊥	G	■ H		■ A	◇■ K ▭	■ C	■ D	■ L ⊥
London Euston ⊖66	d		09 43	09 13	09 13		10 03					09 24	10 23	10 23			09 49			10 43	10 15	10 15	
Northampton 66	d			10 15	10 15							10 38					10 56				11 14	11 14	
Long Buckby	d			10 26	10 26							10 49					11 07				11 25	11 25	
Rugby	d			10 37	10 37		10 51					11 01					11 18				11 36	11 36	
Coventry	a		10 42	10 47	10 47		11 02					11 11	11 22	11 22			11 29			11 42	11 46	11 46	
	d		10 42	10 48	10 48		11 02					11 11	11 22	11 22	11 27		11 30			11 42	11 47	11 47	
Canley	d			10 51	10 51							11 14									11 50	11 50	
Tile Hill	d			10 55	10 55							11 18					11 35				11 54	11 54	
Berkswell	d			10 58	10 58							11 21									11 57	11 57	
Hampton-in-Arden	d			11 02	11 02							11 26									12 01	12 01	
Birmingham International ✈	a		10 53	11 05	11 05		11 13					11 29	11 33	11 33	11 36		11 41			11 53	12 04	12 04	
	d		10 53	11 06	11 06	11 10	11 13			11 19		11 29	11 33	11 33	11 38		11 42	11 46		11 53	12 05	12 05	12 09
Marston Green	d			11 09	11 09							11 32						11 49			12 08	12 08	
Lea Hall	d									11 24								11 52					
Stechford	d									11 27								11 55					
Adderley Park	d									11 30													
BirminghamNewStreet	a		11 05	11 16	11 16	11 21	11 24			11 34		11 41	11 45	11 45	11 48		11 54	12 01		12 04	12 15	12 15	12 22
	d	11 07	11 15		11 21	11 25		11 31	11 34	11 37	11 40			11 52	11 57	12 00	12 04		12 08	12 15		12 20	12 25
Smethwick Rolfe Street	d	11 13									11 46								12 14				
Smethwick Galton Bridge	d	11 15			11 28	11 31					11 48						12 10		12 16			12 27	12 31
Sandwell & Dudley	d	11 17	11 24								11 51					12 08			12 19	12 24			
Dudley Port	d	11 21									11 55								12 22				
Tipton	d	11 23									11 57								12 24				
Coseley	d	11 27								11 48	12 00								12 27				
Wolverhampton	a	11 33	11 37		11 40	11 43		11 47	11 51	11 54	12 05			12 10	12 13	12 18	12 21		12 33	12 37		12 38	12 43
	d				11 41			11 48		11 55					12 14		12 22					12 40	
Penkridge	d									12 04							12 31						
Stafford	a				11 56			12 01		12 11					12 27		12 38					12 55	

		VT	XC	LM	LM	LM	LM	VT	XC	LM	LM	LM	LM	VT	LM	LM	AW	VT	XC	LM	LM	LM
		◇■ ⊠	◇■ F ⊥	G	■ H	■ A	■ I	◇■ ⊠	◇■ J ⊥	G	■ H		■ A	◇■ B ⊠	■ C	■ D	◇ E ⊥	◇■ ⊠	◇■ M ⊥	G	■ H	■ A
London Euston ⊖66	d	11 03					10 24	11 23			10 49			11 43	11 15	11 15		12 03				
Northampton 66	d						11 38				11 56				12 14	12 14						
Long Buckby	d						11 49				12 07				12 25	12 25						
Rugby	d	11 51					12 00				12 18				12 37	12 37		12 51				
Coventry	a	12 02					12 10	12 22			12 29			12 42	12 47	12 47		13 02				
	d	12 02					12 11	12 22	12 27		12 30			12 42	12 47	12 47		13 02				
Canley	d						12 14								12 50	12 50						
Tile Hill	d						12 18				12 35				12 54	12 54						
Berkswell	d						12 21								12 57	12 57						
Hampton-in-Arden	d						12 25								13 02	13 02						
Birmingham International ✈	a	12 13					12 28	12 33	12 36		12 41			12 53	13 05	13 05		13 13				
	d	12 13			12 18		12 29	12 33	12 38		12 42	12 46		12 53	13 05	13 05	13 09	13 13			13 18	
Marston Green	d						12 32					12 49			13 08	13 08						
Lea Hall	d				12 23							12 52									13 23	
Stechford	d				12 26							12 55									13 26	
Adderley Park	d				12 29																13 29	
BirminghamNewStreet	a	12 25			12 34		12 40	12 44	12 48		12 54	13 01		13 04	13 16	13 16	13 22	13 24			13 34	
	d		12 31	12 34	12 37	12 40			12 57	13 00	13 04		13 07	13 15		13 21	13 25		13 31	13 34	13 37	13 40
Smethwick Rolfe Street	d					12 46							13 13									13 46
Smethwick Galton Bridge	d					12 48					13 10		13 15			13 28	13 31					13 48
Sandwell & Dudley	d					12 51				13 08			13 17	13 24								13 51
Dudley Port	d					12 55							13 21									13 55
Tipton	d					12 57							13 23									13 57
Coseley	d				12 50	13 00							13 27								13 50	14 00
Wolverhampton	a		12 47	12 51	12 56	13 06			13 13	13 18	13 21		13 33	13 37		13 39	13 43		13 47	13 51	13 56	14 06
	d		12 48		12 57				13 14		13 22					13 40			13 48		13 57	
Penkridge	d				13 06						13 30										14 06	
Stafford	a		13 01		13 12				13 27		13 36					13 55			14 01		14 12	

A From Walsall
B To Glasgow Central
C To Walsall
D To Crewe
E To Holyhead
F From Bristol Temple Meads to Manchester Piccadilly
G To Shrewsbury
H To Liverpool Lime Street
I To Rugeley Trent Valley
J From Bournemouth to Manchester Piccadilly
K To Edinburgh
L To Aberystwyth
M From Paignton to Manchester Piccadilly

Table T068-F

Northampton - Coventry - Birmingham - Wolverhampton - Stafford

Mondays to Fridays
16 December to 15 May

		LM	VT	XC	LM	LM	LM	LM	VT	LM	LM	AW	VT	XC	LM	LM	LM	LM	VT	XC	LM	LM	LM
		■ A	◇■ ⊠	◇■ B ⊥	C	■ D		E	◇■ F ⊠	■ G	■ H	◇ I ⊥	◇■ ▭	◇■ J ⊥	C	■ D	■ E	■ A	◇■ ▭	◇■ B ⊥	C	■ D	
London Euston ⊖66	d	11 24	12 23			11 49			12 43	12 15	12 15		13 03					12 24	13 23			12 49	
Northampton 66	d	12 38				12 56				13 14	13 14							13 38				13 54	
Long Buckby	d	12 49				13 07				13 25	13 25							13 49				14 05	
Rugby	d	13 00				13 18				13 37	13 37		13 51					14 01				14 18	
Coventry	a	13 10	13 22			13 29			13 42	13 47	13 47		14 02					14 11	14 22			14 29	
	d	13 11	13 22	13 27		13 30			13 42	13 47	13 47		14 02					14 11	14 22	14 27		14 30	
Canley	d	13 14								13 50	13 50							14 14					
Tile Hill	d	13 18				13 35				13 54	13 54							14 18				14 35	
Berkswell	d	13 21								13 57	13 57							14 21					
Hampton-in-Arden	d	13 25								14 02	14 02							14 26					
Birmingham International ✈	a	13 28	13 33	13 36		13 41			13 53	14 05	14 05		14 13					14 29	14 33	14 36		14 41	
	d	13 29	13 33	13 38		13 42	13 46		13 53	14 05	14 05	14 09	14 13			14 18		14 29	14 33	14 38		14 42	14 46
Marston Green	d	13 32					13 49			14 08	14 08							14 32					14 49
Lea Hall	d						13 52									14 23							14 52
Stechford	d						13 55									14 26							14 55
Adderley Park	d															14 29							
BirminghamNewStreet	a	13 40	13 44	13 48		13 51	14 01		14 04	14 16	14 16	14 22	14 26			14 34		14 40	14 45	14 48		14 51	15 01
	d			13 57	14 00	14 04		14 07	14 15		14 21	14 25		14 31	14 34	14 37	14 40			14 57	15 00	15 04	
Smethwick Rolfe Street	d							14 13									14 46						
Smethwick Galton Bridge	d					14 10		14 15			14 28	14 31					14 48					15 10	
Sandwell & Dudley	d				14 08			14 17	14 24								14 51				15 08		
Dudley Port	d							14 21									14 55						
Tipton	d							14 23									14 57						
Coseley	d							14 27								14 50	15 00						
Wolverhampton	a			14 13	14 18	14 21		14 33	14 36		14 39	14 43		14 47	14 51	14 56	15 06			15 13	15 18	15 21	
	d			14 14		14 22					14 40			14 48		14 57				15 14		15 22	
Penkridge	d					14 30										15 06						15 31	
Stafford	a			14 27		14 37					14 54			15 01		15 12				15 27		15 38	

		LM	VT	LM	LM	AW	VT	XC	LM	LM	LM	LM	VT	XC	LM	LM	LM	LM	VT	LM	LM	AW
		E	◇■ K ▭	■ G	■ H	◇ L ⊥	◇■ ▭	◇■ M ⊥	C	■ D	■ E	■ A	◇■ ▭	◇■ B ⊥	C	■ D		E	■ ■ F ▭	■ G	■ H	■ I ⊥
London Euston ⊖66	d		13 43	13 15	13 15		14 03					13 24	14 23			13 49			14 43	14 15	14 15	
Northampton 66	d			14 14	14 14							14 39				14 56				15 14	15 14	
Long Buckby	d			14 25	14 25							14 50				15 07				15 26	15 26	
Rugby	d			14 37	14 37		14 51					15 01				15 18				15 38	15 38	
Coventry	a		14 42	14 47	14 47		15 02					15 11	15 22			15 29			15 42	15 48	15 48	
	d		14 42	14 48	14 48		15 02					15 12	15 22	15 27		15 30			15 42	15 48	15 48	
Canley	d			14 51	14 51							15 15								15 51	15 51	
Tile Hill	d			14 55	14 55							15 18				15 35				15 55	15 55	
Berkswell	d			14 58	14 58							15 21								15 58	15 58	
Hampton-in-Arden	d			15 02	15 02							15 25								16 02	16 02	
Birmingham International ✈	a		14 53	15 05	15 05		15 13					15 28	15 33	15 36		15 41			15 53	16 05	16 05	
	d		14 53	15 06	15 06	15 10	15 13			15 18		15 29	15 33	15 38		15 42	15 46		15 53	16 06	16 06	16 10
Marston Green	d			15 09	15 09							15 32					15 49			16 09	16 09	
Lea Hall	d									15 23							15 52					
Stechford	d									15 26							15 55					
Adderley Park	d									15 29												
BirminghamNewStreet	a		15 04	15 16	15 16	15 21	15 25			15 34		15 40	15 43	15 48		15 51	16 01		16 04	16 17	16 17	16 21
	d	15 07	15 15		15 21	15 25		15 31	15 34	15 37	15 40			15 57	16 00	16 04		16 07	16 15		16 22	16 25
Smethwick Rolfe Street	d	15 13									15 46							16 13				
Smethwick Galton Bridge	d	15 15			15 28	15 31					15 48					16 10		16 15			16 29	16 31
Sandwell & Dudley	d	15 17	15 24								15 51				16 08			16 17	16 24			
Dudley Port	d	15 21									15 55							16 21				
Tipton	d	15 23									15 57							16 23				
Coseley	d	15 27								15 48	16 00							16 27				
Wolverhampton	a	15 33	15 37		15 39	15 43		15 47	15 51	15 54	16 06			16 13	16 18	16 21		16 33	16 37		16 40	16 43
	d				15 40			15 48		15 55				16 14		16 22					16 41	
Penkridge	d									16 04						16 31						
Stafford	a				15 56			16 01		16 10				16 27		16 38					16 55	

A To Rugeley Trent Valley
B From Bournemouth to Manchester Piccadilly
C To Shrewsbury
D To Liverpool Lime Street
E From Walsall
F To Edinburgh
G To Walsall
H To Crewe
I To Aberystwyth
J From Bristol Temple Meads to Manchester Piccadilly
K To Glasgow Central
L To Holyhead
M From Plymouth to Manchester Piccadilly

Table T068-F

Mondays to Fridays
16 December to 15 May

Northampton - Coventry - Birmingham - Wolverhampton - Stafford

Station		VT	XC	LM	LM	LM	LM	VT	XC	LM	LM	LM	LM	VT	LM	AW	VT	XC	LM	LM	LM	LM
		◇1	◇1 A	B	1 C	D	1 E	◇1	◇1 F	B	1 C		1 D	1 G	1 H	◇ I	◇1	◇1 J	B	1 C	D	1 E
London Euston 15 ⊖66	d	15 03					14 24	15 23			14 49			15 43	15 15		16 03					15 24
Northampton 66	d						15 38				15 56				16 14							16 38
Long Buckby	d						15 49				16 07				16 25							16 50
Rugby	d	15 51					16 00				16 18				16 38		16 51					17 01
Coventry	a	16 02					16 10	16 22			16 29			16 42	16 48		17 02					17 11
	d	16 02					16 10	16 22	16 27		16 30			16 42	16 49		17 02					17 12
Canley	d						16 13								16 52							17 15
Tile Hill	d						16 17				16 35				16 56							17 18
Berkswell	d						16 20								16 59							17 21
Hampton-in-Arden	d						16 25								17 03							17 25
Birmingham International ✈	a	16 13					16 28	16 33	16 36		16 41			16 53	17 06		17 13					17 28
	d	16 13			16 18		16 28	16 33	16 38		16 42	16 46		16 53	17 07	17 11	17 13			17 18		17 29
Marston Green	d						16 31					16 49			17 10							17 32
Lea Hall	d				16 23							16 52								17 23		
Stechford	d				16 26							16 55								17 26		
Adderley Park	d				16 29															17 29		
BirminghamNewStreet 12	a	16 25			16 33		16 40	16 44	16 48		16 52	17 01		17 05	17 17	17 22	17 27			17 33		17 40
	d		16 31	16 34	16 37	16 40			16 57	17 00	17 04		17 07	17 15	17 22	17 26		17 31	17 34	17 37	17 40	
Smethwick Rolfe Street	d					16 46							17 13								17 46	
Smethwick Galton Bridge 7	d					16 48					17 10		17 15		17 28	17 32					17 48	
Sandwell & Dudley	d					16 51				17 08			17 17	17 24							17 51	
Dudley Port	d					16 55							17 21							17 47	17 55	
Tipton	d					16 57							17 23							17 49	17 57	
Coseley	d				16 50	17 00							17 27						17 46		18 00	
Wolverhampton 7	a		16 47	16 51	16 56	17 05			17 13	17 18	17 21		17 33	17 37	17 39	17 44		17 47	17 52	17 57	18 06	
	d		16 48		16 57				17 14		17 22				17 40			17 48		17 59		
Penkridge	d				17 06						17 31									18 08		
Stafford	a		17 02		17 13				17 27		17 38				17 56			18 01		18 14		

Station		VT	XC	LM	LM	LM	LM	VT	VT	LM	LM	AW	VT	XC	LM	LM	LM	LM	VT	XC	LM	LM	LM
		◇1	◇1 F	B	1 C		1 D	◇1 H	◇1 K	1 L	1 H	◇ I	◇1	◇1 M	B	1 C	D	1 E	◇1	◇1 F	B	1 H	
London Euston 15 ⊖66	d	16 23			15 49			16 43	16 43	16 15	16 15		17 03					16 30	17 23			16 52	
Northampton 66	d				16 55					17 13	17 13							17 39				17 58	
Long Buckby	d				17 06					17 25	17 25							17 50				18 09	
Rugby	d				17 18					17 36	17 36		17 51					18 01				18 20	
Coventry	a	17 22			17 29			17 42	17 42	17 47	17 47		18 02					18 11	18 22			18 30	
	d	17 22	17 27		17 30			17 42	17 42	17 47	17 47		18 02					18 11	18 22	18 27		18 30	
Canley	d									17 51	17 51							18 14					
Tile Hill	d				17 35					17 54	17 54							18 18				18 35	
Berkswell	d									17 58	17 58							18 21					
Hampton-in-Arden	d									18 01	18 01							18 26					
Birmingham International ✈	a	17 33	17 36		17 42			17 53	17 53	18 05	18 05		18 13					18 29	18 33	18 36		18 42	
	d	17 33	17 38		17 42	17 46		17 53	17 53	18 06	18 06	18 10	18 13			18 18		18 29	18 33	18 38		18 42	18 46
Marston Green	d					17 49				18 08	18 08							18 32					18 49
Lea Hall	d					17 52										18 23							18 52
Stechford	d					17 55										18 26							18 55
Adderley Park	d															18 29							
BirminghamNewStreet 12	a	17 44	17 48		17 52	18 01		18 04	18 05	18 16	18 16	18 21	18 25			18 34		18 40	18 45	18 48		18 52	19 01
	d		17 57	18 00	18 04		18 07	18 15	18 15		18 20	18 25		18 31	18 34	18 37	18 40			18 57	19 00	19 04	
Smethwick Rolfe Street	d						18 13										18 46						
Smethwick Galton Bridge 7	d				18 10		18 15				18 27	18 31					18 48					19 10	
Sandwell & Dudley	d			18 08			18 17	18 24	18 24								18 51				19 08		
Dudley Port	d						18 21										18 55						
Tipton	d						18 23										18 57						
Coseley	d						18 27									18 50	19 00						
Wolverhampton 7	a		18 13	18 18	18 21		18 33	18 36	18 37		18 38	18 44		18 47	18 51	18 56	19 05			19 13	19 18	19 21	
	d		18 14		18 22						18 40			18 48		18 57				19 14		19 22	
Penkridge	d				18 31											19 06						19 30	
Stafford	a		18 27		18 38						18 54			19 01		19 12				19 27		19 37	

A From Bristol Temple Meads to Manchester Piccadilly
B To Shrewsbury
C To Liverpool Lime Street
D From Walsall
E To Rugeley Trent Valley
F From Bournemouth to Manchester Piccadilly
G To Glasgow Central
H To Crewe
I To Aberystwyth
J From Exeter St Davids to Manchester Piccadilly
K To Edinburgh
L To Walsall
M From Paignton to Manchester Piccadilly

NRT DECEMBER 19 EDITION

Table T068-F

Mondays to Fridays
16 December to 15 May

Northampton - Coventry - Birmingham - Wolverhampton - Stafford

Station		LM	VT	LM	AW	LM	VT	XC	LM	LM	LM	LM	VT	XC	LM	LM	LM	LM	LM	VT	LM	AW
		A	◇1 B	1 C	◇ D	1	◇1	◇1 E	F	1 G	1 H	1 A	◇1	◇1 I	1	1 C		F	A	◇1 C	1 C	◇ J
London Euston 15 ⊖66	d		17 43			17 13	18 03				17 23		18 23		17 52					18 43	18 13	
Northampton 66	d					18 20					18 39				18 56						19 09	
Long Buckby	d					18 31					18 50				19 08						19 21	
Rugby	d					18 42	18 51				19 01				19 19						19 36	
Coventry	a		18 42			18 52	19 02				19 11		19 22		19 30					19 42	19 46	
	d		18 42			18 52	19 02				19 11		19 22	19 28	19 31					19 42	19 47	
Canley	d					18 55					19 14										19 50	
Tile Hill	d					18 59					19 18				19 36						19 54	
Berkswell	d					19 02					19 21										19 57	
Hampton-in-Arden	d					19 07					19 26										20 01	
Birmingham International ✈	a		18 53			19 10	19 13				19 29		19 33	19 37	19 42					19 53	20 04	
	d		18 53		19 05	19 10	19 13			19 18	19 29		19 33	19 38	19 43		19 46			19 53	20 05	20 09
Marston Green	d									19 21	19 32						19 49				20 08	
Lea Hall	d									19 24							19 53					
Stechford	d									19 27							19 56					
Adderley Park	d									19 30												
BirminghamNewStreet 12	a		19 05		19 17	19 20	19 24			19 35	19 41		19 44	19 48	19 52		20 03			20 08	20 15	20 22
	d	19 07	19 15	19 20	19 25		19 27	19 31	19 36	19 39		19 42	19 50	19 57		20 00		20 03	20 07	20 15	20 19	20 25
Smethwick Rolfe Street	d	19 13										19 48							20 13			
Smethwick Galton Bridge 7	d	19 15		19 27	19 31							19 50				20 07			20 15		20 27	20 31
Sandwell & Dudley	d	19 17	19 24									19 53	19 59					20 12	20 17	20 24		
Dudley Port	d	19 21										19 57							20 21			
Tipton	d	19 23										19 59							20 23			
Coseley	d	19 27								19 50		20 02							20 26			
Wolverhampton 7	a	19 33	19 37	19 39	19 43		20 00	19 49	19 53	19 56		20 07	20 11	20 13		20 19		20 22	20 33	20 37	20 39	20 43
	d			19 40				19 50		19 57				20 14		20 21				20 37	20 40	
Penkridge	d									20 06						20 30						
Stafford	a			19 57				20 03		20 12				20 27		20 36				20 50	20 54	

Station		VT	XC	LM	LM	LM	LM FO	VT	XC	LM	LM	LM	LM	VT	LM	LM	AW	VT	LM	LM	LM	VT	XC
		1	◇1 E	1 G	A	1 H	1 C	1	◇1 K	F	1 C		A	◇1 C	1 L	1 C	◇ M	◇1	1 G	1 N	1	◇1	◇1 K
London Euston 15 ⊖66	d	19 03				18 21	18 49	19 23			18 52			19 43	19 15	19 15		20 03				20 23	
Northampton 66	d					19 38	19 45				19 55				20 14	20 14							
Long Buckby	d					19 49					20 06				20 26	20 26							
Rugby	d	19 51				20 00	20 05				20 17				20 37	20 37		20 51					
Coventry	a	20 02				20 10		20 22			20 29			20 42	20 47	20 47		21 02				21 22	
	d	20 02				20 11		20 22	20 27		20 30			20 42	20 47	20 47		21 02			21 11	21 22	21 27
Canley	d					20 14									20 50	20 50					21 14		
Tile Hill	d					20 18					20 35				20 54	20 54					21 18		
Berkswell	d					20 21									20 57	20 57					21 21		
Hampton-in-Arden	d					20 25									21 01	21 01					21 25		
Birmingham International ✈	a	20 13				20 28		20 33	20 36		20 41			20 53	21 04	21 04		21 13			21 28	21 33	21 36
	d	20 13		20 18		20 29		20 33	20 38		20 42	20 46		20 53	21 05	21 05	21 09	21 13	21 17		21 29	21 33	21 38
Marston Green	d					20 32						20 49			21 08	21 08					21 32		
Lea Hall	d			20 23								20 52							21 22				
Stechford	d			20 26								20 55							21 24				
Adderley Park	d			20 29															21 28				
BirminghamNewStreet 12	a	20 25		20 34		20 40		20 45	20 48		20 51	21 01		21 05	21 16	21 16	21 21	21 26	21 34		21 41	21 44	21 48
	d		20 31	20 37	20 40			20 50	20 57	21 00	21 04		21 07	21 15		21 21	21 25	21 28	21 37	21 40		21 49	21 57
Smethwick Rolfe Street	d				20 46								21 12							21 45			
Smethwick Galton Bridge 7	d				20 48						21 10		21 15			21 29	21 32			21 48			
Sandwell & Dudley	d				20 50			20 59		21 08			21 18	21 24						21 51		21 59	
Dudley Port	d				20 54								21 22							21 55			
Tipton	d				20 56								21 24							21 57			
Coseley	d			20 50	21 00								21 27						21 50	22 00			
Wolverhampton 7	a		20 47	20 56	21 05			21 10	21 13	21 18	21 22		21 32	21 37		21 40	21 45	21 57	21 56	22 05		22 09	22 13
	d		20 48	20 57					21 14		21 23			21 37		21 41			21 57				22 14
Penkridge	d			21 06							21 32								22 06				
Stafford	a		21 01	21 12			20 56		21 27		21 41			21 53		21 58			22 12				22 27

A From Walsall
B To Glasgow Central
C To Crewe
D To Chester
E From Exeter St Davids to Manchester Piccadilly
F To Shrewsbury
G To Liverpool Lime Street
H To Rugeley Trent Valley
I From Bournemouth to Manchester Piccadilly
J To Aberystwyth
K From Bournemouth to Manchester Piccadilly. to BirminghamNewStreet
L To Walsall
M To Manchester Piccadilly
N From Rugeley Trent Valley

Table T068-F

Northampton - Coventry - Birmingham - Wolverhampton - Stafford

Mondays to Fridays

16 December to 15 May

		LM	VT	LM	LM	LM	XC	VT	LM	LM	LM	LM	XC	AW	LM	LM	VT	LM	AW	LM	XC	LM	LM
		■1	◇■1	■1		■1	◇■1	◇■1				■1	◇■1	◇	■1		◇■1	■1		■1	◇■1	■1	■1
		A		B	C		D		E				F	G	A	E			E	H	I		
			⊡					⊡									⊡						
London Euston 15 ⊖66	d	19 53	20 43			20 16		21 03							20 51		21 43	21 13				21 53	21 54
Northampton 66	d	20 57				21 15									21 57			22 20				22 56	23 19
Long Buckby	d	21 08				21 26									22 08			22 31				23 07	23 30
Rugby	d	21 20				21 38		21 58							22 20			22 42				23 18	23 41
Coventry	a	21 30	21 42			21 48		22 07							22 30		22 45	22 52				23 29	23 51
	d	21 31	21 42			21 49		22 07				22 12	22 27		22 31		22 46	22 53			23 20	23 30	23 52
Canley	d	21 34										22 15			22 34			22 56				23 33	23 55
Tile Hill	d	21 38				21 54						22 19			22 38			23 00				23 37	23 59
Berkswell	d	21 41										22 22			22 41			23 03				23 40	00 02
Hampton-in-Arden	d					22 00						22 26						23 07				23 44	00 07
Birmingham International ✈	a	21 46	21 53			22 03		22 17				22 29	22 36		22 46		22 59	23 10			23 29	23 47	00 10
	d	21 47	21 53			22 04		22 18		22 24		22 30	22 38		22 47		22 59	23 11			23 31	23 48	00 10
Marston Green	d	21 50				22 07						22 33			22 50			23 14				23 51	00 13
Lea Hall	d	21 53								22 28					22 53							23 54	00 17
Stechford	d	21 56								22 31					22 56							23 57	00 19
Adderley Park	d			←						22 34													00 23
BirminghamNewStreet 12	a	22 02	22 05	22 02		22 18		22 30		22 39		22 42	22 48		23 03		23 11	23 22			23 56	00 04	00 28
	d	22 12	22 08	22 12	22 16		22 30	22 33	22 36		22 40			22 52	23 09	23 15	23 18		23 35	23 55			
Smethwick Rolfe Street	d	→			22 21						22 46				23 14					00 01			
Smethwick Galton Bridge 7	d			22 19	22 24						22 49				23 17					00 03			
Sandwell & Dudley	d		22 17	22 22	22 27			22 42			22 52				23 20	23 25	23 32			00 06			
Dudley Port	d				22 31						22 56				23 24					00 10			
Tipton	d				22 33						22 58				23 26					00 12			
Coseley	d			22 28	22 36						23 01				23 29					00 15			
Wolverhampton 7	a		22 28	22 33	22 44		22 47	22 53	22 56		23 07			23 27	23 35	23 40	23 44		00 02	00 21			
	d			22 39			22 48							23 27	23 36								
Penkridge	d			22 49											23 45								
Stafford	a			22 57			23 01							23 43	23 52								

		VT	VT FX	VT FO
		◇■1	◇■1	◇■1
		⊡	⊡	⊡
London Euston 15 ⊖66	d	22 30	23 30	23 30
Northampton 66	d			
Long Buckby	d			
Rugby	d	00 01	01 00	01 07
Coventry	a	00 10	01 13	01 17
	d	00 10	01 13	01 17
Canley	d			
Tile Hill	d			
Berkswell	d			
Hampton-in-Arden	d			
Birmingham International ✈	a	00 20	01 23	01 27
	d	00 20	01 23	01 27
Marston Green	d			
Lea Hall	d			
Stechford	d			
Adderley Park	d			
BirminghamNewStreet 12	a	00 32	01 35	01 39
	d	00 34	01 37	01 42
Smethwick Rolfe Street	d			
Smethwick Galton Bridge 7	d			
Sandwell & Dudley	d			
Dudley Port	d			
Tipton	d			
Coseley	d			
Wolverhampton 7	a	01 00	02 04	02 08
	d			
Penkridge	d			
Stafford	a			

A To Crewe
B From London Euston to Crewe
C From Walsall
D To Manchester Piccadilly
E To Shrewsbury
F From Bournemouth
G To Holyhead
H From Rugeley Trent Valley
I From Reading

Table T068-F

Northampton - Coventry - Birmingham - Wolverhampton - Stafford

Saturdays

21 December to 16 May

		LM	LM	VT	VT	VT	XC	LM	LM	LM	VT	AW	XC	LM	LM	LM	XC	LM	LM	LM	LM	VT	LM
		■1	■1	◇■1	◇■1	◇■1	◇■1	■1	■1	■1	◇■1	◇	◇■1	■1		■1	◇■1		■1		■1	◇■1	■1
		A	B	B	B	C	D	E	F	F	G	H	D	E	I		D	J	K		F	L	F
				⊡	⊡	⊡					⊡	⊼	⊼				⊼					⊡	
London Euston 15 ⊖66	d																						
Northampton 66	d									05 41									05 56		06 04		06 37
Long Buckby	d																		06 07		06 15		
Rugby	d			00 01	01 07					06 02									06 18		06 28		06 57
Coventry	a			00 10	01 17														06 29		06 38		
	d			00 10	01 17			05 37								06 11			06 30		06 39		
Canley	d															06 14			06 33				
Tile Hill	d															06 18			06 37		06 44		
Berkswell	d		00 02													06 21			06 40				
Hampton-in-Arden	d		00 07													06 25					06 50		
Birmingham International ✈	a		00 10	00 20	01 27			05 46								06 28			06 45		06 53		
	d		00 10	00 20	01 27			05 47						06 18		06 29			06 46		06 54		
Marston Green	d		00 13					05 50								06 32			06 49		06 57		
Lea Hall	d		00 17											06 23					06 52				
Stechford	d		00 19											06 26					06 54				
Adderley Park	d		00 23											06 29									
BirminghamNewStreet 12	a		00 28	00 32	01 39			05 58						06 33		06 42			07 00		07 06		
	d			00 34	01 42	05 30	05 57	06 04	06 07		06 15	06 25	06 31	06 36	06 39		06 57	07 00	07 04	07 07	07 12	07 15	
Smethwick Rolfe Street	d	00 01							06 12						06 45					07 13			
Smethwick Galton Bridge 7	d	00 03							06 15			06 31		06 42	06 47				07 10	07 15			
Sandwell & Dudley	d	00 06							06 18		06 24				06 49			07 08		07 18		07 24	
Dudley Port	d	00 10							06 22						06 53					07 21			
Tipton	d	00 12							06 24						06 55					07 23			
Coseley	d	00 15							06 27					06 49	06 59					07 26			
Wolverhampton 7	a	00 21		01 00	02 08	05 47	06 13	06 19	06 32		06 37	06 43	06 47	06 55	07 04		07 13	07 18	07 22	07 31		07 37	
	d					05 48	06 14	06 20	06 33				06 48	06 56			07 14		07 23				
Penkridge	d							06 29						07 05					07 31				
Stafford	a					06 00	06 27	06 36	06 46	06 57			07 01	07 12			07 29		07 38		07 47		07 53

		VT	AW	LM	XC	LM	LM	LM	VT	XC	LM	LM	LM	LM	VT	LM	AW	VT	XC	LM	LM	LM
			■														■					
		◇■1			◇■1	■1			◇■1	◇■1		■1		■1	◇■1	■1		◇■1	◇■1		■1	■1
		M	C	J	D	E	I	N		O	J	E	I	N	G	F	H		P	J	E	N
		⊡	⊼		⊼				⊡	⊼					⊡		⊼	⊡	⊼			
London Euston 15 ⊖66	d								06 23			05 34						07 03				06 24
Northampton 66	d							06 41				06 53		07 14		07 14						07 37
Long Buckby	d											07 05		07 26		07 26						07 47
Rugby	d							07 01				07 18		07 37		07 37		07 51				07 59
Coventry	a							07 10	07 22			07 29		07 47		07 47		08 02				08 09
	d							07 11	07 22	07 27		07 30		07 47		07 47		08 02				08 10
Canley	d							07 14				07 33										08 13
Tile Hill	d							07 18				07 37		07 52		07 52						08 17
Berkswell	d							07 21				07 40										08 20
Hampton-in-Arden	d							07 25						07 59		07 59						08 24
Birmingham International ✈	a							07 28	07 33	07 36		07 45		08 02		08 02		08 13				08 27
	d		07 09			07 18		07 29	07 33	07 38		07 46		08 02		08 02	08 08	08 13			08 18	08 28
Marston Green	d							07 32				07 49		08 05		08 05						08 31
Lea Hall	d					07 23						07 52									08 23	
Stechford	d					07 26						07 55									08 26	
Adderley Park	d					07 29															08 29	
BirminghamNewStreet 12	a		07 21			07 33		07 42	07 45	07 48		08 01		08 14		08 14	08 21	08 24			08 33	08 39
	d	07 21	07 24	07 28	07 31	07 36	07 40			07 57	08 00	08 04	08 07		08 15	08 21	08 25		08 31	08 34	08 37	
Smethwick Rolfe Street	d						07 46						08 13									
Smethwick Galton Bridge 7	d		07 31			07 42	07 48					08 10	08 15			08 28	08 31				08 44	
Sandwell & Dudley	d						07 51				08 08		08 17		08 24							
Dudley Port	d						07 54						08 21									
Tipton	d						07 56						08 23									
Coseley	d					07 49	07 59						08 26								08 50	
Wolverhampton 7	a	07 39	07 43	07 46	07 49	07 55	08 04			08 13	08 18	08 21	08 31		08 37	08 41	08 44		08 47	08 51	08 56	
	d	07 40			07 50	07 56				08 14		08 22				08 41			08 48		08 57	
Penkridge	d					08 05						08 31									09 06	
Stafford	a	07 58			08 03	08 11				08 27		08 38				08 56			09 01		09 13	

A From Rugeley Trent Valley
B From London Euston
C To Holyhead
D To Manchester Piccadilly
E To Liverpool Lime Street
F To Crewe
G To Edinburgh
H To Aberystwyth
I From Walsall
J To Shrewsbury
K From Bletchley to Liverpool Lime Street
L To Glasgow Central
M To Blackpool North
N To Rugeley Trent Valley
O From Southampton Central to Manchester Piccadilly
P From Bristol Temple Meads to Manchester Piccadilly

Table T068-F

Saturdays

21 December to 16 May

Northampton - Coventry - Birmingham - Wolverhampton - Stafford

		LM	VT	XC	LM	LM	LM	VT	LM	LM	AW	VT	XC	LM	LM	LM	LM	VT	XC	LM	LM	LM
		A	◇1	◇1 B	C	1 D	A	◇1 E	1 F	1 G	H	◇1	◇1 I	C	1 D	1 F	A	◇1	◇1 J	C	1 D	A
London Euston ⊖66	d		07 23					07 43				08 03				07 24		08 23			07 49	
Northampton 66	d					07 56			08 14	08 14						08 37					08 55	
Long Buckby	d					08 07			08 25	08 25						08 48					09 06	
Rugby	d					08 18			08 36	08 36		08 51				08 59					09 17	
Coventry	a		08 22			08 29		08 42	08 46	08 46		09 02				09 09		09 22			09 28	
	d		08 22	08 27		08 30		08 42	08 47	08 47		09 02				09 10		09 22	09 27		09 29	
Canley	d					08 33										09 13					09 32	
Tile Hill	d					08 37			08 52	08 52						09 17					09 36	
Berkswell	d					08 40										09 20					09 39	
Hampton-in-Arden	d								08 58	08 58						09 24						
Birmingham International ✈	a		08 33	08 36		08 45		08 53	09 01	09 01		09 13				09 27		09 33	09 36		09 45	
	d		08 33	08 38		08 46		08 53	09 02	09 02	09 08	09 13			09 18	09 28		09 33	09 38		09 45	
Marston Green	d					08 49			09 05	09 05						09 31					09 48	
Lea Hall	d					08 52									09 23						09 52	
Stechford	d					08 55									09 26						09 54	
Adderley Park	d														09 29							
BirminghamNewStreet 12	a		08 45	08 48		09 01		09 04	09 13	09 13	09 19	09 23			09 33	09 39		09 45	09 48		10 00	
	d	08 40		08 57	09 00	09 04	09 07	09 15		09 20	09 25		09 31	09 34	09 37		09 40		09 57	10 00	10 03	10 07
Smethwick Rolfe Street	d	08 46					09 13										09 46					10 13
Smethwick Galton Bridge 7	d	08 48				09 10	09 15			09 27	09 32				09 44		09 48				10 10	10 15
Sandwell & Dudley	d	08 51			09 08		09 17	09 24									09 51			10 08		10 17
Dudley Port	d	08 55					09 21										09 55					10 21
Tipton	d	08 57					09 23										09 57					10 23
Coseley	d	09 00					09 26								09 50		10 00					10 26
Wolverhampton 7	a	09 05		09 13	09 18	09 21	09 31	09 37		09 40	09 44		09 47	09 51	09 56		10 05		10 13	10 18	10 21	10 32
	d			09 14		09 22				09 41			09 48		09 57				10 14		10 22	
Penkridge	d					09 31									10 05						10 31	
Stafford	a			09 27		09 38				09 56			10 03		10 12				10 27		10 38	

		VT	LM	LM	AW	VT	XC	LM	LM	LM	LM	VT	XC	LM	LM	LM	VT	LM	LM	AW	VT	XC	LM
		◇1 K	1 F	1 G	H	◇1	◇1 L	C	1 D	1 F	A	◇1	◇1 J	C	1 D	A	◇1 E	1 M	1 G	◇ N	◇1	◇1 O	C
London Euston ⊖66	d	08 43	08 15	08 15		09 03				08 24		09 23			08 49		09 43	09 15	09 15		10 03		
Northampton 66	d		09 14	09 14						09 37					09 55			10 13	10 13				
Long Buckby	d		09 25	09 25						09 48					10 06			10 25	10 25				
Rugby	d		09 36	09 36		09 51				09 59					10 17			10 36	10 36		10 51		
Coventry	a	09 42	09 46	09 46		10 02				10 09		10 22			10 29		10 42	10 46	10 46		11 02		
	d	09 42	09 47	09 47		10 02				10 10		10 22	10 27		10 30		10 42	10 47	10 47		11 02		
Canley	d									10 13					10 33								
Tile Hill	d		09 52	09 52						10 17					10 37			10 52	10 52				
Berkswell	d									10 20					10 40								
Hampton-in-Arden	d		09 58	09 58						10 24								10 58	10 58				
Birmingham International ✈	a	09 53	10 01	10 01		10 13				10 27		10 33	10 36		10 45		10 53	11 01	11 01		11 13		
	d	09 53	10 02	10 02	10 09	10 13			10 18	10 28		10 33	10 38		10 46		10 53	11 02	11 02	11 08	11 13		
Marston Green	d		10 05	10 05						10 31					10 49			11 05	11 05				
Lea Hall	d								10 23						10 52								
Stechford	d								10 26						10 55								
Adderley Park	d								10 29														
BirminghamNewStreet 12	a	10 04	10 13	10 13	10 20	10 24			10 33	10 39		10 45	10 48		11 01		11 05	11 13	11 13	11 21	11 24		
	d	10 15		10 20	10 25		10 31	10 34	10 37		10 40		10 57	11 00	11 04	11 07	11 15		11 20	11 25		11 31	11 34
Smethwick Rolfe Street	d										10 46					11 13							
Smethwick Galton Bridge 7	d			10 27	10 31						10 48				11 10	11 15			11 27	11 32			
Sandwell & Dudley	d	10 24									10 51			11 08		11 17	11 24						
Dudley Port	d										10 55					11 21							
Tipton	d										10 57					11 23							
Coseley	d								10 48		11 00					11 26							
Wolverhampton 7	a	10 37		10 40	10 44		10 47	10 51	10 54		11 05		11 13	11 18	11 21	11 31	11 37		11 40	11 44		11 47	11 51
	d			10 41			10 48		10 55				11 14		11 22				11 41			11 48	
Penkridge	d								11 03						11 31								
Stafford	a			10 56			11 01		11 10				11 27		11 38				11 56			12 01	

A From Walsall
B From Southampton Central to Manchester Piccadilly
C To Shrewsbury
D To Liverpool Lime Street
E To Glasgow Central
F To Rugeley Trent Valley
G To Crewe
H To Aberystwyth
I From Cardiff Central to Manchester Piccadilly
J From Bournemouth to Manchester Piccadilly
K To Edinburgh
L From Paignton to Manchester Piccadilly
M To Walsall
N To Holyhead
O From Bristol Temple Meads to Manchester Piccadilly

Table T068-F

Saturdays

21 December to 16 May

Northampton - Coventry - Birmingham - Wolverhampton - Stafford

		LM	LM	LM	VT	XC	LM	LM	LM	VT	LM	LM	AW	VT	XC	LM	LM	LM	LM	VT	VT	XC
		1 A	1 B	C	◇1	◇1 D	E	1 A	C	◇1 F	1 G	1 H	I	◇1	◇1 J	E	1 A	1 B	C	◇1	◇1 E	◇1 D
London Euston ⊖66	d		09 24		10 23			09 49		10 43	10 15	10 15		11 03				10 24		11 23	11 23	
Northampton 66	d		10 37					10 56			11 14	11 14						11 37				
Long Buckby	d		10 48					11 07			11 25	11 25						11 48				
Rugby	d		10 59					11 18			11 36	11 36		11 51				11 59				
Coventry	a		11 09		11 22			11 29		11 42	11 46	11 46		12 02				12 09		12 22	12 22	
	d		11 10		11 22	11 27		11 30		11 42	11 47	11 47		12 02				12 10		12 22	12 22	12 27
Canley	d		11 13					11 33										12 13				
Tile Hill	d		11 17					11 37			11 52	11 52						12 17				
Berkswell	d		11 20					11 40										12 20				
Hampton-in-Arden	d		11 24								11 58	11 58						12 24				
Birmingham International ✈	a		11 27		11 33	11 36		11 45		11 53	12 01	12 01		12 13				12 27		12 33	12 33	12 36
	d	11 18	11 28		11 33	11 38		11 46		11 53	12 02	12 02	12 08	12 13			12 18	12 28		12 33	12 33	12 38
Marston Green	d		11 31					11 49			12 05	12 05						12 31				
Lea Hall	d	11 23						11 52									12 23					
Stechford	d	11 26						11 55									12 26					
Adderley Park	d	11 29															12 29					
BirminghamNewStreet 12	a	11 33	11 39		11 45	11 48		12 01		12 04	12 13	12 13	12 21	12 24			12 33	12 39		12 44	12 44	12 48
	d	11 37		11 40		11 57	12 00	12 04	12 07	12 15		12 20	12 25		12 31	12 34	12 37		12 40		12 52	12 57
Smethwick Rolfe Street	d			11 46					12 13										12 46			
Smethwick Galton Bridge 7	d			11 48				12 10	12 15			12 27	12 31						12 48			
Sandwell & Dudley	d			11 51			12 08		12 17	12 24									12 51			
Dudley Port	d			11 55					12 21										12 55			
Tipton	d			11 57					12 23										12 57			
Coseley	d	11 48		12 00					12 26								12 48		13 00			
Wolverhampton 7	a	11 54		12 05		12 13	12 18	12 21	12 31	12 37		12 40	12 44		12 47	12 51	12 54		13 05		13 09	13 13
	d	11 55				12 14		12 22				12 41			12 48		12 55					13 14
Penkridge	d	12 03						12 31									13 03					
Stafford	a	12 09				12 27		12 38				12 55			13 01		13 10					13 27

		LM	LM	LM	VT	LM	LM	AW	VT	XC	LM	LM	LM	LM	VT	XC	LM	LM	LM	VT	LM	LM	AW
		E	1 A	C	◇1 K	1 B	1 H	◇ L	◇1	◇1 M	E	1 A	1 B	C	◇1	◇1 D	E	1 A	C	◇1 F	1 G	1 H	◇ I
London Euston ⊖66	d		10 49		11 43	11 15	11 15		12 03				11 24		12 23			11 49		12 43	12 15	12 15	
Northampton 66	d		11 56			12 15	12 15						12 38					12 51			13 14	13 14	
Long Buckby	d		12 07			12 26	12 26						12 49					13 04			13 25	13 25	
Rugby	d		12 18			12 37	12 37		12 51				12 59					13 17			13 36	13 36	
Coventry	a		12 29		12 42	12 47	12 47		13 02				13 09		13 22			13 28		13 42	13 46	13 46	
	d		12 31		12 42	12 48	12 48		13 02				13 10		13 22	13 27		13 30		13 42	13 47	13 47	
Canley	d		12 34										13 13					13 33					
Tile Hill	d		12 38			12 53	12 53						13 17					13 36			13 52	13 52	
Berkswell	d		12 41										13 20					13 39					
Hampton-in-Arden	d					12 59	12 59						13 24								13 58	13 58	
Birmingham International ✈	a		12 46		12 53	13 02	13 02		13 13				13 27		13 33	13 36		13 45		13 53	14 01	14 01	
	d		12 47		12 53	13 03	13 03	13 08	13 13			13 18	13 28		13 33	13 38		13 45		13 53	14 02	14 02	14 09
Marston Green	d		12 50			13 06	13 06						13 31					13 48			14 05	14 05	
Lea Hall	d		12 53									13 23						13 52					
Stechford	d		12 56									13 26						13 54					
Adderley Park	d											13 29											
BirminghamNewStreet 12	a		13 02		13 04	13 14	13 14	13 21	13 24			13 33	13 39		13 45	13 48		14 00		14 04	14 13	14 13	14 21
	d	13 00	13 04	13 07	13 15		13 21	13 25		13 31	13 34	13 37		13 40		13 57	14 00	14 03	14 07	14 15		14 20	14 25
Smethwick Rolfe Street	d			13 13										13 46					14 13				
Smethwick Galton Bridge 7	d		13 11	13 15			13 28	13 31						13 48				14 10	14 15			14 27	14 31
Sandwell & Dudley	d	13 08		13 17	13 24									13 51			14 08		14 17	14 24			
Dudley Port	d			13 21										13 55					14 21				
Tipton	d			13 23										13 57					14 23				
Coseley	d			13 26								13 48		14 00					14 26				
Wolverhampton 7	a	13 18	13 22	13 32	13 37		13 39	13 44		13 47	13 51	13 54		14 05		14 13	14 18	14 21	14 31	14 37		14 39	14 43
	d		13 22				13 40			13 48		13 55				14 14		14 22				14 40	
Penkridge	d		13 31									14 04						14 30					
Stafford	a		13 38				13 54			14 01		14 11				14 27		14 37				14 57	

A To Liverpool Lime Street
B To Rugeley Trent Valley
C From Walsall
D From Bournemouth to Manchester Piccadilly
E To Shrewsbury
F To Edinburgh
G To Walsall
H To Crewe
I To Aberystwyth
J From Bristol Temple Meads to Manchester Piccadilly
K To Glasgow Central
L To Holyhead
M From Paignton to Manchester Piccadilly

Table T068-F

Saturdays

21 December to 16 May

Northampton - Coventry - Birmingham - Wolverhampton - Stafford

		VT	XC	LM	LM	LM	LM	VT	XC	LM	LM	LM	VT	LM	LM	AW	VT	XC	LM	LM	LM	LM	VT
		◇■	◇■		■	■		◇■	◇■		■		◇■	■	■	■ ◇	◇■	◇■		■		■	◇■
			A	B	C	D	E		F	B	C	E	G	D	H	I		J	B	C	E	D	
London Euston ⊖66	d	13 03				12 24		13 23			12 49		13 43	13 15	13 15		14 03					13 24	14 23
Northampton 66	d					13 37					13 55			14 14	14 14							14 38	
Long Buckby	d					13 48					14 06			14 25	14 25							14 49	
Rugby	d	13 51				13 59					14 18			14 37	14 37		14 51					15 00	
Coventry	a	14 02				14 09		14 22			14 29		14 42	14 47	14 47		15 02					15 10	15 22
	d	14 02				14 10		14 22	14 27		14 30		14 42	14 48	14 48		15 02					15 11	15 22
Canley	d					14 13					14 33											15 14	
Tile Hill	d					14 17					14 37			14 53	14 53							15 18	
Berkswell	d					14 20					14 40											15 21	
Hampton-in-Arden	d					14 24								14 59	14 59							15 25	
Birmingham International ✈	a	14 13				14 27		14 33	14 36		14 45		14 53	15 02	15 02		15 13					15 28	15 33
	d	14 13			14 18	14 28		14 33	14 38		14 46		14 53	15 03	15 03	15 08	15 13			15 18		15 29	15 33
Marston Green	d					14 31					14 49			15 06	15 06							15 32	
Lea Hall	d				14 23						14 52									15 23			
Stechford	d				14 26						14 55									15 26			
Adderley Park	d				14 29															15 29			
BirminghamNewStreet 12	a	14 24			14 33	14 39		14 45	14 48		15 01		15 04	15 14	15 14	15 20	15 24			15 33		15 40	15 44
	d		14 31	14 34	14 37		14 40		14 57	15 00	15 04	15 07	15 15		15 21	15 25		15 31	15 34	15 37	15 40		
Smethwick Rolfe Street	d						14 46					15 13									15 46		
Smethwick Galton Bridge 7	d						14 48				15 10	15 15			15 28	15 31					15 48		
Sandwell & Dudley	d						14 51			15 08		15 17	15 24								15 51		
Dudley Port	d						14 55					15 21									15 55		
Tipton	d						14 57					15 23									15 57		
Coseley	d				14 48		15 00					15 26								15 48	16 00		
Wolverhampton 7	a		14 47	14 51	14 54		15 05		15 13	15 18	15 21	15 31	15 36		15 39	15 43		15 47	15 51	15 54	16 05		
	d		14 48		14 55				15 14		15 22				15 39			15 48		15 55			
Penkridge	d				15 03						15 31									16 03			
Stafford	a		15 01		15 10				15 27		15 38				15 54			16 01		16 10			

		XC	LM	LM	LM	VT	LM	LM	AW	VT	XC	LM	LM	LM	LM	VT	XC	LM	LM	LM	VT	LM	LM
		◇■		■		■	■	■	◇	◇■	◇■		■		■	◇■	◇■		■		■	■	■
		F	B	C	E	K	D	H	L		A	B	C	E	D		F	B	C	E	G	D	H
London Euston ⊖66	d			13 49		14 43	14 15	14 15		15 03					14 24	15 23			14 49		15 43	15 15	15 15
Northampton 66	d			14 55			15 15	15 15							15 38				15 56			16 14	16 14
Long Buckby	d			15 06			15 25	15 25							15 51				16 07			16 25	16 25
Rugby	d			15 19			15 37	15 37		15 51					16 02				16 18			16 37	16 37
Coventry	a			15 30		15 42	15 47	15 47		16 02					16 12	16 22			16 29		16 42	16 47	16 47
	d	15 27		15 31		15 42	15 48	15 48		16 02					16 12	16 22	16 27		16 30		16 42	16 48	16 48
Canley	d			15 34											16 15				16 33				
Tile Hill	d			15 37			15 53	15 53							16 19				16 37			16 53	16 53
Berkswell	d			15 40											16 22				16 40				
Hampton-in-Arden	d						15 59	15 59							16 26							16 59	16 59
Birmingham International ✈	a	15 36		15 46		15 53	16 02	16 02		16 13					16 29	16 33	16 36		16 45		16 53	17 02	17 02
	d	15 38		15 46		15 53	16 03	16 03	16 08	16 13			16 18		16 30	16 33	16 38		16 46		16 53	17 03	17 03
Marston Green	d			15 49			16 06	16 06							16 33				16 49			17 06	17 06
Lea Hall	d			15 52									16 23						16 52				
Stechford	d			15 55									16 26						16 55				
Adderley Park	d												16 29										
BirminghamNewStreet 12	a	15 48		16 01		16 05	16 14	16 14	16 20	16 24			16 33		16 41	16 45	16 48		17 01		17 05	17 14	17 14
	d	15 57	16 00	16 04	16 07	16 15		16 21	16 25		16 31	16 34	16 37	16 40			16 57	17 00	17 04	17 07	17 15		17 21
Smethwick Rolfe Street	d				16 13									16 46						17 13			
Smethwick Galton Bridge 7	d			16 10	16 15			16 28	16 31					16 48					17 10	17 15			17 28
Sandwell & Dudley	d		16 08		16 17	16 24								16 51				17 08		17 17	17 24		
Dudley Port	d				16 21									16 55						17 21			
Tipton	d				16 23									16 57						17 23			
Coseley	d				16 26								16 48	17 00						17 26			
Wolverhampton 7	a	16 13	16 18	16 21	16 31	16 37		16 39	16 43		16 47	16 51	16 54	17 05			17 13	17 18	17 21	17 31	17 37		17 39
	d	16 14		16 22				16 40			16 48		16 55				17 14		17 22				17 40
Penkridge	d			16 30									17 03						17 30				
Stafford	a	16 27		16 37				16 55			17 01		17 10				17 27		17 38				17 57

A From Bristol Temple Meads to Manchester Piccadilly
B To Shrewsbury
C To Liverpool Lime Street
D To Rugeley Trent Valley
E From Walsall
F From Bournemouth to Manchester Piccadilly
G To Glasgow Central
H To Crewe
I To Holyhead
J From Penzance to Manchester Piccadilly
K To Edinburgh
L To Aberystwyth

Table T068-F

Saturdays

21 December to 16 May

Northampton - Coventry - Birmingham - Wolverhampton - Stafford

		AW	VT	XC	LM	LM	LM	LM	VT	XC	LM	LM	LM	VT	LM	LM	AW	VT	XC	LM	LM	LM	LM
		◇	◇■	◇■		■	■		◇■	◇■		■		◇■	■	■	◇	◇■	◇■		■	■	
		A		B	C	D	E	F		G	C	D	F	H	E	I	J		K	C	D	E	F
London Euston ⊖66	d		16 03				15 24		16 23			15 49		16 43	16 15	16 15		17 03				16 24	
Northampton 66	d						16 37					16 55			17 14	17 14						17 37	
Long Buckby	d						16 48					17 06			17 25	17 25						17 48	
Rugby	d		16 51				16 59					17 17			17 37	17 37		17 51				17 59	
Coventry	a		17 02				17 09		17 22			17 28		17 42	17 47	17 47		18 02				18 09	
	d		17 02				17 10		17 22	17 27		17 30		17 42	17 48	17 48		18 02				18 10	
Canley	d						17 13					17 33										18 13	
Tile Hill	d						17 17					17 37			17 53	17 53						18 17	
Berkswell	d						17 20					17 40										18 20	
Hampton-in-Arden	d						17 24								17 59	17 59						18 24	
Birmingham International ✈	a		17 13				17 27		17 33	17 36		17 46		17 53	18 02	18 02		18 13				18 27	
	d	17 08	17 13			17 18	17 28		17 33	17 38		17 46		17 53	18 03	18 03	18 08	18 13			18 18	18 28	
Marston Green	d						17 31					17 49			18 06	18 06						18 31	
Lea Hall	d					17 23						17 53									18 23		
Stechford	d					17 26						17 55									18 26		
Adderley Park	d					17 29															18 29		
BirminghamNewStreet 12	a	17 19	17 24			17 33	17 39		17 45	17 48		18 01		18 04	18 14	18 14	18 19	18 24			18 33	18 39	
	d	17 25		17 31	17 34	17 37		17 40		17 57	18 00	18 04	18 07	18 15		18 21	18 25		18 31	18 34	18 37		18 40
Smethwick Rolfe Street	d							17 46					18 13										18 46
Smethwick Galton Bridge 7	d	17 31						17 48				18 10	18 15			18 28	18 31						18 48
Sandwell & Dudley	d							17 51			18 08		18 17	18 24									18 51
Dudley Port	d							17 55					18 21										18 55
Tipton	d							17 57					18 23										18 57
Coseley	d					17 48		18 00					18 26								18 48		19 00
Wolverhampton 7	a	17 43		17 47	17 51	17 54		18 05		18 13	18 18	18 21	18 31	18 37		18 39	18 43		18 47	18 51	18 54		19 05
	d			17 48		17 55				18 14		18 22				18 40			18 48		18 55		
Penkridge	d					18 03						18 31									19 04		
Stafford	a			18 01		18 10				18 27		18 38				18 55			19 01		19 11		

		VT	XC	LM	LM	LM	VT	LM	LM	AW	XC	LM	VT	LM	VT	LM	LM	VT	XC	LM	LM	LM
		◇■	◇■		■		◇■	■	■	◇	◇■		◇■	■	◇■	■		◇■	◇■		■	
			G	C	D	F	H	E	I	L	M	C	N	D	O	E	F		P	C	D	F
London Euston ⊖66	d	17 23			16 49		17 43	17 15	17 15				18 03			17 24		18 23			17 49	
Northampton 66	d				17 56			18 14	18 14							18 37					18 55	
Long Buckby	d				18 08			18 25	18 25							18 48					19 06	
Rugby	d				18 19			18 37	18 37				18 51			18 59					19 17	
Coventry	a	18 22			18 29		18 42	18 47	18 47				19 02			19 09		19 22			19 28	
	d	18 22	18 27		18 30		18 42	18 48	18 48				19 02			19 10		19 22	19 27		19 31	
Canley	d				18 33											19 13					19 34	
Tile Hill	d				18 37			18 53	18 53							19 17					19 38	
Berkswell	d				18 40											19 20					19 41	
Hampton-in-Arden	d							18 59	18 59							19 24						
Birmingham International ✈	a	18 33	18 36		18 45		18 53	19 02	19 02				19 13			19 27		19 33	19 36		19 46	
	d	18 33	18 38		18 46		18 53	19 03	19 03	19 08			19 13	19 18		19 28		19 33	19 38		19 47	
Marston Green	d				18 49			19 06	19 06							19 31					19 50	
Lea Hall	d				18 52									19 23							19 53	
Stechford	d				18 55									19 26							19 55	
Adderley Park	d													19 29	←							
BirminghamNewStreet 12	a	18 45	18 48		19 01		19 05	19 14	19 14	19 19			19 24	19 33	19 24	19 39		19 44	19 48		20 01	
	d	18 50	18 57	19 00	19 04	19 07	19 15		19 21	19 25	19 31	19 34	19 40	19 37	19 40		19 43	19 50	19 57	20 00	20 04	20 07
Smethwick Rolfe Street	d					19 13							→				19 49					20 13
Smethwick Galton Bridge 7	d				19 10	19 15			19 27	19 31							19 51				20 10	20 15
Sandwell & Dudley	d	18 59		19 08		19 17	19 24								19 49		19 53	19 59		20 08		20 17
Dudley Port	d					19 21											19 57					20 21
Tipton	d					19 23											19 59					20 23
Coseley	d					19 26								19 50			20 02					20 26
Wolverhampton 7	a	19 10	19 13	19 18	19 22	19 32	19 37		19 38	19 43	19 47	19 51		19 56	19 59		20 07	20 11	20 13	20 18	20 21	20 31
	d		19 14		19 22				19 40		19 48			19 57					20 14		20 22	
Penkridge	d				19 31									20 05							20 30	
Stafford	a		19 27		19 38				19 55		20 01			20 11					20 27		20 37	

A To Aberystwyth
B From Paignton to Manchester Piccadilly
C To Shrewsbury
D To Liverpool Lime Street
E To Rugeley Trent Valley
F From Walsall
G From Bournemouth to Manchester Piccadilly
H To Preston
I To Crewe
J To Machynlleth Carr. Sdgs
K From Bristol Temple Meads to Manchester Piccadilly
L To Chester
M From Exeter St Davids to Manchester Piccadilly
N To Wolverhampton
O From London Euston
P From Bournemouth to Manchester Piccadilly. ✠ to BirminghamNewStreet

NRT DECEMBER 19 EDITION

Table T068-F

Saturdays
21 December to 16 May

Northampton - Coventry - Birmingham - Wolverhampton - Stafford

	VT ◇1 A	LM 1	AW ◇ B	XC ◇1 C	LM D		VT ◇1 E	LM 1 F	LM 1 G	LM H	VT ◇1 I	VT ◇1	XC ◇1 J	LM D	LM 1		LM 1 K	LM 1 A	VT ◇1	AW ◇ L	LM D	LM 1 A	LM 1 K	LM 1
London Euston 15 ⊖66 d	18 43	18 15					19 03		18 24			19 23			18 49			19 10	19 43					19 20
Northampton 66 d		19 14							19 37						19 56			20 04						20 30
Long Buckby d		19 25							19 48						20 08			20 15						20 42
Rugby d		19 37					19 51		19 59						20 19			20 26						20 53
Coventry a	19 42	19 47					20 02		20 09			20 22			20 30			20 36	20 49					21 05
d	19 42	19 47					20 02		20 10			20 22	20 27		20 31			20 37	20 49					21 06
Canley d									20 13						20 34			20 40						21 09
Tile Hill d		19 52							20 17						20 38			20 44						21 13
Berkswell d									20 20						20 41			20 47						21 16
Hampton-in-Arden d		19 59							20 24									20 51						21 20
Birmingham International ✈ a	19 53	20 02					20 13		20 27			20 33	20 37		20 46			20 54	21 00					21 23
d	19 53	20 02	20 08				20 13	20 18	20 28			20 33	20 38		20 47			20 55	21 00	21 08		21 18		21 24
Marston Green d		20 05							20 31						20 50			20 58						21 27
Lea Hall d								20 23							20 53							21 23		21 30
Stechford d								20 26							20 56							21 26		21 33
Adderley Park d								20 29			←											21 29		
BirminghamNewStreet 12 a	20 06	20 14	20 20				20 24	20 33	20 39		20 24	20 45	20 48		21 02			21 06	21 11	21 22		21 33		21 41
d	20 15		20 25	20 31	20 34		20 43	20 37		20 40	20 43	20 50	20 57	21 01			21 04	21 13	21 17	21 25	21 32	21 36	21 39	
Smethwick Rolfe Street d							→			20 46							21 10						21 44	
Smethwick Galton Bridge 7 d			20 31							20 48							21 12	21 20		21 31			21 47	
Sandwell & Dudley d	20 24									20 51	20 55	20 59		21 09			21 15						21 50	
Dudley Port d										20 55							21 19						21 54	
Tipton d										20 57							21 21						21 56	
Coseley d								20 48		21 00							21 24					21 47	21 59	
Wolverhampton 7 a	20 37		20 43	20 47	20 51			20 54		21 06	21 09	21 12	21 17	21 22			21 29	21 32	21 35	21 43	21 49	21 54	22 05	
d	20 37			20 48				20 55					21 18					21 33				21 59		
Penkridge d								21 04														22 08		
Stafford a	20 51			21 01				21 10					21 31					21 46				22 15		

	XC ◇1 J		LM 1	LM D	LM H	VT ◇1	LM 1	XC ◇1 M	XC ◇1 N	AW ◇ A	LM 1 A		LM 1 K	LM 1	VT ◇1	XC ◇1 O	LM 1	LM D	VT ◇1	AW D	LM		LM 1	LM 1
London Euston 15 ⊖66 d			19 30			20 25	19 47								21 03		20 39		21 42				21 09	21 31
Northampton 66 d			20 57				21 18										21 56						22 40	22 53
Long Buckby d			21 07				21 28										22 07						22 51	23 03
Rugby d			21 18				21 39								22 13		22 18		22 53				23 02	23 14
Coventry a			21 29			21 36	21 49								22 23		22 29		23 02				23 13	23 25
d	21 27		21 30			21 36	21 50	22 02						22 09	22 24	22 27	22 30		23 03				23 14	23 26
Canley d			21 33											22 12			22 33							23 29
Tile Hill d			21 37				21 55							22 16			22 37						23 19	23 33
Berkswell d			21 40											22 19			22 40							23 36
Hampton-in-Arden d							22 01							22 23									23 25	23 40
Birmingham International ✈ a	21 36		21 45			21 49	22 04	22 11						22 26	22 33	22 36	22 45		23 13				23 28	23 43
d	21 38		21 46			21 50	22 05	22 12			22 18			22 27	22 34	22 38	22 46		23 13				23 29	23 44
Marston Green d			21 49				22 08							22 30			22 49						23 32	23 47
Lea Hall d			21 52								22 23						22 52							23 50
Stechford d			21 55								22 26			22 34										23 53
Adderley Park d											22 29													23 56
BirminghamNewStreet 12 a	21 48		22 01			22 05	22 18	22 22			22 34			22 41	22 45	22 48	22 59		23 24				23 43	00 02
d	21 57			22 03	22 07	22 16			22 31	22 35	22 38		22 41		22 48			23 08	23 27	23 35	23 38			
Smethwick Rolfe Street d					22 13								22 46					23 14			23 44			
Smethwick Galton Bridge 7 d					22 15								22 49					23 16			23 46			
Sandwell & Dudley d				22 11	22 18	22 25							22 52		22 57			23 19	23 36		23 49			
Dudley Port d					22 22								22 56					23 23			23 52			
Tipton d					22 24								22 58					23 25			23 54			
Coseley d					22 27								23 01					23 28			23 57			
Wolverhampton 7 a	22 13			22 22	22 32	22 37			22 47	22 53	22 55		23 06		23 09			23 34	23 47	23 54	00 01			
d	22 14								22 48		22 59													
Penkridge d											23 08													
Stafford a	22 27								23 01		23 14													

A To Crewe
B To Aberystwyth
C From Bristol Temple Meads to Manchester Piccadilly
D To Shrewsbury
E To Wolverhampton
F To Liverpool Lime Street
G To Rugeley Trent Valley
H From Walsall
I From London Euston
J From Bournemouth to Manchester Piccadilly. ✠ to BirminghamNewStreet
K From Rugeley Trent Valley
L To Chester
M From Reading
N To Manchester Piccadilly
O From Bournemouth

NRT DECEMBER 19 EDITION

Table T068-F

Sundays
15 December to 10 May

Northampton - Coventry - Birmingham - Wolverhampton - Stafford

	LM 1 A	LM B	LM 1 A	VT ◇1 C	XC ◇1 D		LM	LM	VT ◇1 E	LM B	LM 1 F	LM G	LM 1 A	XC ◇1 D	AW ◇ H		LM I	VT ◇1 J	LM B	LM 1 F	LM 1 A	LM 1 A	VT ◇1	LM 1 K
London Euston 15 ⊖66 d																				07 52			08 50	
Northampton 66 d																				09 26		09 30		
Long Buckby d																				09 37		09 41		
Rugby d											08 53									09 48		09 52	10 14	
Coventry a											09 04									09 59			10 23	
d							08 37				09 06	09 11								10 00	10 11		10 24	
Canley d							08 40					09 14									10 14			
Tile Hill d							08 44				09 11	09 18									10 18			
Berkswell d							08 47					09 21									10 21			
Hampton-in-Arden d							08 51					09 25									10 25			
Birmingham International ✈ a							08 54				09 18	09 28								10 09	10 28		10 34	
d							08 55	09 03			09 19	09 29	09 41		09 51					10 09	10 29		10 34	
Marston Green d							08 58	09 06			09 22	09 32								10 12	10 32			
Lea Hall d								09 09												10 16				
Stechford d								09 12												10 18				
Adderley Park d								09 15												10 22				←
BirminghamNewStreet 12 a							09 06	09 20			09 30	09 40	09 50		10 02					10 26	10 40		10 45	10 40
d	08 25	08 28	08 39	08 45	09 01		09 09		09 20	09 30	09 42		09 53	10 01	10 04		10 07	10 20	10 26	10 42	10 57		10 48	10 57
Smethwick Rolfe Street d		08 34					09 15										10 13				→			
Smethwick Galton Bridge 7 d		08 37	08 45				09 17				09 49				10 10		10 15		10 32	10 49				
Sandwell & Dudley d		08 40	08 48				09 19			09 38							10 18		10 36				10 59	
Dudley Port d		08 44					09 23										10 21							
Tipton d		08 46					09 25										10 23							
Coseley d	08 38	08 49					09 29										10 26			10 55				
Wolverhampton 7 a	08 45	08 54	08 58	09 03	09 17		09 34		09 37	09 48	10 00		10 08	10 17	10 22		10 31	10 37	10 46	11 01			11 10	11 13
d	08 51		08 59	09 04	09 18						10 00		10 09	10 18						11 02				11 14
Penkridge d	09 02		09 07								10 09									11 11				
Stafford a	09 08		09 14	09 18	09 31						10 15		10 22	10 31						11 18		10 47		11 27

	XC ◇1 L		AW ◇ M	LM 1 N	LM 1	LM I	LM 1 A	LM 1 O	VT ◇1 E	LM B	LM 1 P		LM 1 A	VT ◇1	XC ◇1 Q	LM B	LM I	LM 1	LM 1	VT ◇1 J	LM 1 A		AW ◇ H	LM 1 F
London Euston 15 ⊖66 d				08 24			08 55							09 50				09 24	09 55		10 01			
Northampton 66 d				09 59	10 10		10 28				10 37							11 00	11 11		11 30			11 34
Long Buckby d				10 10	10 21		10 38											11 11	11 22		11 40			11 45
Rugby d				10 21	10 32		10 50				10 56			11 14				11 22	11 34		11 52			11 56
Coventry a				10 32	10 42						11 06			11 22				11 33	11 45					12 06
d	10 27			10 33	10 42						11 07		11 10	11 24	11 27			11 34	11 46					12 07
Canley d				10 36														11 37						
Tile Hill d				10 40									11 15					11 41						
Berkswell d				10 43														11 44						
Hampton-in-Arden d				10 47														11 48						
Birmingham International ✈ a	10 37			10 50	10 53						11 16		11 22	11 33	11 37			11 51	11 55					12 16
d	10 38		10 48	10 51	10 55						11 18		11 22	11 34	11 38			11 52	11 57				12 07	12 18
Marston Green d				10 54									11 25					11 55						
Lea Hall d													11 29											
Stechford d													11 31											
Adderley Park d								←					11 35											
BirminghamNewStreet 12 a	10 49		11 00	11 02	11 05			11 02			11 27		11 40	11 46	11 49			12 03	12 06				12 20	12 27
d	11 01		11 04	11 15		11 07		11 15	11 20	11 26	11 40		11 43	11 49	11 57	12 00	12 03	12 12		12 20			12 23	12 35
Smethwick Rolfe Street d				→		11 13											12 09							
Smethwick Galton Bridge 7 d			11 12			11 15		11 22			11 47					12 06	12 11	12 19					12 31	12 42
Sandwell & Dudley d						11 18				11 34				11 58		12 10	12 14							
Dudley Port d						11 21											12 17							
Tipton d						11 23											12 19							
Coseley d						11 26					11 53						12 22							12 48
Wolverhampton 7 a	11 17		11 24			11 30		11 33	11 37	11 44	11 59		12 04	12 11	12 14	12 20	12 27	12 30		12 37			12 42	12 54
d	11 18							11 34			12 00		12 04		12 15			12 31						12 55
Penkridge d											12 10													13 04
Stafford a	11 31						11 43	11 48			12 16		12 20		12 29			12 45			12 44			13 10

A To Crewe
B To Shrewsbury
C To Preston
D To Manchester Piccadilly
E To Glasgow Central
F To Liverpool Lime Street
G To Rugeley Trent Valley
H To Aberystwyth
I From Walsall
J To Edinburgh
K From Coventry to Crewe
L From Reading to Manchester Piccadilly
M To Chester
N To Stafford
O From London Euston
P From Milton Keynes Central to Liverpool Lime Street
Q From Southampton Central to Manchester Piccadilly

Table T068-F

Sundays

15 December to 10 May

Northampton - Coventry - Birmingham - Wolverhampton - Stafford

		LM	VT	XC	LM	LM	LM	LM	VT	LM	AW	VT	XC	LM	LM	VT	XC	LM	LM	VT	LM	LM
		■ A	◇■	◇■ B	C	D	■	■	◇■ E	■ A	◇ F	◇■	◇■ G	■ H	■ A	◇■	◇■ B	C	■	◇■ I	■	D
London Euston ⊖66	d		10 49				10 31			10 53		11 49				12 20			11 24	12 40	12 08	
Northampton 66	d						11 58	12 12		12 17				12 34					12 55		13 15	
Long Buckby	d						12 09	12 24		12 28				12 45					13 06		13 26	
Rugby	d		12 14				12 20	12 35		12 39		12 51		12 56					13 17		13 37	
Coventry	a		12 23				12 31	12 45				13 00		13 06		13 22			13 29	13 42	13 47	
	d	12 11	12 25	12 27			12 32	12 45				13 01		13 08	13 11	13 22	13 28		13 31	13 42	13 47	
Canley	d						12 35												13 34			
Tile Hill	d	12 16					12 39								13 16				13 38			
Berkswell	d						12 42												13 41			
Hampton-in-Arden	d						12 46												13 45			
Birmingham International	a	12 23	12 34	12 37			12 49	12 54				13 10		13 17	13 23	13 33	13 37		13 48	13 53	13 56	
	d	12 23	12 35	12 38			12 50	12 56			13 07	13 11		13 18	13 23	13 33	13 38		13 49	13 53	13 58	
Marston Green	d	12 26					12 53								13 26				13 52			
Lea Hall	d	12 30													13 30							
Stechford	d	12 32													13 32							
Adderley Park	d	12 36													13 36							
BirminghamNewStreet	a	12 41	12 45	12 49			13 01	13 05			13 19	13 22		13 32	13 41	13 44	13 48		14 00	14 05	14 07	
	d	12 47	12 50	12 57	13 00	13 05	13 15		13 20		13 23		13 31	13 35	13 44	13 47	13 57	14 00	14 05	14 15		14 08
Smethwick Rolfe Street	d					13 11														→		14 14
Smethwick Galton Bridge	d				13 07	13 13	13 22				13 31			13 42				14 06	14 11			14 16
Sandwell & Dudley	d		12 59		13 10	13 16										13 56		14 10				14 19
Dudley Port	d					13 19																14 22
Tipton	d					13 21																14 24
Coseley	d					13 24								13 48								14 27
Wolverhampton	a	13 02	13 10	13 13	13 20	13 29	13 33		13 37		13 42		13 47	13 54	14 00	14 07	14 13	14 20	14 24			14 32
	d	13 03		13 14			13 33						13 48	13 55	14 01		14 14		14 27			
Penkridge	d													14 04								
Stafford	a	13 17		13 27			13 47			13 29			14 01	14 11	14 15		14 27		14 41			

		VT	AW	VT	XC	LM	LM	VT	XC	LM	LM	VT	LM	LM	VT	XC	AW	VT	XC	LM	LM	VT	XC
		◇■ J	■ K	◇■	◇■ L	■ H	■ A	◇■	◇■ B	C	■	◇■ E	■	D	◇■ M	◇■ N	◇ F	◇■	◇■ O	■ H	■ A	◇■	◇■ B
London Euston ⊖66	d			13 00		12 31		13 20			12 34	13 40	13 08					14 00		13 32		14 20	
Northampton 66	d					13 34					13 55		14 15							14 35			
Long Buckby	d					13 45					14 06		14 26							14 46			
Rugby	d			13 51		13 56					14 17		14 37					14 51		14 57			
Coventry	a			14 02		14 07		14 22			14 29	14 43	14 47					15 02		15 08		15 22	
	d			14 02		14 08	14 11	14 22	14 27		14 30	14 43	14 47			14 54		15 02		15 09	15 12	15 22	15 27
Canley	d										14 33												
Tile Hill	d						14 16				14 37										15 17		
Berkswell	d										14 40												
Hampton-in-Arden	d										14 44												
Birmingham International	a			14 13		14 17	14 23	14 33	14 36		14 47	14 53	14 56			15 03		15 13		15 18	15 24	15 32	15 36
	d		14 07	14 13		14 18	14 23	14 33	14 38		14 48	14 54	14 58			15 04	15 08	15 13		15 19	15 24	15 32	15 38
Marston Green	d						14 26				14 51										15 27		
Lea Hall	d						14 30														15 31		
Stechford	d						14 32														15 33		
Adderley Park	d	←					14 36								←						15 37		
BirminghamNewStreet	a	14 05	14 20	14 23		14 30	14 41	14 44	14 48		15 00	15 05	15 07		15 05	15 14	15 20	15 23		15 31	15 42	15 45	15 48
	d	14 15	14 23		14 31	14 35	14 53		14 57	15 00	15 05	15 15		15 08	15 15		15 23		15 31	15 35	15 53		15 57
Smethwick Rolfe Street	d											→		15 14									
Smethwick Galton Bridge	d		14 31			14 42				15 06	15 12			15 16			15 31			15 42			
Sandwell & Dudley	d	14 24								15 09				15 19	15 26								
Dudley Port	d													15 22									
Tipton	d													15 24									
Coseley	d					14 48								15 27						15 48			
Wolverhampton	a	14 37	14 44		14 47	14 54	15 08		15 13	15 19	15 26			15 32	15 36		15 43		15 47	15 54	16 08		16 13
	d				14 48	14 55	15 09		15 14		15 27								15 48	15 55	16 09		16 14
Penkridge	d					15 04														16 04			
Stafford	a				15 01	15 11	15 22		15 27		15 41								16 01	16 11	16 22		16 27

A To Crewe
B From Bournemouth to Manchester Piccadilly
C To Shrewsbury
D From Walsall
E To Glasgow Central
F To Chester
G To Manchester Piccadilly
H To Liverpool Lime Street
I To Edinburgh
J From London Euston to Edinburgh
K To Aberystwyth
L From Paignton to Manchester Piccadilly
M From London Euston to Glasgow Central
N From Reading to Newcastle
O From Plymouth to Manchester Piccadilly

Table T068-F

Sundays

15 December to 10 May

Northampton - Coventry - Birmingham - Wolverhampton - Stafford

		LM	LM	VT	LM	LM	VT	XC	AW	VT	XC	LM	LM	VT	XC	LM	LM	VT	LM	LM	VT	XC
		A	■	◇■ B	■	C	◇■ D	◇■ E	■ F	◇■	◇■ G	■ H	■ I	◇■	◇■ J	A	■	◇■ K	■	C	◇■ L	◇■ M
London Euston ⊖66	d		13 34	14 40	14 08					15 00		14 31		15 20			14 34	15 40	15 06			
Northampton 66	d		14 55		15 15							15 34					15 55		16 15			
Long Buckby	d		15 06		15 26							15 45					16 06		16 26			
Rugby	d		15 17		15 37					15 51		15 56					16 17		16 37			
Coventry	a		15 29	15 42	15 47					16 02		16 07		16 22			16 29	16 42	16 47			
	d		15 30	15 42	15 47			15 54		16 02		16 08	16 11	16 22	16 27		16 30	16 42	16 47			16 54
Canley	d		15 33														16 33					
Tile Hill	d		15 37										16 16				16 37					
Berkswell	d		15 40														16 40					
Hampton-in-Arden	d		15 44														16 44					
Birmingham International	a		15 47	15 53	15 56			16 03		16 12		16 17	16 23	16 33	16 36		16 47	16 52	16 56			17 03
	d		15 48	15 53	15 58			16 04	16 08	16 12		16 18	16 23	16 33	16 38		16 48	16 53	16 57			17 04
Marston Green	d		15 51										16 26				16 51					
Lea Hall	d												16 30									
Stechford	d												16 32									
Adderley Park	d						←						16 36								←	
BirminghamNewStreet	a		16 00	16 05	16 07		16 05	16 14	16 20	16 22		16 29	16 41	16 45	16 48		17 00	17 04	17 07		17 04	17 14
	d	16 00	16 05	16 15		16 08	16 15		16 24		16 31	16 35	16 53		16 57	17 00	17 05	17 15		17 08	17 15	
Smethwick Rolfe Street	d			→		16 14												→		17 14		
Smethwick Galton Bridge	d	16 06	16 12			16 16			16 31			16 42					17 11			17 16		
Sandwell & Dudley	d	16 09				16 19	16 24									17 08				17 19	17 26	
Dudley Port	d					16 22														17 22		
Tipton	d					16 24														17 24		
Coseley	d					16 27						16 48								17 27		
Wolverhampton	a	16 19	16 26			16 32	16 37		16 44		16 47	16 54	17 08		17 13	17 18	17 22			17 32	17 37	
	d		16 27								16 48	16 55	17 09		17 14		17 23					
Penkridge	d											17 04										
Stafford	a		16 41								17 01	17 11	17 22		17 27		17 37					

		AW	VT	XC	LM	LM	VT	XC	LM	LM	VT	LM	LM	VT	XC	AW	VT	XC	LM	LM	VT	XC	LM
		◇ N	◇■	◇■ O	■ H	■ I	◇■	◇■ J	A	■	◇■ B	■	C	◇■ D	◇■ E	◇ F	◇■	◇■ P	■ H	■ I	◇■	◇■ J	A
London Euston ⊖66	d		16 00		15 31		16 20			15 34	16 40	16 06					17 00		16 32		17 20		
Northampton 66	d				16 34					16 55		17 15							17 34				
Long Buckby	d				16 45					17 06		17 26							17 45				
Rugby	d		16 51		16 56					17 17		17 37					17 51		17 56				
Coventry	a		17 02		17 07		17 22			17 29	17 42	17 47					18 02		18 07		18 22		
	d		17 02		17 08	17 11	17 22	17 27		17 30	17 42	17 47			17 54		18 02		18 08	18 11	18 22	18 27	
Canley	d									17 33													
Tile Hill	d					17 16				17 37										18 16			
Berkswell	d									17 40													
Hampton-in-Arden	d									17 44													
Birmingham International	a		17 13		17 17	17 23	17 33	17 36		17 47	17 53	17 56			18 03		18 13		18 17	18 23	18 33	18 36	
	d	17 08	17 13		17 18	17 23	17 33	17 38		17 48	17 53	17 57			18 04	18 08	18 13		18 18	18 23	18 33	18 38	
Marston Green	d					17 26				17 51										18 26			
Lea Hall	d					17 30														18 30			
Stechford	d					17 32														18 32			
Adderley Park	d					17 36								←						18 36			
BirminghamNewStreet	a	17 21	17 23		17 30	17 42	17 45	17 48		18 00	18 05	18 06		18 05	18 14	18 20	18 23		18 30	18 41	18 45	18 48	
	d	17 24		17 31	17 35	17 52		17 57	18 03	18 06	18 15		18 09	18 15		18 23		18 31	18 35	18 53		18 57	19 00
Smethwick Rolfe Street	d										→		18 15										
Smethwick Galton Bridge	d	17 31			17 42				18 10	18 14			18 17			18 31			18 42				19 06
Sandwell & Dudley	d								18 13				18 20	18 24									19 10
Dudley Port	d												18 23										
Tipton	d												18 25										
Coseley	d				17 48								18 28						18 48				
Wolverhampton	a	17 43		17 47	17 54	18 07		18 13	18 23	18 28			18 32	18 37		18 43		18 47	18 54	19 08		19 13	19 20
	d			17 48	17 55	18 08		18 14		18 30								18 48	18 55	19 09		19 14	
Penkridge	d				18 04														19 04				
Stafford	a			18 01	18 11	18 20		18 27		18 44								19 01	19 11	19 22		19 27	

A To Shrewsbury
B To Edinburgh
C From Walsall
D From London Euston to Edinburgh
E From Reading to Newcastle
F To Aberystwyth
G From Plymouth to Manchester Piccadilly
H To Liverpool Lime Street
I To Crewe
J From Bournemouth to Manchester Piccadilly
K To Glasgow Central
L From London Euston to Glasgow Central
M From Reading to Edinburgh
N To Holyhead
O From Bristol Temple Meads to Manchester Piccadilly
P From Penzance to Manchester Piccadilly

Table T068-F

Sundays
15 December to 10 May

Northampton - Coventry - Birmingham - Wolverhampton - Stafford

		LM	VT	LM	LM	VT	XC	AW	XC	VT		LM	VT	LM	VT	XC	LM	LM	LM	VT		LM	XC	AW	VT
		A	B		C	D	E	F	G	H		I	J	A		K	L	A	C	A			M	N	
London Euston ⊖66	d	16 34	17 40	17 06						18 00		17 32			18 20			17 34		18 40		18 06			19 00
Northampton 66	d	17 55		18 16								18 34						18 55				19 07			
Long Buckby	d	18 06		18 27								18 45						19 06				19 18			
Rugby	d	18 17		18 38						18 51		18 56						19 17				19 37			19 51
Coventry	a	18 29	18 42	18 48						19 02		19 07			19 22			19 29		19 42		19 47			20 02
	d	18 30	18 42	18 48			18 54			19 02		19 08		19 11	19 22	19 27		19 30		19 42		19 47	19 54		20 02
Canley	d	18 33																19 33							
Tile Hill	d	18 37												19 16				19 37							
Berkswell	d	18 40																19 40							
Hampton-in-Arden	d	18 44																19 44							
Birmingham International ✈	a	18 47	18 53	18 57			19 03			19 13		19 17		19 23	19 33	19 36		19 47		19 53		19 56	20 03		20 13
	d	18 48	18 53	18 58			19 04	19 09		19 13		19 18		19 23	19 33	19 38		19 48		19 53		20 00	20 04	20 08	20 13
Marston Green	d	18 51												19 26				19 51							
Lea Hall	d													19 30											
Stechford	d													19 32											
Adderley Park	d					←							←	19 35											
BirminghamNewStreet	a	19 00	19 04	19 07		19 04	19 14	19 21		19 23		19 30	19 23	19 41	19 44	19 48		20 01		20 05		20 09	20 14	20 20	20 23
	d	19 05	19 15		19 08	19 15		19 24	19 31	19 38		19 35	19 38	19 54		19 57	20 00	20 05	20 08	20 15				20 24	20 27
Smethwick Rolfe Street	d		→		19 14					→									20 14						
Smethwick Galton Bridge	d	19 12			19 16			19 32				19 42						20 12	20 16					20 31	
Sandwell & Dudley	d				19 19	19 24							19 48				20 08		20 19	20 24					20 36
Dudley Port	d				19 22														20 22						
Tipton	d				19 24														20 24						
Coseley	d				19 27							19 48					20 14		20 27						
Wolverhampton	a	19 23			19 32	19 37		19 44	19 47			19 54	19 59	20 10		20 13	20 20	20 25	20 32	20 37				20 44	20 48
	d	19 24							19 48			19 55		20 11		20 14		20 26		20 37					
Penkridge	d											20 04													
Stafford	a	19 38							20 01			20 11		20 24		20 28		20 40		20 51					

		XC	LM	LM	VT	XC		LM	LM	LM	VT	LM	XC	AW	VT	LM		LM	VT	XC	LM	LM	LM	LM	VT
		G	A	A		K		A	L	C	O	A	M	F		I		A		P	Q		L	C	
London Euston ⊖66	d		18 31		19 20			18 34			19 40	19 11			20 00	19 31			20 18			19 34			20 38
Northampton 66	d		19 34					19 55				20 09				20 34						20 55			
Long Buckby	d		19 45					20 06				20 20				20 45						21 06			
Rugby	d		19 57					20 17				20 37			20 51	20 57						21 17			
Coventry	a		20 07		20 22			20 29			20 42	20 47			21 02	21 07			21 20			21 29			21 46
	d		20 08	20 11	20 22	20 27		20 30			20 42	20 48	20 54		21 02	21 08		21 11	21 20	21 27		21 30			21 46
Canley	d							20 33														21 33			
Tile Hill	d			20 16				20 37										21 16				21 37			
Berkswell	d							20 40														21 40			
Hampton-in-Arden	d							20 44														21 44			
Birmingham International ✈	a		20 17	20 22	20 33	20 36		20 47			20 53	20 58	21 03		21 13	21 17		21 23	21 30	21 36		21 47			21 56
	d		20 18	20 23	20 33	20 38		20 48			20 53	20 58	21 04	21 08	21 13	21 18		21 23	21 31	21 38		21 48			21 57
Marston Green	d			20 26				20 51										21 26				21 51			
Lea Hall	d			20 29														21 30							
Stechford	d			20 32														21 32							
Adderley Park	d			20 35														21 36			←				
BirminghamNewStreet	a		20 30	20 40	20 45	20 48		20 59			21 05	21 08	21 15	21 19	21 23	21 32		21 41	21 44	21 48	21 41	21 59			22 09
	d	20 31	20 40	20 43	20 49	20 57		21 02	21 05	21 08	21 15	21 20		21 23		21 42		22 00	21 47	21 57	22 00		22 05	22 08	22 16
Smethwick Rolfe Street	d									21 14								→						22 14	
Smethwick Galton Bridge	d		20 47					21 08	21 12	21 16				21 31		21 49					22 07		22 12	22 16	
Sandwell & Dudley	d				20 58				21 15	21 19	21 24								21 56				22 15	22 19	22 25
Dudley Port	d									21 22														22 23	
Tipton	d									21 24														22 25	
Coseley	d		20 53							21 27						21 55							22 21	22 28	
Wolverhampton	a	20 51	20 59	21 03	21 10	21 13		21 19	21 26	21 32	21 37	21 40		21 43		22 01			22 08	22 13	22 18		22 28	22 33	22 36
	d	20 52	21 00	21 09		21 14		21 20			21 37	21 46				22 02				22 14	22 21				
Penkridge	d		21 09													22 11					22 29				
Stafford	a	21 05	21 16	21 23		21 27		21 35			21 55	22 00				22 18				22 27	22 36				

A To Crewe
B To Glasgow Central
C From Walsall
D From London Euston to Glasgow Central
E From Reading to Newcastle
F To Chester
G From Bristol Temple Meads to Manchester Piccadilly
H To Wolverhampton
I To Liverpool Lime Street
J From London Euston
K From Bournemouth to Manchester Piccadilly. 🍴 to BirminghamNewStreet
L To Shrewsbury
M From Reading
N To Aberystwyth
O To Preston
P From Bournemouth to Manchester Piccadilly
Q From Coventry to Crewe

NRT DECEMBER 19 EDITION

Table T068-F

Sundays
15 December to 10 May

Northampton - Coventry - Birmingham - Wolverhampton - Stafford

		XC	AW		LM	VT	XC	AW	LM	LM	XC	AW	LM		LM	VT	LM	VT	LM	VT
		A	B		C		D	E		F	A	B			G		H			
London Euston ⊖66	d					20 54			20 34				21 06		21 31	21 55		22 25	22 01	23 24
Northampton 66	d								21 57				22 37		22 51				23 33	
Long Buckby	d								22 08				22 47		23 02				23 43	
Rugby	d					22 07			22 19				22 58		23 13	23 24	←	23 48	23 54	00s47
Coventry	a					22 16			22 31				23 08		23 23	23 33	23 23	23 57	00 04	00s59
	d	21 54			22 08	22 16	22 24		22 32		22 54		23 09		23 37	23 33	23 37	23 57		
Canley	d								22 35						→		23 40			
Tile Hill	d								22 39								23 44			
Berkswell	d								22 42								23 47			
Hampton-in-Arden	d								22 46								23 51			
Birmingham International ✈	a	22 03			22 17	22 26	22 33		22 49		23 03		23 18			23 43	23 54	00 07		01s09
	d	22 04	22 11		22 17	22 27	22 34	22 40	22 50		23 04	23 08	23 18			23 44	23 55	00 08		
Marston Green	d				22 20				22 53				23 22				23 58			
Lea Hall	d				22 24								23 25							
Stechford	d				22 26								23 28							
Adderley Park	d				22 30								23 31							
BirminghamNewStreet	a	22 14	22 22		22 35	22 39	22 44	22 51	23 02		23 14	23 22	23 36			23 56	00 07	00 19		01s22
	d		22 24			22 42		22 55		23 07		23 25	23 39			23 59		00 22		
Smethwick Rolfe Street	d									23 13			23 45							
Smethwick Galton Bridge	d		22 31					23 02		23 15		23 33	23 47							
Sandwell & Dudley	d					22 51				23 18			23 50							
Dudley Port	d									23 22			23 54							
Tipton	d									23 24			23 56							
Coseley	d									23 27			23 59							
Wolverhampton	a		22 43			23 02		23 15		23 32		23 45	00 04			00 15		00 39		01 42
	d							23 15												
Penkridge	d																			
Stafford	a							23 31												

A From Reading
B To Shrewsbury
C To Rugeley Trent Valley
D From Bournemouth
E To Chester
F From Walsall
G To Birmingham New Street
H From London Euston

Table T068-R

Mondays to Fridays

16 December to 15 May

Stafford - Wolverhampton - Birmingham - Coventry - Northampton

Miles	Station		LM MX A	LM MX A	LM MX B	LM MX	LM ■	LM	VT ◇■ ⊠	LM ■	VT ◇■ ⊠	VT ◇■ ⊠	LM ■	LM	XC ◇■ C ⊼	AW D	VT ◇■ ⊠	LM ■	LM	AW E	VT ◇■ ⊠	LM ■	LM ■ F
0	**Stafford**	d														05 24							
5¾	Penkridge	d																					
10¼	**Wolverhampton ■**	a														05 40							
—		d							05 00			05 24		05 35		05 40	05 45	05 53		05 59	06 04		
18½	Coseley	d												05 40									
20	Tipton	d												05 43									
20¾	Dudley Port	d												05 45									
22¾	Sandwell & Dudley	d										05 34		05 49			05 55	06 02			06 15		
24	Smethwick Galton Bridge ■	d												05 52						06 10			
24¾	Smethwick Rolfe Street	d												05 54									
28	**BirminghamNewStreet ■**	a							05 25			05 43		06 00		06 07	06 05	06 10		06 17	06 24		
—		d			00 23	00 40		05 24	05 29	05 33	05 45	05 50			06 04		06 10	06 13	06 19	06 36	06 30		06 33
30	Adderley Park	d				00 44														→			
32	Stechford	d			00 30	00 48		05 30										06 20	06 26				
33	Lea Hall	d		00 01	00 32	00 50		05 33										06 23	06 29				
34½	Marston Green	d		00 03	00 35	00 54				05 41								06 26					06 42
36¼	**Birmingham International**	a		00 06	00 38	00 57		05 37	05 38	05 44	05 54	05 59			06 13		06 19	06 29	06 34		06 39		06 45
—		d		00 07	00 39	00 58			05 40	05 44	05 55	06 00			06 14		06 20	06 30			06 40		06 45
38¼	Hampton-in-Arden	d		00 10	00 42	01 01				05 48								06 33					06 49
41½	Berkswell	d			00 47	01 06				05 52								06 38					
43½	Tile Hill	d	00 02	00 16	00 51	01 09				05 56								06 41					06 55
45½	Canley	d	00 05		00 54	01 12				05 59								06 44					
47¼	**Coventry**	a	00 08	00 22	00 56	01 15			05 50	06 02	06 05	06 10			06 24		06 30	06 47			06 50		07 01
—		d							05 51	06 02	06 06	06 11	05 38				06 31	06 48			06 51	06 22	07 02
60¾	Rugby	d					05 15		06 03	06 13	06 20		05 49					06 59				06 33	07 12
70	Long Buckby	d					05 24			06 22			05 59					07 11				06 43	07 22
79½	**Northampton** 66	a					05 36			06 34	06 39		06 13					07 24				06 54	07 33
—	London Euston ■ ⊖66	a					06 45		07 05	07 38	07 28	07 13	07 22				07 33	08 38			07 53	08 01	08 28

Station		AW G	LM	LM H	VT ◇■ ⊠	LM ■	XC ◇■ I ⊼	VT ◇■ ⊠	LM	LM ■ J	LM G	LM ■ K	VT ◇■ ⊠	VT ◇■ ⊠	LM ■ L	AW ◇ D	XC ◇■ M ⊼	LM ■ L	LM N	VT ◇■ G ⊠	LM ■ O	LM G
Stafford	d						06 25			06 31		06 44					07 01				07 10	
Penkridge	d									06 37											07 16	
Wolverhampton ■	a						06 38			06 48		06 58					07 14				07 26	
	d			06 14	06 27		06 39	06 45		06 48	06 52	07 01	07 05			07 12	07 16		07 19	07 24	07 28	07 33
Coseley	d			06 19						06 53	06 58								07 24			
Tipton	d			06 22							07 01								07 27			
Dudley Port	d			06 25							07 03								07 29			
Sandwell & Dudley	d			06 28	06 38			06 56			07 07		07 15						07 33		07 40	07 44
Smethwick Galton Bridge ■	d			06 31							07 10	07 14				07 23			07 36		07 44	
Smethwick Rolfe Street	d	←		06 34							07 12								07 38			
BirminghamNewStreet ■	a	06 17		06 40	06 47		06 55	07 07		07 10	07 18	07 23	07 25			07 31	07 33		07 44	07 47	07 50	07 55
	d	06 36	06 39		06 50	06 54	07 04	07 10	07 13	07 16			07 30		07 33	07 36		07 39		07 50	07 54	
Adderley Park	d		06 44															07 44				
Stechford	d		06 47							07 23								07 47				
Lea Hall	d		06 50							07 26								07 50				
Marston Green	d					07 02			07 21						07 41						08 02	
Birmingham International	a	06 50	06 55		06 59	07 05	07 13	07 19	07 25	07 30					07 44	07 50		07 55		07 59	08 05	
	d				07 00	07 05	07 14	07 20		07 31				07 42	07 45					08 00	08 05	
Hampton-in-Arden	d					07 08									07 48							
Berkswell	d					07 13									07 53						08 11	
Tile Hill	d									07 39					07 56						08 14	
Canley	d					07 17									07 59						08 17	
Coventry	a				07 10	07 21	07 24	07 30		07 43				07 52	08 03					08 10	08 21	
	d				07 11	07 22		07 31		07 48				07 53	08 04					08 11	08 21	
Rugby	d					07 32				07 59					08 14					08 22	08 39	
Long Buckby	d					07 41				08 09					08 24						08 48	
Northampton 66	a					07 54				08 21					08 36						09 00	
London Euston ■ ⊖66	a				08 16	09 11		08 31		09 24			08 43	08 50	09 29					09 15	10 17	

A From Birmingham New Street
B From Bromsgrove
C To Bournemouth
D From Chester
E From Shrewsbury to Birmingham International
F From Walsall
G From Shrewsbury
H From Shrewsbury Abbey Frgte Cs
I From Manchester Piccadilly to Bournemouth. ⊼ from BirminghamNewStreet
J From Crewe
K From Crewe to Walsall
L From Rugeley Trent Valley
M From Manchester Piccadilly to Bristol Temple Meads
N To Four Oaks
O From Liverpool Lime Street

Table T068-R

Mondays to Fridays

16 December to 15 May

Stafford - Wolverhampton - Birmingham - Coventry - Northampton

Station		VT ◇■ A ⊠	XC ◇■ B ⊼	LM ■ C	VT ◇■ D ⊠	LM ■ E	LM ■	LM	LM ■ F	LM ■ G	LM H	VT ◇■ ⊠	LM ■	AW ◇ I	XC ◇■ J ⊼	LM ■ K	LM L	VT ◇■ ⊠	LM ■ M	LM H	XC ■ N ⊼	VT ◇■ O ⊠	LM ■ K
Stafford	d			07 15	07 24				07 41	07 47					08 03				08 11		08 26		
Penkridge	d								07 47										08 17				
Wolverhampton ■	a			07 29	07 40				07 58	08 01					08 16				08 27		08 39		
	d	07 37		07 40	07 45		07 49		07 58	08 03	08 07			08 11	08 17		08 22		08 30	08 36	08 40	08 45	
Coseley	d			07 45			07 54		08 04								08 27						
Tipton	d			07 48			07 58										08 30						
Dudley Port	d			07 51			08 00										08 32						
Sandwell & Dudley	d				07 57		08 04				08 16						08 36			08 44		08 55	
Smethwick Galton Bridge ■	d			07 55			08 06			08 13				08 23			08 39		08 42				
Smethwick Rolfe Street	d			07 57		←	08 08										08 41						
BirminghamNewStreet ■	a	07 56		08 04	08 07	08 04	08 15		08 18	08 21	08 25			08 31	08 33		08 47		08 50	08 53	08 57	09 05	
	d		08 04	08 14	08 10	08 14		08 18				08 30	08 33	08 36		08 39		08 50	08 54		09 04	09 10	09 13
Adderley Park	d			→												08 43							
Stechford	d							08 24								08 47							
Lea Hall	d							08 27								08 49							
Marston Green	d					08 22		08 30					08 41						09 02				09 21
Birmingham International	a		08 13		08 19	08 25		08 34				08 39	08 44	08 50		08 55		08 59	09 05		09 13	09 19	09 24
	d		08 14		08 20	08 25						08 40	08 45					09 00	09 05		09 14	09 20	09 28
Hampton-in-Arden	d					08 28							08 48										09 31
Berkswell	d					08 33													09 11				09 37
Tile Hill	d					08 36							08 54						09 14				09 40
Canley	d					08 40													09 17				09 43
Coventry	a		08 24		08 30	08 44						08 50	09 00					09 10	09 20		09 24	09 30	09 46
	d				08 31	08 48						08 51	09 00					09 11	09 25			09 31	09 47
Rugby	d					08 58							09 11					09 23	09 36				09 58
Long Buckby	d					09 08							09 21						09 46				10 09
Northampton 66	a					09 20							09 33						09 59				10 21
London Euston ■ ⊖66	a				09 33	10 23						09 53	10 44					10 13	11 18			10 33	11 25

Station		LM P	LM H	LM	VT ◇■ ⊠	LM ■ M	LM ■ E	AW ◇ E	XC ◇■ Q ⊼	LM ■ K	LM ■ L	VT ◇■ ⊠	LM ■ M	LM H	XC ◇■ N ⊼	VT ◇■ R ⊠	VT ◇■ S ⊠	LM ■ K	LM P	LM	LM H	VT ◇■ ⊠
Stafford	d					08 38	08 45		09 02				09 10		09 26							
Penkridge	d					08 44							09 16									
Wolverhampton ■	a					08 59	09 02		09 15				09 26		09 39							
	d	08 48	08 57			09 02	09 06	09 11	09 17		09 22		09 31	09 35	09 40	09 45	09 45		09 48		09 56	
Coseley	d	08 53				09 07					09 27								09 53			
Tipton	d	08 56									09 30								09 56			
Dudley Port	d	08 58									09 32								09 58			
Sandwell & Dudley	d	09 02									09 36			09 44		09 55	09 55		10 02			
Smethwick Galton Bridge ■	d	09 05					09 17	09 22			09 39		09 42						10 05			
Smethwick Rolfe Street	d	09 07									09 41								10 07			
BirminghamNewStreet ■	a	09 14	09 17			09 21	09 25	09 31	09 33		09 47		09 50	09 53	09 58	10 05	10 05		10 14		10 18	
	d			09 19	09 30	09 33		09 36		09 39		09 50	09 54		10 04	10 10	10 10	10 14		10 17		10 30
Adderley Park	d									09 43												
Stechford	d			09 25						09 46										10 23		
Lea Hall	d			09 28						09 49										10 26		
Marston Green	d			09 31		09 41							10 02					10 22		10 29		
Birmingham International	a			09 34	09 39	09 44		09 50		09 54		09 59	10 05		10 13	10 19	10 19	10 25		10 33		10 39
	d				09 40	09 45						10 00	10 05		10 14	10 20	10 20	10 28				10 40
Hampton-in-Arden	d					09 48												10 31				
Berkswell	d												10 11					10 37				
Tile Hill	d					09 54							10 14					10 40				
Canley	d												10 17					10 43				
Coventry	a				09 50	09 59						10 10	10 20		10 24	10 30	10 30	10 47				10 50
	d				09 51	10 01						10 11	10 22			10 31	10 31	10 49				10 51
Rugby	d					10 12						10 23	10 32					10 59				
Long Buckby	d					10 23							10 42					11 09				
Northampton 66	a					10 35							10 54					11 21				
London Euston ■ ⊖66	a				10 56	11 30						11 14	12 16			11 34	11 36	12 24				11 56

A From Preston
B From Nottingham to Bournemouth
C From Crewe to London Euston
D From Manchester Piccadilly
E From Crewe
F From Liverpool Lime Street to Rugeley Trent Valley
G From Crewe to Walsall
H From Shrewsbury
I From Aberystwyth
J From Manchester Piccadilly to Bristol Temple Meads
K From Rugeley Trent Valley
L To Walsall
M From Liverpool Lime Street
N From Manchester Piccadilly to Bournemouth
O From Lancaster
P To Rugeley Trent Valley
Q From Manchester Piccadilly to Paignton
R until 14 February. From Glasgow Central
S from 17 February. From Glasgow Central

Table T068-R

Mondays to Fridays

16 December to 15 May

Stafford - Wolverhampton - Birmingham - Coventry - Northampton

Station		LM 1 A	LM 1 B	AW C	XC ◇1 D	LM 1 E	LM 1 F	VT ◇1	LM 1 A	LM G	XC ◇1 H	VT FX ◇1 I	VT FO ◇1 I	LM J	LM 1 E	LM G	LM	VT ◇1	LM 1 A	LM 1 B	AW ◇ G	XC ◇1 K
Stafford	d	09 39	09 45		10 03				10 10		10 24								10 40	10 49		11 03
Penkridge	d	09 45							10 16										10 46			
Wolverhampton 7	a	09 58	10 02		10 16				10 26		10 37								10 58	11 05		11 16
	d	09 59	10 06	10 10	10 17		10 22		10 31	10 35	10 42	10 45	10 45	10 48		10 56			10 59	11 07	11 11	11 17
Coseley	d	10 04					10 27							10 53					11 04			
Tipton	d						10 30							10 56								
Dudley Port	d						10 32							10 58								
Sandwell & Dudley	d						10 36			10 44		10 55	10 55	11 02								
Smethwick Galton Bridge 7	d		10 17	10 21			10 39		10 43					11 05						11 18	11 22	
Smethwick Rolfe Street	d						10 41							11 07								
BirminghamNewStreet 12	a	10 21	10 25	10 32	10 33		10 47		10 50	10 53	10 58	11 05	11 05	11 13		11 16			11 20	11 26	11 30	11 33
	d	10 33		10 36		10 39		10 50	10 54		11 04	11 10	11 10		11 14		11 17	11 30	11 33		11 36	
Adderley Park	d					10 43																
Stechford	d					10 47											11 23					
Lea Hall	d					10 49											11 26					
Marston Green	d	10 41							11 02						11 23		11 29		11 42			
Birmingham International	a	10 44		10 50		10 55		10 59	11 05		11 13	11 19	11 19		11 26		11 33	11 39	11 45		11 51	
	d	10 45						11 00	11 05		11 14	11 20	11 20		11 27			11 40	11 45			
Hampton-in-Arden	d	10 48													11 30				11 49			
Berkswell	d								11 11						11 35							
Tile Hill	d	10 54							11 14						11 38				11 55			
Canley	d								11 17						11 41							
Coventry	a	10 59						11 10	11 20		11 24	11 30	11 30		11 45			11 50	12 01			
	d	11 01						11 11	11 22			11 31	11 31		11 49			11 51	12 01			
Rugby	d	11 12						11 23	11 32						12 00				12 12			
Long Buckby	d	11 21							11 42						12 10				12 21			
Northampton 66	a	11 33							11 54						12 22				12 33			
London Euston 15 ⊖66	a	12 29						12 14	13 17			12 33	12 35		13 24			12 55	13 30			

Station		LM 1 E	LM	VT ◇1	LM 1 A	LM G	XC ◇1 H	VT ◇1 L	LM J	LM 1 E	LM	LM G	VT ◇1	LM 1 A	LM 1 B	AW ◇ M	XC ◇1 D	LM 1 E	LM F	VT ◇1	LM 1 A	LM G	XC ◇1 H
Stafford	d				11 10		11 28							11 40	11 45		12 03				12 10		12 28
Penkridge	d				11 16									11 46							12 16		
Wolverhampton 7	a				11 26		11 41							11 58	12 02		12 16				12 26		12 41
	d		11 22		11 31	11 34	11 42	11 45	11 48			11 58		12 01	12 07	12 11	12 17		12 22		12 30	12 35	12 42
Coseley	d		11 27						11 53					12 06					12 27				
Tipton	d		11 30						11 56										12 30				
Dudley Port	d		11 32						11 58										12 32				
Sandwell & Dudley	d		11 36			11 44		11 55	12 02										12 36			12 43	
Smethwick Galton Bridge 7	d		11 39		11 43				12 05						12 17	12 22			12 39		12 43		
Smethwick Rolfe Street	d		11 41						12 07										12 41				
BirminghamNewStreet 12	a		11 47		11 50	11 53	11 59	12 05	12 13			12 18		12 21	12 25	12 31	12 33		12 47		12 50	12 54	12 59
	d	11 39		11 50	11 54		12 04	12 10		12 14	12 17		12 30	12 33		12 36		12 39		12 50	12 54		13 04
Adderley Park	d	11 44																12 43					
Stechford	d	11 47									12 23							12 47					
Lea Hall	d	11 49									12 26							12 49					
Marston Green	d				12 02					12 22	12 29			12 41							13 02		
Birmingham International	a	11 55		11 59	12 05		12 13	12 19		12 25	12 33		12 39	12 44		12 50		12 55		12 59	13 05		13 13
	d			12 00	12 05		12 14	12 20		12 29			12 40	12 44						13 00	13 05		13 14
Hampton-in-Arden	d									12 32				12 47									
Berkswell	d				12 11					12 37											13 11		
Tile Hill	d				12 14					12 41				12 54							13 14		
Canley	d				12 17					12 44											13 17		
Coventry	a			12 10	12 21		12 24	12 30		12 48			12 50	12 59						13 10	13 21		13 24
	d			12 11	12 21			12 31		12 49			12 51	13 01						13 11	13 22		
Rugby	d			12 23	12 32					13 00				13 12						13 23	13 32		
Long Buckby	d				12 41					13 10				13 21							13 42		
Northampton 66	a				12 54					13 21				13 34							13 54		
London Euston 15 ⊖66	a			13 14	14 17			13 33		14 24			13 58	14 30						14 14	15 17		

A From Liverpool Lime Street
B From Crewe
C From Barmouth
D From Manchester Piccadilly to Bristol Temple Meads
E From Rugeley Trent Valley
F To Walsall
G From Shrewsbury
H From Manchester Piccadilly to Bournemouth
I From Edinburgh
J To Rugeley Trent Valley
K From Manchester Piccadilly to Exeter St Davids
L From Glasgow Central
M From Pwllheli

Table T068-R

Mondays to Fridays

16 December to 15 May

Stafford - Wolverhampton - Birmingham - Coventry - Northampton

Station		VT WX ◇1 A	VT WO ◇1 A	LM B	LM 1 C	LM D	LM	VT ◇1	LM 1 E	LM 1 F	AW ◇ G	XC ◇1 H	LM 1 C	LM 1 I	VT ◇1	LM 1 E	LM D	XC ◇1 J	VT ◇1 K	LM B	LM 1 C	LM D
Stafford	d								12 40	12 45		13 01				13 11		13 28				
Penkridge	d								12 46							13 17						
Wolverhampton 7	a								12 58	13 02		13 16				13 28		13 41				
	d	12 45	12 45	12 48		12 56			12 59	13 07	13 12	13 17		13 22		13 32	13 35	13 42	13 45	13 48		13 56
Coseley	d			12 53					13 04					13 27						13 53		
Tipton	d			12 56										13 30						13 56		
Dudley Port	d			12 58										13 32						13 58		
Sandwell & Dudley	d	12 55	12 55	13 02										13 36			13 44		13 55	14 02		
Smethwick Galton Bridge 7	d			13 05						13 18	13 23			13 39		13 43				14 05		
Smethwick Rolfe Street	d			13 07										13 41						14 07		
BirminghamNewStreet 12	a	13 05	13 05	13 13		13 16			13 20	13 25	13 30	13 33		13 47		13 50	13 53	13 59	14 05	14 13		14 16
	d	13 10	13 10		13 14		13 17	13 30	13 33		13 36		13 39		13 50	13 54		14 04	14 10		14 14	
Adderley Park	d												13 43									
Stechford	d						13 25						13 47									
Lea Hall	d						13 28						13 49									
Marston Green	d				13 22		13 31		13 41							14 02					14 22	
Birmingham International	a	13 19	13 19		13 25		13 35	13 39	13 44		13 50		13 55		13 59	14 05		14 13	14 19		14 25	
	d	13 20	13 20		13 25			13 40	13 45						14 00	14 06		14 14	14 20		14 25	
Hampton-in-Arden	d				13 28				13 48												14 28	
Berkswell	d				13 33											14 11					14 33	
Tile Hill	d				13 36				13 54							14 15					14 36	
Canley	d				13 40											14 18					14 40	
Coventry	a	13 30	13 30		13 44			13 50	13 59						14 10	14 21		14 24	14 30		14 44	
	d	13 31	13 31		13 49			13 51	14 01						14 11	14 22			14 31		14 48	
Rugby	d				13 59				14 12						14 26	14 32					14 59	
Long Buckby	d				14 09				14 21							14 42					15 09	
Northampton 66	a				14 21				14 33							14 54					15 21	
London Euston 15 ⊖66	a	14 33	14 36		15 22			14 55	15 31						15 16	16 17			15 34		16 25	

Station		LM	VT ◇1	LM 1 E	LM 1 F	AW ◇ L	XC ◇1 H	LM 1 C	LM 1 I	VT ◇1	LM 1 E	LM D	XC ◇1 J	VT ◇1 M	VT ◇1 N	LM B	LM 1 C	LM D	LM	VT ◇1	LM 1 E	LM 1 F	AW ◇ G
Stafford	d			13 41	13 45		14 03				14 10		14 25								14 40	14 46	
Penkridge	d			13 47							14 16										14 46		
Wolverhampton 7	a			13 58	14 02		14 16				14 26		14 38								14 58	15 02	
	d			13 59	14 07	14 12	14 17		14 22		14 31	14 34	14 39	14 45	14 45	14 48		14 56			14 59	15 07	15 11
Coseley	d			14 04					14 27							14 53					15 04		
Tipton	d								14 30							14 56							
Dudley Port	d								14 32							14 58							
Sandwell & Dudley	d								14 36			14 43		14 55	14 55	15 02							
Smethwick Galton Bridge 7	d				14 18	14 23			14 39		14 42					15 05						15 18	15 22
Smethwick Rolfe Street	d								14 41							15 07							
BirminghamNewStreet 12	a			14 20	14 25	14 31	14 33		14 47		14 50	14 53	14 59	15 05	15 05	15 13		15 16			15 20	15 25	15 31
	d	14 17	14 30	14 33		14 36		14 39		14 50	14 54		15 04	15 10	15 10		15 14		15 17	15 30	15 33		15 36
Adderley Park	d							14 44															
Stechford	d	14 24						14 47											15 23				
Lea Hall	d	14 27						14 50											15 26				
Marston Green	d	14 30		14 41							15 02						15 22		15 29		15 41		
Birmingham International	a	14 34	14 39	14 44		14 50		14 55		14 59	15 05		15 13	15 19	15 19		15 25		15 33	15 39	15 44		15 50
	d		14 40	14 44						15 00	15 05		15 14	15 20	15 20		15 29			15 40	15 44		
Hampton-in-Arden	d			14 47													15 32				15 47		
Berkswell	d										15 11						15 38						
Tile Hill	d			14 54							15 14						15 41				15 54		
Canley	d										15 17						15 44						
Coventry	a		14 50	14 59						15 10	15 20		15 24	15 30	15 30		15 48			15 50	15 59		
	d		14 51	15 01						15 11	15 21			15 31	15 31		15 49			15 51	16 01		
Rugby	d			15 12						15 23	15 31						15 59				16 11		
Long Buckby	d			15 21							15 41						16 09				16 21		
Northampton 66	a			15 33							15 51						16 23				16 33		
London Euston 15 ⊖66	a		15 56	16 29						16 13	16 46			16 32	16 33		17 25			16 56	17 31		

A From Edinburgh
B To Rugeley Trent Valley
C From Rugeley Trent Valley
D From Shrewsbury
E From Liverpool Lime Street
F From Crewe
G From Holyhead
H From Manchester Piccadilly to Exeter St Davids
I To Walsall
J From Manchester Piccadilly to Bournemouth
K From Glasgow Central
L From Pwllheli
M until 14 February. From Edinburgh
N from 17 February. From Edinburgh

Table T068-R

Stafford - Wolverhampton - Birmingham - Coventry - Northampton

Mondays to Fridays
16 December to 15 May

		XC	LM	LM	VT	LM	LM	XC	VT	LM	LM	LM	LM	VT	LM	LM	VT	AW	XC	LM	LM	VT	LM
		◇1 A ⊼	1 B	1 C	◇1 ⊡	1 D	E	◇1 F ⊼	◇1 G ⊡	H	1 B		E	◇1 E ⊡	1 D	1 I	◇1 ⊡	◇ J ⊼	◇1 K ⊼	1 B	1 C	◇1 ⊡	1 D
Stafford	d	15 03				15 12		15 28							15 41	15 45			16 03				16 11
Penkridge	d					15 18									15 47								16 16
Wolverhampton 7	a	15 16				15 28		15 41							15 58	16 05			16 16				16 27
	d	15 17		15 22		15 31	15 35	15 42	15 45	15 48			16 01	16 03	15 58	16 07		16 11	16 17		16 22		16 31
Coseley	d			15 27						15 53					16 03						16 27		
Tipton	d			15 30						15 56											16 30		
Dudley Port	d			15 32						15 58											16 32		
Sandwell & Dudley	d			15 36			15 44		15 55	16 02											16 36		
Smethwick Galton Bridge 7	d			15 39		15 43				16 05					16 09			16 22			16 39		16 42
Smethwick Rolfe Street	d			15 41						16 07											16 41		
BirminghamNewStreet 12	a	15 33		15 47		15 50	15 53	15 58	16 04	16 13			16 27	16 21	16 17	16 24		16 31	16 33		16 47		16 50
	d		15 39		15 50	15 54		16 04	16 10		16 14	16 18		16 30	16 33		16 30	16 36		16 39		16 50	16 54
Adderley Park	d		15 43																	16 44			
Stechford	d		15 47									16 24								16 47			
Lea Hall	d		15 49									16 27								16 50			
Marston Green	d					16 02					16 22	16 30			16 41								17 02
Birmingham International ✈	a		15 55		15 59	16 05		16 13	16 19		16 25	16 34		16 39	16 44		16 39	16 50		16 55		16 59	17 05
	d				16 00	16 05		16 14	16 20		16 29			16 40	16 44		16 40					17 00	17 05
Hampton-in-Arden	d										16 32				16 47								
Berkswell	d					16 11					16 38												17 11
Tile Hill	d					16 14					16 41				16 54								17 14
Canley	d					16 17					16 44												17 17
Coventry	a				16 10	16 20		16 24	16 30		16 47			16 50	16 59		16 50					17 10	17 20
	d				16 11	16 21			16 31		16 48			16 51	17 01		16 51					17 11	17 22
Rugby	d				16 23	16 32					16 58				17 15							17 23	17 32
Long Buckby	d					16 42					17 08				17 26								17 42
Northampton 66	a					16 56					17 20				17 38								17 55
London Euston 15 ⊖66	a				17 14	17 46			17 34		18 25			17 56	18 30		17 56					18 14	18 47

		LM	XC	VT	LM	LM	LM	LM	VT	LM	LM	AW	XC	LM	LM	VT	LM	LM	XC	VT	LM	LM	LM
		E	◇1 F ⊼	◇1 L ⊡	H	1 B	E		◇1 ⊠	1 D	1 I	■ M ⊼	◇1 N ⊼	1 B	C	◇1 ⊠	1 D	E	◇1 F ⊼	◇1 G ⊡	H	1 B	E
Stafford	d		16 25							16 39	16 45		17 03				17 10		17 25				
Penkridge	d									16 45							17 16						
Wolverhampton 7	a		16 38							16 58	17 02		17 16				17 26		17 38				
	d	16 34	16 39	16 45	16 48		16 56			17 00	17 07	17 11	17 17		17 22		17 30	17 34	17 39	17 45	17 48		17 57
Coseley	d				16 53					17 05					17 27						17 53		
Tipton	d				16 56										17 30						17 56		
Dudley Port	d				16 58										17 32						17 58		
Sandwell & Dudley	d	16 43		16 55	17 02										17 36			17 43		17 55	18 02		
Smethwick Galton Bridge 7	d				17 05						17 18	17 22			17 39		17 42				18 05		
Smethwick Rolfe Street	d				17 07										17 41						18 07		
BirminghamNewStreet 12	a	16 53	16 58	17 05	17 13		17 16			17 21	17 25	17 31	17 33		17 47		17 50	17 53	17 59	18 05	18 13		18 17
	d		17 04	17 10		17 14		17 18	17 30	17 33		17 36		17 39		17 50	17 54		18 04	18 10		18 14	
Adderley Park	d							17 23						17 43									
Stechford	d					17 20								17 47									
Lea Hall	d							17 27						17 49									
Marston Green	d							17 30		17 41							18 02					18 22	
Birmingham International ✈	a		17 13	17 19		17 25		17 34	17 39	17 44		17 50		17 55		17 59	18 05		18 13	18 19		18 25	
	d		17 14	17 20		17 27			17 40	17 44						18 00	18 05		18 14	18 20		18 29	
Hampton-in-Arden	d					17 30				17 47												18 32	
Berkswell	d					17 35											18 11					18 38	
Tile Hill	d					17 39				17 54							18 14					18 41	
Canley	d					17 42											18 17					18 44	
Coventry	a		17 24	17 30		17 45			17 50	17 59						18 10	18 20		18 24	18 30		18 47	
	d			17 31		17 48			17 51	18 01						18 11	18 22			18 31		18 48	
Rugby	d					17 58				18 13						18 23	18 32					18 58	
Long Buckby	d					18 08				18 22							18 42					19 08	
Northampton 66	a					18 23				18 34							18 54					19 20	
London Euston 15 ⊖66	a			18 33		19 25			18 56	19 30						19 13	19 45			19 33		20 25	

A From Manchester Piccadilly to Paignton
B From Rugeley Trent Valley
C To Walsall
D From Liverpool Lime Street
E From Shrewsbury
F From Manchester Piccadilly to Bournemouth
G From Glasgow Central
H To Rugeley Trent Valley
I From Crewe
J From Pwllheli
K From Manchester Piccadilly to Exeter St Davids
L From Edinburgh
M From Holyhead
N From Manchester Piccadilly to Bristol Temple Meads

Table T068-R

Stafford - Wolverhampton - Birmingham - Coventry - Northampton

Mondays to Fridays
16 December to 15 May

		LM	VT	LM	LM	AW	XC	LM	LM	VT	LM	LM	XC	VT	LM	LM	LM	LM	LM	VT	LM	AW	XC
			◇1 ⊠	1 A	1 B	◇ C ⊼	◇1 D ⊼	1 E	F	◇1 ⊠	1 A	G	◇1 H ⊼	■ 1 I ⊡	1 E	J		G	1 K	◇1 ⊡	1 B	◇ L ⊼	◇1 M ⊼
Stafford	d			17 42	17 46		18 03				18 09		18 27						18 41		18 46		19 01
Penkridge	d			17 47							18 15								18 47				
Wolverhampton 7	a			17 58	18 02		18 16				18 25		18 40						18 58		19 03		19 14
	d			18 01	18 06	18 11	18 17		18 22		18 30	18 35	18 41	18 45		18 48		18 55	18 59		19 07	19 12	19 17
Coseley	d			18 06					18 27							18 53			19 04				
Tipton	d								18 30							18 56							
Dudley Port	d								18 32							18 58							
Sandwell & Dudley	d								18 36			18 44		18 55		19 02							
Smethwick Galton Bridge 7	d				18 17	18 22			18 39		18 43					19 05					19 19	19 23	
Smethwick Rolfe Street	d								18 41							19 07							
BirminghamNewStreet 12	a			18 21	18 25	18 31	18 33		18 47		18 50	18 53	18 57	19 05		19 13		19 16	19 19		19 26	19 31	19 33
	d	18 17	18 30	18 33		18 36		18 40		18 50	18 54		19 04	19 10	19 13		19 16			19 30	19 33	19 36	
Adderley Park	d			18 37				18 44															
Stechford	d	18 23						18 48									19 22						
Lea Hall	d	18 26						18 50									19 25						
Marston Green	d	18 29		18 42							19 02				19 22		19 28				19 41		
Birmingham International ✈	a	18 33	18 39	18 45		18 50		18 56		18 59	19 05		19 13	19 19	19 25		19 32			19 39	19 44	19 50	
	d		18 40	18 46						19 00	19 05		19 14	19 20	19 29					19 40	19 44		
Hampton-in-Arden	d			18 49											19 32						19 47		
Berkswell	d										19 11				19 38								
Tile Hill	d			18 55							19 14				19 41						19 54		
Canley	d										19 17				19 44								
Coventry	a		18 50	19 01						19 10	19 20		19 24	19 30	19 47					19 50	19 59		
	d		18 51	19 01						19 11	19 21			19 31	19 48					19 51	20 01		
Rugby	d			19 12						19 23	19 32				19 58					20 04	20 12		
Long Buckby	d			19 22							19 42				20 08						20 24		
Northampton 66	a			19 37							19 55				20 20						20 37		
London Euston 15 ⊖66	a		19 55	20 30						20 15	21 17			20 33	21 27					20 57	21 30		

		LM	LM	LM	LM	XC	VT	LM	LM	LM	LM	LM	LM	AW	XC	LM	LM	VT	LM	LM	XC	VT
		1 E		1 A	G	◇1 H ⊼	◇1 N ⊠	1 E		G		1 A	1 B	◇ O ⊼	◇1 P ⊼		F	◇1 ⊡	1 A	G	◇1 Q ⊼	■ 1 I ⊠
Stafford	d			19 10		19 27						19 40	19 45		20 03				20 16		20 26	
Penkridge	d			19 16								19 46							20 22			
Wolverhampton 7	a			19 27		19 40						19 58	20 02		20 16				20 32		20 41	
	d		19 22	19 30	19 36	19 41	19 45		19 48	19 56		19 59	20 07	20 11	20 17		20 22		20 33	20 35	20 42	20 46
Coseley	d		19 27						19 53			20 04					20 27					
Tipton	d		19 30						19 56								20 30					
Dudley Port	d		19 32						19 58								20 32					
Sandwell & Dudley	d		19 36		19 45		19 55		20 02								20 36			20 44		20 56
Smethwick Galton Bridge 7	d		19 39	19 43					20 05				20 18	20 22			20 39		20 43			
Smethwick Rolfe Street	d		19 41						20 07								20 41					
BirminghamNewStreet 12	a		19 47	19 50	19 54	19 57	20 05		20 14	20 16		20 20	20 25	20 31	20 33		20 47		20 50	20 53	20 58	21 04
	d	19 39		19 54		20 04	20 10	20 14			20 17	20 33		20 36		20 39		20 50	20 54		21 04	21 10
Adderley Park	d	19 43														20 44						
Stechford	d	19 47									20 23					20 47						
Lea Hall	d	19 49									20 26					20 50						
Marston Green	d			20 02				20 22			20 29	20 42							21 02			
Birmingham International ✈	a	19 54		20 05		20 13	20 19	20 25			20 33	20 45		20 50		20 55		20 59	21 05		21 13	21 19
	d			20 06		20 14	20 20	20 25				20 45						21 00	21 05		21 14	21 20
Hampton-in-Arden	d							20 28				20 48										
Berkswell	d			20 11				20 33											21 11			
Tile Hill	d			20 15				20 36				20 55							21 14			
Canley	d			20 18				20 40				20 58							21 17			
Coventry	a			20 21		20 24	20 30	20 46				21 01						21 10	21 20		21 24	21 30
	d			20 22			20 31					21 02						21 11	21 21			21 31
Rugby	d			20 33								21 14						21 23	21 31			
Long Buckby	d			20 43								21 24							21 41			
Northampton 66	a			20 55								21 35							21 54			
London Euston 15 ⊖66	a			21 53			21 36					22 53						22 12	23 23			22 41

A From Liverpool Lime Street
B From Crewe
C From Pwllheli
D From Manchester Piccadilly to Cardiff Central
E From Rugeley Trent Valley
F To Walsall
G From Shrewsbury
H From Manchester Piccadilly to Bournemouth
I From Edinburgh
J To Rugeley Trent Valley
K From Liverpool Lime Street to Walsall
L From Holyhead
M From Manchester Piccadilly to Plymouth
N From Glasgow Central
O From Aberystwyth
P From Manchester Piccadilly to Bristol Temple Meads
Q From Manchester Piccadilly to Southampton Central. ⊼ to BirminghamNewStreet

Table T068-R

Mondays to Fridays

16 December to 15 May

Stafford - Wolverhampton - Birmingham - Coventry - Northampton

Station		LM ■	LM A	LM ■ B	LM	LM ■ C	XC ◇■ D	LM	LM ■ C	LM ■ B	VT ◇■ E ☒	LM F	XC ◇■ D	XC ◇■ G	VT ◇■	LM ■	LM ■ A	LM ■ B	AW ◇ H	LM ■ C	LM ■ I	LM ■ J	LM
Stafford	d			20 40		20 48	21 03		21 03	21 09	21 15		21 29					21 40		21 49		21 59	
Penkridge	d			20 46						21 16								21 46					
Wolverhampton 7	a			20 57		21 02	21 16			21 26	21 30		21 42					21 57				22 14	
	d		20 49	21 02		21 06	21 17	21 20		21 29	21 33	21 37	21 43		21 46		21 50	22 01	22 12			22 17	22 20
Coseley	d		20 54	21 07				21 25									21 55					22 22	22 25
Tipton	d		20 57					21 28									21 58						22 28
Dudley Port	d		20 59					21 30									22 00						22 30
Sandwell & Dudley	d		21 03					21 34				21 46			21 55		22 04						22 34
Smethwick Galton Bridge 7	d		21 06			21 17		21 36		21 40							22 07		22 23			22 28	22 37
Smethwick Rolfe Street	d		21 08					21 38															22 39
BirminghamNewStreet 12	a		21 14	21 21		21 25	21 33	21 45		21 48	21 54	21 57	22 00		22 06		22 14	22 18	22 32			22 39	22 45
	d	21 14			21 24	21 34				21 54				22 04	22 10	22 14					22 33		
Adderley Park	d				21 28																		
Stechford	d	21 20			21 32											22 20							
Lea Hall	d	21 23			21 34											22 23							
Marston Green	d	21 26				21 42				22 02						22 26					22 41		
Birmingham International	a	21 29			21 39	21 45				22 05				22 13	22 19	22 29					22 44		
	d	21 30				21 45				22 05				22 14	22 20	22 30					22 44		
Hampton-in-Arden	d	21 33				21 48										22 33					22 47		
Berkswell	d	21 38								22 11						22 38					22 52		
Tile Hill	d	21 41				21 55				22 14						22 41					22 55		
Canley	d	21 44								22 17						22 44					22 58		
Coventry	a	21 49				21 59				22 20				22 24	22 30	22 47					23 01		
	d					22 01				22 22					22 31	22 48					23 02		
Rugby	d					22 12			21 59	22 32					22 45	23 00				22 42	23 13		
Long Buckby	d					22 22			22 09	22 42						23 10				22 51	23 22		
Northampton 66	a					22 35			22 21	22 54						23 21				23 03	23 35		
London Euston 15 ⊖66	a									00 26					00 01	00 54							

Station		VT ◇■ K	VT FX ◇■ L ☒	LM ■	XC ◇■ D	VT ◇■ L ☒	LM	AW ◇ M	LM ■ B	LM ■	LM	XC ◇■ D	LM	LM F	LM
Stafford	d				22 28				22 37			23 06			
Penkridge	d								22 43						
Wolverhampton 7	a				22 41				22 58			23 19			
	d	22 29	22 33		22 42	22 45		22 55	22 59	23 02		23 20		23 35	23 39
Coseley	d									23 07					23 44
Tipton	d									23 10					23 48
Dudley Port	d									23 12					23 50
Sandwell & Dudley	d					22 55				23 16					23 54
Smethwick Galton Bridge 7	d								23 09	23 19					23 57
Smethwick Rolfe Street	d									23 21					23 59
BirminghamNewStreet 12	a	22 48	22 52		22 59	23 06		23 28	23 15	23 27		23 37		23 50	00 06
	d			22 55		23 10	23 14				23 34		23 50		
Adderley Park	d						23 19								
Stechford	d						23 22				23 41		23 58		
Lea Hall	d						23 25				23 43		00 01		
Marston Green	d			23 03			23 27				23 47		00 03		
Birmingham International	a			23 06		23 19	23 30				23 50		00 06		
	d			23 06		23 20	23 31				23 51		00 07		
Hampton-in-Arden	d						23 34				23 54		00 10		
Berkswell	d			23 12			23 39				23 59				
Tile Hill	d			23 15			23 42				00 02		00 16		
Canley	d			23 18			23 45				00 05				
Coventry	a			23 21		23 30	23 49				00 08		00 22		
	d			23 22		23 31									
Rugby	d			23 32		23 44									
Long Buckby	d			23 42											
Northampton 66	a			23 56		00s05									
London Euston 15 ⊖66	a					01 13									

A To Rugeley Trent Valley
B From Liverpool Lime Street
C From Crewe
D From Manchester Piccadilly
E From Glasgow Central
F From Shrewsbury
G To Reading
H From Pwllheli
I From Rugeley Trent Valley
J From Crewe to Walsall
K From Bangor (Gwynedd)
L From Edinburgh
M From Holyhead

NRT DECEMBER 19 EDITION

Table T068-R

Saturdays

21 December to 16 May

Stafford - Wolverhampton - Birmingham - Coventry - Northampton

Station		LM A	LM A	LM B	LM	LM ■	VT ◇■	LM	AW C	XC ◇■ D	VT ◇■	LM ■	AW E	VT ◇■	LM ■	AW F	LM	LM F	VT ◇■	LM ■	XC ◇■ G	VT ◇■	LM ■ H
Stafford	d								05 25												06 28		
Penkridge	d																						
Wolverhampton 7	a								05 40												06 41		
	d							05 27	05 40		05 45		06 02	06 06				06 19	06 27		06 42	06 45	
Coseley	d							05 32										06 25					
Tipton	d							05 35										06 28					
Dudley Port	d							05 37										06 30					
Sandwell & Dudley	d							05 41			05 55			06 17				06 33	06 37			06 56	
Smethwick Galton Bridge 7	d							05 44					06 13					06 36					
Smethwick Rolfe Street	d							05 46								←		06 38					
BirminghamNewStreet 12	a							05 54	05 59		06 05		06 21	06 26		06 21		06 44	06 47		06 58	07 06	
	d			00 23	00 40	05 33	05 50			06 04	06 10	06 14	06 36	06 30	06 33	06 36	06 39		06 50	06 54	07 04	07 10	07 16
Adderley Park	d				00 44								→				06 44						
Stechford	d			00 30	00 48							06 20					06 47						07 22
Lea Hall	d		00 01	00 32	00 50							06 23					06 50						07 25
Marston Green	d		00 03	00 35	00 54	05 41						06 26			06 41					07 02			07 28
Birmingham International	a		00 06	00 38	00 57	05 44	06 00			06 13	06 19	06 29		06 39	06 44	06 50	06 55		06 59	07 05	07 13	07 19	07 31
	d		00 07	00 39	00 58	05 44	06 00			06 14	06 20	06 30		06 40	06 45				07 00	07 05	07 14	07 20	07 31
Hampton-in-Arden	d		00 10	00 42	01 01	05 48						06 33			06 48								07 34
Berkswell	d			00 47	01 06	05 52						06 38								07 11			07 39
Tile Hill	d	00 02	00 16	00 51	01 09	05 56						06 41			06 54					07 14			07 42
Canley	d	00 05		00 54	01 12	05 59						06 44								07 17			07 45
Coventry	a	00 08	00 22	00 56	01 15	06 02	06 11			06 24	06 30	06 47		06 49	07 00				07 10	07 20	07 24	07 30	07 48
	d					06 02	06 11				06 31	06 48		06 51	07 01				07 11	07 21		07 31	07 48
Rugby	d					06 13	06 23					06 59			07 12				07 23	07 31			08 00
Long Buckby	d					06 22						07 08			07 22					07 41			08 10
Northampton 66	a					06 34						07 20			07 34					07 53			08 22
London Euston 15 ⊖66	a					07 39	07 13				07 36	08 20		07 53	08 31				08 17	09 17		08 34	09 24

Station		LM F	LM ■ I	VT ◇■	LM ■ I	AW F	XC ◇■ J	LM H	LM K	VT ◇■	LM ■ L	LM F	XC ◇■ M	VT ◇■ N	LM ■ H	LM K	LM F	VT ◇■	LM ■ L	LM ■ I	AW ◇ O	XC ◇■ J
Stafford	d		06 36		06 45		07 03				07 09								07 38	07 51		08 03
Penkridge	d		06 42								07 15								07 44			
Wolverhampton 7	a		06 56		07 04		07 16				07 25								07 54	08 06		08 16
	d	06 47	06 57	07 05	07 09	07 12	07 17		07 20	07 25	07 31	07 36		07 45		07 50	07 56		08 00	08 07	08 11	08 17
Coseley	d	06 53	07 02						07 25							07 55			08 05			
Tipton	d	06 56							07 28							07 58						
Dudley Port	d	06 59							07 30							08 00						
Sandwell & Dudley	d	07 03		07 15					07 33			07 46		07 55		08 04						
Smethwick Galton Bridge 7	d	07 06			07 20	07 23			07 36		07 42					08 07				08 17	08 23	
Smethwick Rolfe Street	d	07 09							07 38							08 09						
BirminghamNewStreet 12	a	07 18	07 22	07 25	07 28	07 32	07 34		07 44	07 47	07 50	07 55		08 05		08 15	08 18		08 21	08 25	08 31	08 33
	d			07 30	07 34	07 37		07 40		07 50	07 54		08 04	08 10	08 14			08 30		08 33	08 36	
Adderley Park	d							07 44														
Stechford	d							07 47							08 20							
Lea Hall	d							07 50							08 23							
Marston Green	d				07 42						08 02				08 26					08 41		
Birmingham International	a			07 39	07 45	07 50		07 54		07 59	08 05		08 13	08 19	08 29			08 39		08 44	08 50	
	d			07 40	07 45					08 00	08 05		08 14	08 20	08 30			08 40		08 45		
Hampton-in-Arden	d				07 48										08 33					08 48		
Berkswell	d										08 11				08 38							
Tile Hill	d				07 55						08 14				08 41					08 54		
Canley	d										08 17				08 44							
Coventry	a			07 50	08 00					08 10	08 20		08 24	08 30	08 47			08 50		08 59		
	d			07 51	08 01					08 11	08 21			08 31	08 48			08 51		09 01		
Rugby	d				08 12					08 23	08 32				08 59					09 12		
Long Buckby	d				08 21						08 41				09 08					09 21		
Northampton 66	a				08 33						08 57				09 20					09 33		
London Euston 15 ⊖66	a			08 53	09 33					09 13	10 17			09 36	10 25			09 57		10 30		

A From Birmingham New Street
B From Bromsgrove
C From Chester
D To Bournemouth
E From Shrewsbury to Birmingham International
F From Shrewsbury
G From Manchester Piccadilly to Bournemouth. from BirminghamNewStreet
H From Rugeley Trent Valley
I From Crewe
J From Manchester Piccadilly to Bristol Temple Meads
K To Walsall
L From Liverpool Lime Street
M From Nottingham to Bournemouth
N From Preston
O From Aberystwyth

Table T068-R

Saturdays

21 December to 16 May

Stafford - Wolverhampton - Birmingham - Coventry - Northampton

		LM A	LM B	VT	LM C	LM D	XC E	VT F	VT	LM B	LM A	LM D	VT D	LM C	LM G	VT	AW H	XC I	LM A	LM B	VT	LM C
Stafford	d				08 10		08 28							08 38	08 46			09 03				09 09
Penkridge	d				08 16									08 44								09 15
Wolverhampton	a				08 26		08 41							08 57	09 03			09 16				09 26
	d		08 22		08 30	08 36	08 42	08 45		08 48		09 00	09 03	08 57	09 06		09 12	09 17		09 22		09 29
Coseley	d		08 27							08 53				09 02						09 27		
Tipton	d		08 30							08 56										09 30		
Dudley Port	d		08 32							08 58										09 32		
Sandwell & Dudley	d		08 36			08 45		08 55		09 02										09 36		
Smethwick Galton Bridge	d		08 39		08 43					09 05				09 08			09 24			09 39		09 43
Smethwick Rolfe Street	d		08 41							09 07										09 41		
BirminghamNewStreet	a		08 47		08 50	08 54	08 58	09 06		09 13		09 26	09 19	09 16	09 22		09 31	09 33		09 47		09 50
	d	08 40		08 50	08 54		09 04		09 10		09 14		09 30	09 33		09 30	09 36		09 39		09 50	09 54
Adderley Park	d	08 44																	09 43			
Stechford	d	08 47									09 20								09 46			
Lea Hall	d	08 50									09 23								09 49			
Marston Green	d				09 02						09 26			09 41								10 02
Birmingham International	a	08 55		08 59	09 05		09 13		09 19		09 29		09 39	09 44		09 39	09 51		09 54		09 59	10 05
	d			09 00	09 05		09 14		09 20		09 30		09 40	09 44		09 40					10 00	10 05
Hampton-in-Arden	d										09 33			09 47								
Berkswell	d				09 11						09 38											10 11
Tile Hill	d				09 14						09 41			09 54								10 14
Canley	d				09 17						09 44											10 17
Coventry	a			09 10	09 20		09 24		09 30		09 47		09 50	09 59		09 50					10 10	10 20
	d			09 11	09 21				09 31		09 48		09 51	10 01		09 51					10 11	10 21
Rugby	d			09 23	09 32						09 59			10 12							10 23	10 32
Long Buckby	d				09 41						10 08			10 21								10 41
Northampton 66	a				09 53						10 20			10 33								10 53
London Euston ⊖66	a			10 15	11 17				10 33		11 25		10 57	11 30		10 57					11 13	12 17

		LM D	XC E	VT J	LM B	LM A	LM D	VT	LM C	LM G	AW K	XC L	LM A	LM B	VT	LM C	LM D	XC E	VT M	LM B	LM A	LM D	VT
Stafford	d		09 28						09 39	09 45		10 03				10 10		10 28					
Penkridge	d								09 45							10 16							
Wolverhampton	a		09 41						09 58	10 02		10 16				10 27		10 41					
	d	09 34	09 42	09 45	09 48		09 56		10 00	10 06	10 10	10 17		10 22		10 32	10 35	10 42	10 45	10 48		10 56	
Coseley	d				09 53				10 05					10 27						10 53			
Tipton	d				09 56									10 30						10 56			
Dudley Port	d				09 58									10 32						10 58			
Sandwell & Dudley	d	09 44		09 55	10 02									10 36			10 44		10 55	11 02			
Smethwick Galton Bridge	d				10 05					10 17	10 21			10 39		10 43				11 05			
Smethwick Rolfe Street	d				10 07									10 41						11 07			
BirminghamNewStreet	a	09 54	09 58	10 05	10 13		10 17		10 20	10 25	10 31	10 33		10 47		10 50	10 53	10 58	11 05	11 13		11 17	
	d		10 04	10 10		10 14		10 30	10 33		10 36		10 40		10 50	10 54		11 04	11 10		11 14		11 30
Adderley Park	d												10 44										
Stechford	d					10 20							10 47								11 20		
Lea Hall	d					10 23							10 50								11 23		
Marston Green	d					10 26			10 41							11 02					11 26		
Birmingham International	a		10 13	10 19		10 29		10 39	10 44		10 50		10 55		10 59	11 05		11 13	11 19		11 29		11 39
	d		10 14	10 20		10 30		10 40	10 45						11 00	11 05		11 14	11 20		11 30		11 40
Hampton-in-Arden	d					10 33			10 48												11 33		
Berkswell	d					10 38										11 11					11 38		
Tile Hill	d					10 41			10 54							11 14					11 41		
Canley	d					10 44										11 17					11 44		
Coventry	a		10 24	10 30		10 47		10 50	10 59						11 10	11 20		11 24	11 30		11 47		11 50
	d			10 31		10 48		10 51	11 01						11 11	11 21			11 31		11 48		11 51
Rugby	d					10 59			11 12						11 22	11 32					11 59		
Long Buckby	d					11 08			11 21							11 41					12 08		
Northampton 66	a					11 20			11 33							11 55					12 20		
London Euston ⊖66	a			11 33		12 24		11 55	12 30						12 12	13 17			12 33		13 24		12 56

A From Rugeley Trent Valley
B To Walsall
C From Liverpool Lime Street
D From Shrewsbury
E From Manchester Piccadilly to Bournemouth
F From Lancaster
G From Crewe
H From Holyhead
I From Manchester Piccadilly to Paignton
J From Glasgow Central
K From Barmouth
L From Manchester Piccadilly to Bristol Temple Meads
M From Edinburgh

Table T068-R

Saturdays

21 December to 16 May

Stafford - Wolverhampton - Birmingham - Coventry - Northampton

		LM A	LM B	AW C	XC D	LM E	LM F	VT	LM A	LM G	XC H	VT I	LM F	LM E	LM G	VT	LM A	LM B	AW J	XC D	LM E	LM F
Stafford	d	10 38	10 45		11 03				11 10		11 28						11 40	11 45		12 03		
Penkridge	d	10 46							11 16								11 46					
Wolverhampton	a	10 58	11 03		11 16				11 26		11 41						11 58	12 03		12 16		
	d	11 00	11 06	11 13	11 17		11 22		11 32	11 35	11 42	11 45	11 48		11 56		12 00	12 06	12 11	12 17		12 22
Coseley	d	11 05					11 27						11 53				12 05					12 27
Tipton	d						11 30						11 56									12 30
Dudley Port	d						11 32						11 58									12 32
Sandwell & Dudley	d						11 36			11 44		11 55	12 02									12 36
Smethwick Galton Bridge	d		11 17	11 24			11 39		11 43				12 05					12 17	12 23			12 39
Smethwick Rolfe Street	d						11 41						12 07									12 41
BirminghamNewStreet	a	11 20	11 25	11 31	11 33		11 47		11 50	11 53	11 58	12 05	12 13		12 17		12 20	12 25	12 31	12 33		12 47
	d	11 33		11 36		11 40		11 50	11 54		12 04	12 10		12 14		12 30	12 33		12 36		12 40	
Adderley Park	d					11 44															12 44	
Stechford	d					11 48								12 20							12 47	
Lea Hall	d					11 50								12 23							12 50	
Marston Green	d	11 41							12 02					12 26			12 41					
Birmingham International	a	11 44		11 50		11 56		11 59	12 05		12 13	12 19		12 29		12 39	12 44		12 50		12 55	
	d	11 45						12 00	12 05		12 14	12 20		12 30		12 40	12 45					
Hampton-in-Arden	d	11 48												12 33			12 48					
Berkswell	d								12 11					12 38								
Tile Hill	d	11 54							12 14					12 41			12 54					
Canley	d								12 17					12 44								
Coventry	a	11 59						12 10	12 20		12 24	12 30		12 47		12 50	12 59					
	d	12 01						12 11	12 21			12 31		12 48		12 51	13 01					
Rugby	d	12 12						12 23	12 32					12 59			13 12					
Long Buckby	d	12 21							12 41					13 08			13 21					
Northampton 66	a	12 33							12 53					13 20			13 33					
London Euston ⊖66	a	13 30						13 14	14 18			13 33		14 24		13 58	14 30					

		VT	LM A	LM G	XC H	VT K	LM F	LM E	LM G	VT	LM A	LM B	AW C	XC L	LM E	LM F	VT	LM A	LM G	XC H	VT I	LM E	LM F
Stafford	d		12 09		12 28						12 40	12 45		13 03				13 10		13 28			
Penkridge	d		12 15								12 46							13 16					
Wolverhampton	a		12 26		12 41						12 58	13 01		13 16				13 27		13 41			
	d		12 31	12 34	12 42	12 45	12 48		12 56		13 00	13 06	13 12	13 17		13 23		13 31	13 34	13 42	13 45		13 48
Coseley	d						12 53				13 05					13 28							13 53
Tipton	d						12 56									13 31							13 56
Dudley Port	d						12 58									13 33							13 58
Sandwell & Dudley	d			12 43		12 55	13 02									13 37			13 44		13 55		14 02
Smethwick Galton Bridge	d		12 43				13 05					13 17	13 23			13 40		13 44					14 05
Smethwick Rolfe Street	d						13 07									13 42							14 07
BirminghamNewStreet	a		12 50	12 53	12 58	13 05	13 13		13 17		13 20	13 25	13 31	13 33		13 48		13 51	13 54	13 58	14 05		14 14
	d	12 50	12 54		13 04	13 10		13 14		13 30	13 33		13 36		13 40		13 50	13 54		14 04	14 10	14 14	
Adderley Park	d														13 44								
Stechford	d							13 20							13 47							14 20	
Lea Hall	d							13 23							13 50							14 23	
Marston Green	d		13 02					13 26			13 41							14 02				14 26	
Birmingham International	a	12 59	13 05		13 13	13 19		13 29		13 39	13 44		13 50		13 55		13 59	14 05		14 13	14 19	14 29	
	d	13 00	13 05		13 14	13 20		13 30		13 40	13 44						14 00	14 05		14 14	14 20	14 30	
Hampton-in-Arden	d							13 33			13 47											14 33	
Berkswell	d		13 11					13 38										14 11				14 38	
Tile Hill	d		13 14					13 41			13 54							14 14				14 41	
Canley	d		13 17					13 44										14 17				14 44	
Coventry	a	13 10	13 20		13 24	13 30		13 47		13 50	13 59						14 10	14 20		14 24	14 30	14 47	
	d	13 11	13 21			13 31		13 48		13 51	14 01						14 11	14 21			14 31	14 48	
Rugby	d	13 23	13 32					13 59			14 12						14 26	14 32				15 01	
Long Buckby	d		13 41					14 08			14 22							14 41				15 10	
Northampton 66	a		13 53					14 20			14 34							14 53				15 22	
London Euston ⊖66	a	14 13	15 17			14 33		15 20		14 55	15 31						15 16	16 19			15 34	16 24	

A From Liverpool Lime Street
B From Crewe
C From Holyhead
D From Manchester Piccadilly to Bristol Temple Meads
E From Rugeley Trent Valley
F To Walsall
G From Shrewsbury
H From Manchester Piccadilly to Bournemouth
I From Glasgow Central
J From Pwllheli
K From Edinburgh
L From Manchester Piccadilly to Exeter St Davids

Table T068-R

Saturdays

21 December to 16 May

Stafford - Wolverhampton - Birmingham - Coventry - Northampton

Station		LM A	VT	LM B	LM C	AW D	XC E	LM F	LM G	VT	LM B	LM A	XC H	VT I	LM G	LM F	LM A	VT	LM B	LM C	AW J	XC K
Stafford	d			13 40	13 45		14 03				14 09		14 28						14 38	14 45		15 03
Penkridge	d			13 46							14 15								14 46			
Wolverhampton	a			13 58	14 02		14 16				14 26		14 41						15 00	15 04		15 16
	d	13 56		14 00	14 06	14 12	14 17		14 22		14 31	14 36	14 42	14 45	14 48		14 56		15 01	15 06	15 12	15 17
Coseley	d			14 05					14 27						14 53				15 06			
Tipton	d								14 30						14 56							
Dudley Port	d								14 32						14 58							
Sandwell & Dudley	d								14 36			14 45		14 55	15 02							
Smethwick Galton Bridge	d				14 17	14 23			14 39		14 43				15 05					15 17	15 23	
Smethwick Rolfe Street	d								14 41						15 07							
BirminghamNewStreet	a	14 17		14 20	14 25	14 30	14 34		14 47		14 50	14 55	14 58	15 05	15 13		15 17		15 20	15 25	15 30	15 33
	d		14 30	14 33		14 36		14 40		14 50	14 54		15 04	15 10		15 14		15 30	15 33		15 36	
Adderley Park	d							14 44														
Stechford	d							14 47								15 20						
Lea Hall	d							14 50								15 23						
Marston Green	d			14 41							15 02					15 26			15 41			
Birmingham International	a		14 39	14 44		14 50		14 55		14 59	15 05		15 13	15 19		15 29		15 39	15 44		15 50	
	d		14 40	14 45						15 00	15 05		15 14	15 20		15 30		15 40	15 44			
Hampton-in-Arden	d			14 48												15 33			15 47			
Berkswell	d										15 11					15 38						
Tile Hill	d			14 54							15 14					15 41			15 54			
Canley	d										15 17					15 44						
Coventry	a		14 50	14 59						15 10	15 20		15 24	15 30		15 47		15 50	15 59			
	d		14 51	15 01						15 11	15 21			15 31		15 48		15 51	16 01			
Rugby	d			15 12						15 22	15 32					15 59			16 12			
Long Buckby	d			15 21							15 41					16 08			16 21			
Northampton 66	a			15 33							15 53					16 20			16 33			
London Euston ⊖66	a		15 55	16 30						16 13	17 17			16 33		17 24		16 55	17 30			

Station		LM F	LM G	VT	LM B	LM A	XC H	VT L	LM G	LM F	LM A	VT A	LM B	LM C	VT	AW D	XC E	LM F	LM G	VT	LM B	LM A	XC H
Stafford	d				15 08		15 28						15 39	15 45			16 03				16 09		16 28
Penkridge	d				15 14								15 45								16 15		
Wolverhampton	a				15 25		15 41						15 58	16 05			16 16				16 25		16 41
	d		15 22		15 30	15 34	15 42	15 45	15 48		16 00	16 03	15 58	16 07		16 12	16 17		16 22		16 31	16 34	16 42
Coseley	d		15 27						15 53				16 03						16 27				
Tipton	d		15 30						15 56										16 30				
Dudley Port	d		15 32						15 58										16 32				
Sandwell & Dudley	d		15 36			15 43		15 55	16 02										16 36			16 43	
Smethwick Galton Bridge	d		15 39		15 43				16 05							16 24			16 39		16 43		
Smethwick Rolfe Street	d		15 41						16 07										16 41				
BirminghamNewStreet	a		15 47		15 50	15 52	15 58	16 05	16 13		16 27	16 22	16 17	16 24		16 31	16 33		16 47		16 50	16 53	16 58
	d	15 40		15 50	15 54		16 04	16 10		16 14		16 30	16 33		16 30	16 36		16 40		16 50	16 54		17 04
Adderley Park	d	15 44																16 44					
Stechford	d	15 47								16 20								16 47					
Lea Hall	d	15 50								16 23								16 50					
Marston Green	d				16 02					16 26			16 41								17 02		
Birmingham International	a	15 55		15 59	16 05		16 13	16 19		16 29		16 39	16 44		16 39	16 49		16 55		16 59	17 05		17 13
	d			16 00	16 05		16 14	16 20		16 30		16 40	16 44		16 40					17 00	17 05		17 14
Hampton-in-Arden	d									16 33			16 47										
Berkswell	d				16 11					16 38											17 11		
Tile Hill	d				16 14					16 41			16 54								17 14		
Canley	d				16 17					16 44											17 17		
Coventry	a			16 10	16 20		16 24	16 30		16 47		16 50	16 59		16 50					17 10	17 20		17 24
	d			16 11	16 21			16 31		16 48		16 51	17 01		16 51					17 11	17 21		
Rugby	d			16 23	16 32					16 59			17 15							17 23	17 32		
Long Buckby	d				16 43					17 08			17 26								17 41		
Northampton 66	a				16 57					17 20			17 38								17 53		
London Euston ⊖66	a			17 13	18 17			17 33		18 24		17 55	18 30		17 55					18 13	19 17		

A From Shrewsbury
B From Liverpool Lime Street
C From Crewe
D From Pwllheli
E From Manchester Piccadilly to Bristol Temple Meads
F From Rugeley Trent Valley
G To Walsall
H From Manchester Piccadilly to Bournemouth
I From Edinburgh
J From Holyhead
K From Manchester Piccadilly to Paignton
L From Glasgow Central

NRT DECEMBER 19 EDITION

Table T068-R

Saturdays

21 December to 16 May

Stafford - Wolverhampton - Birmingham - Coventry - Northampton

Station		VT A	LM B	LM C	LM D	VT	LM E	LM F	AW G	XC H	LM C	LM B	VT	LM E	LM D	XC I	VT J	LM B	LM C	LM D	VT
Stafford	d						16 40	16 47		17 03				17 08		17 25					
Penkridge	d						16 46							17 14							
Wolverhampton	a						16 58	17 03		17 16				17 25		17 38					
	d	16 45	16 48		16 56		17 00	17 06	17 11	17 17		17 22		17 30	17 34	17 42	17 45	17 48		17 56	
Coseley	d		16 53				17 05					17 27						17 53			
Tipton	d		16 56									17 30						17 56			
Dudley Port	d		16 58									17 32						17 58			
Sandwell & Dudley	d	16 55	17 02									17 36			17 43		17 55	18 02			
Smethwick Galton Bridge	d		17 05				17 12	17 17	17 22			17 39		17 43				18 05			
Smethwick Rolfe Street	d		17 07									17 41						18 07			
BirminghamNewStreet	a	17 05	17 13		17 17		17 20	17 26	17 31	17 33		17 47		17 50	17 53	17 58	18 05	18 13		18 16	
	d	17 10		17 14		17 30	17 33		17 36		17 40		17 50	17 54		18 04	18 10		18 14		18 30
Adderley Park	d			17 18							17 44										
Stechford	d			17 22							17 47								18 20		
Lea Hall	d			17 24							17 50								18 23		
Marston Green	d			17 27			17 42							18 02					18 26		
Birmingham International	a	17 19		17 30		17 39	17 45		17 50		17 55		17 59	18 05		18 13	18 19		18 29		18 39
	d	17 20		17 31		17 40	17 45						18 00	18 05		18 14	18 20		18 30		18 40
Hampton-in-Arden	d			17 34			17 48												18 33		
Berkswell	d			17 39										18 11					18 38		
Tile Hill	d			17 42			17 54							18 14					18 41		
Canley	d			17 45										18 17					18 44		
Coventry	a	17 30		17 48		17 50	18 00						18 10	18 20		18 24	18 30		18 47		18 50
	d	17 31		17 49		17 51	18 01						18 11	18 21			18 31		18 48		18 51
Rugby	d			17 59			18 12						18 23	18 32					18 59		
Long Buckby	d			18 08			18 22							18 41					19 08		
Northampton 66	a			18 21			18 37							18 53					19 20		
London Euston ⊖66	a	18 33		19 26		18 59	19 31						19 14	20 17			19 34		20 45		19 55

Station		LM K	LM L	AW M	XC N	LM C	LM B	VT	LM E	LM D	XC I	VT A	LM B	LM C	LM D	LM E	LM F	LM F	AW G	XC O	LM C	LM B	LM E
Stafford	d	17 39	17 45		18 03				18 08		18 28					18 39	18 46	18 55		19 03			19 09
Penkridge	d	17 46							18 14							18 46							19 15
Wolverhampton	a	17 58	18 02		18 16				18 25		18 41					18 58	19 03			19 16			19 26
	d	18 00	18 06	18 11	18 17		18 21		18 29	18 34	18 42	18 45	18 48		18 56	19 00	19 06		19 12	19 17		19 21	19 29
Coseley	d	18 05					18 26						18 53			19 05						19 26	
Tipton	d						18 29						18 56									19 29	
Dudley Port	d						18 31						18 58									19 31	
Sandwell & Dudley	d						18 35				18 43	18 55	19 02									19 35	
Smethwick Galton Bridge	d		18 17	18 22			18 38		18 42				19 05				19 17		19 23			19 38	19 41
Smethwick Rolfe Street	d						18 40						19 07									19 40	
BirminghamNewStreet	a	18 20	18 25	18 31	18 33		18 46		18 49	18 52	18 58	19 05	19 13		19 17	19 20	19 25		19 30	19 33		19 46	19 49
	d	18 33		18 36		18 40		18 50	18 54		19 04	19 10		19 14		19 33			19 36		19 40		19 54
Adderley Park	d					18 44															19 44		
Stechford	d					18 47								19 20							19 48		
Lea Hall	d					18 50								19 23							19 50		
Marston Green	d	18 41							19 02					19 26		19 41							20 02
Birmingham International	a	18 44		18 49		18 55		18 59	19 05		19 13	19 19		19 29		19 44			19 50		19 56		20 05
	d	18 44						19 00	19 05		19 14	19 20		19 30		19 44							20 05
Hampton-in-Arden	d	18 47												19 33		19 47							
Berkswell	d								19 11					19 38									20 11
Tile Hill	d	18 54							19 14					19 41		19 54							20 14
Canley	d								19 17					19 44									20 17
Coventry	a	18 59						19 10	19 20		19 24	19 30		19 47		19 59							20 20
	d	19 01						19 11	19 21			19 31		19 48		20 01							20 21
Rugby	d	19 12						19 23	19 32			19 43		19 59		20 12		19 51					20 32
Long Buckby	d	19 21							19 41					20 08		20 21							20 41
Northampton 66	a	19 33							19 53					20 20		20 35		20 11					20 53
London Euston ⊖66	a							20 23	21 10			20 55		21 34		21 54							22 12

A From Edinburgh
B To Walsall
C From Rugeley Trent Valley
D From Shrewsbury
E From Liverpool Lime Street
F From Crewe
G From Holyhead
H From Manchester Piccadilly to Bristol Temple Meads
I From Manchester Piccadilly to Bournemouth
J From Glasgow Central
K From Liverpool Lime Street to Milton Keynes Central
L From Crewe to Milton Keynes Central
M From Pwllheli
N From Manchester Piccadilly to Cardiff Central
O From Manchester Piccadilly to Plymouth

Table T068-R

Saturdays
21 December to 16 May

Stafford - Wolverhampton - Birmingham - Coventry - Northampton

		LM	XC	VT	LM	LM	LM	LM	LM	LM		AW	XC	LM	LM	LM	LM	XC	VT	LM		LM	LM	LM	LM
			◇■	◇■	■			■	■	■		◇	◇■	■		■		◇■	◇■			■		■	■
		A	B	C	D		A	E	F	F		G	H			E	A	I	J	K			A	E	L
			🍴	☕								🍴	🍴					🍴	☕						
Stafford	d		19 28					19 41	19 46	19 52			20 03			20 11		20 28						20 40	20 45
Penkridge	d							19 47								20 17								20 46	
Wolverhampton 7	a		19 41					19 58	20 02				20 16			20 28		20 41						20 58	21 03
	d	19 31	19 42	19 45		19 48	19 56	20 00	20 08			20 12	20 17		20 21	20 31	20 37	20 42	20 45	20 48			20 55	21 00	21 04
Coseley	d					19 53		20 05							20 26					20 53				21 05	
Tipton	d					19 56									20 29					20 56					
Dudley Port	d					19 58									20 31					20 58					
Sandwell & Dudley	d	19 43		19 55		20 02									20 35		20 46		20 55	21 02					
Smethwick Galton Bridge 7	d					20 05			20 19			20 23			20 38	20 43				21 05					21 15
Smethwick Rolfe Street	d					20 07									20 40					21 07					
BirminghamNewStreet 12	a	19 52	19 58	20 05		20 14	20 17	20 20	20 26			20 31	20 33		20 47	20 50	20 55	20 58	21 05	21 13			21 16	21 20	21 24
	d		20 04	20 10	20 14			20 33				20 36		20 39		20 54		21 04	21 10			21 14			21 34 →
Adderley Park	d													20 44											
Stechford	d				20 20									20 47								21 20			
Lea Hall	d				20 23									20 50								21 23			
Marston Green	d				20 26			20 41								21 02						21 26			
Birmingham International	a		20 13	20 19	20 29			20 44				20 49		20 55		21 05		21 13	21 19			21 29			
	d		20 14	20 20	20 30			20 44								21 05		21 14	21 20			21 30			
Hampton-in-Arden	d				20 33			20 47														21 33			
Berkswell	d				20 38											21 11						21 38			
Tile Hill	d				20 41			20 54								21 14						21 41			
Canley	d				20 44											21 17						21 44			
Coventry	a		20 24	20 30	20 47			20 59								21 20		21 24	21 30			21 49			
	d			20 31	20 48			21 01								21 21			21 31						
Rugby	d			20 43	20 58			21 12		20 47						21 32			21 44						
Long Buckby	d				21 08			21 24								21 41									
Northampton	66 a				21 23			21 34		21 07						21 53									
London Euston 15	⊖66 a			21 57	22 41			22 53								23 31			22 56						

		VT	VT	LM	XC	LM		LM	LM	VT	LM	XC	LM	LM	LM	LM		AW	XC	LM	LM	LM	LM	VT	LM
		◇■	◇■	■	◇■				■	◇■		◇■	■		■	■		◇	◇■	■		■		◇■	
		M	N	F	O			K	E	C	A	O		K	E	F		P	O					C	A
		☕	☕							☕														☕	
Stafford	d				21 03				21 13			21 28			21 38	21 45			22 03					22 08	
Penkridge	d								21 18						21 44										
Wolverhampton 7	a				21 16				21 30			21 41			21 55	21 59			22 16					22 22	
	d	21 09	21 09		21 17			21 19	21 31	21 35	21 38	21 42		21 49	21 58	22 05		22 12	22 17		22 20			22 26	22 35
Coseley	d							21 24						21 54	22 04						22 25				
Tipton	d							21 27						21 57							22 28				
Dudley Port	d							21 29						21 59							22 30				
Sandwell & Dudley	d	21 19	21 19					21 33			21 48			22 03							22 34				22 44
Smethwick Galton Bridge 7	d							21 36	21 44					22 06		22 17		22 23			22 37				
Smethwick Rolfe Street	d			←				21 38						22 08							22 39				
BirminghamNewStreet 12	a	21 28	21 28	21 24	21 33			21 44	21 50	21 53	21 57	22 00		22 15	22 17	22 25		22 32	22 33		22 45			22 49	22 53
	d	21 30	21 30	21 34		21 39			21 54				22 14							22 34		22 45	22 48		
Adderley Park	d					21 44														22 38					
Stechford	d					21 47							22 20							22 42			22 55		
Lea Hall	d					21 50							22 23										22 57		
Marston Green	d			21 42					22 02				22 26							22 46		22 53	23 01		
Birmingham International	a	21 39	21 39	21 45		21 55			22 05				22 29							22 49		22 56	23 04		
	d	21 40	21 40	21 46					22 05				22 30							22 49		22 57	23 05		
Hampton-in-Arden	d			21 49									22 33							22 52			23 08		
Berkswell	d								22 11				22 38									23 03	23 13		
Tile Hill	d			21 55					22 14				22 41							22 59		23 06	23 16		
Canley	d								22 17				22 44									23 09	23 19		
Coventry	a	21 50	21 50	22 00					22 20				22 47							23 04		23 12	23 22		
	d	21 51	21 51	22 01					22 21				22 48									23 13			
Rugby	d	22 03	22 03	22 12					22 32				22 59									23 24			
Long Buckby	d			22 21					22 41				23 08									23 34			
Northampton	66 a			22 33					22 53				23 21									23 45			
London Euston 15	⊖66 a	23 34	23 35	00 05									00 40												

A From Shrewsbury
B From Manchester Piccadilly to Bournemouth
C From Glasgow Central
D From Rugeley Trent Valley
E From Liverpool Lime Street
F From Crewe
G From Aberystwyth
H From Manchester Piccadilly to Bristol Temple Meads
I From Manchester Piccadilly to Southampton Central. 🍴 to BirminghamNewStreet
J From Edinburgh
K To Rugeley Trent Valley
L From Crewe to London Euston
M until 15 February
N from 22 February
O From Manchester Piccadilly
P From Pwllheli

Table T068-R

Saturdays
21 December to 16 May

Stafford - Wolverhampton - Birmingham - Coventry - Northampton

		VT	XC		LM	LM	LM	LM	AW	LM
		◇■	◇■			■			◇	
		A	B		C	D		E	F	G
		☕								
Stafford	d	22 25	22 30			22 41				
Penkridge	d					22 46				
Wolverhampton 7	a	22 38	22 43			22 57				
	d	22 39	22 44		22 49	22 59			23 09	23 36
Coseley	d				22 54	23 05				
Tipton	d				22 57					
Dudley Port	d				22 59					
Sandwell & Dudley	d				23 03					23 45
Smethwick Galton Bridge 7	d				23 06					
Smethwick Rolfe Street	d				23 08					
BirminghamNewStreet 12	a	22 57	23 00		23 16	23 18			23 30	23 54
	d						23 21	23 27		
Adderley Park	d							23 32		
Stechford	d							23 35		
Lea Hall	d						23 28			
Marston Green	d						23 30			
Birmingham International	a						23 33	23 40		
	d						23 34	23 41		
Hampton-in-Arden	d						23 37			
Berkswell	d						23 41			
Tile Hill	d						23 44	23 48		
Canley	d						23 48			
Coventry	a						23 50	23 53		
	d									
Rugby	d									
Long Buckby	d									
Northampton	66 a									
London Euston 15	⊖66 a									

Sundays
15 December to 10 May

		VT	LM	LM	LM	LM	XC	LM	LM	AW		VT	LM	LM	LM	LM	XC	LM	AW	VT		LM	LM	LM	LM
		◇■	■				◇■		■	◇		◇■		■		■	◇■	■	◇	◇■		■	■	■	■
					H	I	J			G			G	K	I	L	M		G			L	I	L	L
		☕					🍴					☕					🍴		🍴	☕					
Stafford	d															09 11	09 28					09 56		10 20	10 15
Penkridge	d															09 18						10 01			
Wolverhampton 7	a															09 28	09 41					10 12			10 29
	d	08 05			08 16	08 22		08 45		09 00		09 05	09 11	09 18	09 21	09 30	09 42	09 51	09 57	10 05		10 12	10 23		10 31
Coseley	d				08 21	08 27		08 50							09 26								10 28		
Tipton	d					08 30		08 53							09 29								10 31		
Dudley Port	d					08 33		08 56							09 32								10 33		
Sandwell & Dudley	d	08 15			08 28	08 37		09 00				09 15	09 20		09 36	09 40		10 01		10 15			10 37		
Smethwick Galton Bridge 7	d				08 30	08 40		09 03		09 11			09 23		09 39	09 43		10 04	10 08				10 40		
Smethwick Rolfe Street	d					08 42		09 05							09 41								10 42		
BirminghamNewStreet 12	a	08 24			08 41	08 48		09 11		09 18		09 24	09 30	09 34	09 47	09 50	09 58	10 11	10 16	10 24		10 28	10 48		10 51
	d	08 30	08 34	08 38			09 04		09 14	09 20		09 30		09 37		09 54	10 04	10 14	10 20	10 30		10 34			10 54
Adderley Park	d			08 42										09 42								10 38			
Stechford	d			08 46										09 45								10 42			
Lea Hall	d			08 48										09 48								10 44			
Marston Green	d		08 42	08 52					09 22					09 51				10 22				10 48			
Birmingham International	a	08 39	08 45	08 55			09 13		09 25	09 32		09 39		09 54		10 03	10 13	10 25	10 32	10 39		10 51			11 03
	d	08 40	08 46				09 14		09 25			09 40		09 55		10 04	10 14	10 25		10 40		10 51			11 05
Hampton-in-Arden	d								09 28									10 28							
Berkswell	d		08 51						09 33					10 00				10 33							
Tile Hill	d		08 55						09 36					10 04				10 36				10 59			
Canley	d		08 58						09 40					10 07				10 40							
Coventry	a	08 50	09 02				09 24		09 44			09 50		10 11		10 15	10 24	10 44		10 50		11 05			11 14
	d	08 51	09 02						09 44			09 51		10 11		10 16		10 44		10 51					11 15
Rugby	d	09 04	09 13						09 55			10 04		10 22		10 26		10 55		11 04				11 20	11 27
Long Buckby	d		09 22						10 04					10 31		10 36		11 04						11 29	11 36
Northampton	66 a		09 35						10 16					10 42		10 46		11 16						11 41	11 48
London Euston 15	⊖66 a	10 25							11 47			11 31				12 16		12 40		12 25				12 49	12 59

A From Edinburgh
B From Manchester Piccadilly
C To Hednesford
D From Liverpool Lime Street
E From Redditch
F From Holyhead
G From Shrewsbury
H To Rugeley Trent Valley
I To Walsall
J To Bournemouth
K ■ from Coventry
L From Crewe
M From Manchester Piccadilly to Bournemouth

Table T068-R

Sundays

15 December to 10 May

Stafford - Wolverhampton - Birmingham - Coventry - Northampton

		LM A	XC ◇1 B	LM 1 C	LM 1	AW ◇ D	VT ◇1	LM 1 C	LM 1 E	VT ◇1	LM 1 C	LM A	VT ◇1 F	XC ◇1 B	VT ◇1	LM 1 G	LM 1	VT ◇1	XC ◇1 H	LM 1 C	AW I	LM 1 E
Stafford	d		10 28	10 31				10 58			11 12			11 28		11 30				11 53		
Penkridge	d			10 37												11 36						
Wolverhampton 7	a		10 41	10 48				11 12			11 26			11 42		11 47				12 07		
	d	10 35	10 42	10 52		10 56	11 05	11 13	11 21		11 28	11 31	11 36	11 43	11 45	11 48				12 08	12 14	12 17
Coseley	d								11 26													12 22
Tipton	d								11 29													12 25
Dudley Port	d								11 31													12 27
Sandwell & Dudley	d						11 14		11 35			11 42			11 55							12 31
Smethwick Galton Bridge 7	d	10 46		11 02		11 07			11 38			11 45									12 26	12 34
Smethwick Rolfe Street	d								11 40													12 36
BirminghamNewStreet 12	a	10 54	10 59	11 09		11 16	11 25	11 29	11 46		11 49	11 52	11 55	12 00	12 05	12 11				12 27	12 35	12 42
	d		11 04	11 14	11 17	11 20	11 30	11 35		11 50	11 54			12 04	12 10	12 14	12 17	12 30	12 33	12 36	12 41	
Adderley Park	d							11 39												12 41		
Stechford	d							11 43												12 44		
Lea Hall	d							11 45												12 47		
Marston Green	d				11 25			11 49									12 25			12 50		
Birmingham International	a		11 13	11 23	11 28	11 32	11 39	11 52		11 59	12 04			12 13	12 19	12 23	12 28	12 39	12 42	12 53	13 02	
	d		11 14	11 24	11 28		11 40	11 52		12 00	12 05			12 14	12 20	12 25	12 29	12 40	12 43	12 53		
Hampton-in-Arden	d				11 31												12 32					
Berkswell	d				11 36												12 37					
Tile Hill	d				11 39			12 00									12 40			13 01		
Canley	d				11 43												12 43					
Coventry	a		11 24	11 35	11 47		11 50	12 06		12 10	12 15			12 24	12 30	12 36	12 47	12 50	12 53	13 06		
	d			11 36	11 47		11 51			12 11	12 15				12 31	12 37	12 48	12 51				
Rugby	d			11 47	11 58		12 05			12 25	12 27					12 47	12 58					
Long Buckby	d			11 57	12 08						12 36					12 57	13 08					
Northampton 66	a			12 09	12 19						12 48					13 09	13 20					
London Euston 15 ⊖66	a			13 18	13 40		13 04			13 17	14 01				13 38	14 24	14 40	13 57				

		VT ◇1	LM 1	VT ◇1 F	LM A	XC ◇1 B	VT ◇1	LM 1	LM 1 G	VT ◇1	LM 1 C	AW ◇ D	LM 1 E	VT ◇1	LM 1	LM A	XC ◇1 B	VT ◇1 J	LM 1	LM 1 G	VT ◇1	XC ◇1 K	AW L
Stafford	d		12 12			12 28			12 38		12 53				13 13		13 28			13 38			
Penkridge	d								12 44											13 44			
Wolverhampton 7	a		12 26			12 41			12 55		13 07				13 27		13 41			13 55			
	d		12 29	12 33	12 36	12 42	12 45		12 57		13 08	13 12	13 21		13 34	13 36	13 42	13 45		13 57			14 07
Coseley	d												13 26										
Tipton	d												13 29										
Dudley Port	d												13 31										
Sandwell & Dudley	d				12 46		12 55						13 35			13 46		13 55					
Smethwick Galton Bridge 7	d								13 07			13 23	13 38							14 07			14 17
Smethwick Rolfe Street	d												13 40										
BirminghamNewStreet 12	a		12 46	12 50	12 55	12 58	13 05		13 14		13 24	13 30	13 46		13 50	13 56	13 58	14 05		14 14			14 26
	d	12 50	12 54			13 04	13 10	13 14	13 17	13 30	13 35	13 39		13 50	13 54		14 04	14 10	14 14	14 17	14 30	14 33	14 39
Adderley Park	d										13 40												→
Stechford	d										13 43												
Lea Hall	d										13 46												
Marston Green	d								13 25		13 49									14 25			
Birmingham International	a	12 59	13 04			13 13	13 19	13 23	13 28	13 39	13 52	13 57		13 59	14 04		14 13	14 19	14 23	14 28	14 39	14 42	
	d	13 00	13 05			13 14	13 20	13 24	13 28	13 40	13 52			14 00	14 05		14 14	14 20	14 24	14 28	14 40	14 43	
Hampton-in-Arden	d								13 31											14 31			
Berkswell	d								13 36											14 36			
Tile Hill	d								13 39		14 00									14 39			
Canley	d								13 43											14 43			
Coventry	a	13 10	13 17			13 24	13 30	13 36	13 47	13 50	14 05			14 10	14 17		14 24	14 30	14 36	14 47	14 50	14 53	
	d	13 11	13 17				13 31	13 37	13 47	13 51				14 11	14 17			14 31	14 37	14 47	14 51		
Rugby	d	13 27	13 28					13 47	13 58					14 22	14 28				14 47	14 58			
Long Buckby	d		13 37					13 57	14 07						14 37				14 57	15 07			
Northampton 66	a		13 48					14 09	14 19						14 48				15 09	15 19			
London Euston 15 ⊖66	a	14 19	15 01				14 36	15 18	15 40	14 57				15 15	16 01			15 37	16 18	16 40	15 57		

A From Shrewsbury
B From Manchester Piccadilly to Bournemouth
C From Crewe
D From Chester
E To Walsall
F From Preston
G From Liverpool Lime Street
H To Reading
I From Aberystwyth
J From Lancaster
K From Derby to Reading
L From Pwllheli to Birmingham International

Table T068-R

Sundays

15 December to 10 May

Stafford - Wolverhampton - Birmingham - Coventry - Northampton

		LM 1 A	AW B	XC ◇1 C	LM 1 D	VT ◇1 E	VT ◇1 F	LM 1	LM G	XC ◇1 H	VT ◇1 I	LM 1	LM 1 J	VT ◇1	AW ◇ K	LM 1 A	AW ◇ L	XC ◇1 M	LM 1 D	VT ◇1	LM 1	LM G	XC ◇1 H
Stafford	d	13 53		14 03				14 12		14 28			14 40			14 53		15 03			15 12		15 28
Penkridge	d												14 46										
Wolverhampton 7	a	14 10		14 16				14 26		14 41			14 56			15 11		15 16			15 26		15 41
	d	14 11		14 17	14 22			14 32	14 37	14 42	14 45		14 57		15 07	15 11		15 17	15 22		15 32	15 37	15 42
Coseley	d				14 27														15 27				
Tipton	d				14 30														15 30				
Dudley Port	d				14 32														15 32				
Sandwell & Dudley	d				14 36				14 46		14 55								15 36			15 46	
Smethwick Galton Bridge 7	d				14 39			14 42					15 07		15 18				15 39		15 42		
Smethwick Rolfe Street	d		←		14 41												←		15 41				
BirminghamNewStreet 12	a	14 27	14 26	14 33	14 47			14 50	14 55	14 58	15 05		15 14		15 26	15 27	15 26	15 33	15 47		15 50	15 57	15 58
	d	14 36	14 39			14 50	14 50	14 54		15 04	15 10	15 14	15 17	15 30	15 39	15 35	15 39			15 50	15 54		16 04
Adderley Park	d	14 40													→	15 40							
Stechford	d	14 44														15 43							
Lea Hall	d	14 46														15 46							
Marston Green	d	14 49											15 25			15 49							
Birmingham International	a	14 52	15 00			14 59	14 59	15 04		15 13	15 19	15 23	15 28	15 39		15 52	15 57			15 59	16 04		16 13
	d	14 53				15 00	15 00	15 05		15 14	15 20	15 24	15 28	15 40		15 52				16 00	16 05		16 14
Hampton-in-Arden	d												15 31										
Berkswell	d												15 36										
Tile Hill	d	15 00											15 39			16 00							
Canley	d												15 43										
Coventry	a	15 07				15 10	15 10	15 17		15 24	15 30	15 36	15 47	15 50		16 06				16 10	16 17		16 24
	d					15 11	15 11	15 17			15 31	15 37	15 47	15 51						16 11	16 17		
Rugby	d					15 25	15 25	15 28				15 47	15 58							16 24	16 28		
Long Buckby	d							15 37				15 57	16 07								16 37		
Northampton 66	a							15 48				16 09	16 19								16 48		
London Euston 15 ⊖66	a					16 18	16 20	17 01			16 37	17 18	17 40	16 57						17 17	18 01		

		VT ◇1 N	LM 1	LM 1 J	VT ◇1 G	VT ◇1	XC ◇1 O	AW P	LM 1 A	AW B	XC ◇1 M	LM 1 D	VT ◇1	LM 1	LM G	XC ◇1 H	VT ◇1 I	LM 1	LM 1 J	VT ◇1	LM 1 A	XC ◇1 M	AW ◇ L
Stafford	d			15 40					15 57		16 03			16 12		16 28			16 38		16 57	17 03	
Penkridge	d			15 46															16 44				
Wolverhampton 7	a			15 56					16 11		16 16			16 26		16 41			16 54		17 11	17 16	
	d	15 45		15 57	16 04			16 08	16 12		16 17	16 22		16 31	16 35	16 42	16 45		16 57		17 11	17 17	17 20
Coseley	d											16 27											
Tipton	d											16 30											
Dudley Port	d											16 32											
Sandwell & Dudley	d	15 55										16 36			16 44		16 55						
Smethwick Galton Bridge 7	d			16 07				16 18				16 39		16 42					17 07				17 32
Smethwick Rolfe Street	d									←		16 41											
BirminghamNewStreet 12	a	16 05		16 14	16 20			16 26	16 28	16 26	16 34	16 47		16 50	16 55	16 58	17 05		17 14		17 27	17 34	17 40
	d	16 10	16 14	16 17	16 30	16 30	16 33	16 39	16 36	16 39			16 50	16 54		17 04	17 10	17 14	17 17	17 30	17 36		17 45
Adderley Park	d							→	16 41												17 40		
Stechford	d								16 44												17 44		
Lea Hall	d								16 47												17 46		
Marston Green	d			16 25					16 50										17 25		17 49		
Birmingham International	a	16 19	16 23	16 28	16 39	16 39	16 43		16 53	17 00			16 59	17 04		17 13	17 19	17 23	17 28	17 39	17 52		17 57
	d	16 20	16 24	16 28	16 40	16 40	16 44		16 53				17 00	17 05		17 14	17 20	17 24	17 28	17 40	17 53		
Hampton-in-Arden	d			16 31															17 31				
Berkswell	d			16 36															17 36				
Tile Hill	d			16 39					17 01										17 39		18 00		
Canley	d			16 43															17 43				
Coventry	a	16 30	16 36	16 47	16 50	16 50	16 54		17 06				17 10	17 17		17 24	17 30	17 36	17 47	17 50	18 06		
	d	16 31	16 37	16 47	16 51	16 51							17 11	17 17			17 31	17 37	17 47	17 51			
Rugby	d		16 47	16 58									17 25	17 28				17 50	17 58				
Long Buckby	d		16 57	17 07										17 37				18 00	18 07				
Northampton 66	a		17 09	17 19										17 48				18 12	18 19				
London Euston 15 ⊖66	a	17 36	18 18	18 40	17 57	17 57							18 18	19 01			18 35	19 24	19 40	18 55			

A From Crewe
B From Pwllheli
C From Manchester Piccadilly to Paignton
D To Walsall
E until 16 February
F from 23 February
G From Shrewsbury
H From Manchester Piccadilly to Bournemouth
I From Edinburgh
J From Liverpool Lime Street
K From Chester to Birmingham International
L From Chester
M From Manchester Piccadilly to Bristol Temple Meads
N From Glasgow Central
O From Newcastle to Reading
P From Pwllheli to Birmingham International

Table T068-R

Sundays
15 December to 10 May

Stafford - Wolverhampton - Birmingham - Coventry - Northampton

	LM	VT	LM	LM	XC	VT	VT	LM	LM	VT	XC	AW	LM	AW	XC	LM	VT	LM	LM	XC	VT	LM
	■	◇■	■		◇■	◇■	◇■	■	■	◇■	◇■	■	■	■	◇■	■	◇■	■		◇■	◇■	■
	A			B	C	D	E		F		G	H	I	J	K	A			B	C	L	M
		🍽			🛒	🍽	🍽			🍽	🛒	🛒		🛒	🛒		🍽			🛒	🍽	
Stafford d			17 12		17 25				17 38				17 58		18 03			18 12		18 28		
Penkridge d									17 44													
Wolverhampton 7 a			17 26		17 39				17 55				18 13		18 16			18 26		18 41		
d	17 24		17 31	17 36	17 41	17 45	17 45		17 57			18 09	18 13		18 17	18 24		18 30	18 34	18 42	18 45	
Coseley d	17 29															18 29						
Tipton d	17 32															18 32						
Dudley Port d	17 34															18 34						
Sandwell & Dudley d	17 37			17 45		17 55	17 55									18 37			18 44		18 55	
Smethwick Galton Bridge 7 d	17 40		17 43						18 07			18 21				18 40		18 43				
Smethwick Rolfe Street d	17 42													←		18 42						
BirminghamNewStreet 12 a	17 48		17 51	17 57	17 59	18 05	18 05		18 14			18 31	18 30	18 31	18 33	18 48		18 51	18 55	18 59	19 05	
d		17 50	17 54		18 04	18 10	18 10	18 14	18 17	18 30	18 33	18 39	18 36	18 39			18 50	18 54		19 04	19 10	19 14
Adderley Park d												→	18 40									
Stechford d													18 43									
Lea Hall d													18 46									
Marston Green d									18 25				18 49									
Birmingham International ✈ a		17 59	18 04		18 13	18 19	18 19	18 23	18 28	18 39	18 42		18 52	18 56			18 59	19 04		19 13	19 19	19 23
d		18 00	18 05		18 14	18 20	18 20	18 24	18 28	18 40	18 43		18 52				19 00	19 05		19 14	19 20	19 24
Hampton-in-Arden d									18 31													
Berkswell d									18 36													
Tile Hill d									18 39				19 00									
Canley d									18 43													
Coventry a		18 10	18 15		18 24	18 30	18 30	18 36	18 47	18 50	18 53		19 06				19 10	19 17		19 24	19 30	19 36
d		18 11	18 15			18 31	18 31	18 37	18 47	18 51							19 11	19 18			19 31	19 37
Rugby d		18 25	18 26					18 47	19 00								19 26	19 28				19 47
Long Buckby d			18 35					18 57	19 09									19 38				19 57
Northampton 66 a			18 46					19 08	19 21									19 48				20 09
London Euston 15 ⊖66 a		19 17	20 01			19 36	19 39	20 19	20 40	19 57							20 18	21 14			20 37	

	LM	VT	XC	AW	LM	AW	XC	LM	LM	LM	XC	VT	LM	LM	VT	AW	LM	AW	XC	LM	LM
	■	◇■	◇■	◇	■	◇	◇■	■	■		◇■	◇■	■	■	◇■	◇	■	◇	◇■	■	■
	F		N	O	I	P	Q	A		B	R	S	F			H	I	J	Q	A	I
		🍽	🛒				🛒				🛒	🍽			🍽	🛒		🛒	🛒		
Stafford d	18 38				18 58		19 03		19 12		19 28		19 37				19 58		20 03		20 12
Penkridge d	18 44												19 43								
Wolverhampton 7 a	18 55				19 13		19 16		19 26		19 41		19 54				20 12		20 16		20 26
d	18 57			19 08	19 14		19 17	19 22	19 32	19 37	19 42	19 45	19 54			20 07	20 14		20 17	20 20	20 30
Coseley d								19 27												20 25	
Tipton d								19 30												20 28	
Dudley Port d								19 32												20 30	
Sandwell & Dudley d								19 36		19 45		19 55								20 34	
Smethwick Galton Bridge 7 d	19 07			19 19				19 39	19 42				20 04			20 19				20 37	20 39
Smethwick Rolfe Street d						←		19 41										←		20 39	
BirminghamNewStreet 12 a	19 14			19 28	19 30	19 28	19 33	19 47	19 50	19 55	19 58	20 05	20 11			20 29	20 30	20 29	20 33	20 45	20 48
d	19 17	19 30	19 33	19 39	19 36	19 39			19 54		20 04	20 10	20 14	20 17	20 30	20 39	20 36	20 39			20 54
Adderley Park d				→	19 40											→	20 41				
Stechford d					19 43												20 44				
Lea Hall d					19 46												20 46				
Marston Green d	19 25				19 49									20 25			20 49				
Birmingham International ✈ a	19 28	19 39	19 43		19 52	19 57			20 04		20 13	20 19	20 23	20 28	20 39		20 52	20 58			21 03
d	19 28	19 40	19 44		19 52				20 05		20 14	20 20	20 24	20 28	20 40		20 53				21 05
Hampton-in-Arden d	19 31													20 31							
Berkswell d	19 36												20 30								
Tile Hill d	19 39				20 01									20 37			21 00				
Canley d	19 43													20 41							
Coventry a	19 47	19 50	19 54		20 06				20 17		20 24	20 30	20 37	20 44	20 50		21 06				21 16
d	19 47	19 51							20 18			20 31	20 37	20 44	20 51						21 17
Rugby d	19 58								20 28				20 48	20 55	21 05						21 27
Long Buckby d	20 07								20 38				20 57	21 04							21 37
Northampton 66 a	20 19								20 48				21 09	21 17							21 49
London Euston 15 ⊖66 a	21 43	20 57										21 47		22 47	22 24						

A To Walsall
B From Shrewsbury
C From Manchester Piccadilly to Bournemouth
D until 16 February. From Glasgow Central
E from 23 February. From Glasgow Central
F From Liverpool Lime Street
G From Edinburgh to Reading
H From Pwllheli to Birmingham International
I From Crewe
J From Pwllheli
K From Manchester Piccadilly to Plymouth
L From Edinburgh
M To Milton Keynes Central
N From Newcastle to Reading
O From Chester to Birmingham International
P From Chester
Q From Manchester Piccadilly to Bristol Temple Meads
R From Manchester Piccadilly to Southampton Central
S From Glasgow Central

Table T068-R

Sundays
15 December to 10 May

Stafford - Wolverhampton - Birmingham - Coventry - Northampton

	VT	LM	XC	LM	LM	LM	VT	LM	AW	XC	LM	AW	LM	LM	LM	VT	LM	AW	VT	XC	LM	LM
	◇■		◇■	■	■	■	◇■	■	◇	◇■		◇		■	■	◇■	■	◇	◇■	◇■	■	■
	A	B	C	D	E	F		D	G	H	I	J	B	E	D		D	K	L	M	N	I
	🍽		🛒				🍽					🛒				🍽			🍽			
Stafford d			20 28	20 34	20 39	20 45				21 03		21 13		21 38	21 51		21 52		22 01	22 05		
Penkridge d					20 45									21 44								
Wolverhampton 7 a			20 41		20 55	21 00				21 16		21 32		21 55			22 06		22 13	22 18		
d	20 34	20 38	20 42		20 57	21 01	21 06		21 12	21 17	21 22	21 34	21 36	21 55		22 05	22 08	22 11	22 14	22 20		22 24
Coseley d											21 27											22 29
Tipton d											21 30											22 32
Dudley Port d											21 32											22 34
Sandwell & Dudley d		20 47					21 17				21 36		21 46			22 16						22 38
Smethwick Galton Bridge 7 d					21 07				21 23		21 39	21 45		22 05				22 23				22 41
Smethwick Rolfe Street d								←			21 41											22 43
BirminghamNewStreet 12 a	20 51	20 56	20 58		21 14	21 18	21 26	21 18	21 32	21 33	21 47	21 53	21 55	22 12		22 24	22 30	22 31	22 32	22 36		22 49
d			21 04		21 17	21 34	21 30	21 34	21 39			21 55		22 15		22 30	22 36	22 39			22 48	
Adderley Park d						→		21 38									22 41				22 52	
Stechford d								21 42									22 44				22 56	
Lea Hall d								21 44									22 47				22 58	
Marston Green d					21 25			21 47						22 23			22 50				23 02	
Birmingham International ✈ a			21 13		21 28		21 39	21 50	21 57			22 07		22 26		22 39	22 53	23 01			23 05	
d			21 14		21 28		21 40	21 51						22 26		22 40	22 53				23 05	
Hampton-in-Arden d					21 31									22 29								
Berkswell d					21 36									22 34								
Tile Hill d					21 39									22 37								
Canley d					21 43									22 40								
Coventry a			21 24		21 47		21 50	22 01						22 44		22 50	23 04				23 16	
d					21 47		21 51							22 45		22 51					23 17	
Rugby d				21 31	21 58		22 04							22 55	22 46	23 04					23 27	
Long Buckby d				21 41	22 07									23 05	22 55						23 37	
Northampton 66 a				21 53	22 18									23 16	23 08						23 49	
London Euston 15 ⊖66 a				23 17	23 43		23 23							00 43		00 26						

	VT	VT	LM	LM	LM	LM	LM	XC
	◇■	◇■		■	■	■	■	◇■
	A		B		E	I	D	M
	🍽	🍽						
Stafford d					22 42		22 51	23 04
Penkridge d					22 48			
Wolverhampton 7 a					22 58		23 05	23 17
d	22 33	22 37	22 47		22 59	23 04	23 12	23 18
Coseley d						23 09		
Tipton d						23 12		
Dudley Port d						23 14		
Sandwell & Dudley d		22 48	22 56			23 18	23 22	
Smethwick Galton Bridge 7 d					23 09	23 20	23 25	
Smethwick Rolfe Street d						23 22		
BirminghamNewStreet 12 a	22 52	22 57	23 05		23 16	23 29	23 32	23 35
d		23 00		23 14				
Adderley Park d				23 18				
Stechford d				23 22				
Lea Hall d				23 24				
Marston Green d				23 27				
Birmingham International ✈ a		23 10		23 30				
d		23 10		23 31				
Hampton-in-Arden d				23 34				
Berkswell d				23 39				
Tile Hill d				23 42				
Canley d				23 45				
Coventry a		23 21		23 49				
d		23 21						
Rugby d		23 35						
Long Buckby d								
Northampton 66 a		23s54						
London Euston 15 ⊖66 a		01 03						

A From Edinburgh
B From Shrewsbury
C From Manchester Piccadilly to Reading. 🛒 to BirminghamNewStreet
D From Crewe
E From Liverpool Lime Street
F From Crewe to Coventry
G From Chester
H From Manchester Piccadilly to Bristol Temple Meads
I To Walsall
J From Holyhead
K From Aberystwyth
L From Glasgow Central
M From Manchester Piccadilly
N From Rugeley Trent Valley

Table T069-F

Mondays to Fridays
16 December to 15 May

Lichfield - Birmingham - Longbridge and Redditch

Miles	Miles			LM MX	LM	LM	LM	LM	LM	LM	LM	LM	LM	LM	LM	LM	LM	XC ◇1	LM	LM	LM	LM	LM
0	—	**Lichfield Trent Valley**	d								05 58	06 08		06 19			06 41		06 50		07 10		07 20
1¼	—	**Lichfield City**	d							05 53	06 03	06 12		06 23			06 45		06 54		07 14		07 24
4¼	—	Shenstone	d							05 58		06 17		06 28			06 50				07 19		
6¾	—	Blake Street	d							06 02	06 11	06 20		06 32			06 53		07 02		07 22		07 32
7½	—	Butlers Lane	d							06 04	06 13	06 23		06 34			06 55		07 04		07 24		07 34
8½	—	Four Oaks	d					05 48		06 06	06 16	06 25		06 36	06 46		06 57		07 06	07 16	07 26		07 36
9¾	—	Sutton Coldfield	d	00 02				05 51		06 10	06 20	06 29		06 40	06 50		07 01		07 10	07 20	07 30		07 40
11¼	—	Wylde Green	d					05 54		06 12	06 22	06 31		06 42	06 52		07 03		07 12	07 22	07 32		07 42
11¾	—	Chester Road	d					05 56		06 14	06 24	06 33		06 44	06 54		07 05		07 14	07 24	07 34		07 44
12¾	—	Erdington	d					05 58		06 17	06 27	06 36		06 47	06 57		07 08		07 17	07 27	07 37		07 47
13½	—	Gravelly Hill	d					06 01		06 19	06 29	06 38		06 49	06 59		07 10		07 19	07 29	07 39		07 49
14¾	—	Aston	d					06 04		06 23	06 33	06 42		06 53	07 03		07 14		07 23	07 33	07 43		07 53
16	—	Duddeston	d					06 07		06 26	06 36	06 45			07 06					07 36	07 46		07 56
17½	—	**Birmingham New Street 12**	a	00 16				06 11		06 30	06 42	06 49		07 00	07 11		07 21		07 31	07 40	07 51		08 01
—	—		d		05 45	05 53	06 03	06 13	06 23	06 33	06 45	06 53	06 59	07 03	07 15	07 20	07 23	07 30	07 33	07 43	07 53	08 00	08 03
18½	—	Five Ways	d		05 49	05 57	06 07	06 17	06 27	06 37	06 49	06 57		07 07	07 19		07 27		07 37	07 47	07 57		08 07
19¾	—	University	d		05 53	06 01	06 11	06 21	06 31	06 41	06 53	07 01	07 06	07 11	07 23	07 26	07 31	07a36	07 41	07 51	08 01	08 06	08 11
20¾	—	Selly Oak	d		05 55	06 03	06 13	06 23	06 33	06 43	06 55	07 03		07 13	07 25		07 33		07 43	07 53	08 03		08 13
21¾	—	Bournville	d		05 58	06 06	06 16	06 26	06 36	06 46	06 58	07 06		07 16	07 28		07 36		07 46	07 56	08 06		08 16
22¾	—	Kings Norton	d		06 01	06 09	06 19	06 29	06 39	06 49	07 01	07 09		07 19	07 31		07 39		07 49	07 59	08 09		08 19
24¼	—	Northfield	d		06 04	06 12	06 22	06 32	06 42	06 52	07 04	07 12		07 22	07 34		07 42		07 52	08 02	08 12		08 22
25¼	—	Longbridge	d		06 07	06 15	06 26	06 35	06 46	06 56	07 07	07 15		07 26	07 37		07 46		07 58	08 06	08 15		08 26
27¾	0	Barnt Green	d		06 11	06 19	06 31		06 51		07 11	07 19		07 31		07 39	07 51			08 11	08 19	08 17	08 31
29¾	—	Alvechurch	d		06 16		06 35		06 55		07 15			07 35			07 55			08 15			08 35
33	—	**Redditch**	a		06 21		06 41		07 03		07 21			07 41			08 03			08 21			08 41
—	3½	Bromsgrove	a			06 25		06 44		07 05		07 26	07 21		07 47	07 43			08 07		08 26	08 21	

		LM	LM	XC ◇1	LM	LM	LM	LM	LM	LM	LM	LM	XC ◇1	LM	LM	LM	LM	LM	LM	LM	XC ◇1	LM	LM
Lichfield Trent Valley	d		07 40		07 50				08 10			08 40		08 50			09 10	09 20		09 40		09 50	
Lichfield City	d		07 44		07 54		08 09		08 14	08 22		08 44		08 54			09 14	09 24		09 44		09 54	
Shenstone	d		07 49						08 19	08 27		08 49		08 59				09 29				09 59	
Blake Street	d		07 52		08 02				08 22	08 31		08 52		09 02			09 22	09 32		09 52		10 02	
Butlers Lane	d		07 54		08 04				08 24	08 33		08 54		09 04			09 24	09 34		09 54		10 04	
Four Oaks	d	07 46	07 56		08 07	08 15	08 18		08 26	08 36	08 46	08 56		09 06	09 16		09 27	09 36	09 46	09 57		10 06	10 16
Sutton Coldfield	d	07 50	08 00		08 10	08 18	08 22		08 30	08 40	08 50	09 00		09 10	09 20		09 30	09 40	09 50	10 00		10 10	10 20
Wylde Green	d	07 52	08 02		08 12	08 21	08 24		08 32	08 42	08 52	09 02		09 12	09 22		09 33	09 42	09 52	10 03		10 12	10 22
Chester Road	d	07 54	08 04		08 14	08 23	08 26		08 34	08 44	08 54	09 04		09 14	09 24		09 35	09 44	09 54	10 05		10 14	10 24
Erdington	d	07 57	08 07		08 17	08 26	08 28		08 37	08 47	08 57	09 07		09 17	09 27		09 37	09 47	09 57	10 07		10 17	10 27
Gravelly Hill	d	07 59	08 09		08 19		08 30		08 39	08 49	08 59	09 09		09 19	09 29		09 40	09 49	09 59	10 10		10 19	10 29
Aston	d	08 03	08 13		08 23		08 33		08 43	08 53	09 03	09 13		09 23	09 33		09 43	09 53	10 03	10 13		10 23	10 33
Duddeston	d	08 06	08 16			08 32	08 36		08 47	08 56	09 06				09 36				10 06				10 36
Birmingham New Street 12	a	08 12	08 21		08 31	08 36	08 41		08 51	08 59	09 12	09 21		09 31	09 41		09 50	10 01	10 11	10 21		10 31	10 41
	d	08 15	08 23	08 30	08 33		08 43	08 50	08 53	09 03	09 14	09 23	09 30	09 33	09 43	09 50	09 53	10 03	10 15	10 23	10 30	10 33	10 43
Five Ways	d	08 19	08 27		08 37		08 47		08 57	09 07	09 19	09 27		09 37	09 47		09 57	10 07	10 19	10 27		10 37	10 47
University	d	08 23	08 31	08a36	08 41		08 51	08 56	09 01	09 11	09 23	09 31	09a36	09 41	09 51	09 56	10 01	10 11	10 23	10 31	10a36	10 41	10 51
Selly Oak	d	08 25	08 33		08 43		08 53		09 03	09 13	09 25	09 33		09 43	09 53		10 03	10 13	10 25	10 33		10 43	10 53
Bournville	d	08 28	08 36		08 46		08 56		09 06	09 16	09 28	09 36		09 46	09 56		10 06	10 16	10 28	10 36		10 46	10 56
Kings Norton	d	08 31	08 39		08 49		08 59		09 09	09 19	09 31	09 39		09 49	09 59		10 09	10 19	10 31	10 39		10 49	10 59
Northfield	d	08 34	08 42		08 52		09 02		09 12	09 22	09 34	09 42		09 52	10 02		10 12	10 22	10 34	10 42		10 52	11 02
Longbridge	d	08 37	08 46		08 58		09 06		09 15	09 25	09 37	09 46		09 58	10 06		10 15	10 26	10 37	10 46		10a54	11 06
Barnt Green	d		08 51				09 11		09 19	09 30		09 51			10 11		10 19	10 31		10 51			11 11
Alvechurch	d		08 55				09 16			09 35		09 55			10 15			10 35		10 55			11 16
Redditch	a		09 03				09 21			09 40		10 03			10 21			10 41		11 03			11 21
Bromsgrove	a	08 46			09 07			09 11	09 25		09 46			10 07		10 11	10 25		10 46				

		LM	LM	LM	LM	LM	XC ◇1	LM	LM	LM	LM	LM	LM	LM	XC ◇1	LM	LM	LM	LM	LM	LM	LM
Lichfield Trent Valley	d		10 10	10 20		10 40		10 50			11 11	11 20		11 40		11 50			12 10	12 20		12 40
Lichfield City	d		10 14	10 24		10 44		10 54			11 15	11 24		11 44		11 54			12 14	12 24		12 44
Shenstone	d			10 29				10 59				11 29				11 59				12 29		
Blake Street	d		10 22	10 32		10 52		11 02			11 23	11 32		11 52		12 02			12 22	12 32		12 52
Butlers Lane	d		10 24	10 34		10 54		11 04			11 25	11 34		11 54		12 04			12 24	12 34		12 54
Four Oaks	d		10 27	10 36	10 46	10 57		11 06	11 16		11 28	11 36	11 46	11 57		12 06	12 16		12 27	12 36	12 46	12 57
Sutton Coldfield	d		10 30	10 40	10 50	11 00		11 10	11 20		11 31	11 40	11 50	12 00		12 10	12 20		12 30	12 40	12 50	13 00
Wylde Green	d		10 33	10 42	10 52	11 03		11 12	11 22		11 34	11 42	11 52	12 03		12 12	12 22		12 33	12 42	12 52	13 03
Chester Road	d		10 35	10 44	10 54	11 05		11 14	11 24		11 36	11 44	11 54	12 05		12 14	12 24		12 35	12 44	12 54	13 05
Erdington	d		10 37	10 47	10 57	11 07		11 17	11 27		11 38	11 47	11 57	12 07		12 17	12 27		12 37	12 47	12 57	13 07
Gravelly Hill	d		10 40	10 49	10 59	11 10		11 19	11 29		11 41	11 49	11 59	12 10		12 19	12 29		12 40	12 49	12 59	13 10
Aston	d		10 43	10 53	11 03	11 13		11 23	11 33		11 44	11 53	12 03	12 13		12 23	12 33		12 43	12 53	13 03	13 13
Duddeston	d				11 06				11 36				12 06				12 36				13 06	
Birmingham New Street 12	a		10 50	10 59	11 11	11 21		11 31	11 41		11 50	12 01	12 11	12 21		12 30	12 41		12 50	12 59	13 11	13 21
	d	10 50	10 53	11 03	11 15	11 23	11 30	11 33	11 43	11 50	11 53	12 03	12 15	12 23	12 30	12 33	12 43	12 50	12 53	13 03	13 15	13 23
Five Ways	d		10 57	11 07	11 19	11 27		11 37	11 47		11 57	12 07	12 19	12 27		12 37	12 47		12 57	13 07	13 19	13 27
University	d	10 56	11 01	11 11	11 23	11 31	11a36	11 41	11 51	11 56	12 01	12 11	12 23	12 31	12a36	12 41	12 51	12 56	13 01	13 11	13 23	13 31
Selly Oak	d		11 03	11 13	11 25	11 33		11 43	11 53		12 03	12 13	12 25	12 33		12 43	12 53		13 03	13 13	13 25	13 33
Bournville	d		11 06	11 16	11 28	11 36		11 46	11 56		12 06	12 16	12 28	12 36		12 46	12 56		13 06	13 16	13 28	13 36
Kings Norton	d		11 09	11 19	11 31	11 39		11 49	11 59		12 09	12 19	12 31	12 39		12 49	12 59		13 09	13 19	13 31	13 39
Northfield	d		11 12	11 22	11 34	11 42		11 52	12 02		12 12	12 22	12 34	12 42		12 52	13 02		13 12	13 22	13 34	13 42
Longbridge	d		11 15	11 26	11 37	11 46		11 58	12 06		12 15	12 26	12 37	12 46		12a54	13 06		13 15	13 27	13 37	13 46
Barnt Green	d		11 19	11 31		11 51			12 11		12 19	12 31		12 51			13 11		13 19	13 32		13 51
Alvechurch	d			11 35		11 55			12 15			12 35		12 55			13 15			13 36		13 55
Redditch	a			11 41		12 03			12 21			12 41		13 03			13 21			13 42		14 03
Bromsgrove	a	11 11	11 25		11 46			12 07		12 11	12 25		12 46					13 11	13 25		13 46	

Table T069-F

Mondays to Fridays
16 December to 15 May

Lichfield - Birmingham - Longbridge and Redditch

		XC ◇1	LM	LM	LM	LM	LM	LM	LM	XC ◇1	LM	LM	LM	LM	LM	LM	LM	XC ◇1	LM	LM	LM	LM	LM
Lichfield Trent Valley	d		12 50			13 10	13 20		13 40		13 50			14 10	14 20		14 40		14 50			15 10	15 20
Lichfield City	d		12 54			13 14	13 24		13 44		13 54			14 14	14 24		14 44		14 54			15 14	15 24
Shenstone	d		12 59				13 29				13 59				14 29				14 59				15 29
Blake Street	d		13 02			13 22	13 32		13 52		14 02			14 22	14 32		14 52		15 02			15 22	15 32
Butlers Lane	d		13 04			13 24	13 34		13 54		14 04			14 24	14 34		14 54		15 04			15 24	15 34
Four Oaks	d		13 06	13 16		13 27	13 36	13 46	13 57		14 06	14 16		14 27	14 36	14 46	14 57		15 06	15 16		15 27	15 36
Sutton Coldfield	d		13 10	13 20		13 30	13 40	13 50	14 00		14 10	14 20		14 30	14 40	14 50	15 00		15 10	15 20		15 30	15 40
Wylde Green	d		13 12	13 22		13 33	13 42	13 52	14 03		14 12	14 22		14 33	14 42	14 52	15 03		15 12	15 22		15 33	15 42
Chester Road	d		13 14	13 24		13 35	13 44	13 54	14 05		14 14	14 24		14 35	14 44	14 54	15 05		15 14	15 24		15 35	15 44
Erdington	d		13 17	13 27		13 37	13 47	13 57	14 07		14 17	14 27		14 37	14 47	14 57	15 07		15 17	15 27		15 37	15 47
Gravelly Hill	d		13 19	13 29		13 40	13 49	13 59	14 10		14 19	14 29		14 40	14 49	14 59	15 10		15 19	15 29		15 40	15 49
Aston	d		13 23	13 33		13 43	13 53	14 03	14 13		14 23	14 33		14 43	14 53	15 03	15 13		15 23	15 33		15 43	15 53
Duddeston	d			13 36				14 06				14 36				15 06				15 36			
Birmingham New Street 12	a		13 30	13 41		13 50	14 00	14 11	14 21		14 30	14 41		14 50	15 00	15 11	15 21		15 30	15 41		15 50	16 01
	d	13 30	13 33	13 43	13 50	13 53	14 03	14 15	14 23	14 30	14 33	14 43	14 50	14 53	15 03	15 15	15 23	15 30	15 33	15 43	15 50	15 53	16 03
Five Ways	d		13 37	13 47		13 57	14 07	14 19	14 27		14 37	14 47		14 57	15 07	15 19	15 27		15 37	15 47		15 57	16 07
University	d	13a36	13 41	13 51	13 56	14 01	14 11	14 23	14 31	14a36	14 41	14 51	14 56	15 01	15 11	15 23	15 31	15a36	15 41	15 51	15 56	16 01	16 11
Selly Oak	d		13 43	13 53		14 03	14 13	14 25	14 33		14 43	14 53		15 03	15 13	15 25	15 33		15 43	15 53		16 03	16 13
Bournville	d		13 46	13 56		14 06	14 16	14 28	14 36		14 46	14 56		15 06	15 16	15 28	15 36		15 46	15 56		16 06	16 16
Kings Norton	d		13 49	13 59		14 09	14 19	14 31	14 39		14 49	14 59		15 09	15 19	15 31	15 39		15 49	15 59		16 09	16 19
Northfield	d		13 52	14 02		14 12	14 22	14 34	14 42		14 52	15 02		15 12	15 22	15 34	15 42		15 52	16 02		16 12	16 22
Longbridge	d		13 59	14 06		14 15	14 26	14 37	14 46		14 59	15 06		15 15	15 26	15 37	15 46		15 58	16 06		16 15	16 26
Barnt Green	d			14 11		14 19	14 31		14 51			15 11		15 19	15 31		15 51			16 11		16 19	16 31
Alvechurch	d			14 15			14 35		14 55			15 16			15 35		15 55			16 16			16 35
Redditch	a			14 21			14 41		15 03			15 21			15 41		16 03			16 21			16 41
Bromsgrove	a		14 08		14 11	14 25		14 46			15 08		15 11	15 25		15 46			16 07		16 11	16 25	

		LM	LM	LM	XC ◇1	LM	LM	LM	LM	LM	LM	LM	LM	XC ◇1	LM	LM	LM	LM	LM	LM	LM	LM	LM
Lichfield Trent Valley	d			15 40		15 50			16 10	16 20			16 40		16 50			17 10		17 20			17 40
Lichfield City	d			15 44		15 54			16 14	16 24			16 44		16 54			17 14		17 24			17 45
Shenstone	d					15 59				16 29					16 59					17 29			
Blake Street	d			15 52		16 02			16 22	16 32			16 52		17 02			17 22		17 32			17 52
Butlers Lane	d			15 54		16 04			16 25	16 34			16 54		17 04			17 24		17 34			17 54
Four Oaks	d	15 46		15 57		16 06	16 16		16 27	16 36	16 46		16 57		17 06	17 16		17 27		17 36	17 46		17 56
Sutton Coldfield	d	15 50		16 00		16 10	16 20		16 31	16 40	16 50		17 00		17 10	17 20		17 30		17 40	17 50		18 00
Wylde Green	d	15 52		16 03		16 12	16 22		16 33	16 42	16 52		17 03		17 12	17 22		17 33		17 42	17 52		18 02
Chester Road	d	15 54		16 05		16 14	16 24		16 35	16 44	16 54		17 05		17 14	17 24		17 35		17 44	17 54		18 04
Erdington	d	15 57		16 07		16 17	16 27		16 38	16 47	16 57		17 07		17 17	17 27		17 37		17 47	17 57		18 07
Gravelly Hill	d	15 59		16 10		16 19	16 29		16 40	16 49	16 59		17 10		17 19	17 29		17 40		17 49	17 59		18 09
Aston	d	16 03		16 13		16 23	16 33		16 44	16 53	17 03		17 13		17 23	17 33		17 43		17 53	18 03		18 13
Duddeston	d	16 06					16 36				17 06					17 36					18 06		
Birmingham New Street 12	a	16 10		16 21		16 30	16 41		16 50	17 01	17 11		17 21		17 31	17 41		17 50		18 00	18 11		18 21
	d	16 15	16 20	16 23	16 30	16 33	16 43	16 50	16 53	17 03	17 15	17 20	17 23	17 30	17 33	17 43	17 50	17 53	17 59	18 03	18 15	18 20	18 23
Five Ways	d	16 19		16 27		16 37	16 47		16 57	17 07	17 19		17 27		17 37	17 47		17 57		18 07	18 19		18 27
University	d	16 23	16 26	16 31	16a36	16 41	16 51	16 56	17 01	17 11	17 23	17 26	17 31	17a36	17 41	17 51	17 56	18 01	18 06	18 11	18 23	18 27	18 31
Selly Oak	d	16 25		16 33		16 43	16 53		17 03	17 13	17 25		17 33		17 43	17 53		18 03		18 13	18 25		18 33
Bournville	d	16 28		16 36		16 46	16 56		17 06	17 16	17 28		17 36		17 46	17 56		18 06		18 16	18 28		18 36
Kings Norton	d	16 31		16 39		16 49	16 59		17 09	17 19	17 31		17 39		17 49	17 59		18 09		18 19	18 31		18 39
Northfield	d	16 34		16 42		16 52	17 02		17 12	17 22	17 34		17 42		17 52	18 02		18 12		18 22	18 34		18 42
Longbridge	d	16 36		16 46		16 58	17 06		17 15	17 26	17 36		17 46		17 58	18 06		18 15		18 26	18 36		18 46
Barnt Green	d			16 51			17 11		17 19	17 31			17 51			18 11		18 19		18 31			18 51
Alvechurch	d			16 55			17 15			17 35			17 55			18 15				18 35			18 55
Redditch	a			17 03			17 21			17 41			18 03			18 21				18 41			19 03
Bromsgrove	a	16 46	16 41			17 07		17 11	17 25		17 46	17 41			18 07		18 11	18 26	18 21		18 47	18 41	

		XC ◇1	LM	LM	LM	LM	LM	LM	LM	LM	XC ◇1	LM	LM	LM	LM	LM	LM	LM	XC ◇1	LM	LM	LM
Lichfield Trent Valley	d		17 50			18 10	18 20			18 40		18 50		19 10		19 20		19 40		19 50		20 11
Lichfield City	d		17 54			18 15	18 24			18 44		18 54		19 14		19 24		19 44		19 54		20 15
Shenstone	d		17 59				18 29					18 59				19 29		19 49		19 59		
Blake Street	d		18 02			18 22	18 32			18 52		19 02		19 22		19 32		19 52		20 02		20 22
Butlers Lane	d		18 04			18 24	18 34			18 54		19 04		19 24		19 34		19 54		20 04		20 25
Four Oaks	d		18 06	18 16		18 26	18 36	18 46		18 57		19 06	19 16	19 27		19 36	19 46	19 56		20 07	20 16	20 27
Sutton Coldfield	d		18 10	18 20		18 30	18 40	18 50		19 00		19 10	19 20	19 30		19 40	19 50	20 00		20 11	20 20	20 31
Wylde Green	d		18 12	18 22		18 32	18 42	18 52		19 03		19 12	19 22	19 33		19 42	19 52	20 02		20 13	20 22	20 33
Chester Road	d		18 14	18 24		18 34	18 44	18 54		19 05		19 14	19 24	19 35		19 44	19 54	20 04		20 15	20 24	20 35
Erdington	d		18 17	18 27		18 37	18 47	18 57		19 07		19 17	19 27	19 37		19 47	19 57	20 07		20 18	20 27	20 38
Gravelly Hill	d		18 19	18 29		18 39	18 49	18 59		19 10		19 19	19 29	19 40		19 49	19 59	20 09		20 20	20 29	20 40
Aston	d		18 23	18 33		18 43	18 53	19 03		19 13		19 23	19 33	19 43		19 53	20 03	20 13		20 24	20 32	20 43
Duddeston	d			18 36				19 06					19 36				20 06				20 35	
Birmingham New Street 12	a		18 30	18 41		18 49	19 00	19 11		19 21		19 30	19 41	19 50		20 00	20 12	20 21		20 32	20 41	20 50
	d	18 30	18 33	18 43	18 50	18 53	19 03	19 15	19 20	19 23	19 30	19 33	19 43	19 53	20 00	20 03	20 15	20 23	20 30	20 35	20 43	20 53
Five Ways	d		18 37	18 47		18 57	19 07	19 19		19 27		19 37	19 47	19 57		20 07	20 19	20 27		20 39	20 47	20 57
University	d	18a36	18 41	18 51	18 56	19 01	19 11	19 23	19 26	19 31	19a36	19 41	19 51	20 01	20 06	20 11	20 23	20 31	20a36	20 43	20 51	21 01
Selly Oak	d		18 43	18 53		19 03	19 13	19 25		19 33		19 43	19 53	20 03		20 13	20 25	20 33		20 45	20 53	21 03
Bournville	d		18 46	18 56		19 06	19 16	19 28		19 36		19 46	19 56	20 06		20 16	20 28	20 36		20 48	20 56	21 06
Kings Norton	d		18 49	18 59		19 09	19 19	19 31		19 39		19 49	19 59	20 09		20 19	20 30	20 39		20 51	20 59	21 09
Northfield	d		18 52	19 02		19 12	19 22	19 34		19 42		19 52	20 02	20 12		20 22	20 33	20 42		20 54	21 02	21 12
Longbridge	d		18 59	19 06		19 15	19 26	19 36		19 46		19 58	20 06	20 15		20 32	20 36	20 46		20 57	21 05	21 15
Barnt Green	d			19 11		19 19	19 31			19 51			20 11	20 19		20 37		20 51			21 12	21 19
Alvechurch	d			19 15			19 35			19 55			20 15			20 41		20 55			21 16	
Redditch	a			19 21			19 45			20 03			20 21			20 47		21 03			21 22	
Bromsgrove	a		19 08		19 11	19 25		19 47	19 42			20 07		20 26	20 21		20 45			21 06		21 26

Table T069-F

Mondays to Fridays

16 December to 15 May

Lichfield - Birmingham - Longbridge and Redditch

		LM	LM	LM	LM	XC 1	LM	LM	LM	LM	LM	LM	LM	LM	LM	LM	LM	LM	LM
Lichfield Trent Valley	d		20 22				20 55			21 28		21 58	22 11			22 28	22 48	23 18	23 41
Lichfield City	d		20 26		20 46		20 59	21 16		21 32	21 46	22 02	22 15			22 32	22 52	23 22	23 45
Shenstone	d						21 04			21 37		22 07				22 37	22 57	23 27	23 50
Blake Street	d		20 33		20 53		21 07	21 23		21 40	21 53	22 10	22 22			22 40	23 01	23 30	23 54
Butlers Lane	d		20 36		20 56		21 09	21 26		21 42	21 56	22 12	22 25			22 42	23 03	23 33	23 56
Four Oaks	d		20 38	20 48	20 58		21 12	21 28		21 45	21 58	22 15	22 27			22 45	23 06	23 35	23 59
Sutton Coldfield	d		20 42	20 52	21 02		21 16	21 32		21 49	22 02	22 19	22 31			22 49	23 09	23 39	00 02
Wylde Green	d		20 44	20 54	21 04		21 18	21 34		21 51	22 04	22 21	22 33			22 51	23 12	23 41	
Chester Road	d		20 46	20 56	21 06		21 20	21 36		21 53	22 06	22 23	22 35			22 53	23 14	23 43	
Erdington	d		20 49	20 59	21 09		21 23	21 39		21 56	22 09	22 26	22 38			22 56	23 16	23 46	
Gravelly Hill	d		20 51	21 01	21 11		21 25	21 41		21 58	22 11	22 28	22 40			22 58	23 19	23 48	
Aston	d		20 54	21 05	21 14		21 28	21 44		22 02	22 14	22 32	22 43			23 02	23 22	23 52	
Duddeston	d			21 08			21 31			22 05		22 35				23 05	23 25	23 55	
Birmingham New Street 12	a		21 00	21 12	21 21		21 40	21 51		22 12	22 21	22 41	22 49			23 09	23 30	23 59	00 16
	d	21 00	21 03	21 15	21 23	21 30	21 44	21 54	22 00	22 15	22 23	22 43	22 53	23 00	23 05	23 15	23 33		
Five Ways	d		21 07	21 19	21 27		21 48	21 58		22 19	22 27	22 47	22 57		23 09	23 19	23 37		
University	d	21 06	21 11	21 23	21 31	21a36	21 52	22 02	22 06	22 23	22 31	22 51	23 01	23 06	23 13	23 23	23 41		
Selly Oak	d		21 13	21 25	21 33		21 54	22 04		22 25	22 33	22 53	23 03		23 15	23 25	23 43		
Bournville	d		21 16	21 28	21 36		21 57	22 07		22 28	22 36	22 56	23 06		23 18	23 28	23 46		
Kings Norton	d		21 19	21 31	21 39		22 00	22 10		22 31	22 39	22 59	23 09		23 21	23 31	23 49		
Northfield	d		21 23	21 34	21 42		22 03	22 13		22 34	22 42	23 02	23 12		23 24	23 34	23 52		
Longbridge	d		21 31	21 36	21 46		22 07	22 18		22 37	22 46	23 06	23 16		23 28	23 38	23a54		
Barnt Green	d		21 36		21 51		22 11	22 23			22 51	23 10	23 21			23 43			
Alvechurch	d		21 41		21 55			22 27			22 55		23 26			23 47			
Redditch	a		21 47		22 05			22 37			23 05		23 36			23 53			
Bromsgrove	a	21 21		21 46			22 17		22 22	22 46		23 16		23 20	23 37				

Saturdays

21 December to 16 May

		LM	LM	LM	LM	LM	LM	LM	LM	LM	LM	LM	LM	XC ◇1	LM	LM	LM	LM	LM	LM	LM	XC ◇1	LM
Lichfield Trent Valley	d										06 20		06 40		06 50			07 10	07 20		07 40		07 50
Lichfield City	d										06 24	06 38	06 45		06 54			07 15	07 24		07 45		07 54
Shenstone	d										06 29		06 50		06 59				07 29				07 59
Blake Street	d						06 02				06 32		06 53		07 02			07 22	07 32		07 52		08 02
Butlers Lane	d						06 04				06 34		06 56		07 04			07 25	07 34		07 55		08 05
Four Oaks	d						06 07				06 36	06 48	06 58		07 06	07 16		07 27	07 36	07 46	07 57		08 06
Sutton Coldfield	d	00 02					06 10				06 40	06 51	07 02		07 10	07 20		07 31	07 40	07 50	08 01		08 10
Wylde Green	d						06 12				06 42	06 54	07 04		07 12	07 22		07 33	07 42	07 52	08 03		08 12
Chester Road	d						06 14				06 44	06 56	07 06		07 14	07 24		07 35	07 44	07 54	08 05		08 14
Erdington	d						06 17				06 47	06 58	07 09		07 17	07 27		07 38	07 47	07 57	08 08		08 17
Gravelly Hill	d						06 19				06 49	07 01	07 11		07 19	07 29		07 40	07 49	07 59	08 10		08 19
Aston	d						06 23				06 53	07 03	07 14		07 23	07 32		07 43	07 53	08 03	08 13		08 23
Duddeston	d						06 26				06 56	07 06			07 26	07 35				08 06			
Birmingham New Street 12	a	00 16					06 30				07 01	07 12	07 20		07 31	07 41		07 50	08 00	08 10	08 21		08 31
	d		05 53	06 03	06 10	06 23	06 33	06 43	06 50	06 53	07 03	07 14	07 23	07 30	07 33	07 43	07 50	07 53	08 03	08 14	08 23	08 30	08 33
Five Ways	d		05 57	06 07	06 14	06 27	06 37	06 47		06 57	07 07	07 18	07 27		07 37	07 47		07 57	08 07	08 18	08 27		08 37
University	d		06 01	06 11	06 18	06 31	06 41	06 51	06 56	07 01	07 11	07 22	07 31	07a36	07 41	07 51	07 56	08 01	08 11	08 22	08 31	08a36	08 41
Selly Oak	d		06 03	06 13	06 20	06 33	06 43	06 53		07 03	07 13	07 24	07 33		07 43	07 53		08 03	08 13	08 24	08 33		08 43
Bournville	d		06 06	06 16	06 23	06 36	06 46	06 56		07 06	07 16	07 27	07 36		07 46	07 56		08 06	08 16	08 27	08 36		08 46
Kings Norton	d		06 09	06 19	06 26	06 39	06 49	06 59		07 09	07 19	07 30	07 39		07 49	07 59		08 09	08 19	08 30	08 39		08 49
Northfield	d		06 12	06 22	06 29	06 42	06 52	07 02		07 12	07 22	07 33	07 42		07 52	08 02		08 12	08 22	08 33	08 42		08 52
Longbridge	d		06 15	06 25	06 32	06 45	06 59	07 05		07 15	07 25	07 36	07 45		07 59	08 05		08 15	08 25	08 36	08 45		08 58
Barnt Green	d		06 19	06 30		06 50		07 10		07 19	07 30		07 50			08 10		08 19	08 30		08 50		
Alvechurch	d			06 34		06 54		07 15			07 34		07 54			08 15			08 34		08 54		
Redditch	a			06 41		07 03		07 21			07 41		08 03			08 20			08 41		09 03		
Bromsgrove	a		06 25		06 41		07 08		07 11	07 25		07 46			08 08		08 11	08 25		08 46			09 07

		LM	LM	LM	LM	LM	LM	XC ◇1	LM	LM	LM	LM	LM	LM	LM	XC ◇1	LM	LM	LM	LM	LM	LM	LM
Lichfield Trent Valley	d			08 10	08 20		08 40		08 50			09 10	09 20		09 40		09 50			10 10	10 20		10 40
Lichfield City	d			08 14	08 24		08 44		08 54			09 14	09 24		09 44		09 54			10 14	10 24		10 44
Shenstone	d				08 29				08 59				09 29				09 59				10 29		
Blake Street	d			08 22	08 32		08 52		09 02			09 22	09 32		09 52		10 02			10 22	10 32		10 52
Butlers Lane	d			08 24	08 34		08 54		09 04			09 24	09 34		09 54		10 04			10 24	10 34		10 54
Four Oaks	d	08 16		08 27	08 36	08 46	08 57		09 06	09 16		09 27	09 36	09 46	09 57		10 06	10 16		10 27	10 36	10 46	10 57
Sutton Coldfield	d	08 20		08 30	08 40	08 50	09 00		09 10	09 20		09 30	09 40	09 50	10 00		10 10	10 20		10 30	10 40	10 50	11 00
Wylde Green	d	08 22		08 33	08 42	08 52	09 03		09 12	09 22		09 33	09 42	09 52	10 03		10 12	10 22		10 33	10 42	10 52	11 03
Chester Road	d	08 24		08 35	08 44	08 54	09 05		09 14	09 24		09 35	09 44	09 54	10 05		10 14	10 24		10 35	10 44	10 54	11 05
Erdington	d	08 27		08 37	08 47	08 57	09 07		09 17	09 27		09 37	09 47	09 57	10 07		10 17	10 27		10 37	10 47	10 57	11 07
Gravelly Hill	d	08 29		08 40	08 49	08 59	09 10		09 19	09 29		09 40	09 49	09 59	10 10		10 19	10 29		10 40	10 49	10 59	11 10
Aston	d	08 33		08 43	08 53	09 03	09 13		09 23	09 33		09 43	09 53	10 03	10 13		10 23	10 33		10 43	10 53	11 03	11 13
Duddeston	d	08 36		08 46		09 06	09 16			09 36				10 06				10 36				11 06	
Birmingham New Street 12	a	08 41		08 50	09 00	09 10	09 21		09 31	09 41		09 50	10 00	10 10	10 21		10 31	10 41		10 50	11 00	11 10	11 21
	d	08 43	08 50	08 53	09 03	09 14	09 23	09 30	09 33	09 43	09 50	09 53	10 03	10 14	10 23	10 30	10 33	10 43	10 50	10 53	11 03	11 14	11 23
Five Ways	d	08 47		08 57	09 07	09 18	09 27		09 37	09 47		09 57	10 07	10 18	10 27		10 37	10 47		10 57	11 07	11 18	11 27
University	d	08 51	08 56	09 01	09 11	09 22	09 31	09a36	09 41	09 51	09 56	10 01	10 11	10 22	10 31	10a36	10 41	10 51	10 56	11 01	11 11	11 22	11 31
Selly Oak	d	08 53		09 03	09 13	09 24	09 33		09 43	09 53		10 03	10 13	10 24	10 33		10 43	10 53		11 03	11 13	11 24	11 33
Bournville	d	08 56		09 06	09 16	09 27	09 36		09 46	09 56		10 06	10 16	10 27	10 36		10 46	10 56		11 06	11 16	11 27	11 36
Kings Norton	d	08 59		09 09	09 19	09 30	09 39		09 49	09 59		10 09	10 19	10 30	10 39		10 49	10 59		11 10	11 19	11 30	11 39
Northfield	d	09 02		09 12	09 22	09 33	09 42		09 52	10 02		10 12	10 22	10 33	10 42		10 52	11 02		11 13	11 22	11 33	11 42
Longbridge	d	09 06		09 15	09 25	09 36	09 45		09 59	10 06		10 15	10 25	10 36	10 46		10 59	11 06		11 16	11 25	11 36	11 45
Barnt Green	d	09 11		09 19	09 30		09 50			10 11		10 19	10 30		10 51			11 11		11 21	11 30		11 50
Alvechurch	d	09 15			09 34		09 54			10 15			10 34		10 55			11 15			11 34		11 54
Redditch	a	09 22			09 41		10 03			10 21			10 41		11 03			11 21			11 41		12 03
Bromsgrove	a		09 11	09 25		09 46			10 08		10 11	10 25		10 46			11 08		11 11	11 27		11 46	

Table T069-F

Saturdays

21 December to 16 May

Lichfield - Birmingham - Longbridge and Redditch

		XC ◇1	LM	LM	LM	LM	LM	LM	LM	XC ◇1	LM	LM	LM	LM	LM	LM	LM	XC ◇1	LM	LM	LM	LM
Lichfield Trent Valley	d		10 50			11 10	11 20		11 40		11 50			12 10	12 20		12 40		12 50			13 10
Lichfield City	d		10 54			11 14	11 24		11 44		11 54			12 14	12 24		12 44		12 54			13 14
Shenstone	d		10 59				11 29				11 59				12 29				12 59			
Blake Street	d		11 02			11 22	11 32		11 52		12 02			12 22	12 32		12 52		13 02			13 22
Butlers Lane	d		11 04			11 24	11 34		11 54		12 04			12 24	12 34		12 54		13 04			13 24
Four Oaks	d		11 06	11 16		11 27	11 36	11 46	11 57		12 06	12 16		12 27	12 36	12 46	12 57		13 06	13 16		13 27
Sutton Coldfield	d		11 10	11 20		11 30	11 40	11 50	12 00		12 10	12 20		12 30	12 40	12 50	13 00		13 10	13 20		13 30
Wylde Green	d		11 12	11 22		11 33	11 42	11 52	12 03		12 12	12 22		12 33	12 42	12 52	13 03		13 12	13 22		13 33
Chester Road	d		11 14	11 24		11 35	11 44	11 54	12 05		12 14	12 24		12 35	12 44	12 54	13 05		13 14	13 24		13 35
Erdington	d		11 17	11 27		11 37	11 47	11 57	12 07		12 17	12 27		12 37	12 47	12 57	13 07		13 17	13 27		13 37
Gravelly Hill	d		11 19	11 29		11 40	11 49	11 59	12 10		12 19	12 29		12 40	12 49	12 59	13 10		13 19	13 29		13 40
Aston	d		11 23	11 33		11 43	11 53	12 03	12 13		12 23	12 33		12 43	12 53	13 03	13 13		13 23	13 33		13 43
Duddeston	d			11 36				12 06				12 36				13 06				13 36		
Birmingham New Street 12	a		11 31	11 41		11 50	12 00	12 10	12 21		12 31	12 41		12 50	13 00	13 10	13 21		13 31	13 41		13 50
	d	11 30	11 33	11 43	11 50	11 53	12 03	12 14	12 23	12 30	12 33	12 43	12 50	12 53	13 03	13 14	13 23	13 30	13 33	13 43	13 50	13 53
Five Ways	d		11 37	11 47		11 57	12 07	12 18	12 27		12 37	12 47		12 57	13 07	13 18	13 27		13 37	13 47		13 57
University	d	11a36	11 41	11 51	11 56	12 01	12 11	12 22	12 31	12a36	12 41	12 51	12 56	13 01	13 11	13 22	13 31	13a36	13 41	13 51	13 56	14 01
Selly Oak	d		11 43	11 53		12 03	12 13	12 24	12 33		12 43	12 53		13 03	13 13	13 24	13 33		13 43	13 53		14 03
Bournville	d		11 46	11 56		12 06	12 16	12 27	12 36		12 46	12 56		13 06	13 16	13 27	13 36		13 46	13 56		14 06
Kings Norton	d		11 49	11 59		12 09	12 19	12 30	12 39		12 49	12 59		13 09	13 19	13 30	13 39		13 49	13 59		14 09
Northfield	d		11 52	12 02		12 12	12 22	12 33	12 42		12 52	13 02		13 12	13 22	13 33	13 42		13 52	14 02		14 12
Longbridge	d		11 59	12 06		12 15	12 25	12 36	12 45		12 59	13 06		13 15	13 25	13 36	13 45		13 58	14 06		14 15
Barnt Green	d			12 11		12 19	12 30		12 50			13 11		13 19	13 30		13 50			14 11		14 19
Alvechurch	d			12 15			12 34		12 54			13 15			13 34		13 54			14 15		
Redditch	a			12 21			12 41		13 03			13 21			13 41		14 03			14 21		
Bromsgrove	a		12 08		12 11	12 25		12 46			13 08		13 11	13 25		13 46			14 07		14 11	14 25

		LM	LM	LM	XC ◇1	LM	LM	LM	LM	LM	LM	LM	XC ◇1	LM	LM	LM	LM	LM	LM	LM	LM	XC ◇1	LM
Lichfield Trent Valley	d	13 20		13 40		13 50			14 10	14 20		14 40		14 50			15 10	15 20			15 40		15 50
Lichfield City	d	13 24		13 44		13 54			14 14	14 24		14 44		14 54			15 14	15 24			15 44		15 54
Shenstone	d	13 29				13 59				14 29				14 59				15 29					15 59
Blake Street	d	13 32		13 52		14 02			14 22	14 32		14 52		15 02			15 22	15 32			15 52		16 02
Butlers Lane	d	13 34		13 54		14 04			14 24	14 34		14 54		15 04			15 24	15 34			15 54		16 04
Four Oaks	d	13 36	13 46	13 57		14 06	14 16		14 27	14 36	14 46	14 57		15 06	15 16		15 27	15 36	15 46		15 57		16 06
Sutton Coldfield	d	13 40	13 50	14 00		14 10	14 20		14 30	14 40	14 50	15 00		15 10	15 20		15 30	15 40	15 50		16 00		16 10
Wylde Green	d	13 42	13 52	14 03		14 12	14 22		14 33	14 42	14 52	15 03		15 12	15 22		15 33	15 42	15 52		16 03		16 12
Chester Road	d	13 44	13 54	14 05		14 14	14 24		14 35	14 44	14 54	15 05		15 14	15 24		15 35	15 44	15 54		16 05		16 14
Erdington	d	13 47	13 57	14 07		14 17	14 27		14 37	14 47	14 57	15 07		15 17	15 27		15 37	15 47	15 57		16 07		16 17
Gravelly Hill	d	13 49	13 59	14 10		14 19	14 29		14 40	14 49	14 59	15 10		15 19	15 29		15 40	15 49	15 59		16 10		16 19
Aston	d	13 53	14 03	14 13		14 23	14 33		14 43	14 53	15 03	15 13		15 23	15 33		15 43	15 53	16 03		16 13		16 23
Duddeston	d		14 06				14 36				15 06				15 36				16 06				
Birmingham New Street 12	a	14 00	14 10	14 21		14 31	14 41		14 50	15 00	15 10	15 21		15 31	15 41		15 50	16 00	16 11		16 21		16 31
	d	14 03	14 14	14 23	14 30	14 33	14 43	14 50	14 53	15 03	15 14	15 23	15 30	15 33	15 43	15 50	15 53	16 03	16 15	16 20	16 23	16 30	16 33
Five Ways	d	14 07	14 18	14 27		14 37	14 47		14 57	15 07	15 18	15 27		15 37	15 47		15 57	16 07	16 19		16 27		16 37
University	d	14 11	14 22	14 31	14a36	14 41	14 51	14 56	15 01	15 11	15 22	15 31	15a36	15 41	15 51	15 56	16 01	16 11	16 23		16 31	16a36	16 41
Selly Oak	d	14 13	14 24	14 33		14 43	14 53		15 03	15 13	15 24	15 33		15 43	15 53		16 03	16 13	16 25		16 33		16 43
Bournville	d	14 16	14 27	14 36		14 46	14 56		15 06	15 16	15 27	15 36		15 46	15 56		16 06	16 16	16 28		16 36		16 46
Kings Norton	d	14 19	14 30	14 39		14 49	14 59		15 09	15 19	15 30	15 39		15 49	15 59		16 09	16 19	16 31		16 39		16 49
Northfield	d	14 22	14 33	14 42		14 52	15 02		15 12	15 22	15 33	15 42		15 53	16 02		16 12	16 22	16 34		16 42		16 52
Longbridge	d	14 25	14 36	14 45		14 59	15 06		15 15	15 25	15 36	15 45		15 59	16 06		16 15	16 25	16 37		16 45		16 59
Barnt Green	d	14 30		14 50			15 11		15 19	15 30		15 50			16 11		16 19	16 30			16 50		
Alvechurch	d	14 34		14 54			15 15			15 34		15 54			16 15			16 34			16 54		
Redditch	a	14 41		15 03			15 21			15 41		16 03			16 21			16 41			17 03		
Bromsgrove	a		14 46			15 08		15 11	15 25		15 46			16 08		16 11	16 25		16 46	16 41			17 08

		LM	LM	LM	LM	LM	LM	LM	XC ◇1	LM	LM	LM	LM	LM	LM	LM	XC ◇1	LM	LM	LM	LM	LM
Lichfield Trent Valley	d			16 10	16 20			16 40		16 50			17 10	17 20		17 40		17 50			18 10	18 20
Lichfield City	d			16 14	16 24			16 44		16 54			17 14	17 24		17 44		17 54			18 14	18 24
Shenstone	d				16 29					16 59				17 29				17 59				18 29
Blake Street	d			16 22	16 32			16 52		17 02			17 22	17 32		17 52		18 02			18 22	18 32
Butlers Lane	d			16 24	16 34			16 54		17 04			17 24	17 34		17 54		18 04			18 24	18 34
Four Oaks	d	16 16		16 27	16 36	16 46		16 57		17 06	17 16		17 27	17 36	17 46	17 57		18 06	18 16		18 27	18 36
Sutton Coldfield	d	16 20		16 30	16 40	16 50		17 00		17 10	17 20		17 30	17 40	17 50	18 00		18 10	18 20		18 30	18 40
Wylde Green	d	16 22		16 33	16 42	16 52		17 03		17 12	17 22		17 33	17 42	17 52	18 03		18 12	18 22		18 33	18 42
Chester Road	d	16 24		16 35	16 44	16 54		17 05		17 14	17 24		17 35	17 44	17 54	18 05		18 14	18 24		18 35	18 44
Erdington	d	16 27		16 37	16 47	16 57		17 07		17 17	17 27		17 37	17 47	17 57	18 07		18 17	18 27		18 37	18 47
Gravelly Hill	d	16 29		16 40	16 49	16 59		17 10		17 19	17 29		17 40	17 49	17 59	18 10		18 19	18 29		18 40	18 49
Aston	d	16 33		16 43	16 53	17 03		17 13		17 23	17 33		17 43	17 53	18 03	18 13		18 23	18 33		18 43	18 53
Duddeston	d	16 36				17 06					17 36				18 06				18 36			
Birmingham New Street 12	a	16 41		16 50	17 00	17 10		17 21		17 31	17 41		17 50	18 00	18 10	18 21		18 31	18 41		18 50	19 00
	d	16 43	16 50	16 53	17 03	17 14	17 20	17 23	17 30	17 33	17 43	17 50	17 53	18 03	18 14	18 23	18 30	18 33	18 43	18 50	18 53	19 03
Five Ways	d	16 47		16 57	17 07	17 18		17 27		17 37	17 47		17 57	18 07	18 18	18 27		18 37	18 47		18 57	19 07
University	d	16 51	16 56	17 01	17 11	17 22		17 31	17a36	17 41	17 51	17 56	18 01	18 11	18 22	18 31	18a36	18 41	18 51	18 56	19 01	19 11
Selly Oak	d	16 53		17 03	17 13	17 24		17 33		17 43	17 53		18 03	18 13	18 24	18 33		18 43	18 53		19 03	19 13
Bournville	d	16 56		17 06	17 16	17 27		17 36		17 46	17 56		18 06	18 16	18 27	18 36		18 46	18 56		19 06	19 16
Kings Norton	d	16 59		17 09	17 19	17 30		17 39		17 49	17 59		18 09	18 19	18 30	18 39		18 49	18 59		19 09	19 19
Northfield	d	17 02		17 12	17 22	17 33		17 42		17 52	18 02		18 12	18 22	18 33	18 42		18 52	19 02		19 12	19 22
Longbridge	d	17 06		17 15	17 25	17 36		17 45		17 58	18 06		18 15	18 25	18 36	18 45		18 58	19 05		19 15	19 24
Barnt Green	d	17 11		17 19	17 30			17 50			18 11		18 19	18 30		18 50			19 10		19 19	19 29
Alvechurch	d	17 16			17 34			17 54			18 15			18 34		18 54			19 14			19 33
Redditch	a	17 21			17 41			18 03			18 21			18 41		19 03			19 22			19 42
Bromsgrove	a		17 11	17 25		17 46	17 42			18 07		18 11	18 25		18 46			19 08		19 11	19 25	

Table T069-F

Saturdays
21 December to 16 May

Lichfield - Birmingham - Longbridge and Redditch

		LM	LM	XC ◇1	LM	LM	LM	LM	LM	LM	LM	XC ◇1	LM	LM	LM	LM	LM	LM	LM	LM	LM	LM	LM
Lichfield Trent Valley	d		18 40		18 50			19 10	19 20		19 40		19 51			20 29			21 00		21 31		
Lichfield City	d		18 44		18 54			19 14	19 24		19 44		19 55			20 33			21 04		21 35		
Shenstone	d				18 59				19 29		19 49		20 00			20 38			21 09		21 40		
Blake Street	d		18 52		19 02			19 22	19 32		19 52		20 03			20 41			21 12		21 43		
Butlers Lane	d		18 54		19 04			19 24	19 34		19 54		20 06			20 44			21 15		21 46		
Four Oaks	d	18 46	18 57		19 06	19 16		19 27	19 36	19 46	19 56		20 08		20 26	20 47		20 56	21 18	21 26	21 48		22 00
Sutton Coldfield	d	18 50	19 00		19 10	19 20		19 30	19 40	19 50	20 00		20 12		20 30	20 50		21 00	21 21	21 30	21 52		22 04
Wylde Green	d	18 52	19 03		19 12	19 22		19 33	19 42	19 52	20 02		20 14		20 32	20 53		21 02	21 24	21 32	21 54		22 06
Chester Road	d	18 54	19 05		19 14	19 24		19 35	19 44	19 54	20 04		20 16		20 35	20 55		21 04	21 26	21 34	21 56		22 08
Erdington	d	18 57	19 07		19 17	19 27		19 37	19 47	19 57	20 07		20 19		20 37	20 57		21 07	21 28	21 37	21 59		22 11
Gravelly Hill	d	18 59	19 10		19 19	19 29		19 40	19 49	19 59	20 09		20 21		20 39	21 00		21 09	21 31	21 39	22 01		22 13
Aston	d	19 03	19 13		19 23	19 33		19 43	19 53	20 03	20 13		20 25		20 43	21 03		21 13	21 34	21 43	22 05		22 17
Duddeston	d	19 06				19 36				20 06			20 27		20 46			21 16		21 46			22 20
Birmingham New Street 12	a	19 10	19 21		19 31	19 41		19 50	20 00	20 11	20 20		20 33		20 50	21 09		21 20	21 40	21 50	22 11		22 24
	d	19 14	19 23	19 30	19 33	19 43	19 50	19 53	20 03	20 15	20 23	20 30	20 35	20 50	20 53	21 15	21 20	21 23	21 43	21 53	22 13	22 20	22 27
Five Ways	d	19 18	19 27		19 37	19 47		19 57	20 07	20 19	20 27		20 39		20 57	21 19		21 27	21 47	21 57	22 17		22 31
University	d	19 22	19 31	19a36	19 41	19 51	19 56	20 01	20 11	20 23	20 31	20a36	20 43	20 56	21 01	21 23	21 26	21 31	21 51	22 01	22 21	22 26	22 35
Selly Oak	d	19 24	19 33		19 43	19 53		20 03	20 13	20 25	20 33		20 45		21 03	21 25		21 33	21 53	22 03	22 23		22 37
Bournville	d	19 27	19 36		19 46	19 56		20 06	20 16	20 28	20 36		20 48		21 06	21 28		21 36	21 56	22 06	22 26		22 40
Kings Norton	d	19 30	19 39		19 49	19 59		20 09	20 19	20 31	20 39		20 51		21 09	21 34		21 39	21 59	22 09	22 29		22 43
Northfield	d	19 33	19 42		19 52	20 02		20 12	20 22	20 34	20 42		20 54		21 12	21 37		21 42	22 02	22 12	22 32		22 46
Longbridge	d	19 36	19 45		19 59	20 08		20 15	20 25	20 36	20 46		20 59		21 16	21 39		21 46	22 07	22 16	22 35		22 49
Barnt Green	d		19 50			20 13		20 19	20 30		20 51		21 04		21 21			21 51	22 12	22 21			22 54
Alvechurch	d		19 54			20 17			20 34		20 55				21 25			21 55		22 25			22 58
Redditch	a		20 03			20 26			20 41		21 03				21 35			22 05		22 35			23 04
Bromsgrove	a	19 46			20 08		20 11	20 25		20 46			21 10	21 13		21 49	21 41		22 18		22 44	22 41	

		LM	LM	LM	LM	LM	LM
Lichfield Trent Valley	d	21 59		22 31		23 00	23 20
Lichfield City	d	22 03		22 35		23 04	23 24
Shenstone	d	22 08		22 40		23 09	23 29
Blake Street	d	22 11		22 43		23 12	23 32
Butlers Lane	d	22 14		22 46		23 15	23 35
Four Oaks	d	22 17	22 33	22 48	23 06	23 17	23 38
Sutton Coldfield	d	22 20	22 37	22 52	23 10	23 21	23 41
Wylde Green	d	22 23	22 39	22 54	23 12	23 23	23 44
Chester Road	d	22 25	22 41	22 56	23 14	23 25	23 46
Erdington	d	22 27	22 44	22 59	23 17	23 28	23 48
Gravelly Hill	d	22 30	22 46	23 01	23 19		
Aston	d	22 33	22 50	23 05	23 23		
Duddeston	d		22 53		23 26		
Birmingham New Street 12	a	22 39	22 58	23 12	23 30	23 37	23 58
	d	22 42	23 00	23 16		23 39	
Five Ways	d	22 46	23 04	23 20		23 43	
University	d	22 50	23 08	23 24		23 47	
Selly Oak	d	22 52	23 10	23 26		23 49	
Bournville	d	22 55	23 13	23 29		23 52	
Kings Norton	d	22 58	23 16	23 32		23 55	
Northfield	d	23 01	23 19	23 35		23 58	
Longbridge	d	23a03	23 23	23 38		00a01	
Barnt Green	d		23 27	23 43			
Alvechurch	d		23 32	23 47			
Redditch	a		23 37	23 53			
Bromsgrove	a						

Sundays
15 December to 10 May

		LM	LM	LM	LM	LM	LM	LM	XC ◇1	LM	LM	LM	LM	LM	XC ◇1	LM	LM	LM	LM	LM	LM	XC ◇1	LM
Lichfield Trent Valley	d					09 01				09 31		10 01				10 31		11 01			11 31		
Lichfield City	d					09 05				09 35		10 05				10 35		11 05			11 35		
Shenstone	d					09 10				09 40		10 10				10 40		11 10			11 40		
Blake Street	d					09 13				09 43		10 13				10 43		11 13			11 43		
Butlers Lane	d					09 16				09 46		10 16				10 46		11 16			11 46		
Four Oaks	d					09 18		09 37		09 48		10 18				10 48		11 18			11 48		
Sutton Coldfield	d					09 22		09 41		09 52		10 22				10 52		11 22			11 52		
Wylde Green	d					09 24		09 43		09 54		10 24				10 54		11 24			11 54		
Chester Road	d					09 26		09 45		09 56		10 26				10 56		11 26			11 56		
Erdington	d					09 29		09 48		09 59		10 29				10 59		11 29			11 59		
Gravelly Hill	d					09 31		09 50		10 01		10 31				11 01		11 31			12 01		
Aston	d					09 35		09 54		10 05		10 35				11 05		11 35			12 05		
Duddeston	d					09 38				10 08		10 38				11 08		11 38			12 08		
Birmingham New Street 12	a					09 42		10 00		10 12		10 42				11 12		11 42			12 12		
	d	08 55	09 03	09 15	09 34	09 45	10 00	10 03	10 12	10 15	10 34	10 45	11 00	11 03	11 12	11 15	11 34	11 45	12 00	12 03	12 15	12 30	12 34
Five Ways	d		09 07	09 19	09 38	09 49		10 07		10 19	10 38	10 49		11 07		11 19	11 38	11 49		12 07	12 19		12 38
University	d	09 01	09 11	09 23	09 42	09 53	10 06	10 11	10a18	10 23	10 42	10 53	11 06	11 11	11a18	11 23	11 42	11 53	12 06	12 11	12 23	12a36	12 42
Selly Oak	d		09 13	09 25	09 44	09 55		10 13		10 25	10 44	10 55		11 13		11 25	11 44	11 55		12 13	12 25		12 44
Bournville	d		09 16	09 28	09 47	09 58		10 16		10 28	10 47	10 58		11 16		11 28	11 47	11 58		12 16	12 28		12 47
Kings Norton	d		09 19	09 31	09 50	10 01		10 19		10 31	10 50	11 01		11 19		11 31	11 50	12 01		12 19	12 31		12 50
Northfield	d		09 22	09 34	09 53	10 04		10 22		10 34	10 53	11 04		11 22		11 34	11 53	12 04		12 22	12 34		12 53
Longbridge	d	09 09	09 25	09 37	09 56	10 07		10 27		10 37	10 56	11 07		11 27		11 37	11 58	12 07		12 26	12 37		12 58
Barnt Green	d		09 29	09 42		10 12		10 31		10 42		11 12		11 31		11 42		12 12		12 31	12 42		
Alvechurch	d			09 46		10 16				10 46		11 16				11 46		12 16			12 46		
Redditch	a	09 22		09 52		10 22				10 52		11 22				11 52		12 22			12 52		
Bromsgrove	a		09 35		10 05		10 20	10 37			11 05		11 20	11 37			12 07		12 20	12 37			13 07

Table T069-F

Sundays
15 December to 10 May

Lichfield - Birmingham - Longbridge and Redditch

		LM	LM	LM	LM	XC ◇1	LM	LM	LM	LM	LM	XC ◇1	LM	LM	LM	LM	LM	XC ◇1	LM	LM	LM	LM	LM
Lichfield Trent Valley	d	12 01			12 31			13 01			13 31			14 01			14 31			15 01			15 31
Lichfield City	d	12 05			12 35			13 05			13 35			14 05			14 35			15 05			15 35
Shenstone	d	12 10			12 40			13 10			13 40			14 10			14 40			15 10			15 40
Blake Street	d	12 13			12 43			13 13			13 43			14 13			14 43			15 13			15 43
Butlers Lane	d	12 16			12 46			13 16			13 46			14 16			14 46			15 16			15 46
Four Oaks	d	12 18			12 48			13 18			13 48			14 18			14 48			15 18			15 48
Sutton Coldfield	d	12 22			12 52			13 22			13 52			14 22			14 52			15 22			15 52
Wylde Green	d	12 24			12 54			13 24			13 54			14 24			14 54			15 24			15 54
Chester Road	d	12 26			12 56			13 26			13 56			14 26			14 56			15 26			15 56
Erdington	d	12 29			12 59			13 29			13 59			14 29			14 59			15 29			15 59
Gravelly Hill	d	12 31			13 01			13 31			14 01			14 31			15 01			15 31			16 01
Aston	d	12 35			13 05			13 35			14 05			14 35			15 05			15 35			16 05
Duddeston	d	12 38			13 08			13 38			14 08			14 38			15 08			15 38			16 08
Birmingham New Street 12	a	12 42			13 12			13 42			14 12			14 42			15 12			15 42			16 12
	d	12 45	13 00	13 03	13 15	13 30	13 34	13 45	14 00	14 03	14 15	14 30	14 34	14 45	15 00	15 03	15 15	15 30	15 34	15 45	16 00	16 03	16 15
Five Ways	d	12 49		13 07	13 19		13 38	13 49		14 07	14 19		14 38	14 49		15 07	15 19		15 38	15 49		16 07	16 19
University	d	12 53	13 06	13 11	13 23	13a36	13 42	13 53	14 06	14 11	14 23	14a36	14 42	14 53	15 06	15 11	15 23	15a36	15 42	15 53	16 06	16 11	16 23
Selly Oak	d	12 55		13 13	13 25		13 44	13 55		14 13	14 25		14 44	14 55		15 13	15 25		15 44	15 55		16 13	16 25
Bournville	d	12 58		13 16	13 28		13 47	13 58		14 16	14 28		14 47	14 58		15 16	15 28		15 47	15 58		16 16	16 28
Kings Norton	d	13 01		13 19	13 31		13 50	14 01		14 19	14 31		14 50	15 01		15 19	15 31		15 50	16 01		16 19	16 31
Northfield	d	13 04		13 22	13 34		13 53	14 04		14 22	14 34		14 53	15 04		15 22	15 34		15 53	16 04		16 22	16 34
Longbridge	d	13 07		13 26	13 37		13 58	14 07		14 26	14 37		14 59	15 07		15 26	15 37		15 58	16 07		16 26	16 37
Barnt Green	d	13 12		13 31	13 42			14 12		14 31	14 42			15 12		15 31	15 42			16 12		16 31	16 42
Alvechurch	d	13 16			13 46			14 16			14 46			15 16			15 46			16 16			16 46
Redditch	a	13 22			13 52			14 22			14 52			15 22			15 52			16 22			16 52
Bromsgrove	a		13 20	13 37			14 07		14 20	14 37			15 08		15 20	15 37			16 07		16 20	16 37	

		XC ◇1	LM	LM	LM	LM	LM	XC ◇1	LM	LM	LM	LM	LM	XC ◇1	LM	LM	LM	LM	LM	XC ◇1	LM	LM
Lichfield Trent Valley	d			16 01			16 31			17 01			17 31			18 01			18 31			19 01
Lichfield City	d			16 05			16 35			17 05			17 35			18 05			18 35			19 05
Shenstone	d			16 10			16 40			17 10			17 40			18 10			18 40			19 10
Blake Street	d			16 13			16 43			17 13			17 43			18 13			18 43			19 13
Butlers Lane	d			16 16			16 46			17 16			17 46			18 16			18 46			19 16
Four Oaks	d			16 18			16 48			17 18			17 48			18 18			18 48			19 18
Sutton Coldfield	d			16 22			16 52			17 22			17 52			18 22			18 52			19 22
Wylde Green	d			16 24			16 54			17 24			17 54			18 24			18 54			19 24
Chester Road	d			16 26			16 56			17 26			17 56			18 26			18 56			19 26
Erdington	d			16 29			16 59			17 29			17 59			18 29			18 59			19 29
Gravelly Hill	d			16 31			17 01			17 31			18 01			18 31			19 01			19 31
Aston	d			16 35			17 05			17 35			18 05			18 35			19 05			19 35
Duddeston	d			16 38			17 08			17 38			18 08			18 38			19 08			19 38
Birmingham New Street 12	a			16 42			17 12			17 42			18 12			18 42			19 12			19 42
	d	16 30	16 34	16 45	17 00	17 03	17 15	17 30	17 34	17 45	18 00	18 03	18 15	18 30	18 34	18 45	19 00	19 03	19 15	19 30	19 34	19 45
Five Ways	d		16 38	16 49		17 07	17 19		17 38	17 49		18 07	18 19		18 38	18 49		19 07	19 19		19 38	19 49
University	d	16a36	16 42	16 53	17 06	17 11	17 23	17a36	17 42	17 53	18 06	18 11	18 23	18a36	18 42	18 53	19 06	19 11	19 23	19a36	19 42	19 53
Selly Oak	d		16 44	16 55		17 13	17 25		17 44	17 55		18 13	18 25		18 44	18 55		19 13	19 25		19 44	19 55
Bournville	d		16 47	16 58		17 16	17 28		17 47	17 58		18 16	18 28		18 47	18 58		19 16	19 28		19 47	19 58
Kings Norton	d		16 50	17 01		17 19	17 31		17 50	18 01		18 19	18 31		18 50	19 01		19 19	19 31		19 50	20 01
Northfield	d		16 53	17 04		17 22	17 34		17 53	18 04		18 22	18 34		18 53	19 04		19 22	19 34		19 53	20 04
Longbridge	d		16 59	17 07		17 26	17 37		17 59	18 07		18 26	18 37		18 58	19 07		19 26	19 37		19 58	20 07
Barnt Green	d			17 12		17 31	17 42			18 12		18 31	18 42			19 12		19 31	19 42			20 12
Alvechurch	d			17 16			17 46			18 16			18 46			19 16			19 46			20 16
Redditch	a			17 22			17 52			18 22			18 52			19 22			19 52			20 22
Bromsgrove	a		17 08		17 20	17 37			18 08		18 20	18 37			19 07		19 20	19 37			20 07	

		LM	LM	LM	LM	LM	LM	LM	LM	LM	LM	LM	LM	LM	LM	LM	LM	LM	LM	LM
Lichfield Trent Valley	d			19 31		20 01			20 31		21 01			21 30			22 01		22 31	23 01
Lichfield City	d			19 35		20 05			20 35		21 05			21 34			22 05		22 35	23 05
Shenstone	d			19 40		20 10			20 40		21 10			21 39			22 10		22 40	23 10
Blake Street	d			19 43		20 13			20 43		21 13			21 42			22 13		22 43	23 13
Butlers Lane	d			19 46		20 16			20 46		21 16			21 45			22 16		22 46	23 16
Four Oaks	d			19 48		20 18			20 48		21 18			21 47			22 18		22 48	23 18
Sutton Coldfield	d			19 52		20 22			20 52		21 22			21 51			22 22		22 52	23 22
Wylde Green	d			19 54		20 24			20 54		21 24			21 53			22 24		22 54	23 24
Chester Road	d			19 56		20 26			20 56		21 26			21 55			22 26		22 56	
Erdington	d			19 59		20 29			20 59		21 29			21 58			22 29		22 59	
Gravelly Hill	d			20 01		20 31			21 01		21 31			22 00			22 31		23 01	
Aston	d			20 05		20 35			21 05		21 35			22 04			22 35		23 05	
Duddeston	d			20 08		20 38			21 08		21 38			22 07			22 38		23 08	
Birmingham New Street 12	a			20 12		20 42			21 12		21 42			22 11			22 42		23 12	23 39
	d	20 00	20 03	20 15	20 34	20 45	21 00	21 03	21 15	21 34	21 45	22 00	22 03	22 15	22 30	22 34	22 45	23 03	23 15	
Five Ways	d		20 07	20 19	20 38	20 49		21 07	21 19	21 38	21 49		22 07	22 19		22 38	22 49	23 07	23 19	
University	d	20 06	20 11	20 23	20 42	20 53	21 06	21 11	21 23	21 42	21 53	22 06	22 11	22 23	22 36	22 42	22 53	23 11	23 23	
Selly Oak	d		20 13	20 25	20 44	20 55		21 13	21 25	21 44	21 55		22 13	22 25		22 44	22 55	23 13	23 25	
Bournville	d		20 16	20 28	20 47	20 58		21 16	21 28	21 47	21 58		22 16	22 28		22 47	22 58	23 16	23 28	
Kings Norton	d		20 19	20 31	20 50	21 01		21 19	21 31	21 50	22 01		22 19	22 31		22 50	23 01	23 19	23 31	
Northfield	d		20 22	20 34	20 53	21 04		21 22	21 34	21 53	22 04		22 22	22 34		22 53	23 04	23 22	23 34	
Longbridge	d		20 26	20 37	20 59	21 07		21 26	21 37	21 59	22 07		22 27	22 37		22 58	23 07	23 26	23 37	
Barnt Green	d		20 31	20 42		21 12		21 31	21 42		22 12		22 31	22 42			23 12	23 31	23 42	
Alvechurch	d			20 46		21 16			21 46		22 16			22 46			23 16		23 46	
Redditch	a			20 52		21 22			21 52		22 22			22 52			23 22		23 52	
Bromsgrove	a	20 20	20 37		21 08		21 20	21 37		22 08		22 20	22 37		22 50	23 07		23 37		

Table T069-R

Redditch and Longbridge - Birmingham - Lichfield

Mondays to Fridays
16 December to 15 May

Miles	Miles			LM MX	LM MX	LM	LM	LM	LM	LM	LM	LM		LM	LM	LM	LM	LM	LM	LM	LM	LM		LM	LM
—	0	Bromsgrove	d						06 11	06 21		06 33		06 43		06 51		07 10	07 23			07 31			
0	—	**Redditch**	d								06 12				06 32		06 55				07 12				07 32
3¼	—	Alvechurch	d								06 17				06 37		07 00				07 17				07 37
5¼	3½	Barnt Green	d						06 17		06 23				06 43	06 57	07 07				07 23				07 43
7¾	—	Longbridge	d					06 12	06 22		06 32	06 42			06 52	07 02	07 12	07 19			07 32	07 42			07 52
8¾	—	Northfield	d					06 14	06 24		06 34	06 44			06 54	07 04	07 14	07 21			07 34	07 44			07 54
10¼	—	Kings Norton	d		00 03			06 17	06 27		06 37	06 47			06 57	07 07	07 17	07 24			07 37	07 47			07 57
11¼	—	Bournville	d		00 05			06 19	06 29		06 39	06 49			06 59	07 09	07 19	07 27			07 39	07 49			07 59
12¼	—	Selly Oak	d	00 02	00 08			06 22	06 32		06 42	06 52			07 02	07 12	07 22	07 30			07 42	07 52			08 02
13¼	—	University	d	00 05	00 11			06 25	06 35	06 39	06 45	06 55		07 00	07 05	07 15	07 25	07 32	07 38		07 45	07 55		08 00	08 05
14½	—	Five Ways	d	00 09	00 15			06 28	06 38		06 48	06 58			07 08	07 18	07 28	07 36			07 48	07 58			08 08
15¼	—	**Birmingham New Street 12**	a	00 12	00 19			06 32	06 42	06 48	06 52	07 03		07 10	07 12	07 22	07 34	07 40	07 46		07 52	08 03		08 09	08 12
—			d			05 56	06 25	06 35	06 45		06 55	07 05			07 15	07 25	07 35	07 42		07 47	07 55	08 05			08 15
16¾	—	Duddeston	d			06 00	06 29		06 49						07 19			07 46							08 19
18¼	—	Aston	d			06 03	06 32	06 41	06 52		07 01	07 11			07 22	07 31	07 41	07 49		07 54	08 01	08 11			08 22
19¼	—	Gravelly Hill	d			06 06	06 34	06 44	06 56		07 04	07 14			07 26	07 34	07 44	07 53			08 04	08 14			08 26
20¼	—	Erdington	d			06 09	06 37	06 47	06 59		07 07	07 17			07 29	07 37	07 47			07 59	08 07	08 17			08 29
21¼	—	Chester Road	d			06 11	06 39	06 49	07 01		07 09	07 19			07 31	07 39	07 49			08 01	08 09	08 19			08 31
21¾	—	Wylde Green	d			06 13	06 42	06 52	07 03		07 12	07 22			07 33	07 42	07 52			08 03	08 12	08 22			08 33
23¼	—	Sutton Coldfield	d			06 16	06 45	06 55	07 06		07 15	07 25			07 36	07 45	07 54	08 00		08 06	08 15	08 25			08 36
24¼	—	Four Oaks	d			06 19	06 48	06 58	07a11		07 17	07 28			07a41	07 48		08 03		08a10	08 18	08 28			08a41
25¼	—	Butlers Lane	d			06 22	06 51	07 01			07 21	07 31				07 51		08 06			08 21	08 31			
26¼	—	Blake Street	d			06 24	06 53	07 03			07 23	07 33				07 53		08 08			08 23	08 33			
28¼	—	Shenstone	d			06 28	06 56				07 26					07 56		08 12			08 26	08 36			
31¼	—	**Lichfield City**	d			06 33	07 02	07 12			07 32	07 42				08 02	08a05	08a17			08 32	08 42			
33	—	**Lichfield Trent Valley**	a			06 36	07 05	07 15			07 35	07 45				08 05					08 35	08 45			

		XC ◇1	LM	LM	LM	LM	XC ◇1	LM		LM	LM	LM	LM	LM	LM	LM	XC ◇1	LM		LM	LM	LM	LM	LM	LM
Bromsgrove	d		07 51			08 12				08 31	08 42		08 51		09 08	09 12				09 30		09 54	09 51		10 12
Redditch	d			07 55				08 12				08 32		08 55				09 12			09 32			09 55	
Alvechurch	d			08 00				08 17				08 37		09 00				09 17			09 37			10 00	
Barnt Green	d		07 57	08 07				08 23				08 43	08 57	09 07				09 23			09 43		09 57	10 07	
Longbridge	d		08 02	08 12		08 22		08 32		08 42		08 52	09 02	09 12		09 22		09 32		09 42	09 52		10 02	10 12	10 22
Northfield	d		08 04	08 14		08 24		08 34		08 44		08 54	09 04	09 14		09 24		09 34		09 44	09 54		10 04	10 14	10 24
Kings Norton	d		08 07	08 17		08 27		08 37		08 47		08 57	09 07	09 17		09 27		09 37		09 47	09 57		10 08	10 17	10 27
Bournville	d		08 09	08 19		08 29		08 39		08 49		08 59	09 09	09 19		09 29		09 39		09 49	09 59		10 10	10 19	10 29
Selly Oak	d		08 12	08 22		08 32		08 42		08 52		09 02	09 12	09 22		09 32		09 42		09 52	10 02		10 13	10 22	10 32
University	d	08 09	08 15	08 25	08 30	08 35	08 39	08 45		08 55	09 00	09 05	09 15	09 25	09 30	09 35	09 39	09 45		09 55	10 05	10 11	10 16	10 25	10 35
Five Ways	d		08 18	08 28		08 38		08 48		08 58		09 08	09 18	09 28		09 38		09 48		09 58	10 08		10 19	10 28	10 38
Birmingham New Street 12	a	08 15	08 23	08 33	08 40	08 42	08 45	08 52		09 03	09 09	09 12	09 22	09 33	09 39	09 42	09 45	09 52		10 02	10 12	10 20	10 23	10 33	10 42
	d		08 25	08 35		08 45		08 55		09 05		09 15	09 25	09 35		09 45		09 55		10 05	10 15		10 25	10 35	10 45
Duddeston	d					08 49						09 19				09 49					10 19				10 49
Aston	d		08 31	08 42		08 52		09 01		09 13		09 22	09 31	09 42		09 52		10 01		10 12	10 22		10 31	10 42	10 52
Gravelly Hill	d		08 34	08 44		08 56		09 04		09 15		09 26	09 34	09 44		09 56		10 04		10 14	10 26		10 34	10 44	10 56
Erdington	d		08 37	08 47		08 59		09 07		09 18		09 29	09 37	09 47		09 59		10 07		10 17	10 29		10 37	10 47	10 59
Chester Road	d		08 39	08 49		09 01		09 09		09 20		09 31	09 39	09 49		10 01		10 09		10 19	10 31		10 39	10 49	11 01
Wylde Green	d		08 41	08 52		09 03		09 12		09 23		09 33	09 42	09 52		10 03		10 12		10 22	10 33		10 42	10 52	11 03
Sutton Coldfield	d		08 44	08 55		09 06		09 15		09 26		09 36	09 45	09 55		10 06		10 15		10 25	10 36		10 45	10 55	11 06
Four Oaks	d		08 47	08 58		09a11		09 18		09 29		09a41	09 48	09 58		10a11		10 18		10 28	10a41		10 48	10 58	11a11
Butlers Lane	d		08 50	09 01				09 21		09 32			09 51	10 01				10 21		10 31			10 51	11 01	
Blake Street	d		08 52	09 03				09 23		09 34			09 53	10 03				10 23		10 33			10 53	11 03	
Shenstone	d		08 55					09 26					09 56					10 26					10 56		
Lichfield City	d		09 01	09 11				09 32		09 42			10 02	10 11				10 32		10 41			11 02	11 11	
Lichfield Trent Valley	a		09 05	09 14				09 35		09 45			10 05	10 14				10 35		10 44			11 06	11 14	

		XC ◇1	LM	LM		LM	LM	LM	LM	LM	XC ◇1	LM	LM	LM		LM	LM	LM	LM	XC ◇1	LM	LM	LM	LM	
Bromsgrove	d			10 30		10 43		10 51					11 29	11 43			11 51		12 12			12 30	12 43		
Redditch	d		10 12				10 32		10 55			11 12				11 32		11 55			12 12			12 32	
Alvechurch	d		10 17				10 37		11 00			11 17				11 37		12 00			12 17			12 37	
Barnt Green	d		10 24				10 43	10 57	11 07			11 23				11 43	11 57	12 07			12 23			12 43	
Longbridge	d		10 32	10 42			10 52	11 02	11 12	11 22		11 32	11 42			11 52	12 02	12 12	12 22		12 32	12 42		12 52	
Northfield	d		10 34	10 44			10 54	11 04	11 14	11 24		11 34	11 44			11 54	12 04	12 14	12 24		12 34	12 44		12 54	
Kings Norton	d		10 37	10 47			10 57	11 07	11 17	11 27		11 37	11 47			11 57	12 07	12 17	12 27		12 37	12 47		12 57	
Bournville	d		10 39	10 49			10 59	11 09	11 19	11 29		11 39	11 49			11 59	12 09	12 19	12 29		12 39	12 49		12 59	
Selly Oak	d		10 42	10 52			11 02	11 12	11 22	11 32		11 42	11 52			12 02	12 12	12 22	12 32		12 42	12 52		13 02	
University	d	10 39	10 45	10 55		11 00	11 05	11 15	11 25	11 35	11 39	11 45	11 55	12 00		12 05	12 15	12 25	12 35	12 39	12 45	12 55	13 00	13 05	
Five Ways	d		10 48	10 58			11 08	11 18	11 28	11 38		11 48	11 58			12 08	12 18	12 28	12 38		12 48	12 58		13 08	
Birmingham New Street 12	a	10 45	10 52	11 03		11 09	11 12	11 22	11 33	11 42	11 45	11 52	12 03	12 09		12 12	12 22	12 33	12 42	12 45	12 52	13 02	13 10	13 12	
	d		10 55	11 05			11 15	11 25	11 35	11 45		11 55	12 05			12 15	12 25	12 35	12 45		12 55	13 05		13 15	
Duddeston	d						11 19			11 49						12 19			12 49					13 19	
Aston	d		11 01	11 12			11 22	11 31	11 42	11 52		12 01	12 12			12 22	12 31	12 42	12 52		13 01	13 12		13 22	
Gravelly Hill	d		11 04	11 14			11 26	11 34	11 44	11 56		12 04	12 14			12 26	12 34	12 44	12 56		13 04	13 14		13 26	
Erdington	d		11 07	11 17			11 29	11 37	11 47	11 59		12 07	12 17			12 29	12 37	12 47	12 59		13 07	13 17		13 29	
Chester Road	d		11 09	11 19			11 31	11 39	11 49	12 01		12 09	12 19			12 31	12 39	12 49	13 01		13 09	13 19		13 31	
Wylde Green	d		11 12	11 22			11 33	11 42	11 52	12 03		12 12	12 22			12 33	12 42	12 52	13 03		13 12	13 22		13 33	
Sutton Coldfield	d		11 15	11 25			11 36	11 45	11 55	12 06		12 15	12 25			12 36	12 45	12 55	13 06		13 15	13 25		13 36	
Four Oaks	d		11 18	11 28			11a41	11 48	11 58	12a11		12 18	12 28			12a41	12 48	12 58	13a11		13 18	13 28		13a41	
Butlers Lane	d		11 21	11 31				11 51	12 01			12 21	12 31				12 51	13 01			13 21	13 31			
Blake Street	d		11 23	11 33				11 53	12 03			12 23	12 33				12 53	13 03			13 23	13 33			
Shenstone	d		11 26					11 56				12 26					12 56				13 26				
Lichfield City	d		11 32	11 41				12 02	12 11			12 32	12 41				13 02	13 11			13 32	13 41			
Lichfield Trent Valley	a		11 35	11 44				12 05	12 14			12 35	12 44				13 04	13 14			13 35	13 44			

		LM	LM	LM	XC ◇1	LM	LM	LM	LM	LM		LM	LM	XC ◇1	LM	LM	LM	LM	LM	LM		LM	XC ◇1	LM	LM
Bromsgrove	d	12 51					13 30	13 42		13 51			14 12			14 30	14 43		14 51			15 12			15 30
Redditch	d		12 55			13 12			13 32			13 55			14 12			14 32		14 55				15 12	
Alvechurch	d		13 00			13 17			13 37			14 00			14 17			14 37		15 00				15 17	
Barnt Green	d	12 57	13 07			13 23			13 43	13 57		14 07			14 23			14 43	14 57	15 07				15 23	
Longbridge	d	13 02	13 12	13 22		13 32	13 42		13 52	14 02		14 12	14 22		14 32	14 42		14 52	15 02	15 12		15 22		15 32	15 42
Northfield	d	13 04	13 14	13 24		13 34	13 44		13 54	14 04		14 14	14 24		14 34	14 44		14 54	15 04	15 14		15 24		15 34	15 44
Kings Norton	d	13 07	13 17	13 27		13 37	13 47		13 57	14 07		14 17	14 27		14 37	14 47		14 57	15 07	15 17		15 27		15 37	15 47
Bournville	d	13 09	13 19	13 29		13 39	13 49		13 59	14 09		14 19	14 29		14 39	14 49		14 59	15 09	15 19		15 29		15 39	15 49
Selly Oak	d	13 12	13 22	13 32		13 42	13 52		14 02	14 12		14 22	14 32		14 42	14 52		15 02	15 12	15 22		15 32		15 42	15 52
University	d	13 15	13 25	13 35	13 39	13 45	13 55	14 00	14 05	14 15		14 25	14 35	14 39	14 45	14 55	15 00	15 05	15 15	15 25		15 35	15 38	15 45	15 55
Five Ways	d	13 18	13 28	13 38		13 48	13 58		14 08	14 18		14 28	14 38		14 48	14 58		15 08	15 18	15 28		15 38		15 48	15 58
Birmingham New Street 12	a	13 22	13 32	13 42	13 45	13 52	14 03	14 09	14 12	14 22		14 33	14 42	14 45	14 52	15 03	15 09	15 12	15 22	15 33		15 42	15 44	15 52	16 03
	d	13 25	13 35	13 45		13 55	14 05		14 15	14 25		14 35	14 46		14 55	15 05		15 15	15 25	15 35		15 46		15 55	16 05
Duddeston	d			13 49					14 19				14 50					15 19				15 50			
Aston	d	13 31	13 42	13 52		14 01	14 12		14 22	14 31		14 42	14 53		15 01	15 12		15 22	15 31	15 42		15 53		16 01	16 12
Gravelly Hill	d	13 34	13 44	13 56		14 04	14 14		14 26	14 33		14 44	14 57		15 04	15 14		15 26	15 34	15 44		15 57		16 04	16 14
Erdington	d	13 37	13 47	13 59		14 07	14 17		14 29	14 37		14 47	15 00		15 07	15 17		15 29	15 37	15 47		16 00		16 07	16 17
Chester Road	d	13 39	13 49	14 01		14 09	14 19		14 31	14 39		14 49	15 02		15 09	15 19		15 31	15 39	15 49		16 02		16 09	16 19
Wylde Green	d	13 42	13 52	14 03		14 12	14 22		14 33	14 42		14 52	15 04		15 12	15 22		15 33	15 42	15 52		16 04		16 12	16 22
Sutton Coldfield	d	13 45	13 55	14 06		14 15	14 25		14 36	14 45		14 55	15 07		15 15	15 25		15 36	15 45	15 55		16 07		16 15	16 25
Four Oaks	d	13 48	13 58	14a11		14 18	14 28		14a41	14 48		14 58	15a11		15 18	15 28		15a41	15 48	15 58		16a11		16 18	16 28
Butlers Lane	d	13 51	14 01			14 21	14 31			14 51		15 01			15 21	15 31			15 51	16 01				16 21	16 31
Blake Street	d	13 53	14 03			14 23	14 33			14 53		15 03			15 23	15 33			15 53	16 03				16 23	16 33
Shenstone	d	13 56				14 26				14 56					15 26				15 56					16 26	
Lichfield City	d	14 02	14 11			14 32	14 41			15 02		15 11			15 32	15 41			16 02	16 11				16 32	16 41
Lichfield Trent Valley	a	14 05	14 14			14 35	14 44			15 05		15 14			15 35	15 44			16 05	16 14				16 35	16 44

		LM	LM	LM	LM	LM		XC ◇1	LM	LM	LM	LM	LM	LM	LM	XC ◇1		LM	LM	LM	LM	LM	LM	LM	LM
Bromsgrove	d	15 43		15 51		16 12				16 30	16 43		16 51		17 12				17 30	17 42		17 51		18 07	18 12
Redditch	d		15 32		15 55				16 12			16 32		16 55				17 12			17 32		17 55		
Alvechurch	d		15 37		16 00				16 17			16 37		17 00				17 17			17 37		18 00		
Barnt Green	d		15 43	15 57	16 08				16 23		16 50	16 43	16 57	17 08				17 23			17 43	17 57	18 08		
Longbridge	d		15 52	16 02	16 12	16 22			16 32	16 42		16 52	17 02	17 12	17 22			17 32	17 42		17 52	18 02	18 12		18 22
Northfield	d		15 54	16 04	16 14	16 24			16 34	16 44		16 54	17 04	17 14	17 24			17 34	17 44		17 55	18 04	18 14		18 24
Kings Norton	d		15 57	16 07	16 17	16 27			16 37	16 47		16 57	17 07	17 17	17 27			17 37	17 47		17 58	18 07	18 17		18 27
Bournville	d		15 59	16 09	16 20	16 29			16 39	16 49		16 59	17 09	17 20	17 29			17 39	17 49		18 00	18 09	18 19		18 29
Selly Oak	d		16 02	16 12	16 23	16 32			16 42	16 52		17 02	17 12	17 23	17 32			17 42	17 52		18 03	18 12	18 22		18 32
University	d	16 00	16 05	16 15	16 25	16 35		16 39	16 45	16 55	17 00	17 05	17 15	17 25	17 35	17 39		17 45	17 55	18 00	18 06	18 15	18 25	18 30	18 35
Five Ways	d		16 08	16 18	16 29	16 38			16 48	16 58		17 08	17 18	17 29	17 38			17 48	17 58		18 09	18 18	18 28		18 38
Birmingham New Street 12	a	16 10	16 12	16 22	16 34	16 42		16 45	16 52	17 03	17 10	17 12	17 22	17 33	17 42	17 45		17 52	18 03	18 09	18 13	18 22	18 33	18 37	18 42
	d		16 15	16 25	16 35	16 45			16 55	17 05		17 15	17 25	17 35	17 45			17 55	18 05		18 15	18 25	18 35		18 45
Duddeston	d		16 19			16 49						17 19			17 49						18 19				18 49
Aston	d		16 22	16 31	16 42	16 52			17 01	17 11		17 22	17 32	17 41	17 52			18 01	18 12		18 22	18 31	18 42		18 52
Gravelly Hill	d		16 26	16 34	16 44	16 56			17 04	17 14		17 26	17 35	17 44	17 56			18 04	18 14		18 26	18 34	18 44		18 56
Erdington	d		16 29	16 37	16 47	16 59			17 07	17 17		17 29	17 38	17 47	17 59			18 07	18 17		18 29	18 37	18 47		18 59
Chester Road	d		16 31	16 39	16 49	17 01			17 09	17 19		17 31	17 40	17 49	18 01			18 09	18 19		18 31	18 39	18 49		19 01
Wylde Green	d		16 33	16 42	16 52	17 03			17 12	17 22		17 33	17 43	17 52	18 03			18 12	18 22		18 33	18 42	18 52		19 03
Sutton Coldfield	d		16 36	16 45	16 55	17 06			17 15	17 25		17 36	17 46	17 55	18 06			18 15	18 25		18 36	18 45	18 55		19 06
Four Oaks	d		16a41	16 48	16 58	17a11			17 18	17 28		17a41	17 49	17 58	18a11			18 18	18 28		18a41	18 48	18 59		19a11
Butlers Lane	d			16 51	17 01				17 21	17 31			17 52	18 01				18 21	18 31			18 51	19 01		
Blake Street	d			16 53	17 03				17 23	17 33			17 54	18 03				18 23	18 33			18 53	19 03		
Shenstone	d			16 56					17 26	17 36			17 57	18 06				18 26				18 56			
Lichfield City	d			17 02	17 11				17 32	17 42			18 03	18 12				18 32	18 41			19 02	19 11		
Lichfield Trent Valley	a			17 05	17 14				17 35	17 45			18 06	18 15				18 35	18 44			19 05	19 14		

		XC ◇1		LM	LM	LM	LM	LM	LM	LM	LM	XC ◇1		LM	LM	LM	LM	LM	LM	LM	XC ◇1	LM		LM	LM
Bromsgrove	d				18 31	18 42		18 52		19 08	19 12				19 30		19 47	19 52		20 12				20 31	
Redditch	d			18 12			18 32		18 55					19 12		19 34			19 55			20 12			20 32
Alvechurch	d			18 17			18 37		19 00					19 17		19 39			20 00			20 17			20 37
Barnt Green	d			18 23			18 43	18 58	19 07					19 23		19 45		19 58	20 08			20 23			20 43
Longbridge	d			18 32	18 42		18 52	19 03	19 12		19 22			19 32	19 42	19 52		20 03	20 13	20 22		20 32		20 42	20 52
Northfield	d			18 34	18 44		18 54	19 05	19 14		19 24			19 34	19 44	19 54		20 05	20 14	20 24		20 34		20 44	20 54
Kings Norton	d			18 37	18 47		18 57	19 08	19 17		19 27			19 37	19 47	19 57		20 08	20 17	20 27		20 37		20 48	20 57
Bournville	d			18 39	18 49		18 59	19 10	19 19		19 29			19 38	19 49	19 59		20 10	20 20	20 29		20 38		20 49	20 59
Selly Oak	d			18 42	18 52		19 02	19 13	19 22		19 32			19 42	19 53	20 02		20 13	20 24	20 32		20 42		20 53	21 02
University	d	18 39		18 45	18 55	19 00	19 05	19 16	19 25	19 30	19 35	19 39		19 45	19 55	20 05	20 09	20 16	20 25	20 35	20 39	20 45		20 56	21 05
Five Ways	d			18 48	18 58		19 08	19 19	19 28		19 38			19 48	19 59	20 08		20 20	20 29	20 38		20 48		20 59	21 08
Birmingham New Street 12	a	18 45		18 52	19 03	19 09	19 12	19 23	19 33	19 37	19 42	19 45		19 52	20 03	20 12	20 19	20 23	20 34	20 42	20 45	20 52		21 03	21 12
	d			18 55	19 05		19 15	19 25	19 35		19 45			19 55	20 06	20 15		20 27	20 36			20 55		21 06	
Duddeston	d						19 19	19 30	19 39		19 49			19 59		20 19		20 31				20 59			
Aston	d			19 01	19 11		19 22	19 32	19 42		19 52			20 02	20 12	20 22		20 34	20 41			21 02		21 12	
Gravelly Hill	d			19 04	19 14		19 26	19 35	19 46		19 56			20 05	20 16	20 26		20 37	20 45			21 05		21 15	
Erdington	d			19 07	19 17		19 29	19 38	19 49		19 59			20 08	20 19	20 29		20 40	20 48			21 08		21 18	
Chester Road	d			19 09	19 19		19 31	19 40	19 51		20 01			20 10	20 21	20 31		20 42	20 50			21 10		21 20	
Wylde Green	d			19 12	19 22		19 33	19 43	19 53		20 03			20 13	20 23	20 33		20 44	20 52			21 13		21 22	
Sutton Coldfield	d			19 15	19 25		19 36	19 46	19 56		20 06			20 16	20 26	20 36		20 47	20 55			21 16		21 25	
Four Oaks	d			19 18	19 28		19a41	19 49	20 00		20a11			20 19	20 29	20a40		20 50	20 58			21 19		21 28	
Butlers Lane	d			19 21	19 31			19 52	20 03					20 22	20 32			20 53	21 01			21 22		21 31	
Blake Street	d			19 23	19 33			19 54	20 05					20 24	20 34			20 55	21 03			21 24		21 33	
Shenstone	d			19 26	19 36			19 58	20 09					20 28				20 58				21 28			
Lichfield City	d			19 32	19 42			20 03	20 14					20 33	20a41			21 04	21a11			21 33		21a41	
Lichfield Trent Valley	a			19 35	19 45			20 06	20 17					20 36				21 09				21 36			

Table T069-R

Mondays to Fridays
16 December to 15 May

Redditch and Longbridge - Birmingham - Lichfield

		LM	LM	LM	LM	XC ◇1	LM	LM	LM	LM	LM	LM	LM	LM	LM	LM	LM	LM	LM	LM
Bromsgrove	d	20 50	20 55				21 23	21 34		21 51		22 22	22 29		22 51		23 21		23 42	
Redditch	d			20 55	21 12				21 32		21 57			22 28		22 56		23 27		23 41
Alvechurch	d			21 00	21 17				21 37		22 02			22 33		23 01		23 32		23 46
Barnt Green	d	20 56		21 07	21 23				21 45	21 57	22 08			22 39	22 57	23 07		23 38		23 52
Longbridge	d	21 01		21 12	21 28		21 38	21 43	21 52	22 02	22 12	22 32		22 44	23 02	23 12	23 32	23 42	23 52	23 58
Northfield	d	21 03		21 14	21 30		21 40	21 45	21 54	22 04	22 14	22 34		22 45	23 04	23 14	23 34	23 44	23 54	23 59
Kings Norton	d	21 06		21 18	21 33		21 43	21 49	21 57	22 07	22 18	22 37		22 49	23 07	23 17	23 37	23 47	23 57	00 03
Bournville	d	21 08		21 19	21 34		21 46	21 50	21 59	22 08	22 19	22 39		22 50	23 09	23 18	23 39	23 49	23 59	00 05
Selly Oak	d	21 11		21 23	21 38		21 49	21 54	22 02	22 12	22 22	22 42		22 54	23 12	23 21	23 42	23 52	00 02	00 08
University	d	21 14	21 18	21 26	21 41	21 46	21 51	21 57	22 05	22 15	22 25	22 45	22 49	22 57	23 15	23 25	23 45	23 55	00 05	00 11
Five Ways	d	21 18		21 29	21 44		21 55	22 00	22 08	22 18	22 29	22 48		23 00	23 18	23 28	23 49	23 58	00 09	00 15
Birmingham New Street 12	a	21 21	21 25	21 33	21 48	21 54	21 59	22 04	22 12	22 22	22 32	22 52	22 55	23 04	23 24	23 32	23 53	00 03	00 12	00 19
	d	21 25		21 37	21 52			22 07		22 25	22 35	22 55		23 15	23 40					
Duddeston	d	21 30			21 58					22 29		22 59			23 44					
Aston	d	21 33		21 43	22 01			22 12		22 32	22 40	23 03		23 20	23 47					
Gravelly Hill	d	21 36		21 47	22 04			22 16		22 35	22 44	23 06		23 24	23 50					
Erdington	d	21 39		21 50	22 07			22 19		22 38	22 47	23 09		23 27	23 53					
Chester Road	d	21 41		21 52	22 09			22 21		22 40	22 49	23 11		23 29	23 55					
Wylde Green	d	21 43		21 54	22 12			22 23		22 43	22 51	23 13		23 31	23 57					
Sutton Coldfield	d	21 46		21 57	22 15			22 26		22 46	22 54	23 16		23 34	23 59					
Four Oaks	d	21 49		22 00	22 18			22 29		22 49	22 57	23 19		23 37	00a04					
Butlers Lane	d	21 52		22 03	22 21			22 32		22 52	23 00	23 22		23 40						
Blake Street	d	21 54		22 05	22 23			22 34		22 54	23 02	23 24		23 42						
Shenstone	d	21 57			22 27					22 58	23 06	23 28		23 46						
Lichfield City	d	22 03		22 13	22 32			22a42		23 03	23a11	23 33		23a51						
Lichfield Trent Valley	a	22 06		22 16	22 35					23 06		23 36								

Saturdays
21 December to 16 May

		LM	LM	LM	LM	LM	LM	LM	LM	LM	LM	LM	LM	LM	LM	LM	LM	XC ◇1	LM	LM	LM	LM	LM
Bromsgrove	d							06 11		06 33		06 47	06 51		07 12		07 30			07 47	07 51		08 12
Redditch	d								06 12		06 32			06 55		07 12			07 32			07 55	
Alvechurch	d								06 17		06 37			07 00		07 17			07 37			08 00	
Barnt Green	d							06 17	06 23		06 43		06 57	07 07		07 23			07 43		07 57	08 07	
Longbridge	d						06 13	06 22	06 32	06 43	06 52		07 02	07 12	07 22	07 32	07 42		07 52		08 02	08 12	08 22
Northfield	d						06 15	06 24	06 34	06 45	06 54		07 04	07 14	07 24	07 34	07 44		07 54		08 04	08 14	08 24
Kings Norton	d		00 03				06 18	06 27	06 37	06 48	06 57		07 07	07 17	07 27	07 37	07 47		07 57		08 07	08 17	08 27
Bournville	d		00 05				06 20	06 29	06 39	06 50	06 59		07 09	07 19	07 29	07 39	07 49		07 59		08 09	08 19	08 29
Selly Oak	d	00 02	00 08				06 23	06 32	06 42	06 53	07 02		07 12	07 22	07 32	07 42	07 52		08 02		08 12	08 22	08 32
University	d	00 05	00 11				06 26	06 35	06 45	06 56	07 05	07 09	07 15	07 25	07 35	07 45	07 55	08 00	08 05	08 09	08 15	08 25	08 35
Five Ways	d	00 09	00 15				06 30	06 38	06 49	06 59	07 09		07 19	07 29	07 38	07 49	07 59		08 09		08 19	08 29	08 38
Birmingham New Street 12	a	00 12	00 19				06 33	06 42	06 52	07 03	07 12	07 15	07 22	07 34	07 42	07 52	08 03	08 06	08 12	08 15	08 22	08 33	08 42
	d			05 55	06 07	06 24	06 36	06 45	06 55	07 06	07 15		07 25	07 36	07 45	07 55	08 06		08 15		08 25	08 36	08 45
Duddeston	d			05 59		06 28		06 49	06 59		07 19				07 49				08 19				08 49
Aston	d			06 02	06 13	06 31	06 41	06 52	07 02	07 11	07 22		07 30	07 41	07 52	08 00	08 11		08 22		08 30	08 41	08 52
Gravelly Hill	d			06 06	06 16	06 35	06 45	06 56	07 06	07 15	07 26		07 34	07 45	07 56	08 04	08 15		08 26		08 34	08 45	08 56
Erdington	d			06 09	06 19	06 38	06 48	06 59	07 09	07 18	07 29		07 37	07 48	07 59	08 07	08 18		08 29		08 37	08 48	08 59
Chester Road	d			06 11	06 21	06 40	06 50	07 01	07 11	07 20	07 31		07 39	07 50	08 01	08 09	08 20		08 31		08 39	08 50	09 01
Wylde Green	d			06 13	06 23	06 42	06 52	07 03	07 13	07 22	07 33		07 41	07 52	08 03	08 11	08 22		08 33		08 41	08 52	09 03
Sutton Coldfield	d			06 16	06 26	06 45	06 55	07 06	07 16	07 25	07 36		07 44	07 55	08 06	08 14	08 25		08 36		08 44	08 55	09 06
Four Oaks	d			06 19	06 29	06 48	06 59	07a11	07 19	07 28	07a41		07 47	07 58	08a11	08 17	08 28		08a41		08 47	08 58	09a11
Butlers Lane	d			06 22	06 32	06 51	07 01		07 22	07 31			07 50	08 01		08 20	08 31				08 50	09 01	
Blake Street	d			06 24	06 34	06 53	07 04		07 24	07 33			07 52	08 03		08 22	08 33				08 52	09 03	
Shenstone	d			06 26		06 55			07 26				07 56			08 26					08 56		
Lichfield City	d			06 33	06 42	07 02	07 12		07 33	07 42			08 02	08 11		08 32	08 41				09 02	09 11	
Lichfield Trent Valley	a			06 36	06 46	07 05	07 15		07 36	07 45			08 05	08 14		08 35	08 44				09 05	09 14	

		XC ◇1	LM	LM	LM	LM	LM	LM	LM	XC ◇1	LM	LM	LM	LM	LM	LM	LM	LM	XC ◇1	LM	LM	LM	LM
Bromsgrove	d			08 30	08 43		08 51		09 12			09 30	09 43		09 51		10 12	10 08			10 30	10 43	
Redditch	d		08 12			08 32		08 55			09 12			09 32		09 55				10 12			10 32
Alvechurch	d		08 17			08 37		09 00			09 17			09 37		10 00				10 17			10 37
Barnt Green	d		08 23			08 43	08 57	09 07			09 23			09 43	09 57	10 07				10 23			10 43
Longbridge	d		08 32	08 42		08 52	09 02	09 12	09 22		09 32	09 42		09 52	10 02	10 12	10 22			10 32	10 42		10 52
Northfield	d		08 34	08 44		08 54	09 04	09 14	09 24		09 34	09 44		09 54	10 04	10 14	10 24			10 34	10 44		10 54
Kings Norton	d		08 37	08 47		08 57	09 07	09 17	09 27		09 37	09 47		09 57	10 07	10 17	10 27			10 37	10 47		10 57
Bournville	d		08 39	08 49		08 59	09 09	09 19	09 29		09 39	09 49		09 59	10 09	10 19	10 28			10 39	10 49		10 59
Selly Oak	d		08 42	08 52		09 02	09 12	09 22	09 32		09 42	09 52		10 02	10 12	10 22	10 31			10 42	10 52		11 02
University	d	08 39	08 45	08 55	09 00	09 05	09 15	09 25	09 35	09 39	09 45	09 55	10 00	10 05	10 15	10 25	10 35		10 39	10 45	10 55	11 00	11 05
Five Ways	d		08 49	08 59		09 09	09 19	09 29	09 39		09 49	09 59		10 09	10 19	10 29	10 38			10 49	10 59		11 09
Birmingham New Street 12	a	08 45	08 52	09 03	09 09	09 12	09 22	09 33	09 42	09 45	09 52	10 03	10 09	10 12	10 22	10 33	10 42	10 43	10 45	10 52	11 04	11 09	11 12
	d		08 55	09 06		09 15	09 25	09 36	09 45		09 55	10 06		10 15	10 25	10 36	10 45			10 55	11 06		11 15
Duddeston	d					09 19			09 49					10 19			10 49						11 19
Aston	d		09 00	09 11		09 22	09 30	09 41	09 52		10 00	10 11		10 22	10 30	10 41	10 52			11 00	11 11		11 22
Gravelly Hill	d		09 04	09 15		09 26	09 34	09 45	09 56		10 04	10 15		10 26	10 34	10 45	10 56			11 04	11 15		11 26
Erdington	d		09 07	09 18		09 29	09 37	09 48	09 59		10 07	10 18		10 29	10 37	10 48	10 59			11 07	11 18		11 29
Chester Road	d		09 09	09 20		09 31	09 39	09 50	10 01		10 09	10 20		10 31	10 39	10 50	11 01			11 09	11 20		11 31
Wylde Green	d		09 11	09 22		09 33	09 41	09 52	10 03		10 11	10 22		10 33	10 41	10 52	11 03			11 11	11 22		11 33
Sutton Coldfield	d		09 14	09 25		09 36	09 44	09 55	10 06		10 14	10 25		10 36	10 44	10 55	11 06			11 14	11 25		11 36
Four Oaks	d		09 17	09 28		09a41	09 47	09 58	10a11		10 17	10 28		10a41	10 47	10 58	11a11			11 17	11 28		11a41
Butlers Lane	d		09 20	09 31			09 50	10 01			10 20	10 31			10 50	11 01				11 20	11 31		
Blake Street	d		09 22	09 33			09 52	10 03			10 22	10 33			10 52	11 03				11 22	11 33		
Shenstone	d		09 26				09 56				10 26				10 56					11 26			
Lichfield City	d		09 32	09 41			10 02	10 11			10 32	10 41			11 02	11 11				11 32	11 41		
Lichfield Trent Valley	a		09 35	09 44			10 05	10 14			10 35	10 44			11 05	11 14				11 35	11 44		

Table T069-R

Saturdays
21 December to 16 May

Redditch and Longbridge - Birmingham - Lichfield

		LM	LM	LM	XC ◇1	LM	LM	LM	LM	LM	LM	LM	XC ◇1	LM	LM	LM	LM	LM	LM	LM	XC ◇1	LM
Bromsgrove	d	10 51		11 12			11 32	11 43		11 51		12 12			12 30	12 43		12 51		13 12		
Redditch	d		10 55			11 12			11 32		11 55			12 12			12 32		12 55			13 12
Alvechurch	d		11 00			11 17			11 37		12 00			12 17			12 37		13 00			13 17
Barnt Green	d	10 57	11 07			11 23			11 43	11 57	12 07			12 23			12 43	12 57	13 07			13 26
Longbridge	d	11 02	11 12	11 22		11 32	11 42		11 53	12 02	12 12	12 22		12 32	12 42		12 52	13 02	13 12	13 22		13 32
Northfield	d	11 04	11 14	11 24		11 34	11 44		11 55	12 04	12 14	12 24		12 34	12 44		12 54	13 04	13 14	13 24		13 34
Kings Norton	d	11 07	11 17	11 27		11 37	11 48		11 58	12 07	12 17	12 27		12 37	12 47		12 57	13 07	13 17	13 27		13 37
Bournville	d	11 09	11 19	11 29		11 39	11 50		12 00	12 09	12 19	12 29		12 39	12 49		12 59	13 09	13 19	13 29		13 39
Selly Oak	d	11 12	11 22	11 32		11 42	11 53		12 03	12 12	12 22	12 32		12 42	12 52		13 02	13 12	13 22	13 32		13 42
University	d	11 15	11 25	11 35	11 39	11 45	11 55	12 01	12 05	12 15	12 25	12 35	12 39	12 45	12 55	13 00	13 05	13 15	13 25	13 35	13 39	13 45
Five Ways	d	11 19	11 29	11 39		11 49	11 59		12 09	12 19	12 29	12 39		12 49	12 59		13 09	13 19	13 29	13 39		13 49
Birmingham New Street 12	a	11 22	11 33	11 42	11 45	11 52	12 03	12 11	12 12	12 22	12 33	12 42	12 45	12 52	13 03	13 09	13 12	13 22	13 33	13 42	13 45	13 52
	d	11 25	11 36	11 45		11 55	12 06		12 15	12 25	12 36	12 45		12 55	13 06		13 15	13 25	13 36	13 45		13 55
Duddeston	d			11 49					12 19			12 49					13 19			13 49		
Aston	d	11 30	11 41	11 52		12 00	12 11		12 22	12 30	12 41	12 52		13 00	13 11		13 22	13 30	13 41	13 52		14 00
Gravelly Hill	d	11 34	11 45	11 56		12 04	12 15		12 26	12 34	12 45	12 56		13 04	13 15		13 26	13 34	13 45	13 56		14 04
Erdington	d	11 37	11 48	11 59		12 07	12 18		12 29	12 37	12 48	12 59		13 07	13 18		13 29	13 37	13 48	13 59		14 07
Chester Road	d	11 39	11 50	12 01		12 09	12 20		12 31	12 39	12 50	13 01		13 09	13 20		13 31	13 39	13 50	14 01		14 09
Wylde Green	d	11 41	11 52	12 03		12 11	12 22		12 33	12 41	12 52	13 03		13 11	13 22		13 33	13 41	13 52	14 03		14 11
Sutton Coldfield	d	11 44	11 55	12 06		12 14	12 25		12 36	12 44	12 55	13 06		13 14	13 25		13 36	13 44	13 55	14 06		14 14
Four Oaks	d	11 47	11 58	12a11		12 17	12 28		12a40	12 47	12 58	13a11		13 17	13 28		13a41	13 47	13 58	14a11		14 17
Butlers Lane	d	11 50	12 01			12 20	12 31			12 50	13 01			13 20	13 31			13 50	14 01			14 20
Blake Street	d	11 52	12 03			12 22	12 33			12 52	13 03			13 22	13 33			13 52	14 03			14 22
Shenstone	d	11 56				12 26				12 56				13 26				13 56				14 26
Lichfield City	d	12 02	12 11			12 32	12 41			13 02	13 11			13 32	13 41			14 02	14 11			14 32
Lichfield Trent Valley	a	12 05	12 14			12 35	12 44			13 05	13 14			13 35	13 44			14 05	14 14			14 35

		LM	LM	LM	LM	LM	LM	XC ◇1	LM	LM	LM	LM	LM	LM	LM	XC ◇1	LM	LM	LM	LM	LM	LM	LM
Bromsgrove	d	13 30	13 43		13 51		14 12			14 30	14 43		14 51		15 12			15 30	15 43		15 51		16 12
Redditch	d			13 32		13 55			14 12			14 32		14 55			15 12			15 32		15 55	
Alvechurch	d			13 37		14 00			14 17			14 37		15 00			15 17			15 37		16 00	
Barnt Green	d			13 43	13 57	14 07			14 23			14 43	14 57	15 07			15 23			15 44	15 57	16 07	
Longbridge	d	13 42		13 52	14 02	14 12	14 22		14 32	14 42		14 52	15 02	15 12	15 22		15 32	15 42		15 53	16 02	16 12	16 22
Northfield	d	13 44		13 54	14 04	14 14	14 24		14 34	14 44		14 54	15 04	15 14	15 24		15 34	15 44		15 55	16 04	16 14	16 24
Kings Norton	d	13 47		13 57	14 07	14 17	14 27		14 37	14 47		14 57	15 07	15 17	15 27		15 37	15 47		15 58	16 07	16 17	16 27
Bournville	d	13 49		14 00	14 09	14 19	14 29		14 39	14 49		15 00	15 09	15 19	15 29		15 39	15 49		16 00	16 09	16 19	16 29
Selly Oak	d	13 52		14 03	14 12	14 22	14 32		14 42	14 52		15 03	15 12	15 22	15 32		15 42	15 52		16 03	16 12	16 22	16 32
University	d	13 55	14 00	14 05	14 15	14 25	14 35	14 39	14 45	14 55	15 00	15 05	15 15	15 25	15 35	15 39	15 45	15 55	16 00	16 06	16 15	16 25	16 35
Five Ways	d	13 59		14 09	14 18	14 29	14 39		14 49	14 59		15 09	15 18	15 29	15 39		15 49	15 58		16 10	16 19	16 29	16 39
Birmingham New Street 12	a	14 03	14 09	14 13	14 22	14 33	14 42	14 45	14 52	15 03	15 09	15 13	15 22	15 33	15 42	15 45	15 52	16 03	16 09	16 13	16 22	16 33	16 42
	d	14 06		14 15	14 25	14 36	14 45		14 55	15 06		15 15	15 25	15 36	15 45		15 55	16 05		16 15	16 25	16 36	16 45
Duddeston	d			14 19			14 49					15 19			15 49					16 19			16 49
Aston	d	14 11		14 22	14 30	14 41	14 52		15 00	15 11		15 22	15 30	15 41	15 52		16 00	16 10		16 22	16 30	16 41	16 52
Gravelly Hill	d	14 15		14 26	14 34	14 45	14 56		15 04	15 15		15 26	15 34	15 45	15 56		16 04	16 14		16 26	16 34	16 45	16 56
Erdington	d	14 18		14 29	14 37	14 48	14 59		15 07	15 18		15 29	15 37	15 48	15 59		16 07	16 17		16 29	16 37	16 48	16 59
Chester Road	d	14 20		14 31	14 39	14 50	15 01		15 09	15 20		15 31	15 39	15 50	16 01		16 09	16 19		16 31	16 39	16 50	17 01
Wylde Green	d	14 22		14 33	14 41	14 52	15 03		15 11	15 22		15 33	15 41	15 52	16 03		16 11	16 21		16 33	16 41	16 52	17 03
Sutton Coldfield	d	14 25		14 36	14 44	14 55	15 06		15 14	15 25		15 36	15 44	15 55	16 06		16 14	16 24		16 36	16 44	16 55	17 06
Four Oaks	d	14 28		14a41	14 47	14 58	15a11		15 17	15 28		15a41	15 47	15 58	16a11		16 17	16 27		16a41	16 47	16 58	17a11
Butlers Lane	d	14 31			14 50	15 01			15 20	15 31			15 50	16 01			16 20	16 30			16 50	17 01	
Blake Street	d	14 33			14 52	15 03			15 22	15 33			15 52	16 03			16 22	16 32			16 52	17 03	
Shenstone	d				14 56				15 26				15 56				16 26				16 56		
Lichfield City	d	14 41			15 02	15 11			15 32	15 41			16 02	16 11			16 32	16 41			17 02	17 11	
Lichfield Trent Valley	a	14 44			15 05	15 14			15 35	15 44			16 05	16 14			16 35	16 44			17 05	17 14	

		LM	XC ◇1	LM	LM	LM	LM	LM	LM	LM	XC ◇1	LM	LM	LM	LM	LM	LM	LM	XC ◇1	LM	LM	LM
Bromsgrove	d	16 08			16 30	16 43		16 51		17 12			17 30	17 43		17 51		18 12			18 30	18 43
Redditch	d			16 12			16 32		16 55			17 12			17 32		17 55			18 12		
Alvechurch	d			16 17			16 37		17 00			17 17			17 37		18 00			18 17		
Barnt Green	d			16 23			16 43	16 57	17 08			17 23			17 43	17 57	18 07			18 23		
Longbridge	d			16 32	16 42		16 52	17 02	17 12	17 22		17 32	17 42		17 52	18 02	18 12	18 22		18 32	18 42	
Northfield	d			16 34	16 44		16 54	17 04	17 14	17 24		17 34	17 44		17 54	18 04	18 14	18 24		18 34	18 44	
Kings Norton	d			16 37	16 47		16 57	17 07	17 17	17 27		17 37	17 47		17 57	18 07	18 17	18 27		18 37	18 47	
Bournville	d			16 39	16 49		16 59	17 09	17 20	17 29		17 39	17 49		17 59	18 09	18 19	18 29		18 39	18 49	
Selly Oak	d			16 42	16 52		17 02	17 12	17 23	17 32		17 42	17 52		18 02	18 12	18 22	18 32		18 42	18 52	
University	d		16 39	16 45	16 55	17 00	17 05	17 15	17 25	17 35	17 39	17 45	17 55	17 59	18 05	18 15	18 25	18 35	18 39	18 45	18 55	19 00
Five Ways	d			16 49	16 59		17 09	17 19	17 29	17 38		17 49	17 59		18 09	18 19	18 29	18 39		18 49	18 59	
Birmingham New Street 12	a	16 43	16 45	16 52	17 02	17 09	17 12	17 22	17 34	17 42	17 45	17 52	18 03	18 09	18 12	18 22	18 33	18 42	18 45	18 52	19 03	19 09
	d			16 55	17 05		17 15	17 25	17 36	17 45		17 55	18 06		18 15	18 25	18 36	18 45		18 55	19 06	
Duddeston	d						17 19			17 49					18 19			18 49				
Aston	d			17 00	17 11		17 22	17 30	17 41	17 52		18 00	18 11		18 22	18 30	18 41	18 52		19 00	19 11	
Gravelly Hill	d			17 04	17 15		17 26	17 34	17 45	17 56		18 04	18 15		18 26	18 34	18 45	18 56		19 04	19 15	
Erdington	d			17 07	17 18		17 29	17 37	17 48	17 59		18 07	18 18		18 29	18 37	18 48	18 59		19 07	19 18	
Chester Road	d			17 09	17 20		17 31	17 39	17 50	18 01		18 09	18 20		18 31	18 39	18 50	19 01		19 09	19 20	
Wylde Green	d			17 11	17 22		17 33	17 41	17 52	18 03		18 11	18 22		18 33	18 41	18 52	19 03		19 11	19 22	
Sutton Coldfield	d			17 14	17 25		17 36	17 44	17 55	18 06		18 14	18 25		18 36	18 44	18 55	19 06		19 14	19 25	
Four Oaks	d			17 17	17 28		17a41	17 47	17 58	18a11		18 17	18 28		18a41	18 47	18 58	19a11		19 17	19 28	
Butlers Lane	d			17 20	17 31			17 50	18 01			18 20	18 31			18 50	19 01			19 20	19 31	
Blake Street	d			17 22	17 33			17 52	18 03			18 22	18 33			18 52	19 03			19 22	19 33	
Shenstone	d			17 26				17 56				18 26				18 56				19 26		
Lichfield City	d			17 32	17 41			18 02	18 11			18 32	18 41			19 02	19 11			19 32	19 41	
Lichfield Trent Valley	a			17 35	17 44			18 05	18 14			18 35	18 44			19 05	19 14			19 35	19 44	

Table T069-R

Redditch and Longbridge - Birmingham - Lichfield

Saturdays
21 December to 16 May

		LM	LM	LM	LM	XC ◇1	LM	LM	LM	LM	LM	LM	LM	XC ◇1	LM	LM	LM	LM	LM	LM	LM	LM	XC ◇1
Bromsgrove	d		18 51		19 12			19 30	19 43		19 51		20 13			20 35	20 43		20 51		21 18		
Redditch	d	18 32		18 55			19 12			19 32		19 55			20 17			20 32		20 55		21 25	
Alvechurch	d	18 37		19 00			19 17			19 38		20 00			20 22			20 38		21 00		21 30	
Barnt Green	d	18 43	18 57	19 07			19 23			19 43	19 57	20 08			20 31			20 43	20 57	21 06		21 38	
Longbridge	d	18 52	19 02	19 12	19 22		19 32	19 42		19 52	20 02	20 13	20 22		20 37	20 44		20 52	21 02	21 11	21 28	21 43	
Northfield	d	18 54	19 04	19 14	19 24		19 34	19 44		19 54	20 04	20 15	20 24		20 39	20 45		20 54	21 04	21 12	21 30	21 44	
Kings Norton	d	18 57	19 07	19 17	19 27		19 37	19 47		19 57	20 07	20 18	20 27		20 45	20 49		20 58	21 07	21 16	21 33	21 48	
Bournville	d	18 59	19 09	19 19	19 29		19 39	19 49		19 59	20 09	20 20	20 29		20 47	20 51		21 01	21 09	21 18	21 34	21 50	
Selly Oak	d	19 02	19 12	19 22	19 32		19 42	19 52		20 02	20 12	20 23	20 32		20 50	20 55		21 04	21 12	21 22	21 38	21 54	
University	d	19 05	19 15	19 25	19 35	19 39	19 45	19 55	20 00	20 05	20 15	20 26	20 35	20 39	20 53	20 57	21 00	21 06	21 15	21 24	21 41	21 56	22 00
Five Ways	d	19 09	19 18	19 29	19 38		19 49	19 59		20 09	20 18	20 30	20 38		20 56	21 01		21 10	21 19	21 27	21 44	22 00	
Birmingham New Street 12	a	19 12	19 22	19 32	19 42	19 45	19 52	20 03	20 09	20 12	20 22	20 33	20 43	20 45	21 00	21 05	21 10	21 14	21 22	21 32	21 48	22 05	22 07
	d	19 15		19 36	19 45			20 06		20 17		20 36	20 45			21 08		21 17		21 34	21 51	22 07	
Duddeston	d	19 19			19 49					20 21			20 49					21 21			21 55	22 11	
Aston	d	19 22		19 42	19 52			20 11		20 24		20 41	20 52			21 13		21 24		21 40	21 58	22 14	
Gravelly Hill	d	19 26		19 45	19 56			20 15		20 28		20 45	20 56			21 17		21 28		21 44	22 02	22 18	
Erdington	d	19 29		19 48	19 59			20 17		20 31		20 47	20 59			21 20		21 31		21 47	22 05	22 21	
Chester Road	d	19 31		19 50	20 01			20 19		20 33		20 49	21 01			21 22		21 33		21 49	22 07	22 23	
Wylde Green	d	19 33		19 52	20 03			20 21		20 35		20 51	21 03			21 24		21 35		21 51	22 09	22 25	
Sutton Coldfield	d	19 36		19 55	20 06			20 24		20 38		20 54	21 06			21 27		21 38		21 54	22 12	22 28	
Four Oaks	d	19a41		19 58	20a11			20 28		20a42		20 58	21a10			21 30		21a42		21 57	22a16	22 31	
Butlers Lane	d			20 01				20 31				21 01				21 33				22 00		22 34	
Blake Street	d			20 03				20 33				21 03				21 36				22 02		22 37	
Shenstone	d			20 07				20 37				21 07				21 40				22 06		22 41	
Lichfield City	d			20 12				20 42				21 12				21 45				22 11		22 46	
Lichfield Trent Valley	a			20 15				20 46				21 15				21 48				22 14		22 49	

		LM	LM	LM	XC ◇1	LM	LM	LM	LM	LM	LM	LM
Bromsgrove	d	21 49	21 54			22 27			22 53			
Redditch	d			21 57			22 27	22 44			23 27	23 42
Alvechurch	d			22 02			22 32	22 49			23 32	23 47
Barnt Green	d		22 00	22 08			22 38	22 54	22 59		23 38	23 52
Longbridge	d		22 05	22 12		22 36	22 42	22 59	23 04	23 22	23 42	23 57
Northfield	d		22 07	22 14		22 38	22 44	23 01	23 06	23 24	23 44	23 59
Kings Norton	d		22 10	22 17		22 41	22 48	23 04	23 09	23 27	23 47	00 02
Bournville	d		22 11	22 20		22 44	22 49	23 07	23 11	23 29	23 49	00 05
Selly Oak	d		22 15	22 23		22 47	22 53	23 10	23 14	23 32	23 52	00 07
University	d	22 06	22 18	22 25	22 39	22 49	22 56	23 12	23 17	23 35	23 55	00 10
Five Ways	d		22 21	22 29		22 53	22 59	23 16	23 20	23 39	23 58	00 14
Birmingham New Street 12	a	22 16	22 25	22 32	22 45	22 58	23 04	23 21	23 24	23 43	00 03	00 17
	d		22 28	22 35		23 01	23 15		23 36			
Duddeston	d		22 32			23 05	23 19					
Aston	d		22 35	22 41		23 08	23 22		23 41			
Gravelly Hill	d		22 39	22 44		23 12	23 25		23 45			
Erdington	d		22 42	22 47		23 15	23 28		23 47			
Chester Road	d		22 44	22 49		23 17	23 30		23 49			
Wylde Green	d		22 46	22 51		23 19	23 32		23 51			
Sutton Coldfield	d		22 49	22 54		23 22	23 35		23 54			
Four Oaks	d		22a53	22 58		23 25	23 38		23a58			
Butlers Lane	d			23 01		23 28	23 41					
Blake Street	d			23 03		23 30	23 43					
Shenstone	d			23 07		23 34	23 47					
Lichfield City	d			23 12		23 39	23a53					
Lichfield Trent Valley	a			23 15		23 42						

Sundays
15 December to 10 May

		LM A	LM	LM	LM	LM	LM	LM	LM	LM	LM	LM	LM	LM	LM	LM	LM	LM	LM	LM	XC ◇1	LM	LM
Bromsgrove	d				09 22		09 42		10 12	10 23		10 42		11 12	11 16		11 42		12 08	12 12			12 42
Redditch	d					09 27		09 57			10 27		10 57			11 27		11 57				12 27	
Alvechurch	d					09 32		10 02			10 32		11 02			11 32		12 02				12 32	
Barnt Green	d					09 38	09 48	10 08			10 38	10 48	11 08			11 38	11 48	12 08				12 38	12 48
Longbridge	d			09 10		09 42	09 52	10 12	10 22		10 42	10 52	11 12	11 22		11 42	11 52	12 12		12 22		12 42	12 52
Northfield	d			09 12		09 44	09 54	10 14	10 24		10 44	10 54	11 14	11 24		11 44	11 54	12 14		12 24		12 44	12 54
Kings Norton	d	00 02		09 15		09 47	09 57	10 17	10 27		10 47	10 57	11 17	11 27		11 47	11 57	12 17		12 27		12 47	12 57
Bournville	d	00 05		09 17		09 49	09 59	10 19	10 29		10 49	10 59	11 19	11 29		11 49	11 59	12 19		12 29		12 49	12 59
Selly Oak	d	00 07		09 20		09 52	10 02	10 22	10 32		10 52	11 02	11 22	11 32		11 52	12 02	12 22		12 32		12 52	13 02
University	d	00 10		09 23	09 39	09 55	10 05	10 25	10 35	10 40	10 55	11 05	11 25	11 35	11 39	11 55	12 05	12 25	12 30	12 35	12 39	12 55	13 05
Five Ways	d	00 14		09 26		09 58	10 08	10 28	10 38		10 58	11 08	11 28	11 38		11 59	12 08	12 28		12 38		12 58	13 08
Birmingham New Street 12	a	00 17		09 30	09 45	10 03	10 13	10 33	10 42	10 46	11 03	11 13	11 33	11 42	11 45	12 03	12 13	12 33	12 37	12 42	12 45	13 03	13 13
	d		09 07	09 36		10 06		10 36			11 06		11 36			12 06		12 36				13 06	
Duddeston	d		09 11	09 40		10 10		10 40			11 10		11 40			12 10		12 40				13 10	
Aston	d		09 14	09 43		10 13		10 43			11 13		11 43			12 13		12 43				13 13	
Gravelly Hill	d		09 18	09 47		10 17		10 47			11 17		11 47			12 17		12 47				13 17	
Erdington	d		09 21	09 50		10 20		10 50			11 20		11 50			12 20		12 50				13 20	
Chester Road	d		09 23	09 52		10 22		10 52			11 22		11 52			12 22		12 52				13 22	
Wylde Green	d		09 25	09 54		10 24		10 54			11 24		11 54			12 24		12 54				13 24	
Sutton Coldfield	d		09 28	09 57		10 27		10 57			11 27		11 57			12 27		12 57				13 27	
Four Oaks	d		09 31	10 00		10 30		11 00			11 30		12 00			12 30		13 00				13 30	
Butlers Lane	d		09 34	10 03		10 33		11 03			11 33		12 03			12 33		13 03				13 33	
Blake Street	d		09 36	10 05		10 35		11 05			11 35		12 05			12 35		13 05				13 35	
Shenstone	d		09 40	10 09		10 39		11 09			11 39		12 09			12 39		13 09				13 39	
Lichfield City	d		09 45	10 14		10 44		11 14			11 44		12 14			12 44		13 14				13 44	
Lichfield Trent Valley	a		09 48	10 17		10 47		11 17			11 47		12 17			12 47		13 17				13 47	

A not 15 December

Table T069-R

Redditch and Longbridge - Birmingham - Lichfield

Sundays
15 December to 10 May

		LM	LM	LM	XC ◇1	LM	LM	LM	LM	LM	XC ◇1	LM	LM	LM	LM	LM	XC ◇1	LM	LM	LM	LM	LM	XC ◇1
Bromsgrove	d		13 08	13 12			13 42		14 08	14 12			14 42		15 08	15 12			15 42		16 03	16 12	
Redditch	d	12 57				13 27		13 57				14 27		14 57				15 27		15 57			
Alvechurch	d	13 02				13 32		14 02				14 32		15 02				15 32		16 02			
Barnt Green	d	13 08				13 38	13 48	14 08				14 38	14 48	15 08				15 38	15 48	16 08			
Longbridge	d	13 12		13 22		13 42	13 52	14 12		14 22		14 42	14 52	15 12		15 22		15 42	15 52	16 12		16 22	
Northfield	d	13 14		13 24		13 44	13 54	14 14		14 24		14 44	14 54	15 14		15 24		15 44	15 54	16 14		16 24	
Kings Norton	d	13 17		13 27		13 47	13 57	14 17		14 27		14 47	14 57	15 17		15 27		15 47	15 57	16 17		16 27	
Bournville	d	13 19		13 29		13 49	13 59	14 19		14 29		14 49	14 59	15 19		15 29		15 49	15 59	16 19		16 29	
Selly Oak	d	13 22		13 32		13 52	14 02	14 22		14 32		14 52	15 02	15 22		15 32		15 52	16 02	16 22		16 32	
University	d	13 25	13 30	13 35	13 39	13 55	14 05	14 25	14 30	14 35	14 39	14 55	15 05	15 25	15 30	15 35	15 39	15 55	16 05	16 25	16 30	16 35	16 39
Five Ways	d	13 28		13 38		13 59	14 08	14 28		14 38		14 59	15 08	15 28		15 38		15 59	16 08	16 28		16 38	
Birmingham New Street 12	a	13 33	13 37	13 42	13 45	14 03	14 13	14 33	14 37	14 42	14 45	15 03	15 13	15 33	15 37	15 42	15 45	16 03	16 13	16 33	16 37	16 42	16 45
	d	13 36				14 06		14 36				15 06		15 36				16 06		16 36			
Duddeston	d	13 40				14 10		14 40				15 10		15 40				16 10		16 40			
Aston	d	13 43				14 13		14 43				15 13		15 43				16 13		16 43			
Gravelly Hill	d	13 47				14 17		14 47				15 17		15 47				16 17		16 47			
Erdington	d	13 50				14 20		14 50				15 20		15 50				16 20		16 50			
Chester Road	d	13 52				14 22		14 52				15 22		15 52				16 22		16 52			
Wylde Green	d	13 54				14 24		14 54				15 24		15 54				16 24		16 54			
Sutton Coldfield	d	13 57				14 27		14 57				15 27		15 57				16 27		16 57			
Four Oaks	d	14 00				14 30		15 00				15 30		16 00				16 30		17 00			
Butlers Lane	d	14 03				14 33		15 03				15 33		16 03				16 33		17 03			
Blake Street	d	14 05				14 35		15 05				15 35		16 05				16 35		17 05			
Shenstone	d	14 09				14 39		15 09				15 39		16 09				16 39		17 09			
Lichfield City	d	14 14				14 44		15 14				15 44		16 14				16 44		17 14			
Lichfield Trent Valley	a	14 17				14 47		15 17				15 47		16 17				16 47		17 17			

		LM	LM	LM	LM	LM	XC ◇1	LM	LM	LM	LM	LM	XC ◇1	LM	LM	LM	LM	LM	XC ◇1	LM	LM	LM
Bromsgrove	d		16 42		17 08	17 12			17 42		18 08	18 12			18 42		19 08	19 12			19 42	
Redditch	d	16 27		16 57				17 27		17 57				18 27		18 57				19 27		19 57
Alvechurch	d	16 32		17 02				17 32		18 02				18 32		19 02				19 32		20 02
Barnt Green	d	16 38	16 48	17 08				17 39	17 48	18 08				18 38	18 48	19 08				19 38	19 48	20 08
Longbridge	d	16 42	16 52	17 12		17 22		17 43	17 52	18 12		18 22		18 42	18 52	19 12		19 22		19 42	19 52	20 12
Northfield	d	16 44	16 54	17 14		17 24		17 45	17 54	18 14		18 24		18 44	18 54	19 14		19 24		19 45	19 54	20 14
Kings Norton	d	16 47	16 57	17 17		17 27		17 48	17 57	18 17		18 27		18 47	18 57	19 17		19 27		19 47	19 57	20 17
Bournville	d	16 49	16 59	17 19		17 29		17 50	17 59	18 19		18 29		18 49	18 59	19 19		19 29		19 49	19 59	20 19
Selly Oak	d	16 52	17 02	17 22		17 32		17 53	18 02	18 22		18 32		18 52	19 02	19 22		19 32		19 52	20 02	20 22
University	d	16 55	17 05	17 25	17 30	17 35	17 39	17 56	18 05	18 25	18 30	18 35	18 39	18 55	19 05	19 25	19 30	19 35	19 39	19 55	20 05	20 25
Five Ways	d	16 59	17 08	17 28		17 38		18 00	18 08	18 28		18 38		18 58	19 08	19 28		19 38		19 58	20 08	20 28
Birmingham New Street 12	a	17 03	17 13	17 33	17 37	17 42	17 45	18 04	18 13	18 33	18 37	18 42	18 45	19 03	19 13	19 33	19 37	19 42	19 45	20 03	20 13	20 33
	d	17 06		17 36				18 06		18 36				19 06		19 36				20 06		20 36
Duddeston	d	17 10		17 40				18 10		18 40				19 10		19 40				20 10		20 40
Aston	d	17 13		17 43				18 13		18 43				19 13		19 43				20 13		20 43
Gravelly Hill	d	17 17		17 47				18 17		18 47				19 17		19 47				20 17		20 47
Erdington	d	17 20		17 50				18 20		18 50				19 20		19 50				20 20		20 50
Chester Road	d	17 22		17 52				18 22		18 52				19 22		19 52				20 22		20 52
Wylde Green	d	17 24		17 54				18 24		18 54				19 24		19 54				20 24		20 54
Sutton Coldfield	d	17 27		17 57				18 27		18 57				19 27		19 57				20 27		20 57
Four Oaks	d	17 30		18 00				18 30		19 00				19 30		20 00				20 30		21 00
Butlers Lane	d	17 33		18 03				18 33		19 03				19 33		20 03				20 33		21 03
Blake Street	d	17 35		18 05				18 35		19 05				19 35		20 05				20 35		21 05
Shenstone	d	17 39		18 09				18 39		19 09				19 39		20 09				20 39		21 09
Lichfield City	d	17 44		18 14				18 44		19 14				19 44		20 14				20 44		21 14
Lichfield Trent Valley	a	17 47		18 17				18 47		19 17				19 47		20 17				20 47		21 17

		LM	LM	XC ◇1	LM	LM	LM	LM	LM	XC ◇1	LM	LM	LM	LM	LM	XC ◇1	LM	LM	LM	LM
Bromsgrove	d	20 08	20 12			20 42		21 08	21 12			21 42	21 58		22 12			22 42		23 15
Redditch	d				20 27		20 57				21 27			21 57			22 27		22 57	
Alvechurch	d				20 32		21 02				21 32			22 02			22 32		23 02	
Barnt Green	d				20 38	20 48	21 08				21 38	21 48		22 08			22 38	22 48	23 08	
Longbridge	d		20 22		20 42	20 52	21 12		21 22		21 42	21 52		22 12	22 22		22 42	22 52	23 12	23 25
Northfield	d		20 24		20 44	20 54	21 14		21 24		21 44	21 54		22 14	22 24		22 44	22 54	23 14	23 27
Kings Norton	d		20 27		20 47	20 57	21 17		21 27		21 47	21 57		22 17	22 27		22 47	22 57	23 17	23 30
Bournville	d		20 29		20 49	20 59	21 19		21 29		21 49	21 59		22 19	22 29		22 49	22 59	23 19	23 32
Selly Oak	d		20 32		20 52	21 02	21 22		21 32		21 52	22 02		22 22	22 32		22 52	23 02	23 22	23 35
University	d	20 31	20 35	20 39	20 55	21 05	21 25	21 31	21 35	21 39	21 55	22 05	22 15	22 25	22 35	22 39	22 55	23 05	23 25	23 38
Five Ways	d		20 38		20 58	21 08	21 28		21 38		21 58	22 08		22 28	22 38		22 58	23 08	23 28	23 42
Birmingham New Street 12	a	20 37	20 42	20 45	21 03	21 13	21 33	21 39	21 42	21 45	22 03	22 13	22 21	22 33	22 42	22 45	23 03	23 13	23 33	23 45
	d				21 06		21 36				22 06			22 36			23 06			
Duddeston	d				21 10		21 40				22 10			22 40			23 10			
Aston	d				21 13		21 43				22 13			22 43			23 13			
Gravelly Hill	d				21 17		21 47				22 17			22 47			23 17			
Erdington	d				21 20		21 50				22 20			22 50			23 20			
Chester Road	d				21 22		21 52				22 22			22 52			23 22			
Wylde Green	d				21 24		21 54				22 24			22 54			23 24			
Sutton Coldfield	d				21 27		21 57				22 27			22 57			23 27			
Four Oaks	d				21 30		22 00				22 30			23 00			23 30			
Butlers Lane	d				21 33		22 03				22 33			23 03			23 33			
Blake Street	d				21 35		22 05				22 35			23 05			23 35			
Shenstone	d				21 39		22 09				22 39			23 09			23 39			
Lichfield City	d				21 44		22 14				22 44			23 14			23 44			
Lichfield Trent Valley	a				21 47		22 17				22 47			23 17			23 47			

Table T070-F

Mondays to Fridays

16 December to 15 May

Birmingham - Walsall and Rugeley

Miles			LM	LM	LM	LM	LM	LM	LM	LM	LM	LM	LM	LM	LM	LM	LM	LM	LM	LM	LM	LM	LM
			MX A			1 B		1	B	1 C	D		1 E	1 C	1 F				1 F	1		F	1 F
—	Wolverhampton 7 68	d								07 01			07 58	08 03		08 22	08 48			09 22	09 48		
0	**Birmingham New Street** 12	d		05 26	06 00	06 27	06 42	06 57	07 19	07 27	07 50	07 57	08 21	08 27	08 50	08 57	09 22	09 27	09 46	09 57	10 20	10 27	10 46
1½	Duddeston	d			06 05	06 33		07 02		07 32		08 02		08 33		09 02		09 32		10 01		10 32	
2¾	Aston	d			06 07	06 36		07 05		07 35		08 05		08 36		09 05		09 34		10 05		10 35	
3½	Witton	d			06 10	06 38		07 07		07 37		08 07		08 38		09 07		09 36		10 07		10 37	
4¾	Perry Barr	d			06 12	06 40		07 10		07 40		08 10		08 40		09 10		09 39		10 10		10 40	
5¾	Hamstead	d		05 39	06 15	06 43		07 13		07 43		08 13		08 43		09 13		09 42		10 13		10 43	
8½	Tame Bridge Parkway	d		05 43	06 19	06 47	06 53	07 17	07 34	07 46	08 04	08 17	08 32	08 47	09 05	09 16	09 33	09 46	10 03	10 16	10 32	10 47	11 01
9½	Bescot Stadium	d		05 45	06 21	06 49		07 19		07 48		08 20		08 49		09 19		09 48	10 05	10 19		10 49	11 03
10¾	**Walsall**	a		05 49	06 24	06 54	06 58	07 24	07 39	07 53	08 11	08 25	08 37	08 54	09 10	09 23	09 38	09 53	10 09	10 23	10 37	10 54	11 08
—		d		05 50	06 25		06 59		07 39		08 12		08 38		09 10		09 38		10 09		10 38		11 10
14	Bloxwich	d		05 56	06 31		07 05		07 45		08 18		08 44		09 16		09 44		10 15		10 44		11 16
14½	Bloxwich North	d		05 58	06 33		07 07		07 47		08 20		08 46		09 18		09 46		10 17		10 46		11 18
16¾	Landywood	d		06 01	06 36		07 10		07 51		08 23		08 49		09 22		09 50		10 20		10 49		11 21
18¾	Cannock	d	00 04	06 05	06 40		07 14		07 55		08 27		08 53		09 26		09 54		10 24		10 53		11 25
20¾	Hednesford	d	00a08	06 09	06 44		07 18		07 59		08 31		08 57		09 30		09 58		10 28		10 57		11 29
24¾	Rugeley Town	d		06 15	06 50		07 24		08 05		08 37		09 03		09 36		10 04		10 35		11 04		11 35
26¾	**Rugeley Trent Valley**	a		06 19	06 54		07 28		08 09		08 41		09 07		09 40		10 08		10 39		11 08		11 39

		LM	LM	LM	LM	LM	LM	LM	LM	LM	LM	LM	LM	LM	LM	LM	LM	LM	LM	LM	LM	LM	LM
		1		F	1 F	1 F	1		1 F	1 F			1 F	1 F	1		F	1 F	1 F	1		F	1 F
Wolverhampton 7 68	d	10 22	10 48					11 48			12 22	12 48			13 22	13 48				14 22	14 48		
Birmingham New Street 12	d	10 57	11 20	11 20	11 27	11 47	11 57	12 20	12 27	12 46	12 57	13 21	13 27	13 46	13 57	14 20	14 20	14 27	14 46	14 57	15 21	15 27	15 46
Duddeston	d	11 02			11 32		12 03		12 32		13 02		13 32		14 02			14 32		15 02		15 31	
Aston	d	11 05			11 35		12 06		12 35		13 05		13 35		14 05			14 35		15 05		15 35	
Witton	d	11 07			11 37		12 08		12 37		13 07		13 37		14 07			14 37		15 07		15 37	
Perry Barr	d	11 10			11 40		12 11		12 40		13 10		13 40		14 10			14 40		15 10		15 40	
Hamstead	d	11 13			11 43		12 14		12 43		13 13		13 43		14 13			14 43		15 13		15 43	
Tame Bridge Parkway	d	11 17	11 31	11 31	11 47	12 02	12 18	12 31	12 47	13 01	13 17	13 32	13 47	14 01	14 17	14 31	14 31	14 47	15 01	15 17	15 33	15 46	16 02
Bescot Stadium	d	11 20			11 49	12 05	12 21		12 50	13 03	13 19		13 49	14 03	14 19			14 49	15 04	15 19		15 49	16 04
Walsall	a	11 23	11 36	11 36	11 54	12 09	12 25	12 36	12 56	13 06	13 24	13 37	13 54	14 08	14 24	14 36	14 36	14 54	15 07	15 24	15 40	15 53	16 10
	d		11 37	11 37		12 09		12 37		13 07		13 37		14 08		14 37	14 37		15 08		15 40		16 10
Bloxwich	d		11 43	11 43		12 15		12 43		13 13		13 43		14 14		14 43	14 43		15 14		15 46		16 16
Bloxwich North	d		11 45	11 45		12 17		12 45		13 15		13 45		14 16		14 45	14 45		15 16		15 48		16 18
Landywood	d		11 48	11 48		12 21		12 48		13 18		13 49		14 20		14 49	14 49		15 19		15 52		16 22
Cannock	d		11 52	11 52		12 25		12 52		13 22		13 53		14 24		14 53	14 53		15 23		15 56		16 26
Hednesford	d		11 56	11 56		12 29		12 56		13 26		13 57		14 28		14 57	14 57		15 27		16 00		16 30
Rugeley Town	d		12 02	12 02		12 35		13 03		13 32		14 03		14 34		15 03	15 03		15 34		16 06		16 36
Rugeley Trent Valley	a		12 06	12 06		12 39		13 07		13 36		14 07		14 38		15 07	15 07		15 38		16 10		16 40

		LM	LM	LM	LM	LM	LM	LM	LM	LM	LM	LM	LM	LM	LM	LM	LM	LM	LM	LM	LM	LM
		1		F	F	1 F	1			1 F			F	1 F			1 E	1 F			1 F	
Wolverhampton 7 68	d	15 22	15 48				16 22	16 48			17 22	17 48			18 22	18 48	18 59					20 22
Birmingham New Street 12	d	15 57	16 21	16 21	16 27	16 46	16 57	17 23	17 27	17 45	17 57	18 21	18 26	18 53	18 57	19 19	19 22	19 54	19 57	20 21	20 47	20 57
Duddeston	d	16 02			16 32		17 02		17 32		18 02		18 31		19 02		19 27		20 03	20 25		21 02
Aston	d	16 05			16 35		17 05		17 36		18 05		18 35		19 05		19 29		20 06	20 28		21 05
Witton	d	16 07			16 37		17 07		17 38		18 07		18 37		19 07		19 31		20 08	20 30		21 07
Perry Barr	d	16 10			16 40		17 10		17 41		18 10		18 40		19 10		19 34		20 11	20 33		21 10
Hamstead	d	16 13			16 43		17 13		17 44		18 13		18 43		19 13		19 37		20 14	20 36		21 13
Tame Bridge Parkway	d	16 17	16 32	16 32	16 47	17 01	17 17	17 34	17 48	18 00	18 17	18 32	18 47	19 08	19 17	19 32	19 41	20 08	20 18	20 40	21 01	21 17
Bescot Stadium	d	16 19			16 50	17 03	17 19		17 50	18 03	18 19		18 49	19 13	19 19		19 43	20 10	20 20	20 42	21 06	21 20
Walsall	a	16 24	16 37	16 37	16 54	17 07	17 24	17 39	17 54	18 09	18 24	18 37	18 54	19 17	19 24	19 37	19 48	20 15	20 24	20 46	21 09	21 24
	d		16 38	16 38		17 08		17 40		18 10		18 38		19 18		19 38		20 16		20 46	21 10	
Bloxwich	d		16 44	16 44		17 14		17 46		18 16		18 44		19 24		19 44		20 22		20 52	21 16	
Bloxwich North	d		16 46	16 46		17 16		17 48		18 18		18 46		19 25		19 46		20 24		20 54	21 18	
Landywood	d		16 49	16 49		17 19		17 51		18 21		18 49		19 29		19 50		20 28		20 58	21 23	
Cannock	d		16 53	16 53		17 23		17 55		18 25		18 53		19 33		19 54		20 32		21 02	21 27	
Hednesford	d		16 57	16 57		17 27		17 59		18 29		18 57		19 37		19 58		20 36		21 06	21 31	
Rugeley Town	d		17 04	17 04		17 34		18 06		18 36		19 04		19 43		20 05		20 48		21 12	21 37	
Rugeley Trent Valley	a		17 08	17 08		17 38		18 10		18 40		19 08		19 47		20 09		20 52		21 16	21 41	

		LM	LM	LM	LM	LM	LM
			F		1	1 C	
Wolverhampton 7 68	d	20 49			21 50	22 17	
Birmingham New Street 12	d	21 20	21 30	21 47	22 20	22 45	23 18
Duddeston	d		21 34	21 52		22 50	23 23
Aston	d		21 37	21 55		22 53	23 27
Witton	d		21 39	21 57		22 55	23 29
Perry Barr	d		21 42	21 59		22 57	23 32
Hamstead	d		21 45	22 02		23 00	23 35
Tame Bridge Parkway	d	21 32	21 49	22 06	22 31	23 04	23 39
Bescot Stadium	d		21 52	22 08		23 07	23 41
Walsall	a	21 39	21 55	22 12	22 36	23 12	23 47
	d	21 39		22 12	22 36		23 48
Bloxwich	d	21 45		22 18	22 42		23 53
Bloxwich North	d	21 47		22 20	22 44		23 55
Landywood	d	21 51		22 24	22 48		23 59
Cannock	d	21 55		22 28	22 52		00 04
Hednesford	d	21 59		22 32	22 56		00a08
Rugeley Town	d	22 05		22 39	23 03		
Rugeley Trent Valley	a	22 09		22 43	23 07		

A From Birmingham New Street
B From Northampton
C From Crewe
D From Coventry
E From Liverpool Lime Street
F From London Euston

For connections to Stafford refer to Table T67

Table T070-F

Saturdays

21 December to 16 May

Birmingham - Walsall and Rugeley

		LM	LM	LM	LM	LM	LM	LM	LM	LM	LM	LM	LM	LM	LM	LM	LM	LM	LM	LM	LM	LM	LM
		A						B		B		1 C		B		1 C		C		1 C		C	
Wolverhampton 7 68	d		05 42						07 20		07 50		08 22		08 48		09 22		09 48		10 22		10 48
Birmingham New Street 12	d			06 00	06 27	06 59	07 27	07 51	07 57	08 21	08 27	08 51	08 57	09 20	09 27	09 50	09 57	10 20	10 27	10 50	10 57	11 21	11 27
Duddeston	d			06 04	06 32	07 03	07 32		08 02		08 32		09 02		09 32		10 02		10 32		11 02		11 32
Aston	d			06 07	06 36	07 06	07 35		08 05		08 35		09 05		09 35		10 05		10 35		11 05		11 35
Witton	d			06 09	06 38	07 08	07 37		08 07		08 37		09 07		09 37		10 07		10 37		11 07		11 37
Perry Barr	d			06 12	06 41	07 11	07 40		08 10		08 40		09 10		09 40		10 10		10 40		11 10		11 40
Hamstead	d			06 15	06 44	07 14	07 43		08 13		08 43		09 13		09 43		10 13		10 43		11 13		11 43
Tame Bridge Parkway	d			06 19	06 48	07 18	07 47	08 05	08 17	08 33	08 47	09 05	09 17	09 32	09 47	10 05	10 17	10 32	10 47	11 05	11 17	11 33	11 47
Bescot Stadium	d			06 21	06 51	07 20	07 49	08 07	08 20		08 49		09 19		09 49		10 19		10 49		11 19		11 49
Walsall	a		05 57	06 26	06 56	07 25	07 54	08 12	08 24	08 38	08 54	09 11	09 24	09 38	09 54	10 11	10 24	10 38	10 54	11 11	11 24	11 38	11 54
	d		05 58	06 27	06 58	07 26		08 12		08 38		09 12		09 38		10 12		10 38		11 12		11 38	
Bloxwich	d			06 33	07 03	07 32		08 18		08 44		09 18		09 44		10 18		10 44		11 18		11 44	
Bloxwich North	d			06 35	07 05	07 34		08 20		08 46		09 20		09 46		10 20		10 46		11 20		11 46	
Landywood	d			06 38	07 09	07 37		08 24		08 50		09 23		09 50		10 23		10 50		11 23		11 50	
Cannock	d	00 04		06 42	07 13	07 41		08 28		08 54		09 27		09 54		10 27		10 54		11 27		11 54	
Hednesford	d	00a08		06 46	07 17	07 45		08 32		08 58		09 31		09 58		10 31		10 58		11 31		11 58	
Rugeley Town	d			06 53	07 23	07 52		08 38		09 04		09 38		10 04		10 38		11 04		11 38		12 04	
Rugeley Trent Valley	a		06 22	06 57	07 28	07 56		08 42		09 08		09 42		10 08		10 42		11 08		11 42		12 08	

		LM	LM	LM	LM	LM	LM	LM	LM	LM	LM	LM	LM	LM	LM	LM	LM	LM	LM	LM	LM	LM
		C	1 C		C		C	1 C		C		1 C		C		C	1 C		C		1 C	
Wolverhampton 7 68	d			11 22		11 48			12 22		12 48		13 23		13 48			14 22		14 48		15 22
Birmingham New Street 12	d	11 27	11 50	11 57	12 20	12 27	12 27	12 47	12 57	13 21	13 27	13 50	13 57	14 20	14 27	14 27	14 50	14 57	15 21	15 27	15 50	15 57
Duddeston	d	11 32		12 02		12 32	12 32		13 02		13 32		14 02		14 32	14 32		15 02		15 32		16 02
Aston	d	11 35		12 05		12 35	12 35		13 05		13 35		14 05		14 35	14 35		15 05		15 35		16 05
Witton	d	11 37		12 07		12 37	12 37		13 07		13 37		14 07		14 37	14 37		15 07		15 37		16 07
Perry Barr	d	11 40		12 10		12 40	12 40		13 10		13 40		14 10		14 40	14 40		15 10		15 40		16 10
Hamstead	d	11 43		12 13		12 43	12 43		13 13		13 43		14 13		14 43	14 43		15 13		15 43		16 13
Tame Bridge Parkway	d	11 47	12 05	12 17	12 32	12 47	12 47	13 06	13 17	13 33	13 47	14 05	14 17	14 32	14 47	14 47	15 05	15 17	15 33	15 47	16 05	16 17
Bescot Stadium	d	11 49		12 19		12 49	12 49		13 19		13 49		14 19		14 49	14 49		15 19		15 49		16 19
Walsall	a	11 54	12 11	12 24	12 38	12 54	12 54	13 11	13 24	13 38	13 54	14 11	14 24	14 38	14 54	14 54	15 11	15 24	15 39	15 54	16 11	16 24
	d		12 12		12 38			13 12		13 38		14 12		14 38			15 12		15 39		16 12	
Bloxwich	d		12 18		12 44			13 18		13 44		14 18		14 44			15 18		15 45		16 18	
Bloxwich North	d		12 20		12 46			13 20		13 46		14 20		14 46			15 20		15 47		16 20	
Landywood	d		12 23		12 50			13 23		13 50		14 23		14 50			15 23		15 51		16 23	
Cannock	d		12 27		12 54			13 27		13 54		14 27		14 54			15 27		15 55		16 27	
Hednesford	d		12 31		12 58			13 31		13 58		14 31		14 58			15 31		15 59		16 31	
Rugeley Town	d		12 38		13 04			13 38		14 04		14 38		15 04			15 38		16 05		16 38	
Rugeley Trent Valley	a		12 42		13 08			13 42		14 08		14 42		15 08			15 42		16 09		16 42	

		LM	LM	LM	LM	LM	LM	LM	LM	LM	LM	LM	LM	LM	LM	LM	LM	LM	LM	LM	LM	LM	LM
		C		1 C		C		1 C		C		1 C		C		1 C			1 C	1			
Wolverhampton 7 68	d		15 48		16 22		16 48		17 22		17 48		18 21		18 48		19 21				20 48	21 19	21 49
Birmingham New Street 12	d	16 21	16 27	16 50	16 57	17 21	17 27	17 50	17 57	18 21	18 27	18 53	18 57	19 21	19 27	19 53	19 57	20 21	20 53	20 57	21 20	21 58	22 19
Duddeston	d		16 32		17 02		17 32		18 02		18 32		19 02		19 32		20 02	20 26		21 02	21 25	22 03	
Aston	d		16 35		17 05		17 35		18 05		18 35		19 05		19 35		20 05	20 29		21 05	21 28	22 06	
Witton	d		16 37		17 07		17 37		18 07		18 37		19 07		19 37		20 07	20 31		21 07	21 30	22 08	
Perry Barr	d		16 40		17 09		17 40		18 10		18 40		19 10		19 40		20 10	20 33		21 09	21 32	22 11	
Hamstead	d		16 43		17 13		17 43		18 13		18 43		19 13		19 43		20 13	20 36		21 12	21 35	22 14	
Tame Bridge Parkway	d	16 33	16 47	17 05	17 17	17 33	17 47	18 05	18 17	18 33	18 47	19 06	19 17	19 33	19 47	20 06	20 16	20 40	21 07	21 16	21 39	22 18	22 31
Bescot Stadium	d		16 49		17 19		17 49		18 19		18 49		19 19		19 49		20 19	20 42		21 19	21 41	22 21	
Walsall	a	16 39	16 54	17 11	17 24	17 39	17 54	18 11	18 24	18 39	18 54	19 11	19 24	19 39	19 54	20 11	20 22	20 47	21 12	21 23	21 46	22 26	22 37
	d	16 39		17 12		17 39		18 12		18 39		19 12		19 39		20 12		20 47	21 12		21 46	22 27	22 37
Bloxwich	d	16 45		17 18		17 45		18 18		18 45		19 18		19 45		20 18		20 53	21 18		21 52	22 33	22 43
Bloxwich North	d	16 47		17 20		17 47		18 20		18 47		19 20		19 47		20 20		20 55	21 20		21 54	22 35	22 45
Landywood	d	16 51		17 23		17 51		18 23		18 51		19 23		19 51		20 23		20 59	21 24		21 58	22 38	22 49
Cannock	d	16 55		17 27		17 55		18 27		18 55		19 27		19 55		20 27		21 03	21 28		22 02	22 42	22 53
Hednesford	d	16 59		17 31		17 59		18 31		18 59		19 31		19 59		20 31		21 07	21 32		22 06	22 46	22 57
Rugeley Town	d	17 05		17 38		18 05		18 38		19 05		19 38		20 08		20 38		21 13	21 40		22 12	22 52	23 07
Rugeley Trent Valley	a	17 09		17 42		18 09		18 42		19 09		19 42		20 12		20 42		21 17	21 44		22 16	22 56	23 11

		LM	LM
Wolverhampton 7 68	d		22 49
Birmingham New Street 12	d	22 55	23 18
Duddeston	d	23 00	23 22
Aston	d	23 03	23 25
Witton	d	23 05	23 27
Perry Barr	d	23 08	23 30
Hamstead	d	23 11	23 33
Tame Bridge Parkway	d	23 15	23 37
Bescot Stadium	d	23 17	23 39
Walsall	a	23 22	23 44
	d		23 44
Bloxwich	d		23 50
Bloxwich North	d		23 52
Landywood	d		23 56
Cannock	d		23 59
Hednesford	d		00a03
Rugeley Town	d		
Rugeley Trent Valley	a		

A From Birmingham New Street
B From Northampton
C From London Euston

For connections to Stafford refer to Table T67

Table T070-F

Sundays

15 December to 10 May

Birmingham - Walsall and Rugeley

		LM	LM	LM A	LM	LM	LM ■1	LM	LM ■1	LM	LM ■1	LM	LM ■1	LM	LM ■1	LM	LM ■1	LM	LM ■1	LM	LM ■1	LM	LM ■1
Wolverhampton ■7 68	d	08 16	08 22		09 21		10 23		11 21		12 17		13 21		14 22		15 22		16 22		17 24		18 24
Birmingham New Street ■12	d	08 45	08 57	09 45	09 57	10 46	10 57	11 46	11 57	12 44	12 57	13 47	13 57	14 44	14 57	15 44	15 57	16 45	16 57	17 45	17 57	18 47	18 57
Duddeston	d		09 01		10 02		11 02		12 02		13 02		14 02		15 02		16 02		17 02		18 02		19 02
Aston	d		09 04		10 05		11 05		12 05		13 05		14 05		15 05		16 05		17 05		18 05		19 05
Witton	d		09 06		10 07		11 07		12 07		13 07		14 07		15 07		16 07		17 07		18 07		19 07
Perry Barr	d		09 09		10 10		11 09		12 09		13 09		14 09		15 09		16 09		17 09		18 09		19 09
Hamstead	d		09 12		10 13		11 12		12 12		13 12		14 12		15 12		16 12		17 12		18 12		19 12
Tame Bridge Parkway	d	08 57	09 16	09 57	10 17	11 00	11 16	11 57	12 16	12 58	13 16	13 59	14 16	14 58	15 16	15 57	16 16	17 00	17 16	17 58	18 16	19 01	19 16
Bescot Stadium	d		09 19		10 19		11 18		12 18		13 18		14 18		15 18		16 18		17 18		18 18		19 18
Walsall	a	09 04	09 23	10 04	10 24	11 06	11 23	12 03	12 23	13 05	13 23	14 05	14 23	15 04	15 23	16 03	16 23	17 06	17 23	18 04	18 23	19 07	19 23
	d	09 06		10 06		11 07		12 04		13 06		14 06		15 04		16 03		17 07		18 05		19 07	
Bloxwich	d	09 12		10 12		11 13		12 10		13 12		14 12		15 10		16 09		17 13		18 11		19 13	
Bloxwich North	d	09 14		10 14		11 14		12 12		13 14		14 14		15 12		16 11		17 15		18 13		19 15	
Landywood	d	09 18		10 18		11 18		12 15		13 17		14 17		15 16		16 15		17 18		18 16		19 19	
Cannock	d	09 22		10 22		11 22		12 19		13 21		14 21		15 20		16 18		17 22		18 20		19 23	
Hednesford	d	09 26		10 26		11 26		12 23		13 25		14 25		15 24		16 22		17 26		18 24		19 27	
Rugeley Town	d	09 32		10 32		11 32		12 30		13 32		14 32		15 30		16 29		17 33		18 31		19 33	
Rugeley Trent Valley	a	09 36		10 36		11 36		12 34		13 36		14 36		15 34		16 33		17 37		18 35		19 37	

		LM	LM ■1	LM	LM ■1	LM	LM	LM A	LM ■1	LM ■1
Wolverhampton ■7 68	d		19 22		20 20		21 22		22 24	23 04
Birmingham New Street ■12	d	19 44	19 57	20 53	20 57	21 51	21 57	22 45	22 57	23 32
Duddeston	d		20 02		21 01		22 02		23 02	23 37
Aston	d		20 05		21 04		22 05		23 05	23 40
Witton	d		20 07		21 06		22 07		23 07	23 42
Perry Barr	d		20 09		21 09		22 10		23 09	23 44
Hamstead	d		20 12		21 12		22 13		23 12	23 47
Tame Bridge Parkway	d	19 59	20 16	21 05	21 16	22 03	22 17	22 59	23 16	23 51
Bescot Stadium	d		20 18		21 18		22 20		23 18	23 53
Walsall	a	20 05	20 23	21 11	21 22	22 09	22 26	23 05	23 23	23 57
	d	20 06		21 12		22 10		23 06		
Bloxwich	d	20 12		21 18		22 16		23 12		
Bloxwich North	d	20 14		21 20		22 18		23 14		
Landywood	d	20 17		21 23		22 22		23 17		
Cannock	d	20 21		21 27		22 25		23 21		
Hednesford	d	20 25		21 31		22 29		23 25		
Rugeley Town	d	20 32		21 38		22 36		23 31		
Rugeley Trent Valley	a	20 36		21 42		22 40		23 35		

A From Coventry

For connections to Stafford refer to Table T67

Table T070-R

Mondays to Fridays

16 December to 15 May

Rugeley and Walsall - Birmingham

Miles			LM ■1 A	LM ■1	LM ■1 A	LM ■1 A	LM ■1 B	LM ■1	LM ■1 A	LM	LM ■1 B	LM	LM ■1 A	LM ■1	LM ■1 B	LM	LM ■1 A	LM	LM ■1 B	LM	LM ■1 A	LM	LM ■1 B
0	**Rugeley Trent Valley**	d		06 05	06 28		06 45		07 10		07 44		08 20		08 47		09 21		09 46		10 20		10 46
1½	Rugeley Town	d		06 08	06 31		06 48		07 13		07 47		08 23		08 50		09 24		09 49		10 23		10 49
5½	Hednesford	d		06 15	06 38		06 55		07 20		07 54		08 30		08 57		09 31		09 56		10 30		10 56
7½	Cannock	d		06 18	06 41		06 58		07 23		07 57		08 33		09 00		09 34		09 59		10 33		10 59
9¾	Landywood	d		06 21	06 44		07 01		07 26		08 00		08 36		09 03		09 37		10 02		10 36		11 02
11¾	Bloxwich North	d		06 26	06 49		07 06		07 31		08 05		08 41		09 08		09 42		10 07		10 41		11 07
12¼	Bloxwich	d		06 28	06 51		07 08		07 33		08 07		08 43		09 10		09 44		10 09		10 43		11 09
15½	**Walsall**	a		06 33	06 56		07 14		07 38		08 14		08 48		09 15		09 49		10 14		10 48		11 14
—		d	06 02	06 34	06 57	07 02	07 15	07 31	07 39	08 00	08 15	08 30	08 49	09 01	09 16	09 30	09 50	10 00	10 15	10 33	10 49	11 01	11 15
16¾	Bescot Stadium	d	06 05	06 38		07 05		07 34		08 03		08 34	08 53	09 04		09 33	09 54	10 03		10 36	10 53	11 04	
17¾	Tame Bridge Parkway	d	06 08	06 40	07 03	07 08	07 20	07 37	07 45	08 06	08 20	08 37	08 55	09 07	09 22	09 36	09 56	10 06	10 20	10 39	10 55	11 07	11 21
20½	Hamstead	d	06 11	06 44		07 11		07 40		08 09		08 41		09 10		09 39		10 09		10 42		11 10	
22	Perry Barr	d	06 14	06 47		07 14		07 43		08 12		08 44		09 13		09 42		10 12		10 45		11 13	
22¾	Witton	d	06 16	06 49		07 16		07 45		08 14		08 47		09 15		09 44		10 14		10 47		11 15	
23½	Aston	d	06 19	06 51		07 19		07 49		08 17		08 50		09 18		09 47		10 16		10 50		11 19	
24¾	Duddeston	d	06 21	06 53		07 21		07 51		08 20		08 53		09 21		09 49		10 19		10 52		11 21	
26¼	**Birmingham New Street ■12**	a	06 28	06 58	07 16	07 26	07 37	07 57	08 01	08 28	08 37	08 58	09 10	09 30	09 37	09 55	10 11	10 23	10 37	10 57	11 10	11 29	11 37
—	Wolverhampton ■7 68	a		07 33				08 33		09 07				10 05		10 33		11 09		11 33		12 05	

		LM ■1	LM ■1 A	LM ■1	LM ■1 B	LM ■1	LM ■1 A	LM ■1	LM ■1 B	LM	LM ■1 A	LM ■1	LM ■1 B	LM	LM ■1 A	LM ■1	LM ■1 B	LM ■1 C	LM ■1 A	LM	LM ■1 B	LM ■1
Rugeley Trent Valley	d		11 20		11 46		12 20		12 46		13 20		13 46		14 20		14 46		15 16		15 46	
Rugeley Town	d		11 23		11 49		12 23		12 49		13 23		13 49		14 23		14 49		15 19		15 49	
Hednesford	d		11 30		11 56		12 30		12 56		13 30		13 56		14 30		14 56		15 26		15 56	
Cannock	d		11 33		11 59		12 33		12 59		13 33		13 59		14 33		14 59		15 29		15 59	
Landywood	d		11 36		12 02		12 36		13 02		13 36		14 02		14 36		15 02		15 32		16 02	
Bloxwich North	d		11 41		12 07		12 41		13 07		13 41		14 07		14 41		15 07		15 37		16 07	
Bloxwich	d		11 43		12 09		12 43		13 09		13 43		14 09		14 43		15 09		15 39		16 09	
Walsall	a		11 48		12 14		12 48		13 14		13 48		14 14		14 48		15 14		15 45		16 14	
	d	11 30	11 49	12 01	12 15	12 31	12 49	13 01	13 15	13 31	13 49	14 01	14 15	14 31	14 49	15 01	15 15	15 31	15 46	16 01	16 15	16 31
Bescot Stadium	d	11 33	11 53	12 04		12 34	12 53	13 04		13 34	13 53	14 04		14 34	14 53	15 04		15 34	15 50	16 04		16 34
Tame Bridge Parkway	d	11 36	11 55	12 07	12 20	12 37	12 55	13 07	13 20	13 37	13 55	14 07	14 20	14 37	14 55	15 07	15 21	15 37	15 52	16 07	16 22	16 37
Hamstead	d	11 40		12 10		12 40		13 10		13 40		14 10		14 40		15 10		15 40		16 10		16 40
Perry Barr	d	11 43		12 13		12 43		13 13		13 43		14 13		14 43		15 13		15 43		16 13		16 43
Witton	d	11 45		12 15		12 45		13 15		13 45		14 15		14 45		15 15		15 45		16 15		16 45
Aston	d	11 49		12 19		12 49		13 19		13 49		14 19		14 49		15 19		15 48		16 19		16 49
Duddeston	d	11 52		12 21		12 51		13 21		13 51		14 22		14 51		15 21		15 51		16 21		16 51
Birmingham New Street ■12	a	11 57	12 10	12 28	12 37	12 58	13 10	13 28	13 37	13 57	14 10	14 28	14 37	14 57	15 10	15 28	15 37	15 56	16 07	16 28	16 37	16 56
Wolverhampton ■7 68	a	12 33		13 06		13 33		14 06		14 33		15 06		15 33		16 06		16 33		17 05		17 33

		LM ■1 A	LM	LM ■1 B	LM ■1	LM ■1 A	LM	LM ■1 B	LM	LM ■1 A	LM ■1	LM ■1 B	LM	LM ■1 D	LM	LM	LM	LM ■1	LM	LM	LM ■1 E	LM	LM ■1
Rugeley Trent Valley	d	16 20		16 46		17 20		17 46		18 20		18 47		19 18			20 06	20 34	21 07		21 25		22 00
Rugeley Town	d	16 23		16 49		17 23		17 49		18 23		18 50		19 21			20 09	20 37	21 10		21 28		22 03
Hednesford	d	16 30		16 56		17 30		17 56		18 30		18 57		19 28			20 16	20 44	21 17		21 35		22 10
Cannock	d	16 33		16 59		17 33		17 59		18 33		19 00		19 31			20 19	20 47	21 20		21 38		22 13
Landywood	d	16 36		17 02		17 36		18 02		18 36		19 03		19 34			20 22	20 50	21 23		21 41		22 16
Bloxwich North	d	16 41		17 07		17 41		18 07		18 41		19 08		19 39			20 27	20 55	21 28		21 46		22 21
Bloxwich	d	16 43		17 09		17 43		18 09		18 43		19 10		19 41			20 29	20 57	21 30		21 48		22 23
Walsall	a	16 48		17 16		17 48		18 14		18 48		19 15		19 47			20 35	21 02	21 35		21 54		22 28
	d	16 49	17 01	17 17	17 31	17 49	18 01	18 15	18 31	18 49	19 01	19 16	19 31	19 48	20 01	20 31	20 36	21 03	21 36	21 40	21 55	22 02	22 29
Bescot Stadium	d	16 53	17 04		17 34	17 53	18 04		18 34	18 53	19 04		19 34	19 52	20 05	20 35		21 06		21 45		22 05	
Tame Bridge Parkway	d	16 55	17 07	17 22	17 37	17 55	18 07	18 21	18 37	18 55	19 07	19 21	19 37	19 54	20 07	20 38	20 43	21 09	21 42	21 48	22 02	22 08	22 34
Hamstead	d		17 10		17 40		18 10		18 40		19 10		19 40		20 11	20 41		21 12		21 51		22 11	
Perry Barr	d		17 13		17 43		18 13		18 43		19 13		19 43		20 14	20 44		21 15		21 54		22 14	
Witton	d		17 15		17 45		18 15		18 45		19 15		19 45		20 16	20 46		21 17		21 56		22 16	
Aston	d		17 18		17 49		18 18		18 49		19 18		19 48		20 18	20 49		21 20		21 59		22 20	
Duddeston	d		17 23		17 51		18 20		18 51		19 20		19 50		20 22	20 52		21 22		22 02		22 22	
Birmingham New Street ■12	a	17 10	17 30	17 37	17 56	18 10	18 29	18 37	18 56	19 10	19 28	19 36	19 55	20 10	20 28	20 56	21 01	21 29	21 54	22 08	22 21	22 27	22 45
Wolverhampton ■7 68	a		18 06		18 33		19 05		19 33		20 07		20 33		21 05	21 32		22 05		22 44			

		LM ■1	LM ■1	LM
Rugeley Trent Valley	d	22 37	23 01	
Rugeley Town	d	22 40	23 04	
Hednesford	d	22 47	23 11	
Cannock	d	22 50	23 14	
Landywood	d	22 53	23 17	
Bloxwich North	d	22 58	23 22	
Bloxwich	d	23 00	23 24	
Walsall	a	23 05	23 30	
	d	23 09	23 31	23 40
Bescot Stadium	d	23 13		23 43
Tame Bridge Parkway	d	23 15	23 36	23 46
Hamstead	d	23 19		23 49
Perry Barr	d	23 22		23 52
Witton	d	23 24		23 54
Aston	d	23 26		23 57
Duddeston	d	23 29		23 59
Birmingham New Street ■12	a	23 33	23 50	00 07
Wolverhampton ■7 68	a		00 21	

A To London Euston
B To Birmingham International
C ■1 to Birmingham New Street
D To Coventry
E To Northampton

For connections from Stafford refer to Table T67

Table T070-R

Saturdays
21 December to 16 May

Rugeley and Walsall - Birmingham

		LM	LM	LM 1 A	LM B	LM	LM	LM 1 A	LM	LM 1 B	LM	LM 1 A	LM	LM 1 B	LM	LM 1 A	LM	LM 1 B	LM	LM 1 A	LM	LM 1 B	LM
Rugeley Trent Valley	d		06 00	06 13	06 28			07 17		07 43		08 13		08 47		09 13		09 47		10 13		10 47	
Rugeley Town	d		06 03	06 16	06 31			07 20		07 46		08 16		08 50		09 16		09 50		10 16		10 50	
Hednesford	d		06 10	06 23	06 38			07 27		07 53		08 23		08 57		09 23		09 57		10 23		10 57	
Cannock	d		06 13	06 26	06 41			07 30		07 56		08 26		09 00		09 26		10 00		10 26		11 00	
Landywood	d		06 16	06 30	06 44			07 33		07 59		08 29		09 03		09 29		10 03		10 29		11 03	
Bloxwich North	d		06 21	06 34	06 48			07 38		08 04		08 34		09 08		09 34		10 08		10 34		11 08	
Bloxwich	d		06 23	06 37	06 50			07 40		08 06		08 36		09 10		09 36		10 10		10 36		11 10	
Walsall	a		06 28	06 43	06 56			07 45		08 12		08 41		09 15		09 41		10 15		10 41		11 15	
	d	06 03	06 29	06 45	06 56	07 02	07 31	07 46	08 01	08 13	08 31	08 42	09 01	09 16	09 31	09 42	10 01	10 16	10 31	10 42	11 01	11 16	11 31
Bescot Stadium	d	06 06	06 32			07 05	07 34		08 04		08 34		09 04		09 34		10 04		10 34		11 04		11 34
Tame Bridge Parkway	d	06 09	06 35	06 50	07 01	07 08	07 37	07 51	08 07	08 18	08 37	08 47	09 07	09 21	09 37	09 47	10 07	10 21	10 37	10 47	11 07	11 21	11 37
Hamstead	d	06 12	06 38			07 12	07 40		08 10		08 40		09 10		09 40		10 10		10 40		11 10		11 40
Perry Barr	d	06 15	06 41			07 15	07 43		08 13		08 43		09 13		09 43		10 13		10 43		11 13		11 43
Witton	d	06 17	06 43			07 17	07 45		08 15		08 45		09 15		09 45		10 15		10 45		11 15		11 45
Aston	d	06 19	06 46			07 19	07 48		08 19		08 48		09 18		09 48		10 18		10 48		11 18		11 48
Duddeston	d	06 22	06 48			07 22	07 51		08 21		08 50		09 20		09 50		10 20		10 50		11 20		11 50
Birmingham New Street 12	a	06 26	06 54	07 09	07 15	07 27	07 55	08 08	08 27	08 37	08 55	09 03	09 25	09 36	09 54	10 02	10 27	10 37	10 54	11 02	11 27	11 37	11 54
Wolverhampton 7 68	a	07 04				08 04	08 31		09 05		09 31		10 05		10 32		11 05		11 31		12 05		12 31

		LM 1 A	LM	LM 1 B	LM	LM 1 A	LM	LM 1 B	LM	LM 1 A	LM	LM 1 B	LM	LM 1 A	LM	LM 1 B	LM	LM 1 A	LM	LM 1 B	LM	LM 1 A
Rugeley Trent Valley	d	11 13		11 47		12 13		12 47		13 13		13 47		14 13		14 47		15 13		15 47		16 14
Rugeley Town	d	11 16		11 50		12 16		12 50		13 16		13 50		14 16		14 50		15 16		15 50		16 17
Hednesford	d	11 23		11 57		12 23		12 57		13 23		13 57		14 23		14 57		15 23		15 57		16 24
Cannock	d	11 26		12 00		12 26		13 00		13 26		14 00		14 26		15 00		15 26		16 00		16 27
Landywood	d	11 29		12 03		12 29		13 03		13 29		14 03		14 29		15 03		15 29		16 03		16 30
Bloxwich North	d	11 34		12 08		12 34		13 08		13 34		14 08		14 34		15 08		15 34		16 07		16 35
Bloxwich	d	11 36		12 10		12 36		13 10		13 36		14 10		14 36		15 10		15 36		16 09		16 37
Walsall	a	11 41		12 15		12 41		13 15		13 41		14 15		14 41		15 15		15 41		16 15		16 42
	d	11 42	12 01	12 16	12 31	12 42	13 01	13 16	13 31	13 42	14 01	14 16	14 31	14 42	15 01	15 16	15 31	15 42	16 01	16 16	16 31	16 43
Bescot Stadium	d		12 04		12 34		13 04		13 34		14 04		14 34		15 04		15 34		16 04		16 34	
Tame Bridge Parkway	d	11 47	12 07	12 21	12 37	12 47	13 07	13 21	13 37	13 47	14 07	14 21	14 37	14 47	15 07	15 21	15 37	15 47	16 07	16 21	16 37	16 48
Hamstead	d		12 10		12 40		13 10		13 40		14 10		14 40		15 10		15 40		16 10		16 40	
Perry Barr	d		12 13		12 43		13 13		13 43		14 13		14 43		15 13		15 43		16 14		16 43	
Witton	d		12 15		12 45		13 15		13 45		14 15		14 45		15 15		15 45		16 16		16 45	
Aston	d		12 18		12 48		13 18		13 48		14 18		14 48		15 18		15 48		16 19		16 48	
Duddeston	d		12 20		12 50		13 20		13 50		14 20		14 50		15 20		15 50		16 21		16 50	
Birmingham New Street 12	a	12 02	12 27	12 37	12 54	13 02	13 27	13 37	13 54	14 02	14 27	14 37	14 55	15 02	15 27	15 37	15 54	16 02	16 28	16 37	16 54	17 03
Wolverhampton 7 68	a		13 05		13 32		14 05		14 31		15 05		15 31		16 05		16 31		17 05		17 31	

		LM	LM 1 B	LM	LM 1 A	LM	LM 1 B	LM	LM 1 A	LM	LM 1 B	LM	LM 1 A	LM	LM 1	LM 1	LM 1	LM	LM 1	LM 1	LM 1 C	LM	LM
Rugeley Trent Valley	d		16 47		17 14		17 47		18 14		18 47		19 14		20 03	20 33	20 57		21 33	22 00	22 33	23 04	
Rugeley Town	d		16 50		17 17		17 50		18 17		18 50		19 17		20 06	20 36	21 00		21 36	22 03	22 36	23 07	
Hednesford	d		16 57		17 23		17 57		18 23		18 57		19 24		20 13	20 43	21 07		21 43	22 10	22 43	23 14	
Cannock	d		17 00		17 27		18 00		18 27		19 00		19 27		20 16	20 46	21 10		21 46	22 13	22 46	23 17	
Landywood	d		17 03		17 30		18 03		18 30		19 03		19 30		20 19	20 49	21 13		21 49	22 16	22 49	23 20	
Bloxwich North	d		17 08		17 34		18 08		18 34		19 08		19 35		20 24	20 54	21 18		21 54	22 21	22 54	23 25	
Bloxwich	d		17 10		17 36		18 10		18 36		19 10		19 37		20 26	20 56	21 20		21 56	22 23	22 56	23 27	
Walsall	a		17 15		17 42		18 15		18 42		19 15		19 42		20 31	21 02	21 26		22 01	22 28	23 01	23 32	
	d	17 01	17 16	17 31	17 42	18 01	18 16	18 31	18 42	19 01	19 16	19 31	19 43	20 00	20 32	21 03	21 27	21 31	22 05	22 29	23 02	23 33	23 40
Bescot Stadium	d	17 04		17 34		18 04		18 34		19 04		19 34		20 04	20 35	21 06		21 34	22 08		23 05		23 43
Tame Bridge Parkway	d	17 07	17 21	17 37	17 47	18 07	18 21	18 37	18 47	19 07	19 21	19 37	19 48	20 07	20 38	21 09	21 32	21 37	22 11	22 34	23 08	23 38	23 46
Hamstead	d	17 10		17 40		18 10		18 40		19 10		19 41		20 11	20 41	21 12		21 40	22 14		23 11		23 49
Perry Barr	d	17 13		17 43		18 13		18 43		19 13		19 44		20 14	20 44	21 15		21 43	22 17		23 14		23 52
Witton	d	17 15		17 45		18 15		18 45		19 15		19 47		20 17	20 46	21 17		21 45	22 19		23 16		23 54
Aston	d	17 18		17 48		18 18		18 48		19 18		19 49		20 20	20 49	21 20		21 48	22 22		23 19		23 57
Duddeston	d	17 20		17 50		18 20		18 50		19 20		19 52		20 23	20 51	21 22		21 51	22 24		23 21		23 59
Birmingham New Street 12	a	17 27	17 37	17 54	18 02	18 27	18 37	18 54	19 03	19 27	19 37	19 57	20 03	20 27	20 56	21 28	21 45	21 55	22 29	22 47	23 28	23 49	00 06
Wolverhampton 7 68	a	18 05		18 31		19 05		19 32		20 07		20 31		21 06	21 29	22 05		22 32	23 06				

Sundays
15 December to 10 May

		LM	LM 1	LM	LM 1	LM	LM 1	LM	LM 1	LM	LM 1	LM	LM 1	LM	LM 1	LM	LM 1	LM	LM 1	LM	LM 1	LM	LM 1
Rugeley Trent Valley	d		09 41		10 41		11 41		12 41		13 41		14 41		15 41		16 42		17 46		18 46		19 48
Rugeley Town	d		09 44		10 44		11 44		12 44		13 44		14 44		15 44		16 45		17 49		18 49		19 51
Hednesford	d		09 51		10 51		11 51		12 51		13 51		14 51		15 51		16 52		17 56		18 56		19 58
Cannock	d		09 54		10 54		11 54		12 54		13 54		14 54		15 54		16 55		17 59		18 59		20 01
Landywood	d		09 57		10 57		11 57		12 57		13 57		14 57		15 57		16 58		18 02		19 02		20 04
Bloxwich North	d		10 02		11 02		12 02		13 02		14 02		15 02		16 02		17 03		18 07		19 07		20 09
Bloxwich	d		10 04		11 04		12 04		13 04		14 04		15 04		16 04		17 05		18 09		19 09		20 11
Walsall	a		10 10		11 10		12 10		13 10		14 10		15 10		16 10		17 11		18 15		19 15		20 16
	d	09 28	10 11	10 30	11 11	11 31	12 11	12 31	13 11	13 31	14 11	14 31	15 11	15 30	16 11	16 31	17 12	17 31	18 16	18 31	19 16	19 29	20 17
Bescot Stadium	d	09 32		10 34		11 35		12 35		13 35		14 35		15 34		16 35		17 35		18 35		19 33	
Tame Bridge Parkway	d	09 35	10 16	10 37	11 16	11 38	12 16	12 38	13 16	13 38	14 16	14 38	15 16	15 37	16 16	16 38	17 17	17 38	18 22	18 38	19 22	19 36	20 22
Hamstead	d	09 38		10 40		11 41		12 41		13 41		14 41		15 40		16 41		17 41		18 41		19 39	
Perry Barr	d	09 41		10 43		11 44		12 44		13 44		14 44		15 43		16 44		17 44		18 44		19 42	
Witton	d	09 43		10 45		11 46		12 46		13 46		14 46		15 45		16 46		17 46		18 46		19 44	
Aston	d	09 46		10 48		11 49		12 49		13 49		14 49		15 48		16 49		17 49		18 49		19 48	
Duddeston	d	09 49		10 51		11 52		12 52		13 52		14 52		15 51		16 52		17 52		18 52		19 51	
Birmingham New Street 12	a	09 53	10 31	10 55	11 32	11 56	12 31	12 56	13 34	13 56	14 30	14 56	15 30	15 57	16 31	16 57	17 31	17 56	18 37	18 56	19 38	19 55	20 36
Wolverhampton 7 68	a	10 31		11 30		12 27		13 29		14 32		15 32		16 32		17 32		18 32		19 32		20 32	

A To London Euston
B To Birmingham International
C 1 from Hednesford

For connections from Stafford refer to Table T67

Table T070-R

Sundays
15 December to 10 May

Rugeley and Walsall - Birmingham

		LM	LM 1	LM	LM 1 A	LM	LM	LM
Rugeley Trent Valley	d		20 41		21 50		22 51	
Rugeley Town	d		20 44		21 53		22 54	
Hednesford	d		20 51		22 00		23 01	
Cannock	d		20 54		22 03		23 04	
Landywood	d		20 57		22 06		23 07	
Bloxwich North	d		21 02		22 11		23 12	
Bloxwich	d		21 04		22 13		23 14	
Walsall	a		21 10		22 19		23 20	
	d	20 31	21 11	21 32	22 20	22 32	23 21	23 31
Bescot Stadium	d	20 35		21 36		22 36		23 35
Tame Bridge Parkway	d	20 38	21 16	21 38	22 25	22 38	23 26	23 38
Hamstead	d	20 41		21 42		22 42		23 41
Perry Barr	d	20 44		21 45		22 45		23 44
Witton	d	20 46		21 47		22 47		23 46
Aston	d	20 49		21 49		22 49		23 49
Duddeston	d	20 52		21 52		22 52		23 52
Birmingham New Street 12	a	20 57	21 36	21 56	22 40	22 56	23 39	23 56
Wolverhampton 7 68	a	21 32		22 33		23 32		

A To Northampton

For connections from Stafford refer to Table T67

AVAILABLE FROM MP Middleton Press

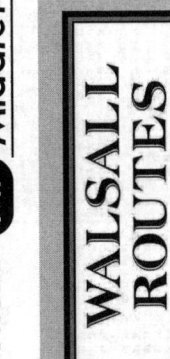

Table T071-F

Mondays to Fridays

16 December to 15 May

Stratford-upon-Avon, Marylebone and Leamington Spa - Birmingham - Stourbridge, Worcester and Hereford

Miles	Miles	Miles			CH MX ◇	CH MX ◇	LM	LM	GW	LM	LM	LM	LM		LM	GW	LM	LM	CH	LM	GW ◇1 ⊼	LM	CH		CH
—	0	—	**Stratford-upon-Avon**	d																			06 06		
—	1	—	Stratford-upon-Avon Parkway	d																			06 10		
—	2¾	—	Wilmcote	d																			06 14		
—	6½	—	Wootton Wawen	d																					
—	8¾	—	Henley-in-Arden	d																					
—	11¼	—	Danzey	d																					
—	13	—	Wood End	d																					
—	14¼	—	The Lakes	d																					
—	15	—	Earlswood (West Midlands)	d																					
—	16	—	Wythall	d																					
—	17	—	Whitlocks End	d													06 27	06 36							
—	18	—	Shirley	d													06 29	06 38							
—	19¼	—	Yardley Wood	d													06 32	06 41							
—	20½	—	Hall Green	d													06 35	06 44							
—	21	—	Spring Road	d													06 38	06 46							
—	—	—	**London Marylebone** [10] ⊖115	d																					
—	—	—	Banbury	d		00 03													06 04						
—	—	0	**Leamington Spa** [8]	a		00 20													06 24				06 46		
—	—	—		d		00 21	05 34					05 47	06 13						06 25			06 31			06 51
—	—	2	Warwick	d	00 03	00 25						05 52							06 30			06 36			06 56
—	—	3¼	Warwick Parkway	d	00 07	00 29						05 55							06 33			06 39			
—	—	6	Hatton	d								05 59										06 43			07a03
—	—	10¼	Lapworth	d								06 04										06 48			
—	—	12¾	Dorridge	d	00 18					05 40	05 53	06 09							06 44			06 54			
—	—	14¾	Widney Manor	d						05 45	05 58	06 13										06 58			
—	—	16¼	Solihull	d	00 24	00 41				05 48	06 02	06 17							06 50			07 02			
—	—	18	Olton	d						05 51	06 05	06 20										07 05			
—	—	19	Acocks Green	d						05 54	06 08	06 22										07 08			
—	22	20	Tyseley	d						05 57		06 25					06 41	06 49				07 10			
—	23	21	Small Heath	d						05 59		06 27					06 43	06 51				07 13			
—	24	—	Bordesley	d																					
—	24¾	—	**Birmingham Moor Street**	d	00a36	00a52				06 04	06 15	06 33					06 48	06 56	07 00			07 19			
—	25¼	—	**Birmingham Snow Hill** ⇌	a						06 06	06 17	06 37					06 50	07 00	07 07			07 21			
—	—	—		d						06 07							06 53	07 03				07 23			
—	26	—	Jewellery Quarter ⇌	d						06 10							06 55	07 05				07 25			
—	28½	—	The Hawthorns ⇌	d						06 14							06 59	07 09				07 29			
—	29	—	Smethwick Galton Bridge [7]	d						06 17							07 02	07 12				07 32			
—	—	—	**Coventry**	a			05 52						06 27												
—	—	—	**Birmingham Intl.** 68 ✈	a																					
0	—	24	**Birmingham New Street** [12] 68	a																					
—	—	—		d											06 59					07 20					
—	30¼	30¼	Langley Green	d						06 20							07 05					07 35			
—	32¼	—	Rowley Regis	d						06 23							07 09	07 18				07 39			
—	33½	—	Old Hill	d						06 26							07 12					07 42			
—	34¾	—	Cradley Heath	d						06 29							07 15	07 23				07 45			
—	36¼	—	Lye	d						06 32							07 18					07 48			
—	37¼	—	**Stourbridge Junction** [2]	d						06 36							07 22	07 29				07 52			
—	39¼	—	Hagley	d						06 39							07 26					07 56			
—	41	—	Blakedown	d						06 42							07 29					07 59			
—	44¼	—	**Kidderminster**	d						06 47							07 34	07a37				08 04			
—	47¾	—	Hartlebury	d													07 39					08 09			
2½	—	—	University	d											07 06					07 26					
10½	—	—	Barnt Green	d																07 39					
13	—	—	Bromsgrove 69	d											07 22					07 44					
19¼	53½	—	Droitwich Spa	d						06 58					07 31		07 47			07 54		08 17			
25	—	—	**Worcester Shrub Hill** [7]	a																08 01		08 24			
—	—	—		d				05 56	06 22							07 53				08 05	08 20	08 32			
25¾	58¾	—	**Worcester Foregate Street** [7]	a				05 58	06 24	07 09					07 41	07 56	07 57			08 07	08 22	08 34			
—	—	—		d				05 59							07 42					08 09	08 23				
32½	—	—	Malvern Link	d				06 08							07 52					08 18	08 32				
33¾	—	—	**Great Malvern**	a				06 10							07 55					08 20	08 34				
—	—	—		d				06 11							08 00										
36½	—	—	Colwall	d				06 16							08 06										
40¾	—	—	Ledbury	a				06 23							08 13										
—	—	—		d				06 25							08 13										
54½	—	—	**Hereford** [7]	a				06 49							08 29										

Table T071-F

Mondays to Fridays

16 December to 15 May

Stratford-upon-Avon, Marylebone and Leamington Spa - Birmingham - Stourbridge, Worcester and Hereford

		LM	LM	LM	LM	LM	LM	LM	XC ◇1 ⊼		CH ◇	LM	XC ◇1 ⊼	LM	LM	LM	GW ◇1 ⊼	LM	LM		LM	LM	LM	CH ◇	CH ◇
Stratford-upon-Avon	d	06 26				06 52						07 20		07 26					07 41						07 33
Stratford-upon-Avon Parkway	d	06 30				06 56						07 24		07 30					07 45						07 37
Wilmcote	d	06 33				06 59													07 48						07 41
Wootton Wawen	d	06x37				07x03													07x52						
Henley-in-Arden	d	06 41				07 07						07 35							07 56						
Danzey	d	06x45				07x11													07x59						
Wood End	d	06x49				07x15													08x02						
The Lakes	d	06x51				07x17													08x05						
Earlswood (West Midlands)	d	06 54				07 20						07 43							08 08						
Wythall	d	06 57				07 23						07 46							08 11						
Whitlocks End	d	07 00				07 26	07 33					07 49				08 07			08 15		08 23				
Shirley	d	07 03				07 29	07 36					07 52				08 10			08 18		08 26				
Yardley Wood	d	07 07				07 32	07 38					07 55				08 12			08 21		08 28				
Hall Green	d	07 10				07 35	07 42					07 58				08 15			08 24		08 32				
Spring Road	d	07 13				07 37	07 44					08 01				08 17			08 27		08 34				
London Marylebone [10] ⊖115	d										06 05													06 17	
Banbury	d								06 57		07 03		07 26											07 49	
Leamington Spa [8]	a								07 14		07 20		07 44											08 08	08 08
	d		07 00					07 08	07 15		07 21		07 45		07 47							08 00	08 02	08 08	
Warwick	d							07 13			07 26				07 51							08 04		08 13	
Warwick Parkway	d							07 16			07 29				07 54							08 07			
Hatton	d							07 20			07 35				07 58							08 11		08a20	
Lapworth	d							07 25							08 03							08 16			
Dorridge	d			07 09				07 34			07 43			07 56	08 07			08 11				08 20			
Widney Manor	d			07 14				07 38			07 47			08 01				08 16				08 25			
Solihull	d			07 17				07 42			07 51			08 04	08 12			08 19				08 28			
Olton	d			07 20				07 45			07 55			08 08				08 22				08 32			
Acocks Green	d			07 23				07 48						08 11				08 25				08 35			
Tyseley	d	07 16		07 26		07 41		07 50						08 14		08 21			08 30			08 39			
Small Heath	d	07 18		07 28		07 43		07 53								08 23			08 32						
Bordesley	d																								
Birmingham Moor Street	d	07 24		07 33		07 48	07 52	07 58			08 03	08 08		08 19	08 24	08 29		08 34	08 38		08 42	08 46			
Birmingham Snow Hill ⇌	a	07 26		07 35		07 50	07 54	08 00			08 10	08 10		08 22	08 26	08 31		08 36	08 40		08 44	08 48			
	d			07 37		07 53		08 02				08 13		08 23		08 33		08 39			08 45				
Jewellery Quarter ⇌	d			07 39		07 55		08 04				08 15		08 25		08 35		08 41			08 48				
The Hawthorns ⇌	d			07 43		07 59		08 08				08 19		08 29		08 39		08 45			08 52				
Smethwick Galton Bridge [7]	d			07 46		08 02		08 11				08 22		08 32		08 42		08 48			08 55				
Coventry	a		07 14						07 26														08 17		
Birmingham Intl. 68 ✈	a								07 36																
Birmingham New Street [12] 68	a								07 48				08 12												
	d				08 00																				
Langley Green	d					08 05		08 14								08 45									
Rowley Regis	d			07 52		08 08		08 18				08 28		08 38		08 48		08 54			09 00				
Old Hill	d					08 12		08 21								08 52									
Cradley Heath	d			07 57		08 15		08 24				08 33		08 43		08 55		09 00			09 05				
Lye	d					08 18		08 27								08 58									
Stourbridge Junction [2]	d			08a03		08 22		08 31				08a40		08a48		09 02		09 07			09a10				
Hagley	d					08 26		08 35								09 06		09 10							
Blakedown	d					08 29		08 38								09 09		09 13							
Kidderminster	d					08 34		08a43								09a13		09 18							
Hartlebury	d					08 39																			
University	d				08 06																				
Barnt Green	d				08 17																				
Bromsgrove 69	d				08 22																				
Droitwich Spa	d				08 32	08 47												09 30							
Worcester Shrub Hill [7]	a																	09 38							
	d																09 15								
Worcester Foregate Street [7]	a				08 40	08 58											09 17								
	d				08 41												09 18								
Malvern Link	d				08 51												09 27								
Great Malvern	a				08 53												09 29								
	d				08 54																				
Colwall	d				08 59																				
Ledbury	a				09 06																				
	d				09 07																				
Hereford [7]	a				09 22																				

Table T071-F

Mondays to Fridays
16 December to 15 May

Stratford-upon-Avon, Marylebone and Leamington Spa - Birmingham - Stourbridge, Worcester and Hereford

Station		XC ◇1 🍴	LM	LM	CH ◇	LM	GW ◇1 🍴	LM	CH	LM	XC ◇1 🍴	LM	LM	GW	LM	LM	CH ◇	LM	XC ◇1 🍴	CH ◇	CH	CH	XC ◇1 🍴
Stratford-upon-Avon	d									08 26											09 00		
Stratford-upon-Avon Parkway	d									08 30											09 04		
Wilmcote	d									08 33											09 07		
Wootton Wawen	d									08x37													
Henley-in-Arden	d									08 41													
Danzey	d									08x45													
Wood End	d									08x49													
The Lakes	d									08x51													
Earlswood (West Midlands)	d									08 54													
Wythall	d									08 57													
Whitlocks End	d					08 37				09 00						09 19							
Shirley	d					08 40				09 03						09 22							
Yardley Wood	d					08 42				09 05						09 24							
Hall Green	d					08 45				09 09						09 27							
Spring Road	d					08 47				09 11						09 29							
London Marylebone 10 ⊖115	d				07 11												07 48			08 14			
Banbury	d	07 57			08 07						08 28						08 50		08 57	09 08			09 33
Leamington Spa 8	a	08 14			08 24						08 44						09 07		09 14	09 25	09 37		09 50
	d	08 15			08 25				08 32		08 50	09 00					09 08		09 15	09 26		09 40	09 51
Warwick	d				08 29				08 38								09 12			09 30		09 45	
Warwick Parkway	d				08 33												09 16			09 34			
Hatton	d								08 44													09a52	
Lapworth	d								08 50														
Dorridge	d			08 25				08 46	08 55				09 10				09 26	09 30					
Widney Manor	d			08 30				08 51					09 15					09 34					
Solihull	d			08 33	08 45			08 54	09 01				09 18				09 31	09 38		09 46			
Olton	d			08 36				08 57					09 21					09 41					
Acocks Green	d			08 39				09 00					09 24					09 43					
Tyseley	d			08 43		08 51		09 02								09 32							
Small Heath	d			08 45		08 52		09 05								09 36							
Bordesley	d																						
Birmingham Moor Street	d			08 50	08 54	08 58		09 09	09a14	09 18			09 33			09 40	09a42	09 50		09 55			
Birmingham Snow Hill 🚊	a			08 52	08 59	09 01		09 12		09 20			09 35			09 42		09 53		10 02			
	d			08 53		09 01		09 13		09 23			09 36			09 43		09 54					
Jewellery Quarter 🚊	d			08 56		09 04		09 15		09 25			09 38			09 46		09 56					
The Hawthorns 🚊	d			09 00		09 08		09 19		09 29			09 42			09 50		10 00					
Smethwick Galton Bridge 7	d			09 03		09 11		09 22		09 32			09 45			09 53		10 03					
Coventry	a	08 26										09 15							09 26				
Birmingham Intl. 68 ✈	a	08 36																	09 36				
Birmingham New Street 12 68	a	08 48									09 18								09 49				10 18
	d		08 50												09 50								
Langley Green	d			09 06						09 35								10 06					
Rowley Regis	d			09 09		09 17		09 28		09 38			09 50			09 58		10 09					
Old Hill	d			09 12						09 42								10 13					
Cradley Heath	d			09 16		09 22		09 33		09 45			09 55			10 03		10 16					
Lye	d			09 19						09 48								10 19					
Stourbridge Junction 2	d			09a22		09 29		09 39		09a52			10 01			10 09		10a22					
Hagley	d					09 33							10 05			10 12							
Blakedown	d					09 36							10 08										
Kidderminster	d					09a40		09 47					10a12			10 18							
Hartlebury	d							09 52															
University	d		08 56												09 56								
Barnt Green	d																						
Bromsgrove 69	d		09 12												10 12								
Droitwich Spa	d		09 22					10 00							10 22	10 30							
Worcester Shrub Hill 7	a																						
	d						09 57							10 13									
Worcester Foregate Street 7	a		09 31				09 59	10 09						10 15	10 30	10 39							
	d		09 32				10 00							10 16	10 32	10 42							
Malvern Link	d		09 42				10 09							10 25	10 42	10 52							
Great Malvern	a		09 44				10 11							10 27	10 44	10 57							
	d		09 45												10 45								
Colwall	d		09 50												10 50								
Ledbury	a		09 57												10 57								
	d		09 59												10 59								
Hereford 7	a		10 14												11 16								

Table T071-F

Mondays to Fridays
16 December to 15 May

Stratford-upon-Avon, Marylebone and Leamington Spa - Birmingham - Stourbridge, Worcester and Hereford

Station		LM	GW ◇1 🍴	LM	LM	LM	CH ◇	LM	XC ◇1 🍴	LM	LM	GW ◇1 🍴	LM	CH ◇	LM	LM	CH	LM	XC ◇1 🍴	LM	CH ◇	LM
Stratford-upon-Avon	d				09 26								10 03					10 26				
Stratford-upon-Avon Parkway	d				09 30								10 07					10 30				
Wilmcote	d				09 33													10 33				
Wootton Wawen	d				09x37													10x37				
Henley-in-Arden	d				09 41													10 41				
Danzey	d				09x45													10x45				
Wood End	d				09x49													10x49				
The Lakes	d				09x51													10x51				
Earlswood (West Midlands)	d				09 54													10 54				
Wythall	d				09 57													10 57				
Whitlocks End	d	09 39			10 00						10 19				10 40			11 00				
Shirley	d	09 41			10 03						10 22				10 42			11 03				
Yardley Wood	d	09 44			10 05						10 24				10 45			11 05				
Hall Green	d	09 47			10 09						10 27				10 48			11 09				
Spring Road	d	09 50			10 11						10 29				10 51			11 11				
London Marylebone 10 ⊖115	d						08 37							09 10							09 40	
Banbury	d						09 40		09 57					10 08					10 28		10 43	
Leamington Spa 8	a						09 57		10 14					10 24					10 44		11 00	
	d						09 58	10 02	10 15					10 25			10 32		10 50		11 01	11 02
Warwick	d						10 03										10 38				11 05	
Warwick Parkway	d						10 07							10 32							11 09	
Hatton	d																10 44					
Lapworth	d																10 50					
Dorridge	d			09 46		10 09	10 18						10 29			10 46	10 55			11 09	11 19	
Widney Manor	d			09 51		10 14							10 33			10 51				11 14		
Solihull	d			09 54		10 17	10 24						10 37	10 45		10 54	11 01			11 17	11 25	
Olton	d			09 57		10 20							10 40			10 57				11 20		
Acocks Green	d			10 00		10 23							10 43			11 00				11 23		
Tyseley	d	09 53		10 02							10 32					11 02						
Small Heath	d	09 55		10 05							10 35					11 05						
Bordesley	d																					
Birmingham Moor Street	d	10 00		10 09	10 18	10 29	10a35				10 39		10 49	10 54	10 59	11 09	11a14	11 18		11 29	11 34	
Birmingham Snow Hill 🚊	a	10 02		10 12	10 20	10 32					10 42		10 52	11 01	11 01	11 12		11 20		11 32	11 41	
	d	10 03		10 13	10 23	10 33					10 43		10 53		11 03	11 13		11 23		11 33		
Jewellery Quarter 🚊	d	10 05		10 15	10 25	10 35					10 45		10 55		11 05	11 15		11 25		11 35		
The Hawthorns 🚊	d	10 09		10 19	10 29	10 39					10 49		10 59		11 09	11 19		11 29		11 39		
Smethwick Galton Bridge 7	d	10 12		10 22	10 32	10 42					10 52		11 02		11 12	11 22		11 32		11 42		
Coventry	a							10 16	10 26													11 16
Birmingham Intl. 68 ✈	a								10 36													
Birmingham New Street 12 68	a								10 48										11 18			
	d									10 50												
Langley Green	d				10 35								11 05					11 35				
Rowley Regis	d	10 18		10 28	10 38	10 48					10 58		11 08		11 18	11 28		11 38		11 48		
Old Hill	d				10 42								11 12					11 42				
Cradley Heath	d	10 23		10 33	10 45	10 53					11 03		11 15		11 23	11 33		11 45		11 53		
Lye	d				10 48								11 18					11 48				
Stourbridge Junction 2	d	10 29		10 39	10a52	10 59					11 09		11a22		11 29	11 39		11a52		11 59		
Hagley	d	10 33				11 03					11 12				11 33					12 03		
Blakedown	d	10 36				11 06									11 36					12 06		
Kidderminster	d	10a40		10 47		11a10					11 18				11a40	11 47				12a10		
Hartlebury	d			10 52												11 52						
University	d									10 56												
Barnt Green	d																					
Bromsgrove 69	d									11 12												
Droitwich Spa	d			11 00						11 22	11 30					12 00						
Worcester Shrub Hill 7	a										11 38											
	d		11 01									11 57										
Worcester Foregate Street 7	a		11 03	11 11						11 30		11 59				12 09						
	d		11 04							11 31		12 00										
Malvern Link	d		11 13							11 41		12 09										
Great Malvern	a		11 15							11 44		12 12										
	d									11 46		12 13										
Colwall	d									11 51		12 19										
Ledbury	a									11 58		12 26										
	d									11 58		12 27										
Hereford 7	a									12 15		12 43										

Table T071-F

Mondays to Fridays

16 December to 15 May

Stratford-upon-Avon, Marylebone and Leamington Spa - Birmingham - Stourbridge, Worcester and Hereford

		CH	XC	GW	LM	LM	LM		CH	CH	XC	LM	LM	LM	LM	CH	LM		XC	LM	LM	LM	CH	LM	GW
		◇	■ 1 ✠	◇					◇	◇	◇ 1 ✠					◇			◇ 1 ✠				◇		◇ 1 ✠
Stratford-upon-Avon	d	10 40					11 03							11 26								12 03			
Stratford-upon-Avon Parkway	d	10 44					11 07							11 30								12 07			
Wilmcote	d	10 47												11 33											
Wootton Wawen	d													11x37											
Henley-in-Arden	d													11 41											
Danzey	d													11x45											
Wood End	d													11x49											
The Lakes	d													11x51											
Earlswood (West Midlands)	d													11 54											
Wythall	d													11 57											
Whitlocks End	d					11 19						11 40		12 00							12 19			12 40	
Shirley	d					11 22						11 42		12 03							12 22			12 42	
Yardley Wood	d					11 24						11 45		12 05							12 24			12 45	
Hall Green	d					11 27						11 48		12 09							12 27			12 48	
Spring Road	d					11 29						11 51		12 11							12 29			12 51	
London Marylebone 10 ⊖115	d								10 10	09 43						10 40							11 10		
Banbury	d		10 57						11 07	11 10	11 31					11 41			11 57				12 07		
Leamington Spa 8	a	11 13	11 14						11 25	11 30	11 47					11 59			12 14				12 25		
	d		11 15						11 26	11 32	11 48					11 59	12 02		12 15				12 26		
Warwick	d									11 37						12 03									
Warwick Parkway	d								11 33							12 07							12 33		
Hatton	d									11a44															
Lapworth	d																								
Dorridge	d						11 29						11 46		12 09	12 17						12 29			
Widney Manor	d						11 33						11 51		12 14							12 33			
Solihull	d						11 37		11 45				11 54		12 17	12 23						12 37	12 45		
Olton	d						11 40						11 57		12 20							12 40			
Acocks Green	d						11 43						12 00		12 23							12 43			
Tyseley	d					11 32							12 02								12 32				
Small Heath	d					11 35							12 05								12 35				
Bordesley	d																								
Birmingham Moor Street	d					11 39	11 49		11a56			11 59	12 09	12 18	12 29	12 34					12 39	12 49	12a56	12 59	
Birmingham Snow Hill ⛴	a					11 42	11 52					12 01	12 12	12 20	12 32	12 41					12 42	12 52		13 01	
	d					11 43	11 53					12 03	12 13	12 23	12 33						12 43	12 53		13 03	
Jewellery Quarter ⛴	d					11 45	11 55					12 05	12 15	12 25	12 35						12 45	12 55		13 05	
The Hawthorns ⛴	d					11 49	11 59					12 09	12 19	12 29	12 39						12 49	12 59		13 09	
Smethwick Galton Bridge 7	d					11 52	12 02					12 12	12 22	12 32	12 42						12 52	13 02		13 12	
Coventry	a		11 26														12 16		12 26						
Birmingham Intl. 68 ✈	a		11 36																12 36						
Birmingham New Street 12 68	a		11 48								12 18								12 48						
	d				11 50															12 50					
Langley Green	d						12 05							12 35								13 05			
Rowley Regis	d					11 58	12 08					12 18	12 28	12 38	12 48						12 58	13 08		13 18	
Old Hill	d						12 12							12 42								13 12			
Cradley Heath	d					12 03	12 15					12 23	12 33	12 45	12 53						13 03	13 15		13 23	
Lye	d						12 18							12 48								13 18			
Stourbridge Junction 2	d					12 09	12a22					12 29	12 39	12a52	12 59						13 09	13a22		13 29	
Hagley	d					12 12						12 33			13 03						13 12			13 33	
Blakedown	d											12 36			13 06									13 36	
Kidderminster	d					12 18						12a40	12 47		13a10						13 18			13a40	
Hartlebury	d												12 52												
University	d				11 56															12 56					
Barnt Green	d																								
Bromsgrove 69	d				12 12															13 12					
Droitwich Spa	d				12 22	12 30							13 00							13 22	13 30				
Worcester Shrub Hill 7	a					12 38							13 10												
	d			12 14									13 13												13 55
Worcester Foregate Street 7	a			12 16	12 30								13 15							13 30	13 40				13 57
	d			12 17	12 32								13 15							13 32					13 58
Malvern Link	d			12 26	12 42								13 24							13 42					14 07
Great Malvern	a			12 28	12 44								13 30							13 44					14 10
	d				12 45															13 45					14 11
Colwall	d				12 50															13 51					14 17
Ledbury	a				12 57															13 57					14 24
	d				12 59															13 59					14 25
Hereford 7	a				13 15															14 15					14 41

Table T071-F

Mondays to Fridays

16 December to 15 May

Stratford-upon-Avon, Marylebone and Leamington Spa - Birmingham - Stourbridge, Worcester and Hereford

		LM	GW		CH	LM	XC	LM	CH	LM	CH	XC	LM		LM	LM	CH	CH	XC	LM	LM	LM	LM		CH
			◇				◇ 1 ✠		◇		◇	◇ 1 ✠					◇	◇	■ 1 ✠						◇
Stratford-upon-Avon	d					12 26					12 43					13 03						13 26			
Stratford-upon-Avon Parkway	d					12 30					12 47					13 07						13 30			
Wilmcote	d					12 33					12 50											13 33			
Wootton Wawen	d					12x37																13x37			
Henley-in-Arden	d					12 41																13 41			
Danzey	d					12x45																13x45			
Wood End	d					12x49																13x49			
The Lakes	d					12x51																13x51			
Earlswood (West Midlands)	d					12 54																13 54			
Wythall	d					12 57																13 57			
Whitlocks End	d					13 00									13 19					13 40		14 00			
Shirley	d					13 03									13 22					13 42		14 03			
Yardley Wood	d					13 05									13 24					13 45		14 05			
Hall Green	d					13 09									13 27					13 48		14 09			
Spring Road	d					13 11									13 29					13 51		14 11			
London Marylebone 10 ⊖115	d								11 40								12 10	11 43							12 40
Banbury	d						12 28		12 40			12 57					13 08	13 10	13 31						13 40
Leamington Spa 8	a						12 44		12 57		13 13	13 14					13 25	13 30	13 48						13 57
	d				12 32		12 50		12 58	13 01		13 15					13 26	13 32	13 50						13 58
Warwick	d				12 38				13 02									13 37							14 02
Warwick Parkway	d								13 06								13 32								14 06
Hatton	d				12 44													13a44							
Lapworth	d				12 50																				
Dorridge	d	12 46			12 55			13 09	13 16							13 29					13 46		14 09		14 16
Widney Manor	d	12 51						13 14								13 33					13 51		14 14		
Solihull	d	12 54			13 01			13 17	13 22							13 37	13 45				13 54		14 17		14 22
Olton	d	12 57						13 20								13 40					13 57		14 20		
Acocks Green	d	13 00						13 23								13 43					14 00		14 23		
Tyseley	d	13 02													13 32						14 02				
Small Heath	d	13 05													13 35						14 05				
Bordesley	d																								
Birmingham Moor Street	d	13 09			13a14	13 18		13 29	13 34						13 39	13 49	13a56			13 59	14 09	14 18	14 29		14 34
Birmingham Snow Hill ⛴	a	13 12				13 20		13 32	13 41						13 42	13 52				14 01	14 12	14 20	14 32		14 41
	d	13 13				13 23		13 33							13 43	13 53				14 03	14 13	14 23	14 33		
Jewellery Quarter ⛴	d	13 15				13 25		13 35							13 45	13 55				14 05	14 15	14 25	14 35		
The Hawthorns ⛴	d	13 19				13 29		13 39							13 49	13 59				14 09	14 19	14 29	14 39		
Smethwick Galton Bridge 7	d	13 22				13 32		13 42							13 52	14 02				14 12	14 22	14 32	14 42		
Coventry	a									13 17		13 26													
Birmingham Intl. 68 ✈	a											13 36													
Birmingham New Street 12 68	a						13 18					13 48							14 18						
	d												13 50												
Langley Green	d					13 35										14 05						14 35			
Rowley Regis	d	13 28				13 38		13 48							13 58	14 08				14 18	14 28	14 38	14 48		
Old Hill	d					13 42										14 12						14 42			
Cradley Heath	d	13 33				13 45		13 53							14 03	14 15				14 23	14 33	14 45	14 53		
Lye	d					13 48										14 18						14 48			
Stourbridge Junction 2	d	13 39				13a52		13 59							14 09	14a22				14 29	14 39	14a52	14 59		
Hagley	d							14 03							14 12					14 33			15 03		
Blakedown	d							14 06												14 36			15 06		
Kidderminster	d	13 47						14a10							14 18					14a40	14 47		15a10		
Hartlebury	d	13 52																			14 52				
University	d												13 56												
Barnt Green	d																								
Bromsgrove 69	d												14 13												
Droitwich Spa	d	14 00											14 23		14 30						15 00				
Worcester Shrub Hill 7	a	14 08													14 40						15 10				
	d		14 13												14 45										
Worcester Foregate Street 7	a		14 15										14 31		14 47										
	d		14 16										14 32		14 47										
Malvern Link	d		14 25										14 42		14 56										
Great Malvern	a		14 29										14 44		14 59										
	d												14 45												
Colwall	d												14 50												
Ledbury	a												14 57												
	d												14 59												
Hereford 7	a												15 14												

Table T071-F

Mondays to Fridays

16 December to 15 May

Stratford-upon-Avon, Marylebone and Leamington Spa - Birmingham - Stourbridge, Worcester and Hereford

		LM	XC	LM	LM	LM	CH	LM	GW	GW	LM	CH	LM	XC	LM	CH	LM	CH	XC	LM	LM	LM	CH
			◇1				◇		◇1	◇				◇1		◇		◇	◇1				◇
Stratford-upon-Avon	d					14 03							14 26					14 40				15 03	
Stratford-upon-Avon Parkway	d					14 07							14 30					14 44				15 07	
Wilmcote	d												14 33					14 47					
Wootton Wawen	d												14x37										
Henley-in-Arden	d												14 41										
Danzey	d												14x45										
Wood End	d												14x49										
The Lakes	d												14x51										
Earlswood (West Midlands)	d												14 54										
Wythall	d												14 57										
Whitlocks End	d				14 19			14 40					15 00								15 19		
Shirley	d				14 22			14 42					15 03								15 22		
Yardley Wood	d				14 24			14 45					15 05								15 24		
Hall Green	d				14 27			14 48					15 09								15 27		
Spring Road	d				14 29			14 51					15 11								15 29		
London Marylebone 10 ⊖115	d						13 10									13 40							14 10
Banbury	d		13 57				14 07							14 31		14 40			14 57				15 07
Leamington Spa 8	a		14 14				14 25							14 47		14 57		15 13	15 14				15 24
	d	14 01	14 15				14 26					14 32		14 50		14 58	15 02		15 15				15 25
Warwick	d											14 38				15 02							
Warwick Parkway	d						14 33									15 06							15 30
Hatton	d											14 44											
Lapworth	d											14 50											
Dorridge	d					14 29					14 46	14 55			15 09	15 16						15 29	
Widney Manor	d					14 33					14 51				15 14							15 33	
Solihull	d					14 37	14 45				14 54	15 01			15 17	15 22						15 37	15 45
Olton	d					14 40					14 57				15 20							15 40	
Acocks Green	d					14 43					15 00				15 23							15 43	
Tyseley	d				14 32						15 02										15 32		
Small Heath	d				14 35						15 05										15 35		
Bordesley	d																						
Birmingham Moor Street	d				14 39	14 49	14a56	14 59			15 09	15a13	15 18		15 29	15 34					15 39	15 49	15a56
Birmingham Snow Hill	a				14 42	14 52		15 01			15 12		15 20		15 32	15 41					15 42	15 52	
	d				14 43	14 53		15 03			15 13		15 23		15 33						15 43	15 53	
Jewellery Quarter	d				14 45	14 55		15 05			15 15		15 25		15 35						15 45	15 55	
The Hawthorns	d				14 50	14 59		15 09			15 19		15 29		15 39						15 49	15 59	
Smethwick Galton Bridge 7	d				14 52	15 02		15 12			15 22		15 32		15 42						15 52	16 02	
Coventry	a	14 19	14 26														15 16		15 26				
Birmingham Intl. 68	a		14 36																15 36				
Birmingham New Street 12 68	a		14 48											15 18					15 48				
	d			14 50																15 50			
Langley Green	d					15 05							15 35									16 05	
Rowley Regis	d				14 58	15 08		15 18			15 28		15 38		15 48						15 58	16 08	
Old Hill	d					15 12							15 42									16 12	
Cradley Heath	d				15 03	15 15		15 23			15 33		15 45		15 53						16 03	16 15	
Lye	d					15 18							15 48									16 18	
Stourbridge Junction 2	d				15 09	15a22		15 29			15 39		15a52		15 59						16 08	16a22	
Hagley	d				15 12			15 33			15 43				16 03						16 12		
Blakedown	d							15 36			15 47				16 06						16 15		
Kidderminster	d				15 18			15a40			15 52				16a10						16 20		
Hartlebury	d										15 57												
University	d			14 56																15 56			
Barnt Green	d																						
Bromsgrove 69	d			15 13																16 12			
Droitwich Spa	d			15 23	15 30						16 06									16 21	16 31		
Worcester Shrub Hill 7	a										16 17												
	d								15 59	16 14	16 21												
Worcester Foregate Street 7	a			15 31	15 39				16 01	16 16	16 25									16 30	16 42		
	d			15 32					16 01	16 17										16 30			
Malvern Link	d			15 42					16 10	16 26										16 40			
Great Malvern	a			15 45					16 12	16 28										16 43			
	d			15 45																16 44			
Colwall	d			15 50																16 49			
Ledbury	a			15 57																16 57			
	d			15 59																16 59			
Hereford 7	a			16 14																17 15			

Table T071-F

Mondays to Fridays

16 December to 15 May

Stratford-upon-Avon, Marylebone and Leamington Spa - Birmingham - Stourbridge, Worcester and Hereford

		CH	XC	LM	LM	LM	LM	LM	CH	LM	XC	GW	LM	GW	LM	LM	LM	CH	LM	LM	GW	CH	LM
		◇	◇1						◇		◇1	◇1		◇1				◇			◇1		
Stratford-upon-Avon	d						15 26									16 03							16 26
Stratford-upon-Avon Parkway	d						15 30									16 07							16 30
Wilmcote	d						15 33																16 33
Wootton Wawen	d						15x37																16x37
Henley-in-Arden	d						15 41																16 41
Danzey	d						15x45																16x45
Wood End	d						15x49																16x49
The Lakes	d						15x51																16x51
Earlswood (West Midlands)	d						15 54																16 54
Wythall	d						15 57																16 57
Whitlocks End	d				15 40		16 00								16 19		16 40						17 00
Shirley	d				15 42		16 03								16 22		16 42						17 03
Yardley Wood	d				15 45		16 05								16 24		16 45						17 05
Hall Green	d				15 48		16 09								16 27		16 48						17 09
Spring Road	d				15 51		16 11								16 29		16 51						17 11
London Marylebone 10 ⊖115	d	13 43							14 40									15 10					
Banbury	d	15 10	15 28						15 42		15 57							16 09					
Leamington Spa 8	a	15 30	15 45						15 59		16 14							16 26					
	d	15 32	15 50						15 59	16 02	16 15							16 26				16 32	
Warwick	d	15 37							16 03													16 38	
Warwick Parkway	d								16 07									16 32					
Hatton	d	15a44																				16 44	
Lapworth	d																					16 50	
Dorridge	d					15 46		16 09	16 17							16 29				16 46		16 55	
Widney Manor	d					15 51		16 14								16 33				16 51			
Solihull	d					15 54		16 17	16 23							16 37		16 45		16 54		17 01	
Olton	d					15 57		16 20								16 40				16 57			
Acocks Green	d					16 00		16 23								16 43				17 00			
Tyseley	d					16 02									16 32		16 54			17 02			
Small Heath	d					16 05									16 35					17 05			
Bordesley	d																						
Birmingham Moor Street	d				15 59	16 09	16 18	16 29	16 34						16 39	16 49	16 59	16 55		17 09		17a14	17 19
Birmingham Snow Hill	a				16 01	16 12	16 20	16 32	16 41						16 42	16 52	17 01	17 02		17 12			17 21
	d				16 03	16 13	16 23	16 33							16 43	16 54	17 03			17 13			17 23
Jewellery Quarter	d				16 05	16 15	16 25	16 35							16 45	16 56	17 05			17 15			17 25
The Hawthorns	d				16 09	16 19	16 29	16 39							16 49	17 00	17 09			17 19			17 29
Smethwick Galton Bridge 7	d				16 12	16 22	16 32	16 42							16 52	17 03	17 12			17 22			17 32
Coventry	a									16 16	16 26												
Birmingham Intl. 68	a										16 36												
Birmingham New Street 12 68	a		16 17								16 48												
	d			16 20									16 50						17 20				
Langley Green	d						16 35									17 06							17 35
Rowley Regis	d				16 18	16 28	16 38	16 48							16 58	17 09	17 18			17 28			17 38
Old Hill	d						16 42									17 13							17 42
Cradley Heath	d				16 23	16 33	16 45	16 53							17 03	17 16	17 23			17 33			17 45
Lye	d						16 48									17 19							17 48
Stourbridge Junction 2	d				16 29	16 39	16a52	16 59							17 10	17a22	17 29			17 39			17a52
Hagley	d				16 33			17 03							17 13		17 33			17 43			
Blakedown	d				16 36			17 06							17 17		17 36			17 47			
Kidderminster	d				16a40	16 47		17a10							17 24		17a40			17 52			
Hartlebury	d					16 52									17 29								
University	d			16 26									16 56						17 26				
Barnt Green	d																						
Bromsgrove 69	d			16 42									17 12						17 42				
Droitwich Spa	d			16 52		17 00							17 22		17 37				17 52	18 04			
Worcester Shrub Hill 7	a			16 58									17 29		17 45				18 01	18 12			
	d			17 03								17 10	17 32	17 38					18 05		18 15		
Worcester Foregate Street 7	a			17 05		17 09						17 12	17 34	17 40					18 07		18 17		
	d			17 06									17 35						18 08		18 18		
Malvern Link	d			17 15									17 44						18 17		18 28		
Great Malvern	a			17 17									17 46						18 19		18 30		
	d												17 47						18 20				
Colwall	d												17 52						18 25				
Ledbury	a												17 59						18 32				
	d												18 00						18 32				
Hereford 7	a												18 17						18 47				

Table T071-F

Mondays to Fridays

16 December to 15 May

Stratford-upon-Avon, Marylebone and Leamington Spa - Birmingham - Stourbridge, Worcester and Hereford

		XC	LM	GW	LM	LM	LM	CH	LM	XC	LM	LM	CH	LM	GW	LM	CH	LM	XC	LM	LM	CH
		◇[1]						◇		◇[1]			◇		◇[1]		◇		◇[1]			◇
		🛒								🛒					🛒				🛒			
Stratford-upon-Avon	d																	17 27				
Stratford-upon-Avon Parkway	d																	17 31				
Wilmcote	d																	17 34				
Wootton Wawen	d																	17x39				
Henley-in-Arden	d																	17 43				
Danzey	d																	17x47				
Wood End	d																	17x50				
The Lakes	d																	17x53				
Earlswood (West Midlands)	d																	17 56				
Wythall	d																	17 58				
Whitlocks End	d		17 06				17 19									17 42		18 01				
Shirley	d		17 10				17 22									17 44		18 04				
Yardley Wood	d		17 13				17 24									17 47		18 07				
Hall Green	d		17 16				17 27									17 50		18 10				
Spring Road	d		17 18				17 29									17 52		18 12				
London Marylebone [10] ⊖115	d							15 40					16 15				16 21					16 47
Banbury	d	16 28						16 40		16 58			17 08				17 24		17 32			17 47
Leamington Spa [8]	a	16 44						16 57		17 14			17 25				17 41		17 50			18 04
	d	16 50						16 58	17 01	17 15			17 26				17 41		17 51	18 00		18 04
Warwick	d							17 02														18 08
Warwick Parkway	d							17 06					17 33				17 47					18 12
Hatton	d																					
Lapworth	d																					
Dorridge	d					17 09		17 16				17 28					17 57				18 04	18 22
Widney Manor	d					17 14						17 33									18 08	
Solihull	d					17 17		17 22				17 36	17 45				18 02				18 12	18 27
Olton	d					17 20						17 39									18 15	
Acocks Green	d					17 23						17 42									18 18	
Tyseley	d					17 25	17 34									17 56					18 21	
Small Heath	d					17 28	17 36									17 58					18 24	
Bordesley	d																					
Birmingham Moor Street	d		17 26			17 32	17 41	17 37				17 49	17 55			18 03	18 12	18 18			18 28	18a38
Birmingham Snow Hill 🚋	a		17 28			17 35	17 43	17 44				17 51	17 57			18 05	18 21	18 21			18 30	
	d		17 30			17 36	17 43					17 53	17 59			18 08		18 23			18 31	
Jewellery Quarter 🚋	d		17 32			17 39	17 47					17 56				18 10		18 25			18 33	
The Hawthorns 🚋	d		17 37			17 43	17 51					18 00				18 14		18 29			18 38	
Smethwick Galton Bridge [7]	d		17 40			17 46	17 54					18 03				18 17		18 32			18 41	
Coventry	a								17 16	17 26										18 15		
Birmingham Intl. 68 ✈	a									17 36												
Birmingham New Street [12] 68	a	17 18								17 48									18 18			
	d				17 50						17 59			18 20								
Langley Green	d						17 57									18 20		18 37			18 44	
Rowley Regis	d		17 45			17 51	18 00					18 09	18 15			18 24		18 41			18 47	
Old Hill	d						18 03									18 27		18 44			18 50	
Cradley Heath	d		17 50			17 57	18 07					18 14				18 30		18 47			18 54	
Lye	d						18 10									18 33		18 50			18 57	
Stourbridge Junction [2]	d		17a56			18 02	18 14					18 20	18 27			18 37		18 54			19a02	
Hagley	d					18 06	18 17					18 24				18 41		18 58				
Blakedown	d					18 09	18 21					18 27				18 44		19 01				
Kidderminster	d					18 14	18a27					18 32	18a44			18 54		19a07				
Hartlebury	d					18 19						18 37				18 59						
University	d				17 56						18 06			18 27								
Barnt Green	d																					
Bromsgrove 69	d				18 12						18 22			18 42								
Droitwich Spa	d				18 22	18 27					18 34	18 46		18 52		19 08						
Worcester Shrub Hill [7]	a				18 31						18 42	18 58				19 17						
	d			18 21	18 34										19 05	19 23						
Worcester Foregate Street [7]	a			18 23	18 36	18 38								19 01	19 07	19 25						
	d				18 37									19 02	19 08	19 26						
Malvern Link	d				18 46									19 11	19 22	19 34						
Great Malvern	a				18 48									19 14	19 24	19 37						
	d				18 49									19 14								
Colwall	d				18 54									19 19								
Ledbury	a				19 02									19 26								
	d				19 04									19 27								
Hereford [7]	a				19 19									19 42								

Table T071-F

Mondays to Fridays

16 December to 15 May

Stratford-upon-Avon, Marylebone and Leamington Spa - Birmingham - Stourbridge, Worcester and Hereford

		CH	CH	XC	LM	GW	LM	LM	CH	CH	XC	LM	LM	LM	GW	LM	GW	LM	LM	CH	XC	LM	GW
		◇		◇[1]		◇[1]				◇	◇[1]				◇[1]					◇	◇[1]		◇[1]
						A																	
				🛒		🛒					🛒				🛒						🛒		🛒
Stratford-upon-Avon	d	17 36					17 55							18 27					18 51				
Stratford-upon-Avon Parkway	d	17 40					17 59							18 31					18 55				
Wilmcote	d	17 43												18 34					18 58				
Wootton Wawen	d													18x39					19x03				
Henley-in-Arden	d						18 07							18 43					19 07				
Danzey	d													18x47									
Wood End	d													18x50									
The Lakes	d													18x53									
Earlswood (West Midlands)	d													18 56									
Wythall	d													18 58									
Whitlocks End	d						18 18						18 45	19 01					19 17				
Shirley	d						18 21						18 47	19 04					19 19				
Yardley Wood	d						18 24						18 50	19 07					19 22				
Hall Green	d						18 27						18 53	19 10					19 25				
Spring Road	d						18 29						18 56	19 12					19 28				
London Marylebone [10] ⊖115	d								16 24	17 15										17 46			
Banbury	d			17 57					18 02	18 09	18 28									18 48	18 58		
Leamington Spa [8]	a	18 09		18 14					18 21	18 26	18 45									19 05	19 15		
	d		18 11	18 15					18 22	18 27	18 50	19 02								19 05	19 16		
Warwick	d		18 16						18 26											19 09			
Warwick Parkway	d									18 34										19 13			
Hatton	d		18a23						18 39														
Lapworth	d								18 46														
Dorridge	d							18 24	18 51	18 45								19 00		19 23			
Widney Manor	d							18 29										19 06					
Solihull	d							18 32	18 57	18 50								19 09		19 29			
Olton	d							18 35										19 12					
Acocks Green	d							18 38										19 15					
Tyseley	d						18 32	18 40					18 59					19 17					
Small Heath	d						18 36	18 43										19 20					
Bordesley	d																						
Birmingham Moor Street	d						18 40	18 48	19 08	19 00			19 04	19 19				19 24	19 35	19 39			
Birmingham Snow Hill 🚋	a						18 43	18 50	19 15	19 02			19 06	19 22				19 26	19 37	19 46			
	d						18 44	18 53		19 04			19 10					19 28	19 43				
Jewellery Quarter 🚋	d						18 47	18 55					19 12					19 30	19 45				
The Hawthorns 🚋	d						18 51	18 59					19 16					19 34	19 49				
Smethwick Galton Bridge [7]	d						18 54	19 02					19 19					19 37	19 52				
Coventry	a			18 26								19 16									19 27		
Birmingham Intl. 68 ✈	a			18 36																	19 37		
Birmingham New Street [12] 68	a			18 48							19 18										19 48		
	d				18 50											19 20						20 00	
Langley Green	d							19 05					19 22					19 40	19 55				
Rowley Regis	d						18 59	19 09		19 17			19 25					19 44	19 59				
Old Hill	d							19 12					19 28					19 47	20 02				
Cradley Heath	d						19 05	19 15					19 32					19 50	20 05				
Lye	d							19 18					19 35					19 53	20 08				
Stourbridge Junction [2]	d						19 10	19a22		19 28			19 39					19 57	20 12				
Hagley	d						19 14						19 43					20 01	20 16				
Blakedown	d						19 17						19 46					20 04	20 19				
Kidderminster	d						19 22			19a41			19a50					20 09	20a24				
Hartlebury	d																	20 14					
University	d				18 56											19 26						20 06	
Barnt Green	d																						
Bromsgrove 69	d				19 13											19 42						20 21	
Droitwich Spa	d				19 23		19 33									19 53		20 22				20 31	
Worcester Shrub Hill [7]	a				19 30											20 05						20 39	
	d					19 34									20 05	20 13	20 21						21 04
Worcester Foregate Street [7]	a					19 36	19 43								20 07	20 15	20 23	20 31					21 06
	d					19 37										20 16	20 24						21 07
Malvern Link	d					19 46										20 25	20 36						21 16
Great Malvern	a					19 49										20 28	20 38						21 18
	d					19 50										20 28							21 24
Colwall	d					19 56										20 34							21 30
Ledbury	a					20 03										20 41							21 38
	d					20 08										20 42							21 47
Hereford [7]	a					20 25										20 58							22 04

A The Cathedrals Express

Table T071-F

Mondays to Fridays
16 December to 15 May

Stratford-upon-Avon, Marylebone and Leamington Spa - Birmingham - Stourbridge, Worcester and Hereford

		LM	CH		XC	LM	LM	LM	LM	CH	LM	XC	LM		CH	GW	LM	CH	LM	LM	XC	LM	LM		CH
			◇		◇1 ⌶					◇		◇1 ⌶			◇	◇1 ⌶		◇			◇1				◇
Stratford-upon-Avon	d	19 03							19 26											20 26					
Stratford-upon-Avon Parkway	d	19 07							19 30											20 30					
Wilmcote	d								19 33											20 33					
Wootton Wawen	d								19x37											20x37					
Henley-in-Arden	d								19 41											20 41					
Danzey	d								19x45											20x45					
Wood End	d								19x49											20x49					
The Lakes	d								19x51											20x51					
Earlswood (West Midlands)	d								19 54											20 54					
Wythall	d								19 57											20 57					
Whitlocks End	d						19 45		20 00								20 34			21 00					
Shirley	d						19 48		20 03								20 37			21 03					
Yardley Wood	d						19 50		20 05								20 39			21 05					
Hall Green	d						19 54		20 09								20 43			21 09					
Spring Road	d						19 56		20 11								20 45			21 11					
London Marylebone 10 ⊖115	d		18 15							18 47					18 24			19 15							19 47
Banbury	d		19 09		19 29					19 50		19 57			20 06			20 16			20 28				20 47
Leamington Spa 8	a		19 27		19 46					20 08		20 14			20 25			20 34			20 44				21 04
	d		19 28		19 50	20 02				20 09		20 15			20 26			20 34			20 50	21 01			21 04
Warwick	d									20 13															21 08
Warwick Parkway	d		19 35							20 17					20 31			20 40							21 12
Hatton	d														20a38										21 17
Lapworth	d	19 25																							21 23
Dorridge	d	19 30	19 45					19 51		20 27	20 30							20 50	20 52				21 18		21 28
Widney Manor	d	19 35						19 56			20 35								20 57				21 23		
Solihull	d	19 38	19 51					19 59		20 33	20 38							20 55	21 00				21 26		21 34
Olton	d	19 41						20 02			20 41								21 03				21 29		
Acocks Green	d	19 44						20 04			20 43								21 05				21 32		
Tyseley	d	19 47					19 59	20 07	20 14								20 48		21 08						
Small Heath	d	19 49					20 01	20 09	20 17								20 51								
Bordesley	d																								
Birmingham Moor Street	d	19 54	20 02				20 07	20 14	20 26	20 42	20 50						20 56	21a06	21 13	21 18			21 38		21 44
Birmingham Snow Hill	a	19 56	20 04				20 09	20 16	20 28	20 49	20 52						20 58		21 15	21 20			21 41		21 51
	d	19 58	20 06					20 23			20 53						21 00			21 23			21 43		
Jewellery Quarter	d	20 00						20 25			20 56						21 02			21 25			21 45		
The Hawthorns	d	20 04	20 13					20 29			21 00						21 06			21 29			21 49		
Smethwick Galton Bridge 7	d	20 07	20 17					20 32			21 03						21 09			21 32			21 52		
Coventry	a					20 16						20 26										21 16			
Birmingham Intl. 68 ✈	a											20 36													
Birmingham New Street 12 68	a				20 18							20 48									21 23				
	d												21 00												
Langley Green	d	20 10						20 35									21 12			21 35					
Rowley Regis	d	20 14	20 23					20 39			21 08						21 16			21 39			21 58		
Old Hill	d	20 17						20 42									21 19			21 42					
Cradley Heath	d	20 20						20 45			21 14						21 22			21 45			22 03		
Lye	d	20 23						20 48									21 25			21 48					
Stourbridge Junction 2	d	20 27	20 34					20 52			21 19						21 29			21 52			22 09		
Hagley	d	20 31						20 56			21 23						21 33			21 56			22 13		
Blakedown	d	20 34						20 59			21 26						21 36			21 59			22 16		
Kidderminster	d	20 39	20a48					21a03			21a31						21 41			22a03			22 21		
Hartlebury	d																21 46								
University	d												21 06												
Barnt Green	d																								
Bromsgrove 69	d												21 21												
Droitwich Spa	d	20 50											21 31				21 54						22 39		
Worcester Shrub Hill 7	a	21 08															22 01								
	d															22 01	22 08								
Worcester Foregate Street 7	a												21 39			22 03	22 10						22 48		
	d												21 41			22 04									
Malvern Link	d												21 51			22 13									
Great Malvern	a												21 54			22 15									
	d												22 00			22 28									
Colwall	d												22 05			22 34									
Ledbury	a												22 13			22 41									
	d												22 19			22 42									
Hereford 7	a												22 34			22 58									

Table T071-F

Mondays to Fridays
16 December to 15 May

Stratford-upon-Avon, Marylebone and Leamington Spa - Birmingham - Stourbridge, Worcester and Hereford

		XC	LM	GW	LM	CH	LM	XC	LM		CH	LM	LM	CH	XC	LM	CH	LM	CH		LM	LM	CH	XC	CH	CH	LM	CH	CH
		◇1 ⌶		◇1 ⌶		◇		◇1			◇			◇	◇1		◇		◇				◇	◇1	◇			◇	◇
Stratford-upon-Avon	d						21 26							21 39								22 33				23 15	23 30		
Stratford-upon-Avon Parkway	d						21 30							21 43								22 37					23 34		
Wilmcote	d						21 33							21 47								22 40							
Wootton Wawen	d																												
Henley-in-Arden	d						21 39															22 46							
Danzey	d																												
Wood End	d						21x46																						
The Lakes	d						21x48																						
Earlswood (West Midlands)	d						21 51																						
Wythall	d						21 54															22 56							
Whitlocks End	d				21 32		21 57											22 34				22 58							
Shirley	d				21 35		22 00											22 37				23 01							
Yardley Wood	d				21 37		22 02											22 39				23 03							
Hall Green	d				21 41		22 06											22 43				23 06							
Spring Road	d				21 43		22 08											22 45				23 08							
London Marylebone 10 ⊖115	d					20 10					20 37						20 43		21 10				21 40		22 10			22 36	23 07
Banbury	d	20 57				21 12		21 30			21 39				21 57		22 01		22 14				22 41	22 48	23 13			23 41	00 33
Leamington Spa 8	a	21 14				21 29		21 47			21 56			22 09	22 13		22 19		22 31				22 58	23 04	23 31	23 38		23 58	00 20
	d	21 15				21 30		21 50			21 57		22 06		22 15		22 20		22 31				22 59	23 09	23 31			23 59	00 21
Warwick	d										22 01						22 24						23 03					00 03	00 25
Warwick Parkway	d					21 36					22 05								22 38				23 07		23 37			00 07	00 29
Hatton	d																22a31						23 12						
Lapworth	d																						23 18						
Dorridge	d								22 01		22 15	22 25									22 49		23 23					00 18	
Widney Manor	d								22 06			22 30									22 54		23 27						
Solihull	d					21 49			22 09		22 21	22 33							22 51		22 57		23 31		23 49			00 24	00 41
Olton	d								22 12			22 36									23 00								
Acocks Green	d								22 15			22 39									23 03								
Tyseley	d				21 46		22 11		22 18									22 48				23 12							
Small Heath	d				21 49		22 13		22 20									22 52				23 14							
Bordesley	d																												
Birmingham Moor Street	d				21 54	22 04	22 18		22 25		22 31	22 46						22 57	23 03		23 10	23 19	23a42		00a01		00s05	00a36	00a52
Birmingham Snow Hill	a				21 56	22 08	22 20		22 27		22 38	22 48						22 59	23 05		23 12	23 21					00 08		
	d				22 00	22 10	22 23		22 35									23 01	23 15										
Jewellery Quarter	d				22 02		22 25		22 37									23 03	23 18										
The Hawthorns	d				22 06	22 17	22 29		22 41									23 07	23 22										
Smethwick Galton Bridge 7	d				22 09	22 20	22 32		22 44									23 10	23 25										
Coventry	a	21 26											22 21		22 26									23 20					
Birmingham Intl. 68 ✈	a	21 36													22 36									23 29					
Birmingham New Street 12 68	a	21 48						22 18							22 48									23 56					
	d		22 00													23 00													
Langley Green	d				22 12		22 35											23 13	23 29										
Rowley Regis	d				22 16	22 25	22 39		22 50									23 17	23 33										
Old Hill	d				22 19		22 42											23 20	23 36										
Cradley Heath	d				22 22	22 31	22 45		22 55									23 23	23 40										
Lye	d				22 25		22 48											23 26	23 43										
Stourbridge Junction 2	d				22 29	22 37	22a51		23 01									23 30	23a49										
Hagley	d				22 33				23 05									23 33											
Blakedown	d				22 36				23 08									23 36											
Kidderminster	d				22 41	22a50			23a12									23 41											
Hartlebury	d				22 46													23 46											
University	d		22 06													23 06													
Barnt Green	d																												
Bromsgrove 69	d		22 23													23 21													
Droitwich Spa	d		22 33		22 54											23 31		23 54											
Worcester Shrub Hill 7	a		22 41		23 01											23 38		00 05											
	d			22 56	23 08																								
Worcester Foregate Street 7	a			22 58	23 10																								
	d			22 59	23 10																								
Malvern Link	d			23 08	23 19																								
Great Malvern	a			23 10	23 23																								
	d																												
Colwall	d																												
Ledbury	a																												
	d																												
Hereford 7	a																												

Table T071-F

Saturdays
21 December to 16 May

Stratford-upon-Avon, Marylebone and Leamington Spa - Birmingham - Stourbridge, Worcester and Hereford

Station		CH ◇	CH ◇	CH	LM	LM	LM	LM	LM	LM	GW ◇1	CH	LM	LM	LM	XC ◇1	LM	LM	LM	LM	CH	XC ◇1	LM
Stratford-upon-Avon	d																			07 00			
Stratford-upon-Avon Parkway	d																			07 04			
Wilmcote	d																			07 07			
Wootton Wawen	d																			07x11			
Henley-in-Arden	d																			07 15			
Danzey	d																			07x19			
Wood End	d																			07x23			
The Lakes	d																			07x25			
Earlswood (West Midlands)	d																			07 28			
Wythall	d																			07 31			
Whitlocks End	d																	07 03		07 33			07 42
Shirley	d																	07 05		07 36			07 45
Yardley Wood	d																	07 08		07 39			07 47
Hall Green	d																	07 11		07 42			07 51
Spring Road	d																	07 14		07 44			07 53
London Marylebone 10 ⊖115	d			00 20																			
Banbury	d		00 03	01 35								06 00				06 57					07 03	07 32	
Leamington Spa 8	a		00 20	01 56								06 20				07 14					07 20	07 49	
	d		00 21		05 34		06 08					06 21		06 29	07 02	07 15					07 21	07 50	
Warwick	d	00 03	00 25									06 25		06 33							07 25		
Warwick Parkway	d	00 07	00 29									06 28		06 36							07 29		
Hatton	d											06 34		06 40							07 34		
Lapworth	d											06 39		06 46									
Dorridge	d	00 18										06 44		06 50					07 26		07 42		
Widney Manor	d													06 54					07 31				
Solihull	d	00 24	00 41									06 49		06 58					07 34		07 48		
Olton	d													07 01					07 37				
Acocks Green	d													07 04					07 40				
Tyseley	d													07 06				07 17	07 42	07 48			07 56
Small Heath	d													07 09				07 19	07 45	07 50			07 59
Bordesley	d																						
Birmingham Moor Street	d	00a36	00a52							06 33		07a00	07 01	07 14				07 24	07 49	07 55	08a00		08 05
Birmingham Snow Hill	a									06 35			07 03	07 17				07 26	07 52	07 57			08 07
	d									06 37			07 05					07 28	07 53	08 03			
Jewellery Quarter	d									06 39			07 07					07 30	07 55	08 05			
The Hawthorns	d									06 43			07 11					07 34	07 59	08 09			
Smethwick Galton Bridge 7	d									06 46			07 14					07 37	08 02	08 12			
Coventry	a				05 49		06 22								07 16	07 26							
Birmingham Intl. 68 ✈	a															07 36							
Birmingham New Street 12 68	a															07 48						08 18	
	d								06 50								07 50						
Langley Green	d									06 49			07 17					07 40		08 15			
Rowley Regis	d									06 52			07 20					07 43	08 08	08 19			
Old Hill	d									06 56			07 24					07 47		08 22			
Cradley Heath	d									06 59			07 27					07 50	08 13	08 25			
Lye	d									07 02			07 30					07 53		08 28			
Stourbridge Junction 2	d									07 06			07 34					07a57	08 19	08 32			
Hagley	d									07 09			07 37						08 23	08 36			
Blakedown	d									07 12			07 40						08 26	08 39			
Kidderminster	d									07 17			07 45						08 31	08a43			
Hartlebury	d									07 22													
University	d								06 56								07 56						
Barnt Green	d																						
Bromsgrove 69	d								07 13								08 13						
Droitwich Spa	d								07 23	07 31			07 56				08 23		08 42				
Worcester Shrub Hill 7	a									07 41			08 05										
	d					05 47		06 30			08 03		08 12										
Worcester Foregate Street 7	a					05 49		06 32	07 31		08 05		08 14				08 31		08 51				
	d					05 50		06 32	07 32		08 06		08 14				08 32						
Malvern Link	d					05 59		06 42	07 42		08 15		08 29				08 42						
Great Malvern	a					06 01		06 44	07 44		08 18		08 34				08 44						
	d							06 45	07 45								08 45						
Colwall	d							06 50	07 50								08 50						
Ledbury	a							06 57	07 57								08 57						
	d							06 59	07 59								08 59						
Hereford 7	a							07 19	08 15								09 14						

Table T071-F

Saturdays
21 December to 16 May

Stratford-upon-Avon, Marylebone and Leamington Spa - Birmingham - Stourbridge, Worcester and Hereford

Station		LM	LM	LM	GW ◇1	LM	LM	XC ◇1	LM	LM	CH ◇	CH ◇	CH	GW ◇1	LM	CH	LM	XC ◇1	LM	XC ◇1	LM	GW	LM
Stratford-upon-Avon	d			07 43								07 56					08 26						
Stratford-upon-Avon Parkway	d			07 47								08 00					08 30						
Wilmcote	d			07 50								08 03					08 33						
Wootton Wawen	d			07x54													08x37						
Henley-in-Arden	d			07 58													08 41						
Danzey	d			08x02													08x45						
Wood End	d			08x05													08x49						
The Lakes	d			08x08													08x51						
Earlswood (West Midlands)	d			08 11													08 54						
Wythall	d			08 14													08 57						
Whitlocks End	d			08 16						08 35							09 00						
Shirley	d			08 19						08 38							09 03						
Yardley Wood	d			08 22						08 40							09 05						
Hall Green	d			08 25						08 43							09 09						
Spring Road	d			08 27						08 45							09 11						
London Marylebone 10 ⊖115	d										07 00												
Banbury	d							07 57			08 04					08 14		08 30		08 57			
Leamington Spa 8	a							08 14			08 22	08 28				08 33		08 47		09 14			
	d					07 56	08 03	08 15			08 23		08 30			08 34		08 50	09 00	09 15			
Warwick	d					08 00							08 34			08 38							
Warwick Parkway	d					08 03					08 29					08 41							
Hatton	d					08 07							08a42			08 46							
Lapworth	d					08 12										08 52							
Dorridge	d		08 07			08 21					08 40				08 46	08 57					09 09		
Widney Manor	d		08 12			08 25									08 51						09 14		
Solihull	d		08 15			08 29					08 47				08 54	09 03					09 17		
Olton	d		08 18			08 32									08 57						09 20		
Acocks Green	d		08 21			08 35									09 00						09 23		
Tyseley	d		08 24	08 31		08 37				08 48					09 02								
Small Heath	d			08 33		08 40				08 51					09 05								
Bordesley	d																						
Birmingham Moor Street	d		08 29	08 38		08 45				08 55	09 00				09 09	09a15	09 18				09 29		
Birmingham Snow Hill	a		08 31	08 40		08 47				08 58	09 07				09 12		09 20				09 32		
	d	08 23	08 33	08 41		08 53				09 03					09 13		09 23				09 33		
Jewellery Quarter	d	08 25	08 35	08 43		08 55				09 05					09 15		09 25				09 35		
The Hawthorns	d	08 29	08 39	08 47		08 59				09 09					09 19		09 29				09 39		
Smethwick Galton Bridge 7	d	08 32	08 42	08 50		09 02				09 12					09 22		09 32				09 42		
Coventry	a						08 17	08 26											09 14	09 26			
Birmingham Intl. 68 ✈	a							08 36												09 36			
Birmingham New Street 12 68	a							08 48										09 18		09 48			
	d								08 50														09 50
Langley Green	d	08 35	08 45			09 05											09 35						
Rowley Regis	d	08 39	08 48	08 56		09 08				09 18					09 28		09 38				09 48		
Old Hill	d	08 42	08 52			09 12											09 42						
Cradley Heath	d	08 45	08 55	09 01		09 15				09 23					09 33		09 45				09 53		
Lye	d	08 48	08 58			09 18											09 48						
Stourbridge Junction 2	d	08a52	09a02	09 07		09 22				09 29					09 39		09a52				09 59		
Hagley	d					09 25				09 33											10 03		
Blakedown	d					09 28				09 36											10 06		
Kidderminster	d			09a14		09 33				09a40					09 47						10a10		
Hartlebury	d														09 52								
University	d								08 56														09 56
Barnt Green	d																						
Bromsgrove 69	d								09 12														10 13
Droitwich Spa	d					09 44			09 22						10 00								10 23
Worcester Shrub Hill 7	a					09 52																	
	d				09 13									10 02								10 18	
Worcester Foregate Street 7	a				09 15				09 30					10 04	10 09							10 20	10 31
	d				09 16				09 32					10 05								10 21	10 32
Malvern Link	d				09 25				09 42					10 14								10 30	10 42
Great Malvern	a				09 28				09 44					10 17								10 32	10 44
	d								09 45														10 45
Colwall	d								09 50														10 50
Ledbury	a								09 57														10 57
	d								09 59														10 59
Hereford 7	a								10 14														11 14

Table T071-F

Saturdays

21 December to 16 May

Stratford-upon-Avon, Marylebone and Leamington Spa - Birmingham - Stourbridge, Worcester and Hereford

		LM		LM	LM	CH	LM	LM	XC	LM	CH	LM		XC	GW	LM	LM	GW	LM	CH	LM	LM		CH	LM
						◇			◇1 ✠		◇			◇1 ✠	◇1 ✠			◇1 ✠		◇					
Stratford-upon-Avon	d			09 03				09 26											10 03						10 26
Stratford-upon-Avon Parkway	d			09 07				09 30											10 07						10 30
Wilmcote	d							09 33																	10 33
Wootton Wawen	d							09x37																	10x37
Henley-in-Arden	d							09 41																	10 41
Danzey	d							09x45																	10x45
Wood End	d							09x49																	10x49
The Lakes	d							09x51																	10x51
Earlswood (West Midlands)	d							09 54																	10 54
Wythall	d							09 57																	10 57
Whitlocks End	d	09 19			09 40			10 00									10 19				10 40				11 00
Shirley	d	09 22			09 42			10 03									10 22				10 42				11 03
Yardley Wood	d	09 24			09 45			10 05									10 24				10 45				11 05
Hall Green	d	09 27			09 48			10 09									10 27				10 48				11 09
Spring Road	d	09 29			09 51			10 11									10 29				10 51				11 11
London Marylebone 10 ⊖115	d					08 10					08 40									09 10					
Banbury	d					09 10			09 28		09 40			09 57						10 07					
Leamington Spa 8	a					09 27			09 44		09 57			10 14						10 24					
	d					09 28			09 50		09 58	10 02		10 15						10 25				10 32	
Warwick	d					09 32					10 02													10 37	
Warwick Parkway	d					09 35					10 06									10 31					
Hatton	d																							10 43	
Lapworth	d																							10 49	
Dorridge	d			09 29		09 45	09 46			10 09	10 16								10 29			10 46		10 54	
Widney Manor	d			09 33			09 51			10 14									10 33			10 51			
Solihull	d			09 37		09 51	09 54			10 17	10 22								10 37	10 43		10 54		11 00	
Olton	d			09 40			09 57			10 20									10 40			10 57			
Acocks Green	d			09 43			10 00			10 23									10 43			11 00			
Tyseley	d	09 32					10 02										10 32					11 02			
Small Heath	d	09 35					10 05										10 35					11 05			
Bordesley	d																								
Birmingham Moor Street	d	09 39		09 49	09 58	10 02	10 09	10 18		10 29	10 34						10 39		10 49	10a54	10 59	11 09		11a14	11 18
Birmingham Snow Hill	a	09 42		09 52	10 00	10 09	10 12	10 20		10 32	10 41						10 42		10 52		11 01	11 12			11 20
	d	09 43		09 53	10 03		10 13	10 23		10 33							10 43		10 53		11 03	11 13			11 23
Jewellery Quarter	d	09 45		09 55	10 05		10 15	10 25		10 35							10 45		10 55		11 05	11 15			11 25
The Hawthorns	d	09 49		09 59	10 09		10 19	10 29		10 39							10 49		10 59		11 09	11 19			11 29
Smethwick Galton Bridge 7	d	09 52		10 02	10 12		10 22	10 32		10 42							10 52		11 02		11 12	11 22			11 32
Coventry	a											10 16		10 26											
Birmingham Intl. 68 ✈	a													10 36											
Birmingham New Street 12 68	a								10 18					10 48											
	d															10 50									
Langley Green	d			10 05				10 35											11 05						11 35
Rowley Regis	d	09 58		10 08	10 18		10 28	10 38		10 48							10 58		11 08		11 18	11 28			11 38
Old Hill	d			10 12				10 42											11 12						11 42
Cradley Heath	d	10 03		10 15	10 23		10 33	10 45		10 53							11 03		11 15		11 23	11 33			11 45
Lye	d			10 18				10 48											11 18						11 48
Stourbridge Junction 2	d	10 09		10a22	10 29		10 39	10a52		10 59							11 09		11a22		11 29	11 39			11a52
Hagley	d	10 12			10 33					11 03							11 12				11 33				
Blakedown	d				10 36					11 06											11 36				
Kidderminster	d	10 18			10a40		10 47			11a10							11 18				11a40	11 47			
Hartlebury	d						10 52															11 52			
University	d															10 56									
Barnt Green	d																								
Bromsgrove 69	d															11 13									
Droitwich Spa	d	10 30					11 00									11 23	11 30					12 00			
Worcester Shrub Hill 7	a	10 38															11 38								
	d														11 10			11 58							
Worcester Foregate Street 7	a						11 09								11 12	11 31		12 00				12 09			
	d						11 10								11 17	11 32		12 01							
Malvern Link	d						11 19								11 29	11 42		12 09							
Great Malvern	a						11 23								11 33	11 44		12 12							
	d															11 45		12 13							
Colwall	d															11 50		12 18							
Ledbury	a															11 57		12 25							
	d															11 59		12 27							
Hereford 7	a															12 14		12 44							

Table T071-F

Saturdays

21 December to 16 May

Stratford-upon-Avon, Marylebone and Leamington Spa - Birmingham - Stourbridge, Worcester and Hereford

		XC	LM	CH	LM	CH	XC	GW		LM	LM	LM	CH	CH	XC	LM	LM	LM		LM	CH	LM	XC	GW	LM
		◇1 ✠		◇		◇	◇1 ✠	◇					◇	◇	◇1 ✠						◇		◇1 ✠	◇1 ✠	
Stratford-upon-Avon	d					10 40						11 03						11 26							
Stratford-upon-Avon Parkway	d					10 44						11 07						11 30							
Wilmcote	d					10 47												11 33							
Wootton Wawen	d																	11x37							
Henley-in-Arden	d																	11 41							
Danzey	d																	11x45							
Wood End	d																	11x49							
The Lakes	d																	11x51							
Earlswood (West Midlands)	d																	11 54							
Wythall	d																	11 57							
Whitlocks End	d										11 19					11 40		12 00							
Shirley	d										11 22					11 42		12 03							
Yardley Wood	d										11 24					11 45		12 05							
Hall Green	d										11 27					11 48		12 09							
Spring Road	d										11 29					11 51		12 11							
London Marylebone 10 ⊖115	d			09 40									10 10	09 43							10 40				
Banbury	d	10 28		10 37			10 57						11 07	11 10	11 28						11 43		11 57		
Leamington Spa 8	a	10 44		10 54		11 13	11 14						11 24	11 30	11 44						12 00		12 14		
	d	10 50		10 55	11 02		11 15						11 25	11 32	11 50						12 01	12 02	12 15		
Warwick	d			10 59										11 37							12 05				
Warwick Parkway	d			11 03									11 32								12 09				
Hatton	d													11a44											
Lapworth	d																								
Dorridge	d		11 09	11 14								11 29					11 46			12 09	12 19				
Widney Manor	d		11 14									11 33					11 51			12 14					
Solihull	d		11 17	11 21								11 37	11 45				11 54			12 17	12 25				
Olton	d		11 20									11 40					11 57			12 20					
Acocks Green	d		11 23									11 43					12 00			12 23					
Tyseley	d										11 32						12 02								
Small Heath	d										11 35						12 05								
Bordesley	d																								
Birmingham Moor Street	d		11 29	11 34							11 39	11 49	11a56			11 59	12 09	12 18		12 29	12 34				
Birmingham Snow Hill	a		11 32	11 41							11 42	11 52				12 01	12 12	12 20		12 32	12 41				
	d		11 33								11 43	11 53				12 03	12 13	12 23		12 33					
Jewellery Quarter	d		11 35								11 45	11 55				12 05	12 15	12 25		12 35					
The Hawthorns	d		11 39								11 49	11 59				12 09	12 19	12 29		12 39					
Smethwick Galton Bridge 7	d		11 42								11 52	12 02				12 12	12 22	12 32		12 42					
Coventry	a				11 16		11 26															12 16	12 26		
Birmingham Intl. 68 ✈	a						11 36																12 36		
Birmingham New Street 68	a	11 18					11 48								12 18								12 48		
	d									11 50															12 50
Langley Green	d											12 05						12 35							
Rowley Regis	d		11 48								11 58	12 08				12 18	12 28	12 38		12 48					
Old Hill	d											12 12						12 42							
Cradley Heath	d		11 53								12 03	12 15				12 23	12 33	12 45		12 53					
Lye	d											12 18						12 48							
Stourbridge Junction 2	d		11 59								12 09	12a22				12 29	12 39	12a52		12 59					
Hagley	d		12 03								12 12					12 33				13 03					
Blakedown	d		12 06													12 36				13 06					
Kidderminster	d		12a10								12 18					12a40	12 47			13a10					
Hartlebury	d																12 52								
University	d									11 56															12 56
Barnt Green	d																								
Bromsgrove 69	d									12 13															13 13
Droitwich Spa	d									12 23	12 30						13 00								13 23
Worcester Shrub Hill 7	a																								
	d							12 15																13 10	
Worcester Foregate Street 7	a							12 17		12 31	12 39						13 09							13 13	13 31
	d							12 18		12 32							13 10								13 32
Malvern Link	d							12 27		12 42							13 19								13 42
Great Malvern	a							12 31		12 44							13 23								13 44
	d									12 45															13 45
Colwall	d									12 50															13 50
Ledbury	a									12 57															13 57
	d									12 59															13 59
Hereford 7	a									13 14															14 14

Table T071-F

Saturdays
21 December to 16 May

Stratford-upon-Avon, Marylebone and Leamington Spa - Birmingham - Stourbridge, Worcester and Hereford

		LM	GW ◇1	LM	CH ◇	LM	LM	CH	LM	XC ◇1	LM	CH ◇	LM	XC ◇1	CH	GW ◇	LM	LM	LM	CH ◇	CH	XC ◇1
Stratford-upon-Avon	d			12 03					12 26						12 40				13 03			
Stratford-upon-Avon Parkway	d			12 07					12 30						12 44				13 07			
Wilmcote	d								12 33						12 47							
Wootton Wawen	d								12x37													
Henley-in-Arden	d								12 41													
Danzey	d								12x45													
Wood End	d								12x49													
The Lakes	d								12x51													
Earlswood (West Midlands)	d								12 54													
Wythall	d								12 57													
Whitlocks End	d	12 19				12 40			13 00									13 18				
Shirley	d	12 22				12 42			13 03									13 21				
Yardley Wood	d	12 24				12 45			13 05									13 23				
Hall Green	d	12 27				12 48			13 09									13 26				
Spring Road	d	12 29				12 51			13 11									13 28				
London Marylebone 10 ⊖115	d				11 10							11 40								12 10		
Banbury	d				12 08					12 28		12 37		12 57						13 07		13 28
Leamington Spa 8	a				12 24					12 44		12 54		13 14	13 17					13 24		13 44
	d				12 26			12 32		12 50		12 55	13 02	13 15						13 25	13 32	13 50
Warwick	d							12 37				12 59									13 37	
Warwick Parkway	d				12 34							13 03								13 32		
Hatton	d							12 43													13a44	
Lapworth	d							12 49														
Dorridge	d			12 29			12 46	12 54			13 09	13 15							13 29			
Widney Manor	d			12 33			12 51				13 14								13 33			
Solihull	d			12 37	12 46		12 54	13 00			13 17	13 21							13 37	13 45		
Olton	d			12 40			12 57				13 20								13 40			
Acocks Green	d			12 43			13 00				13 23								13 43			
Tyseley	d	12 32					13 02											13 31				
Small Heath	d	12 35					13 05											13 34				
Bordesley	d																	13 36				
Birmingham Moor Street	d	12 39		12 49	12a56	12 59	13 09	13a14	13 18		13 29	13 34						13 39	13 49	13a56		
Birmingham Snow Hill	a	12 42		12 52		13 01	13 12		13 20		13 32	13 41						13 42	13 52			
	d	12 43		12 53		13 03	13 13		13 23		13 33							13 43	13 53			
Jewellery Quarter	d	12 45		12 55		13 05	13 15		13 25		13 35							13 45	13 55			
The Hawthorns	d	12 49		12 59		13 09	13 19		13 29		13 39							13 49	13 59			
Smethwick Galton Bridge 7	d	12 52		13 02		13 12	13 22		13 32		13 42							13 52	14 02			
Coventry	a												13 16	13 26								
Birmingham Intl. 68 ✈	a													13 36								
Birmingham New Street 12 68	a									13 18				13 48								14 18
	d																13 50					
Langley Green	d			13 05					13 35										14 05			
Rowley Regis	d	12 58		13 08		13 18	13 28		13 38		13 48							13 58	14 08			
Old Hill	d			13 12					13 42										14 12			
Cradley Heath	d	13 03		13 15		13 23	13 33		13 45		13 53							14 03	14 15			
Lye	d			13 18					13 48										14 18			
Stourbridge Junction 2	d	13 09		13a22		13 29	13 39		13a52		13 59							14 09	14a22			
Hagley	d	13 12				13 33					14 03							14 12				
Blakedown	d					13 36					14 06											
Kidderminster	d	13 18				13a40	13 47				14a10							14 18				
Hartlebury	d						13 52															
University	d																13 56					
Barnt Green	d																					
Bromsgrove 69	d																14 12					
Droitwich Spa	d	13 30					14 00										14 22	14 29				
Worcester Shrub Hill 7	a	13 38																14 39				
	d		13 56													14 14		14 44				
Worcester Foregate Street 7	a		13 59				14 09									14 16	14 30	14 46				
	d		14 00													14 17	14 32	14 46				
Malvern Link	d		14 09													14 26	14 42	14 55				
Great Malvern	a		14 11													14 30	14 44	14 59				
	d		14 12														14 45					
Colwall	d		14 18														14 50					
Ledbury	a		14 25														14 57					
	d		14 26														14 59					
Hereford 7	a		14 44														15 14					

Table T071-F

Saturdays
21 December to 16 May

Stratford-upon-Avon, Marylebone and Leamington Spa - Birmingham - Stourbridge, Worcester and Hereford

		LM	LM	LM	LM	CH ◇	LM	XC ◇1	GW ◇1	LM	LM	GW ◇1	LM	CH ◇	LM	LM	CH	LM	XC ◇1	LM	CH ◇	LM	CH ◇
Stratford-upon-Avon	d			13 26									14 03					14 26					14 40
Stratford-upon-Avon Parkway	d			13 30									14 07					14 30					14 44
Wilmcote	d			13 33														14 33					14 47
Wootton Wawen	d			13x37														14x37					
Henley-in-Arden	d			13 41														14 41					
Danzey	d			13x45														14x45					
Wood End	d			13x49														14x49					
The Lakes	d			13x51														14x51					
Earlswood (West Midlands)	d			13 54														14 54					
Wythall	d			13 57														14 57					
Whitlocks End	d	13 40		14 00							14 19				14 40			15 00					
Shirley	d	13 42		14 03							14 22				14 42			15 03					
Yardley Wood	d	13 45		14 05							14 24				14 45			15 05					
Hall Green	d	13 48		14 09							14 27				14 48			15 09					
Spring Road	d	13 51		14 11							14 29				14 51			15 11					
London Marylebone 10 ⊖115	d					12 40								13 10							13 40		
Banbury	d					13 37		13 57						14 09					14 28		14 37		
Leamington Spa 8	a					13 54		14 14						14 25					14 44		14 54		15 13
	d					13 55	14 02	14 15						14 27			14 32		14 50		14 55	15 02	
Warwick	d					13 59											14 37				14 59		
Warwick Parkway	d					14 03								14 33							15 03		
Hatton	d																14 43						
Lapworth	d																14 49						
Dorridge	d		13 46		14 09	14 13							14 29			14 46	14 54			15 09	15 13		
Widney Manor	d		13 51		14 14								14 33			14 51				15 14			
Solihull	d		13 54		14 17	14 21							14 37	14 45		14 54	15 00			15 17	15 21		
Olton	d		13 57		14 20								14 40			14 57				15 20			
Acocks Green	d		14 00		14 23								14 43			15 00				15 23			
Tyseley	d		14 02								14 32					15 02							
Small Heath	d		14 05								14 35					15 05							
Bordesley	d																						
Birmingham Moor Street	d	13 59	14 09	14 18	14 29	14 34					14 39		14 49	14a56	14 59	15 09	15a14	15 18		15 29	15 34		
Birmingham Snow Hill	a	14 01	14 12	14 20	14 32	14 41					14 42		14 52		15 01	15 12		15 20		15 32	15 41		
	d	14 03	14 13	14 23	14 33						14 43		14 53		15 03	15 13		15 23		15 33			
Jewellery Quarter	d	14 05	14 15	14 25	14 35						14 45		14 55		15 05	15 15		15 25		15 35			
The Hawthorns	d	14 09	14 19	14 29	14 39						14 49		14 59		15 09	15 19		15 29		15 39			
Smethwick Galton Bridge 7	d	14 12	14 22	14 32	14 42						14 52		15 02		15 12	15 22		15 32		15 42			
Coventry	a						14 16	14 26														15 16	
Birmingham Intl. 68 ✈	a							14 36															
Birmingham New Street 12 68	a							14 48											15 18				
	d									14 50													
Langley Green	d			14 35									15 05					15 35					
Rowley Regis	d	14 18	14 28	14 38	14 48						14 58		15 08		15 18	15 28		15 38		15 48			
Old Hill	d			14 42									15 12					15 42					
Cradley Heath	d	14 23	14 33	14 45	14 53						15 03		15 15		15 23	15 33		15 45		15 53			
Lye	d			14 48									15 18					15 48					
Stourbridge Junction 2	d	14 29	14 39	14a52	14 59						15 09		15a22		15 29	15 39		15a52		15 59			
Hagley	d	14 33			15 03						15 12				15 33					16 03			
Blakedown	d	14 36			15 06										15 36					16 06			
Kidderminster	d	14a40	14 47		15a10						15 18				15a40	15 47				16a10			
Hartlebury	d		14 52													15 52							
University	d									14 56													
Barnt Green	d																						
Bromsgrove 69	d									15 13													
Droitwich Spa	d		15 00							15 23	15 30					16 00							
Worcester Shrub Hill 7	a										15 38												
	d								15 14			16 03											
Worcester Foregate Street 7	a		15 09						15 17	15 31		16 05				16 09							
	d									15 32		16 06											
Malvern Link	d									15 42		16 15											
Great Malvern	a									15 44		16 18											
	d									15 45													
Colwall	d									15 50													
Ledbury	a									15 57													
	d									15 59													
Hereford 7	a									16 14													

Table T071-F

Saturdays

21 December to 16 May

Stratford-upon-Avon, Marylebone and Leamington Spa - Birmingham - Stourbridge, Worcester and Hereford

Station		XC	GW	LM	LM	LM	CH	CH	XC	LM	GW	LM	LM	LM	LM	CH	LM	XC	LM	LM	LM	CH	LM
		◇**1** 🛒	◇				◇	◇	◇**1** 🛒		◇**1** 🛒					◇		◇**1** 🛒				◇	
Stratford-upon-Avon	d					15 03								15 26							16 03		
Stratford-upon-Avon Parkway	d					15 07								15 30							16 07		
Wilmcote	d													15 33									
Wootton Wawen	d													15x37									
Henley-in-Arden	d													15 41									
Danzey	d													15x45									
Wood End	d													15x49									
The Lakes	d													15x51									
Earlswood (West Midlands)	d													15 54									
Wythall	d													15 57									
Whitlocks End	d				15 19					15 40				16 00						16 19			16 40
Shirley	d				15 22					15 42				16 03						16 22			16 42
Yardley Wood	d				15 24					15 45				16 05						16 24			16 45
Hall Green	d				15 27					15 48				16 09						16 27			16 48
Spring Road	d				15 29					15 51				16 11						16 29			16 51
London Marylebone **10** ⊖115	d						14 10	13 43								14 40						15 10	
Banbury	d	14 57					15 07	15 10	15 28							15 37		15 57				16 09	
Leamington Spa **8**	a	15 14					15 24	15 30	15 44							15 55		16 14				16 25	
	d	15 15					15 25	15 32	15 50							15 55	16 02	16 15				16 26	
Warwick	d							15 37								15 59							
Warwick Parkway	d						15 32									16 03						16 33	
Hatton	d							15a44															
Lapworth	d																						
Dorridge	d					15 29							15 46		16 09	16 13					16 29		
Widney Manor	d					15 33							15 51		16 14						16 33		
Solihull	d					15 37	15 45						15 54		16 17	16 21					16 37	16 45	
Olton	d					15 40							15 57		16 20						16 40		
Acocks Green	d					15 43							16 00		16 23						16 43		
Tyseley	d				15 32								16 02							16 32			
Small Heath	d				15 35								16 05							16 35			
Bordesley	d																						
Birmingham Moor Street	d				15 39	15 49	15a56			15 59			16 09	16 18	16 29	16 34				16 39	16 49	16a56	16 59
Birmingham Snow Hill 🚊	a				15 42	15 52				16 01			16 12	16 20	16 32	16 41				16 42	16 52		17 01
	d				15 43	15 53				16 03			16 13	16 23	16 33					16 43	16 53		17 03
Jewellery Quarter 🚊	d				15 45	15 55				16 05			16 15	16 25	16 35					16 45	16 55		17 05
The Hawthorns 🚊	d				15 49	15 59				16 09			16 19	16 29	16 39					16 49	16 59		17 09
Smethwick Galton Bridge **7**	d				15 52	16 02				16 12			16 22	16 32	16 42					16 52	17 02		17 12
Coventry	a	15 26															16 16	16 26					
Birmingham Intl. 68 ✈	a	15 36																16 36					
Birmingham New Street **12** 68	a	15 48							16 18									16 48					
	d			15 50								16 20							16 50				
Langley Green	d					16 05								16 35							17 05		
Rowley Regis	d				15 58	16 08				16 18			16 28	16 38	16 48					16 58	17 08		17 18
Old Hill	d					16 12								16 42							17 12		
Cradley Heath	d				16 03	16 15				16 23			16 33	16 45	16 53					17 03	17 15		17 23
Lye	d					16 18								16 48							17 18		
Stourbridge Junction **2**	d				16 09	16a22				16 29			16 39	16a52	16 59					17 09	17a22		17 29
Hagley	d				16 12					16 33					17 03					17 12			17 33
Blakedown	d									16 36					17 06								17 36
Kidderminster	d				16 18					16a40			16 47		17a10					17 18			17a40
Hartlebury	d												16 52										
University	d			15 56															16 56				
Barnt Green	d																						
Bromsgrove 69	d			16 12								16 42							17 13				
Droitwich Spa	d			16 22	16 30							16 52	17 00						17 23	17 30			
Worcester Shrub Hill **7**	a											17 01											
	d		16 14								17 00												
Worcester Foregate Street **7**	a		16 16	16 30	16 39						17 03		17 09						17 31	17 39			
	d		16 18	16 32							17 03		17 16						17 32				
Malvern Link	d		16 28	16 42							17 13		17 25						17 42				
Great Malvern	a		16 32	16 44							17 16		17 29						17 45				
	d			16 45															17 45				
Colwall	d			16 50															17 50				
Ledbury	a			16 57															17 57				
	d			16 59															17 59				
Hereford **7**	a			17 14															18 14				

Table T071-F

Saturdays

21 December to 16 May

Stratford-upon-Avon, Marylebone and Leamington Spa - Birmingham - Stourbridge, Worcester and Hereford

Station		LM	GW	LM	GW	CH	LM	XC	LM	LM	CH	LM	CH	XC	LM	LM	CH	CH	XC	LM	LM	GW
			◇**1** 🛒					◇**1** 🛒			◇		◇	◇**1** 🛒			◇	◇	◇**1** 🛒			◇**1** 🛒
Stratford-upon-Avon	d						16 26						16 40			17 03						
Stratford-upon-Avon Parkway	d						16 30						16 44			17 07						
Wilmcote	d						16 33						16 47									
Wootton Wawen	d						16x37															
Henley-in-Arden	d						16 41															
Danzey	d						16x45															
Wood End	d						16x49															
The Lakes	d						16x51															
Earlswood (West Midlands)	d						16 54															
Wythall	d						16 57															
Whitlocks End	d						17 00								17 19					17 40		
Shirley	d						17 03								17 22					17 42		
Yardley Wood	d						17 05								17 24					17 45		
Hall Green	d						17 09								17 27					17 48		
Spring Road	d						17 11								17 29					17 51		
London Marylebone **10** ⊖115	d										15 40						16 10	15 43				
Banbury	d							16 28			16 37			16 57			17 07	17 10	17 28			
Leamington Spa **8**	a							16 44			16 54		17 13	17 14			17 24	17 30	17 44			
	d					16 32		16 50			16 55	17 02		17 15			17 25	17 32	17 50			
Warwick	d					16 37					16 59							17 37				
Warwick Parkway	d										17 03						17 32					
Hatton	d					16 43												17a44				
Lapworth	d					16 49																
Dorridge	d			16 46		16 54				17 09	17 13					17 29					17 46	
Widney Manor	d			16 51						17 14						17 33					17 51	
Solihull	d			16 54		17 00				17 17	17 21					17 37	17 45				17 54	
Olton	d			16 57						17 20						17 40					17 57	
Acocks Green	d			17 00						17 23						17 43					18 00	
Tyseley	d			17 02											17 32						18 02	
Small Heath	d			17 05											17 35						18 05	
Bordesley	d																					
Birmingham Moor Street	d			17 09		17a14	17 18			17 29	17 34				17 39	17 49	17a56			17 59	18 09	
Birmingham Snow Hill 🚊	a			17 12			17 20			17 32	17 41				17 42	17 52				18 01	18 12	
	d			17 13			17 23			17 33					17 43	17 53				18 03	18 13	
Jewellery Quarter 🚊	d			17 15			17 25			17 35					17 45	17 55				18 05	18 15	
The Hawthorns 🚊	d			17 19			17 29			17 39					17 49	17 59				18 09	18 19	
Smethwick Galton Bridge **7**	d			17 22			17 32			17 42					17 52	18 02				18 12	18 22	
Coventry	a											17 16		17 26								
Birmingham Intl. 68 ✈	a													17 36								
Birmingham New Street **12** 68	a							17 18						17 48					18 18			
	d	17 20							17 50													
Langley Green	d						17 35									18 05					18 25	
Rowley Regis	d			17 28			17 38			17 48					17 58	18 08				18 18	18 28	
Old Hill	d						17 42									18 12					18 32	
Cradley Heath	d			17 33			17 45			17 53					18 03	18 15				18 23	18 35	
Lye	d						17 48									18 18					18 38	
Stourbridge Junction **2**	d			17 41			17a52			17 59					18 09	18a22				18a28	18a42	
Hagley	d									18 03					18 13							
Blakedown	d									18 06					18 16							
Kidderminster	d			17 51						18 12					18 22							
Hartlebury	d			17 56						18 17					18 27							
University	d								17 56													
Barnt Green	d																					
Bromsgrove 69	d	17 43							18 12													
Droitwich Spa	d	17 52		18 04					18 22	18 27					18 37							
Worcester Shrub Hill **7**	a			18 16					18 29	18 35												
	d		18 09		18 16				18 32													18 59
Worcester Foregate Street **7**	a	18 00	18 11		18 18				18 34						18 46							19 01
	d	18 03	18 12						18 35													19 02
Malvern Link	d	18 12							18 45													19 11
Great Malvern	a	18 15	18 25						18 47													19 13
	d								18 48													19 14
Colwall	d								18 53													19 20
Ledbury	a								19 00													19 27
	d								19 01													19 28
Hereford **7**	a								19 16													19 46

Table T071-F

Saturdays

21 December to 16 May

Stratford-upon-Avon, Marylebone and Leamington Spa - Birmingham - Stourbridge, Worcester and Hereford

		LM	LM	CH	LM	LM	XC	LM	LM	GW	LM	CH	CH	LM	XC	GW	LM	CH	LM	LM	CH	XC	LM
				◇			◇1			◇1		◇			◇1			◇			◇	◇1	
Stratford-upon-Avon	d	17 26			17 54									18 26							18 42		
Stratford-upon-Avon Parkway	d	17 30			17 58									18 30							18 46		
Wilmcote	d	17 33			18 01									18 33							18 49		
Wootton Wawen	d	17x37												18x37									
Henley-in-Arden	d	17 41			18 08									18 41									
Danzey	d	17x45												18x45									
Wood End	d	17x49												18x49									
The Lakes	d	17x51												18x51									
Earlswood (West Midlands)	d	17 54												18 55									
Wythall	d	17 57												18 57									
Whitlocks End	d	18 00			18 19						18 36			19 00									
Shirley	d	18 03			18 22						18 39			19 02									
Yardley Wood	d	18 05			18 24						18 41			19 05									
Hall Green	d	18 09			18 27						18 45			19 08									
Spring Road	d	18 11			18 29						18 47			19 11									
London Marylebone 10 ⊖115	d			16 40								17 10						17 40					
Banbury	d			17 37			17 57					18 09			18 28			18 37				18 57	
Leamington Spa 8	a			17 54			18 14					18 25			18 44			18 54			19 13	19 14	
	d			17 55		18 02	18 15					18 27	18 32		18 50			18 55		19 02		19 15	
Warwick	d			17 59									18 37					18 59					
Warwick Parkway	d			18 03								18 34						19 03					
Hatton	d												18 43										
Lapworth	d												18 49										
Dorridge	d		18 09	18 13					18 30				18 54				19 00	19 13	19 16				
Widney Manor	d		18 14						18 34								19 06		19 21				
Solihull	d		18 17	18 21					18 38			18 48	19 01				19 09	19 19	19 24				
Olton	d		18 20						18 41								19 12		19 27				
Acocks Green	d		18 23						18 43								19 15		19 30				
Tyseley	d				18 32												19 17		19 32				
Small Heath	d				18 35												19 20		19 35				
Bordesley	d																						
Birmingham Moor Street	d	18 19	18 29	18 34	18 39				18 50		18 55	19 00	19a12	19 18			19 24	19 30	19 39				
Birmingham Snow Hill 🚊	a	18 21	18 32	18 41	18 43				18 52		18 58	19 02		19 20			19 27	19 37	19 42				
	d	18 23	18 33						18 53			19 05					19 29		19 43				
Jewellery Quarter 🚊	d	18 25	18 36						18 56								19 32		19 45				
The Hawthorns 🚊	d	18 29	18 40						19 00								19 36		19 49				
Smethwick Galton Bridge 7	d	18 32	18 43						19 03								19 39		19 52				
Coventry	a					18 16	18 26													19 16		19 26	
Birmingham Intl. 68 ✈	a						18 36															19 36	
Birmingham New Street 12 68	a						18 48								19 18							19 48	
	d							18 50															19 50
Langley Green	d		18 46						19 06								19 42						
Rowley Regis	d	18 38	18 49						19 09			19 18					19 45		19 58				
Old Hill	d		18 52						19 12								19 48						
Cradley Heath	d	18 43	18 56						19 16								19 52		20 03				
Lye	d		18 59						19 19								19 55						
Stourbridge Junction 2	d	18 49	19 03						19 23			19 30					19 59		20 09				
Hagley	d	18 52	19 06						19 26								20 03		20 13				
Blakedown	d	18 55	19 09						19 29								20 06		20 16				
Kidderminster	d	19 00	19a14						19 34			19a44					20 11		20a20				
Hartlebury	d	19 05															20 16						
University	d							18 56															19 56
Barnt Green	d																						
Bromsgrove 69	d							19 13															20 12
Droitwich Spa	d	19 14						19 23	19 46								20 27						20 22
Worcester Shrub Hill 7	a	19 22							19 54								20 35						
	d	19 25								20 07						20 19							
Worcester Foregate Street 7	a	19 27						19 31		20 10						20 21							20 30
	d							19 32								20 22							20 35
Malvern Link	d							19 42								20 31							20 45
Great Malvern	a							19 44								20 33							20 47
	d							19 45															20 48
Colwall	d							19 50															20 54
Ledbury	a							19 58															21 01
	d							19 59															21 01
Hereford 7	a							20 14															21 17

Table T071-F

Saturdays

21 December to 16 May

Stratford-upon-Avon, Marylebone and Leamington Spa - Birmingham - Stourbridge, Worcester and Hereford

		LM	CH	CH	XC	LM	LM	CH	LM	LM	XC	LM	GW	LM	LM	GW	LM	CH	CH	LM	XC	LM
			◇	◇	◇1			◇			◇1		◇1			◇1		◇			◇1	
Stratford-upon-Avon	d	18 48					19 26		19 53											20 26		
Stratford-upon-Avon Parkway	d	18 52					19 30		19 57											20 30		
Wilmcote	d	18 55					19 33		20 00											20 33		
Wootton Wawen	d	19x00					19x37													20x37		
Henley-in-Arden	d	19 04					19 41		20 07											20 41		
Danzey	d	19x08					19x45													20x45		
Wood End	d	19x11					19x49													20x49		
The Lakes	d	19x14					19x51													20x51		
Earlswood (West Midlands)	d	19 17					19 54													20 54		
Wythall	d	19 20					19 57													20 57		
Whitlocks End	d	19 23					20 00		20 18								20 32			21 00		
Shirley	d	19 26					20 03		20 21								20 35			21 03		
Yardley Wood	d	19 28					20 05		20 23								20 37			21 05		
Hall Green	d	19 32					20 09		20 26								20 41			21 09		
Spring Road	d	19 34					20 11		20 28								20 43			21 11		
London Marylebone 10 ⊖115	d		18 10	17 43				18 40										19 10				
Banbury	d		19 07	19 10	19 28			19 37			19 57							20 09			20 29	
Leamington Spa 8	a		19 24	19 30	19 44			19 54			20 14							20 26			20 46	
	d		19 26	19 32	19 50			19 55		20 02	20 15							20 27	20 32		20 50	
Warwick	d			19 37				19 59											20 37			
Warwick Parkway	d		19 33					20 03										20 33				
Hatton	d			19a44															20 43			
Lapworth	d																		20 49			
Dorridge	d					19 48		20 13				20 19							20 54			21 03
Widney Manor	d					19 53						20 24										21 08
Solihull	d		19 47			19 56		20 19				20 27						20 47	20 59			21 11
Olton	d					19 59						20 30										21 14
Acocks Green	d					20 02						20 33										21 17
Tyseley	d	19 37					20 14										20 46					21 19
Small Heath	d	19 40					20 17										20 49					
Bordesley	d																					
Birmingham Moor Street	d	19 47	20 00			20 09	20 21	20a30	20 35			20 39					20 54	20a58	21a13	21 18		21 24
Birmingham Snow Hill 🚊	a	19 49	20 07			20 11	20 24		20 38			20 42					20 56			21 20		21 27
	d	19 56					20 25					20 43					20 59			21 23		
Jewellery Quarter 🚊	d	19 58					20 27					20 45					21 01			21 25		
The Hawthorns 🚊	d	20 02					20 31					20 49					21 05			21 29		
Smethwick Galton Bridge 7	d	20 05					20 34					20 52					21 08			21 32		
Coventry	a									20 16	20 26											
Birmingham Intl. 68 ✈	a										20 37											
Birmingham New Street 12 68	a				20 18						20 48										21 18	
	d													20 50	21 20							
Langley Green	d	20 08					20 37										21 11			21 35		
Rowley Regis	d	20 11					20 41					20 58					21 15			21 39		
Old Hill	d	20 15					20 44										21 18			21 42		
Cradley Heath	d	20 18					20 47					21 03					21 21			21 45		
Lye	d	20 21					20 50										21 24			21 48		
Stourbridge Junction 2	d	20 25					20 54					21 09					21 28			21 52		
Hagley	d	20 28					20 58					21 13					21 32			21 56		
Blakedown	d	20 31										21 16					21 35					
Kidderminster	d	20 36					21a03					21a20					21 42			22 02		
Hartlebury	d																21 47			22 07		
University	d													20 56	21 26							
Barnt Green	d																					
Bromsgrove 69	d													21 14	21 41							
Droitwich Spa	d	20 48												21 28	21 54		21 58			22 16		
Worcester Shrub Hill 7	a	20 56															22 06			22 24		
	d	20 59											21 15			22 05						
Worcester Foregate Street 7	a	21 01											21 17	21 37	22 02	22 07						
	d	21 01											21 18	21 38	22 03	22 12						
Malvern Link	d	21 10											21 27	21 48	22 12	22 22						
Great Malvern	a	21 15											21 29	21 51	22 14	22 25						
	d												21 32		22 16							
Colwall	d												21 38		22 21							
Ledbury	a												21 46		22 28							
	d												21 49		22 30							
Hereford 7	a												22 06		22 45							

Table T071-F

Saturdays
21 December to 16 May

Stratford-upon-Avon, Marylebone and Leamington Spa - Birmingham - Stourbridge, Worcester and Hereford

		CH	LM	LM	XC	CH	LM	CH	CH	LM		LM	XC	LM	CH	LM	LM	XC	CH	CH		XC	LM	CH	LM
		◇			◇1			◇					◇1		◇			◇1	◇			◇1		◇	
Stratford-upon-Avon	d					20 43						21 26								22 15			22 33		23 30
Stratford-upon-Avon Parkway	d					20 47						21 30											22 37		23 34
Wilmcote	d					20 50						21 33											22 40		
Wootton Wawen	d																								
Henley-in-Arden	d											21 40											22 47		
Danzey	d																								
Wood End	d											21x46													
The Lakes	d											21x48													
Earlswood (West Midlands)	d											21 51													
Wythall	d											21 54											22 56		
Whitlocks End	d						21 31					21 57											22 59		
Shirley	d						21 34					22 00											23 02		
Yardley Wood	d						21 36					22 02											23 04		
Hall Green	d						21 40					22 06											23 07		
Spring Road	d						21 42					22 08											23 09		
London Marylebone 10 ⊖115	d	19 40						20 10							20 40				21 10					22 10	
Banbury	d	20 37			20 57			21 07					21 28		21 37			21 57	22 10			22 28		23 10	
Leamington Spa 8	a	20 55			21 14	21 17		21 24					21 44		21 54			22 14	22 27	22 40		22 44		23 27	
	d	20 55		21 02	21 15			21 25	21 32				21 50		21 55		22 01	22 15	22 28			22 50		23 28	
Warwick	d	20 59							21 37						21 59				22 32					23 32	
Warwick Parkway	d	21 03						21 32							22 03				22 36					23 37	
Hatton	d								21a44										22 41						
Lapworth	d																		22 46						
Dorridge	d	21 13	21 18											22 03	22 13	22 33			22 51					23 47	
Widney Manor	d		21 23											22 08		22 37			22 55						
Solihull	d	21 19	21 26					21 45						22 11	22 19	22 41			22 58					23 53	
Olton	d		21 29											22 14		22 44									
Acocks Green	d		21 32											22 17		22 47									
Tyseley	d						21 45					22 11				22 49							23 12		
Small Heath	d						21 48					22 13				22 52							23 15		
Bordesley	d																								
Birmingham Moor Street	d	21 28	21 38				21 52	21a57				22 18		22 24	22 28	22 56			23 07				23 19	00a04	00s07
Birmingham Snow Hill	a	21 30	21 41				21 55					22 20		22 26	22 35	22 59			23 14				23 22		00 10
	d	21 33	21 43				21 56					22 23				23 00							23 23		
Jewellery Quarter	d		21 45				21 58					22 25				23 03							23 25		
The Hawthorns	d		21 49				22 02					22 29				23 07							23 29		
Smethwick Galton Bridge 7	d		21 52				22 05					22 32				23 10							23 32		
Coventry	a			21 16	21 26								22 01				22 15	22 26							
Birmingham Intl. 68	a				21 36								22 11					22 36							
Birmingham New Street 12 68	a				21 48								22 22					22 48				23 18			
	d									22 20															
Langley Green	d		21 55				22 08					22 35				23 13							23 35		
Rowley Regis	d	21 45	21 59				22 11					22 39				23 16							23 38		
Old Hill	d		22 02				22 15					22 42				23 19							23 42		
Cradley Heath	d	21 51	22 05				22 18					22 45				23 23							23 45		
Lye	d		22 08				22 21					22 48				23 26							23 48		
Stourbridge Junction 2	d	21 59	22 12				22 25					22 52				23 30							23a52		
Hagley	d		22 16				22 28					22 56				23 33									
Blakedown	d		22 19				22 31					22 59				23 36									
Kidderminster	d	22a12	22a24				22 36					23 04				23 41									
Hartlebury	d						22 41					23 09				23 46									
University	d									22 26															
Barnt Green	d																								
Bromsgrove 69	d									22 41															
Droitwich Spa	d						22 50			22 54		23 18				23 54									
Worcester Shrub Hill 7	a						23 00					23 26				00 05									
	d																								
Worcester Foregate Street 7	a									23 02															
	d									23 03															
Malvern Link	d									23 12															
Great Malvern	a									23 14															
	d																								
Colwall	d																								
Ledbury	a																								
	d																								
Hereford 7	a																								

Table T071-F

Sundays
15 December to 10 May

Stratford-upon-Avon, Marylebone and Leamington Spa - Birmingham - Stourbridge, Worcester and Hereford

		LM	LM	LM	GW	LM	LM	LM	GW	LM		CH	LM	LM	CH	XC	LM	CH	CH	GW		LM	CH	LM	LM
					◇1				◇1			◇			◇	◇1		◇		◇1			◇		
Stratford-upon-Avon	d									09 27					09 38							10 27			
Stratford-upon-Avon Parkway	d									09 31					09 41							10 31			
Wilmcote	d									09 34					09 44							10 34			
Wootton Wawen	d									09x38												10x38			
Henley-in-Arden	d									09 42												10 43			
Danzey	d																								
Wood End	d																								
The Lakes	d									09x49												10x49			
Earlswood (West Midlands)	d									09 52												10 52			
Wythall	d									09 54												10 55			
Whitlocks End	d					09 07				09 57												10 57			
Shirley	d					09 10				10 00												11 00			
Yardley Wood	d					09 12				10 02												11 03			
Hall Green	d					09 15				10 06												11 06			
Spring Road	d					09 17				10 08												11 08			
London Marylebone 10 ⊖115	d											08 15						09 10					09 40		
Banbury	d											09 29				09 57		10 07					10 37		
Leamington Spa 8	a											09 46			10 05	10 14		10 24					10 54		
	d											09 47		10 00		10 15		10 25	10 32				10 55		11 00
Warwick	d											09 51							10 38				10 59		
Warwick Parkway	d											09 55						10 32					11 03		
Hatton	d											10 00							10 44						
Lapworth	d											10 06							10 50						
Dorridge	d	08 57					09 27					10 11	10 27						10 55				11 13	11 27	
Widney Manor	d	09 02					09 32						10 32											11 32	
Solihull	d	09 05					09 35					10 16	10 35					10 45	11 01				11 19	11 35	
Olton	d	09 08					09 38						10 38											11 38	
Acocks Green	d	09 11					09 41						10 41											11 41	
Tyseley	d									10 11												11 11			
Small Heath	d																								
Bordesley	d																								
Birmingham Moor Street	d	09 18				09 24	09 50			10 16		10 25	10 48					10 54	11a13			11 16	11 28	11 48	
Birmingham Snow Hill	a	09 20				09 27	09 52			10 19		10 32	10 50					11 01				11 19	11 35	11 50	
	d					09 29				10 22			10 52									11 22		11 52	
Jewellery Quarter	d					09 31				10 24			10 54									11 24		11 54	
The Hawthorns	d					09 35				10 28			10 58									11 28		11 58	
Smethwick Galton Bridge 7	d					09 38				10 31			11 01									11 31		12 01	
Coventry	a													10 16		10 26									11 16
Birmingham Intl. 68	a															10 37									
Birmingham New Street 12 68	a															10 49									
	d							10 00									11 00								
Langley Green	d												11 04											12 04	
Rowley Regis	d					09 44				10 37			11 07									11 37		12 07	
Old Hill	d												11 10											12 10	
Cradley Heath	d					09 49				10 42			11 14									11 42		12 14	
Lye	d												11 17											12 17	
Stourbridge Junction 2	d					09 55				10 47			11a21									11 47		12a21	
Hagley	d					09 58				10 51												11 51			
Blakedown	d									10 54												11 54			
Kidderminster	d					10 04				10 59												11 59			
Hartlebury	d																								
University	d							10 06									11 06								
Barnt Green	d																								
Bromsgrove 69	d							10 20									11 20								
Droitwich Spa	d					10 18		10 30		11 11							11 29					12 11			
Worcester Shrub Hill 7	a					10 25		10 38		11 19												12 19			
	d		08 58	09 43	10 13	10 30		10 42	11 10	11 33										12 09					
Worcester Foregate Street 7	a		09 00	09 46	10 15	10 32		10 44	11 12	11 35							11 39			12 12					
	d		09 01	09 46	10 16	10 32		10 45	11 14	11 36										12 13					
Malvern Link	d		09 10	09 55	10 25	10 41		10 54	11 23	11 45										12 22					
Great Malvern	a		09 12	10 00	10 27	10 43		10 56	11 25	11 47										12 24					
	d		09 13					11 01												12 28					
Colwall	d		09 18					11 06												12 34					
Ledbury	a		09 24					11 13												12 41					
	d		09 25					11 13												12 44					
Hereford 7	a		09 43					11 29												13 00					

Table T071-F

Sundays

15 December to 10 May

Stratford-upon-Avon, Marylebone and Leamington Spa - Birmingham - Stourbridge, Worcester and Hereford

		XC ◇1 ⊤	LM	CH ◇	CH ◇	LM		CH ◇	LM	LM	XC ◇1 ⊤	LM	CH ◇	CH	LM	CH ◇		LM	XC ◇1 ⊤	LM	CH ◇	CH ◇	CH ◇	GW ◇1 ⊤	LM
Stratford-upon-Avon	d					11 27									12 27							12 57			
Stratford-upon-Avon Parkway	d					11 31									12 31							13 01			
Wilmcote	d					11 34									12 34							13 04			
Wootton Wawen	d					11x38									12x38										
Henley-in-Arden	d					11 43									12 43										
Danzey	d																								
Wood End	d																								
The Lakes	d					11x49									12x49										
Earlswood (West Midlands)	d					11 52									12 52										
Wythall	d					11 55									12 55										
Whitlocks End	d					11 57									12 57										
Shirley	d					12 00									13 00										
Yardley Wood	d					12 03									13 03										
Hall Green	d					12 06									13 06										
Spring Road	d					12 08									13 08										
London Marylebone 10 ⊖115	d			10 10	09 43			10 40					11 10			11 40					12 10		11 43		
Banbury	d	10 57		11 07	11 11			11 37			11 57		12 07			12 37			12 58		13 07		13 10		
Leamington Spa 8	a	11 14		11 24	11 30			11 54			12 14		12 24			12 54			13 15		13 24	13 27	13 30		
	d	11 15		11 25	11 32			11 55		12 00	12 15		12 25	12 32		12 55			13 16	13 19	13 25		13 32		
Warwick	d				11 38			11 59						12 38		12 59							13 37		
Warwick Parkway	d			11 32				12 03					12 32			13 03					13 32				
Hatton	d				11a45									12 44									13a44		
Lapworth	d													12 50											
Dorridge	d							12 13	12 27					12 55		13 14		13 27							
Widney Manor	d								12 32									13 32							
Solihull	d			11 45				12 19	12 35				12 45	13 01		13 20		13 35			13 45				
Olton	d								12 38									13 38							
Acocks Green	d								12 41									13 41							
Tyseley	d					12 11									13 11										
Small Heath	d																								
Bordesley	d																								
Birmingham Moor Street	d			11a56		12 16		12 28	12 48				12a56	13a13	13 16	13 30		13 48			13a56				
Birmingham Snow Hill	a					12 19		12 35	12 50						13 19	13 37		13 50							
	d					12 22			12 52						13 22			13 52							
Jewellery Quarter	d					12 24			12 54						13 24			13 54							
The Hawthorns	d					12 28			12 58						13 28			13 58							
Smethwick Galton Bridge 7	d					12 31			13 01						13 31			14 01							
Coventry	a	11 26								12 16	12 26								13 27	13 39					
Birmingham Intl. 68 ✈	a	11 37									12 37								13 37						
Birmingham New Street 12 68	a	11 49									12 49								13 48						
	d		12 00									13 00													
Langley Green	d								13 04									14 04							
Rowley Regis	d					12 37			13 07						13 37			14 07							
Old Hill	d								13 10									14 10							
Cradley Heath	d					12 42			13 14						13 42			14 14							
Lye	d								13 17									14 17							
Stourbridge Junction 2	d					12 47			13a21						13 47			14a21							
Hagley	d					12 51									13 51										
Blakedown	d					12 54																			
Kidderminster	d					12 59									13 57										
Hartlebury	d																								
University	d		12 06									13 06													
Barnt Green	d																								
Bromsgrove 69	d		12 20									13 20													
Droitwich Spa	d		12 32			13 11						13 29			14 08										
Worcester Shrub Hill 7	a		12 40																						
	d		12 47																					14 16	14 31
Worcester Foregate Street 7	a		12 49			13 20						13 39			14 17									14 19	14 33
	d		12 50																					14 20	14 34
Malvern Link	d		12 59																					14 29	14 43
Great Malvern	a		13 01																					14 31	14 45
	d		13 02																					14 32	
Colwall	d		13 07																					14 38	
Ledbury	a		13 14																					14 45	
	d		13 15																					14 48	
Hereford 7	a		13 32																					15 04	

Table T071-F

Sundays

15 December to 10 May

Stratford-upon-Avon, Marylebone and Leamington Spa - Birmingham - Stourbridge, Worcester and Hereford

		LM		LM	XC ◇1 ⊤	CH ◇	LM	XC ◇1 ⊤	LM	LM	CH ◇	CH		XC ◇1 ⊤	LM	CH ◇	LM	CH ◇	XC ◇1 ⊤	LM	CH ◇	CH ◇		GW ◇1 ⊤	LM
Stratford-upon-Avon	d			13 27											14 27			14 43							
Stratford-upon-Avon Parkway	d			13 31											14 31			14 47							
Wilmcote	d			13 34											14 34			14 50							
Wootton Wawen	d			13x38											14x38										
Henley-in-Arden	d			13 43											14 43										
Danzey	d																								
Wood End	d																								
The Lakes	d			13x49											14x49										
Earlswood (West Midlands)	d			13 52											14 52										
Wythall	d			13 55											14 55										
Whitlocks End	d			13 57											14 57										
Shirley	d			14 00											15 00										
Yardley Wood	d			14 03											15 03										
Hall Green	d			14 06											15 06										
Spring Road	d			14 08											15 08										
London Marylebone 10 ⊖115	d					12 40					13 10					13 40					14 10	13 43			
Banbury	d				13 34	13 39		13 57			14 08			14 24		14 39			14 57		15 07	15 10			
Leamington Spa 8	a				13 51	13 56		14 14			14 25			14 41		14 56		15 13	15 14		15 24	15 30			
	d				13 52	13 57		14 15		14 19	14 26	14 32		14 42		14 57			15 15	15 19	15 25	15 32			
Warwick	d					14 01						14 38				15 01						15 37			
Warwick Parkway	d					14 05					14 32					15 05					15 32				
Hatton	d											14 44										15a44			
Lapworth	d											14 50													
Dorridge	d					14 15	14 27					14 55				15 15	15 27								
Widney Manor	d						14 32										15 32								
Solihull	d					14 21	14 35				14 45	15 01				15 21	15 35				15 45				
Olton	d						14 38										15 38								
Acocks Green	d						14 41										15 41								
Tyseley	d			14 11											15 11										
Small Heath	d																								
Bordesley	d																								
Birmingham Moor Street	d			14 16		14 30	14 48				14a56	15a13			15 16	15 30	15 48				15a56				
Birmingham Snow Hill	a			14 19		14 37	14 50								15 19	15 37	15 50								
	d			14 22			14 52								15 22		15 52								
Jewellery Quarter	d			14 24			14 54								15 24		15 54								
The Hawthorns	d			14 28			14 58								15 28		15 58								
Smethwick Galton Bridge 7	d			14 31			15 01								15 31		16 01								
Coventry	a							14 26		14 39				14 53					15 26	15 39					
Birmingham Intl. 68 ✈	a							14 36						15 03					15 36						
Birmingham New Street 12 68	a				14 18			14 48						15 14					15 48						
	d	14 00							15 00																16 00
Langley Green	d						15 04										16 04								
Rowley Regis	d			14 37			15 07								15 37		16 07								
Old Hill	d						15 10										16 10								
Cradley Heath	d			14 42			15 14								15 42		16 14								
Lye	d						15 17										16 17								
Stourbridge Junction 2	d			14 47			15a21								15 47		16a21								
Hagley	d			14 51											15 51										
Blakedown	d			14 54																					
Kidderminster	d			14 59											15 57										
Hartlebury	d																								
University	d	14 06							15 06																16 06
Barnt Green	d																								
Bromsgrove 69	d	14 20							15 20																16 21
Droitwich Spa	d	14 32		15 11					15 31						16 08										16 31
Worcester Shrub Hill 7	a	14 39							15 37																16 38
	d	14 48							15 52															16 15	16 47
Worcester Foregate Street 7	a	14 50		15 20					15 54						16 17									16 18	16 49
	d	14 51							15 55															16 19	16 50
Malvern Link	d	15 00							16 04															16 28	16 59
Great Malvern	a	15 02							16 06															16 30	17 01
	d	15 03							16 07															16 31	17 02
Colwall	d	15 08							16 12															16 36	17 07
Ledbury	a	15 15							16 19															16 43	17 14
	d	15 15							16 19															16 44	17 15
Hereford 7	a	15 31							16 35															17 01	17 33

Table T071-F

Sundays
15 December to 10 May

Stratford-upon-Avon, Marylebone and Leamington Spa - Birmingham - Stourbridge, Worcester and Hereford

		XC ◇1 🛒	LM	CH ◇	LM	XC ◇1 🛒	LM	LM		CH ◇	LM	GW ◇1 🛒	CH	XC ◇1 🛒	LM	CH ◇	LM	CH ◇		XC ◇1 🛒	LM	LM	CH ◇	CH ◇	XC ◇1 🛒
Stratford-upon-Avon	d		15 27												16 27			16 43							
Stratford-upon-Avon Parkway	d		15 31												16 31			16 47							
Wilmcote	d		15 34												16 34			16 50							
Wootton Wawen	d		15x38												16x38										
Henley-in-Arden	d		15 43												16 43										
Danzey	d																								
Wood End	d																								
The Lakes	d		15x49												16x49										
Earlswood (West Midlands)	d		15 52												16 52										
Wythall	d		15 55												16 55										
Whitlocks End	d		15 57												16 57										
Shirley	d		16 00												17 00										
Yardley Wood	d		16 03												17 03										
Hall Green	d		16 06												17 06										
Spring Road	d		16 08												17 08										
London Marylebone 10 ⊖115	d			14 40						15 10						15 40							16 10	15 43	
Banbury	d	15 24		15 39		15 57				16 08				16 24		16 39				16 57			17 08	17 10	17 24
Leamington Spa 8	a	15 41		15 56		16 14				16 25				16 41		16 56		17 13		17 14			17 25	17 30	17 41
	d	15 42		15 57		16 15		16 19		16 26			16 32	16 42		16 57				17 15		17 19	17 26	17 32	17 42
Warwick	d			16 01									16 38			17 01								17 37	
Warwick Parkway	d			16 05						16 32						17 05							17 32		
Hatton	d												16 44											17a44	
Lapworth	d												16 50												
Dorridge	d			16 15	16 27								16 55			17 15	17 27								
Widney Manor	d				16 32												17 32								
Solihull	d			16 21	16 35					16 45			17 01			17 21	17 35						17 45		
Olton	d				16 38												17 38								
Acocks Green	d				16 41												17 41								
Tyseley	d		16 11												17 11										
Small Heath	d																								
Bordesley	d																								
Birmingham Moor Street	d		16 16	16 30	16 48					16a56	17 02		17a13		17 16	17 30	17 48						17a56		
Birmingham Snow Hill 🚊	a		16 19	16 37	16 50						17 04				17 19	17 37	17 50								
	d		16 22		16 51						17 06				17 22		17 52								
Jewellery Quarter 🚊	d		16 24		16 53										17 24		17 54								
The Hawthorns 🚊	d		16 28		16 57										17 28		17 58								
Smethwick Galton Bridge 7	d		16 31		17 00										17 31		18 01								
Coventry	a	15 53				16 26		16 39						16 53						17 26		17 39			17 53
Birmingham Intl. 68 ✈	a	16 03				16 36								17 03						17 36					18 03
Birmingham New Street 12 68	a	16 14				16 48								17 14						17 48					18 14
	d						17 00														18 00				
Langley Green	d				17 03												18 04								
Rowley Regis	d		16 37		17 06										17 37		18 07								
Old Hill	d				17 09												18 10								
Cradley Heath	d		16 42		17 13										17 42		18 14								
Lye	d				17 16												18 17								
Stourbridge Junction 2	d		16 47		17a20						17 24				17 47		18a21								
Hagley	d		16 51								17 27				17 51										
Blakedown	d																								
Kidderminster	d		16 57								17 33				17 59										
Hartlebury	d																								
University	d						17 06														18 06				
Barnt Green	d																								
Bromsgrove 69	d						17 20														18 20				
Droitwich Spa	d		17 08				17 31				17 45				18 11						18 32				
Worcester Shrub Hill 7	a						17 39				17 52										18 41				
	d											18 01									18 48				
Worcester Foregate Street 7	a		17 17									18 03			18 21						18 50				
	d											18 05									18 51				
Malvern Link	d											18 14									19 00				
Great Malvern	a											18 16									19 02				
	d											18 29									19 03				
Colwall	d											18 35									19 08				
Ledbury	a											18 42									19 15				
	d											18 44									19 15				
Hereford 7	a											19 00									19 32				

Table T071-F

Sundays
15 December to 10 May

Stratford-upon-Avon, Marylebone and Leamington Spa - Birmingham - Stourbridge, Worcester and Hereford

		LM	CH ◇	LM		XC ◇1 🛒	LM	LM	CH ◇	CH	XC ◇1 🛒	GW ◇1 🛒	LM	CH ◇		XC ◇1 🛒	LM	CH	LM	CH ◇	CH ◇	XC ◇1 🛒	GW ◇1 🛒	LM
Stratford-upon-Avon	d	17 27											18 27					18 44						19 27
Stratford-upon-Avon Parkway	d	17 31											18 31					18 48						19 31
Wilmcote	d	17 34											18 34					18 51						19 34
Wootton Wawen	d	17x38											18x38											19x38
Henley-in-Arden	d	17 43											18 43											19 43
Danzey	d																							
Wood End	d																							
The Lakes	d	17x49											18x49											19x49
Earlswood (West Midlands)	d																							
Wythall	d	17 53											18 53											19 53
Whitlocks End	d	17 56											18 56											19 56
Shirley	d	17 59											18 59											19 59
Yardley Wood	d	18 01											19 01											20 01
Hall Green	d	18 05											19 05											20 05
Spring Road	d	18 07											19 07											20 07
London Marylebone 10 ⊖115	d		16 40						17 10					17 40						18 10	17 43			
Banbury	d		17 39			17 57			18 08		18 24			18 39		18 57				19 07	19 10	19 24		
Leamington Spa 8	a		17 56			18 14			18 25		18 41			18 56		19 14		19 18		19 24	19 30	19 41		
	d		17 57			18 15		18 19	18 26	18 32	18 42			18 57		19 15			19 19	19 25	19 32	19 42		
Warwick	d		18 01							18 38				19 01							19 37			
Warwick Parkway	d		18 05						18 32					19 05						19 32				
Hatton	d									18 44											19a44			
Lapworth	d									18 50														
Dorridge	d		18 15	18 27						18 55				19 15										
Widney Manor	d			18 32						18 59														
Solihull	d		18 21	18 35					18 45	19 02				19 21						19 45				
Olton	d			18 38																				
Acocks Green	d			18 41																				
Tyseley	d	18 10											19 10											20 10
Small Heath	d																							
Bordesley	d																							
Birmingham Moor Street	d	18 15	18 30	18 48					18a56	19a13			19 15	19 30						19 55				20 15
Birmingham Snow Hill 🚊	a	18 17	18 37	18 50									19 17	19 37						19 57				20 17
	d	18 22											19 22							19 59				20 22
Jewellery Quarter 🚊	d	18 24											19 24											20 24
The Hawthorns 🚊	d	18 28											19 28											20 28
Smethwick Galton Bridge 7	d	18 31											19 31											20 31
Coventry	a					18 26		18 39			18 53					19 26			19 40			19 53		
Birmingham Intl. 68 ✈	a					18 36					19 03					19 36						20 03		
Birmingham New Street 12 68	a					18 48					19 14					19 48						20 14		
	d						19 00										20 00							
Langley Green	d																							
Rowley Regis	d	18 37											19 37							20 12				20 37
Old Hill	d																							
Cradley Heath	d	18 42											19 42											20 42
Lye	d																							
Stourbridge Junction 2	d	18 47											19 47							20 23				20 47
Hagley	d	18 51											19 51											20 51
Blakedown	d	18 54																						
Kidderminster	d	18 59											19 57							20a36				20 57
Hartlebury	d																							
University	d						19 06										20 06							
Barnt Green	d																							
Bromsgrove 69	d						19 20										20 20							
Droitwich Spa	d	19 11					19 31						20 09				20 30							21 09
Worcester Shrub Hill 7	a	19 19					19 39						20 17				20 44							21 17
	d						19 48					20 00					20 59						21 06	21 22
Worcester Foregate Street 7	a						19 50					20 02					21 01						21 08	21 24
	d						19 51					20 03											21 09	21 24
Malvern Link	d						20 00					20 12											21 18	21 33
Great Malvern	a						20 02					20 14											21 21	21 36
	d						20 03																21 26	
Colwall	d						20 08																21 32	
Ledbury	a						20 15																21 39	
	d						20 15																21 41	
Hereford 7	a						20 31																21 58	

Table T071-F

Sundays
15 December to 10 May

Stratford-upon-Avon, Marylebone and Leamington Spa - Birmingham - Stourbridge, Worcester and Hereford

		CH	XC	LM	LM	CH	XC	CH	CH	XC		LM	GW	LM	CH	LM	XC	LM	CH	XC		LM	LM	CH	XC	CH
		◇	◇■ ✕			◇	◇■	◇	◇	◇■			◇■ ✕		◇		◇■		◇	◇■				◇	◇■	◇
Stratford-upon-Avon	d								20 38																	
Stratford-upon-Avon Parkway	d								20 42																	
Wilmcote	d								20 45																	
Wootton Wawen	d																									
Henley-in-Arden	d																									
Danzey	d																									
Wood End	d																									
The Lakes	d																									
Earlswood (West Midlands)	d																									
Wythall	d																									
Whitlocks End	d																									
Shirley	d																									
Yardley Wood	d																									
Hall Green	d																									
Spring Road	d																									
London Marylebone ■ ⊖115	d	18 40				19 10		19 40							20 10				20 40					21 10		22 08
Banbury	d	19 39	19 57			20 08	20 24	20 39		20 57					21 08		21 24		21 39	21 54				22 08	22 24	23 09
Leamington Spa ■	a	19 56	20 14			20 25	20 41	20 56	21 07	21 14					21 25		21 41		21 56	22 11				22 25	22 41	23 26
	d	19 57	20 15		20 19	20 26	20 42	20 57		21 15		21 19			21 26		21 42		21 57	22 12		22 19		22 26	22 42	23 27
Warwick	d	20 01						21 01											22 01					22 30		23 31
Warwick Parkway	d	20 05				20 32		21 05							21 32				22 05					22 34		23 34
Hatton	d							21 10																22 40		
Lapworth	d							21 16																22 46		
Dorridge	d	20 15						21 21											22 15					22 51		23 44
Widney Manor	d							21 25																22 54		
Solihull	d	20 21				20 45		21 29							21 45				22 21					22 58		23 50
Olton	d																									
Acocks Green	d																									
Tyseley	d																									
Small Heath	d																									
Bordesley	d																									
Birmingham Moor Street	d	20 30				20a56		21 38						21 43	21a56				22 30				22 51	23 07		23 59
Birmingham Snow Hill ⇋	a	20 37						21 40						21 45					22 32				22 53	23 14		00 07
	d							21 42						21 46					22 34				22 55			
Jewellery Quarter ⇋	d													21 48									22 57			
The Hawthorns ⇋	d													21 52									23 01			
Smethwick Galton Bridge ■	d													21 55									23 04			
Coventry	a		20 26		20 40		20 53			21 26		21 40					21 53			22 23		22 37			22 53	
Birmingham Intl. 68 ✈	a		20 36				21 03			21 36							22 03			22 33					23 03	
Birmingham New Street ■ 68	a		20 48				21 15			21 48							22 14			22 44					23 14	
	d			21 00												22 00		22 30								
Langley Green	d																									
Rowley Regis	d							21 54						22 00					22 46				23 10			
Old Hill	d																									
Cradley Heath	d							21 59						22 05					22 51				23 15			
Lye	d																									
Stourbridge Junction ■	d							22 05						22 10					22 57				23 22			
Hagley	d													22 14									23 25			
Blakedown	d																									
Kidderminster	d							22a18						22 20					23a10				23 31			
Hartlebury	d																									
University	d			21 06												22 06		22 36								
Barnt Green	d																									
Bromsgrove 69	d			21 20												22 20		22 50								
Droitwich Spa	d			21 30										22 31		22 36		23 00					23 43			
Worcester Shrub Hill ■	a			21 38										22 39		22 45		23 08					23 51			
	d			21 41									22 04			22 51										
Worcester Foregate Street ■	a			21 43									22 06			22 53										
	d			21 44									22 08			22 54										
Malvern Link	d			21 53									22 17			23 03										
Great Malvern	a			21 55									22 19			23 05										
	d			21 56																						
Colwall	d			22 01																						
Ledbury	a			22 08																						
	d			22 09																						
Hereford ■	a			22 27																						

Table T071-R

Mondays to Fridays
16 December to 15 May

Hereford, Worcester and Stourbridge - Birmingham - Leamington Spa, Marylebone and Stratford-upon-Avon

Miles	Miles	Miles			LM MX	CH MX	CH	CH	LM	XC	CH	CH	CH		LM	XC	CH	LM	LM	GW	LM	GW	LM		CH
							◇	◇		◇■ ✕	◇					◇■	◇			◇■ ✕		◇■ ✕			◇
0	—	—	**Hereford** ■	d																04 48		05 23			
13¾	—	—	Ledbury	a																05 04		05 39			
—	—	—		d																05 05		05 40			
18	—	—	Colwall	d																05 13		05 47			
20¾	—	—	**Great Malvern**	a																05 17		05 51			
—	—	—		d																05 18	05 43	05 52			
22	—	—	Malvern Link	d																05 21	05 46	05 56			
28¾	0	—	**Worcester Foregate Street** ■	a																05 30	05 55	06 05			
—	—	—		d																05 31	06 02	06 06			
29½	—	—	**Worcester Shrub Hill** ■	a																05 34		06 09			
—	—	—		d															05 30						
34¼	5½	—	Droitwich Spa	d															05 38		06 11				
40½	—	—	Bromsgrove 69	d																	06 21				
44	—	—	Barnt Green	d																					
52	—	—	University	d																	06 39				
—	11	—	Hartlebury	d																					
—	14¾	—	**Kidderminster**	d															05 48						06 09
—	17¾	—	Blakedown	d																					
—	19¾	—	Hagley	d																					
—	21½	—	**Stourbridge Junction** ■	d															05 56						06 18
—	22¾	—	Lye	d															06 00						
—	24	—	Cradley Heath	d															06 03						
—	25½	—	Old Hill	d															06 07						
—	26¾	—	Rowley Regis	d															06 10						06 30
—	28½	0	Langley Green	d															06 13						
54½	—	6¼	**Birmingham New Street** ■ 68	a																	06 48				
—	—	—		d						06 04						06 33									
—	—	—	**Birmingham Intl.** 68 ✈	d						06 14															
—	—	—	**Coventry**	d						06 25					06 41										
—	29½	—	Smethwick Galton Bridge ■	d															06 17						06 38
—	30¼	—	The Hawthorns ⇋	d															06 19						06 42
—	32¾	—	Jewellery Quarter ⇋	d															06 23						
—	33½	—	**Birmingham Snow Hill** ⇋	a															06 27						06 48
—	—	—		d					05 53									06 30	06 35				06 40		06 50
—	34	—	**Birmingham Moor Street**	d			05 15	05 42	05 56		06 10						06 28	06 33	06 38				06 43		06 55
—	34¾	—	Bordesley	d																					
—	35¾	9¼	Small Heath	d					05 59									06 36	06 42				06 46		
—	36¾	10¼	Tyseley	d					06 02									06 39	06 45				06 49		
—	—	11¼	Acocks Green	d					06 05										06 48						
—	—	12¾	Olton	d					06 07										06 51						
—	—	14	Solihull	d			05 24	05 51	06 11		06 19						06 38		06 54						07 04
—	—	15½	Widney Manor	d					06 14										06 57						
—	—	17½	Dorridge	d				05 56	06 18		06 24						06 50		07a02						
—	—	20	Lapworth	d					06 22																
—	—	24¼	Hatton	d		00 05						06 32													
—	—	27	Warwick Parkway	d		00 10	05 36	06 05			06 34						06 59								07 18
—	—	28¼	Warwick	d	00 01	00 13		06 08				06 40					07 02								
—	—	30¼	**Leamington Spa** ■	a	00 06	00 17	05 41	06 12		06 36	06 40	06 46			06 55	06 58	07 06								07 23
—	—	—		d		00 18	05 41	06 13		06 37	06 41		06 51			07 00	07 06								07 24
—	—	—	Banbury	d		00a41	05 59	06 31		06a53	06 59					07a16	07 24								
—	—	—	**London Marylebone** ■ ⊖115	a			07 03	07 35			08 02						08 33								08 34
—	37¾	—	Spring Road	d														06 42					06 52		
—	38¼	—	Hall Green	d														06 44					06 54		
—	39½	—	Yardley Wood	d														06 47					06 57		
—	40¾	—	Shirley	d														06 50					07 00		
—	41¾	—	Whitlocks End	d														06 53					07 03		
—	42¾	—	Wythall	d														06 56					07 05		
—	43¾	—	Earlswood (West Midlands)	d																			07 08		
—	44½	—	The Lakes	d																			07x10		
—	45¾	—	Wood End	d																			07x12		
—	47½	—	Danzey	d																			07x15		
—	50¼	—	Henley-in-Arden	d														07 06					07 20		
—	52¼	—	Wootton Wawen	d																			07x23		
—	56	—	Wilmcote	d					06 40				07 20										07 28		
—	57¾	—	Stratford-upon-Avon Parkway	a					06 43				07 22					07 15					07 31		
—	58¾	—	**Stratford-upon-Avon**	a					06 48				07 31					07 21					07 36		

Table T071-R

Mondays to Fridays
16 December to 15 May

Hereford, Worcester and Stourbridge - Birmingham - Leamington Spa, Marylebone and Stratford-upon-Avon

		XC	LM	LM	CH	LM	LM	XC	CH	CH	CH	LM	LM	LM	LM	LM	CH	LM	LM	GW	LM	XC	CH
		◇1 ⊥			◇			◇1 ⊥	◇	◇							◇					◇1 ⊥	◇
Hereford 7	d																						
Ledbury	a																						
	d																						
Colwall	d																						
Great Malvern	a																				06 47		
	d																				06 50		
Malvern Link	d																				06 58		
Worcester Foregate Street 7	a																			06 53	06 59		
	d																			06 55	07 01		
Worcester Shrub Hill 7	a											06 12	06 25		06 30				06 49		07 05		
	d											06 20	06 33		06 39				07 03		07 13		
Droitwich Spa	d												06 43								07 23		
Bromsgrove 69	d																						
Barnt Green	d																						
University	d												07 00								07 38		
Hartlebury	d											06 27			06 46				07 10				
Kidderminster	d			06 19								06 33			06 51		07 10		07 16				07 30
Blakedown	d											06 37			06 56				07 20				
Hagley	d											06 41			06 59				07 24				
Stourbridge Junction 2	d		06 24	06 28	06 41	06 45						06 50			07 04	07 10	07 21		07 28				07 38
Lye	d		06 28	06 32								06 54				07 14			07 32				
Cradley Heath	d		06 31	06 35		06 51						06 57			07 11	07 17			07 35				07 44
Old Hill	d		06 34	06 39								07 00				07 21			07 38				
Rowley Regis	d		06 38	06 42	06 52	06 56						07 04			07 17	07 24	07 30		07 42				07 51
Langley Green	d		06 41	06 45								07 07				07 28			07 45				
Birmingham New Street 12 68	a												07 10								07 46		
	d	07 04						07 33														08 04	
Birmingham Intl. 68 ✈	d	07 14																				08 14	
Coventry	d	07 25					07 40															08 25	
Smethwick Galton Bridge 7	d		06 44	06 49		07 03						07 10			07 23	07 31	07 38		07 48				07 57
The Hawthorns	d		06 46	06 51		07 05						07 12			07 25	07 33			07 50				08 00
Jewellery Quarter	d		06 50	06 55		07 09						07 16			07 30	07 37	07 45		07 57				
Birmingham Snow Hill	a		06 54	07 00	07 05	07 13						07 22			07 34	07 41	07 48		08 03				08 07
	d		06 56	07 01	07 07	07 15					07 19	07 25		07 35	07 40	07 46	07 50	07 59	08 04				08 08
Birmingham Moor Street	d		06 59	07 04	07 11	07 18					07 22	07 28		07 38	07 43	07 49	07 54	08 02	08 07				08 11
Bordesley	d																						
Small Heath	d		07 02									07 31		07 41					08 10				
Tyseley	d		07 05									07 34		07 45	07 48	07 55			08 14				
Acocks Green	d		07 08			07 24					07 29				07 51								
Olton	d		07 11			07 27					07 32				07 54								
Solihull	d		07 15		07 22	07 30					07 36				07 57		08 04	08 13					08 20
Widney Manor	d		07 18			07 34					07 40				08 01								
Dorridge	d		07 22		07 29	07 38					07 52				08a06			08a19					08 25
Lapworth	d		07 25								07 56												
Hatton	d		07 30							07 55	08 02												
Warwick Parkway	d		07 34		07 40					08 00							08 17						08 35
Warwick	d		07 37							08 04	08 07												08 38
Leamington Spa 8	a	07 36	07 41		07 46	07 52	07 55	07 58		08 08	08 16						08 22					08 36	08 42
	d	07 37			07 47			08 00	08 08	08 09							08 23					08 37	08 43
Banbury	d	07a53			08 06			08a16		08 28							08 41					08a53	09 02
London Marylebone 10 ⊖115	a				09 07					09 35							09 38						09 59
Spring Road	d			07 10								07 37		07 47		07 58			08 16				
Hall Green	d			07 13								07 39		07 50		08 00			08 19				
Yardley Wood	d			07 15								07 42		07 52		08 03			08 21				
Shirley	d			07 19								07 45		07 56		08 09			08 25				
Whitlocks End	d			07a21								07 48		07a58		08a11			08a28				
Wythall	d											07 51											
Earlswood (West Midlands)	d											07 53											
The Lakes	d											07x56											
Wood End	d											07x58											
Danzey	d											08x01											
Henley-in-Arden	d											08 06											
Wootton Wawen	d											08x09											
Wilmcote	d								08 35			08 15											
Stratford-upon-Avon Parkway	a								08 37			08 18											
Stratford-upon-Avon	a								08 46			08 23											

Table T071-R

Mondays to Fridays
16 December to 15 May

Hereford, Worcester and Stourbridge - Birmingham - Leamington Spa, Marylebone and Stratford-upon-Avon

		LM	LM	GW	LM	XC	CH	LM	LM	LM	LM	CH	LM	LM	XC	LM	CH	CH	CH	LM	LM	LM	XC
				◇1 A ⊥		◇1 ⊥	◇					◇			■1 ⊥				◇				◇1 ⊥
Hereford 7	d			06 43							07 09					07 32							
Ledbury	a			06 59							07 24					07 49							
	d			07 00							07 25					07 50							
Colwall	d			07 08							07 31					07 57							
Great Malvern	a			07 12							07 36					08 01							
	d		07 02	07 13							07 36					08 07							
Malvern Link	d		07 05	07 16							07 39					08 10							
Worcester Foregate Street 7	a		07 14	07 25							07 48					08 18							
	d	07 14	07 16	07 26							07 48			08 02		08 24							
Worcester Shrub Hill 7	a		07 18	07 29							07 51												
	d		07 23						07 35		07 54												
Droitwich Spa	d	07 23	07 33						07 43		08 02			08 11		08 33							
Bromsgrove 69	d															08 42							
Barnt Green	d																						
University	d		08 00								08 30					09 00							
Hartlebury	d	07 30												08 18									
Kidderminster	d	07 36						07 49	07 54			08 09		08 24									
Blakedown	d	07 40							07 59			08 14		08 28									
Hagley	d	07 44							08 03			08 19		08 31									
Stourbridge Junction 2	d	07 48						07 57	08 07	08 15		08 23		08 35						08 44	08 57		
Lye	d							08 01		08 19				08 39							09 01		
Cradley Heath	d	07 54						08 04	08 13	08 22		08 29		08 42						08 50	09 04		
Old Hill	d							08 07		08 25				08 46							09 07		
Rowley Regis	d	07 59						08 11	08 19	08 29		08 35		08 49						08 55	09 11		
Langley Green	d							08 14		08 32				08 52							09 14		
Birmingham New Street 12 68	a		08 09								08 40					09 09							
	d					08 33									09 04								09 33
Birmingham Intl. 68 ✈	d														09 14							09 37	
Coventry	d				08 35										09 25								
Smethwick Galton Bridge 7	d	08 05						08 17	08 25	08 35		08 41		08 56						09 01	09 17		
The Hawthorns	d	08 07						08 19	08 28	08 37		08 44		08 58						09 03	09 19		
Jewellery Quarter	d	08 11						08 23	08 32	08 41		08 49		09 02						09 07	09 23		
Birmingham Snow Hill	a	08 15						08 26	08 35	08 45		08 51		09 07						09 12	09 26		
	d	08 17					08 22	08 28	08 37	08 47		08 52	08 59	09 08					09 12	09 17	09 28		
Birmingham Moor Street	d	08 20					08 25	08 31	08 40	08 50		08 55	09 02	09 11					09 15	09 20	09 31		
Bordesley	d																						
Small Heath	d								08 43					09 14									
Tyseley	d								08 46					09 18									
Acocks Green	d	08 26							08 49				09 08							09 26			
Olton	d	08 29							08 52				09 11							09 29			
Solihull	d	08 32					08 37		08 56			09 07	09 14						09 24	09 32			
Widney Manor	d	08 36							08 59				09 18							09 36			
Dorridge	d	08a41					08 52		09a05				09 22						09 29	09a41			
Lapworth	d																						
Hatton	d																09 21						
Warwick Parkway	d						09 02					09 19							09 39				
Warwick	d						09 06										09 28		09 42				
Leamington Spa 8	a				08 53	08 58	09 11					09 24			09 36		09 37		09 46			09 53	10 03
	d					09 00	09 12					09 25			09 37			09 40	09 46				10 04
Banbury	d					09a16	09 31					09 44			09a53				10 04				10a20
London Marylebone 10 ⊖115	a						10 36					10 40							11 08				
Spring Road	d							08 37		08 56				09 20							09 37		
Hall Green	d							08 39		08 59				09 23							09 39		
Yardley Wood	d							08 42		09 01				09 25							09 42		
Shirley	d							08 45		09 05				09 29							09 45		
Whitlocks End	d							08 48		09a07				09a31							09 48		
Wythall	d							08 51													09 51		
Earlswood (West Midlands)	d							08 53													09 53		
The Lakes	d							08x56													09x56		
Wood End	d							08x58													09x58		
Danzey	d							09x01													10x01		
Henley-in-Arden	d							09 06													10 06		
Wootton Wawen	d							09x09													10x09		
Wilmcote	d							09 15										10 06			10 15		
Stratford-upon-Avon Parkway	a							09 18					09 38					10 08			10 18		
Stratford-upon-Avon	a							09 21					09 42					10 17			10 23		

A The Cathedrals Express

Table T071-R

Mondays to Fridays
16 December to 15 May

Hereford, Worcester and Stourbridge - Birmingham - Leamington Spa, Marylebone and Stratford-upon-Avon

Station			CH ◇	LM	LM	LM	CH ◇	LM	XC ◇1	GW	LM		LM	GW ◇1	LM	CH ◇	LM	LM	LM	LM	GW ◇1		LM	XC ◇1	CH ◇
Hereford [7]	d														08 45										
Ledbury	a														09 03										
	d														09 06										
Colwall	d														09 13										
Great Malvern	a														09 17										
	d							08 36						08 56	09 18						09 54				
Malvern Link	d							08 39						08 59	09 21						09 57				
Worcester Foregate Street [7]	a							08 47						09 08	09 30						10 06				
	d					08 39		08 50		08 55			09 03	09 09	09 31						10 07				
Worcester Shrub Hill [7]	a					08 41				08 57				09 12	09 33						10 10				
	d					08 45									09 36					09 52					
Droitwich Spa	d					08 53		08 59					09 12		09 43					10 00					
Bromsgrove 69	d							09 08							09 54										
Barnt Green	d																								
University	d							09 30							10 11										
Hartlebury	d												09 19												
Kidderminster	d			08 57		09 06							09 25				09 36		09 55	10 10					
Blakedown	d			09 01		09 10							09 29				09 40		09 59						
Hagley	d			09 05		09 14							09 33				09 44		10 03						
Stourbridge Junction [2]	d			09 09	09 15	09 19					09 27		09 37				09 48	09 57	10 07	10 18					
Lye	d										09 31							10 01							
Cradley Heath	d			09 14	09 20	09 25					09 34		09 43				09 54	10 04	10 13	10 24					
Old Hill	d										09 37							10 07							
Rowley Regis	d			09 20	09 26	09 30					09 41		09 48				09 59	10 11	10 18	10 29					
Langley Green	d										09 44							10 14							
Birmingham New Street [12] 68	a							09 39							10 20										
	d								10 04																
Birmingham Intl. 68 ✈	d								10 14															10 33	
Coventry	d								10 25														10 37		
Smethwick Galton Bridge [7]	d			09 25	09 31	09 36					09 47		09 54				10 05	10 17	10 24	10 35					
The Hawthorns	d			09 27		09 38					09 49		09 56				10 07	10 19	10 26	10 37					
Jewellery Quarter	d			09 31		09 42					09 53		10 00				10 11	10 23	10 30	10 41					
Birmingham Snow Hill	a			09 35	09 38	09 46					09 56		10 04				10 15	10 26	10 34	10 45					
	d			09 37		09 47					09 58		10 07			10 12	10 17	10 28	10 37	10 47					
Birmingham Moor Street	d		09 34	09 40		09 50	09 55				10 01		10 10			10 15	10 20	10 31	10 40	10 50					
Bordesley	d																								
Small Heath	d			09 43									10 13						10 43						
Tyseley	d			09 47									10 17						10 47						
Acocks Green	d			09 49							10 07						10 26		10 49						
Olton	d			09 52							10 10						10 28		10 52						
Solihull	d		09 43	09 56			10 04				10 13					10 24	10 32		10 56						
Widney Manor	d			09 59							10 17						10 36		10 59						
Dorridge	d		09 51	10a04							10 21					10 29	10a41		11a04						
Lapworth	d		09 55																						
Hatton	d		10 00																						11 00
Warwick Parkway	d						10 16									10 39									
Warwick	d		10 06													10 42									11 08
Leamington Spa [8]	a		10 17				10 21		10 36							10 46							10 53	10 58	11 13
	d						10 22		10 37							10 46								11 00	11 15
Banbury	d						10 40		10a53							11 04								11a17	11 48
London Marylebone [10] ⊖115	a						11 40									12 08									13 05
Spring Road	d					09 56							10 19					10 37		10 56					
Hall Green	d					09 59							10 22					10 39		10 59					
Yardley Wood	d					10 01							10 24					10 42		11 01					
Shirley	d					10 05							10 28					10 45		11 05					
Whitlocks End	d					10a07							10a30					10 48		11a07					
Wythall	d																	10 51							
Earlswood (West Midlands)	d																	10 53							
The Lakes	d																	10x56							
Wood End	d																	10x58							
Danzey	d																	11x01							
Henley-in-Arden	d																	11 06							
Wootton Wawen	d																	11x09							
Wilmcote	d																	11 15							
Stratford-upon-Avon Parkway	a										10 37							11 18							
Stratford-upon-Avon	a										10 41							11 23							

Table T071-R

Mondays to Fridays
16 December to 15 May

Hereford, Worcester and Stourbridge - Birmingham - Leamington Spa, Marylebone and Stratford-upon-Avon

Station		CH ◇	LM	LM	CH ◇	XC ◇1	CH ◇		LM	LM	LM	LM	XC ◇1	CH	LM	LM	CH ◇		GW ◇	GW ◇1	LM	LM	XC ◇1	CH ◇	LM
Hereford [7]	d										09 39														
Ledbury	a										09 56														
	d										09 58														
Colwall	d										10 05														
Great Malvern	a										10 10														
	d										10 10								10 41	10 58					
Malvern Link	d										10 13								10 44	11 01					
Worcester Foregate Street [7]	a										10 22								10 52	11 10					
	d								10 16		10 24								10 53	11 11					11 16
Worcester Shrub Hill [7]	a																		10 55	11 14					
	d															10 52									
Droitwich Spa	d								10 25		10 33					11 00									11 25
Bromsgrove 69	d										10 43														
Barnt Green	d																								
University	d										11 00														
Hartlebury	d								10 32																11 32
Kidderminster	d			10 26					10 38						10 55	11 10						11 25			11 38
Blakedown	d			10 30											10 59							11 29			
Hagley	d			10 34					10 44						11 03							11 33			11 44
Stourbridge Junction [2]	d		10 28	10 38					10 48	10 57					11 07	11 18					11 27	11 37			11 48
Lye	d		10 31							11 01											11 31				
Cradley Heath	d		10 34	10 44					10 54	11 04					11 13	11 24					11 34	11 43			11 54
Old Hill	d		10 37							11 07											11 37				
Rowley Regis	d		10 41	10 49					10 59	11 11					11 18	11 29					11 41	11 48			11 59
Langley Green	d		10 44							11 14											11 44				
Birmingham New Street [12] 68	a										11 09														
	d					11 04							11 33										12 04		
Birmingham Intl. 68 ✈	d					11 14																	12 14		
Coventry	d					11 25						11 40											12 25		
Smethwick Galton Bridge [7]	d		10 47	10 55					11 05	11 17					11 24	11 35					11 47	11 54			12 05
The Hawthorns	d		10 49	10 57					11 07	11 19					11 26	11 37					11 49	11 56			12 07
Jewellery Quarter	d		10 53	11 01					11 11	11 23					11 30	11 41					11 53	12 00			12 11
Birmingham Snow Hill	a		10 56	11 05					11 15	11 26					11 34	11 45					11 56	12 04			12 15
	d		10 58	11 07			11 12		11 17	11 28					11 37	11 47					11 58	12 07		12 12	12 17
Birmingham Moor Street	d	10 55	11 01	11 10			11 15		11 20	11 31				11 34	11 40	11 50	11 55				12 01	12 10		12 15	12 20
Bordesley	d																								
Small Heath	d			11 13											11 43							12 13			
Tyseley	d			11 17											11 47							12 17			
Acocks Green	d		11 07						11 26						11 49						12 07				12 26
Olton	d		11 10						11 29						11 52						12 10				12 29
Solihull	d	11 04	11 13				11 24		11 32					11 43	11 56		12 04				12 13			12 24	12 32
Widney Manor	d		11 17						11 36						11 59						12 17				12 36
Dorridge	d		11 21				11 29		11a41					11 52	12a04						12 21			12 29	12a41
Lapworth	d													11 56											
Hatton	d													12 01											
Warwick Parkway	d	11 17					11 39										12 16							12 39	
Warwick	d						11 42							12 07										12 42	
Leamington Spa [8]	a	11 22				11 36	11 46					11 55	12 01	12 17			12 22						12 36	12 46	
	d	11 23			11 32	11 37	11 46						12 03				12 22						12 37	12 46	
Banbury	d	11 40				11a53	12 04						12a19				12 40						12a53	13 04	
London Marylebone [10] ⊖115	a	12 43					13 09										13 43							14 09	
Spring Road	d			11 19						11 37						11 56						12 19			
Hall Green	d			11 22						11 39						11 59						12 22			
Yardley Wood	d			11 24						11 42						12 01						12 24			
Shirley	d			11 28						11 45						12 05						12 28			
Whitlocks End	d			11a30						11 48						12a07						12a30			
Wythall	d									11 51															
Earlswood (West Midlands)	d									11 53															
The Lakes	d									11x56															
Wood End	d									11x58															
Danzey	d									12x01															
Henley-in-Arden	d									12 06															
Wootton Wawen	d									12x09															
Wilmcote	d				11 55					12 15															
Stratford-upon-Avon Parkway	a		11 37		11 57					12 18											12 37				
Stratford-upon-Avon	a		11 41		12 06					12 23											12 41				

Table T071-R

Mondays to Fridays
16 December to 15 May

Hereford, Worcester and Stourbridge - Birmingham - Leamington Spa, Marylebone and Stratford-upon-Avon

		LM	LM	LM	LM	GW	LM	XC	CH	CH	LM	LM	CH	XC	CH	LM	LM	LM	LM	XC	CH	LM
						◇1		◇1	◇	◇			◇	◇1	◇					◇1		
Hereford [7]	d		10 39															11 39				
Ledbury	a		10 56															11 55				
	d		10 58															11 58				
Colwall	d		11 05															12 05				
Great Malvern	a		11 10															12 10				
	d		11 10		11 35	11 55												12 10				
Malvern Link	d		11 13		11 38	11 58												12 13				
Worcester Foregate Street [7]	a		11 22		11 48	12 07												12 22				
	d		11 24		11 51	12 08										12 16		12 24				
Worcester Shrub Hill [7]	a					12 11																
	d																					
Droitwich Spa	d		11 33		12 00											12 25		12 33				
Bromsgrove 69	d		11 43															12 43				
Barnt Green	d																					
University	d		12 00															13 00				
Hartlebury	d															12 32						
Kidderminster	d			11 55	12 10							12 25				12 38						12 55
Blakedown	d			11 59								12 29										12 59
Hagley	d			12 03								12 33				12 44						13 03
Stourbridge Junction [2]	d	11 57		12 07	12 18						12 27	12 37				12 48	12 57					13 07
Lye	d	12 01									12 31						13 01					
Cradley Heath	d	12 04		12 13	12 24						12 34	12 43				12 54	13 04					13 13
Old Hill	d	12 07									12 37						13 07					
Rowley Regis	d	12 11		12 18	12 29						12 41	12 48				12 59	13 11					13 18
Langley Green	d	12 14									12 44						13 14					
Birmingham New Street [12] 68	a		12 09															13 10				
	d							12 33						13 04						13 33		
Birmingham Intl. 68 ✈	d													13 14								
Coventry	d						12 38							13 25					13 37			
Smethwick Galton Bridge [7]	d	12 17		12 24	12 35						12 47	12 54				13 05	13 17					13 24
The Hawthorns	d	12 19		12 26	12 37						12 49	12 56				13 07	13 19					13 26
Jewellery Quarter	d	12 23		12 30	12 41						12 53	13 00				13 11	13 23					13 30
Birmingham Snow Hill	a	12 26		12 34	12 45						12 56	13 04				13 15	13 26					13 34
	d	12 28		12 37	12 47						12 58	13 07			13 12	13 17	13 28					13 37
Birmingham Moor Street	d	12 31		12 40	12 50					12 55	13 01	13 10			13 15	13 20	13 31				13 34	13 40
Bordesley	d																					
Small Heath	d			12 43								13 13										13 43
Tyseley	d			12 47								13 17										13 47
Acocks Green	d			12 49							13 07					13 26						13 49
Olton	d			12 52							13 10					13 29						13 52
Solihull	d			12 56						13 04	13 13				13 24	13 32					13 43	13 56
Widney Manor	d			12 59							13 17					13 36						13 59
Dorridge	d			13a04							13 21				13 30	13a41					13 51	14a04
Lapworth	d																				13 54	
Hatton	d								13 00												14 00	
Warwick Parkway	d									13 17					13 40							
Warwick	d								13 08						13 44						14 05	
Leamington Spa [8]	a						12 55	12 58	13 13	13 22				13 36	13 48				13 53	14 01	14 17	
	d							13 00	13 15	13 23			13 32	13 37	13 49					14 03		
Banbury	d							13a19	13 45	13 41				13a53	14 07					14a19		
London Marylebone [10] ⊖115	a								15 05	14 43					15 09							
Spring Road	d	12 37			12 56							13 19					13 37					
Hall Green	d	12 39			12 59							13 22					13 39					
Yardley Wood	d	12 42			13 01							13 24					13 42					
Shirley	d	12 45			13 05							13 28					13 45					
Whitlocks End	d	12 48			13a07							13a30					13 48					
Wythall	d	12 51															13 51					
Earlswood (West Midlands)	d	12 53															13 53					
The Lakes	d	12x56															13x56					
Wood End	d	12x58															13x58					
Danzey	d	13x01															14x01					
Henley-in-Arden	d	13 06															14 06					
Wootton Wawen	d	13x09															14x09					
Wilmcote	d	13 15											13 59				14 15					
Stratford-upon-Avon Parkway	a	13 18									13 37		14 01				14 18					
Stratford-upon-Avon	a	13 23									13 41		14 10				14 23					

Table T071-R

Mondays to Fridays
16 December to 15 May

Hereford, Worcester and Stourbridge - Birmingham - Leamington Spa, Marylebone and Stratford-upon-Avon

		LM	CH	GW	LM	LM	XC	CH	LM	LM	LM	LM	LM	GW	LM	XC	CH	CH	LM	LM	CH	XC	CH
			◇	◇			◇1	◇						◇1		◇1	◇	◇			◇	◇1	◇
Hereford [7]	d										12 39			13 18									
Ledbury	a										12 57			13 34									
	d										12 58			13 35									
Colwall	d										13 05			13 42									
Great Malvern	a										13 10			13 46									
	d			12 42							13 10			13 47									
Malvern Link	d			12 45							13 13			13 51									
Worcester Foregate Street [7]	a			12 53							13 22			14 05									
	d			12 54							13 24		13 51	14 06									
Worcester Shrub Hill [7]	a			12 56										14 09									
	d	12 51							13 17														
Droitwich Spa	d	13 00							13 25		13 33		14 00										
Bromsgrove 69	d										13 42												
Barnt Green	d																						
University	d										14 00												
Hartlebury	d								13 32														
Kidderminster	d	13 10				13 25			13 38			13 55	14 10							14 25			
Blakedown	d					13 29						13 59								14 29			
Hagley	d					13 33			13 44			14 03								14 33			
Stourbridge Junction [2]	d	13 18			13 27	13 37			13 48	13 57		14 07	14 18						14 27	14 37			
Lye	d				13 31					14 01									14 31				
Cradley Heath	d	13 24			13 34	13 43			13 54	14 04		14 13	14 24						14 34	14 43			
Old Hill	d				13 37					14 07									14 37				
Rowley Regis	d	13 29			13 41	13 48			13 59	14 11		14 18	14 29						14 41	14 48			
Langley Green	d				13 44					14 14									14 44				
Birmingham New Street [12] 68	a										14 09												
	d						14 04									14 33						15 04	
Birmingham Intl. 68 ✈	d						14 14															15 14	
Coventry	d						14 25								14 35							15 25	
Smethwick Galton Bridge [7]	d	13 35			13 47	13 54			14 05	14 17		14 24	14 35						14 47	14 54			
The Hawthorns	d	13 37			13 49	13 56			14 07	14 19		14 26	14 37						14 49	14 56			
Jewellery Quarter	d	13 41			13 53	14 00			14 11	14 23		14 30	14 41						14 53	15 00			
Birmingham Snow Hill	a	13 45			13 56	14 04			14 15	14 26		14 34	14 45						14 56	15 04			
	d	13 47			13 58	14 07		14 12	14 17	14 28		14 37	14 47						14 58	15 07			15 12
Birmingham Moor Street	d	13 50	13 55		14 01	14 10		14 15	14 20	14 31		14 40	14 50					14 55	15 01	15 10			15 15
Bordesley	d																						
Small Heath	d					14 13						14 43								15 13			
Tyseley	d					14 17						14 47								15 17			
Acocks Green	d				14 07				14 26			14 49							15 07				
Olton	d				14 10				14 29			14 52							15 10				
Solihull	d		14 04		14 13			14 24	14 32			14 56						15 04	15 13				15 24
Widney Manor	d				14 17				14 36			14 59							15 17				
Dorridge	d				14 21			14 29	14a41			15a04							15 21				15 30
Lapworth	d																						
Hatton	d																15 00						
Warwick Parkway	d		14 16					14 39										15 16					15 40
Warwick	d							14 42									15 08						15 43
Leamington Spa [8]	a		14 21				14 36	14 46							14 52	14 58	15 13	15 21				15 36	15 47
	d		14 22				14 37	14 46								15 00	15 15	15 22			15 32	15 37	15 47
Banbury	d		14 40				14a53	15 04								15a16	15 48	15 42				15a53	16 05
London Marylebone [10] ⊖115	a		15 40					16 08									17 09	16 42					17 12
Spring Road	d	13 56				14 19				14 37			14 56							15 19			
Hall Green	d	13 59				14 22				14 39			14 59							15 22			
Yardley Wood	d	14 01				14 24				14 42			15 01							15 24			
Shirley	d	14 05				14 28				14 45			15 05							15 28			
Whitlocks End	d	14a07				14a30				14 48			15a07							15a30			
Wythall	d									14 51													
Earlswood (West Midlands)	d									14 53													
The Lakes	d									14x56													
Wood End	d									14x58													
Danzey	d									15x01													
Henley-in-Arden	d									15 06													
Wootton Wawen	d									15x09													
Wilmcote	d									15 15											15 59		
Stratford-upon-Avon Parkway	a				14 37					15 18									15 37		16 01		
Stratford-upon-Avon	a				14 41					15 23									15 41		16 10		

Table T071-R

Mondays to Fridays
16 December to 15 May

Hereford, Worcester and Stourbridge - Birmingham - Leamington Spa, Marylebone and Stratford-upon-Avon

Station		LM	LM	LM	LM	XC	CH	LM	LM	CH	GW	LM	LM	XC	CH	LM	LM	LM	LM	LM	LM	GW	LM
						◇[1]				◇	◇			◇[1]	◇							◇[1]	
Hereford [7]	d			13 41														14 39				15 18	
Ledbury	a			13 58														14 57				15 34	
	d			14 00														14 58				15 35	
Colwall	d			14 05														15 05				15 42	
Great Malvern	a			14 10														15 10				15 46	
	d	14 00		14 10							14 41							15 10			15 21	15 55	
Malvern Link	d	14 03		14 13							14 44							15 13			15 24	15 58	
Worcester Foregate Street [7]	a	14 12		14 23							14 52							15 22			15 33	16 07	
	d	14 16		14 24							14 53							15 24			15 33	16 08	
Worcester Shrub Hill [7]	a										14 55										15 36	16 11	
	d								14 52							15 17					15 47		
Droitwich Spa	d	14 25		14 33					15 00							15 25		15 33			15 55		
Bromsgrove 69	d			14 43														15 43					
Barnt Green	d																						
University	d			15 00														16 00					
Hartlebury	d	14 32														15 32							
Kidderminster	d	14 38						14 55	15 10				15 25			15 38				15 55	16 06		
Blakedown	d							14 59					15 29			15 42				15 59	16 10		
Hagley	d	14 44						15 03					15 33			15 46				16 03	16 14		
Stourbridge Junction [2]	d	14 48	14 57					15 07	15 18			15 27	15 37			15 50	15 57			16 07	16 18		
Lye	d		15 01									15 31					16 01						
Cradley Heath	d	14 54	15 04					15 13	15 24			15 34	15 43			15 55	16 04			16 13	16 24		
Old Hill	d		15 07									15 37					16 07						
Rowley Regis	d	14 59	15 11					15 18	15 29			15 41	15 48			16 00	16 11			16 18	16 29		
Langley Green	d		15 14									15 44					16 14						
Birmingham New Street [12] 68	a			15 09														16 10					
	d					15 33								16 04									
Birmingham Intl. 68 ✈	d													16 14									
Coventry	d				15 37									16 25									16 37
Smethwick Galton Bridge [7]	d	15 05	15 17					15 24	15 35			15 47	15 54			16 06	16 17			16 24	16 35		
The Hawthorns	d	15 07	15 19					15 26	15 37			15 49	15 56			16 08	16 19			16 26	16 37		
Jewellery Quarter	d	15 11	15 23					15 30	15 41			15 53	16 00			16 12	16 23			16 30	16 41		
Birmingham Snow Hill	a	15 15	15 26					15 34	15 45			15 56	16 04			16 16	16 26			16 34	16 45		
	d	15 17	15 28					15 37	15 47			15 58	16 07		16 12	16 17	16 28		16 32	16 37	16 47		
Birmingham Moor Street	d	15 20	15 31				15 34	15 40	15 50	15 55		16 01	16 10		16 15	16 20	16 31		16 35	16 40	16 50		
Bordesley	d																						
Small Heath	d							15 43					16 13						16 38	16 43	16 54		
Tyseley	d							15 47					16 17				16 36		16 42	16 47	16 57		
Acocks Green	d	15 26						15 49				16 07				16 26				16 49			
Olton	d	15 29						15 52				16 10				16 29				16 52			
Solihull	d	15 32					15 43	15 56		16 04		16 13			16 24	16 32				16 56			
Widney Manor	d	15 36						15 59				16 17				16 36				16 59			
Dorridge	d	15a41					15 52	16a04				16a22			16 29	16a41				17a04			
Lapworth	d						15 56																
Hatton	d						16 01																
Warwick Parkway	d									16 17					16 39								
Warwick	d						16 07								16 42								
Leamington Spa [8]	a				15 54	16 02	16 18			16 22				16 36	16 46								16 53
	d					16 03				16 23				16 37	16 46								
Banbury	d					16a20				16 41				16a53	17 04								
London Marylebone [10] ⊖115	a									17 45					18 13								
Spring Road	d		15 37						15 56				16 19				16 38		16 44		16 59		
Hall Green	d		15 39						15 59				16 22				16 41		16 47		17 02		
Yardley Wood	d		15 42						16 01				16 24				16 43		16 49		17 04		
Shirley	d		15 45						16 05				16 28				16 46		16 53		17 08		
Whitlocks End	d		15 48						16a07				16a30				16 49		16a55		17a10		
Wythall	d		15 51														16 52						
Earlswood (West Midlands)	d		15 53														16 54						
The Lakes	d		15x56														16x57						
Wood End	d		15x58														16x59						
Danzey	d		16x01														17x02						
Henley-in-Arden	d		16 06														17 07						
Wootton Wawen	d		16x09														17x10						
Wilmcote	d		16 15														17 16						
Stratford-upon-Avon Parkway	a		16 18														17 19						
Stratford-upon-Avon	a		16 23														17 24						

Table T071-R

Mondays to Fridays
16 December to 15 May

Hereford, Worcester and Stourbridge - Birmingham - Leamington Spa, Marylebone and Stratford-upon-Avon

Station		XC	CH	LM	LM	XC	CH	LM	LM	XC	CH	LM	LM	LM	CH	CH	LM	LM	GW	LM	GW	CH
		◇[1]	◇			◇[1]	◇			◇[1]					◇				◇[1]			◇
Hereford [7]	d													15 39								
Ledbury	a													15 56								
	d													15 58								
Colwall	d													16 05								
Great Malvern	a													16 10								
	d													16 10					16 30		16 44	
Malvern Link	d													16 13					16 33		16 47	
Worcester Foregate Street [7]	a													16 22					16 42		16 55	
	d											16 13		16 22				16 34	16 43	16 47	16 56	
Worcester Shrub Hill [7]	a																	16 36	16 46		16 58	
	d																	16 40				
Droitwich Spa	d											16 22		16 33				16 48		16 55		
Bromsgrove 69	d													16 43								
Barnt Green	d													16 50								
University	d													17 00								
Hartlebury	d											16 29						16 55				
Kidderminster	d				16 23							16 35					16 53	17 01		17 06		
Blakedown	d				16 27							16 40					16 57			17 10		
Hagley	d				16 31							16 44					17 01			17 14		
Stourbridge Junction [2]	d			16 27	16 35							16 48	16 57				17 05	17 12		17 18		
Lye	d			16 31									17 01									
Cradley Heath	d			16 34	16 41							16 54	17 04				17 11	17 18		17 24		
Old Hill	d			16 37									17 07									
Rowley Regis	d			16 41	16 46							16 59	17 11				17 16	17 23		17 29		
Langley Green	d			16 44									17 14									
Birmingham New Street [12] 68	a													17 10								
	d	16 33				17 04				17 33												
Birmingham Intl. 68 ✈	d					17 14																
Coventry	d					17 25			17 37													
Smethwick Galton Bridge [7]	d			16 47	16 52							17 05	17 17				17 22	17 29		17 35		
The Hawthorns	d			16 49	16 54							17 09	17 19				17 24	17 31		17 37		
Jewellery Quarter	d			16 53	16 58							17 13	17 23				17 28	17 35		17 41		
Birmingham Snow Hill	a			16 56	17 01							17 18	17 26				17 32	17 39		17 45		
	d		16 52	16 58	17 03		17 07	17 14				17 22	17 28				17 36	17 42		17 47		17 52
Birmingham Moor Street	d		16 55	17 01	17 06		17 10	17 17			17 21	17 25	17 31				17 39	17 45		17 50		17 55
Bordesley	d																					
Small Heath	d							17 20									17 42	17 49		17 53		
Tyseley	d			17 06				17 24					17 36				17 47	17 52		17 57		
Acocks Green	d			17 09								17 31					17 49	17 55				
Olton	d			17 11								17 34					17 52	17 57				
Solihull	d		17 04	17 15			17 19				17 30	17 37					17 56	18 01				18 06
Widney Manor	d			17 18			17 22					17 41					17 59	18 04				
Dorridge	d			17a23			17 26				17 35	17a48					18 03	18a09				18 12
Lapworth	d										17 39						18 07					
Hatton	d										17 45				17 58		18 12					
Warwick Parkway	d		17 16				17 36										18 16					18 22
Warwick	d		17 19				17 39				17 51				18 05		18 19					
Leamington Spa [8]	a	16 58	17 23			17 36	17 43		17 51	18 00	18 01				18 09		18 26					18 28
	d	17 00	17 23			17 37	17 43			18 01					18 09	18 11						18 28
Banbury	d	17a16	17 41			17a54	18 04			18a17					18 28							18 46
London Marylebone [10] ⊖115	a		18 39				19 14								19 41							19 44
Spring Road	d				17 12			17 26					17 38							17 59		
Hall Green	d				17 15			17 29					17 41							18 02		
Yardley Wood	d				17 17			17 31					17 43							18 04		
Shirley	d				17 21			17 35					17 46							18 08		
Whitlocks End	d				17 23			17a38					17 49							18 10		
Wythall	d				17 26								17 52							18 13		
Earlswood (West Midlands)	d												17 54							18 15		
The Lakes	d												17x57							18x18		
Wood End	d												17x59							18x20		
Danzey	d												18x02							18x23		
Henley-in-Arden	d				17 36								18 07							18 28		
Wootton Wawen	d												18x10							18x31		
Wilmcote	d												18 16			18 44				18 37		
Stratford-upon-Avon Parkway	a				17 46								18 19			18 46				18 40		
Stratford-upon-Avon	a				17 49								18 24			18 51				18 43		

Table T071-R

Mondays to Fridays
16 December to 15 May

Hereford, Worcester and Stourbridge - Birmingham - Leamington Spa, Marylebone and Stratford-upon-Avon

		LM	LM	XC	CH	LM	LM	LM	GW	LM	LM	XC	LM	CH	LM	LM	LM	GW	XC	LM	LM	CH	LM
				◇1	◇				◇1			◇1		◇				◇1	◇1			◇	
Hereford 7	d							16 39												17 39			
Ledbury	a							16 57												17 56			
	d							16 57												17 58			
Colwall	d							17 04												18 05			
Great Malvern	a							17 08												18 09			
	d							17 09					17 33							18 10			
Malvern Link	d							17 12					17 36							18 13			
Worcester Foregate Street 7	a							17 20					17 44							18 23			
	d					17 15		17 24	17 27				17 48					17 57		18 24			
Worcester Shrub Hill 7	a								17 30									18 00					
	d																17 55						
Droitwich Spa	d					17 25		17 33					17 58				18 05			18 33			
Bromsgrove 69	d							17 42					18 07							18 42			
Barnt Green	d																						
University	d							18 00					18 30							19 00			
Hartlebury	d					17 32																	
Kidderminster	d		17 25			17 38									18 00		18 15						18 38
Blakedown	d		17 29			17 42									18 05								18 42
Hagley	d		17 33			17 46									18 08		18 21						18 46
Stourbridge Junction 2	d	17 27	17 37			17 50	17 57			18 07					18 12		18 25						18 50
Lye	d	17 31					18 01										18 29						18 54
Cradley Heath	d	17 34	17 43			17 56	18 04			18 13					18 18		18 32						18 57
Old Hill	d	17 37					18 07										18 36						19 00
Rowley Regis	d	17 41	17 48			18 01	18 11			18 18					18 24		18 39						19 04
Langley Green	d	17 44					18 14										18 42						19 07
Birmingham New Street 12 68	a							18 09					18 37							19 09			
	d			18 04								18 33							19 04				
Birmingham Intl. 68 ✈	d			18 14															19 14				
Coventry	d			18 25							18 37								19 25		19 37		
Smethwick Galton Bridge 7	d	17 47	17 54			18 07	18 17			18 24					18 29		18 46						19 10
The Hawthorns	d	17 49	17 56			18 09	18 19			18 26					18 31		18 48						19 12
Jewellery Quarter	d	17 53	18 00			18 13	18 23			18 30					18 35		18 52						19 16
Birmingham Snow Hill	a	17 56	18 04			18 17	18 26			18 34					18 39		18 55						19 20
	d	17 58	18 07		18 12	18 22	18 28			18 36				18 40	18 46	18 50	18 57					19 17	19 22
Birmingham Moor Street	d	18 01	18 10		18 15	18 25	18 31			18 39				18 43	18 49	18 53	19 00					19 20	19 25
Bordesley	d																						
Small Heath	d	18 04	18 13				18 34									18 56	19 03						
Tyseley	d	18 08	18 17				18 37									19 00	19 07						
Acocks Green	d	18 10				18 31									18 56	19 02							19 31
Olton	d	18 13				18 34									18 58	19 05							19 34
Solihull	d	18 17			18 24	18 37								18 52	19 02	19 09						19 29	19 37
Widney Manor	d	18 20				18 41									19 05	19 12							19 41
Dorridge	d	18 24			18 29	18a48								18 57	19 09	19a18						19 34	19a48
Lapworth	d	18 28			18 34										19 13							19 38	
Hatton	d				18 40										19 18							19 44	
Warwick Parkway	d				18 45									19 07	19 22							19 49	
Warwick	d				18 48										19 25							19 52	
Leamington Spa 8	a			18 36	18 52						18 56	18 59		19 12	19 30				19 36		19 52	19 56	
	d			18 37	18 53							19 01		19 12					19 37			19 57	
Banbury	d			18a54	19 13							19a17		19 30					19a53			20 16	
London Marylebone 10 ⊖115	a				20 23									20 37								21 35	
Spring Road	d		18 19				18 40			18 46							19 09						
Hall Green	d		18 22				18 42			18 48							19 12						
Yardley Wood	d		18 24				18 45			18 51							19 14						
Shirley	d		18 28				18 48			18 54							19 18						
Whitlocks End	d		18a30				18 51			18a57							19a20						
Wythall	d						18 53																
Earlswood (West Midlands)	d						18 56																
The Lakes	d						18x58																
Wood End	d						19x00																
Danzey	d						19x02																
Henley-in-Arden	d						19 07																
Wootton Wawen	d						19x10																
Wilmcote	d						19 16																
Stratford-upon-Avon Parkway	a	18 55					19 19																
Stratford-upon-Avon	a	18 59					19 23																

Table T071-R

Mondays to Fridays
16 December to 15 May

Hereford, Worcester and Stourbridge - Birmingham - Leamington Spa, Marylebone and Stratford-upon-Avon

		LM	LM	LM	XC	LM	GW	GW	CH	XC	LM	CH	LM	LM	LM	LM	GW	LM	XC	XC	LM	CH
					◇1			◇1	◇	◇1		◇					◇1		◇1	◇1		◇
Hereford 7	d										18 48											
Ledbury	a										19 03											
	d										19 04											
Colwall	d										19 10											
Great Malvern	a										19 14											
	d							19 04			19 15						19 46					
Malvern Link	d							19 07			19 18						19 49					
Worcester Foregate Street 7	a							19 16			19 26						19 58					
	d			18 41			18 53	19 17			19 28					19 48	19 59					
Worcester Shrub Hill 7	a						18 55	19 20									20 02					
	d		18 37			18 50																
Droitwich Spa	d		18 45	18 50		18 58					19 37					19 57						
Bromsgrove 69	d					19 08					19 47											
Barnt Green	d																					
University	d					19 30					20 09											
Hartlebury	d			18 57												20 04						
Kidderminster	d		18 55	19 07										19 45	20 06	20 10						
Blakedown	d		18 59	19 11										19 49		20 15						
Hagley	d		19 03	19 15										19 53	20 12	20 18						
Stourbridge Junction 2	d		19 06	19 19										19 57	20 17	20 25						
Lye	d			19 23										20 01		20 29						
Cradley Heath	d		19 13	19 26										20 04	20 23	20 32						
Old Hill	d			19 29										20 07		20 35						
Rowley Regis	d		19 18	19 33										20 11	20 28	20 39						
Langley Green	d			19 36										20 14		20 42						
Birmingham New Street 12 68	a					19 37					20 19											
	d				19 33					20 04									20 33	21 04		
Birmingham Intl. 68 ✈	d									20 14										21 14		
Coventry	d									20 25								20 37		21 25	21 36	
Smethwick Galton Bridge 7	d		19 24	19 39										20 17	20 34	20 45						
The Hawthorns	d		19 26	19 41										20 19	20 36	20 47						
Jewellery Quarter	d		19 30	19 45										20 23	20 40	20 51						
Birmingham Snow Hill	a		19 38	19 51										20 26	20 44	20 55						
	d	19 28	19 46	19 54								20 15	20 19	20 28	20 46	21 02						21 10
Birmingham Moor Street	d	19 31	19 49	20 01								20 18	20 22	20 31	20 49	21 05						21 18
Bordesley	d																					
Small Heath	d	19 34	19 52	20 04										20 34	20 52	21 08						
Tyseley	d	19 37	19 55	20 08										20 37	20 55	21 12						
Acocks Green	d		19 58										20 28		20 58							
Olton	d		20 01										20 31		21 01							
Solihull	d		20 05									20 27	20 35		21 05							21 27
Widney Manor	d		20 08										20 38		21 08							
Dorridge	d		20a14									20 32	20a42		21a13							21 32
Lapworth	d																					21 36
Hatton	d																					21 42
Warwick Parkway	d											20 42										21 47
Warwick	d											20 45										21 50
Leamington Spa 8	a				20 00					20 36		20 50						20 53	20 58	21 36	21 50	21 54
	d				20 02				20 26	20 37		20 50							21 00	21 37		21 56
Banbury	d				20a18					20a53		21 13							21a16	21a53		22 13
London Marylebone 10 ⊖115	a											22 12										23 12
Spring Road	d	19 40		20 10										20 40		21 14						
Hall Green	d	19 42		20 13										20 42		21 17						
Yardley Wood	d	19 45		20 15										20 45		21 19						
Shirley	d	19 48		20 19										20 48		21 23						
Whitlocks End	d	19 51		20a21										20 51		21a25						
Wythall	d	19 53												20 53								
Earlswood (West Midlands)	d	19 56												20 56								
The Lakes	d	19x58												20x58								
Wood End	d	20x00												21x00								
Danzey	d	20x02												21x02								
Henley-in-Arden	d	20 07												21 07								
Wootton Wawen	d	20x10												21x10								
Wilmcote	d	20 15							20 48					21 15								
Stratford-upon-Avon Parkway	a	20 18							20 50					21 18								
Stratford-upon-Avon	a	20 23							20 54					21 23								

Table T071-R

Mondays to Fridays

16 December to 15 May

Hereford, Worcester and Stourbridge - Birmingham - Leamington Spa, Marylebone and Stratford-upon-Avon

Station		LM	LM	LM	LM	LM	GW	LM	GW	LM	CH	LM	CH	XC	LM	CH	LM	LM	LM	LM	CH	LM	LM
							◇1 ✠				◇		◇	◇1									
Hereford 7	d			19 50				20 21		20 56										21 28			
Ledbury	a			20 06				20 38		21 12										21 45			
	d			20 09				20 41		21 14										21 45			
Colwall	d			20 15				20 48		21 20										21 52			
Great Malvern	a			20 20				20 52		21 25										21 56			
	d		20 09	20 20				20 53	21 16	21 25										21 57			
Malvern Link	d		20 11	20 23				20 56	21 19	21 28										22 00			
Worcester Foregate Street 7	a		20 21	20 31				21 13	21 27	21 36										22 09			
	d		20 22	20 32		20 51	20 58	21 14	21 29	21 37										22 10			
Worcester Shrub Hill 7	a			20 34			21 01	21 16	21 31	21 39													
	d			20 37															21 54				
Droitwich Spa	d		20 31	20 45		21 00													22 02	22 19			
Bromsgrove 69	d			20 55																22 29			
Barnt Green	d																						
University	d			21 18																22 49			
Hartlebury	d		20 38			21 07																	
Kidderminster	d		20 44		21 05	21 13											21 45		22 13				
Blakedown	d		20 48			21 17											21 49		22 17				
Hagley	d		20 52		21 11	21 21											21 53		22 21				
Stourbridge Junction 2	d		20 57		21 15	21 25											21 57		22 25				
Lye	d		21 01			21 29											22 01		22 29				
Cradley Heath	d		21 04		21 21	21 32											22 04		22 32				
Old Hill	d		21 07			21 35											22 07		22 35				
Rowley Regis	d		21 11		21 27	21 39											22 11		22 39				
Langley Green	d		21 14			21 42											22 14		22 42				
Birmingham New Street 12 68	a			21 25																22 55			
	d													22 04									
Birmingham Intl. 68 ✈	d													22 14									
Coventry	d													22 25	22 43							23 43	
Smethwick Galton Bridge 7	d		21 17		21 32	21 45											22 17		22 45				
The Hawthorns 🚊	d		21 19		21 34	21 47											22 19		22 47				
Jewellery Quarter 🚊	d		21 23		21 38	21 51											22 23		22 51				
Birmingham Snow Hill 🚊	a		21 26		21 42	21 55											22 26		22 56				
	d	21 21	21 28		21 48	21 57						22 07				22 12	22 28	22 53	22 57				23 19
Birmingham Moor Street	d	21 24	21 31		21 51	22 00						22 10				22 15	22 31	22 56	23 00				23 22
Bordesley	d																						
Small Heath	d		21 34		21 54	22 03											22 34	22 59	23 03				23 25
Tyseley	d		21 37		21 57	22 07										22 20	22 37	23 02	23 09				23 29
Acocks Green	d	21 30			22 00							22 17				22 23		23 05					23 31
Olton	d	21 33			22 03							22 20				22 26		23 08					23 34
Solihull	d	21 36			22 07							22 24				22 30		23 12					23 38
Widney Manor	d	21 39			22 10							22 27				22 33		23 15					23 41
Dorridge	d	21a44			22a16							22a32				22 37		23a20					23 45
Lapworth	d															22 41							23 49
Hatton	d										21 59					22 47							23 54
Warwick Parkway	d															22 52							23 58
Warwick	d										22 05					22 55					23 34		00 01
Leamington Spa 8	a										22 09			22 36	22 57	22 59					23 38	23 58	00 06
	d										22 10		22 20	22 37		23 00					23 39		
Banbury	d										22 29			22a53		23a23					23a57		
London Marylebone 10 ⊖115	a										23 54												
Spring Road	d		21 40			22 09											22 40		23 11				
Hall Green	d		21 42			22 12											22 42		23 14				
Yardley Wood	d		21 45			22 14											22 45		23 16				
Shirley	d		21 48			22 18											22 48		23 20				
Whitlocks End	d		21 51			22a20											22 51		23a22				
Wythall	d		21 53														22 53						
Earlswood (West Midlands)	d		21 56														22 56						
The Lakes	d		21x58														22x58						
Wood End	d		22x00														23x00						
Danzey	d		22x02														23x02						
Henley-in-Arden	d		22 07														23 07						
Wootton Wawen	d		22x10														23x10						
Wilmcote	d		22 15										22 43				23 15						
Stratford-upon-Avon Parkway	a		22 18										22 45				23 18						
Stratford-upon-Avon	a		22 23										22 56				23 23						

Table T071-R

Mondays to Fridays

16 December to 15 May

Hereford, Worcester and Stourbridge - Birmingham - Leamington Spa, Marylebone and Stratford-upon-Avon

Station		LM	CH	LM	GW	LM
					◇1 ✠	
Hereford 7	d				22 00	22 59
Ledbury	a				22 17	23 15
	d				22 17	23 15
Colwall	d				22 24	23 22
Great Malvern	a				22 28	23 26
	d				22 29	23 27
Malvern Link	d				22 32	23 30
Worcester Foregate Street 7	a				22 41	23 39
	d			22 17	22 41	23 40
Worcester Shrub Hill 7	a			22 19	22 44	23 47
	d			22 27		
Droitwich Spa	d			22 35		
Bromsgrove 69	d					
Barnt Green	d					
University	d					
Hartlebury	d			22 42		
Kidderminster	d			22 48		
Blakedown	d			22 52		
Hagley	d			22 56		
Stourbridge Junction 2	d	22 56		23 00		
Lye	d			23 04		
Cradley Heath	d	23 02		23 07		
Old Hill	d			23 10		
Rowley Regis	d	23 08		23 14		
Langley Green	d			23 17		
Birmingham New Street 12 68	a					
	d					
Birmingham Intl. 68 ✈	d					
Coventry	d					
Smethwick Galton Bridge 7	d	23 13		23 20		
The Hawthorns 🚊	d	23 16		23 22		
Jewellery Quarter 🚊	d	23 19		23 26		
Birmingham Snow Hill 🚊	a	23 22		23 33		
	d		23 30	23 34		
Birmingham Moor Street	d		23 33	23 37		
Bordesley	d					
Small Heath	d			23 40		
Tyseley	d		23 38	23 44		
Acocks Green	d		23 41			
Olton	d		23 44			
Solihull	d		23 48			
Widney Manor	d		23 51			
Dorridge	d		23 55			
Lapworth	d		23 59			
Hatton	d		00 05			
Warwick Parkway	d		00 10			
Warwick	d		00 13			
Leamington Spa 8	a		00 17			
	d		00 18			
Banbury	d		00a41			
London Marylebone 10 ⊖115	a					
Spring Road	d			23 46		
Hall Green	d			23 49		
Yardley Wood	d			23 51		
Shirley	d			23 55		
Whitlocks End	d			23a57		
Wythall	d					
Earlswood (West Midlands)	d					
The Lakes	d					
Wood End	d					
Danzey	d					
Henley-in-Arden	d					
Wootton Wawen	d					
Wilmcote	d					
Stratford-upon-Avon Parkway	a					
Stratford-upon-Avon	a					

Table T071-R

Saturdays
21 December to 16 May

Hereford, Worcester and Stourbridge - Birmingham - Leamington Spa, Marylebone and Stratford-upon-Avon

		LM	CH	LM	XC	CH	LM	XC	CH	LM		LM	XC	GW	LM	CH	LM	LM	XC	CH		LM	LM	CH	LM
					◇1 🛒	◇		◇1	◇				◇1 🛒	◇1		◇			◇1 🛒					◇	
Hereford 7	d																								
Ledbury	a																								
	d																								
Colwall	d																								
Great Malvern	a																								
	d													05 53									06 17		
Malvern Link	d													05 57									06 20		
Worcester Foregate Street 7	a													06 06									06 27		
	d													06 07									06 28		
Worcester Shrub Hill 7	a													06 10											
	d									05 43		06 07										06 21			
Droitwich Spa	d									05 51		06 15										06 29	06 37		
Bromsgrove 69	d																						06 47		
Barnt Green	d																								
University	d																						07 09		
Hartlebury	d									05 58												06 36			
Kidderminster	d									06 04						06 37						06 43		07 12	
Blakedown	d									06 08												06 47			
Hagley	d									06 12												06 51			
Stourbridge Junction 2	d									06 16						06 45						06 57		07 22	
Lye	d									06 20												07 01			
Cradley Heath	d									06 23						06 51						07 04			
Old Hill	d									06 26												07 08			
Rowley Regis	d									06 30						06 57						07 11		07 33	
Langley Green	d									06 33												07 14			
Birmingham New Street 12 68	a											06 45											07 15		
	d				06 04			06 33					07 04						07 33						
Birmingham Intl. 68 ✈	d				06 14								07 14												
Coventry	d			05 46	06 25		06 40						07 25					07 37							
Smethwick Galton Bridge 7	d									06 36						07 02						07 18		07 41	
The Hawthorns 🚋	d									06 38						07 05						07 20		07 44	
Jewellery Quarter 🚋	d									06 42												07 24			
Birmingham Snow Hill 🚋	a									06 45						07 11						07 28		07 49	
	d					06 12			06 46	06 50					07 02	07 12	07 25					07 37		07 51	07 58
Birmingham Moor Street	d					06 15			06 49	06 53					07 05	07 15	07 28			07 34		07 40		07 55	08 01
Bordesley	d																								
Small Heath	d									06 56					07 08		07 31								
Tyseley	d									06 59					07 11		07 34								
Acocks Green	d									07 02												07 47			08 07
Olton	d									07 05												07 50			08 10
Solihull	d					06 24			07 02	07 09						07 24				07 42		07 53		08 05	08 13
Widney Manor	d									07 12												07 57			08 17
Dorridge	d					06 29				07a17						07 29				07 53		08a02			08 21
Lapworth	d					06 33														07 57					
Hatton	d		00 05			06 39														08 03					
Warwick Parkway	d		00 10			06 44			07 14							07 39								08 18	
Warwick	d	00 01	00 13			06 47										07 42				08 09					
Leamington Spa 8	a	00 06	00 17	06 05	06 36	06 51	06 56	06 58	07 19				07 36			07 46		07 53	08 00	08 19				08 23	
	d		00 18		06 37	06 52		07 00	07 20				07 37			07 46			08 01					08 24	
Banbury	d		00a41		06a55	07 10		07a16	07 39				07a53			08 04			08a19					08 44	
London Marylebone 10 ⊖115	a					08 14			08 42							09 11								09 41	
Spring Road	d														07 14		07 37								
Hall Green	d														07 16		07 39								
Yardley Wood	d														07 19		07 42								
Shirley	d														07 22		07 45								
Whitlocks End	d														07a25		07 48								
Wythall	d																07 51								
Earlswood (West Midlands)	d																07 53								
The Lakes	d																07x56								
Wood End	d																07x58								
Danzey	d																08x01								
Henley-in-Arden	d																08 06								
Wootton Wawen	d																08x09								
Wilmcote	d																08 15								
Stratford-upon-Avon Parkway	a																08 18								08 37
Stratford-upon-Avon	a																08 21								08 41

Table T071-R

Saturdays
21 December to 16 May

Hereford, Worcester and Stourbridge - Birmingham - Leamington Spa, Marylebone and Stratford-upon-Avon

		LM	GW	CH	CH	XC		LM	CH	LM	LM	LM	LM	GW	LM	XC		CH	LM	LM	XC	CH	LM	LM	LM
			◇1 🛒	◇		◇1 🛒			◇					◇1 🛒		◇1 🛒		◇			◇1 🛒	◇			
Hereford 7	d		06 18					06 39						07 12											07 37
Ledbury	a		06 34					06 56						07 28											07 53
	d		06 35					06 59						07 29											07 58
Colwall	d		06 43					07 06						07 37											08 05
Great Malvern	a		06 47					07 10						07 41											08 09
	d		06 52					07 11						07 42											08 10
Malvern Link	d		06 55					07 14						07 45											08 13
Worcester Foregate Street 7	a		07 04					07 22						07 54											08 23
	d		07 06					07 23					07 47	07 55											08 24
Worcester Shrub Hill 7	a		07 09					07 25						07 58											
	d	07 01						07 31															08 15		
Droitwich Spa	d	07 09						07 39					07 56										08 23		08 33
Bromsgrove 69	d							07 47																	08 43
Barnt Green	d																								
University	d							08 09																	09 00
Hartlebury	d	07 16																					08 31		
Kidderminster	d	07 22									07 47		08 06					08 13					08 36		
Blakedown	d	07 26									07 51		08 11										08 41		
Hagley	d	07 30									07 55		08 14										08 44		
Stourbridge Junction 2	d	07 35									07 59	08 05	08 19					08 24		08 35			08 48	08 57	
Lye	d	07 39										08 09								08 39				09 01	
Cradley Heath	d	07 42									08 04	08 12	08 25					08 30		08 42			08 54	09 04	
Old Hill	d	07 45										08 15								08 45				09 07	
Rowley Regis	d	07 49									08 10	08 19	08 30					08 36		08 49			08 59	09 11	
Langley Green	d	07 52										08 22								08 52				09 14	
Birmingham New Street 12 68	a							08 15																	09 09
	d					08 04										08 33					09 04				
Birmingham Intl. 68 ✈	d					08 14															09 14				
Coventry	d					08 25									08 37						09 25				
Smethwick Galton Bridge 7	d	07 55									08 16	08 25	08 36					08 42		08 55			09 05	09 17	
The Hawthorns 🚋	d	07 57									08 18	08 27	08 38					08 45		08 57			09 07	09 19	
Jewellery Quarter 🚋	d	08 01									08 22	08 31	08 42							09 01			09 11	09 23	
Birmingham Snow Hill 🚋	a	08 05									08 26	08 35	08 45					08 51		09 05			09 15	09 26	
	d	08 07								08 17	08 28	08 37	08 47					08 53	08 58	09 07		09 12	09 17	09 28	
Birmingham Moor Street	d	08 10							08 15	08 20	08 31	08 40	08 50					08 56	09 01	09 10		09 15	09 20	09 31	
Bordesley	d																								
Small Heath	d	08 13										08 43								09 13					
Tyseley	d	08 17										08 47								09 17					
Acocks Green	d									08 26		08 49							09 07				09 26		
Olton	d									08 29		08 52							09 10				09 29		
Solihull	d								08 24	08 32		08 56						09 05	09 13			09 24	09 32		
Widney Manor	d									08 36		08 59							09 17				09 36		
Dorridge	d								08 29	08a41		09a04							09 21			09 29	09a41		
Lapworth	d																								
Hatton	d			08 17																					
Warwick Parkway	d								08 39									09 16				09 39			
Warwick	d			08 24					08 42													09 42			
Leamington Spa 8	a			08 28		08 36			08 46						08 54	08 58		09 21			09 36	09 46			
	d			08 29	08 30	08 37			08 46							09 00		09 22			09 37	09 46			
Banbury	d			08 48		08a53			09 04							09a16		09 40			09a54	10 05			
London Marylebone 10 ⊖115	a			10 05					10 11									10 41				11 11			
Spring Road	d	08 19									08 37		08 56							09 19				09 37	
Hall Green	d	08 22									08 39		08 59							09 22				09 39	
Yardley Wood	d	08 24									08 42		09 01							09 24				09 42	
Shirley	d	08 28									08 45		09 05							09 28				09 45	
Whitlocks End	d	08a30									08 48		09a07							09a30				09 48	
Wythall	d										08 51													09 51	
Earlswood (West Midlands)	d										08 53													09 53	
The Lakes	d										08x56													09x56	
Wood End	d										08x58													09x58	
Danzey	d										09x01													10x01	
Henley-in-Arden	d										09 06													10 06	
Wootton Wawen	d										09x09													10x09	
Wilmcote	d				08 58						09 15													10 15	
Stratford-upon-Avon Parkway	a				09 01						09 18								09 38					10 18	
Stratford-upon-Avon	a				09 12						09 23								09 42					10 23	

Hereford, Worcester and Stourbridge - Birmingham - Leamington Spa, Marylebone and Stratford-upon-Avon

		GW ◇■		LM	XC ◇■	CH	LM	LM	CH ◇	LM	LM	GW ◇■		XC ◇■	CH ◇	LM	LM	LM	LM	LM	XC ◇■	LM		LM	GW ◇■
Hereford ■	d																	08 39							
Ledbury	a																	08 56							
	d																	08 58							
Colwall	d																	09 05							
Great Malvern	a																	09 10							
	d											08 48				09 00		09 10							09 58
Malvern Link	d											08 52				09 02		09 13							10 02
Worcester Foregate Street ■	a											09 01				09 12		09 22							10 11
	d	08 25								08 56		09 02				09 16		09 24						09 51	10 12
Worcester Shrub Hill ■	a	08 28										09 05													10 15
	d																					09 44			
Droitwich Spa	d									09 05						09 25		09 33				09 52		10 00	
Bromsgrove 69	d																	09 43				10 08			
Barnt Green	d																								
University	d																	10 00							
Hartlebury	d															09 32									
Kidderminster	d							09 00	09 10	09 16	09 25					09 38			09 55					10 10	
Blakedown	d							09 04			09 29								09 59						
Hagley	d							09 08			09 33					09 44			10 03						
Stourbridge Junction ■	d						09 07	09 13	09 20	09 27	09 37					09 48	09 57		10 07					10 18	
Lye	d									09 31							10 01								
Cradley Heath	d						09 13	09 19		09 34	09 43					09 54	10 04		10 13					10 24	
Old Hill	d									09 37							10 07								
Rowley Regis	d						09 18	09 24	09 31	09 41	09 48					09 59	10 11		10 18					10 30	
Langley Green	d									09 44							10 14								
Birmingham New Street ■ 68	a																	10 09				10 43			
	d				09 33									10 04							10 33				
Birmingham Intl. 68 ✈	d													10 14											
Coventry	d			09 37										10 25						10 37					
Smethwick Galton Bridge ■	d						09 24	09 30	09 39	09 47	09 54					10 05	10 17		10 24					10 35	
The Hawthorns	d						09 26	09 32	09 42	09 49	09 56					10 07	10 19		10 26					10 37	
Jewellery Quarter	d						09 30	09 36		09 53	10 00					10 11	10 23		10 30					10 41	
Birmingham Snow Hill	a						09 34	09 40	09 50	09 56	10 04					10 15	10 26		10 34					10 45	
	d						09 37	09 47	09 51	09 58	10 07				10 12	10 17	10 28		10 37					10 47	
Birmingham Moor Street	d					09 34	09 40	09 50	09 55	10 01	10 10				10 15	10 20	10 31		10 40					10 50	
Bordesley	d																								
Small Heath	d						09 43				10 13								10 43						
Tyseley	d						09 47				10 17								10 47						
Acocks Green	d						09 49			10 07						10 26			10 49						
Olton	d						09 52			10 10						10 29			10 52						
Solihull	d					09 43	09 56		10 06	10 13					10 24	10 32			10 56						
Widney Manor	d						09 59			10 17						10 36			10 59						
Dorridge	d					09 54	10a04			10 21					10 29	10a41			11a04						
Lapworth	d					09 58																			
Hatton	d					10 04																			
Warwick Parkway	d								10 20						10 39										
Warwick	d					10 10									10 42										
Leamington Spa ■	a			09 53	10 01	10 19			10 25					10 36	10 46					10 53	10 58				
	d				10 03				10 26					10 37	10 46						11 00				
Banbury	d				10a19				10 45					10a53	11 05						11a16				
London Marylebone ■ ⊖115	a								11 45						12 11										
Spring Road	d							09 56			10 19						10 37							10 56	
Hall Green	d							09 59			10 22						10 39							10 59	
Yardley Wood	d							10 01			10 24						10 42							11 01	
Shirley	d							10 05			10 28						10 45							11 05	
Whitlocks End	d							10a07			10a30						10 48							11a07	
Wythall	d																10 51								
Earlswood (West Midlands)	d																10 53								
The Lakes	d																10x56								
Wood End	d																10x58								
Danzey	d																11x01								
Henley-in-Arden	d																11 06								
Wootton Wawen	d																11x09								
Wilmcote	d																11 15								
Stratford-upon-Avon Parkway	a									10 37							11 18								
Stratford-upon-Avon	a									10 41							11 23								

Hereford, Worcester and Stourbridge - Birmingham - Leamington Spa, Marylebone and Stratford-upon-Avon

		CH ◇	CH ◇	LM	LM	CH ◇	XC ◇■	CH ◇		LM	LM	LM	LM	XC ◇■	CH	LM	LM	CH ◇		GW ◇■	GW ◇	LM	LM	XC ◇■	CH ◇
Hereford ■	d											09 38													
Ledbury	a											09 55													
	d											09 58													
Colwall	d											10 05													
Great Malvern	a											10 10													
	d											10 10								10 40	10 52				
Malvern Link	d											10 13								10 44	10 55				
Worcester Foregate Street ■	a											10 22								10 53	11 04				
	d									10 16		10 24								10 54	11 05				
Worcester Shrub Hill ■	a																			10 57	11 07				
	d																10 52								
Droitwich Spa	d									10 25		10 33					11 00								
Bromsgrove 69	d											10 43													
Barnt Green	d																								
University	d											11 00													
Hartlebury	d									10 32															
Kidderminster	d				10 25					10 38						10 55	11 10						11 25		
Blakedown	d				10 29											10 59							11 29		
Hagley	d				10 33					10 44						11 03							11 33		
Stourbridge Junction ■	d			10 27	10 37					10 48	10 57					11 07	11 18					11 27	11 37		
Lye	d			10 31							11 01											11 31			
Cradley Heath	d			10 34	10 43					10 54	11 04					11 13	11 24					11 34	11 43		
Old Hill	d			10 37							11 07											11 37			
Rowley Regis	d			10 41	10 48					10 59	11 11					11 18	11 30					11 41	11 48		
Langley Green	d			10 44							11 14											11 44			
Birmingham New Street ■ 68	a											11 09													
	d						11 04							11 33										12 04	
Birmingham Intl. 68 ✈	d						11 14																	12 14	
Coventry	d						11 25						11 37											12 25	
Smethwick Galton Bridge ■	d			10 47	10 54					11 05	11 17					11 24	11 35					11 47	11 54		
The Hawthorns	d			10 49	10 56					11 07	11 19					11 26	11 37					11 49	11 56		
Jewellery Quarter	d			10 53	11 00					11 11	11 23					11 30	11 41					11 53	12 00		
Birmingham Snow Hill	a			10 56	11 04					11 15	11 26					11 34	11 45					11 56	12 04		
	d			10 58	11 07			11 12		11 17	11 28					11 37	11 47					11 58	12 07		12 12
Birmingham Moor Street	d		10 55	11 01	11 10			11 15		11 20	11 31				11 34	11 40	11 50	11 55				12 01	12 10		12 15
Bordesley	d																								
Small Heath	d				11 13											11 43							12 13		
Tyseley	d				11 17											11 47							12 17		
Acocks Green	d			11 07						11 26						11 49						12 07			
Olton	d			11 10						11 29						11 52						12 10			
Solihull	d		11 04	11 13				11 24		11 32					11 43	11 56		12 04				12 13			12 24
Widney Manor	d			11 17						11 36						11 59						12 17			
Dorridge	d			11 21				11 29		11a41					11 54	12a04						12 21			12 29
Lapworth	d														11 58										
Hatton	d	11 01													12 04										
Warwick Parkway	d		11 16					11 39										12 17							12 39
Warwick	d	11 08						11 42							12 09										12 42
Leamington Spa ■	a	11 13	11 21				11 36	11 46					11 53	12 01	12 19			12 22						12 36	12 46
	d	11 15	11 21			11 32	11 37	11 46						12 03				12 23						12 37	12 46
Banbury	d	11 43	11 39				11a53	12 05						12a19				12 42						12a53	13 05
London Marylebone ■ ⊖115	a	13 07	12 41					13 11										13 41							14 11
Spring Road	d				11 19						11 37						11 56						12 19		
Hall Green	d				11 22						11 39						11 59						12 22		
Yardley Wood	d				11 24						11 42						12 01						12 24		
Shirley	d				11 28						11 45						12 05						12 28		
Whitlocks End	d				11a30						11 48						12a07						12a30		
Wythall	d										11 51														
Earlswood (West Midlands)	d										11 53														
The Lakes	d										11x56														
Wood End	d										11x58														
Danzey	d										12x01														
Henley-in-Arden	d										12 06														
Wootton Wawen	d										12x09														
Wilmcote	d										12 15														
Stratford-upon-Avon Parkway	a			11 37		11 57					12 18											12 37			
Stratford-upon-Avon	a			11 41		12 06					12 23											12 41			

Table T071-R

Saturdays

21 December to 16 May

Hereford, Worcester and Stourbridge - Birmingham - Leamington Spa, Marylebone and Stratford-upon-Avon

		LM	LM	LM	LM	LM	GW	LM	XC	CH	CH	LM	LM	CH	XC	CH	LM	LM	LM	LM	XC	CH
							◇1		◇1		◇				◇1	◇					◇1	
Hereford 7	d			10 39															11 39			
Ledbury	a			10 56															11 56			
	d			10 58															11 58			
Colwall	d			11 05															12 05			
Great Malvern	a			11 10															12 10			
	d			11 10		11 35	11 55												12 10			
Malvern Link	d			11 13		11 37	11 59												12 13			
Worcester Foregate Street 7	a			11 22		11 47	12 08												12 22			
	d			11 24		11 51	12 09										12 16		12 24			
Worcester Shrub Hill 7	a						12 12															
	d	11 17																				
Droitwich Spa	d	11 25		11 33		12 00											12 25		12 33			
Bromsgrove 69	d			11 43															12 43			
Barnt Green	d																					
University	d			12 01															13 00			
Hartlebury	d	11 32															12 32					
Kidderminster	d	11 38			11 55	12 10							12 25				12 38					
Blakedown	d				11 59								12 29									
Hagley	d	11 44			12 03								12 33				12 44					
Stourbridge Junction 2	d	11 48	11 57		12 07	12 18						12 27	12 37				12 48	12 57				
Lye	d		12 01									12 31						13 01				
Cradley Heath	d	11 54	12 04		12 13	12 24						12 34	12 43				12 54	13 04				
Old Hill	d		12 07									12 37						13 07				
Rowley Regis	d	11 59	12 11		12 18	12 30						12 41	12 48				12 59	13 11				
Langley Green	d		12 14									12 44						13 14				
Birmingham New Street 12 68	a			12 11															13 09			
	d								12 33						13 04						13 33	
Birmingham Intl. 68 ✈	d														13 14							
Coventry	d							12 37							13 25					13 38		
Smethwick Galton Bridge 7	d	12 05	12 17		12 24	12 35						12 47	12 54				13 05	13 17				
The Hawthorns	d	12 07	12 19		12 26	12 37						12 49	12 56				13 07	13 19				
Jewellery Quarter	d	12 11	12 23		12 30	12 41						12 53	13 00				13 11	13 23				
Birmingham Snow Hill	a	12 15	12 26		12 34	12 45						12 56	13 04				13 15	13 26				
	d	12 17	12 28		12 37	12 47						12 58	13 07			13 12	13 17	13 28				
Birmingham Moor Street	d	12 20	12 31		12 40	12 50					12 55	13 01	13 10			13 15	13 20	13 31				13 34
Bordesley	d																					
Small Heath	d				12 43								13 13									
Tyseley	d				12 47								13 17									
Acocks Green	d	12 26			12 49							13 07					13 26					
Olton	d	12 29			12 52							13 10					13 29					
Solihull	d	12 32			12 56						13 04	13 13				13 24	13 32					13 43
Widney Manor	d	12 36			12 59							13 17					13 36					
Dorridge	d	12a41			13a04							13 21				13 29	13a41					13 54
Lapworth	d																					13 59
Hatton	d									13 01												14 04
Warwick Parkway	d										13 16					13 38						
Warwick	d									13 08						13 41						14 09
Leamington Spa 8	a							12 56	12 58	13 17	13 21				13 36	13 45				13 55	14 01	14 17
	d								13 00		13 22			13 32	13 37	13 46					14 03	
Banbury	d								13a16		13 40				13a53	14 07					14a19	
London Marylebone 10 ⊖115	a										14 41					15 11						
Spring Road	d		12 37			12 56							13 19					13 37				
Hall Green	d		12 39			12 59							13 22					13 39				
Yardley Wood	d		12 42			13 01							13 24					13 42				
Shirley	d		12 45			13 05							13 28					13 45				
Whitlocks End	d		12 48			13a07							13a30					13 48				
Wythall	d		12 51															13 51				
Earlswood (West Midlands)	d		12 53															13 53				
The Lakes	d		12x56															13x56				
Wood End	d		12x58															13x58				
Danzey	d		13x01															14x01				
Henley-in-Arden	d		13 06															14 06				
Wootton Wawen	d		13x09															14x09				
Wilmcote	d		13 15											13 57				14 15				
Stratford-upon-Avon Parkway	a		13 18									13 37		14 00				14 18				
Stratford-upon-Avon	a		13 23									13 41		14 09				14 23				

NRT DECEMBER 19 EDITION

Table T071-R

Saturdays

21 December to 16 May

Hereford, Worcester and Stourbridge - Birmingham - Leamington Spa, Marylebone and Stratford-upon-Avon

		LM	LM	CH	GW	GW	LM	LM	XC	CH	LM	LM	LM	LM	LM	GW	LM	XC	CH	CH	LM	LM	CH
				◇	◇	◇1			◇1	◇						◇1		◇1	◇	◇			◇
Hereford 7	d												12 39			13 18							
Ledbury	a												12 56			13 34							
	d												12 58			13 35							
Colwall	d												13 05			13 43							
Great Malvern	a												13 10			13 47							
	d				12 43								13 10		13 37	13 55							
Malvern Link	d				12 46								13 13		13 39	13 58							
Worcester Foregate Street 7	a				12 55								13 22		13 48	14 07							
	d		12 51		12 56	13 05							13 24		13 51	14 08							
Worcester Shrub Hill 7	a				12 58	13 08										14 11							
	d										13 17												
Droitwich Spa	d		13 00								13 25		13 33		14 00								
Bromsgrove 69	d												13 43										
Barnt Green	d																						
University	d												14 00										
Hartlebury	d										13 32												
Kidderminster	d	12 55	13 10					13 25			13 38			13 55	14 10							14 25	
Blakedown	d	12 59						13 29						13 59								14 29	
Hagley	d	13 03						13 33			13 44			14 03								14 33	
Stourbridge Junction 2	d	13 07	13 18				13 27	13 37			13 48	13 57		14 07	14 18						14 27	14 37	
Lye	d						13 31					14 01									14 31		
Cradley Heath	d	13 13	13 24				13 34	13 43			13 54	14 04		14 13	14 24						14 34	14 43	
Old Hill	d						13 37					14 07									14 37		
Rowley Regis	d	13 18	13 30				13 41	13 48			13 59	14 11		14 18	14 30						14 41	14 48	
Langley Green	d						13 44					14 14									14 44		
Birmingham New Street 12 68	a												14 09										
	d								14 04									14 33					
Birmingham Intl. 68 ✈	d								14 14														
Coventry	d								14 25								14 37						
Smethwick Galton Bridge 7	d	13 24	13 35				13 47	13 54			14 05	14 17		14 24	14 35						14 47	14 54	
The Hawthorns	d	13 26	13 37				13 49	13 56			14 07	14 19		14 26	14 37						14 49	14 56	
Jewellery Quarter	d	13 30	13 41				13 53	14 00			14 11	14 23		14 30	14 41						14 53	15 00	
Birmingham Snow Hill	a	13 34	13 45				13 56	14 04			14 15	14 26		14 34	14 45						14 56	15 04	
	d	13 37	13 47				13 58	14 07		14 12	14 17	14 28		14 37	14 47						14 58	15 07	
Birmingham Moor Street	d	13 40	13 50	13 55			14 01	14 10		14 15	14 20	14 31		14 40	14 50					14 55	15 01	15 10	
Bordesley	d																						
Small Heath	d	13 43						14 13						14 43								15 13	
Tyseley	d	13 47						14 17						14 47								15 17	
Acocks Green	d	13 49					14 07				14 26			14 49							15 07		
Olton	d	13 52					14 10				14 29			14 52							15 10		
Solihull	d	13 56		14 04			14 13			14 24	14 32			14 56						15 04	15 13		
Widney Manor	d	13 59					14 17				14 36			14 59							15 17		
Dorridge	d	14a04					14 21			14 29	14a41			15a04							15 21		
Lapworth	d																						
Hatton	d																		15 01				
Warwick Parkway	d			14 16						14 39										15 16			
Warwick	d									14 42									15 08				
Leamington Spa 8	a			14 21					14 36	14 46							14 54	14 58	15 13	15 21			
	d			14 22					14 37	14 46								15 00	15 15	15 22			15 32
Banbury	d			14 41					14a55	15 05								15a20	15 46	15 41			
London Marylebone 10 ⊖115	a			15 41						16 11									17 06	16 46			
Spring Road	d		13 56					14 19				14 37			14 56							15 19	
Hall Green	d		13 59					14 22				14 39			14 59							15 22	
Yardley Wood	d		14 01					14 24				14 42			15 01							15 24	
Shirley	d		14 05					14 28				14 45			15 05							15 28	
Whitlocks End	d		14a07					14a30				14 48			15a07							15a30	
Wythall	d											14 51											
Earlswood (West Midlands)	d											14 53											
The Lakes	d											14x56											
Wood End	d											14x58											
Danzey	d											15x01											
Henley-in-Arden	d											15 06											
Wootton Wawen	d											15x09											
Wilmcote	d											15 15											15 58
Stratford-upon-Avon Parkway	a						14 37					15 18									15 37		16 00
Stratford-upon-Avon	a						14 41					15 23									15 41		16 09

Table T071-R

Saturdays
21 December to 16 May

Hereford, Worcester and Stourbridge - Birmingham - Leamington Spa, Marylebone and Stratford-upon-Avon

	XC	CH	LM	LM	LM	LM	XC	CH	LM	LM	CH	GW	GW	LM	LM	XC	CH	LM	LM	LM	LM	LM
	◇1	◇					◇1				◇	◇	◇1			◇1	◇					
Hereford 7 d					13 39															14 39		
Ledbury a					13 55															14 55		
d					13 58															14 58		
Colwall d					14 05															15 05		
Great Malvern a					14 10															15 10		
d					14 10							14 43								15 10		
Malvern Link d					14 13							14 46								15 13		
Worcester Foregate Street 7 a					14 22							14 55								15 22		
d			14 16		14 24							14 56	15 08					15 16		15 24		
Worcester Shrub Hill 7 a												14 58	15 11									
d										14 52												
Droitwich Spa d			14 25		14 33					15 00								15 25		15 33		
Bromsgrove 69 d					14 43															15 43		
Barnt Green d																						
University d					15 00															16 00		
Hartlebury d			14 32															15 32				
Kidderminster d			14 38						14 55	15 10					15 25			15 38			15 55	
Blakedown d									14 59						15 29						15 59	
Hagley d			14 44						15 03						15 33			15 44			16 03	
Stourbridge Junction 2 d			14 48	14 57					15 07	15 18				15 27	15 37			15 48	15 57		16 07	
Lye d				15 01										15 31					16 01			
Cradley Heath d			14 54	15 04					15 13	15 24				15 34	15 43			15 54	16 04		16 13	
Old Hill d				15 07										15 37					16 07			
Rowley Regis d			14 59	15 11					15 18	15 30				15 41	15 48			15 59	16 11		16 18	
Langley Green d				15 14										15 44					16 14			
Birmingham New Street 12 68 a					15 09															16 09		
d	15 04						15 33									16 04						
Birmingham Intl. 68 ✈ d	15 14															16 14						
Coventry d	15 25					15 37										16 25						16 37
Smethwick Galton Bridge 7 d			15 05	15 17					15 24	15 35				15 47	15 54			16 05	16 17		16 24	
The Hawthorns d			15 07	15 19					15 26	15 37				15 49	15 56			16 07	16 19		16 26	
Jewellery Quarter d			15 11	15 23					15 30	15 41				15 53	16 00			16 11	16 23		16 30	
Birmingham Snow Hill a			15 15	15 26					15 34	15 45				15 56	16 04			16 15	16 26		16 34	
d		15 12	15 17	15 28					15 37	15 47				15 58	16 07		16 12	16 17	16 28		16 37	
Birmingham Moor Street d		15 15	15 20	15 31				15 34	15 40	15 50	15 55			16 01	16 10		16 15	16 20	16 31		16 40	
Bordesley d																						
Small Heath d									15 43						16 13						16 43	
Tyseley d									15 47						16 17				16 36		16 47	
Acocks Green d			15 26						15 49					16 07				16 26			16 49	
Olton d			15 29						15 52					16 10				16 29			16 52	
Solihull d		15 24	15 32					15 43	15 56		16 04			16 13			16 24	16 32			16 56	
Widney Manor d			15 36						15 59					16 17				16 36			16 59	
Dorridge d		15 29	15a41					15 54	16a04					16 21			16 29	16a41			17a04	
Lapworth d								15 59														
Hatton d								16 04														
Warwick Parkway d		15 39									16 16						16 39					
Warwick d		15 42						16 09									16 42					
Leamington Spa 8 a	15 36	15 46				15 53	16 01	16 17			16 21					16 36	16 46					16 53
d	15 37	15 46					16 03				16 22					16 37	16 46					
Banbury d	15a53	16 05					16a19				16 41					16a53	17 05					
London Marylebone 10 ⊖115 a		17 11									17 41						18 11					
Spring Road d				15 37						15 56					16 19				16 38			
Hall Green d				15 39						15 59					16 22				16 41			
Yardley Wood d				15 42						16 01					16 24				16 43			
Shirley d				15 45						16 05					16 28				16 46			
Whitlocks End d				15 48						16a07					16a30				16 49			
Wythall d				15 51															16 52			
Earlswood (West Midlands) d				15 53															16 54			
The Lakes d				15x56															16x56			
Wood End d				15x58															16x58			
Danzey d				16x01															17x01			
Henley-in-Arden d				16 06															17 06			
Wootton Wawen d				16x09															17x09			
Wilmcote d				16 15															17 15			
Stratford-upon-Avon Parkway a				16 18										16 37					17 18			
Stratford-upon-Avon a				16 23										16 41					17 23			

Table T071-R

Saturdays
21 December to 16 May

Hereford, Worcester and Stourbridge - Birmingham - Leamington Spa, Marylebone and Stratford-upon-Avon

	XC	LM	LM	GW	CH	CH	LM	LM	CH	XC	CH	LM	LM	LM	LM	XC	CH	LM	LM	GW	GW
	◇1			◇1	◇	◇			◇	◇1	◇					◇1				◇1	
Hereford 7 d				15 13										15 39							
Ledbury a				15 29										15 55							
d				15 30										15 58							
Colwall d				15 38										16 05							
Great Malvern a				15 42										16 10							
d			15 33	15 43										16 10						16 40	16 55
Malvern Link d			15 35	15 46										16 13						16 44	16 58
Worcester Foregate Street 7 a			15 45	15 55										16 22						16 53	17 11
d			15 51	15 56								16 14		16 24					16 47	16 54	17 11
Worcester Shrub Hill 7 a				15 59																16 57	17 14
d		15 44																			
Droitwich Spa d		15 52	16 00									16 23		16 33					16 56		
Bromsgrove 69 d		16 08												16 43							
Barnt Green d																					
University d														17 00							
Hartlebury d												16 31									
Kidderminster d			16 10					16 25				16 36						16 55	17 06		
Blakedown d								16 29				16 41						16 59	17 11		
Hagley d								16 32				16 44						17 03	17 14		
Stourbridge Junction 2 d			16 18				16 27	16 37				16 48	16 57					17 07	17 18		
Lye d							16 31						17 01								
Cradley Heath d			16 24				16 34	16 43				16 54	17 04					17 13	17 24		
Old Hill d							16 37						17 07								
Rowley Regis d			16 30				16 41	16 48				16 59	17 11					17 18	17 29		
Langley Green d							16 44						17 14								
Birmingham New Street 12 68 a		16 43												17 09							
d	16 33									17 04						17 33					
Birmingham Intl. 68 ✈ d										17 14											
Coventry d										17 25					17 37						
Smethwick Galton Bridge 7 d			16 35				16 47	16 54				17 05	17 17					17 24	17 35		
The Hawthorns d			16 37				16 49	16 56				17 07	17 19					17 26	17 37		
Jewellery Quarter d			16 41				16 53	17 00				17 11	17 23					17 30	17 41		
Birmingham Snow Hill a			16 45				16 56	17 03				17 15	17 26					17 34	17 45		
d			16 47				16 58	17 07			17 12	17 17	17 28					17 37	17 47		
Birmingham Moor Street d			16 50			16 55	17 01	17 10			17 15	17 20	17 31				17 34	17 40	17 50		
Bordesley d																					
Small Heath d			16 53					17 13										17 43	17 53		
Tyseley d			16 57					17 17					17 36					17 47	17 57		
Acocks Green d							17 07					17 26						17 49			
Olton d							17 10					17 29						17 52			
Solihull d						17 04	17 13				17 24	17 32					17 43	17 56			
Widney Manor d							17 17					17 36						17 59			
Dorridge d							17 21				17 29	17a41					17 54	18a04			
Lapworth d																	17 59				
Hatton d					17 01												18 04				
Warwick Parkway d						17 16					17 39										
Warwick d					17 08						17 42						18 09				
Leamington Spa 8 a	16 58				17 13	17 21				17 36	17 46				17 53	18 01	18 17				
d	17 00				17 15	17 22			17 32	17 37	17 46					18 02					
Banbury d	17a16				17 45	17 41				17a53	18 05					18a18					
London Marylebone 10 ⊖115 a					19 07	18 41					19 11										
Spring Road d			16 59					17 19					17 38						17 59		
Hall Green d			17 02					17 22					17 41						18 02		
Yardley Wood d			17 04					17 24					17 43						18 04		
Shirley d			17 08					17 28					17 47						18 08		
Whitlocks End d			17a10					17a30					17 49						18 10		
Wythall d													17 52						18 13		
Earlswood (West Midlands) d													17 54						18 15		
The Lakes d													17x56						18x18		
Wood End d													17x58						18x20		
Danzey d													18x01						18x23		
Henley-in-Arden d													18 06						18 28		
Wootton Wawen d													18x09						18x31		
Wilmcote d									17 56				18 15						18 37		
Stratford-upon-Avon Parkway a							17 37		17 58				18 18						18 40		
Stratford-upon-Avon a							17 41		18 07				18 21						18 43		

Table T071-R

Saturdays
21 December to 16 May

Hereford, Worcester and Stourbridge - Birmingham - Leamington Spa, Marylebone and Stratford-upon-Avon

		CH	LM	LM	XC	CH	LM	LM	LM	LM	GW	LM	XC	LM	CH	CH	LM	CH	XC	CH	LM	LM	LM
		◇			◇1	◇					◇1		◇1		◇	◇		◇	◇1	◇			
Hereford 7	d								16 39														17 39
Ledbury	a								16 56														17 55
	d								16 58														17 58
Colwall	d								17 05														18 05
Great Malvern	a								17 10														18 10
	d								17 10		17 40										17 51		18 10
Malvern Link	d								17 13		17 44										17 53		18 13
Worcester Foregate Street 7	a								17 22		17 53										18 03		18 22
	d								17 24	17 44	17 54										18 04		18 24
Worcester Shrub Hill 7	a										17 57										18 06		
	d						17 15														18 10		
Droitwich Spa	d						17 24		17 33	17 53											18 18		18 33
Bromsgrove 69	d								17 43														18 43
Barnt Green	d																						
University	d								17 59														19 00
Hartlebury	d						17 31																
Kidderminster	d			17 25			17 36			18 03											18 37		
Blakedown	d			17 29			17 41			18 08											18 41		
Hagley	d			17 33			17 44			18 11											18 45		
Stourbridge Junction 2	d		17 27	17 37			17 48	17 57		18 15							18 27				18 50	18 57	
Lye	d		17 31					18 01									18 31					19 01	
Cradley Heath	d		17 34	17 43			17 54	18 04		18 21							18 34				18 56	19 04	
Old Hill	d		17 37					18 07									18 37					19 07	
Rowley Regis	d		17 41	17 48			18 00	18 11		18 27							18 41				19 01	19 11	
Langley Green	d		17 44					18 14									18 44					19 14	
Birmingham New Street 12 68	a								18 09														19 09
	d				18 04								18 33						19 04				
Birmingham Intl. 68 ✈	d				18 14														19 14				
Coventry	d				18 25							18 37							19 25				
Smethwick Galton Bridge 7	d		17 47	17 54			18 05	18 17		18 32							18 47				19 07	19 17	
The Hawthorns	d		17 49	17 56			18 07	18 19		18 34							18 49				19 09	19 19	
Jewellery Quarter	d		17 53	18 00			18 11	18 23		18 38							18 53				19 13	19 23	
Birmingham Snow Hill	a		17 56	18 04			18 15	18 26		18 42							18 58				19 16	19 26	
	d		17 57	18 07		18 12	18 17	18 28		18 43				18 47			19 02			19 12	19 17	19 28	
Birmingham Moor Street	d	17 55	18 00	18 10		18 15	18 20	18 31		18 46				18 50		18 55	19 05			19 15	19 20	19 31	
Bordesley	d																						
Small Heath	d		18 04	18 13			18 23							18 53			19 08				19 23	19 34	
Tyseley	d		18 07	18 17			18 26							18 57			19 12				19 27	19 37	
Acocks Green	d		18 10				18 29			18 52											19 29		
Olton	d		18 13				18 31			18 55											19 32		
Solihull	d	18 04	18 16			18 24	18 35			18 58						19 05				19 24	19 36		
Widney Manor	d		18 20				18 38			19 01											19 39		
Dorridge	d		18a25			18 29	18a43			19a08										19 29	19a44		
Lapworth	d																						
Hatton	d														19 01								
Warwick Parkway	d	18 16				18 39										19 17				19 39			
Warwick	d					18 42									19 08					19 42			
Leamington Spa 8	a	18 21			18 36	18 46						18 53	18 58		19 13	19 22			19 36	19 46			
	d	18 22			18 37	18 46							19 00		19 15	19 23		19 32	19 37	19 46			
Banbury	d	18 41			18a53	19 05							19a16		19 46	19 41			19a53	20 05			
London Marylebone 10 ⊖115	a	19 41				20 11									21 07	20 41				21 11			
Spring Road	d			18 19				18 37						18 59			19 14					19 40	
Hall Green	d			18 22				18 39						19 02			19 17					19 42	
Yardley Wood	d			18 24				18 42						19 04			19 19					19 45	
Shirley	d			18 28				18 45						19 08			19 23					19 48	
Whitlocks End	d			18a30				18 48						19 11			19a25					19 51	
Wythall	d							18 51						19 13								19 53	
Earlswood (West Midlands)	d							18 53						19 16								19 56	
The Lakes	d							18x56						19x18								19x58	
Wood End	d							18x58						19x21								20x00	
Danzey	d							19x01						19x24								20x02	
Henley-in-Arden	d							19 06						19 29								20 07	
Wootton Wawen	d							19x09						19x32								20x10	
Wilmcote	d							19 15						19 37				19 56				20 15	
Stratford-upon-Avon Parkway	a							19 18						19 40				19 58				20 18	
Stratford-upon-Avon	a							19 23						19 44				20 07				20 23	

NRT DECEMBER 19 EDITION

Table T071-R

Saturdays
21 December to 16 May

Hereford, Worcester and Stourbridge - Birmingham - Leamington Spa, Marylebone and Stratford-upon-Avon

		LM	XC	CH	LM	CH	LM	GW	GW	XC	LM	CH	LM	LM	LM	XC	CH	CH	LM	LM	GW	CH
			◇1			◇			◇1	◇1		◇				◇1					◇1	
Hereford 7	d										18 42											
Ledbury	a										18 58											
	d										19 01											
Colwall	d										19 06											
Great Malvern	a										19 10											
	d							18 42	19 00		19 11											
Malvern Link	d								19 04		19 14											
Worcester Foregate Street 7	a							18 52	19 13		19 23											
	d						18 51	18 53	19 14		19 24									19 51	20 02	
Worcester Shrub Hill 7	a							18 55	19 17												20 05	
	d																					
Droitwich Spa	d						19 00				19 33									20 00		
Bromsgrove 69	d										19 43											
Barnt Green	d																					
University	d										20 00											
Hartlebury	d						19 07													20 07		
Kidderminster	d				18 57		19 13							19 43					20 06	20 13		
Blakedown	d				19 01		19 17							19 47						20 17		
Hagley	d				19 05		19 21							19 51					20 12	20 21		
Stourbridge Junction 2	d				19 09		19 25							19 57					20 17	20 25		
Lye	d						19 29							20 01						20 29		
Cradley Heath	d				19 15		19 32							20 04					20 23	20 32		
Old Hill	d						19 35							20 07						20 35		
Rowley Regis	d				19 20		19 39							20 11					20 28	20 39		
Langley Green	d						19 42							20 14						20 42		
Birmingham New Street 12 68	a										20 09											
	d		19 33							20 04						20 33						
Birmingham Intl. 68 ✈	d									20 14												
Coventry	d	19 37								20 25					20 37							
Smethwick Galton Bridge 7	d				19 26		19 45							20 17					20 34	20 45		
The Hawthorns	d				19 28		19 47							20 19					20 36	20 47		
Jewellery Quarter	d				19 32		19 51							20 23					20 40	20 51		
Birmingham Snow Hill	a				19 36		19 55							20 26					20 44	20 55		
	d				19 39		19 57					20 12	20 16	20 28					20 49	20 57		
Birmingham Moor Street	d			19 34	19 42	19 55	20 00					20 15	20 19	20 31				20 45	20 52	21 00		
Bordesley	d																					
Small Heath	d						20 03						20 22	20 34						21 03		
Tyseley	d						20 08						20 25	20 37						21 07		
Acocks Green	d				19 48								20 28						20 58			
Olton	d				19 51								20 31						21 01			
Solihull	d			19 43	19 54	20 04						20 24	20 35					20 55	21 05			
Widney Manor	d				19 58								20 38						21 08			
Dorridge	d			19 54	20a05							20 29	20a43					21 01	21a13			
Lapworth	d			19 59																		
Hatton	d			20 04													21 02					
Warwick Parkway	d					20 16						20 39						21 13				
Warwick	d			20 09								20 42					21 08	21 17				
Leamington Spa 8	a	19 53	20 01	20 17		20 21				20 36		20 46			20 53	20 58	21 17	21 21				
	d		20 02			20 22				20 37		20 46				21 00		21 22				21 32
Banbury	d		20a18			20 41				20a54		21 05				21a16		21 40				
London Marylebone 10 ⊖115	a					21 41						22 11						22 41				
Spring Road	d						20 10							20 40						21 09		
Hall Green	d						20 13							20 42						21 12		
Yardley Wood	d						20 15							20 45						21 14		
Shirley	d						20 19							20 48						21 18		
Whitlocks End	d						20a21							20 51						21a20		
Wythall	d													20 53								
Earlswood (West Midlands)	d													20 56								
The Lakes	d													20x58								
Wood End	d													21x00								
Danzey	d													21x02								
Henley-in-Arden	d													21 07								
Wootton Wawen	d													21x10								
Wilmcote	d													21 15								21 56
Stratford-upon-Avon Parkway	a													21 18								21 58
Stratford-upon-Avon	a													21 23								22 07

Table T071-R

Saturdays
21 December to 16 May

Hereford, Worcester and Stourbridge - Birmingham - Leamington Spa, Marylebone and Stratford-upon-Avon

		XC	LM	LM	CH	LM	LM	LM	LM	GW	LM	GW	CH	LM	CH	LM	LM	LM	LM	LM	GW	LM
		◇1			◇					◇1											1	
										🍴												
Hereford 7	d		19 40							20 20	20 35							21 31				22 50
Ledbury	a		19 56							20 36	20 52							21 48				23 05
	d		19 59							20 38	21 01							21 54				23 06
Colwall	d		20 05							20 46	21 08							22 00				23 12
Great Malvern	a		20 10							20 50	21 12							22 04				23 16
	d		20 10							20 55	21 13	21 24					21 35	22 05			22 42	23 17
Malvern Link	d		20 13							20 58	21 16	21 27					21 37	22 08			22 46	23 20
Worcester Foregate Street 7	a		20 22							21 07	21 24	21 36					21 47	22 17			22 55	23 28
	d		20 24							21 09	21 25	21 37					21 47	22 18			22 56	23 29
Worcester Shrub Hill 7	a									21 12	21 27	21 39					21 50	22 21			22 59	23 36
	d								20 50		21 30						21 54			22 44		
Droitwich Spa	d		20 33						20 58		21 38						22 02			22 52		
Bromsgrove 69	d		20 43								21 49											
Barnt Green	d																					
University	d		21 00								22 06											
Hartlebury	d								21 07											22 59		
Kidderminster	d					20 46		21 05	21 13							21 46	22 13		22 45	23 05		
Blakedown	d								21 17								22 17			23 10		
Hagley	d					20 52		21 11	21 21							21 52	22 21		22 51	23 14		
Stourbridge Junction 2	d					20 57		21 15	21 25							21 57	22 25		22 56	23 18		
Lye	d					21 01			21 29							22 01	22 29		23 00			
Cradley Heath	d					21 04		21 21	21 32							22 04	22 32		23 03			
Old Hill	d					21 07			21 35							22 07	22 35		23 06			
Rowley Regis	d					21 11		21 27	21 39							22 11	22 39		23 10			
Langley Green	d					21 14			21 42							22 14	22 42		23 13			
Birmingham New Street 12 68	a		21 10								22 16											
	d	21 04																				
Birmingham Intl. 68 ✈	d	21 14																				
Coventry	d	21 25		21 37										22 45								
Smethwick Galton Bridge 7	d					21 17		21 32	21 45							22 17	22 45		23 16			
The Hawthorns	d					21 19		21 34	21 47							22 19	22 47		23 18			
Jewellery Quarter	d					21 23		21 38	21 51							22 23	22 51		23 22			
Birmingham Snow Hill	a					21 26		21 42	21 55							22 26	22 55		23 25	23 36		
	d					21 28	21 35	21 49	21 57							22 28	22 57		23 27	23 37		
Birmingham Moor Street	d				21 18	21 31	21 38	21 52	22 00						22 18	22 31	23 00		23 30	23 40		
Bordesley	d																					
Small Heath	d					21 34			22 03							22 34	23 03		23 33	23 43		
Tyseley	d					21 37			22 07						22 23	22 37	23 07		23 36	23 47		
Acocks Green	d						21 45	21 58							22 26		23 09			23 49		
Olton	d						21 48	22 01							22 29		23 12			23 52		
Solihull	d				21 27		21 52	22 05							22 33		23 16			23 56		
Widney Manor	d				21 30		21 55	22 08							22 36		23 19			23 59		
Dorridge	d				21 34		22 00	22a13							22 40		23 23			00 03		
Lapworth	d				21 38										22 44		23 26			00 06		
Hatton	d				21 44										22 50		23 32			00 12		
Warwick Parkway	d				21 49										22 55		23 35			00 15		
Warwick	d				21 52								22 35		22 58		23 38			00 18		
Leamington Spa 8	a	21 36		21 53	21 56		22 12						22 40	22 59	23 03		23 44			00 25		
	d	21 37			21 57								22 41		23 04							
Banbury	d	21a53			22 16								23a02		23a26							
London Marylebone 10 ⊖115	a				23 48																	
Spring Road	d					21 40			22 09							22 40			23 39			
Hall Green	d					21 42			22 12							22 42			23 41			
Yardley Wood	d					21 45			22 14							22 45			23 44			
Shirley	d					21 48			22 18							22 48			23 47			
Whitlocks End	d					21 51			22a20							22 51			23a51			
Wythall	d					21 53										22 53						
Earlswood (West Midlands)	d					21 56										22 56						
The Lakes	d					21x58										22x58						
Wood End	d					22x00										23x00						
Danzey	d					22x02										23x02						
Henley-in-Arden	d					22 07										23 07						
Wootton Wawen	d					22x10										23x10						
Wilmcote	d					22 15										23 15						
Stratford-upon-Avon Parkway	a					22 18										23 18						
Stratford-upon-Avon	a					22 23										23 23						

Table T071-R

Sundays
15 December to 10 May

Hereford, Worcester and Stourbridge - Birmingham - Leamington Spa, Marylebone and Stratford-upon-Avon

		LM	GW	CH	LM	LM	CH	LM	XC	LM	GW	CH	LM	CH	CH	CH	LM	XC	CH	LM	LM	GW	LM
			◇1	◇			◇		◇1		◇1	◇		◇		◇		◇1	◇			◇1	
		A																					
			🍴						🍴		🍴							🍴				🍴	
Hereford 7	d																						
Ledbury	a																						
	d																						
Colwall	d																						
Great Malvern	a																						
	d										08 56									09 07		09 53	
Malvern Link	d										08 58									09 09		09 55	
Worcester Foregate Street 7	a										09 07									09 19		10 04	
	d		08 15							08 53	09 09									09 20		10 06	
Worcester Shrub Hill 7	a		08 18							08 55	09 11									09 22		10 08	
	d									09 05										09 26	10 05		
Droitwich Spa	d									09 13										09 35	10 13		
Bromsgrove 69	d									09 22											10 23		
Barnt Green	d																						
University	d									09 39											10 40		
Hartlebury	d																						
Kidderminster	d																		09 40	09 45			
Blakedown	d																			09 49			
Hagley	d																			09 53			
Stourbridge Junction 2	d																		09 48	09 57			
Lye	d																						
Cradley Heath	d																		09 54	10 03			
Old Hill	d																						
Rowley Regis	d																		10 00	10 08			
Langley Green	d																						
Birmingham New Street 12 68	a									09 45											10 46		
	d								09 04									10 04					
Birmingham Intl. 68 ✈	d								09 14									10 14					
Coventry	d								09 25									10 25					10 36
Smethwick Galton Bridge 7	d																			10 13			
The Hawthorns	d																			10 15			
Jewellery Quarter	d																			10 19			
Birmingham Snow Hill	a																		10 11	10 22			
	d				08 37	08 41		08 57				09 12	09 27				09 57		10 12	10 27			
Birmingham Moor Street	d			08 25		08 44	08 55	09 00				09 15	09 30		09 41	09 55	10 00		10 15	10 30			
Bordesley	d																						
Small Heath	d																						
Tyseley	d					08 49							09 35							10 35			
Acocks Green	d							09 06									10 06						
Olton	d							09 09									10 09						
Solihull	d			08 34			09 04	09 12				09 24			09 50	10 04	10 12		10 24				
Widney Manor	d							09 16									10 16						
Dorridge	d	00 03		08 39				09a21				09 29			09 54		10a21		10 29				
Lapworth	d	00 06													09 59								
Hatton	d	00 12												09 55	10 04								
Warwick Parkway	d	00 15		08 49			09 16					09 39				10 16			10 39				
Warwick	d	00 18		08 52								09 42		10 01	10 09				10 42				
Leamington Spa 8	a	00 25		08 57			09 21		09 36			09 46		10 05	10 17	10 21		10 36	10 46				10 55
	d			08 58			09 22		09 37			09 46		10 06		10 22		10 37	10 46				
Banbury	d			09 16			09 40		09a53			10 07		10 24		10 40		10a53	11 07				
London Marylebone 10 ⊖115	a			10 18			10 41					11 09		11 39		11 42			12 10				
Spring Road	d					08 51							09 37							10 37			
Hall Green	d					08 54							09 40							10 40			
Yardley Wood	d					08 56							09 42							10 42			
Shirley	d					09 00							09 45							10 45			
Whitlocks End	d					09a02							09 48							10 48			
Wythall	d												09 51							10 51			
Earlswood (West Midlands)	d												09 53							10 53			
The Lakes	d												09x55							10x55			
Wood End	d																						
Danzey	d																						
Henley-in-Arden	d												10 03							11 03			
Wootton Wawen	d												10x05							11x05			
Wilmcote	d												10 11							11 11			
Stratford-upon-Avon Parkway	a				09 08								10 14							11 14			
Stratford-upon-Avon	a				09 11								10 17							11 17			

A not 15 December

Table T071-R

Sundays
15 December to 10 May

Hereford, Worcester and Stourbridge - Birmingham - Leamington Spa, Marylebone and Stratford-upon-Avon

		CH ◇	LM	CH ◇	XC ◇1	CH ◇	LM	LM	GW ◇1	LM	CH	CH ◇	LM	XC ◇1	CH ◇	LM	LM	XC ◇1	LM	GW ◇1	CH ◇	LM	CH ◇
Hereford 7	d							10 05															
Ledbury	a							10 22															
	d							10 22															
Colwall	d							10 29															
Great Malvern	a							10 33															
	d						10 14	10 34	10 50							11 08				11 50			
Malvern Link	d						10 16	10 38	10 53							11 10				11 53			
Worcester Foregate Street 7	a						10 25	10 51	11 02							11 21				12 02			
	d						10 26	10 51	11 04							11 22			11 49	12 04			
Worcester Shrub Hill 7	a							10 54	11 06							11 24				12 06			
	d							10 58								11 28							
Droitwich Spa	d						10 35	11 06								11 37			11 58				
Bromsgrove 69	d							11 16											12 08				
Barnt Green	d																						
University	d							11 39											12 30				
Hartlebury	d																						
Kidderminster	d		10 14				10 45					11 13				11 47							
Blakedown	d		10 18																				
Hagley	d		10 22				10 51									11 53							
Stourbridge Junction 2	d		10 26				10 57					11 22	11 26			11 57						12 26	
Lye	d		10 30										11 30									12 30	
Cradley Heath	d		10 33				11 03						11 33			12 03						12 33	
Old Hill	d		10 36										11 36									12 36	
Rowley Regis	d		10 40				11 08					11 33	11 40			12 08						12 40	
Langley Green	d		10 43										11 43									12 43	
Birmingham New Street 12 68	a							11 45											12 37				
	d				11 04									12 04				12 33					
Birmingham Intl. 68 ✈	d				11 14									12 14				12 43					
Coventry	d				11 25					11 36				12 25			12 36	12 55					
Smethwick Galton Bridge 7	d		10 46				11 13						11 46			12 13						12 46	
The Hawthorns	d		10 48				11 15						11 48			12 15						12 48	
Jewellery Quarter	d		10 52				11 19						11 52			12 19						12 52	
Birmingham Snow Hill	a		10 55				11 22					11 44	11 55			12 22						12 55	
	d		10 57			11 12	11 27					11 49	11 57		12 12	12 27						12 57	
Birmingham Moor Street	d	10 55	11 00			11 15	11 30				11 41	11 55	12 00		12 15	12 30					12 55	13 00	
Bordesley	d																						
Small Heath	d																						
Tyseley	d						11 35									12 35							
Acocks Green	d		11 06										12 06									13 06	
Olton	d		11 09										12 09									13 09	
Solihull	d	11 04	11 12			11 24					11 50	12 04	12 12		12 24						13 04	13 12	
Widney Manor	d		11 16										12 16									13 16	
Dorridge	d		11a21			11 29					11 54		12a21		12 29							13a22	
Lapworth	d										11 59												13 14
Hatton	d										12 04												
Warwick Parkway	d	11 16				11 39						12 16			12 39						13 15		
Warwick	d					11 42					12 09				12 42						13 18		13 22
Leamington Spa 8	a	11 21			11 36	11 46				11 55	12 17	12 22		12 36	12 46		12 55	13 06			13 22		13 27
	d	11 22		11 32	11 37	11 46						12 22		12 37	12 46			13 09			13 23		13 27
Banbury	d	11 40			11a53	12 07						12 40		12a53	13 07			13a25			13 40		13 47
London Marylebone 10 ⊖115	a	12 40				13 10						13 40			14 10						14 40		15 06
Spring Road	d						11 37									12 37							
Hall Green	d						11 40									12 40							
Yardley Wood	d						11 42									12 42							
Shirley	d						11 45									12 45							
Whitlocks End	d						11 48									12 48							
Wythall	d						11 51									12 51							
Earlswood (West Midlands)	d						11 53									12 53							
The Lakes	d						11x55									12x55							
Wood End	d																						
Danzey	d																						
Henley-in-Arden	d						12 03									13 03							
Wootton Wawen	d						12x05									13x05							
Wilmcote	d			11 55			12 11									13 11							
Stratford-upon-Avon Parkway	a			11 57			12 14									13 14							
Stratford-upon-Avon	a			12 07			12 17									13 17							

Table T071-R

Sundays
15 December to 10 May

Hereford, Worcester and Stourbridge - Birmingham - Leamington Spa, Marylebone and Stratford-upon-Avon

		CH ◇	XC ◇1	CH ◇	LM	XC ◇1	LM	LM	CH	CH ◇	LM	XC ◇1	CH ◇	LM	LM	XC ◇1	LM	GW ◇1	CH ◇	CH ◇	LM	CH ◇
Hereford 7	d						12 02											13 27				
Ledbury	a						12 18											13 44				
	d						12 18											13 45				
Colwall	d						12 25											13 53				
Great Malvern	a						12 29											13 57				
	d				12 07		12 30											13 58				
Malvern Link	d				12 09		12 33											14 01				
Worcester Foregate Street 7	a				12 20		12 41											14 09				
	d				12 21		12 42							13 26			13 49	14 11				
Worcester Shrub Hill 7	a				12 23		12 44											14 14				
	d				12 26		12 50															
Droitwich Spa	d				12 35		12 58							13 35			13 58					
Bromsgrove 69	d						13 08										14 08					
Barnt Green	d																					
University	d						13 30										14 30					
Hartlebury	d																					
Kidderminster	d				12 45									13 45								
Blakedown	d				12 49																	
Hagley	d				12 53									13 51								
Stourbridge Junction 2	d				12 57						13 26			13 57							14 26	
Lye	d										13 30										14 30	
Cradley Heath	d				13 03						13 33			14 03							14 33	
Old Hill	d										13 36										14 36	
Rowley Regis	d				13 08						13 40			14 08							14 40	
Langley Green	d										13 43										14 43	
Birmingham New Street 12 68	a						13 37										14 37					
	d		13 04			13 33						14 04				14 33						
Birmingham Intl. 68 ✈	d		13 14									14 14				14 43						
Coventry	d		13 25					13 47				14 25			14 47	14 55						
Smethwick Galton Bridge 7	d				13 13						13 46			14 13							14 46	
The Hawthorns	d				13 15						13 48			14 15							14 48	
Jewellery Quarter	d				13 19						13 52			14 19							14 52	
Birmingham Snow Hill	a				13 22						13 56			14 22							14 55	
	d			13 12	13 27						13 57		14 12	14 27							14 57	
Birmingham Moor Street	d			13 15	13 30				13 42	13 55	14 00		14 15	14 30						14 55	15 00	
Bordesley	d																					
Small Heath	d																					
Tyseley	d				13 35									14 35								
Acocks Green	d										14 06										15 06	
Olton	d										14 09										15 09	
Solihull	d			13 24					13 51	14 04	14 12		14 24							15 04	15 12	
Widney Manor	d										14 16										15 16	
Dorridge	d			13 29					13 56		14a21		14 29								15a22	
Lapworth	d								14 00													
Hatton	d								14 06										15 00			
Warwick Parkway	d			13 39						14 16			14 39							15 16		
Warwick	d			13 42					14 10				14 42						15 08			
Leamington Spa 8	a		13 36	13 46		13 58		14 04	14 18	14 22		14 36	14 46		15 03	15 07			15 13	15 22		
	d	13 32	13 37	13 46		14 00				14 23		14 37	14 46			15 09			15 15	15 23		15 32
Banbury	d		13a53	14 07		14a16				14 40		14a53	15 07			15a25			15 45	15 41		
London Marylebone 10 ⊖115	a			15 10						15 40			16 10						17 05	16 40		
Spring Road	d				13 37									14 37								
Hall Green	d				13 40									14 40								
Yardley Wood	d				13 42									14 42								
Shirley	d				13 45									14 45								
Whitlocks End	d				13 48									14 48								
Wythall	d				13 51									14 51								
Earlswood (West Midlands)	d				13 53									14 53								
The Lakes	d				13x55									14x55								
Wood End	d																					
Danzey	d																					
Henley-in-Arden	d				14 03									15 03								
Wootton Wawen	d				14x05									15x05								
Wilmcote	d	13 54			14 11									15 11								15 54
Stratford-upon-Avon Parkway	a	13 56			14 14									15 14								15 56
Stratford-upon-Avon	a	14 06			14 17									15 17								16 06

Table T071-R

Sundays

15 December to 10 May

Hereford, Worcester and Stourbridge - Birmingham - Leamington Spa, Marylebone and Stratford-upon-Avon

		XC	CH	LM	XC	LM	LM	CH	CH	LM	XC	CH	LM	LM	XC	LM	LM	GW	CH	CH	LM	CH	XC
		◇1 ✕	◇		◇1 ✕				◇		◇1 ✕	◇			◇1 ✕			◇1 ✕	◇	◇		◇	◇1 ✕
Hereford [7]	d					14 02												15 29					
Ledbury	a					14 18												15 46					
	d					14 19												15 46					
Colwall	d					14 26												15 53					
Great Malvern	a					14 30												15 57					
	d					14 31											15 32	15 58					
Malvern Link	d					14 34											15 35	16 01					
Worcester Foregate Street [7]	a					14 42											15 43	16 09					
	d			14 26		14 43							15 28				15 45	16 11					
Worcester Shrub Hill [7]	a					14 45												16 14					
	d					14 50										15 39							
Droitwich Spa	d			14 35		14 58							15 37			15 47	15 54						
Bromsgrove 69	d					15 08										16 03							
Barnt Green	d																						
University	d					15 30										16 30							
Hartlebury	d																						
Kidderminster	d			14 45									15 47				16 05						
Blakedown	d			14 49													16 10						
Hagley	d			14 53									15 53				16 13						
Stourbridge Junction [2]	d			14 57						15 26			15 57				16 17				16 26		
Lye	d									15 30											16 30		
Cradley Heath	d			15 03						15 33			16 03								16 33		
Old Hill	d									15 36											16 36		
Rowley Regis	d			15 08						15 40			16 08								16 40		
Langley Green	d									15 43											16 43		
Birmingham New Street [12] 68	a					15 37										16 37							
	d	15 04			15 33						16 04				16 33								17 04
Birmingham Intl. 68 ✈	d	15 14									16 14				16 44								17 14
Coventry	d	15 25					15 47				16 25			16 47	16 55								17 25
Smethwick Galton Bridge [7]	d			15 13						15 46			16 13				16 30				16 46		
The Hawthorns	d			15 15						15 48			16 15								16 48		
Jewellery Quarter	d			15 19						15 52			16 19								16 52		
Birmingham Snow Hill	a			15 22						15 55			16 23				16 37				16 55		
	d		15 12	15 27						15 57		16 12	16 27				16 43				16 57		
Birmingham Moor Street	d		15 15	15 30				15 42	15 55	16 00		16 15	16 30				16a45			16 55	17 00		
Bordesley	d																						
Small Heath	d																						
Tyseley	d			15 35									16 35										
Acocks Green	d									16 06											17 06		
Olton	d									16 09											17 09		
Solihull	d		15 24					15 51	16 04	16 12		16 24								17 04	17 12		
Widney Manor	d									16 16											17 16		
Dorridge	d		15 29					15 56		16a21		16 29									17a22		
Lapworth	d							16 00															
Hatton	d							16 05											17 00				
Warwick Parkway	d		15 39						16 16			16 39								17 16			
Warwick	d		15 42					16 11				16 42							17 08				
Leamington Spa [8]	a	15 36	15 46		15 58		16 04	16 18	16 22		16 36	16 46		17 03	17 07				17 13	17 22			17 36
	d	15 37	15 46		16 00				16 23		16 37	16 46			17 09				17 15	17 23		17 32	17 37
Banbury	d	15a53	16 07		16a16				16 40		16a53	17 07			17a25				17 45	17 41			17a53
London Marylebone [10] ⊖115	a		17 10						17 40			18 10							19 05	18 40			
Spring Road	d			15 37									16 37										
Hall Green	d			15 40									16 40										
Yardley Wood	d			15 42									16 42										
Shirley	d			15 45									16 45										
Whitlocks End	d			15 48									16 48										
Wythall	d			15 51									16 51										
Earlswood (West Midlands)	d			15 53									16 53										
The Lakes	d			15x55									16x55										
Wood End	d																						
Danzey	d																						
Henley-in-Arden	d			16 03									17 03										
Wootton Wawen	d			16x05									17x05										
Wilmcote	d			16 11									17 11									17 54	
Stratford-upon-Avon Parkway	a			16 14									17 14									17 56	
Stratford-upon-Avon	a			16 17									17 17									18 05	

Table T071-R

Sundays

15 December to 10 May

Hereford, Worcester and Stourbridge - Birmingham - Leamington Spa, Marylebone and Stratford-upon-Avon

		CH	LM	XC	LM	LM	CH	CH	LM	XC	CH	LM	LM	XC	LM	GW	CH	CH	CH	XC	CH	LM
		◇		◇1 ✕				◇		◇1 ✕	◇			◇1 ✕		◇1 ✕		◇	◇	◇1 ✕	◇	
Hereford [7]	d				15 54										16 56	17 28						
Ledbury	a				16 12										17 13	17 45						
	d				16 19										17 15	17 46						
Colwall	d				16 26										17 21	17 54						
Great Malvern	a				16 30										17 26	17 58						
	d				16 31										17 31	17 59						
Malvern Link	d				16 34										17 34	18 03						
Worcester Foregate Street [7]	a				16 42										17 42	18 11						
	d		16 26		16 43							17 27			17 43	18 13						18 26
Worcester Shrub Hill [7]	a				16 45										17 45	18 16						
	d				16 50										17 50							
Droitwich Spa	d		16 35		16 58							17 36			17 58							18 35
Bromsgrove 69	d				17 08										18 08							
Barnt Green	d																					
University	d				17 30										18 30							
Hartlebury	d																					
Kidderminster	d		16 45									17 46										18 45
Blakedown	d											17 51										
Hagley	d		16 51									17 55										18 51
Stourbridge Junction [2]	d		16 57						17 26			17 59										18 55
Lye	d								17 30													
Cradley Heath	d		17 03						17 33			18 05										19 01
Old Hill	d								17 36													
Rowley Regis	d		17 08						17 40			18 10										19 06
Langley Green	d								17 43													
Birmingham New Street [12] 68	a				17 37										18 37							
	d			17 33						18 04				18 33						19 04		
Birmingham Intl. 68 ✈	d									18 14				18 43						19 14		
Coventry	d					17 47				18 25			18 47	18 55						19 25		
Smethwick Galton Bridge [7]	d		17 13						17 46			18 15										19 12
The Hawthorns	d		17 15						17 48			18 17										19 14
Jewellery Quarter	d		17 19						17 52			18 21										19 18
Birmingham Snow Hill	a		17 22						17 55			18 24										19 21
	d	17 12	17 27						17 57		18 12	18 27									19 12	19 22
Birmingham Moor Street	d	17 15	17 30				17 42	17 55	18 00		18 15	18 30						18 55			19 15	19a24
Bordesley	d																					
Small Heath	d																					
Tyseley	d		17 35									18 35										
Acocks Green	d								18 06													
Olton	d								18 09													
Solihull	d	17 24					17 51	18 04	18 12		18 24							19 04			19 24	
Widney Manor	d								18 16													
Dorridge	d	17 29					17 56		18a21		18 29										19 29	
Lapworth	d						18 00															
Hatton	d						18 05										19 02					
Warwick Parkway	d	17 39						18 16			18 39							19 16			19 39	
Warwick	d	17 42					18 10				18 42						19 08				19 42	
Leamington Spa [8]	a	17 46		17 58		18 04	18 18	18 23		18 36	18 46		19 03	19 07			19 18	19 22		19 36	19 46	
	d	17 46		18 00				18 23		18 37	18 46			19 09				19 23	19 32	19 37	19 46	
Banbury	d	18 07		18a16				18 41		18a53	19 07			19a25				19 41		19a53	20 07	
London Marylebone [10] ⊖115	a	19 10						19 40			20 10							20 42			21 10	
Spring Road	d		17 37									18 37										
Hall Green	d		17 40									18 40										
Yardley Wood	d		17 42									18 42										
Shirley	d		17 45									18 45										
Whitlocks End	d		17 48									18 48										
Wythall	d		17 51									18 51										
Earlswood (West Midlands)	d																					
The Lakes	d		17x53									18x53										
Wood End	d																					
Danzey	d																					
Henley-in-Arden	d		18 01									19 01										
Wootton Wawen	d		18x03									19x03										
Wilmcote	d		18 09									19 09							19 54			
Stratford-upon-Avon Parkway	a		18 12									19 12							19 56			
Stratford-upon-Avon	a		18 15									19 15							20 05			

Table T071-R

Sundays
15 December to 10 May

Hereford, Worcester and Stourbridge - Birmingham - Leamington Spa, Marylebone and Stratford-upon-Avon

		LM	XC	LM	CH	XC	CH	LM	XC	LM	GW	LM	CH	XC	CH	LM	LM	GW	LM	LM	LM	LM	LM	LM
			◇■ ⌶		◇	◇■ ⌶	◇		◇■		◇■ ⌶		◇	◇■	◇			◇■ ⌶						
Hereford ■	d			18 03							19 28						19 56			21 00			22 39	
Ledbury	a			18 19							19 46						20 13			21 16			22 56	
	d			18 19							19 47						20 17			21 17			22 58	
Colwall	d			18 26							19 54						20 24			21 23			23 05	
Great Malvern	a			18 30							19 58						20 28			21 27			23 09	
	d			18 31							19 59						20 29	20 40		21 28		22 10	23 10	
Malvern Link	d			18 34							20 02						20 32	20 43		21 31		22 12	23 12	
Worcester Foregate Street ■	a			18 42							20 10						20 40	20 52		21 39		22 22	23 22	
	d			18 43							20 12						20 41	20 53	21 18	21 40		22 23	23 23	
Worcester Shrub Hill ■	a			18 45							20 15						20 43	20 56	21 20			22 25	23 27	
	d			18 50				19 38		19 50						20 38	20 50		21 25			22 29		
Droitwich Spa	d			18 58				19 46		19 58						20 46	20 58		21 33	21 49		22 37		
Bromsgrove 69	d			19 08						20 08							21 08			21 58				
Barnt Green	d																							
University	d			19 30						20 31							21 31			22 15				
Hartlebury	d																							
Kidderminster	d							19 56								20 56			21 43			22 47		
Blakedown	d																							
Hagley	d							20 03								21 03			21 49			22 53		
Stourbridge Junction ■	d							20 07								21 07			21 53			22 57		
Lye	d																							
Cradley Heath	d							20 13								21 13			21 59			23 03		
Old Hill	d																							
Rowley Regis	d							20 18								21 18			22 04			23 08		
Langley Green	d																							
Birmingham New Street ■ 68	a			19 37						20 37							21 39			22 21				
	d		19 33			20 04			20 33					21 04										
Birmingham Intl. 68 ✈	d		19 44			20 14								21 14										
Coventry	d	19 49	19 55			20 25						20 47		21 25							21 57			22 57
Smethwick Galton Bridge ■	d							20 23								21 23			22 09			23 14		
The Hawthorns	d							20 25								21 25			22 11			23 16		
Jewellery Quarter	d							20 29								21 29			22 15			23 20		
Birmingham Snow Hill	a							20 33								21 33			22 19			23 25		
	d						20 12	20 34							21 15	21 34			22 21					
Birmingham Moor Street	d				19 38		20 15	20a37							21 18	21a37			22a23					
Bordesley	d																							
Small Heath	d																							
Tyseley	d																							
Acocks Green	d																							
Olton	d																							
Solihull	d				19 47		20 24								21 27									
Widney Manor	d				19 50										21 30									
Dorridge	d				19 54		20 29								21 34									
Lapworth	d				19 58																			
Hatton	d				20 04								20 56											
Warwick Parkway	d						20 39								21 44									
Warwick	d				20 09		20 42						21 03		21 47									
Leamington Spa ■	a	20 05	20 09		20 14	20 36	20 46		20 58			21 04	21 07	21 36	21 51						22 15			23 15
	d		20 10		20 16	20 37	20 46		21 00				21 08	21 37	21 52									
Banbury	d		20a26		20 36	20a53	21 07		21a17				21 28	21a53	22 15									
London Marylebone ■ ⊖115	a				21 53		22 13						22 53		23 42									
Spring Road	d																							
Hall Green	d																							
Yardley Wood	d																							
Shirley	d																							
Whitlocks End	d																							
Wythall	d																							
Earlswood (West Midlands)	d																							
The Lakes	d																							
Wood End	d																							
Danzey	d																							
Henley-in-Arden	d																							
Wootton Wawen	d																							
Wilmcote	d																							
Stratford-upon-Avon Parkway	a																							
Stratford-upon-Avon	a																							

Table T072-F

Mondays to Fridays
16 December to 15 May

Stourbridge Junction - Stourbridge Town

Miles			LM	LM	LM	LM	LM	LM	and at the same minutes past each hour until	LM	LM	LM	LM	LM	LM	LM	LM	LM	LM	LM
0	Stourbridge Junction ■	d	05 45	05 55	06 05	06 15	06 25	06 35		21 45	21 55	22 05	22 15	22 25	22 35	22 45	23 05	23 15	23 35	23 54
0¾	Stourbridge Town	a	05 48	05 58	06 08	06 18	06 28	06 38		21 48	21 58	22 08	22 18	22 28	22 38	22 48	23 08	23 18	23 38	23 57

Saturdays
21 December to 16 May

		LM	LM	LM	LM	LM	LM	and at the same minutes past each hour until	LM	LM	LM	LM	LM	LM	LM	LM	LM	LM	LM
Stourbridge Junction ■	d	05 45	05 55	06 05	06 15	06 25	06 35		21 45	21 55	22 05	22 15	22 25	22 35	22 55	23 05	23 15	23 35	23 54
Stourbridge Town	a	05 48	05 58	06 08	06 18	06 28	06 38		21 48	21 58	22 08	22 18	22 28	22 38	22 58	23 08	23 18	23 38	23 57

Sundays
15 December to 10 May

		LM	LM	LM	and every 15 minutes until	LM	LM	LM
Stourbridge Junction ■	d	09 40	09 50	10 00		19 30	19 40	19 55
Stourbridge Town	a	09 43	09 53	10 03		19 33	19 43	19 58

Table T072-R

Mondays to Fridays
16 December to 15 May

Stourbridge Town - Stourbridge Junction

Miles			LM	LM	LM	LM	LM	LM	and at the same minutes past each hour until	LM	LM	LM	LM	LM	LM	LM	LM	LM	LM	LM
0	Stourbridge Town	d	05 50	06 00	06 10	06 20	06 30	06 40		21 50	22 00	22 10	22 20	22 30	22 40	22 50	23 10	23 20	23 40	23 59
0¾	Stourbridge Junction ■	a	05 53	06 03	06 13	06 23	06 33	06 43		21 53	22 03	22 13	22 23	22 33	22 43	22 53	23 13	23 23	23 43	00 02

Saturdays
21 December to 16 May

		LM	LM	LM	LM	LM	LM	and at the same minutes past each hour until	LM	LM	LM	LM	LM	LM	LM	LM	LM	LM
Stourbridge Town	d	05 50	06 00	06 10	06 20	06 30	06 40		21 50	22 00	22 10	22 20	22 30	22 40	23 00	23 10	23 20	23 40
Stourbridge Junction ■	a	05 53	06 03	06 13	06 23	06 33	06 43		21 53	22 03	22 13	22 23	22 33	22 43	23 03	23 13	23 23	23 43

Sundays
15 December to 10 May

		LM	LM	LM	LM	and every 15 minutes until	LM	LM	LM
Stourbridge Town	d	00 01	09 45	09 55	10 05		19 35	19 45	20 00
Stourbridge Junction ■	a	00 04	09 48	09 58	10 08		19 38	19 48	20 03

Table T074-F

Birmingham - Wolverhampton - Telford - Shrewsbury

Mondays to Fridays
16 December to 15 May

Miles	Station	LM MX A	AW MO B	AW MX A	AW MX	LM	AW ◇ C	LM	LM	AW ◇ D	LM	LM	AW ■ C	LM	LM	AW ◇ C	LM	LM	AW ◇ C	LM	LM	AW ◇ E
—	Birmingham International 68 d									07 09			08 08			09 10			10 09			11 10
0	Birmingham New Street 68 d						06 25	06 33	07 00	07 23	07 26	08 00	08 25	08 35	09 00	09 25	09 34	10 00	10 25	10 34	11 00	11 25
4	Smethwick Galton Bridge 68 d						06 31			07 29	07 33		08 31			09 31			10 31			11 31
5¼	Sandwell & Dudley 68 d								07 08			08 08			09 08			10 08			11 08	
13	Wolverhampton 68 d			00 03	00 22	06 10	06 43	06 52	07 19	07 43	07 46	08 18	08 44	08 52	09 19	09 43	09 52	10 19	10 43	10 52	11 19	11 44
17	Bilbrook d			00 09		06 16		06 58	07 25		07 52	08 24			09 25			10 25			11 25	
17½	Codsall d			00 12		06 19		07 01	07 28		07 55	08 27		08 59	09 28		09 59	10 28		10 58	11 28	
20¾	Albrighton d		00 02	00 16		06 24		07 06	07 32		08 00	08 31			09 32			10 32			11 32	
22¼	Cosford d		00 05	00 20		06 27		07 09	07 36		08 03	08 35			09 36			10 36			11 36	
25½	Shifnal d	00 03	00 10	00 25		06 32		07 14	07 41		08 08	08 40		09 09	09 41		10 08	10 41		11 07	11 41	
28½	Telford Central d	00 09	00 16	00 31	00 38	06 38	07 01	07 20	07 47	08 00	08 14	08 45	09 00	09 15	09 47	10 00	10 14	10 46	11 00	11 12	11 47	12 01
29½	Oakengates d	00 11	00 18	00 33		06 40		07 22	07 49		08 17	08 47			09 49			10 48			11 49	
32½	Wellington (Shropshire) d	00 17	00 24	00 38	00 46	06 46	07 07	07 28	07 55	08 08	08 23	08 53	09 07	09 22	09 55	10 07	10 20	10 54	11 07	11 18	11 55	12 07
43	Shrewsbury a	00 30	00 39	00 53	01 01	07 00	07 23	07 42	08 08	08 22	08 36	09 06	09 22	09 36	10 08	10 22	10 36	11 07	11 21	11 31	12 08	12 21

Station	LM	VT ◇■ F ⊠	LM	AW ■ C	LM	LM	AW ◇ E	LM	LM	AW ◇ C	LM	LM	AW ◇ E	LM	LM	AW ■ C	LM	LM	AW ◇ C	LM	LM	AW ◇ C
Birmingham International 68 d		11 33		12 09			13 09			14 09			15 10			16 10			17 11			18 10
Birmingham New Street 68 d	11 34	11 52	12 00	12 25	12 34	13 00	13 25	13 34	14 00	14 25	14 34	15 00	15 25	15 34	16 00	16 25	16 34	17 00	17 26	17 34	18 00	18 25
Smethwick Galton Bridge 68 d				12 31			13 31			14 31			15 31			16 31			17 32			18 31
Sandwell & Dudley 68 d			12 08			13 08			14 08			15 08			16 08			17 08			18 08	
Wolverhampton 68 d	11 52	12 11	12 19	12 43	12 52	13 19	13 43	13 52	14 19	14 43	14 52	15 19	15 43	15 52	16 19	16 43	16 52	17 19	17 44	17 53	18 19	18 44
Bilbrook d			12 25			13 25			14 25			15 25			16 25			17 25		17 59	18 25	
Codsall d	11 58		12 28		12 58	13 28		13 58	14 28		14 59	15 28		15 58	16 28		16 58	17 28		18 02	18 28	
Albrighton d			12 32			13 32			14 32			15 32			16 32			17 32		18 06	18 32	
Cosford d			12 36			13 36			14 36			15 36			16 36			17 36		18 10	18 36	
Shifnal d	12 07		12 41		13 07	13 41		14 07	14 41		15 08	15 41		16 07	16 41		17 07	17 41		18 14	18 41	
Telford Central d	12 13	12 29	12 47	13 01	13 13	13 46	14 00	14 13	14 47	15 00	15 14	15 47	16 00	16 14	16 47	17 00	17 13	17 47	18 01	18 20	18 47	19 01
Oakengates d			12 49			13 49			14 49			15 49			16 49			17 49		18 22	18 49	
Wellington (Shropshire) d	12 19	12 36	12 55	13 08	13 19	13 54	14 07	14 19	14 55	15 07	15 22	15 55	16 06	16 21	16 55	17 07	17 20	17 55	18 07	18 28	18 55	19 08
Shrewsbury a	12 32	12 50	13 08	13 22	13 32	14 07	14 21	14 32	15 08	15 22	15 36	16 08	16 20	16 36	17 08	17 20	17 36	18 08	18 21	18 40	19 08	19 23

Station	LM	LM	AW ◇ G	LM	VT ◇■ F ⊠	LM	AW FO ◇ C	AW FX ◇ C	LM	AW ◇ H	LM	LM	AW
Birmingham International 68 d			19 05		19 33		20 09	20 09		21 09			
Birmingham New Street 68 d	18 34	19 00	19 25	19 36	19 50	20 03	20 25	20 25	21 00	21 25	22 36	23 15	23 35
Smethwick Galton Bridge 68 d			19 31				20 31	20 31		21 32			
Sandwell & Dudley 68 d		19 08			19 59	20 12			21 08			23 25	
Wolverhampton 68 d	18 52	19 19	19 43	19 54	20 18	20 25	20 43	20 43	21 19	21 45	22 58	23 41	00 03
Bilbrook d		19 25		20 00		20 31			21 25		23 04	23 47	00 09
Codsall d	18 58	19 28		20 02		20 34			21 28		23 07	23 50	00 12
Albrighton d		19 32		20 07		20 38			21 32		23 11	23 54	00 16
Cosford d		19 36		20 10		20 41			21 36		23 15	23 58	00 20
Shifnal d	19 07	19 41		20 15		20 46			21 41		23 19	00 03	00 25
Telford Central d	19 13	19 47	20 00	20 21	20 35	20 52	21 00	21 00	21 47	22 02	23 25	00 09	00 31
Oakengates d		19 49				20 54			21 49		23 27	00 11	00 33
Wellington (Shropshire) d	19 20	19 55	20 07	20 27	20 42	21 00	21 06	21 07	21 55	22 10	23 33	00 17	00 38
Shrewsbury a	19 36	20 08	20 22	20 40	20 55	21 14	21 20	21 21	22 12	22 24	23 46	00 30	00 53

Saturdays
21 December to 16 May

Station	LM A	AW A	AW	AW ◇ C	LM	AW ■ E	LM	LM	AW ■ C	LM	LM	AW ■ C	LM	LM	AW ■ C	LM	LM	AW ◇ E	LM	LM	AW ■ C	LM
Birmingham International 68 d						07 09			08 08			09 08			10 09			11 08			12 08	
Birmingham New Street 68 d				06 25	07 00	07 24	07 28	08 00	08 25	08 34	09 00	09 25	09 34	10 00	10 25	10 34	11 00	11 25	11 34	12 00	12 25	12 34
Smethwick Galton Bridge 68 d				06 31		07 31			08 31			09 32			10 31			11 32			12 31	
Sandwell & Dudley 68 d					07 08			08 08			09 08			10 08			11 08			12 08		
Wolverhampton 68 d		00 03	00 22	06 43	07 19	07 43	07 46	08 19	08 44	08 52	09 19	09 44	09 52	10 19	10 44	10 52	11 19	11 44	11 52	12 19	12 44	12 52
Bilbrook d		00 09			07 25		07 54	08 25			09 25			10 25			11 25			12 25		
Codsall d		00 12			07 28		07 56	08 28		08 58	09 28		09 58	10 28		10 58	11 28		11 58	12 27		12 58
Albrighton d		00 16			07 32		08 01	08 32			09 32			10 32			11 32			12 32		
Cosford d		00 20			07 36		08 04	08 36			09 36			10 35			11 36			12 35		
Shifnal d	00 03	00 25			07 41		08 09	08 41		09 07	09 41		10 07	10 40		11 07	11 41		12 07	12 40		13 07
Telford Central d	00 09	00 31	00 38	06 59	07 47	08 00	08 15	08 47	09 01	09 13	09 47	10 00	10 13	10 46	11 00	11 12	11 47	12 00	12 13	12 45	13 00	13 13
Oakengates d	00 11	00 33			07 49		08 17	08 49			09 49			10 48			11 49			12 47		
Wellington (Shropshire) d	00 17	00 38	00 45	07 06	07 55	08 07	08 23	08 55	09 08	09 19	09 55	10 07	10 19	10 54	11 07	11 19	11 55	12 07	12 19	12 52	13 07	13 19
Shrewsbury a	00 30	00 53	01 00	07 21	08 08	08 21	08 36	09 08	09 21	09 36	10 08	10 21	10 32	11 07	11 20	11 32	12 08	12 21	12 32	13 05	13 20	13 33

A From Birmingham New Street
B From Birmingham International
C To Aberystwyth
D To Llandudno
E To Holyhead
F From London Euston
G To Chester
H To Manchester Piccadilly

Table T074-F

Birmingham - Wolverhampton - Telford - Shrewsbury

Saturdays
21 December to 16 May

Station	VT ◇■ A	LM	AW ◇ B	LM	LM	AW ◇ C	LM	LM	AW ■ B	LM	LM	AW ◇ C	LM	LM	AW ◇ C	LM	LM	AW ◇ D	LM	LM	AW ◇ E
Birmingham International 68 d	12 33		13 08			14 09			15 08			16 08			17 08			18 08			19 08
Birmingham New Street 68 d	12 52	13 00	13 25	13 34	14 00	14 25	14 34	15 00	15 25	15 34	16 00	16 25	16 34	17 00	17 25	17 34	18 00	18 25	18 34	19 00	19 25
Smethwick Galton Bridge 68 d			13 31			14 31			15 31			16 31			17 31			18 31			19 31
Sandwell & Dudley 68 d		13 08			14 08			15 08			16 08			17 08			18 08			19 08	
Wolverhampton 68 d	13 10	13 19	13 44	13 51	14 19	14 43	14 52	15 19	15 43	15 52	16 19	16 43	16 52	17 19	17 43	17 52	18 19	18 43	18 52	19 18	19 43
Bilbrook d		13 25			14 25			15 25			16 25			17 25			18 25			19 24	
Codsall d		13 28		13 58	14 28		14 58	15 28		15 58	16 27		16 59	17 28		17 59	18 28		18 58	19 27	
Albrighton d		13 32			14 32			15 32			16 32			17 32			18 32			19 32	
Cosford d		13 36			14 36			15 36			16 35			17 36			18 36			19 35	
Shifnal d		13 41		14 07	14 41		15 07	15 41		16 07	16 40		17 08	17 41		18 08	18 41		19 07	19 40	
Telford Central d	13 34	13 47	14 01	14 12	14 47	15 00	15 13	15 47	16 00	16 13	16 46	17 00	17 14	17 47	18 00	18 14	18 47	19 00	19 13	19 46	20 01
Oakengates d		13 49			14 49			15 49			16 49			17 49			18 49			19 48	
Wellington (Shropshire) d	13 41	13 55	14 07	14 19	14 55	15 07	15 19	15 55	16 06	16 19	16 54	17 08	17 21	17 55	18 07	18 21	18 55	19 08	19 19	19 54	20 07
Shrewsbury a	13 54	14 08	14 21	14 32	15 08	15 21	15 36	16 08	16 20	16 32	17 07	17 23	17 34	18 08	18 21	18 34	19 08	19 22	19 36	20 07	20 21

Station	LM	VT ◇■ A	LM	AW ◇ C	LM	LM	AW ◇ E	LM	LM	AW ◇ F	LM	AW
Birmingham International 68 d		19 33		20 08			21 08					
Birmingham New Street 68 d	19 34	19 50	20 00	20 25	20 34	21 01	21 25	21 32	22 03	22 35	23 08	23 35
Smethwick Galton Bridge 68 d				20 31			21 31				23 16	
Sandwell & Dudley 68 d		19 59	20 08			21 09			22 11		23 19	
Wolverhampton 68 d	19 52	20 19	20 25	20 43	20 52	21 22	21 43	21 50	22 23	22 53	23 35	23 54
Bilbrook d			20 31			21 28			22 29			00 01
Codsall d	19 59		20 33		20 58	21 31		21 57	22 32			00 04
Albrighton d			20 38			21 35			22 36			00 08
Cosford d			20 41			21 39			22 40			00 12
Shifnal d	20 08		20 46		21 07	21 44		22 06	22 45			00 17
Telford Central d	20 14	20 36	20 51	20 59	21 13	21 49	22 01	22 11	22 51	23 09	23 51	00 22
Oakengates d			20 54			21 52			22 53			00 25
Wellington (Shropshire) d	20 21	20 43	20 59	21 07	21 20	21 58	22 08	22 18	22 59	23 16	23 58	00 30
Shrewsbury a	20 35	20 56	21 14	21 21	21 38	22 11	22 23	22 31	23 12	23 30	00 11	00 45

Sundays
15 December to 10 May

Station	AW G	AW ◇	LM	LM	AW ◇ C	LM	AW ◇ E	LM	LM	AW ◇ C	LM	AW ◇ E	LM	AW ■ C	LM	AW ◇ E	LM	AW ■ C	LM	AW ◇ B	LM	AW ◇ C
Birmingham International 68 d					09 51		10 48			12 07		13 07		14 07		15 08		16 08		17 08		18 08
Birmingham New Street 68 d			08 28	09 30	10 04	10 26	11 04	11 26	12 00	12 23	13 00	13 23	14 00	14 23	15 00	15 23	16 00	16 24	17 00	17 24	18 03	18 23
Smethwick Galton Bridge 68 d			08 37		10 10	10 32	11 12		12 06	12 31	13 07	13 31	14 06	14 31	15 06	15 31	16 06	16 31		17 31	18 10	18 31
Sandwell & Dudley 68 d			08 40	09 38		10 36		11 34	12 10		13 10		14 10		15 09		16 09		17 08		18 13	
Wolverhampton 68 d		00 20	08 55	09 49	10 22	10 46	11 24	11 44	12 21	12 42	13 21	13 42	14 20	14 44	15 20	15 44	16 20	16 44	17 19	17 44	18 23	18 43
Bilbrook d	00 01		09 03	09 55	10 28	10 52	11 31	11 50	12 27		13 27		14 26		15 26		16 26		17 25		18 29	
Codsall d	00 04		09 05	09 57	10 31	10 55	11 33	11 52	12 29		13 29		14 29		15 28		16 28		17 27		18 32	
Albrighton d	00 08		09 10	10 02	10 35	10 59	11 38	11 57	12 34		13 34		14 33		15 33		16 33		17 32		18 36	
Cosford d	00 12		09 13	10 05	10 39	11 02	11 42	12 00	12 37		13 37		14 36		15 36		16 36		17 35		18 39	
Shifnal d	00 17		09 18	10 10	10 44	11 07	11 47	12 05	12 42		13 42		14 41		15 41		16 41		17 40		18 44	
Telford Central d	00 22	00 37	09 23	10 15	10 49	11 13	11 52	12 10	12 47	12 59	13 47	13 58	14 47	15 02	15 46	16 00	16 46	17 01	17 45	18 01	18 50	19 00
Oakengates d	00 25		09 25	10 17	10 51	11 15	11 55	12 12	12 49		13 49		14 49		15 48		16 48		17 47		18 52	
Wellington (Shropshire) d	00 30	00 44	09 30	10 22	10 57	11 20	12 01	12 17	12 54	13 06	13 54	14 05	14 54	15 09	15 53	16 08	16 53	17 08	17 53	18 07	18 57	19 07
Shrewsbury a	00 45	00 59	09 43	10 35	11 12	11 33	12 15	12 30	13 09	13 20	14 09	14 19	15 09	15 23	16 08	16 25	17 08	17 23	18 08	18 21	19 12	19 21

Station	LM	AW ◇ E	LM	AW ◇ C	VT ◇■ A	LM	AW ◇ E	LM	AW	AW
Birmingham International 68 d		19 09		20 08	20 13		21 08		22 11	23 08
Birmingham New Street 68 d	19 00	19 24	20 00	20 24	20 27	21 05	21 23	22 05	22 24	23 25
Smethwick Galton Bridge 68 d	19 06	19 32		20 31		21 12	21 31	22 12	22 31	23 33
Sandwell & Dudley 68 d	19 10		20 08		20 36	21 15		22 15		
Wolverhampton 68 d	19 21	19 44	20 21	20 44	20 56	21 27	21 43	22 29	22 43	23 49
Bilbrook d	19 27		20 27			21 33	21 49	22 35	22 49	23 55
Codsall d	19 29		20 29			21 35	21 52	22 37	22 51	23 57
Albrighton d	19 34		20 34			21 40	21 56	22 42	22 56	00 02
Cosford d	19 37		20 37			21 43	22 00	22 45	22 59	00 05
Shifnal d	19 42		20 42			21 48	22 05	22 50	23 04	00 10
Telford Central d	19 47	20 01	20 47	21 01	21 13	21 53	22 10	22 55	23 10	00 16
Oakengates d	19 49		20 49			21 55	22 12	22 57	23 12	00 18
Wellington (Shropshire) d	19 54	20 08	20 55	21 08	21 20	22 00	22 17	23 02	23 17	00 24
Shrewsbury a	20 07	20 22	21 12	21 22	21 35	22 13	22 31	23 15	23 30	00 39

A From London Euston
B To Holyhead
C To Aberystwyth
D To Machynlleth Carr. Sdgs
E To Chester
F To Crewe
G not 15 December. From Birmingham New Street

Table T074-R

Mondays to Fridays
16 December to 15 May

Shrewsbury - Telford - Wolverhampton - Birmingham

Miles	Station		AW MX ◇ A	AW	LM B	LM	AW ◇ A	VT ◇[1] C	LM	LM	AW ◇ D	LM	LM	AW ◇ E	LM	LM	AW ■ F	LM	LM	AW ◇	LM	LM	AW ◇ G
0	**Shrewsbury**	d		05 18	05 24	05 59	06 33	06 39	06 51	07 14	07 33	07 47	08 13	08 33	08 41	09 11	09 33	09 41	10 13	10 33	10 43	11 12	11 34
10½	Wellington (Shropshire)	d		05 32	05 37	06 11	06 47	06 53	07 03	07 27	07 47	07 59	08 26	08 47	08 53	09 24	09 47	09 54	10 25	10 47	10 55	11 25	11 47
13½	Oakengates	d			05 42	06 16				07 32		08 04			08 58			09 59			11 00		
14½	**Telford Central**	d		05 38	05 45	06 19	06 53	07 00	07 09	07 36	07 53	08 07	08 32	08 53	09 01	09 31	09 53	10 02	10 31	10 54	11 03	11 31	11 53
17½	Shifnal	d			05 50	06 25			07 14	07 41		08 13	08 37		09 07	09 36		10 08	10 36		11 07	11 36	
20¾	Cosford	d			05 55	06 29				07 46		08 17			09 11			10 12			11 12		
22¼	Albrighton	d	00 01		05 58	06 33			07 21	07 50		08 20			09 15			10 16			11 15		
25½	Codsall	d	00 06		06 03	06 38				07 55		08 26	08 47		09 20	09 46		10 21	10 46		11 21	11 46	
26	Bilbrook	d	00 08		06 06	06 41				07 58		08 28			09 23			10 24			11 23		
30	**Wolverhampton** [7] 68	a	00 17	05 59	06 13	06 51	07 12	07 17	07 32	08 05	08 11	08 35	08 55	09 11	09 30	09 54	10 10	10 31	10 54	11 11	11 30	11 54	12 11
37¾	Sandwell & Dudley 68	a			06 27	07 07			07 44	08 15		08 44			09 43			10 43			11 44		
39	Smethwick Galton Bridge [5] 68	a		06 10	06 31	07 10	07 23				08 22			09 22			10 21			11 22			12 22
43	**Birmingham New Street** [12] 68	a		06 17	06 40	07 18	07 31	07 47	07 55	08 25	08 31	08 53	09 17	09 31	09 53	10 18	10 32	10 53	11 16	11 30	11 53	12 18	12 31
—	Birmingham International 68	a		06 50			07 50	07 59			08 50			09 50			10 50			11 51			12 50

Station		LM	LM	AW ◇ H	LM	LM	AW ◇ G	LM	LM	AW ◇ H	LM	LM	VT ◇[1] C	AW ◇ G	LM	LM	AW ■ H	LM	LM	AW ◇ G	LM	LM
Shrewsbury	d	11 45	12 13	12 33	12 41	13 13	13 34	13 41	14 12	14 33	14 41	15 13	15 24	15 32	15 41	16 13	16 33	16 41	17 13	17 33	17 41	18 13
Wellington (Shropshire)	d	11 57	12 25	12 47	12 53	13 25	13 47	13 53	14 25	14 47	14 53	15 25	15 38	15 45	15 53	16 25	16 47	16 53	17 25	17 47	17 53	18 25
Oakengates	d	12 02			12 58			13 58			14 58				15 58			16 58			17 58	
Telford Central	d	12 05	12 31	12 53	13 01	13 31	13 54	14 01	14 31	14 53	15 01	15 31	15 44	15 53	16 01	16 31	16 53	17 01	17 31	17 53	18 01	18 31
Shifnal	d	12 11	12 36		13 07	13 36		14 07	14 36		15 07	15 36			16 07	16 36		17 07	17 36		18 07	18 36
Cosford	d	12 15			13 11			14 11			15 11				16 11			17 11			18 11	
Albrighton	d	12 19			13 15			14 15			15 15				16 15			17 15			18 14	
Codsall	d	12 24	12 46		13 20	13 46		14 20	14 46		15 20	15 46			16 20	16 46		17 20	17 46		18 20	18 46
Bilbrook	d	12 27			13 23			14 23			15 23				16 23			17 23			18 22	
Wolverhampton [7] 68	a	12 34	12 54	13 12	13 31	13 54	14 12	14 30	14 54	15 11	15 31	15 54	16 01	16 10	16 30	16 54	17 11	17 30	17 54	18 11	18 29	18 54
Sandwell & Dudley 68	a	12 43			13 44			14 43			15 43				16 43			17 43			18 43	
Smethwick Galton Bridge [5] 68	a			13 23			14 23			15 22				16 22			17 22			18 22		
Birmingham New Street [12] 68	a	12 54	13 16	13 30	13 53	14 16	14 31	14 53	15 16	15 31	15 53	16 27	16 21	16 31	16 53	17 16	17 31	17 53	18 17	18 31	18 53	19 16
Birmingham International 68	a			13 50			14 50			15 50			16 39	16 50			17 50			18 50		

Station		AW ◇ H	LM	LM	AW ◇ D	LM	LM	AW ◇ G	LM	AW ◇ H	LM	AW ◇ A
Shrewsbury	d	18 33	18 47	19 13	19 33	19 46	20 45	21 33	21 56	22 18	22 45	23 26
Wellington (Shropshire)	d	18 47	18 59	19 25	19 47	19 58	20 57	21 47	22 08	22 32	22 57	23 40
Oakengates	d		19 04			20 03	21 02		22 13		23 02	23 44
Telford Central	d	18 53	19 07	19 31	19 53	20 06	21 07	21 53	22 16	22 38	23 05	23 48
Shifnal	d		19 13	19 36		20 12	21 13		22 22		23 11	23 53
Cosford	d		19 17			20 16	21 17		22 26		23 15	23 58
Albrighton	d		19 21			20 20	21 21		22 30		23 19	00 01
Codsall	d		19 26	19 46		20 25	21 26		22 35		23 24	00 06
Bilbrook	d		19 29			20 28	21 29		22 37		23 27	00 08
Wolverhampton [7] 68	a	19 12	19 36	19 54	20 11	20 35	21 36	22 12	22 48	22 55	23 34	00 17
Sandwell & Dudley 68	a		19 45			20 44	21 46					
Smethwick Galton Bridge [5] 68	a	19 23			20 22			22 23				
Birmingham New Street [12] 68	a	19 31	19 54	20 16	20 31	20 53	21 57	22 32		23 28	23 50	
Birmingham International 68	a	19 50			20 50							

Saturdays
21 December to 16 May

Station		AW ◇ A	AW	LM	LM	AW	LM	LM	AW ◇ D	LM	LM	VT ◇[1] C	AW ◇ H	LM	LM	AW ■ F	LM	LM	AW ■ H	LM	LM	AW ■ G	LM
Shrewsbury	d		05 19	05 31	05 55	06 33	06 48	07 08	07 32	07 39	08 13	08 19	08 33	08 41	09 13	09 32	09 41	10 13	10 34	10 42	11 12	11 33	11 41
Wellington (Shropshire)	d		05 33	05 43	06 10	06 47	07 00	07 20	07 46	07 54	08 25	08 33	08 47	08 53	09 25	09 46	09 53	10 25	10 48	10 54	11 25	11 47	11 53
Oakengates	d			05 48	06 15		07 05			07 59				08 58			09 58			10 59			11 58
Telford Central	d		05 42	05 51	06 18	06 53	07 08	07 26	07 53	08 07	08 31	08 40	08 53	09 01	09 31	09 52	10 01	10 31	10 55	11 02	11 31	11 53	12 01
Shifnal	d			05 56	06 24		07 13	07 31		08 13	08 36			09 07	09 36		10 07	10 36		11 08	11 36		12 07
Cosford	d			06 01	06 28		07 18			08 17				09 11			10 11			11 12			12 11
Albrighton	d	00 01		06 04	06 32		07 21			08 21				09 15			10 15			11 15			12 15
Codsall	d	00 06		06 09	06 37		07 26	07 41		08 26	08 46			09 20	09 46		10 20	10 46		11 20	11 46		12 20
Bilbrook	d	00 08		06 12	06 40		07 29			08 29				09 23			10 23			11 23			12 23
Wolverhampton [7] 68	a	00 17	06 02	06 19	06 47	07 12	07 36	07 49	08 11	08 36	08 54	09 00	09 12	09 30	09 54	10 09	10 30	10 54	11 13	11 30	11 54	12 11	12 30
Sandwell & Dudley 68	a			06 32	07 02		07 45			08 45				09 43			10 43			11 43			12 43
Smethwick Galton Bridge [5] 68	a		06 13	06 36	07 06	07 23			08 22				09 23			10 21			11 24			12 22	
Birmingham New Street [12] 68	a		06 21	06 44	07 18	07 32	07 55	08 18	08 31	08 54	09 26	09 19	09 31	09 54	10 17	10 31	10 53	11 17	11 31	11 53	12 17	12 31	12 53
Birmingham International 68	a		06 50			07 50			08 50			09 39	09 51			10 50			11 50			12 50	

A From Chester
B From Shrewsbury Abbey Frgte Cs
C To London Euston
D From Aberystwyth
E From Crewe
F From Barmouth
G From Pwllheli
H From Holyhead

Table T074-R

Saturdays
21 December to 16 May

Shrewsbury - Telford - Wolverhampton - Birmingham

Station		LM	AW ■ A	LM	LM	AW ■ B	LM	LM	AW ■ A	LM	LM	VT ◇[1] C	AW ◇ B	LM	LM	AW ■ A	LM	LM	AW ◇ B	LM	LM	AW ■ A
Shrewsbury	d	12 13	12 34	12 41	13 13	13 35	13 44	14 13	14 34	14 41	15 13	15 24	15 32	15 41	16 13	16 34	16 41	17 12	17 30	17 41	18 13	18 30
Wellington (Shropshire)	d	12 25	12 47	12 53	13 25	13 49	13 56	14 25	14 47	14 53	15 25	15 38	15 46	15 53	16 25	16 48	16 53	17 25	17 45	17 53	18 25	18 44
Oakengates	d			12 58			14 01			14 58				15 58			16 58			17 58		
Telford Central	d	12 31	12 54	13 01	13 31	13 55	14 04	14 31	14 54	15 01	15 31	15 44	15 53	16 01	16 31	16 54	17 01	17 31	17 53	18 01	18 31	18 52
Shifnal	d	12 36		13 07	13 36		14 10	14 36		15 07	15 36			16 07	16 36		17 07	17 36		18 07	18 36	
Cosford	d			13 11			14 14			15 11				16 11			17 11			18 11		
Albrighton	d			13 15			14 18			15 15				16 15			17 15			18 15		
Codsall	d	12 46		13 20	13 46		14 23	14 46		15 20	15 46			16 20	16 46		17 20	17 46		18 20	18 46	
Bilbrook	d			13 23			14 26			15 23				16 23			17 23			18 23		
Wolverhampton [7] 68	a	12 54	13 12	13 30	13 54	14 12	14 36	14 54	15 12	15 30	15 54	16 01	16 11	16 30	16 54	17 11	17 30	17 54	18 11	18 30	18 54	19 12
Sandwell & Dudley 68	a			13 43			14 45			15 43				16 43			17 43			18 43		
Smethwick Galton Bridge [5] 68	a		13 22			14 23			15 23				16 23			17 22			18 22			19 23
Birmingham New Street [12] 68	a	13 17	13 31	13 54	14 17	14 30	14 55	15 17	15 30	15 52	16 27	16 22	16 31	16 53	17 17	17 31	17 53	18 16	18 31	18 52	19 17	19 30
Birmingham International 68	a		13 50			14 50			15 50			16 39	16 49			17 50			18 49			19 50

Station		LM	LM	AW ◇ D	LM	LM	LM	AW ◇ B	LM	AW ◇ A	LM	AW ◇ E
Shrewsbury	d	18 41	19 13	19 32	19 47	20 13	20 48	21 34	21 46	22 31	22 47	23 26
Wellington (Shropshire)	d	18 53	19 25	19 46	19 59	20 25	21 01	21 47	21 58	22 45	22 59	23 40
Oakengates	d	18 58			20 04		21 05		22 03		23 04	23 45
Telford Central	d	19 01	19 31	19 53	20 07	20 31	21 08	21 53	22 06	22 51	23 07	23 48
Shifnal	d	19 07	19 36		20 13	20 36	21 14		22 12		23 13	23 53
Cosford	d	19 11			20 17		21 18		22 16		23 17	23 58
Albrighton	d	19 15			20 21		21 22		22 20		23 21	00 02
Codsall	d	19 20	19 46		20 26	20 46	21 27		22 25		23 26	00 07
Bilbrook	d	19 23			20 29		21 30		22 28		23 29	00 09
Wolverhampton [7] 68	a	19 31	19 54	20 11	20 37	20 54	21 38	22 12	22 35	23 09	23 36	00 17
Sandwell & Dudley 68	a	19 42			20 46		21 48		22 44		23 45	
Smethwick Galton Bridge [5] 68	a			20 23				22 23				
Birmingham New Street [12] 68	a	19 52	20 17	20 31	20 55	21 16	21 57	22 32	22 53	23 30	23 54	
Birmingham International 68	a			20 49								

Sundays
15 December to 10 May

Station		AW ◇ F	AW ◇	LM	AW ◇	LM	AW ◇ E	LM	AW ■ D	LM	AW ◇ E	LM	AW ■ B	LM	AW ◇ E	LM	VT ◇[1] C	AW ■ B	LM	AW ◇ E	LM	AW ■ B	LM
Shrewsbury	d		08 10	08 24	09 07	09 48	10 18	10 42	11 36	11 42	12 33	12 48	13 31	13 47	14 31	14 48	15 24	15 32	15 47	16 38	16 47	17 33	17 43
Wellington (Shropshire)	d		08 24	08 36	09 21	10 00	10 32	10 54	11 49	11 55	12 47	13 00	13 44	13 59	14 44	15 00	15 38	15 45	15 59	16 52	16 59	17 47	17 56
Oakengates	d		08 28	08 41	09 25	10 05		10 59		12 00		13 05		14 04		15 05			16 04		17 04		18 01
Telford Central	d		08 31	08 44	09 28	10 08	10 38	11 02	11 55	12 03	12 54	13 08	13 50	14 07	14 51	15 08	15 44	15 51	16 07	16 59	17 07	17 53	18 04
Shifnal	d		08 36	08 49	09 33	10 13		11 07		12 08		13 13		14 12		15 13			16 12		17 12		18 09
Cosford	d		08 41	08 53	09 38	10 17		11 12		12 12		13 17		14 16		15 17			16 16		17 16		18 13
Albrighton	d	00 02	08 44	08 56	09 41	10 20		11 15		12 15		13 20		14 19		15 20			16 19		17 19		18 16
Codsall	d	00 07	08 50	09 02	09 47	10 26		11 20		12 21		13 26		14 25		15 26			16 25		17 25		18 22
Bilbrook	d	00 09	08 52	09 04	09 49	10 28		11 22		12 23		13 28		14 27		15 28			16 27		17 27		18 24
Wolverhampton [7] 68	a	00 17	09 00	09 11	09 57	10 35	10 56	11 29	12 12	12 30	13 11	13 35	14 07	14 36	15 07	15 37	16 01	16 07	16 35	17 20	17 36	18 09	18 31
Sandwell & Dudley 68	a			09 20				11 42		12 46		13 45		14 45		15 46			16 44		17 45		18 44
Smethwick Galton Bridge [5] 68	a		09 11	09 23	10 08	10 46	11 07	11 45	12 25		13 23		14 17		15 17			16 18		17 31		18 20	
Birmingham New Street [12] 68	a		09 18	09 30	10 16	10 54	11 16	11 52	12 35	12 55	13 30	13 56	14 26	14 55	15 26	15 57	16 20	16 26	16 55	17 40	17 57	18 31	18 55
Birmingham International 68	a		09 32		10 32		11 32		13 02		13 57		15 00		15 57		16 39	17 00		17 57		18 56	

Station		AW ◇ E	LM	AW ◇ B	LM	AW ◇ E	LM	AW ◇ D	LM	AW ◇ E
Shrewsbury	d	18 31	18 47	19 30	19 47	20 22	20 46	21 33	21 56	22 24
Wellington (Shropshire)	d	18 45	18 59	19 45	19 59	20 36	20 59	21 47	22 08	22 38
Oakengates	d		19 04		20 04	20 41	21 04		22 13	22 43
Telford Central	d	18 51	19 07	19 51	20 07	20 44	21 07	21 53	22 16	22 46
Shifnal	d		19 12		20 12	20 49	21 12		22 21	22 51
Cosford	d		19 16		20 16	20 54	21 16		22 25	22 56
Albrighton	d		19 19		20 19	20 57	21 19		22 28	22 59
Codsall	d		19 25		20 25	21 02	21 25		22 34	23 05
Bilbrook	d		19 27		20 27	21 04	21 27		22 36	23 07
Wolverhampton [7] 68	a	19 08	19 36	20 07	20 36	21 12	21 36	22 11	22 43	23 15
Sandwell & Dudley 68	a		19 45		20 47		21 46		22 56	
Smethwick Galton Bridge [5] 68	a	19 19		20 18		21 23		22 22		
Birmingham New Street [12] 68	a	19 28	19 55	20 29	20 56	21 32	21 55	22 31	23 05	
Birmingham International 68	a	19 57		20 58		21 57		23 01		

A From Holyhead
B From Pwllheli
C To London Euston
D From Aberystwyth
E From Chester
F not 15 December. From Chester

Table T075-F

Birmingham - Shrewsbury - Chester - Holyhead

Mondays to Fridays

16 December to 15 May

Miles	Miles		AW MX A	AW	AW ◇ B	VT ◇ 1	AW	AW ◇	AW ◇ 🍴	AW ■ ☒	AW ◇ 🍴	AW ◇ 🍴	AW ◇ 🍴	AW ■ ☒	AW ◇ 🍴	AW ◇ 🍴	AW ◇ 🍴	AW ■ 🍴	AW ◇	AW ◇ B	AW ■ ☒	AW FO
0	—	Birmingham International 68 ✈ d							07 09		09 10		11 10		13 09		15 10		17 11			
8¼	—	**Birmingham New Street** 12 74,68 d							07 23		09 25		11 25		13 25		15 25		17 26			
12½	—	Smethwick Galton Bridge 5 74,68 d							07 29		09 31		11 31		13 31		15 31		17 32			
20¾	—	**Wolverhampton** 7 68,74 d							07 43		09 43		11 44		13 43		15 43		17 44			
35¾	—	Telford Central 74 d							08 00		10 00		12 01		14 00		16 00		18 01			
39¾	—	Wellington (Shropshire) 74 d							08 08		10 07		12 07		14 07		16 06		18 07			
—	0	**Cardiff Central** 7 131 d						05 12		07 02		09 22		11 24		13 22		15 22			17 16	
—	11¾	Newport (South Wales) 131 d						05 31		07 16		09 36		11 39		13 37		15 37			17 31	
—	55¾	Hereford 131 d						06 25		08 07		10 29		12 33		14 29		16 28			18 25	
50	106	**Shrewsbury** 74 a						07 25	08 22	08 59	10 22	11 22	12 21	13 22	14 21	15 24	16 20	17 24	18 21		19 09	
—	—	d		05 20	05 59		07 00	07 25	08 25	09 01	10 25	11 25	12 26	13 25	14 25	15 29	16 24	17 25	18 26		19 09	19 27
68	124	Gobowen d		05 39	06 16		07 19	07 43	08 43		10 43	11 42	12 44	13 43	14 43	15 46	16 43	17 43	18 44			19 45
71	127	Chirk d	00 03	05 44	06 22		07 24	07 48	08 48		10 48	11 48	12 49	13 49	14 48	15 52	16 48	17 48	18 49			19 50
75½	131½	Ruabon d	00 10	05 51	06 28		07 31	07 55	08 55		10 55	11 54	12 56	13 56	14 55	15 58	16 55	17 55	18 56			19 57
80¼	136¼	Wrexham General a	00 16	06 00	06 34		07 41	08 01	09 02	09 29	11 02	12 01	13 03	14 05	15 01	16 04	17 02	18 03	19 03		19 38	20 04
—	—	d	00 16	06 05	06 35	07 03		08 01	09 02	09 30	11 02	12 01	13 03	14 05	15 01	16 05	17 02	18 04	19 03	19 09	19 38	20 04
92¼	148¼	**Chester** 81 a	00 35	06 26	07 00	07 20		08 20	09 20	09 48	11 21	12 20	13 21	14 23	15 20	16 24	17 22	18 22	19 22	19 27	19 58	20 24
104¼	160¼	Flint 81 a						08 37	09 38		11 37	12 35	13 37	14 39	15 36	16 40	17 40	18 40	19 46		20 14	
118¾	174¾	Prestatyn 81 a						08 50	09 50		11 50	12 48	13 49	14 54	15 50	16 52	17 53	18 52	19 59			
122¾	178¾	Rhyl 81 a						08 56	09 56		11 56	12 55	13 55	15 00	15 57	16 58	18 00	18 58	20 05		20 30	
132¾	188¾	Colwyn Bay 81 a						09 10	10 10		12 11	13 06	14 05	15 11	16 06	17 09	18 14	19 12	20 19		20 42	
136¾	192¾	Llandudno Junction 81 a						09 16	10 17	10 31	12 18	13 13	14 14	15 20	16 14	17 16	18 21	19 18	20 28		20 51	
139¾	195¾	Llandudno 81 a						09 27	10 28										20 40			
158	214	Bangor (Gwynedd) 81 a								10 50	12 42	13 30	14 36	15 37	16 43	17 40	18 49	19 37			21 09	
182¾	238¾	**Holyhead** 81 a								11 20	13 21	14 14	15 17	16 06	17 15	18 21	19 17	20 20			21 41	

	AW FX	AW ◇	AW FX ◇	AW FO ◇	AW ◇ C	AW
Birmingham International 68 ✈ d		19 05			21 09	
Birmingham New Street 12 74,68 d		19 25			21 25	
Smethwick Galton Bridge 5 74,68 d		19 31			21 32	
Wolverhampton 7 68,74 d		19 43			21 45	
Telford Central 74 d		20 00			22 02	
Wellington (Shropshire) 74 d		20 07			22 10	
Cardiff Central 7 131 d			19 34	19 34		
Newport (South Wales) 131 d			19 50	19 50		
Hereford 131 d			20 41	20 42		
Shrewsbury 74 a		20 22	21 38	21 38	22 24	
d	19 27	20 28	21 41	21 44	22 25	23 40
Gobowen d	19 45	20 46	21 58	22 02	22 43	23 58
Chirk d	19 50	20 51	22 04	22 07	22 48	00 03
Ruabon d	19 57	20 58	22 10	22 14	22 54	00 10
Wrexham General a	20 04	21 05	22 17	22 20	23 01	00 16
d	20 04	21 05	22 17	22 20	23 01	00 16
Chester 81 a	20 25	21 23	22 37	22 41	23 20	00 35
Flint 81 a			23 10	23 10		
Prestatyn 81 a			23 23	23 23		
Rhyl 81 a			23 30	23 30		
Colwyn Bay 81 a			23 44	23 44		
Llandudno Junction 81 a			23 51	23 51		
Llandudno 81 a						
Bangor (Gwynedd) 81 a			00 15	00 14		
Holyhead 81 a			00 43	00 43		

A From Shrewsbury

B To Liverpool Lime Street

C To Manchester Piccadilly

Table T075-F

Birmingham - Shrewsbury - Chester - Holyhead

Saturdays

21 December to 16 May

	AW A	AW	AW ◇ B	AW C	AW ◇	AW ■ 🍴	AW ◇ 🍴	AW ■ 🍴	AW ◇ 🍴	AW ◇ 🍴	AW ■ D 🍴	AW ◇ 🍴	AW ◇ D 🍴	AW ■ 🍴	AW ■ D 🍴	AW ◇	AW ◇ B	AW	AW ■ 🍴	AW ◇	AW ◇	AW ◇
Birmingham International 68 ✈ d						07 09		09 08		11 08		13 08		15 08		17 08				19 08		21 08
Birmingham New Street 12 74,68 d						07 24		09 25		11 25		13 25		15 25		17 25				19 25		21 25
Smethwick Galton Bridge 5 74,68 d						07 31		09 32		11 32		13 31		15 31		17 31				19 31		21 31
Wolverhampton 7 68,74 d						07 43		09 44		11 44		13 44		15 43		17 43				19 43		21 43
Telford Central 74 d						08 00		10 00		12 00		14 01		16 00		18 00				20 01		22 01
Wellington (Shropshire) 74 d						08 07		10 07		12 07		14 07		16 06		18 07				20 07		22 08
Cardiff Central 7 131 d					05 21		07 22		09 23		11 12		13 21		15 23				17 23		19 34	
Newport (South Wales) 131 d					05 34		07 37		09 38		11 37		13 36		15 38				17 36		19 48	
Hereford 131 d					06 26		08 30		10 30		12 28		14 27		16 29				18 27		20 40	
Shrewsbury 74 a					07 23	08 21	09 24	10 21	11 24	12 21	13 21	14 21	15 25	16 20	17 22	18 21			19 21	20 21	21 37	22 23
d		05 15		06 10	07 25	08 25	09 26	10 25	11 25	12 25	13 25	14 24	15 30	16 25	17 26	18 25			19 28	20 26	21 39	22 24
Gobowen d		05 36		06 29	07 42	08 43	09 43	10 43	11 42	12 43	13 42	14 42	15 47	16 43	17 43	18 43			19 45	20 44	21 56	22 42
Chirk d	00 03	05 42		06 34	07 48	08 48	09 49	10 49	11 48	12 49	13 48	14 48	15 53	16 48	17 49	18 49			19 51	20 49	22 02	22 47
Ruabon d	00 10	05 49		06 41	07 54	08 55	09 55	10 55	11 54	12 55	13 54	14 54	15 59	16 55	17 55	18 55			19 57	20 56	22 08	22 54
Wrexham General a	00 16	05 56		06 49	08 01	09 02	10 02	11 02	12 00	13 01	14 01	15 01	16 05	17 02	18 02	19 02			20 03	21 02	22 15	23 01
d	00 16	05 58	06 19	06 50	08 01	09 02	10 02	11 02	12 01	13 02	14 01	15 02	16 06	17 02	18 02	19 02	19 10	19 48	20 04	21 02	22 15	23 01
Chester 81 a	00 35	06 18	06 39	07 10	08 20	09 21	10 20	11 22	12 19	13 20	14 20	15 21	16 24	17 19	18 20	19 22	19 29	20 07	20 24	21 21	22 34	23 21
Flint 81 a					08 36	09 38	10 36	11 38	12 35	13 37	14 36	15 37	16 40	17 38	18 38	19 41			20 46		22 52	
Prestatyn 81 a					08 49	09 53	10 48	11 51	12 49	13 50	14 48	15 50	16 52	17 51	18 50	19 54			20 59		23 05	
Rhyl 81 a					08 56	09 59	10 55	11 58	12 56	13 57	14 55	15 57	16 58	17 58	18 56	20 01			21 06		23 12	
Colwyn Bay 81 a					09 06	10 11	11 06	12 07	13 07	14 06	15 07	16 06	17 09	18 12	19 07	20 15			21 19		23 26	
Llandudno Junction 81 a					09 14	10 19	11 13	12 16	13 16	14 15	15 15	16 15	17 16	18 19	19 14	20 22			21 26		23 36	
Llandudno 81 a																						
Bangor (Gwynedd) 81 a					09 37	10 37	11 37	12 33	13 33	14 38	15 32	16 39	17 40	18 43	19 34	20 49			21 43			
Holyhead 81 a					10 13	11 10	12 09	13 12	14 13	15 09	16 12	17 11	18 18	19 13	20 17	21 28			22 24			

	AW
Birmingham International 68 ✈ d	
Birmingham New Street 12 74,68 d	
Smethwick Galton Bridge 5 74,68 d	
Wolverhampton 7 68,74 d	
Telford Central 74 d	
Wellington (Shropshire) 74 d	
Cardiff Central 7 131 d	
Newport (South Wales) 131 d	
Hereford 131 d	
Shrewsbury 74 a	
d	23 33
Gobowen d	23 53
Chirk d	23 59
Ruabon d	00 05
Wrexham General a	00 12
d	00 14
Chester 81 a	00 33
Flint 81 a	
Prestatyn 81 a	
Rhyl 81 a	
Colwyn Bay 81 a	
Llandudno Junction 81 a	
Llandudno 81 a	
Bangor (Gwynedd) 81 a	
Holyhead 81 a	

Sundays

15 December to 10 May

	AW E	AW ◇	AW ◇ 🍴	AW ◇ 🍴	AW ■ 🍴	AW ◇ 🍴	AW ■ 🍴	AW ◇ 🍴	AW ◇	AW ◇	AW ◇
Birmingham International 68 ✈ d			10 48	13 07		15 08		17 08	19 09		
Birmingham New Street 12 74,68 d			11 04	13 23		15 23		17 24	19 24		
Smethwick Galton Bridge 5 74,68 d			11 12	13 31		15 31		17 31	19 32		
Wolverhampton 7 68,74 d			11 24	13 42		15 44		17 44	19 44		
Telford Central 74 d			11 52	13 58		16 00		18 01	20 01		
Wellington (Shropshire) 74 d			12 01	14 05		16 08		18 07	20 08		
Cardiff Central 7 131 d					13 25		15 17				
Newport (South Wales) 131 d					13 39		15 32				
Hereford 131 d					14 35		16 31				
Shrewsbury 74 a			12 15	14 19	15 29	16 25	17 27	18 21	20 22		
d		10 16	12 18	14 20	15 33	16 30	17 31	18 24	20 24		
Gobowen d		10 34	12 36	14 38	15 51	16 48	17 49	18 42	20 42		
Chirk d		10 39	12 41	14 43	15 56	16 53	17 54	18 47	20 47		
Ruabon d	00 05	10 46	12 48	14 50	16 03	17 00	18 01	18 54	20 54		
Wrexham General a	00 12	10 53	12 55	14 57	16 10	17 07	18 08	19 00	21 01		
d	00 14	10 53	12 55	14 57	16 10	17 07	18 08	19 00	21 01	22 35	23 37
Chester 81 a	00 33	11 12	13 14	15 18	16 29	17 26	18 26		21 20	22 54	23 57
Flint 81 a					16 50		18 44	19 50			
Prestatyn 81 a					17 03		18 57	20 02			
Rhyl 81 a					17 10		19 04	20 08			
Colwyn Bay 81 a					17 24		19 18	20 22			
Llandudno Junction 81 a					17 31		19 24	20 30			
Llandudno 81 a											
Bangor (Gwynedd) 81 a					17 54		19 48	20 52			
Holyhead 81 a					18 38		20 18	21 26			

A From Shrewsbury

B To Liverpool Lime Street

C To Manchester Piccadilly

D From Maesteg

E not 15 December. From Shrewsbury

Table T075-R

Mondays to Fridays
16 December to 15 May

Holyhead - Chester - Shrewsbury - Birmingham

Miles	Miles			AW	AW	AW	AW	AW	AW	AW	AW	AW	AW	AW	AW	AW	AW	AW	AW	AW	AW	VT	AW
				◇		◇	■ ⊠	◇ A	◇	■ 🍴	◇ 🍴	◇ 🍴	■ B 🍴	■ ⊠	◇ 🍴	■ 🍴	◇ 🍴	◇ 🍴	■ ⊠	◇ C	◇	◇[1] D ⊠	
0	0	**Holyhead**	81 d			04 25	05 34		06 28		08 05	09 23	10 40	11 34	11 48	13 27	14 36	15 38	16 51		17 31		
24¾	24¾	Bangor (Gwynedd)	81 d			04 57	06 02		07 06		09 02	10 02	11 09	12 01	12 21	14 06	15 04	16 17	17 18		18 10		
43	43	Llandudno	81 d							08 30													
46	46	Llandudno Junction	81 d			05 15	06 20		07 25	08 39	09 25	10 25	11 27	12 19	12 44	14 31	15 28	16 40	17 36		18 33		
50	50	Colwyn Bay	81 d			05 21	06 28		07 31	08 45	09 31	10 31	11 33	12 27	12 50	14 37	15 34	16 46					
60½	60½	Rhyl	81 d			05 30	06 39		07 40	08 55	09 40	10 41	11 42	12 38	13 00	14 47	15 43	16 55					
64	64	Prestatyn	81 d			05 36			07 46		09 46	10 47	11 48	12 44	13 05	14 52	15 49	17 01					
78	78	Flint	81 d			05 49	06 56		07 59		09 59	11 00	12 01	12 58	13 18	15 06	16 02	17 14					
90½	90½	**Chester**	81 d	05 35	05 45	06 20	07 16		08 19	09 28	10 21	11 36	12 19	13 16	13 38	15 36	16 23	17 34	18 22	18 32	19 17	20 21	
102½	102½	Wrexham General	a	05 50	06 03	06 35	07 32		08 34	09 45	10 35	11 51	12 34	13 31	13 53	15 50	16 37	17 49	18 36	18 48	19 32	20 38	
—	—		d	05 50		06 35	07 35	07 50	08 35	09 45	10 36	11 51	12 35	13 31	13 53	15 51	16 37	17 50	18 37		19 32		20 49
107¼	107¼	Ruabon	a	05 57		06 41		07 58	08 42	09 51	10 42	11 58	12 41	13 38	14 00	15 57	16 44	17 56	18 44		19 39		20 56
111¾	111¾	Chirk	a	06 03		06 48		08 04	08 48	09 58	10 49	12 04	12 48	13 45	14 06	16 04	16 50	18 03	18 51		19 45		21 02
114¾	114¾	Gobowen	a	06 09		06 53		08 10	08 54	10 03	10 54	12 10	12 53	13 50	14 12	16 09	16 56	18 08	18 56		19 51		21 08
132¾	132¾	**Shrewsbury**	74 a	06 28		07 14	08 06	08 28	09 13	10 23	11 14	12 29	13 13	14 16	14 31	16 30	17 15	18 28	19 21		20 13		21 29
—	183½	Hereford	131 a			08 10	08 56		10 10		12 07		14 10	15 07			18 13		20 15				
—	227	Newport (South Wales)	131 a			09 01	09 43		11 00	11 53	12 58		14 56	15 58			19 06		21 06				
—	238¾	**Cardiff Central** [7]	131 a			09 15	09 58		11 16	12 06	13 15		15 11	16 15			19 20		21 24				
143	—	Wellington (Shropshire)	74 a	06 47				08 47				12 46			14 47	16 46		18 47					
147	—	Telford Central	74 a	06 53				08 53				12 53			14 53	16 53		18 53					
162½	—	**Wolverhampton** [7] 68,74 ⛴	a	07 12				09 11				13 12			15 11	17 11		19 12					
170½	—	Smethwick Galton Bridge [5] 74,68 ✈	a	07 23				09 22				13 23			15 22	17 22		19 23					
174½	—	**Birmingham New Street** [12] 74,68	a	07 31				09 31				13 30			15 31	17 31		19 31					
182¾	—	Birmingham International	68 a	07 50				09 50				13 50			15 50	17 50		19 50					

		AW	AW	AW
		FX ◇	◇	◇
Holyhead	81 d		19 22	
Bangor (Gwynedd)	81 d		20 00	
Llandudno	81 d			
Llandudno Junction	81 d		20 23	
Colwyn Bay	81 d		20 29	
Rhyl	81 d		20 38	
Prestatyn	81 d		20 44	
Flint	81 d		20 57	
Chester	81 d	20 55	21 18	22 32
Wrexham General	a		21 32	22 47
	d		21 33	22 47
Ruabon	a		21 40	22 54
Chirk	a		21 46	23 00
Gobowen	a		21 52	23 05
Shrewsbury	74 a	22 08	22 13	23 25
Hereford	131 a	23 08		
Newport (South Wales)	131 a	00 02		
Cardiff Central [7]	131 a	00 20		
Wellington (Shropshire)	74 a		22 32	23 40
Telford Central	74 a		22 37	23 48
Wolverhampton [7] 68,74 ⛴	a		22 55	00 17
Smethwick Galton Bridge [5] 74,68 ✈	a			
Birmingham New Street [12] 74,68	a		23 28	
Birmingham International	68 a			

Saturdays
21 December to 16 May

		AW	AW	AW	AW	AW	AW	AW	AW	AW	AW	AW	AW	AW	AW	AW	AW	AW	AW	AW
			◇ E	◇	◇ E	■	◇ E 🍴	■ 🍴	■ 🍴	■ 🍴	◇ E 🍴	■ 🍴	◇ 🍴	■ 🍴	◇ C	◇ 🍴	◇		◇	◇
Holyhead	81 d		04 25	05 23	06 35	07 15	08 20	09 29	10 33	11 28	12 39	13 28	14 27	15 26		16 52	17 32		19 22	
Bangor (Gwynedd)	81 d		04 57	06 02	07 07	08 02	09 01	10 08	11 05	12 08	13 07	14 07	14 55	16 06		17 20	18 11		20 01	
Llandudno	81 d																			
Llandudno Junction	81 d		05 15	06 25	07 25	08 25	09 25	10 31	11 23	12 33	13 25	14 25	15 18	16 30		17 38	18 34		20 24	
Colwyn Bay	81 d		05 21	06 31	07 31	08 31	09 31	10 37	11 29	12 39	13 31	14 31	15 24	16 36		17 44	18 40		20 30	
Rhyl	81 d		05 30	06 41	07 40	08 41	09 40	10 47	11 39	12 50	13 40	14 41	15 35	16 46		17 54	18 50		20 40	
Prestatyn	81 d		05 36	06 47	07 46	08 47	09 46	10 53	11 45	12 56	13 46	14 47	15 40	16 52		18 00	18 56		20 46	
Flint	81 d		05 49	07 00	07 59	09 00	09 59	11 06	11 58	13 10	13 59	15 00	15 53	17 05		18 13	19 09		20 59	
Chester	81 d	05 30	06 20	07 30	08 20	09 30	10 19	11 36	12 19	13 35	14 19	15 36	16 22	17 30	18 24	18 33	19 34	20 26	21 30	22 30
Wrexham General	a	05 48	06 35	07 45	08 35	09 44	10 34	11 50	12 34	13 49	14 33	15 51	16 37	17 45	18 40	18 47	19 46	20 42	21 45	22 47
	d		06 35	07 45	08 35	09 46	10 34	11 51	12 34	13 51	14 35	15 51	16 37	17 45		18 47	19 46	20 42	21 45	22 47
Ruabon	a		06 41	07 52	08 41	09 52	10 40	11 57	12 40	13 57	14 40	15 58	16 43	17 52		18 54	19 53	20 50	21 52	22 53
Chirk	a		06 48	07 58	08 48	09 58	10 47	12 04	12 47	14 04	14 46	16 04	16 50	17 58		19 00	19 59	20 56	21 58	23 00
Gobowen	a		06 53	08 04	08 53	10 04	10 52	12 09	12 52	14 09	14 52	16 10	16 55	18 04		19 06	20 05	21 02	22 04	23 05
Shrewsbury	74 a		07 13	08 24	09 13	10 29	11 12	12 30	13 12	14 29	15 11	16 30	17 15	18 23		19 25	20 26	21 23	22 24	23 25
Hereford	131 a		08 11		10 07		12 07		14 09		16 03		18 06			20 21				
Newport (South Wales)	131 a		09 05		11 01		12 57		15 05		16 53		18 56			21 15				
Cardiff Central [7]	131 a		09 21		11 17		13 14		15 24		17 09		19 09			21 34				
Wellington (Shropshire)	74 a			08 47		10 48		12 47		14 47		16 48		18 44					22 45	23 40
Telford Central	74 a			08 53		10 54		12 53		14 53		16 53		18 50					22 50	23 48
Wolverhampton [7] 68,74 ⛴	a			09 12		11 13		13 12		15 12		17 11		19 12					23 09	00 17
Smethwick Galton Bridge [5] 74,68 ✈	a			09 23		11 24		13 22		15 23		17 22		19 23						
Birmingham New Street [12] 74,68	a			09 31		11 31		13 31		15 30		17 31		19 30					23 30	
Birmingham International	68 a			09 51		11 50		13 50		15 50		17 50		19 50						

A ◇ from Shrewsbury
B To Llanelli
C From Liverpool Lime Street
D From London Euston
E To Maesteg

Table T075-R

Sundays
15 December to 10 May

Holyhead - Chester - Shrewsbury - Birmingham

		AW	AW	AW	AW	AW	AW	AW	AW	AW	AW	AW
		◇	◇ 🍴	◇ 🍴	■ 🍴	◇ 🍴	◇	◇	■ 🍴	◇	◇	◇
Holyhead	81 d				10 20				16 25			
Bangor (Gwynedd)	81 d				10 59				17 04			
Llandudno	81 d											
Llandudno Junction	81 d				11 22				17 25			
Colwyn Bay	81 d				11 28				17 31			
Rhyl	81 d				11 41				17 44			
Prestatyn	81 d				11 46				17 49			
Flint	81 d				12 00				18 03			
Chester	81 d	08 12	09 24	11 32	12 29	13 35	15 40	17 31	18 25	19 25	21 28	22 05
Wrexham General	a	08 32	09 39	11 48	12 44	13 50	15 56	17 47	18 41	19 40	21 45	22 22
	d		09 39	11 48	12 44	13 50	15 56	17 48	18 41	19 43	21 45	
Ruabon	a		09 45	11 55	12 50	13 57	16 02	17 55	18 48	19 49	21 51	
Chirk	a		09 52	12 01	12 57	14 03	16 09	18 02	18 54	19 55	21 58	
Gobowen	a		09 57	12 07	13 02	14 09	16 14	18 07	19 00	20 01	22 03	
Shrewsbury	74 a		10 17	12 28	13 23	14 28	16 34	18 30	19 19	20 21	22 23	
Hereford	131 a				14 22				20 19			
Newport (South Wales)	131 a				15 12				21 13			
Cardiff Central [7]	131 a				15 26				21 32			
Wellington (Shropshire)	74 a		10 32	12 46		14 44	16 52	18 45		20 36	22 38	
Telford Central	74 a		10 38	12 53		14 50	16 58	18 50		20 44	22 46	
Wolverhampton [7] 68,74 ⛴	a		10 56	13 11		15 07	17 20	19 08		21 12	23 15	
Smethwick Galton Bridge [5] 74,68 ✈	a		11 07	13 23		15 17	17 31	19 19		21 23		
Birmingham New Street [12] 74,68	a		11 16	13 30		15 26	17 40	19 28		21 32		
Birmingham International	68 a		11 32	13 57		15 57	17 57	19 57		21 57		

Table T076-F

Mondays to Fridays
16 December to 15 May

Birmingham - Shrewsbury - Aberystwyth, Barmouth - Pwllheli

Miles	Miles			AW	AW	AW	AW	AW	AW	AW	AW	AW		AW	AW		AW		AW		AW	AW	
							◇		◇ ⌶	◇ ⌶	◇	■ ⌶		◇ ⌶	◇ ⌶		■ ⌶		◇ ⌶			■ ⌶	
—	—	Birmingham International 68 ✈	d									08 08		09 10	10 09		12 09		14 09			16 10	
0	—	**Birmingham New Street** 12 74,68	d							06 25		08 25		09 25	10 25		12 25		14 25			16 25	
4	—	Smethwick Galton Bridge 5 74,68	d							06 31		08 31		09 31	10 31		12 31		14 31			16 31	
12¾	—	**Wolverhampton** 7 68,74	d							06 43		08 44		09 43	10 43		12 43		14 43			16 43	
28¾	—	Telford Central 74	d							07 01		09 00		10 00	11 00		13 01		15 00			17 00	
32¾	—	Wellington (Shropshire) 74	d							07 07		09 07		10 07	11 07		13 08		15 07			17 07	
42¾	—	**Shrewsbury** 74	a							07 23		09 22		10 22	11 21		13 22		15 22			17 20	
—	—		d						06 25	07 27		09 30		10 29	11 27		13 28		15 28			17 28	
62½	—	Welshpool	d						06 48	07 49		09 52		10 51	11 49		13 51		15 52			17 51	
76½	—	Newtown (Powys)	d						07 03	08 04		10 07		11 06	12 04		14 06		16 07			18 06	
82	—	Caersws	d						07 10	08 11		10 14		11 13	12 11		14 13		16 14			18 13	
103¾	0	**Machynlleth** 4	a						07 42	08 43		10 45		11 41	12 42		14 44		16 45			18 42	
—	—		d	04 52	05 07	05 45	06 43	06 47	07 47	08 48	08 52	10 50	10 55	11 42	12 47	12 51	14 49	14 56	16 50	16 55	18 01	18 48	19 04
107¾	4	Dovey Junction 4	d	04 58	05 13	05 54	06 49	06 55	07 55	08 55	08 58	10 56	11 01	11 54	12 55	12 57	14 55	15 02	16 56	17 01		18 56	19 10
116	—	Borth	d	05 08		06 04		07 05	08 05	09 05		11 06		12 04	13 05		15 05		17 06			19 06	
124¼	—	**Aberystwyth**	a	05 24		06 20		07 21	08 21	09 21		11 21		12 20	13 20		15 20		17 21		18 27	19 20	
—	9	Penhelig	d		05x22		06x58				09x07		11x10			13x06		15x11		17x10			19x19
—	10	Aberdovey	d		05 26		07 02				09 11		11 14			13 10		15 15		17 14			19 23
—	13½	Tywyn	a		05 34		07 12				09 21		11 24			13 20		15 25		17 25			19 33
—	—		d		05 34		07 14				09 29		11 30			13 25		15 26		17 29			19 33
—	16	Tonfanau	d		05x38		07x17				09x33		11x33			13x29		15x30		17x32			19x36
—	20	Llwyngwril	d		05x44		07x24				09x39		11x40			13x35		15x36		17x39			19x43
—	22¾	Fairbourne	d		05 53		07 32				09 48		11 49			13 44		15 45		17 47			19 51
—	23¾	Morfa Mawddach	d		05x54		07x34				09x49		11x50			13x45		15x46		17x49			19x53
—	25½	**Barmouth**	a		06 06		07 47				10 01		12 01			13 57		15 58		18 00			20 04
—	—		d				07 47				10 01		12 01			13 57		15 58		18 00			20 04
—	26¾	Llanaber	d				07x50				10x04		12x04			14x00		16x01		18x03			20x07
—	29¼	Talybont	d				07x55				10x09		12x09			14x05		16x06		18x08			20x12
—	30¼	Dyffryn Ardudwy	d				07x58				10x12		12x12			14x08		16x09		18x11			20x15
—	32½	Llanbedr	d				08x02				10x16		12x16			14x12		16x13		18x15			20x19
—	33¼	Pensarn	d				08x04				10x18		12x18			14x14		16x15		18x17			20x21
—	34	Llandanwg	d				08x06				10x20		12x20			14x16		16x17		18x19			20x23
—	35¾	Harlech	a				08 14				10 28		12 28			14 24		16 25		18 27			20 30
—	—		d				08 25				10 28		12 28			14 31		16 28		18 33			20 30
—	38½	Tygwyn	d				08x29				10x31		12x31			14x35		16x31		18x36			20x34
—	39¼	Talsarnau	d				08x31				10x34		12x34			14x37		16x34		18x39			20x36
—	40½	Llandecwyn	d				08x34				10x37		12x37			14x40		16x37		18x42			20x39
—	41¼	Penrhyndeudraeth	d				08 38				10 41		12 41			14 44		16 41		18 46			20 43
—	42½	Minffordd	d				08 42				10 44		12 44			14 48		16 44		18 49			20 47
—	44½	Porthmadog	a				08 50				10 53		12 53			14 56		16 53		18 57			20 55
—	—		d				08 50				10 53		12 53			14 56		16 53		18 57			20 55
—	49½	Criccieth	d				08 57				11 00		13 00			15 03		17 00		19 05			21 03
—	54	Penychain	d				09x03				11x06		13x06			15x09		17x06		19x11			21x08
—	55½	Abererch	d				09x07				11x10		13x10			15x13		17x09		19x15			21x11
—	57½	**Pwllheli**	a				09 13				11 15		13 16			15 20		17 18		19 21			21 18

For connections from London Euston refer to Table T66

For connections from Manchester Piccadilly and Crewe refer to Table T131

Table T076-F

Mondays to Fridays
16 December to 15 May

Birmingham - Shrewsbury - Aberystwyth, Barmouth - Pwllheli

		AW	AW	AW	AW	AW FO	AW FX
		◇ A ⌶	◇	◇	◇	◇	◇
Birmingham International 68 ✈	d	17 11	18 10			20 09	20 09
Birmingham New Street 12 74,68	d	17 26	18 25			20 25	20 25
Smethwick Galton Bridge 5 74,68	d	17 32	18 31			20 31	20 31
Wolverhampton 7 68,74	d	17 44	18 44			20 43	20 43
Telford Central 74	d	18 01	19 01			21 00	21 00
Wellington (Shropshire) 74	d	18 07	19 08			21 06	21 07
Shrewsbury 74	a	18 21	19 23			21 20	21 21
	d	18 31	19 30		20 32	21 50	21 50
Welshpool	d	18 53	19 52		20 54	22 12	22 12
Newtown (Powys)	d	19 08	20 07		21 09	22 27	22 27
Caersws	d	19 15	20 14		21 17	22 34	22 34
Machynlleth 4	a	19 46	20 48		21 44	23 04	23 04
	d	19 47	20 49	21 47	21 50	23 06	23 06
Dovey Junction 4	d	19 55	20 57	21 53	21 58	23 12	23 12
Borth	d	20 05	21 07		22 08	23 22	23 22
Aberystwyth	a	20 20	21 21		22 22	23 36	23 36
Penhelig	d			22x02			
Aberdovey	d			22 06			
Tywyn	a			22 16			
	d			22 16			
Tonfanau	d			22x20			
Llwyngwril	d			22x26			
Fairbourne	d			22 35			
Morfa Mawddach	d			22x36			
Barmouth	a			22 47			
	d			22 47			
Llanaber	d			22x51			
Talybont	d			22x55			
Dyffryn Ardudwy	d			22x57			
Llanbedr	d			23x01			
Pensarn	d			23x03			
Llandanwg	d			23x05			
Harlech	a			23 13			
	d			23 13			
Tygwyn	d			23x17			
Talsarnau	d			23x19			
Llandecwyn	d			23x22			
Penrhyndeudraeth	d			23 26			
Minffordd	d			23 30			
Porthmadog	a			23 38			
	d			23 38			
Criccieth	d			23 46			
Penychain	d			23x51			
Abererch	d			23x54			
Pwllheli	a			00 01			

A ⌶ from Shrewsbury

For connections from London Euston refer to Table T66

For connections from Manchester Piccadilly and Crewe refer to Table T131

Table T076-F

Saturdays
21 December to 16 May

Birmingham - Shrewsbury - Aberystwyth, Barmouth - Pwllheli

		AW	AW	AW	AW	AW	AW	AW		AW	AW		AW	AW		AW		AW			AW	AW		AW	AW
					◇		◇	◇		◇	■		■ ◇ A	■		■		◇				◇		◇ B	◇ C
							⊼	⊼			⊼		⊼	⊼		⊼		⊼				⊼		⊼	
Birmingham International 68 ✈	d										08 08		09 08	10 09		12 08		14 09				16 08		17 08	18 08
Birmingham New Street [12] 74,68	d							06 25			08 25		09 25	10 25		12 25		14 25				16 25		17 25	18 25
Smethwick Galton Bridge [5] 74,68	d							06 31			08 31		09 32	10 31		12 31		14 31				16 31		17 31	18 31
Wolverhampton [7] 68,74	d							06 43			08 44		09 44	10 44		12 44		14 43				16 43		17 43	18 43
Telford Central 74	d							06 59			09 01		10 00	11 00		13 00		15 00				17 00		18 00	19 00
Wellington (Shropshire) 74	d							07 06			09 08		10 07	11 07		13 07		15 07				17 08		18 07	19 08
Shrewsbury 74	a							07 21			09 21		10 21	11 20		13 20		15 21				17 23		18 21	19 22
	d						06 25	07 29			09 29		10 29	11 29		13 29		15 30				17 27		18 27	19 30
Welshpool	d						06 47	07 52			09 52		10 51	11 51		13 51		15 52				17 49		18 49	19 52
Newtown (Powys)	d						07 02	08 07			10 07		11 06	12 06		14 06		16 07				18 04		19 04	20 07
Caersws	d						07 09	08 14			10 14		11 13	12 13		14 13		16 14				18 11		19 11	20 14
Machynlleth [4]	a						07 41	08 45			10 45		11 42	12 44		14 44		16 45				18 42		19 44	20 48
	d	04 52	05 07	05 47	06 43	06 47	07 46	08 49		08 53	10 50	10 55	11 46	12 49	12 52	14 49	14 56	16 50	16 55		18 01	18 48	19 04	19 46	
Dovey Junction [4]	d	04 58	05 13	05 55	06 49	06 55	07 55	08 56		08 59	10 56	11 01	11 55	12 57	12 58	14 55	15 02	16 56	17 01			18 56	19 10	19 55	
Borth	d	05 08		06 05		07 05	08 05	09 06			11 06		12 05	13 07		15 05		17 06				19 06		20 05	
Aberystwyth	a	05 24		06 21		07 21	08 20	09 21			11 21		12 20	13 21		15 20		17 21			18 29	19 21		20 21	
Penhelig	d		05x22		06x58					09x08		11x10			13x07		15x11		17x10				19x19		
Aberdovey	d		05 26		07 02					09 12		11 14			13 11		15 15		17 14				19 23		
Tywyn	a		05 34		07 12					09 21		11 24			13 20		15 25		17 25				19 33		
	d		05 34		07 14					09 29		11 30			13 24		15 25		17 29				19 33		
Tonfanau	d		05x38		07x17					09x33		11x33			13x28		15x29		17x32				19x36		
Llwyngwril	d		05x44		07x24					09x39		11x40			13x34		15x35		17x39				19x43		
Fairbourne	d		05 53		07 32					09 48		11 48			13 43		15 44		17 47				19 51		
Morfa Mawddach	d		05x54		07x34					09x49		11x50			13x44		15x45		17x49				19x53		
Barmouth	a		06 06		07 47					10 01		12 01			13 56		15 57		18 00				20 04		
	d				07 47					10 01		12 01			13 56		15 57		18 00				20 04		
Llanaber	d				07x50					10x04		12x04			13x59		16x00		18x03				20x07		
Talybont	d				07x55					10x09		12x09			14x04		16x05		18x08				20x12		
Dyffryn Ardudwy	d				07x58					10x12		12x12			14x07		16x08		18x11				20x15		
Llanbedr	d				08x02					10x16		12x16			14x11		16x12		18x15				20x19		
Pensarn	d				08x04					10x18		12x18			14x13		16x14		18x17				20x21		
Llandanwg	d				08x06					10x20		12x20			14x15		16x16		18x19				20x23		
Harlech	a				08 14					10 28		12 29			14 23		16 24		18 27				20 30		
	d				08 25					10 28		12 29			14 31		16 29		18 33				20 30		
Tygwyn	d				08x29					10x31		12x32			14x35		16x32		18x36				20x34		
Talsarnau	d				08x31					10x34		12x35			14x37		16x35		18x39				20x36		
Llandecwyn	d				08x34					10x37		12x38			14x40		16x38		18x42				20x39		
Penrhyndeudraeth	d				08 38					10 41		12 42			14 44		16 42		18 46				20 43		
Minffordd	d				08 42					10 44		12 45			14 48		16 45		18 49				20 47		
Porthmadog	a				08 50					10 53		12 54			14 56		16 53		18 57				20 55		
	d				08 50					10 53		12 54			14 56		16 53		18 57				20 55		
Criccieth	d				08 57					11 00		13 01			15 03		17 01		19 05				21 03		
Penychain	d				09x03					11x06		13x07			15x09		17x06		19x10				21x08		
Abererch	d				09x07					11x10		13x11			15x13		17x10		19x14				21x11		
Pwllheli	a				09 13					11 15		13 17			15 20		17 16		19 19				21 18		

A ◇ from Shrewsbury ■ to Shrewsbury
B ⊼ from Shrewsbury
C To Machynlleth Carr. Sdgs

For connections from London Euston refer to Table T66

For connections from Manchester Piccadilly and Crewe refer to Table T131

NRT DECEMBER 19 EDITION

Table T076-F

Saturdays
21 December to 16 May

Birmingham - Shrewsbury - Aberystwyth, Barmouth - Pwllheli

		AW	AW		AW
		◇	◇		◇
Birmingham International 68 ✈	d	18 08			20 08
Birmingham New Street [12] 74,68	d	18 25			20 25
Smethwick Galton Bridge [5] 74,68	d	18 31			20 31
Wolverhampton [7] 68,74	d	18 43			20 43
Telford Central 74	d	19 00			20 59
Wellington (Shropshire) 74	d	19 08			21 07
Shrewsbury 74	a	19 22			21 21
	d	19 30	20 31		21 43
Welshpool	d	19 52	20 54		22 05
Newtown (Powys)	d	20 07	21 09		22 20
Caersws	d	20 14	21 16		22 27
Machynlleth [4]	a	20 48	21 43		22 57
	d	20 53	21 47	21 50	23 03
Dovey Junction [4]	d	21 01	21 53	21 58	23 09
Borth	d	21 11		22 08	23 19
Aberystwyth	a	21 25		22 22	23 35
Penhelig	d		22x02		
Aberdovey	d		22 06		
Tywyn	a		22 16		
	d		22 17		
Tonfanau	d		22x20		
Llwyngwril	d		22x27		
Fairbourne	d		22 35		
Morfa Mawddach	d		22x37		
Barmouth	a		22 48		
	d		22 48		
Llanaber	d		22x51		
Talybont	d		22x55		
Dyffryn Ardudwy	d		22x58		
Llanbedr	d		23x02		
Pensarn	d		23x04		
Llandanwg	d		23x06		
Harlech	a		23 13		
	d		23 14		
Tygwyn	d		23x17		
Talsarnau	d		23x19		
Llandecwyn	d		23x22		
Penrhyndeudraeth	d		23 27		
Minffordd	d		23 30		
Porthmadog	a		23 38		
	d		23 38		
Criccieth	d		23 46		
Penychain	d		23x51		
Abererch	d		23x54		
Pwllheli	a		00 01		

For connections from London Euston refer to Table T66

For connections from Manchester Piccadilly and Crewe refer to Table T131

Table T076-F

Sundays

15 December to 10 May

Birmingham - Shrewsbury - Aberystwyth, Barmouth - Pwllheli

		AW	AW	AW	AW	AW	AW	AW		AW	AW		AW	AW		AW	AW		AW	AW	AW
														■			■				
		◇	◇		◇	◇	◇ Ŧ	◇ Ŧ		◇	◇ Ŧ		◇ Ŧ	Ŧ		◇ Ŧ	Ŧ		◇ Ŧ	◇	◇
Birmingham International 68 ✈	d							09 51			12 07			14 07			16 08			18 08	20 08
Birmingham New Street [12] 74,68	d							10 04			12 23			14 23			16 24			18 23	20 24
Smethwick Galton Bridge [5] 74,68	d							10 10			12 31			14 31			16 31			18 31	20 31
Wolverhampton [7] 68,74 🚋	d							10 22			12 42			14 44			16 44			18 43	20 44
Telford Central 74	d							10 49			12 59			15 02			17 01			19 00	21 01
Wellington (Shropshire) 74	d							10 57			13 06			15 09			17 08			19 07	21 08
Shrewsbury 74	a							11 12			13 20			15 23			17 23			19 21	21 22
	d						10 27	11 28			13 28		14 29	15 28		16 29	17 27		18 28	19 27	21 28
Welshpool	d						10 49	11 50			13 50		14 50	15 51		16 51	17 49		18 50	19 49	21 50
Newtown (Powys)	d						11 04	12 05			14 05		15 06	16 06		17 06	18 04		19 05	20 04	22 05
Caersws	d						11 11	12 12			14 13		15 14	16 13		17 13	18 12		19 12	20 11	22 13
Machynlleth [4]	a						11 43	12 43			14 45		15 45	16 42		17 42	18 43		19 41	20 42	22 40
	d	07 50	08 49	09 47	10 05	10 49	11 43	12 48	12 51	13 50	14 49	14 53	15 46	16 47	16 50	17 43	18 48	18 55	19 42	20 47	22 45
Dovey Junction [4]	d	07 56	08 56	09 55	10 11	10 58	11 56	12 56	13 00	13 57	14 57	14 59	15 55	16 56	16 56	17 55	18 56	19 01	19 56	20 55	22 51
Borth	d	08 06	09 06	10 05		11 08	12 06	13 06		14 07	15 07		16 05	17 06		18 05	19 06		20 06	21 05	23 01
Aberystwyth	a	08 21	09 21	10 19		11 23	12 18	13 21		14 23	15 21		16 20	17 23		18 21	19 20		20 20	21 20	23 15
Penhelig	d				10x20				13x09			15x08			17x05			19x10			
Aberdovey	d				10 24				13 13			15 12			17 09			19 14			
Tywyn	a				10 30				13 20			15 19			17 18			19 21			
	d				10 30				13 24			15 31			17 29			19 24			
Tonfanau	d				10x33				13x28			15x34			17x32			19x28			
Llwyngwril	d				10x40				13x35			15x41			17x39			19x35			
Fairbourne	d				10 49				13 43			15 49			17 47			19 43			
Morfa Mawddach	d				10x51				13x44			15x51			17x49			19x44			
Barmouth	a				10 59				13 56			15 59			17 59			19 53			
	d				10 59				13 56			15 59			17 59			19 53			
Llanaber	d				11x03				13x59			16x03			18x02			19x56			
Talybont	d				11x07				14x04			16x07			18x07			20x01			
Dyffryn Ardudwy	d				11x11				14x07			16x11			18x10			20x04			
Llanbedr	d				11x15				14x11			16x15			18x14			20x08			
Pensarn	d				11x18				14x14			16x18			18x17			20x11			
Llandanwg	d				11x20				14x16			16x20			18x19			20x13			
Harlech	a				11 26				14 23			16 26			18 26			20 20			
	d				11 28				14 31			16 26			18 32			20 23			
Tygwyn	d				11x31				14x35			16x29			18x35			20x27			
Talsarnau	d				11x34				14x38			16x32			18x38			20x30			
Llandecwyn	d				11x37				14x41			16x35			18x41			20x33			
Penrhyndeudraeth	d				11 41				14 45			16 39			18 45			20 37			
Minffordd	d				11 45				14 48			16 43			18 49			20 40			
Porthmadog	a				11 51				14 56			16 49			18 57			20 46			
	d				11 55				14 56			16 49			18 57			20 46			
Criccieth	d				12 02				15 03			16 56			19 04			20 54			
Penychain	d				12x08				15x09			17x02			19x10			21x00			
Abererch	d				12x12				15x13			17x06			19x14			21x03			
Pwllheli	a				12 19				15 20			17 13			19 20			21 11			

For connections from London Euston refer to Table T66

For connections from Manchester Piccadilly and Crewe refer to Table T131

Table T076-R

Mondays to Fridays

16 December to 15 May

Pwllheli - Barmouth, Aberystwyth - Shrewsbury - Birmingham

Miles	Miles			AW MX	AW	AW	AW	AW	AW	AW	AW	AW	AW	AW	AW	AW	AW	AW	AW	AW	AW	AW	AW
							■	■															
				A	◇	Ŧ	◇ B Ŧ	Ŧ	◇	◇ Ŧ	◇ C Ŧ	◇ Ŧ	◇ C Ŧ	◇ Ŧ	◇ Ŧ	◇ C Ŧ	◇ Ŧ	◇ C Ŧ	◇ Ŧ	◇	◇ Ŧ	◇ Ŧ	◇ D Ŧ
—	0	**Pwllheli**	d						06 29		07 24		09 34			11 37		13 38		15 37			
—	1¾	Abererch	d						06x32		07x27		09x37			11x40		13x41		15x40			
—	3¾	Penychain	d						06x36		07x31		09x41			11x44		13x45		15x44			
—	7¾	Criccieth	d						06 43		07 38		09 48			11 51		13 52		15 51			
—	12¾	Porthmadog	a						06 52		07 47		09 57			12 00		14 01		16 00			
—	—		d						06 53		07 47		09 57			12 01		14 02		16 01			
—	15	Minffordd	d						06 57		07 52		10 01			12 05		14 06		16 05			
—	16¼	Penrhyndeudraeth	d						07 01		07 56		10 05			12 09		14 10		16 09			
—	17	Llandecwyn	d						07x03		07x58		10x07			12x11		14x12		16x11			
—	18¼	Talsarnau	d						07x05		08x00		10x09			12x13		14x14		16x13			
—	19	Tygwyn	d						07x08		08x03		10x12			12x16		14x17		16x16			
—	21½	Harlech	a						07 17		08 11		10 22			12 26		14 27		16 26			
—	—		d						07 17		08 21		10 29			12 28		14 28		16 29			
—	23½	Llandanwg	d						07x22		08x25		10x34			12x33		14x33		16x34			
—	24¼	Pensarn	d						07x24		08x28		10x36			12x35		14x35		16x36			
—	30½	Llanbedr	d						07x27		08x30		10x39			12x38		14x38		16x39			
—	27	Dyffryn Ardudwy	d						07x31		08x34		10x43			12x42		14x42		16x43			
—	28¼	Talybont	d						07x34		08x37		10x46			12x45		14x45		16x46			
—	25	Llanaber	d						07x38		08x42		10x50			12x49		14x49		16x50			
—	32	**Barmouth**	a						07 44		08 47		10 56			12 55		14 55		16 56			
—	—		d				06 45		07 49		08 52		10 59			12 55		14 55		16 56			
—	33¾	Morfa Mawddach	d				06x49		07x53		08x56		11x03			12x59		14x59		17x00			
—	34¾	Fairbourne	d				06 53		07 57		09 00		11 07			13 03		15 03		17 04			
—	37¼	Llwyngwril	d				06x59		08x04		09x06		11x14			13x09		15x09		17x10			
—	41½	Tonfanau	d				07x06		08x11		09x13		11x21			13x16		15x16		17x17			
—	44¼	Tywyn	a				07 14		08 17		09 22		11 29			13 25		15 26		17 26			
—	—		d				07 14		08 17		09 27		11 30			13 25		15 26		17 27			
—	47½	Aberdovey	d				07 20		08 23		09 33		11 36			13 31		15 32		17 33			
—	48½	Penhelig	d				07x23		08x25		09x35		11x38			13x33		15x35		17x35			
0	—	**Aberystwyth**	d		05 29	06 30		07 29		08 30		09 30		11 29	12 30		13 30		15 30		17 28	18 32	18 32
8¼	—	Borth	d		05 43	06 44		07 43		08 44		09 44		11 43	12 44		13 44		15 44		17 42	18 46	18 46
16½	53½	Dovey Junction [4]	d	00 04	05 53	06 54	07 36	07 53	08 38	08 58	09 48	09 54	11 50	11 53	12 57	13 46	13 54	15 47	15 54	17 48	17 52	18 56	18 56
20½	57½	**Machynlleth** [4]	a	00 13	06 01	07 02	07 43	08 01	08 46	09 06	09 55	10 02	11 58	12 02	13 05	13 52	14 02	15 55	16 02	17 56	18 00	19 05	19 05
—	—		d		06 02	07 04	08 05			09 06	10 08		12 05		13 06	14 07		16 08			18 05	19 09	
42¼	—	Caersws	d		06 28	07 31	08 32			09 33	10 35		12 32		13 33	14 34		16 35			18 34	19 36	
47¾	—	Newtown (Powys)	d		06 35	07 38	08 39			09 40	10 42		12 39		13 40	14 41		16 42			18 41	19 43	
61¾	—	Welshpool	d		06 50	07 52	08 54			09 55	10 56		12 54		13 54	14 55		16 56			18 56	19 57	
81½	—	**Shrewsbury** 74	a		07 13	08 16	09 18			10 19	11 20		13 20		14 18	15 19		17 20			19 20	20 20	
—	—		d		07 33		09 33				11 34		13 34			15 32		17 33			19 33		
92	—	Wellington (Shropshire) 74	d		07 47		09 47				11 47		13 47			15 45		17 47			19 47		
96	—	Telford Central 74	d		07 53		09 53				11 53		13 54			15 53		17 53			19 53		
112	—	**Wolverhampton** [7] 68,74 🚋	a		08 11		10 10				12 11		14 12			16 10		18 11			20 11		
120¾	—	Smethwick Galton Bridge [5] 68,74	a		08 22		10 21				12 22		14 23			16 22		18 22			20 22		
124¾	—	**Birmingham New Street** [12] 74,68	a		08 31		10 32				12 31		14 31			16 31		18 31			20 31		
—	—	Birmingham International 68 ✈	a		08 50		10 50				12 50		14 50			16 50		18 50			20 50		

A From Aberystwyth

B Ŧ ■ from Machynlleth ◇ to Machynlleth

C Ŧ from Machynlleth

D To Pwllheli

For connections to London Euston refer to Table T66

For connections to Crewe and Manchester Piccadilly refer to Table T131

Table T076-R

Mondays to Fridays

16 December to 15 May

Pwllheli - Barmouth, Aberystwyth - Shrewsbury - Birmingham

		AW	AW	AW	AW	AW	AW	AW
		◇	◇			◇		
Pwllheli	d	17 42				20 26		
Abererch	d	17x45				20x29		
Penychain	d	17x49				20x33		
Criccieth	d	17 56				20 40		
Porthmadog	a	18 05				20 49		
	d	18 06				20 55		
Minffordd	d	18 10				20 59		
Penrhyndeudraeth	d	18 14				21 03		
Llandecwyn	d	18x16				21x05		
Talsarnau	d	18x18				21x07		
Tygwyn	d	18x21				21x10		
Harlech	a	18 30				21 19		
	d	18 30				21 19		
Llandanwg	d	18x36				21x24		
Pensarn	d	18x37				21x26		
Llanbedr	d	18x40				21x29		
Dyffryn Ardudwy	d	18x44				21x33		
Talybont	d	18x47				21x36		
Llanaber	d	18x51				21x41		
Barmouth	a	18 57				21 46		
	d	18 57				21 46		
Morfa Mawddach	d	19x01				21x50		
Fairbourne	d	19 05				21 54		
Llwyngwril	d	19x12				22x01		
Tonfanau	d	19x19				22x08		
Tywyn	a	19 27				22 16		
	d	19 34				22 17		
Aberdovey	d	19 40				22 23		
Penhelig	d	19x43				22x25		
Aberystwyth	d		19 30	20 30	21 30		22 30	23 40
Borth	d		19 44	20 44	21 44		22 44	23 54
Dovey Junction 4	d	19 56	19 59	20 55	21 56	22 38	22 54	00 04
Machynlleth 4	a	20 04	20 07	21 04	22 05	22 45	23 03	00 13
	d	20 11						
Caersws	d	20 38						
Newtown (Powys)	d	20 45						
Welshpool	d	21 00						
Shrewsbury 74	a	21 25						
	d	21 33						
Wellington (Shropshire) 74	d	21 47						
Telford Central 74	d	21 53						
Wolverhampton 7 68,74	a	22 12						
Smethwick Galton Bridge 5 68,74	a	22 23						
Birmingham New Street 12 74,68	a	22 32						
Birmingham International 68 ✈	a							

For connections to London Euston refer to Table T66

For connections to Crewe and Manchester Piccadilly refer to Table T131

NRT DECEMBER 19 EDITION

Table T076-R

Saturdays

21 December to 16 May

Pwllheli - Barmouth, Aberystwyth - Shrewsbury - Birmingham

		AW	AW	AW	AW	AW	AW	AW	AW	AW	AW	AW	AW	AW	AW	AW	AW	AW	AW	AW	AW	AW	AW
					■	■			■	■	■	■	■										
			◇		◇		◇	◇	◇		◇	◇		◇	◇	◇	◇	◇	◇	◇	◇	◇	◇
		A			B				B		B	B			C		C						
				⌶	⌶	⌶		⌶	⌶	⌶	⌶	⌶	⌶	⌶	⌶	⌶	⌶	⌶		⌶	⌶		
Pwllheli	d						06 29		07 24		07 24	09 34			11 37		13 38		15 37			17 42	
Abererch	d						06x32		07x27		07x27	09x37			11x40		13x41		15x40			17x45	
Penychain	d						06x36		07x31		07x31	09x41			11x44		13x45		15x44			17x49	
Criccieth	d						06 43		07 38		07 38	09 48			11 51		13 52		15 51			17 56	
Porthmadog	a						06 52		07 47		07 47	09 57			12 00		14 01		16 00			18 05	
	d						06 53		07 47		07 47	09 58			12 01		14 02		16 01			18 06	
Minffordd	d						06 57		07 52		07 52	10 02			12 05		14 06		16 05			18 10	
Penrhyndeudraeth	d						07 01		07 56		07 56	10 06			12 09		14 10		16 09			18 14	
Llandecwyn	d						07x03		07x58		07x58	10x08			12x11		14x12		16x11			18x16	
Talsarnau	d						07x05		08x00		08x00	10x10			12x13		14x14		16x13			18x18	
Tygwyn	d						07x08		08x03		08x03	10x13			12x16		14x17		16x16			18x21	
Harlech	a						07 17		08 11		08 11	10 23			12 24		14 27		16 26			18 30	
	d						07 17		08 21		08 21	10 28			12 28		14 28		16 29			18 30	
Llandanwg	d						07x22		08x25		08x25	10x33			12x33		14x33		16x34			18x36	
Pensarn	d						07x24		08x28		08x28	10x35			12x35		14x35		16x36			18x37	
Llanbedr	d						07x27		08x30		08x30	10x38			12x38		14x38		16x39			18x40	
Dyffryn Ardudwy	d						07x31		08x34		08x34	10x42			12x42		14x42		16x43			18x44	
Talybont	d						07x34		08x37		08x37	10x45			12x45		14x45		16x46			18x47	
Llanaber	d						07x38		08x42		08x42	10x49			12x49		14x49		16x50			18x51	
Barmouth	a						07 44		08 47		08 47	10 55			12 55		14 55		16 56			18 57	
	d				06 45		07 49		08 52		08 52	10 59			12 55		14 55		16 56			18 57	
Morfa Mawddach	d				06x49		07x53		08x56		08x56	11x03			12x59		14x59		17x00			19x01	
Fairbourne	d				06 53		07 57		09 00		09 00	11 07			13 03		15 03		17 04			19 05	
Llwyngwril	d				06x59		08x04		09x06		09x06	11x14			13x10		15x09		17x10			19x12	
Tonfanau	d				07x06		08x11		09x13		09x13	11x21			13x17		15x16		17x17			19x19	
Tywyn	a				07 14		08 17		09 22		09 22	11 29			13 25		15 26		17 26			19 27	
	d				07 14		08 17		09 27		09 27	11 30			13 25		15 26		17 27			19 35	
Aberdovey	d				07 20		08 23		09 33		09 33	11 36			13 31		15 32		17 33			19 41	
Penhelig	d				07x23		08x25		09x35		09x35	11x39			13x33		15x35		17x35			19x43	
Aberystwyth	d		05 30	06 30		07 30		08 30		09 30			11 30	12 30		13 30		15 30		17 28	18 32		19 30
Borth	d		05 44	06 44		07 44		08 44		09 44			11 44	12 44		13 44		15 44		17 42	18 46		19 44
Dovey Junction 4	d	00 04	05 54	06 54	07 36	07 54	08 38	08 59	09 48	09 54	09 48	11 52	11 55	12 58	13 46	13 54	15 47	15 54	17 48	17 52	18 56	19 56	19 59
Machynlleth 4	a	00 13	06 02	07 02	07 43	08 05	08 48	09 07	09 54	10 02	09 54	11 58	12 03	13 06	13 53	14 02	15 53	16 02	17 56	18 00	19 04	20 04	20 07
	d		06 03	07 03	08 08			09 08	10 08		12 07		12 07	13 06	14 07		16 08			18 05	19 05	20 11	
Caersws	d		06 30	07 30	08 35			09 35	10 35		12 34		12 34	13 33	14 34		16 35			18 32	19 32	20 38	
Newtown (Powys)	d		06 37	07 37	08 42			09 42	10 42		12 41		12 41	13 40	14 41		16 42			18 39	19 39	20 45	
Welshpool	d		06 51	07 52	08 56			09 56	10 56		12 55		12 55	13 55	14 55		16 56			18 55	19 54	21 02	
Shrewsbury 74	a		07 14	08 18	09 20			10 19	11 19		13 19		13 19	14 18	15 18		17 19			19 19	20 19	21 25	
	d		07 32		09 32				11 33		13 35		13 35		15 32		17 30			19 32		21 34	
Wellington (Shropshire) 74	d		07 46		09 46				11 47		13 49		13 49		15 46		17 45			19 46		21 47	
Telford Central 74	d		07 53		09 52				11 53		13 55		13 55		15 53		17 53			19 53		21 53	
Wolverhampton 7 68,74	a		08 11		10 09				12 11		14 12		14 12		16 11		18 11			20 11		22 12	
Smethwick Galton Bridge 5 68,74	a		08 22		10 21				12 22		14 23		14 23		16 23		18 22			20 23		22 23	
Birmingham New Street 12 74,68	a		08 31		10 31				12 31		14 30		14 30		16 31		18 31			20 31		22 32	
Birmingham International 68 ✈	a		08 50		10 50				12 50		14 50		14 50		16 49		18 49			20 49			

A From Aberystwyth

B ⌶ ■ from Machynlleth ◇ to Machynlleth

C ⌶ from Machynlleth

For connections to London Euston refer to Table T66

For connections to Crewe and Manchester Piccadilly refer to Table T131

Table T076-R

Saturdays
21 December to 16 May

Pwllheli - Barmouth, Aberystwyth - Shrewsbury - Birmingham

		AW	AW	AW ◇	AW	AW
Pwllheli	d			20 26		
Abererch	d			20x29		
Penychain	d			20x33		
Criccieth	d			20 40		
Porthmadog	a			20 49		
	d			20 56		
Minffordd	d			21 01		
Penrhyndeudraeth	d			21 04		
Llandecwyn	d			21x06		
Talsarnau	d			21x09		
Tygwyn	d			21x11		
Harlech	a			21 20		
	d			21 20		
Llandanwg	d			21x24		
Pensarn	d			21x27		
Llanbedr	d			21x29		
Dyffryn Ardudwy	d			21x33		
Talybont	d			21x36		
Llanaber	d			21x41		
Barmouth	a			21 47		
	d			21 47		
Morfa Mawddach	d			21x51		
Fairbourne	d			21 55		
Llwyngwril	d			22x02		
Tonfanau	d			22x09		
Tywyn	a			22 17		
	d			22 17		
Aberdovey	d			22 23		
Penhelig	d			22x25		
Aberystwyth	d	20 36	21 33		22 30	23 38
Borth	d	20 50	21 47		22 44	23 52
Dovey Junction [4]	d	21 01	21 58	22 38	22 54	00 02
Machynlleth [4]	a	21 09	22 06	22 45	23 01	00 11
	d					
Caersws	d					
Newtown (Powys)	d					
Welshpool	d					
Shrewsbury 74	a					
	d					
Wellington (Shropshire) 74	d					
Telford Central 74	d					
Wolverhampton [7] 68,74 🚊	a					
Smethwick Galton Bridge [5] 68,74	a					
Birmingham New Street [12] 74,68	a					
Birmingham International 68 ✈	a					

For connections to London Euston refer to Table T66

For connections to Crewe and Manchester Piccadilly refer to Table T131

Table T076-R

Sundays
15 December to 10 May

Pwllheli - Barmouth, Aberystwyth - Shrewsbury - Birmingham

		AW A	AW ◇	AW ■ 🛒	AW ◇	AW ◇	AW ■ ◇ B 🛒	AW ■ 🛒	AW ◇ 🛒	AW ◇	AW ■ ◇ B 🛒	AW ■ 🛒	AW ◇ 🛒	AW ◇	AW ■ ◇ B 🛒	AW ■ 🛒	AW ◇ 🛒	AW ◇	AW ◇ C 🛒	AW ◇ 🛒	AW ◇	AW ◇	AW ◇	AW ◇	AW ◇	AW ◇
Pwllheli	d					09 34	09⌇34			11 28	11⌇28			13 40	13⌇40			15 33	15⌇33			17 36				
Abererch	d					09x37	09x37			11x31	11x31			13x43	13x43			15x36	15x36			17x39				
Penychain	d					09x41	09x41			11x35	11x35			13x47	13x47			15x40	15x40			17x43				
Criccieth	d					09 48	09⌇48			11 42	11⌇42			13 54	13⌇54			15 47	15⌇47			17 50				
Porthmadog	a					09 57	09⌇57			11 52	11⌇52			14 03	14⌇03			15 56	15⌇56			18 00				
	d					09 58	09⌇58			11 57	11⌇57			14 06	14⌇06			15 57	15⌇57			18 00				
Minffordd	d					10 02	10⌇02			12 01	12⌇01			14 10	14⌇10			16 01	16⌇01			18 05				
Penrhyndeudraeth	d					10 06	10⌇06			12 05	12⌇05			14 14	14⌇14			16 05	16⌇05			18 09				
Llandecwyn	d					10x08	10x08			12x07	12x07			14x16	14x16			16x07	16x07			18x11				
Talsarnau	d					10x10	10x10			12x09	12x09			14x18	14x18			16x09	16x09			18x13				
Tygwyn	d					10x13	10x13			12x12	12x12			14x21	14x21			16x12	16x12			18x16				
Harlech	a					10 23	10⌇23			12 19	12⌇19			14 28	14⌇28			16 22	16⌇22			18 23				
	d					10 28	10⌇28			12 21	12⌇21			14 34	14⌇34			16 29	16⌇29			18 27				
Llandanwg	d					10x33	10x33			12x25	12x25			14x38	14x38			16x34	16x34			18x31				
Pensarn	d					10x35	10x35			12x28	12x28			14x41	14x41			16x36	16x36			18x33				
Llanbedr	d					10x38	10x38			12x30	12x30			14x43	14x43			16x39	16x39			18x36				
Dyffryn Ardudwy	d					10x42	10x42			12x34	12x34			14x47	14x47			16x43	16x43			18x40				
Talybont	d					10x45	10x45			12x37	12x37			14x50	14x50			16x46	16x46			18x43				
Llanaber	d					10x49	10x49			12x42	12x42			14x55	14x55			16x50	16x50			18x48				
Barmouth	a					10 55	10⌇55			12 48	12⌇48			15 01	15⌇01			16 56	16⌇56			18 54				
	d					11 01	11⌇01			12 50	12⌇50			15 01	15⌇01			16 56	16⌇56			18 54				
Morfa Mawddach	d					11x05	11x05			12x54	12x54			15x05	15x05			17x00	17x00			18x59				
Fairbourne	d					11 09	11⌇09			12 58	12⌇58			15 09	15⌇09			17 04	17⌇04			19 03				
Llwyngwril	d					11x16	11x16			13x05	13x05			15x15	15x15			17x10	17x10			19x09				
Tonfanau	d					11x23	11x23			13x12	13x12			15x22	15x22			17x17	17x17			19x17				
Tywyn	a					11 30	11⌇30			13 19	13⌇19			15 28	15⌇28			17 26	17⌇26			19 23				
	d					11 30	11⌇30			13 20	13⌇20			15 28	15⌇28			17 27	17⌇27			19 24				
Aberdovey	d					11 36	11⌇36			13 26	13⌇26			15 36	15⌇36			17 33	17⌇33			19 30				
Penhelig	d					11x39	11x39			13x29	13x29			15x38	15x38			17x35	17x35			19x33				
Aberystwyth	d		08 30	09 30	10 30		⌇	11 30	12 29		⌇	13 30	14 30		⌇	15 28	16 30		⌇	17 28	18 30		19 30	20 30	21 30	23 20
Borth	d		08 44	09 43	10 44		⌇	11 43	12 43		⌇	13 43	14 44		⌇	15 43	16 44		⌇	17 43	18 43		19 44	20 44	21 44	23 34
Dovey Junction [4]	d	00⌇02	08 58	09 53	10 56	11 51	11⌇51	11 54	12 57	13 41	13⌇41	13 57	14 59	15 51	15⌇51	15 54	16 56	17 49	17⌇49	17 53	19 02	19 48	19 54	20 55	21 55	23 44
Machynlleth [4]	a	00⌇11	09 06	10 01	11 04	11 58	11⌇58	12 02	13 05	13 49	13⌇49	14 04	15 07	15 59	15⌇59	16 01	17 03	17 57	17⌇57	18 01	19 10	19 55	20 02	21 04	22 04	23 53
	d		09 07	10 06	11 05		12⌇06	12 06	13 06		14⌇07	14 07	15 08		16⌇05	16 05	17 03		18⌇05	18 05			20 05			
Caersws	d		09 34	10 33	11 32		12⌇33	12 33	13 33		14⌇34	14 34	15 35		16⌇34	16 34	17 34		18⌇32	18 32			20 32			
Newtown (Powys)	d		09 41	10 40	11 39		12⌇40	12 40	13 40		14⌇41	14 41	15 42		16⌇41	16 41	17 41		18⌇39	18 39			20 39			
Welshpool	d		09 56	10 54	11 54		12⌇54	12 54	13 54		14⌇56	14 56	15 56		16⌇55	16 55	17 55		18⌇54	18 54			20 53			
Shrewsbury 74	a		10 21	11 18	12 20		13⌇18	13 18	14 19		15⌇19	15 19	16 20		17⌇19	17 19	18 19		19⌇18	19 18			21 18			
	d			11 36			13⌇31	13 31			15⌇32	15 32			17⌇33	17 33			19⌇30	19 30			21 33			
Wellington (Shropshire) 74	d			11 49			13⌇44	13 44			15⌇45	15 45			17⌇47	17 47			19⌇45	19 45			21 47			
Telford Central 74	d			11 55			13⌇50	13 50			15⌇51	15 51			17⌇53	17 53			19⌇51	19 51			21 53			
Wolverhampton [7] 68,74 🚊	a			12 12			14⌇07	14 07			16⌇07	16 07			18⌇09	18 09			20⌇07	20 07			22 11			
Smethwick Galton Bridge [5] 68,74	a			12 25			14⌇17	14 17			16⌇18	16 18			18⌇20	18 20			20⌇18	20 18			22 22			
Birmingham New Street [12] 74,68	a			12 35			14⌇26	14 26			16⌇26	16 26			18⌇31	18 31			20⌇29	20 29			22 31			
Birmingham International 68 ✈	a			13 02			15⌇00	15 00			17⌇00	17 00			18⌇56	18 56			20⌇58	20 58			23 01			

A not 15 December. From Aberystwyth

B until 29 March. 🛒 ■ from Machynlleth ◇ to Machynlleth

C until 29 March. 🛒 from Machynlleth

For connections to London Euston refer to Table T66

For connections to Crewe and Manchester Piccadilly refer to Table T131

Table T078-F

Mondays to Saturdays

16 December to 16 May

Sheffield, Chinley, Marple and Romiley Manchester and Manchester Airport

Miles	Miles	Miles			NT SO ◇ A	NT MSX ◇ A	NT MX ◇ A	TP SO ◇1 B	TP MSX ◇1 B	TP MO ◇1	TP SO ◇1 A	TP MSX ◇1 A	TP ◇1	NT SO C	NT SX C	NT SO	NT SX	NT SX C	NT SO C	NT SX	TP ◇1 D	NT SO	NT SX
0	—	—	**Sheffield 7**	d				03 24	03 24	03 45			05 09								06 09		
4¾	—	—	Dore & Totley	d									05 15								06 15		
9¾	—	—	Grindleford	d																			
11¼	—	—	Hathersage	d																			
13	—	—	Bamford	d																			
14¾	—	—	Hope (Derbyshire)	d																			
20	—	—	Edale	d			00 01																
25½	—	0	**Chinley**	d			00 09																
—	—	8½	Hazel Grove 86	a																			
—	—	—	Stockport 86	a			00 26														06 53		
29¼	—	—	New Mills Central	d												06 00	06 06					06 30	06 32
30¾	—	—	Strines	d												06 03	06 09					06 33	06 35
33	—	—	**Marple**	d												06 06	06 12					06 36	06 38
—	0	—	**Rose Hill Marple**	d																06 20			
34¾	2	—	**Romiley**	d												06 10	06 16			06 26		06 40	06 42
—	3¼	—	Woodley	d																06 29			
—	4¾	—	Hyde Central	d																06 32			
—	6	—	Hyde North	d																06 35			
—	7¾	—	Guide Bridge	d										06 13	06 14			06 36	06 39	06 40			
—	9	—	Fairfield	d																06 43			
—	10	—	Gorton	d										06 16	06 17				06 42	06 46			
35½	—	—	Bredbury	d												06 14	06 20					06 43	06 45
36½	—	—	Brinnington	d												06 16	06 23					06 46	06 48
38½	—	—	Reddish North	d	00 02	00 02										06 20	06 27					06 50	06 52
39¼	—	—	Ryder Brow	d	00 03	00 03										06 22	06 29					06 52	06 54
39½	—	—	Belle Vue	d	00 05	00 05										06 24	06 30					06 53	06 55
40½	11	—	Ashburys	d	00 08	00 08								06 19	06 20	06 27	06 35	06 41	06 45	06 49		06 57	06 58
41½	12	—	Ardwick	d							←	←											
42	12½	8¾	**Manchester Piccadilly 10**	a	00 18	00 20	00 36	04 52	04 52	04 37	04 52	04 52	06 03	06 25	06 26	06 33	06 40	06 47	06 52	06 58	07 02	07 02	07 04
—	—	—	**Manchester Airport 85**	a				→	→	05 16	05 13	05 16	06 27								07 27		

		NT SX	NT SX C	NT SO C	NT SX	NT SO	EM SX ◇ E	EM SO ◇ E	NT	NT SX C	NT SO C	NT SX	TP ◇1 F	NT SX G	NT SO	NT	NT SX	NT SO C	NT SX	NT SX G	NT SX ◇ H	NT SO ◇	NT SX ◇ A
Sheffield 7	d						06 18	06 20					07 07								07 10	07 14	
Dore & Totley	d						06 25	06 27					07 14								07 20	07 21	←
Grindleford	d						06 33	06 35													07 28	07 28	07 28
Hathersage	d						06 38	06 39													→	07 32	07 32
Bamford	d						06 42	06 43														07 36	07 36
Hope (Derbyshire)	d						06 46	06 47														07 39	07 40
Edale	d						06 53	06 54														07 47	07 47
Chinley	d				06 48	06 48	07 01	07 02														07 55	07 56
Hazel Grove 86	a																						
Stockport 86	a						07 25	07 26					07 52										
New Mills Central	d				06 55	06 55						07 26			07 35		07 44		07 50			08 03	08 04
Strines	d				06 58	06 58											07 47						
Marple	d				07 02	07 02						07 31			07 40		07 50		07 57			08 08	08 09
Rose Hill Marple	d	06 44							07 13							07 45							
Romiley	d	06 49			07 09	07 09			07 19			07 35			07 44	07 50	07 54		08 01			08 12	08 13
Woodley	d	06 52							07 22							07 53							
Hyde Central	d	06 56							07 25							07 57							
Hyde North	d	06 58							07 28							07 59							
Guide Bridge	d	07 03	07 07	07 12					07 32	07 39	07 42			07 53		08 04		08 12		08 13			
Fairfield	d	07 06							07 35														
Gorton	d	07 08		07 15					07 38					07 56		08 08				08 17			
Bredbury	d				07 12	07 12						07 38			07 47		07 57		08 04			08 15	
Brinnington	d				07 14	07 14						07 41			07 50		08 00		08 07			08 17	
Reddish North	d				07 18	07 18						07 45			07 54		08 04		08 11			08 21	
Ryder Brow	d											07 47			07 56				08 13				
Belle Vue	d																		08 14				
Ashburys	d		07 13	07 18	07 24	07 24			07 41	07 45	07 47	07 52		07 59	08 00			08 17	08 18	08 20			08 24
Ardwick	d		07 15									07 54			08 03								
Manchester Piccadilly 10	a	07 17	07 19	07 24	07 31	07 34	07 38	07 39	07 46	07 51	07 53	07 58	08 02	08 06	08 07	08 15	08 13	08 23	08 23	08 26		08 34	08 34
Manchester Airport 85	a												08 26										

A From Sheffield
B To Manchester Airport
C From Hadfield
D From Doncaster
E From Nottingham to Liverpool Lime Street
F From Cleethorpes
G From Manchester Piccadilly
H To Manchester Piccadilly

Table T078-F

Mondays to Saturdays

16 December to 16 May

Sheffield, Chinley, Marple and Romiley Manchester and Manchester Airport

		EM SX ◇ A	EM SO ◇ A	NT SO	NT SX B	NT SX	NT SO C	TP ◇1 D	NT SX	NT SX B	NT SO	NT SO	NT SX	NT SX	NT SO C	NT SX B	NT SO ◇	NT SO	NT SX	NT SX ◇	EM ◇ A	NT C
Sheffield 7	d	07 32	07 32					08 08									08 13			08 33	08 42	
Dore & Totley	d	07 39	07 39					08 14									08 20					
Grindleford	d																08 27					
Hathersage	d																08 31					
Bamford	d																08 35					
Hope (Derbyshire)	d																08 38					
Edale	d																08 46			08 57		
Chinley	d	08 03	08 04														08 54			09 05		
Hazel Grove 86	a	08 16	08 16																			
Stockport 86	a	08 25	08 25					08 52													09 25	
New Mills Central	d								08 27		08 34						09 02			09 12		
Strines	d								08 30		08 37											
Marple	d								08 33		08 41			08 54			09 07			09 18		
Rose Hill Marple	d			08 14		08 20						08 45	08 45					09 13	09 13			
Romiley	d			08 20		08 26			08 37		08 45	08 50	08 50	08 58			09 11	09 18	09 18	09 21		
Woodley	d			08 23		08 29						08 53	08 53					09 22	09 22			
Hyde Central	d			08 27		08 32						08 57	08 57					09 25	09 25			
Hyde North	d					08 35						08 59	08 59					09 28	09 28			
Guide Bridge	d			08 33	08 34	08 39	08 42			08 50		09 04	09 04		09 12	09 12		09 32	09 32			09 41
Fairfield	d			08 36		08 42												09 35	09 35			
Gorton	d			08 39		08 45				08 54		09 08	09 08					09 38	09 38			
Bredbury	d								08 40		08 48			09 01			09 14			09 24		
Brinnington	d								08 43		08 51			09 03			09 16			09 27		
Reddish North	d								08 47		08 55			09 07			09 20			09 30		
Ryder Brow	d								08 49		08 57			09 09								
Belle Vue	d								08 50		08 58											
Ashburys	d			08 42	08 40	08 49	08 47		08 55	08 59	09 02			09 13	09 17	09 18		09 41	09 41			09 49
Ardwick	d																					
Manchester Piccadilly 10	a	08 37	08 37	08 47	08 46	08 54	08 53	09 02	09 02	09 07	09 07	09 15	09 17	09 19	09 24	09 24	09 34	09 46	09 48	09 41	09 37	09 54
Manchester Airport 85	a							09 25														

		TP ◇1 D	NT	NT	NT C	NT SO ◇	NT SX ◇	EM MSX ◇ E	EM MSO ◇ E	NT SO	NT SX	NT C	TP ◇1 D	NT	NT	NT C	NT ◇	EM ◇ E	NT	NT C	TP ◇1 D	NT	NT
Sheffield 7	d	09 11				09 14	09 14	09 42	09 42				10 11				10 14	10 42			11 11		
Dore & Totley	d					09 21	09 21										10 21						
Grindleford	d					09 29	09 29										10 29						
Hathersage	d					09 32	09 32										10 32						
Bamford	d					09 36	09 36										10 36						
Hope (Derbyshire)	d					09 40	09 40										10 40						
Edale	d					09 47	09 47										10 47						
Chinley	d					09 55	09 55										10 55						
Hazel Grove 86	a																						
Stockport 86	a	09 53						10 25	10 26				10 52					11 25			11 52		
New Mills Central	d		09 34			10 03	10 03							10 34			11 03					11 34	
Strines	d		09 37											10 37								11 37	
Marple	d		09 41			10 08	10 08							10 41			11 08					11 41	
Rose Hill Marple	d			09 45						10 14	10 20				10 45				11 14				11 45
Romiley	d		09 45	09 50		10 12	10 12			10 19	10 25			10 45	10 50		11 12		11 19			11 45	11 50
Woodley	d			09 53						10 22	10 28				10 53				11 22				11 53
Hyde Central	d			09 57						10 26	10 31				10 57				11 26				11 57
Hyde North	d			09 59											10 59								11 59
Guide Bridge	d			10 04	10 12					10 32	10 37	10 42			11 04	11 12			11 32	11 42			12 04
Fairfield	d									10 35	10 40								11 35				
Gorton	d			10 08						10 38	10 43				11 08				11 38				12 08
Bredbury	d		09 48			10 15	10 15							10 48			11 15					11 48	
Brinnington	d		09 51			10 17	10 17							10 51			11 17					11 51	
Reddish North	d		09 55			10 21	10 21							10 55			11 21					11 55	
Ryder Brow	d		09 57											10 57								11 57	
Belle Vue	d		09 58											10 58								11 58	
Ashburys	d		10 02		10 17					10 41		10 48		11 02		11 17			11 41	11 47		12 02	
Ardwick	d																						
Manchester Piccadilly 10	a	10 02	10 07	10 15	10 23	10 32	10 34	10 37	10 37	10 46	10 53	10 55	11 02	11 07	11 15	11 23	11 32	11 37	11 46	11 53	12 02	12 07	12 15
Manchester Airport 85	a	10 25											11 25								12 25		

A From Nottingham to Liverpool Lime Street
B From Manchester Piccadilly
C From Hadfield
D From Cleethorpes
E From Norwich to Liverpool Lime Street

Table T078-F

Mondays to Saturdays
16 December to 16 May

Sheffield, Chinley, Marple and Romiley Manchester and Manchester Airport

Station		NT A	NT SO ◇	NT SX ◇	EM ◇ B	NT	NT A	TP ◇1 C	NT	NT	NT A	NT SO ◇	NT SX ◇	EM ◇ B	NT	NT A	TP ◇1 C	NT	NT	NT SO A	NT SX A	NT SX ◇	NT SO ◇
Sheffield 7	d		11 14	11 14	11 42			12 11				12 14	12 14	12 42			13 11					13 14	13 14
Dore & Totley	d		11 21	11 21								12 21	12 21										13 21
Grindleford	d		11 28	11 29								12 28	12 29									13 26	13 28
Hathersage	d		11 32	11 32								12 32	12 32										13 32
Bamford	d		11 36	11 36								12 36	12 36									13 32	13 36
Hope (Derbyshire)	d		11 39	11 39								12 39	12 39									13 35	13 39
Edale	d		11 47	11 47								12 47	12 47										13 47
Chinley	d		11 55	11 55								12 55	12 55									13 48	13 55
Hazel Grove 86	a																						
Stockport 86	a				12 25			12 52						13 25			13 52						
New Mills Central	d		12 03	12 03					12 34			13 03	13 03					13 34				14 00	14 03
Strines	d								12 37									13 37					
Marple	d		12 08	12 08					12 41			13 08	13 08					13 41				14 05	14 08
Rose Hill Marple	d					12 14				12 45					13 14				13 45				
Romiley	d		12 12	12 12		12 19			12 45	12 50		13 12	13 12		13 19			13 45	13 50			14 10	14 12
Woodley	d					12 22				12 53					13 22				13 53				
Hyde Central	d					12 26				12 57					13 26				13 57				
Hyde North	d									12 59									13 59				
Guide Bridge	d	12 12				12 32	12 42			13 04	13 12				13 32	13 42			14 04	14 12	14 12		
Fairfield	d					12 35									13 35								
Gorton	d					12 38				13 08					13 38				14 08				
Bredbury	d		12 15	12 15					12 48			13 15	13 15					13 48				14 14	14 15
Brinnington	d		12 18	12 17					12 51			13 17	13 17					13 51				14 16	14 17
Reddish North	d		12 21	12 21					12 55			13 21	13 21					13 55				14 20	14 21
Ryder Brow	d								12 57									13 57					
Belle Vue	d								12 58									13 58					
Ashburys	d	12 17				12 41	12 47		13 02		13 17				13 41	13 47		14 02		14 17	14 18		
Ardwick	d																						
Manchester Piccadilly 10	a	12 23	12 32	12 32	12 37	12 46	12 53	13 02	13 07	13 15	13 23	13 32	13 32	13 37	13 46	13 53	14 02	14 07	14 15	14 23	14 25	14 31	14 32
Manchester Airport 85	a							13 25									14 25						

Station		EM ◇ B	NT	NT SO A	NT SX A	TP ◇1 C	NT SX	NT SO	NT	NT SO A	NT SX A	NT ◇	EM ◇ B	NT	NT A	TP ◇1 C	NT	NT SO	NT SO A	NT SX A	NT SX	NT SO ◇	NT SX
Sheffield 7	d	13 42				14 11						14 14	14 42			15 11						15 14	
Dore & Totley	d											14 21										15 21	
Grindleford	d											14 29										15 28	
Hathersage	d											14 32										15 32	
Bamford	d											14 36										15 36	
Hope (Derbyshire)	d											14 40										15 39	
Edale	d											14 47										15 47	
Chinley	d											14 57										15 55	
Hazel Grove 86	a																						
Stockport 86	a	14 25				14 52							15 25			15 52							
New Mills Central	d						14 32	14 34				15 04					15 34					16 02	16 05
Strines	d						14 35	14 37									15 37						16 08
Marple	d						14 39	14 41				15 10					15 41					16 07	16 12
Rose Hill Marple	d		14 14						14 45					15 14				15 45			15 56		
Romiley	d		14 19				14 43	14 45	14 51			15 13		15 19			15 45	15 50			16 01	16 11	16 16
Woodley	d		14 22						14 54					15 22				15 54			16 05		
Hyde Central	d		14 26						14 58					15 26				15 57			16 08		
Hyde North	d								15 00									16 00			16 11		
Guide Bridge	d		14 32	14 42	14 44				15 05	15 12	15 14			15 32	15 42			16 04	16 11	16 11	16 16		
Fairfield	d		14 35											15 35									
Gorton	d		14 38						15 09					15 38				16 08			16 20		
Bredbury	d						14 46	14 48				15 16					15 48					16 14	16 19
Brinnington	d						14 49	14 51				15 19					15 51					16 17	16 22
Reddish North	d						14 53	14 55				15 23					15 55					16 20	16 26
Ryder Brow	d						14 55	14 57									15 57						16 28
Belle Vue	d						14 56	14 58									15 58						16 29
Ashburys	d		14 41	14 47	14 50		15 01	15 02		15 17	15 19			15 41	15 47		16 02		16 17	16 17			
Ardwick	d																						
Manchester Piccadilly 10	a	14 37	14 46	14 53	14 56	15 02	15 07	15 07	15 16	15 23	15 26	15 34	15 37	15 46	15 53	16 02	16 07	16 15	16 23	16 24	16 27	16 31	16 37
Manchester Airport 85	a					15 25										16 25							

A From Hadfield
B From Norwich to Liverpool Lime Street
C From Cleethorpes

Table T078-F

Mondays to Saturdays
16 December to 16 May

Sheffield, Chinley, Marple and Romiley Manchester and Manchester Airport

Station		EM ◇ A	NT	NT B	NT SO	NT SX ◇	TP ◇1 C	NT SX	NT SO	NT SX B	NT SO B	NT SO ◇	NT SX ◇	EM ◇ A	NT SO	NT SX	NT SO B	NT SX D	TP ◇1 C	NT SX D	NT SX	NT SO	NT
Sheffield 7	d	15 42				15 45	16 11					16 14	16 14	16 42					17 11				
Dore & Totley	d					15 53						16 21	16 21										
Grindleford	d											16 29	16 28										
Hathersage	d					16 03						16 32	16 32										
Bamford	d											16 36	16 35										
Hope (Derbyshire)	d					16 08						16 40	16 39										
Edale	d											16 47	16 46										
Chinley	d					16 21						16 55	16 55										
Hazel Grove 86	a																						
Stockport 86	a	16 25					16 52							17 25					17 52				
New Mills Central	d				16 27	16 28						17 03	17 03								17 37	17 37	
Strines	d				16 30																17 40	17 40	
Marple	d				16 33	16 33						17 08	17 08								17 43	17 43	
Rose Hill Marple	d		16 14					16 45	16 45						17 14	17 20							17 45
Romiley	d		16 19		16 37	16 37		16 50	16 50			17 11	17 11		17 19	17 25					17 47	17 47	17 50
Woodley	d		16 22					16 53	16 53						17 22	17 28							17 55
Hyde Central	d		16 26					16 57	16 57						17 26	17 32							17 58
Hyde North	d							16 59	16 59														18 01
Guide Bridge	d		16 32	16 42				17 04	17 04	17 11	17 11				17 32	17 38	17 41	17 41		17 51			18 05
Fairfield	d		16 35												17 35	17 41							
Gorton	d		16 38					17 08	17 08						17 38	17 43							18 09
Bredbury	d				16 40	16 40						17 14	17 14								17 50	17 50	
Brinnington	d				16 43	16 43						17 17	17 17								17 53	17 53	
Reddish North	d				16 47	16 47						17 20	17 21								17 57	17 57	
Ryder Brow	d				16 49	16 49															18 00	18 00	
Belle Vue	d																				18 03	18 03	
Ashburys	d		16 42	16 47	16 55	16 55				17 16	17 16				17 41	17 46	17 46	17 51		17 57	18 07	18 08	
Ardwick	d																						
Manchester Piccadilly 10	a	16 37	16 48	16 53	17 02	17 02	17 02	17 15	17 16	17 22	17 23	17 31	17 34	17 37	17 46	17 53	17 53	17 58	18 02	18 04	18 12	18 13	18 16
Manchester Airport 85	a						17 25												18 25				

Station		NT SO B	NT SX D	NT ◇	EM SO ◇ A	EM SX ◇ A	NT SO	NT SX	NT SX D	NT SO B	NT SX D	TP ◇1 C	NT SX	NT SO	NT	NT D	NT SO ◇	NT SX ◇	EM SO ◇ A	EM SX ◇ A	NT	NT B
Sheffield 7	d			17 14	17 38	17 39						18 11					18 14	18 14	18 37	18 42		
Dore & Totley	d			17 21													18 21	18 21				
Grindleford	d			17 29													18 29	18 29				
Hathersage	d			17 32													18 32	18 32				
Bamford	d			17 36													18 36	18 36				
Hope (Derbyshire)	d			17 40													18 40	18 40				
Edale	d			17 47													18 47	18 47				
Chinley	d			17 55													18 55	18 55				
Hazel Grove 86	a																					
Stockport 86	a				18 25	18 25						18 52							19 25	19 25		
New Mills Central	d			18 03									18 36	18 36			19 03	19 03				
Strines	d												18 39	18 39								
Marple	d			18 08									18 42	18 42			19 08	19 08				
Rose Hill Marple	d						18 14	18 11							18 45						19 14	
Romiley	d			18 11			18 19	18 22					18 46	18 46	18 50		19 11	19 11			19 19	
Woodley	d						18 22								18 53						19 22	
Hyde Central	d						18 26								18 57						19 26	
Hyde North	d														18 59							
Guide Bridge	d	18 11	18 17				18 32		18 35	18 41	18 50				19 04	19 12					19 32	19 42
Fairfield	d						18 35														19 35	
Gorton	d						18 38								19 08						19 38	
Bredbury	d			18 14				18 25					18 50	18 50			19 14	19 14				
Brinnington	d			18 17				18 28					18 53	18 53			19 17	19 17				
Reddish North	d			18 20				18 32					18 57	18 57			19 20	19 20				
Ryder Brow	d							18 34						18 59								
Belle Vue	d							18 35						19 01								
Ashburys	d	18 16	18 22				18 41	18 39	18 42	18 47	18 56			19 07		19 17					19 41	19 47
Ardwick	d																					
Manchester Piccadilly 10	a	18 23	18 29	18 31	18 37	18 37	18 46	18 46	18 48	18 53	19 01	19 03	19 09	19 12	19 16	19 23	19 31	19 34	19 37	19 37	19 46	19 53
Manchester Airport 85	a											19 25										

A From Norwich to Liverpool Lime Street
B From Hadfield
C From Cleethorpes
D From Manchester Piccadilly

Table T078-F

Mondays to Saturdays
16 December to 16 May

Sheffield, Chinley, Marple and Romiley Manchester and Manchester Airport

		TP	NT	NT	NT	EM	EM	NT	NT	TP	NT	NT	NT	EM	EM	NT	NT	TP	NT	TP	NT	NT	NT
						SO	SX							SO	SX			SO		SX			
		◇1			◇	◇	◇			◇1			◇	◇	◇			◇1		◇1		◇	
		A		B		C	C		B	A		B		D	D		B	A		A	B		B
Sheffield 7	d	19 11			19 14	19 42	19 42			20 11			20 14	20 34	20 39			21 11		21 11		21 14	
Dore & Totley	d				19 21								20 21										
Grindleford	d				19 29																	21 27	
Hathersage	d				19 32								20 31									21 31	
Bamford	d				19 36																	21 34	
Hope (Derbyshire)	d				19 40								20 37									21 38	
Edale	d				19 47								20 44									21 45	
Chinley	d				19 55								20 52									21 53	
Hazel Grove 86	a																						
Stockport 86	a	19 52				20 25	20 25			20 52				21 19	21 25			21 52		21 52			
New Mills Central	d		19 34		20 03						20 34		21 00						21 31			22 01	
Strines	d		19 37								20 37								21 34				
Marple	d		19 41		20 08						20 41		21 05						21 38			22 06	
Rose Hill Marple	d							20 13								21 13							
Romiley	d		19 45		20 11			20 19			20 45		21 08			21 19			21 41			22 10	
Woodley	d							20 22								21 22							
Hyde Central	d							20 25								21 25							
Hyde North	d							20 28								21 28							
Guide Bridge	d			20 12				20 32	20 42			21 11				21 32	21 42				22 11		22 42
Fairfield	d							20 35								21 35							
Gorton	d							20 38				21 14				21 38					22 14		
Bredbury	d		19 48		20 14						20 48		21 11						21 44			22 13	
Brinnington	d		19 51		20 17						20 51		21 14						21 47			22 15	
Reddish North	d		19 55		20 20						20 55		21 17						21 50			22 19	
Ryder Brow	d		19 57								20 57								21 52				
Belle Vue	d		19 58								20 58								21 54				
Ashburys	d		20 02	20 17				20 41	20 47		21 02	21 17				21 41	21 47		21 57		22 17		22 48
Ardwick	d																						
Manchester Piccadilly 10	a	20 02	20 07	20 23	20 31	20 37	20 38	20 46	20 53	21 02	21 07	21 23	21 28	21 29	21 36	21 46	21 55	22 04	22 04	22 08	22 24	22 32	22 53
Manchester Airport 85	a	20 25								21 25													

		NT	TP	NT	NT	NT	NT	NT	NT	NT
					SO	SX	SO	FO	FSX	SX
			◇1		◇			◇	◇	◇
			A	B						
Sheffield 7	d		22 10		22 24			22 47	22 47	23 27
Dore & Totley	d				22 31			22 54	22 54	23 34
Grindleford	d				22 38			23 02	23 02	23 42
Hathersage	d				22 42			23 06	23 06	23 46
Bamford	d				22 46			23 10	23 10	23 50
Hope (Derbyshire)	d				22 49			23 13	23 13	23 54
Edale	d				22 56			23 21	23 21	00 01
Chinley	d				23 04			23 29	23 29	00 09
Hazel Grove 86	a									
Stockport 86	a		22 52							00 26
New Mills Central	d	22 26			23 12	23 15	23 36	23 39	23 39	
Strines	d	22 29				23 18	23 39	23 44	23 44	
Marple	d	22 32			23 17	23 21	23 42	23 48	23 48	
Rose Hill Marple	d									
Romiley	d	22 36			23 21	23 25	23 46	23 52	23 52	
Woodley	d									
Hyde Central	d									
Hyde North	d									
Guide Bridge	d			23 12						
Fairfield	d									
Gorton	d			23 15						
Bredbury	d	22 39			23 24	23 28	23 49	23 55	23 55	
Brinnington	d	22 42			23 26	23 31	23 52	23 57	23 57	
Reddish North	d	22 46			23 30	23 35	23 56	00 02	00 02	
Ryder Brow	d	22 48				23 37	23 58	00 03	00 03	
Belle Vue	d	22 49				23 38	23 59	00 05	00 05	
Ashburys	d	22 53		23 18		23 42	00 04	00 08	00 08	
Ardwick	d									
Manchester Piccadilly 10	a	22 58	23 02	23 24	23 41	23 47	00 09	00 18	00 20	00 36
Manchester Airport 85	a		23 25							

A From Cleethorpes
B From Hadfield
C From Norwich to Liverpool Lime Street
D From Norwich

Table T078-F

Sundays
15 December to 10 May

Sheffield, Chinley, Marple and Romiley Manchester and Manchester Airport

		NT	TP	NT	NT	TP	NT	NT	NT	TP	NT	NT	NT	EM	NT	NT	TP	NT	NT	NT	NT	EM	NT
			◇1	◇	◇	◇1		◇		◇1			◇	◇			◇1			◇	◇	◇	
		A		B	C		D		E	F	G	H		I	G	H	J	G	H	B	C	I	H
Sheffield 7	d		07 51	08 14	08 14	09 11		09 14		10 14			10 17	10 41			11 11			11 15	11 15	11 39	
Dore & Totley	d			08 20	08 20			09 21					10 23	10 48						11 22	11 22		
Grindleford	d			08 27	08 27			09 28					10 30							11 29	11 29		
Hathersage	d			08 31	08 31			09 32					10 34							11 32	11 32		
Bamford	d			08 35	08 35			09 36					10 38							11 36	11 36		
Hope (Derbyshire)	d			08 38	08 38			09 39					10 41							11 40	11 40		
Edale	d			08 46	08 46			09 47					10 49							11 47	11 47		
Chinley	d			08 54	08 54			09 55					10 57							11 55	11 55		
Hazel Grove 86	a																						
Stockport 86	a		08 34			09 53				10 55				11 26			11 56					12 25	
New Mills Central	d			09 01	09 01			10 02					11 04							12 03	12 07		
Strines	d			09 04	09 04			10 05					11 07							12 06	12 10		
Marple	d			09 08	09 08			10 09					11 11							12 10	12 14		
Rose Hill Marple	d																						
Romiley	d			09 12	09 12			10 13					11 14							12 14	12 18		
Woodley	d																						
Hyde Central	d																						
Hyde North	d																						
Guide Bridge	d						10 14		10 38		11 10	11 12			11 42	11 42		12 12	12 12				12 42
Fairfield	d																						
Gorton	d						10 17		10 41		11 13	11 15				11 45		12 15	12 16				
Bredbury	d			09 15	09 15			10 16					11 17							12 17	12 22		
Brinnington	d			09 18	09 18			10 19					11 20							12 20	12 25		
Reddish North	d			09 21	09 21			10 22					11 23							12 23	12 29		
Ryder Brow	d																						
Belle Vue	d																						
Ashburys	d	00 04					10 20		10 44		11 16	11 18				11 48		12 18	12 19				
Ardwick	d																						
Manchester Piccadilly 10	a	00 09	08 43	09 33	09 35	10 03	10 25	10 33	10 51	11 06	11 22	11 25	11 34	11 38	11 52	11 54	12 10	12 25	12 26	12 34	12 43	12 37	12 52
Manchester Airport 85	a		09 03			10 28				11 26							12 31						

		NT	TP	NT	NT	EM	NT	TP	NT	NT	EM	NT	TP	NT	NT	EM	NT	TP	NT	NT	EM	NT
			◇1		◇	◇		◇1		◇	◇		◇1		◇	◇		◇1		◇	◇	
		G	J	D		I	D	J	D		I	D	J	D		K	D	J	D		I	D
Sheffield 7	d		12 11		12 14	12 39		13 10		13 14	13 38		14 11		14 14	14 37		15 11		15 14	15 43	
Dore & Totley	d				12 23					13 20					14 20					15 20		
Grindleford	d				12 30					13 28					14 27					15 27		
Hathersage	d				12 33					13 32					14 31					15 31		
Bamford	d				12 37					13 36					14 35					15 35		
Hope (Derbyshire)	d				12 41					13 39					14 38					15 38		
Edale	d				12 48					13 47					14 46					15 46		
Chinley	d				12 56					13 55					14 54					15 54		
Hazel Grove 86	a																					
Stockport 86	a		12 52			13 25		13 54			14 26		14 53			15 25		15 53			16 25	
New Mills Central	d				13 04					14 02					15 01					16 01		
Strines	d				13 07					14 05					15 04					16 04		
Marple	d				13 10					14 09					15 08					16 08		
Rose Hill Marple	d																					
Romiley	d				13 14					14 13					15 12					16 12		
Woodley	d																					
Hyde Central	d																					
Hyde North	d																					
Guide Bridge	d	12 42		13 12			13 42		14 12			14 42		15 12			15 42		16 12			16 42
Fairfield	d																					
Gorton	d	12 45		13 15			13 45		14 15			14 45		15 15			15 45		16 15			16 45
Bredbury	d				13 17					14 16					15 15					16 15		
Brinnington	d				13 19					14 19					15 18					16 18		
Reddish North	d				13 23					14 22					15 21					16 21		
Ryder Brow	d																					
Belle Vue	d																					
Ashburys	d	12 48		13 18			13 48		14 18			14 52		15 18			15 52		16 18			16 48
Ardwick	d																					
Manchester Piccadilly 10	a	12 54	13 04	13 24	13 34	13 37	13 54	14 03	14 24	14 33	14 37	14 58	15 03	15 24	15 34	15 37	15 58	16 02	16 24	16 33	16 37	16 54
Manchester Airport 85	a		13 26					14 25					15 25					16 25				

A not 15 December. From New Mills Central
B from 5 April
C until 29 March
D From Hadfield
E From Manchester Piccadilly
F From Doncaster
G from 5 April. From Hadfield
H until 29 March. From Hadfield
I From Nottingham to Liverpool Lime Street
J From Cleethorpes
K From Norwich to Liverpool Lime Street

Table T078-F

Sundays

15 December to 10 May

Sheffield, Chinley, Marple and Romiley Manchester and Manchester Airport

		TP	NT	NT	EM	NT	TP	NT	NT	EM	NT	TP	NT	NT	EM	NT	TP	NT	NT	EM	NT	TP
		◇1		◇	◇		◇1		◇	◇		◇1		◇	◇		◇1		◇	◇		◇1
		A	B		C	B	A	B		D	B	A	B		D	B	A	B		E	B	A
Sheffield 7	d	16 10		16 14	16 39		17 10		17 14	17 44		18 11		18 14	18 37		19 11		19 14	19 35		20 11
Dore & Totley	d			16 20					17 20					18 20					19 20			
Grindleford	d			16 27					17 27					18 27					19 27			
Hathersage	d			16 31					17 31					18 31					19 31			
Bamford	d			16 35					17 35					18 35					19 35			
Hope (Derbyshire)	d			16 38					17 38					18 38					19 38			
Edale	d			16 46					17 46					18 46					19 46			
Chinley	d			16 54					17 54					18 54					19 54			
Hazel Grove 86	a																					
Stockport 86	a	16 53			17 28		17 53			18 25		18 53			19 25		19 53			20 26		20 53
New Mills Central	d			17 01					18 01					19 01					20 01			
Strines	d			17 04					18 04					19 04					20 04			
Marple	d			17 08					18 08					19 08					20 08			
Rose Hill Marple	d																					
Romiley	d			17 12					18 12					19 12					20 12			
Woodley	d																					
Hyde Central	d																					
Hyde North	d																					
Guide Bridge	d		17 12			17 42		18 12			18 42		19 12			19 42		20 12			20 42	
Fairfield	d																					
Gorton	d		17 15			17 45		18 15			18 45		19 15			19 45		20 15			20 45	
Bredbury	d			17 15					18 15					19 15					20 15			
Brinnington	d			17 18					18 18					19 18					20 18			
Reddish North	d			17 21					18 21					19 21					20 21			
Ryder Brow	d																					
Belle Vue	d																					
Ashburys	d		17 18			17 48		18 18			18 52		19 18			19 48		20 18			20 50	
Ardwick	d																					
Manchester Piccadilly 10	a	17 02	17 24	17 33	17 38	17 54	18 03	18 24	18 33	18 37	18 58	19 03	19 24	19 33	19 37	19 54	20 03	20 24	20 32	20 38	20 56	21 04
Manchester Airport 85	a	17 25					18 25					19 25					20 25					21 25

		NT	NT	EM	TP	NT	NT	TP	NT
			◇	◇	◇1		◇	◇1	◇
		B		E	A	B		A	
Sheffield 7	d		20 14	20 35	21 11		21 32	22 13	22 16
Dore & Totley	d		20 20						22 23
Grindleford	d		20 27						22 30
Hathersage	d		20 31						22 34
Bamford	d		20 35						22 38
Hope (Derbyshire)	d		20 38						22 41
Edale	d		20 46						22 49
Chinley	d		20 54						22 57
Hazel Grove 86	a								
Stockport 86	a			21 25	21 56			23 03	
New Mills Central	d		21 04						23 04
Strines	d		21 07						23 07
Marple	d		21 11						23 11
Rose Hill Marple	d								
Romiley	d		21 15						23 15
Woodley	d								
Hyde Central	d								
Hyde North	d								
Guide Bridge	d	21 12				22 11			
Fairfield	d								
Gorton	d	21 15				22 14			
Bredbury	d		21 18						23 18
Brinnington	d		21 21						23 21
Reddish North	d		21 24						23 24
Ryder Brow	d								
Belle Vue	d								
Ashburys	d	21 18				22 17			23 32
Ardwick	d								
Manchester Piccadilly 10	a	21 24	21 35	21 36	22 05	22 23	22 34	23 19	23 37
Manchester Airport 85	a				22 25				

A From Cleethorpes
B From Hadfield
C From Peterborough to Liverpool Lime Street
D From Norwich to Liverpool Lime Street
E From Norwich

Table T078-R

Mondays to Saturdays

16 December to 16 May

Manchester Airport and Manchester Romiley, Marple, Chinley and Sheffield

Miles	Miles	Miles			NT SX	NT	NT SX	NT SO	NT	TP	NT SX	NT SO	NT	NT SX	NT SO	NT	NT SX	NT SX	NT SO	NT SX	NT SX	NT SO	NT SX
						◇				◇1				◇	◇								◇
					A		A	A		B	A	A	C			D	E		A	E	C	C	F
—	—	—	**Manchester Airport** 85	d						05 54													
0	0	—	**Manchester Piccadilly 10**	a						06 12													
				d	05 32	05 46	05 52	06 03	06 11	06 15	06 24	06 30	06 34	06 38	06 39		06 47	06 49	07 03	07 07	07 09	07 10	07 11
0½	0½	—	Ardwick	d																			
1½	1½	—	Ashburys	d	05 36		05 56	06 07	06 15		06 28	06 34	06 38				06 51		07 07	07 11			07 15
2¼	—	—	Belle Vue	d					06 17														
2¾	—	—	Ryder Brow	d					06 19									06 55					
3¾	—	—	Reddish North	d					06 22					06 47	06 47			06 58					07 21
5½	—	—	Brinnington	d					06 25					06 51	06 51			07 02					07 24
6½	—	—	Bredbury	d					06 28					06 54	06 54			07 05					07 28
—	2½	—	Gorton	d									06 41								07 16	07 16	
—	3½	—	Fairfield	d									06 43							07 15	→		
—	4¾	—	Guide Bridge	a	05 41		06 01	06 12			06 33	06 39	06 46				06 56		07 12	07 18		07 20	
—	—	—		d									06 46									07 21	
—	6½	—	Hyde North	d									06 50									07 25	
—	7¾	—	Hyde Central	d									06 53									07 28	
—	9¼	—	Woodley	d									06 56			←						07 31	
7¾	10½	—	**Romiley**	d					06 31				07 00	06 57	06 57	07 00		07 08				07 34	07 31
—	12½	—	Rose Hill Marple	a									→			07 05						→	
9	—	—	**Marple**	d					06 35					07 00	07 00			07 12					07 35
11¼	—	—	Strines	d														07 16					
12¾	—	—	New Mills Central	a					06 40					07 06	07 06			07 19					07 40
				d										07 06	07 06								07 41
—	—	—	Stockport 86	d		05 56				06 26													
—	—	0	Hazel Grove 86	d		06 04																	
16½	—	8½	**Chinley**	d		06 15								07 13	07 13								07 48
22	—	—	Edale	d		06 23								07 22	07 22								07 57
27¼	—	—	Hope (Derbyshire)	d		06 30								07 29	07 29								08 04
29	—	—	Bamford	d		06 33								07 32	07 32								08 07
30¾	—	—	Hathersage	d		06 37								07 36	07 36								08 10
32¼	—	—	Grindleford	d		06 41								07 40	07 40								08 14
37¾	—	—	Dore & Totley	d		06 50								07 57	07 57								08 24
42	—	—	**Sheffield 7**	a		06 56				07 06				08 04	08 04								→

		NT SO	NT SX	TP	NT SX	NT SO	NT SX	NT SO	NT SX	NT SO	NT SX	EM SO	EM SX	NT SX	NT SO	NT	NT	TP	NT	NT	NT	EM SO	EM SX
				◇1	◇							◇	◇		◇			◇1				◇	◇
		D	D	B	D		E	A				G	G	E		A		B		A		G	G
Manchester Airport 85	d			06 53														07 53					
Manchester Piccadilly 10	a			07 11														08 11					
	d			07 18		07 19	07 26	07 33	07 35	07 35	07 40	07 42	07 42	07 42	07 49	08 03	08 10	08 19	08 19	08 33	08 40	08 43	08 43
Ardwick	d																						
Ashburys	d					07 23	07 30	07 37			07 44			07 46		08 07			08 24	08 37	08 44		
Belle Vue	d					07 25					07 46												
Ryder Brow	d					07 27					07 48								08 27				
Reddish North	d					07 30					07 51				07 57				08 30				
Brinnington	d					07 33					07 55				08 01				08 33				
Bredbury	d		←			07 36					07 58				08 04				08 36				
Gorton	d		07 16						07 41	07 42							08 16				08 47		
Fairfield	d								07 43	07 45											08 49		
Guide Bridge	a		07 21				07 35	07 42	07 46	07 48				07 51		08 12	08 20			08 42	08 52		
	d		07 21						07 46	07 48							08 20				08 52		
Hyde North	d		07 25														08 24						
Hyde Central	d		07 28						07 52	07 53							08 27				08 57		
Woodley	d	←	07 31						07 55	07 56							08 30				09 00		
Romiley	d	07 34	07 35			07 39			07 58	08 00	08 02				08 07		08 34		08 39		09 03		
Rose Hill Marple	a	07 39	07 40						08 03	08 05							08 39				09 08		
Marple	d					07 43					08 06				08 10				08 43				
Strines	d										08 10								08 47				
New Mills Central	a					07 48					08 13				08 16				08 50				
	d														08 16								
Stockport 86	d			07 28								07 56	07 54					08 28				08 55	08 54
Hazel Grove 86	d																						
Chinley	d														08 24								
Edale	d														08 32								
Hope (Derbyshire)	d														08 39								
Bamford	d														08 42								
Hathersage	d														08 46								
Grindleford	d				←										08 50								
Dore & Totley	d			08 05	08 24							08 28	08 28		08 59								
Sheffield 7	a			08 10	08 32							08 35	08 36		09 05			09 09				09 34	09 35

A To Hadfield
B To Cleethorpes
C To Rose Hill Marple
D From Manchester Piccadilly
E To Manchester Piccadilly
F To Sheffield
G From Liverpool Lime Street to Norwich

Table T078-R

Mondays to Saturdays

16 December to 16 May

Manchester Airport and Manchester Romiley, Marple, Chinley and Sheffield

Station		NT ◇	NT A	NT SX	NT SO	TP ◇1 B ⚒	NT	NT A	NT SO C	EM SO ◇ D	NT SX ◇	NT SO E	EM SX ◇ D	NT SX C	NT SO ◇	NT SX E	NT A	NT	TP ◇1 B ⚒	NT	NT A	NT
Manchester Airport 85	d					08 53													09 53			
Manchester Piccadilly 10	a					09 11													10 11			
	d	08 49	09 03	09 10	09 10	09 18	09 20	09 33	09 39	09 42	09 42		09 43	09 44	09 49		10 03	10 10	10 18	10 19	10 33	10 40
Ardwick	d																					
Ashburys	d		09 07				09 24	09 37						09 48			10 07			10 23	10 37	10 44
Belle Vue	d						09 26													10 25		
Ryder Brow	d						09 28													10 27		
Reddish North	d	08 57					09 31				09 50				09 57					10 30		
Brinnington	d	09 01					09 34				09 53				10 01					10 34		
Bredbury	d	09 04					09 37				09 56				10 04					10 37		
Gorton	d			09 16	09 16				09 45					09 51				10 16				10 47
Fairfield	d								09 47					09 53								10 49
Guide Bridge	a		09 12	09 20	09 20			09 42	09 50					09 56			10 12	10 20			10 42	10 52
	d			09 20	09 20				09 52					09 56				10 20				10 52
Hyde North	d			09 24	09 24				09 56					10 00				10 24				
Hyde Central	d			09 27	09 27				09 58					10 03				10 27				10 57
Woodley	d			09 30	09 30				10 01			←		10 06		←		10 30				11 00
Romiley	d	09 07		09 33	09 34		09 40		10 04		09 59	10 04		10 09	10 07	10 09		10 34		10 40		11 03
Rose Hill Marple	a			09 38	09 39				→			10 09		→		10 16		10 39				11 08
Marple	d	09 11					09 44				10 03				10 11					10 44		
Strines	d						09 48													10 48		
New Mills Central	a	09 16					09 51				10 08				10 16					10 51		
	d	09 17									10 08				10 16							
Stockport 86	d					09 28				09 54			09 54						10 28			
Hazel Grove 86	d																					
Chinley	d	09 23									10 15				10 24							
Edale	d	09 32									10 24				10 32							
Hope (Derbyshire)	d	09 38									10 31				10 39							
Bamford	d	09 42									10 35				10 42							
Hathersage	d	09 45									10 39				10 46							
Grindleford	d	09 49									10 43				10 50							
Dore & Totley	d	09 58									10 58				10 59							
Sheffield 7	a	10 05				10 09				10 34	11 04		10 34		11 05				11 08			

Station		EM SX ◇ D	EM SO ◇ D	NT ◇	NT A	NT	TP ◇1 B ⚒	NT	NT A	NT	EM ◇ D	NT SX ◇	NT SO ◇	NT A	NT	TP ◇1 B ⚒	NT	NT A	NT	EM SX ◇ D	EM SO ◇ D	NT ◇	NT A
Manchester Airport 85	d						10 53									11 53							
Manchester Piccadilly 10	a						11 11									12 11							
	d	10 42	10 42	10 49	11 03	11 10	11 18	11 19	11 33	11 40	11 42	11 49	11 49	12 03	12 10	12 18	12 19	12 33	12 40	12 42	12 42	12 49	13 03
Ardwick	d																						
Ashburys	d				11 07			11 23	11 37	11 44				12 07			12 23	12 37	12 44				13 07
Belle Vue	d							11 25									12 25						
Ryder Brow	d							11 27									12 27						
Reddish North	d			10 57				11 30				11 57	11 57				12 30					12 57	
Brinnington	d			11 01				11 34				12 01	12 01				12 34					13 00	
Bredbury	d			11 04				11 37				12 04	12 04				12 37					13 03	
Gorton	d					11 16				11 47					12 16				12 47				
Fairfield	d									11 49									12 49				
Guide Bridge	a				11 12	11 20			11 42	11 52				12 12	12 20			12 42	12 52				13 12
	d					11 22				11 52					12 20				12 52				
Hyde North	d					11 26									12 24								
Hyde Central	d					11 29				11 57					12 27				12 57				
Woodley	d					11 32				12 00					12 30				13 00				
Romiley	d			11 07		11 35		11 40		12 03		12 07	12 07		12 34		12 40		13 03			13 07	
Rose Hill Marple	a					11 40				12 08					12 39				13 08				
Marple	d			11 10				11 44				12 10	12 10				12 44					13 10	
Strines	d							11 48									12 48						
New Mills Central	a			11 16				11 51				12 16	12 16				12 51					13 16	
	d			11 16								12 16	12 16									13 16	
Stockport 86	d	10 54	10 55				11 28				11 54					12 28				12 55	12 55		
Hazel Grove 86	d																						
Chinley	d			11 23								12 24	12 24									13 23	
Edale	d			11 32								12 32	12 32									13 32	
Hope (Derbyshire)	d			11 38								12 39	12 39									13 38	
Bamford	d			11 42								12 42	12 42									13 42	
Hathersage	d			11 45								12 45	12 46									13 45	
Grindleford	d			11 49								12 49	12 50									13 49	
Dore & Totley	d			11 58								12 58	12 59									13 58	
Sheffield 7	a	11 35	11 36	12 04			12 08				12 35	13 04	13 05			13 08				13 34	13 36	14 04	

A To Hadfield
B To Cleethorpes
C To Rose Hill Marple
D From Liverpool Lime Street to Norwich
E From Manchester Piccadilly

NRT DECEMBER 19 EDITION

Table T078-R

Mondays to Saturdays

16 December to 16 May

Manchester Airport and Manchester Romiley, Marple, Chinley and Sheffield

Station		NT	TP ◇1 A ⚒	NT	NT B	NT	EM SX ◇ C	EM SO ◇ C	NT SX ◇	NT SO ◇	NT B	NT	TP ◇1 A ⚒	NT SX	NT SO	NT B	NT	EM SX ◇ C	EM SO ◇ C	NT ◇	NT B	NT	TP ◇1 A ⚒
Manchester Airport 85	d		12 53										13 53										14 53
Manchester Piccadilly 10	a		13 11										14 11										15 11
	d	13 10	13 18	13 19	13 33	13 40	13 42	13 42	13 49	13 49	14 03	14 10	14 18	14 19	14 19	14 33	14 40	14 42	14 42	14 49	15 03	15 10	15 18
Ardwick	d																						
Ashburys	d			13 23	13 37	13 44					14 07			14 23	14 23	14 37	14 44				15 07		
Belle Vue	d			13 25										14 25	14 25								
Ryder Brow	d			13 27										14 27	14 27								
Reddish North	d			13 30					13 57	13 57				14 30	14 30					14 57			
Brinnington	d			13 34					14 01	14 01				14 34	14 34					15 01			
Bredbury	d			13 37					14 04	14 04				14 37	14 37					15 04			
Gorton	d	13 16				13 47						14 16					14 47					15 16	
Fairfield	d					13 49											14 49						
Guide Bridge	a	13 20			13 42	13 52					14 12	14 20				14 42	14 52				15 12	15 20	
	d	13 20				13 52						14 20					14 52					15 20	
Hyde North	d	13 24										14 24										15 24	
Hyde Central	d	13 27				13 57						14 27					14 57					15 27	
Woodley	d	13 30				14 00						14 30					15 00					15 30	
Romiley	d	13 34		13 40		14 03			14 07	14 07		14 34		14 40	14 41		15 03			15 07		15 34	
Rose Hill Marple	a	13 39				14 08						14 39					15 08					15 39	
Marple	d			13 44					14 10	14 10				14 44	14 45					15 10			
Strines	d			13 48										14 48	14 49								
New Mills Central	a			13 51					14 16	14 16				14 51	14 53					15 16			
	d								14 16	14 16										15 16			
Stockport 86	d		13 28				13 54	13 55					14 28					14 54	14 55				15 28
Hazel Grove 86	d																						
Chinley	d								14 23	14 24										15 23			
Edale	d								14 32	14 32										15 32			
Hope (Derbyshire)	d								14 38	14 39										15 38			
Bamford	d								14 42	14 42										15 42			
Hathersage	d								14 45	14 46										15 45			
Grindleford	d								14 49	14 50										15 49			
Dore & Totley	d								14 58	14 59										15 58			
Sheffield 7	a		14 08				14 35	14 36	15 04	15 05			15 08					15 34	15 36	16 04			16 08

Station		NT	NT B	NT	EM SX ◇ C	EM SO ◇ C	NT ◇	NT B	NT	TP ◇1 A ⚒	NT SO	NT SX	NT SX D	NT SO B	NT SX	NT	EM SO ◇ C	EM SX ◇ C	NT SX D	NT SO ◇	NT SX ◇	NT SO B
Manchester Airport 85	d									15 53												
Manchester Piccadilly 10	a									16 11												
	d	15 19	15 33	15 40	15 42	15 42	15 49	16 03	16 10	16 18	16 19	16 20	16 32	16 33	16 35	16 37	16 42	16 42	16 44	16 49	16 49	17 03
Ardwick	d															16 40						
Ashburys	d	15 23	15 37	15 44				16 07			16 23	16 24	16 36	16 37		16 42			16 48			17 07
Belle Vue	d	15 25									16 25	16 26										
Ryder Brow	d	15 27									16 27	16 28			16 42							
Reddish North	d	15 30					15 57				16 30	16 31			16 45					16 57	16 57	
Brinnington	d	15 34					16 01				16 34	16 35			16 48					17 01	17 01	
Bredbury	d	15 37					16 04				16 37	16 38			16 52					17 04	17 04	
Gorton	d			15 47					16 16										16 51			
Fairfield	d			15 49												16 46						
Guide Bridge	a		15 42	15 52				16 12	16 20				16 41	16 42		16 49			16 55			17 12
	d			15 52					16 20							16 50						
Hyde North	d								16 24							16 54						
Hyde Central	d			15 57					16 27							16 57						
Woodley	d			16 00					16 30							17 00						
Romiley	d	15 40		16 03			16 07		16 34		16 40	16 41			16 55	17 03				17 08	17 08	
Rose Hill Marple	a			16 08					16 39							17 08						
Marple	d	15 44					16 10				16 44	16 45			16 59					17 11	17 11	
Strines	d	15 48									16 48	16 49										
New Mills Central	a	15 51					16 16				16 51	16 52			17 04					17 17	17 17	
	d						16 16													17 17	17 17	
Stockport 86	d				15 54	15 55				16 28							16 55	16 54				
Hazel Grove 86	d																					
Chinley	d						16 24										17 10	17 09		17 24	17 24	
Edale	d						16 32													17 33	17 33	
Hope (Derbyshire)	d						16 39													17 39	17 39	
Bamford	d						16 42													17 42	17 42	
Hathersage	d						16 45													17 46	17 46	
Grindleford	d						16 49													17 50	17 50	
Dore & Totley	d						16 58										17 31	17 31		17 59	17 59	
Sheffield 7	a				16 34	16 35	17 04			17 09							17 37	17 39		18 06	18 10	

A To Cleethorpes
B To Hadfield
C From Liverpool Lime Street to Norwich
D To Manchester Piccadilly

Table T078-R

Manchester Airport and Manchester Romiley, Marple, Chinley and Sheffield

Mondays to Saturdays
16 December to 16 May

		NT SX	NT	TP	NT	NT SX	NT SX	NT SO	NT SO	NT SX	EM SO	EM SX	NT SX	NT SO	NT SX	NT SO	NT SX	NT SO	NT SX	TP	NT SX	NT SO	NT SX
		A		◇1 B 🍴		A		C			◇ D	◇ D	A	◇	◇	C	A			◇1 B 🍴			
Manchester Airport 85	d			16 53																17 53			
Manchester Piccadilly 10	a			17 11																18 11			
	d	17 07	17 10	17 18	17 19	17 26	17 32	17 32	17 35	17 38	17 42	17 42	17 42	17 49	17 49	18 03	18 06	18 10	18 11	18 18	18 19	18 19	18 27
Ardwick	d																18 09						
Ashburys	d	17 11			17 23	17 30		17 36	17 39				17 46			18 07	18 12				18 23	18 23	18 31
Belle Vue	d				17 25																	18 25	18 34
Ryder Brow	d				17 27																	18 27	18 36
Reddish North	d				17 30		17 40							17 57	17 58						18 28	18 30	18 39
Brinnington	d				17 33		17 44							18 01	18 01						18 32	18 33	18 42
Bredbury	d				17 36		17 47							18 04	18 04						18 36	18 36	18 46
Gorton	d		17 16						17 42	17 44			17 49					18 16	18 17				
Fairfield	d		17 18			17 34												18 18	18 19				
Guide Bridge	a	17 16	17 21			17 37		17 41	17 46	17 48			17 53			18 12	18 17	18 21	18 22				
	d		17 21						17 46	17 49								18 21	18 22				
Hyde North	d		17 25						17 50	17 53								18 25	18 26				
Hyde Central	d		17 28						17 53	17 56								18 28	18 29				
Woodley	d		17 31						17 57	17 59								18 31	18 32				
Romiley	d		17 35		17 39		17 50		18 00	18 02				18 07	18 07			18 34	18 35		18 39	18 39	18 49
Rose Hill Marple	a		17 40						18 05	18 07								18 39	18 40				
Marple	d				17 43		17 54							18 11	18 11						18 43	18 43	18 53
Strines	d				17 47		17 58															18 47	18 57
New Mills Central	a				17 50		18 02							18 16	18 16						18 48	18 50	19 00
	d													18 17	18 16						18 49		
Stockport 86	d			17 28							17 55	17 55								18 28			
Hazel Grove 86	d																						
Chinley	d										18 10	18 09		18 24	18 24						18a56		
Edale	d													18 32	18 32								
Hope (Derbyshire)	d													18 39	18 39								
Bamford	d													18 42	18 42								
Hathersage	d													18 46	18 46								
Grindleford	d													18 50	18 50								
Dore & Totley	d			18 04								18 36		18 58	18 58					19 03			
Sheffield 7	a			18 10							18 37	18 47		19 04	19 05					19 08			

		NT	NT	EM SO	EM SX	NT	NT	NT	TP	NT	NT	NT	EM SO	EM SX	NT SX	NT SO	NT	NT SO	NT SX	TP	NT	NT
		C		◇ E	◇ E	◇	C		◇1 B		C		◇ D	◇ D	◇	◇	C			◇1 B		C
Manchester Airport 85	d								18 53											19 53		
Manchester Piccadilly 10	a								19 11											20 11		
	d	18 32	18 34	18 42	18 43	18 49	19 03	19 10	19 18	19 19	19 33	19 40	19 42	19 42	19 49	19 49	20 03	20 10	20 11	20 18	20 19	20 33
Ardwick	d																					
Ashburys	d	18 36	18 38				19 07			19 23	19 37	19 44					20 07				20 23	20 37
Belle Vue	d									19 25												
Ryder Brow	d									19 27											20 26	
Reddish North	d					18 57				19 30					19 57	19 57					20 29	
Brinnington	d					19 01				19 33					20 01	20 01					20 32	
Bredbury	d					19 04				19 36					20 04	20 04					20 35	
Gorton	d	18 38	18 41					19 16				19 47						20 16	20 17			
Fairfield	d		18 43									19 49										
Guide Bridge	a	18 42	18 46				19 12	19 20			19 42	19 52					20 12	20 20	20 21			20 42
	d		18 46					19 20				19 52						20 20	20 21			
Hyde North	d		18 51					19 24										20 24	20 25			
Hyde Central	d		18 54					19 27				19 57						20 27	20 28			
Woodley	d		18 57					19 30				20 00						20 30	20 31			
Romiley	d		19 01			19 07		19 34		19 39		20 03			20 07	20 07		20 34	20 35		20 38	
Rose Hill Marple	a		19 06					19 39				20 08						20 39	20 40			
Marple	d					19 11				19 43					20 11	20 10					20 42	
Strines	d																				20 46	
New Mills Central	a					19 16				19 48					20 16	20 16					20 49	
	d					19 17									20 17	20 16						
Stockport 86	d			18 55	18 54				19 28				19 55	19 54						20 28		
Hazel Grove 86	d																					
Chinley	d					19 24									20 24	20 24						
Edale	d					19 32										20 32						
Hope (Derbyshire)	d					19 39										20 39						
Bamford	d					19 42										20 42						
Hathersage	d					19 46										20 46						
Grindleford	d					19 50										20 50						
Dore & Totley	d					19 58			20 03						20 49	20 59				21 03		
Sheffield 7	a			19 35	19 35	20 05			20 08				20 35	20 37	20 57	21 05				21 08		

A To Manchester Piccadilly
B To Cleethorpes
C To Hadfield
D From Liverpool Lime Street to Nottingham
E From Liverpool Lime Street to Norwich

Table T078-R

Manchester Airport and Manchester Romiley, Marple, Chinley and Sheffield

Mondays to Saturdays
16 December to 16 May

		EM SO	EM SX	NT	NT	NT	TP	NT SO	NT SX	NT	EM SO	NT SX	NT SO	NT	TP SO	TP SX	EM SX	EM SO	NT	NT	NT	NT	TP SX
		◇ A	◇ A	◇	B		◇1 C	◇	◇	B	◇ A			B	◇1 D	◇1 D	◇ A	◇ A	B			E	◇1
Manchester Airport 85	d						20 53								21 53	21 53							23 30
Manchester Piccadilly 10	a						21 13								22 12	22 15							23 45
	d	20 42	20 42	20 49	21 03	21 09	21 18	21 19	21 19	21 33	21 41	21 49	21 49	22 00	22 17	22 20	22 28	22 29	22 30	22 40	23 26	23 29	23 50
Ardwick	d																						
Ashburys	d				21 07					21 37		21 55	21 55	22 04					22 34	22 44	23 30	23 33	
Belle Vue	d								21 25				21 57							22 46	23 33		
Ryder Brow	d								21 27				21 59							22 48	23 35		
Reddish North	d			20 57				21 27	21 30			22 00	22 02							22 51	23 37		
Brinnington	d			21 01				21 31	21 33			22 03	22 06							22 54	23 41		
Bredbury	d			21 04				21 34	21 37			22 07	22 09							22 57	23 44		
Gorton	d					21 15								22 06					22 36			23 35	
Fairfield	d					21 17																	
Guide Bridge	a				21 12	21 20				21 42				22 10					22 40			23 39	
	d					21 20																	
Hyde North	d					21 24																	
Hyde Central	d					21 27																	
Woodley	d					21 30																	
Romiley	d			21 07		21 34		21 38	21 40			22 10	22 12							23 00	23 47		
Rose Hill Marple	a					21 39																	
Marple	d			21 10				21 42	21 44			22 14	22 16							23 04	23 51		
Strines	d							21 46	21 48											23 08	23 55		
New Mills Central	a			21 16				21 50	21 51			22 19	22 21							23 11	23 58		
	d			21 16				21 50	21 52														
Stockport 86	d	20 55	20 53				21 28				21 52						22 39	22 38					
Hazel Grove 86	d																						
Chinley	d			21 23				21 56	22 12								22 54	22 53					
Edale	d			21 31													23 02	23 01					
Hope (Derbyshire)	d			21 38					22 25								23 08	23 07					
Bamford	d			21 41					22 28								23 11	23 11					
Hathersage	d			21 44					22 32								23 15	23 15					
Grindleford	d			21 48													23 19	23 19					
Dore & Totley	d			21 56			22 03	22 21	22 46								23 28	23 28					
Sheffield 7	a	21 34	21 35	22 09			22 08	22 28	22 52		22 31				23 07	23 09	23 36	23 35					01 20

Sundays
15 December to 10 May

		NT	NT	TP	TP	TP	NT	NT	TP	TP	NT	NT	NT	NT	NT	TP	NT	NT	NT	TP	NT	NT	NT
		◇ F	◇ G	◇1 H 🍴	◇1 I 🍴	◇1 J 🍴	◇ F	G	◇1 K 🍴	◇1 J 🍴	L	◇ G	◇ F	M	N	◇1 C 🍴	B	◇	B	◇1 C 🍴	M	N	◇
Manchester Airport 85	d			07 51	07 51				08 46							09 56				10 55			
Manchester Piccadilly 10	a			08 08	08 09				09 03							10 10				11 15			
	d	07 42	07 43	08 13	08 13	08 13	08 29	08 45	09 10	09 10	09 29	09 31	09 45	09 59	10 03	10 14	10 33	10 45	11 03	11 19	11 26	11 33	11 45
Ardwick	d																						
Ashburys	d										09 33			10 03	10 07		10 37		11 07		11 30	11 37	11 49
Belle Vue	d																						
Ryder Brow	d																						
Reddish North	d	07 50	07 51				08 37	08 53				09 39	09 53					10 53					11 54
Brinnington	d	07 54	07 55				08 40	08 56				09 43	09 56					10 56					11 57
Bredbury	d	07 57	07 58				08 43	08 59				09 46	09 59					10 59					12 00
Gorton	d										09 36			10 05	10 09		10 39		11 09		11 33	11 39	
Fairfield	d																						
Guide Bridge	a										09 39			10 09	10 13		10 43		11 13		11 37	11 43	
	d																						
Hyde North	d																						
Hyde Central	d																						
Woodley	d																						
Romiley	d	08 01	08 02				08 46	09 02				09 49	10 02					11 02					12 03
Rose Hill Marple	a																						
Marple	d	08 04	08 05				08 50	09 06				09 52	10 06					11 06					12 07
Strines	d	08 08	08 09				08 54	09 10				09 56	10 10					11 10					12 11
New Mills Central	a	08 12	08 13				08 58	09 13				10 00	10 13					11 13					12 14
	d	08 12	08 13				08 58	09 14				10 00	10 13					11 13					12 14
Stockport 86	d			08 23	08 23	08 23			09 19	09 19						10 23				11 29			
Hazel Grove 86	d																						
Chinley	d	08 21	08 21				09 06	09 21				10 07	10 21					11 21					12 22
Edale	d	08 30	08 30				09 15	09 30				10 16	10 29					11 30					12 30
Hope (Derbyshire)	d	08 37	08 37				09 22	09 37				10 23	10 36					11 37					12 37
Bamford	d	08 41	08 41				09 25	09 40				10 26	10 39					11 40					12 40
Hathersage	d	08 45	08 45				09 29	09 44				10 30	10 43					11 44					12 44
Grindleford	d	08 49	08 49				09 33	09 47				10 33	10 47					11 47					12 47
Dore & Totley	d	08 58	08 58				09 41	09 56				10 42	10 55					11 56					12 56
Sheffield 7	a	09 04	09 04	09 08	09 08	09 08	09 48	10 02	10 08	10 08		10 48	11 02			11 05		12 02		12 09			13 02

A From Liverpool Lime Street to Nottingham
B To Hadfield
C To Cleethorpes
D To Doncaster
E To Glossop
F from 5 April
G until 29 March
H from 5 April. To Cleethorpes
I until 16 February. To Cleethorpes
J from 23 February until 29 March. To Cleethorpes
K until 16 February, from 5 April. To Cleethorpes
L To Manchester Piccadilly
M from 5 April. To Hadfield
N until 29 March. To Hadfield

Table T078-R

Sundays
15 December to 10 May

Manchester Airport and Manchester Romiley, Marple, Chinley and Sheffield

		NT A	NT B	TP ◇1 C	NT B	NT A	EM ◇ D	NT ◇ E	NT ◇ F	NT B	NT A	TP ◇1 C	NT G	EM ◇ H	NT ◇	NT G	TP ◇1 C	NT G	EM ◇ H	NT ◇	NT G	TP ◇1 C	NT G
Manchester Airport 85	d			11 56								12 56					13 56					14 56	
Manchester Piccadilly 10	a			12 12								13 14					14 13					15 13	
	d	12 01	12 02	12 19	12 30	12 33	12 43	12 45	12 52	13 00	13 03	13 20	13 33	13 43	13 43	14 03	14 19	14 33	14 43	14 45	15 03	15 18	15 33
Ardwick	d																						
Ashburys	d	12 05	12 07		12 34	12 37		12 49		13 04	13 07		13 37			14 07		14 37			15 07		15 37
Belle Vue	d																						
Ryder Brow	d																						
Reddish North	d							12 54							13 51					14 53			
Brinnington	d							12 57							13 55					14 56			
Bredbury	d							13 00	13 03						13 58					14 59			
Gorton	d	12 07	12 09		12 36	12 39				13 07	13 09		13 39			14 09		14 39			15 09		15 39
Fairfield	d																						
Guide Bridge	a	12 11	12 13		12 40	12 43				13 10	13 13		13 43			14 13		14 43			15 13		15 43
	d																						
Hyde North	d																						
Hyde Central	d																						
Woodley	d																						
Romiley	d							13 03	13 06						14 01					15 02			
Rose Hill Marple	a																						
Marple	d							13 07	13 09						14 04					15 06			
Strines	d							13 11							14 08					15 10			
New Mills Central	a							13 14	13 15						14 12					15 13			
	d							13 14	13 15						14 12					15 13			
Stockport 86	d			12 28			12 55					13 29		13 51			14 28		14 54			15 28	
Hazel Grove 86	d																						
Chinley	d							13 22	13 22						14 19					15 21			
Edale	d							13 30	13 31						14 28					15 30			
Hope (Derbyshire)	d							13 37	13 37						14 34					15 37			
Bamford	d							13 40	13 40						14 37					15 40			
Hathersage	d							13 44	13 44						14 41					15 44			
Grindleford	d							13 47	13 47						14 45					15 47			
Dore & Totley	d							13 56	13 56						14 53					15 56			
Sheffield 7	a			13 08			13 37	14 02	14 02			14 09		14 37	15 01		15 08		15 34	16 02		16 08	

		EM ◇ H	NT ◇	NT G	TP ◇1 C	NT G	EM ◇ H	NT ◇	NT G	TP ◇1 C	NT G	EM ◇ I	NT ◇	NT G	TP ◇1 C	NT G	EM ◇ H	NT ◇	NT G	TP ◇1 C	NT G	EM ◇ I
Manchester Airport 85	d				15 56					16 56					17 56					18 56		
Manchester Piccadilly 10	a				16 13					17 13					18 13					19 13		
	d	15 43	15 45	16 03	16 19	16 32	16 43	16 45	17 03	17 19	17 33	17 43	17 45	18 03	18 19	18 33	18 43	18 45	19 03	19 19	19 33	19 43
Ardwick	d																					
Ashburys	d			16 07		16 36			17 07		17 37			18 07		18 37			19 07		19 37	
Belle Vue	d																					
Ryder Brow	d																					
Reddish North	d		15 53					16 53					17 53					18 53				
Brinnington	d		15 56					16 57					17 56					18 56				
Bredbury	d		15 59					17 00					17 59					18 59				
Gorton	d			16 09		16 38			17 09		17 39			18 09		18 39			19 09		19 39	
Fairfield	d																					
Guide Bridge	a			16 13		16 42			17 13		17 43			18 13		18 43			19 13		19 43	
	d																					
Hyde North	d																					
Hyde Central	d																					
Woodley	d																					
Romiley	d		16 02					17 03					18 02					19 02				
Rose Hill Marple	a																					
Marple	d		16 06					17 06					18 06					19 06				
Strines	d		16 10					17 10					18 10					19 10				
New Mills Central	a		16 13					17 14					18 13					19 13				
	d		16 13					17 14					18 13					19 13				
Stockport 86	d	15 54			16 28		16 54			17 28		17 54			18 28		18 53			19 28		19 54
Hazel Grove 86	d																					
Chinley	d		16 21					17 21					18 21					19 21				
Edale	d		16 30					17 30					18 30					19 30				
Hope (Derbyshire)	d		16 37					17 37					18 37					19 37				
Bamford	d		16 40					17 40					18 40					19 40				
Hathersage	d		16 44					17 44					18 44					19 44				
Grindleford	d		16 47					17 47					18 47					19 47				
Dore & Totley	d		16 56					17 55		18 03			18 56		19 03			19 56		20 03		
Sheffield 7	a	16 38	17 02		17 08		17 35	18 03		18 09		18 36	19 02		19 09		19 35	20 02		20 09		20 35

A from 5 April. To Hadfield
B until 29 March. To Hadfield
C To Cleethorpes
D To Norwich
E from 5 April
F until 29 March
G To Hadfield
H From Liverpool Lime Street to Norwich
I From Liverpool Lime Street to Nottingham

Table T078-R

Sundays
15 December to 10 May

Manchester Airport and Manchester Romiley, Marple, Chinley and Sheffield

		NT ◇	NT A	TP ◇1 B	NT ◇	EM ◇ C	NT A	TP ◇1 B	NT ◇	EM ◇ C	TP ◇1 D	TP ◇1
Manchester Airport 85	d			19 56				20 55			21 56	22 56
Manchester Piccadilly 10	a			20 13				21 13			22 13	23 12
	d	19 45	20 03	20 18	20 42	20 43	21 02	21 19	21 45	22 13	22 19	23 20
Ardwick	d											
Ashburys	d		20 07				21 06					
Belle Vue	d											
Ryder Brow	d											
Reddish North	d	19 53			20 50				21 53			
Brinnington	d	19 57			20 53				21 56			
Bredbury	d	20 00			20 56				21 59			
Gorton	d		20 09				21 08					
Fairfield	d											
Guide Bridge	a		20 13				21 12					
	d											
Hyde North	d											
Hyde Central	d											
Woodley	d											
Romiley	d	20 03			20 59				22 02			
Rose Hill Marple	a											
Marple	d	20 06			21 03				22 06			
Strines	d	20 10			21 07				22 10			
New Mills Central	a	20 14			21 10				22 13			
	d	20 14			21 10				22 13			
Stockport 86	d			20 28		20 53		21 28		22 30	22 27	23 28
Hazel Grove 86	d											
Chinley	d	20 21			21 18				22 21	22 46		
Edale	d	20 30			21 26				22 30	22 54		
Hope (Derbyshire)	d	20 37			21 33				22 37	22 59		
Bamford	d	20 40			21 36				22 40	23 02		
Hathersage	d	20 44			21 39				22 44	23 05		
Grindleford	d	20 47			21 43				22 47	23 12		
Dore & Totley	d	20 56		21 03	21 51			22 05	22 56	23 18		
Sheffield 7	a	21 02		21 09	22 00	21 34		22 11	23 02	23 26	23 09	00 10

A To Hadfield
B To Cleethorpes
C From Liverpool Lime Street to Nottingham
D To Doncaster

Table T078A

Mondays to Fridays
16 December to 15 May

Stockport - Reddish South - Denton and Stalybridge

Miles			
0	Stockport	84,86	d
1½	Reddish South		d
3½	Denton		d
5	Guide Bridge	78,79	d
7½	Stalybridge	39	a
—	Stalybridge		d
—	Guide Bridge		d
—	Denton		d
—	Reddish South		d
—	Stockport		a

Saturdays
21 December to 16 May

			NT	NT
Stockport	84,86	d		09 45
Reddish South		d		09 50
Denton		d		09 56
Guide Bridge	78,79	d		10 00
Stalybridge	39	a		10 05
Stalybridge		d	08 46	
Guide Bridge		d	08 51	
Denton		d	08 56	
Reddish South		d	09 00	
Stockport		a	09 08	

No Sunday Service

Table T079-F

Manchester - Glossop and Hadfield

Mondays to Fridays
16 December to 15 May

Miles	Miles			NT	NT	NT	NT	NT	NT	NT	NT	NT		NT	NT	NT	NT	NT	NT	NT	NT
0	—	**Manchester Picc.** 10	78 d	05 32	05 52	06 24	06 47	07 07	07 26	07 42	08 03	08 33	and every 30 minutes until	16 03	16 32	16 44	17 07	17 26	17 42	18 06	18 32
0½	—	Ardwick	78 d																	18 09	
1½	—	Ashburys	78 d	05 36	05 56	06 28	06 51	07 11	07 30	07 46	08 07	08 37		16 07	16 36	16 48	17 11	17 30	17 46	18 12	18 36
2½	—	Gorton	78 d													16 51			17 49		18 38
4¾	—	Guide Bridge	78 d	05 41	06 01	06 33	06 56	07 18	07 35	07 51	08 12	08 42		16 12	16 41	16 56	17 16	17 37	17 53	18 17	18 42
6¾	—	Flowery Field	d		06 04	06 36	06 59	07 21	07 38	07 55	08 15	08 45		16 15	16 45	16 59	17 20	17 40	17 56	18 20	18 45
7½	—	Newton for Hyde	d		06 07	06 39	07 02	07 23	07 41	07 57	08 18	08 47		16 17	16 48	17 02	17 23	17 42	17 59	18 22	18 47
8½	—	Godley	d		06 10	06 41	07 04	07 25	07 43	08 00	08 20	08 49		16 19	16 50	17 04	17 26	17 44	18 01	18 25	18 49
9	—	Hattersley	d		06 12	06 44	07 07	07 28	07 46	08 02	08 23	08 51		16 21	16 53	17 07	17 29	17 47	18 04	18 27	18 51
10	—	Broadbottom	d		06 16	06 47	07 10	07 31	07 49	08 05	08 26	08 54		16 24	16 56	17 10	17 33	17 49	18 07	18 31	18 54
12¼	0	Dinting 3	d		06 22	06 53	07 16	07 37	07 59	08 11	08 33	08 59		16 29	17 02	17 16	17 39	17 55	18 13	18 37	18 59
13¼	—	**Glossop**	a		06 25	06 56						09 03		16 33	17 05	17 19	17 43	17 58	18 16	18 40	19 03
—	—		d		06 28	06 59						09 05		16 35	17 08	17 22	17 46	18 03	18 20	18 43	19 05
15	0¾	**Hadfield**	a	05 55	06 34	07 05	07 19	07 40	08 02	08 14	08 36	09 11		16 41	17 14	17 28	17 52	18 09	18 26	18 49	19 11

		NT		NT	NT	NT	NT
Manchester Picc. 10	78 d	19 03	and every 30 minutes until	21 33	22 00	22 30	23 29
Ardwick	78 d						
Ashburys	78 d	19 07		21 37	22 04	22 34	23 33
Gorton	78 d				22 06	22 36	23 35
Guide Bridge	78 d	19 12		21 42	22 10	22 40	23 39
Flowery Field	d	19 15		21 45	22 13	22 43	23 42
Newton for Hyde	d	19 17		21 47	22 15	22 45	23 44
Godley	d	19 19		21 49	22 17	22 47	23 46
Hattersley	d	19 21		21 51	22 19	22 49	23 48
Broadbottom	d	19 24		21 54	22 22	22 52	23 50
Dinting 3	d	19 29		21 59	22 29	23 00	23 56
Glossop	a	19 33		22 03	22 33	23 04	
	d	19 35		22 05	22 35	23 06	
Hadfield	a	19 41		22 11	22 41	23 12	23 58

Saturdays
21 December to 16 May

		NT	NT	NT		NT	NT	NT	NT	NT		NT	NT	NT	NT
Manchester Picc. 10	78 d	06 03	06 30	07 03	and every 30 minutes until	17 03	17 32	18 03	18 32	19 03	and every 30 minutes until	21 33	22 00	22 30	23 29
Ardwick	78 d														
Ashburys	78 d	06 07	06 34	07 07		17 07	17 36	18 07	18 36	19 07		21 37	22 04	22 34	23 33
Gorton	78 d								18 38				22 06	22 36	23 35
Guide Bridge	78 d	06 12	06 39	07 12		17 12	17 41	18 12	18 42	19 12		21 42	22 10	22 40	23 39
Flowery Field	d	06 15	06 43	07 15		17 15	17 44	18 15	18 45	19 15		21 45	22 13	22 43	23 42
Newton for Hyde	d	06 17	06 45	07 17		17 17	17 47	18 17	18 47	19 17		21 47	22 15	22 45	23 44
Godley	d	06 19	06 47	07 19		17 19	17 49	18 19	18 49	19 19		21 49	22 17	22 47	23 46
Hattersley	d	06 21	06 49	07 21		17 21	17 51	18 21	18 51	19 21		21 51	22 19	22 49	23 48
Broadbottom	d	06 24	06 52	07 24		17 24	17 54	18 24	18 54	19 24		21 54	22 22	22 52	23 50
Dinting 3	d	06 29	06 59	07 29		17 29	17 59	18 29	18 59	19 29		21 59	22 29	23 00	23 56
Glossop	a	06 33	07 03	07 33		17 33	18 03	18 33	19 03	19 33		22 03	22 33	23 04	
	d	06 35	07 05	07 35		17 35	18 05	18 35	19 05	19 35		22 05	22 35	23 06	
Hadfield	a	06 41	07 11	07 41		17 41	18 11	18 41	19 11	19 41		22 11	22 41	23 12	23 58

Sundays
15 December to 10 May

		NT	NT A	NT B	NT	NT	NT A	NT B	NT A	NT B	NT B	NT A	NT B	NT A	NT		NT	NT	NT		NT
Manchester Picc. 10	78 d	09 29	09 59	10 03	10 33	11 03	11 26	11 33	12 01	12 02	12 30	12 33	13 00	13 03	13 33	and every 30 minutes until	16 03	16 32	17 03	and every 30 minutes until	20 03
Ardwick	78 d																				
Ashburys	78 d	09 33	10 03	10 07	10 37	11 07	11 30	11 37	12 05	12 07	12 34	12 37	13 04	13 07	13 37		16 07	16 36	17 07		20 07
Gorton	78 d	09 36	10 05	10 09	10 39	11 09	11 33	11 39	12 07	12 09	12 36	12 39	13 07	13 09	13 39		16 09	16 38	17 09		20 09
Guide Bridge	78 d	09 44	10 11	10 13	10 43	11 13	11 41	11 43	12 12	12 13	12 43	12 43	13 10	13 13	13 43		16 13	16 42	17 13		20 13
Flowery Field	d	09 47	10 14	10 16	10 46	11 16	11 44	11 46	12 15	12 16	12 46	12 46	13 14	13 16	13 46		16 16	16 45	17 16		20 16
Newton for Hyde	d	09 50	10 16	10 18	10 48	11 18	11 46	11 48	12 17	12 18	12 48	12 48	13 16	13 18	13 48		16 18	16 47	17 18		20 18
Godley	d	09 52	10 18	10 20	10 50	11 20	11 48	11 50	12 19	12 20	12 50	12 50	13 19	13 20	13 50		16 20	16 49	17 20		20 20
Hattersley	d	09 55	10 20	10 22	10 52	11 22	11 50	11 52	12 21	12 22	12 52	12 52	13 21	13 22	13 52		16 22	16 51	17 22		20 22
Broadbottom	d	09 58	10 22	10 24	10 54	11 24	11 52	11 54	12 23	12 24	12 54	12 54	13 24	13 24	13 54		16 24	16 53	17 24		20 24
Dinting 3	d	10 04	10 28	10 30	11 00	11 30	12 00	12 00	12 30	12 30	13 00	13 00	13 30	13 30	14 00		16 30	17 00	17 30		20 30
Glossop	a		10 31	10 33	11 03	11 33	12 03	12 03	12 33	12 33	13 03	13 03	13 33	13 33	14 03		16 33	17 03	17 33		20 33
	d		10 34	10 36	11 06	11 36	12 06	12 06	12 36	12 36	13 06	13 06	13 36	13 36	14 06		16 36	17 06	17 36		20 36
Hadfield	a	10 06	10 40	10 42	11 12	11 42	12 12	12 12	12 42	12 42	13 12	13 12	13 42	13 42	14 12		16 42	17 12	17 42		20 42

		NT
Manchester Picc. 10	78 d	21 02
Ardwick	78 d	
Ashburys	78 d	21 06
Gorton	78 d	21 08
Guide Bridge	78 d	21 12
Flowery Field	d	21 15
Newton for Hyde	d	21 17
Godley	d	21 19
Hattersley	d	21 21
Broadbottom	d	21 23
Dinting 3	d	21 29
Glossop	a	21 32
	d	21 35
Hadfield	a	21 41

A from 5 April
B until 29 March

Table T079-R

Hadfield and Glossop - Manchester

Mondays to Fridays
16 December to 15 May

Miles	Miles			NT MX	NT	NT	NT	NT	NT	NT	NT	NT	NT	NT	NT	NT	NT		NT	NT	NT	NT
0	0	**Hadfield**	d	00 01	05 45	06 05	06 37	07 08	07 21	07 42	08 04	08 17	08 39	09 14	09 44	10 14	10 44	and every 30 minutes until	13 14	13 44	14 14	14 44
1¾	—	**Glossop**	a	00 06	05 50	06 11	06 43	07 14	07 27	07 48	08 10	08 23	08 45	09 19	09 49	10 19	10 49		13 19	13 49	14 19	14 49
—	—		d		05 54	06 13	06 45	07 17	07 30	07 51	08 13	08 25	08 49	09 22	09 52	10 22	10 52		13 22	13 52	14 22	14 52
2¾	0¾	Dinting 3	d		05 57	06 17	06 49	07 21	07 34	07 55	08 17	08 29	08 53	09 25	09 55	10 25	10 55		13 25	13 55	14 25	14 55
5	—	Broadbottom	d		06 01	06 22	06 54	07 26	07 38	07 59	08 21	08 34	08 57	09 29	09 59	10 29	10 59		13 29	13 59	14 29	14 59
6	—	Hattersley	d		06 04	06 24	06 56	07 28	07 41	08 02	08 24	08 37	09 00	09 32	10 02	10 32	11 02		13 32	14 02	14 32	15 02
6½	—	Godley	d		06 06	06 27	06 59	07 31	07 43	08 04	08 26	08 39	09 03	09 34	10 04	10 34	11 04		13 34	14 04	14 34	15 04
7½	—	Newton for Hyde	d		06 08	06 29	07 01	07 33	07 45	08 07	08 28	08 42	09 05	09 36	10 06	10 36	11 06		13 36	14 06	14 36	15 06
8¼	—	Flowery Field	d		06 10	06 32	07 03	07 35	07 48	08 09	08 31	08 45	09 08	09 38	10 08	10 38	11 08		13 38	14 08	14 38	15 08
10¼	—	Guide Bridge	78 a		06 13	06 35	07 07	07 39	07 53	08 12	08 34	08 50	09 11	09 41	10 12	10 42	11 12		13 42	14 12	14 44	15 14
12½	—	Gorton	78 a		06 17				07 56	08 16		08 54										
13½	—	Ashburys	78 a		06 20	06 41	07 13	07 44	07 59	08 20	08 39	08 59	09 18	09 49	10 17	10 48	11 17		13 47	14 17	14 50	15 19
14½	—	Ardwick	78 a				07 15															
15	—	**Manchester Picc.** 10	78 a		06 26	06 47	07 19	07 51	08 06	08 26	08 46	09 07	09 24	09 54	10 23	10 55	11 23		13 53	14 25	14 56	15 26

		NT	NT	NT	NT	NT	NT	NT	NT	NT	NT	NT	NT	NT	NT	NT	NT	NT	NT
Hadfield	d	15 14	15 44	16 14	16 44	17 19	17 31	17 56	18 14	18 29	18 52	19 14	19 44	20 14	20 44	21 14	21 44	22 14	22 45
Glossop	a	15 19	15 49	16 19	16 49							19 19	19 49	20 19	20 49	21 19	21 49	22 19	22 50
	d	15 22	15 52	16 22	16 52							19 22	19 52	20 22	20 52	21 22	21 52	22 22	22 53
Dinting 3	d	15 25	15 55	16 25	16 55	17 22	17 34	17 59	18 17	18 32	18 55	19 25	19 55	20 25	20 55	21 25	21 55	22 25	22 56
Broadbottom	d	15 29	15 59	16 29	16 59	17 26	17 38	18 03	18 21	18 36	18 59	19 29	19 59	20 29	20 59	21 29	21 59	22 29	23 00
Hattersley	d	15 32	16 02	16 32	17 02	17 29	17 41	18 06	18 24	18 39	19 02	19 32	20 02	20 32	21 02	21 32	22 02	22 32	23 03
Godley	d	15 34	16 04	16 34	17 04	17 31	17 43	18 08	18 26	18 41	19 04	19 34	20 04	20 34	21 04	21 34	22 04	22 34	23 05
Newton for Hyde	d	15 36	16 06	16 36	17 06	17 34	17 45	18 11	18 28	18 44	19 07	19 36	20 06	20 36	21 06	21 36	22 06	22 36	23 07
Flowery Field	d	15 38	16 08	16 38	17 08	17 36	17 48	18 13	18 31	18 46	19 09	19 38	20 08	20 38	21 08	21 38	22 08	22 38	23 09
Guide Bridge	78 a	15 42	16 11	16 42	17 11	17 41	17 51	18 17	18 34	18 50	19 12	19 42	20 12	20 42	21 11	21 42	22 11	22 42	23 12
Gorton	78 a														21 14		22 14		23 15
Ashburys	78 a	15 47	16 17	16 47	17 16	17 50	17 57	18 22	18 42	18 56	19 17	19 47	20 17	20 47	21 17	21 47	22 17	22 48	23 18
Ardwick	78 a																		
Manchester Picc. 10	78 a	15 53	16 24	16 53	17 22	17 58	18 04	18 29	18 48	19 01	19 23	19 53	20 23	20 53	21 23	21 55	22 24	22 53	23 24

Saturdays
21 December to 16 May

		NT	NT	NT	NT	NT	NT	NT	NT	NT	NT	NT	NT		NT	NT	NT	NT	NT	NT	NT
Hadfield	d	00 01	05 45	06 11	06 44	07 14	07 44	08 14	08 44	09 14	09 44	10 14	10 44	and every 30 minutes until	15 14	15 44	16 14	16 44	17 14	17 44	18 14
Glossop	a	00 06	05 50	06 16	06 49	07 19	07 49	08 19	08 49	09 19	09 49	10 19	10 49		15 19	15 49	16 19	16 49	17 19	17 49	18 19
	d		05 53	06 19	06 52	07 22	07 52	08 22	08 52	09 22	09 52	10 22	10 52		15 22	15 52	16 22	16 52	17 22	17 52	18 22
Dinting 3	d		05 56	06 22	06 55	07 25	07 55	08 25	08 55	09 25	09 55	10 25	10 55		15 25	15 55	16 25	16 55	17 25	17 55	18 25
Broadbottom	d		06 00	06 26	06 59	07 29	07 59	08 29	08 59	09 29	09 59	10 29	10 59		15 29	15 59	16 29	16 59	17 29	17 59	18 29
Hattersley	d		06 03	06 29	07 02	07 32	08 02	08 32	09 02	09 32	10 02	10 32	11 02		15 32	16 02	16 32	17 02	17 32	18 02	18 32
Godley	d		06 05	06 31	07 04	07 34	08 04	08 34	09 04	09 34	10 04	10 34	11 04		15 34	16 04	16 34	17 04	17 34	18 04	18 34
Newton for Hyde	d		06 07	06 33	07 06	07 36	08 06	08 36	09 06	09 36	10 06	10 36	11 06		15 36	16 06	16 36	17 06	17 36	18 06	18 36
Flowery Field	d		06 09	06 35	07 08	07 38	08 08	08 38	09 08	09 38	10 08	10 38	11 08		15 38	16 08	16 38	17 08	17 38	18 08	18 38
Guide Bridge	78 a		06 12	06 39	07 12	07 42	08 12	08 42	09 12	09 41	10 12	10 42	11 12		15 42	16 11	16 42	17 11	17 41	18 11	18 41
Gorton	78 a		06 16	06 42	07 15																
Ashburys	78 a		06 19	06 45	07 18	07 47	08 17	08 47	09 17	09 49	10 17	10 48	11 17		15 47	16 17	16 47	17 16	17 46	18 16	18 47
Ardwick	78 a																				
Manchester Picc. 10	78 a		06 25	06 52	07 24	07 53	08 23	08 53	09 24	09 54	10 23	10 55	11 23		15 53	16 23	16 53	17 23	17 53	18 23	18 53

		NT		NT	NT	NT	NT	NT	NT
Hadfield	d	18 44	and every 30 minutes until	20 14	20 44	21 14	21 44	22 14	22 45
Glossop	a	18 49		20 19	20 49	21 19	21 49	22 19	22 50
	d	18 52		20 22	20 52	21 22	21 52	22 22	22 53
Dinting 3	d	18 55		20 25	20 55	21 25	21 55	22 25	22 56
Broadbottom	d	18 59		20 29	20 59	21 29	21 59	22 29	23 00
Hattersley	d	19 02		20 32	21 02	21 32	22 02	22 32	23 03
Godley	d	19 04		20 34	21 04	21 34	22 04	22 34	23 05
Newton for Hyde	d	19 06		20 36	21 06	21 36	22 06	22 36	23 07
Flowery Field	d	19 08		20 38	21 08	21 38	22 08	22 38	23 09
Guide Bridge	78 a	19 12		20 42	21 11	21 42	22 11	22 42	23 12
Gorton	78 a				21 14		22 14		23 15
Ashburys	78 a	19 17		20 47	21 17	21 47	22 17	22 48	23 18
Ardwick	78 a								
Manchester Picc. 10	78 a	19 23		20 53	21 23	21 55	22 24	22 53	23 24

A not 15 December
B from 5 April
C until 29 March

Table T079-R

Hadfield and Glossop - Manchester

Sundays

15 December to 10 May

		NT A	NT	NT	NT B	NT C	NT B	NT C	NT B	NT C	NT C	NT B	NT	NT	NT	NT	NT	NT	NT		NT	NT
Hadfield	d	00 01	09 47	10 11	10 43	10 45	11 15	11 15	11 45	11 45	12 15	12 15	12 45	13 15	13 45	14 15	14 45	15 15	15 45		17 45	18 15
Glossop	a	00 06	09 52	10 16	10 48	10 50	11 20	11 20	11 50	11 50	12 20	12 20	12 50	13 20	13 50	14 20	14 50	15 20	15 50		17 50	18 20
	d		09 55	10 19	10 51	10 53	11 23	11 23	11 53	11 53	12 23	12 23	12 53	13 23	13 53	14 23	14 53	15 23	15 53		17 53	18 23
Dinting ■	d		09 58	10 22	10 54	10 56	11 26	11 26	11 56	11 56	12 26	12 26	12 56	13 26	13 56	14 26	14 56	15 26	15 56	and	17 56	18 26
Broadbottom	d		10 02	10 26	10 58	11 00	11 30	11 30	12 00	12 00	12 30	12 30	13 00	13 30	14 00	14 30	15 00	15 30	16 00	every 30	18 00	18 30
Hattersley	d		10 05	10 29	11 01	11 03	11 33	11 33	12 03	12 03	12 33	12 33	13 03	13 33	14 03	14 33	15 03	15 33	16 03	minutes	18 03	18 33
Godley	d		10 07	10 31	11 03	11 05	11 35	11 35	12 05	12 05	12 35	12 35	13 05	13 35	14 05	14 35	15 05	15 35	16 05	until	18 05	18 35
Newton for Hyde	d		10 09	10 33	11 05	11 07	11 37	11 37	12 07	12 07	12 37	12 37	13 07	13 37	14 07	14 37	15 07	15 37	16 07		18 07	18 37
Flowery Field	d		10 11	10 35	11 07	11 09	11 39	11 39	12 09	12 09	12 39	12 39	13 09	13 39	14 09	14 39	15 09	15 39	16 09		18 09	18 39
Guide Bridge 78	a		10 14	10 38	11 10	11 12	11 42	11 42	12 12	12 12	12 42	12 42	13 12	13 42	14 12	14 42	15 12	15 42	16 12		18 12	18 42
Gorton 78	a		10 17	10 41	11 13	11 15		11 45	12 15	12 16		12 45	13 15	13 45	14 15	14 45	15 15	15 45	16 15		18 15	18 45
Ashburys 78	a		10 20	10 44	11 16	11 18		11 48	12 18	12 18		12 48	13 18	13 48	14 18	14 52	15 18	15 52	16 18		18 18	18 52
Ardwick 78	a																					
Manchester Picc. ■ 78	a		10 25	10 51	11 22	11 25	11 52	11 54	12 25	12 26	12 52	12 54	13 24	13 54	14 24	14 58	15 24	15 58	16 24		18 24	18 58

A not 15 December B from 5 April C until 29 March

		NT	NT	NT	NT	NT	NT
Hadfield	d	18 45	19 15	19 45	20 15	20 45	21 44
Glossop	a	18 50	19 20	19 50	20 20	20 50	21 49
	d	18 53	19 23	19 53	20 23	20 53	21 52
Dinting ■	d	18 56	19 26	19 56	20 26	20 56	21 55
Broadbottom	d	19 00	19 30	20 00	20 30	21 00	21 59
Hattersley	d	19 03	19 33	20 03	20 33	21 03	22 02
Godley	d	19 05	19 35	20 05	20 35	21 05	22 04
Newton for Hyde	d	19 07	19 37	20 07	20 37	21 07	22 06
Flowery Field	d	19 09	19 39	20 09	20 39	21 09	22 08
Guide Bridge 78	a	19 12	19 42	20 12	20 42	21 12	22 11
Gorton 78	a	19 15	19 45	20 15	20 45	21 15	22 14
Ashburys 78	a	19 18	19 48	20 18	20 50	21 18	22 17
Ardwick 78	a						
Manchester Picc. ■ 78	a	19 24	19 54	20 24	20 56	21 24	22 23

NRT DECEMBER 19 EDITION

Table T081-F

Mondays to Fridays

16 December to 15 May

London and Birmingham - Crewe and Liverpool / Manchester - Chester and North Wales

Miles	Miles			AW MX ◇ A	AW MX B	AW MO ◇ C	AW MO ◇ D	AW MO ◇ B	AW MX ◇ A	AW MO ◇ A	AW MX ◇ E	AW MX	NT F	AW	AW	AW	AW	AW ◇ G	NT ◇	AW ◇ H	NT ◇ I	NT ■	VT ◇■ ⊠
—	—	London Euston ■ ⊖65	d																				
—	—	Birmingham New Street ■ 65	d																				05 30
—	—	Manchester Airport 84,85 ✈	d															05 33					
—	—	Cardiff Central ■ 131	d																				
0	—	**Crewe** ■	d			00 01			00 07	00 10	00 15											06 16	06 23
—	0	**Manchester Pic'dilly** ■ 90	d									00 32						05 48		06 50		07 22	
—	0½	**Manchester Oxford Road** 90	d															05 51		06 53		07 25	
—	—	**Manchester Victoria** 90	d																06 14		07 07		
—	16¼	Newton-le-Willows 90	d															06 09	06 35	07 13	07 30	07 48	
—	18	Earlestown ■ 90	d										05 32					06 12	06 38	07 17	07 33	07 50	
—	22	Warrington Bank Quay 90	d										05 42					06 21	06 46	07 25	07 45		
—	27	Runcorn East	d					00 03					05 50					06 28		07 32			
—	—	**Liverpool Lime Street** 91	d																			08a25	
—	—	**Liverpool South Parkway** 91	d																				
—	—	Runcorn 91	a																				
—	30¼	Frodsham	d		00 02			00 08					05 55					06 33		07 37			
—	32¾	Helsby	d		00 06			00 12					05a59					06 38		07 41			
21	40¼	**Chester**	a		00 17	00 23		00 25	00 26	00 34	00 38	01 37						06 51	07 11	07 54	08 09		06 43
—	—		d					00 38			00 40							06 55		07 55			06 43
29	—	Shotton	d															→		→			
33½	—	Flint	d					00 51			00 53												06 56
47½	—	Prestatyn	d					01 04			01 06												07 09
51	—	Rhyl	d					01 10			01 12												07 15
55¼	—	Abergele & Pensarn	d																				
61½	—	Colwyn Bay	d					01 21			01 23												07 26
65½	0	**Llandudno Junction**	a					01 28			01 30												07 31
—	—		d					01 28			01 30			05 40	06 13	06 51	07 31						07 32
—	1¼	Deganwy	d											05x43	06x16	06x54	07x34						
—	3	**Llandudno**	a											05 49	06 21	06 59	07 41						
66½	—	Conwy	d																				
70¾	—	Penmaenmawr	d	00x01			00x03																
73¼	—	Llanfairfechan	d	00x05			00x07																
80¾	—	**Bangor (Gwynedd)**	a	00 15			00 16	01 45			01 47												07 48
—	—		d	00 15			00 17	01 45			01 47												07 49
84½	—	Llanfairpwll	d																				
93½	—	Bodorgan	d																				
96¼	—	Ty Croes	d																				
98	—	Rhosneigr	d																				
102	—	Valley	d																				
105½	—	**Holyhead** ■	a	00 43			00 51	02 13			02 15												08 19

		AW ◇ J	AW ◇	AW	LM ■ K	AW	NT	AW ◇ B	AW ◇	AW ◇	NT	AW ■	AW ◇ L	NT ◇ I	NT ◇	VT ◇■ K ⊠	LM ■ M	LM ■ N	AW ◇ O	NT ◇ I	NT ◇	AW	LM ■ M
London Euston ■ ⊖65	d															05 27							
Birmingham New Street ■ 65	d				06 02												06 36	07 04					07 36
Manchester Airport 84,85 ✈	d																						
Cardiff Central ■ 131	d									05 12													
Crewe ■	d		06 56		06 58	07 11									07 13	07 28	07 33	07 59			08 16	08 23	08 32
Manchester Pic'dilly ■ 90	d						06 14				07 09	07 50			08 23				08 52		09 22		
Manchester Oxford Road 90	d											07 55			08 26				08 55		09 26		
Manchester Victoria 90	d													08 07						09 07			
Newton-le-Willows 90	d											08 17		08 28	08 48				09 16	09 30	09 48		
Earlestown ■ 90	d											08 20		08 31	08 50				09 20	09 33	09 51		
Warrington Bank Quay 90	d											08 27		08 45					09 27	09 47			
Runcorn East	d											08 34							09 34	09 54			
Liverpool Lime Street 91	d								07 16						09a25						10a28		
Liverpool South Parkway 91	d								07 27														
Runcorn 91	a				07 23				07 35							07 45	07 59	08 24					08 52
Frodsham	d								07 45			08 39							09 39	09 59			
Helsby	d	←						←	07 50			08 43							09 43				
Chester	a	06 51	07 19			07 35	07 42	07 54	08 05	08 20	08 38	08 56		09 09					09 56	10 16		08 48	
	d	06 55	07 21					07 55		08 23		08 57							09 57				
Shotton	d		07 30					08 04		08 32									10 05				
Flint	d	07 08	07 36					08 10		08 38		09 09							→				
Prestatyn	d	07 21	07 49					08 23		08 50		09 22											
Rhyl	d	07 27	07 55					08 29		08 56		09 28											
Abergele & Pensarn	d		08 01					08 35		09 02													
Colwyn Bay	d	07 38	08 09					08 43		09 10		09 38											
Llandudno Junction	a	07 45	08 16					08 51		09 16		09 45											
	d	07 45	08 17	08 19						09 17		09 46	09 50										
Deganwy	d	07x49		08x22						09x20			09x53										
Llandudno	a	07 55		08 29						09 27			09 59										
Conwy	d		08x20									09x49											
Penmaenmawr	d		08x26									09x55											
Llanfairfechan	d		08x30									09x59											
Bangor (Gwynedd)	a		08 39									10 08											
	d		08 39									10 08											
Llanfairpwll	d		08x46																				
Bodorgan	d		08x56																				
Ty Croes	d		09x01																				
Rhosneigr	d		09x04																				
Valley	d		09x10																				
Holyhead ■	a		09 21									10 35											

A From Cardiff Central
B From Manchester Piccadilly
C From Birmingham International
D From Crewe
E From Birmingham New Street
F From Liverpool Lime Street to Ellesmere Port
G To Llandudno
H To Llandudno Junction
I From Leeds
J From Manchester Airport
K To Liverpool Lime Street
L From Blaenau Ffestiniog
M From Birmingham International to Liverpool Lime Street
N From Milton Keynes Central to Liverpool Lime Street
O To Holyhead

Table T081-F

Mondays to Fridays

16 December to 15 May

London and Birmingham - Crewe and Liverpool / Manchester - Chester and North Wales

Station		AW ◇	VT ◇1 A ⊠	VT ◇1 ⊠	NT	AW ◇ B ⌶	LM 1 A	AW ■ ⊠	AW ◇ C ⌶	AW ◇ D ⌶	NT ◇ E	NT ◇	AW	AW ◇	LM 1 F	VT ◇1 A ⊠	AW	VT ◇1 ⊠	AW	LM 1 A	NT	AW ◇ G ⌶
London Euston 15 ⊖65	d		07 07	07 10			05 34									08 07		08 10		06 34		
Birmingham New Street 12 65	d					07 23	08 04								08 38					09 04		
Manchester Airport 84,85 ✈	d																					
Cardiff Central 7 131	d							07 02														10 35
Crewe 10	d		08 43	08 47			08 58					09 16	09 25		09 33		09 42	09 50		09 58		
Manchester Pic'dilly 10 90 ⇌	d				07 41					09 52		10 22									08 41	10 52
Manchester Oxford Road 90	d									09u56		10 25										10 55
Manchester Victoria 90	d										10 07											
Newton-le-Willows 90	d									10 16	10 28	10 47										11 15
Earlestown 8 90	d									10 20	10 31	10 50										11 18
Warrington Bank Quay 90	d									10 31	10 44											11 26
Runcorn East	d									10 38												11 33
Liverpool Lime Street 91	d	08 36										11a28		09 13								
Liverpool South Parkway 91	d	08 46												09 23								
Runcorn 91	a	08 54	09 00				09 22							09 33	09 53	10 00				10 25		
Frodsham	d	09 03								10 44				09 47								11 38
Helsby	d	09 08								10 49				09 52								11 42
Chester	a	09 23		09 08	09 12	09 20		09 48	←	11 02	11 08		09 50	10 07			10 03	10 10			10 10	11 55
	d					09 24		09 52		11 03							10 05	10 14				11 56
Shotton	d					09 32			10 05	→							10 13					→
Flint	d					09 38			10 11								10 19	10 27				
Prestatyn	d					09 51			10 24								10 32	10 40				
Rhyl	d					09 57			10 30								10 38	10 46				
Abergele & Pensarn	d					10 03											10 44					
Colwyn Bay	d					10 11			10 39								10 52	10 58				
Llandudno Junction	a					10 17		10 31	10 46								10 59	11 03				
	d					10 18		10 32	10 46								10 59	11 04	11 28			
Deganwy	d					10x21											11x03		11x31			
Llandudno	a					10 28											11 09		11 38			
Conwy	d																					
Penmaenmawr	d																					
Llanfairfechan	d																					
Bangor (Gwynedd)	a							10 50	11 03									11 22				
	d							10 50	11 03									11 24				
Llanfairpwll	d								11x10													
Bodorgan	d								11x20													
Ty Croes	d								11x25													
Rhosneigr	d								11x28													
Valley	d								11x34													
Holyhead 30	a							11 20	11 43									11 53				

Station		NT ◇ E	NT ◇	AW	AW ◇ C ⌶	LM 1 F	NT	AW ◇	VT ◇1 A ⊠	VT ◇1 ⊠	AW ◇ B ⌶	AW ◇ H	LM 1 A	AW ◇ I ⌶	NT ◇	AW	AW ◇ J ⌶	AW	LM 1 F	AW ◇	VT ◇1 A ⊠	VT ◇1 ⊠	LM 1 A
London Euston 15 ⊖65	d								09 07	09 10			07 49								10 07	10 10	08 49
Birmingham New Street 12 65	d					09 37					09 25		10 04						10 37				11 04
Manchester Airport 84,85 ✈	d													11 35									
Cardiff Central 7 131	d																						
Crewe 10	d		10 16	10 25		10 33			10 43	10 47			10 59		11 17	11 24			11 33		11 43	11 47	11 58
Manchester Pic'dilly 10 90 ⇌	d		11 22				09 41							11 52	12 22								
Manchester Oxford Road 90	d		11 26											11 56	12 26								
Manchester Victoria 90	d	11 07																					
Newton-le-Willows 90	d	11 27	11 47											12 17	12 47								
Earlestown 8 90	d	11 30	11 50											12 20	12 49								
Warrington Bank Quay 90	d	11 39												12 28									
Runcorn East	d													→									
Liverpool Lime Street 91	d		12a24					10 36							13a24					11 36			
Liverpool South Parkway 91	d							10 47												11 46			
Runcorn 91	a					10 51		10 55	11 01				11 22						11 53	11 54	12 00		12 24
Frodsham	d							11 04												12 04			
Helsby	d				←			11 09									←			12 09			
Chester	a	12 05		10 50	11 02		11 12	11 24		11 12	11 21					11 49	11 55			12 24		12 08	
	d				11 03					11 13	11 25						11 56						
Shotton	d																12 05						
Flint	d										11 38						12 11						
Prestatyn	d				11 26						11 51						12 23						
Rhyl	d				11 33					11 41	11 57						12 29						
Abergele & Pensarn	d										12 03						12 35						
Colwyn Bay	d									11 52	12 11						12 43						
Llandudno Junction	a				11 47					11 58	12 18						12 51						
	d				11 48					12 00	12 19	12 36						12 58					
Deganwy	d											12x39						13x01					
Llandudno	a											12 46						13 06					
Conwy	d										12x22												
Penmaenmawr	d										12x28												
Llanfairfechan	d										12x33												
Bangor (Gwynedd)	a				12 04					12 19	12 42												
	d				12 05					12 19	12 42												
Llanfairpwll	d										12x49												
Bodorgan	d										12x59												
Ty Croes	d										13x04												
Rhosneigr	d										13x07												
Valley	d										13x13												
Holyhead 30	a				12 34					12 52	13 21												

A To Liverpool Lime Street
B From Birmingham International
C From Manchester Piccadilly
D To Holyhead
E From Leeds
F From Birmingham International to Liverpool Lime Street
G To Llandudno Junction
H From Blaenau Ffestiniog
I To Llandudno
J From Manchester Airport

Table T081-F

Mondays to Fridays

16 December to 15 May

London and Birmingham - Crewe and Liverpool / Manchester - Chester and North Wales

Station		NT	AW ◇ ⌶	AW ◇ A ⌶	NT ◇ B	AW ◇ C ⌶	NT ◇ B	NT ◇	AW	LM 1 D	AW ◇	VT ◇1 E ⊠	VT ◇1 ⊠	NT	AW ◇ F ⌶	AW	AW ◇ A ⌶	LM 1 E	AW ◇ C ⌶	NT ◇ B	NT ◇	AW	AW ◇
London Euston 15 ⊖65	d											11 07	11 10					09 49					
Birmingham New Street 12 65	d									11 37					11 25			12 04					
Manchester Airport 84,85 ✈	d					12 35													13 35				
Cardiff Central 7 131	d		09 22																				
Crewe 10	d							12 17	12 24	12 32		12 43	12 47					12 59			13 18	13 24	
Manchester Pic'dilly 10 90 ⇌	d	10 41				12 52		13 22						11 41					13 52		14 22		
Manchester Oxford Road 90	d					12 55		13 26											13 55		14 26		
Manchester Victoria 90	d				12 07		13 07													14 07			
Newton-le-Willows 90	d					13 15	13 27	13 48											14 16	14 26	14 47		
Earlestown 8 90	d			←		13 19	13 30	13 51											14 19	14 29	14 49		
Warrington Bank Quay 90	d			12 28	12 35	13 27	13 45												14 28	14 37			
Runcorn East	d			12 35		13 34													14 35				
Liverpool Lime Street 91	d							14a28			12 36										15a24		13 36
Liverpool South Parkway 91	d										12 47												13 47
Runcorn 91	a									12 53	12 55	13 00						13 22					13 55
Frodsham	d			12 39		13 39					13 04								14 40				14 04
Helsby	d			12 43		13 43					13 08								14 44				14 09
Chester	a	12 10	12 20	12 56	13 04	13 56	14 09		12 49		13 23		13 08	13 09	13 21		←		14 57	15 05		13 49	14 24
	d		12 23	12 57		13 57									13 25				14 57				
Shotton	d			13 06		14 06											14 06		15 06				
Flint	d		12 36	13 12		→									13 37		14 12		→				
Prestatyn	d		12 49	13 26											13 50		14 26						
Rhyl	d		12 56	13 32											13 57		14 32						
Abergele & Pensarn	d			13 38													14 38						
Colwyn Bay	d		13 06	13 46											14 07		14 46						
Llandudno Junction	a		13 13	13 53											14 14		14 53						
	d		13 14	13 53											14 14	14 28	14 53						
Deganwy	d			13x57												14x31	14x57						
Llandudno	a			14 02												14 38	15 03						
Conwy	d														14x18								
Penmaenmawr	d														14x24								
Llanfairfechan	d														14x28								
Bangor (Gwynedd)	a		13 30												14 36								
	d		13 34												14 38								
Llanfairpwll	d		13x42												14x44								
Bodorgan	d		13x52												14x54								
Ty Croes	d		13x56												14x59								
Rhosneigr	d		13x59												15x02								
Valley	d		14x05												15x08								
Holyhead 30	a		14 14												15 17								

Station		LM 1 D	VT ◇1 E ⊠	VT ◇1 ⊠	LM 1 E	NT	AW ■ ⊠	AW ◇ A ⌶	AW ◇ G	AW ◇ C ⌶	NT ◇	AW	LM 1 D	AW ◇	VT ◇1 E	VT ◇1	NT	AW ◇ F ⌶	AW ◇ A ⌶	LM 1 E	NT ◇ B	AW ◇ C ⌶
London Euston 15 ⊖65	d		12 07	12 10	10 49										13 07	13 10				11 49		
Birmingham New Street 12 65	d	12 37			13 04								13 37					13 25		14 04		
Manchester Airport 84,85 ✈	d									14 35												15 35
Cardiff Central 7 131	d						11 24															
Crewe 10	d	13 34	13 43	13 50	13 57						14 16	14 24	14 34		14 43	14 48				14 58		
Manchester Pic'dilly 10 90 ⇌	d					12 41				14 52	15 22						13 41					15 52
Manchester Oxford Road 90	d									14 55	15 26											15 55
Manchester Victoria 90	d																				15 07	
Newton-le-Willows 90	d									15 16	15 47											16 15
Earlestown 8 90	d									15 19	15 49								←			16 18
Warrington Bank Quay 90	d									15 28									15 28		15 39	16 26
Runcorn East	d									→									15 35			16 33
Liverpool Lime Street 91	d										16a26			14 36								
Liverpool South Parkway 91	d													14 47								
Runcorn 91	a	13 56	14 00		14 23								14 54	14 55	15 00					15 22		
Frodsham	d													15 04					15 39			16 38
Helsby	d													15 09					15 43			16 42
Chester	a			14 11		14 12	14 23	←				14 49		15 24		15 08	15 10	15 20	15 56		16 05	16 55
	d						14 27											15 24	15 57			16 55
Shotton	d							15 06											16 06			17 04
Flint	d						14 41	15 12										15 38	16 12			→
Prestatyn	d						14 55	15 24										15 51	16 24			
Rhyl	d						15 02	15 30										15 57	16 30			
Abergele & Pensarn	d							15 36											16 36			
Colwyn Bay	d						15 12	15 44										16 07	16 44			
Llandudno Junction	a						15 20	15 51										16 14	16 51			
	d						15 20	15 52	16 05									16 20	16 52			
Deganwy	d							15x55	16x08										16x56			
Llandudno	a							16 02	16 15										17 03			
Conwy	d																	16x23				
Penmaenmawr	d																	16x30				
Llanfairfechan	d																	16x34				
Bangor (Gwynedd)	a						15 37											16 43				
	d						15 38											16 44				
Llanfairpwll	d																					
Bodorgan	d																					
Ty Croes	d																					
Rhosneigr	d																					
Valley	d																					
Holyhead 30	a						16 06											17 15				

A From Manchester Airport
B From Leeds
C To Llandudno
D From Birmingham International to Liverpool Lime Street
E To Liverpool Lime Street
F From Birmingham International
G From Blaenau Ffestiniog

Table T081-F

Mondays to Fridays
16 December to 15 May

London and Birmingham - Crewe and Liverpool / Manchester - Chester and North Wales

Station		NT	NT	AW	LM	AW	VT	VT	LM	NT	AW	AW	AW	AW	NT	AW	NT	AW	LM	AW	VT	VT	NT
		◇ A	◇		■1 B	◇	◇■1 C ⊡	◇■1 ⊡	■1 C		◇ 🛒	◇ D 🛒		■ E 🛒	◇ F		◇		■1 B	◇	◇■1 C ⊡	◇■1 ⊡	
London Euston ■15 ⊖65	d						14 07	14 10	12 49												15 07	15 10	
Birmingham New Street ■12 65	d				14 37														15 37				
Manchester Airport 84,85 ✈	d																						
Cardiff Central ■7 131	d										13 22												
Crewe ■10	d		15 16	15 24	15 34		15 43	15 47	15 58								16 16	16 24	16 32		16 43	16 47	
Manchester Pic'dilly ■10 90	d		16 22							14 41				16 50		17 15	17 23						15 41
Manchester Oxford Road 90	d		16 26											16u54		17 18	17 26						
Manchester Victoria 90	d	16 07													17 07								
Newton-le-Willows 90	d	16 27	16 47											17 16		17 36	17 48						
Earlestown ■8 90	d	16 30	16 49											17 19		17 39	17 50						
Warrington Bank Quay 90	d	16 39												17 29	17 36	17 47							
Runcorn East	d	16 47												17 37	17 46	17 54							
Liverpool Lime Street 91	d		17a23			15 36											18a28			16 36			
Liverpool South Parkway 91	d					15 47														16 47			
Runcorn 91	a				15 51	15 55	16 00		16 25										16 52	16 55	17 00		
Frodsham	d	16 52				16 04								17 43	17 51	18 02				17 04			
Helsby	d					16 09								17 48	17a55	18 07				17 09			
Chester	a	17 06		15 49		16 26		16 08		16 10	16 24	←		18 02		18 19		16 49		17 24		17 08	17 11
	d										16 28			18 03									
Shotton	d											17 04											
Flint	d										16 40	17 10											
Prestatyn	d										16 53	17 24		18 27									
Rhyl	d										16 59	17 30		→									
Abergele & Pensarn	d											17 36											
Colwyn Bay	d										17 09	17 44											
Llandudno Junction	a										17 16	17 51											
	d										17 17	17 51	18 26										
Deganwy	d											17x55	18x29										
Llandudno	a											18 01	18 36										
Conwy	d										17x20												
Penmaenmawr	d										17x26												
Llanfairfechan	d										17x31												
Bangor (Gwynedd)	a										17 40												
	d										17 40												
Llanfairpwll	d										17x47												
Bodorgan	d										17x57												
Ty Croes	d										18x02												
Rhosneigr	d										18x05												
Valley	d										18x11												
Holyhead ■30	a										18 21												

Station		AW	AW	AW	LM	AW	LM	AW	VT	VT	LM	NT	AW	AW	AW	AW	AW	LM	VT	AW	NT	NT
		◇ G 🛒	◇ H	■ I 🛒	■1 C		■1 B	◇ J	◇■1 C ⊡	◇■1 ⊡	■1 C		■ 🛒		■ 🛒		◇	■1 B	◇■1 C ⊠	■ K		◇ A
London Euston ■15 ⊖65	d				13 49				16 07	16 10	14 49								17 07			
Birmingham New Street ■12 65	d	15 25			16 04		16 37				17 04							17 37				
Manchester Airport 84,85 ✈	d																					
Cardiff Central ■7 131	d												15 22							16 22		
Crewe ■10	d				16 58	17 24	17 33		17 43	17 48	17 58			18 24				18 36	18 44	18 45		
Manchester Pic'dilly ■10 90	d											16 41			17 52						17 41	
Manchester Oxford Road 90	d														17 55							
Manchester Victoria 90	d																					18 07
Newton-le-Willows 90	d														18 17							18 28
Earlestown ■8 90	d														18 20							18 30
Warrington Bank Quay 90	d														18 28							18 40
Runcorn East	d														18 35							18 48
Liverpool Lime Street 91	d							17 37									18 37					
Liverpool South Parkway 91	d							17 48									18 48					
Runcorn 91	a				17 24		17 52	17 57	18 00		18 24						18 56	19 00	19 01			
Frodsham	d							18 11							18 40		19 08					18 54
Helsby	d							18 16							18 45		19 13					18 58
Chester	a	17 22				17 49		18 30		18 07		18 10	18 22	18 49	18 58		19 28			19 05	19 09	19 14
	d	17 26								18 09			18 26		18 58							
Shotton	d	17 35											18 34		19 07							
Flint	d	17 41		←						18 23			18 40		19 13							
Prestatyn	d	17 54		18 27						18 36			18 53		19 25							
Rhyl	d	18 00		18 33						18 42			18 59		19 31							
Abergele & Pensarn	d	18 06											19 05									
Colwyn Bay	d	18 14		18 43						18 53			19 13		19 42							
Llandudno Junction	a	18 21		18 50						18 58			19 18		19 49							
	d	18 26	18 41	18 51						19 00			19 19		19 53	19 56						
Deganwy	d		18x44	18x56												19x59						
Llandudno	a		18 49	19 02												20 04						
Conwy	d	18x29													19x57							
Penmaenmawr	d	18x35													20x03							
Llanfairfechan	d	18x40													20x07							
Bangor (Gwynedd)	a	18 49								19 18			19 37		20 16							
	d	18 49											19 37		20 17							
Llanfairpwll	d												19x44									
Bodorgan	d												19x54									
Ty Croes	d												19x59									
Rhosneigr	d												20x02									
Valley	d												20x08									
Holyhead ■30	a	19 17											20 20		20 46							

A From Leeds
B From Birmingham International to Liverpool Lime Street
C To Liverpool Lime Street
D From Manchester Airport
E To Llandudno
F From Leeds to Ellesmere Port
G From Birmingham International
H From Blaenau Ffestiniog
I From Manchester Piccadilly
J To Wrexham General
K From Swansea

NRT DECEMBER 19 EDITION

Table T081-F

Mondays to Fridays
16 December to 15 May

London and Birmingham - Crewe and Liverpool / Manchester - Chester and North Wales

Station		VT	VT	AW	LM	VT	AW	NT	AW	NT	NT	AW	AW	AW	LM	VT	NT	VT	VT	VT	VT	AW	AW
		◇■1 ⊠	◇■1 ⊠	◇ A	■1 B	◇■1 B ⊠		◇ C		◇ C	◇		■ ⊠		■1 D	◇■1 B ⊠		◇■1 E ⊠	◇■1	◇■1 B ⊠	■ ■1 B ⊡	◇	◇ F
London Euston ■15 ⊖65	d	17 10	17 10		15 49	17 33										18 07		18 10		18 33	19 07		
Birmingham New Street ■12 65	d			17 26	18 04										18 37								
Manchester Airport 84,85 ✈	d																						
Cardiff Central ■7 131	d												17 16										
Crewe ■10	d	18 56	18 56		18 59	19 16					19 17	19 24			19 33	19 43		19 54		20 16			
Manchester Pic'dilly ■10 90	d						18 53		19 52		20 22						18 41						
Manchester Oxford Road 90	d						18 56		19 55		20 26												
Manchester Victoria 90	d							19 07		20 07													
Newton-le-Willows 90	d						19 18	19 26	20 17	20 26	20 48												
Earlestown ■8 90	d						19 22	19 28	20 20	20 33	20 50												
Warrington Bank Quay 90	d						19 30	19 43	20 27	20 43													
Runcorn East	d						19 37		20 34														
Liverpool Lime Street 91	d										21a27												
Liverpool South Parkway 91	d																						
Runcorn 91	a				19 23	19 35									19 57	20 00				20 33	20 50		
Frodsham	d						19 41		20 38														
Helsby	d						19 45		20 42														
Chester	a	19 15	19 15	19 22			19 57	20 07	20 55	21 07		19 49	19 58				20 10	20 13					
	d		19 23	19 32									20 02						20 26			20 34	
Shotton	d			19 41																		20 43	
Flint	d		19 36	19 47									20 14									20 49	
Prestatyn	d		19 49	20 00																		21 02	
Rhyl	d		19 55	20 06									20 31						20 53			21 08	
Abergele & Pensarn	d			20 12																		21 14	
Colwyn Bay	d		20 06	20 20									20 44						21 04			21 22	
Llandudno Junction	a		20 11	20 28									20 51						21 09			21 29	
	d		20 12	20 30									20 52	20 58					21 10			21 30	21 32
Deganwy	d			20x33										21x01									21x35
Llandudno	a			20 40										21 09									21 43
Conwy	d																					21x33	
Penmaenmawr	d																					21x39	
Llanfairfechan	d																					21x43	
Bangor (Gwynedd)	a		20 27										21 09						21 25			21 52	
	d		20 29										21 09						21 27			21 52	
Llanfairpwll	d																					21x58	
Bodorgan	d																					22x08	
Ty Croes	d																					22x13	
Rhosneigr	d																					22x16	
Valley	d																					22x21	
Holyhead ■30	a		21 00										21 41						21 56			22 32	

Station		AW	LM	AW FX	NT	VT	VT	AW	AW	AW	LM	AW	VT	NT	NT	AW	AW FX	AW FO	VT	AW	AW	NT	AW
			■1 D	■ G 🛒		■ ■1 ⊡	■ ■1 ⊡	◇ A	◇		■1 D	◇	◇■1 ⊡		◇ C	◇	◇	◇	◇■1 B ⊡				
London Euston ■15 ⊖65	d					19 10	19 10						20 10						20 07				
Birmingham New Street ■12 65	d		19 39					19 25			20 37										21 32		
Manchester Airport 84,85 ✈	d									20 34													
Cardiff Central ■7 131	d			18 22													19 34	19 34					
Crewe ■10	d	20 24	20 35	20 47		20 54	20 54				21 33	21 36	21 48						21 48	22 24			
Manchester Pic'dilly ■10 90	d				19 40					20 51				20 41							21 50	21 40	22 12
Manchester Oxford Road 90	d									20 54											21 53		22 15
Manchester Victoria 90	d														21 08								
Newton-le-Willows 90	d									21 12					21 26						22 11		22 38
Earlestown ■8 90	d									21 16					21 39						22 15		22 41
Warrington Bank Quay 90	d									21 27					21 50						22 24		22 49
Runcorn East	d									21 34											22 31		22 56
Liverpool Lime Street 91	d								20 38							21 40							
Liverpool South Parkway 91	d								20 50							21 51							
Runcorn 91	a		20 57						20 59		21 57					21 59			22 06				
Frodsham	d								21 08	21 38						22 08					22 35		23 01
Helsby	d								21 12	21 42						22 13					22 39		23 05
Chester	a	20 49		21 07	21 10	21 19	21 19	21 23	21 31	21 56		21 57	22 11	22 12	22 16	22 28	22 37	22 41		22 48	22 51	23 15	23 19
	d						21 25					22 04					22 56	22 56					
Shotton	d											22 13					23 05	23 05					
Flint	d						21 38					22 19					23 11	23 11					
Prestatyn	d						21 51					22 32					23 24	23 24					
Rhyl	d						21 57					22 38					23 30	23 30					
Abergele & Pensarn	d											22 44					23 36	23 36					
Colwyn Bay	d						22 08					22 52					23 44	23 44					
Llandudno Junction	a						22 13					22 59					23 51	23 51					
	d						22 15					23 00					23 52	23 52					
Deganwy	d																						
Llandudno	a																						
Conwy	d											23x03					23x55	23x55					
Penmaenmawr	d											23x09					00x01	00x01					
Llanfairfechan	d											23x14					00x05	00x05					
Bangor (Gwynedd)	a						22 30					23 24					00 15	00 14					
	d						22 31					23 24					00 15	00 14					
Llanfairpwll	d											23x31											
Bodorgan	d											23x41											
Ty Croes	d											23x46											
Rhosneigr	d											23x49											
Valley	d											23x55											
Holyhead ■30	a						23 01					00 04					00 43	00 43					

A From Birmingham International
B To Liverpool Lime Street
C From Leeds
D From Birmingham International to Liverpool Lime Street
E To Wrexham General
F From Blaenau Ffestiniog
G From Llanelli

Table T081-F

London and Birmingham - Crewe and Liverpool / Manchester - Chester and North Wales

Mondays to Fridays
16 December to 15 May

Station		AW	LM	AW	VT	AW	AW	NT	AW	AW	AW	NT
		◇ A	1 B	◇	◇1 C		◇			◇	◇	
London Euston 15 ⊖65	d				21 07							
Birmingham New Street 12 65	d	21 25	21 37								22 52	
Manchester Airport 84,85 ✈	d											
Cardiff Central 7 131	d									21 15		
Crewe 10	d		22 37		22 53	23 30				00 07	00 15	
Manchester Pic'dilly 10 90	d							22 41	23 14			23 41
Manchester Oxford Road 90	d								23 17			
Manchester Victoria 90	d											
Newton-le-Willows 90	d								23 36			
Earlestown 8 90	d								23 39			
Warrington Bank Quay 90	d								23 48			
Runcorn East	d								23 55			
Liverpool Lime Street 91	d			22 39			23 23					
Liverpool South Parkway 91	d			22 53			23 34					
Runcorn 91	a		23 00	23 01	23 11		23 42					
Frodsham	d			23 11			23 51		00 02			
Helsby	d			23 16			23 55		00 06			
Chester	a	23 20		23 32		23 53	00 10	00 13	00 17	00 26	00 38	01 09
	d										00 40	
Shotton	d											
Flint	d										00 53	
Prestatyn	d										01 06	
Rhyl	d										01 12	
Abergele & Pensarn	d											
Colwyn Bay	d										01 23	
Llandudno Junction	a										01 30	
	d										01 30	
Deganwy	d											
Llandudno	a											
Conwy	d											
Penmaenmawr	d											
Llanfairfechan	d											
Bangor (Gwynedd)	a										01 47	
	d										01 47	
Llanfairpwll	d											
Bodorgan	d											
Ty Croes	d											
Rhosneigr	d											
Valley	d											
Holyhead 30	a										02 15	

Saturdays
21 December to 16 May

Station		AW	AW	AW	AW	AW	NT	AW	AW	AW	AW	NT	AW	NT	NT	VT	AW	LM	AW	AW	NT	AW	NT
		◇ D	E	◇ D	◇ F		G				◇ H	◇	◇ H	◇ I	◇	◇1	◇ J	1 K	◇			◇ H	◇ I
London Euston 15 ⊖65	d																						
Birmingham New Street 12 65	d															05 30		06 04					
Manchester Airport 84,85 ✈	d										05 33												
Cardiff Central 7 131	d																						
Crewe 10	d			00 07	00 15										06 16	06 22		06 58	07 03				
Manchester Pic'dilly 10 90	d					00 32					05 47		06 50		07 22						06 13	07 52	
Manchester Oxford Road 90	d										05 50		06 53		07 25							07 55	
Manchester Victoria 90	d											06 14		07 07									08 07
Newton-le-Willows 90	d										06 08	06 35	07 13	07 31	07 49							08 17	08 28
Earlestown 8 90	d						05 32				06 11	06 38	07 16	07 34	07 51							08 20	08 31
Warrington Bank Quay 90	d						05 42				06 25	06 46	07 24	07 45								08 29	08 43
Runcorn East	d						05 50				06 32		07 31									08 37	
Liverpool Lime Street 91	d														08a23								
Liverpool South Parkway 91	d																						
Runcorn 91	a																	07 24					
Frodsham	d		00 02				05 55				06 37		07 35									08 42	
Helsby	d		00 06				05a59				06 42		07 39				←					08 46	
Chester	a		00 17	00 26	00 38	01 37					06 55	07 10	07 52	08 09		06 42	06 55		07 24		07 40	08 59	09 08
	d				00 40						06 56		07 55			06 44	06 56		07 26			09 00	
Shotton	d										→		→				07 05					09 09	
Flint	d				00 53											06 57	07 11		07 39			→	
Prestatyn	d				01 06											07 10	07 24		07 52				
Rhyl	d				01 12											07 15	07 30		07 58				
Abergele & Pensarn	d																07 36						
Colwyn Bay	d				01 23											07 26	07 44		08 09				
Llandudno Junction	a				01 30											07 31	07 51		08 16				
	d				01 30			06 13	06 51	07 31						07 32	07 52		08 16	08 28			
Deganwy	d							06x16	06x54	07x34							07x56			08x31			
Llandudno	a							06 23	07 01	07 41							08 02			08 38			
Conwy	d																		08x19				
Penmaenmawr	d	00x01																	08x25				
Llanfairfechan	d	00x05																	08x29				
Bangor (Gwynedd)	a	00 14			01 47											07 48			08 38				
	d	00 14			01 47											07 49			08 39				
Llanfairpwll	d																		08x45				
Bodorgan	d																		08x55				
Ty Croes	d																		09x00				
Rhosneigr	d																		09x03				
Valley	d																		09x09				
Holyhead 30	a	00 43			02 15											08 19			09 20				

A From Birmingham International to Manchester Piccadilly
B From Birmingham International to Liverpool Lime Street
C To Liverpool Lime Street
D From Cardiff Central
E From Manchester Piccadilly
F From Birmingham New Street
G From Liverpool Lime Street to Ellesmere Port
H To Llandudno
I From Leeds
J From Manchester Airport
K From Coventry to Liverpool Lime Street

Table T081-F

London and Birmingham - Crewe and Liverpool / Manchester - Chester and North Wales

Saturdays
21 December to 16 May

Station		NT	AW	AW	AW	AW	AW	AW	LM	LM	NT	AW	AW	NT	NT	AW	NT	AW	AW	AW	LM	AW	VT
		◇		◇ A	◇	◇		◇ A	1 B	1 C		◇ D	◇ E	◇ F	◇			G		◇ A	1 B	◇	◇1 H
London Euston 15 ⊖65	d																						07 07
Birmingham New Street 12 65	d								06 36	07 04								07 24			07 36		
Manchester Airport 84,85 ✈	d																						
Cardiff Central 7 131	d					05 21																	
Crewe 10	d	07 13	07 22						07 33	07 58					08 16	08 24					08 32		08 43
Manchester Pic'dilly 10 90	d	08 23									07 08		08 52		09 22		07 41						
Manchester Oxford Road 90	d	08 26											08 55		09 26								
Manchester Victoria 90	d													09 07									
Newton-le-Willows 90	d	08 48											09 17	09 30	09 48								
Earlestown 8 90	d	08 50											09 20	09 33	09 51								
Warrington Bank Quay 90	d												09 28	09 46									
Runcorn East	d												09 35	09 53									
Liverpool Lime Street 91	d	09a25			07 13										10a28							08 37	
Liverpool South Parkway 91	d				07 27																	08 48	
Runcorn 91	a				07 37				07 59	08 23											08 53	08 56	09 00
Frodsham	d				07 45								09 39	09 58								09 05	
Helsby	d			←	07 49								09 43									09 10	
Chester	a		07 47	07 52	08 05	08 20		←			08 38		09 56	10 16		08 49	09 12	09 21		←		09 25	
	d			07 55		08 24							09 57					09 25					
Shotton	d			08 04				09 09					10 06							10 06			
Flint	d			08 10		08 37		09 15					→					09 38		10 12			
Prestatyn	d			08 23		08 50		09 28										09 53		10 25			
Rhyl	d			08 29		08 56		09 34										09 59		10 31			
Abergele & Pensarn	d			08 35				09 40												10 37			
Colwyn Bay	d			08 43		09 07		09 48										10 12		10 45			
Llandudno Junction	a			08 50		09 14		09 55										10 19		10 52			
	d			08 51		09 14	09 28	09 55				10 07						10 20	10 28	10 53			
Deganwy	d			08x55			09x31	09x59				10x10							10x31	10x57			
Llandudno	a			09 01			09 38	10 06				10 16							10 38	11 03			
Conwy	d					09x18																	
Penmaenmawr	d					09x24																	
Llanfairfechan	d					09x28																	
Bangor (Gwynedd)	a					09 37												10 37					
	d					09 38												10 37					
Llanfairpwll	d																	10x44					
Bodorgan	d					09x53																	
Ty Croes	d					09x57																	
Rhosneigr	d					10x00																	
Valley	d																	11x02					
Holyhead 30	a					10 13												11 10					

Station		LM	AW	NT	NT	AW	AW	LM	VT	VT	NT	AW	AW	AW	LM	AW	NT	NT	AW	LM	NT	AW
		1 H	E	◇ F	◇		◇	1 B	◇1 H	◇1		◇		I	1 J	K	◇ F	◇		1 B		◇
London Euston 15 ⊖65	d	05 34							08 07	08 10												
Birmingham New Street 12 65	d	08 04						08 37							09 04					09 37		
Manchester Airport 84,85 ✈	d		09 35													10 35						
Cardiff Central 7 131	d											07 22										
Crewe 10	d	08 57			09 16	09 24		09 33	09 43	09 48					09 59			10 16	10 24	10 33		
Manchester Pic'dilly 10 90	d		09 52		10 22						08 41					10 52		11 22			09 41	
Manchester Oxford Road 90	d		09 55		10 25											10 55		11 26				
Manchester Victoria 90	d			10 07													11 07					
Newton-le-Willows 90	d		10 15	10 28	10 47											11 15	11 27	11 47				
Earlestown 8 90	d		10 18	10 31	10 50											11 18	11 30	11 50				
Warrington Bank Quay 90	d		10 27	10 39												11 27	11 39					
Runcorn East	d		10 34													11 34						
Liverpool Lime Street 91	d				11a28		09 13											12a24				10 37
Liverpool South Parkway 91	d						09 23															10 48
Runcorn 91	a	09 22					09 33	09 52	10 00						10 25					10 54		10 56
Frodsham	d		10 38				09 47									11 38						11 05
Helsby	d		10 42				09 52									11 42						11 10
Chester	a		10 55	11 05		09 49	10 09			10 09	10 10	10 20		←		11 55	12 05		10 49		11 12	11 25
	d		10 56									10 24				11 56						
Shotton	d		11 05											11 05		→						
Flint	d		→									10 36		11 11								
Prestatyn	d											10 50		11 24								
Rhyl	d											10 56		11 30								
Abergele & Pensarn	d													11 36								
Colwyn Bay	d											11 06		11 44								
Llandudno Junction	a											11 13		11 51								
	d											11 14	11 26	11 52								
Deganwy	d												11x29	11x56								
Llandudno	a												11 36	12 02								
Conwy	d											11x17										
Penmaenmawr	d											11x23										
Llanfairfechan	d											11x28										
Bangor (Gwynedd)	a											11 37										
	d											11 37										
Llanfairpwll	d																					
Bodorgan	d																					
Ty Croes	d																					
Rhosneigr	d																					
Valley	d																					
Holyhead 30	a											12 09										

A From Manchester Piccadilly
B From Birmingham International to Liverpool Lime Street
C From Bletchley to Liverpool Lime Street
D From Blaenau Ffestiniog
E To Llandudno
F From Leeds
G From Birmingham International
H To Liverpool Lime Street
I From Manchester Airport
J From Northampton to Liverpool Lime Street
K To Bangor (Gwynedd)

Table T081-F

Saturdays

21 December to 16 May

London and Birmingham - Crewe and Liverpool / Manchester - Chester and North Wales

	VT ◇■ A	VT ◇■	AW ■ B	AW	LM ■ A	AW ◇ C	AW ■ D	NT ◇	AW	AW ■ E	AW	LM ■ F	NT	AW ◇	VT ◇■ A	VT ◇■	LM ■ A	AW ◇	AW ■ E	NT ◇ G	AW ◇ D	NT ◇ G
London Euston ⊖65 d	09 07	09 10			07 49										10 07	10 10	08 49					
Birmingham New Street 65 d			09 25		10 03							10 37					11 04					
Manchester Airport 84,85 ✈ d							11 35														12 35	
Cardiff Central 131 d																		09 23				
Crewe d	10 45	10 48			10 58			11 17	11 24			11 31			11 43	11 54	11 58					
Manchester Pic'dilly 90 d							11 52	12 22					10 41								12 52	
Manchester Oxford Road 90 d							11 55	12 26													12 55	
Manchester Victoria 90 d																				12 07		13 07
Newton-le-Willows 90 d							12 16	12 47													13 15	13 27
Earlestown 90 d							12 19	12 49											←		13 18	13 30
Warrington Bank Quay 90 d							12 28												12 28	12 35	13 27	13 45
Runcorn East d							→												12 35		13 34	
Liverpool Lime Street 91 d								13a24						11 38								
Liverpool South Parkway 91 d														11 49								
Runcorn 91 a	11 01				11 24							11 52		11 57	12 00		12 24					
Frodsham d														12 07					12 40		13 38	
Helsby d										←				12 12					12 44		13 42	
Chester a		11 12	11 22						11 49	11 55			12 10	12 27		12 15		12 19	12 57	13 04	13 55	14 09
d		11 15	11 26							11 56								12 23	12 57		13 56	
Shotton d										12 05									13 06		14 05	
Flint d			11 39							12 11								12 36	13 12		→	
Prestatyn d			11 52							12 24								12 50	13 26			
Rhyl d		11 42	11 58							12 30								12 57	13 32			
Abergele & Pensarn d										12 36									13 38			
Colwyn Bay d		11 53	12 09							12 44								13 09	13 46			
Llandudno Junction a		11 59	12 16							12 51								13 16	13 53			
d		12 00	12 16	12 25		12 35				12 53	12 57							13 16	13 53			
Deganwy d				12x28		12x38					13x00								13x57			
Llandudno a				12 35		12 45					13 07								14 03			
Conwy d										12x56												
Penmaenmawr d										13x02												
Llanfairfechan d										13x06												
Bangor (Gwynedd) a		12 15	12 33							13 15								13 33				
d		12 16	12 33															13 33				
Llanfairpwll d			12x40															13x40				
Bodorgan d			12x50															13x50				
Ty Croes d			12x55															13x55				
Rhosneigr d			12x58															13x58				
Valley d			13x04															14x04				
Holyhead a		12 46	13 12															14 13				

	NT ◇	AW	LM ■ F	AW ◇	VT ◇■ A	VT ◇■	NT	AW ◇ B	AW	AW ◇ E	LM ■ A	AW ◇ D	NT ◇ G	NT ◇	AW	LM ■ F	NT	AW ◇	VT ◇■ A	VT ◇■	LM ■ A
London Euston ⊖65 d					11 07	11 10					09 49								12 07	12 10	10 49
Birmingham New Street 65 d			11 37					11 25			12 04					12 37					13 04
Manchester Airport 84,85 ✈ d												13 35									
Cardiff Central 131 d																					
Crewe d	12 17	12 24	12 30		12 44	12 47					12 59			13 18	13 24	13 30			13 43	13 51	13 58
Manchester Pic'dilly 90 d	13 22						11 41					13 52		14 22			12 41				
Manchester Oxford Road 90 d	13 26											13 55		14 26							
Manchester Victoria 90 d													14 07								
Newton-le-Willows 90 d	13 48											14 16	14 26	14 47							
Earlestown 90 d	13 51											14 19	14 29	14 49							
Warrington Bank Quay 90 d												14 28	14 39								
Runcorn East d												14 35									
Liverpool Lime Street 91 d	14a29			12 38										15a24				13 38			
Liverpool South Parkway 91 d				12 49														13 49			
Runcorn 91 a			12 51	12 57	13 00						13 22					13 51		13 58	14 00		14 24
Frodsham d				13 07								14 39						14 07			
Helsby d				13 12								14 43						14 11			
Chester a		12 49		13 28		13 09	13 10	13 20		←		14 56	15 05		13 49		14 12	14 26		14 13	
d								13 25				14 57									
Shotton d										14 05		15 06									
Flint d								13 38		14 11		→									
Prestatyn d								13 51		14 24											
Rhyl d								13 58		14 30											
Abergele & Pensarn d										14 36											
Colwyn Bay d								14 08		14 44											
Llandudno Junction a								14 15		14 51											
d								14 15	14 28	14 52											
Deganwy d									14x31	14x56											
Llandudno a									14 38	15 02											
Conwy d								14x19													
Penmaenmawr d								14x25													
Llanfairfechan d								14x29													
Bangor (Gwynedd) a								14 38													
d								14 39													
Llanfairpwll d																					
Bodorgan d																					
Ty Croes d																					
Rhosneigr d																					
Valley d																					
Holyhead a								15 09													

A To Liverpool Lime Street
B From Birmingham International
C From Blaenau Ffestiniog
D To Llandudno
E From Manchester Airport
F From Birmingham International to Liverpool Lime Street
G From Leeds

NRT DECEMBER 19 EDITION

Table T081-F

Saturdays

21 December to 16 May

London and Birmingham - Crewe and Liverpool / Manchester - Chester and North Wales

	AW ■ A	AW	AW ◇ B	AW ◇ C	AW ◇ D	NT ◇	AW	LM ■ E	AW ◇	VT ◇■ F	VT ◇■	NT	AW ◇ G	AW	AW ◇ B	LM ■ F	NT ◇ H	AW ◇ D	NT ◇ H	NT ◇	AW	LM ■ E
London Euston ⊖65 d										13 07	13 10					11 49						
Birmingham New Street 65 d								13 37					13 25			14 03						14 37
Manchester Airport 84,85 ✈ d					14 35													15 35				
Cardiff Central 131 d	11 12																					
Crewe d						14 16	14 24	14 31		14 43	14 48					14 59				15 16	15 24	15 31
Manchester Pic'dilly 90 d					14 52	15 22						13 41						15 52		16 22		
Manchester Oxford Road 90 d					14 55	15 26												15 55		16 26		
Manchester Victoria 90 d																	15 07		16 07			
Newton-le-Willows 90 d					15 15	15 47												16 15	16 28	16 47		
Earlestown 90 d					15 18	15 49									←			16 19	16 31	16 49		
Warrington Bank Quay 90 d					15 26										15 26		15 40	16 27	16 40			
Runcorn East d					→										15 33			16 34	16 48			
Liverpool Lime Street 91 d						16a26			14 38											17a23		
Liverpool South Parkway 91 d									14 49													
Runcorn 91 a								14 54	14 58	15 00						15 23						15 52
Frodsham d									15 08						15 37			16 38	16 53			
Helsby d									15 12						15 41			16 42				
Chester a	14 20		←				14 49		15 28		15 07	15 14	15 21		15 54		16 16	16 55	17 07		15 49	
d	14 24												15 25		15 55			16 56				
Shotton d			15 06												16 04			→				
Flint d	14 36		15 12										15 38		16 10							
Prestatyn d	14 50		15 25										15 51		16 23							
Rhyl d	14 57		15 31										15 58		16 29							
Abergele & Pensarn d			15 37												16 35							
Colwyn Bay d	15 08		15 45										16 08		16 43							
Llandudno Junction a	15 15		15 52										16 15		16 50							
d	15 16	15 30	15 53	16 05									16 15	16 26	16 51							
Deganwy d		15x33	15x57	16x08										16x29	16x55							
Llandudno a		15 40	16 03	16 15										16 36	17 02							
Conwy d													16x19									
Penmaenmawr d													16x25									
Llanfairfechan d													16x30									
Bangor (Gwynedd) a	15 32												16 39									
d	15 33												16 39									
Llanfairpwll d	15x40																					
Bodorgan d	15x50																					
Ty Croes d	15x54																					
Rhosneigr d	15x57																					
Valley d	16x03																					
Holyhead a	16 12												17 11									

	AW ◇	VT ◇■ F	VT ◇■	LM ■ F	NT	AW ◇ A	AW	AW ◇ D	NT ◇	AW	AW ◇ B	LM ■ E	AW ◇	VT ◇■ F	VT ◇■	AW ■ G	AW	LM ■ F	NT	NT ◇ H	AW ◇ C	AW ◇ B
London Euston ⊖65 d		14 07	14 10	12 49										15 07	15 10			13 49				
Birmingham New Street 65 d				15 04								15 37				15 25		16 04				
Manchester Airport 84,85 ✈ d								16 35														
Cardiff Central 131 d						13 21																
Crewe d		15 43	15 47	15 59					16 16	16 24		16 31		16 43	16 47			16 59				
Manchester Pic'dilly 90 d					14 41			16 52	17 23										15 41			
Manchester Oxford Road 90 d								16 55	17 26													
Manchester Victoria 90 d																				17 07		
Newton-le-Willows 90 d								17 15	17 48													
Earlestown 90 d								17 18	17 50													
Warrington Bank Quay 90 d								17 27												17 35		
Runcorn East d								17 34												17 43		
Liverpool Lime Street 91 d	15 38								18a28				16 38									
Liverpool South Parkway 91 d	15 49												16 49									
Runcorn 91 a	15 58	16 00		16 25								16 51	16 58	17 00				17 24				
Frodsham d	16 10							17 38					17 07							17 48		
Helsby d	16 14							17 42			←		17 12							17 53		
Chester a	16 30		16 08		16 10	16 24		17 55		16 49	16 55		17 27		17 08	17 19			17 27	18 05		←
d			16 10			16 28		17 56			16 56					17 24						
Shotton d								18 05			17 05					17 33						18 05
Flint d			16 23			16 40		→			17 11					17 39						18 11
Prestatyn d			16 37			16 53					17 24					17 52						18 24
Rhyl d			16 43			16 59					17 30					17 58						18 30
Abergele & Pensarn d											17 36					18 04						18 36
Colwyn Bay d			16 54			17 09					17 44					18 12						18 44
Llandudno Junction a			16 59			17 16					17 51					18 19						18 51
d			17 00			17 17	17 28				17 52					18 20	18 26				18 41	18 52
Deganwy d							17x31				17x56						18x29				18x44	18x56
Llandudno a							17 38				18 02						18 36				18 51	19 02
Conwy d						17x20										18x23						
Penmaenmawr d						17x26										18x30						
Llanfairfechan d						17x31										18x34						
Bangor (Gwynedd) a			17 15			17 40										18 43						
d			17 17			17 40										18 44						
Llanfairpwll d						17x47																
Bodorgan d						17x57																
Ty Croes d						18x01																
Rhosneigr d						18x04																
Valley d						18x10																
Holyhead a			17 46			18 18										19 13						

A From Maesteg
B From Manchester Airport
C From Blaenau Ffestiniog
D To Llandudno
E From Birmingham International to Liverpool Lime Street
F To Liverpool Lime Street
G From Birmingham International
H From Leeds

Table T081-F

Saturdays

21 December to 16 May

London and Birmingham - Crewe and Liverpool / Manchester - Chester and North Wales

	AW	NT	NT	AW	LM	AW	VT	VT	LM	VT	NT	AW	AW	AW	NT	NT	AW	AW	LM	NT	AW
	◇ A	◇ B	◇		1 C	◇ D	◇1 E	◇1	1 E	◇1 E		F			◇ B	◇		◇ G	1 C		◇
London Euston 15 ⊖65 d							16 07	16 10	14 49	16 33											
Birmingham New Street 12 65 d					16 37				17 04										17 37		
Manchester Airport 84,85 ✈ d	17 35													18 35							
Cardiff Central 7 131 d												15 23									
Crewe 10 d			17 16	17 24	17 31		17 43	17 48	17 59							18 16	18 24		18 31		
Manchester Pic'dilly 10 90 d	17 52		18 22								16 41			18 53		19 22				17 41	
Manchester Oxford Road 90 d	17 56		18 26											18 56		19 26					
Manchester Victoria 90 d		18 07													19 07						
Newton-le-Willows 90 d	18 16	18 29	18 48											19 17	19 26	19 48					
Earlestown 8 90 d	18 19	18 32	18 50											19 21	19 29	19 50					
Warrington Bank Quay 90 d	18 27	18 44												19 29	19 39						
Runcorn East d	18 34	18 52												19 36							
Liverpool Lime Street 91 d			19a25			17 37										20a29					18 38
Liverpool South Parkway 91 d						17 48															18 49
Runcorn 91 a					17 52	17 56	18 00		18 24	18 31									18 51		18 57
Frodsham d	18 38	18 57				18 05								19 41							19 06
Helsby d	18 42	19 02				18 10								19 45				←			19 11
Chester a	18 55	19 14		17 49		18 23		18 08			18 10	18 20		19 57	20 05		18 49	18 55		19 09	19 27
d	18 56							18 15				18 24						18 56			
Shotton d	→											18 32						19 05			
Flint d								18 28				18 38						19 11			
Prestatyn d								18 41				18 51						19 24			
Rhyl d								18 47				18 57						19 30			
Abergele & Pensarn d																		19 36			
Colwyn Bay d								18 58				19 07						19 44			
Llandudno Junction a								19 03				19 14						19 51			
d								19 04				19 16	19 28					19 52			
Deganwy d													19x31					19x56			
Llandudno a													19 38					20 03			
Conwy d																					
Penmaenmawr d																					
Llanfairfechan d																					
Bangor (Gwynedd) a								19 19				19 34									
d								19 21				19 34									
Llanfairpwll d												19x41									
Bodorgan d												19x51									
Ty Croes d												19x56									
Rhosneigr d												19x59									
Valley d												20x05									
Holyhead 30 a								19 50				20 17									

	VT	VT	VT	AW	AW	LM	AW	NT	NT	AW	LM	VT	VT	LM	VT	NT	AW	AW	AW	NT	AW	LM
	◇1 E	◇1	◇1	◇ H		1 E		◇ B	◇		1 C	◇1 E	◇1	1 E	◇1 E			◇ I			◇ H	1 C
London Euston 15 ⊖65 d	17 07	17 10	17 10			15 49						18 07	18 10	16 49	18 33							
Birmingham New Street 12 65 d				17 25		18 04					18 37			19 04							19 25	19 37
Manchester Airport 84,85 ✈ d																						
Cardiff Central 7 131 d																	17 23					
Crewe 10 d	18 47	18 50	18 50			18 59			19 17	19 24	19 32	19 43	19 47	19 59					20 24			20 33
Manchester Pic'dilly 10 90 d							19 52		20 22							18 41				19 41		
Manchester Oxford Road 90 d							19 55		20 26													
Manchester Victoria 90 d								20 07														
Newton-le-Willows 90 d							20 17	20 26	20 48													
Earlestown 8 90 d							20 21	20 29	20 50													
Warrington Bank Quay 90 d							20 30	20 42														
Runcorn East d							20 37															
Liverpool Lime Street 91 d									21a25													
Liverpool South Parkway 91 d																						
Runcorn 91 a	19 04					19 23					19 53	20 00		20 22	20 31							20 58
Frodsham d							20 42															
Helsby d							20 46															
Chester a		19 09	19 09	19 22			20 59	21 06		19 49			20 08			20 09	20 24		20 49	21 10	21 21	
d			19 16	19 27													20 32					
Shotton d				19 36													20 41					
Flint d			19 29	19 42													20 47					
Prestatyn d			19 43	19 55													21 00					
Rhyl d			19 49	20 01													21 06					
Abergele & Pensarn d				20 07																		
Colwyn Bay d			20 00	20 15													21 19					
Llandudno Junction a			20 05	20 22													21 26					
d			20 06	20 27	20 30												21 27	21 32				
Deganwy d					20x33													21x35				
Llandudno a					20 40													21 43				
Conwy d				20x30																		
Penmaenmawr d				20x36																		
Llanfairfechan d				20x40																		
Bangor (Gwynedd) a			20 21	20 49													21 43					
d			20 23	20 49													21 44					
Llanfairpwll d				20x56													21x51					
Bodorgan d				21x06													22x01					
Ty Croes d				21x11													22x05					
Rhosneigr d				21x14													22x08					
Valley d				21x20													22x14					
Holyhead 30 a			20 52	21 28													22 24					

A To Llandudno
B From Leeds
C From Birmingham International to Liverpool Lime Street
D To Wrexham General
E To Liverpool Lime Street
F From Maesteg
G From Manchester Airport
H From Birmingham International
I From Blaenau Ffestiniog

Table T081-F

Saturdays

21 December to 16 May

London and Birmingham - Crewe and Liverpool / Manchester - Chester and North Wales

	AW	VT	LM	AW	AW	LM	AW	NT	NT	AW	AW	AW	VT	AW	AW	AW	NT	AW	AW	AW	NT
	◇	◇1 A	1 A	◇		1 B			◇ C	◇	◇		◇1 A			◇			◇ D		
London Euston 15 ⊖65 d		19 07	17 49										20 11								
Birmingham New Street 12 65 d			20 04			20 37													21 25		
Manchester Airport 84,85 ✈ d					20 34																
Cardiff Central 7 131 d											19 34										
Crewe 10 d		20 47	20 58	21 00		21 30	21 36						22 06	22 24						23 21	
Manchester Pic'dilly 10 90 d					20 51			20 41							21 51		21 37	22 12			22 40
Manchester Oxford Road 90 d					20 54										21 54			22 15			
Manchester Victoria 90 d									21 08												
Newton-le-Willows 90 d					21 12				21 26						22 13			22 33			
Earlestown 8 90 d					21 17				21 39						22 16			22 36			
Warrington Bank Quay 90 d					21 30				21 50						22 25			22 44			
Runcorn East d					21 37										22 32			22 52			
Liverpool Lime Street 91 d	20 38									21 40						22 20					
Liverpool South Parkway 91 d	20 49									21 51						22 30					
Runcorn 91 a	20 58	21 05	21 21			21 51				21 59			22 24			22 38					
Frodsham d	21 07				21 41					22 08					22 36	22 47		22 57			
Helsby d	21 12				21 45					22 13					22 40	22 51		23 01			
Chester a	21 27			21 22	21 58		22 00	22 12	22 18	22 28	22 34			22 48	22 54	23 06	23 11	23 14	23 21	23 43	00 09
d				21 26							22 38										
Shotton d				21 35							22 47										
Flint d				21 41							22 53										
Prestatyn d				21 54							23 06										
Rhyl d				22 00							23 12										
Abergele & Pensarn d				22 06							23 18										
Colwyn Bay d				22 14							23 26										
Llandudno Junction a				22 21							23 36										
d				22 22								23 48									
Deganwy d																					
Llandudno a																					
Conwy d				22x25																	
Penmaenmawr d				22x32																	
Llanfairfechan d				22x36																	
Bangor (Gwynedd) a				22 45								00 13									
d				22 46								00 13									
Llanfairpwll d																					
Bodorgan d																					
Ty Croes d																					
Rhosneigr d																					
Valley d																					
Holyhead 30 a				23 17								00 48									

	AW	AW	NT
		◇	
London Euston 15 ⊖65 d			
Birmingham New Street 12 65 d			
Manchester Airport 84,85 ✈ d			
Cardiff Central 7 131 d		20 55	
Crewe 10 d		23 57	
Manchester Pic'dilly 10 90 d	23 14		23 41
Manchester Oxford Road 90 d	23 17		
Manchester Victoria 90 d			
Newton-le-Willows 90 d	23 36		
Earlestown 8 90 d	23 39		
Warrington Bank Quay 90 d	23 48		
Runcorn East d	23 55		
Liverpool Lime Street 91 d			
Liverpool South Parkway 91 d			
Runcorn 91 a			
Frodsham d	23 59		
Helsby d	00 03		
Chester a	00 16	00 23	01 07
d			
Shotton d			
Flint d			
Prestatyn d			
Rhyl d			
Abergele & Pensarn d			
Colwyn Bay d			
Llandudno Junction a			
d			
Deganwy d			
Llandudno a			
Conwy d			
Penmaenmawr d			
Llanfairfechan d			
Bangor (Gwynedd) a			
d			
Llanfairpwll d			
Bodorgan d			
Ty Croes d			
Rhosneigr d			
Valley d			
Holyhead 30 a			

A To Liverpool Lime Street
B From Birmingham International to Liverpool Lime Street
C From Leeds
D From Birmingham International

Table T081-F

Sundays

15 December to 10 May

London and Birmingham - Crewe and Liverpool / Manchester - Chester and North Wales

	AW	AW	AW	AW	AW	AW	AW	AW	VT		NT	LM	AW	AW	VT	AW	AW	AW	AW		AW	AW	VT	LM
					◇			◇	◇1			1	◇		◇1			◇	◇		◇		◇1	1
	A	B							C			D							E				C	C
		🚌	🚌						☕						☕								☕	
London Euston 15 ⊖65 d									08 16														09 16	07 52
Birmingham New Street 12 65 d												09 42												10 42
Manchester Airport 84,85 ✈ d																								
Cardiff Central 7 131 d																								
Crewe 10 d					09 25		10 07		10 30			10 36			10 42		11 05				11 27		11 37	11 41
Manchester Pic'dilly 10 90 d			07 18								09 04		09 48											
Manchester Oxford Road 90 d			07 33										09 51											
Manchester Victoria 90 d																								
Newton-le-Willows 90 d			08 03										10 09											
Earlestown 8 90 d			08 13										10 12											
Warrington Bank Quay 90 d			08 38										10 20											
Runcorn East d			08 58										10 27											
Liverpool Lime Street 91 d								09 45										10 49						
Liverpool South Parkway 91 d								09 56										11 01						
Runcorn 91 a								10 04	10 48			11 01						11 09					11 54	12 03
Frodsham d			09 13					10 13					10 32					11 18						
Helsby d	00 03		09 18					10 17					10 36					11 22						
Chester a	00 16		09 38		09 48		10 30	10 33			10 39		10 49		11 02		11 30	11 39			11 47			
d					09 48										11 07						12 03			
Shotton d					09 57																12 12			
Flint d					10 03																12 18			
Prestatyn d					10 17										11 31						12 31			
Rhyl d					10 23										11 37						12 37			
Abergele & Pensarn d					10 29																			
Colwyn Bay d					10 37										11 48						12 48			
Llandudno Junction a					10 44										11 53						12 55			
d				10 03	10 44	10 50								11 25	11 54	12 00			12 42		12 55	12 58		
Deganwy d				10x06		10x53								11x28		12x03			12x45			13x01		
Llandudno a				10 13		11 00								11 35		12 10			12 52			13 08		
Conwy d					10x47																			
Penmaenmawr d					10x53																			
Llanfairfechan d					10x57																			
Bangor (Gwynedd) a					11 06										12 09						13 12			
d		00 13			11 07										12 11						13 12			
Llanfairpwll d					11x13																			
Bodorgan d					11x23																			
Ty Croes d					11x28																			
Rhosneigr d					11x31																			
Valley d					11x37																			
Holyhead 30 a		00 48			11 49										12 40						13 40			

	AW	AW	NT	NT	AW		AW	AW	AW	VT	AW	AW	LM	AW	AW		VT	AW	AW	LM	VT	AW	AW	NT
	◇				◇			◇		◇1	◇	◇	1		◇		◇1	■		1	◇1	◇		
			F	G						C		H	I				C			J	C			
	⌶									☕	⌶	⌶					☕	⌶			☕	⌶		
London Euston 15 ⊖65 d										10 16							11 16				12 05			
Birmingham New Street 12 65 d												11 04	11 40							12 35				
Manchester Airport 84,85 ✈ d																								
Cardiff Central 7 131 d																								
Crewe 10 d		11 55						12 27		12 34			12 37	12 54			13 15	13 27		13 31	13 45		13 57	
Manchester Pic'dilly 10 90 d	10 52		11 00	11 01							11 56											12 56		13 06
Manchester Oxford Road 90 d	10 57										11 59											12 59		
Manchester Victoria 90 d																								
Newton-le-Willows 90 d	11 14										12 18											13 18		
Earlestown 8 90 d	11 17										12 21											13 23		
Warrington Bank Quay 90 d	11 26										12 30											13 32		
Runcorn East d	11 33										12 37											13 39		
Liverpool Lime Street 91 d					11 56										12 57									
Liverpool South Parkway 91 d					12 07										13 08									
Runcorn 91 a					12 15					12 51			13 02		13 16		13 32			13 53	14 02			
Frodsham d	11 38				12 24						12 42				13 25							13 43		
Helsby d	11 42				12 28						12 46				13 29							13 47		
Chester a	11 55	12 18	12 30	12 30	12 44			12 53			12 58	13 14		13 17	13 45			13 51				13 59	14 20	14 35
d								13 02										14 04						
Shotton d								13 11										14 13						
Flint d								13 17										14 19						
Prestatyn d								13 30										14 32						
Rhyl d								13 36										14 38						
Abergele & Pensarn d								13 42										14 44						
Colwyn Bay d								13 50										14 52						
Llandudno Junction a								13 57										14 59						
d							13 40	13 58	14 04									15 00	15 02					
Deganwy d							13x43		14x07										15x05					
Llandudno a							13 50		14 14										15 12					
Conwy d								14x01																
Penmaenmawr d								14x07																
Llanfairfechan d								14x11																
Bangor (Gwynedd) a								14 20										15 16						
d								14 20										15 17						
Llanfairpwll d																		15x24						
Bodorgan d																		15x34						
Ty Croes d																		15x38						
Rhosneigr d																		15x41						
Valley d																		15x47						
Holyhead 30 a								14 52										15 55						

A not 15 December. From Manchester Piccadilly
B not 15 December. From Llandudno Junction
C To Liverpool Lime Street
D From Rugby to Liverpool Lime Street
E From Blaenau Ffestiniog
F from 5 April
G until 29 March
H From Birmingham International
I From Milton Keynes Central to Liverpool Lime Street
J From Northampton to Liverpool Lime Street

Table T081-F

Sundays

15 December to 10 May

London and Birmingham - Crewe and Liverpool / Manchester - Chester and North Wales

	AW		LM	AW	AW	AW	VT	AW	AW	AW	AW		AW	AW	AW	LM	VT	AW	AW	AW	AW		NT	AW
	◇		1		■		◇1	◇	◇		◇			■		1	◇1	◇		■				◇
			A		B		C		D							C	C							
					⌶		☕	⌶	⌶								☕	⌶		⌶				
London Euston 15 ⊖65 d							13 05									12 31	14 05							
Birmingham New Street 12 65 d			13 35						13 23							14 35								
Manchester Airport 84,85 ✈ d																								
Cardiff Central 7 131 d																				13 25				
Crewe 10 d			14 31		14 34		14 45			14 57				15 27		15 31	15 45		15 57					
Manchester Pic'dilly 10 90 d								13 57										14 57					15 06	
Manchester Oxford Road 90 d								14 00										15 00						
Manchester Victoria 90 d																								
Newton-le-Willows 90 d								14 18										15 18						
Earlestown 8 90 d								14 21										15 21						
Warrington Bank Quay 90 d								14 27										15 28						
Runcorn East d								14 34										15 35						
Liverpool Lime Street 91 d	13 57										14 57													15 57
Liverpool South Parkway 91 d	14 08										15 08													16 08
Runcorn 91 a	14 16		14 57				15 02				15 16					15 54	16 02							16 16
Frodsham d	14 25							14 39			15 25							15 40						16 25
Helsby d	14 29							14 43			15 29							15 44						16 29
Chester a	14 45				14 54			14 55	15 18	15 20	15 45			15 50				15 57	16 23	16 29			16 39	16 45
d					15 02									16 02						16 36				
Shotton d					15 11									16 11						16 45				
Flint d					15 17									16 17						16 51				
Prestatyn d					15 30									16 30						17 04				
Rhyl d					15 36									16 36						17 10				
Abergele & Pensarn d					15 42									16 42						17 16				
Colwyn Bay d					15 50									16 50						17 24				
Llandudno Junction a					15 57									16 57						17 31				
d				15 30	15 58	16 04							16 39	16 58	17 05					17 32	17 40			
Deganwy d				15x33		16x07							16x42		17x08						17x43			
Llandudno a				15 40		16 14							16 49		17 15						17 50			
Conwy d					16x01															17x35				
Penmaenmawr d					16x07															17x41				
Llanfairfechan d					16x11															17x45				
Bangor (Gwynedd) a					16 20									17 14						17 54				
d					16 20									17 15						17 56				
Llanfairpwll d														17x21						18x02				
Bodorgan d														17x31						18x12				
Ty Croes d														17x35						18x17				
Rhosneigr d														17x38						18x21				
Valley d														17x44						18x27				
Holyhead 30 a					16 53									17 55						18 38				

	AW	AW	LM	VT	AW	VT	AW		AW	LM	AW	AW	VT	VT	AW	NT	AW		AW	LM	VT	AW	VT	VT
	■	◇	1	◇1	◇	◇1	◇		◇	1	◇	■	◇1	◇1	■		◇		◇	1	◇1	◇	◇1	◇1
		E	C	C			D			C			C							C	C			
				☕	⌶	☕	⌶				⌶		☕	☕	⌶						☕	⌶	☕	☕
London Euston 15 ⊖65 d			13 32	15 05		15 08				14 31			16 05	16 08						15 31	17 05		17 08	17 08
Birmingham New Street 12 65 d			15 35				15 23			16 35										17 35				
Manchester Airport 84,85 ✈ d																								
Cardiff Central 7 131 d															15 17									
Crewe 10 d	16 27		16 31	16 45		16 51				17 32		17 35	17 46	17 50					18 27	18 31	18 46		19 00	19 00
Manchester Pic'dilly 10 90 d					15 57						16 57					17 06						17 57		
Manchester Oxford Road 90 d					16 00						17 00											18 00		
Manchester Victoria 90 d																								
Newton-le-Willows 90 d					16 18						17 18											18 18		
Earlestown 8 90 d					16 21						17 21											18 21		
Warrington Bank Quay 90 d					16 27						17 27											18 27		
Runcorn East d					16 34						17 34											18 34		
Liverpool Lime Street 91 d									16 56								17 56							
Liverpool South Parkway 91 d									17 07								18 07							
Runcorn 91 a			16 57	17 02					17 15	17 57			18 02				18 15			18 57	19 02			
Frodsham d					16 39				17 24		17 39						18 23					18 39		
Helsby d					16 43				17 28		17 43						18 27					18 43		
Chester a	16 51				16 56	17 10	17 26		17 45		17 56	17 59		18 10	18 26	18 34	18 43		18 46			18 56	19 18	19 19
d	17 02											18 02			18 30				18 52				19 29	
Shotton d	17 11											18 11			18 39				19 01					
Flint d	17 17											18 17			18 45				19 07				19 42	
Prestatyn d	17 30											18 30			18 58				19 21				19 55	
Rhyl d	17 36											18 36			19 04				19 27				20 02	
Abergele & Pensarn d	17 42											18 42			19 10				19 33					
Colwyn Bay d	17 50											18 50			19 18				19 41				20 13	
Llandudno Junction a	17 57											18 57			19 24				19 48				20 18	
d	17 58	18 31										18 58			19 26				19 48				20 19	
Deganwy d		18x34																						
Llandudno a		18 41																						
Conwy d	18x01														19x29				19x52					
Penmaenmawr d	18x07														19x35				19x58					
Llanfairfechan d	18x11														19x40				20x02					
Bangor (Gwynedd) a	18 20											19 14			19 48				20 11				20 34	
d	18 20											19 15			19 49				20 12				20 36	
Llanfairpwll d												19x21												
Bodorgan d												19x31												
Ty Croes d												19x35												
Rhosneigr d												19x38												
Valley d												19x44												
Holyhead 30 a	18 54											19 54			20 18				20 44				21 03	

A From Northampton to Liverpool Lime Street
B ⌶ from Chester
C To Liverpool Lime Street
D From Birmingham International
E From Blaenau Ffestiniog

Table T081-F

Sundays

15 December to 10 May

London and Birmingham - Crewe and Liverpool / Manchester - Chester and North Wales

Station	AW ◇ A	AW ◇	AW	LM ■ B	VT ◇■ B	AW ◇	VT ◇■	VT ◇■	AW ◇ C	NT	AW ◇	AW	LM ■ B	VT ◇■ B	AW ◇	VT ◇■	AW ◇ A	AW ◇	AW ◇	AW ◇	AW ◇
London Euston 15 ⊖65 d				16 32	18 05		18 08	18 08					17 32	19 05		19 08					
Birmingham New Street 12 65 d	17 24			18 35									19 35				19 24				
Manchester Airport 84,85 ✈ d																					
Cardiff Central 7 131 d																					
Crewe 10 d			19 26	19 31	19 45		19 50	19 50				20 27	20 35	20 49		20 53			21 28		
Manchester Pic'dilly 10 90 d						18 57				19 06					19 57					20 54	
Manchester Oxford Road 90 d						19 00									20 00					20 57	
Manchester Victoria 90 d																					
Newton-le-Willows 90 d						19 18									20 18					21 15	
Earlestown 8 90 d						19 21									20 21					21 18	
Warrington Bank Quay 90 d						19 30									20 31					21 27	
Runcorn East d						19 37									20 38					21 34	
Liverpool Lime Street 91 d		18 57									19 57							20 57			21 37
Liverpool South Parkway 91 d		19 08									20 08							21 08			21 48
Runcorn 91 a		19 16		19 54	20 02						20 16		21 00	21 06				21 16			21 56
Frodsham d		19 25				19 41					20 25				20 43			21 25		21 39	22 05
Helsby d		19 29				19 45					20 29				20 47			21 29		21 43	22 09
Chester a		19 45	19 49			19 59	20 10	20 12		20 34	20 45	20 50			21 00	21 12	21 20	21 45	21 52	21 55	22 26
d								20 16								21 15			22 01		
Shotton d	19 44																		22 10		
Flint d	19 50							20 29								21 28			22 16		
Prestatyn d	20 03							20 43								21 42			22 29		
Rhyl d	20 09							20 49								21 48			22 35		
Abergele & Pensarn d	20 15																		22 41		
Colwyn Bay d	20 23							21 00								21 59			22 49		
Llandudno Junction a	20 30							21 05								22 04			22 56		
d	20 30							21 06	21 25							22 05			22 57		
Deganwy d									21x28												
Llandudno a									21 35												
Conwy d	20x33																				
Penmaenmawr d	20x39																				
Llanfairfechan d	20x43																				
Bangor (Gwynedd) a	20 52							21 21								22 20			23 13		
d	20 53							21 23								22 22			23 14		
Llanfairpwll d																			23x21		
Bodorgan d																			23x31		
Ty Croes d																			23x35		
Rhosneigr d																			23x38		
Valley d																			23x44		
Holyhead 30 a	21 26							21 52								22 51			23 55		

Station	VT ◇■ B	VT ◇■ B	AW	NT	AW ◇	LM ■ B	AW ◇	AW ◇ A	AW ◇	AW ◇	AW	AW ◇	VT ◇■ B	AW ◇ A	AW ◇	AW ◇
London Euston 15 ⊖65 d	20 05	20 08				19 31							21 21			
Birmingham New Street 12 65 d						21 42		21 23						22 55		
Manchester Airport 84,85 ✈ d																
Cardiff Central 7 131 d																21 10
Crewe 10 d	21 46	21 55	22 03		22 29	22 40		23 08			23 39		23 47	00 01		00 10
Manchester Pic'dilly 10 90 d				21 06			21 57			22 57					23 25	
Manchester Oxford Road 90 d							22 00			23 00					23 28	
Manchester Victoria 90 d																
Newton-le-Willows 90 d							22 17			23 21					23 46	
Earlestown 8 90 d							22 20			23 24					23 49	
Warrington Bank Quay 90 d							22 27			23 31					23 56	
Runcorn East d							22 34			23 38					00 03	
Liverpool Lime Street 91 d									22 57			23 18				
Liverpool South Parkway 91 d									23 08			23 29				
Runcorn 91 a	22 03	22 12				23 05			23 16			23 38	00 06			
Frodsham d							22 38		23 25	23 42		23 51			00 08	
Helsby d							22 42		23 29	23 46		23 56			00 12	
Chester a			22 27	22 35	22 53		22 55	23 33	23 45	23 59	00 01	00 11		00 23	00 25	00 34
d					23 02										00 38	
Shotton d					23 11											
Flint d					23 17										00 51	
Prestatyn d					23 30										01 04	
Rhyl d					23 36										01 10	
Abergele & Pensarn d																
Colwyn Bay d					23 47										01 21	
Llandudno Junction a					23 54										01 28	
d					23 54										01 28	
Deganwy d																
Llandudno a																
Conwy d					23x57											
Penmaenmawr d					00x03											
Llanfairfechan d					00x07											
Bangor (Gwynedd) a					00 16										01 45	
d					00 17										01 45	
Llanfairpwll d																
Bodorgan d																
Ty Croes d																
Rhosneigr d																
Valley d																
Holyhead 30 a					00 51										02 13	

A From Birmingham International
B To Liverpool Lime Street
C From Blaenau Ffestiniog

Table T081-R

Mondays to Fridays

16 December to 15 May

North Wales and Chester - Manchester / Liverpool and Crewe - Birmingham and London

Miles	Miles	Station	AW	AW	AW	AW ◇ A	AW	AW	AW	NT	LM ■ B	LM ■ C	AW ◇	NT ◇ D	AW ◇	VT ◇■	AW ◇	AW	AW	NT	LM ■ B	AW ◇ E
0	—	**Holyhead** 30 d													04 25	04 48						
3½	—	Valley d													04x31							
7½	—	Rhosneigr d																				
9¼	—	Ty Croes d																				
12	—	Bodorgan d																				
21	—	Llanfairpwll d													04x48							
24¾	—	**Bangor (Gwynedd)** a													04 56	05 14						
—	—	d													04 57	05 14						
32¼	—	Llanfairfechan d																				
34¾	—	Penmaenmawr d																				
39	—	Conwy d																				
—	0	**Llandudno** d																05 53				
—	1¾	Deganwy d																05x57				
40	3	**Llandudno Junction** a													05 14	05 32		06 02				
—	—	d					04 38								05 15	05 32	05 46					
44	—	Colwyn Bay d					04 44								05 21	05 38	05 52					
50¼	—	Abergele & Pensarn d					04 51															
54½	—	Rhyl d					04 57								05 30	05 49	06 02					
58	—	Prestatyn d					05 02								05 36		06 08					
72	—	Flint d					05 16								05 49		06 21					
76¼	—	Shotton d					05 22										06 27					
84¼	0	**Chester** a					05 35								06 08	06 17	06 41					
—	—	d	03 34	04 22	04 59	05 35	05 37	05 38	05 51	05 56			06 07	06 17	06 20	06 26	06 43		06 45	06 51		07 03
—	7½	Helsby d						05 47					06 17	06 26			06 52					07 12
—	10	Frodsham d						05 51					06 22	06 31			06 57					07 16
—	—	Runcorn 91 a											06 35									07 29
—	—	**Liverpool South Parkway** 91 d									06 20	06 42	06 44								07 15	07 42
—	—	**Liverpool Lime Street** 91 a											07 01									07 59
—	13¼	Runcorn East d						05 56						06 36			07 02					
—	18¼	Warrington Bank Quay 90 a						06 06						06 45			07 10					
—	22¼	Earlestown 8 90 a						06 13						06 52			07 18					
—	24	Newton-le-Willows 90 a						06 16						06 55			07 20					
—	—	**Manchester Victoria** 90 a												07 17								
—	39¾	**Manchester Oxford Road** 90 a						06 36									07 42					
—	40¼	**Manchester Pic'dilly** 10 90 a	04 44					06 42		07 26							07 48			08 17		
105½	—	**Crewe** 10 a		04 46	05 21		05 58		06 13		06 48	07 15				06 47			07 08		07 50	
—	—	Cardiff Central 7 131 a													09 15							
—	—	Manchester Airport 84,85 ✈ a	05 02																			
—	—	Birmingham New Street 12 65 a		06 07		07 31					07 50	08 18									08 50	
—	—	London Euston 15 ⊖65 a									10 17					08 34					11 18	

Station	AW ◇	AW ■ ⊠	VT ◇■ ⊠	NT ◇ F	AW ◇	LM ■ B	AW ◇	AW	LM ■ B	NT ◇ B	NT	AW ◇	AW ◇	NT ◇ D	VT ◇■ ⊠	AW ◇	AW	LM ■ B	AW	LM ■ B	NT ◇ B	NT
Holyhead 30 d	05 11	05 34	05 51										06 28		06 55							
Valley d	05x17												06x34									
Rhosneigr d													06x40									
Ty Croes d													06x43									
Bodorgan d													06x48									
Llanfairpwll d	05x35												06x57									
Bangor (Gwynedd) a	05 43	06 02	06 17										07 06		07 21							
d	05 43	06 02	06 18										07 06		07 22							
Llanfairfechan d	05x51																					
Penmaenmawr d	05x55																					
Conwy d	06x01																					
Llandudno d							06 41	07 08								07 45	08 02					
Deganwy d							06x45	07x12								07x49	08x06					
Llandudno Junction a	06 06	06 20	06 35				06 50	07 18					07 24		07 39	07 54	08 12					
d	06 07	06 20	06 36				06 51						07 25		07 40	07 54						
Colwyn Bay d	06 13	06 28	06 42				06 57						07 31		07 47	08 00						
Abergele & Pensarn d	06 20						07 05									08 07						
Rhyl d	06 26	06 39	06 53				07 12						07 40		07 58	08 13						
Prestatyn d	06 31		06 58				07 18						07 46		08 04	08 19						
Flint d	06 45	06 56	07 12				07 33						07 59		08 17	08 32						
Shotton d	06 51						07 40									08 38						
Chester a	07 05	07 12	07 26				07 53						08 16		08 31	08 51						
d	07 12	07 16	07 35		07 38		07 53				08 02	08 11	08 19	08 21	08 35	08 52			08 52			09 02
Helsby d	07 22			07 31	07 49							08 20		08 30		09 01						
Frodsham d	07 26				07 54							08 24		08 35		09 05						
Runcorn 91 a												08 35										
Liverpool South Parkway 91 d						07 44			08 15	08 26		08 43						08 43		09 15	09 26	
Liverpool Lime Street 91 a												09 01										
Runcorn East d	07 31				08 00									08 40		09 11						
Warrington Bank Quay 90 a	07 39			07 46	08 10									08 49		09 20						
Earlestown 8 90 a	07 47				08 22									08 56		09 28						
Newton-le-Willows 90 a	07 49			07 55	08 26									08 59		09 30						
Manchester Victoria 90 a				08 18										09 19								
Manchester Oxford Road 90 a	08 09				08s49					09 07						09 50					10 07	
Manchester Pic'dilly 10 90 a	08 12				08 54					09 11	09 30					09 54					10 11	10 30
Crewe 10 a			07 54			08 16	08 19		08 48						08 54			09 18	09 18	09 48		
Cardiff Central 7 131 a		09 58											11 16									
Manchester Airport 84,85 ✈ a										09 32						10 19					10 32	
Birmingham New Street 12 65 a						09 21			09 50									10 21		10 50		
London Euston 15 ⊖65 a			09 39			11 30			12 16						10 37			12 29		13 17		

A To Birmingham International
B From Liverpool Lime Street
C From Liverpool Lime Street to Rugeley Trent Valley
D To Leeds
E From Shrewsbury
F From Ellesmere Port to Leeds

Table T081-R

Mondays to Fridays
16 December to 15 May

North Wales and Chester - Manchester / Liverpool and Crewe - Birmingham and London

		AW	NT	LM	AW	AW	VT	AW	AW	LM	NT	NT	LM	AW	AW	NT	VT FX	VT FX	VT FO	AW	AW	AW
		◇	◇ A	■ B	◇	■ ⊼	◇■ ⊠	◇ ⊼		■ B	◇ B		■ B	◇	◇ ⊼	◇ A	◇■ C ⊠	◇■ D ⊠	◇■ ⊠	◇ ⊼	◇ E	
Holyhead 30	d	07 15													08 05		08 55	08 55	08 55			
Valley	d	07x21													08x11							
Rhosneigr	d	07x27													08x17							
Ty Croes	d	07x30													08x20							
Bodorgan	d	07x35													08x25							
Llanfairpwll	d	07x44													08x34							
Bangor (Gwynedd)	a	07 53													08 43		09 21	09 21	09 21			
	d	08 02													09 02		09 22	09 22	09 22			
Llanfairfechan	d	08x10													09x10							
Penmaenmawr	d	08x14													09x14							
Conwy	d	08x20													09x20							
Llandudno	d					08 30														09 45	10 08	
Deganwy	d					08x34														09x49	10x12	
Llandudno Junction	a	08 24				08 39									09 24		09 39	09 39	09 39	09 54	10 19	
	d	08 25				08 39		08 54							09 25		09 40	09 40	09 40	09 54		
Colwyn Bay	d	08 31				08 45		09 00							09 31		09 47	09 47	09 47	10 00		
Abergele & Pensarn	d							09 07												10 07		
Rhyl	d	08 41				08 55		09 13							09 40		09 58	09 58	09 58	10 13		
Prestatyn	d	08 47						09 19							09 46		10 04	10 04	10 04	10 19		
Flint	d	09 00						09 32							09 59		10 17	10 17	10 17	10 32		
Shotton	d							09 38												10 38		
Chester	a	09 16				09 25		09 51							10 18		10 31	10 31	10 31	10 51		
	d	09 17	09 21		09 27	09 28	09 35	09 52	09 54			10 02		10 12	10 21	10 23	10 35	10 35	10 35	10 52		10 55
Helsby	d				09 38			10 01						10 21						11 01		
Frodsham	d				09 43			10 05						10 26						11 05		
Runcorn 91	a				09 56									10 37								
Liverpool South Parkway 91	d			09 45	10 06					10 15	10 26		10 43	10 45								
Liverpool Lime Street 91	a				10 20									11 04								
Runcorn East	d							10 11												11 11		
Warrington Bank Quay 90	a		09 45					10 19								10 46				11 19		
Earlestown 5 90	a		09 54					10 28								10 54				11 28		
Newton-le-Willows 90	a		09 57					10 30								10 57				11 30		
Manchester Victoria 90	a		10 18													11 18						
Manchester Oxford Road 90	a							10 50			11 07									11 51		
Manchester Pic'dilly 10 90	a							10 54			11 11	11 30								11 55		
Crewe 10	a	09 39		10 16			09 54		10 19	10 48			11 16				10 54	10 54	10 54			11 19
Cardiff Central 7 131	a					12 06									13 15							
Manchester Airport 84,85	a							11 19			11 32									12 19		
Birmingham New Street 12 65	a			11 20						11 50			12 21									
London Euston 15 ⊖65	a			13 30			11 37			14 17			14 30				12 36	12 37	12 38			

		LM	NT	NT	NT	LM	AW	VT	VT	AW	AW	AW	AW	LM	NT	NT	AW	NT	LM	AW	VT WX	VT WO	AW
		■ B	◇ B		◇ A	■ B	◇	◇■ F ⊡	◇■ D ⊡	◇ G ⊼	◇ ⊼			■ B	◇ B		■ H ⊼	◇ A	■ B	◇	◇■ ⊡	◇■ ⊡	◇ ⊼
Holyhead 30	d									09 23							10 40						
Valley	d									09x29							10x46						
Rhosneigr	d									09x34													
Ty Croes	d									09x38													
Bodorgan	d									09x42													
Llanfairpwll	d									09x52													
Bangor (Gwynedd)	a									10 01							11 08						
	d									10 02							11 09						
Llanfairfechan	d									10x10													
Penmaenmawr	d									10x14													
Conwy	d									10x20													
Llandudno	d										10 44	11 13											11 44
Deganwy	d										10x48	11x17											11x48
Llandudno Junction	a									10 24	10 53	11 22					11 26						11 53
	d									10 25	10 53						11 27						11 53
Colwyn Bay	d									10 31	10 59						11 33						11 59
Abergele & Pensarn	d										11 06												12 06
Rhyl	d									10 41	11 12						11 42						12 12
Prestatyn	d									10 47	11 18						11 48						12 18
Flint	d									11 00	11 31						12 01						12 31
Shotton	d										11 37												12 37
Chester	a									11 17	11 50						12 16						12 50
	d			11 02	11 24		11 32	11 35	11 35	11 36	11 52		11 54			12 02	12 19	12 24		12 30	12 35	12 35	12 52
Helsby	d						11 41				12 01									12 39			13 01
Frodsham	d						11 46				12 06									12 44			13 05
Runcorn 91	a						11 57													12 56			
Liverpool South Parkway 91	d	11 15	11 26			11 43	12 07							12 16	12 27				12 43	13 06			
Liverpool Lime Street 91	a						12 21													13 20			
Runcorn East	d										12 11												13 11
Warrington Bank Quay 90	a				11 47						12 20							12 47					13 19
Earlestown 5 90	a				11 54						12 28							12 54					13 28
Newton-le-Willows 90	a				11 57						12 30							12 57					13 30
Manchester Victoria 90	a				12 18													13 18					
Manchester Oxford Road 90	a		12 07								12 50				13 07								13 50
Manchester Pic'dilly 10 90	a		12 11	12 30							12 54				13 11	13 30							13 54
Crewe 10	a	11 49				12 17		11 54	11 54				12 19	12 48					13 17		12 54	12 54	
Cardiff Central 7 131	a																15 11						
Manchester Airport 84,85	a		12 32								13 19				13 32								14 19
Birmingham New Street 12 65	a	12 50				13 20				13 30				13 50					14 20				
London Euston 15 ⊖65	a	15 17				15 31		13 36	13 37					16 17					16 29		14 36	14 39	

A To Leeds
B From Liverpool Lime Street
C until 13 February
D from 17 February
E To Blaenau Ffestiniog
F until 14 February
G To Birmingham International
H To Llanelli

Table T081-R

Mondays to Fridays
16 December to 15 May

North Wales and Chester - Manchester / Liverpool and Crewe - Birmingham and London

		AW	LM	NT	NT	AW	NT	LM	AW	VT	AW	AW	AW	AW	AW	LM	VT	NT	NT	NT	LM	AW	VT
			■ A	◇ A		■ ⊠	◇ B	■ A	◇	◇■ ⊡	◇ C ⊼	◇ ⊼			◇ D	■ A	◇■ ⊡	◇ A		◇ B	■ A	◇	◇■ ⊡
Holyhead 30	d					11 34					11 48						12 53						
Valley	d										11x54												
Rhosneigr	d																						
Ty Croes	d																						
Bodorgan	d																						
Llanfairpwll	d										12x12												
Bangor (Gwynedd)	a					12 01					12 21						13 19						
	d					12 01					12 21						13 21						
Llanfairfechan	d										12x29												
Penmaenmawr	d										12x33												
Conwy	d										12x39												
Llandudno	d												12 47	13 09									
Deganwy	d												12x51	13x13									
Llandudno Junction	a					12 19					12 44		12 57	13 19			13 37						
	d					12 19					12 44	12 54					13 39						
Colwyn Bay	d					12 27					12 50	13 00					13 45						
Abergele & Pensarn	d											13 07											
Rhyl	d					12 38					13 00	13 13					13 56						
Prestatyn	d					12 44					13 05	13 19					14 01						
Flint	d					12 58					13 18	13 32					14 15						
Shotton	d											13 38											
Chester	a					13 13					13 34	13 51											
	d	12 53			13 02	13 16	13 21		13 27	13 35	13 38	13 52			13 53				14 02	14 20		14 27	14 35
Helsby	d								13 36			14 01										14 36	
Frodsham	d								13 40			14 05										14 40	
Runcorn 91	a								13 51													14 51	
Liverpool South Parkway 91	d		13 15	13 26				13 43	14 00							14 15		14 26			14 41	15 00	
Liverpool Lime Street 91	a								14 14													15 14	
Runcorn East	d											14 11											
Warrington Bank Quay 90	a						13 46					14 21								14 46			
Earlestown 5 90	a						13 54					14 28								14 54			
Newton-le-Willows 90	a						13 57					14 31								14 57			
Manchester Victoria 90	a						14 18													15 18			
Manchester Oxford Road 90	a			14 07								14 50						15 07					
Manchester Pic'dilly 10 90	a			14 11	14 30							14 54						15 11	15 30				
Crewe 10	a	13 18	13 46					14 17		13 54					14 18	14 49	14 54				15 17		14 54
Cardiff Central 7 131	a					16 15																	
Manchester Airport 84,85	a			14 32								15 19						15 32					
Birmingham New Street 12 65	a		14 50					15 20			15 31					15 50					16 17		
London Euston 15 ⊖65	a		16 46					17 31		15 37						17 46	16 36				18 30		16 36

		AW	AW	AW	LM	NT	NT	NT	LM	AW	AW	VT	AW	AW	AW	LM	NT	NT	NT	AW	AW	LM
		◇ ⊼			■ A	◇ A		◇ B	■ A	◇	■ C ⊼	◇■ ⊡	■ E ⊼	◇ ⊼		■ A	◇ A		◇ B	◇ ⊼	◇ ⊼	■ A
Holyhead 30	d	13 07									13 27	13 58									14 36	
Valley	d										13x33											
Rhosneigr	d										13x39											
Ty Croes	d										13x43											
Bodorgan	d										13x47											
Llanfairpwll	d										13x58											
Bangor (Gwynedd)	a	13 34									14 06	14 24									15 03	
	d	13 34									14 06	14 25									15 04	
Llanfairfechan	d										14x15										15x12	
Penmaenmawr	d										14x19										15x16	
Conwy	d										14x26										15x22	
Llandudno	d		14 08											14 40						15 08		
Deganwy	d		14x12											14x44						15x12		
Llandudno Junction	a	13 52	14 18								14 30	14 42		14 49						15 17	15 26	
	d	13 52									14 31	14 43		14 49						15 17	15 28	
Colwyn Bay	d	13 59									14 37	14 50		14 55						15 23	15 34	
Abergele & Pensarn	d	14 07												15 02						15 29		
Rhyl	d	14 14									14 47	15 00		15 08						15 35	15 43	
Prestatyn	d	14 20									14 52			15 14						15 41	15 49	
Flint	d	14 33									15 06			15 27						15 54	16 02	
Shotton	d										15 11		←	15 33						16 00		
Chester	a	14 48									15 25	15 28	15 25	15 47						16 15	16 19	
	d	14 49		14 53			15 02	15 17		15 32	15 36	15 35	15 36	15 49	15 53			16 02	16 14	16 20	16 23	
Helsby	d	14 59								15 41	→			15 58						16 30		
Frodsham	d	15 04								15 45				16 03						16 34		
Runcorn 91	a									15 56												
Liverpool South Parkway 91	d				15 15	15 26			15 43	16 05						16 15	16 26					16 43
Liverpool Lime Street 91	a									16 19												
Runcorn East	d	15 10												16 08						16 40		
Warrington Bank Quay 90	a	15 19						15 41						16 19					16 40	16 49		
Earlestown 5 90	a	15 28						15 51						16 28					16 52	16 57		
Newton-le-Willows 90	a							15 54						16 30					16 54	16 59		
Manchester Victoria 90	a							16 18											17 18			
Manchester Oxford Road 90	a					16 07								16 50			17 08			17 20		
Manchester Pic'dilly 10 90	a	15 54				16 11	16 30							16 54			17 11	17 30		17 24		
Crewe 10	a			15 18	15 51				16 17			15 54			16 18	16 49						17 21
Cardiff Central 7 131	a																				19 20	
Manchester Airport 84,85	a					16 30											17 30					
Birmingham New Street 12 65	a				16 50				17 21				17 31			17 50						18 21
London Euston 15 ⊖65	a				18 47				19 30			17 37				19 45						20 30

A From Liverpool Lime Street
B To Leeds
C To Birmingham International
D To Blaenau Ffestiniog
E From Holyhead to Birmingham International

Table T081-R

North Wales and Chester - Manchester / Liverpool and Crewe - Birmingham and London

		AW ◇	VT ◇■	AW	LM ■ A	NT ◇ A	NT	NT ◇ B	AW ■	AW	AW ◇ C	LM ■ D	AW ◇	AW ◇ E	VT ◇■ ⊠	AW	LM ■ A	NT ◇ A	NT	AW ◇	AW ■ ⊠	AW	NT F
Holyhead 30	d													15 38							16 51		
Valley	d													15x44									
Rhosneigr	d													15x49									
Ty Croes	d													15x53									
Bodorgan	d													15x57									
Llanfairpwll	d													16x07									
Bangor (Gwynedd)	a													16 16							17 18		
	d													16 17							17 18		
Llanfairfechan	d													16x25									
Penmaenmawr	d													16x29									
Conwy	d													16x35									
Llandudno	d								16 06		16 20									17 07		18 08	
Deganwy	d								16x10		16x24									17x11		18x12	
Llandudno Junction	a								16 15		16 29			16 39						17 16	17 36	18 18	
	d								16 15	16 25				16 40						17 17	17 36		
Colwyn Bay	d								16 21	16 31				16 46						17 23			
Abergele & Pensarn	d								16 27											17 29			
Rhyl	d								16 33	16 43				16 55						17 35			
Prestatyn	d								16 38	16 48				17 01						17 41			
Flint	d								16 52	17 02				17 14						17 54			
Shotton	d								16 58											18 00			
Chester	a								17 12	17 17				17 30						18 14	18 18		
	d	16 30	16 35	16 55			17 02	17 16	17 22				17 30	17 34	17 35	17 54			18 01	18 16	18 22		
Helsby	d	16 39							17 31				17 40							18 25			18 34
Frodsham	d	16 44							17 36				17 45							18 30			
Runcorn	91 a	16 56											17 57										
Liverpool South Parkway	91 d	17 06			17 15	17 26						17 44	18 06				18 15	18 26					
Liverpool Lime Street	91 a	17 20											18 22										
Runcorn East	d								17 41											18 35			18 42
Warrington Bank Quay	90 a							17 39	17 50											18 46			18 52
Earlestown 8	90 a							17 51	17 58											18 56			19 00
Newton-le-Willows	90 a							17 54	18 02											18 58			19 03
Manchester Victoria	90 a							18 18															19 25
Manchester Oxford Road	90 a					18 08			18 24									19 07		19 20			
Manchester Pic'dilly 10	90 ⇌ a					18 11	18 30		18 27									19 11	19 30	19 24			
Crewe 10	a		16 54	17 20	17 48							18 16			17 54	18 19	18 48						
Cardiff Central 7	131 a																				21 24		
Manchester Airport	84,85 ✈ a					18 32												19 32					
Birmingham New Street 12	65 a				18 50							19 19		19 31			19 50						
London Euston 15	⊖65 a		18 36		21 17										19 37		21 53						

		LM ■ A	AW ◇	AW	LM ■ A	NT ◇ A	NT	AW ◇ G	NT ◇ B	LM ■ A	AW ◇ H	AW	VT ◇■	AW ◇	AW ◇ C	AW	LM ■ A	NT ◇ A	NT	AW ◇	NT ◇ B	LM ■ A
Holyhead 30	d							17 31												18 23		
Valley	d							17x37												18x29		
Rhosneigr	d							17x42												18x34		
Ty Croes	d							17x46												18x38		
Bodorgan	d							17x50												18x42		
Llanfairpwll	d							18x00												18x53		
Bangor (Gwynedd)	a							18 09												19 01		
	d							18 10												19 02		
Llanfairfechan	d							18x18												19x10		
Penmaenmawr	d							18x22												19x14		
Conwy	d							18x28												19x20		
Llandudno	d													18 44	19 05							
Deganwy	d													18x48	19x09							
Llandudno Junction	a							18 32						18 53	19 14					19 25		
	d							18 33				18 39		18 53						19 26		
Colwyn Bay	d											18 45		18 59						19 32		
Abergele & Pensarn	d													19 06								
Rhyl	d											18 55		19 12						19 42		
Prestatyn	d											19 01		19 18						19 48		
Flint	d											19 14		19 31						20 01		
Shotton	d													19 37								
Chester	a							19 13				19 30		19 50						20 18		
	d		18 51	18 54			19 00		19 20		19 28		19 35	19 52		19 54			20 01	20 19	20 20	
Helsby	d		19 00								19 37			20 01							20 29	
Frodsham	d		19 05								19 41			20 05							20 34	
Runcorn	91 a										19 51											
Liverpool South Parkway	91 d	18 44			19 21	19 24				19 44	19 59						20 16	20 23				20 45
Liverpool Lime Street	91 a										20 15											
Runcorn East	d		19 10											20 11							20 39	
Warrington Bank Quay	90 a		19 19						19 43					20 19							20 48	
Earlestown 8	90 a		19 28						19 52					20 28							20 55	
Newton-le-Willows	90 a		19 31						19 57					20 30							20 58	
Manchester Victoria	90 a								20 17												21 17	
Manchester Oxford Road	90 a		19 50			20 08								20 51				21 08				
Manchester Pic'dilly 10	90 ⇌ a		19 54			20 11	20 30							20 56				21 11	21 35			
Crewe 10	a	19 17		19 19	19 53					20 16			19 54			20 19	20 47			20 41		21 17
Cardiff Central 7	131 a																					
Manchester Airport	84,85 ✈ a		20 19			20 30								21 17				21 31				
Birmingham New Street 12	65 a	20 20			20 50					21 21							21 48					22 18
London Euston 15	⊖65 a	22 53			23 23								21 39				00 26					

A From Liverpool Lime Street
B To Leeds
C To Blaenau Ffestiniog
D From Liverpool Lime Street to Walsall
E To Birmingham International
F From Ellesmere Port
G To Shrewsbury
H From Wrexham General

Table T081-R

North Wales and Chester - Manchester / Liverpool and Crewe - Birmingham and London

		NT A	AW ◇	AW ◇	AW	AW	AW FO ◇	AW FX ◇	NT	LM ■ A	AW ◇	AW ◇	VT ◇■	AW ◇	AW	NT ◇ A	NT	NT ◇	AW ◇	LM ■ A	AW ◇	NT	AW
Holyhead 30	d										19 22								20 32				
Valley	d										19x28												
Rhosneigr	d										19x33												
Ty Croes	d										19x37												
Bodorgan	d										19x41												
Llanfairpwll	d										19x51												
Bangor (Gwynedd)	a										19 59								20 59				
	d										20 00		20 20						21 01				
Llanfairfechan	d										20x08								21x09				
Penmaenmawr	d										20x12								21x13				
Conwy	d										20x18								21x19				
Llandudno	d			19 35		20 09								20 43	21 11								21 45
Deganwy	d			19x41		20x13								20x47	21x15								21x49
Llandudno Junction	a			19 46		20 19					20 22		20 36	20 52	21 22				21 23				21 54
	d			19 46							20 23		20 38	20 52					21 28				21 55
Colwyn Bay	d			19 53							20 29		20 44	20 58					21 34				22 01
Abergele & Pensarn	d			20 01										21 05					21 41				22 09
Rhyl	d			20 08							20 38		20 55	21 11					21 47				22 16
Prestatyn	d			20 14							20 44		21 01	21 17					21 52				22 22
Flint	d			20 27							20 57		21 14	21 30					22 06				22 37
Shotton	d										21 02			21 36					22 12				22 44
Chester	a			20 44							21 14		21 28	21 49					22 25				22 58
	d		20 36	20 45	20 52		20 55	20 55	21 02		21 18	21 25	21 35	21 52			22 01	22 13	22 30		22 30	22 52	23 01
Helsby	d		20 45		21 01							21 34		22 01							22 39		
Frodsham	d		20 50		21 06							21 39		22 06							22 44		
Runcorn	91 a		21 03									21 50									22 55		
Liverpool South Parkway	91 d	21 09	21 14							21 44		22 01				22 35				22 47	23 06		
Liverpool Lime Street	91 a		21 30									22 16									23 20		
Runcorn East	d				21 11									22 11				22 30					
Warrington Bank Quay	90 a				21 20									22 19				22 38					
Earlestown 8	90 a				21 27									22 27				22 52					
Newton-le-Willows	90 a				21 30									22 30				22 54					
Manchester Victoria	90 a																	23 18					
Manchester Oxford Road	90 a	22 11			21 49									22 51		23 16							
Manchester Pic'dilly 10	90 ⇌ a	22 15			21 53				22 33					22 55		23 20	23 27					00 26	
Crewe 10	a			21 07			21 18	21 20		22 15			21 54						22 52	23 25			23 28
Cardiff Central 7	131 a							00 20															
Manchester Airport	84,85 ✈ a	22 31														23 35							
Birmingham New Street 12	65 a									23 15	23 28		22 48										
London Euston 15	⊖65 a																						

		AW ◇ B	LM ■ A
Holyhead 30	d		
Valley	d		
Rhosneigr	d		
Ty Croes	d		
Bodorgan	d		
Llanfairpwll	d		
Bangor (Gwynedd)	a		
	d		
Llanfairfechan	d		
Penmaenmawr	d		
Conwy	d		
Llandudno	d		
Deganwy	d		
Llandudno Junction	a		
	d		
Colwyn Bay	d		
Abergele & Pensarn	d		
Rhyl	d		
Prestatyn	d		
Flint	d		
Shotton	d		
Chester	a		
	d	23 22	
Helsby	d	23 32	
Frodsham	d	23 36	
Runcorn	91 a		
Liverpool South Parkway	91 d		23 45
Liverpool Lime Street	91 a		
Runcorn East	d	23 42	
Warrington Bank Quay	90 a	23 51	
Earlestown 8	90 a	23 59	
Newton-le-Willows	90 a	00 03	
Manchester Victoria	90 a		
Manchester Oxford Road	90 a		
Manchester Pic'dilly 10	90 ⇌ a	00 25	
Crewe 10	a		00 23
Cardiff Central 7	131 a		
Manchester Airport	84,85 ✈ a		
Birmingham New Street 12	65 a		
London Euston 15	⊖65 a		

A From Liverpool Lime Street
B From Birmingham International

Table T081-R

Saturdays

21 December to 16 May

North Wales and Chester - Manchester / Liverpool and Crewe - Birmingham and London

		AW	AW	AW	AW	AW	AW	LM	NT	NT		AW	AW	AW	NT	AW	LM	LM	AW	NT		AW	VT	NT	LM
								■ A	◇ A			◇	◇	◇ B	◇ C		■ A	■ A	◇ D			E	◇■ 🛒	◇ C	■ A
Holyhead [30]	d													04 25											
Valley	d													04x32											
Rhosneigr	d																								
Ty Croes	d																								
Bodorgan	d																								
Llanfairpwll	d													04x49											
Bangor (Gwynedd)	a													04 56											
	d													04 57											
Llanfairfechan	d																								
Penmaenmawr	d																								
Conwy	d																								
Llandudno	d																								
Deganwy	d																								
Llandudno Junction	a													05 14											
	d				04 38									05 15		05 32									
Colwyn Bay	d				04 44									05 21		05 38									
Abergele & Pensarn	d				04 51											05 46									
Rhyl	d				04 57									05 30		05 53									
Prestatyn	d				05 02									05 36		05 59									
Flint	d				05 16									05 49		06 14									
Shotton	d				05 22											06 21									
Chester	a				05 35									06 06		06 34									
	d	03 36	04 22	04 55	05 36	05 38	05 51			05 56		06 04	06 13	06 20	06 22	06 35			06 43	06 51		07 12	07 17	07 20	
Helsby	d					05 47						06 13	06 22						06 52			07 21		07 29	
Frodsham	d					05 52						06 18	06 26						06 57			07 25		07 34	
Runcorn 91	a											06 28							07 08						
Liverpool South Parkway 91	d							06 20	06 24			06 37					06 44	07 15	07 17						07 45
Liverpool Lime Street 91	a											06 51							07 31						
Runcorn East	d					05 57							06 32									07 31		07 39	
Warrington Bank Quay 90	a					06 06							06 40		06 45							07 39		07 48	
Earlestown [6] 90	a					06 15							06 47		06 53							07 46		07 55	
Newton-le-Willows 90	a					06 18							06 50		06 56							07 49		07 58	
Manchester Victoria 90	a														07 17									08 18	
Manchester Oxford Road 90	a					06 41			07 05				07 13									08 08			
Manchester Pic'dilly [10] 90 ⇌	a	04 41				06 44			07 08	07 26			07 18							08 17		08 16			
Crewe [10]	a		04 45	05 18	05 57		06 14	06 47								07 01	07 13	07 47					07 36		08 17
Cardiff Central [7] 131	a													09 21											
Manchester Airport 84,85 ✈	a	05 03							07 28																
Birmingham New Street [12] 65	a		05 59					07 50									08 21	08 50							09 16
London Euston [15] ⊖65	a							10 17									10 30	11 17					09 28		11 30

		AW	AW	AW	AW	LM		NT	NT	AW	AW	NT	VT	AW	AW	LM		AW	LM	NT	NT	NT	LM	AW	AW
		◇ F	◇			■ A		◇ A		◇	◇ B	◇ C	◇■ 🛒	◇		■ A			■ A	◇ A		◇ C	■ A	■ F	◇
Holyhead [30]	d	05 23									06 35		06 52											07 15	
Valley	d	05x29									06x41													07x21	
Rhosneigr	d	05x34																						07x26	
Ty Croes	d	05x38																						07x30	
Bodorgan	d	05x42																						07x34	
Llanfairpwll	d	05x52									06x58													07x44	
Bangor (Gwynedd)	a	06 01									07 06		07 18											07 53	
	d	06 02									07 07		07 20											08 02	
Llanfairfechan	d	06x10																						08x10	
Penmaenmawr	d	06x14																						08x14	
Conwy	d	06x20																						08x20	
Llandudno	d		06 34	07 08										07 45	08 08										
Deganwy	d		06x38	07x12										07x49	08x12										
Llandudno Junction	a	06 24	06 43	07 18							07 24		07 36	07 54	08 18									08 24	
	d	06 25	06 44								07 25		07 38	07 54										08 25	
Colwyn Bay	d	06 31	06 50								07 31		07 44	08 00										08 31	
Abergele & Pensarn	d		06 57											08 07											
Rhyl	d	06 41	07 03								07 40		07 55	08 13										08 41	
Prestatyn	d	06 47	07 08								07 46		08 01	08 19										08 47	
Flint	d	07 00	07 21								07 59		08 15	08 32										09 00	
Shotton	d		07 27											08 38											
Chester	a	07 18	07 40								08 16		08 28	08 51										09 17	
	d	07 30	07 41		07 54				08 02	08 10	08 20	08 21	08 35	08 52				08 54			09 02	09 21		09 30	09 30
Helsby	d		07 50							08 19		08 30		09 01											09 39
Frodsham	d		07 54							08 23		08 35		09 05											09 44
Runcorn 91	a									08 34															09 56
Liverpool South Parkway 91	d					08 18		08 26		08 43						08 44			09 18	09 26			09 42		10 05
Liverpool Lime Street 91	a									08 58															10 19
Runcorn East	d		08 00									08 40		09 11											
Warrington Bank Quay 90	a		08 09									08 49		09 19								09 45			
Earlestown [6] 90	a		08 29									08 56		09 28								09 54			
Newton-le-Willows 90	a		08 32									08 59		09 30								09 57			
Manchester Victoria 90	a											09 19										10 18			
Manchester Oxford Road 90	a		08 50					09 07						09 50						10 07					
Manchester Pic'dilly [10] 90 ⇌	a		08 54					09 11	09 30					09 54						10 11	10 30				
Crewe [10]	a				08 19	08 48							08 54			09 17		09 19	09 48				10 15		
Cardiff Central [7] 131	a										11 17														
Manchester Airport 84,85 ✈	a		09 19					09 32						10 19						10 32					
Birmingham New Street [12] 65	a	09 31				09 50										10 20			10 50				11 20	11 31	
London Euston [15] ⊖65	a					12 17							10 36			12 30			13 17				13 30		

A From Liverpool Lime Street
B To Maesteg
C To Leeds
D From Wrexham General
E From Shrewsbury
F To Birmingham International

NRT DECEMBER 19 EDITION

Table T081-R

Saturdays

21 December to 16 May

North Wales and Chester - Manchester / Liverpool and Crewe - Birmingham and London

		VT		AW	AW	AW	LM	NT	NT	LM	AW	AW		NT	VT	AW	AW	AW	LM	NT	NT	NT		LM	AW
		◇■ 🛒		◇ 🚲			■ A	◇ A		■ A	◇	◇ B 🚲		◇ C	◇■ 🛒	■ 🚲			■ A	◇ A		◇ C		■ A	◇
Holyhead [30]	d	07 55										08 20			08 55										
Valley	d											08x26													
Rhosneigr	d											08x32													
Ty Croes	d											08x35													
Bodorgan	d											08x40													
Llanfairpwll	d											08x49													
Bangor (Gwynedd)	a	08 21										08 58			09 21										
	d	08 22										09 01			09 22										
Llanfairfechan	d											09x09													
Penmaenmawr	d											09x13													
Conwy	d											09x20													
Llandudno	d			08 45	09 08											09 45	10 10								
Deganwy	d			08x49	09x12											09x49	10x14								
Llandudno Junction	a	08 39		08 54	09 18							09 24			09 39	09 54	10 20								
	d	08 40		08 54								09 25			09 40	09 54									
Colwyn Bay	d	08 47		09 00								09 31			09 47	10 00									
Abergele & Pensarn	d			09 07												10 07									
Rhyl	d	08 58		09 13								09 40			09 58	10 13									
Prestatyn	d	09 04		09 19								09 46			10 03	10 19									
Flint	d	09 17		09 32								09 59				10 32									
Shotton	d			09 38												10 38									
Chester	a	09 31		09 51								10 15			10 28	10 51									
	d	09 35		09 52		09 54			10 02		10 12	10 19		10 23	10 35	10 52		10 54			11 02	11 24			11 32
Helsby	d			10 01							10 21					11 01									11 41
Frodsham	d			10 05							10 26					11 05									11 45
Runcorn 91	a										10 37														11 56
Liverpool South Parkway 91	d						10 18	10 26		10 44	10 47								11 18	11 26				11 45	12 05
Liverpool Lime Street 91	a										11 04														12 19
Runcorn East	d			10 11												11 11									
Warrington Bank Quay 90	a			10 19										10 46		11 19						11 47			
Earlestown [6] 90	a			10 28										10 54		11 28						11 54			
Newton-le-Willows 90	a			10 30										10 57		11 30						11 57			
Manchester Victoria 90	a													11 18								12 18			
Manchester Oxford Road 90	a			10 50				11 07								11 51				12 07					
Manchester Pic'dilly [10] 90 ⇌	a			10 54				11 11	11 30							11 55				12 11	12 30				
Crewe [10]	a	09 54				10 19	10 47			11 17					10 54			11 19	11 46					12 18	
Cardiff Central [7] 131	a											13 14													
Manchester Airport 84,85 ✈	a			11 19				11 32								12 19				12 32					
Birmingham New Street [12] 65	a						11 50			12 20									12 50					13 20	
London Euston [15] ⊖65	a	11 36					14 18			14 30					12 36				15 17					15 31	

		VT	AW	AW	AW	AW	AW	LM		NT	NT	AW	NT	LM	AW	VT	AW	AW		AW	LM	NT	NT	NT	LM
		◇■ 🛒	■ D 🚲	◇ E	◇ 🚲			■ A		◇ A		■ 🚲	◇ C	■ A	◇	◇■ 🛒	◇ 🚲				■ A	◇ A		◇ C	■ A
Holyhead [30]	d		09 29									10 33													
Valley	d		09x35									10x39													
Rhosneigr	d		09x40																						
Ty Croes	d		09x44																						
Bodorgan	d		09x48																						
Llanfairpwll	d		09x58									10x56													
Bangor (Gwynedd)	a		10 07									11 04													
	d		10 08									11 05													
Llanfairfechan	d		10x16																						
Penmaenmawr	d		10x20																						
Conwy	d		10x26																						
Llandudno	d			10 22	10 44	11 08											11 44	12 08							
Deganwy	d			10x26	10x48	11x12											11x48	12x12							
Llandudno Junction	a		10 30	10 33	10 53	11 18						11 22					11 53	12 18							
	d		10 31		10 53							11 23					11 53								
Colwyn Bay	d		10 37		10 59							11 29					11 59								
Abergele & Pensarn	d				11 06												12 06								
Rhyl	d		10 47		11 12							11 39					12 12								
Prestatyn	d		10 53		11 18							11 45					12 18								
Flint	d		11 06		11 31							11 58					12 31								
Shotton	d				11 37												12 37								
Chester	a		11 26		11 50							12 14					12 50								
	d	11 35	11 36		11 52		11 54				12 02	12 19	12 24		12 30	12 35	12 51			12 54			13 02	13 21	
Helsby	d				12 01										12 39		13 00								
Frodsham	d				12 06										12 44		13 05								
Runcorn 91	a														12 54										
Liverpool South Parkway 91	d							12 18		12 27				12 45	13 04						13 16	13 26			13 45
Liverpool Lime Street 91	a														13 18										
Runcorn East	d				12 11												13 11								
Warrington Bank Quay 90	a				12 20								12 47				13 20							13 44	
Earlestown [6] 90	a				12 28								12 54				13 28							13 54	
Newton-le-Willows 90	a				12 30								12 57				13 30							13 57	
Manchester Victoria 90	a												13 18											14 18	
Manchester Oxford Road 90	a				12 50					13 07							13 50					14 07			
Manchester Pic'dilly [10] 90 ⇌	a				12 54					13 11	13 30						13 54					14 11	14 30		
Crewe [10]	a	11 54					12 19	12 47						13 17		12 54				13 19	13 45				14 16
Cardiff Central [7] 131	a											15 24													
Manchester Airport 84,85 ✈	a				13 19					13 32							14 19					14 32			
Birmingham New Street [12] 65	a		13 31					13 51						14 20							14 50				15 20
London Euston [15] ⊖65	a	13 36						16 19						16 30		14 36					17 17				17 30

A From Liverpool Lime Street
B To Maesteg
C To Leeds
D To Birmingham International
E To Blaenau Ffestiniog

Table T081-R

Saturdays
21 December to 16 May

North Wales and Chester - Manchester / Liverpool and Crewe - Birmingham and London

	AW	AW	VT	AW	AW	AW	AW	LM	NT	NT	AW	NT	LM	AW	VT	AW	AW	AW	LM	NT	NT
	◇	■ A ⊼	◇■1 ⊐	◇ ⊼		◇ B		■1 C	◇ C		◇ D ⊼	◇ E	■1 C	◇	◇■1 ⊐	◇ ⊼			■1 C	◇ C	
Holyhead [30] d		11 28									12 39										
Valley d		11x34																			
Rhosneigr d		11x40																			
Ty Croes d		11x44																			
Bodorgan d		11x48																			
Llanfairpwll d		11x59																			
Bangor (Gwynedd) a		12 08									13 06										
d		12 08									13 07					13 33					
Llanfairfechan d		12x17														13x41					
Penmaenmawr d		12x22														13x45					
Conwy d		12x28														13x51					
Llandudno d				12 40	12 46	13 08											14 08				
Deganwy d				12x44	12x50	13x12											14x12				
Llandudno Junction a		12 32		12 50	12 56	13 19					13 24					13 56	14 18				
d		12 33		12 53							13 25					13 56					
Colwyn Bay d		12 39		12 59							13 31					14 02					
Abergele & Pensarn d				13 06												14 09					
Rhyl d		12 50		13 12							13 40					14 15					
Prestatyn d		12 56		13 18							13 46					14 21					
Flint d		13 10		13 31							13 59					14 34					
Shotton d				13 37												14 40					
Chester a		13 29		13 50							14 16					14 53					
d	13 30	13 35	13 35	13 52			13 54			14 02	14 19	14 20		14 27	14 35	14 54		14 54			15 02
Helsby d	13 39			14 02										14 36		15 03					
Frodsham d	13 44			14 06										14 40		15 07					
Runcorn 91 a	13 55													14 51							
Liverpool South Parkway 91 d	14 04							14 17	14 26				14 45	14 59					15 17	15 26	
Liverpool Lime Street 91 a	14 18													15 14							
Runcorn East d				14 12												15 13					
Warrington Bank Quay 90 a				14 21								14 47				15 21					
Earlestown [8] 90 a				14 28								14 54				15 28					
Newton-le-Willows 90 a				14 31								14 57				15 31					
Manchester Victoria 90 a												15 18									
Manchester Oxford Road 90 a				14 50					15 07							15 50				16 07	
Manchester Pic'dilly [10] 90 a				14 54					15 11	15 30						15 55				16 11	16 30
Crewe [10] a			13 54				14 19	14 45					15 17		14 54			15 19	15 46		
Cardiff Central [7] 131 a											17 09										
Manchester Airport 84,85 a				15 19					15 32							16 19				16 32	
Birmingham New Street [12] 65 a		15 30						15 50					16 17						16 50		
London Euston [15] ⊖65 a			15 37					18 17					18 30		16 36				19 17		

	NT	LM	AW	AW	VT	AW	AW	AW	LM	NT	NT	NT	AW	AW	LM	AW	VT	AW	AW	AW	LM	NT
	◇ E	■1 C	◇	■ A ⊼	◇■1 ⊐	■ F ⊼	◇ ⊼		■1 C	◇ C		◇ E	◇ ⊼		■1 G	◇	◇■1 ⊐	◇ ⊼			■1 C	◇ C
Holyhead [30] d				13 28	13 58								14 27									
Valley d				13x34																		
Rhosneigr d				13x39																		
Ty Croes d				13x43																		
Bodorgan d				13x47																		
Llanfairpwll d				13x57																		
Bangor (Gwynedd) a				14 06	14 24								14 54									
d				14 07	14 25								14 55									
Llanfairfechan d													15x03									
Penmaenmawr d													15x07									
Conwy d													15x13									
Llandudno d							14 42							15 08				15 44	16 07			
Deganwy d							14x46							15x12				15x48	16x11			
Llandudno Junction a				14 24	14 42		14 51						15 17	15 18				15 53	16 17			
d				14 25	14 43		14 51						15 18					15 53				
Colwyn Bay d				14 31	14 50		14 57						15 24					15 59				
Abergele & Pensarn d							15 04											16 06				
Rhyl d				14 41	15 00		15 10						15 35					16 12				
Prestatyn d				14 47			15 16						15 40					16 18				
Flint d				15 00			15 29						15 53					16 31				
Shotton d						←	15 35											16 37				
Chester a				15 18	15 27	15 18	15 48						16 10					16 50				
d	15 17		15 32	15 36	15 35	15 36	15 49	15 54			16 02	16 20	16 22			16 30	16 35	16 52		16 55		
Helsby d			15 41	→			15 58									16 39		17 01				
Frodsham d			15 45				16 03									16 44		17 06				
Runcorn 91 a			15 56													16 55						
Liverpool South Parkway 91 d		15 43	16 05						16 17	16 26					16 45	17 04					17 17	17 26
Liverpool Lime Street 91 a			16 19													17 19						
Runcorn East d							16 08											17 11				
Warrington Bank Quay 90 a	15 41						16 19					16 44						17 20				
Earlestown [8] 90 a	15 51						16 28					16 51						17 28				
Newton-le-Willows 90 a	15 54						16 30					16 54						17 30				
Manchester Victoria 90 a	16 18											17 18										
Manchester Oxford Road 90 a							16 50			17 08								17 50				18 08
Manchester Pic'dilly [10] 90 a							16 54			17 11	17 30							17 54				18 11
Crewe [10] a		16 17			15 54			16 19	16 46						17 18		16 54			17 20	17 48	
Cardiff Central [7] 131 a													19 09									
Manchester Airport 84,85 a							17 19			17 32								18 19				18 32
Birmingham New Street [12] 65 a		17 20				17 31			17 50						18 20						18 49	
London Euston [15] ⊖65 a		19 31			17 36				20 17								18 36				21 10	

A To Birmingham International
B To Blaenau Ffestiniog
C From Liverpool Lime Street
D To Maesteg
E To Leeds
F From Holyhead to Birmingham International
G From Liverpool Lime Street to Milton Keynes Central

Table T081-R

Saturdays
21 December to 16 May

North Wales and Chester - Manchester / Liverpool and Crewe - Birmingham and London

	NT	NT	LM	AW	AW	AW	VT	AW	AW	AW	LM	NT	NT	NT	AW	AW	AW	LM	AW	LM	NT	NT
		◇ A	■1 B	■ C ⊼	◇	◇ D	◇■1 ⊐	◇ ⊼			■1 B	◇ B		◇ A	◇ ⊼	◇ ⊼		■1 B		■1 B	◇ B	
Holyhead [30] d				15 26											16 52							
Valley d				15x32																		
Rhosneigr d				15x38																		
Ty Croes d				15x42																		
Bodorgan d				15x46																		
Llanfairpwll d				15x57																		
Bangor (Gwynedd) a				16 06											17 19							
d				16 06											17 20							
Llanfairfechan d				16x14																		
Penmaenmawr d				16x18																		
Conwy d				16x24																		
Llandudno d						16 20		16 44	17 08							17 44	18 08					
Deganwy d						16x24		16x48	17x12							17x48	18x12					
Llandudno Junction a				16 29		16 31		16 53	17 18						17 37	17 53	18 18					
d				16 30				16 53							17 38	17 53						
Colwyn Bay d				16 36				16 59							17 44	17 59						
Abergele & Pensarn d								17 06								18 06						
Rhyl d				16 46				17 12							17 54	18 12						
Prestatyn d				16 52				17 18							18 00	18 18						
Flint d				17 05				17 31							18 13	18 31						
Shotton d								17 37								18 37						
Chester a				17 24				17 50							18 29	18 50						
d	17 02	17 20		17 30	17 31		17 35	17 51		17 53			18 01	18 24	18 33	18 52			18 54			19 00
Helsby d					17 41			18 00						18 33		19 01						
Frodsham d					17 46			18 05								19 06						
Runcorn 91 a					17 56																	
Liverpool South Parkway 91 d			17 44		18 06						18 16	18 26						18 44		19 21	19 24	
Liverpool Lime Street 91 a					18 20																	
Runcorn East d								18 11								19 11						
Warrington Bank Quay 90 a		17 43						18 19						18 48		19 20						
Earlestown [8] 90 a		17 51						18 26						18 55		19 29						
Newton-le-Willows 90 a		17 54						18 29						18 58		19 31						
Manchester Victoria 90 a		18 18												19 17								
Manchester Oxford Road 90 a								18 50				19 07				19 50					20 07	
Manchester Pic'dilly [10] 90 a	18 30							18 53				19 11	19 30			19 54					20 11	20 30
Crewe [10] a			18 18				17 54			18 18	18 48							19 16	19 19	19 51		
Cardiff Central [7] 131 a															21 34							
Manchester Airport 84,85 a												19 32				20 19					20 30	
Birmingham New Street [12] 65 a			19 20	19 30							19 49							20 20		20 50		
London Euston [15] ⊖65 a			21 54								22 12							22 53		23 31		

	NT	AW	LM	AW	AW	AW	AW	AW	AW	LM	NT	NT	AW	NT	LM	AW	VT	AW	AW	AW	LM
	◇ A	◇ E	■1 B	◇ F		◇	◇ D			■1 G	◇ B		◇	◇ A	■1 B	◇	◇ ⊐	◇			■1 B
Holyhead [30] d		17 32											18 25								
Valley d		17x38											18x32								
Rhosneigr d		17x43											18x37								
Ty Croes d		17x47											18x41								
Bodorgan d		17x51											18x46								
Llanfairpwll d		18x01											18x56								
Bangor (Gwynedd) a		18 10											19 03								
d		18 11											19 04								
Llanfairfechan d		18x19											19x12								
Penmaenmawr d		18x23											19x16								
Conwy d		18x29											19x22								
Llandudno d						18 44	19 03	19 13										19 42	20 08		
Deganwy d						18x48	19x07	19x17										19x46	20x12		
Llandudno Junction a		18 33				18 53	19 11	19 22					19 26					19 51	20 17		
d		18 34				18 53							19 27					19 51			
Colwyn Bay d		18 40				18 59							19 33					19 57			
Abergele & Pensarn d						19 06												20 04			
Rhyl d		18 50				19 12							19 43					20 10			
Prestatyn d		18 56				19 18							19 49					20 16			
Flint d		19 09				19 31							20 02					20 29			
Shotton d						19 37												20 35			
Chester a		19 26				19 50							20 19					20 48			
d	19 20			19 31	19 37	19 51			19 54			20 01	20 20	20 20		20 30	20 35	20 50		20 54	
Helsby d				19 41		20 01								20 29		20 39		20 59			
Frodsham d				19 46		20 05								20 34		20 43		21 04			
Runcorn 91 a				19 57												20 54					
Liverpool South Parkway 91 d			19 45	20 09						20 14	20 23				20 45	21 03					21 26
Liverpool Lime Street 91 a				20 24												21 17					
Runcorn East d						20 11								20 39				21 11			
Warrington Bank Quay 90 a	19 43					20 19								20 48				21 20			
Earlestown [8] 90 a	19 52					20 27								20 55				21 27			
Newton-le-Willows 90 a	19 57					20 29								20 58				21 30			
Manchester Victoria 90 a	20 17													21 17							
Manchester Oxford Road 90 a						20 51					21 08							21 49			
Manchester Pic'dilly [10] 90 a						20 56					21 11	21 33						21 55			
Crewe [10] a			20 17		20 00				20 19	20 51			20 41		21 16		20 54			21 19	22 00
Cardiff Central [7] 131 a																					
Manchester Airport 84,85 a											21 31										
Birmingham New Street [12] 65 a			21 20							21 50					22 17						
London Euston [15] ⊖65 a																					

A To Leeds
B From Liverpool Lime Street
C To Birmingham International
D To Blaenau Ffestiniog
E To Shrewsbury
F From Wrexham General
G From Liverpool Lime Street to Northampton

Table T081-R

Saturdays
21 December to 16 May

North Wales and Chester - Manchester / Liverpool and Crewe - Birmingham and London

		NT	NT	LM	AW	AW	AW	AW	LM	NT	NT	AW	NT	AW	AW
		◇ A		■ A	◇	◇			■ A	◇ A		◇		◇	
Holyhead [30]	d				19 22							20 37			
Valley	d				19x28										
Rhosneigr	d				19x33										
Ty Croes	d				19x37										
Bodorgan	d				19x41										
Llanfairpwll	d				19x51										
Bangor (Gwynedd)	a				20 00							21 06			
	d				20 01							21 06			
Llanfairfechan	d				20x09							21x14			
Penmaenmawr	d				20x13							21x18			
Conwy	d				20x19							21x24			
Llandudno	d						20 43							21 45	
Deganwy	d						20x47							21x49	
Llandudno Junction	a				20 23		20 52					21 29		21 54	
	d				20 24		20 52					21 29		21 55	
Colwyn Bay	d				20 30		20 58					21 35		22 01	
Abergele & Pensarn	d						21 05					21 42		22 09	
Rhyl	d				20 40		21 11					21 48		22 16	
Prestatyn	d				20 46		21 17					21 54		22 22	
Flint	d				20 59		21 30					22 07		22 37	
Shotton	d						21 36					22 13		22 44	
Chester	a				21 17		21 48					22 26		22 57	
	d		21 01		21 30	21 30		21 53			22 01	22 27	22 48	23 01	23 22
Helsby	d					21 39		22 02							23 31
Frodsham	d					21 44		22 06							23 35
Runcorn	91 a					21 55									
Liverpool South Parkway	91 d	21 40		21 44		22 05			22 14	22 35					
Liverpool Lime Street	91 a					22 19									
Runcorn East	d							22 12							23 41
Warrington Bank Quay	90 a							22 20							23 50
Earlestown [8]	90 a							22 27							23 58
Newton-le-Willows	90 a							22 31							00 01
Manchester Victoria	90 a														
Manchester Oxford Road	90 a	22 20						22 51		23 16					
Manchester Pic'dilly [10]	90 ⇌ a	22 24	22 28					22 55		23 20	23 31		00 17		00 23
Crewe [10]	a			22 20					22 44			22 50		23 27	
Cardiff Central [7]	131 a														
Manchester Airport	84,85 ✈ a	22 40								23 38					
Birmingham New Street [12]	65 a			23 18	23 30										
London Euston [15]	⊖65 a														

Sundays
15 December to 10 May

		NT	AW	AW	AW	NT	NT	NT	AW	AW	AW	AW	AW	LM	NT	AW	AW	AW	NT	NT	AW	NT	VT
		◇ A	◇		◇	◇ A	B	C	◇ D ✕	◇		◇ ✕		■ A	◇ A	◇ ✕	◇	◇	◇ E	B		C	◇■ 🍴
Holyhead [30]	d											07 50					08 45						
Valley	d											07 56											
Rhosneigr	d											08 02											
Ty Croes	d											08 05											
Bodorgan	d											08 10											
Llanfairpwll	d											08 19											
Bangor (Gwynedd)	a											08 28					09 12						
	d											08 28					09 13						
Llanfairfechan	d											08x36											
Penmaenmawr	d											08x40											
Conwy	d											08x46											
Llandudno	d																						
Deganwy	d																						
Llandudno Junction	a											08 51					09 30						
	d											08 51					09 35						
Colwyn Bay	d											08 57					09 41						
Abergele & Pensarn	d																09 48						
Rhyl	d											09 08					09 54						
Prestatyn	d																09 59						
Flint	d																10 13						
Shotton	d											09 28					10 19						
Chester	a											09 41					10 32						
	d		08 31	08 38	08 41		09 04	09 04	09 24	09 31	09 39	09 42	09 57			10 36	10 39	10 47		10 56	10 57	10 58	11 28
Helsby	d		08 40		08 50					09 40		09 51				10 45		10 56					
Frodsham	d		08 45		08 54					09 45		09 55				10 49		11 01					
Runcorn	91 a		08 55							09 55								11 11					
Liverpool South Parkway	91 d	08 31	09 04			09 26				10 04				10 22	10 26			11 20	11 26				
Liverpool Lime Street	91 a		09 18							10 18								11 33					
Runcorn East	d				08 59							10 00				10 54							
Warrington Bank Quay	90 a				09 08							10 10				11 04							
Earlestown [8]	90 a				09 16							10 17				11 12							
Newton-le-Willows	90 a				09 19							10 20				11 15							
Manchester Victoria	90 a																						
Manchester Oxford Road	90 a	09 07			09 38	10 06						10 40			11 06	11 35			12 05				
Manchester Pic'dilly [10]	90 ⇌ a	09 11			09 43	10 11	10 31	10 32				10 46			11 10	11 40			12 09	12 26		12 36	
Crewe [10]	a			09 02							10 04		10 22	10 55			11 03				11 22		11 47
Cardiff Central [7]	131 a																						
Manchester Airport	84,85 ✈ a	09 28				10 31									11 28				12 26				
Birmingham New Street [12]	65 a								11 16					12 11									
London Euston [15]	⊖65 a													14 24									13 42

A From Liverpool Lime Street
B until 29 March
C from 5 April
D To Birmingham International
E from 5 April. From Liverpool Lime Street

NRT DECEMBER 19 EDITION

Table T081-R

Sundays
15 December to 10 May

North Wales and Chester - Manchester / Liverpool and Crewe - Birmingham and London

		LM	AW	AW	AW	AW	AW	AW	AW	AW	VT	AW	AW	NT	NT	AW	LM	AW	AW	NT	NT	AW	VT
		■ A	◇ B ✕	◇ ✕	◇ C		◇			■ ✕	◇■ 🍴			◇ D	◇ E	◇ ✕	■ A	◇		◇ A			◇■ 🍴
Holyhead [30]	d									10 20	10 55												11 50
Valley	d									10x26													
Rhosneigr	d									10x31													
Ty Croes	d									10x35													
Bodorgan	d									10x39													
Llanfairpwll	d									10x49													
Bangor (Gwynedd)	a									10 58	11 21												12 16
	d									10 59	11 22												12 17
Llanfairfechan	d									11x07													
Penmaenmawr	d									11x11													
Conwy	d									11x17													
Llandudno	d				10 22	11 07						11 40	12 18										
Deganwy	d				10x26	11x11						11x44	12x22										
Llandudno Junction	a				10 31	11 17				11 21	11 38	11 50	12 28										12 34
	d			10 25						11 22	11 40												12 35
Colwyn Bay	d			10 31						11 28	11 46												12 42
Abergele & Pensarn	d			10 38						11 35													
Rhyl	d			10 44						11 41	11 57												12 53
Prestatyn	d			10 50						11 46	12 03												12 59
Flint	d			11 03						12 00	12 16												
Shotton	d			11 09						12 06													
Chester	a			11 23						12 21	12 30												13 23
	d		11 32	11 36			11 47	11 57	12 23	12 29	12 33					12 36		12 47	12 59		12 59	13 22	13 30
Helsby	d			11 45			11 56									12 45		12 56					
Frodsham	d			11 49			12 01									12 49		13 01					
Runcorn	91 a						12 11											13 11					
Liverpool South Parkway	91 d	11 45					12 21							12 26	12 26		12 43	13 21		13 26			
Liverpool Lime Street	91 a						12 35											13 35					
Runcorn East	d			11 54												12 54							
Warrington Bank Quay	90 a			12 03												13 03							
Earlestown [8]	90 a			12 11												13 11							
Newton-le-Willows	90 a			12 14												13 13							
Manchester Victoria	90 a																						
Manchester Oxford Road	90 a			12 33										13 07	13 07	13 33				14 07			
Manchester Pic'dilly [10]	90 ⇌ a			12 40										13 11	13 11	13 37				14 11	14 35		
Crewe [10]	a	12 17						12 22	12 45		12 53						13 17		13 20			13 44	13 50
Cardiff Central [7]	131 a									15 26													
Manchester Airport	84,85 ✈ a													13 27	13 28					14 27			
Birmingham New Street [12]	65 a	13 14	13 30														14 14						
London Euston [15]	⊖65 a	15 40									14 40						16 40						15 41

		VT	AW	LM	AW	AW	AW	AW	VT	VT	AW	AW	AW	NT	AW	LM	AW	NT	NT	VT	AW	AW
		◇■ 🍴		■ A	◇ B ✕	◇	◇		◇■ 🍴	◇■ 🍴	◇ C			◇ A	◇ ✕	■ A	◇	◇ A		◇■ 🍴	◇ ✕	
Holyhead [30]	d								12 50											13 55		
Valley	d																					
Rhosneigr	d																					
Ty Croes	d																					
Bodorgan	d																					
Llanfairpwll	d																					
Bangor (Gwynedd)	a								13 16											14 21		
	d								13 18											14 22		
Llanfairfechan	d																					
Penmaenmawr	d																					
Conwy	d																					
Llandudno	d		13 17								13 28	13 52	14 20									15 14
Deganwy	d		13x21								13x32	13x56	14x24									15x18
Llandudno Junction	a		13 27						13 34		13 37	14 02	14 30							14 39		15 24
	d								13 36											14 40		
Colwyn Bay	d								13 42											14 46		
Abergele & Pensarn	d																					
Rhyl	d								13 53											14 57		
Prestatyn	d								13 59											15 03		
Flint	d								14 13													
Shotton	d																					
Chester	a								14 26											15 30		
	d	13 30			13 35	13 36	13 47	14 24	14 33	14 33					14 36		14 47		15 04	15 32	15 36	
Helsby	d					13 45	13 56								14 45		14 56				15 45	
Frodsham	d					13 49	14 01								14 49		15 01				15 49	
Runcorn	91 a						14 11										15 11					
Liverpool South Parkway	91 d			13 45			14 20							14 26		14 43	15 20	15 26				
Liverpool Lime Street	91 a						14 34										15 36					
Runcorn East	d					13 54									14 54						15 54	
Warrington Bank Quay	90 a					14 03									15 03						16 03	
Earlestown [8]	90 a					14 11									15 11						16 11	
Newton-le-Willows	90 a					14 13									15 13						16 13	
Manchester Victoria	90 a																					
Manchester Oxford Road	90 a					14 34								15 07	15 33			16 07			16 33	
Manchester Pic'dilly [10]	90 ⇌ a					14 40								15 11	15 40			16 11	16 40		16 40	
Crewe [10]	a	13 50		14 17				14 50	14 54	14 54						15 17				15 52		
Cardiff Central [7]	131 a																					
Manchester Airport	84,85 ✈ a													15 27				16 27				
Birmingham New Street [12]	65 a			15 14	15 26											16 14						
London Euston [15]	⊖65 a	15 41		17 40					16 40	16 40						18 40				17 40		

A From Liverpool Lime Street
B To Birmingham International
C To Blaenau Ffestiniog
D from 5 April. From Liverpool Lime Street
E until 29 March. From Liverpool Lime Street

Table T081-R

Sundays

15 December to 10 May

North Wales and Chester - Manchester / Liverpool and Crewe - Birmingham and London

Station		LM	AW	AW	AW	NT	AW	AW		AW	LM	AW	AW	NT	NT	AW	AW	AW		AW	VT	VT	AW	LM	AW
		■1	◇	◇		◇		◇			■1	◇		◇		◇				◇	◇■1	◇■1	◇	■1	◇
		A	B			A					A			A						B	C	D		A	
								⫪													🍽	🍽	⫪		
Holyhead 30	d							14 30								15 30									
Valley	d							14x37																	
Rhosneigr	d							14x42																	
Ty Croes	d							14x46																	
Bodorgan	d							14x51																	
Llanfairpwll	d							15x01																	
Bangor (Gwynedd)	a							15 09								15 57									
	d							15 09								15 58									
Llanfairfechan	d															16x06									
Penmaenmawr	d															16x10									
Conwy	d															16x16									
Llandudno	d									15 44							16 16	16 52							
Deganwy	d									15x48							16x20	16x56							
Llandudno Junction	a							15 29		15 54						16 20	16 26	17 02							
	d							15 34								16 25									
Colwyn Bay	d							15 40								16 31									
Abergele & Pensarn	d							15 47								16 38									
Rhyl	d							15 53								16 44									
Prestatyn	d							15 58								16 49									
Flint	d							16 12								17 03									
Shotton	d							16 18								17 09									
Chester	a							16 34								17 22									
	d		15 40	15 47	15 57		16 27	16 36				16 47	16 57		17 07	17 22				17 31	17 35	17 35	17 36		17 47
Helsby	d			15 56				16 45				16 56											17 45		17 56
Frodsham	d			16 01				16 49				17 01											17 49		18 01
Runcorn 91	a			16 11								17 11													18 11
Liverpool South Parkway 91	d	15 45		16 20		16 24					16 43	17 20		17 26										17 45	18 21
Liverpool Lime Street 91	a			16 34								17 34													18 35
Runcorn East	d							16 54															17 54		
Warrington Bank Quay 90	a							17 03															18 03		
Earlestown 8 90	a							17 11															18 11		
Newton-le-Willows 90	a							17 13															18 13		
Manchester Victoria 90	a																								
Manchester Oxford Road 90	a					17 07		17 33						18 07									18 33		
Manchester Pic'dilly 10 90 ⛴	a					17 11		17 40						18 11	18 38								18 37		
Crewe 10	a	16 17			16 20		16 52				17 17		17 20			17 43					17 53	17 53		18 17	
Cardiff Central 7 131	a																								
Manchester Airport 84,85 ✈	a					17 27								18 27											
Birmingham New Street 12 65	a	17 14	17 40								18 14									19 28				19 14	
London Euston 15 ⊖65	a	19 40									20 40										19 41	19 42		21 43	

Station		AW	AW	VT		AW	AW	NT	AW	LM	AW	AW	NT	NT		AW	AW	AW	VT	AW	LM	AW	AW	AW
			■	◇■1				◇	◇	■1	◇		◇			◇	■	◇	◇	◇	■1	◇		◇
								A		E			A			B		F			A			B
			⫪	🍽															🍽					⫪
Holyhead 30	d		16 25														17 34							18 26
Valley	d		16x31																					18x32
Rhosneigr	d		16x36																					18x37
Ty Croes	d		16x40																					18x41
Bodorgan	d		16x44																					18x45
Llanfairpwll	d		16x54																					18x55
Bangor (Gwynedd)	a		17 03														18 02							19 04
	d		17 04														18 03							19 05
Llanfairfechan	d																18x11							
Penmaenmawr	d																18x15							
Conwy	d																18x21							
Llandudno	d					17 20	18 05											18 59						
Deganwy	d					17x24	18x09											19 03						
Llandudno Junction	a		17 21			17 30	18 15										18 25	19 08						19 22
	d		17 25														18 26							19 24
Colwyn Bay	d		17 31														18 32							19 30
Abergele & Pensarn	d		17 38														18 39							19 37
Rhyl	d		17 44														18 45							19 43
Prestatyn	d		17 49														18 50							19 48
Flint	d		18 03														19 03							20 02
Shotton	d		18 11														19 09							20 10
Chester	a		18 23														19 21							20 22
	d	17 58	18 25	18 35					18 36		18 44	19 01		19 05		19 25	19 27		19 35	19 36		19 47	19 52	20 27
Helsby	d								18 45		18 53									19 45		19 56		
Frodsham	d								18 49		18 58									19 49		20 01		
Runcorn 91	a										19 09											20 10		
Liverpool South Parkway 91	d							18 26		18 42	19 21		19 26								19 42	20 21		
Liverpool Lime Street 91	a										19 38											20 35		
Runcorn East	d								18 54											19 54				
Warrington Bank Quay 90	a								19 03											20 03				
Earlestown 8 90	a								19 11											20 11				
Newton-le-Willows 90	a								19 13											20 13				
Manchester Victoria 90	a																							
Manchester Oxford Road 90	a							19 07	19 33				20 06							20 33				
Manchester Pic'dilly 10 90 ⛴	a							19 11	19 37				20 10	20 38						20 40				
Crewe 10	a	18 19		18 53						19 17		19 23					19 49		19 56		20 17		20 14	20 49
Cardiff Central 7 131	a		21 32																					
Manchester Airport 84,85 ✈	a							19 27					20 29											
Birmingham New Street 12 65	a									20 11						21 32					21 14			21 53
London Euston 15 ⊖65	a			20 41																	23 43			

A From Liverpool Lime Street
B To Birmingham International
C until 16 February
D from 23 February
E From Liverpool Lime Street to Northampton
F To Blaenau Ffestiniog

Table T081-R

Sundays

15 December to 10 May

North Wales and Chester - Manchester / Liverpool and Crewe - Birmingham and London

Station		NT	AW	VT	LM	AW	AW	NT	NT	AW		AW	AW	LM	NT	AW	AW	AW	AW	AW		AW	LM
		◇	◇	◇	■1	◇		◇		◇		◇		■1	◇	◇	◇	◇	◇	◇		◇	■1
		A			A			A						A	A								A
				🍽						⫪													
Holyhead 30	d									19 37									20 35			21 40	
Valley	d									19x43									20x41				
Rhosneigr	d									19x48									20x46				
Ty Croes	d									19x52									20x50				
Bodorgan	d									19x56									20x54				
Llanfairpwll	d									20 06									21x04				
Bangor (Gwynedd)	a									20 15									21 13			22 08	
	d									20 16									21 14			22 09	
Llanfairfechan	d									20x24									21x22				
Penmaenmawr	d									20x28									21x26				
Conwy	d									20x34									21x32				
Llandudno	d																						
Deganwy	d																						
Llandudno Junction	a									20 38									21 36			22 26	
	d									20 39									21 37			22 27	
Colwyn Bay	d									20 45									21 43			22 33	
Abergele & Pensarn	d									20 51									21 50				
Rhyl	d									20 56									21 56			22 43	
Prestatyn	d									21 02									22 01			22 49	
Flint	d									21 15									22 15			23 02	
Shotton	d									21 20									22 21				
Chester	a									21 34									22 35			23 18	
	d		20 36	20 37		20 47	20 53		20 59	21 38		21 43	21 52			21 54	22 06	22 28	22 38	23 00			
Helsby	d		20 45			20 56						21 52				22 03	22 15	22 37					
Frodsham	d		20 49			21 01						21 56				22 08	22 19	22 42					
Runcorn 91	a					21 11										22 18		22 52					
Liverpool South Parkway 91	d	20 26			20 45	21 20		21 30						21 44	22 26	22 27		23 01					23 49
Liverpool Lime Street 91	a					21 34										22 41		23 15					
Runcorn East	d		20 55									22 01					22 24						
Warrington Bank Quay 90	a		21 03									22 11					22 33						
Earlestown 8 90	a		21 10									22 18					22 41						
Newton-le-Willows 90	a		21 13									22 21					22 43						
Manchester Victoria 90	a																						
Manchester Oxford Road 90	a	21 07	21 34					22 11				22 40			23 08		23 03						
Manchester Pic'dilly 10 90 ⛴	a	21 11	21 40					22 15	22 28			22 48			23 13		23 06						
Crewe 10	a			20 56	21 15		21 14			22 00			22 15	22 20					23 01	23 23			00 30
Cardiff Central 7 131	a																						
Manchester Airport 84,85 ✈	a	21 26						22 30							23 30								
Birmingham New Street 12 65	a				22 12									23 16									
London Euston 15 ⊖65	a				00 43																		

A From Liverpool Lime Street

Table T082-F

Mondays to Fridays

16 December to 15 May

Manchester - Bolton - Wigan, Kirkby, Southport, Preston, Blackpool North and Barrow-in-Furness

Miles	Miles	Miles	Miles	Miles			NT MX ◇ A	NT MX ◇ B	NT MX C	NT MX ◇ B	NT D	NT	TP MO ◇1 E	TP MX ◇1 E	NT ◇	NT	NT F	NT	NT	NT ◇ G	NT ◇	NT	NT ◇	NT
0	0	0	—	—	**Manchester Airport** 85	d									04 46						05 24		05 42	
1½	1½	1½	—	—	Heald Green 85	d									04 50						05 28		05 46	
—	—	—	—	—	**Alderley Edge**	d																		
—	—	—	—	—	Stockport 84	d																		
9¾	9¾	9¾	—	—	**Manchester Piccadilly** 10	d				00 09			04 57	04 57	05 04						05 44		06 01	
10¼	10¼	10¼	—	—	**Manchester Oxford Road**	d									05 08						05 47		06 05	
10½	10½	10½	—	—	Deansgate	d																	06 07	
—	—	—	—	—	Rochdale 41	d																		
—	—	—	0	—	**Manchester Victoria**	d										05 33	05 37					05 54		06 05
—	—	—	0¾	—	Salford Central	d										05 36	05 40					05 57		06 08
12	12	12	1¾	—	**Salford Crescent**	a									05 13	05 39	05 45					06 00	06 10	06 13
—	—	—	—	—		d									05 13	05 40	05 45					06 00	06 11	06 14
—	—	—	5¾	—	Swinton	d																		
—	—	—	6½	—	Moorside	d																		
—	—	—	8¼	—	Walkden	d																		
—	—	—	11¾	—	Atherton	d			00 04															
—	—	—	13	—	Hag Fold	d			00 06															
—	—	—	13¾	—	Daisy Hill	d			00 10															
15	15	15	—	—	Clifton	d																		
18	18	18	—	—	Kearsley	d																06 08		
18¾	18	18¾	—	—	Farnworth	d																06 10		
19¾	19¾	19¾	—	—	Moses Gate	d																06 12		
21	21	21	—	—	**Bolton**	a									05 22		05 58					06 16	06 20	06 24
—	—	—	—	—		d									05 23							06 16	06 20	06 25
—	—	25½	—	—	Westhoughton	d																06 24		
—	—	28	15¾	—	Hindley	d			00 15													06 28		
—	—	29½	17¼	0	Ince	d			00 18															
—	—	—	—	0¾	**Wigan North Western**	a															06 15	06 37		
—	—	30½	18¼	—	**Wigan Wallgate**	a			00 23							06 02								
—	—	—	—	—		d										06 04			06 37					
—	—	—	20	—	Pemberton	d										06 08								
—	—	—	22	—	Orrell	d										06 12								
—	—	—	23¼	—	Upholland	d										06 15								
—	—	—	25¼	—	Rainford	d										06 21								
—	—	—	30½	—	**Kirkby**	a										06 29								
—	—	33¼	—	—	Gathurst	d													06 41					
—	—	35	—	—	Appley Bridge	d													06 45					
—	—	37¼	—	—	Parbold	d													06 49					
—	—	38¾	—	—	Hoscar	d													06 52					
—	—	40¼	—	—	Burscough Bridge	d													06 56					
—	—	41½	—	—	New Lane	d													06 58					
—	—	43½	—	—	Bescar Lane	d													07 02					
—	—	46¾	—	—	Meols Cop	d													07 07					
—	—	48	—	—	**Southport**	a													07 14					
24	24	—	—	—	Lostock	d																		06 29
26	26	—	—	—	Horwich Parkway	d									05 29								06 27	06 33
27½	27½	—	—	—	Blackrod	d																		06 36
29½	29½	—	—	—	Adlington (Lancashire)	d	00 03																	06 40
33½	33½	—	—	—	Chorley	d	00 08								05 36								06 34	06 45
36	36	—	—	—	Buckshaw Parkway	d	00 11								05 40								06 38	06 48
37	37	—	—	—	Leyland	d	00 16																06 46	06 54
41	41	—	—	—	**Preston** 8 65,97	a	00 23			00 59			05 33	05 34	05 50						06 31		06 52	07 00
—	—	—	—	—		d	00 24			01 01		05 19	05 36	05 36	05 52						06 47		06 53	
48¾	—	—	—	—	Kirkham & Wesham 97	a				01 10					06 01								07 02	
55¼	—	—	—	—	Poulton-le-Fylde 97	a	00 40			01 18					06 09								07 11	
57¼	—	—	—	—	Layton 97	a				01 22					06 13								07 15	
58½	—	—	—	—	**Blackpool North** 97	a	00 46			01 27					06 18								07 19	
—	62	—	—	—	**Lancaster** 6 65	a						05 39	05 51	05 51							07 04			
—	—	—	—	—		d					05 30	05 39	05 51	05 51				05 59		06 48	07 06			
—	81	—	—	—	Oxenholme Lake District 65	a							06 04	06 04				06 18						
—	91	—	—	—	Windermere 83	a												06 39						
—	68	—	—	—	Carnforth	d					05a39	05 49								06a59	07 16			
—	71¾	—	—	—	Silverdale	d						05 54									07 21			
—	74	—	—	—	Arnside	d						05 59									07 26			
—	77¼	—	—	—	Grange-over-Sands	d						06 05									07 32			
—	79½	—	—	—	Kents Bank	d		00 04				06 08									07 35			
—	81½	—	—	—	Cark	d		00 08				06 12									07 39			
—	87½	—	—	—	Ulverston	d		00 16				06 21									07 47			
—	90¾	—	—	—	Dalton	d		00 24				06 29									07 55			
—	95	—	—	—	Roose	d		00 30				06 35									08 01			
—	96¾	—	—	—	**Barrow-in-Furness**	a		00 37				06 42									08 09			

A From Manchester Piccadilly
B From Manchester Airport
C From Blackburn
D To Morecambe; Parliamentary Train
E To Glasgow Central
F To Clitheroe
G To Leeds

Table T082-F

Mondays to Fridays

16 December to 15 May

Manchester - Bolton - Wigan, Kirkby, Southport, Preston, Blackpool North and Barrow-in-Furness

		NT	TP ◇1 A	NT B	NT	NT C	NT ◇ D	NT	NT ◇	NT	NT E	NT	NT F	NT	TP ◇1 G	NT	NT ◇ H	NT ◇	NT	NT	NT I	NT C
Manchester Airport 85	d		06 07						06 40						07 07			07 25				
Heald Green 85	d								06 44									07 29				
Alderley Edge	d											06 48							07 29			
Stockport 84	d			06 14								07 03					07 15					
Manchester Piccadilly 10	d		06 26	06 30					07 01			07 17			07 26		07 30	07 43	07a56			
Manchester Oxford Road	d		06 29	06 33					07 04			07 20			07 30		07 34	07 47				
Deansgate	d			06 36					07 07			07 22					07 36					
Rochdale 41	d	05 53					06 39				06 42		07 09								07 18	
Manchester Victoria	d	06 15			06 37	06 50	06 55	07 00		07 05	07 08		07 25							07 36	07 41	07 49
Salford Central	d	06 18			06 40	06 53	06 58	07 03		07 08	07 11		07 28							07 40	07 44	07 52
Salford Crescent	a	06 21		06 41	06 44	06 56	07 01	07 06	07 11	07 11	07 18	07 26	07 31				07 40			07 43	07 48	07 56
	d	06 22		06 41	06 45	06 57	07 01	07 07	07 11	07 14	07 18	07 27	07 32				07 40			07 44	07 48	07 57
Swinton	d	06 28			06 52			07 13												07 51		
Moorside	d				06 54			07 16												07 54		
Walkden	d	06 33			06 58		07 10	07 19					07 40							07 58		
Atherton	d	06 39			07 04		07 16	07 25					07 46							08 04		
Hag Fold	d	06 41			07 06			07 28												08 07		
Daisy Hill	d	06 44			07 10		07 19	07 31					07 50							08 10		
Clifton	d																					
Kearsley	d					07 04																08 04
Farnworth	d					07 06																08 07
Moses Gate	d					07 09																08 09
Bolton	a			06 50		07 12			07 20	07 24	07 30	07 36					07 50				08 00	08 13
	d		06u42	06 51		07 13			07 21	07 25		07 37					07 50					08 13
Westhoughton	d					07 21						07 44										08 21
Hindley	d	06 49			07 14	07 28		07 35				07 49	07 55							08 15		08 26
Ince	d	06 52						07 38												08 19		
Wigan North Western	a					07 33												08 16				
Wigan Wallgate	a	06 55			07 19		07 29	07 41				07 54	08 02							08 22		08 31
	d	06 57			07 21			07 43				07 55								08 23		08 32
Pemberton	d	07 01						07 47												08 27		
Orrell	d	07 05						07 51												08 32		
Upholland	d	07 08						07 54												08 35		
Rainford	d	07 12						07 58												08 39		
Kirkby	a	07 22						08 08												08 49		
Gathurst	d				07 25							08 00										08 37
Appley Bridge	d				07 29							08 04										08 41
Parbold	d				07 34							08 08										08 45
Hoscar	d											08 11										
Burscough Bridge	d				07 39							08 14										08 50
New Lane	d											08 17										
Bescar Lane	d											08 20										
Meols Cop	d				07 47							08 26										08 58
Southport	a				07 54							08 33										09 05
Lostock	d			06 56						07 29							07 55					
Horwich Parkway	d			06 59					07 27	07 33							07 58					
Blackrod	d			07 02						07 36							08 00					
Adlington (Lancashire)	d			07 06						07 40							08 04					
Chorley	d			07 10					07 35	07 45							08 08					
Buckshaw Parkway	d			07 20					07 38	07 48							08 11					
Leyland	d			07 28						07 54							08 17					
Preston 8 65,97	a		07 02	07 35					07 50	08 00					08 01		08 23	08 40				
	d		07 03	07 38					07 52						08 02		08 25	08 42				
Kirkham & Wesham 97	a								08 02													
Poulton-le-Fylde 97	a			07 56					08 11								08 40					
Layton 97	a								08 15													
Blackpool North 97	a			08 02					08 19								08 47					
Lancaster 6 65	a		07 18												08 17			08 59				
	d		07 19											07 36		08 23		09 00				
Oxenholme Lake District 65	a		07 32																			
Windermere 83	a																					
Carnforth	d													07 45		08 32		09 10				
Silverdale	d													07 51		08 38		09 16				
Arnside	d													07 55		08 42		09 20				
Grange-over-Sands	d													08 01		08 48		09 26				
Kents Bank	d													08 05				09 30				
Cark	d													08 09		08 54		09 34				
Ulverston	d													08 17		09 02		09 42				
Dalton	d													08 26		09 10		09 50				
Roose	d													08 32				09 56				
Barrow-in-Furness	a													08 39		09 22		10 03				

A To Edinburgh
B From Hazel Grove
C From Stalybridge
D From Leeds
E To Blackburn
F From Blackburn
G To Glasgow Central
H From Stoke-on-Trent
I To Clitheroe

Table T082-F

Mondays to Fridays
16 December to 15 May

Manchester - Bolton - Wigan, Kirkby, Southport, Preston, Blackpool North and Barrow-in-Furness

	NT	NT	NT	NT	NT	NT	TP	NT	NT	NT	NT	NT	NT	NT	NT	NT	NT	NT	NT	NT	TP	NT
	◇	◇					◇[1]			◇		◇	◇			◇					◇[1]	
	A			B		C	D	E	F		G	A			B	H	I	J		K	L	C
Manchester Airport 85 ✈ d		07 42					08 07			08 27			08 41								09 07	
Heald Green 85 d		07 47								08 31			08 45									
Alderley Edge d					07 49														08 49			
Stockport 84 d					08 04			08 11											09 06			
Manchester Piccadilly [10] d		08 01			08 18		08 27	08 31		08 47			09 01						09 18		09 26	
Manchester Oxford Road d		08 04			08 21		08 30	08 34		08 51			09 04						09 21		09 30	
Deansgate d		08 06						08 36					09 07									
Rochdale 41 d	07 37			07 42		08 07			08 14			08 39			08 42							09 09
Manchester Victoria d	07 54		08 05	08 09		08 26			08 39		08 50	08 55		09 05	09 08			09 13				09 26
Salford Central d	07 57		08 08	08 12		08 29			08 42		08 53	08 58		09 08	09 12			09 17				09 29
Salford Crescent a	08 00	08 10	08 11	08 18	08 26	08 32		08 40	08 46		08 56	09 01	09 11	09 11	09 18			09 21	09 26			09 32
d	08 01	08 10	08 14	08 18	08 27	08 33		08 41	08 46		08 57	09 01	09 11	09 14	09 18			09 22	09 26			09 33
Swinton d	08 07					08 40												09 29				09 39
Moorside d						08 42												09 31				
Walkden d	08 12					08 46						09 10						09 35				09 44
Atherton d	08 18					08 52						09 16						09 41				09 50
Hag Fold d	08 21					08 55												09 44				09 53
Daisy Hill d	08 24					08 58						09 19						09 47				09 56
Clifton d																						
Kearsley d											09 04											
Farnworth d											09 07											
Moses Gate d											09 10											
Bolton a		08 19	08 23	08 30	08 36			08 50	08 59		09 13		09 20	09 24	09 30				09 35			
d		08 20	08 24		08 37			08 51			09 14		09 21	09 25					09 36		09u44	
Westhoughton d					08 44						09 22								09 43	←		
Hindley d	08 30				08 48	09 03					09 28							09 52	09 48	09 52		10 01
Ince d	08 33					09 06												→		09 55		
Wigan North Western a						09 12				09 18		09 30										
Wigan Wallgate a	08 38				08 53						09 34								09 53	09 58		10 08
d					08 55						09 36								09 54	10 00		
Pemberton d																				10 04		
Orrell d																				10 08		
Upholland d																				10 11		
Rainford d																				10 15		
Kirkby a																				10 25		
Gathurst d					08 59						09 40								09 59			
Appley Bridge d					09 03						09 44								10 03			
Parbold d					09 08						09 49								10 07			
Hoscar d											09 52											
Burscough Bridge d					09 13						09 55								10 12			
New Lane d											09 58											
Bescar Lane d											10 01											
Meols Cop d					09 21						10 07								10 20			
Southport a					09 28						10 14								10 27			
Lostock d			08 28					08 55						09 29								
Horwich Parkway d		08 26	08 32					08 59					09 27	09 33								
Blackrod d			08 35											09 36								
Adlington (Lancashire) d			08 39											09 40								
Chorley d		08 34	08 44					09 07					09 35	09 45								
Buckshaw Parkway d		08 37	08 47					09 11					09 38	09 48								
Leyland d			08 53					09 17						09 54								
Preston [8] 65,97 a		08 49	08 59				09 02	09 23		09 43			09 49	10 00							10 04	
d		08 51					09 04	09 25		09 44			09 51								10 06	
Kirkham & Wesham 97 a		09 00											10 00									
Poulton-le-Fylde 97 a		09 10						09 40					10 08									
Layton 97 a		09 14											10 12									
Blackpool North 97 a		09 19						09 46					10 17									
Lancaster [6] 65 a							09 19														10 21	
d							09 20									09 41	10 13				10 22	
Oxenholme Lake District 65 a							09 33			10 20											10 35	
Windermere 83 a										10 49												
Carnforth d																09a50	10 22					
Silverdale d																	10 28					
Arnside d																	10 32					
Grange-over-Sands d																	10 38					
Kents Bank d																	10 42					
Cark d																	10 46					
Ulverston d																	10 54					
Dalton d																	11 02					
Roose d																	11 08					
Barrow-in-Furness a																	11 16					

A From Leeds
B To Blackburn
C From Blackburn
D To Edinburgh
E From Hazel Grove
F To Clitheroe
G From Stalybridge
H To Leeds
I To Carlisle
J To Kirkby
K From Manchester Victoria
L To Glasgow Central

Table T082-F

Mondays to Fridays
16 December to 15 May

Manchester - Bolton - Wigan, Kirkby, Southport, Preston, Blackpool North and Barrow-in-Furness

	NT	NT	NT	NT	NT	NT	NT	NT	NT	NT	NT	NT	TP	NT	NT	NT	NT	NT	NT	NT	NT
				◇	◇	◇	◇						◇[1]				◇		◇	◇	
	A	B	C	D	E				F	G		H	I	J	A	B		C	D		
Manchester Airport 85 ✈ d						09 28	09 43						10 07				10 28			10 45	
Heald Green 85 d						09 32	09 47										10 32			10 49	
Alderley Edge d											09 50										
Stockport 84 d	09 11										10 06				10 13						
Manchester Piccadilly [10] d	09 30					09 47	10 01				10 18		10 26		10 30		10 47			11 01	
Manchester Oxford Road d	09 34					09 51	10 04				10 21		10 30		10 34		10 50			11 04	
Deansgate d	09 37						10 07								10 37					11 07	
Rochdale 41 d		09 14		09 39					09 42					10 09		10 18			10 39		
Manchester Victoria d		09 39	09 50	09 55				10 05	10 08	10 13				10 26		10 41		10 50	10 55		11 05
Salford Central d		09 42	09 53	09 58				10 08	10 12	10 17				10 29		10 44		10 53	10 58		11 08
Salford Crescent a	09 41	09 46	09 56	10 01			10 10	10 11	10 18	10 21	10 26			10 32	10 40	10 47		10 56	11 01	11 10	11 11
d	09 41	09 46	09 57	10 02			10 11	10 15	10 18	10 22	10 26			10 33	10 41	10 48		10 57	11 01	11 11	11 14
Swinton d										10 29				10 39							
Moorside d										10 31											
Walkden d				10 10						10 35				10 44					11 10		
Atherton d				10 16						10 41				10 50					11 16		
Hag Fold d										10 44				10 53							
Daisy Hill d				10 19						10 47				10 56					11 19		
Clifton d																					
Kearsley d			10 04															11 04			
Farnworth d			10 07															11 07			
Moses Gate d			10 10															11 10			
Bolton a	09 50	09 59	10 13				10 20	10 24	10 30		10 35				10 50	11 00		11 13		11 20	11 24
d	09 51		10 14				10 20	10 25			10 36				10 50			11 14		11 20	11 25
Westhoughton d			10 22								10 43	←						11 22			
Hindley d			10 28							10 52	10 48	10 52		11 01				11 28			
Ince d										→		10 55									
Wigan North Western a						10 20											11 20				
Wigan Wallgate a			10 34	10 29							10 53	10 58		11 08				11 34	11 29		
d			10 36								10 54	11 00						11 36			
Pemberton d												11 04									
Orrell d												11 08									
Upholland d												11 11									
Rainford d												11 15									
Kirkby a												11 25									
Gathurst d			10 40								10 59							11 41			
Appley Bridge d			10 44								11 03							11 44			
Parbold d			10 49								11 07							11 49			
Hoscar d																		11 52			
Burscough Bridge d			10 54								11 12							11 55			
New Lane d																		11 58			
Bescar Lane d																		12 01			
Meols Cop d			11 02								11 20							12 07			
Southport a			11 09								11 27							12 14			
Lostock d	09 55							10 29							10 55						11 29
Horwich Parkway d	09 59						10 27	10 33							10 58					11 27	11 33
Blackrod d								10 36													11 36
Adlington (Lancashire) d								10 40													11 40
Chorley d	10 07						10 35	10 45							11 06					11 35	11 45
Buckshaw Parkway d	10 10						10 38	10 48							11 09					11 39	11 48
Leyland d	10 16							10 54							11 16						11 54
Preston [8] 65,97 a	10 23					10 43	10 49	11 00					11 02		11 22		11 42			11 50	12 00
d	10 25					10 44	10 51								11 24		11 44			11 52	
Kirkham & Wesham 97 a							11 00													12 01	
Poulton-le-Fylde 97 a	10 40						11 10								11 39					12 09	
Layton 97 a							11 14													12 13	
Blackpool North 97 a	10 47						11 19								11 45					12 18	
Lancaster [6] 65 a						11 02											12 02				
d					10 46	11 02											12 02				
Oxenholme Lake District 65 a																					
Windermere 83 a																					
Carnforth d					10a55	11 12											12 12				
Silverdale d																	12 18				
Arnside d						11 21											12 22				
Grange-over-Sands d						11 27											12 28				
Kents Bank d																	12 32				
Cark d						11 33											12 36				
Ulverston d						11 41											12 44				
Dalton d																	12 52				
Roose d																	12 58				
Barrow-in-Furness a						12 00											13 05				

A From Hazel Grove
B To Clitheroe
C From Stalybridge
D From Leeds
E From Morecambe to Leeds
F To Blackburn
G To Kirkby
H From Manchester Victoria
I To Edinburgh
J From Blackburn

Table T082-F

Mondays to Fridays

16 December to 15 May

Manchester - Bolton - Wigan, Kirkby, Southport, Preston, Blackpool North and Barrow-in-Furness

	NT A	NT B	NT	NT C	TP ◇■ D ✠	NT E	NT F	NT G	NT ◇	NT H	NT ◇ I	NT ◇	NT	NT A	NT ◇ J	NT K	NT B	NT	NT C	TP ◇■ L ✠	NT E	NT F
Manchester Airport 85 ✈ d					11 07				11 28			11 45								12 07		
Heald Green 85 d									11 32			11 49										
Alderley Edge d			10 49															11 49				
Stockport 84 d			11 05				11 11											12 05				12 12
Manchester Piccadilly 10 d			11 18		11 26		11 30		11 47			12 01						12 18		12 26		12 30
Manchester Oxford Road d			11 21		11 30		11 34		11 51			12 04						12 21		12 30		12 34
Deansgate d							11 37					12 07										12 37
Rochdale 41 d	10 42					11 09		11 18			11 39			11 42							12 09	
Manchester Victoria d	11 08	11 13				11 26		11 41		11 48	11 55		12 05	12 08			12 13				12 26	
Salford Central d	11 12	11 17				11 29		11 44		11 51	11 58		12 08	12 12			12 17				12 29	
Salford Crescent a	11 18	11 21	11 26			11 32	11 40	11 48		11 54	12 01	12 10	12 11	12 18			12 21	12 26			12 32	12 40
d	11 18	11 22	11 26			11 33	11 41	11 48		11 57	12 01	12 11	12 14	12 18			12 22	12 26			12 33	12 41
Swinton d		11 29				11 39											12 29				12 39	
Moorside d		11 31															12 31					
Walkden d		11 35				11 44					12 10						12 35				12 44	
Atherton d		11 41				11 50					12 16						12 41				12 50	
Hag Fold d		11 44				11 53											12 44				12 53	
Daisy Hill d		11 47				11 56					12 19						12 47				12 56	
Clifton d																						
Kearsley d										12 04												
Farnworth d										12 07												
Moses Gate d										12 10												
Bolton a	11 30		11 35				11 50	12 00		12 13		12 20	12 24	12 30				12 35				12 50
d			11 36				11 50			12 14		12 20	12 25					12 36		12u44		12 50
Westhoughton d			11 43	←						12 22								12 43	←			
Hindley d		11 52	11 48	11 52		12 01				12 28							12 52	12 48	12 52		13 01	
Ince d		→		11 55													→		12 55			
Wigan North Western a									12 18												13 09	
Wigan Wallgate a			11 53	11 58		12 08				12 34	12 29							12 53	12 58			
d			11 54	12 00						12 36								12 54	13 00			
Pemberton d				12 04															13 04			
Orrell d				12 08															13 08			
Upholland d				12 11															13 11			
Rainford d				12 17															13 15			
Kirkby a				12 25															13 25			
Gathurst d			11 59							12 40								12 59				
Appley Bridge d			12 03							12 44								13 03				
Parbold d			12 07							12 49								13 07				
Hoscar d																						
Burscough Bridge d			12 12							12 54								13 12				
New Lane d																						
Bescar Lane d																						
Meols Cop d			12 20							13 02								13 20				
Southport a			12 27							13 09								13 27				
Lostock d							11 55						12 29									12 55
Horwich Parkway d							11 58					12 27	12 33									12 58
Blackrod d													12 36									
Adlington (Lancashire) d													12 40									
Chorley d							12 06					12 35	12 45									13 06
Buckshaw Parkway d							12 09					12 38	12 48									13 09
Leyland d							12 15						12 57									13 16
Preston 8 65,97 a					12 02		12 23		12 36			12 49	13 03							13 03		13 23
d					12 03		12 24		12 46			12 51								13 05		13 24
Kirkham & Wesham 97 a												13 00										
Poulton-le-Fylde 97 a							12 40					13 08										13 40
Layton 97 a												13 12										
Blackpool North 97 a							12 46					13 16										13 46
Lancaster 6 65 a					12 18															13 20		
d					12 19										12 45	13 13				13 21		
Oxenholme Lake District 65 a					12 32				13 31											13 34		
Windermere 83 a									13 53													
Carnforth d															12a54	13 22						
Silverdale d																13 28						
Arnside d																13 32						
Grange-over-Sands d																13 38						
Kents Bank d																13 42						
Cark d																13 46						
Ulverston d																13 54						
Dalton d																14 02						
Roose d																14 08						
Barrow-in-Furness a																14 16						

A To Blackburn
B To Kirkby
C From Manchester Victoria
D To Glasgow Central
E From Blackburn
F From Hazel Grove
G To Clitheroe
H From Stalybridge
I From Leeds
J From Morecambe to Leeds
K To Carlisle
L To Edinburgh

Table T082-F

Mondays to Fridays

16 December to 15 May

Manchester - Bolton - Wigan, Kirkby, Southport, Preston, Blackpool North and Barrow-in-Furness

	NT A	NT ◇	NT B	NT ◇ C	NT ◇	NT	NT D	NT E	NT	NT F	TP ◇■ G ✠	NT H	NT I	NT A	NT B	NT ◇ J	NT ◇	NT ◇ C	NT ◇	NT	NT D	NT E
Manchester Airport 85 ✈ d		12 28			12 45						13 07						13 28		13 45			
Heald Green 85 d		12 32			12 49												13 32		13 49			
Alderley Edge d									12 49													
Stockport 84 d									13 06				13 12									
Manchester Piccadilly 10 d		12 47			13 01				13 18		13 26		13 30				13 47		14 01			
Manchester Oxford Road d		12 50			13 04				13 21		13 30		13 34				13 51		14 04			
Deansgate d					13 07								13 37						14 07			
Rochdale 41 d	12 18			12 39			12 42					13 09		13 18				13 39			13 34	
Manchester Victoria d	12 41		12 50	12 55		13 05	13 07	13 13				13 26		13 41	13 49			13 55		14 05	14 08	14 13
Salford Central d	12 44		12 53	12 58		13 08	13 12	13 17				13 29		13 44	13 52			13 58		14 08	14 12	14 17
Salford Crescent a	12 48		12 56	13 01	13 10	13 11	13 18	13 21	13 26			13 32	13 42	13 48	13 56			14 01	14 10	14 11	14 18	14 21
d	12 48		12 57	13 01	13 11	13 14	13 18	13 22	13 27			13 33	13 42	13 48	13 57			14 02	14 11	14 14	14 18	14 22
Swinton d								13 29				13 39										14 29
Moorside d								13 31														14 31
Walkden d				13 10				13 35				13 44						14 10				14 35
Atherton d				13 16				13 41				13 50						14 16				14 41
Hag Fold d								13 43				13 53										14 44
Daisy Hill d				13 19				13 47				13 56						14 19				14 47
Clifton d																						
Kearsley d			13 04												14 04							
Farnworth d			13 07												14 07							
Moses Gate d			13 10												14 10							
Bolton a	13 00		13 13		13 20	13 24	13 30		13 36				13 51	14 00	14 13				14 20	14 24	14 30	
d			13 14		13 20	13 25			13 36		13u44		13 52		14 14				14 20	14 25		
Westhoughton d			13 22						13 44	←					14 22							
Hindley d			13 28					13 52	13 48	13 52		14 01			14 28							14 52
Ince d								→		13 55												→
Wigan North Western a		13 17															14 18	14 30				
Wigan Wallgate a			13 34	13 29					13 53	13 58		14 08			14 34							
d			13 36						13 54	14 00					14 36							
Pemberton d										14 04												
Orrell d										14 08												
Upholland d										14 11												
Rainford d										14 15												
Kirkby a										14 25												
Gathurst d			13 40						13 59						14 40							
Appley Bridge d			13 44						14 03						14 44							
Parbold d			13 49						14 07						14 49							
Hoscar d			13 52																			
Burscough Bridge d			13 55						14 12						14 54							
New Lane d			13 58																			
Bescar Lane d			14 01																			
Meols Cop d			14 07						14 20						15 02							
Southport a			14 14						14 27						15 09							
Lostock d						13 29							13 56							14 29		
Horwich Parkway d					13 27	13 33							14 00						14 27	14 33		
Blackrod d						13 36														14 36		
Adlington (Lancashire) d						13 40														14 40		
Chorley d					13 35	13 45							14 08						14 34	14 44		
Buckshaw Parkway d					13 38	13 48							14 11						14 38	14 48		
Leyland d						13 54							14 17							14 53		
Preston 8 65,97 a		13 43			13 49	14 00					14 03		14 23				14 43		14 49	15 00		
d		13 44			13 51						14 05		14 25				14 45		14 50			
Kirkham & Wesham 97 a					14 00														14 59			
Poulton-le-Fylde 97 a					14 10								14 40						15 10			
Layton 97 a					14 14														15 14			
Blackpool North 97 a					14 19								14 46						15 19			
Lancaster 6 65 a		14 02									14 20						15 02					
d		14 02									14 21					14 48	15 03					
Oxenholme Lake District 65 a											14 33											
Windermere 83 a																						
Carnforth d		14 12														14a57	15 12					
Silverdale d		14 17															15 18					
Arnside d		14 22															15 22					
Grange-over-Sands d		14 28															15 28					
Kents Bank d		14 31															15 32					
Cark d		14 35															15 36					
Ulverston d		14 43															15 44					
Dalton d		14 51															15 52					
Roose d		14 57															15 58					
Barrow-in-Furness a		15 05															16 05					

A To Clitheroe
B From Stalybridge
C From Leeds
D To Blackburn
E To Kirkby
F From Manchester Victoria
G To Glasgow Central
H From Blackburn
I From Hazel Grove
J From Morecambe to Leeds

Table T082-F

Mondays to Fridays
16 December to 15 May

Manchester - Bolton - Wigan, Kirkby, Southport, Preston, Blackpool North and Barrow-in-Furness

Station		NT	NT	TP	NT	NT	NT	NT	NT	NT	NT	NT	NT	NT	NT	NT	NT	TP	NT	NT	NT	NT
			A	◇1 B	C	D	E	F	◇ G	H	◇	◇		I	J		A	◇1 K	C	D	E	◇
Manchester Airport 85	d			14 07							14 28	14 45						15 07				15 28
Heald Green 85	d										14 32	14 49										15 32
Alderley Edge	d	13 49														14 49						
Stockport 84	d	14 06				14 11										15 05				15 11		
Manchester Piccadilly 10	d	14 18		14 26		14 30					14 47	15 01				15 18		15 26		15 30		15 47
Manchester Oxford Road	d	14 21		14 30		14 34					14 51	15 04				15 21		15 30		15 34		15 50
Deansgate	d					14 37						15 07								15 37		
Rochdale 41	d				14 09		14 18		14 39					14 42					15 09		15 18	
Manchester Victoria	d				14 26		14 41	14 50	14 55				15 05	15 08	15 13				15 26		15 41	
Salford Central	d				14 29		14 44	14 53	14 58				15 08	15 12	15 17				15 29		15 44	
Salford Crescent	a	14 26			14 32	14 41	14 48	14 56	15 01			15 10	15 11	15 18	15 21	15 26			15 32	15 41	15 48	
	d	14 26			14 33	14 41	14 49	14 57	15 01			15 11	15 14	15 18	15 22	15 26			15 33	15 41	15 48	
Swinton	d				14 39										15 29				15 39			
Moorside	d														15 31							
Walkden	d				14 44				15 10						15 35				15 44			
Atherton	d				14 50				15 16						15 41				15 50			
Hag Fold	d				14 53										15 44				15 53			
Daisy Hill	d				14 56				15 19						15 47				15 56			
Clifton	d																					
Kearsley	d							15 04														
Farnworth	d							15 07														
Moses Gate	d							15 10														
Bolton	a	14 35				14 50	15 00	15 13				15 20	15 24	15 30		15 35				15 50	16 00	
	d	14 36				14 51		15 14				15 20	15 25			15 36				15 51		
Westhoughton	d	14 43	←					15 22								15 43	←					
Hindley	d	14 48	14 52		15 01			15 28							15 52	15 48	15 52		16 01			
Ince	d		14 55												→		15 55					
Wigan North Western	a										15 18											16 18
Wigan Wallgate	a	14 53	14 58		15 08			15 34	15 29							15 53	15 58		16 08			
	d	14 54	15 00					15 36								15 54	16 00					
Pemberton	d		15 04														16 04					
Orrell	d		15 08														16 08					
Upholland	d		15 11														16 11					
Rainford	d		15 15														16 15					
Kirkby	a		15 25														16 25					
Gathurst	d	14 59						15 40								15 59						
Appley Bridge	d	15 03						15 44								16 03						
Parbold	d	15 07						15 49								16 07						
Hoscar	d							15 52														
Burscough Bridge	d	15 12						15 55								16 12						
New Lane	d							15 58														
Bescar Lane	d							16 01														
Meols Cop	d	15 20						16 07								16 20						
Southport	a	15 27						16 14								16 27						
Lostock	d					14 56							15 29							15 56		
Horwich Parkway	d					14 59						15 27	15 33							15 59		
Blackrod	d												15 36									
Adlington (Lancashire)	d												15 40									
Chorley	d					15 07						15 35	15 45							16 07		
Buckshaw Parkway	d					15 10						15 38	15 48							16 11		
Leyland	d					15 14							15 54							16 17		
Preston 8 65,97	a			15 02		15 23					15 43	15 49	16 00					16 02		16 23		16 42
	d			15 03		15 24				15 32	15 45	15 51						16 03		16 24		16 45
Kirkham & Wesham 97	a											16 02										
Poulton-le-Fylde 97	a					15 40						16 10								16 40		
Layton 97	a											16 14								16 44		
Blackpool North 97	a					15 46						16 19								16 48		
Lancaster 6 65	a			15 18						15 52								16 18				17 02
	d			15 19						16 13								16 19				17 02
Oxenholme Lake District 65	a			15 32							16 30							16 33				
Windermere 83	a										16 53											
Carnforth	d									16 22												17 12
Silverdale	d									16 28												17 17
Arnside	d									16 32												17 21
Grange-over-Sands	d									16 38												17 27
Kents Bank	d									16 42												17 30
Cark	d									16 46												17 34
Ulverston	d									16 54												17 42
Dalton	d									17 02												17 50
Roose	d									17 08												17 56
Barrow-in-Furness	a									17 16												18 02

A From Manchester Victoria
B To Edinburgh
C From Blackburn
D From Hazel Grove
E To Clitheroe
F From Stalybridge
G From Leeds
H To Carlisle
I To Blackburn
J To Kirkby
K To Glasgow Central

Table T082-F

Mondays to Fridays
16 December to 15 May

Manchester - Bolton - Wigan, Kirkby, Southport, Preston, Blackpool North and Barrow-in-Furness

Station		NT	NT	NT	NT	NT	NT	NT	NT	TP	NT	NT	NT	NT	NT	NT	NT	NT	NT	NT	NT	NT	NT
		A	◇ B	◇		C	D		E	◇1 F	G	H	C	A	◇ B		◇ I	◇	◇		J	D	
Manchester Airport 85	d			15 45						16 07								16 29	16 42				
Heald Green 85	d			15 49														16 33	16 46				
Alderley Edge	d							15 50															16 50
Stockport 84	d							16 06				16 12											17 06
Manchester Piccadilly 10	d			16 01				16 18		16 26		16 30						16 54	17 02				17 19
Manchester Oxford Road	d			16 04				16 21		16 30		16 34						16 59	17 05				
Deansgate	d			16 07								16 37							17 07				17 22
Rochdale 41	d		15 39			15 42					16 09		16 18		16 39						16 33		
Manchester Victoria	d	15 50	15 55		16 05	16 08	16 13				16 26		16 41	16 50	16 55					17 05	17 08	17 13	
Salford Central	d	15 53	15 58		16 08	16 12	16 17				16 29		16 44	16 53	16 58					17 08	17 12	17 17	
Salford Crescent	a	15 56	16 01	16 10	16 11	16 18	16 21	16 27			16 32	16 40	16 47	16 56	17 01				17 11	17 11	17 15	17 21	17 26
	d	15 57	16 01	16 11	16 14	16 18	16 22	16 28			16 33	16 41	16 48	16 57	17 02				17 11	17 14	17 18	17 22	17 26
Swinton	d						16 29				16 39											17 29	
Moorside	d						16 32															17 31	
Walkden	d		16 10				16 36				16 44				17 10							17 35	
Atherton	d		16 16				16 42				16 50				17 16							17 41	
Hag Fold	d						16 45				16 53											17 44	
Daisy Hill	d		16 19				16 48				16 56				17 20							17 47	
Clifton	d																						
Kearsley	d	16 04												17 04									
Farnworth	d	16 07												17 07							17 27		
Moses Gate	d	16 10												17 09									
Bolton	a	16 13		16 20	16 24	16 30		16 37				16 50	16 59	17 13				17 17	17 21	17 25	17 32		17 35
	d	16 14		16 20	16 25			16 38				16 50		17 13				17 17	17 21	17 25			17 36
Westhoughton	d	16 22						16 45	←					17 22									17 44
Hindley	d	16 28					16 53	16 50	16 53		17 01			17 29								17 52	17 48
Ince	d						→		16 56													→	
Wigan North Western	a										17 09												
Wigan Wallgate	a	16 34	16 29					16 55	17 00					17 35	17 30								17 53
	d	16 36						16 56	17 01					17 37									17 55
Pemberton	d								17 05														
Orrell	d								17 10														
Upholland	d								17 13														
Rainford	d								17 17														
Kirkby	a								17 27														
Gathurst	d	16 40						17 01						17 41									17 59
Appley Bridge	d	16 44						17 05						17 45									18 03
Parbold	d	16 49						17 10						17 50									18 08
Hoscar	d													17 53									
Burscough Bridge	d	16 54						17 15						17 56									18 13
New Lane	d													17 59									
Bescar Lane	d													18 02									
Meols Cop	d	17 02						17 23						18 08									18 21
Southport	a	17 09						17 30						18 15									18 28
Lostock	d			16 25	16 29							16 55							17 27	17 30			
Horwich Parkway	d			16 29	16 33							16 59							17 30	17 34			
Blackrod	d				16 36							17 02								17 37			
Adlington (Lancashire)	d				16 40							17 05								17 40			
Chorley	d			16 36	16 45							17 10						17 31	17 38	17 45			
Buckshaw Parkway	d			16 40	16 48							17 21							17 41	17 49			
Leyland	d				16 54							17 28								17 54			
Preston 8 65,97	a			16 51	16 59					17 03		17 34						17 43	17 52	18 00			
	d			16 53						17 05		17 37						17 45	17 54				
Kirkham & Wesham 97	a			17 02								17 46							18 05				
Poulton-le-Fylde 97	a			17 10								17 54							18 13				
Layton 97	a			17 14								17 58							18 17				
Blackpool North 97	a			17 19								18 02							18 22				
Lancaster 6 65	a									17 21								18 02					
	d									17 22						17 38	17 45	18 03					
Oxenholme Lake District 65	a									17 35													
Windermere 83	a																						
Carnforth	d															17 47	17a54	18 12					
Silverdale	d															17 52		18 18					
Arnside	d															17 57		18 22					
Grange-over-Sands	d															18 03		18 28					
Kents Bank	d															18 06		18 32					
Cark	d															18 10		18 36					
Ulverston	d															18 18		18 44					
Dalton	d															18 26		18 52					
Roose	d															18 32		18 58					
Barrow-in-Furness	a															18 40		19 05					

A From Stalybridge
B From Leeds
C To Clitheroe
D To Kirkby
E From Manchester Victoria
F To Edinburgh
G From Blackburn
H From Hazel Grove
I From Morecambe to Leeds
J To Blackburn

Table T082-F

Mondays to Fridays
16 December to 15 May

Manchester - Bolton - Wigan, Kirkby, Southport, Preston, Blackpool North and Barrow-in-Furness

Station		NT A	TP ◇1 B	NT C	NT D	NT ◇	NT	NT E	NT F	NT ◇ G	NT ◇	NT	NT	NT H	NT	NT C	NT	NT I	TP ◇1 J	NT D	NT E	NT ◇
Manchester Airport 85 ✈	d		17 07			17 27					17 42								18 07			18 28
Heald Green 85	d					17 31					17 46											18 32
Alderley Edge	d														17 49							
Stockport 84	d				17 12										18 05					18 12		
Manchester Piccadilly 10	d		17 27		17 31	17 47					18 03				18 18				18 26	18 30		18 47
Manchester Oxford Road	d		17 30		17 34	17 51					18 06				18 21				18 30	18 34		18 51
Deansgate	d				17 37						18 08									18 37		
Rochdale 41	d			17 09				17 19		17 39				17 54		18 09					18 18	
Manchester Victoria	d			17 26			17 36	17 41	17 47	17 55		18 05	18 12	18 17		18 26					18 41	
Salford Central	d			17 29			17 40	17 44	17 51	17 58		18 08	18 15	18 20		18 29					18 44	
Salford Crescent	a			17 32	17 40		17 44	17 48	17 54	18 01	18 11	18 11	18 19	18 23	18 26	18 32				18 40	18 48	
	d			17 33	17 41		17 45	17 48	17 57	18 01	18 12	18 15	18 19	18 24	18 27	18 33				18 41	18 48	
Swinton	d			17 40			17 52						18 26			18 39						
Moorside	d						17 54						18 29									
Walkden	d			17 45			17 58			18 10			18 33			18 44						
Atherton	d			17 51			18 04			18 16			18 38			18 50						
Hag Fold	d			17 54			18 07						18 41			18 53						
Daisy Hill	d			17 57			18 11			18 19			18 44			18 56						
Clifton	d								18 01													
Kearsley	d								18 06													
Farnworth	d								18 09													
Moses Gate	d								18 12													
Bolton	a				17 50			18 00	18 15		18 21	18 25		18 35	18 36					18 50	19 00	
	d				17 50				18 16		18 21	18 25			18 36					18 50		
Westhoughton	d	←							18 24						18 46							
Hindley	d	17 52		18 02			18 16		18 28						18 52	19 01						
Ince	d	17 55					18 19								18 55							
Wigan North Western	a					18 19																19 19
Wigan Wallgate	a	17 58		18 09			18 22		18 34	18 29			18 54		18 59	19 06						
	d	18 00					18 24		18 37						19 01	19 08						
Pemberton	d	18 04														19 12						
Orrell	d	18 08														19 16						
Upholland	d	18 11														19 19						
Rainford	d	18 15														19 23						
Kirkby	a	18 25														19 33						
Gathurst	d						18 28		18 41						19 05							
Appley Bridge	d						18 32		18 45						19 09							
Parbold	d						18 37		18 50						19 14							
Hoscar	d																					
Burscough Bridge	d						18 42		18 55						19 19							
New Lane	d																					
Bescar Lane	d																					
Meols Cop	d						18 50		19 03						19 27							
Southport	a						18 57		19 10						19 34							
Lostock	d				17 55						18 26	18 30								18 55		
Horwich Parkway	d				17 58						18 29	18 33								18 58		
Blackrod	d				18 00							18 36								19 00		
Adlington (Lancashire)	d				18 04							18 40								19 04		
Chorley	d				18 08						18 36	18 45								19 08		
Buckshaw Parkway	d				18 12						18 40	18 48								19 11		
Leyland	d				18 18							18 54								19 18		
Preston 8 65,97	a		18 02		18 24	18 42					18 51	19 00							19 04	19 24		19 43
	d		18 04		18 26	18 45					18 52								19 05	19 26		19 44
Kirkham & Wesham 97	a				18 34						19 01											
Poulton-le-Fylde 97	a				18 43						19 10									19 41		
Layton 97	a				18 47						19 14											
Blackpool North 97	a				18 51						19 18									19 47		
Lancaster 6 65	a		18 19																19 20			20 03
	d		18 20														18 35	19 13	19 21			20 04
Oxenholme Lake District 65	a		18 33			19 21													19 34			
Windermere 83	a					19 43																
Carnforth	d																18 44	19 22				20 13
Silverdale	d																18 50	19 28				20 19
Arnside	d																18 54	19 32				20 23
Grange-over-Sands	d																19 00	19 38				20 29
Kents Bank	d																19 04	19 42				20 33
Cark	d																19 08	19 46				20 37
Ulverston	d																19 16	19 54				20 45
Dalton	d																19 24	20 02				20 53
Roose	d																19 30	20 08				20 59
Barrow-in-Furness	a																19 38	20 16				21 06

A From Manchester Victoria
B To Glasgow Central
C From Blackburn
D From Hazel Grove
E To Clitheroe
F From Stalybridge
G From Leeds
H To Blackburn
I To Carlisle
J To Edinburgh

Table T082-F

Mondays to Fridays
16 December to 15 May

Manchester - Bolton - Wigan, Kirkby, Southport, Preston, Blackpool North and Barrow-in-Furness

Station		NT A	NT ◇ B	NT ◇	NT	NT C	NT D	NT	NT E	TP ◇1 F	NT G	NT H	NT C	NT ◇ I	NT ◇	NT J	NT ◇ B	NT A	NT ◇	TP ◇1 K	NT	NT L	NT M
Manchester Airport 85 ✈	d			18 45						19 07					19 28				19 44				
Heald Green 85	d			18 49											19 32				19 48				
Alderley Edge	d							18 49															
Stockport 84	d							19 06				19 12											
Manchester Piccadilly 10	d			19 01				19 18		19 26		19 30			19 47				20 03				
Manchester Oxford Road	d			19 04				19 21		19 30		19 34			19 51				20 06				
Deansgate	d			19 06								19 37							20 08				
Rochdale 41	d		18 39			18 42					19 09		19 18				19 39					19 42	
Manchester Victoria	d	18 49	18 55		19 05	19 09	19 14				19 26		19 41			19 49	19 55				20 05	20 09	20 15
Salford Central	d	18 53	18 58		19 08	19 13	19 17				19 29		19 44			19 52	19 58				20 08	20 13	20 18
Salford Crescent	a	18 56	19 01	19 10	19 11	19 18	19 21	19 26			19 32	19 40	19 48			19 55	20 01		20 11		20 11	20 18	20 21
	d	18 57	19 01	19 10	19 14	19 18	19 22	19 28			19 33	19 41	19 48			19 57	20 01		20 12		20 15	20 18	20 22
Swinton	d						19 29				19 39												20 29
Moorside	d						19 31																20 31
Walkden	d		19 10				19 35				19 44						20 10						20 35
Atherton	d		19 16				19 41				19 50						20 16						20 41
Hag Fold	d						19 44				19 53												20 44
Daisy Hill	d		19 19				19 47				19 56						20 19						20 47
Clifton	d																						
Kearsley	d	19 04														20 04							
Farnworth	d	19 07														20 07							
Moses Gate	d	19 10														20 09							
Bolton	a	19 13		19 19	19 24	19 30		19 37				19 50	20 00			20 13			20 21		20 25	20 30	
	d	19 14		19 20	19 25			19 37		19u44		19 50				20 13			20 21		20 25		
Westhoughton	d	19 22						19 45	←							20 21		←					
Hindley	d	19 28					19 53	19 49	19 53		20 01					20 31	20 24	20 31					20 52
Ince	d						→		19 56							→							→
Wigan North Western	a		19 30						20 02						20 17								
Wigan Wallgate	a	19 34						19 54			20 08						20 31	20 38					
	d	19 36						19 55															
Pemberton	d																						
Orrell	d																						
Upholland	d																						
Rainford	d																						
Kirkby	a																						
Gathurst	d	19 40						20 00															
Appley Bridge	d	19 44						20 04															
Parbold	d	19 49						20 08															
Hoscar	d	19 52																					
Burscough Bridge	d	19 55						20 13															
New Lane	d	19 58																					
Bescar Lane	d	20 01																					
Meols Cop	d	20 07						20 21															
Southport	a	20 14						20 28															
Lostock	d				19 29							19 55									20 30		
Horwich Parkway	d			19 27	19 33							19 58							20 28		20 33		
Blackrod	d				19 36																20 36		
Adlington (Lancashire)	d				19 40																20 40		
Chorley	d			19 35	19 45							20 06							20 35		20 45		
Buckshaw Parkway	d			19 38	19 48							20 10							20 38		20 48		
Leyland	d				19 55							20 18									20 52		
Preston 8 65,97	a			19 49	20 01					20 04		20 24			20 42				20 49		21 02		
	d			19 51	20 03					20 06		20 26			20 44				20 51	20 59			
Kirkham & Wesham 97	a			20 00	20 12														21 00				
Poulton-le-Fylde 97	a			20 10	20 20							20 41							21 08				
Layton 97	a			20 14															21 12				
Blackpool North 97	a			20 18	20 28							20 47							21 17				
Lancaster 6 65	a									20 21					21 01					21 15			
	d									20 22				20 30	21 02					21 15			
Oxenholme Lake District 65	a									20 35										21 30			
Windermere 83	a																						
Carnforth	d													20a40	21 11								
Silverdale	d														21 16								
Arnside	d														21 20								
Grange-over-Sands	d														21 25								
Kents Bank	d														21 29								
Cark	d														21 33								
Ulverston	d														21 40								
Dalton	d														21 48								
Roose	d														21 54								
Barrow-in-Furness	a														22 01								

A From Stalybridge
B From Leeds
C To Clitheroe
D To Wigan North Western
E From Manchester Victoria
F To Glasgow Central
G From Blackburn
H From Hazel Grove
I From Morecambe to Leeds
J From Stalybridge to Wigan Wallgate
K From Liverpool Lime Street
L To Blackburn
M To Wigan Wallgate

Table T082-F

Mondays to Fridays
16 December to 15 May

Manchester - Bolton - Wigan, Kirkby, Southport, Preston, Blackpool North and Barrow-in-Furness

		NT	NT A	TP ◇1 B	NT C	NT D	NT E	NT F	NT ◇ G	NT ◇	NT H	NT C	NT I	NT	TP ◇1 J	NT D	NT E	NT F	NT ◇ G	NT ◇	NT E	NT ◇	NT F
Manchester Airport 85	d			20 07						20 42					21 06					21 43		22 10	
Heald Green 85	d									20 46													
Alderley Edge	d	19 47																					
Stockport 84	d	20 03				20 12										21 13							
Manchester Piccadilly 10	d	20 18		20 26		20 30				21 02					21 22	21 31				22 01		22 26	
Manchester Oxford Road	d	20 21		20 30		20 34				21 05					21 25	21 34				22 04			
Deansgate	d					20 37				21 07						21 37				22 07			
Rochdale 41	d				20 09		20 18		20 39		20 42	21 09					21 18		21 39		21 42		
Manchester Victoria	d				20 26		20 41	20 50	20 55		21 08	21 26					21 40	21 49	21 55		22 16		22 21
Salford Central	d				20 29		20 44	20 53	20 58		21 12	21 29					21 43	21 53	22 00		22 19		22 24
Salford Crescent	a	20 26			20 32	20 41	20 48	20 56	21 01	21 11	21 19	21 33				21 40	21 47	21 56	22 03	22 10	22 22		22 27
	d	20 27			20 33	20 41	20 48	20 57	21 02	21 11	21 19	21 34				21 41	21 47	21 56	22 04	22 11	22 23		22 28
Swinton	d				20 39				21 09			21 40							22 11				
Moorside	d											21 43											
Walkden	d				20 44				21 14			21 47							22 16				
Atherton	d				20 50				21 20			21 52							22 22				
Hag Fold	d				20 53							21 55											
Daisy Hill	d				20 56				21 24			21 58							22 26				
Clifton	d																						
Kearsley	d							21 04										22 04					
Farnworth	d							21 07										22 06					
Moses Gate	d							21 09										22 08					
Bolton	a	20 36				20 50	21 00	21 13		21 20	21 32					21 51	21 59	22 12		22 20	22 34		22 38
	d	20 37		20u44		20 51		21 13		21 21					21u39	21 51		22 12		22 20			22 39
Westhoughton	d	20 44	←					21 21										22 20					22 46
Hindley	d	20 48	20 52		21 01			21 25	21 28			22 03						22 25					22 51
Ince	d		20 55									22 06											
Wigan North Western	a				21 09			21 32	21 36										22 37			22 57	22 58
Wigan Wallgate	a	20 53	21 00									22 11						22 30					
	d	20 55																22 31					
Pemberton	d																						
Orrell	d																						
Upholland	d																						
Rainford	d																						
Kirkby	a																						
Gathurst	d	20 59																22 36					
Appley Bridge	d	21 03																22 40					
Parbold	d	21 08																22 44					
Hoscar	d	21 11																					
Burscough Bridge	d	21 14																22 49					
New Lane	d	21 17																					
Bescar Lane	d	21 20																					
Meols Cop	d	21 26																22 57					
Southport	a	21 33																23 04					
Lostock	d					20 55										21 56							
Horwich Parkway	d					20 58				21 27						21 59				22 27			
Blackrod	d					21 01										22 01							
Adlington (Lancashire)	d					21 04										22 05							
Chorley	d					21 09				21 34						22 09				22 34			
Buckshaw Parkway	d					21 12				21 38						22 12				22 38			
Leyland	d					21 18										22 20							
Preston 8 65,97	a			21 03		21 24				21 49					21 59	22 26				22 49		23 14	
	d			21 05		21 27				21 50					22 01	22 27				22 51		23 15	
Kirkham & Wesham 97	a									21 59										23 00			
Poulton-le-Fylde 97	a					21 42				22 08						22 43				23 08			
Layton 97	a									22 12										23 12			
Blackpool North 97	a					21 48				22 16						22 49				23 17			
Lancaster 6 65	a			21 20											22 19							23 33	
	d			21 21									21 30	22 09	22 20							23 33	
Oxenholme Lake District 65	a			21 34											22 33								
Windermere 83	a																						
Carnforth	d												21a40	22 18								23 43	
Silverdale	d													22 24								23 48	
Arnside	d													22 28								23 53	
Grange-over-Sands	d													22 34								23 59	
Kents Bank	d													22 38								00 04	
Cark	d													22 42								00 08	
Ulverston	d													22 50								00 16	
Dalton	d													22 58								00 24	
Roose	d													23 04								00 30	
Barrow-in-Furness	a													23 12								00 37	

A From Manchester Victoria
B To Edinburgh
C From Blackburn
D From Hazel Grove
E To Clitheroe
F From Stalybridge
G From Leeds
H To Blackburn
I To Skipton
J To Glasgow Central

Table T082-F

Mondays to Fridays
16 December to 15 May

Manchester - Bolton - Wigan, Kirkby, Southport, Preston, Blackpool North and Barrow-in-Furness

		NT A	NT B	NT C	NT ◇	NT D	TP ◇1 E	NT C	NT ◇	NT B	NT ◇
Manchester Airport 85	d				22 34		23 10				23 47
Heald Green 85	d				22 38						23 51
Alderley Edge	d										
Stockport 84	d	22 13									
Manchester Piccadilly 10	d	22 30			22 54		23 26		23 30		00 09
Manchester Oxford Road	d	22 35			23 00		23 30		23 34		
Deansgate	d	22 37			23 02				23 36		
Rochdale 41	d		22 14			22 43				23 11	
Manchester Victoria	d		22 40	22 51		23 07		23 19		23 37	
Salford Central	d		22 43	22 54		23 12		23 22		23 40	
Salford Crescent	a	22 42	22 46	22 57	23 05	23 16		23 26	23 40	23 43	
	d	22 42	22 47	22 58	23 06	23 17		23 27	23 40	23 44	
Swinton	d		22 54							23 51	
Moorside	d		22 56							23 53	
Walkden	d		23 00							23 58	
Atherton	d		23 06							00 04	
Hag Fold	d		23 09							00 06	
Daisy Hill	d		23 12							00 10	
Clifton	d										
Kearsley	d			23 05				23 34			
Farnworth	d			23 08				23 36			
Moses Gate	d			23 10				23 39			
Bolton	a	22 51		23 14	23 18	23 28		23 42	23 49		
	d	22 52		23 14	23 18			23 43	23 50		
Westhoughton	d			23 22				23 50			
Hindley	d		23 17	23 27				23 56		00 15	
Ince	d		23 20							00 18	
Wigan North Western	a										
Wigan Wallgate	a		23 23	23 34				00 01		00 23	
	d		23 25								
Pemberton	d										
Orrell	d										
Upholland	d										
Rainford	d										
Kirkby	a										
Gathurst	d		23 29								
Appley Bridge	d		23 33								
Parbold	d		23 37								
Hoscar	d										
Burscough Bridge	d		23 42								
New Lane	d										
Bescar Lane	d										
Meols Cop	d		23 50								
Southport	a		23 57								
Lostock	d	22 56							23 54		
Horwich Parkway	d	22 59			23 25				23 57		
Blackrod	d	23 02							23 58		
Adlington (Lancashire)	d	23 05							00 03		
Chorley	d	23 10			23 33				00 08		
Buckshaw Parkway	d	23 13			23 36				00 11		
Leyland	d	23 19			23 43				00 16		
Preston 8 65,97	a	23 25			23 51		00 13		00 23		00 59
	d	23 30			23 55				00 24		01 01
Kirkham & Wesham 97	a				00 05						01 10
Poulton-le-Fylde 97	a	23 46			00 14				00 40		01 18
Layton 97	a				00 18						01 22
Blackpool North 97	a	23 52			00 23				00 46		01 27
Lancaster 6 65	a										
	d										
Oxenholme Lake District 65	a										
Windermere 83	a										
Carnforth	d										
Silverdale	d										
Arnside	d										
Grange-over-Sands	d										
Kents Bank	d										
Cark	d										
Ulverston	d										
Dalton	d										
Roose	d										
Barrow-in-Furness	a										

A From Hazel Grove
B From Blackburn
C From Stalybridge
D To Blackburn
E To Carlisle

Table T082-F

Saturdays

21 December to 16 May

Manchester - Bolton - Wigan, Kirkby, Southport, Preston, Blackpool North and Barrow-in-Furness

		NT ◇ A	NT ◇ B	NT C	NT ◇ B	NT	NT D	NT	TP ◇1 E	NT ◇	NT	NT F	NT	NT	NT ◇ G	NT ◇	NT	NT ◇	NT	NT	TP ◇1 H	NT I	NT
Manchester Airport 85	d									04 46						05 22		05 42			06 07		
Heald Green 85	d									04 50						05 26		05 46					
Alderley Edge	d																						
Stockport 84	d																					06 14	
Manchester Piccadilly	d				00 09				05 00	05 04						05 42		06 01			06 26	06 30	
Manchester Oxford Road	d									05 08						05 45		06 05			06 29	06 33	
Deansgate	d																	06 07				06 36	
Rochdale 41	d																			05 53			
Manchester Victoria	d					00 25					05 33	05 37					05 54		06 06	06 15			06 37
Salford Central	d										05 36	05 40					05 57		06 10	06 18			06 40
Salford Crescent	a					00 29				05 13	05 39	05 45					06 00	06 10	06 13	06 21		06 41	06 44
	d					00 30				05 13	05 40	05 45					06 00	06 11	06 14	06 22		06 41	06 45
Swinton	d																			06 28			06 52
Moorside	d																						06 54
Walkden	d																			06 33			06 58
Atherton	d			00 04																06 39			07 04
Hag Fold	d			00 06																06 41			07 06
Daisy Hill	d			00 10																06 44			07 10
Clifton	d																						
Kearsley	d																06 08						
Farnworth	d																06 10						
Moses Gate	d																06 12						
Bolton	a					00 39				05 22		05 58					06 16	06 20	06 24			06 50	
	d					00 39				05 23							06 16	06 20	06 25		06u42	06 51	
Westhoughton	d																06 24						
Hindley	d			00 15													06 28			06 49			07 14
Ince	d			00 18																06 52			
Wigan North Western	a															06 15	06 37						
Wigan Wallgate	a			00 23							06 02									06 55			07 19
	d										06 04			06 37						06 57			07 21
Pemberton	d										06 08									07 01			
Orrell	d										06 12									07 05			
Upholland	d										06 15									07 08			
Rainford	d										06 21									07 12			
Kirkby	a										06 29									07 22			
Gathurst	d													06 41									07 25
Appley Bridge	d													06 45									07 29
Parbold	d													06 49									07 34
Hoscar	d													06 52									
Burscough Bridge	d													06 56									07 39
New Lane	d													06 58									
Bescar Lane	d													07 02									
Meols Cop	d													07 07									07 47
Southport	a													07 14									07 54
Lostock	d																		06 29			06 56	
Horwich Parkway	d									05 29								06 27	06 33			06 59	
Blackrod	d																		06 36			07 02	
Adlington (Lancashire)	d	00 03																	06 40			07 06	
Chorley	d	00 08								05 36								06 34	06 45			07 10	
Buckshaw Parkway	d	00 11								05 40								06 38	06 48			07 20	
Leyland	d	00 16																06 46	06 54			07 28	
Preston 8 65,97	a	00 23			00 59	01 04			05 33	05 50						06 31		06 51	07 00		07 02	07 35	
	d	00 24			01 01			05 19	05 36	05 52						06 47		06 53			07 03	07 41	
Kirkham & Wesham 97	a				01 10					06 01								07 02					
Poulton-le-Fylde 97	a	00 40			01 18					06 09								07 10				07 57	
Layton 97	a				01 22					06 13								07 14					
Blackpool North 97	a	00 46			01 27					06 18								07 19				08 03	
Lancaster 8 65	a							05 39	05 51							07 04					07 18		
	d						05 30	05 39	05 51				05 59		06 48	07 06					07 19		
Oxenholme Lake District 65	a								06 04				06 18								07 32		
Windermere 83	a												06 39										
Carnforth	d						05a39	05 49							06a59	07 16							
Silverdale	d							05 54								07 21							
Arnside	d							05 59								07 26							
Grange-over-Sands	d							06 05								07 32							
Kents Bank	d		00 04					06 08								07 35							
Cark	d		00 08					06 12								07 39							
Ulverston	d		00 16					06 21								07 47							
Dalton	d		00 24					06 29								07 55							
Roose	d		00 30					06 35								08 01							
Barrow-in-Furness	a		00 37					06 42								08 09							

A From Manchester Piccadilly
B From Manchester Airport
C From Blackburn
D To Morecambe; Parliamentary Train
E To Glasgow Central
F To Clitheroe
G To Leeds
H To Edinburgh
I From Hazel Grove

Table T082-F

Saturdays

21 December to 16 May

Manchester - Bolton - Wigan, Kirkby, Southport, Preston, Blackpool North and Barrow-in-Furness

		NT A	NT ◇ B	NT	NT ◇	NT	NT C	NT	NT D	NT	TP ◇1 E	NT	NT ◇ F	NT ◇	NT	NT G	NT A	NT ◇ B	NT ◇	NT	NT C	NT	NT D
Manchester Airport 85	d				06 40						07 07			07 25					07 43				
Heald Green 85	d				06 44									07 29					07 47				
Alderley Edge	d							06 48														07 49	
Stockport 84	d							07 03					07 15									08 04	
Manchester Piccadilly	d				07 01			07 17			07 26		07 30	07 43					08 01			08 18	
Manchester Oxford Road	d				07 04			07 20			07 30		07 34	07 47					08 04			08 21	
Deansgate	d				07 07			07 22					07 36						08 06				
Rochdale 41	d		06 39				06 42		07 09							07 18		07 37			07 42		08 07
Manchester Victoria	d	06 50	06 55	07 00		07 05	07 08		07 25						07 36	07 41	07 49	07 54		08 05	08 09		08 26
Salford Central	d	06 53	06 58	07 03		07 08	07 11		07 28						07 40	07 44	07 52	07 57		08 08	08 12		08 29
Salford Crescent	a	06 56	07 01	07 06	07 11	07 11	07 18	07 26	07 31				07 40		07 43	07 48	07 56	08 00	08 10	08 11	08 18	08 26	08 32
	d	06 57	07 01	07 07	07 11	07 14	07 18	07 27	07 32				07 40		07 44	07 48	07 57	08 00	08 10	08 14	08 18	08 27	08 33
Swinton	d			07 13											07 51			08 07					08 40
Moorside	d			07 16											07 54								08 42
Walkden	d		07 10	07 19					07 40						07 58			08 12					08 46
Atherton	d		07 16	07 25					07 46						08 04			08 18					08 52
Hag Fold	d			07 28											08 07			08 20					08 55
Daisy Hill	d		07 19	07 31					07 50						08 10			08 24					08 58
Clifton	d																						
Kearsley	d	07 04															08 04						
Farnworth	d	07 06															08 07						
Moses Gate	d	07 09															08 09						
Bolton	a	07 12			07 20	07 24	07 30	07 36					07 50			08 00	08 13		08 19	08 24	08 30	08 36	
	d	07 13			07 21	07 25		07 37					07 50				08 13		08 20	08 25		08 37	
Westhoughton	d	07 21						07 44									08 21					08 44	
Hindley	d	07 28		07 35				07 49	07 55						08 15		08 26	08 30				08 48	09 03
Ince	d			07 38											08 19			08 33					09 06
Wigan North Western	a	07 33												08 16									09 12
Wigan Wallgate	a		07 29	07 41				07 54	08 02						08 22		08 31	08 38				08 53	
	d			07 43				07 55							08 23		08 32					08 55	
Pemberton	d			07 47											08 27								
Orrell	d			07 51											08 32								
Upholland	d			07 54											08 35								
Rainford	d			07 58											08 39								
Kirkby	a			08 08											08 49								
Gathurst	d							08 00									08 37					08 59	
Appley Bridge	d							08 04									08 41					09 03	
Parbold	d							08 08									08 45					09 08	
Hoscar	d							08 11															
Burscough Bridge	d							08 14									08 50					09 13	
New Lane	d							08 17															
Bescar Lane	d							08 20															
Meols Cop	d							08 26									08 58					09 21	
Southport	a							08 33									09 05					09 28	
Lostock	d					07 29							07 55							08 29			
Horwich Parkway	d				07 27	07 33							07 58						08 26	08 33			
Blackrod	d					07 36							08 00							08 36			
Adlington (Lancashire)	d					07 40							08 04							08 40			
Chorley	d				07 35	07 45							08 08						08 34	08 45			
Buckshaw Parkway	d				07 38	07 48							08 11						08 37	08 48			
Leyland	d					07 54							08 17							08 54			
Preston 8 65,97	a				07 50	08 00					08 01		08 23	08 39					08 49	09 00			
	d				07 52						08 02		08 25	08 42					08 51				
Kirkham & Wesham 97	a				08 02														09 00				
Poulton-le-Fylde 97	a				08 11								08 40						09 10				
Layton 97	a				08 15														09 14				
Blackpool North 97	a				08 19								08 47						09 19				
Lancaster 8 65	a										08 17			08 59									
	d									07 36		08 23		09 00									
Oxenholme Lake District 65	a																						
Windermere 83	a																						
Carnforth	d									07 45		08 32		09 10									
Silverdale	d									07 51		08 38		09 16									
Arnside	d									07 55		08 42		09 20									
Grange-over-Sands	d									08 01		08 48		09 26									
Kents Bank	d									08 05		08 52		09 30									
Cark	d									08 09		08 56		09 34									
Ulverston	d									08 17		09 04		09 42									
Dalton	d									08 26		09 13		09 50									
Roose	d									08 32		09 19		09 56									
Barrow-in-Furness	a									08 39		09 26		10 03									

A From Stalybridge
B From Leeds
C To Blackburn
D From Blackburn
E To Glasgow Central
F From Stoke-on-Trent
G To Clitheroe

Table T082-F

Saturdays
21 December to 16 May

Manchester - Bolton - Wigan, Kirkby, Southport, Preston, Blackpool North and Barrow-in-Furness

		TP ◇1 A	NT B	NT C	NT ◇	NT D	NT ◇ E	NT ◇	NT	NT F	NT ◇ G	NT H	NT I	NT	NT J	TP ◇1 K	NT L	NT B	NT C	NT D	NT ◇ E	NT ◇ M
Manchester Airport 85	d	08 07			08 27			08 44								09 07						
Heald Green 85	d				08 31			08 48														
Alderley Edge	d													08 49								
Stockport 84	d		08 11											09 06				09 11				
Manchester Piccadilly 10	d	08 27	08 31		08 47			09 02						09 18		09 26		09 30				
Manchester Oxford Road	d	08 30	08 34		08 51			09 05						09 21		09 30		09 34				
Deansgate	d		08 36					09 07										09 37				
Rochdale 41	d			08 14			08 39			08 42							09 09		09 14		09 39	
Manchester Victoria	d			08 39		08 50	08 55		09 05	09 08			09 13				09 26		09 39	09 50	09 55	
Salford Central	d			08 42		08 53	08 58		09 08	09 12			09 17				09 29		09 42	09 53	09 58	
Salford Crescent	a		08 40	08 46		08 56	09 01	09 11	09 11	09 18			09 21	09 26			09 32	09 41	09 46	09 56	10 01	
	d		08 41	08 46		08 57	09 01	09 11	09 14	09 18			09 22	09 26			09 33	09 41	09 46	09 57	10 02	
Swinton	d												09 29				09 39					
Moorside	d												09 31									
Walkden	d						09 10						09 35				09 44				10 10	
Atherton	d						09 16						09 41				09 50				10 16	
Hag Fold	d												09 44				09 53					
Daisy Hill	d						09 19						09 47				09 56				10 19	
Clifton	d																					
Kearsley	d					09 04														10 04		
Farnworth	d					09 07														10 07		
Moses Gate	d					09 10														10 10		
Bolton	a		08 50	08 59		09 13		09 20	09 24	09 30				09 35				09 50	09 59	10 13		
	d	08u44	08 51			09 14		09 21	09 25					09 36		09u44		09 51		10 14		
Westhoughton	d					09 22								09 43	←					10 22		
Hindley	d					09 28							09 52	09 48	09 52		10 01			10 28		
Ince	d												→		09 55							
Wigan North Western	a				09 18		09 30															
Wigan Wallgate	a					09 34								09 53	09 58		10 08			10 34	10 29	
	d					09 36								09 54	10 00					10 36		
Pemberton	d														10 04							
Orrell	d														10 08							
Upholland	d														10 11							
Rainford	d														10 15							
Kirkby	a														10 25							
Gathurst	d					09 40								09 59						10 40		
Appley Bridge	d					09 44								10 03						10 44		
Parbold	d					09 49								10 07						10 49		
Hoscar	d					09 52																
Burscough Bridge	d					09 55								10 12						10 54		
New Lane	d					09 58																
Bescar Lane	d					10 01																
Meols Cop	d					10 07								10 20						11 02		
Southport	a					10 14								10 27						11 09		
Lostock	d		08 55						09 29									09 55				
Horwich Parkway	d		08 59					09 27	09 33									09 59				
Blackrod	d								09 36													
Adlington (Lancashire)	d								09 40													
Chorley	d		09 07					09 35	09 45									10 07				
Buckshaw Parkway	d		09 11					09 38	09 48									10 10				
Leyland	d		09 17						09 54									10 16				
Preston 8 65,97	a	09 03	09 23		09 43			09 54	10 00							10 04		10 23				
	d	09 05	09 25		09 44			09 56								10 05		10 25				
Kirkham & Wesham 97	a							10 05														
Poulton-le-Fylde 97	a		09 40					10 13										10 40				
Layton 97	a							10 17														
Blackpool North 97	a		09 46					10 22										10 47				
Lancaster 6 65	a	09 20														10 20						
	d	09 21									09 41	10 13				10 21						10 46
Oxenholme Lake District 65	a	09 34			10 32											10 34						
Windermere 83	a				10 52																	
Carnforth	d										09a50	10 22										10a55
Silverdale	d											10 28										
Arnside	d											10 32										
Grange-over-Sands	d											10 38										
Kents Bank	d											10 42										
Cark	d											10 46										
Ulverston	d											10 54										
Dalton	d											11 02										
Roose	d											11 08										
Barrow-in-Furness	a											11 16										

A To Edinburgh
B From Hazel Grove
C To Clitheroe
D From Stalybridge
E From Leeds
F To Blackburn
G To Leeds
H To Carlisle
I To Kirkby
J From Manchester Victoria
K To Glasgow Central
L From Blackburn
M From Morecambe to Leeds

Table T082-F

Saturdays
21 December to 16 May

Manchester - Bolton - Wigan, Kirkby, Southport, Preston, Blackpool North and Barrow-in-Furness

		NT ◇	NT ◇	NT	NT A	NT B	NT	NT C	TP ◇1 D	NT E	NT F	NT G	NT ◇	NT H	NT ◇ I	NT ◇	NT	NT A	NT B	NT	NT C	TP ◇1 J	NT E
Manchester Airport 85	d	09 28	09 45						10 07				10 28			10 45						11 07	
Heald Green 85	d	09 32	09 49										10 32			10 49							
Alderley Edge	d						09 50													10 49			
Stockport 84	d						10 06				10 13									11 05			
Manchester Piccadilly 10	d	09 47	10 01				10 18		10 26		10 30		10 47			11 01				11 18		11 26	
Manchester Oxford Road	d	09 51	10 04				10 21		10 30		10 34		10 50			11 04				11 21		11 30	
Deansgate	d		10 07								10 37					11 07							
Rochdale 41	d				09 42					10 09		10 18			10 39			10 42					11 09
Manchester Victoria	d			10 05	10 08	10 13				10 26		10 41		10 50	10 55		11 05	11 08	11 13				11 26
Salford Central	d			10 08	10 12	10 17				10 29		10 44		10 53	10 58		11 08	11 12	11 17				11 29
Salford Crescent	a		10 10	10 11	10 18	10 21	10 26			10 32	10 40	10 47		10 56	11 01	11 10	11 11	11 18	11 21	11 26			11 32
	d		10 11	10 15	10 18	10 22	10 26			10 33	10 41	10 48		10 57	11 01	11 11	11 14	11 18	11 22	11 26			11 33
Swinton	d					10 29				10 39									11 29				11 39
Moorside	d					10 31													11 31				
Walkden	d					10 35				10 44					11 10				11 35				11 44
Atherton	d					10 41				10 50					11 16				11 41				11 50
Hag Fold	d					10 44				10 53									11 44				11 53
Daisy Hill	d					10 47				10 56					11 19				11 47				11 56
Clifton	d																						
Kearsley	d													11 04									
Farnworth	d													11 07									
Moses Gate	d													11 10									
Bolton	a		10 20	10 24	10 30		10 35				10 50	11 00		11 13		11 20	11 24	11 30		11 35			
	d		10 20	10 25			10 36				10 50			11 14		11 20	11 25			11 36			
Westhoughton	d						10 43	←						11 22						11 43	←		
Hindley	d					10 52	10 48	10 52		11 01				11 28					11 52	11 48	11 52		12 01
Ince	d					→		10 55											→		11 55		
Wigan North Western	a	10 20											11 20										
Wigan Wallgate	a						10 53	10 58		11 08				11 34	11 29					11 53	11 58		12 08
	d						10 54	11 00						11 36						11 54	12 00		
Pemberton	d							11 04													12 04		
Orrell	d							11 08													12 08		
Upholland	d							11 11													12 11		
Rainford	d							11 15													12 17		
Kirkby	a							11 25													12 25		
Gathurst	d						10 59							11 41						11 59			
Appley Bridge	d						11 03							11 44						12 03			
Parbold	d						11 07							11 49						12 07			
Hoscar	d													11 52									
Burscough Bridge	d						11 12							11 55						12 12			
New Lane	d													11 58									
Bescar Lane	d													12 01									
Meols Cop	d						11 20							12 07						12 20			
Southport	a						11 27							12 14						12 27			
Lostock	d			10 29							10 55						11 29						
Horwich Parkway	d		10 27	10 33							10 58					11 27	11 33						
Blackrod	d			10 36													11 36						
Adlington (Lancashire)	d			10 40													11 40						
Chorley	d		10 35	10 45							11 06					11 35	11 45						
Buckshaw Parkway	d		10 38	10 48							11 09					11 39	11 48						
Leyland	d			10 54							11 16						11 54						
Preston 8 65,97	a	10 43	10 49	11 00					11 02		11 22		11 42			11 50	12 00					12 02	
	d	10 44	10 51								11 24		11 44			11 52						12 03	
Kirkham & Wesham 97	a		11 00													12 01							
Poulton-le-Fylde 97	a		11 10								11 39					12 10							
Layton 97	a		11 14													12 14							
Blackpool North 97	a		11 19								11 45					12 19							
Lancaster 6 65	a	11 02											12 02									12 18	
	d	11 02											12 02									12 19	
Oxenholme Lake District 65	a																					12 32	
Windermere 83	a																						
Carnforth	d	11 12											12 12										
Silverdale	d												12 18										
Arnside	d	11 21											12 22										
Grange-over-Sands	d	11 27											12 28										
Kents Bank	d												12 32										
Cark	d	11 33											12 36										
Ulverston	d	11 41											12 44										
Dalton	d												12 52										
Roose	d												12 58										
Barrow-in-Furness	a	12 00											13 05										

A To Blackburn
B To Kirkby
C From Manchester Victoria
D To Edinburgh
E From Blackburn
F From Hazel Grove
G To Clitheroe
H From Stalybridge
I From Leeds
J To Glasgow Central

Table T082-F

Saturdays

21 December to 16 May

Manchester - Bolton - Wigan, Kirkby, Southport, Preston, Blackpool North and Barrow-in-Furness

Station		NT A	NT B	NT C	NT ◇ D	NT ◇ E	NT F	NT ◇	NT ◇	NT	NT G	NT H	NT	NT I	TP ◇1 J	NT K	NT A	NT B	NT ◇	NT C	NT ◇ D	NT ◇
Manchester Airport 85	d							11 28	11 45						12 07				12 28			12 45
Heald Green 85	d							11 32	11 49										12 32			12 49
Alderley Edge	d												11 49									
Stockport 84	d	11 11											12 05				12 12					
Manchester Piccadilly 10	d	11 30						11 47	12 01				12 18		12 26		12 30		12 47			13 01
Manchester Oxford Road	d	11 34						11 51	12 04				12 21		12 30		12 34		12 50			13 04
Deansgate	d	11 37							12 07								12 37					13 07
Rochdale 41	d		11 22		11 39						11 42					12 09		12 18			12 39	
Manchester Victoria	d		11 45	11 48	11 55					12 05	12 08	12 13				12 26		12 41		12 50	12 55	
Salford Central	d		11 48	11 51	11 58					12 08	12 12	12 17				12 29		12 44		12 53	12 58	
Salford Crescent	a	11 40	11 51	11 54	12 01				12 10	12 11	12 18	12 21	12 26			12 32	12 40	12 48		12 56	13 01	13 10
	d	11 41	11 52	11 57	12 01				12 11	12 14	12 18	12 22	12 26			12 33	12 41	12 48		12 57	13 01	13 11
Swinton	d											12 29				12 39						
Moorside	d											12 31										
Walkden	d				12 10							12 35				12 44					13 10	
Atherton	d				12 16							12 41				12 50					13 16	
Hag Fold	d											12 44				12 53						
Daisy Hill	d				12 19							12 47				12 56					13 19	
Clifton	d																					
Kearsley	d			12 04																13 04		
Farnworth	d			12 07																13 07		
Moses Gate	d			12 10																13 10		
Bolton	a	11 50	12 03	12 13					12 20	12 24	12 30		12 35				12 50	13 00		13 13		13 20
	d	11 50		12 14					12 20	12 25			12 36		12u44		12 50			13 14		13 20
Westhoughton	d			12 22									12 43	←						13 22		
Hindley	d			12 28								12 52	12 48	12 52		13 01				13 28		
Ince	d											→		12 55								
Wigan North Western	a							12 18								13 09			13 19			
Wigan Wallgate	a			12 34	12 29								12 53	12 58						13 34	13 29	
	d			12 36									12 54	13 00						13 36		
Pemberton	d													13 04								
Orrell	d													13 08								
Upholland	d													13 11								
Rainford	d													13 15								
Kirkby	a													13 25								
Gathurst	d			12 40									12 59							13 40		
Appley Bridge	d			12 44									13 03							13 44		
Parbold	d			12 49									13 07							13 49		
Hoscar	d																			13 52		
Burscough Bridge	d			12 54									13 12							13 55		
New Lane	d																			13 58		
Bescar Lane	d																			14 01		
Meols Cop	d			13 02									13 20							14 07		
Southport	a			13 09									13 27							14 14		
Lostock	d	11 55								12 29							12 55					
Horwich Parkway	d	11 58							12 27	12 33							12 58					13 27
Blackrod	d									12 36												
Adlington (Lancashire)	d									12 40												
Chorley	d	12 06							12 35	12 45							13 06					13 35
Buckshaw Parkway	d	12 09							12 38	12 48							13 09					13 38
Leyland	d	12 15								12 57							13 16					
Preston 8 65,97	a	12 23						12 42	12 49	13 03					13 03		13 23		13 43			13 49
	d	12 24						12 45	12 51						13 05		13 24		13 44			13 51
Kirkham & Wesham 97	a								13 00													14 00
Poulton-le-Fylde 97	a	12 40							13 08								13 40					14 10
Layton 97	a								13 12													14 14
Blackpool North 97	a	12 46							13 16								13 46					14 19
Lancaster 6 65	a							13 04							13 20				14 02			
	d					12 45	13 01	13 12							13 21				14 02			
Oxenholme Lake District 65	a							13 31							13 34							
Windermere 83	a							13 54														
Carnforth	d					12a54	13 10												14 12			
Silverdale	d						13 16												14 17			
Arnside	d						13 20												14 22			
Grange-over-Sands	d						13 26												14 28			
Kents Bank	d						13 30												14 31			
Cark	d						13 34												14 35			
Ulverston	d						13 42												14 43			
Dalton	d						13 51												14 51			
Roose	d						13 57												14 57			
Barrow-in-Furness	a						14 04												15 05			

A From Hazel Grove
B To Clitheroe
C From Stalybridge
D From Leeds
E From Morecambe to Leeds
F To Carlisle
G To Blackburn
H To Kirkby
I From Manchester Victoria
J To Edinburgh
K From Blackburn

Table T082-F

Saturdays

21 December to 16 May

Manchester - Bolton - Wigan, Kirkby, Southport, Preston, Blackpool North and Barrow-in-Furness

Station		NT	NT A	NT B	NT	NT C	TP ◇1 D	NT E	NT F	NT G	NT H	NT ◇ I	NT ◇	NT ◇ J	NT ◇	NT	NT A	NT B	NT	NT C	TP ◇1 K	NT E	NT F
Manchester Airport 85	d						13 07						13 28		13 45						14 07		
Heald Green 85	d												13 32		13 49								
Alderley Edge	d				12 49														13 49				
Stockport 84	d				13 06				13 12										14 06				14 11
Manchester Piccadilly 10	d				13 18		13 26		13 30				13 47		14 01				14 17		14 26		14 30
Manchester Oxford Road	d				13 21		13 30		13 34				13 50		14 04				14 20		14 30		14 34
Deansgate	d								13 37						14 07								14 37
Rochdale 41	d		12 42					13 09		13 18				13 39			13 34					14 09	
Manchester Victoria	d	13 05	13 07	13 13				13 26		13 41	13 49			13 55		14 05	14 08	14 13				14 26	
Salford Central	d	13 08	13 12	13 17				13 29		13 44	13 52			13 58		14 08	14 12	14 17				14 29	
Salford Crescent	a	13 11	13 18	13 21	13 26			13 32	13 41	13 48	13 56			14 01	14 10	14 11	14 18	14 21	14 26			14 32	14 41
	d	13 14	13 18	13 22	13 27			13 33	13 41	13 48	13 57			14 02	14 11	14 14	14 18	14 22	14 26			14 33	14 41
Swinton	d			13 29				13 39										14 29				14 39	
Moorside	d			13 31														14 31					
Walkden	d			13 35				13 44						14 10				14 35				14 44	
Atherton	d			13 41				13 50						14 16				14 41				14 50	
Hag Fold	d			13 43				13 53										14 44				14 53	
Daisy Hill	d			13 47				13 56						14 19				14 47				14 56	
Clifton	d																						
Kearsley	d										14 04												
Farnworth	d										14 07												
Moses Gate	d										14 10												
Bolton	a	13 24	13 30		13 36				13 50	14 00	14 13				14 20	14 24	14 30		14 35				14 50
	d	13 25			13 36		13u44		13 51		14 14				14 20	14 25			14 36				14 51
Westhoughton	d				13 44	←					14 22								14 43	←			
Hindley	d			13 52	13 48	13 52		14 01			14 28							14 52	14 48	14 52		15 01	
Ince	d			→		13 55												→		14 55			
Wigan North Western	a												14 17	14 30									
Wigan Wallgate	a				13 53	13 58		14 08			14 34								14 53	14 58		15 08	
	d				13 54	14 00					14 36								14 54	15 00			
Pemberton	d					14 04														15 04			
Orrell	d					14 08														15 08			
Upholland	d					14 11														15 11			
Rainford	d					14 15														15 15			
Kirkby	a					14 25														15 25			
Gathurst	d				13 59						14 40								14 59				
Appley Bridge	d				14 03						14 44								15 03				
Parbold	d				14 07						14 49								15 07				
Hoscar	d																						
Burscough Bridge	d				14 12						14 54								15 12				
New Lane	d																						
Bescar Lane	d																						
Meols Cop	d				14 20						15 02								15 20				
Southport	a				14 27						15 09								15 27				
Lostock	d	13 29							13 55							14 29							14 56
Horwich Parkway	d	13 33							13 59						14 27	14 33							14 59
Blackrod	d	13 36														14 36							
Adlington (Lancashire)	d	13 40														14 40							
Chorley	d	13 45							14 07						14 34	14 44							15 07
Buckshaw Parkway	d	13 48							14 10						14 38	14 48							15 10
Leyland	d	13 54							14 16							14 54							15 14
Preston 8 65,97	a	14 00					14 04		14 23				14 43		14 49	15 00					15 02		15 23
	d						14 05		14 24				14 45		14 50						15 03		15 24
Kirkham & Wesham 97	a														14 59								
Poulton-le-Fylde 97	a								14 40						15 10								15 40
Layton 97	a														15 14								
Blackpool North 97	a								14 46						15 19								15 46
Lancaster 6 65	a						14 20						15 02								15 18		
	d						14 21					14 47	15 03								15 19		
Oxenholme Lake District 65	a						14 33														15 32		
Windermere 83	a																						
Carnforth	d											14a56	15 12										
Silverdale	d												15 18										
Arnside	d												15 22										
Grange-over-Sands	d												15 28										
Kents Bank	d												15 32										
Cark	d												15 36										
Ulverston	d												15 44										
Dalton	d												15 52										
Roose	d												15 58										
Barrow-in-Furness	a												16 05										

A To Blackburn
B To Kirkby
C From Manchester Victoria
D To Glasgow Central
E From Blackburn
F From Hazel Grove
G To Clitheroe
H From Stalybridge
I From Morecambe to Leeds
J From Leeds
K To Edinburgh

Table T082-F

Saturdays
21 December to 16 May

Manchester - Bolton - Wigan, Kirkby, Southport, Preston, Blackpool North and Barrow-in-Furness

Station		NT A	NT B	NT ◇ C	NT D	NT ◇	NT ◇	NT	NT E	NT F	NT	NT G	TP ◇1 H ⌶	NT I	NT J	NT A	NT ◇	NT B	NT ◇ C	NT ◇	NT	NT A	NT F
Manchester Airport 85 ✈	d					14 28	14 45						15 07				15 28			15 45			
Heald Green 85	d					14 32	14 49										15 32			15 49			
Alderley Edge	d										14 49												
Stockport 84	d										15 05				15 11								
Manchester Piccadilly 10	d					14 47	15 01				15 18		15 26		15 30		15 47			16 01			
Manchester Oxford Road	d					14 51	15 04				15 21		15 30		15 34		15 50			16 04			
Deansgate	d						15 07								15 37					16 07			
Rochdale 41	d	14 18		14 39					14 42					15 09		15 18			15 39			15 42	
Manchester Victoria	d	14 41	14 50	14 55				15 05	15 08	15 13				15 26		15 41		15 50	15 55		16 05	16 08	16 13
Salford Central	d	14 44	14 53	14 58				15 08	15 12	15 17				15 29		15 44		15 53	15 58		16 08	16 12	16 17
Salford Crescent	a	14 48	14 56	15 01			15 10	15 11	15 18	15 21	15 26			15 32	15 41	15 48		15 56	16 01	16 10	16 11	16 18	16 21
	d	14 49	14 57	15 01			15 11	15 14	15 18	15 22	15 26			15 33	15 41	15 48		15 57	16 01	16 11	16 14	16 18	16 22
Swinton	d									15 29				15 39									16 29
Moorside	d									15 31													16 32
Walkden	d			15 10						15 35				15 44					16 10				16 36
Atherton	d			15 16						15 41				15 50					16 16				16 42
Hag Fold	d									15 44				15 53									16 45
Daisy Hill	d			15 19						15 47				15 56					16 19				16 48
Clifton	d																						
Kearsley	d		15 04															16 04					
Farnworth	d		15 07															16 07					
Moses Gate	d		15 10															16 10					
Bolton	a	15 00	15 13				15 20	15 24	15 30		15 35				15 50	16 00		16 13		16 20	16 24	16 30	
	d		15 14				15 20	15 25			15 36				15 51			16 14		16 20	16 25		
Westhoughton	d		15 22								15 43	←						16 22					
Hindley	d		15 28							15 52	15 48	15 52		16 01				16 28					16 53
Ince	d									→		15 55											→
Wigan North Western	a					15 18											16 18						
Wigan Wallgate	a		15 34	15 29							15 53	15 58		16 08				16 34	16 29				
	d		15 36								15 54	16 00						16 36					
Pemberton	d											16 04											
Orrell	d											16 08											
Upholland	d											16 11											
Rainford	d											16 15											
Kirkby	a											16 25											
Gathurst	d		15 40								15 59							16 40					
Appley Bridge	d		15 44								16 03							16 44					
Parbold	d		15 49								16 07							16 49					
Hoscar	d		15 52																				
Burscough Bridge	d		15 55								16 12							16 54					
New Lane	d		15 58																				
Bescar Lane	d		16 01																				
Meols Cop	d		16 07								16 20							17 02					
Southport	a		16 14								16 27							17 09					
Lostock	d							15 29							15 56					16 25	16 29		
Horwich Parkway	d						15 27	15 33							15 59					16 29	16 33		
Blackrod	d							15 36													16 36		
Adlington (Lancashire)	d							15 40													16 40		
Chorley	d						15 35	15 45							16 07					16 36	16 44		
Buckshaw Parkway	d						15 38	15 48							16 11					16 40	16 48		
Leyland	d							15 54							16 17						16 54		
Preston 8 65,97	a					15 43	15 49	16 00					16 02		16 23		16 42			16 51	17 00		
	d				15 32	15 45	15 51						16 03		16 24		16 45			16 53			
Kirkham & Wesham 97	a						16 00													17 02			
Poulton-le-Fylde 97	a						16 09								16 40					17 10			
Layton 97	a						16 13								16 44					17 14			
Blackpool North 97	a						16 17								16 48					17 19			
Lancaster 8 65	a				15 52								16 18				17 02						
	d				16 13								16 19				17 02						
Oxenholme Lake District 65	a					16 30							16 33										
Windermere 83	a					16 53																	
Carnforth	d				16 22												17 12						
Silverdale	d				16 28												17 17						
Arnside	d				16 32												17 21						
Grange-over-Sands	d				16 38												17 27						
Kents Bank	d				16 42												17 30						
Cark	d				16 46												17 34						
Ulverston	d				16 54												17 42						
Dalton	d				17 02												17 50						
Roose	d				17 08												17 56						
Barrow-in-Furness	a				17 16												18 02						

A To Clitheroe
B From Stalybridge
C From Leeds
D To Carlisle
E To Blackburn
F To Kirkby
G From Manchester Victoria
H To Glasgow Central
I From Blackburn
J From Hazel Grove

Table T082-F

Saturdays
21 December to 16 May

Manchester - Bolton - Wigan, Kirkby, Southport, Preston, Blackpool North and Barrow-in-Furness

Station		NT	NT A	TP ◇1 B ⌶	NT C	NT D	NT E	NT F	NT ◇ G	NT	NT ◇ H	NT ◇	NT ◇	NT	NT I	NT J	NT	NT A	TP ◇1 K ⌶	NT C	NT D	NT ◇
Manchester Airport 85 ✈	d			16 07								16 28	16 45						17 07			17 28
Heald Green 85	d											16 32	16 49									17 32
Alderley Edge	d	15 50															16 50					
Stockport 84	d	16 06				16 12											17 06				17 12	
Manchester Piccadilly 10	d	16 18		16 26		16 30						16 47	17 02				17 19		17 27		17 31	17 47
Manchester Oxford Road	d	16 21		16 30		16 34						16 51	17 05						17 30		17 34	17 51
Deansgate	d					16 37							17 07				17 22				17 37	
Rochdale 41	d				16 09		16 18		16 39						16 42					17 09		
Manchester Victoria	d				16 26		16 41	16 50	16 55					17 05	17 08	17 13				17 26		
Salford Central	d				16 29		16 44	16 53	16 58					17 08	17 12	17 17				17 29		
Salford Crescent	a	16 27			16 32	16 40	16 47	16 56	17 01				17 11	17 11	17 18	17 21	17 26			17 32	17 40	
	d	16 28			16 33	16 41	16 48	16 57	17 02				17 11	17 14	17 18	17 22	17 26			17 33	17 41	
Swinton	d				16 39											17 29				17 40		
Moorside	d															17 31						
Walkden	d				16 44				17 10							17 35				17 45		
Atherton	d				16 50				17 16							17 41				17 51		
Hag Fold	d				16 53											17 44				17 54		
Daisy Hill	d				16 56				17 20							17 47				17 57		
Clifton	d																					
Kearsley	d							17 04														
Farnworth	d							17 07							17 27							
Moses Gate	d							17 09														
Bolton	a	16 37				16 50	16 59	17 13					17 21	17 25	17 32		17 35				17 50	
	d	16 38		16u44		16 50		17 13					17 21	17 25			17 36				17 50	
Westhoughton	d	16 45	←					17 22									17 44	←				
Hindley	d	16 50	16 53		17 01			17 29								17 52	17 48	17 52		18 02		
Ince	d		16 56													→		17 55				
Wigan North Western	a				17 09							17 17										18 19
Wigan Wallgate	a	16 55	17 00					17 35	17 30								17 53	17 58		18 09		
	d	16 56	17 01					17 37									17 55	18 00				
Pemberton	d		17 05															18 04				
Orrell	d		17 10															18 08				
Upholland	d		17 13															18 11				
Rainford	d		17 17															18 15				
Kirkby	a		17 27															18 25				
Gathurst	d	17 01						17 41									17 59					
Appley Bridge	d	17 05						17 45									18 03					
Parbold	d	17 10						17 50									18 08					
Hoscar	d							17 53														
Burscough Bridge	d	17 15						17 56									18 13					
New Lane	d							17 59														
Bescar Lane	d							18 02														
Meols Cop	d	17 23						18 08									18 21					
Southport	a	17 30						18 15									18 28					
Lostock	d					16 55							17 27	17 30							17 55	
Horwich Parkway	d					16 59							17 30	17 34							17 58	
Blackrod	d					17 02								17 37							18 00	
Adlington (Lancashire)	d					17 05								17 40							18 04	
Chorley	d					17 10							17 38	17 45							18 08	
Buckshaw Parkway	d					17 21							17 41	17 49							18 12	
Leyland	d					17 28								17 54							18 18	
Preston 8 65,97	a			17 04		17 34						17 43	17 52	18 00					18 02		18 24	18 42
	d			17 05		17 37						17 45	17 54						18 04		18 26	18 44
Kirkham & Wesham 97	a					17 46							18 03								18 34	
Poulton-le-Fylde 97	a					17 54							18 12								18 43	
Layton 97	a					17 58							18 16								18 47	
Blackpool North 97	a					18 02							18 20								18 51	
Lancaster 8 65	a			17 20								18 02							18 19			
	d			17 21						17 38	17 45	18 03							18 20			
Oxenholme Lake District 65	a			17 34															18 33			19 20
Windermere 83	a																					19 42
Carnforth	d									17 47	17a54	18 12										
Silverdale	d									17 52		18 18										
Arnside	d									17 57		18 22										
Grange-over-Sands	d									18 03		18 28										
Kents Bank	d									18 06		18 32										
Cark	d									18 10		18 36										
Ulverston	d									18 18		18 44										
Dalton	d									18 26		18 52										
Roose	d									18 32		18 58										
Barrow-in-Furness	a									18 40		19 05										

A From Manchester Victoria
B To Edinburgh
C From Blackburn
D From Hazel Grove
E To Clitheroe
F From Stalybridge
G From Leeds
H From Morecambe to Leeds
I To Blackburn
J To Kirkby
K To Glasgow Central

Table T082-F

Saturdays
21 December to 16 May

Manchester - Bolton - Wigan, Kirkby, Southport, Preston, Blackpool North and Barrow-in-Furness

Station		NT	NT	NT	NT	NT	NT	NT	NT	NT	NT	NT	NT	TP	NT	NT	NT	NT	NT	NT	NT	NT	NT
			A	B	◇ C	◇			D		E		F	◇1 G ✠	H	A	◇	B	◇ C	◇	I	A	J
Manchester Airport 85	d					17 45								18 07			18 28			18 45			
Heald Green 85	d					17 49											18 32			18 49			
Alderley Edge	d									17 49													
Stockport 84	d									18 05					18 12								
Manchester Piccadilly 10	d					18 01				18 18				18 26	18 30		18 47			19 01			
Manchester Oxford Road	d					18 04				18 21				18 30	18 34		18 51			19 04			
Deansgate	d					18 07									18 37					19 06			
Rochdale 41	d		17 19		17 39				17 54		18 09					18 18			18 39			18 42	
Manchester Victoria	d	17 36	17 41	17 47	17 55		18 05	18 12	18 17		18 26					18 41		18 49	18 55		19 05	19 09	19 14
Salford Central	d	17 40	17 44	17 51	17 58		18 08	18 15	18 20		18 29					18 44		18 53	18 58		19 08	19 13	19 17
Salford Crescent	a	17 44	17 48	17 54	18 01	18 10	18 11	18 19	18 23	18 27	18 32				18 40	18 48		18 56	19 01	19 10	19 11	19 18	19 21
	d	17 45	17 48	17 57	18 01	18 11	18 15	18 19	18 24	18 28	18 33				18 41	18 48		18 57	19 01	19 10	19 14	19 18	19 22
Swinton	d	17 52						18 26			18 39												19 29
Moorside	d	17 54						18 29															19 31
Walkden	d	17 58			18 10			18 33			18 44								19 10				19 35
Atherton	d	18 04			18 16			18 38			18 50								19 16				19 41
Hag Fold	d	18 07						18 41			18 53												19 44
Daisy Hill	d	18 11			18 19			18 44			18 56								19 19				19 47
Clifton	d			18 01																			
Kearsley	d			18 06														19 04					
Farnworth	d			18 09														19 07					
Moses Gate	d			18 12														19 10					
Bolton	a		18 00	18 15		18 20	18 25		18 35	18 38					18 50	19 00		19 13		19 19	19 24	19 30	
	d			18 16		18 20	18 25			18 39				18u44	18 50			19 14		19 20	19 25		
Westhoughton	d			18 24						18 47								19 22					
Hindley	d	18 16		18 28						18 52	19 01							19 28					19 53
Ince	d	18 19								18 55													→
Wigan North Western	a																19 19		19 30				
Wigan Wallgate	a	18 22		18 34	18 29			18 54		19 00	19 06							19 34					
	d	18 24		18 37						19 01	19 08							19 36					
Pemberton	d										19 12												
Orrell	d										19 16												
Upholland	d										19 19												
Rainford	d										19 23												
Kirkby	a										19 33												
Gathurst	d	18 28		18 41						19 06								19 40					
Appley Bridge	d	18 32		18 45						19 10								19 44					
Parbold	d	18 37		18 50						19 14								19 49					
Hoscar	d																	19 52					
Burscough Bridge	d	18 42		18 55						19 19								19 55					
New Lane	d																	19 58					
Bescar Lane	d																	20 01					
Meols Cop	d	18 50		19 03						19 27								20 07					
Southport	a	18 57		19 10						19 35								20 16					
Lostock	d					18 25	18 30								18 55						19 29		
Horwich Parkway	d					18 29	18 33								18 58					19 27	→		
Blackrod	d						18 36								19 00								
Adlington (Lancashire)	d						18 40								19 04								
Chorley	d					18 36	18 45								19 08					19 35			
Buckshaw Parkway	d					18 40	18 48								19 11					19 38			
Leyland	d						18 54								19 18								
Preston 8 65,97	a					18 51	19 00							19 04	19 24		19 43			19 49			
	d					18 52								19 05	19 26		19 44			19 51			
Kirkham & Wesham 97	a					19 01														20 00			
Poulton-le-Fylde 97	a					19 10									19 41					20 10			
Layton 97	a					19 14														20 14			
Blackpool North 97	a					19 19									19 47					20 18			
Lancaster 6 65	a													19 20			20 02						
	d											18 35	19 13	19 21			20 03						
Oxenholme Lake District 65	a													19 34									
Windermere 83	a																						
Carnforth	d											18 44	19 22				20 12						
Silverdale	d											18 50	19 28				20 18						
Arnside	d											18 54	19 32				20 22						
Grange-over-Sands	d											19 00	19 38				20 28						
Kents Bank	d											19 04	19 42				20 32						
Cark	d											19 08	19 46				20 36						
Ulverston	d											19 16	19 54				20 44						
Dalton	d											19 24	20 02				20 52						
Roose	d											19 30	20 08				20 58						
Barrow-in-Furness	a											19 38	20 16				21 05						

A To Clitheroe
B From Stalybridge
C From Leeds
D To Blackburn
E From Blackburn
F To Millom
G To Edinburgh
H From Hazel Grove
I To Blackpool North
J To Wigan North Western

Table T082-F

Saturdays
21 December to 16 May

Manchester - Bolton - Wigan, Kirkby, Southport, Preston, Blackpool North and Barrow-in-Furness

Station		NT	NT	TP	NT	NT	NT	NT	NT	NT	NT	NT	NT	NT	NT	NT	NT	NT	NT	NT	NT	NT
			A	◇1 B ✠	A	C	D	E	◇ F	◇	G	H	I	◇ J	K	◇		L	M		A	C
Manchester Airport 85	d			19 07						19 28						19 42						
Heald Green 85	d									19 32						19 49						
Alderley Edge	d	18 49																		19 49		
Stockport 84	d	19 06					19 12													20 05		
Manchester Piccadilly 10	d	19 17		19 26			19 30			19 47						20 01				20 18		
Manchester Oxford Road	d	19 20		19 30			19 34			19 51						20 04				20 21		
Deansgate	d						19 37									20 07						
Rochdale 41	d					19 09		19 18						19 39				19 42				20 09
Manchester Victoria	d					19 26		19 41					19 49	19 55			20 05	20 09	20 15			20 26
Salford Central	d					19 29		19 44					19 52	19 58			20 08	20 13	20 18			20 29
Salford Crescent	a	19 26				19 32	19 40	19 48					19 55	20 01		20 10	20 11	20 18	20 21	20 26		20 32
	d	19 28				19 33	19 41	19 48					19 57	20 01		20 11	20 15	20 18	20 22	20 27		20 33
Swinton	d					19 39													20 29			20 39
Moorside	d																		20 31			
Walkden	d					19 44								20 10					20 35			20 44
Atherton	d					19 50								20 16					20 41			20 50
Hag Fold	d					19 53													20 44			20 53
Daisy Hill	d					19 56								20 19					20 47			20 56
Clifton	d																					
Kearsley	d												20 04									
Farnworth	d												20 07									
Moses Gate	d												20 09									
Bolton	a	19 37					19 50	20 00					20 13			20 20	20 25	20 30		20 36		
	d	19 37		19u44			19 50						20 13			20 20	20 25			20 37		
Westhoughton	d	19 45	←										20 21		←					20 44	←	
Hindley	d	19 49	19 53			20 01							20 31	20 24	20 31				20 52	20 48	20 52	21 01
Ince	d		19 56										→						→		20 55	
Wigan North Western	a		20 02							20 17												21 09
Wigan Wallgate	a	19 54				20 08								20 31	20 38					20 53	21 00	
	d	19 55																		20 55		
Pemberton	d																					
Orrell	d																					
Upholland	d																					
Rainford	d																					
Kirkby	a																					
Gathurst	d	20 00																		20 59		
Appley Bridge	d	20 04																		21 03		
Parbold	d	20 08																		21 08		
Hoscar	d																			21 11		
Burscough Bridge	d	20 13																		21 14		
New Lane	d																			21 17		
Bescar Lane	d																			21 20		
Meols Cop	d	20 21																		21 26		
Southport	a	20 28			←															21 33		
Lostock	d				19 29		19 55										20 30					
Horwich Parkway	d				19 33		19 58									20 27	20 33					
Blackrod	d				19 36												20 36					
Adlington (Lancashire)	d				19 40												20 40					
Chorley	d				19 45		20 06									20 35	20 45					
Buckshaw Parkway	d				19 48		20 10									20 38	20 48					
Leyland	d				19 58		20 18										20 52					
Preston 8 65,97	a			20 03	20 04		20 24			20 42						20 49	21 00					
	d			20 05	20 06		20 26			20 44						20 51						
Kirkham & Wesham 97	a				20 15											21 00						
Poulton-le-Fylde 97	a				20 24		20 41									21 08						
Layton 97	a															21 12						
Blackpool North 97	a				20 31		20 47									21 17						
Lancaster 6 65	a			20 20						21 02												
	d			20 21					20 30	21 02	21 30	22 26										
Oxenholme Lake District 65	a			20 34																		
Windermere 83	a																					
Carnforth	d								20a40	21 12	21a40	22 35										
Silverdale	d									21 17		22 41										
Arnside	d									21 22		22 45										
Grange-over-Sands	d									21 28		22 51										
Kents Bank	d									21 31		22 55										
Cark	d									21 35		22 59										
Ulverston	d									21 43		23 07										
Dalton	d									21 51		23 15										
Roose	d									21 57		23 21										
Barrow-in-Furness	a									22 05		23 29										

A From Manchester Victoria
B To Edinburgh
C From Blackburn
D From Hazel Grove
E To Clitheroe
F From Morecambe to Leeds
G To Skipton
H from 11 January until 15 February, from 4 April
I From Stalybridge to Wigan Wallgate
J From Leeds
K From Stalybridge
L To Blackburn
M To Wigan Wallgate

Table T082-F

21 December to 16 May

Manchester - Bolton - Wigan, Kirkby, Southport, Preston, Blackpool North and Barrow-in-Furness

		NT	NT	NT	NT	NT	NT	NT	NT	NT	NT	NT	NT	NT	NT	NT	NT	NT	NT	NT	NT	NT	NT
					◇	◇							◇	◇		◇							◇
		A	B	C	D		E	F	G	A	B	C	D		B		C	H	G	A	F	C	
Manchester Airport 85 ⇌✈	d					20 42								21 41		22 10			22 10				22 30
Heald Green 85	d					20 46																	22 34
Alderley Edge	d																						
Stockport 84	d	20 12								21 13										22 13			
Manchester Piccadilly 10 ⇌	d	20 30				21 02				21 31				21 59		22 26			22 26	22 30			22 54
Manchester Oxford Road	d	20 34				21 05				21 34				22 02		22 29			22 29	22 35			23 00
Deansgate ⇌	d	20 37				21 07				21 37				22 05						22 37			23 02
Rochdale 41	d		20 18		20 39		20 42	21 09			21 18		21 39		21 42						22 14		
Manchester Victoria ⇌	d		20 41	20 50	20 55		21 08	21 26			21 40	21 49	21 55		22 16		22 21				22 40	22 51	
Salford Central	d		20 44	20 53	20 58		21 12	21 29			21 43	21 53	22 00		22 19		22 24				22 43	22 54	
Salford Crescent	a	20 41	20 48	20 56	21 01	21 11	21 19	21 32		21 40	21 47	21 56	22 03	22 08	22 22		22 27			22 41	22 46	22 57	23 05
	d	20 41	20 48	20 57	21 02	21 11	21 19	21 33		21 41	21 47	21 56	22 04	22 09	22 23		22 28			22 41	22 47	22 58	23 06
Swinton	d				21 09			21 39					22 11								22 54		
Moorside	d							21 42													22 56		
Walkden	d				21 14			21 46					22 16								23 00		
Atherton	d				21 20			21 51					22 22								23 06		
Hag Fold	d							21 54													23 09		
Daisy Hill	d				21 24			21 57					22 26								23 12		
Clifton	d																						
Kearsley	d			21 04								22 04										23 05	
Farnworth	d			21 07								22 06										23 08	
Moses Gate	d			21 09								22 08										23 10	
Bolton	a	20 50	21 00	21 13		21 20	21 32			21 51	21 59	22 12		22 18	22 34		22 38			22 50		23 14	23 18
	d	20 51		21 13		21 21				21 51		22 12		22 18			22 39			22 51		23 14	23 18
Westhoughton	d			21 21								22 20					22 46					23 22	
Hindley	d			21 25	21 28			22 02				22 25					22 51				23 17	23 27	
Ince	d							22 05													23 20		
Wigan North Western	a			21 33	21 36								22 37				22 58						
Wigan Wallgate	a							22 10				22 30									23 23	23 34	
	d											22 31									23 25		
Pemberton	d																						
Orrell	d																						
Upholland	d																						
Rainford	d																						
Kirkby	a																						
Gathurst	d											22 36									23 29		
Appley Bridge	d											22 40									23 33		
Parbold	d											22 44									23 37		
Hoscar	d																						
Burscough Bridge	d											22 49									23 42		
New Lane	d																						
Bescar Lane	d																						
Meols Cop	d											22 57									23 50		
Southport	a											23 04									23 57		
Lostock	d	20 55								21 56										22 55			
Horwich Parkway	d	20 58				21 27				21 59				22 25						22 58			23 25
Blackrod	d	21 01								22 01										23 01			
Adlington (Lancashire)	d	21 04								22 05										23 04			
Chorley	d	21 09				21 35				22 09				22 32						23 09			23 33
Buckshaw Parkway	d	21 12				21 39				22 12				22 36						23 12			23 36
Leyland	d	21 18								22 20										23 18			23 43
Preston 8 65,97	a	21 24				21 54				22 26				22 48		23 09			23 09	23 24			23 51
	d	21 27				21 56			22 11	22 27				22 50					23 10	23 26			23 55
Kirkham & Wesham 97	a					22 05								22 59									00 04
Poulton-le-Fylde 97	a	21 42				22 13				22 43				23 07						23 41			00 13
Layton 97	a					22 17								23 11									00 17
Blackpool North 97	a	21 48				22 22				22 49				23 16						23 47			00 22
Lancaster 6 65	a								22 31										23 28				
	d								22 32									23 28	23 28				
Oxenholme Lake District 65	a																						
Windermere 83	a																						
Carnforth	d								22 41									23 37	23 38				
Silverdale	d								22 47									23 43	23 43				
Arnside	d								22 51									23 48	23 48				
Grange-over-Sands	d								22 57									23 54	23 54				
Kents Bank	d								23 01									23 57	23 58				
Cark	d								23 05									00 02	00 02				
Ulverston	d								23 13									00 10	00 10				
Dalton	d								23 21									00 18	00 19				
Roose	d								23 27									00 24	00 25				
Barrow-in-Furness	a								23 35									00 32	00 33				

A From Hazel Grove
B To Clitheroe
C From Stalybridge
D From Leeds
E To Blackburn
F From Blackburn
G from 22 February until 28 March
H from 11 January until 15 February, from 4 April

Table T082-F

21 December to 16 May

Manchester - Bolton - Wigan, Kirkby, Southport, Preston, Blackpool North and Barrow-in-Furness

		NT	NT	NT	NT	NT
					◇	
		A	B			
Manchester Airport 85 ⇌✈	d					23 28
Heald Green 85	d					23 32
Alderley Edge	d					
Stockport 84	d					
Manchester Piccadilly 10 ⇌	d				23 30	23 51
Manchester Oxford Road	d				23 33	23 54
Deansgate ⇌	d				23 36	23 56
Rochdale 41	d	22 43				
Manchester Victoria ⇌	d	23 07	23 16	23 20		
Salford Central	d	23 12	23 19	23 23		
Salford Crescent	a	23 16	23 22	23 26	23 39	00 01
	d	23 17	23 23	23 27	23 40	00 02
Swinton	d			23 33		
Moorside	d			23 36		
Walkden	d			23 40		
Atherton	d			23 45		
Hag Fold	d			23 48		
Daisy Hill	d			23 51		
Clifton	d					
Kearsley	d		23 30			
Farnworth	d		23 32			
Moses Gate	d		23 35			
Bolton	a	23 28	23 38		23 49	00 12
	d		23 39		23 49	
Westhoughton	d		23 46			
Hindley	d		23 51	23 56		
Ince	d			23 59		
Wigan North Western	a					
Wigan Wallgate	a		23 57	00 04		
	d					
Pemberton	d					
Orrell	d					
Upholland	d					
Rainford	d					
Kirkby	a					
Gathurst	d					
Appley Bridge	d					
Parbold	d					
Hoscar	d					
Burscough Bridge	d					
New Lane	d					
Bescar Lane	d					
Meols Cop	d					
Southport	a					
Lostock	d				23 54	
Horwich Parkway	d				23 57	
Blackrod	d				23 59	
Adlington (Lancashire)	d				00 03	
Chorley	d				00 07	
Buckshaw Parkway	d				00 10	
Leyland	d				00 16	
Preston 8 65,97	a				00 24	
	d				00 25	
Kirkham & Wesham 97	a					
Poulton-le-Fylde 97	a				00 41	
Layton 97	a					
Blackpool North 97	a				00 47	
Lancaster 6 65	a					
	d					
Oxenholme Lake District 65	a					
Windermere 83	a					
Carnforth	d					
Silverdale	d					
Arnside	d					
Grange-over-Sands	d					
Kents Bank	d					
Cark	d					
Ulverston	d					
Dalton	d					
Roose	d					
Barrow-in-Furness	a					

A To Blackburn
B From Stalybridge

Table T082-F

Sundays
15 December to 10 May

Manchester - Bolton - Wigan, Kirkby, Southport, Preston, Blackpool North and Barrow-in-Furness

		NT	NT	NT	NT	NT	NT	NT	NT	NT	NT	NT	NT	NT	NT	NT	TP	NT	NT	NT	NT	NT	NT
					◇			◇	◇	◇	◇						◇1			◇	◇	◇	
		A	B	C	D	🚌	E	F	G	H	I			J	I	E	K	L 🚌	M	G	F		N
Manchester Airport 85 ✈	d					05 30			07 39	07 40										08 33		08 41	
Heald Green 85	d								07 43	07 44												08 45	
Alderley Edge	d																						
Stockport 84	d																						
Manchester Piccadilly 10	d					05 55		07 58	08 00	08 00							08 43			08 53	08 53	09 01	
Manchester Oxford Road	d							08 03	08 03	08 03										08 56	08 56	09 04	
Deansgate	d							08 05	08 06	08 06												09 07	
Rochdale 41	d																						
Manchester Victoria	d						07 55				08 04	08 20	08 25	08 30	08 31	08 41							09 20
Salford Central	d											08 23	08 28	08 33	08 34	08 44							09 23
Salford Crescent	a						08 01	08 09	08 09	08 09	08 09	08 26	08 31	08 36	08 37	08 47						09 13	09 26
	d	00 02					08 02	08 10	08 10	08 10	08 10	08 27	08 32	08 37	08 37	08 48						09 13	09 27
Swinton	d												08 39										
Moorside	d												08 42										
Walkden	d												08 46										
Atherton	d												08 51										
Hag Fold	d												08 54										
Daisy Hill	d												08 58										
Clifton	d																						
Kearsley	d																						
Farnworth	d																						
Moses Gate	d																						
Bolton	a	00 12				06s20	08 14	08 19	08 19	08 19	08 19	08 37		08 46	08 46	08 59						09 22	09 37
	d							08 19	08 19	08 19	08 19	08 38		08 47	08 47		09u03					09 23	09 38
Westhoughton	d											08 45											09 45
Hindley	d											08 51	09 02										09 51
Ince	d												09 05										
Wigan North Western	a											08 57								09 22	09 22		09 57
Wigan Wallgate	a												09 08										
	d												09 10										
Pemberton	d																						
Orrell	d																						
Upholland	d																						
Rainford	d																						
Kirkby	a																						
Gathurst	d												09 14										
Appley Bridge	d												09 18										
Parbold	d												09 22										
Hoscar	d																						
Burscough Bridge	d												09 27										
New Lane	d																						
Bescar Lane	d																						
Meols Cop	d												09 35										
Southport	a												09 43										
Lostock	d							08 24	08 24	08 24	08 24			08 51	08 51								
Horwich Parkway	d							08 28	08 28	08 28	08 28			08 55	08 55							09 29	
Blackrod	d							08 31	08 31	08 31	08 31			08 58	08 58								
Adlington (Lancashire)	d				00 03			08 35	08 35	08 35	08 35			09 02	09 02								
Chorley	d				00 07			08 40	08 40	08 40	08 40			09 06	09 06							09 36	
Buckshaw Parkway	d				00 10			08 44	08 44	08 44	08 44			09 10	09 10							09 40	
Leyland	d				00 16			08 47	08 47	08 47	08 47			09 14	09 14								
Preston 8 65,97	a				00 24	06s55		08 55	08 55	08 55	08 55			09 22	09 22		09 22			09 40	09 40	09 53	
	d				00 25			08 57	08 57	08 57	08 57			09 24	09 24		09 24			09 48	09 48	09 54	
Kirkham & Wesham 97	a							09 06	09 06	09 06	09 06			09 33	09 33							10 03	
Poulton-le-Fylde 97	a				00 41			09 14	09 14	09 14	09 14			09 41	09 41							10 12	
Layton 97	a													09 45	09 45								
Blackpool North 97	a				00 47	07 35		09 20	09 20	09 20	09 20			09 50	09 50							10 18	
Lancaster 8 65	a																09 39			10 05	10 05		
	d																09 40	09 45		10 06	10 06		
Oxenholme Lake District 65	a																09 53			10 23	10 23		
Windermere 83	a																			10 51	10 51		
Carnforth	d																	10a10	10 20				
Silverdale	d																		10 26				
Arnside	d																		10 30				
Grange-over-Sands	d																		10 36				
Kents Bank	d																		10 40				
Cark	d		00 02	00 02															10 44				
Ulverston	d		00 10	00 10															10 52				
Dalton	d		00 18	00 19															11 00				
Roose	d		00 24	00 25															11 06				
Barrow-in-Furness	a		00 32	00 33															11 14				

A not 15 December. From Manchester Airport
B from 12 January until 16 February, from 5 April. From Lancaster
C from 23 February until 29 March. From Manchester Airport
D not 15 December. From Manchester Piccadilly
E To Clitheroe
F from 23 February until 29 March
G until 5 January
H from 5 April
I from 12 January until 16 February
J until 5 January, from 23 February
K until 5 January, from 23 February until 29 March. To Edinburgh
L from 12 January until 16 February, from 5 April
M from 12 January until 16 February, from 5 April. To Carlisle
N From Stalybridge

NRT DECEMBER 19 EDITION

Table T082-F

Sundays
15 December to 10 May

Manchester - Bolton - Wigan, Kirkby, Southport, Preston, Blackpool North and Barrow-in-Furness

		NT	NT	TP	TP	NT	NT	NT	NT	NT	NT	NT	NT	NT	NT	TP	NT	NT	NT	NT	NT	NT	NT
				◇1	◇1		◇		◇	◇	◇	◇	◇			◇1				◇	◇		
		A	B	C	D	E	F		G	H	I	J	K	L	A	M	E	K	J			L	A
Manchester Airport 85 ✈	d			09 05	09 05					09 35	09 35	09 43	09 43			10 10				10 32			
Heald Green 85	d											09 47	09 48							10 36			
Alderley Edge	d																						
Stockport 84	d																						
Manchester Piccadilly 10	d			09 22	09 22					09 52	09 53	10 01	10 01			10 26				10 54			
Manchester Oxford Road	d			09 27	09 27					09 57	09 57	10 04	10 04			10 30				10 59	11 03		
Deansgate	d											10 08	10 08								11 06		
Rochdale 41	d	09 03													10 03								11 03
Manchester Victoria	d	09 26				09 45		09 51						10 19	10 25		10 45	10 51	10 51			11 19	11 25
Salford Central	d	09 29				09 48		09 54						10 22	10 29		10 48	10 54	10 54			11 22	11 29
Salford Crescent	a	09 32				09 51		09 57				10 11	10 12	10 25	10 32		10 51	10 57	10 57	11 05	11 09	11 25	11 32
	d	09 32				09 52		09 57				10 12	10 13	10 26	10 32		10 52	10 57	10 58	11 06	11 10	11 26	11 32
Swinton	d	09 39													10 39								11 39
Moorside	d	09 42													10 42								11 42
Walkden	d	09 46													10 46								11 46
Atherton	d	09 51													10 51								11 51
Hag Fold	d	09 54													10 54								11 54
Daisy Hill	d	09 58													10 58								11 58
Clifton	d																						
Kearsley	d																						
Farnworth	d																						
Moses Gate	d																						
Bolton	a					10 04		10 06				10 21	10 22	10 36			11 04	11 06	11 07		11 19	11 36	
	d			09u44	09u44			10 07				10 21	10 22	10 37		10u44		11 07	11 07		11 19	11 37	
Westhoughton	d													10 44								11 44	
Hindley	d	10 02												10 50	11 02							11 50	12 02
Ince	d	10 05													11 05								12 05
Wigan North Western	a									10 28	10 28			10 56								11 56	
Wigan Wallgate	a	10 08													11 08								12 08
	d	10 10													11 10								12 10
Pemberton	d																						
Orrell	d																						
Upholland	d																						
Rainford	d																						
Kirkby	a																						
Gathurst	d	10 14													11 14								12 14
Appley Bridge	d	10 18													11 18								12 18
Parbold	d	10 22													11 22								12 22
Hoscar	d																						
Burscough Bridge	d	10 27													11 27								12 27
New Lane	d																						
Bescar Lane	d																						
Meols Cop	d	10 35													11 35								12 35
Southport	a	10 43													11 43								12 43
Lostock	d							10 11															
Horwich Parkway	d							10 15				10 28	10 29					11 13	11 14		11 26		
Blackrod	d							10 18										11 16	11 17				
Adlington (Lancashire)	d							10 22										11 20	11 21				
Chorley	d							10 26				10 35	10 36					11 25	11 25		11 34		
Buckshaw Parkway	d							10 30				10 39	10 40					11 28	11 29		11 38		
Leyland	d							10 34										11 32	11 33				
Preston 8 65,97	a			10 03	10 03			10 42		10 44	10 44	10 48	10 51			11 04		11 44	11 44	11 43	11 49		
	d			10 05	10 19		10 30	10 43		10 46	10 46	10 50	10 52			11 09		11 46	11 46	11 47	11 51		
Kirkham & Wesham 97	a							10 52				10 59	11 01					11 55	11 55		12 00		
Poulton-le-Fylde 97	a							11 01				11 07	11 10					12 03	12 03		12 08		
Layton 97	a							11 05										12 07	12 07				
Blackpool North 97	a							11 09				11 14	11 16					12 12	12 12		12 15		
Lancaster 8 65	a			10 20	10 34		10 47			11 03	11 03					11 24				12 04			
	d		10 11	10 21			10 48		11 02	11 06	11 06					11 25				12 05			
Oxenholme Lake District 65	a			10 34			11 05									11 38							
Windermere 83	a						11 28																
Carnforth	d		10 20						11a12	11 15	11 15									12 14			
Silverdale	d		10 26							11 21	11 21									12 19			
Arnside	d		10 30							11 25	11 25									12 24			
Grange-over-Sands	d		10 36							11 31	11 31									12 30			
Kents Bank	d		10 40							11 35	11 35												
Cark	d		10 44							11 39	11 39									12 36			
Ulverston	d		10 52							11 47	11 47									12 44			
Dalton	d		11 00							11 55	11 55									12 52			
Roose	d		11 06							12 01	12 01												
Barrow-in-Furness	a		11 14							12 08	12 08									13 04			

A From Blackburn
B until 5 January, from 23 February until 29 March. To Carlisle
C until 5 January, from 23 February until 29 March. To Glasgow Central
D from 12 January until 16 February, from 5 April. To Glasgow Central
E To Clitheroe
F from 12 January until 16 February, from 5 April
G From Morecambe to Leeds
H until 5 January, from 5 April
I from 12 January until 29 March
J until 29 March
K from 5 April
L From Stalybridge
M To Edinburgh

Table T082-F

Sundays
15 December to 10 May

Manchester - Bolton - Wigan, Kirkby, Southport, Preston, Blackpool North and Barrow-in-Furness

	TP ◇1 A ✠	NT ◇ B	NT ◇ C	NT ◇ D	NT E	NT	NT ◇	NT F	NT G	NT H	TP ◇1 I ✠	NT E	NT	NT ◇	NT ◇ J	NT ◇	TP ◇1 A ✠	NT F	NT G	NT ◇	NT E
Manchester Airport 85 ✈ d	11 10			11 31												12 41	13 10			13 30	
Heald Green 85 d				11 35												12 45				13 34	
Alderley Edge d																					
Stockport 84 d		11 14																			
Manchester Piccadilly 10 ⇌ d	11 25	11 30		11 50												13 01	13 26			13 48	
Manchester Oxford Road d	11 29	11a32	11 53	11 53			12 02							13 03		13 06	13 30			13 51	
Deansgate ⇌ d							12 05							13 06							
Rochdale 41 d									12 03										13 03		
Manchester Victoria ⇌ d					11 45	11 51		12 19	12 25		12 31	12 45	12 51					13 19	13 25		13 45
Salford Central d					11 48	11 54		12 22	12 29			12 48	12 54					13 22	13 29		13 48
Salford Crescent a					11 51	11 57	12 08	12 25	12 32			12 51	12 57	13 10				13 25	13 32		13 51
d					11 52	11 57	12 09	12 26	12 32			12 52	12 57	13 10				13 26	13 32		13 52
Swinton d									12 39										13 39		
Moorside d									12 42										13 42		
Walkden d									12 46										13 46		
Atherton d									12 51										13 51		
Hag Fold d									12 54										13 54		
Daisy Hill d									12 58										13 58		
Clifton d																					
Kearsley d																					
Farnworth d																					
Moses Gate d																					
Bolton a					12 04	12 06	12 18	12 36				13 04	13 06	13 19				13 36			14 04
d	11u44					12 07	12 18	12 37			12u44		13 07	13 20				13 37			
Westhoughton d								12 44										13 44			
Hindley d								12 50	13 02									13 50	14 02		
Ince d									13 05										14 05		
Wigan North Western a			12 19	12 19				12 56								13 32		13 56		14 19	
Wigan Wallgate a									13 08										14 08		
d									13 10										14 10		
Pemberton d																					
Orrell d																					
Upholland d																					
Rainford d																					
Kirkby a																					
Gathurst d									13 14										14 14		
Appley Bridge d									13 18										14 18		
Parbold d									13 22										14 22		
Hoscar d																					
Burscough Bridge d									13 27										14 27		
New Lane d																					
Bescar Lane d																					
Meols Cop d									13 35										14 35		
Southport a									13 43										14 43		
Lostock d						12 12							13 12								
Horwich Parkway d						12 16	12 25						13 16	13 26							
Blackrod d						12 20							13 20								
Adlington (Lancashire) d						12 24							13 24								
Chorley d						12 29	12 32						13 29	13 33							
Buckshaw Parkway d						12 32	12 36						13 33	13 37							
Leyland d						12 39							13 40								
Preston 8 65,97 a	12 04		12 42	12 42		12 45	12 50				13 04		13 46	13 51		13 55	14 02			14 38	
d	12 05		12 44	12 44		12 47	12 52				13 05		13 48	13 53		13 59	14 04			14 46	
Kirkham & Wesham 97 a						12 56	13 01						13 57	14 02							
Poulton-le-Fylde 97 a						13 04	13 09						14 05	14 10							
Layton 97 a						13 08							14 09								
Blackpool North 97 a						13 12	13 15						14 13	14 16							
Lancaster 8 65 a	12 20										13 20					14 16	14 20			15 04	
d	12 21									13 13	13 21				13 44	14 17	14 22			15 04	
Oxenholme Lake District 65 a	12 34		13 31	13 31							13 34						14 35				
Windermere 83 a			13 54	13 54																	
Carnforth d										13 22					13a54	14 26				15 14	
Silverdale d										13 28						14 32				15 19	
Arnside d										13 32						14 37				15 24	
Grange-over-Sands d										13 38						14 43				15 30	
Kents Bank d										13 42						14 46				15 33	
Cark d										13 46						14 50				15 37	
Ulverston d										13 54						14 58				15 45	
Dalton d										14 02						15 06				15 54	
Roose d										14 08						15 12				16 00	
Barrow-in-Furness a										14 16						15 20				16 07	

A To Glasgow Central
B From Stoke-on-Trent
C until 29 March
D from 5 April
E To Clitheroe
F From Stalybridge
G From Blackburn
H To Carlisle
I To Edinburgh
J From Heysham Harbour to Leeds

Table T082-F

Sundays
15 December to 10 May

Manchester - Bolton - Wigan, Kirkby, Southport, Preston, Blackpool North and Barrow-in-Furness

	NT	NT ◇	NT A	NT B	TP ◇1 C ✠	NT ◇ D	NT ◇	NT E	NT	NT ◇	NT A	NT B	NT F	TP ◇1 G ✠	NT E	NT ◇ H	NT	NT ◇	NT ◇ I	NT A	NT B	TP ◇1 C ✠
Manchester Airport 85 ✈ d		13 44			14 10		14 30			14 45				15 10		15 30		15 45				16 10
Heald Green 85 d		13 49					14 34			14 49						15 34		15 49				
Alderley Edge d																						
Stockport 84 d																						
Manchester Piccadilly 10 ⇌ d		14 01			14 26		14 48			15 01				15 26		15 48		16 01				16 26
Manchester Oxford Road d		14 04			14 30		14 51			15 04				15 31		15 51		16 05				16 30
Deansgate ⇌ d		14 06								15 06								16 07				
Rochdale 41 d				14 03								15 03									16 03	
Manchester Victoria ⇌ d	13 51		14 20	14 25				14 45	14 51		15 20	15 25			15 45		15 51			16 20	16 25	
Salford Central d	13 54		14 23	14 29				14 48	14 54		15 23	15 29			15 48		15 54			16 23	16 29	
Salford Crescent a	13 57	14 10	14 26	14 32				14 51	14 57	15 10	15 26	15 32			15 51		15 57	16 10		16 26	16 32	
d	13 57	14 10	14 27	14 32				14 52	14 57	15 10	15 27	15 32			15 52		15 57	16 11		16 27	16 32	
Swinton d				14 39								15 39									16 39	
Moorside d				14 42								15 42									16 42	
Walkden d				14 46								15 46									16 46	
Atherton d				14 51								15 51									16 51	
Hag Fold d				14 54								15 54									16 54	
Daisy Hill d				14 58								15 58									16 58	
Clifton d																						
Kearsley d																						
Farnworth d																						
Moses Gate d																						
Bolton a	14 06	14 19	14 37					15 04	15 06	15 19	15 37				16 04		16 06	16 20		16 37		
d	14 07	14 20	14 38		14u44				15 07	15 20	15 38			15u45			16 07	16 20		16 38		16u44
Westhoughton d			14 45								15 45									16 45		
Hindley d			14 51	15 02							15 51	16 02								16 51	17 02	
Ince d				15 05								16 05									17 05	
Wigan North Western a			14 57				15 18				15 57					16 18				16 57		
Wigan Wallgate a				15 08								16 08									17 08	
d				15 10								16 10									17 10	
Pemberton d																						
Orrell d																						
Upholland d																						
Rainford d																						
Kirkby a																						
Gathurst d				15 14								16 14									17 14	
Appley Bridge d				15 18								16 18									17 18	
Parbold d				15 22								16 22									17 22	
Hoscar d																						
Burscough Bridge d				15 27								16 27									17 27	
New Lane d																						
Bescar Lane d																						
Meols Cop d				15 35								16 35									17 35	
Southport a				15 43								16 43									17 43	
Lostock d	14 12								15 12								16 12					
Horwich Parkway d	14 16	14 26							15 15	15 26							16 15	16 27				
Blackrod d	14 20								15 18								16 18					
Adlington (Lancashire) d	14 24								15 23								16 22					
Chorley d	14 29	14 34							15 28	15 34							16 27	16 35				
Buckshaw Parkway d	14 33	14 37							15 32	15 37							16 31	16 39				
Leyland d									15 36								16 35		⟵			
Preston 8 65,97 a	14 46	14 51			15 03		15 36		15 47	15 52				16 04		16 38	16 48	16 53	16 38			17 04
d	14 48	14 53			15 05		15 47		15 49	15 54				16 06		16 57	16 50	16 55	16 57			17 05
Kirkham & Wesham 97 a	14 57	15 02							15 58	16 03						⟶	16 59	17 04				
Poulton-le-Fylde 97 a	15 05	15 10							16 06	16 11							17 07	17 12				
Layton 97 a	15 08								16 10								17 11					
Blackpool North 97 a	15 13	15 16							16 14	16 17							17 15	17 18				
Lancaster 8 65 a					15 20									16 21					17 14			17 20
d						15 52							16 03	16 22					17 15			17 21
Oxenholme Lake District 65 a							16 29							16 35								17 34
Windermere 83 a							16 53															
Carnforth d						16a01							16 12						17 24			
Silverdale d													16 18						17 29			
Arnside d													16 22						17 34			
Grange-over-Sands d													16 28						17 40			
Kents Bank d													16 32						17 43			
Cark d													16 36						17 47			
Ulverston d													16 44						17 55			
Dalton d													16 52						18 03			
Roose d													16 58						18 09			
Barrow-in-Furness a													17 06						18 17			

A From Stalybridge
B From Blackburn
C To Edinburgh
D From Morecambe to Leeds
E To Clitheroe
F To Carlisle
G To Glasgow Central
H To Barrow-in-Furness
I From Manchester Airport

Table T082-F

Sundays

15 December to 10 May

Manchester - Bolton - Wigan, Kirkby, Southport, Preston, Blackpool North and Barrow-in-Furness

	NT A	NT ◇ B	NT ◇	NT	NT ◇	NT C	NT D	TP ◇1 E ✠	NT	NT ◇ F	NT	NT A	NT ◇	NT C	NT D	TP ◇1 G ✠	NT ◇ H	NT ◇	NT A	NT	NT ◇
Manchester Airport 85 ✈ d			16 30		16 45			17 10		17 30			17 45			18 10		18 30			18 45
Heald Green 85 d			16 34		16 49					17 34			17 49					18 34			18 49
Alderley Edge d																					
Stockport 84 d																					
Manchester Piccadilly 10 ⇌ d			16 48		17 01			17 26		17 48			18 01			18 26		18 48			19 01
Manchester Oxford Road d			16 51		17 04			17 30		17 51			18 04			18 30		18 51			19 05
Deansgate ⇌ d					17 07								18 06								19 07
Rochdale 41 d							17 03								18 03						
Manchester Victoria ⇌ d	16 45			16 51		17 20	17 25				17 49	17 59		18 20	18 25				18 45	18 51	
Salford Central d	16 48			16 54		17 23	17 29				17 52	18 02		18 23	18 29				18 48	18 54	
Salford Crescent a	16 51			16 57	17 10	17 26	17 32				17 55	18 05	18 10	18 26	18 32				18 51	18 57	19 10
d	16 52			16 57	17 11	17 27	17 32				17 55	18 05	18 10	18 27	18 32				18 52	18 57	19 11
Swinton d							17 39								18 39						
Moorside d							17 42								18 42						
Walkden d							17 46								18 46						
Atherton d							17 51								18 51						
Hag Fold d							17 54								18 54						
Daisy Hill d							17 58								18 58						
Clifton d																					
Kearsley d																					
Farnworth d																					
Moses Gate d																					
Bolton a	17 04			17 06	17 20	17 37					18 04	18 17	18 19	18 37					19 04	19 06	19 20
d				17 07	17 20	17 38		17u45			18 05		18 20	18 38		18u43				19 07	19 20
Westhoughton d						17 45								18 45							
Hindley d						17 51	18 02							18 51	19 02						
Ince d							18 05								19 05						
Wigan North Western a			17 18			17 57				18 18				18 57				19 18			
Wigan Wallgate a							18 08								19 08						
d							18 10								19 10						
Pemberton d																					
Orrell d																					
Upholland d																					
Rainford d																					
Kirkby a																					
Gathurst d							18 14								19 14						
Appley Bridge d							18 18								19 18						
Parbold d							18 22								19 22						
Hoscar d																					
Burscough Bridge d							18 27								19 27						
New Lane d																					
Bescar Lane d																					
Meols Cop d							18 35								19 35						
Southport a							18 43								19 43						
Lostock d				17 12							18 09									19 11	
Horwich Parkway d				17 15	17 27						18 13		18 26							19 15	19 27
Blackrod d				17 18							18 16									19 18	
Adlington (Lancashire) d				17 22							18 20									19 22	
Chorley d				17 27	17 34						18 25		18 34							19 26	19 34
Buckshaw Parkway d				17 30	17 38						18 28		18 37							19 30	19 38
Leyland d				17 35							18 33						←			19 35	
Preston 8 65,97 a			17 37	17 46	17 51			18 04		18 36	18 45		18 50			19 03	18 36	19 36		19 46	19 51
d			17 46	17 47	17 52			18 07		19 08	18 47		18 52			19 04	19 08	19 47		19 47	19 52
Kirkham & Wesham 97 a				17 56	18 01					→	18 56		19 01							19 56	20 01
Poulton-le-Fylde 97 a				18 05	18 10						19 04		19 09							20 05	20 10
Layton 97 a				18 09							19 08									20 09	
Blackpool North 97 a				18 13	18 16						19 13		19 16							20 13	20 17
Lancaster 6 65 a			18 04					18 22								19 19		20 04			
d		17 51	18 04					18 23	19 03							19 20		20 05			
Oxenholme Lake District 65 a								18 36								19 33	19 40				
Windermere 83 a																	20 02				
Carnforth d		18a00	18 13						19 12									20 14			
Silverdale d			18 19						19 18									20 19			
Arnside d			18 23						19 22									20 24			
Grange-over-Sands d			18 29						19 28									20 30			
Kents Bank d			18 33						19 32									20 34			
Cark d			18 37						19 36									20 38			
Ulverston d			18 45						19 44									20 46			
Dalton d			18 53						19 52									20 54			
Roose d			18 59						19 58									21 01			
Barrow-in-Furness a			19 07						20 06									21 08			

A To Clitheroe
B From Morecambe to Leeds
C From Stalybridge
D From Blackburn
E To Glasgow Central
F To Windermere
G To Edinburgh
H From Manchester Airport

NRT DECEMBER 19 EDITION

Table T082-F

Sundays

15 December to 10 May

Manchester - Bolton - Wigan, Kirkby, Southport, Preston, Blackpool North and Barrow-in-Furness

	NT A	NT B	NT ◇ C	TP ◇1 D ✠	NT ◇	NT E	NT	NT ◇	TP ◇1 F ✠	NT A	NT B	NT	NT ◇	TP ◇1 G ✠	TP ◇1 H ✠	NT E	NT A	NT B	NT	NT ◇	NT E	NT A
Manchester Airport 85 ✈ d				19 10	19 30			19 45	20 10				20 45	21 10	21 10					21 45		
Heald Green 85 d					19 34			19 49					20 49							21 49		
Alderley Edge d																						
Stockport 84 d																						
Manchester Piccadilly 10 ⇌ d				19 26	19 48			20 01	20 26				21 02	21 26	21 26					22 01		
Manchester Oxford Road d				19 29	19 51			20 05	20 30				21 05	21 30	21 30					22 05		
Deansgate ⇌ d								20 07					21 07							22 07		
Rochdale 41 d		19 03									20 03							21 09				
Manchester Victoria ⇌ d	19 20	19 25				19 45	19 51			20 20	20 25	20 51				21 12	21 19	21 32	21 48		22 07	22 19
Salford Central d	19 23	19 29				19 48	19 54			20 23	20 29	20 54				21 15	21 22	21 35	21 51		22 10	22 22
Salford Crescent a	19 26	19 32				19 51	19 57	20 10		20 26	20 32	20 57	21 10			21 18	21 25	21 38	21 54	22 10	22 14	22 25
d	19 27	19 32				19 52	19 57	20 11		20 27	20 32	20 57	21 11			21 19	21 26	21 39	21 54	22 11	22 14	22 26
Swinton d		19 39									20 39							21 45				
Moorside d		19 42									20 42							21 48				
Walkden d		19 46									20 46							21 52				
Atherton d		19 51									20 51							21 58				
Hag Fold d		19 54									20 54							22 01				
Daisy Hill d		19 58									20 58							22 04				
Clifton d																						
Kearsley d																						
Farnworth d																						
Moses Gate d																						
Bolton a	19 37					20 04	20 06	20 20		20 37		21 06	21 20			21 31	21 36		22 03	22 20	22 26	22 36
d	19 38			19u44			20 07	20 20		20 38		21 07	21 20				21 37		22 04	22 20		22 37
Westhoughton d	19 45									20 45							21 44					22 44
Hindley d	19 51	20 02								20 51	21 02						21 50	22 10				22 50
Ince d		20 05									21 05							22 13				
Wigan North Western a	19 57				20 20					20 57							21 56					22 56
Wigan Wallgate a		20 08									21 08							22 16				
d		20 10									21 10							22 17				
Pemberton d																						
Orrell d																						
Upholland d																						
Rainford d																						
Kirkby a																						
Gathurst d		20 14									21 14							22 22				
Appley Bridge d		20 18									21 18							22 26				
Parbold d		20 22									21 22							22 30				
Hoscar d																						
Burscough Bridge d		20 27									21 27							22 35				
New Lane d																						
Bescar Lane d																						
Meols Cop d		20 35									21 35							22 43				
Southport a		20 43									21 43							22 50				
Lostock d							20 11					21 11							22 08			
Horwich Parkway d							20 15	20 27				21 15	21 27						22 12	22 27		
Blackrod d							20 18					21 18							22 15			
Adlington (Lancashire) d							20 22					21 22							22 19			
Chorley d							20 26	20 34				21 26	21 34						22 24	22 34		
Buckshaw Parkway d							20 30	20 38				21 30	21 38						22 27	22 38		
Leyland d							20 35					21 35							22 34			
Preston 8 65,97 a				20 06	20 38		20 46	20 51	21 01			21 45	21 48	22 01	22 01				22 46	22 48		
d				20 07	20 46		20 47	20 52	21 03			21 47	21 50	22 03					22 47	22 49		
Kirkham & Wesham 97 a							20 56	21 01				21 56	21 59						22 56	23 00		
Poulton-le-Fylde 97 a							21 05	21 10				22 04	22 09						23 05	23 10		
Layton 97 a							21 09					22 08							23 09			
Blackpool North 97 a							21 14	21 16				22 13	22 16						23 13	23 16		
Lancaster 6 65 a				20 22	21 05				21 18													
d			20 18	20 23	21 13				21 19													
Oxenholme Lake District 65 a				20 38					21 33					22 28								
Windermere 83 a																						
Carnforth d			20a28		21 22																	
Silverdale d					21 28																	
Arnside d					21 32																	
Grange-over-Sands d					21 38																	
Kents Bank d					21 42																	
Cark d					21 46																	
Ulverston d					21 54																	
Dalton d					22 02																	
Roose d					22 08																	
Barrow-in-Furness a					22 15																	

A From Stalybridge
B From Blackburn
C From Morecambe to Leeds
D To Glasgow Central
E To Clitheroe
F To Edinburgh
G until 5 January, from 23 February until 29 March. To Glasgow Central
H from 12 January until 16 February, from 5 April. To Carlisle

Table T082-F

Sundays 15 December to 10 May

Manchester - Bolton - Wigan, Kirkby, Southport, Preston, Blackpool North and Barrow-in-Furness

		NT	NT	NT	TP	NT	NT
				◇	◇1		
					A	B	C
Manchester Airport 85	d			22 46	23 01		
Heald Green 85	d			22 50			
Alderley Edge	d						
Stockport 84	d						
Manchester Piccadilly 10	d			23 01	23 15		
Manchester Oxford Road	d			23 05	23 19		
Deansgate	d			23 07			
Rochdale 41	d						
Manchester Victoria	d		22 49			23 14	23 19
Salford Central	d		22 52			23 17	23 22
Salford Crescent	a		22 55	23 11		23 20	23 25
	d		22 55	23 11		23 21	23 26
Swinton	d						
Moorside	d						
Walkden	d						
Atherton	d						
Hag Fold	d						
Daisy Hill	d						
Clifton	d						
Kearsley	d						
Farnworth	d						
Moses Gate	d						
Bolton	a		23 04	23 20		23 33	23 36
	d		23 05	23 21			23 37
Westhoughton	d						23 44
Hindley	d						23 50
Ince	d						
Wigan North Western	a						
Wigan Wallgate	a						23 56
	d						
Pemberton	d						
Orrell	d						
Upholland	d						
Rainford	d						
Kirkby	a						
Gathurst	d						
Appley Bridge	d						
Parbold	d						
Hoscar	d						
Burscough Bridge	d						
New Lane	d						
Bescar Lane	d						
Meols Cop	d						
Southport	a						
Lostock	d		23 09	23 25			
Horwich Parkway	d		23 13	23 29			
Blackrod	d		23 16	23 32			
Adlington (Lancashire)	d		23 20				
Chorley	d		23 25	23 38			
Buckshaw Parkway	d		23 28	23 42			
Leyland	d		23 37	23 48			
Preston 8 65,97	a		23 42	23 55	23 58		
	d		23 43	23 57			
Kirkham & Wesham 97	a		23 52	00 06			
Poulton-le-Fylde 97	a		00 01	00 14			
Layton 97	a		00 05				
Blackpool North 97	a		00 10	00 21			
Lancaster 6 65	a						
	d	22 20					
Oxenholme Lake District 65	a						
Windermere 83	a						
Carnforth	d	22 29					
Silverdale	d	22 34					
Arnside	d	22 39					
Grange-over-Sands	d	22 45					
Kents Bank	d	22 48					
Cark	d	22 52					
Ulverston	d	23 00					
Dalton	d	23 08					
Roose	d	23 14					
Barrow-in-Furness	a	23 22					

A To Carlisle
B To Blackburn
C From Stalybridge

Table T082-R

Mondays to Fridays 16 December to 15 May

Barrow-in-Furness, Blackpool North, Preston, Southport, Kirkby and Wigan - Bolton - Manchester

Miles	Miles	Miles	Miles	Miles			NT MX	NT MO	NT MX	TP TW FO	TP ThO	TP MO	NT	NT	NT	NT	NT	NT	NT	NT	NT	NT	NT	TP
									◇	◇1	◇1	◇1	◇	◇		◇					◇		◇	◇1
							A	B	C	D	D					E	F		G			H		
—	0	—	—	—	**Barrow-in-Furness**	d															04 53			
—	1¾	—	—	—	Roose	d																		
—	6	—	—	—	Dalton	d																		
—	9¼	—	—	—	Ulverston	d															05 09			
—	15¼	—	—	—	Cark	d																		
—	17¼	—	—	—	Kents Bank	d																		
—	19½	—	—	—	Grange-over-Sands	d															05 21			
—	22¾	—	—	—	Arnside	d															05 27			
—	25	—	—	—	Silverdale	d																		
—	28¾	—	—	—	Carnforth	d															05 37			
—	—	—	—	—	Windermere 83	d																		
—	—	—	—	—	Oxenholme Lake District 65	d																		
—	34¼	—	—	—	**Lancaster** 6 65	a															05 45			
—	—	—	—	—		d															05 46			06 28
0	—	—	—	—	**Blackpool North** 97	d							03 33	04 44			05 22						05 56	
1¼	—	—	—	—	Layton 97	d											05 25							
3¼	—	—	—	—	Poulton-le-Fylde 97	d								04 50			05 28						06 01	
9¾	—	—	—	—	Kirkham & Wesham 97	d											05 37							
—	55¾	—	—	—	**Preston** 8 65,97	a							03 55	05 08			05 48				06 06		06 19	06 46
—	—	—	—	—		d				00 47	00 47	01 06	03 57	05 10			05 49			06 03	06 08		06 21	06 47
21½	59¾	—	—	—	Leyland	d											05 54			06 09			06 26	
23¾	62	—	—	—	Buckshaw Parkway	d								05 17			05 59			06 14			06 30	
26	64¼	—	—	—	Chorley	d								05 21			06 03			06 18			06 34	
29	67¼	—	—	—	Adlington (Lancashire)	d			00 02											06 23			06 38	
31	69¼	—	—	—	Blackrod	d			00 06											06 27			06 42	
32½	70¾	—	—	—	Horwich Parkway	d			00 09					05 29			06 11			06 31			06 46	
34½	72¾	—	—	—	Lostock	d			00 13								06 15			06 35			06 49	
—	—	0	—	—	**Southport**	d																		
—	—	1¼	—	—	Meols Cop	d																		
—	—	4½	—	—	Bescar Lane	d																		
—	—	6½	—	—	New Lane	d																		
—	—	7¾	—	—	Burscough Bridge	d																		
—	—	9¼	—	—	Hoscar	d																		
—	—	10¾	—	—	Parbold	d																		
—	—	13	—	—	Appley Bridge	d																		
—	—	14¾	—	—	Gathurst	d																		
—	—	—	0	—	**Kirkby**	d																		
—	—	—	5¼	—	Rainford	d																		
—	—	—	7¼	—	Upholland	d																		
—	—	—	8½	—	Orrell	d																		
—	—	—	10½	—	Pemberton	d																		
—	—	17½	12¼	—	**Wigan Wallgate**	a																		
—	—	—	—	—		d												06 01	06 08					
—	—	—	—	0	**Wigan North Western**	d									05 50	05 56					06 23			
—	—	18½	13¼	0¾	Ince	d												06 04						
—	—	20	14¾	—	Hindley	d									05 56			06 08	06 13					
—	—	22½	—	—	Westhoughton	d									06 01				06 18					
37½	75¾	27	—	—	**Bolton**	a			00 18					05 36	06 09		06 20		06 26	06 40			06 54	
—	—	—	—	—		d			00 18					05 37	06 09		06 21		06 26	06 40		06 49	06 55	
38¼	76½	27¾	—	—	Moses Gate	d													06 29					
39¾	78	29¼	—	—	Farnworth	d													06 31					
40½	78¾	30	—	—	Kearsley	d													06 33					
43½	81¾	33	—	—	Clifton	d																		
—	—	—	17¼	—	Daisy Hill	d										06 05		06 12						
—	—	—	17½	—	Hag Fold	d												06 15						
—	—	—	18¾	—	Atherton	d										06 10		06 18						
—	—	—	22¼	—	Walkden	d										06 16		06 24						
—	—	—	24	—	Moorside	d												06 28						
—	—	—	24¾	—	Swinton	d												06 31						
46½	84¾	36	28¾	—	**Salford Crescent**	a			00 30					05 48	06 21	06 27	06 33	06 39	06 44	06 52		07 01	07 06	
—	—	—	—	—		d		00 01	00 31					05 49	06 22	06 28	06 33	06 40	06 45	06 53		07 01	07 06	
—	—	—	29¾	—	Salford Central	d	00 02	00 05								06 31		06 43	06 47	06 56		07 05		
—	—	—	30½	—	**Manchester Victoria**	a	00 05	00 08								06 35		06 46	06 50	06 59		07 09		
—	—	—	—	—	Rochdale 41	a										06 50						07 31		
48	86¼	37½	—	—	Deansgate	a									06 29								07 10	
48¼	86½	37¾	—	—	**Manchester Oxford Road**	a								05 53	06 32		06 40				06 52		07 12	07 20
48¾	87	38¼	—	—	**Manchester Piccadilly** 10	a			00 40	01 40	01 42	01 45	04 46	05 57	06 36		06 46				06 57		07 15	07 24
—	—	—	—	—	Stockport 84	a									06 53		07 01							
—	—	—	—	—	**Alderley Edge**	a									07 13									
57	95¼	46½	—	—	Heald Green 85	a			00 54					06 14							07 13		07 27	
58½	96¾	48	—	—	**Manchester Airport** 85	a			00 59	01 59		02 02	05 04	06 19							07 18		07 32	07 48

A From Clitheroe
B From Southport
C From Blackpool North
D From Edinburgh
E To Leeds
F To Hazel Grove
G To Stalybridge
H From Blackburn

Table T082-R

Mondays to Fridays

16 December to 15 May

Barrow-in-Furness, Blackpool North, Preston, Southport, Kirkby and Wigan - Bolton - Manchester

		NT A	NT	NT	NT ◇ B	NT C	NT	NT D	NT E	NT	TP ◇1 F 🍴	NT ◇	NT	NT G	NT C	NT ◇	TP MX ◇1 H 🍴	TP MO ◇1 H 🍴	NT	NT	NT ◇ B	NT C
Barrow-in-Furness	d											05 48	06 11									
Roose	d											05 52	06 15									
Dalton	d											05 58	06 21									
Ulverston	d											06 06	06 30									
Cark	d											06 14	06 37									
Kents Bank	d											06 18	06 41									
Grange-over-Sands	d											06 22	06 45									
Arnside	d											06 27	06 51									
Silverdale	d											06 32	06 56									
Carnforth	d	06 22										06 40	07 03									
Windermere 83	d																					
Oxenholme Lake District 65	d										06 27						07 08	07 08				
Lancaster 6 65	a	06 31									06 44	06 50	07 15				07 22	07 22				
	d										06 45	06 50					07 23	07 23				
Blackpool North 97	d								06 32							06 53						
Layton 97	d								06 35							06 56						
Poulton-le-Fylde 97	d								06 39							07 00						
Kirkham & Wesham 97	d								06 48							07 09						
Preston 8 65,97	a								06 58		07 03	07 08				07 19	07 40	07 40				
	d								07 00	07 04	07 05	07 11				07 21	07 46	07 47				
Leyland	d									07 10						07 26						
Buckshaw Parkway	d								07 08	07 15						07 31						
Chorley	d								07 12	07 19						07 34						
Adlington (Lancashire)	d								07 17	07 24						07 39						
Blackrod	d								07 20	07 28						07 42						
Horwich Parkway	d								07 24	07 32						07 46						
Lostock	d								07 27	07 36						07 49						
Southport	d			06 17				06 34						06 48						07 17		
Meols Cop	d			06 22				06 40						06 53						07 22		
Bescar Lane	d													06 58								
New Lane	d													07 02								
Burscough Bridge	d			06 31				06 48						07 05						07 31		
Hoscar	d													07 08								
Parbold	d			06 36				06 53						07 11						07 36		
Appley Bridge	d			06 40				06 57						07 16						07 40		
Gathurst	d			06 44				07 01						07 19						07 44		
Kirkby	d						06 36															
Rainford	d						06 44															
Upholland	d						06 48															
Orrell	d						06 52															
Pemberton	d						06 55															
Wigan Wallgate	a			06 49			07 00	07 06						07 24						07 49		
	d			06 50			07 01	07 07						07 25						07 50	07 56	
Wigan North Western	d		06 43		06 56						07a17	07 26							07 42			
Ince	d						07 04												07 45			
Hindley	d			06 56			07 08	07 12						07 31					07 49	07 56		
Westhoughton	d			07 01				07 17												08 01		
Bolton	a			07 09				07 25	07 32	07 41						07 54				08 09		
	d			07 10		07 17		07 25	07 34	07 41					07 49	07 55				08 09		08 17
Moses Gate	d							07 28														
Farnworth	d							07 30														08 21
Kearsley	d					07 22		07 32														
Clifton	d							07 37														
Daisy Hill	d		06 51		07 05		07 13							07 35					07 53		08 04	
Hag Fold	d		06 54				07 16												07 56			
Atherton	d		06 57		07 09		07 19							07 39					07 59		08 08	
Walkden	d		07 03		07 15		07 25							07 45					08 04		08 14	
Moorside	d		07 07				07 29												08 08			
Swinton	d		07 10				07 32												08 10			
Salford Crescent	a		07 18	07 22	07 27	07 32	07 39	07 44	07 47	07 53				07 56	08 02	08 06			08 17	08 21	08 26	08 32
	d		07 18	07 22	07 27	07 33	07 40	07 44	07 48	07 53				07 57	08 02	08 06			08 18	08 22	08 26	08 33
Salford Central	d		07 21		07 30	07 36	07 43	07 47		07 56				08 00	08 06				08 21		08 29	08 36
Manchester Victoria ⇌	a		07 24		07 33	07 41	07 46	07 50		07 59				08 03	08 08				08 24		08 32	08 41
Rochdale 41	a				07 49	08 04								08 17	08 30						08 51	09 04
Deansgate ⇌	a			07 26												08 10				08 25		
Manchester Oxford Road	a			07 28					07 52			07 56				08 12	08 20	08 20		08 28		
Manchester Piccadilly 10 ⇌	a			07 36					07 56			08 00				08 16	08 24	08 24		08 33		
Stockport 84	a			07 51					08 06											08 51		
Alderley Edge	a			08 08																09 08		
Heald Green 85	a											08 16				08 28						
Manchester Airport 85 ⇌✈	a											08 20				08 32	08 47	08 47				

A From Skipton
B To Leeds
C From Clitheroe
D To Stalybridge
E To Hazel Grove
F From Carlisle to Liverpool Lime Street
G To Blackburn
H From Glasgow Central

Table T082-R

Mondays to Fridays

16 December to 15 May

Barrow-in-Furness, Blackpool North, Preston, Southport, Kirkby and Wigan - Bolton - Manchester

		NT A	NT	NT B	NT	NT WO ◇	NT WX ◇	NT	NT C	NT D	NT ◇	TP ◇1 E 🍴	NT	NT	NT ◇ F	NT G	NT A	NT B	NT	NT ◇	NT C	NT ◇ H	NT D
Barrow-in-Furness	d					06 47	06 47	07 08												07 46			
Roose	d					06 51	06 51	07 12												07 50			
Dalton	d					06 57	06 57	07 18												07 56			
Ulverston	d					07 05	07 05	07 27												08 05			
Cark	d					07 13	07 13	07 34												08 12			
Kents Bank	d							07 38															
Grange-over-Sands	d					07 20	07 20	07 42												08 19			
Arnside	d					07 25	07 25	07 49												08 25			
Silverdale	d					07 30	07 30	07 54												08 30			
Carnforth	d					07 37	07 37	08 01												08 37		09 04	
Windermere 83	d																						
Oxenholme Lake District 65	d											08 13											
Lancaster 6 65	a					07 45	07 45	08 12				08 27								08 45		09 13	
	d					07 46	07 46					08 28								08 46			
Blackpool North 97	d	07 23									07 45						08 23						
Layton 97	d	07 26									07 48						08 26						
Poulton-le-Fylde 97	d	07 30									07 52						08 30						
Kirkham & Wesham 97	d	07 39									08 01						08 39						
Preston 8 65,97	a	07 50				08 06	08 06				08 11	08 46					08 51			09 06			
	d	07 51			08 04	08 08	08 08				08 23	08 47					08 55		09 04	09 08			
Leyland	d	07 56			08 10						08 28								09 10				
Buckshaw Parkway	d	07 59			08 15						08 33						09 03		09 15				
Chorley	d	08 03			08 19						08 37						09 07		09 18				
Adlington (Lancashire)	d	08 07			08 24														09 22				
Blackrod	d	08 10			08 28														09 26				
Horwich Parkway	d	08 14			08 32						08 45						09 15		09 30				
Lostock	d	08 17			08 36						08 49								09 34				
Southport	d			07 30										08 17				08 36					
Meols Cop	d			07 35										08 22				08 41					
Bescar Lane	d			07 40																			
New Lane	d			07 44																			
Burscough Bridge	d			07 47										08 31				08 50					
Hoscar	d			07 50																			
Parbold	d			07 54										08 36				08 54					
Appley Bridge	d			07 58										08 40				08 59					
Gathurst	d			08 02										08 44				09 02					
Kirkby	d		07 36										08 18										
Rainford	d		07 44										08 26										
Upholland	d		07 48										08 30										
Orrell	d		07 52										08 34										
Pemberton	d		07 55										08 37										
Wigan Wallgate	a		08 00	08 06									08 42	08 49				09 07					
	d		08 01	08 08					08 22				08 44	08 50	08 56			09 08					
Wigan North Western	d					08 23	08 23													09 23	09 23		
Ince	d		08 04																				
Hindley	d		08 08	08 13					08 27					08 56				09 13			09 28		
Westhoughton	d			08 18										09 01				09 18					
Bolton	a	08 22		08 26	08 41						08 54			09 10			09 22	09 26	09 39				
	d	08 22		08 26	08 41					08 49	08 54			09 10		09 17	09 22	09 26	09 39				09 49
Moses Gate	d			08 29												09 20		09 29					
Farnworth	d			08 32														09 32					
Kearsley	d			08 34														09 34					
Clifton	d																						
Daisy Hill	d		08 13						08 32				08 52		09 04						09 32		
Hag Fold	d		08 16						08 35				08 55								09 35		
Atherton	d		08 19						08 38				08 57		09 08						09 38		
Walkden	d		08 25						08 44				09 03		09 14						09 44		
Moorside	d												09 07										
Swinton	d		08 30						08 49				09 09								09 49		
Salford Crescent	a	08 36	08 39	08 44	08 53				08 56	09 01	09 05		09 17	09 21	09 26	09 32	09 36	09 44	09 53		09 56		10 01
	d	08 36	08 40	08 45	08 53				08 57	09 01	09 06		09 18	09 22	09 26	09 33	09 36	09 45	09 53		09 57		10 01
Salford Central	d		08 42	08 47	08 56				08 59	09 04			09 21		09 29	09 36		09 47	09 56		09 59		10 04
Manchester Victoria ⇌	a		08 46	08 50	08 59				09 02	09 07			09 24		09 32	09 41		09 50	09 59		10 02		10 07
Rochdale 41	a								09 17	09 29					09 50	10 04					10 17		10 29
Deansgate ⇌	a										09 09			09 29									
Manchester Oxford Road	a	08 41				08 54	08 55				09 11	09 20		09 32			09 41			09 54			
Manchester Piccadilly 10 ⇌	a	08 45				08 58	08 59				09 15	09 24		09 36			09 45			09 58			
Stockport 84	a	09 02												09 51			10 02						
Alderley Edge	a													10 08									
Heald Green 85	a					09 13	09 13				09 30									10 12			
Manchester Airport 85 ⇌✈	a					09 18	09 18				09 35	09 49								10 18			

A To Hazel Grove
B To Stalybridge
C To Blackburn
D From Blackburn
E From Edinburgh
F To Leeds
G From Clitheroe
H From Leeds

Table T082-R

Mondays to Fridays
16 December to 15 May

Barrow-in-Furness, Blackpool North, Preston, Southport, Kirkby and Wigan - Bolton - Manchester

		NT ◇	TP ◇■ A ✠	NT	NT ◇ B	NT C	NT D	NT	NT E	NT	NT ◇	NT ◇ F	NT G	NT H	NT ◇	TP ◇■ I ✠	TP ◇■ J ✠	NT K	NT	NT ◇ B	NT C	NT D
Barrow-in-Furness	d										08 46							09 58				
Roose	d										08 50							10 02				
Dalton	d										08 56							10 08				
Ulverston	d										09 04							10 17				
Cark	d										09 12							10 24				
Kents Bank	d										09 16							10 28				
Grange-over-Sands	d										09 20							10 32				
Arnside	d										09 25							10 39				
Silverdale	d										09 30							10 43				
Carnforth	d										09 39	09 57						10 56				
Windermere 83	d																					
Oxenholme Lake District 65	d		09 11													10 03	10 13					
Lancaster [6] 65	a		09 25								09 47	10 06				10 18	10 27	11 07				
	d		09 26								09 47					10 18	10 28					
Blackpool North 97	d	08 58					09 27								09 58							10 27
Layton 97	d						09 30															10 30
Poulton-le-Fylde 97	d	09 03					09 34								10 03							10 34
Kirkham & Wesham 97	d						09 43															10 43
Preston [8] 65,97	a	09 21	09 44				09 53				10 08				10 21	10 38	10 45					10 53
	d	09 23	09 45				09 55			10 04	10 10				10 24	10 39	10 47					10 55
Leyland	d	09 28								10 10					10 29							
Buckshaw Parkway	d	09 33					10 03			10 15					10 33							11 03
Chorley	d	09 37					10 07			10 19					10 37							11 07
Adlington (Lancashire)	d									10 24												
Blackrod	d									10 28												
Horwich Parkway	d	09 45					10 15			10 32					10 45							11 15
Lostock	d	09 49								10 36					10 49							
Southport	d			09 17					09 31										10 17			
Meols Cop	d			09 22					09 36										10 22			
Bescar Lane	d								09 41													
New Lane	d								09 45													
Burscough Bridge	d			09 31					09 48										10 31			
Hoscar	d								09 51													
Parbold	d			09 36					09 54										10 36			
Appley Bridge	d			09 40					09 59										10 40			
Gathurst	d			09 44					10 02										10 44			
Kirkby	d							09 35														
Rainford	d							09 43														
Upholland	d							09 47														
Orrell	d							09 51														
Pemberton	d							09 54														
Wigan Wallgate	a			09 48				09 59	10 07										10 48			
	d			09 50				10 01	10 08				10 23						10 50	10 56		
Wigan North Western	d				09 54						10 24					10a52						
Ince	d							10 04														
Hindley	d			09 55				10 07	10 13				10 28						10 55			
Westhoughton	d			10 00					10 18										11 00			
Bolton	a	09 54	10s03	10 09			10 22		10 26	10 41					10 54		11s05		11 09			11 22
	d	09 54		10 10		10 19	10 22		10 26	10 41				10 49	10 54				11 10		11 19	11 22
Moses Gate	d								10 29													
Farnworth	d								10 32													
Kearsley	d								10 34													
Clifton	d																					
Daisy Hill	d				10 04			10 12					10 32							11 04		
Hag Fold	d							10 15					10 35									
Atherton	d				10 08			10 18					10 38							11 08		
Walkden	d				10 14			10 24					10 44							11 14		
Moorside	d							10 28														
Swinton	d							10 31					10 49									
Salford Crescent	a	10 05		10 21	10 26	10 32	10 36	10 39	10 44	10 53			10 56	11 01	11 05				11 21	11 26	11 32	11 36
	d	10 06		10 22	10 26	10 33	10 36	10 40	10 45	10 53			10 57	11 01	11 06				11 22	11 26	11 33	11 36
Salford Central	d				10 29	10 36		10 43	10 47	10 56			10 59	11 04						11 29	11 36	
Manchester Victoria ⇌	a				10 32	10 41		10 46	10 50	10 59			11 02	11 07						11 32	11 40	
Rochdale 41	a				10 50	11 04							11 17	11 29						11 49	12 01	
Deansgate ⇌	a	10 09		10 29											11 09				11 29			
Manchester Oxford Road	a	10 11	10 20	10 32			10 41				10 54				11 11		11 20		11 32			11 41
Manchester Piccadilly [10] ⇌	a	10 15	10 24	10 36			10 45				10 58				11 15		11 24		11 36			11 45
Stockport 84	a			10 51			11 02												11 51			12 02
Alderley Edge	a			11 08															12 08			
Heald Green 85	a	10 30									11 12				11 30							
Manchester Airport 85 ⇌✈	a	10 35	10 46								11 18				11 35		11 46					

A From Glasgow Central
B To Leeds
C From Clitheroe
D To Hazel Grove
E To Stalybridge
F From Leeds to Morecambe
G To Blackburn
H From Blackburn
I From Glasgow Central to Liverpool Lime Street
J From Edinburgh
K From Carlisle

Table T082-R

Mondays to Fridays
16 December to 15 May

Barrow-in-Furness, Blackpool North, Preston, Southport, Kirkby and Wigan - Bolton - Manchester

		NT ◇	NT	NT A	NT	NT B	NT C	NT ◇	TP ◇■ D ✠	NT	NT ◇ E	NT F	NT G	NT	NT A	NT	NT ◇	NT ◇ H	NT B	NT C	NT ◇	TP ◇■ I ✠	NT
Barrow-in-Furness	d																10 46						
Roose	d																10 50						
Dalton	d																10 56						
Ulverston	d																11 04						
Cark	d																11 12						
Kents Bank	d																11 16						
Grange-over-Sands	d																11 20						
Arnside	d																11 25						
Silverdale	d																11 30						
Carnforth	d																11 37	12 01					
Windermere 83	d	09 56																					
Oxenholme Lake District 65	d	10 17							11 13													12 14	
Lancaster [6] 65	a								11 27								11 45	12 10				12 28	
	d								11 28								11 46					12 29	
Blackpool North 97	d							10 57					11 27								11 58		
Layton 97	d												11 30										
Poulton-le-Fylde 97	d							11 03					11 34								12 03		
Kirkham & Wesham 97	d												11 43										
Preston [8] 65,97	a	10 52						11 21	11 46				11 53				12 06				12 21	12 46	
	d	11 02			11 04			11 24	11 47				11 55			12 04	12 08				12 23	12 48	
Leyland	d				11 10			11 29								12 10					12 28		
Buckshaw Parkway	d				11 15			11 34					12 03			12 15					12 33		
Chorley	d				11 19			11 37					12 07			12 19					12 37		
Adlington (Lancashire)	d				11 24											12 23							
Blackrod	d				11 28											12 27							
Horwich Parkway	d				11 32			11 45					12 15			12 31					12 45		
Lostock	d				11 35			11 49								12 35					12 49		
Southport	d			10 36						11 17					11 31								12 17
Meols Cop	d			10 41						11 22					11 36								12 22
Bescar Lane	d														11 41								
New Lane	d														11 45								
Burscough Bridge	d			10 50						11 31					11 48								12 31
Hoscar	d														11 51								
Parbold	d			10 54						11 36					11 54								12 36
Appley Bridge	d			10 59						11 40					11 59								12 40
Gathurst	d			11 02						11 44					12 02								12 44
Kirkby	d		10 35											11 35									
Rainford	d		10 43											11 43									
Upholland	d		10 47											11 47									
Orrell	d		10 51											11 51									
Pemberton	d		10 54											11 54									
Wigan Wallgate	a		10 59	11 07						11 48				11 59	12 07								12 48
	d		11 01	11 08		11 23				11 50	11 56			12 01	12 08				12 23				12 50
Wigan North Western	d	11 18															12 25						
Ince	d		11 04											12 04									
Hindley	d		11 07	11 13		11 28				11 55				12 07	12 13				12 28				12 55
Westhoughton	d			11 18						12 00					12 18								13 00
Bolton	a			11 26	11 40			11 54	12s05	12 09			12 22		12 26	12 40					12 54		13 10
	d			11 26	11 41		11 49	11 54		12 10		12 19	12 22		12 26	12 41				12 49	12 54		13 11
Moses Gate	d			11 29											12 29								
Farnworth	d			11 32											12 32								
Kearsley	d			11 34											12 34								
Clifton	d																						
Daisy Hill	d		11 12			11 32					12 04			12 12					12 32				
Hag Fold	d		11 15			11 35								12 15					12 35				
Atherton	d		11 18			11 38					12 08			12 18					12 38				
Walkden	d		11 24			11 44					12 14			12 24					12 44				
Moorside	d		11 28											12 28									
Swinton	d		11 31			11 49								12 31					12 49				
Salford Crescent	a		11 39	11 44	11 52	11 56	12 01	12 05		12 21	12 26	12 32	12 36	12 39	12 44	12 52			12 56	13 00	13 05		13 22
	d		11 40	11 45	11 53	11 57	12 02	12 06		12 22	12 26	12 33	12 36	12 40	12 45	12 53			12 57	13 01	13 06		13 22
Salford Central	d		11 43	11 47	11 56	12 00	12 05				12 29	12 36		12 43	12 47	12 56			12 59	13 04			
Manchester Victoria ⇌	a		11 46	11 50	11 59	12 03	12 08				12 32	12 41		12 46	12 50	12 59			13 02	13 07			
Rochdale 41	a					12 17	12 29				12 50	13 04							13 17	13 29			
Deansgate ⇌	a							12 09		12 29											13 09		13 29
Manchester Oxford Road	a	11 54						12 11	12 20	12 32			12 41				12 54				13 11	13 20	13 32
Manchester Piccadilly [10] ⇌	a	11 58						12 15	12 24	12 36			12 45				12 58				13 15	13 24	13 36
Stockport 84	a									12 51			13 02										13 51
Alderley Edge	a									13 08													14 08
Heald Green 85	a	12 12						12 29									13 12				13 30		
Manchester Airport 85 ⇌✈	a	12 17						12 35	12 46								13 18				13 35	13 46	

A To Stalybridge
B To Blackburn
C From Blackburn
D From Glasgow Central
E To Leeds
F From Clitheroe
G To Hazel Grove
H From Leeds to Morecambe
I From Edinburgh

Table T082-R

Mondays to Fridays
16 December to 15 May

Barrow-in-Furness, Blackpool North, Preston, Southport, Kirkby and Wigan - Bolton - Manchester

Station		NT ◇ A	NT B	NT C	NT	NT D	NT	NT ◇	NT E	NT F	NT ◇	TP ◇1 G ⌶	NT	NT ◇ A	NT B	NT C	NT	NT D	NT	NT ◇	NT H	NT ◇ I	NT E
Barrow-in-Furness	d							11 46													12 50		
Roose	d							11 50													12 54		
Dalton	d							11 56													13 00		
Ulverston	d							12 04													13 08		
Cark	d							12 12													13 16		
Kents Bank	d							12 16													13 20		
Grange-over-Sands	d							12 20													13 24		
Arnside	d							12 25													13 30		
Silverdale	d							12 30													13 35		
Carnforth	d							12 37													13 42	14 01	
Windermere 83	d																			13 06			
Oxenholme Lake District 65	d											13 12								13 27			
Lancaster 6 65	a							12 45				13 27								13 44	13 53	14 09	
	d							12 46				13 28								13 45			
Blackpool North 97	d			12 27							12 58					13 27							
Layton 97	d			12 30												13 30							
Poulton-le-Fylde 97	d			12 34							13 03					13 34							
Kirkham & Wesham 97	d			12 43												13 43							
Preston 8 65,97	a			12 53				13 06			13 21	13 46				13 53				14 06			
	d			12 55			13 07	13 12			13 23	13 47				13 55			14 04	14 08			
Leyland	d						13 13				13 28								14 10				
Buckshaw Parkway	d			13 03			13 17				13 33					14 03			14 15				
Chorley	d			13 07			13 21				13 37					14 07			14 19				
Adlington (Lancashire)	d						13 25												14 24				
Blackrod	d						13 29												14 28				
Horwich Parkway	d			13 15			13 33				13 45					14 15			14 32				
Lostock	d						13 36				13 49								14 36				
Southport	d					12 36							13 17					13 31					
Meols Cop	d					12 41							13 22					13 36					
Bescar Lane	d																	13 41					
New Lane	d																	13 45					
Burscough Bridge	d					12 50							13 31					13 48					
Hoscar	d																	13 51					
Parbold	d					12 54							13 36					13 54					
Appley Bridge	d					12 59							13 40					13 59					
Gathurst	d					13 02							13 44					14 02					
Kirkby	d				12 35												13 35						
Rainford	d				12 43												13 43						
Upholland	d				12 47												13 47						
Orrell	d				12 51												13 51						
Pemberton	d				12 54												13 54						
Wigan Wallgate	a				12 59	13 07							13 48				13 59	14 07					
	d	12 56			13 01	13 08							13 50	13 56			14 01	14 08					14 23
Wigan North Western	d								13 23											14 24			
Ince	d				13 04												14 04						
Hindley	d				13 07	13 13			13 28				13 55				14 07	14 13					14 28
Westhoughton	d					13 18							14 00					14 18					
Bolton	a			13 22		13 26	13 41				13 54	14s05	14 09			14 22		14 26	14 41				
	d		13 19	13 22		13 26	13 42			13 49	13 54		14 10		14 18	14 22		14 26	14 41				
Moses Gate	d					13 29												14 29					
Farnworth	d					13 32												14 32					
Kearsley	d					13 34												14 34					
Clifton	d																						
Daisy Hill	d	13 04			13 12				13 32					14 04			14 12						14 32
Hag Fold	d				13 15				13 35								14 15						14 35
Atherton	d	13 08			13 18				13 38					14 08			14 18						14 38
Walkden	d	13 14			13 24				13 44					14 14			14 24						14 44
Moorside	d				13 28												14 28						
Swinton	d				13 31				13 49								14 31						14 49
Salford Crescent	a	13 26	13 32	13 36	13 39	13 44	13 53		13 56	14 00	14 05		14 21	14 26	14 32	14 36	14 39	14 44	14 53				14 56
	d	13 26	13 33	13 36	13 40	13 45	13 53		13 57	14 01	14 06		14 22	14 26	14 32	14 36	14 40	14 45	14 53				14 57
Salford Central	d	13 29	13 36		13 43	13 47	13 56		13 59	14 04				14 29	14 37		14 43	14 47	14 56				14 59
Manchester Victoria ⇌	a	13 32	13 41		13 46	13 50	13 59		14 02	14 07				14 32	14 41		14 46	14 50	14 59				15 02
Rochdale 41	a	13 50	14 04						14 17	14 29				14 49	15 09								15 17
Deansgate ⇌	a										14 09		14 29										
Manchester Oxford Road	a			13 41				13 54			14 11	14 19	14 32			14 41				14 54			
Manchester Piccadilly 10 ⇌	a			13 45				13 58			14 15	14 24	14 36			14 45				14 58			
Stockport 84	a			14 02									14 51			15 02							
Alderley Edge	a												15 08										
Heald Green 85	a							14 12			14 30									15 12			
Manchester Airport 85 ⇌✈	a							14 18			14 35	14 46								15 18			

A To Leeds
B From Clitheroe
C To Hazel Grove
D To Stalybridge
E To Blackburn
F From Blackburn
G From Glasgow Central
H From Carlisle
I From Leeds to Morecambe

Table T082-R

Mondays to Fridays
16 December to 15 May

Barrow-in-Furness, Blackpool North, Preston, Southport, Kirkby and Wigan - Bolton - Manchester

Station		NT A	NT ◇	NT ◇ B	TP ◇1 C ⌶	TP ◇1 D ⌶	NT	NT ◇ B	NT E	NT F	NT	NT G	NT	NT ◇	NT H	NT A	NT ◇	TP ◇1 I ⌶	NT	NT ◇ B	NT E	NT F
Barrow-in-Furness	d													13 53								
Roose	d																					
Dalton	d																					
Ulverston	d													14 09								
Cark	d																					
Kents Bank	d																					
Grange-over-Sands	d													14 21								
Arnside	d													14 27								
Silverdale	d																					
Carnforth	d													14 37								
Windermere 83	d																					
Oxenholme Lake District 65	d				14 06	14 12												15 13				
Lancaster 6 65	a				14 22	14 26								14 46				15 27				
	d				14 23	14 28								14 47				15 28				
Blackpool North 97	d		13 58							14 27							14 58					15 27
Layton 97	d									14 30												15 30
Poulton-le-Fylde 97	d		14 03							14 34							15 03					15 34
Kirkham & Wesham 97	d									14 43												15 43
Preston 8 65,97	a		14 21		14 41	14 45				14 53				15 07			15 21	15 45				15 53
	d		14 23		14 43	14 47				14 55			15 04	15 09			15 23	15 47				15 55
Leyland	d		14 28										15 10				15 28					
Buckshaw Parkway	d		14 33							15 02			15 15				15 33					16 03
Chorley	d		14 37							15 06			15 19				15 37					16 07
Adlington (Lancashire)	d												15 24									
Blackrod	d												15 28									
Horwich Parkway	d		14 45							15 14			15 32				15 45					16 15
Lostock	d		14 49										15 36				15 49					
Southport	d						14 17					14 36							15 17			
Meols Cop	d						14 22					14 41							15 22			
Bescar Lane	d																					
New Lane	d																					
Burscough Bridge	d						14 31					14 50							15 31			
Hoscar	d																					
Parbold	d						14 36					14 54							15 36			
Appley Bridge	d						14 40					14 59							15 40			
Gathurst	d						14 44					15 02							15 44			
Kirkby	d										14 35											
Rainford	d										14 43											
Upholland	d										14 47											
Orrell	d										14 51											
Pemberton	d										14 54											
Wigan Wallgate	a						14 48	←			14 59	15 07							15 48			
	d						14 50				15 01	15 08			15 23				15 50	15 56		
Wigan North Western	d			14 54	14a56			14 54						15 24								
Ince	d			→							15 04											
Hindley	d						14 55				15 07	15 13			15 28				15 55			
Westhoughton	d						15 00					15 18							16 00			
Bolton	a		14 54			15s05	15 09			15 21		15 26	15 41				15 54	16s05	16 09			16 22
	d	14 49	14 54				15 10		15 19	15 22		15 26	15 41			15 49	15 54		16 10		16 19	16 22
Moses Gate	d											15 29										
Farnworth	d											15 32										
Kearsley	d											15 34										
Clifton	d																					
Daisy Hill	d							15 04			15 12				15 32					16 04		
Hag Fold	d										15 15				15 35							
Atherton	d							15 08			15 18				15 38					16 08		
Walkden	d							15 14			15 24				15 44					16 14		
Moorside	d										15 28											
Swinton	d										15 31				15 49							
Salford Crescent	a	15 00	15 05				15 21	15 26	15 32	15 36	15 39	15 44	15 53		15 56	16 00	16 05		16 21	16 28	16 32	16 36
	d	15 01	15 06				15 22	15 26	15 33	15 36	15 40	15 45	15 53		15 57	16 01	16 06		16 22	16 28	16 33	16 36
Salford Central	d	15 04						15 29	15 37		15 43	15 47	15 56		15 59	16 04				16 32	16 36	
Manchester Victoria ⇌	a	15 07						15 32	15 40		15 46	15 50	15 59		16 02	16 07				16 35	16 41	
Rochdale 41	a	15 29						15 49	16 02						16 17	16 29				16 50	17 04	
Deansgate ⇌	a		15 09				15 29										16 09		16 29			16 40
Manchester Oxford Road	a		15 11			15 19	15 32			15 41				15 54			16 11	16 20	16 32			16 42
Manchester Piccadilly 10 ⇌	a		15 15			15 24	15 36			15 45				15 58			16 15	16 24	16 36			16 45
Stockport 84	a						15 51			16 02									16 51			17 02
Alderley Edge	a						16 08												17 08			
Heald Green 85	a		15 30											16 12			16 29					
Manchester Airport 85 ⇌✈	a		15 35			15 46								16 17			16 33	16 48				

A From Blackburn
B To Leeds
C From Glasgow Central to Liverpool Lime Street
D From Edinburgh
E From Clitheroe
F To Hazel Grove
G To Stalybridge
H To Blackburn
I From Glasgow Central

Table T082-R

Mondays to Fridays
16 December to 15 May

Barrow-in-Furness, Blackpool North, Preston, Southport, Kirkby and Wigan - Bolton - Manchester

		NT	NT A	NT	NT ◇	NT ◇ B	NT C	NT D	NT ◇	TP ◇1 E	NT F	NT	NT ◇ G	NT H	NT I	NT	NT A	NT	NT ◇	NT C	NT D	NT ◇	TP ◇1 J
Barrow-in-Furness	d				14 46						15 50												
Roose	d				14 50						15 54												
Dalton	d				14 56						16 00												
Ulverston	d				15 04						16 08												
Cark	d				15 12						16 16												
Kents Bank	d				15 16						16 20												
Grange-over-Sands	d				15 20						16 24												
Arnside	d				15 25						16 30												
Silverdale	d				15 30						16 35												
Carnforth	d				15 37	15 59					16 42												
Windermere 83	d																		16 00				
Oxenholme Lake District 65	d																		16 28				17 10
Lancaster 6 65	a				15 45	16 08					16 52												17 24
	d				15 46					16 30													17 27
Blackpool North 97	d								15 58						16 27							16 53	
Layton 97	d														16 30							16 56	
Poulton-le-Fylde 97	d								16 03						16 34							17 00	
Kirkham & Wesham 97	d														16 43							17 09	
Preston 8 65,97	a				16 06				16 21	16 48					16 53				17 02			17 19	17 44
	d			16 04	16 08				16 23	16 49					16 55			17 04	17 08			17 21	17 46
Leyland	d			16 10					16 28									17 10				17 26	
Buckshaw Parkway	d			16 15					16 33						17 03			17 15				17 31	
Chorley	d			16 19					16 37						17 07			17 19				17 34	
Adlington (Lancashire)	d			16 24														17 24				17 39	
Blackrod	d			16 28														17 28				17 42	
Horwich Parkway	d			16 32					16 45						17 15			17 32				17 46	
Lostock	d			16 36					16 49									17 36				17 49	
Southport	d		15 31									16 15					16 36						
Meols Cop	d		15 36									16 20					16 41						
Bescar Lane	d		15 41																				
New Lane	d		15 45																				
Burscough Bridge	d		15 48									16 29					16 50						
Hoscar	d		15 51																				
Parbold	d		15 54									16 33					16 54						
Appley Bridge	d		15 59									16 38					16 59						
Gathurst	d		16 02									16 41					17 02						
Kirkby	d	15 35														16 36							
Rainford	d	15 43														16 44							
Upholland	d	15 47														16 48							
Orrell	d	15 51														16 52							
Pemberton	d	15 54														16 55							
Wigan Wallgate	a	15 59	16 07									16 46				17 01	17 07						
	d	16 01	16 08				16 23					16 47	16 55			17 03	17 08						
Wigan North Western	d				16 23															17 23			
Ince	d	16 04														17 06							
Hindley	d	16 07	16 13				16 28						17 00			17 09				17 28			
Westhoughton	d		16 18									16 56	17 05				17 17						
Bolton	a		16 26	16 41					16 54			17 04	17 13		17 21		17 25	17 41				17 54	18s04
	d		16 26	16 41				16 49	16 54			17 10	17 14	17 19	17 22		17 26	17 41			17 49	17 55	
Moses Gate	d		16 29														17 29						
Farnworth	d		16 32														17 31						
Kearsley	d		16 34														17 33						
Clifton	d																						
Daisy Hill	d	16 12					16 32									17 14				17 32			
Hag Fold	d	16 15					16 35									17 17				17 35			
Atherton	d	16 18					16 38									17 20				17 38			
Walkden	d	16 24					16 44									17 26				17 44			
Moorside	d	16 28														17 29							
Swinton	d	16 31					16 49									17 32				17 49			
Salford Crescent	a	16 39	16 44	16 53			16 56	17 00	17 05			17 22	17 25	17 32	17 35	17 40	17 44	17 53		17 56	18 01	18 06	
	d	16 40	16 45	16 53			16 57	17 01	17 06			17 22	17 26	17 32	17 36	17 40	17 44	17 53		17 57	18 01	18 06	
Salford Central	d	16 43	16 47	16 56			16 59	17 04					17 29	17 36		17 43	17 47	17 56		17 59	18 04		
Manchester Victoria	a	16 46	16 50	16 59			17 02	17 07					17 32	17 41		17 46	17 50	17 59		18 02	18 07		
Rochdale 41	a						17 17	17 29					17 50	18 04						18 17	18 29		
Deansgate	a								17 09			17 29			17 39							18 10	
Manchester Oxford Road	a				16 54				17 11	17 22		17 32			17 41				17 54			18 12	18 19
Manchester Piccadilly 10	a				16 58				17 15	17 27		17 36			17 45				17 58			18 15	18 23
Stockport 84	a											17 51			18 02								
Alderley Edge	a											18 08											
Heald Green 85	a				17 12				17 29										18 12			18 29	
Manchester Airport 85	a				17 17				17 33	17 48									18 17			18 35	18 46

A To Stalybridge
B From Leeds to Morecambe
C To Blackburn
D From Blackburn
E From Edinburgh
F From Carlisle
G To Leeds
H From Clitheroe
I To Hazel Grove
J From Glasgow Central

Table T082-R

Mondays to Fridays
16 December to 15 May

Barrow-in-Furness, Blackpool North, Preston, Southport, Kirkby and Wigan - Bolton - Manchester

		NT	NT ◇ A	NT B	NT C	NT	NT D	NT	NT ◇	NT	NT E	NT B	NT ◇	TP ◇1 F	NT	NT ◇ A	NT B	NT C	NT	NT D	NT	TP ◇1 G
Barrow-in-Furness	d								16 45	17 19												
Roose	d								16 49	17 23												
Dalton	d								16 56	17 29												
Ulverston	d								17 04	17 37												
Cark	d								17 12	17 45												
Kents Bank	d								17 16													
Grange-over-Sands	d								17 20	17 52												
Arnside	d								17 25	17 58												
Silverdale	d								17 30	18 03												
Carnforth	d								17 37	18 10												
Windermere 83	d																					
Oxenholme Lake District 65	d													18 14								
Lancaster 6 65	a								17 45	18 20				18 28								
	d								17 46					18 29								18 55
Blackpool North 97	d				17 27								17 56					18 27				
Layton 97	d				17 30													18 30				
Poulton-le-Fylde 97	d				17 34								18 01					18 34				
Kirkham & Wesham 97	d				17 43													18 43				
Preston 8 65,97	a				17 53				18 06				18 19	18 47				18 53				19 13
	d				17 55			18 04	18 08				18 21	18 48				18 55			19 08	
Leyland	d							18 10					18 26								19 13	
Buckshaw Parkway	d				18 03			18 15					18 30					19 03			19 17	
Chorley	d				18 07			18 19					18 34					19 07			19 21	
Adlington (Lancashire)	d							18 24					18 38								19 25	
Blackrod	d							18 28					18 42								19 29	
Horwich Parkway	d				18 15			18 32					18 45					19 15			19 32	
Lostock	d							18 36					18 49								19 36	
Southport	d	17 16					17 31								18 17					18 36		
Meols Cop	d	17 21					17 36								18 22					18 41		
Bescar Lane	d						17 41															
New Lane	d						17 45															
Burscough Bridge	d	17 30					17 48								18 31					18 50		
Hoscar	d						17 51															
Parbold	d	17 35					17 54								18 36					18 54		
Appley Bridge	d	17 39					17 59								18 40					18 59		
Gathurst	d	17 43					18 02								18 44					19 02		
Kirkby	d					17 35													18 35			
Rainford	d					17 43													18 43			
Upholland	d					17 47													18 47			
Orrell	d					17 51													18 51			
Pemberton	d					17 54													18 54			
Wigan Wallgate	a	17 47				17 59	18 07								18 48				19 00	19 07		
	d	17 49	17 56			18 01	18 08				18 23				18 50	18 56			19 02	19 08		
Wigan North Western	d								18 23													
Ince	d	17 52				18 04													19 05			
Hindley	d	17 56				18 07	18 13				18 28				18 55				19 08	19 13		
Westhoughton	d	18 01					18 18								19 00					19 18		
Bolton	a	18 09			18 22		18 26	18 41					18 54		19 10			19 21		19 26	19 41	
	d	18 10		18 18	18 22		18 26	18 41				18 49	18 54		19 10		19 18	19 22		19 26	19 41	
Moses Gate	d						18 29													19 29		
Farnworth	d						18 32													19 32		
Kearsley	d						18 34													19 34		
Clifton	d																					
Daisy Hill	d		18 04			18 12					18 32					19 04			19 13			
Hag Fold	d					18 15					18 35								19 16			
Atherton	d		18 08			18 18					18 38					19 08			19 19			
Walkden	d		18 14			18 24					18 44					19 14			19 25			
Moorside	d					18 28													19 29			
Swinton	d					18 31					18 49								19 32			
Salford Crescent	a	18 22	18 27	18 32	18 36	18 39	18 44	18 53			18 56	19 01	19 05		19 21	19 26	19 31	19 35	19 39	19 44	19 53	
	d	18 23	18 28	18 33	18 36	18 40	18 45	18 53			18 57	19 01	19 06		19 22	19 26	19 32	19 35	19 40	19 45	19 53	
Salford Central	d		18 31	18 36		18 43	18 47	18 56			18 59	19 04				19 29	19 35		19 43	19 47	19 56	
Manchester Victoria	a		18 34	18 41		18 46	18 50	18 59			19 02	19 07				19 32	19 40		19 46	19 50	19 59	
Rochdale 41	a		18 50	19 04							19 17	19 29				19 49	20 03					
Deansgate	a	18 29			18 40								19 09		19 29							
Manchester Oxford Road	a	18 32			18 42				18 54				19 11	19 22	19 32			19 40				
Manchester Piccadilly 10	a	18 36			18 45				18 58				19 15	19 27	19 36			19 45				
Stockport 84	a	18 51			19 02										19 51			20 02				
Alderley Edge	a	19 08													20 08							
Heald Green 85	a								19 12				19 29									
Manchester Airport 85	a								19 17				19 35	19 50								

A To Leeds
B From Clitheroe
C To Hazel Grove
D To Stalybridge
E To Blackburn
F From Edinburgh
G From Glasgow Central to Liverpool Lime Street

Table T082-R

Mondays to Fridays
16 December to 15 May

Barrow-in-Furness, Blackpool North, Preston, Southport, Kirkby and Wigan - Bolton - Manchester

	NT	NT ◇ A	NT B	NT C	NT ◇	TP ◇1 D 🍴	NT	NT ◇ E	NT F	NT G	NT H	NT ◇	NT	NT B	NT ◇	TP ◇1 I 🍴	NT	NT	NT F	NT G	NT ◇	NT ◇ J
Barrow-in-Furness d	18 04												18 55								19 43	
Roose d	18 08												18 59								19 47	
Dalton d	18 14												19 05								19 53	
Ulverston d	18 23												19 13								20 02	
Cark d	18 30												19 21								20 09	
Kents Bank d	18 34												19 25								20 13	
Grange-over-Sands d	18 38												19 29								20 17	
Arnside d	18 44												19 35								20 23	
Silverdale d	18 49												19 40								20 28	
Carnforth d	18 56	19 15											19 47								20 35	21 05
Windermere 83 d												18 55										
Oxenholme Lake District 65 d						19 13						19 16				20 13						
Lancaster 6 65 a	19 06	19 24				19 28						19 33	19 55			20 27					20 43	21 14
d						19 29						19 33	19 56			20 29					20 44	
Blackpool North 97 d					18 57					19 25					19 58					20 24		
Layton 97 d										19 28										20 27		
Poulton-le-Fylde 97 d					19 03					19 32					20 03					20 31		
Kirkham & Wesham 97 d										19 41										20 40		
Preston 8 65,97 a					19 21	19 46				19 51		19 54	20 19		20 21	20 46				20 51	21 04	
d					19 23	19 48				19 53		20 11			20 23	20 48				20 52	21 06	
Leyland d					19 28										20 28							
Buckshaw Parkway d					19 33					20 01					20 33					21 00		
Chorley d					19 37					20 05					20 37					21 04		
Adlington (Lancashire) d										20 09										21 09		
Blackrod d										20 12										21 12		
Horwich Parkway d					19 45					20 15					20 45					21 15		
Lostock d					19 49										20 49							
Southport d							19 17										20 13					
Meols Cop d							19 22										20 18					
Bescar Lane d																	20 23					
New Lane d																	20 27					
Burscough Bridge d							19 31										20 30					
Hoscar d																	20 33					
Parbold d							19 36										20 37					
Appley Bridge d							19 40										20 41					
Gathurst d							19 44										20 45					
Kirkby d														19 46								
Rainford d														19 54								
Upholland d														19 58								
Orrell d														20 02								
Pemberton d														20 05								
Wigan Wallgate a							19 48							20 10			20 49					
d			19 23				19 50							20 19			20 51	20 56				
Wigan North Western d								19 56			20 08	20 27										
Ince d														20 22								
Hindley d			19 28				19 55				20 13			20 26			20 56					
Westhoughton d							20 00				20 18						21 01					
Bolton a					19 54	20s06	20 09			20 22	20 26				20 54		21 09			21 21		
d				19 49	19 54		20 10		20 18	20 22	20 26				20 54		21 10		21 18	21 22		
Moses Gate d											20 29											
Farnworth d											20 32											
Kearsley d											20 34											
Clifton d																						
Daisy Hill d			19 32					20 05						20 30				21 04				
Hag Fold d			19 35											20 33								
Atherton d			19 38					20 09						20 36				21 08				
Walkden d			19 44					20 15						20 42				21 14				
Moorside d														20 46								
Swinton d			19 49											20 49								
Salford Crescent a			19 56	20 02	20 05		20 21	20 27	20 31	20 35	20 44			20 56	21 05		21 21	21 26	21 30	21 33		
d			19 57	20 02	20 06		20 21	20 27	20 32	20 35	20 45			20 57	21 06		21 22	21 26	21 30	21 34		
Salford Central d			19 59	20 05				20 30	20 36		20 47			21 00			21 24	21 29	21 33			
Manchester Victoria ⇌ a			20 02	20 08				20 33	20 41		20 50			21 03			21 27	21 32	21 36			
Rochdale 41 a			20 17	20 30				20 50	21 04					21 17					22 00			
Deansgate ⇌ a					20 09		20 29								21 09							
Manchester Oxford Road a					20 11	20 20	20 31			20 41		20 55			21 11	21 20				21 38	21 42	
Manchester Piccadilly 10 ⇌ a					20 15	20 24	20 35			20 45		20 59			21 15	21 24				21 42	21 47	
Stockport 84 a							20 49			21 02										21 56		
Alderley Edge a							21 07															
Heald Green 85 a					20 29							21 15			21 29							
Manchester Airport 85 ⇌✈ a					20 33	20 48						21 20			21 36	21 41					22 03	

A From Leeds to Morecambe
B To Blackburn
C From Blackburn
D From Glasgow Central
E To Leeds
F From Clitheroe
G To Hazel Grove
H To Stalybridge
I From Edinburgh
J From Leeds

Table T082-R

Mondays to Fridays
16 December to 15 May

Barrow-in-Furness, Blackpool North, Preston, Southport, Kirkby and Wigan - Bolton - Manchester

	NT A	NT ◇	TP ◇1 B 🍴	NT	NT	NT	NT C	NT ◇	TP ◇1 D 🍴	NT A	NT	NT ◇	NT E	NT F	NT	NT C	NT ◇	NT
Barrow-in-Furness d				20 42									21 45					
Roose d				20 46									21 49					
Dalton d				20 52									21 55					
Ulverston d				21 01									22 04					
Cark d				21 08									22 11					
Kents Bank d				21 12									22 15					
Grange-over-Sands d				21 16									22 19					
Arnside d				21 22									22 26					
Silverdale d				21 27									22 30					
Carnforth d				21 34									22 38					
Windermere 83 d																		22 45
Oxenholme Lake District 65 d			21 09						22 11									23 06
Lancaster 6 65 a			21 23	21 46					22 25				22 46					23 23
d			21 24						22 26				22 46	23 03				23 24
Blackpool North 97 d		20 58						21 21				22 21					23 13	
Layton 97 d								21 24				22 24					23 16	
Poulton-le-Fylde 97 d		21 03						21 28				22 28					23 20	
Kirkham & Wesham 97 d								21 37				22 37					23 29	
Preston 8 65,97 a		21 21	21 41					21 48	22 44			22 47	23 09	23 24			23 40	23 50
d		21 23	21 43					21 50	22 45			22 49					23 45	
Leyland d		21 28						21 55				22 54					23 50	
Buckshaw Parkway d		21 33						21 59				22 58					23 54	
Chorley d		21 37						22 03				23 02					23 58	
Adlington (Lancashire) d								22 08				23 07					00 02	
Blackrod d								22 11				23 10					00 06	
Horwich Parkway d		21 45						22 15				23 14					00 09	
Lostock d		21 49						22 19				23 18					00 13	
Southport d						21 14					22 18				23 10			
Meols Cop d						21 19					22 23				23 15			
Bescar Lane d											22 28							
New Lane d											22 32							
Burscough Bridge d						21 28					22 35				23 24			
Hoscar d											22 38							
Parbold d						21 32					22 41				23 28			
Appley Bridge d						21 37					22 46				23 33			
Gathurst d						21 40					22 49				23 36			
Kirkby d																		
Rainford d																		
Upholland d																		
Orrell d																		
Pemberton d																		
Wigan Wallgate a						21 45					22 54				23 43			
d	21 15					21 46					22 55							
Wigan North Western d					21 38					22 50								
Ince d					21 42						22 58							
Hindley d	21 21				21 46	21 52				22 56	23 02							
Westhoughton d	21 26					21 56				23 00								
Bolton a	21 34	21 54				22 04		22 24	23s03	23 08		23 23					00 18	
d	21 34	21 54				22 05	22 19	22 24		23 09		23 23				23 46	00 18	
Moses Gate d	21 37					22 08												
Farnworth d	21 39					22 10												
Kearsley d	21 41					22 12												
Clifton d																		
Daisy Hill d					21 50						23 06							
Hag Fold d					21 53						23 09							
Atherton d					21 56						23 11							
Walkden d					22 02						23 17							
Moorside d					22 06						23 20							
Swinton d					22 09						23 23							
Salford Crescent a	21 52	22 05			22 16	22 22	22 32	22 36		23 21	23 32	23 34				23 57	00 30	
d	21 53	22 06			22 17	22 23	22 33	22 36		23 21	23 33	23 35				23 59	00 31	
Salford Central d	21 57				22 20	22 25	22 36			23 24	23 36					00 02		
Manchester Victoria ⇌ a	22 00				22 24	22 28	22 40			23 27	23 39					00 05		
Rochdale 41 a																		
Deansgate ⇌ a		22 12																
Manchester Oxford Road a		22 14						22 42	23 19			23 39						
Manchester Piccadilly 10 ⇌ a		22 19	22 23					22 46	23 24			23 43					00 40	
Stockport 84 a																		
Alderley Edge a																		
Heald Green 85 a		22 34						23 01				00 04					00 54	
Manchester Airport 85 ⇌✈ a		22 38	22 45					23 06	23 46			00 11					00 59	

A To Stalybridge
B From Glasgow Central
C From Clitheroe
D From Edinburgh
E From Carlisle
F From Morecambe

Table T082-R

Saturdays

21 December to 16 May

Barrow-in-Furness, Blackpool North, Preston, Southport, Kirkby and Wigan - Bolton - Manchester

		NT	NT	TP	NT	NT	NT	NT	NT	NT	NT	NT	NT	NT	NT	TP	NT	NT	NT	NT	NT	NT	NT
		A	◇ B	◇1 C 🚲	◇	◇		◇ D	E		F		◇	G	◇	◇1	H			◇ D	A		F
Barrow-in-Furness	d												04 53										
Roose	d																						
Dalton	d																						
Ulverston	d												05 09										
Cark	d																						
Kents Bank	d																						
Grange-over-Sands	d												05 21										
Arnside	d												05 27										
Silverdale	d																						
Carnforth	d												05 37				06 21						
Windermere 83	d																						
Oxenholme Lake District 65	d																						
Lancaster 6 65	a												05 45				06 32						
	d												05 46			06 28							
Blackpool North 97	d				03 33	04 29			05 23						05 56								
Layton 97	d								05 26														
Poulton-le-Fylde 97	d					04 35			05 30						06 01								
Kirkham & Wesham 97	d								05 39														
Preston 8 65,97	a				03 55	04 53			05 49				06 04		06 19	06 46							
	d			00 47	03 56	04 55			05 51			06 03	06 06		06 21	06 47							
Leyland	d								05 56			06 09			06 26								
Buckshaw Parkway	d					05 02			06 01			06 14			06 30								
Chorley	d					05 06			06 05			06 18			06 34								
Adlington (Lancashire)	d		00 02									06 23											
Blackrod	d		00 06									06 27											
Horwich Parkway	d		00 09			05 14			06 12			06 31			06 41								
Lostock	d		00 13						06 16			06 35			06 45								
Southport	d																		06 17				06 34
Meols Cop	d																		06 22				06 40
Bescar Lane	d																						
New Lane	d																						
Burscough Bridge	d																		06 31				06 48
Hoscar	d																						
Parbold	d																		06 36				06 53
Appley Bridge	d																		06 40				06 57
Gathurst	d																		06 44				07 01
Kirkby	d																					06 36	
Rainford	d																					06 44	
Upholland	d																					06 48	
Orrell	d																					06 52	
Pemberton	d																					06 55	
Wigan Wallgate	a																		06 49			07 00	07 06
	d									06 01	06 08								06 50			07 01	07 07
Wigan North Western	d						05 50	05 56					06 23					06 43		06 56			
Ince	d									06 04												07 04	
Hindley	d						05 56			06 08	06 13								06 56			07 08	07 12
Westhoughton	d						06 01				06 18								07 01				07 17
Bolton	a		00 18			05 21	06 09		06 21		06 26	06 40			06 50				07 09				07 25
	d		00 18			05 23	06 09		06 21		06 26	06 40		06 47	06 51				07 10		07 17		07 25
Moses Gate	d										06 29												07 28
Farnworth	d										06 31												07 30
Kearsley	d										06 33										07 22		07 32
Clifton	d																						07 37
Daisy Hill	d							06 05		06 12								06 51		07 05		07 13	
Hag Fold	d									06 15								06 54				07 16	
Atherton	d							06 10		06 18								06 57		07 09		07 19	
Walkden	d							06 16		06 24								07 03		07 15		07 25	
Moorside	d									06 28								07 07				07 29	
Swinton	d									06 31								07 10				07 32	
Salford Crescent	a		00 30			05 34	06 21	06 27	06 35	06 39	06 44	06 52		06 59	07 02			07 18	07 22	07 27	07 32	07 39	07 44
	d		00 31			05 35	06 22	06 28	06 36	06 40	06 45	06 53		06 59	07 03			07 18	07 22	07 27	07 33	07 40	07 44
Salford Central	d	00 02						06 31		06 43	06 47	06 56		07 04				07 21		07 30	07 36	07 43	07 47
Manchester Victoria	a	00 05						06 34		06 46	06 50	06 59		07 07				07 24		07 33	07 41	07 46	07 50
Rochdale 41	a							06 50						07 29						07 49	08 04		
Deansgate	a						06 29								07 06				07 26				
Manchester Oxford Road	a					05 40	06 32		06 43				06 52		07 08	07 20			07 28				
Manchester Piccadilly 10	a		00 40	01 40	04 45	05 44	06 36		06 48				06 57		07 13	07 25			07 36				
Stockport 84	a						06 53		07 02										07 50				
Alderley Edge	a						07 09												08 08				
Heald Green 85	a		00 54			06 01							07 13		07 27								
Manchester Airport 85	a		00 59	01 59	05 03	06 06							07 18		07 32	07 49							

A From Clitheroe
B From Blackpool North
C From Edinburgh
D To Leeds
E To Hazel Grove
F To Stalybridge
G From Blackburn
H From Skipton

Table T082-R

Saturdays

21 December to 16 May

Barrow-in-Furness, Blackpool North, Preston, Southport, Kirkby and Wigan - Bolton - Manchester

		NT	NT	NT	NT	NT	NT	NT	TP	NT	NT	NT	NT	NT	NT	NT	NT	NT	NT	NT	NT	NT	TP
		A		◇		B	C	◇	◇1 D 🚲			◇ E	C	A		F		◇		B	G	◇	◇1 H 🚲
Barrow-in-Furness	d			05 48	06 11													06 47	07 08				
Roose	d			05 52	06 15													06 51	07 12				
Dalton	d			05 58	06 21													06 57	07 18				
Ulverston	d			06 06	06 30													07 05	07 27				
Cark	d			06 14	06 37													07 13	07 34				
Kents Bank	d			06 18	06 41														07 38				
Grange-over-Sands	d			06 22	06 45													07 20	07 42				
Arnside	d			06 27	06 51													07 25	07 49				
Silverdale	d			06 32	06 56													07 30	07 54				
Carnforth	d			06 41	07 03													07 37	08 01				
Windermere 83	d																						
Oxenholme Lake District 65	d								07 08														08 14
Lancaster 6 65	a			06 50	07 15				07 22										07 45	08 12				08 28
	d			06 50					07 23										07 46					08 29
Blackpool North 97	d	06 32						06 53						07 23								07 55	
Layton 97	d	06 35						06 56						07 26								07 58	
Poulton-le-Fylde 97	d	06 39						07 00						07 30								08 02	
Kirkham & Wesham 97	d	06 48						07 09						07 39								08 11	
Preston 8 65,97	a	06 58		07 11				07 19	07 40					07 50				08 06				08 21	08 46
	d	07 00	07 04	07 12				07 21	07 45					07 51			08 04	08 08				08 23	08 48
Leyland	d		07 10					07 26						07 56			08 10					08 28	
Buckshaw Parkway	d	07 08	07 15					07 31						07 59			08 15					08 33	
Chorley	d	07 12	07 19					07 34						08 03			08 19					08 37	
Adlington (Lancashire)	d	07 17	07 24					07 39						08 07			08 24						
Blackrod	d	07 20	07 28					07 42						08 10			08 28						
Horwich Parkway	d	07 24	07 32					07 46						08 14			08 32					08 45	
Lostock	d	07 27	07 36					07 49						08 17			08 36					08 49	
Southport	d					06 48					07 17					07 30							
Meols Cop	d					06 53					07 22					07 35							
Bescar Lane	d					06 58										07 40							
New Lane	d					07 02										07 44							
Burscough Bridge	d					07 05					07 31					07 47							
Hoscar	d					07 08										07 50							
Parbold	d					07 11					07 36					07 54							
Appley Bridge	d					07 16					07 40					07 58							
Gathurst	d					07 19					07 44					08 02							
Kirkby	d														07 36								
Rainford	d														07 44								
Upholland	d														07 48								
Orrell	d														07 52								
Pemberton	d														07 55								
Wigan Wallgate	a					07 24					07 49				08 00	08 06							
	d					07 25					07 50	07 56			08 01	08 08				08 22			
Wigan North Western	d			07 26						07 42							08 23					
Ince	d									07 45					08 04								
Hindley	d					07 31				07 49	07 56				08 08	08 13				08 27			
Westhoughton	d										08 01					08 18							
Bolton	a	07 32	07 41					07 54	08s03		08 09			08 22		08 26	08 41					08 54	09s06
	d	07 34	07 41				07 49	07 55			08 09		08 17	08 22		08 26	08 41				08 49	08 54	
Moses Gate	d															08 29							
Farnworth	d												08 21			08 32							
Kearsley	d															08 34							
Clifton	d																						
Daisy Hill	d					07 35				07 53		08 04			08 13					08 32			
Hag Fold	d									07 56					08 16					08 35			
Atherton	d					07 39				07 59		08 08			08 19					08 38			
Walkden	d					07 45				08 04		08 14			08 25					08 44			
Moorside	d									08 08													
Swinton	d									08 10					08 30					08 49			
Salford Crescent	a	07 47	07 53			07 56	08 02	08 06		08 17	08 21	08 26	08 32	08 36	08 39	08 44	08 53			08 56	09 01	09 05	
	d	07 48	07 53			07 57	08 02	08 06		08 18	08 22	08 26	08 33	08 36	08 40	08 45	08 53			08 57	09 01	09 06	
Salford Central	d		07 56			08 00	08 06			08 21		08 29	08 36		08 42	08 47	08 56			08 59	09 04		
Manchester Victoria	a		07 59			08 03	08 08			08 24		08 32	08 41		08 46	08 50	08 59			09 02	09 07		
Rochdale 41	a					08 17	08 30					08 51	09 04							09 17	09 29		
Deansgate	a							08 10			08 25											09 09	
Manchester Oxford Road	a	07 52		07 57				08 12	08 20		08 28			08 41				08 55				09 11	09 20
Manchester Piccadilly 10	a	07 56		08 01				08 16	08 24		08 33			08 45				08 59				09 15	09 24
Stockport 84	a	08 06									08 51			09 02									
Alderley Edge	a										09 08												
Heald Green 85	a			08 16				08 28									09 13				09 30	
Manchester Airport 85	a			08 21				08 32	08 44								09 18				09 35	09 46

A To Hazel Grove
B To Blackburn
C From Clitheroe
D From Glasgow Central
E To Leeds
F To Stalybridge
G From Blackburn
H From Edinburgh

Table T082-R

Saturdays
21 December to 16 May

Barrow-in-Furness, Blackpool North, Preston, Southport, Kirkby and Wigan - Bolton - Manchester

Station		NT	NT	NT ◇ A	NT B	NT C	NT D	NT	NT ◇	NT E	NT ◇ F	NT G	NT ◇	TP ◇1 H ✠	NT	NT ◇ A	NT B	NT C	NT	NT D	NT	NT ◇
Barrow-in-Furness	d								07 46													08 46
Roose	d								07 50													08 50
Dalton	d								07 56													08 56
Ulverston	d								08 05													09 04
Cark	d								08 12													09 12
Kents Bank	d																					09 16
Grange-over-Sands	d								08 19													09 20
Arnside	d								08 25													09 25
Silverdale	d								08 30													09 30
Carnforth	d								08 37		09 04											09 39
Windermere 83	d																					
Oxenholme Lake District 65	d													09 13								
Lancaster [8] 65	a								08 45		09 13			09 27								09 47
	d								08 46					09 28								09 47
Blackpool North 97	d					08 27							08 58					09 27				
Layton 97	d					08 30												09 30				
Poulton-le-Fylde 97	d					08 34							09 03					09 34				
Kirkham & Wesham 97	d					08 43												09 43				
Preston [8] 65,97	a					08 53			09 06				09 21	09 45				09 53				10 08
	d					08 55		09 04	09 08				09 23	09 47				09 55			10 04	10 10
Leyland	d							09 10					09 28								10 10	
Buckshaw Parkway	d					09 03		09 15					09 33					10 03			10 15	
Chorley	d					09 07		09 18					09 37					10 07			10 19	
Adlington (Lancashire)	d							09 22													10 24	
Blackrod	d							09 26													10 28	
Horwich Parkway	d					09 15		09 30					09 45					10 15			10 32	
Lostock	d							09 34					09 49								10 36	
Southport	d		08 17				08 36								09 17					09 31		
Meols Cop	d		08 22				08 41								09 22					09 36		
Bescar Lane	d																			09 41		
New Lane	d																			09 45		
Burscough Bridge	d		08 31				08 50								09 31					09 48		
Hoscar	d																			09 51		
Parbold	d		08 36				08 54								09 36					09 54		
Appley Bridge	d		08 40				08 59								09 40					09 59		
Gathurst	d		08 44				09 02								09 44					10 02		
Kirkby	d	08 18																	09 35			
Rainford	d	08 26																	09 43			
Upholland	d	08 30																	09 47			
Orrell	d	08 34																	09 51			
Pemberton	d	08 37																	09 54			
Wigan Wallgate	a	08 42	08 49				09 07								09 48				09 59	10 07		
	d	08 44	08 50	08 56			09 08								09 50				10 01	10 08		
Wigan North Western	d								09 23	09 23						09 54						10 24
Ince	d																		10 04			
Hindley	d		08 56				09 13			09 28					09 55				10 07	10 13		
Westhoughton	d		09 01				09 18								10 00					10 18		
Bolton	a		09 10			09 22	09 26	09 39					09 54	10s05	10 09			10 22		10 26	10 41	
	d		09 10		09 17	09 22	09 26	09 39				09 49	09 54		10 10		10 19	10 22		10 26	10 41	
Moses Gate	d				09 20		09 29													10 29		
Farnworth	d						09 32													10 32		
Kearsley	d						09 34													10 34		
Clifton	d																					
Daisy Hill	d	08 52		09 04						09 32						10 04			10 12			
Hag Fold	d	08 55								09 35									10 15			
Atherton	d	08 57		09 08						09 38						10 08			10 18			
Walkden	d	09 03		09 14						09 44						10 14			10 24			
Moorside	d	09 07																	10 28			
Swinton	d	09 09								09 49									10 31			
Salford Crescent	a	09 17	09 21	09 26	09 32	09 36	09 44	09 53		09 56		10 01	10 05		10 21	10 26	10 32	10 36	10 39	10 44	10 53	
	d	09 18	09 22	09 26	09 33	09 36	09 45	09 53		09 57		10 01	10 06		10 22	10 26	10 33	10 36	10 40	10 45	10 53	
Salford Central	d	09 21		09 29	09 36		09 47	09 56		09 59		10 04				10 29	10 36		10 43	10 47	10 56	
Manchester Victoria ⇌	a	09 24		09 32	09 41		09 50	09 59		10 02		10 07				10 32	10 41		10 46	10 50	10 59	
Rochdale 41	a			09 50	10 04					10 17		10 29				10 50	11 04					
Deansgate ⇌	a		09 29										10 09		10 29							
Manchester Oxford Road	a		09 32			09 41			09 54				10 11	10 20	10 32			10 41				10 54
Manchester Piccadilly [10] ⇌	a		09 36			09 45			09 58				10 15	10 24	10 36			10 45				10 58
Stockport 84	a		09 51			10 02									10 51			11 02				
Alderley Edge	a		10 08												11 08							
Heald Green 85	a								10 12				10 30									11 12
Manchester Airport 85 ⇌✈	a								10 18				10 35	10 46								11 18

A To Leeds
B From Clitheroe
C To Hazel Grove
D To Stalybridge
E To Blackburn
F From Leeds
G From Blackburn
H From Glasgow Central

Table T082-R

Saturdays
21 December to 16 May

Barrow-in-Furness, Blackpool North, Preston, Southport, Kirkby and Wigan - Bolton - Manchester

Station		NT ◇ A	NT B	NT C	NT ◇	TP ◇1 D ✠	TP ◇1 E ✠	NT F	NT	NT ◇ G	NT H	NT I	NT	NT J	NT	NT ◇	NT B	NT C	NT ◇	TP ◇1 K ✠	NT	NT ◇ G	NT H
Barrow-in-Furness	d							09 58															
Roose	d							10 02															
Dalton	d							10 08															
Ulverston	d							10 17															
Cark	d							10 24															
Kents Bank	d							10 28															
Grange-over-Sands	d							10 32															
Arnside	d							10 39															
Silverdale	d							10 43															
Carnforth	d	09 57						10 56															
Windermere 83	d															10 08							
Oxenholme Lake District 65	d					10 12	10 17									10 29				11 15			
Lancaster [8] 65	a	10 06				10 26	10 32	11 07												11 29			
	d					10 27	10 32													11 30			
Blackpool North 97	d				09 58							10 27							10 57				
Layton 97	d											10 30											
Poulton-le-Fylde 97	d				10 03							10 34							11 03				
Kirkham & Wesham 97	d											10 43											
Preston [8] 65,97	a				10 21	10 45	10 51					10 53				11 04			11 21	11 47			
	d				10 23	10 47						10 55			11 04	11 08			11 22	11 49			
Leyland	d				10 28										11 10				11 28				
Buckshaw Parkway	d				10 33							11 03			11 15				11 33				
Chorley	d				10 37							11 07			11 19				11 37				
Adlington (Lancashire)	d														11 24								
Blackrod	d														11 28								
Horwich Parkway	d				10 45							11 15			11 32				11 45				
Lostock	d				10 49										11 35				11 49				
Southport	d								10 17					10 36							11 17		
Meols Cop	d								10 22					10 41							11 22		
Bescar Lane	d																						
New Lane	d																						
Burscough Bridge	d								10 31					10 50							11 31		
Hoscar	d																						
Parbold	d								10 36					10 54							11 36		
Appley Bridge	d								10 40					10 59							11 40		
Gathurst	d								10 44					11 02							11 44		
Kirkby	d												10 35										
Rainford	d												10 43										
Upholland	d												10 47										
Orrell	d												10 51										
Pemberton	d												10 54										
Wigan Wallgate	a								10 48				10 59	11 07							11 48		
	d		10 23						10 50	10 56			11 01	11 08			11 23				11 50	11 56	
Wigan North Western	d															11 23							
Ince	d												11 04										
Hindley	d		10 28						10 55				11 07	11 13			11 28				11 55		
Westhoughton	d								11 00					11 18							12 00		
Bolton	a				10 54	11s05			11 09			11 22		11 26	11 40				11 54		12 10		
	d			10 49	10 54				11 10		11 19	11 22		11 26	11 41			11 49	11 54		12 11		12 19
Moses Gate	d													11 29									
Farnworth	d													11 32									
Kearsley	d													11 34									
Clifton	d																						
Daisy Hill	d		10 32							11 04			11 12				11 32					12 04	
Hag Fold	d		10 35										11 15				11 35						
Atherton	d		10 38							11 08			11 18				11 38					12 08	
Walkden	d		10 44							11 14			11 24				11 44					12 14	
Moorside	d												11 28										
Swinton	d		10 49										11 31				11 49						
Salford Crescent	a		10 56	11 01	11 05				11 21	11 26	11 32	11 36	11 39	11 44	11 52		11 56	12 01	12 05		12 22	12 26	12 32
	d		10 57	11 01	11 06				11 22	11 26	11 33	11 36	11 40	11 45	11 53		11 57	12 02	12 06		12 22	12 26	12 33
Salford Central	d		10 59	11 04						11 29	11 36		11 43	11 47	11 56		12 00	12 05				12 29	12 36
Manchester Victoria ⇌	a		11 02	11 07						11 32	11 40		11 46	11 50	11 59		12 03	12 08				12 32	12 41
Rochdale 41	a		11 17	11 29						11 49	12 01						12 17	12 29				12 50	13 04
Deansgate ⇌	a				11 09				11 29										12 09		12 29		
Manchester Oxford Road	a				11 11	11 20			11 32			11 41				11 54			12 11	12 20	12 32		
Manchester Piccadilly [10] ⇌	a				11 15	11 24			11 36			11 45				11 58			12 15	12 24	12 36		
Stockport 84	a								11 51			12 02									12 51		
Alderley Edge	a								12 08												13 08		
Heald Green 85	a				11 30											12 12			12 29				
Manchester Airport 85 ⇌✈	a				11 35	11 46										12 18			12 35	12 46			

A From Leeds to Morecambe
B To Blackburn
C From Blackburn
D From Edinburgh
E From Glasgow Central to Liverpool Lime Street
F From Carlisle
G To Leeds
H From Clitheroe
I To Hazel Grove
J To Stalybridge
K From Glasgow Central

Table T082-R

Saturdays

21 December to 16 May

Barrow-in-Furness, Blackpool North, Preston, Southport, Kirkby and Wigan - Bolton - Manchester

Station		NT A	NT	NT B	NT	NT ◇	NT ◇ C	NT D	NT E	NT ◇	TP ◇1 F ⌶	NT	NT ◇ G	NT H	NT A	NT	NT B	NT	NT ◇	NT D	NT E	NT ◇
Barrow-in-Furness	d					10 46													11 46			
Roose	d					10 50													11 50			
Dalton	d					10 56													11 56			
Ulverston	d					11 04													12 04			
Cark	d					11 12													12 12			
Kents Bank	d					11 16													12 16			
Grange-over-Sands	d					11 20													12 20			
Arnside	d					11 25													12 25			
Silverdale	d					11 30													12 30			
Carnforth	d					11 37	12 01												12 37			
Windermere 83	d																					
Oxenholme Lake District 65	d										12 15											
Lancaster 65	a					11 45	12 10				12 29								12 45			
	d					11 46					12 30								12 46			
Blackpool North 97	d	11 27								11 58					12 27							12 58
Layton 97	d	11 30													12 30							
Poulton-le-Fylde 97	d	11 34								12 03					12 34							13 03
Kirkham & Wesham 97	d	11 43													12 43							
Preston 65,97	a	11 53				12 06				12 21	12 47				12 53				13 06			13 21
	d	11 55			12 04	12 08				12 23	12 49				12 55			13 07	13 12			13 23
Leyland	d				12 10					12 28								13 13				13 28
Buckshaw Parkway	d	12 03			12 15					12 33					13 03			13 17				13 33
Chorley	d	12 07			12 19					12 37					13 07			13 21				13 37
Adlington (Lancashire)	d				12 23													13 25				
Blackrod	d				12 27													13 29				
Horwich Parkway	d	12 15			12 31					12 45					13 15			13 33				13 45
Lostock	d				12 35					12 49								13 36				13 49
Southport	d			11 31								12 17					12 36					
Meols Cop	d			11 36								12 22					12 41					
Bescar Lane	d			11 41																		
New Lane	d			11 45																		
Burscough Bridge	d			11 48								12 31					12 50					
Hoscar	d			11 51																		
Parbold	d			11 54								12 36					12 54					
Appley Bridge	d			11 59								12 40					12 59					
Gathurst	d			12 02								12 44					13 02					
Kirkby	d		11 35													12 35						
Rainford	d		11 43													12 43						
Upholland	d		11 47													12 47						
Orrell	d		11 51													12 51						
Pemberton	d		11 54													12 54						
Wigan Wallgate	a		11 59	12 07								12 48				12 59	13 07					
	d		12 01	12 08				12 23				12 50	12 56			13 01	13 08					
Wigan North Western	d					12 25														13 23		
Ince	d		12 04													13 04						
Hindley	d		12 07	12 13				12 28				12 55				13 07	13 13			13 28		
Westhoughton	d			12 18								13 00					13 18					
Bolton	a	12 22		12 26	12 40					12 54		13 10			13 22		13 26	13 41				13 54
	d	12 22		12 26	12 41				12 49	12 54		13 11		13 19	13 22		13 26	13 42			13 49	13 54
Moses Gate	d			12 29													13 29					
Farnworth	d			12 32													13 32					
Kearsley	d			12 34													13 34					
Clifton	d																					
Daisy Hill	d		12 12					12 32					13 04			13 12				13 32		
Hag Fold	d		12 15					12 35								13 15				13 35		
Atherton	d		12 18					12 38					13 08			13 18				13 38		
Walkden	d		12 24					12 44					13 14			13 24				13 44		
Moorside	d		12 28													13 28						
Swinton	d		12 31					12 49								13 31				13 49		
Salford Crescent	a	12 36	12 39	12 44	12 52			12 56	13 00	13 05		13 22	13 26	13 32	13 36	13 39	13 44	13 53		13 56	14 00	14 05
	d	12 36	12 40	12 45	12 53			12 57	13 01	13 06		13 22	13 26	13 33	13 36	13 40	13 45	13 53		13 57	14 01	14 06
Salford Central	d		12 43	12 47	12 56			12 59	13 04				13 29	13 36		13 43	13 47	13 56		13 59	14 04	
Manchester Victoria ⇌	a		12 46	12 50	12 59			13 02	13 07				13 32	13 41		13 46	13 50	13 59		14 02	14 07	
Rochdale 41	a							13 17	13 29				13 50	14 04						14 17	14 29	
Deansgate ⇌	a									13 09		13 29										14 09
Manchester Oxford Road	a	12 41				12 54				13 11	13 20	13 32			13 41				13 54			14 11
Manchester Piccadilly 10 ⇌	a	12 45				12 58				13 15	13 24	13 36			13 45				13 58			14 15
Stockport 84	a	13 02										13 51			14 02							
Alderley Edge	a											14 08										
Heald Green 85	a					13 12				13 30									14 12			14 30
Manchester Airport 85 ⇌✈	a					13 18				13 35	13 46								14 18			14 35

A To Hazel Grove
B To Stalybridge
C From Leeds to Morecambe
D To Blackburn
E From Blackburn
F From Edinburgh
G To Leeds
H From Clitheroe

Table T082-R

Saturdays

21 December to 16 May

Barrow-in-Furness, Blackpool North, Preston, Southport, Kirkby and Wigan - Bolton - Manchester

Station		TP ◇1 A ⌶	NT	NT ◇ B	NT C	NT D	NT	NT E	NT	NT ◇	NT F	NT ◇ G	NT H	NT I	NT ◇	NT ◇ B	TP ◇1 J ⌶	TP ◇1 K ⌶	NT	NT ◇ B	NT C	NT D	NT
Barrow-in-Furness	d										12 50												
Roose	d										12 54												
Dalton	d										13 00												
Ulverston	d										13 08												
Cark	d										13 16												
Kents Bank	d										13 20												
Grange-over-Sands	d										13 24												
Arnside	d										13 30												
Silverdale	d										13 35												
Carnforth	d										13 42	14 01											
Windermere 83	d									13 06													
Oxenholme Lake District 65	d	13 13								13 28							14 08	14 14					
Lancaster 65	a	13 27								13 44	13 53	14 09					14 23	14 28					
	d	13 28								13 45							14 23	14 29					
Blackpool North 97	d					13 27									13 58							14 27	
Layton 97	d					13 30																14 30	
Poulton-le-Fylde 97	d					13 34									14 03							14 34	
Kirkham & Wesham 97	d					13 43																14 43	
Preston 65,97	a	13 45				13 53				14 05					14 21		14 42	14 46				14 53	
	d	13 47				13 55			14 04	14 08					14 23		14 43	14 48				14 55	
Leyland	d								14 10						14 28								
Buckshaw Parkway	d					14 03			14 15						14 33							15 02	
Chorley	d					14 07			14 19						14 37							15 06	
Adlington (Lancashire)	d								14 24														
Blackrod	d								14 28														
Horwich Parkway	d					14 15			14 32						14 45							15 14	
Lostock	d								14 36						14 49								
Southport	d		13 17					13 31											14 17				
Meols Cop	d		13 22					13 36											14 22				
Bescar Lane	d							13 41															
New Lane	d							13 45															
Burscough Bridge	d		13 31					13 48											14 31				
Hoscar	d							13 51															
Parbold	d		13 36					13 54											14 36				
Appley Bridge	d		13 40					13 59											14 40				
Gathurst	d		13 44					14 02											14 44				
Kirkby	d						13 35																14 35
Rainford	d						13 43																14 43
Upholland	d						13 47																14 47
Orrell	d						13 51																14 51
Pemberton	d						13 54																14 54
Wigan Wallgate	a		13 48				13 59	14 07											14 48	←			14 59
	d		13 50	13 56			14 01	14 08					14 23						14 50				15 01
Wigan North Western	d									14 24						14 54	14a56			14 54			
Ince	d						14 04									→							15 04
Hindley	d		13 55				14 07	14 13					14 28						14 55				15 07
Westhoughton	d		14 00					14 18											15 00				
Bolton	a	14s05	14 09			14 22		14 26	14 41						14 54			15s06	15 10			15 21	
	d		14 10		14 18	14 22		14 26	14 41					14 49	14 54				15 10		15 19	15 22	
Moses Gate	d							14 29															
Farnworth	d							14 32															
Kearsley	d							14 34															
Clifton	d																						
Daisy Hill	d			14 04			14 12						14 32							15 04			15 12
Hag Fold	d						14 15						14 35										15 15
Atherton	d			14 08			14 18						14 38							15 08			15 18
Walkden	d			14 14			14 24						14 44							15 14			15 24
Moorside	d						14 28																15 28
Swinton	d						14 31						14 49										15 31
Salford Crescent	a		14 21	14 26	14 32	14 36	14 39	14 44	14 53				14 56	15 00	15 05				15 21	15 26	15 32	15 36	15 39
	d		14 21	14 26	14 32	14 36	14 40	14 45	14 53				14 57	15 01	15 06				15 22	15 26	15 33	15 36	15 40
Salford Central	d			14 29	14 37		14 43	14 47	14 56				14 59	15 04						15 29	15 37		15 43
Manchester Victoria ⇌	a			14 32	14 41		14 46	14 50	14 59				15 02	15 07						15 32	15 40		15 46
Rochdale 41	a			14 49	15 09								15 17	15 29						15 49	16 02		
Deansgate ⇌	a		14 29												15 09				15 29				
Manchester Oxford Road	a	14 19	14 32			14 41				14 54					15 11			15 20	15 32			15 41	
Manchester Piccadilly 10 ⇌	a	14 24	14 36			14 45				14 58					15 15			15 24	15 36			15 45	
Stockport 84	a		14 51			15 02													15 51			16 02	
Alderley Edge	a		15 08																16 08				
Heald Green 85	a									15 12					15 30								
Manchester Airport 85 ⇌✈	a	14 46								15 18					15 35			15 46					

A From Glasgow Central
B To Leeds
C From Clitheroe
D To Hazel Grove
E To Stalybridge
F From Carlisle
G From Leeds to Morecambe
H To Blackburn
I From Blackburn
J From Glasgow Central to Liverpool Lime Street
K From Edinburgh

Table T082-R

Saturdays

21 December to 16 May

Barrow-in-Furness, Blackpool North, Preston, Southport, Kirkby and Wigan - Bolton - Manchester

	NT	NT	NT	NT	NT	NT	TP	NT	NT	NT	NT	NT	NT	NT	NT	NT	NT	NT	NT	TP	NT	NT
			◇			◇	◇1		◇						◇	◇			◇	◇1		◇
	A			B	C		D ✠		E	F	G		A			H	B	C		I ✠		E
Barrow-in-Furness d			13 53												14 46							
Roose d															14 50							
Dalton d															14 56							
Ulverston d			14 09												15 04							
Cark d															15 12							
Kents Bank d															15 16							
Grange-over-Sands d			14 21												15 20							
Arnside d			14 27												15 25							
Silverdale d															15 30							
Carnforth d			14 37												15 37	15 59						
Windermere 83 d																						
Oxenholme Lake District 65 d							15 12															
Lancaster 6 65 a			14 46				15 26								15 45	16 08						
d			14 47				15 27								15 46					16 27		
Blackpool North 97 d						14 58					15 27								15 58			
Layton 97 d											15 30											
Poulton-le-Fylde 97 d						15 03					15 34								16 03			
Kirkham & Wesham 97 d											15 43											
Preston 8 65,97 a			15 08			15 21	15 45				15 53				16 06				16 21	16 45		
d		15 04	15 10			15 23	15 46				15 55			16 04	16 08				16 23	16 46		
Leyland d		15 10				15 28								16 10					16 28			
Buckshaw Parkway d		15 15				15 33					16 03			16 15					16 33			
Chorley d		15 19				15 37					16 07			16 19					16 37			
Adlington (Lancashire) d		15 24												16 24								
Blackrod d		15 28												16 28								
Horwich Parkway d		15 32				15 45					16 15			16 32					16 45			
Lostock d		15 36				15 49								16 36					16 49			
Southport d	14 36							15 17					15 31								16 17	
Meols Cop d	14 41							15 22					15 36								16 22	
Bescar Lane d													15 41									
New Lane d													15 45									
Burscough Bridge d	14 50							15 31					15 48								16 31	
Hoscar d													15 51									
Parbold d	14 54							15 36					15 54								16 36	
Appley Bridge d	14 59							15 40					15 59								16 40	
Gathurst d	15 02							15 44					16 02								16 44	
Kirkby d												15 35										
Rainford d												15 43										
Upholland d												15 47										
Orrell d												15 51										
Pemberton d												15 54										
Wigan Wallgate a	15 07							15 48				15 59	16 07								16 48	
d	15 08			15 23				15 50	15 56			16 01	16 08				16 23				16 50	16 56
Wigan North Western d			15 24												16 23							
Ince d												16 04										
Hindley d	15 13			15 28				15 55				16 07	16 13				16 28				16 55	
Westhoughton d	15 18							16 00					16 18								17 00	
Bolton a	15 26	15 41				15 54	16s04	16 09			16 22		16 26	16 41					16 54	17s04	17 10	
d	15 26	15 41			15 49	15 54		16 10		16 19	16 22		16 26	16 41				16 49	16 54		17 10	
Moses Gate d	15 29												16 29									
Farnworth d	15 32												16 32									
Kearsley d	15 34												16 34									
Clifton d																						
Daisy Hill d				15 32					16 04			16 12					16 32					17 04
Hag Fold d				15 35								16 15					16 35					
Atherton d				15 38					16 08			16 18					16 38					17 08
Walkden d				15 44					16 14			16 24					16 44					17 14
Moorside d												16 28										
Swinton d				15 49								16 31					16 49					
Salford Crescent a	15 44	15 53		15 56	16 00	16 05		16 21	16 28	16 32	16 36	16 39	16 44	16 53			16 56	17 00	17 05		17 22	17 26
d	15 45	15 53		15 57	16 01	16 06		16 22	16 28	16 33	16 36	16 40	16 45	16 53			16 57	17 01	17 06		17 22	17 26
Salford Central d	15 47	15 56		15 59	16 04				16 32	16 36		16 43	16 47	16 56			16 59	17 04				17 29
Manchester Victoria ⇌ a	15 50	15 59		16 02	16 07				16 35	16 41		16 46	16 50	16 59			17 02	17 07				17 32
Rochdale 41 a				16 17	16 29				16 50	17 10							17 17	17 29				17 50
Deansgate ⇌ a						16 09		16 29			16 40								17 09		17 29	
Manchester Oxford Road a			15 54			16 11	16 20	16 32			16 42				16 54				17 11	17 20	17 32	
Manchester Piccadilly 10 ⇌ a			15 58			16 15	16 24	16 36			16 45				16 58				17 15	17 24	17 36	
Stockport 84 a								16 51			17 02										17 51	
Alderley Edge a								17 08													18 08	
Heald Green 85 a			16 12			16 29									17 12				17 29			
Manchester Airport 85 ⇌✈ a			16 18			16 35	16 46								17 18				17 35	17 46		

A To Stalybridge
B To Blackburn
C From Blackburn
D From Glasgow Central
E To Leeds
F From Clitheroe
G To Hazel Grove
H From Leeds to Morecambe
I From Edinburgh

Table T082-R

Saturdays

21 December to 16 May

Barrow-in-Furness, Blackpool North, Preston, Southport, Kirkby and Wigan - Bolton - Manchester

	NT	NT	NT	NT	NT	NT	NT	NT	NT	NT	TP	NT	NT	NT	NT	NT	NT	NT	NT	NT	NT
						◇				◇	◇1		◇						◇		
	A	B		C			D	E	F		G ✠		H	A	B		C				D
Barrow-in-Furness d								15 50											16 45	17 19	
Roose d								15 54											16 49	17 23	
Dalton d								16 00											16 56	17 29	
Ulverston d								16 08											17 04	17 37	
Cark d								16 16											17 12	17 45	
Kents Bank d								16 20											17 16		
Grange-over-Sands d								16 24											17 20	17 52	
Arnside d								16 30											17 25	17 58	
Silverdale d								16 35											17 30	18 03	
Carnforth d								16 42											17 37	18 10	
Windermere 83 d						16 00															
Oxenholme Lake District 65 d						16 27					17 12										
Lancaster 6 65 a						16 43		16 52			17 26								17 45	18 20	
d						16 45					17 27								17 46		
Blackpool North 97 d		16 27								16 53					17 27						
Layton 97 d		16 30								16 56					17 30						
Poulton-le-Fylde 97 d		16 34								17 00					17 34						
Kirkham & Wesham 97 d		16 43								17 09					17 43						
Preston 8 65,97 a		16 53				17 06				17 19	17 44				17 53				18 06		
d		16 55			17 04	17 08				17 21	17 46				17 55			18 04	18 08		
Leyland d					17 10					17 26								18 10			
Buckshaw Parkway d		17 03			17 15					17 31					18 03			18 15			
Chorley d		17 07			17 19					17 34					18 07			18 19			
Adlington (Lancashire) d					17 24					17 39								18 24			
Blackrod d					17 28					17 42								18 28			
Horwich Parkway d		17 15			17 32					17 46					18 15			18 32			
Lostock d					17 36					17 49								18 36			
Southport d				16 36								17 16					17 31				
Meols Cop d				16 41								17 21					17 36				
Bescar Lane d																	17 41				
New Lane d																	17 45				
Burscough Bridge d				16 50								17 30					17 48				
Hoscar d																	17 51				
Parbold d				16 54								17 35					17 54				
Appley Bridge d				16 59								17 39					17 59				
Gathurst d				17 02								17 43					18 02				
Kirkby d			16 36													17 35					
Rainford d			16 44													17 43					
Upholland d			16 48													17 47					
Orrell d			16 52													17 51					
Pemberton d			16 55													17 54					
Wigan Wallgate a			17 01	17 07								17 47				17 59	18 07				
d			17 03	17 08								17 49	17 56			18 01	18 08				18 23
Wigan North Western d						17 23	17 23												18 23		
Ince d			17 06									17 52				18 04					
Hindley d			17 09				17 28					17 56				18 07	18 13				18 28
Westhoughton d				17 17								18 01					18 18				
Bolton a		17 21		17 25	17 41					17 54	18s04	18 09			18 22		18 26	18 41			
d	17 19	17 22		17 26	17 41				17 49	17 55		18 10		18 18	18 22		18 26	18 41			
Moses Gate d				17 29													18 29				
Farnworth d				17 31													18 32				
Kearsley d				17 33													18 34				
Clifton d																					
Daisy Hill d			17 14				17 32						18 04			18 12					18 32
Hag Fold d			17 17				17 35									18 15					18 35
Atherton d			17 20				17 38						18 08			18 18					18 38
Walkden d			17 26				17 44						18 14			18 24					18 44
Moorside d			17 29													18 28					
Swinton d			17 32				17 49									18 31					18 49
Salford Crescent a	17 32	17 35	17 40	17 44	17 53		17 56		18 01	18 06		18 22	18 27	18 32	18 36	18 39	18 44	18 53			18 56
d	17 32	17 36	17 40	17 44	17 53		17 57		18 01	18 06		18 23	18 28	18 33	18 36	18 40	18 45	18 53			18 57
Salford Central d	17 36		17 43	17 47	17 56		17 59		18 04				18 31	18 36		18 43	18 47	18 56			18 59
Manchester Victoria ⇌ a	17 41		17 46	17 50	17 59		18 02		18 07				18 34	18 41		18 46	18 50	18 59			19 02
Rochdale 41 a	18 04						18 17		18 29				18 50	19 04							19 17
Deansgate ⇌ a		17 39								18 10		18 29			18 40						
Manchester Oxford Road a		17 41				17 55				18 12	18 19	18 32			18 42				18 54		
Manchester Piccadilly 10 ⇌ a		17 45				17 59				18 15	18 23	18 36			18 45				18 58		
Stockport 84 a		18 02										18 51			19 02						
Alderley Edge a												19 08									
Heald Green 85 a						18 13				18 29									19 12		
Manchester Airport 85 ⇌✈ a						18 18				18 35	18 46								19 17		

A From Clitheroe
B To Hazel Grove
C To Stalybridge
D To Blackburn
E From Carlisle
F From Blackburn
G From Glasgow Central
H To Leeds

Table T082-R

Saturdays

21 December to 16 May

Barrow-in-Furness, Blackpool North, Preston, Southport, Kirkby and Wigan - Bolton - Manchester

		NT	NT	TP	NT	NT	NT	NT	NT	NT	NT	TP	NT	NT	NT	NT	NT	TP	NT	NT	NT	NT	NT
			◇	◇■		◇						◇■		◇			◇	◇■		◇			
		A		B		C	A	D		E		F		G	H	I		J		C	A	D	E
Barrow-in-Furness	d												18 04										
Roose	d												18 08										
Dalton	d												18 14										
Ulverston	d												18 23										
Cark	d												18 30										
Kents Bank	d												18 34										
Grange-over-Sands	d												18 38										
Arnside	d												18 44										
Silverdale	d												18 49										
Carnforth	d												18 56	19 10									
Windermere 83	d																						
Oxenholme Lake District 65	d			18 14														19 12					
Lancaster ■ 65	a			18 28									19 06	19 19				19 26					
	d			18 29								18 54						19 27					
Blackpool North 97	d		17 56					18 27									18 56					19 25	
Layton 97	d							18 30														19 28	
Poulton-le-Fylde 97	d		18 01					18 34									19 02					19 32	
Kirkham & Wesham 97	d							18 43														19 41	
Preston ■ 65,97	a		18 19	18 47				18 53				19 13					19 21	19 45				19 51	
	d		18 21	18 48				18 55			19 08						19 23	19 47				19 53	
Leyland	d		18 26								19 13						19 28						
Buckshaw Parkway	d		18 30					19 03			19 17						19 33					20 01	
Chorley	d		18 34					19 07			19 21						19 37					20 05	
Adlington (Lancashire)	d		18 38								19 25											20 09	
Blackrod	d		18 42								19 29											20 12	
Horwich Parkway	d		18 45					19 15			19 32						19 45					20 15	
Lostock	d		18 49								19 36						19 49						
Southport	d				18 17					18 36									19 17				
Meols Cop	d				18 22					18 41									19 22				
Bescar Lane	d																						
New Lane	d																						
Burscough Bridge	d				18 31					18 50									19 31				
Hoscar	d																						
Parbold	d				18 36					18 54									19 36				
Appley Bridge	d				18 40					18 59									19 40				
Gathurst	d				18 44					19 02									19 44				
Kirkby	d								18 35														
Rainford	d								18 43														
Upholland	d								18 47														
Orrell	d								18 51														
Pemberton	d								18 54														
Wigan Wallgate	a				18 48				19 00	19 07									19 48				
	d				18 50	18 56			19 02	19 08					19 23				19 50				
Wigan North Western	d																			19 56			20 08
Ince	d								19 05														
Hindley	d				18 55				19 08	19 13					19 28				19 55				20 13
Westhoughton	d				19 00					19 18									20 00				20 18
Bolton	a		18 54		19 10			19 21		19 26	19 41						19 54	20s05	20 09			20 22	20 26
	d	18 49	18 54		19 10		19 18	19 22		19 26	19 41					19 49	19 54		20 10		20 18	20 22	20 26
Moses Gate	d									19 29													20 29
Farnworth	d									19 32													20 32
Kearsley	d									19 34													20 34
Clifton	d																						
Daisy Hill	d					19 04			19 13						19 32					20 05			
Hag Fold	d								19 16						19 35								
Atherton	d					19 08			19 19						19 38					20 09			
Walkden	d					19 14			19 25						19 44					20 15			
Moorside	d								19 29														
Swinton	d								19 32						19 49								
Salford Crescent	a	19 01	19 05		19 21	19 26	19 31	19 35	19 39	19 44	19 53				19 56	20 02	20 05		20 21	20 27	20 31	20 35	20 44
	d	19 01	19 06		19 22	19 26	19 32	19 35	19 40	19 45	19 53				19 57	20 02	20 06		20 21	20 27	20 32	20 35	20 45
Salford Central	d	19 04				19 29	19 35		19 43	19 47	19 56				19 59	20 05				20 30	20 36		20 47
Manchester Victoria ⇌	a	19 07				19 32	19 40		19 46	19 50	19 59				20 02	20 08				20 33	20 41		20 50
Rochdale 41	a	19 29				19 49	20 03								20 17	20 30				20 50	21 04		
Deansgate ⇌	a		19 09		19 29												20 09		20 29				
Manchester Oxford Road	a		19 11	19 19	19 32			19 41									20 11	20 20	20 31			20 41	
Manchester Piccadilly ■ ⇌	a		19 15	19 24	19 36			19 45									20 15	20 24	20 35			20 45	
Stockport 84	a				19 51			20 02											20 51			21 02	
Alderley Edge	a				20 08														21 08				
Heald Green 85	a		19 29														20 29						
Manchester Airport 85 ⇌✈	a		19 35	19 48													20 34	20 48					

A From Clitheroe
B From Edinburgh
C To Leeds
D To Hazel Grove
E To Stalybridge
F From Glasgow Central to Liverpool Lime Street
G From Leeds to Morecambe
H To Blackburn
I From Blackburn
J From Glasgow Central

Table T082-R

Saturdays

21 December to 16 May

Barrow-in-Furness, Blackpool North, Preston, Southport, Kirkby and Wigan - Bolton - Manchester

		NT	NT	NT	NT	TP	NT	NT	NT	NT	NT	NT	NT	TP	NT	NT	NT	NT	NT	NT	NT	NT
		◇		◇		◇■					◇		◇	◇■	◇					◇		
			A			B			C	D		E		F	G	H		E	C		I	H
Barrow-in-Furness	d				19 03						19 34										20 42	20 42
Roose	d				19 07						19 38										20 46	20 46
Dalton	d				19 13						19 44										20 52	20 52
Ulverston	d				19 21						19 53										21 01	21 01
Cark	d				19 29						20 00										21 08	21 08
Kents Bank	d				19 33						20 04										21 12	21 12
Grange-over-Sands	d				19 37						20 08										21 16	21 16
Arnside	d				19 43						20 14										21 22	21 22
Silverdale	d				19 47						20 19										21 27	21 27
Carnforth	d				19 55						20 26				21 09						21 34	21 34
Windermere 83	d	18 55														20 43						
Oxenholme Lake District 65	d	19 17				20 13								20 56		21 02						
Lancaster ■ 65	a	19 33			20 03	20 27					20 34			21 10	21 17	21 26					21 42	21 46
	d	19 34			20 03	20 28					20 35			21 11							21 43	
Blackpool North 97	d			19 58						20 24			20 58							21 21		
Layton 97	d									20 27										21 24		
Poulton-le-Fylde 97	d			20 03						20 31			21 03							21 28		
Kirkham & Wesham 97	d									20 40										21 37		
Preston ■ 65,97	a	19 55		20 21	20 26	20 45				20 51	20 56		21 21	21 29						21 48	22 05	
	d	20 09		20 23		20 47				20 53	21 05		21 23	21 36						21 49		
Leyland	d			20 28									21 28							21 55		
Buckshaw Parkway	d			20 33						21 01			21 33							21 59		
Chorley	d			20 37						21 04			21 37							22 03		
Adlington (Lancashire)	d									21 09										22 08		
Blackrod	d									21 12										22 11		
Horwich Parkway	d			20 45						21 15			21 45							22 15		
Lostock	d			20 49									21 49							22 19		
Southport	d						20 13											21 14				
Meols Cop	d						20 18											21 19				
Bescar Lane	d						20 23															
New Lane	d						20 27															
Burscough Bridge	d						20 30											21 28				
Hoscar	d						20 33															
Parbold	d						20 37											21 32				
Appley Bridge	d						20 41											21 37				
Gathurst	d						20 45											21 40				
Kirkby	d		19 46																			
Rainford	d		19 54																			
Upholland	d		19 58																			
Orrell	d		20 02																			
Pemberton	d		20 05																			
Wigan Wallgate	a		20 10				20 49											21 45				
	d		20 19				20 51	20 56				21 15						21 46				
Wigan North Western	d	20 25															21 38					
Ince	d		20 22														21 42					
Hindley	d		20 26				20 56					21 21					21 46	21 52				
Westhoughton	d						21 01					21 26						21 56				
Bolton	a			20 54		21s05	21 09			21 21		21 34	21 54					22 04		22 24		
	d			20 54			21 10		21 18	21 22		21 34	21 54					22 05	22 19	22 24		
Moses Gate	d											21 37						22 08				
Farnworth	d											21 39						22 10				
Kearsley	d											21 41						22 12				
Clifton	d																					
Daisy Hill	d		20 30					21 04									21 50					
Hag Fold	d		20 33														21 53					
Atherton	d		20 36					21 08									21 56					
Walkden	d		20 42					21 14									22 02					
Moorside	d		20 46														22 06					
Swinton	d		20 49														22 09					
Salford Crescent	a		20 56	21 05			21 21	21 26	21 30	21 33		21 52	22 05				22 16	22 22	22 32	22 36		
	d		20 57	21 06			21 22	21 26	21 30	21 34		21 54	22 06				22 17	22 23	22 33	22 36		
Salford Central	d		21 00				21 24	21 29	21 33			22 01					22 20	22 25	22 41			
Manchester Victoria ⇌	a		21 03				21 27	21 32	21 36			22 04					22 23	22 28	22 45			
Rochdale 41	a		21 17						22 00													
Deansgate ⇌	a			21 09									22 09									
Manchester Oxford Road	a	20 55		21 11		21 20				21 38	21 42		22 11	22 13						22 42		
Manchester Piccadilly ■ ⇌	a	20 59		21 15		21 24				21 44	21 48		22 15	22 19						22 47		
Stockport 84	a									22 02												
Alderley Edge	a																					
Heald Green 85	a	21 15		21 29									22 30							23 02		
Manchester Airport 85 ⇌✈	a	21 20		21 34		21 47					22 04		22 34	22 39						23 06		

A To Blackburn
B From Edinburgh
C From Clitheroe
D To Hazel Grove
E To Stalybridge
F From Glasgow Central
G From Leeds
H from 11 January until 15 February, from 4 April
I from 22 February until 28 March

Table T082-R

Saturdays
21 December to 16 May

Barrow-in-Furness, Blackpool North, Preston, Southport, Kirkby and Wigan - Bolton - Manchester

Station		NT A	NT	NT ◇	NT B	NT C	NT	NT D	NT ◇ B	NT ◇ E	NT 🚌	NT B	NT 🚌
Barrow-in-Furness	d				21 46	21 46							
Roose	d				21 50	21 50							
Dalton	d				21 56	21 56							
Ulverston	d				22 04	22 04							
Cark	d				22 12	22 12							
Kents Bank	d				22 16	22 16							
Grange-over-Sands	d				22 20	22 20							
Arnside	d				22 26	22 26							
Silverdale	d				22 30	22 30							
Carnforth	d				22 38	22 38							
Windermere 83	d											22 26	22 25
Oxenholme Lake District 65	d											22 47	23 10
Lancaster 6 65	a				22 46	22 49						23 05	23 55
	d				22 46						22 55	23 06	23 55
Blackpool North 97	d			22 21					23 02	23 02			
Layton 97	d			22 24					23 05	23 05			
Poulton-le-Fylde 97	d			22 28					23 09	23 09			
Kirkham & Wesham 97	d			22 37					23 18	23 18			
Preston 8 65,97	a			22 47	23 09				23 28	23 28	23 35	23 29	00 35
	d			22 49					23 30	23 30			
Leyland	d			22 54					23 35	23 35			
Buckshaw Parkway	d			22 58					23 39	23 40			
Chorley	d			23 02					23 43	23 43			
Adlington (Lancashire)	d			23 07					23 48	23 48			
Blackrod	d			23 10					23 51	23 51			
Horwich Parkway	d			23 14					23 55	23 55			
Lostock	d			23 18					23 59	23 59			
Southport	d		22 18				23 10						
Meols Cop	d		22 23				23 15						
Bescar Lane	d		22 28										
New Lane	d		22 32										
Burscough Bridge	d		22 35				23 24						
Hoscar	d		22 38										
Parbold	d		22 41				23 28						
Appley Bridge	d		22 46				23 33						
Gathurst	d		22 49				23 36						
Kirkby	d												
Rainford	d												
Upholland	d												
Orrell	d												
Pemberton	d												
Wigan Wallgate	a		22 54				23 43						
	d		22 55										
Wigan North Western	d	22 50											
Ince	d		22 58										
Hindley	d	22 56	23 02										
Westhoughton	d	23 00											
Bolton	a	23 08		23 23					00 04	00 04			
	d	23 09		23 23				23 46	00 04	00 04			
Moses Gate	d												
Farnworth	d												
Kearsley	d												
Clifton	d												
Daisy Hill	d		23 06										
Hag Fold	d		23 09										
Atherton	d		23 11										
Walkden	d		23 17										
Moorside	d		23 20										
Swinton	d		23 23										
Salford Crescent	a	23 21	23 32	23 34				23 57	00 16	00 16			
	d	23 21	23 33	23 35				00 01	00 17	00 17			
Salford Central	d	23 24	23 36										
Manchester Victoria 🚋	a	23 27	23 39					00 07					
Rochdale 41	a												
Deansgate 🚋	a												
Manchester Oxford Road	a			23 39									
Manchester Piccadilly 10 🚋	a			23 43					00 26	00 26			
Stockport 84	a												
Alderley Edge	a												
Heald Green 85	a			00 05					00 39	00 39			
Manchester Airport 85 🚋✈	a			00 10					00 44	00 44			

A To Stalybridge
B from 22 February until 28 March
C from 11 January until 15 February, from 4 April
D From Clitheroe
E until 15 February, from 4 April

NRT DECEMBER 19 EDITION

Table T082-R

Sundays
15 December to 10 May

Barrow-in-Furness, Blackpool North, Preston, Southport, Kirkby and Wigan - Bolton - Manchester

Station		NT A	NT ◇ B	NT 🚌	NT 🚌	NT C	NT D	NT ◇ E	NT ◇ F	NT G	NT	NT C	TP ◇[1] H	NT ◇ I	NT ◇ J	NT D	NT ◇	NT K	NT	NT C	NT ◇ J	NT ◇ L	NT ◇ F
Barrow-in-Furness	d																					08 40	
Roose	d																					08 44	
Dalton	d																					08 50	
Ulverston	d																					08 58	
Cark	d																					09 06	
Kents Bank	d																					09 10	
Grange-over-Sands	d																					09 14	
Arnside	d																					09 20	
Silverdale	d																					09 24	
Carnforth	d																					09 32	
Windermere 83	d																						
Oxenholme Lake District 65	d																						
Lancaster 6 65	a																					09 40	
	d																					09 40	
Blackpool North 97	d			03 20	05 20			07 52	07 52		08 21						09 00		09 21				
Layton 97	d										08 24								09 24				
Poulton-le-Fylde 97	d										08 27						09 06		09 28				
Kirkham & Wesham 97	d										08 36						09 15		09 37				
Preston 8 65,97	a							08 14	08 14		08 47						09 25		09 47			10 02	
	d			04u00	06u00			08 18	08 18		08 48		08 54	09 12	09 12		09 27		09 49		10 08	10 08	10 08
Leyland	d										08 54								09 56				
Buckshaw Parkway	d							08 25	08 25		08 58						09 34		10 00				
Chorley	d							08 29	08 29		09 02						09 38		10 04				
Adlington (Lancashire)	d										09 07								10 08				
Blackrod	d										09 10								10 12				
Horwich Parkway	d							08 37	08 37		09 14						09 46		10 16				
Lostock	d										09 18								10 19				
Southport	d											08 42								09 38			
Meols Cop	d											08 48								09 44			
Bescar Lane	d																						
New Lane	d																						
Burscough Bridge	d											08 56								09 52			
Hoscar	d																						
Parbold	d											09 01								09 57			
Appley Bridge	d											09 05								10 01			
Gathurst	d											09 09								10 05			
Kirkby	d																						
Rainford	d																						
Upholland	d																						
Orrell	d																						
Pemberton	d																						
Wigan Wallgate	a											09 14								10 10			
	d					08 12						09 15								10 15			
Wigan North Western	d						08 20						09a07	09 26	09 26	09 27					10 24	10 24	10 24
Ince	d					08 15						09 18								10 18			
Hindley	d					08 18	08 26					09 22				09 32				10 22			
Westhoughton	d						08 31									09 37							
Bolton	a						08 39	08 44	08 44		09 23					09 45	09 53		10 24				
	d		00 04	04u35	06u35		08 39	08 45	08 45	09 19	09 23					09 45	09 53	10 19	10 25				
Moses Gate	d																						
Farnworth	d																						
Kearsley	d																						
Clifton	d																						
Daisy Hill	d					08 23						09 26								10 26			
Hag Fold	d					08 26						09 29								10 29			
Atherton	d					08 29						09 32								10 32			
Walkden	d					08 34						09 37								10 37			
Moorside	d					08 38						09 41								10 41			
Swinton	d					08 41						09 44								10 44			
Salford Crescent	a		00 16			08 51	08 55			09 32	09 35	09 51				09 57	10 05	10 33	10 37	10 51			
	d	00 01	00 17			08 52	08 55			09 32	09 36	09 52				09 58	10 05	10 33	10 37	10 52			
Salford Central	d					08 54	08 58			09 35	09 38	09 55				10 01		10 36	10 41	10 55			
Manchester Victoria 🚋	a	00 07				08 57	09 01			09 38	09 41	09 58				10 05		10 39	10 44	10 59			
Rochdale 41	a					09 19						10 20								11 21			
Deansgate 🚋	a							09 00	09 02								10 09						
Manchester Oxford Road	a							09 02	09 04					09 57	09 57		10 13				10 53	10 55	10 55
Manchester Piccadilly 10 🚋	a		00 26	05b00	07b00									10 00	10 00						11 01		
Stockport 84	a																						
Alderley Edge	a																						
Heald Green 85	a		00 39											10 18	10 19						11 16		
Manchester Airport 85 🚋✈	a		00 44	05 25	07 25									10 22	10 23						11 21		

A not 15 December. From Clitheroe
B not 15 December. From Blackpool North
C To Blackburn
D To Stalybridge
E until 5 January, from 23 February
F from 12 January until 16 February
G From Blackburn
H To Liverpool Lime Street
I until 29 March
J from 5 April
K From Clitheroe
L until 5 January, from 23 February until 29 March
b Stops to pick up only

Table T082-R

Sundays

15 December to 10 May

Barrow-in-Furness, Blackpool North, Preston, Southport, Kirkby and Wigan - Bolton - Manchester

		NT A	NT B	NT C	NT ◇ D	NT ◇	NT E	NT	TP ◇1 F	NT ◇	NT G	NT A	NT ◇	NT E	NT	TP ◇1 H	TP ◇1 I	NT ◇ J	NT ◇ K	NT G	NT ◇ L	NT A	NT ◇ J
Barrow-in-Furness	d		09 05	09 05						09 47								10 47	10 47				
Roose	d			09 09						09 51								10 51	10 51				
Dalton	d			09 15						09 57								10 57	10 57				
Ulverston	d		09 22	09 24						10 05								11 06	11 06				
Cark	d			09 31						10 13								11 13	11 13				
Kents Bank	d			09 35						10 17								11 17	11 17				
Grange-over-Sands	d		09 34	09 39						10 21								11 21	11 21				
Arnside	d		09 40	09 45						10 27								11 27	11 27				
Silverdale	d			09 50						10 31								11 32	11 32				
Carnforth	d		09 51	09a57	10 16					10 39								11 40	11 40		12 10		
Windermere 83	d																						
Oxenholme Lake District 65	d								10 26							11 13	11 23						
Lancaster 6 65	a		10 01		10 27				10 41	10 47						11 27	11 37	11 48	11 48		12 19		
	d								10 42	10 47						11 28	11 38	11 49	11 49				
Blackpool North 97	d					10 00		10 15					11 00		11 20								12 00
Layton 97	d							10 18							11 23								
Poulton-le-Fylde 97	d					10 06		10 21					11 06		11 26								12 06
Kirkham & Wesham 97	d					10 15		10 30					11 15		11 35								12 15
Preston 8 65,97	a					10 25		10 41	11 01	11 08			11 25		11 48	11 46	11 56	12 09	12 09				12 25
	d					10 27		10 42	11 02	11 09			11 27		11 51	11 57	11 57	12 11	12 11				12 27
Leyland	d							10 47							11 56								
Buckshaw Parkway	d					10 34		10 52					11 34		12 00								12 34
Chorley	d					10 38		10 56					11 38		12 04			12 22	12 22				12 38
Adlington (Lancashire)	d							11 00							12 09								
Blackrod	d							11 04							12 12								
Horwich Parkway	d					10 46		11 08					11 46		12 16								12 46
Lostock	d							11 11							12 20								
Southport	d										10 38									11 38			
Meols Cop	d										10 44									11 44			
Bescar Lane	d																						
New Lane	d																						
Burscough Bridge	d										10 52									11 52			
Hoscar	d																						
Parbold	d										10 57									11 57			
Appley Bridge	d										11 01									12 01			
Gathurst	d										11 05									12 05			
Kirkby	d																						
Rainford	d																						
Upholland	d																						
Orrell	d																						
Pemberton	d																						
Wigan Wallgate	a										11 10									12 10			
	d										11 15									12 15			
Wigan North Western	d	10 27								11 24		11 27										12 27	
Ince	d										11 18									12 18			
Hindley	d	10 32									11 22	11 32								12 22		12 32	
Westhoughton	d	10 37										11 37										12 37	
Bolton	a	10 45				10 53		11 16				11 45	11 53		12 25			12 34	12 34			12 45	12 53
	d	10 45				10 53	11 19	11 22				11 45	11 53	12 19	12 25			12 35	12 35			12 45	12 53
Moses Gate	d																						
Farnworth	d																						
Kearsley	d																						
Clifton	d																						
Daisy Hill	d										11 26									12 26			
Hag Fold	d										11 29									12 29			
Atherton	d										11 32									12 32			
Walkden	d										11 37									12 37			
Moorside	d										11 41									12 41			
Swinton	d										11 44									12 44			
Salford Crescent	a	10 57				11 05	11 33	11 36			11 51	11 57	12 05	12 33	12 37			12 47	12 47	12 51		12 57	13 05
	d	10 58				11 05	11 33	11 37			11 52	11 58	12 05	12 33	12 37			12 47	12 47	12 52		12 58	13 05
Salford Central	d	11 01					11 36	11 41			11 55	12 01		12 36	12 41					12 55		13 01	
Manchester Victoria ⇌	a	11 05					11 39	11 44	11 50		12 00	12 05		12 39	12 44					13 00		13 04	
Rochdale 41	a										12 21									13 22			
Deansgate ⇌	a					11 09							12 09										13 09
Manchester Oxford Road	a					11 13				11 56			12 11					12 52	12 52				13 11
Manchester Piccadilly 10 ⇌	a									12 01						12 40	12 40	12 56	12 56				13 15
Stockport 84	a																						
Alderley Edge	a																						
Heald Green 85	a									12 15								13 10	13 12				13 27
Manchester Airport 85 ⇌✈	a									12 20						13 00	13 00	13 17	13 17				13 31

A To Stalybridge
B until 5 January, from 23 February until 29 March
C from 12 January until 16 February, from 5 April
D From Leeds to Morecambe
E From Clitheroe
F until 5 January, from 23 February until 29 March. From Glasgow Central
G To Blackburn
H until 5 January, from 23 February until 29 March. From Edinburgh
I from 12 January until 16 February, from 5 April. From Edinburgh
J from 5 April
K until 29 March
L From Leeds to Heysham Harbour

Table T082-R

Sundays

15 December to 10 May

Barrow-in-Furness, Blackpool North, Preston, Southport, Kirkby and Wigan - Bolton - Manchester

		NT ◇ A	TP ◇1 B	NT C	NT	TP ◇1 D	NT ◇	NT E	NT F	NT ◇	TP ◇1 G	NT C	NT	NT ◇	NT H	NT I	NT E	NT F	NT ◇	TP ◇1 B	NT C	NT
Barrow-in-Furness	d						11 37								12 53	13 17						
Roose	d						11 41								12 57	13 21						
Dalton	d						11 47								13 03	13 27						
Ulverston	d						11 56								13 11	13 35						
Cark	d						12 03															
Kents Bank	d						12 07															
Grange-over-Sands	d						12 11								13 24	13 48						
Arnside	d						12 17								13 30	13 54						
Silverdale	d						12 22								13 35	13 59						
Carnforth	d						12 30								13 42	14 06						
Windermere 83	d													13 08								
Oxenholme Lake District 65	d		12 13			12 18					13 12			13 28						14 12		
Lancaster 6 65	a		12 27			12 32	12 38				13 26			13 45	13 52	14 21				14 26		
	d		12 28			12 33	12 39				13 27			13 46						14 27		
Blackpool North 97	d	12 00			12 20					13 00			13 21						14 00			14 19
Layton 97	d				12 23								13 24									14 22
Poulton-le-Fylde 97	d	12 06			12 26					13 06			13 27						14 06			14 25
Kirkham & Wesham 97	d	12 15			12 35					13 15			13 36						14 15			14 34
Preston 8 65,97	a	12 25	12 45		12 46	12 52	13 00			13 25	13 44		13 47	14 07					14 25	14 45		14 45
	d	12 27	12 47		12 50	12 54	13 09			13 27	13 46		13 49	14 10					14 27	14 46		14 49
Leyland	d				12 55								13 54									14 54
Buckshaw Parkway	d	12 34			12 59					13 34			14 00						14 34			14 59
Chorley	d	12 38			13 03					13 38			14 04						14 38			15 03
Adlington (Lancashire)	d				13 07								14 08									15 08
Blackrod	d				13 11								14 12									15 11
Horwich Parkway	d	12 46			13 15					13 46			14 16						14 46			15 15
Lostock	d				13 19								14 19									15 19
Southport	d							12 38									13 38					
Meols Cop	d							12 44									13 44					
Bescar Lane	d																					
New Lane	d																					
Burscough Bridge	d							12 52									13 52					
Hoscar	d																					
Parbold	d							12 57									13 57					
Appley Bridge	d							13 01									14 01					
Gathurst	d							13 05									14 05					
Kirkby	d																					
Rainford	d																					
Upholland	d																					
Orrell	d																					
Pemberton	d																					
Wigan Wallgate	a							13 10									14 10					
	d							13 15									14 15					
Wigan North Western	d					13a07	13 23		13 26					14 24				14 27				
Ince	d							13 18									14 18					
Hindley	d							13 22	13 31								14 22	14 32				
Westhoughton	d								13 36									14 37				
Bolton	a	12 53	13s05		13 24				13 44	13 53	14s05		14 24					14 45	14 53	15s04		15 24
	d	12 53		13 19	13 24				13 44	13 53		14 19	14 25					14 45	14 53		15 19	15 25
Moses Gate	d																					
Farnworth	d																					
Kearsley	d																					
Clifton	d																					
Daisy Hill	d							13 26									14 26					
Hag Fold	d							13 29									14 29					
Atherton	d							13 32									14 32					
Walkden	d							13 37									14 37					
Moorside	d							13 41									14 41					
Swinton	d							13 44									14 44					
Salford Crescent	a	13 05		13 33	13 36			13 51	13 56	14 05		14 33	14 36				14 51	14 57	15 05		15 33	15 36
	d	13 05		13 33	13 37			13 52	13 57	14 05		14 33	14 37				14 52	14 58	15 05		15 33	15 37
Salford Central	d			13 36	13 41			13 55	14 02			14 36	14 41				14 55	15 01			15 36	15 41
Manchester Victoria ⇌	a			13 39	13 44			14 00	14 05			14 39	14 44				14 58	15 05			15 39	15 44
Rochdale 41	a							14 22									15 22					
Deansgate ⇌	a	13 09								14 09									15 09			
Manchester Oxford Road	a	13 11	13 21				13 56			14 11	14 22			14 57					15 11	15 20		
Manchester Piccadilly 10 ⇌	a	13 16	13 25				14 00			14 15	14 26			15 01					15 15	15 24		
Stockport 84	a																					
Alderley Edge	a																					
Heald Green 85	a	13 28					14 14			14 27				15 14					15 27			
Manchester Airport 85 ⇌✈	a	13 32	13 42				14 18			14 31	14 42			15 19					15 31	15 42		

A until 29 March
B From Edinburgh
C From Clitheroe
D From Glasgow Central to Liverpool Lime Street
E To Blackburn
F To Stalybridge
G From Glasgow Central
H until 5 January, from 23 February until 29 March. From Carlisle
I from 12 January until 16 February, from 5 April. From Carlisle

Table T082-R

Sundays
15 December to 10 May

Barrow-in-Furness, Blackpool North, Preston, Southport, Kirkby and Wigan - Bolton - Manchester

		NT	NT	NT	NT	NT	TP	NT	NT	NT	NT	NT	NT	TP	TP	NT	NT	NT	NT	NT	NT	NT	NT
		◇		◇		◇	◇1			◇			◇	◇1	◇1			◇			◇		◇
			A	B	C		D 🍴	E			A	C		F 🍴	G 🍴	E			H	A	B	C	
Barrow-in-Furness	d	13 47								14 44									15 50				
Roose	d	13 51								14 48									15 54				
Dalton	d	13 57								14 54									16 00				
Ulverston	d	14 05								15 02									16 08				
Cark	d	14 13								15 10									16 16				
Kents Bank	d	14 17								15 14									16 20				
Grange-over-Sands	d	14 21								15 18									16 24				
Arnside	d	14 27								15 24									16 30				
Silverdale	d	14 31								15 28									16 35				
Carnforth	d	14 39		15 10						15 36									16 42		17 10		
Windermere	83 d																	15 53					
Oxenholme Lake District	65 d						15 14							16 02	16 12			16 15					
Lancaster 6	65 a	14 47		15 21			15 28			15 44				16 16	16 26			16 33	16 52		17 21		
	d	14 47					15 29			15 47				16 17	16 27			16 46					
Blackpool North	97 d					15 00			15 20				16 00				16 19						17 00
Layton	97 d								15 23								16 22						
Poulton-le-Fylde	97 d					15 06			15 26				16 06				16 25						17 06
Kirkham & Wesham	97 d					15 15			15 35				16 15				16 34						17 15
Preston 8	65,97 a	15 08				15 25	15 46		15 47	16 08			16 25	16 36	16 44		16 45	17 06					17 25
	d	15 09				15 27	15 48		15 51	16 09			16 27	16 38	16 46		16 46	17 09					17 27
Leyland	d								15 56								16 52						
Buckshaw Parkway	d					15 34			16 00				16 34				16 57						17 34
Chorley	d					15 38			16 04				16 38				17 01						17 38
Adlington (Lancashire)	d								16 09								17 05						
Blackrod	d								16 12								17 09						
Horwich Parkway	d					15 46			16 16				16 46				17 13						17 46
Lostock	d								16 20								17 16						
Southport	d		14 38								15 38									16 38			
Meols Cop	d		14 44								15 44									16 44			
Bescar Lane	d																						
New Lane	d																						
Burscough Bridge	d		14 52								15 52									16 52			
Hoscar	d																						
Parbold	d		14 57								15 57									16 57			
Appley Bridge	d		15 01								16 01									17 01			
Gathurst	d		15 05								16 05									17 05			
Kirkby	d																						
Rainford	d																						
Upholland	d																						
Orrell	d																						
Pemberton	d																						
Wigan Wallgate	a		15 10								16 10									17 10			
	d		15 15								16 15									17 15			
Wigan North Western	d	15 23			15 27					16 23		16 27		16a50				17 23				17 27	
Ince	d		15 18								16 18									17 18			
Hindley	d		15 22		15 32						16 22	16 32								17 22		17 32	
Westhoughton	d				15 37							16 37										17 37	
Bolton	a				15 45	15 53	16s06		16 25			16 45	16 53		17s04		17 21					17 45	17 53
	d				15 45	15 53		16 19	16 25			16 45	16 53			17 19	17 23					17 45	17 53
Moses Gate	d																						
Farnworth	d																						
Kearsley	d																						
Clifton	d																						
Daisy Hill	d		15 26								16 26									17 26			
Hag Fold	d		15 29								16 29									17 29			
Atherton	d		15 32								16 32									17 32			
Walkden	d		15 37								16 37									17 37			
Moorside	d		15 41								16 41									17 41			
Swinton	d		15 44								16 44									17 44			
Salford Crescent	a		15 51		15 57	16 05		16 33	16 37		16 51	16 57	17 05			17 33	17 36			17 51		17 57	18 05
	d		15 52		15 58	16 05		16 33	16 37		16 52	16 58	17 06			17 33	17 37			17 52		17 58	18 05
Salford Central	d		15 55		16 01			16 36	16 41		16 55	17 01				17 36	17 41			17 55		18 01	
Manchester Victoria ⇌	a		16 00		16 05			16 39	16 44		17 00	17 05				17 39	17 44			18 00		18 05	
Rochdale	41 a		16 22								17 22									18 22			
Deansgate ⇌	a					16 09							17 09										18 09
Manchester Oxford Road	a	15 54				16 11	16 20			16 54			17 11		17 20			17 58					18 11
Manchester Piccadilly 10 ⇌	a	16 01				16 15	16 24			17 01			17 15		17 24			18 01					18 15
Stockport	84 a																						
Alderley Edge	a																						
Heald Green	85 a	16 15				16 27				17 15			17 27					18 15					18 27
Manchester Airport	85 ⇌✈ a	16 19				16 31	16 42			17 19			17 31		17 42			18 19					18 31

A To Blackburn
B From Leeds to Morecambe
C To Stalybridge
D From Glasgow Central
E From Clitheroe
F From Glasgow Central to Liverpool Lime Street
G From Edinburgh
H From Carlisle

NRT DECEMBER 19 EDITION

Table T082-R

Sundays
15 December to 10 May

Barrow-in-Furness, Blackpool North, Preston, Southport, Kirkby and Wigan - Bolton - Manchester

		NT	TP	NT	NT	NT	NT	NT	NT	TP	NT	NT	NT	NT	NT	NT	NT	TP	NT	NT	NT	NT
			◇1			◇			◇	◇1					◇		◇	◇1		◇		
		A	B 🍴	C	D		E	F		G 🍴	C	H		E	I	F		B 🍴				E
Barrow-in-Furness	d					16 44						17 46									18 51	
Roose	d					16 48						17 50									18 55	
Dalton	d					16 54						17 56									19 01	
Ulverston	d					17 02						18 05									19 09	
Cark	d					17 10						18 12									19 17	
Kents Bank	d					17 14						18 16									19 21	
Grange-over-Sands	d					17 18						18 20									19 25	
Arnside	d					17 24						18 27									19 31	
Silverdale	d					17 28						18 32									19 35	
Carnforth	d					17 36						18 41			19 08						19 43	
Windermere	83 d																			19 01		
Oxenholme Lake District	65 d		17 14							18 14								19 13		19 23		
Lancaster 6	65 a		17 28			17 44				18 28		18 50			19 21			19 27			19 51	
	d		17 29			17 47				18 29								19 28			19 51	
Blackpool North	97 d	17 20							18 00				18 21				19 00		19 20			
Layton	97 d	17 23											18 24						19 23			
Poulton-le-Fylde	97 d	17 26							18 06				18 27				19 06		19 26			
Kirkham & Wesham	97 d	17 35							18 15				18 36				19 15		19 35			
Preston 8	65,97 a	17 46	17 47		←	18 08			18 25	18 46			18 48				19 25	19 46	19 46	19 59	20 14	
	d	17 47	17 48			18 09			18 27	18 48			18 49				19 27	19 47	19 47	20 09		
Leyland	d	17 56			17 56								18 56						19 53			
Buckshaw Parkway	d	→			18 01				18 34				19 02				19 34		19 59			
Chorley	d				18 05				18 38				19 05				19 38		20 03			
Adlington (Lancashire)	d				18 09								19 10						20 08			
Blackrod	d				18 13								19 13						20 11			
Horwich Parkway	d				18 17				18 46				19 17				19 46		20 15			
Lostock	d				18 20								19 20						20 19			
Southport	d						17 38							18 38								19 38
Meols Cop	d						17 44							18 44								19 44
Bescar Lane	d																					
New Lane	d																					
Burscough Bridge	d						17 52							18 52								19 52
Hoscar	d																					
Parbold	d						17 57							18 57								19 57
Appley Bridge	d						18 01							19 01								20 01
Gathurst	d						18 05							19 05								20 05
Kirkby	d																					
Rainford	d																					
Upholland	d																					
Orrell	d																					
Pemberton	d																					
Wigan Wallgate	a						18 10							19 10								20 10
	d						18 15							19 15								20 15
Wigan North Western	d					18 23		18 27								19 27				20 23		
Ince	d						18 18							19 18								20 18
Hindley	d						18 22	18 32						19 22		19 32						20 22
Westhoughton	d							18 37								19 37						
Bolton	a		18s06		18 25			18 45	18 53	19s06			19 25			19 45	19 53	20s05	20 24			
	d			18 19	18 26			18 45	18 53		19 21		19 26			19 45	19 53		20 24			
Moses Gate	d																					
Farnworth	d																					
Kearsley	d																					
Clifton	d																					
Daisy Hill	d						18 26							19 26								20 26
Hag Fold	d						18 29							19 29								20 29
Atherton	d						18 32							19 32								20 32
Walkden	d						18 37							19 37								20 37
Moorside	d						18 41							19 41								20 41
Swinton	d						18 44							19 44								20 44
Salford Crescent	a			18 33	18 37		18 51	18 57	19 05		19 33		19 37	19 51		19 57	20 05		20 35			20 51
	d			18 33	18 37		18 52	18 58	19 05		19 33		19 37	19 52		19 58	20 05		20 36			20 52
Salford Central	d			18 36	18 41		18 55	19 01			19 36		19 41	19 55		20 01			20 40			20 55
Manchester Victoria ⇌	a			18 39	18 44		19 00	19 04			19 39		19 44	20 00		20 05			20 43			21 00
Rochdale	41 a						19 22							20 22								21 22
Deansgate ⇌	a								19 09								20 09					
Manchester Oxford Road	a		18 21			18 54			19 11	19 21							20 11	20 20		20 55		
Manchester Piccadilly 10 ⇌	a		18 25			19 01			19 15	19 25							20 15	20 24		20 59		
Stockport	84 a																					
Alderley Edge	a																					
Heald Green	85 a					19 15			19 27								20 28			21 12		
Manchester Airport	85 ⇌✈ a		18 42			19 19			19 31	19 42							20 32	20 44		21 17		

A To Manchester Victoria
B From Glasgow Central
C From Clitheroe
D From Blackpool North
E To Blackburn
F To Stalybridge
G From Edinburgh
H From Carlisle
I From Leeds to Morecambe

Table T082-R

Sundays
15 December to 10 May

Barrow-in-Furness, Blackpool North, Preston, Southport, Kirkby and Wigan - Bolton - Manchester

		NT	NT	NT	TP	NT	NT	NT	NT	NT	NT	TP	NT	NT	TP	NT	NT	NT	NT	TP	NT	NT	NT	NT	NT
				◇	◇1			◇			◇	◇1			◇1				◇	◇1					
		A	B		C	B			D	A		E	B		F			A		C		G	B		
Barrow-in-Furness	d							19 47								20 46									
Roose	d							19 51								20 50									
Dalton	d							19 57								20 56									
Ulverston	d							20 05								21 05									
Cark	d							20 13								21 12									
Kents Bank	d							20 17								21 16									
Grange-over-Sands	d							20 21								21 20									
Arnside	d							20 27								21 26									
Silverdale	d							20 31								21 31									
Carnforth	d							20 39								21 38									
Windermere 83	d																					21 44			
Oxenholme Lake District 65	d				20 14							20 53			21 17					22 12		22 16			
Lancaster 6 65	a				20 28			20 47				21 11			21 31	21 48				22 26		22 34			
	d				20 29			20 47				21 12			21 32					22 27		22 35			
Blackpool North 97	d			20 00			20 21				20 59			21 22					21 59		22 22				
Layton 97	d						20 24							21 25							22 25				
Poulton-le-Fylde 97	d			20 06			20 27				21 05			21 28					22 05		22 28				
Kirkham & Wesham 97	d			20 15			20 36				21 14			21 37					22 14		22 37				
Preston 8 65,97	a			20 25	20 46		20 49	21 08			21 24	21 30		21 48	21 50				22 24	22 45	22 48	22 57			
	d			20 27	20 48		20 51	21 09			21 26	21 32		21 51	21 51				22 26	22 46	22 49				
Leyland	d						20 56							21 58							22 55				
Buckshaw Parkway	d			20 34			21 01				21 33			22 02					22 34		22 59				
Chorley	d			20 38			21 04				21 37			22 06					22 38		23 03				
Adlington (Lancashire)	d						21 09							22 10							23 08				
Blackrod	d						21 12							22 14							23 11				
Horwich Parkway	d			20 46			21 16				21 45			22 17					22 46		23 15				
Lostock	d						21 19							22 21							23 19				
Southport	d								20 38								21 38								22 54
Meols Cop	d								20 44								21 44								22 59
Bescar Lane	d																								
New Lane	d																								
Burscough Bridge	d								20 52								21 52								23 08
Hoscar	d																								
Parbold	d								20 57								21 57								23 12
Appley Bridge	d								21 01								22 01								23 17
Gathurst	d								21 05								22 05								23 20
Kirkby	d																								
Rainford	d																								
Upholland	d																								
Orrell	d																								
Pemberton	d																								
Wigan Wallgate	a								21 10								22 10								23 25
	d								21 15								22 15								23 26
Wigan North Western	d	20 27						21 23		21 27		21a44						22 27						23 21	
Ince	d								21 18								22 18								23 29
Hindley	d	20 32							21 22	21 32							22 22	22 32						23 26	23 33
Westhoughton	d	20 37								21 37								22 37						23 31	
Bolton	a	20 45		20 53	21s06		21 24			21 45	21 52			22 26				22 45	22 53	23s04	23 24			23 40	
	d	20 45	20 49	20 53		21 19	21 25			21 45	21 52		22 19	22 26				22 45	22 53		23 24		23 36	23 40	
Moses Gate	d																								
Farnworth	d																								
Kearsley	d																								
Clifton	d																								
Daisy Hill	d								21 26								22 26								23 37
Hag Fold	d								21 29								22 29								23 40
Atherton	d								21 32								22 32								23 43
Walkden	d								21 37								22 37								23 48
Moorside	d								21 41								22 41								23 52
Swinton	d								21 44								22 44								23 54
Salford Crescent	a	20 57	21 01	21 05		21 33	21 36		21 51	21 57	22 04		22 33	22 37			22 51	22 57	23 05		23 36		23 48	23 52	00 01
	d	20 58	21 01	21 05		21 33	21 37		21 52	21 58	22 06		22 33	22 38			22 52	22 58	23 05		23 37		23 48	23 53	00 01
Salford Central	a	21 01	21 05			21 36	21 41		21 55	22 01			22 36	22 42			22 55	23 01			23 39		23 51	23 56	00 05
Manchester Victoria ⇌	a	21 05	21 08			21 39	21 44		22 00	22 05			22 39	22 45			23 00	23 04			23 42		23 54	23 59	00 08
Rochdale 41	a								22 22								23 23								
Deansgate ⇌	a			21 09							22 12								23 09						
Manchester Oxford Road	a			21 11	21 20			21 51			22 14				22 23				23 11	23 19					
Manchester Piccadilly 10 ⇌	a			21 15	21 23			21 55			22 19				22 27				23 17	23 23					
Stockport 84	a																								
Alderley Edge	a																								
Heald Green 85	a			21 27				22 09			22 31								23 30						
Manchester Airport 85 ⇌✈	a			21 31	21 42			22 13			22 36				22 43				23 35	23 40					

A To Stalybridge
B From Clitheroe
C From Edinburgh
D To Blackburn
E From Glasgow Central to Liverpool Lime Street
F From Glasgow Central
G until 29 March

Table T083-F

Oxenholme - Lake District - Windermere

Mondays to Fridays
16 December to 15 May

Miles			NT	NT	NT	NT	NT	NT	NT	NT	NT	NT	NT	NT	NT	NT	NT	NT	NT
							◇			◇			◇			◇			
			A				B			B			B			B			
0	**Oxenholme Lake District**	d	06 19	07 28	08 27	09 30	10 27	11 21	12 39	13 32	14 38	15 32	16 31	17 42	18 29	19 22	20 18	21 20	22 19
2¼	Kendal	d	06 23	07 32	08 31	09 34	10 31	11 25	12 43	13 36	14 42	15 37	16 36	17 46	18 33	19 27	20 22	21 24	22 23
4	Burneside	d	06 27	07 36	08 35	09 38	10 35	11 29	12 47	13 40		15 41	16 40	17 50	18 37	19 31	20 26	21 28	22 27
6½	Staveley	d	06 33	07 43	08 41	09 45	10 42	11 36	12 54	13 47		15 48	16 46	17 57	18 44	19 37	20 33	21 35	22 34
10	**Windermere**	a	06 39	07 49	08 47	09 51	10 49	11 42	13 00	13 53	14 55	15 54	16 53	18 03	18 50	19 43	20 39	21 41	22 40

Saturdays
21 December to 16 May

		NT	NT	NT	NT	NT	NT	NT	NT	NT	NT	NT	NT	NT	NT	NT	NT	NT	NT	NT
						◇			◇			◇			◇					
		A				B			B			B			B			C		C
																	🚌		🚌	
Oxenholme Lake District	d	06 19	07 28	08 27	09 40	10 33	11 21	12 39	13 32	14 38	15 32	16 31	17 36	18 29	19 21	20 18	21 15	21 16	22 00	22 01
Kendal	d	06 23	07 32	08 31	09 44	10 38	11 25	12 43	13 37	14 42	15 37	16 36	17 40	18 33	19 26	20 22	21 25	21 20	22 10	22 05
Burneside	d	06 27	07 36	08 35	09 48		11 29	12 47	13 41		15 41	16 40	17 44	18 37	19 30	20 26	21 35	21 24	22 20	22 09
Staveley	d	06 33	07 43	08 41	09 55		11 36	12 54	13 47		15 48	16 46	17 51	18 44	19 36	20 33	21 45	21 30	22 30	22 16
Windermere	a	06 39	07 49	08 47	10 01	10 52	11 42	13 00	13 54	14 55	15 54	16 53	17 57	18 50	19 42	20 39	21 55	21 36	22 40	22 22

Sundays
15 December to 10 May

		NT	NT	NT	NT	NT	NT	NT	NT	NT	NT	NT	NT	NT	NT	NT	NT
			◇	◇				◇			◇		◇				
		D 🚌	E	F	G			B			B		B			H	I
Oxenholme Lake District	d	09 45	10 30	11 07	11 18	12 01	12 47	13 32	14 23	15 28	16 31	17 39	18 30	19 41	20 28	21 17	21 18
Kendal	d	09 55	10 34	11 11	11 22	12 05	12 51	13 37	14 27	15 32	16 35	17 43	18 34	19 45	20 32	21 21	21 22
Burneside	d	10 05	10 38	11 15				13 41	14 31	15 36	16 39		18 38	19 49	20 36		21 26
Staveley	d	10 15	10 44	11 21				13 47	14 38	15 43	16 45		18 45	19 55	20 43		21 33
Windermere	a	10 25	10 51	11 28	11 35	12 19	13 04	13 54	14 44	15 49	16 53	17 56	18 51	20 02	20 49	21 34	21 39

A From Lancaster
B From Manchester Airport
C from 22 February until 28 March
D from 12 January until 16 February, from 5 April
E until 5 January, from 23 February until 29 March. From Manchester Airport
F from 12 January until 16 February, from 5 April. From Preston
G until 5 January, from 23 February until 29 March
H from 5 April
I until 29 March

Table T083-R

Windermere - Oxenholme - Lake District

Mondays to Fridays
16 December to 15 May

Miles			NT	NT	NT	NT	NT	NT	NT	NT	NT	NT	NT	NT	NT	NT	NT	NT	NT
						◇			◇			◇			◇				
						A			A			A			A				B
0	**Windermere**	d	06 43	07 55	08 51	09 56	10 57	11 47	13 06	13 58	14 59	16 00	17 06	18 07	18 55	19 48	20 44	21 46	22 45
3½	Staveley	d	06 49	08 01		10 02	11 03	11 53	13 12	14 04	15 05	16 06	17 12		19 01	19 54	20 50	21 52	22 51
6	Burneside	d	06 54	08 06		10 07	11 08	11 58	13 17	14 09	15 10	16 11	17 17		19 06	19 59	20 55	21 57	22 56
7¾	Kendal	d	06 58	08 10	09 03	10 10	11 12	12 02	13 21	14 13	15 14	16 14	17 21	18 19	19 10	20 03	20 59	22 01	22 59
10	**Oxenholme Lake District**	a	07 03	08 15	09 08	10 15	11 17	12 07	13 26	14 18	15 19	16 19	17 26	18 24	19 15	20 08	21 04	22 06	23 04

Saturdays
21 December to 16 May

		NT	NT	NT	NT	NT	NT	NT	NT	NT	NT	NT	NT	NT	NT	NT	NT	NT	NT	NT	NT
					◇			◇			◇			◇							
					A			A			A			A		C	D	D		B	E
																			🚌	🚌	
Windermere	d	06 43	07 55	08 51	10 08	10 57	11 47	13 06	13 58	14 59	16 00	17 06	18 01	18 55	19 48	20 43	20 44	21 40	21 40	22 25	22 26
Staveley	d	06 49	08 01		10 14	11 03	11 53	13 12	14 04	15 05	16 06	17 12	18 07	19 01	19 54		20 50		21 50	22 35	22 32
Burneside	d	06 54	08 06		10 19	11 08	11 58	13 17	14 09	15 10	16 11	17 17	18 12	19 06	19 59		20 55		22 00	22 45	22 37
Kendal	d	06 58	08 10	09 03	10 22	11 12	12 02	13 21	14 13	15 14	16 14	17 21	18 16	19 10	20 03	20 55	20 59	21 52	22 10	22 55	22 40
Oxenholme Lake District	a	07 03	08 15	09 08	10 27	11 17	12 07	13 26	14 18	15 19	16 19	17 26	18 21	19 15	20 08	21 00	21 04	21 57	22 25	23 10	22 45

Sundays
15 December to 10 May

		NT	NT	NT	NT	NT	NT	NT	NT	NT	NT	NT	NT	NT	NT	NT
						◇			◇			◇				
		F 🚌	G			A			A			A			H	I
Windermere	d	10 30	10 55	11 40	12 23	13 08	13 58	14 49	15 53	17 09	18 00	19 01	20 06	20 53	21 38	21 44
Staveley	d	10 40	11 01		12 29		14 04	14 55	15 59	17 15	18 06	19 07		20 59		21 50
Burneside	d	10 50	11 06		12 34		14 09	15 00	16 04	17 20	18 11	19 12		21 04		21 55
Kendal	d	11 00	11 09	11 52	12 38	13 20	14 13	15 04	16 08	17 24	18 15	19 16	20 18	21 08	21 50	21 59
Oxenholme Lake District	a	11 15	11 14	11 57	12 43	13 25	14 18	15 09	16 13	17 29	18 20	19 21	20 23	21 13	21 55	22 04

A To Manchester Airport
B To Preston
C from 11 January until 15 February, from 4 April. To Lancaster
D from 22 February until 28 March
E from 22 February until 28 March. To Preston
F from 12 January until 16 February, from 5 April
G until 5 January, from 23 February until 29 March
H from 5 April. To Preston
I until 29 March. To Preston

Table T084-F

Mondays to Fridays
16 December to 15 May

Stoke-on-Trent and Crewe - Manchester Airport, Stockport and Manchester

Miles	Miles	Miles		VT MO ◇1 A	NT MX B	NT MX ◇ C	NT MX	NT D	NT	VT ◇1	NT	NT E	TP ◇1 F	NT D	AW	NT G	NT H	NT B	XC ◇1	NT E	EM ◇ I	NT G
—	—	—	London Euston ⊖65 d																			
—	—	—	Birmingham New Street 68 d																05 57			
—	—	—	Wolverhampton 68 d																06 14			
—	—	—	Stafford 65,67 d																06 28			
0	—	—	**Stoke-on-Trent** 50 d																06 45			
3	—	—	Longport 50 d																			
6¼	—	—	Kidsgrove 50 d																			
—	0	—	**Crewe** d				00 44		05 44	06 11				06 16	06 27							
—	4¾	—	Sandbach d						05 51					06 23								
—	8½	—	Holmes Chapel d						05 56					06 28								
—	10½	—	Goostrey d						06 00													
—	14¼	—	Chelford d						06 05													
—	17¼	—	Alderley Edge d						06 09					06 38			06 48					
—	19	0	**Wilmslow** d					05 41	06 13	06 27				06 42	06 44		06 51					
—	—	2	Styal d					05 44						06 46								
—	—	4¼	**Manchester Airport** a				01 07	05 55						06 54								
—	20½	—	Handforth d						06 16								06 54					
11¾	—	—	Congleton d																06 58			
19¾	—	—	**Macclesfield** a																07 05			
—	—	—	d								06 17								07 06			
22½	—	—	Prestbury d								06 22											
24½	—	—	Adlington (Cheshire) d								06 25											
26½	—	—	Poynton d								06 28											
28	—	—	Bramhall d								06 31											
29½	22¾	—	Cheadle Hulme d						06 20		06 35						06 58					
31¼	25	—	**Stockport** a						06 25	06 36	06 39				06 55		07 03		07 19			
—	—	—	d	00 04	00 13	00 26			06 27	06 37	06 40	06 45	06 54		06 55	06 58	07 03	07 16	07 20	07 21	07 25	07 30
31¾	26½	—	Heaton Chapel d						06 31		06 43					07 02	07 07			07 24		
34¾	28	—	Levenshulme d						06 34		06 46					07 05	07 10			07 28		
37¾	31	—	**Manchester Picc.** 85,89 a	00 13	00 26	00 36	01 28	06 20	06 45	06 48	06 53	06 56	07 02	07 21	07 08	07 14	07 15	07 26	07 30	07 36	07 38	07 39
38¼	31½	—	**Manchester Oxford Road** 85,89 a					06 24						07 24			07 19				07 42	
38¾	32	—	Deansgate 85,89 a					06 27						07 27			07 22					

	NT	VT ◇1	NT ◇	NT	NT E	XC ◇1	TP ◇1 J	NT ◇ D	NT ◇ D	AW ◇ K	NT H	NT B	XC ◇1	VT ◇1	NT ◇	NT E	EM ◇ I	NT	VT ◇1	NT ◇	NT E	XC ◇1
London Euston ⊖65 d														06 16					06 36			
Birmingham New Street 68 d						06 30							06 53									07 31
Wolverhampton 68 d						06 48							07 10									07 49
Stafford 65,67 d						07 02							07 24									08 03
Stoke-on-Trent 50 d			06 58			07 20								07 45	07 25					07 56		08 20
Longport 50 d																				08 00		
Kidsgrove 50 d			07 06												07 35					08 05		
Crewe d	06 48	07 10							07 13	07 27			07 45					07 48	08 11			
Sandbach d	06 55								07 20									07 55				
Holmes Chapel d	07 00								07 25									08 00				
Goostrey d	07 03								07 29									08 03				
Chelford d	07 08								07 34									08 08				
Alderley Edge d	07 13			07 29					07 39		07 49							08 13				
Wilmslow d	07 16	07 26		07 32				07 48	07 42	07 47	07 52		08 01					08 16	08 27			
Styal d									07 46													
Manchester Airport a									07 55													
Handforth d	07 19			07 35							07 55							08 19				
Congleton d			07 12												07 41					08 12		
Macclesfield a			07 19			07 37								08 01	07 48					08 19		08 36
d			07 20			07 38								08 02	07 49					08 19		08 37
Prestbury d			07 24												07 53					08 23		
Adlington (Cheshire) d			07 27																	08 26		
Poynton d			07 30												07 58					08 30		
Bramhall d			07 33												08 00					08 33		
Cheadle Hulme d	07 24		07 37	07 40							07 59				08 04			08 24		08 37		
Stockport a	07 28	07 36	07 41			07 49				07 59	08 04		08 13	08 17	08 14			08 28	08 35	08 41		08 49
d	07 29	07 37	07 42		07 46	07 50	07 53			08 00	08 04	08 08	08 14	08 18	08 17	08 20	08 25	08 29	08 36	08 42	08 46	08 50
Heaton Chapel d	07 32			07 47							08 08					08 24		08 32				
Levenshulme d	07 35			07 50							08 11					08 27		08 35				
Manchester Picc. 85,89 a	07 43	07 46	07 52	07 56	07 56	08 00	08 02	08 07	08 21	08 10	08 17	08 17	08 23	08 27	08 30	08 36	08 37	08 43	08 46	08 52	08 56	09 00
Manchester Oxford Road 85,89 a								08 11	08 25		08 20						08 41					
Deansgate 85,89 a									08 28													

A From London Euston
B From Chester
C From Sheffield
D To Liverpool Lime Street
E From Buxton
F From Doncaster to Manchester Airport
G From Hazel Grove
H To Southport
I From Nottingham to Liverpool Lime Street
J From Cleethorpes to Manchester Airport
K From Cardiff Central

NRT DECEMBER 19 EDITION

Table T084-F

Mondays to Fridays
16 December to 15 May

Stoke-on-Trent and Crewe - Manchester Airport, Stockport and Manchester

	TP ◇1 A	VT ◇1	NT ◇ B	AW ◇ C	NT D	XC ◇1 E	VT ◇1	NT F	NT G	EM ◇ H	NT	VT ◇1 I	VT ◇1 J	NT ◇	NT K	XC ◇1 L	TP ◇1 A	VT ◇1	NT ◇ B	AW ◇ M	NT D	XC ◇1 E
London Euston ⊖65 d		06 55					07 20					07 33	07 35					08 00				
Birmingham New Street 68 d						07 57										08 31						08 57
Wolverhampton 68 d						08 14										08 48						09 14
Stafford 65,67 d						08 28										09 02						09 28
Stoke-on-Trent 50 d		08 25				08 44	08 48							08 56		09 20		09 25				09 44
Longport 50 d																						
Kidsgrove 50 d														09 04								
Crewe d			08 16	08 28							08 48	09 11	09 11						09 16	09 29		
Sandbach d			08 23								08 55								09 23			
Holmes Chapel d			08 28								09 00								09 28			
Goostrey d											09 03											
Chelford d											09 08											
Alderley Edge d			08 38		08 49						09 13								09 38		09 50	
Wilmslow d			08 42	08 48	08 52						09 16	09 27	09 27						09 42	09 49	09 53	
Styal d			08 46																09 46			
Manchester Airport a			08 55																09 55			
Handforth d					08 55						09 19										09 56	
Congleton d														09 10								
Macclesfield a		08 41				09 01								09 17		09 36		09 41				10 01
d		08 41				09 02								09 18		09 37		09 41				10 02
Prestbury d														09 22								
Adlington (Cheshire) d														09 25								
Poynton d														09 28								
Bramhall d														09 31								
Cheadle Hulme d					09 00						09 24			09 36							10 01	
Stockport a		08 54		08 59	09 05	09 13	09 16				09 28	09 35	09 35	09 40		09 49		09 54		09 59	10 05	10 13
d	08 53	08 56		08 59	09 06	09 14	09 17	09 17	09 20	09 25	09 29	09 36	09 36	09 41	09 45	09 50	09 53	09 56		09 59	10 06	10 14
Heaton Chapel d									09 24		09 32			09 44								
Levenshulme d								09 23			09 35				09 50							
Manchester Picc. 85,89 a	09 02	09 05	09 21	09 12	09 17	09 24	09 27	09 30	09 36	09 37	09 43	09 46	09 46	09 52	09 56	10 00	10 02	10 05	10 20	10 11	10 16	10 24
Manchester Oxford Road 85,89 a			09 24		09 20					09 41									10 24		10 20	
Deansgate 85,89 a			09 28																10 27			

	VT ◇1	NT F	NT G	EM MX ◇ N	EM MO ◇ N	NT	VT ◇1	NT ◇	NT G	XC ◇1 C	TP ◇1 A	VT ◇1	NT ◇ B	AW M	NT D	XC ◇1 O	VT ◇1	NT F	NT G	EM ◇ N	NT
London Euston ⊖65 d	08 20						08 40					09 00					09 20				
Birmingham New Street 68 d										09 31						09 57					
Wolverhampton 68 d										09 48						10 14					
Stafford 65,67 d										10 02						10 28					
Stoke-on-Trent 50 d	09 48							09 56		10 20		10 25				10 44	10 48				
Longport 50 d																					
Kidsgrove 50 d								10 04													
Crewe d						09 48	10 11						10 16	10 30							10 48
Sandbach d						09 55							10 23								10 55
Holmes Chapel d						10 00							10 28								11 00
Goostrey d						10 03															11 03
Chelford d						10 08															11 08
Alderley Edge d						10 13							10 38		10 49						11 13
Wilmslow d						10 16	10 27						10 42	10 48	10 52						11 16
Styal d													10 45								
Manchester Airport a													10 55								
Handforth d						10 19									10 55						11 19
Congleton d								10 10													
Macclesfield a								10 17		10 36		10 41				11 01					
d								10 18		10 37		10 41				11 02					
Prestbury d								10 22													
Adlington (Cheshire) d								10 25													
Poynton d								10 29													
Bramhall d								10 31													
Cheadle Hulme d						10 24		10 36							11 00						11 24
Stockport a	10 16					10 28	10 35	10 40		10 49		10 54		10 59	11 04	11 13	11 16				11 28
d	10 17	10 18	10 21	10 25	10 26	10 29	10 36	10 41	10 45	10 50	10 53	10 56		10 59	11 05	11 14	11 17	11 17	11 20	11 25	11 29
Heaton Chapel d			10 25			10 32		10 44											11 24		11 32
Levenshulme d			10 28			10 35			10 50										11 27		11 35
Manchester Picc. 85,89 a	10 27	10 30	10 36	10 37	10 37	10 43	10 46	10 52	10 57	11 00	11 02	11 05	11 21	11 11	11 16	11 24	11 27	11 30	11 36	11 37	11 43
Manchester Oxford Road 85,89 a				10 41	10 41								11 24		11 20					11 41	
Deansgate 85,89 a													11 28								

A From Cleethorpes to Manchester Airport
B To Liverpool Lime Street
C From Cardiff Central
D To Southport
E From Southampton Central
F From Chester
G From Buxton
H From Nottingham to Liverpool Lime Street
I from 17 February
J until 14 February
K From Hazel Grove
L From Bristol Temple Meads
M From Carmarthen
N From Norwich to Liverpool Lime Street
O From Bournemouth

Table T084-F

Mondays to Fridays

16 December to 15 May

Stoke-on-Trent and Crewe - Manchester Airport, Stockport and Manchester

	VT	NT	NT	XC	TP	VT	NT	AW	NT	XC	VT	NT	NT	EM	NT	VT	NT	NT	XC	TP	VT	NT
	◇1 ⊠	◇	A	◇1 B	◇1 C	◇1 ⊠	◇ D	◇ E	F	◇1 G	◇1 ⊠	H	A	◇ I		◇1 ⊠	◇	A	◇1 J	◇1 C	◇1 ⊠	◇ D
London Euston 15 ⊖65 d	09 40					10 00					10 20					10 40					11 00	
Birmingham New Street 12 68 d				10 31						10 57									11 31			
Wolverhampton 7 68 d				10 48						11 14									11 48			
Stafford 65,67 d				11 02						11 28									12 02			
Stoke-on-Trent 50 d		10 56		11 20		11 25				11 44	11 48						11 56		12 20		12 25	
Longport 50 d																						
Kidsgrove 50 d		11 04															12 04					
Crewe 10 d	11 11						11 17	11 30							11 48	12 11						12 17
Sandbach d							11 24								11 55							12 24
Holmes Chapel d							11 29								12 00							12 29
Goostrey d															12 03							
Chelford d															12 08							
Alderley Edge d							11 38		11 49						12 13							12 38
Wilmslow d	11 27						11 42	11 49	11 52						12 16	12 27						12 42
Styal d							11 45															12 46
Manchester Airport ✈ a							11 55															12 55
Handforth d									11 55						12 19							
Congleton d		11 10															12 10					
Macclesfield a		11 17		11 36		11 41				12 01							12 17		12 36		12 41	
d		11 18		11 37		11 41				12 02							12 18		12 37		12 41	
Prestbury d		11 22															12 22					
Adlington (Cheshire) d		11 25															12 25					
Poynton d		11 29															12 28					
Bramhall d		11 31															12 31					
Cheadle Hulme d		11 35							11 59						12 24		12 35					
Stockport a	11 35	11 39		11 49		11 54		11 59	12 04	12 13	12 16				12 28	12 35	12 40		12 49		12 54	
d	11 36	11 40	11 45	11 50	11 53	11 56		11 59	12 05	12 14	12 17	12 17	12 20	12 25	12 29	12 36	12 40	12 45	12 50	12 53	12 56	
Heaton Chapel d		11 43											12 24		12 32		12 44					
Levenshulme d			11 50										12 27		12 35			12 50				
Manchester Picc. 10 85,89 a	11 46	11 52	11 56	12 00	12 02	12 05	12 21	12 13	12 17	12 24	12 27	12 30	12 36	12 37	12 43	12 46	12 52	12 56	13 00	13 02	13 05	13 21
Manchester Oxford Road 85,89 a							12 24		12 20					12 41								13 24
Deansgate 85,89 a							12 28															13 28

	AW	NT	XC	VT	NT	NT	EM	NT	VT	NT	NT	XC	TP	VT	NT	AW	NT	XC	VT	NT	NT
	■ E	F	■ ◇1 G	◇1 ⊠	H	A	◇ I		◇1 ⊠	◇	A	◇1 J	◇1 C	◇1 ⊠	◇ D	■ K	F	◇1 G	◇1 ⊠	H	A
London Euston 15 ⊖65 d				11 20					11 40					12 00					12 20		
Birmingham New Street 12 68 d			11 57									12 31						12 57			
Wolverhampton 7 68 d			12 14									12 48						13 14			
Stafford 65,67 d			12 28									13 02						13 28			
Stoke-on-Trent 50 d			12 44	12 48						12 57		13 20		13 25				13 44	13 48		
Longport 50 d																					
Kidsgrove 50 d										13 05											
Crewe 10 d	12 30							12 48	13 11						13 18	13 30					
Sandbach d								12 55							13 25						
Holmes Chapel d								13 00							13 30						
Goostrey d								13 03													
Chelford d								13 08													
Alderley Edge d		12 49						13 13							13 39		13 49				
Wilmslow d	12 49	12 52						13 16	13 27						13 43	13 49	13 52				
Styal d															13 46						
Manchester Airport ✈ a															13 55						
Handforth d		12 55						13 19									13 55				
Congleton d										13 11											
Macclesfield a			13 01							13 18		13 36		13 41				14 01			
d			13 02							13 19		13 37		13 41				14 02			
Prestbury d										13 23											
Adlington (Cheshire) d										13 26											
Poynton d										13 30											
Bramhall d										13 32											
Cheadle Hulme d		12 59						13 24		13 36							13 58				
Stockport a	12 59	13 05	13 13	13 16				13 28	13 35	13 42		13 49		13 54		13 58	14 05	14 13	14 16		
d	12 59	13 06	13 14	13 17	13 17	13 20	13 25	13 29	13 36	13 42	13 45	13 50	13 53	13 56		13 59	14 06	14 14	14 17	14 17	14 20
Heaton Chapel d						13 24		13 32													14 24
Levenshulme d						13 27		13 35			13 50										14 27
Manchester Picc. 10 85,89 a	13 13	13 17	13 24	13 27	13 30	13 36	13 37	13 43	13 46	13 52	13 56	14 00	14 02	14 05	14 21	14 13	14 17	14 24	14 27	14 30	14 36
Manchester Oxford Road 85,89 a		13 20					13 41								14 24		14 20				
Deansgate 85,89 a															14 28						

A From Buxton
B From Paignton
C From Cleethorpes to Manchester Airport
D To Liverpool Lime Street
E From Milford Haven
F To Southport
G From Bournemouth
H From Chester
I From Norwich to Liverpool Lime Street
J From Bristol Temple Meads
K From Fishguard Harbour

Table T084-F

Mondays to Fridays

16 December to 15 May

Stoke-on-Trent and Crewe - Manchester Airport, Stockport and Manchester

	EM	NT	VT	NT	NT	XC	TP	VT	NT	AW	NT	XC	VT	NT	NT	EM	NT	VT	NT	NT	XC	TP
	◇ A		◇1 ⊠	◇	B	◇1 C	◇1 D	◇1	◇ E	■ F	G	◇1 H	◇1	I	B	◇ A		◇1	◇	B	◇1 J	◇1 D
London Euston 15 ⊖65 d			12 40					13 00					13 20					13 40				
Birmingham New Street 12 68 d						13 31						13 57									14 31	
Wolverhampton 7 68 d						13 48						14 14									14 48	
Stafford 65,67 d						14 02						14 28									15 02	
Stoke-on-Trent 50 d				13 56		14 20		14 25				14 44	14 48						14 56		15 20	
Longport 50 d																						
Kidsgrove 50 d				14 04															15 04			
Crewe 10 d		13 48	14 11						14 16	14 30							14 48	15 11				
Sandbach d		13 55							14 23								14 55					
Holmes Chapel d		14 00							14 28								15 00					
Goostrey d		14 03															15 03					
Chelford d		14 08															15 08					
Alderley Edge d		14 13							14 38		14 49						15 13					
Wilmslow d		14 16	14 27						14 42	14 49	14 52						15 16	15 27				
Styal d									14 46													
Manchester Airport ✈ a									14 55													
Handforth d		14 19									14 55						15 19					
Congleton d				14 10															15 10			
Macclesfield a				14 17		14 36		14 41				15 01							15 17		15 36	
d				14 18		14 37		14 41				15 02							15 18		15 37	
Prestbury d				14 22															15 22			
Adlington (Cheshire) d				14 25															15 25			
Poynton d				14 29															15 29			
Bramhall d				14 31															15 31			
Cheadle Hulme d		14 24		14 35							14 59						15 24		15 35			
Stockport a		14 28	14 35	14 40		14 49		14 54		14 59	15 04	15 13	15 16				15 28	15 35	15 40		15 49	
d	14 25	14 29	14 36	14 40	14 45	14 50	14 53	14 56		14 59	15 05	15 14	15 17	15 17	15 20	15 25	15 29	15 36	15 40	15 45	15 50	15 53
Heaton Chapel d		14 32		14 44											15 24		15 32		15 44			
Levenshulme d		14 35			14 50										15 27		15 35			15 50		
Manchester Picc. 10 85,89 a	14 37	14 43	14 46	14 52	14 56	15 00	15 02	15 05	15 21	15 13	15 17	15 24	15 27	15 30	15 36	15 37	15 43	15 46	15 52	15 56	16 00	16 02
Manchester Oxford Road 85,89 a	14 41								15 24		15 20					15 41						
Deansgate 85,89 a									15 28													

	VT	NT	AW	NT	XC	VT	NT	NT	EM	NT	VT	NT	NT	XC	TP	VT	NT	AW	NT	XC	VT	NT
	◇1	◇ E	◇ K	G	◇1 H	◇1	I	B	◇ A		◇1	◇	B	◇1 L	◇1 D	◇1	◇ E	■ M	G	◇1 H	◇1	I
London Euston 15 ⊖65 d	14 00					14 20					14 40					15 00					15 20	
Birmingham New Street 12 68 d					14 57									15 31						15 57		
Wolverhampton 7 68 d					15 14									15 48						16 14		
Stafford 65,67 d					15 28									16 02						16 28		
Stoke-on-Trent 50 d	15 25				15 44	15 48						15 56		16 20		16 25				16 44	16 48	
Longport 50 d																						
Kidsgrove 50 d												16 04										
Crewe 10 d		15 16	15 30							15 48	16 11						16 16	16 30				
Sandbach d		15 23								15 55							16 23					
Holmes Chapel d		15 28								16 00							16 28					
Goostrey d										16 03												
Chelford d										16 08												
Alderley Edge d		15 38		15 50						16 13							16 38		16 50			
Wilmslow d		15 42	15 49	15 53						16 16	16 27						16 42	16 49	16 53			
Styal d		15 46															16 46					
Manchester Airport ✈ a		15 55															16 55					
Handforth d				15 56						16 19									16 56			
Congleton d												16 10										
Macclesfield a	15 41				16 01							16 17		16 36		16 41				17 01	17 05	
d	15 41				16 02							16 18		16 37		16 41				17 02	17 06	
Prestbury d												16 22										
Adlington (Cheshire) d												16 25										
Poynton d												16 29										
Bramhall d												16 31										
Cheadle Hulme d				16 01						16 24		16 35							17 00			
Stockport a	15 54		15 59	16 06	16 13	16 16				16 28	16 35	16 40		16 49		16 54		16 59	17 05	17 13	17 17	
d	15 56		15 59	16 06	16 14	16 17	16 17	16 20	16 25	16 29	16 36	16 40	16 45	16 50	16 53	16 56		16 59	17 06	17 14	17 18	17 17
Heaton Chapel d								16 24		16 32		16 44										
Levenshulme d								16 27		16 35			16 50									
Manchester Picc. 10 85,89 a	16 05	16 21	16 13	16 17	16 24	16 27	16 30	16 36	16 37	16 43	16 46	16 52	16 56	17 00	17 02	17 05	17 21	17 13	17 17	17 24	17 28	17 30
Manchester Oxford Road 85,89 a		16 24		16 20					16 41								17 25					
Deansgate 85,89 a		16 28															17 28		17 22			

A From Norwich to Liverpool Lime Street
B From Buxton
C From Paignton
D From Cleethorpes to Manchester Airport
E To Liverpool Lime Street
F From Cardiff Central
G To Southport
H From Bournemouth
I From Chester
J From Bristol Temple Meads
K From Carmarthen
L From Plymouth
M From Milford Haven

Table T084-F

Mondays to Fridays

16 December to 15 May

Stoke-on-Trent and Crewe - Manchester Airport, Stockport and Manchester

		NT	EM	NT	VT	NT	NT	XC	TP	VT		NT	AW	NT	XC	VT	NT	NT	EM	NT		VT	NT	NT
		A	◇ B		◇1 ☕	◇	A	◇1 C 🍴	◇1 D 🍴	◇1 ☕		◇	■ E 🍴	F	◇1 G 🍴	◇1 ☕	H	A	◇ B			◇1 ☕	◇	A
London Euston ■15 ⊖65 d					15 40					16 00						16 20						16 40		
Birmingham New Street ■12 68 d								16 31							16 57									
Wolverhampton ■7 68 ⛴ d								16 48							17 14									
Stafford 65,67 d								17 03							17 28									
Stoke-on-Trent 50 d						16 57		17 20		17 25					17 44	17 48							17 56	
Longport 50 d																								
Kidsgrove 50 d						17 05																	18 04	
Crewe ■10 d				16 48	17 11							17 16	17 30							17 48		18 11		
Sandbach d				16 55								17 23								17 55				
Holmes Chapel d				17 00								17 28								18 00				
Goostrey d				17 03																18 03				
Chelford d				17 08																18 08				
Alderley Edge d				17 13								17 38		17 49						18 13				
Wilmslow d				17 16	17 27							17 42	17 49	17 52						18 16		18 27		
Styal d												17 46												
Manchester Airport ✈ a												17 53												
Handforth d				17 19										17 55						18 19				
Congleton d						17 11																	18 10	
Macclesfield a						17 18		17 36		17 41					18 01								18 17	
d						17 19		17 37		17 41					18 02								18 18	
Prestbury d						17 23																	18 22	
Adlington (Cheshire) d						17 26																	18 25	
Poynton d						17 30																	18 29	
Bramhall d						17 32																	18 31	
Cheadle Hulme d				17 24		17 36								17 59						18 24			18 36	
Stockport a				17 28	17 35	17 40		17 49		17 54			17 59	18 04	18 13	18 16				18 28		18 35	18 40	
d		17 20	17 25	17 29	17 36	17 41	17 45	17 50	17 53	17 56			17 59	18 05	18 14	18 17	18 17	18 20	18 25	18 29		18 36	18 41	18 45
Heaton Chapel d		17 24		17 32		17 44												18 24		18 32			18 44	
Levenshulme d		17 27		17 35			17 50											18 27		18 35				18 50
Manchester Picc. ■10 85,89 ⛴ a		17 36	17 37	17 43	17 46	17 53	17 56	18 00	18 02	18 05		18 21	18 13	18 17	18 24	18 27	18 30	18 36	18 37	18 43		18 46	18 53	18 56
Manchester Oxford Road 85,89 a			17 41											18 20					18 41					
Deansgate 85,89 ⛴ a																								

	XC	TP	VT	NT	AW	NT		XC	VT	NT	EM	NT	VT	NT	NT	XC		TP	VT	NT	NT	AW	XC	VT
	◇1 I 🍴	◇1 D 🍴	◇1 ⊠	◇	■ J 🍴	F		◇1 G 🍴	◇1 ⊠	H	◇ B		◇1 ⊠	◇	A	◇1 K 🍴		◇1 D	◇1 ⊠	F	◇ L	■ E 🍴	◇1 G 🍴	◇1 ⊠
London Euston ■15 ⊖65 d			17 00						17 20				17 40						18 00					18 20
Birmingham New Street ■12 68 d	17 31							17 57								18 31							18 57	
Wolverhampton ■7 68 ⛴ d	17 48							18 14								18 48							19 14	
Stafford 65,67 d	18 02							18 28								19 02							19 28	
Stoke-on-Trent 50 d	18 20		18 25					18 44	18 48					18 58		19 20			19 25				19 44	19 48
Longport 50 d																								
Kidsgrove 50 d														19 06										
Crewe ■10 d				18 17	18 30							18 48	19 11								19 17	19 37		
Sandbach d				18 24								18 55									19 24			
Holmes Chapel d				18 29								19 00									19 29			
Goostrey d												19 03												
Chelford d												19 08												
Alderley Edge d				18 39		18 49						19 13								19 47	19 38			
Wilmslow d				18 42	18 49	18 52						19 16	19 27							19 50	19 43	19 57		
Styal d				18 46																	19 46			
Manchester Airport ✈ a				18 53																	19 54			
Handforth d						18 55						19 19								19 53				
Congleton d														19 12										
Macclesfield a	18 36		18 41					19 01						19 19		19 36			19 41				20 01	
d	18 37		18 41					19 02						19 20		19 37			19 41				20 02	
Prestbury d														19 24										
Adlington (Cheshire) d														19 27										
Poynton d														19 30										
Bramhall d														19 33										
Cheadle Hulme d						18 59						19 24		19 37						19 56				
Stockport a	18 49		18 54		18 59	19 04		19 13	19 16			19 28	19 35	19 41		19 49			19 54	20 02		20 07	20 13	20 16
d	18 50	18 53	18 56		18 59	19 06		19 14	19 17	19 17	19 25	19 29	19 36	19 42	19 46	19 50		19 53	19 56	20 03		20 07	20 14	20 17
Heaton Chapel d																				20 06				
Levenshulme d																				20 09				
Manchester Picc. ■10 85,89 ⛴ a	19 00	19 03	19 05	19 21	19 13	19 17		19 24	19 27	19 30	19 37	19 39	19 45	19 52	19 56	20 00		20 02	20 05	20 17	20 21	20 19	20 24	20 27
Manchester Oxford Road 85,89 a						19 20					19 41									20 20	20 24			
Deansgate 85,89 ⛴ a																					20 28			

A From Buxton
B From Norwich to Liverpool Lime Street
C From Bristol Temple Meads
D From Cleethorpes to Manchester Airport
E From Carmarthen
F To Southport
G From Bournemouth
H From Chester
I From Exeter St Davids
J From Milford Haven
K From Paignton
L To Liverpool Lime Street

NRT DECEMBER 19 EDITION

Table T084-F

Mondays to Fridays

16 December to 15 May

Stoke-on-Trent and Crewe - Manchester Airport, Stockport and Manchester

	NT	EM		NT	NT	VT	NT	XC	TP	VT	AW	VT ThFO		NT	XC	VT	NT	EM	NT	NT	VT	NT		XC
	A	◇ B			C	◇1 ⊠	◇	◇1 D 🍴	◇1 E	■ 1 ☕	■ F 🍴	◇1 ☕		G	◇1 H 🍴	■ 1 ☕	A	◇ I		C	◇1 ☕	◇		◇1 D 🍴
London Euston ■15 ⊖65 d						18 40				19 00		18 57				19 20					19 40			
Birmingham New Street ■12 68 d								19 31							19 57									20 31
Wolverhampton ■7 68 ⛴ d								19 50							20 14									20 48
Stafford 65,67 d								20 04							20 28						21 04			21 02
Stoke-on-Trent 50 d							19 58	20 20		20 25					20 44	20 50						20 58		21 20
Longport 50 d																								
Kidsgrove 50 d							20 06															21 06		
Crewe ■10 d				19 48		20 18					20 24	20s33							20 48		21 23			
Sandbach d				19 55															20 55					
Holmes Chapel d				20 00															21 00					
Goostrey d				20 03															21 03					
Chelford d				20 08															21 08					
Alderley Edge d				20 13															21 13					
Wilmslow d				20 16		20 33					20 42			20 43					21 16		21 38			
Styal d														20 46										
Manchester Airport ✈ a														20 54										
Handforth d				20 19															21 19					
Congleton d							20 12															21 12		
Macclesfield a							20 19	20 36							21 01	21 06						21 19		21 36
d							20 20	20 37							21 02	21 07						21 20		21 37
Prestbury d							20 24															21 24		
Adlington (Cheshire) d							20 27															21 27		
Poynton d							20 30															21 30		
Bramhall d							20 33															21 33		
Cheadle Hulme d				20 24			20 37												21 24			21 37		
Stockport a				20 28		20 42	20 41	20 49		20 54	20 53				21 13	21 19			21 28			21 41		21 49
d	20 18	20 25		20 29	20 35	20 43	20 42	20 50	20 53	20 55	20 53				21 14	21 20	21 21	21 26	21 29	21 35		21 42		21 50
Heaton Chapel d				20 32															21 32			21 45		
Levenshulme d				20 35															21 35			21 49		
Manchester Picc. ■10 85,89 ⛴ a	20 30	20 38		20 43	20 46	20 52	20 55	20 59	21 02	21 05	21 07	21 09		21 16	21 24	21 28	21 35	21 36	21 42	21 48	21 54	21 56		22 00
Manchester Oxford Road 85,89 a		20 41												21 20										
Deansgate 85,89 ⛴ a														21 29										

	VT	TP	AW	NT	XC	NT	NT	VT		NT	TP	VT	NT	XC	NT	NT FO	NT	NT		AW MWO	AW TThO	AW FO	VT	NT
	◇1 ☕	◇1 J	◇ K 🍴	G	◇1 H	A		◇1 ☕		C	◇1 E	◇1 ☕	G	◇1 H	A	◇	L			◇ M	◇ M	◇ M	◇1 ☕	C
London Euston ■15 ⊖65 d	20 00							20 40				21 00											21 40	
Birmingham New Street ■12 68 d					20 57									21 57										
Wolverhampton ■7 68 ⛴ d					21 14									22 14										
Stafford 65,67 d					21 28									22 28										
Stoke-on-Trent 50 d	21 26				21 45							22 28		22 44		22 20							23 08	
Longport 50 d																								
Kidsgrove 50 d																22 27								
Crewe ■10 d			21 35				21 48	22 11												23 08	23 08	23 08		
Sandbach d							21 56																	
Holmes Chapel d							22 01																	
Goostrey d							22 04																	
Chelford d							22 09																	
Alderley Edge d							22 14																	
Wilmslow d			21 52	21 42			22 17	22 27					22 34					23 10		23 26	23 26	23 26		
Styal d				21 45									22 37											
Manchester Airport ✈ a				21 53									22 47					23 20						
Handforth d							22 20																	
Congleton d																22 34								
Macclesfield a	21 41				22 01							22 44		23 01		22 41							23 24	
d	21 42				22 02							22 44		23 02		22 49							23 24	
Prestbury d																22 53								
Adlington (Cheshire) d																22 56								
Poynton d																22 59								
Bramhall d																23 02								
Cheadle Hulme d							22 25									23 06								
Stockport a	21 54		22 01		22 15		22 29	22 35				22 58		23 13		23 10				23 34	23 35	23 35	23 38	
d	21 55	21 56	22 02		22 16	22 18	22 30	22 36		22 41	22 53	22 59		23 14	23 17	23 13	23 20			23 35	23 35	23 35	23 39	23 45
Heaton Chapel d							22 33			22 45						23 16	23 23							
Levenshulme d							22 36			22 49						23 19	23 26							
Manchester Picc. ■10 85,89 ⛴ a	22 03	22 08	22 15	22 17	22 25	22 33	22 43	22 46		22 58	23 02	23 08	23 20	23 24	23 27	23 30	23 35	23 42		23 48	23 49	23 50	23 50	23 55
Manchester Oxford Road 85,89 a				22 20									23 24											
Deansgate 85,89 ⛴ a				22 33									23 27											

A From Chester
B From Norwich to Liverpool Lime Street
C From Buxton
D From Exeter St Davids
E From Cleethorpes to Manchester Airport
F From Milford Haven
G To Liverpool Lime Street
H From Bournemouth
I From Norwich
J From Cleethorpes
K From Carmarthen
L From Hazel Grove
M From Cardiff Central

Table T084-F

Stoke-on-Trent and Crewe - Manchester Airport, Stockport and Manchester

Mondays to Fridays
16 December to 15 May

		NT	XC	AW	VT
			◇1	◇ A	◇1
London Euston 15 ⊖65	d				23 00
Birmingham New Street 12 68	d		22 30	21 25	
Wolverhampton 7 68	d		22 48	21 45	
Stafford 65,67	d		23 02		
Stoke-on-Trent 50	d		23 20		01s18
Longport 50	d				
Kidsgrove 50	d				
Crewe 10	d	23 12			
Sandbach	d	23 19			
Holmes Chapel	d	23 24			
Goostrey	d	23 27			
Chelford	d	23 32			
Alderley Edge	d	23 37			
Wilmslow	d	23 40			
Styal	d				
Manchester Airport	a				
Handforth	d	23 43			
Congleton	d				
Macclesfield	a				01s34
	d				
Prestbury	d				
Adlington (Cheshire)	d				
Poynton	d				
Bramhall	d				
Cheadle Hulme	d	23 48			
Stockport	a	23 52			01s48
	d	23 53			
Heaton Chapel	d	23 56			
Levenshulme	d	23 59			
Manchester Picc. 10 85,89	a	00 06	00 15	00 25	01 59
Manchester Oxford Road 85,89	a				
Deansgate 85,89	a				

Saturdays
21 December to 16 May

		NT	NT	NT	NT	NT	NT	NT	TP	NT	AW	NT	NT	XC	NT	EM	NT	NT	NT	XC	TP	NT	AW
		B	◇ C		D			E	◇1 F	◇ D		G	B	◇1	E	◇ H		◇	E	◇1	◇1 I	◇ D	◇ J
London Euston 15 ⊖65	d																						
Birmingham New Street 12 68	d													05 57						06 31			
Wolverhampton 7 68	d													06 14						06 48			
Stafford 65,67	d													06 28						07 02			
Stoke-on-Trent 50	d													06 44				06 58		07 20			
Longport 50	d																						
Kidsgrove 50	d																	07 06					
Crewe 10	d			00 44		05 44				06 16	06 27						06 48					07 13	07 27
Sandbach	d					05 51				06 23							06 55					07 20	
Holmes Chapel	d					05 56				06 28							07 00					07 25	
Goostrey	d					06 00											07 03					07 29	
Chelford	d					06 05											07 08					07 34	
Alderley Edge	d					06 09				06 38		06 48					07 13					07 39	
Wilmslow	d				05 41	06 13				06 42	06 44	06 51					07 16					07 42	07 46
Styal	d				05 44					06 46												07 46	
Manchester Airport	a			01 07	05 55					06 54												07 55	
Handforth	d					06 16						06 54					07 19						
Congleton	d													06 57				07 12					
Macclesfield	a													07 04				07 19		07 36			
	d						06 16							07 05				07 20		07 37			
Prestbury	d						06 20											07 24					
Adlington (Cheshire)	d						06 23											07 27					
Poynton	d						06 27											07 30					
Bramhall	d						06 30											07 33					
Cheadle Hulme	d					06 20	06 34					06 58					07 24	07 37					
Stockport	a					06 25	06 38				06 55	07 03		07 19			07 28	07 41		07 49			07 59
	d	00 13	00 26			06 27	06 39	06 45	06 53		06 55	07 03	07 16	07 20	07 21	07 26	07 29	07 42	07 46	07 50	07 52		07 59
Heaton Chapel	d					06 31	06 42					07 07			07 25		07 32						
Levenshulme	d					06 34	06 45					07 10			07 28		07 35						
Manchester Picc. 10 85,89	a	00 26	00 36	01 28	06 20	06 44	06 53	06 56	07 02	07 20	07 07	07 15	07 26	07 31	07 36	07 39	07 43	07 52	07 56	07 59	08 02	08 21	08 10
Manchester Oxford Road 85,89	a				06 24					07 24		07 19				07 42						08 25	
Deansgate 85,89	a				06 27					07 27		07 22										08 28	

A From Birmingham International
B From Chester
C From Sheffield
D To Liverpool Lime Street
E From Buxton
F From Doncaster to Manchester Airport
G To Southport
H From Nottingham to Liverpool Lime Street
I From Cleethorpes to Manchester Airport
J From Cardiff Central

Table T084-F

Stoke-on-Trent and Crewe - Manchester Airport, Stockport and Manchester

Saturdays
21 December to 16 May

		NT	NT	XC	NT	EM	NT	VT	NT	NT	XC	TP	VT	NT	AW	NT	XC	VT	NT	NT	EM	NT	VT
		A	B	◇1	C	◇ D		◇1	◇	C	◇1	◇1 E	◇1	◇ F	◇ G	A	◇1 H	◇1	B	C	◇ D		◇1 I
London Euston 15 ⊖65	d							06 36					06 55					07 20					07 33
Birmingham New Street 12 68	d			06 57							07 31						07 57						
Wolverhampton 7 68	d			07 14							07 50						08 14						
Stafford 65,67	d			07 31							08 04						08 28						
Stoke-on-Trent 50	d								07 56		08 20		08 25				08 44	08 48					
Longport 50	d								08 00														
Kidsgrove 50	d								08 05														
Crewe 10	d			07 52			07 55	08 11						08 16	08 28							08 48	09 11
Sandbach	d						08 02							08 23								08 55	
Holmes Chapel	d						08 07							08 28								09 00	
Goostrey	d																					09 03	
Chelford	d																					09 08	
Alderley Edge	d	07 49					08 16							08 38		08 49						09 13	
Wilmslow	d	07 52		08 08			08 19	08 27						08 42	08 47	08 52						09 16	09 27
Styal	d													08 46									
Manchester Airport	a													08 55									
Handforth	d	07 55					08 22									08 55						09 19	
Congleton	d								08 12														
Macclesfield	a								08 19		08 36		08 41				09 01						
	d								08 19		08 37		08 41				09 02						
Prestbury	d								08 23														
Adlington (Cheshire)	d								08 26														
Poynton	d								08 30														
Bramhall	d								08 33														
Cheadle Hulme	d	07 59					08 27		08 37							09 00						09 24	
Stockport	a	08 04		08 16			08 31	08 35	08 41		08 49		08 54		08 59	09 05	09 13	09 16				09 28	09 35
	d	08 04	08 08	08 16	08 20	08 25	08 32	08 36	08 42	08 45	08 50	08 53	08 56		08 59	09 06	09 14	09 17	09 17	09 20	09 25	09 29	09 36
Heaton Chapel	d	08 08			08 24															09 24		09 32	
Levenshulme	d	08 11			08 27														09 23			09 35	
Manchester Picc. 10 85,89	a	08 17	08 17	08 29	08 36	08 37	08 43	08 46	08 52	08 56	08 59	09 02	09 05	09 21	09 13	09 17	09 24	09 27	09 30	09 36	09 37	09 43	09 46
Manchester Oxford Road 85,89	a	08 20				08 41								09 24		09 20					09 41		
Deansgate 85,89	a													09 28									

		VT	NT	NT	XC	TP	VT	NT	AW	NT	XC	VT	NT	NT	EM	NT	VT	NT	NT	XC	TP	VT
		◇1 J	◇	K	◇1 L	◇1 E	◇1	◇ F	◇ M	A	◇1 H	◇1	B	C	◇ N		◇1	◇	C	◇1 G	◇1 E	◇1
London Euston 15 ⊖65	d	07 35					08 00					08 20					08 40					09 00
Birmingham New Street 12 68	d				08 31						08 57									09 31		
Wolverhampton 7 68	d				08 48						09 14									09 48		
Stafford 65,67	d				09 02						09 28									10 04		
Stoke-on-Trent 50	d		08 56		09 20		09 25				09 44	09 48						09 56		10 20		10 25
Longport 50	d																					
Kidsgrove 50	d		09 04															10 04				
Crewe 10	d	09 11						09 16	09 30							09 48	10 11					
Sandbach	d							09 23								09 55						
Holmes Chapel	d							09 28								10 00						
Goostrey	d															10 03						
Chelford	d															10 08						
Alderley Edge	d							09 38		09 50						10 13						
Wilmslow	d	09 27						09 42	09 48	09 53						10 16	10 27					
Styal	d							09 46														
Manchester Airport	a							09 55														
Handforth	d									09 56						10 19						
Congleton	d		09 10															10 10				
Macclesfield	a		09 17		09 36		09 41				10 01							10 17		10 36		10 41
	d		09 18		09 37		09 41				10 02							10 18		10 37		10 41
Prestbury	d		09 22															10 22				
Adlington (Cheshire)	d		09 25															10 25				
Poynton	d		09 29															10 29				
Bramhall	d		09 31															10 31				
Cheadle Hulme	d		09 36							10 01						10 24		10 36				
Stockport	a	09 35	09 40		09 49		09 54		10 00	10 05	10 13	10 16				10 28	10 35	10 40		10 49		10 54
	d	09 36	09 41	09 45	09 50	09 53	09 56		10 00	10 06	10 14	10 17	10 18	10 21	10 26	10 29	10 36	10 41	10 45	10 50	10 53	10 56
Heaton Chapel	d		09 44											10 25		10 32		10 44				
Levenshulme	d			09 50										10 28		10 35			10 50			
Manchester Picc. 10 85,89	a	09 46	09 52	09 56	10 00	10 02	10 05	10 20	10 14	10 16	10 24	10 27	10 30	10 36	10 37	10 43	10 46	10 52	10 57	11 00	11 02	11 05
Manchester Oxford Road 85,89	a							10 24		10 20					10 41							
Deansgate 85,89	a							10 27														

A To Southport
B From Chester
C From Buxton
D From Nottingham to Liverpool Lime Street
E From Cleethorpes to Manchester Airport
F To Liverpool Lime Street
G From Cardiff Central
H From Southampton Central
I from 22 February
J until 15 February
K From Hazel Grove
L From Bristol Temple Meads
M From Carmarthen
N From Norwich to Liverpool Lime Street

Table T084-F

Saturdays

21 December to 16 May

Stoke-on-Trent and Crewe - Manchester Airport, Stockport and Manchester

Station		NT	AW	NT	XC	VT	NT	NT	EM	NT	VT	NT	NT	XC	TP	VT	NT	AW	NT	XC	VT	NT	NT
		◇ A	■ B	C	◇1 D	◇1	E	F	◇ G		◇1	◇	F	◇1 H	◇1 I	◇1	◇ A	■ J	C	◇1 D	◇1	E	F
London Euston [15] ⊖65	d					09 20					09 40					10 00					10 20		
Birmingham New Street [12] 68	d				09 57									10 31						10 57			
Wolverhampton [7] 68	d				10 14									10 48						11 14			
Stafford 65,67	d				10 28									11 02						11 28			
Stoke-on-Trent 50	d				10 44	10 48						10 56		11 20		11 25				11 44	11 48		
Longport 50	d																						
Kidsgrove 50	d											11 04											
Crewe [10]	d	10 16	10 30							10 48	11 11						11 17	11 30					
Sandbach	d	10 23								10 55							11 24						
Holmes Chapel	d	10 28								11 00							11 29						
Goostrey	d									11 03													
Chelford	d									11 08													
Alderley Edge	d	10 38		10 49						11 13							11 38		11 49				
Wilmslow	d	10 42	10 48	10 52						11 16	11 27						11 42	11 49	11 52				
Styal	d	10 45															11 45						
Manchester Airport	a	10 55															11 55						
Handforth	d			10 55						11 19									11 55				
Congleton	d											11 10											
Macclesfield	a				11 01							11 17		11 36		11 41				12 01			
	d				11 02							11 18		11 37		11 41				12 02			
Prestbury	d											11 22											
Adlington (Cheshire)	d											11 25											
Poynton	d											11 29											
Bramhall	d											11 31											
Cheadle Hulme	d			11 00						11 24		11 36							11 59				
Stockport	a		10 59	11 04	11 13	11 16				11 28	11 35	11 40		11 49		11 54		11 59	12 04	12 13	12 16		
	d		10 59	11 05	11 14	11 17	11 17	11 20	11 26	11 29	11 36	11 41	11 45	11 50	11 53	11 56		11 59	12 05	12 14	12 17	12 17	12 20
Heaton Chapel	d							11 24		11 32		11 44											12 24
Levenshulme	d							11 27		11 35			11 50										12 27
Manchester Picc. [10] 85,89	a	11 21	11 13	11 16	11 24	11 27	11 30	11 36	11 37	11 43	11 46	11 52	11 56	12 00	12 02	12 05	12 21	12 12	12 17	12 24	12 27	12 30	12 36
Manchester Oxford Road 85,89	a	11 24		11 20					11 41								12 24		12 20				
Deansgate 85,89	a	11 28															12 28						

Station		EM	NT	VT	NT	NT	XC	TP	VT	NT	AW	NT	XC	VT	NT	NT	EM	NT	VT	NT	NT	XC
		◇ G		◇1	◇	F	◇1 K	◇1 I	◇1	◇ A	◇ J	C	◇1 D	◇1	E	F	◇ G		◇1	◇	F	◇1 K
London Euston [15] ⊖65	d			10 40					11 00					11 20					11 40			
Birmingham New Street [12] 68	d						11 31						11 57									12 31
Wolverhampton [7] 68	d						11 48						12 14									12 48
Stafford 65,67	d						12 02						12 28									13 02
Stoke-on-Trent 50	d				11 56		12 20		12 25				12 44	12 48						12 56		13 20
Longport 50	d																					
Kidsgrove 50	d				12 04															13 04		
Crewe [10]	d		11 48	12 11						12 17	12 30							12 48	13 11			
Sandbach	d		11 55							12 24								12 55				
Holmes Chapel	d		12 00							12 29								13 00				
Goostrey	d		12 03															13 03				
Chelford	d		12 08															13 08				
Alderley Edge	d		12 13							12 38		12 49						13 13				
Wilmslow	d		12 16	12 27						12 42	12 49	12 52						13 16	13 27			
Styal	d									12 46												
Manchester Airport	a									12 55												
Handforth	d		12 19									12 55						13 19				
Congleton	d				12 10															13 10		
Macclesfield	a				12 17		12 36		12 41				13 01							13 17		13 36
	d				12 18		12 37		12 41				13 02							13 18		13 37
Prestbury	d				12 22															13 22		
Adlington (Cheshire)	d				12 25															13 25		
Poynton	d				12 28															13 28		
Bramhall	d				12 31															13 31		
Cheadle Hulme	d		12 24		12 36							12 59						13 24		13 36		
Stockport	a		12 28	12 35	12 40		12 49		12 54		12 59	13 05	13 13	13 16				13 28	13 35	13 40		13 49
	d	12 26	12 29	12 36	12 41	12 45	12 50	12 53	12 56		12 59	13 06	13 14	13 17	13 17	13 20	13 26	13 29	13 36	13 41	13 45	13 50
Heaton Chapel	d		12 32		12 44											13 24		13 32		13 44		
Levenshulme	d		12 35			12 50										13 27		13 35			13 50	
Manchester Picc. [10] 85,89	a	12 37	12 43	12 46	12 52	12 56	13 00	13 02	13 05	13 21	13 13	13 17	13 24	13 27	13 30	13 36	13 37	13 43	13 46	13 52	13 56	14 00
Manchester Oxford Road 85,89	a	12 41								13 24		13 20					13 41					
Deansgate 85,89	a									13 28												

A To Liverpool Lime Street
B From Carmarthen
C To Southport
D From Bournemouth
E From Chester
F From Buxton
G From Norwich to Liverpool Lime Street
H From Paignton
I From Cleethorpes to Manchester Airport
J From Milford Haven
K From Bristol Temple Meads

Table T084-F

Saturdays

21 December to 16 May

Stoke-on-Trent and Crewe - Manchester Airport, Stockport and Manchester

Station		TP	VT	NT	AW	NT	XC	VT	NT	NT	EM	NT	VT	NT	NT	XC	TP	VT	NT	AW	NT	XC	VT
		◇1 A	◇1	◇ B	◇ C	D	◇1 E	◇1	F	G	◇ H		◇1	◇	G	◇1 I	◇1 A	◇1	◇ B	■ J	D	◇1 E	◇1
London Euston [15] ⊖65	d		12 00					12 20					12 40					13 00					13 20
Birmingham New Street [12] 68	d						12 57									13 31						13 57	
Wolverhampton [7] 68	d						13 14									13 48						14 14	
Stafford 65,67	d						13 28									14 02						14 28	
Stoke-on-Trent 50	d		13 25				13 44	13 48						13 56		14 20		14 25				14 44	14 48
Longport 50	d																						
Kidsgrove 50	d													14 04									
Crewe [10]	d			13 18	13 30							13 48	14 11						14 16	14 30			
Sandbach	d			13 25								13 55							14 23				
Holmes Chapel	d			13 30								14 00							14 28				
Goostrey	d											14 03											
Chelford	d											14 08											
Alderley Edge	d			13 39		13 49						14 13							14 38		14 49		
Wilmslow	d			13 43	13 48	13 52						14 16	14 27						14 42	14 48	14 52		
Styal	d			13 46															14 46				
Manchester Airport	a			13 55															14 55				
Handforth	d					13 55						14 19									14 55		
Congleton	d													14 10									
Macclesfield	a		13 41				14 01							14 17		14 36		14 41				15 01	
	d		13 41				14 02							14 18		14 37		14 41				15 02	
Prestbury	d													14 22									
Adlington (Cheshire)	d													14 25									
Poynton	d													14 29									
Bramhall	d													14 31									
Cheadle Hulme	d					13 58						14 24		14 36							14 59		
Stockport	a		13 54		13 59	14 05	14 13	14 16				14 28	14 35			14 49		14 54		15 00	15 04	15 13	15 16
	d	13 53	13 56		13 59	14 06	14 14	14 17	14 17	14 20	14 26	14 29	14 36		14 45	14 50	14 53	14 56		15 00	15 05	15 14	15 17
Heaton Chapel	d									14 24		14 32		14 43									
Levenshulme	d									14 27		14 35		14 46	14 50								
Manchester Picc. [10] 85,89	a	14 02	14 05	14 21	14 14	14 16	14 24	14 27	14 30	14 36	14 37	14 43	14 46	14 52	14 56	15 00	15 02	15 05	15 21	15 15	15 17	15 24	15 27
Manchester Oxford Road 85,89	a			14 24		14 19					14 41								15 24		15 20		
Deansgate 85,89	a			14 28															15 28				

Station		NT	NT	EM	NT	VT	NT	NT	XC	TP	VT	NT	AW	NT	XC	VT	NT	NT	EM	NT	VT	NT	NT
		F	G	◇ H		◇1	◇	G	◇1 K	◇1 A	◇1	◇ B	■ L	D	◇1 E	◇1	F	G	◇ H		◇1	◇	G
London Euston [15] ⊖65	d					13 40					14 00					14 20					14 40		
Birmingham New Street [12] 68	d								14 31						14 57								
Wolverhampton [7] 68	d								14 48						15 14								
Stafford 65,67	d								15 02						15 28								
Stoke-on-Trent 50	d						14 56		15 20		15 25				15 44	15 48						15 58	
Longport 50	d																						
Kidsgrove 50	d						15 04															16 06	
Crewe [10]	d				14 48	15 11						15 16	15 30							15 48	16 11		
Sandbach	d				14 55							15 23								15 55			
Holmes Chapel	d				15 00							15 28								16 00			
Goostrey	d				15 03															16 03			
Chelford	d				15 08															16 08			
Alderley Edge	d				15 13							15 38		15 50						16 13			
Wilmslow	d				15 16	15 27						15 42	15 47	15 53						16 16	16 27		
Styal	d											15 46											
Manchester Airport	a											15 55											
Handforth	d				15 19									15 56						16 19			
Congleton	d						15 10															16 12	
Macclesfield	a						15 17		15 36		15 41				16 01							16 19	
	d						15 18		15 37		15 41				16 02							16 20	
Prestbury	d						15 22															16 24	
Adlington (Cheshire)	d						15 25															16 27	
Poynton	d						15 29															16 30	
Bramhall	d						15 31															16 33	
Cheadle Hulme	d				15 24		15 36							16 01						16 24		16 37	
Stockport	a				15 28	15 35	15 40		15 49		15 54		16 00	16 06	16 13	16 16				16 28	16 35		
	d	15 17	15 20	15 26	15 29	15 36	15 41	15 45	15 50	15 53	15 56		16 00	16 06	16 14	16 17	16 17	16 20	16 26	16 29	16 36		16 46
Heaton Chapel	d		15 24		15 32		15 44											16 24		16 32			
Levenshulme	d		15 27		15 35			15 50										16 27		16 35			
Manchester Picc. [10] 85,89	a	15 30	15 36	15 37	15 43	15 46	15 52	15 56	16 00	16 02	16 05	16 21	16 15	16 17	16 24	16 27	16 30	16 36	16 37	16 43	16 46	16 52	16 56
Manchester Oxford Road 85,89	a			15 41								16 24		16 20					16 41				
Deansgate 85,89	a											16 28											

A From Cleethorpes to Manchester Airport
B To Liverpool Lime Street
C From Fishguard Harbour
D To Southport
E From Bournemouth
F From Chester
G From Buxton
H From Norwich to Liverpool Lime Street
I From Paignton
J From Milford Haven
K From Bristol Temple Meads
L From Carmarthen

Table T084-F

Saturdays

21 December to 16 May

Stoke-on-Trent and Crewe - Manchester Airport, Stockport and Manchester

		XC	TP	VT	NT	AW	NT	XC	VT	NT	NT	EM	NT	VT	NT	NT	XC	TP	VT	NT	AW	NT
		◇1 A	◇1 B	◇1	◇ C	D	E	◇1 F	◇1	G	H	◇ I		◇1	◇	H	◇1 J	◇1 B	◇1	◇ C	◇ K	E
London Euston 15 ⊖65	d			15 00					15 20					15 40					16 00			
Birmingham New Street 12 68	d	15 31						15 57									16 31					
Wolverhampton 7 68	d	15 48						16 14									16 48					
Stafford 65,67	d	16 02						16 28									17 02					
Stoke-on-Trent 50	d	16 20		16 25				16 44	16 48						16 56		17 20		17 25			
Longport 50	d																					
Kidsgrove 50	d														17 04							
Crewe 10	d				16 16	16 30							16 48	17 11						17 16	17 30	
Sandbach	d				16 23								16 55							17 23		
Holmes Chapel	d				16 28								17 00							17 28		
Goostrey	d												17 03									
Chelford	d												17 08									
Alderley Edge	d				16 38		16 50						17 13							17 38		17 49
Wilmslow	d				16 42	16 48	16 53						17 16	17 27						17 42	17 48	17 52
Styal	d				16 46															17 46		
Manchester Airport ✈	a				16 55															17 55		
Handforth	d						16 56						17 19									17 55
Congleton	d														17 10							
Macclesfield	a	16 36		16 41				17 01							17 17		17 36		17 41			
	d	16 37		16 41				17 02							17 18		17 37		17 41			
Prestbury	d														17 22							
Adlington (Cheshire)	d														17 25							
Poynton	d														17 29							
Bramhall	d														17 31							
Cheadle Hulme	d						17 00						17 24		17 36							17 59
Stockport	a	16 49		16 54		17 00	17 05	17 13	17 16				17 28	17 35	17 40		17 49		17 54		18 00	18 04
	d	16 50	16 53	16 56		17 00	17 06	17 14	17 17	17 17	17 20	17 26	17 29	17 36	17 41	17 45	17 50	17 53	17 56		18 00	18 05
Heaton Chapel	d										17 24		17 32		17 44							
Levenshulme	d										17 27		17 35			17 50						
Manchester Picc. 10 85,89	a	17 00	17 02	17 05	17 21	17 14	17 17	17 24	17 27	17 30	17 36	17 37	17 43	17 46	17 53	17 56	18 00	18 02	18 05	18 21	18 15	18 17
Manchester Oxford Road 85,89	a				17 25							17 41								18 25		18 20
Deansgate 85,89	a				17 28		17 22													18 28		

		XC	VT	NT	NT	EM	NT	VT	NT	NT	XC	TP	VT	NT	AW	NT	XC	VT	NT	EM	NT	VT	NT
		◇1 F	◇1	G	H	◇ I		◇1	◇	H	◇1 L	◇1 B	◇1	◇ C	D	E	◇1 F	◇1	G	◇ I		◇1	◇
London Euston 15 ⊖65	d		16 20					16 40					17 00					17 20				17 40	
Birmingham New Street 12 68	d	16 57									17 31						17 57						
Wolverhampton 7 68	d	17 14									17 48						18 14						
Stafford 65,67	d	17 28									18 02						18 28						
Stoke-on-Trent 50	d	17 44	17 48						17 56		18 20		18 25				18 44	18 48					18 58
Longport 50	d																						
Kidsgrove 50	d								18 04														19 06
Crewe 10	d						17 48	18 11						18 16	18 30						18 48	19 11	
Sandbach	d						17 55							18 23							18 55		
Holmes Chapel	d						18 00							18 28							19 00		
Goostrey	d						18 03														19 03		
Chelford	d						18 08														19 08		
Alderley Edge	d						18 13							18 38		18 49					19 13		
Wilmslow	d						18 16	18 27						18 42	18 48	18 52					19 16	19 27	
Styal	d													18 46									
Manchester Airport ✈	a													18 55									
Handforth	d						18 19									18 55					19 19		
Congleton	d								18 10														19 12
Macclesfield	a	18 01							18 17		18 36		18 41				19 01						19 19
	d	18 02							18 18		18 37		18 41				19 02						19 20
Prestbury	d								18 22														19 24
Adlington (Cheshire)	d								18 25														19 27
Poynton	d								18 29														19 30
Bramhall	d								18 31														19 33
Cheadle Hulme	d						18 24		18 36							18 59					19 24		19 37
Stockport	a	18 13	18 16				18 28	18 35	18 40		18 49		18 54		19 00	19 04	19 13	19 16			19 28	19 35	19 41
	d	18 14	18 17	18 17	18 21	18 26	18 29	18 36	18 41	18 46	18 50	18 53	18 56		19 00	19 06	19 14	19 17	19 17	19 26	19 29	19 36	19 42
Heaton Chapel	d				18 24		18 32		18 44												19 32		
Levenshulme	d				18 27		18 35			18 50											19 35		
Manchester Picc. 10 85,89	a	18 24	18 27	18 30	18 36	18 37	18 43	18 46	18 53	18 57	19 01	19 03	19 05	19 21	19 15	19 16	19 24	19 27	19 30	19 37	19 43	19 45	19 52
Manchester Oxford Road 85,89	a					18 41								19 24		19 19				19 41			
Deansgate 85,89	a													19 28									

A From Penzance
B From Cleethorpes to Manchester Airport
C To Liverpool Lime Street
D From Milford Haven
E To Southport
F From Bournemouth
G From Chester
H From Buxton
I From Norwich to Liverpool Lime Street
J From Bristol Temple Meads
K From Carmarthen
L From Paignton

Table T084-F

Saturdays

21 December to 16 May

Stoke-on-Trent and Crewe - Manchester Airport, Stockport and Manchester

		NT	XC	TP	VT	NT	AW	NT	XC	VT	NT	EM	NT	VT	NT	NT	XC	TP	VT	AW	NT	XC
		A	◇1 B	◇1 C	◇1	◇ D	E	F	◇1 G	◇1	H	◇ I		◇1	A	◇	◇1 J	◇1 C	◇1	K	D	◇1 G
London Euston 15 ⊖65	d				18 00					18 20				18 40					19 00			
Birmingham New Street 12 68	d		18 31						18 57								19 31					19 57
Wolverhampton 7 68	d		18 48						19 14								19 48					20 14
Stafford 65,67	d		19 02						19 28								20 02					20 28
Stoke-on-Trent 50	d		19 20		19 25				19 44	19 48						19 58	20 20		20 25			20 44
Longport 50	d																					
Kidsgrove 50	d															20 06						
Crewe 10	d					19 17	19 30						19 48	20 12						20 30		
Sandbach	d					19 24							19 55									
Holmes Chapel	d					19 29							20 00									
Goostrey	d												20 03									
Chelford	d												20 08									
Alderley Edge	d					19 38		19 49					20 13									
Wilmslow	d					19 43	19 48	19 52					20 16	20 28						20 47	20 43	
Styal	d					19 46															20 46	
Manchester Airport ✈	a					19 54															20 54	
Handforth	d							19 55					20 19									
Congleton	d															20 12						
Macclesfield	a		19 36		19 41				20 01							20 19	20 36		20 41			21 01
	d		19 37		19 41				20 02							20 20	20 37		20 41			21 02
Prestbury	d															20 24						
Adlington (Cheshire)	d															20 27						
Poynton	d															20 30						
Bramhall	d															20 33						
Cheadle Hulme	d							19 58					20 24			20 37						
Stockport	a		19 49		19 54		19 59	20 04	20 13	20 16			20 28	20 36		20 41	20 49		20 54	21 00		21 13
	d	19 46	19 50	19 53	19 56		19 59	20 05	20 14	20 17	20 18	20 26	20 29	20 37	20 35	20 42	20 50	20 53	20 56	21 00		21 14
Heaton Chapel	d												20 32									
Levenshulme	d												20 35									
Manchester Picc. 10 85,89	a	19 56	20 00	20 02	20 05	20 21	20 13	20 17	20 24	20 27	20 30	20 37	20 43	20 45	20 46	20 55	20 59	21 02	21 04	21 15	21 16	21 24
Manchester Oxford Road 85,89	a					20 24		20 20				20 41									21 19	
Deansgate 85,89	a					20 28															21 29	

		EM	VT	NT	NT	NT	VT	NT	XC	TP	AW	NT	NT	XC	NT	VT	NT	TP	NT	NT	XC	NT	NT
		◇ L	◇1	H		A	◇1	◇	◇1 B	◇1 M	◇ E	D	H	◇1 G		◇1	A	◇1 C	D	◇	◇1 G	H	N
London Euston 15 ⊖65	d		19 20				19 40									20 20							
Birmingham New Street 12 68	d								20 31					20 57							21 57		
Wolverhampton 7 68	d								20 48					21 18							22 14		
Stafford 65,67	d								21 02					21 32							22 28		
Stoke-on-Trent 50	d		20 48					20 58	21 20					21 48		22 07				22 29	22 44		
Longport 50	d																						
Kidsgrove 50	d							21 06												22 37			
Crewe 10	d				20 48		21 20				21 30				21 48								
Sandbach	d				20 55										21 56								
Holmes Chapel	d				21 00										22 01								
Goostrey	d				21 03										22 04								
Chelford	d				21 08										22 09								
Alderley Edge	d				21 13										22 14								
Wilmslow	d				21 16		21 35				21 48	21 42			22 17				22 42				
Styal	d											21 45							22 45				
Manchester Airport ✈	a											21 53							22 53				
Handforth	d				21 19										22 20								
Congleton	d							21 12												22 43			
Macclesfield	a							21 19	21 36					22 05		22 24				22 50	23 01		
	d							21 20	21 37					22 06		22 24				22 51	23 02		
Prestbury	d							21 24												22 55			
Adlington (Cheshire)	d							21 27												22 58			
Poynton	d							21 30												23 01			
Bramhall	d							21 33												23 04			
Cheadle Hulme	d				21 24			21 37							22 25					23 07			
Stockport	a		21 21		21 28		21 44	21 41	21 49		21 58			22 17	22 29	22 37				23 11	23 13		
	d	21 20	21 22	21 17	21 29	21 36	21 45	21 42	21 50	21 53	21 58		22 17	22 21	22 30	22 38	22 42	22 53		23 14	23 14	23 18	23 22
Heaton Chapel	d			21 22	21 32			21 45							22 33		22 46						23 26
Levenshulme	d			21 25	21 35			21 49							22 36		22 50						23 29
Manchester Picc. 10 85,89	a	21 29	21 32	21 33	21 43	21 46	21 53	21 56	22 00	22 04	22 13	22 17	22 28	22 33	22 44	22 50	22 59	23 02	23 20	23 26	23 29	23 31	23 36
Manchester Oxford Road 85,89	a											22 20							23 24				
Deansgate 85,89	a											22 33							23 27				

A From Buxton
B From Bristol Temple Meads
C From Cleethorpes to Manchester Airport
D To Liverpool Lime Street
E From Carmarthen
F To Southport
G From Bournemouth
H From Chester
I From Norwich to Liverpool Lime Street
J From Exeter St Davids
K From Milford Haven
L From Norwich
M From Cleethorpes
N From Hazel Grove

Table T084-F

Saturdays
21 December to 16 May

Stoke-on-Trent and Crewe - Manchester Airport, Stockport and Manchester

	VT	NT	AW	NT	NT	XC
	◇1		◇ A	B		◇1
London Euston 15 ⊖65 d	21 01					
Birmingham New Street 12 68 d						22 31
Wolverhampton 7 68 d						22 48
Stafford 65,67 d	22 35					23 02
Stoke-on-Trent 50 d						23 20
Longport 50 d						
Kidsgrove 50 d						
Crewe 10 d	23 00		23 06		23 12	
Sandbach d					23 19	
Holmes Chapel d					23 24	
Goostrey d					23 27	
Chelford d					23 32	
Alderley Edge d					23 37	
Wilmslow d	23 16	23 22	23 24		23 40	
Styal d						
Manchester Airport a						
Handforth d					23 43	
Congleton d						
Macclesfield a						23 38
d						23 39
Prestbury d						
Adlington (Cheshire) d						
Poynton d						
Bramhall d						
Cheadle Hulme d					23 48	
Stockport a	23 26		23 35		23 52	23 53
d	23 27		23 35	23 42	23 53	23 54
Heaton Chapel d					23 56	
Levenshulme d					23 59	
Manchester Picc. 10 85,89 a	23 39	23 42	23 49	23 57	00 06	00 10
Manchester Oxford Road 85,89 a						
Deansgate 85,89 a						

Sundays
15 December to 10 May

	NT	TP	AW	NT	NT	NT	NT	TP	AW	NT	NT	NT	NT	NT	XC	NT	NT	VT	NT	VT	TP	AW
	C	◇1 D	◇	B	E	◇	B	◇1 D	◇	E	◇ F	◇ G	H	I	◇1	◇ G	◇ F	◇1	B	◇1	◇1 J	◇ K
London Euston 15 ⊖65 d																		08 10		08 20		
Birmingham New Street 12 68 d															09 01							
Wolverhampton 7 68 d															09 18							
Stafford 65,67 d															09 32							
Stoke-on-Trent 50 d											09 30	09 30			09 52					10 21		
Longport 50 d																						
Kidsgrove 50 d											09 38	09 38										
Crewe 10 d			08 30			08 58			09 29							09 56	09 56	10 19				10 28
Sandbach d						09 05										10 03	10 03					
Holmes Chapel d						09 09										10 07	10 07					
Goostrey d						09 12										10 10	10 10					
Chelford d						09 17										10 15	10 15					
Alderley Edge d						09 21			09 47							10 19	10 19					
Wilmslow d			08 49		08 38	09 24			09 50	09 43						10 22	10 22	10 34				10 47
Styal d					08 41					09 46												
Manchester Airport a					08 50					09 54												
Handforth d						09 27										10 25	10 25					
Congleton d											09 44	09 44										
Macclesfield a											09 51	09 51			10 09					10 36		
d											09 52	09 52			10 10					10 38		
Prestbury d											09 56	09 56										
Adlington (Cheshire) d											09 59	09 59										
Poynton d											10 02	10 02										
Bramhall d											10 05	10 05										
Cheadle Hulme d						09 32					10 08	10 08				10 30	10 30					
Stockport a						09 36					10 13	10 13			10 22	10 34	10 34	10 43		10 50		11 00
d	00 07	08 35		09 00		09 37	09 43	09 53			10 13	10 13	10 19	10 19	10 27	10 35	10 35	10 44	10 46	10 52	10 56	11 00
Heaton Chapel d				09 04							10 17	10 17										
Levenshulme d				09 07							10 21	10 21										
Manchester Picc. 10 85,89 a	00 17	08 43	09 13	09 13	09 16	09 48	09 54	10 03	10 11	10 20	10 28	10 29	10 31	10 32	10 38	10 47	10 48	10 53	10 56	11 00	11 06	11 16
Manchester Oxford Road 85,89 a					09 20					10 24												
Deansgate 85,89 a					09 23					10 27												

A From Cardiff Central
B From Buxton
C not 15 December. From Chester
D From Sheffield to Manchester Airport
E To Liverpool Lime Street
F until 29 March
G from 5 April
H until 29 March. From Chester
I from 5 April. From Chester
J From Doncaster to Manchester Airport
K From Shrewsbury

Table T084-F

Sundays
15 December to 10 May

Stoke-on-Trent and Crewe - Manchester Airport, Stockport and Manchester

	NT	NT	XC	EM	NT	NT	NT	VT	AW	TP	NT	NT	NT	EM	XC	XC	NT	NT	TP	VT	AW	NT
	A	◇	◇1	◇ B	◇ C	◇ D	E	◇1	◇ F	◇1 G	A	H	I	◇ B	◇1 J	◇1 K	◇	E	◇1 G	◇1	L	A
London Euston 15 ⊖65 d								09 20												10 19		
Birmingham New Street 12 68 d			10 01												11 01	11 01						
Wolverhampton 7 68 d			10 18												11 18	11 18						
Stafford 65,67 d			10 33												11 33	11 33						
Stoke-on-Trent 50 d		10 30	10 52					11 23							11 52	11 52				12 25		
Longport 50 d																						
Kidsgrove 50 d		10 38																				
Crewe 10 d					10 55	10 55			11 23								11 58				12 28	
Sandbach d					11 02	11 02											12 05					
Holmes Chapel d					11 06	11 06											12 09					
Goostrey d					11 09	11 09											12 12					
Chelford d					11 14	11 14											12 17					
Alderley Edge d					11 18	11 18											12 21					
Wilmslow d	10 40				11 21	11 21			11 43		11 38						12 24				12 48	12 44
Styal d	10 43										11 41											12 47
Manchester Airport a	10 51										11 49											12 55
Handforth d					11 24	11 24											12 27					
Congleton d		10 44																				
Macclesfield a		10 51	11 08					11 38							12 08	12 08				12 40		
d		10 52	11 09					11 39							12 09	12 09				12 42		
Prestbury d		10 56																				
Adlington (Cheshire) d		10 59																				
Poynton d		11 02																				
Bramhall d		11 05																				
Cheadle Hulme d		11 09			11 29	11 29											12 32					
Stockport a		11 13	11 22		11 33	11 33		11 52							12 24	12 24	12 36			12 55	13 00	
d		11 14	11 23	11 26	11 34	11 34	11 44	11 53		11 57		12 13	12 18	12 26	12 30	12 30	12 37	12 43	12 53	12 56	13 00	
Heaton Chapel d		11 18											12 22									
Levenshulme d		11 21											12 26									
Manchester Picc. 10 85,89 a	11 19	11 28	11 33	11 38	11 46	11 49	11 56	12 04	12 07	12 10	12 21	12 26	12 36	12 37	12 40	12 42	12 47	12 56	13 04	13 05	13 15	13 21
Manchester Oxford Road 85,89 a	11 23	11 32		11 41							12 24			12 41								13 24
Deansgate 85,89 a	11 26										12 28											13 29

	XC	EM	NT	VT	NT	TP	NT	NT	XC	VT	NT	EM	NT	VT	NT	XC	TP	VT	AW	NT	XC
	◇1 M	◇ B	◇	◇1	E	◇1 G	A	◇	◇1 N	◇1	O	◇ B	◇	◇1	E	◇1	◇1 G	◇1	◇ L	A	◇1 N
London Euston 15 ⊖65 d				11 19						12 17				12 37				12 57			
Birmingham New Street 12 68 d	11 57								12 57							13 31					13 57
Wolverhampton 7 68 d	12 15								13 14							13 48					14 14
Stafford 65,67 d	12 30								13 28							14 02					14 28
Stoke-on-Trent 50 d	12 46			13 11				13 25	13 44	13 50						14 20		14 26			14 44
Longport 50 d																					
Kidsgrove 50 d								13 33													
Crewe 10 d			12 57										13 56	14 13					14 30		
Sandbach d			13 04										14 03								
Holmes Chapel d			13 08										14 07								
Goostrey d			13 11										14 10								
Chelford d			13 16										14 15								
Alderley Edge d			13 20										14 19								
Wilmslow d			13 23				13 44						14 22	14 28					14 50	14 39	
Styal d							13 47													14 42	
Manchester Airport a							13 56													14 50	
Handforth d			13 26										14 25								
Congleton d								13 39													
Macclesfield a	13 04			13 26				13 46	14 04							14 36		14 42			15 01
d	13 05			13 28				13 47	14 05							14 37		14 42			15 02
Prestbury d								13 51													
Adlington (Cheshire) d								13 54													
Poynton d								13 57													
Bramhall d								14 00													
Cheadle Hulme d			13 31					14 04					14 30								
Stockport a	13 16		13 35	13 41				14 08	14 16	14 22			14 34	14 38		14 50		14 55	15 02		15 14
d	13 17	13 26	13 36	13 42	13 49	13 54		14 13	14 17	14 23	14 21	14 27	14 35	14 39	14 45	14 51	14 54	14 56	15 03		15 15
Heaton Chapel d								14 17			14 25										
Levenshulme d								14 20			14 28										
Manchester Picc. 10 85,89 a	13 28	13 37	13 47	13 50	13 59	14 03	14 21	14 28	14 29	14 32	14 35	14 37	14 44	14 48	14 55	14 59	15 03	15 06	15 15	15 21	15 24
Manchester Oxford Road 85,89 a		13 41					14 24					14 41								15 24	
Deansgate 85,89 a							14 28													15 28	

A To Liverpool Lime Street
B From Nottingham to Liverpool Lime Street
C until 29 March
D from 5 April
E From Buxton
F From Cardiff Central
G From Cleethorpes to Manchester Airport
H until 29 March. From Chester
I from 5 April. From Chester
J from 5 April. From Reading
K until 29 March. From Reading
L From Swansea
M From Southampton Central
N From Bournemouth
O From Chester

Table T084-F

Sundays

15 December to 10 May

Stoke-on-Trent and Crewe - Manchester Airport, Stockport and Manchester

	VT	EM	NT	VT	NT	XC	TP	VT	AW	NT	XC	VT	EM	NT	NT	VT	NT	XC	TP	VT	AW	NT
	◇■	◇ A	◇	◇■	B	◇■ C	◇■ D	◇■	◇ E	F	◇■ G	◇■	◇ H	I	◇	◇■	B	◇■ J	◇■ D	◇■	■ K	F
London Euston ⊖65 d	13 17			13 37				13 57				14 17				14 37				14 57		
Birmingham New Street 68 d						14 31					14 57							15 31				
Wolverhampton 68 d						14 48					15 14							15 48				
Stafford 65,67 d						15 02					15 28							16 02				
Stoke-on-Trent 50 d	14 50					15 20		15 26			15 46	15 50						16 20		16 27		
Longport 50 d																						
Kidsgrove 50 d																						
Crewe d			14 56	15 13					15 28						15 56	16 13					16 30	
Sandbach d			15 03												16 03							
Holmes Chapel d			15 07												16 07							
Goostrey d			15 10												16 10							
Chelford d			15 15												16 15							
Alderley Edge d			15 19												16 19							
Wilmslow d			15 22	15 29					15 49	15 44					16 22	16 29					16 49	16 44
Styal d										15 47												16 47
Manchester Airport ✈ a										15 55												16 55
Handforth d			15 25												16 25							
Congleton d																						
Macclesfield a						15 36		15 42			16 04							16 36		16 42		
d						15 37		15 42			16 05							16 37		16 42		
Prestbury d																						
Adlington (Cheshire) d																						
Poynton d																						
Bramhall d																						
Cheadle Hulme d			15 30												16 30							
Stockport a	15 20		15 34	15 38		15 50		15 55	16 00		16 16	16 23			16 34	16 38		16 50		16 56	17 00	
d	15 21	15 26	15 35	15 39	15 43	15 51	15 54	15 56	16 00		16 17	16 24	16 26	16 28	16 35	16 39	16 43	16 51	16 54	16 57	17 00	
Heaton Chapel d																						
Levenshulme d																						
Manchester Picc. 85,89 a	15 31	15 37	15 45	15 48	15 54	15 59	16 02	16 05	16 14	16 21	16 29	16 32	16 37	16 40	16 45	16 48	16 54	16 59	17 02	17 06	17 17	17 21
Manchester Oxford Road 85,89 a		15 41								16 24			16 41									17 24
Deansgate 85,89 a										16 28												17 28

	XC	NT	VT	EM	NT	VT	NT	XC	TP	VT	AW	NT	XC	VT	EM	NT	NT	VT	NT	XC	TP
	◇■ G	◇	◇■	◇ L	◇	◇■	B	◇■ J	◇■ D	◇■	■ M	F	◇■ G	◇■	◇ A	I	◇	◇■	B	◇■ N	◇■ D
London Euston ⊖65 d			15 17			15 37				15 57				16 17				16 37			
Birmingham New Street 68 d	15 57							16 31					16 57							17 31	
Wolverhampton 68 d	16 14							16 48					17 14							17 48	
Stafford 65,67 d	16 28							17 02					17 28							18 02	
Stoke-on-Trent 50 d	16 47	16 30	16 53					17 20		17 26			17 47	17 50						18 20	
Longport 50 d																					
Kidsgrove 50 d		16 38																			
Crewe d					16 56	17 13					17 30						17 56	18 13			
Sandbach d					17 03												18 03				
Holmes Chapel d					17 07												18 07				
Goostrey d					17 10												18 10				
Chelford d					17 15												18 15				
Alderley Edge d					17 19												18 19				
Wilmslow d					17 22	17 29					17 49	17 44					18 22	18 29			
Styal d												17 47									
Manchester Airport ✈ a												17 55									
Handforth d					17 25												18 25				
Congleton d		16 44																			
Macclesfield a	17 04	16 51						17 36		17 42			18 04							18 36	
d	17 05	16 52						17 37		17 42			18 05							18 37	
Prestbury d		16 56																			
Adlington (Cheshire) d		16 59																			
Poynton d		17 02																			
Bramhall d		17 05																			
Cheadle Hulme d		17 09			17 30												18 30				
Stockport a	17 16	17 14	17 23		17 34	17 38		17 50		17 55	18 01		18 16	18 23			18 34	18 38		18 50	
d	17 17	17 14	17 24	17 29	17 35	17 39	17 43	17 51	17 54	17 56	18 01		18 17	18 24	18 26	18 29	18 35	18 39	18 43	18 51	18 54
Heaton Chapel d		17 18																			
Levenshulme d		17 21																			
Manchester Picc. 85,89 a	17 29	17 30	17 32	17 38	17 44	17 48	17 54	17 59	18 03	18 05	18 18	18 21	18 29	18 32	18 37	18 38	18 45	18 48	18 54	18 59	19 03
Manchester Oxford Road 85,89 a				17 41								18 24			18 41						
Deansgate 85,89 a												18 28									

A From Norwich to Liverpool Lime Street
B From Buxton
C From Paignton
D From Cleethorpes to Manchester Airport
E From Carmarthen
F To Liverpool Lime Street
G From Bournemouth
H From Nottingham to Liverpool Lime Street
I From Chester
J From Plymouth
K From Swansea
L From Peterborough to Liverpool Lime Street
M From Milford Haven
N From Bristol Temple Meads

Table T084-F

Sundays

15 December to 10 May

Stoke-on-Trent and Crewe - Manchester Airport, Stockport and Manchester

	VT	AW	NT	XC	VT	EM	NT	VT	NT	XC	TP	VT	AW	NT	XC	VT	NT	EM	NT	VT	NT	XC
	◇■	■ A	B	◇■ C	◇■	◇ D	◇	◇■	E	◇■ F	◇■ G	◇■	■ H	B	◇■ C	◇■	I	◇ J	◇	◇■	E	◇■ K
London Euston ⊖65 d	16 57				17 17			17 37				17 57				18 17				18 37		
Birmingham New Street 68 d				17 57						18 31					18 57							19 31
Wolverhampton 68 d				18 14						18 48					19 14							19 48
Stafford 65,67 d				18 28						19 02					19 28							20 02
Stoke-on-Trent 50 d	18 26			18 45	18 50					19 20		19 26			19 46	19 50						20 20
Longport 50 d																						
Kidsgrove 50 d																						
Crewe d		18 31					18 56	19 13					19 31						19 56	20 13		
Sandbach d							19 03												20 03			
Holmes Chapel d							19 07												20 07			
Goostrey d							19 10												20 10			
Chelford d							19 15												20 15			
Alderley Edge d							19 19												20 19			
Wilmslow d		18 49	18 44				19 22	19 29					19 49	19 44					20 22	20 29		
Styal d			18 47											19 47								
Manchester Airport ✈ a			18 55											19 55								
Handforth d							19 25												20 25			
Congleton d																						
Macclesfield a	18 42			19 04						19 36		19 42			20 04							20 36
d	18 42			19 05						19 37		19 42			20 05							20 37
Prestbury d																						
Adlington (Cheshire) d																						
Poynton d																						
Bramhall d																						
Cheadle Hulme d							19 30												20 30			
Stockport a	18 56	19 00		19 17	19 23		19 34	19 38		19 50		19 56	20 00		20 16	20 23			20 34	20 38		20 50
d	18 57	19 00		19 18	19 24	19 26	19 35	19 39	19 43	19 51	19 54	19 57	20 00		20 17	20 24	20 21	20 27	20 35	20 39	20 43	20 51
Heaton Chapel d																	20 25					
Levenshulme d																	20 28					
Manchester Picc. 85,89 a	19 06	19 16	19 21	19 29	19 32	19 37	19 44	19 48	19 54	19 59	20 03	20 06	20 16	20 21	20 28	20 32	20 38	20 38	20 47	20 48	20 54	21 00
Manchester Oxford Road 85,89 a			19 24			19 42								20 24								
Deansgate 85,89 a			19 28											20 28								

	TP	VT	AW	NT	NT	XC	VT	EM	NT	VT	NT	XC	TP	VT	NT	AW	XC	NT	VT	NT	VT	NT
	◇■ G	◇■	■ A	B	◇	◇■ C	◇■	◇ J		◇■	E	◇■ K	◇■ G	◇■	B	■ H	◇■ C	I	◇■		◇■	E
London Euston ⊖65 d		18 57					19 17			19 37				19 57					20 15		20 35	
Birmingham New Street 68 d						19 57						20 31					20 57					
Wolverhampton 68 d						20 14						20 52					21 14					
Stafford 65,67 d						20 29						21 06					21 28				22 03	
Stoke-on-Trent 50 d		20 26			20 30	20 45	20 50					21 21		21 26			21 45		21 50			
Longport 50 d																						
Kidsgrove 50 d					20 38																	
Crewe d			20 32						20 55	21 13						21 31				21 55	22 22	
Sandbach d									21 02											22 02		
Holmes Chapel d									21 06											22 06		
Goostrey d									21 09											22 09		
Chelford d									21 14											22 14		
Alderley Edge d									21 18							21 48				22 18		
Wilmslow d			20 50	20 44					21 21	21 29					21 43	21 52				22 21	22 37	
Styal d				20 47											21 46							
Manchester Airport ✈ a				20 55											21 55							
Handforth d									21 24											22 24		
Congleton d					20 44																	
Macclesfield a		20 42			20 51	21 03						21 39		21 43			22 03					
d		20 42			20 52	21 04						21 40		21 43			22 04					
Prestbury d					20 56																	
Adlington (Cheshire) d					20 59																	
Poynton d					21 02																	
Bramhall d					21 05																	
Cheadle Hulme d					21 09				21 29											22 29		
Stockport a		20 56	21 01		21 13	21 15	21 19		21 33	21 38		21 52		21 59		22 04	22 15		22 21	22 33	22 46	
d	20 54	20 57	21 01		21 14	21 16	21 20	21 25	21 34	21 39	21 45	21 53	21 56	22 00		22 04	22 16	22 19	22 22	22 34	22 47	22 50
Heaton Chapel d					21 17															22 37		
Levenshulme d					21 21															22 40		
Manchester Picc. 85,89 a	21 04	21 06	21 15	21 17	21 29	21 29	21 31	21 36	21 43	21 49	21 55	22 02	22 05	22 09	22 18	22 19	22 26	22 28	22 31	22 47	22 55	23 00
Manchester Oxford Road 85,89 a				21 20											22 21							
Deansgate 85,89 a				21 29											22 31							

A From Swansea
B To Liverpool Lime Street
C From Bournemouth
D From Norwich to Liverpool Lime Street
E From Buxton
F From Penzance
G From Cleethorpes to Manchester Airport
H From Milford Haven
I From Chester
J From Norwich
K From Bristol Temple Meads

Table T084-F

Sundays
15 December to 10 May

Stoke-on-Trent and Crewe - Manchester Airport, Stockport and Manchester

	TP	XC	NT	NT	NT	NT	VT	VT
	◇■	◇■				◇	◇■	◇■
	A	B	C		D		🛏	🛏
London Euston 15 ⊖65 d							21 25	21 51
Birmingham New Street 12 68 d		21 57						
Wolverhampton 7 68 d		22 14						
Stafford 65,67 d		22 28						23s54
Stoke-on-Trent 50 d		22 44				23 00	23 33	
Longport 50 d								
Kidsgrove 50 d						23 08		
Crewe 10 d				22 56				00s16
Sandbach d				23 03				
Holmes Chapel d				23 07				
Goostrey d				23 10				
Chelford d				23 15				
Alderley Edge d				23 19				
Wilmslow d			22 54	23 22				
Styal d			22 57					
Manchester Airport ✈ a			23 05					
Handforth d				23 25				
Congleton d						23 14		
Macclesfield a		23 01				23 21	23 49	
d		23 02				23 22	23 50	
Prestbury d						23 26		
Adlington (Cheshire) d						23 29		
Poynton d						23 32		
Bramhall d						23 35		
Cheadle Hulme d				23 30		23 39		
Stockport a		23 14		23 34		23 44	00 03	00s39
d	23 03	23 15		23 35	23 45	23 44	00 04	
Heaton Chapel d				23 38		23 48		
Levenshulme d				23 41		23 51		
Manchester Picc. 10 85,89 a	23 19	23 24	23 31	23 49	23 54	23 58	00 13	00 48
Manchester Oxford Road 85,89 a			23 35					
Deansgate 85,89 a			23 38					

A From Cleethorpes
B From Bournemouth
C To Liverpool Lime Street
D From Buxton

Table T084-R

Mondays to Fridays
16 December to 15 May

Manchester, Stockport and Manchester Airport - Crewe and Stoke-on-Trent

Miles	Miles	Miles		NT MX	VT	XC	NT	NT	NT	VT	XC	NT	VT	VT	AW	NT	VT	VT	NT	XC	VT	XC
					◇■	◇■			◇	◇■	◇■		◇■	◇■	◇	◇	◇■	◇■		◇■	◇■	■
				A	⊠	B				⊠	C 🍴		⊠	⊠	D 🍴		⊠	⊠		C 🍴	⊠	B 🍴
0	0	—	Deansgate 85,89 d																			
0½	0½	—	**Manchester Oxford Road** 85,89 d																			
1	1	—	**Manchester Picc.** 10 85,89 d		05 05	05 11	05 19		05 38	05 55	06 00	06 03	06 10	06 27	06 30	06 32	06 35	06 43	06 58	07 05	07 15	07 27
4	4	—	Levenshulme d													06 37			07 04			
5½	5½	—	Heaton Chapel d									06 10				06 40			07 07			
7	7	—	**Stockport** a		05 11				05 48	06 02	06 07	06 14	06 17	06 35	06 39	06 44	06 42	06 50	07 10	07 12	07 22	07 35
—	—	—	d		05 13				05 48	06 03	06 08	06 14	06 18	06 36	06 39	06 44	06 43	06 51	07 19	07 13	07 23	07 36
9¼	9¼	—	Cheadle Hulme d						05 52			06 20				06 51			07 24			
9¾	—	—	Bramhall d						05 56							06 54						
12¼	—	—	Poynton d						05 59							06 57						
14¼	—	—	Adlington (Cheshire) d						06 03							07 01						
16¼	—	—	Prestbury d						06 06							07 04						
19	—	—	**Macclesfield** a						06 09				06 31	06 47		07 07	06 55			07 25		07 48
—	—	—	d					06 00	06 10				06 31	06 48		07 08	06 56			07 26		07 49
27	—	—	Congleton d					06 07	06 19							07 15						
—	11½	—	Handforth d									06 24							07 28			
—	—	0	**Manchester Airport** ✈ d				05 45															
—	—	2¼	Styal d				05 49															
—	13	4	**Wilmslow** d	00 02			05 53			06 11	06 16	06 28			06 47			06 59	07 31			
—	14¾	—	Alderley Edge d	00 06			05 56					06 31							07 34			
—	17¾	—	Chelford d	00 10			06 01					06 35							07 39			
—	21½	—	Goostrey d	00 15			06 06					06 40							07 44			
—	23½	—	Holmes Chapel d	00 19			06 09					06 44							07 48			
—	27¼	—	Sandbach d	00 24			06 14					06 49							07 53			
—	32	—	**Crewe** 10 a	00 32	05 33	05 43	06 23			06 27	06 37	06 58			07 08			07 16	08 01			
32½	—	—	Kidsgrove 50 a						06 25							07 21						
35¾	—	—	Longport 50 a																			
38¾	—	—	**Stoke-on-Trent** 50 a			06 05		06 20	06 35				06 46	07 04		07 30	07 11			07 43	07 49	08 05
—	—	—	Stafford 65,67 a		05 54	06 22					06 58			07 22				07 35		08 00		08 23
—	—	—	Wolverhampton 7 68 a			06 38					07 14			07 40						08 16		08 39
—	—	—	Birmingham New Street 12 68 a			06 55					07 33			08 07						08 33		08 57
—	—	—	London Euston 15 ⊖65 a		07 25					08 10			08 20	09 33			08 46	08 53			09 20	

	AW	VT	NT	VT	NT	XC	VT	XC	AW	VT	NT	VT	NT	XC	VT	XC	AW	VT	VT	NT	VT	NT
	◇	◇■	◇	◇■		◇■	◇■	◇■	◇	◇■	◇	◇■		◇■	◇■	◇■	◇	◇■	◇■	◇	◇■	
	E 🍴	⊠		⊠		F 🍴	⊠	B 🍴	D 🍴	⊠		⊠		C 🍴	⊠	B 🍴	E 🍴	G ⊠	H ⊠		⊠	
Deansgate 85,89 d																						
Manchester Oxford Road 85,89 d																						
Manchester Picc. 10 85,89 d	07 30	07 35	07 47	07 55	08 02	08 05	08 15	08 27	08 31	08 35	08 44	08 55	09 01	09 05	09 15	09 27	09 31	09 35	09 35	09 44	09 55	10 01
Levenshulme d					08 08								09 07									10 07
Heaton Chapel d					08 11								09 10									10 10
Stockport a	07 39	07 42	07 55	08 03	08 15	08 12	08 23	08 35	08 39	08 42	08 56	09 03	09 13	09 12	09 22	09 35	09 39	09 42	09 42	09 56	10 03	10 13
d	07 39	07 43	07 56	08 04	08 19	08 13	08 23	08 36	08 39	08 43	08 57	09 04	09 14	09 13	09 23	09 36	09 39	09 43	09 43	09 57	10 04	10 14
Cheadle Hulme d			08 00		08 23						09 01		09 21							10 01		10 21
Bramhall d			08 03								09 04									10 04		
Poynton d			08 06								09 07									10 07		
Adlington (Cheshire) d			08 09								09 10									10 10		
Prestbury d			08 12								09 13									10 13		
Macclesfield a		07 55	08 16			08 25		08 48		08 55	09 17			09 25		09 48		09 55	09 55	10 17		
d		07 56	08 16			08 26		08 49		08 56	09 17			09 26		09 49		09 56	09 56	10 17		
Congleton d			08 23								09 24									10 24		
Handforth d					08 27								09 25									10 25
Manchester Airport ✈ d																						
Styal d																						
Wilmslow d	07 47			08 11	08 30				08 47			09 11	09 28				09 47				10 11	10 28
Alderley Edge d					08 33								09 31									10 31
Chelford d					08 38								09 36									10 36
Goostrey d					08 43								09 41									10 41
Holmes Chapel d					08 46								09 44									10 44
Sandbach d					08 52								09 50									10 50
Crewe 10 a	08 08			08 27	09 00				09 08			09 28	09 58				10 07				10 27	10 58
Kidsgrove 50 a			08 29								09 30									10 30		
Longport 50 a																						
Stoke-on-Trent 50 a		08 11	08 38			08 43	08 49	09 05		09 11	09 39			09 43	09 49	10 05		10 11	10 11	10 39		
Stafford 65,67 a						09 00		09 22						10 00		10 23						
Wolverhampton 7 68 a						09 15		09 39						10 16		10 37						
Birmingham New Street 12 68 a						09 33		09 58						10 33		10 58						
London Euston 15 ⊖65 a		09 49		10 16			10 26			10 51		11 07			11 20			11 40	11 41		12 02	

A From Manchester Piccadilly
B To Bournemouth
C To Bristol Temple Meads
D To Milford Haven
E To Carmarthen
F To Paignton
G until 14 February
H from 17 February

Table T084-R

Mondays to Fridays
16 December to 15 May

Manchester, Stockport and Manchester Airport - Crewe and Stoke-on-Trent

	XC	VT	XC	AW	VT FX	VT FX	VT FO	NT	VT	NT	XC	VT	XC	AW	VT	NT	VT	NT	XC	VT	XC
	◇1 A	◇1 ⊠	◇1 B	◇ C	◇1 D ⊠	◇1 E ⊠	◇1 ⊠	◇	◇1 ⊠		◇1 F	◇1	◇1 B	◇ G	◇1	◇	◇1 ⊠		◇1 A	◇1	◇1 B
Deansgate 85,89 d																					
Manchester Oxford Road 85,89 d																					
Manchester Picc. 85,89 d	10 05	10 15	10 27	10 31	10 35	10 35	10 35	10 44	10 55	11 01	11 05	11 15	11 27	11 31	11 35	11 44	11 55	12 01	12 05	12 15	12 27
Levenshulme d										11 07								12 07			
Heaton Chapel d										11 10								12 10			
Stockport a	10 12	10 22	10 35	10 39	10 42	10 42	10 42	10 56	11 03	11 13	11 12	11 22	11 35	11 39	11 42	11 56	12 03	12 13	12 12	12 22	12 35
d	10 13	10 23	10 36	10 39	10 43	10 43	10 43	10 57	11 04	11 14	11 13	11 23	11 36	11 39	11 43	11 57	12 04	12 14	12 13	12 23	12 36
Cheadle Hulme d								11 01		11 21						12 01		12 21			
Bramhall d								11 04								12 04					
Poynton d								11 07								12 07					
Adlington (Cheshire) d								11 10								12 10					
Prestbury d								11 13								12 13					
Macclesfield a	10 25		10 48		10 55	10 55	10 55	11 17			11 25		11 48		11 55	12 17			12 25		12 48
d	10 26		10 49		10 56	10 56	10 56	11 17			11 26		11 49		11 56	12 17			12 26		12 49
Congleton d								11 24								12 24					
Handforth d										11 25								12 25			
Manchester Airport d																					
Styal d																					
Wilmslow d				10 47					11 11	11 28				11 47			12 11	12 28			
Alderley Edge d										11 31								12 31			
Chelford d										11 36								12 36			
Goostrey d										11 41								12 41			
Holmes Chapel d										11 44								12 44			
Sandbach d										11 50								12 50			
Crewe 10 a				11 07					11 27	11 58				12 07			12 27	12 58			
Kidsgrove 50 a								11 30								12 30					
Longport 50 a																					
Stoke-on-Trent 50 a	10 43	10 49	11 05		11 11	11 11	11 11	11 39			11 43	11 49	12 06		12 11	12 39			12 43	12 49	13 05
Stafford 65,67 a	11 00		11 24								12 00		12 25						13 00		13 24
Wolverhampton 7 68 a	11 16		11 41								12 16		12 41						13 16		13 41
Birmingham New Street 12 68 a	11 33		11 59								12 33		12 59						13 33		13 59
London Euston 15 ⊖65 a		12 20			12 39	12 40	12 41		13 02			13 20			13 40		14 06			14 20	

	AW	VT WX	VT WO	NT	VT	NT	XC	VT	XC	AW	VT	NT	VT	NT	XC	VT	XC	AW	VT	NT	VT	NT
	C	◇1	◇1	◇	◇1		◇1 A	◇1	◇1 B	H	◇1	◇	◇1		◇1 I	◇1	◇1 B	C	◇1	◇	◇1	
Deansgate 85,89 d																						
Manchester Oxford Road 85,89 d																						
Manchester Picc. 85,89 d	12 31	12 35	12 35	12 44	12 55	13 01	13 05	13 15	13 27	13 31	13 35	13 44	13 55	14 01	14 05	14 15	14 27	14 31	14 35	14 44	14 55	15 01
Levenshulme d						13 07								14 07								15 07
Heaton Chapel d						13 10								14 10								15 10
Stockport a	12 39	12 42	12 42	12 56	13 03	13 13	13 12	13 22	13 35	13 39	13 42	13 56	14 03	14 13	14 12	14 22	14 35	14 39	14 42	14 56	15 03	15 13
d	12 39	12 43	12 43	12 57	13 04	13 14	13 13	13 23	13 36	13 39	13 43	13 57	14 04	14 14	14 13	14 23	14 36	14 39	14 43	14 57	15 04	15 14
Cheadle Hulme d				13 01		13 21						14 01		14 20						15 01		15 20
Bramhall d				13 04								14 04								15 04		
Poynton d				13 07								14 07								15 07		
Adlington (Cheshire) d				13 10								14 10								15 10		
Prestbury d				13 13								14 13								15 13		
Macclesfield a		12 55	12 55	13 17			13 25		13 48		13 55	14 17			14 25		14 48		14 55	15 17		
d		12 56	12 56	13 17			13 26		13 49		13 56	14 17			14 26		14 49		14 56	15 17		
Congleton d				13 24								14 24								15 24		
Handforth d						13 25								14 24								15 24
Manchester Airport d																						
Styal d																						
Wilmslow d	12 47				13 11	13 28				13 47			14 11	14 27				14 47			15 11	15 27
Alderley Edge d						13 31								14 30								15 30
Chelford d						13 36								14 35								15 35
Goostrey d						13 41								14 40								15 40
Holmes Chapel d						13 44								14 43								15 43
Sandbach d						13 50								14 49								15 49
Crewe 10 a	13 09				13 27	13 58				14 07			14 27	14 57				15 07			15 27	15 57
Kidsgrove 50 a				13 30								14 30								15 30		
Longport 50 a																						
Stoke-on-Trent 50 a		13 11	13 11	13 39			13 43	13 49	14 05		14 11	14 39			14 43	14 49	15 05		15 11	15 39		
Stafford 65,67 a							14 00		14 23						15 00		15 24					
Wolverhampton 7 68 a							14 16		14 38						15 16		15 41					
Birmingham New Street 12 68 a							14 33		14 59						15 33		15 58					
London Euston 15 ⊖65 a		14 39	14 42		15 07			15 25			15 40		16 06			16 20			16 40		17 03	

A To Exeter St Davids
B To Bournemouth
C To Milford Haven
D until 13 February
E from 17 February
F To Bristol Temple Meads
G To Carmarthen
H To Tenby
I To Paignton

Table T084-R

Mondays to Fridays
16 December to 15 May

Manchester, Stockport and Manchester Airport - Crewe and Stoke-on-Trent

	XC	VT	XC	AW	VT	NT	VT	NT	XC	VT	XC	AW	VT	NT	VT	NT	XC	VT	NT	XC	AW	VT
	◇1 A	◇1	◇1 B	C	◇1	◇	◇1		◇1 D	◇1	◇1 B	E	◇1	◇	◇1		◇1 F	◇1 ⊠		◇1 B	F	◇1 ⊠
Deansgate 85,89 d																						
Manchester Oxford Road 85,89 d																						
Manchester Picc. 85,89 d	15 05	15 15	15 27	15 31	15 35	15 44	15 55	16 01	16 05	16 15	16 27	16 31	16 35	16 44	16 55	17 01	17 05	17 15	17 21	17 27	17 31	17 35
Levenshulme d								16 07								17 07						
Heaton Chapel d								16 10								17 10						
Stockport a	15 12	15 22	15 35	15 39	15 42	15 56	16 03	16 13	16 12	16 22	16 35	16 39	16 42	16 56	17 03	17 13	17 12	17 22	17 30	17 35	17 39	17 42
d	15 13	15 23	15 36	15 39	15 43	15 57	16 04	16 14	16 13	16 23	16 36	16 39	16 43	16 57	17 04	17 14	17 13	17 23	17 31	17 36	17 39	17 43
Cheadle Hulme d						16 01		16 21						17 01		17 22			17 35			
Bramhall d						16 04								17 04					17 38			
Poynton d						16 07								17 07					17 41			
Adlington (Cheshire) d						16 10								17 10								
Prestbury d						16 13								17 13								
Macclesfield a	15 25		15 48		15 55	16 17			16 25		16 48		16 55	17 17			17 25		17 47			17 55
d	15 26		15 49		15 56	16 17			16 26		16 49		16 56	17 17			17 26		17 48			17 56
Congleton d						16 24								17 24					17 55			
Handforth d								16 25								17 26						
Manchester Airport d																						
Styal d																						
Wilmslow d				15 47			16 11	16 28				16 47			17 11	17 29				17 44	17 49	
Alderley Edge d								16 31								17 32						
Chelford d								16 36								17 37						
Goostrey d								16 41								17 42						
Holmes Chapel d								16 44								17 45						
Sandbach d								16 50								17 51						
Crewe 10 a				16 07			16 27	16 58				17 07			17 27	17 59				18 05	18 09	
Kidsgrove 50 a						16 30								17 30								
Longport 50 a																						
Stoke-on-Trent 50 a	15 43	15 49	16 05		16 11	16 39			16 43	16 49	17 05		17 11	17 39			17 43	17 49	18 08			18 11
Stafford 65,67 a	16 00		16 24						17 00		17 23						18 00			18 25		
Wolverhampton 7 68 a	16 16		16 38						17 16		17 38						18 16			18 40		
Birmingham New Street 12 68 a	16 33		16 58						17 33		17 59						18 33			18 57		
London Euston 15 ⊖65 a		17 21			17 40		18 06			18 20			18 39		19 06			19 20				19 41

	NT	VT	NT	XC	VT	XC	AW	VT	NT	VT	VT	NT	NT	XC	VT	XC	AW	NT	NT	VT	NT
	◇	◇1 ⊠		◇1 G	◇1 ⊠	◇1 B	◇ C	◇1 ⊠	◇	◇1 H ⊠	◇1 I ⊠	◇		◇1 D	◇1	◇1 J	◇ F		◇	◇1	◇
Deansgate 85,89 d																					
Manchester Oxford Road 85,89 d																					
Manchester Picc. 85,89 d	17 44	17 55	18 01	18 05	18 15	18 27	18 31	18 55	18 34	18 35	18 35	18 44	19 00	19 05	19 15	19 27	19 31	19 35	19 44	19 55	20 01
Levenshulme d			18 07										19 06								20 07
Heaton Chapel d			18 10										19 09								20 10
Stockport a	17 56	18 03	18 13	18 12	18 22	18 35	18 39	19 03		18 42	18 42	18 56	19 12	19 12	19 22	19 35	19 40		19 56	20 03	20 13
d	17 57	18 04	18 14	18 13	18 23	18 36	18 39	19 04		18 43	18 43	18 57	19 13	19 13	19 23	19 36	19 40		19 57	20 04	20 14
Cheadle Hulme d	18 01		18 21									19 01	19 20						20 01		20 21
Bramhall d	18 04											19 04							20 04		
Poynton d	18 07											19 07							20 07		
Adlington (Cheshire) d	18 10											19 10							20 10		
Prestbury d	18 13											19 13							20 13		
Macclesfield a	18 17			18 25						18 55	18 55	19 17		19 25	19 35	19 48			20 17		
d	18 17			18 26						18 56	18 56	19 17		19 26	19 36	19 49			20 17		
Congleton d	18 24					18 54						19 24							20 24		
Handforth d			18 25										19 24								20 25
Manchester Airport d									19 03									20 03			
Styal d									19 10									20 07			
Wilmslow d		18 11	18 28				18 47	19 11	19 16				19 27				19 47	20a11		20 11	20 28
Alderley Edge d			18 31						19 19				19 30								20 31
Chelford d			18 36										19 35								20 36
Goostrey d			18 41										19 40								20 41
Holmes Chapel d			18 44						19 28				19 43								20 44
Sandbach d			18 50						19 33				19 49								20 50
Crewe 10 a		18 27	18 58				19 07	19 27	19 43				19 57				20 08			20 27	20 58
Kidsgrove 50 a	18 30											19 30							20 30		
Longport 50 a																					
Stoke-on-Trent 50 a	18 39			18 43	18 49	19 06				19 11	19 11	19 39		19 43	19 51	20 05			20 39		
Stafford 65,67 a				19 00		19 23								20 00		20 24				20 46	
Wolverhampton 7 68 a				19 14		19 40								20 16		20 41					
Birmingham New Street 12 68 a				19 33		19 57								20 33		20 58					
London Euston 15 ⊖65 a		20 07			20 21			21 05		20 39	20 41				21 23					22 09	

A To Exeter St Davids
B To Bournemouth
C To Carmarthen
D To Bristol Temple Meads
E To Milford Haven
F To Cardiff Central
G To Plymouth
H until 14 February
I from 17 February
J To Southampton Central

Table T084-R

Mondays to Fridays
16 December to 15 May

Manchester, Stockport and Manchester Airport - Crewe and Stoke-on-Trent

	XC	VT	XC	AW	NT	NT	VT	XC	AW	NT	NT	XC	NT	AW	NT
	◇1	◇1	◇1	FO ◇ A	◇		◇1	◇1	◇ B	◇		◇1	◇	◇ B	
Deansgate 85,89 d															
Manchester Oxford Road 85,89 d															
Manchester Picc. 10 85,89 d	20 05	20 15	20 27	20 31	20 44	21 01	21 15	21 27	21 36	21 43	22 01	22 07	22 18	22 36	23 38
Levenshulme d						21 07					22 07				23 44
Heaton Chapel d						21 10					22 10				23 47
Stockport a	20 12	20 22	20 35	20 40	20 56	21 13	21 22	21 35	21 45	21 57	22 13	22 14	22 27	22 45	23 50
d	20 13	20 23	20 36	20 41	20 57	21 14	21 23	21 36	21 45	21 57	22 14	22 17	22 28	22 45	23 51
Cheadle Hulme d					21 01	21 21				22 01	22 18		22 32		23 55
Bramhall d					21 04					22 04			22 36		
Poynton d					21 07					22 07			22 39		
Adlington (Cheshire) d					21 11					22 11			22 43		
Prestbury d					21 14					22 14			22 47		
Macclesfield a	20 25	20 35	20 48		21 17		21 35	21 48		22 17		22 28	22 52		
d	20 26	20 36	20 49		21 18		21 36	21 49		22 18		22 29	22 53		
Congleton d					21 25					22 25			23 00		
Handforth d						21 25					22 22				23 59
Manchester Airport d															
Styal d															
Wilmslow d				20 49		21 28			21 52		22 25			22 53	00 02
Alderley Edge d						21 31					22 28				00 06
Chelford d						21 36					22 33				00 10
Goostrey d						21 41					22 38				00 15
Holmes Chapel d						21 44					22 41				00 19
Sandbach d						21 50					22 47				00 24
Crewe 10 a				21 15		21 58			22 12		22 55			23 12	00 32
Kidsgrove 50 a					21 31					22 31			23 06		
Longport 50 a															
Stoke-on-Trent 50 a	20 43	20 51	21 06		21 40		21 51	22 05		22 40		22 46	23 15		
Stafford 65,67 a	21 00		21 23					22 22				23 03			
Wolverhampton 7 68 a	21 16		21 42					22 41				23 19			
Birmingham New Street 12 68 a	21 33		22 00					22 59				23 37			
London Euston 15 ⊖65 a		22 30					23 48								

Saturdays
21 December to 16 May

	NT	XC	VT	NT	NT	NT	VT	XC	NT	VT	AW	VT	NT	VT	NT	XC	VT	XC	AW	VT	NT	VT
	C	◇1 D	◇1			◇	◇1	◇1 E		◇1	◇ F	◇1	◇	◇1		◇1 E	◇1	◇1 D	◇ G	◇1	◇	◇1
Deansgate 85,89 d																						
Manchester Oxford Road 85,89 d																						
Manchester Picc. 10 85,89 d		05 11	05 25	05 16		05 38	05 55	06 00	06 04	06 10	06 30	06 35	06 44	06 55	07 00	07 05	07 15	07 27	07 31	07 35	07 44	07 55
Levenshulme d															07 06							
Heaton Chapel d									06 11						07 09							
Stockport a			05 33			05 48	06 02	06 07	06 15	06 18	06 39	06 42	06 52	07 03	07 12	07 12	07 22	07 35	07 40	07 42	07 55	08 03
d			05 34			05 48	06 03	06 08	06 15	06 19	06 39	06 43	06 57	07 04	07 19	07 13	07 23	07 36	07 40	07 43	07 56	08 04
Cheadle Hulme d						05 52			06 19				07 01		07 24						08 00	
Bramhall d						05 56							07 04								08 03	
Poynton d						05 59							07 07								08 06	
Adlington (Cheshire) d						06 03							07 11								08 09	
Prestbury d						06 06							07 14								08 12	
Macclesfield a						06 09		06 20		06 30		06 55	07 17			07 25		07 48		07 55	08 16	
d					06 00	06 10		06 21		06 31		06 56	07 18			07 26		07 49		07 56	08 16	
Congleton d					06 07	06 19							07 25								08 23	
Handforth d									06 23						07 28							
Manchester Airport d				05 45																		
Styal d				05 49																		
Wilmslow d	00 02		05 41	05 53			06 11		06 27		06 47			07 11	07 31				07 47			08 11
Alderley Edge d	00 06			05 56					06 30						07 34							
Chelford d	00 10			06 01					06 34						07 39							
Goostrey d	00 15			06 06					06 39						07 44							
Holmes Chapel d	00 19			06 09					06 43						07 48							
Sandbach d	00 24			06 14					06 48						07 53							
Crewe 10 a	00 32	05 42	05 57	06 23			06 27		06 56		07 06			07 27	08 01				08 07			08 27
Kidsgrove 50 a						06 25							07 31								08 29	
Longport 50 a																						
Stoke-on-Trent 50 a		06 05			06 20	06 35		06 38		06 46		07 11	07 40			07 43	07 49	08 05		08 11	08 38	
Stafford 65,67 a		06 22	06 17					06 55								08 00		08 24				
Wolverhampton 7 68 a		06 41						07 16								08 16		08 41				
Birmingham New Street 12 68 a		06 58						07 34								08 33		08 58				
London Euston 15 ⊖65 a			07 50				08 07			08 23		08 44		09 01			09 21			09 40		10 08

A To Cardiff Central
B To Shrewsbury
C From Manchester Piccadilly
D To Bournemouth
E To Bristol Temple Meads
F To Milford Haven
G To Carmarthen

NRT DECEMBER 19 EDITION

Table T084-R

Saturdays
21 December to 16 May

Manchester, Stockport and Manchester Airport - Crewe and Stoke-on-Trent

	NT	XC	VT	XC	AW	VT	NT	VT	NT	XC	VT	XC	AW	VT	NT	VT	NT	XC	VT	XC	AW	VT
		◇1 A	◇1	◇1 B	C	◇1	◇	◇1		◇1 D	◇1	◇1 B	◇ E	◇1	◇	◇1		◇1 D	◇1	◇1 B	C	◇1
Deansgate 85,89 d																						
Manchester Oxford Road 85,89 d																						
Manchester Picc. 10 85,89 d	08 02	08 05	08 15	08 27	08 30	08 35	08 44	08 55	09 01	09 05	09 15	09 27	09 31	09 35	09 44	09 55	10 01	10 05	10 15	10 27	10 31	10 35
Levenshulme d	08 08								09 07								10 07					
Heaton Chapel d	08 11								09 10								10 10					
Stockport a	08 14	08 12	08 23	08 35	08 39	08 42	08 56	09 03	09 13	09 12	09 22	09 35	09 40	09 42	09 56	10 03	10 13	10 12	10 22	10 35	10 39	10 42
d	08 19	08 13	08 23	08 36	08 39	08 43	08 57	09 04	09 14	09 13	09 23	09 36	09 40	09 43	09 57	10 04	10 14	10 13	10 23	10 36	10 40	10 43
Cheadle Hulme d	08 23						09 01		09 21						10 01		10 21					
Bramhall d							09 04								10 04							
Poynton d							09 07								10 07							
Adlington (Cheshire) d							09 10								10 10							
Prestbury d							09 13								10 13							
Macclesfield a		08 25		08 48		08 55	09 17			09 25		09 48		09 55	10 17			10 25		10 48		10 55
d		08 26		08 49		08 56	09 17			09 26		09 49		09 56	10 17			10 26		10 49		10 56
Congleton d							09 24								10 24							
Handforth d	08 27								09 25								10 25					
Manchester Airport d																						
Styal d																						
Wilmslow d	08 30				08 47			09 11	09 28				09 47			10 11	10 28				10 47	
Alderley Edge d	08 33								09 31								10 31					
Chelford d	08 38								09 36								10 36					
Goostrey d	08 43								09 41								10 41					
Holmes Chapel d	08 46								09 44								10 44					
Sandbach d	08 52								09 50								10 50					
Crewe 10 a	09 00				09 07			09 28	09 58				10 07			10 27	10 58				11 07	
Kidsgrove 50 a							09 30								10 30							
Longport 50 a																						
Stoke-on-Trent 50 a		08 43	08 49	09 05		09 11	09 39			09 43	09 49	10 05		10 11	10 39			10 43	10 49	11 05		11 11
Stafford 65,67 a		09 00		09 22						10 00		10 22						11 00		11 25		
Wolverhampton 7 68 a		09 16		09 41						10 16		10 41						11 16		11 41		
Birmingham New Street 12 68 a		09 33		09 58						10 33		10 58						11 33		11 58		
London Euston 15 ⊖65 a			10 21			10 41		11 04			11 20			11 39		12 01			12 20			12 40

	NT	VT	NT	XC	VT	XC	AW	VT	NT	VT	NT	XC	VT	XC	AW	VT	NT	VT	NT	XC	VT
	◇	◇1		◇1 D	◇1	◇1 B	◇ E	◇1	◇	◇1		◇1 F	◇1	◇1 B	C	◇1	◇	◇1		◇1 D	◇1
Deansgate 85,89 d																					
Manchester Oxford Road 85,89 d																					
Manchester Picc. 10 85,89 d	10 44	10 55	11 01	11 05	11 15	11 27	11 31	11 35	11 44	11 55	12 01	12 05	12 15	12 27	12 31	12 35	12 44	12 55	13 01	13 05	13 15
Levenshulme d			11 07								12 07								13 07		
Heaton Chapel d			11 10								12 10								13 10		
Stockport a	10 56	11 03	11 13	11 12	11 22	11 35	11 39	11 42	11 56	12 03	12 13	12 12	12 22	12 35	12 39	12 42	12 56	13 03	13 13	13 12	13 22
d	10 57	11 04	11 14	11 13	11 23	11 36	11 39	11 43	11 57	12 04	12 14	12 13	12 23	12 36	12 39	12 43	12 57	13 04	13 14	13 13	13 23
Cheadle Hulme d	11 01		11 21						12 01		12 22						13 01		13 21		
Bramhall d	11 04								12 04								13 04				
Poynton d	11 07								12 07								13 07				
Adlington (Cheshire) d	11 10								12 10								13 10				
Prestbury d	11 13								12 13								13 13				
Macclesfield a	11 17			11 25		11 48		11 55	12 17			12 25		12 48		12 55	13 17			13 25	
d	11 17			11 26		11 49		11 56	12 17			12 26		12 49		12 56	13 17			13 26	
Congleton d	11 24								12 24								13 24				
Handforth d			11 25								12 26								13 25		
Manchester Airport d																					
Styal d																					
Wilmslow d		11 11	11 28				11 47			12 11	12 29				12 47			13 11	13 28		
Alderley Edge d			11 31								12 32								13 31		
Chelford d			11 36								12 37								13 36		
Goostrey d			11 41								12 42								13 41		
Holmes Chapel d			11 44								12 45								13 44		
Sandbach d			11 50								12 51								13 50		
Crewe 10 a		11 27	11 58				12 07			12 27	12 59				13 07			13 27	13 58		
Kidsgrove 50 a	11 30								12 30								13 30				
Longport 50 a																					
Stoke-on-Trent 50 a	11 39			11 43	11 49	12 05		12 11	12 39			12 43	12 49	13 05		13 11	13 39			13 43	13 49
Stafford 65,67 a				12 00		12 23						13 00		13 22						14 00	
Wolverhampton 7 68 a				12 16		12 41						13 16		13 41						14 16	
Birmingham New Street 12 68 a				12 33		12 58						13 33		13 58						14 34	
London Euston 15 ⊖65 a		13 03			13 21			13 39		14 04			14 20			14 41		15 07			15 23

A To Paignton
B To Bournemouth
C To Milford Haven
D To Bristol Temple Meads
E To Carmarthen
F To Exeter St Davids

Table T084-R

Saturdays
21 December to 16 May

Manchester, Stockport and Manchester Airport - Crewe and Stoke-on-Trent

	XC	AW	VT	NT	VT	NT	XC	VT	XC	AW	VT	NT	VT	NT	XC	VT	XC	AW	VT	NT	VT	NT
	◇1 A ✕	■ B ✕	◇1 ☕	◇	◇1 ☕		◇1 C ✕	◇1 ☕	◇1 A ✕	■ D ✕	◇1 ☕	◇	◇1 ☕		◇1 E ✕	◇1 ☕	◇1 A ✕	■ B ✕	◇1 ☕	◇	◇1 ☕	
Deansgate 85,89 ⇌ d																						
Manchester Oxford Road 85,89 d																						
Manchester Picc. 10 85,89 ⇌ d	13 27	13 31	13 35	13 44	13 55	14 01	14 05	14 15	14 27	14 31	14 35	14 44	14 55	15 01	15 05	15 15	15 27	15 31	15 35	15 44	15 55	16 01
Levenshulme d						14 07								15 07								16 07
Heaton Chapel d						14 10								15 10								16 10
Stockport a	13 35	13 39	13 42	13 55	14 03	14 13	14 12	14 22	14 35	14 39	14 42	14 56	15 03	15 13	15 12	15 22	15 35	15 39	15 42	15 56	16 03	16 13
d	13 36	13 39	13 43	13 57	14 04	14 14	14 13	14 23	14 36	14 39	14 43	14 57	15 04	15 14	15 13	15 23	15 36	15 39	15 43	15 57	16 04	16 14
Cheadle Hulme d				14 01		14 20						15 01		15 20						16 01		16 21
Bramhall d				14 04								15 04								16 04		
Poynton d				14 07								15 07								16 07		
Adlington (Cheshire) d				14 10								15 10								16 10		
Prestbury d				14 13								15 13								16 13		
Macclesfield a	13 48		13 55	14 17			14 25		14 48		14 55	15 17			15 25		15 48		15 55	16 17		
d	13 49		13 56	14 17			14 26		14 49		14 56	15 17			15 26		15 49		15 56	16 17		
Congleton d				14 24								15 24								16 24		
Handforth d						14 24								15 24								16 25
Manchester Airport ✈ d																						
Styal d																						
Wilmslow d		13 47			14 11	14 27				14 47			15 11	15 27				15 47			16 11	16 28
Alderley Edge d						14 30								15 30								16 31
Chelford d						14 35								15 35								16 36
Goostrey d						14 40								15 40								16 41
Holmes Chapel d						14 43								15 43								16 44
Sandbach d						14 49								15 49								16 50
Crewe 10 a		14 07			14 27	14 57				15 07			15 27	15 57				16 07			16 27	16 58
Kidsgrove 50 a				14 30								15 30								16 30		
Longport 50 a																						
Stoke-on-Trent 50 a	14 05		14 11	14 39			14 43	14 49	15 05		15 11	15 39			15 43	15 49	16 05		16 11	16 39		
Stafford 65,67 a	14 24						15 00		15 25						16 00		16 23					
Wolverhampton 7 68 ⇌ a	14 41						15 16		15 41						16 16		16 41					
Birmingham New Street 12 68 a	14 58						15 33		15 58						16 33		16 58					
London Euston 15 ⊖65 a			15 40		16 04			16 21			16 40		17 03			17 21			17 41		18 02	

	XC	VT	XC	AW	VT	NT	VT	NT	XC	VT	XC	AW	VT	NT	VT	NT	XC	VT	XC	AW	VT
	◇1 E ✕	◇1 ☕	◇1 A ✕	■ D ✕	◇1 ☕	◇	◇1 ☕		◇1 F ✕	◇1 ☕	◇1 A ✕	■ F ✕	◇1 ☕	◇	◇1 ☕		◇1 G ✕	◇1 ☕	◇1 A ✕	◇ H	◇1 ☕
Deansgate 85,89 ⇌ d																					
Manchester Oxford Road 85,89 d																					
Manchester Picc. 10 85,89 ⇌ d	16 05	16 15	16 27	16 31	16 35	16 44	16 55	17 01	17 05	17 15	17 27	17 31	17 35	17 44	17 55	18 01	18 05	18 15	18 27	18 31	18 35
Levenshulme d								17 07								18 07					
Heaton Chapel d								17 10								18 10					
Stockport a	16 12	16 22	16 35	16 39	16 42	16 56	17 03	17 13	17 12	17 22	17 35	17 39	17 42	17 56	18 02	18 13	18 12	18 22	18 35	18 39	18 42
d	16 13	16 23	16 36	16 39	16 43	16 57	17 04	17 14	17 13	17 23	17 36	17 39	17 43	17 57	18 03	18 14	18 13	18 23	18 36	18 39	18 43
Cheadle Hulme d						17 01		17 22						18 01		18 21					
Bramhall d						17 04								18 04							
Poynton d						17 07								18 07							
Adlington (Cheshire) d						17 10								18 10							
Prestbury d						17 13								18 13							
Macclesfield a	16 25		16 48		16 55	17 17			17 25				17 55	18 17			18 25				18 55
d	16 26		16 49		16 56	17 17			17 26				17 56	18 17			18 26				18 56
Congleton d						17 24					17 54			18 24					18 54		
Handforth d								17 26								18 25					
Manchester Airport ✈ d																					
Styal d																					
Wilmslow d				16 47			17 11	17 29				17 47			18 11	18 28				18 47	
Alderley Edge d								17 32								18 31					
Chelford d								17 37								18 36					
Goostrey d								17 42								18 41					
Holmes Chapel d								17 45								18 44					
Sandbach d								17 51								18 50					
Crewe 10 a				17 07			17 27	17 59				18 07			18 26	18 58				19 09	
Kidsgrove 50 a						17 30								18 30							
Longport 50 a																					
Stoke-on-Trent 50 a	16 43	16 49	17 05		17 11	17 39			17 43	17 49	18 06		18 11	18 39			18 43	18 49	19 06		19 11
Stafford 65,67 a	17 00		17 24						18 00		18 23						19 00		19 23		
Wolverhampton 7 68 ⇌ a	17 16		17 38						18 16		18 41						19 16		19 41		
Birmingham New Street 12 68 a	17 33		17 58						18 33		18 58						19 33		19 58		
London Euston 15 ⊖65 a		18 20			18 41		19 03			19 22			19 38		20 01			20 34			20 59

A To Bournemouth
B To Pembroke Dock
C To Paignton
D To Milford Haven
E To Bristol Temple Meads
F To Cardiff Central
G To Plymouth
H To Carmarthen

Table T084-R

Saturdays
21 December to 16 May

Manchester, Stockport and Manchester Airport - Crewe and Stoke-on-Trent

	NT	VT	NT	XC	XC	AW	VT	NT	NT	XC	XC	AW	VT	NT	NT	XC	XC	AW	NT	NT	AW	NT
	◇	◇1 ☕		◇1 A ✕	◇1 B ✕	◇ C	◇1 ☕	◇	◇	◇1	◇1	◇ C	◇1 ☕	◇		◇1	◇1	◇ D	◇		◇ D	
Deansgate 85,89 ⇌ d																						
Manchester Oxford Road 85,89 d																						
Manchester Picc. 10 85,89 ⇌ d	18 44	18 55	19 01	19 05	19 27	19 31	19 35	19 44	20 01	20 05	20 27	20 30	20 35	20 44	21 01	21 05	21 27	21 33	21 43	22 01	22 35	23 38
Levenshulme d			19 07						20 07						21 07					22 07		23 44
Heaton Chapel d			19 10						20 10						21 10					22 10		23 47
Stockport a	18 56	19 03	19 13	19 12	19 35	19 40	19 42	19 56	20 13	20 12	20 35	20 39	20 42	20 57	21 13	21 12	21 35	21 43	21 57	22 13	22 45	23 50
d	18 57	19 04	19 14	19 13	19 36	19 40	19 43	19 57	20 14	20 13	20 36	20 39	20 43	20 57	21 17	21 13	21 36	21 43	21 57	22 14	22 45	23 51
Cheadle Hulme d	19 01		19 21					20 01	20 21					21 01	21 22				22 01	22 18		23 55
Bramhall d	19 04							20 04						21 04					22 04			
Poynton d	19 07							20 07						21 07					22 07			
Adlington (Cheshire) d	19 10							20 10						21 11					22 11			
Prestbury d	19 13							20 13						21 14					22 14			
Macclesfield a	19 17			19 25	19 48		19 55	20 17		20 25	20 48		20 55	21 17		21 25	21 48		22 17			
d	19 17			19 26	19 49		19 56	20 17		20 26	20 49		20 56	21 18		21 26	21 49		22 18			
Congleton d	19 24							20 24						21 25					22 25			
Handforth d			19 25						20 25						21 26					22 22		23 59
Manchester Airport ✈ d																						
Styal d																						
Wilmslow d		19 11	19 28			19 47			20 28			20 47			21 29			21 53		22 25	22 53	00 02
Alderley Edge d			19 31						20 31						21 32					22 28		00 06
Chelford d			19 36						20 36						21 37					22 33		00 10
Goostrey d			19 41						20 41						21 42					22 38		00 15
Holmes Chapel d			19 44						20 44						21 45					22 41		00 19
Sandbach d			19 50						20 50						21 51					22 47		00 24
Crewe 10 a		19 27	19 58			20 07			20 58			21 07			21 59			22 12		22 55	23 12	00 32
Kidsgrove 50 a	19 30							20 30						21 31					22 31			
Longport 50 a																						
Stoke-on-Trent 50 a	19 39			19 43	20 05		20 11	20 39		20 43	21 05		21 11	21 40		21 43	22 05		22 40			
Stafford 65,67 a				20 00	20 24					21 00	21 22					22 00	22 22					
Wolverhampton 7 68 ⇌ a				20 16	20 41					21 16	21 41					22 16	22 43					
Birmingham New Street 12 68 a				20 33	20 58					21 33	22 00					22 33	23 00					
London Euston 15 ⊖65 a		21 23					22 01						23 00									

Sundays
15 December to 10 May

	NT	VT	NT	VT	NT	XC	NT	NT	NT	VT	XC	AW	NT	NT	VT	XC	AW	AW	VT	NT	VT	XC
	E	◇1 ☕		◇1 ☕	F	◇1 G ✕	H	◇	◇	◇1 ☕	◇1 G ✕	■ I ✕	◇ J	◇ K	◇1 ☕	◇1 G ✕	■ L ✕	■ M ✕	◇1 ☕	◇	◇1 ☕	◇1 G ✕
Deansgate 85,89 ⇌ d																						
Manchester Oxford Road 85,89 d																						
Manchester Picc. 10 85,89 ⇌ d		08 05	08 09	08 20	08 23	08 27	08 30	08 53	08 59	09 20	09 27	09 30	09 55	09 55	10 20	10 27	10 31	10 31	10 35	11 06	11 15	11 27
Levenshulme d																						
Heaton Chapel d																						
Stockport a		08 13	08 17	08 28		08 34		09 02	09 08	09 28	09 34	09 40	10 03	10 04	10 28	10 35	10 39	10 40	10 45	11 16	11 24	11 35
d		08 14	08 21	08 28		08 35		09 02	09 08	09 28	09 35	09 41	10 06	10 06	10 29	10 35	10 40	10 40	10 46	11 16	11 24	11 35
Cheadle Hulme d			08 25					09 06	09 13				10 12	10 12						11 22		
Bramhall d								09 09														
Poynton d								09 12														
Adlington (Cheshire) d								09 16														
Prestbury d								09 19														
Macclesfield a				08 41				09 22		09 40	09 47					10 48			10 57			11 48
d				08 41				09 23		09 40	09 48					10 48			10 57			11 48
Congleton d								09 30														
Handforth d			08 29						09 17				10 16	10 16						11 26		
Manchester Airport ✈ d					08 51		09 11															
Styal d					08 56		09 16															
Wilmslow d	00 02	08 22	08 32		08a59	08 43	09a19		09 20			09 49	10 19	10 19	10 37		10 48	10 48		11 29		
Alderley Edge d	00 06		08 35						09 23			09 53	10 22	10 22						11 32		
Chelford d	00 10								09 27				10 26	10 26								
Goostrey d	00 15								09 31				10 31	10 31								
Holmes Chapel d	00 19								09 34				10 34	10 34						11 40		
Sandbach d	00 24		08 46						09 39				10 39	10 39						11 45		
Crewe 10 a	00 32	08 39	08 54			09 01			09 47			10 12	10 47	10 47	10 53		11 09	11 09		11 53		
Kidsgrove 50 a								09 36														
Longport 50 a																						
Stoke-on-Trent 50 a				08 57				09 45		09 59	10 05					11 06			11 14		11 51	12 06
Stafford 65,67 a		09 01				09 24					10 22					11 23						12 24
Wolverhampton 7 68 ⇌ a						09 41					10 41					11 42						12 41
Birmingham New Street 12 68 a						09 58					10 59					12 00						12 58
London Euston 15 ⊖65 a		10 56		11 01						12 06					12 53				12 57		13 28	

A To Bristol Temple Meads
B To Southampton Central
C To Cardiff Central
D To Shrewsbury
E not 15 December. From Manchester Piccadilly
F from 23 February
G To Bournemouth
H until 16 February
I To Swansea
J until 29 March
K from 5 April
L until 29 March. To Milford Haven
M from 5 April. To Milford Haven

Table T084-R

Sundays

15 December to 10 May

Manchester, Stockport and Manchester Airport - Crewe and Stoke-on-Trent

	AW	VT	NT	VT	NT	NT	VT	XC	AW	VT	VT	XC	NT	VT	XC	AW	VT	VT	XC	NT	VT	XC
	■ A	◇1	◇	◇1	◇ B	◇ C	◇1	◇1 D	■ E	◇1	◇1	◇1 F	◇	◇1	◇1 D	■ A	◇1	◇1	◇1 G	◇	◇1	◇1 D
Deansgate 85,89 d																						
Manchester Oxford Road 85,89 d			11 42																			
Manchester Picc. 10 85,89 d	11 30	11 35	11 46	11 55	12 01	12 02	12 15	12 27	12 32	12 35	12 55	13 05	13 08	13 15	13 27	13 30	13 35	13 55	14 05	14 08	14 15	14 27
Levenshulme d																						
Heaton Chapel d																						
Stockport a	11 40	11 44	11 55	12 04	12 10	12 10	12 21	12 35	12 42	12 42	13 04	13 12	13 17	13 22	13 36	13 39	13 42	14 03	14 12	14 17	14 22	14 34
d	11 43	11 44	11 56	12 05	12 11	12 11	12 21	12 35	12 43	12 43	13 05	13 13	13 18	13 23	13 37	13 40	13 42	14 05	14 13	14 18	14 22	14 35
Cheadle Hulme d			12 00		12 15	12 15							13 22							14 22		
Bramhall d			12 03																			
Poynton d			12 06																			
Adlington (Cheshire) d			12 10																			
Prestbury d			12 13																			
Macclesfield a		11 57	12 17					12 48		12 57		13 25			13 49		13 55		14 25			14 47
d		11 57	12 17					12 48		12 57		13 26			13 50		13 55		14 26			14 48
Congleton d			12 25																			
Handforth d					12 19	12 19							13 26							14 26		
Manchester Airport ✈ d																						
Styal d																						
Wilmslow d	11 52			12 13	12 22	12 22			12 50		13 13		13 29			13 48		14 12		14 29		
Alderley Edge d					12 25	12 25							13 32							14 32		
Chelford d					12 29	12 29							13 36							14 36		
Goostrey d					12 34	12 34							13 40							14 40		
Holmes Chapel d					12 37	12 37							13 43							14 43		
Sandbach d					12 41	12 41							13 48							14 48		
Crewe 10 a	12 12			12 29	12 49	12 49			13 10		13 29		14 00			14 09		14 28		15 00		
Kidsgrove 50 a			12 31																			
Longport 50 a																						
Stoke-on-Trent 50 a		12 14	12 40				12 47	13 06		13 14		13 44		13 50	14 06		14 12		14 44		14 49	15 05
Stafford 65,67 a								13 24				14 00			14 24				15 00			15 23
Wolverhampton 7 68 a								13 41				14 16			14 41				15 16			15 41
Birmingham New Street 12 68 a								13 58				14 33			14 58				15 33			15 58
London Euston 15 ⊖65 a		13 45		14 09			14 26			14 46	15 06			15 25			15 46	16 06			16 26	

	AW	VT	NT	VT	XC	NT	VT	XC	AW	VT	VT	XC	NT	VT	XC	AW	VT	VT	XC	NT	VT
	■ H	◇1	◇	◇1	◇1 G	◇	◇1	◇1 D	■ A	◇1	◇1	◇1 G	◇	◇1	◇1 D	■ A	◇1	◇1	◇1 I	◇	◇1
Deansgate 85,89 d																					
Manchester Oxford Road 85,89 d																					
Manchester Picc. 10 85,89 d	14 30	14 35	14 46	14 55	15 05	15 08	15 15	15 27	15 30	15 35	15 55	16 05	16 08	16 15	16 27	16 30	16 35	16 55	17 05	17 08	17 15
Levenshulme d																					
Heaton Chapel d																					
Stockport a	14 39	14 42	14 57	15 03	15 12	15 17	15 22	15 35	15 40	15 42	16 02	16 12	16 17	16 22	16 34	16 40	16 42	17 02	17 12	17 17	17 22
d	14 40	14 42	14 57	15 04	15 13	15 18	15 22	15 36	15 40	15 42	16 03	16 13	16 18	16 23	16 36	16 40	16 42	17 03	17 13	17 18	17 22
Cheadle Hulme d			15 01			15 22							16 22							17 23	
Bramhall d			15 04																		
Poynton d			15 07																		
Adlington (Cheshire) d			15 11																		
Prestbury d			15 14																		
Macclesfield a		14 55	15 17		15 25			15 48		15 55		16 25			16 48		16 55		17 25		
d		14 55	15 18		15 26			15 49		15 55		16 26			16 50		16 55		17 26		
Congleton d			15 25																		
Handforth d						15 26							16 26							17 27	
Manchester Airport ✈ d																					
Styal d																					
Wilmslow d	14 48			15 12		15 29			15 48		16 11		16 29			16 48		17 11		17 30	
Alderley Edge d						15 32							16 32							17 33	
Chelford d						15 36							16 36							17 37	
Goostrey d						15 40							16 40							17 42	
Holmes Chapel d						15 43							16 43							17 45	
Sandbach d						15 48							16 48							17 50	
Crewe 10 a	15 09			15 28		16 00			16 08		16 27		17 00			17 08		17 27		18 00	
Kidsgrove 50 a			15 31																		
Longport 50 a																					
Stoke-on-Trent 50 a		15 12	15 40		15 44		15 49	16 05		16 12		16 44		16 48	17 06		17 12		17 44		17 49
Stafford 65,67 a					16 00			16 23				17 00			17 24				18 00		
Wolverhampton 7 68 a					16 16			16 41				17 16			17 39				18 16		
Birmingham New Street 12 68 a					16 34			16 58				17 34			17 59				18 33		
London Euston 15 ⊖65 a		16 45		17 07			17 27			17 45	18 06			18 27			18 46	19 05			19 26

A To Swansea
B until 29 March
C from 5 April
D To Bournemouth
E To Milford Haven
F To Paignton
G To Bristol Temple Meads
H To Cardiff Canton Sidings
I To Plymouth

Table T084-R

Sundays

15 December to 10 May

Manchester, Stockport and Manchester Airport - Crewe and Stoke-on-Trent

	XC	AW	VT	VT	XC	NT	VT	XC	AW	VT	NT	VT	XC	NT	VT	VT	XC	AW	VT	XC	NT	VT
	◇1 A	■ B	◇1	◇1	◇1 C	◇	◇1	◇1 D	■ E	◇1	◇	◇1	◇1 C	◇	◇1 F	◇1 G	◇1 H	◇ B	◇1	◇1 C	◇	◇1
Deansgate 85,89 d																						
Manchester Oxford Road 85,89 d																						
Manchester Picc. 10 85,89 d	17 27	17 30	17 35	17 55	18 05	18 09	18 15	18 27	18 30	18 35	18 46	18 55	19 05	19 08	19 15	19 15	19 27	19 30	19 35	20 05	20 08	20 21
Levenshulme d																						
Heaton Chapel d																						
Stockport a	17 34	17 40	17 42	18 02	18 12	18 18	18 22	18 34	18 40	18 42	18 57	19 02	19 12	19 17	19 22	19 22	19 34	19 40	19 41	20 12	20 17	20 27
d	17 35	17 40	17 42	18 03	18 13	18 19	18 22	18 35	18 40	18 42	18 57	19 03	19 13	19 18	19 22	19 22	19 35	19 40	19 41	20 13	20 18	20 27
Cheadle Hulme d						18 23					19 01			19 22							20 23	
Bramhall d											19 04											
Poynton d											19 07											
Adlington (Cheshire) d											19 11											
Prestbury d											19 14											
Macclesfield a	17 47		17 55		18 25			18 47		18 55	19 17		19 25				19 47		19 54	20 25		20 40
d	17 48		17 55		18 26			18 48		18 55	19 18		19 26				19 48		19 54	20 26		20 40
Congleton d											19 25											
Handforth d						18 27								19 26							20 27	
Manchester Airport ✈ d																						
Styal d																						
Wilmslow d		17 48		18 11		18 30			18 48			19 11		19 29				19 48			20 30	
Alderley Edge d						18 33								19 32							20 33	
Chelford d						18 37								19 36							20 37	
Goostrey d						18 42								19 40							20 41	
Holmes Chapel d						18 45								19 43							20 44	
Sandbach d						18 50								19 48							20 49	
Crewe 10 a		18 09		18 27		19 00			19 09			19 27		20 00				20 09			21 00	
Kidsgrove 50 a											19 32											
Longport 50 a																						
Stoke-on-Trent 50 a	18 05		18 12		18 45		18 50	19 05		19 12	19 41		19 45		19 49	19 49	20 05		20 11	20 43		20 57
Stafford 65,67 a	18 25				19 01			19 22					20 01				20 22			21 00		
Wolverhampton 7 68 a	18 41				19 16			19 41					20 16				20 41			21 16		
Birmingham New Street 12 68 a	18 59				19 33			19 58					20 33				20 58			21 33		
London Euston 15 ⊖65 a			19 46	20 06			20 26			20 45		21 10			21 31	21 32			22 01			22 56

	NT	AW	VT	XC	NT	AW	NT	XC	NT	AW	NT
	◇	◇ I	◇1	◇1			◇	◇1			
Deansgate 85,89 d											
Manchester Oxford Road 85,89 d											
Manchester Picc. 10 85,89 d	20 24	20 30	20 55	21 05	21 12	21 35	21 47	22 05	22 15	22 35	23 00
Levenshulme d											
Heaton Chapel d											
Stockport a	20 32	20 38	21 03	21 12	21 20	21 45	21 58	22 12	22 24		23 08
d	20 33	20 40	21 03	21 13	21 23	21 47	21 59	22 13	22 24		23 10
Cheadle Hulme d	20 37				21 27		22 03		22 28		23 14
Bramhall d	20 40						22 06				
Poynton d	20 43						22 09				
Adlington (Cheshire) d	20 47						22 12				
Prestbury d	20 50						22 15				
Macclesfield a	20 54		21 16	21 25			22 19	22 25			
d	20 54		21 16	21 26			22 29	22 26			
Congleton d	21 02						22 36				
Handforth d					21 31				22 32		23 18
Manchester Airport ✈ d											
Styal d											
Wilmslow d		20 48			21 34	21 57			22 35	22 50	23 21
Alderley Edge d					21 37				22 38	22 54	23 24
Chelford d					21 41				22 42		23 28
Goostrey d					21 45				22 47		23 33
Holmes Chapel d					21 48				22 50		23 36
Sandbach d					21 53				22 55		23 41
Crewe 10 a		21 09			22 03	22 17			23 03	23 14	23 49
Kidsgrove 50 a	21 08						22 42				
Longport 50 a											
Stoke-on-Trent 50 a	21 17		21 33	21 45			22 51	22 43			
Stafford 65,67 a				22 04				23 00			
Wolverhampton 7 68 a				22 18				23 17			
Birmingham New Street 12 68 a				22 36				23 35			
London Euston 15 ⊖65 a			23 47								

A To Bournemouth
B To Swansea
C To Bristol Temple Meads
D To Southampton Central
E To Carmarthen
F until 16 February
G from 23 February
H To Reading
I To Cardiff Central

Table T085-F

Manchester Airport - Manchester

Mondays to Fridays
16 December to 15 May

Miles	Station		NT MX	NT MX	TP	NT MX	TP	NT	NT	TP	NT		AW	TP	NT	TP	NT	TP	TP	TP	NT		TP	NT	TP
			◇		◇1		◇1 🛒	◇		◇1 🛒	◇		◇	◇1	◇	◇1		◇1 🛒	◇1	◇1 🛒	◇		◇1 🛒	■	◇1 🛒
—	Crewe 10	84 d				00 44																		06 16	
—	Wilmslow	84 d															05 41							06 42	
0	**Manchester Airport**	d		00 22	00 38	01 13	04 22	04 46	05 07	05 19	05 24		05 33	05 37	05 42	05 54	05 59	06 07	06 15	06 35	06 40		06 53	06 58	07 07
1½	Heald Green	d						04 50			05 28				05 46		06 03				06 44			07 02	
4	Gatley	d													05 49		06 06			06 41	06 47			07 05	
5¼	East Didsbury	d									05 32						06 08		06 22					07 07	
6¼	Burnage	d									05 35						06 11				06 50			07 10	
7¼	Mauldeth Road	d	00 01												05 53		06 13				06 53			07 12	
—	**Manchester Piccadilly 10**	a	00 08	00 40	00 51	01 28	04 35	05 02	05 19	05 33	05 43		05 48	05 56	06 00	06 12	06 20	06 24	06 32	06 54	06 59		07 11	07 21	07 25
—		d						05 04	05 22	05 34	05 44		05 48	05 57	06 01		06 22	06 26	06 34	06 56	07 01			07 22	07 26
—	**Manchester Oxford Rd.**	a						05 06	05 24	05 36	05 46		05 51	05 59	06 03		06 24	06 28	06 36	06 58	07 03			07 24	07 28
—	Deansgate	a													06 07		06 27				07 07			07 27	
—	**Manchester Victoria**	a								05 45				06 10					06 45	07 11					

Station		TP	NT	NT	TP	TP	NT		TP	TP	NT	TP	NT	TP	NT	TP	TP		NT	TP	NT	TP	NT	TP	TP
		◇1 🛒	◇	◇	◇1 🛒	◇1 🛒	◇		◇1 🛒	◇1 🛒	◇	◇1 🛒	◇	◇1 🛒	◇	◇1 🛒	◇1 🛒		◇	◇1 🛒	◇	◇1 🛒	◇	◇1 🛒	◇1 🛒
Crewe 10	84 d						07 13								08 16								09 16		
Wilmslow	84 d						07 42								08 42								09 42		
Manchester Airport	d	07 10	07 25	07 42	07 47	07 53	07 59		08 07	08 10	08 27	08 35	08 41	08 53	08 59	09 07	09 10		09 28	09 36	09 43	09 53	09 59	10 07	10 10
Heald Green	d		07 29	07 47			08 03				08 31		08 45		09 03				09 32		09 47		10 03		
Gatley	d				07 53		08 06					08 41			09 06					09 42			10 06		
East Didsbury	d	07 18	07 33				08 08			08 18	08 35				09 08		09 18						10 08		
Burnage	d			07 52			08 11				08 38				09 11				09 37				10 11		
Mauldeth Road	d						08 13						08 51		09 13								10 13		
Manchester Piccadilly 10	a	07 33	07 42	07 59	08 03	08 11	08 21		08 25	08 33	08 46	08 54	08 59	09 11	09 21	09 25	09 33		09 46	09 55	09 59	10 11	10 20	10 25	10 33
	d	07 34	07 43	08 01	08 05		08 23		08 27	08 35	08 47	08 56	09 01		09 22	09 26	09 34		09 47	09 57	10 01		10 22	10 26	10 34
Manchester Oxford Rd.	a	07 36	07 45	08 03	08 07		08 25		08 29	08 37	08 49	08 58	09 03		09 24	09 28	09 36		09 49	09 59	10 03		10 24	10 28	10 36
Deansgate	a			08 06			08 28						09 07		09 28						10 06		10 27		
Manchester Victoria	a	07 43			08 14					08 45		09 12					09 44			10 11					10 44

Station		NT	AW		TP	NT	TP	NT	TP	TP	NT	AW	TP		NT	TP	NT	TP	TP	NT	AW	TP	NT		TP
		◇	◇ 🛒		◇1 🛒	◇	◇1 🛒	◇	◇1 🛒	◇1 🛒	◇	◇ 🛒	◇1 🛒		◇	◇1 🛒	◇	◇1 🛒	◇1 🛒	◇	◇ 🛒	◇1 🛒	◇		◇1 🛒
Crewe 10	84 d							10 16									11 17								
Wilmslow	84 d							10 42									11 42								
Manchester Airport	d	10 28	10 35		10 40	10 45	10 53	10 59	11 07	11 10	11 28	11 35	11 40		11 45	11 53	11 59	12 07	12 10	12 28	12 35	12 40	12 45		12 53
Heald Green	d	10 32				10 49		11 03			11 32				11 49		12 03			12 32			12 49		
Gatley	d				10 46			11 06					11 46				12 06					12 46			
East Didsbury	d		10 42					11 08				11 42					12 08				12 42				
Burnage	d	10 37						11 11			11 37						12 11			12 37					
Mauldeth Road	d							11 13									12 13								
Manchester Piccadilly 10	a	10 46	10 51		10 55	10 59	11 11	11 21	11 25	11 33	11 46	11 51	11 55		11 59	12 11	12 21	12 25	12 33	12 46	12 51	12 55	12 59		13 11
	d	10 47	10 52		10 57	11 01		11 22	11 26	11 34	11 47	11 52	11 57		12 01		12 22	12 26	12 34	12 47	12 52	12 57	13 01		
Manchester Oxford Rd.	a	10 49	10 55		10 59	11 03		11 24	11 28	11 36	11 49	11 55	11 59		12 03		12 24	12 28	12 36	12 49	12 55	12 59	13 03		
Deansgate	a					11 06		11 28							12 06		12 28						13 06		
Manchester Victoria	a				11 11					11 44			12 10						12 44			13 13			

Station		NT	TP	TP	NT	AW	TP	NT	TP		NT	TP	TP	NT	AW	TP	NT	TP	NT		TP	TP	NT	AW	TP
		◇	◇1 🛒	◇1 🛒	◇	◇ 🛒	◇1 🛒	◇	◇1 🛒		◇	◇1 🛒	◇1 🛒	◇	◇ 🛒	◇1 🛒	◇	◇1 🛒	◇		◇1 🛒	◇1 🛒	◇	◇ 🛒	◇1 🛒
Crewe 10	84 d	12 17									13 18								14 16						
Wilmslow	84 d	12 42									13 43								14 42						
Manchester Airport	d	12 59	13 07	13 10	13 28	13 35	13 40	13 45	13 53		13 59	14 07	14 10	14 28	14 35	14 40	14 45	14 53	14 59		15 07	15 10	15 28	15 35	15 40
Heald Green	d	13 03			13 32			13 49			14 03			14 32			14 49		15 03				15 32		
Gatley	d	13 06					13 46				14 06					14 46			15 06						15 46
East Didsbury	d	13 08				13 42					14 08				14 42				15 08					15 42	
Burnage	d	13 11			13 38						14 11			14 37					15 11				15 37		
Mauldeth Road	d	13 13									14 13								15 13						
Manchester Piccadilly 10	a	13 21	13 25	13 33	13 46	13 51	13 55	13 59	14 11		14 21	14 25	14 33	14 46	14 51	14 55	14 59	15 11	15 21		15 25	15 33	15 46	15 51	15 55
	d	13 22	13 26	13 34	13 47	13 52	13 57	14 01			14 22	14 26	14 34	14 47	14 52	14 57	15 01		15 22		15 26	15 34	15 47	15 52	15 57
Manchester Oxford Rd.	a	13 24	13 28	13 36	13 49	13 55	13 59	14 03			14 24	14 28	14 36	14 49	14 55	14 59	15 03		15 24		15 28	15 36	15 49	15 55	15 59
Deansgate	a	13 28						14 06			14 28						15 06		15 28						
Manchester Victoria	a			13 44			14 10						14 44			15 11						15 44			16 10

Station		TP	NT	TP	TP		NT	TP	TP	NT	TP	TP	NT	TP	TP		NT	TP	TP	NT	TP	NT	TP	NT	TP
		◇1 🛒	◇	◇1 🛒	◇1 🛒		◇	◇1 🛒	◇1 🛒	◇	◇1 🛒	◇1 🛒	◇	◇1 🛒	◇1 🛒		◇	◇1 🛒	◇1 🛒	◇	◇1	◇	◇1	◇	◇1 🛒
Crewe 10	84 d		15 16							16 16							17 16							18 17	
Wilmslow	84 d		15 42							16 42							17 42							18 42	
Manchester Airport	d	15 53	15 59	16 07	16 10		16 29	16 34	16 53	16 59	17 07	17 10	17 27	17 34	17 53		17 59	18 07	18 10	18 28	18 37	18 45	18 53	18 59	19 07
Heald Green	d		16 03				16 33			17 03			17 31				18 03			18 32		18 49		19 03	
Gatley	d		16 06					16 40		17 06				17 42			18 06				18 43			19 06	
East Didsbury	d		16 08		16 18					17 08		17 18	17 35				18 08		18 18					19 08	
Burnage	d		16 11				16 39			17 11			17 38				18 11			18 37				19 11	
Mauldeth Road	d		16 13							17 13							18 13							19 13	
Manchester Piccadilly 10	a	16 11	16 21	16 25	16 33		16 52	16 55	17 11	17 21	17 25	17 33	17 46	17 56	18 11		18 21	18 25	18 33	18 46	18 55	18 59	19 11	19 21	19 25
	d		16 22	16 26	16 34		16 54	16 57		17 23	17 27	17 35	17 47	17 58				18 26	18 34	18 47	18 57	19 01			19 26
Manchester Oxford Rd.	a		16 24	16 28	16 36		16 56	16 59		17 25	17 29	17 37	17 49	18 00				18 28	18 36	18 49	18 59	19 03			19 28
Deansgate	a		16 28							17 28												19 06			
Manchester Victoria	a				16 44			17 10				17 44		18 13					18 44		19 11				

Table T085-F

Manchester Airport - Manchester

Mondays to Fridays
16 December to 15 May

Station		TP	NT	TP	NT	TP	NT		TP	TP	AW	NT	TP	NT	TP	AW	TP		NT	TP	NT	NT	NT	TP	NT
		◇1	◇	◇1	◇	◇1	◇		◇1 🛒	◇1		◇	◇1		◇1 🛒		◇1		◇	◇1		◇	◇	◇1 🛒	
Crewe 10	84 d						19 17																		
Wilmslow	84 d						19 43							20 43							21 42				22 34
Manchester Airport	d	19 10	19 28	19 38	19 44	19 53	19 59		20 07	20 10	20 34	20 42	20 53	20 58	21 06	21 32	21 35		21 43	21 53	21 59	22 10	22 34	22 39	23 01
Heald Green	d		19 32		19 48		20 03					20 46		21 02							22 03		22 38		23 05
Gatley	d			19 44			20 06							21 05			21 41				22 06		22 41		23 08
East Didsbury	d	19 18					20 08					20 50		21 07							22 08				
Burnage	d		19 37				20 11						21 01							22 01			22 44		23 11
Mauldeth Road	d						20 13					20 54	21 04							22 04					23 14
Manchester Piccadilly 10	a	19 33	19 46	19 57	20 01	20 11	20 21		20 25	20 33	20 50	21 00	21 13	21 16	21 20	21 49	21 53		21 59	22 15	22 17	22 25	22 52	22 56	23 20
	d	19 34	19 47	19 59	20 03		20 22		20 26	20 34	20 51	21 02		21 18	21 22	21 50	21 55		22 01		22 18		22 54	22 58	23 22
Manchester Oxford Rd.	a	19 36	19 49	20 01	20 05		20 24		20 28	20 36	20 54	21 04		21 20	21 24	21 53	21 57		22 03		22 20		22 56	23 00	23 24
Deansgate	a				20 08		20 28					21 07		21 29					22 06		22 33		23 02		23 27
Manchester Victoria	a	19 44		20 14						20 44							22 11							23 13	

Station		TP	NT		TP	TP	NT
		◇1 🛒			◇1	◇1	◇
Crewe 10	84 d						
Wilmslow	84 d		23 10				
Manchester Airport	d	23 10	23 24		23 30	23 40	23 47
Heald Green	d						23 51
Gatley	d						23 54
East Didsbury	d						23 56
Burnage	d		23 32				23 59
Mauldeth Road	d						00 01
Manchester Piccadilly 10	a	23 24	23 42		23 45	23 54	00 08
	d	23 26				23 55	
Manchester Oxford Rd.	a	23 28				23 57	
Deansgate	a						
Manchester Victoria	a					00 04	

Saturdays
21 December to 16 May

Station		NT	NT	TP	NT	TP	NT	NT	TP	NT		AW	TP	NT	TP	NT	TP	TP	TP	NT		TP	NT	TP	TP
		◇		◇1		◇1 🛒	◇		◇1 🛒	◇		◇	◇1	◇	◇1		◇1 🛒	◇1	◇1 🛒	◇		◇1 🛒	◇	◇1 🛒	◇1 🛒
Crewe 10	84 d				00 44																		06 16		
Wilmslow	84 d															05 41							06 42		
Manchester Airport	d		00 22	00 38	01 13	04 22	04 46	05 07	05 19	05 22		05 33	05 37	05 42	05 54	05 59	06 07	06 10	06 35	06 40		06 53	06 58	07 07	07 10
Heald Green	d						04 50			05 26				05 46		06 03				06 44			07 02		
Gatley	d													05 49		06 06			06 41	06 47			07 05		
East Didsbury	d									05 30						06 08		06 17					07 07		07 18
Burnage	d									05 33						06 11				06 50			07 10		
Mauldeth Road	d	00 01												05 53		06 13				06 53			07 12		
Manchester Piccadilly 10	a	00 08	00 40	00 52	01 28	04 35	05 02	05 19	05 33	05 41		05 47	05 56	06 00	06 12	06 20	06 24	06 32	06 54	06 59		07 11	07 20	07 25	07 33
	d						05 04	05 22	05 34	05 42		05 47	05 57	06 01		06 22	06 26	06 34	06 56	07 01			07 22	07 26	07 34
Manchester Oxford Rd.	a						05 06	05 24	05 36	05 44		05 50	05 59	06 03		06 24	06 28	06 36	06 58	07 03			07 24	07 28	07 36
Deansgate	a													06 07		06 27				07 07			07 27		
Manchester Victoria	a								05 45				06 06					06 45	07 11						07 43

Station		NT	TP	NT	TP	NT		TP	TP	NT	TP	NT	TP	NT	TP	TP		NT	AW	TP	NT	TP	NT	TP	TP
		◇	◇1 🛒	◇	◇1 🛒	◇		◇1 🛒	◇1 🛒	◇	◇1 🛒	◇	◇1 🛒	◇	◇1 🛒	◇1 🛒		◇	■ 🛒	◇1 🛒	◇	◇1 🛒	◇	◇1 🛒	◇1 🛒
Crewe 10	84 d					07 13								08 16									09 16		
Wilmslow	84 d					07 42								08 42									09 42		
Manchester Airport	d	07 25	07 35	07 43	07 53	07 59		08 07	08 10	08 27	08 35	08 44	08 53	08 59	09 07	09 10		09 28	09 35	09 40	09 45	09 53	09 59	10 07	10 10
Heald Green	d	07 29		07 47		08 03				08 31		08 48		09 03				09 32			09 49		10 03		
Gatley	d		07 41			08 06					08 41			09 06						09 46			10 06		
East Didsbury	d	07 33				08 08			08 18	08 35				09 08		09 18			09 42				10 08		
Burnage	d			07 52		08 11				08 38				09 11				09 37					10 11		
Mauldeth Road	d					08 13						08 54		09 13									10 13		
Manchester Piccadilly 10	a	07 42	07 54	07 59	08 11	08 21		08 25	08 33	08 46	08 54	09 00	09 11	09 21	09 25	09 33		09 46	09 51	09 55	09 59	10 11	10 20	10 25	10 33
	d	07 43	07 56	08 01		08 23		08 27	08 35	08 47	08 56	09 02		09 22	09 26	09 34		09 47	09 52	09 57	10 01		10 22	10 26	10 34
Manchester Oxford Rd.	a	07 45	07 58	08 03		08 25		08 29	08 37	08 49	08 58	09 04		09 24	09 28	09 36		09 49	09 55	09 59	10 03		10 24	10 28	10 36
Deansgate	a			08 06		08 28						09 07		09 28							10 06		10 27		
Manchester Victoria	a		08 11						08 45		09 12					09 44				10 11					10 44

Station		NT		AW	TP	NT	TP	NT	TP	TP	NT	AW		TP	NT	TP	NT	TP	TP	NT	AW	TP		NT	TP
		◇		■ 🛒	◇1 🛒	◇	◇1 🛒	◇	◇1 🛒	◇1 🛒	◇	■ 🛒		◇1 🛒	◇	◇1 🛒	◇	◇1 🛒	◇1 🛒	◇	◇ 🛒	◇1 🛒		◇	◇1 🛒
Crewe 10	84 d							10 16									11 17								
Wilmslow	84 d							10 42									11 42								
Manchester Airport	d	10 28		10 35	10 40	10 45	10 53	10 59	11 07	11 10	11 28	11 35		11 40	11 45	11 53	11 59	12 07	12 10	12 28	12 35	12 40		12 45	12 53
Heald Green	d	10 32				10 49		11 03			11 32				11 49		12 03			12 32				12 49	
Gatley	d				10 46			11 06						11 46			12 06					12 46			
East Didsbury	d			10 42				11 08				11 42					12 08				12 42				
Burnage	d	10 37						11 11			11 37						12 11			12 37					
Mauldeth Road	d							11 13									12 13								
Manchester Piccadilly 10	a	10 46		10 51	10 55	10 59	11 11	11 21	11 25	11 33	11 46	11 51		11 55	11 59	12 11	12 21	12 25	12 33	12 46	12 51	12 55		12 59	13 11
	d	10 47		10 52	10 57	11 01		11 22	11 26	11 34	11 47	11 52		11 57	12 01		12 22	12 26	12 34	12 47	12 52	12 57		13 01	
Manchester Oxford Rd.	a	10 49		10 55	10 59	11 03		11 24	11 28	11 36	11 50	11 55		11 59	12 03		12 24	12 28	12 36	12 49	12 55	12 59		13 03	
Deansgate	a					11 06		11 28							12 06		12 28							13 06	
Manchester Victoria	a				11 11					11 44				12 10					12 44			13 10			

Table T085-F

Manchester Airport - Manchester

Saturdays

21 December to 16 May

	NT	TP	TP	NT	AW	TP	NT	TP	NT	TP	TP	NT	AW	TP	NT	TP	NT	TP	TP	NT	AW
	◇	◇1 🛒	◇1 🛒	◇	◇ 🛒	◇1 🛒	◇	◇1 🛒	◇	◇1 🛒	◇1 🛒	◇	◇ 🛒	◇1 🛒	◇	◇1 🛒	◇	◇1 🛒	◇1 🛒	◇	◇ 🛒
Crewe 10 84 d	12 17								13 18								14 16				
Wilmslow 84 d	12 42								13 43								14 42				
Manchester Airport ✈ d	12 59	13 07	13 10	13 28	13 35	13 40	13 45	13 53	13 59	14 07	14 10	14 28	14 35	14 40	14 45	14 53	14 59	15 07	15 10	15 28	15 35
Heald Green d	13 03			13 32			13 49		14 03			14 32			14 49		15 03			15 32	
Gatley d	13 06					13 46			14 06					14 46			15 06				
East Didsbury d	13 08				13 42				14 08				14 42				15 08				15 42
Burnage d	13 11			13 37					14 11			14 38					15 11			15 37	
Mauldeth Road d	13 13								14 13								15 13				
Manchester Piccadilly 10 🚊 a	13 21	13 25	13 33	13 45	13 51	13 55	13 59	14 11	14 21	14 25	14 33	14 46	14 51	14 55	14 59	15 11	15 21	15 25	15 33	15 46	15 51
d	13 22	13 26	13 34	13 47	13 52	13 57	14 01		14 22	14 26	14 34	14 47	14 52	14 57	15 01		15 22	15 26	15 34	15 47	15 52
Manchester Oxford Rd. a	13 24	13 28	13 36	13 49	13 55	13 59	14 03		14 24	14 28	14 36	14 49	14 55	14 59	15 03		15 24	15 28	15 36	15 49	15 55
Deansgate 🚊 a	13 28						14 06		14 28						15 06		15 28				
Manchester Victoria a			13 44			14 10					14 44			15 11					15 44		

	TP	TP	NT	TP	TP	NT	AW	TP	TP	NT	TP	TP	NT	AW	TP	TP	NT	TP	TP	NT	AW	TP
	◇1 🛒	◇1 🛒	◇	◇1 🛒	◇1 🛒	◇	◇ 🛒	◇1 🛒	◇1 🛒	◇	◇1 🛒	◇1 🛒	◇	◇ 🛒	◇1 🛒	◇1 🛒	◇	◇1 🛒	◇1 🛒	◇	◇	◇1
Crewe 10 84 d			15 16							16 16							17 16					
Wilmslow 84 d			15 42							16 42							17 42					
Manchester Airport ✈ d	15 40	15 53	15 59	16 07	16 10	16 28	16 35	16 40	16 53	16 59	17 07	17 10	17 28	17 35	17 40	17 53	17 59	18 07	18 10	18 28	18 35	18 40
Heald Green d			16 03			16 32				17 03			17 32				18 03			18 32		
Gatley d	15 46		16 06					16 46		17 06					17 46		18 06					18 46
East Didsbury d			16 08		16 18		16 42			17 08		17 18		17 42			18 08		18 18		18 42	
Burnage d			16 11			16 37				17 11			17 37				18 11			18 37		
Mauldeth Road d			16 13							17 13							18 13					
Manchester Piccadilly 10 🚊 a	15 55	16 11	16 21	16 25	16 33	16 46	16 51	16 55	17 11	17 21	17 25	17 33	17 46	17 51	17 56	18 11	18 21	18 25	18 33	18 46	18 52	18 55
d	15 57		16 22	16 26	16 34	16 47	16 52	16 57		17 23	17 27	17 35	17 47	17 52	17 57		18 22	18 26	18 34	18 47	18 53	18 57
Manchester Oxford Rd. a	15 59		16 24	16 28	16 36	16 49	16 55	16 59		17 25	17 29	17 37	17 49	17 55	17 59		18 25	18 28	18 36	18 49	18 56	18 59
Deansgate 🚊 a			16 28							17 28							18 28					
Manchester Victoria a	16 10				16 44			17 10				17 44			18 11				18 44			19 11

	NT	TP	NT	TP	TP	NT	TP	NT	TP	NT	TP	AW	NT	TP	NT	TP	NT	TP	NT	NT	NT	TP
	◇	◇1	◇	◇1 🛒	◇1	◇	◇1	◇	◇1	◇	◇1		◇	◇1		◇1	◇	◇1			◇	◇1
Crewe 10 84 d			18 16							19 17												
Wilmslow 84 d			18 42							19 43					20 43				21 42			
Manchester Airport ✈ d	18 45	18 53	18 59	19 07	19 10	19 28	19 36	19 42	19 53	19 59	20 10	20 34	20 42	20 53	20 58	21 35	21 41	21 53	21 59	22 10	22 30	22 40
Heald Green d	18 49		19 03			19 32		19 49		20 03			20 46		21 02				22 03		22 34	
Gatley d			19 06				19 42			20 06					21 05	21 41			22 06		22 38	
East Didsbury d			19 08		19 18					20 08			20 50		21 07				22 08			
Burnage d			19 11			19 37				20 11				21 01				22 01			22 42	
Mauldeth Road d			19 13							20 13			20 54	21 04				22 04				
Manchester Piccadilly 10 🚊 a	18 59	19 11	19 21	19 25	19 33	19 46	19 54	19 59	20 11	20 21	20 33	20 50	21 00	21 13	21 16	21 53	21 57	22 12	22 17	22 25	22 52	22 59
d	19 01		19 22	19 26	19 34	19 47	19 55	20 01		20 22	20 34	20 51	21 02		21 17	21 55	21 59		22 18	22 26	22 54	23 01
Manchester Oxford Rd. a	19 03		19 24	19 28	19 36	19 49	19 57	20 03		20 24	20 36	20 54	21 04		21 19	21 57	22 01		22 20	22 28	22 56	23 03
Deansgate 🚊 a	19 06		19 28					20 06		20 28			21 07		21 29		22 04		22 33		23 02	
Manchester Victoria a					19 44		20 10				20 44					22 11						23 11

	NT	TP	NT	TP	TP
		A 🚌		◇1 B	◇1 A
Crewe 10 84 d					
Wilmslow 84 d	22 42				
Manchester Airport ✈ d	22 59	23 20	23 28	23 40	23 40
Heald Green d	23 03		23 32		
Gatley d	23 06		23 35		
East Didsbury d	23 08		23 37		
Burnage d	23 11		23 40		
Mauldeth Road d	23 13		23 42		
Manchester Piccadilly 10 🚊 a	23 20	23 45	23 49	23 53	23 57
d	23 22		23 51	23 55	
Manchester Oxford Rd. a	23 24		23 53	23 57	
Deansgate 🚊 a	23 27		23 56		
Manchester Victoria a				00 04	

Sundays

15 December to 10 May

	TP	TP	TP	TP	TP	NT	NT	NT	TP	TP	NT	NT	NT	TP	TP	TP	TP	TP	TP	TP	TP	NT
	◇1 C	D 🚌	D 🚌	◇1 C	D 🚌	🚌	D 🚌	C	D 🚌	◇1 C 🛒	E 🚌	F	G	D 🚌	◇1 C 🛒	D 🚌	◇1 H 🛒	◇1 I 🛒	◇1 F 🛒	◇1 G 🛒	◇1 F 🛒	J 🚌
Crewe 10 84 d																						
Wilmslow 84 d																						
Manchester Airport ✈ d	00 38	01 00	03 30	04 22	05 20	05 30	05 50	05 54	06 05	06 27	06 50	06 51	06 51	07 00	07 27	07 35	07 40	07 46	07 51	07 51	07 56	08 00
Heald Green d							05 55	05 58			06 55		06 55									08 05
Gatley d							06 03	06 01			07 03		06 58									08 13
East Didsbury d							06 11	06 03			07 11		07 00									08 21
Burnage d							06 16	06 06			07 16		07 03									08 26
Mauldeth Road d							06 21	06 08			07 21		07 05									08 31
Manchester Piccadilly 10 🚊 a	00 52	01 25	03 55	04 36	05 45	05 55	06 32	06 16	06 30	06 41	07 32	07 05	07 15	07 25	07 41	08 00	07 58	08 00	08 08	08 09	08 12	08 42
d																		08 05			08 19	
Manchester Oxford Rd. a																		08 07			08 21	
Deansgate 🚊 a																						
Manchester Victoria a																		08 14			08 28	

A from 22 February until 28 March
B until 15 February, from 4 April
C until 16 February, from 5 April
D from 23 February until 29 March
E from 23 February
F from 5 April
G until 16 February
H from 12 January until 16 February
I until 5 January
J until 29 March

Table T085-F

Manchester Airport - Manchester

Sundays

15 December to 10 May

	NT	NT	TP	NT	TP	NT	TP	TP	NT	NT	NT	NT	TP	NT	TP	TP	TP	NT	TP	NT	TP
	A	◇ B	C 🚌	◇	◇1 D 🛒		◇1 🛒	◇1 D 🛒	◇ E	◇ F	◇ G	◇ A	◇1 🛒		◇1 🛒	◇1 G 🛒	◇1 A 🛒	◇	◇1 🛒		◇1 🛒
Crewe 10 84 d																					
Wilmslow 84 d						08 38								09 43						10 40	
Manchester Airport ✈ d	08 01	08 33	08 35	08 41	08 46	08 54	09 05	09 14	09 35	09 35	09 43	09 43	09 56	09 59	10 10	10 13	10 13	10 32	10 55	10 58	11 10
Heald Green d	08 05			08 45		08 58					09 47	09 48		10 03				10 36		11 02	
Gatley d	08 08					09 01								10 06						11 05	
East Didsbury d	08 11					09 03								10 08				10 41		11 08	
Burnage d	08 13					09 06								10 11						11 10	
Mauldeth Road d	08 16					09 08								10 13						11 13	
Manchester Piccadilly 10 🚊 a	08 22	08 51	09 00	08 59	09 03	09 16	09 20	09 32	09 50	09 51	09 59	09 59	10 10	10 20	10 24	10 34	10 35	10 50	11 15	11 19	11 23
d	08 24	08 53		09 01		09 18	09 22	09 35	09 52	09 53	10 01	10 01		10 22	10 26	10 36	10 37	10 54		11 21	11 25
Manchester Oxford Rd. a	08 26	08 55		09 03		09 20	09 24	09 37	09 54	09 55	10 03	10 03		10 24	10 28	10 38	10 39	10 56		11 23	11 27
Deansgate 🚊 a	08 29			09 06		09 23					10 06	10 06		10 27						11 26	
Manchester Victoria a								09 44								10 44	10 45				

	NT	TP	TP	NT	TP	TP	NT	TP	NT	TP	TP	NT	TP	NT	TP	NT	TP	TP	NT	TP	NT	TP
	◇ A	◇1 🛒	◇1 🛒		◇1 🛒	◇1 🛒	◇	◇1 🛒		◇1 🛒	◇1 🛒	◇	◇1 🛒	◇	◇1 🛒		◇1 🛒	◇1 🛒	◇	◇1 🛒	◇	◇1 🛒
Crewe 10 84 d																						
Wilmslow 84 d				11 38					12 44							13 44						
Manchester Airport ✈ d	11 31	11 37	11 56	11 59	12 13	12 33	12 41	12 56	12 59	13 10	13 13	13 30	13 36	13 44	13 56	13 59	14 10	14 13	14 30	14 36	14 45	14 56
Heald Green d	11 35			12 03			12 45		13 03			13 34		13 49		14 03			14 34		14 49	
Gatley d		11 43		12 06		12 39			13 06				13 42			14 06				14 42		
East Didsbury d	11 39			12 09			12 50		13 08			13 38				14 09			14 38			
Burnage d				12 11					13 11							14 11						
Mauldeth Road d				12 14					13 13							14 14						
Manchester Piccadilly 10 🚊 a	11 48	11 59	12 12	12 21	12 33	12 49	12 59	13 14	13 21	13 25	13 33	13 47	13 51	13 59	14 13	14 21	14 25	14 33	14 47	14 51	14 59	15 13
d	11 50	12 01		12 22	12 34	12 51	13 01		13 22	13 26	13 35	13 48	13 53	14 01		14 22	14 26	14 35	14 48	14 53	15 01	
Manchester Oxford Rd. a	11 52	12 03		12 24	12 37	12 53	13 03		13 24	13 28	13 37	13 50	13 55	14 03		14 24	14 28	14 37	14 50	14 55	15 03	
Deansgate 🚊 a				12 28					13 29					14 06		14 28					15 06	
Manchester Victoria a		12 13			12 45	13 01					13 44		14 04					14 44		15 04		

	NT	TP	TP	NT	TP	NT	TP	NT	TP	TP	NT	TP	NT	TP	NT	TP	TP	NT	TP	NT	TP
		◇1 🛒	◇1 🛒	◇	◇1 🛒	◇	◇1 🛒		◇1 🛒	◇1 🛒	◇	◇1 🛒	◇	◇1 🛒		◇1 🛒	◇1 🛒	◇	◇1 🛒	◇	◇1 🛒
Crewe 10 84 d																					
Wilmslow 84 d	14 39							15 44							16 44						
Manchester Airport ✈ d	14 59	15 10	15 13	15 30	15 36	15 45	15 56	15 59	16 10	16 13	16 30	16 36	16 45	16 56	16 59	17 10	17 13	17 30	17 36	17 45	17 56
Heald Green d	15 03			15 34		15 49		16 03			16 34		16 49		17 03			17 34		17 49	
Gatley d	15 06				15 42			16 06				16 42			17 06				17 42		
East Didsbury d	15 09			15 38				16 09			16 38				17 09			17 38			
Burnage d	15 11							16 11							17 11						
Mauldeth Road d	15 14							16 14							17 14						
Manchester Piccadilly 10 🚊 a	15 21	15 25	15 33	15 47	15 51	16 00	16 13	16 21	16 25	16 33	16 47	16 51	16 59	17 13	17 21	17 25	17 33	17 47	17 51	17 59	18 13
d	15 22	15 26	15 34	15 48	15 53	16 01		16 22	16 26	16 34	16 48	16 53	17 01		17 22	17 26	17 34	17 48	17 53	18 01	
Manchester Oxford Rd. a	15 24	15 28	15 36	15 50	15 55	16 03		16 24	16 28	16 36	16 50	16 55	17 03		17 24	17 28	17 37	17 50	17 55	18 03	
Deansgate 🚊 a	15 28					16 07		16 28					17 06		17 28					18 06	
Manchester Victoria a			15 44		16 04					16 45		17 04					17 45		18 04		

	NT	TP	TP	NT	TP	NT	TP	NT	TP	TP	NT	TP	NT	TP	NT	TP	TP	NT	TP	NT	TP	TP
		◇1 🛒	◇1 🛒	◇	◇1	◇	◇1		◇1 🛒	◇1	◇	◇1	◇	◇1		◇1 🛒	◇1	◇	◇1		◇1 🛒	◇1
Crewe 10 84 d																						
Wilmslow 84 d	17 44							18 44							19 44					20 44		
Manchester Airport ✈ d	17 59	18 10	18 13	18 30	18 36	18 45	18 56	18 59	19 10	19 13	19 30	19 36	19 45	19 56	19 59	20 10	20 13	20 45	20 55	20 59	21 10	21 36
Heald Green d	18 03			18 34		18 49		19 03			19 34		19 49		20 03			20 49		21 03		
Gatley d	18 06				18 42			19 06				19 42			20 06					21 06		21 42
East Didsbury d	18 09			18 38				19 09			19 38				20 09					21 08		
Burnage d	18 11							19 11							20 11				21 02			
Mauldeth Road d	18 14							19 14							20 14				21 05			
Manchester Piccadilly 10 🚊 a	18 21	18 25	18 33	18 47	18 51	19 00	19 13	19 21	19 25	19 33	19 47	19 51	20 00	20 13	20 21	20 25	20 33	21 00	21 13	21 17	21 23	21 51
d	18 22	18 26	18 35	18 48	18 53	19 01		19 22	19 26	19 35	19 48	19 53	20 01		20 22	20 26	20 35	21 02		21 18	21 26	21 53
Manchester Oxford Rd. a	18 24	18 28	18 37	18 50	18 55	19 03		19 24	19 28	19 37	19 50	19 55	20 03		20 24	20 28	20 37	21 04		21 20	21 28	21 55
Deansgate 🚊 a	18 28					19 07		19 28					20 07		20 28			21 07		21 29		
Manchester Victoria a			18 45		19 04					19 45		20 04					20 44					22 04

	NT	TP	NT	TP	TP	TP	NT	TP
	◇	◇1		◇1	◇1	◇1 🛒		◇1
Crewe 10 84 d								
Wilmslow 84 d			21 43				22 54	
Manchester Airport ✈ d	21 45	21 56	21 59	22 37	22 56	23 01	23 09	23 35
Heald Green d	21 49		22 03				23 13	
Gatley d			22 06				23 16	
East Didsbury d			22 08				23 19	
Burnage d		22 03					23 21	
Mauldeth Road d		22 06					23 24	
Manchester Piccadilly 10 🚊 a	21 59	22 13	22 18	22 50	23 12	23 14	23 31	23 47
d	22 01		22 19	22 51		23 15	23 33	23 49
Manchester Oxford Rd. a	22 03		22 21	22 53		23 17	23 35	23 51
Deansgate 🚊 a	22 07		22 31				23 38	
Manchester Victoria a				23 00				23 58

A from 5 April
B until 5 January
C from 23 February until 29 March
D until 16 February, from 5 April
E until 5 January, from 5 April
F from 12 January until 29 March
G until 29 March

Table T085-R

Manchester - Manchester Airport

Mondays to Fridays

16 December to 15 May

Miles			TP MX	TP MO	TP MO	TP MX	NT MO	TP TW FO	TP MO	TP	NT	NT	AW	NT	TP	TP	NT	TP	NT	TP	TP	NT	TP
			◇1	◇1	◇1 ⊼	◇1 ⊼		◇1 ⊼	◇1 ⊼	◇1		◇		◇	◇1	◇1		◇1	◇	◇1	◇1	◇	◇1
—	Manchester Victoria	d			00 24	00 26												05 39			06 10		06 39
—	Deansgate 84,89	d					00 25															06 19	
—	Manchester Oxford Rd. 84,89	d		00 01			00 32											05 46	05 55		06 16	06 22	06 50
0	Manchester Piccadilly 10	a		00 04	00 31	00 34	00 35											05 49	05 57		06 20	06 24	06 53
—		d	00 03	00 05	00 32	00 36	00 36	01 44	01 46	03 43	03 46	04 14	04 46	04 49	04 57	05 00	05 19	05 50	05 59	06 08	06 20	06 26	06 55
3½	Mauldeth Road	d					00 42										05 26		06 05			06 32	
4½	Burnage	d					00 45										05 28		06 07			06 35	
5½	East Didsbury	d					00 47										05 31			06 17		06 37	
6¾	Gatley	d					00 50										05 33	06 02	06 11			06 40	07 04
8¼	Heald Green	d					00 53										05 36		06 14			06 43	
9¾	Manchester Airport	a	00 19	00 20	00 47	00 51	00 57	01 59	02 02	03 59	04 00	04 27	05 02	05 04	05 13	05 16	05 41	06 13	06 19	06 27	06 41	06 47	07 16
—	Wilmslow 84	a															05 53					07 12	
—	Crewe 10 84	a															06 23					07 42	

		NT	TP	TP	TP	NT	TP	NT	TP	TP	TP	NT	TP	NT WO	NT WX	TP	TP	TP	NT	TP	AW	NT
		◇	◇1	◇1	◇1	◇	◇1	◇	◇1 ⊼	◇1 ⊼	◇1 ⊼	◇	◇1 ⊼	◇	◇	◇1	◇1 ⊼	◇1 ⊼	◇	◇1 ⊼	◇	◇
Manchester Victoria	d			07 10			07 39			08 10			08 39				09 10			09 39		
Deansgate 84,89	d					07 22						08 22							09 23			
Manchester Oxford Rd. 84,89	d	06 55		07 16	07 21	07 25	07 46	07 58		08 16	08 21	08 26	08 47	08 56	08 56		09 16	09 22	09 26	09 47	09 51	09 56
Manchester Piccadilly 10	a	06 57		07 20	07 24	07 29	07 49	08 00		08 20	08 24	08 28	08 49	08 58	08 59		09 19	09 24	09 28	09 49	09 54	09 58
	d	06 59	07 07	07 21	07 26	07 31	07 50	08 02	08 07	08 21	08 26	08 30	08 51	09 00	09 00	09 07	09 20	09 26	09 30	09 51	09 55	10 00
Mauldeth Road	d	07 05				07 37		08 08				08 37							09 36			
Burnage	d	07 08				07 39		08 10				08 39		09 07	09 07				09 39			10 07
East Didsbury	d		07 17			07 42				08 31		08 42					09 30		09 41		10 04	
Gatley	d					07 44	08 02					08 44	09 02						09 44	10 02		
Heald Green	d	07 13				07 47		08 16				08 47		09 13	09 13				09 47			10 13
Manchester Airport	a	07 18	07 27	07 41	07 48	07 52	08 16	08 20	08 26	08 41	08 47	08 52	09 16	09 18	09 18	09 25	09 41	09 49	09 52	10 13	10 19	10 18
Wilmslow 84	a					08 14						09 13							10 15			
Crewe 10 84	a					08 42						09 42							10 44			

		TP	TP	TP	NT	TP	AW	NT	TP	TP	TP	NT	TP	AW	NT	TP	TP	TP	NT	TP	AW	NT	TP
		◇1 ⊼	◇1 ⊼	◇1 ⊼	◇	◇1 ⊼	◇ ⊼	◇	◇1 ⊼	◇1 ⊼	◇1 ⊼	◇	◇1 ⊼	◇ ⊼	◇	◇1 ⊼	◇1 ⊼	◇1 ⊼	◇	◇1 ⊼	◇ ⊼	◇	◇1 ⊼
Manchester Victoria	d		10 10			10 39				11 09			11 40				12 10			12 39			
Deansgate 84,89	d				10 22							11 22							12 22				
Manchester Oxford Rd. 84,89	d		10 16	10 21	10 25	10 47	10 51	10 56		11 16	11 21	11 25	11 47	11 51	11 55		12 16	12 21	12 25	12 47	12 51	12 56	
Manchester Piccadilly 10	a		10 19	10 24	10 28	10 49	10 54	10 58		11 19	11 24	11 28	11 49	11 55	11 58		12 19	12 24	12 28	12 49	12 54	12 58	
	d	10 07	10 20	10 25	10 30	10 51	10 55	11 00	11 07	11 20	11 25	11 30	11 51	11 55	11 59	12 07	12 20	12 25	12 30	12 51	12 55	13 00	13 07
Mauldeth Road	d				10 37							11 36							12 37				
Burnage	d				10 39			11 07				11 39			12 06				12 39			13 07	
East Didsbury	d				10 42		11 04					11 41		12 04					12 42		13 05		
Gatley	d				10 44	11 02						11 44	12 02						12 44	13 02			
Heald Green	d				10 47			11 13				11 47			12 12				12 47			13 13	
Manchester Airport	a	10 25	10 41	10 46	10 52	11 13	11 19	11 18	11 25	11 41	11 46	11 52	12 13	12 19	12 17	12 25	12 41	12 46	12 52	13 13	13 19	13 18	13 25
Wilmslow 84	a				11 15							12 14							13 15				
Crewe 10 84	a				11 44							12 42							13 43				

		TP	TP	NT	TP	AW	NT	TP	TP	TP	NT	TP	AW	NT	TP	TP	TP	NT	TP	NT	TP	TP	TP
		◇1 ⊼	◇1 ⊼	◇	◇1 ⊼	◇ ⊼	◇	◇1 ⊼	◇1 ⊼	◇1 ⊼	◇	◇1 ⊼	◇ ⊼	◇	◇1 ⊼	◇1 ⊼	◇1 ⊼	◇	◇1 ⊼	◇	◇1 ⊼	◇1 ⊼	◇1 ⊼
Manchester Victoria	d	13 10			13 39				14 10			14 40				15 10			15 40			16 10	
Deansgate 84,89	d			13 22							14 22							15 22					
Manchester Oxford Rd. 84,89	d	13 16	13 21	13 25	13 47	13 51	13 56		14 16	14 21	14 25	14 47	14 51	14 56		15 16	15 21	15 25	15 47	15 56		16 16	16 21
Manchester Piccadilly 10	a	13 20	13 24	13 28	13 49	13 54	13 58		14 19	14 24	14 28	14 49	14 54	14 58		15 19	15 24	15 28	15 49	15 58		16 19	16 24
	d	13 20	13 25	13 30	13 51	13 55	14 00	14 07	14 20	14 25	14 30	14 51	14 55	15 00	15 07	15 20	15 25	15 29	15 51	16 00	16 07	16 20	16 25
Mauldeth Road	d			13 36							14 36							15 36					
Burnage	d			13 38			14 07				14 38			15 07				15 39		16 07			
East Didsbury	d			13 41		14 04					14 41		15 04					15 41				16 30	
Gatley	d			13 43	14 02						14 43	15 02						15 44	16 02				
Heald Green	d			13 46			14 13				14 46			15 13				15 47		16 13			
Manchester Airport	a	13 41	13 46	13 52	14 13	14 19	14 18	14 25	14 41	14 46	14 52	15 13	15 19	15 18	15 25	15 41	15 46	15 52	16 13	16 17	16 25	16 40	16 48
Wilmslow 84	a			14 15							15 15							16 15					
Crewe 10 84	a			14 42							15 42							16 42					

		NT	TP	NT	TP	TP	TP	NT	TP	NT	TP	TP	TP	NT	TP	NT	TP	TP	TP	NT	TP	AW
		◇	◇1 ⊼	◇	◇1 ⊼	◇1 ⊼	◇1 ⊼	◇	◇1 ⊼	◇	◇1 ⊼	◇1 ⊼	◇1 ⊼	◇	◇1 ⊼	◇	◇1 ⊼	◇1 ⊼	◇1 ⊼		◇1 ⊼	◇
Manchester Victoria	d		16 39			17 10			17 39			18 10			18 39			19 10			19 39	
Deansgate 84,89	d	16 22						17 24														
Manchester Oxford Rd. 84,89	d	16 25	16 47	16 56		17 16	17 24	17 28	17 47	17 56		18 16	18 21		18 47	18 56		19 16	19 24		19 47	19 51
Manchester Piccadilly 10	a	16 28	16 49	16 58		17 19	17 27	17 31	17 49	17 58		18 19	18 23		18 49	18 58		19 19	19 27		19 49	19 54
	d	16 29	16 51	17 00	17 07	17 20	17 29	17 33	17 51	18 00	18 07	18 20	18 25	18 34	18 51	19 00	19 07	19 20	19 29	19 35	19 51	19 55
Mauldeth Road	d	16 36						17 39						18 41						19 42		
Burnage	d	16 39		17 07				17 42		18 07				18 44		19 07				19 45		
East Didsbury	d	16 41				17 30		17 44				18 30		18 46				19 30		19 48		
Gatley	d	16 44	17 02					17 47	18 02					18 49	19 02					19 50	20 02	
Heald Green	d	16 47		17 13				17 50		18 13				18 52		19 13				19 53		
Manchester Airport	a	16 52	17 16	17 17	17 25	17 40	17 48	17 57	18 14	18 17	18 25	18 41	18 46	18 57	19 16	19 17	19 25	19 42	19 50	19 58	20 13	20 19
Wilmslow 84	a	17 16						18 15						19 14						20 11		
Crewe 10 84	a	17 43						18 43						19 43								

Table T085-R

Manchester - Manchester Airport

Mondays to Fridays

16 December to 15 May

		TP	TP	TP	NT	TP	AW	NT	TP	TP	NT	NT	TP	TP	NT	TP	TP	TP	NT	TP
		◇1	◇1 ⊼	◇1 ⊼		◇1	◇	◇	◇1	◇1 ⊼		◇	◇1	◇1 ⊼		◇1	◇1	◇1 ⊼		◇1
Manchester Victoria	d		20 10			20 39							21 56				22 55			23 52
Deansgate 84,89	d				20 23						21 22				22 25				23 25	
Manchester Oxford Rd. 84,89	d		20 16	20 21	20 26	20 47	20 52	20 57		21 21	21 24	21 44	22 03		22 28		23 02	23 21	23 28	23 59
Manchester Piccadilly 10	a		20 19	20 24	20 28	20 49	20 56	20 59		21 24	21 28	21 47	22 06		22 31		23 05	23 24	23 31	00 01
	d	20 07	20 20	20 25	20 30	20 51	20 56	21 01	21 09	21 25	21 29	21 49	22 07	22 24	22 32	23 09	23 12	23 25	23 33	00 03
Mauldeth Road	d				20 36						21 36				22 38				23 40	
Burnage	d				20 38			21 08			21 38				22 41				23 42	
East Didsbury	d				20 41						21 41				22 43				23 45	
Gatley	d				20 43	21 02		21 12			21 44				22 46				23 47	
Heald Green	d				20 46			21 15			21 48				22 49				23 51	
Manchester Airport	a	20 25	20 40	20 48	20 51	21 11	21 17	21 20	21 25	21 41	21 57	22 03	22 22	22 45	22 53	23 25	23 28	23 46	23 56	00 19
Wilmslow 84	a				21 10						22 12				23 06					
Crewe 10 84	a																			

Saturdays

21 December to 16 May

		TP	TP	TP	TP	NT	NT	TP	AW	NT	TP	NT	NT	TP	TP	TP	NT	TP	NT	TP	TP	TP	NT
		◇1	◇1 ⊼	◇1 ⊼	◇1		◇	◇1		◇	◇1		◇	◇1	◇1	◇1	◇	◇1	◇	◇1	◇1	◇1	◇
Manchester Victoria	d		00 26											05 37		06 10		06 39			07 10		
Deansgate 84,89	d																06 19						07 22
Manchester Oxford Rd. 84,89	d												05 41	05 46		06 16	06 22	06 50	06 55		07 16	07 21	07 25
Manchester Piccadilly 10	a		00 34										05 44	05 49		06 20	06 24	06 53	06 57		07 20	07 25	07 29
	d	00 03	00 36	01 44	03 34	03 46	04 14	04 34	04 46	04 49	04 55	05 16	05 45	05 50	06 08	06 20	06 26	06 55	06 59	07 07	07 21	07 27	07 31
Mauldeth Road	d											05 23	05 52				06 32		07 05				07 37
Burnage	d											05 25	05 54				06 35		07 08				07 39
East Didsbury	d											05 28			06 17		06 37			07 17			07 42
Gatley	d											05 30	05 58	06 02			06 40	07 04					07 44
Heald Green	d											05 33	06 01				06 43		07 13				07 47
Manchester Airport	a	00 19	00 51	01 59	03 51	04 00	04 27	04 52	05 03	05 03	05 13	05 38	06 06	06 13	06 27	06 41	06 47	07 16	07 18	07 27	07 41	07 49	07 52
Wilmslow 84	a											05 53					07 12						08 14
Crewe 10 84	a											06 23					07 44						08 42

		TP	NT	TP	TP	TP	NT	TP	AW	NT	TP	TP	TP	NT	TP	AW	NT	TP	TP	TP	NT	TP	AW
		◇1	◇	◇1 ⊼	◇1 ⊼	◇1 ⊼	◇	◇1 ⊼	◇	◇	◇1	◇1 ⊼	◇1 ⊼	◇	◇1 ⊼	◇	◇	◇1 ⊼	◇1 ⊼	◇1 ⊼	◇	◇1 ⊼	◇ ⊼
Manchester Victoria	d	07 39			08 10			08 39				09 10			09 39				10 10			10 39	
Deansgate 84,89	d						08 22							09 23							10 22		
Manchester Oxford Rd. 84,89	d	07 46	07 58		08 16	08 21	08 26	08 47	08 51	08 56		09 16	09 22	09 26	09 47	09 51	09 56		10 16	10 21	10 25	10 47	10 51
Manchester Piccadilly 10	a	07 49	08 01		08 20	08 24	08 28	08 49	08 54	08 59		09 19	09 24	09 28	09 49	09 54	09 58		10 19	10 24	10 28	10 49	10 54
	d	07 50	08 02	08 07	08 21	08 26	08 30	08 51	08 55	09 00	09 07	09 20	09 26	09 30	09 51	09 55	10 00	10 07	10 20	10 25	10 30	10 51	10 55
Mauldeth Road	d		08 08				08 37							09 36							10 37		
Burnage	d		08 11				08 40			09 07				09 39			10 07				10 39		
East Didsbury	d				08 31		08 42		09 03			09 30		09 41		10 04					10 42		11 04
Gatley	d	08 02					08 45	09 02						09 44	10 02						10 44	11 02	
Heald Green	d		08 16				08 48			09 13				09 47			10 13				10 47		
Manchester Airport	a	08 16	08 21	08 26	08 41	08 44	08 52	09 13	09 19	09 18	09 25	09 41	09 46	09 52	10 13	10 19	10 18	10 25	10 41	10 46	10 52	11 13	11 19
Wilmslow 84	a						09 15							10 15							11 15		
Crewe 10 84	a						09 42							10 44							11 44		

		NT	TP	TP	TP	NT	TP	AW	NT	TP	TP	TP	NT	TP	AW	NT	TP	TP	TP	NT	TP	AW
		◇	◇1 ⊼	◇1 ⊼	◇1 ⊼	◇	◇1 ⊼	■ ⊼	◇	◇1 ⊼	◇1 ⊼	◇1 ⊼	◇	◇1 ⊼	◇ ⊼	◇	◇1 ⊼	◇1 ⊼	◇1 ⊼	◇	◇1 ⊼	◇ ⊼
Manchester Victoria	d			11 09			11 40				12 10			12 39				13 10			13 39	
Deansgate 84,89	d					11 22							12 22							13 22		
Manchester Oxford Rd. 84,89	d	10 56		11 16	11 21	11 25	11 47	11 51	11 56		12 16	12 21	12 25	12 47	12 51	12 56		13 16	13 21	13 25	13 47	13 51
Manchester Piccadilly 10	a	10 58		11 19	11 24	11 28	11 49	11 55	11 58		12 19	12 24	12 28	12 49	12 54	12 58		13 20	13 24	13 28	13 49	13 54
	d	11 00	11 07	11 20	11 25	11 30	11 51	11 55	12 00	12 07	12 20	12 25	12 30	12 51	12 55	13 00	13 07	13 20	13 25	13 29	13 51	13 55
Mauldeth Road	d					11 36							12 37							13 36		
Burnage	d	11 07				11 39			12 07				12 39			13 07				13 38		
East Didsbury	d					11 41		12 04					12 42		13 05					13 41		14 04
Gatley	d					11 44	12 02						12 44	13 02						13 43	14 02	
Heald Green	d	11 13				11 47			12 13				12 47			13 13				13 46		
Manchester Airport	a	11 18	11 25	11 41	11 46	11 52	12 13	12 19	12 18	12 25	12 41	12 46	12 52	13 13	13 19	13 18	13 25	13 41	13 46	13 52	14 13	14 19
Wilmslow 84	a					12 14							13 15							14 15		
Crewe 10 84	a					12 42							13 43							14 42		

		NT	TP	TP	TP	NT	TP	AW	NT	TP	TP	TP	NT	TP	AW	NT	TP	TP	TP	NT	TP	AW	NT
		◇	◇1 ⊼	◇1 ⊼	◇1 ⊼	◇	◇1 ⊼	◇ ⊼	◇	◇1 ⊼	◇1 ⊼	◇1 ⊼	◇	◇1 ⊼	◇ ⊼	◇	◇1 ⊼	◇1 ⊼	◇1 ⊼	◇	◇1 ⊼	◇ ⊼	◇
Manchester Victoria	d			14 10			14 40				15 10			15 40				16 10			16 39		
Deansgate 84,89	d					14 22							15 22							16 22			
Manchester Oxford Rd. 84,89	d	13 56		14 16	14 21	14 25	14 47	14 51	14 56		15 16	15 21	15 25	15 47	15 51	15 56		16 16	16 21	16 25	16 47	16 51	16 56
Manchester Piccadilly 10	a	13 58		14 19	14 24	14 28	14 49	14 54	14 58		15 19	15 24	15 28	15 49	15 55	15 58		16 19	16 24	16 28	16 49	16 54	16 58
	d	14 00	14 07	14 20	14 25	14 30	14 51	14 55	15 00	15 07	15 20	15 25	15 29	15 51	15 55	16 00	16 07	16 20	16 25	16 29	16 51	16 55	17 00
Mauldeth Road	d					14 36							15 36							16 36			
Burnage	d	14 07				14 38			15 07				15 39			16 07				16 39			17 07
East Didsbury	d					14 41		15 04					15 41		16 05			16 30		16 41		17 04	
Gatley	d					14 43	15 02						15 44	16 02						16 44	17 02		
Heald Green	d	14 13				14 46			15 13				15 47			16 13				16 47			17 13
Manchester Airport	a	14 18	14 25	14 41	14 46	14 52	15 13	15 19	15 18	15 25	15 41	15 46	15 52	16 13	16 19	16 18	16 25	16 41	16 46	16 52	17 13	17 19	17 18
Wilmslow 84	a					15 15							16 15							17 16			
Crewe 10 84	a					15 42							16 42							17 43			

Table T085-R

Saturdays

21 December to 16 May

Manchester - Manchester Airport

Station		TP ◇1 🛒	TP ◇1 🛒	TP ◇1 🛒	NT ◇	TP ◇1 🛒	AW ◇ 🛒	NT ◇	TP ◇1 🛒	TP ◇1 🛒	TP ◇1 🛒	NT ◇	TP ◇1 🛒	NT ◇	TP ◇1 🛒	TP ◇1 🛒	TP ◇1 🛒	NT ◇ A	TP ◇1 🛒	AW ◇ 🛒	TP ◇1	TP ◇1 🛒	TP ◇1 🛒
Manchester Victoria	d		17 10			17 39				18 10			18 39			19 10			19 39			20 10	
Deansgate 84,89	d				17 22							18 23						19 25					
Manchester Oxford Rd. 84,89	d		17 16	17 21	17 25	17 47	17 51	17 57		18 16	18 21	18 26	18 47	18 56		19 16	19 21	19 28	19 47	19 51		20 16	20 21
Manchester Piccadilly [10]	a		17 19	17 24	17 28	17 49	17 54	17 59		18 19	18 23	18 29	18 49	18 58		19 19	19 24	19 30	19 49	19 54		20 19	20 24
	d	17 07	17 20	17 25	17 29	17 51	17 55	18 01	18 07	18 20	18 25	18 31	18 51	19 00	19 07	19 20	19 25	19 32	19 51	19 55	20 07	20 20	20 25
Mauldeth Road	d				17 37							18 37						19 38					
Burnage	d				17 39			18 08				18 39		19 07				19 40					
East Didsbury	d		17 30		17 42		18 04			18 30		18 42				19 30		19 43					
Gatley	d				17 44	18 02						18 44	19 02					19 45	20 02				
Heald Green	d				17 47			18 13				18 47		19 13				19 52					
Manchester Airport	a	17 25	17 40	17 46	17 52	18 14	18 19	18 18	18 25	18 41	18 46	18 52	19 16	19 17	19 25	19 42	19 48	19 57	20 13	20 19	20 25	20 40	20 48
Wilmslow 84	a				18 16							19 14						20 11					
Crewe [10] 84	a				18 43							19 42											

Station		NT	TP ◇1	NT ◇	TP ◇1	TP ◇1 🛒	NT	NT ◇	TP ◇1	TP ◇1 🛒	NT	TP ◇1	TP ◇1	NT	TP ◇1
Manchester Victoria	d		20 39						21 56			22 55			23 52
Deansgate 84,89	d	20 23					21 22				22 25			23 25	
Manchester Oxford Rd. 84,89	d	20 26	20 47	20 57		21 21	21 25	21 45	22 03	22 16	22 28	23 01		23 28	23 59
Manchester Piccadilly [10]	a	20 28	20 49	20 59		21 24	21 28	21 48	22 06	22 19	22 32	23 04		23 32	00 01
	d	20 30	20 51	21 01	21 09	21 25	21 29	21 50	22 07	22 20	22 33	23 05	23 09	23 34	00 03
Mauldeth Road	d	20 36					21 35				22 39			23 40	
Burnage	d	20 38		21 08			21 38				22 42			23 42	
East Didsbury	d	20 41					21 40				22 44			23 45	
Gatley	d	20 43	21 02	21 12			21 43				22 47			23 47	
Heald Green	d	20 51		21 15			21 51				22 50			23 51	
Manchester Airport	a	20 57	21 11	21 20	21 25	21 47	21 57	22 04	22 22	22 39	22 56	23 20	23 25	23 56	00 19
Wilmslow 84	a	21 10					22 11				23 12				
Crewe [10] 84	a														

Sundays

15 December to 10 May

Station		TP ◇1 B	TP ◇1 C 🛒	TP D 🚌	TP ◇1 E	TP D 🚌	NT 🚌	TP ◇1 E	NT E	NT D 🚌	NT D 🚌	NT E	TP ◇1 E	NT 🚌	NT F 🚌	NT G	NT H	NT G	TP ◇1 H	TP ◇1 G	TP D 🚌	NT F	NT H
Manchester Victoria	d																						
Deansgate 84,89	d																						
Manchester Oxford Rd. 84,89	d																						
Manchester Piccadilly [10]	a																						
	d	00 03	00 33	00 40	03 47	03 55	05u00	05 21	05 24	05 25	06 20	06 21	06 44	07u00	07 20	07 29	07 35	07 36	07 42	07 42	07 45	08 23	08 30
Mauldeth Road	d								05 31	05 36	06 31	06 28			07 31		07 42	07 43				08 30	
Burnage	d								05 34	05 41	06 36	06 31			07 36		07 45	07 46				08 32	
East Didsbury	d								05 37	05 47	06 42	06 34			07 42		07 47	07 48				08 35	08 39
Gatley	d								05 39	05 52	06 47	06 36			07 47		07 50	07 51				08 37	08 42
Heald Green	d								05 42	06 00	06 55	06 39			07 55		07 53	07 54				08 40	08 45
Manchester Airport	a	00 19	00 49	01 05	04 02	04 20	05 25	05 37	05 48	06 05	07 00	06 45	07 00	07 25	08 00	07 48	07 58	08 00	08 03	08 07	08 10	08 46	08 53
Wilmslow 84	a																					08 59	09 19
Crewe [10] 84	a																						

Station		TP ◇1 🛒	TP ◇1 I 🛒	TP ◇1 J 🛒	NT	NT ◇ K	NT ◇ G	TP ◇1 K 🛒	TP ◇1 G 🛒	NT K	NT G	NT ◇ G	TP ◇1	TP ◇1 🛒	NT	TP ◇1 🛒	NT ◇	TP ◇1	TP ◇1 G 🛒	TP ◇1 K 🛒	NT	TP ◇1	TP ◇1 🛒
Manchester Victoria	d		08 44											11 10		11 40			12 10	12 10			12 39
Deansgate 84,89	d									10 24	10 25				11 23						12 22		
Manchester Oxford Rd. 84,89	d		08 51		09 13	09 58	09 58			10 27	10 29	10 59		11 16	11 26	11 47	11 59		12 16	12 16	12 25		12 47
Manchester Piccadilly [10]	a		08 53		09 15	10 00	10 00			10 29	10 31	11 01		11 20	11 29	11 49	12 01		12 20	12 20	12 28		12 49
	d	08 47	08 56	08 56	09 17	10 05	10 07	10 10	10 11	10 40	10 40	11 03	11 09	11 21	11 33	11 52	12 04	12 13	12 20	12 21	12 30	12 42	12 53
Mauldeth Road	d				09 23					10 47	10 47				11 40						12 37		
Burnage	d				09 26					10 49	10 49				11 42						12 39		
East Didsbury	d				09 28	10 13	10 14			10 52	10 52	11 12			11 45						12 42		
Gatley	d				09 31					10 54	10 54				11 47	12 03					12 44		13 04
Heald Green	d				09 34	10 18	10 19			10 57	10 57	11 16			11 51		12 16				12 47		
Manchester Airport	a	09 03	09 12	09 12	09 39	10 22	10 23	10 28	10 28	11 02	11 02	11 21	11 26	11 38	11 57	12 14	12 20	12 31	12 39	12 39	12 52	13 00	13 16
Wilmslow 84	a				09 56					11 14	11 14				12 12						13 10		
Crewe [10] 84	a																						

A ◇ from Manchester Piccadilly
B not 15 December
C from 22 December until 16 February, from 5 April
D from 23 February until 29 March
E until 16 February, from 5 April
F from 23 February
G from 5 April
H until 16 February
I until 5 January, from 5 April
J from 12 January until 16 February
K until 29 March

Table T085-R

Sundays

15 December to 10 May

Manchester - Manchester Airport

Station		NT ◇ A	NT ◇ B	TP ◇1	NT ◇ A	NT ◇ B	TP ◇1 A 🛒	TP ◇1 B 🛒	TP ◇1 🛒	NT	TP ◇1 🛒	NT ◇	TP ◇1	NT ◇	TP ◇1 🛒	TP ◇1 🛒	NT	TP ◇1 🛒	NT ◇	TP ◇1	NT ◇	TP ◇1 🛒	TP ◇1 🛒
Manchester Victoria	d						13 10	13 10			13 39				14 10			14 39				15 10	
Deansgate 84,89	d				13 09	13 09				13 23				14 09			14 25				15 09		
Manchester Oxford Rd. 84,89	d	12 53	12 53		13 12	13 12	13 16	13 16	13 22	13 27	13 47	13 58		14 12	14 16	14 23	14 28	14 47	14 58		15 12	15 16	15 22
Manchester Piccadilly [10]	a	12 56	12 56		13 15	13 16	13 20	13 20	13 25	13 29	13 50	14 00		14 15	14 20	14 26	14 30	14 50	15 01		15 15	15 20	15 24
	d	12 58	13 00	13 09	13 17	13 18	13 20	13 21	13 27	13 31	13 51	14 02	14 09	14 17	14 20	14 28	14 32	14 51	15 02	15 09	15 17	15 20	15 26
Mauldeth Road	d									13 37							14 39						
Burnage	d									13 40							14 42						
East Didsbury	d	13 06	13 07							13 42		14 09					14 45		15 10				
Gatley	d									13 45	14 02						14 48	15 02					
Heald Green	d	13 11	13 12		13 27	13 28				13 48		14 14		14 27			14 56		15 14		15 27		
Manchester Airport	a	13 17	13 17	13 26	13 31	13 32	13 36	13 37	13 42	13 52	14 16	14 18	14 25	14 31	14 36	14 42	15 03	15 16	15 19	15 25	15 31	15 36	15 42
Wilmslow 84	a									14 11							15 15						
Crewe [10] 84	a																						

Station		NT	TP ◇1 🛒	NT ◇	TP ◇1	NT ◇	TP ◇1 🛒	TP ◇1 🛒	NT	TP ◇1 🛒	NT ◇	TP ◇1	NT ◇	TP ◇1 🛒	TP ◇1 🛒	NT	TP ◇1 🛒	NT ◇	TP ◇1	NT ◇	TP ◇1 🛒	TP ◇1 🛒
Manchester Victoria	d		15 40				16 11			16 39				17 10			17 39				18 10	
Deansgate 84,89	d	15 22				16 09			16 23				17 09			17 23				18 09		
Manchester Oxford Rd. 84,89	d	15 25	15 47	15 59		16 12	16 17	16 22	16 26	16 47	16 59		17 13	17 16	17 22	17 26	17 47	17 59		18 12	18 16	18 22
Manchester Piccadilly [10]	a	15 28	15 50	16 01		16 15	16 20	16 24	16 29	16 49	17 01		17 15	17 20	17 24	17 28	17 50	18 01		18 15	18 20	18 25
	d	15 30	15 51	16 03	16 09	16 17	16 21	16 26	16 30	16 51	17 03	17 09	17 17	17 20	17 26	17 30	17 51	18 03	18 09	18 17	18 20	18 26
Mauldeth Road	d	15 36							16 36							17 36						
Burnage	d	15 38							16 39							17 39						
East Didsbury	d	15 41		16 10					16 41		17 10					17 41		18 10				
Gatley	d	15 43	16 02						16 44	17 01						17 44	18 02					
Heald Green	d	15 46		16 15		16 27			16 47		17 15		17 27			17 47		18 15		18 27		
Manchester Airport	a	15 51	16 16	16 19	16 25	16 31	16 37	16 42	16 52	17 16	17 19	17 25	17 31	17 36	17 42	17 52	18 16	18 19	18 25	18 31	18 36	18 42
Wilmslow 84	a	16 10							17 10							18 10						
Crewe [10] 84	a																					

Station		NT	TP ◇1 🛒	NT ◇	TP ◇1	NT ◇	TP ◇1 🛒	TP ◇1 🛒	NT	TP ◇1 🛒	TP ◇1	NT ◇	TP ◇1 🛒	TP ◇1 🛒	NT	TP ◇1	NT ◇	TP ◇1	NT ◇	TP ◇1 🛒	NT	AW	NT ◇
Manchester Victoria	d		18 39				19 10			19 39			20 10			20 39							
Deansgate 84,89	d	18 23				19 09			19 23			20 09			20 23				21 09		21 23		
Manchester Oxford Rd. 84,89	d	18 26	18 47	18 59		19 12	19 16	19 22	19 26	19 47		20 12	20 16	20 22	20 26	20 47	20 56		21 12	21 21	21 26		21 53
Manchester Piccadilly [10]	a	18 29	18 50	19 01		19 15	19 20	19 25	19 29	19 50		20 15	20 20	20 24	20 28	20 50	20 59		21 15	21 23	21 28		21 55
	d	18 30	18 51	19 03	19 09	19 17	19 20	19 26	19 30	19 51	20 09	20 17	20 20	20 26	20 30	20 51	21 00	21 09	21 17	21 25	21 30	21 35	21 57
Mauldeth Road	d	18 36							19 36						20 36						21 36		
Burnage	d	18 39							19 39						20 39						21 38		
East Didsbury	d	18 41		19 10					19 41						20 41		21 08				21 41		22 04
Gatley	d	18 44	19 02						19 44	20 02					20 44	21 02					21 44		
Heald Green	d	18 47		19 15		19 27			19 47			20 28			20 47		21 12		21 27		21 47		22 09
Manchester Airport	a	18 52	19 16	19 19	19 25	19 31	19 36	19 42	19 52	20 16	20 25	20 32	20 37	20 44	20 52	21 16	21 17	21 25	21 31	21 42	21 52		22 13
Wilmslow 84	a	19 10							20 10						21 10						22 10	21 57	
Crewe [10] 84	a																					22 17	

Station		TP ◇1	TP ◇1	NT ◇	TP ◇1 🛒	NT	AW	TP ◇1	NT ◇	TP ◇1 🛒	NT	TP ◇1
Manchester Victoria	d	21 54						22 56				23 54
Deansgate 84,89	d			22 12		22 25			23 09		23 22	
Manchester Oxford Rd. 84,89	d	22 01		22 16	22 24	22 28		23 05	23 14	23 20	23 25	00 01
Manchester Piccadilly [10]	a	22 04		22 19	22 27	22 31		23 09	23 17	23 23	23 28	00 04
	d	22 05	22 09	22 21	22 28	22 32	22 35	23 11	23 19	23 24	23 29	00 05
Mauldeth Road	d					22 38					23 35	
Burnage	d					22 41					23 38	
East Didsbury	d					22 43					23 40	
Gatley	d					22 46					23 43	
Heald Green	d			22 31		22 49			23 30		23 46	
Manchester Airport	a	22 22	22 25	22 36	22 43	22 53		23 26	23 35	23 40	23 51	00 20
Wilmslow 84	a					23 12	22 50				00 09	
Crewe [10] 84	a						23 14					

A from 5 April
B until 29 March

Table T086-F

Buxton and Hazel Grove - Manchester

Mondays to Fridays
16 December to 15 May

Miles	Station	NT A	NT	NT	NT	NT	NT	NT A	NT	EM ◇ B	NT	NT A	NT	NT	NT A	NT	NT	NT A	NT	NT	NT A	NT
0	**Buxton** d		06 00		06 33		07 01		07 36		08 00		08 34			09 34	10 02		10 34	11 02		11 34
3	Dove Holes d		06 06		06 39				07 42				08 40			09 40						11 40
5¼	Chapel-en-le-Frith d		06 12		06 45		07 11		07 48		08 10		08 45			09 46	10 12		10 44	11 12		11 46
9½	Whaley Bridge d		06 18		06 51		07 17		07 54		08 17		08 51			09 52	10 18		10 50	11 18		11 52
10¾	Furness Vale d		06 21		06 54		07 21		07 57		08 20		08 55			09 55			10 54			11 55
11½	New Mills Newtown d		06 25		06 58		07 24		08 01		08 24		08 58			09 59	10 23		10 57	11 23		11 59
13¼	Disley d		06 28		07 01		07 28		08 04		08 27		09 02			10 02	10 27		11 01	11 27		12 02
14¾	Middlewood d		06 32		07 05				08 08				09 05						11 05			
17	**Hazel Grove** a		06 36		07 09		07 35		08 12		08 34		09 10			10 09	10 34		11 09	11 34		12 09
—	d	06 06	06 37	06 50	07 10	07 21	07 35	08 02	08 13	08 17	08 35	09 03	09 10	09 35	10 03	10 10	10 35	11 03	11 10	11 35	12 03	12 10
18	Woodsmoor d	06 08		06 52	07 13	07 23	07 38	08 04			08 38	09 05	09 13	09 38	10 05	10 13	10 38	11 05	11 13	11 38	12 05	12 13
18¾	Davenport d	06 10		06 54	07 15	07 25	07 40	08 06			08 40	09 07	09 16	09 40	10 07	10 15	10 40	11 07	11 15	11 40	12 07	12 15
19¾	**Stockport** 84 a	06 14	06 45	06 58	07 20	07 30	07 45	08 10	08 20	08 25	08 45	09 11	09 20	09 45	10 12	10 21	10 45	11 11	11 20	11 45	12 11	12 20
21¼	Heaton Chapel 84 a	06 18		07 02	07 24			08 14	08 24			09 15	09 24		10 16	10 25		11 15	11 24		12 15	12 24
22¾	Levenshulme 84 a	06 22		07 05	07 28			08 18	08 27			09 19		09 50	10 20	10 28	10 50	11 19	11 27	11 50	12 19	12 27
25¾	**Manchester Picc.** 84 a	06 28	06 56	07 14	07 36	07 39	07 56	08 29	08 36	08 37	08 56	09 29	09 36	09 56	10 29	10 36	10 57	11 29	11 36	11 56	12 29	12 36
—	Manchester Oxford Road a	06 32						08 33		08 41		09 32			10 32			11 32			12 32	
—	Deansgate a	06 36						08 36				09 37			10 36			11 36			12 36	

Station	NT	NT A	NT	NT	NT A	NT	NT	NT A	NT	NT	NT A	NT	NT	NT A	NT	NT	NT A	NT	NT	NT A	NT	NT A
Buxton d	12 02		12 34	13 02		13 34	14 02		14 34	15 02		15 34	16 00		16 36	17 00		17 35	18 00		19 00	
Dove Holes d						13 40						15 40				17 06			18 06			
Chapel-en-le-Frith d	12 12		12 44	13 12		13 46	14 12		14 44	15 12		15 46	16 10		16 46	17 11		17 45	18 11		19 10	
Whaley Bridge d	12 18		12 50	13 18		13 52	14 18		14 50	15 18		15 52	16 16		16 52	17 17		17 51	18 17		19 16	
Furness Vale d			12 54			13 55			14 54			15 55	16 19		16 55	17 21		17 54	18 21		19 20	
New Mills Newtown d	12 23		12 57	13 23		13 59	14 23		14 57	15 23		15 59	16 23		16 59	17 24		17 58	18 24		19 23	
Disley d	12 27		13 01	13 27		14 02	14 27		15 01	15 27		16 02	16 26		17 02	17 27		18 01	18 27		19 26	
Middlewood d			13 05						15 05				16 30					18 05			19 30	
Hazel Grove a	12 34		13 09	13 34		14 09	14 34		15 09	15 34		16 09	16 34		17 09	17 34		18 09	18 34		19 34	
d	12 35	13 03	13 10	13 35	14 03	14 10	14 35	15 03	15 10	15 35	16 03	16 10	16 35	17 03	17 10	17 35	18 03	18 10	18 35	19 03	19 35	20 03
Woodsmoor d	12 38	13 05	13 13	13 38	14 05	14 13	14 38	15 05	15 13	15 38	16 05	16 13	16 38	17 05	17 13	17 38	18 05	18 13	18 38	19 05	19 38	20 05
Davenport d	12 40	13 07	13 15	13 40	14 07	14 15	14 40	15 07	15 15	15 40	16 07	16 15	16 40	17 07	17 15	17 40	18 07	18 15	18 40	19 07	19 40	20 07
Stockport 84 a	12 45	13 11	13 20	13 45	14 11	14 20	14 45	15 11	15 20	15 45	16 11	16 20	16 45	17 11	17 20	17 45	18 11	18 20	18 45	19 11	19 45	20 11
Heaton Chapel 84 a		13 15	13 24		14 15	14 24		15 15	15 24		16 15	16 24		17 15	17 24		18 15	18 24		19 15		20 15
Levenshulme 84 a	12 50	13 19	13 27	13 50	14 19	14 27	14 50	15 19	15 27	15 50	16 19	16 27	16 50	17 19	17 27	17 50	18 19	18 27	18 50	19 19		20 19
Manchester Picc. 84 a	12 56	13 29	13 36	13 56	14 29	14 36	14 56	15 29	15 36	15 56	16 29	16 36	16 56	17 29	17 36	17 56	18 29	18 36	18 56	19 29	19 56	20 29
Manchester Oxford Road a		13 32			14 32			15 32			16 32			17 33			18 32			19 32		20 32
Deansgate a		13 36			14 36			15 36			16 36			17 36			18 36			19 36		20 37

Station	NT	NT A	NT	NT A	NT	NT	NT
Buxton d	19 48		20 51		21 54		22 59
Dove Holes d	19 54				22 00		23 05
Chapel-en-le-Frith d	19 59		21 01		22 05		23 10
Whaley Bridge d	20 06		21 07		22 11		23 16
Furness Vale d	20 09		21 11		22 15		23 20
New Mills Newtown d	20 13		21 14		22 18		23 23
Disley d	20 16		21 17		22 21		23 27
Middlewood d	20 20		21 21		22 25		23 30
Hazel Grove a	20 24		21 25		22 29		23 35
d	20 25	21 03	21 26	22 03	22 30	23 08	23 35
Woodsmoor d	20 27	21 05	21 28	22 05	22 33	23 10	23 38
Davenport d	20 30	21 07	21 31	22 07	22 35	23 13	23 40
Stockport 84 a	20 34	21 11	21 35	22 11	22 40	23 17	23 45
Heaton Chapel 84 a		21 16		22 17	22 44	23 23	
Levenshulme 84 a		21 20		22 20	22 48	23 26	
Manchester Picc. 84 a	20 46	21 29	21 48	22 29	22 58	23 35	23 55
Manchester Oxford Road a		21 33		22 32			
Deansgate a		21 36		22 37			

Saturdays
21 December to 16 May

Station	NT A	NT	NT	NT	NT A	NT	EM ◇ B	NT	NT A	NT	NT	NT A	NT	NT	NT A	NT	NT	NT A	NT	NT	NT A	NT
Buxton d		06 00	06 33	07 01		07 36		08 00		08 34			09 34	10 02		10 34	11 02		11 34	12 02		12 34
Dove Holes d		06 06	06 39			07 42				08 40			09 40						11 40			
Chapel-en-le-Frith d		06 12	06 45	07 11		07 48		08 10		08 45			09 46	10 12		10 44	11 12		11 46	12 12		12 44
Whaley Bridge d		06 18	06 51	07 17		07 54		08 17		08 51			09 52	10 18		10 50	11 18		11 52	12 18		12 50
Furness Vale d		06 21	06 54	07 21		07 57		08 20		08 55			09 55			10 54			11 55			12 54
New Mills Newtown d		06 25	06 58	07 24		08 01		08 24		08 58			09 59	10 23		10 57	11 23		11 59	12 23		12 57
Disley d		06 28	07 01	07 28		08 04		08 27		09 02			10 02	10 27		11 01	11 27		12 02	12 27		13 01
Middlewood d		06 32	07 05			08 08				09 05						11 05						13 05
Hazel Grove a		06 36	07 09	07 35		08 12		08 34		09 10			10 09	10 34		11 09	11 34		12 09	12 34		13 09
d	06 06	06 37	07 10	07 35	08 02	08 13	08 17	08 35	09 03	09 10	09 35	10 03	10 10	10 35	11 03	11 10	11 35	12 03	12 10	12 35	13 03	13 10
Woodsmoor d	06 08		07 13	07 38	08 04			08 38	09 05	09 13	09 38	10 05	10 13	10 38	11 05	11 13	11 38	12 05	12 13	12 38	13 05	13 13
Davenport d	06 10		07 15	07 40	08 06			08 40	09 07	09 16	09 40	10 07	10 15	10 40	11 07	11 15	11 40	12 07	12 15	12 40	13 07	13 15
Stockport 84 a	06 14	06 45	07 21	07 45	08 10	08 20	08 25	08 45	09 11	09 20	09 45	10 12	10 21	10 45	11 11	11 20	11 45	12 11	12 20	12 45	13 11	13 20
Heaton Chapel 84 a	06 18		07 25		08 14	08 24			09 15	09 24		10 16	10 25		11 15	11 24		12 15	12 24		13 15	13 24
Levenshulme 84 a	06 22		07 28		08 18	08 27			09 19		09 50	10 20	10 28	10 50	11 19	11 27	11 50	12 19	12 27	12 50	13 19	13 27
Manchester Picc. 84 a	06 28	06 56	07 36	07 56	08 29	08 36	08 37	08 56	09 29	09 36	09 56	10 29	10 36	10 57	11 29	11 36	11 56	12 29	12 36	12 56	13 29	13 36
Manchester Oxford Road a	06 32				08 33		08 41		09 32			10 32			11 32			12 32			13 32	
Deansgate a	06 36				08 36				09 36			10 36			11 36			12 36			13 36	

A To Blackpool North

B From Nottingham to Liverpool Lime Street

Table T086-F

Buxton and Hazel Grove - Manchester

Saturdays
21 December to 16 May

Station	NT	NT A	NT	NT	NT A	NT	NT	NT A	NT	NT	NT A	NT	NT	NT A	NT	NT	NT A	NT	NT A	NT	NT A
Buxton d	13 02		13 34	14 02		14 34	15 02		15 34	16 00		16 36	17 00		17 35	18 00		19 00		19 48	
Dove Holes d			13 40						15 40				17 06			18 06				19 54	
Chapel-en-le-Frith d	13 12		13 46	14 12		14 44	15 12		15 46	16 10		16 46	17 11		17 45	18 11		19 10		19 59	
Whaley Bridge d	13 18		13 52	14 18		14 50	15 18		15 52	16 16		16 52	17 17		17 51	18 17		19 16		20 06	
Furness Vale d			13 55			14 54			15 55	16 19		16 55	17 21		17 54	18 21		19 20		20 09	
New Mills Newtown d	13 23		13 59	14 23		14 57	15 23		15 59	16 23		16 59	17 24		17 58	18 24		19 23		20 13	
Disley d	13 27		14 02	14 27		15 01	15 27		16 02	16 26		17 02	17 27		18 01	18 27		19 26		20 16	
Middlewood d						15 05				16 30					18 05			19 30		20 20	
Hazel Grove a	13 34		14 09	14 34		15 09	15 34		16 09	16 34		17 09	17 34		18 09	18 34		19 34		20 24	
d	13 35	14 03	14 10	14 35	15 03	15 10	15 35	16 03	16 10	16 35	17 03	17 10	17 35	18 03	18 10	18 35	19 03	19 35	20 03	20 25	21 03
Woodsmoor d	13 38	14 05	14 13	14 38	15 05	15 13	15 38	16 05	16 13	16 38	17 05	17 13	17 38	18 05	18 13	18 38	19 05	19 38	20 05	20 27	21 05
Davenport d	13 40	14 07	14 15	14 40	15 07	15 15	15 40	16 07	16 15	16 40	17 07	17 15	17 40	18 07	18 15	18 40	19 07	19 40	20 07	20 30	21 07
Stockport 84 a	13 45	14 11	14 20	14 45	15 11	15 20	15 45	16 11	16 20	16 45	17 11	17 20	17 45	18 11	18 20	18 45	19 11	19 45	20 11	20 34	21 11
Heaton Chapel 84 a		14 15	14 24		15 15	15 24		16 15	16 24		17 15	17 24		18 15	18 24		19 15		20 15		21 16
Levenshulme 84 a	13 50	14 19	14 27	14 50	15 19	15 27	15 50	16 19	16 27		17 19	17 27	17 50	18 19	18 27	18 50	19 19		20 19		21 20
Manchester Picc. 84 a	13 56	14 29	14 36	14 56	15 29	15 36	15 56	16 29	16 36	16 56	17 29	17 36	17 56	18 29	18 36	18 57	19 29	19 56	20 29	20 46	21 29
Manchester Oxford Road a		14 32			15 32			16 32			17 33			18 32			19 32		20 32		21 33
Deansgate a		14 36			15 36			16 36			17 36			18 36			19 36		20 37		21 36

Station	NT	NT A	NT	NT	NT
Buxton d	20 52		21 54		22 56
Dove Holes d			22 00		23 02
Chapel-en-le-Frith d	21 02		22 05		23 07
Whaley Bridge d	21 08		22 11		23 13
Furness Vale d	21 12		22 15		23 17
New Mills Newtown d	21 15		22 18		23 20
Disley d	21 18		22 21		23 24
Middlewood d	21 22		22 25		23 27
Hazel Grove a	21 26		22 29		23 32
d	21 27	22 03	22 30	23 13	23 32
Woodsmoor d	21 29	22 05	22 33	23 15	23 35
Davenport d	21 31	22 07	22 35	23 18	23 37
Stockport 84 a	21 36	22 11	22 41	23 22	23 42
Heaton Chapel 84 a		22 17	22 45	23 26	
Levenshulme 84 a		22 20	22 49	23 29	
Manchester Picc. 84 a	21 46	22 29	22 59	23 36	23 57
Manchester Oxford Road a		22 32			
Deansgate a		22 37			

Sundays
15 December to 10 May

Station	NT	NT	NT	NT	NT	NT	NT	NT	NT	NT	NT	NT	NT	NT	NT	NT
Buxton d	08 14	08 56	10 03	10 59	11 59	13 00	13 58	14 58	15 58	16 58	17 58	18 58	19 58	21 00	22 05	22 59
Dove Holes d	08 20	09 02		11 05		13 06		15 04		17 04		19 04		21 06		23 05
Chapel-en-le-Frith d	08 25	09 07	10 12	11 10	12 08	13 11	14 07	15 09	16 07	17 09	18 07	19 09	20 07	21 11	22 14	23 10
Whaley Bridge d	08 32	09 14	10 19	11 17	12 15	13 18	14 14	15 15	16 14	17 15	18 14	19 15	20 14	21 18	22 21	23 17
Furness Vale d	08 35	09 17	10 22	11 20	12 18	13 21	14 17	15 18	16 17	17 18	18 17	19 18	20 17	21 21	22 24	23 20
New Mills Newtown d	08 38	09 20	10 25	11 23	12 21	13 24	14 20	15 21	16 20	17 21	18 20	19 21	20 20	21 24	22 27	23 23
Disley d	08 42	09 24	10 29	11 27	12 25	13 28	14 24	15 25	16 24	17 25	18 24	19 25	20 24	21 28	22 31	23 27
Middlewood d	08 45	09 27	10 32		12 28		14 27		16 27		18 27		20 27		22 34	23 30
Hazel Grove a	08 49	09 32	10 37	11 34	12 33	13 35	14 32	15 32	16 32	17 32	18 32	19 32	20 32	21 35	22 39	23 35
d	08 50	09 32	10 37	11 34	12 33	13 35	14 32	15 32	16 32	17 32	18 32	19 32	20 32	21 35	22 39	23 35
Woodsmoor d	08 53	09 35	10 40	11 37	12 36	13 38	14 35	15 35	16 35	17 35	18 35	19 35	20 35	21 38	22 42	23 38
Davenport d	08 55	09 37	10 42	11 39	12 38	13 43	14 37	15 37	16 37	17 37	18 37	19 37	20 37	21 40	22 44	23 40
Stockport 84 a	09 00	09 42	10 46	11 43	12 42	13 49	14 42	15 42	16 42	17 42	18 42	19 42	20 42	21 44	22 50	23 44
Heaton Chapel 84 a	09 04															
Levenshulme 84 a	09 07															
Manchester Picc. 84 a	09 13	09 54	10 56	11 56	12 56	13 59	14 55	15 54	16 54	17 54	18 54	19 54	20 54	21 55	23 00	23 54
Manchester Oxford Road a																
Deansgate a																

A To Blackpool North

Table T086-R

Mondays to Fridays

16 December to 15 May

Manchester - Hazel Grove and Buxton

Miles			NT ◇ A	NT	NT B	NT	NT	NT B	NT	NT	NT B	NT	NT	NT B	NT	NT	NT B	NT	NT	NT B	NT	NT	NT B
—	Deansgate	d																					
—	Manchester Oxford Road	d			06 44			07 54			08 43			09 43			10 43			11 42			12 42
0	**Manchester Picc.** 10 84	d	05 46	06 24	06 48	06 51	07 24	07 58	08 08	08 24	08 47	09 08	09 24	09 47	10 08	10 24	10 47	11 08	11 24	11 47	12 08	12 24	12 47
3	Levenshulme 84	d		06 30	06 54		07 30			08 30	08 55		09 30	09 55		10 30	10 55		11 30	11 55		12 30	12 55
4½	Heaton Chapel 84	d		06 33	06 57		07 33			08 33	08 58		09 33	09 58		10 33	10 58		11 33	11 58		12 33	12 58
6	**Stockport** 84	d	05 56	06 37	07 01	07 06	07 37	08 07	08 22	08 37	09 02	09 18	09 37	10 02	10 18	10 37	11 02	11 18	11 37	12 02	12 18	12 37	13 02
7	Davenport	d		06 41	07 05		07 41	08 11	08 26	08 41	09 06	09 22	09 41	10 06	10 22	10 41	11 06	11 22	11 41	12 06	12 22	12 41	13 06
7¾	Woodsmoor	d		06 46	07 07		07 43	08 13		08 44	09 09	09 24	09 43	10 09	10 24	10 43	11 09	11 24	11 43	12 09	12 24	12 43	13 09
8¾	**Hazel Grove**	a	06 03	06 49	07 09	07 15	07 46	08 15	08 29	08 47	09 11	09 27	09 46	10 11	10 27	10 46	11 11	11 27	11 46	12 11	12 27	12 46	13 11
—		d		06 50			07 48		08 30	08 47		09 27	09 47		10 27	10 47		11 27	11 47		12 27	12 47	
11	Middlewood	d		06 54						08 52			09 51						11 51				
12½	Disley	d		06 58			07 55		08 37	08 56		09 34	09 55		10 34	10 54		11 34	11 55		12 34	12 54	
14¼	New Mills Newtown	d		07 02			07 59		08 41	09 00		09 38	09 59		10 38	10 58		11 38	11 59		12 38	12 58	
15½	Furness Vale	d		07 05			08 02		08 44	09 03		09 41	10 03			11 01			12 03			13 01	
16¾	Whaley Bridge	d		07 08			08 05		08 47	09 06		09 44	10 06		10 44	11 04		11 44	12 06		12 44	13 04	
20½	Chapel-en-le-Frith	d		07 16			08 13		08 54	09 13		09 51	10 13		10 51	11 12		11 51	12 15		12 51	13 12	
22¾	Dove Holes	d		07 21						09 18						11 17						13 17	
25¾	**Buxton**	a		07 29			08 24		09 06	09 26		10 03	10 25		11 02	11 25		12 02	12 27		13 02	13 25	

		NT	NT	NT B	NT	NT	NT B	NT	NT	NT B	NT	NT	NT B	NT	NT	NT B	NT	NT	NT B	NT	NT	NT B
Deansgate	d												16 40			17 39			18 40			
Manchester Oxford Road	d			13 42			14 43			15 43			16 43			17 43			18 43			19 43
Manchester Picc. 10 84	d	13 08	13 24	13 47	14 08	14 24	14 47	15 08	15 24	15 47	16 08	16 24	16 47	17 08	17 24	17 47	18 08	18 24	18 47	19 12	19 24	19 47
Levenshulme 84	d		13 30	13 55		14 30	14 55		15 30	15 55		16 30	16 55		17 30	17 55		18 30	18 55		19 30	19 55
Heaton Chapel 84	d		13 33	13 58		14 33	14 58		15 33	15 58		16 33	16 58		17 33	17 58		18 33	18 58		19 33	19 58
Stockport 84	d	13 18	13 37	14 02	14 19	14 37	15 02	15 18	15 37	16 02	16 18	16 37	17 02	17 18	17 37	18 02	18 18	18 37	19 02	19 22	19 37	20 02
Davenport	d	13 22	13 41	14 06	14 23	14 41	15 06	15 22	15 41	16 06	16 22	16 41	17 06		17 41	18 06	18 22	18 41	19 06		19 41	20 06
Woodsmoor	d	13 24	13 43	14 09	14 25	14 43	15 09	15 24	15 43	16 09	16 24	16 43	17 09		17 44	18 09	18 24	18 43	19 09		19 43	20 09
Hazel Grove	a	13 27	13 46	14 11	14 28	14 46	15 11	15 27	15 46	16 11	16 27	16 46	17 11	17 25	17 47	18 11	18 27	18 46	19 11	19 29	19 46	20 11
	d	13 27	13 47		14 28	14 47		15 27	15 47		16 27	16 47		17 25	17 47		18 27	18 47		19 29	19 47	
Middlewood	d		13 51						15 51			16 51			17 52			18 51				
Disley	d	13 34	13 55		14 35	14 54		15 34	15 55		16 34	16 56		17 33	17 56		18 34	18 56		19 36	19 54	
New Mills Newtown	d	13 38	13 59		14 39	14 58		15 38	15 59		16 38	17 00		17 37	18 00		18 38	19 00		19 40	19 58	
Furness Vale	d		14 03			15 01			16 03		16 41	17 03		17 40	18 04		18 41	19 03		19 43	20 01	
Whaley Bridge	d	13 44	14 06		14 44	15 04		15 44	16 06		16 45	17 07		17 44	18 07		18 44	19 06		19 46	20 04	
Chapel-en-le-Frith	d	13 51	14 13		14 51	15 12		15 51	16 13		16 52	17 14		17 51	18 15		18 51	19 14		19 53	20 12	
Dove Holes	d					15 17						17 19			18 20			19 19			20 17	
Buxton	a	14 02	14 25		15 03	15 25		16 02	16 25		17 03	17 27		18 02	18 29		19 03	19 27		20 04	20 25	

		NT	NT B	NT	NT B	NT	NT	NT
Deansgate	d							
Manchester Oxford Road	d		20 43		21 40			
Manchester Picc. 10 84	d	20 24	20 47	21 24	21 44	22 10	23 11	23 24
Levenshulme 84	d	20 30	20 56	21 30	21 49	22 16		23 30
Heaton Chapel 84	d	20 33	20 59	21 33	21 52	22 19		23 33
Stockport 84	d	20 37	21 03	21 37	21 56	22 23	23 21	23 37
Davenport	d	20 41	21 07	21 41	22 00	22 27		23 40
Woodsmoor	d	20 43	21 09	21 43	22 03	22 29		23 43
Hazel Grove	a	20 46	21 11	21 46	22 05	22 32	23 28	23 45
	d	20 47		21 47		22 33	23 28	
Middlewood	d	20 51				22 37	23 33	
Disley	d	20 55		21 54		22 41	23 37	
New Mills Newtown	d	20 59		21 58		22 45	23 41	
Furness Vale	d	21 03		22 01		22 48	23 44	
Whaley Bridge	d	21 06		22 04		22 51	23 47	
Chapel-en-le-Frith	d	21 13		22 12		22 58	23 54	
Dove Holes	d			22 17			23 59	
Buxton	a	21 25		22 25		23 10	00 07	

Saturdays

21 December to 16 May

		NT ◇ A	NT	NT B	NT	NT B	NT	NT	NT B	NT	NT	NT B	NT	NT	NT B	NT	NT	NT B	NT	NT	NT B	NT	NT
Deansgate	d																						
Manchester Oxford Road	d			06 46		07 54			08 43			09 43			10 43			11 42			12 42		
Manchester Picc. 10 84	d	05 46	06 24	06 50	07 22	07 58	08 08	08 24	08 47	09 08	09 24	09 47	10 08	10 24	10 47	11 08	11 24	11 47	12 08	12 24	12 47	13 08	13 24
Levenshulme 84	d		06 30	06 56	07 30			08 30	08 55		09 30	09 55		10 30	10 55		11 30	11 55		12 30	12 55		13 30
Heaton Chapel 84	d		06 33	06 59	07 33			08 33	08 58		09 33	09 58		10 33	10 58		11 33	11 58		12 33	12 58		13 33
Stockport 84	d	05 56	06 37	07 03	07 37	08 07	08 22	08 37	09 02	09 18	09 37	10 02	10 18	10 37	11 02	11 18	11 37	12 02	12 18	12 37	13 02	13 18	13 37
Davenport	d		06 41	07 07	07 41	08 11	08 26	08 41	09 06	09 22	09 41	10 06	10 22	10 41	11 06	11 22	11 41	12 06	12 22	12 41	13 06	13 22	13 41
Woodsmoor	d		06 43	07 09	07 43	08 13		08 44	09 09	09 24	09 43	10 09	10 24	10 43	11 09	11 24	11 43	12 09	12 24	12 43	13 09	13 24	13 43
Hazel Grove	a	06 03	06 46	07 11	07 46	08 15	08 29	08 47	09 11	09 27	09 46	10 11	10 27	10 46	11 11	11 27	11 46	12 11	12 27	12 46	13 11	13 27	13 46
	d		06 47		07 47		08 30	08 47		09 27	09 47		10 27	10 47		11 27	11 47		12 27	12 47		13 27	13 47
Middlewood	d		06 51					08 52			09 51						11 51						13 51
Disley	d		06 55		07 54		08 37	08 56		09 34	09 55		10 34	10 54		11 34	11 55		12 34	12 54		13 34	13 55
New Mills Newtown	d		06 59		07 58		08 41	09 00		09 38	09 59		10 38	10 58		11 38	11 59		12 38	12 58		13 38	13 59
Furness Vale	d		07 02		08 01		08 44	09 03		09 41	10 03			11 01			12 03			13 01			14 03
Whaley Bridge	d		07 05		08 04		08 47	09 06		09 44	10 06		10 44	11 04		11 44	12 06		12 44	13 04		13 44	14 06
Chapel-en-le-Frith	d		07 13		08 11		08 54	09 13		09 51	10 13		10 51	11 12		11 51	12 13		12 51	13 12		13 51	14 13
Dove Holes	d		07 18					09 18						11 17						13 17			
Buxton	a		07 26		08 23		09 06	09 26		10 03	10 25		11 02	11 25		12 02	12 25		13 02	13 25		14 02	14 25

A To Sheffield

B From Blackpool North

Table T086-R

Saturdays

21 December to 16 May

Manchester - Hazel Grove and Buxton

		NT A	NT	NT	NT A	NT	NT	NT A	NT	NT	NT A	NT	NT	NT A	NT	NT	NT A	NT	NT	NT A	NT	NT A
Deansgate	d										16 40			17 39			18 40					
Manchester Oxford Road	d	13 42			14 43			15 43			16 43			17 43			18 43			19 42		20 43
Manchester Picc. 10 84	d	13 47	14 08	14 24	14 47	15 11	15 24	15 47	16 08	16 24	16 47	17 08	17 24	17 47	18 09	18 24	18 47	19 08	19 24	19 47	20 24	20 47
Levenshulme 84	d	13 55		14 30	14 55		15 30	15 55		16 30	16 55		17 30	17 55		18 30	18 55		19 30	19 55	20 30	20 56
Heaton Chapel 84	d	13 58		14 33	14 58		15 33	15 58		16 33	16 58		17 33	17 58		18 33	18 58		19 33	19 58	20 33	20 59
Stockport 84	d	14 02	14 18	14 37	15 02	15 21	15 37	16 02	16 18	16 37	17 02	17 18	17 37	18 02	18 19	18 37	19 02	19 18	19 37	20 02	20 37	21 03
Davenport	d	14 06	14 22	14 41	15 06	15 25	15 41	16 06	16 22	16 41	17 06		17 41	18 06	18 23	18 41	19 06		19 41	20 06	20 41	21 07
Woodsmoor	d	14 09	14 24	14 43	15 09	15 27	15 43	16 09	16 24	16 43	17 09		17 44	18 09	18 25	18 43	19 09		19 43	20 09	20 43	21 09
Hazel Grove	a	14 11	14 27	14 46	15 11	15 30	15 46	16 11	16 27	16 46	17 11	17 25	17 47	18 11	18 28	18 46	19 11	19 25	19 46	20 11	20 46	21 11
	d		14 27	14 47		15 30	15 47		16 27	16 47		17 25	17 47		18 28	18 47		19 26	19 47		20 47	
Middlewood	d						15 51			16 51			17 52			18 51					20 51	
Disley	d		14 34	14 54		15 37	15 55		16 34	16 56		17 32	17 56		18 35	18 56		19 33	19 54		20 55	
New Mills Newtown	d		14 38	14 58		15 41	15 59		16 38	17 00		17 36	18 00		18 39	19 00		19 37	19 58		20 59	
Furness Vale	d			15 01			16 03		16 41	17 03		17 39	18 04		18 42	19 03		19 40	20 01		21 03	
Whaley Bridge	d		14 44	15 04		15 47	16 06		16 45	17 07		17 42	18 07		18 45	19 06		19 43	20 04		21 06	
Chapel-en-le-Frith	d		14 51	15 12		15 54	16 13		16 52	17 14		17 49	18 15		18 52	19 14		19 50	20 12		21 13	
Dove Holes	d			15 17						17 19			18 20			19 19			20 17			
Buxton	a		15 02	15 25		16 05	16 25		17 03	17 27		18 01	18 28		19 04	19 27		20 01	20 25		21 25	

		NT	NT A	NT	NT	NT
Deansgate	d					
Manchester Oxford Road	d		21 40			
Manchester Picc. 10 84	d	21 24	21 46	22 10	23 07	23 17
Levenshulme 84	d	21 30	21 56	22 16		23 23
Heaton Chapel 84	d	21 33	21 59	22 19		23 26
Stockport 84	d	21 37	22 04	22 23	23 17	23 30
Davenport	d	21 41	22 08	22 27	23 21	
Woodsmoor	d	21 43	22 10	22 29	23 23	
Hazel Grove	a	21 46	22 12	22 32	23 26	23 36
	d	21 47		22 33	23 26	
Middlewood	d			22 37	23 31	
Disley	d	21 54		22 41	23 35	
New Mills Newtown	d	21 58		22 45	23 39	
Furness Vale	d	22 01		22 48	23 42	
Whaley Bridge	d	22 04		22 51	23 45	
Chapel-en-le-Frith	d	22 12		22 58	23 52	
Dove Holes	d	22 17			23 57	
Buxton	a	22 25		23 10	00 05	

Sundays

15 December to 10 May

		NT	NT	NT B	NT C	NT	NT B	NT C	NT	NT	NT	NT	NT	NT	NT	NT	NT	NT
Deansgate	d																	
Manchester Oxford Road	d																	
Manchester Picc. 10 84	d	08 50	09 45	10 43	10 45	11 49	12 48	12 50	13 51	14 49	15 49	16 49	17 49	18 49	19 49	20 49	21 50	22 48
Levenshulme 84	d	08 56		10 49	10 51	11 55	12 54	12 56	13 57	14 55	15 55	16 55	17 55	18 55	19 55	20 55	21 56	22 54
Heaton Chapel 84	d	08 59		10 52	10 54	11 58	12 57	12 59	14 00	14 58	15 58	16 58	17 58	18 58	19 58	20 58	21 59	22 57
Stockport 84	d	09 03	09 55	10 56	10 58	12 02	13 02	13 03	14 04	15 02	16 02	17 02	18 02	19 02	20 02	21 02	22 03	23 01
Davenport	d	09 07	09 59	11 00	11 02	12 06	13 06	13 07	14 08	15 06	16 06	17 06	18 06	19 06	20 06	21 06	22 07	23 05
Woodsmoor	d	09 09	10 01	11 02	11 04	12 08	13 08	13 09	14 10	15 08	16 08	17 08	18 08	19 08	20 08	21 08	22 09	23 07
Hazel Grove	a	09 12	10 04	11 05	11 07	12 11	13 11	13 12	14 13	15 11	16 11	17 11	18 11	19 11	20 11	21 11	22 12	23 10
	d	09 12	10 04	11 06	11 08	12 12	13 12	13 13	14 13	15 11	16 11	17 11	18 11	19 11	20 11	21 11	22 12	23 10
Middlewood	d	09 17	10 09			12 16			14 18		16 16		18 16		20 16		22 17	23 15
Disley	d	09 21	10 13	11 13	11 15	12 20	13 19	13 20	14 22	15 18	16 20	17 18	18 20	19 18	20 20	21 18	22 21	23 19
New Mills Newtown	d	09 25	10 17	11 17	11 19	12 24	13 23	13 24	14 26	15 22	16 24	17 22	18 24	19 22	20 24	21 22	22 25	23 23
Furness Vale	d	09 27	10 19	11 19	11 21	12 27	13 25	13 26	14 28	15 25	16 26	17 25	18 26	19 25	20 26	21 25	22 27	23 25
Whaley Bridge	d	09 31	10 23	11 23	11 25	12 30	13 29	13 30	14 32	15 28	16 30	17 28	18 30	19 28	20 30	21 28	22 31	23 29
Chapel-en-le-Frith	d	09 38	10 30	11 30	11 32	12 37	13 36	13 37	14 39	15 35	16 37	17 35	18 37	19 35	20 37	21 35	22 38	23 36
Dove Holes	d	09 43		11 35	11 37		13 41	13 42		15 40		17 40		19 40		21 40		23 41
Buxton	a	09 51	10 41	11 43	11 45	12 49	13 49	13 50	14 50	15 48	16 48	17 48	18 48	19 48	20 48	21 48	22 49	23 49

A From Blackpool North

B from 5 April

C until 29 March

Table T088-F

Manchester - Northwich and Chester

Mondays to Fridays
16 December to 15 May

Miles			NT MX	NT MX	NT	NT	NT	NT	NT	NT	NT	NT	NT	NT	NT	NT	NT	NT	NT	NT	NT	NT	NT
0	**Manchester Picc.** 10 ... 81 ⇌	d			06 14	07 09	07 41		08 41	09 41	10 41	11 41	12 41	13 41	14 41	15 41	16 41		17 41		18 41	19 40	20 41
6½	**Stockport**	d			06 23	07 18	07 51	08 18	08 52	09 52	10 52	11 52	12 52	13 52	14 52	15 52	16 52	17 18	17 52	18 18	18 52	19 52	20 54
14¾	Navigation Road ⇌	d		00 08	06 37	07 34	08 07	08 33	09 07	10 07	11 07	12 07	13 07	14 07	15 07	16 07	17 07	17 33	18 07	18 33	19 07	20 08	21 09
15¼	**Altrincham** ⇌	a		00 10	06 39	07 36	08 09	08 35	09 09	10 09	11 09	12 09	13 09	14 09	15 09	16 09	17 09	17 35	18 09	18 35	19 09	20 10	21 11
—		d		00 11	06 40	07 36	08 10	08 36	09 10	10 10	11 10	12 10	13 10	14 10	15 10	16 10	17 10	17 36	18 10	18 36	19 10	20 10	21 12
16	Hale	d		00 13	06 43	07 39	08 14	08 39	09 13	10 13	11 13	12 12	13 13	14 13	15 13	16 13	17 13	17 39	18 12	18 39	19 12	20 13	21 14
17¾	Ashley	d		00 17	06 46	07 43	08 19	08 42	09 16	10 16	11 16	12 16	13 16	14 16	15 16	16 16	17 16	17 42	18 16	18 42	19 16	20 16	21 18
18¾	Mobberley	d		00 20	06 50	07 47	08 24	08 46	09 20	10 20	11 20	12 19	13 20	14 20	15 20	16 20	17 20	17 46	18 19	18 46	19 19	20 20	21 21
22¼	Knutsford	d		00 25	06 55	07 52	08 28	08 51	09 25	10 25	11 25	12 24	13 25	14 25	15 25	16 25	17 25	17 51	18 24	18 51	19 24	20 24	21 26
24¾	Plumley	d		00 30	06 59	07 56	08 32	08 55	09 29	10 29	11 29	12 28	13 29	14 29	15 29	16 29	17 29	17 55	18 29	18 55	19 29	20 29	21 30
26¾	Lostock Gralam	d		00 33	07 03	08 00	08 36	08 59	09 33	10 33	11 33	12 32	13 33	14 33	15 33	16 33	17 33	17 59	18 32	18 59	19 32	20 32	21 34
28¼	**Northwich**	d		00 38	07 07	08 05	08 41	09 03	09 37	10 37	11 37	12 36	13 37	14 37	15 37	16 37	17 37	18 03	18 37	19 03	19 37	20 37	21 38
30	Greenbank	d		00 43	07 13	08 10	08 46	09 09	09 43	10 43	11 43	12 42	13 43	14 43	15 43	16 43	17 43	18 09	18 42	19 09	19 42	20 42	21 43
32¾	Cuddington	d		00 48	07 18	08 15	08 51	09 14	09 48	10 48	11 48	12 47	13 48	14 48	15 48	16 48	17 48	18 14	18 47	19 14	19 47	20 47	21 48
35¾	Delamere	d		00 53	07 23	08 20	08 55	09 19	09 53	10 53	11 53	12 52	13 53	14 53	15 53	16 53	17 53	18 19	18 52	19 19	19 52	20 52	21 53
38¾	Mouldsworth	d	00 01	00 58	07 28	08 26	09 00	09 24	09 58	10 58	11 58	12 57	13 58	14 58	15 58	16 58	17 58	18 24	18 57	19 24	19 57	20 57	21 58
45¼	**Chester** ... 81	a	00 13	01 09	07 42	08 38	09 12	09 36	10 10	11 12	12 10	13 09	14 12	15 10	16 10	17 11	18 10	18 36	19 09	19 38	20 10	21 10	22 12

		NT	NT	NT
Manchester Picc. 10 ... 81 ⇌	d	21 40	22 41	23 41
Stockport	d	21 52	22 56	23 54
Navigation Road ⇌	d	22 07	23 13	00 08
Altrincham ⇌	a	22 09	23 15	00 10
	d	22 10	23 15	00 11
Hale	d	22 12	23 18	00 13
Ashley	d	22 16	23 21	00 17
Mobberley	d	22 19	23 24	00 20
Knutsford	d	22 24	23 29	00 25
Plumley	d	22 29	23 33	00 30
Lostock Gralam	d	22 32	23 37	00 33
Northwich	d	22 37	23 41	00 38
Greenbank	d	22 42	23 46	00 43
Cuddington	d	22 47	23 51	00 48
Delamere	d	22 52	23 56	00 53
Mouldsworth	d	23 04	00 01	00 58
Chester ... 81	a	23 15	00 13	01 09

Saturdays
21 December to 16 May

		NT	NT	NT	NT	NT	NT	NT	NT	NT	NT	NT	NT	NT	NT	NT	NT	NT	NT	NT	NT	NT
Manchester Picc. 10 ... 81 ⇌	d			06 13	07 08	07 41	08 41	09 41	10 41	11 41	12 41	13 41	14 41	15 41	16 41	17 41	18 41	19 41	20 41	21 37	22 40	23 41
Stockport	d			06 22	07 19	07 51	08 52	09 52	10 52	11 52	12 52	13 52	14 52	15 52	16 52	17 52	18 52	19 52	20 52	21 52	22 51	23 50
Navigation Road ⇌	d		00 08	06 37	07 34	08 07	09 07	10 07	11 10	12 07	13 07	14 12	15 07	16 13	17 07	18 07	19 07	20 08	21 07	22 07	23 07	00 06
Altrincham ⇌	a		00 10	06 39	07 36	08 09	09 09	10 09	11 12	12 09	13 09	14 14	15 09	16 15	17 09	18 09	19 09	20 10	21 09	22 09	23 09	00 08
	d		00 11	06 40	07 37	08 09	09 10	10 10	11 12	12 10	13 10	14 15	15 10	16 15	17 10	18 10	19 10	20 10	21 10	22 10	23 10	00 08
Hale	d		00 13	06 43	07 40	08 12	09 13	10 13	11 15	12 13	13 13	14 17	15 13	16 18	17 13	18 12	19 12	20 13	21 12	22 12	23 12	00 11
Ashley	d		00 17	06 46	07 44	08 15	09 16	10 16	11 18	12 16	13 16	14 21	15 16	16 22	17 16	18 16	19 16	20 16	21 16	22 16	23 16	00 14
Mobberley	d		00 20	06 50	07 47	08 19	09 20	10 20	11 22	12 20	13 20	14 24	15 20	16 26	17 20	18 19	19 19	20 20	21 19	22 19	23 19	00 18
Knutsford	d		00 25	06 55	07 52	08 24	09 25	10 25	11 26	12 25	13 25	14 29	15 25	16 31	17 25	18 24	19 24	20 24	21 24	22 24	23 24	00 23
Plumley	d		00 30	06 59	07 57	08 28	09 29	10 29	11 31	12 29	13 29	14 34	15 29	16 36	17 29	18 29	19 29	20 29	21 29	22 29	23 29	00 27
Lostock Gralam	d		00 33	07 03	08 01	08 32	09 33	10 33	11 34	12 33	13 33	14 37	15 33	16 40	17 33	18 32	19 32	20 32	21 32	22 32	23 32	00 31
Northwich	d		00 38	07 07	08 05	08 36	09 37	10 37	11 39	12 37	13 37	14 41	15 37	16 44	17 37	18 37	19 37	20 37	21 37	22 37	23 37	00 35
Greenbank	d		00 43	07 13	08 11	08 42	09 43	10 43	11 44	12 43	13 43	14 46	15 43	16 50	17 43	18 42	19 42	20 42	21 42	22 42	23 42	00 40
Cuddington	d		00 48	07 18	08 16	08 47	09 48	10 48	11 49	12 48	13 48	14 51	15 48	16 55	17 48	18 47	19 47	20 47	21 47	22 47	23 47	00 45
Delamere	d		00 53	07 23	08 20	08 51	09 53	10 53	11 53	12 53	13 53	14 56	15 53	17 00	17 53	18 52	19 52	20 52	21 52	22 52	23 52	00 50
Mouldsworth	d	00 01	00 58	07 28	08 26	08 56	09 58	10 58	11 58	12 58	13 58	15 01	15 58	17 14	17 58	18 57	19 57	20 57	21 58	23 00	23 57	00 55
Chester ... 81	a	00 13	01 09	07 40	08 38	09 12	10 10	11 12	12 10	13 10	14 12	15 14	16 10	17 27	18 10	19 09	20 09	21 10	22 12	23 11	00 09	01 07

Sundays
15 December to 10 May

		NT A	NT	NT B	NT C	NT	NT	NT	NT	NT
Manchester Picc. 10 ... 81 ⇌	d		09 04	11 00	11 01	13 06	15 06	17 06	19 06	21 06
Stockport	d		09 20	11 11	11 13	13 15	15 19	17 17	19 17	21 18
Navigation Road ⇌	d	00 06	09 34	11 27	11 27	13 32	15 34	17 31	19 31	21 33
Altrincham ⇌	a	00 08	09 36	11 29	11 29	13 34	15 36	17 33	19 33	21 35
	d	00 08	09 37	11 29	11 29	13 34	15 37	17 34	19 34	21 35
Hale	d	00 11	09 39	11 32	11 32	13 37	15 39	17 36	19 36	21 38
Ashley	d	00 14	09 43	11 36	11 36	13 41	15 43	17 40	19 40	21 42
Mobberley	d	00 18	09 47	11 39	11 39	13 44	15 47	17 44	19 44	21 45
Knutsford	d	00 23	09 52	11 44	11 44	13 49	15 52	17 49	19 49	21 50
Plumley	d	00 27	09 56	11 49	11 49	13 54	15 56	17 53	19 53	21 55
Lostock Gralam	d	00 31	10 00	11 53	11 53	13 58	16 00	17 57	19 57	21 59
Northwich	d	00 35	10 05	11 57	11 57	14 02	16 05	18 02	20 02	22 03
Greenbank	d	00 40	10 10	12 03	12 03	14 08	16 10	18 07	20 07	22 09
Cuddington	d	00 45	10 15	12 08	12 08	14 13	16 15	18 12	20 12	22 14
Delamere	d	00 50	10 20	12 13	12 13	14 18	16 20	18 17	20 17	22 19
Mouldsworth	d	00 55	10 26	12 19	12 19	14 24	16 26	18 23	20 23	22 25
Chester ... 81	a	01 07	10 39	12 30	12 30	14 35	16 39	18 34	20 34	22 35

A not 15 December B from 5 April C until 29 March

Table T088-R

Chester and Northwich - Manchester

Mondays to Fridays
16 December to 15 May

Miles			NT	NT	NT	NT	NT	NT	NT		NT	NT	NT	NT	NT	NT	NT
0	**Chester** ... 81	d	05 56	06 21	06 51	07 15	08 02	09 02	10 02	and hourly until	17 02	18 01	19 00	20 01	21 02	22 01	22 52
6½	Mouldsworth	d	06 08	06 32	07 03	07 31	08 13	09 14	10 13		17 13	18 13	19 12	20 12	21 14	22 13	23 04
9½	Delamere	d	06 13	06 38	07 08	07 37	08 18	09 18	10 18		17 18	18 18	19 17	20 17	21 19	22 18	23 10
12½	Cuddington	d	06 18	06 42	07 13	07 42	08 23	09 23	10 23		17 23	18 23	19 22	20 22	21 23	22 23	23 14
15¼	Greenbank	d	06 23	06 47	07 18	07 47	08 27	09 27	10 27		17 27	18 27	19 26	20 26	21 28	22 27	23 19
17	**Northwich**	d	06 28	06 53	07 23	07 52	08 33	09 33	10 33		17 33	18 33	19 32	20 32	21 33	22 33	23 25
18½	Lostock Gralam	d	06 31	06 57	07 26	07 56	08 36	09 36	10 36		17 36	18 36	19 35	20 35	21 36	22 36	23 28
20½	Plumley	d	06 35	07 01	07 30	08 00	08 39	09 39	10 39		17 39	18 39	19 38	20 38	21 40	22 39	23 31
23	Knutsford	d	06 40	07 07	07 35	08 05	08 44	09 44	10 44		17 44	18 44	19 44	20 44	21 45	22 44	23 37
26¾	Mobberley	d	06 45	07 12	07 40	08 10	08 49	09 49	10 49		17 49	18 49	19 48	20 48	21 50	22 49	23 41
27½	Ashley	d	06 48	07 16	07 43	08 14	08 52	09 52	10 52		17 52	18 52	19 52	20 52	21 53	22 52	23 45
29¼	Hale	d	06 52	07 20	07 47	08 18	08 56	09 56	10 56		17 56	18 56	19 56	20 56	21 57	22 56	23 49
30	**Altrincham** ⇌	a	06 56	07 23	07 51	08 22	08 59	09 59	10 59		17 59	18 59	19 59	20 59	22 01	22 59	23 52
—		d	06 56	07 25	07 51	08 22	09 00	10 00	11 00		18 00	19 00	20 00	21 00	22 01	23 00	23 53
30½	Navigation Road ⇌	d	06 59	07 27	07 53	08 25	09 02	10 02	11 02		18 02	19 02	20 02	21 02	22 03	23 02	23 55
38¾	**Stockport**	a	07 15	07 46	08 08	08 39	09 16	10 16	11 16		18 16	19 16	20 16	21 16	22 18	23 16	00 12
44¾	**Manchester Picc.** 10 ... 81 ⇌	a	07 26		08 17		09 30	10 30	11 30		18 30	19 30	20 30	21 35	22 33	23 27	00 26

Saturdays
21 December to 16 May

		NT	NT	NT		NT	NT	NT	NT	NT	NT	NT	NT	NT	NT
Chester ... 81	d	05 56	06 51	08 02	and hourly until	14 02	15 02	16 02	17 02	18 01	19 00	20 01	21 01	22 01	22 48
Mouldsworth	d	06 08	07 03	08 13		14 13	15 14	16 13	17 13	18 13	19 12	20 12	21 12	22 13	22 59
Delamere	d	06 13	07 08	08 18		14 18	15 19	16 18	17 18	18 18	19 17	20 17	21 17	22 18	23 05
Cuddington	d	06 18	07 13	08 23		14 23	15 24	16 23	17 23	18 23	19 22	20 22	21 22	22 23	23 09
Greenbank	d	06 23	07 18	08 27		14 27	15 28	16 27	17 27	18 27	19 26	20 26	21 26	22 27	23 14
Northwich	d	06 28	07 23	08 33		14 33	15 34	16 33	17 33	18 33	19 32	20 32	21 32	22 33	23 20
Lostock Gralam	d	06 31	07 26	08 36		14 36	15 37	16 36	17 36	18 36	19 35	20 35	21 35	22 36	23 23
Plumley	d	06 35	07 30	08 39		14 39	15 40	16 39	17 39	18 39	19 38	20 38	21 38	22 39	23 26
Knutsford	d	06 40	07 35	08 44		14 44	15 45	16 44	17 44	18 44	19 44	20 44	21 44	22 44	23 32
Mobberley	d	06 45	07 40	08 49		14 49	15 50	16 49	17 49	18 49	19 48	20 48	21 48	22 49	23 36
Ashley	d	06 48	07 43	08 52		14 52	15 53	16 52	17 52	18 52	19 52	20 52	21 52	22 52	23 40
Hale	d	06 52	07 47	08 56		14 56	15 57	16 56	17 56	18 56	19 56	20 56	21 56	22 56	23 44
Altrincham ⇌	a	06 56	07 51	08 59		14 59	16 00	16 59	17 59	18 59	19 59	20 59	21 59	22 59	23 47
	d	06 56	07 51	09 00		15 00	16 01	17 00	18 00	19 00	20 00	21 00	22 00	23 00	23 48
Navigation Road ⇌	d	06 59	07 53	09 02		15 02	16 03	17 02	18 02	19 02	20 02	21 02	22 02	23 02	23 50
Stockport	a	07 15	08 08	09 16		15 16	16 17	17 16	18 16	19 16	20 16	21 16	22 16	23 17	00 06
Manchester Picc. 10 ... 81 ⇌	a	07 26	08 17	09 30		15 30	16 30	17 30	18 30	19 30	20 30	21 33	22 28	23 31	00 17

Sundays
15 December to 10 May

		NT A	NT B	NT A	NT B	NT	NT	NT	NT	NT
Chester ... 81	d	09 04	09 04	10 56	10 58	12 59	15 04	17 07	19 05	20 59
Mouldsworth	d	09 15	09 15	11 07	11 10	13 10	15 15	17 18	19 16	21 10
Delamere	d	09 20	09 20	11 13	11 16	13 16	15 21	17 23	19 22	21 16
Cuddington	d	09 25	09 25	11 17	11 20	13 20	15 25	17 28	19 26	21 20
Greenbank	d	09 29	09 29	11 22	11 25	13 25	15 30	17 33	19 31	21 25
Northwich	d	09 35	09 35	11 28	11 31	13 31	15 36	17 38	19 37	21 31
Lostock Gralam	d	09 38	09 38	11 31	11 34	13 34	15 39	17 41	19 40	21 34
Plumley	d	09 41	09 41	11 35	11 38	13 38	15 43	17 45	19 44	21 38
Knutsford	d	09 47	09 47	11 40	11 43	13 43	15 48	17 50	19 49	21 43
Mobberley	d	09 51	09 51	11 45	11 48	13 48	15 53	17 54	19 53	21 48
Ashley	d	09 55	09 55	11 48	11 51	13 51	15 56	17 58	19 57	21 51
Hale	d	09 58	09 58	11 52	11 55	13 55	16 00	18 02	20 00	21 55
Altrincham ⇌	a	10 02	10 02	11 56	11 59	13 59	16 04	18 05	20 04	21 59
	d	10 02	10 02	11 56	11 59	13 59	16 04	18 06	20 04	21 59
Navigation Road ⇌	d	10 04	10 04	11 58	12 02	14 02	16 07	18 08	20 06	22 02
Stockport	a	10 19	10 19	12 13	12 16	14 17	16 28	18 29	20 21	22 17
Manchester Picc. 10 ... 81 ⇌	a	10 31	10 32	12 26	12 36	14 35	16 40	18 38	20 38	22 28

A until 29 March B from 5 April

Table T089-F

Mondays to Fridays
16 December to 15 May

Manchester Airport and Manchester - Warrington Central - Liverpool

Miles		NT MX A	NT	NT	AW ◇ B	NT ◇	NT	NT C	NT	NT	AW ◇ D	NT ◇	NT	NT ■ E	EM ◇ F	AW ◇ B	NT	NT ◇ C	NT	NT ◇ E	EM ◇ F	NT
0	Manchester Airport 85 d		05 07			05 51		05 59				06 50		06 58						07 59		
—	Sheffield 78 d														06 18						07 32	
—	Stockport 84 d														07 25						08 25	
9¾	Manchester Picc 84,85 d		05 22			06 09		06 22				07 09		07 22	07 39			08 09		08 23	08 38	
10½	Manchester Oxford Road 84,85 d		05 27			06 13	06 22	06 25		06 49		07 12		07 25	07 42		07 49	08 12	08 16	08 26	08 42	08 46
10¾	Deansgate 84,85 d						06 24	06 28		06 52				07 27			07 51			08 28		08 48
13¾	Trafford Park d						06 30												08 22			
14½	Humphrey Park d						06 32															
15½	Urmston d						06 34			06 59							07 58		08 25			08 55
16	Chassen Road d						06 36												08 27			
16¾	Flixton d						06 39										08 01		08 30			
19	Irlam d						06 43			07 05							08 05		08 34			09 01
20¼	Glazebrook d						06 46										08 08					
23	Birchwood d					06 28	06 51			07 12		07 26					08 13	08 27	08 40			09 07
24½	Padgate d	00 01					06 54										08 16		08 43			
26½	Warrington Central a	00 05				06 33	06 58			07 18		07 31			07 58		08 19	08 32	08 46		08 58	09 12
—	d	00 05		05 57		06 33	06 58		07 10			07 31	07 40		07 58		08 20	08 32	08 47		08 58	09 12
28¾	Sankey for Penketh d												07 45									
32¼	Widnes d	00 15		06 07			07 08		07 20				07 51		08 06		08 30		08 56		09 06	09 22
34	Hough Green d	00 19		06 10			07 11		07 24				07 54		08 10		08 33		09 00			09 26
36½	Halewood d	00 23		06 14			07 15		07 28				07 58				08 37					09 30
37½	Hunts Cross 103 d	00 26		06 18			07 19		07 31				08 01		08s15		08 40					09 33
39	L'pool Sth Parkway 91,103 d	00 32		06 23	06 44	06 52	07 24		07 37		07 42	07 50	08 06		08 20	08 43	08 48	08 53	09 08		09 15	09 39
40	West Allerton 91 a			06 26			07 27		07 40				08 09				08 51		09 11			09 42
40½	Mossley Hill 91 a			06 29			07 30		07 43				08 12				08 53		09 14			09 44
43¼	Edge Hill 90,91 a		06 22	06 35			07 35	07 19	07 49				08 19	08 20			08 59			09 21		09 50
44½	Liverpool Lime Street 90,91 a	00 47	06 29	06 39	07 01	07 03	07 39	07 25	07 53		07 59	08 01	08 23	08 25	08 34	09 01	09 03	09 06	09 23	09 25	09 28	09 58

	NT ◇	AW ◇ B	NT	NT ◇ E	EM ◇ F	NT	NT ◇	AW ◇ B	NT	NT ◇ E	EM MX ◇ G	EM MO ◇ G	NT	NT ◇	AW ◇ B	NT	NT ◇ E	EM ◇ G	NT	NT ◇	AW ◇ B	NT
Manchester Airport 85 d				08 59			09 48			09 59				10 49			10 59			11 49		
Sheffield 78 d					08 42						09 42	09 42						10 42				
Stockport 84 d					09 25						10 25	10 26						11 25				
Manchester Picc 84,85 d				09 22	09 39		10 09			10 22	10 38	10 38		11 09			11 22	11 38		12 09		
Manchester Oxford Road 84,85 d	09 12		09 16	09 26	09 42	09 46	10 13		10 16	10 25	10 42	10 42	10 46	11 13		11 16	11 26	11 42	11 46	12 12		12 16
Deansgate 84,85 d				09 28		09 48				10 28			10 48				11 28		11 48			
Trafford Park d			09 22													11 22						
Humphrey Park d			09 24													11 24						
Urmston d			09 27			09 56			10 23				10 56			11 26			11 55			12 23
Chassen Road d									10 25													12 25
Flixton d			09 30						10 28							11 29						12 28
Irlam d			09 34			10 02			10 32				11 02			11 34			12 01			12 32
Glazebrook d									10 35													12 35
Birchwood d	09 26		09 40			10 07	10 27		10 40				11 07	11 27		11 39			12 07	12 26		12 40
Padgate d			09 43						10 43							11 42						12 43
Warrington Central a	09 31		09 46		09 58	10 12	10 32		10 46		10 58	10 58	11 12	11 32		11 46		11 58	12 12	12 31		12 46
d	09 32		09 47		09 58	10 13	10 32		10 47		10 58	10 58	11 13	11 33		11 46		11 58	12 12	12 32		12 47
Sankey for Penketh d																						
Widnes d			09 56		10 06	10 23			10 56		11 06	11 06	11 23			11 56		12 06	12 22			12 56
Hough Green d			10 00			10 26			11 00				11 26			12 00			12 26			13 00
Halewood d						10 30							11 30						12 30			
Hunts Cross 103 d						10 33							11 33						12 33			
L'pool Sth Parkway 91,103 d	09 50	10 06	10 08		10 15	10 39	10 51	10 45	11 07		11 15	11 15	11 39	11 51	12 07	12 09		12 16	12 39	12 51	13 06	13 08
West Allerton 91 a			10 12			10 42			11 11				11 42			12 13			12 42			13 11
Mossley Hill 91 a			10 14			10 45			11 14				11 45			12 15			12 45			13 14
Edge Hill 90,91 a				10 21		10 50				11 24			11 50				12 20		12 50			
Liverpool Lime Street 90,91 a	10 03	10 20	10 23	10 28	10 31	10 58	11 03	11 04	11 24	11 28	11 32	11 32	11 58	12 03	12 21	12 24	12 24	12 32	12 59	13 02	13 20	13 23

	NT ◇ E	EM ◇ G	NT	NT ◇	AW ◇ B	NT	NT ◇ E	EM ◇ G	NT	NT ◇	AW ◇ B	NT	NT ◇ E	EM ◇ G	NT	NT ◇	AW ◇ B	NT	NT ◇ E	EM ◇ G	NT
Manchester Airport 85 d	11 59			12 49			12 59			13 49			13 59			14 49			14 59		
Sheffield 78 d		11 42						12 42						13 42						14 42	
Stockport 84 d		12 25						13 25						14 25						15 25	
Manchester Picc 84,85 d	12 22	12 38		13 09			13 22	13 38		14 09			14 22	14 38		15 09			15 22	15 38	
Manchester Oxford Road 84,85 d	12 26	12 42	12 46	13 12		13 16	13 26	13 42	13 46	14 13		14 16	14 26	14 42	14 46	15 13		15 16	15 26	15 42	15 46
Deansgate 84,85 d	12 28		12 48				13 28		13 48				14 28		14 48				15 28		15 48
Trafford Park d						13 22												15 22			
Humphrey Park d						13 24												15 24			
Urmston d			12 56			13 27			13 56			14 23			14 56			15 27			15 56
Chassen Road d												14 25									
Flixton d						13 30						14 28						15 30			
Irlam d			13 02			13 34			14 02			14 32			15 02			15 34			16 02
Glazebrook d												14 35									
Birchwood d			13 07	13 26		13 40			14 07	14 27		14 40			15 07	15 27		15 40			16 07
Padgate d						13 43						14 43						15 43			
Warrington Central a		12 58	13 12	13 31		13 46		13 58	14 12	14 32		14 46		14 58	15 12	15 32		15 46		15 58	16 12
d		12 58	13 13	13 32		13 47		13 58	14 13	14 32		14 47		14 58	15 13	15 32		15 47		15 58	16 13
Sankey for Penketh d																					
Widnes d		13 06	13 23			13 57		14 06	14 23			14 56		15 06	15 23			15 56		16 06	16 23
Hough Green d			13 26			14 00			14 26			15 00			15 26			16 00			16 26
Halewood d			13 30						14 30						15 30						16 30
Hunts Cross 103 d			13 33						14 33						15 33						16 33
L'pool Sth Parkway 91,103 d		13 15	13 39	13 50	14 00	14 07		14 15	14 39	14 51	15 00	15 07		15 15	15 39	15 51	16 05	16 08		16 15	16 39
West Allerton 91 a			13 42			14 12			14 42			15 11			15 42			16 11			16 42
Mossley Hill 91 a			13 45			14 14			14 45			15 14			15 45			16 14			16 45
Edge Hill 90,91 a	13 20		13 50				14 24		14 50				15 20		15 52				16 22		16 50
Liverpool Lime Street 90,91 a	13 24	13 32	13 58	14 01	14 14	14 24	14 28	14 32	14 58	15 02	15 14	15 23	15 24	15 32	15 58	16 03	16 19	16 23	16 26	16 32	16 58

A From Manchester Oxford Road
B From Chester
C From Wilmslow
D From Shrewsbury
E From Crewe
F From Nottingham
G From Norwich

NRT DECEMBER 19 EDITION

Table T089-F

Mondays to Fridays
16 December to 15 May

Manchester Airport and Manchester - Warrington Central - Liverpool

	NT ◇	AW ◇ A	NT	NT ◇ B	EM ◇ C	NT	NT ◇	AW ◇ A	NT	NT ◇ B	EM ◇ C	NT	NT ◇	NT	EM ◇ C	NT	NT ◇	AW ◇ D	NT	EM ◇ C	NT	NT ◇
Manchester Airport 85 d	15 49			15 59			16 48			16 59			17 48				18 49					19 50
Sheffield 78 d					15 42						16 42				17 39					18 42		
Stockport 84 d					16 25						17 25				18 25					19 25		
Manchester Picc 84,85 d	16 09			16 22	16 38		17 10			17 23	17 38		18 09		18 38		19 09			19 38		20 09
Manchester Oxford Road 84,85 d	16 12		16 16	16 26	16 42	16 46	17 13		17 16	17 26	17 42	17 46	18 13	18 16	18 42	18 46	19 12		19 16	19 42	19 46	20 12
Deansgate 84,85 d				16 28		16 48				17 29		17 48				18 48					19 48	
Trafford Park d						16 54			17 22			17 54		18 22		18 54					19 54	
Humphrey Park d									17 24			17 56		18 24		18 56					19 56	
Urmston d			16 23			16 58			17 27			17 59		18 27		18 58			19 25		19 59	
Chassen Road d			16 25						17 29			18 01		18 29		19 00			19 27			
Flixton d			16 28			17 01			17 32			18 04		18 31		19 03			19 29			
Irlam d			16 32			17 05			17 37		17 53	18 09		18 36		19 07			19 34		20 04	
Glazebrook d			16 35						17 40			18 12				19 10					20 07	
Birchwood d	16 27		16 40			17 11	17 28		17 45		17 58	18 16	18 27	18 42		19 14	19 27				20 12	20 27
Padgate d			16 43			17 14			17 48			18 19				19 17					20 15	
Warrington Central a	16 32		16 46		16 58	17 17	17 33		17 51		18 03	18 23	18 32	18 47	18 58	19 21	19 32		19 42	19 58	20 18	20 32
d	16 32		16 47		16 58	17 18	17 33		17 52		18 04	18 23	18 33	18 47	18 58	19 21	19 32		19 43	19 58	20 19	20 32
Sankey for Penketh d									17 57													
Widnes d			16 56		17 06	17 28			18 03		18 12			18 57	19 06		19 42			20 06	20 29	
Hough Green d			17 00			17 31			18 06			18 35		19 01		19 33			19 52		20 32	
Halewood d						17 35			18 10					19 05		19 37					20 36	
Hunts Cross 103 d						17 38			18 13			18 40		19 08	19 13	19 40					20 39	
L'pool Sth Parkway 91,103 d	16 51	17 06	17 08		17 15	17 46	17 52	18 06	18 19		18 23	18 47	18 51	19 16	19 20	19 47	19 53	19 59	20 04	20 17	20 46	20 53
West Allerton 91 a			17 12			17 49			18 21			18 50		19 19		19 50			20 07			
Mossley Hill 91 a			17 15			17 52			18 24			18 52		19 23		19 53			20 10		20 50	
Edge Hill 90,91 a				17 18		17 57			18 33	18 24		19 02		19 30					20 19		20 56	
Liverpool Lime Street 90,91 a	17 04	17 20	17 24	17 23	17 32	18 02	18 05	18 22	18 41	18 28	18 36	19 06	19 03	19 35	19 35	20 02	20 05	20 15	20 24	20 34	21 00	21 05

	NT	NT ◇ B	AW ◇ A	EM ◇ C	NT	NT ◇	AW ◇ A	NT E	NT	NT ◇	AW ◇ A	NT E	NT	NT ◇	NT E	NT
Manchester Airport 85 d		19 59				20 47		20 58		21 48		21 59		22 49	23 01	
Sheffield 78 d				19 42												
Stockport 84 d				20 25												
Manchester Picc 84,85 d		20 22		20 38		21 11		21 18		22 08		22 18		23 09	23 22	
Manchester Oxford Road 84,85 d	20 16	20 26		20 42	20 47	21 14		21 27	21 45	22 11		22 31	22 43	23 13	23 25	23 28
Deansgate 84,85 d		20 28			20 49			21 29	21 47			22 34	22 45		23 28	23 30
Trafford Park d					20 55				21 53							23 36
Humphrey Park d					20 57				21 55							23 38
Urmston d	20 24				21 00				21 58				22 52			23 41
Chassen Road d	20 26								22 00							23 43
Flixton d	20 28								22 02							23 46
Irlam d	20 33				21 05				22 06				22 58			23 51
Glazebrook d					21 08				22 09							23 54
Birchwood d	20 39				21 13	21 29			22 14	22 26			23 04	23 28		23 58
Padgate d					21 16				22 17							00 01
Warrington Central a	20 44			20 58	21 19	21 34			22 20	22 31			23 09	23 33		00 05
d	20 44			20 59	21 20	21 34			22 21	22 31			23 09	23 34		00 05
Sankey for Penketh d																
Widnes d	20 54			21 06	21 30					22 41			23 19			00 15
Hough Green d	20 58				21 33				22 32				23 23			00 19
Halewood d					21 37				22 36				23 27			00 23
Hunts Cross 103 d					21 40				22 39				23 30			00 26
L'pool Sth Parkway 91,103 d	21 10		21 14	21 20	21 46	21 54	22 01		22 50	22 53	23 06		23 37	23 53		00 32
West Allerton 91 a	21 12								22 52				23 39			
Mossley Hill 91 a	21 15				21 50				22 55				23 42			
Edge Hill 90,91 a		21 22			21 57			22 19	23 04			23 27	23 48		00 20	
Liverpool Lime Street 90,91 a	21 24	21 27	21 30	21 36	22 02	22 05	22 16	22 26	23 09	23 05	23 20	23 33	23 53	00 05	00 26	00 47

Saturdays
21 December to 16 May

	NT F	NT	NT	AW ◇ A	NT ◇	NT	NT E	AW ◇ D	NT	NT	NT ◇	NT ◇ B	NT	EM ◇ G	AW ◇ A	NT	NT ◇	NT	NT ◇ B	EM ◇ G	NT	NT ◇
Manchester Airport 85 d		05 07			05 51		05 59				06 50	06 58					07 48		07 59			
Sheffield 78 d														06 20						07 32		
Stockport 84 d														07 26						08 25		
Manchester Picc 84,85 d		05 22			06 09		06 22				07 09	07 22		07 39			08 09		08 23	08 38		
Manchester Oxford Road 84,85 d		05 27			06 13	06 22	06 25			06 49	07 12	07 25		07 42		07 49	08 12	08 16	08 26	08 42	08 46	09 12
Deansgate 84,85 d						06 24	06 28			06 52		07 27				07 51			08 28		08 48	
Trafford Park d						06 30												08 22				
Humphrey Park d						06 32																
Urmston d						06 34				06 59						07 58		08 25			08 55	
Chassen Road d						06 36												08 27				
Flixton d						06 39										08 01		08 30				
Irlam d						06 43				07 05						08 05		08 34			09 01	
Glazebrook d						06 46										08 08						
Birchwood d					06 28	06 51				07 12	07 26					08 13	08 27	08 40			09 07	09 26
Padgate d	00 01					06 54										08 16		08 43				
Warrington Central a	00 05				06 33	06 58				07 18	07 31			07 58		08 19	08 32	08 46		08 58	09 12	09 31
d	00 05		05 57		06 33	06 58			07 10		07 31		07 40	07 58		08 20	08 32	08 47		08 58	09 12	09 32
Sankey for Penketh d													07 45									
Widnes d	00 15		06 07			07 08			07 20				07 51	08 06		08 30		08 56		09 06	09 22	
Hough Green d	00 19		06 10			07 11			07 24				07 54	08 10		08 33		09 00			09 26	
Halewood d	00 23		06 14			07 15			07 28				07 58			08 37					09 30	
Hunts Cross 103 d	00 26		06 18			07 19			07 31				08 01	08s15		08 40					09 33	
L'pool Sth Parkway 91,103 d	00 32		06 23	06 37	06 52	07 24		07 17	07 37		07 50		08 06	08 20	08 43	08 46	08 51	09 08		09 15	09 39	09 50
West Allerton 91 a			06 26			07 27			07 40				08 09			08 49		09 11			09 42	
Mossley Hill 91 a			06 29			07 30			07 43				08 12			08 52		09 14			09 44	
Edge Hill 90,91 a		06 22	06 35			07 35	07 19		07 49			08 18	08 19			08 57			09 21		09 50	
Liverpool Lime Street 90,91 a	00 47	06 29	06 39	06 51	07 03	07 39	07 25	07 31	07 53		08 01	08 23	08 23	08 33	08 58	09 02	09 07	09 23	09 25	09 30	09 58	10 03

A From Chester
B From Crewe
C From Norwich
D From Wrexham General
E From Wilmslow
F From Manchester Oxford Road
G From Nottingham

Manchester Airport and Manchester - Warrington Central - Liverpool

Saturdays
21 December to 16 May

	AW ◇ A	NT	NT ◇ B	EM ◇ C	NT	AW ◇ A	NT ◇	NT	NT ◇ B	EM ◇ D	NT	NT ◇	AW ◇ A	NT	NT ◇ B	EM ◇ D	NT	NT ◇	AW ◇ A	NT	NT ◇ B	EM ◇ D
Manchester Airport 85 d			08 59				09 49		09 59			10 49			10 59			11 49			11 59	
Sheffield 78 d				08 42						09 42						10 42						11 42
Stockport 84 d				09 25						10 26						11 26						12 26
ManchesterPicc 84,85 d			09 22	09 38			10 09		10 22	10 38		11 09			11 22	11 38		12 09			12 22	12 38
Manchester Oxford Road 84,85 d		09 16	09 26	09 42	09 46		10 13	10 16	10 25	10 42	10 46	11 13		11 16	11 26	11 42	11 46	12 12		12 16	12 26	12 42
Deansgate 84,85 d			09 28		09 48				10 28		10 48				11 28		11 48				12 28	
Trafford Park d		09 22												11 22								
Humphrey Park d		09 24												11 24								
Urmston d		09 27			09 56			10 23			10 56			11 26			11 55			12 23		
Chassen Road d								10 25												12 25		
Flixton d		09 30						10 28						11 29						12 28		
Irlam d		09 34			10 02			10 32			11 02			11 34			12 01			12 32		
Glazebrook d								10 35												12 35		
Birchwood d		09 40			10 07		10 27	10 40			11 07	11 27		11 39			12 07	12 27		12 40		
Padgate d		09 43						10 43						11 42						12 43		
Warrington Central a		09 46		09 58	10 12		10 32	10 46		10 58	11 12	11 32		11 46		11 58	12 12	12 32		12 46		12 58
d		09 47		09 58	10 13		10 32	10 47		10 58	11 13	11 33		11 46		11 58	12 12	12 32		12 47		12 58
Sankey for Penketh d																						
Widnes d		09 56		10 06	10 23			10 56		11 06	11 23			11 56		12 06	12 22			12 56		13 06
Hough Green d		10 00			10 26			11 00			11 26			12 00			12 26			13 00		
Halewood d					10 30						11 30						12 30					
Hunts Cross 103 d					10 33						11 33						12 33					
L'pool Sth Parkway 91,103 d	10 05	10 08		10 15	10 39	10 47	10 51	11 07		11 15	11 39	11 52	12 05	12 08		12 15	12 39	12 53	13 04	13 07		13 15
West Allerton 91 a		10 12			10 42			11 11			11 42			12 11			12 42			13 11		
Mossley Hill 91 a		10 14			10 45			11 14			11 45			12 14			12 45			13 14		
Edge Hill 90,91 a			10 21		10 50				11 24		11 50				12 20		12 50				13 20	
Liverpool Lime Street 90,91 a	10 19	10 23	10 28	10 30	10 58	11 04	11 04	11 24	11 28	11 32	11 58	12 04	12 19	12 23	12 24	12 32	12 58	13 04	13 18	13 23	13 24	13 32

	NT	NT ◇	AW ◇ A	NT	NT ◇ B	EM ◇ D	NT	NT ◇	AW ◇ A	NT	NT ◇ B	EM ◇ D	NT	NT ◇	AW ◇ A	NT	NT ◇ B	EM ◇ D	NT	NT ◇	AW ◇ A
Manchester Airport 85 d		12 49			12 59			13 49			13 59			14 49			14 59			15 49	
Sheffield 78 d						12 42						13 42						14 42			
Stockport 84 d						13 26						14 26						15 26			
ManchesterPicc 84,85 d		13 09			13 22	13 38		14 09			14 22	14 38		15 09			15 22	15 38		16 09	
Manchester Oxford Road 84,85 d	12 46	13 12		13 16	13 26	13 42	13 46	14 13		14 16	14 26	14 42	14 46	15 13		15 16	15 26	15 42	15 46	16 12	
Deansgate 84,85 d	12 48				13 28		13 48				14 28		14 48				15 28		15 48		
Trafford Park d				13 22												15 22					
Humphrey Park d				13 24												15 24					
Urmston d	12 56			13 27			13 56			14 23			14 56			15 27			15 56		
Chassen Road d										14 25											
Flixton d				13 30						14 28						15 30					
Irlam d	13 02			13 34			14 02			14 32			15 02			15 34			16 02		
Glazebrook d										14 35											
Birchwood d	13 07	13 26		13 40			14 07	14 27		14 40			15 07	15 27		15 40			16 07	16 27	
Padgate d				13 43						14 43						15 43					
Warrington Central a	13 12	13 31		13 46		13 58	14 12	14 32		14 46		14 58	15 12	15 32		15 46		15 58	16 12	16 32	
d	13 13	13 32		13 47		13 58	14 13	14 32		14 47		14 58	15 13	15 32		15 47		15 58	16 13	16 32	
Sankey for Penketh d																					
Widnes d	13 23			13 57		14 06	14 23			14 56		15 06	15 23			15 56		16 06	16 23		
Hough Green d	13 26			14 00			14 26			15 00			15 26			16 00			16 26		
Halewood d	13 30						14 30						15 30						16 30		
Hunts Cross 103 d	13 33						14 33						15 33						16 33		
L'pool Sth Parkway 91,103 d	13 39	13 52	14 04	14 07		14 15	14 39	14 52	14 59	15 07		15 15	15 39	15 52	16 05	16 08		16 15	16 39	16 53	17 04
West Allerton 91 a	13 42			14 12			14 42			15 11			15 42			16 11			16 42		
Mossley Hill 91 a	13 45			14 14			14 45			15 14			15 45			16 14			16 45		
Edge Hill 90,91 a	13 50				14 24		14 50				15 20		15 52				16 22		16 50		
Liverpool Lime Street 90,91 a	13 58	14 03	14 18	14 24	14 29	14 32	14 59	15 05	15 14	15 23	15 24	15 30	15 58	16 03	16 19	16 23	16 26	16 32	16 58	17 04	17 19

	NT	NT ◇ B	EM ◇ D	NT	NT ◇	AW ◇ A	NT	NT ◇ B	EM ◇ D	NT	NT ◇	NT	NT ◇ B	EM ◇ D	NT	NT ◇	NT	AW ◇ E	NT ◇ B	EM ◇ D	NT	NT ◇
Manchester Airport 85 d		15 59			16 49			16 59			17 49		17 59			18 49			18 59			19 50
Sheffield 78 d			15 42						16 42					17 38						18 37		
Stockport 84 d			16 26						17 26					18 26						19 26		
ManchesterPicc 84,85 d		16 22	16 38		17 09			17 23	17 38		18 09		18 22	18 38		19 09			19 22	19 38		20 09
Manchester Oxford Road 84,85 d	16 16	16 26	16 42	16 46	17 12		17 16	17 26	17 42	17 46	18 13	18 16	18 26	18 42	18 46	19 12	19 16		19 26	19 42	19 46	20 12
Deansgate 84,85 d		16 28		16 48				17 29		17 48			18 28		18 48				19 28		19 48	
Trafford Park d				16 54			17 22			17 54		18 22			18 54						19 54	
Humphrey Park d							17 24			17 56		18 24			18 56						19 56	
Urmston d	16 23			16 58			17 27			17 59		18 27			18 58		19 23				19 59	
Chassen Road d	16 25						17 29			18 01		18 29			19 00		19 25					
Flixton d	16 28			17 01			17 32			18 04		18 31			19 03		19 28					
Irlam d	16 32			17 05			17 37		17 53	18 09		18 36			19 07		19 33				20 04	
Glazebrook d	16 35						17 40			18 12					19 10						20 07	
Birchwood d	16 40			17 11	17 27		17 45		17 58	18 16	18 27	18 42			19 14	19 27					20 12	20 27
Padgate d	16 43			17 14			17 48			18 19					19 17						20 15	
Warrington Central a	16 46		16 58	17 17	17 32		17 51		18 03	18 23	18 32	18 47		18 58	19 21	19 32	19 41			19 58	20 18	20 32
d	16 47		16 58	17 18	17 32		17 52		18 04	18 23	18 33	18 47		18 58	19 21	19 32	19 41			19 58	20 19	20 32
Sankey for Penketh d							17 57															
Widnes d	16 56		17 06	17 28			18 03		18 12			18 57		19 06		19 42				20 06	20 29	
Hough Green d	17 00			17 31			18 06			18 35		19 01			19 33		19 51				20 32	
Halewood d				17 35			18 10					19 05			19 37						20 36	
Hunts Cross 103 d				17 38			18 13			18 40		19 08		19 13	19 40						20 39	
L'pool Sth Parkway 91,103 d	17 08		17 15	17 46	17 52	18 06	18 19		18 23	18 47	18 52	19 16		19 19	19 47	19 53	19 58	20 09		20 18	20 46	20 53
West Allerton 91 a	17 12			17 49			18 21			18 50		19 19			19 50		20 03					
Mossley Hill 91 a	17 15			17 52			18 24			18 52		19 23			19 53		20 05				20 50	
Edge Hill 90,91 a		17 18		17 57			18 33	18 24		19 03		19 29	19 21				20 11		20 22		20 56	
Liverpool Lime Street 90,91 a	17 24	17 23	17 32	18 02	18 05	18 20	18 37	18 28	18 36	19 07	19 04	19 34	19 25	19 35	20 02	20 05	20 16	20 24	20 29	20 33	21 00	21 04

A From Chester
B From Crewe
C From Nottingham
D From Norwich
E From Wrexham General

Manchester Airport and Manchester - Warrington Central - Liverpool

Saturdays
21 December to 16 May

	AW ◇ A	NT	NT ◇ B	EM ◇ C	NT	NT ◇	AW ◇ A	NT D	NT	NT ◇	NT D	NT	NT ◇	NT	NT D
Manchester Airport 85 d			19 59			20 49		20 58		21 48	21 59		22 49		22 59
Sheffield 78 d				19 42											
Stockport 84 d				20 26											
ManchesterPicc 84,85 d			20 22	20 38		21 11		21 17		22 08	22 18		23 09		23 22
Manchester Oxford Road 84,85 d		20 17	20 26	20 42	20 46	21 14		21 27	21 45	22 11	22 31	22 43	23 12	23 20	23 25
Deansgate 84,85 d			20 28		20 48			21 29	21 47		22 34	22 45		23 22	23 28
Trafford Park d					20 54				21 53					23 28	
Humphrey Park d					20 56				21 55					23 30	
Urmston d		20 24			20 59				21 58			22 52		23 33	
Chassen Road d		20 26							22 00					23 35	
Flixton d		20 29							22 02					23 38	
Irlam d		20 34			21 04				22 06			22 58		23 43	
Glazebrook d					21 07				22 09					23 46	
Birchwood d		20 39			21 12	21 29			22 14	22 26		23 04	23 28	23 51	
Padgate d					21 15				22 17					23 54	
Warrington Central a		20 44		20 58	21 18	21 34			22 20	22 31		23 09	23 33	23 57	
d		20 45		20 58	21 19	21 34			22 21	22 31		23 09	23 34	23 58	
Sankey for Penketh d															
Widnes d		20 54		21 06	21 29					22 41		23 19		00 08	
Hough Green d		20 58			21 32				22 32			23 23		00 11	
Halewood d					21 36				22 36			23 27		00 15	
Hunts Cross 103 d					21 39				22 39			23 30		00 19	
L'pool Sth Parkway 91,103 d	21 03	21 07		21 20	21 46	21 54	22 05		22 50	22 53		23 37	23 53	00 24	
West Allerton 91 a		21 10							22 52			23 39			
Mossley Hill 91 a		21 13			21 50				22 55			23 42			
Edge Hill 90,91 a			21 21		21 57			22 19	23 04		23 24	23 50			00 19
Liverpool Lime Street 90,91 a	21 17	21 24	21 25	21 32	22 02	22 07	22 19	22 23	23 09	23 05	23 29	23 55	00 05	00 36	00 26

Sundays
15 December to 10 May

	NT E	NT F	NT G	NT ◇ G	AW ◇ A	NT H	NT I	NT G	NT F	AW ◇ A	NT D	NT	NT ◇ I	NT ◇ J	NT D	AW ◇ A	NT	NT ◇	NT D	EM ◇ K	AW ◇ A	NT
Manchester Airport 85 d							08 01				08 54				09 59			10 52	10 58			
Sheffield 78 d																				10 41		
Stockport 84 d																				11 26		
ManchesterPicc 84,85 d						08 24	08 24				09 18				10 22			11 11	11 21	11 38		
Manchester Oxford Road 84,85 d		07 40	07 46	08 17		08 27	08 27	08 39			09 21	09 46	10 18	10 20	10 25		10 43	11 14	11 24	11 42		11 46
Deansgate 84,85 d		07 44	07 48			08 29	08 29	08 41			09 23	09 48			10 28		10 45		11 27			11 48
Trafford Park d																						
Humphrey Park d																						
Urmston d		07 59	07 55					08 49				09 55					10 52					11 55
Chassen Road d																						
Flixton d		08 05	07 58					08 52				09 58					10 55					11 58
Irlam d		08 26	08 02					08 57				10 02					10 59					12 02
Glazebrook d																						
Birchwood d		08 46	08 07	08 31				09 03				10 07	10 32	10 34			11 04	11 28				12 07
Padgate d																						
Warrington Central a		08 58	08 12	08 36				09 08				10 12	10 37	10 39			11 09	11 33		11 58		12 12
d			08 13	08 37				09 08	09 08			10 13	10 38	10 40			11 10	11 34		11 59		12 13
Sankey for Penketh d																						
Widnes d	00 08		08 23					09 18	09 18			10 23					11 20			12 06		12 23
Hough Green d	00 11		08 26					09 22	09 22			10 26					11 23					12 26
Halewood d	00 15		08 30					09 27	09 27			10 30					11 27					12 30
Hunts Cross 103 d	00 19		08 33					09 31	09 31			10 33					11 30					12 33
L'pool Sth Parkway 91,103 d	00 24		08 39	08 58	09 04			09 37	09 37	10 04		10 39	11 01	11 01		11 20	11 36	11 53		12 17	12 21	12 39
West Allerton 91 a			08 42					09 40	09 40			10 42					11 39					12 42
Mossley Hill 91 a			08 44					09 42	09 42			10 44					11 41					12 44
Edge Hill 90,91 a																						
Liverpool Lime Street 90,91 a	00 36		08 53	09 09	09 18	09 30	09 31	09 51	09 51	10 18	10 24	10 53	11 12	11 12	11 25	11 33	11 51	12 04	12 25	12 30	12 35	12 54

A From Chester
B From Crewe
C From Norwich
D From Wilmslow
E not 15 December. From Manchester Oxford Road
F from 12 January until 16 February
G until 5 January, from 23 February
H until 5 January, from 23 February until 29 March
I from 5 April
J until 29 March
K From Nottingham

Table T089-F

Sundays
15 December to 10 May

Manchester Airport and Manchester - Warrington Central - Liverpool

	NT		NT	EM	AW	NT	NT	NT	NT	EM	AW		NT	NT	NT	EM	AW	NT	NT	NT	EM		AW	NT
	◇		A	◇ B	◇ C		◇ D	◇ E	A	◇ B	◇ C			◇	A	◇ B	◇ C		◇	A	◇ F		◇ C	
Manchester Airport 85 d	11 53		11 59				12 48		12 59					13 53	13 59				14 53	14 59				
Sheffield 7 78 d				11 39						12 39						13 38					14 37			
Stockport 84 d				12 26						13 26						14 27					15 26			
ManchesterPicc 10 84,85 d	12 09		12 22	12 38			13 07		13 22	13 38				14 10	14 22	14 38			15 09	15 22	15 38			
Manchester Oxford Road 84,85 d	12 12		12 26	12 42		12 46	13 10	13 13	13 26	13 42			13 46	14 13	14 26	14 42		14 46	15 13	15 26	15 42			15 46
Deansgate 84,85 d			12 28			12 48			13 29				13 48		14 28			14 48		15 28				15 48
Trafford Park d																								
Humphrey Park d																								
Urmston d						12 55							13 55					14 55						15 55
Chassen Road d																								
Flixton d						12 58							13 58					14 58						15 58
Irlam d						13 02							14 02					15 02						16 02
Glazebrook d																								
Birchwood d	12 26					13 07	13 24	13 27					14 07	14 27				15 07	15 27					16 07
Padgate d																								
Warrington Central a	12 31			12 58		13 12	13 29	13 32		13 58			14 12	14 32		14 58		15 12	15 32		15 58			16 12
d	12 32			12 59		13 13	13 30	13 32		13 58			14 13	14 33		14 58		15 13	15 32		15 58			16 13
Sankey for Penketh d																								
Widnes d				13 06		13 22				14 06			14 23			15 06		15 23			16 06			16 23
Hough Green d						13 26							14 26					15 26						16 26
Halewood d						13 30							14 30					15 30						16 30
Hunts Cross 103 d						13 33							14 33					15 33						16 33
L'pool Sth Parkway 7 91,103 d	12 51			13 17	13 21	13 38	13 49	13 51		14 16	14 20		14 39	14 52		15 16	15 20	15 39	15 51		16 16		16 20	16 39
West Allerton 91 a						13 41							14 42					15 42						16 42
Mossley Hill 91 a						13 44							14 44					15 44						16 44
Edge Hill 90,91 a																								
Liverpool Lime Street 10 90,91 a	13 02		13 25	13 31	13 35	13 53	14 00	14 02	14 25	14 32	14 34		14 56	15 03	15 25	15 30	15 36	15 56	16 02	16 25	16 28		16 34	16 53

	NT	NT	EM	AW	NT	NT	NT		EM	AW	NT	NT	NT	EM	AW	NT	NT		NT	EM	AW	NT	NT	NT
	◇	A	◇ B	◇ C		◇	A		◇ G	◇ C		◇	A	◇ F	◇ C		◇		A	◇ F	◇ C		◇	A
Manchester Airport 85 d	15 53	15 59				16 53	16 59					17 53	17 59				18 53		18 59				19 52	19 59
Sheffield 7 78 d			15 43						16 39					17 44						18 37				
Stockport 84 d			16 26						17 29					18 26						19 26				
ManchesterPicc 10 84,85 d	16 09	16 22	16 38			17 09	17 22		17 38			18 11	18 22	18 38			19 09		19 22	19 39			20 07	20 22
Manchester Oxford Road 84,85 d	16 13	16 26	16 42		16 46	17 13	17 26		17 42		17 46	18 15	18 26	18 42		18 46	19 13		19 26	19 43		19 46	20 11	20 26
Deansgate 84,85 d		16 28			16 48		17 28				17 48		18 28			18 48			19 28			19 48		20 28
Trafford Park d																								
Humphrey Park d																								
Urmston d					16 55						17 55					18 55						19 55		
Chassen Road d																								
Flixton d					16 58						17 58					18 58						19 58		
Irlam d					17 02						18 02					19 02						20 02		
Glazebrook d																								
Birchwood d	16 27				17 07	17 27					18 07	18 29				19 07	19 27					20 07	20 25	
Padgate d																								
Warrington Central a	16 32		16 58		17 12	17 32			17 58		18 12	18 34		18 58		19 12	19 32			19 59		20 12	20 30	
d	16 32		16 58		17 13	17 32			17 59		18 13	18 34		18 58		19 13	19 32			19 59		20 13	20 30	
Sankey for Penketh d																								
Widnes d			17 06		17 23				18 06		18 23			19 06		19 23				20 07		20 23		
Hough Green d					17 26						18 26					19 26						20 26		
Halewood d					17 30						18 30					19 30						20 30		
Hunts Cross 103 d					17 33						18 33					19 33						20 33		
L'pool Sth Parkway 7 91,103 d	16 51		17 16	17 20	17 39	17 51			18 17	18 21	18 39	18 53		19 17	19 21	19 39	19 51			20 17	20 21	20 39	20 49	
West Allerton 91 a					17 42						18 42					19 42						20 42		
Mossley Hill 91 a					17 44						18 44					19 44						20 44		
Edge Hill 90,91 a																								
Liverpool Lime Street 10 90,91 a	17 02	17 23	17 32	17 34	17 53	18 02	18 25		18 30	18 35	18 53	19 04	19 25	19 30	19 38	19 53	20 02		20 25	20 31	20 35	20 53	21 00	21 23

	AW	NT	NT		NT	AW	NT	NT	AW	NT	NT	NT	NT
	◇ C		◇		A	◇ C		◇	◇ C	A		◇	A
Manchester Airport 85 d			20 51		20 59			21 53		21 59		22 52	23 09
Sheffield 7 78 d													
Stockport 84 d													
ManchesterPicc 10 84,85 d			21 09		21 18			22 09		22 19		23 09	23 33
Manchester Oxford Road 84,85 d		20 46	21 12		21 27		21 45	22 13		22 29	22 44	23 13	23 36
Deansgate 84,85 d		20 48			21 29		21 47			22 32	22 46		23 38
Trafford Park d													
Humphrey Park d													
Urmston d		20 55					21 54				22 53		
Chassen Road d													
Flixton d		20 58					21 57				22 56		
Irlam d		21 02					22 01				23 00		
Glazebrook d													
Birchwood d		21 07	21 26				22 07	22 27			23 06	23 27	
Padgate d													
Warrington Central a		21 12	21 31				22 12	22 32			23 11	23 32	
d		21 13	21 32				22 12	22 32			23 11	23 32	
Sankey for Penketh d													
Widnes d		21 23					22 22				23 21		
Hough Green d		21 26					22 26				23 25		
Halewood d		21 30					22 30				23 29		
Hunts Cross 103 d		21 33					22 33				23 33		
L'pool Sth Parkway 7 91,103 d	21 20	21 39	21 51			22 27	22 38	22 51	23 01		23 39	23 51	
West Allerton 91 a		21 42					22 41				23 42		
Mossley Hill 91 a		21 44					22 44				23 44		
Edge Hill 90,91 a													
Liverpool Lime Street 10 90,91 a	21 34	21 53	22 02		22 24	22 41	22 53	23 02	23 15	23 27	23 54	00 05	00 35

A From Wilmslow
B From Nottingham
C From Chester
D from 5 April
E until 29 March
F From Norwich
G From Peterborough

NRT DECEMBER 19 EDITION

Table T089-R

Mondays to Fridays
16 December to 15 May

Liverpool - Warrington Central - Manchester and Manchester Airport

Miles		NT MX	NT	NT	NT	NT	NT	NT	NT	EM		NT	NT	NT	NT	NT	EM	NT	NT	NT		NT	EM	NT
		A	◇	◇ B			◇ C		◇ B	◇ D				◇		◇ B	◇ D		◇			◇ B	◇ D	
0	**Liverpool Lime Street 10 90,91** d		03 37	05 24		05 49	06 13	06 20	06 27	06 47			06 50	07 09	07 19	07 27	07 42	07 45	08 16	08 19		08 27	08 52	08 55
1¼	Edge Hill 90,91 d			05 28		05 53			06 31				06 54		07 23	07 31				08 23		08 31		08 59
3¾	Mossley Hill 91 d					05 58		06 28					06 59		07 28			07 54		08 28				09 04
4½	West Allerton 91 d					06 01		06 31					07 01		07 31			07 56		08 31				09 07
5½	L'pool Sth Parkway 7 91,103 d					06 04	06 24	06 34		06 58			07 04	07 19	07 34		07 53	08 00	08 26	08 34			09 03	09 10
7	Hunts Cross 103 d					06 07							07 08				07 59	08 04						09 13
8	Halewood d					06 10							07 11					08 07						09 16
10½	Hough Green d	00 03				06 14		06 40					07 15		07 41			08 11		08 41				09 20
12¼	Widnes d	00 07				06 18		06 44		07 07			07 19	07 28			08 05	08 15		08 44			09 11	09 24
15¾	Sankey for Penketh d																	08 20						
18¾	**Warrington Central** a	00 17				06 28	06 41	06 54		07 15			07 29	07 38	07 53		08 13	08 25	08 44	08 54			09 18	09 34
—	d	00 18			06 00		06 41	06 54		07 15		07 23		07 39	07 53		08 13	08 26	08 45	08 55			09 19	09 35
20	Padgate d				06 03			06 58				07 26			07 57					08 58				
21½	Birchwood d				06 06		06 46	07 01		07 20		07 30		07 44	08 00		08 18	08 31	08 50	09 02				09 39
24¼	Glazebrook d				06 11			07 06				07 35			08 05					09 07				
25½	Irlam d				06 14		06 52	07 09				07 38		07 51	08 09			08 38		09 10				09 46
27¾	Flixton d				06 18			07 13				07 42			08 13			08 42		09 14				
28½	Chassen Road d				06 20			07 15				07 44			08 15			08 44		09 16				
29	Urmston d				06 22		06 57	07 17				07 47			08 18			08 46		09 18				09 51
30	Humphrey Park d				06 25			07 20				07 50			08 21			08 49		09 21				
30¾	Trafford Park d				06 28			07 23				07 53			08 24			08 52		09 24				
33¾	Deansgate 84,85 a			06 19	06 36			07 31	07 22			08 01			08 32	08 22		09 00		09 32		09 23		10 02
34	**Manchester Oxford Road 84,85** a			06 21	06 38		07 08	07 33	07 24	07 38		08 03		08 05	08 34	08 24	08 38	09 03	09 07	09 35		09 25	09 39	10 04
34¾	**ManchesterPicc 10** 84,85 a	00 38	04 12	06 24			07 11		07 29	07 41						08 28	08 41		09 11			09 28	09 41	
—	Stockport 84 a									07 54							08 54						09 54	
—	Sheffield 7 78 a									08 36							09 35						10 34	
44½	**Manchester Airport 85,84** a		04 27	06 47					07 52							08 52			09 32			09 52		

	NT	NT	NT	EM	NT	NT		NT	NT	EM	NT	NT	NT	NT	EM	NT		NT	NT	NT	EM	NT	NT	NT
	◇		◇ B	◇ D		◇			◇ B	◇ D		◇		◇ B	◇ D			◇		◇ B	◇ D		◇	
Liverpool Lime Street 10 90,91 d	09 16	09 19	09 27	09 51	09 55	10 16		10 20	10 27	10 51	10 55	11 16	11 19	11 27	11 51	11 55		12 16	12 19	12 27	12 51	12 55	13 16	13 19
Edge Hill 90,91 d			09 31		09 59				10 31		10 59			11 31		11 59				12 31		12 59		
Mossley Hill 91 d		09 28			10 04			10 28			11 04		11 28			12 04			12 28			13 04		13 28
West Allerton 91 d		09 31			10 07			10 31			11 07		11 31			12 07			12 31			13 07		13 31
L'pool Sth Parkway 7 91,103 d	09 26	09 34		10 02	10 10	10 26		10 34		11 02	11 10	11 26	11 34		12 02	12 10		12 27	12 34		13 02	13 10	13 26	13 34
Hunts Cross 103 d					10 13						11 13					12 13						13 13		
Halewood d					10 16						11 16					12 16						13 16		
Hough Green d		09 41			10 20			10 41			11 20		11 41			12 20			12 41			13 20		13 41
Widnes d		09 45		10 10	10 24			10 45		11 10	11 24		11 45		12 10	12 24			12 45		13 10	13 24		13 45
Sankey for Penketh d																								
Warrington Central a	09 44	09 53		10 18	10 34	10 44		10 53		11 18	11 34	11 44	11 53		12 18	12 34		12 44	12 53		13 18	13 34	13 44	13 53
d	09 45	09 55		10 18	10 35	10 45		10 55		11 18	11 35	11 45	11 55		12 18	12 35		12 45	12 55		13 18	13 35	13 45	13 55
Padgate d		09 59						10 59					11 59						12 59					13 59
Birchwood d	09 50	10 03			10 39	10 50		11 03			11 39	11 50	12 03			12 39		12 50	13 03			13 39	13 50	14 03
Glazebrook d								11 08											13 08					
Irlam d		10 09			10 46			11 11			11 46		12 09			12 46			13 11			13 46		14 09
Flixton d		10 13						11 15					12 13						13 15					14 13
Chassen Road d								11 17											13 17					
Urmston d		10 17			10 51			11 20			11 51		12 17			12 51			13 20			13 51		14 17
Humphrey Park d		10 20											12 20											14 20
Trafford Park d		10 22											12 22											14 22
Deansgate 84,85 a		10 32	10 22		11 01			11 32	11 22		12 01		12 32	12 22		13 01			13 32	13 22		14 01		14 32
Manchester Oxford Road 84,85 a	10 07	10 35	10 24	10 38	11 03	11 07		11 34	11 24	11 38	12 03	12 07	12 35	12 24	12 38	13 03		13 07	13 35	13 24	13 38	14 03	14 07	14 35
ManchesterPicc 10 84,85 a	10 11		10 28	10 41		11 11			11 28	11 41		12 11		12 28	12 41			13 11		13 28	13 41		14 11	
Stockport 84 a				10 54						11 54					12 54						13 54			
Sheffield 7 78 a				11 35						12 35					13 34						14 35			
Manchester Airport 85,84 a	10 32		10 52			11 32			11 52			12 32		12 52				13 32		13 52			14 32	

	NT	EM		NT	NT	NT	NT	EM	NT	NT	NT	NT		EM	NT	NT	NT	NT	NT	EM	NT	NT		NT
	◇ B	◇ D			◇		◇ B	◇ D		◇		◇ B		◇ D		E	◇		◇ B	◇ F		◇		
Liverpool Lime Street 10 90,91 d	13 27	13 51		13 55	14 16	14 19	14 27	14 51	14 55	15 16	15 19	15 27		15 51	15 55	16 01	16 16	16 19	16 27	16 50	16 55	17 15		17 19
Edge Hill 90,91 d	13 31			13 59			14 31		14 59			15 31			15 59	16a05			16 31		16 59			
Mossley Hill 91 d				14 04		14 28			15 04		15 28				16 04			16 28			17 04			17 27
West Allerton 91 d				14 07		14 31			15 07		15 31				16 07			16 31			17 07			17 30
L'pool Sth Parkway 7 91,103 d		14 02		14 10	14 26	14 34		15 02	15 10	15 26	15 34			16 02	16 10		16 26	16 34		17 01	17 10	17 26		17 33
Hunts Cross 103 d				14 13					15 13						16 14						17 13			17 36
Halewood d				14 16					15 16						16 17						17 16			17 39
Hough Green d				14 20		14 41			15 20		15 41				16 21			16 41			17 20			17 44
Widnes d		14 10		14 24		14 45		15 10	15 24		15 45			16 10	16 25			16 45		17 09	17 24			17 47
Sankey for Penketh d																								17 52
Warrington Central a		14 18		14 34	14 44	14 53		15 18	15 34	15 44	15 53			16 18	16 35		16 44	16 53		17 17	17 34	17 43		17 57
d		14 18		14 35	14 45	14 55		15 18	15 35	15 45	15 55			16 18	16 35		16 45	16 56		17 17	17 35	17 44		17 59
Padgate d						14 59					15 59							17 00						18 02
Birchwood d				14 39	14 50	15 03			15 39	15 50	16 03				16 40		16 50	17 04			17 39	17 49		18 05
Glazebrook d						15 08												17 09						
Irlam d				14 46		15 11			15 46		16 09				16 46			17 12			17 46			18 11
Flixton d						15 15					16 13							17 16						18 15
Chassen Road d						15 17												17 18						
Urmston d				14 51		15 20			15 51		16 17				16 51			17 21			17 51			18 19
Humphrey Park d											16 20													18 22
Trafford Park d											16 22													18 24
Deansgate 84,85 a	14 22			15 01		15 32	15 22		16 01		16 32	16 22			17 01			17 32	17 23		18 01			18 32
Manchester Oxford Road 84,85 a	14 24	14 38		15 03	15 07	15 35	15 24	15 38	16 03	16 07	16 35	16 24		16 38	17 03		17 08	17 35	17 26	17 38	18 03	18 08		18 35
ManchesterPicc 10 84,85 a	14 28	14 41			15 11		15 28	15 41		16 11		16 28		16 41			17 11		17 31	17 41		18 11		
Stockport 84 a		14 54						15 54						16 54						17 54				
Sheffield 7 78 a		15 34						16 34						17 39						18 47				
Manchester Airport 85,84 a	14 52				15 32		15 52			16 30		16 52					17 30		17 57			18 32		

A From Liverpool Lime Street
B To Crewe
C To Wilmslow
D To Norwich
E To Earlestown
F To Nottingham

Table T089-R

Liverpool - Warrington Central - Manchester and Manchester Airport

Mondays to Fridays

16 December to 15 May

	EM ◇ A	NT	NT ◇	NT	EM ◇ B	NT	NT ◇	NT	NT C	EM ◇ B	NT	NT ◇	NT	NT C	NT	NT C	EM ◇ B	NT	NT ◇	NT	NT
Liverpool Lime Street 90,91 d	17 51	17 55	18 16	18 20	18 51	18 55	19 14	19 20	19 28	19 51	19 56	20 13	20 26	20 27	20 55	21 28	21 37	21 55	22 24	22 29	23 38
Edge Hill 90,91 d		17 59				18 59			19 32		20 00			20 31	20 59	21 32		21 59		22 33	23 42
Mossley Hill 91 d		18 04		18 28		19 04		19 28			20 05		20 34		21 04			22 04			23 47
West Allerton 91 d		18 07		18 31		19 07		19 31			20 08		20 37		21 06			22 07			23 50
L'pool Sth Parkway 91,103 d	18 02	18 10	18 26	18 34	19 02	19 10	19 24	19 34		20 02	20 11	20 23	20 40		21 09		21 47	22 10	22 35		23 53
Hunts Cross 103 d		18 13		18 38		19 13					20 14				21 13			22 13			23 56
Halewood d		18 16		18 41		19 16					20 17				21 15			22 16			23 59
Hough Green d		18 20		18 45		19 20		19 41			20 21		20 46		21 19			22 20			00 03
Widnes d	18 10	18 24		18 48	19 10	19 24		19 45		20 10	20 25		20 50		21 23		21 56	22 24			00 07
Sankey for Penketh d																					
Warrington Central a	18 18	18 34	18 44	18 58	19 18	19 34	19 44	19 53		20 18	20 35	20 44	20 58		21 33		22 03	22 34	22 53		00 17
d	18 18	18 35	18 45	18 59	19 18	19 35	19 45	19 55		20 18	20 35	20 45	20 58		21 33		22 04	22 35	22 54		00 18
Padgate d				19 02				19 59			20 39		21 02		21 36			22 38			
Birchwood d		18 39	18 50	19 05		19 39	19 50	20 02			20 42	20 50	21 05		21 39			22 41	22 59		
Glazebrook d				19 10		19 44		20 07					21 10		21 44			22 46			
Irlam d		18 46		19 14		19 48		20 10			20 48		21 14		21 47			22 50			
Flixton d				19 18				20 14					21 18		21 51			22 54			
Chassen Road d				19 20									21 20		21 53			22 56			
Urmston d		18 51		19 22		19 53		20 18			20 53		21 22		21 56			22 58			
Humphrey Park d								20 21							21 58			23 01			
Trafford Park d								20 23							22 01			23 04			
Deansgate 84,85 a				19 32		20 03		20 32	20 23		21 03		21 33	21 22	22 09	22 25		23 12		23 25	
Manchester Oxford Road 84,85 a	18 38	19 02	19 07	19 34	19 38	20 05	20 08	20 35	20 25	20 38	21 05	21 08	21 35	21 24	22 11	22 27	22 24	23 14	23 16	23 27	
ManchesterPicc 84,85 a	18 41		19 11		19 41		20 11		20 28	20 41		21 11		21 28	22 15	22 31	22 27		23 20	23 31	00 38
Stockport 84 a	18 54				19 54					20 52							22 38				
Sheffield 78 a	19 35				20 37					21 35							23 36				
Manchester Airport 85,84 a			19 32				20 30		20 51			21 31		21 57	22 31	22 53			23 35	23 56	

Saturdays

21 December to 16 May

	NT D	NT ◇	NT ◇ E	NT	NT	NT ◇	NT	NT ◇ E	EM ◇ A	NT	NT	NT ◇	NT	NT ◇ E	EM ◇ A	NT	NT ◇	NT	NT ◇ E	EM ◇ A	NT	NT ◇
Liverpool Lime Street 90,91 d		03 37	05 24		05 49	06 13	06 20	06 27	06 47		06 50	07 09	07 19	07 27	07 42	07 45	08 16	08 19	08 27	08 52	08 55	09 16
Edge Hill 90,91 d			05 28		05 53			06 31			06 54		07 23	07 31				08 23	08 31		08 59	
Mossley Hill 91 d					05 58		06 28				06 59		07 28			07 54		08 28			09 04	
West Allerton 91 d					06 01		06 31				07 01		07 31			07 56		08 31			09 07	
L'pool Sth Parkway 91,103 d					06 04	06 24	06 34		06 58		07 04	07 19	07 34		07 52	08 00	08 26	08 34		09 02	09 10	09 26
Hunts Cross 103 d					06 07						07 08				07 59	08 04					09 13	
Halewood d					06 10						07 11					08 07					09 16	
Hough Green d	00 03				06 14		06 40				07 15		07 41			08 11		08 41			09 20	
Widnes d	00 07				06 18		06 44		07 07		07 19	07 28			08 05	08 15		08 44		09 10	09 24	
Sankey for Penketh d																08 20						
Warrington Central a	00 17				06 28	06 38	06 54		07 15		07 29	07 38	07 53		08 13	08 25	08 44	08 54		09 18	09 34	09 44
d	00 18			06 00		06 38	06 54		07 15	07 23		07 39	07 53		08 13	08 26	08 45	08 55		09 18	09 35	09 45
Padgate d				06 03			06 58			07 26			07 57					08 58				
Birchwood d				06 06		06 43	07 01		07 20	07 30		07 44	08 00		08 18	08 31	08 50	09 02			09 39	09 50
Glazebrook d				06 11			07 06			07 35			08 05					09 07				
Irlam d				06 14		06 49	07 09			07 38		07 51	08 09			08 38		09 10			09 46	
Flixton d				06 18			07 13			07 42			08 13			08 42		09 14				
Chassen Road d				06 20			07 15			07 44			08 15			08 44		09 16				
Urmston d				06 22		06 54	07 17			07 47			08 18			08 46		09 18			09 51	
Humphrey Park d				06 25			07 20			07 50			08 21			08 49		09 21				
Trafford Park d				06 28			07 23			07 52			08 24			08 52		09 24				
Deansgate 84,85 a			06 19	06 36			07 31	07 22		08 00			08 32	08 22		09 00		09 32	09 23		10 02	
Manchester Oxford Road 84,85 a			06 21	06 38		07 05	07 33	07 24	07 38	08 02		08 05	08 34	08 24	08 38	09 03	09 07	09 35	09 25	09 38	10 04	10 07
ManchesterPicc 84,85 a	00 38	04 12	06 24			07 08		07 29	07 41					08 28	08 41		09 11		09 28	09 41		10 11
Stockport 84 a									07 55						08 54					09 54		
Sheffield 78 a									08 35						09 34					10 34		
Manchester Airport 85,84 a		04 27	06 47			07 28		07 52						08 52			09 32		09 52			10 32

	NT	NT ◇ E	EM ◇ A	NT	NT ◇	NT	NT ◇ E	EM ◇ A	NT	NT ◇	NT	NT ◇ E	EM ◇ A	NT	NT ◇	NT	NT ◇ E	EM ◇ A	NT	NT ◇	NT	NT ◇ E
Liverpool Lime Street 90,91 d	09 19	09 27	09 51	09 55	10 16	10 20	10 27	10 51	10 55	11 16	11 19	11 27	11 51	11 55	12 16	12 19	12 27	12 51	12 55	13 16	13 19	13 27
Edge Hill 90,91 d		09 31		09 59			10 31		10 59			11 31		11 59			12 31		12 59			13 31
Mossley Hill 91 d	09 28			10 04		10 28			11 04		11 28			12 04		12 28			13 04		13 28	
West Allerton 91 d	09 31			10 07		10 31			11 07		11 31			12 07		12 31			13 07		13 31	
L'pool Sth Parkway 91,103 d	09 34		10 02	10 10	10 26	10 34		11 02	11 10	11 26	11 34		12 02	12 10	12 27	12 34		13 02	13 10	13 26	13 34	
Hunts Cross 103 d				10 13					11 13					12 13					13 13			
Halewood d				10 16					11 16					12 16					13 16			
Hough Green d	09 41			10 20		10 41			11 20		11 41			12 20		12 41			13 20		13 41	
Widnes d	09 45		10 10	10 24		10 45		11 10	11 24		11 45		12 10	12 24		12 45		13 10	13 24		13 45	
Sankey for Penketh d																						
Warrington Central a	09 53		10 18	10 34	10 44	10 53		11 18	11 34	11 44	11 53		12 18	12 34	12 44	12 53		13 18	13 34	13 44	13 53	
d	09 55		10 18	10 35	10 45	10 55		11 18	11 35	11 45	11 55		12 18	12 35	12 45	12 55		13 18	13 35	13 45	13 55	
Padgate d	09 59					10 59					11 59					12 59					13 59	
Birchwood d	10 03			10 39	10 50	11 03			11 39	11 50	12 03			12 39	12 50	13 03			13 39	13 50	14 03	
Glazebrook d						11 08										13 08						
Irlam d	10 09			10 46		11 11			11 46		12 09			12 46		13 11			13 46		14 09	
Flixton d	10 13					11 15					12 13					13 15					14 13	
Chassen Road d						11 17										13 17						
Urmston d	10 17			10 51		11 20			11 51		12 17			12 51		13 20			13 51		14 17	
Humphrey Park d	10 20										12 20										14 20	
Trafford Park d	10 22										12 22										14 22	
Deansgate 84,85 a	10 32	10 22		11 01		11 32	11 22		12 01		12 32	12 22		13 01		13 32	13 22		14 01		14 32	14 22
Manchester Oxford Road 84,85 a	10 35	10 24	10 38	11 03	11 07	11 34	11 24	11 38	12 03	12 07	12 35	12 24	12 38	13 03	13 07	13 35	13 24	13 38	14 03	14 07	14 35	14 24
ManchesterPicc 84,85 a		10 28	10 41		11 11		11 28	11 41		12 11		12 28	12 41		13 11		13 28	13 41		14 11		14 28
Stockport 84 a			10 54					11 54					12 54					13 55				
Sheffield 78 a			11 36					12 35					13 36					14 36				
Manchester Airport 85,84 a		10 52			11 32		11 52			12 32		12 52			13 32		13 52			14 32		14 52

A To Norwich
B To Nottingham
C To Wilmslow
D From Liverpool Lime Street
E To Crewe

Table T089-R

Saturdays

21 December to 16 May

Liverpool - Warrington Central - Manchester and Manchester Airport

	EM ◇ A	NT	NT ◇	NT	NT ◇ B	EM ◇ A	NT	NT ◇	NT	NT ◇ B	EM ◇ A	NT	NT ◇	NT	NT ◇ B	EM ◇ C	NT	NT ◇	NT	NT ◇ B	EM ◇ A
Liverpool Lime Street 90,91 d	13 51	13 55	14 16	14 19	14 27	14 51	14 55	15 16	15 19	15 27	15 51	15 55	16 16	16 19	16 27	16 51	16 55	17 15	17 19	17 28	17 51
Edge Hill 90,91 d		13 59			14 31		14 59			15 31		15 59			16 31		16 59			17 32	
Mossley Hill 91 d		14 04		14 28			15 04		15 28			16 04		16 28			17 04		17 27		
West Allerton 91 d		14 07		14 31			15 07		15 31			16 07		16 31			17 07		17 30		
L'pool Sth Parkway 91,103 d	14 02	14 10	14 26	14 34		15 02	15 10	15 26	15 34		16 02	16 10	16 26	16 34		17 02	17 10	17 26	17 33		18 02
Hunts Cross 103 d		14 13					15 13					16 14					17 13		17 36		
Halewood d		14 16					15 16					16 17					17 16		17 39		
Hough Green d		14 20		14 41			15 20		15 41			16 21		16 41			17 20		17 44		
Widnes d	14 10	14 24		14 45		15 10	15 24		15 45		16 10	16 25		16 45		17 10	17 24		17 47		18 10
Sankey for Penketh d																			17 52		
Warrington Central a	14 18	14 34	14 44	14 53		15 18	15 34	15 44	15 53		16 18	16 35	16 44	16 53		17 18	17 34	17 43	17 57		18 18
d	14 18	14 35	14 45	14 55		15 18	15 35	15 45	15 55		16 18	16 35	16 45	16 56		17 18	17 35	17 44	17 59		18 18
Padgate d				14 59					15 59					17 00					18 02		
Birchwood d		14 39	14 50	15 03			15 39	15 50	16 03			16 40	16 50	17 04			17 39	17 49	18 05		
Glazebrook d				15 08										17 09							
Irlam d		14 46		15 11			15 46		16 09			16 46		17 12			17 46		18 11		
Flixton d				15 15					16 13					17 16					18 15		
Chassen Road d				15 17										17 18							
Urmston d		14 51		15 20			15 51		16 17			16 51		17 21			17 51		18 19		
Humphrey Park d									16 20										18 22		
Trafford Park d									16 22										18 24		
Deansgate 84,85 a		15 01		15 32	15 22		16 01		16 32	16 22		17 01		17 32	17 22		18 01		18 32	18 23	
Manchester Oxford Road 84,85 a	14 38	15 03	15 07	15 35	15 24	15 38	16 03	16 07	16 35	16 24	16 38	17 03	17 08	17 35	17 24	17 38	18 03	18 08	18 35	18 25	18 38
ManchesterPicc 84,85 a	14 41		15 11		15 28	15 41		16 11		16 28	16 41		17 11		17 28	17 41		18 11		18 29	18 41
Stockport 84 a	14 55					15 55					16 55					17 55					18 55
Sheffield 78 a	15 36					16 35					17 37					18 37					19 35
Manchester Airport 85,84 a			15 32		15 52			16 32		16 52			17 32		17 52			18 32		18 52	

	NT	NT ◇	NT	NT ◇ D	EM ◇ C	NT	NT ◇	NT	NT E	EM ◇ C	NT	NT ◇	NT	NT E	EM ◇ C	NT	NT ◇	NT E	EM ◇ C	NT	NT ◇	NT
Liverpool Lime Street 90,91 d	17 55	18 15	18 20	18 29	18 51	18 55	19 14	19 20	19 28	19 52	19 56	20 12	20 26	20 27	20 49	20 56	21 29	21 29	21 37	21 55	22 24	22 29
Edge Hill 90,91 d	17 59			18 33		18 59			19 32		20 00			20 31		21 00		21 33		21 59		22 33
Mossley Hill 91 d	18 04		18 28			19 04		19 28			20 05		20 34			21 05				22 04		
West Allerton 91 d	18 07		18 31			19 07		19 31			20 08		20 37			21 07				22 07		
L'pool Sth Parkway 91,103 d	18 10	18 26	18 34		19 02	19 10	19 24	19 34		20 02	20 11	20 23	20 40		21 00	21 10	21 40		21 47	22 10	22 35	
Hunts Cross 103 d	18 13		18 38			19 13					20 14					21 15				22 13		
Halewood d	18 16		18 41			19 16					20 17					21 17				22 16		
Hough Green d	18 20		18 45			19 20		19 41			20 21		20 46			21 21				22 20		
Widnes d	18 24		18 48		19 10	19 24		19 45		20 10	20 25		20 50		21 08	21 25			21 56	22 24		
Sankey for Penketh d																						
Warrington Central a	18 34	18 44	18 58		19 18	19 34	19 44	19 53		20 18	20 35	20 44	20 58		21 16	21 35	21 57		22 03	22 34	22 53	
d	18 35	18 45	18 59		19 18	19 35	19 45	19 55		20 18	20 35	20 45	20 58		21 16	21 35	21 58		22 04	22 35	22 54	
Padgate d			19 02					19 59			20 39		21 02			21 38				22 38		
Birchwood d	18 39	18 50	19 05			19 39	19 50	20 02			20 42	20 50	21 05			21 41	22 03			22 41	22 59	
Glazebrook d			19 10			19 44		20 07					21 10			21 46				22 46		
Irlam d	18 46		19 14			19 48		20 10			20 48		21 14			21 50				22 50		
Flixton d			19 18					20 14					21 18			21 54				22 54		
Chassen Road d			19 20										21 20			21 56				22 56		
Urmston d	18 51		19 22			19 53		20 18			20 53		21 22			21 58				22 58		
Humphrey Park d								20 21								22 01				23 01		
Trafford Park d								20 23								22 04				23 04		
Deansgate 84,85 a			19 32	19 25		20 03		20 32	20 23		21 03		21 32	21 22		22 12		22 25		23 12		23 25
Manchester Oxford Road 84,85 a	19 02	19 07	19 34	19 27	19 38	20 05	20 07	20 35	20 25	20 38	21 05	21 08	21 34	21 24	21 37	22 14	22 20	22 27	22 25	23 14	23 16	23 27
ManchesterPicc 84,85 a		19 11		19 30	19 41		20 11		20 28	20 41		21 11		21 28	21 40		22 24	22 32	22 28		23 20	23 32
Stockport 84 a					19 54					20 54					21 51				22 38			
Sheffield 78 a					20 35					21 34					22 31				23 35			
Manchester Airport 85,84 a		19 32		19 57			20 30		20 57			21 31		21 57			22 40	22 56			23 38	23 56

	NT
Liverpool Lime Street 90,91 d	23 38
Edge Hill 90,91 d	23 42
Mossley Hill 91 d	23 47
West Allerton 91 d	23 50
L'pool Sth Parkway 91,103 d	23 53
Hunts Cross 103 d	23 56
Halewood d	23 59
Hough Green d	00 03
Widnes d	00 07
Sankey for Penketh d	
Warrington Central a	00 17
d	00 18
Padgate d	
Birchwood d	
Glazebrook d	
Irlam d	
Flixton d	
Chassen Road d	
Urmston d	
Humphrey Park d	
Trafford Park d	
Deansgate 84,85 a	
Manchester Oxford Road 84,85 a	
ManchesterPicc 84,85 a	00 38
Stockport 84 a	
Sheffield 78 a	
Manchester Airport 85,84 a	

A To Norwich
B To Crewe
C To Nottingham
D To Wilmslow. ◇ from ManchesterPicc
E To Wilmslow

Table T089-R

Sundays

15 December to 10 May

Liverpool - Warrington Central - Manchester and Manchester Airport

Station		NT A	NT B	NT ◇	NT	NT ◇	NT	NT C	NT D	NT ◇	NT	NT B	NT ◇ E	NT ◇ F	NT	NT B	NT ◇ F	NT ◇ E	NT	NT B	EM ◇ G	NT ◇	NT
Liverpool Lime Street 10 90,91	d		08 15	08 21	08 25	09 16	09 26	09 30	09 30	10 16	10 27	10 31	11 16	11 16	11 26	11 29	12 16	12 16	12 25	12 30	12 52	13 16	13 26
Edge Hill 90,91	d																						
Mossley Hill 91	d				08 33		09 34				10 35				11 34				12 33				13 34
West Allerton 91	d				08 35		09 36				10 37				11 36				12 35				13 36
L'pool Sth Parkway 7 91,103	d			08 31	08 40	09 26	09 40			10 26	10 41		11 26	11 26	11 40		12 26	12 26	12 39		13 03	13 26	13 40
Hunts Cross 103	d				08 43		09 43				10 44				11 43				12 43				13 43
Halewood	d				08 46		09 46				10 47				11 46				12 46				13 46
Hough Green	d	00 03			08 50		09 50				10 51				11 50				12 50				13 50
Widnes	d	00 07			08 54		09 53				10 55				11 54				12 54		13 11		13 54
Sankey for Penketh	d																						
Warrington Central	a	00 17		08 45	09 04	09 43	10 03			10 43	11 05		11 43	11 43	12 04		12 43	12 43	13 04		13 18	13 43	14 04
	d	00 18		08 46	09 05	09 44	10 04			10 44	11 05		11 44	11 44	12 04		12 44	12 44	13 04		13 19	13 44	14 04
Padgate	d																						
Birchwood	d			08 50	09 09	09 49	10 08			10 49	11 10		11 48	11 48	12 09		12 48	12 48	13 09			13 49	14 09
Glazebrook	d																						
Irlam	d				09 15		10 14				11 16				12 15				13 15				14 15
Flixton	d				09 19		10 18				11 20				12 19				13 19				14 19
Chassen Road	d																						
Urmston	d				09 22		10 21				11 23				12 22				13 22				14 22
Humphrey Park	d																						
Trafford Park	d																						
Deansgate 84,85	a				09 32		10 31	10 24	10 25		11 35	11 23			12 33	12 22			13 33	13 23			14 34
Manchester Oxford Road 84,85	a		09 12	09 07	09 34	10 06	10 33	10 26	10 27	11 06	11 37	11 25	12 05	12 05	12 35	12 24	13 07	13 07	13 35	13 25	13 39	14 07	14 36
ManchesterPicc 10 84,85	a	00 38	09 15	09 11		10 11		10 29	10 31	11 10		11 29		12 09		12 28	13 11	13 11		13 29	13 41	14 11	
Stockport 84	a																				13 51		
Sheffield 7 78	a																				14 37		
Manchester Airport 85,84	a		09 39	09 28		10 31		11 02	11 02	11 28		11 57		12 26		12 52	13 27	13 28		13 52		14 27	

Station		NT B	EM ◇ G	NT ◇	NT	NT B	EM ◇ G	NT ◇	NT	NT B	EM ◇ G	NT ◇	NT	NT B	EM ◇ H	NT ◇	NT	NT B	EM ◇ G	NT ◇	NT	NT B	EM ◇ H
Liverpool Lime Street 10 90,91	d	13 29	13 52	14 16	14 25	14 29	14 52	15 16	15 26	15 29	15 52	16 14	16 25	16 29	16 52	17 16	17 26	17 29	17 52	18 16	18 25	18 29	18 52
Edge Hill 90,91	d																						
Mossley Hill 91	d				14 33				15 34				16 33				17 34				18 33		
West Allerton 91	d				14 35				15 36				16 35				17 36				18 35		
L'pool Sth Parkway 7 91,103	d		14 03	14 26	14 39		15 03	15 26	15 40		16 03	16 24	16 39		17 03	17 26	17 40		18 03	18 26	18 39		19 03
Hunts Cross 103	d				14 43				15 43				16 43				17 43				18 43		
Halewood	d				14 46				15 46				16 46				17 46				18 46		
Hough Green	d				14 50				15 50				16 50				17 50				18 50		
Widnes	d		14 11		14 54		15 11		15 54		16 11		16 54		17 11		17 54		18 11		18 54		19 11
Sankey for Penketh	d																						
Warrington Central	a		14 19	14 43	15 04		15 18	15 43	16 04		16 19	16 43	17 04		17 18	17 43	18 04		18 19	18 43	19 04		19 19
	d		14 19	14 44	15 04		15 19	15 44	16 04		16 19	16 44	17 04		17 19	17 44	18 04		18 19	18 44	19 04		19 19
Padgate	d																						
Birchwood	d			14 49	15 09			15 49	16 09			16 49	17 09			17 49	18 09			18 49	19 09		
Glazebrook	d																						
Irlam	d				15 15				16 15				17 15				18 15				19 15		
Flixton	d				15 19				16 19				17 19				18 19				19 19		
Chassen Road	d																						
Urmston	d				15 22				16 22				17 22				18 22				19 22		
Humphrey Park	d																						
Trafford Park	d																						
Deansgate 84,85	a	14 24			15 33	15 22			16 34	16 23			17 33	17 23			18 34	18 23			19 34	19 23	
Manchester Oxford Road 84,85	a	14 27	14 39	15 07	15 35	15 24	15 39	16 07	16 36	16 25	16 39	17 07	17 35	17 25	17 39	18 07	18 36	18 25	18 39	19 07	19 36	19 25	19 39
ManchesterPicc 10 84,85	a	14 30	14 42	15 11		15 28	15 41	16 11		16 29	16 42	17 11		17 28	17 41	18 11		18 29	18 42	19 11		19 29	19 42
Stockport 84	a		14 51				15 52				16 52				17 52				18 52				19 51
Sheffield 7 78	a		15 34				16 38				17 35				18 36				19 35				20 35
Manchester Airport 85,84	a	15 03		15 27		15 51		16 27		16 52		17 27		17 52		18 27		18 52		19 27		19 52	

Station		NT ◇	NT	NT B	EM ◇ H	NT ◇	NT	NT B	EM ◇ H	NT ◇	NT	NT B	NT ◇	NT	NT B	NT
Liverpool Lime Street 10 90,91	d	19 16	19 25	19 29	19 52	20 16	20 26	20 29	21 16	21 19	21 26	21 29	22 16	22 26	22 29	23 30
Edge Hill 90,91	d															
Mossley Hill 91	d		19 33				20 34				21 34			22 34		
West Allerton 91	d		19 35				20 36				21 36			22 36		
L'pool Sth Parkway 7 91,103	d	19 26	19 39		20 03	20 26	20 40		21 26	21 30	21 40		22 26	22 40		
Hunts Cross 103	d		19 43				20 43				21 43			22 43		
Halewood	d		19 46				20 46				21 46			22 46		
Hough Green	d		19 50				20 50				21 50			22 50		
Widnes	d		19 54		20 11		20 54		21 35		21 53			22 54		
Sankey for Penketh	d															
Warrington Central	a	19 43	20 04		20 19	20 43	21 04		21 42	21 48	22 03		22 44	23 04		
	d	19 44	20 04		20 19	20 44	21 04		21 43	21 49	22 04		22 45	23 04		
Padgate	d															
Birchwood	d	19 49	20 09			20 49	21 09			21 53	22 08		22 50	23 09		
Glazebrook	d															
Irlam	d		20 15				21 15				22 14			23 15		
Flixton	d		20 19				21 19				22 18			23 19		
Chassen Road	d															
Urmston	d		20 22				21 22				22 21			23 22		
Humphrey Park	d															
Trafford Park	d															
Deansgate 84,85	a		20 34	20 23			21 35	21 23			22 31	22 25		23 33	23 22	00 25
Manchester Oxford Road 84,85	a	20 06	20 36	20 25	20 39	21 07	21 37	21 25	22 07	22 11	22 33	22 27	23 08	23 35	23 24	00 27
ManchesterPicc 10 84,85	a	20 10		20 28	20 42	21 11		21 28	22 10	22 15		22 31	23 13		23 28	00 35
Stockport 84	a				20 52				22 22							
Sheffield 7 78	a				21 34				23 26							
Manchester Airport 85,84	a	20 29		20 52		21 26		21 52		22 30		22 53	23 30		23 51	00 57

A not 15 December. From Liverpool Lime Street
B To Wilmslow
C until 29 March. To Wilmslow
D from 5 April. To Wilmslow
E until 29 March
F from 5 April
G To Norwich
H To Nottingham

NRT DECEMBER 19 EDITION

Table T090-F

Mondays to Fridays

16 December to 15 May

Manchester Airport, Manchester, Preston, Wigan and Newton-le-Willows - St Helens and Liverpool

Miles	Miles	Miles	Miles	Station		NT	NT ◇	NT A	NT ◇	NT ■ B	NT ◇ B	NT ◇ B	NT ◇	NT ◇ B	NT ◇	NT ◇ B	NT ◇	NT ◇ B	NT ◇	NT ◇ B	NT ◇	NT ◇ B	NT ◇
—	—	—	0	**Manchester Airport** 85	d	05 07	05 51	05 59	06 50	06 58	07 59	08 59	09 48	09 59	10 49	10 59	11 49	11 59	12 49	12 59	13 49	13 59	14 49
—	—	—	9¾	**Manchester Piccadilly** 10	d	05 22	06 09	06 22	07 09	07 22	08 23	09 22	10 09	10 22	11 09	11 22	12 09	12 22	13 09	13 22	14 09	14 22	15 09
—	—	—	10½	**Manchester Oxford Road**	d	05 27	06 13	06 25	07 12	07 25	08 26	09 26	10 13	10 25	11 13	11 26	12 12	12 26	13 12	13 26	14 13	14 26	15 13
0	—	—	—	**Manchester Victoria**	d																		
4	—	—	14½	Eccles	d	05 35		06 35		07 34	08 35	09 35		10 34		11 34		12 34		13 35		14 34	
5	—	—	15½	Patricroft	d	05 37		06 37		07 37	08 37	09 37		10 37		11 37		12 36		13 38		14 36	
—	—	—	—	Blackpool North 97	d																		
—	0	0	—	**Preston** 8 65,82	d																		
—	4	4	—	Leyland 82	d																		
—	6¾	6¾	—	Euxton Balshaw Lane	d																		
—	15	15	—	**Wigan North Western** 65	a																		
—	—	—	—		d																		
15½	—	22	26	**Newton-le-Willows**	d	05 48		06 48		07 48	08 48	09 48		10 47		11 47		12 47		13 48		14 47	
—	—	—	—	Warrington Bank Quay	d																		
17	—	23½	27½	Earlestown 8	d	05 50		06 50		07 50	08 50	09 51		10 50		11 50		12 49		13 51		14 49	
—	—	—	—	Warrington Bank Quay	a																		
19¾	—	26¼	30¼	**St Helens Junction**	d	05 55		06 54		07 55	08 54	09 55		10 54		11 54		12 53		13 55		14 53	
21	—	27½	31½	Lea Green	d	05 58		06 57		07 58	08 57	09 58		10 57		11 57		12 56		13 58		14 56	
22¾	—	29¼	33¼	Rainhill	d	06 02		07 01		08 02	09 01	10 01		11 00		12 00		13 00		14 01		15 00	
24¼	—	30¾	34¾	Whiston	d	06 05		07 04		08 06	09 04	10 04		11 03		12 03		13 03		14 04		15 03	
—	18¾	—	—	Bryn	d																		
—	20	—	—	Garswood	d																		
—	23¾	—	—	**St Helens Central**	a																		
—	—	—	—		d																		
—	25¼	—	—	Thatto Heath	d																		
—	26¼	—	—	Eccleston Park	d																		
—	27¼	—	—	Prescot	d																		
26¼	29½	32¾	36¾	Huyton	d	06 09		07 08		08 11	09 10	10 10		11 09		12 09		13 09		14 10		15 09	
26¾	30	33¼	37¼	Roby	d	06 11		07 10			09 12	10 12		11 15		12 11		13 11		14 15		15 11	
28¼	31½	34¾	38¾	Broad Green	d	06 14		07 13			09 15	10 15		11 18		12 14		13 14		14 18		15 14	
29¼	32½	35¾	39¾	Wavertree Technology Park	d	06 17		07 16		08 17	09 18	10 18		11 21		12 17		13 17		14 21		15 17	
30	33¼	36½	40½	Edge Hill 91	d	06 22		07 19		08 20	09 21	10 21		11 24		12 20		13 20		14 24		15 20	
31¼	35	38¼	42¼	**Liverpool Lime Street** 10 91	a	06 29	07 03	07 25	08 01	08 25	09 25	10 28	11 03	11 28	12 03	12 24	13 02	13 24	14 01	14 28	15 02	15 24	16 03

Station		NT ◇ B	NT ◇	NT ◇ B	NT ◇	NT ◇ B	NT ◇	NT ◇	NT ◇	NT ◇ B	NT ◇	NT A	NT ◇	NT A	NT ◇	NT A
Manchester Airport 85	d	14 59	15 49	15 59	16 48	16 59	17 48	18 49	19 50	19 59	20 47	20 58	21 48	21 59	22 49	23 01
Manchester Piccadilly 10	d	15 22	16 09	16 22	17 10	17 23	18 09	19 09	20 09	20 22	21 11	21 18	22 08	22 18	23 09	23 22
Manchester Oxford Road	d	15 26	16 12	16 26	17 13	17 26	18 13	19 12	20 12	20 26	21 14	21 27	22 11	22 31	23 13	23 25
Manchester Victoria	d															
Eccles	d	15 34		16 34		17 35				20 35		21 36		22 41		23 35
Patricroft	d	15 36		16 36		17 37				20 37		21 38		22 44		23 37
Blackpool North 97	d															
Preston 8 65,82	d															
Leyland 82	d															
Euxton Balshaw Lane	d															
Wigan North Western 65	a															
	d															
Newton-le-Willows	d	15 47		16 47		17 48				20 48		21 49		22 56		23 48
Warrington Bank Quay	d															
Earlestown 8	d	15 49		16 49		17 50				20 50		21 51		22 59		23 50
Warrington Bank Quay	a															
St Helens Junction	d	15 53		16 53		17 55				20 54		21 55		23 03		23 55
Lea Green	d	15 56		16 56		17 58				20 57		21 58		23 06		23 58
Rainhill	d	16 00		17 00		18 02				21 01		22 02		23 09		00 02
Whiston	d	16 03		17 03		18 06				21 04		22 05		23 12		00 05
Bryn	d															
Garswood	d															
St Helens Central	a															
	d															
Thatto Heath	d															
Eccleston Park	d															
Prescot	d															
Huyton	d	16 09		17 07		18 13				21 08		22 08		23 16		00 09
Roby	d	16 13		17 09		18 15				21 10		22 10		23 18		00 11
Broad Green	d	16 16		17 12		18 18				21 15		22 13		23 21		00 14
Wavertree Technology Park	d	16 19		17 15		18 21				21 18		22 16		23 24		00 17
Edge Hill 91	d	16 22		17 18		18 24				21 22		22 19		23 27		00 20
Liverpool Lime Street 10 91	a	16 26	17 04	17 23	18 05	18 28	19 03	20 05	21 05	21 27	22 05	22 26	23 05	23 33	00 05	00 26

A From Wilmslow
B From Crewe

Table T090-F

Saturdays
21 December to 16 May

Manchester Airport, Manchester, Preston, Wigan and Newton-le-Willows - St Helens and Liverpool

	NT	NT	NT	NT	NT	NT	NT	NT	NT	NT	NT
		◇	A	◇	◇ B	◇	◇ B	◇ B	◇	◇ B	◇
Manchester Airport 85 d	05 07	05 51	05 59	06 50	06 58	07 48	07 59	08 59	09 49	09 59	10 49
Manchester Piccadilly d	05 22	06 09	06 22	07 09	07 22	08 09	08 23	09 22	10 09	10 22	11 09
Manchester Oxford Road d	05 27	06 13	06 25	07 12	07 25	08 12	08 26	09 26	10 13	10 25	11 13
Manchester Victoria d											
Eccles d	05 35		06 35		07 36		08 35	09 35		10 34	
Patricroft d	05 37		06 37		07 38		08 37	09 37		10 37	
Blackpool North 97 d											
Preston 65,82 d											
Leyland 82 d											
Euxton Balshaw Lane d											
Wigan North Western 65 a											
d											
Newton-le-Willows d	05 48		06 48		07 49		08 48	09 48		10 47	
Warrington Bank Quay d											
Earlestown d	05 50		06 50		07 51		08 50	09 51		10 50	
Warrington Bank Quay a											
St Helens Junction d	05 55		06 54		07 55		08 54	09 55		10 54	
Lea Green d	05 58		06 57		07 58		08 57	09 58		10 57	
Rainhill d	06 02		07 01		08 02		09 01	10 01		11 00	
Whiston d	06 05		07 04		08 05		09 04	10 04		11 03	
Bryn d											
Garswood d											
St Helens Central a											
d											
Thatto Heath d											
Eccleston Park d											
Prescot d											
Huyton d	06 09		07 08		08 09		09 10	10 10		11 09	
Roby d	06 11		07 10				09 12	10 12		11 15	
Broad Green d	06 14		07 13				09 15	10 15		11 18	
Wavertree Technology Park d	06 17		07 16		08 15		09 18	10 18		11 21	
Edge Hill 91 d	06 22		07 19		08 18		09 21	10 21		11 24	
Liverpool Lime Street 91 a	06 29	07 03	07 25	08 01	08 23	09 07	09 25	10 28	11 04	11 28	12 04

	NT	NT	NT	NT	NT	NT	NT	NT	NT	NT	NT
	◇ B	◇	◇ B	◇	◇ B	◇	◇ B	◇	◇ B	◇	◇ B
Manchester Airport 85 d	10 59	11 49	11 59	12 49	12 59	13 49	13 59	14 49	14 59	15 49	15 59
Manchester Piccadilly d	11 22	12 09	12 22	13 09	13 22	14 09	14 22	15 09	15 22	16 09	16 22
Manchester Oxford Road d	11 26	12 12	12 26	13 12	13 26	14 13	14 26	15 13	15 26	16 12	16 26
Manchester Victoria d											
Eccles d	11 34		12 34		13 35		14 34		15 34		16 34
Patricroft d	11 37		12 36		13 38		14 36		15 36		16 36
Blackpool North 97 d											
Preston 65,82 d											
Leyland 82 d											
Euxton Balshaw Lane d											
Wigan North Western 65 a											
d											
Newton-le-Willows d	11 47		12 47		13 48		14 47		15 47		16 47
Warrington Bank Quay d											
Earlestown d	11 50		12 49		13 51		14 49		15 49		16 49
Warrington Bank Quay a											
St Helens Junction d	11 54		12 53		13 55		14 53		15 53		16 53
Lea Green d	11 57		12 56		13 58		14 56		15 56		16 56
Rainhill d	12 00		13 00		14 01		15 00		16 00		17 00
Whiston d	12 03		13 03		14 04		15 03		16 03		17 03
Bryn d											
Garswood d											
St Helens Central a											
d											
Thatto Heath d											
Eccleston Park d											
Prescot d											
Huyton d	12 09		13 09		14 10		15 09		16 09		17 07
Roby d	12 11		13 11		14 15		15 11		16 13		17 09
Broad Green d	12 14		13 14		14 18		15 14		16 16		17 12
Wavertree Technology Park d	12 17		13 17		14 21		15 17		16 19		17 15
Edge Hill 91 d	12 20		13 20		14 24		15 20		16 22		17 18
Liverpool Lime Street 91 a	12 24	13 04	13 24	14 03	14 29	15 05	15 24	16 03	16 26	17 04	17 23

	NT	NT	NT	NT	NT	NT	NT	NT	NT	NT	NT	NT	NT	NT
	◇	◇ B	◇	◇ B	◇	◇ B	◇	◇ B	◇	A	◇	A	◇	A
Manchester Airport 85 d	16 49	16 59	17 49	17 59	18 49	18 59	19 50	19 59	20 49	20 58	21 48	21 59	22 49	22 59
Manchester Piccadilly d	17 09	17 23	18 09	18 22	19 09	19 22	20 09	20 22	21 11	21 17	22 08	22 18	23 09	23 22
Manchester Oxford Road d	17 12	17 26	18 13	18 26	19 12	19 26	20 12	20 26	21 14	21 27	22 11	22 31	23 12	23 25
Manchester Victoria d														
Eccles d		17 35		18 35		19 35		20 35		21 35		22 40		23 34
Patricroft d		17 37		18 37		19 37		20 37		21 37		22 42		23 37
Blackpool North 97 d														
Preston 65,82 d														
Leyland 82 d														
Euxton Balshaw Lane d														
Wigan North Western 65 a														
d														
Newton-le-Willows d		17 48		18 48		19 48		20 48		21 48		22 53		23 47
Warrington Bank Quay d														
Earlestown d		17 50		18 50		19 50		20 50		21 50		22 55		23 50
Warrington Bank Quay a														
St Helens Junction d		17 55		18 54		19 54		20 54		21 54		22 59		23 54
Lea Green d		17 58		18 57		19 57		20 57		21 57		23 02		23 57
Rainhill d		18 02		19 01		20 01		21 01		22 01		23 06		00 01
Whiston d		18 06		19 04		20 04		21 04		22 04		23 09		00 04
Bryn d														
Garswood d														
St Helens Central a														
d														
Thatto Heath d														
Eccleston Park d														
Prescot d														
Huyton d		18 13		19 09		20 11		21 08		22 08		23 13		00 08
Roby d		18 15		19 11		20 13		21 10		22 10		23 15		00 10
Broad Green d		18 18		19 14		20 16		21 15		22 13		23 18		00 13
Wavertree Technology Park d		18 21		19 18		20 19		21 18		22 16		23 21		00 16
Edge Hill 91 d		18 24		19 21		20 22		21 21		22 19		23 24		00 19
Liverpool Lime Street 91 a	18 05	18 28	19 04	19 25	20 05	20 29	21 04	21 25	22 07	22 23	23 05	23 29	00 05	00 26

A From Wilmslow
B From Crewe

Table T090-F

Sundays
15 December to 10 May

Manchester Airport, Manchester, Preston, Wigan and Newton-le-Willows - St Helens and Liverpool

	NT	NT	NT	NT	NT	NT	NT	NT	NT	NT	NT
	A	B	B	◇	B	◇	B	◇ A	B	◇	B
Manchester Airport 85 d	08 01	08 54	09 59	10 52	10 58	11 53	11 59	12 48	12 59	13 53	13 59
Manchester Piccadilly d	08 24	09 18	10 22	11 11	11 21	12 09	12 22	13 07	13 22	14 10	14 22
Manchester Oxford Road d	08 27	09 21	10 25	11 14	11 24	12 12	12 26	13 10	13 26	14 13	14 26
Manchester Victoria d											
Eccles d	08 35	09 32	10 35		11 35		12 35		13 36		14 36
Patricroft d	08 37	09 34	10 38		11 38		12 38		13 38		14 38
Blackpool North 97 d											
Preston 65,82 d											
Leyland 82 d											
Euxton Balshaw Lane d											
Wigan North Western 65 a											
d											
Newton-le-Willows d	08 48	09 45	10 48		11 48		12 48		13 49		14 49
Warrington Bank Quay d											
Earlestown d	08 50	09 47	10 51		11 51		12 51		13 51		14 51
Warrington Bank Quay a											
St Helens Junction d	08 54	09 51	10 55		11 55		12 55		13 55		14 55
Lea Green d	08 57	09 54	10 58		11 58		12 58		13 58		14 58
Rainhill d	09 01	09 58	11 01		12 01		13 01		14 02		15 02
Whiston d	09 04	10 01	11 04		12 04		13 04		14 05		15 05
Bryn d											
Garswood d											
St Helens Central a											
d											
Thatto Heath d											
Eccleston Park d											
Prescot d											
Huyton d	09 13	10 05	11 08		12 08		13 08		14 09		15 09
Roby d	09 15	10 07	11 10		12 10		13 10		14 11		15 11
Broad Green d	09 18	10 10	11 13		12 13		13 13		14 14		15 14
Wavertree Technology Park d	09 21	10 13	11 16		12 16		13 16		14 17		15 17
Edge Hill 91 d											
Liverpool Lime Street 91 a	09 31	10 24	11 25	12 04	12 25	13 02	13 25	14 00	14 25	15 03	15 25

	NT	NT	NT	NT	NT	NT	NT	NT	NT	NT	NT
	◇	B	◇	B	◇	B	◇	B	◇	B	◇
Manchester Airport 85 d	14 53	14 59	15 53	15 59	16 53	16 59	17 53	17 59	18 53	18 59	19 52
Manchester Piccadilly d	15 09	15 22	16 09	16 22	17 09	17 22	18 11	18 22	19 09	19 22	20 07
Manchester Oxford Road d	15 13	15 26	16 13	16 26	17 13	17 26	18 15	18 26	19 13	19 26	20 11
Manchester Victoria d											
Eccles d		15 36		16 34		17 36		18 35		19 35	
Patricroft d		15 38		16 36		17 38		18 38		19 38	
Blackpool North 97 d											
Preston 65,82 d											
Leyland 82 d											
Euxton Balshaw Lane d											
Wigan North Western 65 a											
d											
Newton-le-Willows d		15 49		16 47		17 49		18 48		19 48	
Warrington Bank Quay d											
Earlestown d		15 51		16 49		17 51		18 51		19 51	
Warrington Bank Quay a											
St Helens Junction d		15 55		16 53		17 55		18 55		19 55	
Lea Green d		15 58		16 56		17 58		18 58		19 58	
Rainhill d		16 02		17 00		18 02		19 01		20 01	
Whiston d		16 05		17 03		18 05		19 04		20 04	
Bryn d											
Garswood d											
St Helens Central a											
d											
Thatto Heath d											
Eccleston Park d											
Prescot d											
Huyton d		16 09		17 07		18 09		19 08		20 08	
Roby d		16 11		17 09		18 11		19 10		20 10	
Broad Green d		16 14		17 12		18 14		19 13		20 13	
Wavertree Technology Park d		16 17		17 15		18 17		19 16		20 16	
Edge Hill 91 d											
Liverpool Lime Street 91 a	16 02	16 25	17 02	17 23	18 02	18 25	19 04	19 25	20 02	20 25	21 00

	NT	NT	NT	NT	NT	NT	NT
	B	◇	B	◇	B	◇	B
Manchester Airport 85 d	19 59	20 51	20 59	21 53	21 59	22 52	23 09
Manchester Piccadilly d	20 22	21 09	21 18	22 09	22 19	23 09	23 33
Manchester Oxford Road d	20 26	21 12	21 27	22 13	22 29	23 13	23 36
Manchester Victoria d							
Eccles d	20 34		21 35		22 37		23 43
Patricroft d	20 36		21 37		22 40		23 46
Blackpool North 97 d							
Preston 65,82 d							
Leyland 82 d							
Euxton Balshaw Lane d							
Wigan North Western 65 a							
d							
Newton-le-Willows d	20 47		21 48		22 50		23 56
Warrington Bank Quay d							
Earlestown d	20 49		21 50		22 53		23 59
Warrington Bank Quay a							
St Helens Junction d	20 53		21 54		22 57		00 03
Lea Green d	20 56		21 57		23 00		00 06
Rainhill d	21 00		22 01		23 03		00 09
Whiston d	21 03		22 04		23 06		00 12
Bryn d							
Garswood d							
St Helens Central a							
d							
Thatto Heath d							
Eccleston Park d							
Prescot d							
Huyton d	21 07		22 08		23 10		00 16
Roby d	21 09		22 11		23 12		00 18
Broad Green d	21 12		22 14		23 15		00 21
Wavertree Technology Park d	21 15		22 17		23 19		00 24
Edge Hill 91 d							
Liverpool Lime Street 91 a	21 23	22 02	22 24	23 02	23 27	00 05	00 35

A from 5 April
B From Wilmslow

Table T090-R

Mondays to Fridays
16 December to 15 May

Liverpool and St Helens - Newton-le-Willows, Wigan, Preston, Manchester and Manchester Airport

Miles	Miles	Miles	Miles			NT	NT	NT	NT	NT	NT	NT	NT	NT	NT	NT	NT	NT	NT	NT	NT	NT	NT
						MX	◇	◇	◇	◇	◇	◇	◇	◇	◇	◇	◇	◇	◇	◇	◇	◇	◇
						A		B	C	B	B	C		B		D	B		C	B		C	B
0	0	0	—	Liverpool Lime Street 91	d		03 37	05 24		06 27	07 27		08 16	08 27	09 16		09 27	10 16		10 27	11 16		11 27
1¼	1¼	1¼	—	Edge Hill 91	d			05 28		06 31	07 31			08 31			09 31			10 31			11 31
2½	2½	2½	—	Wavertree Technology Park	d			05 30		06 33	07 33			08 33			09 33			10 33			11 33
3½	3½	3½	—	Broad Green	d			05 33		06 36	07 36			08 37			09 36			10 36			11 36
5	5	5	—	Roby	d			05 36		06 39	07 39			08 40			09 39			10 39			11 39
5½	5½	5½	—	Huyton	d			05 38		06 41	07 41			08 42			09 41			10 41			11 41
—	7¾	—	—	Prescot	d																		
—	8¾	—	—	Eccleston Park	d																		
—	9¾	—	—	Thatto Heath	d																		
—	11¼	—	—	St Helens Central	a																		
—	—	—	—		d																		
—	15	—	—	Garswood	d																		
—	16¼	—	—	Bryn	d																		
7½	—	7½	—	Whiston	d			05 42		06 45	07 45			08 46			09 45			10 45			11 45
9	—	9	—	Rainhill	d			05 45		06 48	07 48			08 49			09 48			10 48			11 48
10¾	—	10¾	—	Lea Green	d			05 48		06 51	07 51			08 52			09 51			10 51			11 51
12	—	12	—	St Helens Junction	d			05 51		06 54	07 54			08 56			09 54			10 54			11 54
—	—	—	—	Warrington Bank Quay	d																		
14¾	—	14¾	—	Earlestown	d			05 55		06 58	07 58			09 00			09 58			10 58			11 58
—	—	—	—	Warrington Bank Quay	a																		
16¼	—	16¼	0	Newton-le-Willows	d			05 58		07 01	08 01			09 02			10 01			11 01			12 01
—	20	23¼	—	Wigan North Western 65,82	a																		
—	—	—	—		d	00 04			06 15			08 16				09 19			10 20			11 21	
—	28¼	31½	—	Euxton Balshaw Lane	d	00 13																	
—	31	34¼	—	Leyland 82	d	00 17																	
—	35	38¼	—	Preston 65,82	d	00a25			06a31			08a40				09a43			10a43			11a42	
—	52½	—	—	Blackpool North 97	d																		
26¾	—	—	10½	Patricroft	d			06 09		07 12	08 12			09 13			10 12			11 12			12 12
27¾	—	—	11½	Eccles	d			06 11		07 14	08 14			09 16			10 14			11 14			12 14
31¾	—	—	—	Manchester Victoria	d																		
—	—	—	15¾	Manchester Oxford Road	d			06 22		07 25	08 26		09 09	09 26	10 09		10 25	11 09		11 25	12 09		12 25
—	—	—	16¼	Manchester Piccadilly	d		04 14	06 26		07 31	08 30		09 13	09 30	10 13		10 30	11 13		11 30	12 13		12 30
—	—	—	26	Manchester Airport 85	a		04 27	06 47		07 52	08 52		09 32	09 52	10 32		10 52	11 32		11 52	12 32		12 52
—	—	—	—	Scarborough	a																		

		NT	NT	NT	NT	NT	NT	NT	NT	NT	NT	NT	NT	NT	NT	NT	NT	NT	NT	NT	NT	NT	NT
		◇	◇	◇	◇	◇	◇	◇	◇	◇	◇	◇	◇	◇	◇	◇	◇	◇	◇	◇	◇		◇
			D	B		C	B		C	B		D	B		C	B			D		C	E	
Liverpool Lime Street 91	d	12 16		12 27	13 16		13 27	14 16		14 27	15 16		15 27	16 16		16 27	17 15	18 16		19 14		19 28	20 13
Edge Hill 91	d			12 31			13 31			14 31			15 31			16 31						19 32	
Wavertree Technology Park	d			12 33			13 33			14 33			15 33			16 33						19 34	
Broad Green	d			12 36			13 36			14 36			15 36			16 36						19 37	
Roby	d			12 39			13 39			14 39			15 39			16 39						19 40	
Huyton	d			12 41			13 41			14 41			15 41			16 42						19 42	
Prescot	d																						
Eccleston Park	d																						
Thatto Heath	d																						
St Helens Central	a																						
	d																						
Garswood	d																						
Bryn	d																						
Whiston	d			12 45			13 45			14 45			15 45			16 45						19 46	
Rainhill	d			12 48			13 48			14 48			15 48			16 49						19 49	
Lea Green	d			12 51			13 51			14 51			15 51			16 52						19 52	
St Helens Junction	d			12 54			13 54			14 54			15 54			16 56						19 55	
Warrington Bank Quay	d																						
Earlestown	d			12 58			13 58			14 58			15 58			17 00						19 59	
Warrington Bank Quay	a																						
Newton-le-Willows	d			13 01			14 01			15 01			16 01			17 02						20 02	
Wigan North Western 65,82	a																						
	d		12 18			13 18			14 18			15 20			16 18				18 20		19 20		
Euxton Balshaw Lane	d																						
Leyland 82	d																						
Preston 65,82	d		12a36			13a43			14a43			15a43			16a42				18a42		19a43		
Blackpool North 97	d																						
Patricroft	d			13 12			14 12			15 12			16 12			17 13						20 13	
Eccles	d			13 14			14 14			15 14			16 14			17 16						20 15	
Manchester Victoria	d																						
Manchester Oxford Road	d	13 09		13 25	14 09		14 25	15 09		15 25	16 09		16 25	17 09		17 28	18 09	19 08		20 09		20 26	21 09
Manchester Piccadilly	d	13 13		13 30	14 13		14 30	15 13		15 29	16 13		16 29	17 13		17 33	18 13	19 12		20 13		20 30	21 13
Manchester Airport 85	a	13 32		13 52	14 32		14 52	15 32		15 52	16 30		16 52	17 30		17 57	18 32	19 32		20 30		20 51	21 31
Scarborough	a																						

A From Liverpool Lime Street
B To Crewe
C From Manchester Airport to Barrow-in-Furness
D From Manchester Airport to Windermere
E To Wilmslow

NRT DECEMBER 19 EDITION

Table T090-R

Mondays to Fridays
16 December to 15 May

Liverpool and St Helens - Newton-le-Willows, Wigan, Preston, Manchester and Manchester Airport

		NT	NT	NT	NT	NT	NT	NT
		◇				◇		◇
		A	B		B			A
Liverpool Lime Street 91	d		20 27	20 55	21 28	22 24	22 29	
Edge Hill 91	d		20 31	20 59	21 32		22 33	
Wavertree Technology Park	d		20 33		21 34		22 35	
Broad Green	d		20 36		21 38		22 38	
Roby	d		20 39		21 41		22 41	
Huyton	d		20 41		21 43		22 43	
Prescot	d							
Eccleston Park	d							
Thatto Heath	d							
St Helens Central	a							
	d							
Garswood	d							
Bryn	d							
Whiston	d		20 45		21 46		22 47	
Rainhill	d		20 48		21 49		22 50	
Lea Green	d		20 51		21 53		22 53	
St Helens Junction	d		20 54		21 56		22 56	
Warrington Bank Quay	d							
Earlestown	d		20 58		22 00		23 00	
Warrington Bank Quay	a							
Newton-le-Willows	d		21 01		22 03		23 03	
Wigan North Western 65,82	a							
	d	20 18						22 58
Euxton Balshaw Lane	d							
Leyland 82	d							
Preston 65,82	d	20a42						23a14
Blackpool North 97	d							
Patricroft	d		21 12		22 13		23 14	
Eccles	d		21 14		22 16		23 16	
Manchester Victoria	d							
Manchester Oxford Road	d		21 24	22 12	22 28	23 17	23 28	
Manchester Piccadilly	d		21 29	22 16	22 32	23 21	23 33	
Manchester Airport 85	a		21 57	22 31	22 53	23 35	23 56	
Scarborough	a							

Saturdays
21 December to 16 May

		NT	NT	NT	NT	NT	NT	NT	NT	NT	NT	NT	NT	NT	NT	NT	NT	NT	NT	NT	NT	NT	NT
			◇	◇	◇	◇	◇	◇	◇	◇	◇	◇	◇	◇	◇	◇	◇	◇	◇	◇	◇	◇	◇
		C		D		A	D	D	A		D		E	D		A	D		A	D		E	D
Liverpool Lime Street 91	d		03 37	05 24	06 13		06 27	07 27		08 16	08 27	09 16		09 27	10 16		10 27	11 16		11 27	12 16		12 27
Edge Hill 91	d			05 28			06 31	07 31			08 31			09 31			10 31			11 31			12 31
Wavertree Technology Park	d			05 30			06 33	07 33			08 33			09 33			10 33			11 33			12 33
Broad Green	d			05 33			06 36	07 36			08 37			09 36			10 36			11 36			12 36
Roby	d			05 36			06 39	07 39			08 40			09 39			10 39			11 39			12 39
Huyton	d			05 38			06 41	07 41			08 42			09 41			10 41			11 41			12 41
Prescot	d																						
Eccleston Park	d																						
Thatto Heath	d																						
St Helens Central	a																						
	d																						
Garswood	d																						
Bryn	d																						
Whiston	d			05 42			06 45	07 45			08 46			09 45			10 45			11 45			12 45
Rainhill	d			05 45			06 48	07 48			08 49			09 48			10 48			11 48			12 48
Lea Green	d			05 48			06 51	07 51			08 52			09 51			10 51			11 51			12 51
St Helens Junction	d			05 51			06 54	07 54			08 56			09 54			10 54			11 54			12 54
Warrington Bank Quay	d																						
Earlestown	d			05 55			06 58	07 58			09 00			09 58			10 58			11 58			12 58
Warrington Bank Quay	a																						
Newton-le-Willows	d			05 58			07 01	08 01			09 02			10 01			11 01			12 01			13 01
Wigan North Western 65,82	a																						
	d	00 04				06 15			08 16				09 19			10 20			11 21			12 18	
Euxton Balshaw Lane	d	00 13																					
Leyland 82	d	00 17																					
Preston 65,82	d	00a25				06a31			08a39				09a43			10a43			11a42			12a42	
Blackpool North 97	d																						
Patricroft	d			06 09			07 12	08 12			09 13			10 12			11 12			12 12			13 12
Eccles	d			06 11			07 14	08 14			09 16			10 14			11 14			12 14			13 14
Manchester Victoria	d																						
Manchester Oxford Road	d			06 22	07 06		07 25	08 26		09 09	09 26	10 09		10 25	11 09		11 25	12 09		12 25	13 09		13 25
Manchester Piccadilly	d		04 14	06 26	07 11		07 31	08 30		09 13	09 30	10 13		10 30	11 13		11 30	12 13		12 30	13 13		13 29
Manchester Airport 85	a		04 27	06 47	07 28		07 52	08 52		09 32	09 52	10 32		10 52	11 32		11 52	12 32		12 52	13 32		13 52
Scarborough	a																						

A From Manchester Airport to Barrow-in-Furness
B To Wilmslow
C From Liverpool Lime Street
D To Crewe
E From Manchester Airport to Windermere

Table T090-R

Saturdays

21 December to 16 May

Liverpool and St Helens - Newton-le-Willows, Wigan, Preston, Manchester and Manchester Airport

Station		NT ◇	NT ◇ A	NT ◇ B	NT ◇	NT ◇ A	NT ◇ B	NT ◇	NT ◇ C	NT ◇ B	NT ◇	NT ◇ A	NT ◇ B	NT ◇	NT ◇ A	NT ◇ B	NT ◇	NT ◇ C	NT ◇ D	NT ◇	NT ◇ A	NT E	NT ◇
Liverpool Lime Street 10 91	d	13 16		13 27	14 16		14 27	15 16		15 27	16 16		16 27	17 15		17 28	18 15		18 29	19 14		19 28	20 12
Edge Hill 91	d			13 31			14 31			15 31			16 31			17 32			18 33			19 32	
Wavertree Technology Park	d			13 33			14 33			15 33			16 33			17 34			18 35			19 34	
Broad Green	d			13 36			14 36			15 36			16 36			17 38			18 39			19 37	
Roby	d			13 39			14 39			15 39			16 39			17 41			18 42			19 40	
Huyton	d			13 41			14 41			15 41			16 41			17 43			18 44			19 42	
Prescot	d																						
Eccleston Park	d																						
Thatto Heath	d																						
St Helens Central	a																						
	d																						
Garswood	d																						
Bryn	d																						
Whiston	d			13 45			14 45			15 45			16 45			17 46			18 47			19 46	
Rainhill	d			13 48			14 48			15 48			16 48			17 49			18 50			19 49	
Lea Green	d			13 51			14 51			15 51			16 51			17 53			18 54			19 52	
St Helens Junction	d			13 54			14 54			15 54			16 54			17 56			18 57			19 55	
Warrington Bank Quay	d																						
Earlestown 8	d			13 58			14 58			15 58			16 58			18 00			19 01			19 59	
Warrington Bank Quay	a																						
Newton-le-Willows	d			14 01			15 01			16 01			17 01			18 03			19 04			20 02	
Wigan North Western 65,82	a																						
	d		13 19			14 18			15 20			16 18			17 20			18 20			19 20		
Euxton Balshaw Lane	d																						
Leyland 82	d																						
Preston 8 65,82	d		13a43			14a43			15a43			16a42			17a43			18a42			19a43		
Blackpool North 97	d																						
Patricroft	d			14 12			15 12			16 12			17 12			18 13			19 14			20 13	
Eccles	d			14 14			15 14			16 14			17 15			18 16			19 16			20 15	
Manchester Victoria	d																						
Manchester Oxford Road	d	14 09		14 25	15 09		15 25	16 09		16 25	17 09		17 25	18 09		18 26	19 08		19 28	20 09		20 26	21 09
Manchester Piccadilly 10	d	14 13		14 30	15 13		15 29	16 13		16 29	17 13		17 29	18 13		18 31	19 12		19 32	20 13		20 30	21 13
Manchester Airport 85	a	14 32		14 52	15 32		15 52	16 32		16 52	17 32		17 52	18 32		18 52	19 32		19 57	20 30		20 57	21 31
Scarborough	a																						

Station		NT ◇ A	NT E	NT ◇	NT E	NT ◇	NT
Liverpool Lime Street 10 91	d		20 27	21 29	21 29	22 24	22 29
Edge Hill 91	d		20 31		21 33		22 33
Wavertree Technology Park	d		20 33		21 35		22 35
Broad Green	d		20 36		21 38		22 38
Roby	d		20 39		21 41		22 41
Huyton	d		20 41		21 43		22 43
Prescot	d						
Eccleston Park	d						
Thatto Heath	d						
St Helens Central	a						
	d						
Garswood	d						
Bryn	d						
Whiston	d		20 45		21 47		22 47
Rainhill	d		20 48		21 50		22 50
Lea Green	d		20 51		21 53		22 53
St Helens Junction	d		20 54		21 56		22 56
Warrington Bank Quay	d						
Earlestown 8	d		20 58		22 00		23 00
Warrington Bank Quay	a						
Newton-le-Willows	d		21 01		22 03		23 03
Wigan North Western 65,82	a						
	d	20 18					
Euxton Balshaw Lane	d						
Leyland 82	d						
Preston 8 65,82	d	20a42					
Blackpool North 97	d						
Patricroft	d		21 12		22 14		23 14
Eccles	d		21 14		22 16		23 16
Manchester Victoria	d						
Manchester Oxford Road	d		21 25	22 21	22 28	23 17	23 28
Manchester Piccadilly 10	d		21 29	22 25	22 33	23 21	23 34
Manchester Airport 85	a		21 57	22 40	22 56	23 38	23 56
Scarborough	a						

A From Manchester Airport to Barrow-in-Furness
B To Crewe
C From Manchester Airport to Windermere
D To Wilmslow. ◇ from Manchester Piccadilly
E To Wilmslow

Table T090-R

Sundays

15 December to 10 May

Liverpool and St Helens - Newton-le-Willows, Wigan, Preston, Manchester and Manchester Airport

Station		NT ◇ A	NT ◇ B	NT ◇ C	NT ◇ B	NT ◇ B	NT ◇ C	NT ◇ B	NT ◇ B	NT ◇ C	NT ◇ B	NT ◇ B	NT D	NT ◇	NT E	NT ◇	NT F	NT G	NT ◇	NT D	NT ◇ H	NT D	NT ◇ H
Liverpool Lime Street 10 91	d												08 15	08 21		09 16	09 30	09 30	10 16	10 31	11 16	11 29	12 16
Edge Hill 91	d														←								
Wavertree Technology Park	d												08 22		08 22		09 36	09 36		10 37		11 34	
Broad Green	d												→		08 25		09 39	09 39		10 39		11 37	
Roby	d														08 28		09 42	09 42		10 42		11 40	
Huyton	d														08 30		09 44	09 44		10 44		11 42	
Prescot	d																						
Eccleston Park	d																						
Thatto Heath	d																						
St Helens Central	a																						
	d																						
Garswood	d																						
Bryn	d																						
Whiston	d														08 34		09 48	09 48		10 47		11 46	
Rainhill	d														08 37		09 51	09 51		10 50		11 49	
Lea Green	d														08 40		09 54	09 54		10 54		11 52	
St Helens Junction	d														08 44		09 57	09 57		10 57		11 55	
Warrington Bank Quay	d																						
Earlestown 8	d														08 48		10 01	10 01		11 01		11 59	
Warrington Bank Quay	a																						
Newton-le-Willows	d														08 51		10 04	10 04		11 03		12 02	
Wigan North Western 65,82	a																						
	d	09 22	10 28	12 20	13 33	14 21	15 18	16 22	17 19	18 18	19 18	20 21											
Euxton Balshaw Lane	d																						
Leyland 82	d																						
Preston 8 65,82	d	09a40	10a44	12a42	13a55	14a38	15a36	16a38	17a37	18a36	19a36	20a38											
Blackpool North 97	d																						
Patricroft	d														09 01		10 14	10 14		11 13		12 12	
Eccles	d														09 03		10 16	10 16		11 16		12 14	
Manchester Victoria	d																						
Manchester Oxford Road	d													09 09	09 13	10 09	10 27	10 29	11 07	11 26	12 06	12 25	13 08
Manchester Piccadilly 10	d													09 13	09 17	10 17	10 40	10 40	11 12	11 33	12 12	12 30	13 13
Manchester Airport 85	a													09 28	09 39	10 31	11 02	11 02	11 28	11 57	12 26	12 52	13 27
Scarborough	a																						

Station		NT ◇ I	NT D	NT ◇	NT D	NT ◇	NT D	NT ◇	NT D	NT ◇	NT D	NT ◇	NT D	NT ◇	NT D	NT ◇	NT D	NT ◇	NT D	NT ◇	NT D	NT ◇	NT D	NT
Liverpool Lime Street 10 91	d	12 16	12 30	13 16	13 29	14 16	14 29	15 16	15 29	16 14	16 29	17 16	17 29	18 16	18 29	19 16	19 29	20 16	20 29	21 19	21 29	22 16	22 29	23 30
Edge Hill 91	d																							
Wavertree Technology Park	d		12 35		13 35		14 34		15 34		16 34		17 34		18 34		19 34		20 34		21 34		22 34	23 35
Broad Green	d		12 38		13 38		14 37		15 37		16 37		17 37		18 37		19 37		20 37		21 37		22 37	23 38
Roby	d		12 41		13 41		14 40		15 40		16 40		17 40		18 40		19 40		20 40		21 40		22 40	23 41
Huyton	d		12 43		13 43		14 42		15 42		16 42		17 42		18 42		19 42		20 42		21 42		22 42	23 43
Prescot	d																							
Eccleston Park	d																							
Thatto Heath	d																							
St Helens Central	a																							
	d																							
Garswood	d																							
Bryn	d																							
Whiston	d		12 46		13 46		14 45		15 45		16 45		17 45		18 46		19 46		20 46		21 45		22 45	23 47
Rainhill	d		12 49		13 49		14 48		15 48		16 48		17 48		18 49		19 49		20 49		21 48		22 48	23 50
Lea Green	d		12 53		13 53		14 52		15 52		16 52		17 52		18 52		19 52		20 52		21 52		22 52	23 53
St Helens Junction	d		12 56		13 56		14 55		15 55		16 55		17 55		18 55		19 55		20 55		21 55		22 55	23 56
Warrington Bank Quay	d																							
Earlestown 8	d		13 01		14 00		14 59		15 59		16 59		17 59		18 59		19 59		20 59		21 59		22 59	00 02
Warrington Bank Quay	a																							
Newton-le-Willows	d		13 03		14 03		15 01		16 01		17 02		18 02		19 02		20 02		21 02		22 01		23 01	00 05
Wigan North Western 65,82	a																							
	d																							
Euxton Balshaw Lane	d																							
Leyland 82	d																							
Preston 8 65,82	d																							
Blackpool North 97	d																							
Patricroft	d		13 13		14 13		15 12		16 12		17 13		18 13		19 13		20 13		21 13		22 12		23 12	00 15
Eccles	d		13 16		14 16		15 15		16 15		17 15		18 15		19 15		20 15		21 15		22 15		23 15	00 17
Manchester Victoria	d																							
Manchester Oxford Road	d	13 08	13 27	14 08	14 28	15 08	15 25	16 08	16 26	17 08	17 26	18 08	18 26	19 08	19 26	20 08	20 26	21 08	21 26	22 12	22 28	23 09	23 25	00 32
Manchester Piccadilly 10	d	13 14	13 31	14 13	14 32	15 13	15 30	16 13	16 30	17 13	17 30	18 13	18 30	19 13	19 30	20 13	20 30	21 13	21 30	22 17	22 32	23 15	23 29	00 36
Manchester Airport 85	a	13 28	13 52	14 27	15 03	15 27	15 51	16 27	16 52	17 27	17 52	18 27	18 52	19 27	19 52	20 29	20 52	21 26	21 52	22 30	22 53	23 30	23 51	00 57
Scarborough	a																							

A until 5 January, from 23 February until 29 March. From Manchester Airport to Windermere
B From Manchester Airport to Barrow-in-Furness
C From Manchester Airport to Windermere
D To Wilmslow
E From Liverpool Lime Street to Wilmslow
F until 29 March. To Wilmslow
G from 5 April. To Wilmslow
H from 5 April
I until 29 March

Table T091-F

Mondays to Fridays

16 December to 15 May

Crewe and Runcorn - Liverpool

Miles	Station		VT MO	NT MX	LM	NT	LM	AW	NT	LM	NT		LM	NT	AW	NT	VT	NT	LM	EM	LM		LM	AW	NT
—	London Euston ⊖65	d														05 27								
—	Coventry	d																		06 30		06 43		
—	Birmingham New Street 65	d										06 02						06 36		07 04		07 20		
—	Chester	d						06 07							07 03									08 11	
0	Crewe	65 d			05 40		06 04			06 33			06 58				07 28		07 33		07 59		08a33		
7½	Winsford	d					06 13			06 41			07 06						07 42		08 06				
11¾	Hartford	d					06 18			06 45			07 10						07 47		08 11				
14½	Acton Bridge	d					06 22			06 50			07 15						07 51		08 16				
22½	Runcorn	a			05 59		06 30	06 35		06 58			07 23		07 29		07 45		07 59		08 24			08 35	
—		d	00 06		06 00		06 31	06 35		06 58			07 23		07 29		07 45		08 00		08 25			08 35	
30	Liverpool South Parkway	a			06 07		06 39	06 44		07 07			07 32		07 42				08 09		08 35			08 43	
—		d		00 32	06 08	06 23	06 40	06 44	06 52	07 07	07 24		07 32	07 37	07 42	07 50		08 06	08 09	08 20	08 35			08 43	08 48
31	West Allerton	d				06 26					07 27			07 40				08 09							08 51
31¾	Mossley Hill	d				06 29					07 30			07 43				08 12							08 53
34½	Edge Hill	90 d				06 35					07 35			07 49				08 19							08 59
35½	Liverpool Lime Street	90 a	00 29	00 47	06 19	06 39	06 54	07 01	07 03	07 16	07 39		07 42	07 53	07 59	08 01	08 04	08 23	08 19	08 34	08 44			09 01	09 03

Station		NT	LM	LM	LM	LM	VT		NT	EM	LM	NT	NT	LM	AW	LM	LM		LM	VT	NT	EM	LM	NT	AW
London Euston ⊖65	d			05 34		06 34	07 07									←			07 49	08 07					
Coventry	d			07 30		08 30								←		08 30			09 30						
Birmingham New Street 65	d		07 36	08 04	08 38	→								08 38		09 04	09 37		10 04						
Chester	d				→						←				09 27										10 12
Crewe	65 d		08 32	08 58			08 43				08 58			09 33		09 58	10 33		10 59						
Winsford	d			→							09 07					10 07			→						
Hartford	d		08 42								09 12			09 44		10 11									
Acton Bridge	d															10 16							←		
Runcorn	a		08 52				09 00				09 22			09 53	09 56	10 25	10 51			10 00			10 25		10 37
	d		08 53				09 00				09 22			09 53	09 56	10 25	10 52			10 00			10 25		10 37
Liverpool South Parkway	a		09 00								09 31			10 02	10 05	→	→						10 33		10 45
	d	08 53	09 01						09 08	09 15	09 31	09 39	09 50	10 02	10 06						10 08	10 15	10 33	10 39	10 45
West Allerton	d								09 11			09 42									10 12			10 42	
Mossley Hill	d								09 14			09 44									10 14			10 45	
Edge Hill	90 d											09 50												10 50	
Liverpool Lime Street	90 a	09 06	09 11				09 20		09 23	09 28	09 40	09 58	10 03	10 12	10 20					10 20	10 23	10 31	10 43	10 58	11 04

Station		NT	LM		LM	LM	VT MO	VT MX	NT	EM	LM	NT	NT		LM	AW	LM	LM	VT	NT	EM	LM	NT		NT
London Euston ⊖65	d					08 49	09 07	09 07										09 49	10 07						
Coventry	d					10 30												11 30							
Birmingham New Street 65	d				10 37	11 04											11 37	12 04							
Chester	d										←				←	11 32						←			
Crewe	65 d				11 33	11 58	10 43	10 43			10 59				11 33		12 32	12 59	11 43			11 58			
Winsford	d				→	→					11 07						→	→				12 07			
Hartford	d										11 12				11 44							12 12			
Acton Bridge	d		←																			12 16			
Runcorn	a		10 51				11 01	11 01			11 22				11 53	11 57			12 00			12 24			
	d		10 52				11 01	11 01			11 22				11 54	11 57			12 00			12 25			
Liverpool South Parkway	a		11 00								11 31				12 02	12 07						12 33			
	d	10 51	11 01						11 07	11 15	11 31	11 39	11 51		12 03	12 07				12 09	12 16	12 34	12 39		12 51
West Allerton	d								11 11			11 42								12 13			12 42		
Mossley Hill	d								11 14			11 45								12 15			12 45		
Edge Hill	90 d											11 51											12 50		
Liverpool Lime Street	90 a	11 03	11 10				11 19	11 20	11 24	11 32	11 40	11 58	12 03		12 12	12 21			12 21	12 24	12 32	12 43	12 59		13 02

Station		LM	AW	LM	LM	VT	NT	EM	LM		NT	NT	AW	LM	LM	LM	VT	NT	EM		LM	NT	NT	AW	LM
London Euston ⊖65	d				10 49	11 07										11 49	12 07								
Coventry	d				12 30											13 30									
Birmingham New Street 65	d			12 37	13 04										13 37	14 04									
Chester	d	←	12 30						←				13 27	←							←			14 27	←
Crewe	65 d	12 32		13 34	13 57	12 43			12 59					13 34	14 34	14 58	13 43				13 57				14 34
Winsford	d			→	→				13 07						→	→					14 08				
Hartford	d	12 43							13 12					13 45							14 13				14 44
Acton Bridge	d													13 49											
Runcorn	a	12 53	12 56			13 00			13 22				13 51	13 56			14 00				14 23			14 51	14 54
	d	12 53	12 56			13 00			13 22				13 51	13 57			14 00				14 24			14 51	14 55
Liverpool South Parkway	a	13 02	13 06						13 30				14 00	14 04							14 31			15 00	15 04
	d	13 02	13 06				13 08	13 15	13 30		13 39	13 50	14 00	14 05				14 07	14 15		14 32	14 39	14 51	15 00	15 05
West Allerton	d						13 11				13 42							14 12				14 42			
Mossley Hill	d						13 14				13 45							14 14				14 45			
Edge Hill	90 d										13 50											14 50			
Liverpool Lime Street	90 a	13 11	13 20			13 20	13 23	13 32	13 40		13 58	14 01	14 14	14 14			14 19	14 24	14 32		14 42	14 58	15 02	15 14	15 14

Table T091-F

Mondays to Fridays

16 December to 15 May

Crewe and Runcorn - Liverpool

Station			LM	LM	VT	NT	EM	LM	NT	NT	LM		AW	LM	LM	VT	NT	EM	LM	NT	NT		LM	AW	LM
London Euston ⊖65	d			12 49	13 07										13 49	14 07									
Coventry	d			14 30											15 30										
Birmingham New Street 65	d		14 37	15 04										15 37	16 04										16 37
Chester	d							←			←		15 32						←				←	16 30	
Crewe	65 d		15 34	15 58	14 43			14 58			15 34			16 32	16 58	15 43			15 58				16 32		17 33
Winsford	d		→	→				15 07						→	→				16 07						→
Hartford	d							15 12											16 12				16 42		
Acton Bridge	d																		16 17						
Runcorn	a				15 00			15 22			15 51		15 56			16 00			16 25				16 52	16 56	
	d				15 00			15 22			15 52		15 56			16 00			16 25				16 53	16 56	
Liverpool South Parkway	a							15 31			16 00		16 05						16 33				17 01	17 06	
	d					15 07	15 15	15 31	15 39	15 51	16 01		16 05				16 08	16 15	16 33	16 39	16 51		17 02	17 06	
West Allerton	d					15 11			15 42								16 11			16 42					
Mossley Hill	d					15 14			15 45								16 14			16 45					
Edge Hill	90 d								15 52											16 50					
Liverpool Lime Street	90 a				15 19	15 23	15 32	15 40	15 58	16 03	16 10		16 19			16 20	16 23	16 32	16 43	16 58	17 04		17 11	17 20	

Station		LM	VT	NT	EM	LM	NT		NT	LM	AW	LM	LM	VT	NT	EM	LM		NT	NT	LM	VT	NT	EM	LM
London Euston ⊖65	d	14 49	15 07										15 49	16 07								17 07			←
Coventry	d	16 30											17 30								←				17 30
Birmingham New Street 65	d	17 04										17 37	→								17 37				18 04
Chester	d					←				←	17 30	→					←								
Crewe	65 d	17 58	16 43			16 58				17 33				17 43			17 58				18 36	18 44			18 59
Winsford	d	→				17 07											18 06				18 44				19 07
Hartford	d					17 11				17 43							18 11				18 48				19 12
Acton Bridge	d					17 16											18 16				18 53				
Runcorn	a		17 00			17 24				17 52	17 57			18 00			18 24				19 00	19 01			19 23
	d		17 00			17 24				17 53	17 57			18 00			18 24				19 01	19 01			19 23
Liverpool South Parkway	a					17 32				18 02	18 06						18 32				19 09				19 32
	d			17 08	17 15	17 32	17 46		17 52	18 03	18 06				18 19	18 23	18 32		18 47	18 51	19 10		19 16	19 20	19 32
West Allerton	d			17 12			17 49								18 22				18 50				19 19		
Mossley Hill	d			17 15			17 52								18 25				18 52				19 23		
Edge Hill	90 d						17 57								18 33				19 02				19 30		
Liverpool Lime Street	90 a		17 20	17 24	17 32	17 42	18 02		18 05	18 12	18 22			18 20	18 41	18 36	18 44		19 06	19 03	19 19	19 22	19 35	19 35	19 41

Station		VT	NT		NT	AW	NT	LM	VT	EM	VT	NT	NT		VT	LM	NT	AW	EM	NT	NT	AW	LM		VT
London Euston ⊖65	d	17 33							18 07		18 33				19 07										20 07
Coventry	d																								
Birmingham New Street 65	d							18 37								19 39							20 37		
Chester	d					19 28												20 36				21 25			
Crewe	65 d	19 16						19 33	19 43		20 16					20 35							21 33		21 48
Winsford	d							19 42								20 42							21 40		
Hartford	d							19 47								20 48							21 45		
Acton Bridge	d																						21 50		
Runcorn	a	19 35				19 51		19 57	20 00		20 33				20 50	20 57		21 03				21 50	21 57		22 06
	d	19 35				19 51		19 58	20 00		20 33				20 50	20 58		21 04				21 51	21 58		22 06
Liverpool South Parkway	a					19 59		20 06								21 06		21 14				22 00	22 05		
	d		19 47		19 53	19 59	20 04	20 07		20 17		20 46	20 53			21 07	21 10	21 14	21 20	21 46	21 54	22 01	22 06		
West Allerton	d		19 50				20 08										21 12								
Mossley Hill	d		19 53				20 11					20 50					21 15			21 50					
Edge Hill	90 d						20 19					20 56								21 57					
Liverpool Lime Street	90 a	19 52	20 02		20 05	20 15	20 24	20 16	20 20	20 34	20 53	21 00	21 05		21 08	21 17	21 24	21 30	21 36	22 02	22 05	22 16	22 16		22 23

Station		NT	NT	AW	LM	VT	NT	NT
London Euston ⊖65	d					21 07		
Coventry	d							
Birmingham New Street 65	d				21 37			
Chester	d			22 30				
Crewe	65 d				22 37	22 53		
Winsford	d				22 43			
Hartford	d				22 49			
Acton Bridge	d				22 53			
Runcorn	a			22 55	23 00	23 11		
	d			22 55	23 01	23 11		
Liverpool South Parkway	a			23 06	23 09			
	d	22 50	22 53	23 06	23 10		23 37	23 53
West Allerton	d	22 53					23 40	
Mossley Hill	d	22 56					23 43	
Edge Hill	90 d	23 04					23 48	
Liverpool Lime Street	90 a	23 09	23 05	23 20	23 20	23 33	23 53	00 05

Table T091-F

Crewe and Runcorn - Liverpool

Saturdays
21 December to 16 May

	NT	LM ■	NT	AW ◇	LM ■	NT ◇	LM ■	AW ◇	NT	LM ■	NT	NT ◇	NT	LM ■	EM ◇	LM ■	LM ■	AW ◇	NT	NT ◇	LM ■	LM ■
London Euston ⊖65 d																						05 34
Coventry d										05 37						06 30	06 39					07 30
Birmingham New Street 12 65 d										06 04				06 36		07 04	07 12				07 36	→
Chester d				06 04				06 43										08 10				
Crewe 10 65 d		05 48			06 15		06 33			06 58				07 33		07 58	08a31				08 32	
Winsford d							06 42			07 06				07 41		08 06						
Hartford d							06 46			07 11				07 46		08 11					08 43	
Acton Bridge d							06 51			07 16				07 51		08 15						
Runcorn a		06 07		06 28	06 34		07 00	07 08		07 24				07 59		08 23		08 34			08 53	
d		06 07		06 28	06 34		07 00	07 08		07 24				07 59		08 24		08 34			08 53	
Liverpool South Parkway 7 ✈ a		06 16		06 37	06 43		07 09	07 17		07 33				08 10		08 31		08 43			09 02	
d	00 32	06 16	06 23	06 37	06 43	06 52	07 09	07 17	07 24	07 33	07 37	07 50	08 06	08 10	08 20	08 32		08 43	08 46	08 51	09 02	
West Allerton d			06 26						07 27		07 40		08 09						08 49			
Mossley Hill d			06 29						07 30		07 43		08 12						08 52			
Edge Hill 90 d			06 35						07 35		07 49		08 19						08 57			
Liverpool Lime Street 10 90 a	00 47	06 25	06 39	06 51	06 54	07 03	07 20	07 31	07 39	07 43	07 53	08 01	08 23	08 19	08 33	08 42		08 58	09 02	09 07	09 11	

	VT ◇■	NT	EM ◇	LM ■	NT	LM ■	NT ◇	LM ■	AW ◇	LM ■	LM ■	LM ■	LM ■	VT ◇■	NT	EM ◇	LM ■	NT	AW ◇	NT ◇	LM ■
London Euston ⊖65 d	07 07			←									07 49	08 07							
Coventry d				07 30		07 47				08 30	08 47		09 29								
Birmingham New Street 12 65 d				08 04		08 21		08 37		09 04	09 20	09 37	10 03								
Chester d									09 30								←		10 12		←
Crewe 10 65 d	08 43			08 57		09a35		09 33		09 59	10a36	10 33	10 58	09 43			09 59				10 33
Winsford d				09 07						→		→	→				10 08				
Hartford d				09 12				09 43									10 13				10 44
Acton Bridge d																	10 17				
Runcorn a	09 00			09 22				09 52	09 56					10 00			10 25		10 37		10 54
d	09 00			09 22				09 53	09 56					10 00			10 26		10 38		10 54
Liverpool South Parkway 7 ✈ a				09 31				10 00	10 05								10 33		10 47		11 03
d		09 08	09 15	09 31	09 39		09 50	10 01	10 05						10 08	10 15	10 34	10 39	10 47	10 51	11 03
West Allerton d		09 11			09 42										10 12			10 42			
Mossley Hill d		09 14			09 44										10 14			10 45			
Edge Hill 90 d					09 50													10 50			
Liverpool Lime Street 10 90 a	09 20	09 23	09 30	09 40	09 58		10 03	10 12	10 19					10 19	10 23	10 30	10 44	10 58	11 04	11 04	11 12

	LM ■	LM ■	VT ◇■	NT	EM ◇	LM ■	NT	NT ◇	LM ■	AW ◇	LM ■	LM ■	VT ◇■	NT	EM ◇	LM ■	NT	NT ◇	LM ■	AW ◇	LM ■	LM ■
London Euston ⊖65 d		08 49	09 07									09 49	10 07									10 49
Coventry d		10 30										11 30										12 31
Birmingham New Street 12 65 d	10 37	11 04									11 37	12 04									12 37	13 04
Chester d						←			←	11 32						←			←	12 30		
Crewe 10 65 d	11 31	11 58	10 45			10 58			11 31		12 30	12 59	11 43			11 58			12 30		13 30	13 58
Winsford d	→	→				11 07					→	→				12 07					→	→
Hartford d						11 12			11 42							12 12			12 41			
Acton Bridge d						11 16										12 16						
Runcorn a			11 01			11 24			11 52	11 56			12 00			12 24			12 51	12 54		
d			11 01			11 25			11 52	11 56			12 00			12 25			12 51	12 54		
Liverpool South Parkway 7 ✈ a						11 32			12 01	12 05						12 32			13 00	13 04		
d				11 07	11 15	11 33	11 39	11 52	12 01	12 05				12 08	12 15	12 33	12 39	12 53	13 00	13 04		
West Allerton d				11 11			11 42							12 11			12 42					
Mossley Hill d				11 14			11 45							12 14			12 45					
Edge Hill 90 d							11 51										12 51					
Liverpool Lime Street 10 90 a			11 20	11 24	11 32	11 43	11 58	12 04	12 10	12 19			12 19	12 23	12 32	12 43	12 58	13 04	13 09	13 18		

	VT ◇■	NT	EM ◇	LM ■	NT	NT ◇	LM ■	AW ◇	LM ■	LM ■	VT ◇■	NT	EM ◇	LM ■	NT	NT ◇	AW ◇	LM ■	LM ■	LM ■	VT ◇■
London Euston ⊖65 d	11 07									11 49	12 07									12 49	13 07
Coventry d										13 30										14 30	
Birmingham New Street 12 65 d									13 37	14 03									14 37	15 04	
Chester d				←			←	13 30						←			14 27	←			
Crewe 10 65 d	12 44			12 59			13 30		14 31	14 59	13 43			13 58				14 31	15 31	15 59	14 43
Winsford d				13 07					→	→				14 07					→	→	
Hartford d				13 12			13 41							14 12				14 42			
Acton Bridge d														14 16							
Runcorn a	13 00			13 22			13 51	13 55			14 00			14 24			14 51	14 54			15 00
d	13 00			13 23			13 51	13 55			14 00			14 25			14 51	14 55			15 00
Liverpool South Parkway 7 ✈ a				13 31			13 59	14 04						14 32			14 59	15 03			
d		13 07	13 15	13 32	13 39	13 52	13 59	14 04				14 07	14 15	14 33	14 39	14 52	14 59	15 04			
West Allerton d		13 11			13 42							14 12			14 42						
Mossley Hill d		13 14			13 45							14 14			14 45						
Edge Hill 90 d					13 50										14 50						
Liverpool Lime Street 10 90 a	13 19	13 23	13 32	13 41	13 58	14 03	14 09	14 18			14 19	14 24	14 32	14 43	14 59	15 05	15 14	15 14			15 19

Table T091-F

Crewe and Runcorn - Liverpool

Saturdays
21 December to 16 May

	NT	EM ◇	LM ■	NT	NT ◇	LM ■	AW ◇	LM ■	LM ■	VT ◇■	NT	EM ◇	LM ■	NT	NT ◇	LM ■	AW ◇	LM ■	LM ■	VT ◇■	NT	EM ◇
London Euston ⊖65 d									13 49	14 07									14 49	15 07		
Coventry d									15 31										16 30			
Birmingham New Street 12 65 d								15 37	16 04									16 37	17 04			
Chester d			←			←	15 32						←			←	16 30					
Crewe 10 65 d			14 59			15 31		16 31	16 59	15 43			15 59			16 31		17 31	17 59	16 43		
Winsford d			15 08					→	→				16 07					→	→			
Hartford d			15 13			15 42							16 12			16 42						
Acton Bridge d													16 16									
Runcorn a			15 23			15 52	15 56			16 00			16 25			16 51	16 55			17 00		
d			15 23			15 52	15 56			16 00			16 25			16 51	16 55			17 00		
Liverpool South Parkway 7 ✈ a			15 32			16 01	16 05						16 33			17 00	17 04					
d	15 07	15 15	15 32	15 39	15 52	16 01	16 05				16 08	16 15	16 33	16 39	16 53	17 00	17 04				17 08	17 15
West Allerton d	15 11			15 42							16 11			16 42							17 12	
Mossley Hill d	15 14			15 45							16 14			16 45							17 15	
Edge Hill 90 d				15 52										16 50								
Liverpool Lime Street 10 90 a	15 23	15 30	15 42	15 58	16 03	16 10	16 19			16 19	16 23	16 32	16 43	16 58	17 04	17 10	17 19			17 20	17 24	17 32

	LM ■	NT	NT ◇	LM ■	AW ◇	LM ■	LM ■	VT ◇■	NT	EM ◇	LM ■	VT ◇■	NT	NT ◇	LM ■	LM ■	LM ■	VT ◇■	NT	EM ◇	LM ■
London Euston ⊖65 d							15 49	16 07				16 33					16 49	17 07			
Coventry d							17 30										18 30				
Birmingham New Street 12 65 d						17 37	18 04									18 37	19 04				
Chester d	←			←	17 31						←				←						←
Crewe 10 65 d	16 59			17 31		18 31	18 59	17 43			17 59				18 31	19 32	19 59	18 47			18 59
Winsford d	17 07					→	→				18 07					→	→				19 08
Hartford d	17 12			17 42							18 11				18 42						19 13
Acton Bridge d	17 16										18 16										
Runcorn a	17 24			17 52	17 56			18 00			18 24	18 31			18 51			19 04			19 23
d	17 25			17 52	17 56			18 00			18 24	18 31			18 51			19 04			19 24
Liverpool South Parkway 7 ✈ a	17 33			18 01	18 06						18 32				19 00						19 32
d	17 34	17 46	17 52	18 01	18 06				18 19	18 23	18 32		18 47	18 52	19 00				19 16	19 19	19 33
West Allerton d		17 49							18 22				18 50						19 19		
Mossley Hill d		17 52							18 25				18 52						19 23		
Edge Hill 90 d		17 57							18 33				19 03						19 29		
Liverpool Lime Street 10 90 a	17 43	18 02	18 05	18 10	18 20			18 20	18 37	18 36	18 42	18 51	19 07	19 04	19 10			19 22	19 34	19 35	19 42

	NT	NT ◇	NT	LM ■	AW ◇	LM ■	LM ■	VT ◇■	EM ◇	LM ■	VT ◇■	NT	NT ◇	AW ◇	NT	LM ■	VT ◇■	EM ◇	LM ■	NT	NT ◇	LM ■
London Euston ⊖65 d							17 49	18 07			18 33						19 07		←			
Coventry d							19 31									←			19 31			
Birmingham New Street 12 65 d						19 37	→									19 37			20 04			20 37
Chester d				←	19 31	→				←				20 30								
Crewe 10 65 d				19 32				19 43		19 59						20 33	20 47		20 58			21 30
Winsford d										20 07						20 40			21 06			
Hartford d				19 43												20 46			21 11			21 41
Acton Bridge d										20 14						20 50						
Runcorn a				19 53	19 57			20 00		20 22	20 31			20 54		20 58	21 05		21 21			21 51
d				19 53	19 57			20 00		20 23	20 32			20 54		20 59	21 05		21 21			21 51
Liverpool South Parkway 7 ✈ a				20 02	20 09					20 31				21 03		21 08			21 30			22 00
d	19 47	19 53	19 58	20 02	20 09				20 18	20 31		20 46	20 53	21 03	21 07	21 09		21 20	21 30	21 46	21 54	22 00
West Allerton d	19 50		20 03												21 10							
Mossley Hill d	19 53		20 05									20 50			21 13					21 50		
Edge Hill 90 d			20 11									20 56								21 57		
Liverpool Lime Street 10 90 a	20 02	20 05	20 16	20 11	20 24			20 18	20 33	20 41	20 51	21 00	21 04	21 17	21 24	21 18	21 27	21 32	21 39	22 02	22 07	22 09

	AW ◇	VT ◇■	NT	NT ◇	NT	NT ◇
London Euston ⊖65 d		20 11				
Coventry d						
Birmingham New Street 12 65 d						
Chester d	21 30					
Crewe 10 65 d		22 06				
Winsford d						
Hartford d						
Acton Bridge d						
Runcorn a	21 55	22 24				
d	21 55	22 24				
Liverpool South Parkway 7 ✈ a	22 05					
d	22 05		22 50	22 53	23 37	23 53
West Allerton d			22 53		23 40	
Mossley Hill d			22 56		23 43	
Edge Hill 90 d			23 04		23 50	
Liverpool Lime Street 10 90 a	22 19	22 41	23 09	23 05	23 55	00 05

Table T091-F

Sundays
15 December to 10 May

Crewe and Runcorn - Liverpool

Station		NT	NT	NT	AW	NT	LM	AW	NT	LM	LM	VT	NT	LM	AW	NT	NT	VT	LM	LM	EM	AW	NT
		A	B	◇ B	◇		■	◇		■	■	◇■ ☕	◇	■	◇		◇	◇■ ☕	■	■	◇	◇	
London Euston ⊖65	d										07 52	08 16						09 16	←				
Coventry	d									09 06	10 00			←					10 00	10 11			
Birmingham New Street ■ 65	d									09 42	→			09 42					10 42	10 57			
Chester	d				08 31			09 31		→					10 47							11 47	
Crewe ■ 65	d						09 20					10 30		10 36				11 37	11 41	12a06			
Winsford	d						09 27							10 43					11 48				
Hartford	d						09 32							10 48					11 53				
Acton Bridge	d						09 37							10 53									
Runcorn	a				08 55		09 45	09 55				10 48		11 01	11 11			11 54	12 03			12 11	
	d				08 55		09 46	09 55				10 48		11 02	11 11			11 54	12 04			12 11	
Liverpool South Parkway ■ ✈	a				09 04		09 54	10 04						11 10	11 20				12 12			12 21	
	d	00 24	08 39	08 58	09 04	09 37	09 55	10 04	10 39				11 01	11 11	11 20	11 36	11 53		12 13		12 17	12 21	12 39
West Allerton	d		08 42			09 40			10 42							11 39							12 42
Mossley Hill	d		08 44			09 42			10 44							11 41							12 44
Edge Hill 90	d																						
Liverpool Lime Street ■ 90	a	00 36	08 53	09 09	09 18	09 51	10 05	10 18	10 53			11 05	11 12	11 20	11 33	11 51	12 04	12 11	12 22		12 30	12 35	12 54

Station		NT	VT	LM	LM	EM	AW	NT	VT	NT	NT	LM	VT	LM	EM	AW	NT	NT	LM	LM	LM	VT
		◇	◇■ ☕	■	■	◇	◇		◇■ ☕	◇ C	◇ D	■	◇■ ☕	■	◇	◇		◇	■	■	■	◇■ ☕
London Euston ⊖65	d		10 16						11 16				12 05								12 31	13 05
Coventry	d			11 07	11 10							12 07		12 11					13 08	13 11	14 08	
Birmingham New Street ■ 65	d			11 40	11 43							12 35		12 47					13 35	13 44	→	
Chester	d						12 47									13 47						
Crewe ■ 65	d		12 34	12 37	12a59				13 15			13 31	13 45	13a56					14 31	14a54		14 45
Winsford	d			12 45								13 38							14 39			
Hartford	d			12 50								13 43							14 44			
Acton Bridge	d			12 54															14 49			
Runcorn	a		12 51	13 02			13 11		13 32			13 53	14 02			14 11			14 57			15 02
	d		12 51	13 03			13 11		13 32			13 54	14 02			14 11			14 57			15 02
Liverpool South Parkway ■ ✈	a			13 11			13 21					14 02				14 20			15 06			
	d	12 51		13 12		13 17	13 21	13 38		13 49	13 51	14 03			14 16	14 20	14 39	14 52	15 06			
West Allerton	d							13 41									14 42					
Mossley Hill	d							13 44									14 44					
Edge Hill 90	d																					
Liverpool Lime Street ■ 90	a	13 02	13 08	13 21		13 31	13 35	13 53	13 55	14 00	14 02	14 12	14 20		14 32	14 34	14 56	15 03	15 15			15 20

Station		EM	AW	NT	NT	LM	LM	LM	VT	EM	AW	NT	NT	LM	LM	LM	VT	EM	AW	NT	NT	LM	LM
		◇	◇		◇	■	■	■	◇■ ☕	◇	◇		◇	■	■	■	◇■ ☕	◇	◇		◇	■	■
London Euston ⊖65	d					←		13 32	14 05					←		14 31	15 05					←	
Coventry	d					14 08	14 11	15 09						15 09	15 12	16 08						16 08	16 11
Birmingham New Street ■ 65	d					14 35	14 53	→						15 35	15 53	→						16 35	16 53
Chester	d		14 47								15 47								16 47				
Crewe ■ 65	d					15 31	16a05		15 45					16 31	17a05		16 45					17 32	18a05
Winsford	d					15 39								16 39								17 39	
Hartford	d					15 44								16 44								17 44	
Acton Bridge	d													16 49								17 49	
Runcorn	a		15 11			15 54			16 02		16 11			16 57			17 02		17 11			17 57	
	d		15 11			15 54			16 02		16 11			16 57			17 02		17 11			17 57	
Liverpool South Parkway ■ ✈	a		15 20			16 03					16 20			17 06					17 20			18 06	
	d	15 16	15 20	15 39	15 51	16 03				16 16	16 20	16 39	16 51	17 06				17 16	17 20	17 39	17 51	18 06	
West Allerton	d			15 42								16 42								17 42			
Mossley Hill	d			15 44								16 44								17 44			
Edge Hill 90	d																						
Liverpool Lime Street ■ 90	a	15 30	15 36	15 56	16 02	16 12			16 23	16 28	16 34	16 53	17 02	17 15			17 21	17 32	17 34	17 53	18 02	18 15	

Station		LM	VT	EM	AW	NT	NT	LM	LM	LM	VT	EM	AW	NT	NT	LM	LM	LM	VT	EM	AW	NT
		■	◇■ ☕	◇	◇		◇	■	■	■	◇■ ☕	◇	◇		◇	■	■	■	◇■ ☕	◇	◇	
London Euston ⊖65	d	15 31	16 05					←		16 32	17 05					←		17 32	18 05			
Coventry	d	17 08						17 08	17 11	18 08						18 08	18 11	19 08				
Birmingham New Street ■ 65	d	→						17 35	17 52	→						18 35	18 53	→				
Chester	d				17 47								18 44								19 47	
Crewe ■ 65	d		17 46					18 31	19a05		18 46					19 31	20a08		19 45			
Winsford	d							18 39								19 39						
Hartford	d							18 44								19 44						
Acton Bridge	d							18 49														
Runcorn	a		18 02		18 11			18 57			19 02		19 09			19 54			20 02		20 10	
	d		18 02		18 11			18 57			19 02		19 09			19 54			20 02		20 11	
Liverpool South Parkway ■ ✈	a				18 21			19 06					19 21			20 03					20 21	
	d			18 17	18 21	18 39	18 53	19 06				19 17	19 21	19 39	19 51	20 03				20 17	20 21	20 39
West Allerton	d					18 42								19 42								20 42
Mossley Hill	d					18 44								19 44								20 44
Edge Hill 90	d																					
Liverpool Lime Street ■ 90	a		18 21	18 30	18 35	18 53	19 04	19 15			19 21	19 30	19 38	19 53	20 02	20 12			20 20	20 31	20 35	20 53

A not 15 December
B until 5 January, from 23 February
C from 5 April
D until 29 March

NRT DECEMBER 19 EDITION

Table T091-F

Sundays
15 December to 10 May

Crewe and Runcorn - Liverpool

Station		NT	LM	VT	LM	LM	AW	NT	NT	LM	VT	VT	AW	NT	NT	AW	LM	NT	LM	NT	VT	LM
		◇	■	◇■ ☕	■	■	◇		◇	■	◇■ ☕	◇■ ☕	◇		◇	◇	■		■	◇	◇■ ☕	■
London Euston ⊖65	d		←	19 05						19 31	20 05	20 08					←				21 21	22 01
Coventry	d		19 08		19 11	20 11				21 08							21 08		21 11			00a04
Birmingham New Street ■ 65	d		19 35		19 54	20 43				→							21 42		22 00			
Chester	d						20 47						21 54			22 28						
Crewe ■ 65	d		20 35	20 49	21a06	22a05					21 46	21 55					22 40		23a15		23 47	
Winsford	d		20 42														22 47					
Hartford	d		20 47														22 52					
Acton Bridge	d		20 52														22 57					
Runcorn	a		21 00	21 06			21 11				22 03	22 12	22 18			22 52	23 05				00 06	
	d		21 01	21 06			21 11				22 03	22 12	22 18			22 52	23 06				00 06	
Liverpool South Parkway ■ ✈	a		21 09				21 20						22 27			23 01	23 16					
	d	20 49	21 10				21 20	21 39	21 51				22 27	22 38	22 51	23 01	23 16	23 39		23 51		
West Allerton	d							21 42						22 41				23 42				
Mossley Hill	d							21 44						22 44				23 44				
Edge Hill 90	d																					
Liverpool Lime Street ■ 90	a	21 00	21 19	21 23			21 34	21 53	22 02		22 20	22 29	22 41	22 53	23 02	23 15	23 29	23 54		00 05	00 29	

AVAILABLE FROM MP Middleton Press

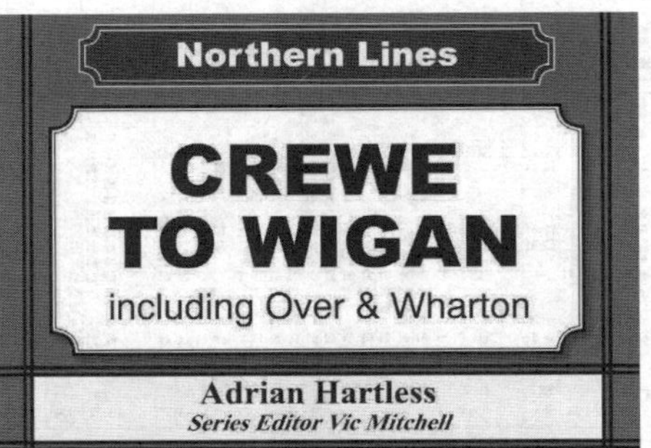

Northern Lines
CREWE
TO WIGAN
including Over & Wharton
Adrian Hartless
Series Editor Vic Mitchell

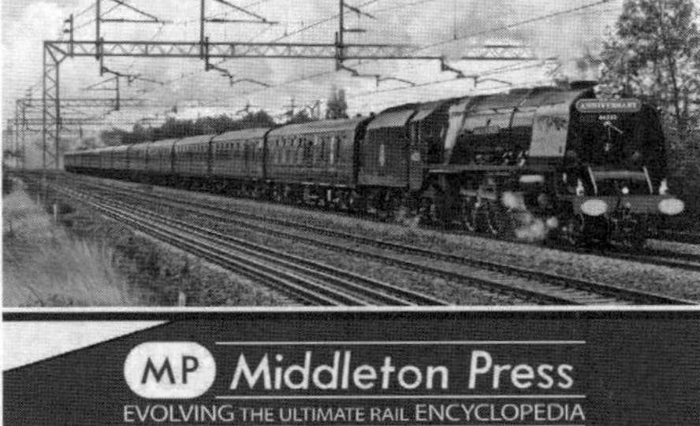

MP Middleton Press
EVOLVING THE ULTIMATE RAIL ENCYCLOPEDIA

Table T091-R

Liverpool - Runcorn and Crewe

Mondays to Fridays
16 December to 15 May

Miles		LM MX	LM MO	NT	VT	NT	VT	LM	NT	NT	NT	LM	EM	NT	VT	LM	NT	AW	NT	NT	LM	EM
		1	1	◇	◇1 ⊠		◇1 ⊠	1	◇		◇	1	◇		◇1 ⊠	1	◇	◇		◇	1	◇
0	**Liverpool Lime Street** 10 90 d			05 24	05 26	05 49	06 05	06 10	06 13	06 20	06 27	06 32	06 47	06 50	07 00	07 05	07 09	07 16	07 19	07 27	07 35	07 42
1¼	Edge Hill 90 d			05 28		05 53					06 31			06 54					07 23	07 31		
3¾	Mossley Hill d					05 58				06 28				06 59					07 28			
4½	West Allerton d					06 01				06 31				07 01					07 31			
5½	**Liverpool South Parkway** 7 ✈ a					06 04		06 20	06 24	06 34		06 41	06 58	07 04		07 15	07 19	07 26	07 34		07 44	07 52
—	d							06 20				06 42				07 15		07 27			07 44	
13	**Runcorn** a				05 42		06 20	06 27				06 49				07 22		07 35			07 52	
—	d				05 43		06 21	06 28				06 49			07u15	07 23		07 35			07 52	
21	Acton Bridge d	00 01	00 09									06 58				07 32						
23¾	Hartford d	00 06	00 14					06 37				07 03				07 37					08 02	
28	Winsford d	00 10	00 19									07 07				07 42					08 07	
35½	**Crewe** 10 65 a	00 23	00 30	07 42	06 00			06 48			08 42	07 15				07 50				09 42	08 16	
—	Chester a																	08 05				
—	**Birmingham New Street** 12 65 a							07 50				08 18				08 50					09 21	
—	**Coventry** a							08 21								09 20					09 59	
—	**London Euston** ⊖65 a				07 50		08 23	10 17							09 03	11 18					11 30	

	NT	VT	LM	NT	NT	NT	LM	AW	VT	EM	NT	LM	AW	NT	NT	NT	LM	VT	EM	NT	LM
		◇1 ⊠	1	◇			1	◇	◇1 ⊠	◇		1	◇	◇		◇	1	◇1 ⊠	◇		1
Liverpool Lime Street 10 90 d	07 45	07 47	08 05	08 16	08 19	08 27	08 33	08 36	08 47	08 52	08 55	09 05	09 13	09 16	09 19	09 27	09 35	09 47	09 51	09 55	10 05
Edge Hill 90 d					08 23	08 31					08 59					09 31				09 59	
Mossley Hill d	07 54				08 28						09 04				09 28					10 04	
West Allerton d	07 56				08 31						09 07				09 31					10 07	
Liverpool South Parkway 7 ✈ a	07 59		08 15	08 26	08 34		08 42	08 46		09 02	09 10	09 14	09 23	09 26	09 34		09 44		10 01	10 10	10 14
d			08 15				08 43	08 46				09 15	09 23				09 45				10 15
Runcorn a		08 02	08 22				08 50	08 54	09 02			09 22	09 33				09 52	10 02			10 22
d		08 03	08 25				08 50	08 55	09 03			09 26	09 35				09 52	10 03			10 26
Acton Bridge d			08 36				09 01														
Hartford d							09 06					09 37					10 02				10 37
Winsford d							09 10										10 07				
Crewe 10 65 a		08 21	08 48			10 44	09 18		09 22			09 48				11 44	10 16	10 21			10 48
Chester a								09 23					10 07								
Birmingham New Street 12 65 a			09 50				10 21					10 50					11 20				11 50
Coventry a			10 20				10 59					11 20					12 01				12 21
London Euston ⊖65 a		09 59	12 16				12 29		11 00			13 17					13 30	11 59			14 17

	NT	NT	NT	LM	AW	VT	EM	NT	LM	NT	NT	NT	LM	AW	VT	EM	NT	LM	NT	NT	NT	LM
	◇		◇	1	◇	◇1 ⊠	◇		1		◇	◇	1	◇	◇1 ☕	◇		1		◇	◇	1
Liverpool Lime Street 10 90 d	10 16	10 20	10 27	10 33	10 36	10 47	10 51	10 55	11 05	11 16	11 19	11 27	11 33	11 36	11 47	11 51	11 55	12 05	12 16	12 19	12 27	12 33
Edge Hill 90 d			10 31					10 59				11 31					11 59				12 31	
Mossley Hill d		10 28						11 04			11 28						12 04			12 28		
West Allerton d		10 31						11 07			11 31						12 07			12 31		
Liverpool South Parkway 7 ✈ a	10 26	10 34		10 42	10 46		11 01	11 10	11 15	11 26	11 34		11 42	11 46		12 01	12 10	12 15	12 27	12 34		12 42
d				10 43	10 47				11 15				11 43	11 46				12 16				12 43
Runcorn a				10 50	10 55	11 02			11 22				11 50	11 54	12 02			12 23				12 50
d				10 50	10 55	11 03			11 23				11 50	11 55	12 03			12 23				12 50
Acton Bridge d									11 34													13 00
Hartford d				11 02					11 38				12 04					12 37				13 05
Winsford d				11 07									12 08									13 09
Crewe 10 65 a			12 42	11 16		11 21			11 49			13 43	12 17		12 21			12 48			14 42	13 17
Chester a					11 24									12 24								
Birmingham New Street 12 65 a				12 21					12 50				13 20					13 50				14 20
Coventry a				12 59					13 21				13 59					14 21				14 59
London Euston ⊖65 a				14 30		12 59			15 17				15 31		14 03			16 17				16 29

	AW	VT	VT	EM	NT	LM	NT	NT	NT	LM	AW	VT	EM	NT	LM	NT	NT	NT	LM	AW	VT	EM
	◇	◇1 A ☕	◇1 B ☕	◇		1	◇		◇	1	◇	◇1 ☕	◇		1	◇		◇	1	◇	◇1 ☕	◇
Liverpool Lime Street 10 90 d	12 36	12 47	12 47	12 51	12 55	13 05	13 16	13 19	13 27	13 33	13 36	13 47	13 51	13 55	14 05	14 16	14 19	14 27	14 31	14 36	14 47	14 51
Edge Hill 90 d					12 59				13 31					13 59				14 31				
Mossley Hill d					13 04			13 28						14 04			14 28					
West Allerton d					13 07			13 31						14 07			14 31					
Liverpool South Parkway 7 ✈ a	12 46			13 01	13 10	13 15	13 26	13 34		13 42	13 46		14 01	14 10	14 15	14 26	14 34		14 41	14 46		15 01
d	12 47					13 15				13 43	13 47				14 15				14 41	14 47		
Runcorn a	12 55	13 02	13 02			13 22				13 50	13 55	14 02			14 24				14 48	14 55	15 02	
d	12 55	13 03	13 03			13 23				13 50	13 55	14 03			14 25				14 49	14 55	15 03	
Acton Bridge d																			14 58			
Hartford d						13 35				14 02					14 38				15 02			
Winsford d										14 07									15 07			
Crewe 10 65 a		13 22	13 22			13 46			15 42	14 17		14 22			14 49			16 42	15 17		15 21	
Chester a	13 23										14 24									15 24		
Birmingham New Street 12 65 a						14 50				15 20					15 50				16 17			
Coventry a						15 20				15 59					16 20				16 59			
London Euston ⊖65 a		15 03	15 04			16 46				17 31		16 03			17 46				18 30		16 59	

A until 14 February B from 17 February

Table T091-R

Liverpool - Runcorn and Crewe

Mondays to Fridays
16 December to 15 May

	NT	LM	NT	NT	NT	LM	AW	VT	EM	NT	NT	LM	NT	NT	NT	LM	AW	VT	VT	EM	NT	LM
		1	◇		◇	1	◇	◇1 ☕	◇			1	◇		◇	1	◇	◇1 A ☕	◇1 B ☕	◇		1
Liverpool Lime Street 10 90 d	14 55	15 05	15 16	15 19	15 27	15 33	15 36	15 47	15 51	15 55	16 01	16 05	16 16	16 19	16 27	16 33	16 36	16 47	16 47	16 50	16 55	17 05
Edge Hill 90 d	14 59				15 31					15 59	16a05				16 31						16 59	
Mossley Hill d	15 04			15 28						16 04				16 28							17 04	
West Allerton d	15 07			15 31						16 07				16 31							17 07	
Liverpool South Parkway 7 ✈ a	15 10	15 15	15 26	15 34		15 42	15 46		16 01	16 10		16 15	16 26	16 34		16 42	16 46			17 00	17 10	17 15
d		15 15				15 43	15 47					16 15				16 43	16 47					17 15
Runcorn a		15 22				15 50	15 55	16 02				16 22				16 50	16 55	17 02	17 02			17 22
d		15 24				15 50	15 55	16 03				16 23				16 51	16 55	17 03	17 03			17 23
Acton Bridge d		15 36										16 34				17 03						
Hartford d		15 40				16 02						16 38				17 07						17 35
Winsford d						16 07																17 40
Crewe 10 65 a		15 51			17 43	16 17		16 22				16 49			18 43	17 21						17 48
Chester a							16 26										17 24					
Birmingham New Street 12 65 a		16 50				17 21						17 50				18 21						18 50
Coventry a		17 20				17 59						18 20				19 01						19 20
London Euston ⊖65 a		18 47				19 30		18 03				19 45				20 30		18 59	19 02			21 17

	NT	NT	LM	AW	VT	EM	NT	LM	NT	NT	LM	AW	VT	EM	NT	LM	NT	NT	NT	LM	VT
	◇		1	◇	◇1 ⊠	◇		1	◇		1	◇	◇1 ⊠	◇		1	◇			1	◇1 ☕
Liverpool Lime Street 10 90 d	17 15	17 19	17 34	17 37	17 47	17 51	17 55	18 05	18 16	18 20	18 34	18 37	18 47	18 51	18 55	19 11	19 14	19 20	19 28	19 34	19 47
Edge Hill 90 d							17 59								18 59				19a32		
Mossley Hill d		17 27					18 04			18 28					19 04			19 28			
West Allerton d		17 30					18 07			18 31					19 07			19 31			
Liverpool South Parkway 7 ✈ a	17 25	17 33	17 43	17 48		18 01	18 10	18 15	18 26	18 34	18 43	18 47		19 01	19 10	19 20	19 24	19 34		19 43	
d			17 44	17 48				18 15			18 44	18 48				19 21				19 44	
Runcorn a			17 51	17 57	18 02			18 22			18 52	18 56	19 02			19 29				19 51	20 02
d			17 51	17 59	18 03			18 23			18 52	18 56	19 03			19 29				19 51	20 03
Acton Bridge d			18 00													19 41					
Hartford d			18 04					18 36			19 02									20 04	
Winsford d			18 09					18 40			19 07									20 08	
Crewe 10 65 a			18 16		18 22			18 48			19 17		19 21			19 53				20 16	20 22
Chester a				18 30								19 28									
Birmingham New Street 12 65 a			19 19					19 50			20 20					20 50				21 21	
Coventry a								20 21			21 01					21 20					
London Euston ⊖65 a					20 03			21 53			22 53		21 02			23 23					22 04

	EM	NT	LM	NT	NT	NT	LM	AW	VT	NT	NT	LM	EM	AW	NT	NT	NT	LM	AW	AW	LM	NT
	◇		1	◇			1	◇	◇1 ☕			1	◇	◇		◇		1	◇	◇	1	
Liverpool Lime Street 10 90 d	19 51	19 56	20 06	20 13	20 26	20 27	20 35	20 38	20 48	20 55	21 28	21 34	21 37	21 40	21 55	22 24	22 29	22 35	22 39	23 23	23 35	23 38
Edge Hill 90 d		20 00				20a31				20 59	21a32				21 59		22a33					23 42
Mossley Hill d		20 05			20 34					21 04					22 04							23 47
West Allerton d		20 08			20 37					21 06					22 07							23 50
Liverpool South Parkway 7 ✈ a	20 01	20 11	20 16	20 23	20 40		20 44	20 50		21 09		21 43	21 47	21 50	22 10	22 35		22 46	22 52	23 33	23 44	23 53
d			20 16				20 45	20 50				21 44		21 51				22 47	22 53	23 34	23 45	
Runcorn a			20 23				20 52	20 59	21 03			21 51		21 59				22 55	23 01	23 42	23 52	
d			20 24				20 52	20 59	21 04			21 51		21 59				22 55	23 02	23 42	23 52	
Acton Bridge d																		23 04			00 01	
Hartford d							21 04					22 03						23 09			00 06	
Winsford d							21 09					22 07						23 13			00 10	
Crewe 10 65 a			20 47				21 17		21 23			22 15						23 25			00 23	
Chester a								21 31						22 28					23 32	00 10		
Birmingham New Street 12 65 a			21 48				22 18					23 15										
Coventry a			22 20																			
London Euston ⊖65 a			00 26						23 44													

Saturdays
21 December to 16 May

	LM	NT	VT	NT	LM	NT	NT	NT	LM	VT	EM	NT	LM	NT	AW	VT	AW	NT	NT	LM	EM	NT
	1	◇	◇1 ☕		1	◇		◇	1	◇1 ☕	◇		1	◇	◇	◇1 ☕	◇		◇	1	◇	
Liverpool Lime Street 10 90 d		05 24	05 46	05 49	06 10	06 13	06 20	06 27	06 34	06 44	06 47	06 50	07 05	07 09	07 13	07 16		07 19	07 27	07 35	07 42	07 45
Edge Hill 90 d		05 28		05 53				06 31				06 54						07 23	07 31			
Mossley Hill d				05 58			06 28					06 59						07 28				07 54
West Allerton d				06 01			06 31					07 01					←	07 31				07 56
Liverpool South Parkway 7 ✈ a				06 04	06 19	06 23	06 34		06 43		06 58	07 04	07 15	07 19	07 24		07 24	07 34		07 44	07 52	07 59
d					06 20				06 44				07 15		07 27		07 27			07 45		
Runcorn a			06 02		06 27				06 51	07 00			07 22		→	07 32	07 37			07 52		
d			06 03		06 27				06 51	07 01			07 23			07 33	07 37			07 52		
Acton Bridge d	00 01												07 32									
Hartford d	00 06								07 01				07 36							08 02		
Winsford d	00 10								07 06											08 07		
Crewe 10 65 a	00 23	07 44			06 47			08 42	07 13	07 19			07 47			07 54			09 42	08 17		
Chester a																	08 05					
Birmingham New Street 12 65 a					07 50				08 21				08 50							09 16		
Coventry a					08 20				08 59				09 20							09 59		
London Euston ⊖65 a			08 02		10 17				10 30	08 56			11 17			09 44				11 30		

A until 14 February B from 17 February

Table T091-R

Saturdays
21 December to 16 May

Liverpool - Runcorn and Crewe

	VT	LM	NT	NT	NT	LM	AW	VT	EM	NT	LM	AW	NT	NT	NT	LM	VT	EM	NT	LM	NT
Liverpool Lime Street 90 d	07 47	08 07	08 16	08 19	08 27	08 34	08 37	08 47	08 52	08 55	09 04	09 13	09 16	09 19	09 27	09 32	09 47	09 51	09 55	10 05	10 16
Edge Hill 90 d				08 23	08 31					08 59					09 31				09 59		
Mossley Hill d				08 28						09 04				09 28					10 04		
West Allerton d				08 31						09 07				09 31					10 07		
Liverpool South Parkway a		08 17	08 26	08 34		08 43	08 47		09 02	09 10	09 17	09 23	09 26	09 34		09 41		10 01	10 10	10 17	10 26
d		08 18				08 44	08 48				09 18	09 23				09 42				10 18	
Runcorn a	08 02	08 25				08 51	08 56	09 02			09 25	09 33				09 49	10 02			10 25	
d	08 03	08 25				08 51	08 56	09 03			09 27	09 35				09 49	10 03			10 26	
Acton Bridge d		08 34				09 00															
Hartford d						09 04					09 38					09 59				10 37	
Winsford d						09 09										10 05					
Crewe 65 a	08 21	08 48			10 44	09 17		09 22			09 48				11 44	10 15	10 21			10 47	
Chester a							09 25					10 09									
Birmingham New Street 65 a		09 50				10 20					10 50					11 20				11 50	
Coventry a		10 20				10 59					11 20					11 59				12 20	
London Euston ⊖65 a	10 03	12 17				12 30		11 01			13 17					13 30	11 58			14 18	

	NT	NT	LM	AW	VT	EM	NT	LM	NT	NT	NT	LM	AW	VT	EM	NT	LM	NT	NT	NT	LM	AW
Liverpool Lime Street 90 d	10 20	10 27	10 34	10 37	10 47	10 51	10 55	11 05	11 16	11 19	11 27	11 35	11 38	11 47	11 51	11 55	12 05	12 16	12 19	12 27	12 35	12 38
Edge Hill 90 d		10 31					10 59				11 31					11 59				12 31		
Mossley Hill d	10 28						11 04			11 28						12 04			12 28			
West Allerton d	10 31						11 07			11 31						12 07			12 31			
Liverpool South Parkway a	10 34		10 43	10 47		11 01	11 10	11 17	11 26	11 34		11 44	11 48		12 01	12 10	12 17	12 27	12 34		12 44	12 48
d			10 44	10 48				11 18				11 45	11 49				12 18				12 45	12 49
Runcorn a			10 51	10 56	11 02			11 25				11 52	11 57	12 02			12 25				12 52	12 57
d			10 51	10 56	11 03			11 26				11 52	11 57	12 03			12 27				12 52	12 58
Acton Bridge d			11 00																		13 01	
Hartford d			11 05					11 36				12 04					12 37				13 06	
Winsford d			11 09									12 09									13 10	
Crewe 65 a		12 42	11 17		11 21			11 46			13 43	12 18		12 21			12 47			14 42	13 17	
Chester a				11 25									12 27									13 28
Birmingham New Street 65 a			12 20					12 50				13 20					13 51				14 20	
Coventry a			12 59					13 20				13 59					14 20				14 59	
London Euston ⊖65 a			14 30		13 00			15 17				15 31		14 01			16 19				16 30	

	VT	EM	NT	LM	NT	NT	NT	LM	AW	VT	EM	NT	LM	NT	NT	NT	LM	AW	VT	EM	NT
Liverpool Lime Street 90 d	12 47	12 51	12 55	13 05	13 16	13 19	13 27	13 35	13 38	13 47	13 51	13 55	14 05	14 16	14 19	14 27	14 35	14 38	14 47	14 51	14 55
Edge Hill 90 d			12 59				13 31					13 59				14 31					14 59
Mossley Hill d			13 04			13 28						14 04			14 28						15 04
West Allerton d			13 07			13 31						14 07			14 31						15 07
Liverpool South Parkway a		13 01	13 10	13 16	13 26	13 34		13 44	13 48		14 01	14 10	14 16	14 26	14 34		14 44	14 48		15 01	15 10
d				13 16				13 45	13 49				14 17				14 45	14 49			
Runcorn a	13 02			13 24				13 52	13 58	14 02			14 25				14 52	14 58	15 02		
d	13 03			13 25				13 52	13 58	14 03			14 25				14 52	14 58	15 03		
Acton Bridge d																					
Hartford d				13 35				14 02					14 35				15 02				
Winsford d								14 07									15 08				
Crewe 65 a	13 22			13 45			15 42	14 16		14 23			14 45			16 42	15 17		15 21		
Chester a									14 26									15 28			
Birmingham New Street 65 a				14 50				15 20					15 50				16 17				
Coventry a				15 20				15 59					16 20				16 59				
London Euston ⊖65 a	14 59			17 17				17 30		16 01			18 17				18 30		16 59		

	LM	NT	NT	NT	LM	AW	VT	EM	NT	LM	NT	NT	NT	LM	AW	VT	EM	NT	LM	NT	NT	NT
Liverpool Lime Street 90 d	15 05	15 16	15 19	15 27	15 33	15 38	15 47	15 51	15 55	16 05	16 16	16 19	16 27	16 35	16 38	16 47	16 51	16 55	17 05	17 15	17 19	17 28
Edge Hill 90 d				15 31					15 59				16 31					16 59				17 32
Mossley Hill d			15 28						16 04			16 28						17 04			17 27	
West Allerton d			15 31						16 07			16 31						17 07			17 30	
Liverpool South Parkway a	15 17	15 26	15 34		15 42	15 48		16 01	16 10	16 16	16 26	16 34		16 44	16 48		17 01	17 10	17 17	17 25	17 33	
d	15 17				15 43	15 49				16 17				16 45	16 49				17 17			
Runcorn a	15 25				15 50	15 58	16 02			16 25				16 52	16 58	17 02			17 25			
d	15 26				15 50	15 58	16 03			16 25				16 52	16 58	17 03			17 26			
Acton Bridge d					15 59									17 01								
Hartford d	15 36				16 04					16 36				17 06					17 36			
Winsford d					16 08														17 40			
Crewe 65 a	15 46			17 43	16 17		16 20			16 46			18 43	17 18		17 22			17 48			19 42
Chester a						16 30									17 27							
Birmingham New Street 65 a	16 50				17 20					17 50				18 20					18 49			
Coventry a	17 20				18 00					18 20				18 59					19 20			
London Euston ⊖65 a	19 17				19 31		17 59			20 17						19 07			21 10			

Table T091-R

Saturdays
21 December to 16 May

Liverpool - Runcorn and Crewe

	LM	AW	VT	EM	NT	LM	NT	NT	NT	LM	AW	VT	EM	NT	LM	NT	NT	NT	LM	VT	EM
Liverpool Lime Street 90 d	17 34	17 37	17 47	17 51	17 55	18 06	18 15	18 20	18 29	18 34	18 38	18 47	18 51	18 55	19 11	19 14	19 20	19 28	19 35	19 48	19 52
Edge Hill 90 d					17 59				18a33					18 59				19a32			
Mossley Hill d					18 04			18 28						19 04			19 28				
West Allerton d					18 07			18 31						19 07			19 31				
Liverpool South Parkway a	17 43	17 47		18 01	18 10	18 15	18 26	18 34		18 43	18 48		19 01	19 10	19 20	19 24	19 34		19 44		20 02
d	17 44	17 48				18 16				18 44	18 49				19 21				19 45		
Runcorn a	17 51	17 56	18 02			18 23				18 51	18 57	19 02			19 29				19 52	20 04	
d	17 51	17 56	18 03			18 23				18 51	18 57	19 03			19 30				19 52	20 05	
Acton Bridge d	18 00														19 39						
Hartford d	18 05					18 36				19 01									20 03		
Winsford d						18 40				19 06									20 08		
Crewe 65 a	18 18					18 48				19 16		19 21			19 51				20 17	20 22	
Chester a		18 23									19 27										
Birmingham New Street 65 a	19 20					19 49				20 20					20 50				21 20		
Coventry a	19 59					20 20				20 59					21 20						
London Euston ⊖65 a	21 54		19 58			22 12				22 53		21 13			23 31					22 18	

	NT	LM	NT	NT	NT	LM	AW	EM	NT	LM	NT	NT	LM	EM	AW	NT	LM	AW	NT	NT	NT
Liverpool Lime Street 90 d	19 56	20 04	20 12	20 26	20 27	20 35	20 38	20 49	20 56	21 15	21 29	21 29	21 34	21 37	21 40	21 55	22 03	22 20	22 24	22 29	23 38
Edge Hill 90 d	20 00				20a31				21 00			21a33				21 59				22a33	23 42
Mossley Hill d	20 05			20 34					21 05							22 04					23 47
West Allerton d	20 08			20 37					21 07							22 07					23 50
Liverpool South Parkway a	20 11	20 14	20 23	20 40		20 44	20 48	20 59	21 10	21 25	21 40		21 43	21 47	21 51	22 10	22 13	22 30	22 35		23 53
d		20 14				20 45	20 49			21 26			21 44		21 51		22 14	22 30			
Runcorn a		20 21				20 52	20 58			21 33			21 51		21 59		22 21	22 38			
d		20 22				20 52	20 59			21 34			21 51		22 00		22 21	22 38			
Acton Bridge d										21 43			22 03								
Hartford d		20 31				21 02				21 47			22 07				22 31				
Winsford d		20 36				21 07				21 51			22 12				22 36				
Crewe 65 a		20 51				21 16				22 00			22 20				22 44				
Chester a							21 27								22 28			23 06			
Birmingham New Street 65 a		21 50				22 17							23 18								
Coventry a		22 20																			
London Euston ⊖65 a																					

Sundays
15 December to 10 May

	VT	NT	NT	VT	NT	NT	VT	AW	LM	NT	NT	VT	AW	NT	NT	LM	VT	AW	NT	NT	LM	VT
Liverpool Lime Street 90 d	08 18	08 21	08 25	08 38	09 16	09 26	09 38	09 45	10 12	10 16	10 27	10 38	10 49	11 16	11 26	11 35	11 47	11 56	12 16	12 25	12 33	12 47
Edge Hill 90 d																						
Mossley Hill d			08 33			09 34					10 35				11 34					12 33		
West Allerton d			08 35			09 36					10 37				11 36					12 35		
Liverpool South Parkway a		08 31	08 38		09 26	09 39		09 55	10 21	10 26	10 40		11 00	11 26	11 39	11 44		12 06	12 26	12 38	12 42	
d								09 56	10 22				11 01			11 45		12 07			12 43	
Runcorn a	08 34			08 53			09 53	10 04	10 29			10 53	11 09			11 52	12 04	12 15			12 50	13 04
d	08 35			08 54			09 54	10 04	10 29			10 54	11 09			11 52	12 05	12 15			12 50	13 05
Acton Bridge d									10 38												12 59	
Hartford d									10 42							12 02					13 04	
Winsford d									10 47							12 07					13 08	
Crewe 65 a	08 52			09 11			10 12		10 55			11 12				12 17	12 21				13 17	13 21
Chester a								10 33					11 39					12 44				
Birmingham New Street 65 a									12 11							13 14					14 14	
Coventry a									12 36							13 47					14 47	
London Euston ⊖65 a	11 04			11 34			12 29		14 24			13 09				15 40	14 03				16 40	15 03

	EM	AW	NT	NT	LM	VT	EM	AW	NT	NT	LM	VT	EM	AW	NT	NT	LM	VT	EM	AW	NT	VT
Liverpool Lime Street 90 d	12 52	12 57	13 16	13 26	13 35	13 47	13 52	13 57	14 16	14 25	14 32	14 47	14 52	14 57	15 16	15 26	15 35	15 47	15 52	15 57	16 14	16 19
Edge Hill 90 d																						
Mossley Hill d				13 34						14 33						15 34						
West Allerton d				13 36						14 35						15 36						
Liverpool South Parkway a	13 02	13 07	13 26	13 39	13 44		14 02	14 07	14 26	14 38	14 42		15 02	15 07	15 26	15 39	15 44		16 02	16 07	16 24	
d		13 08			13 45			14 08			14 43			15 08			15 45			16 08		
Runcorn a		13 16			13 52	14 04		14 16			14 50	15 04		15 16			15 52	16 04		16 16		16 34
d		13 16			13 52	14 05		14 16			14 50	15 05		15 16			15 52	16 05		16 16		16 35
Acton Bridge d											14 59											
Hartford d					14 02						15 04						16 02					
Winsford d					14 07						15 08						16 07					
Crewe 65 a					14 17	14 21					15 17	15 21					16 17	16 21				16 51
Chester a		13 45						14 45						15 45						16 45		
Birmingham New Street 65 a					15 14						16 14						17 14					
Coventry a					15 47						16 47						17 47					
London Euston ⊖65 a					17 40	16 03					18 40	17 04					19 40	18 03				18 39

Table T091-R

Sundays

15 December to 10 May

Liverpool - Runcorn and Crewe

			NT	LM	VT	EM	AW	NT	NT	LM	VT	EM	AW	NT	NT	LM	VT	EM	AW	NT	NT	LM	VT	EM
				■1	◇■1	◇	◇	◇		■1	◇■1	◇	◇	◇		■1	◇■1	◇	◇	◇		■1	◇■1	◇
Liverpool Lime Street [10]	90	d	16 25	16 32	16 47	16 52	16 56	17 16	17 26	17 35	17 47	17 52	17 56	18 16	18 25	18 32	18 47	18 52	18 57	19 16	19 25	19 32	19 47	19 52
Edge Hill	90	d																						
Mossley Hill		d	16 33						17 34						18 33						19 33			
West Allerton		d	16 35						17 36						18 35						19 35			
Liverpool South Parkway [7] ✈		a	16 38	16 42		17 02	17 06	17 26	17 39	17 44		18 02	18 06	18 26	18 38	18 42		19 02	19 07	19 26	19 38	19 42		20 02
		d		16 43			17 07			17 45			18 07			18 42			19 08			19 42		
Runcorn		a		16 50	17 04		17 15			17 52	18 04		18 15			18 49	19 04		19 16			19 49	20 03	
		d		16 50	17 05		17 15			17 52	18 05		18 15			18 50	19 05		19 16			19 50	20 04	
Acton Bridge		d		16 59												18 59						19 59		
Hartford		d		17 04						18 02						19 03						20 03		
Winsford		d		17 08						18 07						19 08						20 08		
Crewe [10]	65	a		17 17	17 21					18 17	18 21					19 17	19 21					20 17	20 22	
Chester		a					17 45						18 43						19 45					
Birmingham New Street [12]	65	a		18 14						19 14						20 11						21 14		
Coventry		a		18 47						19 47						20 37						21 47		
London Euston	⊖65	a		20 40	19 02					21 43	20 03						21 02					23 43	22 27	

			AW	NT	NT	LM	VT	AW	EM	NT	NT	LM	AW	NT	NT	AW	AW	LM
			◇	◇		■1	◇■1	◇	◇	◇		■1	◇	◇		◇	◇	■1
Liverpool Lime Street [10]	90	d	19 57	20 16	20 26	20 35	20 47	20 57	21 16	21 19	21 26	21 34	21 37	22 16	22 26	22 57	23 18	23 39
Edge Hill	90	d																
Mossley Hill		d			20 34						21 34				22 34			
West Allerton		d			20 36						21 36				22 36			
Liverpool South Parkway [7] ✈		a	20 07	20 26	20 39	20 44		21 07	21 26	21 30	21 39	21 43	21 47	22 26	22 39	23 07	23 28	23 48
		d	20 08			20 45		21 08				21 44	21 48			23 08	23 29	23 49
Runcorn		a	20 16			20 52	21 02	21 16				21 51	21 56			23 16	23 38	23 58
		d	20 16			20 52	21 03	21 16				21 51	21 56			23 16	23 41	23 59
Acton Bridge		d										22 01						00 09
Hartford		d				21 02						22 05						00 14
Winsford		d				21 07						22 10						00 19
Crewe [10]	65	a				21 15	21 22					22 20						00 30
Chester		a	20 45					21 45					22 26			23 45	00 11	
Birmingham New Street [12]	65	a				22 12						23 16						
Coventry		a				22 44												
London Euston	⊖65	a				00 43	23 53											

Table T094-F

Mondays to Fridays

16 December to 15 May

Manchester and Bolton - Blackburn - Clitheroe

Miles				NT	NT	NT	NT	NT	NT	NT	NT	NT	NT	NT	NT	NT	NT	NT	NT	NT	NT	NT	NT	NT
0	**Manchester Victoria**	82 ⇌	d		05 37		07 08	07 41	08 09	08 39	09 08	09 39	10 08	10 41	11 08	11 41	12 08	12 41	13 07	13 41	14 08	14 41	15 08	15 41
0¾	Salford Central	82	d		05 40		07 11	07 44	08 12	08 42	09 12	09 42	10 12	10 44	11 12	11 44	12 12	12 44	13 12	13 44	14 12	14 44	15 12	15 44
—	Manchester Piccadilly [10]	82 ⇌	d																					
1¾	Salford Crescent	82	d		05 45		07 18	07 48	08 18	08 46	09 18	09 46	10 18	10 48	11 18	11 48	12 18	12 48	13 18	13 48	14 18	14 49	15 18	15 48
10¾	**Bolton**	82	d		05 59		07 31	08 00	08 31	09 00	09 31	10 00	10 31	11 00	11 31	12 00	12 31	13 00	13 30	14 00	14 31	15 01	15 31	16 00
12½	Hall I' Th' Wood		d		06 04		07 36	08 06	08 36	09 06	09 36	10 06	10 36	11 06	11 36	12 06	12 36	13 06	13 36	14 06	14 36	15 06	15 36	16 06
13½	Bromley Cross		d		06 09		07 41	08 10	08 41	09 10	09 41	10 10	10 41	11 10	11 41	12 10	12 41	13 10	13 40	14 10	14 41	15 11	15 41	16 10
16½	Entwistle		d		06x16			08x17		09x17		10x17		11x17		12x17		13x17		14x17		15x17		16x17
20¼	Darwen		a		06 23		07 52	08 23	08 52	09 23	09 52	10 23	10 52	11 23	11 52	12 23	12 52	13 23	13 52	14 23	14 52	15 24	15 52	16 23
—			d		06 25		07 55	08 25	08 55	09 25	09 55	10 25	10 55	11 25	11 55	12 25	12 57	13 25	13 54	14 25	14 55	15 25	15 55	16 25
—	Blackpool North	97	d																					
—	Preston [8]	97	d																					
24½	**Blackburn**		a		06 32		08 07	08 32	09 07	09 32	10 08	10 32	11 06	11 32	12 06	12 32	13 07	13 32	14 05	14 32	15 06	15 33	16 05	16 32
—			d	06 11	06 33	07 32		08 33		09 33		10 33		11 33		12 33		13 34		14 33		15 33		16 33
27¼	Ramsgreave & Wilpshire		d	06 17	06 39	07 38		08 39		09 39		10 39		11 39		12 39		13 40		14 39		15 39		16 39
29¾	Langho		d	06 22	06 44	07 43		08 44		09 44		10 44		11 44		12 44		13 45		14 44		15 44		16 44
31¾	Whalley		d	06 26	06 48	07 47		08 48		09 48		10 48		11 48		12 48		13 49		14 48		15 48		16 48
34¼	**Clitheroe**		a	06 34	06 56	07 55		08 56		09 56		10 56		11 56		12 56		13 57		14 56		15 57		16 56

			NT	NT	NT	NT	NT	NT	NT	NT	NT	NT	NT	NT	NT	NT
Manchester Victoria	82 ⇌	d	16 08	16 41	17 08	17 41	18 17	18 41	19 09	19 41	20 09	20 41	21 08	21 40	22 16	23 07
Salford Central	82	d	16 12	16 44	17 12	17 44	18 20	18 44	19 13	19 44	20 13	20 44	21 12	21 43	22 19	23 12
Manchester Piccadilly [10]	82 ⇌	d														
Salford Crescent	82	d	16 18	16 48	17 18	17 48	18 24	18 48	19 18	19 48	20 18	20 48	21 19	21 47	22 23	23 17
Bolton	82	d	16 31	17 00	17 33	18 00	18 36	19 00	19 31	20 00	20 31	21 00	21 32	21 59	22 35	23 29
Hall I' Th' Wood		d	16 36	17 05	17 38	18 06	18 41	19 06	19 36	20 06	20 36	21 06	21 38	22 05	22 40	23 34
Bromley Cross		d	16 41	17 10	17 42	18 10	18 44	19 10	19 41	20 10	20 41	21 10	21 41	22 10	22 43	23 39
Entwistle		d		17x16	17x48	18x17		19x17		20x17		21x17		22x16	22x50	23x45
Darwen		a	16 52	17 23	17 55	18 23	18 55	19 23	19 52	20 23	20 52	21 23	21 53	22 23	22 56	23 52
		d	16 55	17 25	17 55	18 25	18 56	19 25	19 55	20 25	20 55	21 25	21 55	22 24	22 57	23 53
Blackpool North	97	d														
Preston [8]	97	d														
Blackburn		a	17 07	17 32	18 06	18 32	19 07	19 32	20 06	20 32	21 05	21 32	22 05	22 31	23 04	00 02
		d	17 09	17 33		18 33		19 33	20 08	20 33		21 33		22 32	23 05	
Ramsgreave & Wilpshire		d	17 15	17 39		18 39		19 39	20 14	20 39		21 39		22 38	23 11	
Langho		d	17 20	17 44		18 44		19 44	20 19	20 44		21 44		22 43	23 16	
Whalley		d	17 24	17 48		18 48		19 48	20 23	20 48		21 48		22 47	23 20	
Clitheroe		a	17 32	17 56		18 56		19 56	20 31	20 56		21 56		22 55	23 28	

Saturdays

21 December to 16 May

			NT	NT	NT	NT	NT	NT	NT	NT	NT	NT	NT	NT	NT	NT	NT	NT	NT	NT	NT	NT	NT	NT
Manchester Victoria	82 ⇌	d		05 37		07 08	07 41	08 09	08 39	09 08	09 39	10 08	10 41	11 08	11 45	12 08	12 41	13 07	13 41	14 08	14 41	15 08	15 41	16 08
Salford Central	82	d		05 40		07 11	07 44	08 12	08 42	09 12	09 42	10 12	10 44	11 12	11 48	12 12	12 44	13 12	13 44	14 12	14 44	15 12	15 44	16 12
Manchester Piccadilly [10]	82 ⇌	d																						
Salford Crescent	82	d		05 45		07 18	07 48	08 18	08 46	09 18	09 46	10 18	10 48	11 18	11 52	12 18	12 48	13 18	13 48	14 18	14 49	15 18	15 48	16 18
Bolton	82	d		05 59		07 31	08 00	08 31	09 00	09 31	10 00	10 31	11 00	11 31	12 04	12 31	13 00	13 30	14 00	14 31	15 01	15 31	16 00	16 31
Hall I' Th' Wood		d		06 04		07 36	08 06	08 36	09 06	09 36	10 06	10 36	11 06	11 36	12 09	12 36	13 06	13 36	14 06	14 36	15 06	15 36	16 06	16 36
Bromley Cross		d		06 09		07 41	08 10	08 41	09 10	09 41	10 10	10 41	11 10	11 41	12 12	12 41	13 10	13 40	14 10	14 41	15 11	15 41	16 10	16 41
Entwistle		d		06x16			08x17		09x17		10x17		11x17		12x19		13x17		14x17		15x17		16x17	
Darwen		a		06 23		07 52	08 23	08 52	09 23	09 52	10 23	10 52	11 23	11 52	12 25	12 52	13 23	13 52	14 23	14 52	15 24	15 52	16 23	16 52
		d		06 25		07 55	08 25	08 55	09 25	09 55	10 25	10 55	11 25	11 55	12 26	12 57	13 25	13 54	14 25	14 55	15 25	15 55	16 25	16 55
Blackpool North	97	d																						
Preston [8]	97	d																						
Blackburn		a		06 32		08 07	08 32	09 07	09 32	10 08	10 32	11 06	11 32	12 06	12 33	13 07	13 32	14 05	14 32	15 06	15 33	16 05	16 32	17 07
		d	06 11	06 33	07 32		08 33		09 33		10 33		11 33		12 34		13 34		14 33		15 33		16 33	17 09
Ramsgreave & Wilpshire		d	06 17	06 39	07 38		08 39		09 39		10 39		11 39		12 40		13 40		14 39		15 39		16 39	17 15
Langho		d	06 22	06 44	07 43		08 44		09 44		10 44		11 44		12 45		13 45		14 44		15 44		16 44	17 20
Whalley		d	06 26	06 48	07 47		08 48		09 48		10 48		11 48		12 49		13 49		14 48		15 48		16 48	17 24
Clitheroe		a	06 34	06 56	07 55		08 56		09 56		10 56		11 56		12 57		13 57		14 56		15 57		16 56	17 32

			NT	NT	NT	NT	NT	NT	NT	NT	NT	NT	NT	NT	NT
Manchester Victoria	82 ⇌	d	16 41	17 08	17 41	18 17	18 41	19 09	19 41	20 09	20 41	21 08	21 40	22 16	23 07
Salford Central	82	d	16 44	17 12	17 44	18 20	18 44	19 13	19 44	20 13	20 44	21 12	21 43	22 19	23 12
Manchester Piccadilly [10]	82 ⇌	d													
Salford Crescent	82	d	16 48	17 18	17 48	18 24	18 48	19 18	19 48	20 18	20 48	21 19	21 47	22 23	23 17
Bolton	82	d	17 00	17 33	18 00	18 36	19 00	19 31	20 00	20 31	21 00	21 32	21 59	22 35	23 29
Hall I' Th' Wood		d	17 05	17 38	18 06	18 41	19 06	19 36	20 06	20 36	21 06	21 38	22 05	22 40	23 34
Bromley Cross		d	17 10	17 42	18 10	18 44	19 10	19 41	20 10	20 41	21 10	21 41	22 10	22 43	23 39
Entwistle		d	17x16	17x48	18x17		19x17		20x17		21x17		22x16	22x50	23x45
Darwen		a	17 23	17 55	18 23	18 55	19 23	19 52	20 23	20 52	21 23	21 53	22 23	22 56	23 52
		d	17 25	17 55	18 25	18 56	19 25	19 55	20 25	20 55	21 25	21 55	22 24	22 57	23 53
Blackpool North	97	d													
Preston [8]	97	d													
Blackburn		a	17 32	18 06	18 32	19 07	19 32	20 06	20 32	21 05	21 32	22 05	22 31	23 04	00 02
		d	17 33		18 33		19 33	20 08	20 33		21 33		22 32	23 05	
Ramsgreave & Wilpshire		d	17 39		18 39		19 39	20 14	20 39		21 39		22 38	23 11	
Langho		d	17 44		18 44		19 44	20 19	20 44		21 44		22 43	23 16	
Whalley		d	17 48		18 48		19 48	20 23	20 48		21 48		22 47	23 20	
Clitheroe		a	17 56		18 56		19 56	20 31	20 56		21 56		22 55	23 28	

Table T094-F

Sundays
15 December to 10 May

Manchester and Bolton - Blackburn - Clitheroe

		NT	NT A	NT	NT		NT	NT B	NT	NT	NT	NT	NT	NT	NT	NT
Manchester Victoria 82	d	07 55		08 41	09 45		14 45		15 45	16 45	17 59	18 45	19 45	21 12	22 07	23 14
Salford Central 82	d			08 44	09 48		14 48		15 48	16 48	18 02	18 48	19 48	21 15	22 10	23 17
Manchester Piccadilly 10 82	d															
Salford Crescent 82	d	08 02		08 48	09 52		14 52		15 52	16 52	18 05	18 52	19 52	21 19	22 14	23 21
Bolton 82	d	08 15		09 00	10 04		15 04		16 04	17 04	18 19	19 04	20 04	21 32	22 26	23 36
Hall I' Th' Wood	d	08 20		09 05	10 09		15 09		16 09	17 09	18 24	19 09	20 09	21 37	22 31	23 41
Bromley Cross	d	08 23		09 09	10 12	and	15 12		16 12	17 12	18 27	19 12	20 12	21 41	22 34	23 44
Entwistle	d	08x29		09x16	10x19	hourly	15x19		16x19	17x19	18x34	19x19	20x19	21x48		23x50
Darwen	a	08 36		09 22	10 25	until	15 25		16 25	17 25	18 40	19 25	20 25	21 54	22 46	23 57
	d	08 36		09 23	10 26		15 26		16 26	17 26	18 41	19 26	20 26	21 55	22 46	23 57
Blackpool North 97	d		08 12													
Preston 8 97	d		08 39					15 29								
Blackburn	a	08 43	08 59	09 32	10 33		15 33	15 50	16 33	17 33	18 48	19 33	20 33	22 04	22 53	00 05
	d	08 44	09 00	09 38	10 34		15 34	15 51	16 34	17 34	18 49	19 34	20 34	22 05	22 54	
Ramsgreave & Wilpshire	d	08 50	09 06	09 47	10 40		15 40	15 57	16 40	17 40	18 55	19 40	20 40	22 11	23 00	
Langho	d	08 55	09 11	09 52	10 45		15 45	16 01	16 45	17 45	19 00	19 45	20 45	22 16	23 05	
Whalley	d	08 59	09 15	09 56	10 49		15 49	16 05	16 49	17 49	19 04	19 49	20 49	22 20	23 09	
Clitheroe	a	09 07	09 21	10 04	10 57		15 57	16 12	16 57	17 57	19 12	19 57	20 57	22 28	23 17	

A Arrives Hellifield 0947
B Arrives Hellifield 1635

AVAILABLE FROM MP Middleton Press

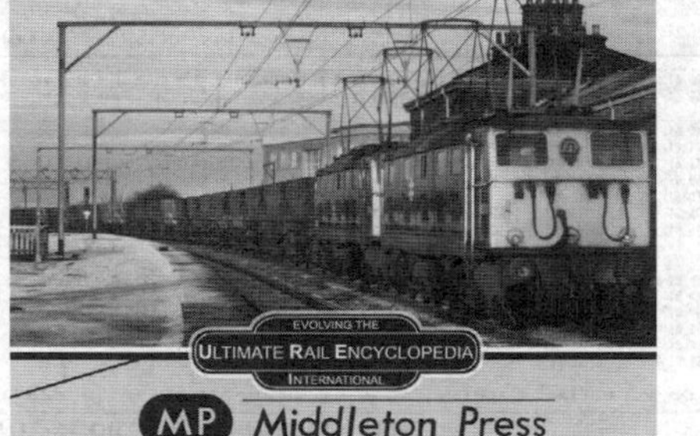

Table T094-R

Mondays to Fridays
16 December to 15 May

Clitheroe - Blackburn - Bolton and Manchester

Miles			NT	NT	NT	NT	NT	NT	NT	NT	NT	NT	NT	NT	NT	NT	NT	NT	NT	NT	NT	NT	NT
0	**Clitheroe**	d			06 25		06 49	07 25			08 25			09 25			10 25			11 25			12 25
2½	Whalley	d			06 31		06 55	07 31			08 31			09 31			10 31			11 31			12 31
4½	Langho	d			06 36		07 00	07 36			08 36			09 36			10 36			11 36			12 36
7	Ramsgreave & Wilpshire	d			06 40		07 04	07 40			08 40			09 40			10 40			11 40			12 40
9¾	**Blackburn**	a			06 47		07 11	07 47			08 47			09 47			10 47			11 47			12 47
—		d	06 16	06 19	06 48	07 14	07 18	07 48	08 18	08 19	08 48	09 18	09 19	09 48	10 18	10 19	10 48	11 17	11 19	11 48	12 18	12 19	12 48
—	Preston 8 97	a																					
—	Blackpool North 97	a																					
14	Darwen	a	06 23		06 55		07 25	07 55	08 25		08 55	09 25		09 55	10 25		10 55	11 24		11 55	12 25		12 55
—		d	06 27		06 56		07 27	07 56	08 27		08 56	09 27		09 56	10 27		10 56	11 27		11 56	12 27		12 56
17¾	Entwistle	d	06x34		07x03		07x34	08x03			09x03			10x03			11x03			12x03			13x03
20¼	Bromley Cross	d	06 40		07 09		07 40	08 09	08 40		09 08	09 40		10 09	10 40		11 09	11 40		12 09	12 40		13 09
21¼	Hall I' Th' Wood	d	06 43		07 12		07 43	08 12	08 43		09 11	09 43		10 12	10 43		11 12	11 43		12 12	12 43		13 12
23½	**Bolton** 82	a	06 48		07 17		07 48	08 17	08 48		09 16	09 48		10 17	10 48		11 17	11 49		12 17	12 48		13 17
32½	Salford Crescent 82	a	07 01		07 32		08 02	08 32	09 01		09 32	10 01		10 32	11 01		11 32	12 01		12 32	13 00		13 32
—	Manchester Piccadilly 10 82	a																					
33½	Salford Central 82	a	07 05		07 36		08 05	08 35	09 04		09 35	10 04		10 36	11 04		11 36	12 04		12 36	13 04		13 36
34¼	**Manchester Victoria** 82	a	07 09	07 24	07 41	08 24	08 08	08 41	09 07	09 24	09 41	10 07	10 24	10 41	11 07	11 24	11 40	12 08	12 24	12 41	13 07	13 24	13 41

		NT	NT	NT	NT	NT	NT	NT	NT	NT	NT	NT	NT	NT	NT	NT	NT	NT	NT	NT	NT	NT
Clitheroe	d			13 23			14 25			15 25			16 25			17 25	17 53		18 25			19 10
Whalley	d			13 29			14 31			15 31			16 31			17 31	17 59		18 31			19 16
Langho	d			13 34			14 36			15 36			16 36			17 36	18 04		18 36			19 21
Ramsgreave & Wilpshire	d			13 38			14 40			15 40			16 40			17 40	18 08		18 40			19 25
Blackburn	a			13 45			14 47			15 47			16 47			17 47	18 16		18 47			19 32
	d	13 17	13 19	13 47	14 17	14 19	14 48	15 18	15 19	15 48	16 17	16 18	16 48	17 18	17 19	17 48	18 18	18 19	18 48	19 8	19 19	19 46
Preston 8 97	a																					
Blackpool North 97	a																					
Darwen	a	13 24		13 54	14 24		14 55	15 25		15 55		16 25	16 55	17 25		17 56	18 25		18 55	19 25		19 53
	d	13 27		13 56	14 27		14 56	15 27		15 56		16 27	16 56	17 28		17 56	18 28		18 56	19 27		19 56
Entwistle	d			14x03			15x03			16x03			17x03			18x03			19x03			20x03
Bromley Cross	d	13 40		14 09	14 40		15 09	15 40		16 09		16 40	17 09	17 40		18 09	18 40		19 09	19 40		20 09
Hall I' Th' Wood	d	13 43		14 12	14 43		15 12	15 43		16 12		16 43	17 12	17 43		18 12	18 43		19 12	19 43		20 12
Bolton 82	a	13 48		14 17	14 48		15 17	15 48		16 17		16 48	17 17	17 48		18 17	18 48		19 17	19 48		20 17
Salford Crescent 82	a	14 00		14 32	15 00		15 32	16 00		16 32		17 00	17 32	18 01		18 32	19 01		19 31	20 02		20 31
Manchester Piccadilly 10 82	a																					
Salford Central 82	a	14 04		14 35	15 04		15 37	16 04		16 36		17 04	17 36	18 04		18 36	19 04		19 35	20 05		20 35
Manchester Victoria 82	a	14 07	14 24	14 41	15 07	15 24	15 40	16 07	16 24	16 41	17 24	17 07	17 41	18 07	18 24	18 41	19 07	19 24	19 40	20 08	20 24	20 41

		NT	NT	NT	NT	NT	NT	NT	NT
Clitheroe	d		20 25		21 25		22 54		23 39
Whalley	d		20 31		21 31		23 00		23 45
Langho	d		20 36		21 36		23 05		23 50
Ramsgreave & Wilpshire	d		20 40		21 40		23 09		23 54
Blackburn	a		20 47		21 47		23 17		00 01
	d	20 17	20 48	21 20	21 48	22 19	23 17	23 19	
Preston 8 97	a								
Blackpool North 97	a								
Darwen	a		20 55		21 55		23 25		
	d		20 56		21 56		23 25		
Entwistle	d		21x03		22x03		23x32		
Bromley Cross	d		21 09		22 09		23 38		
Hall I' Th' Wood	d		21 12		22 12		23 40		
Bolton 82	a		21 17		22 17		23 45		
Salford Crescent 82	a		21 30		22 32		23 57		
Manchester Piccadilly 10 82	a								
Salford Central 82	a		21 33		22 36		00 01		
Manchester Victoria 82	a	21 23	21 36	22 29	22 40	23 33	00 05	00 23	

Saturdays
21 December to 16 May

		NT	NT	NT	NT	NT	NT	NT	NT	NT	NT	NT	NT	NT	NT	NT	NT	NT	NT	NT	NT	NT	NT
Clitheroe	d			06 25		06 49	07 25			08 25			09 25			10 25			11 25			12 25	
Whalley	d			06 31		06 55	07 31			08 31			09 31			10 31			11 31			12 31	
Langho	d			06 36		07 00	07 36			08 36			09 36			10 36			11 36			12 36	
Ramsgreave & Wilpshire	d			06 40		07 04	07 40			08 40			09 40			10 40			11 40			12 40	
Blackburn	a			06 47		07 11	07 47			08 47			09 47			10 47			11 47			12 47	
	d	06 16	06 19	06 48	07 14	07 18	07 48	08 18	08 19	08 48	09 18	09 19	09 48	10 18	10 19	10 48	11 17	11 19	11 48	12 18	12 19	12 48	13 17
Preston 8 97	a																						
Blackpool North 97	a																						
Darwen	a	06 23		06 55		07 25	07 55	08 25		08 55	09 25		09 55	10 25		10 55	11 24		11 55	12 25		12 55	13 24
	d	06 25		06 56		07 27	07 56	08 27		08 56	09 27		09 56	10 27		10 56	11 27		11 56	12 27		12 56	13 27
Entwistle	d	06x32		07x03		07x34	08x03			09x03			10x03			11x03			12x03			13x03	
Bromley Cross	d	06 38		07 09		07 40	08 09	08 40		09 08	09 40		10 09	10 40		11 09	11 40		12 09	12 40		13 09	13 40
Hall I' Th' Wood	d	06 41		07 12		07 43	08 12	08 43		09 11	09 43		10 12	10 43		11 12	11 43		12 12	12 43		13 12	13 43
Bolton 82	a	06 46		07 17		07 48	08 17	08 48		09 16	09 48		10 17	10 48		11 17	11 49		12 17	12 48		13 17	13 48
Salford Crescent 82	a	06 59		07 32		08 02	08 32	09 01		09 32	10 01		10 32	11 01		11 32	12 01		12 32	13 00		13 32	14 00
Manchester Piccadilly 10 82	a																						
Salford Central 82	a	07 02		07 36		08 05	08 35	09 04		09 35	10 04		10 36	11 04		11 36	12 04		12 36	13 04		13 36	14 04
Manchester Victoria 82	a	07 07	07 24	07 41	08 24	08 08	08 41	09 07	09 24	09 41	10 07	10 24	10 41	11 07	11 24	11 40	12 08	12 24	12 41	13 07	13 24	13 41	14 07

Table T094-R

Saturdays

21 December to 16 May

Clitheroe - Blackburn - Bolton and Manchester

	NT	NT	NT	NT	NT	NT	NT	NT	NT	NT	NT	NT	NT	NT	NT	NT	NT	NT	NT	NT	NT
Clitheroe d		13 23			14 25			15 25			16 25			17 25	17 53		18 25			19 10	
Whalley d		13 29			14 31			15 31			16 31			17 31	17 59		18 31			19 16	
Langho d		13 34			14 36			15 36			16 36			17 36	18 04		18 36			19 21	
Ramsgreave & Wilpshire d		13 38			14 40			15 40			16 40			17 40	18 08		18 40			19 25	
Blackburn a		13 45			14 47			15 47			16 47			17 47	18 16		18 47			19 32	
d	13 19	13 47	14 17	14 19	14 48	15 18	15 19	15 48	16 17	16 18	16 48	17 18	17 19	17 48	18 18	18 19	18 48	19 18	19 19	19 46	20 17
Preston 8 97 a																					
Blackpool North 97 a																					
Darwen a		13 54	14 24		14 55	15 25		15 55		16 25	16 55	17 25		17 56	18 25		18 55	19 25		19 53	
d		13 56	14 27		14 56	15 27		15 56		16 27	16 56	17 28		17 56	18 28		18 56	19 27		19 56	
Entwistle d		14x03			15x03			16x03			17x03			18x03			19x03			20x03	
Bromley Cross d		14 09	14 40		15 09	15 40		16 09		16 40	17 09	17 40		18 09	18 40		19 09	19 40		20 09	
Hall I' Th' Wood d		14 12	14 43		15 12	15 43		16 12		16 43	17 12	17 43		18 12	18 43		19 12	19 43		20 12	
Bolton 82 a		14 17	14 48		15 17	15 48		16 17		16 48	17 17	17 48		18 17	18 48		19 17	19 48		20 17	
Salford Crescent 82 a		14 32	15 00		15 32	16 00		16 32		17 00	17 32	18 01		18 32	19 01		19 31	20 02		20 31	
Manchester Piccadilly 10 82 ⛴ a																					
Salford Central 82 a		14 35	15 04		15 37	16 04		16 36		17 04	17 36	18 04		18 36	19 04		19 35	20 05		20 35	
Manchester Victoria 82 ⛴ a	14 24	14 41	15 07	15 24	15 40	16 07	16 24	16 41	17 24	17 07	17 41	18 07	18 24	18 41	19 07	19 24	19 40	20 08	20 24	20 41	21 23

	NT	NT	NT	NT	NT	NT	NT
Clitheroe d	20 25		21 25		22 54		23 39
Whalley d	20 31		21 31		23 00		23 45
Langho d	20 36		21 36		23 05		23 50
Ramsgreave & Wilpshire d	20 40		21 40		23 09		23 54
Blackburn a	20 47		21 47		23 17		00 01
d	20 48	21 20	21 48	22 19	23 17	23 19	
Preston 8 97 a							
Blackpool North 97 a							
Darwen a	20 55		21 55		23 25		
d	20 56		21 56		23 25		
Entwistle d	21x03		22x03		23x32		
Bromley Cross d	21 09		22 09		23 38		
Hall I' Th' Wood d	21 12		22 12		23 40		
Bolton 82 a	21 17		22 17		23 45		
Salford Crescent 82 a	21 30		22 32		23 57		
Manchester Piccadilly 10 82 ⛴ a							
Salford Central 82 a	21 33		22 36				
Manchester Victoria 82 ⛴ a	21 36	22 29	22 45	23 33	00 07	00 23	

Sundays

15 December to 10 May

	NT	NT	NT	NT	NT	NT	NT	NT	NT	NT A	NT	NT		NT	NT	NT	NT B	NT	NT	NT	NT
Clitheroe d						09 25		10 25		10 58	11 25		and at the same minutes past each hour until	16 25		17 25	17 37		18 25		
Whalley d						09 31		10 31		11 04	11 31			16 31		17 31	17 43		18 31		
Langho d						09 36		10 36		11 09	11 36			16 36		17 36	17 48		18 36		
Ramsgreave & Wilpshire d						09 40		10 40		11 14	11 40			16 40		17 40	17 52		18 40		
Blackburn a						09 47		10 47		11 25	11 47			16 47		17 47	18 00		18 47		
d	07 48	08 12	08 30	08 48	09 12	09 48	10 12	10 48	11 12	11 34	11 48	12 12		16 48	17 12	17 48	18 00	18 12	18 50	19 12	20 16
Preston 8 97 a			08 47							11 57							18 21				
Blackpool North 97 a																	18 47				
Darwen a				08 55		09 55		10 55			11 55			16 55		17 55			18 57		
d				08 56		09 56		10 56			11 56			16 56		17 56			18 58		
Entwistle d				09x03		10x03		11x03			12x03			17x03		18x03			19x05		
Bromley Cross d				09 09		10 09		11 09			12 09			17 09		18 09			19 11		
Hall I' Th' Wood d				09 13		10 12		11 12			12 12			17 12		18 12			19 14		
Bolton 82 a				09 18		10 17		11 17			12 17			17 17		18 17			19 19		
Salford Crescent 82 a				09 32		10 33		11 33			12 33			17 33		18 33			19 33		
Manchester Piccadilly 10 82 ⛴ a																					
Salford Central 82 a				09 35		10 36		11 36			12 36			17 36		18 36			19 36		
Manchester Victoria 82 ⛴ a	08 59	09 24		09 38	10 24	10 39	11 24	11 39	12 24		12 39	13 24		17 39	18 24	18 39		19 24	19 39	20 24	21 30

	NT	NT	NT	NT	NT	NT	NT
Clitheroe d	19 47	20 25		21 25			22 45
Whalley d	19 53	20 31		21 31			22 51
Langho d	19 58	20 36		21 36			22 55
Ramsgreave & Wilpshire d	20 02	20 40		21 40			23 00
Blackburn a	20 12	20 47		21 47			23 07
d	20 17	20 48	21 13	21 48	22 13	23 00	23 07
Preston 8 97 a							
Blackpool North 97 a							
Darwen a	20 26	20 55		21 55			23 15
d	20 27	20 56		21 56			23 15
Entwistle d	20x34	21x03		22x03			23x22
Bromley Cross d	20 40	21 09		22 09			23 28
Hall I' Th' Wood d	20 43	21 12		22 12			23 30
Bolton 82 a	20 48	21 17		22 17			23 35
Salford Crescent 82 a	21 01	21 33		22 33			23 48
Manchester Piccadilly 10 82 ⛴ a							
Salford Central 82 a	21 04	21 36		22 36			23 51
Manchester Victoria 82 ⛴ a	21 08	21 39	22 25	22 39	23 25	00 11	23 54

A Departs from Hellifield 1030
B Departs from Hellifield 1715

Table T097-F

Mondays to Fridays

16 December to 15 May

Colne, Burnley, Accrington and Blackburn - Preston - Blackpool

Miles	Miles		NT MX A	NT MX B	NT MX ◇ C	NT MO A	NT MO ◇ C	NT MX ◇ D	NT MO ◇ D	NT MO ◇ E	NT MX ◇ F	NT MX ◇ D	NT ◇ D	NT	NT	NT	NT ◇ D	NT	NT ◇ E	NT	NT	NT G
0	—	**Colne** d												05 22				06 11				
2	—	Nelson d												05 27				06 16				
3¼	—	Brierfield d												05 30				06 19				
5½	—	**Burnley Central** d												05 35				06 24				
6	—	Burnley Barracks d												05x38				06x27				
—	0	Manchester Victoria ⛴ d																		06 00		
—	10½	Rochdale ⛴ d																		06 14		
—	19¼	Todmorden d																		06 29		
—	—	Leeds 10 41 d																				
—	28	Burnley Manchester Road 41 d			00 02															06 45		
7	—	Rose Grove d												05 41				06 30		06 48		
8½	—	Hapton d												05x44				06x33				
10	—	Huncoat d												05 48				06 37				
11¾	34	Accrington d	00 01		00 11									05 52				06 41		06 55		
12½	—	Church & Oswaldtwistle d												05 55				06 44				
14¼	—	Rishton d												05 59				06 48				
18	39½	**Blackburn** a	00 12		00 20									06 04				06 54		07 06		
—	—	Clitheroe 94 d																				
—	—	**Blackburn** d												06 05		06 13		06 54				
19¾	—	Mill Hill (Lancashire) d														06 16		06 57				
20	—	Cherry Tree d														06 18		06 59				
21	—	Pleasington d														06 21		07x02				
26	—	Bamber Bridge d														06 28		07 09				
27¼	—	Lostock Hall d		00 01												06 30		07 11				
30	0	**Preston** 8 a		00 10										06 22		06 39		07 20				
—	—	d								00 17	00 24	01 01	05 52		06 31	06 41	06 53		07 29		07 34	07 38
35¼	5¼	Salwick d																			07 41	
37½	7½	Kirkham & Wesham d						00 06	00 06	00 27		01 10	06 01		06 40		07 03		07 38		07 46	
41	—	Moss Side d													06 46						07 52	
43½	—	Lytham d													06 50						07 56	
44¾	—	Ansdell & Fairhaven d													06 53						07 59	
46¼	—	St Annes-on-the-Sea d													06 57						08 03	
48¼	—	Squires Gate d													07 01						08 06	
49½	—	Blackpool Pleasure Beach d													07 03						08 09	
50	—	**Blackpool South** a													07 06						08 11	
—	14½	Poulton-le-Fylde d				00 02	00 06	00 14	00 15	00 35	00 40	01 18	06 10			06 57	07 11		07 46			07 56
—	16¾	Layton d				00 05		00 18				01 22	06 13				07 15					
—	17½	**Blackpool North** a				00 10	00 13	00 23	00 21	00 41	00 46	01 27	06 18			07 07	07 19		07 52			08 02

	NT ◇ C	NT ◇ D	NT	NT ◇ H	NT	NT ◇ E	NT	NT ◇ C	NT ◇ D	VT ◇1 I 🍴	NT	NT G	NT J	NT ◇ E	NT	NT ◇ C	NT ◇ D	NT	NT G	NT K	NT ◇ E	NT
Colne d			07 09								08 11							09 11				
Nelson d			07 14								08 16							09 16				
Brierfield d			07 17								08 19							09 19				
Burnley Central d			07 22								08 24							09 24				
Burnley Barracks d			07x25								08x27							09x27				
Manchester Victoria ⛴ d					07 04								08 04							09 04		
Rochdale ⛴ d					07 18								08 18							09 18		
Todmorden d					07 35								08 35							09 35		
Leeds 10 41 d	05 57							06 57								07 55						
Burnley Manchester Road 41 d	07 03				07 51			08 04					08 51			09 03				09 51		
Rose Grove d			07 29		07 54						08 30		08 54					09 30		09 54		
Hapton d			07x32								08x33							09x33				
Huncoat d			07 35								08 37							09 37				
Accrington d	07 12		07 40		08 01			08 13			08 41		09 01			09 12		09 41		10 01		
Church & Oswaldtwistle d			07 44								08 44							09 44				
Rishton d			07 48								08 48							09 48				
Blackburn a	07 21		07 54		08 12			08 21			08 54		09 12			09 20		09 54		10 12		
Clitheroe 94 d																						
Blackburn d	07 23		07 54					08 21			08 54					09 21		09 54				
Mill Hill (Lancashire) d	07 26		07 57					08 24			08 57							09 57				
Cherry Tree d			07 59								08 59							09 59				
Pleasington d			08x02								09x02							10x02				
Bamber Bridge d	07 34		08 09					08 33			09 09							10 09				
Lostock Hall d	07 37		08 11					08 35			09 11							10 11				
Preston 8 a	07 45		08 21					08 44			09 21					09 38		10 21				
d	07 47	07 52		08 25		08 30	08 35	08 45	08 51	09 17		09 25		09 30	09 35	09 40	09 51		10 25		10 30	10 35
Salwick d																						
Kirkham & Wesham d		08 03				08 39	08 44		09 02					09 39	09 44		10 00				10 39	10 44
Moss Side d							08 50								09 50							10 50
Lytham d							08 54								09 54							10 54
Ansdell & Fairhaven d							08 57								09 57							10 57
St Annes-on-the-Sea d							09 01								10 01							11 01
Squires Gate d							09 04								10 04							11 04
Blackpool Pleasure Beach d							09 07								10 07							11 07
Blackpool South a							09 09								10 09							11 09
Poulton-le-Fylde d	08 06	08 11		08 41		08 47		09 01	09 11			09 40		09 47		09 56	10 09		10 41		10 47	
Layton d		08 15							09 14								10 12					
Blackpool North a	08 12	08 19		08 47		08 53		09 08	09 19	09 37		09 46		09 53		10 02	10 17		10 47		10 53	

A From Manchester Victoria
B From Colne
C From York
D From Manchester Airport
E From Liverpool Lime Street
F From Manchester Piccadilly
G From Hazel Grove
H From Stoke-on-Trent
I From London Euston
J From Southport
K From Wigan Wallgate

Table T097-F

Mondays to Fridays

16 December to 15 May

Colne, Burnley, Accrington and Blackburn - Preston - Blackpool

Station		NT ◇ A	NT ◇ B	NT	NT C	NT D	VT ◇1 E	NT ◇ F	NT	NT ◇ A	NT ◇ B	NT	NT C	NT G	NT ◇ F	NT	NT ◇ A	NT ◇ B	VT ◇1 E	NT	NT C	NT G
Colne	d			10 11								11 11								12 11		
Nelson	d			10 16								11 16								12 16		
Brierfield	d			10 19								11 19								12 19		
Burnley Central	d			10 24								11 24								12 24		
Burnley Barracks	d			10x26								11x26								12x27		
Manchester Victoria	d					10 04								11 04								12 04
Rochdale	d					10 18								11 18								12 18
Todmorden	d					10 33								11 33								12 33
Leeds 10	41 d	08 57								09 57							10 57					
Burnley Manchester Road	41 d	10 03				10 49				11 03				11 49			12 03					12 49
Rose Grove	d			10 30		10 52						11 30		11 52						12 30		12 52
Hapton	d			10x33								11x33								12x33		
Huncoat	d			10 36								11 36								12 37		
Accrington	d	10 12		10 41		10 59				11 12		11 41		11 59			12 12			12 41		12 59
Church & Oswaldtwistle	d			10 44								11 44								12 44		
Rishton	d			10 47								11 47								12 48		
Blackburn	a	10 20		10 53		11 10				11 20		11 53		12 10			12 20			12 54		13 10
Clitheroe	94 d																					
Blackburn	d	10 21		10 54						11 21		11 54					12 21			12 54		
Mill Hill (Lancashire)	d			10 57								11 57								12 57		
Cherry Tree	d			10 59								11 59								12 59		
Pleasington	d			11x01								12x01								13x02		
Bamber Bridge	d			11 08								12 08								13 09		
Lostock Hall	d			11 11								12 11								13 11		
Preston 8	a	10 38		11 20						11 38		12 20					12 38			13 21		
	d	10 40	10 51		11 24		11 28	11 31	11 35	11 40	11 52		12 24		12 29	12 35	12 40	12 51	13 00		13 24	
Salwick	d																					
Kirkham & Wesham	d		11 02					11 40	11 44		12 01				12 40	12 44		13 00				
Moss Side	d								11 50							12 50						
Lytham	d								11 54							12 54						
Ansdell & Fairhaven	d								11 57							12 57						
St Annes-on-the-Sea	d								12 01							13 01						
Squires Gate	d								12 04							13 04						
Blackpool Pleasure Beach	d								12 07							13 07						
Blackpool South	a								12 09							13 09						
Poulton-le-Fylde	d	10 56	11 10		11 39			11 48		11 56	12 10		12 40		12 48		12 56	13 08			13 40	
Layton	d		11 14								12 14							13 12				
Blackpool North	a	11 02	11 19		11 45		11 49	11 54		12 02	12 18		12 46		12 54		13 02	13 16	13 20		13 46	

Station		NT ◇ F	NT	NT ◇ A	NT ◇ B	NT	NT C	NT G	NT ◇ F	NT	NT ◇ A	NT ◇ B	NT	NT C	NT D	NT ◇ F	NT	NT ◇ A	NT ◇ B	NT	NT C	NT G	NT ◇ F
Colne	d					13 11							14 11							15 11			
Nelson	d					13 16							14 16							15 16			
Brierfield	d					13 19							14 19							15 19			
Burnley Central	d					13 24							14 24							15 24			
Burnley Barracks	d					13x26							14x26							15x27			
Manchester Victoria	d							13 04							14 04							15 04	
Rochdale	d							13 18							14 18							15 18	
Todmorden	d							13 33							14 33							15 33	
Leeds 10	41 d			11 57							12 57							13 57					
Burnley Manchester Road	41 d			13 03				13 49			14 03				14 49			15 03				15 49	
Rose Grove	d					13 30		13 52					14 30		14 52					15 30		15 52	
Hapton	d					13x33							14x33							15x33			
Huncoat	d					13 36							14 36							15 37			
Accrington	d			13 12		13 41		13 59			14 12		14 41		14 59			15 12		15 41		15 59	
Church & Oswaldtwistle	d					13 44							14 44							15 44			
Rishton	d					13 47							14 47							15 48			
Blackburn	a			13 20		13 53		14 10			14 20		14 53		15 10			15 20		15 54		16 10	
Clitheroe	94 d																						
Blackburn	d			13 20		13 54					14 21		14 54					15 21		15 54			
Mill Hill (Lancashire)	d					13 57							14 57							15 57			
Cherry Tree	d					13 59							14 59							15 59			
Pleasington	d					14x01							15x01							16x02			
Bamber Bridge	d					14 08							15 08							16 09			
Lostock Hall	d					14 11							15 11							16 11			
Preston 8	a			13 38		14 20					14 38		15 20					15 38		16 21			
	d	13 29	13 34	13 39	13 51		14 25		14 30	14 35	14 40	14 50		15 24		15 29	15 35	15 40	15 51		16 24		16 30
Salwick	d																		15 58				
Kirkham & Wesham	d	13 39	13 44		14 02				14 39	14 44		15 02				15 39	15 44		16 02				16 39
Moss Side	d		13 50							14 50							15 50						
Lytham	d		13 54							14 54							15 54						
Ansdell & Fairhaven	d		13 57							14 57							15 57						
St Annes-on-the-Sea	d		14 01							15 01							16 01						
Squires Gate	d		14 04							15 04							16 04						
Blackpool Pleasure Beach	d		14 07							15 07							16 07						
Blackpool South	a		14 09							15 09							16 09						
Poulton-le-Fylde	d	13 47		13 55	14 11		14 40		14 47		14 56	15 10		15 40		15 47		15 56	16 11		16 40		16 47
Layton	d				14 15							15 14							16 15		16 44		
Blackpool North	a	13 53		14 02	14 19		14 46		14 53		15 02	15 19		15 46		15 53		16 02	16 19		16 48		16 53

A From York
B From Manchester Airport
C From Hazel Grove
D From Wigan North Western
E From London Euston
F From Liverpool Lime Street
G From Wigan Wallgate

Table T097-F

Mondays to Fridays

16 December to 15 May

Colne, Burnley, Accrington and Blackburn - Preston - Blackpool

Station		NT	NT ◇ A	NT ◇ B	NT	NT ◇ C	NT D	NT	NT E	NT ◇ A	NT ◇ B	NT	NT E	NT D	NT	NT ◇ C	NT ◇ A	NT ◇ B	VT ◇1 F	NT	NT E	NT G	NT ◇ C
Colne	d				16 11							17 11								18 11			
Nelson	d				16 16							17 16								18 16			
Brierfield	d				16 19							17 19								18 19			
Burnley Central	d				16 24							17 24								18 24			
Burnley Barracks	d				16x27							17x27								18x27			
Manchester Victoria	d						16 04							17 04								18 04	
Rochdale	d						16 18							17 18								18 18	
Todmorden	d						16 35							17 35								18 35	
Leeds 10	41 d		14 57							15 57							16 57						
Burnley Manchester Road	41 d		16 03				16 51			17 03				17 51			18 03					18 51	
Rose Grove	d				16 30		16 54					17 30		17 54						18 30		18 54	
Hapton	d				16x33							17x33								18x33			
Huncoat	d				16 37							17 37								18 37			
Accrington	d		16 12		16 41		17 01			17 12		17 41		18 01			18 12			18 41		19 01	
Church & Oswaldtwistle	d				16 44							17 44								18 44			
Rishton	d				16 48							17 48								18 48			
Blackburn	a		16 20		16 54		17 12			17 20		17 54		18 12			18 20			18 54		19 12	
Clitheroe	94 d																						
Blackburn	d		16 21		16 54					17 21		17 54					18 21			18 54			
Mill Hill (Lancashire)	d				16 57							17 57								18 57			
Cherry Tree	d				16 59							17 59								18 59			
Pleasington	d				17x02							18x02								19x02			
Bamber Bridge	d				17 09							18 09								19 09			
Lostock Hall	d				17 11							18 11								19 11			
Preston 8	a		16 39		17 21					17 40		18 21					18 40			19 21			
	d	16 35	16 40	16 53		17 29		17 34	17 37	17 42	17 54		18 26		18 32	18 37	18 43	18 52	19 05		19 26		19 30
Salwick	d										18 01												
Kirkham & Wesham	d	16 44		17 02		17 39		17 44	17 46		18 05		18 35		18 41	18 46		19 02	19 15				19 40
Moss Side	d	16 50						17 50							18 47								
Lytham	d	16 54						17 54							18 52								
Ansdell & Fairhaven	d	16 57						17 57							18 55								
St Annes-on-the-Sea	d	17 01						18 01							18 59								
Squires Gate	d	17 04						18 04							19 02								
Blackpool Pleasure Beach	d	17 07						18 07							19 05								
Blackpool South	a	17 09						18 09							19 08								
Poulton-le-Fylde	d		16 56	17 10		17 47			17 54	17 58	18 14		18 43			18 54	18 59	19 10	19 24		19 41		19 48
Layton	d			17 14					17 58		18 18		18 47					19 14					
Blackpool North	a		17 03	17 19		17 53			18 02	18 06	18 22		18 51			19 00	19 05	19 18	19 30		19 47		19 55

Station		NT	NT ◇ A	NT ◇ B	NT	NT	NT E	NT D	NT ◇ C	NT	NT ◇ A	NT ◇ B	NT	NT E	NT D	NT ◇ C	VT FO ◇1 F	NT	NT ◇ A	NT ◇ B	NT ◇ C	NT E
Colne	d					19 11							20 11									
Nelson	d					19 16							20 16									
Brierfield	d					19 19							20 19									
Burnley Central	d					19 24							20 24									
Burnley Barracks	d					19x27							20x27									
Manchester Victoria	d				19 05			19 04							20 04							
Rochdale	d							19 18							20 18							
Todmorden	d							19 33							20 33							
Leeds 10	41 d		17 57								18 57								19 57			
Burnley Manchester Road	41 d		19 03					19 49			20 03				20 49				21 03			
Rose Grove	d					19 30		19 52					20 30		20 52							
Hapton	d					19x33							20x33									
Huncoat	d					19 37							20 37									
Accrington	d		19 12			19 41		19 59			20 12		20 41		20 59				21 12			
Church & Oswaldtwistle	d					19 44							20 44									
Rishton	d					19 48							20 48									
Blackburn	a		19 20			19 54		20 09			20 20		20 54		21 10				21 20			
Clitheroe	94 d																					
Blackburn	d		19 21			19 54					20 21		20 54						21 21			
Mill Hill (Lancashire)	d					19 57							20 57									
Cherry Tree	d					19 59							20 59									
Pleasington	d					20x02							21x02									
Bamber Bridge	d					20 09							21 09									
Lostock Hall	d					20 11							21 11									
Preston 8	a		19 38		20 01	20 21					20 38		21 21						21 41			
	d	19 35	19 40	19 51	20 03		20 26		20 31	20 36	20 40	20 51		21 27		21 31	21 34	21 38	21 43	21 50	22 22	22 27
Salwick	d																					
Kirkham & Wesham	d	19 44		20 02	20 12				20 40	20 45		21 00				21 40	21 45	21 47		22 00	22 32	
Moss Side	d	19 50								20 51								21 53				
Lytham	d	19 54								20 55								21 57				
Ansdell & Fairhaven	d	19 57								20 58								22 00				
St Annes-on-the-Sea	d	20 01								21 02								22 04				
Squires Gate	d	20 04								21 05								22 07				
Blackpool Pleasure Beach	d	20 07								21 08								22 10				
Blackpool South	a	20 09								21 10								22 12				
Poulton-le-Fylde	d		19 56	20 10	20 21		20 41		20 48		20 56	21 09		21 42		21 48	21 54		21 59	22 08	22 40	22 43
Layton	d			20 14								21 13								22 12		
Blackpool North	a		20 02	20 18	20 28		20 47		20 54		21 04	21 17		21 48		21 54	22 00		22 05	22 16	22 46	22 49

A From York
B From Manchester Airport
C From Liverpool Lime Street
D From Wigan Wallgate
E From Hazel Grove
F From Lo don Euston
G From Wigan North Western

Table T097-F

Mondays to Fridays
16 December to 15 May

Colne, Burnley, Accrington and Blackburn - Preston - Blackpool

	NT	NT	NT A	NT ◇ B	NT ◇ C	NT	NT	NT ◇ D	NT E	NT ◇ B	NT ◇ C	NT	NT	NT ◇ B
Colne d	21 26					22 24						23 11		
Nelson d	21 31					22 29						23 16		
Brierfield d	21 34					22 32						23 19		
Burnley Central d	21 39					22 37						23 24		
Burnley Barracks d	21x42					22x40						23x27		
Manchester Victoria d			21 04				22 04						23 04	
Rochdale d			21 18				22 18						23 18	
Todmorden d			21 36				22 35						23 33	
Leeds 10 41 d				20 57						21 57				22 57
Burnley Manchester Road 41 d			21 52	22 03			22 51			23 03			23 49	00 02
Rose Grove d	21 45		21 55			22 43	22 54					23 30	23 52	
Hapton d	21x48					22x46								
Huncoat d	21 52					22 50								
Accrington d	21 56		22 02	22 12		22 54	23 01			23 12		23 37	00 01	00 11
Church & Oswaldtwistle d	21 59					22 57								
Rishton d	22 03					23 01								
Blackburn a	22 09		22 13	22 20		23 09	23 13			23 20		23 46	00 12	00 20
Clitheroe 94 d														
Blackburn d	22 09			22 21						23 21		23 47		
Mill Hill (Lancashire) d	22 12											23 50		
Cherry Tree d	22 14													
Pleasington d	22x17													
Bamber Bridge d	22 24											23 58		
Lostock Hall d	22 26											00 01		
Preston 8 a	22 36			22 38						23 38		00 10		
d		22 36		22 40	22 51			23 24	23 30	23 40	23 55			
Salwick d														
Kirkham & Wesham d		22 45			23 00			23 33			00 06			
Moss Side d		22 51												
Lytham d		22 56												
Ansdell & Fairhaven d		22 59												
St Annes-on-the-Sea d		23 03												
Squires Gate d		23 06												
Blackpool Pleasure Beach d		23 09												
Blackpool South a		23 11												
Poulton-le-Fylde d				22 57	23 09			23 41	23 46	23 58	00 14			
Layton d					23 13						00 18			
Blackpool North a				23 07	23 17			23 47	23 52	00 04	00 23			

Saturdays
21 December to 16 May

	NT F	NT G	NT ◇ B	NT ◇ C	NT ◇ H	NT ◇ C	NT ◇ C	NT	NT	NT ◇ C	NT	NT	NT ◇ D	NT	NT E	NT	NT ◇ B	NT ◇ C	NT	NT ◇ I	NT	NT ◇ D
Colne d								05 23				06 11							07 09			
Nelson d								05 27				06 16							07 14			
Brierfield d								05 30				06 19							07 17			
Burnley Central d								05 35				06 24							07 22			
Burnley Barracks d								05x37				06x27							07x25			
Manchester Victoria d														06 00							07 04	
Rochdale d														06 14							07 18	
Todmorden d														06 29							07 35	
Leeds 10 41 d																	05 57					
Burnley Manchester Road 41 d			00 02											06 45			07 03				07 51	
Rose Grove d								05 40				06 30		06 48					07 29		07 54	
Hapton d								05x43				06x33							07x32			
Huncoat d								05 46				06 37							07 35			
Accrington d	00 01		00 11					05 51				06 41		06 55			07 12		07 40		08 01	
Church & Oswaldtwistle d								05 53				06 44							07 44			
Rishton d								05 56				06 48							07 48			
Blackburn a	00 12		00 20					06 02				06 54		07 06			07 21		07 54		08 12	
Clitheroe 94 d																						
Blackburn d								06 02	06 13			06 54					07 23		07 54			
Mill Hill (Lancashire) d									06 16			06 57					07 26		07 57			
Cherry Tree d									06 18			06 59							07 59			
Pleasington d									06 21			07x02							08x02			
Bamber Bridge d									06 28			07 09					07 34		08 09			
Lostock Hall d		00 01							06 30			07 11					07 37		08 11			
Preston 8 a		00 10						06 20	06 39			07 20					07 45		08 21			
d					00 24	01 01	05 52		06 41	06 53	06 56		07 29		07 41	07 44	07 47	07 52		08 25		08 30
Salwick d																07 51						
Kirkham & Wesham d				00 06		01 10	06 01			07 02	07 05		07 38			08 00		08 03				08 39
Moss Side d											07 11					08 06						
Lytham d											07 15					08 10						
Ansdell & Fairhaven d											07 18					08 13						
St Annes-on-the-Sea d											07 22					08 17						
Squires Gate d											07 26					08 20						
Blackpool Pleasure Beach d											07 28					08 23						
Blackpool South a											07 31					08 25						
Poulton-le-Fylde d				00 14	00 40	01 18	06 10		06 57	07 11			07 46		07 57		08 06	08 11		08 41		08 47
Layton d				00 18		01 22	06 13			07 14								08 15				
Blackpool North a				00 23	00 46	01 27	06 18		07 07	07 19			07 52		08 03		08 12	08 19		08 47		08 53

A From Kirkby
B From York
C From Manchester Airport
D From Liverpool Lime Street
E From Hazel Grove
F From Manchester Victoria
G From Colne
H From Manchester Piccadilly
I From Stoke-on-Trent

Table T097-F

Saturdays
21 December to 16 May

Colne, Burnley, Accrington and Blackburn - Preston - Blackpool

	NT ◇ A	NT ◇ B	NT	VT ◇1 C	NT	NT D	NT E	NT ◇ F	NT ◇ A	NT	NT ◇ B	NT	NT D	NT G	NT ◇ F	NT ◇ A	NT ◇ B	NT	NT	NT D	NT H	NT ◇ F
Colne d					08 11							09 11							10 11			
Nelson d					08 16							09 16							10 16			
Brierfield d					08 19							09 19							10 19			
Burnley Central d					08 24							09 24							10 24			
Burnley Barracks d					08x27							09x27							10x26			
Manchester Victoria d							08 04							09 04							10 04	
Rochdale d							08 18							09 18							10 18	
Todmorden d							08 35							09 35							10 33	
Leeds 10 41 d	06 57								07 55							08 57						
Burnley Manchester Road 41 d	08 04						08 51		09 03					09 51		10 03					10 49	
Rose Grove d					08 30		08 54					09 30		09 54					10 30		10 52	
Hapton d					08x33							09x33							10x33			
Huncoat d					08 37							09 37							10 36			
Accrington d	08 13				08 41		09 01		09 12			09 41		10 01		10 12			10 41		10 59	
Church & Oswaldtwistle d					08 44							09 44							10 44			
Rishton d					08 48							09 48							10 47			
Blackburn a	08 21				08 54		09 12		09 20			09 54		10 12		10 20			10 53		11 10	
Clitheroe 94 d																						
Blackburn d	08 21				08 54				09 21			09 54				10 21			10 54			
Mill Hill (Lancashire) d	08 24				08 57							09 57							10 57			
Cherry Tree d					08 59							09 59							10 59			
Pleasington d					09x02							10x02							11x01			
Bamber Bridge d	08 33				09 09							10 09							11 08			
Lostock Hall d	08 35				09 11							10 11							11 11			
Preston 8 a	08 44				09 21				09 38			10 21				10 38			11 20			
d	08 45	08 51	08 56	09 11		09 25		09 30	09 40	09 51	09 56		10 25		10 30	10 40	10 51	10 57		11 24		11 31
Salwick d																						
Kirkham & Wesham d		09 02	09 05					09 39		10 00	10 05				10 39		11 02	11 07				11 40
Moss Side d			09 11							10 06								11 13				
Lytham d			09 15							10 10								11 17				
Ansdell & Fairhaven d			09 18							10 13								11 20				
St Annes-on-the-Sea d			09 22							10 17								11 24				
Squires Gate d			09 26							10 21								11 27				
Blackpool Pleasure Beach d			09 28							10 24								11 30				
Blackpool South a			09 31							10 26								11 32				
Poulton-le-Fylde d	09 01	09 11				09 40		09 47	09 56		10 14		10 41		10 47	10 56	11 10			11 39		11 48
Layton d		09 14									10 17						11 14					
Blackpool North a	09 08	09 19		09 32		09 46		09 53	10 02		10 22		10 47		10 53	11 02	11 19			11 45		11 54

	VT ◇1 I	NT ◇ A	NT ◇ B	NT	NT	NT D	NT G	NT ◇ F	NT ◇ A	NT ◇ B	NT	VT ◇1 I	NT	NT D	NT G	NT ◇ F	NT ◇ A	NT ◇ B	NT	NT	NT D
Colne d					11 11								12 11							13 11	
Nelson d					11 16								12 16							13 16	
Brierfield d					11 19								12 19							13 19	
Burnley Central d					11 24								12 24							13 24	
Burnley Barracks d					11x26								12x27							13x26	
Manchester Victoria d							11 04								12 04						
Rochdale d							11 18								12 18						
Todmorden d							11 33								12 33						
Leeds 10 41 d		09 57							10 57								11 57				
Burnley Manchester Road 41 d		11 03					11 49		12 03						12 49		13 03				
Rose Grove d					11 30		11 52						12 30		12 52					13 30	
Hapton d					11x33								12x33							13x33	
Huncoat d					11 36								12 37							13 36	
Accrington d		11 12			11 41		11 59		12 12				12 41		12 59		13 12			13 41	
Church & Oswaldtwistle d					11 44								12 44							13 44	
Rishton d					11 47								12 48							13 47	
Blackburn a		11 20			11 53		12 10		12 20				12 54		13 10		13 20			13 53	
Clitheroe 94 d																					
Blackburn d		11 21			11 54				12 21				12 54				13 20			13 54	
Mill Hill (Lancashire) d					11 57								12 57							13 57	
Cherry Tree d					11 59								12 59							13 59	
Pleasington d					12x01								13x02							14x01	
Bamber Bridge d					12 08								13 09							14 08	
Lostock Hall d					12 11								13 11							14 11	
Preston 8 a		11 38			12 20				12 38				13 21				13 38			14 20	
d	11 34	11 40	11 52	11 57		12 24		12 29	12 40	12 51	12 56	13 00		13 24		13 29	13 39	13 51	13 56		14 24
Salwick d																					
Kirkham & Wesham d			12 02	12 07				12 40		13 00	13 05					13 39		14 02	14 06		
Moss Side d				12 13							13 11								14 12		
Lytham d				12 17							13 15								14 16		
Ansdell & Fairhaven d				12 20							13 18								14 19		
St Annes-on-the-Sea d				12 24							13 22								14 23		
Squires Gate d				12 27							13 26								14 26		
Blackpool Pleasure Beach d				12 30							13 28								14 29		
Blackpool South a				12 32							13 31								14 31		
Poulton-le-Fylde d		11 56	12 11			12 40		12 48	12 56	13 08				13 40		13 47	13 55	14 11			14 40
Layton d			12 15							13 12								14 15			
Blackpool North a	11 57	12 02	12 19			12 46		12 54	13 02	13 16		13 20		13 46		13 53	14 02	14 19			14 46

A From York
B From Manchester Airport
C From Birmingham New Street
D From Hazel Grove
E From Southport
F From Liverpool Lime Street
G From Wigan Wallgate
H From Wigan North Western
I From London Euston

Table T097-F

21 December to 16 May

Colne, Burnley, Accrington and Blackburn - Preston - Blackpool

		NT	NT	NT	NT	NT	NT	NT	NT	NT	NT	NT	NT	NT	NT	NT	NT	NT	NT	NT	NT	NT	NT
		A	◇ B	◇ C	◇ D			E	F	◇ B	◇ C		◇ D		E	A	◇ B	◇ C	◇ D			◇ B	A
Colne	d						14 11							15 11							16 11		
Nelson	d						14 16							15 16							16 16		
Brierfield	d						14 19							15 19							16 19		
Burnley Central	d						14 24							15 24							16 24		
Burnley Barracks	d						14x26							15x27							16x27		
Manchester Victoria	d	13 04							14 04							15 04							16 04
Rochdale	d	13 18							14 18							15 18							16 18
Todmorden	d	13 33							14 33							15 33							16 35
Leeds 10	41 d			12 57							13 57							14 57					
Burnley Manchester Road	41 d	13 49		14 03					14 49		15 03					15 49		16 03					16 51
Rose Grove	d	13 52					14 30		14 52					15 30		15 52					16 30		16 54
Hapton	d						14x33							15x33							16x33		
Huncoat	d						14 36							15 37							16 37		
Accrington	d	13 59		14 12			14 41		14 59		15 12			15 41		15 59		16 12			16 41		17 01
Church & Oswaldtwistle	d						14 44							15 44							16 44		
Rishton	d						14 47							15 48							16 48		
Blackburn	a	14 10		14 20			14 53		15 10		15 20			15 54		16 10		16 20			16 54		17 12
Clitheroe	94 d																						
Blackburn	d			14 21			14 54				15 21			15 54				16 21			16 54		
Mill Hill (Lancashire)	d						14 57							15 57							16 57		
Cherry Tree	d						14 59							15 59							16 59		
Pleasington	d						15x01							16x02							17x02		
Bamber Bridge	d						15 08							16 09							17 09		
Lostock Hall	d						15 11							16 11							17 11		
Preston 8	a			14 38			15 20				15 38			16 21				16 39			17 21		
	d		14 36	14 40	14 50	14 56		15 24		15 29	15 40	15 46	15 51		16 24		16 30	16 40	16 53	16 56		17 29	
Salwick	d											15 53											
Kirkham & Wesham	d		14 46		15 02	15 06				15 39		16 02	16 01				16 39		17 02	17 06		17 39	
Moss Side	d					15 12						16 08								17 12			
Lytham	d					15 16						16 12								17 16			
Ansdell & Fairhaven	d					15 19						16 15								17 19			
St Annes-on-the-Sea	d					15 23						16 19								17 23			
Squires Gate	d					15 26						16 22								17 26			
Blackpool Pleasure Beach	d					15 29						16 25								17 29			
Blackpool South	a					15 31						16 27								17 31			
Poulton-le-Fylde	d		14 54	14 58	15 10			15 40		15 47	15 56		16 09		16 40		16 47	16 56	17 11			17 47	
Layton	d				15 14								16 13		16 44				17 14				
Blackpool North	a		15 01	15 04	15 19			15 46		15 53	16 02		16 17		16 48		16 53	17 03	17 19			17 53	

		NT	NT	NT	NT	NT	NT	NT	NT	NT	NT	NT	NT	NT	NT	NT	NT	NT	NT	NT	NT	NT
		E	◇ C		◇ D		E	A	◇ B	◇ C	◇ D			E	F	◇ B	◇ C	◇ D				E
Colne	d					17 11							18 12								19 11	
Nelson	d					17 16							18 17								19 16	
Brierfield	d					17 19							18 20								19 19	
Burnley Central	d					17 24							18 25								19 24	
Burnley Barracks	d					17x27							18x28								19x27	
Manchester Victoria	d							17 04							18 04					19 05		
Rochdale	d							17 18							18 18							
Todmorden	d							17 35							18 35							
Leeds 10	41 d		15 57							16 57							17 57					
Burnley Manchester Road	41 d		17 03					17 51		18 03					18 51		19 03					
Rose Grove	d					17 30		17 54					18 31		18 54						19 30	
Hapton	d					17x33							18x34								19x33	
Huncoat	d					17 37							18 38								19 37	
Accrington	d		17 12			17 41		18 01		18 12			18 42		19 01		19 12				19 41	
Church & Oswaldtwistle	d					17 44							18 45								19 44	
Rishton	d					17 48							18 49								19 48	
Blackburn	a		17 20			17 54		18 12		18 20			18 55		19 12		19 20				19 54	
Clitheroe	94 d																					
Blackburn	d		17 21			17 54				18 21			18 55				19 21				19 54	
Mill Hill (Lancashire)	d					17 57							18 58								19 57	
Cherry Tree	d					17 59							19 00								19 59	
Pleasington	d					18x02							19x03								20x02	
Bamber Bridge	d					18 09							19 10								20 09	
Lostock Hall	d					18 11							19 12								20 11	
Preston 8	a		17 40			18 21				18 40			19 22				19 38			20 04	20 21	
	d	17 37	17 42	17 49	17 54		18 26		18 38	18 43	18 52	18 56		19 26		19 30	19 40	19 51	19 57	20 06		20 26
Salwick	d			17 56																		
Kirkham & Wesham	d	17 46		18 03	18 04		18 35		18 47		19 02	19 06				19 40		20 02	20 06	20 16		
Moss Side	d			18 09								19 12							20 12			
Lytham	d			18 13								19 16							20 16			
Ansdell & Fairhaven	d			18 16								19 19							20 19			
St Annes-on-the-Sea	d			18 20								19 23							20 23			
Squires Gate	d			18 23								19 26							20 27			
Blackpool Pleasure Beach	d			18 26								19 29							20 29			
Blackpool South	a			18 28								19 31							20 32			
Poulton-le-Fylde	d	17 54	17 58		18 12		18 43		18 55	18 59	19 11			19 41		19 48	19 56	20 10		20 24		20 41
Layton	d	17 58			18 16		18 47				19 14							20 14				
Blackpool North	a	18 02	18 06		18 20		18 51		19 01	19 05	19 19			19 47		19 55	20 02	20 18		20 31		20 47

A From Wigan Wallgate
B From Liverpool Lime Street
C From York
D From Manchester Airport
E From Hazel Grove
F From Wigan North Western

NRT DECEMBER 19 EDITION

Table T097-F

21 December to 16 May

Colne, Burnley, Accrington and Blackburn - Preston - Blackpool

		NT	NT	NT	NT	NT	NT	NT	NT	NT	NT	NT	NT	NT	NT	NT	NT	NT	NT	NT	NT	NT	NT
		A	◇ B	◇ C	◇ D			E	A	◇ B	◇ C	◇ D		◇ B	E		F	◇ C				◇ D	E
Colne	d						20 11									21 26				22 24			
Nelson	d						20 16									21 31				22 29			
Brierfield	d						20 19									21 34				22 32			
Burnley Central	d						20 24									21 39				22 37			
Burnley Barracks	d						20x27									21x42				22x40			
Manchester Victoria	d	19 04							20 04								21 04				22 04		
Rochdale	d	19 18							20 18								21 18				22 18		
Todmorden	d	19 33							20 33								21 36				22 35		
Leeds 10	41 d			18 57							19 57							20 57					
Burnley Manchester Road	41 d	19 49		20 03					20 49		21 03						21 52	22 03			22 51		
Rose Grove	d	19 52					20 30		20 52							21 45	21 55			22 43	22 54		
Hapton	d						20x33									21x48				22x46			
Huncoat	d						20 37									21 52				22 50			
Accrington	d	19 59		20 12			20 41		20 59		21 12					21 56	22 02	22 12		22 54	23 01		
Church & Oswaldtwistle	d						20 44									21 59				22 57			
Rishton	d						20 48									22 03				23 01			
Blackburn	a	20 09		20 20			20 54		21 10		21 20					22 09	22 13	22 20		23 09	23 13		
Clitheroe	94 d																						
Blackburn	d			20 21			20 54				21 21					22 09		22 21					
Mill Hill (Lancashire)	d						20 57									22 12							
Cherry Tree	d						20 59									22 14							
Pleasington	d						21x02									22x17							
Bamber Bridge	d						21 09									22 24							
Lostock Hall	d						21 11									22 26							
Preston 8	a			20 38			21 21				21 39					22 36		22 38					
	d		20 31	20 40	20 51	20 55		21 27		21 31	21 41	21 56	21 59	22 22	22 27			22 40	22 45			22 50	23 26
Salwick	d																						
Kirkham & Wesham	d		20 40		21 00	21 05				21 40		22 05	22 08	22 32					22 54			22 59	
Moss Side	d					21 11							22 14						23 00				
Lytham	d					21 15							22 19						23 05				
Ansdell & Fairhaven	d					21 18							22 22						23 08				
St Annes-on-the-Sea	d					21 22							22a25						23 12				
Squires Gate	d					21 25													23 15				
Blackpool Pleasure Beach	d					21 28													23 18				
Blackpool South	a					21 30													23 20				
Poulton-le-Fylde	d		20 48	20 56	21 09			21 42		21 48	21 57	22 14		22 40	22 43			22 57				23 08	23 41
Layton	d				21 13							22 18										23 12	
Blackpool North	a		20 54	21 04	21 17			21 48		21 54	22 03	22 22		22 46	22 49			23 06				23 16	23 47

		NT	NT	NT	NT	NT	NT	NT
		◇ B	◇ C	◇ D				◇ C
Colne	d				23 11			
Nelson	d				23 16			
Brierfield	d				23 19			
Burnley Central	d				23 24			
Burnley Barracks	d				23x27			
Manchester Victoria	d					22 42	23 04	
Rochdale	d					23 03	23 18	
Todmorden	d					23 15	23 33	
Leeds 10	41 d		21 57					22 57
Burnley Manchester Road	41 d		23 03			23 31	23 49	00 02
Rose Grove	d				23 30	23 34	23 52	
Hapton	d							
Huncoat	d							
Accrington	d		23 12		23 37	23 41	00 01	00 12
Church & Oswaldtwistle	d							
Rishton	d							
Blackburn	a		23 20		23 46	23 52	00 12	00 22
Clitheroe	94 d							
Blackburn	d		23 21		23 47			
Mill Hill (Lancashire)	d				23 50			
Cherry Tree	d							
Pleasington	d							
Bamber Bridge	d				23 58			
Lostock Hall	d				00 01			
Preston 8	a		23 38		00 10			
	d	23 30	23 40	23 55				
Salwick	d							
Kirkham & Wesham	d	23 39		00 05				
Moss Side	d							
Lytham	d							
Ansdell & Fairhaven	d							
St Annes-on-the-Sea	d							
Squires Gate	d							
Blackpool Pleasure Beach	d							
Blackpool South	a							
Poulton-le-Fylde	d	23 47	23 58	00 13				
Layton	d			00 17				
Blackpool North	a	23 53	00 04	00 22				

A From Wigan Wallgate
B From Liverpool Lime Street
C From York
D From Manchester Airport
E From Hazel Grove
F From Kirkby

Table T097-F

Sundays 15 December to 10 May

Colne, Burnley, Accrington and Blackburn - Preston - Blackpool

Station		NT A	NT B	NT ◇ C	NT ◇ D	NT ◇ E	NT	NT ◇ F	NT ◇ G	NT H		NT F	NT	NT ◇ I	NT	NT ◇ J	NT ◇ I	NT	NT K	NT		NT ◇ L	NT ◇ M	NT ◇ I	NT
Colne	d																	09 20							10 21
Nelson	d																	09 26							10 26
Brierfield	d																	09 29							10 29
Burnley Central	d																	09 34							10 34
Burnley Barracks	d																	09x36							10x37
Manchester Victoria ⛴	d							08 04		08 30		08 31	08 33						08 59	09 51					
Rochdale ⛴	d												08 54						09 20						
Todmorden	d												09 09						09 35						
Leeds 10 (41)	d																								
Burnley Manchester Road (41)	d			00 02									09 25						09 51						
Rose Grove	d												09 28					09 40	09 54						10 40
Hapton	d																	09x43							10x43
Huncoat	d																	09 46							10 47
Accrington	d	00 01		00 12									09 36					09 51	10 02						10 51
Church & Oswaldtwistle	d												09 40					09 54	10 04						10 54
Rishton	d																	09 57							10 58
Blackburn	a	00 12		00 22									09 52					10 03	10 16						11 04
Clitheroe (94)	d																								
Blackburn	d																	10 04							11 04
Mill Hill (Lancashire)	d																	10 07							11 07
Cherry Tree	d																	10 09							11 09
Pleasington	d																	10x11							11x12
Bamber Bridge	d																	10 18							11 19
Lostock Hall	d		00 01															10 21							11 26
Preston 8	a		00 10					08 55		09 22		09 22						10 30		10 42					11 34
	d					00 25	08 34	08 57	08 57	09 24		09 24		09 34	09 38	09 54	10 14	10 36		10 43		10 50	10 52	11 22	11 36
Salwick	d																								
Kirkham & Wesham	d				00 05		08 45	09 06	09 06	09 33		09 33		09 44	09 47	10 04	10 24	10 45		10 53		10 59	11 02	11 31	11 45
Moss Side	d						08 51								09 53			10 51							11 51
Lytham	d						08 55								09 57			10 55							11 55
Ansdell & Fairhaven	d						08 58								10 00			10 58							11 58
St Annes-on-the-Sea	d						09 02								10 04			11 02							12 02
Squires Gate	d						09 05								10 08			11 06							12 06
Blackpool Pleasure Beach	d						09 08								10 10			11 08							12 08
Blackpool South	a						09 11								10 14			11 12							12 12
Poulton-le-Fylde	d				00 13	00 41		09 14	09 14	09 42		09 42		09 52		10 12	10 32			11 01		11 08	11 10	11 39	
Layton	d				00 17					09 45		09 45								11 05					
Blackpool North	a				00 22	00 47		09 20	09 20	09 50		09 50		09 58		10 18	10 38			11 09		11 14	11 16	11 45	

Station		NT N	NT ◇ O	NT	NT ◇ P	NT ◇ I		NT	NT N	NT ◇ O	NT	NT ◇ P	NT ◇ I	NT	NT N	NT ◇ O		NT	NT ◇ P	NT ◇ I	NT	NT N	NT ◇ O	NT	NT ◇ J
Colne	d							11 20						12 21							13 21				
Nelson	d							11 25						12 26							13 26				
Brierfield	d							11 28						12 29							13 29				
Burnley Central	d							11 33						12 34							13 34				
Burnley Barracks	d							11x36						12x37							13x37				
Manchester Victoria ⛴	d	10 00		10 51					11 01		11 51				12 01			12 51				13 02		13 51	
Rochdale ⛴	d	10 21							11 21						12 21							13 22			
Todmorden	d	10 36							11 36						12 36							13 37			
Leeds 10 (41)	d		09 52							10 49						11 57							12 57		
Burnley Manchester Road (41)	d	10 52	11 03						11 52	12 00					12 52	13 04						13 53	14 05		
Rose Grove	d	10 55						11 39	11 55					12 40	12 55						13 40	13 56			
Hapton	d							11x42						12x43							13x43				
Huncoat	d							11 46						12 47							13 47				
Accrington	d	11 03	11 12					11 50	12 03	12 10				12 51	13 03	13 13					13 51	14 03	14 14		
Church & Oswaldtwistle	d	11 05						11 53	12 05					12 54	13 05						13 54	14 05			
Rishton	d							11 57						12 58							13 58				
Blackburn	a	11 17	11 21					12 03	12 17	12 20				13 04	13 17	13 21					14 04	14 17	14 22		
Clitheroe (94)	d																								
Blackburn	d		11 22					12 03		12 21				13 04		13 22					14 04		14 23		
Mill Hill (Lancashire)	d							12 06						13 07							14 07				
Cherry Tree	d							12 08						13 09							14 09				
Pleasington	d							12x11						13x12							14x12				
Bamber Bridge	d							12 18						13 19							14 19				
Lostock Hall	d							12 25						13 26							14 26				
Preston 8	a		11 40	11 44				12 33		12 39	12 45			13 34		13 40		13 46			14 34		14 41	14 46	
	d		11 41	11 46	11 51	12 17		12 35		12 42	12 47	12 52	13 17	13 36		13 43		13 48	13 53	14 17	14 36		14 43	14 48	14 53
Salwick	d																								
Kirkham & Wesham	d			11 55	12 00	12 27		12 44			12 56	13 01	13 27	13 45				13 57	14 02	14 27	14 45			14 57	15 02
Moss Side	d							12 50						13 51							14 51				
Lytham	d							12 54						13 55							14 55				
Ansdell & Fairhaven	d							12 57						13 58							14 58				
St Annes-on-the-Sea	d							13 01						14 02							15 02				
Squires Gate	d							13 05						14 06							15 06				
Blackpool Pleasure Beach	d							13 07						14 08							15 08				
Blackpool South	a							13 11						14 12							15 12				
Poulton-le-Fylde	d		11 57	12 04	12 09	12 35				12 58	13 04	13 09	13 35			13 59		14 05	14 10	14 35			14 59	15 05	15 10
Layton	d			12 07							13 08							14 09						15 08	
Blackpool North	a		12 04	12 12	12 15	12 41				13 05	13 12	13 15	13 41			14 06		14 13	14 16	14 41			15 05	15 13	15 16

A not 15 December. From Manchester Victoria
B not 15 December. From Colne
C not 15 December. From York
D not 15 December. From Manchester Airport
E not 15 December. From Manchester Piccadilly
F from 12 January until 16 February
G until 5 January, from 23 February. From Manchester Airport
H until 5 January, from 23 February
I From Liverpool Lime Street
J From Manchester Airport
K From Wigan Wallgate
L until 29 March. From Manchester Airport
M from 5 April. From Manchester Airport
N From Southport
O From York
P From Manchester Oxford Road

Table T097-F

Sundays 15 December to 10 May

Colne, Burnley, Accrington and Blackburn - Preston - Blackpool

Station		NT ◇ A		NT	NT B	NT ◇ C	NT	NT ◇ D	NT ◇ A	NT	NT B	NT ◇ C		NT	NT ◇ D	NT ◇ A	NT	NT B	NT ◇ C	NT	NT ◇ D	NT ◇ A		NT E	NT
Colne	d			14 20						15 21							16 20								17 21
Nelson	d			14 25						15 26							16 25								17 26
Brierfield	d			14 28						15 29							16 28								17 29
Burnley Central	d			14 33						15 34							16 33								17 34
Burnley Barracks	d			14x36						15x37							16x36								17x37
Manchester Victoria ⛴	d				14 02		14 51				15 02			15 51				16 02		16 51					
Rochdale ⛴	d				14 22						15 22							16 22							
Todmorden	d				14 37						15 37							16 37							
Leeds 10 (41)	d					13 57						14 56							15 57						
Burnley Manchester Road (41)	d				14 53	15 08					15 53	16 08						16 53	17 06						
Rose Grove	d			14 39	14 56					15 40	15 56						16 39	16 56							17 40
Hapton	d			14x42						15x43							16x42								17x43
Huncoat	d			14 46						15 47							16 46								17 47
Accrington	d			14 50	15 03	15 17				15 51	16 03	16 17					16 50	17 03	17 15						17 51
Church & Oswaldtwistle	d			14 53	15 05					15 54	16 05						16 53	17 05							17 54
Rishton	d			14 57						15 58							16 57								17 58
Blackburn	a			15 03	15 17	15 25				16 04	16 17	16 25					17 03	17 17	17 23						18 04
Clitheroe (94)	d																							17 37	
Blackburn	d			15 03		15 25				16 04		16 26					17 03		17 24					18 00	18 04
Mill Hill (Lancashire)	d			15 06						16 07							17 06								18 07
Cherry Tree	d			15 08						16 09							17 08								18 09
Pleasington	d			15x11						16x12							17x11								18x12
Bamber Bridge	d			15 18						16 19							17 18							18 10	18 19
Lostock Hall	d			15 25						16 26							17 25							18 13	18 26
Preston 8	a			15 33		15 42	15 47			16 34		16 43		16 48			17 33		17 41	17 46				18 21	18 34
	d	15 20		15 35		15 44	15 49	15 54	16 19	16 36		16 45		16 50	16 55	17 17	17 35		17 42	17 47	17 52	18 17		18 22	18 36
Salwick	d																								
Kirkham & Wesham	d	15 30		15 44			15 58	16 03	16 29	16 45				16 59	17 04	17 27	17 44			17 57	18 02	18 27		18 32	18 45
Moss Side	d			15 50						16 51							17 50								18 51
Lytham	d			15 54						16 55							17 54								18 55
Ansdell & Fairhaven	d			15 57						16 58							17 57								18 58
St Annes-on-the-Sea	d			16 01						17 02							18 01								19 02
Squires Gate	d			16 05						17 06							18 05								19 06
Blackpool Pleasure Beach	d			16 07						17 08							18 07								19 08
Blackpool South	a			16 11						17 12							18 11								19 12
Poulton-le-Fylde	d	15 38				16 00	16 06	16 11	16 37			17 01		17 07	17 12	17 35			17 58	18 05	18 10	18 35		18 40	
Layton	d						16 10							17 11						18 09					
Blackpool North	a	15 44				16 06	16 14	16 17	16 43			17 07		17 15	17 18	17 41			18 05	18 13	18 16	18 41		18 47	

Station		NT B	NT ◇ C	NT	NT ◇ D	NT ◇ A	NT	NT B		NT ◇ C	NT	NT ◇ D	NT ◇ A	NT	NT B	NT ◇ C	NT	NT ◇ D		NT ◇ A	NT	NT B	NT ◇ C	NT	NT ◇ D
Colne	d						18 20							19 21							20 20				
Nelson	d						18 25							19 26							20 25				
Brierfield	d						18 28							19 29							20 28				
Burnley Central	d						18 33							19 34							20 33				
Burnley Barracks	d						18x36							19x37							20x36				
Manchester Victoria ⛴	d	17 02		17 49				18 02			18 51				19 02		19 51					20 02		20 51	
Rochdale ⛴	d	17 22						18 22							19 22							20 22			
Todmorden	d	17 37						18 37							19 37							20 37			
Leeds 10 (41)	d		16 56							17 56						18 56							19 56		
Burnley Manchester Road (41)	d	17 53	18 04					18 53		19 05					19 53	20 05						20 53	21 04		
Rose Grove	d	17 56					18 39	18 56						19 40	19 56						20 39	20 56			
Hapton	d						18x42							19x43							20x42				
Huncoat	d						18 46							19 47							20 46				
Accrington	d	18 03	18 13				18 50	19 03		19 14				19 51	20 03	20 14					20 50	21 03	21 13		
Church & Oswaldtwistle	d	18 05					18 53	19 05						19 54	20 05						20 53	21 05			
Rishton	d						18 57							19 58							20 57				
Blackburn	a	18 17	18 21				19 03	19 17		19 22				20 04	20 17	20 22					21 03	21 17	21 21		
Clitheroe (94)	d																								
Blackburn	d		18 22				19 03			19 23				20 04		20 23					21 03		21 22		
Mill Hill (Lancashire)	d						19 06							20 07							21 06				
Cherry Tree	d						19 08							20 09							21 08				
Pleasington	d						19x11							20x12							21x11				
Bamber Bridge	d						19 18							20 19							21 18				
Lostock Hall	d						19 25							20 26							21 25				
Preston 8	a		18 40	18 45			19 33			19 41	19 46			20 34		20 41	20 46				21 33		21 40	21 45	
	d		18 42	18 47	18 52	19 20	19 35			19 42	19 47	19 52	20 17	20 36		20 42	20 47	20 52		21 19	21 35		21 42	21 47	21 50
Salwick	d																								
Kirkham & Wesham	d			18 56	19 01	19 30	19 44				19 57	20 02	20 27	20 45			20 57	21 02		21 29	21 44			21 56	21 59
Moss Side	d						19 50							20 51							21 50				
Lytham	d						19 54							20 55							21 54				
Ansdell & Fairhaven	d						19 57							20 58							21 57				
St Annes-on-the-Sea	d						20 01							21 02							22 01				
Squires Gate	d						20 05							21 06							22 05				
Blackpool Pleasure Beach	d						20 07							21 08							22 07				
Blackpool South	a						20 11							21 12							22 11				
Poulton-le-Fylde	d		18 58	19 05	19 10	19 38				19 58	20 05	20 10	20 35			20 58	21 05	21 10		21 37			21 58	22 05	22 10
Layton	d			19 08							20 09						21 09							22 08	
Blackpool North	a		19 04	19 13	19 16	19 44				20 05	20 13	20 17	20 41			21 05	21 14	21 16		21 43			22 04	22 13	22 16

A From Liverpool Lime Street
B From Southport
C From York
D From Manchester Airport
E From Hellifield

Table T097-F

Sundays

15 December to 10 May

Colne, Burnley, Accrington and Blackburn - Preston - Blackpool

		NT ◇ A	NT	NT B	NT ◇ C	NT	NT B	NT ◇ D	NT ◇ A	NT	NT ◇ C	NT ◇ D
Colne	d		21 25									
Nelson	d		21 30									
Brierfield	d		21 33									
Burnley Central	d		21 38									
Burnley Barracks	d		21x41									
Manchester Victoria	d			21 02		21 48	22 02			22 49		
Rochdale	d			21 22			22 22					
Todmorden	d			21 37			22 37					
Leeds 10	41 d				20 56						21 56	
Burnley Manchester Road	41 d			21 53	22 05		22 53				23 10	
Rose Grove	d		21 44	21 56			22 56					
Hapton	d		21x47									
Huncoat	d		21 51									
Accrington	d		21 55	22 03	22 14		23 03				23 19	
Church & Oswaldtwistle	d		21 58	22 05			23 05					
Rishton	d		22 02									
Blackburn	a		22 08	22 17	22 22		23 17				23 27	
Clitheroe	94 d											
Blackburn	d		22 08		22 23						23 28	
Mill Hill (Lancashire)	d		22 11									
Cherry Tree	d		22 13									
Pleasington	d		22x16									
Bamber Bridge	d		22 23									
Lostock Hall	d		22 25									
Preston 8	a		22 35		22 41	22 46				23 42	23 46	
	d	22 19			22 42	22 47		22 49	23 14	23 43	23 49	23 57
Salwick	d											
Kirkham & Wesham	d	22 29				22 57		23 01	23 23	23 53		00 06
Moss Side	d											
Lytham	d											
Ansdell & Fairhaven	d											
St Annes-on-the-Sea	d											
Squires Gate	d											
Blackpool Pleasure Beach	d											
Blackpool South	a											
Poulton-le-Fylde	d	22 37			22 58	23 05		23 10	23 32	00 02	00 06	00 15
Layton	d					23 09				00 05		
Blackpool North	a	22 43			23 05	23 13		23 16	23 38	00 10	00 13	00 21

A From Liverpool Lime Street
B From Southport
C From York
D From Manchester Airport

Table T097-R

Mondays to Fridays

16 December to 15 May

Blackpool - Preston - Blackburn, Accrington, Burnley and Colne

Miles	Miles	Miles			NT MX A	NT MX B	NT ◇ C	NT	NT ◇ C	NT ◇ D	NT E	NT	NT F	NT G	NT	NT ◇ C	NT ◇ H	NT I	NT ◇ D	NT	NT J	NT I	NT
—	0	—	**Blackpool North**	d			03 33		04 44	05 19	05 22					05 56	06 03		06 20				
—	1¼	—	Layton	d							05 25												
—	3¼	—	Poulton-le-Fylde	d					04 50	05 25	05 28					06 01	06 08		06 26				
0	—	—	**Blackpool South**	d								05 14								06 14			
0½	—	—	Blackpool Pleasure Beach	d								05 16								06 16			
1¾	—	—	Squires Gate	d								05 18								06 18			
3¼	—	—	St Annes-on-the-Sea	d								05 22								06 22			
5¼	—	—	Ansdell & Fairhaven	d								05 26								06 26			
6½	—	—	Lytham	d								05 29								06 29			
9	—	—	Moss Side	d								05 34								06 34			
12¼	9¾	—	Kirkham & Wesham	d							05 37	05 41					06 17			06 43			
14¾	12¼	—	Salwick	d																06 47			
20	17½	—	**Preston** 8	a			03 55		05 08	05 43	05 48	05 52				06 19	06 27		06 44	06 55			
—	—	—		d				05 05		05 46					05 56				06 46				06 57
22¾	—	—	Lostock Hall	d											06 02								07 03
24	—	—	Bamber Bridge	d											06 05								07 06
29	—	—	Pleasington	d											06x13								07x14
30	—	—	Cherry Tree	d											06 16								07 17
30¾	—	—	Mill Hill (Lancashire)	d											06 19								07 20
32	—	—	**Blackburn**	a				05 22		06 03					06 22				07 02				07 23
—	—	—	Clitheroe	94 a																			
—	—	0	**Blackburn**	d				05 23		06 03			06 16	06 19	06 23			06 48	07 03		07 14	07 18	07 24
35¾	—	—	Rishton	d				05 28							06 28								07 29
37½	—	—	Church & Oswaldtwistle	d				05 31							06 31								07 32
38¼	—	5¼	**Accrington**	d				05 34		06 11				06 27	06 34				07 11		07 21		07 35
40	—	—	Huncoat	d				05 39							06 39								07 40
41½	—	—	Hapton	d				05x42							06x42								07x43
43	—	—	Rose Grove	d				05 45						06 34	06 45						07 28		07 46
—	—	11¼	Burnley Manchester Road	41 a						06 20				06 37					07 19		07 32		
—	—	—	Leeds 10	41 a						07 31									08 26				
—	—	20¾	Todmorden	d										06 55							07 50		
—	—	29	Rochdale	d		00 09								07 09							08 07		
—	—	39½	Manchester Victoria	a		00 23							07 09	07 24				07 41			08 24	08 08	
44	—	—	Burnley Barracks	d				05x48							06x48								07x49
44½	—	—	**Burnley Central**	d				05 51							06 51								07 52
46¾	—	—	Brierfield	d				05 56							06 55								07 57
48	—	—	Nelson	d	00 01			05 59							06 58								08 00
50	—	—	**Colne**	a	00 07			06 06							07 05								08 07

		NT E	NT ◇ C	NT ◇ H	NT I	NT ◇ D	NT E	NT	NT F	NT G	NT	NT ◇ C	NT ◇ H	NT I	NT ◇ D	NT E	NT	NT F	NT G	NT	NT ◇ C	NT ◇ H	NT I
Blackpool North	d	06 32	06 53	07 03		07 20	07 23					07 45	08 04		08 20	08 23					08 58	09 03	
Layton	d	06 35	06 56				07 26					07 48				08 26							
Poulton-le-Fylde	d	06 39	07 00	07 08		07 26	07 30					07 52	08 09		08 26	08 30					09 03	09 08	
Blackpool South	d							07 15									08 17						
Blackpool Pleasure Beach	d							07 17									08 19						
Squires Gate	d							07 19									08 21						
St Annes-on-the-Sea	d							07 23									08 25						
Ansdell & Fairhaven	d							07 27									08 28						
Lytham	d							07 30									08 31						
Moss Side	d							07 35									08 36						
Kirkham & Wesham	d	06 48	07 09	07 17			07 39	07 43				08 01	08 18			08 39	08 44					09 17	
Salwick	d							07 48															
Preston 8	a	06 58	07 19	07 27		07 44	07 50	07 56				08 11	08 28		08 44	08 51	08 54				09 21	09 27	
	d					07 46					07 59				08 45					08 56			
Lostock Hall	d										08 05									09 02			
Bamber Bridge	d										08 08									09 05			
Pleasington	d										08x16									09x13			
Cherry Tree	d										08 19									09 16			
Mill Hill (Lancashire)	d										08 21									09 19			
Blackburn	a					08 03					08 24				09 02					09 22			
Clitheroe	94 a																						
Blackburn	d				07 48	08 03			08 18	08 19	08 25			08 48	09 03			09 18	09 19	09 23			09 48
Rishton	d										08 30									09 28			
Church & Oswaldtwistle	d										08 33									09 31			
Accrington	d					08 11				08 27	08 36				09 11				09 27	09 34			
Huncoat	d										08 40									09 39			
Hapton	d										08x43									09x42			
Rose Grove	d									08 34	08 46								09 34	09 45			
Burnley Manchester Road	41 a					08 20				08 37					09 20				09 37				
Leeds 10	41 a					09 27									10 27								
Todmorden	d									08 55									09 55				
Rochdale	d									09 09									10 09				
Manchester Victoria	a				08 41				09 07	09 24				09 41				10 07	10 24				10 41
Burnley Barracks	d										08x49									09x48			
Burnley Central	d										08 52									09 51			
Brierfield	d										08 57									09 56			
Nelson	d										09 00									09 59			
Colne	a										09 07									10 06			

A From Preston
B From Blackburn
C To Manchester Airport
D To York
E To Hazel Grove
F To Rochdale
G To Wigan Wallgate
H To Liverpool Lime Street
I From Clitheroe to Rochdale
J To Wigan North Western

Table T097-R

Mondays to Fridays

16 December to 15 May

Blackpool - Preston - Blackburn, Accrington, Burnley and Colne

		NT	NT	NT	NT	NT	NT	NT	NT	NT	NT	NT	NT	NT	NT	NT	NT	NT	NT	NT	NT	NT
		◇ A		B	C	D		◇ E	◇ F	G	◇ A		B	C	H		◇ E	◇ F	G	◇ A		B
Blackpool North	d	09 20		09 27				09 58	10 03		10 20		10 27				10 57	11 03		11 20		11 27
Layton	d			09 30									10 30									11 30
Poulton-le-Fylde	d	09 26		09 34				10 03	10 08		10 26		10 34				11 03	11 08		11 26		11 34
Blackpool South	d		09 13									10 13									11 13	
Blackpool Pleasure Beach	d		09 15									10 15									11 15	
Squires Gate	d		09 17									10 17									11 17	
St Annes-on-the-Sea	d		09 21									10 21									11 21	
Ansdell & Fairhaven	d		09 24									10 24									11 24	
Lytham	d		09 27									10 27									11 27	
Moss Side	d		09 32									10 32									11 32	
Kirkham & Wesham	d		09 39	09 43					10 17			10 39	10 43					11 17			11 39	11 43
Salwick	d																					
Preston 8	a	09 44	09 50	09 53				10 21	10 27		10 44	10 50	10 53				11 21	11 27		11 44	11 50	11 53
	d	09 46					09 57				10 46					10 57				11 46		
Lostock Hall	d						10 03									11 03						
Bamber Bridge	d						10 06									11 06						
Pleasington	d						10x14									11x14						
Cherry Tree	d						10 17									11 17						
Mill Hill (Lancashire)	d						10 20									11 20						
Blackburn	a	10 03					10 23				11 02					11 23				12 03		
Clitheroe 94	a																					
Blackburn	d	10 03			10 18	10 19	10 24			10 48	11 03			11 17	11 19	11 24			11 48	12 03		
Rishton	d						10 29									11 29						
Church & Oswaldtwistle	d						10 32									11 32						
Accrington	d	10 11				10 27	10 35				11 11				11 27	11 35				12 11		
Huncoat	d						10 40									11 40						
Hapton	d						10x43									11x43						
Rose Grove	d					10 34	10 46								11 34	11 46						
Burnley Manchester Road 41	a	10 20				10 37					11 19				11 37					12 20		
Leeds 10 41	a	11 27									12 27									13 27		
Todmorden	d					10 55									11 55							
Rochdale	d					11 09									12 09							
Manchester Victoria	a				11 07	11 24				11 40				12 08	12 24				12 41			
Burnley Barracks	d						10x49									11x49						
Burnley Central	d						10 52									11 52						
Brierfield	d						10 57									11 57						
Nelson	d						11 00									12 00						
Colne	a						11 07									12 07						

		NT	NT	NT	NT	NT	NT	NT	NT	NT	NT	NT	NT	NT	NT	NT	NT	NT	NT	NT	NT	NT	NT
		C	D		◇ E	◇ F	G	◇ A		B	C	D		◇ E	◇ F	G	◇ A		B	C	D		◇ E
Blackpool North	d				11 58	12 03		12 20		12 27				12 58	13 06		13 21		13 27				13 58
Layton	d									12 30									13 30				
Poulton-le-Fylde	d				12 03	12 08		12 26		12 34				13 03	13 11		13 27		13 34				14 03
Blackpool South	d								12 13									13 13					
Blackpool Pleasure Beach	d								12 15									13 15					
Squires Gate	d								12 17									13 17					
St Annes-on-the-Sea	d								12 21									13 21					
Ansdell & Fairhaven	d								12 24									13 24					
Lytham	d								12 27									13 27					
Moss Side	d								12 32									13 32					
Kirkham & Wesham	d					12 17			12 39	12 43					13 20			13 39	13 43				
Salwick	d																						
Preston 8	a				12 21	12 27		12 44	12 50	12 53				13 21	13 30		13 45	13 50	13 53				14 21
	d			11 57				12 46					12 54				13 46					13 57	
Lostock Hall	d			12 03									13 01									14 03	
Bamber Bridge	d			12 06									13 06									14 06	
Pleasington	d			12x14									13x14									14x14	
Cherry Tree	d			12 17									13 17									14 17	
Mill Hill (Lancashire)	d			12 20									13 20									14 20	
Blackburn	a			12 23				13 03					13 23				14 02					14 23	
Clitheroe 94	a																						
Blackburn	d	12 18	12 19	12 24			12 48	13 03			13 17	13 19	13 24			13 47	14 03			14 17	14 19	14 24	
Rishton	d			12 29									13 29									14 29	
Church & Oswaldtwistle	d			12 32									13 32									14 32	
Accrington	d		12 27	12 35				13 11				13 27	13 35				14 11				14 27	14 35	
Huncoat	d			12 40									13 40									14 40	
Hapton	d			12x43									13x43									14x43	
Rose Grove	d		12 34	12 46								13 34	13 46								14 34	14 46	
Burnley Manchester Road 41	a		12 37					13 20				13 37					14 19				14 37		
Leeds 10 41	a							14 27									15 27						
Todmorden	d		12 55									13 55									14 55		
Rochdale	d		13 09									14 09									15 09		
Manchester Victoria	a	13 07	13 24				13 41				14 07	14 24				14 41				15 07	15 24		
Burnley Barracks	d			12x49									13x49									14x49	
Burnley Central	d			12 52									13 52									14 52	
Brierfield	d			12 57									13 57									14 57	
Nelson	d			13 00									14 00									15 00	
Colne	a			13 07									14 07									15 07	

A To York
B To Hazel Grove
C To Rochdale
D To Wigan Wallgate
E To Manchester Airport
F To Liverpool Lime Street
G From Clitheroe to Rochdale
H To Wigan North Western

Table T097-R

Mondays to Fridays

16 December to 15 May

Blackpool - Preston - Blackburn, Accrington, Burnley and Colne

		NT	NT	NT	NT	NT	NT	NT	NT	NT	NT	NT	NT	NT	NT	NT	NT	NT	NT	NT	NT	NT	NT
		◇ A	B	◇ C		D	E	F		◇ G	◇ A	B	◇ C		D	H	E		◇ G	◇ A	B	◇ C	
Blackpool North	d	14 03		14 20		14 27				14 58	15 05		15 20		15 27				15 58	16 05		16 20	
Layton	d					14 30									15 30								
Poulton-le-Fylde	d	14 08		14 26		14 34				15 03	15 10		15 26		15 34				16 03	16 10		16 26	
Blackpool South	d				14 13									15 13									16 13
Blackpool Pleasure Beach	d				14 15									15 15									16 15
Squires Gate	d				14 17									15 17									16 17
St Annes-on-the-Sea	d				14 21									15 21									16 21
Ansdell & Fairhaven	d				14 24									15 24									16 24
Lytham	d				14 27									15 27									16 27
Moss Side	d				14 32									15 32									16 32
Kirkham & Wesham	d	14 17			14 39	14 43					15 19			15 39	15 43					16 19			16 39
Salwick	d																						
Preston 8	a	14 27		14 44	14 50	14 53				15 21	15 29		15 44	15 50	15 53				16 21	16 29		16 44	16 50
	d			14 46					14 58				15 46					15 57				16 46	
Lostock Hall	d								15 04									16 03					
Bamber Bridge	d								15 07									16 06					
Pleasington	d								15x14									16x14					
Cherry Tree	d								15 17									16 17					
Mill Hill (Lancashire)	d								15 20									16 20					
Blackburn	a			15 03					15 23				16 02					16 23				17 03	
Clitheroe 94	a																						
Blackburn	d		14 48	15 03			15 18	15 19	15 24			15 48	16 03			16 17	16 18	16 24			16 48	17 03	
Rishton	d								15 29									16 29					
Church & Oswaldtwistle	d								15 32									16 32					
Accrington	d			15 11				15 27	15 35				16 11			16 25		16 35				17 11	
Huncoat	d								15 40									16 40					
Hapton	d								15x43									16x43					
Rose Grove	d							15 34	15 46							16 32		16 46					
Burnley Manchester Road 41	a			15 20				15 37					16 19			16 35						17 20	
Leeds 10 41	a			16 27									17 29									18 27	
Todmorden	d							15 55								16 53							
Rochdale	d							16 09								17 09							
Manchester Victoria	a		15 40				16 07	16 24				16 41				17 24	17 07				17 41		
Burnley Barracks	d								15x49									16x49					
Burnley Central	d								15 52									16 52					
Brierfield	d								15 57									16 57					
Nelson	d								16 00									17 00					
Colne	a								16 07									17 07					

		NT	NT	NT	NT	NT	NT	NT	NT	NT	NT	NT	NT	NT	NT	NT	NT	NT	NT	NT	NT	NT
		D	E	I			◇ G	◇ A	B	◇ C		D	B	H		◇ G	◇ A	B	◇ C		D	E
Blackpool North	d	16 27					16 53	17 03		17 20		17 27				17 56	18 03		18 19		18 27	
Layton	d	16 30					16 56					17 30									18 30	
Poulton-le-Fylde	d	16 34					17 00	17 08		17 26		17 34				18 01	18 08		18 25		18 34	
Blackpool South	d										17 13									18 13		
Blackpool Pleasure Beach	d										17 15									18 15		
Squires Gate	d										17 17									18 17		
St Annes-on-the-Sea	d										17 21									18 21		
Ansdell & Fairhaven	d										17 24									18 24		
Lytham	d										17 27									18 27		
Moss Side	d										17 32									18 32		
Kirkham & Wesham	d	16 43					17 09	17 17			17 39	17 43					18 17			18 39	18 43	
Salwick	d							17 21														
Preston 8	a	16 53					17 19	17 30		17 44	17 50	17 53				18 19	18 27		18 44	18 50	18 53	
	d				16 57	17 14				17 46					17 57				18 46			
Lostock Hall	d				17 03	17 20									18 03							
Bamber Bridge	d				17 06	17 24									18 06							
Pleasington	d				17x14	17x31									18x14							
Cherry Tree	d				17 17	17 35									18 17							
Mill Hill (Lancashire)	d				17 20	17 38									18 20							
Blackburn	a				17 23	17 41				18 03					18 23				19 03			
Clitheroe 94	a																					
Blackburn	d		17 18	17 19	17 24				17 48	18 03			18 18	18 19	18 24			18 48	19 03			19 18
Rishton	d				17 29										18 29							
Church & Oswaldtwistle	d				17 32										18 32							
Accrington	d			17 27	17 35					18 11				18 27	18 35				19 11			
Huncoat	d				17 40										18 40							
Hapton	d				17x43										18x43							
Rose Grove	d			17 34	17 46									18 34	18 46							
Burnley Manchester Road 41	a			17 37						18 20				18 37					19 20			
Leeds 10 41	a									19 27									20 26			
Todmorden	d			17 55										18 55								
Rochdale	d			18 09										19 09								
Manchester Victoria	a		18 07	18 24					18 41				19 07	19 24				19 40				20 08
Burnley Barracks	d				17x49										18x49							
Burnley Central	d				17 52										18 52							
Brierfield	d				17 57										18 57							
Nelson	d				18 00										19 00							
Colne	a				18 07										19 07							

A To Liverpool Lime Street
B From Clitheroe to Rochdale
C To York
D To Hazel Grove
E To Rochdale
F To Wigan North Western
G To Manchester Airport
H To Wigan Wallgate
I To Kirkby

Table T097-R

Mondays to Fridays

16 December to 15 May

Blackpool - Preston - Blackburn, Accrington, Burnley and Colne

	NT	NT	NT	NT	NT	NT	NT	NT	NT	NT	NT	NT	NT	NT	NT	NT	NT	NT	NT	NT	NT	NT
	A		◇ B	◇ C	D	◇ E	F		G		◇ B	◇ C	D	◇ E	F		H		◇ B	◇ C	I	◇ E
Blackpool North d			18 57	19 05		19 20	19 25				19 58	20 03		20 20	20 24				20 58	21 01		21 17
Layton d							19 28								20 27							
Poulton-le-Fylde d			19 03	19 10		19 26	19 32				20 03	20 08		20 26	20 31				21 03	21 07		21 23
Blackpool South d								19 16								20 15						
Blackpool Pleasure Beach d								19 18								20 17						
Squires Gate d								19 21								20 20						
St Annes-on-the-Sea d								19 25								20 24						
Ansdell & Fairhaven d								19 28								20 27						
Lytham d								19 32								20 31						
Moss Side d								19 37								20 36						
Kirkham & Wesham d				19 19			19 41	19 45				20 17			20 40	20 44				21 16		
Salwick d																						
Preston 8 a			19 21	19 29		19 44	19 51	19 55			20 21	20 27		20 44	20 51	20 54			21 21	21 26		21 41
d		18 57				19 46				19 57				20 46				20 57				21 44
Lostock Hall d		19 03								20 04								21 03				
Bamber Bridge d		19 06								20 07								21 06				
Pleasington d		19x14								20x15								21x14				
Cherry Tree d		19 17								20 18								21 17				
Mill Hill (Lancashire) d		19 20								20 20								21 20				
Blackburn a		19 23				20 03				20 24				21 03				21 23				22 01
Clitheroe 94 a																						
Blackburn d	19 19	19 24			19 46	20 03			20 17	20 24			20 48	21 03			21 20	21 24			21 48	22 01
Rishton d		19 29								20 29								21 29				
Church & Oswaldtwistle d		19 32								20 32								21 32				
Accrington d	19 27	19 35				20 11			20 25	20 36				21 11			21 30	21 35				22 09
Huncoat d		19 40								20 40								21 40				
Hapton d		19x43								20x43								21x43				
Rose Grove d	19 34	19 46							20 32	20 46							21 37	21 46				
Burnley Manchester Road 41 a	19 37					20 20			20 35					21 20			21 40					22 18
Leeds 10 41 a						21 28								22 27								23 26
Todmorden d	19 55								20 53								21 58					
Rochdale d	20 09								21 09								22 14					
Manchester Victoria a	20 24				20 41				21 23				21 36				22 29				22 40	
Burnley Barracks d		19x49								20x49								21x49				
Burnley Central d		19 52								20 52								21 52				
Brierfield d		19 57								20 57								21 57				
Nelson d		20 00								21 00								22 00				
Colne a		20 07								21 07								22 07				

	NT	NT	NT	NT	NT	NT	NT	NT	NT	NT	NT	NT	NT	NT
	◇ B		G		◇ J	◇ C	◇ B		I				◇ B	
Blackpool North d	21 21				22 02	22 18	22 21					23 00	23 13	
Layton d	21 24						22 24						23 16	
Poulton-le-Fylde d	21 28					22 23	22 28					23 06	23 20	
Blackpool South d		21 14						22 16						23 24
Blackpool Pleasure Beach d		21 16						22 18						23 26
Squires Gate d		21 18						22 20						23 28
St Annes-on-the-Sea d		21 22						22 24						23 32
Ansdell & Fairhaven d		21 25						22 27						23 35
Lytham d		21 28						22 30						23 38
Moss Side d		21 33						22 35						23 43
Kirkham & Wesham d	21 37	21 40					22 37	22 42					23 29	23 50
Salwick d														
Preston 8 a	21 48	21 51			22 24	22 41	22 47	22 53				23 23	23 40	00 02
d				21 57	22 25						22 57	23 24		
Lostock Hall d				22 03							23 03			
Bamber Bridge d				22 06							23 07			
Pleasington d				22x14							23x14			
Cherry Tree d				22 17							23 18			
Mill Hill (Lancashire) d				22 20							23 20			
Blackburn a				22 23	22 41						23 24	23 42		
Clitheroe 94 a														
Blackburn d			22 19	22 24	22 42				23 17	23 19	23 25			
Rishton d				22 29							23 30			
Church & Oswaldtwistle d				22 32							23 33			
Accrington d			22 27	22 35	22 50					23 27	23 37			
Huncoat d				22 40							23 41			
Hapton d				22x43							23x44			
Rose Grove d			22 34	22 46						23 34	23 47			
Burnley Manchester Road 41 a			22 37		22 58					23 37				
Leeds 10 41 a														
Todmorden d			22 55							23 55				
Rochdale d			23 11							00 09				
Manchester Victoria a			23 33						00 05	00 23				
Burnley Barracks d				22x49							23x50			
Burnley Central d				22 52							23 53			
Brierfield d				22 57							23 57			
Nelson d				23 00							00 01			
Colne a				23 07							00 07			

A To Wigan North Western
B To Manchester Airport
C To Liverpool Lime Street
D From Clitheroe to Rochdale
E To York
F To Hazel Grove
G To Wigan Wallgate
H To Southport
I From Clitheroe
J To Bradford Interchange

Table T097-R

Saturdays

21 December to 16 May

Blackpool - Preston - Blackburn, Accrington, Burnley and Colne

	NT	NT	NT	NT	NT	NT	NT	NT	NT	NT	NT	NT	NT	NT	NT	NT	NT	NT	NT	NT	NT	NT
	A	B	◇ C	◇ C		◇ D	E	F	G			◇ C	◇ H	I	◇ D	J	I		E		◇ C	◇ H
Blackpool North d			03 33	04 29		05 19	05 23					05 56	06 03		06 20				06 32		06 53	07 03
Layton d							05 26												06 35		06 56	
Poulton-le-Fylde d				04 35		05 25	05 30					06 01	06 08		06 26				06 39		07 00	07 08
Blackpool South d											05 35									06 35		
Blackpool Pleasure Beach d											05 37									06 37		
Squires Gate d											05 39									06 39		
St Annes-on-the-Sea d											05 43									06 43		
Ansdell & Fairhaven d											05 47									06 47		
Lytham d											05 50									06 50		
Moss Side d											05 55									06 55		
Kirkham & Wesham d							05 39				06 02		06 17						06 48	07 02	07 09	07 17
Salwick d																				07 06		
Preston 8 a			03 55	04 53		05 43	05 49				06 13	06 19	06 27		06 44				06 58	07 15	07 19	07 27
d					05 05	05 46				05 56					06 46			06 57				
Lostock Hall d										06 02								07 03				
Bamber Bridge d										06 05								07 06				
Pleasington d										06x13								07x14				
Cherry Tree d										06 16								07 17				
Mill Hill (Lancashire) d										06 19								07 20				
Blackburn a					05 22	06 03				06 22					07 02			07 23				
Clitheroe 94 a																						
Blackburn d					05 23	06 03		06 16	06 19	06 23				06 48	07 03	07 14	07 18	07 24				
Rishton d					05 28					06 28								07 29				
Church & Oswaldtwistle d					05 31					06 31								07 32				
Accrington d					05 34	06 11			06 27	06 34					07 11	07 21		07 35				
Huncoat d					05 39					06 39								07 40				
Hapton d					05x42					06x42								07x43				
Rose Grove d					05 45				06 34	06 45						07 28		07 46				
Burnley Manchester Road 41 a						06 20			06 37						07 19	07 32						
Leeds 10 41 a						07 31									08 26							
Todmorden d									06 55							07 50						
Rochdale d		00 09							07 09							08 07						
Manchester Victoria a		00 23						07 07	07 24					07 41		08 24	08 08					
Burnley Barracks d					05x48					06x48								07x49				
Burnley Central d					05 51					06 51								07 52				
Brierfield d					05 56					06 55								07 57				
Nelson d	00 01				05 59					06 58								08 00				
Colne a	00 07				06 06					07 05								08 07				

	NT	NT	NT	NT	NT	NT	NT	NT	NT	NT	NT	NT	NT	NT	NT	NT	NT	NT	NT	NT	NT	NT
	I	◇ D	E	F	G			◇ C	◇ H	I	◇ D	E	F	G			◇ C	◇ H	I	◇ D	E	F
Blackpool North d		07 20	07 23					07 55	08 04		08 20	08 27					08 58	09 03		09 20	09 27	
Layton d			07 26					07 58				08 30									09 30	
Poulton-le-Fylde d		07 26	07 30					08 02	08 09		08 26	08 34					09 03	09 08		09 26	09 34	
Blackpool South d							07 35									08 35						
Blackpool Pleasure Beach d							07 37									08 37						
Squires Gate d							07 39									08 39						
St Annes-on-the-Sea d							07 43									08 43						
Ansdell & Fairhaven d							07 47									08 47						
Lytham d							07 50									08 50						
Moss Side d							07 55									08 55						
Kirkham & Wesham d			07 39				08 02	08 11	08 18			08 43				09 02		09 17			09 43	
Salwick d							08 07															
Preston 8 a		07 44	07 50				08 16	08 21	08 28		08 44	08 53				09 15	09 21	09 27		09 44	09 53	
d		07 46				07 57					08 45				08 56					09 46		
Lostock Hall d						08 03									09 02							
Bamber Bridge d						08 07									09 05							
Pleasington d						08x14									09x13							
Cherry Tree d						08 18									09 16							
Mill Hill (Lancashire) d						08 20									09 19							
Blackburn a		08 03				08 24					09 02				09 22					10 03		
Clitheroe 94 a																						
Blackburn d	07 48	08 03		08 18	08 19	08 24				08 48	09 03		09 18	09 19	09 23				09 48	10 03		10 18
Rishton d						08 29									09 28							
Church & Oswaldtwistle d						08 32									09 31							
Accrington d		08 11			08 27	08 36					09 11			09 27	09 34					10 11		
Huncoat d						08 40									09 39							
Hapton d						08x43									09x42							
Rose Grove d					08 34	08 47								09 34	09 45							
Burnley Manchester Road 41 a		08 20			08 37						09 20			09 37						10 20		
Leeds 10 41 a		09 27									10 27									11 27		
Todmorden d					08 55									09 55								
Rochdale d					09 09									10 09								
Manchester Victoria a	08 41			09 07	09 24					09 41			10 07	10 24					10 41			11 07
Burnley Barracks d						08x50									09x48							
Burnley Central d						08 53									09 51							
Brierfield d						08 57									09 56							
Nelson d						09 01									09 59							
Colne a						09 07									10 06							

A From Preston
B From Blackburn
C To Manchester Airport
D To York
E To Hazel Grove
F To Rochdale
G To Wigan Wallgate
H To Liverpool Lime Street
I From Clitheroe to Rochdale
J To Wigan North Western

Table T097-R

Saturdays
21 December to 16 May

Blackpool - Preston - Blackburn, Accrington, Burnley and Colne

		NT A		NT	NT	NT ◇ B	NT ◇ C	NT D	NT ◇ E	NT F	NT G	NT H		NT	NT	NT ◇ B	NT ◇ C	NT D	NT ◇ E	NT F	NT G	NT A		NT	NT
Blackpool North	d					09 58	10 03		10 20	10 27						10 57	11 03		11 20	11 27					
Layton	d									10 30										11 30					
Poulton-le-Fylde	d					10 03	10 08		10 26	10 34						11 03	11 08		11 26	11 34					
Blackpool South	d				09 35										10 35										11 36
Blackpool Pleasure Beach	d				09 37										10 37										11 38
Squires Gate	d				09 39										10 39										11 40
St Annes-on-the-Sea	d				09 43										10 43										11 44
Ansdell & Fairhaven	d				09 47										10 47										11 47
Lytham	d				09 50										10 50										11 50
Moss Side	d				09 55										10 55										11 55
Kirkham & Wesham	d				10 02		10 17			10 43					11 02		11 17			11 43					12 02
Salwick	d																								
Preston 8	a				10 13	10 21	10 27		10 44	10 53					11 13	11 21	11 27		11 44	11 53					12 13
	d			09 57					10 46					10 57					11 46					11 57	
Lostock Hall	d			10 03										11 03										12 03	
Bamber Bridge	d			10 07										11 07										12 07	
Pleasington	d			10x14										11x14										12x14	
Cherry Tree	d			10 17										11 17										12 17	
Mill Hill (Lancashire)	d			10 20										11 20										12 20	
Blackburn	a			10 23					11 02					11 23					12 03					12 23	
Clitheroe 94	a																								
Blackburn	d	10 19		10 24				10 48	11 03		11 17	11 19		11 24				11 48	12 03		12 18	12 19		12 24	
Rishton	d			10 29										11 29										12 29	
Church & Oswaldtwistle	d			10 32										11 32										12 32	
Accrington	d	10 27		10 35					11 11			11 27		11 35					12 11			12 27		12 35	
Huncoat	d			10 40										11 40										12 40	
Hapton	d			10x43										11x43										12x43	
Rose Grove	d	10 34		10 46								11 34		11 46								12 34		12 46	
Burnley Manchester Road 41	a	10 37							11 19			11 37							12 20			12 37			
Leeds 10 41	a								12 27										13 27						
Todmorden	d	10 55										11 55										12 55			
Rochdale	d	11 09										12 09										13 09			
Manchester Victoria	a	11 24						11 40			12 08	12 24						12 41			13 07	13 24			
Burnley Barracks	d			10x49										11x49										12x49	
Burnley Central	d			10 52										11 52										12 52	
Brierfield	d			10 57										11 57										12 57	
Nelson	d			11 00										12 00										13 00	
Colne	a			11 07										12 07										13 07	

		NT ◇ B	NT ◇ C	NT D	NT ◇ E	NT F	NT G	NT A		NT	NT	NT ◇ B	NT ◇ C	NT D	NT ◇ E	NT F	NT G	NT A		NT	NT	NT ◇ B	NT ◇ C	NT D	NT ◇ E
Blackpool North	d	11 58	12 03		12 20	12 27						12 58	13 06		13 21	13 27						13 58	14 03		14 20
Layton	d					12 30										13 30									
Poulton-le-Fylde	d	12 03	12 08		12 26	12 34						13 03	13 11		13 27	13 34						14 03	14 08		14 26
Blackpool South	d										12 36										13 35				
Blackpool Pleasure Beach	d										12 38										13 37				
Squires Gate	d										12 40										13 39				
St Annes-on-the-Sea	d										12 44										13 43				
Ansdell & Fairhaven	d										12 48										13 47				
Lytham	d										12 51										13 50				
Moss Side	d										12 56										13 55				
Kirkham & Wesham	d		12 17			12 43					13 05		13 20			13 43					14 02		14 17		
Salwick	d																								
Preston 8	a	12 21	12 27		12 44	12 53					13 16	13 21	13 30		13 45	13 53					14 13	14 21	14 27		14 44
	d				12 46					12 57					13 46					13 57					14 46
Lostock Hall	d									13 03										14 03					
Bamber Bridge	d									13 07										14 07					
Pleasington	d									13x14										14x14					
Cherry Tree	d									13 17										14 17					
Mill Hill (Lancashire)	d									13 20										14 20					
Blackburn	a				13 03					13 23					14 02					14 23					15 03
Clitheroe 94	a																								
Blackburn	d			12 48	13 03		13 17	13 19		13 24				13 47	14 03		14 17	14 19		14 24				14 48	15 03
Rishton	d									13 29										14 29					
Church & Oswaldtwistle	d									13 32										14 32					
Accrington	d				13 11			13 27		13 35					14 11			14 27		14 35					15 11
Huncoat	d									13 40										14 40					
Hapton	d									13x43										14x43					
Rose Grove	d							13 34		13 46								14 34		14 46					
Burnley Manchester Road 41	a				13 20			13 37							14 19			14 37							15 20
Leeds 10 41	a				14 27										15 27										16 27
Todmorden	d							13 55										14 55							
Rochdale	d							14 09										15 09							
Manchester Victoria	a			13 41			14 07	14 24						14 41			15 07	15 24						15 40	
Burnley Barracks	d									13x49										14x49					
Burnley Central	d									13 52										14 52					
Brierfield	d									13 57										14 57					
Nelson	d									14 00										15 00					
Colne	a									14 07										15 07					

A To Wigan Wallgate
B To Manchester Airport
C To Liverpool Lime Street
D From Clitheroe to Rochdale
E To York
F To Hazel Grove
G To Rochdale
H To Wigan North Western

Table T097-R

Saturdays
21 December to 16 May

Blackpool - Preston - Blackburn, Accrington, Burnley and Colne

		NT A	NT B	NT C		NT	NT	NT ◇ D	NT ◇ E	NT F	NT ◇ G	NT A	NT H	NT B		NT	NT	NT ◇ D	NT ◇ E	NT F	NT ◇ G	NT A	NT B	NT I
Blackpool North	d	14 27						14 58	15 05		15 20	15 27						15 58	16 05		16 20	16 27		
Layton	d	14 30										15 30										16 30		
Poulton-le-Fylde	d	14 34						15 03	15 10		15 26	15 34						16 03	16 10		16 26	16 34		
Blackpool South	d						14 35										15 35							
Blackpool Pleasure Beach	d						14 37										15 37							
Squires Gate	d						14 39										15 39							
St Annes-on-the-Sea	d						14 43										15 43							
Ansdell & Fairhaven	d						14 47										15 47							
Lytham	d						14 50										15 50							
Moss Side	d						14 55										15 55							
Kirkham & Wesham	d	14 43					15 02		15 19			15 43					16 01		16 19			16 43		
Salwick	d																							
Preston 8	a	14 53					15 13	15 21	15 29		15 44	15 53					16 12	16 21	16 29		16 44	16 53		
	d					14 58					15 46					15 57					16 46			
Lostock Hall	d					15 04										16 03								
Bamber Bridge	d					15 07										16 07								
Pleasington	d					15x14										16x14								
Cherry Tree	d					15 17										16 17								
Mill Hill (Lancashire)	d					15 20										16 20								
Blackburn	a					15 23					16 02					16 23					17 03			
Clitheroe 94	a																							
Blackburn	d		15 18	15 19		15 24				15 48	16 03		16 17	16 18		16 24				16 48	17 03		17 18	17 19
Rishton	d					15 29										16 29								
Church & Oswaldtwistle	d					15 32										16 32								
Accrington	d			15 27		15 35					16 11		16 25			16 35					17 11			17 27
Huncoat	d					15 40										16 40								
Hapton	d					15x43										16x43								
Rose Grove	d			15 34		15 46							16 32			16 46								17 34
Burnley Manchester Road 41	a			15 37							16 19		16 35								17 20			17 37
Leeds 10 41	a										17 28										18 27			
Todmorden	d			15 55									16 53											17 55
Rochdale	d			16 09									17 09											18 09
Manchester Victoria	a		16 07	16 24						16 41			17 24	17 07						17 41			18 07	18 24
Burnley Barracks	d					15x49										16x49								
Burnley Central	d					15 52										16 52								
Brierfield	d					15 57										16 57								
Nelson	d					16 00										17 00								
Colne	a					16 07										17 07								

		NT	NT	NT	NT ◇ D	NT ◇ E	NT F	NT ◇ G	NT A	NT F		NT H	NT	NT	NT ◇ D	NT ◇ E	NT F	NT ◇ G	NT A	NT B		NT C	NT	NT	NT ◇ D
Blackpool North	d				16 53	17 03		17 20	17 27						17 56	18 03		18 21	18 27						18 56
Layton	d				16 56				17 30										18 30						
Poulton-le-Fylde	d				17 00	17 08		17 26	17 34						18 01	18 08		18 27	18 34						19 02
Blackpool South	d		16 35											17 35										18 35	
Blackpool Pleasure Beach	d		16 37											17 37										18 37	
Squires Gate	d		16 39											17 39										18 39	
St Annes-on-the-Sea	d		16 43											17 43										18 43	
Ansdell & Fairhaven	d		16 47											17 47										18 47	
Lytham	d		16 50											17 50										18 50	
Moss Side	d		16 55											17 55										18 55	
Kirkham & Wesham	d		17 02		17 09	17 17			17 43					18 01		18 17			18 43					19 02	
Salwick	d					17 21																			
Preston 8	a		17 13		17 19	17 30		17 44	17 53					18 12	18 19	18 27		18 45	18 53					19 13	19 21
	d	16 58		17 15				17 46					17 57					18 46					18 57		
Lostock Hall	d	17 05		17 21									18 03										19 03		
Bamber Bridge	d	17 08		17 24									18 06										19 07		
Pleasington	d	17x16		17x32									18x14										19x14		
Cherry Tree	d	17 19		17 35									18 17										19 17		
Mill Hill (Lancashire)	d	17 21		17 38									18 20										19 20		
Blackburn	a	17 25		17 42				18 03					18 23					19 03					19 23		
Clitheroe 94	a																								
Blackburn	d	17 25					17 48	18 03		18 18		18 19	18 24				18 48	19 03		19 18		19 19	19 24		
Rishton	d	17 30											18 29										19 29		
Church & Oswaldtwistle	d	17 33											18 32										19 32		
Accrington	d	17 37						18 11				18 27	18 35					19 11				19 27	19 35		
Huncoat	d	17 41											18 40										19 40		
Hapton	d	17x44											18x43										19x43		
Rose Grove	d	17 48										18 34	18 46									19 34	19 46		
Burnley Manchester Road 41	a							18 20				18 37						19 20				19 37			
Leeds 10 41	a							19 27										20 26							
Todmorden	d											18 55										19 55			
Rochdale	d											19 09										20 09			
Manchester Victoria	a						18 41			19 07		19 24					19 40			20 08		20 24			
Burnley Barracks	d	17x51											18x49										19x49		
Burnley Central	d	17 54											18 52										19 52		
Brierfield	d	17 58											18 57										19 57		
Nelson	d	18 02											19 00										20 00		
Colne	a	18 08											19 07										20 07		

A To Hazel Grove
B To Rochdale
C To Wigan North Western
D To Manchester Airport
E To Liverpool Lime Street
F From Clitheroe to Rochdale
G To York
H To Wigan Wallgate
I To Kirkby

Table T097-R

Saturdays

21 December to 16 May

Blackpool - Preston - Blackburn, Accrington, Burnley and Colne

	NT ◇ A	NT B	NT ◇ C	NT D	NT E	NT	NT	NT ◇ F	NT ◇ A	NT B	NT ◇ C	NT D	NT G	NT	NT	NT ◇ F	NT ◇ A	NT H	NT ◇ C	NT ◇ F	NT	NT
Blackpool North d	19 05		19 20	19 25				19 58	20 03		20 20	20 24				20 58	21 01		21 18	21 21		
Layton d				19 28								20 27								21 24		
Poulton-le-Fylde d	19 10		19 26	19 32				20 03	20 08		20 26	20 31				21 03	21 07		21 24	21 28		
Blackpool South d							19 35								20 36							
Blackpool Pleasure Beach d							19 37								20 38							
Squires Gate d							19 39								20 40							
St Annes-on-the-Sea d							19 43								20 44							
Ansdell & Fairhaven d							19 47								20 47							
Lytham d							19 50								20 50							
Moss Side d							19 55								20 55							
Kirkham & Wesham d	19 19			19 41			20 01		20 17			20 40			21 05		21 16			21 37		
Salwick d																						
Preston 8 a	19 29		19 44	19 51			20 12	20 21	20 27		20 44	20 51			21 16	21 21	21 26		21 42	21 48		
d			19 46			19 55					20 46			20 56					21 43			21 57
Lostock Hall d						20 01								21 03								22 03
Bamber Bridge d						20 05								21 06								22 07
Pleasington d						20x12								21x14								22x14
Cherry Tree d						20 15								21 17								22 18
Mill Hill (Lancashire) d						20 18								21 20								22 20
Blackburn a			20 03			20 21					21 03			21 23					22 00			22 24
Clitheroe 94 a																						
Blackburn d		19 46	20 03		20 17	20 22				20 48	21 03		21 20	21 24				21 48	22 00		22 19	22 24
Rishton d						20 27								21 29								22 29
Church & Oswaldtwistle d						20 30								21 32								22 32
Accrington d			20 11		20 25	20 33					21 11		21 30	21 35					22 08		22 27	22 36
Huncoat d						20 38								21 40								22 40
Hapton d						20x41								21x43								22x43
Rose Grove d					20 32	20 44							21 37	21 46							22 34	22 47
Burnley Manchester Road 41 a			20 20		20 35						21 20		21 40						22 17		22 37	
Leeds 10 41 a			21 28								22 26								23 23			
Todmorden d					20 53								21 58								22 55	
Rochdale d					21 09								22 14								23 11	
Manchester Victoria a		20 41			21 23					21 36			22 29					22 45			23 33	
Burnley Barracks d						20x47								21x49								22x50
Burnley Central d						20 50								21 52								22 53
Brierfield d						20 55								21 57								22 57
Nelson d						20 58								22 00								23 01
Colne a						21 05								22 07								23 07

	NT	NT ◇ A	NT ◇ F	NT H	NT	NT	NT	NT ◇ F	NT
Blackpool North d		22 18	22 21					23 02	
Layton d			22 24					23 05	
Poulton-le-Fylde d		22 23	22 28					23 09	
Blackpool South d	21 35								23 24
Blackpool Pleasure Beach d	21 37								23 26
Squires Gate d	21 39								23 28
St Annes-on-the-Sea d	21 43						22 29		23 32
Ansdell & Fairhaven d	21 47						22 32		23 35
Lytham d	21 50						22 35		23 38
Moss Side d	21 55						22 40		23 43
Kirkham & Wesham d	22 02		22 37				22 48	23 18	23 50
Salwick d									
Preston 8 a	22 13	22 41	22 47				22 58	23 28	00 01
d						22 57			
Lostock Hall d						23 03			
Bamber Bridge d						23 07			
Pleasington d						23x14			
Cherry Tree d						23 17			
Mill Hill (Lancashire) d						23 20			
Blackburn a						23 23			
Clitheroe 94 a									
Blackburn d				23 17	23 19	23 24			
Rishton d						23 29			
Church & Oswaldtwistle d						23 32			
Accrington d					23 27	23 35			
Huncoat d						23 40			
Hapton d						23x43			
Rose Grove d					23 34	23 46			
Burnley Manchester Road 41 a					23 37				
Leeds 10 41 a									
Todmorden d					23 55				
Rochdale d					00 09				
Manchester Victoria a				00 07	00 23				
Burnley Barracks d						23x49			
Burnley Central d						23a52			
Brierfield d									
Nelson d									
Colne a									

A To Liverpool Lime Street
B From Clitheroe to Rochdale
C To York
D To Hazel Grove
E To Wigan Wallgate
F To Manchester Airport
G To Southport
H From Clitheroe

NRT DECEMBER 19 EDITION

Table T097-R

Sundays

15 December to 10 May

Blackpool - Preston - Blackburn, Accrington, Burnley and Colne

	NT A	NT	NT ◇ B	NT C	NT	NT ◇ D	NT	NT E	NT	NT ◇ F	NT C	NT	NT ◇ D	NT ◇ B	NT G	NT ◇ F	NT	NT C	NT	NT ◇ D	NT ◇ B	NT G
Blackpool North d			07 52			07 55		08 12	08 21				08 32	09 00		09 18	09 21			09 32	10 00	
Layton d									08 24								09 24					
Poulton-le-Fylde d						08 01		08 18	08 27				08 38	09 06		09 24	09 28			09 38	10 06	
Blackpool South d																			09 16			
Blackpool Pleasure Beach d																			09 18			
Squires Gate d																			09 20			
St Annes-on-the-Sea d																			09 24			
Ansdell & Fairhaven d																			09 28			
Lytham d																			09 31			
Moss Side d																			09 36			
Kirkham & Wesham d						08 10		08 27	08 36				08 47	09 15			09 37		09 43	09 47	10 15	
Salwick d																						
Preston 8 a			08 14			08 21		08 38	08 47				08 57	09 25		09 43	09 47		09 54	09 59	10 25	
d					08 15			08 39	08 48			08 56				09 47	09 49		09 55			
Lostock Hall d					08 21			08 45				09 02							10 06			
Bamber Bridge d					08 24			08 48				09 05							10 09			
Pleasington d												09x13							10x17			
Cherry Tree d												09 16							10 20			
Mill Hill (Lancashire) d												09 19							10 23			
Blackburn a					08 35			08 59				09 22				10 06			10 26			
Clitheroe 94 a								09 21														
Blackburn d		07 48		08 12	08 36		08 48			09 04	09 12	09 23			09 48	10 07		10 12	10 27			10 48
Rishton d												09 28							10 32			
Church & Oswaldtwistle d		07 53		08 17							09 17	09 31						10 17	10 35			
Accrington d		07 56		08 21	08 44					09 12	09 21	09 34				10 15		10 21	10 38			
Huncoat d												09 39							10 43			
Hapton d												09x42							10x46			
Rose Grove d		08 03		08 28	08 51						09 28	09 45						10 28	10 49			
Burnley Manchester Road 41 a		08 07		08 31						09 20	09 31					10 23		10 31				
Leeds 10 41 a										10 32						11 38						
Todmorden d		08 24		08 49							09 49							10 49				
Rochdale d	00 09	08 38		09 03							10 03							11 03				
Manchester Victoria a	00 23	08 59		09 24			09 38		09 41		10 24				10 39		10 44	11 24				11 39
Burnley Barracks d												09x48							10x52			
Burnley Central d					08 56							09 51							10 55			
Brierfield d					09 01							09 56							11 00			
Nelson d					09 04							09 59							11 03			
Colne a					09 11							10 06							11 10			

	NT	NT ◇ F	NT C	NT	NT ◇ D	NT ◇ B	NT G	NT ◇ F	NT	NT C	NT	NT ◇ D	NT ◇ H	NT G	NT ◇ F	NT	NT ◇ D	NT C	NT	NT ◇ H	NT G	NT ◇ F
Blackpool North d	10 15	10 20			10 33	11 00		11 17	11 20			11 32	12 00		12 17	12 20	12 24			13 00		13 17
Layton d	10 18								11 23							12 23						
Poulton-le-Fylde d	10 21	10 27			10 39	11 06		11 23	11 26			11 38	12 06		12 23	12 26	12 30			13 06		13 23
Blackpool South d				10 18							11 16								12 16			
Blackpool Pleasure Beach d				10 20							11 18								12 18			
Squires Gate d				10 22							11 20								12 20			
St Annes-on-the-Sea d				10 26							11 24								12 24			
Ansdell & Fairhaven d				10 29							11 28								12 28			
Lytham d				10 32							11 31								12 31			
Moss Side d				10 37							11 36								12 36			
Kirkham & Wesham d	10 30			10 44	10 48	11 15			11 35		11 43	11 47	12 15			12 35	12 39		12 43	13 15		
Salwick d																						
Preston 8 a	10 41	10 46		10 55	10 59	11 25		11 42	11 48		11 54	11 58	12 25		12 41	12 46	12 51		12 54	13 25		13 41
d	10 42	10 47		10 56				11 43	11 51		11 57				12 42	12 50			12 56			13 42
Lostock Hall d				11 07							12 06								13 07			
Bamber Bridge d				11 10							12 10								13 10			
Pleasington d				11x18							12x17								13x18			
Cherry Tree d				11 21							12 21								13 21			
Mill Hill (Lancashire) d				11 23							12 23								13 24			
Blackburn a		11 06		11 27				12 03			12 27				13 01				13 27			14 03
Clitheroe 94 a																						
Blackburn d		11 07	11 12	11 27			11 48	12 04		12 12	12 27			12 48	13 02			13 12	13 28		13 48	14 04
Rishton d				11 32							12 32								13 33			
Church & Oswaldtwistle d			11 17	11 35						12 17	12 35							13 17	13 36			
Accrington d		11 15	11 21	11 39				12 12		12 21	12 39				13 10			13 21	13 39			14 12
Huncoat d				11 43							12 43								13 44			
Hapton d				11x46							12x46								13x47			
Rose Grove d			11 28	11 50						12 28	12 50							13 28	13 50			
Burnley Manchester Road 41 a		11 23	11 31					12 20		12 31					13 18			13 31				14 20
Leeds 10 41 a		12 36						13 33							14 31							15 35
Todmorden d			11 49							12 49								13 49				
Rochdale d			12 03							13 03								14 03				
Manchester Victoria a	11 44		12 24				12 39		12 44	13 24				13 39		13 44		14 24			14 39	
Burnley Barracks d				11x53							12x53								13x53			
Burnley Central d				11 56							12 56								13 56			
Brierfield d				12 00							13 00								14 01			
Nelson d				12 04							13 04								14 04			
Colne a				12 10							13 10								14 11			

A not 15 December. From Blackburn
B To Manchester Oxford Road
C To Southport
D To Liverpool Lime Street
E To Hellifield
F To York
G From Clitheroe
H To Manchester Airport

Table T097-R

Sundays
15 December to 10 May

Blackpool - Preston - Blackburn, Accrington, Burnley and Colne

		NT		NT A	NT	NT ◇ B	NT ◇ C	NT D	NT ◇ E	NT	NT A	NT		NT ◇ B	NT ◇ C	NT F	NT D	NT ◇ E	NT	NT A	NT	NT ◇ B		NT ◇ C	NT D
Blackpool North	d	13 21				13 32	14 00		14 16	14 19				14 32	15 00			15 17	15 20			15 32		16 00	
Layton	d	13 24								14 22									15 23						
Poulton-le-Fylde	d	13 27				13 38	14 06		14 22	14 25				14 38	15 06			15 23	15 26			15 38		16 06	
Blackpool South	d				13 16							14 16									15 16				
Blackpool Pleasure Beach	d				13 18							14 18									15 18				
Squires Gate	d				13 20							14 20									15 20				
St Annes-on-the-Sea	d				13 24							14 24									15 24				
Ansdell & Fairhaven	d				13 28							14 28									15 28				
Lytham	d				13 31							14 31									15 31				
Moss Side	d				13 36							14 36									15 36				
Kirkham & Wesham	d	13 36			13 43	13 47	14 15			14 34		14 43		14 47	15 15				15 35		15 43	15 47		16 15	
Salwick	d																								
Preston 8	a	13 47			13 54	13 57	14 25		14 40	14 45		14 54		14 58	15 25			15 42	15 47		15 54	15 59		16 25	
	d	13 49			13 56				14 41	14 49		14 56				15 29		15 44	15 51		15 56				
Lostock Hall	d				14 06							15 06				15 36					16 06				
Bamber Bridge	d				14 10							15 10				15 39					16 10				
Pleasington	d				14x17							15x17									16x17				
Cherry Tree	d				14 21							15 21									16 21				
Mill Hill (Lancashire)	d				14 23							15 23									16 23				
Blackburn	a				14 27				15 03			15 27				15 50		16 03			16 27				
Clitheroe 94	a															16 12									
Blackburn	d			14 12	14 27			14 48	15 04		15 12	15 27					15 48	16 04		16 12	16 27				16 48
Rishton	d				14 32							15 32									16 32				
Church & Oswaldtwistle	d			14 17	14 35						15 17	15 35								16 17	16 35				
Accrington	d			14 21	14 39				15 12		15 21	15 39						16 12		16 21	16 39				
Huncoat	d				14 43							15 43									16 43				
Hapton	d				14x46							15x46									16x46				
Rose Grove	d			14 28	14 50						15 28	15 50								16 28	16 50				
Burnley Manchester Road 41	a			14 31					15 20		15 31							16 20		16 31					
Leeds 10 41	a								16 33									17 33							
Todmorden	d			14 49							15 49									16 49					
Rochdale	d			15 03							16 03									17 03					
Manchester Victoria	a	14 44		15 24				15 39		15 44	16 24						16 39		16 44	17 24					17 39
Burnley Barracks	d				14x53							15x53									16x53				
Burnley Central	d				14 56							15 56									16 56				
Brierfield	d				15 00							16 00									17 00				
Nelson	d				15 04							16 04									17 04				
Colne	a				15 10							16 10									17 10				

		NT ◇ E	NT	NT A	NT	NT ◇ B	NT ◇ C	NT D		NT ◇ E	NT	NT A	NT	NT ◇ B	NT ◇ C	NT D	NT ◇ E	NT		NT A	NT	NT ◇ B	NT ◇ C	NT ◇ E	NT
Blackpool North	d	16 16	16 19			16 32	17 00			17 17	17 20			17 32	18 00		18 17	18 21				18 32	19 00	19 17	19 20
Layton	d		16 22								17 23							18 24							19 23
Poulton-le-Fylde	d	16 22	16 25			16 38	17 06			17 23	17 26			17 38	18 06		18 23	18 27				18 38	19 06	19 23	19 26
Blackpool South	d				16 16								17 16								18 16				
Blackpool Pleasure Beach	d				16 18								17 18								18 18				
Squires Gate	d				16 20								17 20								18 20				
St Annes-on-the-Sea	d				16 24								17 24								18 24				
Ansdell & Fairhaven	d				16 28								17 28								18 28				
Lytham	d				16 31								17 31								18 31				
Moss Side	d				16 36								17 36								18 36				
Kirkham & Wesham	d		16 34		16 43	16 47	17 15				17 35		17 43	17 47	18 15			18 36			18 43	18 47	19 15		19 35
Salwick	d																								
Preston 8	a	16 40	16 45		16 54	16 58	17 25			17 41	17 46		17 54	17 57	18 25		18 43	18 48			18 54	18 58	19 25	19 41	19 46
	d	16 41	16 46		16 56					17 42	17 47		17 56				18 44	18 49			18 56			19 42	19 47
Lostock Hall	d				17 06								18 06								19 06				
Bamber Bridge	d				17 10								18 10								19 10				
Pleasington	d				17x17								18x17								19x17				
Cherry Tree	d				17 21								18 21								19 21				
Mill Hill (Lancashire)	d				17 23								18 23								19 23				
Blackburn	a	17 03			17 27					18 03			18 30				19 03				19 27			20 03	
Clitheroe 94	a																								
Blackburn	d	17 04		17 12	17 27			17 48		18 04		18 12	18 31			18 50	19 04			19 12	19 27			20 04	
Rishton	d				17 32								18 38								19 32				
Church & Oswaldtwistle	d			17 17	17 35							18 17	18 41							19 17	19 35				
Accrington	d	17 12		17 21	17 39					18 12		18 21	18 44				19 12			19 21	19 39			20 12	
Huncoat	d				17 43								18 49								19 43				
Hapton	d				17x46								18x52								19x46				
Rose Grove	d			17 28	17 50							18 28	18 55							19 28	19 50				
Burnley Manchester Road 41	a	17 20		17 31						18 20		18 31					19 20			19 31				20 20	
Leeds 10 41	a	18 35								19 32							20 33							21 33	
Todmorden	d			17 49								18 49								19 49					
Rochdale	d			18 03								19 03								20 03					
Manchester Victoria	a		17 44	18 24				18 39			18 44	19 24				19 39		19 44		20 24					20 43
Burnley Barracks	d				17x53								18x58								19x53				
Burnley Central	d				17 56								19 01								19 56				
Brierfield	d				18 00								19 06								20 00				
Nelson	d				18 04								19 09								20 04				
Colne	a				18 10								19 16								20 10				

A To Southport
B To Liverpool Lime Street
C To Manchester Airport
D From Clitheroe
E To York
F To Hellifield

Table T097-R

Sundays
15 December to 10 May

Blackpool - Preston - Blackburn, Accrington, Burnley and Colne

		NT ◇ A	NT B	NT C		NT	NT ◇ D	NT C	NT ◇ E	NT	NT	NT	NT ◇ A	NT ◇ D		NT C	NT ◇ E	NT	NT	NT	NT ◇ D	NT ◇ A	NT	NT	
Blackpool North	d	19 25					20 00		20 17	20 21			20 32	20 59			21 17	21 22			21 59	22 06	22 22		
Layton	d									20 24								21 25					22 25		
Poulton-le-Fylde	d	19 31					20 06		20 23	20 27			20 38	21 05			21 23	21 28			22 05	22 12	22 28		
Blackpool South	d					19 16						20 16								21 18				22 18	
Blackpool Pleasure Beach	d					19 18						20 18								21 20				22 20	
Squires Gate	d					19 20						20 20								21 22				22 22	
St Annes-on-the-Sea	d					19 24						20 24								21 26				22 26	
Ansdell & Fairhaven	d					19 28						20 28								21 30				22 30	
Lytham	d					19 31						20 31								21 33				22 33	
Moss Side	d					19 36						20 36								21 38				22 38	
Kirkham & Wesham	d	19 40				19 44	20 15			20 36		20 43	20 47	21 14				21 37		21 45	22 14	22 21	22 37	22 45	
Salwick	d																								
Preston 8	a	19 51				19 56	20 25		20 41	20 49		20 54	20 59	21 24			21 43	21 48		21 56	22 24	22 31	22 48	22 56	
	d					19 57			20 44	20 51		20 55					21 44	21 51		22 01			22 49		
Lostock Hall	d					20 07						21 07								22 07					
Bamber Bridge	d					20 10						21 11								22 10					
Pleasington	d					20x18						21x18								22x18					
Cherry Tree	d					20 21						21 21								22 21					
Mill Hill (Lancashire)	d					20 23						21 24								22 24					
Blackburn	a					20 27			21 03			21 27					22 01			22 27					
Clitheroe 94	a																								
Blackburn	d		20 16	20 17		20 27		20 48	21 04		21 13	21 28				21 48	22 01		22 13	22 28					
Rishton	d					20 32						21 33								22 33					
Church & Oswaldtwistle	d		20 21			20 35					21 18	21 36							22 18	22 36					
Accrington	d		20 25			20 39			21 12		21 22	21 39					22 11		22 22	22 39					
Huncoat	d					20 43						21 44								22 44					
Hapton	d					20x46						21x47								22x47					
Rose Grove	d		20 32			20 50					21 29	21 50							22 29	22 50					
Burnley Manchester Road 41	a		20 35						21 20		21 32						22 21		22 32						
Leeds 10 41	a								22 41								23 34								
Todmorden	d		20 55								21 50								22 50						
Rochdale	d		21 09								22 04								23 04						
Manchester Victoria	a		21 30	21 08				21 39		21 44	22 25					22 39		22 45	23 25				23 42		
Burnley Barracks	d					20x53						21x53								22x53					
Burnley Central	d					20 56						21 56								22 56					
Brierfield	d					21 00						22 01								23 01					
Nelson	d					21 04						22 04								23 04					
Colne	a					21 10						22 11								23 11					

		NT	NT	NT C
Blackpool North	d		23 01	
Layton	d			
Poulton-le-Fylde	d		23 07	
Blackpool South	d			
Blackpool Pleasure Beach	d			
Squires Gate	d			
St Annes-on-the-Sea	d			
Ansdell & Fairhaven	d			
Lytham	d			
Moss Side	d			
Kirkham & Wesham	d		23 16	
Salwick	d			
Preston 8	a		23 26	
	d			
Lostock Hall	d			
Bamber Bridge	d			
Pleasington	d			
Cherry Tree	d			
Mill Hill (Lancashire)	d			
Blackburn	a			
Clitheroe 94	a			
Blackburn	d	23 00		23 07
Rishton	d			
Church & Oswaldtwistle	d	23 05		
Accrington	d	23 08		
Huncoat	d			
Hapton	d			
Rose Grove	d	23 15		
Burnley Manchester Road 41	a	23 19		
Leeds 10 41	a			
Todmorden	d	23 35		
Rochdale	d	23 49		
Manchester Victoria	a	00 11		23 54
Burnley Barracks	d			
Burnley Central	d			
Brierfield	d			
Nelson	d			
Colne	a			

A To Liverpool Lime Street
B To Southport
C From Clitheroe
D To Manchester Airport
E To York

Table T098-F

Mondays to Fridays
16 December to 15 May

Lancaster - Morecambe and Heysham

Miles	Station			NT	NT	NT	NT	NT	NT	NT	NT	NT	NT	NT	NT	NT	NT	NT	NT	NT	NT	NT	NT	NT
										◇			◇			◇			◇					
				B																				
0	Lancaster	82	d	05 30	06 18	07 23	07 56	08 41	09 28	10 16	10 50	11 28	12 14	12 49	13 52	14 14	14 40	15 25	16 22	16 51	17 12	17 49	18 28	19 05
2½	Bare Lane		d	05 50	06 23	07 28	08 01	08 46	09 33	10 23	10 55	11 33	12 20	12 54	13 57	14 20	14 45	15 30	16 28	16 56	17 18	17 54	18 33	19 10
4¼	Morecambe		a	05 54	06 27	07 32	08 05	08 50	09 37	10 27	10 59	11 37	12 24	12 58	14 01	14 24	14 49	15 34	16 32	17 00	17 22	17 58	18 37	19 14
—			d											13 02										
8¼	Heysham Port	⛴	a											13 17										

Station			NT	NT	NT	NT	NT
			◇				
Lancaster	82	d	19 40	20 38	21 35	22 04	22 37
Bare Lane		d	19 47	20 43	21 40	22 09	22 42
Morecambe		a	19 51	20 47	21 44	22 13	22 46
		d					
Heysham Port	⛴	a					

Saturdays
21 December to 16 May

Station			NT	NT	NT	NT	NT	NT	NT	NT	NT	NT	NT	NT	NT	NT	NT	NT	NT	NT	NT	NT	NT	NT
									◇			◇			◇			◇						◇
			B																					
Lancaster	82	d	05 30	06 18	07 23	07 56	08 41	09 28	10 16	10 50	11 28	12 14	12 49	13 52	14 14	14 51	15 24	16 22	16 51	17 12	17 49	18 28	19 05	19 34
Bare Lane		d	05 50	06 23	07 28	08 01	08 46	09 33	10 23	10 55	11 33	12 20	12 54	13 57	14 20	14 56	15 29	16 28	16 56	17 18	17 54	18 33	19 10	19 41
Morecambe		a	05 54	06 27	07 32	08 05	08 50	09 37	10 27	10 59	11 37	12 24	12 58	14 01	14 24	15 00	15 33	16 32	17 00	17 22	17 58	18 37	19 14	19 45
		d											13 02											
Heysham Port	⛴	a											13 17											

Station			NT	NT	NT	NT
Lancaster	82	d	20 36	21 35	22 06	22 37
Bare Lane		d	20 41	21 40	22 11	22 42
Morecambe		a	20 45	21 44	22 15	22 46
		d				
Heysham Port	⛴	a				

Sundays
15 December to 10 May

Station			NT	NT	NT	NT	NT	NT	NT	NT	NT	NT	NT	NT	NT
				◇		◇			◇		◇		◇		
			A												
Lancaster	82	d	09 30	10 30	11 30	12 30	13 40	14 29	15 23	16 30	17 24	18 32	19 28	20 30	21 30
Bare Lane		d	09 35	10 35	11 35	12 35	13 45	14 34	15 28	16 35	17 30	18 37	19 34	20 35	21 35
Morecambe		a	09 39	10 39	11 39	12 39	13 49	14 38	15 33	16 39	17 34	18 41	19 38	20 39	21 39
		d				12 43									
Heysham Port	⛴	a				12 58									

A until 5 January, from 23 February until 29 March

B *Parliamentary Train;* via Carnforth (Arrives 0539;Departs 0543)

Table T098-R

Mondays to Fridays
16 December to 15 May

Heysham and Morecambe - Lancaster

Miles	Station			NT	NT	NT	NT	NT	NT	NT	NT	NT	NT	NT	NT	NT	NT	NT	NT	NT	NT	NT	NT	NT
										◇			◇			◇					◇			
0	Heysham Port	⛴	d											13 20										
4¼	Morecambe		a											13 35										
—			d	05 58	07 00	07 40	08 23	08 54	09 41	10 33	11 15	11 41	12 32	13 39	14 21	14 32	15 04	15 43	16 38	17 04	17 31	18 13	18 41	19 49
6	Bare Lane		d	06 02	07 04	07 44	08 27	08 58	09 45	10 37	11 19	11 45	12 36	13 43	14 25	14 37	15 08	15 47	16 42	17 08	17 35	18 17	18 45	19 53
8½	Lancaster	82	a	06 08	07 11	07 50	08 33	09 04	09 51	10 42	11 24	11 51	12 42	13 48	14 32	14 43	15 13	15 53	16 47	17 14	17 41	18 24	18 50	20 00

Station			NT	NT	NT	NT	NT
			◇				
Heysham Port	⛴	d					
Morecambe		a					
		d	20 07	20 56	21 48	22 21	22 52
Bare Lane		d	20 11	21 00	21 52	22 25	22 56
Lancaster	82	a	20 17	21 06	21 58	22 31	23 02

Saturdays
21 December to 16 May

Station			NT	NT	NT	NT	NT	NT	NT	NT	NT	NT	NT	NT	NT	NT	NT	NT	NT	NT	NT	NT	NT	NT
									◇			◇			◇					◇				◇
Heysham Port	⛴	d											13 20											
Morecambe		a											13 35											
		d	05 58	07 00	07 40	08 23	08 54	09 41	10 33	11 15	11 41	12 32	13 39	14 22	14 32	15 09	15 43	16 38	17 04	17 31	18 13	18 41	19 41	20 07
Bare Lane		d	06 02	07 04	07 44	08 27	08 58	09 45	10 37	11 19	11 45	12 36	13 43	14 26	14 37	15 13	15 47	16 42	17 08	17 35	18 17	18 45	19 45	20 11
Lancaster	82	a	06 08	07 11	07 50	08 33	09 04	09 51	10 42	11 24	11 51	12 42	13 48	14 33	14 43	15 18	15 53	16 47	17 14	17 41	18 24	18 50	19 51	20 17

Station			NT	NT	NT	NT
Heysham Port	⛴	d				
Morecambe		a				
		d	21 12	21 48	22 20	22 52
Bare Lane		d	21 16	21 52	22 24	22 56
Lancaster	82	a	21 22	21 58	22 30	23 01

Sundays
15 December to 10 May

Station			NT	NT	NT	NT	NT	NT	NT	NT	NT	NT	NT	NT	NT
				◇		◇			◇		◇		◇		
			A												
Heysham Port	⛴	d				13 05									
Morecambe		a				13 20									
		d	10 00	10 49	11 50	13 23	13 57	14 42	15 40	16 57	17 38	18 57	20 04	20 57	22 00
Bare Lane		d	10 04	10 53	11 54	13 27	14 01	14 46	15 44	17 01	17 42	19 01	20 08	21 01	22 04
Lancaster	82	a	10 10	10 58	12 00	13 34	14 07	14 52	15 49	17 07	17 48	19 07	20 13	21 07	22 10

A until 5 January, from 23 February until 29 March

Table T099-F

Mondays to Saturdays

16 December to 16 May

Ormskirk - Preston

Miles			NT	NT	NT SX	NT SO	NT SX	NT SO	NT SX	NT SO	NT SX	NT SO	NT SO	NT SX	NT SO	NT SX	NT SO	NT SX	NT SO	NT SX	NT	NT SX	NT SO
0	**Ormskirk**	d	07 01	08 01	09 01	09 01	10 01	10 01	11 01	11 01	12 01	12 01	13 01	13 01	14 01	14 01	15 01	15 01	16 01	16 01	17 01	18 01	18 01
2½	Burscough Junction	d	07 05	08 05	09 05	09 05	10 05	10 05	11 05	11 05	12 05	12 05	13 05	13 05	14 05	14 05	15 05	15 05	16 05	16 05	17 05	18 05	18 05
5½	Rufford	d	07 11	08 11	09 11	09 11	10 11	10 11	11 11	11 11	12 11	12 11	13 11	13 11	14 11	14 11	15 11	15 11	16 11	16 11	17 11	18 11	18 11
8	Croston	d	07 16	08 16	09 16	09 16	10 16	10 16	11 16	11 16	12 16	12 16	13 16	13 16	14 16	14 16	15 16	15 16	16 16	16 16	17 16	18 16	18 16
15	**Preston 8**	a	07 32	08 33	09 33	09 34	10 33	10 34	11 33	11 34	12 33	12 34	13 31	13 32	14 31	14 33	15 32	15 33	16 31	16 33	17 32	18 30	18 31

		NT SO	NT SX	NT	NT SX	NT SO	NT SO	NT SX	NT
Ormskirk	d	19 01	19 01	20 01	21 01	21 01	22 01	22 01	23 10
Burscough Junction	d	19 05	19 05	20 05	21 05	21 05	22 05	22 05	23 14
Rufford	d	19 11	19 11	20 11	21 11	21 11	22 11	22 11	23 20
Croston	d	19 16	19 16	20 16	21 16	21 16	22 16	22 16	23 25
Preston 8	a	19 31	19 33	20 34	21 34	21 35	22 30	22 31	23 42

For connections from Liverpool Central refer to Table T105

No Sunday Service

NRT DECEMBER 19 EDITION

Table T099-R

Mondays to Saturdays

16 December to 16 May

Preston - Ormskirk

Miles			NT	NT	NT	NT	NT	NT	NT	NT	NT	NT	NT	NT	NT	NT	NT	NT	NT
0	**Preston 8**	d	06 25	07 26	08 26	09 26	10 26	11 26	12 26	13 26	14 26	15 26	16 26	17 26	18 26	19 26	20 26	21 26	22 37
7	Croston	d	06 38	07 39	08 39	09 39	10 39	11 39	12 39	13 39	14 39	15 39	16 39	17 39	18 39	19 40	20 39	21 39	22 49
9½	Rufford	d	06 44	07 44	08 44	09 44	10 44	11 44	12 44	13 44	14 44	15 44	16 44	17 44	18 44	19 45	20 44	21 44	22 54
12½	Burscough Junction	d	06 49	07 50	08 50	09 50	10 50	11 50	12 50	13 50	14 50	15 50	16 50	17 50	18 50	19 51	20 50	21 50	23 00
15	**Ormskirk**	a	06 55	07 56	08 56	09 56	10 56	11 56	12 56	13 56	14 56	15 56	16 56	17 56	18 56	19 57	20 56	21 56	23 06

For connections to Liverpool Central refer to Table T103

No Sunday Service

Table T100-F

Mondays to Fridays

16 December to 15 May

Barrow-in-Furness - Whitehaven and Carlisle

Miles			NT	NT	NT	NT	NT	NT	NT	NT	NT	NT	NT	NT	NT	NT	NT	NT	NT	NT	NT	NT	NT
—	Lancaster 6	82 d								10 13			13 13					16 13				19 13	
0	**Barrow-in-Furness**	d			05 58	06 51	07 50	09 27	10 22	11 18	12 06	13 16	14 17	14 49	15 44	16 15		17 17	18 07	19 12	19 44	20 19	21 10
6	Askam	d			06 08	07 01	08 00	09 37	10 32	11 28	12 16	13 26	14 27	14 59	15 54	16 25		17 28	18 17	19 22	19 54	20 29	21 20
9¼	Kirkby-in-Furness	d			06x12	07x05	08x04	09x41	10x36	11x32	12x20	13x30	14x31	15x03	15x58	16x29		17x32	18x21	19x26	19x58	20x33	21x24
11¼	Foxfield	d			06 16	07 09	08 08	09 45	10 40	11 36	12 24	13 34	14 35	15 07	16 02	16 34		17 36	18 25	19 30	20 02	20 37	21 28
13½	Green Road	d			06x20	07x13	08x11	09x48	10x43	11x40	12x27	13x37	14x39	15x10	16x05	16x37		17x39	18x28	19x33	20x05	20x40	21x32
16	Millom	a			06 26	07 19	08 17	09 54	10 49	11 46	12 33	13 43	14 45	15 16	16 11	16 43		17 45	18 34	19 39	20 12	20 46	21 38
—		d			06 27	07 19	08 18	09 55	10 50	11 46	12 34	13 44	14 45	15 17	16 12	16 44		17 45	18 34	19 40		20 46	
19	Silecroft	d			06x32	07x24	08x23	09x59	10x54	11x51	12x38	13x48	14x49	15x21	16x16	16x48		17x50		19x44		20x51	
24½	Bootle	d			06x39	07x31	08x29	10x06	11x01	11x57	12x45	13x55	14x56	15x28	16x23	16x55		17x56		19x51		20x57	
29¼	Ravenglass for Eskdale	d			06 45	07 37	08 35	10 12	11 07	12 03	12 51	14 01	15 02	15 34	16 29	17 01		18 02	18 49	19 57		21 03	
31	Drigg	d			06x49	07x41	08x38	10x15	11x10	12x06	12x54	14x04	15x05	15x37	16x32	17x04		18x05	18x52	20x00		21x06	
33¼	Seascale	d			06 53	07 45	08 42	10 19	11 14	12 10	12 57	14 07	15 08	15 41	16 35	17 08		18 09	18 56	20 03		21 10	
35	Sellafield	d			07 00	07 53	08 49	10 32	11 22	12 17	13 03	14 13	15 14	15 47	16 41	17a12		18 14	19 00	20 12		21 16	
37	Braystones	d				07x57			11x26		13x07	14x16								20x15			
38¼	Nethertown	d				07x59			11x28		13x09	14x19								20x18			
41¼	St Bees	d			07 13	08 05	09 00	10 42	11 34	12 27	13 28	14 27	15 27	16 00	16 52			18 26	19 12	20 27		21 25	
44¾	Corkickle	d			07 19	08 11	09 05	10 47	11 40	12 32	13 34	14 33	15 33	16 06	16 57			18 32	19 17	20 32		21 31	
45¾	**Whitehaven**	a			07 22	08 14	09 08	10 50	11 43	12 35	13 36	14 36	15 36	16 08	17 00			18 34	19 20	20 36		21 33	
—		d		06 30	07 23	08 16	09 09	10 51	11 45	12 36	13 38	14 38	15 40	16 12	17 01		17 49	18 35	19 21	20 37		21 35	
47	Parton	d		06x33	07x27	08x20	09x13	10x55	11x48		13x41	14x41	15x45	16x15	17x05		17x52	18x39	19x25	20x41		21x38	
50½	Harrington	d		06 42	07 36	08 28	09 21	11 03	11 57		13 50	14 50	15 53	16 24	17 13		18 01	18 47	19 33	20 49		21 47	
52¼	**Workington**	d	05 52	06 48	07 42	08 34	09 27	11 09	12 03	12 53	13 56	14 56	15 59	16 33	17 19		18 07	18 53	19 43	20 55		21 53	
56	Flimby	d	05x56	06x52	07x46	08x39	09x32	11x14	12x07		14x00	15x00	16x04	16x37	17x24		18x11	18x58	19x47	21x00		21x57	
58	Maryport	d	06 00	06 56	07 50	08 43	09 36	11 17	12 11	13 01	14 04	15 05	16 08	16 43	17 28		18 16	19 02	19 53	21 04		22 01	
65½	Aspatria	d	06 10	07 06	08 00	08 53	09 46	11 27	12 21		14 14	15 15	16 18	16 53	17 38		18 26	19 12	20 03	21 14		22 11	
71¾	Wigton	d	06 22	07 18	08 12	09 04	09 57	11 38	12 33	13 22	14 26	15 26	16 29	17 05	17 49		18 37	19 23	20 14	21 25		22 22	
81¼	Dalston	d	06 31	07 27	08 21	09 13	10 06	11 47	12 42		14 35	15 35	16 38	17 14	17 59		18 46	19 32	20 23	21 34		22 31	
85¼	**Carlisle 8**	a	06 42	07 38	08 32	09 24	10 17	11 58	12 53	13 40	14 47	15 46	16 51	17 25	18 10		18 57	19 43	20 34	21 45		22 42	

		NT	NT
Lancaster 6	82 d		
Barrow-in-Furness	d		22 11
Askam	d		22 21
Kirkby-in-Furness	d		22x25
Foxfield	d		22 29
Green Road	d		22x33
Millom	a		22 39
	d		
Silecroft	d		
Bootle	d		
Ravenglass for Eskdale	d		
Drigg	d		
Seascale	d		
Sellafield	d		
Braystones	d		
Nethertown	d		
St Bees	d		
Corkickle	d		
Whitehaven	a		
	d	22 09	
Parton	d	22x12	
Harrington	d	22 21	
Workington	d	22 27	
Flimby	d	22x32	
Maryport	d	22 36	
Aspatria	d	22 46	
Wigton	d	22 57	
Dalston	d	23 06	
Carlisle 8	a	23 17	

Saturdays

21 December to 16 May

		NT	NT	NT	NT	NT	NT	NT	NT	NT	NT	NT	NT	NT	NT	NT	NT	NT	NT	NT	NT	NT	NT
Lancaster 6	82 d								10 13			13 01				16 13				19 13			
Barrow-in-Furness	d			05 58	06 51	07 54	09 17	10 22	11 18	12 06	13 16	14 14	14 49	15 44	16 11	17 17	18 07	18 57	19 44	20 18	21 10		22 11
Askam	d			06 08	07 01	08 04	09 27	10 32	11 28	12 16	13 26	14 24	14 59	15 54	16 21	17 28	18 17	19 07	19 54	20 28	21 20		22 21
Kirkby-in-Furness	d			06x12	07x05	08x08	09x31	10x36	11x32	12x20	13 30	14x28	15x03	15x58	16x25	17x32	18x21	19x11	19x58	20x32	21x24		22x25
Foxfield	d			06 16	07 09	08 12	09 35	10 40	11 36	12 24	13 34	14 32	15 07	16 02	16 29	17 36	18 25	19 15	20 02	20 36	21 28		22 29
Green Road	d			06x20	07x13	08x15	09x38	10x43	11x40	12x27	13 37	14x35	15x10	16x05	16x32	17x39	18x28	19x19	20x05	20x39	21x32		22x33
Millom	a			06 26	07 19	08 21	09 43	10 49	11 46	12 33	13 43	14 41	15 16	16 11	16 38	17 45	18 34	19 25	20 11	20 46	21 38		22 39
	d			06 27	07 19	08 22	09 44	10 50	11 46	12 34	13 44	14 42	15 17	16 12	16 39	17 45	18 34	19 25	20 11				
Silecroft	d			06x32	07x24	08x27	09x48	10x54	11x51	12x38	13 48	14x46	15x21	16x16	16x43	17x50		19x29	20x16				
Bootle	d			06x39	07x31	08x33	09x55	11x01	11x57	12x45	13 55	14x53	15x28	16x23	16x50	17x56		19x36	20x22				
Ravenglass for Eskdale	d			06 45	07 37	08 39	10 01	11 07	12 03	12 51	14 01	14 59	15 34	16 29	16 56	18 02	18 49	19 42	20 28				
Drigg	d			06x49	07x41	08x42	10x04	11x10	12x06	12x54	14 04	15x02	15x37	16x32	16x59	18x05	18x52	19x45	20x31				
Seascale	d			06 53	07 45	08 46	10 08	11 14	12 10	12 57	14 07	15 06	15 41	16 35	17 02	18 09	18 56	19 48	20 35				
Sellafield	d			07 00	07 53	08 52	10 14	11 22	12 17	13 03	14 13	15 12	15 47	16 41	17 08	18 14	19 00	19 53	20 41				
Braystones	d				07x57	08x55		11x26		13x07		15 15			17x11				20x44				
Nethertown	d				07x59	08x58		11x28		13x09		15 18			17x14				20x47				
St Bees	d			07 13	08 05	09 04	10 27	11 34	12 27	13 28	14 26	15 27	16 00	16 52	17 19	18 26	19 12	20 03	20 52				
Corkickle	d			07 19	08 11	09 09	10 33	11 40	12 32	13 34	14 32	15 33	16 06	16 57	17 24	18 32	19 17	20 08	20 57				
Whitehaven	a			07 22	08 14	09 13	10 35	11 43	12 35	13 36	14 34	15 36	16 08	17 00	17 28	18 34	19 20	20 12	21 01				
	d		06 30	07 23	08 16	09 14	10 37	11 45	12 36	13 38	14 38	15 39	16 12	17 01	17 29	18 35	19 21	20 13	21 02			22 09	
Parton	d		06x33	07x27	08x20	09x18	10x40	11x48		13x41	14x41	15x44	16x15	17x05	17x33	18x39	19x25	20x17	21x06			22x12	
Harrington	d		06 42	07 36	08 28	09 27	10 49	11 57		13 50	14 50	15 52	16 24	17 13	17 41	18 47	19 33	20 25	21 14			22 21	
Workington	d	05 48	06 48	07 42	08 34	09 33	10 55	12 03	12 53	13 56	14 56	15 58	16 33	17 19	17 47	18 53	19 43	20 35	21 20			22 27	
Flimby	d	05x52	06x52	07x46	08x39	09x37	10x59	12x07		14x00	15x00	16x03	16x37	17x24	17x52	18x58	19x47	20x40	21x25			22x32	
Maryport	d	05 56	06 56	07 50	08 43	09 41	11 03	12 11	13 01	14 04	15 05	16 07	16 43	17 28	17 56	19 02	19 53	20 44	21a28			22a36	
Aspatria	d	06 06	07 06	08 00	08 53	09 51	11 13	12 21		14 14	15 15	16 17	16 53	17 38	18 06	19 12	20 03	20 54					
Wigton	d	06 18	07 18	08 12	09 04	10 03	11 24	12 33	13 22	14 26	15 26	16 28	17 05	17 49	18 17	19 23	20 14	21 05					
Dalston	d	06 27	07 27	08 21	09 13	10 12	11 33	12 42		14 35	15 35	16 37	17 14	17 59	18 26	19 32	20 23	21 14					
Carlisle 8	a	06 38	07 39	08 32	09 24	10 23	11 44	12 53	13 40	14 47	15 46	16 48	17 25	18 11	18 41	19 43	20 34	21 25					

Table T100-F

Sundays

15 December to 10 May

Barrow-in-Furness - Whitehaven and Carlisle

		NT A	NT	NT A	NT B	NT	NT	NT A	NT B	NT
Lancaster 🅱 82	d							10ʃ11		
Barrow-in-Furness	d		09 05				09 50	11ʃ15	11ʃ15	12 18
Askam	d		09 15				10 00	11ʃ25	11ʃ25	12 28
Kirkby-in-Furness	d		09x19				10x04	11x29	11x29	12x32
Foxfield	d		09 23				10 08	11ʃ33	11ʃ33	12 36
Green Road	d		09x26				10x11	11x37	11x37	12x39
Millom	a		09 33				10 17	11ʃ43	11ʃ43	12 45
	d						10 17	11ʃ43	11ʃ43	12 45
Silecroft	d						10x22	11x47	11x47	12x50
Bootle	d						10x28	11x54	11x54	12x56
Ravenglass for Eskdale	d						10 34	12ʃ00	12ʃ00	13 02
Drigg	d						10x37	12x03	12x03	13x05
Seascale	d						10 41	12ʃ06	12ʃ06	13 09
Sellafield	d						10 46	12ʃ12	12ʃ12	13 15
Braystones	d						10x50	ʃ	ʃ	
Nethertown	d						10x52	ʃ	ʃ	
St Bees	d						11 00	12ʃ25	12ʃ25	13 28
Corkickle	d						11 06	12ʃ30	12ʃ30	13 33
Whitehaven	a						11 09	12ʃ33	12ʃ33	13 37
	d					10 16	11 11	12ʃ34	12ʃ34	13 38
Parton	d					10x20	11x14	12x38	12x38	13x42
Harrington	d					10 28	11 23	12ʃ46	12ʃ46	13 50
Workington	d	08ʃ55		09ʃ40	09ʃ57	10 34	11 29	12ʃ52	12ʃ52	13 58
Flimby	d	09x00		09x45	10x02	10x39	11x33	12x57	12x57	14x03
Maryport	d	09ʃ04		09ʃ49	10ʃ06	10 43	11 37	13ʃ01	13ʃ01	14 08
Aspatria	d	09ʃ14		09ʃ59	10ʃ16	10 53	11 47	13ʃ11	13ʃ11	14 18
Wigton	d	09ʃ25		10ʃ10	10ʃ27	11 04	11 59	13ʃ22	13ʃ22	14 30
Dalston	d	09ʃ34		10ʃ19	10ʃ36	11 13	12 08	13ʃ31	13ʃ31	14 39
Carlisle 🅱	a	09ʃ45		10ʃ30	10ʃ47	11 24	12 19	13ʃ42	13ʃ42	14 50

		NT	NT	NT	NT	NT	NT	NT	NT	NT
Lancaster 🅱 82	d		13 13			16 03				
Barrow-in-Furness	d	13 09	14 17	14 55	15 58	17 17	18 25	19 07		
Askam	d	13 19	14 27	15 05	16 08	17 28	18 35	19 17		
Kirkby-in-Furness	d	13x23		15x09	16x12	17x32	18x39	19x21		
Foxfield	d	13 27		15 13	16 16	17 36	18 43	19 25		
Green Road	d	13x30		15x16	16x19	17x39	18x46	19x28		
Millom	a	13 36	14 41	15 22	16 25	17 45	18 53	19 35		
	d	13 36	14 43	15 23	16 25	17 46				
Silecroft	d	13x41		15x28	16x30	17x50				
Bootle	d	13x47		15x34	16x36	17x57				
Ravenglass for Eskdale	d	13 53	14 58	15 41	16 42	18 03				
Drigg	d	13x56		15x44	16x45	18x06				
Seascale	d	14 00		15 47	16 49	18 09				
Sellafield	d	14 05	15 06	15 51	16 54	18 15				
Braystones	d	14x09			16x58	18x18				
Nethertown	d	14x11			17x00	18x21				
St Bees	d	14 16	15 20	16 01	17 05	18 29				
Corkickle	d	14 21	15 25	16 07	17 10	18 34				
Whitehaven	a	14 25	15 28	16 09	17 14	18 38				
	d	14 26	15 29	16 11	17 16	18 39			19 38	20 30
Parton	d	14x30	15x33	16x14	17x20	18x43			19x41	20x33
Harrington	d	14 38	15 41	16 23	17 28	18 51			19 50	20 42
Workington	d	14 44	15 47	16 29	17 34	18 57			19 56	20 48
Flimby	d	14x49	15x52	16x33	17x39	19x02			20x01	20x53
Maryport	d	14 53	15 56	16 37	17 43	19 06			20 05	20 57
Aspatria	d	15 03	16 06	16 47	17 53	19 16			20 15	21 07
Wigton	d	15 14	16 17	16 59	18 04	19 27			20 26	21 18
Dalston	d	15 23	16 26	17 08	18 13	19 36			20 35	21 27
Carlisle 🅱	a	15 34	16 37	17 19	18 24	19 47			20 46	21 38

A until 5 January, from 23 February until 29 March B from 12 January until 16 February, from 5 April

Table T100-R

Mondays to Fridays

16 December to 15 May

Carlisle and Whitehaven - Barrow-in-Furness

Miles			NT	TP ◇🅱 🍴	NT	NT	NT	NT
0	**Carlisle** 🅱	d		05 48	05 53	06 19	07 10	08 08
4	Dalston	d			06 02	06 27	07 19	08 16
11½	Wigton	d			06 11	06 36	07 31	08 26
19¾	Aspatria	d			06 22	06 48	07 42	08 36
27¼	Maryport	d	05 48		06 33	06 59	07 55	08 48
29¼	Flimby	d	05x51		06x36	07x02	07x58	08x51
33	**Workington**	d	05 58		06 44	07 10	08 06	08 58
34¾	Harrington	d	06 02		06 48	07 14	08 10	09 02
38¼	Parton	d	06x11		06x57	07x24	08x18	09x11
39½	**Whitehaven**	a	06 16		07 02	07 29	08 24	09 16
—		d	06 18		07 04	07 30	08 25	09 18
40½	Corkickle	d	06 20		07 06	07 33	08 28	09 20
44	St Bees	d	06 26		07 12	07 39	08 34	09 28
47	Nethertown	d	06x30					
48¼	Braystones	d	06x33					
50¼	Sellafield	d	06 39		07 24	07 50	08 44	09 39
52	Seascale	d	06 43		07 28	07 54	08 48	09 42
54¼	Drigg	d	06x46		07x31	07x57	08x51	09x45
56	Ravenglass for Eskdale	d	06 50		07 34	08 01	08 54	09 49
60¾	Bootle	d	06x55		07x40	08x07	09x00	09x54
66¼	Silecroft	d	07x02		07x46	08x13	09x06	10x01
69¼	Millom	a	07 08		07 53	08 20	09 13	10 07
—		d	07 09		07 53	08 20	09 14	10 08
71¾	Green Road	d	07x13		07x57	08x24	09x18	10x12
73¾	Foxfield	d	07 17		08 01	08 28	09 22	10 16
76	Kirkby-in-Furness	d	07x21		08x05	08x32	09x26	10x20
79¼	Askam	d	07 26		08 11	08 38	09 31	10 25
85¼	**Barrow-in-Furness**	a	07 41		08 26	08 53	09 47	10 40
—	Lancaster 🅱 82	a		06 44			11 07	

		NT	NT	NT	NT	NT	NT	NT	NT	NT
Carlisle 🅱	d	09 02	10 13	11 07	12 10	13 07	14 08	14 41	15 12	15 59
Dalston	d	09 10	10 22	11 15	12 18	13 15	14 16	14 49	15 20	16 07
Wigton	d	09 20	10 31	11 25	12 27	13 25	14 26	14 58	15 30	16 17
Aspatria	d	09 30	10 42	11 35	12 38	13 35	14 36	15 09	15 40	16 27
Maryport	d	09 41	10 53	11 46	12 49	13 46	14 47	15 20	15 51	16 38
Flimby	d	09x44	10x56	11x49	12x52	13x49	14x50	15x23	15x54	16x41
Workington	d	09 52	11 03	11 57	12 59	13 57	14 58	15 30	16 02	16 48
Harrington	d	09 56	11 07	12 01	13 03	14 01	15 02	15 34	16 06	16 52
Parton	d	10x05	11x16	12x09	13x12	14x09	15x10	15x43	16x14	17x01
Whitehaven	a	10 10	11 21	12 15	13 17	14 15	15 16	15 48	16 20	17 08
	d	10 12	11 23	12 16	13 19	14 16	15 17	15 50	16 21	
Corkickle	d	10 14	11 25	12 19	13 21	14 19	15 20	15 53	16 24	
St Bees	d	10 20	11 33	12 28	13 29	14 30	15 26	15 59	16 30	
Nethertown	d		11x37					16x03		
Braystones	d		11x40					16x05		
Sellafield	d	10 31	11 45	12 38	13 40	14 41	15 37	16 11	16 41	
Seascale	d	10 35	11 49	12 42	13 43	14 44	15 41	16 15	16 44	
Drigg	d	10x38	11x52	12x45	13x46	14x47	15x44	16x18	16x48	
Ravenglass for Eskdale	d	10 42	11 55	12 48	13 50	14 51	15 48	16 22	16 51	
Bootle	d	10x47	12x01	12x54	13x56	14x56	15x53	16x28	16x57	
Silecroft	d	10x54	12x07	13x00	14x02	15x03	16x00	16x35	17x04	
Millom	a	11 00	12 14	13 07	14 09	15 09	16 06	16 41	17 11	
	d	11 01	12 14	13 07	14 09	15 11	16 07	16 42	17 12	
Green Road	d	11x05	12x18	13x11	14x13	15x15	16x11	16x46	17x16	
Foxfield	d	11 09	12 22	13 15	14 17	15 19	16 15	16 50	17 20	
Kirkby-in-Furness	d	11x13	12x26	13x19	14x21	15x23	16x19	16x55	17x25	
Askam	d	11 18	12 31	13 24	14 26	15 28	16 24	17 00	17 30	
Barrow-in-Furness	a	11 35	12 46	13 39	14 41	15 43	16 39	17 14	17 45	
Lancaster 🅱 82	a		13 53			16 52				

		NT	NT	NT	NT	NT	NT
Carlisle 🅱	d		17 07	17 54	19 09	20 00	20 55
Dalston	d		17 15	18 02	19 17	20 08	21 03
Wigton	d		17 25	18 12	19 27	20 18	21 13
Aspatria	d		17 35	18 22	19 37	20 28	21 23
Maryport	d		17 46	18 33	19 48	20 39	21 34
Flimby	d		17x49	18x36	19x51	20x42	21x37
Workington	d		17 57	18 44	19 59	20 50	21 45
Harrington	d		18 01	18 48	20 03	20 54	21 49
Parton	d		18x09	18x56	20x11	21x02	21x57
Whitehaven	a		18 16	19 02	20 16	21 09	22 04
	d		18 18	19 03	20 18		
Corkickle	d		18 20	19 06	20 20		
St Bees	d		18 27	19 14	20 28		
Nethertown	d		18x31		20x32		
Braystones	d		18x34		20x34		
Sellafield	d	17 25	18 40	19 27	20 40		
Seascale	d	17 28	18 43	19 32	20 44		
Drigg	d	17x31		19x35	20x47		
Ravenglass for Eskdale	d	17 35	18 49	19 39	20 50		
Bootle	d	17x41		19x45	20x56		
Silecroft	d	17x47		19x51	21x02		
Millom	a	17 54	19 05	19 58	21 09		
	d	17 54	19 05	20 01	21 09		
Green Road	d	17x58	19x09	20x05	21x13		
Foxfield	d	18 02	19 13	20 09	21 17		
Kirkby-in-Furness	d	18x06	19x17	20x13	21x21		
Askam	d	18 11	19 22	20 19	21 26		
Barrow-in-Furness	a	18 26	19 37	20 36	21 42		
Lancaster 🅱 82	a				22 46		

		NT
Carlisle 🅱	d	22 01
Dalston	d	22 09
Wigton	d	22 19
Aspatria	d	22 29
Maryport	d	22 41
Flimby	d	22x44
Workington	d	22 51
Harrington	d	22 55
Parton	d	23x04
Whitehaven	a	23 10
	d	
Corkickle	d	
St Bees	d	
Nethertown	d	
Braystones	d	
Sellafield	d	
Seascale	d	
Drigg	d	
Ravenglass for Eskdale	d	
Bootle	d	
Silecroft	d	
Millom	a	
	d	
Green Road	d	
Foxfield	d	
Kirkby-in-Furness	d	
Askam	d	
Barrow-in-Furness	a	
Lancaster 🅱 82	a	

Saturdays

21 December to 16 May

		NT	NT	NT	NT	NT	NT	NT	NT	NT
Carlisle 🅱	d		05 53	06 16	07 10	08 13	09 08	10 13	11 07	12 10
Dalston	d		06 02	06 24	07 19	08 21	09 16	10 22	11 15	12 18
Wigton	d		06 11	06 35	07 31	08 31	09 26	10 31	11 25	12 27
Aspatria	d		06 22	06 46	07 42	08 41	09 36	10 42	11 35	12 38
Maryport	d	05 48	06 33	06 59	07 55	08 52	09 47	10 53	11 46	12 49
Flimby	d	05x51	06x36	07x02	07x58		09x50	10x56	11x49	12x52
Workington	d	05 58	06 44	07 10	08 06	09 02	09 58	11 03	11 57	12 59
Harrington	d	06 02	06 48	07 14	08 10	09 06	10 02	11 07	12 01	13 03
Parton	d	06x11	06x57	07x24	08x18	09x14	10x10	11x16	12x09	13x12
Whitehaven	a	06 16	07 02	07 29	08 24	09 20	10 16	11 21	12 15	13 17
	d	06 18	07 04	07 30	08 25	09 21	10 17	11 23	12 16	13 19
Corkickle	d	06 20	07 06	07 33	08 28	09 24	10 20	11 25	12 19	13 21
St Bees	d	06 26	07 12	07 39	08 34	09 32	10 26	11 33	12 28	13 29
Nethertown	d	06x30						11x37	12x32	
Braystones	d	06x33						11x40	12x34	
Sellafield	d	06 39	07 24	07 50	08 44	09 42	10 37	11 45	12 40	13 40
Seascale	d	06 43	07 28	07 54	08 48	09 45	10 41	11 49	12 44	13 43
Drigg	d	06x46	07x31	07x57	08x51	09x48	10x44	11x52	12x47	13x46
Ravenglass for Eskdale	d	06 50	07 34	08 01	08 54	09 52	10 48	11 55	12 50	13 50
Bootle	d	06x55	07x40	08x07	09x00	09x57	10x53	12x01	12x56	13x56
Silecroft	d	07x02	07x46	08x13	09x06	10x04	11x00	12x07	13x02	14x02
Millom	a	07 08	07 53	08 20	09 13	10 10	11 06	12 14	13 09	14 09
	d	07 09	07 53	08 20	09 14	10 10	11 07	12 14	13 09	14 09
Green Road	d	07x13	07x57	08x24	09x18		11x11	12x18	13x13	14x13
Foxfield	d	07 17	08 01	08 28	09 22	10 18	11 15	12 22	13 17	14 17
Kirkby-in-Furness	d	07x21	08x05	08x32	09x26	10x22	11x19	12x26	13x21	14x21
Askam	d	07 26	08 11	08 38	09 31	10 27	11 24	12 31	13 26	14 26
Barrow-in-Furness	a	07 41	08 26	08 53	09 47	10 41	11 39	12 46	13 41	14 41
Lancaster 🅱 82	a				11 07			13 53		

		NT	NT	NT	NT	NT	NT	NT	NT	NT
Carlisle 🅱	d	13 07	14 08	14 41	15 12	16 26	17 07	17 54	18 46	19 09
Dalston	d	13 15	14 16	14 49	15 20	16 34	17 15	18 02	18 54	19 17
Wigton	d	13 25	14 26	14 58	15 30	16 44	17 25	18 12	19 04	19 27
Aspatria	d	13 35	14 36	15 09	15 40	16 54	17 35	18 22	19 14	19 37
Maryport	d	13 46	14 47	15 20	15 51	17 05	17 46	18 33	19 25	19 48
Flimby	d	13x49	14x50	15x23	15x54	17x08	17x49	18x36	19x28	19x51
Workington	d	13 57	14 58	15 30	16 02	17 15	17 57	18 44	19 36	19 59
Harrington	d	14 01	15 02	15 34	16 06	17 20	18 01	18 48	19 40	20 03
Parton	d	14x09	15x10	15x43	16x14	17x29	18x09	18x56	19x49	20x11
Whitehaven	a	14 15	15 16	15 48	16 20	17 35	18 16	19 02	19 56	20 19
	d	14 16	15 17	15 50	16 21	17 36	18 18	19 03		20 20
Corkickle	d	14 19	15 20	15 53	16 24	17 39	18 20	19 06		20 23
St Bees	d	14 30	15 26	15 59	16 30	17 44	18 27	19 14		20 28
Nethertown	d			16x03			18x31			20x32
Braystones	d			16x05			18x34			20x35
Sellafield	d	14 41	15 37	16 11	16 41	17 55	18 40	19 27		20 40
Seascale	d	14 44	15 41	16 15	16 44	17 58	18 43	19 32		20 44
Drigg	d	14x47	15x44	16x18	16x48	18x01		19x35		20x47
Ravenglass for Eskdale	d	14 51	15 48	16 22	16 51	18 05	18 49	19 39		20 50
Bootle	d	14x56	15x53	16x28	16x57	18x11		19x45		20x56
Silecroft	d	15x03	16x00	16x35	17x04	18x17		19x51		21x02
Millom	a	15 09	16 06	16 41	17 11	18 24	19 05	19 58		21 09
	d	15 11	16 07	16 42	17 12	18 25	19 05	20 01		21 09
Green Road	d	15x15	16x11	16x46	17x16	18x29	19x09	20x05		21x13
Foxfield	d	15 19	16 15	16 50	17 20	18 33	19 13	20 09		21 17
Kirkby-in-Furness	d	15x23	16x19	16x55	17x25	18x37	19x17	20x13		21x21
Askam	d	15 28	16 24	17 00	17 30	18 42	19 22	20 19		21 26
Barrow-in-Furness	a	15 43	16 39	17 14	17 45	18 57	19 37	20 36		21 41
Lancaster 🅱 82	a	16 52								

		NT	NT	NT
Carlisle 🅱	d	20 00	21 06	21 49
Dalston	d	20 08	21 14	21 57
Wigton	d	20 18	21 24	22 06
Aspatria	d	20 28	21 34	22 17
Maryport	d	20 39	21 45	22 27
Flimby	d	20x42	21x48	22x31
Workington	d	20 50	21 56	22 37
Harrington	d	20 54	22 00	22 41
Parton	d	21x02	22x08	22x51
Whitehaven	a	21 09	22 15	22 57
	d			
Corkickle	d			
St Bees	d			
Nethertown	d			
Braystones	d			
Sellafield	d			
Seascale	d			
Drigg	d			
Ravenglass for Eskdale	d			
Bootle	d			
Silecroft	d			
Millom	a			
	d			
Green Road	d			
Foxfield	d			
Kirkby-in-Furness	d			
Askam	d			
Barrow-in-Furness	a			
Lancaster 🅱 82	a			

Table T100-R

Sundays
15 December to 10 May

Carlisle and Whitehaven - Barrow-in-Furness

		NT	NT A	NT B	NT A	NT B	NT	NT	NT	NT	NT	NT	NT	NT		NT
Carlisle	d		09 45		10 23	10 41	11 06	12 07	13 24	14 01	15 10	16 16	17 10	18 10		21 10
Dalston	d		09 53		10 32	10 49	11 14	12 15	13 32	14 09	15 18	16 24	17 18	18 18		21 18
Wigton	d		10 02		10 41	10 58	11 24	12 25	13 42	14 19	15 28	16 34	17 28	18 28		21 28
Aspatria	d		10 13		10 52	11 09	11 34	12 35	13 52	14 29	15 38	16 44	17 38	18 38		21 38
Maryport	d	09 17	10 24	10 24	11 03	11 20	11 45	12 46	14 03	14 40	15 49	16 55	17 49	18 49		21 49
Flimby	d	09x20			11x06	11x23	11x48	12x49	14x06	14x43	15x52	16x58	17x52	18x52		21x52
Workington	d	09 27	10 33	10 33	11 13	11 30	11 56	12 58	14 14	14 51	16 00	17 06	18 00	19 00		22 00
Harrington	d	09 31			11 17	11 34	12 00	13 02	14 18	14 55	16 04	17 10	18 04	19 04		22 04
Parton	d	09x40	10x45	10x45	11x26	11x43	12x08	13 10	14x26	15x03	16x12	17x18	18x12	19x12		22x12
Whitehaven	a	09 45	10 50	10 50	11 31	11 48	12 14	13 16	14 32	15 08	16 17	17 24	18 18	19 19		22 19
	d	09 47	10 51	10 51	11 33	11 50	12 15	13 18	14 33	15 10	16 19	17 25	18 19			
Corkickle	d	09 49	10 54	10 54	11 35	11 52	12 18	13 21	14 36	15 12	16 22	17 28	18 22		and hourly until	
St Bees	d	09 55	10 59	10 59	11 41	11 58	12 24	13 27	14 41	15 18	16 29	17 33	18 28			
Nethertown	d	09x59					12x28				16x33		18x32			
Braystones	d	10x01					12x30				16x35		18x34			
Sellafield	d	10 07	11 09	11 09	11 51	12 08	12 36	13 37	14 51	15 28	16 42	17 44	18 40			
Seascale	d	10 11	11 13	11 13	11 54	12 11	12 40	13 40	14 55	15 32	16 46	17 48	18 44			
Drigg	d	10x14	11x16	11x16	11x57	12x14	12x43	13x43		15x35	16x49	17x51	18x47			
Ravenglass for Eskdale	d	10 17	11 19	11 19	12 01	12 18	12 46	13 47	15 01	15 39	16 52	17 54	18 50			
Bootle	d	10x23	11x25	11x25	12x06	12x23	12x52	13x52		15 44	16x58	18x00	18x56			
Silecroft	d	10x29	11x31	11x31	12x13	12x30	12x58	13x59		15x51	17x04	18x06	19x02			
Millom	a	10 36	11 37	11 37	12 19	12 36	13 05	14 05	15 16	15 56	17 11	18 13	19 09			
	d	10 36	11 37	11 37	12 19	12 36	13 05	14 06	15 17	15 56	17 11	18 14	19 09			
Green Road	d	10x40	11x41	11x41	12x23	12x40	13x09	14x10		16x00	17x15	18x18	19x13			
Foxfield	d	10 44	11 45	11 45	12 27	12 44	13 13	14 14	15 24	16 04	17 19	18 22	19 17			
Kirkby-in-Furness	d	10x48	11x49	11x49	12x31	12x48	13x17	14x18	15x28	16x08	17x23	18x26	19x21			
Askam	d	10 53	11 54	11 54	12 36	12 53	13 22	14 23	15 33	16 13	17 28	18 31	19 26			
Barrow-in-Furness	a	11 08	12 09	12 09	12 51	13 08	13 37	14 38	15 48	16 28	17 43	18 46	19 41			
Lancaster 82	a				13 52	14 21			16 52		18 50					

A until 5 January, from 23 February until 29 March   B from 12 January until 16 February, from 5 April

AVAILABLE FROM MP Middleton Press

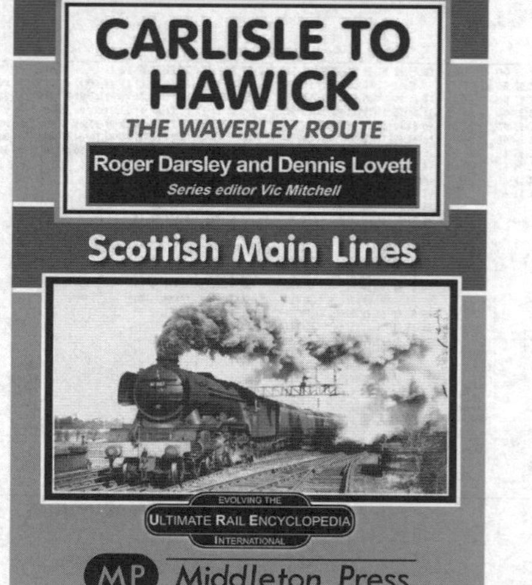

CARLISLE TO HAWICK
THE WAVERLEY ROUTE
Roger Darsley and Dennis Lovett
Series editor Vic Mitchell
Scottish Main Lines
EVOLVING THE
ULTIMATE RAIL ENCYCLOPEDIA
INTERNATIONAL
MP Middleton Press

Table T101-F

Mondays to Fridays
16 December to 15 May

Wrexham - Bidston

Miles			AW	AW	AW	AW	AW	AW	AW	AW	AW	AW	AW	AW	AW	AW
0	**Wrexham Central**	d		07 29	08 31	09 31	10 31	11 31	12 31	13 31	14 31	15 31	16 31	17 44	19 45	21 56
0½	**Wrexham General**	a		07 32	08 34	09 34	10 34	11 34	12 34	13 34	14 34	15 34	16 34	17 47	19 48	21 59
—		d	06 32	07 32	08 34	09 34	10 34	11 34	12 34	13 34	14 34	15 34	16 34	17 47	19 48	21 59
2¼	Gwersyllt	d	06 36	07 36	08 38	09 37	10 37	11 37	12 37	13 37	14 37	15 37	16 37	17 51	19 51	22 02
4	Cefn-y-Bedd	d	06 41	07 40	08 42	09 42	10 42	11 42	12 42	13 42	14 42	15 42	16 42	17 56	19 56	22 07
4¾	Caergwrle	d	06 43	07 42	08 44	09 44	10 44	11 44	12 44	13 44	14 44	15 44	16 44	17 58	19 58	22 09
5¼	Hope (Flintshire)	d	06 45	07 44	08 46	09 46	10 46	11 46	12 46	13 46	14 46	15 46	16 46	18 00	20 00	22 11
7¼	Penyffordd	d	06 49	07 48	08 50	09 50	10 50	11 50	12 50	13 50	14 50	15 50	16 50	18 04	20 04	22 15
8½	Buckley	d	06 52	07 52	08 54	09 53	10 53	11 53	12 53	13 53	14 53	15 53	16 53	18 07	20 07	22 18
10½	Hawarden	d	06 56	07 56	08 58	09 57	10 57	11 57	12 57	13 57	14 57	15 57	16 57	18 11	20 11	22 22
12¾	Shotton High Level	d	07 00	08 00	09 02	10 01	11 01	12 01	13 01	14 01	15 01	16 01	17 01	18 16	20 15	22 26
13¼	Hawarden Bridge	d	07x02	08x02									17x03			
18¾	Neston	d	07 11	08 11	09 12	10 11	11 11	12 11	13 11	14 11	15 11	16 11	17 12	18 26	20 25	22 36
21¼	Heswall	d	07 16	08 16	09 17	10 16	11 16	12 16	13 16	14 16	15 16	16 16	17 17	18 31	20 30	22 41
25½	Upton	d	07 22	08 22	09 23	10 22	11 22	12 22	13 22	14 22	15 22	16 22	17 23	18 37	20 36	22 47
27½	**Bidston**	a	07 30	08 30	09 31	10 30	11 30	12 30	13 30	14 30	15 30	16 30	17 31	18 45	20 44	22 55

Saturdays
21 December to 16 May

		AW	AW	AW	AW	AW	AW	AW	AW	AW	AW	AW	AW	AW
Wrexham Central	d		07 29	08 31	09 31	10 31	11 31	12 31	13 31	14 31	15 31	16 31	17 44	19 45
Wrexham General	a		07 31	08 34	09 34	10 34	11 34	12 34	13 34	14 34	15 34	16 34	17 48	19 48
	d	06 32	07 31	08 34	09 34	10 34	11 34	12 34	13 34	14 34	15 34	16 34	17 48	19 48
Gwersyllt	d	06 36	07 36	08 38	09 37	10 37	11 37	12 37	13 37	14 37	15 37	16 37	17 51	19 51
Cefn-y-Bedd	d	06 41	07 40	08 42	09 42	10 42	11 42	12 42	13 42	14 42	15 42	16 42	17 56	19 56
Caergwrle	d	06 43	07 42	08 44	09 44	10 44	11 44	12 44	13 44	14 44	15 44	16 44	17 58	19 58
Hope (Flintshire)	d	06 45	07 44	08 46	09 46	10 46	11 46	12 46	13 46	14 46	15 46	16 46	18 00	20 00
Penyffordd	d	06 49	07 48	08 50	09 50	10 50	11 50	12 50	13 50	14 50	15 50	16 50	18 04	20 04
Buckley	d	06 52	07 52	08 54	09 53	10 53	11 53	12 53	13 53	14 53	15 53	16 53	18 07	20 07
Hawarden	d	06 56	07 56	08 58	09 57	10 57	11 57	12 57	13 57	14 57	15 57	16 57	18 11	20 11
Shotton High Level	d	07 00	08 00	09 02	10 01	11 01	12 01	13 01	14 01	15 01	16 01	17 01	18 16	20 15
Hawarden Bridge	d	07x02	08x02									17x03		
Neston	d	07 11	08 11	09 12	10 11	11 11	12 11	13 11	14 11	15 11	16 11	17 12	18 26	20 25
Heswall	d	07 16	08 16	09 17	10 16	11 16	12 16	13 16	14 16	15 16	16 16	17 17	18 31	20 30
Upton	d	07 22	08 22	09 23	10 22	11 22	12 22	13 22	14 22	15 22	16 22	17 23	18 37	20 36
Bidston	a	07 30	08 30	09 31	10 30	11 30	12 30	13 30	14 30	15 30	16 30	17 31	18 45	20 44

Sundays
15 December to 10 May

		AW	AW	AW	AW	AW	AW	AW	AW	AW	AW
Wrexham Central	d			11 06	12 06	13 36	15 06	16 06	17 54	18 36	21 06
Wrexham General	a			11 10	12 10	13 40	15 10	16 10	17 57	18 40	21 10
	d	08 41	09 46	11 10	12 10	13 40	15 10	16 10	17 57	18 40	21 10
Gwersyllt	d	08 45	09 49	11 13	12 13	13 43	15 13	16 13	18 02	18 43	21 13
Cefn-y-Bedd	d	08 50	09 54	11 18	12 18	13 48	15 18	16 18	18 06	18 48	21 18
Caergwrle	d	08 52	09 56	11 20	12 20	13 50	15 20	16 20	18 08	18 50	21 20
Hope (Flintshire)	d	08 54	09 58	11 22	12 22	13 52	15 22	16 22	18 10	18 52	21 22
Penyffordd	d	08 58	10 02	11 26	12 26	13 56	15 26	16 26	18 15	18 56	21 26
Buckley	d	09 01	10 05	11 29	12 29	13 59	15 29	16 29	18 18	18 59	21 29
Hawarden	d	09 05	10 09	11 33	12 33	14 03	15 33	16 33	18 22	19 03	21 33
Shotton High Level	d	09 09	10 13	11 37	12 37	14 07	15 37	16 37	18 28	19 07	21 37
Hawarden Bridge	d	09x11	10x15	11x39	12x39	14x09	15x39	16x39	18x29	19x09	21x39
Neston	d	09 20	10 24	11 48	12 48	14 18	15 48	16 48	18 37	19 18	21 48
Heswall	d	09 25	10 29	11 53	12 53	14 23	15 53	16 53	18 42	19 23	21 53
Upton	d	09 31	10 35	11 59	12 59	14 29	15 59	16 59	18 49	19 29	21 59
Bidston	a	09 38	10 42	12 06	13 06	14 36	16 06	17 06	18 57	19 36	22 06

For connections to Liverpool Lime Street refer to Table T106

Table T101-R

Mondays to Fridays
16 December to 15 May

Bidston - Wrexham

Miles			AW	AW	AW	AW	AW	AW	AW	AW	AW	AW	AW	AW	AW	AW	AW
0	**Bidston**	d		07 31	08 31	09 32	10 32	11 32	12 32	13 32	14 32	15 32	16 35	17 45	18 46	20 56	22 56
2	Upton	d		07 34	08 34	09 35	10 35	11 35	12 35	13 35	14 35	15 35	16 38	17 48	18 49	20 59	22 59
6¼	Heswall	d		07 41	08 41	09 42	10 42	11 42	12 42	13 42	14 42	15 42	16 45	17 55	18 56	21 06	23 06
8¾	Neston	d		07 46	08 46	09 47	10 47	11 47	12 47	13 47	14 47	15 47	16 50	18 00	19 01	21 11	23 11
14¼	Hawarden Bridge	d		07x54	08x54								16x58	18x08			
14¾	Shotton High Level	d		07 56	08 56	09 56	10 56	11 56	12 56	13 56	14 56	15 56	17 00	18 10	19 10	21 20	23 21
17½	Hawarden	d		08 01	09 01	10 01	11 01	12 01	13 01	14 01	15 01	16 01	17 05	18 15	19 15	21 25	23 26
19	Buckley	d		08 06	09 06	10 06	11 06	12 06	13 06	14 06	15 06	16 06	17 10	18 20	19 20	21 30	23 31
20¼	Penyffordd	d		08 09	09 09	10 09	11 09	12 09	13 09	14 09	15 09	16 09	17 13	18 23	19 23	21 33	23 34
22¼	Hope (Flintshire)	d		08 13	09 13	10 13	11 13	12 13	13 13	14 13	15 13	16 13	17 17	18 27	19 27	21 37	23 38
22¾	Caergwrle	d		08 15	09 15	10 15	11 15	12 15	13 15	14 15	15 15	16 15	17 19	18 29	19 29	21 39	23 40
23½	Cefn-y-Bedd	d		08 17	09 17	10 17	11 17	12 17	13 17	14 17	15 17	16 17	17 21	18 31	19 31	21 41	23 42
25¼	Gwersyllt	d		08 21	09 21	10 21	11 21	12 21	13 21	14 21	15 21	16 21	17 25	18 35	19 35	21 45	23 46
27	**Wrexham General**	a		08 27	09 27	10 27	11 27	12 27	13 27	14 27	15 27	16 27	17 31	18 41	19 41	21 51	23 54
—		d	07 10	08 27	09 27	10 27	11 27	12 27	13 27	14 27	15 27	16 27	17 31	18 41	19 41	21 51	
27½	**Wrexham Central**	a	07 13	08 32	09 32	10 32	11 32	12 32	13 32	14 32	15 32	16 32	17 36	18 46	19 46	21 56	

Saturdays
21 December to 16 May

		AW	AW	AW	AW	AW	AW	AW	AW	AW	AW	AW	AW	AW	AW	AW
Bidston	d		07 31	08 31	09 32	10 32	11 32	12 32	13 32	14 32	15 32	16 35	17 45	18 46	20 56	22 56
Upton	d		07 34	08 34	09 35	10 35	11 35	12 35	13 35	14 35	15 35	16 38	17 48	18 49	20 59	22 59
Heswall	d		07 41	08 41	09 42	10 42	11 42	12 42	13 42	14 42	15 42	16 45	17 55	18 56	21 06	23 06
Neston	d		07 46	08 46	09 47	10 47	11 47	12 47	13 47	14 47	15 47	16 50	18 00	19 01	21 11	23 11
Hawarden Bridge	d		07x54	08x54								16x58	18x08			
Shotton High Level	d		07 56	08 56	09 56	10 56	11 56	12 56	13 56	14 56	15 56	17 00	18 10	19 10	21 20	23 21
Hawarden	d		08 01	09 01	10 01	11 01	12 01	13 01	14 01	15 01	16 01	17 05	18 15	19 15	21 25	23 26
Buckley	d		08 06	09 06	10 06	11 06	12 06	13 06	14 06	15 06	16 06	17 10	18 20	19 20	21 30	23 31
Penyffordd	d		08 09	09 09	10 09	11 09	12 09	13 09	14 09	15 09	16 09	17 13	18 23	19 23	21 33	23 34
Hope (Flintshire)	d		08 13	09 13	10 13	11 13	12 13	13 13	14 13	15 13	16 13	17 17	18 27	19 27	21 37	23 38
Caergwrle	d		08 15	09 15	10 15	11 15	12 15	13 15	14 15	15 15	16 15	17 19	18 29	19 29	21 39	23 40
Cefn-y-Bedd	d		08 17	09 17	10 17	11 17	12 17	13 17	14 17	15 17	16 17	17 21	18 31	19 31	21 41	23 42
Gwersyllt	d		08 21	09 21	10 21	11 21	12 21	13 21	14 21	15 21	16 21	17 25	18 35	19 35	21 45	23 46
Wrexham General	a		08 27	09 27	10 27	11 27	12 27	13 27	14 27	15 27	16 27	17 31	18 41	19 41	21 51	23 53
	d	07 10	08 27	09 27	10 27	11 27	12 27	13 27	14 27	15 27	16 27	17 31	18 41	19 41	21 51	
Wrexham Central	a	07 13	08 32	09 31	10 31	11 31	12 31	13 31	14 31	15 31	16 31	17 35	18 45	19 45	21 55	

Sundays
15 December to 10 May

		AW	AW	AW	AW	AW	AW	AW	AW	AW	AW
Bidston	d	09 57	10 57	12 27	13 28	14 57	16 30	17 27	19 00	19 57	22 27
Upton	d	10 00	11 00	12 30	13 31	15 00	16 33	17 30	19 03	20 00	22 30
Heswall	d	10 07	11 07	12 37	13 38	15 07	16 40	17 37	19 10	20 07	22 37
Neston	d	10 12	11 12	12 42	13 43	15 12	16 45	17 42	19 15	20 12	22 42
Hawarden Bridge	d	10x20	11x20	12x50	13x51	15x20	16x53	17x50	19x23	20x20	22x50
Shotton High Level	d	10 22	11 22	12 52	13 53	15 22	16 55	17 52	19 25	20 22	22 52
Hawarden	d	10 27	11 27	12 57	13 58	15 27	17 00	17 57	19 30	20 27	22 57
Buckley	d	10 32	11 32	13 02	14 03	15 32	17 05	18 02	19 35	20 32	23 02
Penyffordd	d	10 35	11 35	13 05	14 06	15 35	17 08	18 05	19 38	20 35	23 05
Hope (Flintshire)	d	10 39	11 39	13 09	14 10	15 39	17 12	18 09	19 42	20 39	23 09
Caergwrle	d	10 41	11 41	13 11	14 12	15 41	17 14	18 11	19 44	20 41	23 11
Cefn-y-Bedd	d	10 43	11 43	13 13	14 14	15 43	17 16	18 13	19 46	20 43	23 13
Gwersyllt	d	10 47	11 47	13 17	14 18	15 47	17 20	18 17	19 50	20 47	23 17
Wrexham General	a	10 52	11 54	13 24	14 25	15 54	17 27	18 24	19 56	20 54	23 26
	d	10 53	11 55	13 24	14 25	15 54	17 27	18 24		20 54	
Wrexham Central	a	10 59	11 58	13 27	14 28	15 59	17 30	18 29		20 59	

For connections from Liverpool Lime Street refer to Table T106

NRT DECEMBER 19 EDITION

Table T102-F

Mondays to Saturdays
16 December to 16 May

Llandudno - Blaenau Ffestiniog

Miles				AW SO ◇	AW SX ◇	AW ◇	AW SX ◇	AW SO ◇	AW SO ◇	AW SX ◇	AW ◇	AW SO ◇	AW SX ◇
0	**Llandudno**	81	d				10 08	10 22	13 08	13 09	16 20	19 03	19 05
1¾	Deganwy	81	d				10x12	10x26	13x12	13x13	16x24	19x07	19x09
3	**Llandudno Junction**	81	d	05 30	05 30	07 26	10 33	10 34	13 30	13 30	16 33	19 19	19 23
5	Glan Conwy		d			07x29	10x36	10x37	13x33	13x33	16x36	19x22	19x26
8½	Tal-y-Cafn		d	05 38	05 38	07 35	10 42	10 43	13 39	13 39	16 42	19 28	19 32
11½	Dolgarrog		d			07x40	10x47	10x48	13x44	13x44	16x47	19x33	19x37
14½	North Llanrwst		d			07x47	10x53	10x54	13x50	13x50	16x53	19x39	19x43
15	Llanrwst		d	05 48	05 48	07 49	10 55	10 56	13 52	13 52	16 55	19 41	19 45
18½	Betws-y-Coed		d	05 54	05 54	07 55	11 01	11 02	13 58	13 58	17 01	19 47	19 51
22¾	Pont-y-Pant		d			08x03	11x09	11x10	14x06	14x06	17x09	19x55	19x59
24¼	Dolwyddelan		d			08x06	11x12	11x13	14x09	14x09	17x12	19x58	20x02
26	Roman Bridge		d			08x10	11x16	11x17	14x13	14x13	17x16	20x02	20x06
31	**Blaenau Ffestiniog**		a	06 21	06 24	08 28	11 34	11 35	14 31	14 31	17 34	20 20	20 22

Sundays
15 December to 10 May

			AW ◇	AW ◇	AW ◇	AW ◇
Llandudno	81	d	10 22	13 28		18 59
Deganwy	81	d	10x26	13x32		19 03
Llandudno Junction	81	d	10 32	13 40	16 15	19 15
Glan Conwy		d	10x35	13x43	16x18	19x18
Tal-y-Cafn		d	10 41	13 49	16 24	19 24
Dolgarrog		d	10x46	13x54	16x29	19x29
North Llanrwst		d	10x52	14x00	16x35	19x35
Llanrwst		d	10 54	14 02	16 37	19 37
Betws-y-Coed		d	11 00	14 08	16 43	19 43
Pont-y-Pant		d	11x08	14x16	16x51	19x51
Dolwyddelan		d	11x11	14x19	16x54	19x54
Roman Bridge		d	11x15	14x23	16x58	19x58
Blaenau Ffestiniog		a	11 30	14 38	17 15	20 15

For connections from Crewe, Chester, Rhyl and Bangor (Gwynedd), refer to Table 081

Table T102-R

Mondays to Saturdays
16 December to 16 May

Blaenau Ffestiniog - Llandudno

Miles				AW ◇	AW SX ◇	AW SO ◇	AW SO ◇	AW SX ◇	AW ◇	AW SX ◇	AW SO ◇	AW SO ◇	AW SX ◇
0	**Blaenau Ffestiniog**		d	06 24	08 35	08 46	11 35	11 36	14 57	17 36	17 37	20 23	20 23
5	Roman Bridge		d	06x34	08x45	08x56	11x45	11x46	15x07	17x46	17x47	20x33	20x33
6¾	Dolwyddelan		d	06x37	08x49	09x00	11x49	11x50	15x11	17x50	17x51	20x37	20x37
8¼	Pont-y-Pant		d	06x40	08x52	09x03	11x52	11x53	15x14	17x53	17x54	20x40	20x40
12½	Betws-y-Coed		d	06 50	09 02	09 13	12 02	12 03	15 24	18 03	18 04	20 50	20 50
16	Llanrwst		d	06 56	09 08	09 19	12 08	12 09	15 30	18 09	18 10	20 56	20 56
16½	North Llanrwst		d	06x57	09x09	09x20	12x09	12x10	15x31	18x10	18x11	20x57	20x57
19½	Dolgarrog		d	07x03	09x16	09x27	12x16	12x17	15x38	18x17	18x18	21x04	21x04
22½	Tal-y-Cafn		d	07x09	09x22	09x33	12x22	12x23	15x44	18x23	18x24	21x10	21x10
26	Glan Conwy		d	07x15	09x28	09x39	12x28	12x29	15x50	18x29	18x30	21x16	21x16
28	**Llandudno Junction**	81	a	07 20	09 35	09 46	12 34	12 35	15 56	18 34	18 36	21 20	21 21
29¼	Deganwy	81	a		09x53	10x10	12x38	12x39	16x08	18x44	18x44	21x35	21x35
31	**Llandudno**	81	a		09 59	10 16	12 45	12 46	16 15	18 49	18 51	21 43	21 43

Sundays
15 December to 10 May

			AW ◇	AW ◇	AW ◇	AW ◇
Blaenau Ffestiniog		d	11 45	15 03	17 30	20 24
Roman Bridge		d	11x55	15x13	17x40	20x34
Dolwyddelan		d	11x58	15x16	17x45	20x38
Pont-y-Pant		d	12x01	15x19	17x48	20x41
Betws-y-Coed		d	12 11	15 29	17 57	20 51
Llanrwst		d	12 17	15 35	18 03	20 57
North Llanrwst		d	12x18	15x36	18x05	20x58
Dolgarrog		d	12x24	15x42	18x11	21x05
Tal-y-Cafn		d	12x29	15x48	18x18	21x11
Glan Conwy		d	12x35	15x54	18x23	21x17
Llandudno Junction	81	a	12 41	15 59	18 30	21 23
Deganwy	81	a	12x45		18x34	21x28
Llandudno	81	a	12 52		18 41	21 35

For connections to Bangor (Gwynedd), Rhyl, Chester and Crewe refer to Table 081

Table T103-F

Hunts Cross - Southport

Mondays to Fridays

16 December to 15 May

Miles			ME	ME	ME	ME	ME	ME	ME	ME		ME		ME	ME		ME	ME	ME	ME	ME	ME
0	**Hunts Cross** 89	d					06 01	06 21	06 36	06 51	and every 15 minutes until	15 51		16 06	16 21	and every 15 minutes until	19 21	19 36	19 51	20 06	20 21	20 36
1½	**Liverpool Sth Parkway** 7 89 ✈	d					06 04	06 24	06 39	06 54		15 54		16 10	16 24		19 24	19 39	19 54	20 09	20 24	20 39
2½	Cressington	d					06 07	06 27	06 42	06 57		15 57		16 12	16 27		19 27	19 42	19 57	20 12	20 27	20 42
3¼	Aigburth	d					06 09	06 29	06 44	06 59		15 59		16 14	16 29		19 29	19 44	19 59	20 14	20 29	20 44
4½	St Michaels	d					06 11	06 31	06 46	07 01		16 01		16 17	16 31		19 31	19 46	20 01	20 16	20 31	20 46
5¾	Brunswick	d					06 14	06 34	06 49	07 04		16 04		16 19	16 34		19 34	19 49	20 04	20 19	20 34	20 49
7¼	**Liverpool Central** 10	a					06 23	06 38	06 53	07 08		16 08		16 23	16 38		19 38	19 53	20 08	20 23	20 38	20 53
—		d				06 08	06 23	06 38	06 53	07 08		16 08		16 23	16 38		19 38	19 53	20 08	20 23	20 38	20 53
7¾	**Moorfields** 10	d				06 10	06 25	06 41	06 55	07 11		16 11		16 26	16 41		19 41	19 55	20 11	20 25	20 41	20 55
9¼	Sandhills	d			05 59	06 14	06 29	06 45	06 59	07 15		16 15		16 30	16 45		19 45	19 59	20 15	20 29	20 45	20 59
10	Bank Hall	d			06 02	06 17	06 32	06 47	07 02	07 17		16 17		16 32	16 47		19 47	20 02	20 17	20 32	20 47	21 02
10¾	Bootle Oriel Road	d			06 04	06 19	06 34	06 49	07 04	07 19		16 19		16 34	16 49		19 49	20 04	20 19	20 34	20 49	21 04
11	Bootle New Strand	d			06 06	06 21	06 36	06 51	07 06	07 21		16 21		16 36	16 51		19 51	20 06	20 21	20 36	20 51	21 06
12	Seaforth & Litherland	d			06 08	06 23	06 38	06 53	07 08	07 23		16 23		16 38	16 53		19 53	20 08	20 23	20 38	20 53	21 08
13¼	Waterloo	d			06 10	06 25	06 40	06 55	07 10	07 25		16 25		16 40	16 55		19 55	20 10	20 25	20 40	20 55	21 10
14¼	Blundellsands & Crosby	d			06 13	06 28	06 43	06 58	07 13	07 28		16 28		16 43	16 58		19 58	20 13	20 28	20 43	20 58	21 13
15	Hall Road	d			06 15	06 30	06 45	07 00	07 15	07 30		16 30		16 45	17 00		20 00	20 15	20 30	20 45	21 00	21 15
17	Hightown	d		00 03	06 18	06 33	06 48	07 03	07 18	07 33		16 33		16 48	17 03		20 03	20 18	20 33	20 48	21 03	21 18
19	Formby	d		00 07	06 22	06 37	06 52	07 07	07 22	07 37		16 37		16 52	17 07		20 07	20 22	20 37	20 52	21 07	21 22
20	Freshfield	d		00 09	06 24	06 39	06 54	07 09	07 24	07 39		16 39		16 54	17 09		20 09	20 24	20 39	20 54	21 09	21 24
22¾	Ainsdale	d		00 13	06 28	06 43	06 58	07 13	07 28	07 43		16 43		16 58	17 13		20 13	20 28	20 43	20 58	21 13	21 28
24½	Hillside	d	00 01	00 16	06 31	06 46	07 01	07 16	07 31	07 46		16 46		17 01	17 16		20 16	20 31	20 46	21 01	21 16	21 31
25¼	Birkdale	d	00 03	00 18	06 33	06 48	07 03	07 18	07 33	07 48		16 48		17 03	17 18		20 18	20 33	20 48	21 03	21 18	21 33
26¼	**Southport**	a	00 10	00 25	06 40	06 55	07 10	07 25	07 40	07 55		16 55		17 10	17 25		20 25	20 40	20 55	21 10	21 25	21 40

		ME	ME	ME	ME	ME	ME	ME	ME	ME		ME	ME
Hunts Cross 89	d	20 51	21 06	21 21	21 36	21 51	22 06	22 21	22 36	22 51		23 06	23 21
Liverpool Sth Parkway 7 89 ✈	d	20 54	21 09	21 24	21 39	21 54	22 09	22 24	22 40	22 54		23 09	23 23
Cressington	d	20 57	21 12	21 27	21 42	21 57	22 12	22 27	22 42	22 57		23 12	23 27
Aigburth	d	20 59	21 14	21 29	21 44	21 59	22 14	22 29	22 44	22 59		23 14	23 29
St Michaels	d	21 01	21 16	21 31	21 46	22 01	22 16	22 31	22 47	23 01		23 16	23 30
Brunswick	d	21 04	21 19	21 34	21 49	22 04	22 19	22 34	22 49	23 04		23 19	23 34
Liverpool Central 10	a	21 08	21 23	21 38	21 53	22 08	22 23	22 38	22 53	23 08		23 23	23 38
	d	21 08	21 23	21 38	21 53	22 08	22 23	22 38	22 53	23 08		23 23	23 38
Moorfields 10	d	21 11	21 25	21 41	21 55	22 11	22 25	22 41	22 56	23 11		23 26	23 41
Sandhills	d	21 15	21 29	21 45	21 59	22 15	22 29	22 45	23 00	23 15		23 29	23 44
Bank Hall	d	21 17	21 32	21 47	22 02	22 17	22 32	22 47	23 02	23 17		23 32	23 47
Bootle Oriel Road	d	21 19	21 34	21 49	22 04	22 19	22 34	22 49	23 04	23 19		23 34	23 49
Bootle New Strand	d	21 21	21 36	21 51	22 06	22 21	22 36	22 51	23 06	23 21		23 36	23 51
Seaforth & Litherland	d	21 23	21 38	21 53	22 08	22 23	22 38	22 53	23 08	23 23		23 38	23 53
Waterloo	d	21 25	21 40	21 55	22 10	22 25	22 40	22 55	23 10	23 25		23 40	23 55
Blundellsands & Crosby	d	21 28	21 43	21 58	22 13	22 28	22 43	22 58	23 13	23 28		23 43	23 58
Hall Road	d	21 30	21 45	22 00	22 15	22 30	22 45	23 00	23 15	23 30		23 45	23 59
Hightown	d	21 33	21 48	22 03	22 18	22 33	22 48	23 03	23 18	23 33		23 48	00 03
Formby	d	21 37	21 52	22 07	22 22	22 37	22 52	23 07	23 22	23 37		23 52	00 07
Freshfield	d	21 39	21 54	22 09	22 24	22 39	22 54	23 09	23 24	23 39		23 54	00 09
Ainsdale	d	21 43	21 58	22 13	22 28	22 43	22 58	23 13	23 28	23 43		23 58	00 13
Hillside	d	21 46	22 01	22 16	22 31	22 46	23 01	23 16	23 31	23 46		00 01	00 16
Birkdale	d	21 48	22 03	22 18	22 33	22 48	23 03	23 18	23 33	23 48		00 03	00 18
Southport	a	21 55	22 10	22 25	22 40	22 55	23 10	23 25	23 40	23 55		00 10	00 25

Saturdays

21 December to 16 May

		ME	ME	ME	ME	ME	ME	ME	ME	ME		ME	ME	ME		ME	ME	ME		ME		ME	ME
Hunts Cross 89	d					06 01	06 21	06 36	06 51	07 06		07 21	07 36	07 51	and every 15 minutes until	15 51	16 06	16 21	and every 15 minutes until	19 21		19 36	19 51
Liverpool Sth Parkway 7 89 ✈	d					06 04	06 24	06 39	06 54	07 09		07 24	07 39	07 54		15 54	16 10	16 24		19 24		19 39	19 54
Cressington	d					06 07	06 27	06 42	06 57	07 12		07 27	07 42	07 57		15 57	16 12	16 27		19 27		19 42	19 57
Aigburth	d					06 09	06 29	06 44	06 59	07 14		07 29	07 44	07 59		15 59	16 14	16 29		19 29		19 44	19 59
St Michaels	d					06 11	06 31	06 46	07 01	07 16		07 31	07 46	08 01		16 01	16 17	16 31		19 31		19 46	20 01
Brunswick	d					06 14	06 34	06 49	07 04	07 19		07 34	07 49	08 04		16 04	16 19	16 34		19 34		19 49	20 04
Liverpool Central 10	a					06 23	06 38	06 53	07 08	07 23		07 38	07 53	08 08		16 08	16 23	16 38		19 38		19 53	20 08
	d				06 08	06 23	06 38	06 53	07 08	07 23		07 38	07 53	08 08		16 08	16 23	16 38		19 38		19 53	20 08
Moorfields 10	d				06 10	06 25	06 41	06 55	07 11	07 26		07 41	07 56	08 11		16 11	16 26	16 41		19 41		19 55	20 11
Sandhills	d			05 59	06 14	06 29	06 45	06 59	07 15	07 30		07 45	08 00	08 15		16 15	16 30	16 45		19 45		19 59	20 15
Bank Hall	d			06 02	06 17	06 32	06 47	07 02	07 17	07 32		07 47	08 02	08 17		16 17	16 32	16 47		19 47		20 02	20 17
Bootle Oriel Road	d			06 04	06 19	06 34	06 49	07 04	07 19	07 34		07 49	08 04	08 19		16 19	16 34	16 49		19 49		20 04	20 19
Bootle New Strand	d			06 06	06 21	06 36	06 51	07 06	07 21	07 36		07 51	08 06	08 21		16 21	16 36	16 51		19 51		20 06	20 21
Seaforth & Litherland	d			06 08	06 23	06 38	06 53	07 08	07 23	07 38		07 53	08 08	08 23		16 23	16 38	16 53		19 53		20 08	20 23
Waterloo	d			06 10	06 25	06 40	06 55	07 10	07 25	07 40		07 55	08 10	08 25		16 25	16 40	16 55		19 55		20 10	20 25
Blundellsands & Crosby	d			06 13	06 28	06 43	06 58	07 13	07 28	07 43		07 58	08 13	08 28		16 28	16 43	16 58		19 58		20 13	20 28
Hall Road	d			06 15	06 30	06 45	07 00	07 15	07 30	07 45		08 00	08 15	08 30		16 30	16 45	17 00		20 00		20 15	20 30
Hightown	d		00 03	06 18	06 33	06 48	07 03	07 18	07 33	07 48		08 03	08 18	08 33		16 33	16 48	17 03		20 03		20 18	20 33
Formby	d		00 07	06 22	06 37	06 52	07 07	07 22	07 37	07 52		08 07	08 22	08 37		16 37	16 52	17 07		20 07		20 22	20 37
Freshfield	d		00 09	06 24	06 39	06 54	07 09	07 24	07 39	07 54		08 09	08 24	08 39		16 39	16 54	17 09		20 09		20 24	20 39
Ainsdale	d		00 13	06 28	06 43	06 58	07 13	07 28	07 43	07 58		08 13	08 28	08 43		16 43	16 58	17 13		20 13		20 28	20 43
Hillside	d	00 01	00 16	06 31	06 46	07 01	07 16	07 31	07 46	08 01		08 16	08 31	08 46		16 46	17 01	17 16		20 16		20 31	20 46
Birkdale	d	00 03	00 18	06 33	06 48	07 03	07 18	07 33	07 48	08 03		08 18	08 33	08 48		16 48	17 03	17 18		20 18		20 33	20 48
Southport	a	00 10	00 25	06 40	06 55	07 10	07 25	07 40	07 55	08 10		08 25	08 39	08 55		16 55	17 10	17 25		20 25		20 40	20 55

For alternative services between Liverpool and Sandhills refer to Tables T104 and T105

Table T103-F

Hunts Cross - Southport

Saturdays

21 December to 16 May

		ME	ME	ME	ME	ME	ME	ME		ME	ME	ME	ME	ME	ME	ME
Hunts Cross 89	d	20 06	20 21	20 36	20 51	21 06	21 21	21 36		21 51	22 06	22 21	22 36	22 51	23 06	23 21
Liverpool Sth Parkway 7 89 ✈	d	20 09	20 24	20 39	20 54	21 09	21 24	21 39		21 54	22 09	22 24	22 40	22 54	23 09	23 23
Cressington	d	20 12	20 27	20 42	20 57	21 12	21 27	21 42		21 57	22 12	22 27	22 42	22 57	23 12	23 27
Aigburth	d	20 14	20 29	20 44	20 59	21 14	21 29	21 44		21 59	22 14	22 29	22 44	22 59	23 14	23 29
St Michaels	d	20 16	20 31	20 46	21 01	21 16	21 31	21 46		22 01	22 16	22 31	22 47	23 01	23 16	23 30
Brunswick	d	20 19	20 34	20 49	21 04	21 19	21 34	21 49		22 04	22 19	22 34	22 49	23 04	23 19	23 34
Liverpool Central 10	a	20 23	20 38	20 53	21 08	21 23	21 38	21 53		22 08	22 23	22 38	22 53	23 08	23 23	23 38
	d	20 23	20 38	20 53	21 08	21 23	21 38	21 53		22 08	22 23	22 38	22 53	23 08	23 23	23 38
Moorfields 10	d	20 25	20 41	20 55	21 11	21 25	21 41	21 55		22 11	22 25	22 41	22 56	23 11	23 26	23 41
Sandhills	d	20 29	20 45	20 59	21 15	21 29	21 45	21 59		22 15	22 29	22 45	23 00	23 15	23 29	23 44
Bank Hall	d	20 32	20 47	21 02	21 17	21 32	21 47	22 02		22 17	22 32	22 47	23 02	23 17	23 32	23 47
Bootle Oriel Road	d	20 34	20 49	21 04	21 19	21 34	21 49	22 04		22 19	22 34	22 49	23 04	23 19	23 34	23 49
Bootle New Strand	d	20 36	20 51	21 06	21 21	21 36	21 51	22 06		22 21	22 36	22 51	23 06	23 21	23 36	23 51
Seaforth & Litherland	d	20 38	20 53	21 08	21 23	21 38	21 53	22 08		22 23	22 38	22 53	23 08	23 23	23 38	23 53
Waterloo	d	20 40	20 55	21 10	21 25	21 40	21 55	22 10		22 25	22 40	22 55	23 10	23 25	23 40	23 55
Blundellsands & Crosby	d	20 43	20 58	21 13	21 28	21 43	21 58	22 13		22 28	22 43	22 58	23 13	23 28	23 43	23 58
Hall Road	d	20 45	21 00	21 15	21 30	21 45	22 00	22 15		22 30	22 45	23 00	23 15	23 30	23 45	23 59
Hightown	d	20 48	21 03	21 18	21 33	21 48	22 03	22 18		22 33	22 48	23 03	23 18	23 33	23 48	00 03
Formby	d	20 52	21 07	21 22	21 37	21 52	22 07	22 22		22 37	22 52	23 07	23 22	23 37	23 52	00 07
Freshfield	d	20 54	21 09	21 24	21 39	21 54	22 09	22 24		22 39	22 54	23 09	23 24	23 39	23 54	00 09
Ainsdale	d	20 58	21 13	21 28	21 43	21 58	22 13	22 28		22 43	22 58	23 13	23 28	23 43	23 58	00 13
Hillside	d	21 01	21 16	21 31	21 46	22 01	22 16	22 31		22 46	23 01	23 16	23 31	23 46	00 01	00 16
Birkdale	d	21 03	21 18	21 33	21 48	22 03	22 18	22 33		22 48	23 03	23 18	23 33	23 48	00 03	00 18
Southport	a	21 10	21 25	21 40	21 55	22 10	22 25	22 40		22 55	23 10	23 25	23 40	23 55	00 10	00 25

Sundays

15 December to 10 May

		ME A	ME A	ME	ME		ME	ME
Hunts Cross 89	d				08 06	and every 30 minutes until	23 06	
Liverpool Sth Parkway 7 89 ✈	d				08 09		23 09	
Cressington	d				08 12		23 12	
Aigburth	d				08 14		23 14	
St Michaels	d				08 16		23 16	
Brunswick	d				08 19		23 19	
Liverpool Central 10	a				08 23		23 23	
	d			08 08	08 23		23 23	23 38
Moorfields 10	d			08 10	08 25		23 25	23 40
Sandhills	d			08 14	08 29		23 29	23 44
Bank Hall	d			08 17	08 32		23 32	23 47
Bootle Oriel Road	d			08 19	08 34		23 34	23 49
Bootle New Strand	d			08 21	08 36		23 36	23 51
Seaforth & Litherland	d			08 23	08 38		23 38	23 53
Waterloo	d			08 25	08 40		23 40	23 55
Blundellsands & Crosby	d			08 28	08 43		23 43	23 58
Hall Road	d			08 30	08 45		23 45	23 59
Hightown	d		00 03	08 33	08 48		23 48	00 03
Formby	d		00 07	08 37	08 52		23 52	00 07
Freshfield	d		00 09	08 39	08 54		23 54	00 09
Ainsdale	d		00 13	08 43	08 58		23 58	00 13
Hillside	d	00 01	00 16	08 46	09 01		00 01	00 16
Birkdale	d	00 03	00 18	08 48	09 03		00 03	00 18
Southport	a	00 10	00 25	08 55	09 10		00 10	00 25

A not 15 December

For alternative services between Liverpool and Sandhills refer to Tables T104 and T105

Table T103-R

Mondays to Fridays

16 December to 15 May

Southport - Hunts Cross

Miles	Station		ME	ME	ME	ME	ME	ME	ME		ME	ME	ME		ME	ME	ME	ME		ME
0	**Southport**	d		05 38	05 53	06 08	06 23	06 43	06 58	and every 15 minutes until	07 58	08 13	08 28	and every 15 minutes until	10 28	10 43	10 58	11 13	and every 15 minutes until	15 28
1	Birkdale	d		05 42	05 57	06 12	06 27	06 47	07 02		08 02	08 17	08 32		10 32	10 47	11 02	11 17		15 32
2	Hillside	d		05 44	05 59	06 14	06 29	06 49	07 04		08 04	08 19	08 34		10 34	10 49	11 04	11 19		15 34
3½	Ainsdale	d		05 47	06 02	06 17	06 32	06 52	07 07		08 07	08 22	08 37		10 37	10 52	11 07	11 22		15 37
6¼	Freshfield	d		05 51	06 06	06 21	06 36	06 56	07 11		08 11	08 26	08 41		10 41	10 56	11 11	11 26		15 41
7¼	Formby	d		05 53	06 08	06 23	06 38	06 58	07 13		08 13	08 28	08 43		10 43	10 58	11 13	11 28		15 43
9¾	Hightown	d		05 57	06 12	06 27	06 42	07 02	07 17		08 17	08 32	08 47		10 47	11 02	11 17	11 32		15 47
11¼	Hall Road	d		06 00	06 15	06 30	06 45	07 05	07 20		08 20	08 35	08 50		10 50	11 05	11 20	11 35		15 50
12	Blundellsands & Crosby	d		06 02	06 17	06 32	06 47	07 07	07 22		08 22	08 37	08 52		10 52	11 07	11 22	11 37		15 52
13	Waterloo	d		06 05	06 20	06 35	06 50	07 10	07 25		08 25	08 40	08 55		10 55	11 10	11 25	11 40		15 55
14¼	Seaforth & Litherland	d		06 07	06 22	06 37	06 52	07 12	07 27		08 27	08 42	08 57		10 57	11 12	11 27	11 42		15 57
15¼	Bootle New Strand	d		06 10	06 25	06 40	06 55	07 15	07 30		08 30	08 45	09 00		11 00	11 15	11 30	11 45		16 00
15½	Bootle Oriel Road	d		06 11	06 26	06 41	06 56	07 16	07 31		08 31	08 46	09 01		11 01	11 16	11 31	11 46		16 01
16¼	Bank Hall	d		06 18	06 33	06 48	07 03	07 18	07 33		08 33	08 48	09 03		11 03	11 18	11 33	11 48		16 03
17	Sandhills	d	06 06	06 21	06 36	06 51	07 06	07 21	07 36		08 36	08 51	09 06		11 06	11 21	11 36	11 51		16 06
18½	**Moorfields [10]**	d	06 10	06 25	06 40	06 55	07 10	07 25	07 40		08 40	08 55	09 10		11 10	11 25	11 40	11 55		16 10
19	**Liverpool Central [10]**	a	06 13	06 28	06 43	06 58	07 13	07 28	07 43		08 43	08 58	09 13		11 13	11 28	11 43	11 58		16 13
—		d	06 14	06 29	06 44	06 58	07 13	07 29	07 43		08 43	08 59	09 13		11 13	11 29	11 44	11 58		16 13
20½	Brunswick	d	06 17	06 32	06 47	07 02	07 17	07 32	07 47		08 47	09 02	09 17		11 17	11 32	11 47	12 02		16 17
21¾	St Michaels	d	06 20	06 35	06 50	07 05	07 20	07 35	07 50		08 50	09 05	09 20		11 20	11 35	11 50	12 05		16 20
23	Aigburth	d	06 22	06 37	06 52	07 07	07 22	07 37	07 52		08 52	09 07	09 22		11 22	11 37	11 52	12 07		16 22
23¾	Cressington	d	06 24	06 39	06 54	07 09	07 24	07 39	07 54		08 54	09 09	09 24		11 24	11 39	11 54	12 09		16 24
24¾	**Liverpool Sth Parkway [7] 89 ✈**	d	06 27	06 42	06 57	07 12	07 27	07 42	07 57		08 57	09 12	09 27		11 27	11 42	11 57	12 12		16 27
26¼	**Hunts Cross** 89	a	06 32	06 47	07 02	07 17	07 32	07 47	08 02		09 02	09 17	09 32		11 32	11 47	12 02	12 17		16 32

Station		ME	ME		ME	ME	ME	ME	ME		ME	ME		ME	ME	ME	ME	ME	ME
Southport	d	15 43	15 58	and every 15 minutes until	17 13	17 28	17 43	17 58	18 13	and every 15 minutes until	19 13	19 28	and every 15 minutes until	20 43	20 58	21 13	21 28	21 43	21 58
Birkdale	d	15 47	16 02		17 17	17 32	17 47	18 02	18 17		19 17	19 32		20 47	21 02	21 17	21 32	21 47	22 02
Hillside	d	15 49	16 04		17 19	17 34	17 49	18 04	18 19		19 19	19 34		20 49	21 04	21 19	21 34	21 49	22 04
Ainsdale	d	15 52	16 07		17 22	17 37	17 52	18 07	18 22		19 22	19 37		20 52	21 07	21 22	21 37	21 52	22 07
Freshfield	d	15 56	16 11		17 26	17 41	17 56	18 11	18 26		19 26	19 41		20 56	21 11	21 26	21 41	21 56	22 11
Formby	d	15 58	16 13		17 28	17 43	17 58	18 13	18 28		19 28	19 43		20 58	21 13	21 28	21 43	21 58	22 13
Hightown	d	16 02	16 17		17 32	17 47	18 02	18 17	18 32		19 32	19 47		21 02	21 17	21 32	21 47	22 02	22 17
Hall Road	d	16 05	16 20		17 35	17 50	18 05	18 20	18 35		19 35	19 50		21 05	21 20	21 35	21 50	22 05	22 20
Blundellsands & Crosby	d	16 07	16 22		17 37	17 52	18 07	18 22	18 37		19 37	19 52		21 07	21 22	21 37	21 52	22 07	22 22
Waterloo	d	16 10	16 25		17 40	17 55	18 10	18 25	18 40		19 40	19 55		21 10	21 25	21 40	21 55	22 10	22 25
Seaforth & Litherland	d	16 12	16 27		17 42	17 57	18 12	18 27	18 42		19 42	19 57		21 12	21 27	21 42	21 57	22 12	22 27
Bootle New Strand	d	16 15	16 30		17 45	18 00	18 15	18 30	18 45		19 45	20 00		21 15	21 30	21 45	22 00	22 15	22 30
Bootle Oriel Road	d	16 16	16 31		17 46	18 01	18 16	18 31	18 46		19 46	20 01		21 16	21 31	21 46	22 01	22 16	22 31
Bank Hall	d	16 18	16 33		17 48	18 03	18 18	18 33	18 48		19 48	20 03		21 18	21 33	21 48	22 03	22 18	22 33
Sandhills	d	16 21	16 36		17 51	18 06	18 21	18 36	18 51		19 51	20 06		21 21	21 36	21 51	22 06	22 21	22 36
Moorfields [10]	d	16 25	16 40		17 55	18 10	18 25	18 40	18 55		19 55	20 10		21 25	21 40	21 55	22 10	22 25	22 40
Liverpool Central [10]	a	16 28	16 43		17 58	18 13	18 28	18 43	18 58		19 58	20 13		21 28	21 44	21 58	22 13	22 28	22 43
	d	16 29	16 43		17 58	18 14	18 28	18 43	18 59		19 59	20 13		21 28	21 44	21 58	22 14	22 28	22 44
Brunswick	d	16 32	16 47		18 02	18 17	18 32	18 47	19 02		20 02	20 17		21 32	21 48	22 02	22 17	22 32	22 47
St Michaels	d	16 35	16 50		18 05	18 20	18 35	18 50	19 05		20 05	20 20		21 35	21 50	22 05	22 20	22 35	22 50
Aigburth	d	16 37	16 52		18 07	18 22	18 37	18 52	19 07		20 07	20 22		21 37	21 53	22 07	22 22	22 37	22 52
Cressington	d	16 39	16 54		18 09	18 24	18 39	18 54	19 09		20 09	20 24		21 39	21 55	22 09	22 24	22 39	22 54
Liverpool Sth Parkway [7] 89 ✈	d	16 42	16 57		18 12	18 27	18 42	18 57	19 12		20 12	20 27		21 42	21 57	22 12	22 27	22 42	22 57
Hunts Cross 89	a	16 47	17 02		18 17	18 32	18 47	19 02	19 17		20 17	20 32		21 47	22 02	22 17	22 32	22 47	23 02

Station		ME	ME	ME	ME	ME
Southport	d	22 13	22 28	22 43	22 58	23 18
Birkdale	d	22 17	22 32	22 47	23 02	23 22
Hillside	d	22 19	22 34	22 49	23 04	23 24
Ainsdale	d	22 22	22 37	22 52	23 07	23 27
Freshfield	d	22 26	22 41	22 56	23 11	23 31
Formby	d	22 28	22 43	22 58	23 13	23 33
Hightown	d	22 32	22 47	23 02	23 17	23 37
Hall Road	d	22 35	22 50	23 05	23 20	23 40
Blundellsands & Crosby	d	22 37	22 52	23 07	23 22	23 42
Waterloo	d	22 40	22 55	23 10	23 25	23 45
Seaforth & Litherland	d	22 42	22 57	23 12	23 27	23 47
Bootle New Strand	d	22 45	23 00	23 15	23 30	23 50
Bootle Oriel Road	d	22 46	23 01	23 16	23 31	23 51
Bank Hall	d	22 48	23 03	23 18	23 33	23 53
Sandhills	d	22 51	23 06	23 21	23 36	23 56
Moorfields [10]	d	22 55	23 10	23 25	23 40	23 59
Liverpool Central [10]	a	22 58	23 13	23 28	23 43	00 03
	d	22 58	23 14	23 29	23 44	
Brunswick	d	23 02	23 17	23 32	23 47	
St Michaels	d	23 05	23 20	23 35	23 50	
Aigburth	d	23 07	23 22	23 37	23 52	
Cressington	d	23 09	23 24	23 39	23 54	
Liverpool Sth Parkway [7] 89 ✈	d	23 12	23 27	23 42	23 57	
Hunts Cross 89	a	23 17	23 33	23 49	00 02	

For alternative services between Sandhills and Liverpool refer to Tables T104 and T105

Table T103-R

Saturdays

21 December to 16 May

Southport - Hunts Cross

Station		ME	ME	ME	ME	ME	ME		ME	ME		ME	ME	ME	ME	ME	ME	ME	ME	ME	ME
Southport	d		05 38	05 53	06 08	06 23	06 43	and every 15 minutes until	08 13	08 28	and every 15 minutes until	09 28	09 43	09 58	10 13	10 28	10 43	10 58	11 13	11 28	11 43
Birkdale	d		05 42	05 57	06 12	06 27	06 47		08 17	08 32		09 32	09 47	10 02	10 17	10 32	10 47	11 02	11 17	11 32	11 47
Hillside	d		05 44	05 59	06 14	06 29	06 49		08 19	08 34		09 34	09 49	10 04	10 19	10 34	10 49	11 04	11 19	11 34	11 49
Ainsdale	d		05 47	06 02	06 17	06 32	06 52		08 22	08 37		09 37	09 52	10 07	10 22	10 37	10 52	11 07	11 22	11 37	11 52
Freshfield	d		05 51	06 06	06 21	06 36	06 56		08 26	08 41		09 41	09 56	10 11	10 26	10 41	10 56	11 11	11 26	11 41	11 56
Formby	d		05 53	06 08	06 23	06 38	06 58		08 28	08 43		09 43	09 58	10 13	10 28	10 43	10 58	11 13	11 28	11 43	11 58
Hightown	d		05 57	06 12	06 27	06 42	07 02		08 32	08 47		09 47	10 02	10 17	10 32	10 47	11 02	11 17	11 32	11 47	12 02
Hall Road	d		06 00	06 15	06 30	06 45	07 05		08 35	08 50		09 50	10 05	10 20	10 35	10 50	11 05	11 20	11 35	11 50	12 05
Blundellsands & Crosby	d		06 02	06 17	06 32	06 47	07 07		08 37	08 52		09 52	10 07	10 22	10 37	10 52	11 07	11 22	11 37	11 52	12 07
Waterloo	d		06 05	06 20	06 35	06 50	07 10		08 40	08 55		09 55	10 10	10 25	10 40	10 55	11 10	11 25	11 40	11 55	12 10
Seaforth & Litherland	d		06 07	06 22	06 37	06 52	07 12		08 42	08 57		09 57	10 12	10 27	10 42	10 57	11 12	11 27	11 42	11 57	12 12
Bootle New Strand	d		06 10	06 25	06 40	06 55	07 15		08 45	09 00		10 00	10 15	10 30	10 45	11 00	11 15	11 30	11 45	12 00	12 15
Bootle Oriel Road	d		06 11	06 26	06 41	06 56	07 16		08 46	09 01		10 01	10 16	10 31	10 46	11 01	11 16	11 31	11 46	12 01	12 16
Bank Hall	d		06 18	06 33	06 48	07 03	07 18		08 48	09 03		10 03	10 18	10 33	10 48	11 03	11 18	11 33	11 48	12 03	12 18
Sandhills	d	06 06	06 21	06 36	06 51	07 06	07 21		08 51	09 06		10 06	10 21	10 36	10 51	11 06	11 21	11 36	11 51	12 06	12 21
Moorfields [10]	d	06 10	06 25	06 40	06 55	07 10	07 25		08 55	09 10		10 10	10 25	10 40	10 55	11 10	11 25	11 40	11 55	12 10	12 25
Liverpool Central [10]	a	06 13	06 28	06 43	06 58	07 13	07 28		08 58	09 13		10 13	10 28	10 43	10 58	11 13	11 28	11 43	11 58	12 13	12 28
	d	06 14	06 29	06 44	06 58	07 13	07 29		08 59	09 13		10 13	10 29	10 43	10 58	11 14	11 29	11 44	11 58	12 14	12 28
Brunswick	d	06 17	06 32	06 47	07 02	07 17	07 32		09 02	09 17		10 17	10 32	10 47	11 02	11 17	11 32	11 47	12 02	12 17	12 32
St Michaels	d	06 20	06 35	06 50	07 05	07 20	07 35		09 05	09 20		10 20	10 35	10 50	11 05	11 20	11 35	11 50	12 05	12 20	12 35
Aigburth	d	06 22	06 37	06 52	07 07	07 22	07 37		09 07	09 22		10 22	10 37	10 52	11 07	11 22	11 37	11 52	12 07	12 22	12 37
Cressington	d	06 24	06 39	06 54	07 09	07 24	07 39		09 09	09 24		10 24	10 39	10 54	11 09	11 24	11 39	11 54	12 09	12 24	12 39
Liverpool Sth Parkway [7] 89 ✈	d	06 27	06 42	06 57	07 12	07 27	07 42		09 12	09 27		10 27	10 42	10 57	11 12	11 27	11 42	11 57	12 12	12 27	12 42
Hunts Cross 89	a	06 32	06 47	07 02	07 17	07 32	07 47		09 17	09 32		10 32	10 47	11 02	11 17	11 32	11 47	12 02	12 17	12 32	12 47

Station		ME	ME	ME	ME	ME	ME	ME	ME	ME	ME	ME	ME	ME	ME	ME	ME	ME	ME	ME	ME	ME
Southport	d	11 58	12 13	12 28	12 43	12 58	13 13	13 28	13 43	13 58	14 13	14 28	14 43	14 58	15 13	15 28	15 43	15 58	16 13	16 28	16 43	16 58
Birkdale	d	12 02	12 17	12 32	12 47	13 02	13 17	13 32	13 47	14 02	14 17	14 32	14 47	15 02	15 17	15 32	15 47	16 02	16 17	16 32	16 47	17 02
Hillside	d	12 04	12 19	12 34	12 49	13 04	13 19	13 34	13 49	14 04	14 19	14 34	14 49	15 04	15 19	15 34	15 49	16 04	16 19	16 34	16 49	17 04
Ainsdale	d	12 07	12 22	12 37	12 52	13 07	13 22	13 37	13 52	14 07	14 22	14 37	14 52	15 07	15 22	15 37	15 52	16 07	16 22	16 37	16 52	17 07
Freshfield	d	12 11	12 26	12 41	12 56	13 11	13 26	13 41	13 56	14 11	14 26	14 41	14 56	15 11	15 26	15 41	15 56	16 11	16 26	16 41	16 56	17 11
Formby	d	12 13	12 28	12 43	12 58	13 13	13 28	13 43	13 58	14 13	14 28	14 43	14 58	15 13	15 28	15 43	15 58	16 13	16 28	16 43	16 58	17 13
Hightown	d	12 17	12 32	12 47	13 02	13 17	13 32	13 47	14 02	14 17	14 32	14 47	15 02	15 17	15 32	15 47	16 02	16 17	16 32	16 47	17 02	17 17
Hall Road	d	12 20	12 35	12 50	13 05	13 20	13 35	13 50	14 05	14 20	14 35	14 50	15 05	15 20	15 35	15 50	16 05	16 20	16 35	16 50	17 05	17 20
Blundellsands & Crosby	d	12 22	12 37	12 52	13 07	13 22	13 37	13 52	14 07	14 22	14 37	14 52	15 07	15 22	15 37	15 52	16 07	16 22	16 37	16 52	17 07	17 22
Waterloo	d	12 25	12 40	12 55	13 10	13 25	13 40	13 55	14 10	14 25	14 40	14 55	15 10	15 25	15 40	15 55	16 10	16 25	16 40	16 55	17 10	17 25
Seaforth & Litherland	d	12 27	12 42	12 57	13 12	13 27	13 42	13 57	14 12	14 27	14 42	14 57	15 12	15 27	15 42	15 57	16 12	16 27	16 42	16 57	17 12	17 27
Bootle New Strand	d	12 30	12 45	13 00	13 15	13 30	13 45	14 00	14 15	14 30	14 45	15 00	15 15	15 30	15 45	16 00	16 15	16 30	16 45	17 00	17 15	17 30
Bootle Oriel Road	d	12 31	12 46	13 01	13 16	13 31	13 46	14 01	14 16	14 31	14 46	15 01	15 16	15 31	15 46	16 01	16 16	16 31	16 46	17 01	17 16	17 31
Bank Hall	d	12 33	12 48	13 03	13 18	13 33	13 48	14 03	14 18	14 33	14 48	15 03	15 18	15 33	15 48	16 03	16 18	16 33	16 48	17 03	17 18	17 33
Sandhills	d	12 36	12 51	13 06	13 21	13 36	13 51	14 06	14 21	14 36	14 51	15 06	15 21	15 36	15 51	16 06	16 21	16 36	16 51	17 06	17 21	17 36
Moorfields [10]	d	12 40	12 55	13 10	13 25	13 40	13 55	14 10	14 25	14 40	14 55	15 10	15 25	15 40	15 55	16 10	16 25	16 40	16 55	17 10	17 25	17 40
Liverpool Central [10]	a	12 43	12 58	13 13	13 28	13 43	13 58	14 13	14 28	14 43	14 58	15 13	15 28	15 43	15 58	16 13	16 28	16 43	16 58	17 13	17 28	17 43
	d	12 43	12 58	13 14	13 29	13 43	13 59	14 13	14 29	14 44	14 59	15 13	15 29	15 43	15 58	16 14	16 29	16 43	16 58	17 13	17 29	17 43
Brunswick	d	12 47	13 02	13 17	13 32	13 47	14 02	14 17	14 32	14 47	15 02	15 17	15 32	15 47	16 02	16 17	16 32	16 47	17 02	17 17	17 32	17 47
St Michaels	d	12 50	13 05	13 20	13 35	13 50	14 05	14 20	14 35	14 50	15 05	15 20	15 35	15 50	16 05	16 20	16 35	16 50	17 05	17 20	17 35	17 50
Aigburth	d	12 52	13 07	13 22	13 37	13 52	14 07	14 22	14 37	14 52	15 07	15 22	15 37	15 52	16 07	16 22	16 37	16 52	17 07	17 22	17 37	17 52
Cressington	d	12 54	13 09	13 24	13 39	13 54	14 09	14 24	14 39	14 54	15 09	15 24	15 39	15 54	16 09	16 24	16 39	16 54	17 09	17 24	17 39	17 54
Liverpool Sth Parkway [7] 89 ✈	d	12 57	13 12	13 27	13 42	13 57	14 12	14 27	14 42	14 57	15 12	15 27	15 42	15 57	16 12	16 27	16 42	16 57	17 12	17 27	17 42	17 57
Hunts Cross 89	a	13 02	13 17	13 32	13 47	14 02	14 17	14 32	14 47	15 02	15 17	15 32	15 47	16 02	16 17	16 32	16 47	17 02	17 17	17 32	17 47	18 02

Station		ME	ME	ME	ME	ME	ME	ME	ME	ME	ME	ME	ME	ME	ME	ME	ME	ME	ME	ME	ME	ME	ME
Southport	d	17 13	17 28	17 43	17 58	18 13	18 28	18 43	18 58	19 13	19 28	19 43	19 58	20 13	20 28	20 43	20 58	21 13	21 28	21 43	21 58	22 13	22 28
Birkdale	d	17 17	17 32	17 47	18 02	18 17	18 32	18 47	19 02	19 17	19 32	19 47	20 02	20 17	20 32	20 47	21 02	21 17	21 32	21 47	22 02	22 17	22 32
Hillside	d	17 19	17 34	17 49	18 04	18 19	18 34	18 49	19 04	19 19	19 34	19 49	20 04	20 19	20 34	20 49	21 04	21 19	21 34	21 49	22 04	22 19	22 34
Ainsdale	d	17 22	17 37	17 52	18 07	18 22	18 37	18 52	19 07	19 22	19 37	19 52	20 07	20 22	20 37	20 52	21 07	21 22	21 37	21 52	22 07	22 22	22 37
Freshfield	d	17 26	17 41	17 56	18 11	18 26	18 41	18 56	19 11	19 26	19 41	19 56	20 11	20 26	20 41	20 56	21 11	21 26	21 41	21 56	22 11	22 26	22 41
Formby	d	17 28	17 43	17 58	18 13	18 28	18 43	18 58	19 13	19 28	19 43	19 58	20 13	20 28	20 43	20 58	21 13	21 28	21 43	21 58	22 13	22 28	22 43
Hightown	d	17 32	17 47	18 02	18 17	18 32	18 47	19 02	19 17	19 32	19 47	20 02	20 17	20 32	20 47	21 02	21 17	21 32	21 47	22 02	22 17	22 32	22 47
Hall Road	d	17 35	17 50	18 05	18 20	18 35	18 50	19 05	19 20	19 35	19 50	20 05	20 20	20 35	20 50	21 05	21 20	21 35	21 50	22 05	22 20	22 35	22 50
Blundellsands & Crosby	d	17 37	17 52	18 07	18 22	18 37	18 52	19 07	19 22	19 37	19 52	20 07	20 22	20 37	20 52	21 07	21 22	21 37	21 52	22 07	22 22	22 37	22 52
Waterloo	d	17 40	17 55	18 10	18 25	18 40	18 55	19 10	19 25	19 40	19 55	20 10	20 25	20 40	20 55	21 10	21 25	21 40	21 55	22 10	22 25	22 40	22 55
Seaforth & Litherland	d	17 42	17 57	18 12	18 27	18 42	18 57	19 12	19 27	19 42	19 57	20 12	20 27	20 42	20 57	21 12	21 27	21 42	21 57	22 12	22 27	22 42	22 57
Bootle New Strand	d	17 45	18 00	18 15	18 30	18 45	19 00	19 15	19 30	19 45	20 00	20 15	20 30	20 45	21 00	21 15	21 30	21 45	22 00	22 15	22 30	22 45	23 00
Bootle Oriel Road	d	17 46	18 01	18 16	18 31	18 46	19 01	19 16	19 31	19 46	20 01	20 16	20 31	20 46	21 01	21 16	21 31	21 46	22 01	22 16	22 31	22 46	23 01
Bank Hall	d	17 48	18 03	18 18	18 33	18 48	19 03	19 18	19 33	19 48	20 03	20 18	20 33	20 48	21 03	21 18	21 33	21 48	22 03	22 18	22 33	22 48	23 03
Sandhills	d	17 51	18 06	18 21	18 36	18 51	19 06	19 21	19 36	19 51	20 06	20 21	20 36	20 51	21 06	21 21	21 36	21 51	22 06	22 21	22 36	22 51	23 06
Moorfields [10]	d	17 55	18 10	18 25	18 40	18 55	19 10	19 25	19 40	19 55	20 10	20 25	20 40	20 55	21 10	21 25	21 40	21 55	22 10	22 25	22 40	22 55	23 10
Liverpool Central [10]	a	17 58	18 13	18 28	18 43	18 58	19 13	19 28	19 43	19 58	20 13	20 28	20 43	20 58	21 13	21 28	21 44	21 58	22 13	22 28	22 43	22 58	23 13
	d	17 58	18 14	18 28	18 44	18 58	19 13	19 28	19 43	19 59	20 13	20 29	20 44	20 58	21 13	21 28	21 44	21 58	22 14	22 29	22 44	22 58	23 14
Brunswick	d	18 02	18 17	18 32	18 47	19 02	19 17	19 33	19 47	20 02	20 17	20 32	20 47	21 02	21 17	21 32	21 48	22 02	22 17	22 32	22 47	23 02	23 17
St Michaels	d	18 05	18 20	18 35	18 50	19 05	19 20	19 35	19 50	20 05	20 20	20 35	20 50	21 05	21 20	21 35	21 50	22 05	22 20	22 35	22 50	23 05	23 20
Aigburth	d	18 07	18 22	18 37	18 52	19 07	19 22	19 38	19 52	20 07	20 22	20 37	20 52	21 07	21 22	21 37	21 53	22 07	22 22	22 37	22 52	23 07	23 22
Cressington	d	18 09	18 24	18 39	18 54	19 09	19 24	19 40	19 54	20 09	20 24	20 39	20 54	21 09	21 24	21 39	21 55	22 09	22 24	22 39	22 54	23 09	23 24
Liverpool Sth Parkway [7] 89 ✈	d	18 12	18 27	18 42	18 57	19 12	19 27	19 42	19 57	20 12	20 27	20 42	20 57	21 12	21 27	21 42	21 57	22 12	22 27	22 42	22 57	23 12	23 27
Hunts Cross 89	a	18 17	18 32	18 47	19 02	19 17	19 32	19 48	20 02	20 17	20 32	20 47	21 02	21 17	21 32	21 47	22 02	22 17	22 32	22 47	23 02	23 17	23 32

For alternative services between Sandhills and Liverpool refer to Tables T104 and T105

Table T103-R

Southport - Hunts Cross

Saturdays

21 December to 16 May

		ME	ME	ME
Southport	d	22 43	22 58	23 18
Birkdale	d	22 47	23 02	23 22
Hillside	d	22 49	23 04	23 24
Ainsdale	d	22 52	23 07	23 27
Freshfield	d	22 56	23 11	23 31
Formby	d	22 58	23 13	23 33
Hightown	d	23 02	23 17	23 37
Hall Road	d	23 05	23 20	23 40
Blundellsands & Crosby	d	23 07	23 22	23 42
Waterloo	d	23 10	23 25	23 45
Seaforth & Litherland	d	23 12	23 27	23 47
Bootle New Strand	d	23 15	23 30	23 50
Bootle Oriel Road	d	23 16	23 31	23 51
Bank Hall	d	23 18	23 33	23 53
Sandhills	d	23 21	23 36	23 56
Moorfields 10	d	23 25	23 40	23 59
Liverpool Central 10	a	23 28	23 43	00 03
	d	23 29	23 44	
Brunswick	d	23 32	23 47	
St Michaels	d	23 35	23 50	
Aigburth	d	23 37	23 52	
Cressington	d	23 39	23 54	
Liverpool Sth Parkway 7 89 ✈	d	23 42	23 57	
Hunts Cross 89	a	23 49	00 02	

Sundays

15 December to 10 May

		ME	ME		ME	ME	ME
Southport	d		07 58	and every 30 minutes until	22 28	22 58	23 18
Birkdale	d		08 02		22 32	23 02	23 22
Hillside	d		08 04		22 34	23 04	23 24
Ainsdale	d		08 07		22 37	23 07	23 27
Freshfield	d		08 11		22 41	23 11	23 31
Formby	d		08 13		22 43	23 13	23 33
Hightown	d		08 17		22 47	23 17	23 37
Hall Road	d		08 20		22 50	23 20	23 40
Blundellsands & Crosby	d		08 22		22 52	23 22	23 42
Waterloo	d		08 25		22 55	23 25	23 45
Seaforth & Litherland	d		08 27		22 57	23 27	23 47
Bootle New Strand	d		08 30		23 00	23 30	23 50
Bootle Oriel Road	d		08 31		23 01	23 31	23 51
Bank Hall	d		08 33		23 03	23 33	23 53
Sandhills	d		08 36		23 06	23 36	23 56
Moorfields 10	d		08 40		23 10	23 40	23 59
Liverpool Central 10	a		08 43		23 13	23 44	00 03
	d	08 14	08 44		23 14	23 45	
Brunswick	d	08 17	08 47		23 17	23 48	
St Michaels	d	08 20	08 50		23 20	23 51	
Aigburth	d	08 22	08 52		23 22	23 53	
Cressington	d	08 24	08 54		23 24	23 55	
Liverpool Sth Parkway 7 89 ✈	d	08 27	08 57		23 27	23 58	
Hunts Cross 89	a	08 32	09 02		23 32	00 03	

For alternative services between Sandhills and Liverpool refer to Tables T104 and T105

Table T104-F

Liverpool Central - Kirkby

Mondays to Saturdays

16 December to 16 May

Miles			ME	ME	ME	ME		ME	ME SX	ME SO	ME		ME	ME SX	ME SO	ME		ME
0	**Liverpool Central** 10	d		06 05	06 35	07 05	and every 15 minutes until	09 05	09 20	09 20	09 35	and every 15 minutes until	16 35	16 50	16 50	17 05	and every 15 minutes until	19 35
0½	**Moorfields** 10	d		06 06	06 38	07 08		09 08	09 23	09 23	09 38		16 38	16 53	16 53	17 08		19 38
2	Sandhills	d	00 01	06 10	06 41	07 11		09 11	09 25	09 26	09 41		16 41	16 55	16 56	17 11		19 41
3	Kirkdale	d	00 04	06 14	06 44	07 14		09 14	09 29	09 29	09 44		16 44	16 59	16 59	17 14		19 44
4¼	Rice Lane	d	00 07	06 17	06 47	07 17		09 17	09 32	09 32	09 47		16 47	17 02	17 02	17 17		19 47
5¾	Fazakerley	d	00 10	06 20	06 49	07 20		09 20	09 35	09 35	09 50		16 50	17 05	17 05	17 20		19 50
7½	**Kirkby**	a	00 14	06 23	06 54	07 24		09 24	09 39	09 39	09 54		16 54	17 09	17 09	17 24		19 54

		ME		ME	ME	ME	ME	ME
Liverpool Central 10	d	20 05	and every 30 minutes until	22 05	22 35	23 05	23 35	23 55
Moorfields 10	d	20 08		22 08	22 38	23 08	23 38	23 58
Sandhills	d	20 11		22 11	22 41	23 11	23 41	00 01
Kirkdale	d	20 14		22 14	22 44	23 14	23 44	00 04
Rice Lane	d	20 17		22 17	22 49	23 17	23 47	00 07
Fazakerley	d	20 20		22 20	22 52	23 20	23 50	00 10
Kirkby	a	20 24		22 24	22 56	23 24	23 54	00 14

Sundays

15 December to 10 May

		ME A	ME		ME	ME
Liverpool Central 10	d		08 05	and every 30 minutes until	23 35	23 55
Moorfields 10	d		08 08		23 38	23 58
Sandhills	d	00 01	08 11		23 41	00 01
Kirkdale	d	00 04	08 14		23 44	00 04
Rice Lane	d	00 07	08 17		23 47	00 07
Fazakerley	d	00 10	08 20		23 50	00 10
Kirkby	a	00 14	08 24		23 54	00 14

A not 15 December

For additional trains Liverpool-Kirkdale refer to Table T105

For additional trains between Liverpool and Sandhills refer to Tables T103 and T105

Table T104-R

Kirkby - Liverpool Central

Mondays to Saturdays

16 December to 16 May

Miles			ME		ME	ME		ME	ME SO	ME SX	ME		ME	ME SX	ME SO	ME		ME
0	**Kirkby**	d	05 43	and every 30 minutes until	07 13	07 28	and every 15 minutes until	14 43	14 58	14 58	15 13	and every 15 minutes until	16 43	16 58	16 58	17 13	and every 15 minutes until	19 43
1¾	Fazakerley	d	05 46		07 16	07 31		14 46	15 01	15 01	15 16		16 46	17 01	17 01	17 16		19 46
3¼	Rice Lane	d	05 49		07 19	07 34		14 49	15 04	15 04	15 19		16 49	17 04	17 04	17 19		19 49
4½	Kirkdale	d	05 52		07 22	07 37		14 52	15 07	15 07	15 22		16 52	17 07	17 07	17 22		19 52
5½	Sandhills	d	05 55		07 25	07 40		14 55	15 10	15 10	15 25		16 55	17 10	17 10	17 25		19 55
7	**Moorfields** 10	d	05 58		07 28	07 43		14 58	15 13	15 13	15 28		16 58	17 13	17 14	17 28		19 58
7½	**Liverpool Central** 10	a	06 01		07 31	07 46		15 01	15 16	15 17	15 31		17 01	17 16	17 16	17 31		20 01

		ME		ME
Kirkby	d	20 13	and every 30 minutes until	23 13
Fazakerley	d	20 16		23 16
Rice Lane	d	20 19		23 19
Kirkdale	d	20 22		23 22
Sandhills	d	20 25		23 25
Moorfields 10	d	20 28		23 28
Liverpool Central 10	a	20 31		23 31

Sundays

15 December to 10 May

		ME		ME
Kirkby	d	08 13	and every 30 minutes until	23 13
Fazakerley	d	08 16		23 16
Rice Lane	d	08 19		23 19
Kirkdale	d	08 22		23 22
Sandhills	d	08 25		23 25
Moorfields 10	d	08 28		23 28
Liverpool Central 10	a	08 31		23 31

For additional trains Liverpool-Kirkdale refer to Table T105

For additional trains between Liverpool and Sandhills refer to Tables T103 and T105

Table T105-F

Mondays to Saturdays
16 December to 16 May

Liverpool Central - Ormskirk

Miles			ME MX	ME MO	ME	ME	ME	ME	ME	ME	ME	ME	ME	ME	ME	ME	ME	ME	ME	ME	ME	ME	ME
0	**Liverpool Central** 10	d				06 05	06 08	06 17	06 23	06 32	06 35	06 38	06 47	06 53	07 02	07 05	07 08	07 17	07 20	07 23	07 32	07 35	07 38
0½	**Moorfields** 10	d				06 06	06 10	06 20	06 25	06 35	06 38	06 41	06 50	06 55	07 05	07 08	07 11	07 20	07 23	07 26	07 35	07 38	07 41
2	Sandhills	d			00 01	06 10	06a14	06 23	06a29	06 38	06 41	06a44	06 53	06a59	07 08	07 11	07a14	07 23	07 26	07a29	07 38	07 41	07a44
3	Kirkdale	d			00a04	06a14		06 26		06 41	06a44		06 56		07 11	07a14		07 26	07a29		07 41	07a44	
4¼	Walton	d						06 29		06 44			06 59		07 14			07 29			07 44		
4½	Orrell Park	d	00 01	00 01				06 30		06 45			07 00		07 15			07 30			07 45		
5½	Aintree	d	00 04	00 04				06 33		06 48			07 03		07 18			07 33			07 48		
6¼	Old Roan	d	00 06	00 06				06 35		06 50			07 05		07 20			07 35			07 50		
8	Maghull	d	00 09	00 09				06 38		06 53			07 08		07 23			07 38			07 53		
9	Maghull North	d	00 10	00 11				06 40		06 55			07 10		07 25			07 40			07 55		
10½	Town Green	d	00 15	00 15				06 44		06 59			07 14		07 29			07 44			07 59		
11½	Aughton Park	d	00 16	00 17				06 46		07 01			07 16		07 31			07 46			08 01		
12¾	**Ormskirk**	a	00 22	00 22				06 52		07 07			07 22		07 37			07 52			08 07		

		ME	ME	ME	ME	ME	ME	ME	ME	ME	ME	ME	ME	ME	ME	ME	ME	ME	ME	ME	ME SX	ME SO	ME
Liverpool Central 10	d	07 47	07 50	07 53	08 02	08 05	08 08	08 17	08 20	08 23	08 32	08 35	08 38	08 47	08 50	08 53	09 02	09 05	09 08	09 17	09 20	09 20	09 23
Moorfields 10	d	07 50	07 53	07 56	08 05	08 08	08 11	08 20	08 23	08 26	08 35	08 38	08 41	08 50	08 53	08 56	09 05	09 08	09 11	09 20	09 23	09 23	09 26
Sandhills	d	07 53	07 56	07a59	08 08	08 11	08a14	08 23	08 26	08a29	08 38	08 41	08a44	08 53	08 56	08a59	09 08	09 11	09a14	09 23	09 25	09 26	09a30
Kirkdale	d	07 56	07a59		08 11	08a14		08 26	08a29		08 41	08a44		08 56	08a59		09 11	09a14		09 26	09a28	09a29	
Walton	d	07 59			08 14			08 29			08 44			08 59			09 14			09 29			
Orrell Park	d	08 00			08 15			08 30			08 45			09 00			09 15			09 30			
Aintree	d	08 03			08 18			08 33			08 48			09 03			09 18			09 33			
Old Roan	d	08 05			08 20			08 35			08 50			09 05			09 20			09 35			
Maghull	d	08 08			08 23			08 38			08 53			09 08			09 23			09 38			
Maghull North	d	08 10			08 25			08 40			08 55			09 10			09 25			09 40			
Town Green	d	08 14			08 29			08 44			08 59			09 14			09 29			09 44			
Aughton Park	d	08 16			08 31			08 46			09 01			09 16			09 31			09 46			
Ormskirk	a	08 22			08 37			08 52			09 07			09 22			09 37			09 52			

		ME	ME	ME	ME	ME	ME	ME	ME	ME	ME	ME	ME	ME	ME	ME	ME	ME	ME	ME	ME	ME
Liverpool Central 10	d	09 32	09 35	09 38	09 47	09 50	09 53	10 02	10 05	10 08	10 17	10 20	10 23	10 32	10 35	10 38	10 47	10 50	10 53	11 02	11 05	11 08
Moorfields 10	d	09 35	09 38	09 41	09 50	09 53	09 56	10 05	10 08	10 11	10 20	10 23	10 26	10 35	10 38	10 41	10 50	10 53	10 56	11 05	11 08	11 11
Sandhills	d	09 38	09 41	09a44	09 53	09 56	09a59	10 08	10 11	10a14	10 23	10 26	10a29	10 38	10 41	10a44	10 53	10 56	10a59	11 08	11 11	11a14
Kirkdale	d	09 41	09a44		09 56	09a59		10 11	10a14		10 26	10a29		10 41	10a44		10 56	10a59		11 11	11a14	
Walton	d	09 44			09 59			10 14			10 29			10 44			10 59			11 14		
Orrell Park	d	09 45			10 00			10 15			10 30			10 45			11 00			11 15		
Aintree	d	09 48			10 03			10 18			10 33			10 48			11 03			11 18		
Old Roan	d	09 50			10 05			10 20			10 35			10 50			11 05			11 20		
Maghull	d	09 53			10 08			10 23			10 38			10 53			11 08			11 23		
Maghull North	d	09 55			10 10			10 25			10 40			10 55			11 10			11 25		
Town Green	d	09 59			10 14			10 29			10 44			10 59			11 14			11 29		
Aughton Park	d	10 01			10 16			10 31			10 46			11 01			11 16			11 31		
Ormskirk	a	10 07			10 22			10 37			10 52			11 07			11 22			11 37		

		ME	ME	ME	ME	ME	ME	ME	ME	ME	ME	ME	ME	ME	ME	ME	ME	ME	ME	ME	ME	ME	ME
Liverpool Central 10	d	11 17	11 20	11 23	11 32	11 35	11 38	11 47	11 50	11 53	12 02	12 05	12 08	12 17	12 20	12 23	12 32	12 35	12 38	12 47	12 50	12 53	13 02
Moorfields 10	d	11 20	11 23	11 26	11 35	11 38	11 41	11 50	11 53	11 56	12 05	12 08	12 11	12 20	12 23	12 26	12 35	12 38	12 41	12 50	12 53	12 56	13 05
Sandhills	d	11 23	11 26	11a29	11 38	11 41	11a44	11 53	11 56	11a59	12 08	12 11	12a14	12 23	12 26	12a29	12 38	12 41	12a44	12 53	12 56	12a59	13 08
Kirkdale	d	11 26	11a29		11 41	11a44		11 56	11a59		12 11	12a14		12 26	12a29		12 41	12a44		12 56	12a59		13 11
Walton	d	11 29			11 44			11 59			12 14			12 29			12 44			12 59			13 14
Orrell Park	d	11 30			11 45			12 00			12 15			12 30			12 45			13 00			13 15
Aintree	d	11 33			11 48			12 03			12 18			12 33			12 48			13 03			13 18
Old Roan	d	11 35			11 50			12 05			12 20			12 35			12 50			13 05			13 20
Maghull	d	11 38			11 53			12 08			12 23			12 38			12 53			13 08			13 23
Maghull North	d	11 40			11 55			12 10			12 25			12 40			12 55			13 10			13 25
Town Green	d	11 44			11 59			12 14			12 29			12 44			12 59			13 14			13 29
Aughton Park	d	11 46			12 01			12 16			12 31			12 46			13 01			13 16			13 31
Ormskirk	a	11 52			12 07			12 22			12 37			12 52			13 07			13 22			13 37

		ME	ME	ME	ME	ME	ME	ME	ME	ME	ME	ME	ME	ME	ME	ME	ME	ME	ME	ME	ME	ME	ME
Liverpool Central 10	d	13 05	13 08	13 17	13 20	13 23	13 32	13 35	13 38	13 47	13 50	13 53	14 02	14 05	14 08	14 17	14 20	14 23	14 32	14 35	14 38	14 47	14 50
Moorfields 10	d	13 08	13 11	13 20	13 23	13 26	13 35	13 38	13 41	13 50	13 53	13 56	14 05	14 08	14 11	14 20	14 23	14 26	14 35	14 38	14 41	14 50	14 53
Sandhills	d	13 11	13a14	13 23	13 26	13a29	13 38	13 41	13a44	13 53	13 56	13a59	14 08	14 11	14a14	14 23	14 26	14a29	14 38	14 41	14a44	14 53	14 56
Kirkdale	d	13a14		13 26	13a29		13 41	13a44		13 56	13a59		14 11	14a14		14 26	14a29		14 41	14a44		14 56	14a59
Walton	d			13 29			13 44			13 59			14 14			14 29			14 44			14 59	
Orrell Park	d			13 30			13 45			14 00			14 15			14 30			14 45			15 00	
Aintree	d			13 33			13 48			14 03			14 18			14 33			14 48			15 03	
Old Roan	d			13 35			13 50			14 05			14 20			14 35			14 50			15 05	
Maghull	d			13 38			13 53			14 08			14 23			14 38			14 53			15 08	
Maghull North	d			13 40			13 55			14 10			14 25			14 40			14 55			15 10	
Town Green	d			13 44			13 59			14 14			14 29			14 44			14 59			15 14	
Aughton Park	d			13 46			14 01			14 16			14 31			14 46			15 01			15 16	
Ormskirk	a			13 52			14 07			14 22			14 37			14 52			15 07			15 22	

For additional trains between Liverpool and Kirkdale refer to Table T104

For additional trains between Liverpool and Sandhills refer to Tables T103 and T104

NRT DECEMBER 19 EDITION

Table T105-F

Mondays to Saturdays
16 December to 16 May

Liverpool Central - Ormskirk

		ME	ME	ME	ME	ME	ME	ME	ME	ME	ME	ME	ME	ME	ME	ME	ME	ME	ME	ME	ME	ME	ME
Liverpool Central 10	d	14 53	15 02	15 05	15 08	15 17	15 20	15 23	15 32	15 35	15 38	15 47	15 50	15 53	16 02	16 05	16 08	16 17	16 20	16 23	16 32	16 35	16 38
Moorfields 10	d	14 56	15 05	15 08	15 11	15 20	15 23	15 26	15 35	15 38	15 41	15 50	15 53	15 56	16 05	16 08	16 11	16 20	16 23	16 26	16 35	16 38	16 41
Sandhills	d	14a59	15 08	15 11	15a14	15 23	15 26	15a29	15 38	15 41	15a44	15 53	15 56	15a59	16 08	16 11	16a14	16 23	16 26	16a29	16 38	16 41	16a44
Kirkdale	d		15 11	15a14		15 26	15a29		15 41	15a44		15 56	15a59		16 11	16a14		16 26	16a29		16 41	16a44	
Walton	d		15 14			15 29			15 44			15 59			16 14			16 29			16 44		
Orrell Park	d		15 15			15 30			15 45			16 00			16 15			16 30			16 45		
Aintree	d		15 18			15 33			15 48			16 03			16 18			16 33			16 48		
Old Roan	d		15 20			15 35			15 50			16 05			16 20			16 35			16 50		
Maghull	d		15 23			15 38			15 53			16 08			16 23			16 38			16 53		
Maghull North	d		15 25			15 40			15 55			16 10			16 25			16 40			16 55		
Town Green	d		15 29			15 44			15 59			16 14			16 29			16 44			16 59		
Aughton Park	d		15 31			15 46			16 01			16 16			16 31			16 46			17 01		
Ormskirk	a		15 37			15 52			16 07			16 22			16 37			16 52			17 07		

		ME	ME SX	ME SO	ME	ME	ME	ME	ME	ME	ME	ME	ME	ME	ME	ME	ME	ME	ME	ME	ME	ME
Liverpool Central 10	d	16 47	16 50	16 50	16 53	17 02	17 05	17 08	17 17	17 20	17 23	17 32	17 35	17 38	17 47	17 50	17 53	18 02	18 05	18 08	18 17	18 20
Moorfields 10	d	16 50	16 53	16 53	16 56	17 05	17 08	17 11	17 20	17 23	17 26	17 35	17 38	17 41	17 50	17 53	17 56	18 05	18 08	18 11	18 20	18 23
Sandhills	d	16 53	16 55	16 56	16a59	17 08	17 11	17a14	17 23	17 26	17a29	17 38	17 41	17a44	17 53	17 56	17a59	18 08	18 11	18a14	18 23	18 26
Kirkdale	d	16 56	16a58	16a59		17 11	17a14		17 26	17a29		17 41	17a44		17 56	17a59		18 11	18a14		18 26	18a29
Walton	d	16 59				17 14			17 29			17 44			17 59			18 14			18 29	
Orrell Park	d	17 00				17 15			17 30			17 45			18 00			18 15			18 30	
Aintree	d	17 03				17 18			17 33			17 48			18 03			18 18			18 33	
Old Roan	d	17 05				17 20			17 35			17 50			18 05			18 20			18 35	
Maghull	d	17 08				17 23			17 38			17 53			18 08			18 23			18 38	
Maghull North	d	17 10				17 25			17 40			17 55			18 10			18 25			18 40	
Town Green	d	17 14				17 29			17 44			17 59			18 14			18 29			18 44	
Aughton Park	d	17 16				17 31			17 46			18 01			18 16			18 31			18 46	
Ormskirk	a	17 22				17 37			17 52			18 07			18 22			18 37			18 52	

		ME	ME	ME	ME	ME	ME	ME	ME	ME	ME	ME	ME	ME	ME	ME	ME	ME	ME	ME	ME	ME	ME
Liverpool Central 10	d	18 23	18 32	18 35	18 38	18 47	18 50	18 53	19 02	19 05	19 08	19 17	19 20	19 23	19 35	19 38	19 47	19 53	20 05	20 08	20 17	20 23	20 35
Moorfields 10	d	18 26	18 35	18 38	18 41	18 50	18 53	18 56	19 05	19 08	19 11	19 20	19 23	19 26	19 38	19 41	19 50	19 55	20 08	20 11	20 20	20 25	20 38
Sandhills	d	18a29	18 38	18 41	18a44	18 53	18 56	18a59	19 08	19 11	19a14	19 23	19 26	19a29	19 41	19a44	19 53	19a59	20 11	20a14	20 23	20a29	20 41
Kirkdale	d		18 41	18a44		18 56	18a59		19 11	19a14		19 26	19a29		19a44		19 56		20a14		20 26		20a44
Walton	d		18 44			18 59			19 14			19 29					19 59				20 29		
Orrell Park	d		18 45			19 00			19 15			19 30					20 00				20 30		
Aintree	d		18 48			19 03			19 18			19 33					20 03				20 33		
Old Roan	d		18 50			19 05			19 20			19 35					20 05				20 35		
Maghull	d		18 53			19 08			19 23			19 38					20 08				20 38		
Maghull North	d		18 55			19 10			19 25			19 40					20 10				20 40		
Town Green	d		18 59			19 14			19 29			19 44					20 14				20 44		
Aughton Park	d		19 01			19 16			19 31			19 46					20 16				20 46		
Ormskirk	a		19 07			19 22			19 37			19 52					20 22				20 52		

		ME	ME	ME	ME	ME	ME	ME	ME	ME	ME	ME	ME	ME	ME	ME	ME	ME	ME	ME	ME	ME	ME
Liverpool Central 10	d	20 38	20 47	20 53	21 05	21 08	21 17	21 23	21 35	21 38	21 47	21 53	22 05	22 08	22 17	22 23	22 35	22 38	22 47	22 53	23 05	23 08	23 17
Moorfields 10	d	20 41	20 50	20 55	21 08	21 11	21 20	21 25	21 38	21 41	21 50	21 55	22 08	22 11	22 20	22 25	22 38	22 41	22 50	22 56	23 08	23 11	23 20
Sandhills	d	20a44	20 53	20a59	21 11	21a14	21 23	21a28	21 41	21a44	21 53	21a59	22 11	22a14	22 23	22a29	22 41	22a44	22 53	22a59	23 11	23a14	23 23
Kirkdale	d		20 56		21a14		21 26		21a44		21 56		22a14		22 26		22a44		22 56		23a14		23 26
Walton	d		20 59				21 29				21 59				22 29				22 59				23 29
Orrell Park	d		21 00				21 30				22 00				22 30				23 00				23 30
Aintree	d		21 03				21 33				22 03				22 33				23 03				23 33
Old Roan	d		21 05				21 35				22 05				22 35				23 05				23 35
Maghull	d		21 08				21 38				22 08				22 38				23 08				23 38
Maghull North	d		21 10				21 40				22 10				22 40				23 10				23 40
Town Green	d		21 14				21 44				22 14				22 44				23 14				23 44
Aughton Park	d		21 16				21 46				22 16				22 46				23 16				23 46
Ormskirk	a		21 22				21 52				22 22				22 52				23 22				23 52

		ME	ME	ME	ME	ME
Liverpool Central 10	d	23 23	23 35	23 38	23 47	23 55
Moorfields 10	d	23 26	23 38	23 41	23 50	23 58
Sandhills	d	23a29	23 41	23a44	23 53	00 01
Kirkdale	d		23a44		23 56	00a04
Walton	d				23 59	
Orrell Park	d				00 01	
Aintree	d				00 04	
Old Roan	d				00 06	
Maghull	d				00 09	
Maghull North	d				00 10	
Town Green	d				00 15	
Aughton Park	d				00 16	
Ormskirk	a				00 22	

For additional trains between Liverpool and Kirkdale refer to Table T104

For additional trains between Liverpool and Sandhills refer to Tables T103 and T104

Table T105-F

Sundays

15 December to 10 May

Liverpool Central - Ormskirk

		ME A	ME A	ME	ME	ME	ME	ME	ME	ME	ME		ME	ME	ME	ME	ME	ME	ME	ME	ME	ME	ME
Liverpool Central 10	d			08 05	08 08	08 17	08 23	08 35	08 47	08 53	09 05	and at the same minutes past each hour until	22 17	22 23	22 35	22 47	22 53	23 05	23 17	23 23	23 35	23 38	23 47
Moorfields 10	d			08 08	08 10	08 20	08 25	08 38	08 50	08 55	09 08		22 20	22 25	22 38	22 50	22 55	23 08	23 20	23 25	23 38	23 40	23 50
Sandhills	d		00 01	08 11	08a14	08 23	08a29	08 41	08 53	08a59	09 11		22 23	22a29	22 41	22 53	22a59	23 11	23 23	23a29	23 41	23a44	23 53
Kirkdale	d		00a04	08a14		08 26		08a44	08 56		09a14		22 26		22a44	22 56		23a14	23 26		23a44		23 56
Walton	d					08 29			08 59				22 29			22 59			23 29				23 59
Orrell Park	d	00 01				08 30			09 00				22 30			23 00			23 30				00 01
Aintree	d	00 04				08 33			09 03				22 33			23 03			23 33				00 04
Old Roan	d	00 06				08 35			09 05				22 35			23 05			23 35				00 06
Maghull	d	00 09				08 38			09 08				22 38			23 08			23 38				00 09
Maghull North	d	00 10				08 40			09 10				22 40			23 10			23 40				00 11
Town Green	d	00 15				08 44			09 14				22 44			23 14			23 44				00 15
Aughton Park	d	00 16				08 46			09 16				22 46			23 16			23 46				00 17
Ormskirk	a	00 22				08 52			09 22				22 52			23 22			23 52				00 22

		ME
Liverpool Central 10	d	23 55
Moorfields 10	d	23 58
Sandhills	d	00 01
Kirkdale	d	00a04
Walton	d	
Orrell Park	d	
Aintree	d	
Old Roan	d	
Maghull	d	
Maghull North	d	
Town Green	d	
Aughton Park	d	
Ormskirk	a	

A not 15 December

For additional trains between Liverpool and Kirkdale refer to Table T104

For additional trains between Liverpool and Sandhills refer to Tables T103 and T104

Table T105-R

Mondays to Saturdays

16 December to 16 May

Ormskirk - Liverpool Central

Miles			ME MX	ME MO	ME	ME	ME	ME	ME	ME	ME	ME	ME	ME	ME	ME	ME	ME	ME	ME	ME	ME	ME
0	**Ormskirk**	d					05 49				06 19				06 49			07 04			07 19		
1¼	Aughton Park	d					05 52				06 22				06 52			07 07			07 22		
2¼	Town Green	d					05 54				06 24				06 54			07 09			07 24		
4	Maghull North	d					05 58				06 28				06 58			07 13			07 28		
4¾	Maghull	d					06 01				06 31				07 01			07 16			07 31		
6½	Old Roan	d					06 04				06 34				07 04			07 19			07 34		
7¼	Aintree	d					06 06				06 36				07 06			07 21			07 36		
8¼	Orrell Park	d					06 08				06 38				07 08			07 23			07 38		
8½	Walton	d					06 11				06 41				07 11			07 26			07 41		
9¾	Kirkdale	d	00 02	00 02	05 52		06 14		06 22		06 44		06 52		07 14		07 22	07 29		07 37	07 44		07 52
10¾	Sandhills	d	00 04	00 04	05 55	06 06	06 16	06 21	06 25	06 36	06 46	06 51	06 55	07 06	07 16	07 21	07 25	07 31	07 36	07 40	07 46	07 51	07 55
12¼	**Moorfields** 10	d	00 08	00 08	05 58	06 10	06 20	06 25	06 28	06 40	06 50	06 55	06 58	07 10	07 20	07 25	07 28	07 35	07 40	07 43	07 50	07 55	07 58
12¾	**Liverpool Central** 10	a	00 11	00 12	06 01	06 13	06 23	06 28	06 31	06 43	06 53	06 58	07 01	07 13	07 23	07 28	07 31	07 38	07 43	07 46	07 53	07 58	08 01

		ME	ME	ME	ME	ME	ME	ME	ME	ME	ME	ME	ME	ME	ME	ME	ME	ME	ME	ME	ME	ME
Ormskirk	d	07 34			07 49			08 04			08 19			08 34			08 49			09 04		
Aughton Park	d	07 37			07 52			08 07			08 22			08 37			08 52			09 07		
Town Green	d	07 39			07 54			08 09			08 24			08 39			08 54			09 09		
Maghull North	d	07 43			07 58			08 13			08 28			08 43			08 58			09 13		
Maghull	d	07 46			08 01			08 16			08 31			08 46			09 01			09 16		
Old Roan	d	07 49			08 04			08 19			08 34			08 49			09 04			09 19		
Aintree	d	07 51			08 06			08 21			08 36			08 51			09 06			09 21		
Orrell Park	d	07 53			08 08			08 23			08 38			08 53			09 08			09 23		
Walton	d	07 56			08 11			08 26			08 41			08 56			09 11			09 26		
Kirkdale	d	07 59		08 07	08 14		08 22	08 29		08 37	08 44		08 52	08 59		09 07	09 14		09 22	09 29		09 37
Sandhills	d	08 01	08 06	08 10	08 16	08 21	08 25	08 31	08 36	08 40	08 46	08 51	08 55	09 01	09 06	09 10	09 16	09 21	09 25	09 31	09 36	09 40
Moorfields 10	d	08 05	08 10	08 13	08 20	08 25	08 28	08 35	08 40	08 43	08 50	08 55	08 58	09 05	09 10	09 13	09 20	09 25	09 28	09 35	09 40	09 43
Liverpool Central 10	a	08 08	08 13	08 16	08 23	08 28	08 31	08 38	08 43	08 46	08 53	08 58	09 01	09 08	09 13	09 16	09 23	09 28	09 31	09 38	09 43	09 46

		ME	ME	ME	ME	ME	ME	ME	ME	ME	ME	ME	ME	ME	ME	ME	ME	ME	ME	ME	ME	ME	ME
Ormskirk	d	09 19			09 34			09 49			10 04			10 19			10 34			10 49			11 04
Aughton Park	d	09 22			09 37			09 52			10 07			10 22			10 37			10 52			11 07
Town Green	d	09 24			09 39			09 54			10 09			10 24			10 39			10 54			11 09
Maghull North	d	09 28			09 43			09 58			10 13			10 28			10 43			10 58			11 13
Maghull	d	09 31			09 46			10 01			10 16			10 31			10 46			11 01			11 16
Old Roan	d	09 34			09 49			10 04			10 19			10 34			10 49			11 04			11 19
Aintree	d	09 36			09 51			10 06			10 21			10 36			10 51			11 06			11 21
Orrell Park	d	09 38			09 53			10 08			10 23			10 38			10 53			11 08			11 23
Walton	d	09 41			09 56			10 11			10 26			10 41			10 56			11 11			11 26
Kirkdale	d	09 44		09 52	09 59		10 07	10 14		10 22	10 29		10 37	10 44		10 52	10 59		11 07	11 14		11 22	11 29
Sandhills	d	09 46	09 51	09 55	10 01	10 06	10 10	10 16	10 21	10 25	10 31	10 36	10 40	10 46	10 51	10 55	11 01	11 06	11 10	11 16	11 21	11 25	11 31
Moorfields 10	d	09 50	09 55	09 58	10 05	10 10	10 13	10 20	10 25	10 28	10 35	10 40	10 43	10 50	10 55	10 58	11 05	11 10	11 13	11 20	11 25	11 28	11 35
Liverpool Central 10	a	09 53	09 58	10 01	10 08	10 13	10 16	10 23	10 28	10 31	10 38	10 43	10 46	10 53	10 58	11 01	11 08	11 13	11 16	11 23	11 28	11 31	11 38

		ME	ME	ME	ME	ME	ME	ME	ME	ME	ME	ME	ME	ME	ME	ME	ME	ME	ME	ME	ME	ME	ME
Ormskirk	d			11 19			11 34			11 49			12 04			12 19			12 34			12 49	
Aughton Park	d			11 22			11 37			11 52			12 07			12 22			12 37			12 52	
Town Green	d			11 24			11 39			11 54			12 09			12 24			12 39			12 54	
Maghull North	d			11 28			11 43			11 58			12 13			12 28			12 43			12 58	
Maghull	d			11 31			11 46			12 01			12 16			12 31			12 46			13 01	
Old Roan	d			11 34			11 49			12 04			12 19			12 34			12 49			13 04	
Aintree	d			11 36			11 51			12 06			12 21			12 36			12 51			13 06	
Orrell Park	d			11 38			11 53			12 08			12 23			12 38			12 53			13 08	
Walton	d			11 41			11 56			12 11			12 26			12 41			12 56			13 11	
Kirkdale	d		11 37	11 44		11 52	11 59		12 07	12 14		12 22	12 29		12 37	12 44		12 52	12 59		13 07	13 14	
Sandhills	d	11 36	11 40	11 46	11 51	11 55	12 01	12 06	12 10	12 16	12 21	12 25	12 31	12 36	12 40	12 46	12 51	12 55	13 01	13 06	13 10	13 16	13 21
Moorfields 10	d	11 40	11 43	11 50	11 55	11 58	12 05	12 10	12 13	12 20	12 25	12 28	12 35	12 40	12 43	12 50	12 55	12 58	13 05	13 10	13 13	13 20	13 25
Liverpool Central 10	a	11 43	11 46	11 53	11 58	12 01	12 08	12 13	12 16	12 23	12 28	12 31	12 38	12 43	12 46	12 53	12 58	13 01	13 08	13 13	13 16	13 23	13 28

		ME	ME	ME	ME	ME	ME	ME	ME	ME	ME	ME	ME	ME	ME	ME	ME	ME	ME	ME	ME	ME
Ormskirk	d		13 04			13 19			13 34			13 49			14 04			14 19			14 34	
Aughton Park	d		13 07			13 22			13 37			13 52			14 07			14 22			14 37	
Town Green	d		13 09			13 24			13 39			13 54			14 09			14 24			14 39	
Maghull North	d		13 13			13 28			13 43			13 58			14 13			14 28			14 43	
Maghull	d		13 16			13 31			13 46			14 01			14 16			14 31			14 46	
Old Roan	d		13 19			13 34			13 49			14 04			14 19			14 34			14 49	
Aintree	d		13 21			13 36			13 51			14 06			14 21			14 36			14 51	
Orrell Park	d		13 23			13 38			13 53			14 08			14 23			14 38			14 53	
Walton	d		13 26			13 41			13 56			14 11			14 26			14 41			14 56	
Kirkdale	d	13 22	13 29		13 37	13 44		13 52	13 59		14 07	14 14		14 22	14 29		14 37	14 44		14 52	14 59	
Sandhills	d	13 25	13 31	13 36	13 40	13 46	13 51	13 55	14 01	14 06	14 10	14 16	14 21	14 25	14 31	14 36	14 40	14 46	14 51	14 55	15 01	15 06
Moorfields 10	d	13 28	13 35	13 40	13 43	13 50	13 55	13 58	14 05	14 10	14 13	14 20	14 25	14 28	14 35	14 40	14 43	14 50	14 55	14 58	15 05	15 10
Liverpool Central 10	a	13 31	13 38	13 43	13 46	13 53	13 58	14 01	14 08	14 13	14 16	14 23	14 28	14 31	14 38	14 43	14 46	14 53	14 58	15 01	15 08	15 13

For additional trains between Liverpool and Kirkdale refer to Table T104

For additional trains between Liverpool and Sandhills refer to Tables T103 and T104

Table T105-R

Mondays to Saturdays

16 December to 16 May

Ormskirk - Liverpool Central

		ME SO	ME SX	ME	ME	ME	ME	ME	ME	ME	ME	ME	ME	ME	ME	ME	ME	ME	ME	ME	ME	ME
Ormskirk	d			14 49			15 04			15 19			15 34			15 49			16 04			16 19
Aughton Park	d			14 52			15 07			15 22			15 37			15 52			16 07			16 22
Town Green	d			14 54			15 09			15 24			15 39			15 54			16 09			16 24
Maghull North	d			14 58			15 13			15 28			15 43			15 58			16 13			16 28
Maghull	d			15 01			15 16			15 31			15 46			16 01			16 16			16 31
Old Roan	d			15 04			15 19			15 34			15 49			16 04			16 19			16 34
Aintree	d			15 06			15 21			15 36			15 51			16 06			16 21			16 36
Orrell Park	d			15 08			15 23			15 38			15 53			16 08			16 23			16 38
Walton	d			15 11			15 26			15 41			15 56			16 11			16 26			16 41
Kirkdale	d	15 07	15 07	15 14		15 22	15 29		15 37	15 44		15 52	15 59		16 07	16 14		16 22	16 29		16 37	16 44
Sandhills	d	15 10	15 10	15 16	15 21	15 25	15 31	15 36	15 40	15 46	15 51	15 55	16 01	16 06	16 10	16 16	16 21	16 25	16 31	16 36	16 40	16 46
Moorfields 10	d	15 13	15 13	15 20	15 25	15 28	15 35	15 40	15 43	15 50	15 55	15 58	16 05	16 10	16 13	16 20	16 25	16 28	16 35	16 40	16 43	16 50
Liverpool Central 10	a	15 16	15 17	15 23	15 28	15 31	15 38	15 43	15 46	15 53	15 58	16 01	16 08	16 13	16 16	16 23	16 28	16 31	16 38	16 43	16 46	16 53

		ME	ME	ME	ME	ME SX	ME SO	ME	ME	ME	ME	ME	ME	ME	ME	ME	ME	ME	ME	ME	ME	ME	ME
Ormskirk	d			16 34				16 49			17 04			17 19			17 34			17 49			18 04
Aughton Park	d			16 37				16 52			17 07			17 22			17 37			17 52			18 07
Town Green	d			16 39				16 54			17 09			17 24			17 39			17 54			18 09
Maghull North	d			16 43				16 58			17 13			17 28			17 43			17 58			18 13
Maghull	d			16 46				17 01			17 16			17 31			17 46			18 01			18 16
Old Roan	d			16 49				17 04			17 19			17 34			17 49			18 04			18 19
Aintree	d			16 51				17 06			17 21			17 36			17 51			18 06			18 21
Orrell Park	d			16 53				17 08			17 23			17 38			17 53			18 08			18 23
Walton	d			16 56				17 11			17 26			17 41			17 56			18 11			18 26
Kirkdale	d		16 52	16 59		17 07	17 07	17 14		17 22	17 29		17 37	17 44		17 52	17 59		18 07	18 14		18 22	18 29
Sandhills	d	16 51	16 55	17 01	17 06	17 10	17 10	17 16	17 21	17 25	17 31	17 36	17 40	17 46	17 51	17 55	18 01	18 06	18 10	18 16	18 21	18 25	18 31
Moorfields 10	d	16 55	16 58	17 05	17 10	17 13	17 14	17 20	17 25	17 28	17 35	17 40	17 43	17 50	17 55	17 58	18 05	18 10	18 13	18 20	18 25	18 28	18 35
Liverpool Central 10	a	16 58	17 01	17 08	17 13	17 16	17 16	17 23	17 28	17 31	17 38	17 43	17 46	17 53	17 58	18 01	18 08	18 13	18 16	18 23	18 28	18 31	18 38

		ME	ME	ME	ME	ME	ME	ME	ME	ME	ME	ME	ME	ME	ME	ME	ME	ME	ME SO	ME SX	ME	ME	ME
Ormskirk	d			18 19			18 34			18 49			19 04			19 19			19 34	19 34			
Aughton Park	d			18 22			18 37			18 52			19 07			19 22			19 37	19 37			
Town Green	d			18 24			18 39			18 54			19 09			19 24			19 39	19 39			
Maghull North	d			18 28			18 43			18 58			19 13			19 28			19 43	19 43			
Maghull	d			18 31			18 46			19 01			19 16			19 31			19 46	19 46			
Old Roan	d			18 34			18 49			19 04			19 19			19 34			19 49	19 49			
Aintree	d			18 36			18 51			19 06			19 21			19 36			19 51	19 51			
Orrell Park	d			18 38			18 53			19 08			19 23			19 38			19 53	19 53			
Walton	d			18 41			18 56			19 11			19 26			19 41			19 56	19 56			
Kirkdale	d		18 37	18 44		18 52	18 59		19 07	19 14		19 22	19 29		19 37	19 44		19 52	19 59	19 59			20 22
Sandhills	d	18 36	18 40	18 46	18 51	18 55	19 01	19 06	19 10	19 16	19 21	19 25	19 31	19 36	19 40	19 46	19 51	19 55	20 01	20 01	20 06	20 21	20 25
Moorfields 10	d	18 40	18 43	18 50	18 55	18 58	19 05	19 10	19 13	19 20	19 25	19 28	19 35	19 40	19 43	19 50	19 55	19 58	20 05	20 05	20 10	20 25	20 28
Liverpool Central 10	a	18 43	18 46	18 53	18 58	19 01	19 08	19 13	19 16	19 23	19 28	19 31	19 38	19 43	19 46	19 53	19 58	20 01	20 08	20 11	20 13	20 28	20 31

		ME	ME	ME	ME	ME	ME	ME	ME	ME	ME	ME	ME	ME	ME	ME	ME	ME	ME	ME	ME	ME
Ormskirk	d	20 07				20 37				21 07					21 37				22 07			22 37
Aughton Park	d	20 10				20 40				21 10					21 40				22 10			22 40
Town Green	d	20 12				20 42				21 12					21 42				22 12			22 42
Maghull North	d	20 16				20 46				21 16					21 46				22 16			22 46
Maghull	d	20 19				20 49				21 19					21 49				22 19			22 49
Old Roan	d	20 22				20 52				21 22					21 52				22 22			22 52
Aintree	d	20 24				20 54				21 24					21 54				22 24			22 54
Orrell Park	d	20 26				20 56				21 26					21 56				22 26			22 56
Walton	d	20 29				20 58				21 28					21 58				22 28			22 58
Kirkdale	d	20 32			20 52	21 01			21 22	21 31				21 52	22 01			22 22	22 31		22 52	23 01
Sandhills	d	20 34	20 36	20 51	20 55	21 03	21 06	21 21	21 25	21 33	21 36	21 51	21 55	22 03	22 06	22 21	22 25	22 33	22 36	22 51	22 55	23 03
Moorfields 10	d	20 38	20 40	20 55	20 58	21 07	21 10	21 25	21 28	21 37	21 40	21 55	21 58	22 07	22 10	22 25	22 28	22 37	22 40	22 55	22 58	23 07
Liverpool Central 10	a	20 41	20 43	20 58	21 01	21 11	21 13	21 28	21 31	21 41	21 44	21 58	22 01	22 11	22 13	22 28	22 31	22 41	22 43	22 58	23 01	23 11

		ME	ME	ME	ME	ME	ME	ME
Ormskirk	d				23 07			23 37
Aughton Park	d				23 10			23 40
Town Green	d				23 12			23 42
Maghull North	d				23 16			23 46
Maghull	d				23 19			23 49
Old Roan	d				23 22			23 52
Aintree	d				23 24			23 54
Orrell Park	d				23 26			23 56
Walton	d				23 28			23 59
Kirkdale	d			23 22	23 31			00 02
Sandhills	d	23 06	23 21	23 25	23 33	23 36	23 56	00 04
Moorfields 10	d	23 10	23 25	23 28	23 37	23 40	23 59	00 08
Liverpool Central 10	a	23 13	23 28	23 31	23 41	23 43	00 03	00 11

For additional trains between Liverpool and Kirkdale refer to Table T104

For additional trains between Liverpool and Sandhills refer to Tables T103 and T104

Table T105-R

Sundays

15 December to 10 May

Ormskirk - Liverpool Central

		ME A	ME	ME	ME	ME	ME	ME		ME	ME	ME	ME	ME	ME	ME	ME	ME	ME	ME
Ormskirk	d			08 07			08 37		and at the same minutes past each hour until		22 07			22 37			23 07			23 37
Aughton Park	d			08 10			08 40				22 10			22 40			23 10			23 40
Town Green	d			08 12			08 42				22 12			22 42			23 12			23 42
Maghull North	d			08 16			08 46				22 16			22 46			23 16			23 46
Maghull	d			08 19			08 49				22 19			22 49			23 19			23 49
Old Roan	d			08 22			08 52				22 22			22 52			23 22			23 52
Aintree	d			08 24			08 54				22 24			22 54			23 24			23 54
Orrell Park	d			08 26			08 56				22 26			22 56			23 26			23 56
Walton	d			08 28			08 58				22 28			22 58			23 28			23 59
Kirkdale	d	00 02	08 22	08 31		08 52	09 01			22 22	22 31		22 52	23 01		23 22	23 31			00 02
Sandhills	d	00 04	08 25	08 33	08 36	08 55	09 03	09 06		22 25	22 33	22 36	22 55	23 03	23 06	23 25	23 33	23 36	23 56	00 04
Moorfields 10	d	00 08	08 28	08 37	08 40	08 58	09 07	09 10		22 28	22 37	22 40	22 58	23 07	23 10	23 28	23 37	23 40	23 59	00 08
Liverpool Central 10	a	00 11	08 31	08 41	08 43	09 01	09 11	09 13		22 31	22 41	22 43	23 01	23 11	23 13	23 31	23 42	23 44	00 03	00 12

A not 15 December

For additional trains between Liverpool and Kirkdale refer to Table T104

For additional trains between Liverpool and Sandhills refer to Tables T103 and T104

AVAILABLE FROM MP Middleton Press

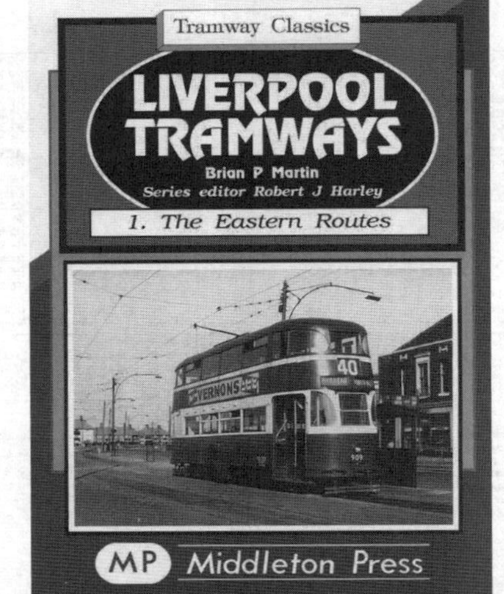

Tramway Classics
LIVERPOOL TRAMWAYS
Brian P Martin
Series editor Robert J Harley
1. The Eastern Routes
MP Middleton Press

Table T106-F

Mondays to Saturdays
16 December to 16 May

Liverpool and Birkenhead - New Brighton and West Kirby

Miles	Miles			ME	ME	ME	ME	ME	ME	ME	ME	ME	ME	ME	ME	ME	ME SO	ME SX	ME	ME	ME	ME	ME
0	0	Moorfields 10	d			06 16	06 21	06 46	06 51	07 16	07 21	07 31	07 36	07 46	07 51	08 01	08 06	08 06	08 16	08 21	08 31	08 36	08 46
0½	0½	Liverpool Lime Street 10	d			06 18	06 23	06 48	06 53	07 18	07 23	07 33	07 38	07 48	07 53	08 03	08 08	08 08	08 18	08 23	08 33	08 38	08 48
1	1	Liverpool Central 10	d			06 20	06 25	06 50	06 55	07 20	07 25	07 35	07 40	07 50	07 55	08 05	08 10	08 10	08 20	08 25	08 35	08 40	08 50
1½	1½	James Street	d			06 22	06 27	06 52	06 57	07 22	07 27	07 37	07 42	07 52	07 57	08 07	08 12	08 12	08 22	08 27	08 37	08 42	08 52
2¾	2¾	Hamilton Square	d			06 25	06 30	06 55	07 00	07 25	07 30	07 40	07 45	07 55	08 00	08 10	08 15	08 15	08 25	08 30	08 40	08 45	08 55
3¼	3¼	Conway Park	d			06 27	06 32	06 57	07 02	07 27	07 32	07 42	07 47	07 57	08 02	08 12	08 17	08 17	08 27	08 32	08 42	08 47	08 57
4	4	Birkenhead Park	d			06 29	06 34	06 59	07 04	07 29	07 34	07 44	07 49	07 59	08 04	08 14	08 19	08 20	08 29	08 34	08 44	08 49	08 59
4¾	4¾	Birkenhead North	d		00 02	06 32	06 37	07 02	07 07	07 32	07 37	07 47	07 52	08 02	08 07	08 17	08 22	08 22	08 32	08 37	08 47	08 52	09 02
—	6¼	Wallasey Village	d		00 07	06 37		07 07		07 37		07 52		08 07		08 22			08 37		08 52		09 07
—	6½	Wallasey Grove Road	d		00 08	06 38		07 08		07 38		07 53		08 08		08 23			08 38		08 53		09 08
—	7¾	**New Brighton**	a		00 13	06 43		07 13		07 43		07 58		08 13		08 28			08 43		08 58		09 13
5¼	—	Bidston	d				06 40		07 10		07 40		07 55		08 10		08 25	08 25		08 40		08 55	
6½	—	Leasowe	d				06 42		07 12		07 42		07 57		08 12		08 27	08 27		08 42		08 57	
7	—	Moreton	d				06 44		07 14		07 44		07 59		08 14		08 29	08 29		08 44		08 59	
8¼	—	Meols	d				06 48		07 18		07 48		08 03		08 18		08 33	08 33		08 48		09 03	
9½	—	Manor Road	d				06 50		07 20		07 50		08 05		08 20		08 35	08 35		08 50		09 05	
10	—	Hoylake	d	00 02			06 52		07 22		07 52		08 07		08 22		08 37	08 37		08 52		09 07	
11¼	—	**West Kirby**	a	00 07			06 57		07 27		07 57		08 12		08 27		08 42	08 42		08 57		09 12	

		ME SX	ME	ME	ME	ME	ME	ME	ME	ME		ME	ME	ME	ME	ME	ME	ME	ME	ME	ME	ME
Moorfields 10	d	08 48	08 51	09 01	09 06	09 16	09 21	09 31	09 36	09 46	and at the same minutes past each hour until	17 51	18 01	18 06	18 16	18 21	18 31	18 36	18 46	18 51	19 01	19 06
Liverpool Lime Street 10	d	08 50	08 53	09 03	09 08	09 18	09 23	09 33	09 38	09 48		17 53	18 03	18 08	18 18	18 23	18 33	18 38	18 48	18 53	19 03	19 08
Liverpool Central 10	d	08 52	08 55	09 05	09 10	09 20	09 25	09 35	09 40	09 50		17 55	18 05	18 10	18 20	18 25	18 35	18 40	18 50	18 55	19 05	19 10
James Street	d	08 54	08 57	09 07	09 12	09 22	09 27	09 37	09 42	09 52		17 57	18 07	18 12	18 22	18 27	18 37	18 42	18 52	18 57	19 07	19 12
Hamilton Square	d	08 57	09 00	09 10	09 15	09 25	09 30	09 40	09 45	09 55		18 00	18 10	18 15	18 25	18 30	18 40	18 45	18 55	19 00	19 10	19 15
Conway Park	d	09 00	09 02	09 12	09 17	09 27	09 32	09 42	09 47	09 57		18 02	18 12	18 17	18 27	18 32	18 42	18 47	18 57	19 02	19 12	19 17
Birkenhead Park	d	09 02	09 04	09 14	09 19	09 29	09 34	09 44	09 49	09 59		18 04	18 14	18 19	18 29	18 34	18 44	18 49	18 59	19 04	19 14	19 19
Birkenhead North	d	09a05	09 07	09 17	09 22	09 32	09 37	09 47	09 52	10 02		18 07	18 17	18 22	18 32	18 37	18 47	18 52	19 02	19 07	19 17	19 22
Wallasey Village	d			09 22		09 37		09 52		10 07			18 22		18 37		18 52		19 07		19 22	
Wallasey Grove Road	d			09 23		09 38		09 53		10 08			18 23		18 38		18 53		19 08		19 23	
New Brighton	a			09 28		09 43		09 58		10 13			18 28		18 43		18 58		19 13		19 28	
Bidston	d		09 10		09 25		09 40		09 55			18 10		18 25		18 40		18 55		19 10		19 25
Leasowe	d		09 12		09 27		09 42		09 57			18 12		18 27		18 42		18 57		19 12		19 27
Moreton	d		09 14		09 29		09 44		09 59			18 14		18 29		18 44		18 59		19 14		19 29
Meols	d		09 18		09 33		09 48		10 03			18 18		18 33		18 48		19 03		19 18		19 33
Manor Road	d		09 20		09 35		09 50		10 05			18 20		18 35		18 50		19 05		19 20		19 35
Hoylake	d		09 22		09 37		09 52		10 07			18 22		18 37		18 52		19 07		19 22		19 37
West Kirby	a		09 27		09 42		09 57		10 12			18 27		18 42		18 57		19 12		19 27		19 42

		ME	ME	ME	ME		ME	ME	ME	ME	ME	ME	ME
Moorfields 10	d	19 16	19 31	19 46	20 01	and at the same minutes past each hour until	22 16	22 31	22 46	23 01	23 16	23 31	23 46
Liverpool Lime Street 10	d	19 18	19 33	19 48	20 03		22 18	22 33	22 48	23 03	23 18	23 33	23 48
Liverpool Central 10	d	19 20	19 35	19 50	20 05		22 20	22 35	22 50	23 05	23 20	23 35	23 50
James Street	d	19 22	19 37	19 52	20 07		22 22	22 37	22 52	23 07	23 22	23 37	23 52
Hamilton Square	d	19 25	19 40	19 55	20 10		22 25	22 40	22 55	23 10	23 25	23 40	23 55
Conway Park	d	19 27	19 42	19 57	20 12		22 27	22 42	22 57	23 12	23 27	23 42	23 57
Birkenhead Park	d	19 29	19 44	19 59	20 14		22 29	22 44	22 59	23 14	23 29	23 44	23 59
Birkenhead North	d	19 32	19 47	20 02	20 17		22 32	22 47	23 02	23 17	23 32	23 47	00 02
Wallasey Village	d	19 37		20 07			22 37		23 07		23 37		00 07
Wallasey Grove Road	d	19 38		20 08			22 38		23 08		23 38		00 08
New Brighton	a	19 43		20 13			22 43		23 13		23 43		00 13
Bidston	d		19 50		20 20			22 50		23 20		23 50	
Leasowe	d		19 52		20 22			22 52		23 22		23 52	
Moreton	d		19 54		20 24			22 54		23 24		23 54	
Meols	d		19 58		20 28			22 58		23 28		23 58	
Manor Road	d		20 00		20 30			23 00		23 30		23 59	
Hoylake	d		20 02		20 32			23 02		23 32		00 02	
West Kirby	a		20 07		20 37			23 07		23 37		00 07	

Sundays
15 December to 10 May

		ME A	ME A	ME	ME	ME	ME		ME	ME	ME	ME	ME	ME	ME	ME
Moorfields 10	d			08 01	08 16	08 31	08 46	and at the same minutes past each hour until	22 01	22 16	22 31	22 46	23 01	23 16	23 31	23 46
Liverpool Lime Street 10	d			08 03	08 18	08 33	08 48		22 03	22 18	22 33	22 48	23 03	23 18	23 33	23 48
Liverpool Central 10	d			08 05	08 20	08 35	08 50		22 05	22 20	22 35	22 50	23 05	23 20	23 35	23 50
James Street	d			08 07	08 22	08 37	08 52		22 07	22 22	22 37	22 52	23 07	23 22	23 37	23 52
Hamilton Square	d			08 10	08 25	08 40	08 55		22 10	22 25	22 40	22 55	23 10	23 25	23 40	23 55
Conway Park	d			08 12	08 27	08 42	08 57		22 12	22 27	22 42	22 57	23 12	23 27	23 42	23 57
Birkenhead Park	d			08 14	08 29	08 44	08 59		22 14	22 29	22 44	22 59	23 14	23 29	23 44	23 59
Birkenhead North	d		00 02	08 17	08 32	08 47	09 02		22 17	22 32	22 47	23 02	23 17	23 32	23 47	00 02
Wallasey Village	d		00 07		08 37		09 07			22 37		23 07		23 37		00 07
Wallasey Grove Road	d		00 08		08 38		09 08			22 38		23 08		23 38		00 08
New Brighton	a		00 13		08 43		09 13			22 43		23 13		23 43		00 13
Bidston	d			08 20		08 50			22 20		22 50		23 20		23 50	
Leasowe	d			08 22		08 52			22 22		22 52		23 22		23 52	
Moreton	d			08 24		08 54			22 24		22 54		23 24		23 54	
Meols	d			08 28		08 58			22 28		22 58		23 28		23 58	
Manor Road	d			08 30		09 00			22 30		23 00		23 30		23 59	
Hoylake	d	00 02		08 32		09 02			22 32		23 02		23 32		00 02	
West Kirby	a	00 07		08 37		09 07			22 37		23 07		23 37		00 07	

A not 15 December

Table T106-R

Mondays to Saturdays
16 December to 16 May

West Kirby and New Brighton - Birkenhead and Liverpool

Miles	Miles			ME	ME	ME	ME	ME	ME	ME	ME	ME	ME	ME	ME		ME	ME	ME	ME	ME	ME	ME
0	—	**West Kirby**	d		05 51		06 21		06 51		07 06		07 21		07 36	and at the same minutes past each hour until		17 51		18 06		18 21	
1	—	Hoylake	d		05 54		06 24		06 54		07 09		07 24		07 39			17 54		18 09		18 24	
1¾	—	Manor Road	d		05 56		06 26		06 56		07 11		07 26		07 41			17 56		18 11		18 26	
3	—	Meols	d		05 58		06 28		06 58		07 13		07 28		07 43			17 58		18 13		18 28	
4¼	—	Moreton	d		06 01		06 31		07 01		07 16		07 31		07 46			18 01		18 16		18 31	
4¾	—	Leasowe	d		06 03		06 33		07 03		07 18		07 33		07 48			18 03		18 18		18 33	
5½	—	Bidston	d		06 06		06 36		07 06		07 21		07 36		07 51			18 06		18 21		18 36	
—	0	**New Brighton**	d	05 53		06 23		06 53		07 08		07 23		07 38			17 53		18 08		18 23		18 38
—	1¼	Wallasey Grove Road	d	05 57		06 27		06 57		07 12		07 27		07 42			17 57		18 12		18 27		18 42
—	1½	Wallasey Village	d	05 59		06 29		06 59		07 14		07 29		07 44			17 59		18 14		18 29		18 44
6½	3	Birkenhead North	d	06 04	06 09	06 34	06 39	07 04	07 09	07 19	07 24	07 34	07 39	07 49	07 54		18 04	18 09	18 19	18 24	18 34	18 39	18 49
7½	3¾	Birkenhead Park	d	06 06	06 11	06 36	06 41	07 06	07 11	07 21	07 26	07 36	07 41	07 51	07 56		18 06	18 11	18 21	18 26	18 36	18 41	18 51
8¼	4½	Conway Park	d	06 09	06 14	06 39	06 44	07 09	07 14	07 24	07 29	07 39	07 44	07 54	07 59		18 09	18 14	18 24	18 29	18 39	18 44	18 54
8¾	5	Hamilton Square	d	06 11	06 16	06 41	06 46	07 11	07 16	07 26	07 31	07 41	07 46	07 56	08 01		18 11	18 16	18 26	18 31	18 41	18 46	18 56
8¾	6¼	James Street	d	06 14	06 19	06 44	06 49	07 14	07 19	07 29	07 34	07 44	07 49	07 59	08 04		18 14	18 19	18 29	18 34	18 44	18 49	18 59
10¼	7¼	Moorfields 10	a	06 16	06 21	06 46	06 51	07 16	07 21	07 31	07 36	07 46	07 51	08 01	08 06		18 16	18 21	18 31	18 36	18 46	18 51	19 01
9¾	7¼	Liverpool Lime Street 10	a	06 18	06 23	06 48	06 53	07 18	07 23	07 33	07 38	07 48	07 53	08 03	08 08		18 18	18 23	18 33	18 38	18 48	18 53	19 03
9¼	6¾	**Liverpool Central** 10	a	06 20	06 25	06 50	06 55	07 20	07 25	07 35	07 40	07 50	07 55	08 05	08 10		18 20	18 25	18 35	18 40	18 50	18 55	19 05

		ME	ME	ME	ME	ME		ME	ME	ME	ME	ME	ME	ME
West Kirby	d	18 36		19 01		19 31	and at the same minutes past each hour until		22 01		22 31		23 01	
Hoylake	d	18 39		19 04		19 34			22 04		22 34		23 04	
Manor Road	d	18 41		19 06		19 36			22 06		22 36		23 06	
Meols	d	18 43		19 08		19 38			22 08		22 38		23 08	
Moreton	d	18 46		19 11		19 41			22 11		22 41		23 11	
Leasowe	d	18 48		19 13		19 43			22 13		22 43		23 13	
Bidston	d	18 51		19 16		19 46			22 16		22 46		23 16	
New Brighton	d		18 53		19 23			21 53		22 23		22 53		23 23
Wallasey Grove Road	d		18 57		19 27			21 57		22 27		22 57		23 27
Wallasey Village	d		18 59		19 29			21 59		22 29		22 59		23 29
Birkenhead North	d	18 54	19 04	19 19	19 34	19 49		22 04	22 19	22 34	22 49	23 04	23 19	23 34
Birkenhead Park	d	18 56	19 06	19 21	19 36	19 51		22 06	22 21	22 36	22 51	23 06	23 21	23 36
Conway Park	d	18 59	19 09	19 24	19 39	19 54		22 09	22 24	22 39	22 54	23 09	23 24	23 39
Hamilton Square	d	19 01	19 11	19 26	19 41	19 56		22 11	22 26	22 41	22 56	23 11	23 26	23 41
James Street	d	19 04	19 14	19 29	19 44	19 59		22 14	22 29	22 44	22 59	23 14	23 29	23 44
Moorfields 10	a	19 06	19 16	19 31	19 46	20 01		22 16	22 31	22 46	23 01	23 16	23 31	23 46
Liverpool Lime Street 10	a	19 08	19 18	19 33	19 48	20 03		22 18	22 33	22 48	23 03	23 18	23 33	23 48
Liverpool Central 10	a	19 10	19 20	19 35	19 50	20 05		22 20	22 35	22 50	23 05	23 20	23 35	23 50

Sundays
15 December to 10 May

		ME	ME	ME	ME		ME	ME	ME	ME	ME	ME	ME
West Kirby	d		08 01		08 31	and at the same minutes past each hour until		22 01		22 31		23 01	
Hoylake	d		08 04		08 34			22 04		22 34		23 04	
Manor Road	d		08 06		08 36			22 06		22 36		23 06	
Meols	d		08 08		08 38			22 08		22 38		23 08	
Moreton	d		08 11		08 41			22 11		22 41		23 11	
Leasowe	d		08 13		08 43			22 13		22 43		23 13	
Bidston	d		08 16		08 46			22 16		22 46		23 16	
New Brighton	d	07 53		08 23			21 53		22 23		22 53		23 23
Wallasey Grove Road	d	07 57		08 27			21 57		22 27		22 57		23 27
Wallasey Village	d	07 59		08 29			21 59		22 29		22 59		23 29
Birkenhead North	d	08 04	08 19	08 34	08 49		22 04	22 19	22 34	22 49	23 04	23 19	23 34
Birkenhead Park	d	08 06	08 21	08 36	08 51		22 06	22 21	22 36	22 51	23 06	23 21	23 36
Conway Park	d	08 09	08 24	08 39	08 54		22 09	22 24	22 39	22 54	23 09	23 24	23 39
Hamilton Square	d	08 11	08 26	08 41	08 56		22 11	22 26	22 41	22 56	23 11	23 26	23 41
James Street	d	08 14	08 29	08 44	08 59		22 14	22 29	22 44	22 59	23 14	23 29	23 44
Moorfields 10	a	08 16	08 31	08 46	09 01		22 16	22 31	22 46	23 01	23 16	23 31	23 46
Liverpool Lime Street 10	a	08 18	08 33	08 48	09 03		22 18	22 33	22 48	23 03	23 18	23 33	23 48
Liverpool Central 10	a	08 20	08 35	08 50	09 05		22 20	22 35	22 50	23 05	23 20	23 35	23 50

Table T107-F

Mondays to Saturdays

16 December to 16 May

Liverpool - Chester & Ellesmere Port

Miles	Miles			ME	ME	ME	ME	ME	ME	ME SO	ME SX	ME	ME SO	ME SX	ME	ME	ME SX	ME SO	ME SX	ME	ME SX	ME	ME SX
0	—	Moorfields 10	d			05 36	05 56	06 06	06 26	06 41	06 41	06 56	07 11	07 11	07 26	07 41	07 53	07 56		08 11	08 19	08 26	08 33
0½	—	Liverpool Lime Street 10	d			05 38	05 58	06 08	06 28	06 43	06 43	06 58	07 13	07 13	07 28	07 43	07 55	07 58		08 13	08 21	08 28	08 35
1	—	Liverpool Central 10	d			05 40	06 00	06 10	06 30	06 45	06 45	07 00	07 15	07 15	07 30	07 45	07 57	08 00		08 15	08 23	08 30	08 37
1½	—	James Street	d			05 42	06 02	06 12	06 32	06 47	06 47	07 02	07 17	07 17	07 32	07 47	07 59	08 02		08 17	08 25	08 32	08 39
2¾	—	Hamilton Square	d			05 45	06 05	06 15	06 35	06 50	06 50	07 05	07 20	07 20	07 35	07 50	08 02	08 05		08 20	08 28	08 35	08 42
3	—	Birkenhead Central	d			05 47	06 07	06 17	06 37	06 52	06 52	07 07	07 22	07 22	07 37	07 52	08 05	08 07		08 22	08 30	08 37	08a44
3¾	—	Green Lane	d			05 49	06 09	06 19	06 39	06 54	06 54	07 09	07 24	07 24	07 39	07 54	08 07	08 09		08 24	08 32	08 39	
4½	—	Rock Ferry	d			05 52	06 12	06 22	06 42	06 57	06 57	07 12	07 27	07 27	07 42	07 57	08 09	08 12		08 27	08 35	08 42	
5½	—	Bebington	d			05 54	06 14	06 24	06 44	06 59	06 59	07 14	07 29	07 29	07 44	07 59	08 12	08 14		08 29	08 37	08 44	
6½	—	Port Sunlight	d		00 01	05 56	06 16	06 26	06 46	07 01	07 01	07 16	07 31	07 31	07 46	08 01	08 14	08 16		08 31	08 39	08 46	
7	—	Spital	d		00 03	05 58	06 18	06 28	06 48	07 03	07 03	07 18	07 33	07 33	07 48	08 03	08 16	08 18		08 33	08 41	08 48	
7¾	—	Bromborough Rake	d		00 05	06 00	06 20	06 30	06 50	07 05	07 05	07 20	07 35	07 35	07 50	08 05	08 18	08 20		08 35	08 43	08 50	
8½	—	Bromborough	d		00 07	06 02	06 22	06 32	06 52	07 07	07 07	07 22	07 37	07 37	07 52	08 07	08 20	08 22		08 37	08 45	08 52	
9	—	Eastham Rake	d		00 10	06 05	06 25	06 35	06 55	07 10	07 10	07 25	07 40	07 40	07 55	08 10	08 22	08 25		08 40	08 48	08 55	
10	0	Hooton	d		00 12	06 07	06 27	06 37	06 57	07 12	07 12	07 27	07 42	07 43	07 57	08 13	08 24	08 27	08 29	08 42	08 50	08 57	
—	1½	Little Sutton	d	00 01			06 31		07 01			07 31			08 01			08 31	08 34			09 01	
—	2½	Overpool	d	00 03			06 33		07 03			07 33			08 03			08 33	08 36			09 03	
—	4	**Ellesmere Port**	a	00 07			06 38		07 08			07 38			08 08			08 38	08 39			09 08	
13	—	Capenhurst	d		00 17	06 12		06 42		07 17	07 17		07 47	07 48		08 18	08 29			08 47	08 55		
16¾	—	Bache	d		00 22	06 17		06 47		07 22	07 22		07 53	07 54		08 24	08 35			08 52	09 00		
18¾	—	**Chester**	a		00 26	06 26		06 56		07 26	07 27		07 56	07 58		08 28	08 38			08 57	09 07		

		ME SO	ME SX	ME SO	ME SO	ME SX	ME	ME SO	ME SX	ME	ME	ME	ME	ME	ME	ME	ME	ME	ME	ME	ME	ME	ME
Moorfields 10	d	08 41	08 41	08 48	08 56	08 56	09 11	09 18	09 19	09 26	09 41	09 48	09 56	10 11	10 18	10 26	10 41	10 48	10 56	11 11	11 18	11 26	11 41
Liverpool Lime Street 10	d	08 43	08 43	08 50	08 58	08 58	09 13	09 20	09 21	09 28	09 43	09 50	09 58	10 13	10 20	10 28	10 43	10 50	10 58	11 13	11 20	11 28	11 43
Liverpool Central 10	d	08 45	08 45	08 52	09 00	09 00	09 15	09 22	09 23	09 30	09 45	09 52	10 00	10 15	10 22	10 30	10 45	10 52	11 00	11 15	11 22	11 30	11 45
James Street	d	08 47	08 47	08 54	09 02	09 02	09 17	09 24	09 25	09 32	09 47	09 54	10 02	10 17	10 24	10 32	10 47	10 54	11 02	11 17	11 24	11 32	11 47
Hamilton Square	d	08 50	08 50	08 57	09 05	09 05	09 20	09 27	09 28	09 35	09 50	09 57	10 05	10 20	10 27	10 35	10 50	10 57	11 05	11 20	11 27	11 35	11 50
Birkenhead Central	d	08 52	08 53	09 00	09 07	09 07	09 22	09 30	09 30	09 37	09 52	10 00	10 07	10 22	10 30	10 37	10 52	11 00	11 07	11 22	11 30	11 37	11 52
Green Lane	d	08 54	08 55	09 02	09 09	09 09	09 24	09 32	09 32	09 39	09 54	10 02	10 09	10 24	10 32	10 39	10 54	11 02	11 09	11 24	11 32	11 39	11 54
Rock Ferry	d	08 57	08 57	09 04	09 12	09 12	09 27	09 34	09 35	09 42	09 57	10 04	10 12	10 27	10 34	10 42	10 57	11 04	11 12	11 27	11 34	11 42	11 57
Bebington	d	08 59	09 00	09 07	09 14	09 14	09 29	09 37	09 37	09 44	09 59	10 07	10 14	10 29	10 37	10 44	10 59	11 07	11 14	11 29	11 37	11 44	11 59
Port Sunlight	d	09 01	09 02	09 09	09 16	09 16	09 31	09 39	09 39	09 46	10 01	10 09	10 16	10 31	10 39	10 46	11 01	11 09	11 16	11 31	11 39	11 46	12 01
Spital	d	09 03	09 04	09 11	09 18	09 18	09 33	09 41	09 41	09 48	10 03	10 11	10 18	10 33	10 41	10 48	11 03	11 11	11 18	11 33	11 41	11 48	12 03
Bromborough Rake	d	09 05	09 06	09 13	09 20	09 20	09 35	09 43	09 43	09 50	10 05	10 13	10 20	10 35	10 43	10 50	11 05	11 13	11 20	11 35	11 43	11 50	12 05
Bromborough	d	09 07	09 08	09 15	09 22	09 22	09 37	09 45	09 45	09 52	10 07	10 15	10 22	10 37	10 45	10 52	11 07	11 15	11 22	11 37	11 45	11 52	12 07
Eastham Rake	d	09 10	09 10	09 17	09 25	09 25	09 40	09 47	09 48	09 55	10 10	10 17	10 25	10 40	10 47	10 55	11 10	11 17	11 25	11 40	11 47	11 55	12 10
Hooton	d	09 12	09 12	09 19	09 27	09 27	09 42	09 49	09 50	09 57	10 12	10 19	10 27	10 42	10 49	10 57	11 12	11 19	11 27	11 42	11 49	11 57	12 12
Little Sutton	d			09 24		09 31		09 54	09 54			10 24			10 54			11 24			11 54		
Overpool	d			09 26		09 33		09 56	09 56			10 26			10 56			11 26			11 56		
Ellesmere Port	a			09 32		09 38		10 00	10 00			10 30			11 00			11 30			12 00		
Capenhurst	d	09 17	09 17				09 47				10 17			10 47			11 17			11 47			12 17
Bache	d	09 22	09 23		09 36		09 52			10 06	10 22		10 36	10 52		11 06	11 22		11 36	11 52		12 06	12 22
Chester	a	09 27	09 27		09 41		09 57			10 11	10 27		10 41	10 57		11 11	11 27		11 41	11 57		12 11	12 27

		ME	ME	ME	ME	ME	ME	ME		ME	ME	ME	ME	ME	ME	ME	ME	ME	ME	ME SX	ME	ME	ME SO
Moorfields 10	d	11 48	11 56	12 11	12 18	12 26	12 41	12 48		14 56	15 11	15 18	15 26	15 41	15 48	15 56	16 11	16 18	16 26	16 33	16 41	16 48	16 56
Liverpool Lime Street 10	d	11 50	11 58	12 13	12 20	12 28	12 43	12 50		14 58	15 13	15 20	15 28	15 43	15 50	15 58	16 13	16 20	16 28	16 35	16 43	16 50	16 58
Liverpool Central 10	d	11 52	12 00	12 15	12 22	12 30	12 45	12 52		15 00	15 15	15 22	15 30	15 45	15 52	16 00	16 15	16 22	16 30	16 37	16 45	16 52	17 00
James Street	d	11 54	12 02	12 17	12 24	12 32	12 47	12 54		15 02	15 17	15 24	15 32	15 47	15 54	16 02	16 17	16 24	16 32	16 39	16 47	16 54	17 02
Hamilton Square	d	11 57	12 05	12 20	12 27	12 35	12 50	12 57		15 05	15 20	15 27	15 35	15 50	15 57	16 05	16 20	16 27	16 35	16 42	16 50	16 57	17 05
Birkenhead Central	d	12 00	12 07	12 22	12 30	12 37	12 52	13 00		15 07	15 22	15 30	15 37	15 52	16 00	16 07	16 22	16 30	16 37	16 45	16 52	17 00	17 07
Green Lane	d	12 02	12 09	12 24	12 32	12 39	12 54	13 02	and at the same minutes past each hour until	15 09	15 24	15 32	15 39	15 54	16 02	16 09	16 24	16 32	16 39	16 47	16 54	17 02	17 09
Rock Ferry	d	12 04	12 12	12 27	12 34	12 42	12 57	13 04		15 12	15 27	15 34	15 42	15 57	16 04	16 12	16 27	16 34	16 42	16 49	16 57	17 04	17 12
Bebington	d	12 07	12 14	12 29	12 37	12 44	12 59	13 07		15 14	15 29	15 37	15 44	15 59	16 07	16 14	16 29	16 37	16 44	16 52	16 59	17 07	17 14
Port Sunlight	d	12 09	12 16	12 31	12 39	12 46	13 01	13 09		15 16	15 31	15 39	15 46	16 01	16 09	16 16	16 31	16 39	16 46	16 54	17 01	17 09	17 16
Spital	d	12 11	12 18	12 33	12 41	12 48	13 03	13 11		15 18	15 33	15 41	15 48	16 03	16 11	16 18	16 33	16 41	16 48	16 56	17 03	17 11	17 18
Bromborough Rake	d	12 13	12 20	12 35	12 43	12 50	13 05	13 13		15 20	15 35	15 43	15 50	16 05	16 13	16 20	16 35	16 43	16 50	16 58	17 05	17 13	17 20
Bromborough	d	12 15	12 22	12 37	12 45	12 52	13 07	13 15		15 22	15 37	15 45	15 52	16 07	16 15	16 22	16 37	16 45	16 52	17 00	17 07	17 15	17 22
Eastham Rake	d	12 17	12 25	12 40	12 47	12 55	13 10	13 17		15 25	15 40	15 47	15 55	16 10	16 17	16 25	16 40	16 47	16 55	17 02	17 10	17 17	17 25
Hooton	d	12 19	12 27	12 42	12 49	12 57	13 12	13 19		15 27	15 42	15 49	15 57	16 12	16 19	16 27	16 42	16 49	16 57	17 04	17 12	17 19	17 27
Little Sutton	d	12 24			12 54			13 24				15 54			16 24			16 54		17 09		17 24	
Overpool	d	12 26			12 56			13 26				15 56			16 26			16 56		17 11		17 26	
Ellesmere Port	a	12 31			13 00			13 30				16 00			16 30			17 00		17 16		17 30	
Capenhurst	d			12 47			13 17				15 47			16 17			16 47				17 17		
Bache	d		12 36	12 52		13 06	13 22			15 36	15 52		16 06	16 22		16 36	16 52		17 06		17 22		17 36
Chester	a		12 41	12 57		13 11	13 27			15 41	15 57		16 11	16 27		16 41	16 57		17 11		17 27		17 41

		ME SX	ME SX	ME	ME	ME SO	ME SX	ME SX	ME	ME	ME	ME	ME	ME	ME	ME	ME	ME	ME	ME	ME	ME
Moorfields 10	d	16 56	17 03	17 11	17 18	17 26	17 26	17 33	17 41	17 48	17 56	18 11	18 18	18 26	18 41	18 48	18 56	19 11	19 26	19 41	19 56	20 11
Liverpool Lime Street 10	d	16 58	17 05	17 13	17 20	17 28	17 28	17 35	17 43	17 50	17 58	18 13	18 20	18 28	18 43	18 50	18 58	19 13	19 28	19 43	19 58	20 13
Liverpool Central 10	d	17 00	17 07	17 15	17 22	17 30	17 30	17 37	17 45	17 52	18 00	18 15	18 22	18 30	18 45	18 52	19 00	19 15	19 30	19 45	20 00	20 15
James Street	d	17 02	17 09	17 17	17 24	17 32	17 32	17 39	17 47	17 54	18 02	18 17	18 24	18 32	18 47	18 54	19 02	19 17	19 32	19 47	20 02	20 17
Hamilton Square	d	17 05	17 12	17 20	17 27	17 35	17 35	17 42	17 50	17 57	18 05	18 20	18 27	18 35	18 50	18 57	19 05	19 20	19 35	19 50	20 05	20 20
Birkenhead Central	d	17 07	17 15	17 22	17 30	17 37	17 37	17 45	17 52	18 00	18 07	18 22	18 30	18 37	18 52	19 00	19 07	19 22	19 37	19 52	20 07	20 22
Green Lane	d	17 09	17 17	17 24	17 32	17 39	17 39	17 47	17 54	18 02	18 09	18 24	18 32	18 39	18 54	19 02	19 09	19 24	19 39	19 54	20 09	20 24
Rock Ferry	d	17 12	17 19	17 27	17 34	17 42	17 42	17 49	17 57	18 04	18 12	18 27	18 34	18 42	18 57	19 04	19 12	19 27	19 42	19 57	20 12	20 27
Bebington	d	17 14	17 22	17 29	17 37	17 44	17 44	17 52	17 59	18 07	18 14	18 29	18 37	18 44	18 59	19 07	19 14	19 29	19 44	19 59	20 14	20 29
Port Sunlight	d	17 16	17 24	17 31	17 39	17 46	17 46	17 54	18 01	18 09	18 16	18 31	18 39	18 46	19 01	19 09	19 16	19 31	19 46	20 01	20 16	20 31
Spital	d	17 18	17 26	17 33	17 41	17 48	17 48	17 56	18 03	18 11	18 18	18 33	18 41	18 48	19 03	19 11	19 18	19 33	19 48	20 03	20 18	20 33
Bromborough Rake	d	17 20	17 28	17 35	17 43	17 50	17 50	17 58	18 05	18 13	18 20	18 35	18 43	18 50	19 05	19 13	19 20	19 35	19 50	20 05	20 20	20 35
Bromborough	d	17 22	17 30	17 37	17 45	17 52	17 52	18 00	18 07	18 15	18 22	18 37	18 45	18 52	19 07	19 15	19 22	19 37	19 52	20 07	20 22	20 37
Eastham Rake	d	17 25	17 32	17 40	17 47	17 55	17 55	18 02	18 10	18 18	18 25	18 40	18 47	18 55	19 10	19 17	19 25	19 40	19 55	20 10	20 25	20 40
Hooton	d	17 27	17 34	17 42	17 49	17 57	17 57	18 04	18 12	18 19	18 27	18 42	18 49	18 57	19 12	19 19	19 27	19 42	19 57	20 12	20 27	20 42
Little Sutton	d		17 39		17 54			18 09		18 24			18 54			19 24			20 01		20 31	
Overpool	d		17 41		17 56			18 11		18 26			18 56			19 26			20 03		20 33	
Ellesmere Port	a		17 46		18 00			18 16		18 30			19 00			19 30			20 08		20 38	
Capenhurst	d	17 32		17 47			18 02		18 17			18 47			19 17			19 47		20 17		20 47
Bache	d	17 37		17 52		18 06	18 07		18 22		18 36	18 52		19 06	19 22		19 36	19 52		20 22		20 52
Chester	a	17 41		17 57		18 11	18 11		18 26		18 39	18 56		19 10	19 26		19 41	19 56		20 26		20 56

Table T107-F

Mondays to Saturdays

16 December to 16 May

Liverpool - Chester & Ellesmere Port

		ME SO	ME SX	ME	ME	ME	ME	ME	ME	ME	ME	ME	ME	ME	ME	ME
Moorfields 10	d	20 26	20 27	20 41	20 56	21 11	21 26	21 41	21 56	22 11	22 26	22 41	22 56	23 11	23 26	23 41
Liverpool Lime Street 10	d	20 28	20 29	20 43	20 58	21 13	21 28	21 43	21 58	22 13	22 28	22 43	22 58	23 13	23 28	23 43
Liverpool Central 10	d	20 30	20 31	20 45	21 00	21 15	21 30	21 45	22 00	22 15	22 30	22 45	23 00	23 15	23 30	23 45
James Street	d	20 32	20 33	20 47	21 02	21 17	21 32	21 47	22 02	22 17	22 32	22 47	23 02	23 17	23 32	23 47
Hamilton Square	d	20 35	20 36	20 50	21 05	21 20	21 35	21 50	22 05	22 20	22 35	22 50	23 05	23 20	23 35	23 50
Birkenhead Central	d	20 37	20 38	20 52	21 07	21 22	21 37	21 52	22 07	22 22	22 37	22 52	23 07	23 22	23 37	23 52
Green Lane	d	20 39	20 40	20 54	21 09	21 24	21 39	21 54	22 09	22 24	22 39	22 54	23 09	23 24	23 39	23 54
Rock Ferry	d	20 42	20 43	20 57	21 12	21 27	21 42	21 57	22 12	22 27	22 42	22 57	23 12	23 27	23 42	23 57
Bebington	d	20 44	20 45	20 59	21 14	21 29	21 44	21 59	22 14	22 29	22 44	22 59	23 14	23 29	23 44	23 59
Port Sunlight	d	20 46	20 47	21 01	21 16	21 31	21 46	22 01	22 16	22 31	22 46	23 01	23 16	23 31	23 46	00 01
Spital	d	20 48	20 49	21 03	21 18	21 33	21 48	22 03	22 18	22 33	22 48	23 03	23 18	23 33	23 48	00 03
Bromborough Rake	d	20 50	20 51	21 05	21 20	21 35	21 50	22 05	22 20	22 35	22 50	23 05	23 20	23 35	23 50	00 05
Bromborough	d	20 52	20 53	21 07	21 22	21 37	21 52	22 07	22 22	22 37	22 52	23 07	23 22	23 37	23 52	00 07
Eastham Rake	d	20 55	20 56	21 10	21 25	21 40	21 55	22 10	22 25	22 40	22 55	23 10	23 25	23 40	23 55	00 10
Hooton	d	20 57	20 58	21 12	21 27	21 42	21 57	22 12	22 27	22 42	22 57	23 12	23 27	23 42	23 57	00 12
Little Sutton	d	21 01	21 02		21 31		22 01		22 31		23 01		23 31		00 01	
Overpool	d	21 03	21 04		21 33		22 03		22 33		23 03		23 33		00 03	
Ellesmere Port	a	21 08	21 09		21 38		22 08		22 38		23 08		23 37		00 07	
Capenhurst	d			21 17		21 47		22 17		22 47		23 17		23 47		00 17
Bache	d			21 22		21 52		22 22		22 52		23 22		23 52		00 22
Chester	a			21 26		21 56		22 26		22 56		23 26		23 56		00 26

Sundays

15 December to 10 May

		ME A	ME A	ME	ME	ME	ME		ME	ME	ME	ME	ME	ME	ME	ME
Moorfields 10	d			07 56	08 11	08 26	08 41		21 56	22 11	22 26	22 41	22 56	23 11	23 26	23 41
Liverpool Lime Street 10	d			07 58	08 13	08 28	08 43		21 58	22 13	22 28	22 43	22 58	23 13	23 28	23 43
Liverpool Central 10	d			08 00	08 15	08 30	08 45		22 00	22 15	22 30	22 45	23 00	23 15	23 30	23 45
James Street	d			08 02	08 17	08 32	08 47		22 02	22 17	22 32	22 47	23 02	23 17	23 32	23 47
Hamilton Square	d			08 05	08 20	08 35	08 50		22 05	22 20	22 35	22 50	23 05	23 20	23 35	23 50
Birkenhead Central	d			08 07	08 22	08 37	08 52		22 07	22 22	22 37	22 52	23 07	23 22	23 37	23 52
Green Lane	d			08 09	08 24	08 39	08 54	and at the same minutes past each hour until	22 09	22 24	22 39	22 54	23 09	23 24	23 39	23 54
Rock Ferry	d			08 12	08 27	08 42	08 57		22 12	22 27	22 42	22 57	23 12	23 27	23 42	23 57
Bebington	d			08 14	08 29	08 44	08 59		22 14	22 29	22 44	22 59	23 14	23 29	23 44	23 59
Port Sunlight	d		00 01	08 16	08 31	08 46	09 01		22 16	22 31	22 46	23 01	23 16	23 31	23 46	00 01
Spital	d		00 03	08 18	08 33	08 48	09 03		22 18	22 33	22 48	23 03	23 18	23 33	23 48	00 03
Bromborough Rake	d		00 05	08 20	08 35	08 50	09 05		22 20	22 35	22 50	23 05	23 20	23 35	23 50	00 05
Bromborough	d		00 07	08 22	08 37	08 52	09 07		22 22	22 37	22 52	23 07	23 22	23 37	23 52	00 07
Eastham Rake	d		00 10	08 25	08 40	08 55	09 10		22 25	22 40	22 55	23 10	23 25	23 40	23 55	00 10
Hooton	d		00 12	08 27	08 42	08 57	09 12		22 27	22 42	22 57	23 12	23 27	23 42	23 57	00 12
Little Sutton	d	00 01		08 31		09 01			22 31		23 01		23 31		00 01	
Overpool	d	00 03		08 33		09 03			22 33		23 03		23 33		00 03	
Ellesmere Port	a	00 07		08 38		09 08			22 38		23 08		23 37		00 07	
Capenhurst	d		00 17		08 47		09 17			22 47		23 17		23 47		00 17
Bache	d		00 22		08 52		09 22			22 52		23 22		23 52		00 22
Chester	a		00 26		08 56		09 26			22 56		23 26		23 56		00 26

A not 15 December

Table T107-R

Mondays to Saturdays

16 December to 16 May

Chester, Ellesmere Port - Liverpool

Miles	Miles			ME	ME	ME	ME	ME	ME	ME	ME SX	ME SO	ME SX	ME SO	ME SX	ME SX	ME	ME SX	ME SO	ME SX	ME SX	ME SO	ME SO
0	—	**Chester**	d			05 55		06 30		07 00			07 22	07 30		07 37		07 52	08 00		08 07		08 15
1½	—	Bache	d			05 58		06 33		07 03			07 26	07 33		07 41		07 56	08 03		08 11		08 18
5¼	—	Capenhurst	d			06 04		06 39		07 09			07 32	07 39		07 47		08 02	08 09		08 17		08 24
—	0	**Ellesmere Port**	d				06 17		06 47		07 17	07 19			07 31		07 49			08 01		08 12	
—	1½	Overpool	d				06 20		06 50		07 20	07 22			07 34		07 52			08 04		08 15	
—	2½	Little Sutton	d				06 22		06 52		07 22	07 24			07 36		07 54			08 06		08 17	
8¼	4	Hooton	d	05 39	05 59	06 09	06 26	06 44	06 56	07 14	07 26	07 29	07 36	07 44	07 44	07 52	07 59	08 06	08 14	08 14	08 21	08 21	08 29
9¼	—	Eastham Rake	d	05 41	06 01	06 11	06 28	06 46	06 58	07 16	07 28	07 31	07 38	07 46	07 46	07 54	08 01	08 08	08 16	08 16	08 23	08 23	08 31
9¾	—	Bromborough	d	05 43	06 03	06 13	06 31	06 48	07 01	07 18	07 31	07 33	07 41	07 48	07 48	07 56	08 03	08 11	08 18	08 18	08 26	08 26	08 33
10½	—	Bromborough Rake	d	05 45	06 05	06 15	06 33	06 50	07 03	07 20	07 33	07 35	07 43	07 50	07 50	07 58	08 05	08 13	08 20	08 20	08 28	08 28	08 35
11¼	—	Spital	d	05 47	06 07	06 17	06 35	06 52	07 05	07 22	07 35	07 37	07 45	07 52	07 52	08 00	08 07	08 15	08 22	08 22	08 30	08 30	08 37
11¾	—	Port Sunlight	d	05 49	06 09	06 19	06 37	06 54	07 07	07 24	07 37	07 39	07 47	07 54	07 54	08 02	08 09	08 17	08 24	08 24	08 32	08 32	08 39
12¾	—	Bebington	d	05 51	06 11	06 21	06 39	06 56	07 09	07 26	07 39	07 41	07 49	07 56	07 56	08 04	08 11	08 19	08 26	08 26	08 34	08 34	08 41
13¾	—	Rock Ferry	d	05 54	06 14	06 24	06 42	06 59	07 12	07 29	07 42	07 44	07 52	07 59	07 59	08 07	08 14	08 22	08 29	08 29	08 37	08 37	08 44
14½	—	Green Lane	d	05 57	06 17	06 27	06 44	07 02	07 14	07 32	07 44	07 47	07 54	08 02	08 02	08 10	08 17	08 24	08 32	08 32	08 39	08 39	08 47
15	—	Birkenhead Central	d	05 59	06 19	06 34	06 49	07 04	07 19	07 34	07 47	07 49	07 57	08 04	08 04	08 12	08 19	08 27	08 34	08 34	08 42	08 42	08 49
15½	—	Hamilton Square	d	06 01	06 21	06 36	06 51	07 06	07 21	07 36	07 49	07 51	07 59	08 06	08 06	08 14	08 21	08 29	08 36	08 36	08 44	08 44	08 51
16¾	—	James Street	d	06 04	06 24	06 39	06 54	07 09	07 24	07 39	07 52	07 54	08 02	08 09	08 09	08 17	08 24	08 32	08 39	08 39	08 47	08 47	08 54
17	—	Moorfields 10	a	06 06	06 26	06 41	06 56	07 11	07 26	07 41	07 53	07 56	08 03	08 11	08 11	08 19	08 26	08 33	08 41	08 41	08 48	08 48	08 56
17½	—	Liverpool Lime Street 10	a	06 08	06 28	06 43	06 58	07 13	07 28	07 43	07 55	07 58	08 05	08 13	08 13	08 21	08 28	08 35	08 43	08 43	08 50	08 50	08 58
18	—	**Liverpool Central** 10	a	06 10	06 30	06 45	07 00	07 15	07 30	07 45	07 57	08 00	08 07	08 15	08 15	08 23	08 30	08 37	08 45	08 45	08 52	08 52	09 00

		ME SX	ME	ME SO	ME SX	ME	ME	ME	ME	ME	ME		ME	ME	ME	ME	ME	ME	ME	ME	ME	ME	ME
Chester	d		08 31			08 45	09 01		09 15	09 31			16 45	17 01		17 15	17 31		17 45	18 01		18 15	18 30
Bache	d		08 35			08 48	09 05		09 18	09 35			16 48	17 05		17 18	17 35		17 48	18 05		18 18	18 33
Capenhurst	d					08 54			09 24				16 54			17 24			17 54			18 24	18 39
Ellesmere Port	d	08 17		08 42	08 42			09 12			09 42				17 12			17 42			18 12		
Overpool	d	08 20		08 45	08 45			09 15			09 45				17 15			17 45			18 15		
Little Sutton	d	08 22		08 47	08 47			09 17			09 47				17 17			17 47			18 17		
Hooton	d	08 29	08 44	08 51	08 52	08 59	09 14	09 21	09 29	09 44	09 51	and at	16 59	17 14	17 21	17 29	17 44	17 51	17 59	18 14	18 21	18 29	18 44
Eastham Rake	d	08 31	08 46	08 53	08 54	09 01	09 16	09 23	09 31	09 46	09 53	the same	17 01	17 16	17 23	17 31	17 46	17 53	18 01	18 16	18 23	18 31	18 46
Bromborough	d	08 33	08 48	08 56	08 56	09 03	09 18	09 26	09 33	09 48	09 56	minutes	17 03	17 18	17 26	17 33	17 48	17 56	18 03	18 18	18 26	18 33	18 48
Bromborough Rake	d	08 35	08 50	08 58	08 58	09 05	09 20	09 28	09 35	09 50	09 58	past	17 05	17 20	17 28	17 35	17 50	17 58	18 05	18 20	18 28	18 35	18 50
Spital	d	08 37	08 52	09 00	09 00	09 07	09 22	09 30	09 37	09 52	10 00	each	17 07	17 22	17 30	17 37	17 52	18 00	18 07	18 22	18 30	18 37	18 52
Port Sunlight	d	08 39	08 54	09 02	09 02	09 09	09 24	09 32	09 39	09 54	10 02	hour until	17 09	17 24	17 32	17 39	17 54	18 02	18 09	18 24	18 32	18 39	18 54
Bebington	d	08 41	08 56	09 04	09 04	09 11	09 26	09 34	09 41	09 56	10 04		17 11	17 26	17 34	17 41	17 56	18 04	18 11	18 26	18 34	18 41	18 56
Rock Ferry	d	08 44	08 59	09 07	09 07	09 14	09 29	09 37	09 44	09 59	10 07		17 14	17 29	17 37	17 44	17 59	18 07	18 14	18 29	18 37	18 44	18 59
Green Lane	d	08 47	09 02	09 09	09 10	09 17	09 32	09 39	09 47	10 02	10 09		17 17	17 32	17 39	17 47	18 02	18 09	18 17	18 32	18 39	18 47	19 02
Birkenhead Central	d	08 49	09 04	09 12	09 12	09 19	09 34	09 42	09 49	10 04	10 12		17 19	17 34	17 42	17 49	18 04	18 12	18 19	18 34	18 42	18 49	19 04
Hamilton Square	d	08 51	09 06	09 14	09 14	09 21	09 36	09 44	09 51	10 06	10 14		17 21	17 36	17 44	17 51	18 06	18 14	18 21	18 36	18 44	18 51	19 06
James Street	d	08 54	09 09	09 17	09 17	09 24	09 39	09 47	09 54	10 09	10 17		17 24	17 39	17 47	17 54	18 09	18 17	18 24	18 39	18 47	18 54	19 09
Moorfields 10	a	08 56	09 11	09 18	09 19	09 26	09 41	09 48	09 56	10 11	10 18		17 26	17 41	17 48	17 56	18 11	18 18	18 26	18 41	18 48	18 56	19 11
Liverpool Lime Street 10	a	08 58	09 13	09 20	09 21	09 28	09 43	09 50	09 58	10 13	10 20		17 28	17 43	17 50	17 58	18 13	18 20	18 28	18 43	18 50	18 58	19 13
Liverpool Central 10	a	09 00	09 15	09 22	09 23	09 30	09 45	09 52	10 00	10 15	10 22		17 30	17 45	17 52	18 00	18 15	18 22	18 30	18 45	18 52	19 00	19 15

		ME	ME	ME	ME	ME SO	ME SX	ME	ME	ME	ME	ME	ME	ME	ME	ME	ME	ME	ME	ME	ME	ME
Chester	d		19 00		19 30			20 00		20 30		21 00		21 30		22 00		22 30		23 00		23 30
Bache	d		19 03		19 33			20 03		20 33		21 03		21 33		22 03		22 33		23 03		23 33
Capenhurst	d		19 09		19 39			20 09		20 39		21 09		21 39		22 09		22 39		23 09		23 39
Ellesmere Port	d	18 46		19 16		19 49	19 49		20 19		20 49		21 19		21 49		22 19		22 49		23 19	
Overpool	d	18 49		19 19		19 52	19 52		20 22		20 52		21 22		21 52		22 22		22 52		23 22	
Little Sutton	d	18 51		19 21		19 54	19 54		20 24		20 54		21 24		21 54		22 24		22 54		23 24	
Hooton	d	18 59	19 14	19 29	19 44	19 59	20 00	20 14	20 29	20 44	20 59	21 14	21 29	21 44	21 59	22 14	22 29	22 44	22 59	23 14	23 29	23a44
Eastham Rake	d	19 01	19 16	19 31	19 46	20 01	20 02	20 16	20 31	20 46	21 01	21 16	21 31	21 46	22 01	22 16	22 31	22 46	23 01	23 16	23 31	
Bromborough	d	19 03	19 18	19 33	19 48	20 03	20 04	20 18	20 33	20 48	21 03	21 18	21 33	21 48	22 03	22 18	22 33	22 48	23 03	23 18	23 33	
Bromborough Rake	d	19 05	19 20	19 35	19 50	20 05	20 06	20 20	20 35	20 50	21 05	21 20	21 35	21 50	22 05	22 20	22 35	22 50	23 05	23 20	23 35	
Spital	d	19 07	19 22	19 37	19 52	20 07	20 08	20 22	20 37	20 52	21 07	21 22	21 37	21 52	22 07	22 22	22 37	22 52	23 07	23 22	23 37	
Port Sunlight	d	19 09	19 24	19 39	19 54	20 09	20 10	20 24	20 39	20 54	21 09	21 24	21 39	21 54	22 09	22 24	22 39	22 54	23 09	23 24	23 39	
Bebington	d	19 11	19 26	19 41	19 56	20 11	20 12	20 26	20 41	20 56	21 11	21 26	21 41	21 56	22 11	22 26	22 41	22 56	23 11	23 26	23 41	
Rock Ferry	d	19 14	19 29	19 44	19 59	20 14	20 15	20 29	20 44	20 59	21 14	21 29	21 44	21 59	22 14	22 29	22 44	22 59	23 14	23 29	23 44	
Green Lane	d	19 17	19 32	19 47	20 02	20 17	20 18	20 32	20 47	21 02	21 17	21 32	21 47	22 02	22 17	22 32	22 47	23 02	23 17	23 32	23 47	
Birkenhead Central	d	19 19	19 34	19 49	20 04	20 19	20 20	20 34	20 49	21 04	21 19	21 34	21 49	22 04	22 19	22 34	22 49	23 04	23 19	23 34	23 49	
Hamilton Square	d	19 21	19 36	19 51	20 06	20 21	20 22	20 36	20 51	21 06	21 21	21 36	21 51	22 06	22 21	22 36	22 51	23 06	23 21	23 36	23 51	
James Street	d	19 24	19 39	19 54	20 09	20 24	20 25	20 39	20 54	21 09	21 24	21 39	21 54	22 09	22 24	22 39	22 54	23 09	23 24	23 39	23 54	
Moorfields 10	a	19 26	19 41	19 56	20 11	20 26	20 27	20 41	20 56	21 11	21 26	21 41	21 56	22 11	22 26	22 41	22 56	23 11	23 26	23 41	23 56	
Liverpool Lime Street 10	a	19 28	19 43	19 58	20 13	20 28	20 29	20 43	20 58	21 13	21 28	21 43	21 58	22 13	22 28	22 43	22 58	23 13	23 28	23 43	23 58	
Liverpool Central 10	a	19 30	19 45	20 00	20 15	20 30	20 31	20 45	21 00	21 15	21 30	21 45	22 00	22 15	22 30	22 45	23 00	23 15	23 30	23 45	23 59	

Sundays

15 December to 10 May

		ME	ME	ME	ME	ME		ME	ME	ME	ME	ME	ME	ME	ME
Chester	d			08 00		08 30			22 00		22 30		23 00		23 30
Bache	d			08 03		08 33			22 03		22 33		23 03		23 33
Capenhurst	d			08 09		08 39			22 09		22 39		23 09		23 39
Ellesmere Port	d		07 49		08 19			21 49		22 19		22 49		23 19	
Overpool	d		07 52		08 22			21 52		22 22		22 52		23 22	
Little Sutton	d		07 54		08 24			21 54		22 24		22 54		23 24	
Hooton	d	07 44	07 59	08 14	08 29	08 44	and at	21 59	22 14	22 29	22 44	22 59	23 14	23 29	23a45
Eastham Rake	d	07 46	08 01	08 16	08 31	08 46	the same	22 01	22 16	22 31	22 46	23 01	23 16	23 31	
Bromborough	d	07 48	08 03	08 18	08 33	08 48	minutes	22 03	22 18	22 33	22 48	23 03	23 18	23 33	
Bromborough Rake	d	07 50	08 05	08 20	08 35	08 50	past	22 05	22 20	22 35	22 50	23 05	23 20	23 35	
Spital	d	07 52	08 07	08 22	08 37	08 52	each	22 07	22 22	22 37	22 52	23 07	23 22	23 37	
Port Sunlight	d	07 54	08 09	08 24	08 39	08 54	hour until	22 09	22 24	22 39	22 54	23 09	23 24	23 39	
Bebington	d	07 56	08 11	08 26	08 41	08 56		22 11	22 26	22 41	22 56	23 11	23 26	23 41	
Rock Ferry	d	07 59	08 14	08 29	08 44	08 59		22 14	22 29	22 44	22 59	23 14	23 29	23 44	
Green Lane	d	08 02	08 17	08 32	08 47	09 02		22 17	22 32	22 47	23 02	23 17	23 32	23 47	
Birkenhead Central	d	08 04	08 19	08 34	08 49	09 04		22 19	22 34	22 49	23 04	23 19	23 34	23 49	
Hamilton Square	d	08 06	08 21	08 36	08 51	09 06		22 21	22 36	22 51	23 06	23 21	23 36	23 51	
James Street	d	08 09	08 24	08 39	08 54	09 09		22 24	22 39	22 54	23 09	23 24	23 39	23 54	
Moorfields 10	a	08 11	08 26	08 41	08 56	09 11		22 26	22 41	22 56	23 11	23 26	23 41	23 56	
Liverpool Lime Street 10	a	08 13	08 28	08 43	08 58	09 13		22 28	22 43	22 58	23 13	23 28	23 43	23 58	
Liverpool Central 10	a	08 15	08 30	08 45	09 00	09 15		22 30	22 45	23 00	23 15	23 30	23 45	23 59	

Table T109-F

Mondays to Fridays

16 December to 15 May

Ellesmere Port - Helsby

Miles			AW A	NT ◇ B	NT	AW ◇ C	AW ◇ D	NT ◇ E	AW ◇ A	NT ◇ B	AW ◇ F	AW ◇ G 🍴	AW ◇ F 🍴	AW ◇ F 🍴
0	**Ellesmere Port**	d			06 22			07 15						
2½	Stanlow & Thornton	d			06 26			07 20						
3¾	Ince & Elton	d			06 29			07 22						
5¼	**Helsby**	d	05 47	06 26	06a32	06 52	07 22	07 31	07 49	08 30	09 01	10 01	11 01	12 01
—	Warrington Bank Quay 81	a	06 06	06 45		07 10	07 39	07 46	08 10	08 49	09 20	10 19	11 19	12 20

		AW ◇ F 🍴	AW ◇ G 🍴	AW ◇ D 🍴	AW ◇ H 🍴	AW ◇ H 🍴	AW ■ H	AW ◇ H 🍴	NT I	AW ◇ J	AW ◇ F	NT ◇ B	AW A
Ellesmere Port	d								18 23				
Stanlow & Thornton	d								18 27				
Ince & Elton	d								18 30				
Helsby	d	13 01	14 01	14 59	15 58	16 30	17 31	18 25	18 34	19 00	20 01	20 29	21 01
Warrington Bank Quay 81	a	13 19	14 21	15 19	16 19	16 49	17 50	18 46	18 52	19 19	20 19	20 48	21 20

		AW ◇ H	AW ◇ K
Ellesmere Port	d		
Stanlow & Thornton	d		
Ince & Elton	d		
Helsby	d	22 01	23 32
Warrington Bank Quay 81	a	22 19	23 51

Saturdays

21 December to 16 May

		AW A	AW ◇ A	NT	AW L	NT	NT ◇ B	AW ◇ F	NT ◇ B	AW ◇ F	AW ◇ F 🍴	AW ■ F 🍴	AW ◇ F 🍴
Ellesmere Port	d			06 22		07 14							
Stanlow & Thornton	d			06 26		07 18							
Ince & Elton	d			06 29		07 21							
Helsby	d	05 47	06 22	06a32	07 21	07a24	07 29	07 50	08 30	09 01	10 01	11 01	12 01
Warrington Bank Quay 81	a	06 06	06 40		07 39		07 48	08 09	08 49	09 19	10 19	11 19	12 20

		AW ◇ F 🍴	AW ◇ F 🍴	AW ◇ M 🍴	AW ◇ F 🍴	AW ◇ F 🍴	AW ◇ H 🍴	NT	NT ◇ B	AW ◇ F 🍴	AW ◇ H	NT ◇ B	AW ◇ H
Ellesmere Port	d							18 19					
Stanlow & Thornton	d							18 23					
Ince & Elton	d							18 26					
Helsby	d	13 00	14 02	15 03	15 58	17 01	18 00	18a29	18 33	19 01	20 01	20 29	20 59
Warrington Bank Quay 81	a	13 20	14 21	15 21	16 19	17 20	18 19		18 48	19 20	20 19	20 48	21 20

		AW A	AW A
Ellesmere Port	d		
Stanlow & Thornton	d		
Ince & Elton	d		
Helsby	d	22 02	23 31
Warrington Bank Quay 81	a	22 20	23 50

A From Chester to Manchester Piccadilly
B From Chester to Leeds
C From Llandudno Junction to Manchester Piccadilly
D From Holyhead to Manchester Piccadilly
E To Leeds
F From Llandudno to Manchester Airport
G From Llandudno Junction to Manchester Airport
H From Llandudno to Manchester Piccadilly
I To Manchester Victoria
J From Chester to Manchester Airport
K From Birmingham International to Manchester Piccadilly
L From Shrewsbury to Manchester Piccadilly
M From Bangor (Gwynedd) to Manchester Airport

No Sunday Service

Table T109-R

Helsby - Ellesmere Port

Mondays to Fridays

16 December to 15 May

Miles			NT	NT	AW	AW	AW	AW	AW	AW	AW	AW	AW
			A		◇ B	◇ C	■ D	◇ D 🛒	◇ D 🛒	◇ E 🛒	◇ B 🛒	◇ B 🛒	◇ B 🛒
—	Warrington Bank Quay 81	d	05 42		06 21	07 25	08 27	09 27	10 31	11 26	12 28	13 27	14 28
0	**Helsby**	d	06 00	06 36	06a37	07a41	08a43	09a43	10a48	11a42	12a43	13a43	14a44
2	Ince & Elton	d	06 03	06 39									
2¾	Stanlow & Thornton	d	06 06	06 41									
5¼	**Ellesmere Port**	a	06 12	06 47									

		AW	AW	AW	NT	AW	AW	NT	AW	AW	AW	AW	AW
		◇ B 🛒	◇ B 🛒	■ F 🛒	◇ G	H	■ D 🛒	◇ I	H	H	J	J	H
Warrington Bank Quay 81	d	15 28	16 26	17 29	17 36	17 47	18 28	18 40	19 30	20 27	21 27	22 24	22 49
Helsby	d	15a43	16a42	17a47	17 55	18a06	18a44	18a58	19a45	20a42	21a42	22a39	23a05
Ince & Elton	d				17 58								
Stanlow & Thornton	d				18 01								
Ellesmere Port	a				18 07								

		AW
		H
Warrington Bank Quay 81	d	23 48
Helsby	d	00a06
Ince & Elton	d	
Stanlow & Thornton	d	
Ellesmere Port	a	

Saturdays

21 December to 16 May

		NT	NT	AW	AW	AW	AW	AW	AW	AW	AW	AW	AW
		A		◇ B	◇ F	◇ F	◇ F 🛒	■ B 🛒	■ K 🛒	■ B 🛒	◇ B 🛒	◇ B 🛒	◇ B 🛒
Warrington Bank Quay 81	d	05 42		06 25	07 24	08 29	09 28	10 27	11 27	12 28	13 27	14 28	15 26
Helsby	d	06 00	06 36	06a42	07a39	08a46	09a43	10a42	11a42	12a44	13a42	14a43	15a41
Ince & Elton	d	06 03	06 39										
Stanlow & Thornton	d	06 06	06 41										
Ellesmere Port	a	06 12	06 47										

		AW	AW	NT	NT	AW	NT	AW	AW	AW	AW	AW	AW
		◇ B 🛒	◇ B 🛒	◇ I		◇ B 🛒	◇ I	J	H	J	H	H	H
Warrington Bank Quay 81	d	16 27	17 27	17 35		18 27	18 44	19 29	20 30	21 30	22 25	22 44	23 48
Helsby	d	16a42	17a42	17a52	18 06	18a42	19a01	19a45	20a46	21a45	22a40	23a01	00a03
Ince & Elton	d				18 09								
Stanlow & Thornton	d				18 11								
Ellesmere Port	a				18 15								

A From Liverpool Lime Street
B From Manchester Airport to Llandudno
C From Manchester Piccadilly to Llandudno Junction
D From Manchester Piccadilly to Holyhead
E From Manchester Airport to Llandudno Junction
F From Manchester Piccadilly to Llandudno
G From Leeds
H From Manchester Piccadilly to Chester
I From Leeds to Chester
J From Manchester Airport to Chester
K From Manchester Airport to Bangor (Gwynedd)

No Sunday Service

NRT DECEMBER 19 EDITION

Table T114-F

London - Amersham and Aylesbury

Mondays to Fridays

16 December to 15 May

Miles			CH	CH	CH	CH	CH	CH	CH	CH	CH	CH	CH	CH	CH	CH	CH	CH	CH	CH	CH	CH	CH
			A	MX A																			
0	**London Marylebone** 10	⊖ d			06 33	06 52	07 26	07 57	08 27	08 57	09 27	09 57	10 27	10 57	11 27	11 57	12 27	12 57	13 27	13 57	14 27	14 57	15 27
9	Harrow-on-the-Hill 3 §	⊖ d		00 09	06 45	07 04	07 39	08 09	08 39	09 09	09 39	10 09	10 39	11 09	11 39	12 09	12 39	13 09	13 39	14 09	14 39	15 09	15 39
17	Rickmansworth §	⊖ d		00 19	06 55	07 14	07 49	08 19	08 49	09 19	09 49	10 19	10 49	11 19	11 49	12 19	12 49	13 19	13 49	14 19	14 49	15 19	15 49
19¾	Chorleywood §	⊖ d		00 24	07 00	07 19	07 54	08 24	08 54	09 24	09 54	10 24	10 54	11 24	11 54	12 24	12 54	13 24	13 54	14 24	14 54	15 24	15 54
21½	Chalfont & Latimer §	⊖ d		00 28	07 04	07 23	07 58	08 28	08 58	09 28	09 58	10 28	10 58	11 28	11 58	12 28	12 58	13 28	13 58	14 28	14 58	15 28	15 58
23½	**Amersham** §	⊖ d	00 02	00 32	07 08	07 27	08 02	08 32	09 02	09 32	10 02	10 32	11 02	11 32	12 02	12 32	13 02	13 32	14 02	14 32	15 02	15 32	16 02
28¾	Great Missenden	d	00 09	00 39	07 15	07 34	08 09	08 39	09 09	09 39	10 09	10 39	11 09	11 39	12 09	12 39	13 09	13 39	14 09	14 39	15 09	15 39	16 09
33¼	Wendover	d	00 15	00 45	07 21	07 40	08 15	08 45	09 15	09 45	10 15	10 45	11 15	11 45	12 15	12 45	13 15	13 45	14 15	14 45	15 15	15 45	16 15
35¼	Stoke Mandeville	d	00 19	00 49	07 25	07 44	08 19	08 49	09 19	09 49	10 19	10 49	11 19	11 49	12 19	12 49	13 19	13 49	14 19	14 49	15 19	15 49	16 19
37¾	**Aylesbury**	d	00a26	00 54	07 30	07 56	08a25	08 54	09a26	09 54	10a26	10 54	11a29	11 54	12a31	12 54	13a26	13 54	14a26	14 54	15a32	15 54	16 26
40½	**Aylesbury Vale Parkway**	a		01 03	07 39	08 04		09 03		10 03		11 03		12 03		13 03		14 03		15 03		16 03	16 34

		CH	CH	CH	CH	CH	CH	CH	CH	CH	CH	CH	CH	CH	CH	CH	CH	CH	CH	CH	CH	CH	CH
London Marylebone 10	⊖ d	15 56	16 12	16 27	16 42	17 11	17 30	17 40	17 58	18 12	18 32	18 43	18 59	19 18	19 32	19 56	20 23	20 57	21 27	21 57	22 27	22 57	23 27
Harrow-on-the-Hill 3 §	⊖ d	16 09	16 24		16 54	17 23		17 54		18 24		18 55	19 11		19 45	20 08	20 35	21 09	21 39	22 09	22 39	23 09	23 39
Rickmansworth §	⊖ d	16 19	16 34		17 04			18 04		18 34			19 22		19 55	20 18	20 45	21 19	21 49	22 19	22 49	23 19	23 49
Chorleywood §	⊖ d	16 24	16 39		17 09	17 37		18 09		18 39		19 10	19 26		20 00	20 23	20 50	21 24	21 54	22 24	22 54	23 24	23 54
Chalfont & Latimer §	⊖ d	16 28	16 43		17 13	17 41		18 13		18 43		19 14	19 30		20 04	20 27	20 54	21 28	21 58	22 28	22 58	23 28	23 58
Amersham §	⊖ d	16 32	16 47	16 57	17 17	17 45		18 17	18 29	18 47		19 18	19 34	19 51	20 08	20 31	20 58	21 32	22 02	22 32	23 02	23 32	00 02
Great Missenden	d	16 39	16 54	17 04	17 24	17 52	18 06	18 24	18 37	18 54	19 08	19 25	19 42	19 58	20 15	20 38	21 05	21 39	22 09	22 39	23 09	23 39	00 09
Wendover	d	16 45	17 00	17 10	17 30	17 58	18 12	18 30	18 43	19 00	19 14	19 31	19 49	20 04	20 21	20 44	21 11	21 45	22 15	22 45	23 15	23 45	00 15
Stoke Mandeville	d	16 49	17 04	17 14	17 34	18 02	18 17	18 34	18 47	19 04	19 19	19 35	19 54	20 09	20 25	20 48	21 15	21 49	22 19	22 49	23 19	23 49	00 19
Aylesbury	d	16a55	17 09	17a21	17 39	18a09	18 24	18a39	18 52	19a11	19 25	19a42	20 03	20a16	20 31	20 53	21a22	21 54	22a26	22 54	23a26	23 54	00a26
Aylesbury Vale Parkway	a		17 18		17 48		18 32		19 01		19 33		20 11		20 39	21 02		22 03		23 03		00 03	

		CH
London Marylebone 10	⊖ d	23 57
Harrow-on-the-Hill 3 §	⊖ d	00 09
Rickmansworth §	⊖ d	00 19
Chorleywood §	⊖ d	00 24
Chalfont & Latimer §	⊖ d	00 28
Amersham §	⊖ d	00 32
Great Missenden	d	00 39
Wendover	d	00 45
Stoke Mandeville	d	00 49
Aylesbury	d	00 54
Aylesbury Vale Parkway	a	01 03

Saturdays

21 December to 16 May

		CH	CH	CH	CH	CH	CH	CH	CH	CH	CH	CH	CH	CH	CH	CH	CH	CH	CH	CH	CH	CH	CH
		A	A																				
London Marylebone 10	⊖ d				07 27	07 57	08 27	08 57	09 27	09 57	10 27	10 57	11 27	11 57	12 27	12 57	13 27	13 57	14 27	14 57	15 27	15 57	16 27
Harrow-on-the-Hill 3 §	⊖ d		00 09		07 39	08 09	08 39	09 09	09 39	10 09	10 39	11 09	11 39	12 09	12 39	13 09	13 39	14 09	14 39	15 09	15 39	16 09	16 39
Rickmansworth §	⊖ d		00 19		07 49	08 19	08 49	09 19	09 49	10 19	10 49	11 19	11 49	12 19	12 49	13 19	13 49	14 19	14 49	15 19	15 49	16 19	16 49
Chorleywood §	⊖ d		00 24		07 54	08 24	08 54	09 24	09 54	10 24	10 54	11 24	11 54	12 24	12 54	13 24	13 54	14 24	14 54	15 24	15 54	16 24	16 54
Chalfont & Latimer §	⊖ d		00 28		07 58	08 28	08 58	09 28	09 58	10 28	10 58	11 28	11 58	12 28	12 58	13 28	13 58	14 28	14 58	15 28	15 58	16 28	16 58
Amersham §	⊖ d	00 02	00 32	07 02	08 02	08 32	09 02	09 32	10 02	10 32	11 02	11 32	12 02	12 32	13 02	13 32	14 02	14 32	15 02	15 32	16 02	16 32	17 02
Great Missenden	d	00 09	00 39	07 09	08 09	08 39	09 09	09 39	10 09	10 39	11 09	11 39	12 09	12 39	13 09	13 39	14 09	14 39	15 09	15 39	16 09	16 39	17 09
Wendover	d	00 15	00 45	07 15	08 15	08 45	09 15	09 45	10 15	10 45	11 15	11 45	12 15	12 45	13 15	13 45	14 15	14 45	15 15	15 45	16 15	16 45	17 15
Stoke Mandeville	d	00 19	00 49	07 19	08 19	08 49	09 19	09 49	10 19	10 49	11 19	11 49	12 19	12 49	13 19	13 49	14 19	14 49	15 19	15 49	16 19	16 49	17 19
Aylesbury	d	00a26	00 54	07a26	08 24	08 54	09 24	09 54	10a26	10 54	11a26	11 54	12a26	12 54	13a26	13 54	14a26	14 54	15a26	15 54	16a26	16 54	17a26
Aylesbury Vale Parkway	a		01 03		08 33	09 03	09 33	10 03		11 03		12 03		13 03		14 03		15 03		16 03		17 03	

		CH	CH	CH	CH	CH	CH	CH	CH	CH	CH	CH	CH	CH	CH	CH
London Marylebone 10	⊖ d	16 57	17 27	17 57	18 27	18 57	19 27	19 57	20 27	20 57	21 27	21 57	22 27	22 57	23 27	23 57
Harrow-on-the-Hill 3 §	⊖ d	17 09	17 39	18 09	18 39	19 09	19 39	20 09	20 39	21 09	21 39	22 09	22 39	23 09	23 39	00 09
Rickmansworth §	⊖ d	17 19	17 49	18 19	18 49	19 19	19 49	20 19	20 49	21 19	21 49	22 19	22 49	23 19	23 49	00 19
Chorleywood §	⊖ d	17 24	17 54	18 24	18 54	19 24	19 54	20 24	20 54	21 24	21 54	22 24	22 54	23 24	23 54	00 24
Chalfont & Latimer §	⊖ d	17 28	17 58	18 28	18 58	19 28	19 58	20 28	20 58	21 28	21 58	22 28	22 58	23 28	23 58	00 28
Amersham §	⊖ d	17 32	18 02	18 32	19 02	19 32	20 02	20 32	21 02	21 32	22 02	22 32	23 02	23 32	00 02	00 32
Great Missenden	d	17 39	18 09	18 39	19 09	19 39	20 09	20 39	21 09	21 39	22 09	22 39	23 09	23 39	00 09	00 39
Wendover	d	17 45	18 15	18 45	19 15	19 45	20 15	20 45	21 15	21 45	22 15	22 45	23 15	23 45	00 15	00 45
Stoke Mandeville	d	17 49	18 19	18 49	19 19	19 49	20 19	20 49	21 19	21 49	22 19	22 49	23 19	23 49	00 19	00 49
Aylesbury	d	17 54	18a26	18 54	19a26	19 54	20a26	20 54	21 24	21 54	22a26	22 54	23 24	23 54	00a26	00a56
Aylesbury Vale Parkway	a	18 03		19 03		20 03		21 03	21 33	22 03		23 03	23 33	00 03		

Sundays

15 December to 10 May

		CH	CH	CH	CH	CH	CH	CH	CH	CH	CH	CH	CH	CH	CH	CH	CH	CH	CH	CH	CH	CH	CH
		B	B																				
London Marylebone 10	⊖ d			07 57	08 57	09 57	10 57	11 57	12 57	13 57	14 57	15 27	15 57	16 27	16 57	17 27	17 57	18 27	18 57	19 27	19 57	20 27	20 57
Harrow-on-the-Hill 3 §	⊖ d		00 09	08 09	09 09	10 09	11 09	12 09	13 09	14 09	15 09	15 39	16 09	16 39	17 09	17 39	18 09	18 39	19 09	19 39	20 09	20 39	21 09
Rickmansworth §	⊖ d		00 19	08 19	09 19	10 19	11 19	12 19	13 19	14 19	15 19	15 49	16 19	16 49	17 19	17 49	18 19	18 49	19 19	19 49	20 19	20 49	21 19
Chorleywood §	⊖ d		00 24	08 24	09 24	10 24	11 24	12 24	13 24	14 24	15 24	15 54	16 24	16 54	17 24	17 54	18 24	18 54	19 24	19 54	20 24	20 54	21 24
Chalfont & Latimer §	⊖ d		00 28	08 28	09 28	10 28	11 28	12 28	13 28	14 28	15 28	15 58	16 28	16 58	17 28	17 58	18 28	18 58	19 28	19 58	20 28	20 58	21 28
Amersham §	⊖ d	00 02	00 32	08 32	09 32	10 32	11 32	12 32	13 32	14 32	15 32	16 02	16 32	17 02	17 32	18 02	18 32	19 02	19 32	20 02	20 32	21 02	21 32
Great Missenden	d	00 09	00 39	08 39	09 39	10 39	11 39	12 39	13 39	14 39	15 39	16 09	16 39	17 09	17 39	18 09	18 39	19 09	19 39	20 09	20 39	21 09	21 39
Wendover	d	00 15	00 45	08 45	09 45	10 45	11 45	12 45	13 45	14 45	15 45	16 15	16 45	17 15	17 45	18 15	18 45	19 15	19 45	20 15	20 45	21 15	21 45
Stoke Mandeville	d	00 19	00 49	08 49	09 49	10 49	11 49	12 49	13 49	14 49	15 49	16 19	16 49	17 19	17 49	18 19	18 49	19 19	19 49	20 19	20 49	21 19	21 49
Aylesbury	d	00a26	00a56	08 54	09 54	10 54	11 54	12 54	13 54	14 54	15 54	16a26	16 54	17a26	17 54	18a26	18 54	19a26	19 54	20a26	20 54	21 24	21 54
Aylesbury Vale Parkway	a			09 03	10 03	11 03	12 03	13 03	14 03	15 03	16 03		17 03		18 03		19 03		20 03		21 03	21 33	22 03

§ London Underground Limited (Metropolitan Line) services operate between Harrow-on-the-Hill, Rickmansworth, Chorleywood, Chalfont & Latimer and Amersham

A From London Marylebone
B not 15 December. From London Marylebone

For additional services between London and Aylesbury refer to Table T115

Table T114-F

Sundays
15 December to 10 May

London - Amersham and Aylesbury

		CH	CH	CH	CH	CH
London Marylebone 10	⊖ d	21 27	21 57	22 27	22 57	23 27
Harrow-on-the-Hill 3 §	⊖ d	21 39	22 09	22 39	23 09	23 39
Rickmansworth §	⊖ d	21 49	22 19	22 49	23 19	23 49
Chorleywood §	⊖ d	21 54	22 24	22 54	23 24	23 54
Chalfont & Latimer §	⊖ d	21 58	22 28	22 58	23 28	23 58
Amersham §	⊖ d	22 02	22 32	23 02	23 32	00 02
Great Missenden	d	22 09	22 39	23 09	23 39	00 09
Wendover	d	22 15	22 45	23 15	23 45	00 15
Stoke Mandeville	d	22 19	22 49	23 19	23 49	00 19
Aylesbury	d	22 24	22a56	23 24	23a56	00a26
Aylesbury Vale Parkway	a	22 33		23 33		

§ London Underground Limited (Metropolitan Line) services operate between Harrow-on-the-Hill, Rickmansworth, Chorleywood, Chalfont & Latimer and Amersham

For additional services between London and Aylesbury refer to Table T115

AVAILABLE FROM MP Middleton Press

RICKMANSWORTH TO AYLESBURY

Including the Chesham Branch

MIDLAND MAIN LINES

Vic Mitchell and Keith Smith

MP Middleton Press

EVOLVING THE ULTIMATE RAIL ENCYCLOPEDIA

Table T114-R

Mondays to Fridays
16 December to 15 May

Aylesbury and Amersham - London

Miles			CH	CH	CH	CH A	CH B	CH		CH	CH	CH	CH	CH	CH A	CH B	CH A	CH B		CH	CH	CH A	CH B	CH A	CH B
0	**Aylesbury Vale Parkway**	d	05 16	05 44		06 19	06 20			06 53		07 25		07 51	08 12	08 13	08 39	08 40			09 18			10 13	10 15
2¾	**Aylesbury**	d	05 21	05 49	06 07	06 24	06 25	06 38		06 58	07 10	07 30	07 41	08 02	08 17	08 18	08 44	08 45		09 02	09 23	09 48	09 50	10 18	10 20
5¼	Stoke Mandeville	d	05 26	05 54	06 11	06 29	06 30	06 43		07 03	07 15	07 35	07 46	08 07	08 22	08 23	08 48	08 49		09 06	09 27	09 52	09 54	10 22	10 24
7¼	Wendover	d	05 30	05 58	06 15	06 33	06 34	06 47		07 07	07 19	07 39	07 50	08 11	08 26	08 27	08 52	08 53		09 10	09 31	09 56	09 58	10 26	10 28
11¾	Great Missenden	d	05 36	06 04	06 21	06 40	06 41	06 53		07 14	07 25	07 46	07 56	08 18	08 32	08 33	08 58	08 59		09 16	09 37	10 02	10 04	10 32	10 34
17	**Amersham** §	⊖ d	05 43	06 11	06 28	06 47	06 48	07 00		07 21	07 32	07 53	08 03	08 25	08 39	08 40	09 05	09 06		09 23	09 44	10 09	10 11	10 39	10 41
19	Chalfont & Latimer §	⊖ d		06 15	06 32			07 04			07 36		08 07		08 43	08 44	09 09	09 10		09 27	09 48	10 13	10 15	10 43	10 45
21¼	Chorleywood §	⊖ d		06 18	06 35			07 07			07 39		08 10		08 46	08 47	09 12	09 13		09 30	09 52	10 16	10 18	10 46	10 48
23½	Rickmansworth §	⊖ d		06 23	06 40			07 12					08 15				09 17	09 18		09 35	09 56	10 21	10 23	10 51	10 53
31½	Harrow-on-the-Hill 3 §	⊖ d	06 01	06 34	06 51			07 23			07 53		08 26	08 46	09 01	09 02	09 28	09 29		09 46	10 08	10 32	10 34	11 02	11 04
40½	**London Marylebone** 10	⊖ a	06 16	06 49	07 07	07 22	07 22	07 38		07 53	08 09	08 27	08 41	09 03	09 17	09 18	09 44	09 45		10 04	10 23	10 50	10 50	11 20	11 20

		CH A	CH B	CH A		CH B	CH A	CH B	CH A	CH B	CH A	CH B	CH A	CH B		CH A	CH B	CH A	CH B	CH A	CH B	CH A	CH B	CH A	
Aylesbury Vale Parkway	d			11 13		11 15			12 13	12 15			13 13	13 15				14 13	14 15			15 13	15 15		
Aylesbury	d	10 48	10 50	11 18		11 20	11 48	11 50	12 18	12 20	12 48	12 50	13 18	13 20		13 48	13 50	14 18	14 20	14 48	14 50	15 18	15 20	15 48	
Stoke Mandeville	d	10 52	10 54	11 22		11 24	11 52	11 54	12 22	12 24	12 52	12 54	13 22	13 24		13 52	13 54	14 22	14 24	14 52	14 54	15 22	15 24	15 52	
Wendover	d	10 56	10 58	11 26		11 28	11 56	11 58	12 26	12 28	12 56	12 58	13 26	13 28		13 56	13 58	14 26	14 28	14 56	14 58	15 26	15 28	15 56	
Great Missenden	d	11 02	11 04	11 32		11 34	12 02	12 04	12 32	12 34	13 02	13 04	13 32	13 34		14 02	14 04	14 32	14 34	15 02	15 04	15 32	15 34	16 02	
Amersham §	⊖ d	11 09	11 11	11 39		11 41	12 09	12 11	12 39	12 41	13 09	13 11	13 39	13 41		14 09	14 11	14 39	14 41	15 09	15 11	15 39	15 41	16 09	
Chalfont & Latimer §	⊖ d	11 13	11 15	11 43		11 45	12 13	12 15	12 43	12 45	13 13	13 15	13 43	13 45		14 13	14 15	14 43	14 45	15 13	15 15	15 43	15 45	16 13	
Chorleywood §	⊖ d	11 16	11 18	11 46		11 48	12 16	12 18	12 46	12 48	13 16	13 18	13 46	13 48		14 16	14 18	14 46	14 48	15 16	15 18	15 46	15 48	16 16	
Rickmansworth §	⊖ d	11 21	11 23	11 51		11 53	12 21	12 23	12 51	12 53	13 21	13 23	13 51	13 53		14 21	14 23	14 51	14 53	15 21	15 23	15 51	15 53	16 21	
Harrow-on-the-Hill 3 §	⊖ d	11 32	11 34	12 02		12 04	12 32	12 34	13 02	13 04	13 32	13 34	14 02	14 04		14 32	14 34	15 02	15 04	15 32	15 34	16 02	16 04	16 32	
London Marylebone 10	⊖ a	11 50	11 50	12 20		12 20	12 50	12 50	13 20	13 20	13 50	13 50	14 20	14 20		14 50	14 50	15 20	15 20	15 50	15 50	16 20	16 21	16 50	

		CH B	CH A	CH B	CH A	CH B	CH	CH	CH	CH		CH	CH	CH A	CH B	CH	CH B	CH A	CH	CH A		CH B	CH A	CH B	CH A
Aylesbury Vale Parkway	d		16 13	16 15			16 43		17 34	18 06			18 42			19 43			20 48	21 13		21 15			
Aylesbury	d	15 50	16 18	16 20	16 30	16 33	16 48	17 15	17 50	18a11		18 20	18 47	19 18	19 20	19 48	20 20	20 21	20 53	21 18		21 20	21 48	21 50	22 48
Stoke Mandeville	d	15 54	16 22	16 24	16 35	16 38	16 52	17 19	17 54			18 25	18 51	19 22	19 24	19 52	20 24	20 25	20 57	21 22		21 24	21 52	21 54	22 52
Wendover	d	15 58	16 26	16 28	16 39	16 42	16 56	17 23	17 58			18 29	18 55	19 26	19 28	19 56	20 28	20 29	21 01	21 26		21 28	21 56	21 58	22 56
Great Missenden	d	16 04	16 32	16 34	16 45	16 48	17 02	17 29	18 04			18 35	19 01	19 32	19 34	20 02	20 34	20 35	21 07	21 32		21 34	22 02	22 04	23 02
Amersham §	⊖ d	16 11	16 39	16 41	16 51	16 54	17 09	17 36	18 11			18 42	19 08	19 39	19 41	20 09	20 41	20 42	21 14	21 39		21 41	22 09	22 11	23 09
Chalfont & Latimer §	⊖ d	16 15	16 43	16 45	16 55	16 58	17 13	17 40	18 15			18 46	19 12	19 43	19 45	20 13	20 45	20 46	21 18	21 43		21 45	22 13	22 15	23 13
Chorleywood §	⊖ d	16 18	16 46	16 48	16 59	17 02	17 16	17 43	18 18			18 49	19 15	19 46	19 48	20 16	20 48	20 49	21 21	21 46		21 48	22 16	22 18	23 16
Rickmansworth §	⊖ d	16 23	16 51	16 53	17 03	17 06	17 21	17 48	18 23			18 54	19 20	19 51	19 53	20 21	20 53	20 54	21 26	21 51		21 53	22 21	22 23	23 21
Harrow-on-the-Hill 3 §	⊖ d	16 34	17 02	17 04	17 16	17 17	17 32	17 59	18 34			19 05	19 31	20 02	20 04	20 32	21 04	21 05	21 37	22 02		22 04	22 32	22 34	23 32
London Marylebone 10	⊖ a	16 50	17 20	17 20	17 32	17 33	17 48	18 15	18 50			19 20	19 48	20 20	20 20	20 49	21 20	21 21	21 53	22 20		22 20	22 50	22 50	23 50

		CH B
Aylesbury Vale Parkway	d	
Aylesbury	d	22 50
Stoke Mandeville	d	22 54
Wendover	d	22 58
Great Missenden	d	23 04
Amersham §	⊖ d	23 11
Chalfont & Latimer §	⊖ d	23 15
Chorleywood §	⊖ d	23 18
Rickmansworth §	⊖ d	23 23
Harrow-on-the-Hill 3 §	⊖ d	23 34
London Marylebone 10	⊖ a	23 50

Saturdays
21 December to 16 May

		CH C	CH D	CH C	CH D	CH C	CH D	CH C	CH D	CH C		CH D	CH C	CH D	CH C	CH D	CH C	CH D	CH C	CH D		CH C	CH D	CH C	CH D
Aylesbury Vale Parkway	d	06 13	06 15			07 13	07 15			08 13		08 15	08 43	08 45	09 13	09 15	09 43	09 45	10 13	10 15				11 13	11 15
Aylesbury	d	06 18	06 20	06 48	06 50	07 18	07 20	07 48	07 50	08 18		08 20	08 48	08 50	09 18	09 20	09 48	09 50	10 18	10 20		10 48	10 50	11 18	11 20
Stoke Mandeville	d	06 22	06 24	06 52	06 54	07 22	07 24	07 52	07 54	08 22		08 24	08 52	08 54	09 22	09 24	09 52	09 54	10 22	10 24		10 52	10 54	11 22	11 24
Wendover	d	06 26	06 28	06 56	06 58	07 26	07 28	07 56	07 58	08 26		08 28	08 56	08 58	09 26	09 28	09 56	09 58	10 26	10 28		10 56	10 58	11 26	11 28
Great Missenden	d	06 32	06 34	07 02	07 04	07 32	07 34	08 02	08 04	08 32		08 34	09 02	09 04	09 32	09 34	10 02	10 04	10 32	10 34		11 02	11 04	11 32	11 34
Amersham §	⊖ d	06 39	06 41	07 09	07 11	07 39	07 41	08 09	08 11	08 39		08 41	09 09	09 11	09 39	09 41	10 09	10 11	10 39	10 41		11 09	11 11	11 39	11 41
Chalfont & Latimer §	⊖ d	06 43	06 45	07 13	07 15	07 43	07 45	08 13	08 15	08 43		08 45	09 13	09 15	09 43	09 45	10 13	10 15	10 43	10 45		11 13	11 15	11 43	11 45
Chorleywood §	⊖ d	06 46	06 48	07 16	07 18	07 46	07 48	08 16	08 18	08 46		08 48	09 16	09 18	09 46	09 48	10 16	10 18	10 46	10 48		11 16	11 18	11 46	11 48
Rickmansworth §	⊖ d	06 51	06 53	07 21	07 23	07 51	07 53	08 21	08 23	08 51		08 53	09 21	09 23	09 51	09 53	10 21	10 23	10 51	10 53		11 21	11 23	11 51	11 53
Harrow-on-the-Hill 3 §	⊖ d	07 02	07 04	07 32	07 34	08 02	08 04	08 32	08 34	09 02		09 04	09 32	09 34	10 02	10 04	10 32	10 34	11 02	11 04		11 32	11 34	12 02	12 04
London Marylebone 10	⊖ a	07 18	07 20	07 50	07 50	08 20	08 20	08 50	08 50	09 20		09 20	09 50	09 50	10 20	10 20	10 50	10 50	11 20	11 20		11 50	11 50	12 20	12 20

		CH C	CH D	CH C	CH D	CH C		CH D	CH C	CH D	CH C	CH D	CH C	CH D	CH C	CH D		CH C	CH D	CH C	CH D	CH C	CH D	CH C	CH D
Aylesbury Vale Parkway	d			12 13	12 15				13 13	13 15			14 13	14 15				15 13	15 15			16 13	16 15		
Aylesbury	d	11 48	11 50	12 18	12 20	12 48		12 50	13 18	13 20	13 48	13 50	14 18	14 20	14 48	14 50		15 18	15 20	15 48	15 50	16 18	16 20	16 48	16 50
Stoke Mandeville	d	11 52	11 54	12 22	12 24	12 52		12 54	13 22	13 24	13 52	13 54	14 22	14 24	14 52	14 54		15 22	15 24	15 52	15 54	16 22	16 24	16 52	16 54
Wendover	d	11 56	11 58	12 26	12 28	12 56		12 58	13 26	13 28	13 56	13 58	14 26	14 28	14 56	14 58		15 26	15 28	15 56	15 58	16 26	16 28	16 56	16 58
Great Missenden	d	12 02	12 04	12 32	12 34	13 02		13 04	13 32	13 34	14 02	14 04	14 32	14 34	15 02	15 04		15 32	15 34	16 02	16 04	16 32	16 34	17 02	17 04
Amersham §	⊖ d	12 09	12 11	12 39	12 41	13 09		13 11	13 39	13 41	14 09	14 11	14 39	14 41	15 09	15 11		15 39	15 41	16 09	16 11	16 39	16 41	17 09	17 11
Chalfont & Latimer §	⊖ d	12 13	12 15	12 43	12 45	13 13		13 15	13 43	13 45	14 13	14 15	14 43	14 45	15 13	15 15		15 43	15 45	16 13	16 15	16 43	16 45	17 13	17 15
Chorleywood §	⊖ d	12 16	12 18	12 46	12 48	13 16		13 18	13 46	13 48	14 16	14 18	14 46	14 48	15 16	15 18		15 46	15 48	16 16	16 18	16 46	16 48	17 16	17 18
Rickmansworth §	⊖ d	12 21	12 23	12 51	12 53	13 21		13 23	13 51	13 53	14 21	14 23	14 51	14 53	15 21	15 23		15 51	15 53	16 21	16 23	16 51	16 53	17 21	17 23
Harrow-on-the-Hill 3 §	⊖ d	12 32	12 34	13 02	13 04	13 32		13 34	14 02	14 04	14 32	14 34	15 02	15 04	15 32	15 34		16 02	16 04	16 32	16 34	17 02	17 04	17 32	17 34
London Marylebone 10	⊖ a	12 50	12 50	13 20	13 20	13 50		13 50	14 20	14 20	14 50	14 50	15 20	15 20	15 50	15 50		16 20	16 20	16 50	16 50	17 20	17 20	17 50	17 50

§ London Underground Limited (Metropolitan Line) services operate between Harrow-on-the-Hill, Rickmansworth, Chorleywood, Chalfont & Latimer and Amersham

A until 20 March
B from 23 March
C until 21 March
D from 28 March

For additional services between London and Aylesbury refer to Table T115

Table T114-R

Saturdays

21 December to 16 May

Aylesbury and Amersham - London

		CH A	CH B	CH A	CH B	CH A	CH B	CH A	CH B	CH A	CH B	CH A	CH B	CH A	CH B	CH A	CH B	CH A	CH B	CH A	CH B	CH A	CH B
Aylesbury Vale Parkway	d	17 13	17 15			18 13	18 15			19 13	19 15			20 13	20 15			21 13	21 15	21 43	21 45	22 13	22 15
Aylesbury	d	17 18	17 20	17 48	17 50	18 18	18 20	18 48	18 50	19 18	19 20	19 48	19 50	20 18	20 20	20 48	20 50	21 18	21 20	21 48	21 50	22 18	22 20
Stoke Mandeville	d	17 22	17 24	17 52	17 54	18 22	18 24	18 52	18 54	19 22	19 24	19 52	19 54	20 22	20 24	20 52	20 54	21 22	21 24	21 52	21 54	22 22	22 24
Wendover	d	17 26	17 28	17 56	17 58	18 26	18 28	18 56	18 58	19 26	19 28	19 56	19 58	20 26	20 28	20 56	20 58	21 26	21 28	21 56	21 58	22 26	22 28
Great Missenden	d	17 32	17 34	18 02	18 04	18 32	18 34	19 02	19 04	19 32	19 34	20 02	20 04	20 32	20 34	21 02	21 04	21 32	21 34	22 02	22 04	22 32	22 34
Amersham §	⊖ d	17 39	17 41	18 09	18 11	18 39	18 41	19 09	19 11	19 39	19 41	20 09	20 11	20 39	20 41	21 09	21 11	21 39	21 41	22 09	22 11	22 39	22 41
Chalfont & Latimer §	⊖ d	17 43	17 45	18 13	18 15	18 43	18 45	19 13	19 15	19 43	19 45	20 13	20 15	20 43	20 45	21 13	21 15	21 43	21 45	22 13	22 15	22 43	22 45
Chorleywood §	⊖ d	17 46	17 48	18 16	18 18	18 46	18 48	19 16	19 18	19 46	19 48	20 16	20 18	20 46	20 48	21 16	21 18	21 46	21 48	22 16	22 18	22 46	22 48
Rickmansworth §	⊖ d	17 51	17 53	18 21	18 23	18 51	18 53	19 21	19 23	19 51	19 53	20 21	20 23	20 51	20 53	21 21	21 23	21 51	21 53	22 21	22 23	22 51	22 53
Harrow-on-the-Hill 3 §	⊖ d	18 02	18 04	18 32	18 34	19 02	19 04	19 32	19 34	20 02	20 04	20 32	20 34	21 02	21 04	21 32	21 34	22 02	22 04	22 32	22 34	23 02	23 04
London Marylebone 10	⊖ a	18 20	18 20	18 50	18 50	19 20	19 20	19 50	19 50	20 20	20 20	20 50	20 50	21 20	21 20	21 50	21 50	22 20	22 20	22 50	22 50	23 18	23 20

		CH A	CH B
Aylesbury Vale Parkway	d		
Aylesbury	d	23 18	23 20
Stoke Mandeville	d	23 22	23 24
Wendover	d	23 26	23 28
Great Missenden	d	23 32	23 34
Amersham §	⊖ d	23a42	23a44
Chalfont & Latimer §	⊖ d		
Chorleywood §	⊖ d		
Rickmansworth §	⊖ d		
Harrow-on-the-Hill 3 §	⊖ d		
London Marylebone 10	⊖ a		

Sundays

15 December to 10 May

		CH C	CH D	CH C	CH D	CH C	CH D	CH C	CH D	CH C	CH D	CH C	CH D	CH C	CH D	CH C	CH D	CH C	CH D	CH C	CH D	CH C	CH D
Aylesbury Vale Parkway	d	07 13	07 15	08 13	08 15			09 13	09 15			10 13	10 15	11 13	11 15	12 13	12 15	13 13	13 15	14 13	14 15	15 13	15 15
Aylesbury	d	07 18	07 20	08 18	08 20	08 48	08 50	09 18	09 20	09 48	09 50	10 18	10 20	11 18	11 20	12 18	12 20	13 18	13 20	14 18	14 20	15 18	15 20
Stoke Mandeville	d	07 22	07 24	08 22	08 24	08 52	08 54	09 22	09 24	09 52	09 54	10 22	10 24	11 22	11 24	12 22	12 24	13 22	13 24	14 22	14 24	15 22	15 24
Wendover	d	07 26	07 28	08 26	08 28	08 56	08 58	09 26	09 28	09 56	09 58	10 26	10 28	11 26	11 28	12 26	12 28	13 26	13 28	14 26	14 28	15 26	15 28
Great Missenden	d	07 32	07 34	08 32	08 34	09 02	09 04	09 32	09 34	10 02	10 04	10 32	10 34	11 32	11 34	12 32	12 34	13 32	13 34	14 32	14 34	15 32	15 34
Amersham §	⊖ d	07 39	07 41	08 39	08 41	09 09	09 11	09 39	09 41	10 09	10 11	10 39	10 41	11 39	11 41	12 39	12 41	13 39	13 41	14 39	14 41	15 39	15 41
Chalfont & Latimer §	⊖ d	07 43	07 45	08 43	08 45	09 13	09 15	09 43	09 45	10 13	10 15	10 43	10 45	11 43	11 45	12 43	12 45	13 43	13 45	14 43	14 45	15 43	15 45
Chorleywood §	⊖ d	07 46	07 48	08 46	08 48	09 16	09 18	09 46	09 48	10 16	10 18	10 46	10 48	11 46	11 48	12 46	12 48	13 46	13 48	14 46	14 48	15 46	15 48
Rickmansworth §	⊖ d	07 51	07 53	08 51	08 53	09 21	09 23	09 51	09 53	10 21	10 23	10 51	10 53	11 51	11 53	12 51	12 53	13 51	13 53	14 51	14 53	15 51	15 53
Harrow-on-the-Hill 3 §	⊖ d	08 02	08 04	09 02	09 04	09 32	09 34	10 02	10 04	10 32	10 34	11 02	11 04	12 02	12 04	13 02	13 04	14 02	14 04	15 02	15 04	16 02	16 04
London Marylebone 10	⊖ a	08 20	08 20	09 18	09 20	09 50	09 50	10 20	10 20	10 50	10 50	11 20	11 20	12 20	12 20	13 20	13 20	14 20	14 20	15 20	15 20	16 20	16 20

		CH C	CH D	CH C	CH D	CH C	CH D	CH C	CH D	CH C	CH D	CH C	CH D	CH C	CH D	CH C	CH D	CH C	CH D	CH C	CH D	CH C	CH D
Aylesbury Vale Parkway	d			16 13	16 15			17 13	17 15			18 13	18 15			19 13	19 15			20 13	20 15		
Aylesbury	d	15 48	15 50	16 18	16 20	16 48	16 50	17 18	17 20	17 48	17 50	18 18	18 20	18 48	18 50	19 18	19 20	19 48	19 50	20 18	20 20	20 48	20 50
Stoke Mandeville	d	15 52	15 54	16 22	16 24	16 52	16 54	17 22	17 24	17 52	17 54	18 22	18 24	18 52	18 54	19 22	19 24	19 52	19 54	20 22	20 24	20 52	20 54
Wendover	d	15 56	15 58	16 26	16 28	16 56	16 58	17 26	17 28	17 56	17 58	18 26	18 28	18 56	18 58	19 26	19 28	19 56	19 58	20 26	20 28	20 56	20 58
Great Missenden	d	16 02	16 04	16 32	16 34	17 02	17 04	17 32	17 34	18 02	18 04	18 32	18 34	19 02	19 04	19 32	19 34	20 02	20 04	20 32	20 34	21 02	21 04
Amersham §	⊖ d	16 09	16 11	16 39	16 41	17 09	17 11	17 39	17 41	18 09	18 11	18 39	18 41	19 09	19 11	19 39	19 41	20 09	20 11	20 39	20 41	21 09	21 11
Chalfont & Latimer §	⊖ d	16 13	16 15	16 43	16 45	17 13	17 15	17 43	17 45	18 13	18 15	18 43	18 45	19 13	19 15	19 43	19 45	20 13	20 15	20 43	20 45	21 13	21 15
Chorleywood §	⊖ d	16 16	16 18	16 46	16 48	17 16	17 18	17 46	17 48	18 16	18 18	18 46	18 48	19 16	19 18	19 46	19 48	20 16	20 18	20 46	20 48	21 16	21 18
Rickmansworth §	⊖ d	16 21	16 23	16 51	16 53	17 21	17 23	17 51	17 53	18 21	18 23	18 51	18 53	19 21	19 23	19 51	19 53	20 21	20 23	20 51	20 53	21 21	21 23
Harrow-on-the-Hill 3 §	⊖ d	16 32	16 34	17 02	17 04	17 32	17 34	18 02	18 04	18 32	18 34	19 02	19 04	19 32	19 34	20 02	20 04	20 32	20 34	21 02	21 04	21 32	21 34
London Marylebone 10	⊖ a	16 50	16 50	17 20	17 20	17 50	17 50	18 20	18 20	18 50	18 50	19 20	19 20	19 48	19 50	20 20	20 20	20 50	20 50	21 20	21 20	21 50	21 50

		CH C	CH D	CH C	CH D	CH C	CH D
Aylesbury Vale Parkway	d	21 13	21 15	21 43	21 45	22 43	22 45
Aylesbury	d	21 18	21 20	21 48	21 50	22 48	22 50
Stoke Mandeville	d	21 22	21 24	21 52	21 54	22 52	22 54
Wendover	d	21 26	21 28	21 56	21 58	22 56	22 58
Great Missenden	d	21 32	21 34	22 02	22 04	23 02	23 04
Amersham §	⊖ d	21 39	21 41	22 09	22 11	23 09	23 11
Chalfont & Latimer §	⊖ d	21 43	21 45	22 13	22 15	23 13	23 15
Chorleywood §	⊖ d	21 46	21 48	22 16	22 18	23 16	23 18
Rickmansworth §	⊖ d	21 51	21 53	22 21	22 23	23 21	23 23
Harrow-on-the-Hill 3 §	⊖ d	22 02	22 04	22 32	22 34	23 32	23 34
London Marylebone 10	⊖ a	22 20	22 20	22 50	22 50	23 48	23 50

§ London Underground Limited (Metropolitan Line) services operate between Harrow-on-the-Hill, Rickmansworth, Chorleywood, Chalfont & Latimer and Amersham

A until 21 March
B from 28 March
C until 15 March
D from 22 March

For additional services between London and Aylesbury refer to Table T115

Table T115-F

Mondays to Fridays

16 December to 15 May

London - High Wycombe, Aylesbury, Oxford Parkway, Banbury, Stratford-upon-Avon, Birmingham Snow Hill and Kidderminster

Miles	Miles	Miles	Miles			CH MX A	CH MX ◇ A	CH MX ◇ A	CH MO ◇ A	CH MX A	CH MO A	CH MX A	CH MX ◇	CH MO A	CH MX	CH MO	CH MX	CH	CH	CH	CH	CH ◇	CH	LM B	CH
0	—	—	—	**London Marylebone** 10 ⊖	d								00 01		00 05	00 05	00 10					06 09	05 50		
6½	—	—	—	Wembley Stadium	d												00 19						06 00		
8	—	—	—	Sudbury & Harrow Road	d																				
8¾	—	—	—	Sudbury Hill Harrow	d																				
9¾	—	—	—	Northolt Park	d												00 24						06 06		
—	—	—	—	West Ealing	d																				
11½	—	—	—	South Ruislip § ⊖	d									00 02			00 28						06 23		
13¼	—	—	—	West Ruislip 3 § ⊖	d									00 06			00 32						06 27		
16	—	—	—	Denham	d									00 10			00 37						06 32		
17	—	—	—	Denham Golf Club	d									00 13									06 35		
18¾	—	—	—	Gerrards Cross 4	d							00 02		00 17	00 24	00 25	00 42					06 28	06 39		
21¼	—	—	—	Seer Green	d									00 21			00 46						06 43		
23	—	—	—	Beaconsfield	d							00 09		00 25	00 30	00 32	00 50					06 34	06 47		
27¾	—	—	—	**High Wycombe** 4	d						00 04	00 15	00 28	00 31	00 36	00 38	00 56		06 05			06 40	06a56		
32¾	—	—	—	Saunderton	d					00 04				00 37			01 02		06 11						
36	0	—	—	**Princes Risborough** 2	d	00 03				00 10	00 14	00 26		00 45	00 45	00 48	01 09		06 16			06 49			
—	1½	—	—	Monks Risborough	d	00 07						00 29		00 48			01 12								
—	3	—	—	Little Kimble	d	00 11						00 33		00 52			01 16								
—	7½	—	—	**Aylesbury**	a	00 21						00 46		01 06			01 29								
44¾	—	—	0	Haddenham & Thame Parkway	d				00 03	00 17	00 21				00 52	00 55			06 23			06 55			
—	—	—	10	Bicester Village	d			00 11	00 18				00 54							05 42	06 25	07 08			
—	—	—	16	Islip	d															05 49		07 15			
—	—	—	18¾	Oxford Parkway 116	a			00 19	00 26				01 03							05 53	06 34	07 18			
—	—	—	21¾	Oxford	a			00 27	00 35				01 12							06 01	06 43	07 30			
54¾	—	—	—	**Bicester North** 3	d					00 30	00 34				01 05	01 08		05 47	06 38						
65¼	—	—	—	Kings Sutton	d					00 42						01 19									
68¾	—	—	—	**Banbury**	d		00 03			00a50	00a52				01a22	01a27		06 04	06a52						
88¾	0	—	—	**Leamington Spa** 4	d		00 21											06 25							06 51
90¾	2	—	—	Warwick	d		00 25											06 30							06 56
92	3¼	—	—	Warwick Parkway	d		00 29											06 33							
94¾	6	—	—	Hatton	d																				07 04
—	7¾	—	—	Claverdon	d																			06x31	07 10
—	11	—	—	Bearley	d																			06x35	
—	12½	—	—	Wilmcote	d																			06 40	07 20
—	14¼	—	—	Stratford-upon-Avon Parkway	a																			06 43	07 22
—	15¼	—	—	**Stratford-upon-Avon**	a																			06 48	07 31
99	—	—	—	Lapworth	d																				
101½	—	—	—	Dorridge	d													06 44							
104¾	—	—	—	Solihull	d		00 41											06 50							
111¼	—	—	—	**Birmingham Moor Street**	a		00 52											06 59							
112	—	—	—	**Birmingham Snow Hill**	a													07 07							
—	—	—	—	Rowley Regis	a																				
—	—	—	—	Cradley Heath	a																				
—	—	—	—	Stourbridge Junction 2	a																				
—	—	—	—	**Kidderminster**	a																				

§ London Underground Limited (Central Line) also operate services between South Ruislip and West Ruislip at frequent intervals

A From London Marylebone
B From Birmingham Snow Hill

For complete services between Banbury and Birmingham, refer to Table T71

For principal services between London and Aylesbury refer to Table T114

Table T115-F

Mondays to Fridays
16 December to 15 May

London - High Wycombe, Aylesbury, Oxford Parkway, Banbury, Stratford-upon-Avon, Birmingham Snow Hill and Kidderminster

Station		CH ◇	LM A	LM B	CH ◇	CH C	CH ◇	CH	CH	CH C	CH ◇	CH ◇	CH	CH	CH	CH	CH	CH ◇	CH ◇	CH	CH	CH C	CH ◇
London Marylebone 10 ⊖	d	06 05			06 17	06 33	06 48		06 40	06 52	07 11	07 14	07 00	07 18	07 26	07 29		07 40	07 48	07 44	07 51	07 57	08 11
Wembley Stadium	d				06 27				06 50				07 09	07 27							08 00		
Sudbury & Harrow Road	d																						
Sudbury Hill Harrow	d												07 13								08 04		
Northolt Park	d				06 32								07 16								08 07		
West Ealing	d																						
South Ruislip § ⊖	d								07 02				07 28							08 02			
West Ruislip 3 § ⊖	d				06 37								07 31	07a40							08 13		
Denham	d				06 42				07 08				07 36							08 09			
Denham Golf Club	d								07 10											08 11			
Gerrards Cross 1	d				06 47		07 05		07 14				07 41			07 48				08 15	08a22		
Seer Green	d				06 52								07 46							08 20			
Beaconsfield	d				06 55		07 11		07 20				07 49			07 54				08 23			
High Wycombe 1	d				07 01		07 17		07 26			07 38	07 55			08a03		08 05	08 14	08a32			
Saunderton	d				07 07								08 01										
Princes Risborough 2	d				07 13		07 25	07 26	07a38				08 07				08 12	08 14					
Monks Risborough	d							07 29									08 16						
Little Kimble	d							07 33									08 20						
Aylesbury	a					07 29		07 43		07 49					08 25		08 30					08 53	
Haddenham & Thame Parkway	d				07 20		07 31						08 13					08 20					
Bicester Village	d						07 44					08 01						08 32					08 53
Islip	d											08 08											
Oxford Parkway 116	a						07 51					08 11						08 39					09 00
Oxford	a						08 01					08 21						08 49					09 10
Bicester North 3	d	06 47			07 33						07 54		08 28						08 36				
Kings Sutton	d	06 57			07 44								08 39										
Banbury	d	07 03			07 49						08 07		08a45						08 50				
Leamington Spa 8	d	07 21			08 08						08 25								09 08				
Warwick	d	07 26			08 13						08 29								09 12				
Warwick Parkway	d	07 29									08 33								09 16				
Hatton	d	07 35			08 21																		
Claverdon	d				08 26																		
Bearley	d				08 31																		
Wilmcote	d		07 28	08 15	08 35																		
Stratford-upon-Avon Parkway	a		07 31	08 18	08 37																		
Stratford-upon-Avon	a		07 36	08 23	08 46																		
Lapworth	d																						
Dorridge	d	07 43																	09 26				
Solihull	d	07 51									08 45								09 31				
Birmingham Moor Street	a	08 02									08 53								09 42				
Birmingham Snow Hill ⛴	a	08 10									08 59												
Rowley Regis	a																						
Cradley Heath	a																						
Stourbridge Junction 2	a																						
Kidderminster	a																						

§ London Underground Limited (Central Line) also operate services between South Ruislip and West Ruislip at frequent intervals

A From Birmingham Snow Hill
B From Worcester Shrub Hill
C To Aylesbury Vale Parkway

For complete services between Banbury and Birmingham, refer to Table T71

For principal services between London and Aylesbury refer to Table T114

Table T115-F

Mondays to Fridays
16 December to 15 May

London - High Wycombe, Aylesbury, Oxford Parkway, Banbury, Stratford-upon-Avon, Birmingham Snow Hill and Kidderminster

Station		CH ◇	CH	CH	CH	LM A	CH	CH	CH ◇	CH ◇	CH	CH	CH	CH B	CH ◇	CH ◇	CH	CH	CH	CH	CH ◇	CH ◇	LM C
London Marylebone 10 ⊖	d	08 14	08 17	08 22	08 27				08 37	08 41	08 44	08 47	08 50	08 57	09 00	09 10	09 13		09 17	09 27	09 35	09 40	
Wembley Stadium	d			08 32									08 59						09 26				
Sudbury & Harrow Road	d																						
Sudbury Hill Harrow	d												09 03										
Northolt Park	d												09 06										
West Ealing	d																						
South Ruislip § ⊖	d												09 13										
West Ruislip 3 § ⊖	d		08 32																09 35				
Denham	d			08 43								09 04											
Denham Golf Club	d											09 06											
Gerrards Cross 1	d		08 39	08 48							09 03	09 10	09a24				09 33		09 42				
Seer Green	d										09 07								09 46				
Beaconsfield	d		08 45								09 11	09 17							09 50			10 02	
High Wycombe 1	d		08 51	09a01						09 07	09 17	09a26				09 36	09 43		09a59		10 00		
Saunderton	d		08 57														09 49						
Princes Risborough 2	d		09 06				09 15				09 26						09a58	10 07					
Monks Risborough	d						09 19											10 11					
Little Kimble	d						09 23											10 15					
Aylesbury	a		09 25		09 26		09 33							09 53				10 25		10 26			
Haddenham & Thame Parkway	d								09 14		09 32				09 38								
Bicester Village	d									09 31					09 52						10 23		
Islip	d														09 58								
Oxford Parkway 116	a									09 38					10 01						10 30		
Oxford	a									09 47					10 10						10 38		
Bicester North 3	d								09 26		09 45											10 29	
Kings Sutton	d										09 56												
Banbury	d	09 08							09 40		10a03					10 08						10 43	
Leamington Spa 8	d	09 26						09 40	09 58							10 25						11 01	
Warwick	d	09 30						09 45	10 03													11 05	
Warwick Parkway	d	09 34							10 07							10 32						11 09	
Hatton	d							09 52															
Claverdon	d							09 57															
Bearley	d							10 02															
Wilmcote	d					09 15		10 06															10 15
Stratford-upon-Avon Parkway	a					09 18		10 08															10 18
Stratford-upon-Avon	a					09 21		10 17															10 23
Lapworth	d																						
Dorridge	d								10 18													11 19	
Solihull	d	09 46							10 24							10 45						11 25	
Birmingham Moor Street	a	09 54							10 35							10 53						11 33	
Birmingham Snow Hill ⛴	a	10 02														11 01						11 41	
Rowley Regis	a																						
Cradley Heath	a																						
Stourbridge Junction 2	a																						
Kidderminster	a																						

§ London Underground Limited (Central Line) also operate services between South Ruislip and West Ruislip at frequent intervals

A From Kidderminster
B To Aylesbury Vale Parkway
C From Stourbridge Junction

For complete services between Banbury and Birmingham, refer to Table T71

For principal services between London and Aylesbury refer to Table T114

Table T115-F

Mondays to Fridays
16 December to 15 May

London - High Wycombe, Aylesbury, Oxford Parkway, Banbury, Stratford-upon-Avon, Birmingham Snow Hill and Kidderminster

Station		LM A	CH ◇ B	CH	CH C	CH ◇	CH ◇	CH ◇ D	CH	CH	CH	CH ◇	CH ◇	CH	CH	CH C	CH ◇	CH ◇	CH	CH	CH	CH ◇	CH ◇
London Marylebone 10 ⊖	d		09 43	09 46	09 57	10 06	10 10		10 13	10 16	10 27	10 35	10 40	10 43	10 46	10 57	11 07	11 10	11 13	11 17	11 27	11 35	11 40
Wembley Stadium	d			09 55						10 25					10 55					11 26			
Sudbury & Harrow Road	d																						
Sudbury Hill Harrow	d			09 59											10 59								
Northolt Park	d			10 02											11 01								
West Ealing	d																						
South Ruislip § ⊖	d									10 32										11 33			
West Ruislip 3 § ⊖	d		09 58												11 06								
Denham	d			10 09											11 11								
Denham Golf Club	d			10 11										11 00									
Gerrards Cross 1	d		10 05	10a18					10 32	10 42				11 04	11a19				11 32	11 42			
Seer Green	d								10 36										11 36				
Beaconsfield	d		10 12						10 40	10 48				11 10					11 40	11 48			
High Wycombe 1	d		10 18				10 36		10 46	10a58		11 00		11 16				11 35	11 46	11a58		12 00	
Saunderton	d								10 53										11 53				
Princes Risborough 2	d		10 27						11 00					11 25					12 00				
Monks Risborough	d								11 03										12 03				
Little Kimble	d																						
Aylesbury	a				10 53				11 18		11 29					11 53			12 19		12 31		
Haddenham & Thame Parkway	d		10 34			10 40								11 32			11 41						
Bicester Village	d					10 54						11 25					11 54					12 23	
Islip	d																					12 29	
Oxford Parkway 116	a					11 02						11 33					12 02					12 32	
Oxford	a					11 09		←				11 39					12 09					12 40	
Bicester North 3	d		10 47					10 47					11 28	11 45									12 27
Kings Sutton	d		→																				
Banbury	d						11 07	11 10					11 41	12a02				12 07					12 40
Leamington Spa 8	d						11 26	11 32					11 59					12 26					12 58
Warwick	d							11 37					12 03										13 02
Warwick Parkway	d						11 33						12 07					12 33					13 06
Hatton	d							11 44															
Claverdon	d																						
Bearley	d																						
Wilmcote	d	11 15						11 55															
Stratford-upon-Avon Parkway	a	11 18						11 57															
Stratford-upon-Avon	a	11 23						12 06															
Lapworth	d																						
Dorridge	d												12 17										13 16
Solihull	d						11 45						12 23					12 45					13 22
Birmingham Moor Street	a						11 56						12 33					12 56					13 33
Birmingham Snow Hill ⛴	a												12 41										13 41
Rowley Regis	a																						
Cradley Heath	a																						
Stourbridge Junction 2	a																						
Kidderminster	a																						

§ London Underground Limited (Central Line) also operate services between South Ruislip and West Ruislip at frequent intervals

A From Stourbridge Junction
B To Stratford-upon-Avon
C To Aylesbury Vale Parkway
D From London Marylebone

For complete services between Banbury and Birmingham, refer to Table T71

For principal services between London and Aylesbury refer to Table T114

Table T115-F

Mondays to Fridays
16 December to 15 May

London - High Wycombe, Aylesbury, Oxford Parkway, Banbury, Stratford-upon-Avon, Birmingham Snow Hill and Kidderminster

Station		LM A	LM A	CH ◇ B	CH	CH E	CH C	CH ◇	CH ◇	CH ◇ D	CH	CH	CH	CH ◇	CH ◇	CH	CH	CH C	CH ◇	CH ◇	CH	CH	CH
London Marylebone 10 ⊖	d			11 43	11 47		11 57	12 07	12 10		12 13	12 17	12 27	12 35	12 40	12 43	12 47	12 57	13 06	13 10	13 13	13 17	13 27
Wembley Stadium	d				11 56							12 26					12 56					13 26	
Sudbury & Harrow Road	d																						
Sudbury Hill Harrow	d				12 00												13 00						
Northolt Park	d				12 02												13 02						
West Ealing	d					11 47																	
South Ruislip § ⊖	d											12 33										13 33	
West Ruislip 3 § ⊖	d				12 07												13 07						
Denham	d				12 12												13 12						
Denham Golf Club	d			12 00												13 00							
Gerrards Cross 1	d			12 04	12a19						12 32	12 42				13 04	13a19				13 32	13 42	
Seer Green	d										12 36										13 36		
Beaconsfield	d			12 10							12 40	12 48				13 10					13 40	13 48	
High Wycombe 1	d			12 16		12a27			12 34		12 47	12a57		12 59		13 16				13 35	13 46	13a57	
Saunderton	d										12 53										13 53		
Princes Risborough 2	d			12 25							13 00					13 25					14 00		
Monks Risborough	d										13 03										14 03		
Little Kimble	d										13 07												
Aylesbury	a						12 53				13 23		13 26					13 53			14 19		14 26
Haddenham & Thame Parkway	d			12 32				12 41								13 32			13 41				
Bicester Village	d							12 55						13 22					13 55				
Islip	d																						
Oxford Parkway 116	a							13 03						13 31					14 03				
Oxford	a							13 10		←				13 37					14 10				
Bicester North 3	d			12 45						12 45					13 27	13 45							
Kings Sutton	d			→						12 55													
Banbury	d								13 08	13 10					13 40	14a02				14 07			
Leamington Spa 8	d								13 26	13 32					13 58					14 26			
Warwick	d									13 37					14 02								
Warwick Parkway	d								13 32						14 06					14 33			
Hatton	d									13 44													
Claverdon	d									13 49													
Bearley	d									13 55													
Wilmcote	d	12 15	13 15							13 59													
Stratford-upon-Avon Parkway	a	12 18	13 18							14 01													
Stratford-upon-Avon	a	12 23	13 23							14 10													
Lapworth	d																						
Dorridge	d														14 16								
Solihull	d								13 45						14 22					14 45			
Birmingham Moor Street	a								13 56						14 33					14 56			
Birmingham Snow Hill ⛴	a														14 41								
Rowley Regis	a																						
Cradley Heath	a																						
Stourbridge Junction 2	a																						
Kidderminster	a																						

§ London Underground Limited (Central Line) also operate services between South Ruislip and West Ruislip at frequent intervals

A From Stourbridge Junction
B To Stratford-upon-Avon
C To Aylesbury Vale Parkway
D From London Marylebone
E Parliamentary Train

For complete services between Banbury and Birmingham, refer to Table T71

For principal services between London and Aylesbury refer to Table T114

Table T115-F

Mondays to Fridays
16 December to 15 May

London - High Wycombe, Aylesbury, Oxford Parkway, Banbury, Stratford-upon-Avon, Birmingham Snow Hill and Kidderminster

		CH	CH	LM		LM	CH	CH	CH	CH	CH	CH	CH	CH	CH	CH	CH	CH	CH	CH		CH	CH	CH	CH
		◇	◇				◇			◇	◇	◇				◇	◇					◇	◇		
				A		A	B		C			D								C					
London Marylebone 10 ⊖	d	13 35	13 40				13 43	13 47	13 57	14 06	14 10		14 13	14 17	14 27	14 35	14 40	14 43	14 47	14 57		15 05	15 10	15 13	15 17
Wembley Stadium	d							13 56						14 26					14 56						15 26
Sudbury & Harrow Road	d																								
Sudbury Hill Harrow	d													14 30											
Northolt Park	d							14 01											15 01						
West Ealing	d																								
South Ruislip § ⊖	d													14 35											15 33
West Ruislip 3 § ⊖	d							14 06											15 06						
Denham	d							14 10											15 10					15 29	
Denham Golf Club	d						14 00												15 12						
Gerrards Cross 1	d						14 04	14a18					14 32	14 44				15 02	15a19					15 34	15 41
Seer Green	d												14 36												15 45
Beaconsfield	d						14 10						14 40	14 50				15 08						15 40	15 49
High Wycombe 1	d	13 59					14 16				14 34		14 46	15a01		15 03		15 14					15 35	15 46	15a59
Saunderton	d												14 53											15 53	
Princes Risborough 2	d						14 25						15 00					15 23						16 00	
Monks Risborough	d												15 03											16 03	
Little Kimble	d												15 07												
Aylesbury	a								14 53				15 20		15 32					15 53				16 19	
Haddenham & Thame Parkway	d						14 32			14 41								15 30					15 48		
Bicester Village	d	14 22								14 54						15 25						15 55			
Islip	d									15 00															
Oxford Parkway 116	a	14 31								15 04						15 33						16 03			
Oxford	a	14 37								15 12		←				15 41						16 11			
Bicester North 3	d		14 27				14 45					14 45					15 29	15 43							
Kings Sutton	d						→											15 56							
Banbury	d		14 40								15 07	15 10					15 42	16a04					16 09		
Leamington Spa 8	d		14 58								15 25	15 32					15 59						16 26		
Warwick	d		15 02									15 37					16 03								
Warwick Parkway	d		15 06								15 30						16 07						16 32		
Hatton	d											15 44													
Claverdon	d											15 49													
Bearley	d											15 55													
Wilmcote	d			14 15		15 15						15 59													
Stratford-upon-Avon Parkway	a			14 18		15 18						16 01													
Stratford-upon-Avon	a			14 23		15 23						16 10													
Lapworth	d																								
Dorridge	d		15 16														16 17								
Solihull	d		15 22								15 45						16 23						16 45		
Birmingham Moor Street	a		15 33								15 56						16 33						16 54		
Birmingham Snow Hill	a		15 41														16 41						17 02		
Rowley Regis	a																								
Cradley Heath	a																								
Stourbridge Junction 2	a																								
Kidderminster	a																								

§ London Underground Limited (Central Line) also operate services between South Ruislip and West Ruislip at frequent intervals

A From Stourbridge Junction
B To Stratford-upon-Avon
C To Aylesbury Vale Parkway
D From London Marylebone

For complete services between Banbury and Birmingham, refer to Table T71

For principal services between London and Aylesbury refer to Table T114

Table T115-F

Mondays to Fridays
16 December to 15 May

London - High Wycombe, Aylesbury, Oxford Parkway, Banbury, Stratford-upon-Avon, Birmingham Snow Hill and Kidderminster

		CH	CH	CH		CH	CH	CH	CH	CH	LM	CH	CH	CH	CH	LM	LM	LM	CH	CH		CH	CH	CH	CH
			◇	◇								◇	◇	◇											◇
		A								A	B					B	B	C	D					A	
London Marylebone 10 ⊖	d	15 27	15 35	15 40		15 43	16 00	15 50	15 56	16 12		16 15	16 18	16 21					16 24	16 27		16 30	16 33	16 42	16 47
Wembley Stadium	d							15 59															16 42		
Sudbury & Harrow Road	d																						16 45		
Sudbury Hill Harrow	d							16 03																	
Northolt Park	d							16 06															16 49		
West Ealing	d																								
South Ruislip § ⊖	d							16 14															16 53		
West Ruislip 3 § ⊖	d					15 57																	16a59		
Denham	d							16 20														16 47			
Denham Golf Club	d							16 22														16 50			
Gerrards Cross 1	d					16 04	16 17	16a28											16 43			16 54			
Seer Green	d																		16 47						
Beaconsfield	d					16 10	16 23							16 42								17 01			
High Wycombe 1	d		16 00			16 16	16 29							16 48					16 55			17a10			
Saunderton	d					16 23													17 02						
Princes Risborough 2	d					16 28								16 56	17 05				17 07						
Monks Risborough	d														17 09										
Little Kimble	d														17 13										
Aylesbury	a	16 24							16 55	17 08					17 23					17 21				17 38	
Haddenham & Thame Parkway	d					16 35	16 42						16 53						17 13						17 22
Bicester Village	d		16 22				16 54						17 06												
Islip	d																								
Oxford Parkway 116	a		16 29				17 01						17 13												
Oxford	a		16 38				17 09						17 21												
Bicester North 3	d			16 27		16 48								17 11					17 26						17 34
Kings Sutton	d																		17 37						
Banbury	d			16 40		17a03						17 08		17 24					→						17 47
Leamington Spa 8	d			16 58								17 26		17 41											18 04
Warwick	d			17 02																					18 08
Warwick Parkway	d			17 06								17 33		17 47											18 12
Hatton	d																								
Claverdon	d																								
Bearley	d																								
Wilmcote	d										16 15					17 16	18 16	18 37							
Stratford-upon-Avon Parkway	a										16 18					17 19	18 19	18 40							
Stratford-upon-Avon	a										16 23					17 24	18 24	18 43							
Lapworth	d																								
Dorridge	d			17 16										17 57											18 22
Solihull	d			17 22								17 45		18 02											18 27
Birmingham Moor Street	a			17 36								17 54		18 10											18 38
Birmingham Snow Hill	a			17 44								17 57		18 21											
Rowley Regis	a											18 13													
Cradley Heath	a																								
Stourbridge Junction 2	a											18 25													
Kidderminster	a											18 44													

§ London Underground Limited (Central Line) also operate services between South Ruislip and West Ruislip at frequent intervals

A To Aylesbury Vale Parkway
B From Stourbridge Junction
C From Worcester Foregate Street
D To Birmingham Snow Hill

For complete services between Banbury and Birmingham, refer to Table T71

For principal services between London and Aylesbury refer to Table T114

Table T115-F

Mondays to Fridays

16 December to 15 May

London - High Wycombe, Aylesbury, Oxford Parkway, Banbury, Stratford-upon-Avon, Birmingham Snow Hill and Kidderminster

		CH ◇	CH	CH		CH	CH	CH	CH A	CH ◇	CH ◇	CH FO	CH FX	CH	CH	CH B	CH	CH	CH ◇	CH ◇		CH	CH B	CH	CH
London Marylebone 10 ⊖	d	16 50	16 53	17 00		16 56	17 11			17 15	17 18	17 21	17 21	17 24	17 27	17 30	17 34	17 40	17 46	17 50		17 53	17 58	18 01	18 04
Wembley Stadium	d			17 10													17 43								18 13
Sudbury & Harrow Road	d														17 38										
Sudbury Hill Harrow	d					17 07																			18 18
Northolt Park	d					17 10									17 42										18 21
West Ealing	d																								
South Ruislip § ⊖	d					17 17									17 50										18 35
West Ruislip 3 § ⊖	d		17 08												17a59									18 16	
Denham	d		17 13											17 41								18 10			
Denham Golf Club	d													17 43											
Gerrards Cross 1	d		17 18	17 23		17a28								17 48			17 56					18 16		18 23	18a45
Seer Green	d			17 27										17 52								18 21			
Beaconsfield	d		17 26	17 31								17 45	17 45				18 02					18 25		18 29	
High Wycombe 1	d	17 13	17 32	17a40								17 53	17 53	18 00			18a11			18 14		18 31		18a38	
Saunderton	d													18 07											
Princes Risborough 2	d	17 22	17 46									18 03	18 03	18 12						18 23		18 42			
Monks Risborough	d		17 50																			18 45			
Little Kimble	d		17 54																			18 49			
Aylesbury	a		18 09				18 09									18 23		18 39				19 02	18 51		
Haddenham & Thame Parkway	d											18 12	18 12						18 23						
Bicester Village	d	17 38									18 04									18 39					
Islip	d	17 44																							
Oxford Parkway 116	a	17 47									18 11									18 46					
Oxford	a	17 56									18 20									18 54					
Bicester North 3	d								←			18 24	18a26	18a32					18 35						
Kings Sutton	d								17 37																
Banbury	d								18 02	18 09		18a42							18 48						
Leamington Spa 8	d							18 11	18 22	18 27									19 05						
Warwick	d							18 16	18 26										19 09						
Warwick Parkway	d									18 34									19 13						
Hatton	d							18 27	18 39																
Claverdon	d							18 33																	
Bearley	d							18 39																	
Wilmcote	d							18 44																	
Stratford-upon-Avon Parkway	a							18 46																	
Stratford-upon-Avon	a							18 51																	
Lapworth	d								18 46																
Dorridge	d								18 51	18 45									19 23						
Solihull	d								18 57	18 50									19 29						
Birmingham Moor Street	a								19 07	18 59									19 38						
Birmingham Snow Hill	a								19 15	19 02									19 46						
Rowley Regis	a									19 15															
Cradley Heath	a																								
Stourbridge Junction 2	a									19 26															
Kidderminster	a									19 41															

§ London Underground Limited (Central Line) also operate services between South Ruislip and West Ruislip at frequent intervals

A From London Marylebone
B To Aylesbury Vale Parkway

For complete services between Banbury and Birmingham, refer to Table T71

For principal services between London and Aylesbury refer to Table T114

NRT DECEMBER 19 EDITION

Table T115-F

Mondays to Fridays

16 December to 15 May

London - High Wycombe, Aylesbury, Oxford Parkway, Banbury, Stratford-upon-Avon, Birmingham Snow Hill and Kidderminster

		CH	CH ◇	CH ◇ A		CH	CH ◇	LM B	LM C	CH ◇	CH	CH D	CH	CH	CH ◇	CH	CH	CH	CH	CH D		CH ◇	CH	CH ◇	CH
London Marylebone 10 ⊖	d	18 12	18 15	18 18		18 21	18 47			18 24	18 28	18 32	18 36	18 43	18 50		18 53	19 03	18 56	18 59		19 15	19 18	19 21	19 24
Wembley Stadium	d										18 37								19 05						
Sudbury & Harrow Road	d										18 40														
Sudbury Hill Harrow	d										18 43														
Northolt Park	d									18 36									19 10						
West Ealing	d																								
South Ruislip § ⊖	d										18 51								19 17						
West Ruislip 3 § ⊖	d										18a57						19 08								
Denham	d									18 44							19 13								
Denham Golf Club	d																		19 23						
Gerrards Cross 1	d									18 49			18 56				19 18	19 23	19a29						19 44
Seer Green	d									18 54							19 22								19 48
Beaconsfield	d					18 44							19 03				19 26	19 31							19 52
High Wycombe 1	d					18 50				19 02			19a12		19 16		19 32	19a39						19 45	19 58
Saunderton	d									19 08															20 04
Princes Risborough 2	d					19 00				19 13					19 25	19 32	19 43								20a12
Monks Risborough	d															19 35									
Little Kimble	d															19 39									
Aylesbury	a	19 11										19 24		19 42		19 49	20 01			20 02			20 16		
Haddenham & Thame Parkway	d			18 54		19 06	19 25																	19 58	
Bicester Village	d			19 07											19 41									20 11	
Islip	d																								
Oxford Parkway 116	a			19 16											19 48									20 18	
Oxford	a			19 23											19 57									20 27	
Bicester North 3	d					19 19	19 37			19 44												20 02			
Kings Sutton	d									19 55															
Banbury	d		19 09			19a39	19 50			20 06												20 16			
Leamington Spa 8	d		19 28				20 09			20 26												20 34			
Warwick	d						20 13																		
Warwick Parkway	d		19 35				20 17			20 31												20 40			
Hatton	d									20 38															
Claverdon	d																								
Bearley	d																								
Wilmcote	d							19 16	20 15	20 48															
Stratford-upon-Avon Parkway	a							19 19	20 18	20 50															
Stratford-upon-Avon	a							19 23	20 23	20 54															
Lapworth	d																								
Dorridge	d		19 45				20 27															20 50			
Solihull	d		19 51				20 33															20 55			
Birmingham Moor Street	a		20 00				20 41															21 06			
Birmingham Snow Hill	a		20 04				20 49																		
Rowley Regis	a		20 22																						
Cradley Heath	a																								
Stourbridge Junction 2	a		20 33																						
Kidderminster	a		20 48																						

§ London Underground Limited (Central Line) also operate services between South Ruislip and West Ruislip at frequent intervals

A The Oxford Flyer
B From Stourbridge Junction
C From Birmingham Snow Hill
D To Aylesbury Vale Parkway

For complete services between Banbury and Birmingham, refer to Table T71

For principal services between London and Aylesbury refer to Table T114

Table T115-F

Mondays to Fridays
16 December to 15 May

London - High Wycombe, Aylesbury, Oxford Parkway, Banbury, Stratford-upon-Avon, Birmingham Snow Hill and Kidderminster

		CH	CH A	CH ◇	CH ◇	CH	CH	CH	CH A	CH ◇	CH ◇	CH	CH	CH	CH ◇	CH ◇	LM B	LM C	CH ◇	CH	CH A	CH ◇	CH ◇
London Marylebone [10] ⊖	d	19 28	19 32	19 47	19 50		19 53	19 36	19 56	20 07	20 10	20 13	20 16	20 23	20 37	20 40			20 43	20 46	20 57	21 06	21 10
Wembley Stadium	d							19 45					20 25							20 55			
Sudbury & Harrow Road	d							19 48															
Sudbury Hill Harrow	d							19 51												20 59			
Northolt Park	d							19 54					20 30							21 02			
West Ealing	d																						
South Ruislip § ⊖	d							20 07					20 34										
West Ruislip [3] § ⊖	d	19 43										20 28								21 07			
Denham	d	19 48										20 33								21 11			
Denham Golf Club	d	19 50																		21 14			
Gerrards Cross [1]	d	19 54					20 12	20a18				20 38	20 42						21 02	21a20			
Seer Green	d						20 17						20 47										
Beaconsfield	d	20 00					20 21					20 44	20 50						21 08				
High Wycombe [1]	d	20a09			20 14		20a30				20 35	20 50	20a59			21 05			21 14				21 36
Saunderton	d											20 56											
Princes Risborough [2]	d			20 17	20 23	20 33						21 04							21 23				
Monks Risborough	d					20 37						21 08											
Little Kimble	d					20 41																	
Aylesbury	a		20 30			20 51			20 52			21 25		21 22							21 53		
Haddenham & Thame Parkway	d			20 23							20 48				21 11				21 30			21 42	
Bicester Village	d				20 39					20 52						21 27						21 55	
Islip	d									20 58													
Oxford Parkway 116	a				20 46					21 02						21 35						22 02	
Oxford	a				20 56					21 11						21 41						22 11	
Bicester North [3]	d			20 34							20 59				21 24				21 43				21 59
Kings Sutton	d																		21 55				
Banbury	d			20 47							21 12				21 39				22 01				22 14
Leamington Spa [8]	d			21 04							21 30				21 57				22 20				22 31
Warwick	d			21 08											22 01				22 24				
Warwick Parkway	d			21 12							21 36				22 05								22 38
Hatton	d			21 17															22 31				
Claverdon	d																		22 36				
Bearley	d																						
Wilmcote	d																21 15	22 15	22 43				
Stratford-upon-Avon Parkway	a																21 18	22 18	22 45				
Stratford-upon-Avon	a																21 23	22 23	22 56				
Lapworth	d			21 23																			
Dorridge	d			21 28											22 15								
Solihull	d			21 34							21 49				22 21								22 51
Birmingham Moor Street	a			21 43							21 57				22 30								23 00
Birmingham Snow Hill	a			21 51							22 08				22 38								23 05
Rowley Regis	a										22 25												23 32
Cradley Heath	a										22 30												23 39
Stourbridge Junction [2]	a										22 36												23 49
Kidderminster	a										22 50												

§ London Underground Limited (Central Line) also operate services between South Ruislip and West Ruislip at frequent intervals

A To Aylesbury Vale Parkway
B From Kidderminster
C From Great Malvern

For complete services between Banbury and Birmingham, refer to Table T71

For principal services between London and Aylesbury refer to Table T114

Table T115-F

Mondays to Fridays
16 December to 15 May

London - High Wycombe, Aylesbury, Oxford Parkway, Banbury, Stratford-upon-Avon, Birmingham Snow Hill and Kidderminster

		CH	CH	CH	CH ◇	CH ◇	CH	CH	CH A	CH FX ◇	CH FO ◇	CH ◇	CH	CH	CH	CH ◇	CH ◇	CH	CH A	CH ◇	CH	CH ◇	LM B
London Marylebone [10] ⊖	d	21 13	21 16	21 27	21 32	21 40	21 43	21 46	21 57	22 05	22 05	22 10	22 13	22 17	22 27	22 36	22 40	22 43	22 57	23 11	23 00	23 07	
Wembley Stadium	d		21 25					21 55						22 26				22 52		23 20	23 09		
Sudbury & Harrow Road	d																						
Sudbury Hill Harrow	d																						
Northolt Park	d							22 00													23 14		
West Ealing	d																						
South Ruislip § ⊖	d		21 32											22 33							23 27		
West Ruislip [3] § ⊖	d							22 05													23 31		
Denham	d		21 38					22 10						22 39									
Denham Golf Club	d							22 12						22 41							23 36		
Gerrards Cross [1]	d	21 32	21 43				22 02	22 16					22 32	22 45				23 05			23 40		
Seer Green	d	21 36											22 36										
Beaconsfield	d	21 40	21 49				22 08	22 22					22 40	22 51				23 11			23 46		
High Wycombe [1]	d	21 46	21a58		21 59	22 04	22 14	22a31				22 35	22 46	23a01		23 02	23 07	23 17		23 40	23 52		
Saunderton	d	21 52											22 52										
Princes Risborough [2]	d	21 59					22 25						22 59					23 26		23 49	00 03		
Monks Risborough	d	22 02											23 02								00 07		
Little Kimble	d	22 06											23 06								00 11		
Aylesbury	a	22 19		22 26			22 43		22 53				23 19		23 26				23 53		00 21		
Haddenham & Thame Parkway	d					22 17						22 48				23 15		23 33		23 56			
Bicester Village	d				22 26					22 52	22 56						23 33			00 11			
Islip	d									22 58	23 02												
Oxford Parkway 116	a				22 34					23 01	23 06						23 41			00 19			
Oxford	a				22 41					23 09	23 13						23 49			00 27			
Bicester North [3]	d					22 28						22 59				23 27		23a47				23 50	
Kings Sutton	d																						
Banbury	d					22 41						23 13				23 41						00 03	
Leamington Spa [8]	d					22 59						23 31				23 59						00 21	
Warwick	d					23 03										00 03						00 25	
Warwick Parkway	d					23 07						23 37				00 07						00 29	
Hatton	d					23 12																	
Claverdon	d																						
Bearley	d																						
Wilmcote	d																						23 15
Stratford-upon-Avon Parkway	a																						23 18
Stratford-upon-Avon	a																						23 23
Lapworth	d					23 18																	
Dorridge	d					23 23										00 18							
Solihull	d					23 31						23 49				00 24						00 41	
Birmingham Moor Street	a					23 42						00 01				00 36						00 52	
Birmingham Snow Hill	a																						
Rowley Regis	a																						
Cradley Heath	a																						
Stourbridge Junction [2]	a																						
Kidderminster	a																						

§ London Underground Limited (Central Line) also operate services between South Ruislip and West Ruislip at frequent intervals

A To Aylesbury Vale Parkway
B From Kidderminster

For complete services between Banbury and Birmingham, refer to Table T71

For principal services between London and Aylesbury refer to Table T114

Table T115-F

Mondays to Fridays
16 December to 15 May

London - High Wycombe, Aylesbury, Oxford Parkway, Banbury, Stratford-upon-Avon, Birmingham Snow Hill and Kidderminster

		CH	CH	CH FX	CH FO	CH A
London Marylebone 10 ⊖	d	23 20	23 27	23 30	23 45	23 57
Wembley Stadium	d	23 29		23 39	23 54	
Sudbury & Harrow Road	d					
Sudbury Hill Harrow	d					
Northolt Park	d			23 44	23 59	
West Ealing	d					
South Ruislip § ⊖	d			23 47	00 02	
West Ruislip 3 § ⊖	d			23 51	00 06	
Denham	d	23 39		23 56	00 11	
Denham Golf Club	d			23 58	00 13	
Gerrards Cross 1	d	23 44		00 02	00 17	
Seer Green	d	23 48				
Beaconsfield	d	23 52		00 09	00 24	
High Wycombe 1	d	23 58		00 15	00 30	
Saunderton	d	00 04				
Princes Risborough 2	d	00 10		00 26	00 41	
Monks Risborough	d			00 29	00 44	
Little Kimble	d			00 33	00 48	
Aylesbury	a		00 26	00 46	01 01	00 53
Haddenham & Thame Parkway	d	00 17				
Bicester Village	d					
Islip	d					
Oxford Parkway 116	a					
Oxford	a					
Bicester North 3	d	00 30				
Kings Sutton	d	00 42				
Banbury	d	00a50				
Leamington Spa 8	d					
Warwick	d					
Warwick Parkway	d					
Hatton	d					
Claverdon	d					
Bearley	d					
Wilmcote	d					
Stratford-upon-Avon Parkway	a					
Stratford-upon-Avon	a					
Lapworth	d					
Dorridge	d					
Solihull	d					
Birmingham Moor Street	a					
Birmingham Snow Hill	a					
Rowley Regis	a					
Cradley Heath	a					
Stourbridge Junction 2	a					
Kidderminster	a					

§ London Underground Limited (Central Line) also operate services between South Ruislip and West Ruislip at frequent intervals

A To Aylesbury Vale Parkway

For complete services between Banbury and Birmingham, refer to Table T71

For principal services between London and Aylesbury refer to Table T114

Table T115-F

Saturdays
21 December to 16 May

London - High Wycombe, Aylesbury, Oxford Parkway, Banbury, Stratford-upon-Avon, Birmingham Snow Hill and Kidderminster

		CH ◇ A	CH A	CH ◇ A	CH A	CH A	CH ◇ A	CH ◇		CH	CH	CH ◇	CH	CH ◇	CH	CH ◇	CH ◇	CH ◇	CH	CH B	CH ◇	CH	CH	CH B
London Marylebone 10 ⊖	d							00 10		00 20	00 25	01 10		05 56	06 13	06 44	07 00	07 06	07 09	07 27	07 40	07 43	07 46	07 57
Wembley Stadium	d										00 34			06 05	06 22				07 18				07 55	
Sudbury & Harrow Road	d																							
Sudbury Hill Harrow	d																							
Northolt Park	d										00 39				06 27				07 23				08 00	
West Ealing	d																							
South Ruislip § ⊖	d					00 02					00 43				06 31				07 26				08 03	
West Ruislip 3 § ⊖	d					00 06					00 47				06 34				07 30				08 07	
Denham	d					00 11					00 52				06 39				07 34				08 11	
Denham Golf Club	d					00 13									06 41				07 37			08 00		
Gerrards Cross 1	d					00 17				00 39	00 57	01 29			06 45				07 41			08 04	08a19	
Seer Green	d										01 01				06 50				07 45			08 09		
Beaconsfield	d					00 24				00 45	01 05	01 35			06 53				07 48			08 12		
High Wycombe 1	d					00 30		00 38		00 51	01 11	01 41	06 12	06 26	06 59	07 07	07 23	07 30	07 54		08 03	08 18		
Saunderton	d				00 04						01 17		06 18		07 06				08 01					
Princes Risborough 2	d		00 03		00 10	00 41				01 00	01 24	01 51	06 24		07 13	07 16	07 32		08 08			08 27		
Monks Risborough	d		00 07			00 44					01 27				07 17				08 11					
Little Kimble	d		00 11			00 48					01 31				07 21				08 15					
Aylesbury	a		00 21			01 01					01 44				07 32				08 26	08 23				08 53
Haddenham & Thame Parkway	d				00 17					01 07		01 59	06 31	06 40		07 22	07 38	07 43				08 34		
Bicester Village	d						00 11	01 05				02 13		06 55		07 34		07 56			08 25			
Islip	d															07 40					08 31			
Oxford Parkway 116	a						00 19	01 13				02 21		07 03		07 43		08 03			08 34			
Oxford	a						00 27	01 22				02 29		07 11		07 51		08 12			08 42			
Bicester North 3	d				00 30					01 20			06 45				07 50					08 47		
Kings Sutton	d				00 42								06 57									08 58		
Banbury	d			00 03	00a50					01 35			07 03				08 04					09a05		
Leamington Spa 8	d			00 21						01a56			07 21				08 23							
Warwick	d	00 03		00 25									07 25											
Warwick Parkway	d	00 07		00 29									07 29				08 29							
Hatton	d												07 34											
Claverdon	d																							
Bearley	d																							
Wilmcote	d																							
Stratford-upon-Avon Parkway	a																							
Stratford-upon-Avon	a																							
Lapworth	d																							
Dorridge	d	00 18											07 42				08 40							
Solihull	d	00 24		00 41									07 48				08 47							
Birmingham Moor Street	a	00 36		00 52									08 00				08 59							
Birmingham Snow Hill	a																09 07							
Rowley Regis	a																							
Cradley Heath	a																							
Stourbridge Junction 2	a																							
Kidderminster	a																							

§ London Underground Limited (Central Line) also operate services between South Ruislip and West Ruislip at frequent intervals

A From London Marylebone
B To Aylesbury Vale Parkway

For complete services between Banbury and Birmingham, refer to Table T71

For principal services between London and Aylesbury refer to Table T114

Table T115-F

London - High Wycombe, Aylesbury, Oxford Parkway, Banbury, Stratford-upon-Avon, Birmingham Snow Hill and Kidderminster

Saturdays
21 December to 16 May

		CH ◇	LM A	CH	CH ◇	CH	CH B	CH ◇	CH ◇	CH	CH	CH B	CH ◇	CH ◇	CH	LM C	CH	CH ◇	CH ◇	LM D	LM D	CH ◇ E	CH
London Marylebone 10 ⊖	d	08 06			08 10	08 13	08 27	08 35	08 40	08 43	08 46	08 57	09 06	09 10	09 13		09 27	09 35	09 40			09 43	09 46
Wembley Stadium	d					08 22					08 55				09 22								09 55
Sudbury & Harrow Road	d																						
Sudbury Hill Harrow	d																						
Northolt Park	d										09 00												10 00
West Ealing	d																						
South Ruislip § ⊖	d										09 03												10 03
West Ruislip 3 § ⊖	d										09 07												10 07
Denham	d					08 32					09 11				09 32								10 11
Denham Golf Club	d									09 00												10 00	
Gerrards Cross 1	d					08 36				09 04	09a19				09 37							10 04	10a19
Seer Green	d					08 41				09 09												10 09	
Beaconsfield	d					08 44				09 12					09 43							10 12	
High Wycombe 1	d				08 34	08 50		08 58		09 18				09 34	09 49			09 58				10 18	
Saunderton	d					08 56									09 56								
Princes Risborough 2	d					09 03				09 27					10 03							10 27	
Monks Risborough	d					09 06									10 06								
Little Kimble	d					09 10									10 10								
Aylesbury	a					09 21	09 23					09 53			10 21		10 26						
Haddenham & Thame Parkway	d	08 40								09 34			09 40									10 34	
Bicester Village	d	08 53						09 22					09 53					10 21					
Islip	d							09 28															
Oxford Parkway 116	a	09 00						09 32					10 00					10 28					
Oxford	a	09 10						09 38					10 10					10 37					
Bicester North 3	d				08 56				09 26	09 47									10 24			10 47	
Kings Sutton	d																					→	
Banbury	d				09 10				09 40	10a02				10 07					10 37				
Leamington Spa 8	d			08 30	09 28				09 58					10 25					10 55				
Warwick	d			08 34	09 32				10 02										10 59				
Warwick Parkway	d				09 35				10 06					10 31					11 03				
Hatton	d			08 42																			
Claverdon	d			08 48																			
Bearley	d			08 53																			
Wilmcote	d		08 15	08 58												09 15				10 15	11 15		
Stratford-upon-Avon Parkway	a		08 18	09 01												09 18				10 18	11 18		
Stratford-upon-Avon	a		08 21	09 12												09 23				10 23	11 23		
Lapworth	d																						
Dorridge	d				09 45				10 16										11 14				
Solihull	d				09 51				10 22					10 43					11 21				
Birmingham Moor Street	a				10 01				10 33					10 54					11 33				
Birmingham Snow Hill ⛴	a				10 09				10 41										11 41				
Rowley Regis	a																						
Cradley Heath	a																						
Stourbridge Junction 2	a																						
Kidderminster	a																						

§ London Underground Limited (Central Line) also operate services between South Ruislip and West Ruislip at frequent intervals

A From Birmingham Snow Hill
B To Aylesbury Vale Parkway
C From Kidderminster
D From Stourbridge Junction
E To Stratford-upon-Avon

For complete services between Banbury and Birmingham, refer to Table T71

For principal services between London and Aylesbury refer to Table T114

Table T115-F

London - High Wycombe, Aylesbury, Oxford Parkway, Banbury, Stratford-upon-Avon, Birmingham Snow Hill and Kidderminster

Saturdays
21 December to 16 May

		CH A	CH ◇	CH ◇	CH ◇ B	CH	CH	CH ◇	CH ◇	CH	CH	CH A	CH ◇	CH ◇	CH	CH	CH ◇	CH ◇	CH	CH	CH A	CH ◇	CH ◇
London Marylebone 10 ⊖	d	09 57	10 06	10 10		10 13	10 27	10 35	10 40	10 43	10 46	10 57	11 06	11 10	11 13	11 27	11 35	11 40	11 43	11 46	11 57	12 06	12 10
Wembley Stadium	d					10 22					10 55				11 22					11 55			
Sudbury & Harrow Road	d																						
Sudbury Hill Harrow	d																						
Northolt Park	d										11 00									12 00			
West Ealing	d																						
South Ruislip § ⊖	d										11 03									12 03			
West Ruislip 3 § ⊖	d										11 07									12 07			
Denham	d					10 32					11 11				11 32					12 11			
Denham Golf Club	d									11 00									12 00				
Gerrards Cross 1	d					10 37				11 04	11a19				11 37				12 04	12a19			
Seer Green	d									11 09									12 09				
Beaconsfield	d					10 43				11 12					11 43				12 12				
High Wycombe 1	d			10 34		10 49		10 59		11 18				11 34	11 49		11 58		12 18				12 34
Saunderton	d					10 55									11 56								
Princes Risborough 2	d					11 02				11 27					12 03				12 27				
Monks Risborough	d					11 05									12 06								
Little Kimble	d														12 10								
Aylesbury	a	10 53				11 19	11 26					11 53			12 21	12 26					12 53		
Haddenham & Thame Parkway	d		10 40							11 34			11 40						12 34			12 40	
Bicester Village	d		10 54					11 23					11 54				12 21					12 54	
Islip	d																12 27						
Oxford Parkway 116	a		11 01					11 30					12 02				12 30					13 01	
Oxford	a		11 10		←			11 39					12 09				12 39					13 10	
Bicester North 3	d				10 47				11 28	11 47								12 24	12 47				
Kings Sutton	d									11 58													
Banbury	d			11 07	11 10				11 43	12a03				12 08				12 37	13a02				13 07
Leamington Spa 8	d			11 25	11 32				12 01					12 26				12 55					13 25
Warwick	d				11 37				12 05									12 59					
Warwick Parkway	d			11 32					12 09					12 34				13 03					13 32
Hatton	d				11 44																		
Claverdon	d																						
Bearley	d				11 52																		
Wilmcote	d																						
Stratford-upon-Avon Parkway	a				11 57																		
Stratford-upon-Avon	a				12 06																		
Lapworth	d																						
Dorridge	d								12 19									13 15					
Solihull	d			11 45					12 25					12 46				13 21					13 45
Birmingham Moor Street	a			11 56					12 33					12 56				13 33					13 56
Birmingham Snow Hill ⛴	a								12 41									13 41					
Rowley Regis	a																						
Cradley Heath	a																						
Stourbridge Junction 2	a																						
Kidderminster	a																						

§ London Underground Limited (Central Line) also operate services between South Ruislip and West Ruislip at frequent intervals

A To Aylesbury Vale Parkway
B From London Marylebone

For complete services between Banbury and Birmingham, refer to Table T71

For principal services between London and Aylesbury refer to Table T114

Table T115-F

Saturdays

21 December to 16 May

London - High Wycombe, Aylesbury, Oxford Parkway, Banbury, Stratford-upon-Avon, Birmingham Snow Hill and Kidderminster

		CH	LM A	CH	CH ◇	LM A	CH	CH ◇	CH	CH	CH B	CH ◇	CH ◇	CH	CH	CH ◇	CH ◇	LM A	LM A	CH ◇ C	CH	CH B	CH ◇
London Marylebone 10 ⊖	d	12 13		12 27	12 35			12 40	12 43	12 46	12 57	13 06	13 10	13 13	13 27	13 35	13 40			13 43	13 46	13 57	14 06
Wembley Stadium	d	12 22								12 55				13 22							13 55		
Sudbury & Harrow Road	d																						
Sudbury Hill Harrow	d																						
Northolt Park	d									13 00											14 00		
West Ealing	d																						
South Ruislip § ⊖	d									13 03											14 03		
West Ruislip 3 § ⊖	d									13 07											14 07		
Denham	d	12 32								13 11				13 32							14 11		
Denham Golf Club	d								13 00											14 00			
Gerrards Cross 1	d	12 37							13 04	13a19				13 37						14 04	14a19		
Seer Green	d								13 09											14 09			
Beaconsfield	d	12 43							13 12					13 43						14 12			
High Wycombe 1	d	12 49			12 58				13 18				13 35	13 49		13 58				14 18			
Saunderton	d	12 56												13 55									
Princes Risborough 2	d	13 03							13 27					14 02						14 27			
Monks Risborough	d	13 06												14 05									
Little Kimble	d	13 10												14 09									
Aylesbury	a	13 21		13 26							13 53			14 20	14 26							14 53	
Haddenham & Thame Parkway	d								13 34			13 40								14 34			14 40
Bicester Village	d				13 21							13 54				14 21							14 53
Islip	d																						
Oxford Parkway 116	a				13 28							14 01				14 28							15 00
Oxford	a				13 37							14 10				14 37							15 10
Bicester North 3	d							13 24	13 47								14 24			14 47			
Kings Sutton	d								13 58											→			
Banbury	d							13 37	14a04				14 09				14 37						
Leamington Spa 8	d						13 32	13 55					14 27				14 55						
Warwick	d						13 37	13 59									14 59						
Warwick Parkway	d							14 03					14 33				15 03						
Hatton	d						13 44																
Claverdon	d						13 49																
Bearley	d						13 54																
Wilmcote	d		12 15			13 15	13 57											14 15	15 15				
Stratford-upon-Avon Parkway	a		12 18			13 18	14 00											14 18	15 18				
Stratford-upon-Avon	a		12 23			13 23	14 09											14 23	15 23				
Lapworth	d																						
Dorridge	d							14 13									15 13						
Solihull	d							14 21					14 45				15 21						
Birmingham Moor Street	a							14 33					14 56				15 33						
Birmingham Snow Hill	a							14 41									15 41						
Rowley Regis	a																						
Cradley Heath	a																						
Stourbridge Junction 2	a																						
Kidderminster	a																						

§ London Underground Limited (Central Line) also operate services between South Ruislip and West Ruislip at frequent intervals

A From Stourbridge Junction
B To Aylesbury Vale Parkway
C To Stratford-upon-Avon

For complete services between Banbury and Birmingham, refer to Table T71

For principal services between London and Aylesbury refer to Table T114

Table T115-F

Saturdays

21 December to 16 May

London - High Wycombe, Aylesbury, Oxford Parkway, Banbury, Stratford-upon-Avon, Birmingham Snow Hill and Kidderminster

		CH ◇	CH ◇ A	CH	CH	CH ◇	CH ◇	CH	CH	CH B	CH ◇	CH ◇	CH	CH	CH ◇	CH ◇	LM C	LM C	CH ◇ D	CH	CH B	CH ◇	CH ◇
London Marylebone 10 ⊖	d	14 10		14 13	14 27	14 35	14 40	14 43	14 46	14 57	15 06	15 10	15 13	15 27	15 35	15 40			15 43	15 46	15 57	16 06	16 10
Wembley Stadium	d			14 22					14 55				15 22							15 55			
Sudbury & Harrow Road	d																						
Sudbury Hill Harrow	d																						
Northolt Park	d								15 00											16 00			
West Ealing	d																						
South Ruislip § ⊖	d								15 03											16 03			
West Ruislip 3 § ⊖	d								15 07											16 07			
Denham	d			14 32					15 11				15 32							16 11			
Denham Golf Club	d							15 00											16 00				
Gerrards Cross 1	d			14 36				15 04	15a19				15 37						16 04	16a19			
Seer Green	d							15 09											16 09				
Beaconsfield	d			14 43				15 12					15 43						16 12				
High Wycombe 1	d	14 34		14 49		14 58		15 18				15 34	15 49		15 58				16 18				16 34
Saunderton	d			14 55									15 55										
Princes Risborough 2	d			15 02				15 27					16 02						16 27				
Monks Risborough	d			15 05									16 05										
Little Kimble	d			15 09									16 09										
Aylesbury	a			15 20	15 26					15 53			16 20	16 26							16 53		
Haddenham & Thame Parkway	d							15 34			15 40								16 34			16 40	
Bicester Village	d					15 21					15 53				16 21							16 53	
Islip	d					15 27																	
Oxford Parkway 116	a					15 30					16 00				16 28							17 00	
Oxford	a		←			15 39					16 10				16 37							17 10	
Bicester North 3	d		14 47				15 24	15 47								16 24			16 47				
Kings Sutton	d							15 58											→				
Banbury	d	15 07	15 10				15 37	16a04				16 09				16 37							17 07
Leamington Spa 8	d	15 25	15 32				15 55					16 26				16 55							17 25
Warwick	d		15 37				15 59									16 59							
Warwick Parkway	d	15 32					16 03					16 33				17 03							17 32
Hatton	d		15 44																				
Claverdon	d		15 49																				
Bearley	d		15 54																				
Wilmcote	d		15 58														16 15	17 15					
Stratford-upon-Avon Parkway	a		16 00														16 18	17 18					
Stratford-upon-Avon	a		16 09														16 23	17 23					
Lapworth	d																						
Dorridge	d						16 13									17 13							
Solihull	d	15 45					16 21					16 45				17 21							17 45
Birmingham Moor Street	a	15 56					16 33					16 56				17 33							17 56
Birmingham Snow Hill	a						16 41									17 41							
Rowley Regis	a																						
Cradley Heath	a																						
Stourbridge Junction 2	a																						
Kidderminster	a																						

§ London Underground Limited (Central Line) also operate services between South Ruislip and West Ruislip at frequent intervals

A From London Marylebone
B To Aylesbury Vale Parkway
C From Stourbridge Junction
D To Stratford-upon-Avon

For complete services between Banbury and Birmingham, refer to Table T71

For principal services between London and Aylesbury refer to Table T114

Table T115-F

Saturdays

21 December to 16 May

London - High Wycombe, Aylesbury, Oxford Parkway, Banbury, Stratford-upon-Avon, Birmingham Snow Hill and Kidderminster

Station		CH ◇ A	CH	CH	CH ◇	CH ◇	CH	CH	CH B	CH ◇	CH ◇	CH	CH	CH ◇	CH ◇	LM C	LM D	LM C	LM E	CH ◇ F	CH	CH B	CH ◇
London Marylebone 10 ⊖	d		16 13	16 27	16 35	16 40	16 43	16 46	16 57	17 06	17 10	17 13	17 27	17 35	17 40					17 43	17 46	17 57	18 06
Wembley Stadium	d		16 22					16 55				17 22									17 55		
Sudbury & Harrow Road	d																						
Sudbury Hill Harrow	d																						
Northolt Park	d							17 00													18 00		
West Ealing	d																						
South Ruislip § ⊖	d							17 03													18 03		
West Ruislip 3 § ⊖	d							17 07													18 07		
Denham	d		16 32					17 11				17 32									18 11		
Denham Golf Club	d						17 00													18 00			
Gerrards Cross 1	d		16 37				17 04	17a19				17 37								18 04	18a19		
Seer Green	d						17 09													18 09			
Beaconsfield	d		16 43				17 12					17 43								18 12			
High Wycombe 1	d		16 49		16 58		17 18				17 34	17 49		17 58						18 18			
Saunderton	d		16 55									17 55											
Princes Risborough 2	d		17 02				17 27					18 02								18 27			
Monks Risborough	d		17 05									18 05											
Little Kimble	d		17 09									18 09											
Aylesbury	a		17 20	17 26					17 53			18 20	18 26									18 53	
Haddenham & Thame Parkway	d						17 34			17 40										18 34			18 40
Bicester Village	d				17 21					17 53				18 21									18 53
Islip	d													18 27									
Oxford Parkway 116	a				17 28					18 00				18 30									19 00
Oxford	a	←			17 37					18 10				18 39									19 10
Bicester North 3	d	16 47				17 24	17 47								18 24					18 47			
Kings Sutton	d						17 58													→			
Banbury	d	17 10				17 37	18a04				18 09				18 37								
Leamington Spa 8	d	17 32				17 55					18 27				18 55								
Warwick	d	17 37				17 59									18 59								
Warwick Parkway	d					18 03					18 34				19 03								
Hatton	d	17 44																					
Claverdon	d	17 49																					
Bearley	d																						
Wilmcote	d	17 56														18 15	18 37	19 15	19 37				
Stratford-upon-Avon Parkway	a	17 58														18 18	18 40	19 18	19 40				
Stratford-upon-Avon	a	18 07														18 21	18 43	19 23	19 44				
Lapworth	d																						
Dorridge	d					18 13									19 13								
Solihull	d					18 21					18 48				19 19								
Birmingham Moor Street	a					18 33					18 58				19 29								
Birmingham Snow Hill	a					18 41					19 02				19 37								
Rowley Regis	a										19 16												
Cradley Heath	a																						
Stourbridge Junction 2	a										19 27												
Kidderminster	a										19 44												

§ London Underground Limited (Central Line) also operate services between South Ruislip and West Ruislip at frequent intervals

A From London Marylebone
B To Aylesbury Vale Parkway
C From Stourbridge Junction
D From Worcester Foregate Street
E From Birmingham Snow Hill
F To Stratford-upon-Avon

For complete services between Banbury and Birmingham, refer to Table T71

For principal services between London and Aylesbury refer to Table T114

Table T115-F

Saturdays

21 December to 16 May

London - High Wycombe, Aylesbury, Oxford Parkway, Banbury, Stratford-upon-Avon, Birmingham Snow Hill and Kidderminster

Station		CH ◇	CH ◇ A	CH	CH	CH ◇	CH ◇	CH	CH	CH B	CH ◇	CH ◇	CH	CH	CH ◇	CH ◇	CH	CH	CH B	CH ◇	CH ◇	CH	LM C
London Marylebone 10 ⊖	d	18 10		18 13	18 27	18 35	18 40	18 43	18 46	18 57	19 06	19 10	19 13	19 27	19 35	19 40	19 43	19 46	19 57	20 06	20 10	20 13	
Wembley Stadium	d			18 22					18 55				19 22					19 55				20 22	
Sudbury & Harrow Road	d																						
Sudbury Hill Harrow	d																						
Northolt Park	d								19 00									20 00					
West Ealing	d																						
South Ruislip § ⊖	d								19 03									20 03					
West Ruislip 3 § ⊖	d								19 07									20 07					
Denham	d			18 32					19 11				19 32					20 11				20 32	
Denham Golf Club	d							19 00									20 00						
Gerrards Cross 1	d			18 37				19 04	19a19				19 37				20 04	20a19				20 37	
Seer Green	d							19 09									20 09						
Beaconsfield	d			18 43				19 12					19 43				20 12					20 43	
High Wycombe 1	d	18 34		18 49		18 58		19 18				19 34	19 49		19 58		20 18				20 34	20 49	
Saunderton	d			18 55									19 55									20 56	
Princes Risborough 2	d			19 02				19 27					20 02				20 27					21 03	
Monks Risborough	d			19 05									20 05									21 06	
Little Kimble	d			19 09									20 09									21 10	
Aylesbury	a			19 20	19 26					19 53			20 20	20 26					20 53			21 21	
Haddenham & Thame Parkway	d							19 34			19 40						20 34			20 40			
Bicester Village	d					19 21					19 53				20 21					20 53			
Islip	d																						
Oxford Parkway 116	a					19 28					20 00				20 28					21 00			
Oxford	a		←			19 37					20 10				20 37					21 10			
Bicester North 3	d		18 47				19 24	19 47								20 24	20 47						
Kings Sutton	d							19 58															
Banbury	d	19 07	19 10				19 37	20a04				20 09				20 37	21a02				21 07		
Leamington Spa 8	d	19 26	19 32				19 55					20 27				20 55					21 25		
Warwick	d		19 37				19 59									20 59							
Warwick Parkway	d	19 33					20 03					20 33				21 03					21 32		
Hatton	d		19 44																				
Claverdon	d		19 49																				
Bearley	d																						
Wilmcote	d		19 56																				20 15
Stratford-upon-Avon Parkway	a		19 58																				20 18
Stratford-upon-Avon	a		20 07																				20 23
Lapworth	d																						
Dorridge	d						20 13									21 13							
Solihull	d	19 47					20 19					20 47				21 19					21 45		
Birmingham Moor Street	a	19 58					20 30					20 58				21 27					21 57		
Birmingham Snow Hill	a	20 07														21 30							
Rowley Regis	a															21 44							
Cradley Heath	a															21 50							
Stourbridge Junction 2	a															21 56							
Kidderminster	a															22 12							

§ London Underground Limited (Central Line) also operate services between South Ruislip and West Ruislip at frequent intervals

A From London Marylebone
B To Aylesbury Vale Parkway
C From Stourbridge Junction

For complete services between Banbury and Birmingham, refer to Table T71

For principal services between London and Aylesbury refer to Table T114

Table T115-F

Saturdays

21 December to 16 May

London - High Wycombe, Aylesbury, Oxford Parkway, Banbury, Stratford-upon-Avon, Birmingham Snow Hill and Kidderminster

		CH	CH	LM	CH	CH	CH	CH	CH	CH	CH	CH	CH	CH	CH	CH	CH	CH	CH	CH	LM	CH	CH
			◇			◇				◇	◇			◇				◇	◇				◇
		A		B					A								A				B	A	
London Marylebone 10 ⊖	d	20 27	20 35			20 40	20 43	20 46	20 57	21 06	21 10	21 13	21 27	21 35	21 40	21 46	21 57	22 06	22 10	22 13		22 27	22 35
Wembley Stadium	d							20 55				21 22				21 55				22 22			22 45
Sudbury & Harrow Road	d																						
Sudbury Hill Harrow	d																						
Northolt Park	d							21 00								22 00				22 27			
West Ealing	d																						
South Ruislip § ⊖	d							21 03								22 03				22 30			
West Ruislip 3 § ⊖	d							21 07								22 07				22 34			
Denham	d							21 11				21 32				22 11				22 38			
Denham Golf Club	d						21 00								21 57					22 41			
Gerrards Cross 1	d						21 04	21a19				21 37			22 01	22a19				22 45			
Seer Green	d						21 09								22 06					22 50			
Beaconsfield	d						21 12					21 43			22 10					22 53			
High Wycombe 1	d		20 58				21 18				21 34	21 49		21 59	22 16				22 34	22 59			23 06
Saunderton	d											21 56			22 23					23 06			
Princes Risborough 2	d						21 27					22 03			22 28					23 13			
Monks Risborough	d											22 06								23 16			
Little Kimble	d											22 10								23 20			
Aylesbury	a	21 23							21 53			22 21	22 26				22 53			23 31		23 23	
Haddenham & Thame Parkway	d						21 34			21 40					22 35			22 40					
Bicester Village	d		21 21							21 53				22 21				22 53					23 33
Islip	d		21 27																				
Oxford Parkway 116	a		21 30							22 00				22 28				23 01					23 41
Oxford	a		21 39							22 09				22 38				23 10					23 47
Bicester North 3	d					21 24	21 47				21 57				22 48				22 57				
Kings Sutton	d						21 58																
Banbury	d					21 37	22a05				22 10				23a07				23 10				
Leamington Spa 8	d				21 32	21 55					22 28								23 28				
Warwick	d				21 37	21 59					22 32								23 32				
Warwick Parkway	d					22 03					22 36								23 37				
Hatton	d				21 44						22 41												
Claverdon	d				21 49																		
Bearley	d																						
Wilmcote	d			21 15	21 56																22 15		
Stratford-upon-Avon Parkway	a			21 18	21 58																22 18		
Stratford-upon-Avon	a			21 23	22 07																22 23		
Lapworth	d										22 46												
Dorridge	d					22 13					22 51								23 47				
Solihull	d					22 19					22 58								23 53				
Birmingham Moor Street	a					22 27					23 06								00 04				
Birmingham Snow Hill ⛴	a					22 35					23 14												
Rowley Regis	a																						
Cradley Heath	a																						
Stourbridge Junction 2	a																						
Kidderminster	a																						

§ London Underground Limited (Central Line) also operate services between South Ruislip and West Ruislip at frequent intervals

A To Aylesbury Vale Parkway
B From Kidderminster

For complete services between Banbury and Birmingham, refer to Table T71

For principal services between London and Aylesbury refer to Table T114

Table T115-F

Saturdays

21 December to 16 May

London - High Wycombe, Aylesbury, Oxford Parkway, Banbury, Stratford-upon-Avon, Birmingham Snow Hill and Kidderminster

		CH	CH	CH	LM	CH	CH	CH	CH	CH
				◇						
			A		B					
London Marylebone 10 ⊖	d	22 40	22 57	23 10		23 15	23 20	23 27	23 45	23 57
Wembley Stadium	d	22 49		23 19		23 24	23 29		23 55	
Sudbury & Harrow Road	d									
Sudbury Hill Harrow	d									
Northolt Park	d						23 34			
West Ealing	d									
South Ruislip § ⊖	d						23 37			
West Ruislip 3 § ⊖	d						23 41			
Denham	d						23 45			
Denham Golf Club	d						23 48			
Gerrards Cross 1	d	23 02				23 37	23 51		00 08	
Seer Green	d						23 56			
Beaconsfield	d	23 08				23 43	23 59		00 15	
High Wycombe 1	d	23 14		23 36		23 49	00 05		00 21	
Saunderton	d						00 11			
Princes Risborough 2	d	23 23				23 59	00 18		00 31	
Monks Risborough	d						00 21			
Little Kimble	d						00 25			
Aylesbury	a		23 53				00 36	00 26		00 56
Haddenham & Thame Parkway	d	23 30				00 06			00 38	
Bicester Village	d			23 59						
Islip	d			00 05						
Oxford Parkway 116	a			00 09						
Oxford	a			00 18						
Bicester North 3	d	23 43				00 19			00 51	
Kings Sutton	d								01 03	
Banbury	d	00a01				00a36			01a11	
Leamington Spa 8	d									
Warwick	d									
Warwick Parkway	d									
Hatton	d									
Claverdon	d									
Bearley	d									
Wilmcote	d				23 15					
Stratford-upon-Avon Parkway	a				23 18					
Stratford-upon-Avon	a				23 23					
Lapworth	d									
Dorridge	d									
Solihull	d									
Birmingham Moor Street	a									
Birmingham Snow Hill ⛴	a									
Rowley Regis	a									
Cradley Heath	a									
Stourbridge Junction 2	a									
Kidderminster	a									

§ London Underground Limited (Central Line) also operate services between South Ruislip and West Ruislip at frequent intervals

A To Aylesbury Vale Parkway
B From Kidderminster

For complete services between Banbury and Birmingham, refer to Table T71

For principal services between London and Aylesbury refer to Table T114

Table T115-F

Sundays

15 December to 10 May

London - High Wycombe, Aylesbury, Oxford Parkway, Banbury, Stratford-upon-Avon, Birmingham Snow Hill and Kidderminster

		CH ◇ A	CH A	CH A	CH A	CH	CH ◇	LM B		LM C	CH D	CH E	CH ◇	CH F	CH ◇	CH	CH	CH E	CH ◇	CH ◇	CH	CH ◇	CH ◇	CH ◇ G
London Marylebone 10 ⊖	d					00 10	07 35				07 50	07 57	08 15		08 35	08 40	08 46	08 57	09 05	09 10	09 13	09 35	09 40	09 43
Wembley Stadium	d					00 19					07 59						08 55				09 22			
Sudbury & Harrow Road	d																							
Sudbury Hill Harrow	d																							
Northolt Park	d					00 24					08 04						09 00							
West Ealing	d																							
South Ruislip § ⊖	d					00 27					08 07						09 03							
West Ruislip 3 § ⊖	d					00 31					08 11						09 07							
Denham	d					00 35					08 15						09 11							
Denham Golf Club	d					00 38					08 18													10 00
Gerrards Cross 1	d				00 08	00 42	07 53				08 22		08 33			09 00	09a19				09 35			10 04
Seer Green	d					00 46					08 27					09 05								10 09
Beaconsfield	d				00 15	00 50	07 59				08 30		08 39			09 08					09 41			10 12
High Wycombe 1	d		00 05		00 21	00 56	08 05				08 36		08 45	←	08 59	09 14				09 34	09 47	09 58		10 18
Saunderton	d		00 11			01 02					08 43			08 43		09 21					09 54			
Princes Risborough 2	d		00 18		00 31	01 09	08 14				→		08 53	09 01		09 26					10 01			10 27
Monks Risborough	d		00 21			01 12								09 04							10 04			
Little Kimble	d		00 25			01 16								09 08							10 08			
Aylesbury	a		00 36			01 27						08 53		09 19				09 53			10 19			
Haddenham & Thame Parkway	d			00 06	00 38		08 21						09 00			09 33			09 39					10 34
Bicester Village	d						08 33								09 22				09 53			10 21		
Islip	d	00 05													09 28							10 27		
Oxford Parkway 116	a	00 09					08 40								09 31				10 00			10 30		
Oxford	a	00 18					08 48								09 39				10 09			10 39		
Bicester North 3	d			00 19	00 51								09 10			09 46							10 24	10 47
Kings Sutton	d				01 03								09 20											→
Banbury	d			00a36	01a11								09 29			10a02				10 07			10 37	
Leamington Spa 8	d												09 47							10 25			10 55	
Warwick	d												09 51										10 59	
Warwick Parkway	d												09 55							10 32			11 03	
Hatton	d												10 00											
Claverdon	d																							
Bearley	d																							
Wilmcote	d							10 11		11 11														
Stratford-upon-Avon Parkway	a							10 14		11 14														
Stratford-upon-Avon	a							10 17		11 17														
Lapworth	d												10 06											
Dorridge	d												10 11										11 13	
Solihull	d												10 16							10 45			11 19	
Birmingham Moor Street	a												10 24							10 53			11 27	
Birmingham Snow Hill	a												10 32							11 01			11 35	
Rowley Regis	a																							
Cradley Heath	a																							
Stourbridge Junction 2	a																							
Kidderminster	a																							

§ London Underground Limited (Central Line) also operate services between South Ruislip and West Ruislip at frequent intervals

A not 15 December. From London Marylebone

B From Birmingham Snow Hill

C From Great Malvern

D To Aylesbury

E To Aylesbury Vale Parkway

F From London Marylebone

G To Stratford-upon-Avon

For complete services between Banbury and Birmingham, refer to Table T71

For principal services between London and Aylesbury refer to Table T114

Table T115-F

Sundays

15 December to 10 May

London - High Wycombe, Aylesbury, Oxford Parkway, Banbury, Stratford-upon-Avon, Birmingham Snow Hill and Kidderminster

		CH	CH A	CH ◇	CH ◇	CH ◇ B	CH	CH ◇		CH ◇	CH	CH	CH A	CH ◇	CH ◇	CH	CH ◇	CH ◇	LM C	LM C	CH ◇ D	CH	CH A	CH ◇
London Marylebone 10 ⊖	d	09 46	09 57	10 05	10 10		10 13	10 35		10 40	10 43	10 46	10 57	11 05	11 10	11 13	11 35	11 40			11 43	11 46	11 57	12 05
Wembley Stadium	d	09 55					10 22					10 55				11 22						11 55		
Sudbury & Harrow Road	d																							
Sudbury Hill Harrow	d																							
Northolt Park	d	10 00										11 00										12 00		
West Ealing	d																							
South Ruislip § ⊖	d	10 03										11 03										12 03		
West Ruislip 3 § ⊖	d											11 07												
Denham	d	10 09										11 11										12 09		
Denham Golf Club	d																				12 00			
Gerrards Cross 1	d	10a16					10 35				11 02	11a19				11 36					12 04	12a16		
Seer Green	d										11 07										12 09			
Beaconsfield	d						10 41				11 10					11 42					12 12			
High Wycombe 1	d				10 34		10 47	10 58			11 16				11 34	11 48	11 58				12 18			
Saunderton	d						10 54									11 55								
Princes Risborough 2	d						11 01				11 25					12 02					12 27			
Monks Risborough	d						11 04									12 05								
Little Kimble	d						11 08									12 09								
Aylesbury	a		10 53				11 19						11 53			12 20							12 53	
Haddenham & Thame Parkway	d			10 39							11 32			11 39							12 34			12 39
Bicester Village	d			10 53				11 21						11 53			12 21							12 53
Islip	d																12 27							
Oxford Parkway 116	a			11 00				11 28						12 00			12 30							13 00
Oxford	a			11 09		←		11 37						12 09			12 39							13 09
Bicester North 3	d					10 47				11 24	11 45							12 24			12 47			
Kings Sutton	d										11 57										→			
Banbury	d				11 07	11 11				11 37	12a02				12 07			12 37						
Leamington Spa 8	d				11 25	11 32				11 55					12 25			12 55						
Warwick	d					11 38				11 59								12 59						
Warwick Parkway	d				11 32					12 03					12 32			13 03						
Hatton	d					11 45																		
Claverdon	d																							
Bearley	d																							
Wilmcote	d					11 55													12 11	13 11				
Stratford-upon-Avon Parkway	a					11 57													12 14	13 14				
Stratford-upon-Avon	a					12 07													12 17	13 17				
Lapworth	d																							
Dorridge	d									12 13								13 14						
Solihull	d				11 45					12 19					12 45			13 20						
Birmingham Moor Street	a				11 56					12 27					12 56			13 29						
Birmingham Snow Hill	a									12 35								13 37						
Rowley Regis	a																							
Cradley Heath	a																							
Stourbridge Junction 2	a																							
Kidderminster	a																							

§ London Underground Limited (Central Line) also operate services between South Ruislip and West Ruislip at frequent intervals

A To Aylesbury Vale Parkway

B From London Marylebone

C From Great Malvern

D To Stratford-upon-Avon

For complete services between Banbury and Birmingham, refer to Table T71

For principal services between London and Aylesbury refer to Table T114

Table T115-F

Sundays
15 December to 10 May

London - High Wycombe, Aylesbury, Oxford Parkway, Banbury, Stratford-upon-Avon, Birmingham Snow Hill and Kidderminster

		CH ◇	CH ◇ A	CH	CH ◇	CH ◇	CH	CH	CH B	CH ◇	CH ◇	CH	CH ◇	CH ◇	LM C	LM D	CH ◇ E	CH	CH B	CH ◇	CH ◇	CH ◇ A	CH
London Marylebone [10] ⊖	d	12 10		12 13	12 35	12 40	12 43	12 46	12 57	13 05	13 10	13 13	13 35	13 40			13 43	13 46	13 57	14 05	14 10		14 13
Wembley Stadium	d			12 22				12 55				13 22						13 55					14 22
Sudbury & Harrow Road	d																						
Sudbury Hill Harrow	d																						
Northolt Park	d							13 00										14 00					
West Ealing	d																						
South Ruislip § ⊖	d							13 03										14 03					
West Ruislip [3] § ⊖	d							13 07															
Denham	d							13 11										14 09					
Denham Golf Club	d																14 00						
Gerrards Cross [1]	d			12 36			13 02	13a19				13 35					14 04	14a16					14 35
Seer Green	d						13 07										14 09						
Beaconsfield	d			12 42		13 01	13 10					13 41		14 01			14 12						14 41
High Wycombe [1]	d	12 34		12 48	12 59		13 16				13 34	13 47	13 59				14 18				14 34		14 47
Saunderton	d			12 55								13 54											14 54
Princes Risborough [2]	d			13 02			13 25					14 01					14 27						15 01
Monks Risborough	d			13 05								14 04											15 04
Little Kimble	d			13 09								14 08											15 08
Aylesbury	a			13 20					13 53			14 19							14 53				15 19
Haddenham & Thame Parkway	d						13 32			13 40							14 34			14 40			
Bicester Village	d				13 22					13 54			14 22							14 53			
Islip	d												14 28										
Oxford Parkway 116	a				13 29					14 01			14 31							15 00			
Oxford	a		←		13 37					14 09			14 39							15 09		←	
Bicester North [3]	d		12 47			13 26	13 45							14 26			14 47					14 47	
Kings Sutton	d						13 57										↪						
Banbury	d	13 07	13 10			13 39	14a03				14 08			14 39							15 07	15 10	
Leamington Spa [8]	d	13 25	13 32			13 57					14 26			14 57							15 25	15 32	
Warwick	d		13 37			14 01								15 01								15 37	
Warwick Parkway	d	13 32				14 05					14 32			15 05							15 32		
Hatton	d		13 44																			15 44	
Claverdon	d																						
Bearley	d																						
Wilmcote	d		13 54												14 11	15 11						15 54	
Stratford-upon-Avon Parkway	a		13 56												14 14	15 14						15 56	
Stratford-upon-Avon	a		14 06												14 17	15 17						16 06	
Lapworth	d																						
Dorridge	d					14 15								15 15									
Solihull	d	13 45				14 21					14 45			15 21							15 45		
Birmingham Moor Street	a	13 56				14 29					14 56			15 29							15 56		
Birmingham Snow Hill	a					14 37								15 37									
Rowley Regis	a																						
Cradley Heath	a																						
Stourbridge Junction [2]	a																						
Kidderminster	a																						

§ London Underground Limited (Central Line) also operate services between South Ruislip and West Ruislip at frequent intervals

A From London Marylebone
B To Aylesbury Vale Parkway
C From Great Malvern
D From Worcester Foregate Street
E To Stratford-upon-Avon

For complete services between Banbury and Birmingham, refer to Table T71

For principal services between London and Aylesbury refer to Table T114

NRT DECEMBER 19 EDITION

Table T115-F

Sundays
15 December to 10 May

London - High Wycombe, Aylesbury, Oxford Parkway, Banbury, Stratford-upon-Avon, Birmingham Snow Hill and Kidderminster

		CH ◇	CH ◇	CH	CH	CH A	CH ◇	CH ◇	CH	CH	CH ◇	CH ◇	LM B	LM B	CH ◇ C	CH	CH A	CH ◇	CH ◇	CH ◇ D	CH	CH	CH ◇
London Marylebone [10] ⊖	d	14 35	14 40	14 43	14 46	14 57	15 05	15 10	15 13	15 27	15 35	15 40			15 43	15 46	15 57	16 05	16 10		16 13	16 27	16 35
Wembley Stadium	d				14 55				15 22							15 55					16 22		
Sudbury & Harrow Road	d																						
Sudbury Hill Harrow	d																						
Northolt Park	d				15 00											16 00							
West Ealing	d																						
South Ruislip § ⊖	d				15 03											16 03							
West Ruislip [3] § ⊖	d				15 07																		
Denham	d				15 11											16 09							
Denham Golf Club	d														16 00								
Gerrards Cross [1]	d			15 02	15a18				15 35						16 04	16a16					16 35		
Seer Green	d			15 07											16 09								
Beaconsfield	d		15 01	15 10					15 41			16 01			16 12						16 41		
High Wycombe [1]	d	14 59		15 16				15 34	15 47		15 59				16 18				16 34		16 47		16 59
Saunderton	d								15 54												16 54		
Princes Risborough [2]	d			15 25					16 01						16 27						17 01		
Monks Risborough	d								16 04												17 04		
Little Kimble	d								16 08												17 08		
Aylesbury	a					15 53			16 19	16 26							16 53				17 19	17 26	
Haddenham & Thame Parkway	d			15 32			15 40								16 34			16 40					
Bicester Village	d	15 21					15 53				16 21							16 53					17 21
Islip	d										16 27												
Oxford Parkway 116	a	15 28					16 00				16 30							17 00					17 28
Oxford	a	15 37					16 09				16 39							17 09		←			17 37
Bicester North [3]	d		15 26	15 45								16 26			16 47					16 47			
Kings Sutton	d			15 57											↪								
Banbury	d		15 39	16a03				16 08				16 39							17 08	17 10			
Leamington Spa [8]	d		15 57					16 26				16 57							17 26	17 32			
Warwick	d		16 01									17 01								17 37			
Warwick Parkway	d		16 05					16 32				17 05							17 32				
Hatton	d																			17 44			
Claverdon	d																						
Bearley	d																						
Wilmcote	d												16 11	17 11						17 54			
Stratford-upon-Avon Parkway	a												16 14	17 14						17 56			
Stratford-upon-Avon	a												16 17	17 17						18 05			
Lapworth	d																						
Dorridge	d		16 15									17 15											
Solihull	d		16 21					16 45				17 21							17 45				
Birmingham Moor Street	a		16 29					16 56				17 29							17 56				
Birmingham Snow Hill	a		16 37									17 37											
Rowley Regis	a																						
Cradley Heath	a																						
Stourbridge Junction [2]	a																						
Kidderminster	a																						

§ London Underground Limited (Central Line) also operate services between South Ruislip and West Ruislip at frequent intervals

A To Aylesbury Vale Parkway
B From Worcester Foregate Street
C To Stratford-upon-Avon
D From London Marylebone

For complete services between Banbury and Birmingham, refer to Table T71

For principal services between London and Aylesbury refer to Table T114

Table T115-F

Sundays

15 December to 10 May

London - High Wycombe, Aylesbury, Oxford Parkway, Banbury, Stratford-upon-Avon, Birmingham Snow Hill and Kidderminster

		CH	CH	CH	CH	CH	CH	CH	CH	CH	CH	LM	LM	CH	CH	CH	CH	CH	CH	CH	CH	CH	CH
		◇			A	◇	◇			◇	◇	B	B	◇ C		A	◇	◇	◇ D			◇	◇
London Marylebone 10 ⊖	d	16 40	16 43	16 46	16 57	17 05	17 10	17 13	17 27	17 35	17 40			17 43	17 46	17 57	18 05	18 10		18 13	18 27	18 35	18 40
Wembley Stadium	d			16 55				17 22							17 55					18 22			
Sudbury & Harrow Road	d																						
Sudbury Hill Harrow	d																						
Northolt Park	d			17 00											18 00								
West Ealing	d																						
South Ruislip § ⊖	d			17 03											18 03								
West Ruislip 3 § ⊖	d			17 07																			
Denham	d			17 11											18 09								
Denham Golf Club	d													18 00									
Gerrards Cross 1	d		17 02	17a18				17 35						18 04	18a16					18 35			
Seer Green	d		17 07											18 09									
Beaconsfield	d	17 01	17 10					17 41			18 01			18 12						18 41			19 01
High Wycombe 1	d		17 16				17 34	17 47		17 59				18 18				18 35		18 47		18 59	
Saunderton	d							17 54												18 54			
Princes Risborough 2	d		17 25					18 01						18 27						19 01			
Monks Risborough	d							18 04												19 04			
Little Kimble	d							18 08												19 08			
Aylesbury	a				17 53			18 19	18 26							18 53				19 19	19 26		
Haddenham & Thame Parkway	d		17 32			17 40								18 34			18 40						
Bicester Village	d					17 53				18 21							18 53					19 21	
Islip	d																						
Oxford Parkway 116	a					18 00				18 28							19 00					19 28	
Oxford	a					18 09				18 37							19 09		←			19 37	
Bicester North 3	d	17 26	17 45								18 26			18 47					18 47				19 26
Kings Sutton	d		17 57											↪									
Banbury	d	17 39	18a03				18 08				18 39							19 07	19 10				19 39
Leamington Spa 8	d	17 57					18 26				18 57							19 25	19 32				19 57
Warwick	d	18 01									19 01								19 37				20 01
Warwick Parkway	d	18 05					18 32				19 05							19 32					20 05
Hatton	d																		19 44				
Claverdon	d																						
Bearley	d																						
Wilmcote	d											18 09	19 09						19 54				
Stratford-upon-Avon Parkway	a											18 12	19 12						19 56				
Stratford-upon-Avon	a											18 15	19 15						20 05				
Lapworth	d																						
Dorridge	d	18 15									19 15												20 15
Solihull	d	18 21					18 45				19 21							19 45					20 21
Birmingham Moor Street	a	18 29					18 56				19 29							19 53					20 29
Birmingham Snow Hill ⇌	a	18 37									19 37							19 57					20 37
Rowley Regis	a																	20 10					
Cradley Heath	a																						
Stourbridge Junction 2	a																	20 21					
Kidderminster	a																	20 36					

§ London Underground Limited (Central Line) also operate services between South Ruislip and West Ruislip at frequent intervals

A To Aylesbury Vale Parkway
B From Worcester Foregate Street
C To Stratford-upon-Avon
D From London Marylebone

For complete services between Banbury and Birmingham, refer to Table T71

For principal services between London and Aylesbury refer to Table T114

Table T115-F

Sundays

15 December to 10 May

London - High Wycombe, Aylesbury, Oxford Parkway, Banbury, Stratford-upon-Avon, Birmingham Snow Hill and Kidderminster

		CH	CH	CH	CH	CH	CH	CH	CH	CH	CH	CH	CH	CH	CH	CH	CH	CH	CH	CH	CH	CH	CH
				A	◇	◇			◇	◇			A	◇	◇		A	◇	◇			A	◇
London Marylebone 10 ⊖	d	18 43	18 46	18 57	19 05	19 10	19 13	19 27	19 35	19 40	19 43	19 47	19 57	20 05	20 10	20 13	20 27	20 35	20 40	20 43	20 47	20 57	21 05
Wembley Stadium	d		18 55				19 22					19 56				20 22					20 56		
Sudbury & Harrow Road	d																						
Sudbury Hill Harrow	d																						
Northolt Park	d		19 00									20 01									21 01		
West Ealing	d																						
South Ruislip § ⊖	d		19 03									20 04									21 04		
West Ruislip 3 § ⊖	d		19 07																		21 08		
Denham	d		19 11									20 10									21 12		
Denham Golf Club	d										20 00												
Gerrards Cross 1	d	19 02	19a18				19 35				20 04	20a17				20 35				21 03	21a19		
Seer Green	d	19 07									20 09									21 08			
Beaconsfield	d	19 10					19 41			20 01	20 12					20 41			21 01	21 11			
High Wycombe 1	d	19 16				19 34	19 47		19 59		20 18				20 34	20 47		20 58		21 17			
Saunderton	d						19 54									20 54							
Princes Risborough 2	d	19 25					20 01				20 27					21 01				21 26			
Monks Risborough	d						20 04									21 04							
Little Kimble	d						20 08									21 08							
Aylesbury	a			19 53			20 19	20 26					20 53			21 19	21 23					21 53	
Haddenham & Thame Parkway	d	19 32			19 40						20 34			20 40						21 33			21 39
Bicester Village	d				19 53				20 21					20 53				21 20					21 51
Islip	d								20 27														
Oxford Parkway 116	a				20 00				20 30					21 00				21 28					21 59
Oxford	a				20 09				20 39					21 09				21 36					22 08
Bicester North 3	d	19 45								20 26	20 47								21 26	21 46			
Kings Sutton	d	19 57																		21 57			
Banbury	d	20a03				20 08				20 39	21a03				21 08				21 39	22a03			
Leamington Spa 8	d					20 26				20 57					21 26				21 57				
Warwick	d									21 01									22 01				
Warwick Parkway	d					20 32				21 05					21 32				22 05				
Hatton	d									21 10													
Claverdon	d																						
Bearley	d																						
Wilmcote	d																						
Stratford-upon-Avon Parkway	a																						
Stratford-upon-Avon	a																						
Lapworth	d									21 16													
Dorridge	d									21 21									22 15				
Solihull	d					20 45				21 29					21 45				22 21				
Birmingham Moor Street	a					20 56				21 37					21 56				22 29				
Birmingham Snow Hill ⇌	a									21 40									22 32				
Rowley Regis	a									21 53									22 45				
Cradley Heath	a									21 59									22 51				
Stourbridge Junction 2	a									22 04									22 56				
Kidderminster	a									22 18									23 10				

§ London Underground Limited (Central Line) also operate services between South Ruislip and West Ruislip at frequent intervals

A To Aylesbury Vale Parkway

For complete services between Banbury and Birmingham, refer to Table T71

For principal services between London and Aylesbury refer to Table T114

Table T115-F

Sundays

15 December to 10 May

London - High Wycombe, Aylesbury, Oxford Parkway, Banbury, Stratford-upon-Avon, Birmingham Snow Hill and Kidderminster

	CH ◇	CH	CH A	CH ◇	CH	CH	CH	CH ◇	CH ◇	CH A	CH	CH	CH	CH ◇	CH	CH	CH
London Marylebone 10 ⊖ d	21 10	21 13	21 27	21 35	21 40	21 45	21 57	22 08	22 15	22 27	22 35	22 45	22 57	23 15	23 27	23 30	23 45
Wembley Stadium d		21 22				21 54						22 55				23 39	23 54
Sudbury & Harrow Road d																	
Sudbury Hill Harrow d																	
Northolt Park d						21 59						23 00					23 59
West Ealing d																	
South Ruislip § ⊖ d						22 02						23 03					00 02
West Ruislip 3 § ⊖ d						22 06						23 07					00 06
Denham d						22 10						23 11					00 10
Denham Golf Club d					21 57							23 14					00 13
Gerrards Cross 1 d		21 35			22 01	22 15					22 54	23 18		23 35		23 52	00 17
Seer Green d					22 06							23 22					00 21
Beaconsfield d		21 41			22 09	22 21					23 00	23 26		23 41		23 58	00 25
High Wycombe 1 d	21 34	21 47		21 59	22 15	22 27		22 34			23 06	23 32		23 47		00 04	00 31
Saunderton d		21 54				22 33						23 38					00 37
Princes Risborough 2 d		22 01			22 24	22 40					23 15	23 45		23 56		00 14	00 45
Monks Risborough d		22 04				22 43						23 48					00 48
Little Kimble d		22 08				22 47						23 52					00 52
Aylesbury a		22 19	22 23			22 58	22 56			23 23		00 03	23 56		00 26		01 06
Haddenham & Thame Parkway d					22 31				22 54		23 22			00 03		00 21	
Bicester Village d				22 21					23 09					00 18			
Islip d				22 27													
Oxford Parkway 116 a				22 30					23 17					00 26			
Oxford a				22 39					23 26					00 35			
Bicester North 3 d					22a47			22 56			23 35					00 34	
Kings Sutton d																	
Banbury d	22 08							23 09			23a52					00a52	
Leamington Spa 8 d	22 26							23 27									
Warwick d	22 30							23 31									
Warwick Parkway d	22 34							23 34									
Hatton d	22 40																
Claverdon d																	
Bearley d																	
Wilmcote d																	
Stratford-upon-Avon Parkway a																	
Stratford-upon-Avon a																	
Lapworth d	22 46																
Dorridge d	22 51							23 44									
Solihull d	22 58							23 50									
Birmingham Moor Street a	23 06							23 58									
Birmingham Snow Hill a	23 14							00 07									
Rowley Regis a																	
Cradley Heath a																	
Stourbridge Junction 2 a																	
Kidderminster a																	

§ London Underground Limited (Central Line) also operate services between South Ruislip and West Ruislip at frequent intervals

A To Aylesbury Vale Parkway

For complete services between Banbury and Birmingham, refer to Table T71

For principal services between London and Aylesbury refer to Table T114

Table T115-R

Mondays to Fridays

16 December to 15 May

Kidderminster, Birmingham Snow Hill, Stratford-upon-Avon, Banbury, Oxford Parkway, Aylesbury, High Wycombe - London

Miles	Miles	Miles	Miles		CH MX A	CH B	CH	CH	CH B	CH	CH	CH ◇	CH ◇	CH	CH	CH C	CH ◇	CH	CH	CH ◇	CH ◇	CH
—	—	—	—	**Kidderminster** d																		
—	—	—	—	Stourbridge Junction 2 d																		
—	—	—	—	Cradley Heath d																		
—	—	—	—	Rowley Regis d																		
0	—	—	—	**Birmingham Snow Hill** d																		
0¼	—	—	—	**Birmingham Moor Street** d									05 15								05 42	
7¼	—	—	—	Solihull d									05 24								05 51	
10½	—	—	—	Dorridge d																	05 56	
13	—	—	—	Lapworth d																		
—	—	0	—	**Stratford-upon-Avon** d																		
—	—	1	—	Stratford-upon-Avon Parkway d																		
—	—	2¾	—	Wilmcote d																		
—	—	4¼	—	Bearley d																		
—	—	7¼	—	Claverdon d																		
17¼	—	9¼	—	Hatton d																		
20	—	12	—	Warwick Parkway d									05 36								06 05	
21¼	—	13¼	—	Warwick d																	06 08	
23¼	—	15¼	—	**Leamington Spa** 8 d									05 41								06 13	
43¼	—	—	—	**Banbury** d				05 17					05 59								06 31	
46¾	—	—	—	Kings Sutton d				05 22													06 36	
57¼	—	—	—	**Bicester North** 3 d				05 33					06 11						06 22		06 46	
—	—	—	0	Oxford d								05 35					06 00			06 25		
—	—	—	3½	Oxford Parkway 116 d								05 42					06 06			06 31		
—	—	—	5¾	Islip d																		
—	—	—	11¾	Bicester Village d								05 52					06 16			06 40		
70¼	—	—	21¾	Haddenham & Thame Parkway d				05 45				06 06	06 22						06 34			
—	0	—	—	**Aylesbury** d		05 21	05 02		05 49	05 35				06 07	06 10	06 24		06 23				06 38
—	4½	—	—	Little Kimble d			05 11			05 44					06 19							
—	6	—	—	Monks Risborough d			05 15			05 48					06 23							
76	7½	—	—	**Princes Risborough** 2 d			05 20			05 54		06 13			06 31		06 36	06a39	06 43			
79¼	—	—	—	Saunderton d			05 25					06 18										
84¼	—	—	—	**High Wycombe** 1 d			05 31	05 59		06 04	06 19	06 25	06 35				06 46		06 54			
89	—	—	—	Beaconsfield d			05 38	06 05		06 11	06 26	06 31			06 46				07 02			
90¾	—	—	—	Seer Green d			05 41			06 14							06 53					
93¼	—	—	—	Gerrards Cross 1 d			05 46	06 11		06 19	06 32	06 37			06 52		06 58					
95	—	—	—	Denham Golf Club d			05 49			06 22							07 01					
96	—	—	—	Denham d			05 52			06 25					06 56					07 13		
98¾	—	—	—	West Ruislip 3 § ⊖ d			05 56				06 49						07 06					
100½	—	—	—	South Ruislip § ⊖ d			06 00			06 31					07 02							
—	—	—	—	West Ealing a																		
102¼	—	—	—	Northolt Park d			06 04			06 35	06 55											
103¼	—	—	—	Sudbury Hill Harrow d							06 58											
104	—	—	—	Sudbury & Harrow Road d							07 01											
105½	—	—	—	Wembley Stadium d	00 06		06 09			06 40	07 04											
112	—	—	—	**London Marylebone** 10 ⊖ a	00 19	06 16	06 19	06 31	06 49	06 51	07 16	07 00	07 03	07 07	07 19	07 22	07 23		07 28	07 29	07 35	07 38

§ London Underground Limited (Central Line) also operate services between South Ruislip and West Ruislip at frequent intervals

A From Aylesbury
B From Aylesbury Vale Parkway
C From Aylesbury Vale Parkway

For complete services between Banbury and Birmingham, refer to Table T71

For principal services between London and Aylesbury refer to Table T114

Table T115-R

Mondays to Fridays

16 December to 15 May

Kidderminster, Birmingham Snow Hill, Stratford-upon-Avon, Banbury, Oxford Parkway, Aylesbury, High Wycombe - London

		CH	CH	CH	CH	CH	CH	LM	LM	CH	LM	LM	CH	CH	CH	CH		CH	CH	CH	CH	CH	CH	CH	CH
					◇	◇										◇				◇	◇				
			A					B	C		D	D				E		A							
Kidderminster	d																				06 09				
Stourbridge Junction 2	d																				06 18				
Cradley Heath	d																								
Rowley Regis	d																				06 30				
Birmingham Snow Hill	d																				06 50				
Birmingham Moor Street	d					06 10														06 28	06 55				
Solihull	d					06 19														06 38	07 04				
Dorridge	d					06 24														06 50					
Lapworth	d																								
Stratford-upon-Avon	d						06 06	06 26	06 52		07 20	07 26													
Stratford-upon-Avon Parkway	d						06 10	06 30	06 56		07a23	07a29													
Wilmcote	d						06 14	06a33	06a59																
Bearley	d																								
Claverdon	d						06 21																		
Hatton	d						06 32																		
Warwick Parkway	d					06 34														06 59	07 18				
Warwick	d						06 40													07 02					
Leamington Spa 8	d					06 41	06a46													07 06	07 24				
Banbury	d					06 59														07 24					
Kings Sutton	d																								
Bicester North 3	d					07 11									07 16					07 40					
Oxford	d				06 43											07 12									
Oxford Parkway 116	d				06 50											07 25									
Islip	d																								
Bicester Village	d				06 59											07 35									
Haddenham & Thame Parkway	d				07 11										07 28					07 52					
Aylesbury	d		06 58	06 46						07 10				07 10				07 30				07 41	07 48		
Little Kimble	d			06 54																			07 56		
Monks Risborough	d			06 58																			08 00		
Princes Risborough 2	d			07 02	07 18									07 27					07 52				08a05		
Saunderton	d			07 07																					
High Wycombe 1	d	07 10		07 14	07 27									07 37	07 42				08 01						08 11
Beaconsfield	d			07 20	07 34										07 49				08 07						08 18
Seer Green	d			07 24											07 52										08 21
Gerrards Cross 1	d	07 21		07 29										07 47	07 57									08 22	08 26
Denham Golf Club	d													07 51											
Denham	d													07 54											08 30
West Ruislip 3 § ⊖	d												07 46											08 29	
South Ruislip § ⊖	d	07 29		07 37																					08 36
West Ealing	a																								
Northolt Park	d	07 33											07 52											08 35	
Sudbury Hill Harrow	d												07 55												
Sudbury & Harrow Road	d												07 58												
Wembley Stadium	d			07 44										08 04											08 43
London Marylebone 10 ⊖	a	07 49	07 53	07 56	07 57	08 02				08 09			08 12	08 16	08 19	08 20		08 27	08 30	08 33	08 34	08 41		08 52	08 55

§ London Underground Limited (Central Line) also operate services between South Ruislip and West Ruislip at frequent intervals

A From Aylesbury Vale Parkway
B To Birmingham Snow Hill
C To Worcester Foregate Street
D To Stourbridge Junction
E The Oxford Flyer

For complete services between Banbury and Birmingham, refer to Table T71

For principal services between London and Aylesbury refer to Table T114

Table T115-R

Mondays to Fridays

16 December to 15 May

Kidderminster, Birmingham Snow Hill, Stratford-upon-Avon, Banbury, Oxford Parkway, Aylesbury, High Wycombe - London

		CH	CH	CH	CH	CH	CH		CH	CH	CH	CH	CH	CH	LM	LM		CH		CH	CH	CH	CH	CH	CH
			◇			◇					◇	◇	◇	◇									◇	◇	
					A		B								C	D		B							
Kidderminster	d													07 10										07 30	
Stourbridge Junction 2	d					06 41								07 21										07 38	
Cradley Heath	d																							07 44	
Rowley Regis	d					06 52								07 30										07 51	
Birmingham Snow Hill	d					07 07								07 50										08 08	
Birmingham Moor Street	d					07 11								07 54										08 11	
Solihull	d					07 22								08 04										08 20	
Dorridge	d					07 29																		08 25	
Lapworth	d																								
Stratford-upon-Avon	d												07 33		07 41	08 26									
Stratford-upon-Avon Parkway	d												07 37		07 45	08 30									
Wilmcote	d												07 41		07a48	08a33									
Bearley	d																								
Claverdon	d												07 49												
Hatton	d												07 55												
Warwick Parkway	d					07 40							08 00	08 17										08 35	
Warwick	d												08 04											08 38	
Leamington Spa 8	d					07 47							08 09	08 23										08 43	
Banbury	d			07 50		08 06							08 28	08 41										09 02	
Kings Sutton	d			07 55																					
Bicester North 3	d			08 07									08 42	08 55											
Oxford	d		07 43								08 02	08 22											08 40		
Oxford Parkway 116	d		07 50								08 08	08 28											08 50		
Islip	d										08 12														
Bicester Village	d		07 59								08 20	08 37											08 59		
Haddenham & Thame Parkway	d		08 11										08 53										09 11		
Aylesbury	d				08 02		08 17											08 44		08 47					09 02
Little Kimble	d																			08 56					
Monks Risborough	d																			09 00					
Princes Risborough 2	d	08 08	08 18								08 42	08 53								09a08			09 18		
Saunderton	d	08 13									08 47														
High Wycombe 1	d	08 19	08 27	08 31						08 40	08 54	09 02	09 06									09 17	09 27		
Beaconsfield	d	08 26								08 47	09 01											09 24			
Seer Green	d									08 50			09 13												
Gerrards Cross 1	d	08 32							08 49	08 55		09 11										09 30			
Denham Golf Club	d								08 53																
Denham	d									08 59													09 38		
West Ruislip 3 § ⊖	d	08 50																			09 26				
South Ruislip § ⊖	d									09 05												09 37			
West Ealing	a																								
Northolt Park	d								09 02												09 32				
Sudbury Hill Harrow	d	08 57																			09 35				
Sudbury & Harrow Road	d								09 06																
Wembley Stadium	d									09 12											09 39				
London Marylebone 10 ⊖	a	09 12	08 58	09 00	09 03	09 07	09 17		09 21	09 25	09 27	09 30	09 35	09 38				09 44			09 52	09 55	09 56	09 59	10 04

§ London Underground Limited (Central Line) also operate services between South Ruislip and West Ruislip at frequent intervals

A From Aylesbury Vale Parkway
B From Aylesbury Vale Parkway
C To Birmingham Snow Hill
D To Stourbridge Junction

For complete services between Banbury and Birmingham, refer to Table T71

For principal services between London and Aylesbury refer to Table T114

Table T115-R

Mondays to Fridays
16 December to 15 May

Kidderminster, Birmingham Snow Hill, Stratford-upon-Avon, Banbury, Oxford Parkway, Aylesbury, High Wycombe - London

		CH	CH	CH	CH	CH	CH	CH	CH	CH	LM	CH	CH	LM	CH	CH	CH	CH	CH	CH	CH	LM	CH
				◇				◇	◇			◇						◇	◇				
					A						B			B						C	D	B	
Kidderminster	d								08 09														
Stourbridge Junction 2	d								08 23														
Cradley Heath	d								08 29														
Rowley Regis	d								08 35														
Birmingham Snow Hill	d							08 22	08 52									09 12					
Birmingham Moor Street	d							08 25	08 55									09 15					
Solihull	d							08 37	09 07									09 24					
Dorridge	d							08 52										09 29					
Lapworth	d																						
Stratford-upon-Avon	d									09 00	09 26			10 03								10 26	
Stratford-upon-Avon Parkway	d									09 04	09 30			10a06								10 30	
Wilmcote	d									09 07	09a33											10a33	
Bearley	d									09 11													
Claverdon	d									09 16													
Hatton	d									09 21													
Warwick Parkway	d							09 02	09 19									09 39					
Warwick	d							09 06		09 28								09 42					
Leamington Spa 8	d							09 12	09 25	09a37								09 46					
Banbury	d					09 07		09 31	09 44									10 04					
Kings Sutton	d					09 12																	
Bicester North 3	d					09 30		09 43										10 16					
Oxford	d			09 10								09 38							10 10				
Oxford Parkway 116	d			09 16								09 45							10 17				
Islip	d											09 49											
Bicester Village	d			09 25								09 57							10 26				
Haddenham & Thame Parkway	d					09 42		09 54										10 27	10 38				
Aylesbury	d				09 23		09 33						09 48							10 18			
Little Kimble	d						09 41																
Monks Risborough	d						09 45																
Princes Risborough 2	d			09 42			09 49										10 16						
Saunderton	d						09 54																
High Wycombe 1	d		09 36	09 52		09 57	10 02	10 07							10 20		10 26		10 51				
Beaconsfield	d		09 43			10 03									10 27		10 32						
Seer Green	d		09 46														10 35						
Gerrards Cross 1	d	09 42	09 51					10 16							10 33		10 40						10 49
Denham Golf Club	d	09 45																					10 52
Denham	d		09 55														10 44						10 55
West Ruislip 3 § ⊖	d						10 29																11 05
South Ruislip § ⊖	d		10 00												10 41						11 02		
West Ealing	a																				11 20		
Northolt Park	d	09 54					10 35																11 11
Sudbury Hill Harrow	d						10 38																11 14
Sudbury & Harrow Road	d						10 41																
Wembley Stadium	d	09 59													10 48								11 18
London Marylebone 10 ⊖	a	10 12	10 18	10 19	10 23	10 32	10 55	10 36	10 40			10 41	10 50		10 59		11 05	11 08	11 18	11 20			11 32

§ London Underground Limited (Central Line) also operate services between South Ruislip and West Ruislip at frequent intervals

A From Aylesbury Vale Parkway
B To Stourbridge Junction
C From Aylesbury Vale Parkway
D Parliamentary Train

For complete services between Banbury and Birmingham, refer to Table T71

For principal services between London and Aylesbury refer to Table T114

NRT DECEMBER 19 EDITION

Table T115-R

Mondays to Fridays
16 December to 15 May

Kidderminster, Birmingham Snow Hill, Stratford-upon-Avon, Banbury, Oxford Parkway, Aylesbury, High Wycombe - London

		CH	CH	CH	CH	CH	CH	CH	CH	CH	CH	CH	CH	CH	LM	LM	CH	CH	LM	CH	CH
			◇	◇				◇	◇				◇	◇			◇				◇
										A			B		C	C			C		D
Kidderminster	d																				
Stourbridge Junction 2	d																				
Cradley Heath	d																				
Rowley Regis	d																				
Birmingham Snow Hill	d							10 12													
Birmingham Moor Street	d		09 55					10 15						10 55							
Solihull	d		10 04					10 24						11 04							
Dorridge	d							10 29													
Lapworth	d																				
Stratford-upon-Avon	d												10 40		11 03	11 26			12 03		
Stratford-upon-Avon Parkway	d												10 44		11a06	11 30			12a06		
Wilmcote	d												10 47			11a33					
Bearley	d												10 51								
Claverdon	d												10 56								
Hatton	d												11 00								
Warwick Parkway	d		10 16					10 39						11 17							
Warwick	d							10 42					11 08								
Leamington Spa 8	d		10 22					10 46					11 15	11 23							←
Banbury	d		10 40				10 45	11 04					11 48	11 40							11 48
Kings Sutton	d						10 50						→								
Bicester North 3	d						11 01	11 16													12 03
Oxford	d			10 41					11 09								11 42				
Oxford Parkway 116	d			10 47					11 15								11 48				
Islip	d																				
Bicester Village	d			10 56					11 24								11 57				
Haddenham & Thame Parkway	d						11 13		11 38												
Aylesbury	d	10 30			10 48					1118		11 29						11 48			
Little Kimble	d											11 37									
Monks Risborough	d	10 41										11 41									
Princes Risborough 2	d	10 45					11 20					11 46									12 20
Saunderton	d	10 50										11 51									
High Wycombe 1	d	10 57	11 10			11 20	11 30		11 51			11 57		12 13						12 20	12 30
Beaconsfield	d	11 03				11 26	11 36					12 03								12 26	12 36
Seer Green	d	11 06										12 06									
Gerrards Cross 1	d	11 11				11 32	11 42				11 49	12 11								12 32	12 42
Denham Golf Club	d										11 52										
Denham	d					11 36					11 55										
West Ruislip 3 § ⊖	d										12 05										
South Ruislip § ⊖	d					11 41														12 39	
West Ealing	a																				
Northolt Park	d										12 11										
Sudbury Hill Harrow	d										12 14										
Sudbury & Harrow Road	d																				
Wembley Stadium	d					11 48					12 18									12 46	
London Marylebone 10 ⊖	a	11 36	11 40	11 46	11 50	11 59	12 05	12 08	12 18	12 20	12 32	12 36		12 43			12 46	12 50		12 59	13 05

§ London Underground Limited (Central Line) also operate services between South Ruislip and West Ruislip at frequent intervals

A From Aylesbury Vale Parkway
B To London Marylebone
C To Stourbridge Junction
D From Stratford-upon-Avon

For complete services between Banbury and Birmingham, refer to Table T71

For principal services between London and Aylesbury refer to Table T114

Table T115-R

Mondays to Fridays
16 December to 15 May

Kidderminster, Birmingham Snow Hill, Stratford-upon-Avon, Banbury, Oxford Parkway, Aylesbury, High Wycombe - London

Station		CH ◇	CH ◇	CH A		LM B	CH	CH	CH ◇	CH ◇	CH		CH	CH	CH ◇	CH ◇		CH A		CH	CH	CH ◇ C	CH ◇	LM B	LM B
Kidderminster	d																								
Stourbridge Junction 2	d																								
Cradley Heath	d																								
Rowley Regis	d																								
Birmingham Snow Hill ⇌	d	11 12													12 12										
Birmingham Moor Street	d	11 15							11 55						12 15								12 55		
Solihull	d	11 24							12 04						12 24								13 04		
Dorridge	d	11 29													12 29										
Lapworth	d																								
Stratford-upon-Avon	d					12 26																12 43		13 03	13 26
Stratford-upon-Avon Parkway	d					12 30																12 47		13a06	13 30
Wilmcote	d					12a33																12 50			13a33
Bearley	d																								
Claverdon	d																								
Hatton	d																					13 00			
Warwick Parkway	d	11 39							12 16						12 39								13 17		
Warwick	d	11 42													12 42							13 08			
Leamington Spa 8	d	11 46							12 22						12 46							13 15	13 23		
Banbury	d	12 04							12 40					12 44	13 04							13 45	13 41		
Kings Sutton	d																					→			
Bicester North 3	d	12 16												13 01	13 17										
Oxford	d		12 11							12 41						13 11									
Oxford Parkway 116	d		12 17							12 47						13 17									
Islip	d																								
Bicester Village	d		12 26							12 56						13 26									
Haddenham & Thame Parkway	d	12 27	12 38											13 13		13 38									
Aylesbury	d			12 18				12 32			12 48							13 18			13 31				
Little Kimble	d																				13 39				
Monks Risborough	d							12 43													13 43				
Princes Risborough 2	d							12 47						13 20							13 47				
Saunderton	d							12 52													13 52				
High Wycombe 1	d		12 51					12 58	13 13				13 20	13 30		13 51					13 58		14 13		
Beaconsfield	d							13 05					13 27	13 36							14 05				
Seer Green	d							13 08													14 08				
Gerrards Cross 1	d						12 49	13 13					13 33	13 42						13 49	14 13				
Denham Golf Club	d						12 52													13 52					
Denham	d						12 55													13 55					
West Ruislip 3 § ⊖	d						13 05													14 05					
South Ruislip § ⊖	d												13 40												
West Ealing	a																								
Northolt Park	d						13 11													14 11					
Sudbury Hill Harrow	d						13 14													14 14					
Sudbury & Harrow Road	d																								
Wembley Stadium	d						13 18						13 47							14 18	14 26				
London Marylebone 10 ⊖	a	13 09	13 18	13 [illegible]0			13 32	13 38	13 43	13 46	13 50		13 59	14 05	14 09	14 18		14 20		14 32	14 40		14 43		

§ London Underground Limited (Central Line) also operate services between South Ruislip and West Ruislip at frequent intervals

A From Aylesbury Vale Parkway
B To Stourbridge Junction
C To London Marylebone

For complete services between Banbury and Birmingham, refer to Table T71

For principal services between London and Aylesbury refer to Table T114

Table T115-R

Mondays to Fridays
16 December to 15 May

Kidderminster, Birmingham Snow Hill, Stratford-upon-Avon, Banbury, Oxford Parkway, Aylesbury, High Wycombe - London

Station		CH ◇	CH		LM A	CH	CH ◇ B	CH ◇	CH ◇	CH C		LM A	CH	CH	CH ◇	CH ◇		CH		CH	CH	CH ◇	CH C		CH ◇
Kidderminster	d																								
Stourbridge Junction 2	d																								
Cradley Heath	d																								
Rowley Regis	d																								
Birmingham Snow Hill ⇌	d							13 12														14 12			
Birmingham Moor Street	d							13 15							13 55							14 15			
Solihull	d							13 24							14 04							14 24			
Dorridge	d							13 30														14 29			
Lapworth	d																								
Stratford-upon-Avon	d				14 03							14 26													
Stratford-upon-Avon Parkway	d				14a06							14 30													
Wilmcote	d											14a33													
Bearley	d																								
Claverdon	d																								
Hatton	d																								
Warwick Parkway	d							13 40							14 16							14 39			
Warwick	d							13 44														14 42			
Leamington Spa 8	d						←	13 49							14 22							14 46			
Banbury	d						13 45	14 07							14 40						14 46	15 04			
Kings Sutton	d						13 50																		
Bicester North 3	d						14 01	14 20													15 00	15 16			
Oxford	d	13 39							14 11							14 41									15 13
Oxford Parkway 116	d	13 45							14 17							14 47									15 19
Islip	d	13 48																							
Bicester Village	d	13 56							14 26							14 56									15 28
Haddenham & Thame Parkway	d						14 13		14 38												15 12				15 40
Aylesbury	d		13 48							14 18				14 31				14 48					15 18		
Little Kimble	d													14 39											
Monks Risborough	d													14 43											
Princes Risborough 2	d						14 20							14 47							15 19				
Saunderton	d													14 52											
High Wycombe 1	d					14 20	14 30		14 51					14 58	15 10					15 20	15 29	15 37			15 53
Beaconsfield	d					14 27	14 36							15 05						15 26	15 35				15 59
Seer Green	d													15 08											
Gerrards Cross 1	d					14 33	14 42						14 49	15 13						15 32	15 41	15 47			
Denham Golf Club	d												14 52												
Denham	d												14 55												
West Ruislip 3 § ⊖	d												15 05												
South Ruislip § ⊖	d					14 40														15 40					
West Ealing	a																								
Northolt Park	d												15 11												
Sudbury Hill Harrow	d												15 14												
Sudbury & Harrow Road	d																								
Wembley Stadium	d					14 47							15 18							15 47					16 12
London Marylebone 10 ⊖	a	14 46	14 50			14 59	15 05	15 09	15 18	15 20			15 32	15 36	15 40	15 43		15 50		15 59	16 05	16 08	16 20		16 24

§ London Underground Limited (Central Line) also operate services between South Ruislip and West Ruislip at frequent intervals

A To Stourbridge Junction
B From Stratford-upon-Avon
C From Aylesbury Vale Parkway

For complete services between Banbury and Birmingham, refer to Table T71

For principal services between London and Aylesbury refer to Table T114

Table T115-R

Mondays to Fridays
16 December to 15 May

Kidderminster, Birmingham Snow Hill, Stratford-upon-Avon, Banbury, Oxford Parkway, Aylesbury, High Wycombe - London

Station		CH	CH	CH ◇ A	CH ◇	LM B	LM B	CH ◇	CH		LM B	CH	CH ◇ C	CH ◇	CH D			CH ◇	LM B	CH		CH	CH	CH ◇	CH E
Kidderminster	d																								
Stourbridge Junction 2	d																								
Cradley Heath	d																								
Rowley Regis	d																								
Birmingham Snow Hill	d													15 12											
Birmingham Moor Street	d				14 55									15 15										15 55	
Solihull	d				15 04									15 24										16 04	
Dorridge	d													15 30											
Lapworth	d																								
Stratford-upon-Avon	d			14 40		15 03	15 26				16 03								16 26						
Stratford-upon-Avon Parkway	d			14 44		15a06	15 30				16a06								16 30						
Wilmcote	d			14 47			15a33												16a33						
Bearley	d			14 51																					
Claverdon	d			14 56																					
Hatton	d			15 00																					
Warwick Parkway	d				15 16									15 40										16 17	
Warwick	d			15 08										15 43											
Leamington Spa 8	d			15 15	15 22								←	15 47										16 23	
Banbury	d			15 48	15 42								15 48	16 05										16 41	
Kings Sutton	d			→																					
Bicester North 3	d												16 03	16 17											
Oxford	d							15 43										16 11							
Oxford Parkway 116	d							15 49										16 17							
Islip	d																								
Bicester Village	d							15 58										16 26							
Haddenham & Thame Parkway	d													16 28				16 38							
Aylesbury	d		15 33						15 48						16 18					16 30		16 29			16 48
Little Kimble	d																					16 37			
Monks Risborough	d		15 44																			16 41			
Princes Risborough 2	d		15 48										16 20									16 46			
Saunderton	d		15 53																			16 51			
High Wycombe 1	d		15 59		16 14							16 21	16 30					16 51				16 57	17 03	17 13	
Beaconsfield	d		16 06									16 28	16 36									17 04	17 10		
Seer Green	d		16 09																				17 13		
Gerrards Cross 1	d	15 53	16 14									16 34	16 42									17 10	17 18		
Denham Golf Club	d	15 56										16 37													
Denham	d	15 59										16 40						17 02							
West Ruislip 3 § ⊖	d	16 09										16 53											17 34		
South Ruislip § ⊖	d		16 21																			17 17			
West Ealing	a																								
Northolt Park	d	16 15																				17 21			
Sudbury Hill Harrow	d	16 18																					17 41		
Sudbury & Harrow Road	d																								
Wembley Stadium	d	16 22										17 02										17 26			
London Marylebone 10 ⊖	a	16 35	16 39		16 42			16 45	16 50			17 16	17 09	17 12	17 20			17 21		17 32		17 39	17 57	17 45	17 48

§ London Underground Limited (Central Line) also operate services between South Ruislip and West Ruislip at frequent intervals

A To London Marylebone
B To Stourbridge Junction
C From Stratford-upon-Avon
D From Aylesbury Vale Parkway
E From Aylesbury Vale Parkway

For complete services between Banbury and Birmingham, refer to Table T71

For principal services between London and Aylesbury refer to Table T114

NRT DECEMBER 19 EDITION

Table T115-R

Mondays to Fridays
16 December to 15 May

Kidderminster, Birmingham Snow Hill, Stratford-upon-Avon, Banbury, Oxford Parkway, Aylesbury, High Wycombe - London

Station		CH ◇	CH	CH	CH ◇	CH	CH ◇	CH	LM A	CH	CH ◇	CH ◇	CH FX ◇	CH B	CH FO ◇	CH		CH	CH	CH ◇	CH ◇	CH	CH	CH	CH
Kidderminster	d																								
Stourbridge Junction 2	d																								
Cradley Heath	d																								
Rowley Regis	d																								
Birmingham Snow Hill	d				16 12							16 52									17 07				
Birmingham Moor Street	d				16 15							16 55									17 10				
Solihull	d				16 24							17 04									17 19				
Dorridge	d				16 29																17 26				
Lapworth	d																								
Stratford-upon-Avon	d								17 27																
Stratford-upon-Avon Parkway	d								17 31																
Wilmcote	d								17a34																
Bearley	d																								
Claverdon	d																								
Hatton	d																								
Warwick Parkway	d				16 39							17 16									17 36				
Warwick	d				16 42							17 19									17 39				
Leamington Spa 8	d				16 46							17 23									17 43				
Banbury	d			16 45	17 04							17 41							17 46		18 04				
Kings Sutton	d			16 50															17 51						
Bicester North 3	d			17 03	17 16														18 03		18 21				
Oxford	d	16 39					17 00				17 23		17 40		17 40					17 57					
Oxford Parkway 116	d	16 45					17 07				17 29		17 46		17 46					18 03					
Islip	d						17 11						17 50		17 50					18 07					
Bicester Village	d	16 57					17 20				17 38		17 58		17 58					18 15					
Haddenham & Thame Parkway	d				17 27						17 50										18 32				
Aylesbury	d					17 15				17 29				17 50								18 20	18 22		
Little Kimble	d									17 38													18 31		
Monks Risborough	d									17 42													18 35		
Princes Risborough 2	d			17 20						17a48	17 57								18 21				18a47		
Saunderton	d			17 25															18 26						
High Wycombe 1	d		17 24	17 31			17 45	17 52			18 06	18 11						18 22	18 33	18 38	18 45				18 51
Beaconsfield	d		17 31	17 38				17 59										18 29		18 45					18 58
Seer Green	d							18 02																	19 01
Gerrards Cross 1	d		17 37	17 44			17 54	18 07										18 35	18 43					18 58	19 06
Denham Golf Club	d		17 40															18 38							
Denham	d		17 43				17 58											18 41						19 02	
West Ruislip 3 § ⊖	d															18 32									
South Ruislip § ⊖	d			17 52			18 04	18 14								18 36			18 50						
West Ealing	a																								
Northolt Park	d							18 18																19 09	
Sudbury Hill Harrow	d															18 41									
Sudbury & Harrow Road	d																								
Wembley Stadium	d		17 54				18 11									18 45		18 51						19 14	
London Marylebone 10 ⊖	a	17 50	18 07	18 10	18 13	18 15	18 26	18 33			18 36	18 39	18 48	18 50	18 53	18 59		19 04	19 08	19 09	19 14	19 20		19 27	19 30

§ London Underground Limited (Central Line) also operate services between South Ruislip and West Ruislip at frequent intervals

A To Kidderminster
B From Aylesbury Vale Parkway

For complete services between Banbury and Birmingham, refer to Table T71

For principal services between London and Aylesbury refer to Table T114

Table T115-R

Mondays to Fridays
16 December to 15 May

Kidderminster, Birmingham Snow Hill, Stratford-upon-Avon, Banbury, Oxford Parkway, Aylesbury, High Wycombe - London

		CH ◇	CH ◇	CH ◇	LM A	LM B	CH C	LM D	LM E	CH	CH	CH FX ◇	CH FO ◇	CH	CH ◇	CH	CH	CH	CH ◇	LM B	CH ◇	CH C	CH
Kidderminster	d																						
Stourbridge Junction 2	d																						
Cradley Heath	d																						
Rowley Regis	d																						
Birmingham Snow Hill	d			17 52											18 12				18 40				
Birmingham Moor Street	d			17 55											18 15				18 43				
Solihull	d			18 06											18 24				18 52				
Dorridge	d			18 12											18 29				18 57				
Lapworth	d														18 34								
Stratford-upon-Avon	d		17 36		17 55	18 27		18 51	19 03							19 12				19 26			
Stratford-upon-Avon Parkway	d		17 40		17a58	18 31		18 55	19a06							19 16				19 30			
Wilmcote	d		17 43			18a34		18a58								19 20				19a33			
Bearley	d		17 47													19 24							
Claverdon	d		17 52													19 29							
Hatton	d		17 58												18 40	19 35							
Warwick Parkway	d			18 22											18 45				19 07				
Warwick	d		18 05												18 48	19a46							
Leamington Spa 8	d		18 09	18 28											18 53				19 12				
Banbury	d		18 28	18 46											19 13				19 30				
Kings Sutton	d														19 18								
Bicester North 3	d		18 45	18 58							19 03				19 29				19 42				
Oxford	d	18 23										19 01	19 01								19 27		
Oxford Parkway 116	d	18 29										19 07	19 07								19 37		
Islip	d											19 10	19 10										
Bicester Village	d	18 38										19 18	19 18								19 47		
Haddenham & Thame Parkway	d	18 50									19 15				19 41				19 53		19 59		
Aylesbury	d						18 47							19 18			19 13					19 48	20 09
Little Kimble	d																						20 18
Monks Risborough	d																19 24						20 22
Princes Risborough 2	d	18 57									19 22						19 34		20 00				20a28
Saunderton	d										19 27												
High Wycombe 1	d	19 06								19 20	19 34						19 44		20 09		20 13		
Beaconsfield	d									19 27							19 50				20 19		
Seer Green	d									19 30													
Gerrards Cross 1	d									19 35							19 56	20 03					
Denham Golf Club	d																	20 06					
Denham	d									19 39								20 09					
West Ruislip 3 § ⊖	d																20 07						
South Ruislip § ⊖	d									19 44								20 15					
West Ealing	a																						
Northolt Park	d																20 13						
Sudbury Hill Harrow	d																	20 19					
Sudbury & Harrow Road	d																						
Wembley Stadium	d									19 51							20 18						
London Marylebone 10 ⊖	a	19 33	19 41	19 44			19 48			20 04	20 08	20 10	20 13	20 20	20 23		20 31	20 34	20 37		20 43	20 49	

§ London Underground Limited (Central Line) also operate services between South Ruislip and West Ruislip at frequent intervals

A To Worcester Foregate Street
B To Birmingham Snow Hill
C From Aylesbury Vale Parkway
D To Kidderminster
E To Worcester Shrub Hill

For complete services between Banbury and Birmingham, refer to Table T71

For principal services between London and Aylesbury refer to Table T114

Table T115-R

Mondays to Fridays
16 December to 15 May

Kidderminster, Birmingham Snow Hill, Stratford-upon-Avon, Banbury, Oxford Parkway, Aylesbury, High Wycombe - London

		CH	CH ◇	CH	LM A	CH	CH ◇	CH ◇	CH B	CH	CH ◇	CH ◇	CH ◇	CH C	LM D	CH	CH	CH	CH ◇	CH	CH
Kidderminster	d																				
Stourbridge Junction 2	d																				
Cradley Heath	d																				
Rowley Regis	d																				
Birmingham Snow Hill	d						19 17					20 15									
Birmingham Moor Street	d						19 20					20 18									
Solihull	d						19 29					20 27									
Dorridge	d						19 34					20 32									
Lapworth	d						19 38														
Stratford-upon-Avon	d				20 26										21 26						
Stratford-upon-Avon Parkway	d				20 30										21 30						
Wilmcote	d				20a33										21a33						
Bearley	d																				
Claverdon	d																				
Hatton	d						19 44														
Warwick Parkway	d						19 49					20 42									
Warwick	d						19 52					20 45									
Leamington Spa 8	d						19 57					20 50									
Banbury	d						20 16					21 13									21 34
Kings Sutton	d																				
Bicester North 3	d						20 30					21 25									21 56
Oxford	d		20 00					20 26			20 55		21 15						21 34		
Oxford Parkway 116	d		20 09					20 32			21 01		21 21						21 41		
Islip	d																				
Bicester Village	d		20 19					20 42			21 10		21 30						21 50		
Haddenham & Thame Parkway	d						20 42	20 54			21 22								22 03		22 09
Aylesbury	d			20 20					20 53					21 18			21 24			21 50	
Little Kimble	d																21 33				
Monks Risborough	d																21 37				
Princes Risborough 2	d		20 36				20 49				21 29						21 48				22 16
Saunderton	d						20 54										21 53				
High Wycombe 1	d	20 17					21 01	21 09		21 19	21 38	21 45					21 59	22 08	22 18		22 26
Beaconsfield	d	20 24					21 07			21 26							22 06	22 15			22 32
Seer Green	d	20 27								21 29							22 09				
Gerrards Cross 1	d	20 32				20 56	21 13			21 34						22 01	22 14	22 21			22 38
Denham Golf Club	d					20 59										22 04					
Denham	d					21 02										22 07					22 42
West Ruislip 3 § ⊖	d	20 39				21 07										22 12		22 33			
South Ruislip § ⊖	d									21 42							22 21				22 48
West Ealing	a																				
Northolt Park	d					21 13										22 18		22 39			
Sudbury Hill Harrow	d																				
Sudbury & Harrow Road	d																				
Wembley Stadium	d	20 48				21 18				21 49						22 23	22 28	22 44			22 55
London Marylebone 10 ⊖	a	21 03	21 10	21 20		21 30	21 35	21 38	21 53	22 02	22 05	22 12	22 18	22 20		22 36	22 41	22 57	22 47	22 50	23 08

§ London Underground Limited (Central Line) also operate services between South Ruislip and West Ruislip at frequent intervals

A To Kidderminster
B From Aylesbury Vale Parkway
C From Aylesbury Vale Parkway
D To Stourbridge Junction

For complete services between Banbury and Birmingham, refer to Table T71

For principal services between London and Aylesbury refer to Table T114

Table T115-R

Mondays to Fridays
16 December to 15 May

Kidderminster, Birmingham Snow Hill, Stratford-upon-Avon, Banbury, Oxford Parkway, Aylesbury, High Wycombe - London

		CH	CH	CH	CH	LM	CH	CH	CH	CH FO	CH	LM
		◇	◇		◇	A	◇			◇		A
Kidderminster	d											
Stourbridge Junction 2	d											
Cradley Heath	d											
Rowley Regis	d											
Birmingham Snow Hill	d	21 10										
Birmingham Moor Street	d	21 18										
Solihull	d	21 27										
Dorridge	d	21 32										
Lapworth	d	21 36										
Stratford-upon-Avon	d				21 39	22 33					23 15	23 30
Stratford-upon-Avon Parkway	d				21 43	22 37						23a33
Wilmcote	d				21 47	22a40						
Bearley	d											
Claverdon	d				21 54							
Hatton	d	21 42			21 59							
Warwick Parkway	d	21 47										
Warwick	d	21 50			22 05						23 34	
Leamington Spa 8	d	21 56			22 10						23 39	
Banbury	d	22 13			22 29						23 58	
Kings Sutton	d				22 34							
Bicester North 3	d	22 25			22 46							
Oxford	d		22 15				22 41		23 15	23 36	00a21	
Oxford Parkway 116	d		22 21				22 47		23 21	23 42		
Islip	d						22 50					
Bicester Village	d		22 30				22 58		23 31	23 52		
Haddenham & Thame Parkway	d		22 42		22 59		23 10		23 44			
Aylesbury	d			22 48				23 16				
Little Kimble	d							23 24				
Monks Risborough	d							23 28				
Princes Risborough 2	d		22 49		23 07			23 32	23 51			
Saunderton	d		22 54									
High Wycombe 1	d	22 45	23 00		23 17		23 23	23 42	00a04	00 18		
Beaconsfield	d		23 07		23 24		23 29	23 48				
Seer Green	d						23 32					
Gerrards Cross 1	d		23 13		23 30		23 36	23 54				
Denham Golf Club	d						23 39					
Denham	d						23 42					
West Ruislip 3 § ⊖	d						23 46					
South Ruislip § ⊖	d						23 50					
West Ealing	a											
Northolt Park	d						23 54					
Sudbury Hill Harrow	d											
Sudbury & Harrow Road	d											
Wembley Stadium	d		23 24				23 59	00 06				
London Marylebone 10 ⊖	a	23 12	23 35	23 50	23 54		00 12	00 19		00 47		

§ London Underground Limited (Central Line) also operate services between South Ruislip and West Ruislip at frequent intervals

A To Birmingham Snow Hill

For complete services between Banbury and Birmingham, refer to Table T71

For principal services between London and Aylesbury refer to Table T114

Table T115-R

Saturdays
21 December to 16 May

Kidderminster, Birmingham Snow Hill, Stratford-upon-Avon, Banbury, Oxford Parkway, Aylesbury, High Wycombe - London

		CH	CH	CH	CH	CH	CH	CH	CH	CH	CH	CH	LM	CH	CH	CH	CH	CH	CH	LM
		A	◇ B			C		◇		◇			D		◇	C	◇		◇	D
Kidderminster	d																			
Stourbridge Junction 2	d																			
Cradley Heath	d																			
Rowley Regis	d																			
Birmingham Snow Hill	d														06 12				06 46	
Birmingham Moor Street	d														06 15				06 49	
Solihull	d														06 24				07 02	
Dorridge	d														06 29					
Lapworth	d														06 33					
Stratford-upon-Avon	d												07 00							07 43
Stratford-upon-Avon Parkway	d												07 04							07 47
Wilmcote	d												07a07							07a50
Bearley	d																			
Claverdon	d																			
Hatton	d														06 39					
Warwick Parkway	d														06 44				07 14	
Warwick	d														06 47					
Leamington Spa 8	d														06 52				07 20	
Banbury	d						06 04		06 19						07 10				07 39	
Kings Sutton	d								06 24											
Bicester North 3	d						06 18		06 35						07 22				07 51	
Oxford	d							06 12		06 37							07 10			
Oxford Parkway 116	d							06 18		06 43							07 16			
Islip	d																07 19			
Bicester Village	d							06 28		06 52							07 27			
Haddenham & Thame Parkway	d						06 30	06 42	06 48						07 33		07 41			
Aylesbury	d			05 15	05 55	06 18					06 48	06 52				07 18		07 32		
Little Kimble	d			05 23	06 03							07 00						07 40		
Monks Risborough	d			05 27	06 07							07 04						07 44		
Princes Risborough 2	d			05 31	06 11		06 37					07 08						07 49		
Saunderton	d			05 36	06 16							07 13						07 54		
High Wycombe 1	d		00 18	05 43	06 23		06 47	06 56	07 02			07 20		07 31	07 46		07 55	08 01	08 11	
Beaconsfield	d			05 50	06 29		06 53		07 08			07 27		07 37				08 07		
Seer Green	d			05 53	06 32							07 30						08 10		
Gerrards Cross 1	d			05 58	06 37		06 59		07 14			07 35		07 43				08 14		
Denham Golf Club	d			06 01	06 41									07 46						
Denham	d			06 04	06 44									07 49				08 18		
West Ruislip 3 § ⊖	d			06 09	06 49							07 42		07 59						
South Ruislip § ⊖	d			06 13	06 53							07 46		08 03						
West Ealing	a																			
Northolt Park	d			06 17	06 57							07 50		08 07						
Sudbury Hill Harrow	d																			
Sudbury & Harrow Road	d																			
Wembley Stadium	d	00 06		06 22	07 02		07 11					07 55		08 12						
London Marylebone 10 ⊖	a	00 19	00 47	06 35	07 15	07 18	07 23	07 24	07 37	07 40	07 50	08 09		08 25	08 14	08 20	08 28	08 39	08 42	

§ London Underground Limited (Central Line) also operate services between South Ruislip and West Ruislip at frequent intervals

A From Aylesbury
B From Oxford
C From Aylesbury Vale Parkway
D To Kidderminster

For complete services between Banbury and Birmingham, refer to Table T71

For principal services between London and Aylesbury refer to Table T114

Table T115-R

Saturdays
21 December to 16 May

Kidderminster, Birmingham Snow Hill, Stratford-upon-Avon, Banbury, Oxford Parkway, Aylesbury, High Wycombe - London

Station		CH	CH ◇	CH	CH ◇	CH ◇	CH A	CH	CH	CH ◇	CH ◇	CH A	CH ◇	CH ◇	LM B	LM B	CH ◇	CH A	LM B
Kidderminster	d				06 37					07 12									
Stourbridge Junction	d				06 45					07 22									
Cradley Heath	d				06 51														
Rowley Regis	d				06 57					07 33									
Birmingham Snow Hill	d				07 12					07 51									
Birmingham Moor Street	d				07 15					07 55				08 15					
Solihull	d				07 24					08 05				08 24					
Dorridge	d				07 29									08 29					
Lapworth	d																		
Stratford-upon-Avon	d												07 56		08 26	09 03			09 26
Stratford-upon-Avon Parkway	d												08 00		08 30	09a06			09 30
Wilmcote	d												08 03		08a33				09a33
Bearley	d																		
Claverdon	d												08 11						
Hatton	d												08 17						
Warwick Parkway	d				07 39					08 18				08 39					
Warwick	d				07 42								08 24	08 42					
Leamington Spa	d				07 46					08 24			08 29	08 46					
Banbury	d			07 44	08 04					08 44			08 48	09 04					
Kings Sutton	d			07 49									08 53						
Bicester North	d			08 00	08 16								09 03	09 16					
Oxford	d		07 36			08 11					08 43						09 09		
Oxford Parkway 116	d		07 44			08 17					08 49						09 15		
Islip	d																09 18		
Bicester Village	d		07 55			08 26					08 58						09 26		
Haddenham & Thame Parkway	d			08 13		08 38							09 14				09 38		
Aylesbury	d	07 48					08 18		08 29			08 48						09 18	
Little Kimble	d								08 37										
Monks Risborough	d								08 41										
Princes Risborough	d			08 20	08 31				08 45				09 21	09 31					
Saunderton	d								08 50										
High Wycombe	d			08 30		08 51			08 57	09 15			09 30				09 51		
Beaconsfield	d			08 36					09 03				09 36						
Seer Green	d								09 06										
Gerrards Cross	d			08 42				08 49	09 11				09 41						
Denham Golf Club	d							08 52											
Denham	d							08 55	09 15										
West Ruislip § ⊖	d							09 05											
South Ruislip § ⊖	d							09 09											
West Ealing	a																		
Northolt Park	d							09 13											
Sudbury Hill Harrow	d																		
Sudbury & Harrow Road	d																		
Wembley Stadium	d			08 54				09 18					09 52						
London Marylebone ⊖	a	08 50	08 53	09 07	09 11	09 18	09 20	09 32	09 36	09 41	09 46	09 50	10 05	10 11			10 18	10 20	

§ London Underground Limited (Central Line) also operate services between South Ruislip and West Ruislip at frequent intervals

A From Aylesbury Vale Parkway
B To Stourbridge Junction

For complete services between Banbury and Birmingham, refer to Table T71

For principal services between London and Aylesbury refer to Table T114

Table T115-R

Saturdays
21 December to 16 May

Kidderminster, Birmingham Snow Hill, Stratford-upon-Avon, Banbury, Oxford Parkway, Aylesbury, High Wycombe - London

Station		CH	CH	CH ◇	CH ◇	CH A	CH	CH ◇	LM B	CH ◇	CH A	LM B	CH	CH	CH	CH ◇	CH ◇	CH	CH	CH ◇
Kidderminster	d			08 13												09 10				
Stourbridge Junction	d			08 24												09 20				
Cradley Heath	d			08 30																
Rowley Regis	d			08 36												09 31				
Birmingham Snow Hill	d			08 53				09 12								09 51				10 12
Birmingham Moor Street	d			08 56				09 15								09 55				10 15
Solihull	d			09 05				09 24								10 06				10 24
Dorridge	d							09 29												10 29
Lapworth	d																			
Stratford-upon-Avon	d								10 03			10 26								
Stratford-upon-Avon Parkway	d								10a06			10 30								
Wilmcote	d											10a33								
Bearley	d																			
Claverdon	d																			
Hatton	d																			
Warwick Parkway	d			09 16				09 39								10 20				10 39
Warwick	d							09 42												10 42
Leamington Spa	d			09 22				09 46								10 26				10 46
Banbury	d			09 40			09 44	10 05							10 24	10 45			10 49	11 05
Kings Sutton	d						09 49								10 31					
Bicester North	d						10 01	10 18							10 42				11 03	11 18
Oxford	d				09 42					10 09							10 44			
Oxford Parkway 116	d				09 48					10 15							10 50			
Islip	d									10 18										
Bicester Village	d				09 57					10 26							10 59			
Haddenham & Thame Parkway	d						10 13			10 38									11 15	
Aylesbury	d		09 29			09 48					10 18			10 29				10 48		
Little Kimble	d		09 37											10 37						
Monks Risborough	d		09 41											10 41						
Princes Risborough	d		09 45				10 20							10 45					11 22	
Saunderton	d		09 50											10 50						
High Wycombe	d		09 57	10 14			10 30			10 51				10 57	11 10	11 18			11 32	
Beaconsfield	d		10 03				10 36							11 03					11 38	
Seer Green	d		10 06											11 06						
Gerrards Cross	d	09 49	10 11				10 42						10 49	11 11					11 44	
Denham Golf Club	d	09 52											10 52							
Denham	d	09 55	10 15										10 55	11 15						
West Ruislip § ⊖	d	10 05											11 05							
South Ruislip § ⊖	d	10 09											11 09							
West Ealing	a																			
Northolt Park	d	10 13											11 13							
Sudbury Hill Harrow	d																			
Sudbury & Harrow Road	d																			
Wembley Stadium	d	10 18					10 54						11 18						11 56	
London Marylebone ⊖	a	10 32	10 36	10 41	10 48	10 50	11 07	11 11		11 18	11 20		11 32	11 36	11 41	11 45	11 49	11 50	12 08	12 11

§ London Underground Limited (Central Line) also operate services between South Ruislip and West Ruislip at frequent intervals

A From Aylesbury Vale Parkway
B To Stourbridge Junction

For complete services between Banbury and Birmingham, refer to Table T71

For principal services between London and Aylesbury refer to Table T114

Table T115-R

Saturdays

21 December to 16 May

Kidderminster, Birmingham Snow Hill, Stratford-upon-Avon, Banbury, Oxford Parkway, Aylesbury, High Wycombe - London

		CH ◇	CH A	CH	CH	CH ◇ B	CH ◇	LM C	LM C	CH ◇	CH	CH ◇ E	CH ◇	LM C	CH ◇	CH A	LM C	CH	CH	CH ◇
Kidderminster	d																			
Stourbridge Junction 2	d																			
Cradley Heath	d																			
Rowley Regis	d																			
Birmingham Snow Hill	d												11 12							
Birmingham Moor Street	d						10 55						11 15							11 55
Solihull	d						11 04						11 24							12 04
Dorridge	d												11 29							
Lapworth	d																			
Stratford-upon-Avon	d					10 40		11 03	11 26					12 03			12 26			
Stratford-upon-Avon Parkway	d					10 44		11a06	11 30					12a06			12 30			
Wilmcote	d					10 47			11a33								12a33			
Bearley	d					10 51														
Claverdon	d					10 56														
Hatton	d					11 01														
Warwick Parkway	d						11 16						11 39							12 17
Warwick	d					11 08							11 42							
Leamington Spa 8	d					11 15	11 21					←	11 46							12 23
Banbury	d					11 43	11 39					11 43	12 05							12 42
Kings Sutton	d					→														
Bicester North 3	d											12 01	12 18							
Oxford	d	11 11								11 42					12 09					
Oxford Parkway 116	d	11 17								11 48					12 15					
Islip	d														12 18					
Bicester Village	d	11 26								11 57					12 26					
Haddenham & Thame Parkway	d	11 38										12 13			12 38					
Aylesbury	d		11 18		11 30						11 48					12 18			12 29	
Little Kimble	d																		12 37	
Monks Risborough	d				11 41														12 41	
Princes Risborough 2	d				11 45							12 20							12 45	
Saunderton	d				11 50														12 50	
High Wycombe 1	d	11 51			11 57		12 14					12 30			12 51				12 57	13 14
Beaconsfield	d				12 03							12 36							13 03	
Seer Green	d				12 06														13 06	
Gerrards Cross 1	d			11 51	12 11							12 42						12 49	13 11	
Denham Golf Club	d			11 54														12 52		
Denham	d			11 57	12 15													12 55	13 15	
West Ruislip 3 § ⊖	d			12 06														13 05		
South Ruislip § ⊖	d			12 10														13 09		
West Ealing	a																			
Northolt Park	d			12 14														13 13		
Sudbury Hill Harrow	d																			
Sudbury & Harrow Road	d																			
Wembley Stadium	d			12 19								12 54						13 18		
London Marylebone 10 ⊖	a	12 19	12 20	12 32	12 36		12 41			12 46	12 50	13 07	13 11		13 18	13 20		13 32	13 36	13 41

§ London Underground Limited (Central Line) also operate services between South Ruislip and West Ruislip at frequent intervals

A From Aylesbury Vale Parkway
B To London Marylebone
C To Stourbridge Junction
E From Stratford-upon-Avon

For complete services between Banbury and Birmingham, refer to Table T71

For principal services between London and Aylesbury refer to Table T114

Table T115-R

Saturdays

21 December to 16 May

Kidderminster, Birmingham Snow Hill, Stratford-upon-Avon, Banbury, Oxford Parkway, Aylesbury, High Wycombe - London

		CH ◇	CH	CH	CH ◇	CH	LM A	CH ◇	CH B	LM A	CH	CH	CH ◇	CH ◇	CH	CH	CH ◇	LM A	CH ◇	CH B
Kidderminster	d																			
Stourbridge Junction 2	d																			
Cradley Heath	d																			
Rowley Regis	d																			
Birmingham Snow Hill	d				12 12												13 12			
Birmingham Moor Street	d				12 15								12 55				13 15			
Solihull	d				12 24								13 04				13 24			
Dorridge	d				12 29												13 29			
Lapworth	d																			
Stratford-upon-Avon	d					12 40	13 03			13 26								14 03		
Stratford-upon-Avon Parkway	d					12 44	13a06			13 30								14a06		
Wilmcote	d					12 47				13a33										
Bearley	d					12 51														
Claverdon	d					12 56														
Hatton	d					13 01														
Warwick Parkway	d				12 39								13 16				13 38			
Warwick	d				12 42	13 08											13 41			
Leamington Spa 8	d				12 46	13a17							13 22				13 46			
Banbury	d			12 46	13 05								13 40			13 47	14 07			
Kings Sutton	d																			
Bicester North 3	d			13 01	13 18											14 02	14 20			
Oxford	d	12 42						13 11						13 43					14 11	
Oxford Parkway 116	d	12 48						13 17						13 49					14 17	
Islip	d																			
Bicester Village	d	12 56						13 26						13 58					14 26	
Haddenham & Thame Parkway	d			13 13				13 38								14 14			14 38	
Aylesbury	d		12 48						13 18			13 29			13 48					14 18
Little Kimble	d											13 37								
Monks Risborough	d											13 41								
Princes Risborough 2	d			13 20								13 45				14 21				
Saunderton	d											13 50								
High Wycombe 1	d			13 30				13 51				13 57	14 14			14 31			14 51	
Beaconsfield	d			13 36								14 03				14 37				
Seer Green	d											14 06								
Gerrards Cross 1	d			13 42							13 49	14 11				14 43				
Denham Golf Club	d										13 52									
Denham	d										13 55	14 15								
West Ruislip 3 § ⊖	d										14 05									
South Ruislip § ⊖	d										14 09									
West Ealing	a																			
Northolt Park	d										14 13									
Sudbury Hill Harrow	d																			
Sudbury & Harrow Road	d																			
Wembley Stadium	d			13 54							14 18					14 55				
London Marylebone 10 ⊖	a	13 46	13 50	14 07	14 11			14 19	14 20		14 32	14 36	14 41	14 46	14 50	15 08	15 11		15 18	15 20

§ London Underground Limited (Central Line) also operate services between South Ruislip and West Ruislip at frequent intervals

A To Stourbridge Junction
B From Aylesbury Vale Parkway

For complete services between Banbury and Birmingham, refer to Table T71

For principal services between London and Aylesbury refer to Table T114

Table T115-R

Saturdays

21 December to 16 May

Kidderminster, Birmingham Snow Hill, Stratford-upon-Avon, Banbury, Oxford Parkway, Aylesbury, High Wycombe - London

		CH	LM	CH	CH	CH	CH	CH	CH	CH	CH	CH	CH	CH	CH	CH	LM	LM	CH	CH
						◇	◇			◇	◇				◇	◇			◇	
		A	B									A			C		B	B		
Kidderminster	d																			
Stourbridge Junction 2	d																			
Cradley Heath	d																			
Rowley Regis	d																			
Birmingham Snow Hill	d									14 12										
Birmingham Moor Street	d					13 55				14 15						14 55				
Solihull	d					14 04				14 24						15 04				
Dorridge	d									14 29										
Lapworth	d																			
Stratford-upon-Avon	d		14 26												14 40		15 03	15 26		
Stratford-upon-Avon Parkway	d		14 30												14 44		15a06	15 30		
Wilmcote	d		14a33												14 47			15a33		
Bearley	d														14 51					
Claverdon	d														14 56					
Hatton	d														15 01					
Warwick Parkway	d					14 16				14 39						15 16				
Warwick	d									14 42					15 08					
Leamington Spa 8	d					14 22				14 46					15 15	15 22				
Banbury	d					14 41			14 44	15 05					15 46	15 41				
Kings Sutton	d								14 49						→					
Bicester North 3	d								15 01	15 18										
Oxford	d						14 42				15 09								15 43	
Oxford Parkway 116	d						14 48				15 15								15 49	
Islip	d										15 18									
Bicester Village	d						14 57				15 26								15 58	
Haddenham & Thame Parkway	d								15 13		15 38									
Aylesbury	d	14 20			14 29			14 48				15 20		15 30						15 48
Little Kimble	d				14 37															
Monks Risborough	d				14 41									15 41						
Princes Risborough 2	d				14 45				15 20					15 45						
Saunderton	d				14 50									15 50						
High Wycombe 1	d				14 57	15 15			15 30		15 51			15 57		16 14				
Beaconsfield	d				15 03				15 36					16 03						
Seer Green	d				15 06									16 06						
Gerrards Cross 1	d			14 50	15 11				15 42				15 49	16 11						
Denham Golf Club	d			14 53									15 52							
Denham	d			14 56	15 15								15 55	16 15						
West Ruislip 3 § ⊖	d			15 05									16 05							
South Ruislip § ⊖	d			15 09									16 09							
West Ealing	a																			
Northolt Park	d			15 13									16 13							
Sudbury Hill Harrow	d																			
Sudbury & Harrow Road	d																			
Wembley Stadium	d			15 18					15 54				16 18							
London Marylebone 10 ⊖	a	15 20		15 32	15 36	15 41	15 47	15 50	16 07	16 11	16 18	16 20	16 32	16 36		16 46			16 49	16 50

§ London Underground Limited (Central Line) also operate services between South Ruislip and West Ruislip at frequent intervals

A From Aylesbury Vale Parkway
B To Stourbridge Junction
C To London Marylebone

For complete services between Banbury and Birmingham, refer to Table T71

For principal services between London and Aylesbury refer to Table T114

Table T115-R

Saturdays

21 December to 16 May

Kidderminster, Birmingham Snow Hill, Stratford-upon-Avon, Banbury, Oxford Parkway, Aylesbury, High Wycombe - London

		CH	CH	LM	CH	CH	LM	CH	CH	CH	CH	CH	CH	CH	CH	CH	CH	CH	CH	CH
		◇	◇		◇					◇	◇			◇	◇				◇	◇
		A		B		C	B									C			D	
Kidderminster	d																			
Stourbridge Junction 2	d																			
Cradley Heath	d																			
Rowley Regis	d																			
Birmingham Snow Hill	d		15 12											16 12						
Birmingham Moor Street	d		15 15							15 55				16 15						16 55
Solihull	d		15 24							16 04				16 24						17 04
Dorridge	d		15 29											16 29						
Lapworth	d																			
Stratford-upon-Avon	d			16 03			16 26												16 40	
Stratford-upon-Avon Parkway	d			16a06			16 30												16 44	
Wilmcote	d						16a33												16 47	
Bearley	d																		16 51	
Claverdon	d																		16 56	
Hatton	d																		17 01	
Warwick Parkway	d		15 39							16 16				16 39						17 16
Warwick	d		15 42											16 42					17 08	
Leamington Spa 8	d	←	15 46							16 22				16 46					17 15	17 22
Banbury	d	15 46	16 05							16 41			16 44	17 05					17 45	17 41
Kings Sutton	d												16 49						→	
Bicester North 3	d	16 01	16 18										17 01	17 18						
Oxford	d				16 11						16 42				17 11					
Oxford Parkway 116	d				16 17						16 48				17 17					
Islip	d																			
Bicester Village	d				16 26						16 57				17 26					
Haddenham & Thame Parkway	d	16 13			16 38								17 13		17 38					
Aylesbury	d					16 18			16 29			16 48				17 18		17 29		
Little Kimble	d								16 37									17 37		
Monks Risborough	d								16 41									17 41		
Princes Risborough 2	d	16 20							16 45				17 20					17 45		
Saunderton	d								16 50									17 50		
High Wycombe 1	d	16 30			16 51				16 57	17 14			17 30		17 51			17 57		18 14
Beaconsfield	d	16 36							17 03				17 36					18 03		
Seer Green	d								17 06									18 06		
Gerrards Cross 1	d	16 42						16 50	17 11				17 42				17 49	18 11		
Denham Golf Club	d							16 53									17 52			
Denham	d							16 56	17 15								17 55	18 15		
West Ruislip 3 § ⊖	d							17 05									18 05			
South Ruislip § ⊖	d							17 09									18 09			
West Ealing	a																			
Northolt Park	d							17 13									18 13			
Sudbury Hill Harrow	d																			
Sudbury & Harrow Road	d																			
Wembley Stadium	d	16 54						17 18					17 54				18 18			
London Marylebone 10 ⊖	a	17 06	17 11		17 18	17 20		17 32	17 36	17 41	17 47	17 50	18 07	18 11	18 18	18 20	18 32	18 36		18 41

§ London Underground Limited (Central Line) also operate services between South Ruislip and West Ruislip at frequent intervals

A From Stratford-upon-Avon
B To Stourbridge Junction
C From Aylesbury Vale Parkway
D To London Marylebone

For complete services between Banbury and Birmingham, refer to Table T71

For principal services between London and Aylesbury refer to Table T114

Table T115-R

Saturdays
21 December to 16 May

Kidderminster, Birmingham Snow Hill, Stratford-upon-Avon, Banbury, Oxford Parkway, Aylesbury, High Wycombe - London

		LM	LM	CH	CH	CH	CH	LM	CH	CH	LM	CH	CH	CH	CH	CH	CH	CH	CH	CH
				◇		◇	◇		◇					◇	◇			◇	◇	
		A	B			C		D		E	D									E
Kidderminster	d																			
Stourbridge Junction [2]	d																			
Cradley Heath	d																			
Rowley Regis	d																			
Birmingham Snow Hill	d						17 12											18 12		
Birmingham Moor Street	d						17 15							17 55				18 15		
Solihull	d						17 24							18 04				18 24		
Dorridge	d						17 29											18 29		
Lapworth	d																			
Stratford-upon-Avon	d	17 03	17 26					17 54			18 26									
Stratford-upon-Avon Parkway	d	17a06	17 30					17 58			18 30									
Wilmcote	d		17a33					18a01			18a33									
Bearley	d																			
Claverdon	d																			
Hatton	d																			
Warwick Parkway	d						17 39							18 16				18 39		
Warwick	d						17 42											18 42		
Leamington Spa [8]	d					←	17 46							18 22				18 46		
Banbury	d					17 45	18 05							18 41			18 44	19 05		
Kings Sutton	d																18 49			
Bicester North [3]	d					18 01	18 18										19 01	19 18		
Oxford	d			17 41					18 09						18 42				19 11	
Oxford Parkway 116	d			17 48					18 15						18 48				19 17	
Islip	d								18 18											
Bicester Village	d			17 57					18 26						18 57				19 26	
Haddenham & Thame Parkway	d					18 13			18 38								19 13		19 38	
Aylesbury	d				17 48					18 18			18 29			18 48				19 18
Little Kimble	d												18 37							
Monks Risborough	d												18 41							
Princes Risborough [2]	d					18 20							18 45				19 20			
Saunderton	d												18 50							
High Wycombe [1]	d					18 30			18 51				18 57	19 14			19 30		19 51	
Beaconsfield	d					18 36							19 03				19 36			
Seer Green	d												19 06							
Gerrards Cross [1]	d					18 42						18 49	19 11				19 42			
Denham Golf Club	d											18 52								
Denham	d											18 55	19 15							
West Ruislip [3] § ⊖	d											19 05								
South Ruislip § ⊖	d											19 09								
West Ealing	a																			
Northolt Park	d											19 13								
Sudbury Hill Harrow	d																			
Sudbury & Harrow Road	d																			
Wembley Stadium	d					18 54						19 18					19 54			
London Marylebone [10] ⊖	a			18 47	18 50	19 07	19 11		19 18	19 20		19 32	19 36	19 41	19 47	19 50	20 07	20 11	20 18	20 20

§ London Underground Limited (Central Line) also operate services between South Ruislip and West Ruislip at frequent intervals

A To Stourbridge Junction
B To Worcester Foregate Street
C From Stratford-upon-Avon
D To Birmingham Snow Hill
E From Aylesbury Vale Parkway

For complete services between Banbury and Birmingham, refer to Table T71

For principal services between London and Aylesbury refer to Table T114

NRT DECEMBER 19 EDITION

Table T115-R

Saturdays
21 December to 16 May

Kidderminster, Birmingham Snow Hill, Stratford-upon-Avon, Banbury, Oxford Parkway, Aylesbury, High Wycombe - London

		CH	CH	CH	CH	LM	CH	LM	CH	CH	CH	CH	LM	CH	CH	LM	CH	CH	CH	CH	CH
					◇		◇		◇		◇	◇		◇					◇	◇	
		A			B	C		D			E		F		G	H					
Kidderminster	d																				
Stourbridge Junction [2]	d																				
Cradley Heath	d																				
Rowley Regis	d																				
Birmingham Snow Hill	d											19 12									
Birmingham Moor Street	d						18 55					19 15							19 55		
Solihull	d						19 05					19 24							20 04		
Dorridge	d											19 29									
Lapworth	d																				
Stratford-upon-Avon	d				18 42	18 48		19 26					19 53			20 26					
Stratford-upon-Avon Parkway	d				18 46	18 52		19 30					19 57			20 30					
Wilmcote	d				18 49	18a55		19a33					20a00			20a33					
Bearley	d																				
Claverdon	d				18 56																
Hatton	d				19 01																
Warwick Parkway	d						19 17					19 39							20 16		
Warwick	d				19 08							19 42									
Leamington Spa [8]	d				19 15		19 23				←	19 46							20 22		
Banbury	d				19 46		19 41				19 46	20 05							20 41		
Kings Sutton	d				→																
Bicester North [3]	d										20 01	20 18									
Oxford	d								19 42					20 11						20 42	
Oxford Parkway 116	d								19 48					20 17						20 48	
Islip	d																				
Bicester Village	d								19 57					20 26						20 57	
Haddenham & Thame Parkway	d										20 13			20 38							
Aylesbury	d	19 20		19 29						19 48					20 18			20 29			20 48
Little Kimble	d			19 37														20 37			
Monks Risborough	d			19 41														20 41			
Princes Risborough [2]	d			19 45							20 20							20 45			
Saunderton	d			19 50														20 50			
High Wycombe [1]	d			19 57			20 14				20 30			20 51				20 57	21 14		
Beaconsfield	d			20 03							20 36							21 03			
Seer Green	d			20 06														21 06			
Gerrards Cross [1]	d		19 49	20 11							20 42						20 49	21 11			
Denham Golf Club	d		19 52														20 52				
Denham	d		19 55	20 15													20 55	21 15			
West Ruislip [3] § ⊖	d		20 05														21 05				
South Ruislip § ⊖	d		20 09														21 09				
West Ealing	a																				
Northolt Park	d		20 13														21 13				
Sudbury Hill Harrow	d																				
Sudbury & Harrow Road	d																				
Wembley Stadium	d		20 18								20 54						21 18				
London Marylebone [10] ⊖	a	20 20	20 32	20 36			20 41		20 48	20 50	21 07	21 11		21 18	21 20		21 32	21 36	21 41	21 47	21 50

§ London Underground Limited (Central Line) also operate services between South Ruislip and West Ruislip at frequent intervals

A From Aylesbury Vale Parkway
B To London Marylebone
C To Great Malvern
D To Kidderminster
E From Stratford-upon-Avon
F To Birmingham Snow Hill
G From Aylesbury Vale Parkway
H To Worcester Shrub Hill

For complete services between Banbury and Birmingham, refer to Table T71

For principal services between London and Aylesbury refer to Table T114

Table T115-R

Kidderminster, Birmingham Snow Hill, Stratford-upon-Avon, Banbury, Oxford Parkway, Aylesbury, High Wycombe - London

Saturdays

21 December to 16 May

		CH	CH	CH ◇	CH	CH ◇	CH	LM	CH	CH	CH	CH ◇	CH	CH	CH	CH ◇	CH	CH ◇	CH	LM	LM A
Kidderminster	d																				
Stourbridge Junction 2	d																				
Cradley Heath	d																				
Rowley Regis	d																				
Birmingham Snow Hill	d			20 12																	
Birmingham Moor Street	d			20 15							20 45							21 18			
Solihull	d			20 24							20 55							21 27			
Dorridge	d			20 29							21 01							21 34			
Lapworth	d																	21 38			
Stratford-upon-Avon	d				20 43			21 26											22 15	22 33	23 30
Stratford-upon-Avon Parkway	d				20 47			21 30												22 37	23a33
Wilmcote	d				20 50			21a33												22a40	
Bearley	d																				
Claverdon	d				20 57																
Hatton	d				21 02													21 44			
Warwick Parkway	d			20 39							21 13							21 49			
Warwick	d			20 42	21 08						21 17							21 52	22 35		
Leamington Spa 8	d			20 46	21a17						21 22							21 57	22 41		
Banbury	d		20 45	21 05							21 40				21 46			22 16	23a02		
Kings Sutton	d		20 50															22 21			
Bicester North 3	d		21 01	21 18							21 52				22 02			22 32			
Oxford	d					21 09						21 42				22 09					
Oxford Parkway 116	d					21 15						21 48				22 15					
Islip	d					21 18										22 18					
Bicester Village	d					21 26						21 57				22 26					
Haddenham & Thame Parkway	d		21 13			21 38						22 09			22 15	22 38		22 43			
Aylesbury	d	20 50					21 18			21 29			21 48	22 18			22 29				
Little Kimble	d									21 37							22 37				
Monks Risborough	d									21 41							22 41				
Princes Risborough 2	d		21 20							21 45					22 22		22a47	22 50			
Saunderton	d									21 50								22 55			
High Wycombe 1	d		21 30			21 51				21 57	22 14	22 22			22 32	22 52		23 02			
Beaconsfield	d		21 36							22 03					22 38	22 58		23 08			
Seer Green	d									22 06								23 11			
Gerrards Cross 1	d		21 42						21 49	22 11					22 44	23 04		23 15			
Denham Golf Club	d								21 52						22 47						
Denham	d								21 55	22 15					22 50			23 19			
West Ruislip 3 § ⊖	d								22 05						22 55			23 24			
South Ruislip § ⊖	d								22 09						22 59			23 28			
West Ealing	a																				
Northolt Park	d								22 13						23 03			23 32			
Sudbury Hill Harrow	d																				
Sudbury & Harrow Road	d																				
Wembley Stadium	d		21 54						22 18						23 08			23 37			
London Marylebone 10 ⊖	a	21 50	22 07	22 11		22 18	22 20		22 32	22 36	22 41	22 49	22 50	23 18	23 22	23 25		23 48			

§ London Underground Limited (Central Line) also operate services between South Ruislip and West Ruislip at frequent intervals

A To Birmingham Snow Hill

For complete services between Banbury and Birmingham, refer to Table T71

For principal services between London and Aylesbury refer to Table T114

Table T115-R

Kidderminster, Birmingham Snow Hill, Stratford-upon-Avon, Banbury, Oxford Parkway, Aylesbury, High Wycombe - London

Sundays

15 December to 10 May

		CH A	CH B	CH	CH	CH ◇	CH A	CH B	CH	CH ◇	CH	CH ◇	CH C	CH D	LM E	CH	CH	CH ◇	CH ◇	CH A	CH B	CH	CH ◇
Kidderminster	d																						
Stourbridge Junction 2	d																						
Cradley Heath	d																						
Rowley Regis	d																						
Birmingham Snow Hill	d																						
Birmingham Moor Street	d																		08 25				08 55
Solihull	d																		08 34				09 04
Dorridge	d																		08 39				
Lapworth	d																						
Stratford-upon-Avon	d														09 27								
Stratford-upon-Avon Parkway	d														09 31								
Wilmcote	d														09a34								
Bearley	d																						
Claverdon	d																						
Hatton	d																						
Warwick Parkway	d																		08 49				09 16
Warwick	d																		08 52				
Leamington Spa 8	d																		08 58				09 22
Banbury	d								07 50								08 49		09 16				09 40
Kings Sutton	d																						
Bicester North 3	d								08 04								09 03		09 29				
Oxford	d					07 43				08 10		08 38						09 01					
Oxford Parkway 116	d					07 49				08 16		08 44						09 07					
Islip	d																	09 11					
Bicester Village	d					07 58				08 25		08 53						09 18					
Haddenham & Thame Parkway	d					08 10			08 16	08 37		09 05					09 15	09 31	09 40				
Aylesbury	d	07 18	07 20	07 20	07 30		08 18	08 20			08 29		08 48	08 50						09 18	09 20	09 32	
Little Kimble	d				07 38						08 37											09 40	
Monks Risborough	d				07 42						08 41											09 44	
Princes Risborough 2	d			07 35	07 46				08 23		08 45						09 22					09 48	
Saunderton	d				07 51						08 51											09 53	
High Wycombe 1	d			07 48	07 57	08 23			08 33	08 50	09 00						09 32	09 44				10 00	10 13
Beaconsfield	d			07 54	08 03				08 39	08 56	09 06						09 38					10 06	
Seer Green	d				08 06				08 42		09 09											10 09	
Gerrards Cross 1	d			08 00	08 11				08 47	09 02	09 14					09 29	09 44					10 14	
Denham Golf Club	d				08 14				08 50														
Denham	d				08 17				08 53							09 33							
West Ruislip 3 § ⊖	d				08 22				08 57							09 37							
South Ruislip § ⊖	d				08 26				09 01							09 41							
West Ealing	a																						
Northolt Park	d				08 30				09 05							09 45							
Sudbury Hill Harrow	d																						
Sudbury & Harrow Road	d																						
Wembley Stadium	d				08 35				09 10		09 26					09 50						10 26	
London Marylebone 10 ⊖	a	08 20	08 20	08 23	08 48	08 51	09 18	09 20	09 23	09 26	09 38	09 42	09 50	09 50		10 03	10 06	10 11	10 18	10 20	10 20	10 38	10 41

§ London Underground Limited (Central Line) also operate services between South Ruislip and West Ruislip at frequent intervals

A until 15 March. From Aylesbury Vale Parkway
B from 22 March. From Aylesbury Vale Parkway
C until 15 March
D from 22 March
E To Great Malvern

For complete services between Banbury and Birmingham, refer to Table T71

For principal services between London and Aylesbury refer to Table T114

Table T115-R

Sundays

15 December to 10 May

Kidderminster, Birmingham Snow Hill, Stratford-upon-Avon, Banbury, Oxford Parkway, Aylesbury, High Wycombe - London

		CH ◇	CH A	CH B	CH	CH	CH ◇	CH ◇	CH C	CH D	CH	CH ◇	CH ◇	LM E	CH ◇	LM F	CH	CH	CH ◇	CH ◇	CH C	CH D	CH
Kidderminster	d																		09 40				
Stourbridge Junction 2	d																		09 48				
Cradley Heath	d																		09 54				
Rowley Regis	d																		10 00				
Birmingham Snow Hill	d						09 12												10 12				
Birmingham Moor Street	d						09 15						09 55						10 15				
Solihull	d						09 24						10 04						10 24				
Dorridge	d						09 29												10 29				
Lapworth	d																						
Stratford-upon-Avon	d											09 38		10 27		11 27							
Stratford-upon-Avon Parkway	d											09 41		10 31		11 31							
Wilmcote	d											09 44		10a34		11a34							
Bearley	d																						
Claverdon	d																						
Hatton	d											09 55											
Warwick Parkway	d						09 39						10 16						10 39				
Warwick	d						09 42					10 01							10 42				
Leamington Spa 8	d						09 46					10 06	10 22						10 46				
Banbury	d					09 44	10 07					10 24	10 40					10 44	11 07				
Kings Sutton	d					09 50												10 50					
Bicester North 3	d					10 02	10 19					10 36						11 02	11 19				
Oxford	d	09 42						10 11							10 42					11 09			
Oxford Parkway 116	d	09 48						10 17							10 48					11 15			
Islip	d																			11 18			
Bicester Village	d	09 57						10 26							10 57					11 26			
Haddenham & Thame Parkway	d					10 14		10 38				10 47						11 14		11 38			
Aylesbury	d		09 48	09 50					10 18	10 20	10 29										11 18	11 20	11 29
Little Kimble	d										10 37												11 37
Monks Risborough	d										10 41												11 41
Princes Risborough 2	d					10 21					10 45	10 54						11 21					11 45
Saunderton	d										10 50												11 50
High Wycombe 1	d					10 31		10 51			10 57	11 03	11 14					11 31		11 51			11 57
Beaconsfield	d					10 37					11 03	11 09						11 37	11 45				12 03
Seer Green	d										11 06												12 06
Gerrards Cross 1	d				10 29	10 43					11 11	11 15					11 29	11 43					12 11
Denham Golf Club	d				10 32																		
Denham	d				10 35												11 33						
West Ruislip 3 § ⊖	d																11 37						
South Ruislip § ⊖	d				10 40												11 41						
West Ealing	a																						
Northolt Park	d				10 44												11 45						
Sudbury Hill Harrow	d																						
Sudbury & Harrow Road	d																						
Wembley Stadium	d				10 49						11 23						11 50						12 23
London Marylebone 10 ⊖	a	10 45	10 50	10 50	11 02	11 06	11 09	11 18	11 20	11 20	11 36	11 39	11 42		11 45		12 02	12 06	12 10	12 18	12 20	12 20	12 36

§ London Underground Limited (Central Line) also operate services between South Ruislip and West Ruislip at frequent intervals

A until 15 March
B from 22 March
C until 15 March. From Aylesbury Vale Parkway
D from 22 March. From Aylesbury Vale Parkway
E To Worcester Shrub Hill
F To Worcester Foregate Street

For complete services between Banbury and Birmingham, refer to Table T71

For principal services between London and Aylesbury refer to Table T114

NRT DECEMBER 19 EDITION

Table T115-R

Sundays

15 December to 10 May

Kidderminster, Birmingham Snow Hill, Stratford-upon-Avon, Banbury, Oxford Parkway, Aylesbury, High Wycombe - London

		CH ◇	CH ◇	LM A	CH	CH	CH ◇	CH ◇	CH B	CH C	CH	CH ◇	CH ◇	CH	CH	CH ◇	CH ◇	CH B	CH C	CH	CH ◇	CH ◇	CH
Kidderminster	d											11 13											
Stourbridge Junction 2	d											11 22											
Cradley Heath	d																						
Rowley Regis	d											11 33											
Birmingham Snow Hill	d						11 12					11 49				12 12							
Birmingham Moor Street	d	10 55					11 15					11 55				12 15					12 55		
Solihull	d	11 04					11 24					12 04				12 24					13 04		
Dorridge	d						11 29									12 29							
Lapworth	d																						
Stratford-upon-Avon	d			12 27																			
Stratford-upon-Avon Parkway	d			12 31																			
Wilmcote	d			12a34																			
Bearley	d																						
Claverdon	d																						
Hatton	d																						
Warwick Parkway	d	11 16					11 39					12 16				12 39					13 15		
Warwick	d						11 42									12 42					13 18		
Leamington Spa 8	d	11 22					11 46					12 22				12 46					13 23		
Banbury	d	11 40				11 44	12 07					12 40			12 44	13 07					13 40		
Kings Sutton	d														12 50								
Bicester North 3	d					12 02	12 19								13 02	13 19							
Oxford	d		11 42					12 11					12 42				13 09					13 42	
Oxford Parkway 116	d		11 48					12 17					12 48				13 15					13 48	
Islip	d																13 18						
Bicester Village	d		11 57					12 26					12 57				13 26					13 57	
Haddenham & Thame Parkway	d					12 14		12 38							13 14		13 38						
Aylesbury	d								12 18	12 20	12 29							13 18	13 20	13 29			
Little Kimble	d										12 37									13 37			
Monks Risborough	d										12 41									13 41			
Princes Risborough 2	d					12 21					12 45				13 21					13 45			
Saunderton	d										12 50									13 50			
High Wycombe 1	d	12 13				12 31		12 51			12 57	13 14			13 31		13 51			13 57	14 13		
Beaconsfield	d					12 37	12 45				13 03				13 37	13 45				14 03			
Seer Green	d										13 06									14 06			
Gerrards Cross 1	d				12 29	12 43					13 11			13 29	13 43					14 11			14 29
Denham Golf Club	d				12 32																		14 32
Denham	d				12 35									13 33									14 35
West Ruislip 3 § ⊖	d													13 37									
South Ruislip § ⊖	d				12 40									13 41									14 40
West Ealing	a																						
Northolt Park	d				12 44									13 45									14 44
Sudbury Hill Harrow	d																						
Sudbury & Harrow Road	d																						
Wembley Stadium	d				12 49						13 23			13 50						14 23			14 49
London Marylebone 10 ⊖	a	12 40	12 43		13 02	13 06	13 10	13 18	13 20	13 20	13 36	13 40	13 45	14 03	14 06	14 10	14 18	14 20	14 20	14 36	14 40	14 43	15 02

§ London Underground Limited (Central Line) also operate services between South Ruislip and West Ruislip at frequent intervals

A To Worcester Foregate Street
B until 15 March. From Aylesbury Vale Parkway
C from 22 March. From Aylesbury Vale Parkway

For complete services between Banbury and Birmingham, refer to Table T71

For principal services between London and Aylesbury refer to Table T114

Table T115-R

Sundays

15 December to 10 May

Kidderminster, Birmingham Snow Hill, Stratford-upon-Avon, Banbury, Oxford Parkway, Aylesbury, High Wycombe - London

		CH ◇	CH ◇	LM A	CH ◇	CH B	CH C	LM A	CH	CH ◇	CH ◇	CH	CH	CH ◇	CH ◇	CH B	CH C	CH	CH ◇ D	CH ◇	LM A	CH ◇	CH E
Kidderminster	d																						
Stourbridge Junction 2	d																						
Cradley Heath	d																						
Rowley Regis	d																						
Birmingham Snow Hill ⛴	d		13 12											14 12									
Birmingham Moor Street	d		13 15							13 55				14 15						14 55			
Solihull	d		13 24							14 04				14 24						15 04			
Dorridge	d		13 29											14 29									
Lapworth	d																						
Stratford-upon-Avon	d	12 57		13 27				14 27											14 43		15 27		
Stratford-upon-Avon Parkway	d	13 01		13 31				14 31											14 47		15 31		
Wilmcote	d	13 04		13a34				14a34											14 50		15a34		
Bearley	d																						
Claverdon	d																						
Hatton	d	13 14																	15 00				
Warwick Parkway	d		13 39							14 16				14 39						15 16			
Warwick	d	13 22	13 42											14 42					15 08				
Leamington Spa 8	d	13 27	13 46							14 23				14 46					15 15	15 23			
Banbury	d	13 47	14 07							14 40			14 45	15 07					15 45	15 41			
Kings Sutton	d												14 50						→				
Bicester North 3	d	14 02	14 19										15 01	15 19									
Oxford	d				14 11						14 41				15 09							15 41	
Oxford Parkway 116	d				14 17						14 47				15 15							15 47	
Islip	d														15 18								
Bicester Village	d				14 26						14 56				15 26							15 56	
Haddenham & Thame Parkway	d	14 14			14 38								15 13		15 38								
Aylesbury	d					14 18	14 20		14 29							15 18	15 20	15 29					15 48
Little Kimble	d								14 37									15 37					
Monks Risborough	d								14 41									15 41					
Princes Risborough 2	d	14 21							14 45				15 20					15 45					
Saunderton	d								14 50									15 50					
High Wycombe 1	d	14 31			14 51				14 57	15 13			15 30		15 51			15 57		16 13			
Beaconsfield	d	14 37	14 45						15 03				15 36	15 45				16 03					
Seer Green	d								15 06									16 06					
Gerrards Cross 1	d	14 43							15 11			15 29	15 42					16 11					
Denham Golf Club	d																						
Denham	d											15 33											
West Ruislip 3 § ⊖	d											15 37											
South Ruislip § ⊖	d											15 41											
West Ealing	a																						
Northolt Park	d											15 45											
Sudbury Hill Harrow	d																						
Sudbury & Harrow Road	d																						
Wembley Stadium	d								15 23			15 50						16 23					
London Marylebone 10 ⊖	a	15 06	15 10		15 18	15 20	15 20		15 36	15 40	15 43	16 03	16 06	16 10	16 18	16 20	16 20	16 36		16 40		16 45	16 50

§ London Underground Limited (Central Line) also operate services between South Ruislip and West Ruislip at frequent intervals

A To Worcester Foregate Street
B until 15 March. From Aylesbury Vale Parkway
C from 22 March. From Aylesbury Vale Parkway
D To London Marylebone
E until 15 March

For complete services between Banbury and Birmingham, refer to Table T71

For principal services between London and Aylesbury refer to Table T114

Table T115-R

Sundays

15 December to 10 May

Kidderminster, Birmingham Snow Hill, Stratford-upon-Avon, Banbury, Oxford Parkway, Aylesbury, High Wycombe - London

		CH A	LM B	CH	CH ◇ C	CH ◇	CH ◇	CH D	CH E	CH	CH ◇	CH ◇	CH F	CH A	CH	CH	CH ◇	CH ◇	CH D	CH E	CH	CH ◇ G	CH ◇
Kidderminster	d																						
Stourbridge Junction 2	d																						
Cradley Heath	d																						
Rowley Regis	d																						
Birmingham Snow Hill ⛴	d					15 12											16 12						
Birmingham Moor Street	d					15 15					15 55						16 15						16 55
Solihull	d					15 24					16 04						16 24						17 04
Dorridge	d					15 29											16 29						
Lapworth	d																						
Stratford-upon-Avon	d		16 27																			16 43	
Stratford-upon-Avon Parkway	d		16 31																			16 47	
Wilmcote	d		16a34																			16 50	
Bearley	d																						
Claverdon	d																						
Hatton	d																					17 00	
Warwick Parkway	d					15 39					16 16						16 39						17 16
Warwick	d					15 42											16 42					17 08	
Leamington Spa 8	d				←	15 46					16 23						16 46					17 15	17 23
Banbury	d				15 45	16 07					16 40					16 45	17 07					17 45	17 41
Kings Sutton	d															16 50						→	
Bicester North 3	d				16 01	16 19										17 01	17 19						
Oxford	d						16 11					16 41						17 09					
Oxford Parkway 116	d						16 17					16 47						17 15					
Islip	d																	17 18					
Bicester Village	d						16 26					16 56						17 26					
Haddenham & Thame Parkway	d				16 13		16 38									17 13		17 38					
Aylesbury	d	15 50						16 18	16 20	16 29			16 48	16 50					17 18	17 20	17 29		
Little Kimble	d									16 37											17 37		
Monks Risborough	d									16 41											17 41		
Princes Risborough 2	d				16 20					16 45						17 20					17 45		
Saunderton	d									16 50											17 50		
High Wycombe 1	d				16 30		16 51			16 57	17 13					17 30		17 51			17 57		18 12
Beaconsfield	d				16 36	16 45				17 03						17 36	17 45				18 03		
Seer Green	d									17 06											18 06		
Gerrards Cross 1	d			16 29	16 42					17 11					17 29	17 42					18 11		
Denham Golf Club	d			16 32																			
Denham	d			16 35											17 33								
West Ruislip 3 § ⊖	d														17 37								
South Ruislip § ⊖	d			16 40											17 41								
West Ealing	a																						
Northolt Park	d			16 44											17 45								
Sudbury Hill Harrow	d																						
Sudbury & Harrow Road	d																						
Wembley Stadium	d			16 49						17 23					17 50						18 23		
London Marylebone 10 ⊖	a	16 50		17 02	17 05	17 10	17 18	17 20	17 20	17 36	17 40	17 43	17 50	17 50	18 03	18 06	18 10	18 17	18 20	18 20	18 36		18 40

§ London Underground Limited (Central Line) also operate services between South Ruislip and West Ruislip at frequent intervals

A from 22 March
B To Worcester Foregate Street
C From Stratford-upon-Avon
D until 15 March. From Aylesbury Vale Parkway
E from 22 March. From Aylesbury Vale Parkway
F until 15 March
G To London Marylebone

For complete services between Banbury and Birmingham, refer to Table T71

For principal services between London and Aylesbury refer to Table T114

Table T115-R

Sundays

15 December to 10 May

Kidderminster, Birmingham Snow Hill, Stratford-upon-Avon, Banbury, Oxford Parkway, Aylesbury, High Wycombe - London

		LM	CH	CH	CH	LM	CH	CH	CH	CH	CH	CH	CH	CH	CH	CH	CH	CH	CH	CH	CH	CH	CH
			◇					◇	◇	◇				◇	◇					◇		◇	
		A		B	C	A		D			E	F				B	C						E
Kidderminster	d																						
Stourbridge Junction 2	d																						
Cradley Heath	d																						
Rowley Regis	d																						
Birmingham Snow Hill	d								17 12											18 12			
Birmingham Moor Street	d								17 15					17 55						18 15			
Solihull	d								17 24					18 04						18 24			
Dorridge	d								17 29											18 29			
Lapworth	d																						
Stratford-upon-Avon	d	17 27				18 27															18 44		
Stratford-upon-Avon Parkway	d	17 31				18 31															18 48		
Wilmcote	d	17a34				18a34															18 51		
Bearley	d																						
Claverdon	d																						
Hatton	d																				19 02		
Warwick Parkway	d								17 39					18 16						18 39			
Warwick	d								17 42											18 42	19 08		
Leamington Spa 8	d							←	17 46					18 23						18 46	19a18		
Banbury	d							17 45	18 07					18 41					18 45	19 07			
Kings Sutton	d																		18 50				
Bicester North 3	d							18 01	18 19										19 01	19 19			
Oxford	d		17 41							18 11					18 41							19 09	
Oxford Parkway 116	d		17 47							18 17					18 47							19 15	
Islip	d																					19 18	
Bicester Village	d		17 56							18 26					18 56							19 26	
Haddenham & Thame Parkway	d							18 13		18 38									19 13			19 38	
Aylesbury	d			17 48	17 50						18 18	18 20	18 29			18 48	18 50						19 18
Little Kimble	d												18 37										
Monks Risborough	d												18 41										
Princes Risborough 2	d							18 20					18 45						19 20				
Saunderton	d												18 50										
High Wycombe 1	d							18 30		18 51			18 57	19 13					19 30			19 51	
Beaconsfield	d							18 36	18 45				19 03						19 36	19 45			
Seer Green	d												19 06										
Gerrards Cross 1	d						18 29	18 42					19 11					19 29	19 42				
Denham Golf Club	d						18 32																
Denham	d						18 35											19 33					
West Ruislip 3 § ⊖	d																	19 37					
South Ruislip § ⊖	d						18 40											19 41					
West Ealing	a																						
Northolt Park	d						18 44											19 45					
Sudbury Hill Harrow	d																						
Sudbury & Harrow Road	d																						
Wembley Stadium	d						18 49						19 23					19 50					
London Marylebone 10 ⊖	a		18 43	18 50	18 50		19 02	19 05	19 10	19 18	19 20	19 20	19 36	19 40	19 45	19 48	19 50	20 03	20 06	20 10		20 17	20 20

§ London Underground Limited (Central Line) also operate services between South Ruislip and West Ruislip at frequent intervals

A To Worcester Shrub Hill
B until 15 March
C from 22 March
D From Stratford-upon-Avon
E until 15 March. From Aylesbury Vale Parkway
F from 22 March. From Aylesbury Vale Parkway

For complete services between Banbury and Birmingham, refer to Table T71

For principal services between London and Aylesbury refer to Table T114

Table T115-R

Sundays

15 December to 10 May

Kidderminster, Birmingham Snow Hill, Stratford-upon-Avon, Banbury, Oxford Parkway, Aylesbury, High Wycombe - London

		CH	LM	CH	CH	CH	CH	CH	CH	CH	CH	CH	CH	CH	CH	CH	CH	CH	CH	CH	CH	CH	CH
					◇	◇				◇	◇						◇	◇		◇	◇		
		A	B				C	D				E	A		C	D						E	A
Kidderminster	d																						
Stourbridge Junction 2	d																						
Cradley Heath	d																						
Rowley Regis	d																						
Birmingham Snow Hill	d									19 12										20 12			
Birmingham Moor Street	d				18 55					19 15							19 38			20 15			
Solihull	d				19 04					19 24							19 47			20 24			
Dorridge	d									19 29							19 54			20 29			
Lapworth	d																19 58						
Stratford-upon-Avon	d		19 27																				
Stratford-upon-Avon Parkway	d		19 31																				
Wilmcote	d		19a34																				
Bearley	d																						
Claverdon	d																						
Hatton	d																20 04						
Warwick Parkway	d				19 16					19 39										20 39			
Warwick	d									19 42							20 09			20 42			
Leamington Spa 8	d				19 23					19 46							20 16			20 46			
Banbury	d				19 41					20 07				20 13			20 36			21 07			
Kings Sutton	d													20 20									
Bicester North 3	d				19 53					20 19				20 32			20 52			21 19			
Oxford	d					19 42					20 11							20 49			21 08		
Oxford Parkway 116	d					19 48					20 17							20 55			21 14		
Islip	d																				21 17		
Bicester Village	d					19 57					20 26							21 04			21 25		
Haddenham & Thame Parkway	d					20 09					20 38			20 44							21 37		
Aylesbury	d	19 20		19 29			19 48	19 50				20 18	20 20		20 48	20 50						21 18	21 20
Little Kimble	d			19 37																			
Monks Risborough	d			19 41																			
Princes Risborough 2	d			19 45	20 07									20 51									
Saunderton	d			19 50										20 56									
High Wycombe 1	d			19 57	20 16						20 51			21 03			21 16				21 50		
Beaconsfield	d			20 03						20 45				21 09			21 22						
Seer Green	d			20 06										21 12									
Gerrards Cross 1	d			20 11					20 32					21 17			21 28		21 35				
Denham Golf Club	d								20 35														
Denham	d								20 38										21 39				
West Ruislip 3 § ⊖	d																		21 43				
South Ruislip § ⊖	d								20 43										21 47				
West Ealing	a																						
Northolt Park	d								20 47										21 51				
Sudbury Hill Harrow	d																						
Sudbury & Harrow Road	d																						
Wembley Stadium	d			20 23					20 52					21 29					21 56				
London Marylebone 10 ⊖	a	20 20		20 36	20 42	20 48	20 50	20 50	21 05	21 10	21 18	21 20	21 20	21 41	21 50	21 50	21 53	21 56	22 09	22 13	22 16	22 20	22 20

§ London Underground Limited (Central Line) also operate services between South Ruislip and West Ruislip at frequent intervals

A from 22 March. From Aylesbury Vale Parkway
B To Great Malvern
C until 15 March
D from 22 March
E until 15 March. From Aylesbury Vale Parkway

For complete services between Banbury and Birmingham, refer to Table T71

For principal services between London and Aylesbury refer to Table T114

Table T115-R

Sundays 15 December to 10 May

Kidderminster, Birmingham Snow Hill, Stratford-upon-Avon, Banbury, Oxford Parkway, Aylesbury, High Wycombe - London

		CH	CH A	CH B	CH ◇	CH ◇	CH ◇	CH	CH ◇	CH A	CH B
Kidderminster	d										
Stourbridge Junction ■	d										
Cradley Heath	d										
Rowley Regis	d										
Birmingham Snow Hill 🚊	d								21 15		
Birmingham Moor Street	d								21 18		
Solihull	d								21 27		
Dorridge	d								21 34		
Lapworth	d										
Stratford-upon-Avon	d				20 38						
Stratford-upon-Avon Parkway	d				20 42						
Wilmcote	d				20 45						
Bearley	d										
Claverdon	d										
Hatton	d				20 56						
Warwick Parkway	d								21 44		
Warwick	d				21 03				21 47		
Leamington Spa ■	d				21 08				21 52		
Banbury	d	21 14			21 28				22 15		
Kings Sutton	d								22 20		
Bicester North ■	d	21 30			21 42				22 31		
Oxford	d					21 54	22 08				
Oxford Parkway 116	d					22 00	22 14				
Islip	d										
Bicester Village	d					22 09	22 23				
Haddenham & Thame Parkway	d	21 43			21 55		22 36		22 42		
Aylesbury	d		21 48	21 50				22 21		22 48	22 50
Little Kimble	d							22 29			
Monks Risborough	d							22 33			
Princes Risborough ■	d	21 50						22a40	22 49		
Saunderton	d	21 55							22 54		
High Wycombe ■	d	22 02			22 13		22 51		23 01		
Beaconsfield	d	22 08			22 19				23 07		
Seer Green	d				22 22				23 10		
Gerrards Cross ■	d	22 14			22 27				23 13		
Denham Golf Club	d	22 17									
Denham	d	22 20							23 17		
West Ruislip ■ § ⊖	d				22 33						
South Ruislip § ⊖	d	22 25							23 23		
West Ealing	a										
Northolt Park	d	22 29									
Sudbury Hill Harrow	d										
Sudbury & Harrow Road	d										
Wembley Stadium	d	22 34							23 29		
London Marylebone [15] ⊖	a	22 47	22 50	22 50	22 53	22 56	23 16		23 42	23 48	23 50

§ London Underground Limited (Central Line) also operate services between South Ruislip and West Ruislip at frequent intervals

A until 15 March. From Aylesbury Vale Parkway
B from 22 March. From Aylesbury Vale Parkway

For complete services between Banbury and Birmingham, refer to Table T71

For principal services between London and Aylesbury refer to Table T114

Table T116-F

Mondays to Fridays 16 December to 15 May

London and Reading - Bedwyn, Oxford, Banbury and Birmingham

Miles	Miles			GW MX	GW MX ◇[1] A 🛒	GW MO B 🚌	GW MX ◇[1] C	CH MX	GW MX	GW MO D	GW MO ◇[1] E 🛒	GW MO 🚌	GW MO C	GW MX C	GW MX	GW MX F	GW MX C	GW MO C	GW MX ◇[1]	GW MO	GW MX	GW	GW	GW [1] 🛒
0	—	**London Paddington** [15] ⊖	d																00 30	00 34	00 34	01 34	03 34	
5¾	—	Ealing Broadway ⊖	d														00 01	00 03		00 42	00 42	01 42	03 42	
18½	—	Slough [3]	d								00 01						00 23	00 25	00 48	01 02	01 05	02 00	04 00	
24¼	—	Maidenhead [3]	d											00 09			00 33	00 33	00 56	01 08	01 16	02 07	04 07	
31	—	Twyford [3]	d							00 04			←	00 19		00 33	00 40	00 40	01 04	01 15	01 23	02 14	04 14	
36	0	**Reading** [7]	a							00 12	00 17		00 12	00 25		00 44	00 47	00 52	01 11	01 22	01 31	02 21	04 21	
—	—		d		00 03		00 07		00 17	00 24	00 19		00 24	00 26					01 13					05 12
—	1	Reading West	d						00s20	→														
—	5¼	Theale	d						00s26															
—	8¾	Aldermaston	d						00s32															
—	10¾	Midgham	d						00s35															
—	13½	Thatcham	d						00s40															
—	16½	Newbury Racecourse	d						00s45															
—	17	**Newbury**	a						00 49															05 27
—	—		d																					05 28
—	22½	Kintbury	d																					05 34
—	25½	Hungerford	d																					05 39
—	30½	**Bedwyn**	a																					05 44
38¾	—	Tilehurst	d										00 28	00 30										
41½	—	Pangbourne	d										00 31	00 34										
44¼	—	Goring & Streatley	d										00 35	00 38										
48½	—	Cholsey	d										00 39	00 42										
53¼	—	**Didcot Parkway**	a		00 16						00s34		00 48	00 50					01 28					
—	—		d	00 11								00 45			00 55				01 31					
55½	—	Appleford	d												00 59									
56¼	—	Culham	d												01 02									
58½	—	Radley	d	00 18		00 14									01 06									
63½	—	**Oxford** 115	a	00 26		00 29	00 35					01 15			01 15				01 44					
—	—		d					00 40																
72¼	—	Tackley	d					00 50																
75¼	—	Heyford	d					00 55																
82¾	—	Kings Sutton	d					01 03																
86¼	—	**Banbury** 71	a					01 11																
106¼	—	Leamington Spa [8]	a																					
115¾	—	Coventry	a																					
126½	—	Birmingham International	a																					
135	—	**Birmingham New Street** [12] 71	a																					

		GW	GW	GW	GW ◇[1] 🛒	GW	GW	GW	GW	GW ◇[1] G 🛒	GW ◇[1] H 🛒	GW I	GW ◇[1] J 🛒	GW	GW	XR	XC ◇[1] K 🛒	GW	GW ◇[1] L 🛒	GW	GW	GW	XR	XC ◇[1] M 🛒
London Paddington [15] ⊖	d				04 59					05 28	05 35		05 45			05 13			05 50				05 43	
Ealing Broadway ⊖	d															05 21							05 53	
Slough [3]	d				05 20											05 46			06 04				06 16	
Maidenhead [3]	d															05 56							06 26	
Twyford [3]	d															06 03							06 33	
Reading [7]	a				05 35					05 51	05 57		06 08			06 11			06 17				06 41	
	d	05 15			05 37	05 38	05 49	05 50			05 59			06 10	06 10		06 15		06 18	06 22	06 37			06 45
Reading West	d	05 18													06 12						06 39			
Theale	d	05 24						05 57							06 18						06 44			
Aldermaston	d	05 29													06 22						06 49			
Midgham	d	05 32													06 25						06 52			
Thatcham	d	05 37						06 05							06 30						06 56			
Newbury Racecourse	d	05 42													06 34						07 00			
Newbury	a	05 45						06 12							06 37						07 04			
	d								06 24													07 22		
Kintbury	d								06 30													07 29		
Hungerford	d								06 35													07 33		
Bedwyn	a								06 41													07 40		
Tilehurst	d					05 43	05 55							06 14						06 26				
Pangbourne	d					05 47	05 59							06 18						06 30				
Goring & Streatley	d					05 51	06 04							06 22						06 35				
Cholsey	d					05 56	06 08							06 26				←		06 40				
Didcot Parkway	a				05 50	06 03	06 16				06 12			06 34						06 47				
	d			05 20	05 51							06 29						06 29		06 48				
Appleford	d											→												
Culham	d			05 25														06 34						
Radley	d			05 29														06 38						
Oxford 115	a			05 37	06 04												06 37	06 46	06 49	07 00				07 06
	d		05 20	05 40													06 39	06 47						07 08
Tackley	d		05 29	05 49														06 56						
Heyford	d		05 34	05 54														07 00						
Kings Sutton	d		05 42	06 02														07 09						
Banbury 71	a		05 48	06 08													06 56	07 14						07 25
Leamington Spa [8]	a																07 14							07 44
Coventry	a																07 26							
Birmingham International	a																07 36							
Birmingham New Street [12] 71	a																07 48							08 12

A From London Paddington to Cardiff Central
B From Didcot Parkway
C From London Paddington
D From London Paddington to Didcot Parkway
E From London Paddington to Bristol Temple Meads
F From Henley-on-Thames
G To Swansea
H To Worcester Shrub Hill
I To Banbury
J To Bristol Temple Meads
K From Southampton Central to Manchester Piccadilly
L To Great Malvern
M From Guildford to Newcastle

For complete services between Banbury and Birmingham, refer to Table T71

Table T116-F

Mondays to Fridays

16 December to 15 May

London and Reading - Bedwyn, Oxford, Banbury and Birmingham

		GW ◇1 🍴	GW A	GW ◇1 B 🍴	GW C	GW ◇1 D 🍴	XR	GW ◇1 E 🍴	GW	XR	GW ◇1 F 🍴	XC ◇1 G 🍴	GW A	GW ◇1 H 🍴	GW	GW C	GW ◇1 D 🍴	XR	GW ◇1 I 🍴	GW ◇1	GW ◇1 J 🍴	GW	XR
London Paddington 15 ⊖	d	06 19	05 56	06 28		06 32	05 58	06 37		06 13	06 48		06 26	06 50			07 02	06 28	07 04	07 07	07 13		06 43
Ealing Broadway ⊖	d		06 04				06 08			06 21			06 34					06 38					06 51
Slough 3	d	06 33	06 26				06 32			06 46			06 55	07 04				07 01					07 16
Maidenhead 3	d		06 32				06 42			06 56			07 01					07 11					07 26
Twyford 3	d		06 39		←		06 49			07 03			07 08			←		07 18					07 33
Reading 7	a	06 46	06 47	06 51	06 47	06 55	06 57	07 00		07 11	07 11		07 15	07 17		07 15	07 25	07 26	07 27	07 32	07 36		07 41
	d	06 47	06 54	06 53	06 54	06 57			07 10			07 14	07 25	07 18		07 25	07 27		07 29	07 34	07 38	07 40	
Reading West	d		→						07 12				→										
Theale	d								07 17											07 41			
Aldermaston	d								07 22														
Midgham	d								07 25														
Thatcham	d								07 29											07 48			
Newbury Racecourse	d								07 33														
Newbury	a								07 37										07 43	07 53			
	d																			07 54			
Kintbury	d																			08 00			
Hungerford	d																			08 04			
Bedwyn	a																			08 10			
Tilehurst	d				06 58											07 29						07 44	
Pangbourne	d				07 02											07 33						07 48	
Goring & Streatley	d				07 06											07 37						07 53	
Cholsey	d				07 10											07 41						07 58	
Didcot Parkway	a	07 01		07 05	07 17	07 11										07 50	07 39				07 50	08 07	
	d	07 02													07 34							08 07	
Appleford	d														07 38							08 12	
Culham	d														07 41							08 14	
Radley	d														07 45							08 18	
Oxford 115	a	07 14										07 37		07 45	07 53							08 26	
	d	07 17										07 39											
Tackley	d																						
Heyford	d																						
Kings Sutton	d																						
Banbury 71	a	07 35										07 56											
Leamington Spa 8	a											08 14											
Coventry	a											08 26											
Birmingham International	a											08 36											
Birmingham New Street 12 71	a											08 48											

		XC ◇1 K 🍴	GW A	GW ◇1 🍴	GW C	GW ◇1 B 🍴	XR	GW ◇1 D 🍴	GW	GW ◇1 L 🍴	XR	XC ◇1 M 🍴	GW A	GW ◇1 H 🍴	GW	GW	GW C	GW ◇1 D 🍴	XR	GW ◇1 E 🍴	GW ◇1 🍴	XR	GW ◇1 J 🍴	GW ◇1 🍴
London Paddington 15 ⊖	d		06 56	07 20		07 28	06 58	07 34		07 48	07 13		07 26	07 50				08 02	07 28	08 04	08 07	07 43	08 18	08 20
Ealing Broadway ⊖	d		07 04				07 08				07 21		07 34						07 38			07 51		
Slough 3	d		07 24	07 34			07 31				07 46		07 54	08 04					08 01			08 16		
Maidenhead 3	d		07 30				07 41				07 56		08 00						08 11			08 26		
Twyford 3	d		07 37		←		07 48				08 03		08 07				←		08 18			08 33		
Reading 7	a		07 44	07 46	07 44	07 51	07 56	07 57		08 10	08 11		08 14	08 17			08 14	08 25	08 26	08 27	08 30	08 41	08 41	08 42
	d	07 45	07 51	07 48	07 51			07 59	08 03			08 15	08 26	08 18		08 22	08 26	08 27			08 35			08 46
Reading West	d		→						08 07				→											
Theale	d								08 12												08 43			
Aldermaston	d								08 17															
Midgham	d								08 20															
Thatcham	d								08 24												08 50			
Newbury Racecourse	d								08 28															
Newbury	a								08 32												08 55			
	d																				08 55			
Kintbury	d																				09 01			
Hungerford	d																				09 05			
Bedwyn	a																				09 11			
Tilehurst	d				07 55											08 26	08 30							
Pangbourne	d				07 59											08 30	08 35							
Goring & Streatley	d				08 03											08 35	08 39							
Cholsey	d				08 07											08 40	08 44							
Didcot Parkway	a				08 15			08 12								08 47	08 52	08 39						09 00
	d														08 34	08 48								09 06
Appleford	d														08 38									
Culham	d															08 53								
Radley	d														08 43									
Oxford 115	a	08 07		08 12								08 38		08 42	08 51	09 03								09 18
	d	08 08										08 39			08 52									
Tackley	d														09 01									
Heyford	d														09 05									
Kings Sutton	d														09 14									
Banbury 71	a	08 25										08 56			09 19									
Leamington Spa 8	a	08 44										09 14												
Coventry	a											09 26												
Birmingham International	a											09 36												
Birmingham New Street 12 71	a	09 18										09 49												

A To Didcot Parkway
B To Cheltenham Spa
C From London Paddington
D To Bristol Temple Meads
E To Penzance
F To Swansea
G From Southampton Central to Manchester Piccadilly
H To Great Malvern
I To Paignton. The Devon Express
J To Cardiff Central
K To Newcastle
L To Swansea. The Saint David
M From Bournemouth to Manchester Piccadilly

For complete services between Banbury and Birmingham, refer to Table T71

Table T116-F

Mondays to Fridays

16 December to 15 May

London and Reading - Bedwyn, Oxford, Banbury and Birmingham

		GW	XC ◇1 A 🍴	GW	GW ◇1 B 🍴	GW	GW ◇1 C 🍴	XR	GW	GW ◇	GW ◇1 D 🍴	GW	XR	XC ◇1 E 🍴	GW F	GW ◇1 G 🍴	GW	GW H	GW ◇1 I 🍴	XR	GW ◇1 J 🍴	GW ◇1 🍴	GW ◇1 K 🍴
London Paddington 15 ⊖	d			07 56	08 28		08 32	07 58	08 06	08 36	08 48		08 13		08 26	08 50			09 02	08 28	09 04	09 07	09 18
Ealing Broadway ⊖	d			08 04				08 08	08 17				08 21		08 34					08 38			
Slough 3	d			08 27				08 31	08 35				08 46		08 54	09 04				09 01			
Maidenhead 3	d			08 36				08 41	08 45				08 56		09 00					09 11			
Twyford 3	d			08 43				08 48	08 52				09 03		09 07			←		09 18			
Reading 7	a			08 50	08 51		08 55	08 56	09 00	09 02	09 10		09 11		09 14	09 16		09 14	09 25	09 26	09 27	09 30	09 40
	d	08 49	08 50	08 53	08 53		08 57			09 08		09 11		09 12	09 23	09 18		09 23	09 27			09 37	
Reading West	d											09 14			→								
Theale	d	08 56										09 20										09 49	
Aldermaston	d											09 25											
Midgham	d											09 28											
Thatcham	d	09 04										09 32										09 58	
Newbury Racecourse	d											09 36											
Newbury	a	09 10								09 23		09 40										10 03	
	d																					10 04	
Kintbury	d																					10 10	
Hungerford	d																					10 14	
Bedwyn	a																					10 21	
Tilehurst	d			08 57														09 27					
Pangbourne	d			09 01														09 31					
Goring & Streatley	d			09 05														09 35					
Cholsey	d			09 09														09 39					
Didcot Parkway	a			09 18	09 05		09 11											09 48	09 39				
	d					09 11											09 37						
Appleford	d																						
Culham	d																						
Radley	d					09 18											09 44						
Oxford 115	a		09 13			09 26								09 38		09 43	09 52						
	d		09 14											09 39									
Tackley	d																						
Heyford	d																						
Kings Sutton	d																						
Banbury 71	a		09 32											09 56									
Leamington Spa 8	a		09 50											10 14									
Coventry	a													10 26									
Birmingham International	a													10 36									
Birmingham New Street 12 71	a		10 18											10 48									

		XR	XC ◇1 L 🍴	GW F	GW ◇1 🍴	GW ◇1 M 🍴	GW	GW H	GW ◇1 C 🍴	GW ◇1 N 🍴	XR	GW ◇1 D 🍴	GW	XC ■ 1 E 🍴	GW F	GW ◇1 O 🍴	GW	GW H	GW ◇1 C 🍴	GW FX ◇1 P 🍴	GW ◇1 🍴	XR	GW ◇1 K 🍴	XC ◇1 A 🍴
London Paddington 15 ⊖	d	08 43		08 56	09 20	09 28			09 32	09 37	09 13	09 48			09 20	09 50			10 02	10 04	10 07	09 43	10 18	
Ealing Broadway ⊖	d	08 51		09 04							09 22				09 33							09 52		
Slough 3	d	09 16		09 24	09 34						09 46				09 54	10 05						10 17		
Maidenhead 3	d	09 26		09 30							09 56				10 00							10 27		
Twyford 3	d	09 33		09 37				←			10 03				10 07			←				10 34		
Reading 7	a	09 41		09 44	09 46	09 51		09 44	09 55	10 00	10 11	10 11			10 14	10 17		10 14	10 25	10 27	10 32	10 41	10 41	
	d		09 45	09 53	09 48	09 52		09 53	09 57	10 02			10 12	10 15	10 23	10 19		10 23	10 27		10 37			10 45
Reading West	d			→									10 14		→									
Theale	d												10 19								10 45			
Aldermaston	d												10 23											
Midgham	d												10 26											
Thatcham	d												10 30								10 54			
Newbury Racecourse	d												10 34											
Newbury	a									10 16			10 38								10 59			
	d																				11 00			
Kintbury	d																				11 06			
Hungerford	d																				11 10			
Bedwyn	a																				11 16			
Tilehurst	d							09 57										10 27						
Pangbourne	d							10 01										10 31						
Goring & Streatley	d							10 05										10 35						
Cholsey	d							10 09										10 39						
Didcot Parkway	a					10 04		10 19	10 11									10 48	10 39					
	d						10 04										10 36							
Appleford	d																							
Culham	d						10 09																	
Radley	d						10 13																	
Oxford 115	a		10 08		10 13		10 23							10 38		10 42	10 48							11 08
	d		10 10											10 39										11 10
Tackley	d																							
Heyford	d																							
Kings Sutton	d																							
Banbury 71	a		10 27											10 56										11 30
Leamington Spa 8	a		10 44											11 14										11 47
Coventry	a													11 26										
Birmingham International	a													11 36										
Birmingham New Street 12 71	a		11 18											11 48										12 18

A From Southampton Central to Newcastle
B To Cheltenham Spa. The Cheltenham Spa Express
C To Bristol Temple Meads
D To Swansea
E From Bournemouth to Manchester Piccadilly
F To Didcot Parkway
G To Great Malvern
H From London Paddington
I To Exeter St Davids
J To Plymouth
K To Cardiff Central
L To Newcastle
M To Cheltenham Spa
N To Paignton. The Torbay Express
O To Hereford
P To Penzance. The Cornish Riviera

For complete services between Banbury and Birmingham, refer to Table T71

London and Reading - Bedwyn, Oxford, Banbury and Birmingham

		GW	GW	GW	GW	GW	GW	GW	GW	GW	XR	XC	GW	GW	GW	GW	GW	GW	GW	GW	XR	XC	GW
		A	◇1 ⊼	◇1 B ⊼		C	◇1 D ⊼	◇1 E ⊼	◇1 F ✕			◇1 G ⊼	A	◇1 H ⊼		◇1 D ⊼	C	◇1 I ⊼	◇1 ⊼	◇1 J ⊼		◇1 K ⊼	A
London Paddington 15 ⊖	d	09 56	10 20	10 28			10 32	10 35	10 48		10 13		10 27	10 50		11 02		11 04	11 07	11 18	10 43		10 56
Ealing Broadway ⊖	d	10 05									10 25		10 35								10 51		11 04
Slough 3	d	10 24	10 34								10 46		10 54	11 04							11 16		11 24
Maidenhead 3	d	10 31									10 56		11 00								11 26		11 30
Twyford 3	d	10 38				←					11 03		11 08				←				11 33		11 37
Reading 7	a	10 45	10 46	10 51		10 45	10 55	10 59	11 10		11 12		11 16	11 16		11 25	11 16	11 27	11 32	11 40	11 41		11 44
	d	10 53	10 49	10 52		10 53	10 57	11 01		11 12		11 15	11 28	11 18		11 27	11 28		11 37			11 45	11 53
Reading West	d	→								11 14			→										→
Theale	d									11 19									11 44				
Aldermaston	d									11 23													
Midgham	d									11 26													
Thatcham	d									11 30									11 52				
Newbury Racecourse	d									11 34													
Newbury	a							11 15		11 38									11 56				
	d																		11 57				
Kintbury	d																		12 03				
Hungerford	d																		12 07				
Bedwyn	a																		12 13				
Tilehurst	d					10 57											11 32						
Pangbourne	d					11 01											11 36						
Goring & Streatley	d					11 05											11 40						
Cholsey	d					11 09											11 44						
Didcot Parkway	a			11 04		11 19	11 11									11 39	11 53						
	d				11 04										11 36								
Appleford	d				11 08																		
Culham	d				11 11																		
Radley	d				11 15																		
Oxford 115	a		11 13		11 23							11 38		11 42	11 48							12 08	
	d				11 24							11 39										12 10	
Tackley	d				11 33																		
Heyford	d				11 37																		
Kings Sutton	d				11 46																		
Banbury 71	a				11 51							11 56										12 27	
Leamington Spa 8	a											12 14										12 44	
Coventry	a											12 26											
Birmingham International	a											12 36											
Birmingham New Street 12 71	a											12 48										13 18	

		GW	GW	GW	GW	GW	GW	XR	GW	GW	XC	GW	GW	GW	GW	GW	GW FX	GW	GW	XR	XC	GW	GW	GW
		◇1 ⊼	◇1 B ⊼		C	◇1 D ⊼	◇		◇1 F ⊼		◇1 G ⊼	A	◇1 L ⊼		C	◇1 D ⊼	◇1 M ✕	◇1 ⊼	◇1 J ⊼		R 1 N ⊼	A	◇1 ⊼	◇1 B ⊼
London Paddington 15 ⊖	d	11 20	11 28			11 32	11 36	11 13	11 48			11 27	11 50			12 02	12 04	12 07	12 18	11 43		11 57	12 20	12 28
Ealing Broadway ⊖	d							11 21				11 35								11 51		12 05		
Slough 3	d	11 34						11 43				11 54	12 04							12 16		12 24	12 34	
Maidenhead 3	d							11 53				12 00								12 26		12 30		
Twyford 3	d				←			12 00				12 07			←					12 33		12 37		
Reading 7	a	11 46	11 51		11 44	11 55	12 03	12 08	12 11			12 14	12 16		12 14	12 25	12 27	12 32	12 40	12 41		12 44	12 46	12 51
	d	11 48	11 52		11 53	11 57	12 04			12 12	12 13	12 23	12 18		12 23	12 27		12 37			12 45	12 53	12 49	12 52
Reading West	d									12 14		→										→		
Theale	d									12 19								12 45						
Aldermaston	d									12 23														
Midgham	d									12 26														
Thatcham	d									12 30								12 52						
Newbury Racecourse	d									12 34														
Newbury	a						12 17			12 38								12 57						
	d																	12 58						
Kintbury	d																	13 04						
Hungerford	d																	13 08						
Bedwyn	a																	13 14						
Tilehurst	d				11 57										12 27									
Pangbourne	d				12 01										12 32									
Goring & Streatley	d				12 05										12 36									
Cholsey	d				12 09										12 41									
Didcot Parkway	a		12 05		12 18	12 11									12 50	12 39								13 04
	d			12 05										12 34										
Appleford	d																							
Culham	d																							
Radley	d			12 12																				
Oxford 115	a	12 13		12 20							12 38		12 42	12 48							13 08		13 13	
	d										12 39										13 10			
Tackley	d																							
Heyford	d																							
Kings Sutton	d																							
Banbury 71	a										12 56										13 30			
Leamington Spa 8	a										13 14										13 48			
Coventry	a										13 26													
Birmingham International	a										13 36													
Birmingham New Street 12 71	a										13 48										14 18			

A To Didcot Parkway
B To Cheltenham Spa
C From London Paddington
D To Bristol Temple Meads
E To Exeter St Davids
F To Swansea
G From Bournemouth to Manchester Piccadilly
H To Worcester Shrub Hill
I To Plymouth. The Mayflower
J To Cardiff Central
K To Newcastle
L To Hereford
M To Penzance. The Royal Duchy
N From Southampton Central to Newcastle

For complete services between Banbury and Birmingham, refer to Table T71

London and Reading - Bedwyn, Oxford, Banbury and Birmingham

		GW	GW	GW	GW	GW	XR	GW	XC	GW	GW	GW	GW	GW	GW FX	GW	GW	XR	XC	GW	GW	GW	GW
			A	◇1 B ⊼	◇1 C ⊼	◇1 D ⊼			◇1 E ⊼	F	◇1 G ⊼		A	◇1 B ⊼	◇1 H ✕	◇1 ⊼	◇1 I ⊼		◇1 J ⊼	F	◇1 ⊼		◇1 K ⊼
London Paddington 15 ⊖	d			12 32	12 36	12 48	12 13			12 26	12 50			13 02	13 04	13 07	13 18	12 43		12 57	13 20		13 28
Ealing Broadway ⊖	d						12 21			12 34								12 51		13 05			
Slough 3	d						12 46			12 54	13 04							13 16		13 24	13 34		
Maidenhead 3	d						12 56			13 00								13 26		13 30			
Twyford 3	d		←				13 03			13 07			←					13 34		13 37			
Reading 7	a		12 44	12 55	12 59	13 10	13 11			13 14	13 16		13 14	13 25	13 27	13 30	13 40	13 42		13 45	13 46		13 51
	d		12 53	12 57	13 01			13 12	13 15	13 23	13 18		13 23	13 27		13 37			13 45	13 53	13 48		13 53
Reading West	d							13 14		→										→			
Theale	d							13 19								13 44							
Aldermaston	d							13 23															
Midgham	d							13 26															
Thatcham	d							13 30								13 52							
Newbury Racecourse	d							13 34															
Newbury	a				13 15			13 38								13 56							
	d															13 57							
Kintbury	d															14 03							
Hungerford	d															14 07							
Bedwyn	a															14 13							
Tilehurst	d		12 57										13 27										
Pangbourne	d		13 01										13 31										
Goring & Streatley	d		13 05										13 35										
Cholsey	d		13 09										13 39										
Didcot Parkway	a		13 20	13 11									13 48	13 39									14 05
	d	13 04										13 36										14 04	
Appleford	d																					14 08	
Culham	d																					14 11	
Radley	d	13 11																				14 15	
Oxford 115	a	13 19							13 38		13 42	13 48							14 08		14 13	14 23	
	d								13 39										14 10			14 24	
Tackley	d																					14 33	
Heyford	d																					14 37	
Kings Sutton	d																					14 46	
Banbury 71	a								13 56										14 30			14 51	
Leamington Spa 8	a								14 14										14 47				
Coventry	a								14 26														
Birmingham International	a								14 36														
Birmingham New Street 12 71	a								14 48										15 18				

		GW	GW	GW	XR	GW	GW	XC	GW	GW	GW	GW	GW	GW FX	GW	GW	XR	XC	GW	GW	GW	GW	GW	GW
		A	◇1 B ⊼	◇		◇1 D ⊼		◇1 E ⊼	F	◇1 L ⊼		A	◇1 B ⊼	◇1 M ⊼	◇1 ⊼	◇1 I ⊼		◇1 N ⊼	F	◇1 ⊼		◇1 K ⊼	A	◇1 B ⊼
London Paddington 15 ⊖	d		13 32	13 34	13 13	13 48			13 27	13 50			14 02	14 04	14 07	14 18	13 43		13 56	14 20		14 28		14 32
Ealing Broadway ⊖	d				13 21				13 35								13 51		14 06					
Slough 3	d				13 46				13 54	14 04							14 16		14 24	14 34				
Maidenhead 3	d				13 56				14 00								14 26		14 30					
Twyford 3	d	←			14 03				14 07			←					14 33		14 37				←	
Reading 7	a	13 45	13 55	14 00	14 11	14 11			14 14	14 16		14 14	14 25	14 27	14 32	14 40	14 41		14 44	14 46		14 51	14 44	14 55
	d	13 53	13 57	14 02			14 12	14 15	14 25	14 18		14 25	14 27		14 37			14 45	14 53	14 48		14 53	14 53	14 57
Reading West	d						14 14		→										→					
Theale	d						14 19								14 44									
Aldermaston	d						14 24																	
Midgham	d						14 27																	
Thatcham	d						14 31								14 52									
Newbury Racecourse	d						14 35																	
Newbury	a			14 15			14 39								14 56									
	d														14 57									
Kintbury	d														15 03									
Hungerford	d														15 07									
Bedwyn	a														15 13									
Tilehurst	d	13 57										14 29											14 57	
Pangbourne	d	14 01										14 33											15 01	
Goring & Streatley	d	14 05										14 37											15 06	
Cholsey	d	14 09										14 41											15 10	
Didcot Parkway	a	14 18	14 11									14 50	14 39									15 05	15 19	15 11
	d										14 36										15 04			
Appleford	d																							
Culham	d																							
Radley	d																				15 11			
Oxford 115	a							14 38		14 42	14 49							15 08		15 13	15 19			
	d							14 39										15 10						
Tackley	d																							
Heyford	d																							
Kings Sutton	d																							
Banbury 71	a							14 56										15 27						
Leamington Spa 8	a							15 14										15 45						
Coventry	a							15 26																
Birmingham International	a							15 36																
Birmingham New Street 12 71	a							15 48										16 17						

A From London Paddington
B To Bristol Temple Meads
C To Exeter St Davids
D To Swansea
E From Bournemouth to Manchester Piccadilly
F To Didcot Parkway
G To Worcester Shrub Hill
H To Plymouth
I To Cardiff Central
J To Newcastle
K To Cheltenham Spa
L To Great Malvern
M To Penzance
N From Southampton Central to Edinburgh

For complete services between Banbury and Birmingham, refer to Table T71

Table T116-F

Mondays to Fridays

16 December to 15 May

London and Reading - Bedwyn, Oxford, Banbury and Birmingham

Station		GW ◇1 A		GW	XR	GW ◇1 B	XC ◇1 C	GW D	GW ◇1 E	GW	GW F	GW ◇1 G	GW FX ◇1 H	GW ◇1	GW ◇1 I	XR	XC ◇1 J	GW D		GW ◇1 E	GW	GW F	GW ◇1 K	GW	GW ◇1 G
London Paddington ⊖	d	14 36			14 13	14 48		14 27	14 50			15 02	15 04	15 07	15 18	14 43		14 57		15 20			15 28		15 32
Ealing Broadway ⊖	d				14 23			14 35								14 51		15 05							
Slough	d				14 46			14 54	15 04							15 16		15 24		15 34					
Maidenhead	d				14 56			15 00								15 26		15 30							
Twyford	d				15 03			15 07			←					15 33		15 37				←			
Reading	a	14 59			15 11	15 11		15 14	15 16		15 14	15 25	15 27	15 31	15 40	15 41		15 44		15 46		15 44	15 51		15 55
	d	15 01		15 10			15 15	15 23	15 18		15 23	15 27		15 37			15 45	15 51		15 48		15 51	15 52	15 55	15 57
Reading West	d			15 12				→										→							
Theale	d			15 17										15 45											
Aldermaston	d			15 22																					
Midgham	d			15 25																					
Thatcham	d			15 29										15 53											
Newbury Racecourse	d			15 33																					
Newbury	a	15 15		15 37										15 58											
	d													15 59											
Kintbury	d													16 05											
Hungerford	d													16 09											
Bedwyn	a													16 15											
Tilehurst	d										15 27											15 55		15 59	
Pangbourne	d										15 31											15 59		16 03	
Goring & Streatley	d										15 35											16 03		16 08	
Cholsey	d										15 39											16 08		16 13	
Didcot Parkway	a										15 48	15 39										16 17	16 04	16 19	16 10
	d									15 36											16 03			16 20	
Appleford	d																				16 07				
Culham	d																				16 10				
Radley	d																				16 14				
Oxford 115	a						15 38		15 42	15 48							16 08			16 12	16 22			16 32	
	d						15 39										16 10				16 24				
Tackley	d																				16 33				
Heyford	d																				16 37				
Kings Sutton	d																				16 46				
Banbury 71	a						15 56										16 27				16 51				
Leamington Spa	a						16 14										16 44								
Coventry	a						16 26																		
Birmingham International	a						16 36																		
Birmingham New Street 71	a						16 48										17 18								

Station		GW ◇	GW ◇1 B	GW	XR	GW	XC ◇1 C	GW ◇1 L	GW	GW ◇1 G		GW FX ◇1 M	GW ◇1	GW ◇1 I	XR	XC ◇1 N	GW D	GW O	GW ◇1	GW P	GW ◇1 K	GW F	GW ◇1 Q	XR	GW R
London Paddington ⊖	d	15 37	15 48		15 13			15 50	15 27	16 02		16 04	16 08	16 18	15 43		15 56		16 20		16 30		16 32	15 58	
Ealing Broadway ⊖	d				15 24				15 35						15 51									16 08	
Slough	d				15 46			16u04	15 59						16 16		16 23		16 34					16 31	
Maidenhead	d				15 56				16 07						16 26		16 30							16 41	
Twyford	d				16 03				16 14						16 33		16 37					←		16 48	
Reading	a	16 02	16 10		16 11				16 21	16 25		16 27	16 31	16 41	16 42		16 45		16 46			16 45	16 55	16 56	
	d	16 04		16 10		16 12	16 15	16u18	16 25	16 27			16 37	16 43		16 45	16 52	16 45	16 48			16 52	16 57		17 01
Reading West	d					16 14											→								
Theale	d					16 19							16 44					16 53							
Aldermaston	d					16 23												16 58							
Midgham	d					16 26																			
Thatcham	d					16 30							16 56					17 04							
Newbury Racecourse	d					16 34												17 20							
Newbury	a	16 19				16 38							17 03					17 22							
	d												17 07					17 23							
Kintbury	d												17 13					→							
Hungerford	d												17 17												
Bedwyn	a												17 23												
Tilehurst	d			16 14					16 29													16 56			
Pangbourne	d			16 18					16 33													17 01			
Goring & Streatley	d			16 23					16 37													17 05			17 09
Cholsey	d			16 28					16 41													17 10			17 14
Didcot Parkway	a			16 35					16 50	16 39				16 55							17 04	17 18	17 10		17 23
	d			16 37																17 03					17 33
Appleford	d																			17 07					→
Culham	d																			17 10					
Radley	d			16 44																17 14					
Oxford 115	a			16 52			16 37	16 41								17 08			17 13	17 22					
	d						16 39									17 10									
Tackley	d																								
Heyford	d																								
Kings Sutton	d																								
Banbury 71	a						16 57									17 31									
Leamington Spa	a						17 14									17 50									
Coventry	a						17 26																		
Birmingham International	a						17 36																		
Birmingham New Street 71	a						17 48									18 18									

A To Plymouth
B To Swansea
C From Bournemouth to Manchester Piccadilly
D To Didcot Parkway
E To Worcester Foregate Street
F From London Paddington
G To Bristol Temple Meads
H To Penzance. The Cornishman
I To Cardiff Central
J To Newcastle
K To Cheltenham Spa
L To Great Malvern
M To Penzance
N From Southampton Central to Newcastle
O To Bedwyn
P To Moreton-in-Marsh
Q To Taunton
R To Banbury

For complete services between Banbury and Birmingham, refer to Table T71

Table T116-F

Mondays to Fridays

16 December to 15 May

London and Reading - Bedwyn, Oxford, Banbury and Birmingham

Station		GW ◇1 A		GW B	GW	GW	XR	GW ◇1 C	XC ◇1 D	GW	GW ◇1 E	XR	GW FX ◇1 F	GW ◇1	GW ◇1 G	XR	GW ◇1 H	GW B		XC ◇1 I	GW	GW ◇1 J	GW ◇1 K	GW	GW ◇1 L
London Paddington ⊖	d	16 38				16 43	16 13	16 48		16 50	17 02	16 28	17 04	17 08	17 17	16 43	16 58					17 28	17 30	17 19	17 34
Ealing Broadway ⊖	d						16 21					16 38				16 53									
Slough	d						16 46					17 01				17 16									
Maidenhead	d						16 56			17 08		17 12				17 26								17 40	
Twyford	d						17 03			17 15		17 20		17 28		17 33								17 47	
Reading	a	17 01				17 09	17 11	17 11		17 22	17 25	17 27	17 27	17 34	17 40	17 41							17 52	17 54	17 57
	d	17 03			17 10	17 11			17 15	17 25	17 27			17 35	17 42					17 43			17 54	17 58	17 59
Reading West	d				17 12																				
Theale	d				17 18									17 42											
Aldermaston	d				17 22																				
Midgham	d				17 25																				
Thatcham	d				17 29									17 50											
Newbury Racecourse	d			←	17 33																				
Newbury	a	17 17		17 22	17 37									17 54											
	d	17 18		17 23										18 02											
Kintbury	d			17 29										18 08											
Hungerford	d	17a27		17 34										18 12											
Bedwyn	a			17 41										18 18											
Tilehurst	d									17 29														18 02	
Pangbourne	d									17 34														18 06	
Goring & Streatley	d									17 38														18 10	
Cholsey	d									17 43								←						18 15	
Didcot Parkway	a					17 27				17 52	17 39				17 54			17 23				18 01	18 07	18 23	
	d																	17 33			17 59				
Appleford	d																	17 38							
Culham	d																	17 40			18 04				
Radley	d																	17 44			18 08				
Oxford 115	a								17 38								17 42	17 52		18 08	18 17				18 21
	d								17 39									17 55		18 10					
Tackley	d																	18 04							
Heyford	d																	18 08							
Kings Sutton	d																	18 17							
Banbury 71	a								17 56									18 22		18 27					
Leamington Spa	a								18 14											18 45					
Coventry	a								18 26																
Birmingham International	a								18 36																
Birmingham New Street 71	a								18 48											19 18					

Station		XR	GW ◇1 M	GW	GW	GW	GW ◇1 C	XR	XC ◇1 D	GW ◇1 N		GW	GW ◇1 E	XR	GW FO 1 O	GW FX 1 O	GW	GW ◇1 P	XR	GW ◇1 G	GW	XC ◇1 Q	GW ◇1	GW ◇1 J	GW
London Paddington ⊖	d	16 58	17 37			17 42	17 47	17 13		17 58			18 02	17 28	18 04	18 04	17 51	18 07	17 43	18 18	17 56		18 28	18 30	
Ealing Broadway ⊖	d	17 08						17 21						17 38					17 51						
Slough	d	17 31						17 46						18 00					18 16		18 21				
Maidenhead	d	17 44	17 54					17 56						18 10			18 16		18 26		18 30				
Twyford	d	17 51						18 03						18 17			18 23	18 28	18 33		18 37				
Reading	a	17 58	18 03			18 08	18 10	18 11					18 24	18 25		18 27	18 30	18 33	18 41	18 41	18 44				
	d		18 04		18 08	18 10			18 15			18 22	18 27		18u29	18 29	18 32	18 38		18 42		18 45			
Reading West	d				18 10																				
Theale	d				18 16													18 46							
Aldermaston	d				18 21																				
Midgham	d				18 24																				
Thatcham	d				18 28													18 54							
Newbury Racecourse	d				18 32																				
Newbury	a		18 19		18 36										18 43	18 43		18 59							
	d			18 28														19 00							
Kintbury	d			18 35														19 07							
Hungerford	d			18 39														19 11							
Bedwyn	a			18 46														19 17							
Tilehurst	d											18 27					18 36								
Pangbourne	d											18 31					18 41								
Goring & Streatley	d											18 36					18 45								
Cholsey	d											18 41					18 50								
Didcot Parkway	a					18 26						18 48	18 39				18 58			18 54				19 04	
	d											18 49													19 05
Appleford	d																								
Culham	d																								
Radley	d											18 56													19 12
Oxford 115	a								18 39	18 43		19 03										19 08	19 12		19 19
	d								18 40													19 10	19 14		19 20
Tackley	d																								19 30
Heyford	d																								19 35
Kings Sutton	d																								
Banbury 71	a								18 57													19 28	19 34		19 46
Leamington Spa	a								19 15													19 46			
Coventry	a								19 27																
Birmingham International	a								19 37																
Birmingham New Street 71	a								19 48													20 18			

A To Exeter St Davids
B From Reading
C To Swansea
D From Bournemouth to Manchester Piccadilly
E To Bristol Temple Meads
F To Penzance
G To Cardiff Central
H To Great Malvern
I To Newcastle
J To Cheltenham Spa
K To Taunton
L To Hereford. The Cathedrals Express
M To Paignton
N To Worcester Foregate Street
O To Penzance. The Golden Hind
P To Frome
Q From Southampton Central to York

For complete services between Banbury and Birmingham, refer to Table T71

Table T116-F

Mondays to Fridays

16 December to 15 May

London and Reading - Bedwyn, Oxford, Banbury and Birmingham

		GW		XR	GW ◇1 A 🍴	GW ◇1 B 🍴	GW	GW	GW	GW ◇1 C 🍴	XR	GW	XC ◇1 D 🍴	GW ◇1 E 🍴	GW	GW	GW ◇1 F 🍴	XR		GW FX ■ ■ G ✕	GW	GW FO ■ ■ H ✕	GW ◇1 🍴	XR	GW ◇1 I 🍴
London Paddington 15 ⊖	d	18 20		17 58	18 34	18 37		18 42		18 47	18 13	18 26		18 58			19 02	18 28		19 04	18 49	19 04	19 07	18 43	19 18
Ealing Broadway ⊖	d			18 08							18 21							18 38						18 53	
Slough 3	d			18 32							18 46	18 51						19 01						19 16	
Maidenhead 3	d	18 39		18 43							18 56	19 00						19 11			19 15			19 26	
Twyford 3	d	18 46		18 50							19 03	19 07						19 18			19 23		19 28	19 33	
Reading 7	a	18 53		18 57	18 57	19 00		19 08		19 10	19 11	19 14					19 25	19 26		19 27	19 30		19 34	19 41	19 41
	d	18 57			18 59	19 05		19 10	19 10				19 15			19 22	19 27			19 30	19 30	19u30	19 35		
Reading West	d								19 12																
Theale	d								19 18														19 42		
Aldermaston	d								19 22																
Midgham	d								19 25																
Thatcham	d								19 30														19 50		
Newbury Racecourse	d								19 34																
Newbury	a					19 20			19 38											19 44		19 44	19 54		
	d					19 22	19 28																19 55		
Kintbury	d						19 35																20 01		
Hungerford	d					19 32	19 39																20 05		
Bedwyn	a					19 37	19 46																20 11		
Tilehurst	d	19 01														19 26					19 35				
Pangbourne	d	19 06														19 31					19 39				
Goring & Streatley	d	19 11														19 36					19 44				
Cholsey	d	19 16														19 41					19 49				
Didcot Parkway	a	19 23			19 12			19 26								19 48	19 39				19 58				
	d														19 37	19 48									
Appleford	d																								
Culham	d															19 54									
Radley	d														19 44										
Oxford 115	a												19 38	19 42	19 52	20 03									
	d												19 39												
Tackley	d																								
Heyford	d																								
Kings Sutton	d																								
Banbury 71	a												19 56												
Leamington Spa 8	a												20 14												
Coventry	a												20 26												
Birmingham International	a												20 36												
Birmingham New Street 12 71	a												20 48												

		GW	GW	XC ◇1	GW ◇1 J 🍴	GW ◇1 🍴	GW	GW	GW ◇1 F 🍴	GW ◇		GW	GW	GW	GW ◇1 I 🍴	XR	XC ◇1 D 🍴	GW ◇1 E 🍴	GW	GW	GW ◇1 F 🍴	GW ◇1 B 🍴	GW ◇1 🍴	XR	XC ◇1
London Paddington 15 ⊖	d		18 56		19 28	19 30		19 20	19 33	19 36				19 35	19 48	19 13		19 50		19 26	20 02	20 04	20 06	19 43	
Ealing Broadway ⊖	d															19 21				19 34				19 51	
Slough 3	d		19 21													19 48		20 04		19 54				20 16	
Maidenhead 3	d		19 30					19 39						19 54		19 59				20 03				20 26	
Twyford 3	d		19 37					19 46						20 02		20 06				20 10				20 33	
Reading 7	a		19 44			19 53		19 55	19 56	20 04				20 09	20 10	20 14		20 17		20 18	20 24	20 26	20 31	20 41	
	d	19 42		19 45		19 55		19 57	19 58	20 06			20 10	20 12			20 15	20 18		20 23	20 27		20 33		20 45
Reading West	d	19 44											20 13												
Theale	d	19 49											20 19										20 40		
Aldermaston	d	19 54											20 23												
Midgham	d	19 57											20 26												
Thatcham	d	20 01											20 31										20 47		
Newbury Racecourse	d	20 05											20 35												
Newbury	a	20 09								20 19			20 38										20 52		
	d											20 24											20 53		
Kintbury	d											20 31											20 59		
Hungerford	d											20 35											21 03		
Bedwyn	a											20 42											21 09		
Tilehurst	d							20 01						20 16						20 27					
Pangbourne	d							20 06						20 21						20 31					
Goring & Streatley	d							20 10						20 25						20 36					
Cholsey	d							20 15						20 30						20 40					
Didcot Parkway	a				20 01			20 23	20 11					20 37						20 50	20 39				
	d						20 10												20 37						
Appleford	d						20 14																		
Culham	d																								
Radley	d						20 19												20 44						
Oxford 115	a			20 08		20 18	20 28										20 38	20 42	20 52						21 08
	d			20 10													20 39		20 55						21 10
Tackley	d																		21 04						
Heyford	d																		21 08						
Kings Sutton	d																		21 17						
Banbury 71	a			20 27													20 56		21 22						21 29
Leamington Spa 8	a			20 44													21 14								21 47
Coventry	a																21 26								
Birmingham International	a																21 36								
Birmingham New Street 12 71	a			21 23													21 48								22 18

A To Weston-super-Mare
B To Plymouth
C To Swansea. Y Cymro/The Welshman
D From Bournemouth to Manchester Piccadilly
E To Hereford
F To Bristol Temple Meads
G To Plymouth. The Armada
H To Penzance. The Armada
I To Swansea
J To Worcester Shrub Hill

For complete services between Banbury and Birmingham, refer to Table T71

Table T116-F

Mondays to Fridays

16 December to 15 May

London and Reading - Bedwyn, Oxford, Banbury and Birmingham

		GW ◇1 🍴		GW	GW ◇1 A 🍴	GW	GW	GW ◇1 B 🍴	GW	GW ◇1 C 🍴	XR	XC ◇1 D	GW E	GW ◇1 F 🍴	GW	GW G	GW ◇1 B 🍴	GW ◇1 H 🍴		GW	XR	GW	GW ◇1 🍴	GW	GW ◇1 A 🍴
London Paddington 15 ⊖	d	20 20		19 56	20 28		20 18	20 32		20 48	20 13		20 26	20 50			21 02	21 04			20 43	20 56	21 15		21 33
Ealing Broadway ⊖	d			20 04							20 21		20 34								20 51	21 04			
Slough 3	d	20 35		20 26							20 46		20 54	21 04							21 16	21 24	21 29		
Maidenhead 3	d			20 34			20 38				20 56		21 00								21 26	21 30	21 35		
Twyford 3	d			20 41			20 45				21 03		21 07			←					21 33	21 37	21 41		
Reading 7	a	20 47		20 49	20 51		20 52	20 55		21 10	21 11		21 14	21 17		21 14	21 25	21 27			21 41	21 45	21 47		21 56
	d	20 49		20 51	20 53			20 57	21 10			21 13	21 23	21 18		21 23	21 27	21 29					21 50		21 57
Reading West	d								21 12				→												
Theale	d								21 17																
Aldermaston	d								21 21																
Midgham	d								21 24																
Thatcham	d								21 28																
Newbury Racecourse	d								21 32																
Newbury	a								21 36									21 43							
	d																			21 52					
Kintbury	d																			21 59					
Hungerford	d																			22 03					
Bedwyn	a																			22 10					
Tilehurst	d			20 56												21 27									
Pangbourne	d			21 00												21 31									
Goring & Streatley	d			21 05												21 35									
Cholsey	d			21 09												21 39									
Didcot Parkway	a			21 18	21 05			21 10								21 47	21 39								22 09
	d					21 06									21 35									22 05	
Appleford	d																								
Culham	d																								
Radley	d					21 14									21 43									22 12	
Oxford 115	a	21 13				21 22						21 36		21 42	21 51								22 14	22 20	
	d											21 37			21 52										
Tackley	d														22 01										
Heyford	d														22 05										
Kings Sutton	d														22 14										
Banbury 71	a											21 54			22 19										
Leamington Spa 8	a											22 13													
Coventry	a											22 26													
Birmingham International	a											22 36													
Birmingham New Street 12 71	a											22 48													

		GW I	XC ◇1	GW FO ◇1 C 🍴	GW	GW	GW FX ◇1 C 🍴	XR	GW	GW ◇1 J 🍴		GW	GW FO ◇1 K 🍴	GW FX ◇1 K 🍴	GW FO ◇1 L 🍴	XR	GW ◇1 🍴	GW	GW FO ◇1 B 🍴	GW FX ◇1 B 🍴	GW	GW FO ◇1	GW FX ◇1	XR	GW
London Paddington 15 ⊖	d			21 48			21 48	21 13	21 26	21 50			22 00	22 00		21 43	22 18	21 57	22 30	22 30		22 20	22 20	22 13	22 27
Ealing Broadway ⊖	d							21 21	21 34							21 51		22 05						22 21	22 35
Slough 3	d							21 46	21 54	22 04						22 16		22 24				22 36	22 39	22 44	22 53
Maidenhead 3	d							21 56	22 00							22 26		22 30				22 42	22 45	22 54	22 59
Twyford 3	d							22 03	22 07						←	22 33		22 37				22 49	22 51	23 01	23 06
Reading 7	a			22 09			22 10	22 11	22 14	22 16			22 21	22 22	22 21	22 41	22 41	22 44	22 52	22 53		22 56	22 58	23 09	23 14
	d	21 59	22 02		22 10					22 18			22 25	22 24	22 25		22 43	22 46	22 59	22 59		23 01	23 01		
Reading West	d				22 14								→									23 04	23 04		
Theale	d				22 19																	23 10	23 10		
Aldermaston	d				22 24																	23 16	23 16		
Midgham	d				22 27																	23 20	23 20		
Thatcham	d				22 31																	23 26	23 26		
Newbury Racecourse	d				22 35																	23 31	23 31		
Newbury	a				22 39																	23 34	23 34		
	d					22 44																23 36	23 36		
Kintbury	d					22 51																23 42	23 42		
Hungerford	d					22 55																23 46	23 46		
Bedwyn	a					23 02																23 51	23 51		
Tilehurst	d	22 03																22 50							
Pangbourne	d	22 07																22 54							
Goring & Streatley	d	22 12																22 58							
Cholsey	d	22 17																23 02							
Didcot Parkway	a	22 23												22 36	22 37			23 10	23 11	23 11					
	d	22 42																			23 18				
Appleford	d																				23 22				
Culham	d																				23 25				
Radley	d																				23 29				
Oxford 115	a	22 56	22 25							22 43							23 06				23 37				
	d		22 30									23 05													
Tackley	d											23 15													
Heyford	d											23 20													
Kings Sutton	d											23 28													
Banbury 71	a		22 47									23 34													
Leamington Spa 8	a		23 04																						
Coventry	a		23 20																						
Birmingham International	a		23 29																						
Birmingham New Street 12 71	a		23 56																						

A To Cheltenham Spa
B To Bristol Temple Meads
C To Swansea
D From Bournemouth
E To Didcot Parkway
F To Great Malvern
G From London Paddington
H To Plymouth
I From Basingstoke
J To Worcester Shrub Hill
K To Exeter St Davids
L From London Paddington to Exeter St Davids

For complete services between Banbury and Birmingham, refer to Table T71

Table T116-F

Mondays to Fridays

16 December to 15 May

London and Reading - Bedwyn, Oxford, Banbury and Birmingham

		GW FO ◇1 A		GW FX ◇1 A	GW ◇1 B	GW	GW	XR	GW ◇1 C	GW ◇1 D	GW ◇1 E	GW	GW
London Paddington 15 ⊖	d	22 48		22 48	22 50		22 41	22 43	23 15	23 32		23 34	23 52
Ealing Broadway ⊖	d						22 49	22 53					00 01
Slough 3	d				23 06		23 10	23 16	23 35			23 56	00 23
Maidenhead 3	d				23 13		23 17	23 26	23 42			00 09	00 33
Twyford 3	d				23 20		23 24	23 33	23 50		←	00 19	00 40
Reading 7	a	23 16		23 17	23 26		23 31	23 41	23 58	00 02	23 58	00 25	00 47
	d	23 18		23 18	23 28		23 32		00 07	00 03	00 07	00 26	
Reading West	d								→				
Theale	d												
Aldermaston	d												
Midgham	d												
Thatcham	d												
Newbury Racecourse	d												
Newbury	a												
	d												
Kintbury	d												
Hungerford	d												
Bedwyn	a												
Tilehurst	d						23 36					00 30	
Pangbourne	d						23 40					00 34	
Goring & Streatley	d						23 44					00 38	
Cholsey	d						23 49					00 42	
Didcot Parkway	a	23 32		23 32			23 56			00 16		00 50	
	d					23 45							
Appleford	d												
Culham	d												
Radley	d												
Oxford 115	a				23 52	23 59					00 35		
	d												
Tackley	d												
Heyford	d												
Kings Sutton	d												
Banbury 71	a												
Leamington Spa 8	a												
Coventry	a												
Birmingham International	a												
Birmingham New Street 12 71	a												

Saturdays

21 December to 16 May

		GW	GW ◇1 F	GW ◇1 E	CH	GW	GW E	GW	GW G	GW E	GW ◇1	GW	GW	GW	GW 1	GW 1		GW ◇1	GW	GW	GW	XR	XC ◇1 H	GW ◇1 I	GW
London Paddington 15 ⊖	d										00 30	00 34	01 34	03 34				05 20				05 13		05 50	
Ealing Broadway ⊖	d									00 01		00 42	01 42	03 42								05 21			
Slough 3	d									00 23	00 48	01 05	02 00	04 00				05 35				05 46		06 04	
Maidenhead 3	d						00 09			00 33	00 56	01 16	02 07	04 07								05 56			
Twyford 3	d						00 19		00 33	00 40	01 04	01 23	02 14	04 14								06 03			
Reading 7	a						00 25		00 44	00 47	01 11	01 31	02 21	04 21				05 48				06 11		06 16	
	d		00 03	00 07		00 17	00 26				01 13				05 08	05 32		05 49		05 55	06 07		06 15	06 18	
Reading West	d					00s20									05 11	05 35					06 09				
Theale	d					00s26									05 17	05 41					06 15				
Aldermaston	d					00s32									05 22	05 47					06 19				
Midgham	d					00s35									05 25	05 52					06 22				
Thatcham	d					00s40									05 30	05 58					06 27				
Newbury Racecourse	d					00s45									05 35	06 03					06 31				
Newbury	a					00 49									05 38	06 06					06 35				
	d														05 38	06 07									
Kintbury	d														05 44	06 14									
Hungerford	d														05 49	06 18									
Bedwyn	a														05 57	06 24									
Tilehurst	d						00 30													05 58					
Pangbourne	d						00 34													06 02					
Goring & Streatley	d						00 38													06 06					
Cholsey	d						00 42													06 11					
Didcot Parkway	a		00 16				00 50				01 28							06 02		06 20				06 33	
	d	00 11						00 55			01 31							06 04	06 07					06 34	06 38
Appleford	d							00 59																	06 42
Culham	d							01 02																	06 44
Radley	d	00 18						01 06																	06 48
Oxford 115	a	00 26		00 35				01 15			01 44							06 18	06 21				06 38	06 47	06 57
	d				00 40														06 23				06 39		
Tackley	d				00 50														06 31						
Heyford	d				00 55														06 36						
Kings Sutton	d				01 03														06 44						
Banbury 71	a				01 11														06 50				06 56		
Leamington Spa 8	a																						07 14		
Coventry	a																						07 26		
Birmingham International	a																						07 36		
Birmingham New Street 12 71	a																						07 48		

A To Swansea
B To Worcestershire Parkway Hl
C To Oxford
D To Cardiff Central
E From London Paddington
F From London Paddington to Cardiff Central
G From Henley-on-Thames
H From Southampton Central to Manchester Piccadilly
I To Great Malvern

For complete services between Banbury and Birmingham, refer to Table T71

NRT DECEMBER 19 EDITION

Table T116-F

Saturdays

21 December to 16 May

London and Reading - Bedwyn, Oxford, Banbury and Birmingham

		GW	GW 1	XR	XC ◇1 A	GW	GW B	GW ◇1		GW ◇1 C	GW D	GW ◇1 E	GW	XR	XC ◇1 F	GW B	GW ◇1 G	GW	GW D	GW ◇1 C	GW ◇1	XR	XC ◇1 H	GW B
London Paddington 15 ⊖	d	05 27		05 43			05 55	06 20		06 29		06 47		06 13		06 27	06 50			06 59	07 07	06 43		06 57
Ealing Broadway ⊖	d	05 35		05 53			06 03							06 21		06 35						06 51		07 05
Slough 3	d	05 56		06 16			06 23	06 34						06 46		06 54	07 04					07 16		07 24
Maidenhead 3	d	06 02		06 26			06 30							06 56		07 00						07 26		07 30
Twyford 3	d	06 09		06 33			06 37				←			07 03		07 07			←			07 33		07 37
Reading 7	a	06 18		06 41			06 44	06 48		06 52	06 44	07 10		07 11		07 14	07 17		07 14	07 22	07 30	07 41		07 44
	d	06 19	06 34		06 47		06 56	06 50		06 54	06 56		07 10		07 15	07 23	07 19		07 23	07 24	07 33		07 46	07 53
Reading West	d						→						07 12			→								→
Theale	d		06 42										07 17								07 40			
Aldermaston	d												07 22											
Midgham	d												07 25											
Thatcham	d		06 50										07 29								07 48			
Newbury Racecourse	d												07 33											
Newbury	a		06 54										07 37								07 53			
	d		06 55																		07 54			
Kintbury	d		07 02																		08 00			
Hungerford	d		07 06																		08 05			
Bedwyn	a		07 13																		08 11			
Tilehurst	d	06 24									07 00								07 27					
Pangbourne	d	06 28									07 04								07 31					
Goring & Streatley	d	06 32									07 08								07 35					
Cholsey	d	06 37									07 12								07 39					
Didcot Parkway	a	06 46						07 04		07 07	07 21								07 48	07 37				
	d					07 02		07 06										07 34						
Appleford	d																							
Culham	d																							
Radley	d					07 09																		
Oxford 115	a				07 10	07 17		07 22							07 38		07 43	07 48					08 10	
	d				07 12										07 39								08 11	
Tackley	d																							
Heyford	d																							
Kings Sutton	d																							
Banbury 71	a				07 31										07 56								08 29	
Leamington Spa 8	a				07 49										08 14								08 47	
Coventry	a														08 26									
Birmingham International	a														08 36									
Birmingham New Street 12 71	a				08 18										08 48								09 18	

		GW ◇1	GW ◇1 C	GW	GW D	GW ◇1 I	GW	GW ◇1 E	XR	XC ◇1 J	GW B	GW ◇1 G	GW	GW D	GW ◇1 C	GW ◇1 K		GW ◇1	GW ◇1 L	XR	XC ◇1 M	GW B	GW ◇1	GW ◇1 N	GW
London Paddington 15 ⊖	d	07 20	07 29			07 32		07 47	07 13		07 27	07 50			07 59	08 03		08 07	08 17	07 42		07 57	08 20	08 29	
Ealing Broadway ⊖	d								07 21		07 35									07 53		08 05			
Slough 3	d	07 34							07 46		07 54	08 04								08 16		08 24	08 34		
Maidenhead 3	d								07 56		08 00									08 26		08 30			
Twyford 3	d				←				08 03		08 07			←						08 33		08 37			
Reading 7	a	07 47	07 52		07 44	07 55		08 10	08 11		08 14	08 17		08 14	08 23	08 26		08 31	08 40	08 41		08 44	08 47	08 52	
	d	07 49			07 53	07 57	08 06			08 15	08 23	08 19		08 23	08 24			08 33	08 42		08 45	08 53	08 49		
Reading West	d						08 08				→											→			
Theale	d						08 13											08 41							
Aldermaston	d						08 18																		
Midgham	d						08 21																		
Thatcham	d						08 25											08 49							
Newbury Racecourse	d						08 28																		
Newbury	a						08 32											08 53							
	d																	08 54							
Kintbury	d																	09 01							
Hungerford	d																	09 05							
Bedwyn	a																	09 11							
Tilehurst	d				07 57									08 27											
Pangbourne	d				08 01									08 31											
Goring & Streatley	d				08 05									08 35											
Cholsey	d				08 09									08 39											
Didcot Parkway	a				08 18	08 10								08 48	08 37				08 55						
	d			08 06									08 34												09 06
Appleford	d																								09 10
Culham	d			08 11																					
Radley	d			08 15																					09 15
Oxford 115	a	08 16		08 23						08 38		08 43	08 48								09 08		09 14		09 23
	d			08 24						08 40											09 10				
Tackley	d			08 32																					
Heyford	d			08 37																					
Kings Sutton	d			08 45																					
Banbury 71	a			08 51						08 57											09 27				
Leamington Spa 8	a									09 14											09 44				
Coventry	a									09 26															
Birmingham International	a									09 36															
Birmingham New Street 12 71	a									09 48											10 18				

A From Guildford to Newcastle
B To Didcot Parkway
C To Bristol Temple Meads
D From London Paddington
E To Swansea
F From Southampton Central to Manchester Piccadilly
G To Great Malvern
H From Bournemouth to Newcastle
I To Cheltenham Spa
J From Bournemouth to Manchester Piccadilly
K To Penzance
L To Cardiff Central
M From Southampton Central to Newcastle
N To Weston-super-Mare

For complete services between Banbury and Birmingham, refer to Table T71

Table T116-F

London and Reading - Bedwyn, Oxford, Banbury and Birmingham

Saturdays

21 December to 16 May

Station		GW A	GW ◇1 B ⚲	GW ◇1 C ⚲	GW	GW ◇1 D ⚲	XR	XC ◇1 E ⚲	GW F	GW ◇1 G ⚲	GW	GW A	GW ◇1 H ⚲	GW ◇1 I ⚲	GW ◇1	GW ◇1 J ⚲	XR	XC ◇1 K ⚲	GW F	GW ◇1	GW ◇1 H ⚲	GW	GW A
London Paddington 15 ⊖	d		08 32	08 35		08 47	08 13		08 27	08 50			08 59	09 03	09 07	09 17	08 43		08 57	09 20	09 29		
Ealing Broadway ⊖	d						08 21		08 35								08 51		09 05				
Slough 3	d						08 46		08 54	09 04							09 16		09 24	09 34			
Maidenhead 3	d						08 56		09 00								09 26		09 30				
Twyford 3	d	←					09 03		09 07			←					09 33		09 37				←
Reading 7	a	08 44	08 55	08 58		09 10	09 11		09 15	09 17		09 15	09 22	09 26	09 30	09 40	09 41		09 44	09 47	09 52		09 44
	d	08 53	08 56	09 00	09 09			09 15	09 23	09 19		09 23	09 24		09 33	09 42		09 45	09 53	09 49			09 53
Reading West	d				09 11				→										→				
Theale	d				09 16										09 41								
Aldermaston	d				09 21																		
Midgham	d				09 24																		
Thatcham	d				09 28										09 49								
Newbury Racecourse	d				09 32																		
Newbury	a			09 14	09 36										09 53								
	d														09 55								
Kintbury	d														10 01								
Hungerford	d														10 06								
Bedwyn	a														10 12								
Tilehurst	d	08 57										09 27											09 57
Pangbourne	d	09 01										09 31											10 01
Goring & Streatley	d	09 05										09 35											10 05
Cholsey	d	09 09										09 39											10 09
Didcot Parkway	a	09 18	09 10									09 49	09 37			09 55							10 19
	d										09 34											10 06	
Appleford	d																						
Culham	d																					10 11	
Radley	d																					10 15	
Oxford 115	a							09 38		09 43	09 48							10 08		10 14		10 23	
	d							09 39										10 10				10 24	
Tackley	d																					10 32	
Heyford	d																					10 37	
Kings Sutton	d																					10 45	
Banbury 71	a							09 56										10 27				10 51	
Leamington Spa 8	a							10 14										10 44					
Coventry	a							10 26															
Birmingham International	a							10 36															
Birmingham New Street 12 71	a							10 48										11 18					

Station		GW ◇1 B ⚲	GW ◇	GW	GW ◇1 D ⚲	XR	XC ◇1 E ⚲	GW F	GW ◇1 L ⚲	GW	GW A	GW ◇1 H ⚲	GW ◇1 M ⚲	GW ◇1	GW ◇1 J ⚲	XR	XC ◇1 N ⚲	GW F	GW ◇1	GW ◇1 H ⚲	GW	GW A	GW ◇1 B ⚲	GW ◇1 C ⚲
London Paddington 15 ⊖	d	09 32	09 37		09 47	09 13		09 27	09 50			09 59	10 02	10 07	10 17	09 43		09 57	10 20	10 29			10 32	10 35
Ealing Broadway ⊖	d					09 21		09 35								09 51		10 05						
Slough 3	d					09 46		09 54	10 04							10 16		10 24	10 34					
Maidenhead 3	d					09 56		10 00								10 26		10 30						
Twyford 3	d					10 03		10 07			←					10 33		10 37				←		
Reading 7	a	09 55	10 02		10 10	10 11		10 14	10 17		10 14	10 22	10 25	10 31	10 40	10 41		10 44	10 47	10 53		10 44	10 55	10 58
	d	09 57	10 04	10 09			10 15	10 23	10 19		10 23	10 24		10 34	10 42		10 45	10 52	10 49			10 52	10 57	11 00
Reading West	d			10 11				→										→						
Theale	d			10 16										10 41										
Aldermaston	d			10 21																				
Midgham	d			10 24																				
Thatcham	d			10 28										10 49										
Newbury Racecourse	d			10 32																				
Newbury	a		10 17	10 36										10 54										11 15
	d													10 55										
Kintbury	d													11 01										
Hungerford	d													11 06										
Bedwyn	a													11 12										
Tilehurst	d										10 27											10 56		
Pangbourne	d										10 31											11 00		
Goring & Streatley	d										10 35											11 04		
Cholsey	d										10 39											11 08		
Didcot Parkway	a	10 10									10 48	10 37			10 55							11 16	11 10	
	d									10 34											11 06			
Appleford	d																				11 10			
Culham	d																							
Radley	d																				11 15			
Oxford 115	a						10 38		10 43	10 48							11 08		11 14		11 23			
	d						10 39										11 10							
Tackley	d																							
Heyford	d																							
Kings Sutton	d																							
Banbury 71	a						10 56										11 27							
Leamington Spa 8	a						11 14										11 44							
Coventry	a						11 26																	
Birmingham International	a						11 36																	
Birmingham New Street 12 71	a						11 48										12 18							

A From London Paddington
B To Cheltenham Spa
C To Exeter St Davids
D To Swansea
E From Bournemouth to Manchester Piccadilly
F To Didcot Parkway
G To Great Malvern
H To Bristol Temple Meads
I To Plymouth
J To Cardiff Central
K To Newcastle
L To Hereford
M To Penzance. The Cornish Riviera
N From Southampton Central to Newcastle

For complete services between Banbury and Birmingham, refer to Table T71

Table T116-F

London and Reading - Bedwyn, Oxford, Banbury and Birmingham

Saturdays

21 December to 16 May

Station		GW	GW ◇1 A ⚲	XR	XC ◇1 B ⚲	GW C	GW ◇1 D ⚲	GW	GW E	GW ◇1 F ⚲	GW ◇1 G ⚲	GW ◇1	GW ◇1 H ⚲	XR	XC ◇1 I ⚲	GW C	GW ◇1	GW ◇1 F ⚲	GW	GW E	GW ◇1 J ⚲	GW ◇	GW
London Paddington 15 ⊖	d		10 47	10 13		10 27	10 50			10 59	11 02	11 07	11 17	10 43		10 56	11 20	11 29			11 32	11 37	
Ealing Broadway ⊖	d			10 21		10 35								10 51		11 04							
Slough 3	d			10 46		10 54	11 04							11 16		11 24	11 35						
Maidenhead 3	d			10 56		11 00								11 26		11 30							
Twyford 3	d			11 03		11 07			←					11 33		11 37				←			
Reading 7	a		11 10	11 11		11 14	11 17		11 14	11 22	11 25	11 31	11 40	11 41		11 44	11 47	11 52		11 44	11 55	12 02	
	d	11 10			11 15	11 23	11 19		11 23	11 24		11 34	11 42		11 45	11 53	11 49			11 53	11 57	12 04	12 10
Reading West	d	11 12				→										→							12 12
Theale	d	11 17										11 41											12 17
Aldermaston	d	11 22																					12 22
Midgham	d	11 25																					12 25
Thatcham	d	11 29										11 49											12 29
Newbury Racecourse	d	11 33																					12 33
Newbury	a	11 37										11 54										12 17	12 37
	d											11 55											
Kintbury	d											12 01											
Hungerford	d											12 06											
Bedwyn	a											12 12											
Tilehurst	d								11 27											11 57			
Pangbourne	d								11 31											12 01			
Goring & Streatley	d								11 35											12 05			
Cholsey	d								11 39											12 09			
Didcot Parkway	a								11 48	11 37			11 55							12 20	12 10		
	d							11 34											12 06				
Appleford	d																						
Culham	d																		12 11				
Radley	d																		12 15				
Oxford 115	a				11 38		11 43	11 48							12 08		12 14		12 23				
	d				11 39										12 10				12 24				
Tackley	d																		12 32				
Heyford	d																		12 37				
Kings Sutton	d																		12 45				
Banbury 71	a				11 56										12 27				12 51				
Leamington Spa 8	a				12 14										12 44								
Coventry	a				12 26																		
Birmingham International	a				12 36																		
Birmingham New Street 12 71	a				12 48										13 18								

Station		GW ◇1 A ⚲	XR	XC ◇1 B ⚲	GW C	GW ◇1 K ⚲	GW	GW E	GW ◇1 F ⚲	GW ◇1 L ⚲	GW ◇1	GW ◇1 H ⚲	XR	XC ◇1 M ⚲	GW C	GW ◇1	GW ◇1 F ⚲	GW	GW E	GW ◇1 J ⚲	GW ◇1 N ⚲	GW	GW ◇1 A ⚲	XR
London Paddington 15 ⊖	d	11 47	11 13		11 27	11 50			11 59	12 02	12 07	12 17	11 43		11 57	12 20	12 29			12 32	12 35		12 47	12 13
Ealing Broadway ⊖	d		11 21		11 35								11 51		12 05									12 21
Slough 3	d		11 46		11 54	12 04							12 16		12 24	12 34								12 46
Maidenhead 3	d		11 56		12 00								12 26		12 30									12 56
Twyford 3	d		12 03		12 07			←					12 33		12 37				←					13 03
Reading 7	a	12 10	12 11		12 14	12 17		12 14	12 22	12 25	12 31	12 40	12 41		12 44	12 47	12 52		12 44	12 55	12 59		13 10	13 11
	d			12 15	12 23	12 19		12 23	12 24		12 35	12 42		12 45	12 53	12 49			12 53	12 57	13 00	13 10		
Reading West	d				→										→							13 12		
Theale	d										12 43											13 17		
Aldermaston	d																					13 22		
Midgham	d																					13 25		
Thatcham	d										12 51											13 29		
Newbury Racecourse	d																					13 33		
Newbury	a										12 56										13 14	13 37		
	d										12 57													
Kintbury	d										13 03													
Hungerford	d										13 08													
Bedwyn	a										13 14													
Tilehurst	d							12 27											12 57					
Pangbourne	d							12 31											13 01					
Goring & Streatley	d							12 35											13 05					
Cholsey	d							12 39											13 09					
Didcot Parkway	a							12 48	12 37			12 55							13 18	13 10				
	d						12 34											13 06						
Appleford	d																	13 10						
Culham	d																							
Radley	d																	13 15						
Oxford 115	a			12 38		12 43	12 48							13 08		13 14		13 23						
	d			12 39										13 10										
Tackley	d																							
Heyford	d																							
Kings Sutton	d																							
Banbury 71	a			12 56										13 27										
Leamington Spa 8	a			13 14										13 44										
Coventry	a			13 26																				
Birmingham International	a			13 36																				
Birmingham New Street 12 71	a			13 48										14 18										

A To Swansea
B From Bournemouth to Manchester Piccadilly
C To Didcot Parkway
D To Worcester Foregate Street
E From London Paddington
F To Bristol Temple Meads
G To Plymouth
H To Cardiff Central
I To Newcastle
J To Cheltenham Spa
K To Hereford
L To Penzance. The Royal Duchy
M From Southampton Central to Newcastle
N To Exeter St Davids

For complete services between Banbury and Birmingham, refer to Table T71

Table T116-F

Saturdays

21 December to 16 May

London and Reading - Bedwyn, Oxford, Banbury and Birmingham

		XC	GW	GW	GW	GW	GW	GW	GW	GW	XR	XC	GW	GW	GW	GW	GW	GW	GW	GW	GW	XR	XC
		◇1		◇1			◇1	◇1	◇1	◇1		◇1		◇1	◇1			◇1	◇		◇1		◇1
		A	B	C		D	E	F		G		H	B		E		D	I			J		A
London Paddington 15 ⊖	d		12 27	12 50			12 59	13 02	13 07	13 17	12 43		12 57	13 20	13 29			13 32	13 37		13 47	13 13	
Ealing Broadway ⊖	d		12 35								12 51		13 05									13 21	
Slough 3	d		12 54	13 04							13 16		13 24	13 34								13 46	
Maidenhead 3	d		13 00								13 26		13 30									13 56	
Twyford 3	d		13 07			←					13 33		13 37				←					14 03	
Reading 7	a		13 14	13 17		13 14	13 22	13 25	13 31	13 40	13 41		13 44	13 47	13 52		13 44	13 55	14 02		14 10	14 11	
	d	13 15	13 23	13 19		13 23	13 24		13 34	13 42		13 45	13 53	13 49			13 53	13 57	14 04	14 10			14 15
Reading West	d		→										→							14 12			
Theale	d								13 41											14 17			
Aldermaston	d																			14 22			
Midgham	d																			14 25			
Thatcham	d								13 49											14 29			
Newbury Racecourse	d																			14 33			
Newbury	a								13 54										14 17	14 37			
	d								13 55														
Kintbury	d								14 01														
Hungerford	d								14 06														
Bedwyn	a								14 12														
Tilehurst	d					13 27											13 57						
Pangbourne	d					13 31											14 01						
Goring & Streatley	d					13 35											14 05						
Cholsey	d					13 39											14 09						
Didcot Parkway	a					13 48	13 37			13 55							14 18	14 10					
	d				13 34											14 06							
Appleford	d																						
Culham	d															14 11							
Radley	d															14 15							
Oxford 115	a	13 38		13 43	13 48							14 08		14 14		14 23							14 38
	d	13 39										14 10				14 24							14 39
Tackley	d															14 32							
Heyford	d															14 37							
Kings Sutton	d															14 45							
Banbury 71	a	13 56										14 27				14 51							14 56
Leamington Spa 8	a	14 14										14 44											15 14
Coventry	a	14 26																					15 26
Birmingham International	a	14 36																					15 36
Birmingham New Street 12 71	a	14 48										15 18											15 48

		GW	GW	GW	GW	GW	GW	GW	GW	XR	XC	GW	GW	GW	GW	GW	GW	GW	GW	GW	XR	XC	GW	GW
			◇1		◇1		◇1	◇1	◇1		◇1		◇1	◇1			◇1	◇1		◇1		◇1		◇1
		B	K		E	D	F		G		L	B		E		D	I	M		J		A	B	K
London Paddington 15 ⊖	d	13 27	13 50		13 59		14 02	14 07	14 17	13 43		13 57	14 20	14 29			14 32	14 35		14 47	14 13		14 27	14 50
Ealing Broadway ⊖	d	13 35								13 51		14 05									14 21		14 35	
Slough 3	d	13 54	14 04							14 16		14 24	14 34								14 46		14 54	15 04
Maidenhead 3	d	14 00								14 26		14 30									14 56		15 00	
Twyford 3	d	14 07				←				14 33		14 37				←					15 03		15 07	
Reading 7	a	14 14	14 17		14 22	14 14	14 25	14 31	14 40	14 41		14 44	14 47	14 53		14 44	14 55	14 58		15 10	15 11		15 14	15 17
	d	14 24	14 19		14 24	14 24		14 34	14 42		14 45	14 53	14 49			14 53	14 57	15 00	15 10			15 15	15 24	15 19
Reading West	d	→										→							15 12				→	
Theale	d							14 41											15 17					
Aldermaston	d																		15 22					
Midgham	d																		15 25					
Thatcham	d							14 49											15 29					
Newbury Racecourse	d																		15 33					
Newbury	a							14 54										15 14	15 37					
	d							14 55																
Kintbury	d							15 01																
Hungerford	d							15 06																
Bedwyn	a							15 12																
Tilehurst	d					14 28										14 57								
Pangbourne	d					14 32										15 01								
Goring & Streatley	d					14 36										15 05								
Cholsey	d					14 40										15 09								
Didcot Parkway	a				14 37	14 49			14 55							15 18	15 10							
	d			14 34											15 06									
Appleford	d														15 10									
Culham	d																							
Radley	d														15 15									
Oxford 115	a		14 43	14 48							15 08		15 14		15 23							15 38		15 43
	d										15 10											15 39		
Tackley	d																							
Heyford	d																							
Kings Sutton	d																							
Banbury 71	a										15 27											15 56		
Leamington Spa 8	a										15 44											16 14		
Coventry	a																					16 26		
Birmingham International	a																					16 36		
Birmingham New Street 12 71	a										16 18											16 48		

A From Bournemouth to Manchester Piccadilly
B To Didcot Parkway
C To Worcester Foregate Street
D From London Paddington
E To Bristol Temple Meads
F To Penzance
G To Cardiff Central
H To Newcastle
I To Cheltenham Spa
J To Swansea
K To Great Malvern
L From Southampton Central to Newcastle
M To Plymouth

For complete services between Banbury and Birmingham, refer to Table T71

NRT DECEMBER 19 EDITION

Table T116-F

Saturdays

21 December to 16 May

London and Reading - Bedwyn, Oxford, Banbury and Birmingham

		GW	GW	GW	GW	GW	GW	XR	XC	GW	GW	GW	GW	GW	GW	GW	GW	GW	XR	XC	GW	GW	GW
			◇1		◇1	◇1	◇1		◇1		◇1	◇1			◇1	◇		◇1		◇1		◇1	
			A	B	C		D		E	F		A		B	G			H		I	F	J	
London Paddington 15 ⊖	d		14 59		15 02	15 07	15 17	14 43		14 57	15 20	15 29			15 32	15 37		15 47	15 13		15 27	15 50	
Ealing Broadway ⊖	d							14 51		15 05									15 21		15 35		
Slough 3	d							15 16		15 24	15 35								15 46		15 54	16 04	
Maidenhead 3	d							15 26		15 30									15 56		16 00		
Twyford 3	d			←				15 33		15 37				←					16 03		16 07		
Reading 7	a		15 22	15 14	15 26	15 31	15 40	15 41		15 44	15 47	15 52		15 44	15 55	16 03		16 10	16 11		16 14	16 17	
	d		15 24	15 24		15 34	15 42		15 45	15 53	15 49			15 53	15 57	16 04	16 10			16 15	16 23	16 18	
Reading West	d									→							16 12				→		
Theale	d					15 41											16 17						
Aldermaston	d																16 22						
Midgham	d																16 25						
Thatcham	d					15 49											16 29						
Newbury Racecourse	d																16 33						
Newbury	a					15 54										16 17	16 37						
	d					15 55																	
Kintbury	d					16 01																	
Hungerford	d					16 06																	
Bedwyn	a					16 12																	
Tilehurst	d			15 28										15 57									
Pangbourne	d			15 32										16 01									
Goring & Streatley	d			15 36										16 05									
Cholsey	d			15 40										16 09									
Didcot Parkway	a		15 37	15 49			15 55							16 18	16 10								
	d	15 34											16 06										16 34
Appleford	d																						
Culham	d												16 11										
Radley	d												16 15										
Oxford 115	a	15 48							16 08		16 14		16 23							16 38		16 43	16 48
	d								16 10				16 24							16 39			
Tackley	d												16 32										
Heyford	d												16 37										
Kings Sutton	d												16 45										
Banbury 71	a								16 27				16 51							16 56			
Leamington Spa 8	a								16 44											17 14			
Coventry	a																			17 26			
Birmingham International	a																			17 36			
Birmingham New Street 12 71	a								17 18											17 48			

		GW	GW	GW	GW	GW	XR	XC	GW	GW	GW	GW	GW	GW	GW	GW	GW	XR	XC	GW	GW	GW	GW	GW
			◇1	◇1	◇1	◇1		◇1		◇1	◇1			◇1	◇1		◇1		◇1		◇1			◇1
		B	A	K		D		L	F		M		B	G	N		H		I	F	O		B	A
London Paddington 15 ⊖	d		16 00	16 03	16 07	16 17	15 43		15 57	16 20	16 29			16 32	16 35		16 47	16 13		16 27	16 50			16 59
Ealing Broadway ⊖	d						15 51		16 05									16 21		16 35				
Slough 3	d						16 16		16 24	16 34								16 46		16 54	17 04			
Maidenhead 3	d						16 26		16 30									16 56		17 00				
Twyford 3	d	←					16 33		16 37				←					17 03		17 07			←	
Reading 7	a	16 14	16 23	16 26	16 31	16 40	16 41		16 44	16 47	16 52		16 44	16 55	16 58		17 10	17 11		17 14	17 17		17 14	17 22
	d	16 23	16 25		16 34	16 42		16 45	16 53	16 49			16 53	16 57	17 00	17 10			17 15	17 23	17 19		17 23	17 24
Reading West	d								→							17 12				→				
Theale	d				16 41											17 18								
Aldermaston	d															17 23								
Midgham	d															17 26								
Thatcham	d				16 49											17 30								
Newbury Racecourse	d															17 34								
Newbury	a				16 54										17 14	17 38								
	d				16 55																			
Kintbury	d				17 01																			
Hungerford	d				17 06																			
Bedwyn	a				17 12																			
Tilehurst	d	16 27											16 57										17 27	
Pangbourne	d	16 31											17 01										17 31	
Goring & Streatley	d	16 35											17 05										17 35	
Cholsey	d	16 39											17 09										17 39	
Didcot Parkway	a	16 48	16 38			16 55							17 18	17 10									17 48	17 37
	d											17 06										17 34		
Appleford	d											17 10												
Culham	d																							
Radley	d											17 15												
Oxford 115	a							17 08		17 14		17 23							17 38		17 43	17 48		
	d							17 10											17 39					
Tackley	d																							
Heyford	d																							
Kings Sutton	d																							
Banbury 71	a							17 27											17 56					
Leamington Spa 8	a							17 44											18 14					
Coventry	a																		18 26					
Birmingham International	a																		18 36					
Birmingham New Street 12 71	a							18 18											18 48					

A To Bristol Temple Meads
B From London Paddington
C To Penzance
D To Cardiff Central
E To Newcastle
F To Didcot Parkway
G To Cheltenham Spa
H To Swansea
I From Bournemouth to Manchester Piccadilly
J To Great Malvern
K To Plymouth
L From Southampton Central to Newcastle
M To Taunton
N To Paignton. The Torbay Express
O To Hereford

For complete services between Banbury and Birmingham, refer to Table T71

Table T116-F

Saturdays

21 December to 16 May

London and Reading - Bedwyn, Oxford, Banbury and Birmingham

Station		GW ◇■ A	GW ◇■	GW ◇■ B	XR	XC ◇■ C	GW D	GW ◇■	GW ◇■ E	GW	GW F	GW ◇■ G	GW ◇	XR	GW ◇■ H	XC ◇■ I	GW D	GW ◇■ J	GW	GW F	GW ◇■ K	GW ◇■ A	GW ◇■
London Paddington ⊖	d	17 03	17 07	17 17	16 43		16 56	17 20	17 29			17 32	17 42	17 13	17 47		17 27	17 50			18 00	18 03	18 07
Ealing Broadway ⊖	d				16 51		17 04							17 21			17 35						
Slough	d				17 16		17 24	17 34						17 46			17 54	18 05					
Maidenhead	d				17 26		17 30							17 56			18 00						
Twyford	d				17 33		17 37				←			18 03			18 07			←			
Reading	a	17 26	17 31	17 40	17 41		17 44	17 47	17 52		17 44	17 55	18 08	18 10	18 10		18 14	18 17		18 14	18 23	18 26	18 31
	d		17 34	17 42		17 45	17 53	17 49			17 53	17 57	18 10			18 15	18 23	18 19		18 23	18 25		18 34
Reading West	d						→						18 12				→						
Theale	d		17 41										18 17										18 41
Aldermaston	d												18 22										
Midgham	d												18 25										
Thatcham	d		17 49										18 29										18 49
Newbury Racecourse	d												18 33										
Newbury	a		17 54										18 37										18 54
	d		17 55																				18 55
Kintbury	d		18 01																				19 01
Hungerford	d		18 06																				19 06
Bedwyn	a		18 12																				19 12
Tilehurst	d										17 57									18 27			
Pangbourne	d										18 01									18 31			
Goring & Streatley	d										18 05									18 35			
Cholsey	d										18 09									18 39			
Didcot Parkway	a			17 55							18 18	18 10								18 48	18 38		
	d									18 06									18 34				
Appleford	d																						
Culham	d									18 11													
Radley	d									18 15													
Oxford 115	a					18 08		18 13		18 23						18 38		18 43	18 48				
	d					18 10				18 24						18 39							
Tackley	d									18 32													
Heyford	d									18 37													
Kings Sutton	d									18 45													
Banbury 71	a					18 27				18 51						18 56							
Leamington Spa	a					18 44										19 14							
Coventry	a															19 26							
Birmingham International	a															19 36							
Birmingham New Street 71	a					19 18										19 48							

Station		GW ◇■ H	XR	XC ◇■ L	GW D	GW ◇■	GW ◇■ M	GW	GW F	GW ◇■ G	GW	GW ◇■ H	XR	XC ◇■ I	GW D	GW ◇■ N	GW	GW F	GW ◇■ K	GW ◇■ O	GW ◇■	GW ◇■ H	XR	XC ◇■
London Paddington ⊖	d	18 17	17 43		17 57	18 20	18 29			18 32		18 47	18 13		18 27	18 50			18 59	19 03	19 07	19 17	18 43	
Ealing Broadway ⊖	d		17 51		18 05								18 21		18 35								18 51	
Slough	d		18 16		18 24	18 34							18 46		18 54	19 04							19 16	
Maidenhead	d		18 26		18 30								18 56		19 00								19 26	
Twyford	d		18 33		18 37				←				19 03		19 07			←					19 33	
Reading	a	18 40	18 41		18 44	18 47	18 52		18 44	18 55		19 10	19 11		19 14	19 17		19 14	19 22	19 26	19 37	19 40	19 41	
	d	18 42		18 45	18 53	18 49			18 53	18 57	19 10			19 15	19 23	19 19		19 23	19 24	19 28	19 40	19 42		19 45
Reading West	d				→						19 12				→									
Theale	d										19 17										19 47			
Aldermaston	d										19 22													
Midgham	d										19 25													
Thatcham	d										19 29										19 56			
Newbury Racecourse	d										19 33													
Newbury	a										19 37									19 42	20 02			
	d																				20 03			
Kintbury	d																				20 09			
Hungerford	d																				20 13			
Bedwyn	a																				20 21			
Tilehurst	d								18 57									19 27						
Pangbourne	d								19 01									19 31						
Goring & Streatley	d								19 05									19 35						
Cholsey	d								19 09									19 39						
Didcot Parkway	a	18 55							19 18	19 10								19 48	19 37			19 55		
	d							19 06									19 34							
Appleford	d							19 10																
Culham	d																							
Radley	d							19 15																
Oxford 115	a			19 08		19 13		19 23						19 38		19 43	19 48							20 10
	d			19 10										19 39			19 50							20 11
Tackley	d																19 58							
Heyford	d																20 03							
Kings Sutton	d																20 11							
Banbury 71	a			19 27										19 56			20 18							20 28
Leamington Spa	a			19 44										20 14										20 46
Coventry	a													20 26										
Birmingham International	a													20 37										
Birmingham New Street 71	a			20 18										20 48										21 18

A To Penzance
B To Carmarthen
C To Newcastle
D To Didcot Parkway
E To Weston-super-Mare
F From London Paddington
G To Cheltenham Spa
H To Swansea
I From Bournemouth to Manchester Piccadilly
J To Worcester Foregate Street
K To Bristol Temple Meads
L From Southampton Central to York
M To Taunton
N To Hereford
O To Plymouth

For complete services between Banbury and Birmingham, refer to Table T71

Table T116-F

Saturdays

21 December to 16 May

London and Reading - Bedwyn, Oxford, Banbury and Birmingham

Station		GW A	GW ◇■	GW ◇■ B	GW	GW C	GW ◇■ D	GW	GW ◇■ E	XR	XC ◇■ F	GW A	GW ◇■ G	GW	GW C	GW ◇■ H	GW ◇■ I	GW ■	GW J	XR	XC ◇■	GW A	GW ◇■
London Paddington ⊖	d	18 57	19 20	19 29			19 32		19 47	19 13		19 27	19 50			19 59	20 03			19 43		19 57	20 20
Ealing Broadway ⊖	d	19 05								19 21		19 35								19 51		20 05	
Slough	d	19 24	19 34							19 46		19 54	20 04							20 16		20 24	20 34
Maidenhead	d	19 30								19 56		20 00								20 26		20 30	
Twyford	d	19 37				←				20 03		20 07			←					20 33		20 37	
Reading	a	19 44	19 47	19 52		19 44	19 55		20 10	20 11		20 14	20 17		20 14	20 22	20 26			20 41		20 44	20 47
	d	19 53	19 49			19 53	19 57	20 10			20 15	20 23	20 19		20 23	20 24	20 28		20 30		20 45	20 53	20 49
Reading West	d	→						20 12				→										→	
Theale	d							20 17															
Aldermaston	d							20 22															
Midgham	d							20 25															
Thatcham	d							20 29															
Newbury Racecourse	d							20 33															
Newbury	a							20 37									20 42						
	d																	20 50					
Kintbury	d																	20 56					
Hungerford	d																	21 00					
Bedwyn	a																	21 09					
Tilehurst	d					19 57									20 27				20 33				
Pangbourne	d					20 01									20 31				20 38				
Goring & Streatley	d					20 05									20 35				20 43				
Cholsey	d					20 09									20 39				20 48				
Didcot Parkway	a					20 18	20 10								20 48	20 37			20 55				
	d				20 04									20 34					21 04				
Appleford	d																		→				
Culham	d				20 10																		
Radley	d				20 14																		
Oxford 115	a		20 16		20 22						20 38		20 43	20 48							21 08		21 14
	d										20 39										21 10		
Tackley	d																						
Heyford	d																						
Kings Sutton	d																						
Banbury 71	a										20 56										21 27		
Leamington Spa	a										21 14										21 44		
Coventry	a										21 26										22 01		
Birmingham International	a										21 36										22 11		
Birmingham New Street 71	a										21 48										22 22		

Station		GW K	GW C	GW ◇■ L	GW ◇■ D	GW	GW ■	GW ◇■ E	XR	XC ◇■ M	GW A	GW ◇■	XR	GW	GW C	XC ◇■	GW	GW A	GW ◇■	GW ◇■ H	GW C	GW	GW ■	XR
London Paddington ⊖	d			20 29	20 32			20 47	20 13		20 27	20 50	20 43					20 57	21 19	21 29				21 13
Ealing Broadway ⊖	d								20 21		20 35		20 51					21 05						21 21
Slough	d								20 46		20 54	21 04	21 16					21 24	21 34					21 46
Maidenhead	d								20 56		21 00		21 26					21 30	21 40					21 56
Twyford	d		←						21 03		21 07		21 33		←			21 37			←			22 03
Reading	a		20 44	20 52	20 55			21 10	21 11		21 14	21 17	21 41		21 14			21 44	21 49	21 52	21 44			22 11
	d		20 53		20 57	21 10				21 15	21 23	21 19			21 23	21 45		21 57	21 50	21 54	21 57	22 10		
Reading West	d					21 12					→							→				22 12		
Theale	d					21 17																22 17		
Aldermaston	d					21 22																22 22		
Midgham	d					21 25																22 25		
Thatcham	d					21 29																22 29		
Newbury Racecourse	d					21 33																22 33		
Newbury	a					21 38																22 38		
	d						21 47																22 45	
Kintbury	d						21 53																22 51	
Hungerford	d						21 57																22 55	
Bedwyn	a						22 06																23 04	
Tilehurst	d		20 57												21 27						22 01			
Pangbourne	d		21 01												21 31						22 05			
Goring & Streatley	d		21 05												21 35						22 09			
Cholsey	d	←	21 09												21 39						22 13			
Didcot Parkway	a	20 55	21 18		21 10										21 48				22 05	22 07	22 22			
	d	21 04												21 34			22 03		22 08					
Appleford	d	21 08																						
Culham	d	21 10																						
Radley	d	21 14															22 10							
Oxford 115	a	21 23								21 38		21 43		21 50		22 08	22 18		22 24					
	d	21 24								21 39						22 10								
Tackley	d	21 32																						
Heyford	d	21 37																						
Kings Sutton	d	21 45																						
Banbury 71	a	21 52								21 56						22 27								
Leamington Spa	a									22 14						22 44								
Coventry	a									22 26														
Birmingham International	a									22 36														
Birmingham New Street 71	a									22 48						23 18								

A To Didcot Parkway
B To Taunton
C From London Paddington
D To Cheltenham Spa
E To Swansea
F From Bournemouth to Manchester Piccadilly
G To Great Malvern
H To Bristol Temple Meads
I To Plymouth
J To Banbury
K From Reading
L To Exeter St Davids
M From Bournemouth

For complete services between Banbury and Birmingham, refer to Table T71

Table T116-F

London and Reading - Bedwyn, Oxford, Banbury and Birmingham

Saturdays
21 December to 16 May

		GW	GW ◇1 A 🍴	GW ◇1 B 🍴	GW	GW	XR	GW C		GW ◇1 D 🍴	GW ◇1	GW E	GW	GW 1	XR	GW	GW 🚌	GW	GW ◇1	XR	GW	GW ◇1 D 🍴	GW ◇1	GW	
London Paddington 15 ⊖	d	21 27	21 49	21 57			21 43	21 57		22 29	22 19				22 13	22 28			22 50	22 43	22 58	23 30	23 33	23 28	
Ealing Broadway ⊖	d	21 35					21 51	22 05							22 21	22 37				22 51	23 06			23 36	
Slough 3	d	21 54	22 03				22 16	22 24			22 35				22 46	22 57			23 08	23 14	23 26		23 48	23 57	
Maidenhead 3	d	22 00					22 26	22 30			22 42				22 56	23 03			23 15	23 24	23 32		23 56	00 08	
Twyford 3	d	22 07					22 33	22 37				←			23 03	23 10				23 31	23 39			00 15	
Reading 7	a	22 14	22 16	22 21			22 41	22 44		22 52	22 53	22 44			23 11	23 17			23 30	23 39	23 46	00 01	00 07	00 22	
	d		22 17	22 22		22 35		23 05		22 54	22 55	23 05	23 10						23 31		23 48	00 02	00 10	00 23	
Reading West	d							→					23 12												
Theale	d												23 17												
Aldermaston	d												23 22												
Midgham	d												23 25												
Thatcham	d												23 29												
Newbury Racecourse	d												23 33												
Newbury	a												23 38												
	d													23 43											
Kintbury	d													23 49											
Hungerford	d													23 53											
Bedwyn	a													00 02											
Tilehurst	d					22 38						23 09									23 52			00 27	
Pangbourne	d					22 43						23 13									23 56			00 31	
Goring & Streatley	d					22 48						23 17									23 59			00 35	
Cholsey	d					22 53						23 21									00 04			00 39	
Didcot Parkway	a		22 32	22 35		23 00				23 07	23 09	23 30							23 46		00 13	00 17	00 24	00 48	
	d		22 33		22 38	23 01					23 11							23 35	23 47				00 26		
Appleford	d																								
Culham	d																								
Radley	d				22 45	23 08												23 42					00 34		
Oxford 115	a		22 46		22 53	23 18					23 25							23 53	00 01				00 43		
	d																23 41								
Tackley	d																00s01								
Heyford	d																00s16								
Kings Sutton	d																								
Banbury 71	a																00 41								
Leamington Spa 8	a																								
Coventry	a																								
Birmingham International	a																								
Birmingham New Street 12 71	a																								

Sundays
15 December to 10 May

		GW F	GW ◇1 G 🍴	GW ◇1 F	GW	GW F	GW 🚌	GW	GW	GW	XR	GW	GW ◇1 H 🍴	GW ◇1 I 🍴	GW ◇1 J 🍴	GW		GW	GW ◇1 K 🍴	GW	GW ◇1 L 🍴	XR	GW ◇1 H 🍴	GW C	GW ◇1 J 🍴
London Paddington 15 ⊖	d							00 30	01 00	06 44	07 00		07 37	07 57	08 00			07 27	08 27		08 33	08 03	08 37	08 24	08 51
Ealing Broadway ⊖	d							00 38	01 08	06 54	07 08							07 35				08 11		08 32	
Slough 3	d							01 00	01 23	07 13	07 30		08 00					07 52				08 36	08 51	08 47	
Maidenhead 3	d					00 08		01 10	01 30	07 22	07 37							08 18				08 46		08 53	
Twyford 3	d					00 15		01 17	01 37	07 30	07 44							08 25				08 53		09 03	
Reading 7	a					00 22		01 24	01 44	07 37	07 52		08 14	08 24	08 29			08 34	08 51		08 57	09 01	09 06	09 11	09 14
	d		00 02	00 10	00 20	00 23						08 10	08 21	08 26	08 29	08 35		08 38	08 53				09 08	09 18	
Reading West	d				00s22							08 13												→	
Theale	d				00s27							08 19				08 43									
Aldermaston	d				00s32							08 23													
Midgham	d				00s35							08 26													
Thatcham	d				00s39							08 30				08 51									
Newbury Racecourse	d				00s44																				
Newbury	a				00 47							08 38		08 40		08 55									
	d															08 56									
Kintbury	d															09 03									
Hungerford	d															09 07									
Bedwyn	a															09 13									
Tilehurst	d					00 27												08 42							
Pangbourne	d					00 31												08 46							
Goring & Streatley	d					00 35												08 50							
Cholsey	d	00 04				00 39												08 54							
Didcot Parkway	a	00 13	00 17	00 24		00 48							08 37		08 46			09 03	09 05				09 23		
	d			00 26			01 00						08 38							09 10			09 29		
Appleford	d						01s10																		
Culham	d						01s20																		
Radley	d			00 34			01s30													09 17					
Oxford 115	a			00 43			01 45						08 49							09 27			09 43		
Tackley	d																								
Heyford	d																								
Kings Sutton	d																								
Banbury 71	a																								
Leamington Spa 8	a																								
Coventry	a																								
Birmingham International	a																								
Birmingham New Street 12 71	a																								

A To Worcester Shrub Hill
B To Cardiff Central
C To Didcot Parkway
D To Bristol Temple Meads
E From London Paddington
F not 15 December. From London Paddington
G not 15 December. From London Paddington to Bristol Temple Meads
H To Great Malvern
I To Penzance
J To Plymouth
K To Cheltenham Spa
L To Swansea

For complete services between Banbury and Birmingham, refer to Table T71

NRT DECEMBER 19 EDITION

Table T116-F

London and Reading - Bedwyn, Oxford, Banbury and Birmingham

Sundays
15 December to 10 May

		XC ◇1 A 🍴	GW B	GW ◇1 C 🍴	XR	GW ◇1	GW ◇1 D	GW ◇1 E 🍴		GW ◇1 F 🍴	GW ◇1 G 🍴	XR	GW H	GW ◇1 I 🍴	XC ◇1 J 🍴	GW B	GW ◇1 K 🍴	GW ◇1 L 🍴	XR	GW ◇	GW ◇1 M 🍴	GW ◇1	GW ◇1 C 🍴	GW ◇1 F 🍴	
London Paddington 15 ⊖	d			09 00	08 33	09 07	09 21	09 29		09 32	09 37	09 03	09 24	09 42			10 00	10 03	09 33	10 05	10 17	10 21	10 29	10 32	
Ealing Broadway ⊖	d				08 41							09 11	09 32						09 41						
Slough 3	d				09 06		09 35					09 36	09 47	09 58					10 06			10 35			
Maidenhead 3	d				09 16	09 23						09 46	09 53						10 16	10 23					
Twyford 3	d		←		09 23							09 53	10 00			←			10 23						
Reading 7	a		09 11	09 23	09 31	09 33	09 45	09 52		09 55	10 00	10 01	10 08	10 10		10 08	10 23	10 26	10 31	10 34	10 40	10 45	10 52	10 55	
	d	09 15	09 18	09 29		09 34	09 47			09 57			10 18	10 10	10 15	10 18	10 24			10 34	10 42	10 47		10 57	
Reading West	d												→							10 37					
Theale	d					09 41														10 42					
Aldermaston	d					09 48														10 46					
Midgham	d					09 53														10 49					
Thatcham	d					09 59														10 53					
Newbury Racecourse	d																			10 57					
Newbury	a					10 05														11 01					
	d					10 06																			
Kintbury	d					10 12																			
Hungerford	d					10 17																			
Bedwyn	a					10 23																			
Tilehurst	d		09 22													10 22									
Pangbourne	d		09 26													10 26									
Goring & Streatley	d		09 30													10 30									
Cholsey	d		09 34													10 34									
Didcot Parkway	a		09 43	09 44			10 01			10 10				10 26		10 43	10 38				10 55	11 01		11 10	
	d						10 03							10 29								11 03			
Appleford	d																								
Culham	d																								
Radley	d						10 10															11 11			
Oxford 115	a	09 38					10 18							10 40	10 38							11 19			
	d	09 39													10 39										
Tackley	d																								
Heyford	d																								
Kings Sutton	d																								
Banbury 71	a	09 56													10 56										
Leamington Spa 8	a	10 14													11 14										
Coventry	a	10 26													11 26										
Birmingham International	a	10 37													11 37										
Birmingham New Street 12 71	a	10 49													11 49										

		GW ◇1 N 🍴	XR	GW ◇1 O 🍴	GW H	GW ◇1 P 🍴	XC ◇1 Q 🍴	GW B	GW ◇1 E 🍴	GW ◇1 K 🍴	XR	GW ◇1	GW ◇1 M 🍴	GW ◇1	GW ◇1 R 🍴	GW ◇1 F 🍴		XR	GW ◇	GW ◇1 G 🍴	GW H	GW ◇1 I 🍴	XC ◇1 Q 🍴	GW B	GW ◇1 E 🍴
London Paddington 15 ⊖	d	10 36	10 03	10 43	10 24	10 46			11 00	11 03	10 33	11 07	11 17	11 21	11 29	11 32		11 03	11 37	11 43	11 24	11 46			12 00
Ealing Broadway ⊖	d		10 11		10 32						10 41							11 11			11 32				
Slough 3	d		10 36		10 47	11 00					11 06			11 35				11 36			11 47	12 00			
Maidenhead 3	d		10 46		10 53						11 16	11 23						11 46			11 53				
Twyford 3	d		10 53		11 00			←			11 23							11 53			12 00			←	
Reading 7	a	10 59	11 01	11 06	11 08	11 12		11 08	11 23	11 26	11 31	11 33	11 40	11 45	11 52	11 55		12 01	12 02	12 06	12 08	12 12		12 08	12 23
	d	11 01			11 18	11 13	11 15	11 18	11 24			11 35	11 42	11 47		11 57			12 04		12 18	12 12	12 15	12 18	12 24
Reading West	d				→																→				
Theale	d											11 42													
Aldermaston	d																								
Midgham	d																								
Thatcham	d											11 50													
Newbury Racecourse	d																								
Newbury	a	11 14										11 55							12 17						
	d											11 56													
Kintbury	d											12 02													
Hungerford	d											12 07													
Bedwyn	a											12 12													
Tilehurst	d							11 22																12 22	
Pangbourne	d							11 26																12 26	
Goring & Streatley	d							11 30																12 30	
Cholsey	d							11 34																12 34	
Didcot Parkway	a					11 27		11 43	11 38				11 55	12 01		12 10						12 26		12 43	12 38
	d					11 29								12 03								12 29			
Appleford	d																								
Culham	d																								
Radley	d													12 11											
Oxford 115	a					11 43	11 38							12 19								12 41	12 39		
	d						11 39																12 40		
Tackley	d																								
Heyford	d																								
Kings Sutton	d																								
Banbury 71	a						11 56																12 57		
Leamington Spa 8	a						12 14																13 15		
Coventry	a						12 26																13 27		
Birmingham International	a						12 37																13 37		
Birmingham New Street 12 71	a						12 49																13 48		

A To Manchester Piccadilly
B From London Paddington
C To Weston-super-Mare
D 1 to Didcot Parkway
E To Bristol Temple Meads
F To Penzance
G To Carmarthen
H To Didcot Parkway
I To Hereford
J From Southampton Central to Manchester Piccadilly
K To Plymouth
L To Penzance
M To Cardiff Central
N To Exeter St Davids
O To Swansea
P To Worcester Shrub Hill
Q From Bournemouth to Manchester Piccadilly
R To Paignton

For complete services between Banbury and Birmingham, refer to Table T71

Table T116-F

London and Reading - Bedwyn, Oxford, Banbury and Birmingham

Sundays

15 December to 10 May

		GW ◇1 A ⌶	XR	GW ◇	GW ◇1 B ⌶	GW ◇1	GW ◇1 C ⌶	XC ◇1 D ⌶	GW ◇1 E ⌶	GW ◇1 F ⌶	XR	GW ◇1 G ⌶	GW H	GW ◇1 I ⌶	XC ◇1 J ⌶	GW K	GW ◇1 L ⌶	GW ◇1 M ⌶	XR	GW ◇1 N	GW ◇1 B ⌶	XC ◇1 O ⌶	GW ◇1 P
London Paddington 15 ⊖	d	12 03	11 33	12 05	12 17	12 21	12 29		12 32	12 36	12 03	12 43	12 24	12 46			13 00	13 03	12 33	13 06	13 17		13 21
Ealing Broadway ⊖	d		11 41								12 11		12 32						12 41				
Slough 3	d		12 06			12 35					12 36		12 47	13 00					13 06				13 35
Maidenhead 3	d		12 16	12 23							12 46		12 55						13 16	13 22			
Twyford 3	d		12 23								12 53		13 00			←			13 23				
Reading 7	a	12 26	12 31	12 34	12 40	12 45	12 52		12 55	12 59	13 01	13 06	13 08	13 12		13 08	13 23	13 26	13 31	13 33	13 40		13 45
	d			12 35	12 42	12 47		12 52	12 57	13 00			13 18	13 13	13 15	13 18	13 24			13 34	13 42	13 42	13 47
Reading West	d			12 37									→										
Theale	d			12 43																13 42			
Aldermaston	d			12 47																			
Midgham	d			12 50																			
Thatcham	d			12 55																13 49			
Newbury Racecourse	d			12 59																			
Newbury	a			13 02						13 14										13 54			
	d																			13 55			
Kintbury	d																			14 02			
Hungerford	d																			14 06			
Bedwyn	a																			14 12			
Tilehurst	d															13 22							
Pangbourne	d															13 26							
Goring & Streatley	d															13 30							
Cholsey	d															13 34							
Didcot Parkway	a				12 55	13 02			13 10					13 27		13 43	13 37				13 55		14 03
	d					13 03								13 29									14 03
Appleford	d																						
Culham	d																						
Radley	d					13 14																	14 10
Oxford 115	a					13 22		13 15						13 43	13 38							14 05	14 19
	d							13 16							13 39							14 06	
Tackley	d																						
Heyford	d																						
Kings Sutton	d																						
Banbury 71	a							13 33							13 56							14 23	
Leamington Spa 8	a							13 51							14 14							14 41	
Coventry	a														14 26							14 53	
Birmingham International	a														14 36							15 03	
Birmingham New Street 12 71	a							14 18							14 48							15 14	

		GW ◇1 L ⌶	GW ◇1 E ⌶	XR	GW ◇	GW ◇1 Q ⌶	GW H	GW ◇1 R ⌶	XC ◇1 J ⌶	GW K	GW ◇1 L ⌶	GW ◇1 A ⌶	XR	GW ◇	GW ◇1 B ⌶	XC ◇1 O ⌶	GW ◇1	GW ◇1 L ⌶	GW ◇1 E ⌶	GW ◇1 F ⌶	XR	GW ◇1 G ⌶	GW H	GW ◇1 I ⌶
London Paddington 15 ⊖	d	13 29	13 32	13 03	13 37	13 43	13 24	13 45			14 00	14 03	13 33	14 05	14 17		14 21	14 29	14 32	14 36	14 03	14 43	14 24	14 46
Ealing Broadway ⊖	d			13 11			13 32						13 41								14 11		14 32	
Slough 3	d			13 36			13 47	14 00					14 06				14 35				14 36		14 47	15 00
Maidenhead 3	d			13 46			13 53						14 16	14 23							14 46		14 53	
Twyford 3	d			13 53			14 00			←			14 23								14 53		15 00	
Reading 7	a	13 52	13 55	14 01	14 02	14 06	14 08	14 12		14 08	14 23	14 26	14 31	14 34	14 40		14 45	14 52	14 55	14 59	15 01	15 06	15 08	15 12
	d		13 57		14 04		14 18	14 12	14 15	14 18	14 24			14 34	14 42	14 42	14 47		14 57	15 00			15 18	15 13
Reading West	d						→							14 36									→	
Theale	d													14 42										
Aldermaston	d													14 46										
Midgham	d													14 50										
Thatcham	d													14 55										
Newbury Racecourse	d													14 58										
Newbury	a				14 17									15 02						15 14				
	d																							
Kintbury	d																							
Hungerford	d																							
Bedwyn	a																							
Tilehurst	d									14 22														
Pangbourne	d									14 26														
Goring & Streatley	d									14 30														
Cholsey	d									14 34														
Didcot Parkway	a		14 10					14 26		14 43	14 38				14 55		15 02		15 10					15 27
	d							14 29									15 04							15 30
Appleford	d																							
Culham	d																							
Radley	d																15 11							
Oxford 115	a							14 40	14 38							15 05	15 19							15 43
	d								14 39							15 06								
Tackley	d																							
Heyford	d																							
Kings Sutton	d																							
Banbury 71	a								14 56							15 23								
Leamington Spa 8	a								15 14							15 41								
Coventry	a								15 26							15 53								
Birmingham International	a								15 36							16 03								
Birmingham New Street 12 71	a								15 48							16 14								

A To Penzance
B To Cardiff Central
C To Weston-super-Mare
D From Guildford to Newcastle
E To Cheltenham Spa
F To Exeter St Davids
G To Swansea
H To Didcot Parkway
I To Worcester Shrub Hill
J From Bournemouth to Manchester Piccadilly
K From London Paddington
L To Bristol Temple Meads
M To Plymouth
N 1 to Reading
O To Newcastle
P 1 to Didcot Parkway
Q To Carmarthen
R To Hereford

For complete services between Banbury and Birmingham, refer to Table T71

Table T116-F

London and Reading - Bedwyn, Oxford, Banbury and Birmingham

Sundays

15 December to 10 May

		XC ◇1 A ⌶	GW B	GW ◇1 C ⌶	GW ◇1 D ⌶	XR	GW ◇1 E	GW ◇1 F ⌶	XC ◇1 G ⌶	GW ◇1	GW ◇1 H ⌶	GW ◇1 I ⌶	XR	GW ◇	GW ◇1 J ⌶	GW K	GW ◇1 L ⌶	XC ◇1 A ⌶	GW B	GW ◇1 C ⌶	GW ◇1 M ⌶	XR	GW ◇
London Paddington 15 ⊖	d			15 00	15 03	14 33	15 07	15 17		15 21	15 29	15 32	15 03	15 36	15 43	15 24	15 46			16 00	16 03	15 33	16 05
Ealing Broadway ⊖	d					14 41							15 11			15 32						15 41	
Slough 3	d					15 06				15 35			15 36			15 47	16 00					16 06	
Maidenhead 3	d					15 16	15 23						15 46			15 53						16 16	16 23
Twyford 3	d		←			15 23							15 53			16 00			←			16 23	
Reading 7	a		15 08	15 23	15 25	15 31	15 32	15 40		15 45	15 52	15 55	16 01	16 02	16 07	16 08	16 12		16 08	16 23	16 26	16 31	16 34
	d	15 15	15 18	15 24			15 34	15 42	15 42	15 47		15 57		16 04		16 18	16 13	16 15	16 18	16 24			16 34
Reading West	d															→							16 36
Theale	d						15 42																16 42
Aldermaston	d																						16 46
Midgham	d																						16 49
Thatcham	d						15 49																16 54
Newbury Racecourse	d																						16 59
Newbury	a						15 54							16 17									17 02
	d						15 55																
Kintbury	d						16 02																
Hungerford	d						16 06																
Bedwyn	a						16 12																
Tilehurst	d		15 22																16 22				
Pangbourne	d		15 26																16 26				
Goring & Streatley	d		15 30																16 30				
Cholsey	d		15 34																16 34				
Didcot Parkway	a		15 43	15 38				15 55		16 01		16 10					16 27		16 43	16 38			
	d									16 03							16 29						
Appleford	d																						
Culham	d																						
Radley	d									16 10													
Oxford 115	a	15 38							16 05	16 20							16 43	16 38					
	d	15 39							16 06									16 39					
Tackley	d																						
Heyford	d																						
Kings Sutton	d																						
Banbury 71	a	15 56							16 23									16 56					
Leamington Spa 8	a	16 14							16 41									17 14					
Coventry	a	16 26							16 53									17 26					
Birmingham International	a	16 36							17 03									17 36					
Birmingham New Street 12 71	a	16 48							17 14									17 48					

		GW ◇1 J ⌶	XC ◇1 N ⌶	GW ◇1	GW ◇1 C ⌶	GW ◇1 I ⌶	GW ◇1 D ⌶	XR	GW ◇1 J ⌶	GW K	GW ◇1 O ⌶	XC ◇1 A ⌶	GW B	GW ◇1 C ⌶	GW ◇1 M ⌶	XR	GW ◇1	GW ◇1 F ⌶	XC ◇1 N ⌶	GW ◇1	GW ◇1 P ⌶	GW ◇1 I ⌶	XR	GW ◇
London Paddington 15 ⊖	d	16 17		16 20	16 29	16 32	16 36	16 03	16 42	16 24	16 46			17 00	17 03	16 33	17 05	17 17		17 21	17 29	17 32	17 03	17 38
Ealing Broadway ⊖	d							16 11		16 32						16 41							17 11	
Slough 3	d			16 35				16 36		16 47	17 00					17 06				17 35			17 36	
Maidenhead 3	d							16 46		16 53						17 16	17 22						17 46	
Twyford 3	d							16 53		17 00			←			17 23							17 53	
Reading 7	a	16 40		16 45	16 52	16 55	16 59	17 01	17 06	17 08	17 12		17 08	17 23	17 26	17 31	17 32	17 40		17 45	17 52	17 55	18 01	18 03
	d	16 42	16 42	16 47		16 57	17 00			17 18	17 13	17 15	17 18	17 24			17 35	17 42	17 42	17 47		17 57		18 04
Reading West	d									→														
Theale	d																17 42							
Aldermaston	d																							
Midgham	d																							
Thatcham	d																17 49							
Newbury Racecourse	d																							
Newbury	a						17 14										17 54							18 17
	d																17 55							
Kintbury	d																18 02							
Hungerford	d																18 06							
Bedwyn	a																18 12							
Tilehurst	d												17 22											
Pangbourne	d												17 26											
Goring & Streatley	d												17 30											
Cholsey	d												17 34											
Didcot Parkway	a	16 55		17 01		17 10					17 27		17 43	17 38				17 55		18 01		18 10		
	d			17 03							17 30									18 03				
Appleford	d																							
Culham	d																							
Radley	d			17 10																18 10				
Oxford 115	a		17 05	17 23							17 43	17 38							18 05	18 20				
	d		17 06									17 39							18 06					
Tackley	d																							
Heyford	d																							
Kings Sutton	d																							
Banbury 71	a		17 23									17 56							18 23					
Leamington Spa 8	a		17 41									18 14							18 41					
Coventry	a		17 53									18 26							18 53					
Birmingham International	a		18 03									18 36							19 03					
Birmingham New Street 12 71	a		18 14									18 48							19 14					

A From Bournemouth to Manchester Piccadilly
B From London Paddington
C To Bristol Temple Meads
D To Plymouth
E 1 to Reading
F To Cardiff Central
G To Edinburgh
H To Taunton
I To Cheltenham Spa
J To Swansea
K To Didcot Parkway
L To Hereford
M To Penzance
N To Newcastle
O To Worcester Shrub Hill
P To Weston-super-Mare

For complete services between Banbury and Birmingham, refer to Table T71

Table T116-F

Sundays

15 December to 10 May

London and Reading - Bedwyn, Oxford, Banbury and Birmingham

Station		GW	GW	GW	XC	GW	GW	GW	XR	GW	GW	XC	GW	GW	GW	GW	XR	GW	GW	GW	XC	GW	GW
		◇1		◇1	◇1		◇1	◇1		◇	◇1	◇1	◇1	◇1	◇1	◇1		◇1		◇1	◇1		◇1
		A	B	C	D	E	F	G			A		H	I	J	F		A	B	K	D	E	L
		🍴		🍴	🍴		🍴	🍴			🍴	🍴		🍴	🍴	🍴		🍴		🍴	🍴		🍴
London Paddington 15 ⊖	d	17 43	17 24	17 46			18 00	18 03	17 33	18 05	18 17		18 21	18 29	18 32	18 36	18 03	18 43	18 24	18 46			19 00
Ealing Broadway ⊖	d		17 32						17 41								18 11		18 32				
Slough 3	d		17 47	18 00					18 06				18 35				18 36		18 47	19 00			
Maidenhead 3	d		17 53						18 16	18 23							18 46		18 53				
Twyford 3	d		18 00			←			18 23								18 53		19 00			←	
Reading 7	a	18 06	18 08	18 12		18 08	18 23	18 26	18 31	18 34	18 40		18 45	18 52	18 55	18 59	19 01	19 06	19 08	19 12		19 08	19 23
	d		18 18	18 13	18 15	18 18	18 24			18 34	18 42	18 42	18 47		18 57	19 00			19 18	19 13	19 15	19 18	19 24
Reading West	d		→							18 36									→				
Theale	d									18 42													
Aldermaston	d									18 46													
Midgham	d									18 49													
Thatcham	d									18 54													
Newbury Racecourse	d									18 58													
Newbury	a									19 02						19 14							
	d																						
Kintbury	d																						
Hungerford	d																						
Bedwyn	a																						
Tilehurst	d					18 22																19 22	
Pangbourne	d					18 26																19 26	
Goring & Streatley	d					18 30																19 30	
Cholsey	d					18 34																19 34	
Didcot Parkway	a			18 27		18 43	18 38				18 55		19 01		19 10					19 27		19 43	19 38
	d			18 28									19 03							19 31			
Appleford	d																						
Culham	d																						
Radley	d												19 10										
Oxford 115	a			18 43	18 38							19 05	19 19							19 43	19 38		
	d				18 39							19 06									19 39		
Tackley	d																						
Heyford	d																						
Kings Sutton	d																						
Banbury 71	a				18 56							19 23									19 56		
Leamington Spa 8	a				19 14							19 41									20 14		
Coventry	a				19 26							19 53									20 26		
Birmingham International	a				19 36							20 03									20 36		
Birmingham New Street 12 71	a				19 48							20 14									20 48		

Station		GW	XR	XC	GW	GW	GW	GW	GW	XR	GW	GW	GW	XC	GW	GW	GW	XR	GW	GW	XC	GW	GW	XR
		◇1		◇1	◇	◇1	◇	◇1	◇1		◇1		◇1	◇1		◇1	◇1			◇1	◇1	◇1	◇1	
		F			M	A	E	L	J		A	B	C	D	E	L	F			N		I	J	
		🍴				🍴		🍴	🍴		🍴		🍴			🍴	🍴			🍴		🍴	🍴	
London Paddington 15 ⊖	d	19 03	18 33		19 05	19 17		19 29	19 32	19 03	19 43	19 24	19 46			20 00	20 03	19 33		20 17		20 29	20 32	20 03
Ealing Broadway ⊖	d		18 41							19 11		19 32						19 41						20 11
Slough 3	d		19 06							19 36		19 47	20 00					20 06						20 36
Maidenhead 3	d		19 16		19 27					19 46		19 53						20 16						20 46
Twyford 3	d		19 23				←			19 53		20 00			←			20 23						20 53
Reading 7	a	19 26	19 31		19 41	19 42	19 41	19 52	19 55	20 01	20 06	20 08	20 12		20 08	20 23	20 26	20 31		20 40		20 52	20 55	21 01
	d			19 39	19 44	19 43	19 44		19 57		20 08	20 18	20 13	20 15	20 18	20 24	20 27		20 42	20 42	20 42		20 57	
Reading West	d				→							→							20 44					
Theale	d						19 52												20 49					
Aldermaston	d																		20 54					
Midgham	d																		20 56					
Thatcham	d						20 00												21 00					
Newbury Racecourse	d																		21 05					
Newbury	a						20 06										20 41		21 08					
	d						20 06																	
Kintbury	d						20 12																	
Hungerford	d						20 17																	
Bedwyn	a						20 24																	
Tilehurst	d														20 22									
Pangbourne	d														20 26									
Goring & Streatley	d														20 30									
Cholsey	d														20 34									
Didcot Parkway	a					19 56			20 10		20 21		20 27		20 43	20 38				20 55			21 10	
	d												20 29											
Appleford	d																							
Culham	d																							
Radley	d												20 37											
Oxford 115	a			20 05									20 45	20 38							21 05			
	d			20 06										20 39							21 06			
Tackley	d																							
Heyford	d																							
Kings Sutton	d																							
Banbury 71	a			20 23										20 56							21 23			
Leamington Spa 8	a			20 41										21 14							21 41			
Coventry	a			20 53										21 26							21 53			
Birmingham International	a			21 03										21 36							22 03			
Birmingham New Street 12 71	a			21 15										21 48							22 14			

A To Swansea
B To Didcot Parkway
C To Great Malvern
D From Bournemouth to Manchester Piccadilly
E From London Paddington
F To Plymouth
G To Penzance
H 1 to Didcot Parkway
I To Weston-super-Mare
J To Cheltenham Spa
K To Hereford
L To Bristol Temple Meads
M To Bedwyn
N To Bristol Parkway

For complete services between Banbury and Birmingham, refer to Table T71

NRT DECEMBER 19 EDITION

Table T116-F

Sundays

15 December to 10 May

London and Reading - Bedwyn, Oxford, Banbury and Birmingham

Station		GW	XC	GW	GW	GW	GW	GW	XR	XC	GW	GW	XR	GW	GW	GW	GW	GW	GW	XR	GW	XR	GW
		◇1	◇1		◇1		◇1	◇1		◇1		◇1			◇1		◇1	◇1					
		A	B	C		D	E	F				E			A		G	E					C
		🍴					🍴	🍴				🍴			🍴			🍴	🚌				
London Paddington 15 ⊖	d	20 43		20 24	20 46		21 00	21 03	20 33			21 29	21 03		21 43	21 24	21 46	22 00		21 33		22 03	22 24
Ealing Broadway ⊖	d			20 32					20 41				21 11			21 32				21 41		22 11	22 32
Slough 3	d			20 47	21 00				21 06				21 36			21 47	21 59			22 06		22 36	22 47
Maidenhead 3	d			20 53					21 16				21 46			21 53				22 16		22 46	22 51
Twyford 3	d			21 00		←			21 23				21 53			22 00				22 23		22 53	22 58
Reading 7	a	21 06		21 07	21 10	21 07	21 23	21 26	21 31			21 52	22 01		22 05	22 08	22 12	22 23		22 31		23 01	23 06
	d	21 08	21 12	21 18	21 14	21 18	21 24			21 42	21 44				22 08	22 11	22 13	22 25			22 44		23 20
Reading West	d			→																	22 46		→
Theale	d										21 51										22 51		
Aldermaston	d																				22 55		
Midgham	d																				22 58		
Thatcham	d										21 59										23 02		
Newbury Racecourse	d																				23 06		
Newbury	a										22 05										23 11		
	d										22 06												
Kintbury	d										22 12												
Hungerford	d										22 17												
Bedwyn	a										22 24												
Tilehurst	d					21 22										22 15							
Pangbourne	d					21 26										22 19							
Goring & Streatley	d					21 30										22 23							
Cholsey	d					21 34										22 27							
Didcot Parkway	a	21 21			21 27	21 42	21 38								22 21	22 36	22 26	22 39					
	d				21 29									21 57			22 29		22 45				
Appleford	d																						
Culham	d																						
Radley	d													22 04					23 10				
Oxford 115	a		21 33		21 43					22 05				22 12			22 42		23 25				
	d		21 36							22 06													
Tackley	d																						
Heyford	d																						
Kings Sutton	d																						
Banbury 71	a		21 53							22 23													
Leamington Spa 8	a		22 11							22 41													
Coventry	a		22 23							22 53													
Birmingham International	a		22 33							23 03													
Birmingham New Street 12 71	a		22 44							23 14													

Station		GW	GW	GW	XR	GW	GW	GW	GW	GW	GW
		◇1				◇1			◇1		
		H	D			E		C	E	D	
		🍴				🍴	🚌		🍴		
London Paddington 15 ⊖	d	22 37			22 33	22 57		23 27	23 33		23 53
Ealing Broadway ⊖	d				22 41			23 35			00 03
Slough 3	d	22 56			23 06			23 50	00 01		00 25
Maidenhead 3	d				23 16			23 56			00 33
Twyford 3	d		←		23 23			00 04		←	00 40
Reading 7	a	23 13	23 06		23 31	23 35		00 12	00 17	00 12	00 52
	d	23 15	23 20	23 22		23 37		00 24	00 19	00 24	
Reading West	d			23 27				→			
Theale	d			23 33							
Aldermaston	d										
Midgham	d										
Thatcham	d			23 42							
Newbury Racecourse	d										
Newbury	a			23 48							
	d										
Kintbury	d										
Hungerford	d										
Bedwyn	a										
Tilehurst	d		23 24							00 28	
Pangbourne	d		23 27							00 31	
Goring & Streatley	d		23 31							00 35	
Cholsey	d		23 36							00 39	
Didcot Parkway	a	23s30	23 45			23s52			00s34	00 48	
	d						23 59				
Appleford	d										
Culham	d										
Radley	d						00 14				
Oxford 115	a						00 29				
	d										
Tackley	d										
Heyford	d										
Kings Sutton	d										
Banbury 71	a										
Leamington Spa 8	a										
Coventry	a										
Birmingham International	a										
Birmingham New Street 12 71	a										

A To Swansea
B From Bournemouth
C To Didcot Parkway
D From London Paddington
E To Bristol Temple Meads
F To Exeter St Davids
G To Worcester Shrub Hill
H To Bristol Parkway

For complete services between Banbury and Birmingham, refer to Table T71

Birmingham, Banbury, Oxford and Bedwyn - Reading and London

Miles	Miles			GW MX A	GW MX	GW MO B	GW MO C	GW MO 🚌	GW MX 1	GW MX ◇1 D 🍴	GW MX E	GW MO ◇	GW MX	GW MX	GW	GW MO 🚌	GW	GW	GW MX	GW MO	GW	GW	GW	GW
0	—	**Birmingham New Street** 12 71	d																					
8½	—	Birmingham International	d																					
19¾	—	Coventry	d																					
28¾	—	Leamington Spa 8	d																					
48¼	—	**Banbury** 71	d																					
52¼	—	Kings Sutton	d																					
59¾	—	Heyford	d																					
62½	—	Tackley	d								00 02													
71½	—	**Oxford** 115	a								00 12													
—	—		d					00 05		00 11				00 45		03 35			03 54				05 00	
76½	—	Radley	d											00 51									05 06	
78¾	—	Culham	d																					
79¾	—	Appleford	d																					
81½	—	**Didcot Parkway**	a					00 30		00 22				01 01		04 00			04 06				05 15	
—	—		d							00 24		00 35		01 02					04 10	04 10		05 12		
86¾	—	Cholsey	d											01 08					04 16	04 16		05 17		
90¼	—	Goring & Streatley	d			00 03								01 13					04 22	04 22		05 22		
93½	—	Pangbourne	d			00 07								01 17					04 27	04 27		05 26		
96¼	—	Tilehurst	d			00 11								01 22					04 32	04 32		05 30		
—	0	**Bedwyn**	d						00 06															
—	5	Hungerford	d																					
—	8	Kintbury	d																					
—	13½	**Newbury**	a						00 15															
—	—		d						00 18															
—	14	Newbury Racecourse	d																					
—	17	Thatcham	d				00 02																	
—	19¾	Midgham	d				00 07																	
—	21¾	Aldermaston	d				00 10																	
—	25¾	Theale	d				00 15																	
—	29½	Reading West	d	00 04			00s23																	
99	30½	**Reading** 7	a	00 08		00 23	00 28		00 36	00 41		00 50		01 27					04 37	04 37		05 35		
—	—		d		00 17	00 24			00 38	00 43		00 54	01 15		02 24		03 54	04 34			05 08	05 36		05 50
104	—	Twyford 3	a		00 22	00 29						01 00	01 20		02 29		04 00	04 41			05 13	05 41		05 55
110¾	—	Maidenhead 3	a		00 29	00 36						01 08	01 27		02 36		04 08	04 49			05 20	05 48		06 01
116½	—	Slough 3	a		00 40	00 45				00 56		01 15	01 34		02 43		04 15	04 57			05 31	06 02		06 07
129¼	—	Ealing Broadway ⊖	a		01 02	01 06						01 31	01 48		03 02		04 36	05 20			05 56	06 25		
135	—	**London Paddington** 15 ⊖	a		01 11	01 15			01 13	01 15		01 42	01 57		03 11		04 46	05 28			06 07	06 34		06 23

		XR	GW F	GW ◇1 G 🍴	GW	XR	GW H	GW ◇1	GW B	GW 1 🍴	XR	GW ◇1 I 🍴	GW ◇1 G 🍴	GW ◇1 🍴	GW ◇1 🍴	GW	GW	GW H	GW ◇1 J 🍴	XR	GW ◇1 K 🍴	GW ◇1 G 🍴	GW B	GW
Birmingham New Street 12 71	d																							
Birmingham International	d																							
Coventry	d																							
Leamington Spa 8	d																							
Banbury 71	d																							
Kings Sutton	d																							
Heyford	d																							
Tackley	d																							
Oxford 115	a																							
	d		05 19							05 40				06 00			06 04				06 32			
Radley	d									05 47							06 10							
Culham	d																06 14							
Appleford	d																06 17							
Didcot Parkway	a		05 31							05 55				06 12			06 23							
	d		05 32	05 45			05 47					06 13		06 16		06 21		06 34	06 35			06 46		
Cholsey	d		05 38				05 52									06 27		06 40						
Goring & Streatley	d		05 43				05 57									06 32		06 45						
Pangbourne	d		05 47				06 01									06 36		06 49						
Tilehurst	d		05 52				06 05									06 41		06 54						
Bedwyn	d							05 34							06 01									
Hungerford	d							05 40							06 07									
Kintbury	d							05 45							06 12									
Newbury	a							05 51							06 18									
	d				05 29			05 52							06 19									06 31
Newbury Racecourse	d				05 31																			06 33
Thatcham	d				05 35			05 56							06 23									06 37
Midgham	d				05 39																			06 42
Aldermaston	d				05 42																			06 45
Theale	d				05 47			06 05							06 31									06 50
Reading West	d				05 54			06 11	←						06 38								←	06 55
Reading 7	a		05 57	05 57	06 00		06 13	06 14	06 13			06 25		06 32	06 41	06 46		06 59	06 47		06 53	06 58	06 59	07 00
	d	05 51		06 00		06 03	06 19	06 15	06 19		06 22	06 29	06 33	06 35	06 42	06 48		07 01	06 50	06 52	06 56	07 01	07 01	
Twyford 3	a	05 57				06 08	→		06 25		06 27				06 47	06 53		→		06 57			07 06	
Maidenhead 3	a	06 04				06 15			06 32		06 34			06 44		07 01				07 04	07 06		07 14	
Slough 3	a	06 14				06 26					06 44			06 50						07 14			07 21	
Ealing Broadway ⊖	a	06 37				06 51					07 07									07 37				
London Paddington 15 ⊖	a	06 47		06 25		07 02		06 38	06 52		07 17	06 54	07 00	07 05	07 08	07 22			07 14	07 47	07 24	07 27	07 40	

A From Bedwyn
B From Didcot Parkway
C From Newbury
D From Hereford
E From Banbury
F To Basingstoke
G From Bristol Temple Meads
H To London Paddington
I From Cheltenham Spa
J From Swansea
K From Worcester Shrub Hill

For complete services between Banbury and Birmingham, refer to Table T71

Birmingham, Banbury, Oxford and Bedwyn - Reading and London

		XR	GW ◇1 A 🍴	GW B	GW B	GW ◇1 C 🍴	XR	GW B	GW	GW ◇1 D 🍴	GW E	GW E	GW ◇1 F 🍴	XR	GW ◇	GW ◇1 G 🍴	GW	GW	GW ◇1 H 🍴	XR	GW	GW B	GW ◇1 🍴
Birmingham New Street 12 71	d																						
Birmingham International	d																						
Coventry	d																						
Leamington Spa 8	d																						
Banbury 71	d								06 04									06 25					
Kings Sutton	d								06 12									06 30					
Heyford	d								06 20									06 38					
Tackley	d								06 24									06 42					
Oxford 115	a								06 35									06 52					
	d								06 37	06 48								06 56					07 07
Radley	d								06 43									07 02					
Culham	d								06 47									07 06					
Appleford	d								06 50									07 09					
Didcot Parkway	a								06 56									07 15					07 19
	d			06 50	07 00				07 04							07 14						07 16	07 21
Cholsey	d			06 55					07 11													07 23	
Goring & Streatley	d			07 00					07 17													07 29	
Pangbourne	d			07 04					07 22													07 34	
Tilehurst	d			07 08					07 27													07 40	
Bedwyn	d		06 26																06 51		07 00		
Hungerford	d		06 33																06 57		07 06		
Kintbury	d		06 38																07 02		07 10		
Newbury	a		06 44																07 08		07 17		
	d		06 45												06 52				07 10				
Newbury Racecourse	d														06 54								
Thatcham	d		06 50												06 58				07 15				
Midgham	d														07 02								
Aldermaston	d														07 05								
Theale	d		07 02												07 10				07 23				
Reading West	d										←	←	←	←	07 17		←		07 29				
Reading 7	a		07 08	07 13	07 14				07 33	07 09	07 14	07 13			07 20	07 27			07 31			07 45	07 33
	d	07 05	07 10	07 18	07 16	07 20	07 22	07 30		07 12	07 16	07 18	07 20	07 22	07 24	07 29	07 30		07 34	07 34		07 47	07 37
Twyford 3	a	07 11		→	→	→	→	→				07 23		07 27			07 35			07 40		→	
Maidenhead 3	a	07 18										07 31		07 34	07 33		07 43			07 47			
Slough 3	a	07 29												07 44			07 50			07 57			
Ealing Broadway ⊖	a	07 52												08 07						08 21			
London Paddington 15 ⊖	a	08 02	07 35							07 39	07 42	07 52	07 44	08 17	07 54	07 59	08 19		08 01	08 32			08 05

		GW ◇1 A 🍴	XC ◇1 I 🍴	GW ◇1 J 🍴	GW E	GW ◇1 K 🍴	XR	GW B	GW	GW ◇1 D 🍴	GW	GW ◇1 A 🍴	GW E	GW ◇1 L 🍴	XC ◇1 M	XR	GW ◇1 N 🍴	GW B	GW ◇1 🍴	GW ◇1 O 🍴	GW E	GW ◇1 F 🍴	XR	GW ◇1 G 🍴
Birmingham New Street 12 71	d		06 04												06 33									
Birmingham International	d		06 14																					
Coventry	d		06 25																					
Leamington Spa 8	d		06 37												07 00									
Banbury 71	d		06 54												07 17									
Kings Sutton	d																							
Heyford	d																							
Tackley	d																							
Oxford 115	a		07 14												07 35									
	d		07 17						07 21	07 32					07 37				07 42	07 53				
Radley	d								07 27															
Culham	d								07 31															
Appleford	d								07 34															
Didcot Parkway	a								07 40										07 55					
	d			07 32				07 34	07 44			07 46						07 52	07 58					08 14
Cholsey	d							07 40	07 50									07 57						
Goring & Streatley	d							07 45	07 55									08 02						
Pangbourne	d							07 49	07 59									08 06						
Tilehurst	d							07 54	08 04									08 10						
Bedwyn	d													07 29										
Hungerford	d													07 36										
Kintbury	d																							
Newbury	a													07 44										
	d										07 25			07 45										
Newbury Racecourse	d										07 27													
Thatcham	d										07 31													
Midgham	d										07 35													
Aldermaston	d										07 38													
Theale	d										07 43													
Reading West	d				←	←					07 50		←				←				←			
Reading 7	a		07 41	07 44	07 45	07 44		07 59	08 10	07 53	07 55	07 58	07 59	08 01	08 03		08 01	08 15	08 10	08 14	08 15			08 26
	d	07 40		07 50	07 47	07 50	07 52	08 01		07 56		08 01	08 01	08 10		08 05	08 10	08 17	08 14	08 17	08 17	08 20	08 22	08 29
Twyford 3	a			→	07 53		07 57	→					08 06	→		08 10		→			08 22		08 27	
Maidenhead 3	a				08 01		08 04						08 13			08 17					08 30		08 34	
Slough 3	a						08 14						08 20			08 27							08 44	
Ealing Broadway ⊖	a						08 37									08 51							09 07	
London Paddington 15 ⊖	a	08 09			08 22	08 16	08 47			08 24		08 27	08 49			09 02	08 36		08 38	08 40	08 52	08 45	09 18	08 54

A From Bristol Temple Meads
B To London Paddington
C From Swansea to London Paddington
D From Hereford
E From Didcot Parkway
F From Swansea
G From Cheltenham Spa
H From Frome
I To Bournemouth
J From Cardiff Central to London Paddington
K From Cardiff Central
L From Plymouth to London Paddington
M To Southampton Central
N From Plymouth
O From Worcester Shrub Hill

For complete services between Banbury and Birmingham, refer to Table T71

Table T116-R

Mondays to Fridays

16 December to 15 May

Birmingham, Banbury, Oxford and Bedwyn - Reading and London

Station		GW		GW	GW	GW ◇1 A ✠	XR	GW B	GW ◇1 ✠	GW ◇1 C ✠	XC ◇1 D ✠	GW ◇1 E ✠	GW F	GW	XR	GW ◇1 G ✠	XR	GW B		GW H	GW ◇1 I ✠	GW F	GW ◇1	GW	XC ◇1 J ✠
Birmingham New Street 12 71	d										07 04														07 33
Birmingham International	d										07 14														
Coventry	d										07 25														
Leamington Spa 8	d										07 37														08 00
Banbury 71	d	07 28							07 45		07 54														08 17
Kings Sutton	d	07 33																							
Heyford	d	07 41																							
Tackley	d	07 45																							
Oxford 115	a	07 56							08 03		08 14														08 39
	d	07 58							08 07		08 16									08 26				08 35	08 41
Radley	d	08 04																		08 33				08 41	
Culham	d	08 08																							
Appleford	d																							08 46	
Didcot Parkway	a	08 15							08 19											08 41				08 52	
	d							08 16	08 20			08 32						08 38			08 46			08 56	
Cholsey	d							08 23										08 43						09 02	
Goring & Streatley	d							08 29										08 48						09 07	
Pangbourne	d							08 34										08 52						09 11	
Tilehurst	d							08 40										08 56						09 16	
Bedwyn	d													07 50									08 31		
Hungerford	d													07 56									08 37		
Kintbury	d													08 00									08 42		
Newbury	a													08 07									08 48		
	d			07 55										08 19		08 36							08 49		
Newbury Racecourse	d			07 58										08 21											
Thatcham	d			08 02										08 26									08 53		
Midgham	d			08 06										08 31											
Aldermaston	d			08 10										08 34											
Theale	d			08 15										08 39									09 01		
Reading West	d			08 22									←	08 48								←			
Reading 7	a			08 27				08 45	08 33		08 42	08 44	08 45	08 51		08 53		09 01			08 58	09 01	09 09	09 22	09 11
	d				08 31	08 33	08 35	08 48	08 35	08 38		08 47	08 48		08 52	08 56	09 03	09 08			09 04	09 08	09 11		
Twyford 8	a				08 36		08 40	→					08 53		08 57		09 08	→				09 13			
Maidenhead 8	a				08 43		08 47						09 00		09 04		09 15					09 21			
Slough 8	a				08 50		08 57								09 14		09 25					09 32			
Ealing Broadway ⊖	a						09 21								09 37		09 50					09 55			
London Paddington 15 ⊖	a				09 09	08 59	09 32		09 01	09 07		09 11	09 26		09 47	09 19	10 02				09 30	10 05	09 35		

Station		GW ◇1 K ✠	GW ◇1 L ✠	GW ◇1 M ✠	XR	GW ◇1 ✠	GW B	GW ◇1 N ✠	GW ◇1 O ✠	GW ◇1 P ✠		GW ◇	GW F	GW	XC ◇1 Q ✠	GW ◇1 R ✠	GW	XR	GW	GW ◇1 N ✠	GW ◇1 S ✠	GW B	GW	XC ◇1 T ✠	GW ◇1 M ✠
Birmingham New Street 12 71	d														08 04									08 33	
Birmingham International	d														08 14										
Coventry	d														08 25										
Leamington Spa 8	d														08 37									09 00	
Banbury 71	d														08 54									09 17	
Kings Sutton	d																								
Heyford	d																								
Tackley	d																								
Oxford 115	a														09 14									09 40	
	d	08 49				09 02								09 06	09 16		09 20			09 32			09 37	09 42	
Radley	d													09 12											
Culham	d													09 16											
Appleford	d																								
Didcot Parkway	a													09 23			09 32						09 49		
	d		09 02				09 09	09 17		09 27				09 27								09 38			
Cholsey	d						09 15							09 33								09 43			
Goring & Streatley	d						09 19							09 38								09 48			
Pangbourne	d						09 23							09 43								09 52			
Tilehurst	d						09 27							09 47								09 56			
Bedwyn	d																								
Hungerford	d																								
Kintbury	d																								
Newbury	a																								
	d											09 19							09 25						
Newbury Racecourse	d																		09 27						
Thatcham	d											09 24							09 31						
Midgham	d																		09 35						
Aldermaston	d																		09 38						
Theale	d											09 32							09 44						
Reading West	d												←						09 50						
Reading 7	a	09 11	09 14			09 24	09 33	09 29		09 39		09 40	09 33	09 53	09 40				09 55	09 55		10 01		10 06	
	d	09 13	09 16	09 20	09 22	09 28	09 45	09 33	09 35	09 42		09 44	09 45			09 47		09 52		09 57	10 03	10 15			10 08
Twyford 8	a				09 27		→						09 50					09 57				→			
Maidenhead 8	a				09 34								09 57					10 04							
Slough 8	a				09 44								10 04					10 14		10 09					
Ealing Broadway ⊖	a				10 08								10 24					10 37							
London Paddington 15 ⊖	a	09 37	09 39	09 44	10 17	09 54		09 57	09 59	10 07		10 09	10 32			10 12		10 47		10 24	10 29				10 34

A From Plymouth. The Armada
B To London Paddington
C From Weston-super-Mare
D From Manchester Piccadilly to Bournemouth
E From Cardiff Central
F From Didcot Parkway
G From Plymouth
H From Worcester Foregate Street
I From Bristol Temple Meads
J From Sheffield
K From Hereford. The Cathedrals Express
L From Swindon
M From Swansea
N From Worcester Shrub Hill
O From Penzance. The Golden Hind
P From Taunton
Q From Nottingham to Bournemouth
R From Swansea. Y Cymro/The Welshman
S From Paignton
T From York to Southampton Central

For complete services between Banbury and Birmingham, refer to Table T71

NRT DECEMBER 19 EDITION

Table T116-R

Mondays to Fridays

16 December to 15 May

Birmingham, Banbury, Oxford and Bedwyn - Reading and London

Station		GW ◇1 ✠		GW A	GW ◇1 B ✠	XR	GW ◇1 ✠	GW C	GW ◇1 D ✠	GW	GW	GW A	GW ◇1 B ✠	XC 1 E ✠	GW ◇1 F ✠	XR	GW ◇	GW ◇1 G ✠		GW ◇1 H ✠	GW	GW	GW ◇1 B ✠	XC ◇1 I ✠	GW ◇1 J ✠
Birmingham New Street 12 71	d													09 04										09 33	
Birmingham International	d													09 14											
Coventry	d													09 25											
Leamington Spa 8	d													09 37										10 04	
Banbury 71	d									09 36				09 54										10 21	
Kings Sutton	d									09 41															
Heyford	d									09 49															
Tackley	d									09 53															
Oxford 115	a									10 03				10 12										10 40	
	d						09 59			10 03				10 16				10 32				10 37		10 42	
Radley	d									10 10															
Culham	d									10 14															
Appleford	d									10 16															
Didcot Parkway	a									10 22												10 49			
	d				10 02			10 13	10 15				10 27								10 38		10 57		
Cholsey	d							10 18													10 43				
Goring & Streatley	d							10 23													10 48				
Pangbourne	d							10 27													10 52				
Tilehurst	d							10 31													10 56				
Bedwyn	d	09 24																							
Hungerford	d	09 30																							
Kintbury	d	09 35																							
Newbury	a	09 41																							
	d	09 50									10 06						10 30								
Newbury Racecourse	d										10 08														
Thatcham	d	09 54									10 12														
Midgham	d										10 16														
Aldermaston	d										10 19														
Theale	d	10 02									10 24														
Reading West	d			←							10 31	←													
Reading 7	a	10 11		10 01	10 14		10 23	10 36	10 27		10 35	10 36	10 39	10 40			10 50	10 54			11 01		11 09	11 10	
	d	10 12		10 15	10 16	10 22	10 26	10 38	10 34			10 38	10 42		10 47	10 52	10 54	10 57		11 04	11 04		11 12		11 16
Twyford 8	a			10 20		10 27		→				10 43				10 57					11 09				
Maidenhead 8	a			10 27		10 34						10 51				11 04					11 18				
Slough 8	a			10 34		10 44	10 38					11 01				11 14		11 08			11 32				
Ealing Broadway ⊖	a			10 51		11 07						11 22				11 37					11 51				
London Paddington 15 ⊖	a	10 37		11 04	10 39	11 17	10 53		10 59			11 35	11 07		11 12	11 47	11 22	11 24		11 29	12 01		11 37		11 39

Station		XR	GW ◇1 ✠	GW ◇1 ✠	GW C	GW ◇1 D ✠	GW A	GW	GW	GW ◇1 K ✠		XC ◇1 E ✠	GW ◇1 B ✠	GW ◇1 L ✠	GW ◇1 M ✠	XR	GW ◇1 G ✠	GW ◇1 H ✠	GW C	GW	XC ◇1 N ✠	GW ◇1 B ✠	GW A	GW ◇1 J ✠	XR
Birmingham New Street 12 71	d											10 04									10 33				
Birmingham International	d											10 14													
Coventry	d											10 25													
Leamington Spa 8	d											10 37									11 00				
Banbury 71	d											10 54									11 18				
Kings Sutton	d																								
Heyford	d																								
Tackley	d																								
Oxford 115	a											11 12									11 40				
	d			11 02					11 07			11 16					11 32			11 37	11 42				
Radley	d								11 13																
Culham	d																								
Appleford	d																								
Didcot Parkway	a								11 22											11 49					
	d				11 08	11 15							11 27						11 33			11 57			
Cholsey	d				11 13														11 38						
Goring & Streatley	d				11 18														11 44						
Pangbourne	d				11 22														11 48						
Tilehurst	d				11 26														11 53						
Bedwyn	d		10 41																						
Hungerford	d		10 47																						
Kintbury	d		10 52																						
Newbury	a		10 58																						
	d		10 59					11 06		11 22															
Newbury Racecourse	d							11 08																	
Thatcham	d		11 03					11 12																	
Midgham	d							11 16																	
Aldermaston	d							11 19																	
Theale	d		11 11					11 24																	
Reading West	d						←	11 31						←									←		
Reading 7	a		11 21	11 24	11 31	11 28	11 31	11 35		11 38		11 39	11 39	11 38			11 54		11 59		12 07	12 09	11 59		
	d	11 19	11 24	11 26	11 36	11 34	11 36			11 43			11 42	11 43	11 48	11 52	11 57	12 04	12 13			12 12	12 13	12 17	12 22
Twyford 8	a	11 24			→		11 41			→						11 57			→				12 18		12 27
Maidenhead 8	a	11 31					11 49									12 04							12 25		12 34
Slough 8	a	11 41		11 38			11 57									12 14	12 08						12 32		12 44
Ealing Broadway ⊖	a	12 04					12 19									12 37							12 49		13 07
London Paddington 15 ⊖	a	12 17	11 52	11 54		11 59	12 31						12 07	12 09	12 11	12 47	12 24	12 29				12 37	13 01	12 40	13 17

A From Didcot Parkway
B From Bristol Temple Meads
C To London Paddington
D From Cheltenham Spa
E From Manchester Piccadilly to Bournemouth
F From Carmarthen. The Red Dragon
G From Great Malvern
H From Penzance
I From Newcastle
J From Cardiff Central
K From Plymouth to London Paddington
L From Plymouth
M From Swansea
N From Newcastle to Southampton Central

For complete services between Banbury and Birmingham, refer to Table T71

Table T116-R

Mondays to Fridays
16 December to 15 May

Birmingham, Banbury, Oxford and Bedwyn - Reading and London

		GW		GW	GW	GW	GW	GW	GW	XC	GW	GW	XR	GW	GW	GW	GW	GW		XC	GW	GW	XR	GW	GW
		◇1		◇1		◇1			◇1	◇1		◇1		◇	◇1	◇1				◇1	◇1	◇1		◇1	◇1
					A	B	C		D	E		F			G	H				I	D	J			
		T		T		T			T	T		T			T	T				T	T	T		T	T
Birmingham New Street 12 71	d									11 04										11 33					
Birmingham International	d									11 14															
Coventry	d									11 25															
Leamington Spa 8	d									11 37										12 03					
Banbury 71	d									11 54										12 20					
Kings Sutton	d																								
Heyford	d																								
Tackley	d																								
Oxford 115	a									12 12										12 41					
	d			12 02				12 07		12 16					12 32			12 37		12 43				13 02	
Radley	d							12 13																	
Culham	d																								
Appleford	d																								
Didcot Parkway	a							12 22										12 49							
	d				12 08	12 16			12 28								12 36				12 57				
Cholsey	d				12 13												12 41								
Goring & Streatley	d				12 18												12 46								
Pangbourne	d				12 22												12 50								
Tilehurst	d				12 26												12 54								
Bedwyn	d	11 41																							12 41
Hungerford	d	11 47																							12 47
Kintbury	d	11 52																							12 52
Newbury	a	11 58																							12 58
	d	11 59									12 09			12 27											13 02
Newbury Racecourse	d										12 12														
Thatcham	d	12 03									12 16														13 06
Midgham	d										12 20														
Aldermaston	d										12 24														
Theale	d	12 11									12 29														13 14
Reading West	d						←				12 39														
Reading 7	a	12 21		12 24	12 33	12 28	12 33		12 40	12 42	12 42			12 45	12 54		13 00			13 06	13 09			13 24	13 24
	d	12 24		12 26	12 38	12 34	12 38		12 42			12 47	12 52	12 54	12 57	13 04	13 08				13 12	13 16	13 22	13 26	13 31
Twyford 3	a				→		12 43						12 57				13 13						13 27		
Maidenhead 3	a						12 51						13 04				13 21						13 34		
Slough 3	a			12 38			13 01						13 14		13 08		13 32						13 44	13 38	
Ealing Broadway ⊖	a						13 21						13 37				13 51						14 08		
London Paddington 15 ⊖	a	12 52		12 54		12 59	13 31		13 07			13 10	13 47	13 22	13 24	13 29	14 01				13 37	13 40	14 17	13 54	13 57

		GW	GW	GW	GW	GW	GW	XC	GW	GW		XR	GW	GW	GW	GW	GW	XC	GW	XR	GW	GW	GW	GW	GW
			◇1				◇1	◇1	◇1	◇1			◇1	◇1			◇1	◇1	◇1		◇1	◇1		◇1	
		A	B	C			D	E	K	F			G	L			D	M	J				A	B	
			T				T	T	R	T			T	T			T	T	T		T	T		T	
Birmingham New Street 12 71	d							12 04										12 33							
Birmingham International	d							12 14																	
Coventry	d							12 25																	
Leamington Spa 8	d							12 37										13 00							
Banbury 71	d				12 34			12 54										13 20							
Kings Sutton	d				12 39																				
Heyford	d				12 50																				
Tackley	d				12 54																				
Oxford 115	a				13 05			13 12										13 40							
	d				13 07			13 16					13 32			13 37		13 42				14 02			14 07
Radley	d				13 13																				14 13
Culham	d				13 17																				
Appleford	d				13 20																				
Didcot Parkway	a				13 26											13 49									14 22
	d	13 06	13 16				13 27								13 39		13 57						14 08	14 16	
Cholsey	d	13 12													13 44								14 13		
Goring & Streatley	d	13 17													13 49								14 18		
Pangbourne	d	13 21													13 53								14 22		
Tilehurst	d	13 26													13 57								14 26		
Bedwyn	d																				13 41				
Hungerford	d																				13 47				
Kintbury	d																				13 52				
Newbury	a																				13 58				
	d					13 10			13 25												13 59				
Newbury Racecourse	d					13 12																			
Thatcham	d					13 16															14 04				
Midgham	d					13 20																			
Aldermaston	d					13 23																			
Theale	d					13 28															14 12				
Reading West	d			←		13 34																			
Reading 7	a	13 31	13 29	13 31		13 38	13 39	13 40	13 41				13 54		14 03		14 09	14 09			14 21	14 24	14 31	14 28	
	d	13 38	13 34	13 38			13 41		13 42	13 47		13 52	13 57	14 04	14 09		14 11		14 18	14 22	14 24	14 26	14 45	14 35	
Twyford 3	a	→		13 43								13 57			14 14					14 27			→		
Maidenhead 3	a			13 51								14 04			14 24					14 35					
Slough 3	a			14 01								14 14	14 08		14 32					14 45		14 38			
Ealing Broadway ⊖	a			14 21								14 37			14 51					15 07					
London Paddington 15 ⊖	a		13 59	14 31			14 07		14 09	14 11		14 47	14 24	14 27	15 01		14 36		14 41	15 17	14 52	14 54		15 01	

A To London Paddington
B From Cheltenham Spa
C From Didcot Parkway
D From Bristol Temple Meads
E From Manchester Piccadilly to Bournemouth
F From Swansea
G From Great Malvern
H From Penzance
I From Edinburgh
J From Cardiff Central
K From Paignton
L From Penzance. The Cornish Riviera
M From Newcastle to Southampton Central

For complete services between Banbury and Birmingham, refer to Table T71

Table T116-R

Mondays to Fridays
16 December to 15 May

Birmingham, Banbury, Oxford and Bedwyn - Reading and London

		GW		GW	XC	GW	GW	XR	GW	GW	GW	GW	GW	XC	GW	GW	XR	GW		GW	GW	GW	GW	GW	GW
		◇1			◇1		◇1		◇	◇1	1			◇1	◇1	◇1		◇1		◇1		◇1			
		A		B	C		D			E	F			G	A	H					I	J	B		
		T			T		T			T	T			T	T	T		T		T		T			
Birmingham New Street 12 71	d				13 04									13 33											
Birmingham International	d				13 14																				
Coventry	d				13 25																				
Leamington Spa 8	d				13 37									14 03											
Banbury 71	d				13 54									14 20											
Kings Sutton	d																								
Heyford	d																								
Tackley	d																								
Oxford 115	a				14 12									14 40											
	d				14 16					14 32			14 37	14 42						15 02				15 07	
Radley	d																							15 13	
Culham	d																							15 17	
Appleford	d																								
Didcot Parkway	a												14 49											15 24	
	d	14 27										14 36			14 57						15 08	15 16			
Cholsey	d											14 41									15 13				
Goring & Streatley	d											14 46									15 18				
Pangbourne	d											14 50									15 22				
Tilehurst	d											14 54									15 26				
Bedwyn	d																	14 41							
Hungerford	d																	14 47							
Kintbury	d																	14 52							
Newbury	a																	14 58							
	d					14 10			14 26									14 59							15 09
Newbury Racecourse	d					14 12																			15 11
Thatcham	d					14 16												15 03							15 15
Midgham	d					14 20																			15 19
Aldermaston	d					14 23																			15 22
Theale	d					14 28												15 11							15 27
Reading West	d			←		14 36																	←		15 33
Reading 7	a	14 39		14 31	14 40	14 40			14 48	14 54		14 59		15 05	15 09			15 21		15 24	15 32	15 29	15 32		15 36
	d	14 42		14 45			14 47	14 52	14 53	14 57	15 04	15 10			15 12	15 17	15 22	15 24		15 27	15 38	15 34	15 38		
Twyford 3	a			14 50				14 57				15 15					15 27				→		15 43		
Maidenhead 3	a			14 57				15 04				15 22					15 34						15 51		
Slough 3	a			15 04				15 14		15 08		15 32					15 44			15 38			16 01		
Ealing Broadway ⊖	a			15 21				15 37				15 51					16 07						16 24		
London Paddington 15 ⊖	a	15 08		15 31			15 12	15 47	15 22	15 24	15 29	16 02			15 36	15 41	16 17	15 52		15 54		15 59	16 36		

		XC	GW	GW	GW	XR	GW	GW	GW	GW		XC	GW	GW	GW	XR	GW	GW	GW	GW	GW	XR	GW	GW	GW
		◇1	◇1	◇1	◇1		◇1	◇1				◇1	◇1		◇1		◇1	◇1		◇1			◇1		◇1
		C	A	D	K		L	M	I			N	A	B	H				I	O			P	B	A
		T	T	T	T		T	T				T	T		T		T	T		T			T		T
Birmingham New Street 12 71	d	14 04										14 33													
Birmingham International	d	14 14																							
Coventry	d	14 25																							
Leamington Spa 8	d	14 37										15 00													
Banbury 71	d	14 54								15 07		15 17													
Kings Sutton	d									15 12															
Heyford	d									15 20															
Tackley	d									15 24															
Oxford 115	a	15 12								15 35		15 40													
	d	15 16					15 32			15 37		15 42						16 02							
Radley	d																								
Culham	d																								
Appleford	d																								
Didcot Parkway	a									15 49															
	d		15 27						15 38				15 57						16 08	16 17					16 27
Cholsey	d								15 43										16 13						
Goring & Streatley	d								15 48										16 18						
Pangbourne	d								15 52										16 22						
Tilehurst	d								15 56										16 26						
Bedwyn	d																15 41								
Hungerford	d																15 47								
Kintbury	d																15 52								
Newbury	a																15 58								
	d				15 29												15 59				16 04				
Newbury Racecourse	d																				16 06				
Thatcham	d																16 03				16 10				
Midgham	d																				16 14				
Aldermaston	d																				16 17				
Theale	d																16 11				16 22				
Reading West	d													←							16 29		←	←	
Reading 7	a	15 39	15 39		15 43		15 54		16 02			16 07	16 09	16 02			16 20	16 24	16 31	16 29	16 32		16 29	16 31	16 39
	d		15 41	15 46	15 48	15 52	15 57	16 04	16 15				16 12	16 15	16 18	16 22	16 25	16 27	16 38	16 34		16 33	16 34	16 38	16 41
Twyford 3	a					15 57			→					16 20		16 27			→	→		16 38		16 43	
Maidenhead 3	a					16 04								16 27		16 34						16 45		16 50	
Slough 3	a					16 14	16 08							16 34		16 44		16 39				16 56		17 00	
Ealing Broadway ⊖	a					16 37								16 55		17 07						17 21		17 25	
London Paddington 15 ⊖	a		16 07	16 09	16 11	16 49	16 24	16 29					16 36	17 04	16 44	17 17	16 54	16 57				17 33	17 00	17 35	17 07

A From Bristol Temple Meads
B From Didcot Parkway
C From Manchester Piccadilly to Bournemouth
D From Swansea
E From Worcester Shrub Hill
F From Penzance. The Cornishman
G From Newcastle
H From Cardiff Central
I To London Paddington
J From Cheltenham Spa
K From Exeter St Davids
L From Hereford
M From Plymouth
N From Newcastle to Southampton Central
O From Cheltenham Spa to London Paddington. The Cheltenham Spa Express
P From Cheltenham Spa. The Cheltenham Spa Express

For complete services between Banbury and Birmingham, refer to Table T71

Table T116-R

Mondays to Fridays

16 December to 15 May

Birmingham, Banbury, Oxford and Bedwyn - Reading and London

		GW		XC ◇1 A	GW ◇1 B	GW ◇1 C	XR	GW ◇ D	GW ◇1 E	GW ◇ F	XR	GW ◇1 G	GW	GW	GW ◇1 H	XC ◇1 I	GW ◇1 J	XR		GW	GW	GW D	GW ◇1 K	GW	XR
Birmingham New Street 12 71	d			15 04												15 33									
Birmingham International	d			15 14																					
Coventry	d			15 25																					
Leamington Spa 8	d			15 37												16 03									
Banbury 71	d			15 54												16 21									
Kings Sutton	d																								
Heyford	d																								
Tackley	d																								
Oxford 115	a			16 12												16 40									
	d	16 07		16 16					16 32					16 37		16 42					17 01				
Radley	d	16 13												16 43											
Culham	d																								
Appleford	d	16 18																							
Didcot Parkway	a	16 24												16 52											
	d	16 28											16 38		16 57							17 08	17 16		
Cholsey	d	16 34											16 43									17 13			
Goring & Streatley	d	16 39											16 48									17 18			
Pangbourne	d	16 43											16 52									17 22			
Tilehurst	d	16 48											16 56									17 26			
Bedwyn	d																			16 41					
Hungerford	d																			16 47					
Kintbury	d																			16 52					
Newbury	a																			16 58					
	d							16 34												16 59				17 05	
Newbury Racecourse	d																							17 07	
Thatcham	d																			17 03				17 11	
Midgham	d																							17 15	
Aldermaston	d																							17 18	
Theale	d																			17 11				17 23	
Reading West	d									←														17 30	
Reading 7	a	16 53		16 41				16 51	16 54	16 51			17 01		17 09	17 09				17 22	17 24	17 32	17 28	17 33	
	d				16 46	16 48	16 52	17 00	16 57	17 00	17 03	17 05	17 06		17 11		17 18	17 22		17 24	17 27	17 41	17 33		17 34
Twyford 3	a						16 57	→			17 08		17 13					17 27				→			17 39
Maidenhead 3	a						17 04				17 15		17 22					17 34							17 46
Slough 3	a						17 14		17 08		17 26		17 30					17 44			17 38				17 57
Ealing Broadway ⊖	a						17 37				17 51		17 55					18 07							18 21
London Paddington 15 ⊖	a				17 09	17 12	17 48		17 24	17 27	18 02	17 29	18 04		17 35		17 41	18 17		17 50	17 54		17 56		18 32

		GW ◇1 L	GW	XC ◇1 A	GW ◇1 H	GW M	GW ◇1 N	GW ◇1 O	XR	GW ◇1 P		GW ◇1 Q	XR	GW	GW	GW ◇1 H	XC ◇1 R	GW ◇1 J	GW	GW ◇1 D	XR	GW	GW ◇1 S	XR	GW D
Birmingham New Street 12 71	d			16 04													16 33								
Birmingham International	d			16 14																					
Coventry	d			16 25																					
Leamington Spa 8	d			16 37													17 00								
Banbury 71	d			16 54													17 17		17 20						
Kings Sutton	d																		17 25						
Heyford	d																		17 33						
Tackley	d																		17 37						
Oxford 115	a			17 14													17 39		17 49						
	d		17 07	17 16								17 32			17 36		17 42			18 02					
Radley	d		17 13												17 42										
Culham	d		17 17																						
Appleford	d														17 47										
Didcot Parkway	a		17 24												17 53										
	d		17 33											17 38		17 57									18 04
Cholsey	d		17 39											17 43											18 09
Goring & Streatley	d		17 44											17 48											18 14
Pangbourne	d		17 48											17 52											18 18
Tilehurst	d		17 53											17 57											18 22
Bedwyn	d																					17 41			
Hungerford	d																					17 47			
Kintbury	d																					17 52			
Newbury	a																					17 58			
	d	17 21																				17 59			
Newbury Racecourse	d																								
Thatcham	d																					18 04			
Midgham	d																								
Aldermaston	d																								
Theale	d																					18 13			
Reading West	d					←	←																←		
Reading 7	a	17 38	17 59	17 39		17 32	17 38					17 56		18 02		18 09	18 11			18 24		18 25	18 24		18 29
	d	17 42			17 40	17 41	17 42	17 50	17 52	17 58		18 00	18 05	18 09		18 12		18 18		18 28	18 22	18 26	18 28	18 33	18 41
Twyford 3	a	→				17 46			17 57				18 10	18 14						→	18 27			18 38	→
Maidenhead 3	a					17 53			18 04				18 17	18 21							18 34			18 45	
Slough 3	a					18 01			18 14			18 11	18 28	18 32							18 44		18 42	18 56	
Ealing Broadway ⊖	a					18 26			18 37				18 51	18 55							19 07			19 21	
London Paddington 15 ⊖	a				18 07	18 34	18 09	18 15	18 48	18 24		18 29	19 02	19 06		18 39		18 41			19 17	18 54	18 59	19 32	

A From Manchester Piccadilly to Bournemouth
B From Swansea
C From Paignton. The Torbay Express
D To London Paddington
E From Worcester Shrub Hill
F From Newbury
G From Penzance. The Royal Duchy
H From Bristol Temple Meads
I From Newcastle
J From Cardiff Central
K From Cheltenham Spa
L From Exeter St Davids to London Paddington
M From Didcot Parkway
N From Exeter St Davids
O From Swansea. The Saint David
P From Plymouth. The Mayflower
Q From Hereford
R From Newcastle to Guildford
S From Oxford

For complete services between Banbury and Birmingham, refer to Table T71

Table T116-R

Mondays to Fridays

16 December to 15 May

Birmingham, Banbury, Oxford and Bedwyn - Reading and London

		GW ◇1 A		GW B	GW	GW	GW ◇1 C	GW ◇1	GW	XC ◇1 D	GW ◇1 E	XR	GW ◇1 F	GW ◇1 G	XR	GW	GW	GW ◇1 C		XC ◇1 H	GW	GW ◇1 I	XR	GW ◇1	GW ◇1 J
Birmingham New Street 12 71	d									17 04										17 33					
Birmingham International	d									17 14															
Coventry	d									17 25															
Leamington Spa 8	d									17 37										18 01					
Banbury 71	d									17 55										18 18					
Kings Sutton	d																								
Heyford	d																								
Tackley	d																								
Oxford 115	a									18 13										18 40					
	d								18 07	18 16				18 32			18 35			18 42					19 02
Radley	d								18 13								18 41								
Culham	d								18 17																
Appleford	d																18 46								
Didcot Parkway	a								18 26								18 52								
	d	18 17					18 27		18 34							18 38		18 57							
Cholsey	d								18 40							18 44									
Goring & Streatley	d								18 45							18 49									
Pangbourne	d								18 49							18 54									
Tilehurst	d								18 54							18 58									
Bedwyn	d					17 53																		18 40	
Hungerford	d					17 59																		18 46	
Kintbury	d					18 03																		18 50	
Newbury	a					18 10																		18 56	
	d				18 04			18 20													18 47			18 57	
Newbury Racecourse	d				18 06																18 49				
Thatcham	d				18 10			18 25													18 53			19 02	
Midgham	d				18 14																18 57				
Aldermaston	d				18 17																19 00				
Theale	d				18 22			18 33													19 05			19 10	
Reading West	d			←	18 29																19 12				
Reading 7	a	18 30		18 29	18 35		18 39	18 41	19 00	18 42				18 57		19 04		19 09		19 10	19 15			19 18	19 24
	d	18 34		18 41			18 43	18 45			18 50	18 52	18 58	19 00	19 04	19 14		19 15				19 18	19 22	19 24	19 27
Twyford 3	a			18 46								18 57			19 09	19 19							19 27		
Maidenhead 3	a			18 55								19 04			19 16	19 26							19 34		
Slough 3	a			19 03								19 14		19 11	19 27	19 35							19 44		19 38
Ealing Broadway ⊖	a			19 33								19 39			19 51	19 56							20 07		
London Paddington 15 ⊖	a	19 01		19 42			19 09	19 12			19 14	19 48	19 24	19 28	20 02	20 06		19 39				19 42	20 17	19 52	19 54

		GW	GW K	GW ◇1 A	GW B	GW	GW ◇1 C	XC ◇1 D	GW ◇1 E	XR		GW ◇1 L	GW ◇1 J	GW K	GW	GW	XC ◇1 H	GW ◇1 C	GW B	XR	GW K	GW ◇1 I	GW ◇1	GW B	GW ◇1 A
Birmingham New Street 12 71	d							18 04									18 33								
Birmingham International	d							18 14																	
Coventry	d							18 25																	
Leamington Spa 8	d							18 37									19 01								
Banbury 71	d					18 36		18 55									19 18						19 44		
Kings Sutton	d					18 41																			
Heyford	d					18 50																			
Tackley	d					18 54																			
Oxford 115	a					19 05		19 14									19 40						20 02		
	d					19 07		19 16					19 32		19 36		19 42						20 06		
Radley	d					19 13									19 42										
Culham	d																								
Appleford	d																								
Didcot Parkway	a					19 22									19 51										
	d		19 04	19 16			19 27		19 33					19 34				19 58			20 03	20 10			20 20
Cholsey	d		19 09											19 39							20 08				
Goring & Streatley	d		19 14											19 44							20 13				
Pangbourne	d		19 18											19 48							20 17				
Tilehurst	d		19 22											19 52							20 21				
Bedwyn	d	19 03																							
Hungerford	d	19 09																							
Kintbury	d	19 13																							
Newbury	a	19 20																							
	d											19 35				19 42									
Newbury Racecourse	d																								
Thatcham	d															19 47									
Midgham	d																								
Aldermaston	d																								
Theale	d															19 55									
Reading West	d				←														←					←	
Reading 7	a		19 27	19 28	19 27		19 39	19 39	19 45			19 52	19 53	19 57		20 03	20 10	20 10	19 57		20 26	20 22	20 28	20 26	20 32
	d		19 38	19 34	19 38		19 41		19 48	19 52		19 53	19 56	20 15				20 12	20 15	20 22	20 34	20 28	20 31	20 34	20 36
Twyford 3	a		→		19 43					19 57				→					20 20	20 27	→			20 39	
Maidenhead 3	a				19 50					20 04									20 27	20 34				20 46	
Slough 3	a				20 01					20 14			20 08						20 34	20 44			20 42	20 54	
Ealing Broadway ⊖	a				20 21					20 37									20 51	21 07				21 18	
London Paddington 15 ⊖	a			19 57	20 30		20 05		20 14	20 47		20 22	20 24					20 36	21 01	21 17		20 54	20 59	21 31	21 01

A From Cheltenham Spa
B From Didcot Parkway
C From Bristol Temple Meads
D From Manchester Piccadilly to Bournemouth
E From Swansea
F From Penzance
G From Great Malvern
H From Newcastle
I From Cardiff Central
J From Worcester Foregate Street
K To London Paddington
L From Plymouth

For complete services between Banbury and Birmingham, refer to Table T71

Table T116-R

Mondays to Fridays
16 December to 15 May

Birmingham, Banbury, Oxford and Bedwyn - Reading and London

		GW		GW ◇1 A 🚲	XC ◇1 B 🚲	GW	GW ◇1 C 🚲	GW	GW ◇	XR	GW ◇1 D 🚲	GW ◇1 E 🚲	GW	GW	XC ◇1 F 🚲	GW ◇1 A 🚲	XR	GW ◇1 🚲		GW ◇1 🚲	GW	GW ◇1 G 🚲	GW	GW	XC ◇1 B 🚲
Birmingham New Street [12] 71	d				19 04										19 33										20 04
Birmingham International	d				19 14																				20 14
Coventry	d				19 25																				20 25
Leamington Spa [8]	d				19 37										20 02										20 37
Banbury 71	d				19 54									20 07	20 19										20 54
Kings Sutton	d													20 12											
Heyford	d													20 20											
Tackley	d													20 24											
Oxford 115	a				20 13									20 34	20 40										21 12
	d	20 10			20 16						20 32			20 37	20 42					21 02			21 07		21 15
Radley	d	20 16																					21 13		
Culham	d	20 20																							
Appleford	d																								
Didcot Parkway	a	20 27												20 49									21 22		
	d			20 27									20 38			20 57					21 04	21 20			
Cholsey	d												20 43								21 09				
Goring & Streatley	d												20 48								21 15				
Pangbourne	d												20 52								21 19				
Tilehurst	d												20 56								21 23				
Bedwyn	d							20 00										20 42							
Hungerford	d							20 06										20 48							
Kintbury	d							20 11										20 52							
Newbury	a							20 18										20 58							
	d					20 14			20 32									21 01						21 10	
Newbury Racecourse	d					20 16																		21 12	
Thatcham	d					20 20												21 05						21 16	
Midgham	d					20 24																		21 20	
Aldermaston	d					20 27																		21 23	
Theale	d					20 32												21 13						21 28	
Reading West	d					20 41																		21 35	
Reading [7]	a			20 39	20 43	20 44			20 48		20 53		21 02		21 06	21 09		21 21		21 24	21 29	21 32		21 38	21 40
	d			20 42			20 46		20 49	20 52	20 56	21 05	21 08			21 12	21 22	21 23		21 26	21 38	21 38			
Twyford [3]	a									20 57			21 13				21 27				21 43				
Maidenhead [3]	a									21 04			21 20				21 34				21 51				
Slough [3]	a									21 14	21 07		21 33				21 44			21 38	22 00				
Ealing Broadway ⊖	a									21 37			21 52				22 07				22 22				
London Paddington [15] ⊖	a			21 08			21 10		21 14	21 47	21 22	21 29	22 01			21 37	22 17	21 52		21 54	22 31	22 06			

		GW ◇1 C 🚲	GW	XR	GW H	GW	GW ◇1 D 🚲	GW ◇1 I 🚲	XC ◇1 J	GW ◇1 A 🚲		GW K	GW	GW ◇1 🚲	XR	GW ◇1 🚲	GW FX ◇1 G 🚲	GW FO ◇1 G 🚲	GW	XC ◇1 L	GW ◇1 C 🚲	GW	GW	XR	GW ◇1 M 🚲
Birmingham New Street [12] 71	d								20 33											21 04					
Birmingham International	d																			21 14					
Coventry	d																			21 25					
Leamington Spa [8]	d								21 00											21 37					
Banbury 71	d								21 17										21 37	21 54					
Kings Sutton	d																		21 42						
Heyford	d																		21 50						
Tackley	d																		21 54						
Oxford 115	a								21 39										22 05	22 13					
	d					21 27	21 32		21 44							22 02			22 06	22 16					22 32
Radley	d																		22 12						
Culham	d																								
Appleford	d																								
Didcot Parkway	a					21 39													22 21						22 44
	d				21 38					21 56							22 15	22 15	22 22						22 45
Cholsey	d				21 43														22 28						
Goring & Streatley	d				21 48														22 33						
Pangbourne	d				21 52														22 37						
Tilehurst	d				21 58														22 42						
Bedwyn	d		21 10											21 41								22 19			
Hungerford	d		21 16											21 47								22 25			
Kintbury	d		21 20											21 51								22 29			
Newbury	a		21 27											21 57								22 36			
	d							21 41					21 46	21 59											
Newbury Racecourse	d												21 48												
Thatcham	d												21 52	22 03											
Midgham	d												21 56												
Aldermaston	d												21 59												
Theale	d												22 03	22 11											
Reading West	d											←	22 10												
Reading [7]	a				22 03		21 53	21 59	22 07	22 08		22 03	22 13	22 21		22 24	22 27	22 29	22 47	22 40					22 57
	d	21 46		21 52	22 15		21 56	22 04		22 10		22 15		22 22	22 22	22 26	22 35	22 35			22 46		22 48	22 52	22 59
Twyford [3]	a			21 57	→							22 20			22 27								22 53	22 57	
Maidenhead [3]	a			22 04								22 27			22 34								23 00	23 04	23 08
Slough [3]	a			22 14			22 07					22 34			22 44	22 38							23 07	23 14	23 18
Ealing Broadway ⊖	a			22 37								22 53			23 07								23 24	23 37	
London Paddington [15] ⊖	a	22 09		22 47			22 24	22 29		22 35		23 03		22 45	23 18	22 54	23 00	23 00			23 09		23 36	23 47	23 44

A From Bristol Temple Meads
B From Manchester Piccadilly to Bournemouth
C From Swansea
D From Great Malvern
E From Penzance
F From Newcastle
G From Cheltenham Spa
H To London Paddington
I From Plymouth
J From Newcastle to Southampton Central
K From Didcot Parkway
L From Manchester Piccadilly to Southampton Central
M From Worcester Foregate Street

For complete services between Banbury and Birmingham, refer to Table T71

Table T116-R

Mondays to Fridays
16 December to 15 May

Birmingham, Banbury, Oxford and Bedwyn - Reading and London

		GW ◇1 A 🚲		GW	GW	GW	GW ◇	GW	XC ◇1	GW	GW ◇1 B 🚲	GW	CH C
Birmingham New Street [12] 71	d								22 04				
Birmingham International	d								22 14				
Coventry	d								22 25				
Leamington Spa [8]	d								22 37				23 39
Banbury 71	d				22 32				22 54	23 45			23 58
Kings Sutton	d				22 37					23 50			
Heyford	d				22 45					23 58			
Tackley	d				22 49					00 02			
Oxford 115	a				22 59				23 12	00 12			00 21
	d			22 47			23 05		23 16				
Radley	d			22 53									
Culham	d			22 57									
Appleford	d			23 00									
Didcot Parkway	a			23 06			23 17						
	d	22 59					23 18	23 22			23 36		
Cholsey	d							23 28					
Goring & Streatley	d							23 32					
Pangbourne	d							23 36					
Tilehurst	d							23 40					
Bedwyn	d											23 17	
Hungerford	d											23 23	
Kintbury	d											23 27	
Newbury	a											23 34	
	d					22 51						23 34	
Newbury Racecourse	d					22 53						23 37	
Thatcham	d					22 57						23 42	
Midgham	d					23 01						23 47	
Aldermaston	d					23 04						23 50	
Theale	d					23 09						23 56	
Reading West	d					23 16						00 04	
Reading [7]	a	23 11				23 19	23 33	23 46	23 50		23 52	00 08	
	d	23 19				23 22	23 36				23 54		
Twyford [3]	a					23 27							
Maidenhead [3]	a					23 34							
Slough [3]	a					23 44	23 56						
Ealing Broadway ⊖	a					00 04							
London Paddington [15] ⊖	a	23 56				00 12	00 18				00 29		

Saturdays
21 December to 16 May

		GW D	GW	GW 1	GW ◇1 E 🚲	GW	GW F	GW	GW	GW	GW	GW	GW	XR	GW	GW ◇1		XR	GW G	GW	GW ◇1 B 🚲	GW H	GW ◇1 I 🚲	XR	GW ◇1 G
Birmingham New Street [12] 71	d																								
Birmingham International	d																								
Coventry	d																								
Leamington Spa [8]	d																								
Banbury 71	d																								
Kings Sutton	d																								
Heyford	d																								
Tackley	d						00 02																		
Oxford 115	a						00 12																		
	d				00 11			00 45		04 00		05 15				05 50				06 07					
Radley	d							00 51				05 21								06 13					
Culham	d											05 25								06 17					
Appleford	d																								
Didcot Parkway	a				00 22			01 01		04 13		05 33				06 02				06 25					
	d				00 24			01 02		04 13					05 44	06 04			06 10		06 28		06 35		
Cholsey	d							01 08							05 49				06 15						
Goring & Streatley	d							01 13							05 54				06 20						
Pangbourne	d							01 17							05 58				06 24						
Tilehurst	d							01 22							06 03				06 28						
Bedwyn	d			00 06																					06 06
Hungerford	d																								06 11
Kintbury	d																								06 16
Newbury	a			00 15																					06 23
	d			00 18																					06 23
Newbury Racecourse	d																								06 25
Thatcham	d																								06 30
Midgham	d																								06 35
Aldermaston	d																								06 38
Theale	d																								06 43
Reading West	d	00 04																				←			06 50
Reading [7]	a	00 08		00 36	00 41			01 28		04 31					06 08	06 17			06 34		06 41	06 34	06 48		06 54
	d		00 17	00 38	00 43	01 15			04 13		04 54		05 45	05 54	06 15	06 20		06 22	06 45		06 42	06 45	06 50	06 52	06 59
Twyford [3]	a		00 22			01 20			04 19		04 59		05 50	05 59	06 20			06 27	→			06 50		06 57	→
Maidenhead [3]	a		00 29			01 27			04 27		05 06		05 57	06 06	06 27			06 34				06 57		07 04	
Slough [3]	a		00 40		00 56	01 34			04 34		05 13		06 04	06 16	06 34	06 31		06 44				07 04		07 14	
Ealing Broadway ⊖	a		01 02			01 51			04 55		05 32		06 23	06 39	06 51			07 07				07 21		07 37	
London Paddington [15] ⊖	a		01 11	01 13	01 15	02 01			05 04		05 40		06 31	06 49	07 01	06 50		07 17			07 06	07 31	07 14	07 48	

A From Penzance
B From Bristol Temple Meads
C From Stratford-upon-Avon
D From Bedwyn
E From Hereford
F From Banbury
G To London Paddington
H From Didcot Parkway
I From Swansea

For complete services between Banbury and Birmingham, refer to Table T71

Table T116-R

Saturdays

21 December to 16 May

Birmingham, Banbury, Oxford and Bedwyn - Reading and London

		GW ◇1	GW ◇1 A	GW B	GW	GW ◇1 C ⚒	GW D	GW ◇1	GW ◇1 E ⚒	XR	GW ◇1	GW B	GW ◇1 F ⚒	GW	GW	GW ◇1 C ⚒	GW D	XC ◇1 G ⚒	GW ◇1 E ⚒	XR	GW ◇1 H	GW B	GW
Birmingham New Street 12 71	d																	06 04					
Birmingham International	d																	06 14					
Coventry	d																	06 25					
Leamington Spa 8	d																	06 37					
Banbury 71	d																	06 56					07 04
Kings Sutton	d																						07 08
Heyford	d																						07 16
Tackley	d																						07 21
Oxford 115	a																	07 14					07 35
	d	06 32			06 40						07 02			07 08				07 16			07 32		07 37
Radley	d													07 14									
Culham	d													07 18									
Appleford	d																						
Didcot Parkway	a				06 53									07 26									07 50
	d			06 38		06 58			07 04			07 08	07 16			07 26						07 38	
Cholsey	d			06 43								07 13										07 43	
Goring & Streatley	d			06 48								07 18										07 48	
Pangbourne	d			06 52								07 22										07 52	
Tilehurst	d			06 56								07 26										07 56	
Bedwyn	d							06 36															
Hungerford	d							06 43															
Kintbury	d							06 48															
Newbury	a							06 54															
	d							06 55							07 10								
Newbury Racecourse	d														07 12								
Thatcham	d							07 00							07 16								
Midgham	d														07 20								
Aldermaston	d														07 23								
Theale	d							07 08							07 28								
Reading West	d		←				←								07 34		←						
Reading 7	a	06 55	06 54	07 01		07 11	07 01	07 16	07 17		07 25	07 32	07 29		07 38	07 40	07 32	07 41			07 54	08 02	
	d	06 56	06 59	07 14		07 12	07 14	07 17	07 20	07 22	07 26	07 45	07 35			07 41	07 45		07 47	07 52	07 56	08 15	
Twyford 3	a			→			07 19			07 27		→					07 50			07 57		→	
Maidenhead 3	a						07 26			07 34							07 57			08 04			
Slough 3	a	07 08					07 33			07 44	07 38						08 04			08 14	08 07		
Ealing Broadway ⊖	a						07 51			08 07							08 21			08 37			
London Paddington 15 ⊖	a	07 25	07 29			07 36	08 01	07 44	07 44	08 17	07 54		08 00			08 06	08 29		08 13	08 47	08 22		

		XC ◇1 I	GW ◇1 J ⚒	GW D	GW ◇1 E ⚒	GW ◇1	XR	GW ◇1	GW B	GW ◇1 F ⚒	GW	XC ◇1 K ⚒	GW	GW ◇1 C ⚒	GW D	GW ◇1 E ⚒	XR	GW ◇1 L ⚒	GW ◇1 M ⚒	GW B	GW	GW ◇1 N ⚒	GW D	XC ◇1 O ⚒
Birmingham New Street 12 71	d	06 33										07 04												07 33
Birmingham International	d											07 14												
Coventry	d											07 25												
Leamington Spa 8	d	07 00										07 37												08 01
Banbury 71	d	07 17										07 54												08 22
Kings Sutton	d																							
Heyford	d																							
Tackley	d																							
Oxford 115	a	07 40										08 12												08 42
	d	07 42						08 02			08 07	08 16						08 32			08 39			08 45
Radley	d										08 13													
Culham	d																							
Appleford	d										08 17													
Didcot Parkway	a										08 24										08 53			
	d		07 55		08 03				08 08	08 17				08 27						08 38		08 55		
Cholsey	d								08 13											08 43				
Goring & Streatley	d								08 18											08 48				
Pangbourne	d								08 22											08 52				
Tilehurst	d								08 26											08 56				
Bedwyn	d					07 36																		
Hungerford	d					07 43																		
Kintbury	d					07 48																		
Newbury	a					07 54																		
	d					07 55							08 13						08 46					
Newbury Racecourse	d												08 15											
Thatcham	d					08 00							08 19											
Midgham	d												08 23											
Aldermaston	d												08 26											
Theale	d					08 08							08 31											
Reading West	d			←									08 37		←								←	
Reading 7	a	08 06	08 08	08 02	08 16	08 16		08 25	08 32	08 30		08 37	08 41	08 41	08 32			08 54	09 01	09 01		09 08	09 01	09 09
	d		08 10	08 15	08 18	08 20	08 22	08 26	08 45	08 35				08 43	08 45	08 47	08 52	08 57	09 06	09 15		09 10	09 15	
Twyford 3	a			08 20			08 27		→						08 50		08 58			→			09 20	
Maidenhead 3	a			08 27			08 34								08 57		09 05						09 28	
Slough 3	a			08 34			08 44	08 38							09 04		09 15	09 08					09 36	
Ealing Broadway ⊖	a			08 53			09 07								09 21		09 38						09 53	
London Paddington 15 ⊖	a		08 36	09 01	08 42	08 45	09 17	08 54		09 00				09 08	09 31	09 11	09 47	09 23	09 30			09 36	10 01	

A From Bedwyn
B To London Paddington
C From Bristol Temple Meads
D From Didcot Parkway
E From Swansea
F From Cheltenham Spa
G To Bournemouth
H From Great Malvern
I To Southampton Central
J From Weston-super-Mare
K From Manchester Piccadilly to Bournemouth
L From Hereford
M From Plymouth
N From Taunton
O From Derby

For complete services between Banbury and Birmingham, refer to Table T71

NRT DECEMBER 19 EDITION

Table T116-R

Saturdays

21 December to 16 May

Birmingham, Banbury, Oxford and Bedwyn - Reading and London

		GW ◇1 A ⚒	XR	GW ◇1	GW ◇1	GW B	GW ◇1 C ⚒	GW	GW	XC ◇1 D ⚒	GW ◇1 E ⚒	GW ◇1 F ⚒	GW G	GW ◇1 A ⚒	XR	GW ◇1 H ⚒	GW ◇1 I ⚒	GW B	GW	XC ◇1 J ⚒	GW ◇1 K ⚒	GW ◇1 L ⚒	GW G
Birmingham New Street 12 71	d									08 04										08 33			
Birmingham International	d									08 14													
Coventry	d									08 25													
Leamington Spa 8	d									08 37										09 00			
Banbury 71	d									08 54									09 09	09 17			
Kings Sutton	d																		09 13				
Heyford	d																		09 21				
Tackley	d																		09 26				
Oxford 115	a									09 12									09 36	09 40			
	d				09 02			09 07		09 16						09 32			09 37	09 42		09 47	
Radley	d							09 13															
Culham	d							09 17															
Appleford	d																						
Didcot Parkway	a							09 25											09 51				
	d	09 03				09 08	09 18				09 26							09 38			09 57		
Cholsey	d					09 13												09 43					
Goring & Streatley	d					09 18												09 48					
Pangbourne	d					09 22												09 52					
Tilehurst	d					09 26												09 56					
Bedwyn	d			08 41																			
Hungerford	d			08 48																			
Kintbury	d			08 53																			
Newbury	a			08 59																			
	d			09 00					09 10														
Newbury Racecourse	d								09 12														
Thatcham	d			09 05					09 16														
Midgham	d								09 20														
Aldermaston	d								09 23														
Theale	d			09 13					09 28														
Reading West	d								09 34				←										←
Reading 7	a	09 16		09 21	09 25	09 31	09 31		09 38	09 40	09 40		09 31			09 54		10 01		10 06	10 10	10 13	10 01
	d	09 17	09 22	09 25	09 27	09 45	09 35				09 41	09 44	09 45	09 47	09 52	09 56	10 05	10 15			10 11	10 14	10 15
Twyford 3	a		09 27			→							09 50		09 57			→					10 20
Maidenhead 3	a		09 34										09 57		10 04								10 27
Slough 3	a		09 44		09 39								10 04		10 14	10 07							10 34
Ealing Broadway ⊖	a		10 07										10 22		10 37								10 51
London Paddington 15 ⊖	a	09 42	10 17	09 53	09 55		10 00				10 06	10 07	10 31	10 11	10 47	10 24	10 29				10 36	10 37	11 02

		GW ◇1 A ⚒	XR	GW ◇1	GW ◇1	GW B	GW ◇1 C ⚒	GW	XC ◇1 M ⚒	GW ◇1 E ⚒	GW G	GW	GW ◇1 N ⚒	GW ◇	XR	GW ◇1 O ⚒	GW ◇1 P ⚒	GW B	GW	XC ◇1 Q ⚒	GW ◇1 E ⚒	GW G	GW ◇1 R ⚒	XR
Birmingham New Street 12 71	d								09 04											09 33				
Birmingham International	d								09 14															
Coventry	d								09 25															
Leamington Spa 8	d								09 37											10 03				
Banbury 71	d								09 55											10 20				
Kings Sutton	d																							
Heyford	d																							
Tackley	d																							
Oxford 115	a								10 13											10 42				
	d				10 02			10 07	10 16							10 32			10 37	10 43				
Radley	d							10 13																
Culham	d																							
Appleford	d							10 17																
Didcot Parkway	a							10 24											10 50					
	d	10 03				10 06	10 17			10 26								10 38			10 55		11 04	
Cholsey	d					10 12												10 43						
Goring & Streatley	d					10 17												10 48						
Pangbourne	d					10 21												10 52						
Tilehurst	d					10 26												10 56						
Bedwyn	d			09 42																				
Hungerford	d			09 49																				
Kintbury	d			09 54																				
Newbury	a			10 00																				
	d			10 01								10 12		10 29										
Newbury Racecourse	d											10 14												
Thatcham	d			10 06								10 18												
Midgham	d											10 22												
Aldermaston	d											10 25												
Theale	d			10 14								10 30												
Reading West	d										←	10 37										←		
Reading 7	a	10 16		10 22	10 25	10 31	10 30		10 39	10 40	10 31	10 41		10 45		10 54		11 01		11 07	11 08	11 01	11 16	
	d	10 20	10 22	10 24	10 27	10 45	10 35			10 42	10 45		10 47	10 49	10 52	10 56	11 05	11 15			11 10	11 15	11 19	11 22
Twyford 3	a		10 27			→					10 50				10 57			→				11 20		11 27
Maidenhead 3	a		10 34								10 57				11 04							11 27		11 34
Slough 3	a		10 44		10 38						11 04				11 14	11 07						11 34		11 44
Ealing Broadway ⊖	a		11 07								11 23				11 37							11 51		12 07
London Paddington 15 ⊖	a	10 45	11 17	10 53	10 54		11 00			11 06	11 31		11 12	11 13	11 47	11 25	11 29				11 36	12 01	11 42	12 17

A From Swansea
B To London Paddington
C From Cheltenham Spa
D From Nottingham to Bournemouth
E From Bristol Temple Meads
F From Plymouth
G From Didcot Parkway
H From Hereford
I From Exeter St Davids
J From York to Southampton Central
K From Taunton
L From Worcester Foregate Street
M From Manchester Piccadilly to Bournemouth
N From Carmarthen
O From Great Malvern
P From Penzance
Q From Newcastle
R From Cardiff Central

For complete services between Banbury and Birmingham, refer to Table T71

Table T116-R

Saturdays 21 December to 16 May

Birmingham, Banbury, Oxford and Bedwyn - Reading and London

		GW ◇1	GW ◇1	GW A	GW ◇1 B ⊥	GW	GW	XC ◇1 C ⊥	GW ◇1 D ⊥	GW ◇1 E ⊥	GW F	GW ◇1 G ⊥	XR	GW ◇1 H ⊥	GW ◇1 I ⊥	GW A	GW	XC ◇1 J ⊥	GW ◇1 D ⊥	GW F	GW ◇1 K ⊥	XR	GW ◇1
Birmingham New Street 12 71	d							10 04										10 33					
Birmingham International	d							10 14															
Coventry	d							10 25															
Leamington Spa 8	d							10 37										11 00					
Banbury 71	d							10 54									11 08	11 17					
Kings Sutton	d																11 12						
Heyford	d																11 20						
Tackley	d																11 25						
Oxford 115	a							11 12									11 35	11 40					
	d		11 00			11 06		11 16						11 32			11 37	11 42					
Radley	d					11 12																	
Culham	d					11 16																	
Appleford	d																						
Didcot Parkway	a					11 25											11 50						
	d			11 06	11 17				11 26							11 38			11 55		12 03		
Cholsey	d			11 12												11 43							
Goring & Streatley	d			11 17												11 48							
Pangbourne	d			11 21												11 52							
Tilehurst	d			11 26												11 57							
Bedwyn	d	10 41																					11 41
Hungerford	d	10 48																					11 48
Kintbury	d	10 53																					11 53
Newbury	a	10 59																					11 59
	d	11 00					11 10			11 24													12 00
Newbury Racecourse	d						11 12																
Thatcham	d	11 05					11 16																12 05
Midgham	d						11 20																
Aldermaston	d						11 23																
Theale	d	11 13					11 28																12 13
Reading West	d						11 34				←									←			
Reading 7	a	11 21	11 23	11 31	11 30		11 37	11 39	11 40	11 41	11 31			11 54		12 02		12 07	12 08	12 02	12 16		12 21
	d	11 24	11 27	11 45	11 35				11 41	11 44	11 45	11 47	11 52	11 57	12 05	12 15			12 10	12 15	12 17	12 22	12 24
Twyford 3	a			→							11 50		11 57			→				12 20		12 27	
Maidenhead 3	a										11 57		12 04							12 27		12 34	
Slough 3	a		11 39								12 04		12 14	12 08						12 34		12 44	
Ealing Broadway ⊖	a										12 21		12 37							12 51		13 07	
London Paddington 15 ⊖	a	11 53	11 54		12 00				12 06	12 08	12 31	12 11	12 47	12 25	12 29				12 36	13 01	12 41	13 17	12 53

		GW ◇1	GW A	GW ◇1 B ⊥	GW	XC ◇1 C ⊥	GW ◇1 L ⊥	GW F	GW	GW ◇1 G ⊥	XR	GW ◇	GW ◇1 H ⊥	GW ◇1 I ⊥	GW A	GW	XC ◇1 M ⊥	GW ◇1 D ⊥	GW F	GW ◇1 K ⊥	XR	GW ◇1	GW ◇1	GW A
Birmingham New Street 12 71	d					11 04											11 33							
Birmingham International	d					11 14																		
Coventry	d					11 25																		
Leamington Spa 8	d					11 37											12 03							
Banbury 71	d					11 54											12 20							
Kings Sutton	d																							
Heyford	d																							
Tackley	d																							
Oxford 115	a					12 13											12 41							
	d	12 02			12 07	12 16							12 32			12 37	12 43						13 02	
Radley	d				12 13																			
Culham	d																							
Appleford	d				12 17																			
Didcot Parkway	a				12 24											12 50								
	d		12 08	12 17			12 26								12 38			12 55		13 03				13 08
Cholsey	d		12 13												12 43									13 13
Goring & Streatley	d		12 18												12 48									13 18
Pangbourne	d		12 22												12 52									13 22
Tilehurst	d		12 26												12 56									13 26
Bedwyn	d																					12 41		
Hungerford	d																					12 48		
Kintbury	d																					12 53		
Newbury	a																					12 59		
	d								12 12			12 32										13 00		
Newbury Racecourse	d								12 14															
Thatcham	d								12 18													13 05		
Midgham	d								12 22															
Aldermaston	d								12 25															
Theale	d								12 30													13 13		
Reading West	d							←	12 37										←					
Reading 7	a	12 25	12 31	12 30		12 39	12 40	12 31	12 41			12 50	12 54		13 01		13 07	13 08	13 01	13 15		13 21	13 25	13 31
	d	12 26	12 45	12 35			12 42	12 45		12 47	12 52	12 54	12 57	13 05	13 15			13 10	13 15	13 17	13 22	13 23	13 26	13 45
Twyford 3	a		→					12 50			12 57				→				13 20		13 27			→
Maidenhead 3	a							12 57			13 04								13 27		13 34			
Slough 3	a	12 38						13 04			13 14		13 08						13 34		13 44		13 38	
Ealing Broadway ⊖	a							13 21			13 37								13 51		14 07			
London Paddington 15 ⊖	a	12 55		13 00			13 08	13 31		13 12	13 47	13 22	13 24	13 29				13 36	14 01	13 40	14 17	13 53	13 55	

A To London Paddington
B From Cheltenham Spa
C From Manchester Piccadilly to Bournemouth
D From Bristol Temple Meads
E From Paignton. The Torbay Express
F From Didcot Parkway
G From Swansea
H From Great Malvern
I From Penzance
J From Newcastle to Southampton Central
K From Cardiff Central
L From Weston-super-Mare
M From Edinburgh

For complete services between Banbury and Birmingham, refer to Table T71

Table T116-R

Saturdays 21 December to 16 May

Birmingham, Banbury, Oxford and Bedwyn - Reading and London

		GW ◇1 A ⊥	GW	GW	XC ◇1 B ⊥	GW ◇1 C ⊥	GW ◇1 D ⊥	GW E	GW ◇1 F ⊥	XR	GW ◇1 G ⊥	GW ◇1 H ⊥	GW I	GW	XC ◇1 J ⊥	GW ◇1 C ⊥	GW E	GW ◇1 K ⊥	XR	GW ◇1	GW ◇1	GW I	GW ◇1 A ⊥
Birmingham New Street 12 71	d				12 04										12 33								
Birmingham International	d				12 14																		
Coventry	d				12 25																		
Leamington Spa 8	d				12 37										13 00								
Banbury 71	d				12 54									13 08	13 17								
Kings Sutton	d													13 12									
Heyford	d													13 20									
Tackley	d													13 25									
Oxford 115	a				13 12									13 35	13 40								
	d		13 07		13 16						13 32			13 37	13 42						14 02		
Radley	d		13 13																				
Culham	d		13 17																				
Appleford	d																						
Didcot Parkway	a		13 24											13 50									
	d	13 17				13 26							13 38			13 55		14 06				14 08	14 20
Cholsey	d												13 43									14 13	
Goring & Streatley	d												13 48									14 18	
Pangbourne	d												13 52									14 22	
Tilehurst	d												13 56									14 26	
Bedwyn	d																			13 41			
Hungerford	d																			13 48			
Kintbury	d																			13 53			
Newbury	a																			13 59			
	d			13 10			13 25													14 00			
Newbury Racecourse	d			13 12																			
Thatcham	d			13 16																14 05			
Midgham	d			13 20																			
Aldermaston	d			13 23																			
Theale	d			13 28																14 13			
Reading West	d			13 34				←									←						
Reading 7	a	13 30		13 38	13 39	13 40	13 42	13 31			13 54		14 02		14 06	14 08	14 02	14 19		14 23	14 25	14 31	14 33
	d	13 35				13 41	13 44	13 45	13 47	13 52	13 56	14 05	14 15			14 10	14 15	14 20	14 22	14 24	14 27	14 45	14 35
Twyford 3	a							13 50		13 57			→				14 20		14 27			→	
Maidenhead 3	a							13 57		14 04							14 27		14 34				
Slough 3	a							14 04		14 14	14 07						14 34		14 44		14 38		
Ealing Broadway ⊖	a							14 21		14 37							14 51		15 07				
London Paddington 15 ⊖	a	14 00				14 06	14 09	14 31	14 11	14 47	14 22	14 29				14 36	15 01	14 44	15 17	14 53	14 55		15 00

		GW	GW ◇1 C ⊥	GW E	XC ◇1 B ⊥	GW	GW ◇1 F ⊥	GW ◇	XR	GW ◇1 L ⊥	GW ◇1 M ⊥	GW I	GW	XC ◇1 N ⊥	GW ◇1 C ⊥	GW E	GW ◇1 K ⊥	XR	GW ◇1	GW ◇1	GW I	GW ◇1 A ⊥	GW	GW
Birmingham New Street 12 71	d				13 04									13 33										
Birmingham International	d				13 14																			
Coventry	d				13 25																			
Leamington Spa 8	d				13 37									14 03										
Banbury 71	d				13 54									14 20										
Kings Sutton	d																							
Heyford	d																							
Tackley	d																							
Oxford 115	a				14 12									14 40										
	d	14 07			14 16					14 31			14 37	14 42						15 02			15 07	
Radley	d	14 13																					15 13	
Culham	d																						15 17	
Appleford	d	14 17																						
Didcot Parkway	a	14 24											14 51										15 24	
	d		14 26									14 37			14 55		15 05				15 08	15 17		
Cholsey	d											14 42									15 13			
Goring & Streatley	d											14 47									15 18			
Pangbourne	d											14 51									15 22			
Tilehurst	d											14 56									15 26			
Bedwyn	d																		14 41					
Hungerford	d																		14 48					
Kintbury	d																		14 53					
Newbury	a																		14 59					
	d					14 11		14 27											15 00					15 10
Newbury Racecourse	d					14 13																		15 12
Thatcham	d					14 17													15 05					15 16
Midgham	d					14 21																		15 20
Aldermaston	d					14 24																		15 23
Theale	d					14 29													15 13					15 28
Reading West	d			←		14 37										←								15 34
Reading 7	a		14 40	14 31	14 40	14 41		14 45		14 53		15 01		15 06	15 08	15 01	15 18		15 21	15 25	15 31	15 30		15 38
	d		14 41	14 45			14 47	14 49	14 52	14 56	15 05	15 15			15 11	15 15	15 19	15 22	15 23	15 26	15 45	15 35		
Twyford 3	a			14 50					14 57			→				15 20		15 27			→			
Maidenhead 3	a			14 57					15 04							15 27		15 34						
Slough 3	a			15 04					15 14	15 07						15 34		15 44		15 38				
Ealing Broadway ⊖	a			15 21					15 37							15 51		16 07						
London Paddington 15 ⊖	a		15 06	15 31			15 11	15 14	15 47	15 22	15 29				15 38	16 01	15 43	16 17	15 53	15 55		16 00		

A From Cheltenham Spa
B From Manchester Piccadilly to Bournemouth
C From Bristol Temple Meads
D From Exeter St Davids
E From Didcot Parkway
F From Swansea
G From Great Malvern
H From Penzance. The Cornish Riviera
I To London Paddington
J From Newcastle to Southampton Central
K From Cardiff Central
L From Worcester Foregate Street
M From Penzance
N From Newcastle

For complete services between Banbury and Birmingham, refer to Table T71

Table T116-R

Saturdays

21 December to 16 May

Birmingham, Banbury, Oxford and Bedwyn - Reading and London

	XC	GW	GW	GW	GW	XR	GW	GW	GW	GW	XC	GW	GW	GW	XR	GW	GW	GW	GW	GW	XC	GW
	◇1	◇1	◇1		◇1		◇1	◇1			◇1	◇1		◇1		◇1	◇1		◇1		◇1	◇1
	A	B	C	D	E		F	G	H		I	B	D	J				H	K		A	B
	🛒	🛒	🛒		🛒		🛒	🛒			🛒	🛒		🛒					🛒		🛒	🛒
Birmingham New Street 12 71 d	14 04										14 33										15 04	
Birmingham International d	14 14																				15 14	
Coventry d	14 25																				15 25	
Leamington Spa 8 d	14 37										15 00										15 37	
Banbury 71 d	14 56									15 08	15 21										15 54	
Kings Sutton d										15 12												
Heyford d										15 20												
Tackley d										15 25												
Oxford 115 a	15 14									15 35	15 40										16 12	
d	15 16						15 32			15 37	15 42						16 02			16 07	16 16	
Radley d																				16 13		
Culham d																						
Appleford d																				16 17		
Didcot Parkway a										15 51										16 24		
d		15 26							15 38			15 55		16 03				16 08	16 17			16 26
Cholsey d									15 43									16 13				
Goring & Streatley d									15 48									16 18				
Pangbourne d									15 52									16 22				
Tilehurst d									15 56									16 26				
Bedwyn d																15 41						
Hungerford d																15 48						
Kintbury d																15 53						
Newbury a																15 59						
d			15 24													16 00						
Newbury Racecourse d																						
Thatcham d																16 05						
Midgham d																						
Aldermaston d																						
Theale d																16 13						
Reading West d				←									←									
Reading 7 a	15 39	15 40	15 41	15 31			15 54		16 01		16 06	16 08	16 01	16 16		16 21	16 26	16 31	16 30		16 39	16 40
d		15 41	15 44	15 45	15 47	15 52	15 56	16 05	16 15			16 11	16 15	16 17	16 22	16 24	16 28	16 45	16 35			16 41
Twyford 3 a				15 50		15 57			→				16 20		16 27			→				
Maidenhead 3 a				15 57		16 04							16 27		16 34							
Slough 3 a				16 04		16 14	16 07						16 34		16 44		16 39					
Ealing Broadway ⊖ a				16 21		16 37							16 51		17 07							
London Paddington 15 ⊖ a		16 06	16 08	16 31	16 11	16 47	16 25	16 30				16 38	17 04	16 41	17 17	16 53	16 54		17 00			17 08

	GW	GW	GW	GW	XR	GW	GW	GW	GW	XC	GW	GW	GW	XR	GW	GW	GW	GW	GW	GW	XC	GW	GW
			◇1	◇		◇1	◇1			◇1	◇1		◇1		◇1			◇1			◇1	◇1	◇1
	D		E			L	M	H		N	B	D	J				H	K			A	B	C
			🛒			🛒	🛒			🛒	🛒		🛒					🛒			🛒	🛒	🛒
Birmingham New Street 12 71 d										15 33											16 04		
Birmingham International d																					16 14		
Coventry d																					16 25		
Leamington Spa 8 d										16 03											16 37		
Banbury 71 d										16 20											16 54		
Kings Sutton d																							
Heyford d																							
Tackley d																							
Oxford 115 a										16 40											17 12		
d						16 32			16 37	16 42						17 02			17 07		17 16		
Radley d																			17 13				
Culham d																			17 17				
Appleford d																							
Didcot Parkway a									16 50										17 24				
d								16 38			16 56		17 03				17 08	17 19				17 26	
Cholsey d								16 43									17 13						
Goring & Streatley d								16 48									17 18						
Pangbourne d								16 52									17 22						
Tilehurst d								16 56									17 26						
Bedwyn d															16 41								
Hungerford d															16 48								
Kintbury d															16 53								
Newbury a															16 59								
d		16 10		16 32											17 00					17 10			17 24
Newbury Racecourse d		16 12																		17 12			
Thatcham d		16 16													17 05					17 16			
Midgham d		16 20																		17 20			
Aldermaston d		16 23																		17 23			
Theale d		16 29													17 13					17 28			
Reading West d	←	16 37										←								17 34			
Reading 7 a	16 31	16 41		16 47		16 54		17 01		17 06	17 10	17 01	17 15		17 21	17 25	17 31	17 32		17 38	17 39	17 40	17 41
d	16 45		16 47	16 49	16 52	16 56	17 05	17 15			17 14	17 15	17 17	17 22	17 23	17 26	17 45	17 35				17 41	17 44
Twyford 3 a	16 50				16 57			→				17 20		17 27			→						
Maidenhead 3 a	16 57				17 04							17 27		17 34									
Slough 3 a	17 04				17 14	17 07						17 34		17 44		17 38							
Ealing Broadway ⊖ a	17 21				17 37							17 51		18 07									
London Paddington 15 ⊖ a	17 31		17 13	17 14	17 47	17 23	17 29				17 38	18 01	17 40	18 17	17 50	17 54		18 01				18 07	18 09

- **A** From Manchester Piccadilly to Bournemouth
- **B** From Bristol Temple Meads
- **C** From Exeter St Davids
- **D** From Didcot Parkway
- **E** From Swansea
- **F** From Hereford
- **G** From Plymouth
- **H** To London Paddington
- **I** From Newcastle to Southampton Central
- **J** From Cardiff Central
- **K** From Cheltenham Spa
- **L** From Worcester Foregate Street
- **M** From Penzance. The Royal Duchy
- **N** From Newcastle

For complete services between Banbury and Birmingham, refer to Table T71

NRT DECEMBER 19 EDITION

Table T116-R

Saturdays

21 December to 16 May

Birmingham, Banbury, Oxford and Bedwyn - Reading and London

	GW	GW	XR	GW	GW	GW	GW	XC	GW	GW	GW	XR	GW	GW	GW	GW	GW	XC	GW	GW	GW	GW
		◇1		◇1	◇1			◇1	◇1		◇1		◇1	◇1		◇1		◇1	◇1			◇1
	A	B		C	D	E		F	G	A	H				E	I		J	G	A		B
		🛒		🛒	🛒			🛒	🛒		🛒					🛒		🛒	🛒			🛒
Birmingham New Street 12 71 d								16 33										17 04				
Birmingham International d																		17 14				
Coventry d																		17 25				
Leamington Spa 8 d								17 00										17 37				
Banbury 71 d							17 08	17 17										17 54				
Kings Sutton d							17 12															
Heyford d							17 20															
Tackley d							17 25															
Oxford 115 a							17 35	17 41										18 12				
d				17 32			17 36	17 43						18 02			18 07	18 16				
Radley d																	18 13					
Culham d																						
Appleford d																	18 17					
Didcot Parkway a							17 50										18 24					
d						17 38			17 56		18 06				18 08	18 19			18 26			
Cholsey d						17 43									18 13							
Goring & Streatley d						17 48									18 18							
Pangbourne d						17 52									18 22							
Tilehurst d						17 56									18 26							
Bedwyn d													17 41									
Hungerford d													17 48									
Kintbury d													17 53									
Newbury a													17 59									
d													18 00								18 13	
Newbury Racecourse d																					18 15	
Thatcham d													18 05								18 19	
Midgham d																					18 23	
Aldermaston d																					18 26	
Theale d													18 13								18 31	
Reading West d	←									←										←	18 38	
Reading 7 a	17 31			17 54		18 01		18 06	18 09	18 01	18 19		18 21	18 25	18 31	18 32		18 39	18 40	18 31	18 41	
d	17 45	17 47	17 52	17 56	18 05	18 15			18 11	18 15	18 20	18 22	18 23	18 26	18 45	18 35			18 42	18 45		18 47
Twyford 3 a	17 50		17 57			→				18 20		18 27			→					18 50		
Maidenhead 3 a	17 57		18 04							18 27		18 34								18 57		
Slough 3 a	18 04		18 14	18 07						18 34		18 44		18 38						19 04		
Ealing Broadway ⊖ a	18 21		18 37							18 51		19 07								19 21		
London Paddington 15 ⊖ a	18 31	18 11	18 47	18 23	18 30				18 36	19 01	18 44	19 17	18 54	18 54		19 00			19 08	19 31		19 11

	XR	GW	GW	GW	GW	XC	GW	GW	GW	XR	GW	GW	GW	GW	GW	GW	XC	GW	GW	GW	XR	GW	GW
		◇1	◇1			◇1	◇1		◇1		◇1	◇1		◇1			◇1	◇1		◇1		◇1	◇1
		K	L	E		M	G	A	H				E	I			J	G	A	B		K	D
		🛒	🛒			🛒	🛒		🛒					🛒			🛒	🛒		🛒		🛒	🛒
Birmingham New Street 12 71 d						17 33											18 04						
Birmingham International d																	18 14						
Coventry d																	18 25						
Leamington Spa 8 d						18 02											18 37						
Banbury 71 d						18 19											18 54						
Kings Sutton d																							
Heyford d																							
Tackley d																							
Oxford 115 a						18 40											19 12						
d		18 32			18 37	18 42						19 02			19 07		19 16					19 32	
Radley d															19 13								
Culham d															19 17								
Appleford d																							
Didcot Parkway a					18 50										19 24								
d				18 38			18 55		19 06				19 08	19 17				19 26					
Cholsey d				18 43									19 13										
Goring & Streatley d				18 48									19 18										
Pangbourne d				18 52									19 22										
Tilehurst d				18 56									19 26										
Bedwyn d											18 41												
Hungerford d											18 48												
Kintbury d											18 53												
Newbury a											18 59												
d											19 00					19 10							19 42
Newbury Racecourse d																19 12							
Thatcham d											19 05					19 16							
Midgham d																19 20							
Aldermaston d																19 23							
Theale d											19 13					19 28							
Reading West d								←								19 34			←				
Reading 7 a		18 54		19 01		19 06	19 08	19 01	19 19		19 21	19 25	19 31	19 30		19 38	19 39	19 40	19 31			19 54	19 59
d	18 52	18 56	19 05	19 15			19 10	19 15	19 20	19 22	19 23	19 26	19 45	19 35				19 41	19 45	19 47	19 52	19 56	20 02
Twyford 3 a	18 57			→				19 20		19 27			→						19 50		19 57		
Maidenhead 3 a	19 04							19 27		19 34									19 57		20 04		
Slough 3 a	19 14	19 07						19 34		19 44		19 38							20 04		20 14	20 07	
Ealing Broadway ⊖ a	19 37							19 51		20 07									20 21		20 37		
London Paddington 15 ⊖ a	19 47	19 24	19 29				19 36	20 01	19 44	20 17	19 51	19 54		20 00				20 06	20 31	20 11	20 47	20 25	20 27

- **A** From Didcot Parkway
- **B** From Swansea
- **C** From Hereford
- **D** From Plymouth
- **E** To London Paddington
- **F** From Newcastle to Guildford
- **G** From Bristol Temple Meads
- **H** From Cardiff Central
- **I** From Cheltenham Spa
- **J** From Manchester Piccadilly to Bournemouth
- **K** From Great Malvern
- **L** From Penzance
- **M** From Newcastle

For complete services between Banbury and Birmingham, refer to Table T71

Table T116-R

Saturdays
21 December to 16 May

Birmingham, Banbury, Oxford and Bedwyn - Reading and London

		GW	GW	XC	GW	GW	GW	XR		GW	GW	GW	GW	GW	GW	XC	GW	GW	XR	GW	GW	GW	XC	GW
				◇■	◇■		◇■			◇■		◇■				◇■	◇■	■		◇■			◇■	◇■
		A		B	C	D					A	E	D			F	G			H	A		B	C
				⌶	⌶							⌶				⌶	⌶			⌶			⌶	⌶
Birmingham New Street 12 71	d			18 33												19 04							19 33	
Birmingham International	d															19 14								
Coventry	d															19 25								
Leamington Spa 8	d			19 00												19 37							20 02	
Banbury 71	d		19 08	19 17												19 54							20 19	
Kings Sutton	d		19 12																					
Heyford	d		19 20																					
Tackley	d		19 25																					
Oxford 115	a		19 35	19 40												20 12							20 40	
	d		19 37	19 42						20 02				20 07		20 16				20 32		20 37	20 42	
Radley	d													20 13										
Culham	d																							
Appleford	d													20 17										
Didcot Parkway	a		19 50											20 24								20 51		
	d	19 38			19 56						20 08	20 20									20 38	20 53		20 55
Cholsey	d	19 43									20 13										20 43	20 58		
Goring & Streatley	d	19 48									20 18										20 48	21 03		
Pangbourne	d	19 52									20 22										20 52	21 08		
Tilehurst	d	19 56									20 26										20 56	21 12		
Bedwyn	d						19 38											20 29						
Hungerford	d						19 45											20 34						
Kintbury	d						19 50											20 39						
Newbury	a						19 56											20 46						
	d						19 57								20 10									
Newbury Racecourse	d														20 12									
Thatcham	d						20 02								20 16									
Midgham	d														20 20									
Aldermaston	d														20 23									
Theale	d						20 10								20 28									
Reading West	d					←							←		20 34									
Reading 7	a	20 01		20 06	20 09	20 01	20 18			20 25	20 31	20 33	20 31		20 38	20 39				20 54	21 01	21 19	21 06	21 08
	d	20 15			20 11	20 15	20 20	20 22		20 27	20 45	20 35	20 45				20 47		20 52	20 56	21 15			21 10
Twyford 3	a	→				20 20		20 27			→		20 50						20 57		→			
Maidenhead 3	a					20 27		20 34					20 57						21 04					
Slough 3	a					20 34		20 44		20 39			21 04						21 14	21 07				
Ealing Broadway ⊖	a					20 51		21 07					21 21						21 37					
London Paddington 15 ⊖	a				20 35	21 01	20 45	21 17		20 55		21 00	21 31				21 11		21 47	21 23				21 35

		GW	GW	XR	GW	GW	GW	GW	GW	GW	GW	XC	GW	GW	XR	GW		GW	XC	GW	GW	GW	XR	GW	GW
			◇■		◇■		◇■	◇■				◇■	■	◇■		◇■			◇■	◇■					◇■
		D	I				J	E	K			F		G		L			M	N	O				
			⌶					⌶				⌶		⌶		⌶			⌶	⌶					
Birmingham New Street 12 71	d											20 04							20 33						
Birmingham International	d											20 14													
Coventry	d											20 25													
Leamington Spa 8	d											20 37							21 00						
Banbury 71	d									20 36		20 55							21 17						
Kings Sutton	d									20 40															
Heyford	d									20 48															
Tackley	d									20 53															
Oxford 115	a									21 05		21 13							21 40						
	d				21 02					21 07		21 16				21 32		21 37	21 42						22 04
Radley	d									21 13															
Culham	d																								
Appleford	d																								
Didcot Parkway	a									21 22								21 50							22 16
	d						21 08	21 19						21 36						21 55				22 04	22 18
Cholsey	d						21 13																	22 09	
Goring & Streatley	d						21 18																	22 13	
Pangbourne	d						21 22																	22 17	
Tilehurst	d						21 26																	22 21	
Bedwyn	d												21 17												
Hungerford	d												21 22												
Kintbury	d												21 27												
Newbury	a												21 34												
	d										21 10											21 50			
Newbury Racecourse	d										21 12											21 52			
Thatcham	d										21 16											21 56			
Midgham	d										21 20											22 00			
Aldermaston	d										21 23											22 03			
Theale	d										21 28											22 08			
Reading West	d	←							←		21 34											22 14			
Reading 7	a	21 01			21 25		21 31	21 32	21 31		21 38	21 39		21 49		21 54			22 07	22 08		22 18		22 27	22 32
	d	21 15	21 20	21 22	21 26	21 30	21 45	21 35	21 45					21 51	21 52	21 56				22 10	22 15		22 22		22 34
Twyford 3	a	21 20		21 27		21 36	→		21 50						21 57						22 20		22 27		
Maidenhead 3	a	21 27		21 34		21 44			21 57						22 04						22 27		22 34		22 42
Slough 3	a	21 34		21 44	21 38	21 51			22 04						22 14	22 07					22 34		22 44		22 49
Ealing Broadway ⊖	a	21 51		22 07		22 11			22 21						22 38						22 53		23 07		
London Paddington 15 ⊖	a	22 01	21 44	22 17	21 54	22 23		22 00	22 32					22 15	22 47	22 25				22 35	23 02		23 17		23 07

A To London Paddington
B From Newcastle
C From Bristol Temple Meads
D From Didcot Parkway
E From Cheltenham Spa
F From Manchester Piccadilly to Bournemouth
G From Swansea
H From Great Malvern
I From Penzance
J not 4 January. To London Paddington
K not 4 January. From Didcot Parkway
L From Worcester Foregate Street
M From Newcastle to Southampton Central
N From Weston-super-Mare
O not 4 January

For complete services between Banbury and Birmingham, refer to Table T71

Table T116-R

Saturdays
21 December to 16 May

Birmingham, Banbury, Oxford and Bedwyn - Reading and London

		GW	GW	XC	GW	GW	XR	GW		GW	GW	GW	GW	GW	GW	GW	GW	GW	GW	GW	GW
			◇■	◇■	■	◇■				◇■			◇■		◇■		◇■		■		
			A	B		C		D		E			F	G			H				
			⌶			⌶				⌶			⌶				⌶				
Birmingham New Street 12 71	d			21 04																	
Birmingham International	d			21 14																	
Coventry	d			21 25																	
Leamington Spa 8	d			21 37																	
Banbury 71	d			21 54							22 08										
Kings Sutton	d										22 12										
Heyford	d										22 20										
Tackley	d										22 25										
Oxford 115	a			22 13							22 37										
	d	22 10		22 16						22 36					23 00	23 08					
Radley	d	22 16														23 14					
Culham	d															23 18					
Appleford	d															23 20					
Didcot Parkway	a	22 25								22 48					23 12	23 27					
	d		22 25			22 30		22 38		22 50			22 55		23 15		23 38			23 45	
Cholsey	d							22 43												23 50	
Goring & Streatley	d							22 48												23 55	
Pangbourne	d							22 52												23 59	
Tilehurst	d							22 56												00 03	
Bedwyn	d				22 17														23 17		
Hungerford	d				22 22														23 22		
Kintbury	d				22 27														23 27		
Newbury	a				22 34														23 34		
	d											22 42									23 42
Newbury Racecourse	d											22 44									23 44
Thatcham	d											22 48									23 48
Midgham	d											22 52									23 52
Aldermaston	d											22 55									23 55
Theale	d											23 00									00 01
Reading West	d											23 06		←							00 07
Reading 7	a		22 38	22 41		22 43		23 01		23 05		23 10	23 10	23 01	23 27		23 51			00 08	00 10
	d		22 39			22 45	22 52	23 19		23 06			23 13	23 19	23 31		23 54	23 58		00 17	
Twyford 3	a						22 57	→						23 24				00 03		00 22	
Maidenhead 3	a						23 04							23 31	23 39			00 10		00 29	
Slough 3	a						23 14			23 19				23 42	23 46			00 17		00 40	
Ealing Broadway ⊖	a						23 37							00 05				00 36		01 04	
London Paddington 15 ⊖	a		23 05			23 10	23 47			23 36			23 41	00 15	00 18		00 30	00 44		01 12	

Sundays
15 December to 10 May

		GW	GW	GW	XR	GW	XR	GW	XR	GW	GW	XR	GW	GW	GW	GW		XR	GW	GW	GW	XR	GW	GW	GW
										◇■	◇■		◇■			◇			◇■	◇■	◇■			◇■	
		I	J										C						K	L	C		D	M	G
													⌶						⌶	⌶	⌶			⌶	
Birmingham New Street 12 71	d																								
Birmingham International	d																								
Coventry	d																								
Leamington Spa 8	d																								
Banbury 71	d																								
Kings Sutton	d																								
Heyford	d																								
Tackley	d																								
Oxford 115	a																								
	d									07 58	08 24				08 42									09 35	
Radley	d														08 50										
Culham	d																								
Appleford	d																								
Didcot Parkway	a									08 09	08 35				08 59									09 45	
	d									08 10	08 37		08 44	08 48					09 14	09 14			09 35	09 46	
Cholsey	d													08 53									09 40		
Goring & Streatley	d									08 17				08 58									09 45		
Pangbourne	d													09 02									09 49		
Tilehurst	d	00 03												09 06									09 53		
Bedwyn	d																								
Hungerford	d																								
Kintbury	d																								
Newbury	a																								
	d															08 48									
Newbury Racecourse	d															08 49									
Thatcham	d															08 53									
Midgham	d															08 57									
Aldermaston	d															09 00									
Theale	d		00 01													09 05									
Reading West	d		00 07													09 12									←
Reading 7	a	00 08	00 10							08 25	08 50		08 57	09 10		09 17			09 27	09 28			09 58	10 00	09 58
	d	00 17		06 25	06 49	07 10	07 55	08 10	08 25	08 31	08 51	08 55	09 00	09 10		09 19		09 25	09 29	09 29	09 41	09 55	10 06	10 01	10 06
Twyford 3	a	00 22		06 30	06 54	07 15	08 00	08 15	08 30			09 00		09 17				09 30				10 00	→		10 11
Maidenhead 3	a	00 29		06 37	07 01	07 22	08 07	08 22	08 37			09 07		09 22		09 27		09 37				10 07			10 20
Slough 3	a	00 40		06 46	07 12	07 29	08 18	08 29	08 48	08 42	09 03	09 18		09 31		09 33		09 48				10 18		10 13	10 29
Ealing Broadway ⊖	a	01 04		07 07	07 37	07 48	08 43	08 47	09 13			09 43		09 47				10 13				10 43			10 46
London Paddington 15 ⊖	a	01 12		07 16	07 48	07 56	08 53	08 55	09 23	08 59	09 21	09 53	09 24	09 55		09 51		10 23	09 53	09 53	10 07	10 53		10 29	10 55

A From Cheltenham Spa
B From Manchester Piccadilly to Southampton Central
C From Bristol Temple Meads
D To London Paddington
E From Hereford
F From Penzance
G From Didcot Parkway
H From Taunton
I not 15 December. From Didcot Parkway
J not 15 December. From Newbury
K from 5 April. From Cardiff Central
L until 29 March. From Cardiff Central
M From Worcester Foregate Street

For complete services between Banbury and Birmingham, refer to Table T71

Table T116-R

Sundays

15 December to 10 May

Birmingham, Banbury, Oxford and Bedwyn - Reading and London

		GW	GW	XR	GW	GW	GW	XC	GW	GW	GW	XR	GW	GW	GW	GW	GW	GW	GW	XR	GW	GW	XC
		◇1	◇1		◇1	◇1	◇1	◇1	◇1	◇1	◇1			◇1		◇1	◇1	◇1	◇1		◇1	◇1	◇1
		A				B	C	D	E	F	G		H	I	J	F	B				C	K	L
		🛒			☕	🛒	🛒	🛒	🛒	🛒	🛒			🛒		🛒	🛒		☕		🛒	🛒	🛒
Birmingham New Street 12 71	d							09 04															10 04
Birmingham International	d							09 14															10 14
Coventry	d							09 25															10 25
Leamington Spa 8	d							09 37															10 37
Banbury 71	d							09 54															10 54
Kings Sutton	d																						
Heyford	d																						
Tackley	d																						
Oxford 115	a							10 12															11 12
	d				09 55			10 16						10 31					10 55				11 16
Radley	d				10 01														11 02				
Culham	d																						
Appleford	d																						
Didcot Parkway	a				10 08									10 44					11 08				
	d	09 56			10 08		10 22						10 35	10 45		10 56	11 01		11 09		11 15		
Cholsey	d												10 40										
Goring & Streatley	d												10 45										
Pangbourne	d												10 49										
Tilehurst	d												10 53										
Bedwyn	d		09 27															10 40					
Hungerford	d		09 33															10 46					
Kintbury	d		09 38															10 51					
Newbury	a		09 44															10 57					
	d		09 45						10 24									10 58				11 19	
Newbury Racecourse	d		09 48																				
Thatcham	d		09 52															11 03					
Midgham	d		09 56																				
Aldermaston	d		10 00																				
Theale	d		10 05															11 11					
Reading West	d		10 10												←								
Reading 7	a	10 09	10 13		10 25		10 34	10 39	10 40				10 58	10 59	10 58	11 09	11 14	11 19	11 24		11 27	11 35	11 39
	d	10 11	10 15	10 23	10 26	10 27	10 35		10 40	10 43	10 53	10 55	11 06	11 00	11 06	11 10	11 16	11 21	11 25	11 25	11 28	11 39	
Twyford 3	a			10 28								11 00	→		11 11					11 30			
Maidenhead 3	a		10 24	10 35								11 07			11 22			11 30		11 37			
Slough 3	a			10 48	10 42							11 18		11 12	11 29				11 38	11 48			
Ealing Broadway ⊖	a			11 13								11 43			11 47					12 13			
London Paddington 15 ⊖	a	10 36	10 41	11 23	11 00	10 52	11 05		11 08	11 11	11 20	11 53		11 29	11 55	11 36	11 39	11 53	11 54	12 23	11 56	12 06	

		GW	GW	XR	GW	GW	GW	GW	GW	GW	GW	GW	XR	GW	XC	GW	GW	GW	GW	XR	GW	GW	GW	GW
		◇1	◇1		◇1		◇1		◇1	◇1	◇	◇1		◇1	◇1	◇1	◇1	◇	◇1			◇1		◇1
		A	B		K	H	I	J	F	B				C	L	F	B		M		H	I	J	A
		🛒	🛒		🛒		🛒		🛒	🛒		☕		🛒	🛒	🛒	🛒		☕			🛒		🛒
Birmingham New Street 12 71	d														11 04									
Birmingham International	d														11 14									
Coventry	d														11 25									
Leamington Spa 8	d														11 37									
Banbury 71	d														11 54									
Kings Sutton	d																							
Heyford	d																							
Tackley	d																							
Oxford 115	a														12 12									
	d						11 31					11 55			12 16							12 31		
Radley	d											12 02												
Culham	d																							
Appleford	d																							
Didcot Parkway	a						11 44					12 08										12 44		
	d					11 35	11 45		11 56	12 04		12 09		12 19							12 35	12 45		12 56
Cholsey	d					11 40															12 40			
Goring & Streatley	d					11 45															12 45			
Pangbourne	d					11 49															12 49			
Tilehurst	d					11 53															12 53			
Bedwyn	d																							
Hungerford	d																							
Kintbury	d																							
Newbury	a																							
	d										11 53							12 27						
Newbury Racecourse	d										11 55													
Thatcham	d										11 59													
Midgham	d										12 03													
Aldermaston	d										12 06													
Theale	d										12 11													
Reading West	d							←			12 17												←	
Reading 7	a					11 58	11 59	11 58	12 09	12 17	12 20	12 24		12 31	12 39			12 44			12 58	12 59	12 58	13 09
	d	11 43	11 50	11 53	11 56	12 06	12 00	12 06	12 11	12 19	12 23	12 25	12 25	12 33		12 39	12 46	12 48	12 55	12 55	13 06	13 00	13 06	13 10
Twyford 3	a			11 58		→		12 11					12 30							13 00	→		13 11	
Maidenhead 3	a			12 07				12 22			12 29		12 37							13 07			13 22	
Slough 3	a			12 18			12 13	12 29				12 38	12 48							13 18		13 13	13 29	
Ealing Broadway ⊖	a			12 43				12 47					13 13							13 43			13 47	
London Paddington 15 ⊖	a	12 09	12 14	12 53	12 23		12 29	12 55	12 36	12 42	12 53	12 54	13 23	12 59		13 07	13 09	13 13	13 23	13 53		13 29	13 55	13 36

A From Weston-super-Mare
B From Swansea
C From Cheltenham Spa
D To Bournemouth
E From Exeter St Davids
F From Bristol Temple Meads
G From Bristol Parkway
H To London Paddington
I From Great Malvern
J From Didcot Parkway
K From Plymouth
L From Manchester Piccadilly to Bournemouth
M From Penzance

For complete services between Banbury and Birmingham, refer to Table T71

Table T116-R

Sundays

15 December to 10 May

Birmingham, Banbury, Oxford and Bedwyn - Reading and London

		GW	GW	GW	GW	XR	GW	XC	GW	GW	XR	GW	GW	GW	GW	XC	GW	GW	GW	GW	XR	GW	XC
		◇1	◇1	◇1	◇1		◇1	◇1	◇1	◇1		◇1		◇1		◇1	◇1	◇1	◇	◇1		◇1	◇1
		A		B			C	D	E	A		F	G	H	I		E	J				C	D
		🛒		🛒			🛒	🛒	🛒	🛒		☕		☕		🛒	🛒	🛒				🛒	🛒
Birmingham New Street 12 71	d							12 04								12 33							13 04
Birmingham International	d							12 14								12 43							13 14
Coventry	d							12 25								12 55							13 25
Leamington Spa 8	d							12 37								13 09							13 37
Banbury 71	d							12 54								13 26							13 54
Kings Sutton	d																						
Heyford	d																						
Tackley	d																						
Oxford 115	a							13 12								13 44							14 12
	d				12 55			13 16						13 31		13 46				13 55			14 16
Radley	d				13 02															14 02			
Culham	d																						
Appleford	d																						
Didcot Parkway	a				13 08									13 44						14 08			
	d	13 04			13 09		13 22						13 35	13 45			13 56	14 05		14 09		14 21	
Cholsey	d												13 40										
Goring & Streatley	d												13 45										
Pangbourne	d												13 49										
Tilehurst	d												13 53										
Bedwyn	d		12 38																				
Hungerford	d		12 43																				
Kintbury	d		12 48																				
Newbury	a		12 54																				
	d		12 55	13 06															13 53				
Newbury Racecourse	d																		13 55				
Thatcham	d		13 00																14 00				
Midgham	d																		14 04				
Aldermaston	d																		14 07				
Theale	d		13 08																14 12				
Reading West	d														←				14 18				
Reading 7	a	13 17	13 17	13 22	13 24		13 34	13 39					13 58	13 59	13 58	14 09	14 09	14 18	14 21	14 24		14 33	14 39
	d	13 19	13 21	13 22	13 25	13 25	13 34		13 42	13 50	13 55	13 58	14 06	14 00	14 06		14 11	14 20	14 23	14 25	14 25	14 34	
Twyford 3	a					13 30					14 00		→		14 11						14 30		
Maidenhead 3	a		13 28			13 37					14 07				14 21				14 31		14 37		
Slough 3	a				13 38	13 48					14 18			14 14	14 28					14 38	14 48		
Ealing Broadway ⊖	a					14 13					14 43				14 47						15 13		
London Paddington 15 ⊖	a	13 44	13 50	13 53	13 57	14 23	13 59		14 06	14 14	14 53	14 23		14 29	14 55		14 36	14 43	14 51	14 57	15 23	14 59	

		GW	GW	GW	XR	GW	GW	GW	GW	XC	GW	GW	GW	GW	XR	GW	GW	XC	GW	GW	XR	GW	GW	GW
		◇1	◇	◇1		◇1		◇1		◇1	◇1	◇1	◇1	◇1		◇1	◇1	◇1	◇1	◇1		◇1		◇1
		E		A		F	G	K	I		L	J				C	M	D	E	A		N	G	O
		🛒		🛒		🛒		🛒		🛒	🛒	🛒				🛒	🛒	🛒	🛒	🛒		🛒		🛒
Birmingham New Street 12 71	d									13 33								14 04						
Birmingham International	d																	14 14						
Coventry	d																	14 25						
Leamington Spa 8	d									14 00								14 37						
Banbury 71	d									14 17								14 54						
Kings Sutton	d																							
Heyford	d																							
Tackley	d																							
Oxford 115	a									14 35								15 12						
	d							14 31		14 37				14 55				15 16						15 31
Radley	d													15 02										
Culham	d																							
Appleford	d																							
Didcot Parkway	a							14 44						15 08										15 44
	d						14 34	14 45			14 56	15 05		15 09		15 21							15 35	15 45
Cholsey	d						14 39																15 40	
Goring & Streatley	d						14 44																15 45	
Pangbourne	d						14 48																15 49	
Tilehurst	d						14 52																15 53	
Bedwyn	d												14 39											
Hungerford	d												14 45											
Kintbury	d												14 50											
Newbury	a												14 56											
	d		14 27										14 57				15 20							
Newbury Racecourse	d																							
Thatcham	d												15 02											
Midgham	d																							
Aldermaston	d																							
Theale	d												15 10											
Reading West	d								←															
Reading 7	a		14 43				14 57	14 59	14 57	15 00	15 09	15 18	15 20	15 24		15 33	15 36	15 39					15 58	15 59
	d	14 39	14 44	14 49	14 55	14 57	15 06	15 00	15 06		15 10	15 19	15 22	15 25	15 25	15 34	15 40		15 43	15 50	15 55	15 58	16 06	16 00
Twyford 3	a				15 00		→		15 11						15 30						16 00		→	
Maidenhead 3	a				15 07				15 22				15 32		15 37						16 07			
Slough 3	a				15 18			15 13	15 29					15 39	15 48						16 18			16 13
Ealing Broadway ⊖	a				15 43				15 47						16 13						16 43			
London Paddington 15 ⊖	a	15 06	15 09	15 12	15 53	15 24		15 32	15 55		15 36	15 42	15 50	15 54	16 23	15 59	16 06		16 09	16 14	16 53	16 24		16 36

A From Swansea
B From Paignton
C From Cheltenham Spa
D From Manchester Piccadilly to Bournemouth
E From Bristol Temple Meads
F From Penzance
G To London Paddington
H From Great Malvern
I From Didcot Parkway
J From Cardiff Central
K From Worcester Shrub Hill
L From Weston-super-Mare
M From Exeter St Davids
N From Plymouth
O From Hereford

For complete services between Banbury and Birmingham, refer to Table T71

Table T116-R

Sundays

15 December to 10 May

Birmingham, Banbury, Oxford and Bedwyn - Reading and London

		GW	XC	GW	GW	GW	GW	XR		GW	XC	GW	GW	GW	XR	GW	GW	GW	GW	XC	GW	GW	GW	GW
			◇1	◇1	◇	◇1	◇1			◇1	◇1	◇1	◇1	◇		◇1		◇1		◇1	◇1	◇1	◇1	◇1
		A	B	C		D				E	F	C	G			H	I	J	A	K	L	D		
			🛒	🛒		🛒	🍴			🛒	🛒	🛒	🛒			🛒		🛒		🛒	🛒	🛒		
Birmingham New Street [12] 71	d		14 33								15 04									15 33				
Birmingham International	d		14 43								15 14													
Coventry	d		14 55								15 25													
Leamington Spa [8]	d		15 09								15 37									16 00				
Banbury 71	d		15 26								15 54									16 17				
Kings Sutton	d																							
Heyford	d																							
Tackley	d																							
Oxford 115	a		15 44								16 12									16 35				
	d		15 46				15 55				16 16							16 31		16 37				16 55
Radley	d						16 02																	17 02
Culham	d																							
Appleford	d																							
Didcot Parkway	a						16 08											16 44						17 08
	d			15 56		16 05	16 09			16 21							16 35	16 45			16 56	17 04		17 09
Cholsey	d																16 40							
Goring & Streatley	d																16 45							
Pangbourne	d																16 49							
Tilehurst	d																16 53							
Bedwyn	d																						16 41	
Hungerford	d																						16 47	
Kintbury	d																						16 52	
Newbury	a																						16 58	
	d				15 46									16 35									16 59	
Newbury Racecourse	d				15 48																			
Thatcham	d				15 52																		17 04	
Midgham	d				15 56																			
Aldermaston	d				15 59																			
Theale	d				16 04																		17 12	
Reading West	d	←			16 10														←					
Reading [7]	a	15 58	16 09	16 09	16 13	16 18	16 24			16 33	16 39			16 50			16 58	16 59	16 58	17 02	17 09	17 17	17 20	17 24
	d	16 06		16 10	16 13	16 20	16 25	16 25		16 34		16 43	16 50	16 51	16 55	16 56	17 06	17 00	17 06		17 11	17 19	17 22	17 25
Twyford [3]	a	16 11						16 30							17 00		→		17 11					
Maidenhead [3]	a	16 22			16 21			16 37							17 07				17 22				17 30	
Slough [3]	a	16 29					16 38	16 48							17 18			17 12	17 29					17 38
Ealing Broadway ⊖	a	16 47						17 13							17 43				17 47					
London Paddington [15] ⊖	a	16 55		16 39	16 44	16 46	16 54	17 23		17 02		17 09	17 14	17 27	17 53	17 21		17 28	17 55		17 37	17 43	17 52	17 55

		XR	GW	GW	XC	GW	GW	XR	GW	GW	GW	GW	XC	GW	GW	GW		GW	XR	GW	XC	GW	GW	GW	XR
			◇1	◇1	◇1	◇1	◇1		◇1		◇1		◇1	◇1	◇1	◇1				◇1	◇1	◇1	◇1	◇	
			E	M	F	C	N		O	I	P	A	Q	O	D					E	F	C	G		
			🛒	🛒	🛒	🛒	🍴		🛒		🛒		🛒	🛒	🛒					🛒	🛒	🛒	🛒		
Birmingham New Street [12] 71	d				16 04								16 33								17 04				
Birmingham International	d				16 14								16 44								17 14				
Coventry	d				16 25								16 55								17 25				
Leamington Spa [8]	d				16 37								17 09								17 37				
Banbury 71	d				16 54								17 26								17 54				
Kings Sutton	d																								
Heyford	d																								
Tackley	d																								
Oxford 115	a				17 12								17 44								18 12				
	d				17 16						17 31		17 46			17 51					18 16				
Radley	d															17 58									
Culham	d																								
Appleford	d																								
Didcot Parkway	a										17 44					18 04									
	d		17 20							17 35	17 45			17 56	18 05	18 07				18 19					
Cholsey	d									17 40															
Goring & Streatley	d									17 45															
Pangbourne	d									17 49															
Tilehurst	d									17 53															
Bedwyn	d																								
Hungerford	d																								
Kintbury	d																								
Newbury	a																								
	d			17 20														17 53						18 30	
Newbury Racecourse	d																	17 55							
Thatcham	d																	17 59							
Midgham	d																	18 02							
Aldermaston	d																	18 05							
Theale	d																	18 10							
Reading West	d											←						18 17							
Reading [7]	a		17 32	17 36	17 39					17 58	17 59	17 58	18 09	18 11	18 18	18 22		18 23		18 31	18 39			18 45	
	d	17 25	17 33	17 40		17 43	17 50	17 55	17 56	18 06	18 00	18 06		18 11	18 19	18 23			18 25	18 31		18 39	18 46	18 49	18 55
Twyford [3]	a	17 30						18 00		→		18 11							18 30						19 00
Maidenhead [3]	a	17 37						18 07				18 22							18 37						19 07
Slough [3]	a	17 48						18 18			18 13	18 29				18 38			18 48						19 18
Ealing Broadway ⊖	a	18 13						18 43				18 47							19 13						19 43
London Paddington [15] ⊖	a	18 23	17 59	18 06		18 08	18 14	18 53	18 23		18 29	18 55		18 38	18 44	18 56			19 23	18 59		19 06	19 09	19 15	19 53

A From Didcot Parkway
B From Derby
C From Bristol Temple Meads
D From Cardiff Central
E From Cheltenham Spa
F From Manchester Piccadilly to Bournemouth
G From Swansea
H From Penzance
I To London Paddington
J From Worcester Shrub Hill
K From Sheffield
L From Weston-super-Mare
M From Exeter St Davids
N From Carmarthen
O From Plymouth
P From Hereford
Q From Newcastle

For complete services between Banbury and Birmingham, refer to Table T71

Table T116-R

Sundays

15 December to 10 May

Birmingham, Banbury, Oxford and Bedwyn - Reading and London

		GW	GW	GW	GW	XC	GW	GW		GW	GW	XR	GW	GW	XC	GW	GW	XR	GW	GW	GW	GW	XC	GW
		◇1		◇1		◇1	◇1	◇1		◇1	◇1		◇1	◇1	◇1	◇1	◇1		◇1		◇1		◇1	◇1
		A	B	C	D	E	F	G					H	I	J	K	L		M	B	N	D	O	K
		🛒		🛒		🛒	🛒	🛒					🛒	🛒	🛒	🛒	🛒		🛒		🛒		🛒	🛒
Birmingham New Street [12] 71	d					17 33									18 04								18 33	
Birmingham International	d														18 14								18 43	
Coventry	d														18 25								18 55	
Leamington Spa [8]	d					18 00									18 37								19 09	
Banbury 71	d					18 17									18 54								19 26	
Kings Sutton	d																							
Heyford	d																							
Tackley	d																							
Oxford 115	a					18 35									19 12								19 44	
	d			18 31		18 37					18 55				19 16						19 31		19 46	
Radley	d										19 02													
Culham	d																							
Appleford	d																							
Didcot Parkway	a			18 44							19 08										19 44			
	d		18 37	18 45			18 56	19 05			19 09		19 19							19 35	19 45			19 56
Cholsey	d		18 42																	19 40				
Goring & Streatley	d		18 47																	19 45				
Pangbourne	d		18 51																	19 49				
Tilehurst	d		18 55																	19 53				
Bedwyn	d									18 40														
Hungerford	d									18 46														
Kintbury	d									18 50														
Newbury	a									18 56														
	d									18 57				19 23										
Newbury Racecourse	d																							
Thatcham	d									19 01														
Midgham	d																							
Aldermaston	d																							
Theale	d									19 09														
Reading West	d				←																	←		
Reading [7]	a		19 00	18 59	19 00	19 06	19 10	19 18		19 18	19 24		19 31	19 38	19 39					19 58	19 59	19 58	20 09	20 09
	d	18 58	19 10	19 00	19 10		19 11	19 19		19 21	19 25	19 25	19 31	19 40		19 43	19 50	19 55	19 58	20 10	20 00	20 10		20 11
Twyford [3]	a		→		19 15							19 30						20 00		→		20 15		
Maidenhead [3]	a				19 22					19 28		19 37						20 07				20 22		
Slough [3]	a			19 13	19 29						19 38	19 48						20 18			20 13	20 28		
Ealing Broadway ⊖	a				19 47							20 13						20 43				20 47		
London Paddington [15] ⊖	a	19 24		19 29	19 55		19 38	19 42		19 51	19 54	20 23	19 56	20 07		20 09	20 14	20 53	20 25		20 29	20 55		20 38

		GW	GW	XR	GW	XC	GW	GW	GW	GW	XR	GW	GW	GW	GW	XC		GW	XR	GW	GW	GW	XC	GW	XR
			◇1		◇1	◇1	◇1	◇1		◇1		◇1	◇1		◇1	◇1		1		◇1		◇1	◇1	◇1	
					H	J	K	M	B	P		A	C	D	Q	E				H		K	R	P	
					🛒	🛒	🛒	🛒		🛒		🛒	🛒		🛒	🛒				🛒		🛒	🛒	🛒	
Birmingham New Street [12] 71	d					19 04										19 33							20 04		
Birmingham International	d					19 14										19 44							20 14		
Coventry	d					19 25										19 55							20 25		
Leamington Spa [8]	d					19 37										20 10							20 37		
Banbury 71	d					19 54										20 27							20 54		
Kings Sutton	d																								
Heyford	d																								
Tackley	d																								
Oxford 115	a					20 12										20 46							21 12		
	d		19 55			20 16							20 32			20 47					21 07		21 16		
Radley	d		20 02																		21 14				
Culham	d																								
Appleford	d																								
Didcot Parkway	a		20 08										20 44								21 22				
	d		20 09		20 19				20 35	20 36			20 45		20 57					21 20		21 26		21 33	
Cholsey	d								20 40																
Goring & Streatley	d								20 45																
Pangbourne	d								20 49																
Tilehurst	d								20 53																
Bedwyn	d																	20 40							
Hungerford	d																	20 46							
Kintbury	d																	20 50							
Newbury	a																	20 57							
	d	19 53																20 57							
Newbury Racecourse	d	19 55																							
Thatcham	d	19 59																21 02							
Midgham	d	20 03																							
Aldermaston	d	20 06																							
Theale	d	20 11																21 10							
Reading West	d	20 18												←											
Reading [7]	a	20 21	20 24		20 31	20 39			20 58	20 49			20 59	20 58	21 10	21 11		21 19		21 32		21 39	21 39	21 46	
	d		20 25	20 25	20 31		20 39	20 40	21 10	20 49	20 55	20 58	21 00	21 10	21 11				21 25	21 33		21 39		21 48	21 55
Twyford [3]	a			20 31					→		21 00			21 15					21 30						22 00
Maidenhead [3]	a			20 38							21 07			21 22					21 37						22 07
Slough [3]	a		20 38	20 48							21 18		21 13	21 29					21 48						22 18
Ealing Broadway ⊖	a			21 13							21 43			21 47					22 13						22 43
London Paddington [15] ⊖	a		20 53	21 23	20 59		21 05	21 10		21 14	21 53	21 23	21 29	21 55	21 38				22 23	21 59		22 10		22 11	22 53

A From Penzance
B To London Paddington
C From Worcester Shrub Hill
D From Didcot Parkway
E From Newcastle
F From Paignton
G From Cardiff Central
H From Cheltenham Spa
I From Exeter St Davids
J From Manchester Piccadilly to Bournemouth
K From Bristol Temple Meads
L From Carmarthen
M From Plymouth
N From Hereford
O From Edinburgh
P From Swansea
Q From Taunton
R From Manchester Piccadilly to Southampton Central

For complete services between Banbury and Birmingham, refer to Table T71

Table T116-R

Sundays
15 December to 10 May

Birmingham, Banbury, Oxford and Bedwyn - Reading and London

		GW	GW	GW	XC	GW	XR	GW	XC	GW	GW	GW	GW	XR	GW	GW	GW	GW	GW	GW	GW
			◇1		◇1			◇1	◇1	◇1	◇1	◇1	◇1				◇1				
		A	B	C	D			E	F	G	H	I	J				K				
Birmingham New Street 12 71	d				20 33				21 04												
Birmingham International	d								21 14												
Coventry	d								21 25												
Leamington Spa 8	d				21 00				21 37												
Banbury 71	d				21 18				21 54												
Kings Sutton	d																				
Heyford	d																				
Tackley	d																				
Oxford 115	a				21 37				22 12												
	d		21 31		21 39				22 16				22 23					23 05			
Radley	d																	23 20			
Culham	d																				
Appleford	d																				
Didcot Parkway	a		21 44										22 38					23 45			
	d	21 35	21 45					22 19		22 25	22 35		22 39		22 45		23 21			23 53	
Cholsey	d	21 40													22 50					23 58	
Goring & Streatley	d	21 45													22 55					00 03	
Pangbourne	d	21 49													22 59					00 07	
Tilehurst	d	21 53													23 03					00 11	
Bedwyn	d															22 35					
Hungerford	d															22 41					
Kintbury	d															22 45					
Newbury	a															22 52					
	d					21 53						22 33				22 53			23 23		23 55
Newbury Racecourse	d					21 55															23 57
Thatcham	d					21 59										22 58			23 28		00 02
Midgham	d					22 02															00 07
Aldermaston	d					22 05															00 10
Theale	d					22 10										23 06			23 36		00 15
Reading West	d			←		22 18															00s23
Reading 7	a	21 58	21 59	21 58	22 02	22 21		22 31	22 39	22 39	22 48	22 49	22 52		23 08	23 15	23 34		23 46	00 23	00 28
	d	22 10	22 00	22 10			22 27	22 31		22 39	22 50	22 51	22 54	22 59	23 10		23 35			00 24	
Twyford 3	a	→		22 15			22 32							23 04	23 15					00 29	
Maidenhead 3	a			22 22			22 39							23 11	23 22					00 36	
Slough 3	a		22 12	22 29			22 50						23 07	23 23	23 31					00 45	
Ealing Broadway ⊖	a			22 47			23 13							23 49	23 56					01 06	
London Paddington 15 ⊖	a		22 29	22 55			23 22	23 03		23 15	23 29	23 35	23 44	23 58	00 04		00 12			01 15	

A To London Paddington
B From Hereford
C From Didcot Parkway
D From Newcastle to Guildford
E From Cheltenham Spa
F From Manchester Piccadilly
G From Weston-super-Mare
H From Carmarthen
I From Penzance
J From Great Malvern
K From Plymouth

For complete services between Banbury and Birmingham, refer to Table T71

NRT DECEMBER 19 EDITION

Table Table T116A-F

Mondays to Fridays
16 December to 15 May

Leamington Spa, Kenilworth - Coventry

		LM	LM	LM	XC	LM	XC	LM	XC	LM	XC	LM	XC	LM	XC	LM	XC	LM	XC	LM	XC	LM	XC
					◇1		◇1		◇1		◇1		1		◇1		◇1		◇1		◇1		◇1
Leamington Spa	d	05 34	06 13	07 00	07 15	08 02	08 15	09 00	09 15	10 02	10 15	11 02	11 15	12 02	12 15	13 01	13 15	14 01	14 15	15 02	15 15	16 02	16 15
Kenilworth	a	05 42	06 19	07 06		08 08		09 06		10 08		11 08		12 08		13 09		14 07		15 08		16 08	
	d	05 42	06 20	07 07		08 09		09 07		10 09		11 09		12 09		13 09		14 08		15 08		16 09	
Coventry	a	05 52	06 27	07 14	07 26	08 17	08 26	09 15	09 26	10 16	10 26	11 16	11 26	12 16	12 26	13 17	13 26	14 19	14 26	15 16	15 26	16 16	16 26

		LM	XC	LM	XC	LM	XC	LM	XC	LM	XC	LM	XC	XC
			◇1		◇1		◇1		◇1		◇1		◇1	◇1
Leamington Spa	d	17 01	17 15	18 00	18 15	19 02	19 16	20 02	20 15	21 01	21 15	22 06	22 15	23 09
Kenilworth	a	17 07		18 06		19 08		20 08		21 07		22 13		
	d	17 08		18 07		19 09		20 09		21 09		22 13		
Coventry	a	17 16	17 26	18 15	18 26	19 16	19 27	20 16	20 26	21 16	21 26	22 21	22 26	23 20

Saturdays
21 December to 16 May

		LM	LM	LM	XC	LM	XC	LM	XC	LM		XC	LM	XC	XC	LM	XC
					◇1		◇1		◇1			◇1		◇1	◇1		◇1
Leamington Spa	d	05 34	06 08	07 02	07 15	08 03	08 15	09 00	09 15	10 02	and at the same minutes past each hour until	20 15	21 02	21 15	21 50	22 01	22 15
Kenilworth	a	05 40	06 14	07 08		08 09		09 06		10 08			21 08			22 07	
	d	05 41	06 15	07 09		08 10		09 07		10 09			21 09			22 08	
Coventry	a	05 49	06 22	07 16	07 26	08 17	08 26	09 14	09 26	10 16		20 26	21 16	21 26	22 01	22 15	22 26

Sundays
15 December to 10 May

		LM	XC	LM	XC	LM	XC	XC	LM	XC	LM	XC		XC	LM	XC	XC	LM	XC	XC	LM	XC	XC
			◇1		◇1		◇1	◇1		◇1		◇1		◇1		◇1	◇1		◇1	◇1		◇1	◇1
Leamington Spa	d	10 00	10 15	11 00	11 15	12 00	12 15	13 16	13 19	14 15	14 19	14 42	and at the same minutes past each hour until	18 15	18 19	18 42	19 15	19 19	19 42	20 15	20 19	20 42	21 15
Kenilworth	a	10 07		11 07		12 07			13 26		14 26				18 26			19 26			20 26		
	d	10 08		11 08		12 08			13 26		14 26				18 26			19 27			20 27		
Coventry	a	10 16	10 26	11 16	11 26	12 16	12 26	13 27	13 39	14 26	14 39	14 53		18 26	18 39	18 53	19 26	19 40	19 53	20 26	20 40	20 53	21 26

		LM	XC	XC	LM	XC
			◇1	◇1		◇1
Leamington Spa	d	21 19	21 42	22 12	22 19	22 42
Kenilworth	a	21 26			22 26	
	d	21 26			22 27	
Coventry	a	21 40	21 53	22 23	22 37	22 53

Table Table T116A-R

Mondays to Fridays

16 December to 15 May

Coventry - Kenilworth and Leamington Spa

Miles			XC	LM	XC	LM	XC	LM		XC	LM	XC	LM	XC	LM	XC	LM	XC		LM	XC	LM	XC	LM	XC
0	Coventry	d	06 25	06 41	07 25	07 40	08 25	08 35		09 25	09 37	10 25	10 37	11 25	11 40	12 25	12 38	13 25		13 37	14 25	14 35	15 25	15 37	16 25
4½	Kenilworth	a		06 48		07 47		08 42			09 44		10 44		11 47		12 48			13 44		14 42		15 44	
—		d		06 48		07 48		08 43			09 45		10 45		11 47		12 48			13 45		14 43		15 45	
9½	Leamington Spa	a	06 36	06 55	07 36	07 55	08 36	08 53		09 36	09 53	10 36	10 53	11 36	11 55	12 36	12 55	13 36		13 53	14 36	14 52	15 36	15 54	16 36

		LM	XC	LM		XC	LM	XC	LM	XC	LM	XC	LM	XC		LM	LM
Coventry	d	16 37	17 25	17 37		18 25	18 37	19 25	19 37	20 25	20 37	21 25	21 36	22 25		22 43	23 43
Kenilworth	a	16 44		17 44			18 44		19 44		20 44		21 43			22 50	23 50
	d	16 45		17 45			18 45		19 45		20 45		21 44			22 51	23 51
Leamington Spa	a	16 53	17 36	17 51		18 36	18 56	19 36	19 52	20 36	20 53	21 36	21 50	22 36		22 57	23 58

Saturdays

21 December to 16 May

		LM	XC	LM	XC	LM	XC	LM	XC	LM		XC	LM	XC	LM	XC	LM	XC	LM	XC		LM
Coventry	d	05 46	06 25	06 40	07 25	07 37	08 25	08 37	09 25	09 37		10 25	10 37	11 25	11 37	12 25	12 37	13 25	13 38	14 25		14 37
Kenilworth	a	05 54		06 47		07 44		08 44		09 44			10 44		11 44		12 49		13 47			14 44
	d	05 54		06 48		07 45		08 45		09 45			10 45		11 45		12 49		13 48			14 45
Leamington Spa	a	06 05	06 36	06 56	07 36	07 53	08 36	08 54	09 36	09 53		10 36	10 53	11 36	11 53	12 36	12 56	13 36	13 55	14 36		14 54

		XC	LM		XC	LM	LM
Coventry	d	15 25	15 37	and at the same minutes past each hour until	21 25	21 37	22 45
Kenilworth	a		15 44			21 44	22 52
	d		15 45			21 45	22 53
Leamington Spa	a	15 36	15 53		21 36	21 53	22 59

Sundays

15 December to 10 May

		XC	XC	LM	XC	LM	XC	LM	XC	XC		LM	XC	LM	XC	XC	LM	XC	LM	XC		XC	LM	XC	LM
Coventry	d	09 25	10 25	10 36	11 25	11 36	12 25	12 36	12 55	13 25		13 47	14 25	14 47	14 55	15 25	15 47	16 25	16 47	16 55		17 25	17 47	18 25	18 47
Kenilworth	a			10 44		11 44		12 44				13 55		14 55			15 55		16 55				17 55		18 55
	d			10 44		11 44		12 44				13 55		14 55			15 55		16 55				17 55		18 55
Leamington Spa	a	09 36	10 36	10 55	11 36	11 55	12 36	12 55	13 06	13 36		14 04	14 36	15 03	15 07	15 36	16 04	16 36	17 03	17 07		17 36	18 04	18 36	19 03

		XC	XC	LM	XC	XC		LM	XC	LM	LM
Coventry	d	18 55	19 25	19 49	19 55	20 25		20 47	21 25	21 57	22 57
Kenilworth	a			19 57				20 55		22 05	23 05
	d			19 57				20 55		22 05	23 05
Leamington Spa	a	19 07	19 36	20 05	20 09	20 36		21 04	21 36	22 15	23 15

Table T117-F

Mondays to Fridays

16 December to 15 May

London - Greenford, Heathrow Airport and Reading

Stopping Services

Miles	Miles	Miles	Miles			GW MO	GW MX	XR MO	XR MX	GW MX	GW MX	GW MO	GW MX	GW MO		GW MX	GW MO	GW MX	GW	XR	GW	HX	XR	XR
0	0	0	0	London Paddington 15 ⊖	d								00 30	00 34		00 34	01 34	01 34	03 34	04 42	04 59			05 02
4¼	4¼	4¼	4¼	Acton Main Line	d																			
5¾	5¾	5¾	5¾	Ealing Broadway ⊖	d						00 01	00 03		00 42		00 42	01 42	01 42	03 42	04 51				05 11
6½	6½	6½	6½	West Ealing	d																			
—	7¼	—	—	Drayton Green	d																			
—	7½	—	—	Castle Bar Park	d																			
—	8¼	—	—	South Greenford	d																			
—	9¼	—	—	Greenford ⊖	a																			
7¼	—	7¼	7¼	Hanwell	d																			
9	—	9	9	Southall	d						00 05	00 09		00 47		00 47	01 46	01 47	03 47	04 55				05 16
10¾	—	10¾	10¾	Hayes & Harlington	d				00 02		00 09	00 13		00 50		00 50	01 50	01 50	03 50	04 59				05 20
—	—	14¾	14¾	HeathrowTermls 2 & 3 2 ⊖ ✈	a															05 06				05 30
—	—	—	—		d															05 08		05 13	05 18	05 33
—	—	16½	—	Heathrow Terminal 4 ⊖ ✈	a															05 16			05 22	05 37
—	—	—	—		d																			
—	—	—	16¼	Heathrow Terminal 5 ⊖ ✈	a																	05 17		
—	—	—	—		d																			
13¼	—	—	—	West Drayton	d				00 06		00 13			00 54		00 54	01 53	01 54	03 54					
14¾	—	—	—	Iver	d				00 09		00 16					00 58								
16¼	—	—	—	Langley	d			00 02	00 11		00 19	00 20		00 58		01 01								
18½	—	—	—	Slough 3	a			00 06	00 15		00 22	00 24	00 48	01 01		01 04	02 00	02 00	04 00		05 19			
—	—	—	—		d			00 06	00 15		00 23	00 25	00 48	01 02		01 05	02 00	02 00	04 00		05 20			
21	—	—	—	Burnham	d						00 26	00 28				01 09								
22½	—	—	—	Taplow	d						00 29					01 12								
24¼	—	—	—	Maidenhead 3	d		00 09	00a13	00a22		00 33	00 33	00 56	01 08		01 16	02 07	02 07	04 07					
31	—	—	—	Twyford 3	d	00 04	00 19			00 33	00 40	00 40	01 04	01 15		01 23	02 14	02 14	04 14					
36	—	—	—	Reading 7	a	00 12	00 25			00 44	00 47	00 52	01 11	01 22		01 31	02 21	02 21	04 21		05 35			
—	—	—	—	Oxford	a								01 44								06 04			

		HX	XR	XR	HX	XR	XR	GW	HX	GW		XR	XR	GW	XR	HX	XR	GW	XR	XR		GW	HX	XR	XR
London Paddington 15 ⊖	d	05 10	05 13	05 17	05 25		05 32	05 35	05 40	05 41		05 43	05 48	05 50		05 55		05 56	05 58	06 02			06 10	06 13	06 18
Acton Main Line	d												05 54												06 24
Ealing Broadway ⊖	d		05 21	05 27			05 41			05 49		05 53	05 57					06 04	06 08	06 11				06 21	06 27
West Ealing	d						05 44			05 52			06 00							06 14		06 27			06 30
Drayton Green	d									05 55												06 29			
Castle Bar Park	d									05 57												06 31			
South Greenford	d									05 59												06 34			
Greenford ⊖	a									06 04												06 39			
Hanwell	d						05 46													06 16					
Southall	d		05 30	05 33			05 50					06 00	06 05						06 13	06 20				06 27	06 35
Hayes & Harlington	d		05 33	05a41			05 54					06 03	06a12					06 12	06 18	06 24				06 30	06a42
HeathrowTermls 2 & 3 2 ⊖ ✈	a	05 26			05 40		06 00		05 55							06 10				06 30			06 25		
	d	05 28			05 41	05 48	06 03		05 58							06 11	06 18			06 33			06 28		
Heathrow Terminal 4 ⊖ ✈	a					05 52	06 07										06 22			06 37					
	d																								
Heathrow Terminal 5 ⊖ ✈	a	05 32			05 46				06 02							06 16							06 32		
	d																								
West Drayton	d		05 37									06 07						06 16	06 21					06 34	
Iver	d		05 40									06 10							06 24					06 38	
Langley	d		05 42									06 12			←				06 27					06 41	
Slough 3	a		05 46									06 16		06 03	06 16			06 22	06 32					06 44	
	d		05 46									06 16		06 04	06 16			06 26	06 32					06 46	
Burnham	d		05 50									→			06 20				06 36					→	
Taplow	d		05 53												06 23				06 39						
Maidenhead 3	d		05 56												06 26			06 32	06 42						
Twyford 3	d		06 03												06 33			06 39	06 49						
Reading 7	a		06 11					05 57						06 17	06 41			06 47	06 57						
Oxford	a													06 49											

For non-stop services between London and Reading refer to Table T116

For non-stop services between London and Heathrow Airport see Table T118

Table T117-F

Mondays to Fridays
16 December to 15 May

London - Greenford, Heathrow Airport and Reading
Stopping Services

Station		GW ◇1		XR	HX ◇1	XR	GW	GW ◇1	XR	XR	GW	HX ◇1		XR	XR	GW ◇1	XR	HX ◇1	XR	GW	XR	XR		GW	HX ◇1
London Paddington ⊖	d	06 19			06 25		06 26	06 28	06 28	06 32		06 40		06 43	06 48	06 50		06 55		06 56	06 58	07 02			07 10
Acton Main Line	d														06 54										
Ealing Broadway ⊖	d						06 34		06 38	06 41				06 51	06 57					07 04	07 08	07 11			
West Ealing	d									06 44	06 57				07 00							07 14		07 27	
Drayton Green	d										06 59													07 29	
Castle Bar Park	d										07 01													07 31	
South Greenford	d										07 04													07 34	
Greenford ⊖	a										07 09													07 39	
Hanwell	d									06 46												07 16			
Southall	d								06 43	06 50				07 00	07 05					07 10	07 13	07 20			
Hayes & Harlington	d						06 43		06 47	06 54				07 03	07a13					07 13	07 17	07 24			
HeathrowTermls 2 & 3 ⊖ ✈	a				06 40					07 00		06 55						07 10				07 30			07 25
	d				06 41	06 48				07 03		06 58						07 11	07 18			07 33			07 28
Heathrow Terminal 4 ⊖ ✈	a					06 52				07 07									07 22			07 37			
	d																								
Heathrow Terminal 5 ⊖ ✈	a				06 46							07 02						07 16							07 32
	d																								
West Drayton	d						06 47		06 50					07 07						07 17	07 20				
Iver	d								06 53					07 10							07 23				
Langley	d			←					06 56					07 12			←				07 26				
Slough	a	06 32		06 44			06 52		07 00					07 16		07 03	07 16			07 23	07 30				
	d	06 33		06 46			06 55		07 01					07 16		07 04	07 16			07 24	07 31				
Burnham	d			06 50					07 04					→			07 20				07 34				
Taplow	d			06 53					07 07								07 23				07 37				
Maidenhead	d			06 56			07 01		07 11								07 26			07 30	07 41				
Twyford	d			07 03			07 08		07 18								07 33			07 37	07 48				
Reading	a	06 46		07 11			07 15	06 51	07 26							07 17	07 41			07 44	07 56				
Oxford	a	07 14														07 45									

Station		XR	XR	GW ◇1	XR	HX ◇1	XR	GW		GW ◇1	XR	XR	GW	HX ◇1	XR	XR	GW ◇1	XR		HX ◇1	XR	GW	XR	XR	GW
London Paddington ⊖	d	07 13	07 18	07 20		07 25		07 26		07 28	07 28	07 32		07 40	07 43	07 48	07 50			07 55		07 56	07 58	08 02	
Acton Main Line	d		07 24													07 54									
Ealing Broadway ⊖	d	07 21	07 27					07 34			07 38	07 41			07 51	07 57						08 04	08 08	08 11	
West Ealing	d		07 30									07 44	07 57			08 00								08 14	08 27
Drayton Green	d												07 59												08 29
Castle Bar Park	d												08 01												08 31
South Greenford	d												08 04												08 34
Greenford ⊖	a												08 09												08 39
Hanwell	d											07 46												08 16	
Southall	d	07 30	07 35					07 40			07 43	07 50			08 00	08 05						08 10	08 13	08 20	
Hayes & Harlington	d	07 33	07a42					07 43			07 47	07 54			08 03	08a12						08 13	08 17	08 24	
HeathrowTermls 2 & 3 ⊖ ✈	a					07 40						08 00		07 55						08 10				08 30	
	d					07 41	07 48					08 03		07 58						08 11	08 18			08 33	
Heathrow Terminal 4 ⊖ ✈	a						07 52					08 07									08 22			08 37	
	d																								
Heathrow Terminal 5 ⊖ ✈	a					07 46								08 02						08 16					
	d																								
West Drayton	d	07 37						07 47			07 50				08 07							08 17	08 20		
Iver	d	07 40									07 53				08 10								08 23		
Langley	d	07 42			←						07 56				08 12			←					08 26		
Slough	a	07 46		07 33	07 46			07 53			08 00				08 16		08 03	08 16				08 23	08 30		
	d	07 46		07 34	07 46			07 54			08 01				08 16		08 04	08 16				08 27	08 31		
Burnham	d	→			07 50						08 04				→			08 20					08 34		
Taplow	d				07 53						08 07							08 23					08 37		
Maidenhead	d				07 56			08 00			08 11							08 26				08 36	08 41		
Twyford	d				08 03			08 07			08 18							08 33				08 43	08 48		
Reading	a			07 46	08 11			08 14		07 51	08 26						08 17	08 41				08 50	08 56		
Oxford	a			08 12													08 42								

For non-stop services between London and Reading refer to Table T116

For non-stop services between London and Heathrow Airport see Table T118

NRT DECEMBER 19 EDITION

Table T117-F

Mondays to Fridays
16 December to 15 May

London - Greenford, Heathrow Airport and Reading
Stopping Services

Station		GW	HX ◇1	XR	XR	GW ◇1	HX ◇1	XR	GW	GW ◇1 A		XR	XR	GW	GW ◇	HX ◇1	XR	XR	GW ◇1	XR		HX ◇1	XR	GW	XR
London Paddington ⊖	d	08 06	08 10	08 13	08 18	08 20	08 25		08 26	08 28		08 28	08 32		08 36	08 40	08 43	08 48	08 50			08 55		08 56	08 58
Acton Main Line	d				08 24													08 54							
Ealing Broadway ⊖	d	08 17		08 21	08 28				08 34			08 38	08 41				08 51	08 57						09 04	09 08
West Ealing	d				08 30								08 44	08 57				09 00							
Drayton Green	d													08 59											
Castle Bar Park	d													09 01											
South Greenford	d													09 04											
Greenford ⊖	a													09 09											
Hanwell	d												08 46												
Southall	d			08 30	08 35							08 43	08 50				09 00	09 05							09 13
Hayes & Harlington	d			08 33	08a42				08 43			08 47	08 54				09 03	09a12						09 12	09 17
HeathrowTermls 2 & 3 ⊖ ✈	a		08 25				08 40						09 00			08 55						09 10			
	d		08 28				08 41	08 48					09 03			08 58						09 11	09 18		
Heathrow Terminal 4 ⊖ ✈	a							08 52					09 07										09 22		
	d																								
Heathrow Terminal 5 ⊖ ✈	a		08 32				08 46									09 02						09 16			
	d																								
West Drayton	d			08 37					08 47			08 50					09 07							09 16	09 20
Iver	d			08 40								08 53					09 10								09 23
Langley	d			08 42								08 56					09 12			←					09 26
Slough	a	08 34		08 46					08 52			09 00					09 16		09 03	09 16				09 22	09 30
	d	08 35		08 46					08 54			09 01					09 16		09 04	09 16				09 24	09 31
Burnham	d			08 50								09 04					→			09 20					09 34
Taplow	d			08 53								09 07								09 23					09 37
Maidenhead	d	08 45		08 56					09 00			09 11								09 26				09 30	09a41
Twyford	d	08 52		09 03					09 07			09 18								09 33				09 37	
Reading	a	09 00		09 11		08 42			09 14	08 51		09 26			09 02				09 16	09 41				09 44	
Oxford	a					09 18													09 43						

Station		XR	GW	HX ◇1	XR	XR		GW ◇1	XR	GW	HX ◇1	XR	GW ◇1	XR	GW	HX ◇1		XR	XR	GW ◇1	XR	HX ◇1	XR	GW	XR
London Paddington ⊖	d	09 02		09 10	09 13	09 18		09 20		09 20	09 25		09 28	09 32		09 40		09 43	09 48	09 50		09 55		09 56	10 02
Acton Main Line	d					09 24													09 54						
Ealing Broadway ⊖	d	09 11			09 22	09 27				09 33				09 41				09 52	09 57					10 05	10 11
West Ealing	d	09 14	09 27			09 30								09 44	09 57				10 00						10 14
Drayton Green	d		09 29												09 59										
Castle Bar Park	d		09 31												10 01										
South Greenford	d		09 34												10 04										
Greenford ⊖	a		09 39												10 09										
Hanwell	d	09 16												09 46											10 16
Southall	d	09 20			09 30	09 34								09 50				10 00	10 05						10 20
Hayes & Harlington	d	09 24			09 33	09a42				09 43				09 54				10 04	10a12					10 12	10 24
HeathrowTermls 2 & 3 ⊖ ✈	a	09 30		09 25							09 40			10 00		09 56						10 10			10 30
	d	09 33		09 28							09 41	09 48		10 03		09 58						10 11	10 18		10 33
Heathrow Terminal 4 ⊖ ✈	a	09 37										09 52		10 07									10 22		10 37
	d																								
Heathrow Terminal 5 ⊖ ✈	a			09 32							09 46					10 02						10 16			
	d																								
West Drayton	d				09 36					09 47								10 07						10 16	
Iver	d				09 39													10 10							
Langley	d				09 42				←									10 13			←				
Slough	a				09 45			09 33	09 45	09 53								10 16		10 03	10 16			10 22	
	d				09 46			09 34	09 46	09 54								10 17		10 05	10 17			10 24	
Burnham	d				→				09 49									→			10 20				
Taplow	d								09 52												10 23				
Maidenhead	d								09 56	10 00											10 27			10 31	
Twyford	d								10 03	10 07											10 34			10 38	
Reading	a							09 46	10 11	10 14			09 51							10 17	10 41			10 45	
Oxford	a							10 13												10 42					

A The Cheltenham Spa Express

For non-stop services between London and Reading refer to Table T116

For non-stop services between London and Heathrow Airport see Table T118

Table T117-F

Mondays to Fridays
16 December to 15 May

London - Greenford, Heathrow Airport and Reading
Stopping Services

	GW	HX ◇1	XR	XR	GW ◇1 ⚲	XR	HX ◇1		XR	GW	GW ◇1 ⚲	XR	GW	GW ◇1 ⚲	HX ◇1	XR	XR		GW ◇1 ⚲	XR	HX ◇1	XR	GW	XR
London Paddington 15 ⊖ d		10 10	10 13	10 18	10 20		10 25			10 27	10 28	10 32		10 35	10 40	10 43	10 48		10 50		10 55		10 56	11 02
Acton Main Line d				10 24													10 54							
Ealing Broadway ⊖ d			10 25	10 28						10 35		10 41				10 51	10 57						11 04	11 11
West Ealing d	10 27			10 31								10 44	10 57				11 00							11 14
Drayton Green d	10 29												10 59											
Castle Bar Park d	10 31												11 01											
South Greenford d	10 34												11 04											
Greenford ⊖ a	10 39												11 09											
Hanwell d												10 46												11 16
Southall d			10 30	10 35								10 50				11 00	11 04							11 20
Hayes & Harlington d			10 33	10a42						10 43		10 54				11 03	11a12						11 13	11 24
HeathrowTermls 2 & 3 2 ⊖ ✈ a		10 25					10 40					11 00			10 55						11 10			11 30
d		10 28					10 41		10 48			11 03			10 58						11 11	11 18		11 33
Heathrow Terminal 4 ⊖ ✈ a									10 52			11 07										11 22		11 37
d																								
Heathrow Terminal 5 ⊖ ✈ a		10 32					10 46								11 02						11 16			
d																								
West Drayton d			10 37							10 47						11 07							11 17	
Iver d			10 40													11 10								
Langley d			10 42			←										11 12				←				
Slough 3 a			10 46		10 33	10 46				10 52						11 16			11 03	11 16			11 22	
d			10 46		10 34	10 46				10 54						11 16			11 04	11 16			11 24	
Burnham d			→			10 50										→				11 20				
Taplow d						10 53														11 23				
Maidenhead 3 d						10 56				11 00										11 26			11 30	
Twyford 3 d						11 03				11 08										11 33			11 37	
Reading 7 a					10 46	11 12				11 16	10 51			10 59					11 16	11 41			11 44	
Oxford a					11 13														11 42					

	GW	HX ◇1	XR		XR	GW ◇1 ⚲	XR	HX ◇1	XR	GW	GW ◇1 ⚲	XR	GW		GW ◇	HX ◇1	XR	XR	GW ◇1 ⚲	XR	HX ◇1	XR	GW	
London Paddington 15 ⊖ d		11 10	11 13		11 18	11 20		11 25		11 27	11 28	11 32			11 36	11 40	11 43	11 48	11 50		11 55		11 57	
Acton Main Line d					11 24													11 54						
Ealing Broadway ⊖ d			11 21		11 27					11 35		11 41					11 51	11 57					12 05	
West Ealing d	11 27				11 30							11 44	11 57					12 00						
Drayton Green d	11 29												11 59											
Castle Bar Park d	11 31												12 01											
South Greenford d	11 34												12 04											
Greenford ⊖ a	11 39												12 09											
Hanwell d												11 46												
Southall d			11 27		11 35							11 50					12 00	12 05						
Hayes & Harlington d			11 30		11a42					11 43		11 54					12 03	12a12					12 13	
HeathrowTermls 2 & 3 2 ⊖ ✈ a		11 25						11 40				12 00				11 56					12 10			
d		11 28						11 41	11 48			12 03				11 58					12 11	12 18		
Heathrow Terminal 4 ⊖ ✈ a									11 52			12 07										12 22		
d																								
Heathrow Terminal 5 ⊖ ✈ a		11 32						11 46								12 02					12 16			
d																								
West Drayton d			11 34							11 47							12 07						12 17	
Iver d			11 37														12 10							
Langley d			11 39				←										12 12			←				
Slough 3 a			11 43			11 33	11 43			11 52							12 16		12 03	12 16			12 22	
d			11 43			11 34	11 43			11 54							12 16		12 04	12 16			12 24	
Burnham d			→				11 47										→			12 20				
Taplow d							11 50													12 23				
Maidenhead 3 d							11 53			12 00										12 26			12 30	
Twyford 3 d							12 00			12 07										12 33			12 37	
Reading 7 a						11 46	12 08			12 14	11 51				12 03				12 16	12 41			12 44	
Oxford a						12 13													12 42					

For non-stop services between London and Reading refer to Table T116

For non-stop services between London and Heathrow Airport see Table T118

Table T117-F

Mondays to Fridays
16 December to 15 May

London - Greenford, Heathrow Airport and Reading
Stopping Services

	XR	HX ◇1	XR	XR	GW		GW ◇1 ⚲	XR	HX ◇1	XR	GW	GW ◇1 ⚲	XR	GW ◇1 ⚲	HX ◇1		XR	XR	GW	GW ◇1 ⚲	XR	HX ◇1	XR	GW
London Paddington 15 ⊖ d	12 02	12 10	12 13	12 18			12 20		12 25		12 26	12 28	12 32	12 36	12 40		12 43	12 48		12 50		12 55		12 57
Acton Main Line d				12 24														12 54						
Ealing Broadway ⊖ d	12 11		12 21	12 27							12 34		12 41				12 51	12 57						13 05
West Ealing d	12 14			12 30	12 31								12 44					13 00	13 01					
Drayton Green d					12 33														13 03					
Castle Bar Park d					12 35														13 05					
South Greenford d					12 38														13 08					
Greenford ⊖ a					12 43														13 13					
Hanwell d	12 16												12 46											
Southall d	12 20		12 30	12 35									12 50				12 58	13 05						
Hayes & Harlington d	12 24		12 33	12a42							12 42		12 54				13 03	13a12						13 12
HeathrowTermls 2 & 3 2 ⊖ ✈ a	12 30	12 25							12 40				13 00		12 55							13 10		
d	12 33	12 28							12 41	12 48			13 03		12 58							13 11	13 18	
Heathrow Terminal 4 ⊖ ✈ a	12 37									12 52			13 07										13 22	
d																								
Heathrow Terminal 5 ⊖ ✈ a		12 32							12 46						13 02							13 16		
d																								
West Drayton d			12 37								12 46						13 07							13 16
Iver d			12 40														13 10							
Langley d			12 42					←									13 12				←			
Slough 3 a			12 46				12 33	12 46			12 52						13 16			13 03	13 16			13 22
d			12 46				12 34	12 46			12 54						13 16			13 04	13 16			13 24
Burnham d			→					12 50									→				13 20			
Taplow d								12 53													13 23			
Maidenhead 3 d								12 56			13 00										13 26			13 30
Twyford 3 d								13 03			13 07										13 34			13 37
Reading 7 a							12 46	13 11			13 14	12 51		12 59						13 16	13 42			13 45
Oxford a							13 13													13 42				

	XR		HX ◇1	XR	XR	GW	GW ◇1 ⚲	XR	HX ◇1	XR	GW		GW ◇1 ⚲	XR	GW	GW ◇	HX ◇1	XR	XR	GW ◇1 ⚲	XR		HX ◇1	XR
London Paddington 15 ⊖ d	13 02		13 10	13 13	13 18		13 20		13 25		13 27		13 28	13 32		13 34	13 40	13 43	13 48	13 50			13 55	
Acton Main Line d					13 24														13 54					
Ealing Broadway ⊖ d	13 11			13 21	13 27						13 35			13 41				13 51	13 57					
West Ealing d	13 14				13 30	13 31								13 44	14 00				14 00					
Drayton Green d						13 33									14 02									
Castle Bar Park d						13 35									14 04									
South Greenford d						13 38									14 07									
Greenford ⊖ a						13 43									14 12									
Hanwell d	13 16													13 46										
Southall d	13 20			13 30	13 35									13 50				14 00	14 05					
Hayes & Harlington d	13 24			13 33	13a42						13 42			13 54				14 03	14a12					
HeathrowTermls 2 & 3 2 ⊖ ✈ a	13 30		13 26						13 40					14 00			13 55						14 10	
d	13 33		13 28						13 41	13 48				14 03			13 58						14 11	14 18
Heathrow Terminal 4 ⊖ ✈ a	13 37									13 52				14 07										14 22
d																								
Heathrow Terminal 5 ⊖ ✈ a			13 32						13 46								14 02						14 16	
d																								
West Drayton d				13 37							13 46							14 07						
Iver d				13 40														14 10						
Langley d				13 42				←										14 12			←			
Slough 3 a				13 46			13 33	13 46			13 52							14 16		14 03	14 16			
d				13 46			13 34	13 46			13 54							14 16		14 04	14 16			
Burnham d				→				13 50										→			14 20			
Taplow d								13 53													14 23			
Maidenhead 3 d								13 56			14 00										14 26			
Twyford 3 d								14 03			14 07										14 33			
Reading 7 a							13 46	14 11			14 14		13 51			14 00				14 16	14 41			
Oxford a							14 13													14 42				

For non-stop services between London and Reading refer to Table T116

For non-stop services between London and Heathrow Airport see Table T118

Table T117-F

Mondays to Fridays
16 December to 15 May

London - Greenford, Heathrow Airport and Reading

Stopping Services

		GW	XR	HX		XR	XR	GW	GW	XR	HX	XR	GW	GW		XR	HX	XR	XR	GW	GW	XR	HX	XR	
				◇1					◇1 🚲		◇1			◇1 🚲			◇1				◇1 🚲		◇1		
London Paddington 15 ⊖	d	13 56	14 02	14 10		14 13	14 18		14 20		14 25		14 27	14 28		14 32	14 40	14 43	14 48		14 50		14 55		
Acton Main Line	d						14 24												14 54						
Ealing Broadway ⊖	d	14 06	14 11			14 23	14 27						14 35			14 41		14 51	14 57						
West Ealing	d		14 14				14 30	14 35								14 44			15 00	15 05					
Drayton Green	d							14 37												15 07					
Castle Bar Park	d							14 39												15 09					
South Greenford	d							14 42												15 12					
Greenford ⊖	a							14 47												15 17					
Hanwell	d		14 16													14 46									
Southall	d		14 20			14 30	14 35									14 50		15 00	15 05						
Hayes & Harlington	d	14 12	14 24			14 33	14a42						14 42			14 54		15 03	15a12						
HeathrowTermls 2 & 3 2 ⊖ ✈	a		14 30	14 25							14 40					15 00	14 55						15 10		
	d		14 33	14 28							14 41	14 48				15 03	14 58						15 11	15 18	
Heathrow Terminal 4 ⊖ ✈	a		14 37									14 52				15 07								15 22	
	d																								
Heathrow Terminal 5 ⊖ ✈	a			14 32							14 46						15 02						15 16		
	d																								
West Drayton	d	14 16				14 37							14 46					15 07							
Iver	d					14 40												15 10							
Langley	d					14 42				←								15 12				←			
Slough 3	a	14 22				14 46			14 33	14 46			14 52					15 16			15 03	15 16			
	d	14 24				14 46			14 34	14 46			14 54					15 16			15 04	15 16			
Burnham	d					→				14 50								→				15 20			
Taplow	d									14 53												15 23			
Maidenhead 3	d	14 30								14 56			15 00									15 26			
Twyford 3	d	14 37								15 03			15 07									15 33			
Reading 7	a	14 44							14 46	15 11			15 14	14 51							15 16	15 41			
Oxford	a								15 13												15 42				

		GW	XR	HX	XR	XR	GW	GW	XR	HX		XR	GW	GW	XR	GW	HX	XR	XR	GW		GW	XR	HX	XR
				◇1				◇1 🚲		◇1				◇1 🚲		◇	◇1					◇1 🚲		◇1	
London Paddington 15 ⊖	d	14 57	15 02	15 10	15 13	15 18		15 20		15 25			15 27	15 28	15 32	15 37	15 40	15 43	15 48			15 50		15 55	
Acton Main Line	d					15 24													15 54						
Ealing Broadway ⊖	d	15 05	15 11		15 24	15 27							15 35		15 41			15 51	15 57						
West Ealing	d		15 14			15 30	15 35								15 44				16 00	16 05					
Drayton Green	d						15 37													16 07					
Castle Bar Park	d						15 39													16 09					
South Greenford	d						15 42													16 12					
Greenford ⊖	a						15 47													16 17					
Hanwell	d		15 16												15 46										
Southall	d		15 20		15 30	15 35									15 50			16 00	16 05						
Hayes & Harlington	d	15 14	15 24		15 33	15a42							15 47		15 54			16 03	16a12						
HeathrowTermls 2 & 3 2 ⊖ ✈	a		15 30	15 25						15 40					16 00		15 55							16 10	
	d		15 33	15 28						15 41		15 48			16 03		15 58							16 11	16 18
Heathrow Terminal 4 ⊖ ✈	a		15 37									15 52			16 07										16 22
	d																								
Heathrow Terminal 5 ⊖ ✈	a			15 32						15 46							16 02							16 16	
	d																								
West Drayton	d	15 18			15 37								15 51					16 07							
Iver	d				15 40													16 10							
Langley	d				15 42				←									16 12					←		
Slough 3	a	15 23			15 46			15 33	15 46				15 57					16 16					16 16		
	d	15 24			15 46			15 34	15 46				15 59					16 16				16u04	16 16		
Burnham	d				→				15 50									→					16 20		
Taplow	d								15 53														16 23		
Maidenhead 3	d	15 30							15 56				16 07										16 26		
Twyford 3	d	15 37							16 03				16 14										16 33		
Reading 7	a	15 44						15 46	16 11				16 21	15 51		16 02						16b18	16 42		
Oxford	a							16 12														16 41			

b Stops to pick up only

For non-stop services between London and Reading refer to Table T116

For non-stop services between London and Heathrow Airport see Table T118

NRT DECEMBER 19 EDITION

Table T117-F

Mondays to Fridays
16 December to 15 May

London - Greenford, Heathrow Airport and Reading

Stopping Services

		GW		XR	XR	HX	XR	XR	GW	GW	XR	HX		XR	XR	XR	GW FX	HX	GW	XR	XR	GW		GW	XR
						◇1				◇1 🚲		◇1					◇1 A 🚲	◇1							
London Paddington 15 ⊖	d	15 56		15 58	16 02	16 10	16 13	16 18		16 20		16 25			16 28	16 32	16 38	16 40	16 43	16 43	16 48			16 50	
Acton Main Line	d							16 24													16 54				
Ealing Broadway ⊖	d			16 08	16 11		16 21	16 27							16 38	16 41				16 53	16 57				
West Ealing	d				16 14			16 30	16 35							16 44					17 00	17 05			
Drayton Green	d								16 37													17 07			
Castle Bar Park	d								16 39													17 09			
South Greenford	d								16 42													17 12			
Greenford ⊖	a								16 47													17 17			
Hanwell	d				16 16											16 46									
Southall	d			16 13	16 20		16 29	16 35							16 43	16 50				17 00	17 05				
Hayes & Harlington	d			16 17	16 24		16 32	16a42							16 47	16 54				17 03	17a12				
HeathrowTermls 2 & 3 2 ⊖ ✈	a				16 30	16 25						16 40				17 00		16 55							
	d				16 33	16 28						16 41		16 48		17 03		16 58							
Heathrow Terminal 4 ⊖ ✈	a				16 37									16 52		17 07									
	d																								
Heathrow Terminal 5 ⊖ ✈	a					16 32						16 46						17 02							
	d																								
West Drayton	d			16 20			16 37								16 50					17 06					
Iver	d			16 23			16 40								16 53					17 09					
Langley	d			16 26			16 42				←				16 56					17 12					←
Slough 3	a	16 20		16 30			16 46			16 33	16 46				17 00					17 15					17 00
	d	16 23		16 31			16 46			16 34	16 46				17 01					17 16					17 01
Burnham	d			16 34			→				16 50				→					→					17 04
Taplow	d			16 37							16 53														17 08
Maidenhead 3	d	16 30		16 41							16 56													17 08	17 12
Twyford 3	d	16 37		16 48							17 03													17 15	17 20
Reading 7	a	16 45		16 56						16 46	17 11						17 01		17 09					17 22	17 27
Oxford	a									17 13															

		XR	HX	XR	GW	XR	XR	HX		XR	XR	GW	GW	XR	XR	HX	XR	GW		XR	XR	GW	HX	GW	XR
			◇1					◇1								◇1						◇1 B 🚲	◇1		
London Paddington 15 ⊖	d		16 55		16 56	16 58	17 02	17 10		17 13	17 18		17 19			17 25		17 27		17 28	17 32	17 34	17 40	17 42	17 43
Acton Main Line	d										17 24														
Ealing Broadway ⊖	d					17 08	17 11			17 21	17 27									17 38	17 41				17 51
West Ealing	d						17 14				17 30	17 35									17 44				
Drayton Green	d											17 37													
Castle Bar Park	d											17 39													
South Greenford	d											17 42													
Greenford ⊖	a											17 47													
Hanwell	d						17 16														17 46				
Southall	d					17 13	17 20			17 30	17 35									17 43	17 50				18 00
Hayes & Harlington	d					17 17	17 24			17 33	17a42									17 47	17 54				18 03
HeathrowTermls 2 & 3 2 ⊖ ✈	a		17 10				17 30	17 25								17 40					18 00		17 55		
	d		17 11	17 18			17 33	17 28								17 41	17 48				18 03		17 58		
Heathrow Terminal 4 ⊖ ✈	a			17 22			17 37										17 52				18 07				
	d																								
Heathrow Terminal 5 ⊖ ✈	a		17 16					17 32								17 46							18 02		
	d																								
West Drayton	d					17 20				17 37										17 50					18 07
Iver	d					17 23				17 40										17 53					18 10
Langley	d	←				17 26				17 42				←	←					17 56					18 12
Slough 3	a	17 15			17 20	17 30				17 46				17 30	17 46			17 50		18 00					18 16
	d	17 16			17 20	17 31				17 46				17 31	17 46			17 50		18 00					18 16
Burnham	d	17 19			17 24	→				→				17 34	17 50			17 54		18 04					→
Taplow	d	17 22												17 37	17 53					18 07					
Maidenhead 3	d	17 26			17a30								17 40	17 44	17 56			18a00		18 10					
Twyford 3	d	17 33											17 47	17 51	18 03					18 17					
Reading 7	a	17 41											17 54	17 58	18 11					18 25		17 57		18 08	
Oxford	a																					18 21			

A until 2 April

B The Cathedrals Express

For non-stop services between London and Reading refer to Table T116

For non-stop services between London and Heathrow Airport see Table T118

Table T117-F

Mondays to Fridays

16 December to 15 May

London - Greenford, Heathrow Airport and Reading

Stopping Services

Station		XR	GW	GW	XR	HX ◇1	XR	GW	XR	XR		HX ◇1	XR	XR	GW	GW	XR	XR	HX ◇1	XR		GW	XR	XR	HX ◇1
London Paddington 15 ⊖	d	17 48		17 51		17 55		17 56	17 58	18 02		18 10	18 13	18 18		18 20			18 25			18 26	18 28	18 32	18 40
Acton Main Line	d	17 54												18 24											
Ealing Broadway ⊖	d	17 57							18 08	18 11			18 21	18 27									18 38	18 41	
West Ealing	d	18 00	18 05							18 14				18 30	18 35									18 44	
Drayton Green	d		18 07												18 37										
Castle Bar Park	d		18 09												18 39										
South Greenford	d		18 12												18 42										
Greenford ⊖	a		18 17												18 47										
Hanwell	d									18 16														18 46	
Southall	d	18 05							18 13	18 20			18 30	18 35									18 43	18 50	
Hayes & Harlington	d	18a12							18 17	18 24			18 33	18a42									18 47	18 54	
HeathrowTermls 2 & 3 2 ⊖ ✈	a					18 10				18 30		18 25							18 40					19 00	18 55
	d					18 11	18 18			18 33		18 28							18 41	18 48				19 03	18 58
Heathrow Terminal 4 ⊖ ✈	a						18 22			18 37										18 52				19 07	
	d																								
Heathrow Terminal 5 ⊖ ✈	a					18 16						18 32							18 46						19 02
	d																								
West Drayton	d								18 20				18 37										18 50		
Iver	d								18 23				18 40										18 53		
Langley	d				←				18 26				18 42				←	←					18 56		
Slough 3	a				18 16			18 20	18 30				18 46				18 30	18 46				18 50	19 00		
	d				18 16			18 21	18 32				18 46				18 32	18 46				18 51	19 01		
Burnham	d				18 20			18 25	→				→				18 36	18 50				18 55	19 04		
Taplow	d				18 23												18 39	18 53					19 07		
Maidenhead 3	d			18 16	18 26			18 30								18 39	18 43	18 56				19 00	19 11		
Twyford 3	d			18 23	18 33			18 37								18 46	18 50	19 03				19 07	19 18		
Reading 7	a			18 30	18 41			18 44								18 53	18 57	19 11				19 14	19 26		
Oxford	a																								

Station		GW	XR	XR	GW	GW		XR	HX ◇1	XR	GW	XR	XR	HX ◇1	XR	XR		GW	GW	HX ◇1	XR	GW	GW ◇1	XR	GW
London Paddington 15 ⊖	d	18 42	18 43	18 48		18 49			18 55		18 56	18 58	19 02	19 10	19 13	19 18			19 20	19 25		19 26	19 30	19 32	19 35
Acton Main Line	d			18 54												19 24									
Ealing Broadway ⊖	d		18 53	18 57								19 08	19 11		19 21	19 27						19 34		19 41	
West Ealing	d			19 00	19 05								19 14			19 30		19 35						19 44	
Drayton Green	d				19 07													19 37							
Castle Bar Park	d				19 09													19 39							
South Greenford	d				19 12													19 42							
Greenford ⊖	a				19 17													19 47							
Hanwell	d												19 16											19 46	
Southall	d		19 00	19 05								19 13	19 20		19 30	19 35						19 40		19 50	
Hayes & Harlington	d		19 03	19a12								19 17	19 24		19 33	19a42						19 43		19 54	
HeathrowTermls 2 & 3 2 ⊖ ✈	a								19 10				19 30	19 25						19 40				20 00	
	d								19 11	19 18			19 33	19 28						19 41	19 48			20 03	
Heathrow Terminal 4 ⊖ ✈	a									19 22			19 37								19 52			20 07	
	d																								
Heathrow Terminal 5 ⊖ ✈	a								19 16					19 32						19 46					
	d																								
West Drayton	d		19 07									19 20			19 37							19 47			
Iver	d		19 10									19 24			19 41										
Langley	d		19 12					←				19 27			19 44										
Slough 3	a		19 16					19 16			19 20	19 31			19 47							19 53			
	d		19 16					19 16			19 21	19 32			19 48							19 54			
Burnham	d		→					19 20			19 25	19 35			→							→			
Taplow	d							19 23				19 38													
Maidenhead 3	d					19 15		19 26			19 30	19a42							19 39						19 54
Twyford 3	d					19 23		19 33			19 37								19 46						20 02
Reading 7	a	19 08				19 30		19 41			19 44								19 55				19 53		20 09
Oxford	a																						20 18		

For non-stop services between London and Reading refer to Table T116

For non-stop services between London and Heathrow Airport see Table T118

Table T117-F

Mondays to Fridays

16 December to 15 May

London - Greenford, Heathrow Airport and Reading

Stopping Services

Station		GW ◇	XR	HX ◇1	XR	XR	GW	GW ◇1		GW	XR	HX ◇1	XR	GW	XR	HX ◇1	XR	XR		GW	GW	GW ◇1	XR	HX ◇1	XR
London Paddington 15 ⊖	d	19 36		19 40	19 43	19 48		19 50				19 55		19 56	20 02	20 10	20 13	20 18			20 18	20 20		20 25	
Acton Main Line	d					19 56												20 24							
Ealing Broadway ⊖	d				19 51	20 00								20 04	20 11		20 21	20 27							
West Ealing	d					20 02	20 05								20 14			20 30		20 39					
Drayton Green	d						20 07													20 41					
Castle Bar Park	d						20 09													20 43					
South Greenford	d						20 12													20 46					
Greenford ⊖	a						20 17													20 51					
Hanwell	d														20 16										
Southall	d				20 00	20 07									20 20		20 30	20 35							
Hayes & Harlington	d				20 03	20a14								20 14	20 24		20 33	20a42							
HeathrowTermls 2 & 3 2 ⊖ ✈	a			19 55								20 10			20 30	20 25								20 40	
	d			19 58								20 11	20 18		20 33	20 28								20 41	20 48
Heathrow Terminal 4 ⊖ ✈	a												20 22		20 37										20 52
	d																								
Heathrow Terminal 5 ⊖ ✈	a			20 02								20 16				20 32								20 46	
	d																								
West Drayton	d				20 07									20 18			20 37								
Iver	d				20 10												20 40								
Langley	d		←		20 12					←	←						20 42						←		
Slough 3	a		19 47		20 16			20 03		19 53	20 16			20 24			20 46					20 34	20 46		
	d		19 48		20 16			20 04		19 54	20 16			20 26			20 46					20 35	20 46		
Burnham	d		19 52		→						20 20						→						20 50		
Taplow	d		19 55								20 23												20 53		
Maidenhead 3	d		19 59							20 03	20 26			20 34							20 38		20 56		
Twyford 3	d		20 06							20 10	20 33			20 41							20 45		21 03		
Reading 7	a	20 04	20 14					20 17		20 18	20 41			20 49							20 52	20 47	21 11		
Oxford	a							20 42														21 13			

Station		GW	GW ◇1	XR		HX ◇1	XR	XR	GW	GW ◇1	XR	HX ◇1	XR	GW		XR	HX ◇1	XR	GW ◇1	XR	XR	GW	HX ◇1	XR	
London Paddington 15 ⊖	d	20 26	20 28	20 32		20 40	20 43	20 48		20 50		20 55		20 56		21 02	21 10	21 13	21 15		21 18		21 25		
Acton Main Line	d							20 54													21 24				
Ealing Broadway ⊖	d	20 34		20 41			20 51	20 57						21 04		21 11		21 21			21 27				
West Ealing	d			20 44				21 00	21 08							21 14					21 30	21 37			
Drayton Green	d								21 10													21 39			
Castle Bar Park	d								21 12													21 41			
South Greenford	d								21 15													21 44			
Greenford ⊖	a								21 20													21 49			
Hanwell	d			20 46												21 16									
Southall	d			20 50			21 00	21 05								21 20		21 30			21 35				
Hayes & Harlington	d	20 42		20 54			21 03	21a12						21 12		21 24		21 33			21a42				
HeathrowTermls 2 & 3 2 ⊖ ✈	a			21 00		20 55						21 10				21 30	21 25						21 40		
	d			21 03		20 58						21 11	21 18			21 33	21 28						21 41	21 48	
Heathrow Terminal 4 ⊖ ✈	a			21 07									21 22			21 37								21 52	
	d																								
Heathrow Terminal 5 ⊖ ✈	a					21 02						21 16					21 32						21 46		
	d																								
West Drayton	d	20 46					21 07							21 16				21 37							
Iver	d						21 10											21 40							
Langley	d						21 12				←							21 42		←					
Slough 3	a	20 53					21 16			21 03	21 16			21 22				21 46	21 28	21 46					
	d	20 54					21 16			21 04	21 16			21 24				21 46	21 29	21 46					
Burnham	d						→				21 20							→		21 50					
Taplow	d										21 23									21 53					
Maidenhead 3	d	21 00									21 26			21 30					21 35	21 56					
Twyford 3	d	21 07									21 33			21 37					21 41	22 03					
Reading 7	a	21 14	20 51							21 17	21 41			21 45					21 47	22 11					
Oxford	a									21 42									22 14						

For non-stop services between London and Reading refer to Table T116

For non-stop services between London and Heathrow Airport see Table T118

Table T117-F

Mondays to Fridays
16 December to 15 May

London - Greenford, Heathrow Airport and Reading
Stopping Services

Station		GW	XR	GW ◇1	HX ◇1	XR		XR	GW ◇1	XR	HX ◇1	XR	GW	XR	HX ◇1	XR		XR	GW ◇1	HX ◇1	XR	GW	XR	HX ◇1	GW
London Paddington 15 ⊖	d	21 26	21 32	21 33	21 40	21 43		21 48	21 50		21 55		21 57	22 02	22 10	22 13		22 18	22 18	22 25		22 27	22 32	22 40	22 41
Acton Main Line	d							21 54										22 24							
Ealing Broadway ⊖	d	21 34	21 41			21 51		21 57					22 05	22 11		22 21		22 27				22 35	22 41		22 49
West Ealing	d		21 44					22 00						22 14				22 30					22 44		
Drayton Green	d																								
Castle Bar Park	d																								
South Greenford	d																								
Greenford ⊖	a																								
Hanwell	d		21 46											22 16									22 46		
Southall	d		21 50			22 00		22 05						22 20		22 28		22 35					22 50		
Hayes & Harlington	d	21 42	21 54			22 03		22a12					22 12	22 24		22 31		22a42				22 42	22 54		22 57
HeathrowTermls 2 & 3 2 ⊖ ✈	a		22 00		21 55						22 10			22 30	22 25					22 40			23 00	22 55	
	d		22 03		21 58						22 11	22 18		22 33	22 28					22 41	22 48		23 03	22 58	
Heathrow Terminal 4 ⊖ ✈	a		22 07									22 22		22 37							22 52		23 07		
	d																								
Heathrow Terminal 5 ⊖ ✈	a				22 02						22 16				22 32					22 46				23 02	
	d																								
West Drayton	d	21 46				22 07							22 16			22 35						22 46			23 03
Iver	d					22 10										22 38									
Langley	d					22 12				←						22 40									
Slough 3	a	21 52				22 16			22 03	22 16			22 22			22 44						22 52			23 10
	d	21 54				22 16			22 04	22 16			22 24			22 44						22 53			23 10
Burnham	d					→				22 20						22 48									→
Taplow	d									22 23						22 51									
Maidenhead 3	d	22 00								22 26			22 30			22 54						22 59			
Twyford 3	d	22 07								22 33			22 37			23 01						23 06			
Reading 7	a	22 14		21 56					22 16	22 41			22 44			23 09			22 41			23 14			
Oxford	a								22 43										23 06						

Station		XR		XR	GW ◇1	GW	XR	HX ◇1	XR	XR	HX ◇1	XR		GW ◇1	XR	XR	HX ◇1	XR	GW	XR	GW
London Paddington 15 ⊖	d	22 43		22 48	22 50			22 55		23 02	23 10	23 13		23 15		23 18	23 25		23 34	23 43	23 52
Acton Main Line	d			22 54												23 24					
Ealing Broadway ⊖	d	22 53		22 57						23 11		23 21				23 27				23 51	00 01
West Ealing	d			23 00						23 14						23 30					
Drayton Green	d																				
Castle Bar Park	d																				
South Greenford	d																				
Greenford ⊖	a																				
Hanwell	d									23 16											
Southall	d	23 00		23 05						23 20		23 28				23 35				23 59	00 05
Hayes & Harlington	d	23 03		23a12						23 24		23 31				23a42				00 02	00 09
HeathrowTermls 2 & 3 2 ⊖ ✈	a							23 10		23 30	23 25						23 40				
	d							23 11	23 18	23 33	23 28						23 41	23 48			
Heathrow Terminal 4 ⊖ ✈	a								23 22	23 37								23 52			
	d																				
Heathrow Terminal 5 ⊖ ✈	a							23 16			23 32						23 46				
	d																				
West Drayton	d	23 07										23 35								00 06	00 13
Iver	d	23 10										23 38								00 09	00 16
Langley	d	23 12				←	←					23 40			←					00 11	00 19
Slough 3	a	23 16			23 05	23 10	23 16					23 44		23 34	23 44				23 56	00 15	00 22
	d	23 16			23 06	23 10	23 16					23 52		23 35	23 52				23 56	00 15	00 23
Burnham	d	→					23 20					→			23 56						00 26
Taplow	d						23 23								23 59						00 29
Maidenhead 3	d				23 13	23 17	23 26							23 42	00a05				00 09	00a22	00 33
Twyford 3	d				23 20	23 24	23 33							23 50					00 19		00 40
Reading 7	a				23 26	23 31	23 41							23 58					00 25		00 47
Oxford	a				23 52									00 35							

For non-stop services between London and Reading refer to Table T116

For non-stop services between London and Heathrow Airport see Table T118

NRT DECEMBER 19 EDITION

Table T117-F

Saturdays
21 December to 16 May

London - Greenford, Heathrow Airport and Reading
Stopping Services

Station		GW	XR	GW	GW	GW ◇1		GW	GW	GW	XR	HX	XR	XR	HX ◇1	XR		XR	GW ◇1	XR	HX ◇1	XR	GW	XR	HX ◇1
London Paddington 15 ⊖	d					00 30		00 34	01 34	03 34	04 42			05 02	05 10	05 13		05 18	05 20		05 25		05 27	05 32	05 40
Acton Main Line	d																								
Ealing Broadway ⊖	d				00 01			00 42	01 42	03 42	04 50			05 11		05 21		05 27					05 35	05 41	
West Ealing	d													05 14										05 44	
Drayton Green	d																								
Castle Bar Park	d																								
South Greenford	d																								
Greenford ⊖	a																								
Hanwell	d													05 16										05 46	
Southall	d				00 05			00 47	01 47	03 47	04 54			05 20		05 30		05 35						05 50	
Hayes & Harlington	d		00 02		00 09			00 50	01 50	03 50	04 58			05 24		05 33		05a42					05 42	05 54	
HeathrowTermls 2 & 3 2 ⊖ ✈	a										05 05			05 30	05 25						05 40			06 00	05 55
	d										05 07	05 13	05 18	05 33	05 27						05 41	05 48		06 03	05 58
Heathrow Terminal 4 ⊖ ✈	a										05 15		05 22	05 37								05 52		06 07	
	d																								
Heathrow Terminal 5 ⊖ ✈	a											05 17			05 31						05 46				06 02
	d																								
West Drayton	d		00 06		00 13			00 54	01 54	03 54						05 37							05 46		
Iver	d		00 09		00 16			00 58								05 40									
Langley	d		00 11		00 19			01 01								05 42				←					
Slough 3	a		00 15		00 22	00 48		01 04	02 00	04 00						05 46			05 35	05 46			05 52		
	d		00 15		00 23	00 48		01 05	02 00	04 00						05 46			05 35	05 46			05 56		
Burnham	d				00 26			01 09								→				05 50					
Taplow	d				00 29			01 12												05 53					
Maidenhead 3	d	00 09	00a22		00 33	00 56		01 16	02 07	04 07										05 56			06 02		
Twyford 3	d	00 19		00 33	00 40	01 04		01 23	02 14	04 14										06 03			06 09		
Reading 7	a	00 25		00 44	00 47	01 11		01 31	02 21	04 21									05 48	06 11			06 18		
Oxford	a					01 44													06 18						

Station		GW		XR	XR	GW ◇1	XR	HX ◇1	XR	GW	XR	GW		HX ◇1	XR	XR	GW ◇1	XR	HX ◇1	XR	GW	XR		GW	HX ◇1
London Paddington 15 ⊖	d	05 41		05 43	05 47	05 50		05 55		05 55	06 02			06 10	06 13	06 18	06 20		06 25		06 27	06 32			06 40
Acton Main Line	d				05 53											06 24									
Ealing Broadway ⊖	d	05 49		05 53	05 57					06 03	06 11				06 21	06 27					06 35	06 41			
West Ealing	d	05 52			05 59						06 14	06 27				06 30						06 44		06 57	
Drayton Green	d	05 55										06 29												06 59	
Castle Bar Park	d	05 57										06 31												07 01	
South Greenford	d	05 59										06 33												07 03	
Greenford ⊖	a	06 05										06 39												07 09	
Hanwell	d										06 16											06 46			
Southall	d			06 00	06 04						06 20				06 30	06 35						06 50			
Hayes & Harlington	d			06 03	06a11					06 12	06 24				06 33	06a42					06 41	06 54			
HeathrowTermls 2 & 3 2 ⊖ ✈	a							06 10			06 30			06 25					06 40			07 00			06 55
	d							06 11	06 18		06 33			06 28					06 41	06 48		07 03			06 58
Heathrow Terminal 4 ⊖ ✈	a								06 22		06 37									06 52		07 07			
	d																								
Heathrow Terminal 5 ⊖ ✈	a							06 16						06 32					06 46						07 02
	d																								
West Drayton	d			06 07						06 16					06 37						06 45				
Iver	d			06 10											06 40										
Langley	d			06 12			←								06 42			←							
Slough 3	a			06 16		06 03	06 16			06 21					06 46		06 33	06 46			06 51				
	d			06 16		06 04	06 16			06 23					06 46		06 34	06 46			06 54				
Burnham	d			→			06 20								→			06 50							
Taplow	d						06 23											06 53							
Maidenhead 3	d						06 26			06 30								06 56			07 00				
Twyford 3	d						06 33			06 37								07 03			07 07				
Reading 7	a					06 16	06 41			06 44							06 48	07 11			07 14				
Oxford	a					06 47											07 22								

For non-stop services between London and Reading refer to Table T116

For non-stop services between London and Heathrow Airport see Table T118

Table T117-F

Saturdays
21 December to 16 May

London - Greenford, Heathrow Airport and Reading

Stopping Services

	XR	XR	GW ◇1 🍴	XR	HX ◇1	XR	GW	XR	GW	HX ◇1	XR	XR	GW ◇1	XR	HX ◇1	XR	GW	XR	GW	GW ◇1 🍴	HX ◇1
London Paddington 15 ⊖ d	06 43	06 48	06 50		06 55		06 57	07 02		07 10	07 13	07 18	07 20		07 25		07 27	07 32		07 32	07 40
Acton Main Line d		06 54										07 24									
Ealing Broadway ⊖ d	06 51	06 57					07 05	07 11			07 21	07 27					07 35	07 41			
West Ealing d		07 00						07 14	07 27			07 30						07 44	07 57		
Drayton Green d									07 29										07 59		
Castle Bar Park d									07 31										08 01		
South Greenford d									07 33										08 03		
Greenford ⊖ a									07 39										08 09		
Hanwell d								07 16										07 46			
Southall d	07 00	07 05						07 20			07 30	07 35						07 50			
Hayes & Harlington d	07 03	07a12					07 11	07 24			07 33	07a42					07 41	07 54			
HeathrowTermls 2 & 3 2 ⊖ ✈ a					07 10			07 30		07 25					07 40			08 00			07 55
d					07 11	07 18		07 33		07 28					07 41	07 48		08 03			07 58
Heathrow Terminal 4 ⊖ ✈ a						07 22		07 37								07 52		08 07			
d																					
Heathrow Terminal 5 ⊖ ✈ a					07 16					07 32					07 46						08 02
d																					
West Drayton d	07 07						07 15				07 37						07 45				
Iver d	07 10										07 40										
Langley d	07 12			←							07 42			←							
Slough 3 a	07 16		07 03	07 16			07 21				07 46		07 33	07 46			07 51				
d	07 16		07 04	07 16			07 24				07 46		07 34	07 46			07 54				
Burnham d	→			07 20							→			07 50							
Taplow d				07 23										07 53							
Maidenhead 3 d				07 26			07 30							07 56			08 00				
Twyford 3 d				07 33			07 37							08 03			08 07				
Reading 7 a			07 17	07 41			07 44						07 47	08 11			08 14			07 55	
Oxford a			07 43										08 16								

	XR	XR	GW ◇1 🍴	XR	HX ◇1	XR	GW	XR	GW	HX ◇1	XR	XR	GW ◇1	XR	HX ◇1	XR	GW	XR	GW	GW ◇1 🍴	GW ◇1 🍴	HX ◇1
London Paddington 15 ⊖ d	07 42	07 48	07 50		07 55		07 57	08 02		08 10	08 13	08 18	08 20		08 25		08 27	08 32		08 32	08 35	08 40
Acton Main Line d		07 54										08 24										
Ealing Broadway ⊖ d	07 53	07 57					08 05	08 11			08 21	08 27					08 35	08 41				
West Ealing d		08 00						08 14	08 27			08 30						08 44	08 57			
Drayton Green d									08 29										08 59			
Castle Bar Park d									08 31										09 01			
South Greenford d									08 33										09 03			
Greenford ⊖ a									08 39										09 09			
Hanwell d								08 16										08 46				
Southall d	08 00	08 05						08 20			08 30	08 35						08 50				
Hayes & Harlington d	08 03	08a12					08 11	08 24			08 33	08a42					08 41	08 54				
HeathrowTermls 2 & 3 2 ⊖ ✈ a					08 10			08 30		08 25					08 40			09 00				08 55
d					08 11	08 18		08 33		08 28					08 41	08 48		09 03				08 58
Heathrow Terminal 4 ⊖ ✈ a						08 22		08 37								08 52		09 07				
d																						
Heathrow Terminal 5 ⊖ ✈ a					08 16					08 32					08 46							09 02
d																						
West Drayton d	08 07						08 15				08 37						08 45					
Iver d	08 10										08 40											
Langley d	08 12			←							08 42			←								
Slough 3 a	08 16		08 03	08 16			08 21				08 46		08 33	08 46			08 51					
d	08 16		08 04	08 16			08 24				08 46		08 34	08 46			08 54					
Burnham d	→			08 20							→			08 50								
Taplow d				08 23										08 53								
Maidenhead 3 d				08 26			08 30							08 56			09 00					
Twyford 3 d				08 33			08 37							09 03			09 07					
Reading 7 a			08 17	08 41			08 44						08 47	09 11			09 15			08 55	08 58	
Oxford a			08 43										09 14									

For non-stop services between London and Reading refer to Table T116

For non-stop services between London and Heathrow Airport see Table T118

Table T117-F

Saturdays
21 December to 16 May

London - Greenford, Heathrow Airport and Reading

Stopping Services

	XR	XR	GW ◇1 🍴	XR	HX ◇1	XR	GW	XR	GW	HX ◇1	XR	XR	GW ◇1	XR	HX ◇1	XR	GW	XR	GW	GW ◇1 🍴	GW ◇
London Paddington 15 ⊖ d	08 43	08 48	08 50		08 55		08 57	09 02		09 10	09 13	09 18	09 20		09 25		09 27	09 32		09 32	09 37
Acton Main Line d		08 54										09 24									
Ealing Broadway ⊖ d	08 51	08 57					09 05	09 11			09 21	09 27					09 35	09 41			
West Ealing d		09 00						09 14	09 27			09 30						09 44	09 57		
Drayton Green d									09 29										09 59		
Castle Bar Park d									09 31										10 01		
South Greenford d									09 33										10 03		
Greenford ⊖ a									09 39										10 09		
Hanwell d								09 16										09 46			
Southall d	09 00	09 05						09 20			09 30	09 35						09 50			
Hayes & Harlington d	09 03	09a12					09 11	09 24			09 33	09a42					09 41	09 54			
HeathrowTermls 2 & 3 2 ⊖ ✈ a					09 10			09 30		09 25					09 40			10 00			
d					09 11	09 18		09 33		09 28					09 41	09 48		10 03			
Heathrow Terminal 4 ⊖ ✈ a						09 22		09 37								09 52		10 07			
d																					
Heathrow Terminal 5 ⊖ ✈ a					09 16					09 32					09 46						
d																					
West Drayton d	09 07						09 15				09 37						09 45				
Iver d	09 10										09 40										
Langley d	09 12			←							09 42			←							
Slough 3 a	09 16		09 03	09 16			09 21				09 46		09 33	09 46			09 51				
d	09 16		09 04	09 16			09 24				09 46		09 34	09 46			09 54				
Burnham d	→			09 20							→			09 50							
Taplow d				09 23										09 53							
Maidenhead 3 d				09 26			09 30							09 56			10 00				
Twyford 3 d				09 33			09 37							10 03			10 07				
Reading 7 a			09 17	09 41			09 44						09 47	10 11			10 14			09 55	10 02
Oxford a			09 43										10 14								

	HX ◇1	XR	XR	GW ◇1 🍴	XR	HX ◇1	XR	GW	XR	GW	HX ◇1	XR	XR	GW ◇1	XR	HX ◇1	XR	GW	XR	GW	GW ◇1 🍴	GW ◇1 🍴
London Paddington 15 ⊖ d	09 40	09 43	09 48	09 50		09 55		09 57	10 02		10 10	10 13	10 18	10 20		10 25		10 27	10 32		10 32	10 35
Acton Main Line d			09 54										10 24									
Ealing Broadway ⊖ d		09 51	09 57					10 05	10 11			10 21	10 27					10 35	10 41			
West Ealing d			10 00						10 14	10 27			10 30						10 44	10 57		
Drayton Green d										10 29										10 59		
Castle Bar Park d										10 31										11 01		
South Greenford d										10 33										11 03		
Greenford ⊖ a										10 39										11 09		
Hanwell d									10 16										10 46			
Southall d		10 00	10 05						10 20			10 30	10 35						10 50			
Hayes & Harlington d		10 03	10a12					10 11	10 24			10 33	10a42					10 41	10 54			
HeathrowTermls 2 & 3 2 ⊖ ✈ a	09 55					10 10			10 30		10 25					10 40			11 00			
d	09 58					10 11	10 18		10 33		10 28					10 41	10 48		11 03			
Heathrow Terminal 4 ⊖ ✈ a							10 22		10 37								10 52		11 07			
d																						
Heathrow Terminal 5 ⊖ ✈ a	10 02					10 16					10 32					10 46						
d																						
West Drayton d		10 07						10 15				10 37						10 45				
Iver d		10 10										10 40										
Langley d		10 12			←							10 42			←							
Slough 3 a		10 16		10 03	10 16			10 21				10 46		10 33	10 46			10 51				
d		10 16		10 04	10 16			10 24				10 46		10 34	10 46			10 54				
Burnham d		→			10 20							→			10 50							
Taplow d					10 23										10 53							
Maidenhead 3 d					10 26			10 30							10 56			11 00				
Twyford 3 d					10 33			10 37							11 03			11 07				
Reading 7 a				10 17	10 41			10 44						10 47	11 11			11 14			10 55	10 58
Oxford a				10 43										11 14								

For non-stop services between London and Reading refer to Table T116

For non-stop services between London and Heathrow Airport see Table T118

Table T117-F

Saturdays

21 December to 16 May

London - Greenford, Heathrow Airport and Reading

Stopping Services

		HX	XR	XR	GW	XR	HX	XR	GW	XR		GW	HX	XR	XR	GW	XR	HX	XR	GW		XR	GW	GW	GW
		◇1			◇1 🍴		◇1						◇1			◇1		◇1						◇1 🍴	◇
London Paddington 15 ⊖	d	10 40	10 43	10 48	10 50		10 55		10 56	11 02			11 10	11 13	11 18	11 20		11 25		11 27		11 32		11 32	11 37
Acton Main Line	d			10 54											11 24										
Ealing Broadway ⊖	d		10 51	10 57					11 04	11 11				11 21	11 27					11 35		11 41			
West Ealing	d			11 00						11 14		11 27			11 30							11 44	11 57		
Drayton Green	d											11 29											11 59		
Castle Bar Park	d											11 31											12 01		
South Greenford	d											11 33											12 03		
Greenford ⊖	a											11 39											12 09		
Hanwell	d									11 16												11 46			
Southall	d		11 00	11 05						11 20				11 30	11 35							11 50			
Hayes & Harlington	d		11 03	11a12					11 12	11 24				11 33	11a42					11 41		11 54			
HeathrowTermls 2 & 3 2 ⊖ ✈	a	10 55					11 10			11 30			11 25					11 40				12 00			
	d	10 58					11 11	11 18		11 33			11 28					11 41	11 48			12 03			
Heathrow Terminal 4 ⊖ ✈	a							11 22		11 37									11 52			12 07			
	d																								
Heathrow Terminal 5 ⊖ ✈	a	11 02					11 16						11 32					11 46							
	d																								
West Drayton	d		11 07						11 16					11 37						11 45					
Iver	d		11 10											11 40											
Langley	d		11 12			←								11 42			←								
Slough 3	a		11 16		11 03	11 16			11 22					11 46		11 34	11 46			11 51					
	d		11 16		11 04	11 16			11 24					11 46		11 35	11 46			11 54					
Burnham	d		→			11 20								→			11 50								
Taplow	d					11 23											11 53								
Maidenhead 3	d					11 26			11 30								11 56			12 00					
Twyford 3	d					11 33			11 37								12 03			12 07					
Reading 7	a				11 17	11 41			11 44							11 47	12 11			12 14				11 55	12 02
Oxford	a				11 43											12 14									

		HX	XR	XR	GW	XR		HX	XR	GW	XR	HX	XR	XR	GW	GW		XR	HX	XR	GW	XR	GW	GW	HX
		◇1			◇1 🍴			◇1				◇1				◇1			◇1				◇1 🍴	◇1 🍴	◇1
London Paddington 15 ⊖	d	11 40	11 43	11 48	11 50			11 55		11 57	12 02	12 10	12 13	12 18		12 20			12 25		12 27	12 32	12 32	12 35	12 40
Acton Main Line	d			11 54										12 24											
Ealing Broadway ⊖	d		11 51	11 57						12 05	12 11		12 21	12 27							12 35	12 41			
West Ealing	d			12 00							12 14			12 30	12 31							12 44			
Drayton Green	d														12 33										
Castle Bar Park	d														12 35										
South Greenford	d														12 37										
Greenford ⊖	a														12 43										
Hanwell	d										12 16											12 46			
Southall	d		12 00	12 05							12 20		12 30	12 35								12 50			
Hayes & Harlington	d		12 03	12a12						12 11	12 24		12 33	12a42							12 41	12 54			
HeathrowTermls 2 & 3 2 ⊖ ✈	a	11 55						12 10			12 30	12 25							12 40			13 00			12 55
	d	11 58						12 11	12 18		12 33	12 28							12 41	12 48		13 03			12 58
Heathrow Terminal 4 ⊖ ✈	a								12 22		12 37									12 52		13 07			
	d																								
Heathrow Terminal 5 ⊖ ✈	a	12 02						12 16				12 32							12 46						13 02
	d																								
West Drayton	d		12 07							12 15			12 37								12 45				
Iver	d		12 10										12 40												
Langley	d		12 12			←							12 42					←							
Slough 3	a		12 16		12 03	12 16				12 21			12 46			12 33		12 46			12 51				
	d		12 16		12 04	12 16				12 24			12 46			12 34		12 46			12 54				
Burnham	d		→			12 20							→					12 50							
Taplow	d					12 23												12 53							
Maidenhead 3	d					12 26				12 30								12 56			13 00				
Twyford 3	d					12 33				12 37								13 03			13 07				
Reading 7	a				12 17	12 41				12 44						12 47		13 11			13 14		12 55	12 59	
Oxford	a				12 43											13 14									

For non-stop services between London and Reading refer to Table T116

For non-stop services between London and Heathrow Airport see Table T118

NRT DECEMBER 19 EDITION

Table T117-F

Saturdays

21 December to 16 May

London - Greenford, Heathrow Airport and Reading

Stopping Services

		XR	XR	GW	GW	XR	HX	XR		GW	XR	HX	XR	XR	GW	GW	XR	HX		XR	GW	XR	GW	GW	HX
					◇1 🍴		◇1					◇1				◇1		◇1					◇1 🍴	◇	◇1
London Paddington 15 ⊖	d	12 43	12 48		12 50		12 55			12 57	13 02	13 10	13 13	13 18		13 20		13 25			13 27	13 32	13 32	13 37	13 40
Acton Main Line	d		12 54											13 24											
Ealing Broadway ⊖	d	12 51	12 57							13 05	13 11		13 21	13 27							13 35	13 41			
West Ealing	d		13 00	13 01							13 14			13 30	13 31							13 44			
Drayton Green	d			13 03											13 33										
Castle Bar Park	d			13 05											13 35										
South Greenford	d			13 07											13 37										
Greenford ⊖	a			13 13											13 43										
Hanwell	d										13 16											13 46			
Southall	d	13 00	13 05								13 20		13 30	13 35								13 50			
Hayes & Harlington	d	13 03	13a12							13 11	13 24		13 33	13a42							13 41	13 54			
HeathrowTermls 2 & 3 2 ⊖ ✈	a						13 10				13 30	13 25						13 40				14 00			13 55
	d						13 11	13 18			13 33	13 28						13 41		13 48		14 03			13 58
Heathrow Terminal 4 ⊖ ✈	a							13 22			13 37									13 52		14 07			
	d																								
Heathrow Terminal 5 ⊖ ✈	a						13 16					13 32						13 46							14 02
	d																								
West Drayton	d	13 07								13 15			13 37								13 45				
Iver	d	13 10											13 40												
Langley	d	13 12				←							13 42				←								
Slough 3	a	13 16			13 03	13 16				13 21			13 46			13 33	13 46				13 51				
	d	13 16			13 04	13 16				13 24			13 46			13 34	13 46				13 54				
Burnham	d	→				13 20							→				13 50								
Taplow	d					13 23											13 53								
Maidenhead 3	d					13 26				13 30							13 56				14 00				
Twyford 3	d					13 33				13 37							14 03				14 07				
Reading 7	a				13 17	13 41				13 44						13 47	14 11				14 14		13 55	14 02	
Oxford	a				13 43											14 14									

		XR	XR	GW		GW	XR	HX	XR	GW	XR	HX	XR	XR		GW	GW	XR	HX	XR	GW	XR	GW	HX	
						◇1 🍴		◇1				◇1					◇1		◇1				◇1 🍴	◇1	
London Paddington 15 ⊖	d	13 43	13 48			13 50		13 55		13 57	14 02	14 10	14 13	14 18			14 20		14 25		14 27	14 32	14 32	14 40	
Acton Main Line	d		13 54											14 24											
Ealing Broadway ⊖	d	13 51	13 57							14 05	14 11		14 21	14 27							14 35	14 41			
West Ealing	d		14 00	14 01							14 14			14 30		14 31						14 44			
Drayton Green	d			14 03												14 33									
Castle Bar Park	d			14 05												14 35									
South Greenford	d			14 07												14 37									
Greenford ⊖	a			14 13												14 43									
Hanwell	d										14 16											14 46			
Southall	d	14 00	14 05								14 20		14 30	14 35								14 50			
Hayes & Harlington	d	14 03	14a12							14 11	14 24		14 33	14a42							14 41	14 54			
HeathrowTermls 2 & 3 2 ⊖ ✈	a							14 10			14 30	14 25							14 40			15 00		14 55	
	d							14 11	14 18		14 33	14 28							14 41	14 48		15 03		14 58	
Heathrow Terminal 4 ⊖ ✈	a								14 22		14 37									14 52		15 07			
	d																								
Heathrow Terminal 5 ⊖ ✈	a							14 16				14 32							14 46					15 02	
	d																								
West Drayton	d	14 07								14 15			14 37								14 45				
Iver	d	14 10											14 40												
Langley	d	14 12					←						14 42					←							
Slough 3	a	14 16				14 03	14 16			14 21			14 46				14 33	14 46			14 51				
	d	14 16				14 04	14 16			14 24			14 46				14 34	14 46			14 54				
Burnham	d	→					14 20						→					14 50							
Taplow	d						14 23											14 53							
Maidenhead 3	d						14 26			14 30								14 56			15 00				
Twyford 3	d						14 33			14 37								15 03			15 07				
Reading 7	a					14 17	14 41			14 44							14 47	15 11			15 14		14 55		
Oxford	a					14 43											15 14								

For non-stop services between London and Reading refer to Table T116

For non-stop services between London and Heathrow Airport see Table T118

Table T117-F

Saturdays

21 December to 16 May

London - Greenford, Heathrow Airport and Reading

Stopping Services

		XR	XR	GW	GW	XR		HX	XR	GW	XR	HX	XR	XR	GW	GW		XR	HX	XR	GW	XR	GW	GW	HX
					◇1 ⚒			◇1				◇1				◇1			◇1				◇1 ⚒	◇	◇1
London Paddington 15 ⊖	d	14 43	14 48		14 50			14 55		14 57	15 02	15 10	15 13	15 18		15 20			15 25		15 27	15 32	15 32	15 37	15 40
Acton Main Line	d		14 54											15 24											
Ealing Broadway ⊖	d	14 51	14 57							15 05	15 11		15 21	15 27							15 35	15 41			
West Ealing	d		15 00	15 01							15 14			15 30	15 31							15 44			
Drayton Green	d			15 03											15 33										
Castle Bar Park	d			15 05											15 35										
South Greenford	d			15 07											15 37										
Greenford ⊖	a			15 13											15 43										
Hanwell	d										15 16											15 46			
Southall	d	15 00	15 05								15 20		15 30	15 35								15 50			
Hayes & Harlington	d	15 03	15a12							15 11	15 24		15 33	15a42							15 41	15 54			
Heathrow Termls 2 & 3 2 ⊖ ✈	a							15 10			15 30	15 25							15 40			16 00			15 55
	d							15 11	15 18		15 33	15 28							15 41	15 48		16 03			15 58
Heathrow Terminal 4 ⊖ ✈	a								15 22		15 37									15 52		16 07			
	d																								
Heathrow Terminal 5 ⊖ ✈	a							15 16				15 32							15 46						16 02
	d																								
West Drayton	d	15 07								15 15			15 37								15 45				
Iver	d	15 10											15 40												
Langley	d	15 12				←							15 42					←							
Slough 3	a	15 16			15 03	15 16				15 21			15 46			15 34		15 46			15 51				
	d	15 16			15 04	15 16				15 24			15 46			15 35		15 46			15 54				
Burnham	d	→				15 20							→					15 50							
Taplow	d					15 23												15 53							
Maidenhead 3	d					15 26				15 30								15 56			16 00				
Twyford 3	d					15 33				15 37								16 03			16 07				
Reading 7	a				15 17	15 41				15 44						15 47		16 11			16 14		15 55	16 03	
Oxford	a				15 43											16 14									

		XR		XR	GW	GW	XR	HX	XR	GW	XR	HX		XR	XR	GW	GW	XR	HX	XR	GW	XR		GW	HX
						◇1 ⚒		◇1				◇1					◇1		◇1					◇1 ⚒	◇1
London Paddington 15 ⊖	d	15 43		15 48		15 50		15 55		15 57	16 02	16 10		16 13	16 18		16 20		16 25		16 27	16 32		16 32	16 40
Acton Main Line	d			15 54											16 24										
Ealing Broadway ⊖	d	15 51		15 57						16 05	16 11			16 21	16 27						16 35	16 41			
West Ealing	d			16 00	16 01						16 14				16 30	16 31						16 44			
Drayton Green	d				16 03											16 33									
Castle Bar Park	d				16 05											16 35									
South Greenford	d				16 07											16 37									
Greenford ⊖	a				16 13											16 43									
Hanwell	d										16 16											16 46			
Southall	d	16 00		16 05							16 20			16 30	16 35							16 50			
Hayes & Harlington	d	16 03		16a12						16 11	16 24			16 33	16a42						16 41	16 54			
Heathrow Termls 2 & 3 2 ⊖ ✈	a							16 10			16 30	16 25							16 40			17 00			16 55
	d							16 11	16 18		16 33	16 28							16 41	16 48		17 03			16 58
Heathrow Terminal 4 ⊖ ✈	a								16 22		16 37									16 52		17 07			
	d																								
Heathrow Terminal 5 ⊖ ✈	a							16 16				16 32							16 46						17 02
	d																								
West Drayton	d	16 07								16 15				16 37							16 45				
Iver	d	16 10												16 40											
Langley	d	16 12					←							16 42				←							
Slough 3	a	16 16				16 03	16 16			16 21				16 46			16 33	16 46			16 51				
	d	16 16				16 04	16 16			16 24				16 46			16 34	16 46			16 54				
Burnham	d	→					16 20							→				16 50							
Taplow	d						16 23											16 53							
Maidenhead 3	d						16 26			16 30								16 56			17 00				
Twyford 3	d						16 33			16 37								17 03			17 07				
Reading 7	a					16 17	16 41			16 44							16 47	17 11			17 14			16 55	
Oxford	a					16 43											17 14								

For non-stop services between London and Reading refer to Table T116

For non-stop services between London and Heathrow Airport see Table T118

Table T117-F

Saturdays

21 December to 16 May

London - Greenford, Heathrow Airport and Reading

Stopping Services

		XR	XR	GW		GW	XR	HX	XR	GW	XR	HX	XR	XR		GW	GW	XR	HX	XR	GW	XR	GW	HX
						◇1 ⚒		◇1				◇1					◇1		◇1				◇1 ⚒	◇1
London Paddington 15 ⊖	d	16 43	16 48			16 50		16 55		16 56	17 02	17 10	17 13	17 18			17 20		17 25		17 27	17 32	17 32	17 40
Acton Main Line	d		16 54											17 24										
Ealing Broadway ⊖	d	16 51	16 57							17 04	17 11		17 21	17 27							17 35	17 41		
West Ealing	d		17 00	17 01							17 14			17 30		17 31						17 44		
Drayton Green	d			17 03												17 33								
Castle Bar Park	d			17 05												17 35								
South Greenford	d			17 07												17 37								
Greenford ⊖	a			17 13												17 43								
Hanwell	d										17 16											17 46		
Southall	d	17 00	17 05								17 20		17 30	17 35								17 50		
Hayes & Harlington	d	17 03	17a12							17 12	17 24		17 33	17a42							17 41	17 54		
Heathrow Termls 2 & 3 2 ⊖ ✈	a							17 10			17 30	17 25							17 40			18 00		17 55
	d							17 11	17 18		17 33	17 28							17 41	17 48		18 03		17 58
Heathrow Terminal 4 ⊖ ✈	a								17 22		17 37									17 52		18 07		
	d																							
Heathrow Terminal 5 ⊖ ✈	a							17 16				17 32							17 46					18 02
	d																							
West Drayton	d	17 07								17 16			17 37								17 45			
Iver	d	17 10											17 40											
Langley	d	17 12					←						17 42					←						
Slough 3	a	17 16				17 03	17 16			17 22			17 46				17 33	17 46			17 51			
	d	17 16				17 04	17 16			17 24			17 46				17 34	17 46			17 54			
Burnham	d	→					17 20						→					17 50						
Taplow	d						17 23											17 53						
Maidenhead 3	d						17 26			17 30								17 56			18 00			
Twyford 3	d						17 33			17 37								18 03			18 07			
Reading 7	a					17 17	17 41			17 44							17 47	18 10			18 14		17 55	
Oxford	a					17 43											18 13							

		GW	XR	XR	GW	GW	XR	HX	XR	GW		XR	HX	XR	XR	GW	GW	XR	HX	XR		GW	XR	GW	HX
		◇				◇1 ⚒		◇1					◇1				◇1		◇1					◇1 ⚒	◇1
London Paddington 15 ⊖	d	17 42	17 43	17 48		17 50		17 55		17 57		18 02	18 10	18 13	18 18		18 20		18 25			18 27	18 32	18 32	18 40
Acton Main Line	d			17 54											18 24										
Ealing Broadway ⊖	d		17 51	17 57						18 05		18 11		18 21	18 27							18 35	18 41		
West Ealing	d			18 00	18 01							18 14			18 30	18 31							18 44		
Drayton Green	d				18 03											18 33									
Castle Bar Park	d				18 05											18 35									
South Greenford	d				18 07											18 37									
Greenford ⊖	a				18 13											18 43									
Hanwell	d											18 16											18 46		
Southall	d		18 00	18 05								18 20		18 30	18 35								18 50		
Hayes & Harlington	d		18 03	18a12						18 11		18 24		18 33	18a42							18 41	18 54		
Heathrow Termls 2 & 3 2 ⊖ ✈	a							18 10				18 30	18 25						18 40				19 00		18 55
	d							18 11	18 18			18 33	18 28						18 41	18 48			19 03		18 58
Heathrow Terminal 4 ⊖ ✈	a								18 22			18 37								18 52			19 07		
	d																								
Heathrow Terminal 5 ⊖ ✈	a							18 16					18 32						18 46						19 02
	d																								
West Drayton	d		18 07							18 15				18 37								18 45			
Iver	d		18 10											18 40											
Langley	d		18 12				←							18 42				←							
Slough 3	a		18 16			18 04	18 16			18 21				18 46			18 33	18 46				18 51			
	d		18 16			18 05	18 16			18 24				18 46			18 34	18 46				18 54			
Burnham	d		→				18 20							→				18 50							
Taplow	d						18 23											18 53							
Maidenhead 3	d						18 26			18 30								18 56				19 00			
Twyford 3	d						18 33			18 37								19 03				19 07			
Reading 7	a	18 08				18 17	18 41			18 44							18 47	19 11				19 14		18 55	
Oxford	a					18 43											19 13								

For non-stop services between London and Reading refer to Table T116

For non-stop services between London and Heathrow Airport see Table T118

Table T117-F

Saturdays
21 December to 16 May

London - Greenford, Heathrow Airport and Reading
Stopping Services

	XR		XR	GW	GW	XR	HX	XR	GW	XR	HX		XR	XR	GW	GW	XR	HX	XR	GW	XR		GW	HX
					◇1 ⊼		◇1				◇1					◇1		◇1					◇1 ⊼	◇1
London Paddington 15 ⊖ d	18 43		18 48		18 50		18 55		18 57	19 02	19 10		19 13	19 18		19 20		19 25		19 27	19 32		19 32	19 40
Acton Main Line d			18 54											19 24										
Ealing Broadway ⊖ d	18 51		18 57						19 05	19 11			19 21	19 27						19 35	19 41			
West Ealing d			19 00	19 01						19 14				19 30	19 31						19 44			
Drayton Green d				19 03											19 33									
Castle Bar Park d				19 05											19 35									
South Greenford d				19 07											19 37									
Greenford ⊖ a				19 13											19 43									
Hanwell d										19 16											19 46			
Southall d	19 00		19 05							19 20			19 30	19 35							19 50			
Hayes & Harlington d	19 03		19a12						19 11	19 24			19 33	19a42						19 41	19 54			
HeathrowTermls 2 & 3 2 ⊖ ✈ a							19 10			19 30	19 25							19 40			20 00			19 55
d							19 11	19 18		19 33	19 28							19 41	19 48		20 03			19 58
Heathrow Terminal 4 ⊖ ✈ a								19 22		19 37									19 52		20 07			
d																								
Heathrow Terminal 5 ⊖ ✈ a							19 16				19 32							19 46						20 02
d																								
West Drayton d	19 07								19 15				19 37							19 45				
Iver d	19 10												19 40											
Langley d	19 12					←							19 42				←							
Slough 3 a	19 16				19 03	19 16			19 21				19 46			19 33	19 46			19 51				
d	19 16				19 04	19 16			19 24				19 46			19 34	19 46			19 54				
Burnham d	→					19 20							→				19 50							
Taplow d						19 23											19 53							
Maidenhead 3 d						19 26			19 30								19 56			20 00				
Twyford 3 d						19 33			19 37								20 03			20 07				
Reading 7 a					19 17	19 41			19 44							19 47	20 11			20 14			19 55	
Oxford a					19 43											20 16								

	XR	XR	GW	GW	XR	HX	XR		GW	XR	HX	XR	XR	GW	GW	XR	HX		XR	GW	XR	GW	HX	XR
				◇1 ⊼		◇1					◇1				◇1		◇1					◇1 ⊼	◇1	
London Paddington 15 ⊖ d	19 43	19 48		19 50		19 55			19 57	20 02	20 10	20 13	20 18		20 20		20 25			20 27	20 32	20 32	20 40	20 43
Acton Main Line d		19 54											20 24											
Ealing Broadway ⊖ d	19 51	19 57							20 05	20 11		20 21	20 27							20 35	20 41			20 51
West Ealing d		20 00	20 01							20 14			20 30	20 31							20 44			
Drayton Green d			20 03											20 33										
Castle Bar Park d			20 05											20 35										
South Greenford d			20 07											20 37										
Greenford ⊖ a			20 13											20 43										
Hanwell d										20 16											20 46			
Southall d	20 00	20 05								20 20		20 30	20 35								20 50			21 00
Hayes & Harlington d	20 03	20a12							20 11	20 24		20 33	20a42							20 41	20 54			21 03
HeathrowTermls 2 & 3 2 ⊖ ✈ a						20 10				20 30	20 25						20 40				21 00		20 55	
d						20 11	20 18			20 33	20 28						20 41		20 48		21 03		20 58	
Heathrow Terminal 4 ⊖ ✈ a							20 22			20 37									20 52		21 07			
d																								
Heathrow Terminal 5 ⊖ ✈ a						20 16					20 32						20 46						21 02	
d																								
West Drayton d	20 07								20 15			20 37								20 45				21 07
Iver d	20 10											20 40												21 10
Langley d	20 12				←							20 42				←								21 12
Slough 3 a	20 16			20 03	20 16				20 21			20 46			20 33	20 46				20 51				21 16
d	20 16			20 04	20 16				20 24			20 46			20 34	20 46				20 54				21 16
Burnham d	→				20 20							→				20 50								→
Taplow d					20 23											20 53								
Maidenhead 3 d					20 26				20 30							20 56				21 00				
Twyford 3 d					20 33				20 37							21 03				21 07				
Reading 7 a				20 17	20 41				20 44						20 47	21 11				21 14		20 55		
Oxford a				20 43											21 14									

For non-stop services between London and Reading refer to Table T116

For non-stop services between London and Heathrow Airport see Table T118

NRT DECEMBER 19 EDITION

Table T117-F

Saturdays
21 December to 16 May

London - Greenford, Heathrow Airport and Reading
Stopping Services

	XR	GW	GW	XR	HX	XR	GW	XR	HX		XR	XR	GW	GW	XR	HX	XR	GW	XR		HX	XR	XR	GW
			◇1		◇1				◇1					◇1		◇1					◇1			◇1 ⊼
London Paddington 15 ⊖ d	20 48		20 50		20 55		20 57	21 02	21 10		21 13	21 18		21 19		21 25		21 27	21 32		21 40	21 43	21 48	21 49
Acton Main Line d	20 54											21 24											21 54	
Ealing Broadway ⊖ d	20 57						21 05	21 11			21 21	21 27						21 35	21 41			21 51	21 57	
West Ealing d	21 00	21 01						21 14				21 30	21 31						21 44				22 00	
Drayton Green d		21 03											21 33											
Castle Bar Park d		21 05											21 35											
South Greenford d		21 07											21 37											
Greenford ⊖ a		21 13											21 43											
Hanwell d								21 16											21 46					
Southall d	21 05							21 20			21 30	21 35							21 50			22 00	22 05	
Hayes & Harlington d	21a12						21 11	21 24			21 33	21a42						21 42	21 54			22 03	22a12	
HeathrowTermls 2 & 3 2 ⊖ ✈ a					21 10			21 30	21 25							21 40			22 00		21 55			
d					21 11	21 18		21 33	21 28							21 41	21 48		22 03		21 58			
Heathrow Terminal 4 ⊖ ✈ a						21 22		21 37									21 52		22 07					
d																								
Heathrow Terminal 5 ⊖ ✈ a					21 16				21 32							21 46					22 02			
d																								
West Drayton d							21 15				21 37							21 46				22 07		
Iver d											21 40											22 10		
Langley d				←							21 42				←							22 12		
Slough 3 a			21 03	21 16			21 21				21 46			21 33	21 46			21 52				22 16		22 02
d			21 04	21 16			21 24				21 46			21 34	21 46			21 54				22 16		22 03
Burnham d				21 20							→				21 50							→		
Taplow d				21 23											21 53									
Maidenhead 3 d				21 26			21 30							21 40	21 56			22 00						
Twyford 3 d				21 33			21 37								22 03			22 07						
Reading 7 a			21 17	21 41			21 44							21 49	22 11			22 14						22 16
Oxford a			21 43											22 24										22 46

	XR	HX	XR	GW	XR		HX	XR	XR	GW	XR	HX	XR	GW	XR		HX	XR	XR	GW	XR	HX	XR	GW
		◇1					◇1			◇1		◇1					◇1			◇1		◇1		
London Paddington 15 ⊖ d		21 55		21 57	22 02		22 10	22 13	22 18	22 19		22 25		22 28	22 32		22 40	22 43	22 48	22 50		22 55		22 58
Acton Main Line d									22 24										22 54					
Ealing Broadway ⊖ d				22 05	22 11			22 21	22 27					22 37	22 41			22 51	22 57					23 06
West Ealing d					22 14				22 30						22 44				23 00					
Drayton Green d																								
Castle Bar Park d																								
South Greenford d																								
Greenford ⊖ a																								
Hanwell d					22 16										22 46									
Southall d					22 20			22 30	22 35						22 50			22 58	23 05					
Hayes & Harlington d				22 12	22 24			22 33	22a42					22 45	22 54			23 01	23a12					23 14
HeathrowTermls 2 & 3 2 ⊖ ✈ a		22 10			22 30		22 25					22 40			23 00		22 55					23 10		
d		22 11	22 18		22 33		22 28					22 41	22 48		23 03		22 58					23 11	23 18	
Heathrow Terminal 4 ⊖ ✈ a			22 22		22 37								22 52		23 07								23 22	
d																								
Heathrow Terminal 5 ⊖ ✈ a		22 16					22 32					22 46					23 02					23 16		
d																								
West Drayton d				22 16				22 37						22 49				23 05						23 18
Iver d								22 40										23 08						
Langley d	←							22 42			←							23 10			←			
Slough 3 a	22 16			22 22				22 46		22 33	22 46			22 55				23 14		23 08	23 14			23 25
d	22 16			22 24				22 46		22 35	22 46			22 57				23 14		23 08	23 14			23 26
Burnham d	22 20							→			22 50							→			23 18			
Taplow d	22 23										22 53										23 21			
Maidenhead 3 d	22 26			22 30						22 42	22 56			23 03						23 15	23 24			23 32
Twyford 3 d	22 33			22 37							23 03			23 10							23 31			23 39
Reading 7 a	22 41			22 44						22 53	23 11			23 17						23 30	23 39			23 46
Oxford a										23 25										00 01				

For non-stop services between London and Reading refer to Table T116

For non-stop services between London and Heathrow Airport see Table T118

Table T117-F

Saturdays
21 December to 16 May

London - Greenford, Heathrow Airport and Reading

Stopping Services

	XR	HX ◇1	XR	XR	HX ◇1	XR	GW	GW ◇1	XR	GW	XR
London Paddington 15 ⊖ d	23 02	23 10	23 13	23 18	23 25		23 28	23 33			23 58
Acton Main Line d				23 25							
Ealing Broadway ⊖ d	23 11		23 21	23 28			23 36				00 07
West Ealing d	23 14			23 31							
Drayton Green d											
Castle Bar Park d											
South Greenford d											
Greenford ⊖ a											
Hanwell d	23 16										
Southall d	23 20		23 28	23 35			23 41				00 15
Hayes & Harlington d	23 24		23 32	23a42			23 44				00 18
HeathrowTermls 2 & 3 2 ⊖ ✈ a	23 30	23 25			23 40						
d	23 33	23 28			23 41	23 48					
Heathrow Terminal 4 ⊖ ✈ a	23 37					23 52					
d											
Heathrow Terminal 5 ⊖ ✈ a		23 32			23 46						
d											
West Drayton d			23 37				23 48				00 22
Iver d			23 41								00 25
Langley d			23 49						←	←	00 27
Slough 3 a			23 52				23 57	23 47	23 52	23 57	00 31
d			23 53				23 57	23 48	23 53	23 57	00 31
Burnham d			→				→		23 56	00 01	
Taplow d									23 59	00 04	
Maidenhead 3 d								23 56	00a03	00 08	00a39
Twyford 3 d										00 15	
Reading 7 a								00 07		00 22	
Oxford a								00 43			

Sundays
15 December to 10 May

	GW A	XR A	GW	GW	HX	HX ◇1	XR	HX ◇1	XR	HX ◇1	XR	HX ◇1	XR	HX ◇	XR	HX ◇1	XR	HX ◇1	XR	GW	HX ◇1	XR
London Paddington 15 ⊖ d			00 30	01 00		05 10	05 11	05 25	05 26	05 40	05 41	05 55		06 10	06 11	06 25		06 40	06 41	06 44	06 55	
Acton Main Line d																						
Ealing Broadway ⊖ d		00 07	00 38	01 08			05 20		05 35		05 50				06 20				06 50	06 54		
West Ealing d																						
Drayton Green d																						
Castle Bar Park d																						
South Greenford d																						
Greenford ⊖ a																						
Hanwell d																						
Southall d		00 15	00 42	01 13			05 24		05 39		05 54				06 24				06 54	06 59		
Hayes & Harlington d		00 18	00 46	01 16			05 28		05 43		05 58				06 28				06 58	07 02		
HeathrowTermls 2 & 3 2 ⊖ ✈ a						05 26	05 35	05 41	05 50	05 56	06 05	06 11		06 26	06 35	06 41		06 56	07 05		07 11	
d					05 13	05 28	05 38	05 43	05 53	05 58	06 08	06 13	06 23	06 28	06 38	06 43	06 53	06 58	07 08		07 13	07 23
Heathrow Terminal 4 ⊖ ✈ a							05 45		06 00		06 15		06 27		06 45		06 57		07 15			07 27
d																						
Heathrow Terminal 5 ⊖ ✈ a					05 17	05 32		05 47		06 02		06 17		06 32		06 47		07 02			07 17	
d																						
West Drayton d		00 22	00 50																			
Iver d		00 25	00 53																			
Langley d		00 27	00 56																	07 08		
Slough 3 a		00 31	00 59	01 23																07 13		
d		00 31	01 00	01 23																07 13		
Burnham d	00 01		01 04																	07 17		
Taplow d	00 04		01 07																			
Maidenhead 3 d	00 08	00a39	01 10	01 30																07 22		
Twyford 3 d	00 15		01 17	01 37																07 30		
Reading 7 a	00 22		01 24	01 44																07 37		
Oxford a																						

A not 15 December

For non-stop services between London and Reading refer to Table T116

For non-stop services between London and Heathrow Airport see Table T118

Table T117-F

Sundays
15 December to 10 May

London - Greenford, Heathrow Airport and Reading

Stopping Services

	XR	HX ◇1	XR	HX ◇1	XR	GW	GW ◇1	HX ◇1	XR	HX ◇1	XR	XR	HX ◇1	XR	HX ◇1	XR	GW	GW ◇1	XR	GW ◇1	XR
London Paddington 15 ⊖ d	07 00	07 10	07 11	07 25		07 27	07 37	07 40	07 41	07 55		08 03	08 10	08 11	08 22		08 24	08 27	08 33	08 37	
Acton Main Line d																					
Ealing Broadway ⊖ d	07 08		07 20			07 35			07 50			08 11		08 20			08 32		08 41		
West Ealing d																					
Drayton Green d																					
Castle Bar Park d																					
South Greenford d																					
Greenford ⊖ a																					
Hanwell d																					
Southall d	07 14		07 24			07 39			07 54			08 19		08 24			08 36		08 49		
Hayes & Harlington d	07 17		07 28			07 43			07 58			08 23		08 28			08 40		08 53		
HeathrowTermls 2 & 3 2 ⊖ ✈ a		07 26	07 35	07 41				07 56	08 05	08 11			08 26	08 35	08 41						
d		07 28	07 38	07 43	07 53			07 58	08 08	08 13	08 23		08 28	08 38	08 43	08 53					
Heathrow Terminal 4 ⊖ ✈ a			07 45		07 57				08 15		08 27			08 45		08 57					
d																					
Heathrow Terminal 5 ⊖ ✈ a		07 32		07 47				08 02		08 17			08 32		08 47						
d																					
West Drayton d	07 21											08 27							08 57		
Iver d	07 24											08 30							09 00		
Langley d	07 26					07 48						08 32							09 02		←
Slough 3 a	07 30					07 52	07 58					08 36					08 47		09 06	08 50	09 06
d	07 30					07 52	08 00					08 36					08 47		09 06	08 51	09 06
Burnham d						07 56						08 40							→		09 10
Taplow d												08 43									09 13
Maidenhead 3 d	07 37					08 18						08 46					08 53				09 16
Twyford 3 d	07 44					08 25						08 53					09 03				09 23
Reading 7 a	07 52					08 34	08 14					09 01					09 11	08 51		09 06	09 31
Oxford a							08 49													09 43	

	HX ◇1	XR	HX ◇1	XR	XR	HX ◇1	XR	GW ◇1 A	XR	GW	HX ◇1	XR	XR	GW ◇1	XR	HX ◇1	XR	GW ◇1	XR	HX ◇1	XR	XR
London Paddington 15 ⊖ d	08 40	08 41	08 55		09 03	09 10	09 11	09 21		09 24	09 25		09 27	09 32	09 33	09 40	09 41	09 42		09 55		09 57
Acton Main Line d													09 33									10 03
Ealing Broadway ⊖ d		08 50			09 11		09 20			09 32			09 36		09 41		09 50					10 06
West Ealing d													09 39									10 09
Drayton Green d																						
Castle Bar Park d																						
South Greenford d																						
Greenford ⊖ a																						
Hanwell d																						
Southall d		08 54			09 19		09 24			09 36			09 45		09 49		09 54					10 15
Hayes & Harlington d		08 58			09 23		09 28			09 40			09a51		09 53		09 58					10a21
HeathrowTermls 2 & 3 2 ⊖ ✈ a	08 56	09 05	09 11			09 26	09 35				09 41					09 56	10 05			10 11		
d	08 58	09 08	09 13	09 23		09 28	09 38				09 43	09 53				09 58	10 08			10 13	10 23	
Heathrow Terminal 4 ⊖ ✈ a		09 15		09 27			09 45					09 57					10 15				10 27	
d																						
Heathrow Terminal 5 ⊖ ✈ a	09 02		09 17			09 32					09 47					10 02				10 17		
d																						
West Drayton d					09 27										09 57							
Iver d					09 30										10 00							
Langley d					09 32				←						10 02				←			
Slough 3 a					09 36			09 33	09 36	09 47					10 06			09 57	10 06			
d					09 36			09 35	09 36	09 47					10 06			09 58	10 06			
Burnham d					→				09 40						→				10 10			
Taplow d									09 43										10 13			
Maidenhead 3 d									09 46	09 53									10 16			
Twyford 3 d									09 53	10 00									10 23			
Reading 7 a								09 45	10 01	10 08				09 55				10 10	10 31			
Oxford a								10 18										10 40				

A 1 to Reading

For non-stop services between London and Reading refer to Table T116

For non-stop services between London and Heathrow Airport see Table T118

Table T117-F

Sundays

15 December to 10 May

London - Greenford, Heathrow Airport and Reading

Stopping Services

		XR	GW ◇	HX ◇1	XR	GW ◇1	XR	GW	HX ◇1	XR		XR	GW ◇1 🚲	XR	GW ◇1 🚲	HX ◇1	XR	GW ◇1 🚲	XR	HX ◇1		XR	XR	XR	HX ◇1
London Paddington 15 ⊖	d	10 03	10 05	10 10	10 11	10 21		10 24	10 25			10 27	10 32	10 33	10 36	10 40	10 41	10 46		10 55			10 57	11 03	11 10
Acton Main Line	d											10 33											11 03		
Ealing Broadway ⊖	d	10 11			10 20			10 32				10 36		10 41			10 50						11 06	11 11	
West Ealing	d											10 39											11 09		
Drayton Green	d																								
Castle Bar Park	d																								
South Greenford	d																								
Greenford ⊖	a																								
Hanwell	d																								
Southall	d	10 19			10 24			10 36				10 45		10 49			10 54						11 15	11 19	
Hayes & Harlington	d	10 23			10 28			10 40				10a51		10 53			10 58						11a21	11 23	
HeathrowTermls 2 & 3 2 ⊖ ✈	a			10 26	10 35				10 41							10 56	11 05			11 11					11 26
	d			10 28	10 38				10 43	10 53						10 58	11 08			11 13		11 23			11 28
Heathrow Terminal 4 ⊖ ✈	a				10 45					10 57							11 15					11 27			
	d																								
Heathrow Terminal 5 ⊖ ✈	a			10 32					10 47							11 02				11 17					11 32
	d																								
West Drayton	d	10 27												10 57										11 27	
Iver	d	10 30												11 00										11 30	
Langley	d	10 32					←							11 02					←					11 32	
Slough 3	a	10 36				10 33	10 36	10 47						11 06				10 59	11 06					11 36	
	d	10 36				10 35	10 36	10 47						11 06				11 00	11 06					11 36	
Burnham	d	→					10 40							→					11 10					→	
Taplow	d						10 43												11 13						
Maidenhead 3	d		10 23				10 46	10 53											11 16						
Twyford 3	d						10 53	11 00											11 23						
Reading 7	a		10 34			10 45	11 01	11 08					10 55		10 59			11 12	11 31						
Oxford	a					11 19												11 43							

		XR	GW ◇1	XR	GW	HX ◇1		XR	XR	GW ◇1 🚲	XR	GW ◇	HX ◇1	XR	GW ◇1 🚲	XR		HX ◇1	XR	XR	XR	GW ◇	HX ◇	XR	GW ◇1
London Paddington 15 ⊖	d	11 11	11 21		11 24	11 25			11 27	11 32	11 33	11 37	11 40	11 41	11 46			11 55		11 57	12 03	12 05	12 10	12 11	12 21
Acton Main Line	d								11 33											12 03					
Ealing Broadway ⊖	d	11 20			11 32				11 36		11 41			11 50						12 06	12 11			12 20	
West Ealing	d								11 39											12 09					
Drayton Green	d																								
Castle Bar Park	d																								
South Greenford	d																								
Greenford ⊖	a																								
Hanwell	d																								
Southall	d	11 27			11 36				11 45		11 49			11 54						12 15	12 19			12 24	
Hayes & Harlington	d	11 31			11 40				11a51		11 53			11 58						12a21	12 23			12 28	
HeathrowTermls 2 & 3 2 ⊖ ✈	a	11 38				11 41							11 56	12 05				12 11					12 26	12 35	
	d	11 41				11 43		11 53					11 58	12 08				12 13	12 23				12 28	12 38	
Heathrow Terminal 4 ⊖ ✈	a	11 48						11 57						12 15					12 27					12 45	
	d																								
Heathrow Terminal 5 ⊖ ✈	a					11 47							12 02					12 17					12 32		
	d																								
West Drayton	d										11 57										12 27				
Iver	d										12 00										12 30				
Langley	d			←							12 02					←					12 32				
Slough 3	a		11 33	11 36	11 47						12 06				11 59	12 06					12 36				12 33
	d		11 35	11 36	11 47						12 06				12 00	12 06					12 36				12 35
Burnham	d			11 40							→					12 10					→				
Taplow	d			11 43												12 13									
Maidenhead 3	d			11 46	11 53											12 16						12 23			
Twyford 3	d			11 53	12 00											12 23									
Reading 7	a		11 45	12 01	12 08					11 55		12 02			12 12	12 31						12 34			12 45
Oxford	a		12 19												12 41										13 22

For non-stop services between London and Reading refer to Table T116

For non-stop services between London and Heathrow Airport see Table T118

Table T117-F

Sundays

15 December to 10 May

London - Greenford, Heathrow Airport and Reading

Stopping Services

		XR	GW	HX ◇	XR	XR	GW ◇1 🚲	XR		GW ◇1 🚲	HX ◇1	XR	GW ◇1 🚲	XR	HX ◇1	XR	XR	XR		HX ◇1	XR	GW ◇1 A	XR	GW	HX ◇1
London Paddington 15 ⊖	d		12 24	12 25		12 27	12 32	12 33		12 36	12 40	12 41	12 46		12 55		12 57	13 03		13 10	13 11	13 21		13 24	13 25
Acton Main Line	d					12 33											13 03								
Ealing Broadway ⊖	d		12 32			12 36		12 41				12 50					13 06	13 11			13 20			13 32	
West Ealing	d					12 39											13 09								
Drayton Green	d																								
Castle Bar Park	d																								
South Greenford	d																								
Greenford ⊖	a																								
Hanwell	d																								
Southall	d		12 36			12 45		12 49				12 54					13 15	13 19			13 24			13 36	
Hayes & Harlington	d		12 40			12a51		12 53				12 58					13a21	13 23			13 28			13 40	
HeathrowTermls 2 & 3 2 ⊖ ✈	a			12 41							12 56	13 05			13 11					13 26	13 35				13 41
	d			12 43	12 53						12 58	13 08			13 13	13 23				13 28	13 38				13 43
Heathrow Terminal 4 ⊖ ✈	a				12 57							13 15				13 27					13 45				
	d																								
Heathrow Terminal 5 ⊖ ✈	a			12 47							13 02				13 17					13 32					13 47
	d																								
West Drayton	d							12 57										13 27							
Iver	d							13 00										13 30							
Langley	d	←						13 02						←				13 32					←		
Slough 3	a	12 36	12 47					13 06					12 59	13 06				13 36				13 33	13 36	13 47	
	d	12 36	12 47					13 06					13 00	13 06				13 36				13 35	13 36	13 47	
Burnham	d	12 40						→						13 10				→					13 40		
Taplow	d	12 43												13 13									13 43		
Maidenhead 3	d	12 46	12 55											13 16									13 46	13 53	
Twyford 3	d	12 53	13 00											13 23									13 53	14 00	
Reading 7	a	13 01	13 08				12 55			12 59			13 12	13 31								13 45	14 01	14 08	
Oxford	a												13 43									14 19			

		XR	XR	GW ◇1 🚲		XR	GW ◇	HX ◇1	XR	GW ◇1 🚲	XR	HX ◇1	XR	XR		XR	GW ◇	HX ◇1	XR	GW ◇1	XR	GW	HX ◇1	XR	
London Paddington 15 ⊖	d		13 27	13 32		13 33	13 37	13 40	13 41	13 45		13 55		13 57		14 03	14 05	14 10	14 11	14 21		14 24	14 25		
Acton Main Line	d		13 33											14 03											
Ealing Broadway ⊖	d		13 36			13 41			13 50					14 06		14 11			14 20			14 32			
West Ealing	d		13 39											14 09											
Drayton Green	d																								
Castle Bar Park	d																								
South Greenford	d																								
Greenford ⊖	a																								
Hanwell	d																								
Southall	d		13 45			13 49			13 54					14 15		14 19			14 24			14 36			
Hayes & Harlington	d		13a51			13 53			13 58					14a21		14 23			14 28			14 40			
HeathrowTermls 2 & 3 2 ⊖ ✈	a							13 56	14 05			14 11						14 26	14 35				14 41		
	d	13 53						13 58	14 08			14 13	14 23					14 28	14 38				14 43	14 54	
Heathrow Terminal 4 ⊖ ✈	a	13 57							14 15				14 27						14 45					14 58	
	d																								
Heathrow Terminal 5 ⊖ ✈	a							14 02				14 17						14 32					14 47		
	d																								
West Drayton	d					13 57										14 27									
Iver	d					14 00										14 30									
Langley	d					14 02					←					14 32					←				
Slough 3	a					14 06				13 59	14 06					14 36				14 33	14 36	14 47			
	d					14 06				14 00	14 06					14 36				14 35	14 36	14 47			
Burnham	d					→					14 10					→					14 40				
Taplow	d										14 13										14 43				
Maidenhead 3	d										14 16						14 23				14 46	14 53			
Twyford 3	d										14 23										14 53	15 00			
Reading 7	a			13 55			14 02			14 12	14 31						14 34			14 45	15 01	15 08			
Oxford	a									14 40										15 19					

A 1 to Reading

For non-stop services between London and Reading refer to Table T116

For non-stop services between London and Heathrow Airport see Table T118

Table T117-F

Sundays

15 December to 10 May

London - Greenford, Heathrow Airport and Reading

Stopping Services

	XR	GW	XR	GW	HX		XR	GW	XR	HX	XR	XR	XR	HX	XR		GW	XR	GW	HX	XR	XR	GW	XR
		◇1		◇1	◇1			◇1		◇1				◇1			◇1			◇1			◇1	
		⚮		⚮				⚮															⚮	
London Paddington 15 ⊖ d	14 27	14 32	14 33	14 36	14 40		14 41	14 46		14 55		14 57	15 03	15 10	15 11		15 21		15 24	15 25		15 27	15 32	15 33
Acton Main Line d	14 33											15 03										15 33		
Ealing Broadway ⊖ d	14 36		14 41				14 50					15 06	15 11		15 20				15 32			15 36		15 41
West Ealing d	14 39											15 09										15 39		
Drayton Green d																								
Castle Bar Park d																								
South Greenford d																								
Greenford ⊖ a																								
Hanwell d																								
Southall d	14 45		14 49				14 54					15 15	15 19		15 24				15 36			15 45		15 49
Hayes & Harlington d	14a51		14 53				14 58					15a21	15 23		15 28				15 40			15a51		15 53
Heathrow Termls 2 & 3 2 ⊖ ✈ a					14 56		15 05			15 11				15 26	15 35					15 41				
d					14 58		15 08			15 13	15 23			15 28	15 38					15 43	15 53			
Heathrow Terminal 4 ⊖ ✈ a							15 15				15 27				15 45						15 57			
d																								
Heathrow Terminal 5 ⊖ ✈ a					15 02					15 17				15 32						15 47				
d																								
West Drayton d			14 57										15 27											15 57
Iver d			15 00										15 30											16 00
Langley d			15 02						←				15 32					←						16 02
Slough 3 a			15 06					14 59	15 06				15 36				15 33	15 36	15 47					16 06
d			15 06					15 00	15 06				15 36				15 35	15 36	15 47					16 06
Burnham d			→						15 10				→					15 40						→
Taplow d									15 13									15 43						
Maidenhead 3 d									15 16									15 46	15 53					
Twyford 3 d									15 23									15 53	16 00					
Reading 7 a		14 55		14 59				15 12	15 31								15 45	16 01	16 08				15 55	
Oxford a								15 43									16 20							

	GW		HX	XR	GW	XR	HX	XR	XR	XR	GW		HX	XR	GW	XR	GW	HX	XR	XR	GW		XR	HX
	◇		◇1		◇1		◇1				◇		◇1		◇1			◇1			◇1			◇1
					⚮																⚮			
London Paddington 15 ⊖ d	15 36		15 40	15 41	15 46		15 55		15 57	16 03	16 05		16 10	16 11	16 20		16 24	16 25		16 27	16 32		16 33	16 40
Acton Main Line d									16 03											16 33				
Ealing Broadway ⊖ d				15 50					16 06	16 11				16 20			16 32			16 36			16 41	
West Ealing d									16 09											16 39				
Drayton Green d																								
Castle Bar Park d																								
South Greenford d																								
Greenford ⊖ a																								
Hanwell d																								
Southall d				15 54					16 15	16 19				16 24			16 36			16 45			16 49	
Hayes & Harlington d				15 58					16a21	16 23				16 28			16 40			16a51			16 53	
Heathrow Termls 2 & 3 2 ⊖ ✈ a			15 56	16 05			16 11						16 26	16 35				16 41						16 56
d			15 58	16 08			16 13	16 23					16 28	16 38				16 43	16 53					16 58
Heathrow Terminal 4 ⊖ ✈ a				16 15				16 27						16 45					16 57					
d																								
Heathrow Terminal 5 ⊖ ✈ a			16 02				16 17						16 32					16 47						17 02
d																								
West Drayton d										16 27													16 57	
Iver d										16 30													17 00	
Langley d						←				16 32						←							17 02	
Slough 3 a					15 59	16 06				16 36					16 33	16 36	16 47						17 06	
d					16 00	16 06				16 36					16 35	16 36	16 47						17 06	
Burnham d						16 10				→						16 40							→	
Taplow d						16 13										16 43								
Maidenhead 3 d						16 16					16 23					16 46	16 53							
Twyford 3 d						16 23										16 53	17 00							
Reading 7 a	16 02				16 12	16 31					16 34				16 45	17 01	17 08				16 55			
Oxford a					16 43										17 23									

For non-stop services between London and Reading refer to Table T116

For non-stop services between London and Heathrow Airport see Table T118

Table T117-F

Sundays

15 December to 10 May

London - Greenford, Heathrow Airport and Reading

Stopping Services

	XR	GW	XR		HX	XR	XR	XR	HX	XR	GW	XR	GW		HX	XR	XR	GW	XR	GW	HX	XR	GW	
		◇1			◇1				◇		◇1				◇			◇1		◇	◇		◇1	
		⚮																⚮					⚮	
London Paddington 15 ⊖ d	16 41	16 46			16 55		16 57	17 03	17 10	17 11	17 21		17 24		17 25		17 27	17 32	17 33	17 38	17 40	17 41	17 46	
Acton Main Line d							17 03										17 33							
Ealing Broadway ⊖ d	16 50						17 06	17 11		17 20			17 32				17 36		17 41			17 50		
West Ealing d							17 09										17 39							
Drayton Green d																								
Castle Bar Park d																								
South Greenford d																								
Greenford ⊖ a																								
Hanwell d																								
Southall d	16 54						17 15	17 19		17 24			17 36				17 45		17 49			17 54		
Hayes & Harlington d	16 58						17a21	17 23		17 28			17 40				17a51		17 53			17 58		
Heathrow Termls 2 & 3 2 ⊖ ✈ a	17 05				17 11				17 26	17 35					17 41						17 56	18 05		
d	17 08				17 13	17 23			17 28	17 38					17 43	17 53					17 58	18 08		
Heathrow Terminal 4 ⊖ ✈ a	17 15					17 27				17 45						17 57						18 15		
d																								
Heathrow Terminal 5 ⊖ ✈ a					17 17				17 32						17 47						18 02			
d																								
West Drayton d								17 27											17 57					
Iver d								17 30											18 00					
Langley d			←					17 32				←							18 02					
Slough 3 a		16 59	17 06					17 36			17 33	17 36	17 47						18 06				17 59	
d		17 00	17 06					17 36			17 35	17 36	17 47						18 06				18 00	
Burnham d			17 10					→				17 40							→					
Taplow d			17 13									17 43												
Maidenhead 3 d			17 16									17 46	17 53											
Twyford 3 d			17 23									17 53	18 00											
Reading 7 a		17 12	17 31								17 45	18 01	18 08					17 55		18 03			18 12	
Oxford a		17 43									18 20												18 43	

	XR	HX	XR	XR	XR	GW	HX	XR	GW		XR	GW	HX	XR	XR	GW	XR	HX	XR		GW	XR	HX	XR
		◇				◇	◇		◇1				◇			◇1		◇			◇1		◇	
									A							⚮					⚮			
London Paddington 15 ⊖ d		17 55		17 57	18 03	18 05	18 10	18 11	18 21			18 24	18 25		18 27	18 32	18 33	18 40	18 41		18 46		18 55	
Acton Main Line d				18 03											18 33									
Ealing Broadway ⊖ d				18 06	18 11			18 20				18 32			18 36		18 41		18 50					
West Ealing d				18 09											18 39									
Drayton Green d																								
Castle Bar Park d																								
South Greenford d																								
Greenford ⊖ a																								
Hanwell d																								
Southall d				18 15	18 19			18 24				18 36			18 45		18 49		18 54					
Hayes & Harlington d				18a21	18 23			18 28				18 40			18a51		18 53		18 58					
Heathrow Termls 2 & 3 2 ⊖ ✈ a		18 11					18 26	18 35					18 41					18 56	19 05				19 11	
d		18 13	18 23				18 28	18 38					18 43	18 53				18 58	19 08				19 13	19 23
Heathrow Terminal 4 ⊖ ✈ a			18 27					18 45						18 57					19 15					19 27
d																								
Heathrow Terminal 5 ⊖ ✈ a		18 17					18 32						18 47					19 02					19 17	
d																								
West Drayton d					18 27												18 57							
Iver d					18 30												19 00							
Langley d	←				18 32						←						19 02					←		
Slough 3 a	18 06				18 36				18 33		18 36	18 47					19 06				18 59	19 06		
d	18 06				18 36				18 35		18 36	18 47					19 06				19 00	19 06		
Burnham d	18 10				→						18 40						→					19 10		
Taplow d	18 13										18 43											19 13		
Maidenhead 3 d	18 16					18 23					18 46	18 53										19 16		
Twyford 3 d	18 23										18 53	19 00										19 23		
Reading 7 a	18 31					18 34			18 45		19 01	19 08				18 55					19 12	19 31		
Oxford a									19 19												19 43			

A 1 to Reading

For non-stop services between London and Reading refer to Table T116

For non-stop services between London and Heathrow Airport see Table T118

Table T117-F

Sundays
15 December to 10 May

London - Greenford, Heathrow Airport and Reading
Stopping Services

		XR		XR	HX	XR	GW	HX	XR	XR	GW	XR		HX	XR	GW	XR	HX	XR	XR	XR	HX		XR	GW
					◇			◇			◇1 🚲			◇		◇1 🚲		◇				◇			◇1 🚲
London Paddington 15 ⊖	d	18 57		19 03	19 10	19 11	19 24	19 25		19 27	19 32	19 33		19 40	19 41	19 46		19 55		19 57	20 03	20 10		20 11	20 17
Acton Main Line	d	19 03								19 33										20 03					
Ealing Broadway ⊖	d	19 06		19 11		19 20	19 32			19 36		19 41			19 50					20 06	20 11			20 20	
West Ealing	d	19 09								19 39										20 09					
Drayton Green	d																								
Castle Bar Park	d																								
South Greenford	d																								
Greenford ⊖	a																								
Hanwell	d																								
Southall	d	19 15		19 19		19 24	19 36			19 45		19 49			19 54					20 15	20 19			20 24	
Hayes & Harlington	d	19a21		19 23		19 28	19 40			19a51		19 53			19 58					20a21	20 23			20 28	
HeathrowTermls 2 & 3 2 ⊖ ✈	a				19 26	19 35		19 41						19 56	20 05			20 11				20 26		20 35	
	d				19 28	19 38		19 43	19 53					19 58	20 08			20 13	20 23			20 28		20 38	
Heathrow Terminal 4 ⊖ ✈	a					19 45			19 57						20 15				20 27					20 45	
	d																								
Heathrow Terminal 5 ⊖ ✈	a				19 32			19 47						20 02				20 17				20 32			
	d																								
West Drayton	d			19 27								19 57									20 27				
Iver	d			19 30								20 00									20 30				
Langley	d			19 32								20 02					←				20 32				
Slough 3	a			19 36			19 47					20 06				19 59	20 06				20 36				
	d			19 36			19 47					20 06				20 00	20 06				20 36				
Burnham	d			19 40								→					20 10				20 40				
Taplow	d			19 43													20 13				20 43				
Maidenhead 3	d			19 46			19 53										20 16				20 46				
Twyford 3	d			19 53			20 00										20 23				20 53				
Reading 7	a			20 01			20 08				19 55					20 12	20 31				21 01				20 40
Oxford	a															20 45									

		GW	HX	XR	XR	GW	XR	HX		XR	GW	HX	XR	GW	XR	XR	HX	XR		GW	HX	XR	XR	HX	XR
			◇			◇1 🚲		◇			◇1	◇		◇1 🚲			◇				◇			◇	
London Paddington 15 ⊖	d	20 24	20 25		20 27	20 32	20 33	20 40		20 41	20 46	20 55		21 03		21 03	21 10	21 11		21 24	21 25		21 33	21 40	21 41
Acton Main Line	d				20 33																				
Ealing Broadway ⊖	d	20 32			20 36		20 41			20 50						21 11		21 20		21 32			21 41		21 50
West Ealing	d				20 39																				
Drayton Green	d																								
Castle Bar Park	d																								
South Greenford	d																								
Greenford ⊖	a																								
Hanwell	d																								
Southall	d	20 36			20 45		20 49			20 54						21 19		21 24		21 36			21 49		21 54
Hayes & Harlington	d	20 40			20a51		20 53			20 58						21 23		21 28		21 40			21 53		21 58
HeathrowTermls 2 & 3 2 ⊖ ✈	a		20 41					20 56		21 05		21 11					21 26	21 35			21 41			21 56	22 05
	d		20 43	20 53				20 58		21 08		21 13	21 23				21 28	21 38			21 43	21 53		21 58	22 08
Heathrow Terminal 4 ⊖ ✈	a			20 57						21 15			21 27					21 45				21 57			22 15
	d																								
Heathrow Terminal 5 ⊖ ✈	a		20 47					21 02				21 17					21 32				21 47			22 02	
	d																								
West Drayton	d						20 57									21 27							21 57		
Iver	d						21 00									21 30							22 00		
Langley	d						21 02								←	21 32							22 02		
Slough 3	a	20 46					21 06				20 58				21 06	21 36				21 46			22 06		
	d	20 47					21 06				21 00				21 06	21 36				21 47			22 06		
Burnham	d						→								21 10	21 40							→		
Taplow	d														21 13	21 43									
Maidenhead 3	d	20 53													21 16	21 46				21 53					
Twyford 3	d	21 00													21 23	21 53				22 00					
Reading 7	a	21 07				20 55					21 10			21 26	21 31	22 01				22 08					
Oxford	a										21 43														

For non-stop services between London and Reading refer to Table T116

For non-stop services between London and Heathrow Airport see Table T118

NRT DECEMBER 19 EDITION

Table T117-F

Sundays
15 December to 10 May

London - Greenford, Heathrow Airport and Reading
Stopping Services

		GW	XR	HX	XR	XR	HX	XR	GW	HX		XR	XR	GW	XR	HX	XR	HX	XR	XR		HX	XR	HX	GW
		◇1		◇			◇			◇				◇1 🚲		◇		◇				◇		◇	
London Paddington 15 ⊖	d	21 46		21 55		22 03	22 10	22 11	22 24	22 25			22 33	22 37		22 40	22 41	22 55		23 00		23 10	23 11	23 25	23 27
Acton Main Line	d																								
Ealing Broadway ⊖	d					22 11		22 20	22 32				22 41				22 50			23 08			23 20		23 35
West Ealing	d																								
Drayton Green	d																								
Castle Bar Park	d																								
South Greenford	d																								
Greenford ⊖	a																								
Hanwell	d																								
Southall	d					22 19		22 24	22 36				22 49				22 54			23 14			23 24		23 39
Hayes & Harlington	d					22 23		22 28	22 40				22 53				22 58			23 17			23 28		23 43
HeathrowTermls 2 & 3 2 ⊖ ✈	a			22 11			22 26	22 35		22 41						22 56	23 05	23 11				23 26	23 35	23 41	
	d			22 13	22 23		22 28	22 38		22 43		22 53				22 58	23 08	23 13	23 23			23 28	23 38	23 43	
Heathrow Terminal 4 ⊖ ✈	a				22 27			22 45				22 57					23 15		23 27				23 45		
	d																								
Heathrow Terminal 5 ⊖ ✈	a			22 17			22 32			22 47						23 02		23 17				23 32		23 47	
	d																								
West Drayton	d					22 27							22 57							23 21					
Iver	d					22 30							23 00							23 24					
Langley	d		←			22 32							23 02		←					23 26					
Slough 3	a	21 58	22 06			22 36			22 46				23 06	22 53	23 06					23 30					23 49
	d	21 59	22 06			22 36			22 47				23 06	22 56	23 06					23 30					23 50
Burnham	d		22 10			22 40							→		23 10					23 34					23 53
Taplow	d		22 13			22 43									23 13					23 37					
Maidenhead 3	d		22 16			22 46			22 51						23 16					23a41					23 56
Twyford 3	d		22 23			22 53			22 58						23 23										00 04
Reading 7	a	22 12	22 31			23 01			23 06					23 13	23 31										00 12
Oxford	a	22 42																							

		XR	GW
London Paddington 15 ⊖	d	23 35	23 53
Acton Main Line	d		
Ealing Broadway ⊖	d	23 43	00 03
West Ealing	d		
Drayton Green	d		
Castle Bar Park	d		
South Greenford	d		
Greenford ⊖	a		
Hanwell	d		
Southall	d	23 49	00 09
Hayes & Harlington	d	23 53	00 13
HeathrowTermls 2 & 3 2 ⊖ ✈	a		
	d		
Heathrow Terminal 4 ⊖ ✈	a		
	d		
Heathrow Terminal 5 ⊖ ✈	a		
	d		
West Drayton	d	23 57	
Iver	d	23 59	
Langley	d	00 02	00 20
Slough 3	a	00 06	00 24
	d	00 06	00 25
Burnham	d		00 28
Taplow	d		
Maidenhead 3	d	00a13	00 33
Twyford 3	d		00 40
Reading 7	a		00 52
Oxford	a		

For non-stop services between London and Reading refer to Table T116

For non-stop services between London and Heathrow Airport see Table T118

Table T117-R

Mondays to Fridays
16 December to 15 May

Reading, Heathrow Airport and Greenford - London

Stopping Services

Miles	Miles	Miles	Miles			GW MX	XR MO	XR MX	XR MO	XR MX	GW MX	GW MO	GW MX ◇[1]	GW MO ◇	GW MX	GW MX	GW	GW	GW	GW MX	HX ◇[1]	HX ◇[1]	XR
—	—	—	—	Oxford	d								00 11			00 45				03 54			
0	—	—	—	**Reading** [7]	d						00 17	00 24	00 43	00 54	01 15	01a27	02 24	03 54	04 34	04a37			
5	—	—	—	**Twyford** [3]	d						00 23	00 30		01 00	01 21		02 30	04 00	04 42				
11¾	—	—	—	**Maidenhead** [3]	d						00 30	00 37		01 08	01 28		02 37	04 08	04 49				
13½	—	—	—	Taplow	d						00 33												
15	—	—	—	Burnham	d						00 37	00 41											
17½	—	—	—	**Slough** [3]	a						00 40	00 45	00 56	01 15	01 34		02 43	04 15	04 57				
—	—	—	—		d						00 41	00 45	00 57	01 16	01 34		02 43	04 16	04 58				
19¾	—	—	—	Langley	d						00 45	00 49							05 01				
21¼	—	—	—	Iver	d														05 04				
22¾	—	—	—	West Drayton	d						00 49	00 54					02 49	04 23	05 07				
—	—	—	0	**Heathrow Terminal 5** ⊖ ✈	a																		
—	—	—	—		d																05 12	05 27	
—	—	0	—	**Heathrow Terminal 4** ⊖ ✈	a																		
—	—	—	—		d				00 01	00 07													05 22
—	—	1½	1½	**Heathrow Termls 2 & 3** [2] ⊖ ✈	a				00 05	00 11											05 16	05 31	05 26
—	—	—	—		d			00 03	00 07	00 13											05 17	05 32	05 28
25¼	—	5½	5½	Hayes & Harlington	d			00 09	00 14	00 19	00 53	00 58		01 25	01 42		02 53	04 27	05 11				05 34
27	—	7½	7¼	Southall	d		00 03	00 13	00 18	00 23	00 57	01 02					02 57	04 31	05 15				05 38
28¾	—	9¼	9	Hanwell	d																		05 41
—	0	—	—	**Greenford** ⊖	d																		
—	1	—	—	South Greenford	d																		
—	1¾	—	—	Castle Bar Park	d																		
—	2	—	—	Drayton Green	d																		
29¾	2½	10	9¾	West Ealing	d																		05 43
30¼	3½	10¾	10½	**Ealing Broadway** ⊖	d	00 04	00 08	00 18	00 23	00 28	01 02	01 07		01 32	01 49		03 02	04 37	05 20				05 46
31¾	5	12¼	12	Acton Main Line	d																		
36	9¼	16½	16¼	**London Paddington** [15] ⊖	a	00 12	00 20	00 31	00 34	00 40	01 11	01 15	01 15	01 42	01 57		03 11	04 46	05 28		05 34	05 50	05 55

		XR	XR	HX ◇[1]	GW	XR	XR	HX ◇[1]	XR	XR	GW	GW	XR	GW	HX ◇[1]	XR	XR	GW	HX ◇[1]	XR	XR	GW	XR
Oxford	d																	05 19					
Reading [7]	d				05 08						05 36	05 50					05 51	05a57			06 03	06 19	
Twyford [3]	d				05 14						05 42	05 56					05 58				06 09	06 26	
Maidenhead [3]	d	05 16			05 21		05 36			05 45	05 50	06 02					06 05				06 16	06 33	
Taplow	d	05 19			05 24		05 39			05 48	05 54						06 08				06 19		
Burnham	d	05 22			05 28		05 42			05 52	05 59						06 11				06 23		
Slough [3]	a	05 25			05 31		05 45			05 55	06 02	06 07					06 14				06 26		
	d	05 26			05 32		05 46			05 56	06 04	06 08					06 15				06 27		
Langley	d	05 30					05 49			06 00							06 18				06 31		
Iver	d	05 33					05 52			06 03							06 21				06 34		
West Drayton	d	05 37					05 55			06 07							06 24				06 37		
Heathrow Terminal 5 ⊖ ✈	a																						
	d			05 42				05 57							06 12				06 27				
Heathrow Terminal 4 ⊖ ✈	a																						
	d		05 41						05 52				06 11							06 22			06 41
Heathrow Termls 2 & 3 [2] ⊖ ✈	a		05 45	05 46				06 01	05 56				06 15		06 16				06 31	06 26			06 45
	d			05 47				06 02	05 58						06 17				06 32	06 28			
Hayes & Harlington	d	05 41			05 45	05 48	05 59		06 04	06 11	06 15					06 18	06 28			06 34	06 41		
Southall	d	05 45			05 49	05 53	06 03		06 08	06 16						06 23	06 32			06 38	06 46		
Hanwell	d								06 11											06 41			
Greenford ⊖	d													06 12									
South Greenford	d													06 16									
Castle Bar Park	d													06 18									
Drayton Green	d													06 20									
West Ealing	d					05 57			06 13					06a23		06 27				06 43			
Ealing Broadway ⊖	d	05 52			05 57	06 00	06 08		06 16	06 22	06 26					06 30	06 38			06 46	06 52		
Acton Main Line	d					06 03										06 33							
London Paddington [15] ⊖	a	06 02		06 02	06 07	06 13	06 17	06 17	06 25	06 32	06 34	06 23			06 32	06 43	06 47		06 47	06 55	07 02	06 52	

For non-stop services between Reading and London refer to Table T116

For non-stop services between London and Heathrow Airport see Table T118

Table T117-R

Mondays to Fridays
16 December to 15 May

Reading, Heathrow Airport and Greenford - London

Stopping Services

		GW	XR	XR	GW ◇[1]	HX ◇[1]	GW ◇[1]	HX ◇[1]	XR	XR	GW	XR	GW	XR	XR	GW ◇[1]	HX ◇[1]	GW	XR	XR	GW	GW ◇[1]
Oxford	d						06 00									06 32					06 37	06 48
Reading [7]	d			06 22	06 29		06 35				06 48				06 52	06 56		07 01		07 05	07a33	07 12
Twyford [3]	d			06 28							06 54				06 58			07 07		07 11		
Maidenhead [3]	d			06 35			06 45			06 45	07 02				07 05	07 07		07 15		07 19		
Taplow	d			06 38						06 48					07 08					07 22		
Burnham	d			06 41						06 52					07 11					07 25		
Slough [3]	a			06 44			06 50			06 55					07 14			07 21		07 29		
	d			06 45			06 51			06 56					07 15			07 22		07 29		
Langley	d			06 48						07 00					07 18					07 33		
Iver	d			06 51						07 03					07 21					07 36		
West Drayton	d			06 54						07 07					07 24					07 39		
Heathrow Terminal 5 ⊖ ✈	a																					
	d					06 42		06 57									07 12					
Heathrow Terminal 4 ⊖ ✈	a																					
	d								06 52			07 11							07 22			
Heathrow Termls 2 & 3 [2] ⊖ ✈	a					06 46		07 01	06 56			07 15					07 16		07 26			
	d					06 47		07 02	06 58								07 17		07 28			
Hayes & Harlington	d		06 48	06 58					07 04	07 11				07 18	07 28				07 34	07 43		
Southall	d		06 53	07 02					07 08	07 16				07 23	07 32				07 38	07 48		
Hanwell	d								07 12										07 41			
Greenford ⊖	d	06 42											07 12									
South Greenford	d	06 46											07 16									
Castle Bar Park	d	06 48											07 18									
Drayton Green	d	06 50											07 20									
West Ealing	d	06a53	06 57						07 14				07a23	07 27					07 43			
Ealing Broadway ⊖	d		07 00	07 08					07 17	07 22				07 30	07 38				07 46	07 53		
Acton Main Line	d		07 03											07 33								
London Paddington [15] ⊖	a		07 13	07 17	06 54	07 02	07 05	07 17	07 26	07 32	07 22			07 43	07 47	07 24	07 32	07 40	07 56	08 02		07 39

		GW	HX ◇[1]	GW	XR	GW	XR	XR	GW ◇	GW ◇[1]	HX ◇[1]	GW	XR	XR	GW ◇[1]	XC ◇[1]	HX ◇[1]	GW	XR	GW	XR	XR	GW
Oxford	d														07 07	07 17							07 21
Reading [7]	d	07 16		07 18				07 22	07 24	07 29		07 30		07 34	07 37	07a41		07 47				07 52	08a10
Twyford [3]	d			07 24				07 28				07 36		07 40				07 54				07 58	
Maidenhead [3]	d			07 32				07 35	07 35			07 44		07 48				08 02				08 05	
Taplow	d							07 38						07 51								08 08	
Burnham	d							07 41						07 54								08 11	
Slough [3]	a							07 44				07 50		07 57								08 14	
	d							07 45				07 51		07 58								08 15	
Langley	d							07 48						08 01								08 18	
Iver	d							07 51						08 04								08 21	
West Drayton	d							07 54						08 07								08 24	
Heathrow Terminal 5 ⊖ ✈	a																						
	d		07 27								07 42						07 57						
Heathrow Terminal 4 ⊖ ✈	a																						
	d				07 41								07 52						08 11				
Heathrow Termls 2 & 3 [2] ⊖ ✈	a		07 31		07 45						07 46		07 56				08 01		08 15				
	d		07 32								07 47		07 58				08 02						
Hayes & Harlington	d						07 48	07 58					08 04	08 11							08 18	08 28	
Southall	d						07 53	08 02					08 08	08 16							08 23	08 32	
Hanwell	d												08 11										
Greenford ⊖	d					07 42														08 12			
South Greenford	d					07 46														08 16			
Castle Bar Park	d					07 48														08 18			
Drayton Green	d					07 50														08 20			
West Ealing	d					07a53	07 57						08 13							08a23	08 27		
Ealing Broadway ⊖	d						08 00	08 08					08 16	08 22							08 30	08 38	
Acton Main Line	d						08 03														08 33		
London Paddington [15] ⊖	a	07 42	07 47	07 52			08 13	08 17	07 54	07 59	08 03	08 19	08 26	08 32	08 05		08 18	08 22			08 43	08 47	

For non-stop services between Reading and London refer to Table T116

For non-stop services between London and Heathrow Airport see Table T118

Table T117-R

Mondays to Fridays

16 December to 15 May

Reading, Heathrow Airport and Greenford - London

Stopping Services

	GW	HX	GW	XC	XR	XR	GW	GW	HX		GW	XR	GW	XR	XR	GW	GW	GW	HX		HX	XR	XR	XC
	◇1 🍴	◇1		◇1			◇1 🍴	◇1 🍴	◇1							◇1 🍴		◇1 🍴	◇1		◇1			◇1 🍴
Oxford d	07 32			07 37			07 42	07 53										08 07						08 16
Reading 7 d	07 56		08 01	08a03		08 05	08 14	08 17			08 17				08 22	08 29	08 31	08 35					08 35	08a42
Twyford 3 d			08 07			08 11					08 23				08 28		08 37						08 41	
Maidenhead 3 d			08 14			08 18					08 31				08 35		08 44						08 48	
Taplow d						08 21									08 38								08 51	
Burnham d						08 24									08 41								08 54	
Slough 3 a			08 20			08 27									08 44		08 50						08 57	
d			08 21			08 28									08 45		08 51						08 58	
Langley d						08 31									08 48								09 01	
Iver d						08 34									08 51								09 04	
West Drayton d						08 37									08 54								09 07	
Heathrow Terminal 5 ⊖ ✈ a																								
d		08 12							08 27										08 42		08 57			
Heathrow Terminal 4 ⊖ ✈ a																								
d					08 22							08 41										08 52		
Heathrow Termls 2 & 3 2 ⊖ ✈ a		08 16			08 26				08 31			08 45							08 46		09 01	08 56		
d		08 17			08 28				08 32										08 47		09 02	08 58		
Hayes & Harlington d					08 34	08 41								08 48	08 58							09 04	09 11	
Southall d					08 38	08 46								08 53	09 02							09 08	09 16	
Hanwell d					08 41																	09 11		
Greenford ⊖ d													08 42											
South Greenford d													08 46											
Castle Bar Park d													08 48											
Drayton Green d													08 50											
West Ealing d					08 43								08a53	08 57								09 13		
Ealing Broadway ⊖ d					08 46	08 52								09 00	09 08							09 16	09 22	
Acton Main Line d														09 03										
London Paddington 15 ⊖ a	08 24	08 33	08 49		08 56	09 02	08 38	08 40	08 47		08 52			09 14	09 18	08 54	09 09	09 01	09 03		09 17	09 25	09 32	

	GW	XR	GW	HX	XR		XR	XR	XR	GW	GW	XC	GW	GW	HX		XR	GW	XR	XR	GW	GW	GW	XC
				◇1								◇1 🍴	◇1 A 🍴	◇1 🍴	◇1						◇1 🍴	◇1 🍴		◇1 🍴
Oxford d											08 35	08 41	08 49								09 02		09 06	09 16
Reading 7 d	08 48						08 52		09 03	09 08	09a22	09a11	09 13	09 16						09 22	09 28	09 33	09a53	09a40
Twyford 3 d	08 54						08 58		09 09	09 15										09 28				
Maidenhead 3 d	09 01						09 05		09 16	09 23										09 35				
Taplow d							09 08		09 19											09 38				
Burnham d							09 11		09 22											09 41				
Slough 3 a							09 14		09 25	09 32										09 44				
d							09 15		09 26	09 33										09 45				
Langley d							09 18		09 30											09 48				
Iver d							09 21		09 32											09 51				
West Drayton d							09 24		09 36	09 41										09 54				
Heathrow Terminal 5 ⊖ ✈ a																								
d				09 12											09 27									
Heathrow Terminal 4 ⊖ ✈ a																								
d		09 11						09 22									09 41							
Heathrow Termls 2 & 3 2 ⊖ ✈ a		09 15		09 16				09 26							09 31		09 45							
d				09 17				09 28							09 32									
Hayes & Harlington d					09 18		09 28	09 35	09 41	09 45									09 48	09 58				
Southall d					09 23		09 32	09 39	09 44	09 49									09 53	10 02				
Hanwell d								09 42																
Greenford ⊖ d			09 12															09 42						
South Greenford d			09 16															09 46						
Castle Bar Park d			09 18															09 48						
Drayton Green d			09 20															09 50						
West Ealing d			09a23		09 27			09 44										09a53	09 57					
Ealing Broadway ⊖ d					09 30		09 38	09 47	09 50	09 55									10 00	10 09				
Acton Main Line d					09 33														10 03					
London Paddington 15 ⊖ a	09 26			09 32	09 43		09 47	09 56	10 02	10 05			09 37	09 39	09 47				10 13	10 17	09 54	09 57		

A The Cathedrals Express

For non-stop services between Reading and London refer to Table T116

For non-stop services between London and Heathrow Airport see Table T118

Table T117-R

Mondays to Fridays

16 December to 15 May

Reading, Heathrow Airport and Greenford - London

Stopping Services

	HX	GW	HX	XR	GW	XR	GW		XR	GW	XC	HX	XR	XR	HX	XR	GW		XR	GW	XR	GW	GW	HX
	◇1	◇	◇1							◇1 🍴	◇1 🍴	◇1			◇1							◇1 🍴	◇1 🍴	◇1
Oxford d										09 32	09 42											09 59		
Reading 7 d		09 44			09 45				09 52	09 57	10a06						10 15				10 22	10 26	10 34	
Twyford 3 d					09 51				09 58								10 21				10 28			
Maidenhead 3 d					09 58				10 05								10 28				10 35			
Taplow d									10 08												10 38			
Burnham d									10 11					←							10 41			
Slough 3 a					10 04				10 14	10 09				10 14			10 34				10 44	10 38		
d					10 04				10 15	10 10				10 15			10 34				10 45	10 39		
Langley d									→					10 18							→			
Iver d														10 21										
West Drayton d					10 10									10 24			10 40							
Heathrow Terminal 5 ⊖ ✈ a																								
d	09 42		09 57									10 12			10 27									10 42
Heathrow Terminal 4 ⊖ ✈ a																								
d				09 52		10 11										10 22			10 41					
Heathrow Termls 2 & 3 2 ⊖ ✈ a	09 46		10 01	09 56		10 15						10 16			10 31	10 26			10 45					10 46
d	09 47		10 02	09 58								10 17			10 32	10 28								10 47
Hayes & Harlington d				10 04	10 14								10 18	10 28		10 34	10 44							
Southall d				10 08									10 23	10 32		10 38								
Hanwell d				10 11												10 41								
Greenford ⊖ d							10 12													10 42				
South Greenford d							10 16													10 46				
Castle Bar Park d							10 18													10 48				
Drayton Green d							10 20													10 50				
West Ealing d				10 13			10a23						10 27			10 43				10a53				
Ealing Broadway ⊖ d				10 16	10 24								10 30	10 38		10 46	10 52							
Acton Main Line d													10 33											
London Paddington 15 ⊖ a	10 02	10 09	10 17	10 25	10 32					10 24		10 32	10 43	10 47	10 47	10 55	11 04					10 53	10 59	11 02

	XR	XR	HX		XR	GW	XC	XR	GW	GW	XR	GW	HX		XR	XR	HX	XR	GW	XC	XR	GW	GW
			◇1				■ 1 🍴		◇	◇1 🍴			◇1				◇1			◇1 🍴		◇1 🍴	◇1 🍴
Oxford d							10 16			10 32										10 42		11 02	
Reading 7 d						10 38	10a40	10 52	10 54	10 57									11 04	11a10	11 19	11 26	11 34
Twyford 3 d						10 45		10 58											11 12		11 25		
Maidenhead 3 d						10 53		11 05											11 25		11 32		
Taplow d								11 08													11 35		
Burnham d		←						11 11								←					11 38		
Slough 3 a		10 44				11 01		11 14		11 08						11 14			11 32		11 41	11 38	
d		10 45				11 02		11 15		11 09						11 15			11 34		11 42	11 39	
Langley d		10 48						→								11 18					→		
Iver d		10 51														11 21							
West Drayton d		10 54				11 09										11 24			11 40				
Heathrow Terminal 5 ⊖ ✈ a																							
d			10 57										11 12				11 27						
Heathrow Terminal 4 ⊖ ✈ a																							
d					10 52						11 11							11 22					
Heathrow Termls 2 & 3 2 ⊖ ✈ a			11 01		10 56						11 15		11 16				11 31	11 26					
d			11 02		10 58								11 17				11 32	11 28					
Hayes & Harlington d	10 48	10 58			11 04	11 15									11 18	11 28		11 34	11 44				
Southall d	10 53	11 02			11 08										11 23	11 32		11 38					
Hanwell d					11 11													11 41					
Greenford ⊖ d												11 12											
South Greenford d												11 16											
Castle Bar Park d												11 18											
Drayton Green d												11 20											
West Ealing d	10 57				11 13							11a23			11 27			11 43					
Ealing Broadway ⊖ d	11 00	11 08			11 16	11 22									11 30	11 38		11 46	11 52				
Acton Main Line d	11 03														11 33								
London Paddington 15 ⊖ a	11 13	11 17	11 17		11 25	11 35			11 22	11 24			11 32		11 43	11 47	11 47	11 55	12 01			11 54	11 59

For non-stop services between Reading and London refer to Table T116

For non-stop services between London and Heathrow Airport see Table T118

Table T117-R

Mondays to Fridays

16 December to 15 May

Reading, Heathrow Airport and Greenford - London

Stopping Services

		XR	HX ◇1	GW	XR	XR		HX ◇1	XR	GW	XC ◇1 ⌶	XR	GW ◇1 ⌶	XC ◇1 ⌶	XR	HX ◇1		GW	XR	XR	HX ◇1	XR	GW	XR	GW
Oxford	d										11 16		11 32	11 42											
Reading [7]	d									11 36	11a39	11 52	11 57	12a07									12 13		
Twyford [3]	d									11 43		11 58											12 19		
Maidenhead [3]	d									11 51		12 05											12 26		
Taplow	d											12 08													
Burnham	d					←						12 11								←					
Slough [3]	a					11 41				11 57		12 14	12 08							12 14			12 32		
	d					11 42				11 58		12 15	12 09							12 15			12 32		
Langley	d					11 45						→								12 18					
Iver	d					11 48														12 21					
West Drayton	d					11 51				12 05										12 24			12 38		
Heathrow Terminal 5 ⊖ ✈	a																								
	d		11 42					11 57								12 12					12 27				
Heathrow Terminal 4 ⊖ ✈	a																								
	d	11 41							11 52						12 11							12 22		12 41	
Heathrow Termls 2 & 3 [2] ⊖ ✈	a	11 45	11 46					12 01	11 56						12 15	12 16					12 31	12 26		12 45	
	d		11 47					12 02	11 58							12 17					12 32	12 28			
Hayes & Harlington	d				11 48	11 55			12 04	12 11									12 18	12 28		12 34	12 42		
Southall	d				11 53	11 59			12 08										12 23	12 32		12 38			
Hanwell	d								12 11													12 41			
Greenford ⊖	d			11 43														12 16							12 46
South Greenford	d			11 47														12 20							12 50
Castle Bar Park	d			11 49														12 22							12 52
Drayton Green	d			11 51														12 24							12 54
West Ealing	d			11a54	11 57				12 13									12a27	12 27			12 43			12a57
Ealing Broadway ⊖	d				12 00	12 05			12 16	12 20									12 30	12 38		12 46	12 52		
Acton Main Line	d				12 03														12 33						
London Paddington [15] ⊖	a		12 02		12 13	12 17		12 17	12 25	12 31			12 24			12 32			12 43	12 47	12 47	12 55	13 01		

		XR		GW ◇1 ⌶	GW ◇1 ⌶	HX ◇1	XR	XR	HX ◇1	XR	GW	XC ◇1 ⌶		XR	GW ◇	GW ◇1 ⌶	XC ◇1 ⌶	XR	HX ◇1	GW	XR	XR		HX ◇1	XR
Oxford	d			12 02								12 16				12 32	12 43								
Reading [7]	d	12 22		12 26	12 34						12 38	12a42		12 52	12 54	12 57	13a06								
Twyford [3]	d	12 28									12 45			12 58											
Maidenhead [3]	d	12 35									12 53			13 05											
Taplow	d	12 38												13 08											
Burnham	d	12 41						←						13 11								←			
Slough [3]	a	12 44		12 38				12 44			13 01			13 14		13 08						13 14			
	d	12 45		12 39				12 45			13 02			13 15		13 09						13 15			
Langley	d	→						12 48						→								13 18			
Iver	d							12 51														13 21			
West Drayton	d							12 54			13 09											13 24			
Heathrow Terminal 5 ⊖ ✈	a																								
	d					12 42			12 57										13 12					13 27	
Heathrow Terminal 4 ⊖ ✈	a																								
	d									12 52								13 11							13 22
Heathrow Termls 2 & 3 [2] ⊖ ✈	a					12 46			13 01	12 56								13 15	13 16					13 31	13 26
	d					12 47			13 02	12 58									13 17					13 32	13 28
Hayes & Harlington	d						12 48	12 58		13 04	13 14										13 18	13 28			13 34
Southall	d						12 53	13 02		13 08											13 23	13 32			13 38
Hanwell	d									13 11															13 41
Greenford ⊖	d																			13 16					
South Greenford	d																			13 20					
Castle Bar Park	d																			13 22					
Drayton Green	d																			13 24					
West Ealing	d						12 57			13 13										13a27	13 27				13 43
Ealing Broadway ⊖	d						13 00	13 08		13 16	13 22										13 30	13 38			13 46
Acton Main Line	d						13 03														13 33				
London Paddington [15] ⊖	a			12 54	12 59	13 02	13 13	13 17	13 17	13 26	13 31				13 22	13 24			13 32		13 43	13 47		13 47	13 55

For non-stop services between Reading and London refer to Table T116

For non-stop services between London and Heathrow Airport see Table T118

Table T117-R

Mondays to Fridays

16 December to 15 May

Reading, Heathrow Airport and Greenford - London

Stopping Services

		GW	XR	GW		XR	GW ◇1 ⌶	GW ◇1 ⌶	HX ◇1	XR	XR	HX ◇1	XR	GW		XC ◇1 ⌶	XR	GW ◇1 ⌶	XC ◇1 ⌶	XR	HX ◇1	XR	XR	GW	
Oxford	d						13 02									13 16		13 32	13 42						
Reading [7]	d	13 08				13 22	13 26	13 34						13 38		13a40	13 52	13 57	14a09						
Twyford [3]	d	13 15				13 28								13 45			13 58								
Maidenhead [3]	d	13 26				13 35								13 53			14 05								
Taplow	d					13 38											14 08								
Burnham	d					13 41					←						14 11						←		
Slough [3]	a	13 32				13 44	13 38				13 44			14 01			14 14	14 08					14 14		
	d	13 32				13 45	13 39				13 45			14 02			14 15	14 09					14 15		
Langley	d					→					13 48						→						14 18		
Iver	d										13 51												14 21		
West Drayton	d	13 39									13 54			14 09									14 24		
Heathrow Terminal 5 ⊖ ✈	a																								
	d								13 42			13 57									14 12				
Heathrow Terminal 4 ⊖ ✈	a																								
	d		13 41										13 52							14 11					
Heathrow Termls 2 & 3 [2] ⊖ ✈	a		13 45						13 46			14 01	13 56							14 15	14 16				
	d								13 47			14 02	13 58								14 17				
Hayes & Harlington	d	13 44								13 48	13 58		14 04	14 14								14 18	14 28		
Southall	d									13 53	14 02		14 08									14 23	14 32		
Hanwell	d												14 11												
Greenford ⊖	d			13 46																				14 20	
South Greenford	d			13 50																				14 24	
Castle Bar Park	d			13 52																				14 26	
Drayton Green	d			13 54																				14 28	
West Ealing	d			13a57						13 57			14 13									14 27		14a31	
Ealing Broadway ⊖	d	13 52								14 00	14 09		14 16	14 22								14 30	14 37		
Acton Main Line	d									14 03												14 33			
London Paddington [15] ⊖	a	14 01					13 54	13 59	14 03	14 13	14 17	14 17	14 25	14 31				14 24			14 32	14 43	14 47		

		HX ◇1	XR	GW	XR	XR	GW ◇1 ⌶	GW ◇1 ⌶	XC ◇1 ⌶	HX ◇1		XR	XR	GW	HX ◇1	XR	GW	XR	XR	GW ◇		GW ◇1 ⌶	XC ◇1 ⌶	HX ◇1	XR
Oxford	d						14 02		14 16													14 32	14 42		
Reading [7]	d			14 09		14 22	14 26	14 35	14a40								14 45		14 52	14 53		14 57	15a05		
Twyford [3]	d			14 18		14 28											14 51		14 58						
Maidenhead [3]	d			14 26		14 35											14 58		15 05						
Taplow	d					14 38													15 08						
Burnham	d					14 41							←						15 11						
Slough [3]	a			14 32		14 45	14 38						14 45				15 04		15 14			15 08			
	d			14 32		14 45	14 39						14 45				15 04		15 15			15 09			
Langley	d					→							14 49						→						
Iver	d												14 51												
West Drayton	d			14 39									14 55				15 10								
Heathrow Terminal 5 ⊖ ✈	a																								
	d	14 27								14 42					14 57									15 12	
Heathrow Terminal 4 ⊖ ✈	a																								
	d		14 22		14 41											14 52		15 11							
Heathrow Termls 2 & 3 [2] ⊖ ✈	a	14 31	14 26		14 45					14 46					15 01	14 56		15 15						15 16	
	d	14 32	14 28							14 47					15 02	14 58								15 17	
Hayes & Harlington	d		14 35	14 44								14 48	14 59			15 04	15 14								15 18
Southall	d		14 39									14 53	15 03			15 08									15 23
Hanwell	d		14 42													15 11									
Greenford ⊖	d													14 50											
South Greenford	d													14 54											
Castle Bar Park	d													14 56											
Drayton Green	d													14 58											
West Ealing	d		14 44									14 57		15a01		15 13									15 27
Ealing Broadway ⊖	d		14 47	14 52								15 00	15 08			15 16	15 22								15 30
Acton Main Line	d											15 03													15 33
London Paddington [15] ⊖	a	14 47	14 56	15 01			14 54	15 01		15 03		15 13	15 17		15 17	15 25	15 31			15 22		15 24		15 32	15 43

For non-stop services between Reading and London refer to Table T116

For non-stop services between London and Heathrow Airport see Table T118

Table T117-R

Mondays to Fridays
16 December to 15 May

Reading, Heathrow Airport and Greenford - London
Stopping Services

		XR		GW	HX ◇1	XR	GW	XR	XR	GW ◇1	GW ◇1	HX ◇1		XR	XR	GW	XR	GW	XC ◇1	GW ◇1	HX ◇1	XR		XR	GW ◇1
Oxford	d									15 02									15 16						15 32
Reading 7	d						15 10		15 22	15 27	15 34							15 38	15a39	15 48				15 52	15 57
Twyford 3	d						15 16		15 28									15 45						15 58	
Maidenhead 3	d						15 26		15 35									15 53						16 05	
Taplow	d								15 38															16 08	
Burnham	d	←							15 41						←									16 11	
Slough 3	a	15 14					15 32		15 44	15 38					15 44			16 01						16 14	16 08
	d	15 15					15 32		15 45	15 39					15 45			16 02						16 15	16 09
Langley	d	15 18							→						15 48									→	
Iver	d	15 21													15 51										
West Drayton	d	15 24					15 39								15 54			16 09							
Heathrow Terminal 5	a																								
	d				15 27							15 42									15 57				
Heathrow Terminal 4	a																								
	d					15 22		15 41									15 52					16 11			
Heathrow Termls 2 & 3	a				15 31	15 26		15 45				15 46					15 56				16 01	16 15			
	d				15 32	15 28						15 47					15 58				16 02				
Hayes & Harlington	d	15 28				15 34	15 44							15 48	15 58		16 04	16 14							
Southall	d	15 32				15 38								15 53	16 02		16 08								
Hanwell	d					15 41											16 11								
Greenford	d			15 20												15 50									
South Greenford	d			15 24												15 54									
Castle Bar Park	d			15 26												15 56									
Drayton Green	d			15 28												15 58									
West Ealing	d			15a31		15 43								15 57		16a01	16 13								
Ealing Broadway	d	15 38				15 46	15 52							16 00	16 08		16 16	16 26							
Acton Main Line	d													16 03											
London Paddington 15	a	15 47			15 47	15 55	16 02			15 54	15 59	16 02		16 13	16 17		16 25	16 36		16 11	16 17				16 24

		XC ◇1	HX ◇1	XR	GW	HX ◇1	XR	XR		XR	GW	XR	XR	GW ◇1	XR	XR	GW	XR		XR	GW ◇1 A	HX ◇1	HX ◇1	GW	GW
Oxford	d	15 42												16 02											16 07
Reading 7	d	16a07									16 15		16 22	16 27						16 33	16 34			16 38	16a53
Twyford 3	d										16 21		16 28							16 39				16 44	
Maidenhead 3	d									16 15	16 28		16 35							16 46				16 54	
Taplow	d									16 18			16 38							16 49					
Burnham	d						←			16 22			16 41			←				16 52					
Slough 3	a						16 14			16 25	16 34		16 44	16 39		16 44				16 56				17 00	
	d						16 15			16 26	16 34		16 45	16 40		16 45				16 56				17 01	
Langley	d						16 18			16 30			→			16 48				17 00					
Iver	d						16 21			16 33						16 51				17 03					
West Drayton	d						16 24			16 37	16 41					16 54				17 07				17 11	
Heathrow Terminal 5	a																								
	d		16 12			16 27																16 42	16 57		
Heathrow Terminal 4	a																								
	d							16 22				16 41						16 52							
Heathrow Termls 2 & 3	a		16 16			16 31		16 26				16 45						16 56				16 46	17 01		
	d		16 17			16 32		16 28										16 58				16 47	17 02		
Hayes & Harlington	d			16 18			16 28	16 34		16 41	16 45				16 48	16 58		17 04		17 11				17 15	
Southall	d			16 23			16 32	16 38		16 46					16 53	17 02		17 08		17 16					
Hanwell	d							16 41										17 11							
Greenford	d				16 20												16 50								
South Greenford	d				16 24												16 54								
Castle Bar Park	d				16 26												16 56								
Drayton Green	d				16 28												16 58								
West Ealing	d			16 27	16a31			16 43							16 57		17a01	17 13							
Ealing Broadway	d			16 30			16 38	16 46		16 52	16 56				17 00	17 08		17 16		17 22				17 26	
Acton Main Line	d			16 33											17 03										
London Paddington 15	a		16 32	16 43		16 48	16 49	16 56		17 02	17 04			16 57	17 13	17 17		17 26		17 33	17 00	17 02	17 17	17 35	

A The Cheltenham Spa Express

For non-stop services between Reading and London refer to Table T116

For non-stop services between London and Heathrow Airport see Table T118

Table T117-R

Mondays to Fridays
16 December to 15 May

Reading, Heathrow Airport and Greenford - London
Stopping Services

		XC ◇1	XR	GW ◇1	GW ◇	XR	HX ◇1	XR	XR	GW		HX ◇1	XR	XR	GW	XC ◇1	XR	GW ◇1	GW ◇1	XR		HX ◇1	XR	XR	GW
Oxford	d	16 16		16 32												16 42		17 01							
Reading 7	d	16a41	16 52	16 57	17 00									17 03	17 06	17a09	17 22	17 27	17 33						
Twyford 3	d		16 58											17 09	17 15		17 28								
Maidenhead 3	d		17 05											17 16	17 24		17 35								
Taplow	d		17 08											17 19			17 38								
Burnham	d		17 11						←					17 22			17 41							←	
Slough 3	a		17 14	17 08					17 14					17 26	17 30		17 44	17 38						17 44	
	d		17 15	17 09					17 15					17 26	17 32		17 45	17 39						17 45	
Langley	d		→						17 18					17 30			→							17 48	
Iver	d								17 21					17 33										17 51	
West Drayton	d								17 24					17 37	17 41									17 54	
Heathrow Terminal 5	a																								
	d						17 12					17 27										17 42			
Heathrow Terminal 4	a																								
	d					17 11							17 22							17 41					
Heathrow Termls 2 & 3	a					17 15	17 16					17 31	17 26							17 45		17 46			
	d						17 17					17 32	17 28									17 47			
Hayes & Harlington	d							17 18	17 28				17 34	17 41	17 45								17 48	17 58	
Southall	d							17 23	17 32				17 38	17 46									17 53	18 02	
Hanwell	d												17 41												
Greenford	d									17 20															17 50
South Greenford	d									17 24															17 54
Castle Bar Park	d									17 26															17 56
Drayton Green	d									17 28															17 58
West Ealing	d							17 27		17a31			17 43										17 57		18a01
Ealing Broadway	d							17 30	17 38				17 46	17 52	17 56								18 00	18 08	
Acton Main Line	d							17 33															18 03		
London Paddington 15	a			17 24	17 27		17 32	17 43	17 48			17 48	17 56	18 02	18 04			17 54	17 56			18 02	18 13	18 17	

		XR	XR	GW	XC ◇1	GW		GW ◇1	HX ◇1	XR	XR	GW ◇1	HX ◇1	XR	GW	HX ◇1		XR	XR	XR	GW	XC ◇1	XR	GW ◇1	XR
Oxford	d			17 07	17 16							17 32										17 42		18 02	
Reading 7	d		17 34	17a59	17a39	17 41		17 42			17 52	18 00								18 05	18 09	18a11	18 22	18 28	
Twyford 3	d		17 40			17 47					17 58									18 11	18 15		18 28		
Maidenhead 3	d		17 47			17 54					18 05									18 18	18 25		18 35		
Taplow	d		17 50								18 08									18 21			18 38		
Burnham	d		17 53								18 11							←		18 24			18 41		
Slough 3	a		17 57			18 01					18 14	18 11						18 14		18 28	18 32		18 44	18 42	
	d		17 57			18 01					18 15	18 12						18 15		18 28	18 32		18 45	18 42	
Langley	d		18 01								→							18 18		18 32			→		
Iver	d		18 04															18 21		18 35					
West Drayton	d		18 07			18 11												18 24		18 38	18 42				
Heathrow Terminal 5	a																								
	d								17 57				18 12			18 27									
Heathrow Terminal 4	a																								
	d	17 52								18 11									18 22						18 41
Heathrow Termls 2 & 3	a	17 56							18 01	18 15			18 16			18 31			18 26						18 45
	d	17 58							18 02				18 17			18 32			18 28						
Hayes & Harlington	d	18 04	18 11			18 15								18 18				18 28	18 34	18 42	18 46				
Southall	d	18 08	18 16											18 23				18 32	18 38	18 46					
Hanwell	d	18 11																	18 41						
Greenford	d														18 20										
South Greenford	d														18 24										
Castle Bar Park	d														18 26										
Drayton Green	d														18 28										
West Ealing	d	18 13												18 27	18a31				18 43						
Ealing Broadway	d	18 16	18 22			18 26								18 30				18 38	18 46	18 52	18 56				
Acton Main Line	d													18 33											
London Paddington 15	a	18 26	18 32			18 34		18 09	18 17			18 29	18 33	18 44		18 47		18 48	18 55	19 02	19 06			18 59	

For non-stop services between Reading and London refer to Table T116

For non-stop services between London and Heathrow Airport see Table T118

Table T117-R

Mondays to Fridays
16 December to 15 May

Reading, Heathrow Airport and Greenford - London

Stopping Services

		XR	XR	GW	XR	XR	GW ◇1 🍴	HX ◇1		XR	GW	GW	XC ◇1 🍴	GW ◇1 🍴	HX ◇1	XR	GW	XR		GW ◇1 🍴	HX ◇1	HX ◇1	XR	XR	XR
Oxford	d											18 07	18 16							18 32					
Reading 7	d					18 33	18 34				18 41	19a00	18a42	18 45				18 52		19 00					19 04
Twyford 3	d					18 39					18 49							18 58							19 10
Maidenhead 3	d					18 46					18 57							19 05							19 17
Taplow	d					18 49												19 08							19 20
Burnham	d		←			18 52												19 11					←		19 23
Slough 3	a		18 44			18 56					19 03							19 14		19 11			19 14		19 27
	d		18 45			18 56					19 05							19 15		19 12			19 15		19 27
Langley	d		18 48			19 00												→					19 18		19 31
Iver	d		18 51			19 03																	19 21		19 34
West Drayton	d		18 54			19 07					19 16												19 24		19 37
Heathrow Terminal 5 ⊖ ✈	a																								
	d							18 42							18 57						19 12	19 27			
Heathrow Terminal 4 ⊖ ✈	a																								
	d				18 52											19 11								19 22	
Heathrow Termls 2 & 3 2 ⊖ ✈	a				18 56			18 46							19 01	19 15					19 16	19 31		19 26	
	d				18 58			18 47							19 02						19 17	19 32		19 28	
Hayes & Harlington	d	18 48	18 58		19 04	19 11				19 18	19 21												19 28	19 34	19 41
Southall	d	18 53	19 02		19 08	19 16				19 23													19 34	19 38	19 46
Hanwell	d				19 11																			19 41	
Greenford ⊖	d			18 50													19 20								
South Greenford	d			18 54													19 24								
Castle Bar Park	d			18 56													19 26								
Drayton Green	d			18 58													19 28								
West Ealing	d	18 57		19a01	19 13					19 27							19a31							19 43	
Ealing Broadway ⊖	d	19 00	19 08		19 16	19 22				19 30	19 33												19 39	19 46	19 52
Acton Main Line	d	19 03								19 33															
London Paddington 15 ⊖	a	19 13	19 17		19 26	19 32	19 01	19 03		19 43	19 42			19 12	19 17					19 28	19 32	19 47	19 48	19 55	20 02

		XC ◇1 🍴	GW	XR		XR	GW ◇1 🍴	GW ◇1 🍴	HX ◇1	XR	XR	GW	HX ◇1	XR		GW	XC ◇1 🍴	XR	GW ◇1 🍴	XC ◇1 🍴	XR	HX ◇1	XR	XR	
Oxford	d	18 42					19 02										19 16		19 32	19 42					
Reading 7	d	19a10	19 14			19 22	19 27	19 34								19 38	19a39	19 52	19 56	20a10					
Twyford 3	d		19 20			19 28										19 44		19 58							
Maidenhead 3	d		19 29			19 35										19 55		20 05							
Taplow	d					19 38												20 08							
Burnham	d					19 41					←							20 11						←	
Slough 3	a		19 35			19 44	19 38				19 44					20 01		20 14	20 08					20 14	
	d		19 35			19 45	19 39				19 45					20 01		20 15	20 09					20 15	
Langley	d					→					19 48							→						20 18	
Iver	d										19 51													20 21	
West Drayton	d		19 41								19 54					20 08								20 24	
Heathrow Terminal 5 ⊖ ✈	a																								
	d								19 42				19 57									20 12			
Heathrow Terminal 4 ⊖ ✈	a																								
	d			19 41										19 52							20 11				
Heathrow Termls 2 & 3 2 ⊖ ✈	a			19 45					19 46				20 01	19 56							20 15	20 16			
	d								19 47				20 02	19 58								20 17			
Hayes & Harlington	d		19 45							19 48	19 58			20 04		20 13							20 18	20 28	
Southall	d									19 53	20 02			20 08									20 23	20 32	
Hanwell	d													20 11											
Greenford ⊖	d											19 50													
South Greenford	d											19 54													
Castle Bar Park	d											19 56													
Drayton Green	d											19 58													
West Ealing	d									19 57		20a01		20 13									20 27		
Ealing Broadway ⊖	d		19 56							20 00	20 08			20 16		20 22							20 30	20 38	
Acton Main Line	d									20 03													20 33		
London Paddington 15 ⊖	a		20 06				19 54	19 57	20 02	20 13	20 17		20 17	20 26		20 30			20 24			20 32	20 43	20 47	

For non-stop services between Reading and London refer to Table T116

For non-stop services between London and Heathrow Airport see Table T118

Table T117-R

Mondays to Fridays
16 December to 15 May

Reading, Heathrow Airport and Greenford - London

Stopping Services

		GW	HX ◇1	XR	GW	XR		XR	GW ◇1 🍴	XR	XR	GW	XR	GW	GW ◇1 🍴	XC ◇1 🍴		HX ◇1	GW ◇	HX ◇1	XR	XR	GW ◇1 🍴	XC ◇1 🍴	HX ◇1
Oxford	d								20 06							20 16							20 32	20 42	
Reading 7	d				20 15			20 22	20 31					20 34	20 36	20a43			20 49			20 52	20 56	21a06	
Twyford 3	d				20 21			20 28						20 40								20 58			
Maidenhead 3	d				20 28			20 35						20 48								21 05			
Taplow	d							20 38														21 08			
Burnham	d							20 41			←											21 11			
Slough 3	a				20 34			20 44	20 42		20 44			20 54								21 14	21 07		
	d				20 34			20 45	20 43		20 45			20 55								21 15	21 08		
Langley	d							→			20 48											→			
Iver	d										20 51														
West Drayton	d				20 40						20 54			21 02											
Heathrow Terminal 5 ⊖ ✈	a																								
	d		20 27															20 42		20 57					21 12
Heathrow Terminal 4 ⊖ ✈	a																								
	d			20 22		20 41							20 52								21 11				
Heathrow Termls 2 & 3 2 ⊖ ✈	a		20 31	20 26		20 45							20 56					20 46		21 01	21 15				21 16
	d		20 32	20 28									20 58					20 47		21 02					21 17
Hayes & Harlington	d			20 34	20 44					20 48	20 58		21 04	21 10											
Southall	d			20 38						20 53	21 02		21 08												
Hanwell	d			20 41									21 11												
Greenford ⊖	d	20 25										20 54													
South Greenford	d	20 29										20 58													
Castle Bar Park	d	20 31										21 00													
Drayton Green	d	20 33										21 02													
West Ealing	d	20a36		20 43						20 57		21a05	21 13												
Ealing Broadway ⊖	d			20 46	20 52					21 00	21 08		21 16	21 19											
Acton Main Line	d									21 03															
London Paddington 15 ⊖	a		20 47	20 55	21 01				20 59	21 13	21 17		21 25	21 31	21 01			21 03	21 14	21 17			21 22		21 32

		XR		XR	GW	HX ◇1	XR	GW	XR	XR	GW ◇1 🍴	HX ◇1		GW ◇1 🍴	XR	XR	HX ◇1	GW	XR	GW	XC ◇1 🍴	XR		GW ◇1 🍴	GW FX ◇1 A 🍴
Oxford	d										21 02										21 15			21 32	
Reading 7	d							21 08		21 22	21 26			21 38						21 38	21a40	21 52		21 56	22 04
Twyford 3	d							21 14		21 28										21 45		21 58			
Maidenhead 3	d							21 27		21 35										21 53		22 05			
Taplow	d									21 38												22 08			
Burnham	d			←						21 41						←						22 11			
Slough 3	a			21 14				21 33		21 44	21 38					21 44				22 00		22 14		22 07	
	d			21 15				21 33		21 45	21 39					21 45				22 01		22 15		22 08	
Langley	d			21 18						→						21 48						→			
Iver	d			21 21												21 51									
West Drayton	d			21 24				21 39								21 54				22 08					
Heathrow Terminal 5 ⊖ ✈	a																								
	d					21 27						21 42					21 57								
Heathrow Terminal 4 ⊖ ✈	a																								
	d						21 22		21 41										21 52						
Heathrow Termls 2 & 3 2 ⊖ ✈	a					21 31	21 26		21 45			21 46					22 01		21 56						
	d					21 32	21 28					21 47					22 02		21 58						
Hayes & Harlington	d	21 18		21 28			21 34	21 43							21 48	21 58			22 04	22 13					
Southall	d	21 23		21 32			21 38	21 47							21 53	22 02			22 08	22 17					
Hanwell	d						21 41												22 11						
Greenford ⊖	d				21 23													21 55							
South Greenford	d				21 27													21 59							
Castle Bar Park	d				21 29													22 01							
Drayton Green	d				21 31													22 03							
West Ealing	d	21 28			21a34		21 43								21 57			22 08	22 13						
Ealing Broadway ⊖	d	21 31		21 38			21 46	21 52							22 00	22 08		22 11	22 16	22 23					
Acton Main Line	d	21 34													22 03										
London Paddington 15 ⊖	a	21 43		21 47		21 47	21 55	22 01			21 54	22 02		22 06	22 13	22 17	22 17	22 23	22 26	22 31				22 24	22 29

A until 2 April

For non-stop services between Reading and London refer to Table T116

For non-stop services between London and Heathrow Airport see Table T118

Table T117-R

Mondays to Fridays

16 December to 15 May

Reading, Heathrow Airport and Greenford - London

Stopping Services

		XC	XR	HX	XR	XR	HX	XR	GW	XR	XR	GW	GW	GW	XC	HX	XR	HX	XR	XR	XR	HX
		◇1		◇1			◇1					◇1 🍴	◇1 🍴		◇1	◇1		◇1				FX ◇1
Oxford	d	21 44										22 02		22 06	22 16							
Reading 7	d	22a07							22 15		22 22	22 26	22 35	22a47	22a40							
Twyford 3	d								22 21		22 28											
Maidenhead 3	d								22 28		22 35											
Taplow	d										22 38											
Burnham	d					←					22 41								←			
Slough 3	a					22 14			22 34		22 44	22 38							22 44			
	d					22 15			22 34		22 45	22 39							22 45			
Langley	d					22 18					→								22 48			
Iver	d					22 21													22 51			
West Drayton	d					22 24			22 40										22 54			
Heathrow Terminal 5 ⊖ ✈	a																					
	d			22 12			22 27									22 42		22 57				23 12
Heathrow Terminal 4 ⊖ ✈	a																					
	d		22 11					22 22		22 41										22 52	23 11	
Heathrow Termls 2 & 3 2 ⊖ ✈	a		22 15	22 16			22 31	22 26		22 45						22 46		23 01		22 56	23 15	23 16
	d			22 17			22 32	22 28								22 47		23 02		22 58		23 17
Hayes & Harlington	d				22 18	22 28		22 34	22 44								22 47		22 58	23 04		
Southall	d				22 23	22 32		22 38	22 48								22 52		23 02	23 08		
Hanwell	d							22 41												23 11		
Greenford ⊖	d																					
South Greenford	d																					
Castle Bar Park	d																					
Drayton Green	d																					
West Ealing	d				22 27			22 43									22 56			23 13		
Ealing Broadway ⊖	d				22 30	22 38		22 46	22 53								22 59		23 08	23 16		
Acton Main Line	d				22 33												23 02					
London Paddington 15 ⊖	a			22 32	22 43	22 47	22 49	22 55	23 03			22 54	23 00			23 02	23 12	23 17	23 18	23 25		23 32

		HX	GW	XR	XR	GW	HX	XR	XR	HX	HX	XR	GW	HX	GW	XC	XR
		FO ◇1				◇1 🍴	◇1			FX ◇1	FO ◇1				◇	◇1	
Oxford	d					22 32									23 05	23 16	
Reading 7	d		22 48		22 52	22 59							23 22		23 36	23a50	
Twyford 3	d		22 54		22 58								23 28				
Maidenhead 3	d		23 01		23 05	23 09							23 35				
Taplow	d				23 08								23 38				
Burnham	d				23 11								23 41				
Slough 3	a		23 07		23 14	23 18							23 44		23 56		
	d		23 07		23 15	23 19							23 45		23 57		
Langley	d				23 18								23 48				
Iver	d				23 21								23 51				
West Drayton	d				23 24												
Heathrow Terminal 5 ⊖ ✈	a																
	d	23 12					23 27			23 42	23 42			23 51			
Heathrow Terminal 4 ⊖ ✈	a																
	d							23 22	23 41								23 57
Heathrow Termls 2 & 3 2 ⊖ ✈	a	23 16					23 31	23 26	23 45	23 46	23 46			23 55			00 01
	d	23 17					23 32	23 28		23 47	23 47			23 57			00 03
Hayes & Harlington	d		23 15	23 18	23 28			23 34				23 48	23 55				00 09
Southall	d		23 19	23 23	23 32			23 38				23 53	23 59				00 13
Hanwell	d							23 41									
Greenford ⊖	d																
South Greenford	d																
Castle Bar Park	d																
Drayton Green	d																
West Ealing	d			23 27				23 43									
Ealing Broadway ⊖	d		23 25	23 30	23 38			23 46				23 58	00 04				00 18
Acton Main Line	d			23 33													
London Paddington 15 ⊖	a	23 33	23 36	23 43	23 47	23 44	23 47	23 55		00 03	00 04	00 10	00 12	00 15	00 18		00 31

For non-stop services between Reading and London refer to Table T116

For non-stop services between London and Heathrow Airport see Table T118

NRT DECEMBER 19 EDITION

Table T117-R

Saturdays

21 December to 16 May

Reading, Heathrow Airport and Greenford - London

Stopping Services

		GW	XR	XR	GW	GW	GW	GW	GW	GW	HX	GW	HX	XR	XR	HX	XR	XR	XR	HX	XR	GW	XR
						◇1 🍴					◇1		◇1			◇1				◇1			
Oxford	d					00 11		00 45		04 00													
Reading 7	d				00 17	00 43	01 15	01a28	04 13	04a31		04 54										05 45	
Twyford 3	d				00 23		01 21		04 19			05 00										05 51	
Maidenhead 3	d				00 30		01 28		04 27			05 07					05 18		05 35			05 58	
Taplow	d				00 33												05 21		05 38				
Burnham	d				00 37												05 24		05 41				
Slough 3	a				00 40	00 56	01 34		04 34			05 13					05 28		05 44			06 04	
	d				00 41	00 57	01 34		04 35			05 13					05 28		05 45			06 04	
Langley	d				00 45												05 32		05 48				
Iver	d																05 35		05 51				
West Drayton	d				00 49				04 42			05 19					05 39		05 54			06 10	
Heathrow Terminal 5 ⊖ ✈	a																						
	d										05 12		05 27			05 42				05 57			
Heathrow Terminal 4 ⊖ ✈	a																						
	d			00 07										05 22	05 41						05 52		06 11
Heathrow Termls 2 & 3 2 ⊖ ✈	a			00 11							05 16		05 31	05 26	05 45	05 46				06 01	05 56		06 15
	d		00 03	00 13							05 17		05 32	05 28		05 47				06 02	05 58		
Hayes & Harlington	d		00 09	00 19	00 53		01 42		04 46			05 23		05 34			05 43	05 48	05 58		06 04	06 14	
Southall	d		00 13	00 23	00 57				04 50			05 27		05 38			05 47	05 53	06 02		06 08	06 18	
Hanwell	d													05 41							06 11		
Greenford ⊖	d																						
South Greenford	d																						
Castle Bar Park	d																						
Drayton Green	d																						
West Ealing	d													05 43				05 57			06 13		
Ealing Broadway ⊖	d	00 04	00 18	00 28	01 02		01 51		04 55			05 32		05 46			05 54	06 00	06 08		06 16	06 23	
Acton Main Line	d																	06 03					
London Paddington 15 ⊖	a	00 12	00 31	00 40	01 11	01 15	02 01		05 04		05 32	05 40	05 48	05 55		06 03	06 04	06 13	06 17	06 18	06 25	06 31	

		GW	HX	XR	HX	XR	GW	GW	XR	GW	XR	GW	HX	XR	XR	HX	XR	GW	XR	GW	XR	GW
			◇1		◇1			◇1					◇1			◇1						◇1
Oxford	d							05 50														06 32
Reading 7	d					05 54	06 15	06 20							06 22			06 45			06 52	06 56
Twyford 3	d					06 00	06 21								06 28			06 51			06 58	
Maidenhead 3	d					06 07	06 28								06 35			06 58			07 05	
Taplow	d					06 10									06 38						07 08	
Burnham	d					06 13				←					06 41						07 11	
Slough 3	a					06 16	06 34	06 31		06 34					06 44			07 04			07 14	07 08
	d					06 17	06 34	06 33		06 34					06 45			07 04			07 15	07 09
Langley	d					06 20	→								06 48						→	
Iver	d					06 23									06 51							
West Drayton	d					06 26				06 40					06 54			07 10				
Heathrow Terminal 5 ⊖ ✈	a																					
	d		06 12		06 27								06 42			06 57						
Heathrow Terminal 4 ⊖ ✈	a																					
	d								06 22		06 41						06 52		07 11			
Heathrow Termls 2 & 3 2 ⊖ ✈	a		06 16		06 31				06 26		06 45		06 46			07 01	06 56		07 15			
	d		06 17		06 32				06 28				06 47			07 02	06 58					
Hayes & Harlington	d			06 18		06 30			06 34	06 44				06 48	06 58		07 04	07 14				
Southall	d			06 23		06 34			06 38					06 53	07 02		07 08					
Hanwell	d								06 41								07 11					
Greenford ⊖	d	06 12										06 42								07 12		
South Greenford	d	06 15										06 45								07 15		
Castle Bar Park	d	06 18										06 48								07 18		
Drayton Green	d	06 20										06 50								07 20		
West Ealing	d	06a23		06 27					06 43			06a53		06 57			07 13			07a23		
Ealing Broadway ⊖	d			06 30		06 40			06 46	06 51				07 00	07 08		07 16	07 21				
Acton Main Line	d			06 33										07 03								
London Paddington 15 ⊖	a		06 33	06 43	06 48	06 49		06 50	06 55	07 01			07 03	07 13	07 17	07 18	07 25	07 31				07 25

For non-stop services between Reading and London refer to Table T116

For non-stop services between London and Heathrow Airport see Table T118

Table T117-R

Saturdays

21 December to 16 May

Reading, Heathrow Airport and Greenford - London

Stopping Services

Station		HX ◇1	XR	XR		HX ◇1	XR	GW	XR	GW	XR	GW ◇1	GW ◇1 ⊼	XC ◇1 ⊼		HX ◇1	XR	XR	HX ◇1	XR	GW	XR	GW	XR	
Oxford	d											07 02		07 16											
Reading 7	d							07 14			07 22	07 26	07 35	07a41							07 45			07 52	
Twyford 3	d							07 20			07 28										07 51			07 58	
Maidenhead 3	d							07 27			07 35										07 58			08 05	
Taplow	d										07 38													08 08	
Burnham	d			←							07 41							←						08 11	
Slough 3	a			07 14				07 33			07 44	07 38						07 44			08 04			08 14	
	d			07 15				07 34			07 45	07 39						07 45			08 04			08 15	
Langley	d			07 18							→							07 48						→	
Iver	d			07 21														07 51							
West Drayton	d			07 24				07 40										07 54			08 10				
Heathrow Terminal 5 ⊖ ✈	a																								
	d	07 12				07 27										07 42			07 57						
Heathrow Terminal 4 ⊖ ✈	a																								
	d						07 22		07 41											07 52		08 11			
Heathrow Termls 2 & 3 2 ⊖ ✈	a	07 16				07 31	07 26		07 45							07 46			08 01	07 56		08 15			
	d	07 17				07 32	07 28									07 47			08 02	07 58					
Hayes & Harlington	d		07 18	07 28			07 34	07 44									07 48	07 58		08 04	08 14				
Southall	d		07 23	07 32			07 38										07 53	08 02		08 08					
Hanwell	d						07 41													08 11					
Greenford ⊖	d									07 42													08 12		
South Greenford	d									07 45													08 15		
Castle Bar Park	d									07 48													08 18		
Drayton Green	d									07 50													08 20		
West Ealing	d		07 27				07 43			07a53							07 57			08 13			08a23		
Ealing Broadway ⊖	d		07 30	07 38			07 46	07 51									08 00	08 08		08 16	08 21				
Acton Main Line	d		07 33														08 03								
London Paddington 15 ⊖	a	07 33	07 43	07 48		07 48	07 55	08 01				07 54	08 00			08 03	08 13	08 17	08 18	08 25	08 29				

Station		GW ◇1	XC ◇1	HX ◇1	XR	XR	HX ◇1	XR	GW	XR		GW	XR	GW ◇1	GW ◇1 ⊼	XC ◇1 ⊼	HX ◇1	XR	XR	HX ◇1		XR	GW	XR	GW
Oxford	d	07 32	07 42											08 02		08 16									
Reading 7	d	07 56	08a06						08 15				08 22	08 26	08 35	08a37							08 45		
Twyford 3	d								08 21				08 28										08 51		
Maidenhead 3	d								08 28				08 35										08 58		
Taplow	d												08 38												
Burnham	d					←							08 41						←						
Slough 3	a	08 07				08 14			08 34				08 44	08 38					08 44				09 04		
	d	08 08				08 15			08 34				08 45	08 39					08 45				09 04		
Langley	d					08 18							→						08 48						
Iver	d					08 21													08 51						
West Drayton	d					08 24			08 40										08 54				09 10		
Heathrow Terminal 5 ⊖ ✈	a																								
	d			08 12			08 27										08 42			08 57					
Heathrow Terminal 4 ⊖ ✈	a																								
	d							08 22		08 41												08 52		09 11	
Heathrow Termls 2 & 3 2 ⊖ ✈	a			08 16			08 31	08 26		08 45							08 46			09 01		08 56		09 15	
	d			08 17			08 32	08 28									08 47			09 02		08 58			
Hayes & Harlington	d				08 18	08 28		08 34	08 44									08 48	08 58			09 04	09 14		
Southall	d				08 23	08 32		08 38										08 53	09 02			09 08			
Hanwell	d							08 41														09 11			
Greenford ⊖	d											08 42													09 12
South Greenford	d											08 45													09 15
Castle Bar Park	d											08 48													09 18
Drayton Green	d											08 50													09 20
West Ealing	d				08 27			08 43				08a53						08 57				09 13			09a23
Ealing Broadway ⊖	d				08 30	08 38		08 46	08 53									09 00	09 08			09 16	09 21		
Acton Main Line	d				08 33													09 03							
London Paddington 15 ⊖	a	08 22		08 33	08 43	08 47	08 48	08 55	09 01					08 54	09 00		09 03	09 13	09 17	09 18		09 25	09 31		

For non-stop services between Reading and London refer to Table T116

For non-stop services between London and Heathrow Airport see Table T118

Table T117-R

Saturdays

21 December to 16 May

Reading, Heathrow Airport and Greenford - London

Stopping Services

Station		XR		GW ◇1 ⊼	XC ◇1 ⊼	HX ◇1	XR	XR	HX ◇1	XR	GW	XR		GW	XR	GW ◇1	GW ◇1 ⊼	XC ◇1 ⊼	HX ◇1	XR	XR	HX ◇1		XR	GW
Oxford	d			08 32	08 45											09 02		09 16							
Reading 7	d	08 52		08 57	09a09						09 15				09 22	09 27	09 35	09a40							09 45
Twyford 3	d	08 59									09 21				09 28										09 51
Maidenhead 3	d	09 06									09 29				09 35										09 58
Taplow	d	09 09													09 38										
Burnham	d	09 12						←							09 41						←				
Slough 3	a	09 15		09 08				09 15			09 36				09 44	09 39					09 44				10 04
	d	09 16		09 09				09 16			09 36				09 45	09 40					09 45				10 04
Langley	d	→						09 19							→						09 48				
Iver	d							09 22													09 51				
West Drayton	d							09 25			09 42										09 54				10 10
Heathrow Terminal 5 ⊖ ✈	a																								
	d					09 12			09 27										09 42			09 57			
Heathrow Terminal 4 ⊖ ✈	a																								
	d									09 22		09 41												09 52	
Heathrow Termls 2 & 3 2 ⊖ ✈	a					09 16			09 31	09 26		09 45							09 46			10 01		09 56	
	d					09 17			09 32	09 28									09 47			10 02		09 58	
Hayes & Harlington	d						09 18	09 29		09 34	09 46									09 48	09 58			10 04	10 14
Southall	d						09 23	09 33		09 38										09 53	10 02			10 08	
Hanwell	d									09 41														10 11	
Greenford ⊖	d													09 42											
South Greenford	d													09 45											
Castle Bar Park	d													09 48											
Drayton Green	d													09 50											
West Ealing	d						09 27			09 43				09a53						09 57				10 13	
Ealing Broadway ⊖	d						09 30	09 39		09 46	09 53									10 00	10 08			10 16	10 22
Acton Main Line	d						09 33													10 03					
London Paddington 15 ⊖	a			09 23		09 34	09 43	09 47	09 48	09 55	10 01					09 55	10 00		10 03	10 13	10 17	10 18		10 25	10 31

Station		XR	GW	XR	GW ◇1 ⊼	GW ◇1 ⊼	XC ◇1 ⊼	HX ◇1		GW ◇1 ⊼	XR	XR	HX ◇1	XR	GW	XR	GW	XR		GW ◇1	GW ◇1 ⊼	XC ◇1 ⊼	HX ◇1	XR	XR
Oxford	d				09 32		09 42			09 47										10 02		10 16			
Reading 7	d			09 52	09 56	10 05	10a06			10 14					10 15			10 22		10 27	10 35	10a39			
Twyford 3	d			09 58											10 21			10 28							
Maidenhead 3	d			10 05											10 28			10 35							
Taplow	d			10 08														10 38							
Burnham	d			10 11								←						10 41							←
Slough 3	a			10 14	10 07							10 14			10 34			10 44		10 38					10 44
	d			10 15	10 08							10 15			10 34			10 45		10 39					10 45
Langley	d			→								10 18						→							10 48
Iver	d											10 21													10 51
West Drayton	d											10 24			10 40										10 54
Heathrow Terminal 5 ⊖ ✈	a																								
	d							10 12					10 27										10 42		
Heathrow Terminal 4 ⊖ ✈	a																								
	d	10 11												10 22		10 41									
Heathrow Termls 2 & 3 2 ⊖ ✈	a	10 15						10 16					10 31	10 26		10 45							10 46		
	d							10 17					10 32	10 28									10 47		
Hayes & Harlington	d										10 18	10 28		10 34	10 44									10 48	10 58
Southall	d										10 23	10 32		10 38										10 53	11 02
Hanwell	d													10 41											
Greenford ⊖	d		10 12														10 42								
South Greenford	d		10 15														10 45								
Castle Bar Park	d		10 18														10 48								
Drayton Green	d		10 20														10 50								
West Ealing	d		10a23								10 27			10 43			10a53							10 57	
Ealing Broadway ⊖	d										10 30	10 38		10 46	10 51									11 00	11 08
Acton Main Line	d										10 33													11 03	
London Paddington 15 ⊖	a				10 24	10 29		10 33		10 37	10 43	10 47	10 48	10 55	11 02					10 54	11 00		11 03	11 13	11 17

For non-stop services between Reading and London refer to Table T116

For non-stop services between London and Heathrow Airport see Table T118

Table T117-R

Saturdays
21 December to 16 May

Reading, Heathrow Airport and Greenford - London

Stopping Services

		XR	GW	GW ◇	HX ◇1	XR	GW	XR	GW ◇1 🍴	XC ◇1 🍴		HX ◇1	XR	XR	HX ◇1	XR	GW	XR	GW	XR		GW ◇1	GW ◇1 🍴	XC ◇1 🍴	HX ◇1
Oxford	d								10 32	10 43												11 00		11 16	
Reading 7	d		10 45	10 49				10 52	10 56	11a07							11 15			11 22		11 27	11 35	11a39	
Twyford 3	d		10 51					10 58									11 21			11 28					
Maidenhead 3	d		10 58					11 05									11 28			11 35					
Taplow	d							11 08												11 38					
Burnham	d							11 11						←						11 41					
Slough 3	a		11 04					11 14	11 07					11 14			11 34			11 44		11 39			
	d		11 04					11 15	11 08					11 15			11 34			11 45		11 40			
Langley	d							→						11 18						→					
Iver	d													11 21											
West Drayton	d		11 10											11 24			11 40								
Heathrow Terminal 5 ⊖ ✈	a																								
	d				10 57							11 12			11 27										11 42
Heathrow Terminal 4 ⊖ ✈	a																								
	d	10 52				11 11										11 22		11 41							
Heathrow Termls 2 & 3 2 ⊖ ✈	a	10 56			11 01	11 15						11 16			11 31	11 26		11 45							11 46
	d	10 58			11 02							11 17			11 32	11 28									11 47
Hayes & Harlington	d	11 04	11 14										11 18	11 28		11 34	11 44								
Southall	d	11 08											11 23	11 32		11 38									
Hanwell	d	11 11														11 41									
Greenford ⊖	d						11 12												11 42						
South Greenford	d						11 15												11 45						
Castle Bar Park	d						11 18												11 48						
Drayton Green	d						11 20												11 50						
West Ealing	d	11 13					11a23						11 27			11 43			11a53						
Ealing Broadway ⊖	d	11 16	11 23										11 30	11 38		11 46	11 51								
Acton Main Line	d												11 33												
London Paddington 15 ⊖	a	11 25	11 31	11 13	11 18				11 25			11 33	11 43	11 47	11 48	11 55	12 01					11 54	12 00		12 03

		XR	XR	HX ◇1	XR	GW		XR	GW	XR	GW ◇1 🍴	XC ◇1 🍴	HX ◇1	XR	XR	HX ◇1		XR	GW	XR	GW	XR	GW ◇1	GW ◇1 🍴	XC ◇1 🍴
Oxford	d										11 32	11 42											12 02		12 16
Reading 7	d					11 45				11 52	11 57	12a07							12 15			12 22	12 26	12 35	12a39
Twyford 3	d					11 51				11 58									12 21			12 28			
Maidenhead 3	d					11 58				12 05									12 28			12 35			
Taplow	d									12 08												12 38			
Burnham	d		←							12 11					←							12 41			
Slough 3	a		11 44			12 04				12 14	12 08				12 14				12 34			12 44	12 38		
	d		11 45			12 04				12 15	12 09				12 15				12 34			12 45	12 39		
Langley	d		11 48							→					12 18							→			
Iver	d		11 51												12 21										
West Drayton	d		11 54			12 10									12 24				12 40						
Heathrow Terminal 5 ⊖ ✈	a																								
	d			11 57									12 12			12 27									
Heathrow Terminal 4 ⊖ ✈	a																								
	d				11 52			12 11										12 22		12 41					
Heathrow Termls 2 & 3 2 ⊖ ✈	a			12 01	11 56			12 15					12 16			12 31		12 26		12 45					
	d			12 02	11 58								12 17			12 32		12 28							
Hayes & Harlington	d	11 48	11 58		12 04	12 14								12 18	12 28			12 34	12 44						
Southall	d	11 53	12 02		12 08									12 23	12 32			12 38							
Hanwell	d				12 11													12 41							
Greenford ⊖	d								12 12												12 46				
South Greenford	d								12 15												12 49				
Castle Bar Park	d								12 18												12 52				
Drayton Green	d								12 20												12 54				
West Ealing	d	11 57			12 13				12a23					12 27				12 43			12a57				
Ealing Broadway ⊖	d	12 00	12 08		12 16	12 21								12 30	12 38			12 46	12 51						
Acton Main Line	d	12 03												12 33											
London Paddington 15 ⊖	a	12 13	12 17	12 18	12 25	12 31					12 25		12 33	12 43	12 47	12 48		12 55	13 01				12 55	13 00	

For non-stop services between Reading and London refer to Table T116

For non-stop services between London and Heathrow Airport see Table T118

Table T117-R

Saturdays
21 December to 16 May

Reading, Heathrow Airport and Greenford - London

Stopping Services

		HX ◇1	XR	XR	HX ◇1	XR	GW	XR		GW	XR	GW ◇	GW ◇1 🍴	XC ◇1 🍴	HX ◇1	XR	XR	HX ◇1		XR	GW	XR	GW	XR	GW ◇1
Oxford	d												12 32	12 43											13 02
Reading 7	d						12 45				12 52	12 54	12 57	13a07							13 15			13 22	13 26
Twyford 3	d						12 51				12 58										13 21			13 28	
Maidenhead 3	d						12 58				13 05										13 28			13 35	
Taplow	d										13 08													13 38	
Burnham	d			←							13 11						←							13 41	
Slough 3	a			12 44			13 04				13 14		13 08				13 14				13 34			13 44	13 38
	d			12 45			13 04				13 15		13 09				13 15				13 34			13 45	13 39
Langley	d			12 48							→						13 18							→	
Iver	d			12 51													13 21								
West Drayton	d			12 54			13 10										13 24				13 40				
Heathrow Terminal 5 ⊖ ✈	a																								
	d	12 42			12 57										13 12			13 27							
Heathrow Terminal 4 ⊖ ✈	a																								
	d					12 52		13 11												13 22		13 41			
Heathrow Termls 2 & 3 2 ⊖ ✈	a	12 46			13 01	12 56		13 15							13 16			13 31		13 26		13 45			
	d	12 47			13 02	12 58									13 17			13 32		13 28					
Hayes & Harlington	d		12 48	12 58		13 04	13 14									13 18	13 28			13 34	13 44				
Southall	d		12 53	13 02		13 08										13 23	13 32			13 38					
Hanwell	d					13 11														13 41					
Greenford ⊖	d									13 16													13 46		
South Greenford	d									13 19													13 49		
Castle Bar Park	d									13 22													13 52		
Drayton Green	d									13 24													13 54		
West Ealing	d		12 57			13 13				13a27						13 27				13 43			13a57		
Ealing Broadway ⊖	d		13 00	13 08		13 16	13 21									13 30	13 38			13 46	13 51				
Acton Main Line	d		13 03													13 33									
London Paddington 15 ⊖	a	13 03	13 13	13 17	13 18	13 25	13 31					13 22	13 24		13 33	13 43	13 47	13 48		13 55	14 01				13 55

		GW ◇1 🍴	XC ◇1 🍴	HX ◇1		GW ◇1 🍴	XR	XR	HX ◇1	XR	GW	XR	GW	XR		GW ◇1 🍴	XC ◇1 🍴	HX ◇1	XR	XR	HX ◇1	XR	GW	XR	
Oxford	d		13 16													13 32	13 42								
Reading 7	d	13 35	13a39			13 44					13 45			13 52		13 56	14a06						14 15		
Twyford 3	d										13 51			13 58									14 21		
Maidenhead 3	d										13 58			14 05									14 28		
Taplow	d													14 08											
Burnham	d							←						14 11						←					
Slough 3	a							13 44			14 04			14 14		14 07				14 14			14 34		
	d							13 45			14 04			14 15		14 08				14 15			14 34		
Langley	d							13 48						→						14 18					
Iver	d							13 51												14 21					
West Drayton	d							13 54			14 10									14 24			14 40		
Heathrow Terminal 5 ⊖ ✈	a																								
	d			13 42					13 57									14 12			14 27				
Heathrow Terminal 4 ⊖ ✈	a																								
	d									13 52		14 11										14 22		14 41	
Heathrow Termls 2 & 3 2 ⊖ ✈	a			13 46					14 01	13 56		14 15						14 16			14 31	14 26		14 45	
	d			13 47					14 02	13 58								14 17			14 32	14 28			
Hayes & Harlington	d						13 48	13 58		14 04	14 14								14 18	14 28		14 34	14 44		
Southall	d						13 53	14 02		14 08									14 23	14 32		14 38			
Hanwell	d									14 11												14 41			
Greenford ⊖	d												14 16												
South Greenford	d												14 19												
Castle Bar Park	d												14 22												
Drayton Green	d												14 24												
West Ealing	d						13 57			14 13			14a27						14 27			14 43			
Ealing Broadway ⊖	d						14 00	14 08		14 16	14 21								14 30	14 38		14 46	14 51		
Acton Main Line	d						14 03												14 33						
London Paddington 15 ⊖	a	14 00		14 03		14 09	14 13	14 17	14 18	14 25	14 31					14 22		14 33	14 43	14 47	14 48	14 55	15 01		

For non-stop services between Reading and London refer to Table T116

For non-stop services between London and Heathrow Airport see Table T118

Table T117-R

Saturdays

21 December to 16 May

Reading, Heathrow Airport and Greenford - London

Stopping Services

		GW	XR	GW ◇1	GW ◇1 ⚒	XC ◇1 ⚒		HX ◇1	XR	XR	XR	GW	GW ◇	HX ◇1	XR	GW		XR	GW ◇1 ⚒	XC ◇1 ⚒	HX ◇1	XR	XR	HX ◇1	XR
Oxford	d			14 02		14 16													14 31	14 42					
Reading 7	d		14 22	14 27	14 35	14a40						14 45	14 49					14 52	14 56	15a06					
Twyford 3	d		14 28									14 51						14 58							
Maidenhead 3	d		14 35									14 58						15 05							
Taplow	d		14 38															15 08							
Burnham	d		14 41							←								15 11					←		
Slough 3	a		14 44	14 38						14 44		15 04						15 14	15 07				15 14		
	d		14 45	14 39						14 45		15 04						15 15	15 08				15 15		
Langley	d		→							14 48								→					15 18		
Iver	d									14 51													15 21		
West Drayton	d									14 54		15 10											15 24		
Heathrow Terminal 5 ⊖ ✈	a																								
	d							14 42						14 57							15 12			15 27	
Heathrow Terminal 4 ⊖ ✈	a																								
	d										14 52				15 11										15 22
Heathrow Termls 2 & 3 2 ⊖ ✈	a							14 46			14 56			15 01	15 15						15 16			15 31	15 26
	d							14 47			14 58			15 02							15 17			15 32	15 28
Hayes & Harlington	d								14 48	14 58	15 04	15 14										15 18	15 28		15 34
Southall	d								14 53	15 02	15 08											15 23	15 32		15 38
Hanwell	d										15 11														15 41
Greenford ⊖	d	14 46														15 16									
South Greenford	d	14 49														15 19									
Castle Bar Park	d	14 52														15 22									
Drayton Green	d	14 54														15 24									
West Ealing	d	14a57							14 57		15 13					15a27						15 27			15 43
Ealing Broadway ⊖	d								15 00	15 08	15 16	15 21										15 30	15 38		15 46
Acton Main Line	d								15 03													15 33			
London Paddington 15 ⊖	a			14 55	15 00			15 03	15 13	15 17	15 25	15 31	15 14	15 18					15 22		15 33	15 43	15 47	15 48	15 55

		GW		XR	GW	XR	GW ◇1	GW ◇1 ⚒	XC ◇1 ⚒	HX ◇1	GW ◇1 ⚒	XR		XR	HX ◇1	XR	GW	XR	GW	XR	GW ◇1 ⚒	XC ◇1 ⚒		HX ◇1	XR
Oxford	d						15 02		15 16												15 32	15 42			
Reading 7	d	15 15				15 22	15 26	15 35	15a39		15 44						15 45			15 52	15 56	16a06			
Twyford 3	d	15 21				15 28											15 51			15 58					
Maidenhead 3	d	15 28				15 35											15 58			16 05					
Taplow	d					15 38														16 08					
Burnham	d					15 41								←						16 11					
Slough 3	a	15 34				15 44	15 38							15 44			16 04			16 14	16 07				
	d	15 34				15 45	15 39							15 45			16 04			16 15	16 08				
Langley	d					→								15 48						→					
Iver	d													15 51											
West Drayton	d	15 40												15 54			16 10								
Heathrow Terminal 5 ⊖ ✈	a																								
	d									15 42					15 57									16 12	
Heathrow Terminal 4 ⊖ ✈	a																								
	d			15 41												15 52		16 11							
Heathrow Termls 2 & 3 2 ⊖ ✈	a			15 45						15 46					16 01	15 56		16 15						16 16	
	d									15 47					16 02	15 58								16 17	
Hayes & Harlington	d	15 44										15 48		15 58		16 04	16 14								16 18
Southall	d											15 53		16 02		16 08									16 23
Hanwell	d															16 11									
Greenford ⊖	d				15 46														16 16						
South Greenford	d				15 49														16 19						
Castle Bar Park	d				15 52														16 22						
Drayton Green	d				15 54														16 24						
West Ealing	d				15a57							15 57				16 13			16a27						16 27
Ealing Broadway ⊖	d	15 51										16 00		16 08		16 16	16 21								16 30
Acton Main Line	d											16 03													16 33
London Paddington 15 ⊖	a	16 01					15 55	16 00		16 03	16 08	16 13		16 17	16 18	16 25	16 31				16 25			16 33	16 43

For non-stop services between Reading and London refer to Table T116

For non-stop services between London and Heathrow Airport see Table T118

Table T117-R

Saturdays

21 December to 16 May

Reading, Heathrow Airport and Greenford - London

Stopping Services

		XR	HX ◇1	XR		GW	XR	GW	XR	GW ◇1	GW ◇1 ⚒	XC ◇1 ⚒	HX ◇1	XR		XR	XR	GW	GW ◇	HX ◇1	XR	GW	XR	GW ◇1 ⚒	
Oxford	d									16 02		16 16												16 32	
Reading 7	d					16 15			16 22	16 28	16 35	16a39						16 45	16 49				16 52	16 56	
Twyford 3	d					16 21			16 28									16 51					16 58		
Maidenhead 3	d					16 28			16 35									16 58					17 05		
Taplow	d								16 38														17 08		
Burnham	d	←							16 41							←							17 11		
Slough 3	a	16 14				16 34			16 44	16 39						16 44		17 04					17 14	17 07	
	d	16 15				16 34			16 45	16 40						16 45		17 04					17 15	17 08	
Langley	d	16 18							→							16 48							→		
Iver	d	16 21														16 51									
West Drayton	d	16 24				16 40										16 54		17 10							
Heathrow Terminal 5 ⊖ ✈	a																								
	d		16 27										16 42							16 57					
Heathrow Terminal 4 ⊖ ✈	a																								
	d			16 22			16 41										16 52				17 11				
Heathrow Termls 2 & 3 2 ⊖ ✈	a		16 31	16 26			16 45						16 46				16 56			17 01	17 15				
	d		16 32	16 28									16 47				16 58			17 02					
Hayes & Harlington	d	16 28		16 34		16 44								16 48		16 58	17 04	17 14							
Southall	d	16 32		16 38										16 53		17 02	17 08								
Hanwell	d			16 41													17 11								
Greenford ⊖	d							16 46														17 16			
South Greenford	d							16 49														17 19			
Castle Bar Park	d							16 52														17 22			
Drayton Green	d							16 54														17 24			
West Ealing	d			16 43				16a57						16 57			17 13					17a27			
Ealing Broadway ⊖	d	16 38		16 46		16 53								17 00		17 08	17 16	17 21							
Acton Main Line	d													17 03											
London Paddington 15 ⊖	a	16 47	16 48	16 55		17 04				16 54	17 00		17 03	17 13		17 17	17 25	17 31	17 14	17 18				17 23	

		XC ◇1 ⚒	HX ◇1	XR	XR	HX ◇1	XR	GW	XR	GW		XR	GW ◇1	GW ◇1 ⚒	XC ◇1 ⚒	HX ◇1	GW ◇1 ⚒	XR	XR	HX ◇1		XR	GW	XR	GW
Oxford	d	16 42											17 02		17 16										
Reading 7	d	17a06						17 15				17 22	17 26	17 35	17a39		17 44						17 45		
Twyford 3	d							17 21				17 28											17 51		
Maidenhead 3	d							17 28				17 35											17 58		
Taplow	d											17 38													
Burnham	d				←							17 41							←						
Slough 3	a				17 14			17 34				17 44	17 38						17 44				18 04		
	d				17 15			17 34				17 45	17 39						17 45				18 04		
Langley	d				17 18							→							17 48						
Iver	d				17 21														17 51						
West Drayton	d				17 24			17 40											17 54				18 10		
Heathrow Terminal 5 ⊖ ✈	a																								
	d		17 12			17 27										17 42				17 57					
Heathrow Terminal 4 ⊖ ✈	a																								
	d						17 22		17 41													17 52		18 11	
Heathrow Termls 2 & 3 2 ⊖ ✈	a		17 16			17 31	17 26		17 45							17 46				18 01		17 56		18 15	
	d		17 17			17 32	17 28									17 47				18 02		17 58			
Hayes & Harlington	d			17 18	17 28		17 34	17 44										17 48	17 58			18 04	18 14		
Southall	d			17 23	17 32		17 38											17 53	18 02			18 08			
Hanwell	d						17 41															18 11			
Greenford ⊖	d									17 46															18 16
South Greenford	d									17 49															18 19
Castle Bar Park	d									17 52															18 22
Drayton Green	d									17 54															18 24
West Ealing	d			17 27			17 43			17a57								17 57				18 13			18a27
Ealing Broadway ⊖	d			17 30	17 38		17 46	17 51										18 00	18 08			18 16	18 21		
Acton Main Line	d			17 33														18 03							
London Paddington 15 ⊖	a		17 33	17 43	17 47	17 48	17 55	18 01					17 54	18 01		18 03	18 09	18 13	18 17	18 18		18 25	18 31		

For non-stop services between Reading and London refer to Table T116

For non-stop services between London and Heathrow Airport see Table T118

Table T117-R

Saturdays
21 December to 16 May

Reading, Heathrow Airport and Greenford - London

Stopping Services

	XR		GW	XC	HX	XR	XR	HX	XR	GW	XR		GW	XR	GW	GW	XC	HX	XR	XR	HX		XR	GW
			◇1 🍴	◇1 🍴	◇1			◇1							◇1	◇1 🍴	◇1 🍴	◇1			◇1			
Oxford d			17 32	17 43											18 02		18 16							
Reading 7 d	17 52		17 56	18a06						18 15				18 22	18 26	18 35	18a39							18 45
Twyford 3 d	17 58									18 21				18 28										18 51
Maidenhead 3 d	18 05									18 28				18 35										18 58
Taplow d	18 08													18 38										
Burnham d	18 11						←							18 41						←				
Slough 3 a	18 14		18 07				18 14			18 34				18 44	18 38					18 44				19 04
d	18 15		18 08				18 15			18 34				18 45	18 39					18 45				19 04
Langley d	→						18 18							→						18 48				
Iver d							18 21													18 51				
West Drayton d							18 24			18 40										18 54				19 10
Heathrow Terminal 5 ⊖ ✈ a																								
d					18 12			18 27										18 42			18 57			
Heathrow Terminal 4 ⊖ ✈ a																								
d									18 22		18 41												18 52	
Heathrow Termls 2 & 3 2 ⊖ ✈ a					18 16			18 31	18 26		18 45							18 46			19 01		18 56	
d					18 17			18 32	18 28									18 47			19 02		18 58	
Hayes & Harlington d						18 18	18 28		18 34	18 44									18 48	18 58			19 04	19 14
Southall d						18 23	18 32		18 38										18 53	19 02			19 08	
Hanwell d									18 41														19 11	
Greenford ⊖ d												18 46												
South Greenford d												18 49												
Castle Bar Park d												18 52												
Drayton Green d												18 54												
West Ealing d						18 27			18 43			18a57							18 57				19 13	
Ealing Broadway ⊖ d						18 30	18 38		18 46	18 51									19 00	19 08			19 16	19 21
Acton Main Line d						18 33													19 03					
London Paddington 15 ⊖ a			18 23		18 33	18 43	18 47	18 48	18 55	19 01					18 54	19 00		19 03	19 13	19 17	19 18		19 25	19 31

	XR	GW	XR	GW	XC	HX	XR		XR	HX	XR	GW	XR	GW	XR	GW	GW		XC	HX	XR	XR	HX	XR
				◇1 🍴	◇1 🍴	◇1				◇1						◇1	◇1 🍴		◇1 🍴	◇1			◇1	
Oxford d				18 32	18 42											19 02			19 16					
Reading 7 d			18 52	18 56	19a06							19 15			19 22	19 26	19 35		19a39					
Twyford 3 d			18 58									19 21			19 28									
Maidenhead 3 d			19 05									19 28			19 35									
Taplow d			19 08												19 38									
Burnham d			19 11						←						19 41							←		
Slough 3 a			19 14	19 07					19 14			19 34			19 44	19 38						19 44		
d			19 15	19 08					19 15			19 34			19 45	19 39						19 45		
Langley d			→						19 18						→							19 48		
Iver d									19 21													19 51		
West Drayton d									19 24			19 40										19 54		
Heathrow Terminal 5 ⊖ ✈ a																								
d						19 12				19 27										19 42			19 57	
Heathrow Terminal 4 ⊖ ✈ a																								
d	19 11										19 22		19 41											19 52
Heathrow Termls 2 & 3 2 ⊖ ✈ a	19 15					19 16				19 31	19 26		19 45							19 46			20 01	19 56
d						19 17				19 32	19 28									19 47			20 02	19 58
Hayes & Harlington d							19 18		19 28		19 34	19 44									19 48	19 58		20 04
Southall d							19 23		19 32		19 38										19 53	20 02		20 08
Hanwell d											19 41													20 11
Greenford ⊖ d		19 16												19 46										
South Greenford d		19 19												19 49										
Castle Bar Park d		19 22												19 52										
Drayton Green d		19 24												19 54										
West Ealing d		19a27					19 27				19 43			19a57							19 57			20 13
Ealing Broadway ⊖ d							19 30		19 38		19 46	19 51									20 00	20 08		20 16
Acton Main Line d							19 33														20 03			
London Paddington 15 ⊖ a				19 24		19 33	19 43		19 47	19 49	19 55	20 01				19 54	20 00			20 03	20 13	20 17	20 18	20 25

For non-stop services between Reading and London refer to Table T116

For non-stop services between London and Heathrow Airport see Table T118

Table T117-R

Saturdays
21 December to 16 May

Reading, Heathrow Airport and Greenford - London

Stopping Services

	GW	XR	GW	XR	GW	XC	HX	XR	XR		HX	XR	GW	XR	GW	XR	GW	GW	XC		HX	XR	XR	HX
					◇1 🍴	◇1 🍴	◇1				◇1						◇1	◇1 🍴	◇1 🍴		◇1			◇1
Oxford d					19 32	19 42											20 02		20 16					
Reading 7 d	19 45			19 52	19 56	20a06							20 15			20 22	20 27	20 35	20a39					
Twyford 3 d	19 51			19 58									20 21			20 28								
Maidenhead 3 d	19 58			20 05									20 28			20 35								
Taplow d				20 08												20 38								
Burnham d				20 11					←							20 41							←	
Slough 3 a	20 04			20 14	20 07				20 14				20 34			20 44	20 39						20 44	
d	20 04			20 15	20 08				20 15				20 34			20 45	20 40						20 45	
Langley d				→					20 18							→							20 48	
Iver d									20 21														20 51	
West Drayton d	20 10								20 24				20 40										20 54	
Heathrow Terminal 5 ⊖ ✈ a																								
d							20 12				20 27										20 42			20 57
Heathrow Terminal 4 ⊖ ✈ a																								
d		20 11										20 22		20 41										
Heathrow Termls 2 & 3 2 ⊖ ✈ a		20 15					20 16				20 31	20 26		20 45							20 46			21 01
d							20 17				20 32	20 28									20 47			21 02
Hayes & Harlington d	20 14							20 18	20 28			20 34	20 44									20 48	20 58	
Southall d								20 23	20 32			20 38										20 53	21 02	
Hanwell d												20 41												
Greenford ⊖ d			20 16												20 46									
South Greenford d			20 19												20 49									
Castle Bar Park d			20 22												20 52									
Drayton Green d			20 24												20 54									
West Ealing d			20a27					20 27				20 43			20a57							20 57		
Ealing Broadway ⊖ d	20 21							20 30	20 38			20 46	20 51									21 00	21 08	
Acton Main Line d								20 33														21 03		
London Paddington 15 ⊖ a	20 31				20 25		20 33	20 43	20 47		20 48	20 55	21 01				20 55	21 00			21 03	21 13	21 17	21 18

	XR	GW	XR	GW	XR		GW	GW	XC	HX	XR	XR	HX	XR	GW		XR	XR	GW	XR	GW	XR	GW	GW
							◇1 🍴		◇1 🍴	◇1			◇1						◇1					◇1 🍴
Oxford d							20 32	20 37	20 42										21 02					
Reading 7 d		20 45			20 52		20 56	21a19	21a06						21 15			21 22	21 26				21 30	21 35
Twyford 3 d		20 51			20 58										21 21			21 28					21 36	
Maidenhead 3 d		20 58			21 05										21 28			21 35					21 44	
Taplow d					21 08													21 38						
Burnham d					21 11							←						21 41				←		
Slough 3 a		21 04			21 14		21 07					21 14			21 34			21 44	21 38			21 44	21 51	
d		21 04			21 15		21 08					21 15			21 34			21 45	21 39			21 45	21 52	
Langley d					→							21 18						→				21 48		
Iver d												21 21										21 51		
West Drayton d		21 10										21 24			21 40							21 54		
Heathrow Terminal 5 ⊖ ✈ a																								
d										21 12			21 27											
Heathrow Terminal 4 ⊖ ✈ a																								
d	20 52		21 11											21 22			21 41							
Heathrow Termls 2 & 3 2 ⊖ ✈ a	20 56		21 15							21 16			21 31	21 26			21 45							
d	20 58									21 17			21 32	21 28										
Hayes & Harlington d	21 04	21 14									21 18	21 28		21 34	21 44					21 48		21 58	22 01	
Southall d	21 08										21 23	21 32		21 38						21 53		22 02		
Hanwell d	21 11													21 41										
Greenford ⊖ d				21 16																	21 50			
South Greenford d				21 19																	21 53			
Castle Bar Park d				21 22																	21 56			
Drayton Green d				21 24																	21 58			
West Ealing d	21 13			21a27							21 27			21 43						21 57	22 00			
Ealing Broadway ⊖ d	21 16	21 21									21 30	21 38		21 46	21 51					22 00	22 03	22 08	22 12	
Acton Main Line d											21 33									22 03				
London Paddington 15 ⊖ a	21 25	21 31					21 23			21 33	21 43	21 47	21 48	21 55	22 01				21 54	22 13	22 13	22 17	22 23	22 00

For non-stop services between Reading and London refer to Table T116

For non-stop services between London and Heathrow Airport see Table T118

Table T117-R

Saturdays

21 December to 16 May

Reading, Heathrow Airport and Greenford - London

Stopping Services

Station		XC	HX	HX	XR	GW	XR	XR		GW	XC	HX	XR	XR	HX	XR	GW	XR		HX	XR	XR	GW	GW	XC
		◇1	◇1	◇1						◇1	◇1	◇1			◇1					◇1			◇1	◇1	◇1
						A											A								
Oxford	d	21 16								21 32	21 42												22 04		22 16
Reading 7	d	21a39				21 45		21 52		21 56	22a07						22 15					22 22	22 34	22 39	22a41
Twyford 3	d					21 51		21 58									22 21					22 28			
Maidenhead 3	d					21 58		22 05									22 28					22 35	22 43		
Taplow	d							22 08														22 38			
Burnham	d							22 11						←								22 41			
Slough 3	a					22 04		22 14		22 07				22 14			22 34					22 44	22 49		
	d					22 04		22 15		22 08				22 15			22 34					22 45	22 50		
Langley	d							→						22 18								22 48			
Iver	d													22 21								22 51			
West Drayton	d					22 10								22 24			22 40					22 54			
Heathrow Terminal 5 ⊖ ✈	a																								
	d		21 42	21 57								22 12			22 27					22 42					
Heathrow Terminal 4 ⊖ ✈	a																								
	d				21 52		22 11									22 22		22 41							
Heathrow Termls 2 & 3 2 ⊖ ✈	a		21 46	22 01	21 56		22 15					22 16			22 31	22 26		22 45		22 46					
	d		21 47	22 03	21 58							22 17			22 33	22 28				22 47					
Hayes & Harlington	d				22 04	22 14							22 18	22 28		22 34	22 44				22 48	22 58			
Southall	d				22 08								22 23	22 32		22 38					22 53	23 02			
Hanwell	d				22 11											22 41									
Greenford ⊖	d																								
South Greenford	d																								
Castle Bar Park	d																								
Drayton Green	d																								
West Ealing	d				22 13								22 27			22 43					22 57				
Ealing Broadway ⊖	d				22 16	22 21							22 30	22 39		22 46	22 53				23 00	23 08			
Acton Main Line	d												22 33								23 03				
London Paddington 15 ⊖	a		22 03	22 19	22 25	22 32				22 25		22 33	22 43	22 47	22 49	22 55	23 02			23 03	23 13	23 17	23 07	23 05	

Station		HX	XR	XR		HX	XR	XR	GW	HX	XR	XR	HX	XR		GW	GW	HX	XR	GW
		◇1				◇1			◇1	◇1			◇1				◇1			
Oxford	d								22 36								23 00			
Reading 7	d							22 52	23 06							23 19	23 31			23 58
Twyford 3	d							22 58								23 25				00 04
Maidenhead 3	d							23 05								23 32	23 41			00 11
Taplow	d							23 08								23 35				
Burnham	d							23 11								23 38				
Slough 3	a							23 14	23 19							23 42	23 46			00 17
	d							23 15	23 20							23 42	23 49			00 17
Langley	d							23 18								23 46				
Iver	d							23 21								23 49				
West Drayton	d							23 24								23 52				00 23
Heathrow Terminal 5 ⊖ ✈	a																			
	d	22 57				23 12				23 27			23 42					23 52		
Heathrow Terminal 4 ⊖ ✈	a																			
	d		22 52	23 11							23 22	23 41							23 57	
Heathrow Termls 2 & 3 2 ⊖ ✈	a	23 01	22 56	23 15		23 16				23 31	23 26	23 45	23 46					23 56	00 01	
	d	23 03	22 58			23 17				23 33	23 28		23 47						00 03	
Hayes & Harlington	d		23 04				23 18	23 28			23 34			23 48		23 56			00 09	00 27
Southall	d		23 08				23 23	23 32			23 38			23 53		00 01			00 13	00 31
Hanwell	d		23 11								23 41									
Greenford ⊖	d																			
South Greenford	d																			
Castle Bar Park	d																			
Drayton Green	d																			
West Ealing	d		23 13				23 27				23 43									
Ealing Broadway ⊖	d		23 16				23 30	23 38			23 46			23 58		00 06			00 18	00 36
Acton Main Line	d						23 33													
London Paddington 15 ⊖	a	23 19	23 25			23 33	23 43	23 47	23 36	23 49	23 55		00 03	00 10		00 15	00 18		00 30	00 44

A not 4 January

For non-stop services between Reading and London refer to Table T116

For non-stop services between London and Heathrow Airport see Table T118

Table T117-R

Sundays

15 December to 10 May

Reading, Heathrow Airport and Greenford - London

Stopping Services

Station		GW	XR	XR	GW	GW	HX		HX		XR	XR	HX	HX	XR	GW	XR	HX	HX		XR	XR	XR	HX
							◇1		◇1				◇1	◇1				◇1	◇1					◇1
		A	A		A	A																		
Oxford	d																							
Reading 7	d					00 17										06 25						06 49		
Twyford 3	d				00 04	00 23										06 31						06 55		
Maidenhead 3	d				00 11	00 30										06 38						07 02		
Taplow	d					00 33																		
Burnham	d					00 37										06 42								
Slough 3	a				00 17	00 40										06 46						07 12		
	d				00 17	00 41										06 46						07 12		
Langley	d					00 45										06 50						07 16		
Iver	d					00 48																07 19		
West Drayton	d				00 23	00 51		and								06 55						07 22		
Heathrow Terminal 5 ⊖ ✈	a							every 15																
	d						05 12	minutes	06 12				06 27	06 42				06 57	07 12					07 27
Heathrow Terminal 4 ⊖ ✈	a							until																
	d			00 07							06 01	06 16			06 31		06 46				07 01		07 16	
Heathrow Termls 2 & 3 2 ⊖ ✈	a			00 11			05 16		06 16		06 05	06 20	06 31	06 46	06 35		06 50	07 01	07 16		07 05		07 20	07 31
	d		00 03	00 13			05 17		06 17		06 07		06 32	06 47	06 37			07 02	07 17		07 07			07 32
Hayes & Harlington	d		00 09	00 22	00 27	00 55					06 14				06 44	06 59					07 14	07 26		
Southall	d	00 01	00 13	00 26	00 31	00 59					06 18				06 48	07 03					07 18	07 30		
Hanwell	d																							
Greenford ⊖	d																							
South Greenford	d																							
Castle Bar Park	d																							
Drayton Green	d																							
West Ealing	d																							
Ealing Broadway ⊖	d	00 06	00 18	00 31	00 36	01 04					06 23				06 53	07 08					07 23	07 37		
Acton Main Line	d																							
London Paddington 15 ⊖	a	00 15	00 30	00 41	00 44	01 12	05 33		06 33		06 34		06 48	07 03	07 07	07 16		07 19	07 33		07 34	07 48		07 48

Station		GW	HX	XR	XR	HX		XR	XR	HX	XR	HX	XR	GW	XR	GW		XR	HX	XR	HX	XR	GW	XR	HX
			◇1			◇1				◇1		◇1				◇1			◇1		◇1		◇1		◇1
Oxford	d															07 58							08 24		
Reading 7	d	07 10											07 55	08 10	08 25	08 31							08 51		
Twyford 3	d	07 16											08 01	08 16	08 31										
Maidenhead 3	d	07 23						07 38					08 08	08 23	08 38										
Taplow	d												08 11		08 41										
Burnham	d												08 14		08 44							←			
Slough 3	a	07 29						07 48					08 18	08 29	08 48	08 42						08 48	09 03		
	d	07 31						07 48					08 18	08 31	08 48	08 43						08 48	09 04		
Langley	d							07 52					08 22		→							08 52			
Iver	d							07 55					08 25									08 55			
West Drayton	d							07 58					08 28									08 58			
Heathrow Terminal 5 ⊖ ✈	a																								
	d		07 42			07 57				08 12		08 27							08 42		08 57				09 12
Heathrow Terminal 4 ⊖ ✈	a																								
	d			07 31	07 46				08 01		08 16							08 31		08 46				09 01	
Heathrow Termls 2 & 3 2 ⊖ ✈	a		07 46	07 35	07 50	08 01			08 05	08 16	08 20	08 31						08 35	08 46	08 50	09 01			09 05	09 16
	d		07 47	07 37		08 02			08 07	08 17		08 32						08 37	08 47		09 02			09 07	09 17
Hayes & Harlington	d	07 39		07 44				08 02	08 14				08 32	08 39				08 44				09 02		09 15	
Southall	d	07 43		07 48				08 06	08 18				08 36	08 42				08 48				09 06		09 19	
Hanwell	d																								
Greenford ⊖	d																								
South Greenford	d																								
Castle Bar Park	d																								
Drayton Green	d																								
West Ealing	d																								
Ealing Broadway ⊖	d	07 48		07 53				08 13	08 23				08 43	08 47				08 53				09 13		09 24	
Acton Main Line	d																								
London Paddington 15 ⊖	a	07 56	08 04	08 05		08 18		08 23	08 34	08 34		08 48	08 53	08 55		08 59		09 04	09 08		09 19	09 23	09 21	09 34	09 36

A not 15 December

For non-stop services between Reading and London refer to Table T116

For non-stop services between London and Heathrow Airport see Table T118

Table T117-R

Sundays
15 December to 10 May

Reading, Heathrow Airport and Greenford - London

Stopping Services

		XR	HX	XR	GW	GW	XR	HX		XR	HX	XR	XR	XR	GW	XR	HX	XR		HX	XR	XR	GW	XR	GW
			◇1			◇		◇1			◇1				◇1 🛒		◇1			◇1					◇1 🍽
Oxford	d														09 35										09 55
Reading 7	d			08 55	09 10	09 19							09 25	09 55	10 01								10 06	10 23	10 26
Twyford 3	d			09 01	09 18								09 31	10 01									10 16	10 29	
Maidenhead 3	d			09 08	09 25	09 28							09 38	10 08									10 23	10 38	
Taplow	d			09 11									09 41	10 11										10 41	
Burnham	d			09 14									09 44	10 14								←		10 44	
Slough 3	a			09 18	09 31	09 33							09 48	10 18	10 13							10 18	10 29	10 48	10 42
	d			09 18	09 31	09 34							09 48	10 18	10 15							10 18	10 31	10 48	10 43
Langley	d			09 22									09 52	→								10 22		→	
Iver	d			09 25									09 55									10 25			
West Drayton	d			09 28									09 58									10 28			
Heathrow Terminal 5 ⊖ ✈	a																								
	d		09 27					09 42			09 57						10 12			10 27					
Heathrow Terminal 4 ⊖ ✈	a																								
	d	09 16					09 31			09 46						10 01		10 16							
Heathrow Termls 2 & 3 2 ⊖ ✈ a		09 20	09 31				09 35	09 46		09 50	10 01					10 05	10 16	10 20		10 31					
	d		09 32				09 37	09 47			10 02					10 07	10 17			10 32					
Hayes & Harlington	d			09 32	09 39		09 45					09 57	10 02			10 15					10 27	10 32	10 38		
Southall	d			09 36	09 42		09 49					10 02	10 06			10 19					10 32	10 36	10 41		
Hanwell	d																								
Greenford ⊖	d																								
South Greenford	d																								
Castle Bar Park	d																								
Drayton Green	d																								
West Ealing	d											10 07									10 37				
Ealing Broadway ⊖	d			09 43	09 47		09 54					10 10	10 13			10 24					10 40	10 43	10 46		
Acton Main Line	d											10 13									10 43				
London Paddington 15 ⊖	a		09 48	09 53	09 55	09 51	10 03	10 03			10 18	10 22	10 23		10 29	10 33	10 34			10 50	10 52	10 53	10 55		11 00

		XR	HX	GW		XC	GW	XR	HX	GW	XR	XR	XR	GW		XR	HX	XR	HX	XR	XR	GW	GW	XR	
			◇1	◇1 🛒		◇1 🛒	◇1 🛒		◇1	◇1 🛒				◇1 🛒			◇1		◇1				◇1 🍽		
Oxford	d					10 16								10 31									10 55		
Reading 7	d			10 35		10a39	10 40			10 53			10 55	11 00								11 06	11 25		
Twyford 3	d												11 01									11 16			
Maidenhead 3	d												11 08									11 23			
Taplow	d												11 11												
Burnham	d											←	11 14								←				
Slough 3	a											10 48	11 18	11 12							11 18	11 29	11 38		
	d											10 48	11 18	11 14							11 18	11 31	11 39		
Langley	d											10 52	→								11 22				
Iver	d											10 55									11 25				
West Drayton	d											10 58									11 28				
Heathrow Terminal 5 ⊖ ✈	a																								
	d		10 42						10 57								11 12		11 27						
Heathrow Terminal 4 ⊖ ✈	a																								
	d	10 31						10 46								11 01		11 16						11 31	
Heathrow Termls 2 & 3 2 ⊖ ✈ a		10 35	10 46					10 50	11 01							11 05	11 16	11 20	11 31					11 35	
	d	10 37	10 47						11 02							11 07	11 17		11 32					11 37	
Hayes & Harlington	d	10 45									10 57	11 02				11 15				11 27	11 32	11 39		11 45	
Southall	d	10 49									11 02	11 06				11 19				11 32	11 36	11 42		11 49	
Hanwell	d																								
Greenford ⊖	d																								
South Greenford	d																								
Castle Bar Park	d																								
Drayton Green	d																								
West Ealing	d										11 07									11 37					
Ealing Broadway ⊖	d	10 54									11 10	11 13				11 24				11 40	11 43	11 47		11 54	
Acton Main Line	d										11 13									11 43					
London Paddington 15 ⊖	a	11 03	11 03	11 05			11 08		11 18	11 20	11 22	11 23		11 29		11 33	11 33		11 50	11 52	11 53	11 55	11 54	12 03	

For non-stop services between Reading and London refer to Table T116

For non-stop services between London and Heathrow Airport see Table T118

NRT DECEMBER 19 EDITION

Table T117-R

Sundays
15 December to 10 May

Reading, Heathrow Airport and Greenford - London

Stopping Services

		XR	XR	GW	XC	XR		HX	XR	HX	GW	XR	HX	XR	HX	XR		XR	GW	GW	GW	XR	XR	XR	GW
				◇1 🛒	◇1 🛒			◇1		◇1	◇1 🛒		◇1		◇1					◇	◇1 🍽				◇1 🛒
Oxford	d				11 16						11 31										11 55				
Reading 7	d		11 25	11 28	11a39	11 53					12 00								12 06	12 23	12 25			12 25	12 33
Twyford 3	d		11 31			11 59													12 16					12 31	
Maidenhead 3	d		11 38			12 08													12 23	12 30				12 38	
Taplow	d		11 41			12 11																		12 41	
Burnham	d		11 44			12 14												←						12 44	
Slough 3	a		11 48			12 18					12 13							12 18	12 29		12 38			12 48	
	d		11 48			12 18					12 14							12 18	12 31		12 39			12 48	
Langley	d		11 52			→												12 22						12 52	
Iver	d		11 55															12 25						12 55	
West Drayton	d		11 58															12 28						12 58	
Heathrow Terminal 5 ⊖ ✈	a																								
	d							11 42		11 57			12 12		12 27										
Heathrow Terminal 4 ⊖ ✈	a																								
	d								11 46			12 01		12 16								12 31			
Heathrow Termls 2 & 3 2 ⊖ ✈ a								11 46	11 50	12 01		12 05	12 16	12 20	12 31							12 35			
	d							11 47		12 02		12 07	12 17		12 32							12 37			
Hayes & Harlington	d	11 57	12 02									12 15				12 27		12 32	12 39			12 45	12 57	13 02	
Southall	d	12 02	12 06									12 19				12 32		12 36	12 42			12 49	13 02	13 06	
Hanwell	d																								
Greenford ⊖	d																								
South Greenford	d																								
Castle Bar Park	d																								
Drayton Green	d																								
West Ealing	d	12 07														12 37							13 07		
Ealing Broadway ⊖	d	12 10	12 13									12 24				12 40		12 43	12 47			12 54	13 10	13 13	
Acton Main Line	d	12 13														12 43							13 13		
London Paddington 15 ⊖	a	12 22	12 23	11 56				12 04		12 18	12 29	12 33	12 33		12 50	12 52		12 53	12 55	12 53	12 54	13 03	13 22	13 23	12 59

		XC		HX	XR	GW	HX	XR	GW	XR	HX	XR		HX	XR	XR	GW	GW	XR	XR	XR	GW		XC	XR
		◇1 🛒		◇1		◇	◇1		◇1 🛒		◇1			◇1				◇1				◇1 🛒		◇1 🛒	
Oxford	d	12 16							12 31									12 55						13 16	
Reading 7	d	12a39				12 48		12 55	13 00								13 06	13 25			13 25	13 34		13a39	13 55
Twyford 3	d							13 01									13 16				13 31				14 01
Maidenhead 3	d							13 08									13 23				13 38				14 08
Taplow	d							13 11													13 41				14 11
Burnham	d							13 14								←					13 44				14 14
Slough 3	a							13 18	13 13							13 18	13 29	13 38			13 48				14 18
	d							13 18	13 14							13 18	13 31	13 39			13 48				14 18
Langley	d							→								13 22					13 52				→
Iver	d															13 25					13 55				
West Drayton	d															13 28					13 58				
Heathrow Terminal 5 ⊖ ✈	a																								
	d			12 42			12 57				13 12			13 27											
Heathrow Terminal 4 ⊖ ✈	a																								
	d				12 46					13 01		13 16							13 31						
Heathrow Termls 2 & 3 2 ⊖ ✈ a				12 46	12 50		13 01			13 05	13 16	13 20		13 31					13 35						
	d			12 47			13 02			13 07	13 17			13 32					13 37						
Hayes & Harlington	d									13 15					13 27	13 32	13 39		13 45	13 57	14 02				
Southall	d									13 19					13 32	13 36	13 42		13 49	14 02	14 06				
Hanwell	d																								
Greenford ⊖	d																								
South Greenford	d																								
Castle Bar Park	d																								
Drayton Green	d																								
West Ealing	d														13 37					14 07					
Ealing Broadway ⊖	d									13 24					13 40	13 43	13 47		13 54	14 10	14 13				
Acton Main Line	d														13 43					14 13					
London Paddington 15 ⊖	a			13 04		13 13	13 18		13 29	13 33	13 34			13 48	13 52	13 53	13 55	13 57	14 03	14 22	14 23	13 59			

For non-stop services between Reading and London refer to Table T116

For non-stop services between London and Heathrow Airport see Table T118

Table T117-R

Sundays

15 December to 10 May

Reading, Heathrow Airport and Greenford - London

Stopping Services

Station		HX	XR	HX	GW	XR	HX	XR	HX	XR	XR	GW	XC	GW	GW	XR	XR	XR	GW	XC	HX	GW
Oxford	d				13 31								13 46		13 55					14 16		
Reading	d				14 00							14 06	14a09	14 23	14 25			14 25	14 34	14a39		14 44
Twyford	d											14 16						14 31				
Maidenhead	d											14 22		14 32				14 38				
Taplow	d																	14 41				
Burnham	d										←							14 44				
Slough	a				14 14						14 18	14 28			14 38			14 48				
	d				14 15						14 18	14 31			14 39			14 48				
Langley	d										14 22							14 52				
Iver	d										14 25							14 55				
West Drayton	d										14 28							14 58				
Heathrow Terminal 5 ⊖ ✈	a																					
	d	13 42		13 57			14 12		14 27												14 42	
Heathrow Terminal 4 ⊖ ✈	a																					
	d		13 46			14 01		14 16								14 31						
Heathrow Termls 2 & 3 ⊖ ✈	a	13 46	13 50	14 01		14 05	14 16	14 20	14 31							14 35					14 46	
	d	13 47		14 02		14 07	14 17		14 32							14 37					14 47	
Hayes & Harlington	d					14 15				14 27	14 32	14 39				14 45	14 57	15 02				
Southall	d					14 19				14 32	14 36	14 42				14 49	15 02	15 06				
Hanwell	d																					
Greenford ⊖	d																					
South Greenford	d																					
Castle Bar Park	d																					
Drayton Green	d																					
West Ealing	d									14 37							15 07					
Ealing Broadway ⊖	d					14 24				14 40	14 43	14 47				14 54	15 10	15 13				
Acton Main Line	d									14 43							15 13					
London Paddington ⊖	a	14 04		14 18	14 29	14 33	14 34		14 48	14 52	14 53	14 55		14 51	14 57	15 03	15 22	15 23	14 59		15 04	15 09

Station		XR	HX	XR	GW	XC	XR	HX	XR	HX	XR	XR	GW	GW	XR	XR	XR	GW	XC	HX	GW	XR	HX
Oxford	d				14 31	14 37								14 55					15 16				
Reading	d			14 55	15 00	15a00							15 06	15 25			15 25	15 34	15a39		15 40		
Twyford	d			15 01									15 16				15 31						
Maidenhead	d			15 08									15 23				15 38						
Taplow	d			15 11													15 41						
Burnham	d			15 14								←					15 44						
Slough	a			15 18	15 13							15 18	15 29	15 39			15 48						
	d			15 18	15 14							15 18	15 31	15 40			15 48						
Langley	d			→								15 22					15 52						
Iver	d											15 25					15 55						
West Drayton	d											15 28					15 58						
Heathrow Terminal 5 ⊖ ✈	a																						
	d		14 57					15 12		15 27										15 42			15 57
Heathrow Terminal 4 ⊖ ✈	a																						
	d	14 47					15 01		15 16						15 31							15 46	
Heathrow Termls 2 & 3 ⊖ ✈	a	14 51	15 01				15 05	15 16	15 20	15 31					15 35					15 46		15 50	16 01
	d		15 02				15 07	15 17		15 32					15 37					15 47			16 02
Hayes & Harlington	d						15 15				15 27	15 32	15 39		15 45	15 57	16 02						
Southall	d						15 19				15 32	15 36	15 42		15 49	16 02	16 06						
Hanwell	d																						
Greenford ⊖	d																						
South Greenford	d																						
Castle Bar Park	d																						
Drayton Green	d																						
West Ealing	d										15 37					16 07							
Ealing Broadway ⊖	d						15 24				15 40	15 43	15 47		15 54	16 10	16 13						
Acton Main Line	d										15 43					16 13							
London Paddington ⊖	a		15 19		15 32		15 33	15 34		15 48	15 52	15 53	15 55	15 54	16 03	16 22	16 23	15 59		16 04	16 06		16 18

For non-stop services between Reading and London refer to Table T116

For non-stop services between London and Heathrow Airport see Table T118

Table T117-R

Sundays

15 December to 10 May

Reading, Heathrow Airport and Greenford - London

Stopping Services

Station		XR	HX	XR	XR	GW	XR	XR	GW	XC	GW	HX	GW	XR	XR	XR	GW	XC	HX	XR	HX	GW
Oxford	d					15 31				15 46			15 55					16 16				
Reading	d				15 55	16 00			16 06	16a09	16 13		16 25			16 25	16 34	16a39				16 51
Twyford	d				16 01				16 16							16 31						
Maidenhead	d				16 08				16 23		16 23					16 38						
Taplow	d				16 11											16 41						
Burnham	d				16 14			←								16 44						
Slough	a				16 18	16 13		16 18	16 29				16 38			16 48						
	d				16 18	16 14		16 18	16 31				16 39			16 48						
Langley	d				→			16 22								16 52						
Iver	d							16 25								16 55						
West Drayton	d							16 28								16 58						
Heathrow Terminal 5 ⊖ ✈	a																					
	d		16 12									16 27							16 42		16 57	
Heathrow Terminal 4 ⊖ ✈	a																					
	d	16 01		16 16										16 31						16 46		
Heathrow Termls 2 & 3 ⊖ ✈	a	16 05	16 16	16 20								16 31		16 35					16 46	16 50	17 01	
	d	16 07	16 17									16 32		16 37					16 47		17 02	
Hayes & Harlington	d	16 15					16 27	16 32	16 39					16 45	16 57	17 02						
Southall	d	16 19					16 32	16 36	16 42					16 49	17 02	17 06						
Hanwell	d																					
Greenford ⊖	d																					
South Greenford	d																					
Castle Bar Park	d																					
Drayton Green	d																					
West Ealing	d						16 37								17 07							
Ealing Broadway ⊖	d	16 24					16 40	16 43	16 47					16 54	17 10	17 13						
Acton Main Line	d						16 43								17 13							
London Paddington ⊖	a	16 33	16 34			16 36	16 52	16 53	16 55		16 44	16 48	16 54	17 03	17 22	17 23	17 02		17 04		17 18	17 27

Station		XR	GW	XC	XR	HX	XR	HX	XR	XR	GW	GW	XR	XR	XR	GW	XC	HX	GW	XR	HX	XR	GW
Oxford	d		16 31	16 37								16 55					17 16						17 31
Reading	d	16 55	17 00	17a02							17 06	17 25			17 25	17 33	17a39		17 40			17 55	18 00
Twyford	d	17 01									17 16				17 31							18 01	
Maidenhead	d	17 08									17 23				17 38							18 08	
Taplow	d	17 11													17 41							18 11	
Burnham	d	17 14								←					17 44							18 14	
Slough	a	17 18	17 12							17 18	17 29	17 38			17 48							18 18	18 13
	d	17 18	17 13							17 18	17 31	17 39			17 48							18 18	18 14
Langley	d	→								17 22					17 52							→	
Iver	d									17 25					17 55								
West Drayton	d									17 28					17 58								
Heathrow Terminal 5 ⊖ ✈	a																						
	d					17 12		17 27										17 42			17 57		
Heathrow Terminal 4 ⊖ ✈	a																						
	d				17 01		17 16						17 31							17 46			
Heathrow Termls 2 & 3 ⊖ ✈	a				17 05	17 16	17 20	17 31					17 35					17 46		17 50	18 01		
	d				17 07	17 17		17 32					17 37					17 47			18 02		
Hayes & Harlington	d				17 15				17 27	17 32	17 39		17 45	17 57	18 02								
Southall	d				17 19				17 32	17 36	17 42		17 49	18 02	18 06								
Hanwell	d																						
Greenford ⊖	d																						
South Greenford	d																						
Castle Bar Park	d																						
Drayton Green	d																						
West Ealing	d								17 37					18 07									
Ealing Broadway ⊖	d				17 24				17 40	17 43	17 47		17 54	18 10	18 13								
Acton Main Line	d								17 43					18 13									
London Paddington ⊖	a		17 28		17 33	17 33		17 48	17 52	17 53	17 55	17 55	18 03	18 22	18 23	17 59		18 04	18 06		18 18		18 29

For non-stop services between Reading and London refer to Table T116

For non-stop services between London and Heathrow Airport see Table T118

Table T117-R

Sundays

15 December to 10 May

Reading, Heathrow Airport and Greenford - London

Stopping Services

		XR	HX	XR	HX	XR	XR	GW	XC	GW		XR	XR	XR	GW	XC	HX	XR	GW	HX		XR	GW	XC	XR
			◇1		◇1				◇1 🍴	◇1					◇1 🍴	◇1 🍴	◇1		◇	◇1			◇1 🍴	◇1 🍴	
Oxford	d								17 46	17 51						18 16							18 31	18 37	
Reading 7	d							18 06	18a09	18 23				18 25	18 31	18a39			18 49			18 55	19 00	19a06	
Twyford 3	d							18 16						18 31								19 01			
Maidenhead 3	d							18 23						18 38								19 08			
Taplow	d													18 41								19 11			
Burnham	d						←							18 44								19 14			
Slough 3	a						18 18	18 29		18 38				18 48								19 18	19 13		
	d						18 18	18 31		18 39				18 48								19 18	19 14		
Langley	d						18 22							18 52								→			
Iver	d						18 25							18 55											
West Drayton	d						18 28							18 58											
Heathrow Terminal 5 ⊖ ✈	a																								
	d		18 12		18 27												18 42			18 57					
Heathrow Terminal 4 ⊖ ✈	a																								
	d	18 01		18 16								18 31						18 46							19 01
Heathrow Termls 2 & 3 2 ⊖ ✈	a	18 05	18 16	18 20	18 31							18 35					18 46	18 50		19 01					19 05
	d	18 07	18 17		18 32							18 37					18 47			19 02					19 07
Hayes & Harlington	d	18 15				18 27	18 32	18 39				18 45	18 57	19 02											19 15
Southall	d	18 19				18 32	18 36	18 42				18 49	19 02	19 06											19 19
Hanwell	d																								
Greenford ⊖	d																								
South Greenford	d																								
Castle Bar Park	d																								
Drayton Green	d																								
West Ealing	d					18 37							19 07												
Ealing Broadway ⊖	d	18 24				18 40	18 43	18 47				18 54	19 10	19 13											19 24
Acton Main Line	d					18 43							19 13												
London Paddington 15 ⊖	a	18 33	18 34		18 48	18 52	18 53	18 55		18 56		19 03	19 22	19 23	18 59		19 03		19 15	19 18			19 29		19 33

		HX	XR	HX	XR	XR		GW	GW	XR	XR	XR	GW	XC	HX	GW		XR	HX	XR	GW	XC	XR	HX	XR
		◇1		◇1					◇1				◇1 🍴	◇1 🍴	◇1	◇1 🍴			◇1		◇1 🍴	◇1 🍴		◇1	
Oxford	d								18 55					19 16							19 31	19 46			
Reading 7	d							19 10	19 25			19 25	19 31	19a39		19 40				19 55	20 00	20a09			
Twyford 3	d							19 16				19 31								20 01					
Maidenhead 3	d							19 23				19 38								20 08					
Taplow	d											19 41								20 11					
Burnham	d					←						19 44								20 14					
Slough 3	a					19 18		19 29	19 38			19 48								20 18	20 13				
	d					19 18		19 31	19 39			19 48								20 18	20 14				
Langley	d					19 22						19 52								→					
Iver	d					19 25						19 55													
West Drayton	d					19 28						19 58													
Heathrow Terminal 5 ⊖ ✈	a																								
	d	19 12		19 27											19 42				19 57					20 12	
Heathrow Terminal 4 ⊖ ✈	a																								
	d		19 16							19 31								19 46					20 01		20 16
Heathrow Termls 2 & 3 2 ⊖ ✈	a	19 16	19 20	19 31						19 35					19 46			19 50	20 01				20 05	20 16	20 20
	d	19 17		19 32						19 37					19 47				20 02				20 07	20 17	
Hayes & Harlington	d				19 27	19 32		19 39		19 45	19 57	20 02											20 15		
Southall	d				19 32	19 36		19 42		19 49	20 02	20 06											20 19		
Hanwell	d																								
Greenford ⊖	d																								
South Greenford	d																								
Castle Bar Park	d																								
Drayton Green	d																								
West Ealing	d				19 37						20 07														
Ealing Broadway ⊖	d				19 40	19 43		19 47		19 54	20 10	20 13											20 24		
Acton Main Line	d				19 43						20 13														
London Paddington 15 ⊖	a	19 34		19 48	19 52	19 53		19 55	19 54	20 03	20 22	20 23	19 56		20 03	20 07			20 18		20 29		20 33	20 33	

For non-stop services between Reading and London refer to Table T116

For non-stop services between London and Heathrow Airport see Table T118

NRT DECEMBER 19 EDITION

Table T117-R

Sundays

15 December to 10 May

Reading, Heathrow Airport and Greenford - London

Stopping Services

		HX	XR	XR	GW	GW	XR	XR		XR	GW	XC	XR	HX	XR	HX	GW	HX		XR	XR	HX	XR	GW	XC
		◇1				◇1					◇1 🍴	◇1 🍴		◇1		◇1	◇1 🍴	◇1				◇1			◇1 🍴
Oxford	d					19 55						20 16					20 32								20 47
Reading 7	d				20 10	20 25				20 25	20 31	20a39	20 55				21 00							21 10	21a11
Twyford 3	d				20 16					20 31			21 01											21 16	
Maidenhead 3	d				20 23					20 38			21 08											21 23	
Taplow	d									20 41			21 11												
Burnham	d			←						20 45			21 14										←		
Slough 3	a			20 18	20 28	20 38				20 48			21 18				21 13						21 18	21 29	
	d			20 18	20 31	20 39				20 49			21 18				21 14						21 18	21 31	
Langley	d			20 22						20 53			→										21 22		
Iver	d			20 25						20 55													21 25		
West Drayton	d			20 28						20 59													21 28		
Heathrow Terminal 5 ⊖ ✈	a																								
	d	20 27												20 42		20 57		21 12				21 27			
Heathrow Terminal 4 ⊖ ✈	a																								
	d						20 31								20 46					21 01	21 16				
Heathrow Termls 2 & 3 2 ⊖ ✈	a	20 31					20 35							20 46	20 50	21 01		21 16		21 05	21 20	21 31			
	d	20 32					20 37							20 47		21 02		21 17		21 07		21 32			
Hayes & Harlington	d		20 27	20 32	20 39		20 45	20 57		21 03										21 15			21 32	21 39	
Southall	d		20 32	20 36	20 42		20 49	21 02		21 07										21 19			21 36	21 42	
Hanwell	d																								
Greenford ⊖	d																								
South Greenford	d																								
Castle Bar Park	d																								
Drayton Green	d																								
West Ealing	d		20 37					21 07																	
Ealing Broadway ⊖	d		20 40	20 43	20 47		20 54	21 10		21 13										21 24			21 43	21 47	
Acton Main Line	d		20 43					21 13																	
London Paddington 15 ⊖	a	20 48	20 52	20 53	20 55	20 53	21 03	21 22		21 23	20 59			21 03		21 18	21 29	21 34		21 35		21 48	21 53	21 55	

		XR	XR	GW		XC	XR	HX	XR	HX	GW	XC	XR	HX		XR	HX	XR	GW	XR	XR	GW	XC	HX	
				◇1 🍴		◇1 🍴		◇1		◇1	◇1 🍴	◇1		◇1			◇1					◇1 🍴	◇1	◇1	
Oxford	d					21 16					21 31	21 39											22 16		
Reading 7	d		21 25	21 33		21a39	21 55				22 00	22a02							22 10		22 27	22 31	22a39		
Twyford 3	d		21 31				22 01												22 16		22 33				
Maidenhead 3	d		21 38				22 08												22 23		22 40				
Taplow	d		21 41				22 11														22 43				
Burnham	d		21 44				22 14											←			22 46				
Slough 3	a		21 48				22 18				22 12							22 18	22 29		22 50				
	d		21 48				22 18				22 13							22 18	22 31		22 50				
Langley	d		21 52				→											22 22			22 54				
Iver	d		21 55															22 25			22 57				
West Drayton	d		21 58															22 28			23 00				
Heathrow Terminal 5 ⊖ ✈	a																								
	d							21 42		21 57				22 12			22 27							22 42	
Heathrow Terminal 4 ⊖ ✈	a																								
	d	21 31							21 46				22 01			22 16				22 31					
Heathrow Termls 2 & 3 2 ⊖ ✈	a	21 35						21 46	21 50	22 01			22 05	22 16		22 20	22 31			22 35				22 46	
	d	21 37						21 47		22 02			22 07	22 17			22 32			22 37				22 47	
Hayes & Harlington	d	21 44	22 02										22 14					22 32	22 39	22 44	23 04				
Southall	d	21 48	22 06										22 18					22 36	22 42	22 48	23 08				
Hanwell	d																								
Greenford ⊖	d																								
South Greenford	d																								
Castle Bar Park	d																								
Drayton Green	d																								
West Ealing	d																								
Ealing Broadway ⊖	d	21 53	22 13										22 23					22 43	22 47	22 53	23 13				
Acton Main Line	d																								
London Paddington 15 ⊖	a	22 04	22 23	21 59				22 03		22 18	22 29		22 34	22 36			22 49	22 53	22 55	23 07	23 22	23 03		23 11	

For non-stop services between Reading and London refer to Table T116

For non-stop services between London and Heathrow Airport see Table T118

Table T117-R

Sundays
15 December to 10 May

Reading, Heathrow Airport and Greenford - London

Stopping Services

Station		XR	HX ◇1	XR	HX ◇1	GW ◇1	XR	HX ◇1	XR	XR	GW	HX ◇1	XR	HX
Oxford	d					22 23								
Reading 7	d					22 54			22 59		23 10			
Twyford 3	d								23 05		23 16			
Maidenhead 3	d								23 13		23 23			
Taplow	d								23 16					
Burnham	d								23 19		23 27			
Slough 3	a					23 07			23 23		23 31			
	d					23 13			23 25		23 34			
Langley	d								23 29		23 39			
Iver	d								23 32					
West Drayton	d								23 36		23 43			
Heathrow Terminal 5 ⊖ ✈	a													
	d		22 57		23 12			23 27				23 42		23 55
Heathrow Terminal 4 ⊖ ✈	a													
	d	22 46		23 01			23 16			23 31			23 46	
Heathrow Termls 2 & 3 2 ⊖ ✈	a	22 50	23 01	23 05	23 16		23 20	23 31		23 35		23 46	23 50	23 59
	d		23 02	23 07	23 17			23 32		23 37		23 47	23 52	
Hayes & Harlington	d			23 14					23 40	23 44	23 47		23 59	
Southall	d			23 18					23 44	23 48	23 51		00 03	
Hanwell	d													
Greenford ⊖	d													
South Greenford	d													
Castle Bar Park	d													
Drayton Green	d													
West Ealing	d													
Ealing Broadway ⊖	d			23 23					23 50	23 53	23 56		00 08	
Acton Main Line	d													
London Paddington 15 ⊖	a		23 24	23 34	23 37	23 44		23 50	23 58	00 04	00 04	00 07	00 20	

For non-stop services between Reading and London refer to Table T116

For non-stop services between London and Heathrow Airport see Table T118

Table T118-F

Mondays to Fridays
16 December to 15 May

London - Heathrow Airport (Heathrow Express Services)

Miles	Miles	Station		XR	HX	XR	HX ◇1	XR	HX ◇1	XR	HX ◇1	XR	HX ◇1	XR	HX ◇1		XR	HX ◇1	XR	HX ◇1	XR	HX ◇1	XR	HX ◇1
0	—	London Paddington 15 ⊖	d	04 42			05 10	05 02	05 25		05 40	05 32	05 55		06 10	and at the same minutes past each hour until	08 02	08 25		08 40	08 32	08 55		09 10
14¾	0	Heathrow Terminals 2 & 3 2 ⊖ ✈	a	05 06			05 26	05 30	05 40		05 55	06 00	06 10		06 25		08 30	08 40		08 55	09 00	09 10		09 25
—	—		d	05 08	05 13	05 18	05 28	05 33	05 41	05 48	05 58	06 03	06 11	06 18	06 28		08 33	08 41	08 48	08 58	09 03	09 11	09 18	09 28
—	1¾	Heathrow Terminal 4 ⊖ ✈	a	05 16		05 22		05 37		05 52		06 07		06 22			08 37		08 52		09 07		09 22	
16¼	—	Heathrow Terminal 5 ⊖ ✈	a		05 17		05 32		05 46		06 02		06 16		06 32			08 46		09 02		09 16		09 32

Station			XR	HX ◇1	XR	HX ◇1	XR	HX ◇1	XR	HX ◇1	XR		HX ◇1	XR	HX ◇1	XR	HX ◇1	XR	HX ◇1	XR	HX ◇1		XR	HX ◇1	XR
London Paddington 15 ⊖	d		09 02	09 25		09 40	09 32	09 55		10 10	10 02		10 25		10 40	10 32	10 55		11 10	11 02	11 25			11 40	11 32
Heathrow Terminals 2 & 3 2 ⊖ ✈	a		09 30	09 40		09 56	10 00	10 10		10 25	10 30		10 40		10 55	11 00	11 10		11 25	11 30	11 40			11 56	12 00
	d		09 33	09 41	09 48	09 58	10 03	10 11	10 18	10 28	10 33		10 41	10 48	10 58	11 03	11 11	11 18	11 28	11 33	11 41		11 48	11 58	12 03
Heathrow Terminal 4 ⊖ ✈	a		09 37		09 52		10 07		10 22		10 37			10 52		11 07		11 22		11 37			11 52		12 07
Heathrow Terminal 5 ⊖ ✈	a			09 46		10 02		10 16		10 32			10 46		11 02		11 16		11 32		11 46			12 02	

Station		HX ◇1	XR	HX ◇1	XR	HX ◇1	XR		HX ◇1	XR	HX ◇1	XR	HX ◇1	XR	HX ◇1	XR	HX ◇1	XR	HX ◇1	XR	HX ◇1	
London Paddington 15 ⊖	d	11 55		12 10	12 02	12 25			12 40	12 32	12 55		13 10	13 02	13 25		13 40	13 32	13 55		14 10	and at the same minutes past each hour until
Heathrow Terminals 2 & 3 2 ⊖ ✈	a	12 10		12 25	12 30	12 40			12 55	13 00	13 10		13 26	13 30	13 40		13 55	14 00	14 10		14 25	
	d	12 11	12 18	12 28	12 33	12 41	12 48		12 58	13 03	13 11	13 18	13 28	13 33	13 41	13 48	13 58	14 03	14 11	14 18	14 28	
Heathrow Terminal 4 ⊖ ✈	a		12 22		12 37		12 52			13 07		13 22		13 37		13 52		14 07		14 22		
Heathrow Terminal 5 ⊖ ✈	a	12 16		12 32		12 46			13 02		13 16		13 32		13 46		14 02		14 16		14 32	

Station		XR	HX ◇1	XR	HX ◇1	XR	HX ◇1	XR	HX ◇1		XR	HX ◇1	XR
London Paddington 15 ⊖	d	22 02	22 25		22 40	22 32	22 55		23 10		23 02	23 25	
Heathrow Terminals 2 & 3 2 ⊖ ✈	a	22 30	22 40		22 55	23 00	23 10		23 25		23 30	23 40	
	d	22 33	22 41	22 48	22 58	23 03	23 11	23 18	23 28		23 33	23 41	23 48
Heathrow Terminal 4 ⊖ ✈	a	22 37		22 52		23 07		23 22			23 37		23 52
Heathrow Terminal 5 ⊖ ✈	a		22 46		23 02		23 16		23 32			23 46	

Saturdays
21 December to 16 May

Station		XR	HX	XR	HX ◇1	XR	HX ◇1	XR	HX ◇1	XR	HX ◇1	XR	HX ◇1		XR	HX ◇1	XR	HX ◇1	XR	HX ◇1	XR	HX ◇1		XR
London Paddington 15 ⊖	d	04 42			05 10	05 02	05 25		05 40	05 32	05 55		06 10	and at the same minutes past each hour until	22 02	22 25		22 40	22 32	22 55		23 10		23 02
Heathrow Terminals 2 & 3 2 ⊖ ✈	a	05 05			05 25	05 30	05 40		05 55	06 00	06 10		06 25		22 30	22 40		22 55	23 00	23 10		23 25		23 30
	d	05 07	05 13	05 18	05 27	05 33	05 41	05 48	05 58	06 03	06 11	06 18	06 28		22 33	22 41	22 48	22 58	23 03	23 11	23 18	23 28		23 33
Heathrow Terminal 4 ⊖ ✈	a	05 15		05 22		05 37		05 52		06 07		06 22			22 37		22 52		23 07		23 22			23 37
Heathrow Terminal 5 ⊖ ✈	a		05 17		05 31		05 46		06 02		06 16		06 32			22 46		23 02		23 16		23 32		

Station		HX ◇1	XR
London Paddington 15 ⊖	d	23 25	
Heathrow Terminals 2 & 3 2 ⊖ ✈	a	23 40	
	d	23 41	23 48
Heathrow Terminal 4 ⊖ ✈	a		23 52
Heathrow Terminal 5 ⊖ ✈	a	23 46	

Sundays
15 December to 10 May

Station		HX	HX ◇1	XR	HX ◇1	XR	HX ◇1	XR	HX ◇1	XR		HX ◇	XR	HX ◇1	XR	HX ◇1	XR	HX ◇1	XR	HX ◇1		XR	HX ◇1	XR	HX ◇1
London Paddington 15 ⊖	d		05 10	05 11	05 25	05 26	05 40	05 41	05 55			06 10	06 11	06 25		06 40	06 41	06 55		07 10		07 11	07 25		07 40
Heathrow Terminals 2 & 3 2 ⊖ ✈	a		05 26	05 35	05 41	05 50	05 56	06 05	06 11			06 26	06 35	06 41		06 56	07 05	07 11		07 26		07 35	07 41		07 56
	d	05 13	05 28	05 38	05 43	05 53	05 58	06 08	06 13	06 23		06 28	06 38	06 43	06 53	06 58	07 08	07 13	07 23	07 28		07 38	07 43	07 53	07 58
Heathrow Terminal 4 ⊖ ✈	a			05 45		06 00		06 15		06 27			06 45		06 57		07 15		07 27			07 45		07 57	
Heathrow Terminal 5 ⊖ ✈	a	05 17	05 32		05 47		06 02		06 17			06 32		06 47		07 02		07 17		07 32			07 47		08 02

Station		XR	HX ◇1	XR	HX ◇1	XR		HX ◇1	XR	HX ◇1	XR	HX ◇1	XR	HX ◇1	XR	HX ◇1		XR	HX ◇1	XR	HX ◇1	XR	HX ◇1	XR	HX ◇1
London Paddington 15 ⊖	d	07 41	07 55		08 10	08 11		08 22		08 40	08 41	08 55		09 10	09 11	09 25			09 40	09 41	09 55		10 10	10 11	10 25
Heathrow Terminals 2 & 3 2 ⊖ ✈	a	08 05	08 11		08 26	08 35		08 41		08 56	09 05	09 11		09 26	09 35	09 41			09 56	10 05	10 11		10 26	10 35	10 41
	d	08 08	08 13	08 23	08 28	08 38		08 43	08 53	08 58	09 08	09 13	09 23	09 28	09 38	09 43		09 53	09 58	10 08	10 13	10 23	10 28	10 38	10 43
Heathrow Terminal 4 ⊖ ✈	a	08 15		08 27		08 45			08 57		09 15		09 27		09 45			09 57		10 15		10 27		10 45	
Heathrow Terminal 5 ⊖ ✈	a		08 17		08 32			08 47		09 02		09 17		09 32		09 47			10 02		10 17		10 32		10 47

For MTR Crossrail services see Table T117

Table T118-F

Sundays
15 December to 10 May

London - Heathrow Airport (Heathrow Express Services)

	XR	HX	XR	HX	XR	HX	XR		HX	XR	HX	XR	HX	XR	HX	XR	HX		XR	HX	XR	HX	XR	HX
		◇1		◇1		◇1			◇1		◇1		◇1		◇		◇			◇1		◇1		◇1
London Paddington 15 ⊖ d		10 40	10 41	10 55		11 10	11 11		11 25		11 40	11 41	11 55		12 10	12 11	12 25			12 40	12 41	12 55		13 10
Heathrow Terminals 2 & 3 2 ⊖ ✈ a		10 56	11 05	11 11		11 26	11 38		11 41		11 56	12 05	12 11		12 26	12 35	12 41			12 56	13 05	13 11		13 26
d	10 53	10 58	11 08	11 13	11 23	11 28	11 41		11 43	11 53	11 58	12 08	12 13	12 23	12 28	12 38	12 43		12 53	12 58	13 08	13 13	13 23	13 28
Heathrow Terminal 4 ⊖ ✈ a	10 57		11 15		11 27		11 48			11 57		12 15		12 27		12 45			12 57		13 15		13 27	
Heathrow Terminal 5 ⊖ ✈ a		11 02		11 17		11 32			11 47		12 02		12 17		12 32		12 47			13 02		13 17		13 32

	XR	HX	XR		HX	XR	HX	XR	HX	XR	HX	XR	HX	XR	HX	XR	HX	XR	HX	XR				
		◇1			◇1		◇1		◇1		◇1		◇1		◇1		◇1		◇1					
London Paddington 15 ⊖ d	13 11	13 25			13 40	13 41	13 55		14 10	14 11	14 25		14 40	14 41	14 55		15 10	15 11	15 25		and at the same minutes past each hour until			
Heathrow Terminals 2 & 3 2 ⊖ ✈ a	13 35	13 41			13 56	14 05	14 11		14 26	14 35	14 41		14 56	15 05	15 11		15 26	15 35	15 41					
d	13 38	13 43	13 53		13 58	14 08	14 13	14 23	14 28	14 38	14 43	14 54	14 58	15 08	15 13	15 23	15 28	15 38	15 43	15 53				
Heathrow Terminal 4 ⊖ ✈ a	13 45		13 57			14 15		14 27		14 45		14 58		15 15		15 27		15 45		15 57				
Heathrow Terminal 5 ⊖ ✈ a		13 47			14 02		14 17		14 32		14 47		15 02		15 17		15 32		15 47					

	HX	XR	HX	XR	HX	XR	HX	XR		HX	XR	HX	XR	HX	XR	HX
	◇		◇		◇		◇			◇		◇		◇		◇
London Paddington 15 ⊖ d	21 40	21 41	21 55		22 10	22 11	22 25			22 40	22 41	22 55		23 10	23 11	23 25
Heathrow Terminals 2 & 3 2 ⊖ ✈ a	21 56	22 05	22 11		22 26	22 35	22 41			22 56	23 05	23 11		23 26	23 35	23 41
d	21 58	22 08	22 13	22 23	22 28	22 38	22 43	22 53		22 58	23 08	23 13	23 23	23 28	23 38	23 43
Heathrow Terminal 4 ⊖ ✈ a		22 15		22 27		22 45		22 57			23 15		23 27		23 45	
Heathrow Terminal 5 ⊖ ✈ a	22 02		22 17		22 32		22 47			23 02		23 17		23 32		23 47

For MTR Crossrail services see Table T117

AVAILABLE FROM MP Middleton Press

NRT DECEMBER 19 EDITION

Table T118-R

Mondays to Fridays
16 December to 15 May

Heathrow Airport (Heathrow Express Services) - London

Miles	Miles		XR MX	XR MO	XR MX	HX	XR	HX	XR		HX	XR	HX	XR	HX	XR	HX	XR	HX		XR	HX	XR	HX
						◇1		◇1			◇1		◇1		◇1		◇1		◇1			◇1		◇1
0	—	Heathrow Terminal 5 ⊖ ✈ d				05 12		05 27			05 42		05 57		06 12		06 27		06 42			06 57		07 12
—	0	Heathrow Terminal 4 ⊖ ✈ d		00 01	00 07		05 22		05 41			05 52		06 11		06 22		06 41			06 52		07 11	
1½	1¾	Heathrow Terminals 2 & 3 2 ⊖ ✈ a		00 05	00 11	05 16	05 26	05 31	05 45		05 46	05 56	06 01	06 15	06 16	06 26	06 31	06 45	06 46		06 56	07 01	07 15	07 16
—	—	d	00 03	00 07	00 13	05 17	05 28	05 32			05 47	05 58	06 02		06 17	06 28	06 32		06 47		06 58	07 02		07 17
16¼	—	London Paddington 15 ⊖ a	00 31	00 34	00 40	05 34	05 55	05 50			06 02	06 25	06 17		06 32	06 55	06 47		07 02		07 26	07 17		07 32

	XR	HX	XR	HX	XR		HX	XR	HX	XR	HX	XR	HX	XR	HX		XR	HX	XR	HX	XR	HX	XR	HX
		◇1		◇1			◇1		◇1		◇1		◇1		◇1			◇1		◇1		◇1		◇1
Heathrow Terminal 5 ⊖ ✈ d		07 27		07 42			07 57		08 12		08 27		08 42		08 57			09 12		09 27		09 42		09 57
Heathrow Terminal 4 ⊖ ✈ d	07 22		07 41		07 52			08 11		08 22		08 41		08 52			09 11		09 22		09 41		09 52	
Heathrow Terminals 2 & 3 2 ⊖ ✈ a	07 26	07 31	07 45	07 46	07 56		08 01	08 15	08 16	08 26	08 31	08 45	08 46	08 56	09 01		09 15	09 16	09 26	09 31	09 45	09 46	09 56	10 01
d	07 28	07 32		07 47	07 58		08 02		08 17	08 28	08 32		08 47	08 58	09 02			09 17	09 28	09 32		09 47	09 58	10 02
London Paddington 15 ⊖ a	07 56	07 47		08 03	08 26		08 18		08 33	08 56	08 47		09 03	09 25	09 17			09 32	09 56	09 47		10 02	10 25	10 17

	XR		HX	XR	HX	XR	HX	XR	HX	XR	HX		XR	HX	XR	HX	XR	HX	XR	HX	XR		HX	XR
			◇1		◇1		◇1		◇1		◇1			◇1		◇1		◇1		◇1			◇1	
Heathrow Terminal 5 ⊖ ✈ d			10 12		10 27		10 42		10 57		11 12			11 27		11 42		11 57		12 12			12 27	
Heathrow Terminal 4 ⊖ ✈ d	10 11			10 22		10 41		10 52		11 11			11 22		11 41		11 52		12 11		12 22			12 41
Heathrow Terminals 2 & 3 2 ⊖ ✈ a	10 15		10 16	10 26	10 31	10 45	10 46	10 56	11 01	11 15	11 16		11 26	11 31	11 45	11 46	11 56	12 01	12 15	12 16	12 26		12 31	12 45
d			10 17	10 28	10 32		10 47	10 58	11 02		11 17		11 28	11 32		11 47	11 58	12 02		12 17	12 28		12 32	
London Paddington 15 ⊖ a			10 32	10 55	10 47		11 02	11 25	11 17		11 32		11 55	11 47		12 02	12 25	12 17		12 32	12 55		12 47	

	HX	XR	HX	XR	HX	XR	HX		XR	HX	XR	HX	XR	HX	XR	HX	XR		HX	XR	HX	XR	HX	XR
	◇1		◇1		◇1		◇1			◇1		◇1		◇1		◇1			◇1		◇1		◇1	
Heathrow Terminal 5 ⊖ ✈ d	12 42		12 57		13 12		13 27			13 42		13 57		14 12		14 27			14 42		14 57		15 12	
Heathrow Terminal 4 ⊖ ✈ d		12 52		13 11		13 22			13 41		13 52		14 11		14 22		14 41			14 52		15 11		15 22
Heathrow Terminals 2 & 3 2 ⊖ ✈ a	12 46	12 56	13 01	13 15	13 16	13 26	13 31		13 45	13 46	13 56	14 01	14 15	14 16	14 26	14 31	14 45		14 46	14 56	15 01	15 15	15 16	15 26
d	12 47	12 58	13 02		13 17	13 28	13 32			13 47	13 58	14 02		14 17	14 28	14 32			14 47	14 58	15 02		15 17	15 28
London Paddington 15 ⊖ a	13 02	13 26	13 17		13 32	13 55	13 47			14 03	14 25	14 17		14 32	14 56	14 47			15 03	15 25	15 17		15 32	15 55

	HX	XR	HX		XR	HX	XR	HX	XR	HX	XR	HX	XR		HX	XR	HX	XR	HX	XR	HX	XR	HX	
	◇1		◇1			◇1		◇1		◇1		◇1			◇1		◇1		◇1		◇1		◇1	
Heathrow Terminal 5 ⊖ ✈ d	15 27		15 42			15 57		16 12		16 27		16 42			16 57		17 12		17 27		17 42		17 57	
Heathrow Terminal 4 ⊖ ✈ d		15 41			15 52		16 11		16 22		16 41		16 52			17 11		17 22		17 41		17 52		
Heathrow Terminals 2 & 3 2 ⊖ ✈ a	15 31	15 45	15 46		15 56	16 01	16 15	16 16	16 26	16 31	16 45	16 46	16 56		17 01	17 15	17 16	17 26	17 31	17 45	17 46	17 56	18 01	
d	15 32		15 47		15 58	16 02		16 17	16 28	16 32		16 47	16 58		17 02		17 17	17 28	17 32		17 47	17 58	18 02	
London Paddington 15 ⊖ a	15 47		16 02		16 25	16 17		16 32	16 56	16 48		17 02	17 26		17 17		17 32	17 56	17 48		18 02	18 26	18 17	

	XR	HX	XR	HX	XR	HX	XR	HX	XR		HX	XR	HX	XR	HX	XR	HX	XR	HX		XR	HX	XR	HX
		◇1		◇1		◇1		◇1			◇1		◇1		◇1		◇1		◇1			◇1		◇1
Heathrow Terminal 5 ⊖ ✈ d		18 12		18 27		18 42		18 57			19 12		19 27		19 42		19 57		20 12			20 27		20 42
Heathrow Terminal 4 ⊖ ✈ d	18 11		18 22		18 41		18 52		19 11			19 22		19 41		19 52		20 11			20 22		20 41	
Heathrow Terminals 2 & 3 2 ⊖ ✈ a	18 15	18 16	18 26	18 31	18 45	18 46	18 56	19 01	19 15		19 16	19 26	19 31	19 45	19 46	19 56	20 01	20 15	20 16		20 26	20 31	20 45	20 46
d		18 17	18 28	18 32		18 47	18 58	19 02			19 17	19 28	19 32		19 47	19 58	20 02		20 17		20 28	20 32		20 47
London Paddington 15 ⊖ a		18 33	18 55	18 47		19 03	19 26	19 17			19 32	19 55	19 47		20 02	20 26	20 17		20 32		20 55	20 47		21 03

	XR	HX	XR	HX	XR		HX	XR	HX	XR	HX	XR	HX	XR	HX		XR	HX	XR	HX	XR	HX FX	HX FO	XR
		◇1		◇1			◇1		◇1		◇1		◇1		◇1			◇1		◇1		◇1	◇1	
Heathrow Terminal 5 ⊖ ✈ d		20 57		21 12			21 27		21 42		21 57		22 12		22 27			22 42		22 57		23 12	23 12	
Heathrow Terminal 4 ⊖ ✈ d	20 52		21 11		21 22			21 41		21 52		22 11		22 22			22 41		22 52		23 11			23 22
Heathrow Terminals 2 & 3 2 ⊖ ✈ a	20 56	21 01	21 15	21 16	21 26		21 31	21 45	21 46	21 56	22 01	22 15	22 16	22 26	22 31		22 45	22 46	22 56	23 01	23 15	23 16	23 16	23 26
d	20 58	21 02		21 17	21 28		21 32		21 47	21 58	22 02		22 17	22 28	22 32			22 47	22 58	23 02		23 17	23 17	23 28
London Paddington 15 ⊖ a	21 25	21 17		21 32	21 55		21 47		22 02	22 26	22 17		22 32	22 55	22 49			23 02	23 25	23 17		23 32	23 33	23 55

	HX		XR	HX FX	HX FO	HX	XR
	◇1			◇1	◇1		
Heathrow Terminal 5 ⊖ ✈ d	23 27			23 42	23 42	23 51	
Heathrow Terminal 4 ⊖ ✈ d			23 41				23 57
Heathrow Terminals 2 & 3 2 ⊖ ✈ a	23 31		23 45	23 46	23 46	23 55	00 01
d	23 32			23 47	23 47	23 57	00 03
London Paddington 15 ⊖ a	23 47			00 03	00 04	00 15	00 31

For MTR Crossrail services see Table T117

Table T118-R

Heathrow Airport (Heathrow Express Services) - London

Saturdays

21 December to 16 May

	XR	XR	HX ◇1	XR	HX ◇1		XR	HX ◇1	XR	HX ◇1	XR	HX ◇1	XR	HX ◇1	XR		HX ◇1	XR	HX ◇1	XR	HX ◇1	XR	HX ◇1	XR
Heathrow Terminal 5 ⊖ ✈ d			05 12		05 27			05 42		05 57		06 12		06 27			06 42		06 57		07 12		07 27	
Heathrow Terminal 4 ⊖ ✈ d		00 07		05 22			05 41		05 52		06 11		06 22		06 41			06 52		07 11		07 22		07 41
Heathrow Terminals 2 & 3 2 ⊖ ✈ a		00 11	05 16	05 26	05 31		05 45	05 46	05 56	06 01	06 15	06 16	06 26	06 31	06 45		06 46	06 56	07 01	07 15	07 16	07 26	07 31	07 45
d	00 03	00 13	05 17	05 28	05 32			05 47	05 58	06 02		06 17	06 28	06 32			06 47	06 58	07 02		07 17	07 28	07 32	
London Paddington 15 ⊖ a	00 31	00 40	05 32	05 55	05 48			06 03	06 25	06 18		06 33	06 55	06 48			07 03	07 25	07 18		07 33	07 55	07 48	

	HX ◇1		XR	HX ◇1	XR	HX ◇1	XR	HX ◇1	XR	HX ◇1	XR		HX ◇1	XR	HX ◇1	XR	HX ◇1	XR	HX ◇1	XR	HX ◇1	XR		
Heathrow Terminal 5 ⊖ ✈ d	07 42			07 57		08 12		08 27		08 42			08 57		09 12		09 27		09 42		09 57			
Heathrow Terminal 4 ⊖ ✈ d			07 52		08 11		08 22		08 41		08 52			09 11		09 22		09 41		09 52		10 11		
Heathrow Terminals 2 & 3 2 ⊖ ✈ a	07 46		07 56	08 01	08 15	08 16	08 26	08 31	08 45	08 46	08 56		09 01	09 15	09 16	09 26	09 31	09 45	09 46	09 56	10 01	10 15		
d	07 47		07 58	08 02		08 17	08 28	08 32		08 47	08 58		09 02		09 17	09 28	09 32		09 47	09 58	10 02			
London Paddington 15 ⊖ a	08 03		08 25	08 18		08 33	08 55	08 48		09 03	09 25		09 18		09 34	09 55	09 48		10 03	10 25	10 18			

	HX ◇1		XR	HX ◇1	XR	HX ◇1	XR	HX ◇1	XR	HX ◇1		XR	HX ◇1	XR	HX ◇1	XR	HX ◇1	XR	HX ◇1	XR		HX ◇1	XR
Heathrow Terminal 5 ⊖ ✈ d	10 12	and at the same minutes past each hour until		18 27		18 42		18 57		19 12			19 27		19 42		19 57		20 12			20 27	
Heathrow Terminal 4 ⊖ ✈ d			18 22		18 41		18 52		19 11			19 22		19 41		19 52		20 11		20 22			20 41
Heathrow Terminals 2 & 3 2 ⊖ ✈ a	10 16		18 26	18 31	18 45	18 46	18 56	19 01	19 15	19 16		19 26	19 31	19 45	19 46	19 56	20 01	20 15	20 16	20 26		20 31	20 45
d	10 17		18 28	18 32		18 47	18 58	19 02		19 17		19 28	19 32		19 47	19 58	20 02		20 17	20 28		20 32	
London Paddington 15 ⊖ a	10 33		18 55	18 48		19 03	19 25	19 18		19 33		19 55	19 49		20 03	20 25	20 18		20 33	20 55		20 48	

	HX ◇1	XR	HX ◇1	XR	HX ◇1	XR	HX ◇1		XR	HX ◇1	XR	HX ◇1	XR	HX ◇1	XR	HX ◇1	XR		HX ◇1	XR	HX ◇1	XR	HX ◇1	XR
Heathrow Terminal 5 ⊖ ✈ d	20 42		20 57		21 12		21 27			21 42		21 57		22 12		22 27			22 42		22 57		23 12	
Heathrow Terminal 4 ⊖ ✈ d		20 52		21 11		21 22			21 41		21 52		22 11		22 22		22 41			22 52		23 11		23 22
Heathrow Terminals 2 & 3 2 ⊖ ✈ a	20 46	20 56	21 01	21 15	21 16	21 26	21 31		21 45	21 46	21 56	22 01	22 15	22 16	22 26	22 31	22 45		22 46	22 56	23 01	23 15	23 16	23 26
d	20 47	20 58	21 02		21 17	21 28	21 32			21 47	21 58	22 03		22 17	22 28	22 33			22 47	22 58	23 03		23 17	23 28
London Paddington 15 ⊖ a	21 03	21 25	21 18		21 33	21 55	21 48			22 03	22 25	22 19		22 33	22 55	22 49			23 03	23 25	23 19		23 33	23 55

	HX ◇1	XR	HX ◇1		HX	XR
Heathrow Terminal 5 ⊖ ✈ d	23 27		23 42		23 52	
Heathrow Terminal 4 ⊖ ✈ d		23 41				23 57
Heathrow Terminals 2 & 3 2 ⊖ ✈ a	23 31	23 45	23 46		23 56	00 01
d	23 33		23 47			00 03
London Paddington 15 ⊖ a	23 49		00 03			00 30

Sundays

15 December to 10 May

	XR A	XR	HX ◇1		HX ◇1	XR	HX ◇1	XR	HX ◇1		XR	HX ◇1	XR	HX ◇1	XR	HX ◇1	XR	HX ◇1	XR		HX ◇1	XR	HX ◇1
Heathrow Terminal 5 ⊖ ✈ d			05 12	and every 15 minutes until	05 57		06 12		06 27			06 42		06 57		07 12		07 27			07 42		07 57
Heathrow Terminal 4 ⊖ ✈ d		00 07				06 01		06 16			06 31		06 46		07 01		07 16		07 31			07 46	
Heathrow Terminals 2 & 3 2 ⊖ ✈ a		00 11	05 16		06 01	06 05	06 16	06 20	06 31		06 35	06 46	06 50	07 01	07 05	07 16	07 20	07 31	07 35		07 46	07 50	08 01
d	00 03	00 13	05 17		06 02	06 07	06 17		06 32		06 37	06 47		07 02	07 07	07 17		07 32	07 37		07 47		08 02
London Paddington 15 ⊖ a	00 30	00 41	05 33		06 18	06 34	06 33		06 48		07 07	07 03		07 19	07 34	07 33		07 48	08 05		08 04		08 18

	XR	HX ◇1	XR	HX ◇1	XR	HX ◇1		XR	HX ◇1	XR	HX ◇1	XR	HX ◇1	XR	HX ◇1	XR		HX ◇1	XR	HX ◇1	XR	HX ◇1	XR	HX ◇1
Heathrow Terminal 5 ⊖ ✈ d		08 12		08 27		08 42			08 57		09 12		09 27		09 42			09 57		10 12		10 27		10 42
Heathrow Terminal 4 ⊖ ✈ d	08 01		08 16		08 31			08 46		09 01		09 16		09 31		09 46			10 01		10 16		10 31	
Heathrow Terminals 2 & 3 2 ⊖ ✈ a	08 05	08 16	08 20	08 31	08 35	08 46		08 50	09 01	09 05	09 16	09 20	09 31	09 35	09 46	09 50		10 01	10 05	10 16	10 20	10 31	10 35	10 46
d	08 07	08 17		08 32	08 37	08 47			09 02	09 07	09 17		09 32	09 37	09 47			10 02	10 07	10 17		10 32	10 37	10 47
London Paddington 15 ⊖ a	08 34	08 34		08 48	09 04	09 08			09 19	09 34	09 36		09 48	10 03	10 03			10 18	10 33	10 34		10 50	11 03	11 03

	XR	HX ◇1		XR	HX ◇1	XR	HX ◇1	XR	HX ◇1	XR	HX ◇1	XR		HX ◇1	XR	HX ◇1	XR	HX ◇1	XR	HX ◇1	XR	HX ◇1		XR
Heathrow Terminal 5 ⊖ ✈ d		10 57			11 12		11 27		11 42		11 57			12 12		12 27		12 42		12 57		13 12		
Heathrow Terminal 4 ⊖ ✈ d	10 46			11 01		11 16		11 31		11 46		12 01			12 16		12 31		12 46		13 01			13 16
Heathrow Terminals 2 & 3 2 ⊖ ✈ a	10 50	11 01		11 05	11 16	11 20	11 31	11 35	11 46	11 50	12 01	12 05		12 16	12 20	12 31	12 35	12 46	12 50	13 01	13 05	13 16		13 20
d		11 02		11 07	11 17		11 32	11 37	11 47		12 02	12 07		12 17		12 32	12 37	12 47		13 02	13 07	13 17		
London Paddington 15 ⊖ a		11 18		11 33	11 33		11 50	12 03	12 04		12 18	12 33		12 33		12 50	13 03	13 04		13 18	13 33	13 34		

A not 15 December

For MTR Crossrail services see Table T117

Table T118-R

Heathrow Airport (Heathrow Express Services) - London

Sundays

15 December to 10 May

	HX ◇1	XR	HX ◇1	XR		HX ◇1	XR	HX ◇1	XR	HX ◇1	XR	HX ◇1	XR	HX ◇1		XR	HX ◇1	XR	HX ◇1	XR	HX ◇1	XR	HX ◇1	XR
Heathrow Terminal 5 ⊖ ✈ d	13 27		13 42			13 57		14 12		14 27		14 42		14 57			15 12		15 27		15 42		15 57	
Heathrow Terminal 4 ⊖ ✈ d		13 31		13 46			14 01		14 16		14 31		14 47			15 01		15 16		15 31		15 46		16 01
Heathrow Terminals 2 & 3 2 ⊖ ✈ a	13 31	13 35	13 46	13 50		14 01	14 05	14 16	14 20	14 31	14 35	14 46	14 51	15 01		15 05	15 16	15 20	15 31	15 35	15 46	15 50	16 01	16 05
d	13 32	13 37	13 47			14 02	14 07	14 17		14 32	14 37	14 47		15 02		15 07	15 17		15 32	15 37	15 47		16 02	16 07
London Paddington 15 ⊖ a	13 48	14 03	14 04			14 18	14 33	14 34		14 48	15 03	15 04		15 19		15 33	15 34		15 48	16 03	16 04		16 18	16 33

		HX ◇1	XR	HX ◇1	XR	HX ◇1	XR	HX ◇1	XR	HX ◇1		XR	HX ◇1	XR	HX ◇1	XR	HX ◇1	XR	HX ◇1	XR		HX ◇1	XR	HX ◇1
Heathrow Terminal 5 ⊖ ✈ d		16 12		16 27		16 42		16 57		17 12			17 27		17 42		17 57		18 12			18 27		18 42
Heathrow Terminal 4 ⊖ ✈ d			16 16		16 31		16 46		17 01			17 16		17 31		17 46		18 01		18 16			18 31	
Heathrow Terminals 2 & 3 2 ⊖ ✈ a		16 16	16 20	16 31	16 35	16 46	16 50	17 01	17 05	17 16		17 20	17 31	17 35	17 46	17 50	18 01	18 05	18 16	18 20		18 31	18 35	18 46
d		16 17		16 32	16 37	16 47		17 02	17 07	17 17			17 32	17 37	17 47		18 02	18 07	18 17			18 32	18 37	18 47
London Paddington 15 ⊖ a		16 34		16 48	17 03	17 04		17 18	17 33	17 33			17 48	18 03	18 04		18 18	18 33	18 34			18 48	19 03	19 03

	XR	HX ◇1	XR	HX ◇1	XR	HX ◇1		XR	HX ◇1	XR	HX ◇1	XR	HX ◇1	XR	HX ◇1	XR		HX ◇1	XR	HX ◇1	XR	HX ◇1	XR	HX ◇1
Heathrow Terminal 5 ⊖ ✈ d		18 57		19 12		19 27			19 42		19 57		20 12		20 27			20 42		20 57		21 12		21 27
Heathrow Terminal 4 ⊖ ✈ d	18 46		19 01		19 16			19 31		19 46		20 01		20 16		20 31			20 46		21 01		21 16	
Heathrow Terminals 2 & 3 2 ⊖ ✈ a	18 50	19 01	19 05	19 16	19 20	19 31		19 35	19 46	19 50	20 01	20 05	20 16	20 20	20 31	20 35		20 46	20 50	21 01	21 05	21 16	21 20	21 31
d		19 02	19 07	19 17		19 32		19 37	19 47		20 02	20 07	20 17		20 32	20 37		20 47		21 02	21 07	21 17		21 32
London Paddington 15 ⊖ a		19 18	19 33	19 34		19 48		20 03	20 03		20 18	20 33	20 33		20 48	21 03		21 03		21 18	21 35	21 34		21 48

	XR	HX ◇1		XR	HX ◇1	XR	HX ◇1	XR	HX ◇1	XR	HX ◇1	XR		HX ◇1	XR	HX ◇1	XR	HX ◇1	XR	HX ◇1	XR	HX		
Heathrow Terminal 5 ⊖ ✈ d		21 42			21 57		22 12		22 27		22 42			22 57		23 12		23 27		23 42		23 55		
Heathrow Terminal 4 ⊖ ✈ d	21 31			21 46		22 01		22 16		22 31		22 46			23 01		23 16		23 31		23 46			
Heathrow Terminals 2 & 3 2 ⊖ ✈ a	21 35	21 46		21 50	22 01	22 05	22 16	22 20	22 31	22 35	22 46	22 50		23 01	23 05	23 16	23 20	23 31	23 35	23 46	23 50	23 59		
d	21 37	21 47			22 02	22 07	22 17		22 32	22 37	22 47			23 02	23 07	23 17		23 32	23 37	23 47	23 52			
London Paddington 15 ⊖ a	22 04	22 03			22 18	22 34	22 36		22 49	23 07	23 11			23 24	23 34	23 37		23 50	00 04	00 07	00 20			

For MTR Crossrail services see Table T117

Table T119-F

Mondays to Fridays

16 December to 15 May

Slough - Windsor & Eton

Miles			GW	GW	GW	GW	GW	GW	GW	GW	GW	GW	GW	GW	GW	and at the same minutes past each hour until	GW	GW	GW	GW	GW	GW
0	Slough 🅂	d	05 30	05 49	06 07	06 26	06 50	07 10	07 30	07 50	08 09	08 30	08 56	09 16	09 36		21 56	22 16	22 36	22 56	23 16	23 40
2¾	Windsor & Eton Central	a	05 36	05 55	06 13	06 32	06 56	07 16	07 36	07 56	08 15	08 36	09 02	09 22	09 42		22 02	22 22	22 42	23 02	23 22	23 46

Saturdays

21 December to 16 May

		GW		GW	GW	GW	GW		GW	GW	GW	GW		GW	GW	GW	GW
Slough 🅂	d	06 14	and every 30 minutes until	08 44	09 16	09 36	09 56	and at the same minutes past each hour until	18 16	18 36	18 56	19 14	and every 30 minutes until	22 14	22 47	23 23	23 53
Windsor & Eton Central	a	06 20		08 50	09 22	09 42	10 02		18 22	18 42	19 02	19 20		22 20	22 53	23 29	23 59

Sundays

15 December to 10 May

		GW		GW	GW	GW	GW		GW	GW	GW	GW		GW
Slough 🅂	d	08 22	and every 30 minutes until	09 52	10 12	10 32	10 52	and at the same minutes past each hour until	18 12	18 32	18 52	19 22	and every 30 minutes until	23 22
Windsor & Eton Central	a	08 28		09 58	10 18	10 38	10 58		18 18	18 38	18 58	19 28		23 28

NRT DECEMBER 19 EDITION

Table T119-R

Mondays to Fridays

16 December to 15 May

Windsor & Eton - Slough

Miles			GW	GW	GW	GW	GW	GW	GW	GW	GW	GW	GW	GW	GW	and at the same minutes past each hour until	GW	GW	GW	GW	GW	GW
0	Windsor & Eton Central	d	05 39	05 58	06 16	06 40	06 59	07 19	07 39	07 59	08 18	08 39	09 05	09 25	09 45		22 05	22 25	22 45	23 05	23 25	23 54
2¾	Slough 🅂	a	05 45	06 04	06 22	06 46	07 05	07 25	07 45	08 05	08 24	08 45	09 11	09 31	09 51		22 11	22 31	22 51	23 11	23 31	00 01

Saturdays

21 December to 16 May

		GW		GW	GW	GW	GW		GW	GW	GW	GW		GW	GW	GW
Windsor & Eton Central	d	06 24	and every 30 minutes until	08 54	09 25	09 45	10 05	and at the same minutes past each hour until	18 25	18 45	19 05	19 24	and every 30 minutes until	22 24	22 57	23 32
Slough 🅂	a	06 30		09 00	09 31	09 51	10 11		18 31	18 51	19 11	19 30		22 30	23 03	23 38

Sundays

15 December to 10 May

		GW	GW		GW	GW	GW	GW		GW	GW	GW	GW		GW
Windsor & Eton Central	d	00 02	08 32	and every 30 minutes until	10 02	10 22	10 42	11 02	and at the same minutes past each hour until	18 22	18 42	19 02	19 32	and every 30 minutes until	23 32
Slough 🅂	a	00 08	08 38		10 08	10 28	10 48	11 08		18 28	18 48	19 08	19 38		23 38

NRT DECEMBER 19 EDITION

Table T120-F

Mondays to Fridays

16 December to 15 May

Maidenhead - Marlow

Miles			GW MX	GW	GW	GW	GW	GW	GW	GW	GW		GW	GW	GW	GW	GW	GW	GW	GW	GW		GW	GW	GW
0	Maidenhead 🅂	d		05 27	05 59		06 31		07 01		07 31			08 01		08 31		09 34	10 34	11 34	12 34		13 34	14 34	15 34
1¼	Furze Platt	d		05 31	06 03		06 35		07 05		07 35			08 05		08 35		09 38	10 38	11 38	12 38		13 38	14 38	15 38
3	Cookham	d		05 34	06 06		06 38		07 08		07 38			08 08		08 38		09 41	10 41	11 41	12 41		13 41	14 41	15 41
4½	Bourne End 🅂	a		05 38	06 10		06 42		07 12		07 42			08 12		08 42		09 45	10 45	11 45	12 45		13 45	14 45	15 45
—		d	00 03	05 42		06 16		06 46		07 16			07 46		08 16		08 46	09 49	10 49	11 49	12 49		13 49	14 49	15 49
7¼	Marlow	a	00 11	05 50		06 23		06 53		07 23			07 53		08 23		08 53	09 57	10 57	11 57	12 57		13 57	14 57	15 57

		GW	GW	GW	GW	GW	GW		GW	GW	GW	GW	GW	GW	GW	GW	GW		GW	GW	GW	GW	GW
Maidenhead 🅂	d	16 37	17 14		17 44		18 20			18 50		19 20		19 50		20 20			20 50		21 42	22 49	23 48
Furze Platt	d	16 41	17 18		17 48		18 24			18 54		19 24		19 54		20 24			20 54		21 46	22 52	23 52
Cookham	d	16 44	17 21		17 51		18 27			18 57		19 27		19 57		20 27			20 57		21 49	22 56	23 55
Bourne End 🅂	a	16 48	17 25		17 55		18 31			19 01		19 31		20 01		20 31			21 01		21 53	23 00	23 59
	d	16 52		17 29		17 58			18 35		19 05		19 35		20 05		20 35			21 05	21 57	23 04	00 03
Marlow	a	17 00		17 36		18 05			18 42		19 12		19 42		20 12		20 42			21 12	22 05	23 12	00 11

Saturdays

21 December to 16 May

		GW	GW	GW	GW	GW	GW	GW	GW	GW		GW	GW	GW	GW	GW	GW	GW	GW	GW		GW
Maidenhead 🅂	d		06 34	07 34	08 34	09 34	10 34	11 34	12 34	13 34		14 34	15 34	16 34	17 34	18 34	19 34	20 34	21 43	22 47		23 45
Furze Platt	d		06 37	07 37	08 37	09 37	10 37	11 37	12 37	13 37		14 37	15 37	16 37	17 37	18 37	19 37	20 37	21 46	22 50		23 48
Cookham	d		06 41	07 41	08 41	09 41	10 41	11 41	12 41	13 41		14 41	15 41	16 41	17 41	18 41	19 41	20 41	21 50	22 54		23 52
Bourne End 🅂	a		06 45	07 45	08 45	09 45	10 45	11 45	12 45	13 45		14 45	15 45	16 45	17 45	18 45	19 45	20 45	21 54	22 58		23 56
	d	00 03	06 49	07 49	08 49	09 49	10 49	11 49	12 49	13 49		14 49	15 49	16 49	17 49	18 49	19 49	20 49	21 58	23 02		23 59
Marlow	a	00 11	06 57	07 57	08 57	09 57	10 57	11 57	12 57	13 57		14 57	15 57	16 57	17 57	18 57	19 57	20 57	22 06	23 10		00 08

Sundays

15 December to 10 May

		GW	GW	GW	GW	GW	GW	GW	GW	GW		GW	GW	GW	GW	GW
Maidenhead 🅂	d	08 26	09 26	10 26	11 26	12 26	13 26	14 26	15 26	16 26		17 26	18 26	19 26	20 26	21 35
Furze Platt	d	08 30	09 30	10 30	11 30	12 30	13 30	14 30	15 30	16 30		17 30	18 30	19 30	20 30	21 39
Cookham	d	08 33	09 33	10 33	11 33	12 33	13 33	14 33	15 33	16 33		17 33	18 33	19 33	20 33	21 42
Bourne End 🅂	a	08 38	09 38	10 38	11 38	12 38	13 38	14 38	15 38	16 38		17 38	18 38	19 38	20 38	21 47
	d	08 42	09 42	10 42	11 42	12 42	13 42	14 42	15 42	16 42		17 42	18 42	19 42	20 42	21 51
Marlow	a	08 49	09 49	10 49	11 49	12 49	13 49	14 49	15 49	16 49		17 49	18 49	19 49	20 49	21 58

Table T120-R

Mondays to Fridays

16 December to 15 May

Marlow - Maidenhead

Miles			GW MX	GW	GW	GW	GW	GW		GW	GW	GW	GW	GW	GW	GW	GW	GW		GW	GW	GW	GW	GW	GW
0	Marlow	d	00 14	06 06		06 36		07 06			07 36		08 06		08 36		08 56	10 00		11 06	12 00	13 00	14 00	15 00	16 00
2¾	Bourne End 🅂	a	00 21	06 13		06 43		07 13			07 43		08 13		08 43		09 03	10 07		11 13	12 07	13 07	14 07	15 07	16 07
—		d	00 25		06 16		06 46			07 16		07 46		08 16		08 46	09 07	10 11		11 17	12 11	13 11	14 11	15 11	16 11
4¼	Cookham	d	00 28		06 19		06 49			07 19		07 49		08 19		08 49	09 11	10 15		11 21	12 15	13 15	14 15	15 15	16 15
6	Furze Platt	d	00 32		06 23		06 53			07 23		07 53		08 23		08 53	09 14	10 18		11 24	12 18	13 18	14 18	15 18	16 18
7¼	Maidenhead 🅂	a	00 37		06 27		06 57			07 27		07 57		08 27		08 57	09 19	10 23		11 29	12 23	13 23	14 23	15 23	16 23

		GW	GW	GW		GW	GW	GW	GW	GW	GW	GW	GW	GW		GW	GW	GW	GW	GW	GW	GW
Marlow	d	17 18		17 47			18 24		18 47		19 24		19 54			20 24		20 54		21 15	22 08	23 15
Bourne End 🅂	a	17 25		17 54			18 31		18 54		19 31		20 01			20 31		21 01		21 22	22 15	23 22
	d		17 29			18 00		18 35		19 05		19 35		20 05			20 35		21 05	21 26	22 19	23 26
Cookham	d		17 32			18 03		18 38		19 08		19 38		20 08			20 38		21 08	21 30	22 23	23 29
Furze Platt	d		17 36			18 07		18 42		19 12		19 42		20 12			20 42		21 12	21 33	22 26	23 33
Maidenhead 🅂	a		17 40			18 11		18 46		19 16		19 46		20 16			20 46		21 16	21 38	22 31	23 38

Saturdays

21 December to 16 May

		GW	GW	GW	GW	GW	GW	GW	GW	GW		GW	GW	GW	GW	GW	GW	GW	GW	GW
Marlow	d	00 14	07 00	08 00	09 00	10 00	11 00	12 00	13 00	14 00		15 00	16 00	17 00	18 00	19 00	20 00	21 00	22 09	23 14
Bourne End 🅂	a	00 21	07 07	08 07	09 07	10 07	11 07	12 07	13 07	14 07		15 07	16 07	17 07	18 07	19 07	20 07	21 07	22 16	23 21
	d	00 25	07 11	08 11	09 11	10 11	11 11	12 11	13 11	14 11		15 11	16 11	17 11	18 11	19 11	20 11	21 11	22 20	23 25
Cookham	d	00 28	07 14	08 14	09 14	10 14	11 14	12 14	13 14	14 14		15 14	16 14	17 14	18 14	19 14	20 14	21 14	22 23	23 28
Furze Platt	d	00 32	07 18	08 18	09 18	10 18	11 18	12 18	13 18	14 18		15 18	16 18	17 18	18 18	19 18	20 18	21 18	22 27	23 32
Maidenhead 🅂	a	00 37	07 23	08 23	09 23	10 23	11 23	12 23	13 23	14 23		15 23	16 23	17 23	18 23	19 23	20 23	21 23	22 32	23 37

Sundays

15 December to 10 May

		GW	GW	GW	GW	GW	GW	GW	GW	GW		GW	GW	GW	GW	GW	GW
Marlow	d	00 12	08 55	09 55	10 55	11 55	12 55	13 55	14 55	15 55		16 55	17 55	18 55	19 55	20 55	22 02
Bourne End 🅂	a	00 19	09 02	10 02	11 02	12 02	13 02	14 02	15 02	16 02		17 02	18 02	19 02	20 02	21 02	22 09
	d	00 23	09 06	10 06	11 06	12 06	13 06	14 06	15 06	16 06		17 06	18 06	19 06	20 06	21 06	22 13
Cookham	d	00 26	09 10	10 10	11 10	12 10	13 10	14 10	15 10	16 10		17 10	18 10	19 10	20 10	21 10	22 17
Furze Platt	d	00 30	09 14	10 14	11 14	12 14	13 14	14 14	15 14	16 14		17 14	18 14	19 14	20 14	21 14	22 21
Maidenhead 🅂	a	00 35	09 18	10 18	11 18	12 18	13 18	14 18	15 18	16 18		17 18	18 18	19 18	20 18	21 18	22 25

Table T121-F

Twyford - Henley-on-Thames

Mondays to Fridays
16 December to 15 May

Miles			GW MX	GW	GW	GW	GW	GW	GW	GW	GW	GW		GW	GW	GW	GW	GW	GW	GW	GW	GW	GW
0	Twyford [3]	d	00 03	05 49	06 20	06 51	07 21	07 52	08 22	08 56	09 26	10 12	and every 30 minutes until	16 12	16 43	17 21	17 52	18 27	18 57	19 28	19 58	20 29	20 59
1¾	Wargrave	d	00 07	05 53	06 24	06 55	07 25	07 56	08 26	09 00	09 30	10 16		16 16	16 47	17 25	17 56	18 31	19 01	19 32	20 02	20 33	21 03
2¾	Shiplake	d	00 10	05 56	06 27	06 58	07 28	07 59	08 29	09 03	09 33	10 19		16 19	16 50	17 28	17 59	18 34	19 04	19 35	20 05	20 36	21 06
4½	Henley-on-Thames	a	00 15	06 01	06 32	07 03	07 33	08 04	08 34	09 08	09 38	10 24		16 24	16 55	17 33	18 04	18 39	19 09	19 40	20 10	20 41	21 11

		GW	GW	GW	GW
Twyford [3]	d	21 46	22 16	22 56	23 30
Wargrave	d	21 50	22 20	23 00	23 34
Shiplake	d	21 53	22 23	23 03	23 37
Henley-on-Thames	a	21 58	22 28	23 08	23 42

Saturdays
21 December to 16 May

		GW	GW	GW	GW	GW		GW	GW	GW	GW	GW	GW
Twyford [3]	d	00 03	06 53	07 53	08 42	09 16	and every 30 minutes until	19 46	20 42	21 42	22 42	23 13	23 43
Wargrave	d	00 07	06 57	07 57	08 46	09 20		19 50	20 46	21 46	22 46	23 17	23 47
Shiplake	d	00 10	07 00	08 00	08 49	09 23		19 53	20 49	21 49	22 49	23 20	23 50
Henley-on-Thames	a	00 15	07 05	08 05	08 54	09 28		19 58	20 54	21 54	22 54	23 25	23 55

Sundays
15 December to 10 May

		GW	GW	GW		GW	GW	GW	GW
Twyford [3]	d	08 38	09 38	10 15	and every 30 minutes until	18 45	19 45	20 45	21 45
Wargrave	d	08 42	09 42	10 19		18 49	19 49	20 49	21 49
Shiplake	d	08 45	09 45	10 22		18 52	19 52	20 52	21 52
Henley-on-Thames	a	08 50	09 50	10 27		18 57	19 57	20 57	21 57

NRT DECEMBER 19 EDITION

Table T121-R

Henley-on-Thames - Twyford

Mondays to Fridays
16 December to 15 May

Miles			GW MX	GW	GW	GW	GW	GW	GW	GW	GW	GW		GW	GW	GW	GW	GW	GW	GW	GW	GW
0	Henley-on-Thames	d	00 18	06 05	06 35	07 06	07 36	08 07	08 37	09 11	09 41	10 27	and every 30 minutes until	16 27	17 05	17 36	18 07	18 42	19 12	19 43	20 13	20 44
1¾	Shiplake	d	00 22	06 09	06 39	07 10	07 40	08 11	08 41	09 15	09 45	10 31		16 31	17 09	17 40	18 11	18 46	19 16	19 47	20 17	20 48
2¾	Wargrave	d	00 25	06 12	06 42	07 13	07 43	08 14	08 44	09 18	09 48	10 34		16 34	17 12	17 43	18 14	18 49	19 19	19 50	20 20	20 51
4½	Twyford [3]	a	00 30	06 17	06 47	07 18	07 48	08 19	08 49	09 23	09 53	10 39		16 39	17 17	17 48	18 19	18 54	19 24	19 55	20 25	20 56

		GW	GW	GW	GW	GW
Henley-on-Thames	d	21 16	22 01	22 31	23 11	23 46
Shiplake	d	21 20	22 05	22 35	23 15	23 50
Wargrave	d	21 23	22 08	22 38	23 18	23 53
Twyford [3]	a	21 28	22 13	22 43	23 23	23 59

Saturdays
21 December to 16 May

		GW	GW	GW	GW		GW	GW	GW	GW	GW	GW	GW
Henley-on-Thames	d	00 18	07 22	08 22	09 01	and every 30 minutes until	19 31	20 04	21 04	22 04	22 58	23 28	23 58
Shiplake	d	00 22	07 26	08 26	09 05		19 35	20 08	21 08	22 08	23 02	23 32	00 02
Wargrave	d	00 25	07 29	08 29	09 08		19 38	20 11	21 11	22 11	23 05	23 35	00 05
Twyford [3]	a	00 30	07 34	08 34	09 13		19 43	20 16	21 16	22 16	23 10	23 40	00 10

Sundays
15 December to 10 May

		GW A	GW	GW		GW	GW	GW	GW
Henley-on-Thames	d		09 00	10 00	and every 30 minutes until	19 00	20 00	21 00	22 00
Shiplake	d	00 02	09 04	10 04		19 04	20 04	21 04	22 04
Wargrave	d	00 05	09 07	10 07		19 07	20 07	21 07	22 07
Twyford [3]	a	00 10	09 12	10 12		19 12	20 12	21 12	22 12

A not 15 December

Table T122-F

Reading - Basingstoke

Mondays to Fridays
16 December to 15 May

Miles			GW	GW	GW	GW	GW	GW	GW	GW	XC	GW	XC	GW	XC	GW	GW	GW	XC	GW	XC	GW	XC
											◇[1] ⚲		◇[1] ⚲		◇[1] ⚲				◇[1] ⚲		◇[1] ⚲		[B] [1] ⚲
0	Reading [7]	d	05 18	05 40	06 00	06 18	06 40	06 57	07 16	07 37	07 52	08 00	08 19	08 24	08 48	08 55	08 58	09 32	09 49	10 05	10 19	10 32	10 50
1	Reading West	d	05 21	05 43	06 03	06 22	06 43	07 00	07 19	07 40		08 03		08 27			09 02	09 35		10 08		10 36	
7¼	Mortimer	d	05 31	05 53	06 13	06 32	06 53	07 11	07 29	07 50		08 13		08 37			09 12	09 45		10 18		10 46	
10½	Bramley (Hants)	d	05 36	05 58	06 18	06 37	06 58	07 17	07 35	07 55		08 18		08 42			09 17	09 50		10 23		10 52	
15½	Basingstoke	a	05 45	06 08	06 27	06 47	07 07	07 27	07 47	08 04	08 11	08 27	08 41	08 53	09 10	09 16	09 32	10 00	10 09	10 32	10 42	11 00	11 09

		GW	GW	XC	GW	XC	GW	XC	GW	GW	XC	GW	XC	GW	XC	GW	GW	XC	GW	XC	GW	XC	GW
				◇[1] ⚲		◇[1] ⚲		◇[1] ⚲			◇[1] ⚲		◇[1] ⚲		◇[1] ⚲			◇[1] ⚲		◇[1] ⚲		◇[1] ⚲	
Reading [7]	d	11 07	11 32	11 49	12 07	12 19	12 32	12 50	13 07	13 32	13 49	14 07	14 19	14 32	14 49	15 05	15 32	15 49	16 07	16 19	16 33	16 52	16 55
Reading West	d	11 10	11 35		12 10		12 36		13 10	13 35		14 11		14 35		15 08	15 35		16 10		16 36		
Mortimer	d	11 20	11 45		12 20		12 46		13 20	13 45		14 21		14 45		15 18	15 45		16 20		16 45		17 08
Bramley (Hants)	d	11 25	11 50		12 25		12 51		13 25	13 50		14 26		14 50		15 23	15 50		16 25		16 50		17 13
Basingstoke	a	11 34	11 59	12 10	12 34	12 42	13 01	13 09	13 34	13 59	14 10	14 34	14 41	15 03	15 10	15 32	15 59	16 10	16 34	16 42	17 03	17 10	17 22

		GW	GW	XC	GW	GW	GW	XC	GW	GW	XC	GW	GW	XC	GW	GW	XC	GW	XC	XC	GW	GW
				◇[1] ⚲				◇[1] ⚲			◇[1] ⚲			◇[1]			◇[1]		◇[1]	◇[1]		
Reading [7]	d	17 15	17 39	17 52	18 00	18 13	18 32	18 52	19 00	19 21	19 49	19 57	20 22	20 49	20 52	21 22	21 52	22 05	22 23	22 49	22 52	23 34
Reading West	d	17 18	17 42		18 03	18 16	18 35		19 03	19 24		20 00	20 25		20 56	21 25		22 08			22 55	23 37
Mortimer	d	17 28	17 52		18 14	18 26	18 45		19 13	19 34		20 10	20 35		21 06	21 35		22 18			23 05	23 47
Bramley (Hants)	d	17 33	17 57		18 20	18 31	18 50		19 18	19 39		20 15	20 39		21 11	21 40		22 23			23 10	23 52
Basingstoke	a	17 43	18 05	18 09	18 29	18 41	18 59	19 09	19 27	19 48	20 09	20 24	20 48	21 09	21 19	21 49	22 09	22 32	22 41	23 07	23 19	00 01

Saturdays
21 December to 16 May

		GW		GW	XC	GW	XC	GW	XC	GW	GW	XC	GW	XC	GW	XC	GW	GW	XC	GW	XC	GW
					◇[1] ⚲		◇[1] ⚲		◇[1] ⚲			◇[1] ⚲		◇[1] ⚲		◇[1] ⚲			◇[1] ⚲		◇[1] ⚲	
Reading [7]	d	05 52	and every 30 minutes until	07 22	07 49	07 52	08 19	08 22	08 49	08 52	09 22	09 49	09 52	10 19	10 22	10 49	10 54	11 22	11 49	11 52	12 19	12 22
Reading West	d	05 56		07 26		07 56		08 26		08 56	09 26		09 56		10 26		10 58	11 26		11 56		12 26
Mortimer	d	06 06		07 36		08 06		08 36		09 06	09 36		10 06		10 36		11 09	11 36		12 06		12 36
Bramley (Hants)	d	06 11		07 41		08 11		08 41		09 11	09 41		10 11		10 41		11 14	11 41		12 11		12 41
Basingstoke	a	06 19		07 49	08 08	08 19	08 40	08 49	09 11	09 19	09 49	10 09	10 19	10 40	10 49	11 10	11 22	11 49	12 09	12 19	12 40	12 49

		XC	GW	GW	XC	GW	XC	GW	XC	GW	GW	XC	GW	XC	GW	XC	GW	GW	XC	GW	GW	
		◇[1] ⚲			◇[1] ⚲		◇[1] ⚲		◇[1] ⚲			◇[1] ⚲		◇[1] ⚲		◇[1] ⚲			◇[1] ⚲			
Reading [7]	d	12 49	12 52	13 22	13 49	13 52	14 19	14 22	14 49	14 52	15 22	15 49	15 52	16 19	16 22	16 49	16 52	17 22	17 49	17 52	18 22	and at the same minutes past each hour until
Reading West	d		12 56	13 26		13 56		14 26		14 56	15 26		15 56		16 26		16 56	17 26		17 56	18 26	
Mortimer	d		13 06	13 37		14 06		14 36		15 06	15 36		16 06		16 36		17 06	17 36		18 06	18 36	
Bramley (Hants)	d		13 11	13 42		14 11		14 41		15 11	15 41		16 11		16 41		17 11	17 42		18 11	18 41	
Basingstoke	a	13 09	13 19	13 50	14 09	14 19	14 40	14 49	15 09	15 19	15 49	16 09	16 19	16 40	16 49	17 09	17 19	17 50	18 09	18 19	18 49	

		XC	GW	GW	XC	GW	XC	GW	XC	GW
		◇[1]			◇[1]		◇[1]		◇[1]	
Reading [7]	d	20 49	20 52	21 22	21 49	21 52	22 19	22 22	22 52	23 05
Reading West	d		20 56	21 26		21 56		22 26		23 09
Mortimer	d		21 06	21 36		22 06		22 36		23 19
Bramley (Hants)	d		21 11	21 41		22 11		22 41		23 24
Basingstoke	a	21 09	21 19	21 49	22 10	22 19	22 41	22 49	23 09	23 32

Sundays
15 December to 10 May

		GW	GW	SW	GW	XC	SW	GW	XC	SW	GW	XC	SW	GW	XC	SW		GW	XC	SW	GW	XC
				◇[1]		◇[1] ⚲	◇[1]		◇[1] ⚲	◇[1]		◇[1] ⚲	◇[1]		◇[1] ⚲	◇[1]			◇[1] ⚲	◇[1]		◇[1] ⚲
Reading [7]	d	07 38	08 38	09 12	09 38	09 52	10 12	10 38	10 52	11 12	11 38	11 52	12 12	12 38	12 52	13 12	and at the same minutes past each hour until	15 38	15 52	16 12	16 38	16 52
Reading West	d	07 41	08 41		09 41			10 41			11 41			12 41				15 41			16 41	
Mortimer	d	07 51	08 51		09 51			10 51			11 51			12 51				15 51			16 51	
Bramley (Hants)	d	07 56	08 56		09 56			10 56			11 56			12 56				15 56			16 56	
Basingstoke	a	08 04	09 04	09 32	10 04	10 10	10 32	11 04	11 09	11 30	12 04	12 09	12 31	13 04	13 09	13 30		16 04	16 09	16 30	17 04	17 09

		SW	GW	XC		GW	XC	GW	GW
		◇[1]		◇[1] ⚲			◇[1]		
Reading [7]	d	17 12	17 38	17 52	and at the same minutes past each hour until	21 38	21 52	22 38	23 38
Reading West	d		17 41			21 41		22 41	23 41
Mortimer	d		17 51			21 51		22 51	23 51
Bramley (Hants)	d		17 56			21 56		22 56	23 56
Basingstoke	a	17 31	18 04	18 09		22 04	22 09	23 04	00 04

Table T122-R

Mondays to Fridays
16 December to 15 May

Basingstoke - Reading

Miles			GW MX	GW MO	XC	GW	GW	GW		XC	GW	GW	GW	XC	GW	GW	XC	GW		XC	GW	GW	XC	GW	XC
0	Basingstoke	d	00 05	00 07	05 49	06 04	06 23	06 31		06 49	07 03	07 21	07 40	07 51	07 56	08 08	08 28	08 36		08 49	09 00	09 20	09 49	09 54	10 20
5	Bramley (Hants)	d	00 11	00 14		06 11	06 30	06 38			07 10	07 28	07 48		08 03	08 15		08 43			09 07	09 27		10 00	
8¼	Mortimer	d	00 16	00 19		06 16	06 36	06 43			07 15	07 33	07 53		08 08	08 20		08 48			09 12	09 32		10 05	
14½	Reading West	d	00 26	00 27		06 26	06 47				07 25	07 43	08 03		08 18	08 30		08 58			09 22	09 42		10 14	
15½	Reading 7	a	00 30	00 32	06 05	06 29	06 51	06 56		07 06	07 28	07 46	08 06	08 09	08 22	08 33	08 44	09 02		09 05	09 26	09 45	10 06	10 18	10 37

		GW	XC	GW		GW	XC	GW	XC	GW	XC	GW	GW	XC		GW	XC	GW	XC	GW	GW	XC	GW	XC
Basingstoke	d	10 26	10 49	10 53		11 23	11 49	11 53	12 19	12 23	12 49	12 53	13 23	13 49		13 55	14 19	14 23	14 49	14 59	15 26	15 49	15 54	16 19
Bramley (Hants)	d	10 33		11 00		11 30		11 59		12 29		13 00	13 30			14 01		14 30		15 06	15 33		16 00	
Mortimer	d	10 38		11 05		11 35		12 04		12 34		13 05	13 35			14 06		14 35		15 11	15 38		16 05	
Reading West	d	10 51		11 14		11 45		12 13		12 45		13 14	13 45			14 15		14 45		15 21	15 48		16 14	
Reading 7	a	10 54	11 06	11 18		11 48	12 06	12 16	12 36	12 49	13 07	13 18	13 52	14 06		14 18	14 36	14 51	15 06	15 25	15 52	16 09	16 17	16 38

		GW	XC	GW	GW	GW	XC	GW	XC	GW		GW	XC	GW	GW	GW	XC	GW	GW	XC		GW	GW	GW	SW
Basingstoke	d	16 25	16 49	16 59	17 18	17 32	17 49	17 55	18 19	18 25		18 37	18 49	18 53	19 07	19 34	19 49	20 05	20 35	20 49		21 01	21 31	22 13	22 33
Bramley (Hants)	d	16 31		17 05	17 25	17 39		18 02		18 31		18 44			19 14	19 41		20 12	20 42			21 08	21 38	22 20	
Mortimer	d	16 36		17 10	17 30			18 06		18 36		18 49			19 19	19 46		20 17	20 47			21 13	21 43	22 25	
Reading West	d	16 45		17 22	17 43			18 15		18 45		18 59			19 29	19 57		20 27	21 01			21 23	21 53	22 35	
Reading 7	a	16 49	17 05	17 25	17 46	17 55	18 07	18 20	18 38	18 49		19 04	19 06	19 11	19 33	20 00	20 06	20 30	21 04	21 07		21 26	21 56	22 40	22 50

		GW	GW
Basingstoke	d	22 38	23 23
Bramley (Hants)	d	22 45	23 30
Mortimer	d	22 50	23 35
Reading West	d	23 00	23 44
Reading 7	a	23 03	23 48

Saturdays
21 December to 16 May

		GW	XC	GW	XC	GW	XC	GW	XC	GW		XC	GW	XC	GW	GW	XC	GW	XC	GW		XC	GW	GW	XC
Basingstoke	d	00 05	05 40	06 35	06 51	07 01	07 26	07 31	07 51	08 01		08 20	08 31	08 51	09 01	09 31	09 51	10 05	10 20	10 40		10 51	11 01	11 31	11 51
Bramley (Hants)	d	00 12		06 42		07 08		07 38		08 08			08 38		09 08	09 38		10 12		10 47			11 08	11 38	
Mortimer	d	00 17		06 47		07 13		07 43		08 13			08 43		09 13	09 43		10 17		10 52			11 13	11 43	
Reading West	d	00 26		06 57		07 23		07 53		08 23			08 53		09 23	09 53		10 27		11 02			11 24	11 53	
Reading 7	a	00 30	06 00	07 00	07 08	07 26	07 41	07 57	08 08	08 26		08 37	08 56	09 09	09 27	09 56	10 08	10 31	10 37	11 05		11 09	11 27	11 56	12 08

		GW	XC	GW	XC	GW		GW	XC	GW	XC	GW	XC	GW	GW	XC		GW	XC	GW	XC	GW	GW	XC	GW
Basingstoke	d	12 01	12 20	12 31	12 51	13 06		13 31	13 51	14 07	14 20	14 31	14 51	15 01	15 31	15 51		16 01	16 20	16 31	16 51	17 01	17 31	17 51	18 01
Bramley (Hants)	d	12 08		12 38		13 13		13 38		14 14		14 38		15 08	15 38			16 08		16 38		17 08	17 38		18 08
Mortimer	d	12 13		12 43		13 18		13 43		14 19		14 43		15 13	15 43			16 13		16 43		17 13	17 43		18 13
Reading West	d	12 23		12 53		13 28		13 53		14 29		14 53		15 24	15 53			16 23		16 53		17 24	17 53		18 23
Reading 7	a	12 26	12 37	12 56	13 09	13 32		13 56	14 08	14 32	14 37	14 56	15 09	15 27	15 56	16 08		16 26	16 37	16 56	17 09	17 27	17 56	18 07	18 26

		XC		GW	XC	GW	GW	XC	GW	GW	XC	GW		GW		GW	GW
Basingstoke	d	18 20		18 31	18 51	19 01	19 31	19 51	20 01	20 31	20 51	21 01	and every 30 minutes until	22 31		23 00	23 40
Bramley (Hants)	d			18 38		19 08	19 38		20 08	20 38		21 08		22 38		23 07	23 47
Mortimer	d			18 43		19 13	19 43		20 13	20 43		21 13		22 43		23 12	23 52
Reading West	d			18 53		19 23	19 53		20 23	20 53		21 23		22 53		23 22	00 02
Reading 7	a	18 37		18 56	19 08	19 26	19 56	20 08	20 26	20 56	21 08	21 26		22 56		23 25	00 05

Sundays
15 December to 10 May

		GW A	GW	SW	GW	SW	XC	GW	SW	XC		GW	SW	XC	GW	SW	XC	GW	SW	XC		GW	SW	XC	GW
Basingstoke	d		08 07	08 28	09 07	09 28	09 51	10 07	10 28	10 51		11 07	11 28	11 51	12 07	12 28	12 51	13 07	13 28	13 51		14 07	14 28	14 51	15 07
Bramley (Hants)	d		08 14		09 14			10 14				11 14			12 14			13 14				14 14			15 14
Mortimer	d		08 18		09 19			10 18				11 18			12 18			13 18				14 18			15 18
Reading West	d	00 02	08 29		09 29			10 27				11 27			12 28			13 28				14 28			15 28
Reading 7	a	00 05	08 32	08 45	09 32	09 45	10 08	10 32	10 45	11 10		11 32	11 45	12 07	12 32	12 45	13 09	13 32	13 45	14 07		14 32	14 49	15 10	15 32

A not 15 December

Table T122-R

Sundays
15 December to 10 May

Basingstoke - Reading

		SW	XC	GW	SW	XC	GW	XC		GW	XC	GW	XC	GW	XC	GW	GW	GW
Basingstoke	d	15 28	15 51	16 07	16 28	16 51	17 07	17 51		18 07	18 51	19 07	19 51	20 07	20 51	21 07	22 07	23 07
Bramley (Hants)	d			16 14			17 14			18 14		19 14		20 14		21 14	22 14	23 14
Mortimer	d			16 18			17 18			18 18		19 18		20 18		21 18	22 18	23 18
Reading West	d			16 28			17 28			18 28		19 28		20 28		21 28	22 28	23 28
Reading 7	a	15 45	16 07	16 32	16 45	17 09	17 32	18 07		18 32	19 09	19 32	20 07	20 32	21 07	21 32	22 32	23 32

AVAILABLE FROM MP Middleton Press

Table T123-F

Mondays to Fridays

16 December to 15 May

Brighton, Portsmouth and Weymouth - Bristol, Cardiff, Gloucester and Great Malvern

Miles	Miles	Miles	Miles	Miles			GW	GW	GW	GW	GW	GW	GW	GW	GW		SW	GW	SW	GW	GW	GW	GW	GW	GW
									◇1 A ᴫ	◇1 ᴫ			◇ B	◇1 C ᴫ			◇1	◇ D	◇1 E			■	◇1 C ᴫ	◇	
—	—	0	—	—	Brighton 10	d																			
—	—	1½	—	—	Hove 2	d																			
—	—	6	—	—	Shoreham-by-Sea	d																			
—	—	10½	—	—	Worthing 4	d																			
—	—	22½	—	—	Barnham	d																			
—	—	28¾	—	—	**Chichester** 4	d																			
—	—	37½	—	—	Havant 30	d																			
0	—	—	—	—	**Portsmouth Harbour** ⛴	d																06 01			
0¾	—	—	—	—	Portsmouth & Southsea	d																06 05			
1¾	—	—	—	—	Fratton 3	d																06 09			
5½	—	41¾	—	—	Cosham	d																06 16			
11¼	—	47½	—	—	Fareham	a																06 24			
—	—	—	—	—		d																06 25			
25¾	—	62¼	—	—	**Southampton Central** 3 ⛴	d																06 47			
34	—	70¼	—	—	Romsey	d																07 00			
50½	—	86¾	—	—	**Salisbury** 3	a																07 18			
—	—	—	—	—		d					06 10						06 40					07 19			
70¼	—	106½	—	—	Warminster	d					06 29						07 02				07 28	07 38			
73½	—	109¾	—	—	Dilton Marsh	d					06x33										07x32	07x42			
—	0	—	0	—	**Weymouth**	d							05 28											06 44	
—	2½	—	2½	—	Upwey	d							05 33											06 49	
—	7	—	7	—	Dorchester West	d							05 41											06 57	
—	14¾	—	14¾	—	Maiden Newton	d							05 53											07 09	
—	21¼	—	21¼	—	Chetnole	d							06x01											07x17	
—	23¼	—	23¼	—	Yetminster	d							06x05											07x20	
—	24¼	—	24¼	—	Thornford	d							06x08											07x22	
—	27½	—	27½	—	Yeovil Pen Mill	d							06 18						06 55					07 32	
—	39¼	—	39¼	—	Castle Cary	a							06 31						07 08					07 45	
—	—	—	—	—		d							06 32	06 41					07 10				07 39	07 47	
—	42¾	—	42¾	—	Bruton	d							06 37						07 15					07 52	
—	53¼	—	53¼	—	Frome	d				06 12		06 42	06 50					←	07 27					08 04	
75	59	111¾	59	0	**Westbury** 2	a				06 22	06 38	06 51	07 07	07 00			07 10	07 07	07 36		07 37	07 47	07 58	08 13	
—	—	—	—	—		d	05 17	05 58	05 59	06 23	06 41	06 55	07 20	07 01	07 03		07 11	07 20		07 36	07 41	08 00	08 00	08 15	08 41
—	—	—	—	—	London Paddington 15 ⊖	a			07 35	08 01			→	08 36									09 19		
79	63	115¾	63	4	Trowbridge	d	05 23	06 04			06 47	07 02			07 09		07 17	07 27		07 42	07 47	08 06		08 22	08 47
82¼	66¼	118½	66¼	—	Bradford-on-Avon	d		06 10			06 53	07 08					07 23	07 33			07 53	08 12		08 28	08 53
83½	67¾	119¾	67¾	—	Avoncliff	d		06 13			06 56	07 11						07 36			07 56			08 31	08 56
84½	68½	120¾	68½	—	Freshford	d		06 16			06 59	07 14						07 38			07 59	08 17		08 33	08 59
91½	75¾	128	75¾	—	Bath Spa 7	a		06 27			07 13	07 24					07 36	07 49			08 09	08 28		08 44	09 09
—	—	—	—	9½	Melksham	d	05 33								07 19					07 52					
—	—	—	—	15¾	Chippenham	a	05 42								07 30					08 01					
—	—	—	—	32½	Swindon	a	05 59								07 47					08 19					
92½	76¾	129	76¾	—	Oldfield Park	a		06 30			07 17	07 28					07 40	07 52			08 13	08 32		08 47	09 13
98½	82¾	134¾	82¾	—	Keynsham	a		06 37			07 24	07 35					07 47	07 59			08 20	08 39		08 57	09 20
103	87¼	139½	87¼	—	**Bristol Temple Meads** 10	a		06 48			07 34	07 43					07 55	08 08			08 28	08 48		09 05	09 29
107½	91¾	144	91¾	—	Filton Abbey Wood	a		07 04			07 45	08 00						08 27			08 45	09 03			09 45
—	—	145½	93¾	—	Bristol Parkway	d					07 54										08 51				09 50
—	—	151¼	99½	—	Yate	d					08 03										09 00				09 59
—	—	162¼	110	—	Cam & Dursley	d					08 16										09 12				10 11
—	—	175¼	123	—	Gloucester	d					08a31				08 56						09 35				10a29
—	—	181¾	129½	—	Cheltenham Spa	d									09a05						09 46				
—	—	189	137	—	Ashchurch for Tewkesbury	d															09 54				
—	—	203¾	151½	—	Worcester Shrub Hill	d															10 13				
—	—	204½	152¼	—	Worcester Foregate Street	d															10 16				
—	—	211¼	159	—	Malvern Link	d															10 25				
—	—	212½	160¼	—	Great Malvern	a															10 27				
119½	119½	—	—	—	Severn Tunnel Jn	a		07 16																	
129½	113½	—	—	—	Newport (South Wales) 2	a		07 28				08 29										09 28			
141¼	125¼	—	—	—	**Cardiff Central** 7	a		07 42				08 45										09 45			

A From Bristol Temple Meads
B To Filton Abbey Wood
C From Plymouth
D From Weymouth
E To London Waterloo

For connections from Bristol Parkway and Cardiff Central to Swansea refer to Table T128

For connections from Castle Cary, Westbury and Bristol Temple Meads to Exeter and Plymouth refer to Table T135

For connections from Salisbury to Yeovil Junction and Exeter refer to Table T160

For connections from Bournemouth to Southampton Central, Weymouth and Upwey refer to Table T158

For additional bus connections between Yeovil Junction and Yeovil Pen Mill refer to Table T123A

Table T123-F

Mondays to Fridays

16 December to 15 May

Brighton, Portsmouth and Weymouth - Bristol, Cardiff, Gloucester and Great Malvern

		GW	GW	GW	GW	SW	GW	GW	GW	GW		GW	SW	SW	GW	GW	GW	GW	GW	GW		GW	GW	GW
		◇	◇1 A ᴫ	◇		◇1 B	◇		◇	◇1 C ᴫ		◇	◇1 D	◇1 E	◇ F ᴫ	◇		◇	◇1 G ᴫ	◇		◇	◇	
Brighton 10	d														09 00									
Hove 2	d														09 04									
Shoreham-by-Sea	d														09 13									
Worthing 4	d														09 22									
Barnham	d														09 38									
Chichester 4	d														09 46									
Havant 30	d														09 57									
Portsmouth Harbour ⛴	d	07 21					08 23					09 23				10 23				11 23			12 23	
Portsmouth & Southsea	d	07 25					08 27					09 27				10 27				11 27			12 27	
Fratton 3	d	07 29					08 31					09 31				10 31				11 31			12 31	
Cosham	d	07 37					08 39					09 39			10 05	10 39				11 39			12 39	
Fareham	a	07 44					08 46					09 46			10 12	10 46				11 46			12 46	
	d	07 45					08 47					09 47			10 15	10 47				11 47			12 47	
Southampton Central 3 ⛴	d	08 10		08 23			09 11					10 11			10 42	11 11				12 11		12 27	13 11	
Romsey	d	08 21		08 34			09 22					10 22			10 53	11 22				12 22		12 38	13 22	
Salisbury 3	a	08 39		08 52			09 40					10 40			11 11	11 40				12 40		12 56	13 40	
	d	08 41		09 03		09 24	09 42					10 42	10 52		11 12	11 42				12 42		13 07	13 42	
Warminster	d	09 00		09 22		09 44	10 01	10 12				11 01	11 12		11 32	12 01				13 01		13 26	14 01	
Dilton Marsh	d			09x26				10x16														13x30		
Weymouth	d								08 49									11 11						
Upwey	d								08 54									11 16						
Dorchester West	d								09 02									11 24						
Maiden Newton	d								09 14									11 40						
Chetnole	d								09x22									11x47						
Yetminster	d								09x25									11x50						
Thornford	d								09x27									11x53						
Yeovil Pen Mill	d								09 37					10 45				12 01						
Castle Cary	a								09 50					10 58				12 15						
	d		08 52						09 51	10 25				11 04				12 15	12 21					
Bruton	d								09 56					11 09				12 20						
Frome	d								10 15					11 21				12 32						
Westbury 2	a	09 08	09 11	09 31		09 52	10 09	10 20	10 24	10 44		11 09	11 20	11 30	11 40	12 09		12 41	12 47	13 09		13 35	14 09	
	d	09 10	09 13	09 40	09 45		10 11		10 37	10 45		11 11	11 21		11 41	12 11	12 16	12 42	12 48	13 11		13 41	14 11	14 16
London Paddington 15 ⊖	a		10 29							12 09									14 09					
Trowbridge	d	09 16		09 46	09 51		10 17		10 43			11 17	11 27		11 47	12 17	12 22	12 49		13 17		13 47	14 17	14 22
Bradford-on-Avon	d	09 22		09 52			10 23		10 49			11 23	11 33		11 53	12 23		12 56		13 23		13 53	14 23	
Avoncliff	d			09 56					10 52						11 56			12 59				13 56		
Freshford	d			09 59					10 55						11 59			13 01				13 59		
Bath Spa 7	a	09 34		10 09			10 35		11 05			11 35	11 45		12 09	12 35		13 14		13 35		14 09	14 35	
Melksham	d				10 01												12 32							14 32
Chippenham	a				10 10												12 41							14 41
Swindon	a				10 33												12 59							15 00
Oldfield Park	a			10 13					11 09				11 49		12 13			13 18				14 13		
Keynsham	a			10 20					11 16				11 56		12 20			13 25				14 20		
Bristol Temple Meads 10	a	09 51		10 29			10 51		11 29			11 50	12 05		12 30	12 49		13 35		13 51		14 29	14 49	
Filton Abbey Wood	a	10 03		10 45			11 04		11 44			12 03			12 46	13 04		13 45		14 04		14 45	15 04	
Bristol Parkway	d			10 50					11 50						12 50			13 50				14 51		
Yate	d			10 59					11 58						12 59			13 59				15 00		
Cam & Dursley	d			11 11					12 10						13 12			14 11				15 13		
Gloucester	d			11 37					12a27						13 36			14a27				15 36		
Cheltenham Spa	d			11 48											13 47							15 47		
Ashchurch for Tewkesbury	d			11 56											13 55							15 55		
Worcester Shrub Hill	d			12 14											14 13							16 14		
Worcester Foregate Street	d			12 17											14 16							16 17		
Malvern Link	d			12 26											14 25							16 26		
Great Malvern	a			12 28											14 29							16 28		
Severn Tunnel Jn	a																							
Newport (South Wales) 2	a	10 33					11 30					12 30				13 29				14 30			15 30	
Cardiff Central 7	a	10 47					11 46					12 44				13 43				14 46			15 44	

A From Paignton
B From London Waterloo to Yeovil Pen Mill
C From Plymouth
D From London Waterloo
E To London Waterloo
F ᴫ from Salisbury to Bristol Temple Meads
G From Paignton. ᴫ to Westbury

For connections from Bristol Parkway and Cardiff Central to Swansea refer to Table T128

For connections from Castle Cary, Westbury and Bristol Temple Meads to Exeter and Plymouth refer to Table T135

For connections from Salisbury to Yeovil Junction and Exeter refer to Table T160

For connections from Bournemouth to Southampton Central, Weymouth and Upwey refer to Table T158

For additional bus connections between Yeovil Junction and Yeovil Pen Mill refer to Table T123A

Table T123-F

Mondays to Fridays
16 December to 15 May

Brighton, Portsmouth and Weymouth - Bristol, Cardiff, Gloucester and Great Malvern

		SW ◇1 A	GW	GW ◇	GW ◇1 B 🍴	SW ◇1 C 🍴	GW	GW ◇	GW	SW ◇1 D	GW ◇1 E 🍴	GW ■	GW	GW ◇	GW ◇1 B 🍴	GW ■	SW ◇1 D	GW	GW ■	GW F	SW ◇1 A	GW G	GW
Brighton 10	d																						
Hove 2	d																						
Shoreham-by-Sea	d																						
Worthing 4	d																						
Barnham	d																						
Chichester 4	d																						
Havant 30	d																						
Portsmouth Harbour ⛴	d							13 23				14 23				15 23			16 23				
Portsmouth & Southsea	d							13 27				14 27				15 27			16 27				
Fratton 3	d							13 31				14 31				15 31			16 31				
Cosham	d							13 39				14 39				15 39			16 39				
Fareham	a							13 46				14 46				15 46			16 46				
	d							13 47				14 47				15 47			16 47				
Southampton Central 3 ⛴	d							14 11				15 11				16 10			17 11				
Romsey	d							14 22				15 22				16 22			17 22				
Salisbury 3	a							14 40				15 40				16 40			17 40				
	d	13 52				14 24		14 42				15 42				16 42			17 42		18 01		
Warminster	d	14 12				14 44		15 01	15 30			16 01				17 01		17 30	18 01	18 15	18 21		
Dilton Marsh	d								15x34									17x34		18x19			
Weymouth	d			13 12										14 55									
Upwey	d			13 17										15 00									
Dorchester West	d			13 25										15 08									
Maiden Newton	d			13 38										15 26									
Chetnole	d			13x45										15x34									
Yetminster	d			13x48										15x37									
Thornford	d			13x51										15x39									
Yeovil Pen Mill	d			13 59						15 02				15 49			16 53						
Castle Cary	a			14 13						15 13				16 02			17 06						
	d			14 13	14 24					15 14				16 06	16 23		17 07						
Bruton	d			14 18						15 19				16 11			17 12						
Frome	d			14 30			14 54			15 31				16 23			17 24					←	
Westbury 2	a	14 20		14 40	14 46	14 52	15 03	15 09	15 39	15 41		16 09		16 32	16 44	17 09	17 33	17 39	18 09	18 24	18 29	18 24	
	d	14 21	14 26	14 41	14 47			15 11	15 41		15 58	16 11	16 25	16 41	16 46	17 11		17 44	18 11	18 36	18 30	18 36	18 39
London Paddington 15 ⊖	a				16 11						17 12				18 09					→			
Trowbridge	d	14 27	14 32	14 48				15 17	15 47			16 17	16 31	16 47		17 17		17 50	18 17		18 36	18 42	18 45
Bradford-on-Avon	d	14 33	14 39	14 54				15 23	15 53			16 23		16 53		17 23		17 56	18 23		18 42	18 48	
Avoncliff	d		14 42	14 57					15 56					16 56				17 59				18 51	
Freshford	d		14 45	14 59					15 59					16 59				18 02				18 54	
Bath Spa 7	a	14 45	15 00	15 10				15 35	16 09			16 35		17 09		17 35		18 18	18 35		18 56	19 04	
Melksham	d												16 41										18 55
Chippenham	a												16 50										19 04
Swindon	a												17 07										19 21
Oldfield Park	a	14 49	15 04	15 14					16 13					17 13				18 21				19 08	
Keynsham	a	14 56	15 11	15 20					16 20					17 20				18 28				19 15	
Bristol Temple Meads 10	a	15 05	15 19	15 29				15 49	16 29			16 50		17 29		17 50		18 37	18 50		19 15	19 23	
Filton Abbey Wood	a		15 39	15 45				16 03	16 45			17 06		17 45		18 03		18 48	19 03			19 49	
Bristol Parkway	d			15 51					16 51					17 51				18 56				19a54	
Yate	d			16 00					17 00					18 00				19 05					
Cam & Dursley	d			16 12					17 12					18 12				19 17					
Gloucester	d			16a29					17 39					18a30				19 39					
Cheltenham Spa	d								17 50									19 50					
Ashchurch for Tewkesbury	d								17 58									19 58					
Worcester Shrub Hill	d								18 21									20 21					
Worcester Foregate Street	d								18a23									20 24					
Malvern Link	d																	20 36					
Great Malvern	a																	20 38					
Severn Tunnel Jn	a											17 19				18 20			19 19				
Newport (South Wales) 2	a							16 30				17 31				18 32			19 32				
Cardiff Central 7	a							16 44				17 45				18 46			19 47				

A From London Waterloo
B From Exeter St Davids
C From London Waterloo to Yeovil Pen Mill
D From Yeovil Junction to London Waterloo
E From Paignton. The Torbay Express
F To Bristol Parkway
G From Warminster

For connections from Bristol Parkway and Cardiff Central to Swansea refer to Table T128

For connections from Castle Cary, Westbury and Bristol Temple Meads to Exeter and Plymouth refer to Table T135

For connections from Salisbury to Yeovil Junction and Exeter refer to Table T160

For connections from Bournemouth to Southampton Central, Weymouth and Upwey refer to Table T158

For additional bus connections between Yeovil Junction and Yeovil Pen Mill refer to Table T123A

Table T123-F

Mondays to Fridays
16 December to 15 May

Brighton, Portsmouth and Weymouth - Bristol, Cardiff, Gloucester and Great Malvern

		GW ◇	GW ◇1 A 🍴	GW ◇	GW ◇	GW	GW ◇	SW ◇1 B	GW 1	SW ◇1 C	GW	GW ◇1 A 🍴	GW FX ◇	GW FO ◇	GW	SW ◇1 B	GW FO ◇	GW FX ◇	GW FO ◇	GW FX ◇	SW ◇1 D	GW
Brighton 10	d				17 02																	
Hove 2	d				17 06																	
Shoreham-by-Sea	d				17 12																	
Worthing 4	d				17 23																	
Barnham	d				17 39																	
Chichester 4	d				17 47																	
Havant 30	d				17 58																	
Portsmouth Harbour ⛴	d			17 23			18 24						19 23	19 23					20 23	20 23		
Portsmouth & Southsea	d			17 27			18 29						19 27	19 27					20 27	20 27		
Fratton 3	d			17 31			18 33						19 31	19 31					20 31	20 31		
Cosham	d			17 39	18 04		18 40						19 39	19 39								
Fareham	a			17 46	18 12		18 48						19 46	19 46					20 44	20 44		
	d			17 47	18 13		18 49						19 47	19 47					20 45	20 45		
Southampton Central 3 ⛴	d			18 10	18 43		19 11						20 10	20 10					21 11	21 11		21 22
Romsey	d			18 22	18 54		19 23						20 22	20 22					21 22	21 22		21 33
Salisbury 3	a			18 40	19 12		19 41						20 40	20 40					21 40	21 40		21 51
	d			18 42	19 13		19 42	18 23		19 58			20 42	20 42		20 57			21 42	21 42		21 56
Warminster	d			19 01	19 31		20 01			20 18			21 01	21 01		21 17			22 01	22 01		22 13
Dilton Marsh	d																					22x19
Weymouth	d	17 23															20 15	20 15				
Upwey	d	17 28															20 20	20 20				
Dorchester West	d	17 36															20 28	20 28				
Maiden Newton	d	17 48															20 40	20 40				
Chetnole	d	17x56															20x48	20x48				
Yetminster	d	17x59															20x51	20x51				
Thornford	d	18x01															20x53	20x53				
Yeovil Pen Mill	d	18 12						19 26									21 03	21 03				
Castle Cary	a	18 26						19 39									21 16	21 16				
	d	18 26	18 39					19 40				20 43					21 17	21 17			21 41	
Bruton	d	18 31						19 45									21 22	21 22			21 46	
Frome	d	18 43						19 57	20 15						21 06		21 34	21 34			21 58	
Westbury 2	a	18 52	18 58	19 09	19 39		20 10	20 15	20 25	20 30		21 04	21 09	21 09	21 15	21 25	21 44	21 44	22 09	22 09	22 12	22 24
	d	18 53	19 00	19 11	19 41	20 06	20 12				20 41	21 06	21 11	21 11		21 25	21 48	21 48	22 12	22 12		
London Paddington 15 ⊖	a		20 22									22 29										
Trowbridge	d	19 00		19 17	19 47	20 12	20 18				20 47		21 17	21 17		21 31	21 55	21 55	22 18	22 18		
Bradford-on-Avon	d	19 06		19 23	19 53		20 24				20 53		21 23	21 23		21 37	22 01	22 01	22 24	22 24		
Avoncliff	d	19 09									20 56						22 04	22 04				
Freshford	d	19 11									20 59						22 06	22 06				
Bath Spa 7	a	19 30		19 35	20 05		20 36				21 09		21 35	21 35		21 50	22 17	22 17	22 36	22 36		
Melksham	d					20 22																
Chippenham	a					20 31																
Swindon	a					20 49																
Oldfield Park	a	19 33			20 09						21 13						22 21	22 21				
Keynsham	a	19 40			20 16						21 20					21 58	22 28	22 28				
Bristol Temple Meads 10	a	19 49		19 53	20 25		20 50				21 29		21 51	21 51		22 06	22 36	22 36	22 50	22 50		
Filton Abbey Wood	a			20 04	20 50		21 04				21 48		22 02	22 02				22 52	23 04	23 04		
Bristol Parkway	d				20a56						21a53							23 00				
Yate	d																	23 08				
Cam & Dursley	d																	23 20				
Gloucester	d					21 56												23a38				
Cheltenham Spa	d					22a05																
Ashchurch for Tewkesbury	d																					
Worcester Shrub Hill	d																					
Worcester Foregate Street	d																					
Malvern Link	d																					
Great Malvern	a																					
Severn Tunnel Jn	a			20 20			21 19						22 18	22 19					23 20	23 20		
Newport (South Wales) 2	a			20 31			21 31						22 38	22 32					23 31	23 37		
Cardiff Central 7	a			20 45			21 45						22 58	22 46					23 45	23 57		

A From Plymouth
B From London Waterloo
C To Castle Cary
D To Salisbury

For connections from Bristol Parkway and Cardiff Central to Swansea refer to Table T128

For connections from Castle Cary, Westbury and Bristol Temple Meads to Exeter and Plymouth refer to Table T135

For connections from Salisbury to Yeovil Junction and Exeter refer to Table T160

For connections from Bournemouth to Southampton Central, Weymouth and Upwey refer to Table T158

For additional bus connections between Yeovil Junction and Yeovil Pen Mill refer to Table T123A

Table T123-F

Mondays to Fridays

16 December to 15 May

Brighton, Portsmouth and Weymouth - Bristol, Cardiff, Gloucester and Great Malvern

Station		GW	GW FX	GW FO
Brighton 10	d			
Hove 2	d			
Shoreham-by-Sea	d			
Worthing 4	d			
Barnham	d			
Chichester 4	d			
Havant 30	d			
Portsmouth Harbour ⛴	d		21 23	21 23
Portsmouth & Southsea	d		21 27	21 27
Fratton 3	d		21 31	21 31
Cosham	d			
Fareham	a		21 44	21 44
	d		21 47	21 47
Southampton Central 8 ⛴	d		22 22	22 22
Romsey	d		22 35	22 35
Salisbury 8	a		22 53	22 53
	d		22 59	22 59
Warminster	d		23 19	23 19
Dilton Marsh	d		23x23	23x23
Weymouth	d			
Upwey	d			
Dorchester West	d			
Maiden Newton	d			
Chetnole	d			
Yetminster	d			
Thornford	d			
Yeovil Pen Mill	d			
Castle Cary	a			
	d			
Bruton	d			
Frome	d			
Westbury 2	a		23 29	23 29
	d	22 41	23 34	23 34
London Paddington 15 ⊖	a			
Trowbridge	d	22 47	23 40	23 40
Bradford-on-Avon	d	22 53	23 46	23 46
Avoncliff	d	22 56		
Freshford	d	22 59		
Bath Spa 7	a	23 09	00 01	00 02
Melksham	d			
Chippenham	a			
Swindon	a			
Oldfield Park	a	23 13		
Keynsham	a	23 20		
Bristol Temple Meads 10	a	23 29	00 15	00 15
Filton Abbey Wood	a			
Bristol Parkway	d			
Yate	d			
Cam & Dursley	d			
Gloucester	d			
Cheltenham Spa	d			
Ashchurch for Tewkesbury	d			
Worcester Shrub Hill	d			
Worcester Foregate Street	d			
Malvern Link	d			
Great Malvern	a			
Severn Tunnel Jn	a			
Newport (South Wales) 2	a			
Cardiff Central 7	a			

For connections from Bristol Parkway and Cardiff Central to Swansea refer to Table T128

For connections from Castle Cary, Westbury and Bristol Temple Meads to Exeter and Plymouth refer to Table T135

For connections from Salisbury to Yeovil Junction and Exeter refer to Table T160

For connections from Bournemouth to Southampton Central, Weymouth and Upwey refer to Table T158

For additional bus connections between Yeovil Junction and Yeovil Pen Mill refer to Table T123A

Table T123-F

Saturdays

21 December to 16 May

Brighton, Portsmouth and Weymouth - Bristol, Cardiff, Gloucester and Great Malvern

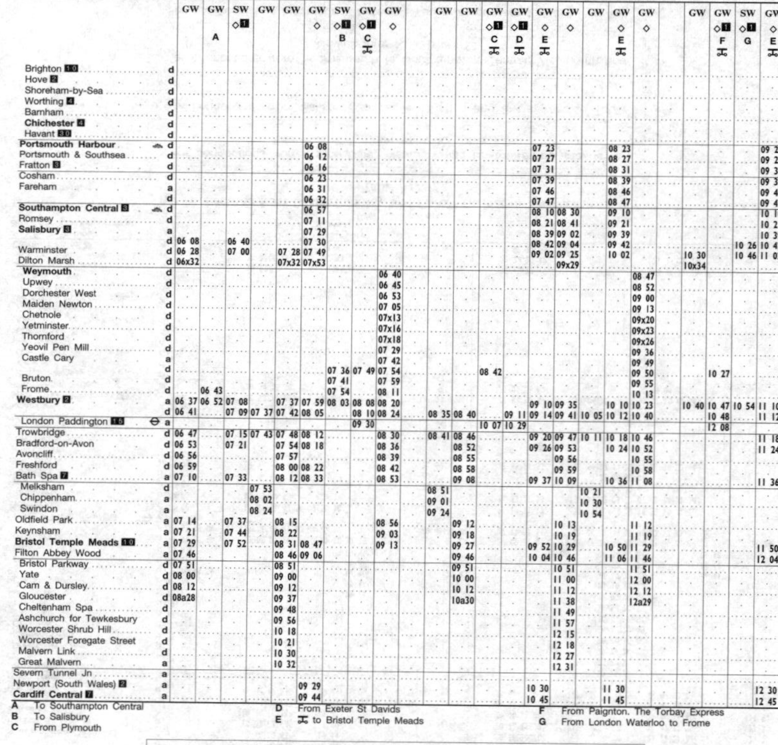

Station		GW	GW A	SW ◇1	GW	GW	GW ◇	SW ◇1 B	GW ◇1 C ⌶	GW ◇	GW	GW	GW ◇1 C ⌶	GW ◇1 D ⌶	GW ◇ E ⌶	GW ◇	GW	GW ◇ E ⌶	GW ◇	GW	GW ◇1 F ⌶	SW ◇1 G	GW ◇ E ⌶
Brighton 10	d																						
Hove 2	d																						
Shoreham-by-Sea	d																						
Worthing 4	d																						
Barnham	d																						
Chichester 4	d																						
Havant 30	d																						
Portsmouth Harbour ⛴	d						06 08								07 23			08 23					09 23
Portsmouth & Southsea	d						06 12								07 27			08 27					09 27
Fratton 3	d						06 16								07 31			08 31					09 31
Cosham	d						06 23								07 39			08 39					09 39
Fareham	a						06 31								07 46			08 46					09 46
	d						06 32								07 47			08 47					09 47
Southampton Central 8 ⛴	d						06 57								08 10	08 30		09 10					10 10
Romsey	d						07 11								08 21	08 41		09 21					10 21
Salisbury 8	a						07 29								08 39	09 02		09 39					10 39
	d	06 08		06 40			07 30								08 42	09 04		09 42				10 26	10 42
Warminster	d	06 28		07 00		07 28	07 49								09 02	09 25		10 02		10 30		10 46	11 02
Dilton Marsh	d	06x32				07x32	07x53									09x29				10x34			
Weymouth	d									06 40									08 47				
Upwey	d									06 45									08 52				
Dorchester West	d									06 53									09 00				
Maiden Newton	d									07 05									09 13				
Chetnole	d									07x13									09x20				
Yetminster	d									07x16									09x23				
Thornford	d									07x18									09x26				
Yeovil Pen Mill	d									07 29									09 36				
Castle Cary	a									07 42									09 49				
	d							07 36	07 49	07 54			08 42						09 50		10 27		
Bruton	d							07 41		07 59									09 55				
Frome	d		06 43					07 54		08 11									10 13				
Westbury 2	a	06 37	06 52	07 08		07 37	07 59	08 03	08 08	08 20					09 10	09 35		10 10	10 23	10 40	10 47	10 54	11 10
	d	06 41		07 09	07 37	07 42	08 05		08 10	08 24	08 35	08 40		09 11	09 14	09 41	10 05	10 12	10 40		10 48		11 12
London Paddington 15 ⊖	a								09 30				10 07	10 29							12 08		
Trowbridge	d	06 47		07 15	07 43	07 48	08 12			08 30	08 41	08 46			09 20	09 47	10 11	10 18	10 46				11 18
Bradford-on-Avon	d	06 53		07 21		07 54	08 18			08 36		08 52			09 26	09 53		10 24	10 52				11 24
Avoncliff	d	06 56				07 57				08 39		08 55				09 56			10 55				
Freshford	d	06 59				08 00	08 22			08 42		08 58				09 59			10 58				
Bath Spa 7	a	07 10		07 33		08 12	08 33			08 53		09 08			09 37	10 09		10 36	11 08				11 36
Melksham	d				07 53						08 51						10 21						
Chippenham	a				08 02						09 01						10 30						
Swindon	a				08 24						09 24						10 54						
Oldfield Park	a	07 14		07 37		08 15				08 56		09 12				10 13			11 12				
Keynsham	a	07 21		07 44		08 22				09 03		09 18				10 19			11 19				
Bristol Temple Meads 10	a	07 29		07 52		08 31	08 47			09 13		09 27			09 52	10 29		10 50	11 29				11 50
Filton Abbey Wood	a	07 46				08 46	09 06					09 46			10 04	10 46		11 06	11 46				12 04
Bristol Parkway	d	07 51				08 51						09 51				10 51			11 51				
Yate	d	08 00				09 00						10 00				11 00			12 00				
Cam & Dursley	d	08 12				09 12						10 12				11 12			12 12				
Gloucester	d	08a28				09 37						10a30				11 38			12a29				
Cheltenham Spa	d					09 48										11 49							
Ashchurch for Tewkesbury	d					09 56										11 57							
Worcester Shrub Hill	d					10 18										12 15							
Worcester Foregate Street	d					10 21										12 18							
Malvern Link	d					10 30										12 27							
Great Malvern	a					10 32										12 31							
Severn Tunnel Jn	a																						
Newport (South Wales) 2	a						09 29								10 30			11 30					12 30
Cardiff Central 7	a						09 44								10 45			11 45					12 45

A To Southampton Central
B To Salisbury
C From Plymouth
D From Exeter St Davids
E ⌶ to Bristol Temple Meads
F From Paignton. The Torbay Express
G From London Waterloo to Frome

For connections from Bristol Parkway and Cardiff Central to Swansea refer to Table T128

For connections from Castle Cary, Westbury and Bristol Temple Meads to Exeter and Plymouth refer to Table T135

For connections from Salisbury to Yeovil Junction and Exeter refer to Table T160

For connections from Bournemouth to Southampton Central, Weymouth and Upwey refer to Table T158

For additional bus connections between Yeovil Junction and Yeovil Pen Mill refer to Table T123A

Table T123-F

Saturdays

21 December to 16 May

Brighton, Portsmouth and Weymouth - Bristol, Cardiff, Gloucester and Great Malvern

		SW A	SW ◇1 B	GW ◇	GW	GW ◇ C		GW ◇	GW ◇1 D	GW ◇	GW ◇	SW 1	GW	GW ◇	SW ◇1 A	GW ◇	GW ◇1 D	GW	GW E	GW ◇	GW	GW ◇	GW	GW ◇	GW ◇1 D
Brighton 10	d			09 00																					
Hove 2	d			09 04																					
Shoreham-by-Sea	d			09 13																					
Worthing 4	d			09 23																					
Barnham	d			09 43																					
Chichester 4	d			09 51																					
Havant 10	d			10 03																					
Portsmouth Harbour ⛴	d					10 23				11 23				12 23						13 23		14 23			
Portsmouth & Southsea	d					10 27				11 27				12 27						13 27		14 27			
Fratton 3	d					10 31				11 31				12 31						13 31		14 31			
Cosham	d			10 11		10 39				11 39				12 39						13 39		14 39			
Fareham	a			10 19		10 46				11 46				12 46						13 46		14 46			
	d			10 20		10 47				11 47				12 47						13 47		14 47			
Southampton Central 8 ⛴	d			10 42		11 10				12 10	12 27			13 10						14 10		15 10			
Romsey	d			10 54		11 21				12 21	12 38			13 21						14 21		15 21			
Salisbury 8	a			11 12		11 39				12 39	12 59			13 39						14 39		15 39			
	d	10 52		11 13		11 42				12 42	13 07			13 42	13 52					14 42		15 42			
Warminster	d	11 12		11 32		12 02				13 02	13 27			14 02	14 12					15 02	15 30	16 02			
Dilton Marsh	d										13x31										15x34				
Weymouth	d							11 10				12 10				13 10								14 55	
Upwey	d							11 15				12 15				13 15								15 00	
Dorchester West	d							11 23				12 23				13 23								15 08	
Maiden Newton	d							11 36				12 34				13 36								15 21	
Chetnole	d							11x43								13x43								15x28	
Yetminster	d							11x46								13x46								15x31	
Thornford	d							11x49								13x49								15x34	
Yeovil Pen Mill	d							11 58				12 50				13 58								15 43	
Castle Cary	a							12 12								14 12								15 57	
	d							12 13	12 28							14 13	14 28							16 06	16 28
Bruton	d							12 18								14 19								16 12	
Frome	d		11 30					12 30								14 31			14 58					16 26	
Westbury 2	a	11 20	11 39	11 40		12 10		12 40	12 48	13 10	13 36			14 10	14 20	14 40	14 47		15 07	15 10	15 39	16 10		16 36	16 47
	d	11 21		11 41	12 05	12 12		12 42	12 49	13 12	13 41		14 07	14 12	14 21	14 41	14 48	15 00		15 12	15 40	16 12	16 32	16 41	16 48
London Paddington 15 ⊖	a								14 09								16 08								18 09
Trowbridge	d	11 27		11 48	12 11	12 18		12 49		13 18	13 47		14 13	14 18	14 27	14 47		15 06		15 18	15 46	16 18	16 38	16 47	
Bradford-on-Avon	d	11 33		11 54		12 24		12 55		13 24	13 53			14 24	14 33	14 53				15 24	15 52	16 24		16 53	
Avoncliff	d			11 57				12 58			13 56					14 56					15 55			16 56	
Freshford	d			11 59				13 00			13 59					14 59					15 58			16 59	
Bath Spa 7	a	11 52		12 10		12 36		13 11		13 36	14 09			14 36	14 51	15 09				15 36	16 08	16 36		17 09	
Melksham	d				12 21								14 23					15 16					16 48		
Chippenham	a				12 30								14 32					15 27					17 00		
Swindon	a				12 48								14 54					15 48					17 24		
Oldfield Park	a	11 56		12 14				13 14			14 13				14 55	15 13					16 12			17 13	
Keynsham	a	12 03		12 21				13 21			14 19				15 02	15 19					16 19			17 19	
Bristol Temple Meads 10	a	12 12		12 29		12 53		13 30		13 50	14 29			14 50	15 10	15 29				15 50	16 28	16 50		17 29	
Filton Abbey Wood	a			12 46		13 06		13 46		14 04	14 46			15 06		15 46				16 04	16 46	17 06		17 46	
Bristol Parkway	d			12 51				13 51			14 51					15 51					16 51			17 51	
Yate	d			13 00				14 00			15 00					16 00					17 00			18 00	
Cam & Dursley	d			13 12				14 12			15 12					16 12					17 12			18 12	
Gloucester	d			13 38				14a30			15 37					16a28					17 38			18a30	
Cheltenham Spa	d			13 49							15 48										17 49				
Ashchurch for Tewkesbury	d			13 57							15 56										17 57				
Worcester Shrub Hill	d			14 14							16 14										18 16				
Worcester Foregate Street	d			14 17							16 18										18a18				
Malvern Link	d			14 26							16 28														
Great Malvern	a			14 30							16 32														
Severn Tunnel Jn	a																					17 19			
Newport (South Wales) 2	a					13 30				14 30				15 30						16 30		17 31			
Cardiff Central 7	a					13 45				14 45				15 46						16 46		17 46			

A From London Waterloo
B To Salisbury
C to Bristol Temple Meads
D From Exeter St Davids
E To Warminster

For connections from Bristol Parkway and Cardiff Central to Swansea refer to Table T128

For connections from Castle Cary, Westbury and Bristol Temple Meads to Exeter and Plymouth refer to Table T135

For connections from Salisbury to Yeovil Junction and Exeter refer to Table T160

For connections from Bournemouth to Southampton Central, Weymouth and Upwey refer to Table T158

For additional bus connections between Yeovil Junction and Yeovil Pen Mill refer to Table T123A

Table T123-F

Saturdays

21 December to 16 May

Brighton, Portsmouth and Weymouth - Bristol, Cardiff, Gloucester and Great Malvern

		GW ◇	SW 1	GW	GW ◇	SW ◇1 A	GW	GW	GW ◇	GW ◇1 B	GW ◇	GW ◇		SW ◇1 C	GW ◇	GW ◇1 D	GW	GW	GW ◇	SW ◇1 A	GW	GW ◇		GW	GW 1
Brighton 10	d											17 00													
Hove 2	d											17 04													
Shoreham-by-Sea	d											17 13													
Worthing 4	d											17 23													
Barnham	d											17 42													
Chichester 4	d											17 50													
Havant 10	d											18 05													
Portsmouth Harbour ⛴	d	15 23			16 23						17 23				18 23				19 23			20 23			21 23
Portsmouth & Southsea	d	15 27			16 27						17 27				18 27				19 27			20 27			21 27
Fratton 3	d	15 31			16 31						17 31				18 31				19 31			20 31			21 31
Cosham	d	15 39			16 39						17 39	18 12			18 39				19 39						
Fareham	a	15 46			16 46						17 46	18 20			18 46				19 46			20 45			21 44
	d	15 47			16 47						17 47	18 21			18 47				19 47			20 47			21 45
Southampton Central 8 ⛴	d	16 10			17 10						18 10	18 45			19 10				20 10			21 12		21 32	22 24
Romsey	d	16 21			17 21						18 21	18 56			19 21				20 21			21 23		21 43	22 36
Salisbury 8	a	16 39			17 39						18 39	19 14			19 39				20 39			21 41		22 01	22 55
	d	16 42			17 42	17 56					18 42	19 15		19 27	19 42				20 42	20 57		21 42		22 04	22 58
Warminster	d	17 02		17 30	18 02	18 16					19 02	19 35		19 46	20 02				21 02	21 17		22 03		22 24	23 18
Dilton Marsh	d			17x34								19x39												22x28	23x22
Weymouth	d		16 54						17 28												20 20				
Upwey	d		16 59						17 33												20 25				
Dorchester West	d		17 07						17 41												20 33				
Maiden Newton	d		17 18						17 54												20 46				
Chetnole	d								18x01												20x53				
Yetminster	d								18x04												20x56				
Thornford	d								18x07												20x59				
Yeovil Pen Mill	d		17 34						18 16												21 08				
Castle Cary	a								18 30												21 22				
	d								18 30	18 44						20 06					21 22				
Bruton	d								18 36												21 28				
Frome	d								18 49									20 52			21 40				
Westbury 2	a	17 10		17 39	18 11	18 24			18 58	19 03	19 10	19 44		19 54	20 11	20 25		21 02	21 10	21 25	21 49	22 11		22 34	23 29
	d	17 12		17 41	18 12	18 25	18 35	18 41	18 59	19 06	19 12	19 45			20 12	20 27	20 41		21 12	21 25	21 50	22 12		22 41	
London Paddington 15 ⊖	a									20 27						21 44									
Trowbridge	d	17 18		17 47	18 18	18 31	18 41	18 47	19 05		19 18	19 52			20 18		20 47		21 18	21 31	21 56	22 18		22 47	
Bradford-on-Avon	d	17 24		17 53	18 24	18 37		18 53	19 11		19 24	19 58			20 24		20 53		21 24	21 37	22 02	22 24		22 53	
Avoncliff	d			17 56				18 56	19 14								20 56				22 05			22 56	
Freshford	d			17 59				18 59	19 17								20 59				22 08			22 59	
Bath Spa 7	a	17 36		18 09	18 36	18 52		19 09	19 28		19 36	20 10			20 36		21 10		21 36	21 52	22 18	22 36		23 10	
Melksham	d						18 51																		
Chippenham	a						19 00																		
Swindon	a						19 24																		
Oldfield Park	a			18 13		18 56		19 13	19 32			20 14					21 14				22 22			23 14	
Keynsham	a			18 19		19 03		19 19	19 39			20 21					21 21			22 00	22 29			23 21	
Bristol Temple Meads 10	a	17 50		18 30	18 50	19 12		19 28	19 49		19 51	20 31			20 50		21 30		21 51	22 08	22 39	22 50		23 30	
Filton Abbey Wood	a	18 04		18 46	19 04			19 46			20 04				21 04				22 07			23 02			
Bristol Parkway	d			18 51				19 51																	
Yate	d			19 00				20 00																	
Cam & Dursley	d			19 12				20 12																	
Gloucester	d			19 38				20 36																	
Cheltenham Spa	d			19 50				20a46																	
Ashchurch for Tewkesbury	d			19 58																					
Worcester Shrub Hill	d			20 19																					
Worcester Foregate Street	d			20 22																					
Malvern Link	d			20 31																					
Great Malvern	a			20 33																					
Severn Tunnel Jn	a	18 19			19 19						20 20				21 20				22 23			23 17			
Newport (South Wales) 2	a	18 31			19 31						20 31				21 31				22 40			23 35			
Cardiff Central 7	a	18 46			19 47						20 46				21 46				23 00			23 55			

A From London Waterloo
B From Plymouth
C From London Waterloo to Yeovil Junction
D From Penzance

For connections from Bristol Parkway and Cardiff Central to Swansea refer to Table T128

For connections from Castle Cary, Westbury and Bristol Temple Meads to Exeter and Plymouth refer to Table T135

For connections from Salisbury to Yeovil Junction and Exeter refer to Table T160

For connections from Bournemouth to Southampton Central, Weymouth and Upwey refer to Table T158

For additional bus connections between Yeovil Junction and Yeovil Pen Mill refer to Table T123A

Table T123-F

Sundays

15 December to 10 May

Brighton, Portsmouth and Weymouth - Bristol, Cardiff, Gloucester and Great Malvern

Station		GW	GW	GW	GW	GW	GW	SW	GW	GW		GW	GW	SW	GW	GW	GW	GW	GW	SW		GW	GW	GW	GW
			◇ A	◇ B	◇ C	◇ D	◇1 E ✠	◇1 F		◇1 G ✠		■	◇1 G ✠	◇1 H		◇1 I ✠	◇	◇	◇	◇1 H		◇1 E ✠		◇	◇
Brighton 10	d																		11 10						
Hove 2	d																		11 14						
Shoreham-by-Sea	d																		11 21						
Worthing 4	d																		11 31						
Barnham	d																		11 56						
Chichester 4	d																		12 04						
Havant 30	d																		12 15						
Portsmouth Harbour ⛴	d											09 08						11 08						13 08	
Portsmouth & Southsea	d											09 12						11 12						13 12	
Fratton 3	d											09 16						11 15						13 16	
Cosham	d											09 23						11 23	12 25					13 23	
Fareham	a											09 31						11 31	12 33					13 31	
	d											09 32						11 32	12 34					13 32	
Southampton Central 3 ⛴	d											09 56						11 57	12 56					13 57	
Romsey	d											10 08						12 08	13 07					14 08	
Salisbury 3	a											10 24						12 26	13 25					14 26	
	d											10 26		10 55				12 27	13 25	13 55				14 27	
Warminster	d	08 11										10 51		11 15				12 44	13 44	14 15				14 44	
Dilton Marsh	d	08x16										10x56												14x50	
Weymouth	d				08 07												11 00								14 08
Upwey	d																11 05								14 13
Dorchester West	d				08 19												11 13								14 21
Maiden Newton	d				08 31												11 27								14 33
Chetnole	d				08 40												11x35								14x41
Yetminster	d				08 43												11x38								14x44
Thornford	d				08 45												11x40								14x46
Yeovil Pen Mill	d				08 54			09 57									11 50								15 00
Castle Cary	a				09 07			10 10									12 02								15 13
	d				09 08		09 21	10 12		10 21						12 09	12 13					14 24			15 14
Bruton	d				09 13			10 17									12 18								15 19
Frome	d				09 25	09 27		10 30							11 30		12 30								15 31
Westbury 2	a	08 19			09 34	09 36	09 41	10 39		10 43		11 00		11 23	11 39	12 29	12 39	12 54	13 58	14 23		14 42		14 56	15 40
	d	08 20	08 48	08 48	09 46	09 46	09 48		10 44	10 44		11 01	11 12	11 24	11 40	12 30	12 41	13 00	13 58	14 24		14 45	14 50	15 00	15 41
London Paddington 15 ⊖	a						11 08			12 06			12 23			13 53						16 06			
Trowbridge	d	08 26	08 54	08 54	09 52	09 52			10 49			11 07		11 30	11 46		12 47	13 07	14 05	14 30			14 55	15 06	15 47
Bradford-on-Avon	d		09 00	09 00	09 58	09 58						11 13		11 36	11 52			13 13	14 11	14 36				15 12	15 53
Avoncliff	d		09 04	09 04	10 01	10 01									11 56				14 14						15 56
Freshford	d		09 07	09 07	10 04	10 04									11 59				14 16						15 59
Bath Spa 7	a		09 17	09 17	10 15	10 15						11 28		11 52	12 09			13 27	14 27	14 54				15 24	16 09
Melksham	d	08 37							11 00								12 56						15 06		
Chippenham	a	08 46							11 09								13 05						15 17		
Swindon	a	09 03							11 28								13 23						15 34		
Oldfield Park	a		09 21	09 21	10 18	10 18						11 31		11 56	12 13			13 30	14 30	14 58				15 30	16 12
Keynsham	a		09 28	09 28	10 25	10 25						11 38		12 03	12 20			13 37	14 38	15 05				15 37	16 20
Bristol Temple Meads 10	a		09 39	09 39	10 36	10 36						11 48		12 11	12 29			13 45	14 47	15 13				15 46	16 29
Filton Abbey Wood	a		09 51	09 57	10 50	10 50						12 02						14 00	15 01					16 04	
Bristol Parkway	d																								
Yate	d																								
Cam & Dursley	d																								
Gloucester	d																								
Cheltenham Spa	d																								
Ashchurch for Tewkesbury	d																								
Worcester Shrub Hill	d																								
Worcester Foregate Street	d																								
Malvern Link	d																								
Great Malvern	a																								
Severn Tunnel Jn	a		10 10	10 13	11 02	11 02						12 20						14 14	15 14					16 18	
Newport (South Wales) 2	a		10 21	10 24	11 13	11 13						12 32						14 26	15 29					16 29	
Cardiff Central 7	a		10 35	10 38	11 28	11 28						12 45						14 42	15 42					16 44	

A from 12 January
B until 5 January
C from 5 April
D until 29 March
E From Exeter St Davids
F From Yeovil Junction to Salisbury
G From Plymouth
H From London Waterloo
I From Paignton

For connections from Bristol Parkway and Cardiff Central to Swansea refer to Table T128

For connections from Castle Cary, Westbury and Bristol Temple Meads to Exeter and Plymouth refer to Table T135

For connections from Salisbury to Yeovil Junction and Exeter refer to Table T160

For connections from Bournemouth to Southampton Central, Weymouth and Upwey refer to Table T158

For additional bus connections between Yeovil Junction and Yeovil Pen Mill refer to Table T123A

Table T123-F

Sundays

15 December to 10 May

Brighton, Portsmouth and Weymouth - Bristol, Cardiff, Gloucester and Great Malvern

Station		GW	GW	GW	GW	GW		SW	GW	GW	GW	SW	GW	GW	GW	SW		GW	GW	GW	SW	GW	GW	GW	GW	GW		GW
		◇	◇1 A ✠		■	◇		◇1 B	◇	◇		◇1 C	◇1 A ✠	◇	◇	◇1 D		◇1 E ✠	◇		◇1 F	◇	◇		◇	◇1 G ✠		
Brighton 10	d									15 47												17 46						
Hove 2	d									15 51												17 50						
Shoreham-by-Sea	d									15 57												17 56						
Worthing 4	d									16 09												18 08						
Barnham	d									16 27												18 27						
Chichester 4	d									16 35												18 35						
Havant 30	d									16 44												18 50						
Portsmouth Harbour ⛴	d	14 08			15 08				16 08					17 08					18 08				19 08		20 08			22 05
Portsmouth & Southsea	d	14 12			15 12				16 12					17 12					18 12				19 12		20 12			22 12
Fratton 3	d	14 16			15 16				16 16					17 16					18 16				19 16		20 16			22 16
Cosham	d	14 23			15 23				16 23	16 51				17 23					18 23			18 57	19 23					
Fareham	a	14 31			15 31				16 31	16 59				17 31					18 31			19 04	19 31		20 31			22 31
	d	14 32			15 32				16 32	16 59				17 32					18 32			19 05	19 32		20 32			22 32
Southampton Central 3 ⛴	d	14 57			15 57				16 57	17 22				17 57					18 57			19 28	19 57		20 56			22 57
Romsey	d	15 08			16 08				17 08	17 39				18 08					19 08			19 40	20 08		21 08			23 08
Salisbury 3	a	15 26			16 26				17 26	17 57				18 26					19 26			19 58	20 26		21 26			23 26
	d	15 27			16 27			17 16	17 27	17 58				18 28		19 21			19 27		19 55	20 01	20 27		21 27			23 27
Warminster	d	15 48			16 44			17 36	17 44	18 18				18 48		19 41			19 50		20 15	20 22	20 44		21 44			23 48
Dilton Marsh	d	15x50			16x50					18x23												20x27			21x53			23x53
Weymouth	d					16 10									17 56									20 09				
Upwey	d					16 15									18 01									20 14				
Dorchester West	d					16 23									18 09									20 22				
Maiden Newton	d					16 35									18 21									20 34				
Chetnole	d					16x43									18x29									20x42				
Yetminster	d					16x46									18x32									20x45				
Thornford	d					16x48									18x34									20x47				
Yeovil Pen Mill	d					16 58									18 44									20 57				
Castle Cary	a					17 10									18 56									21 09				
	d		16 24			17 13							18 24		19 05									21 10		21 37		
Bruton	d					17 18									19 11									21 16				
Frome	d					17 30						18 33			19 23									21 28				
Westbury 2	a	15 56	16 42		16 56	17 39		17 44	17 57	18 26		18 42	18 45	18 56	19 32	19 49			19 59		20 23	20 31	20 56	21 38	21 55	21 56		23 57
	d	16 04	16 45	16 50	17 00	17 40			18 01	18 28	18 35		18 47	18 59	19 32			19 54	20 00	20 18	20 23	20 32	21 02	21 39	21 58	21 58		
London Paddington 15 ⊖	a		18 06										20 07					21 10								23 35		
Trowbridge	d	16 10		16 55	17 06	17 47			18 07	18 34	18 41			19 04	19 38				20 06	20 23	20 29	20 39	21 06	21 46	22 05			
Bradford-on-Avon	d	16 16			17 12	17 53			18 13	18 40				19 10	19 44				20 12		20 35	20 45	21 12	21 52	22 11			
Avoncliff	d								18 16						19 47							20 48		21 55				
Freshford	d								18 19						19 50							20 50		21 58				
Bath Spa 7	a	16 28			17 27	18 03			18 30	18 51				19 25	20 01				20 26		20 52	21 01	21 25	22 08	22 24			
Melksham	d			17 06							18 51									20 34								
Chippenham	a			17 17							19 00									20 43								
Swindon	a			17 34							19 17									21 00								
Oldfield Park	a				17 31	18 08				18 56					20 04							21 05		22 12				
Keynsham	a				17 38	18 16				19 03					20 11						21 00	21 11		22 19				
Bristol Temple Meads 10	a	16 41			17 46	18 26			18 44	19 12				19 39	20 22				20 41		21 08	21 20	21 40	22 30	22 38			
Filton Abbey Wood	a	16 57			18 01				19 01					19 49					20 52				21 50		22 51			
Bristol Parkway	d																											
Yate	d																											
Cam & Dursley	d																											
Gloucester	d																											
Cheltenham Spa	d																											
Ashchurch for Tewkesbury	d																											
Worcester Shrub Hill	d																											
Worcester Foregate Street	d																											
Malvern Link	d																											
Great Malvern	a																											
Severn Tunnel Jn	a	17 18			18 17				19 18					20 02					21 05				22 07		23 04			
Newport (South Wales) 2	a	17 31			18 29				19 29					20 13					21 18				22 18		23 16			
Cardiff Central 7	a	17 45			18 43				19 43					20 29					21 31				22 33		23 29			

A From Exeter St Davids
B From Reading to Frome
C To Salisbury
D From London Waterloo to Yeovil Pen Mill
E From Plymouth
F From London Waterloo
G From Penzance

For connections from Bristol Parkway and Cardiff Central to Swansea refer to Table T128

For connections from Castle Cary, Westbury and Bristol Temple Meads to Exeter and Plymouth refer to Table T135

For connections from Salisbury to Yeovil Junction and Exeter refer to Table T160

For connections from Bournemouth to Southampton Central, Weymouth and Upwey refer to Table T158

For additional bus connections between Yeovil Junction and Yeovil Pen Mill refer to Table T123A

Table T123-R

Mondays to Fridays

16 December to 15 May

Great Malvern, Gloucester, Cardiff and Bristol - Weymouth, Portsmouth and Brighton

Miles	Miles	Miles	Miles	Miles			GW	GW	GW	GW	GW	GW	GW	GW	GW	SW	GW	GW	GW	GW	GW	GW	SW	GW
							MX A		◇	◇ 1 B 🍴		◇	◇			◇ 1 C	◇	◇ 1 D 🍴		■		◇	◇ 1 E	
0	0	—	—	—	**Cardiff Central** [7]	d											06 30			07 28				
11¾	11¾	—	—	—	Newport (South Wales) [2]	d											06 44			07 42				
21¾	21¾	—	—	—	Severn Tunnel Jn	d											06 54			07 52				
—	—	0	0	—	Great Malvern	d																		
—	—	1¼	1¼	—	Malvern Link	d																		
—	—	8	8	—	Worcester Foregate Street	d																		
—	—	8½	8½	—	Worcester Shrub Hill	d																07 08		
—	—	23¼	23¼	—	Ashchurch for Tewkesbury	d																07 24		
—	—	30½	30½	—	Cheltenham Spa	d																07 34		
—	—	37	37	—	Gloucester	d																07 46		
—	—	50	50	—	Cam & Dursley	d																08 00		
—	—	60¾	60¾	—	Yate	d																08 13		
—	—	67	67	—	Bristol Parkway	d									06 12							08 22		
33¾	33¾	68½	68½	—	Filton Abbey Wood	d									06 16		07 12			08 07		08 26		08 51
38¼	38¼	73	73	—	**Bristol Temple Meads** [10]	d			05 00	05 10		05 51			06 39		07 24		07 38	08 19		08 41	08 49	09 04
42¾	42¾	77½	77½	—	Keynsham	d						05 58			06 46				07 45	08 27		08 49	08 56	09 11
48¾	48¾	83½	83½	—	Oldfield Park	d						06 05			06 53				07 52	08 34		08 56	09 03	09 18
—	—	—	—	0	Swindon	d								06 11							08 44			
—	—	—	—	16¾	Chippenham	d								06 27							08 59			
—	—	—	—	23	Melksham	d								06 36							09 09			
49¾	49¾	84½	84½	—	**Bath Spa** [7]	d	00 03		05 13			06 08			06 56		07 37		07 55	08 38		09 01	09 07	09 21
56¾	56¾	91¾	91¾	—	Freshford	d	00 12					06 18			07 05				08 04			09 10		
57¾	57¾	92½	92½	—	Avoncliff	d	00 14					06 20			07 08				08 07			09 12		
59	59	94	94	—	Bradford-on-Avon	d	00 18		05 25	05 35		06 24			07 12		07 49		08 11	08 50		09 16	09 24	09 33
62¼	62¼	97¼	97¼	28½	Trowbridge	d	00 25		05 32	05 41		06 31		06 46	07 18		07 56		08 19	08 57	09 18	09 23	09 29	09 40
—	—	—	—	—	London Paddington [15] ⊖	d												07 04						
66¼	66¼	101¼	101¼	32½	**Westbury** [2]	a	00 32		05 39	05 49		06 38		06 53	07 25		08 03	08 20	08 26	09 04	09 25	09 30	09 37	09 49
—	—	—	—	—		d	00 33	05 24	05 49		06 25	06 40	06 48	06 54		07 40	08 05	08 21		09 05		09 33	09 40	09 51
—	72	—	107	—	Frome	d	00a42				06a34		06 58									09 43		
—	82½	—	117½	—	Bruton	d							07 09									09 54		
—	86	—	121	—	Castle Cary	a							07 14					08 40				09 59		
—	—	—	—	—		d							07 15									10 00		
—	97¾	—	132¾	—	Yeovil Pen Mill	d							07 33									10 14		
—	101	—	135¾	—	Thornford	d							07x37									10x19		
—	102	—	137	—	Yetminster	d							07x40									10x22		
—	104	—	139	—	Chetnole	d							07x44									10x26		
—	110½	—	145½	—	Maiden Newton	d							07 56									10 38		
—	118¼	—	153¼	—	Dorchester West	d							08 07									10 48		
—	122¾	—	157¾	—	Upwey	a							08 14									10 56		
—	125¼	—	160¼	—	**Weymouth**	a							08 19									11 01		
67¾	—	102½	—	—	Dilton Marsh	d								06x56										09x53
71	—	105¾	—	—	Warminster	d		05 32	05 57			06 48		07 03		07 48	08 13			09 13			09 48	10a00
90¾	—	125½	—	—	**Salisbury** [3]	a		05 51	06 16			07 09		07 23		08 10	08 32			09 32			10 09	
—	—	—	—	—		d			06 19			07 11		07 35			08 33			09 33				
107¼	—	142¼	—	—	Romsey	d			06 37			07 29		07 54			08 52			09 52				
115½	—	150¼	—	—	**Southampton Central** [3]	a			06 47			07 40		08 08			09 02			10 02				
130	—	165	—	—	Fareham	a			07 11			08 02					09 33			10 28				
—	—	—	—	—		d			07 12			08 03					09 34			10 29				
135¾	—	170¼	—	—	Cosham	a			07 19			08 11					09 41			10 36				
139½	—	—	—	—	Fratton [3]	a			07 26			08 18					09 49			10 43				
140½	—	—	—	—	Portsmouth & Southsea	a			07 30			08 21					09 52			10 47				
141¼	—	—	—	—	**Portsmouth Harbour**	a			07 38			08 26					09 56			10 51				
—	—	174¾	—	—	Havant [3]	a																		
—	—	183¾	—	—	**Chichester** [4]	a																		
—	—	190	—	—	Barnham	a																		
—	—	201¾	—	—	Worthing [4]	a																		
—	—	206½	—	—	Shoreham-by-Sea	a																		
—	—	211	—	—	Hove [2]	a																		
—	—	212½	—	—	Brighton [10]	a																		

A From Bristol Temple Meads
B To London Paddington
C From Yeovil Pen Mill to London Waterloo
D To Paignton. The Devon Express
E To London Waterloo

For connections from Swansea to Cardiff Central and Bristol Parkway refer to Table T128

For connections from Plymouth and Exeter to Bristol Temple Meads, Westbury and Castle Cary, refer to Table T135

For connections from Exeter and Yeovil Junction to Salisbury refer to Table T160

For connections from Upwey, Weymouth and Southampton Central to Bournemouth refer to Table T158

For additional bus connections between Yeovil Junction and Yeovil Pen Mill refer to Table T123A

Table T123-R

Mondays to Fridays

16 December to 15 May

Great Malvern, Gloucester, Cardiff and Bristol - Weymouth, Portsmouth and Brighton

		SW	GW	GW	GW	GW	GW	GW	SW	GW	GW	GW	GW	GW	GW	SW	GW	GW	GW	GW	SW	GW
		◇ 1 A	◇	◇	◇ 1 B 🍴	◇			◇ 1 C		◇ 1 D 🍴	◇	◇	◇	◇	◇ 1 E 🍴	◇ 1 D 🍴		◇		◇ 1 A 🍴	◇
Cardiff Central [7]	d		08 27			09 27						10 30		11 30					12 30			13 30
Newport (South Wales) [2]	d		08 41			09 41						10 44		11 44					12 44			13 44
Severn Tunnel Jn	d		08 51			09 51																
Great Malvern	d														10 41							
Malvern Link	d														10 44							
Worcester Foregate Street	d							08 55							10 53							
Worcester Shrub Hill	d							08 58							10 56							
Ashchurch for Tewkesbury	d							09 14							11 13							
Cheltenham Spa	d							09 23							11 22							
Gloucester	d			08 42				09 41					10 42		11 40					12 42		
Cam & Dursley	d			08 55				09 54					10 54		11 53					12 54		
Yate	d			09 08				10 07					11 07		12 06					13 07		
Bristol Parkway	d			09 19				10 16					11 16		12 16					13 16		
Filton Abbey Wood	d		09 07	09 23		10 06		10 20				11 07	11 19	12 07	12 20				13 07	13 20		14 07
Bristol Temple Meads [10]	d		09 23	09 45		10 23		10 47				11 22	11 45	12 22	12 42	12 49			13 22	13 45		14 22
Keynsham	d			09 53				10 54					11 52		12 49	12 56				13 52		
Oldfield Park	d			10 00				11 01					11 59		12 56	13 03				13 59		
Swindon	d									11 05								13 14				
Chippenham	d									11 20								13 29				
Melksham	d									11 30								13 39				
Bath Spa [7]	d		09 36	10 03		10 36		11 05				11 35	12 03	12 35	13 00	13 07			13 35	14 03		14 35
Freshford	d			10 12				11 14					12 12		13 09					14 12		
Avoncliff	d			10 15				11 17					12 14		13 12					14 14		
Bradford-on-Avon	d		09 48	10 19		10 48		11 21				11 47	12 18	12 48	13 16	13 23			13 47	14 18		14 47
Trowbridge	d		09 55	10 25		10 55		11 27		11 39		11 54	12 25	12 55	13 22	13 30		13 48	13 54	14 25		14 54
London Paddington [15] ⊖	d				09 37						10 35						12 36					
Westbury [2]	a		10 02	10 32	10 54	11 02		11 34		11 46	11 52	12 01	12 32	13 02	13 29	13 37	13 52	13 55	14 01	14 32		15 01
	d	09 56	10 05	10 33	10 56	11 05	11 11		11 36		11 54	12 03	12 33	13 03	13 33	13 40	13 53		14 03	14 36	14 55	15 03
Frome	d	10 05		10 43									12 43							14a45	15 04	
Bruton	d	10 17		10 54									12 54								15 16	
Castle Cary	a	10 21		10 59	11 15						12 13		12 59				14 12				15 21	
	d	10 22		11 01									12 59								15 22	
Yeovil Pen Mill	d	10a36		11 15									13 12								15a33	
Thornford	d			11x19									13x17									
Yetminster	d			11x22									13x20									
Chetnole	d			11x26									13x24									
Maiden Newton	d			11 38									13 36									
Dorchester West	d			11 53									13 53									
Upwey	a			12 01									14 01									
Weymouth	a			12 06									14 06									
Dilton Marsh	d						11x13								13x36							
Warminster	d		10 13			11 13	11 20		11 48			12 11		13 11	13 43	13 48			14 11			15 11
Salisbury [3]	a		10 32			11 32	11 40		12 09			12 30		13 30	14 02	14 10			14 30			15 30
	d		10 33			11 33	11 42					12 32		13 32	14 04				14 32			15 32
Romsey	d		10 52			11 52	12 00					12 51		13 51	14 22				14 51			15 51
Southampton Central [3]	a		11 02			12 02	12 11					13 02		14 01	14 32				15 02			16 02
Fareham	a		11 28			12 28						13 27		14 27	14 56				15 27			16 27
	d		11 29			12 29						13 28		14 28	14 57				15 28			16 28
Cosham	a		11 36			12 36						13 35		14 35	15 05				15 35			16 35
Fratton [3]	a		11 43			12 43						13 42		14 42					15 42			16 42
Portsmouth & Southsea	a		11 47			12 47						13 46		14 46					15 46			16 48
Portsmouth Harbour	a		11 51			12 51						13 50		14 50					15 50			16 52
Havant [3]	a														15 11							
Chichester [4]	a														15 25							
Barnham	a														15 36							
Worthing [4]	a														15 54							
Shoreham-by-Sea	a														16 00							
Hove [2]	a														16 09							
Brighton [10]	a														16 13							

A From London Waterloo
B To Paignton. The Torbay Express
C From Yeovil Pen Mill to London Waterloo
D To Exeter St Davids
E To London Waterloo

For connections from Swansea to Cardiff Central and Bristol Parkway refer to Table T128

For connections from Plymouth and Exeter to Bristol Temple Meads, Westbury and Castle Cary, refer to Table T135

For connections from Exeter and Yeovil Junction to Salisbury refer to Table T160

For connections from Upwey, Weymouth and Southampton Central to Bournemouth refer to Table T158

For additional bus connections between Yeovil Junction and Yeovil Pen Mill refer to Table T123A

Table T123-R

Mondays to Fridays
16 December to 15 May

Great Malvern, Gloucester, Cardiff and Bristol - Weymouth, Portsmouth and Brighton

		GW	GW	SW	GW	GW	GW	GW	SW	GW	GW	GW	SW	GW	GW	GW	GW	GW	GW	GW	GW	GW	GW
			◇	◇[1] A		◇[1] B ⊥	◇		◇[1] C	◇		◇	◇[1] A		◇[1] D ⊥	■		◇		◇[1] E ⊥	■		
Cardiff Central [7]	d						14 30			15 30						16 27					17 30		
Newport (South Wales) [2]	d						14 44			15 44						16 41					17 44		
Severn Tunnel Jn	d															16 51					17 54		
Great Malvern	d		12 42									14 41										16 44	
Malvern Link	d		12 45									14 44										16 47	
Worcester Foregate Street	d		12 54									14 53										16 56	
Worcester Shrub Hill	d		12 57									14 56										16 59	
Ashchurch for Tewkesbury	d		13 13									15 13										17 15	
Cheltenham Spa	d		13 22									15 22										17 24	
Gloucester	d		13 37					14 41				15 38						16 42				17 42	17 50
Cam & Dursley	d		13 50					14 54				15 51						16 54				17 54	
Yate	d		14 03					15 07				16 05						17 07				18 07	
Bristol Parkway	d		14 13					15 16				16 14		16 45				17 16	17 45			18 16	
Filton Abbey Wood	d		14 17				15 07	15 20		16 07		16 18		16 51		17 06		17 20	17 49		18 11	18 20	
Bristol Temple Meads [10]	d		14 45				15 22	15 44	15 50	16 22		16 45		17 09		17 22		17 45	18 05		18 24	18 43	
Keynsham	d		14 52					15 51	15 57			16 52		17 16				17 52	18 12			18 50	
Oldfield Park	d		14 59					15 58	16 04			16 59		17 23				17 59	18 19			18 57	
Swindon	d				15 14												17 36						18 51
Chippenham	d				15 29												17 51						19 06
Melksham	d				15 39												18 01						19 16
Bath Spa [7]	d		15 03				15 35	16 02	16 08	16 36		17 02		17 27		17 35		18 03	18 23		18 37	19 01	
Freshford	d		15 12					16 11				17 11		17 36				18 12	18 32			19 10	
Avoncliff	d		15 14					16 14				17 14						18 14	18 35			19 13	
Bradford-on-Avon	d		15 18				15 47	16 18	16 25	16 48		17 18		17 40		17 47		18 18	18 39		18 50	19 17	
Trowbridge	d		15 25		15 48		15 54	16 24	16 31	16 54		17 24		17 47		17 56	18 10	18 25	18 45		18 56	19 23	19 28
London Paddington [15] ⊖	d					14 36									16 38					17 37			
Westbury [2]	a		15 32		15 55	15 57	16 02	16 31	16 38	17 01		17 31		17 54	17 57	18 03	18 17	18 32	18 52	18 57	19 04	19 31	19 35
	d	15 11	15 33	15 42		15 58	16 06		16 40	17 03	17 11	17 33	17 45	17 55	17 59	18 05		18 33		18 59	19 05		19 36
Frome	d		15 43									17 43						18 50					
Bruton	d		15 54									17 54						19 01					
Castle Cary	a		15 59			16 17						17 59			18 18			19 05		19 18			
	d		16 05									17 59						19 06					
Yeovil Pen Mill	d		16 19									18 13						19 20					
Thornford	d		16x23									18x18						19x24					
Yetminster	d		16x26									18x21						19x27					
Chetnole	d		16x30									18x25						19x31					
Maiden Newton	d		16 42									18 37						19 43					
Dorchester West	d		16 53									18 47						19 54					
Upwey	a		17 01									18 55						20 01					
Weymouth	a		17 06									19 00						20 06					
Dilton Marsh	d	15x13									17x13			17x59									19x39
Warminster	d	15a20		15 50			16 14		16 48	17 11	17a20		17 54	18a04		18 13					19 13		19 46
Salisbury [3]	a			16 12			16 33		17 08	17 30			18 17			18 32					19 32		20 05
	d						16 34			17 32						18 33					19 33		20 07
Romsey	d						16 53			17 51						18 52					19 52		20 25
Southampton Central [3]	a						17 03			18 02						19 02					20 02		20 36
Fareham	a						17 27			18 27						19 28					20 28		
	d						17 28			18 28						19 29					20 29		
Cosham	a						17 36			18 35						19 36							
Fratton [3]	a						17 43			18 45						19 43					20 43		
Portsmouth & Southsea	a						17 48			18 50						19 47					20 46		
Portsmouth Harbour	a						17 52			18 54						19 51					20 50		
Havant [3]	a																						
Chichester [4]	a																						
Barnham	a																						
Worthing [4]	a																						
Shoreham-by-Sea	a																						
Hove [2]	a																						
Brighton [10]	a																						

A From Yeovil Junction to London Waterloo
B To Plymouth
C To London Waterloo
D To Exeter St Davids
E To Paignton

For connections from Swansea to Cardiff Central and Bristol Parkway refer to Table T128

For connections from Plymouth and Exeter to Bristol Temple Meads, Westbury and Castle Cary, refer to Table T135

For connections from Exeter and Yeovil Junction to Salisbury refer to Table T160

For connections from Upwey, Weymouth and Southampton Central to Bournemouth refer to Table T158

For additional bus connections between Yeovil Junction and Yeovil Pen Mill refer to Table T123A

Table T123-R

Mondays to Fridays
16 December to 15 May

Great Malvern, Gloucester, Cardiff and Bristol - Weymouth, Portsmouth and Brighton

		GW	GW	GW	SW	SW	GW	GW	GW	GW	GW	GW	SW	GW	SW	GW	GW
		◇[1] ⊥	◇	◇[1] A ⊥	◇[1] B	◇[1] C		◇	◇[1] A ⊥		◇	◇	◇[1] D	◇[1] A ⊥	◇[1]		
Cardiff Central [7]	d		18 30					19 30				20 30					
Newport (South Wales) [2]	d		18 44					19 44				20 44					
Severn Tunnel Jn	d		18 54														
Great Malvern	d																
Malvern Link	d																
Worcester Foregate Street	d																
Worcester Shrub Hill	d																
Ashchurch for Tewkesbury	d																
Cheltenham Spa	d																
Gloucester	d						18 42										
Cam & Dursley	d						18 54										
Yate	d						19 07										
Bristol Parkway	d						19 16				20 30						
Filton Abbey Wood	d		19 11				19 20	20 07			20 34	21 07					
Bristol Temple Meads [10]	d		19 23		19 35		19 41	20 24			20 46	21 23			22 25	22 53	23 45
Keynsham	d				19 42		19 50				20 53				22 32	23 00	23 52
Oldfield Park	d						19 57				21 00					23 07	23 59
Swindon	d									20 45							
Chippenham	d									21 00							
Melksham	d									21 10							
Bath Spa [7]	d		19 37		19 51		20 01	20 37			21 03	21 37			22 41	23 11	00 03
Freshford	d						20 10				21 12					23 20	00 12
Avoncliff	d						20 12				21 15					23 22	00 14
Bradford-on-Avon	d		19 49		20 02		20 16	20 49			21 19	21 49			22 52	23 26	00 18
Trowbridge	d		19 55		20 08		20 23	20 56		21 19	21 25	21 56			22 58	23 33	00 25
London Paddington [15] ⊖	d	18 07		18 37					20 04					21 04			
Westbury [2]	a	19 44	20 02	20 06	20 15		20 31	21 03	21 16	21 26	21 32	22 03		22 20	23 05	23 40	00 32
	d	19 57	20 05	20 08	20 16	20 34	20 39	21 05	21 17		21 34	22 04	22 18	22 21	23 07		00 33
Frome	d	20a07				20 43	20a48				21 43						00a42
Bruton	d					20 55					21 55						
Castle Cary	a			20 27		20 59			21 36		21 59			22 40			
	d										22 01						
Yeovil Pen Mill	d										22 15						
Thornford	d										22x19						
Yetminster	d										22x22						
Chetnole	d										22x26						
Maiden Newton	d										22 38						
Dorchester West	d										22 49						
Upwey	a										22 56						
Weymouth	a										23 01						
Dilton Marsh	d											22x07					
Warminster	d		20 13		20 24			21 13				22 13	22 26		23 14		
Salisbury [3]	a		20 32		20 44			21 32				22 33	22 46		23 37		
	d		20 33					21 33				22 34					
Romsey	d		20 52					21 52				22 53					
Southampton Central [3]	a		21 02					22 02				23 05					
Fareham	a		21 25					22 43				23 31					
	d		21 26					22 44				23 32					
Cosham	a																
Fratton [3]	a		21 40					22 57				23 45					
Portsmouth & Southsea	a		21 43					23 00				23 48					
Portsmouth Harbour	a		21 49					23 04				23 53					
Havant [3]	a																
Chichester [4]	a																
Barnham	a																
Worthing [4]	a																
Shoreham-by-Sea	a																
Hove [2]	a																
Brighton [10]	a																

A To Plymouth
B To London Waterloo
C From Salisbury
D From Castle Cary

For connections from Swansea to Cardiff Central and Bristol Parkway refer to Table T128

For connections from Plymouth and Exeter to Bristol Temple Meads, Westbury and Castle Cary, refer to Table T135

For connections from Exeter and Yeovil Junction to Salisbury refer to Table T160

For connections from Upwey, Weymouth and Southampton Central to Bournemouth refer to Table T158

For additional bus connections between Yeovil Junction and Yeovil Pen Mill refer to Table T123A

Table T123-R

Saturdays
21 December to 16 May

Great Malvern, Gloucester, Cardiff and Bristol - Weymouth, Portsmouth and Brighton

Station		GW A	GW	GW	GW ◇	GW	GW B	GW	GW ◇	SW ◇1 C	SW 1	GW	GW ◇	GW ◇	GW	SW ◇1 D	GW ◇1 E ⊼	GW ◇	GW	GW ◇		SW ◇1 F	GW ◇ G ⊼	GW	GW
Cardiff Central 7	d								06 29				07 27					08 27					09 28		
Newport (South Wales) 2	d								06 44				07 41					08 41					09 42		
Severn Tunnel Jn	d								06 54				07 51					08 51					09 52		
Great Malvern	d																								
Malvern Link	d																								
Worcester Foregate Street	d																								
Worcester Shrub Hill	d													06 52											08 58
Ashchurch for Tewkesbury	d													07 08											09 14
Cheltenham Spa	d													07 18											09 23
Gloucester	d													07 40						08 42					09 41
Cam & Dursley	d													07 53						08 55					09 54
Yate	d													08 06						09 08					10 08
Bristol Parkway	d							06 19						08 15						09 18					10 17
Filton Abbey Wood	d							06 23	07 09				08 06	08 19				09 06		09 21			10 07		10 21
Bristol Temple Meads 10	d				05 40			06 40	07 21			07 40	08 22	08 40		08 50		09 22		09 40			10 22		10 43
Keynsham	d				05 47			06 47				07 47		08 47		08 57				09 47					10 50
Oldfield Park	d				05 54			06 54				07 54		08 54		09 04				09 54					10 57
Swindon	d														08 45										
Chippenham	d														09 01										
Melksham	d														09 10										
Bath Spa 7	d	00 03			05 58			06 57	07 34			07 58	08 35	08 57		09 08		09 35		09 58			10 35		11 01
Freshford	d	00 12			06 07			07 07				08 07		09 07						10 07					11 10
Avoncliff	d	00 14			06 10			07 09				08 10		09 09						10 10					11 13
Bradford-on-Avon	d	00 18			06 14			07 13	07 46			08 14	08 47	09 13		09 22		09 47		10 14			10 47		11 17
Trowbridge	d	00 25			06 20			07 20	07 52			08 20	08 54	09 20	09 25	09 28		09 54		10 20			10 54		11 23
London Paddington 15 ⊖	d																08 35								
Westbury 2	a	00 32			06 30			07 27	07 59			08 27	09 01	09 27	09 33	09 37	09 51	10 01		10 27			11 01		11 31
	d	00 33	05 24	06 01	06 43	06 45	07 03		08 02	08 10			09 02	09 30		09 40	09 53	10 02	10 12	10 29		10 57	11 02	11 12	
Frome	d	00a42				06 54								09 39						10 39		11a06			
Bruton	d					07 06								09 51						10 51					
Castle Cary	a					07 10								09 55			10 12			10 55					
	d					07 11								09 56						10 56					
Yeovil Pen Mill	d					07 30					09 50			10 10						11 10					
Thornford	d					07x34								10x14						11x14					
Yetminster	d					07x37								10x17						11x17					
Chetnole	d					07x41								10x21						11x21					
Maiden Newton	d					07 53					10 08			10 34						11 34					
Dorchester West	d					08 04					10 18			10 44						11 53					
Upwey	a					08 12					10 24			10 52						12 01					
Weymouth	a					08 18					10 29			10 58						12 07					
Dilton Marsh	d						07x05												10x14					11x14	
Warminster	d		05 32	06 09	06 52		07 12		08 10	08 18			09 10			09 48		10 10	10a22				11 10	11 21	
Salisbury 3	a		05 53	06 30	07 13		07 34		08 32	08 37			09 32			10 09		10 32					11 32	11 43	
	d			06 32	07 24		07 36		08 33				09 33					10 33					11 33	11 44	
Romsey	d			06 50	07 43		07 54		08 52				09 51					10 51					11 51	12 04	
Southampton Central 3	a			07 02	07 55		08 08		09 02				10 03					11 03					12 03	12 21	
Fareham	a			07 27	08 24				09 27				10 27					11 27					12 27		
	d			07 28	08 25				09 28				10 28					11 28					12 28		
Cosham	a			07 35	08 32				09 35				10 35					11 35					12 35		
Fratton 3	a			07 42	08 40				09 43				10 42					11 42					12 42		
Portsmouth & Southsea	a			07 46	08 45				09 46				10 46					11 46					12 46		
Portsmouth Harbour	a			07 50	08 49				09 51				10 50					11 50					12 50		
Havant 3	a																								
Chichester 4	a																								
Barnham	a																								
Worthing 4	a																								
Shoreham-by-Sea	a																								
Hove 2	a																								
Brighton 10	a																								

A From Bristol Temple Meads
B From Frome
C From Castle Cary
D To London Waterloo
E To Exeter St Davids
F From London Waterloo
G ⊼ from Bristol Temple Meads

For connections from Swansea to Cardiff Central and Bristol Parkway refer to Table T128

For connections from Plymouth and Exeter to Bristol Temple Meads, Westbury and Castle Cary, refer to Table T135

For connections from Exeter and Yeovil Junction to Salisbury refer to Table T160

For connections from Upwey, Weymouth and Southampton Central to Bournemouth refer to Table T158

For additional bus connections between Yeovil Junction and Yeovil Pen Mill refer to Table T123A

Table T123-R

Saturdays
21 December to 16 May

Great Malvern, Gloucester, Cardiff and Bristol - Weymouth, Portsmouth and Brighton

Station		SW ◇1 A	GW	GW ◇1 B ⊼	GW ◇ C ⊼	GW ◇		GW ◇ C ⊼	GW ◇	SW ◇1 D ⊼	GW	GW ◇1 B ⊼	GW ◇ C ⊼	SW 1	GW	GW ◇	GW A	GW ◇	GW	GW ◇1 E ⊼	GW ◇	GW	SW ◇1 D	GW	GW ◇
Cardiff Central 7	d				10 30			11 30					12 27			13 30					14 30				15 30
Newport (South Wales) 2	d				10 44			11 44					12 41			13 44					14 44				15 44
Severn Tunnel Jn	d																								
Great Malvern	d								10 52									12 43							
Malvern Link	d								10 55									12 46							
Worcester Foregate Street	d								11 05									12 56							
Worcester Shrub Hill	d								11 09									12 59							
Ashchurch for Tewkesbury	d								11 25									13 15							
Cheltenham Spa	d								11 34									13 24							
Gloucester	d					10 42			11 46						12 42			13 42				14 42			
Cam & Dursley	d					10 55			11 59						12 55			13 55				14 55			
Yate	d					11 08			12 13						13 08			14 08				15 08			
Bristol Parkway	d					11 18			12 22						13 18			14 18				15 18			
Filton Abbey Wood	d				11 07	11 21		12 07	12 25				13 04		13 21	14 07		14 21			15 07	15 21			16 10
Bristol Temple Meads 10	d				11 22	11 40		12 22	12 40	12 48			13 22		13 45	14 22		14 40			15 22	15 40	15 50		16 22
Keynsham	d					11 47			12 47	12 55					13 52			14 47				15 47	15 57		
Oldfield Park	d					11 54			12 54	13 02					13 59			14 54				15 53	16 04		
Swindon	d		11 04								13 04								15 04					16 01	
Chippenham	d		11 20								13 20								15 22					16 16	
Melksham	d		11 29								13 29								15 33					16 26	
Bath Spa 7	d				11 35	11 58		12 35	12 58	13 06			13 35		14 03	14 35		14 58			15 35	15 57	16 08		16 35
Freshford	d					12 07			13 07						14 12			15 07				16 06			
Avoncliff	d					12 10			13 10						14 15			15 10				16 09			
Bradford-on-Avon	d				11 47	12 14		12 47	13 14	13 20			13 47		14 19	14 47		15 14			15 47	16 13	16 25		16 47
Trowbridge	d		11 39		11 54	12 20		12 54	13 20	13 27	13 39		13 54		14 25	14 54		15 20	15 42		15 54	16 19	16 31	16 36	16 54
London Paddington 15 ⊖	d			10 35								12 35								14 35					
Westbury 2	a		11 47	11 52	12 01	12 27		13 01	13 27	13 34	13 47	13 51	14 01		14 32	15 01		15 27	15 49	15 52	16 01	16 27	16 38	16 43	17 01
	d	11 43		11 53	12 02	12 29		13 02	13 30	13 38		13 53	14 02		14 36	15 02	15 12	15 29		15 54	16 02		16 40		17 02
Frome	d					12 39									14a45			15 38							
Bruton	d					12 50												15 50							
Castle Cary	a			12 12		12 55						14 12						15 54		16 13					
	d					12 56												15 58							
Yeovil Pen Mill	d					13 10								14 26				16 12							
Thornford	d					13x14												16x17							
Yetminster	d					13x17												16x20							
Chetnole	d					13x21												16x24							
Maiden Newton	d					13 35								14 44				16 36							
Dorchester West	d					13 53								14 54				16 54							
Upwey	a					14 01								15 01				17 02							
Weymouth	a					14 07								15 06				17 08							
Dilton Marsh	d								13x32								15x14								
Warminster	d	11 50			12 10			13 10	13 39	13 46			14 10			15 10	15a22				16 10		16 48		17 10
Salisbury 3	a	12 11			12 32			13 32	14 00	14 07			14 32			15 32					16 32		17 09		17 32
	d				12 33			13 33	14 01				14 33			15 33					16 33				17 33
Romsey	d				12 51			13 51	14 21				14 51			15 51					16 51				17 51
Southampton Central 3	a				13 03			14 03	14 32				15 03			16 03					17 03				18 03
Fareham	a				13 27			14 27	14 55				15 27			16 27					17 27				18 27
	d				13 28			14 28	14 56				15 28			16 28					17 28				18 28
Cosham	a				13 35			14 35	15 03				15 35			16 35					17 35				18 35
Fratton 3	a				13 42			14 42					15 42			16 42					17 42				18 42
Portsmouth & Southsea	a				13 46			14 46					15 46			16 46					17 46				18 46
Portsmouth Harbour	a				13 50			14 50					15 50			16 50					17 50				18 50
Havant 3	a								15 10																
Chichester 4	a								15 21																
Barnham	a								15 29																
Worthing 4	a								15 49																
Shoreham-by-Sea	a								15 59																
Hove 2	a								16 12																
Brighton 10	a								16 18																

A From Frome
B To Exeter St Davids
C ⊼ from Bristol Temple Meads
D To London Waterloo
E To Plymouth

For connections from Swansea to Cardiff Central and Bristol Parkway refer to Table T128

For connections from Plymouth and Exeter to Bristol Temple Meads, Westbury and Castle Cary, refer to Table T135

For connections from Exeter and Yeovil Junction to Salisbury refer to Table T160

For connections from Upwey, Weymouth and Southampton Central to Bournemouth refer to Table T158

For additional bus connections between Yeovil Junction and Yeovil Pen Mill refer to Table T123A

Table T123-R

Great Malvern, Gloucester, Cardiff and Bristol - Weymouth, Portsmouth and Brighton

Saturdays

21 December to 16 May

		GW	GW ◇	GW ◇1 A ✕	GW ◇	GW	GW ◇	GW ◇	GW	SW ◇1 B	GW ◇	GW	GW ◇1 C ✕	SW ◇1 D	GW	GW ◇	GW ◇1 C ✕	GW ◇	GW	GW ◇	GW	SW ◇1	GW
Cardiff Central 7	d				16 27			17 27			18 27					19 30				20 30			
Newport (South Wales) 2	d				16 41			17 41			18 41					19 44				20 44			
Severn Tunnel Jn	d				16 51			17 51			18 51												
Great Malvern	d		14 43						16 55														
Malvern Link	d		14 46						16 58														
Worcester Foregate Street	d		14 56						17 11														
Worcester Shrub Hill	d		14 59						17 14														
Ashchurch for Tewkesbury	d		15 15						17 30														
Cheltenham Spa	d		15 24						17 40														
Gloucester	d		15 42				16 42		17 50						18 42								
Cam & Dursley	d		15 55				16 55		18 03						18 55								
Yate	d		16 08				17 08		18 16						19 08								
Bristol Parkway	d		16 18				17 18		18 26						19 18			20 10					
Filton Abbey Wood	d		16 21		17 06		17 21	18 06	18 29		19 06				19 22	20 07		20 15		21 07			
Bristol Temple Meads 10	d		16 45		17 22		17 43	18 22	18 45		19 22			19 35	19 42	20 22		20 44		21 22	22 03	22 23	23 12
Keynsham	d		16 52				17 50		18 52					19 42	19 49			20 51			22 10	22 30	23 19
Oldfield Park	d		16 59				17 57		18 59					19 49	19 56			20 58			22 17		23 26
Swindon	d					17 33						19 33							21 07				
Chippenham	d					17 48						19 48							21 22				
Melksham	d					17 58						19 58							21 32				
Bath Spa 7	d		17 03		17 35		18 01	18 35	19 03		19 35			19 54	20 03	20 35		21 01		21 35	22 21	22 39	23 29
Freshford	d		17 12				18 10		19 12						20 12			21 11			22 30		23 38
Avoncliff	d		17 15				18 13		19 15						20 15			21 13			22 33		23 41
Bradford-on-Avon	d		17 19		17 47		18 17	18 47	19 19		19 47			20 10	20 19	20 47		21 17		21 47	22 37	22 50	23 45
Trowbridge	d		17 25		17 54	18 07	18 23	18 54	19 25		19 54	20 07		20 17	20 25	20 54		21 24	21 41	21 54	22 43	22 56	23 51
London Paddington 15 ⊖	d			16 35									19 03				20 03						
Westbury 2	a		17 32	17 51	18 01	18 15	18 30	19 01	19 32		20 01	20 15	20 20	20 24	20 32	21 01	21 20	21 31	21 49	22 01	22 51	23 03	23 58
	d	17 11	17 34	17 52	18 02		18 32	19 02	19 38	19 58	20 03		20 21	20 24	20 33	21 03	21 21	21 32		22 03		23 05	23 59
Frome	d		17 43				18 41			20 07					20a43			21 46					00a10
Bruton	d		17 54				18 53			20 19								21 57					
Castle Cary	a		17 59	18 11			18 57			20 23			20 40				21 40	22 02					
	d		17 59				18 58			20 24								22 02					
Yeovil Pen Mill	d		18 18				19 12			20a38								22 18					
Thornford	d		18x23				19x16											22x23					
Yetminster	d		18x26				19x19											22x26					
Chetnole	d		18x30				19x23											22x30					
Maiden Newton	d		18 42				19 35											22 42					
Dorchester West	d		18 53				19 53											22 52					
Upwey	a		19 01				20 01											23 00					
Weymouth	a		19 08				20 09											23 08					
Dilton Marsh	d	17x13							19x40											22x05			
Warminster	d	17a21			18 10			19 10	19 47		20 11			20 32		21 11				22 12		23 12	
Salisbury 3	a				18 32			19 32	20 09		20 32			20 51		21 32				22 34		23 33	
	d				18 33			19 33	20 10		20 33					21 33				22 35			
Romsey	d				18 51			19 51	20 28		20 52					21 52				22 53			
Southampton Central 3	a				19 03			20 03	20 40		21 03					22 02				23 04			
Fareham	a				19 27			20 27			21 27					22 26				23 27			
	d				19 28			20 28			21 28					22 27				23 28			
Cosham	a				19 35																		
Fratton 3	a				19 42			20 42			21 42					22 41				23 41			
Portsmouth & Southsea	a				19 46			20 45			21 46					22 45				23 45			
Portsmouth Harbour	a				19 50			20 49			21 50					22 50				23 49			
Havant 3	a																						
Chichester 4	a																						
Barnham	a																						
Worthing 4	a																						
Shoreham-by-Sea	a																						
Hove 2	a																						
Brighton 10	a																						

A To Paignton. The Torbay Express
B From London Waterloo to Yeovil Junction
C To Plymouth
D To Basingstoke

For connections from Swansea to Cardiff Central and Bristol Parkway refer to Table T128

For connections from Plymouth and Exeter to Bristol Temple Meads, Westbury and Castle Cary, refer to Table T135

For connections from Exeter and Yeovil Junction to Salisbury refer to Table T160

For connections from Upwey, Weymouth and Southampton Central to Bournemouth refer to Table T158

For additional bus connections between Yeovil Junction and Yeovil Pen Mill refer to Table T123A

Table T123-R

Great Malvern, Gloucester, Cardiff and Bristol - Weymouth, Portsmouth and Brighton

Sundays

15 December to 10 May

		GW	GW ◇	GW ◇1 A ✕	GW	GW ◇	GW ◇1 B ✕	GW ◇	SW ◇1 C	GW ◇ D	GW ◇ E	GW	GW ◇1 F ✕	GW ◇	GW	GW ■ ◇ G	SW ◇1	GW ◇1 F ✕	GW ◇	GW ◇	GW ◇	GW ◇1 F ✕	GW ◇
Cardiff Central 7	d					08 10				09 13	09 20			10 13		11 13			12 13		13 13		14 13
Newport (South Wales) 2	d					08 28				09 31	09 38			10 27		11 27			12 26		13 26		14 25
Severn Tunnel Jn	d					08 46				09 48	09 48			10 37		11 37			12 36		13 37		14 33
Great Malvern	d																						
Malvern Link	d																						
Worcester Foregate Street	d																						
Worcester Shrub Hill	d																						
Ashchurch for Tewkesbury	d																						
Cheltenham Spa	d																						
Gloucester	d																						
Cam & Dursley	d																						
Yate	d																						
Bristol Parkway	d																						
Filton Abbey Wood	d					09 00				10 00	10 00			10 50		11 50			12 53		13 50		14 50
Bristol Temple Meads 10	d		08 19			09 20		09 34						11 10		12 10	13 04		13 10		14 09		15 10
Keynsham	d		08 26					09 41						11 16		12 17	13 11		13 17		14 17		15 17
Oldfield Park	d		08 33					09 48						11 23		12 24	13 18		13 24		14 24		15 23
Swindon	d				09 12										11 41					13 41			
Chippenham	d				09 27										11 56					13 56			
Melksham	d				09 37										12 06					14 05			
Bath Spa 7	d		08 37			09 32		09 52		10 32	10 32			11 26		12 27	13 22		13 27		14 28		15 27
Freshford	d		08 47					10 01								12 37					14 37		
Avoncliff	d		08 49					10 03								12 40					14 40		
Bradford-on-Avon	d		08 53			09 45		10 07		10 45	10 45			11 39		12 44	13 34		13 40		14 44		15 40
Trowbridge	d		09 00		09 46	09 52		10 14		10 52	10 52			11 47	12 15	12 50	13 40		13 48	14 14	14 50		15 47
London Paddington 15 ⊖	d			07 57			08 51						10 36					12 36				14 36	
Westbury 2	a		09 06	09 17	09 52	09 59	10 03	10 20		10 58	10 58		11 51	11 54	12 21	12 56	13 47	13 51	13 54	14 20	14 56	15 51	15 54
	d	07 55	09 07	09 19		10 00	10 04	10 21	10 43	11 01	11 01	11 15	11 52	12 01		13 01	13 50	13 52	14 01	14 22	15 02	15 52	16 03
Frome	d		09 18					10 31				11a24								14 30			
Bruton	d		09 29					10 42												14 41			
Castle Cary	a		09 33	09 37			10 23	10 45					12 10					14 10		14 45		16 10	
	d		09 34					10 47												14 46			
Yeovil Pen Mill	d		09 51					11 02												15 01			
Thornford	d		09x56					11x07												15x07			
Yetminster	d		09x59					11x10												15x10			
Chetnole	d		10x03					11x14												15x14			
Maiden Newton	d		10 17					11 30												15 25			
Dorchester West	d		10 29					11 41												15 36			
Upwey	a		10 36					11 49												15 44			
Weymouth	a		10 42					11 54												15 49			
Dilton Marsh	d					10x03								12x04					14x04				16x06
Warminster	d	08a02				10 09			10 51	11 08	11 08			12 10		13 08	13 58		14 10		15 08		16 12
Salisbury 3	a					10 33			11 12	11 32	11 32			12 32		13 32	14 19		14 34		15 32		16 32
	d					10 33				11 32	11 32			12 32		13 32			14 36		15 32		16 32
Romsey	d					10 51				11 50	11 50			12 50		13 50			14 54		15 51		16 50
Southampton Central 3	a					11 03				12 03	12 03			13 03		14 03			15 03		16 04		17 03
Fareham	a					11 26				12 26	12 26			13 29		14 26			15 27		16 27		17 26
	d					11 26				12 26	12 26			13 30		14 26			15 28		16 27		17 26
Cosham	a					11 34				12 34	12 34			13 37		14 34			15 36		16 34		17 34
Fratton 3	a					11 40				12 40	12 40					14 40					16 40		17 40
Portsmouth & Southsea	a					11 44				12 44	12 44					14 44					16 45		17 44
Portsmouth Harbour	a					11 51				12 51	12 51					14 51					16 51		17 51
Havant 3	a													13 45					15 42				
Chichester 4	a													13 57					15 57				
Barnham	a													14 08					16 05				
Worthing 4	a													14 30					16 23				
Shoreham-by-Sea	a													14 36					16 31				
Hove 2	a													14 43					16 37				
Brighton 10	a													14 49					16 44				

A To Penzance
B To Plymouth
C From Yeovil Junction
D until 29 March
E from 5 April
F To Exeter St Davids
G ◇ from Bristol Temple Meads ■ to Bristol Temple Meads

For connections from Swansea to Cardiff Central and Bristol Parkway refer to Table T128

For connections from Plymouth and Exeter to Bristol Temple Meads, Westbury and Castle Cary, refer to Table T135

For connections from Exeter and Yeovil Junction to Salisbury refer to Table T160

For connections from Upwey, Weymouth and Southampton Central to Bournemouth refer to Table T158

For additional bus connections between Yeovil Junction and Yeovil Pen Mill refer to Table T123A

Table T123-R

Sundays
15 December to 10 May

Great Malvern, Gloucester, Cardiff and Bristol - Weymouth, Portsmouth and Brighton

		GW	SW	GW	SW	GW	GW	GW	GW	GW	SW	GW	GW	GW	SW	GW	GW	GW	GW	GW	GW	GW	SW	GW	GW
			◇■ A	◇	◇■ B	◇■ C ✠	◇	◇		◇ D	◇■ E	◇	◇	◇■ C ✠	◇■ F	◇		◇	◇■ C ✠			◇	◇■		◇
Cardiff Central 7	d			15 13			16 13	16 36				17 13	17 40			18 12		19 13				20 30			22 15
Newport (South Wales) 2	d			15 27			16 27	16 51				17 27	17 54			18 26		19 27				20 44			22 28
Severn Tunnel Jn	d			15 37			16 37					17 37				18 37		19 37				20 54			22 35
Great Malvern	d																								
Malvern Link	d																								
Worcester Foregate Street	d																								
Worcester Shrub Hill	d																								
Ashchurch for Tewkesbury	d																								
Cheltenham Spa	d																								
Gloucester	d																								
Cam & Dursley	d																								
Yate	d																								
Bristol Parkway	d																								
Filton Abbey Wood	d			15 52			16 50	17 14				17 50	18 18			18 50		19 51				21 09			22 54
Bristol Temple Meads 10	d		16 04	16 10			17 10	17 40		17 45		18 15	18 40			19 15		20 15		20 48		21 25	21 35	22 25	23 15
Keynsham	d		16 11	16 17			17 17			17 52			18 47					20 22		20 55			21 42	22 32	
Oldfield Park	d		16 18	16 24			17 24			17 59			18 54					20 29		21 02				22 39	
Swindon	d	15 46							17 44								19 27				21 10				
Chippenham	d	16 01							17 59								19 42				21 25				
Melksham	d	16 11							18 09								19 52				21 35				
Bath Spa 7	d		16 22	16 27			17 30	17 52		18 02		18 28	18 58			19 26		20 32		21 05		21 38	21 51	22 42	23 29
Freshford	d			16 37						18 13								20 42		21 16				22 53	
Avoncliff	d			16 40						18 15								20 45		21 19				22 56	
Bradford-on-Avon	d		16 34	16 44			17 43	18 05		18 19		18 40	19 10			19 38		20 49		21 23		21 50	22 02	23 00	23 41
Trowbridge	d	16 20	16 40	16 50			17 50	18 12	18 18	18 26		18 50	19 16			19 46	20 01	20 55		21 29	21 44	21 57	22 08	23 06	23 48
London Paddington 15 ⊖	d					16 36								18 36					20 03						
Westbury 2	a	16 26	16 47	16 58		17 51	17 58	18 19	18 25	18 33		18 57	19 25	19 51		19 53	20 09	21 02	21 18	21 36	21 51	22 04	22 15	23 13	23 55
	d		16 50	17 01	17 48	17 51	18 01	18 20		18 33	18 50	19 01	19 25	19 51	19 55	19 59		21 03	21 20	21 37		22 05	22 17		23 56
Frome	d				17a57					18 42					20 05					21 47					
Bruton	d									18 54					20 16					21 58					
Castle Cary	a					18 10				18 58				20 09	20 21				21 38	22 03					
	d									18 59					20 21					22 03					
Yeovil Pen Mill	d									19 13					20a36					22 19					
Thornford	d									19x18										22x24					
Yetminster	d									19x21										22x27					
Chetnole	d									19x25										22x31					
Maiden Newton	d									19 37										22 43					
Dorchester West	d									19 48										22 53					
Upwey	a									19 56										23 01					
Weymouth	a									20 04										23 06					
Dilton Marsh	d			17x04				18x23								20x02									23x59
Warminster	d		16 58	17 10			18 08	18 29			18 58	19 08	19 32			20 08		21 10				22 13	22 24		00a05
Salisbury 3	a		17 19	17 32			18 32	18 52			19 19	19 32	19 54			20 32		21 32				22 34	22 45		
	d			17 32			18 32	18 56				19 32	19 57			20 32		21 32				22 36			
Romsey	d			17 50			18 50	19 14				19 50	20 15			20 50		21 49				22 54			
Southampton Central 3	a			18 03			19 03	19 27				20 03	20 27			21 03		22 02				23 05			
Fareham	a			18 26			19 24	19 53				20 24	20 58			21 24		22 26				23 29			
	d			18 26			19 26	19 54				20 26	20 59			21 26		22 27				23 30			
Cosham	a			18 34			19 34	20 02																	
Fratton 3	a			18 40			19 40					20 40	21 12			21 40		22 39				23 43			
Portsmouth & Southsea	a			18 44			19 44					20 44	21 17			21 43		22 44				23 46			
Portsmouth Harbour	a			18 53			19 51					20 50	21 22			21 48		22 51				23 50			
Havant 3	a							20 10																	
Chichester 4	a							20 21																	
Barnham	a							20 29																	
Worthing 4	a							20 50																	
Shoreham-by-Sea	a							20 57																	
Hove 2	a							21 05																	
Brighton 10	a							21 10																	

A To London Waterloo
B From Reading
C To Plymouth
D From Weston-super-Mare
E From Frome
F From London Waterloo

For connections from Swansea to Cardiff Central and Bristol Parkway refer to Table T128

For connections from Plymouth and Exeter to Bristol Temple Meads, Westbury and Castle Cary, refer to Table T135

For connections from Exeter and Yeovil Junction to Salisbury refer to Table T160

For connections from Upwey, Weymouth and Southampton Central to Bournemouth refer to Table T158

For additional bus connections between Yeovil Junction and Yeovil Pen Mill refer to Table T123A

Table T123A-F

Mondays to Saturdays
16 December to 16 May

Yeovil Pen Mill - Yeovil Junction

Miles			SW SX ◇■	SW SX ◇■	SW SX ■	SW SO ◇■	SW SX ◇■	SW SX ■	SW SX ◇■	SW SX ■	SW SO ◇■	SW SX ■	SW SO ◇■
0	Yeovil Pen Mill	d	05 41	07 11	12 38	12 55	13 44	14 32	15 44	16 35	17 39	20 30	20 39
—	Yeovil Bus Station	d											
1¾	Yeovil Junction	a	05 46	07 16	12 43	13 00	13 49	14 37	15 49	16 40	17 44	20 35	20 45
—		d											

Sundays
15 December to 10 May

		SW ◇■
Yeovil Pen Mill	d	15 43
Yeovil Bus Station	d	
Yeovil Junction	a	15 48
	d	

NRT DECEMBER 19 EDITION

Table T123A-R

Mondays to Saturdays
16 December to 16 May

Yeovil Junction - Yeovil Pen Mill

Miles			SW SO ◇■	SW SX ◇■ ✠	SW SX ■	SW SO ◇■	SW SX ◇■	SW SX ◇■	SW SX ◇■	SW SX ◇■	SW SX ◇■	SW SX ◇■	SW SX ◇■ ✠
0	Yeovil Junction	d	09 35	12 19	13 20	14 16	14 18	14 50	16 20	16 46	19 17	20 21	21 17
—	Yeovil Bus Station	d											
1¾	Yeovil Pen Mill	a	09 45	12 24	13 27	14 21	14 25	14 55	16 28	16 51	19 25	20 28	21 24

Sundays
15 December to 10 May

		SW ◇■	SW ◇■
Yeovil Junction	d	09 50	15 16
Yeovil Bus Station	d		
Yeovil Pen Mill	a	09 55	15 21

Table T124-F

Mondays to Saturdays

16 December to 16 May

Cardiff Queen Street to Cardiff Bay

Miles			AW	AW	AW	AW	AW	and at the same minutes past each hour until	AW	AW	AW	AW	AW	AW	AW
0	Cardiff Queen Street [3]	d	06 36	06 48	07 00	07 12	07 24		22 36	22 48	23 00	23 12	23 24	23 36	23 48
1	Cardiff Bay	a	06 40	06 52	07 04	07 16	07 28		22 40	22 52	23 04	23 16	23 28	23 40	23 52

Sundays

15 December to 10 May

		AW	AW	AW	AW	AW	and at the same minutes past each hour until	AW	AW	AW	AW	AW
Cardiff Queen Street [3]	d	09 00	09 12	09 24	09 36	09 48		18 00	18 12	18 24	18 36	18 48
Cardiff Bay	a	09 04	09 16	09 28	09 40	09 52		18 04	18 16	18 28	18 40	18 52

When events are being held at the Principality Stadium, services are subject to alteration. Please check times before travelling.

NRT DECEMBER 19 EDITION

Table T124-R

Mondays to Saturdays

16 December to 16 May

Cardiff Bay to Cardiff Queen Street

Miles			AW	AW	AW	AW	AW	and at the same minutes past each hour until	AW	AW	AW	AW	AW	AW	AW	AW	AW	AW SX	AW SO	AW	AW	AW
0	Cardiff Bay	d	06 42	06 54	07 06	07 18	07 30		11 42	11 54	12 06	12 18	12 30	12 42	12 54	13 06	13 18	13 30	13 30	13 42	13 54	14 06
1	Cardiff Queen Street [3]	a	06 46	06 58	07 10	07 22	07 34		11 46	11 58	12 10	12 22	12 34	12 46	12 58	13 10	13 22	13 33	13 34	13 46	13 58	14 10

		AW	AW	AW	AW	AW	AW	AW	AW	AW	AW SX	AW SO	AW	AW	AW	AW	AW	AW	AW	AW	AW	AW	AW
Cardiff Bay	d	14 18	14 30	14 42	14 54	15 06	15 18	15 30	15 42	15 54	16 06	16 06	16 18	16 30	16 42	16 54	17 06	17 18	17 30	17 42	17 54	18 06	18 18
Cardiff Queen Street [3]	a	14 22	14 34	14 46	14 58	15 10	15 22	15 34	15 46	15 58	16 09	16 10	16 22	16 34	16 46	16 58	17 10	17 22	17 34	17 46	17 58	18 10	18 22

		AW	AW	AW	AW	AW	AW	AW SX	AW SO	AW SX	AW SO	AW	AW	AW	AW	AW	and at the same minutes past each hour until	AW	AW	AW	AW	AW
Cardiff Bay	d	18 30	18 42	18 54	19 06	19 18	19 30	19 42	19 42	19 54	19 54	20 06	20 18	20 30	20 42	20 54		23 06	23 18	23 30	23 42	23 54
Cardiff Queen Street [3]	a	18 34	18 46	18 58	19 10	19 22	19 34	19 45	19 46	19 57	19 58	20 10	20 22	20 34	20 46	20 58		23 10	23 22	23 34	23 46	23 58

Sundays

15 December to 10 May

		AW	AW	AW	AW	AW	AW	AW	AW	and at the same minutes past each hour until	AW	AW	AW	AW	AW	AW	AW
Cardiff Bay	d	09 06	09 18	09 30	09 42	09 54	10 06	10 18	10 30		17 42	17 54	18 06	18 18	18 30	18 42	18 54
Cardiff Queen Street [3]	a	09 10	09 22	09 33	09 46	09 58	10 10	10 22	10 34		17 46	17 58	18 10	18 22	18 34	18 46	18 58

When events are being held at the Principality Stadium, services are subject to alteration. Please check times before travelling.

Table T125-F

Mondays to Fridays

16 December to 15 May

London - Swindon, Cheltenham Spa, Bristol, Weston-super-Mare and South Wales

Miles	Miles	Miles			GW MX	GW MX	GW MX	GW MO	GW	GW	GW	GW	GW	GW	GW	GW	GW	GW	GW	GW	GW	GW	GW
						◇1	◇1	◇1		◇1	◇1	◇1	◇1	◇1	◇1		◇1	◇1	◇1	◇1	◇1		◇1
					A	B	B	C	D							E					F	G	
						⌶	⌶	⌶		⌶	⌶	⌶	⌶	⌶	⌶		⌶	⌶	⌶	⌶	⌶		⌶
0	0	0	LonPaddington [15] ⊖117,116	d						05 28	05 35	05 45	06 28	06 32	06 48		07 02	07 13	07 28	07 34	07 48		08 02
18½	18½	18½	Slough [3] 117,116	d				00 01															
36	36	36	Reading [7] 117,116	d			00 03	00 19		05 53	05 59	06 10	06 53	06 57	07 13		07 27	07 38	07 52	07 59	08 12		08 27
53¼	53¼	53¼	Didcot Parkway 116	d			00 18	00s34			06 13		07 07	07 12			07 41	07 52		08 13			08 41
77¼	77¼	77¼	Swindon	a			00 34	00s52		06 18	06 30	06 33	07 23	07 28	07 38		07 56	08 07	08 19	08 28	08 37		08 56
—	—	—		d			00 36		06 11	06 21	06 32	06 39	07 29	07 30	07 41	07 54	07 59	08 10	08 21	08 30	08 40	08 44	08 59
—	—	91	Kemble	d							06 44		07 41			08 07			08 34				
—	—	102¼	Stroud	d	00 10						07 00		07 57			08 22			08 49				
—	—	105	Stonehouse	d	00 15						07 05		08 02			08 27			08 54				
—	—	113¾	Gloucester [7]	a	00 29						07 16		08 17			08 48			09 09				
—	—	120¼	Cheltenham Spa [4]	a	00 43						07 32		08 31			09 05			09 25				
—	—	—	Worcester Shrub Hill	a							07 58												
—	94	—	Chippenham	d			00 48	01s04	06a26	06 33		06 51		07 42			08 11			08 42		08a59	09 11
—	107	—	Bath Spa [7]	a			00 59	01s16		06 43		07 06		07 53			08 21			08 53			09 21
111¾	—	—	Bristol Parkway [7]	a											08 02			08 31			09 01		
—	—	—		d		00 15									08 04			08 33			09 03		
117¾	118½	—	Bristol Temple Meads [10]	a			01 12	01 31		06 58		07 22		08 13			08 36			09 10			09 36
—	137½	—	Weston-super-Mare	a																			
—	164¼	—	Taunton	a																			
133½	—	—	Newport (South Wales)	a		00 40	01s54			07 49					08 23			08 53			09 22		
145¼	—	—	Cardiff Central [7] 128	a		00 58	02 13			08 03					08 37			09 07			09 38		
165½	—	—	Bridgend 128	a		01 19				08 24					09 01						09 59		
177¾	—	—	Port Talbot Parkway 128	a		01 42				08 38					09 15						10 13		
183¼	—	—	Neath 128	a		01 50				08 45					09 22						10 21		
192¾	—	—	Swansea 128	a		02 03				08 58					09 34						10 34		

		GW	GW	GW	GW	GW	GW	GW	GW	GW	GW	GW	GW	GW	GW	GW	GW	GW	GW	GW	GW	GW	GW
		◇1	◇1	◇1	◇1	◇1	◇1	◇1	◇1	◇1	◇1	◇1		◇1	◇1	◇1	◇1	◇1	◇1	◇1	◇1	◇1	◇1
			H			I							G				J						
		⌶	⌶	⌶	⌶	⌶	⌶	⌶	⌶	⌶	⌶	⌶		⌶	⌶	⌶	✕⌶	⌶	⌶	⌶	⌶	⌶	⌶
LonPaddington [15] ⊖117,116	d	08 18	08 28	08 32	08 48	09 02	09 15	09 18	09 28	09 32	09 48	10 02		10 18	10 28	10 32	10 48	11 02	11 18	11 28	11 32	11 48	12 02
Slough [3] 117,116	d																						
Reading [7] 117,116	d	08 43	08 53	08 57	09 12	09 27		09 42	09 52	09 57	10 13	10 27		10 43	10 52	10 57	11 12	11 27	11 42	11 52	11 57	12 13	12 27
Didcot Parkway 116	d		09 07	09 12		09 41			10 06	10 12		10 41			11 06	11 12		11 41		12 07	12 12		12 41
Swindon	a	09 08	09 23	09 28	09 37	09 56		10 07	10 23	10 27	10 38	10 56		11 08	11 23	11 27	11 37	11 56	12 07	12 23	12 28	12 38	12 56
	d	09 11	09 29	09 30	09 40	09 59		10 10	10 28	10 30	10 41	10 59	11 05	11 11	11 28	11 30	11 40	11 59	12 10	12 28	12 30	12 41	12 59
Kemble	d		09 42						10 41						11 41					12 41			
Stroud	d		09 58						10 57						11 56					12 57			
Stonehouse	d		10 03						11 02						12 01					13 02			
Gloucester [7]	a		10 14						11 14						12 12					13 14			
Cheltenham Spa [4]	a		10 30						11 30						12 27					13 31			
Worcester Shrub Hill	a																						
Chippenham	d			09 42		10 13				10 42		11 11	11a20			11 42		12 11			12 42		13 11
Bath Spa [7]	a			09 53		10 24				10 52		11 21				11 52		12 21			12 53		13 21
Bristol Parkway [7]	a	09 32			10 01		10 23	10 31			11 02			11 32			12 01		12 31			13 02	
	d	09 35			10 03		10 26	10 33			11 04			11 34			12 03		12 33			13 04	
Bristol Temple Meads [10]	a			10 07		10 37	10 36			11 07		11 39				12 10		12 36			13 10		13 40
Weston-super-Mare	a					11 07																	
Taunton	a					11 28																	
Newport (South Wales)	a	09 54			10 21			10 51			11 24			11 56			12 25		13 02			13 24	
Cardiff Central [7] 128	a	10 09			10 37			11 05			11 39			12 11			12 39		13 17			13 39	
Bridgend 128	a				10 58						12 01						13 01					14 01	
Port Talbot Parkway 128	a				11 10						12 14						13 15					14 15	
Neath 128	a				11 17						12 21						13 22					14 22	
Swansea 128	a				11 29						12 34						13 34					14 34	

A From Swindon
B From London Paddington
C From London Paddington. ⊡ from Chippenham ⌶ to Chippenham
D To Southampton Central
E From Westbury
F The Saint David
G To Westbury
H The Cheltenham Spa Express
I To Exeter St Davids
J ✕ to Cardiff Central ⌶ from Cardiff Central

For connections to/from:
Oxford - refer to Table T116; Gatwick Airport - refer to Table T148; Table T117 for Services via London Paddington

For principal services between: London & Taunton - refer to Table T135; London & Worcester - refer to Table T126

Table T125-F

Mondays to Fridays

16 December to 15 May

London - Swindon, Cheltenham Spa, Bristol, Weston-super-Mare and South Wales

Station			GW ◇1 🛒	GW A	GW ◇1 🛒	GW ◇1 🛒	GW ◇1 🛒	GW ◇1 🛒	GW ◇1 🛒	GW ◇1 🛒	GW ◇1 🛒	GW ◇1 🛒	GW ◇1 🛒	GW ◇1 🛒	GW ◇1 🛒	GW A	GW ◇1 🛒	GW ◇1 🛒	GW ◇1 🛒	GW ◇1 🛒	GW ◇1 🛒	GW ◇1 🛒	GW ◇1 🛒
LonPaddington 15	⊖117,116	d	12 18		12 28	12 32	12 45	12 48	13 02	13 18	13 28	13 32	13 48	14 02	14 18		14 28	14 32	14 45	14 48	15 02	15 18	15 28
Slough 3	117,116	d																					
Reading 7	117,116	d	12 42		12 52	12 57		13 12	13 27	13 42	13 53	13 57	14 13	14 27	14 42		14 53	14 57		15 13	15 27	15 42	15 52
Didcot Parkway	116	d			13 06	13 12			13 41		14 07	14 12		14 41			15 07	15 12			15 41		16 06
Swindon		a	13 07		13 23	13 27		13 37	13 56	14 07	14 23	14 28	14 38	14 56	15 07		15 23	15 28		15 38	15 57	16 07	16 23
		d	13 10	13 14	13 28	13 30		13 40	13 59	14 10	14 28	14 30	14 41	14 59	15 10	15 14	15 28	15 30		15 41	16 00	16 10	16 28
Kemble		d			13 41						14 41						15 41						16 41
Stroud		d			13 57						14 57						15 57						16 57
Stonehouse		d			14 02						15 02						16 02						17 02
Gloucester 7		a			14 14						15 14						16 16						17 14
Cheltenham Spa 4		a			14 27						15 28						16 32						17 31
Worcester Shrub Hill		a																					
Chippenham		d		13a29		13 43			14 11			14 42		15 11		15a29		15 42			16 12		
Bath Spa 7		a				13 56			14 21			14 53		15 21				15 53			16 22		
Bristol Parkway 7		a	13 31				13 53	14 01		14 31			15 02		15 31				15 58	16 02		16 31	
		d	13 33				13 55	14 03		14 33			15 04		15 33				16 01	16 05		16 33	
Bristol Temple Meads 10		a				14 12	14 04		14 36			15 09		15 36				16 08	16 09		16 38		
Weston-super-Mare		a					14 31												16 41				
Taunton		a																					
Newport (South Wales)		a	13 55					14 23		14 59			15 22		15 52					16 23		16 54	
Cardiff Central 7	128	a	14 09					14 39		15 17			15 36		16 07					16 35		17 07	
Bridgend	128	a						15 04					15 59							17 05			
Port Talbot Parkway	128	a						15 17					16 13							17 19			
Neath	128	a						15 24					16 20							17 26			
Swansea	128	a						15 37					16 33							17 39			

Station			GW ◇1 🛒	GW ◇1 🛒	GW ◇1 🛒	GW ◇1 🛒	GW ◇1 B 🛒	GW ◇1 🛒	GW ◇1 🛒	GW ◇1 🛒	GW A	GW ◇1 🛒	GW ◇1 🛒	GW ◇1 🛒	GW ◇1 🛒	GW ◇1 🛒	GW ◇1 🛒	GW ◇1 🛒	GW ◇1 🛒	GW ◇1 C 🛒	GW D	GW ◇1 🛒	GW ◇1 E 🛒	GW ◇1 🛒
LonPaddington 15	⊖117,116	d	15 32	15 45	15 48	16 02	16 15	16 18	16 30	16 32		16 48	17 00	17 02	17 15	17 17	17 28	17 30	17 47	18 00		18 02	18 16	18 18
Slough 3	117,116	d																						
Reading 7	117,116	d	15 57		16 12	16 27		16 43		16 57		17 13		17 27		17 42		17 54	18 12			18 27		18 42
Didcot Parkway	116	d	16 11			16 41		16 57	17 06	17 11				17 41		17 56	18 04	18 08				18 41		18 57
Swindon		a	16 27		16 37	16 56		17 12	17 25	17 29		17 38		17 57		18 11	18 21	18 25	18 37			18 56		19 12
		d	16 29		16 40	16 59		17 15	17 28	17 32	17 36	17 42		17 59		18 14	18 24	18 28	18 40		18 51	18 59		19 15
Kemble		d							17 41								18 37							
Stroud		d							17 57								18 53							
Stonehouse		d							18 02								18 58							
Gloucester 7		a							18 15								19 16							
Cheltenham Spa 4		a							18 30								19 32							
Worcester Shrub Hill		a																						
Chippenham		d	16 41			17 11				17 44	17a51		18 00	18 11				18 40		19 00	19a06	19 12		
Bath Spa 7		a	16 52			17 21				17 54			18 11	18 22				18 50		19 13		19 23		
Bristol Parkway 7		a		16 53	17 01		17 23	17 36				18 03			18 24	18 35			19 01				19 25	19 36
		d		16 55	17 04		17 26	17 39				18 05			18 26	18 38			19 03				19 28	19 39
Bristol Temple Meads 10		a	17 06	17 04		17 36				18 08			18 27	18 41				19 08		19 27		19 37		
Weston-super-Mare		a		17 44						18 44								19 44						
Taunton		a								19 15								20 15						
Newport (South Wales)		a			17 25		17 44	18 00				18 23			18 44	18 59			19 21				19 46	19 57
Cardiff Central 7	128	a			17 39		17 57	18 14				18 37			18 57	19 15			19 38				19 59	20 12
Bridgend	128	a			18 00		18 20					18 58			19 19				19 59				20 21	
Port Talbot Parkway	128	a			18 14		18 34					19 13			19 33				20 13				20 35	
Neath	128	a			18 21		18 41					19 20			19 40				20 20				20 42	
Swansea	128	a			18 33		18 54					19 33			19 52				20 32				20 55	

A To Westbury
B The Capitals United
C The Bristolian
D From Gloucester to Southampton Central
E To Carmarthen. The Red Dragon

For connections to/from:
Oxford - refer to Table T116; Gatwick Airport - refer to Table T148; Table T117 for Services via London Paddington

For principal services between: London & Taunton - refer to Table T135; London & Worcester - refer to Table T126

Table T125-F

Mondays to Fridays

16 December to 15 May

London - Swindon, Cheltenham Spa, Bristol, Weston-super-Mare and South Wales

Station			XC ◇1 A 🛒	GW ◇1 🛒	GW ◇1 🛒	GW ◇1 B 🛒	GW ◇1 🛒	GW ◇1 🛒	GW ◇1 🛒	GW ◇1 🛒	GW ◇1 🛒	GW ◇1 🛒	GW ◇1 🛒	GW C	GW D	GW ◇1 🛒	GW ◇1 🛒	GW ◇1 🛒	GW FO ◇1 🛒	GW FX ◇1 🛒	GW ◇1 🛒	GW ◇1 🛒	GW FO ◇1 🛒	GW FX ◇1 🛒
LonPaddington 15	⊖117,116	d		18 30	18 34	18 47	19 00	19 02	19 15	19 18	19 28	19 33	19 48			20 02	20 28	20 32	20 48	20 48	21 02	21 33	21 48	21 48
Slough 3	117,116	d																						
Reading 7	117,116	d			18 59	19 12		19 27		19 43		19 58	20 12			20 27	20 53	20 57	21 12	21 12	21 27	21 57	22 12	22 12
Didcot Parkway	116	d		19 06	19 13			19 41			20 04	20 12				20 41	21 07	21 12			21 41	22 11		
Swindon		a		19 23	19 28	19 37		19 57		20 08	20 20	20 27	20 37			20 56	21 23	21 28	21 37	21 37	21 56	22 28	22 37	22 37
		d		19 25	19 31	19 40		19 59		20 11	20 23	20 30	20 40	20 45	20 54	20 59	21 26	21 30	21 40	21 40	21 59	22 30	22 40	22 40
Kemble		d		19 38							20 36				21 07		21 39					22 43		
Stroud		d		19 54							20 52				21 22		21 55					22 58		
Stonehouse		d		19 59							20 57				21 27		22 00					23 03		
Gloucester 7		a		20 14							21 16				21 42		22 15					23 16		
Cheltenham Spa 4		a		20 31							21 32				22 05		22 34					23 32		
Worcester Shrub Hill		a									22 09													
Chippenham		d			19 43		20 00	20 11				20 42		21a00		21 11		21 42			22 11			
Bath Spa 7		a			19 53		20 12	20 22				20 52				21 21		21 56			22 22			
Bristol Parkway 7		a				20 01			20 23	20 32			21 02						22 01	22 01			23 01	23 01
		d	19 57			20 03			20 26	20 35			21 04						22 03	22 03			23 02	23 02
Bristol Temple Meads 10		a	20 07		20 07		20 30	20 37	20 35			21 07				21 37		22 12			22 45			
Weston-super-Mare		a			20 45				21 11															
Taunton		a																						
Newport (South Wales)		a	20 46			20 24				20 57			21 22						22 24	22 31			23 21	23 27
Cardiff Central 7	128	a	21 02			20 37				21 15			21 40						22 39	22 48			23 35	23 45
Bridgend	128	a				20 58				21 45			22 00						23 08	23 08			00 11	00 11
Port Talbot Parkway	128	a				21 12				21 59			22 14						23 22	23 22			00 23	00 23
Neath	128	a				21 19				22 06			22 22						23 30	23 30			00 31	00 31
Swansea	128	a				21 31				22 19			22 35						23 43	23 43			00 44	00 44

Station			GW FX ◇1 E 🛒	GW FO ◇1 E 🛒	GW FO ◇1 🛒	GW FX ◇1 🛒	GW	GW FO ◇1 🛒	GW FX ◇1 🛒	GW ◇1 🛒
LonPaddington 15	⊖117,116	d	22 00	22 00	22 30	22 30		22 48	22 48	23 32
Slough 3	117,116	d								
Reading 7	117,116	d	22 24	22 25	22 59	22 59		23 18	23 18	00 03
Didcot Parkway	116	d	22 39	22 39	23 13	23 13		23 34	23 34	00 18
Swindon		a	22 55	22 55	23 28	23 29		23 49	23 49	00 34
		d	22 57	22 57	23 31	23 32	23 42	23 52	23 52	00 36
Kemble		d					23 55			
Stroud		d					00 10			
Stonehouse		d					00 15			
Gloucester 7		a					00 29			
Cheltenham Spa 4		a					00 43			
Worcester Shrub Hill		a								
Chippenham		d	23 12	23 12	23 43	23 44				00 48
Bath Spa 7		a	23 22	23 22	23 53	23 54				00 59
Bristol Parkway 7		a						00 13	00 13	
		d						00 15	00 15	
Bristol Temple Meads 10		a	23 36	23 36	00 08	00 09				01 12
Weston-super-Mare		a	00s16	00s16						
Taunton		a	00s45	00s45						
Newport (South Wales)		a						00 34	00 40	01s54
Cardiff Central 7	128	a						00 47	00 58	02 13
Bridgend	128	a						01 08	01 19	
Port Talbot Parkway	128	a						01 31	01 42	
Neath	128	a						01 39	01 50	
Swansea	128	a						01 52	02 03	

A From Manchester Piccadilly. 🛒 to Bristol Temple Meads
B Y Cymro/The Welshman
C To Westbury
D From Westbury
E To Exeter St Davids

For connections to/from:
Oxford - refer to Table T116; Gatwick Airport - refer to Table T148; Table T117 for Services via London Paddington

For principal services between: London & Taunton - refer to Table T135; London & Worcester - refer to Table T126

Table T125-F

Saturdays

21 December to 16 May

London - Swindon, Cheltenham Spa, Bristol, Weston-super-Mare and South Wales

	GW	GW	GW	GW	GW	GW	GW	GW	GW	GW	GW	GW	GW	GW	GW	GW	GW	GW	GW	GW	GW	GW
		◇1	◇1	◇1	◇1	◇1	◇1	◇1	◇1	◇1	◇1		◇1	◇1	◇1	◇1	◇1	◇1	◇1	◇1	◇1	◇1
	A	B	B			C						D										
LonPaddington 15 ⊖117,116 d				06 29			06 47	06 59	07 29	07 32	07 47		07 59	08 17	08 29	08 32	08 47	08 59	09 17	09 29	09 32	09 47
Slough 3 117,116 d																						
Reading 7 117,116 d			00 03	06 54			07 12	07 24	07 54	07 57	08 12		08 24	08 42	08 54	08 56	09 12	09 24	09 42	09 54	09 57	10 12
Didcot Parkway 116 d			00 18	07 08				07 38		08 11			08 38	08 56		09 11		09 38	09 56		10 11	
Swindon a			00 34	07 24			07 38	07 54	08 20	08 28	08 38		08 55	09 12	09 20	09 28	09 38	09 54	10 12	10 20	10 28	10 38
d			00 36	07 26	07 29		07 40	07 56	08 22	08 29	08 40	08 45	08 56	09 14	09 22	09 30	09 40	09 56	10 14	10 22	10 29	10 40
Kemble d					07 42					08 41						09 42					10 41	
Stroud d	00 10				07 57					08 56						09 57					10 56	
Stonehouse d	00 15				08 02					09 01						10 01					11 01	
Gloucester 7 a	00 29				08 14					09 13						10 14					11 14	
Cheltenham Spa 4 a	00 43				08 28					09 28						10 29					11 31	
Worcester Shrub Hill a																						
Chippenham d			00 48	07 38				08 08	08 34			09a00	09 08		09 34			10 08		10 34		
Bath Spa 7 a			00 59	07 49				08 19	08 45				09 20		09 45			10 19		10 45		
Bristol Parkway 7 a							08 02				09 02			09 36			10 02		10 36			11 02
d		00 15				07 25	08 04				09 04			09 38			10 04		10 38			11 04
Bristol Temple Meads 10 a			01 12	08 04				08 37	09 00				09 37		10 04			10 37		11 04		
Weston-super-Mare a															10 28							
Taunton a																						
Newport (South Wales) a		00 34	01s54			07 44	08 25				09 23			09 57			10 24		10 57			11 23
Cardiff Central 7 128 a		00 47	02 13			07 58	08 38				09 39			10 12			10 40		11 11			11 37
Bridgend 128 a		01 08				08 19	09 00				10 03						11 02					12 02
Port Talbot Parkway 128 a		01 31				08 33	09 14				10 17						11 16					12 16
Neath 128 a		01 39				08 40	09 22				10 24						11 24					12 24
Swansea 128 a		01 52				08 54	09 36				10 37						11 37					12 37

	GW	GW	GW	GW	GW	GW	GW	GW	GW	GW	GW	GW	GW	GW	GW	GW	GW	GW	GW	GW	GW
	◇1		◇1	◇1	◇1	◇1	◇1	◇1	◇1	◇1	◇1	◇1		◇1	◇1	◇1	◇1	◇1	◇1	◇1	◇1
		D											D								
LonPaddington 15 ⊖117,116 d	09 59		10 17	10 29	10 32	10 47	10 59	11 17	11 29	11 32	11 47	11 59		12 17	12 29	12 32	12 47	12 59	13 17	13 29	13 32
Slough 3 117,116 d																					
Reading 7 117,116 d	10 24		10 42	10 54	10 57	11 12	11 24	11 42	11 54	11 57	12 12	12 24		12 42	12 54	12 57	13 12	13 24	13 42	13 54	13 57
Didcot Parkway 116 d	10 38		10 56		11 11		11 38	11 56		12 11		12 38		12 56		13 11		13 38	13 56		14 11
Swindon a	10 54		11 12	11 21	11 29	11 38	11 54	12 12	12 20	12 28	12 38	12 54		13 15	13 20	13 28	13 38	13 54	14 12	14 20	14 28
d	10 56	11 04	11 14	11 22	11 30	11 40	11 56	12 14	12 22	12 30	12 40	12 56	13 04	13 16	13 22	13 30	13 40	13 56	14 14	14 22	14 29
Kemble d					11 42					12 42						13 42					14 41
Stroud d					11 57					12 57						13 58					14 57
Stonehouse d					12 02					13 02						14 03					15 01
Gloucester 7 a					12 14					13 15						14 15					15 13
Cheltenham Spa 4 a					12 29					13 31						14 28					15 27
Worcester Shrub Hill a																					
Chippenham d	11 08	11a19		11 34			12 08		12 34			13 08	13a19		13 35			14 08		14 34	
Bath Spa 7 a	11 19			11 46			12 19		12 45			13 19			13 49			14 19		14 45	
Bristol Parkway 7 a			11 36			12 02		12 36			13 02			13 39			14 02		14 36		
d			11 38			12 04		12 38			13 04			13 40			14 04		14 39		
Bristol Temple Meads 10 a	11 34			12 04			12 37		13 04			13 37			14 04			14 37		15 04	
Weston-super-Mare a																					
Taunton a																					
Newport (South Wales) a			11 57			12 23		13 01			13 23			14 00			14 23		15 00		
Cardiff Central 7 128 a			12 13			12 39		13 18			13 38			14 14			14 37		15 17		
Bridgend 128 a						13 01					14 02						15 02				
Port Talbot Parkway 128 a						13 15					14 16						15 16				
Neath 128 a						13 23					14 24						15 24				
Swansea 128 a						13 36					14 37						15 37				

A From Swindon
B From London Paddington
C From Bristol Temple Meads
D To Westbury

For connections to/from:
Oxford - refer to Table T116; Gatwick Airport - refer to Table T148; Table T117 for Services via London Paddington

For principal services between: London & Taunton - refer to Table T135; London & Worcester - refer to Table T126

Table T125-F

Saturdays

21 December to 16 May

London - Swindon, Cheltenham Spa, Bristol, Weston-super-Mare and South Wales

	GW	GW	GW	GW	GW	GW	GW	GW	GW	GW	GW	GW	GW	GW	GW	GW	GW	GW	GW	GW	GW
	◇1	◇1		◇1	◇1	◇1	◇1	◇1		◇1	◇1	◇1	◇1	◇1	◇1	◇1	◇1		◇1	◇1	◇1
			A						A									A			B
LonPaddington 15 ⊖117,116 d	13 47	13 59		14 17	14 29	14 32	14 47	14 59		15 17	15 29	15 32	15 47	16 00	16 17	16 29	16 32		16 47	16 59	17 17
Slough 3 117,116 d																					
Reading 7 117,116 d	14 12	14 24		14 42	14 54	14 57	15 12	15 24		15 42	15 54	15 57	16 12	16 25	16 42	16 54	16 57		17 12	17 24	17 42
Didcot Parkway 116 d		14 38		14 56		15 11		15 38		15 56		16 11		16 39	16 56		17 11			17 38	17 56
Swindon a	14 38	14 55		15 12	15 21	15 29	15 38	15 54		16 12	16 20	16 28	16 38	16 55	17 12	17 20	17 28		17 38	17 58	18 12
d	14 40	14 58	15 04	15 14	15 22	15 29	15 40	15 56	16 01	16 14	16 22	16 29	16 40	16 57	17 14	17 22	17 29	17 33	17 40	18 00	18 14
Kemble d						15 42						16 41					17 41				
Stroud d						15 57						16 56					17 56				
Stonehouse d						16 02						17 01					18 01				
Gloucester 7 a						16 15						17 13					18 14				
Cheltenham Spa 4 a						16 31						17 27					18 31				
Worcester Shrub Hill a																					
Chippenham d		15 10	15a19		15 34			16 08	16a16		16 34			17 09		17 34		17a48		18 12	
Bath Spa 7 a		15 21			15 46			16 19			16 45			17 20		17 45				18 23	
Bristol Parkway 7 a	15 02			15 36			16 02			16 36			17 02		17 36				18 02		18 37
d	15 04			15 38			16 04			16 38			17 04		17 38				18 04		18 38
Bristol Temple Meads 10 a		15 37			16 04			16 37			17 04			17 37		18 03				18 37	
Weston-super-Mare a																18 38					
Taunton a																19 08					
Newport (South Wales) a	15 23			15 58			16 23			16 57			17 23		17 58				18 23		19 00
Cardiff Central 7 128 a	15 40			16 14			16 37			17 12			17 38		18 12				18 36		19 14
Bridgend 128 a	16 06						17 03						17 57						19 02		19 39
Port Talbot Parkway 128 a	16 20						17 17						18 11						19 16		19 53
Neath 128 a	16 27						17 24						18 19						19 23		20 00
Swansea 128 a	16 40						17 37						18 32						19 36		20 13

	GW	GW	GW	GW	GW	GW	GW	GW	XC	GW	GW	GW	GW	GW	GW	GW	GW	GW	GW	GW	GW	GW
	◇1	◇1	◇1	◇1	◇1	◇1	◇1		◇1	◇1	◇1	◇1	◇1	◇1	◇1	◇1		◇1	◇1	◇1	◇1	
								A	C								A	D				
LonPaddington 15 ⊖117,116 d	17 29	17 32	17 47	18 00	18 17	18 29	18 32			18 47	18 59	19 17	19 29	19 32	19 47	19 59		20 29	20 32	20 47	21 29	
Slough 3 117,116 d																						
Reading 7 117,116 d	17 54	17 57	18 12	18 25	18 42	18 54	18 57			19 12	19 24	19 42	19 54	19 57	20 12	20 24		20 54	20 57	21 12	21 54	
Didcot Parkway 116 d		18 11		18 39	18 56		19 11				19 38	19 56		20 11		20 38			21 11		22 08	
Swindon a	18 21	18 29	18 38	18 55	19 12	19 20	19 28			19 38	19 54	20 12	20 20	20 28	20 38	20 54		21 20	21 28	21 38	22 24	
d	18 22	18 30	18 40	18 57	19 14	19 22	19 30	19 33		19 40	19 56	20 14	20 22	20 29	20 40	20 56	21 07	21 22	21 30	21 40	22 26	22 41
Kemble d		18 43					19 42							20 41					21 42			22 54
Stroud d		18 58					19 57							20 56					21 57			23 09
Stonehouse d		19 03					20 02							21 01					22 02			23 14
Gloucester 7 a		19 16					20 15							21 13					22 14			23 29
Cheltenham Spa 4 a		19 32					20 32							21 28					22 28			
Worcester Shrub Hill a																						
Chippenham d	18 34			19 09		19 34		19a48			20 08		20 34			21 08	21a22	21 34			22 38	
Bath Spa 7 a	18 46			19 20		19 45					20 19		20 46			21 19		21 46			22 49	
Bristol Parkway 7 a			19 02		19 36					20 02		20 36			21 02					22 02		
d			19 04		19 40				20 00	20 04		20 38			21 04					22 04		
Bristol Temple Meads 10 a	18 59			19 35		20 03			20 09		20 35		21 00			21 37		21 59			23 05	
Weston-super-Mare a	19 40					20 37							21 39					22s35				
Taunton a						21 08							22 09					23 04				
Newport (South Wales) a			19 23		19 59				20 46	20 23		20 57			21 24					22 30		
Cardiff Central 7 128 a			19 40		20 13				21 00	20 39		21 10			21 37					22 47		
Bridgend 128 a			20 00		20 33					20 59		21 31			21 57					23 09		
Port Talbot Parkway 128 a			20 14		20 47					21 13		21 45			22 11					23 26		
Neath 128 a			20 21		20 54					21 20		21 52			22 18					23 37		
Swansea 128 a			20 34		21 08					21 33		22 05			22 31					23 53		

A To Westbury
B To Carmarthen
C From Manchester Piccadilly. to Bristol Temple Meads
D To Exeter St Davids

For connections to/from:
Oxford - refer to Table T116; Gatwick Airport - refer to Table T148; Table T117 for Services via London Paddington

For principal services between: London & Taunton - refer to Table T135; London & Worcester - refer to Table T126

Table T125-F

Saturdays
21 December to 16 May

London - Swindon, Cheltenham Spa, Bristol, Weston-super-Mare and South Wales

		GW	GW	GW
		◇1	◇1	◇1
		⌶	⌶	⌶
LonPaddington 15 ⊖117,116	d	21 57	22 29	23 30
Slough 3 117,116	d			
Reading 7 117,116	d	22 22	22 54	00 02
Didcot Parkway 116	d	22 36	23 08	00 18
Swindon	a	22 53	23 24	00 36
	d	22 54	23 26	00 37
Kemble	d			
Stroud	d			
Stonehouse	d			
Gloucester 7	a			
Cheltenham Spa 4	a			
Worcester Shrub Hill	a			
Chippenham	d		23 38	00 49
Bath Spa 7	a		23 49	01 01
Bristol Parkway 7	a	23 16		
	d	23 18		
Bristol Temple Meads 10	a		00 05	01 15
Weston-super-Mare	a			
Taunton	a			
Newport (South Wales)	a	23 44		
Cardiff Central 7 128	a	00 04		
Bridgend 128	a			
Port Talbot Parkway 128	a			
Neath 128	a			
Swansea 128	a			

Sundays
15 December to 10 May

		GW	GW	GW	GW	GW	GW	GW	GW	GW	GW	GW	GW	GW	GW	GW	GW	GW	GW	GW	GW	GW	GW
		◇1	◇1		◇1	◇1	◇1	◇1	◇1	◇1	◇1	◇1	◇1	◇1	◇1		◇1	◇1	◇1	◇1	◇1	◇1	◇1
		A	B	C		D				E	B					C			F		G	H	
		⌶	⌶		⌶	R⌶	⌶	⌶	⌶	R⌶	⌶	⌶	⌶	⌶	⌶		⌶	⌶	⌶	⌶	⌶	R⌶	⌶
LonPaddington 15 ⊖117,116	d		08 00		08 27	08 33	09 00	09 29	09 32	09 37	10 00	10 17	10 29	10 32	10 43		11 00	11 17	11 29	11 32	11 43	12 00	12 17
Slough 3 117,116	d																						
Reading 7 117,116	d	00 02	08 29		08 53	08 58	09 29	09 53	09 57	10 03	10 24	10 42	10 53	10 57	11 08		11 24	11 42	11 53	11 57	12 08	12 24	12 42
Didcot Parkway 116	d	00 18	08 47		09 07		09 45		10 11		10 39	10 56		11 11			11 39	11 56		12 11		12 39	12 56
Swindon	a	00 36	09 03		09 25	09 29	10 01	10 19	10 29	10 32	10 54	11 12	11 19	11 29	11 34		11 54	12 12	12 19	12 29	12 34	12 54	13 12
	d	00 37	09 05	09 12	09 25	09 30	10 02	10 21	10 29	10 34	10 56	11 14	11 21	11 29	11 36	11 41	11 56	12 14	12 21	12 29	12 36	12 56	13 14
Kemble	d				09 38				10 42					11 42						12 42			
Stroud	d				09 54				10 58					11 57						12 57			
Stonehouse	d				09 57				11 01					12 00						13 00			
Gloucester 7	a				10 16				11 19					12 17						13 16			
Cheltenham Spa 4	a				10 30				11 34					12 32						13 31			
Worcester Shrub Hill	a																						
Chippenham	d	00 49	09 17	09a27			10 14	10 33			11 09		11 33			11a56	12 07		12 33			13 07	
Bath Spa 7	a	01 01	09 28				10 26	10 44			11 20		11 44				12 20		12 45			13 20	
Bristol Parkway 7	a					09 51				10 55		11 36			11 57			12 35			12 57		13 35
	d					09 53				10 57		11 37			11 58			12 36			12 58		13 37
Bristol Temple Meads 10	a	01 15	09 47				10 41	11 00			11 38		12 00				12 33		13 04			13 37	
Weston-super-Mare	a						11 03						12 33										
Taunton	a		10 29								12 16								13 45				
Newport (South Wales)	a					10 10				11 18		11 58			12 18			12 57			13 18		13 54
Cardiff Central 7 128	a					10 24				11 32		12 11			12 32			13 11			13 32		14 11
Bridgend 128	a					10 52				11 52					12 53						13 54		
Port Talbot Parkway 128	a					11 06				12 06					13 07						14 10		
Neath 128	a					11 14				12 15					13 15						14 18		
Swansea 128	a					11 27				12 28					13 28						14 31		

A not 15 December. From London Paddington
B To Plymouth
C To Westbury
D R from Cardiff Central ⌶ to Cardiff Central
E To Carmarthen. R from Cardiff Central ⌶ to Cardiff Central
F To Paignton
G To Carmarthen
H R from Didcot Parkway to Chippenham ⌶ to Didcot Parkway ⌶ from Chippenham

For connections to/from:
Oxford - refer to Table T116; Gatwick Airport - refer to Table T148; Table T117 for Services via London Paddington

For principal services between: London & Taunton - refer to Table T135; London & Worcester - refer to Table T126

Table T125-F

Sundays
15 December to 10 May

London - Swindon, Cheltenham Spa, Bristol, Weston-super-Mare and South Wales

		GW	GW	GW	GW	GW	GW	GW	GW	GW	GW	GW	GW	GW	GW	GW	GW	GW	GW	GW	GW	GW
		◇1	◇1	◇1	◇	◇1	◇1	◇1	◇1	◇1	◇1	◇1	◇1	◇1	◇1		◇1	◇1	◇1	◇1	◇1	◇1
					A	B				C	D					E						B
		⌶	⌶	⌶		R⌶	⌶	⌶	⌶	⌶	R⌶	⌶	⌶	⌶	⌶		⌶	⌶	⌶	⌶	⌶	R⌶
LonPaddington 15 ⊖117,116	d	12 29	12 32	12 43		13 00	13 17	13 29	13 32	13 43	14 00	14 17	14 29	14 32	14 43		15 00	15 17	15 29	15 32	15 43	16 00
Slough 3 117,116	d																					
Reading 7 117,116	d	12 53	12 57	13 08		13 24	13 42	13 53	13 57	14 08	14 24	14 42	14 53	14 57	15 08		15 24	15 42	15 53	15 57	16 08	16 24
Didcot Parkway 116	d		13 11			13 39	13 56		14 11		14 39	14 56		15 11			15 39	15 56		16 11		16 39
Swindon	a	13 19	13 29	13 34		13 53	14 12	14 19	14 29	14 33	14 54	15 12	15 19	15 29	15 34		15 54	16 12	16 19	16 29	16 35	16 54
	d	13 21	13 29	13 36	13 41	13 55	14 14	14 21	14 29	14 35	14 56	15 13	15 21	15 29	15 36	15 46	15 56	16 14	16 21	16 29	16 37	16 56
Kemble	d		13 42						14 42					15 42						16 42		
Stroud	d		13 58						14 57					15 57						16 57		
Stonehouse	d		14 01						15 00					16 00						17 00		
Gloucester 7	a		14 17						15 16					16 16						17 16		
Cheltenham Spa 4	a		14 31						15 31					16 32						17 32		
Worcester Shrub Hill	a																					
Chippenham	d	13 33			13a56	14 08		14 33			15 08		15 33			16a01	16 08		16 33			17 08
Bath Spa 7	a	13 44				14 19		14 44			15 19		15 44				16 20		16 44			17 20
Bristol Parkway 7	a			13 57			14 35			14 58		15 35			15 59			16 35			16 59	
	d			13 58			14 36			15 00		15 36			16 00			16 37			17 01	
Bristol Temple Meads 10	a	13 59				14 37		14 59			15 38		15 59				16 37		17 00			17 37
Weston-super-Mare	a	14 29																	17 33			
Taunton	a																		18 04			
Newport (South Wales)	a			14 18			14 56			15 18		15 56			16 21			16 54			17 23	
Cardiff Central 7 128	a			14 30			15 10			15 32		16 10			16 32			17 10			17 38	
Bridgend 128	a			14 52						15 53					16 58						17 59	
Port Talbot Parkway 128	a			15 06						16 07					17 14						18 13	
Neath 128	a			15 14						16 15					17 23						18 21	
Swansea 128	a			15 27						16 28					17 36						18 33	

		GW	GW	GW	GW	GW	GW	GW	GW	GW	GW	GW	GW	GW	GW	GW	GW	GW	GW	GW	GW	GW	GW
		◇1	◇1	◇1	◇1		◇1	◇1	◇1	◇1	◇1	◇1	◇1	◇1		◇1	◇1	◇1	◇1	◇1	◇1	◇1	◇1
		F				E	B					G	F		E				H			F	
		R⌶	⌶	⌶	⌶		R⌶	⌶	⌶	⌶	⌶	⌶	R⌶	⌶		⌶	⌶	⌶	R⌶	⌶	⌶	R⌶	⌶
LonPaddington 15 ⊖117,116	d	16 17	16 29	16 32	16 42		17 00	17 17	17 29	17 32	17 43	18 00	18 17	18 29		18 32	18 43	19 00	19 17	19 29	19 32	19 43	20 00
Slough 3 117,116	d																						
Reading 7 117,116	d	16 42	16 53	16 57	17 08		17 24	17 42	17 53	17 57	18 08	18 24	18 42	18 53		18 57	19 07	19 24	19 43	19 53	19 57	20 08	20 24
Didcot Parkway 116	d	16 56		17 11			17 39	17 56		18 11		18 39	18 56			19 11		19 39	19 57		20 11	20 22	20 39
Swindon	a	17 12	17 19	17 29	17 35		17 54	18 12	18 19	18 29	18 34	18 54	19 12	19 19		19 29	19 34	19 54	20 14	20 19	20 29	20 38	20 54
	d	17 14	17 21	17 29	17 36	17 44	17 56	18 14	18 21	18 29	18 36	18 56	19 14	19 21	19 27	19 29	19 35	19 56	20 15	20 21	20 29	20 40	20 56
Kemble	d			17 42						18 42						19 42					20 42		
Stroud	d			17 57						18 57						19 57					20 58		
Stonehouse	d			18 00						19 00						20 01					21 01		
Gloucester 7	a			18 18						19 16						20 16					21 18		
Cheltenham Spa 4	a			18 32						19 31						20 32					21 33		
Worcester Shrub Hill	a																						
Chippenham	d		17 33			17a59	18 08		18 33			19 08		19 32	19a42			20 08		20 33			21 08
Bath Spa 7	a		17 44				18 20		18 44			19 20		19 44				20 20		20 44			21 20
Bristol Parkway 7	a	17 35			17 57			18 35			18 57		19 35				19 56		20 36			21 01	
	d	17 37			17 59			18 37			18 58		19 36				19 58		20 39			21 02	
Bristol Temple Meads 10	a		17 59				18 37		18 59			19 34		19 58				20 37		21 04			21 34
Weston-super-Mare	a								19 38					20 32									
Taunton	a											20 09											
Newport (South Wales)	a	17 57			18 18			18 54			19 18		19 56				20 18		20 59			21 19	
Cardiff Central 7 128	a	18 10			18 32			19 10			19 33		20 10				20 33		21 16			21 34	
Bridgend 128	a	18 31			18 52						19 53		20 30				20 53		21 35			21 54	
Port Talbot Parkway 128	a	18 45			19 06						20 07		20 44				21 07		21 49			22 08	
Neath 128	a	18 52			19 15						20 16		20 52				21 16		21 56			22 17	
Swansea 128	a	19 05			19 28						20 29		21 05				21 32		22 08			22 30	

A To Weymouth
B R from Didcot Parkway to Chippenham ⌶ to Didcot Parkway ⌶ from Chippenham
C To Carmarthen
D R from Didcot Parkway ⌶ to Didcot Parkway
E To Westbury
F R from Didcot Parkway to Cardiff Central ⌶ to Didcot Parkway ⌶ from Cardiff Central
G To Plymouth
H R from Cardiff Central ⌶ to Cardiff Central

For connections to/from:
Oxford - refer to Table T116; Gatwick Airport - refer to Table T148; Table T117 for Services via London Paddington

For principal services between: London & Taunton - refer to Table T135; London & Worcester - refer to Table T126

Table T125-F

Sundays

15 December to 10 May

London - Swindon, Cheltenham Spa, Bristol, Weston-super-Mare and South Wales

	GW	GW	GW	GW	GW	GW	GW	GW	GW	GW	GW	GW	GW
		◇1	◇1	◇1	◇1	◇1	◇1	◇1	◇1	◇1	◇1	◇1	◇1
	A				B			C					D
		⊼	⊼	⊼	🍽⊼	⊼	⊼	🍽⊼	⊼	⊼	⊼	⊼	🍽⊼
LonPaddington [15] ⊖117,116 d		20 17	20 29	20 32	20 43	21 00	21 29	21 43	22 00		22 37	22 57	23 33
Slough [3] 117,116 d											22 56		00 01
Reading [7] 117,116 d		20 42	20 53	20 57	21 08	21 24	21 53	22 08	22 25		23 15	23 37	00 19
Didcot Parkway 116 d		20 56		21 11	21 22	21 39		22 22	22 39		23s30	23s52	00s34
Swindon a		21 12	21 19	21 29	21 38	21 54	22 19	22 38	22 55		23s48	00s11	00s52
d	21 10	21 15	21 21	21 29	21 40	21 56	22 21	22 40	22 56	23 09			
Kemble d				21 42						23 21			
Stroud d				21 57						23 36			
Stonehouse d				22 01						23 40			
Gloucester [7] a				22 19						23 57			
Cheltenham Spa [4] a				22 33						00 12			
Worcester Shrub Hill a													
Chippenham d	21a25		21 33			22 08	22 33		23 08			00s24	01s04
Bath Spa [7] a			21 48			22 19	22 44		23 19			00s35	01s16
Bristol Parkway [7] a		21 37			22 03			23 01			00 11		
d					22 05			23 02					
Bristol Temple Meads [10] a			22 04			22 36	23 01		23 35			00 50	01 31
Weston-super-Mare a			22 36										
Taunton a													
Newport (South Wales) a					22 21			23 19					
Cardiff Central [7] 128 a					22 35			23 34					
Bridgend 128 a					22 56			23 54					
Port Talbot Parkway 128 a					23 09			00 09					
Neath 128 a					23 17			00 17					
Swansea 128 a					23 30			00 30					

A To Westbury
B 🍽 from Cardiff Central ⊼ to Cardiff Central
C 🍽 from Didcot Parkway to Cardiff Central ⊼ to Didcot Parkway ⊼ from Cardiff Central
D 🍽 from Chippenham ⊼ to Chippenham

For connections to/from:
Oxford - refer to Table T116; Gatwick Airport - refer to Table T148; Table T117 for Services via London Paddington

For principal services between: London & Taunton - refer to Table T135; London & Worcester - refer to Table T126

Table T125-R

Mondays to Fridays

16 December to 15 May

South Wales, Weston-super-Mare, Bristol, Cheltenham Spa and Swindon - London

Miles	Miles	Miles		GW	GW	GW	GW	GW	GW	GW	GW	GW	GW	GW	GW	GW	GW	GW	GW	GW	GW	GW
				◇1	◇1		◇1	◇1	◇1	◇1	◇1	◇1	◇1	◇1	◇1	◇1	◇1		◇1	◇1	◇1	◇1
						A											B	C	D			
				⊼	⊼		⊼	⊼	⊼	⊼	⊼	⊼	⊼	⊼	⊼	⊼	⊼		✕⊼	⊼	⊼	⊼
0	—	—	**Swansea** 128 d					03 46			04 58				05 28				05 57			
9½	—	—	Neath 128 d					03 58			05 10				05 40				06 09			
15	—	—	Port Talbot Parkway 128 d					04 05			05 17				05 47				06 16			
27¼	—	—	Bridgend 128 d					04 26			05 31				06 01				06 30			
47½	—	—	**Cardiff Central** [7] 128 d					05 07			05 56			06 15	06 25				06 53			07 13
59¼	—	—	Newport (South Wales) d					05 25			06 08			06 28	06 37				07 05			07 25
—	0	—	Taunton d																			
—	26¾	—	Weston-super-Mare d														06 20				06 48	
—	45¾	—	**Bristol Temple Meads** [10] d	04 53			05 25		05 46	06 00			06 30			06 49	07 00				07 28	
81	—	—	Bristol Parkway [7] a	05 02				05 51			06 28			06 48	06 57				07 25			07 49
—	—	—	d	05 03				05 53			06 29			06 50	07 02				07 27			07 50
—	57¼	—	Bath Spa [7] d				05 37		06 02	06 14			06 43			07 02	07 13				07 43	
—	70	—	Chippenham d			05 43	05 51		06 15	06 27			06 55			07 15	07 26	07 31			07 56	
—	—	—	Worcester Shrub Hill d																			
—	—	0	**Cheltenham Spa** [4] d		04 56							05 53								06 48		
—	—	6½	Gloucester [7] d		05 10							06 08								07 04		
—	—	15½	Stonehouse d		05 21							06 20								07 19		
—	—	18	Stroud d		05 26							06 26								07 24		
—	—	29¼	Kemble d		05 42							06 42								07 40		
115½	86¾	43	**Swindon** a	05 25	05 55	05 59	06 03	06 15	06 28		06 51	06 55	07 08	07 14		07 27	07 38	07 47	07 50	07 53	08 09	08 14
—	—	—	d	05 27	05 56		06 05	06 17	06 29		06 53	06 57	07 09	07 15		07 29	07 40		07 52	07 57	08 11	08 15
139½	110¾	67	Didcot Parkway 116 a	05 44	06 12			06 34	06 45			07 12		07 31		07 44				08 12		08 30
156¾	128	84½	**Reading** [7] 117,116 a	05 57	06 25		06 29	06 47	06 58		07 18	07 27	07 37	07 44		07 58			08 18	08 26	08 36	08 44
174¼	145½	101¾	Slough [3] 117,116 a																			
192¾	164	120¼	**LonPaddington** [15] ⊖117,116 a	06 25	06 54		07 00	07 14	07 27	07 29	07 44	07 59	08 09	08 16	08 14	08 27	08 29		08 45	08 54	09 07	09 11

	GW	GW	GW	GW	GW	GW	GW	GW	GW	GW	GW	GW	GW	GW	GW	GW	GW	GW	GW	GW	GW	GW
	◇1		◇1	◇1	◇1	◇1	◇1	◇1	◇1	◇1	◇1	◇1	◇1	◇1		◇1	◇1	◇1	◇1	◇1	◇1	◇1
	E	A							F					G	A							
	⊼		⊼	⊼	⊼	⊼	⊼	⊼	⊼	⊼	⊼	⊼	⊼	⊼		⊼	⊼	⊼	⊼	⊼	⊼	⊼
Swansea 128 d	06 28					06 58			07 20	07 44				08 22						09 22		
Neath 128 d	06 40					07 10			07 32	07 56				08 34						09 34		
Port Talbot Parkway 128 d	06 47					07 17			07 39	08 03				08 41						09 41		
Bridgend 128 d	07 01					07 31			07 53	08 17				08 55						09 55		
Cardiff Central [7] 128 d	07 24					07 55			08 18	08 41				09 18			09 51			10 18		10 41
Newport (South Wales) d	07 36					08 09			08 30	08 53				09 31			10 03			10 33		10 53
Taunton d				06 55				07 22														
Weston-super-Mare d				07 24				07 54														
Bristol Temple Meads [10] d			07 49	08 00				08 30			09 00		09 30			10 00			10 30		11 00	
Bristol Parkway [7] a	07 58					08 29			08 54	09 14				09 54			10 24			10 54		11 18
d	08 01					08 29			08 55	09 14				09 56			10 25			10 56		11 23
Bath Spa [7] d			08 02	08 13				08 43			09 13		09 43			10 13			10 43		11 13	
Chippenham d		08 02	08 15	08 26				08 56			09 26		09 56		10 14	10 26			10 56		11 26	
Worcester Shrub Hill d							07 25															
Cheltenham Spa [4] d							07 58					08 58						09 58				
Gloucester [7] d							08 12					09 11						10 12				
Stonehouse d							08 25					09 22						10 24				
Stroud d							08 30					09 27						10 29				
Kemble d							08 46					09 42						10 44				
Swindon a		08 19	08 27			08 52	08 59	09 09	09 18	09 37	09 41	09 55	10 09	10 19	10 33	10 38	10 47	10 57	11 08	11 19	11 38	11 47
d			08 29		08 45	08 53	09 00	09 10	09 19	09 38	09 45	09 57	10 10	10 20		10 40	10 49	10 59	11 10	11 21	11 40	11 49
Didcot Parkway 116 a			08 44		09 00		09 16	09 26			10 01	10 13	10 26			10 56		11 14	11 26		11 56	
Reading [7] 117,116 a			08 58		09 14	09 19	09 29	09 39	09 44	10 06	10 14	10 27	10 39	10 45		11 09	11 14	11 28	11 39	11 45	12 09	12 15
Slough [3] 117,116 a																						
LonPaddington [15] ⊖117,116 a	09 14		09 30	09 28	09 39	09 44	09 57	10 07	10 12	10 34	10 39	10 59	11 07	11 12		11 37	11 39	11 59	12 07	12 11	12 37	12 40

A From Westbury
B The Bristolian
C From Westbury to Cheltenham Spa
D ✕ to Cardiff Central ⊼ from Cardiff Central
E The Capitals United
F Y Cymro/The Welshman
G From Carmarthen. The Red Dragon

For connections to/from:
Oxford - refer to Table T116; Gatwick Airport - refer to Table T148; Table T117 for Services via London Paddington

For principal services between: London & Taunton - refer to Table T135; London & Worcester - refer to Table T126

Table T125-R

Mondays to Fridays

16 December to 15 May

South Wales, Weston-super-Mare, Bristol, Cheltenham Spa and Swindon - London

	GW ◇1	GW ◇1	GW ◇1	GW ◇1	GW ◇1	GW ◇1	GW A	GW ◇1	GW ◇1	GW ◇1	GW ◇1	GW ◇1	GW ◇1	GW ◇1	GW ◇1	GW ◇1	GW ◇1	GW A	GW ◇1	GW ◇1	GW ◇1	GW ◇1
Swansea 128 d			10 22						11 22					12 22						13 22		
Neath 128 d			10 34						11 34					12 34						13 33		
Port Talbot Parkway 128 d			10 41						11 41					12 41						13 40		
Bridgend 128 d			10 55						11 55					12 55						13 55		
Cardiff Central 7 128 d			11 18		11 51				12 18		12 54			13 18		13 53				14 18		14 54
Newport (South Wales) d			11 30		12 03				12 30		13 07			13 30		14 05				14 30		15 07
Taunton d																						
Weston-super-Mare d																						
Bristol Temple Meads 10 d		11 30		12 00				12 30		13 00			13 30		14 00				14 30		15 00	
Bristol Parkway 7 a			11 53		12 23				12 53		13 27			13 54		14 25				14 54		15 27
d			11 55		12 24				12 55		13 27			13 55		14 26				14 55		15 27
Bath Spa 7 d		11 43		12 13				12 43		13 13			13 43		14 13				14 43		15 13	
Chippenham d		11 56		12 26			12 42	12 56		13 26			13 56		14 26			14 42	14 56		15 26	
Worcester Shrub Hill d																						
Cheltenham Spa 4 d	10 58					11 58						12 58					13 58					
Gloucester 7 d	11 10					12 13						13 12					14 12					
Stonehouse d	11 22					12 25						13 24					14 24					
Stroud d	11 27					12 30						13 29					14 29					
Kemble d	11 43					12 45						13 45					14 45					
Swindon a	11 56	12 08	12 17	12 38	12 46	12 58	12 59	13 09	13 18	13 38	13 50	13 58	14 08	14 18	14 38	14 48	14 58	15 00	15 08	15 18	15 38	15 50
d	11 58	12 10	12 19	12 40	12 48	13 00		13 10	13 19	13 40	13 51	13 59	14 10	14 19	14 40	14 50	14 59		15 10	15 19	15 40	15 51
Didcot Parkway 116 a	12 14	12 27		12 56		13 15		13 26		13 56		14 15	14 26		14 56		15 15		15 26		15 56	
Reading 7 117,116 a	12 28	12 40	12 45	13 09	13 13	13 29		13 39	13 44	14 09	14 16	14 28	14 39	14 44	15 09	15 14	15 29		15 39	15 45	16 09	16 16
Slough 3 117,116 a																						
LonPaddington 15 ⊖117,116 a	12 59	13 07	13 10	13 37	13 40	13 59		14 07	14 11	14 36	14 41	15 01	15 08	15 12	15 36	15 41	15 59		16 07	16 09	16 36	16 44

	GW ◇1 B	GW ◇1	GW ◇1	GW ◇1	GW ◇1	GW ◇1	GW A	GW ◇1	GW ◇1 C	GW ◇1	GW ◇1	GW ◇1	GW ◇1	GW ◇1	GW D	GW ◇1	GW ◇1	GW ◇1	GW ◇1	GW ◇1	GW A	GW ◇1
Swansea 128 d			14 22						15 22					16 22						17 22		
Neath 128 d			14 33						15 33					16 34						17 34		
Port Talbot Parkway 128 d			14 40						15 40					16 41						17 41		
Bridgend 128 d			14 53						15 55					16 55						17 55		
Cardiff Central 7 128 d			15 18		15 54				16 18		16 54			17 20			17 54			18 18		
Newport (South Wales) d			15 30		16 07				16 30		17 07			17 35			18 07			18 30		
Taunton d																						
Weston-super-Mare d																						
Bristol Temple Meads 10 d		15 30		16 00				16 30		17 00			17 30			18 00			18 30			19 00
Bristol Parkway 7 a			15 54		16 27				16 54		17 27			17 55			18 27			18 51		
d			15 55		16 27				16 55		17 27			17 55			18 27			18 52		
Bath Spa 7 d		15 43		16 14				16 43		17 13			17 43			18 13			18 43			19 13
Chippenham d		15 56		16 26			16 51	16 57		17 26			17 56			18 26			18 56		19 05	19 26
Worcester Shrub Hill d																						
Cheltenham Spa 4 d	14 58					15 58						16 58						17 58				
Gloucester 7 d	15 12					16 12						17 12			17 50			18 11				
Stonehouse d	15 24					16 23						17 24			18 02			18 23				
Stroud d	15 29					16 28						17 29			18 07			18 28				
Kemble d	15 45					16 44						17 45			18 20			18 43				
Swindon a	15 58	16 08	16 18	16 39	16 50	16 57	17 07	17 11	17 18	17 39	17 50	17 58	18 08	18 18	18 34	18 38	18 50	18 56	19 09	19 15	19 21	19 38
d	16 00	16 10	16 19	16 40	16 51	16 59		17 13	17 19	17 41	17 51	17 59	18 10	18 19		18 40	18 51	18 59	19 10	19 16		19 40
Didcot Parkway 116 a	16 15	16 26		16 56		17 15				17 56		18 16	18 26			18 56		19 15	19 26	19 32		19 57
Reading 7 117,116 a	16 29	16 39	16 44	17 09	17 16	17 28		17 38	17 45	18 09	18 16	18 30	18 39	18 46		19 09	19 16	19 28	19 39	19 45		20 10
Slough 3 117,116 a																						
LonPaddington 15 ⊖117,116 a	17 00	17 07	17 09	17 35	17 41	17 56		18 07	18 15	18 39	18 41	19 01	19 09	19 14		19 39	19 42	19 57	20 05	20 14		20 36

A From Westbury
B The Cheltenham Spa Express
C The Saint David
D To Southampton Central

For connections to/from:
Oxford - refer to Table T116; Gatwick Airport - refer to Table T148; Table T117 for Services via London Paddington

For principal services between: London & Taunton - refer to Table T135; London & Worcester - refer to Table T126

Table T125-R

Mondays to Fridays

16 December to 15 May

South Wales, Weston-super-Mare, Bristol, Cheltenham Spa and Swindon - London

	GW ◇1	GW ◇1	GW ◇1	GW ◇1	GW ◇1	GW A	GW ◇1	GW ◇1	GW	GW ◇1	GW FX ◇1	GW FO ◇1	GW ◇1	GW ◇1 B	GW FX ◇1	GW FO ◇1	GW	GW ◇1
Swansea 128 d				18 22				19 22					20 22		21 22	21 22		
Neath 128 d				18 34				19 34					20 34		21 34	21 34		
Port Talbot Parkway 128 d				18 41				19 41					20 41		21 41	21 41		
Bridgend 128 d				18 55				19 55					20 55		21 55	21 55		
Cardiff Central 7 128 d	18 50			19 18				20 21					21 20		22 18	22 19		
Newport (South Wales) d	19 05			19 30				20 33					21 32		22 35	22 31		
Taunton d														21 16				
Weston-super-Mare d									20 10									
Bristol Temple Meads 10 d			19 30		20 00				20 45	21 00				22 00				22 40
Bristol Parkway 7 a	19 25			19 50				20 53	21 00				21 52		23 04	22 52		
d	19 29			19 52				20 54	21 01				21 53					
Bath Spa 7 d			19 43		20 13					21 13				22 13				22 53
Chippenham d			19 56		20 26	20 32				21 25				22 26				23 05
Worcester Shrub Hill d									22a27									
Cheltenham Spa 4 d		18 58					19 58				20 58	20 58					22 16	
Gloucester 7 d		19 12					20 16				21 11	21 11					22 28	
Stonehouse d		19 24					20 28				21 23	21 23					22 39	
Stroud d		19 29					20 33				21 28	21 28					22 44	
Kemble d		19 45					20 49				21 43	21 43					22 58	
Swindon a	19 51	19 58	20 08	20 15	20 38	20 49	21 02	21 16		21 38	21 56	21 56	22 17	22 38			23 12	23 18
d	19 53	20 03	20 10	20 18	20 40		21 03	21 18		21 39	21 58	21 58	22 19	22 41				23 19
Didcot Parkway 116 a	20 08	20 18	20 26		20 56		21 19			21 55	22 13	22 13		22 58				23 35
Reading 7 117,116 a	20 22	20 32	20 39	20 44	21 09		21 32	21 43		22 08	22 27	22 29	22 43	23 11				23 52
Slough 3 117,116 a																		
LonPaddington 15 ⊖117,116 a	20 54	21 01	21 08	21 10	21 37		22 06	22 09		22 35	23 00	23 00	23 09	23 56				00 29

Saturdays

21 December to 16 May

	GW ◇1	GW ◇1	GW ◇1	GW ◇1	GW ◇1	GW ◇1	GW ◇1	GW ◇1	GW ◇1	GW ◇1	GW ◇1	GW ◇1	GW C	GW ◇1	GW ◇1	GW ◇1	GW ◇1	GW ◇1	GW C	GW ◇1	GW ◇1	GW ◇1
Swansea 128 d		03 59		04 48			05 22		05 52			06 20			06 44			07 22			07 40	
Neath 128 d		04 11		05 00			05 34		06 04			06 32			06 56			07 34			07 52	
Port Talbot Parkway 128 d		04 18		05 07			05 41		06 11			06 39			07 03			07 41			08 00	
Bridgend 128 d		04 32		05 21			05 55		06 25			06 53			07 17			07 55			08 17	
Cardiff Central 7 128 d		05 14		05 44			06 20		06 48			07 18			07 41			08 20			08 41	
Newport (South Wales) d		05 26		05 56			06 32		07 00			07 32			07 56			08 32			08 55	
Taunton d														06 57						07 57		
Weston-super-Mare d								06 20						07 27						08 28		
Bristol Temple Meads 10 d	05 30		06 00			06 30		06 57			07 30			07 57			08 30			09 01		
Bristol Parkway 7 a		05 53		06 16			06 52		07 20			07 54			08 20			08 54			09 15	
d		05 54		06 18			06 55		07 22			07 56			08 21			08 56			09 21	
Bath Spa 7 d	05 43		06 13			06 43		07 10			07 43			08 10			08 43			09 14		
Chippenham d	05 56		06 26			06 55		07 23			07 56		08 05	08 23			08 55		09 05	09 26		
Worcester Shrub Hill d																						
Cheltenham Spa 4 d					05 40					06 49						07 58						08 58
Gloucester 7 d					05 56					07 12						08 14						09 13
Stonehouse d					06 08					07 24						08 26						09 25
Stroud d					06 13					07 29						08 31						09 30
Kemble d					06 28					07 45						08 47						09 46
Swindon a	06 08	06 16	06 38	06 44	06 41	07 08	07 17	07 35	07 44	07 58	08 08	08 18	08 24	08 35	08 44	09 00	09 09	09 18	09 24	09 39	09 44	09 59
d	06 11	06 18	06 41	06 47	07 00	07 10	07 20	07 38	07 46	08 01	08 10	08 20		08 38	08 46	09 01	09 10	09 20		09 40	09 46	10 01
Didcot Parkway 116 a	06 26	06 33	06 56	07 02	07 15	07 26		07 53	08 01	08 16	08 26			08 53	09 01	09 17	09 26			09 56	10 01	10 16
Reading 7 117,116 a	06 41	06 48	07 11	07 17	07 29	07 40	07 45	08 08	08 16	08 30	08 41	08 45		09 08	09 16	09 31	09 40	09 45		10 10	10 16	10 30
Slough 3 117,116 a																						
LonPaddington 15 ⊖117,116 a	07 06	07 14	07 36	07 44	08 00	08 06	08 13	08 36	08 42	09 00	09 08	09 11		09 36	09 42	10 00	10 06	10 11		10 36	10 45	11 00

A From Westbury to Cheltenham Spa
B From Penzance
C From Westbury

For connections to/from:
Oxford - refer to Table T116; Gatwick Airport - refer to Table T148; Table T117 for Services via London Paddington

For principal services between: London & Taunton - refer to Table T135; London & Worcester - refer to Table T126

Table T125-R

Saturdays

21 December to 16 May

South Wales, Weston-super-Mare, Bristol, Cheltenham Spa and Swindon - London

			GW ◇1	GW ◇1 A	GW ◇1	GW ◇1	GW B	GW ◇1	GW ◇1	GW ◇1	GW ◇1	GW ◇1	GW ◇1	GW ◇1	GW ◇1	GW ◇1	GW ◇1	GW B	GW ◇1	GW ◇1	GW ◇1	GW ◇1	GW ◇1
Swansea	128	d		08 22						09 23					10 22						11 22		
Neath	128	d		08 34						09 35					10 34						11 35		
Port Talbot Parkway	128	d		08 41						09 42					10 41						11 44		
Bridgend	128	d		08 55						09 56					10 55						11 57		
Cardiff Central 7	128	d		09 19		09 50				10 19		10 41			11 19		11 41				12 20		12 49
Newport (South Wales)		d		09 32		10 03				10 32		10 54			11 32		11 54				12 32		13 04
Taunton		d																					
Weston-super-Mare		d												11 03									
Bristol Temple Meads 10		d	09 30		09 57				10 30		10 57			11 30		11 57				12 30		12 57	
Bristol Parkway 7		a		09 54		10 23				10 55		11 14			11 54		12 15				12 54		13 25
		d		09 56		10 24				10 56		11 19			11 56		12 19				12 56		13 25
Bath Spa 7		d	09 44		10 10				10 43		11 10			11 43		12 10				12 43		13 12	
Chippenham		d	09 57		10 23		10 36		10 56		11 23			11 56		12 23		12 32		12 56		13 24	
Worcester Shrub Hill		d																					
Cheltenham Spa 4		d						09 58					10 58						11 58				
Gloucester 7		d						10 14					11 14						12 13				
Stonehouse		d						10 26					11 26						12 25				
Stroud		d						10 31					11 31						12 30				
Kemble		d						10 46					11 46						12 46				
Swindon		a	10 09	10 18	10 35	10 46	10 54	10 59	11 08	11 18	11 35	11 42	11 59	12 08	12 18	12 35	12 42	12 48	12 59	13 08	13 18	13 37	13 48
		d	10 11	10 20	10 38	10 48		11 01	11 10	11 20	11 38	11 46	12 01	12 10	12 20	12 38	12 46		13 01	13 10	13 20	13 38	13 49
Didcot Parkway	116	a	10 26		10 53	11 03		11 16	11 26		11 53	12 01	12 16	12 26		12 53	13 01		13 16	13 26		13 54	14 05
Reading 7	117,116	a	10 40	10 45	11 08	11 16		11 30	11 40	11 45	12 08	12 16	12 30	12 40	12 45	13 08	13 15		13 30	13 40	13 45	14 08	14 19
Slough 3	117,116	a																					
LonPaddington 15	⊖117,116	a	11 06	11 12	11 36	11 42		12 00	12 06	12 11	12 36	12 41	13 00	13 08	13 12	13 36	13 40		14 00	14 06	14 11	14 36	14 44

			GW ◇1	GW ◇1	GW ◇1	GW ◇1	GW ◇1	GW B	GW ◇1	GW ◇1	GW ◇1	GW ◇1	GW ◇1	GW B	GW ◇1	GW ◇1	GW ◇1	GW ◇1	GW ◇1	GW ◇1	GW ◇1	GW ◇1	GW B	GW ◇1
Swansea	128	d			12 22						13 24						14 23					15 23		
Neath	128	d			12 34						13 36						14 35					15 34		
Port Talbot Parkway	128	d			12 41						13 43						14 42					15 43		
Bridgend	128	d			12 55						13 57						14 56					15 57		
Cardiff Central 7	128	d			13 18		13 50				14 21		14 41				15 19		15 41			16 22		
Newport (South Wales)		d			13 32		14 03				14 33		14 54				15 31		15 54			16 35		
Taunton		d																						
Weston-super-Mare		d																						
Bristol Temple Meads 10		d		13 30		13 57				14 30		14 57				15 30		15 58			16 30			16 57
Bristol Parkway 7		a			13 54		14 24				14 54		15 15				15 54		16 15			16 55		
		d			13 56		14 24				14 56		15 19				15 56		16 19			16 56		
Bath Spa 7		d		13 43		14 10				14 43		15 10				15 43		16 14			16 43			17 10
Chippenham		d		13 56		14 23		14 36		14 56		15 23		15 30		15 56		16 27			16 56		17 05	17 23
Worcester Shrub Hill		d																						
Cheltenham Spa 4		d	12 58						13 58						14 58					15 58				
Gloucester 7		d	13 16						14 13						15 13					16 16				
Stonehouse		d	13 29						14 25						15 25					16 27				
Stroud		d	13 34						14 30						15 30					16 32				
Kemble		d	13 49						14 46						15 46					16 48				
Swindon		a	14 02	14 08	14 18	14 35	14 47	14 54	14 59	15 08	15 18	15 35	15 41	15 48	15 59	16 08	16 18	16 39	16 44	17 01	17 08	17 18	17 24	17 37
		d	14 04	14 10	14 20	14 38	14 48		15 01	15 10	15 20	15 38	15 46		16 01	16 10	16 20	16 41	16 46	17 02	17 10	17 20		17 39
Didcot Parkway	116	a	14 19	14 26		14 53	15 04		15 16	15 26		15 53	16 01		16 16	16 26		16 56	17 02	17 18	17 26			17 54
Reading 7	117,116	a	14 33	14 40	14 45	15 08	15 18		15 30	15 40	15 45	16 08	16 16		16 30	16 40	16 45	17 10	17 15	17 32	17 40	17 45		18 09
Slough 3	117,116	a																						
LonPaddington 15	⊖117,116	a	15 00	15 06	15 11	15 38	15 43		16 00	16 06	16 11	16 38	16 41		17 00	17 08	17 13	17 38	17 40	18 01	18 07	18 11		18 36

A From Carmarthen

B From Westbury

For connections to/from:
Oxford - refer to Table T116; Gatwick Airport - refer to Table T148; Table T117 for Services via London Paddington

For principal services between: London & Taunton - refer to Table T135; London & Worcester - refer to Table T126

Table T125-R

Saturdays

21 December to 16 May

South Wales, Weston-super-Mare, Bristol, Cheltenham Spa and Swindon - London

			GW ◇1	GW ◇1	GW ◇1	GW ◇1	GW ◇1	GW ◇1	GW ◇1	GW ◇1	GW ◇1	GW A	GW ◇1	GW ◇1	GW ◇1	GW ◇1	GW ◇1	GW ◇1	GW ◇1	GW ◇1	GW ◇1	GW	GW ◇1 B	GW ◇1
Swansea	128	d				16 22					17 26				18 22			19 26						
Neath	128	d				16 34					17 38				18 34			19 38						
Port Talbot Parkway	128	d				16 41					17 45				18 41			19 45						
Bridgend	128	d				16 55					17 59				18 55			19 59						
Cardiff Central 7	128	d	16 51			17 19		17 51			18 22				19 19			20 23						
Newport (South Wales)		d	17 03			17 31		18 03			18 34				19 32			20 35						
Taunton		d																					21 20	21 40
Weston-super-Mare		d																	20 27					22 10
Bristol Temple Meads 10		d			17 30		17 57			18 30			19 00			19 57			20 57		21 30		21 57	22 40
Bristol Parkway 7		a	17 24			17 54		18 23			18 54				19 54			20 55						
		d	17 24			17 56		18 25			18 56				19 56			20 56						
Bath Spa 7		d			17 43		18 10			18 43			19 13			20 10			21 10		21 43		22 10	22 55
Chippenham		d			17 56		18 23			18 56		19 05	19 25			20 23			21 23		21 56		22 23	23 08
Worcester Shrub Hill		d																						
Cheltenham Spa 4		d		16 58					17 58					19 00			19 58			21 00		21 31		
Gloucester 7		d		17 16					18 15					19 17			20 16			21 22		21 44		
Stonehouse		d		17 28					18 26					19 29			20 28			21 34		21 56		
Stroud		d		17 33					18 31					19 34			20 33			21 39		22 01		
Kemble		d		17 48					18 46					19 49			20 48			21 54		22 15		
Swindon		a	17 47	18 01	18 08	18 18	18 35	18 48	18 59	19 08	19 18	19 24	19 38	20 02	20 18	20 35	21 01	21 18	21 35	22 07	22 08	22 29	22 35	23 20
		d	17 49	18 03	18 10	18 20	18 38	18 49	19 01	19 10	19 20		19 39	20 04	20 20	20 38	21 03	21 20	21 38	22 08	22 13		22 38	23 22
Didcot Parkway	116	a	18 04	18 18	18 26		18 53	19 05	19 16	19 26			19 55	20 19		20 53	21 18	21 35	21 53	22 24	22 28		22 53	23 37
Reading 7	117,116	a	18 19	18 32	18 40	18 45	19 08	19 19	19 30	19 40	19 45		20 09	20 33	20 45	21 08	21 32	21 49	22 08	22 38	22 43		23 10	23 51
Slough 3	117,116	a																						
LonPaddington 15	⊖117,116	a	18 44	19 00	19 08	19 11	19 36	19 44	20 00	20 06	20 11		20 35	21 00	21 11	21 35	22 00	22 15	22 35	23 05	23 10		23 41	00 30

Sundays

15 December to 10 May

			GW ◇1	GW ◇1 C	GW ◇1 D	GW E	GW ◇1	GW ◇1	GW ◇1	GW ◇1	GW ◇1	GW ◇1	GW ◇1	GW ◇1	GW ◇1	GW ◇1	GW ◇1	GW A	GW ◇1	GW ◇1	GW ◇1	GW ◇1	GW ◇1	GW ◇1
Swansea	128	d							07 53					08 37			09 22			09 52			10 22	
Neath	128	d							08 05					08 49			09 34			10 04			10 34	
Port Talbot Parkway	128	d							08 11					08 55			09 40			10 10			10 40	
Bridgend	128	d							08 26					09 13			09 55			10 25			10 55	
Cardiff Central 7	128	d		07 50	07 50				08 50					09 35			10 20			10 50			11 20	
Newport (South Wales)		d		08 07	08 07				09 07					09 54			10 32			11 03			11 32	
Taunton		d																						
Weston-super-Mare		d						08 26								09 55								11 32
Bristol Temple Meads 10		d	07 45				08 30	09 00			09 30		10 00			10 30			11 00			11 30		12 00
Bristol Parkway 7		a		08 32	08 32				09 32					10 19			10 54			11 22			11 54	
		d		08 34	08 34				09 36			10 03		10 21			10 55			11 24			11 55	
Bath Spa 7		d	07 58				08 43	09 13			09 43		10 13			10 43			11 13			11 43		12 13
Chippenham		d	08 11			08 47	08 56	09 26			09 56		10 25			10 56		11 11	11 26			11 56		12 26
Worcester Shrub Hill		d																						
Cheltenham Spa 4		d								08 58					09 50						10 54			
Gloucester 7		d								09 13					10 05						11 17			
Stonehouse		d								09 26					10 18						11 27			
Stroud		d								09 32					10 24						11 33			
Kemble		d								09 47					10 39						11 47			
Swindon		a	08 23	08 56	08 56	09 03	09 08	09 38	09 58	10 01	10 08	10 25	10 38	10 43	10 53	11 09	11 18	11 28	11 38	11 46	12 01	12 08	12 18	12 38
		d	08 26	08 58	08 58		09 10	09 40	10 00	10 04	10 09	10 26	10 39	10 45	10 55	11 10	11 20		11 40	11 48	12 01	12 10	12 19	12 39
Didcot Parkway	116	a	08 42	09 13	09 13			09 55		10 21			10 55	11 00	11 13				11 55	12 03	12 18			12 55
Reading 7	117,116	a	08 57	09 27	09 28		09 37	10 09	10 25	10 34	10 38	10 52	11 09	11 14	11 27	11 39	11 45		12 09	12 17	12 31	12 38	12 45	13 09
Slough 3	117,116	a																						
LonPaddington 15	⊖117,116	a	09 24	09 53	09 53		10 07	10 36	10 52	11 05	11 11	11 20	11 36	11 39	11 56	12 09	12 14		12 36	12 42	12 59	13 07	13 09	13 36

A From Westbury

B From Penzance

C from 5 April

D until 29 March

E From Warminster

For connections to/from:
Oxford - refer to Table T116; Gatwick Airport - refer to Table T148; Table T117 for Services via London Paddington

For principal services between: London & Taunton - refer to Table T135; London & Worcester - refer to Table T126

Table T125-R

Sundays
15 December to 10 May

South Wales, Weston-super-Mare, Bristol, Cheltenham Spa and Swindon - London

		GW		GW	GW	GW	GW	GW	GW	GW	GW	GW		GW	GW	GW	GW	GW	GW	GW	GW	GW		GW	GW
		◇1		◇1	◇1	◇1	◇	◇1	◇1	◇1	◇1	◇1		◇1	◇1	◇1	◇1	◇1		◇1	◇1	◇1		◇1	◇1
							A												B						
		🍴		🍴	🍴	🍴		🍴	🍴	🍴	🍴	🍴		🍴	🍴	🍴	🍴	🍴		🍴	🍴	🍴		🍴	🍴
Swansea	128 d	10 51				11 22						12 22						13 22							14 22
Neath	128 d	11 03				11 33						12 34						13 34							14 34
Port Talbot Parkway	128 d	11 09				11 40						12 40						13 40							14 40
Bridgend	128 d	11 24				11 53						12 55						13 54							14 55
Cardiff Central 7	128 d	11 50				12 20			12 50			13 20			13 41			14 20			14 50				15 20
Newport (South Wales)	d	12 03				12 32			13 04			13 32			13 55			14 33			15 03				15 35
Taunton	d																								
Weston-super-Mare	d													13 25											
Bristol Temple Meads 10	d				12 30			13 00			13 30			14 00			14 30			15 00				15 30	
Bristol Parkway 7	a	12 22				12 54			13 23			13 54			14 18			14 54			15 23				15 54
	d	12 23				12 55			13 25			13 55			14 24			14 55			15 25				15 55
Bath Spa 7	d				12 43			13 13			13 43			14 13			14 43			15 13				15 43	
Chippenham	d				12 56		13 05	13 26			13 56			14 26			14 56		15 18	15 26				15 55	
Worcester Shrub Hill	d																								
Cheltenham Spa 4	d			11 55						13 01						14 01						14 58			
Gloucester 7	d			12 16						13 16						14 16						15 14			
Stonehouse	d			12 29						13 29						14 29						15 28			
Stroud	d			12 35						13 35						14 35						15 34			
Kemble	d			12 50						13 49						14 49						15 49			
Swindon	a	12 46		13 04	13 08	13 18	13 23	13 38	13 47	14 03	14 08	14 19		14 38	14 46	15 03	15 08	15 19	15 34	15 38	15 47	16 03		16 08	16 19
	d	12 48		13 04	13 12	13 20		13 40	13 49	14 04	14 10	14 20		14 40	14 48	15 04	15 09	15 20		15 39	15 49	16 03		16 09	16 21
Didcot Parkway	116 a	13 03		13 21				13 55	14 04	14 20				14 55	15 03	15 20				15 55	16 04	16 20			
Reading 7	117,116 a	13 17		13 34	13 38	13 45		14 09	14 18	14 33	14 35	14 46		15 09	15 18	15 33	15 39	15 46		16 09	16 18	16 33		16 38	16 46
Slough 3	117,116 a																								
LonPaddington 15	⊖117,116 a	13 44		13 59	14 06	14 14		14 36	14 43	14 59	15 06	15 12		15 36	15 42	15 59	16 09	16 14		16 39	16 46	17 02		17 09	17 14

		GW	GW	GW	GW	GW	GW	GW		GW	GW	GW	GW	GW	GW	GW	GW	GW		GW	GW	GW	GW	GW	GW
		◇1	◇1	◇1	◇1	◇1		◇1		◇1	◇1	◇1	◇1	◇1	◇1	◇1	◇1			◇1	◇1	◇1	◇1	◇1	◇1
						C	B	D						E				B		C					F
		🍴	🍴	🍴	🍴	🍽		🍴		🍴	🍴	🍴	🍴	🍴	🍴	🍴	🍴			🍴	🍴	🍴	🍴	🍴	🍽🍴
Swansea	128 d					15 17							16 22							17 22				18 22	
Neath	128 d					15 29							16 34							17 34				18 34	
Port Talbot Parkway	128 d					15 35							16 40							17 40				18 40	
Bridgend	128 d					15 50							16 55							17 55				18 55	
Cardiff Central 7	128 d		15 50			16 20				16 50			17 20		17 50					18 20				19 20	
Newport (South Wales)	d		16 03			16 32				17 04			17 32		18 03					18 33				19 33	
Taunton	d							16 16						17 03											18 58
Weston-super-Mare	d	15 26												17 33											19 26
Bristol Temple Meads 10	d	16 00			16 30			17 00				17 30		18 00			18 30				19 00		19 30		20 01
Bristol Parkway 7	a		16 22			16 54				17 23			17 54		18 24					18 54				19 54	
	d		16 24			16 55				17 25			17 55		18 25					18 58				19 55	
Bath Spa 7	d	16 13			16 43			17 13				17 43		18 13			18 43				19 13		19 43		20 14
Chippenham	d	16 26			16 56		17 18	17 24				17 55		18 26			18 56	19 01			19 26		19 55		20 27
Worcester Shrub Hill	d																								
Cheltenham Spa 4	d			15 58							17 00					18 00						19 00			
Gloucester 7	d			16 15							17 15					18 15						19 16			
Stonehouse	d			16 28							17 28					18 28						19 28			
Stroud	d			16 34							17 33					18 33						19 33			
Kemble	d			16 48							17 48					18 47						19 48			
Swindon	a	16 38	16 46	17 02	17 08	17 19	17 34	17 38		17 47	18 01	18 08	18 18	18 38	18 47	19 01	19 09	19 17		19 21	19 38	20 01	20 08	20 18	20 38
	d	16 40	16 48	17 02	17 09	17 20		17 39		17 48	18 02	18 09	18 19	18 39	18 48	19 01	19 09			19 23	19 40	20 02	20 09	20 19	20 39
Didcot Parkway	116 a	16 55	17 03	17 19				17 55		18 04	18 18			18 55	19 04	19 18					19 55	20 18		20 35	20 56
Reading 7	117,116 a	17 09	17 17	17 32	17 38	17 46		18 11		18 18	18 31	18 38	18 45	19 10	19 18	19 31	19 38			19 48	20 09	20 31	20 38	20 49	21 10
Slough 3	117,116 a																								
LonPaddington 15	⊖117,116 a	17 37	17 43	17 59	18 08	18 14		18 38		18 44	18 59	19 06	19 09	19 38	19 42	19 56	20 09			20 14	20 38	20 59	21 05	21 14	21 38

A From Weymouth
B From Westbury
C From Carmarthen
D From Plymouth
E From Paignton
F 🍽 from Bristol Temple Meads to Chippenham 🍴 to Bristol Temple Meads 🍴 from Chippenham

For connections to/from:
Oxford - refer to Table T116; Gatwick Airport - refer to Table T148; Table T117 for Services via London Paddington

For principal services between: London & Taunton - refer to Table T135; London & Worcester - refer to Table T126

Table T125-R

Sundays
15 December to 10 May

South Wales, Weston-super-Mare, Bristol, Cheltenham Spa and Swindon - London

		GW	GW	GW		GW	GW	GW	GW	GW	GW
			◇1	◇1		◇1	◇1	◇1	◇1	◇1	1
		A							B	C	
			🍴	🍴		🍴	🍴	🍴	🍴	🍴	
Swansea	128 d					19 22			20 19		
Neath	128 d					19 34			20 31		
Port Talbot Parkway	128 d					19 40			20 37		
Bridgend	128 d					19 55			20 52		
Cardiff Central 7	128 d					20 20			21 20		
Newport (South Wales)	d					20 32			21 32		
Taunton	d									21 42	
Weston-super-Mare	d							21 05			
Bristol Temple Meads 10	d			20 30				21 30		22 20	
Bristol Parkway 7	a					20 51			21 53		
	d					20 52			21 54		
Bath Spa 7	d			20 43				21 43		22 34	
Chippenham	d	20 44		20 56				21 55		22 47	
Worcester Shrub Hill	d										
Cheltenham Spa 4	d		19 58				20 58				21 58
Gloucester 7	d		20 16				21 13				22 13
Stonehouse	d		20 29				21 26				22 26
Stroud	d		20 34				21 32				22 31
Kemble	d		20 48				21 47				22 46
Swindon	a	21 00	21 02	21 08		21 15	22 01	22 08	22 17	22 59	22 59
	d		21 03	21 10		21 17	22 01	22 09	22 19	23 04	
Didcot Parkway	116 a		21 19	21 25		21 32	22 18	22 24	22 34	23 20	
Reading 7	117,116 a		21 32	21 39		21 46	22 31	22 39	22 48	23 34	
Slough 3	117,116 a										
LonPaddington 15	⊖117,116 a		21 59	22 10		22 11	23 03	23 15	23 29	00 12	

A From Westbury
B From Carmarthen
C From Plymouth

For connections to/from:
Oxford - refer to Table T116; Gatwick Airport - refer to Table T148; Table T117 for Services via London Paddington

For principal services between: London & Taunton - refer to Table T135; London & Worcester - refer to Table T126

Table T126-F

London and Oxford - Worcester and Hereford

Mondays to Fridays
16 December to 15 May

Miles		GW	GW	GW	GW	GW	GW	GW	GW	GW	GW	GW	GW	GW	GW	GW	GW	GW	GW	GW	GW	GW
		MX ◇[1] A		◇[1] 🛒	◇[1] 🛒	◇[1] 🛒	◇[1] 🛒	◇[1] 🛒	◇[1] 🛒	◇[1] 🛒	◇[1] 🛒	◇[1] 🛒	◇[1] 🛒	◇[1] 🛒	◇[1] 🛒		◇[1] 🛒	◇[1] B 🛒	◇[1] 🛒	◇[1] 🛒	◇[1] 🛒	◇[1] 🛒
0	London Paddington [15] ⊖116,125,135 d			05 50	06 50	07 50	08 50	09 50	10 50	11 50	12 50	13 50	14 50	15 20	15 50		16 58	17 34	17 58	18 58	19 50	20 50
18½	Slough [3] 116,125,135 d			06 04	07 04	08 04	09 04	10 05	11 04	12 04	13 04	14 04	15 04	15 34	16u04						20 04	21 04
36	Reading [7] 116,125,135 d			06 18	07 18	08 18	09 18	10 19	11 18	12 18	13 18	14 18	15 18	15 48	16u18			17 59			20 18	21 18
53¼	Didcot Parkway 116,125 d															17 03						
63½	Oxford 116 d		05 10	06 52	07 48	08 44	09 45	10 45	11 44	12 45	13 45	14 45	15 45	16 15	16 44	17 23	17 45	18 24	18 46	19 44	20 43	21 43
70½	Hanborough d	00 11		07 02	07 58	08 55	09 55	10 55	11 59	12 55	13 55	14 55	15 55	16 29	16 55	17 32	17 55	18 34	18 59	19 55	20 55	21 53
71½	Combe d															17 35						
75	Finstock d															17 41						
76¾	Charlbury a	00 18		07 09	08 04	09 01	10 02	11 02	12 05	13 02	14 02	15 02	16 02	16 36	17 01	17 45	18 02	18 41	19 06	20 01	21 02	22 00
—	d	00 19		07 10	08 05	09 02	10 03	11 03	12 06	13 03	14 03	15 03	16 03	16 37	17 02	17 45	18 03	18 42	19 07	20 02	21 03	22 00
80½	Ascott-under-Wychwood d															17 51						
81½	Shipton d															17 54			19 13			
84¾	Kingham d	00 28		07 19	08 14	09 11	10 12	11 12	12 15	13 12	14 12	15 12	16 12	16 46	17 11	17 59	18 14	18 51	19 18	20 11	21 12	22 09
91¾	Moreton-in-Marsh a	00 35	05 35	07 26	08 21	09 18	10 19	11 19	12 22	13 19	14 19	15 19	16 19	16 53	17 18	18 07	18 21	18 58	19 25	20 18	21 19	22 16
—	d	00 36	05 35	07 27	08 22	09 19	10 20	11 20	12 23	13 20	14 20	15 20	16 20	16 54	17 19		18 22	18 59	19 26	20 19	21 20	22 16
101¼	Honeybourne d	00 47	05 46	07 38	08 33		10 31		12 34		14 31		16 31	17 05	17 30		18 33		19 36	20 30	21 31	22 27
106¼	Evesham a	00 53	05 53	07 43	08 39	09 33	10 36	11 34	12 40	13 34	14 36	15 34	16 36	17 10	17 36		18 38	19 13	19 42	20 36	21 36	22 32
—	d	00 54	05 53	07 51	08 42	09 34	10 37	11 35	12 41	13 35	14 37	15 35	16 37	17 11	17 50		18 39	19 14	19 42	20 37	21 37	22 33
112½	Pershore d	01a00	06 01	07 58	08 49	09 41	10 44	11 42	12 48		14 44	15 42	16 44	17 18	17 57		18 46		19 49	20 44	21 44	22 39
120½	Worcester Shrub Hill [7] a		06 21	08 19	09 05	09 57	11 00	11 56	13 04	13 54	15 00	15 58	17 05	17 37	18 12		19 02	19 33	20 04	20 59	22 00	22 55
121¼	Worcester Foregate Street [7] a		06 24	08 22	09 17	09 59	11 03	11 59		13 57		16 01	17 12	17 40	18 17		19 07	19 36	20 07	21 06	22 03	22 58
128	Malvern Link a			08 31	09 26	10 08	11 12	12 08		14 06		16 09			18 27		19 21	19 45		21 15	22 12	23 07
128¾	Great Malvern a			08 34	09 29	10 11	11 15	12 12		14 10		16 12			18 30		19 24	19 49		21 18	22 15	23 10
131¾	Colwall a							12 18		14 16								19 55		21 29	22 33	
136	Ledbury a							12 26		14 24								20 03		21 38	22 41	
149¾	Hereford [7] a							12 43		14 41								20 25		22 04	22 58	

	GW	GW
	◇[1] 🛒	◇[1] C
London Paddington [15] ⊖116,125,135 d	21 50	22 50
Slough [3] 116,125,135 d	22 04	23 06
Reading [7] 116,125,135 d	22 18	23 28
Didcot Parkway 116,125 d		
Oxford 116 d	22 45	23 59
Hanborough d	22 55	00 11
Combe d		
Finstock d		
Charlbury a	23 02	00 18
d	23 03	00 19
Ascott-under-Wychwood d		
Shipton d	23 09	
Kingham d	23 14	00 28
Moreton-in-Marsh a	23 21	00 35
d	23 22	00 36
Honeybourne d	23 33	00 47
Evesham a	23 39	00 53
d	23 40	00 54
Pershore d	23 47	01a00
Worcester Shrub Hill [7] a	00 02	
Worcester Foregate Street [7] a		
Malvern Link a		
Great Malvern a		
Colwall a		
Ledbury a		
Hereford [7] a		

A From London Paddington to Worcestershire Parkway Hl
B The Cathedrals Express
C To Worcestershire Parkway Hl

For additional services between London and Worcester refer to Table T125

Table T126-F

London and Oxford - Worcester and Hereford

Saturdays
21 December to 16 May

	GW	GW	GW	GW	GW	GW	GW	GW	GW	GW	GW	GW	GW	GW	GW	GW	GW
	◇[1] A	◇[1] 🛒	◇[1] 🛒	◇[1] 🛒	◇[1] 🛒	◇[1] 🛒	◇[1] 🛒	◇[1] 🛒	◇[1] 🛒	◇[1] 🛒	◇[1] 🛒	◇[1] 🛒	◇[1] 🛒	◇[1] 🛒	◇[1] 🛒	◇[1] 🛒	◇[1] 🛒
London Paddington [15] ⊖116,125,135 d		05 50	06 50	07 50	08 50	09 50	10 50	11 50	12 50	13 50	14 50	15 50	16 50	17 50	18 50	19 50	21 49
Slough [3] 116,125,135 d		06 04	07 04	08 04	09 04	10 04	11 04	12 04	13 04	14 04	15 04	16 04	17 04	18 05	19 04	20 04	22 03
Reading [7] 116,125,135 d		06 18	07 19	08 19	09 19	10 19	11 19	12 19	13 19	14 19	15 19	16 18	17 19	18 19	19 19	20 19	22 17
Didcot Parkway 116,125 d		06 34															22 33
Oxford 116 d		06 48	07 45	08 45	09 45	10 45	11 45	12 45	13 45	14 45	15 45	16 45	17 45	18 44	19 45	20 45	22 48
Hanborough d	00 11	06 58	07 55	08 56	09 55	10 55	11 57	12 55	13 55	14 57	15 55	16 55	17 55	18 55	19 55	20 55	22 58
Combe d																	
Finstock d																	
Charlbury a	00 18	07 05	08 02	09 03	10 02	11 02	12 04	13 02	14 02	15 03	16 02	17 02	18 01	19 01	20 02	21 02	23 05
d	00 19	07 06	08 03	09 04	10 03	11 03	12 05	13 03	14 03	15 04	16 03	17 03	18 02	19 02	20 03	21 03	23 06
Ascott-under-Wychwood d																	
Shipton d									14 09					19 08		21 09	23 12
Kingham d	00 28	07 15	08 12	09 13	10 12	11 12	12 14	13 12	14 14	15 13	16 12	17 12	18 11	19 13	20 12	21 14	23 17
Moreton-in-Marsh a	00 35	07 22	08 19	09 20	10 19	11 19	12 21	13 19	14 21	15 20	16 19	17 19	18 18	19 20	20 19	21 21	23 24
d	00 36	07 23	08 20	09 21	10 20	11 20	12 22	13 20	14 22	15 21	16 20	17 20	18 19	19 21	20 20	21 22	23 25
Honeybourne d	00 47	07 33	08 31	09 31	10 31		12 33	13 31	14 33	15 32	16 31	17 31	18 30	19 32	20 31	21 33	23 36
Evesham a	00 53	07 39	08 36	09 37	10 36	11 34	12 38	13 36	14 39	15 38	16 36	17 36	18 35	19 37	20 36	21 39	23 42
d	00 54	07 40	08 49	09 38	10 37	11 35	12 39	13 37	14 40	15 39	16 37	17 37	18 36	19 38	20 37	21 40	23 43
Pershore d	01a00	07 46	08 56	09 45	10 44	11 42	12 46		14 47	15 46	16 44	17 44	18 43	19 45	20 44	21 47	23 50
Worcester Shrub Hill [7] a		08 02	09 12	10 01	11 00	11 57	13 02	13 55	15 03	16 02	17 00	18 00	18 58	20 01	21 14	22 03	00 06
Worcester Foregate Street [7] a		08 05	09 15	10 04	11 12	12 00	13 13	13 59	15 17	16 05	17 03	18 11	19 01	20 10	21 17	22 07	
Malvern Link a		08 14	09 24	10 13	11 29	12 09		14 08		16 14	17 12		19 10		21 26	22 21	
Great Malvern a		08 18	09 28	10 17	11 33	12 12		14 11		16 18	17 16	18 25	19 13		21 29	22 25	
Colwall a						12 18		14 17					19 19		21 37		
Ledbury a						12 25		14 25					19 27		21 46		
Hereford [7] a						12 44		14 44					19 46		22 06		

Sundays
15 December to 10 May

	GW	GW	GW	GW	GW	GW	GW	GW	GW	GW	GW	GW	GW	GW
	◇[1] 🛒	◇[1] 🛒	◇[1] 🛒	◇[1] 🛒	◇[1] 🛒	◇[1] 🛒	◇[1] 🛒	◇[1] 🛒	◇[1] 🛒	◇[1] 🛒	◇[1] 🛒	◇[1] 🛒	◇[1] 🛒	◇[1]
London Paddington [15] ⊖116,125,135 d	07 37	08 37	09 42	10 46	11 46	12 46	13 45	14 46	15 46	16 46	17 46	18 46	19 46	21 46
Slough [3] 116,125,135 d	08 00	08 51	09 58	11 00	12 00	13 00	14 00	15 00	16 00	17 00	18 00	19 00	20 00	21 59
Reading [7] 116,125,135 d	08 21	09 08	10 10	11 13	12 12	13 13	14 12	15 13	16 13	17 13	18 13	19 13	20 13	22 13
Didcot Parkway 116,125 d	08 38	09 29	10 29	11 29	12 29	13 29	14 29	15 30	16 29	17 30	18 28	19 31	20 29	22 29
Oxford 116 d	08 51	09 44	10 41	11 44	12 43	13 44	14 41	15 44	16 44	17 45	18 44	19 45	20 46	22 43
Hanborough d	09 02	09 54	10 53	11 54	12 55	13 54	14 53	15 54	16 55	17 55	18 54	19 56	20 56	22 54
Combe d														
Finstock d														
Charlbury a	09 09	09 59	10 59	12 00	13 00	14 00	14 59	16 00	17 00	18 00	18 59	20 00	21 02	23 00
d	09 10	10 00	11 00	12 01	13 01	14 01	15 00	16 01	17 01	18 01	19 00	20 01	21 03	23 01
Ascott-under-Wychwood d														
Shipton d														
Kingham d	09 19	10 09	11 09	12 10	13 10	14 10	15 09	16 10	17 10	18 10	19 09	20 10	21 12	23 10
Moreton-in-Marsh a	09 26	10 17	11 17	12 18	13 18	14 18	15 17	16 18	17 17	18 18	19 17	20 17	21 20	23 18
d	09 27	10 18	11 18	12 19	13 19	14 19	15 18	16 19	17 18	18 19	19 18	20 18	21 21	23 18
Honeybourne d	09 38	10 28	11 31		13 32		15 31		17 31	18 31	19 30	20 31	21 33	23 29
Evesham a	09 43	10 34	11 36	12 32	13 38	14 32	15 36	16 32	17 36	18 35	19 34	20 37	21 36	23 35
d	09 44	10 37	11 37	12 35	13 39	14 36	15 37	16 35	17 38	18 38	19 37	20 38	21 40	23 35
Pershore d	09 51	10 44	11 44	12 42	13 46	14 43	15 44	16 42	17 45	18 45	19 44	20 45	21 47	23 43
Worcester Shrub Hill [7] a	10 09	11 04	12 00	12 57	14 01	14 57	16 00	16 57	18 00	18 59	19 59	21 02	22 03	23 59
Worcester Foregate Street [7] a	10 15	11 12	12 12		14 19		16 18		18 03		20 02	21 08	22 06	
Malvern Link a	10 24	11 22	12 21		14 28		16 27		18 13		20 11	21 17	22 16	
Great Malvern a	10 27	11 25	12 24		14 31		16 30		18 16		20 14	21 21	22 19	
Colwall a			12 33		14 37		16 36		18 34			21 31		
Ledbury a			12 41		14 45		16 43		18 42			21 39		
Hereford [7] a			13 00		15 04		17 01		19 00			21 58		

A From London Paddington to Worcestershire Parkway Hl

For additional services between London and Worcester refer to Table T125

Table T126-R

Hereford and Worcester - Oxford and London

Mondays to Fridays
16 December to 15 May

Miles			GW	GW	GW	GW	GW	GW	GW	GW	GW	GW	GW	GW	GW	GW	GW	GW	GW	GW	GW	GW	GW
			◇1	◇1	◇1	◇1		◇1	◇1	◇1	◇1	◇1	◇1	◇1	◇1	◇1	◇1	◇1	◇1	◇1		◇1	◇1
								A															
			⊥	⊥	⊥	⊥		⊥	⊥	⊥	⊥	⊥	⊥	⊥	⊥	⊥	⊥	⊥	⊥	⊥		⊥	⊥
0	**Hereford** [7]	d		04 48	05 23			06 43							13 18		15 18						
13¾	Ledbury	d		05 05	05 40			07 00							13 35		15 35						
18	Colwall	d		05 13	05 47			07 08							13 42		15 42						
20½	Great Malvern	d		05 18	05 52			07 13		08 56	09 54	10 58	11 55		13 47		15 55	16 30				19 04	19 46
21¾	Malvern Link	d		05 21	05 56			07 16		08 59	09 57	11 01	11 58		13 51		15 58	16 33				19 07	19 49
28½	**Worcester Foregate Street** [7]	d		05 31	06 06		06 53	07 26		09 09	10 07	11 11	12 08		14 06		16 08	16 43	17 27	17 57		19 17	19 59
29¾	**Worcester Shrub Hill** [7]	d	05 11	05 35	06 10	06 43	07 02	07 30	08 13	09 14	10 14	11 15	12 15	13 18	14 10	15 20	16 14	16 51	17 32	18 02		19 21	20 03
37	Pershore	d	05 25		06 24		07 11	07 44	08 27	09 28	10 28	11 29	12 29		14 24		16 28	17 05	17 44	18 17		19 35	20 17
43	Evesham	a	05 31	05 52	06 30	07 00	07 18	07 51	08 34	09 34	10 35	11 35	12 36	13 35	14 31	15 35	16 34	17 12	17 50	18 23		19 41	20 24
—		d	05 32	05 54	06 36	07 01	07 22	07 52	08 35	09 35	10 36	11 37	12 37	13 36	14 33	15 36	16 35	17 13	18 00	18 24		19 42	20 25
48	Honeybourne	d	05 39		06 43		07 29	07 59	08 42	09 42	10 43	11 44	12 44	13 43	14 40		16 42	17 20	18 08	18 31			20 32
58	Moreton-in-Marsh	a	05 50	06 08	06 54	07 15	07 40	08 09	08 52	09 53	10 53	11 54	12 54	13 54	14 50	15 50	16 53	17 30	18 18	18 42		19 56	20 42
—		d	05 51	06 09	06 55	07 16	07 41	08 10	08 53	09 54	10 54	11 55	12 55	13 55	14 51	15 51	16 54	17 39	18 22	18 46	19 10	19 56	20 43
65	Kingham	d	05 59	06 17	07 03	07 24	07 49	08 18	09 01	10 02	11 02	12 03	13 03	14 03	14 59	15 59	17 02	17 47	18 31	18 54	19 18	20 04	20 51
68	Shipton	d					07 53														19 23		
69¼	Ascott-under-Wychwood	d					07 56																
73	Charlbury	a	06 07	06 25	07 11	07 32	08 02	08 26	09 09	10 10	11 10	12 11	13 11	14 11	15 07	16 07	17 10	17 55	18 39	19 02	19 29	20 12	20 59
—		d	06 08	06 26	07 12	07 33	08 05	08 27	09 10	10 11	11 11	12 12	13 12	14 12	15 08	16 08	17 11	18 03	18 41	19 09	19 30	20 13	21 10
74¾	Finstock	d					08 08																
78¾	Combe	d					08 13																
79¾	Hanborough	d	06 15	06 34	07 19	07 40	08 17	08 35	09 18	10 18	11 19	12 20	13 20	14 19	15 16	16 15	17 18	18 10		19 16	19 37	20 20	21 18
86¾	**Oxford** 116	a	06 25	06 46	07 29	07 51	08 26	08 44	09 30	10 28	11 28	12 29	13 29	14 29	15 25	16 25	17 28	18 25	19 00	19 30	19 50	20 30	21 30
96½	Didcot Parkway 125,116	a					08 41																
113¾	Reading [7] 135,125,116	a	06 53	07 09	07 53	08 14		09 11	09 55	10 54	11 54	12 54	13 54	14 54	15 54	16 54	17 56	18 57	19 24	19 53		20 53	21 53
131¼	Slough [3] 135,125,116	a							10 09	11 08	12 08	13 08	14 08	15 08	16 08	17 08	18 11	19 11	19 38	20 08		21 07	22 07
149¾	**London Paddington** [15] ⊖135,125,116	a	07 24	07 39	08 24	08 40		09 37	10 24	11 24	12 24	13 24	14 24	15 24	16 24	17 24	18 29	19 28	19 54	20 24		21 22	22 24

		GW	GW
		◇1	◇1
		⊥	⊥
Hereford [7]	d		22 00
Ledbury	d		22 17
Colwall	d		22 24
Great Malvern	d		22 29
Malvern Link	d		22 32
Worcester Foregate Street [7]	d	20 58	22 41
Worcester Shrub Hill [7]	d	21 02	22 50
Pershore	d	21 16	23 04
Evesham	a	21 23	23 11
	d	21 26	23 12
Honeybourne	d	21 33	23 19
Moreton-in-Marsh	a	21 44	23 29
	d	21 50	23 30
Kingham	d	21 58	23 38
Shipton	d		
Ascott-under-Wychwood	d		
Charlbury	a	22 06	23 46
	d	22 13	23 47
Finstock	d		
Combe	d		
Hanborough	d	22 20	23 55
Oxford 116	a	22 30	00 08
Didcot Parkway 125,116	a	22 44	00 22
Reading [7] 135,125,116	a	22 57	00 41
Slough [3] 135,125,116	a	23 18	00 56
London Paddington [15] ⊖135,125,116	a	23 44	01 15

Saturdays
21 December to 16 May

		GW	GW	GW	GW	GW	GW	GW	GW	GW	GW	GW	GW	GW	GW	GW	GW	GW	GW
		◇1	◇1	◇1	◇1	◇1	◇1	◇1	◇1	◇1	◇1	◇1	◇1	◇1	◇1	◇1	◇1	◇1	1
			⊥	⊥	⊥	⊥	⊥	⊥	⊥	⊥	⊥	⊥	⊥	⊥	⊥	⊥	⊥	⊥	
Hereford [7]	d		06 18	07 12							13 18		15 13					20 20	
Ledbury	d		06 35	07 29							13 35		15 30					20 38	
Colwall	d		06 43	07 37							13 43		15 38					20 46	
Great Malvern	d	05 53	06 52	07 42		08 48	09 58	10 40	11 55		13 55		15 43	16 40	17 40	19 00		20 55	22 42
Malvern Link	d	05 57	06 55	07 45		08 52	10 02	10 44	11 59		13 58		15 46	16 44	17 44	19 04		20 58	22 46
Worcester Foregate Street [7]	d	06 07	07 06	07 55	08 25	09 02	10 12	10 54	12 09	13 05	14 08	15 08	15 56	16 54	17 54	19 14	20 02	21 09	22 56
Worcester Shrub Hill [7]	d	06 11	07 10	08 00	08 29	09 10	10 16	11 00	12 13	13 10	14 13	15 13	16 10	16 58	18 02	19 18	20 13	21 13	23 02
Pershore	d	06 25	07 24	08 16	08 43	09 24	10 30	11 16	12 27	13 24	14 27	15 27	16 24	17 14	18 18	19 30	20 27	21 27	23 16
Evesham	a	06 32	07 31	08 22	08 50	09 30	10 37	11 22	12 34	13 31	14 34	15 34	16 31	17 20	18 24	19 36	20 34	21 33	23 24
	d	06 36	07 33	08 30	08 52	09 33	10 38	11 36	12 36	13 33	14 36	15 36	16 33	17 36	18 36	19 37	20 36	21 35	
Honeybourne	d	06 43	07 40	08 37	08 59	09 40	10 45	11 43	12 43	13 40	14 43	15 43	16 40	17 43	18 43	19 44	20 43	21 42	
Moreton-in-Marsh	a	06 53	07 50	08 47	09 09	09 50	10 55	11 53	12 53	13 50	14 53	15 53	16 50	17 53	18 53	19 55	20 53	21 52	
	d	06 55	07 52	08 49	09 10	09 52	10 56	11 55	12 55	13 52	14 55	15 55	16 52	17 55	18 55	19 56	20 55	21 54	
Kingham	d	07 03	08 00	08 57	09 18	10 00	11 04	12 03	13 03	14 00	15 03	16 03	17 00	18 03	19 03	20 04	21 03	22 02	
Shipton	d		08 05			10 05				14 05			17 05						
Ascott-under-Wychwood	d																		
Charlbury	a	07 11	08 11	09 05	09 26	10 11	11 12	12 11	13 11	14 11	15 11	16 11	17 11	18 11	19 11	20 12	21 11	22 10	
	d	07 12	08 12	09 06	09 27	10 12	11 13	12 12	13 12	14 12	15 12	16 12	17 12	18 12	19 12	20 13	21 12	22 11	
Finstock	d																		
Combe	d																		
Hanborough	d	07 19	08 19	09 13	09 35	10 19	11 21	12 19	13 19	14 19	15 19	16 19	17 19	18 19	19 19	20 20	21 19	22 18	
Oxford 116	a	07 29	08 29	09 23	09 45	10 29	11 30	12 29	13 29	14 29	15 29	16 29	17 29	18 29	19 29	20 30	21 29	22 29	
Didcot Parkway 125,116	a																	22 48	
Reading [7] 135,125,116	a	07 54	08 54	09 54	10 13	10 54	11 54	12 54	13 54	14 53	15 54	16 54	17 54	18 54	19 54	20 54	21 54	23 05	
Slough [3] 135,125,116	a	08 07	09 08	10 07		11 07	12 08	13 08	14 07	15 07	16 07	17 07	18 07	19 07	20 07	21 07	22 07	23 19	
London Paddington [15] ⊖135,125,116	a	08 22	09 23	10 24	10 37	11 25	12 25	13 24	14 22	15 22	16 25	17 23	18 23	19 24	20 25	21 23	22 25	23 36	

A The Cathedrals Express

Table T126-R

Sundays
15 December to 10 May

Hereford and Worcester - Oxford and London

		GW	GW	GW	GW	GW	GW	GW	GW	GW	GW	GW	GW	GW	GW
		◇1	◇1	◇1	◇1	◇1	◇1	◇1	◇1	◇1	◇1	◇1	◇1	◇1	◇1
						A									
		⊥	⊥	⊥	⊥	⊡⊥	⊥	⊥	⊥	⊥	⊥	⊥	⊥	⊥	⊥
Hereford [7]	d							13 27		15 29		17 28		19 28	
Ledbury	d							13 45		15 46		17 46		19 47	
Colwall	d							13 53		15 53		17 54		19 54	
Great Malvern	d		08 56	09 53	10 50	11 50		13 58		15 58		17 59		19 59	20 40
Malvern Link	d		08 58	09 55	10 53	11 53		14 01		16 01		18 03		20 02	20 43
Worcester Foregate Street [7]	d	08 15	09 09	10 06	11 04	12 04		14 11		16 11		18 13		20 12	20 53
Worcester Shrub Hill [7]	d	08 21	09 12	10 13	11 06	12 11	13 16	14 15	15 18	16 15	17 18	18 17	19 18	20 16	20 57
Pershore	d	08 34	09 26	10 25	11 20	12 25	13 27	14 30	15 29	16 29	17 29	18 31	19 30	20 31	21 12
Evesham	a	08 41	09 32	10 31	11 26	12 31	13 34	14 36	15 36	16 36	17 36	18 37	19 36	20 37	21 18
	d	08 42	09 34	10 34	11 31	12 35	13 35	14 37	15 37	16 37	17 37	18 38	19 37	20 38	21 19
Honeybourne	d	08 48	09 41	10 41	11 36	12 40	13 42	14 44	15 44	16 44	17 44	18 45	19 44	20 45	21 26
Moreton-in-Marsh	a	08 59	09 50	10 50	11 46	12 50	13 52	14 55	15 55	16 54	17 55	18 56	19 55	20 56	21 37
	d	09 00	09 51	10 51	11 47	12 51	13 53	14 56	15 56	16 55	17 56	18 57	19 56	20 57	21 38
Kingham	d	09 08	09 59	10 59	11 54	12 58	14 01	15 04	16 04	17 03	18 04	19 05	20 04	21 05	21 46
Shipton	d														
Ascott-under-Wychwood	d														
Charlbury	a	09 16	10 11	11 11	12 02	13 06	14 09	15 12	16 12	17 11	18 12	19 13	20 12	21 13	21 54
	d	09 17	10 12	11 12	12 02	13 06	14 10	15 12	16 13	17 11	18 13	19 13	20 13	21 13	21 55
Finstock	d														
Combe	d														
Hanborough	d	09 24	10 19	11 19	12 10	13 14	14 18	15 18	16 20	17 18	18 20		20 20	21 19	22 02
Oxford 116	a	09 34	10 28	11 28	12 22	13 26	14 27	15 28	16 29	17 29	18 29	19 28	20 31	21 31	22 21
Didcot Parkway 125,116	a	09 45	10 44	11 44	12 44	13 44	14 44	15 44	16 44	17 44	18 44	19 44	20 44	21 44	22 38
Reading [7] 135,125,116	a	10 00	10 59	11 59	12 59	13 59	14 59	15 59	16 59	17 59	18 59	19 59	20 59	21 59	22 52
Slough [3] 135,125,116	a	10 13	11 12	12 13	13 13	14 14	15 13	16 13	17 12	18 13	19 13	20 13	21 13	22 12	23 07
London Paddington [15] ⊖135,125,116	a	10 29	11 29	12 29	13 29	14 29	15 32	16 36	17 28	18 29	19 29	20 29	21 29	22 29	23 44

A ⊡ from Oxford ⊥ to Oxford

For additional services between Worcester and London refer to Table T125

Table T127-F

Mondays to Fridays
16 December to 15 May

Cardiff Central - Ebbw Vale Town

Miles			AW	AW	AW	AW	AW	AW	AW	AW	AW	AW	AW	AW	AW	AW	AW	AW	AW FO	AW FX
—	Newport (South Wales)	d																		
0	**Cardiff Central** 7	d	06 34	07 38	08 33	09 34	10 34	11 34	12 34	13 34	14 34	15 34	16 34	17 34	18 34	19 38	20 34	21 34	23 05	23 05
—	Pye Corner	d	06 53	07 57	08 52	09 53	10 53	11 53	12 53	13 53	14 53	15 53	16 53	17 53	18 53	19 57	20 53	21 53	23 27	23 28
14	Rogerstone	d	06 57	08 01	08 56	09 57	10 57	11 57	12 57	13 57	14 57	15 57	16 57	17 57	18 57	20 01	20 57	21 57	23 31	23 32
15¼	Risca & Pontymister	d	07 01	08 05	09 00	10 00	11 00	12 00	13 00	14 00	15 00	16 00	17 00	18 01	19 00	20 04	21 01	22 01	23 34	23 35
17¼	Cross Keys	d	07 06	08 10	09 05	10 06	11 06	12 06	13 06	14 06	15 06	16 06	17 06	18 06	19 06	20 10	21 06	22 06	23 40	23 41
20¾	Newbridge (Ebbw Vale)	d	07 14	08 18	09 13	10 14	11 14	12 14	13 14	14 14	15 14	16 14	17 14	18 14	19 14	20 18	21 14	22 14	23 48	23 49
23½	Llanhilleth	d	07 20	08 24	09 19	10 20	11 20	12 20	13 20	14 20	15 20	16 20	17 20	18 20	19 20	20 24	21 20	22 20	23 54	23 55
28¾	**Ebbw Vale Parkway**	a	07 29	08 33	09 28	10 28	11 28	12 28	13 28	14 28	15 28	16 28	17 28	18 29	19 28	20 32	21 29	22 29	00 02	00 03
—	Ebbw Vale Town	a	07 36	08 39	09 34	10 35	11 35	12 35	13 33	14 35	15 35	16 35	17 35	18 36	19 33	20 39	21 35	22 35	00 08	00 09

Saturdays
21 December to 16 May

		AW	AW ◇	AW	AW	AW	AW	AW	AW	AW	AW	AW	AW	AW	AW	AW	AW	AW
Newport (South Wales)	d																	
Cardiff Central 7	d	06 33	07 36	08 34	09 34	10 34	11 34	12 34	13 34	14 34	15 34	16 34	17 34	18 34	19 38	20 34	21 34	23 02
Pye Corner	d	06 53	07 56	08 53	09 53	10 53	11 53	12 53	13 53	14 53	15 53	16 53	17 53	18 53	19 57	20 53	21 53	23 24
Rogerstone	d	06 57	08 00	08 57	09 57	10 57	11 57	12 57	13 57	14 57	15 57	16 57	17 57	18 57	20 01	20 57	21 57	23 28
Risca & Pontymister	d	07 00	08 04	09 01	10 00	11 01	12 01	13 01	14 01	15 01	16 01	17 01	18 01	19 01	20 05	21 01	22 01	23 31
Cross Keys	d	07 06	08 09	09 06	10 06	11 06	12 06	13 06	14 06	15 06	16 06	17 06	18 06	19 06	20 10	21 06	22 06	23 37
Newbridge (Ebbw Vale)	d	07 14	08 17	09 14	10 14	11 14	12 14	13 14	14 14	15 14	16 14	17 14	18 14	19 14	20 18	21 14	22 14	23 45
Llanhilleth	d	07 20	08 23	09 20	10 20	11 20	12 20	13 20	14 20	15 20	16 20	17 20	18 20	19 20	20 24	21 20	22 20	23 51
Ebbw Vale Parkway	a	07 28	08 32	09 29	10 28	11 29	12 29	13 29	14 29	15 29	16 29	17 29	18 29	19 29	20 33	21 29	22 29	23 59
Ebbw Vale Town	a	07 35	08 38	09 35	10 35	11 35	12 35	13 35	14 35	15 35	16 35	17 35	18 35	19 35	20 39	21 35	22 35	00 06

Sundays
15 December to 10 May

		AW	AW	AW	AW	AW	AW	AW
Newport (South Wales)	d							
Cardiff Central 7	d	07 38	09 22	11 30	13 55	16 29	19 02	21 30
Pye Corner	d	07 58	09 43	11 50	14 16	16 51	19 22	21 50
Rogerstone	d	08 02	09 47	11 54	14 19	16 55	19 26	21 54
Risca & Pontymister	d	08 06	09 50	11 57	14 23	16 59	19 30	21 58
Cross Keys	d	08 12	09 56	12 02	14 28	17 04	19 36	22 04
Newbridge (Ebbw Vale)	d	08 20	10 04	12 10	14 37	17 13	19 44	22 12
Llanhilleth	d	08 27	10 10	12 16	14 43	17 19	19 51	22 19
Ebbw Vale Parkway	a	08 35	10 18	12 25	14 51	17 28	19 59	22 28
Ebbw Vale Town	a	08 43	10 26	12 32	14 56	17 36	20 07	22 35

Table T127-R

Mondays to Fridays
16 December to 15 May

Ebbw Vale Town - Cardiff Central

Miles			AW	AW	AW	AW	AW	AW	AW	AW	AW	AW	AW	AW	AW	AW	AW	AW	AW FO	AW FX
—	Ebbw Vale Town	d	06 35	07 37	08 40	09 38	10 37	11 37	12 37	13 37	14 37	15 37	16 37	17 37	18 40	19 37	20 41	21 37	22 37	22 37
0	**Ebbw Vale Parkway**	d	06 38	07 40	08 43	09 41	10 40	11 40	12 40	13 40	14 40	15 40	16 40	17 40	18 43	19 40	20 44	21 40	22 40	22 40
5¼	Llanhilleth	d	06 46	07 48	08 51	09 49	10 48	11 48	12 48	13 48	14 48	15 48	16 48	17 48	18 51	19 48	20 52	21 48	22 48	22 48
8	Newbridge (Ebbw Vale)	d	06 52	07 54	08 57	09 55	10 54	11 54	12 54	13 54	14 54	15 54	16 54	17 54	18 57	19 54	20 58	21 54	22 54	22 54
11½	Cross Keys	d	07 00	08 02	09 05	10 03	11 02	12 02	13 02	14 02	15 02	16 02	17 02	18 02	19 05	20 02	21 06	22 02	23 02	23 02
13½	Risca & Pontymister	d	07 05	08 07	09 10	10 08	11 07	12 07	13 07	14 07	15 07	16 07	17 07	18 07	19 10	20 07	21 11	22 07	23 07	23 07
14¾	Rogerstone	d	07 09	08 11	09 14	10 12	11 11	12 11	13 11	14 11	15 11	16 11	17 11	18 11	19 14	20 11	21 15	22 11	23 11	23 11
—	Pye Corner	d	07 13	08 15	09 18	10 16	11 15	12 15	13 15	14 15	15 15	16 15	17 15	18 15	19 18	20 15	21 19	22 15	23 15	23 15
28¾	**Cardiff Central** 7	a	07 32	08 35	09 36	10 36	11 36	12 35	13 36	14 36	15 35	16 33	17 34	18 37	19 38	20 34	21 39	22 41	23 38	23 40
—	Newport (South Wales)	a																		

Saturdays
21 December to 16 May

		AW	AW	AW	AW	AW	AW	AW	AW	AW	AW	AW	AW	AW	AW	AW	AW	AW
Ebbw Vale Town	d	06 37	07 37	08 40	09 37	10 37	11 37	12 37	13 37	14 37	15 37	16 37	17 37	18 37	19 37	20 41	21 37	22 37
Ebbw Vale Parkway	d	06 40	07 40	08 43	09 40	10 40	11 40	12 40	13 40	14 40	15 40	16 40	17 40	18 40	19 40	20 44	21 40	22 40
Llanhilleth	d	06 48	07 48	08 51	09 48	10 48	11 49	12 48	13 48	14 48	15 48	16 49	17 48	18 48	19 49	20 52	21 48	22 48
Newbridge (Ebbw Vale)	d	06 54	07 54	08 57	09 54	10 54	11 55	12 54	13 54	14 54	15 54	16 55	17 54	18 54	19 56	20 58	21 54	22 54
Cross Keys	d	07 02	08 02	09 05	10 02	11 02	12 03	13 02	14 02	15 02	16 02	17 03	18 02	19 02	20 04	21 06	22 02	23 02
Risca & Pontymister	d	07 07	08 07	09 10	10 08	11 07	12 08	13 07	14 07	15 07	16 07	17 08	18 07	19 07	20 09	21 16	22 07	23 07
Rogerstone	d	07 11	08 11	09 14	10 12	11 11	12 12	13 11	14 11	15 11	16 11	17 12	18 11	19 11	20 13	21 20	22 11	23 11
Pye Corner	d	07 15	08 15	09 18	10 16	11 15	12 16	13 15	14 15	15 15	16 15	17 16	18 15	19 15	20 17	21 24	22 15	23 15
Cardiff Central 7	a	07 35	08 34	09 37	10 36	11 37	12 36	13 36	14 35	15 34	16 35	17 35	18 33	19 43	20 36	21 45	22 37	23 38
Newport (South Wales)	a																	

Sundays
15 December to 10 May

		AW	AW	AW	AW	AW	AW	AW
Ebbw Vale Town	d	08 49	10 27	12 33	15 01	17 42	20 08	22 37
Ebbw Vale Parkway	d	08 52	10 30	12 36	15 04	17 45	20 11	22 40
Llanhilleth	d	09 01	10 39	12 45	15 13	17 54	20 19	22 48
Newbridge (Ebbw Vale)	d	09 07	10 45	12 51	15 19	18 01	20 25	22 54
Cross Keys	d	09 15	10 53	12 59	15 27	18 09	20 33	23 02
Risca & Pontymister	d	09 20	10 58	13 04	15 32	18 14	20 38	23 07
Rogerstone	d	09 24	11 02	13 08	15 36	18 18	20 41	23 10
Pye Corner	d	09 28	11 05	13 11	15 40	18 22	20 45	23 14
Cardiff Central 7	a	09 49	11 22	13 28	16 01	18 39	21 03	23 42
Newport (South Wales)	a							

Table T128-F

Mondays to Fridays
16 December to 15 May

Cardiff - Maesteg, Swansea and West Wales

Miles	Miles			AW MO ◇	AW MX ◇	AW MX	AW MX ◇	GW MO ◇1 ⌶	GW MX ◇1 ⌶	GW MX ◇1 ⌶	AW	AW ◇	AW	AW	AW ◇	AW ◇	AW	AW ◇	AW ◇	AW ◇	AW ◇	AW ◇	AW ◇
—	—	London Paddington 15 ⊖	d																				
—	—	Reading 7	d																				
—	—	Manchester Piccadilly 10	d																				
—	—	Gloucester 7	d																		05 49		
—	—	Bristol Parkway 7	d							00 15													
—	—	Newport (South Wales)	d							00 43											06 43		
0	—	**Cardiff Central** 7	d							01 01								05 35	05 53	06 37	07 03		07 16
11	—	Pontyclun	d															05 51			07 15		
14	—	Llanharan	d															05 56			07 20		
16¼	—	Pencoed	d															06 01			07 24		
20¼	0	Bridgend	d						00 12	01 20								06 07	06 18	07 03	07 32		07 36
—	1	Wildmill	d																06 20		07 35		
—	2¼	Sarn	d																06 23		07 38		
—	3	Tondu	d																06 27		07 41		
—	7	Garth (Mid Glamorgan)	d																06 36		07 51		
—	7¾	Maesteg (Ewenny Road)	d																06 39		07 53		
—	8¼	Maesteg	a																06 42		07 57		
26¼	—	Pyle	d															06 14		07 12			07 44
32½	—	Port Talbot Parkway	d				00 01	00 10	00 24	01 43								06 22		07 20			07 53
34½	—	Baglan	d				00 05											06 24		07 24			07 56
36¼	—	Briton Ferry	d				00 09											06 28		07 28			08 00
38	—	Neath	d				00 13	00 18	00 32	01 51								06 32		07 32			08 04
41¾	—	Skewen	d				00 16											06 35		07 35			08 07
43½	—	Llansamlet	d				00 20											06 39		07 40			08 11
47½	—	**Swansea**	a				00 29	00 30	00 44	02 03								06 48		07 49			08 19
—	—		d			00 10	00 45								05 45	06 04		06 51		07 53		08 16	
53	—	Gowerton	d			00 21	00 56								05 56	06 15		07 02		08 05			
58¾	—	Llanelli	a			00 29	01 04								06 04	06 23		07 10		08 12		08 33	
—	—		d	00 01		00 29	01 04								06 05			07 10		08 12		08 33	
62¾	—	Pembrey & Burry Port	d	00 07		00 34	01s10								06 11			07 16		08 17			
68	—	Kidwelly	d	00x14		00x41	01s16								06x19			07x22		08x24			
72¼	—	Ferryside	d	00x20		00x47	01s22								06x25			07x28		08x30			
79¼	—	**Carmarthen**	a	00 33		01 01	01 36								06 39			07 42		08 43			
—	—		d				01 39				04 50	05 30	05 50	06 00	06 41			07 46		08 46			
93¼	0	Whitland	a				01 55				05 06	05 47	06 06	06 15	06 59			08 02		09 02		09 12	
—	—		d				01 55				05 06	05 47	06 06	06 15	06 59			08 02		09 04		09 12	
—	5¼	Narberth	d									05x56			07x08					09x13			
—	10¾	Kilgetty	d									06x05			07x17					09x23			
—	11½	Saundersfoot	d									06x07			07x19					09x25			
—	15¾	**Tenby**	a									06 15			07 27					09 33			
—	—		d									06 24			07 32					09 43			
—	17	Penally	d									06x27			07x35					09x46			
—	20¼	Manorbier	d									06 33			07 42					09 53			
—	23¾	Lamphey	d									06x41			07x49					10x00			
—	25¼	Pembroke	d									06 44			07 52					10 03			
—	27¼	**Pembroke Dock**	a									06 56			08 07					10 13			
98¾	—	Clunderwen	d								05x13		06x13	06x21				08x09				09x19	
105¼	0	Clarbeston Road	d				02x08				05x20		06x20	06x29			07 20	08x16				09x27	
—	5¼	Haverfordwest	d								05 31			06 37				08 25					
—	10	Johnston	d		00x07						05x39			06x45				08x33					
—	14	**Milford Haven**	a		00 20						05 52			06 58				08 43					
—	—	Fishguard & Goodwick	a				02 27						06 39				07 38					09 46	
121	—	**Fishguard Harbour** 30 ⛴	a				02 32						06 45				07 44					09 52	
—	—		d																				
—	—	Rosslare Harbour ⛴	a																				

When events are being held at the Principality Stadium, services are subject to alteration. Please check times before travelling.

Ferry service between Fishguard Harbour and Rosslare Harbour is operated by Stena Line

Table T128-F

Mondays to Fridays

16 December to 15 May

Cardiff - Maesteg, Swansea and West Wales

Station		AW	AW	GW	AW	AW	AW	AW	GW	AW	AW	AW	AW	GW	AW	AW	AW	AW	GW	AW	AW	AW	AW
						MX	MO									■							
			◇	◇1	◇	◇	◇		◇1	◇	◇	◇	◇	◇1 A	◇		◇	◇	◇1	◇	◇	◇	◇
			⚲	⚲	⚲				⚲	⚲				⚲	⚲		⚲		⚲	⚲	⚲		
London Paddington 15 ⊖	d			05 28					06 48					07 48					08 48				
Reading 7	d			05 53					07 13					08 12					09 12				
Manchester Piccadilly 10	d																06 30			07 30			
Gloucester 7	d												07 58					08 57					
Bristol Parkway 7	d			07 28					08 04					09 03					10 03				
Newport (South Wales)	d		07 33	07 52		08 03	08 03		08 26	08 41			08 50	09 25			09 39	09 51	10 24	10 30			
Cardiff Central 7	d	07 33	07 50	08 06		08 19	08 21	08 36	08 42	09 04		09 12	09 16	09 41			10 04	10 16	10 40	10 47		11 12	11 16
Pontyclun	d					08 31	08 33						09 28					10 28					11 29
Llanharan	d					08 36	08 38						09 32					10 33					11 34
Pencoed	d					08 41	08 43						09 36					10 37					11 38
Bridgend	d	07a53	08 10	08 25		08 47	08 49	08a56	09 02	09 24		09 32	09 42	10 00			10 24	10 44	10 59	11 06		11 32	11 48
Wildmill	d					08 49	08 51						09 45					10 46					11 51
Sarn	d					08 52	08 54						09 48					10 49					11 54
Tondu	d					08 56	08 58						09 51					10 53					11 57
Garth (Mid Glamorgan)	d					09 05	09 07						09 59					11 02					12 06
Maesteg (Ewenny Road)	d					09 08	09 10						10 02					11 05					12 09
Maesteg	a					09 10	09 12						10 05					11 07					12 11
Pyle	d		08 18									09 40										11 40	
Port Talbot Parkway	d		08 26	08 39					09 15	09 36		09 49		10 14			10 35		11 10	11 18		11 47	
Baglan	d		08 28									09 52										11 51	
Briton Ferry	d		08 32									09 56										11 54	
Neath	d		08 36	08 46					09 22	09 43		10 00		10 22			10 42		11 17	11 25		11 58	
Skewen	d		08 39									10 03										12 02	
Llansamlet	d		08 43									10 07										12 06	
Swansea	a		08 52	08 58					09 34	09 56		10 17		10 34			10 56		11 29	11 38		12 16	
	d		09 11		09 30					10 03					11 00		11 10			11 42	12 00	12 17	
Gowerton	d		09 22		09 41					10 14							11 21				12 11	12 28	
Llanelli	a		09 29		09 49					10 21					11 16		11 28			11 58	12 19	12 36	
	d		09 30							10 22					11 17		11 29			11 59	12 20		
Pembrey & Burry Port	d		09 36							10 28							11 34			12 05	12 26		
Kidwelly	d		09x42							10x34										12x11			
Ferryside	d		09x47							10x39										12x16			
Carmarthen	a		10 00							10 51							11 55			12 29	12 49		
	d		10 05								10 56						11 56				12 51		
Whitland	a		10 20								11 13				11 52		12 11				13 08		
	d		10 20								11 13				11 52		12 11				13 08		
Narberth	d										11x22										13x17		
Kilgetty	d										11x32										13x27		
Saundersfoot	d										11x34										13x29		
Tenby	a										11 42										13 37		
	d										11 49										13 45		
Penally	d										11x52										13x48		
Manorbier	d										11 58										13 54		
Lamphey	d										12x06										14x02		
Pembroke	d										12 09										14 05		
Pembroke Dock	a										12 22										14 17		
Clunderwen	d		10x26														12x17						
Clarbeston Road	d		10x34												12x05		12x24						
Haverfordwest	d		10 42														12 34						
Johnston	d		10x50														12x41						
Milford Haven	a		11 05														12 52						
Fishguard & Goodwick	a														12 23								
Fishguard Harbour 30 ⛴	a														12 30								
	d															13 10							
Rosslare Harbour ⛴	a															16 25							

A The Saint David

When events are being held at the Principality Stadium, services are subject to alteration. Please check times before travelling.

Ferry service between Fishguard Harbour and Rosslare Harbour is operated by Stena Line

NRT DECEMBER 19 EDITION

Table T128-F

Mondays to Fridays

16 December to 15 May

Cardiff - Maesteg, Swansea and West Wales

Station		GW	AW	AW	AW	GW	AW	AW	AW	AW	AW	GW	AW	AW	AW	AW	AW	GW	AW	AW	AW	GW
																				■		
		◇1	◇	◇		◇1 A	◇	◇	◇	◇	◇	◇1	◇	◇	◇		◇	◇1	◇		◇	◇1
		⚲	⚲			✕⚲	⚲	⚲			⚲	⚲	⚲	⚲			⚲	⚲	⚲	⚲		⚲
London Paddington 15 ⊖	d	09 48				10 48						11 48						12 48				13 48
Reading 7	d	10 13				11 12						12 13						13 12				14 13
Manchester Piccadilly 10	d		08 31				09 31				10 31						11 31					
Gloucester 7	d			10 53																	13 59	
Bristol Parkway 7	d	11 04				12 03						13 04						14 03				15 04
Newport (South Wales)	d	11 26	11 22	11 49		12 27	12 23				13 23	13 27					14 22	14 26		14 56	14 51	15 25
Cardiff Central 7	d	11 43	11 46	12 18	12 36	12 42	12 45		13 12	13 16	13 38	13 42			14 16	14 36	14 39	14 43		15 14	15 17	15 39
Pontyclun	d			12 30						13 28					14 30						15 29	
Llanharan	d			12 35						13 33					14 35						15 34	
Pencoed	d			12 39						13 37					14 39						15 39	
Bridgend	d	12 01	12 07	12 47	12a56	13 02	13 08		13 32	13 43	13 57	14 02			14 46	14a56	15 00	15 04		15 33	15 45	16 00
Wildmill	d			12 49						13 46					14 48						15 47	
Sarn	d			12 52						13 49					14 51						15 50	
Tondu	d			12 56						13 52					14 55						15 54	
Garth (Mid Glamorgan)	d			13 05						14 02					15 04						16 03	
Maesteg (Ewenny Road)	d			13 08						14 04					15 07						16 06	
Maesteg	a			13 11						14 08					15 10						16 08	
Pyle	d								13 40											15 40		
Port Talbot Parkway	d	12 15	12 20			13 15	13 19		13 49		14 09	14 15					15 11	15 18		15 47		16 14
Baglan	d								13 52											15 51		
Briton Ferry	d								13 56											15 54		
Neath	d	12 22	12 27			13 22	13 27		14 00		14 16	14 22					15 18	15 25		15 58		16 21
Skewen	d								14 03											16 02		
Llansamlet	d								14 07					←						16 06		
Swansea	a	12 34	12 40			13 34	13 40		14 15		14 29	14 34		14 29			15 32	15 37		16 15		16 33
	d		12 43				13 43	14 00			14 40		14 35	14 40			15 35		16 00	16 18		
Gowerton	d		12 54				13 54				→			14 51			15 46		16 11	16 30		
Llanelli	a		13 01				14 01	14 17					14 52	14 59			15 54		16 19	16 36		
	d		13 02				14 02	14 17						14 59			15 54		16 19			
Pembrey & Burry Port	d		13 08				14 08	14 23						15 05			16 00		16 25			
Kidwelly	d						14x14										16x06					
Ferryside	d						14x19										16x12					
Carmarthen	a		13 28				14 31	14 48						15 26			16 26		16 48			
	d		13 30					14 51						15 29					16 51			
Whitland	a		13 46					15 08						15 45					17 08			
	d		13 46					15 08						15 45					17 08			
Narberth	d							15x17											17x17			
Kilgetty	d							15x27											17x27			
Saundersfoot	d							15x29											17x29			
Tenby	a							15 37											17 37			
	d							15 45											17 45			
Penally	d							15x48											17x48			
Manorbier	d							15 54											17 54			
Lamphey	d							16x02											18x02			
Pembroke	d							16 05											18 05			
Pembroke Dock	a							16 17											18 18			
Clunderwen	d		13x52											15x51								
Clarbeston Road	d		14x00											15x59								
Haverfordwest	d		14 08											16 07								
Johnston	d		14x16											16x15								
Milford Haven	a		14 26											16 26								
Fishguard & Goodwick	a																					
Fishguard Harbour 30 ⛴	a																					
	d																					
Rosslare Harbour ⛴	a																					

A ✕ to Cardiff Central ⚲ from Cardiff Central

When events are being held at the Principality Stadium, services are subject to alteration. Please check times before travelling.

Ferry service between Fishguard Harbour and Rosslare Harbour is operated by Stena Line

Table T128-F

Mondays to Fridays

16 December to 15 May

Cardiff - Maesteg, Swansea and West Wales

Station		AW	AW	AW	AW	AW	GW	AW	AW	AW	AW	GW	AW	GW	AW	AW	GW	AW	GW	AW	AW	AW	GW
		■ ⊥	◇ ⊥	◇		⊥	◇1 ⊥	■ ⊥	◇		◇	◇1 ⊥	■ ⊥	◇1 A ⊥	◇	◇	◇1 ⊥		◇1 ⊥	■ ⊥		◇	◇1 ⊥
London Paddington [15] ⊖	d						14 48					15 48		16 15			16 48		17 15				17 47
Reading [7]	d						15 13					16 12					17 13						18 12
Manchester Piccadilly [10]	d	12 31						13 31					14 31							15 31			
Gloucester [7]	d															17 00						18 00	
Bristol Parkway [7]	d						16 05					17 04		17 26			18 05		18 26				19 03
Newport (South Wales)	d	15 22					16 25	16 41				17 27	17 22	17 46		17 54	18 25		18 46	18 41		18 54	19 24
Cardiff Central [7]	d	15 45	16 04	16 18	16 36		16 43	17 04		17 23		17 42	17 46	18 01	18 06	18 16	18 40		19 01	19 04		19 12	19 41
Pontyclun	d			16 30	16 48					17 36					18 18	18 28						19 24	
Llanharan	d			16 35				17 19		17 41						18 33						19 29	
Pencoed	d			16 39	16 55					17 45					18 25	18 37						19 33	
Bridgend	d	16 06	16 23	16 46	17a01		17 06	17 27		17 50		18 01	18 06	18 21	18 31	18 45	18 59		19 20	19 24		19 41	20 00
Wildmill	d			16 49						17 53						18 47						19 43	
Sarn	d			16 52						17 56						18 50						19 46	
Tondu	d			16 55						17 59						18 54						19 50	
Garth (Mid Glamorgan)	d			17 05						18 09						19 03						19 59	
Maesteg (Ewenny Road)	d			17 07						18 11						19 06						20 02	
Maesteg	a			17 11						18 15						19 09						20 05	
Pyle	d		16 31					17 36					18 14		18 39					19 31			
Port Talbot Parkway	d	16 18	16 40				17 20	17 43				18 14	18 21	18 35	18 48		19 14		19 34	19 38			20 13
Baglan	d							17 46							18 51					19 42			
Briton Ferry	d							17 50							18 55					19 45			
Neath	d	16 26	16 47				17 27	17 54				18 21	18 28	18 42	18 59		19 21		19 41	19 49			20 20
Skewen	d							17 58							19 02					19 54			
Llansamlet	d							18 02							19 06					19 58			
Swansea	a	16 39	17 01				17 39	18 10				18 33	18 41	18 54	19 15		19 33		19 52	20 07			20 32
	d	16 43	17 10			17 38		18 14			18 27		18 45					19 35		20 11			
Gowerton	d	16 54	17 21			17 49		18 25			18 38		18 56					19 46		20 22			
Llanelli	a	17 01	17 29			17 57		18 32			18 46		19 04					19 54		20 30			
	d	17 02	17 29			17 58		18 33					19 04					19 55		20 30			
Pembrey & Burry Port	d	17 08	17 35			18 04		18 38					19 10					20 01		20 36			
Kidwelly	d	17x14	17x42			18x11		18x44										20x08					
Ferryside	d	17x19	17x48			18x17		18x50										20x14					
Carmarthen	a	17 32	18 01			18 32		19 03					19 32					20 29		20 58			
	d	17 36	18 05					19 05					19 35								21 03		
Whitland	a	17 51	18 20					19 21					19 51								21 19		
	d	17 51	18 20					19 22					19 51								21 19		
Narberth	d							19x31															
Kilgetty	d							19x41															
Saundersfoot	d							19x44															
Tenby	a							19 51															
	d								20 05														
Penally	d								20x08														
Manorbier	d								20 14														
Lamphey	d								20x22														
Pembroke	d								20 25														
Pembroke Dock	a								20 36														
Clunderwen	d	17x57	18x26										19x58								21x26		
Clarbeston Road	d	18x05	18x34										20x05								21x34		
Haverfordwest	d	18 13											20 14										
Johnston	d	18x21											20x22										
Milford Haven	a	18 31											20 32										
Fishguard & Goodwick	a		18 52																		21 52		
Fishguard Harbour [30] ⛴	a		18 57																		21 59		
	d																						
Rosslare Harbour ⛴	a																						

A The Capitals United

When events are being held at the Principality Stadium, services are subject to alteration. Please check times before travelling.

Ferry service between Fishguard Harbour and Rosslare Harbour is operated by Stena Line

Table T128-F

Mondays to Fridays

16 December to 15 May

Cardiff - Maesteg, Swansea and West Wales

Station		AW	AW	GW	AW	GW	AW	AW FO	AW FX	AW FO	AW	GW	GW	AW FO	AW FX	AW FO	AW	GW FO	GW FX	AW	GW FO	GW FX	GW FO	GW FX
		◇	■ ⊥	◇1 A ⊥	◇	◇1 B ⊥	[B]	◇	◇	◇	◇	◇1 ⊥	◇1 ⊥	◇	◇	◇	◇	◇1 ⊥	◇1 ⊥	◇	◇1 ⊥	◇1 ⊥	◇1 ⊥	◇1 ⊥
London Paddington [15] ⊖	d			18 16		18 47						19 18	19 48					20 48	20 48		21 48	21 48	22 48	22 48
Reading [7]	d					19 12						19 43	20 12					21 12	21 12		22 12	22 12	23 18	23 18
Manchester Piccadilly [10]	d		16 31											18 31	18 31									
Gloucester [7]	d				19 00						20 00													
Bristol Parkway [7]	d			19 28		20 03						20 35	21 04					22 03	22 03		23 02	23 02	00 15	00 15
Newport (South Wales)	d		19 30	19 48	19 54	20 26					20 54	21 00	21 25	21 53	21 53			22 26	22 32		23 24	23 30	00 36	00 43
Cardiff Central [7]	d		19 47	20 03	20 15	20 40		21 08	21 08		21 13	21 24	21 42	22 10	22 18		22 36	22 50	22 50	23 15	23 49	23 49	00 50	01 01
Pontyclun	d				20 27						21 25			22 23	22 30					23 29				
Llanharan	d				20 32						21 30			22 27	22 35					23 34				
Pencoed	d				20 36						21 34			22 31	22 39					23 39				
Bridgend	d		20 07	20 22	20 43	20 59		21 28	21 28		21 41	21 46	22 01	22 37	22 45		22 59	23 09	23 09	23 45	00 12	00 12	01 09	01 20
Wildmill	d				20 45						21 43						23 01							
Sarn	d				20 48						21 46						23 04							
Tondu	d				20 52						21 50						23 08							
Garth (Mid Glamorgan)	d				21 02						21 59						23 17							
Maesteg (Ewenny Road)	d				21 04						22 02						23 20							
Maesteg	a				21 08						22 05						23 23							
Pyle	d							21 35	21 37											23 53				
Port Talbot Parkway	d		20 19	20 36		21 12		21 45	21 46			22 00	22 15	22 49	22 58			23 23	23 23	00 01	00 24	00 24	01 32	01 43
Baglan	d																			00 05				
Briton Ferry	d																			00 09				
Neath	d		20 26	20 43		21 19		21 52	21 54			22 07	22 23	22 56				23 31	23 31	00 13	00 32	00 32	01 40	01 51
Skewen	d																			00 16				
Llansamlet	d																			00 20				
Swansea	a		20 41	20 55		21 31		22 07	22 08			22 19	22 35	23 10				23 43	23 43	00 29	00 44	00 44	01 52	02 03
	d		20 43	21 05				22 27	22 27					23 13						00 45				
Gowerton	d		20 55					22 38	22 38					23 24		←				00 56				
Llanelli	a		21 02	21 21				22 45	22 46					23 32	23 28	23 32				01 04				
	d		21 03	21 22				22 46	22 46					23 32	23 29	23 32				01 04				
Pembrey & Burry Port	d		21 09	21 29				22 51	22 52					→	23 34	23 38				01s10				
Kidwelly	d		21x15					22x57	22x58						23x40	23x44				01s16				
Ferryside	d		21x21					23x03	23x04	←					23x46	23x50				01s22				
Carmarthen	a		21 34	21 51				23 20	23 19	23 20					23 59	00 07				01 36				
	d	21 10	21 42					23 21	23 21	23 21										01 39				
Whitland	a	21 26	21 58					→	23 37	23 37										01 55				
	d	21 26	21 58						23 37	23 37										01 55				
Narberth	d	21x34																						
Kilgetty	d	21x43																						
Saundersfoot	d	21x45																						
Tenby	a	21 53																						
	d	21 54																						
Penally	d	21x57																						
Manorbier	d	22 03																						
Lamphey	d	22x10																						
Pembroke	d	22 13																						
Pembroke Dock	a	22 25																						
Clunderwen	d		22x04						23x43	23x43														
Clarbeston Road	d		22x12						23x51	23x51										02x08				
Haverfordwest	d		22 23						23 59	23 59														
Johnston	d		22x31						00x07	00x07														
Milford Haven	a		22 41						00 20	00 21														
Fishguard & Goodwick	a																			02 27				
Fishguard Harbour [30] ⛴	a																			02 32				
	d						23 45																	
Rosslare Harbour ⛴	a						04 00																	

A The Red Dragon

B Y Cymro/The Welshman

When events are being held at the Principality Stadium, services are subject to alteration. Please check times before travelling.

Ferry service between Fishguard Harbour and Rosslare Harbour is operated by Stena Line

Table T128-F

Saturdays

21 December to 16 May

Cardiff - Maesteg, Swansea and West Wales

	AW	AW	AW	GW	GW	AW	AW	AW	AW	AW	AW	AW	AW	AW	AW	AW	AW	AW	AW	AW	GW	AW
	◇		◇	◇[1] 🍴	◇[1] 🍴	◇		◇			◇		◇	◇	◇	◇	◇		◇	◇ 🍴	◇[1] 🍴	◇ 🍴
London Paddington [15] ⊖ d																						
Reading [7] d																						
Manchester Piccadilly [10] d																						
Gloucester [7] d																05 50						
Bristol Parkway [7] d					00 15																07 25	
Newport (South Wales) d					00 36											06 44				07 40	07 46	
Cardiff Central [7] d					00 50								05 36	05 49	06 42	07 04	07 16	07 36		07 55	08 01	
Pontyclun d													05 50	06 01		07 16						
Llanharan d													05 56	06 06		07 21						
Pencoed d													06 00	06 11		07 25						
Bridgend d				00 12	01 09								06 07	06 18	07 03	07 32	07 37	07a57		08 14	08 20	
Wildmill d														06 20		07 35						
Sarn d														06 23		07 38						
Tondu d														06 27		07 41						
Garth (Mid Glamorgan) d														06 36		07 51						
Maesteg (Ewenny Road) d														06 39		07 53						
Maesteg a														06 42		07 57						
Pyle d													06 15		07 11		07 45					
Port Talbot Parkway d			00 01	00 24	01 32								06 23		07 19		07 54			08 27	08 34	
Baglan d			00 05										06 27		07 23		07 57					
Briton Ferry d			00 09										06 30		07 26		08 01					
Neath d			00 13	00 32	01 40								06 34		07 30		08 04			08 34	08 41	
Skewen d			00 16										06 38		07 34		08 08					
Llansamlet d			00 20										06 42		07 38		08 13					
Swansea a			00 29	00 44	01 52								06 52		07 47		08 22			08 48	08 54	
d		00 10	00 45			04 31					05 45		06 54		07 52					09 02		09 15
Gowerton d		00 21	00 56			04 42					05 56		07 05		08 04					09 16		09 26
Llanelli a		00 29	01 04			04 50					06 04		07 13		08 11					09 23		09 34
d		00 29	01 04								06 05		07 13		08 12					09 23		
Pembrey & Burry Port d		00 34	01s10								06 11		07 19		08 17					09 29		
Kidwelly d		00x41	01s16								06x18		07x25		08x24					09x35		
Ferryside d		00x47	01s22								06x24		07x31		08x30					09x41		
Carmarthen a		01 01	01 36								06 39		07 46		08 44					09 54		
d			01 39				04 50	05 30	05 50	06 00	06 41		07 47		08 46					09 57		
Whitland a			01 55				05 06	05 47	06 06	06 15	06 58		08 03		09 03					10 14		
d			01 55				05 06	05 47	06 06	06 15	06 59		08 03		09 07				09 08	10 14		
Narberth d								05x56			07x08				09x16							
Kilgetty d								06x06			07x17				09x25							
Saundersfoot d								06x08			07x19				09x27							
Tenby a								06 16			07 27				09 36							
d								06 24			07 32				09 42							
Penally d								06x27			07x35				09x45							
Manorbier d								06 33			07 41				09 52							
Lamphey d								06x41			07x49				09x59							
Pembroke d								06 44			07 52				10 02							
Pembroke Dock a								06 56			08 04				10 14							
Clunderwen d							05x13		06x13	06x21			08x10						09x15	10x20		
Clarbeston Road d			02x08				05x20		06x21	06x29		07 20	08x17						09x23	10x28		
Haverfordwest d							05 32			06 37			08 26							10 36		
Johnston d	00x07						05x40			06x45			08x34							10x44		
Milford Haven a	00 21						05 52			06 57			08 46							10 58		
Fishguard & Goodwick a			02 27						06 40			07 38							09 42			
Fishguard Harbour [30] ⛴ a			02 32						06 46			07 44							09 48			
d																						
Rosslare Harbour ⛴🚌 a																						

When events are being held at the Principality Stadium, services are subject to alteration. Please check times before travelling.

Ferry service between Fishguard Harbour and Rosslare Harbour is operated by Stena Line

Table T128-F

Saturdays

21 December to 16 May

Cardiff - Maesteg, Swansea and West Wales

	AW	AW	GW	AW	AW	AW	AW	AW	GW	AW	AW	AW	AW	AW	GW	AW	AW	AW	AW	AW	GW	AW
	◇		◇[1] 🍴	◇ 🍴	◇	◇	◇		◇[1] 🍴	◇ 🍴	R	◇ 🍴	◇		◇[1] 🍴	◇ 🍴	◇ 🍴	◇	◇		◇[1] 🍴	R 🍴
London Paddington [15] ⊖ d			06 47						07 47						08 47						09 47	
Reading [7] d			07 12						08 12						09 12						10 12	
Manchester Piccadilly [10] d												06 30					07 31					08 30
Gloucester [7] d													08 59									
Bristol Parkway [7] d			08 04						09 04						10 04						11 04	
Newport (South Wales) d			08 26	08 39			09 05		09 26			09 41	09 53		10 25		10 47		11 03		11 25	11 37
Cardiff Central [7] d	08 22	08 35	08 41	09 02		09 11	09 21	09 37	09 45			10 00	10 15	10 37	10 42		11 07	11 13	11 18	11 37	11 41	12 04
Pontyclun d	08 34						09 33						10 30						11 30			
Llanharan d	08 39						09 38						10 35						11 35			
Pencoed d	08 43						09 42						10 39						11 40			
Bridgend d	08 49	08a56	09 01	09 21		09 31	09 49	09a58	10 04			10 20	10 47	10a58	11 03		11 27	11 34	11 47	11a58	12 03	12 24
Wildmill d	08 52						09 52						10 49						11 50			
Sarn d	08 55						09 55						10 52						11 53			
Tondu d	08 58												10 56						11 57			
Garth (Mid Glamorgan) d	09 07						10 08						11 05						12 06			
Maesteg (Ewenny Road) d	09 10						10 10						11 08						12 09			
Maesteg a	09 14						10 13						11 11						12 12			
Pyle d						09 39												11 42				
Port Talbot Parkway d			09 15	09 34		09 48			10 18			10 32			11 17		11 40	11 51			12 17	12 36
Baglan d						09 51												11 54				
Briton Ferry d						09 55												11 58				
Neath d			09 23	09 41		09 59			10 25			10 39			11 25		11 47	12 02			12 25	12 43
Skewen d						10 02												12 05				
Llansamlet d						10 06												12 09				
Swansea a			09 36	09 55		10 16			10 37			10 53			11 37		12 00	12 18			12 37	12 57
d				10 03						11 00		11 05				11 50	12 05					13 03
Gowerton d				10 14								11 17					12 16					13 14
Llanelli a				10 21						11 16		11 25				12 09	12 23					13 21
d				10 21						11 17		11 25				12 12	12 24					13 22
Pembrey & Burry Port d				10 27								11 31				12 18	12 30					13 28
Kidwelly d				10x33													12x36					
Ferryside d				10x39													12x41					
Carmarthen a				10 50								11 52				12 43	12 53					13 48
d					10 55							11 53				12 58						13 51
Whitland a					11 11					11 52		12 09				13 14						14 07
d					11 11					11 52		12 16				13 14						14 07
Narberth d					11x20											13x23						
Kilgetty d					11x30											13x33						
Saundersfoot d					11x32											13x35						
Tenby a					11 40											13 43						
d					11 45											13 45						
Penally d					11x48											13x48						
Manorbier d					11 54											13 54						
Lamphey d					12x02											14x02						
Pembroke d					12 05											14 05						
Pembroke Dock a					12 15											14 18						
Clunderwen d												12x22										14x13
Clarbeston Road d										12x05		12x30										14x21
Haverfordwest d												12 38										14 29
Johnston d												12x46										14x37
Milford Haven a												13 01										14 52
Fishguard & Goodwick a										12 23												
Fishguard Harbour [30] ⛴ a										12 30												
d											13 10											
Rosslare Harbour ⛴🚌 a											16 25											

When events are being held at the Principality Stadium, services are subject to alteration. Please check times before travelling.

Ferry service between Fishguard Harbour and Rosslare Harbour is operated by Stena Line

Table T128-F

Saturdays

21 December to 16 May

Cardiff - Maesteg, Swansea and West Wales

		AW	AW	AW	GW	AW	AW	AW	AW	AW	AW	GW	AW	AW	AW	GW	AW	AW	AW	AW	AW	AW
		◇		◇ ⚯	◇1 ⚯	◇ ⚯	◇ ⚯	◇	◇ ⚯	◇		◇1 ⚯	■ ⚯	◇		◇1 ⚯	◇ ⚯	◇ ⚯	◇	◇		■ ⚯
London Paddington 15 ⊖	d				10 47							11 47				12 47						
Reading 7	d				11 12							12 12				13 12						
Manchester Piccadilly 10	d						09 31						10 31				11 31					12 31
Gloucester 7	d	10 53																		13 58		
Bristol Parkway 7	d				12 04							13 04				14 04						
Newport (South Wales)	d	11 47			12 25		12 40		12 57			13 25	13 37			14 25	14 40		14 56	14 52		15 22
Cardiff Central 7	d	12 18	12 36		12 41		13 04	13 10	13 15	13 15	13 36	13 41	14 04	14 16	14 35	14 43	15 04		15 14	15 18	15 35	15 40
Pontyclun	d	12 30							13 27	13 27				14 28						15 30		
Llanharan	d	12 35							13 32	13 32				14 33						15 35		
Pencoed	d	12 39							13 36	13 36				14 37						15 39		
Bridgend	d	12 47	12a57		13 02		13 24	13 32	13 43	13 43	13a58	14 03	14 24	14 43	14a56	15 03	15 24		15 35	15 46	15a56	16 01
Wildmill	d	12 49							13 45	13 45				14 46						15 48		
Sarn	d	12 52							13 48	13 48				14 49						15 51		
Tondu	d	12 56							13 52	13 52				14 52						15 55		
Garth (Mid Glamorgan)	d	13 05							14 02	14 02				15 02						16 05		
Maesteg (Ewenny Road)	d	13 08							14 05	14 05				15 04						16 07		
Maesteg	a	13 11							14 08	14 08				15 08						16 10		
Pyle	d							13 40											15 43			
Port Talbot Parkway	d				13 16		13 37	13 49				14 17	14 36			15 17	15 36		15 51			16 14
Baglan	d							13 52											15 55			
Briton Ferry	d							13 56											15 58			
Neath	d				13 24		13 44	14 00				14 25	14 43			15 25	15 43		16 02			16 21
Skewen	d							14 03											16 07			
Llansamlet	d							14 07											16 11			
Swansea	a				13 36		13 58	14 17				14 37	14 56			15 37	15 57		16 21			16 35
	d			13 12		13 50	14 05						15 00				16 00	16 09	16 27			16 38
Gowerton	d			13 23			14 16						15 12				16 11	16 21	16 38			16 49
Llanelli	a			13 31		14 07	14 23						15 19				16 19	16 29	16 46			16 56
	d					14 07	14 24						15 20				16 19	16 29				16 57
Pembrey & Burry Port	d					14 14	14 30						15 26				16 25	16 36				17 03
Kidwelly	d						14x36										16x31					17x09
Ferryside	d						14x42										16x37					17x14
Carmarthen	a					14 42	14 53						15 46				16 53	16 59				17 27
	d					14 58							15 49					17 00				17 31
Whitland	a					15 14							16 04					17 17				17 46
	d					15 14							16 04					17 17				17 46
Narberth	d					15x23												17x26				
Kilgetty	d					15x33												17x35				
Saundersfoot	d					15x35												17x37				
Tenby	a					15 43												17 45				
	d					15 45												17 47				
Penally	d					15x48												17x50				
Manorbier	d					15 54												17 57				
Lamphey	d					16x02												18x04				
Pembroke	d					16 05												18 07				
Pembroke Dock	a					16 18												18 20				
Clunderwen	d												16x10									17x52
Clarbeston Road	d												16x18									18x00
Haverfordwest	d												16 26									18 08
Johnston	d												16x34									18x16
Milford Haven	a												16 49									18 31
Fishguard & Goodwick	a																					
Fishguard Harbour 30 ⛴	a																					
	d																					
Rosslare Harbour ⛴	a																					

When events are being held at the Principality Stadium, services are subject to alteration. Please check times before travelling.

Ferry service between Fishguard Harbour and Rosslare Harbour is operated by Stena Line

Table T128-F

Saturdays

21 December to 16 May

Cardiff - Maesteg, Swansea and West Wales

		GW	AW	AW	AW	GW	AW	AW	AW	AW	GW	AW	AW	AW	AW	GW	AW	AW	AW	GW	AW	GW	AW
		◇1 ⚯	◇ ⚯	◇		◇1 ⚯	⚯	■ ⚯	◇ ⚯	◇	◇1 ⚯		■ ⚯	◇		◇1 ⚯		■ ⚯		◇1 ⚯	◇	◇1 ⚯	■ ⚯
London Paddington 15 ⊖	d	13 47				14 47					15 47					16 47				17 17		17 47	
Reading 7	d	14 12				15 12					16 12					17 12				17 42		18 12	
Manchester Piccadilly 10	d							13 31					14 31					15 31					16 31
Gloucester 7	d		14 42											16 58							17 46		
Bristol Parkway 7	d	15 04				16 04					17 04					18 04				18 38		19 04	
Newport (South Wales)	d	15 26	15 37			16 25		16 39	16 54		17 24		17 37	17 52		18 24		18 42		19 02	18 39	19 24	19 38
Cardiff Central 7	d	15 44	16 02	16 18	16 36	16 40		17 04	17 15		17 39	17 43	18 04	18 15	18 34	18 39		19 03		19 16	19 07	19 42	20 01
Pontyclun	d			16 30					17 27					18 29							19 19		
Llanharan	d			16 35					17 32					18 34							19 24		
Pencoed	d			16 39					17 36					18 38							19 29		
Bridgend	d	16 07	16 22	16 46	16a57	17 04		17 25	17 42		17 58	18 03	18 25	18 46	18a57	19 03		19 23		19 40	19 46	20 01	20 20
Wildmill	d			16 48					17 45					18 49							19 49		
Sarn	d			16 51					17 48					18 52							19 52		
Tondu	d			16 55					17 51					18 55							19 55		
Garth (Mid Glamorgan)	d			17 05					18 01					19 05							20 05		
Maesteg (Ewenny Road)	d			17 07					18 03					19 07							20 07		
Maesteg	a			17 11					18 06					19 11							20 11		
Pyle	d		16 30					17 32				18 12	18 33					19 30					
Port Talbot Parkway	d	16 21	16 39			17 18		17 40			18 12	18 21	18 41			19 17		19 38		19 54		20 15	20 32
Baglan	d							17 43				18 25						19 42					
Briton Ferry	d							17 47				18 28						19 45					
Neath	d	16 28	16 47			17 25		17 51			18 20	18 32	18 49			19 24		19 49		20 01		20 22	
Skewen	d							17 55				18 36						19 54					
Llansamlet	d							17 59				18 40						19 58					
Swansea	a	16 40	17 00			17 37		18 07			18 32	18 51	19 03			19 36		20 07		20 13		20 34	
	d		17 04				17 50	18 11		18 17			19 05				19 40	20 13		20 23			
Gowerton	d		17 15				18 01	18 22		18 29			19 16				19 51	20 24					
Llanelli	a		17 23				18 09	18 30		18 37			19 24				19 59	20 31		20 39			21 03
	d		17 23				18 10	18 30					19 24				20 00	20 32		20 41			21 03
Pembrey & Burry Port	d		17 29				18 16	18 36					19 30				20 06	20 37		20 48			21 09
Kidwelly	d		17x35				18x23	18x43									20x13						21x15
Ferryside	d		17x41				18x29	18x49									20x19						21x20
Carmarthen	a		17 54				18 47	19 02					19 52				20 34	20 58		21 10			21 34
	d		18 03					19 05					19 57					21 00	21 07				22 03
Whitland	a		18 18					19 21					20 13					21 16	21 23				22 18
	d		18 19					19 21					20 13					21 16	21 23				22 18
Narberth	d							19x31										21x24					
Kilgetty	d							19x41										21x33					
Saundersfoot	d							19x43										21x35					
Tenby	a							19 53										21 42					
	d							19 53										21 44					
Penally	d							19x56										21x47					
Manorbier	d							20 03										21 53					
Lamphey	d							20x10										22x00					
Pembroke	d							20 13										22 03					
Pembroke Dock	a							20 25										22 18					
Clunderwen	d		18x26										20x20										22x24
Clarbeston Road	d		18x33										20x27						21x36				22x32
Haverfordwest	d												20 36										22 40
Johnston	d												20x44										22x48
Milford Haven	a												20 59										23 03
Fishguard & Goodwick	a		18 52																21 55				
Fishguard Harbour 30 ⛴	a		18 57																22 03				
	d																						
Rosslare Harbour ⛴	a																						

When events are being held at the Principality Stadium, services are subject to alteration. Please check times before travelling.

Ferry service between Fishguard Harbour and Rosslare Harbour is operated by Stena Line

Table T128-F

Saturdays
21 December to 16 May

Cardiff - Maesteg, Swansea and West Wales

		GW	AW	GW	AW	GW	AW	GW	AW	AW	GW	AW
		◇[1] ⊤	◇	◇[1] ⊤	◇	◇[1] ⊤	◇	◇[1] ⊤	◇	◇	◇[1] ⊤	[B]
London Paddington [15] ⊖	d	18 17		18 47		19 17		19 47			20 47	
Reading [7]	d	18 42		19 12		19 42		20 12			21 12	
Manchester Piccadilly [10]	d								18 31			
Gloucester [7]	d		18 58									
Bristol Parkway [7]	d	19 40		20 04		20 38		21 04			22 04	
Newport (South Wales)	d	20 01	19 52	20 25		20 58		21 25	21 45		22 31	
Cardiff Central [7]	d	20 15	20 19	20 41	21 04	21 13	21 17	21 39	22 08	22 37	22 50	
Pontyclun	d		20 31				21 29		22 21	22 49		
Llanharan	d		20 36				21 34		22 25	22 54		
Pencoed	d		20 40				21 38		22 29	22 58		
Bridgend	d	20 34	20 47	21 00	21 24	21 32	21 45	21 58	22 35	23 05	23 10	
Wildmill	d		20 49				21 47					
Sarn	d		20 52				21 50					
Tondu	d		20 56				21 54					
Garth (Mid Glamorgan)	d		21 06				22 04					
Maesteg (Ewenny Road)	d		21 08				22 06					
Maesteg	a		21 12				22 10					
Pyle	d				21 31					23 13		
Port Talbot Parkway	d	20 48		21 14	21 40	21 46		22 12	22 47	23 21	23 27	
Baglan	d									23 25		
Briton Ferry	d									23 28		
Neath	d	20 55		21 21	21 47	21 53		22 19	22 54	23 32	23 38	
Skewen	d									23 36		
Llansamlet	d									23 40		
Swansea	a	21 08		21 33	21 59	22 05		22 31	23 08	23 50	23 53	
	d				22 26				23 10	23 53		
Gowerton	d				22 38				23 21	00 04		
Llanelli	a				22 45				23 29	00 12		
	d				22 46				23 29	00 12		
Pembrey & Burry Port	d				22 52				23 35	00 18		
Kidwelly	d				22x58				23x41	00x25		
Ferryside	d				23x04				23x46	00x31		
Carmarthen	a				23 21				00 03	00 46		
	d											
Whitland	a											
	d											
Narberth	d											
Kilgetty	d											
Saundersfoot	d											
Tenby	a											
	d											
Penally	d											
Manorbier	d											
Lamphey	d											
Pembroke	d											
Pembroke Dock	a											
Clunderwen	d											
Clarbeston Road	d											
Haverfordwest	d											
Johnston	d											
Milford Haven	a											
Fishguard & Goodwick	a											
Fishguard Harbour [30] ⛴	a											
	d										23 45	
Rosslare Harbour ⛴	a										04 00	

When events are being held at the Principality Stadium, services are subject to alteration. Please check times before travelling.

Ferry service between Fishguard Harbour and Rosslare Harbour is operated by Stena Line

Table T128-F

Sundays
15 December to 10 May

Cardiff - Maesteg, Swansea and West Wales

		AW	AW	AW	AW	AW	AW	AW	AW	AW	GW	AW	GW	AW	GW	AW	AW	GW	AW	GW	AW	AW	GW
		◇ A	🚌	◇	◇	◇	◇	[B]	◇ ⊤	◇	◇[1] B ⊏⊤	◇ ⊤	◇[1] B ⊏⊤	◇	◇[1] ⊤	◇	■ ⊤	◇[1] ⊤	■ ⊤	◇[1] ⊤	◇	■ ⊤	◇[1] ⊤
London Paddington [15] ⊖	d										08 33		09 37		10 43			11 43		12 43			13 43
Reading [7]	d										08 58		10 03		11 08			12 08		13 08			14 08
Manchester Piccadilly [10]	d																09 30		10 31			11 30	
Gloucester [7]	d																						
Bristol Parkway [7]	d										09 53		10 57		11 58			12 58		13 58			15 00
Newport (South Wales)	d								09 33		10 10	10 59	11 18		12 18		13 06	13 18	13 41	14 20		14 35	15 18
Cardiff Central [7]	d								09 57		10 34	11 18	11 34	12 05	12 35		13 21	13 35	14 06	14 35		14 51	15 35
Pontyclun	d								10 09					12 18									
Llanharan	d								10 14					12 23									
Pencoed	d								10 18					12 28									
Bridgend	d								10 24		10 53	11 38	11 53	12 35	12 54		13 42	13 55	14 28	14 53		15 11	15 54
Wildmill	d																						
Sarn	d																						
Tondu	d																						
Garth (Mid Glamorgan)	d																						
Maesteg (Ewenny Road)	d																						
Maesteg	a																						
Pyle	d								10 32					12 43			13 51		14 36			15 18	
Port Talbot Parkway	d								10 41		11 07	11 52	12 07	12 51	13 08		13 59	14 11	14 45	15 07		15 27	16 08
Baglan	d																						
Briton Ferry	d																						
Neath	d								10 49		11 15	12 00	12 16		13 16		14 07	14 19	14 53	15 15		15 34	16 16
Skewen	d																						
Llansamlet	d																						
Swansea	a								11 01		11 27	12 12	12 28		13 28		14 20	14 31	15 07	15 27		15 48	16 28
	d			00 10			10 43		11 05	11 11		12 17	12 36			14 02		14 38	15 26		15 36		16 36
Gowerton	d	00 04		00s21					11 16	11 23		12 28				14 13			15 37		15 47		
Llanelli	a	00 12		00s29			10 59		11 24	11 31		12 36	12 52	13 24		14 21		14 55	15 46		15 55		16 52
	d	00 12					11 00		11 24			12 36	12 53	13 25		14 22		14 56	15 47				16 53
Pembrey & Burry Port	d	00 18		00s35			11 06		11 30			12 42	13 00	13 31		14 28		15 03	15 53				16 59
Kidwelly	d	00x25		00s42					11x37			12x48				14x35							
Ferryside	d	00x31		00s48					11x43			12x54				14x41							
Carmarthen	a	00 46		01 02			11 26		11 58			13 08	13 27	13 54		14 55		15 24	16 16				17 21
	d		00 57		09 55	10 19	11 32		12 05			13 10		13 57		14 57			16 20				
Whitland	a		01 17		10 12	10 36	11 48		12 21			13 26		14 13		15 14			16 37				
	d		01 17		10 12	10 36	11 48		12 22			13 27		14 13		15 14			16 37				
Narberth	d					10x45										15x23							
Kilgetty	d					10x54										15x33							
Saundersfoot	d					10x56										15x35							
Tenby	a					11 04										15 43							
	d					11 11										15 44							
Penally	d					11x14										15x47							
Manorbier	d					11 20										15 53							
Lamphey	d					11x28										16x01							
Pembroke	d					11 31										16 04							
Pembroke Dock	a					11 42										16 17							
Clunderwen	d				10x19				12x30					14x20					16x45				
Clarbeston Road	d				10x27		12x01		12x39			13x40		14x27					16x53				
Haverfordwest	d				10 36				12 47					14 36					17 01				
Johnston	d				10x44				12x56					14x44					17x10				
Milford Haven	a				10 55				13 07					14 54					17 22				
Fishguard & Goodwick	a		02 07				12 19					13 59											
Fishguard Harbour [30] ⛴	a		02 12				12 28					14 05											
	d							13 10															
Rosslare Harbour ⛴	a							16 25															

A not 15 December

B ⊏ from Cardiff Central ⊤ to Cardiff Central

When events are being held at the Principality Stadium, services are subject to alteration. Please check times before travelling.

Ferry service between Fishguard Harbour and Rosslare Harbour is operated by Stena Line

Table T128-F

Sundays

15 December to 10 May

Cardiff - Maesteg, Swansea and West Wales

		AW	AW	GW	AW	GW	AW	AW	AW	GW	GW	AW	GW	AW	AW	AW	GW	AW	GW	AW	GW	GW	AW
		◇	■ ✠	◇1 ✠	■ ✠	◇1 ✠	◇	■ ✠	◇	◇1 A ⊡✠	◇1 ✠	■ ✠	◇1 ✠	■ ✠	◇	■	◇1 A ⊡✠	◇	◇1 ✠	■ ✠	◇1 B ⊡✠	◇1 A ⊡✠	■
London Paddington 15 ⊖	d			14 43		15 43				16 17	16 42		17 43				18 17		18 43		19 17	19 43	
Reading 7	d			15 08		16 08				16 42	17 08		18 08				18 42		19 07		19 43	20 08	
Manchester Piccadilly 10	d		12 32		13 30			14 30				15 30		16 30						17 30			18 30
Gloucester 7	d																						
Bristol Parkway 7	d			16 00		17 01				17 37	17 59		18 58				19 36		19 58		20 39	21 02	
Newport (South Wales)	d		15 42	16 22	16 40	17 23		17 40		17 58	18 18	18 37	19 19	19 36			19 58		20 19	20 29	20 59	21 20	21 29
Cardiff Central 7	d		16 02	16 35	17 06	17 41		18 00		18 13	18 34	19 02	19 35	19 54			20 12	20 18	20 35	20 50	21 17	21 36	21 49
Pontyclun	d																						
Llanharan	d																						
Pencoed	d																						
Bridgend	d		16 23	16 59	17 27	18 00		18 22		18 32	18 53	19 23	19 54	20 15			20 31	20 38	20 54	21 11	21 36	21 55	22 09
Wildmill	d																						
Sarn	d																						
Tondu	d																						
Garth (Mid Glamorgan)	d																						
Maesteg (Ewenny Road)	d																						
Maesteg	a																						
Pyle	d		16 32		17 35			18 30				19 30		20 22				20 47		21 18			22 16
Port Talbot Parkway	d		16 40	17 15	17 44	18 13		18 38		18 46	19 07	19 39	20 08	20 30			20 45	20 54	21 08	21 26	21 49	22 09	22 24
Baglan	d																						
Briton Ferry	d																						
Neath	d		16 48	17 24	17 53	18 21		18 46		18 53	19 16	19 46	20 17	20 37			20 53	21 02	21 17	21 33	21 56	22 18	22 31
Skewen	d																						
Llansamlet	d																						
Swansea	a		17 03	17 36	18 08	18 33		19 01		19 05	19 28	20 02	20 29	20 52			21 05	21 16	21 32	21 49	22 08	22 30	22 46
	d	16 42	17 07				18 35	19 14							20 58			21 19					22 49
Gowerton	d	16 53	17 19				18 46	19 26							21 09			21 30					23 00
Llanelli	a	17 00	17 27				18 54	19 34							21 17			21 38					23 08
	d	17 02	17 29				18 55	19 34							21 18			21 39					23 08
Pembrey & Burry Port	d	17 08	17 35				19 01	19 41							21 23			21 45					23 14
Kidwelly	d	17x15					19x08								21x30								23x20
Ferryside	d	17x21					19x14								21x36								23x26
Carmarthen	a	17 36	18 00				19 30	20 05							21 49			22 09					23 42
	d	17 37	18 06				19 33	20 11							21 51			22 11					
Whitland	a	17 54	18 23				19 50	20 28							22 07			22 27					
	d	17 54	18 24				19 50	20 32	20 37						22 07			22 27					
Narberth	d	18x03							20x46														
Kilgetty	d	18x13							20x55														
Saundersfoot	d	18x15							20x57														
Tenby	a	18 23							21 05														
	d	18 23							21 06														
Penally	d	18x26							21x09														
Manorbier	d	18 33							21 15														
Lamphey	d	18x40							21x23														
Pembroke	d	18 44							21 26														
Pembroke Dock	a	18 54							21 37														
Clunderwen	d		18x31				19x58	20x40										22x35					
Clarbeston Road	d		18x39				20x06	20x48							22x20			22x43					
Haverfordwest	d		18 49				20a15	20 56										22 51					
Johnston	d		18x57					21x05										23x00					
Milford Haven	a		19 12					21 20										23 10					
Fishguard & Goodwick	a														22 39								
Fishguard Harbour 30 ⛴	a														22 46								
	d															23 45							
Rosslare Harbour ⛴	a															04 00							

A ⊡ from Bristol Parkway to Cardiff Central ✠ to Reading ✠ from Cardiff Central

B ⊡ from Cardiff Central ✠ to Cardiff Central

When events are being held at the Principality Stadium, services are subject to alteration. Please check times before travelling.

Ferry service between Fishguard Harbour and Rosslare Harbour is operated by Stena Line

Table T128-F

Sundays

15 December to 10 May

Cardiff - Maesteg, Swansea and West Wales

		AW	GW	AW	GW
		◇	◇1 A ⊡✠	◇	◇1 B ⊡✠
London Paddington 15 ⊖	d		20 43		21 43
Reading 7	d		21 08		22 08
Manchester Piccadilly 10	d			19 30	
Gloucester 7	d				
Bristol Parkway 7	d		22 05		23 02
Newport (South Wales)	d		22 21	22 41	23 20
Cardiff Central 7	d	22 30	22 38	23 02	23 36
Pontyclun	d				
Llanharan	d				
Pencoed	d				
Bridgend	d	22 50	22 56	23 23	23 55
Wildmill	d				
Sarn	d				
Tondu	d				
Garth (Mid Glamorgan)	d				
Maesteg (Ewenny Road)	d				
Maesteg	a				
Pyle	d			23 31	
Port Talbot Parkway	d	23 04	23 10	23 40	00 10
Baglan	d				
Briton Ferry	d				
Neath	d	23 12	23 18	23 48	00 18
Skewen	d				
Llansamlet	d				
Swansea	a	23 25	23 30	00 02	00 30
	d	23 40			
Gowerton	d	23 52			
Llanelli	a	23 59			
	d	00 01			
Pembrey & Burry Port	d	00 07			
Kidwelly	d	00x14			
Ferryside	d	00x20			
Carmarthen	a	00 33			
	d				
Whitland	a				
	d				
Narberth	d				
Kilgetty	d				
Saundersfoot	d				
Tenby	a				
	d				
Penally	d				
Manorbier	d				
Lamphey	d				
Pembroke	d				
Pembroke Dock	a				
Clunderwen	d				
Clarbeston Road	d				
Haverfordwest	d				
Johnston	d				
Milford Haven	a				
Fishguard & Goodwick	a				
Fishguard Harbour 30 ⛴	a				
	d				
Rosslare Harbour ⛴	a				

A ⊡ from Cardiff Central ✠ to Cardiff Central

B ⊡ from Bristol Parkway to Cardiff Central ✠ to Reading ✠ from Cardiff Central

When events are being held at the Principality Stadium, services are subject to alteration. Please check times before travelling.

Ferry service between Fishguard Harbour and Rosslare Harbour is operated by Stena Line

Table T128-R

Mondays to Fridays

16 December to 15 May

West Wales, Swansea and Maesteg - Cardiff

Miles	Miles			AW MO	AW MX	AW	GW	AW MX	AW	GW	GW	AW	GW	GW	AW	AW	GW	AW	GW	AW	GW	AW	AW
				◇		◇	◇1 ⊼		◇	◇1 ⊼	◇1 ⊼	◇ ⊼	◇1 A ✕⊼	◇1 B ⊼		■ ⊼	◇1 ⊼	◇	◇1 C ⊼		◇1 ⊼	◇ ⊼	
—	—	Rosslare Harbour ⛴	d																				
0	—	**Fishguard Harbour** 30 ⛴	a																				
—	—		d					02 37															06 50
—	—	Fishguard & Goodwick	d					02 40															06 53
—	0	**Milford Haven**	d		00 21																	05 54	
—	4	Johnston	d		00x29																	06x02	
—	8¾	Haverfordwest	d		00 36																	06 09	
15¾	14	Clarbeston Road	d		00x44			02x59														06x17	07a14
22¼	—	Clunderwen	d		00x51																	06x24	
—	0	**Pembroke Dock**	d																				
—	2	Pembroke	d																				
—	3½	Lamphey	d																				
—	7	Manorbier	d																				
—	10¼	Penally	d																				
—	11½	**Tenby**	a																				
—	—		d																				
—	15¾	Saundersfoot	d																				
—	16½	Kilgetty	d																				
—	22	Narberth	d																				
27¾	27¼	Whitland	a		00 57			03 11														06 31	
—	—		d		00 57			03 11														06 31	
41¼	—	**Carmarthen**	a		01 16			03 29														06 47	
—	—		d			02 59			04 47			05 00				05 46		06 15				06 50	
48¾	—	Ferryside	d													05x56		06x25				07x00	
53	—	Kidwelly	d													06x01		06x31				07x05	
58¼	—	Pembrey & Burry Port	d						05 06			05 18				06 08		06 37				07 12	
62¼	—	Llanelli	a			03 22			05 13			05 24				06 14		06 44				07 18	
—	—		d			03 22						05 25				06 15		06 44				07 19	
68	—	Gowerton	d													06 22		06 51				07 25	
73½	—	**Swansea**	a			03 41										06 35		07 05				07 39	
—	—		d				03 46			04 58	05 28		05 57	06 28		06 38	06 58	07 07	07 20		07 44	07 49	
77½	—	Llansamlet	d													06 44							
79¼	—	Skewen	d													06 48							
83	—	Neath	d				03 58			05 10	05 40		06 09	06 40		06 52	07 10	07 18	07 32		07 56	08 01	
84¾	—	Briton Ferry	d													06 56							
86½	—	Baglan	d													06 59							
88½	—	Port Talbot Parkway	d				04 05			05 17	05 47	05 58	06 16	06 47		07 03	07 17	07 25	07 39		08 03	08 08	
94¾	—	Pyle	d									06 06				07 11		07 33				08 15	
—	0	Maesteg	d												06 44								
—	0½	Maesteg (Ewenny Road)	d												06 46								
—	1¼	Garth (Mid Glamorgan)	d												06 49								
—	5¼	Tondu	d												06 57								
—	6	Sarn	d												07 00								
—	7¼	Wildmill	d												07 03								
100¾	8¾	Bridgend	d	00 07			04 26			05 31	06 01	06 13	06 30	07 01	07 07	07 19	07 31	07 41	07 53	08 04	08 17	08 23	
104¾	—	Pencoed	d									06 20			07 13	07 25				08 10			
107	—	Llanharan	d									06 24			07 18			07 49				08 30	
110	—	Pontyclun	d									06 29			07 24	07 33				08 18			
121	—	**Cardiff Central** 7	a	00 34			05 07			05 51	06 21	06 43	06 50	07 21	07 38	07 47	07 51	08 05	08 13	08 32	08 37	08 48	
—	—	Newport (South Wales)	a				05 24			06 06	06 35	06 59	07 03	07 34		08 03	08 06		08 28		08 52	09 03	
—	—	Bristol Parkway 7	a				05 51			06 28	06 57		07 25	07 58			08 29		08 54		09 14		
—	—	Gloucester 7	a																				
—	—	Manchester Piccadilly 10	a									10 11				11 11						12 13	
—	—	Reading 7	a				06 47			07 18			08 18				09 19		09 44		10 06		
—	—	London Paddington 15 ⊖	a				07 14			07 44	08 14		08 45	09 14			09 44		10 12		10 34		

A ✕ to Cardiff Central ⊼ from Cardiff Central   B The Capitals United   C Y Cymro/The Welshman

When events are being held at the Principality Stadium, services are subject to alteration. Please check times before travelling.

Ferry service between Fishguard Harbour and Rosslare Harbour is operated by Stena Line

Table T128-R

Mondays to Fridays

16 December to 15 May

West Wales, Swansea and Maesteg - Cardiff

		AW	AW	GW	AW	AW	AW	AW	AW	GW	AW	AW	AW	GW	AW	AW	AW	AW	GW	AW	AW	AW	AW
		◇	◇	◇1 A ⊼		■ ⊼	◇ ⊼	◇	◇	◇1 ⊼	■ ⊼	◇	◇	◇1 ⊼	■ ⊼	◇	◇	◇ ⊼	◇1 ⊼		B		◇ ⊼
Rosslare Harbour ⛴	d																				08 00		
Fishguard Harbour 30 ⛴	a																				11 15		
	d										07 50									09 54			
Fishguard & Goodwick	d										07 53									09 57			
Milford Haven	d					07 04									09 09								
Johnston	d					07x12									09x17								
Haverfordwest	d					07 19									09 24								
Clarbeston Road	d					07x27					08x11				09x32					10x17			
Clunderwen	d					07x34					08x19				09x40					10x25			
Pembroke Dock	d						06 59											09 09					
Pembroke	d						07 07											09 17					
Lamphey	d						07x10											09x20					
Manorbier	d						07 18											09 29					
Penally	d						07x23											09x34					
Tenby	a						07 27											09 37					
	d						07 29											09 40					
Saundersfoot	d						07x36											09x48					
Kilgetty	d						07x38											09x50					
Narberth	d						07x48											10x00					
Whitland	a					07 40	07 56				08 26				09 47			10 09		10 32			
	d					07 40	07 56				08 26				09 47			10 09		10 32			
Carmarthen	a					07 57	08 14				08 45				10 04			10 28		10 50			
	d			07 23		08 01	08 15				08 58				10 08			10 31					11 01
Ferryside	d			07 35		08x11	08x25				09x08												11x11
Kidwelly	d			07 41		08x16	08x31				09x14												11x18
Pembrey & Burry Port	d			07 48		08 23	08 37				09 21				10 25			10 50					11 24
Llanelli	a			07 56		08 29	08 44				09 27				10 32			10 57					11 31
	d	07 46		07 57		08 30	08 44				09 28	09 39			10 32			10 58					11 31
Gowerton	d	07 54				08 36					09 35	09 46						11 05					11 38
Swansea	a	08 09		08 14		08 50	09 01				09 49	10 02			10 50			11 22					11 51
	d			08 22		08 53			09 06	09 22	09 55	10 08		10 22	10 55		11 05		11 22				11 55
Llansamlet	d								09 13								11 12						
Skewen	d								09 17								11 16						
Neath	d			08 34		09 04			09 21	09 34	10 06			10 34	11 06		11 20		11 34				12 06
Briton Ferry	d								09 24								11 23						
Baglan	d								09 28								11 27						
Port Talbot Parkway	d			08 41		09 11			09 32	09 41	10 13			10 41	11 13		11 31		11 41				12 13
Pyle	d								09 39								11 38						
Maesteg	d		08 04					09 16					10 16			11 15							
Maesteg (Ewenny Road)	d		08 06					09 18					10 18			11 17							
Garth (Mid Glamorgan)	d		08 09					09 21					10 21			11 20							
Tondu	d		08 18					09 30					10 30			11 28							
Sarn	d		08 21					09 33					10 33			11 31							
Wildmill	d		08 23					09 35					10 35			11 34							
Bridgend	d		08 27	08 55	09 09	09 23		09 39	09 48	09 55	10 27	10 36	10 41	10 55	11 27	11 39	11 46		11 55			12 07	12 25
Pencoed	d		08 33					09 45					10 47			11 44							
Llanharan	d							09 49					10 51			11 48							
Pontyclun	d		08 40					09 53					10 55			11 52							
Cardiff Central 7	a		08 54	09 15	09 32	09 49		10 07	10 13	10 15	10 49	11 07	11 12	11 15	11 48	12 08	12 12		12 15			12 32	12 47
Newport (South Wales)	a		09 22	09 29		10 18		10 23	10 28	10 31	11 04			11 28		12 24			12 28				13 02
Bristol Parkway 7	a			09 54						10 54				11 53					12 53				
Gloucester 7	a		10 15					11 13								13 16							
Manchester Piccadilly 10	a					13 13					14 13												16 13
Reading 7	a			10 45						11 45				12 45					13 44				
London Paddington 15 ⊖	a			11 12						12 11				13 10					14 11				

A The Red Dragon

When events are being held at the Principality Stadium, services are subject to alteration. Please check times before travelling.

Ferry service between Fishguard Harbour and Rosslare Harbour is operated by Stena Line

Table T128-R

Mondays to Fridays

16 December to 15 May

West Wales, Swansea and Maesteg - Cardiff

		AW	GW	AW	AW	AW	AW	AW	GW	AW	AW	AW	GW	AW	AW	AW	AW	AW	AW	GW	AW	AW
		◇	◇1 ✠		■ ✠	◇	◇	◇ ✠	◇1 ✠	■ ✠	◇ ✠	◇	◇1 ✠	■ ✠		■ ✠	◇	■	◇ ✠	◇1 A ✠		■ ✠
Rosslare Harbour ⛴	d																					
Fishguard Harbour 30 ⛴	a																					
	d													12 50								
Fishguard & Goodwick	d													12 53								
Milford Haven	d				11 10											13 08						
Johnston	d				11x18											13x16						
Haverfordwest	d				11 25											13 23						
Clarbeston Road	d				11x33									13x12		13x31						
Clunderwen	d				11x40											13x38						
Pembroke Dock	d							11 09											13 09			
Pembroke	d							11 17											13 17			
Lamphey	d							11x20											13x20			
Manorbier	d							11 29											13 29			
Penally	d							11x34											13x34			
Tenby	a							11 38											13 38			
	d							11 44											13 42			
Saundersfoot	d							11x52											13x50			
Kilgetty	d							11x54											13x52			
Narberth	d							12x04											14x02			
Whitland	a				11 47			12 16						13 25		13 44			14 11			
	d				11 47			12 16						13 25		13 44			14 11			
Carmarthen	a				12 04			12 35						13 42		14 01			14 31			
	d				12 08			12 36		13 00				13 49		14 05			14 34			15 02
Ferryside	d									13x10												15x12
Kidwelly	d									13x17												15x17
Pembrey & Burry Port	d				12 26			12 55		13 23						14 23			14 53			15 24
Llanelli	a				12 32			13 02		13 30				14 11		14 29			15 00			15 30
	d				12 33		12 43	13 03		13 30	13 56			14 11		14 30			15 00			15 31
Gowerton	d				12 39		12 50			13 37	14 03					14 36						15 37
Swansea	a				12 53		13 03	13 21		13 50	14 20					14 50			15 18			15 51
	d		12 22		12 56		13 05		13 22	13 55			14 22			14 55		15 05		15 22		15 55
Llansamlet	d						13 12											15 12				
Skewen	d						13 16											15 16				
Neath	d		12 34		13 07		13 20		13 33	14 06			14 33			15 06		15 20		15 33		16 06
Briton Ferry	d						13 24											15 23				
Baglan	d						13 27											15 27				
Port Talbot Parkway	d		12 41		13 14		13 31		13 40	14 13			14 40	14 45		15 13		15 31		15 40		16 13
Pyle	d						13 39											15 38				
Maesteg	d	12 17				13 15						14 15					15 15					
Maesteg (Ewenny Road)	d	12 19				13 17						14 17					15 17					
Garth (Mid Glamorgan)	d	12 22				13 20						14 20					15 20					
Tondu	d	12 31				13 29						14 29					15 29					
Sarn	d	12 34				13 32						14 32					15 32					
Wildmill	d	12 36				13 34						14 34					15 34					
Bridgend	d	12 40	12 55	13 07	13 28	13 38	13 48		13 55	14 26		14 39	14 53	15 00	15 09	15 26	15 38	15 48		15 55	16 07	16 25
Pencoed	d	12 46				13 44						14 45					15 44					
Llanharan	d	12 50				13 48						14 49					15 48					
Pontyclun	d	12 54				13 52						14 53					15 52					
Cardiff Central 7	a	13 09	13 15	13 30	13 49	14 08	14 11		14 15	14 47		15 08	15 14	15 26	15 32	15 47	16 07	16 13		16 15	16 29	16 47
Newport (South Wales)	a	13 24	13 28		14 18				14 28	15 02		15 22	15 28			16 02	16 23	16 35		16 28		17 01
Bristol Parkway 7	a		13 54						14 54				15 54							16 54		
Gloucester 7	a	14 15										16 13					17 17					
Manchester Piccadilly 10	a				17 13					18 13						19 13						20 19
Reading 7	a		14 44						15 45				16 44							17 45		
London Paddington 15 ⊖	a		15 12						16 09				17 09							18 15		

A The Saint David

When events are being held at the Principality Stadium, services are subject to alteration. Please check times before travelling.

Ferry service between Fishguard Harbour and Rosslare Harbour is operated by Stena Line

Table T128-R

Mondays to Fridays

16 December to 15 May

West Wales, Swansea and Maesteg - Cardiff

		AW	GW	AW	AW	AW	AW	AW	GW	AW FO	AW FX	AW	AW	GW	AW	AW FO	AW FX	AW	GW	AW	AW	AW	AW
		◇	◇1 ✠		■ ✠	◇	■ ✠	◇ ✠	◇1 ✠	◇ ✠	◇ ✠	◇ ✠	◇	◇1 ✠		◇	◇	◇	◇1 ✠	◇		B	◇
Rosslare Harbour ⛴	d																					18 10	
Fishguard Harbour 30 ⛴	a																					21 25	
	d																				19 08		
Fishguard & Goodwick	d																				19 11		
Milford Haven	d				15 07											17 11	17 11						
Johnston	d				15x15											17x19	17x19						
Haverfordwest	d				15 22											17 26	17 26						
Clarbeston Road	d				15x30											17x34	17x34				19x30		
Clunderwen	d				15x37											17x41	17x41						
Pembroke Dock	d							15 09										17 09					19 19
Pembroke	d							15 17										17 17					19 27
Lamphey	d							15x20										17x20					19x31
Manorbier	d							15 29										17 29					19 39
Penally	d							15x34										17x34					19x44
Tenby	a							15 38										17 38					19 48
	d							15 40										17 40					
Saundersfoot	d							15x48										17x48					
Kilgetty	d							15x50										17x50					
Narberth	d							16x00										18x00					
Whitland	a				15 44			16 09								17 47	17 47	18 09			19 43		
	d				15 44			16 09								17 47	17 47	18 09			19 43		
Carmarthen	a				16 01			16 28								18 03	18 04	18 28			20 02		
	d				16 05			16 30		16 56	16 56					18 08	18 08	18 32		18 50			
Ferryside	d									17x06	17x06					18x18	18x18			19x00			
Kidwelly	d									17x12	17x12					18x23	18x23			19x06			
Pembrey & Burry Port	d				16 23			16 49		17 19	17 19					18 30	18 30	18 51		19 14			
Llanelli	a				16 29			16 56		17 24	17 25					18 35	18 36	18 58		19 21			
	d				16 30		16 45	16 57		17 26	17 26	17 52				18 36	18 37	18 58		19 21			
Gowerton	d				16 36			17 04		17 33	17 33	17 59				18 43	18 43	19 06		19 29			
Swansea	a				16 50		17 04	17 18		17 45	17 46	18 14				18 56	18 57	19 21		19 44			
	d		16 22		16 55		17 05		17 22	17 50	17 50			18 22		19 05	19 05		19 22	19 51			
Llansamlet	d						17 11			17 56	17 56					19 11	19 11						
Skewen	d						17 15			18 00	18 00					19 15	19 15						
Neath	d		16 34		17 06		17 19		17 34	18 04	18 04			18 34		19 19	19 19		19 34	20 02			
Briton Ferry	d						17 23			18 08	18 08					19 23	19 23						
Baglan	d						17 26			18 11	18 11					19 26	19 26						
Port Talbot Parkway	d		16 41		17 13		17 30		17 41	18 15	18 15			18 41		19 30	19 30		19 41	20 09			
Pyle	d						17 37			18 22	18 22					19 37	19 37						
Maesteg	d	16 15				17 14							18 20		19 14								
Maesteg (Ewenny Road)	d	16 17				17 16							18 22		19 16								
Garth (Mid Glamorgan)	d	16 20				17 19							18 25		19 19								
Tondu	d	16 28				17 28							18 34		19 28								
Sarn	d	16 31				17 31							18 37		19 31								
Wildmill	d	16 34				17 33							18 39		19 33								
Bridgend	d	16 38	16 55	17 11	17 25	17 37	17 45		17 55	18 30	18 30		18 43	18 55	19 37	19 47	19 47		19 55	20 23			
Pencoed	d	16 43				17 43							18 49		19 43								
Llanharan	d	16 47				17 47							18 52		19 46								
Pontyclun	d	16 51				17 51							18 57		19 51								
Cardiff Central 7	a	17 05	17 15	17 33	17 48	18 05	18 09		18 15	18 53	18 53		19 12	19 15	20 04	20 08	20 08		20 17	20 44			
Newport (South Wales)	a	17 20	17 32		18 02	18 20	18 35		18 28	19 08	19 08			19 29					20 31				
Bristol Parkway 7	a		17 55						18 51					19 50					20 53				
Gloucester 7	a	18 13				19 11																	
Manchester Piccadilly 10	a				21 07					22 15	22 15												
Reading 7	a		18 46						19 45					20 44					21 43				
London Paddington 15 ⊖	a		19 14						20 14					21 10					22 09				

When events are being held at the Principality Stadium, services are subject to alteration. Please check times before travelling.

Ferry service between Fishguard Harbour and Rosslare Harbour is operated by Stena Line

Table T128-R

Mondays to Fridays

16 December to 15 May

West Wales, Swansea and Maesteg - Cardiff

		AW	GW	AW	AW	GW FO	GW FX	AW FO	AW FX	AW	AW	AW FO	AW FX	AW	AW	AW	AW
		◇	◇1 ⊼	◇	◇	◇1 ⊼	◇1 ⊼	◇	◇		◇	◇	◇	◇		◇	
Rosslare Harbour	d																
Fishguard Harbour 30	a																
	d														22 13		
Fishguard & Goodwick	d														22 16		
Milford Haven	d			19 16						20 38							23 20
Johnston	d			19x24						20x46							23x28
Haverfordwest	d			19 31						20 53							23 35
Clarbeston Road	d			19x39						21x01					22x35		23x43
Clunderwen	d			19x46						21x08					22x42		23x50
Pembroke Dock	d										21 09					22 27	
Pembroke	d										21 17					22 35	
Lamphey	d										21x20					22x38	
Manorbier	d										21 29					22 46	
Penally	d										21x34					22x52	
Tenby	a										21 38					22 56	
	d							19 59	19 59		21 55					22 57	
Saundersfoot	d							20x07	20x07		22x03					23x05	
Kilgetty	d							20x09	20x09		22x05					23x07	
Narberth	d							20x19	20x19		22x15					23x16	
Whitland	a			19 52				20 28	20 28	21 15	22 24				22 50	23 25	23 57
	d			19 52				20 28	20 28	21 15	22 24				22 50	23 25	23 57
Carmarthen	a			20 09				20 45	20 45	21 33	22 43				23 08	23 43	00 15
	d			20 11				20 49	20 49						23 10		
Ferryside	d							20x59	20x59						23x20		
Kidwelly	d							21x04	21x05						23x26		
Pembrey & Burry Port	d			20 29				21 11	21 12						23 33		
Llanelli	a			20 35				21 18	21 19						23 40		
	d			20 36				21 18	21 19					22 01	23 41		
Gowerton	d			20 42				21 26	21 27					22 08	23 48		
Swansea	a			20 56				21 40	21 41					22 23	00 06		
	d		20 22	21 00		21 22	21 22	21 45	21 45					22 32			
Llansamlet	d							21 52	21 52					22 39			
Skewen	d							21 56	21 56					22 43			
Neath	d		20 34	21 11		21 34	21 34	22 00	22 00					22 47			
Briton Ferry	d							22 03	22 03					22 51			
Baglan	d							22 07	22 07					22 54			
Port Talbot Parkway	d		20 41	21 18		21 41	21 41	22 11	22 11					22 58			
Pyle	d							22 19	22 19					23 07			
Maesteg	d	20 15			21 15							22 15	22 15				
Maesteg (Ewenny Road)	d	20 17			21 17							22 17	22 17				
Garth (Mid Glamorgan)	d	20 20			21 20							22 20	22 20				
Tondu	d	20 29			21 29							22 29	22 29				
Sarn	d	20 32			21 32							22 32	22 32				
Wildmill	d	20 34			21 34							22 34	22 34				
Bridgend	d	20 38	20 55	21 31	21 38	21 55	21 55	22 29	22 29			22 38	22 38	23 15			
Pencoed	d	20 44			21 44							22 44	22 44				
Llanharan	d	20 48			21 48							22 48	22 48				
Pontyclun	d	20 52			21 52							22 52	22 52				
Cardiff Central 7	a	21 06	21 15	21 58	22 10	22 15	22 15	22 55	22 55			23 09	23 09	23 39			
Newport (South Wales)	a	21 24	21 31			22 29	22 34					23 35	23 40				
Bristol Parkway 7	a		21 52			22 52	23 04										
Gloucester 7	a	22 17										00 32	00 40				
Manchester Piccadilly 10	a																
Reading 7	a		22 43														
London Paddington 15 ⊖	a		23 09														

When events are being held at the Principality Stadium, services are subject to alteration. Please check times before travelling.

Ferry service between Fishguard Harbour and Rosslare Harbour is operated by Stena Line

NRT DECEMBER 19 EDITION

Table T128-R

Saturdays

21 December to 16 May

West Wales, Swansea and Maesteg - Cardiff

		AW	AW	GW	AW	GW	GW	AW	GW	GW	AW	GW	AW	AW	GW	AW	GW	AW	AW	AW	GW	AW	AW
			◇	◇1 ⊼		◇1 ⊼	◇1 ⊼	◇ ⊼	◇1 ⊼	◇1 ⊼	◇	◇1 ⊼	■ ⊼		◇1 ⊼		◇1 ⊼	■ ⊼		◇	◇1 ⊼		◇ ⊼
Rosslare Harbour	d																						
Fishguard Harbour 30	a																						
	d				02 37														06 50				
Fishguard & Goodwick	d				02 40														06 53				
Milford Haven	d	00 21																05 55					07 06
Johnston	d	00x29																06x03					07x14
Haverfordwest	d	00 36																06 10					07 21
Clarbeston Road	d	00x44			02x59													06x18	07a14				07x29
Clunderwen	d	00x51																06x25					07x36
Pembroke Dock	d																						
Pembroke	d																						
Lamphey	d																						
Manorbier	d																						
Penally	d																						
Tenby	a																						
	d																						
Saundersfoot	d																						
Kilgetty	d																						
Narberth	d																						
Whitland	a	00 57			03 11													06 31					07 42
	d	00 57			03 11													06 31					07 42
Carmarthen	a	01 16			03 29													06 47					07 57
	d		02 44					05 03					05 55	06 15				06 50			07 21		08 01
Ferryside	d												06x05	06x25				07x00			07 33		08x11
Kidwelly	d												06x10	06x30				07x05			07 39		08x16
Pembrey & Burry Port	d							05 21					06 17	06 37				07 12			07 46		08 23
Llanelli	a		03 07					05 27					06 23	06 43				07 18			07 54		08 29
	d		03 07					05 28					06 24	06 44				07 19			07 56		08 30
Gowerton	d												06 30	06 51				07 25					08 36
Swansea	a		03 26										06 44	07 04				07 39			08 12		08 50
	d			03 59		04 48	05 22		05 52	06 20		06 44	06 49	07 06	07 22		07 40	07 47			08 22		08 54
Llansamlet	d													07 13									
Skewen	d													07 17									
Neath	d			04 11		05 00	05 34		06 04	06 32		06 56	07 01	07 21	07 34		07 52	07 58			08 34		09 06
Briton Ferry	d													07 24									
Baglan	d													07 28									
Port Talbot Parkway	d			04 18		05 07	05 41	06 01	06 11	06 39		07 03	07 08	07 32	07 41		08 00	08 05			08 41		09 13
Pyle	d							06 07					07 14	07 40				08 12					09 21
Maesteg	d										06 44									08 05			
Maesteg (Ewenny Road)	d										06 46									08 08			
Garth (Mid Glamorgan)	d										06 49									08 11			
Tondu	d										06 58									08 20			
Sarn	d										07 01									08 23			
Wildmill	d										07 03									08 26			
Bridgend	d			04 32		05 21	05 55	06 15	06 25	06 53	07 07	07 17	07 22	07 49	07 55	08 07	08 17	08 22		08 30	08 55	09 11	09 29
Pencoed	d							06 21			07 13			08 02				08 28					
Llanharan	d							06 24					07 29	08 05						08 37			
Pontyclun	d							06 29			07 20			08 10				08 35					
Cardiff Central 7	a			04 53		05 42	06 16	06 43	06 46	07 16	07 35	07 38	07 46	08 27	08 16	08 30	08 39	08 50		08 56	09 16	09 33	09 50
Newport (South Wales)	a			05 24		05 54	06 30	07 05	06 58	07 28		07 55	08 05		08 30		08 53	09 05		09 19	09 29		10 08
Bristol Parkway 7	a			05 53		06 16	06 52		07 20	07 54		08 20			08 54		09 15				09 54		
Gloucester 7	a																			10 13			
Manchester Piccadilly 10	a							10 14					11 13					12 12					13 13
Reading 7	a			06 48		07 17	07 45		08 16	08 45		09 16			09 45		10 16				10 45		
London Paddington 15 ⊖	a			07 14		07 44	08 13		08 42	09 11		09 42			10 11		10 45				11 12		

When events are being held at the Principality Stadium, services are subject to alteration. Please check times before travelling.

Ferry service between Fishguard Harbour and Rosslare Harbour is operated by Stena Line

Table T128-R

Saturdays

21 December to 16 May

West Wales, Swansea and Maesteg - Cardiff

		AW ◇ 🍴	AW ◇	AW ◇	GW ◇1 🍴	AW		AW ◇	AW ◇ 🍴	AW ■ 🍴	GW ◇1 🍴	AW	AW ■ 🍴	AW ◇	AW ◇	AW ◇ 🍴		GW ◇1 🍴	AW	AW ■	AW	AW ■ 🍴	AW ◇ 🍴	GW ◇1 🍴	AW
Rosslare Harbour ⛴	d																			08 00					
Fishguard Harbour 30 ⛴	a																			11 15					
	d								07 50										09 53						
Fishguard & Goodwick	d								07 53										09 56						
Milford Haven	d												09 10												
Johnston	d												09x18												
Haverfordwest	d												09 25												
Clarbeston Road	d								08x11				09x33						10x14						
Clunderwen	d								08x19				09x40						10x22						
Pembroke Dock	d	06 59														09 09									
Pembroke	d	07 07														09 17									
Lamphey	d	07x10														09x20									
Manorbier	d	07 17														09 29									
Penally	d	07x23														09x34									
Tenby	a	07 26														09 38									
	d	07 29														09 39									
Saundersfoot	d	07x36														09x47									
Kilgetty	d	07x38														09x49									
Narberth	d	07x47														09x59									
Whitland	a	07 55							08 26				09 47			10 07			10 29						
	d	07 55							08 26				09 47			10 07			10 29						
Carmarthen	a	08 12							08 45				10 05			10 26			10 47						
	d	08 14							09 00				10 08			10 27						11 07			
Ferryside	d	08x24							09x10													11x17			
Kidwelly	d	08x30							09x15													11x23			
Pembrey & Burry Port	d	08 36							09 21				10 26			10 47						11 30			
Llanelli	a	08 42							09 28				10 32			10 54						11 36			
	d	08 43						09 00	09 28				10 33			10 54						11 37			
Gowerton	d							09 08	09 35							11 02						11 44			
Swansea	a	09 02						09 24	09 50				10 51			11 17						11 57			
	d			09 05	09 23			09 34	09 54		10 22		10 55		11 10			11 22				12 00		12 22	
Llansamlet	d			09 12											11 17										
Skewen	d			09 16											11 21										
Neath	d			09 20	09 35			09 46	10 06		10 34		11 06		11 25			11 35				12 11		12 34	
Briton Ferry	d			09 23											11 28										
Baglan	d			09 27											11 32										
Port Talbot Parkway	d			09 31	09 42			09 53	10 13		10 41		11 13		11 36			11 44				12 18		12 41	
Pyle	d			09 38				10 02	10 20				11 21		11 43										
Maesteg	d		09 15							10 18				11 15									12 18		
Maesteg (Ewenny Road)	d		09 17							10 20				11 17									12 20		
Garth (Mid Glamorgan)	d		09 20							10 23				11 20									12 23		
Tondu	d		09 29											11 28									12 32		
Sarn	d		09 32							10 35				11 31									12 35		
Wildmill	d		09 34							10 37				11 34									12 37		
Bridgend	d		09 38	09 51	09 56	10 10		10 14	10 28	10 41	10 55	11 11	11 29	11 38	11 51			11 57			12 10	12 32	12 41	12 55	13 09
Pencoed	d		09 44							10 47				11 43									12 47		
Llanharan	d		09 47							10 51				11 47									12 51		
Pontyclun	d		09 52							10 55				11 51									12 55		
Cardiff Central 7	a		10 06	10 14	10 17	10 32		10 38	10 49	11 10	11 16	11 32	11 50	12 06	12 14			12 18			12 32	12 53	13 10	13 16	13 31
Newport (South Wales)	a		10 21	10 38	10 29				11 08	11 26	11 29		12 08	12 20				12 30				13 08	13 35	13 30	
Bristol Parkway 7	a				10 55						11 54							12 54						13 54	
Gloucester 7	a		11 12											13 11											
Manchester Piccadilly 10	a								14 14				15 15									16 15			
Reading 7	a				11 45						12 45							13 45						14 45	
London Paddington 15 ⊖	a				12 11						13 12							14 11						15 11	

When events are being held at the Principality Stadium, services are subject to alteration. Please check times before travelling.

Ferry service between Fishguard Harbour and Rosslare Harbour is operated by Stena Line

Table T128-R

Saturdays

21 December to 16 May

West Wales, Swansea and Maesteg - Cardiff

		AW ■ 🍴		AW ◇	AW ◇ 🍴	AW ◇ 🍴	GW ◇1 🍴	AW	AW ◇ 🍴	AW ■ 🍴	AW ■ 🍴	GW ◇1 🍴		AW	AW ■ 🍴	AW ◇	AW ◇	AW ◇ 🍴	GW ◇1 🍴	AW	AW ■ 🍴	AW ◇		GW ◇1 🍴	AW
Rosslare Harbour ⛴	d																								
Fishguard Harbour 30 ⛴	a																								
	d										12 43														
Fishguard & Goodwick	d										12 46														
Milford Haven	d	11 07													13 08										
Johnston	d	11x15													13x16										
Haverfordwest	d	11 22													13 23										
Clarbeston Road	d	11x30									13x05				13x31										
Clunderwen	d	11x37													13x38										
Pembroke Dock	d					11 09												13 09							
Pembroke	d					11 17												13 17							
Lamphey	d					11x20												13x20							
Manorbier	d					11 29												13 29							
Penally	d					11x34												13x34							
Tenby	a					11 38												13 38							
	d					11 42												13 44							
Saundersfoot	d					11x50												13x52							
Kilgetty	d					11x52												13x54							
Narberth	d					12x02												14x04							
Whitland	a	11 43				12 11					13 17				13 44			14 13							
	d	11 44				12 11					13 17				13 44			14 13							
Carmarthen	a	12 01				12 29					13 34				14 01			14 31							
	d	12 04				12 32			13 00		13 38				14 05			14 33			15 01				
Ferryside	d								13x10		13x48										15x11				
Kidwelly	d								13x16		13x53										15x17				
Pembrey & Burry Port	d	12 22				12 51			13 23		14 00				14 23			14 52			15 24				
Llanelli	a	12 29				12 58			13 29		14 06				14 29			14 59			15 30				
	d	12 29			12 43	12 59			13 30		14 07				14 30			14 59			15 31				
Gowerton	d	12 36							13 37						14 36						15 38				
Swansea	a	12 49			13 02	13 18			13 51						14 50			15 17			15 51				
	d	12 53			13 07		13 24		14 00			14 23			14 55		15 08		15 23		15 55			16 22	
Llansamlet	d				13 14												15 15								
Skewen	d				13 18												15 19								
Neath	d	13 04			13 22		13 36		14 11			14 35			15 06		15 23		15 34		16 06			16 34	
Briton Ferry	d				13 26												15 26								
Baglan	d				13 29												15 30								
Port Talbot Parkway	d	13 11			13 33		13 43		14 18		14 34	14 42			15 13		15 34		15 43		16 13			16 41	
Pyle	d	13 19			13 41												15 41				16 21				
Maesteg	d			13 15						14 15						15 17						16 15			
Maesteg (Ewenny Road)	d			13 17						14 17						15 19						16 17			
Garth (Mid Glamorgan)	d			13 20						14 20						15 22						16 20			
Tondu	d			13 29						14 29						15 29						16 28			
Sarn	d			13 32						14 32						15 32						16 31			
Wildmill	d			13 34						14 34						15 36						16 34			
Bridgend	d	13 27		13 38	13 49		13 57	14 10	14 31	14 38	14 48	14 56		15 07	15 26	15 39	15 51		15 57	16 08	16 29	16 38		16 55	17 07
Pencoed	d			13 44						14 44						15 44						16 43			
Llanharan	d			13 48						14 47						15 48						16 47			
Pontyclun	d			13 52						14 52						15 52						16 51			
Cardiff Central 7	a	13 49		14 08	14 11		14 18	14 32	14 53	15 04	15 09	15 17		15 32	15 47	16 06	16 13		16 18	16 31	16 50	17 06		17 16	17 29
Newport (South Wales)	a	14 08			14 28		14 31		15 08	15 37		15 29			16 08	16 20	16 30		16 33		17 08	17 21		17 29	
Bristol Parkway 7	a						14 54					15 54							16 55					17 54	
Gloucester 7	a															17 12						18 13			
Manchester Piccadilly 10	a	17 14							18 15						19 15						20 13				
Reading 7	a						15 45					16 45							17 45					18 45	
London Paddington 15 ⊖	a						16 11					17 13							18 11					19 11	

When events are being held at the Principality Stadium, services are subject to alteration. Please check times before travelling.

Ferry service between Fishguard Harbour and Rosslare Harbour is operated by Stena Line

Table T128-R

Saturdays

21 December to 16 May

West Wales, Swansea and Maesteg - Cardiff

		AW	AW	AW	AW	GW	AW	AW		AW	GW	AW	AW	AW	AW	AW	GW	AW		AW	AW	AW	AW	AW	AW
		[B] 🛒	◇	◇	◇ 🛒	◇1 🛒	◇ 🛒	◇ 🛒		◇	◇1 🛒		◇	◇	◇	◇	◇1 🛒	◇			[B]	◇	◇	◇	◇
Rosslare Harbour ⛴🚌	d																				18 10				
Fishguard Harbour 30 ⛴	a																				21 25				
	d																			19 02					
Fishguard & Goodwick	d																			19 05					
Milford Haven	d	15 08											17 08										19 10		
Johnston	d	15x16											17x16										19x18		
Haverfordwest	d	15 23											17 23										19 25		
Clarbeston Road	d	15x31											17x31							19x24			19x33		
Clunderwen	d	15x38											17x38										19x40		
Pembroke Dock	d				15 09											17 12									19 19
Pembroke	d				15 17											17 20									19 27
Lamphey	d				15x20											17x23									19x31
Manorbier	d				15 29											17 32									19 38
Penally	d				15x34											17x37									19x44
Tenby	a				15 38											17 41									19 49
	d				15 44											17 45									19 53
Saundersfoot	d				15x52											17x53									20x00
Kilgetty	d				15x54											17x55									20x02
Narberth	d				16x04											18x05									20x12
Whitland	a	15 44			16 12								17 44			18 13				19 37			19 46		20 21
	d	15 44			16 12								17 44			18 13				19 37			19 46		20 21
Carmarthen	a	16 01			16 30								18 02			18 32				19 55			20 04		20 40
	d	16 05			16 32		17 00						18 07			18 33		18 54					20 07		20 45
Ferryside	d						17x10						18x17					19x04							20x56
Kidwelly	d						17x16						18x23					19x10							21x02
Pembrey & Burry Port	d	16 23			16 52		17 23						18 30			18 52		19 18					20 25		21 09
Llanelli	a	16 29			16 59		17 29						18 36			18 59		19 25					20 31		21 16
	d	16 30		16 50	16 59		17 30	17 41					18 37			19 00		19 25					20 32		21 16
Gowerton	d	16 36			17 06		17 37	17 48					18 43			19 07		19 33					20 38		21 24
Swansea	a	16 50		17 09	17 21		17 50	18 02					18 57			19 21		19 48					20 52		21 38
	d	16 55		17 12		17 26	17 55				18 22		19 00		19 10		19 26	19 52					20 55		21 43
Llansamlet	d			17 19											19 17										21 50
Skewen	d			17 23											19 21										21 54
Neath	d	17 06		17 27		17 38	18 06				18 34		19 11		19 25		19 38	20 03					21 06		21 58
Briton Ferry	d			17 30											19 28										22 01
Baglan	d			17 34											19 32										22 05
Port Talbot Parkway	d	17 13		17 38		17 45	18 13				18 41		19 18		19 36		19 45	20 10					21 13		22 09
Pyle	d	17 21		17 45			18 19								19 43										22 17
Maesteg	d		17 13							18 20				19 16								20 16		21 15	
Maesteg (Ewenny Road)	d		17 15							18 22				19 18								20 18		21 17	
Garth (Mid Glamorgan)	d		17 18							18 25				19 21								20 21		21 20	
Tondu	d		17 27							18 34				19 30								20 30		21 29	
Sarn	d		17 30							18 37				19 33								20 33		21 32	
Wildmill	d		17 32							18 39				19 35								20 35		21 34	
Bridgend	d	17 29	17 36	17 54		17 59	18 27			18 43	18 55	19 10	19 30	19 39	19 52		19 59	20 25				20 39	21 27	21 38	22 26
Pencoed	d		17 42							18 49			19 36									20 45		21 44	
Llanharan	d		17 46							18 53			19 39									20 49		21 48	
Pontyclun	d		17 50							18 57			19 44									20 53		21 52	
Cardiff Central 7	a	17 50	18 04	18 16		18 20	18 48			19 13	19 16	19 33	19 59	20 02	20 16		20 20	20 47				21 08	21 49	22 13	22 50
Newport (South Wales)	a	18 09	18 21			18 32	19 04				19 29						20 33					21 26	22 11		
Bristol Parkway 7	a					18 54					19 54						20 55								
Gloucester 7	a		19 14																			22 20			
Manchester Piccadilly 10	a	21 15					22 13																		
Reading 7	a					19 45					20 45						21 49								
London Paddington 15 ⊖	a					20 11					21 11						22 15								

When events are being held at the Principality Stadium, services are subject to alteration. Please check times before travelling.

Ferry service between Fishguard Harbour and Rosslare Harbour is operated by Stena Line

Table T128-R

Saturdays

21 December to 16 May

West Wales, Swansea and Maesteg - Cardiff

		AW	AW	AW		AW	AW	AW	AW	AW
			◇	◇		◇	◇		◇	
Rosslare Harbour ⛴🚌	d									
Fishguard Harbour 30 ⛴	a									
	d							22 15		
Fishguard & Goodwick	d							22 18		
Milford Haven	d	21 18								23 18
Johnston	d	21x26								23x26
Haverfordwest	d	21 33								23 33
Clarbeston Road	d	21x41						22x37		23x41
Clunderwen	d	21x48						22x45		23x48
Pembroke Dock	d		21 09						22 18	
Pembroke	d		21 17						22 26	
Lamphey	d		21x20						22x29	
Manorbier	d		21 29						22 37	
Penally	d		21x34						22x43	
Tenby	a		21 38						22 47	
	d		21 44						22 47	
Saundersfoot	d		21x52						22x55	
Kilgetty	d		21x54						22x57	
Narberth	d		22x04						23x06	
Whitland	a	21 55	22 13					22 52	23 15	23 54
	d	21 55	22 13					22 52	23 15	23 54
Carmarthen	a	22 13	22 32					23 09	23 33	00 13
	d							23 11		
Ferryside	d							23x21		
Kidwelly	d							23x26		
Pembrey & Burry Port	d							23 33		
Llanelli	a							23 39		
	d			21 39				23 40		
Gowerton	d			21 47				23 47		
Swansea	a			22 04				00 01		
	d						22 20			
Llansamlet	d						22 27			
Skewen	d						22 31			
Neath	d						22 35			
Briton Ferry	d						22 38			
Baglan	d						22 42			
Port Talbot Parkway	d						22 46			
Pyle	d						22 54			
Maesteg	d					22 18				
Maesteg (Ewenny Road)	d					22 20				
Garth (Mid Glamorgan)	d					22 23				
Tondu	d					22 32				
Sarn	d					22 35				
Wildmill	d					22 37				
Bridgend	d					22 41	23 03			
Pencoed	d					22 47				
Llanharan	d					22 51				
Pontyclun	d					22 55				
Cardiff Central 7	a					23 11	23 25			
Newport (South Wales)	a					23 35				
Bristol Parkway 7	a									
Gloucester 7	a					00 40				
Manchester Piccadilly 10	a									
Reading 7	a									
London Paddington 15 ⊖	a									

When events are being held at the Principality Stadium, services are subject to alteration. Please check times before travelling.

Ferry service between Fishguard Harbour and Rosslare Harbour is operated by Stena Line

Table T128-R

West Wales, Swansea and Maesteg - Cardiff

Sundays
15 December to 10 May

		AW	GW	AW	AW	GW	GW	GW	AW	GW	AW	AW	GW	GW	AW	AW	GW	AW	GW	AW	AW	AW	GW
		🚌	◇1 🛒	R	■	◇1 🛒	◇1 🛒	◇1 🛒	◇	◇1 🛒	◇ 🛒	◇	◇1 🛒	◇1 🛒	◇ 🛒	◇	◇1 🛒	■ 🛒	◇1 🛒	■ 🛒	◇	◇	◇1 🛒
Rosslare Harbour ⛴	d			08 00																			
Fishguard Harbour 30 ⛴	a			11 15																			
	d	02 17																				12 40	
Fishguard & Goodwick	d	02 22																				12 43	
Milford Haven	d																			11 24			
Johnston	d																			11x32			
Haverfordwest	d																			11 39			
Clarbeston Road	d																			11x48		13x02	
Clunderwen	d																			11x55			
Pembroke Dock	d																				12 00		
Pembroke	d																				12 08		
Lamphey	d																				12x11		
Manorbier	d																				12 20		
Penally	d																				12x25		
Tenby	a																				12 29		
	d																				12 30		
Saundersfoot	d																				12x38		
Kilgetty	d																				12x40		
Narberth	d																				12x50		
Whitland	a	03 12																		12 03	12 59	13 15	
	d	03 12																		12 03	13 00	13 15	
Carmarthen	a	03 32																		12 21	13 18	13 33	
	d								09 34			09 43			10 29	10 53				12 25	13 20	13 38	
Ferryside	d											09x53				11x03					13x30		
Kidwelly	d											09x59				11x09					13x36		
Pembrey & Burry Port	d								09 52			10 06			10 48	11 17				12 45	13 43		
Llanelli	a								09 58			10 13			10 55	11 24				12 52	13 50	14 01	
	d								09 59			10 14			10 56	11 24				12 52	13 51	14 01	
Gowerton	d											10 21			11 03	11 32				13 00	13 59		
Swansea	a								10 16			10 36			11 19	11 47				13 20	14 15		
	d		07 53		08 22	08 37	09 22	09 52		10 22	10 30		10 51	11 22	11 34		12 22	12 49	13 22	13 43			14 22
Llansamlet	d																						
Skewen	d																						
Neath	d		08 05		08 33	08 49	09 34	10 04		10 34	10 41		11 03	11 33	11 45		12 34	13 00	13 34	13 54			14 34
Briton Ferry	d																						
Baglan	d																						
Port Talbot Parkway	d		08 11		08 41	08 55	09 40	10 10		10 40	10 50		11 09	11 40	11 52		12 40	13 07	13 40	14 02			14 40
Pyle	d				08 48						10 57				12 00			13 14		14 10			
Maesteg	d																						
Maesteg (Ewenny Road)	d																						
Garth (Mid Glamorgan)	d																						
Tondu	d																						
Sarn	d																						
Wildmill	d																						
Bridgend	d		08 26		08 57	09 13	09 55	10 25		10 55	11 07		11 24	11 53	12 09		12 55	13 23	13 54	14 18		14 45	14 55
Pencoed	d																						
Llanharan	d																						
Pontyclun	d																						
Cardiff Central 7	a		08 47		09 20	09 34	10 16	10 46		11 16	11 30		11 45	12 14	12 33		13 16	13 49	14 16	14 45		15 08	15 16
Newport (South Wales)	a		09 05		09 47	09 51	10 29	11 01		11 29	11 50		12 01	12 30	12 49		13 29	14 04	14 29	15 08			15 34
Bristol Parkway 7	a		09 32			10 19	10 54	11 22		11 54			12 22	12 54			13 54		14 54				15 54
Gloucester 7	a																						
Manchester Piccadilly 10	a				13 15						15 15				16 14			17 17		18 18			
Reading 7	a		10 25			11 14	11 45	12 17		12 45			13 17	13 45			14 46		15 46				16 46
London Paddington 15 ⊖	a		10 52			11 39	12 14	12 42		13 09			13 44	14 14			15 12		16 14				17 14

When events are being held at the Principality Stadium, services are subject to alteration. Please check times before travelling.

Ferry service between Fishguard Harbour and Rosslare Harbour is operated by Stena Line

Table T128-R

West Wales, Swansea and Maesteg - Cardiff

Sundays
15 December to 10 May

		AW	GW	AW	AW	GW	AW	AW	GW	AW	AW	AW	GW	AW	AW	GW	AW	GW	AW	AW	AW	AW	AW
		■ 🛒	◇1 A 🚌🛒	■ 🛒	◇	◇1 🛒	◇	■ 🛒	◇1 🛒	■ 🛒	■ 🛒	R	◇1 🛒	◇	◇	◇1 🛒	◇	◇1 🛒	◇	◇	◇	◇	◇
Rosslare Harbour ⛴	d											18 10											
Fishguard Harbour 30 ⛴	a											21 25											
	d						14 22																
Fishguard & Goodwick	d						14 25																
Milford Haven	d			13 29						15 29	15 29						17 40				19 40		
Johnston	d			13x37						15x37	15x37						17x48				19x48		
Haverfordwest	d			13 44						15 44	15 44						17 55				19 55		
Clarbeston Road	d			13x53			14x44			15x53	15x53						18x03				20x03		
Clunderwen	d			14x00						16x00	16x00						18x10				20x10		
Pembroke Dock	d														16 28					19 01			
Pembroke	d														16 36					19 09			
Lamphey	d														16x39					19x12			
Manorbier	d														16 48					19 21			
Penally	d														16x53					19x26			
Tenby	a														16 57					19 30			
	d														16 58					19 31			
Saundersfoot	d														17x06					19x39			
Kilgetty	d														17x08					19x41			
Narberth	d														17x18					19x51			
Whitland	a			14 08			14 57			16 08	16 08				17 27		18 17			20 00	20 17		
	d			14 08			14 57			16 09	16 09				17 27		18 17			20 00	20 18		
Carmarthen	a			14 29			15 15			16 29	16 29				17 46		18 35			20 18	20 35		
	d		14 19	14 34			15 38		16 22	16 35	16 35				17 50			19 21		20 21		21 15	21 15
Ferryside	d		14 31				15x49		16 33	16x46	16x46				18x00			19 32		20x31			
Kidwelly	d		14 37				15x55		16 40	16x52	16x52				18x06			19 39		20x37			
Pembrey & Burry Port	d		14 44	14 54			16 02		16 47	16 59	16 59				18 14			19 46		20 45		21 34	21 34
Llanelli	a		14 52	15 00			16 09		16 54	17 06	17 06				18 21			19 53		20 52		21 41	21 41
	d		14 54	15 01	15 41		16 09		16 55	17 07	17 07				18 22			19 54	20 04	20 52		21 41	21 41
Gowerton	d			15 09	15 50		16 17			17 14	17 14				18 30				20 11	21 00		21 48	21 48
Swansea	a		15 10	15 26	16 03		16 33		17 14	17 31	17 31				18 47			20 12	20 25	21 20		22 03	22 03
	d	14 56	15 17	15 31		16 22		16 52	17 22	17 37	17 37		18 22	18 40		19 22		20 19	20 40			22 10	22 10
Llansamlet	d																						
Skewen	d																						
Neath	d	15 07	15 29	15 42		16 34		17 03	17 34	17 48	17 48		18 34	18 51		19 34		20 31	20 51			22 21	22 21
Briton Ferry	d																						
Baglan	d																						
Port Talbot Parkway	d	15 14	15 35	15 49		16 40		17 11	17 40	17 55	17 55		18 40	18 59		19 40		20 37	20 58			22 28	22 28
Pyle	d	15 21		15 57				17 18		18 03	18 03			19 06								22 37	22 37
Maesteg	d																						
Maesteg (Ewenny Road)	d																						
Garth (Mid Glamorgan)	d																						
Tondu	d																						
Sarn	d																						
Wildmill	d																						
Bridgend	d	15 29	15 50	16 05		16 55		17 26	17 55	18 11	18 11		18 55	19 15		19 55		20 52	21 14			22 45	22 45
Pencoed	d			16 11																			
Llanharan	d			16 16																			
Pontyclun	d			16 21																			
Cardiff Central 7	a	15 51	16 11	16 35		17 16		17 49	18 16	18 35	18 35		19 16	19 38		20 16		21 13	21 37			23 11	23 11
Newport (South Wales)	a	16 12	16 30	16 54		17 29		18 07	18 29		18 53		19 29	19 55		20 29		21 30				23 37	
Bristol Parkway 7	a		16 54			17 54			18 54				19 54			20 51		21 53					
Gloucester 7	a																						
Manchester Piccadilly 10	a	19 16		20 16				21 15			22 19												
Reading 7	a		17 46			18 45			19 48				20 49			21 46		22 48					
London Paddington 15 ⊖	a		18 14			19 09			20 14				21 14			22 11		23 29					

A 🚌 from Swansea 🛒 to Swansea

When events are being held at the Principality Stadium, services are subject to alteration. Please check times before travelling.

Ferry service between Fishguard Harbour and Rosslare Harbour is operated by Stena Line

Table T128-R

Sundays
15 December to 10 May

West Wales, Swansea and Maesteg - Cardiff

		AW ◇	AW ◇	AW ◇	AW ◇
Rosslare Harbour	d				
Fishguard Harbour	a				
	d			23 03	
Fishguard & Goodwick	d			23 06	
Milford Haven	d	21 35			23 15
Johnston	d	21x43			23x23
Haverfordwest	d	21 50			23 30
Clarbeston Road	d	21x59		23x25	23x39
Clunderwen	d	22x06			23x46
Pembroke Dock	d		22 01		
Pembroke	d		22 09		
Lamphey	d		22x12		
Manorbier	d		22 21		
Penally	d		22x26		
Tenby	a		22 30		
	d		22 31		
Saundersfoot	d		22x39		
Kilgetty	d		22x41		
Narberth	d		22x51		
Whitland	a	22 13	23 00	23 38	23 54
	d	22 13	23 00	23 38	23 54
Carmarthen	a	22 30	23 21	23 56	00 15
	d	22 35		23 59	
Ferryside	d	22x45			
Kidwelly	d	22x51			
Pembrey & Burry Port	d	22 58			
Llanelli	a	23 05			
	d	23 05			
Gowerton	d	23 13			
Swansea	a	23 27		00 39	
	d	23 33			
Llansamlet	d				
Skewen	d				
Neath	d	23 44			
Briton Ferry	d				
Baglan	d				
Port Talbot Parkway	d	23 51			
Pyle	d	23 59			
Maesteg	d				
Maesteg (Ewenny Road)	d				
Garth (Mid Glamorgan)	d				
Tondu	d				
Sarn	d				
Wildmill	d				
Bridgend	d	00 07			
Pencoed	d				
Llanharan	d				
Pontyclun	d				
Cardiff Central	a	00 34			
Newport (South Wales)	a				
Bristol Parkway	a				
Gloucester	a				
Manchester Piccadilly	a				
Reading	a				
London Paddington	a				

When events are being held at the Principality Stadium, services are subject to alteration. Please check times before travelling.

Ferry service between Fishguard Harbour and Rosslare Harbour is operated by Stena Line

NRT DECEMBER 19 EDITION

Table T129-F

Mondays to Fridays
16 December to 15 May

Shrewsbury - Swansea

Miles			AW ◇	AW ◇	AW ◇	AW ◇	AW ◇	AW ◇
0	**Shrewsbury**	d	04 46		05 56	10 09	14 05	18 24
12¾	Church Stretton	d	05 04		06 14	10 27	14 23	18 42
20	Craven Arms	d	05 15		06 26	10 37	14 34	18 54
22½	Broome	d			06x31	10x42	14x39	18x59
25	Hopton Heath	d			06x35	10x46	14x43	19x03
28	Bucknell	d			06x40	10x51	14x48	19x08
32¼	Knighton	a	05 35		06 48	11 00	14 56	19 16
—		d	05 37		06 56	11 01	14 58	19 18
34¾	Knucklas	d			07x01	11x06	15x02	19x22
38¾	Llangynllo	d			07x09	11x14	15x10	19x30
41¾	Llanbister Road	d			07x14	11x19	15x15	19x35
45¼	Dolau	d			07x20	11x25	15x21	19x41
48½	Pen-y-bont	d			07x24	11x29	15x26	19x46
51¾	Llandrindod	a	06 12		07 35	11 40	15 37	19 57
—		d			07 37	11 57	15 43	19 58
57½	Builth Road	d			07x45	12x05	15x51	20x07
59½	Cilmeri	d			07x49	12x09	15x55	20x10
63	Garth (Powys)	d			07x54	12x14	16x00	20x16
64¾	Llangammarch	d			07x58	12x18	16x04	20x20
68	Llanwrtyd	a			08 05	12 26	16 12	20 28
—		d			08 11	12 28	16 25	20 32
70¾	Sugar Loaf	d			08x16	12x33	16x30	20x38
74¾	Cynghordy	d			08x23	12x40	16x37	20x45
79½	Llandovery	a			08 34	12 52	16 49	20 56
—		d		06 44	08 36	12 53	16 50	20 58
83¼	Llanwrda	d		06x50	08x41	12x58	16x55	21x03
85	Llangadog	d		06x54	08x45	13x02	16x59	21x07
90¾	Llandeilo	a		07 04	08 55	13 13	17 10	21 18
—		d		07 05	08 58	13 15	17 12	21 19
91½	Ffairfach	d		07 08	09 00	13 17	17 14	21 22
95½	Llandybie	d		07x14	09x07	13x24	17x21	21x28
97¼	Ammanford	d		07x19	09x11	13x28	17x25	21x33
98½	Pantyffynnon	d		07 23	09 15	13 32	17 29	21 37
103¼	Pontarddulais	d		07x29	09x21	13x38	17x35	21x43
105½	Llangennech	d		07x33	09x26	13x43	17x40	21x47
107½	Bynea	d		07x37	09x29	13x46	17x43	21x51
110¼	Llanelli	a		07 44	09 36	13 53	17 50	21 58
116	Gowerton	a		07 54	09 46	14 03	17 59	22 08
121½	**Swansea**	a		08 09	10 02	14 20	18 14	22 23

Saturdays
21 December to 16 May

		AW ◇	AW ◇	AW ◇	AW ◇
Shrewsbury	d	05 15	09 00	13 58	17 57
Church Stretton	d	05 33	09 19	14 16	18 13
Craven Arms	d	05 47	09 29	14 26	18 24
Broome	d	05x52	09x34	14x31	18x29
Hopton Heath	d	05x55	09x38	14x35	18x33
Bucknell	d	06x00	09x43	14x40	18x38
Knighton	a	06 09	09 52	14 49	18 47
	d	06 10	09 53	14 50	18 48
Knucklas	d	06x15	09x58	14x55	18x53
Llangynllo	d	06x22	10x06	15x03	19x01
Llanbister Road	d	06x27	10x11	15x08	19x06
Dolau	d	06x33	10x17	15x14	19x12
Pen-y-bont	d	06x37	10x21	15x18	19x16
Llandrindod	a	06 48	10 32	15 29	19 27
	d	06 56	10 34	15 42	19 30
Builth Road	d	07x04	10x42	15x50	19x38
Cilmeri	d	07x07	10x46	15x54	19x42
Garth (Powys)	d	07x12	10x51	15x59	19x47
Llangammarch	d	07x15	10x55	16x03	19x51
Llanwrtyd	a	07 23	11 03	16 11	19 59
	d	07 25	11 09	16 13	20 10
Sugar Loaf	d	07x30	11x14	16x18	20x16
Cynghordy	d	07x36	11x21	16x25	20x23
Llandovery	a	07 48	11 33	16 37	20 34
	d	07 49	11 34	16 38	20 36
Llanwrda	d	07x54	11x39	16x43	20x41
Llangadog	d	07x57	11x43	16x47	20x45
Llandeilo	a	08 08	11 54	16 58	20 56
	d	08 10	11 56	17 00	20 57
Ffairfach	d	08 12	11 58	17 02	21 00
Llandybie	d	08x19	12x05	17x09	21x06
Ammanford	d	08x23	12x09	17x13	21x11
Pantyffynnon	d	08 27	12 13	17 17	21 15
Pontarddulais	d	08x33	12x19	17x23	21x21
Llangennech	d	08x38	12x24	17x28	21x26
Bynea	d	08x41	12x27	17x31	21x30
Llanelli	a	08 51	12 38	17 38	21 36
Gowerton	a	09 07		17 48	21 47
Swansea	a	09 24	13 02	18 02	22 04

When events are being held at the Principality Stadium, services are subject to alteration. Please check times before travelling.

Table T129-F

Sundays
15 December to 10 May

Shrewsbury - Swansea

		AW ◇	AW ◇
Shrewsbury	d	12 04	16 20
Church Stretton	d	12 22	16 39
Craven Arms	d	12 33	16 49
Broome	d	12x39	16x54
Hopton Heath	d	12x43	16x58
Bucknell	d	12x48	17x03
Knighton	a	12 56	17 12
	d	12 57	17 13
Knucklas	d	13x03	17x18
Llangynllo	d	13x11	17x26
Llanbister Road	d	13x16	17x31
Dolau	d	13x22	17x37
Pen-y-bont	d	13x26	17x41
Llandrindod	a	13 36	17 52
	d	13 41	18 05
Builth Road	d	13x50	18x14
Cilmeri	d	13x54	18x17
Garth (Powys)	d	13x59	18x23
Llangammarch	d	14x03	18x27
Llanwrtyd	a	14 10	18 35
	d	14 12	18 36
Sugar Loaf	d	14x18	18x42
Cynghordy	d	14x25	18x49
Llandovery	a	14 36	19 00
	d	14 37	19 02
Llanwrda	d	14x43	19x07
Llangadog	d	14x47	19x11
Llandeilo	a	14 57	19 22
	d	14 59	19 23
Ffairfach	d	15 01	19 26
Llandybie	d	15x09	19x32
Ammanford	d	15x13	19x37
Pantyffynnon	d	15 16	19 41
Pontarddulais	d	15x23	19x47
Llangennech	d	15x28	19x51
Bynea	d	15x31	19x55
Llanelli	a	15 37	20 02
Gowerton	a	15 50	20 11
Swansea	a	16 03	20 25

When events are being held at the Principality Stadium, services are subject to alteration. Please check times before travelling.

Table T129-R

SUNDAY RETURN TIMES

Sundays
15 December to 10 May

Swansea - Shrewsbury

		AW ◇	AW ◇
Swansea	d	11 11	15 36
Gowerton	d	11 23	15 47
Llanelli	d	11 34	15 58
Bynea	d	11x38	16x02
Llangennech	d	11x42	16x06
Pontarddulais	d	11x46	16x10
Pantyffynnon	d	11 55	16 18
Ammanford	d	11 58	16 21
Llandybie	d	12 02	16 26
Ffairfach	d	12x09	16x32
Llandeilo	a	12 13	16 37
	d	12 15	16 38
Llangadog	d	12 24	16 48
Llanwrda	d	12 28	16 51
Llandovery	a	12 35	16 59
	d	12 37	17 00
Cynghordy	d	12x44	17x08
Sugar Loaf	d	12x53	17x16
Llanwrtyd	a	13 01	17 24
	d	13 02	17 26
Llangammarch	d	13x07	17x31
Garth (Powys)	d	13x11	17x35
Cilmeri	d	13x17	17x40
Builth Road	d	13x20	17x44
Llandrindod	a	13 34	17 57
	d	13 43	17 59
Pen-y-bont	d	13x50	18x05
Dolau	d	13 56	18 11
Llanbister Road	d	14x01	18x16
Llangynllo	d	14x06	18x22
Knucklas	d	14x13	18x28
Knighton	a	14 20	18 36
	d	14 22	18 37
Bucknell	d	14 28	18 43
Hopton Heath	d	14x31	18x47
Broome	d	14x36	18x51
Craven Arms	a	14 44	18 59
Church Stretton	a	14 57	19 12
Shrewsbury	a	15 13	19 35

Table T129-R

Mondays to Fridays
16 December to 15 May

Swansea - Shrewsbury

Miles			AW ◇	AW ◇	AW ◇	AW ◇ 🛒	AW ◇ 🛒	AW ◇
0	**Swansea**	d			06 04	09 30	14 35	18 27
5½	Gowerton	d			06 15	09 41		18 38
11¼	Llanelli	d	05 16		06 25	09 51	14 53	18 48
14	Bynea	d	05x20		06x29	09x55	14x57	18x52
16	Llangennech	d	05x24		06x33	09x59	15x01	18x56
18¼	Pontarddulais	d	05x29		06x38	10x03	15x06	19x00
23	Pantyffynnon	d	05 37		06 46	10 12	15 14	19 09
24¼	Ammanford	d	05 40		06 49	10 15	15 17	19 12
26	Llandybie	d	05 45		06 54	10 19	15 22	19 16
30	Ffairfach	d	05x51		07x00	10x26	15x28	19x23
30¾	Llandeilo	a	05 56		07 05	10 30	15 33	19 27
—		d	05 57		07 08	10 32	15 34	19 29
36½	Llangadog	d	06 07		07 18	10 41	15 44	19 38
38¼	Llanwrda	d	06 10		07 21	10 45	15 47	19 42
42	Llandovery	a	06 19		07 29	10 52	15 55	19 49
—		d			07 30	10 54	15 56	19 51
46¾	Cynghordy	d			07x38	11x01	16x04	19x58
49½	Sugar Loaf	d			07x46	11x10	16x12	20x07
53½	Llanwrtyd	a			07 54	11 18	16 20	20 15
—		d			08 12	11 19	16 26	20 33
56¾	Llangammarch	d			08x17	11x24	16x31	20x38
58½	Garth (Powys)	d			08x21	11x28	16x35	20x42
62	Cilmeri	d			08x26	11x34	16x40	20x48
64	Builth Road	d			08x30	11x37	16x44	20x51
69¾	Llandrindod	a			08 43	11 51	16 57	21 05
—		d		06 18	08 45	12 01	16 59	21 19
73¼	Pen-y-bont	d		06x25	08x51	12x08	17x05	21x26
76¼	Dolau	d		06 30	08 57	12 14	17 11	21 32
79¾	Llanbister Road	d		06x36	09x02	12x19	17x16	21x37
82¾	Llangynllo	d		06x42	09x08	12x24	17x22	21x42
86¾	Knucklas	d		06x48	09x14	12x31	17x28	21x49
89¼	Knighton	a		06 55	09 22	12 38	17 36	21 56
—		d		07 03	09 23	12 41	17 37	21 58
93½	Bucknell	d		07 09	09 29	12 47	17 43	22 04
96½	Hopton Heath	d		07x14	09x33	12x50	17x47	22x07
99	Broome	d		07x18	09x37	12x55	17x51	22x12
101½	Craven Arms	a		07 27	09 46	13 04	18 00	22 20
108¾	Church Stretton	a		07 42	09 58	13 17	18 12	22 35
121½	**Shrewsbury**	a		07 58	10 15	13 33	18 28	22 53

Saturdays
21 December to 16 May

		AW ◇	AW ◇ 🛒	AW ◇ 🛒	AW ◇
Swansea	d	04 31	09 15	13 12	18 17
Gowerton	d	04 42	09 26	13 23	18 29
Llanelli	d	04 52	09 36	13 34	18 42
Bynea	d	04x56	09x40	13x38	18x45
Llangennech	d	04x59	09x44	13x42	18x49
Pontarddulais	d	05x03	09x48	13x47	18x53
Pantyffynnon	d	05 12	09 57	13 55	19 01
Ammanford	d	05 15	10 00	13 58	19 04
Llandybie	d	05 19	10 04	14 03	19 09
Ffairfach	d	05x25	10x11	14x09	19x15
Llandeilo	a	05 30	10 15	14 14	19 19
	d	05 31	10 17	14 15	19 21
Llangadog	d	05 41	10 26	14 25	19 30
Llanwrda	d	05 44	10 30	14 28	19 34
Llandovery	a	05 52	10 37	14 36	19 41
	d	05 53	10 39	14 37	19 43
Cynghordy	d	06x00	10x46	14x45	19x50
Sugar Loaf	d	06x08	10x55	14x53	19x58
Llanwrtyd	a	06 16	11 02	15 01	20 06
	d	06 18	11 08	15 03	20 10
Llangammarch	d	06x22	11x13	15x08	20x15
Garth (Powys)	d	06x26	11x17	15x12	20x19
Cilmeri	d	06x31	11x23	15x17	20x24
Builth Road	d	06x34	11x26	15x21	20x27
Llandrindod	a	06 46	11 40	15 34	20 40
	d	06 55	11 41	15 42	20 42
Pen-y-bont	d	07x01	11x48	15x49	20x48
Dolau	d	07x06	11 54	15 55	20 54
Llanbister Road	d	07x12	11x59	16x00	20x58
Llangynllo	d	07x17	12x05	16x05	21x03
Knucklas	d	07x23	12x11	16x12	21x09
Knighton	a	07 30	12 18	16 19	21 17
	d	07 32	12 19	16 21	21 18
Bucknell	d	07 38	12 25	16 27	21 24
Hopton Heath	d	07x41	12x28	16x30	21x27
Broome	d	07x45	12x32	16x35	21x31
Craven Arms	a	07 54	12 40	16 43	21 40
Church Stretton	a	08 06	12 53	16 56	21 52
Shrewsbury	a	08 24	13 10	17 12	22 09

When events are being held at the Principality Stadium, services are subject to alteration. Please check times before travelling.

← **See Sunday times, left.**

Table T130-F

Mondays to Fridays

16 December to 15 May

Treherbert, Aberdare, Merthyr, Pontypridd, Rhymney and Coryton - Cardiff, Penarth, Barry, Barry Island and Bridgend

Miles	Miles	Miles	Miles	Miles			AW MX A	AW	AW	AW	AW	AW	AW	AW	AW	AW	AW	AW	AW B	AW	AW	AW C	AW D	AW
0	—	—	—	—	**Treherbert**	d										05 42					06 16	06 16		
0½	—	—	—	—	Ynyswen	d										05 44					06 18	06 18		
1¼	—	—	—	—	Treorchy	d										05 47					06 21	06 21		
2¾	—	—	—	—	Ton Pentre	d										05 50					06 24	06 24		
3¼	—	—	—	—	Ystrad Rhondda	a										05 52					06 26	06 26		
—	—	—	—	—		d										05 54					06 28	06 28		
4½	—	—	—	—	Llwynypia	d										05 56					06 30	06 30		
5½	—	—	—	—	Tonypandy	d										05 59					06 33	06 33		
6	—	—	—	—	Dinas Rhondda	d										06 01					06 35	06 35		
7½	—	—	—	—	Porth	a										06 04					06 38	06 38		
—	—	—	—	—		d										06 05					06 39	06 39		
8¾	—	—	—	—	Trehafod	d										06 08					06 42	06 42		
—	—	0	—	—	**Merthyr Tydfil**	d														06 08				
—	—	1½	—	—	Pentre-bach	d														06 12				
—	—	2¾	—	—	Troed Y Rhiw	d														06 15				
—	—	4½	—	—	Merthyr Vale	a														06 18				
—	—	—	—	—		d														06 20				
—	—	6¾	—	—	Quakers Yard	d														06 25				
—	—	—	—	0	**Aberdare**	d												05 51						06 22
—	—	—	—	1½	Cwmbach	d												05 54						06 25
—	—	—	—	2¾	Fernhill	d												06 02						06 28
—	—	—	—	3¾	Mountain Ash	a												06 05						06 32
—	—	—	—	—		d												06 06						06 34
—	—	—	—	5	Penrhiwceiber	d												06 09						06 37
—	—	8¾	—	7¾	Abercynon	d												06 16		06 30				06 45
10¾	—	11½	—	11	**Pontypridd** 3	a										06 14		06 24		06 38	06 48	06 48		06 54
						d					05 18					06 15		06 24		06 38	06 48	06 48		06 54
11½	—	—	—	—	Trefforest	d					05 21					06 18		06 27		06 41	06 51	06 51		06 57
14	—	—	—	—	Trefforest Estate	d					05 25									06 45				
16¼	—	—	—	—	Taffs Well	d					05 29					06 25		06 34		06 49	06 58	06 58		07 04
18¾	—	—	0	—	Radyr 3	a					05 33					06 29		06 38		06 53	07 02	07 02		07 08
—	—	—	—	—		d					05 33					06 29		06 38		06 53	07 02	07 02	07 03	07 08
—	—	—	1½	—	Danescourt	d																	07 07	
—	—	—	2	—	Fairwater	d																	07 09	
—	—	—	2¼	—	Waun-gron Park	d																	07 11	
—	—	—	3¾	—	Ninian Park	d																	07 14	
19¼	—	—	—	—	Llandaf	d					05 36					06 32		06 41		06 56	07 05	07 05		07 11
21¾	—	—	—	—	Cathays	d					05 40					06 36		06 46		07 01	07 10	07 10		07 16
—	0	—	—	—	**Rhymney** 3	d																		
—	1	—	—	—	Pontlottyn	d																		
—	3½	—	—	—	Tir-phil	d																		
—	4½	—	—	—	Brithdir	d																		
—	6	—	—	—	Bargoed	a																		
—	—	—	—	—		d																		
—	6½	—	—	—	Gilfach Fargoed	d																		
—	7½	—	—	—	Pengam	d																		
—	9¼	—	—	—	Hengoed	d																		
—	10½	—	—	—	Ystrad Mynach	d																		
—	13	—	—	—	Llanbradach	d																		
—	14¼	—	—	—	Energlyn & Churchill Park	d																		
—	15	—	—	—	Aber	d																		
—	15¾	—	—	—	Caerphilly	d									06 11									
—	18¼	—	—	—	Lisvane & Thornhill	d									06 15									
—	19¼	—	—	—	Llanishen	d									06 17									
—	20¼	—	—	—	Heath High Level	d									06 20									
—	—	0	—	—	**Coryton**	d													06 45					
—	—	0½	—	—	Whitchurch (Cardiff)	d													06 46					
—	—	0¾	—	—	Rhiwbina	d													06 48					
—	—	1¼	—	—	Birchgrove	d													06 50					
—	—	1½	—	—	Ty Glas	d													06 51					
—	—	2¼	—	—	Heath Low Level	d													06 54					
22½	22¾	4¾	—	—	**Cardiff Queen Street** 3	a					05 45				06 26	06 41		06 50	07 00	07 05	07 14	07 14		07 20
—	—	—	—	—		d	00 01				05 45				06 26	06 41		06 50	07 01	07 05	07 14	07 14		07 21
23	23¼	—	4¾	—	**Cardiff Central** 7	a	00 05				05 49				06 30	06 46		06 55	07 05	07 09	07 18	07 18	07 20	07 25
—	—	—	—	—		d		05 20	05 42	05 46	05 55	06 16	06 25	06 36	06 41		06 55	07 01		07 10	07 21			07 25
24	24¼	—	—	—	Grangetown	d		05 24	05 46	05 50	05 59	06 20	06 29	06 40	06 45		06 59	07 05		07 14				07 29
—	26¾	—	—	—	Dingle Road	d				05 54		06 24		06 44				07 11						
—	27	—	—	—	**Penarth**	a				05 59		06 29		06 49				07 16			07 31			
25¾	—	—	—	—	Cogan	d		05 28	05 49		06 03		06 33		06 48		07 03			07 18				07 33
26½	—	—	—	—	Eastbrook	d		05 30	05 52		06 05		06 35		06 51		07 05			07 20				07 35
27½	—	—	—	—	Dinas Powys	d		05 32	05 54		06 07		06 37		06 53		07 07			07 22				07 37
29½	—	—	—	—	Cadoxton	d		05 36	05 58		06 11		06 41		06 57		07 11			07 26				07 41
30¼	—	—	—	—	Barry Docks	d		05 39	06 01		06 14		06 44		07 00		07 14			07 29				07 44
31½	—	0	—	—	**Barry** 3	d		05 43	06 05		06 18		06 48		07 05		07 18			07 33				07 48
32¼	—	—	—	—	**Barry Island**	a		05 48			06 24		06 54				07 24			07 39				07 54
—	—	3¼	—	—	Rhoose Cardiff Int Airport ✈	d			06 12						07 12									
—	—	9¾	—	—	Llantwit Major	d			06 23						07 22									
—	—	19	—	—	**Bridgend**	a			06 39						07 39									

A From Cardiff Bay
B To Radyr
C To Treherbert
D To Coryton

When events are being held at the Principality Stadium, services are subject to alteration. Please check times before travelling.

For connections to Cardiff Bay please refer to Table T124

Table T130-F

Mondays to Fridays

16 December to 15 May

Treherbert, Aberdare, Merthyr, Pontypridd, Rhymney and Coryton - Cardiff, Penarth, Barry, Barry Island and Bridgend

		AW	AW A	AW		AW	AW B	AW	AW	AW	AW A	AW	AW	AW B	AW	AW	AW	AW	AW A	AW	AW B	AW
Treherbert	d							06 46							07 16							07 45
Ynyswen	d							06 48							07 18							07 47
Treorchy	d							06 51							07 21							07 51
Ton Pentre	d							06 54							07 24							07 54
Ystrad Rhondda	a							06 56							07 26							07 56
	d							06 58							07 28							07 58
Llwynypia	d							07 00							07 30							08 00
Tonypandy	d							07 03							07 33							08 03
Dinas Rhondda	d							07 05							07 36							08 05
Porth	a							07 08							07 39							08 08
	d							07 09							07 40							08 09
Trehafod	d							07 12							07 43							08 12
Merthyr Tydfil	d			06 38								07 08								07 38		
Pentre-bach	d			06 42								07 12								07 42		
Troed Y Rhiw	d			06 45								07 15								07 45		
Merthyr Vale	a			06 48								07 18								07 48		
	d			06 50								07 20								07 50		
Quakers Yard	d			06 55								07 25								07 55		
Aberdare	d								06 52							07 22						
Cwmbach	d								06 55							07 25						
Fernhill	d								06 58							07 28						
Mountain Ash	a								07 02							07 32						
	d								07 04							07 34						
Penrhiwceiber	d								07 07							07 37						
Abercynon	d			07 00					07 15			07 30				07 45				08 00		
Pontypridd 3	a			07 07				07 19	07 24			07 38			07 49	07 55				08 08		08 19
	d			07 08				07 19	07 24			07 38			07 49	07 55				08 08		08 19
Trefforest	d			07 11				07 22	07 27			07 41			07 52	07 58				08 11		08 22
Trefforest Estate	d			07 15								07 45								08 15		
Taffs Well	d			07 19				07 29	07 34			07 49			07 59	08 05				08 19		08 29
Radyr 3	a			07 23				07 33	07 38			07 53			08 03	08 09				08 23		08 33
	d			07 23			07 33	07 33	07 38			07 53		08 03	08 03	08 09	08 13			08 23	08 33	08 33
Danescourt	d						07 37							08 07							08 37	
Fairwater	d						07 39							08 09							08 39	
Waun-gron Park	d						07 41							08 11							08 41	
Ninian Park	d						07 44							08 14							08 44	
Llandaf	d			07 26				07 36	07 41			07 56			08 06		08 16			08 26		08 36
Cathays	d			07 31				07 40	07 46			08 01			08 11	08 15	08 20			08 31		08 41
Rhymney 3	d	06 30								07 00								07 24				
Pontlottyn	d	06 33								07 03								07 27				
Tir-phil	d	06 38								07 08								07 31				
Brithdir	d	06 40								07 10								07 34				
Bargoed	a	06 44								07 15								07 39				
	d	06 44				07 02				07 15			07 32					07 43				
Gilfach Fargoed	d	06 47				07 04				07 18								07 46				
Pengam	d	06 49				07 07				07 20			07 37					07 49				
Hengoed	d	06 53				07 10				07 24			07 40					07 53				
Ystrad Mynach	d	06 56				07 13				07 27			07 43					07 56				
Llanbradach	d	07 01				07 18				07 31			07 48					08 01				
Energlyn & Churchill Park	d	07 04								07 35								08 05				
Aber	d	07 07				07 22				07 38			07 52					08 08				
Caerphilly	d	07 10				07 25				07 40			07 55					08 11				
Lisvane & Thornhill	d	07 14				07 29				07 45			07 59					08 16				
Llanishen	d	07 16				07 31				07 47			08 01					08 18				
Heath High Level	d	07 19				07 34				07 50			08 04					08 21				
Coryton	d		07 15								07 45								08 15			
Whitchurch (Cardiff)	d		07 16								07 46								08 16			
Rhiwbina	d		07 18								07 48								08 18			
Birchgrove	d		07 20								07 50								08 20			
Ty Glas	d		07 21								07 51								08 21			
Heath Low Level	d		07 24								07 54								08 24			
Cardiff Queen Street 3	a	07 25	07 31	07 35		07 40		07 45	07 50	07 56	08 00	08 05	08 10		08 15	08 20	08 25	08 28	08 31	08 35		08 45
	d	07 26	07 31	07 35		07 41		07 46	07 51	07 56	08 01	08 06	08 11		08 15	08 20	08 25	08 28	08 32	08 36		08 46
Cardiff Central 7	a	07 30	07 35	07 38		07 45	07 50	07 51	07 55	08 00	08 05	08 10	08 15	08 20	08 21	08 24	08 29	08 32	08 36	08 40	08 50	08 50
	d	07 32		07 42	07 51	07 46			07 55	08 01		08 10	08 18			08 25		08 33		08 41		
Grangetown	d	07 36		07 46		07 50			07 59	08 06		08 14	08 22			08 29		08 37		08 45		
Dingle Road	d	07 42				07 56				08 11			08 27					08 41				
Penarth	a	07 46				08 01				08 15			08 30					08 46				
Cogan	d			07 49					08 03			08 18				08 33				08 48		
Eastbrook	d			07 52					08 05			08 20				08 35				08 51		
Dinas Powys	d			07 54					08 07			08 22				08 37				08 53		
Cadoxton	d			07 58					08 11			08 26				08 41				08 57		
Barry Docks	d			08 01					08 14			08 29				08 44				09 00		
Barry 3	d			08 05	08a09				08 18			08 33				08 48				09 05		
Barry Island	a								08 24			08 39				08 53						
Rhoose Cardiff Int Airport ✈	d			08 12																09 12		
Llantwit Major	d			08 22																09 22		
Bridgend	a			08 39																09 39		

A To Radyr
B To Coryton

When events are being held at the Principality Stadium, services are subject to alteration. Please check times before travelling.

For connections to Cardiff Bay please refer to Table T124

Table T130-F

Mondays to Fridays

16 December to 15 May

Treherbert, Aberdare, Merthyr, Pontypridd, Rhymney and Coryton - Cardiff, Penarth, Barry, Barry Island and Bridgend

		AW	AW	AW A	AW	AW	AW B	AW	AW	AW	AW A	AW	AW	AW B	AW	AW	AW	AW A	AW	AW	AW	AW B	AW
Treherbert	d							08 16							08 46						09 16		
Ynyswen	d							08 18							08 48						09 18		
Treorchy	d							08 21							08 51						09 21		
Ton Pentre	d							08 24							08 54						09 24		
Ystrad Rhondda	a							08 26							08 56						09 26		
	d							08 28							08 58						09 28		
Llwynypia	d							08 30							09 00						09 30		
Tonypandy	d							08 33							09 03						09 33		
Dinas Rhondda	d							08 35							09 05						09 35		
Porth	a							08 38							09 08						09 38		
	d							08 39							09 09						09 39		
Trehafod	d							08 42							09 12						09 42		
Merthyr Tydfil	d				08 08							08 38							09 08				
Pentre-bach	d				08 12							08 42							09 12				
Troed Y Rhiw	d				08 15							08 45							09 15				
Merthyr Vale	a				08 18							08 48							09 18				
	d				08 20							08 50							09 20				
Quakers Yard	d				08 25							08 55							09 25				
Aberdare	d	07 52							08 22							08 52							09 22
Cwmbach	d	07 55							08 25							08 55							09 25
Fernhill	d	07 58							08 28							08 58							09 28
Mountain Ash	a	08 02							08 32							09 02							09 32
	d	08 04							08 34							09 04							09 34
Penrhiwceiber	d	08 07							08 37							09 07							09 37
Abercynon	d	08 15			08 30				08 45			09 00				09 15			09 30				09 45
Pontypridd 3	a	08 24			08 38			08 49	08 54			09 08			09 19	09 24			09 38		09 49		09 54
	d	08 24			08 38			08 49	08 54			09 08			09 19	09 24			09 38		09 49		09 54
Trefforest	d	08 27			08 41			08 52	08 57			09 11			09 22	09 27			09 41		09 52		09 57
Trefforest Estate	d				08 45							09 15							09 45				
Taffs Well	d	08 34			08 49			08 59	09 04			09 19			09 29	09 34			09 49		09 59		10 04
Radyr 3	a	08 38			08 53			09 03	09 08			09 23			09 33	09 38			09 53		10 03		10 08
	d	08 38			08 53		09 03	09 03	09 08			09 23		09 33	09 33	09 38			09 53		10 03	10 03	10 08
Danescourt	d						09 07							09 37								10 07	
Fairwater	d						09 09							09 39								10 09	
Waun-gron Park	d						09 11							09 41								10 11	
Ninian Park	d						09 14							09 44								10 14	
Llandaf	d	08 41			08 56			09 06	09 11			09 26			09 36	09 41			09 56		10 06		10 11
Cathays	d	08 46			09 01			09 11	09 16			09 31			09 40	09 46			10 01		10 10		10 16
Rhymney 3	d									08 33													
Pontlottyn	d									08 36													
Tir-phil	d									08 40													
Brithdir	d									08 43													
Bargoed	a									08 47													
	d		08 14			08 32				08 47			09 00				09 17			09 32			
Gilfach Fargoed	d		08 17														09 19						
Pengam	d		08 19			08 37				08 52			09 04				09 22			09 37			
Hengoed	d		08 23			08 40				08 55			09 08				09 25			09 40			
Ystrad Mynach	d		08 26			08 43				08 58			09 11				09 28			09 43			
Llanbradach	d		08 30			08 48				09 03			09 15				09 33			09 48			
Energlyn & Churchill Park	d		08 34										09 19										
Aber	d		08 36			08 52				09 07			09 21				09 37			09 52			
Caerphilly	d		08 40			08 55				09 10			09 25				09 40			09 55			
Lisvane & Thornhill	d		08 44			08 59				09 14			09 29				09 44			09 59			
Llanishen	d		08 46			09 01				09 16			09 31				09 46			10 01			
Heath High Level	d		08 49			09 04				09 19			09 34				09 49			10 04			
Coryton	d			08 45							09 15							09 45					
Whitchurch (Cardiff)	d			08 46							09 16							09 46					
Rhiwbina	d			08 48							09 18							09 48					
Birchgrove	d			08 50							09 20							09 50					
Ty Glas	d			08 51							09 21							09 51					
Heath Low Level	d			08 54							09 24							09 54					
Cardiff Queen Street 3	a	08 50	08 55	09 00	09 05	09 10		09 15	09 20	09 25	09 30	09 35	09 40		09 45	09 50	09 55	10 00	10 05	10 10	10 15		10 20
	d	08 51	08 56	09 01	09 06	09 11		09 16	09 21	09 26	09 31	09 36	09 41		09 46	09 51	09 56	10 01	10 06	10 11	10 16		10 21
Cardiff Central 7	a	08 55	09 00	09 05	09 10	09 15	09 20	09 21	09 25	09 30	09 35	09 40	09 45	09 50	09 51	09 55	10 00	10 05	10 10	10 15	10 20	10 20	10 25
	d	08 55	09 01		09 10	09 16			09 25	09 31		09 41	09 46			09 55	10 01		10 10	10 16			10 25
Grangetown	d	08 59	09 05		09 14	09 22			09 29	09 37		09 45	09 50			09 59	10 07		10 14	10 22			10 29
Dingle Road	d		09 11			09 26				09 41			09 56				10 11			10 26			
Penarth	a		09 16			09 31				09 46			10 01				10 16			10 31			
Cogan	d	09 03			09 18				09 33			09 48				10 03			10 18				10 33
Eastbrook	d	09 05			09 20				09 35			09 51				10 05			10 20				10 35
Dinas Powys	d	09 07			09 22				09 37			09 53				10 07			10 22				10 37
Cadoxton	d	09 11			09 26				09 41			09 57				10 11			10 26				10 41
Barry Docks	d	09 14			09 29				09 44			10 00				10 14			10 29				10 44
Barry 3	d	09 18			09 33				09 48			10 05				10 18			10 33				10 48
Barry Island	a	09 24			09 39				09 54							10 24			10 39				10 54
Rhoose Cardiff Int Airport ✈	d											10 12											
Llantwit Major	d											10 22											
Bridgend	a											10 39											

A To Radyr B To Coryton

When events are being held at the Principality Stadium, services are subject to alteration. Please check times before travelling.

For connections to Cardiff Bay please refer to Table T124

Table T130-F

Mondays to Fridays

16 December to 15 May

Treherbert, Aberdare, Merthyr, Pontypridd, Rhymney and Coryton - Cardiff, Penarth, Barry, Barry Island and Bridgend

		AW	AW A	AW	AW	AW B	AW	AW	AW	AW	AW A	AW	AW	AW B	AW	AW	AW	AW A	AW	AW	AW B	AW
Treherbert	d						09 46										10 16					10 46
Ynyswen	d						09 48										10 18					10 48
Treorchy	d						09 51										10 21					10 51
Ton Pentre	d						09 54										10 24					10 54
Ystrad Rhondda	a						09 56										10 26					10 56
	d						09 58										10 28					10 58
Llwynypia	d						10 00										10 30					11 00
Tonypandy	d						10 03										10 33					11 03
Dinas Rhondda	d						10 05										10 35					11 05
Porth	a						10 08										10 38					11 08
	d						10 09										10 52					11 09
Trehafod	d						10 12										10 55					11 12
Merthyr Tydfil	d			09 38					10 04										10 38			
Pentre-bach	d			09 42					10 08										10 42			
Troed Y Rhiw	d			09 45					10 11										10 45			
Merthyr Vale	a			09 48					10 14										10 48			
	d			09 50					10 15										10 52			
Quakers Yard	d			09 55					10 21										10 57			
Aberdare	d							09 52							10 22							
Cwmbach	d							09 55							10 25							
Fernhill	d							09 58							10 28							
Mountain Ash	a							10 02							10 32							
	d							10 04							10 34							
Penrhiwceiber	d							10 07							10 37							
Abercynon	d			10 00				10 15	10 25						10 45				11 01			
Pontypridd 3	a			10 08			10 19	10 24	10 33						10 54		11 01		11 08			11 19
	d			10 08			10 19	10 24				10 39			10 54		11 04		11 08			11 19
Trefforest	d			10 11			10 22	10 27				10 42			10 57		11 07		11 11			11 22
Trefforest Estate	d			10 15															11 15			
Taffs Well	d			10 19			10 29	10 34				10 49			11 04		11 14		11 19			11 29
Radyr 3	a			10 23			10 33	10 38				10 53			11 08		11 19		11 23			11 33
	d			10 23		10 33	10 33	10 38				10 53		11 03	11 08		11 21		11 23		11 33	11 33
Danescourt	d					10 37								11 07							11 37	
Fairwater	d					10 39								11 09							11 39	
Waun-gron Park	d					10 41								11 11							11 41	
Ninian Park	d					10 44								11 14							11 44	
Llandaf	d			10 26			10 36	10 41				10 56			11 11				11 26			11 36
Cathays	d			10 31			10 40	10 46				11 01			11 16				11 31			11 40
Rhymney 3	d	09 27														10 27						
Pontlottyn	d	09 30														10 30						
Tir-phil	d	09 35														10 35						
Brithdir	d	09 37														10 37						
Bargoed	a	09 43														10 43						
	d	09 44			10 00					10 17			10 32			10 44				11 00		
Gilfach Fargoed	d									10 19												
Pengam	d	09 49			10 04					10 22			10 37			10 49				11 04		
Hengoed	d	09 53			10 08					10 25			10 40			10 53				11 08		
Ystrad Mynach	d	09 56			10 11					10 28			10 43			10 56				11 11		
Llanbradach	d	10 00			10 15					10 33			10 48			11 00				11 15		
Energlyn & Churchill Park	d	10 04			10 19											11 04				11 19		
Aber	d	10 06			10 21					10 37			10 52			11 06				11 21		
Caerphilly	d	10 10			10 25					10 40			10 55			11 10				11 25		
Lisvane & Thornhill	d	10 14			10 29					10 44			10 59			11 14				11 29		
Llanishen	d	10 16			10 31					10 46			11 01			11 16				11 31		
Heath High Level	d	10 19			10 34					10 49			11 04			11 19				11 34		
Coryton	d		10 15								10 45							11 15				
Whitchurch (Cardiff)	d		10 16								10 46							11 16				
Rhiwbina	d		10 18								10 48							11 18				
Birchgrove	d		10 20								10 50							11 20				
Ty Glas	d		10 21								10 51							11 21				
Heath Low Level	d		10 24								10 54							11 24				
Cardiff Queen Street 3	a	10 25	10 30	10 35	10 40		10 45	10 50		10 55	11 00	11 05	11 10		11 20	11 25		11 30	11 35	11 40		11 45
	d	10 26	10 31	10 36	10 41		10 46	10 51		10 56	11 01	11 06	11 11		11 21	11 26		11 31	11 36	11 41		11 46
Cardiff Central 7	a	10 30	10 35	10 40	10 45	10 50	10 51	10 55		11 00	11 05	11 10	11 15	11 20	11 25	11 30	11 33	11 35	11 40	11 45	11 50	11 51
	d	10 31		10 41	10 46			10 55		11 01		11 10	11 16		11 25	11 31			11 41	11 46		
Grangetown	d	10 37		10 45	10 50			10 59		11 05		11 14	11 22		11 29	11 37			11 45	11 52		
Dingle Road	d	10 41			10 56					11 11			11 26			11 41				11 56		
Penarth	a	10 46			11 01					11 16			11 31			11 46				12 01		
Cogan	d			10 48				11 03				11 18			11 33				11 48			
Eastbrook	d			10 51				11 05				11 20			11 35				11 51			
Dinas Powys	d			10 53				11 07				11 22			11 37				11 53			
Cadoxton	d			10 57				11 11				11 26			11 41				11 57			
Barry Docks	d			11 00				11 14				11 29			11 44				12 00			
Barry 3	d			11 05				11 18				11 33			11 48				12 05			
Barry Island	a							11 24				11 39			11 54							
Rhoose Cardiff Int Airport ✈	d			11 12															12 12			
Llantwit Major	d			11 22															12 22			
Bridgend	a			11 39															12 39			

A To Radyr B To Coryton

When events are being held at the Principality Stadium, services are subject to alteration. Please check times before travelling.

For connections to Cardiff Bay please refer to Table T124

Table T130-F

Mondays to Fridays

16 December to 15 May

Treherbert, Aberdare, Merthyr, Pontypridd, Rhymney and Coryton - Cardiff, Penarth, Barry, Barry Island and Bridgend

		AW	AW	AW A	AW	AW	AW B	AW	AW		AW	AW A	AW	AW	AW B	AW	AW	AW	AW A		AW	AW	AW B	AW	AW
Treherbert	d							11 16								11 46								12 16	
Ynyswen	d							11 18								11 48								12 18	
Treorchy	d							11 21								11 51								12 21	
Ton Pentre	d							11 24								11 54								12 24	
Ystrad Rhondda	a							11 26								11 56								12 26	
	d							11 28								11 58								12 28	
Llwynypia	d							11 30								12 00								12 30	
Tonypandy	d							11 33								12 03								12 33	
Dinas Rhondda	d							11 35								12 05								12 35	
Porth	a							11 38								12 08								12 38	
	d							11 39								12 09								12 39	
Trehafod	d							11 42								12 12								12 42	
Merthyr Tydfil	d				11 08								11 38								12 08				
Pentre-bach	d				11 12								11 42								12 12				
Troed Y Rhiw	d				11 15								11 45								12 15				
Merthyr Vale	a				11 18								11 48								12 18				
	d				11 20								11 50								12 20				
Quakers Yard	d				11 25								11 55								12 25				
Aberdare	d	10 52							11 22																12 22
Cwmbach	d	10 55							11 25																12 25
Fernhill	d	10 58							11 28																12 28
Mountain Ash	a	11 02							11 32																12 32
	d	11 04							11 34																12 34
Penrhiwceiber	d	11 07							11 37																12 37
Abercynon	d	11 15			11 30				11 45				12 00								12 30				12 45
Pontypridd 3	a	11 23			11 38			11 49	11 54				12 08			12 19					12 38			12 49	12 54
	d	11 24			11 38			11 49	11 54				12 08			12 19					12 38			12 49	12 54
Trefforest	d	11 27			11 41			11 52	11 57				12 11			12 22					12 41			12 52	12 57
Trefforest Estate	d				11 45								12 15								12 45				
Taffs Well	d	11 34			11 49			11 59	12 04				12 19			12 29					12 49			12 59	13 04
Radyr 3	a	11 38			11 53			12 03	12 08				12 23			12 33					12 53			13 03	13 08
	d	11 38			11 53		12 03	12 03	12 08				12 23		12 33	12 33					12 53		13 03	13 03	13 08
Danescourt	d						12 07								12 37								13 07		
Fairwater	d						12 09								12 39								13 09		
Waun-gron Park	d						12 11								12 41								13 11		
Ninian Park	d						12 14								12 44								13 14		
Llandaf	d	11 41			11 56			12 06	12 11				12 26			12 36					12 56			13 06	13 11
Cathays	d	11 46			12 01			12 10	12 16				12 31			12 40					13 01			13 10	13 16
Rhymney 3	d										11 27														
Pontlottyn	d										11 30														
Tir-phil	d										11 35														
Brithdir	d										11 37														
Bargoed	a										11 43														
	d		11 17			11 32					11 44			12 00				12 17				12 32			
Gilfach Fargoed	d		11 19															12 19							
Pengam	d		11 22			11 37					11 49			12 04				12 22				12 37			
Hengoed	d		11 25			11 40					11 53			12 08				12 25				12 40			
Ystrad Mynach	d		11 28			11 43					11 56			12 11				12 28				12 43			
Llanbradach	d		11 33			11 48					12 00			12 15				12 33				12 48			
Energlyn & Churchill Park	d										12 04			12 19											
Aber	d		11 37			11 52					12 06			12 21				12 37				12 52			
Caerphilly	d		11 40			11 55					12 10			12 25				12 40				12 55			
Lisvane & Thornhill	d		11 44			11 59					12 14			12 29				12 44				12 59			
Llanishen	d		11 46			12 01					12 16			12 31				12 46				13 01			
Heath High Level	d		11 49			12 04					12 19			12 34				12 49				13 04			
Coryton	d			11 45								12 15							12 45						
Whitchurch (Cardiff)	d			11 46								12 16							12 46						
Rhiwbina	d			11 48								12 18							12 48						
Birchgrove	d			11 50								12 20							12 50						
Ty Glas	d			11 51								12 21							12 51						
Heath Low Level	d			11 54								12 24							12 54						
Cardiff Queen Street 3	a	11 50	11 55	12 00	12 05	12 10		12 15	12 20		12 25	12 30	12 35	12 40		12 45		12 55	13 00		13 05	13 10		13 15	13 20
	d	11 51	11 56	12 01	12 06	12 11		12 16	12 20		12 26	12 31	12 36	12 41		12 46		12 56	13 01		13 06	13 11		13 16	13 21
Cardiff Central 7	a	11 55	12 00	12 05	12 10	12 15	12 20	12 21	12 24		12 30	12 35	12 40	12 45	12 50	12 51		13 00	13 05		13 11	13 15	13 20	13 21	13 25
	d	11 55	12 01		12 10	12 16		12 27			12 31		12 41	12 46			12 55	13 01				13 16			13 25
Grangetown	d	11 59	12 07		12 14	12 22					12 37		12 45	12 52			12 59	13 07				13 22			13 29
Dingle Road	d		12 11			12 26					12 41			12 56				13 11				13 26			
Penarth	a		12 16			12 31					12 46			13 01				13 16				13 31			
Cogan	d	12 03			12 18				12 33				12 48				13 03								13 33
Eastbrook	d	12 05			12 20				12 36				12 51				13 05								13 35
Dinas Powys	d	12 07			12 22				12 38				12 53				13 07								13 37
Cadoxton	d	12 11			12 26				12 42				12 57				13 11								13 41
Barry Docks	d	12 14			12 29				12 44				13 00				13 14								13 44
Barry 3	d	12 18			12 33				12 48				13 05				13 18								13 48
Barry Island	a	12 24			12 39				12 54								13 24								13 54
Rhoose Cardiff Int Airport ✈	d												13 12												
Llantwit Major	d												13 22												
Bridgend	a												13 39												

A To Radyr **B** To Coryton

When events are being held at the Principality Stadium, services are subject to alteration. Please check times before travelling.

For connections to Cardiff Bay please refer to Table T124

Table T130-F

Mondays to Fridays

16 December to 15 May

Treherbert, Aberdare, Merthyr, Pontypridd, Rhymney and Coryton - Cardiff, Penarth, Barry, Barry Island and Bridgend

		AW	AW A	AW	AW		AW B	AW	AW	AW	AW A	AW	AW	AW	AW		AW B	AW	AW A	AW	AW	AW	AW B	AW	AW
Treherbert	d							12 46							13 16							13 44			
Ynyswen	d							12 48							13 18							13 46			
Treorchy	d							12 51							13 21							13 51			
Ton Pentre	d							12 54							13 24							13 54			
Ystrad Rhondda	a							12 56							13 26							13 56			
	d							12 58							13 28							13 58			
Llwynypia	d							13 00							13 30							14 00			
Tonypandy	d							13 03							13 33							14 03			
Dinas Rhondda	d							13 05							13 35							14 05			
Porth	a							13 08							13 38							14 08			
	d							13 09							13 39							14 09			
Trehafod	d							13 12							13 42							14 12			
Merthyr Tydfil	d			12 38									13 08							13 38					
Pentre-bach	d			12 42									13 12							13 42					
Troed Y Rhiw	d			12 45									13 15							13 45					
Merthyr Vale	a			12 48									13 18							13 48					
	d			12 50									13 20							13 50					
Quakers Yard	d			12 55									13 25							13 55					
Aberdare	d								12 52															13 52	
Cwmbach	d								12 55															13 55	
Fernhill	d								12 58															13 58	
Mountain Ash	a								13 02															14 02	
	d								13 04															14 04	
Penrhiwceiber	d								13 07															14 07	
Abercynon	d			13 00					13 15				13 30					13 45		14 00				14 15	
Pontypridd 3	a			13 08				13 19	13 24				13 38		13 49			13 54		14 08		14 19		14 24	
	d			13 08				13 19	13 24				13 38		13 49			13 54		14 08		14 19		14 24	
Trefforest	d			13 11				13 22	13 27				13 41		13 52			13 57		14 11		14 22		14 27	
Trefforest Estate	d			13 15									13 45							14 15					
Taffs Well	d			13 19				13 29	13 34				13 49		13 59			14 04		14 19		14 29		14 34	
Radyr 3	a			13 23				13 33	13 38				13 53		14 03			14 08		14 23		14 33		14 38	
	d			13 23			13 33	13 33	13 38				13 53		14 03		14 03	14 08		14 23		14 33	14 33	14 38	
Danescourt	d						13 37										14 07						14 37		
Fairwater	d						13 39										14 09						14 39		
Waun-gron Park	d						13 41										14 11						14 41		
Ninian Park	d						13 44										14 14						14 44		
Llandaf	d			13 26				13 36	13 41				13 56		14 06			14 11		14 26		14 36		14 41	
Cathays	d			13 31				13 40	13 46				14 01		14 10			14 16		14 31		14 40		14 46	
Rhymney 3	d	12 27																							
Pontlottyn	d	12 30																							
Tir-phil	d	12 35																							
Brithdir	d	12 37																							
Bargoed	a	12 43																							
	d	12 44			13 00					13 17				13 32							14 00				14 17
Gilfach Fargoed	d									13 19															14 19
Pengam	d	12 49			13 04					13 22				13 37							14 04				14 22
Hengoed	d	12 53			13 08					13 25				13 40							14 08				14 25
Ystrad Mynach	d	12 56			13 11					13 28				13 43							14 11				14 28
Llanbradach	d	13 00			13 15					13 33				13 48							14 15				14 33
Energlyn & Churchill Park	d	13 04			13 19																14 19				
Aber	d	13 06			13 21					13 37				13 52							14 21				14 37
Caerphilly	d	13 10			13 25					13 40				13 55							14 25				14 40
Lisvane & Thornhill	d	13 14			13 29					13 44				13 59							14 29				14 44
Llanishen	d	13 16			13 31					13 46				14 01							14 31				14 46
Heath High Level	d	13 19			13 34					13 49				14 04							14 34				14 49
Coryton	d		13 15								13 45								14 15						
Whitchurch (Cardiff)	d		13 16								13 46								14 16						
Rhiwbina	d		13 18								13 48								14 18						
Birchgrove	d		13 20								13 50								14 20						
Ty Glas	d		13 21								13 51								14 21						
Heath Low Level	d		13 24								13 54								14 24						
Cardiff Queen Street 3	a	13 25	13 30	13 35	13 40			13 45	13 50	13 55	14 00		14 05	14 10	14 15			14 20	14 30	14 35	14 40	14 45		14 50	14 55
	d	13 26	13 31	13 36	13 41			13 46	13 51	13 56	14 01		14 06	14 11	14 15			14 21	14 31	14 36	14 41	14 46		14 51	14 56
Cardiff Central 7	a	13 30	13 35	13 40	13 45		13 50	13 51	13 55	14 00	14 05		14 11	14 15	14 19		14 20	14 25	14 35	14 40	14 45	14 50	14 50	14 55	15 00
	d	13 31		13 41	13 46				13 55	14 01		14 10		14 16				14 25		14 41	14 46			14 55	15 01
Grangetown	d	13 35		13 45	13 50				13 59	14 05		14 14		14 20				14 29		14 45	14 50			14 59	15 05
Dingle Road	d	13 41			13 56					14 11				14 26							14 56				15 11
Penarth	a	13 46			14 01					14 16				14 31							15 01				15 16
Cogan	d			13 48					14 03			14 18						14 33		14 48				15 03	
Eastbrook	d			13 51					14 05			14 20						14 35		14 51				15 05	
Dinas Powys	d			13 53					14 07			14 22						14 37		14 53				15 07	
Cadoxton	d			13 57					14 11			14 26						14 41		14 57				15 11	
Barry Docks	d			14 00					14 14			14 29						14 44		15 00				15 14	
Barry 3	d			14 05					14 18			14 33						14 48		15 05				15 18	
Barry Island	a								14 24			14 39						14 54						15 24	
Rhoose Cardiff Int Airport ✈	d			14 12																15 12					
Llantwit Major	d			14 22																15 22					
Bridgend	a			14 39																15 39					

A To Radyr **B** To Coryton

When events are being held at the Principality Stadium, services are subject to alteration. Please check times before travelling.

For connections to Cardiff Bay please refer to Table T124

Table T130-F

Mondays to Fridays
16 December to 15 May

Treherbert, Aberdare, Merthyr, Pontypridd, Rhymney and Coryton - Cardiff, Penarth, Barry, Barry Island and Bridgend

		AW A	AW	AW	AW B	AW	AW	AW	AW A	AW	AW	AW B	AW	AW	AW	AW A	AW	AW	AW B	AW	AW	AW A
Treherbert	d							14 16					14 46							15 16		
Ynyswen	d							14 18					14 48							15 18		
Treorchy	d							14 21					14 51							15 21		
Ton Pentre	d							14 24					14 54							15 24		
Ystrad Rhondda	a							14 26					14 56							15 26		
	d							14 28					14 58							15 28		
Llwynypia	d							14 30					15 00							15 30		
Tonypandy	d							14 33					15 03							15 33		
Dinas Rhondda	d							14 35					15 05							15 35		
Porth	a							14 38					15 08							15 38		
	d							14 52					15 09							15 39		
Trehafod	d							14 55					15 12							15 42		
Merthyr Tydfil	d		14 08							14 38							15 08					
Pentre-bach	d		14 12							14 42							15 12					
Troed Y Rhiw	d		14 15							14 45							15 15					
Merthyr Vale	a		14 18							14 48							15 18					
	d		14 20							14 50							15 20					
Quakers Yard	d		14 25							14 55							15 25					
Aberdare	d					14 22								14 52							15 22	
Cwmbach	d					14 25								14 55							15 25	
Fernhill	d					14 28								14 58							15 28	
Mountain Ash	a					14 32								15 02							15 32	
	d					14 34								15 04							15 34	
Penrhiwceiber	d					14 37								15 07							15 37	
Abercynon	d		14 30			14 45				15 00				15 15			15 30				15 45	
Pontypridd 3	a		14 38			14 54		15 02		15 08			15 19	15 24			15 38			15 49	15 54	
	d		14 38			14 54		15 04		15 08			15 19	15 24			15 38			15 49	15 54	
Trefforest	d		14 41			14 57		15 07		15 11			15 22	15 27			15 41			15 52	15 57	
Trefforest Estate	d		14 45							15 15							15 45					
Taffs Well	d		14 49			15 04		15 14		15 19			15 29	15 34			15 49			15 59	16 04	
Radyr 3	a		14 53			15 08		15 19		15 23			15 33	15 38			15 53			16 03	16 08	
	d		14 53		15 03	15 08		15 21		15 23		15 33	15 33	15 38			15 53		16 03	16 03	16 08	
Danescourt	d				15 07							15 37							16 07			
Fairwater	d				15 09							15 39							16 09			
Waun-gron Park	d				15 11							15 41							16 11			
Ninian Park	d				15 14							15 44							16 14			
Llandaf	d		14 56			15 11				15 26			15 36	15 41			15 56			16 06	16 11	
Cathays	d		15 01			15 16				15 31			15 40	15 46			16 01			16 10	16 16	
Rhymney 3	d						14 27															
Pontlottyn	d						14 30															
Tir-phil	d						14 35															
Brithdir	d						14 37															
Bargoed	a						14 43															
	d			14 32			14 44				15 00				15 17			15 32				
Gilfach Fargoed	d														15 19							
Pengam	d			14 37			14 49				15 04				15 22			15 37				
Hengoed	d			14 40			14 53				15 08				15 25			15 40				
Ystrad Mynach	d			14 43			14 56				15 11				15 28			15 43				
Llanbradach	d			14 48			15 00				15 15				15 33			15 48				
Energlyn & Churchill Park	d						15 04				15 19											
Aber	d			14 52			15 06				15 21				15 37			15 52				
Caerphilly	d			14 55			15 10				15 25				15 40			15 55				
Lisvane & Thornhill	d			14 59			15 14				15 29				15 44			15 59				
Llanishen	d			15 01			15 16				15 31				15 46			16 01				
Heath High Level	d			15 04			15 19				15 34				15 49			16 04				
Coryton	d	14 45							15 15							15 45						16 15
Whitchurch (Cardiff)	d	14 46							15 16							15 46						16 16
Rhiwbina	d	14 48							15 18							15 48						16 18
Birchgrove	d	14 50							15 20							15 50						16 20
Ty Glas	d	14 51							15 21							15 51						16 21
Heath Low Level	d	14 54							15 24							15 54						16 24
Cardiff Queen Street 3	a	15 00	15 05	15 10		15 20	15 25		15 30	15 35	15 40		15 45	15 50	15 55	16 00	16 05	16 10		16 15	16 20	16 30
	d	15 01	15 06	15 11		15 21	15 26		15 31	15 36	15 41		15 46	15 51	15 56	16 01	16 06	16 11		16 16	16 21	16 31
Cardiff Central 7	a	15 06	15 10	15 15	15 20	15 25	15 30	15 33	15 35	15 40	15 45	15 50	15 51	15 55	16 00	16 06	16 10	16 15	16 20	16 21	16 25	16 35
	d		15 10	15 16		15 25	15 31			15 41	15 46			15 55	16 01		16 10	16 16			16 25	
Grangetown	d		15 14	15 20		15 29	15 35			15 45	15 50			15 59	16 05		16 14	16 20			16 29	
Dingle Road	d			15 26			15 41				15 56				16 11			16 26				
Penarth	a			15 31			15 46				16 01				16 16			16 31				
Cogan	d		15 18			15 33				15 48				16 03			16 18				16 33	
Eastbrook	d		15 20			15 35				15 51				16 05			16 20				16 35	
Dinas Powys	d		15 22			15 37				15 53				16 07			16 22				16 37	
Cadoxton	d		15 26			15 41				15 57				16 11			16 26				16 41	
Barry Docks	d		15 29			15 44				16 00				16 14			16 29				16 44	
Barry 3	d		15 33			15 48				16 05				16 18			16 33				16 48	
Barry Island	a		15 39			15 54								16 24			16 39				16 54	
Rhoose Cardiff Int Airport ✈	d									16 12												
Llantwit Major	d									16 22												
Bridgend	a									16 39												

A To Radyr **B** To Coryton

When events are being held at the Principality Stadium, services are subject to alteration. Please check times before travelling.

For connections to Cardiff Bay please refer to Table T124

Table T130-F

Mondays to Fridays
16 December to 15 May

Treherbert, Aberdare, Merthyr, Pontypridd, Rhymney and Coryton - Cardiff, Penarth, Barry, Barry Island and Bridgend

		AW	AW	AW	AW A	AW	AW	AW B	AW	AW	AW A	AW	AW	AW	AW B	AW	AW	AW A	AW	AW	AW	AW B	AW
Treherbert	d			15 44								16 16							16 46				
Ynyswen	d			15 46								16 18							16 48				
Treorchy	d			15 51								16 21							16 51				
Ton Pentre	d			15 54								16 24							16 54				
Ystrad Rhondda	a			15 56								16 26							16 56				
	d			15 58								16 28							16 58				
Llwynypia	d			16 00								16 30							17 00				
Tonypandy	d			16 03								16 33							17 03				
Dinas Rhondda	d			16 05								16 35							17 05				
Porth	a			16 08								16 38							17 08				
	d			16 09								16 39							17 09				
Trehafod	d			16 12								16 42							17 12				
Merthyr Tydfil	d	15 38							16 08							16 38							17 08
Pentre-bach	d	15 42							16 12							16 42							17 12
Troed Y Rhiw	d	15 45							16 15							16 45							17 15
Merthyr Vale	a	15 48							16 18							16 48							17 18
	d	15 50							16 20							16 50							17 20
Quakers Yard	d	15 55							16 25							16 55							17 25
Aberdare	d					15 52							16 22							16 52			
Cwmbach	d					15 55							16 25							16 55			
Fernhill	d					15 58							16 28							16 58			
Mountain Ash	a					16 02							16 32							17 02			
	d					16 04							16 34							17 04			
Penrhiwceiber	d					16 07							16 37							17 07			
Abercynon	d	16 00				16 15			16 30				16 45			17 00				17 15			17 30
Pontypridd 3	a	16 08		16 19		16 24			16 38			16 49	16 54			17 08			17 19	17 24			17 38
	d	16 08		16 19		16 24			16 38			16 49	16 54			17 08			17 19	17 24			17 38
Trefforest	d	16 11		16 22		16 27			16 41			16 52	16 57			17 11			17 22	17 27			17 41
Trefforest Estate	d	16 15							16 45							17 15							17 45
Taffs Well	d	16 19		16 29		16 34			16 49			16 59	17 04			17 19			17 29	17 34			17 49
Radyr 3	a	16 23		16 33		16 38			16 53			17 03	17 08			17 23			17 33	17 38			17 53
	d	16 23		16 33	16 33	16 38			16 53		17 03	17 03	17 08			17 23		17 33	17 33	17 38			17 53
Danescourt	d				16 37						17 07							17 37					
Fairwater	d				16 39						17 09							17 39					
Waun-gron Park	d				16 41						17 11							17 41					
Ninian Park	d				16 44						17 14							17 44					
Llandaf	d	16 26		16 36		16 41			16 56			17 06	17 11			17 26			17 36	17 41			17 56
Cathays	d	16 31		16 40		16 46			17 01			17 10	17 16			17 31			17 40	17 46			18 01
Rhymney 3	d													16 27									
Pontlottyn	d													16 30									
Tir-phil	d													16 35									
Brithdir	d													16 37									
Bargoed	a													16 43									
	d		16 00				16 17			16 32				16 44			17 00				17 17		
Gilfach Fargoed	d						16 19														17 19		
Pengam	d		16 04				16 22			16 37				16 49			17 04				17 22		
Hengoed	d		16 08				16 25			16 40				16 53			17 08				17 25		
Ystrad Mynach	d		16 11				16 28			16 43				16 56			17 11				17 28		
Llanbradach	d		16 15				16 33			16 48				17 00			17 15				17 33		
Energlyn & Churchill Park	d		16 19											17 04			17 19						
Aber	d		16 21				16 37			16 52				17 06			17 21				17 37		
Caerphilly	d		16 25				16 40			16 55				17 10			17 25				17 40		
Lisvane & Thornhill	d		16 29				16 44			16 59				17 14			17 29				17 44		
Llanishen	d		16 31				16 46			17 01				17 16			17 31				17 46		
Heath High Level	d		16 34				16 49			17 04				17 19			17 34				17 49		
Coryton	d							16 45							17 15							17 45	
Whitchurch (Cardiff)	d							16 46							17 16							17 46	
Rhiwbina	d							16 48							17 18							17 48	
Birchgrove	d							16 50							17 20							17 50	
Ty Glas	d							16 51							17 21							17 51	
Heath Low Level	d							16 54							17 24							17 54	
Cardiff Queen Street 3	a	16 35	16 40	16 45		16 50	16 55	17 00	17 05	17 10		17 15	17 20	17 25	17 30	17 35	17 40		17 45	17 50	17 55	18 00	18 05
	d	16 36	16 41	16 46		16 51	16 56	17 01	17 06	17 11		17 16	17 21	17 26	17 31	17 36	17 41		17 46	17 51	17 56	18 01	18 06
Cardiff Central 7	a	16 40	16 45	16 49	16 50	16 55	17 00	17 05	17 10	17 15	17 20	17 21	17 25	17 30	17 35	17 40	17 45	17 50	17 51	17 55	18 00	18 05	18 10
	d	16 41	16 46			16 55	17 01		17 10	17 16			17 25	17 31		17 41	17 46			17 55	18 01		18 10
Grangetown	d	16 45	16 50			16 59	17 05		17 14	17 20			17 29	17 35		17 45	17 50			17 59	18 05		18 14
Dingle Road	d		16 56				17 11			17 26				17 41			17 56				18 11		
Penarth	a		17 01				17 14			17 31				17 46			18 01				18 16		
Cogan	d	16 48				17 03			17 18				17 33			17 48				18 03			18 18
Eastbrook	d	16 51				17 05			17 20				17 35			17 51				18 05			18 20
Dinas Powys	d	16 53				17 07			17 22				17 37			17 53				18 07			18 22
Cadoxton	d	16 57				17 11			17 26				17 41			17 57				18 11			18 26
Barry Docks	d	17 00				17 14			17 29				17 44			18 00				18 14			18 29
Barry 3	d	17 05				17 18			17 33				17 48			18 05				18 18			18 33
Barry Island	a					17 24			17 39				17 54							18 24			18 39
Rhoose Cardiff Int Airport ✈	d	17 12														18 12							
Llantwit Major	d	17 22														18 22							
Bridgend	a	17 39														18 39							

A To Coryton **B** To Radyr

When events are being held at the Principality Stadium, services are subject to alteration. Please check times before travelling.

For connections to Cardiff Bay please refer to Table T124

Table T130-F

Mondays to Fridays
16 December to 15 May

Treherbert, Aberdare, Merthyr, Pontypridd, Rhymney and Coryton - Cardiff, Penarth, Barry, Barry Island and Bridgend

		AW	AW A	AW	AW	AW	AW B	AW	AW A	AW	AW	AW	AW	AW	AW	AW	AW	AW	AW	AW B	AW	AW
Treherbert	d			17 16						17 46						18 16						18 46
Ynyswen	d			17 18						17 48						18 18						18 48
Treorchy	d			17 21						17 51						18 21						18 51
Ton Pentre	d			17 24						17 54						18 24						18 54
Ystrad Rhondda	a			17 26						17 56						18 26						18 56
	d			17 28						17 58						18 28						18 58
Llwynypia	d			17 30						18 00						18 30						19 00
Tonypandy	d			17 33						18 03						18 33						19 03
Dinas Rhondda	d			17 35						18 05						18 35						19 05
Porth	a			17 38						18 08						18 38						19 08
	d			17 39						18 09						18 39						19 09
Trehafod	d			17 42						18 12						18 42						19 12
Merthyr Tydfil	d							17 38						18 08							18 38	
Pentre-bach	d							17 42						18 12							18 42	
Troed Y Rhiw	d							17 45						18 15							18 45	
Merthyr Vale	a							17 48						18 18							18 48	
	d							17 50						18 20							18 50	
Quakers Yard	d							17 55						18 25							18 55	
Aberdare	d				17 22						17 52						18 22					
Cwmbach	d				17 25						17 55						18 25					
Fernhill	d				17 28						17 58						18 28					
Mountain Ash	a				17 32						18 02						18 32					
	d				17 34						18 04						18 34					
Penrhiwceiber	d				17 37						18 07						18 37					
Abercynon	d				17 45			18 00			18 15			18 30			18 45				19 00	
Pontypridd ■	a			17 49	17 54			18 08		18 19	18 24			18 38		18 49	18 54				19 08	19 19
	d			17 49	17 54			18 08		18 19	18 24			18 38		18 49	18 54				19 08	19 19
Trefforest	d			17 52	17 57			18 11		18 22	18 27			18 41		18 52	18 57				19 11	19 22
Trefforest Estate	d							18 15						18 45							19 15	
Taffs Well	d			17 59	18 04			18 19		18 29	18 34			18 49		18 59	19 04				19 19	19 29
Radyr ■	a			18 03	18 08			18 23		18 33	18 38			18 53		19 03	19 08				19 23	19 33
	d		18 03	18 03	18 08			18 23	18 33	18 33	18 38			18 53	19 03	19 03	19 08				19 23	19 33
Danescourt	d		18 07						18 37						19 07							
Fairwater	d		18 09						18 39						19 09							
Waun-gron Park	d		18 11						18 41						19 11							
Ninian Park	d		18 14						18 44						19 14							
Llandaf	d			18 06	18 11			18 26		18 36	18 41			18 56		19 06	19 11				19 26	19 36
Cathays	d			18 10	18 16			18 31		18 40	18 46			19 01		19 10	19 16				19 31	19 40
Rhymney ■	d					17 27																
Pontlottyn	d					17 30																
Tir-phil	d					17 35																
Brithdir	d					17 37																
Bargoed	a					17 43																
	d	17 32				17 44						18 15										
Gilfach Fargoed	d											18 18										
Pengam	d	17 37				17 49						18 20										
Hengoed	d	17 40				17 53						18 24										
Ystrad Mynach	d	17 43				17 56						18 27										
Llanbradach	d	17 48				18 00						18 31										
Energlyn & Churchill Park	d					18 04						18 35										
Aber	d	17 52				18 06						18 37										
Caerphilly	d	17 55				18 10						18 40										
Lisvane & Thornhill	d	17 59				18 14						18 44										
Llanishen	d	18 01				18 16						18 46										
Heath High Level	d	18 04				18 19						18 49										
Coryton	d						18 15						18 45							19 15		
Whitchurch (Cardiff)	d						18 16						18 46							19 16		
Rhiwbina	d						18 18						18 48							19 18		
Birchgrove	d						18 20						18 50							19 20		
Ty Glas	d						18 21						18 51							19 21		
Heath Low Level	d						18 24						18 54							19 24		
Cardiff Queen Street ■	a	18 10		18 15	18 20	18 25	18 30	18 35		18 45	18 50	18 55	19 00	19 05		19 15	19 20			19 31	19 36	19 45
	d	18 11		18 16	18 21	18 26	18 31	18 36		18 45	18 51	18 56	19 01	19 06		19 15	19 20			19 32	19 37	19 45
Cardiff Central ■	a	18 15	18 20	18 21	18 25	18 30	18 35	18 40	18 50	18 51	18 55	19 00	19 05	19 11	19 21	19 22	19 24			19 36	19 41	19 51
	d	18 16			18 25	18 31		18 41			18 55	19 01						19 25	19 31		19 41	
Grangetown	d	18 20			18 29	18 35		18 45			18 59	19 05						19 29	19 37		19 45	
Dingle Road	d	18 26				18 41						19 11							19 41			
Penarth	a	18 31				18 46						19 16							19 46			
Cogan	d				18 33			18 48			19 03							19 33			19 49	
Eastbrook	d				18 35			18 51			19 05							19 35			19 51	
Dinas Powys	d				18 37			18 53			19 07							19 37			19 53	
Cadoxton	d				18 41			18 57			19 11							19 41			19 58	
Barry Docks	d				18 44			19 00			19 14							19 44			20 00	
Barry ■	d				18 48			19 05			19 18							19 48			20 05	
Barry Island	a				18 54						19 24							19 54				
Rhoose Cardiff Int Airport ✈	d							19 12													20 12	
Llantwit Major	d							19 22													20 22	
Bridgend	a							19 39													20 39	

A To Coryton
B To Radyr

When events are being held at the Principality Stadium, services are subject to alteration. Please check times before travelling.

For connections to Cardiff Bay please refer to Table T124

Table T130-F

Mondays to Fridays
16 December to 15 May

Treherbert, Aberdare, Merthyr, Pontypridd, Rhymney and Coryton - Cardiff, Penarth, Barry, Barry Island and Bridgend

		AW	AW	AW	AW	AW	AW	AW A	AW	AW	AW	AW	AW	AW	AW	AW	AW	AW	AW A	AW	AW	AW	AW B
Treherbert	d				19 16						19 46					20 16							
Ynyswen	d				19 18						19 48					20 18							
Treorchy	d				19 21						19 51					20 21							
Ton Pentre	d				19 24						19 54					20 24							
Ystrad Rhondda	a				19 26						19 56					20 26							
	d				19 28						19 58					20 28							
Llwynypia	d				19 30						20 00					20 30							
Tonypandy	d				19 33						20 03					20 33							
Dinas Rhondda	d				19 35						20 05					20 35							
Porth	a				19 38						20 08					20 38							
	d				19 39						20 09					20 39							
Trehafod	d				19 42						20 12					20 42							
Merthyr Tydfil	d			19 08					19 38											20 38			
Pentre-bach	d			19 12					19 42											20 42			
Troed Y Rhiw	d			19 15					19 45											20 45			
Merthyr Vale	a			19 18					19 48											20 48			
	d			19 20					19 50											20 50			
Quakers Yard	d			19 25					19 55											20 55			
Aberdare	d	18 52										19 52					20 22				20 52		
Cwmbach	d	18 55										19 55					20 25				20 55		
Fernhill	d	18 58										19 58					20 28				20 58		
Mountain Ash	a	19 02										20 03					20 32				21 02		
	d	19 04										20 07					20 34				21 04		
Penrhiwceiber	d	19 07										20 10					20 37				21 07		
Abercynon	d	19 15		19 30			19 45		20 00			20 16					20 45			21 00	21 15		
Pontypridd ■	a	19 24		19 38	19 49		19 53		20 08		20 19	20 24				20 49	20 54			21 08	21 24		
	d	19 24		19 38	19 49		19 54		20 08		20 19	20 24				20 49	20 54			21 08	21 24		
Trefforest	d	19 27		19 41	19 52		19 57		20 11		20 22	20 27				20 52	20 57			21 11	21 27		
Trefforest Estate	d			19 45					20 15											21 15			
Taffs Well	d	19 34		19 49	19 59		20 04		20 19		20 29	20 34				20 59	21 04			21 19	21 34		
Radyr ■	a	19 38		19 53	20 03		20 08		20 23		20 33	20 38				21 03	21 08			21 23	21 38		
	d	19 38		19 53	20 03	20 04	20 08		20 23		20 33	20 38			21 03	21 03	21 08			21 23	21 38		22 03
Danescourt	d					20 08									21 07								22 07
Fairwater	d					20 10									21 09								22 09
Waun-gron Park	d					20 12									21 11								22 11
Ninian Park	d					20 15									21 14								22 14
Llandaf	d	19 41		19 56	20 06		20 11		20 26		20 36	20 41				21 06	21 11			21 26	21 41		
Cathays	d	19 46		20 01	20 10		20 16		20 31		20 40	20 46				21 10	21 16			21 31	21 46		
Rhymney ■	d													20 00									
Pontlottyn	d													20 03									
Tir-phil	d													20 08									
Brithdir	d													20 10									
Bargoed	a													20 15									
	d													20 15									
Gilfach Fargoed	d													20 18									
Pengam	d													20 21									
Hengoed	d													20 24									
Ystrad Mynach	d													20 27								21 39	
Llanbradach	d													20 32								21 43	
Energlyn & Churchill Park	d													20 36									
Aber	d													20 38								21 48	
Caerphilly	d		19 40							20 26				20 42								21 51	
Lisvane & Thornhill	d		19 44							20 30				20 46								21 55	
Llanishen	d		19 46							20 32				20 48								21 57	
Heath High Level	d		19 49							20 35				20 51								22 00	
Coryton	d							20 15											21 15				
Whitchurch (Cardiff)	d							20 16											21 16				
Rhiwbina	d							20 18											21 18				
Birchgrove	d							20 20											21 20				
Ty Glas	d							20 21											21 21				
Heath Low Level	d							20 24											21 24				
Cardiff Queen Street ■	a	19 50	19 55	20 05	20 15		20 20	20 30	20 35	20 41	20 46	20 50		20 57		21 15	21 20		21 30	21 35	21 50	22 06	
	d	19 51	19 56	20 06	20 15		20 21	20 31	20 36	20 42	20 46	20 51		21 00		21 16	21 21		21 31	21 36	21 51	22 06	
Cardiff Central ■	a	19 56	20 00	20 10	20 20	20 24	20 26	20 35	20 40	20 46	20 51	20 55		21 04	21 20	21 21	21 26		21 35	21 40	21 55	22 10	22 20
	d	20 03		20 10	20 31				20 41				21 06	21 10				21 32		21 41	21 56	22 10	
Grangetown	d	20 07		20 14	20 37				20 45				21 10	21 14				21 36		21 45	22 00	22 14	
Dingle Road	d	20 11			20 41								21 14					21 41			22 04		
Penarth	a	20 16			20 46								21 19					21 46			22 09		
Cogan	d			20 18					20 48					21 18						21 48		22 18	
Eastbrook	d			20 20					20 51					21 20						21 51		22 20	
Dinas Powys	d			20 22					20 53					21 22						21 53		22 22	
Cadoxton	d			20 26					20 57					21 26						21 57		22 26	
Barry Docks	d			20 29					21 00					21 29						22 00		22 29	
Barry ■	d			20 33					21 07					21 33						22 05		22 33	
Barry Island	a			20 39										21 39								22 39	
Rhoose Cardiff Int Airport ✈	d								21 14											22 12			
Llantwit Major	d								21 24											22 22			
Bridgend	a								21 39											22 39			

A To Radyr
B To Coryton

When events are being held at the Principality Stadium, services are subject to alteration. Please check times before travelling.

For connections to Cardiff Bay please refer to Table T124

Table T130-F

Mondays to Fridays

16 December to 15 May

Treherbert, Aberdare, Merthyr, Pontypridd, Rhymney and Coryton - Cardiff, Penarth, Barry, Barry Island and Bridgend

		AW	AW	AW	AW	AW	AW	AW	AW	AW
Treherbert	d	21 16								
Ynyswen	d	21 18								
Treorchy	d	21 21								
Ton Pentre	d	21 24								
Ystrad Rhondda	a	21 26								
	d	21 28								
Llwynypia	d	21 30								
Tonypandy	d	21 33								
Dinas Rhondda	d	21 35								
Porth	a	21 38								
	d	21 39								
Trehafod	d	21 42								
Merthyr Tydfil	d			21 38					22 38	
Pentre-bach	d			21 42					22 42	
Troed Y Rhiw	d			21 45					22 45	
Merthyr Vale	a			21 48					22 48	
	d			21 50					22 50	
Quakers Yard	d			21 55					22 55	
Aberdare	d					21 52				22 51
Cwmbach	d					21 55				22 54
Fernhill	d					21 58				22 58
Mountain Ash	a					22 02				23 02
	d					22 04				23 04
Penrhiwceiber	d					22 07				23 08
Abercynon	d			22 00		22 15			23 00	23 14
Pontypridd 3	a	21 49		22 08		22 24			23 08	23 24
	d	21 49		22 08		22 24			23 08	
Trefforest	d	21 52		22 11		22 27			23 11	
Trefforest Estate	d			22 15					23 15	
Taffs Well	d	21 59		22 19		22 34			23 19	
Radyr 3	a	22 03		22 23		22 38			23 23	
	d	22 03		22 23		22 38		23 14	23 23	
Danescourt	d									
Fairwater	d									
Waun-gron Park	d									
Ninian Park	d									
Llandaf	d	22 06		22 26		22 41		23 16	23 26	
Cathays	d	22 10		22 31		22 46		23 20	23 31	
Rhymney 3	d		21 36							
Pontlottyn	d		21 39							
Tir-phil	d		21 44							
Brithdir	d		21 46							
Bargoed	a		21 50							
	d		21 50							
Gilfach Fargoed	d		21 53							
Pengam	d		21 55							
Hengoed	d		21 59							
Ystrad Mynach	d		22 02							
Llanbradach	d		22 06							
Energlyn & Churchill Park	d		22 10							
Aber	d		22 12							
Caerphilly	d		22 15		22 29					
Lisvane & Thornhill	d		22 19							
Llanishen	d		22 21							
Heath High Level	d		22 24							
Coryton	d						22 45			
Whitchurch (Cardiff)	d						22 46			
Rhiwbina	d						22 48			
Birchgrove	d						22 50			
Ty Glas	d						22 51			
Heath Low Level	d						22 54			
Cardiff Queen Street 3	a	22 15	22 30	22 35	22 40	22 51	23 00	23 25	23 35	
	d	22 16	22 31	22 36	22 41	22 54	23 01	23 25	23 36	
Cardiff Central 7	a	22 21	22 35	22 40	22 46	23 04	23 05	23 29	23 41	
	d		22 36	22 43		23 11		23 30		
Grangetown	d		22 40	22 47		23 15		23 34		
Dingle Road	d		22 44			23 19				
Penarth	a		22 49			23 24				
Cogan	d			22 50				23 37		
Eastbrook	d			22 53				23 40		
Dinas Powys	d			22 55				23 42		
Cadoxton	d			22 59				23 46		
Barry Docks	d			23 02				23 49		
Barry 3	d			23 06				23 53		
Barry Island	a							23 59		
Rhoose Cardiff Int Airport ✈	d			23 13						
Llantwit Major	d			23 23						
Bridgend	a			23 39						

When events are being held at the Principality Stadium, services are subject to alteration. Please check times before travelling.

For connections to Cardiff Bay please refer to Table T124

Table T130-F

Saturdays

21 December to 16 May

Treherbert, Aberdare, Merthyr, Pontypridd, Rhymney and Coryton - Cardiff, Penarth, Barry, Barry Island and Bridgend

		AW A	AW	AW B	AW	AW	AW	AW	AW	AW	AW	AW C	AW	AW D	AW	AW E	AW	AW F	AW	AW	AW D	AW	AW
Treherbert	d												05 47				06 16						
Ynyswen	d												05 49				06 18						
Treorchy	d												05 51				06 21						
Ton Pentre	d												05 54				06 24						
Ystrad Rhondda	a												05 56				06 26						
	d												05 58				06 28						
Llwynypia	d												06 00				06 30						
Tonypandy	d												06 03				06 33						
Dinas Rhondda	d												06 05				06 35						
Porth	a												06 08				06 38						
	d												06 09				06 39						
Trehafod	d												06 12				06 42						
Merthyr Tydfil	d																					06 38	
Pentre-bach	d																					06 42	
Troed Y Rhiw	d																					06 45	
Merthyr Vale	a																					06 48	
	d																					06 50	
Quakers Yard	d																					06 55	
Aberdare	d																		06 22				
Cwmbach	d																		06 25				
Fernhill	d																		06 28				
Mountain Ash	a																		06 32				
	d																		06 34				
Penrhiwceiber	d																		06 37				
Abercynon	d																		06 45			07 00	
Pontypridd 3	a												06 19				06 48		06 54			07 07	
	d						05 18						06 19				06 48		06 54			07 08	
Trefforest	d						05 21						06 22				06 51		06 57			07 11	
Trefforest Estate	d						05 25															07 15	
Taffs Well	d						05 29						06 29			06 53	06 58	←	07 04			07 19	
Radyr 3	a						05 33						06 33			06 58	07 02	06 58	07 08			07 23	
	d						05 33						06 33			07 03	07 02	07 03	07 08			07 23	
Danescourt	d															→		07 07					
Fairwater	d																	07 09					
Waun-gron Park	d																	07 11					
Ninian Park	d																	07 14					
Llandaf	d						05 36						06 36				07 05		07 11			07 26	
Cathays	d						05 40						06 40				07 09		07 16			07 31	
Rhymney 3	d																			06 30			
Pontlottyn	d																			06 33			
Tir-phil	d																			06 38			
Brithdir	d																			06 41			
Bargoed	a																			06 44			
	d																			06 45			07 02
Gilfach Fargoed	d																			06 47			07 04
Pengam	d																			06 50			07 07
Hengoed	d																			06 53			07 10
Ystrad Mynach	d																			06 56			07 13
Llanbradach	d																			07 01			07 18
Energlyn & Churchill Park	d																			07 05			
Aber	d																			07 07			07 22
Caerphilly	d										06 11									07 10			07 25
Lisvane & Thornhill	d										06 15									07 14			07 29
Llanishen	d										06 17									07 16			07 31
Heath High Level	d										06 20									07 19			07 34
Coryton	d													06 45							07 15		
Whitchurch (Cardiff)	d													06 46							07 16		
Rhiwbina	d													06 48							07 18		
Birchgrove	d													06 50							07 20		
Ty Glas	d													06 51							07 21		
Heath Low Level	d													06 54							07 24		
Cardiff Queen Street 3	a						05 45				06 26		06 45	07 00			07 14		07 20	07 25	07 30	07 35	07 40
	d	00 01					05 45				06 26		06 45	07 01			07 14		07 21	07 26	07 31	07 36	07 41
Cardiff Central 7	a	00 05					05 49				06 30		06 49	07 05			07 18	07 20	07 25	07 30	07 35	07 40	07 45
	d		05 20		05 43	05 46	05 55	06 16	06 24	06 36	06 41	06 56	07 01		07 10		07 19		07 25	07 31		07 41	07 46
Grangetown	d		05 24	05 24	05 47	05 50	05 59	06 20	06 29	06 40	06 45	07 00	07 05		07 14		07 23		07 29	07 38		07 45	07 50
Dingle Road	d					05 54		06 24		06 44			07 11				07 27			07 42			07 56
Penarth	a					05 58		06 29		06 49			07 15				07 30			07 46			08 01
Cogan	d		05 28	05 28	05 50		06 03		06 33		06 48	07 04			07 18				07 33			07 48	
Eastbrook	d		05 30	05 30	05 53		06 05		06 35		06 51	07 06			07 20				07 35			07 51	
Dinas Powys	d		05 32	05 32	05 55		06 07		06 37		06 53	07 08			07 22				07 37			07 53	
Cadoxton	d		05 36	05 36	05 59		06 11		06 41		06 57	07 12			07 26				07 41			07 57	
Barry Docks	d		05 39	05 39	06 02		06 14		06 44		07 00	07 15			07 29				07 44			08 00	
Barry 3	d		05 43	05 43	06 07		06 18		06 48		07 05	07 19			07 33				07 48			08 05	
Barry Island	a		05 48	05 48			06 24		06 54			07 23			07 39				07 54				
Rhoose Cardiff Int Airport ✈	d				06 14						07 12											08 12	
Llantwit Major	d				06 24						07 22											08 22	
Bridgend	a				06 40						07 39											08 39	

A From Cardiff Bay
B From Cardiff Canton Sidings
C From Hereford
D To Radyr
E To Coryton
F From Taffs Well to Coryton

When events are being held at the Principality Stadium, services are subject to alteration. Please check times before travelling.

For connections to Cardiff Bay please refer to Table T124

Table T130-F

Saturdays
21 December to 16 May

Treherbert, Aberdare, Merthyr, Pontypridd, Rhymney and Coryton - Cardiff, Penarth, Barry, Barry Island and Bridgend

		AW A	AW	AW	AW	AW B	AW	AW	AW A	AW	AW	AW	AW B	AW	AW A	AW	AW	AW	AW B	AW	AW	AW A	AW
Treherbert	d		06 46							07 16						07 46							08 16
Ynyswen	d		06 48							07 18						07 48							08 18
Treorchy	d		06 51							07 21						07 51							08 21
Ton Pentre	d		06 54							07 24						07 54							08 24
Ystrad Rhondda	a		06 56							07 26						07 56							08 26
	d		06 58							07 28						07 58							08 28
Llwynypia	d		07 00							07 30						08 00							08 30
Tonypandy	d		07 03							07 33						08 03							08 33
Dinas Rhondda	d		07 05							07 35						08 05							08 35
Porth	a		07 08							07 38						08 08							08 38
	d		07 09							07 39						08 09							08 39
Trehafod	d		07 12							07 42						08 12							08 42
Merthyr Tydfil	d						07 08							07 38						08 08			
Pentre-bach	d						07 12							07 42						08 12			
Troed Y Rhiw	d						07 15							07 45						08 15			
Merthyr Vale	a						07 18							07 48						08 18			
	d						07 20							07 50						08 20			
Quakers Yard	d						07 25							07 55						08 25			
Aberdare	d			06 52							07 22						07 52						
Cwmbach	d			06 55							07 25						07 55						
Fernhill	d			06 58							07 28						07 58						
Mountain Ash	a			07 02							07 32						08 02						
	d			07 04							07 34						08 04						
Penrhiwceiber	d			07 07							07 37						08 07						
Abercynon	d			07 15			07 30				07 45			08 00			08 15			08 30			
Pontypridd 3	a		07 19	07 24			07 38			07 49	07 54			08 08		08 19	08 24			08 38			08 49
	d		07 19	07 24			07 38			07 49	07 54			08 08		08 19	08 24			08 38			08 49
Trefforest	d		07 22	07 27			07 41			07 52	07 57			08 11		08 22	08 27			08 41			08 52
Trefforest Estate	d						07 45							08 15						08 45			
Taffs Well	d		07 29	07 34			07 49			07 59	08 04			08 19		08 29	08 34			08 49			08 59
Radyr 3	a		07 33	07 38			07 53			08 03	08 08			08 23		08 33	08 38			08 53			09 03
	d	07 33	07 33	07 38			07 53		08 03	08 03	08 08			08 23	08 33	08 33	08 38			08 53		09 03	09 03
Danescourt	d	07 37							08 07						08 37							09 07	
Fairwater	d	07 39							08 09						08 39							09 09	
Waun-gron Park	d	07 41							08 11						08 41							09 11	
Ninian Park	d	07 44							08 14						08 44							09 14	
Llandaf	d		07 36	07 41			07 56			08 06	08 11			08 26		08 36	08 41			08 56			09 06
Cathays	d		07 40	07 46			08 01			08 10	08 16			08 31		08 40	08 46			09 01			09 10
Rhymney 3	d				07 00							07 24											
Pontlottyn	d				07 03							07 27											
Tir-phil	d				07 08							07 32											
Brithdir	d				07 10							07 34											
Bargoed	a				07 15							07 40											
	d				07 15			07 32				07 43						08 14			08 32		
Gilfach Fargoed	d				07 18							07 45						08 17					
Pengam	d				07 20			07 37				07 48						08 19			08 37		
Hengoed	d				07 24			07 40				07 52						08 23			08 40		
Ystrad Mynach	d				07 27			07 43				07 55						08 26			08 43		
Llanbradach	d				07 31			07 48				08 00						08 30			08 48		
Energlyn & Churchill Park	d				07 35							08 03						08 34					
Aber	d				07 37			07 52				08 06						08 36			08 52		
Caerphilly	d				07 40			07 55				08 10						08 40			08 55		
Lisvane & Thornhill	d				07 44			07 59				08 14						08 44			08 59		
Llanishen	d				07 46			08 01				08 16						08 46			09 01		
Heath High Level	d				07 49			08 04				08 19						08 49			09 04		
Coryton	d					07 45							08 15						08 45				
Whitchurch (Cardiff)	d					07 46							08 16						08 46				
Rhiwbina	d					07 48							08 18						08 48				
Birchgrove	d					07 50							08 20						08 50				
Ty Glas	d					07 51							08 21						08 51				
Heath Low Level	d					07 54							08 24						08 54				
Cardiff Queen Street 3	a		07 45	07 50	07 55	08 00	08 05	08 10		08 15	08 20	08 25	08 30	08 35		08 45	08 50	08 55	09 00	09 05	09 10		09 15
	d		07 46	07 51	07 56	08 01	08 06	08 11		08 15	08 21	08 26	08 31	08 36		08 46	08 51	08 56	09 01	09 06	09 11		09 16
Cardiff Central 7	a	07 50	07 51	07 55	08 00	08 05	08 10	08 15	08 19	08 20	08 25	08 30	08 35	08 40	08 50	08 50	08 55	09 00	09 05	09 10	09 15	09 20	09 21
	d			07 55	08 01		08 10	08 18			08 25	08 31		08 41			08 55	09 01		09 10	09 16		
Grangetown	d			07 59	08 05		08 14	08 22			08 29	08 35		08 45			08 59	09 05		09 14	09 20		
Dingle Road	d				08 11			08 27				08 41						09 11			09 26		
Penarth	a				08 16			08 30				08 45						09 16			09 31		
Cogan	d			08 03			08 18				08 33			08 48			09 03			09 18			
Eastbrook	d			08 05			08 20				08 35			08 51			09 05			09 20			
Dinas Powys	d			08 07			08 22				08 37			08 53			09 07			09 22			
Cadoxton	d			08 11			08 26				08 41			08 57			09 11			09 26			
Barry Docks	d			08 14			08 29				08 44			09 00			09 14			09 29			
Barry 3	d			08 18			08 33				08 48			09 05			09 18			09 33			
Barry Island	a			08 24			08 39				08 54						09 24			09 39			
Rhoose Cardiff Int Airport ✈	d													09 12									
Llantwit Major	d													09 22									
Bridgend	a													09 39									

A To Coryton
B To Radyr

When events are being held at the Principality Stadium, services are subject to alteration. Please check times before travelling.

For connections to Cardiff Bay please refer to Table T124

Table T130-F

Saturdays
21 December to 16 May

Treherbert, Aberdare, Merthyr, Pontypridd, Rhymney and Coryton - Cardiff, Penarth, Barry, Barry Island and Bridgend

		AW	AW	AW A	AW	AW	AW B	AW	AW	AW	AW A	AW	AW	AW B	AW	AW	AW	AW A	AW	AW	AW	AW B
Treherbert	d							08 46							09 16						09 46	
Ynyswen	d							08 48							09 18						09 48	
Treorchy	d							08 51							09 21						09 51	
Ton Pentre	d							08 54							09 24						09 54	
Ystrad Rhondda	a							08 56							09 26						09 56	
	d							08 58							09 28						09 58	
Llwynypia	d							09 00							09 30						10 00	
Tonypandy	d							09 03							09 33						10 03	
Dinas Rhondda	d							09 05							09 35						10 05	
Porth	a							09 08							09 38						10 08	
	d							09 09							09 39						10 09	
Trehafod	d							09 12							09 42						10 12	
Merthyr Tydfil	d				08 38							09 08							09 38			
Pentre-bach	d				08 42							09 12							09 42			
Troed Y Rhiw	d				08 45							09 15							09 45			
Merthyr Vale	a				08 48							09 18							09 48			
	d				08 50							09 20							09 50			
Quakers Yard	d				08 55							09 25							09 55			
Aberdare	d	08 22							08 52							09 22						
Cwmbach	d	08 25							08 55							09 25						
Fernhill	d	08 28							08 58							09 28						
Mountain Ash	a	08 32							09 02							09 32						
	d	08 34							09 04							09 34						
Penrhiwceiber	d	08 37							09 07							09 37						
Abercynon	d	08 45			09 00				09 15			09 30				09 45			10 00			
Pontypridd 3	a	08 54			09 08			09 19	09 24			09 38			09 49	09 54			10 08		10 19	
	d	08 54			09 08			09 19	09 24			09 38			09 49	09 54			10 08		10 19	
Trefforest	d	08 57			09 11			09 22	09 27			09 41			09 52	09 57			10 11		10 22	
Trefforest Estate	d				09 15							09 45							10 15			
Taffs Well	d	09 04			09 19			09 29	09 34			09 49			09 59	10 04			10 19		10 29	
Radyr 3	a	09 08			09 23			09 33	09 38			09 53			10 03	10 08			10 23		10 33	
	d	09 08			09 23		09 33	09 33	09 38			09 53		10 03	10 03	10 08			10 23		10 33	10 33
Danescourt	d						09 37							10 07								10 37
Fairwater	d						09 39							10 09								10 39
Waun-gron Park	d						09 41							10 11								10 41
Ninian Park	d						09 44							10 14								10 44
Llandaf	d	09 11			09 26			09 36	09 41			09 56			10 06	10 11			10 26		10 36	
Cathays	d	09 16			09 31			09 40	09 46			10 01			10 10	10 16			10 31		10 40	
Rhymney 3	d		08 33														09 27					
Pontlottyn	d		08 36														09 30					
Tir-phil	d		08 40														09 35					
Brithdir	d		08 43														09 37					
Bargoed	a		08 47														09 43					
	d		08 47			09 00				09 17			09 32				09 44			10 00		
Gilfach Fargoed	d									09 19												
Pengam	d		08 52			09 04				09 22			09 37				09 49			10 04		
Hengoed	d		08 55			09 09				09 25			09 40				09 53			10 08		
Ystrad Mynach	d		08 58			09 12				09 28			09 43				09 56			10 11		
Llanbradach	d		09 03			09 16				09 33			09 48				10 00			10 15		
Energlyn & Churchill Park	d					09 20											10 04			10 19		
Aber	d		09 07			09 22				09 37			09 52				10 06			10 21		
Caerphilly	d		09 10			09 26				09 40			09 55				10 10			10 25		
Lisvane & Thornhill	d		09 14			09 30				09 44			09 59				10 14			10 29		
Llanishen	d		09 16			09 32				09 46			10 01				10 16			10 31		
Heath High Level	d		09 19			09 35				09 49			10 04				10 19			10 34		
Coryton	d			09 15							09 45							10 15				
Whitchurch (Cardiff)	d			09 16							09 46							10 16				
Rhiwbina	d			09 18							09 48							10 18				
Birchgrove	d			09 20							09 50							10 20				
Ty Glas	d			09 21							09 51							10 21				
Heath Low Level	d			09 24							09 54							10 24				
Cardiff Queen Street 3	a	09 20	09 25	09 30	09 35	09 42		09 45	09 50	09 55	10 00	10 05	10 10		10 15	10 20	10 25	10 30	10 35	10 40	10 45	
	d	09 21	09 26	09 31	09 36	09 43		09 46	09 51	09 56	10 01	10 06	10 11		10 16	10 21	10 26	10 31	10 36	10 41	10 46	
Cardiff Central 7	a	09 25	09 30	09 35	09 40	09 47	09 50	09 51	09 55	10 00	10 05	10 10	10 15	10 20	10 21	10 25	10 30	10 35	10 40	10 45	10 51	10 51
	d	09 25	09 31		09 40	09 48			09 55	10 01		10 10	10 16			10 25	10 31		10 41	10 48		
Grangetown	d	09 29	09 35		09 45	09 52			09 59	10 05		10 14	10 20			10 29	10 35		10 45	10 54		
Dingle Road	d		09 41			09 56				10 11			10 26				10 41			10 58		
Penarth	a		09 46			10 01				10 16			10 31				10 46			11 01		
Cogan	d	09 33			09 48				10 03			10 18				10 33			10 48			
Eastbrook	d	09 35			09 51				10 05			10 20				10 35			10 51			
Dinas Powys	d	09 37			09 53				10 07			10 22				10 37			10 53			
Cadoxton	d	09 41			09 57				10 11			10 26				10 41			10 57			
Barry Docks	d	09 44			10 00				10 14			10 29				10 44			11 00			
Barry 3	d	09 48			10 05				10 18			10 33				10 48			11 05			
Barry Island	a	09 54							10 24			10 39				10 54						
Rhoose Cardiff Int Airport ✈	d				10 12														11 12			
Llantwit Major	d				10 22														11 22			
Bridgend	a				10 39														11 39			

A To Radyr
B To Coryton

When events are being held at the Principality Stadium, services are subject to alteration. Please check times before travelling.

For connections to Cardiff Bay please refer to Table T124

Table T130-F

Saturdays

21 December to 16 May

Treherbert, Aberdare, Merthyr, Pontypridd, Rhymney and Coryton - Cardiff, Penarth, Barry, Barry Island and Bridgend

		AW	AW	AW	AW A	AW	AW	AW B	AW	AW	AW	AW A	AW	AW	AW B	AW	AW	AW	AW A	AW	AW	AW B	AW
Treherbert	d										10 16					10 46							11 16
Ynyswen	d										10 18					10 48							11 18
Treorchy	d										10 21					10 51							11 21
Ton Pentre	d										10 24					10 54							11 24
Ystrad Rhondda	a										10 26					10 56							11 26
	d										10 28					10 58							11 28
Llwynypia	d										10 30					11 00							11 30
Tonypandy	d										10 33					11 03							11 33
Dinas Rhondda	d										10 35					11 05							11 35
Porth	a										10 38					11 08							11 38
	d										10 52					11 09							11 39
Trehafod	d										10 55					11 12							11 42
Merthyr Tydfil	d		10 04										10 38							11 08			
Pentre-bach	d		10 08										10 42							11 12			
Troed Y Rhiw	d		10 11										10 45							11 15			
Merthyr Vale	a		10 14										10 48							11 18			
	d		10 15										10 53							11 20			
Quakers Yard	d		10 21										10 58							11 25			
Aberdare	d	09 52							10 22								10 52						
Cwmbach	d	09 55							10 25								10 55						
Fernhill	d	09 58							10 28								10 58						
Mountain Ash	a	10 02							10 32								11 02						
	d	10 04							10 34								11 04						
Penrhiwceiber	d	10 07							10 37								11 07						
Abercynon	d	10 15	10 25						10 45				11 02				11 15			11 30			
Pontypridd 3	a	10 24	10 33						10 54		11 01		11 09			11 19	11 23			11 38			11 49
	d	10 24				10 39			10 54		11 04		11 09			11 19	11 24			11 38			11 49
Trefforest	d	10 27				10 42			10 57		11 07		11 12			11 22	11 27			11 41			11 52
Trefforest Estate	d												11 16							11 45			
Taffs Well	d	10 34				10 49			11 04		11 14		11 20			11 29	11 34			11 49			11 59
Radyr 3	a	10 38				10 53			11 08		11 19		11 23			11 33	11 38			11 53			12 03
	d	10 38				10 53		11 03	11 08		11 21		11 23		11 33	11 33	11 38			11 53		12 03	12 03
Danescourt	d							11 07							11 37							12 07	
Fairwater	d							11 09							11 39							12 09	
Waun-gron Park	d							11 11							11 41							12 11	
Ninian Park	d							11 14							11 44							12 14	
Llandaf	d	10 41				10 56			11 11				11 26			11 36	11 41			11 56			12 06
Cathays	d	10 46				11 01			11 16				11 31			11 40	11 46			12 01			12 10
Rhymney 3	d									10 27													
Pontlottyn	d									10 30													
Tir-phil	d									10 35													
Brithdir	d									10 37													
Bargoed	a									10 43													
	d			10 17			10 32			10 44				11 00				11 17			11 32		
Gilfach Fargoed	d			10 19														11 19					
Pengam	d			10 22			10 37			10 49				11 04				11 22			11 37		
Hengoed	d			10 25			10 40			10 53				11 08				11 25			11 40		
Ystrad Mynach	d			10 28			10 43			10 56				11 11				11 28			11 43		
Llanbradach	d			10 33			10 48			11 00				11 15				11 33			11 48		
Energlyn & Churchill Park	d									11 04				11 19									
Aber	d			10 37			10 52			11 06				11 21				11 37			11 52		
Caerphilly	d			10 40			10 55			11 10				11 25				11 40			11 55		
Lisvane & Thornhill	d			10 44			10 59			11 14				11 29				11 44			11 59		
Llanishen	d			10 46			11 01			11 16				11 31				11 46			12 01		
Heath High Level	d			10 49			11 04			11 19				11 34				11 49			12 04		
Coryton	d				10 45							11 15							11 45				
Whitchurch (Cardiff)	d				10 46							11 16							11 46				
Rhiwbina	d				10 48							11 18							11 48				
Birchgrove	d				10 50							11 20							11 50				
Ty Glas	d				10 51							11 21							11 51				
Heath Low Level	d				10 54							11 24							11 54				
Cardiff Queen Street 3	a	10 50		10 55	11 00	11 05	11 10		11 20	11 25		11 29	11 35	11 40		11 45	11 50	11 55	12 00	12 05	12 10		12 15
	d	10 51		10 56	11 01	11 06	11 11		11 21	11 26		11 31	11 36	11 41		11 46	11 51	11 56	12 01	12 06	12 11		12 16
Cardiff Central 7	a	10 55		11 00	11 05	11 10	11 15	11 20	11 25	11 30	11 33	11 34	11 40	11 45	11 49	11 51	11 55	12 00	12 05	12 10	12 15	12 20	12 21
	d	10 55		11 01		11 10	11 16		11 25	11 31			11 41	11 46			11 55	12 01		12 10	12 16		
Grangetown	d	10 59		11 05		11 14	11 20		11 29	11 35			11 45	11 50			11 59	12 05		12 14	12 20		
Dingle Road	d			11 11			11 26			11 41				11 56				12 11			12 26		
Penarth	a			11 16			11 31			11 46				12 01				12 16			12 31		
Cogan	d	11 03				11 18			11 33				11 48				12 03			12 18			
Eastbrook	d	11 05				11 20			11 35				11 51				12 05			12 20			
Dinas Powys	d	11 07				11 22			11 37				11 53				12 07			12 22			
Cadoxton	d	11 11				11 26			11 41				11 57				12 11			12 26			
Barry Docks	d	11 14				11 29			11 44				12 00				12 14			12 29			
Barry 3	d	11 18				11 33			11 48				12 05				12 18			12 33			
Barry Island	a	11 24				11 39			11 54								12 24			12 39			
Rhoose Cardiff Int Airport ✈	d												12 12										
Llantwit Major	d												12 22										
Bridgend	a												12 39										

A To Radyr
B To Coryton

When events are being held at the Principality Stadium, services are subject to alteration. Please check times before travelling.

For connections to Cardiff Bay please refer to Table T124

Table T130-F

Saturdays

21 December to 16 May

Treherbert, Aberdare, Merthyr, Pontypridd, Rhymney and Coryton - Cardiff, Penarth, Barry, Barry Island and Bridgend

		AW	AW	AW A	AW	AW	AW B	AW	AW	AW A	AW	AW	AW B	AW	AW	AW	AW A	AW	AW	AW B	AW	AW
Treherbert	d							11 46						12 16							12 46	
Ynyswen	d							11 48						12 18							12 48	
Treorchy	d							11 51						12 21							12 51	
Ton Pentre	d							11 54						12 24							12 54	
Ystrad Rhondda	a							11 56						12 26							12 56	
	d							11 58						12 28							12 58	
Llwynypia	d							12 00						12 30							13 00	
Tonypandy	d							12 03						12 33							13 03	
Dinas Rhondda	d							12 05						12 35							13 05	
Porth	a							12 08						12 38							13 08	
	d							12 09						12 39							13 09	
Trehafod	d							12 12						12 42							13 12	
Merthyr Tydfil	d				11 38						12 08							12 38				
Pentre-bach	d				11 42						12 12							12 42				
Troed Y Rhiw	d				11 45						12 15							12 45				
Merthyr Vale	a				11 48						12 18							12 48				
	d				11 50						12 20							12 50				
Quakers Yard	d				11 55						12 25							12 55				
Aberdare	d	11 22													12 22							12 52
Cwmbach	d	11 25													12 25							12 55
Fernhill	d	11 28													12 28							12 58
Mountain Ash	a	11 32													12 32							13 02
	d	11 34													12 34							13 04
Penrhiwceiber	d	11 37													12 37							13 07
Abercynon	d	11 45			12 00						12 30				12 45			13 00				13 15
Pontypridd 3	a	11 54			12 08			12 19			12 38			12 49	12 54			13 08			13 19	13 24
	d	11 54			12 08			12 19			12 38			12 49	12 54			13 08			13 19	13 24
Trefforest	d	11 57			12 11			12 22			12 41			12 52	12 57			13 11			13 22	13 27
Trefforest Estate	d				12 15						12 45							13 15				
Taffs Well	d	12 04			12 19			12 29			12 49			12 59	13 04			13 19			13 29	13 34
Radyr 3	a	12 08			12 23			12 33			12 53			13 03	13 08			13 23			13 33	13 38
	d	12 08			12 23		12 33	12 33			12 53		13 03	13 03	13 08			13 23		13 33	13 33	13 38
Danescourt	d						12 37						13 07							13 37		
Fairwater	d						12 39						13 09							13 39		
Waun-gron Park	d						12 41						13 11							13 41		
Ninian Park	d						12 44						13 14							13 44		
Llandaf	d	12 11			12 26			12 36			12 56			13 06	13 11			13 26			13 36	13 41
Cathays	d	12 16			12 31			12 40			13 01			13 10	13 16			13 31			13 40	13 46
Rhymney 3	d		11 27													12 27						
Pontlottyn	d		11 30													12 30						
Tir-phil	d		11 35													12 35						
Brithdir	d		11 37													12 37						
Bargoed	a		11 43													12 43						
	d		11 44			12 00			12 17			12 32				12 44			13 00			
Gilfach Fargoed	d								12 19													
Pengam	d		11 49			12 04			12 22			12 37				12 49			13 04			
Hengoed	d		11 53			12 08			12 25			12 40				12 53			13 08			
Ystrad Mynach	d		11 56			12 11			12 28			12 43				12 56			13 11			
Llanbradach	d		12 00			12 15			12 33			12 48				13 00			13 15			
Energlyn & Churchill Park	d		12 04			12 19										13 04			13 19			
Aber	d		12 06			12 21			12 37			12 52				13 06			13 21			
Caerphilly	d		12 10			12 25			12 40			12 55				13 10			13 25			
Lisvane & Thornhill	d		12 14			12 29			12 44			12 59				13 14			13 29			
Llanishen	d		12 16			12 31			12 46			13 01				13 16			13 31			
Heath High Level	d		12 19			12 34			12 49			13 04				13 19			13 34			
Coryton	d			12 15						12 45							13 15					
Whitchurch (Cardiff)	d			12 16						12 46							13 16					
Rhiwbina	d			12 18						12 48							13 18					
Birchgrove	d			12 20						12 50							13 20					
Ty Glas	d			12 21						12 51							13 21					
Heath Low Level	d			12 24						12 54							13 24					
Cardiff Queen Street 3	a	12 20	12 25	12 30	12 35	12 40		12 45	12 55	13 00	13 05	13 10		13 15	13 20	13 25	13 30	13 35	13 40		13 45	13 50
	d	12 21	12 26	12 31	12 36	12 41		12 46	12 56	13 01	13 06	13 11		13 16	13 21	13 26	13 31	13 36	13 41		13 46	13 51
Cardiff Central 7	a	12 25	12 30	12 35	12 40	12 45	12 50	12 51	13 00	13 05	13 10	13 15	13 20	13 21	13 25	13 30	13 35	13 40	13 45	13 50	13 51	13 55
	d	12 25	12 31		12 41	12 46		12 55	13 01		13 10	13 16			13 25	13 31		13 41	13 46			13 55
Grangetown	d	12 29	12 35		12 45	12 50		12 59	13 05		13 14	13 20			13 29	13 35		13 45	13 50			13 59
Dingle Road	d		12 41			12 56			13 11			13 26				13 41			13 56			
Penarth	a		12 46			13 01			13 16			13 31				13 44			14 01			
Cogan	d	12 33			12 48			13 03			13 18				13 33			13 48				14 03
Eastbrook	d	12 35			12 51			13 05			13 20				13 35			13 51				14 05
Dinas Powys	d	12 37			12 53			13 07			13 22				13 37			13 53				14 07
Cadoxton	d	12 41			12 57			13 11			13 26				13 41			13 57				14 11
Barry Docks	d	12 44			13 00			13 14			13 29				13 44			14 00				14 14
Barry 3	d	12 48			13 05			13 18			13 33				13 48			14 05				14 18
Barry Island	a	12 54						13 24			13 39				13 54							14 24
Rhoose Cardiff Int Airport ✈	d				13 12													14 12				
Llantwit Major	d				13 22													14 22				
Bridgend	a				13 39													14 39				

A To Radyr
B To Coryton

When events are being held at the Principality Stadium, services are subject to alteration. Please check times before travelling.

For connections to Cardiff Bay please refer to Table T124

Table T130-F

Saturdays
21 December to 16 May

Treherbert, Aberdare, Merthyr, Pontypridd, Rhymney and Coryton - Cardiff, Penarth, Barry, Barry Island and Bridgend

		AW	AW A	AW	AW	AW B	AW	AW	AW	AW A		AW	AW	AW B	AW	AW	AW	AW A	AW	AW		AW B	AW	AW	AW
Treherbert	d						13 16								13 46										14 16
Ynyswen	d						13 18								13 48										14 18
Treorchy	d						13 21								13 51										14 21
Ton Pentre	d						13 24								13 54										14 24
Ystrad Rhondda	a						13 26								13 56										14 26
	d						13 28								13 58										14 28
Llwynypia	d						13 30								14 00										14 30
Tonypandy	d						13 33								14 03										14 33
Dinas Rhondda	d						13 35								14 05										14 35
Porth	a						13 38								14 08										14 38
	d						13 39								14 09										14 52
Trehafod	d						13 42								14 12										14 55
Merthyr Tydfil	d			13 08								13 38							14 08						
Pentre-bach	d			13 12								13 42							14 12						
Troed Y Rhiw	d			13 15								13 45							14 15						
Merthyr Vale	a			13 18								13 48							14 18						
	d			13 20								13 50							14 20						
Quakers Yard	d			13 25								13 55							14 25						
Aberdare	d															13 52						14 22			
Cwmbach	d															13 55						14 25			
Fernhill	d															13 58						14 28			
Mountain Ash	a															14 02						14 32			
	d															14 04						14 34			
Penrhiwceiber	d															14 07						14 37			
Abercynon	d			13 30				13 45				14 00				14 15			14 30				14 45		
Pontypridd	a			13 38			13 49	13 54				14 08			14 19	14 24			14 38				14 54		15 01
	d			13 38			13 49	13 54				14 08			14 19	14 24			14 38				14 54		15 04
Trefforest	d			13 41			13 52	13 57				14 11			14 22	14 27			14 41				14 57		15 07
Trefforest Estate	d			13 45								14 15							14 45						
Taffs Well	d			13 49			13 59	14 04				14 19			14 29	14 34			14 49				15 04		15 14
Radyr	a			13 53			14 03	14 08				14 23			14 33	14 38			14 53				15 08		15 19
	d			13 53		14 03	14 03	14 08				14 23		14 33	14 33	14 38			14 53			15 03	15 08		15 21
Danescourt	d					14 07								14 37								15 07			
Fairwater	d					14 09								14 39								15 09			
Waun-gron Park	d					14 11								14 41								15 11			
Ninian Park	d					14 14								14 44								15 14			
Llandaf	d			13 56			14 06	14 11				14 26			14 36	14 41			14 56				15 11		
Cathays	d			14 01			14 10	14 16				14 31			14 40	14 46			15 01				15 16		
Rhymney	d								13 27															14 27	
Pontlottyn	d								13 30															14 30	
Tir-phil	d								13 35															14 35	
Brithdir	d								13 37															14 37	
Bargoed	a								13 43															14 43	
	d	13 17			13 32				13 44				14 00				14 17			14 32				14 44	
Gilfach Fargoed	d	13 19															14 19								
Pengam	d	13 22			13 37				13 49				14 04				14 22			14 37				14 49	
Hengoed	d	13 25			13 40				13 53				14 08				14 25			14 40				14 53	
Ystrad Mynach	d	13 28			13 43				13 56				14 11				14 28			14 43				14 56	
Llanbradach	d	13 33			13 48				14 00				14 15				14 33			14 48				15 00	
Energlyn & Churchill Park	d								14 04				14 19											15 04	
Aber	d	13 37			13 52				14 06				14 21				14 37			14 52				15 06	
Caerphilly	d	13 40			13 55				14 10				14 25				14 40			14 55				15 10	
Lisvane & Thornhill	d	13 44			13 59				14 14				14 29				14 44			14 59				15 14	
Llanishen	d	13 46			14 01				14 16				14 31				14 46			15 01				15 16	
Heath High Level	d	13 49			14 04				14 19				14 34				14 49			15 04				15 19	
Coryton	d		13 45							14 15								14 45							
Whitchurch (Cardiff)	d		13 46							14 16								14 46							
Rhiwbina	d		13 48							14 18								14 48							
Birchgrove	d		13 50							14 20								14 50							
Ty Glas	d		13 51							14 21								14 51							
Heath Low Level	d		13 54							14 24								14 54							
Cardiff Queen Street	a	13 55	14 00	14 05	14 10		14 15	14 20	14 25	14 30		14 35	14 40		14 45	14 50	14 55	15 00	15 05	15 10			15 20	15 25	
	d	13 56	14 01	14 06	14 11		14 16	14 21	14 26	14 31		14 36	14 41		14 46	14 51	14 56	15 01	15 06	15 11			15 21	15 26	
Cardiff Central	a	14 00	14 05	14 10	14 15	14 20	14 21	14 25	14 30	14 35		14 40	14 45	14 50	14 51	14 55	15 00	15 05	15 10	15 15		15 20	15 25	15 30	15 33
	d	14 01		14 10	14 16			14 25	14 31			14 41	14 46			14 55	15 01		15 10	15 16			15 25	15 31	
Grangetown	d	14 05		14 14	14 20			14 29	14 35			14 45	14 50			14 59	15 05		15 14	15 20			15 29	15 35	
Dingle Road	d	14 11			14 26				14 41				14 56				15 11			15 26				15 41	
Penarth	a	14 16			14 31				14 46				15 01				15 16			15 31				15 46	
Cogan	d			14 18				14 33				14 48				15 03			15 18				15 33		
Eastbrook	d			14 20				14 35				14 51				15 05			15 20				15 35		
Dinas Powys	d			14 22				14 37				14 53				15 07			15 22				15 37		
Cadoxton	d			14 26				14 41				14 57				15 11			15 26				15 41		
Barry Docks	d			14 29				14 44				15 00				15 14			15 29				15 44		
Barry	d			14 33				14 48				15 05				15 18			15 33				15 48		
Barry Island	a			14 39				14 54								15 24			15 39				15 54		
Rhoose Cardiff Int Airport ✈	d											15 12													
Llantwit Major	d											15 22													
Bridgend	a											15 39													

A To Radyr B To Coryton

When events are being held at the Principality Stadium, services are subject to alteration. Please check times before travelling.

For connections to Cardiff Bay please refer to Table T124

NRT DECEMBER 19 EDITION

Table T130-F

Saturdays
21 December to 16 May

Treherbert, Aberdare, Merthyr, Pontypridd, Rhymney and Coryton - Cardiff, Penarth, Barry, Barry Island and Bridgend

		AW A	AW	AW	AW B	AW		AW	AW	AW A	AW	AW	AW B	AW	AW	AW A		AW	AW	AW B	AW	AW	AW	AW A	AW
Treherbert	d					14 46								15 16							15 46				
Ynyswen	d					14 48								15 18							15 48				
Treorchy	d					14 51								15 21							15 51				
Ton Pentre	d					14 54								15 24							15 54				
Ystrad Rhondda	a					14 56								15 26							15 56				
	d					14 58								15 28							15 58				
Llwynypia	d					15 00								15 30							16 00				
Tonypandy	d					15 03								15 33							16 03				
Dinas Rhondda	d					15 05								15 35							16 05				
Porth	a					15 08								15 38							16 08				
	d					15 09								15 39							16 09				
Trehafod	d					15 12								15 42							16 12				
Merthyr Tydfil	d		14 38								15 08							15 38							16 08
Pentre-bach	d		14 42								15 12							15 42							16 12
Troed Y Rhiw	d		14 45								15 15							15 45							16 15
Merthyr Vale	a		14 48								15 18							15 48							16 18
	d		14 50								15 20							15 50							16 20
Quakers Yard	d		14 55								15 25							15 55							16 25
Aberdare	d							14 52							15 22							15 52			
Cwmbach	d							14 55							15 25							15 55			
Fernhill	d							14 58							15 28							15 58			
Mountain Ash	a							15 02							15 32							16 02			
	d							15 04							15 34							16 04			
Penrhiwceiber	d							15 07							15 37							16 07			
Abercynon	d		15 00					15 15			15 30				15 45			16 00				16 15			16 30
Pontypridd	a		15 08			15 19		15 24			15 38			15 49	15 54			16 08			16 19	16 24			16 38
	d		15 08			15 19		15 24			15 38			15 49	15 54			16 08			16 19	16 24			16 38
Trefforest	d		15 11			15 22		15 27			15 41			15 52	15 57			16 11			16 22	16 27			16 41
Trefforest Estate	d		15 15								15 45							16 15							16 45
Taffs Well	d		15 19			15 29		15 34			15 49			15 59	16 04			16 19			16 29	16 34			16 49
Radyr	a		15 23			15 33		15 38			15 53			16 03	16 08			16 23			16 33	16 38			16 53
	d		15 23		15 33	15 33		15 38			15 53		16 03	16 03	16 08			16 23		16 33	16 33	16 38			16 53
Danescourt	d				15 37								16 07							16 37					
Fairwater	d				15 39								16 09							16 39					
Waun-gron Park	d				15 41								16 11							16 41					
Ninian Park	d				15 44								16 14							16 44					
Llandaf	d		15 26			15 36		15 41			15 56			16 06	16 11			16 26			16 36	16 41			16 56
Cathays	d		15 31			15 40		15 46			16 01			16 10	16 16			16 31			16 40	16 46			17 01
Rhymney	d																								
Pontlottyn	d																								
Tir-phil	d																								
Brithdir	d																								
Bargoed	a																								
	d			15 00					15 17			15 32							16 00				16 17		
Gilfach Fargoed	d								15 19														16 19		
Pengam	d			15 04					15 22			15 37							16 04				16 22		
Hengoed	d			15 08					15 25			15 40							16 08				16 25		
Ystrad Mynach	d			15 11					15 28			15 43							16 11				16 28		
Llanbradach	d			15 15					15 33			15 48							16 15				16 33		
Energlyn & Churchill Park	d			15 19															16 19						
Aber	d			15 21					15 37			15 52							16 21				16 37		
Caerphilly	d			15 25					15 40			15 55							16 25				16 40		
Lisvane & Thornhill	d			15 29					15 44			15 59							16 29				16 44		
Llanishen	d			15 31					15 46			16 01							16 31				16 46		
Heath High Level	d			15 34					15 49			16 04							16 34				16 49		
Coryton	d	15 15								15 45						16 15								16 45	
Whitchurch (Cardiff)	d	15 16								15 46						16 16								16 46	
Rhiwbina	d	15 18								15 48						16 18								16 48	
Birchgrove	d	15 20								15 50						16 20								16 50	
Ty Glas	d	15 21								15 51						16 21								16 51	
Heath Low Level	d	15 24								15 54						16 24								16 54	
Cardiff Queen Street	a	15 30	15 35	15 40		15 45		15 50	15 55	16 00	16 05	16 10		16 15	16 20	16 30		16 35	16 40		16 45	16 50	16 55	17 00	17 05
	d	15 31	15 36	15 41		15 46		15 51	15 56	16 01	16 06	16 11		16 16	16 21	16 31		16 36	16 41		16 46	16 51	16 56	17 01	17 06
Cardiff Central	a	15 35	15 40	15 45	15 50	15 51		15 55	16 00	16 06	16 10	16 15	16 20	16 21	16 25	16 35		16 40	16 45	16 50	16 51	16 55	17 00	17 05	17 10
	d		15 41	15 46				15 55	16 03		16 10	16 16			16 25			16 41	16 46			16 55	17 01		17 10
Grangetown	d		15 45	15 50				15 59	16 08		16 14	16 20			16 29			16 45	16 50			16 59	17 05		17 14
Dingle Road	d			15 56					16 12			16 26							16 56				17 11		
Penarth	a			16 01					16 14			16 31							17 01				17 16		
Cogan	d		15 48					16 03			16 18				16 33			16 48				17 03			17 18
Eastbrook	d		15 51					16 05			16 20				16 35			16 51				17 05			17 20
Dinas Powys	d		15 53					16 07			16 22				16 37			16 53				17 07			17 22
Cadoxton	d		15 57					16 11			16 26				16 41			16 57				17 11			17 26
Barry Docks	d		16 00					16 14			16 29				16 44			17 00				17 14			17 29
Barry	d		16 05					16 18			16 33				16 48			17 05				17 18			17 33
Barry Island	a							16 24			16 39				16 54							17 24			17 39
Rhoose Cardiff Int Airport ✈	d		16 12															17 12							
Llantwit Major	d		16 22															17 22							
Bridgend	a		16 40															17 39							

A To Radyr B To Coryton

When events are being held at the Principality Stadium, services are subject to alteration. Please check times before travelling.

For connections to Cardiff Bay please refer to Table T124

Table T130-F

Saturdays

21 December to 16 May

Treherbert, Aberdare, Merthyr, Pontypridd, Rhymney and Coryton - Cardiff, Penarth, Barry, Barry Island and Bridgend

		AW	AW A	AW	AW	AW	AW B	AW	AW	AW A	AW	AW	AW	AW B	AW	AW	AW A	AW	AW	AW	AW B	AW
Treherbert	d			16 16							16 46							17 16				
Ynyswen	d			16 18							16 48							17 18				
Treorchy	d			16 21							16 51							17 21				
Ton Pentre	d			16 24							16 54							17 24				
Ystrad Rhondda	a			16 26							16 56							17 26				
	d			16 28							16 58							17 28				
Llwynypia	d			16 30							17 00							17 30				
Tonypandy	d			16 33							17 03							17 33				
Dinas Rhondda	d			16 35							17 05							17 35				
Porth	a			16 38							17 08							17 38				
	d			16 39							17 09							17 39				
Trehafod	d			16 42							17 12							17 42				
Merthyr Tydfil	d							16 38							17 08							17 38
Pentre-bach	d							16 42							17 12							17 42
Troed Y Rhiw	d							16 45							17 15							17 45
Merthyr Vale	a							16 48							17 18							17 48
	d							16 50							17 20							17 50
Quakers Yard	d							16 55							17 25							17 55
Aberdare	d				16 22							16 52							17 22			
Cwmbach	d				16 25							16 55							17 25			
Fernhill	d				16 28							16 58							17 28			
Mountain Ash	a				16 32							17 02							17 32			
	d				16 34							17 04							17 34			
Penrhiwceiber	d				16 37							17 07							17 37			
Abercynon	d				16 45			17 00				17 15			17 30				17 45			18 00
Pontypridd 3	a			16 49	16 54			17 08			17 19	17 24			17 38			17 49	17 54			18 08
	d			16 49	16 54			17 08			17 19	17 24			17 38			17 49	17 54			18 08
Trefforest	d			16 52	16 57			17 11			17 22	17 27			17 41			17 52	17 57			18 11
Trefforest Estate	d							17 15							17 45							18 15
Taffs Well	d			16 59	17 04			17 19			17 29	17 34			17 49			17 59	18 04			18 19
Radyr 3	a			17 03	17 08			17 23			17 33	17 38			17 53			18 03	18 08			18 23
	d		17 03	17 03	17 08			17 23		17 33	17 33	17 38			17 53		18 03	18 03	18 08			18 23
Danescourt	d		17 07							17 37							18 07					
Fairwater	d		17 09							17 39							18 09					
Waun-gron Park	d		17 11							17 41							18 11					
Ninian Park	d		17 14							17 44							18 14					
Llandaf	d			17 06	17 11			17 26			17 36	17 41			17 56			18 06	18 11			18 26
Cathays	d			17 10	17 16			17 31			17 40	17 46			18 01			18 10	18 16			18 31
Rhymney 3	d					16 27														17 27		
Pontlottyn	d					16 30														17 30		
Tir-phil	d					16 35														17 35		
Brithdir	d					16 37														17 37		
Bargoed	a					16 43														17 43		
	d	16 32				16 44			17 00				17 17			17 32				17 44		
Gilfach Fargoed	d												17 19									
Pengam	d	16 37				16 49			17 04				17 22			17 37				17 49		
Hengoed	d	16 40				16 53			17 08				17 25			17 40				17 53		
Ystrad Mynach	d	16 43				16 56			17 11				17 28			17 43				17 56		
Llanbradach	d	16 48				17 00			17 15				17 33			17 48				18 00		
Energlyn & Churchill Park	d					17 04			17 19											18 04		
Aber	d	16 52				17 06			17 21				17 37			17 52				18 06		
Caerphilly	d	16 55				17 10			17 25				17 40			17 55				18 10		
Lisvane & Thornhill	d	16 59				17 14			17 29				17 44			17 59				18 14		
Llanishen	d	17 01				17 16			17 31				17 46			18 01				18 16		
Heath High Level	d	17 04				17 19			17 34				17 49			18 04				18 19		
Coryton	d						17 15							17 45							18 15	
Whitchurch (Cardiff)	d						17 16							17 46							18 16	
Rhiwbina	d						17 18							17 48							18 18	
Birchgrove	d						17 20							17 50							18 20	
Ty Glas	d						17 21							17 51							18 21	
Heath Low Level	d						17 24							17 54							18 24	
Cardiff Queen Street 3	a	17 10		17 15	17 20	17 25	17 30	17 35	17 40		17 45	17 50	17 55	18 00	18 05	18 10		18 15	18 20	18 25	18 30	18 35
	d	17 11		17 16	17 21	17 26	17 31	17 36	17 41		17 46	17 51	17 56	18 01	18 06	18 11		18 16	18 21	18 26	18 31	18 36
Cardiff Central 7	a	17 15	17 20	17 21	17 25	17 30	17 35	17 40	17 45	17 50	17 51	17 55	18 00	18 06	18 10	18 15	18 20	18 21	18 25	18 30	18 35	18 40
	d	17 16			17 25	17 31		17 41	17 46			17 55	18 01		18 10	18 16			18 25	18 31		18 41
Grangetown	d	17 20			17 29	17 35		17 45	17 50			17 59	18 05		18 14	18 20			18 29	18 35		18 45
Dingle Road	d	17 26				17 41			17 56				18 11			18 26				18 41		
Penarth	a	17 31				17 46			18 01				18 16			18 31				18 46		
Cogan	d				17 33			17 48				18 03			18 18				18 33			18 48
Eastbrook	d				17 35			17 51				18 05			18 20				18 35			18 51
Dinas Powys	d				17 37			17 53				18 07			18 22				18 37			18 53
Cadoxton	d				17 41			17 57				18 11			18 26				18 41			18 57
Barry Docks	d				17 44			18 00				18 14			18 29				18 44			19 00
Barry 3	d				17 48			18 05				18 18			18 33				18 48			19 05
Barry Island	a				17 54							18 24			18 39				18 54			
Rhoose Cardiff Int Airport ✈	d							18 12														19 12
Llantwit Major	d							18 22														19 22
Bridgend	a							18 39														19 39

A To Coryton **B** To Radyr

When events are being held at the Principality Stadium, services are subject to alteration. Please check times before travelling.

For connections to Cardiff Bay please refer to Table T124

Table T130-F

Saturdays

21 December to 16 May

Treherbert, Aberdare, Merthyr, Pontypridd, Rhymney and Coryton - Cardiff, Penarth, Barry, Barry Island and Bridgend

		AW A	AW	AW	AW	AW	AW	AW B	AW	AW	AW C	AW D	AW	AW	AW	AW	AW	AW	AW	AW	AW D	AW	AW
Treherbert	d		17 46					18 16						18 46				19 16					
Ynyswen	d		17 48					18 18						18 48				19 18					
Treorchy	d		17 51					18 21						18 51				19 21					
Ton Pentre	d		17 54					18 24						18 54				19 24					
Ystrad Rhondda	a		17 56					18 26						18 56				19 26					
	d		17 58					18 28						18 58				19 28					
Llwynypia	d		18 00					18 30						19 00				19 30					
Tonypandy	d		18 03					18 33						19 03				19 33					
Dinas Rhondda	d		18 05					18 35						19 05				19 35					
Porth	a		18 08					18 38						19 08				19 38					
	d		18 09					18 39						19 09				19 39					
Trehafod	d		18 12					18 42						19 12				19 42					
Merthyr Tydfil	d						18 08						18 38				19 08					19 38	
Pentre-bach	d						18 12						18 42				19 12					19 42	
Troed Y Rhiw	d						18 15						18 45				19 15					19 45	
Merthyr Vale	a						18 18						18 48				19 18					19 48	
	d						18 20						18 50				19 20					19 50	
Quakers Yard	d						18 25						18 55				19 25					19 55	
Aberdare	d			17 52						18 22					18 52								
Cwmbach	d			17 55						18 25					18 55								
Fernhill	d			17 58						18 28					18 58								
Mountain Ash	a			18 02						18 32					19 02								
	d			18 04						18 34					19 04								
Penrhiwceiber	d			18 07						18 37					19 07								
Abercynon	d			18 15			18 30			18 45			19 00		19 15		19 30			19 45		20 00	
Pontypridd 3	a		18 19	18 24			18 38	18 49		18 54			19 08	19 19	19 24		19 38	19 49		19 54		20 08	
	d		18 19	18 24			18 38	18 49		18 54			19 08	19 19	19 24		19 38	19 49		19 54		20 08	
Trefforest	d		18 22	18 27			18 41	18 52		18 57			19 11	19 22	19 27		19 41	19 52		19 57		20 11	
Trefforest Estate	d						18 45						19 15				19 45					20 15	
Taffs Well	d		18 29	18 34			18 49	18 59		19 04			19 19	19 29	19 34		19 49	19 59		20 04		20 19	
Radyr 3	a		18 33	18 38			18 53	19 03		19 08			19 23	19 33	19 38		19 53	20 03		20 08		20 23	
	d	18 33	18 33	18 38			18 53	19 03	19 03	19 08			19 23	19 33	19 38		19 53	20 03	20 04	20 08		20 23	
Danescourt	d	18 37							19 07										20 08				
Fairwater	d	18 39							19 09										20 10				
Waun-gron Park	d	18 41							19 11										20 12				
Ninian Park	d	18 44							19 14										20 15				
Llandaf	d		18 36	18 41			18 56	19 06		19 11			19 26	19 36	19 41		19 56	20 06		20 11		20 26	
Cathays	d		18 40	18 46			19 01	19 10		19 16			19 31	19 40	19 46		20 01	20 10		20 16		20 31	
Rhymney 3	d																						
Pontlottyn	d																						
Tir-phil	d																						
Brithdir	d																						
Bargoed	a																						
	d				18 15																		
Gilfach Fargoed	d				18 18																		
Pengam	d				18 20																		
Hengoed	d				18 24																		
Ystrad Mynach	d				18 27																		
Llanbradach	d				18 31																		
Energlyn & Churchill Park	d				18 35																		
Aber	d				18 37																		
Caerphilly	d				18 40											19 40							20 26
Lisvane & Thornhill	d				18 44											19 44							20 30
Llanishen	d				18 46											19 46							20 32
Heath High Level	d				18 49											19 49							20 35
Coryton	d					18 45						19 15									20 15		
Whitchurch (Cardiff)	d					18 46						19 16									20 16		
Rhiwbina	d					18 48						19 18									20 18		
Birchgrove	d					18 50						19 20									20 20		
Ty Glas	d					18 51						19 21									20 21		
Heath Low Level	d					18 54						19 24									20 24		
Cardiff Queen Street 3	a		18 45	18 50	18 55	19 00	19 05	19 15		19 20	←	19 31	19 36	19 45	19 50	19 55	20 05	20 15		20 20	20 30	20 35	20 41
	d		18 46	18 51	18 56	19 01	19 06	19 16		19 21		19 32	19 37	19 46	19 51	19 56	20 06	20 16		20 21	20 31	20 36	20 42
Cardiff Central 7	a	18 50	18 51	18 55	19 00	19 05	19 11	19 20	19 21	19 25	19 20	19 36	19 41	19 51	19 56	20 00	20 10	20 21	20 24	20 26	20 35	20 40	20 46
	d			18 55	19 01			19 31		19 25	19 31		19 41		20 03		20 10			20 31		20 41	
Grangetown	d			18 59	19 05			→		19 29	19 35		19 45		20 07		20 14			20 35		20 45	
Dingle Road	d				19 11						19 41				20 11					20 41			
Penarth	a				19 16						19 46				20 16					20 46			
Cogan	d			19 03						19 33			19 49				20 18					20 48	
Eastbrook	d			19 05						19 35			19 51				20 20					20 51	
Dinas Powys	d			19 07						19 37			19 53				20 22					20 53	
Cadoxton	d			19 11						19 41			19 58				20 26					20 57	
Barry Docks	d			19 14						19 44			20 00				20 29					21 00	
Barry 3	d			19 18						19 48			20 05				20 33					21 07	
Barry Island	a			19 24						19 54							20 39						
Rhoose Cardiff Int Airport ✈	d												20 12									21 14	
Llantwit Major	d												20 22									21 24	
Bridgend	a												20 39									21 41	

A To Coryton
B To Penarth
C From Treherbert
D To Radyr

When events are being held at the Principality Stadium, services are subject to alteration. Please check times before travelling.

For connections to Cardiff Bay please refer to Table T124

Table T130-F

Saturdays

21 December to 16 May

Treherbert, Aberdare, Merthyr, Pontypridd, Rhymney and Coryton - Cardiff, Penarth, Barry, Barry Island and Bridgend

		AW	AW A	AW	AW B	AW	AW	AW	AW	AW C	AW	AW	AW	AW D	AW	AW	AW	AW	AW	AW	AW	AW	AW	AW E
Treherbert	d	19 46					20 16								21 16									
Ynyswen	d	19 48					20 18								21 18									
Treorchy	d	19 51					20 21								21 21									
Ton Pentre	d	19 54					20 24								21 24									
Ystrad Rhondda	a	19 56					20 26								21 26									
	d	19 58					20 28								21 28									
Llwynypia	d	20 00					20 30								21 30									
Tonypandy	d	20 03					20 33								21 33									
Dinas Rhondda	d	20 05					20 35								21 35									
Porth	a	20 08					20 38								21 38									
	d	20 09					20 39								21 39									
Trehafod	d	20 12					20 42								21 42									
Merthyr Tydfil	d										20 38						21 38					22 38		
Pentre-bach	d										20 42						21 42					22 42		
Troed Y Rhiw	d										20 45						21 45					22 45		
Merthyr Vale	a										20 48						21 48					22 48		
	d										20 50						21 50					22 50		
Quakers Yard	d										20 55						21 55					22 55		
Aberdare	d		19 52					20 22				20 52							21 52				22 51	
Cwmbach	d		19 55					20 25				20 55							21 55				22 54	
Fernhill	d		19 58					20 28				20 58							21 58				22 58	
Mountain Ash	a		20 02					20 32				21 02							22 02				23 02	
	d		20 07					20 34				21 04							22 04				23 04	
Penrhiwceiber	d		20 10					20 37				21 07							22 07				23 08	
Abercynon	d		20 16					20 45			21 00	21 15					22 00		22 15			23 00	23 14	
Pontypridd 3	a	20 19	20 24				20 49	20 54			21 08	21 24			21 49		22 08		22 24			23 08	23 24	
	d	20 19	20 24				20 49	20 54			21 08	21 24			21 49		22 08		22 24			23 08		
Trefforest	d	20 22	20 27				20 52	20 57			21 11	21 27			21 52		22 11		22 27			23 11		
Trefforest Estate	d										21 15						22 15					23 15		
Taffs Well	d	20 29	20 34				20 59	21 04			21 19	21 34			21 59		22 19		22 34			23 19		
Radyr 3	a	20 33	20 38				21 03	21 08			21 23	21 38			22 03		22 23		22 38			23 23		
	d	20 33	20 38			21 03	21 03	21 08			21 23	21 38		22 03	22 03		22 23		22 38		23 14	23 23		
Danescourt	d					21 07								22 07										
Fairwater	d					21 09								22 09										
Waun-gron Park	d					21 11								22 11										
Ninian Park	d					21 14								22 14										
Llandaf	d	20 36	20 41				21 06	21 11			21 26	21 41			22 06		22 26		22 41		23 16	23 26		
Cathays	d	20 40	20 46				21 10	21 16			21 31	21 46			22 10		22 31		22 46		23 20	23 31		
Rhymney 3	d			20 00												21 36								
Pontlottyn	d			20 03												21 39								
Tir-phil	d			20 08												21 44								
Brithdir	d			20 10												21 46								
Bargoed	a			20 15												21 50								
	d			20 15												21 50								
Gilfach Fargoed	d			20 17												21 53								
Pengam	d			20 20												21 55								
Hengoed	d			20 23												21 59								
Ystrad Mynach	d			20 27									21 39			22 02								
Llanbradach	d			20 31									21 43			22 06								
Energlyn & Churchill Park	d			20 35												22 10								
Aber	d			20 37									21 48			22 12								
Caerphilly	d			20 40									21 51			22 15		22 29						
Lisvane & Thornhill	d			20 45									21 55			22 19								
Llanishen	d			20 47									21 57			22 21								
Heath High Level	d			20 50									22 00			22 24								
Coryton	d									21 15										22 45				
Whitchurch (Cardiff)	d									21 16										22 46				
Rhiwbina	d									21 18										22 48				
Birchgrove	d									21 20										22 50				
Ty Glas	d									21 21										22 51				
Heath Low Level	d									21 24										22 54				
Cardiff Queen Street 3	a	20 46	20 50	20 56	←		21 15	21 20		21 30	21 35	21 50	22 06		22 15	22 30	22 35	22 40	22 51	23 00	23 25	23 35		
	d	20 46	20 51	20 56			21 16	21 21		21 31	21 36	21 51	22 06		22 16	22 31	22 36	22 40	22 54	23 01	23 25	23 36		23 58
Cardiff Central 7	a	20 51	20 56	21 01	20 56	21 20	21 21	21 26		21 35	21 40	21 56	22 10	22 19	22 21	22 35	22 40	22 44	22 59	23 05	23 29	23 39		00 03
	d		21 10	21 06	21 10				21 32		21 41	22 05	22 10			22 36			23 11		23 31			
Grangetown	d		→	21 10	21 14				21 36		21 45	22 09	22 14			22 40			23 15		23 35			
Dingle Road	d			21 14					21 41			22 13				22 44			23 19					
Penarth	a			21 19					21 46			22 18				22 49			23 24					
Cogan	d				21 17						21 48		22 18								23 38			
Eastbrook	d				21 20						21 51		22 20								23 41			
Dinas Powys	d				21 22						21 53		22 22								23 43			
Cadoxton	d				21 26						21 57		22 26								23 47			
Barry Docks	d				21 28						22 00		22 29								23 50			
Barry 3	d				21 33						22 05		22 33								23 54			
Barry Island	a				21 38								22 39								23 59			
Rhoose Cardiff Int Airport ✈	d										22 12													
Llantwit Major	d										22 22													
Bridgend	a										22 39													

A To Barry Island
B From Aberdare
C To Radyr
D To Coryton
E From Cardiff Bay

When events are being held at the Principality Stadium, services are subject to alteration. Please check times before travelling.

For connections to Cardiff Bay please refer to Table T124

NRT DECEMBER 19 EDITION

Table T130-F

Sundays

15 December to 10 May

Treherbert, Aberdare, Merthyr, Pontypridd, Rhymney and Coryton - Cardiff, Penarth, Barry, Barry Island and Bridgend

		AW	AW	AW	AW	AW	AW	AW	AW	AW	AW	AW	AW	AW	AW	AW	AW	AW	AW	AW	AW	AW	AW
Treherbert	d				08 17			09 16						10 17			11 17					12 17	
Ynyswen	d				08 19			09 18						10 19			11 19					12 19	
Treorchy	d				08 21			09 21						10 21			11 21					12 21	
Ton Pentre	d				08 23			09 24						10 23			11 23					12 23	
Ystrad Rhondda	a				08 26			09 26						10 26			11 26					12 26	
	d				08 28			09 28						10 28			11 28					12 28	
Llwynypia	d				08 30			09 30						10 30			11 30					12 30	
Tonypandy	d				08 33			09 33						10 33			11 33					12 33	
Dinas Rhondda	d				08 35			09 35						10 35			11 35					12 35	
Porth	a				08 38			09 38						10 38			11 38					12 38	
	d				08 39			09 39						10 39			11 39					12 39	
Trehafod	d				08 42			09 42						10 42			11 42					12 42	
Merthyr Tydfil	d										09 38								11 38				
Pentre-bach	d										09 42								11 42				
Troed Y Rhiw	d										09 45								11 45				
Merthyr Vale	a										09 48								11 48				
	d										09 50								11 50				
Quakers Yard	d										09 55								11 55				
Aberdare	d						08 53					09 53				10 53				11 53			
Cwmbach	d						08 56					09 56				10 56				11 56			
Fernhill	d						09 00					10 00				11 00				12 00			
Mountain Ash	a						09 04					10 04				11 04				12 04			
	d						09 04					10 04				11 04				12 04			
Penrhiwceiber	d						09 08					10 08				11 08				12 08			
Abercynon	d						09 15				10 00	10 15				11 14			12 00	12 15			
Pontypridd 3	a				08 49		09 23	09 49			10 08	10 24		10 49		11 24	11 49		12 08	12 24		12 49	
	d				08 50		09 24	09 49			10 09	10 24		10 49		11 24	11 49		12 09	12 24		12 49	
Trefforest	d				08 53		09 27	09 52			10 12	10 27		10 52		11 27	11 52		12 12	12 27		12 52	
Trefforest Estate	d																						
Taffs Well	d				09 00		09 34	09 59			10 20	10 34		10 59		11 34	11 59		12 20	12 34		12 59	
Radyr 3	a				09 04		09 38	10 03			10 23	10 38		11 03		11 38	12 03		12 23	12 38		13 03	
	d				09 04		09 38	10 03			10 23	10 38		11 03		11 38	12 03		12 23	12 38		13 03	
Danescourt	d																						
Fairwater	d																						
Waun-gron Park	d																						
Ninian Park	d																						
Llandaf	d				09 07		09 41	10 06			10 26	10 41		11 06		11 41	12 06		12 26	12 41		13 06	
Cathays	d				09 11		09 46	10 10			10 31	10 46		11 10		11 46	12 11		12 31	12 46		13 11	
Rhymney 3	d												10 10								12 11		
Pontlottyn	d												10 13								12 14		
Tir-phil	d												10 17								12 19		
Brithdir	d												10 20								12 21		
Bargoed	a												10 24								12 26		
	d												10 25								12 26		
Gilfach Fargoed	d												10 27								12 29		
Pengam	d												10 30								12 31		
Hengoed	d												10 33								12 35		
Ystrad Mynach	d												10 36								12 38		
Llanbradach	d												10 41								12 42		
Energlyn & Churchill Park	d												10 44								12 46		
Aber	d												10 47								12 48		
Caerphilly	d					09 10				10 10			10 50		11 10			12 10			12 52		13 10
Lisvane & Thornhill	d					09 14				10 14			10 55		11 14			12 14			12 56		13 14
Llanishen	d					09 16				10 16			10 57		11 16			12 16			12 58		13 16
Heath High Level	d					09 19				10 19			11 00		11 19			12 19			13 01		13 19
Coryton	d																						
Whitchurch (Cardiff)	d																						
Rhiwbina	d																						
Birchgrove	d																						
Ty Glas	d																						
Heath Low Level	d																						
Cardiff Queen Street 3	a				09 16	09 25	09 50	10 15		10 25	10 35	10 50	11 06	11 15	11 25	11 50	12 15	12 25	12 35	12 50	13 07	13 16	13 25
	d				09 16	09 26	09 51	10 16		10 26	10 36	10 51	11 06	11 15	11 26	11 51	12 16	12 26	12 36	12 51	13 08	13 16	13 26
Cardiff Central 7	a				09 21	09 30	09 55	10 20		10 30	10 40	10 55	11 10	11 20	11 30	11 55	12 20	12 30	12 40	12 55	13 12	13 20	13 30
	d	08 25	08 41	09 18	09 25		09 55		10 25		10 41	10 55	11 16	11 25		11 55	12 25		12 41	12 55	13 18	13 25	
Grangetown	d	08 29	08 45	09 22	09 29		09 59		10 29		10 45	10 59	11 20	11 29		11 59	12 29		12 45	12 59	13 22	13 29	
Dingle Road	d			09 26									11 24								13 26		
Penarth	a			09 31									11 29								13 31		
Cogan	d	08 33	08 48		09 33		10 03		10 33		10 48	11 03		11 33		12 03	12 33		12 48	13 03		13 33	
Eastbrook	d	08 35	08 51		09 35		10 05		10 35		10 51	11 05		11 35		12 05	12 35		12 51	13 05		13 35	
Dinas Powys	d	08 37	08 53		09 37		10 07		10 37		10 53	11 07		11 37		12 07	12 37		12 53	13 07		13 37	
Cadoxton	d	08 41	08 57		09 41		10 11		10 41		10 57	11 11		11 41		12 11	12 41		12 57	13 11		13 41	
Barry Docks	d	08 44	09 00		09 44		10 14		10 44		11 00	11 14		11 44		12 14	12 44		13 00	13 14		13 44	
Barry 3	d	08 48	09 05		09 48		10 18		10 48		11 05	11 18		11 48		12 18	12 48		13 05	13 18		13 48	
Barry Island	a	08 53			09 54		10 24		10 54			11 24		11 54		12 24	12 54			13 24		13 54	
Rhoose Cardiff Int Airport ✈	d		09 12								11 12								13 12				
Llantwit Major	d		09 22								11 22								13 22				
Bridgend	a		09 37								11 39								13 39				

When events are being held at the Principality Stadium, services are subject to alteration. Please check times before travelling.

For connections to Cardiff Bay please refer to Table T124

Table T130-F

Sundays

15 December to 10 May

Treherbert, Aberdare, Merthyr, Pontypridd, Rhymney and Coryton - Cardiff, Penarth, Barry, Barry Island and Bridgend

		AW	AW	AW	AW	AW		AW	AW	AW	AW	AW	AW	AW	AW	AW		AW	AW	AW	AW	AW	AW	AW	AW
Treherbert	d		13 17						14 17			15 17						16 17			17 17				
Ynyswen	d		13 19						14 19			15 19						16 19			17 19				
Treorchy	d		13 21						14 21			15 21						16 21			17 21				
Ton Pentre	d		13 23						14 23			15 23						16 23			17 23				
Ystrad Rhondda	a		13 26						14 26			15 26						16 26			17 26				
	d		13 28						14 28			15 28						16 28			17 28				
Llwynypia	d		13 30						14 30			15 30						16 30			17 30				
Tonypandy	d		13 33						14 33			15 33						16 33			17 33				
Dinas Rhondda	d		13 35						14 35			15 35						16 35			17 35				
Porth	a		13 38						14 38			15 38						16 38			17 38				
	d		13 39						14 39			15 39						16 39			17 39				
Trehafod	d		13 42						14 42			15 42						16 42			17 42				
Merthyr Tydfil	d				13 38									15 38									17 38		
Pentre-bach	d				13 42									15 42									17 42		
Troed Y Rhiw	d				13 45									15 45									17 45		
Merthyr Vale	a				13 48									15 48									17 48		
	d				13 50									15 50									17 50		
Quakers Yard	d				13 55									15 55									17 55		
Aberdare	d	12 53									14 53									16 53				17 53	
Cwmbach	d	12 56									14 56									16 56				17 56	
Fernhill	d	13 00									15 00									17 00				18 00	
Mountain Ash	a	13 04									15 04									17 04				18 05	
	d	13 04									15 04									17 04				18 05	
Penrhiwceiber	d	13 08									15 08									17 08				18 09	
Abercynon	d	13 14			14 00						15 14			16 00						17 14			18 00	18 15	
Pontypridd [3]	a	13 24	13 49		14 08				14 49		15 24	15 49		16 08				16 49		17 24	17 49		18 08	18 24	
	d	13 24	13 49		14 09				14 49		15 24	15 49		16 09				16 49		17 24	17 49		18 09	18 24	
Trefforest	d	13 27	13 52		14 12				14 52		15 27	15 52		16 12				16 52		17 27	17 52		18 12	18 27	
Trefforest Estate	d																								
Taffs Well	d	13 34	13 59		14 20				14 59		15 34	15 59		16 20				16 59		17 34	17 59		18 20	18 34	
Radyr [3]	a	13 38	14 03		14 23				15 03		15 38	16 03		16 23				17 03		17 38	18 03		18 23	18 38	
	d	13 38	14 03		14 23				15 03		15 38	16 03		16 23				17 03		17 38	18 03		18 23	18 38	
Danescourt	d																								
Fairwater	d																								
Waun-gron Park	d																								
Ninian Park	d																								
Llandaf	d	13 41	14 06		14 26				15 06		15 41	16 06		16 26				17 06		17 41	18 06		18 26	18 41	
Cathays	d	13 46	14 10		14 31				15 10		15 46	16 10		16 31				17 10		17 46	18 10		18 31	18 46	
Rhymney [3]	d							14 11								16 11									18 11
Pontlottyn	d							14 14								16 14									18 14
Tir-phil	d							14 19								16 19									18 19
Brithdir	d							14 21								16 21									18 21
Bargoed	a							14 26								16 26									18 26
	d							14 26								16 26									18 26
Gilfach Fargoed	d							14 29								16 29									18 29
Pengam	d							14 31								16 31									18 31
Hengoed	d							14 35								16 35									18 35
Ystrad Mynach	d							14 38								16 38									18 38
Llanbradach	d							14 42								16 42									18 42
Energlyn & Churchill Park	d							14 46								16 46									18 46
Aber	d							14 48								16 48									18 48
Caerphilly	d			14 10				14 52		15 10			16 10			16 52			17 10			18 10			18 52
Lisvane & Thornhill	d			14 14				14 56		15 14			16 14			16 56			17 14			18 14			18 56
Llanishen	d			14 16				14 58		15 16			16 16			16 58			17 16			18 16			18 58
Heath High Level	d			14 19				15 01		15 19			16 19			17 01			17 19			18 19			19 01
Coryton	d																								
Whitchurch (Cardiff)	d																								
Rhiwbina	d																								
Birchgrove	d																								
Ty Glas	d																								
Heath Low Level	d																								
Cardiff Queen Street [3]	a	13 50	14 15	14 25	14 35			15 07	15 15	15 25	15 50	16 15	16 25	16 35		17 07		17 15	17 25	17 50	18 15	18 25	18 35	18 50	19 07
	d	13 51	14 16	14 26	14 36			15 08	15 16	15 26	15 51	16 16	16 26	16 36		17 08		17 16	17 26	17 51	18 16	18 26	18 36	18 51	19 08
Cardiff Central [7]	a	13 55	14 20	14 30	14 40			15 12	15 20	15 30	15 55	16 20	16 30	16 40		17 12		17 20	17 30	17 55	18 20	18 30	18 40	18 55	19 12
	d	13 55	14 25		14 41	14 55		15 16	15 25		15 55	16 25		16 41	16 55	17 16		17 25		17 55	18 25		18 42	18 55	19 16
Grangetown	d	13 59	14 29		14 45	14 59		15 20	15 29		15 59	16 29		16 45	16 59	17 20		17 29		17 59	18 29		18 46	18 59	19 20
Dingle Road	d							15 24								17 24									19 24
Penarth	a							15 29								17 29									19 30
Cogan	d	14 03	14 33		14 48	15 03			15 33		16 03	16 33		16 48	17 03			17 33		18 03	18 33		18 50	19 03	
Eastbrook	d	14 05	14 35		14 51	15 05			15 35		16 05	16 35		16 51	17 05			17 35		18 05	18 35		18 52	19 05	
Dinas Powys	d	14 07	14 37		14 53	15 07			15 37		16 07	16 37		16 53	17 07			17 37		18 07	18 37		18 54	19 07	
Cadoxton	d	14 11	14 41		14 57	15 11			15 41		16 11	16 41		16 57	17 11			17 41		18 11	18 41		18 59	19 11	
Barry Docks	d	14 14	14 44		15 00	15 14			15 44		16 14	16 44		17 00	17 14			17 44		18 14	18 44		19 01	19 14	
Barry [3]	d	14 18	14 48		15 05	15 18			15 48		16 18	16 48		17 05	17 18			17 48		18 18	18 48		19 06	19 18	
Barry Island	a	14 24	14 54			15 24			15 54		16 24	16 54			17 24			17 54		18 24	18 54			19 24	
Rhoose Cardiff Int Airport ✈	d				15 12									17 12									19 13		
Llantwit Major	d				15 22									17 22									19 23		
Bridgend	a				15 39									17 39									19 39		

When events are being held at the Principality Stadium, services are subject to alteration. Please check times before travelling.

For connections to Cardiff Bay please refer to Table T124

Table T130-F

Sundays

15 December to 10 May

Treherbert, Aberdare, Merthyr, Pontypridd, Rhymney and Coryton - Cardiff, Penarth, Barry, Barry Island and Bridgend

		AW		AW	AW	AW	AW	AW	AW	AW	AW	AW		AW	AW	AW
Treherbert	d	18 17				19 16						20 17			21 17	
Ynyswen	d	18 19				19 18						20 19			21 19	
Treorchy	d	18 21				19 21						20 21			21 21	
Ton Pentre	d	18 23				19 24						20 23			21 23	
Ystrad Rhondda	a	18 26				19 26						20 26			21 26	
	d	18 28				19 28						20 28			21 28	
Llwynypia	d	18 30				19 30						20 30			21 30	
Tonypandy	d	18 33				19 33						20 33			21 33	
Dinas Rhondda	d	18 35				19 35						20 35			21 35	
Porth	a	18 38				19 38						20 38			21 38	
	d	18 39				19 39						20 39			21 39	
Trehafod	d	18 42				19 42						20 42			21 42	
Merthyr Tydfil	d									19 38						21 38
Pentre-bach	d									19 42						21 42
Troed Y Rhiw	d									19 45						21 45
Merthyr Vale	a									19 48						21 48
	d									19 50						21 50
Quakers Yard	d									19 55						21 55
Aberdare	d				18 54						19 53			20 53		
Cwmbach	d				18 57						19 56			20 56		
Fernhill	d				19 01						20 00			21 00		
Mountain Ash	a				19 05						20 04			21 04		
	d				19 06						20 05			21 04		
Penrhiwceiber	d				19 10						20 09			21 08		
Abercynon	d				19 16					20 00	20 15			21 15		22 00
Pontypridd [3]	a	18 49			19 24	19 49				20 08	20 24	20 49		21 23	21 49	22 08
	d	18 49			19 24	19 49				20 09	20 24	20 49		21 24	21 49	22 09
Trefforest	d	18 52			19 27	19 52				20 12	20 27	20 52		21 27	21 52	22 12
Trefforest Estate	d															
Taffs Well	d	18 59			19 34	19 59				20 20	20 34	20 59		21 34	21 59	22 20
Radyr [3]	a	19 03			19 38	20 03				20 23	20 38	21 03		21 38	22 03	22 23
	d	19 03			19 38	20 03				20 23	20 38	21 03		21 38	22 03	22 23
Danescourt	d															
Fairwater	d															
Waun-gron Park	d															
Ninian Park	d															
Llandaf	d	19 06			19 41	20 06				20 26	20 41	21 06		21 41	22 06	22 26
Cathays	d	19 10			19 46	20 10				20 31	20 46	21 10		21 46	22 10	22 31
Rhymney [3]	d						19 22									
Pontlottyn	d						19 25									
Tir-phil	d						19 30									
Brithdir	d						19 32									
Bargoed	a						19 37									
	d						19 37									
Gilfach Fargoed	d						19 39									
Pengam	d						19 42									
Hengoed	d						19 45									
Ystrad Mynach	d						19 49									
Llanbradach	d						19 53									
Energlyn & Churchill Park	d						19 57									
Aber	d						19 59									
Caerphilly	d			19 10			20 03	20 10								
Lisvane & Thornhill	d			19 14			20 08	20 14								
Llanishen	d			19 16			20 10	20 16								
Heath High Level	d			19 19			20 13	20 19								
Coryton	d															
Whitchurch (Cardiff)	d															
Rhiwbina	d															
Birchgrove	d															
Ty Glas	d															
Heath Low Level	d															
Cardiff Queen Street [3]	a	19 15		19 25	19 50	20 15	20 20	20 25		20 35	20 50	21 15		21 50	22 15	22 35
	d	19 16		19 26	19 51	20 15	20 21	20 26		20 36	20 51	21 16		21 51	22 16	22 36
Cardiff Central [7]	a	19 20		19 30	19 55	20 19	20 24	20 30		20 40	20 55	21 21		21 56	22 21	22 41
	d	19 25			19 55		20 25		20 32	20 41	20 55	21 25			22 25	
Grangetown	d	19 29			19 59		20 29		20 36	20 45	20 59	21 29			22 29	
Dingle Road	d								20 41							
Penarth	a								20 46							
Cogan	d	19 33			20 03		20 33			20 48	21 03	21 33			22 33	
Eastbrook	d	19 35			20 05		20 35			20 51	21 05	21 35			22 35	
Dinas Powys	d	19 37			20 07		20 37			20 53	21 07	21 37			22 37	
Cadoxton	d	19 41			20 11		20 41			20 57	21 11	21 41			22 41	
Barry Docks	d	19 44			20 14		20 44			21 00	21 14	21 44			22 44	
Barry [3]	d	19 48			20 18		20 48			21 05	21 18	21 48			22 48	
Barry Island	a	19 54			20 24		20 54				21 24	21 54			22 54	
Rhoose Cardiff Int Airport ✈	d									21 12						
Llantwit Major	d									21 22						
Bridgend	a									21 39						

When events are being held at the Principality Stadium, services are subject to alteration. Please check times before travelling.

For connections to Cardiff Bay please refer to Table T124

Table T130-R

Mondays to Fridays

16 December to 15 May

Bridgend, Barry Island, Barry, Penarth and Cardiff - Coryton, Rhymney, Pontypridd, Merthyr, Aberdare and Treherbert

Miles	Miles	Miles	Miles	Miles			AW	AW	AW	AW	AW	AW	AW	AW	AW	AW	AW	AW	AW	AW	AW	AW	AW	AW
—	—	0	—	—	**Bridgend**	d												05 42						
—	—	9¼	—	—	Llantwit Major	d												05 56						
—	—	15¾	—	—	Rhoose Cardiff Int Airport ✈	d												06 06						
0	—	—	—	—	**Barry Island**	d		05 15						05 51							06 26			
0¾	—	19	—	—	**Barry** [3]	d		05 19						05 55				06 15			06 30			
2	—	—	—	—	Barry Docks	d		05 22						05 58				06 18			06 33			
2¾	—	—	—	—	Cadoxton	d		05 25						06 01				06 21			06 36			
4¾	—	—	—	—	Dinas Powys	d		05 29						06 05				06 25			06 40			
5¾	—	—	—	—	Eastbrook	d		05 32						06 08				06 28			06 43			
6½	—	—	—	—	Cogan	d		05 34						06 10				06 30			06 45			
—	0	—	—	—	**Penarth**	d							06 02						06 32					
—	0¼	—	—	—	Dingle Road	d							06 04						06 34					
8¼	2¾	—	—	—	Grangetown	d		05 38					06 08	06 14				06 34	06 38		06 49			
9¼	3¾	—	0	—	**Cardiff Central** [7]	a		05 44					06 14	06 20				06 40	06 45		06 55			
—	—	—	—	—		d	05 26	05 46	05 52		05 56	06 11	06 15	06 21	06 26	06 32	06 36	06 41	06 46	06 52	06 56	07 06	07 06	07 11
9¾	4¼	0½	—	—	**Cardiff Queen Street** [3]	a	05 30	05 50	05 56		06 00	06 15	06 20	06 25	06 30	06 36	06 40	06 45	06 50	06 55	07 00	07 10		07 15
—	—	—	—	—		d	05 30	05 50	05 56		06 00	06 15	06 20	06 25	06 30	06 36	06 40	06 45	06 50	06 56	07 00	07 10		07 15
—	—	3	—	—	Heath Low Level	d			06 01					06 30						07 01				
—	4½	—	—	—	Ty Glas	d			06 03					06 33						07 04				
—	—	4¼	—	—	Birchgrove	d			06 05					06 34						07 05				
—	—	4¾	—	—	Rhiwbina	d			06 07					06 36						07 07				
—	—	5	—	—	Whitchurch (Cardiff)	d			06 08					06 38						07 09				
—	—	5½	—	—	**Coryton**	a			06 13					06 43						07 13				
—	6¾	—	—	—	Heath High Level	d		05 55					06 25						06 55					
—	7¾	—	—	—	Llanishen	d		05 58					06 28						06 58					
—	8¾	—	—	—	Lisvane & Thornhill	d		06 00					06 30						07 00					
—	11¼	—	—	—	Caerphilly	d		06a08					06 36						07 06					
—	12	—	—	—	Aber	d							06 38						07 08					
—	12¾	—	—	—	Energlyn & Churchill Park	d																		
—	14	—	—	—	Llanbradach	d							06 42						07 12					
—	16¾	—	—	—	Ystrad Mynach	d							06 47						07 17					
—	17¾	—	—	—	Hengoed	d							06 50						07 20					
—	19½	—	—	—	Pengam	d							06 53						07 23					
—	20½	—	—	—	Gilfach Fargoed	d																		
—	21	—	—	—	Bargoed	a							07 00						07 30					
—	—	—	—	—		d																		
—	22½	—	—	—	Brithdir	d																		
—	23½	—	—	—	Tir-phil	d																		
—	26	—	—	—	Pontlottyn	d																		
—	27	—	—	—	**Rhymney** [3]	a																		
10½	—	—	—	—	Cathays	d	05 33				06 03	06 18			06 33	06 38	06 43	06 48			07 03	07 12		07 18
13	—	—	—	—	Llandaf	d	05 37				06 07	06 22			06 37	06 43	06 47	06 52			07 07	07 17		07 22
—	—	—	1	—	Ninian Park	d																	07 10	
—	—	—	2½	—	Waun-gron Park	d																	07 13	
—	—	—	2¾	—	Fairwater	d																	07 15	
—	—	—	3¼	—	Danescourt	d																	07 17	
14	—	—	4¾	—	Radyr [3]	a	05 41				06 11	06 26			06 41	06 47	06 50	06 56			07 11	07 20	07 24	07 26
—	—	—	—	—		d	05 41				06 11	06 26			06 41		06 50	06 56			07 11	07 20		07 26
16	—	—	—	—	Taffs Well	d	05 45				06 15	06 30			06 45		06 54	07 00			07 15	07 24		07 30
18¼	—	—	—	—	Trefforest Estate	d	05 49				06 19				06 49						07 19			
20¾	—	—	—	—	Trefforest	d	05 53				06 23	06 37			06 53		07 01	07 07			07 23	07 31		07 37
21¾	—	0	—	0	**Pontypridd** [3]	a	05 57				06 28	06 41			06 58		07 05	07 11			07 28	07 35		07 41
—	—	—	—	—		d	06 00			06 11	06 28	06 42			06 58		07 05	07 12			07 28	07 35		07 42
—	—	3¼	—	3¼	Abercynon	d	06 07			06 19	06 35	06 49			07 05			07 19			07 35			07 49
—	—	—	—	6	Penrhiwceiber	d				06 24		06 55						07 25						07 55
—	—	—	—	7¼	Mountain Ash	a				06 30		07 00						07 30						07 59
—	—	—	—	—		d				06 33		07 03						07 33						08 03
—	—	—	—	8¼	Fernhill	d				06 36		07 06						07 36						08 06
—	—	—	—	9½	Cwmbach	d				06 40		07 10						07 40						08 10
—	—	—	—	11	**Aberdare**	a				06 46		07 16						07 46						08 16
—	—	4¾	—	—	Quakers Yard	d	06 11				06 39				07 09						07 39			
—	—	7	—	—	Merthyr Vale	a	06 16				06 44				07 14						07 44			
—	—	—	—	—		d	06 17				06 47				07 17						07 47			
—	—	8¾	—	—	Troed Y Rhiw	d	06 21				06 51				07 21						07 51			
—	—	10	—	—	Pentre-bach	d	06 24				06 54				07 24						07 54			
—	—	11½	—	—	**Merthyr Tydfil**	a	06 31				07 01				07 31						08 01			
23½	—	—	—	—	Trehafod	d											07 10					07 40		
24¾	—	—	—	—	Porth	a											07 13					07 43		
—	—	—	—	—		d											07 14					07 44		
26¼	—	—	—	—	Dinas Rhondda	d											07 18					07 48		
26¾	—	—	—	—	Tonypandy	d											07 20					07 50		
27¾	—	—	—	—	Llwynypia	d											07 22					07 52		
29	—	—	—	—	Ystrad Rhondda	a											07 25					07 55		
—	—	—	—	—		d											07 29					07 59		
29½	—	—	—	—	Ton Pentre	d											07 31					08 02		
30¾	—	—	—	—	Treorchy	d											07 34					08 06		
31¾	—	—	—	—	Ynyswen	d											07 37					08 09		
32¼	—	—	—	—	**Treherbert**	a											07 43					08 13		

When events are being held at the Principality Stadium, services are subject to alteration. Please check times before travelling.

For connections to Cardiff Bay please refer to Table T124

NRT DECEMBER 19 EDITION

Table T130-R

Mondays to Fridays

16 December to 15 May

Bridgend, Barry Island, Barry, Penarth and Cardiff - Coryton, Rhymney, Pontypridd, Merthyr, Aberdare and Treherbert

		AW	AW	AW	AW	AW	AW	AW	AW	AW	AW	AW	AW	AW	AW	AW	AW	AW	AW	AW	AW	AW
Bridgend	d							06 42														
Llantwit Major	d							06 56														
Rhoose Cardiff Int Airport ✈	d							07 06														
Barry Island	d			06 56							07 26					07 41			07 56			
Barry [3]	d			07 00				07 15			07 30					07 45			08 00			
Barry Docks	d			07 03				07 18			07 33					07 48			08 03			
Cadoxton	d			07 06				07 21			07 36					07 51			08 06			
Dinas Powys	d			07 10				07 25			07 40					07 55			08 10			
Eastbrook	d			07 13				07 28			07 43					07 58			08 13			
Cogan	d			07 15				07 30			07 45					08 00			08 15			
Penarth	d	07 02			07 18				07 34				07 47				08 03			08 18		
Dingle Road	d	07 04			07 20				07 36				07 49				08 05			08 20		
Grangetown	d	07 08		07 19	07 24			07 34	07 40		07 49		07 54			08 04	08 09		08 19	08 24		
Cardiff Central [7]	a	07 14		07 25	07 30			07 40	07 46		07 55		08 01			08 10	08 15		08 25	08 30		
	d	07 16	07 21	07 26	07 31	07 35	07 36	07 41	07 46	07 51	07 56	07 57	08 01	08 05	08 06	08 11	08 16	08 21	08 26	08 31	08 35	08 37
Cardiff Queen Street [3]	a	07 20	07 25	07 30	07 35	07 39		07 45	07 50	07 56	08 00		08 05	08 09		08 15	08 20	08 25	08 30	08 35	08 39	
	d	07 20	07 26	07 30	07 35	07 39		07 45	07 50	07 56	08 01		08 05	08 09		08 15	08 20	08 25	08 30	08 35	08 39	
Heath Low Level	d		07 31							08 01								08 30				
Ty Glas	d		07 34							08 03								08 33				
Birchgrove	d		07 35							08 05								08 34				
Rhiwbina	d		07 37							08 07								08 36				
Whitchurch (Cardiff)	d		07 39							08 08								08 38				
Coryton	a		07 43							08 13								08 43				
Heath High Level	d	07 25			07 40				07 55				08 10				08 25			08 40		
Llanishen	d	07 28			07 43				07 58				08 13				08 28			08 43		
Lisvane & Thornhill	d	07 31			07 45				08 00				08 16				08 30			08 45		
Caerphilly	d	07 37			07 51				08 06				08 22				08 37			08 51		
Aber	d	07 39			07 53				08 08				08 24				08 39			08 53		
Energlyn & Churchill Park	d	07 42											08 27				08 41					
Llanbradach	d	07 46			07 57				08 12				08 31				08 45			08 57		
Ystrad Mynach	d	07 52			08 02				08 17				08 37				08 50			09 02		
Hengoed	d	07 55			08 05				08 20				08 40				08 53			09 05		
Pengam	d	07 58			08 08				08 23				08 44				08 56			09 08		
Gilfach Fargoed	d												08 47									
Bargoed	a	08 05			08 14				08 30				08 52				09 02			09 15		
	d				08 14												09 02					
Brithdir	d				08 18												09 05					
Tir-phil	d				08 21												09 08					
Pontlottyn	d				08 25												09 13					
Rhymney [3]	a				08 31												09 18					
Cathays	d			07 33		07 42		07 48			08 03			08 12		08 18			08 33		08 42	
Llandaf	d			07 37		07 46		07 52			08 08			08 16		08 22			08 37		08 46	
Ninian Park	d						07 40								08 10							08 41
Waun-gron Park	d						07 43								08 13							08 44
Fairwater	d						07 45								08 15							08 46
Danescourt	d						07 47								08 17							08 48
Radyr [3]	a			07 41		07 50	07 54	07 56			08 12	08 10		08 20	08 24	08 26			08 41		08 50	08 54
	d			07 41		07 50		07 56			08 12			08 20		08 26			08 41		08 50	
Taffs Well	d			07 45		07 54		08 00			08 16			08 24		08 30			08 45		08 54	
Trefforest Estate	d			07 49							08 20								08 49			
Trefforest	d			07 53		08 01		08 07			08 24			08 31		08 37			08 53		09 01	
Pontypridd [3]	a			07 57		08 05		08 11			08 29			08 35		08 41			08 58		09 05	
	d			07 58		08 05		08 12			08 29			08 35		08 42			08 58		09 05	
Abercynon	d			08 05				08 19			08 36					08 49			09 05			
Penrhiwceiber	d							08 25								08 55						
Mountain Ash	a							08 30								09 00						
	d							08 33								09 03						
Fernhill	d							08 36								09 06						
Cwmbach	d							08 40								09 10						
Aberdare	a							08 46								09 16						
Quakers Yard	d			08 09							08 40								09 09			
Merthyr Vale	a			08 14							08 45								09 14			
	d			08 17							08 47								09 17			
Troed Y Rhiw	d			08 21							08 51								09 21			
Pentre-bach	d			08 24							08 54								09 24			
Merthyr Tydfil	a			08 31							09 01								09 31			
Trehafod	d					08 10								08 40							09 10	
Porth	a					08 13								08 43							09 13	
	d					08 14								08 44							09 14	
Dinas Rhondda	d					08 18								08 48							09 18	
Tonypandy	d					08 20								08 50							09 20	
Llwynypia	d					08 22								08 52							09 22	
Ystrad Rhondda	a					08 25								08 55							09 25	
	d					08 29								08 59							09 29	
Ton Pentre	d					08 31								09 01							09 31	
Treorchy	d					08 34								09 04							09 34	
Ynyswen	d					08 37								09 07							09 37	
Treherbert	a					08 42								09 12							09 42	

When events are being held at the Principality Stadium, services are subject to alteration. Please check times before travelling.

For connections to Cardiff Bay please refer to Table T124

Table T130-R

Mondays to Fridays
16 December to 15 May

Bridgend, Barry Island, Barry, Penarth and Cardiff - Coryton, Rhymney, Pontypridd, Merthyr, Aberdare and Treherbert

Station		AW	AW	AW	AW	AW	AW	AW	AW	AW	AW	AW	AW	AW	AW	AW	AW	AW	AW	AW	AW	AW	AW
Bridgend	d		07 42														08 42						
Llantwit Major	d		07 56														08 56						
Rhoose Cardiff Int Airport ✈	d		08 06														09 06						
Barry Island	d					08 26				08 41			08 56							09 27			
Barry [3]	d	08 13	08 21			08 30				08 45			09 00				09 15			09 31			
Barry Docks	d	08 16	08 24			08 33				08 48			09 03				09 18			09 34			
Cadoxton	d	08 19	08 27			08 36				08 51			09 06				09 21			09 37			
Dinas Powys	d	08 23				08 40				08 55			09 10				09 25			09 41			
Eastbrook	d	08 26				08 43				08 58			09 13				09 28			09 44			
Cogan	d	08 29				08 45				09 00			09 15				09 30			09 46			
Penarth	d			08 33			08 48							09 18				09 33				09 48	
Dingle Road	d			08 35			08 50							09 20				09 35				09 50	
Grangetown	d			08 39		08 49	08 54			09 04			09 19	09 24			09 34	09 39		09 50		09 54	
Cardiff Central [7]	a	08 40	08 41	08 45		08 55	09 00			09 10			09 25	09 30			09 40	09 45		09 56		10 00	
	d		08 42	08 46	08 51	08 56	09 01	09 05	09 06	09 11	09 16	09 21	09 26	09 31	09 35	09 36	09 41	09 46	09 51	09 56		10 01	10 05
Cardiff Queen Street [3]	a		08 46	08 50	08 55	09 00	09 05	09 09		09 15	09 20	09 25	09 30	09 35	09 39		09 45	09 50	09 55	10 00		10 05	10 09
	d		08 46	08 50	08 55	09 00	09 05	09 09		09 15	09 20	09 25	09 30	09 35	09 39		09 45	09 50	09 55	10 00		10 05	10 09
Heath Low Level	d				09 00							09 30							10 00				
Ty Glas	d				09 03							09 33							10 03				
Birchgrove	d				09 04							09 34							10 04				
Rhiwbina	d				09 06							09 36							10 06				
Whitchurch (Cardiff)	d				09 08							09 38							10 08				
Coryton	a				09 13							09 43							10 13				
Heath High Level	d			08 55			09 10				09 25			09 40				09 55				10 10	
Llanishen	d			08 58			09 13				09 28			09 43				09 58				10 13	
Lisvane & Thornhill	d			09 00			09 16				09 30			09 45				10 00				10 16	
Caerphilly	d			09 06			09 22				09 37			09 51				10 06				10 22	
Aber	d			09 08			09 24				09 39			09 53				10 08				10 24	
Energlyn & Churchill Park	d						09 27				09 41											10 27	
Llanbradach	d			09 12			09 31				09 45			09 57				10 12				10 31	
Ystrad Mynach	d			09 17			09 37				09 50			10 02				10 17				10 37	
Hengoed	d			09 20			09 40				09 53			10 05				10 20				10 40	
Pengam	d			09 23			09 44				09 56			10 08				10 23				10 44	
Gilfach Fargoed	d						09 47															10 47	
Bargoed	a			09 30			09 52				10 02			10 15				10 30				10 52	
	d										10 02												
Brithdir	d										10 05												
Tir-phil	d										10 08												
Pontlottyn	d										10 13												
Rhymney [3]	a										10 18												
Cathays	d		08 48			09 03		09 12		09 18			09 33		09 42		09 48			10 03			10 12
Llandaf	d		08 53			09 07		09 16		09 22			09 37		09 46		09 52			10 07			10 16
Ninian Park	d								09 11							09 40							
Waun-gron Park	d								09 14							09 43							
Fairwater	d								09 16							09 45							
Danescourt	d								09 18							09 47							
Radyr [3]	a		08 56			09 11		09 20	09 24	09 26			09 41		09 50	09 54	09 56			10 11			10 20
	d		08 56			09 11		09 20		09 26			09 41		09 50		09 56			10 11			10 20
Taffs Well	d		09 00			09 15		09 24		09 30			09 45		09 54		10 00			10 15			10 24
Trefforest Estate	d					09 19							09 49										
Trefforest	d		09 07			09 23		09 31		09 37			09 53		10 01		10 07			10 21			10 31
Pontypridd [3]	a		09 11			09 28		09 35		09 41			09 58		10 05		10 10			10 32			10 35
	d		09 12			09 28		09 35		09 42			09 58		10 05		10 12				10 34		10 35
Abercynon	d		09 19			09 35				09 49			10 05				10 19				10 40		
Penrhiwceiber	d		09 25							09 55							10 25						
Mountain Ash	a		09 30							10 00							10 30						
	d		09 33							10 03							10 33						
Fernhill	d		09 36							10 06							10 36						
Cwmbach	d		09 40							10 10							10 40						
Aberdare	a		09 46							10 16							10 46						
Quakers Yard	d					09 39							10 09								10 44		
Merthyr Vale	a					09 44							10 14								10 49		
	d					09 47							10 17								10 51		
Troed Y Rhiw	d					09 51							10 21								10 55		
Pentre-bach	d					09 54							10 24								10 58		
Merthyr Tydfil	a					10 01							10 31								11 06		
Trehafod	d							09 40							10 10								10 40
Porth	a							09 43							10 13								10 43
	d							09 44							10 14								10 44
Dinas Rhondda	d							09 48							10 18								10 48
Tonypandy	d							09 50							10 20								10 50
Llwynypia	d							09 52							10 22								10 52
Ystrad Rhondda	a							09 55							10 25								10 55
	d							09 59							10 29								10 59
Ton Pentre	d							10 01							10 31								11 01
Treorchy	d							10 04							10 34								11 04
Ynyswen	d							10 07							10 37								11 07
Treherbert	a							10 12							10 42								11 12

When events are being held at the Principality Stadium, services are subject to alteration. Please check times before travelling.

For connections to Cardiff Bay please refer to Table T124

Table T130-R

Mondays to Fridays
16 December to 15 May

Bridgend, Barry Island, Barry, Penarth and Cardiff - Coryton, Rhymney, Pontypridd, Merthyr, Aberdare and Treherbert

Station		AW	AW	AW	AW	AW	AW	AW	AW	AW	AW	AW	AW	AW	AW	AW	AW	AW	AW	AW	AW	AW
Bridgend	d									09 42												
Llantwit Major	d									09 56												
Rhoose Cardiff Int Airport ✈	d									10 06												
Barry Island	d		09 41			09 56								10 26				10 41			10 56	
Barry [3]	d		09 45			10 00				10 15				10 30				10 45			11 00	
Barry Docks	d		09 48			10 03				10 18				10 33				10 48			11 03	
Cadoxton	d		09 51			10 06				10 21				10 36				10 51			11 06	
Dinas Powys	d		09 55			10 10				10 25				10 40				10 55			11 10	
Eastbrook	d		09 58			10 13				10 28				10 43				10 58			11 13	
Cogan	d		10 00			10 15				10 30				10 45				11 00			11 15	
Penarth	d			10 03			10 18				10 33					10 48			11 03			11 18
Dingle Road	d			10 05			10 20				10 35					10 50			11 05			11 20
Grangetown	d		10 04	10 09		10 19	10 24			10 34	10 40			10 49		10 54		11 04	11 09		11 19	11 24
Cardiff Central [7]	a		10 10	10 15		10 25	10 30			10 41	10 45			10 55		11 00		11 10	11 15		11 25	11 30
	d	10 06	10 11	10 16	10 21	10 26	10 31	10 35	10 36		10 46	10 51	10 55	10 56		11 01	11 07	11 11	11 16	11 21	11 26	11 31
Cardiff Queen Street [3]	a		10 15	10 20	10 25	10 30	10 35	10 39			10 50	10 55		11 00		11 05		11 15	11 20	11 25	11 30	11 35
	d		10 15	10 20	10 25	10 30	10 35	10 39			10 50	10 55		11 00		11 05		11 15	11 20	11 25	11 30	11 35
Heath Low Level	d				10 30							11 00								11 30		
Ty Glas	d				10 33							11 03								11 33		
Birchgrove	d				10 34							11 04								11 34		
Rhiwbina	d				10 36							11 06								11 36		
Whitchurch (Cardiff)	d				10 38							11 08								11 38		
Coryton	a				10 43							11 13								11 43		
Heath High Level	d			10 25			10 40				10 55					11 10			11 25			11 40
Llanishen	d			10 28			10 43				10 58					11 13			11 28			11 43
Lisvane & Thornhill	d			10 30			10 45				11 00					11 16			11 30			11 45
Caerphilly	d			10 37			10 51				11 06					11 22			11 37			11 51
Aber	d			10 39			10 53				11 08					11 24			11 39			11 53
Energlyn & Churchill Park	d			10 41												11 27			11 41			
Llanbradach	d			10 45			10 57				11 12					11 31			11 45			11 57
Ystrad Mynach	d			10 50			11 02				11 17					11 37			11 50			12 02
Hengoed	d			10 53			11 05				11 20					11 40			11 53			12 05
Pengam	d			10 56			11 08				11 23					11 44			11 56			12 08
Gilfach Fargoed	d															11 47						
Bargoed	a			11 02			11 15				11 30					11 52			12 02			12 15
	d			11 02															12 02			
Brithdir	d			11 05															12 05			
Tir-phil	d			11 08															12 08			
Pontlottyn	d			11 13															12 13			
Rhymney [3]	a			11 18															12 18			
Cathays	d		10 18			10 33		10 42						11 03				11 18			11 33	
Llandaf	d		10 22			10 37		10 46						11 07				11 22			11 37	
Ninian Park	d	10 10							10 41								11 11					
Waun-gron Park	d	10 13							10 44								11 14					
Fairwater	d	10 15							10 46								11 16					
Danescourt	d	10 17							10 48						←		11 18					
Radyr [3]	a	10 24	10 26			10 41		10 50	10 54				11 08	11 11	11 08		11 24	11 26			11 41	
	d		10 26			10 41		10 50					11 20	11 11	11 20			11 26			11 41	
Taffs Well	d		10 30			10 45		10 54					→	11 15	11 24			11 30			11 45	
Trefforest Estate	d					10 49								11 19							11 49	
Trefforest	d		10 37			10 53		11 01						11 23	11 31			11 37			11 53	
Pontypridd [3]	a		10 41			10 58		11 05						11 28	11 34			11 41			11 58	
	d		10 42			10 58		11 05						11 28	11 35			11 42			11 58	
Abercynon	d		10 49			11 05								11 35				11 49			12 05	
Penrhiwceiber	d		10 55															11 55				
Mountain Ash	a		11 00															12 00				
	d		11 03															12 03				
Fernhill	d		11 06															12 06				
Cwmbach	d		11 10															12 10				
Aberdare	a		11 16															12 16				
Quakers Yard	d					11 09								11 39							12 09	
Merthyr Vale	a					11 14								11 44							12 14	
	d					11 17								11 47							12 17	
Troed Y Rhiw	d					11 21								11 51							12 21	
Pentre-bach	d					11 24								11 54							12 24	
Merthyr Tydfil	a					11 31								12 01							12 31	
Trehafod	d							11 10							11 40							
Porth	a							11 13							11 43							
	d							11 14							11 44							
Dinas Rhondda	d							11 18							11 48							
Tonypandy	d							11 20							11 50							
Llwynypia	d							11 22							11 52							
Ystrad Rhondda	a							11 25							11 55							
	d							11 29							11 59							
Ton Pentre	d							11 31							12 01							
Treorchy	d							11 34							12 04							
Ynyswen	d							11 37							12 07							
Treherbert	a							11 42							12 12							

When events are being held at the Principality Stadium, services are subject to alteration. Please check times before travelling.

For connections to Cardiff Bay please refer to Table T124

Table T130-R

Mondays to Fridays

16 December to 15 May

Bridgend, Barry Island, Barry, Penarth and Cardiff - Coryton, Rhymney, Pontypridd, Merthyr, Aberdare and Treherbert

Station		AW	AW	AW	AW	AW	AW	AW	AW	AW	AW	AW	AW	AW	AW	AW	AW	AW	AW	AW	AW	AW	AW
Bridgend	d			10 42														11 42					
Llantwit Major	d			10 56														11 56					
Rhoose Cardiff Int Airport ✈	d			11 06														12 06					
Barry Island	d						11 26				11 41			11 56								12 26	
Barry 3	d			11 15			11 30				11 45			12 00				12 15				12 30	
Barry Docks	d			11 18			11 33				11 48			12 03				12 18				12 33	
Cadoxton	d			11 21			11 36				11 51			12 06				12 21				12 36	
Dinas Powys	d			11 25			11 40				11 55			12 10				12 25				12 40	
Eastbrook	d			11 28			11 43				11 58			12 13				12 28				12 43	
Cogan	d			11 30			11 45				12 00			12 15				12 30				12 45	
Penarth	d				11 33			11 48				12 03			12 18					12 33			12 48
Dingle Road	d				11 35			11 50				12 05			12 20					12 35			12 50
Grangetown	d			11 34	11 39		11 49	11 54			12 04	12 09		12 19	12 24			12 34		12 39		12 49	12 54
Cardiff Central 7	a			11 40	11 45		11 55	12 01			12 11	12 15		12 25	12 30			12 40		12 45		12 55	13 00
	d	11 35	11 36	11 41	11 46	11 51	11 56	12 01	12 05	12 07	12 11	12 16	12 21	12 26	12 31	12 35	12 36		12 41	12 46	12 51	12 56	13 01
Cardiff Queen Street 3	a	11 39		11 45	11 50	11 55	12 00	12 05	12 09		12 15	12 20	12 25	12 30	12 35	12 39			12 45	12 50	12 55	13 00	13 05
	d	11 39		11 45	11 50	11 55	12 00	12 05	12 09		12 15	12 20	12 25	12 30	12 35	12 39			12 45	12 50	12 55	13 00	13 05
Heath Low Level	d					12 00							12 30								13 00		
Ty Glas	d					12 03							12 33								13 03		
Birchgrove	d					12 04							12 34								13 04		
Rhiwbina	d					12 06							12 36								13 06		
Whitchurch (Cardiff)	d					12 08							12 38								13 08		
Coryton	a					12 13							12 43								13 13		
Heath High Level	d				11 55			12 10				12 25			12 40					12 55			13 10
Llanishen	d				11 58			12 13				12 28			12 43					12 58			13 13
Lisvane & Thornhill	d				12 00			12 16				12 30			12 45					13 00			13 16
Caerphilly	d				12 06			12 22				12 37			12 51					13 06			13 22
Aber	d				12 08			12 24				12 39			12 53					13 08			13 24
Energlyn & Churchill Park	d							12 27				12 41											13 27
Llanbradach	d				12 12			12 31				12 45			12 57					13 12			13 31
Ystrad Mynach	d				12 17			12 37				12 50			13 02					13 17			13 37
Hengoed	d				12 20			12 40				12 53			13 05					13 20			13 40
Pengam	d				12 23			12 44				12 56			13 08					13 23			13 44
Gilfach Fargoed	d							12 47															13 47
Bargoed	a				12 30			12 52				13 02			13 15					13 30			13 52
	d											13 02											
Brithdir	d											13 05											
Tir-phil	d											13 08											
Pontlottyn	d											13 13											
Rhymney 3	a											13 18											
Cathays	d	11 42		11 48			12 03		12 12		12 18			12 33		12 42			12 48			13 03	
Llandaf	d	11 46		11 52			12 07		12 16		12 22			12 37		12 46			12 52			13 07	
Ninian Park	d		11 41							12 11							12 40						
Waun-gron Park	d		11 44							12 14							12 43						
Fairwater	d		11 46							12 16							12 45						
Danescourt	d		11 48							12 18							12 47						
Radyr 3	a	11 50	11 54	11 56			12 11		12 20	12 25	12 25			12 41		12 50	12 54		12 56			13 11	
	d	11 50		11 56			12 11		12 20		12 25			12 41		12 50			12 56			13 11	
Taffs Well	d	11 54		12 00			12 15		12 24		12 29			12 45		12 54			13 00			13 15	
Trefforest Estate	d						12 19							12 49								13 19	
Trefforest	d	12 01		12 07			12 23		12 31		12 36			12 53		13 01			13 07			13 23	
Pontypridd 3	a	12 05		12 11			12 28		12 35		12 41			12 58		13 05			13 11			13 28	
	d	12 05		12 12			12 28		12 35					12 58		13 05			13 12			13 28	
Abercynon	d			12 20			12 35							13 05					13 19			13 35	
Penrhiwceiber	d			12 26															13 25				
Mountain Ash	a			12 31															13 30				
	d			12 33															13 33				
Fernhill	d			12 36															13 36				
Cwmbach	d			12 40															13 40				
Aberdare	a			12 46															13 46				
Quakers Yard	d						12 39							13 09								13 39	
Merthyr Vale	a						12 44							13 14								13 44	
	d						12 47							13 17								13 47	
Troed Y Rhiw	d						12 51							13 21								13 51	
Pentre-bach	d						12 54							13 24								13 54	
Merthyr Tydfil	a						13 01							13 31								14 01	
Trehafod	d	12 10							12 40							13 10							
Porth	a	12 13							12 43							13 13							
	d	12 14							12 44							13 14							
Dinas Rhondda	d	12 18							12 48							13 18							
Tonypandy	d	12 20							12 50							13 20							
Llwynypia	d	12 22							12 52							13 22							
Ystrad Rhondda	a	12 25							12 55							13 25							
	d	12 29							12 59							13 29							
Ton Pentre	d	12 31							13 01							13 31							
Treorchy	d	12 34							13 04							13 34							
Ynyswen	d	12 37							13 07							13 37							
Treherbert	a	12 42							13 12							13 42							

When events are being held at the Principality Stadium, services are subject to alteration. Please check times before travelling.

For connections to Cardiff Bay please refer to Table T124

Table T130-R

Mondays to Fridays

16 December to 15 May

Bridgend, Barry Island, Barry, Penarth and Cardiff - Coryton, Rhymney, Pontypridd, Merthyr, Aberdare and Treherbert

Station		AW	AW	AW	AW	AW	AW	AW	AW	AW	AW	AW	AW	AW	AW	AW	AW	AW	AW	AW	AW	AW	AW
Bridgend	d										12 42												
Llantwit Major	d										12 56												
Rhoose Cardiff Int Airport ✈	d										13 06												
Barry Island	d			12 41			12 56							13 26							13 56		
Barry 3	d			12 45			13 00				13 15			13 30							14 00		
Barry Docks	d			12 48			13 03				13 18			13 33							14 03		
Cadoxton	d			12 51			13 06				13 21			13 36							14 06		
Dinas Powys	d			12 55			13 10				13 25			13 40							14 10		
Eastbrook	d			12 58			13 13				13 28			13 43							14 13		
Cogan	d			13 00			13 15				13 30			13 45							14 15		
Penarth	d				13 03			13 18				13 33			13 48				14 03			14 18	
Dingle Road	d				13 05			13 20				13 35			13 50				14 05			14 20	
Grangetown	d			13 04	13 09		13 19	13 24			13 34	13 39		13 49	13 54				14 09		14 19	14 24	
Cardiff Central 7	a			13 10	13 16		13 25	13 30			13 40	13 45		13 55	14 00				14 15		14 25	14 30	
	d	13 05	13 06	13 11	13 16	13 21	13 26	13 31	13 35	13 36	13 41	13 46	13 51	13 56	14 01	14 05	14 06	14 13	14 16	14 21	14 26	14 31	14 35
Cardiff Queen Street 3	a	13 09		13 15	13 20	13 25	13 30	13 35	13 39		13 45	13 50	13 55	14 00	14 05	14 09		14 16	14 20	14 25	14 30	14 35	14 39
	d	13 09		13 15	13 20	13 25	13 30	13 35	13 39		13 45	13 50	13 55	14 00	14 05	14 09		14 17	14 20	14 25	14 30	14 35	14 39
Heath Low Level	d					13 30							14 00							14 30			
Ty Glas	d					13 33							14 03							14 33			
Birchgrove	d					13 34							14 04							14 34			
Rhiwbina	d					13 36							14 06							14 36			
Whitchurch (Cardiff)	d					13 38							14 08							14 38			
Coryton	a					13 43							14 13							14 43			
Heath High Level	d				13 25			13 40				13 55			14 10				14 25			14 40	
Llanishen	d				13 28			13 43				13 58			14 13				14 28			14 43	
Lisvane & Thornhill	d				13 30			13 45				14 00			14 16				14 30			14 45	
Caerphilly	d				13 37			13 51				14 06			14 22				14 37			14 51	
Aber	d				13 39			13 53				14 08			14 24				14 39			14 53	
Energlyn & Churchill Park	d				13 41										14 27				14 41				
Llanbradach	d				13 45			13 57				14 12			14 31				14 45			14 57	
Ystrad Mynach	d				13 50			14 02				14 17			14 37				14 50			15 02	
Hengoed	d				13 53			14 05				14 20			14 40				14 53			15 05	
Pengam	d				13 56			14 08				14 23			14 44				14 56			15 08	
Gilfach Fargoed	d														14 47								
Bargoed	a				14 02			14 15				14 30			14 52				15 02			15 15	
	d				14 02														15 02				
Brithdir	d				14 05														15 05				
Tir-phil	d				14 08														15 08				
Pontlottyn	d				14 13														15 13				
Rhymney 3	a				14 18														15 18				
Cathays	d	13 12		13 18			13 33		13 42		13 48			14 03		14 12		14 19			14 33		14 42
Llandaf	d	13 16		13 22			13 37		13 46		13 52			14 07		14 16		14 24			14 37		14 46
Ninian Park	d		13 10							13 40							14 10						
Waun-gron Park	d		13 13							13 43							14 13						
Fairwater	d		13 15							13 45							14 15						
Danescourt	d		13 17							13 47							14 17						
Radyr 3	a	13 20	13 24	13 26			13 41		13 50	13 54	13 56			14 11		14 20	14 24	14 28			14 41		14 50
	d	13 20		13 26			13 41		13 50		13 56			14 11		14 20		14 28			14 41		14 50
Taffs Well	d	13 24		13 30			13 45		13 54		14 00			14 15		14 24		14 32			14 45		14 54
Trefforest Estate	d						13 49							14 19							14 49		
Trefforest	d	13 31		13 37			13 53		14 01		14 07			14 23		14 31		14 39			14 53		15 01
Pontypridd 3	a	13 35		13 41			13 58		14 05		14 11			14 28		14 35		14 43			14 58		15 05
	d	13 35		13 42			13 58		14 05		14 12			14 28		14 35		14 43			14 58		15 05
Abercynon	d			13 49			14 05				14 19			14 35				14 50			15 05		
Penrhiwceiber	d			13 55							14 25							14 56					
Mountain Ash	a			14 00							14 30							15 01					
	d			14 03							14 33							15 03					
Fernhill	d			14 06							14 36							15 06					
Cwmbach	d			14 10							14 40							15 10					
Aberdare	a			14 16							14 46							15 16					
Quakers Yard	d						14 09							14 39							15 09		
Merthyr Vale	a						14 14							14 44							15 14		
	d						14 17							14 47							15 17		
Troed Y Rhiw	d						14 21							14 51							15 21		
Pentre-bach	d						14 24							14 54							15 24		
Merthyr Tydfil	a						14 31							15 01							15 31		
Trehafod	d	13 40							14 10							14 40							15 10
Porth	a	13 43							14 13							14 43							15 13
	d	13 44							14 14							14 44							15 14
Dinas Rhondda	d	13 48							14 18							14 48							15 18
Tonypandy	d	13 50							14 20							14 50							15 20
Llwynypia	d	13 52							14 22							14 52							15 22
Ystrad Rhondda	a	13 55							14 25							14 55							15 25
	d	13 59							14 29							14 59							15 29
Ton Pentre	d	14 01							14 31							15 01							15 31
Treorchy	d	14 04							14 34							15 04							15 34
Ynyswen	d	14 07							14 37							15 07							15 37
Treherbert	a	14 12							14 42							15 12							15 42

When events are being held at the Principality Stadium, services are subject to alteration. Please check times before travelling.

For connections to Cardiff Bay please refer to Table T124

Table T130-R

Mondays to Fridays
16 December to 15 May

Bridgend, Barry Island, Barry, Penarth and Cardiff - Coryton, Rhymney, Pontypridd, Merthyr, Aberdare and Treherbert

		AW	AW	AW	AW	AW	AW	AW	AW	AW	AW	AW	AW	AW	AW	AW	AW	AW	AW	AW	AW	AW
Bridgend	d		13 42																14 42			
Llantwit Major	d		13 56																14 56			
Rhoose Cardiff Int Airport ✈	d		14 06																15 06			
Barry Island	d							14 26				14 41			14 56							15 26
Barry 3	d		14 15					14 30				14 45			15 00				15 15			15 30
Barry Docks	d		14 18					14 33				14 48			15 04				15 18			15 33
Cadoxton	d		14 21					14 36				14 51			15 09				15 21			15 36
Dinas Powys	d		14 25					14 40				14 55			15 13				15 25			15 40
Eastbrook	d		14 28					14 43				14 58			15 15				15 28			15 43
Cogan	d		14 30					14 45				15 00			15 17				15 30			15 45
Penarth	d				14 33								15 03			15 18				15 33		
Dingle Road	d				14 35								15 05			15 20				15 35		
Grangetown	d				14 39			14 49				15 04	15 09		15 21	15 24			15 34	15 39		15 49
Cardiff Central 7	a		14 38		14 45			14 55				15 10	15 15		15 26	15 30			15 40	15 45		15 55
	d	14 36	14 42	14 42	14 46	14 51	14 52	14 56		15 01	15 07	15 11	15 16	15 21	15 26	15 31	15 35	15 36	15 41	15 46	15 51	15 56
Cardiff Queen Street 3	a		14 46	14 46	14 49	14 55		15 00		15 05		15 15	15 20	15 25	15 30	15 35	15 39		15 45	15 50	15 55	16 00
	d		14 46	14 46	14 50	14 55		15 00		15 05		15 15	15 20	15 25	15 30	15 35	15 39		15 45	15 50	15 55	16 00
Heath Low Level	d					15 00								15 30							16 00	
Ty Glas	d					15 03								15 33							16 03	
Birchgrove	d					15 04								15 34							16 04	
Rhiwbina	d					15 06								15 36							16 06	
Whitchurch (Cardiff)	d					15 08								15 38							16 08	
Coryton	a					15 13								15 43							16 13	
Heath High Level	d				14 55					15 10			15 25			15 40				15 55		
Llanishen	d				14 58					15 13			15 28			15 43				15 58		
Lisvane & Thornhill	d				15 00					15 16			15 30			15 45				16 00		
Caerphilly	d				15 06					15 22			15 37			15 51				16 06		
Aber	d				15 08					15 24			15 39			15 53				16 08		
Energlyn & Churchill Park	d									15 27			15 41									
Llanbradach	d				15 12					15 31			15 45			15 57				16 12		
Ystrad Mynach	d				15 17					15 37			15 50			16 02				16 17		
Hengoed	d				15 20					15 40			15 53			16 05				16 20		
Pengam	d				15 23					15 44			15 56			16 08				16 23		
Gilfach Fargoed	d									15 47												
Bargoed	a				15 28					15 52			16 02			16 15				16 30		
	d												16 02									
Brithdir	d												16 05									
Tir-phil	d												16 08									
Pontlottyn	d												16 13									
Rhymney 3	a												16 20									
Cathays	d		14 48	14 48				15 03				15 18			15 33		15 42		15 48			16 03
Llandaf	d		14 53	14 53				15 07				15 22			15 37		15 46		15 52			16 07
Ninian Park	d	14 40									15 11							15 40				
Waun-gron Park	d	14 43									15 14							15 43				
Fairwater	d	14 45									15 16							15 45				
Danescourt	d	14 47							←		15 18							15 47				
Radyr 3	a	14 54	14 57	14 57			15 07	15 11	15 07		15 24	15 26			15 41		15 50	15 54	15 56			16 11
	d		14 57	14 57			15 20	15 11	15 20			15 26			15 41		15 50		15 56			16 11
Taffs Well	d		15 01	15 01			→	15 15	15 24			15 30			15 45		15 54		16 00			16 15
Trefforest Estate	d							15 19							15 49							16 19
Trefforest	d		15 08	15 08				15 23	15 31			15 37			15 53		16 01		16 07			16 23
Pontypridd 3	a		15 12	15 12				15 28	15 34			15 41			15 58		16 05		16 11			16 28
	d		15 12	15 12				15 28	15 35			15 42			15 58		16 05		16 12			16 28
Abercynon	d		15 19	15 19				15 35				15 49			16 05				16 19			16 35
Penrhiwceiber	d		15 25	15 25								15 55							16 25			
Mountain Ash	a		15 31	15 31								16 00							16 30			
	d		15 33	15 33								16 03							16 33			
Fernhill	d		15 36	15 36								16 06							16 36			
Cwmbach	d		15 40	15 40								16 10							16 40			
Aberdare	a		15 46	15 46								16 16							16 46			
Quakers Yard	d							15 39							16 09							16 39
Merthyr Vale	a							15 44							16 14							16 44
	d							15 47							16 17							16 47
Troed Y Rhiw	d							15 51							16 21							16 51
Pentre-bach	d							15 54							16 24							16 54
Merthyr Tydfil	a							16 01							16 31							17 01
Trehafod	d								15 40								16 10					
Porth	a								15 43								16 13					
	d								15 44								16 14					
Dinas Rhondda	d								15 48								16 18					
Tonypandy	d								15 50								16 20					
Llwynypia	d								15 52								16 22					
Ystrad Rhondda	a								15 55								16 25					
	d								15 59								16 29					
Ton Pentre	d								16 01								16 31					
Treorchy	d								16 04								16 34					
Ynyswen	d								16 07								16 37					
Treherbert	a								16 12								16 42					

When events are being held at the Principality Stadium, services are subject to alteration. Please check times before travelling.

For connections to Cardiff Bay please refer to Table T124

Table T130-R

Mondays to Fridays
16 December to 15 May

Bridgend, Barry Island, Barry, Penarth and Cardiff - Coryton, Rhymney, Pontypridd, Merthyr, Aberdare and Treherbert

		AW	AW	AW	AW	AW	AW	AW	AW	AW	AW	AW	AW	AW	AW	AW	AW	AW	AW	AW	AW	AW	AW
Bridgend	d											15 42											
Llantwit Major	d											15 56											
Rhoose Cardiff Int Airport ✈	d											16 06											
Barry Island	d				15 41			15 56							16 26				16 41			16 56	
Barry 3	d				15 45			16 00				16 15			16 30				16 45			17 00	
Barry Docks	d				15 48			16 03				16 18			16 33				16 48			17 03	
Cadoxton	d				15 51			16 06				16 21			16 36				16 51			17 06	
Dinas Powys	d				15 55			16 10				16 25			16 40				16 55			17 10	
Eastbrook	d				15 58			16 13				16 28			16 43				16 58			17 13	
Cogan	d				16 00			16 15				16 30			16 45				17 00			17 15	
Penarth	d	15 48				16 03			16 18				16 33							17 03			17 18
Dingle Road	d	15 50				16 05			16 20				16 35							17 05			17 20
Grangetown	d	15 54			16 04	16 09		16 19	16 24			16 34	16 39		16 49				17 04	17 09		17 19	17 24
Cardiff Central 7	a	16 00			16 10	16 15		16 25	16 30			16 40	16 45		16 55				17 10	17 15		17 25	17 30
	d	16 01	16 05	16 06	16 11	16 16	16 21	16 26	16 31	16 35	16 36	16 41	16 46	16 51	16 56	17 01	17 05	17 06	17 11	17 16	17 21	17 26	17 31
Cardiff Queen Street 3	a	16 05	16 09		16 15	16 20	16 25	16 30	16 35	16 39		16 45	16 50	16 55	17 00	17 05	17 09		17 15	17 20	17 25	17 30	17 35
	d	16 05	16 09		16 15	16 20	16 25	16 30	16 35	16 39		16 45	16 50	16 55	17 00	17 06	17 09		17 15	17 20	17 25	17 30	17 35
Heath Low Level	d						16 30							17 00							17 30		
Ty Glas	d						16 33							17 03							17 33		
Birchgrove	d						16 34							17 04							17 34		
Rhiwbina	d						16 36							17 06							17 36		
Whitchurch (Cardiff)	d						16 38							17 08							17 38		
Coryton	a						16 43							17 13							17 43		
Heath High Level	d	16 10				16 25			16 40				16 55			17 10				17 25			17 40
Llanishen	d	16 13				16 28			16 43				16 58			17 14				17 28			17 44
Lisvane & Thornhill	d	16 16				16 30			16 45				17 00			17 17				17 31			17 47
Caerphilly	d	16 22				16 37			16 51				17 06			17 22				17 37			17 53
Aber	d	16 24				16 39			16 53				17 08			17 24				17 39			17 55
Energlyn & Churchill Park	d	16 27				16 41										17 27				17 41			17 58
Llanbradach	d	16 31				16 45			16 57				17 12			17 31				17 45			18 02
Ystrad Mynach	d	16 37				16 50			17 02				17 17			17 37				17 50			18 08
Hengoed	d	16 40				16 53			17 05				17 20			17 40				17 53			18 11
Pengam	d	16 44				16 56			17 08				17 23			17 44				17 56			18 15
Gilfach Fargoed	d	16 47																					18 18
Bargoed	a	16 52				17 02			17 15				17 30			17 50				18 03			18 22
	d					17 02										17 51							18 23
Brithdir	d					17 05										17 54							18 26
Tir-phil	d					17 08										17 58							18 30
Pontlottyn	d					17 13										18 02							18 34
Rhymney 3	a					17 18										18 07							18 40
Cathays	d		16 12		16 18			16 33		16 42		16 48			17 03		17 12		17 18			17 33	
Llandaf	d		16 16		16 22			16 37		16 46		16 52			17 07		17 16		17 22			17 37	
Ninian Park	d			16 11							16 40							17 10					
Waun-gron Park	d			16 14							16 43							17 13					
Fairwater	d			16 16							16 45							17 15					
Danescourt	d			16 18							16 47							17 17					
Radyr 3	a		16 20	16 24	16 26			16 41		16 50	16 54	16 56			17 11		17 20	17 24	17 26			17 41	
	d		16 20		16 26			16 41		16 50		16 56			17 11		17 20		17 26			17 41	
Taffs Well	d		16 24		16 30			16 45		16 54		17 00			17 15		17 24		17 30			17 45	
Trefforest Estate	d							16 49							17 19							17 49	
Trefforest	d		16 31		16 37			16 53		17 01		17 07			17 23		17 31		17 37			17 53	
Pontypridd 3	a		16 35		16 41			16 58		17 05		17 11			17 28		17 35		17 41			17 58	
	d		16 35		16 42			16 58		17 05		17 12			17 28		17 35		17 42			17 58	
Abercynon	d				16 49			17 05				17 19			17 35				17 49			18 05	
Penrhiwceiber	d				16 55							17 25							17 55				
Mountain Ash	a				17 00							17 30							18 00				
	d				17 03							17 33							18 03				
Fernhill	d				17 06							17 36							18 06				
Cwmbach	d				17 10							17 40							18 10				
Aberdare	a				17 16							17 46							18 16				
Quakers Yard	d							17 09							17 39							18 09	
Merthyr Vale	a							17 14							17 44							18 14	
	d							17 17							17 47							18 17	
Troed Y Rhiw	d							17 21							17 51							18 21	
Pentre-bach	d							17 24							17 54							18 24	
Merthyr Tydfil	a							17 31							18 01							18 31	
Trehafod	d		16 40							17 10							17 40						
Porth	a		16 43							17 13							17 43						
	d		16 44							17 14							17 44						
Dinas Rhondda	d		16 48							17 18							17 48						
Tonypandy	d		16 50							17 20							17 50						
Llwynypia	d		16 52							17 22							17 52						
Ystrad Rhondda	a		16 55							17 25							17 55						
	d		16 59							17 29							17 59						
Ton Pentre	d		17 01							17 31							18 01						
Treorchy	d		17 04							17 34							18 04						
Ynyswen	d		17 07							17 37							18 07						
Treherbert	a		17 12							17 42							18 12						

When events are being held at the Principality Stadium, services are subject to alteration. Please check times before travelling.

For connections to Cardiff Bay please refer to Table T124

Table T130-R

Mondays to Fridays
16 December to 15 May

Bridgend, Barry Island, Barry, Penarth and Cardiff - Coryton, Rhymney, Pontypridd, Merthyr, Aberdare and Treherbert

		AW	AW		AW	AW	AW	AW	AW	AW	AW	AW	AW		AW	AW	AW	AW	AW	AW	AW	AW	AW		AW
Bridgend	d				16 42																17 42				
Llantwit Major	d				16 56																17 56				
Rhoose Cardiff Int Airport ✈	d				17 06																18 06				
Barry Island	d								17 26				17 41				17 56								18 26
Barry 3	d				17 15				17 30				17 45				18 00				18 15				18 31
Barry Docks	d				17 18				17 33				17 48				18 03				18 18				18 34
Cadoxton	d				17 21				17 36				17 51				18 06				18 21				18 37
Dinas Powys	d				17 25				17 40				17 55				18 10				18 25				18 41
Eastbrook	d				17 28				17 43				17 58				18 13				18 28				18 43
Cogan	d				17 30				17 45				18 00				18 15				18 30				18 46
Penarth	d						17 33			17 48					18 03			18 18				18 33			
Dingle Road	d						17 35			17 50					18 05			18 20				18 35			
Grangetown	d				17 34		17 39		17 49	17 54			18 04		18 09		18 19	18 24			18 34	18 39			18 50
Cardiff Central 7	a				17 40		17 49		17 55	18 00			18 10		18 15		18 25	18 30			18 40	18 46			18 57
	d	17 35	17 36		17 41	17 46		17 51	17 56	18 01	18 05	18 06	18 11		18 16	18 21	18 26	18 31	18 35	18 36	18 42		18 51		
Cardiff Queen Street 3	a	17 39			17 45	17 50		17 55	18 00	18 05	18 09		18 15		18 20	18 25	18 30	18 35	18 39		18 46		18 55		
	d	17 39			17 45	17 50		17 55	18 00	18 05	18 09		18 15		18 20	18 25	18 30	18 35	18 39		18 46		18 56		
Heath Low Level	d							18 00								18 30							19 01		
Ty Glas	d							18 03								18 33							19 03		
Birchgrove	d							18 04								18 34							19 05		
Rhiwbina	d							18 06								18 36							19 07		
Whitchurch (Cardiff)	d							18 08								18 38							19 08		
Coryton	a							18 13								18 43							19 13		
Heath High Level	d					17 55				18 10					18 25			18 40							
Llanishen	d					17 59				18 13					18 28			18 43							
Lisvane & Thornhill	d					18 02				18 15					18 30			18 45							
Caerphilly	d					18 08				18 21					18 36			18 52							
Aber	d					18 11				18 23					18 38			18 54							
Energlyn & Churchill Park	d					18 14									18 41			18 56							
Llanbradach	d					18 18				18 27					18 44			19 00							
Ystrad Mynach	d					18 24				18 32					18a52			19 05							
Hengoed	d					18 27				18 35								19 08							
Pengam	d					18 31				18 38								19 11							
Gilfach Fargoed	d									18 41								19 14							
Bargoed	a					18 37				18 47								19 19							
	d					18 37												19 19							
Brithdir	d					18 41												19 23							
Tir-phil	d					18 46												19 26							
Pontlottyn	d					18 51												19 30							
Rhymney 3	a					18 57												19 35							
Cathays	d	17 42			17 48				18 03		18 12		18 18				18 33		18 42		18 49				
Llandaf	d	17 46			17 52				18 07		18 16		18 22				18 37		18 46		18 53				
Ninian Park	d		17 40									18 10								18 40					
Waun-gron Park	d		17 43									18 13								18 43					
Fairwater	d		17 45									18 15								18 45					
Danescourt	d		17 47									18 17								18 47					
Radyr 3	a	17 50	17 54		17 56				18 11		18 20	18 24	18 26				18 41		18 50	18 54	18 57				
	d	17 50			17 56				18 11		18 20		18 26				18 41		18 50		18 57				
Taffs Well	d	17 54			18 00				18 15		18 24		18 30				18 45		18 54		19 01				
Trefforest Estate	d								18 19								18 49								
Trefforest	d	18 01			18 07				18 23		18 31		18 37				18 53		19 01		19 08				
Pontypridd 3	a	18 05			18 11				18 28		18 35		18 41				18 58		19 05		19 12				
	d	18 05			18 12				18 28		18 35		18 42				18 58		19 05		19 13				
Abercynon	d				18 19				18 35				18 49				19 05				19 20				
Penrhiwceiber	d				18 25								18 55								19 25				
Mountain Ash	a				18 30								19 00								19 30				
	d				18 33								19 03								19 30				
Fernhill	d				18 36								19 06								19 32				
Cwmbach	d				18 40								19 10								19 45				
Aberdare	a				18 46								19 16								19 49				
Quakers Yard	d								18 39								19 09								
Merthyr Vale	a								18 44								19 14								
	d								18 47								19 17								
Troed Y Rhiw	d								18 51								19 21								
Pentre-bach	d								18 54								19 24								
Merthyr Tydfil	a								19 01								19 31								
Trehafod	d	18 10									18 40								19 10						
Porth	a	18 13									18 43								19 13						
	d	18 14									18 44								19 14						
Dinas Rhondda	d	18 18									18 48								19 18						
Tonypandy	d	18 20									18 50								19 20						
Llwynypia	d	18 22									18 52								19 22						
Ystrad Rhondda	a	18 26									18 55								19 25						
	d	18 29									18 59								19 29						
Ton Pentre	d	18 31									19 01								19 31						
Treorchy	d	18 34									19 04								19 34						
Ynyswen	d	18 37									19 07								19 37						
Treherbert	a	18 42									19 12								19 42						

When events are being held at the Principality Stadium, services are subject to alteration. Please check times before travelling.

For connections to Cardiff Bay please refer to Table T124

Table T130-R

Mondays to Fridays
16 December to 15 May

Bridgend, Barry Island, Barry, Penarth and Cardiff - Coryton, Rhymney, Pontypridd, Merthyr, Aberdare and Treherbert

		AW	AW	AW	AW	AW	AW	AW	AW		AW	AW	AW	AW	AW	AW	AW	AW	AW		AW	AW	AW	AW	AW
Bridgend	d							18 42								19 42									20 42
Llantwit Major	d							18 56								19 56									20 56
Rhoose Cardiff Int Airport ✈	d							19 06								20 06									21 06
Barry Island	d			18 41	18 56						19 26		19 56								20 56				
Barry 3	d			18 45	19 00			19 15			19 30		20 00			20 15					21 00				21 15
Barry Docks	d			18 48	19 03			19 18			19 33		20 03			20 18					21 03				21 18
Cadoxton	d			18 51	19 06			19 21			19 36		20 06			20 21					21 06				21 21
Dinas Powys	d			18 55	19 10			19 25			19 40		20 10			20 25					21 10				21 25
Eastbrook	d			18 58	19 13			19 28			19 43		20 13			20 28					21 13				21 28
Cogan	d			19 00	19 15			19 30			19 45		20 15			20 30					21 15				21 30
Penarth	d	18 48				19 18						19 48		20 18				20 48						21 23	
Dingle Road	d	18 50				19 20						19 50		20 20				20 50						21 25	
Grangetown	d	18 54		19 04	19 19	19 24		19 34			19 49	19 54	20 19	20 24		20 34		20 54			21 19			21 29	21 34
Cardiff Central 7	a	19 00		19 10	19 25	19 30		19 40			19 55	20 00	20 26	20 31		20 40		21 00			21 25			21 41	21 43
	d	19 01	19 05	19 11	19 26	19 31	19 36	19 43	19 51		20 01	20 06	20 27	20 31	20 36	20 41	20 52	21 01	21 05		21 27	21 32	21 36		21 43
Cardiff Queen Street 3	a	19 05	19 09	19 15	19 30	19 35		19 47	19 55		20 05	20 10	20 31	20 35		20 45	20 56	21 05	21 09		21 31	21 36			21 47
	d	19 05	19 09	19 15	19 30	19 36		19 47	19 55		20 05	20 10	20 31	20 35		20 45	20 56	21 05	21 09		21 31	21 36			21 47
Heath Low Level	d								20 00								21 01								
Ty Glas	d								20 03								21 03								
Birchgrove	d								20 04								21 05								
Rhiwbina	d								20 06								21 07								
Whitchurch (Cardiff)	d								20 08								21 08								
Coryton	a								20 13								21 13								
Heath High Level	d	19 10				19 40					20 10			20 40				21 11				21 41			
Llanishen	d	19 13				19 43					20 13			20 43				21 14				21 44			
Lisvane & Thornhill	d	19 15				19 46					20 16			20 45				21 16				21 46			
Caerphilly	d	19a23				19 52					20a24			20 51				21 22				21 53			
Aber	d					19 54								20 53				21 24				21 55			
Energlyn & Churchill Park	d					19 57								20 55				21 26				21 57			
Llanbradach	d					20 00								20 59				21 30				22 01			
Ystrad Mynach	d					20 06								21 04				21a36				22 06			
Hengoed	d					20 08								21 07								22 09			
Pengam	d					20 12								21 10								22 12			
Gilfach Fargoed	d					20 15								21 13								22 15			
Bargoed	a					20 19								21 18								22 20			
	d					20 19								21 18								22 20			
Brithdir	d					20 23								21 22								22 24			
Tir-phil	d					20 26								21 25								22 27			
Pontlottyn	d					20 30								21 29								22 31			
Rhymney 3	a					20 35								21 35								22 36			
Cathays	d		19 12	19 18	19 33			19 50				20 13	20 34			20 48			21 12		21 34				21 50
Llandaf	d		19 16	19 22	19 37			19 54				20 17	20 38			20 52			21 16		21 38				21 54
Ninian Park	d						19 40								20 40								21 40		
Waun-gron Park	d						19 43								20 43								21 43		
Fairwater	d						19 45								20 45								21 45		
Danescourt	d						19 47								20 47								21 47		
Radyr 3	a		19 20	19 26	19 41		19 54	19 58				20 20	20 42		20 54	20 56			21 20		21 42		21 54		21 58
	d		19 20	19 26	19 41			19 58				20 20	20 42			20 56			21 20		21 42				21 58
Taffs Well	d		19 24	19 30	19 45			20 02				20 24	20 46			21 00			21 24		21 46				22 02
Trefforest Estate	d				19 49								20 50								21 50				
Trefforest	d		19 31	19 37	19 53			20 09				20 31	20 54			21 07			21 31		21 54				22 09
Pontypridd 3	a		19 35	19 41	19 58			20 13				20 35	20 58			21 11			21 35		21 59				22 13
	d		19 35	19 42	19 58			20 13				20 35	20 59			21 12			21 35		21 59				22 14
Abercynon	d			19 53	20 05			20 21					21 06			21 19					22 06				22 21
Penrhiwceiber	d			19 59				20 27								21 25									22 27
Mountain Ash	a			20 04				20 32								21 29									22 31
	d			20 04				20 33								21 29									22 31
Fernhill	d			20 06				20 36								21 32									22 34
Cwmbach	d			20 10				20 40								21 36									22 38
Aberdare	a			20 16				20 46								21 42									22 44
Quakers Yard	d				20 09								21 10								22 10				
Merthyr Vale	a				20 14								21 15								22 15				
	d				20 15								21 16								22 16				
Troed Y Rhiw	d				20 19								21 20								22 20				
Pentre-bach	d				20 22								21 23								22 23				
Merthyr Tydfil	a				20 30								21 31								22 31				
Trehafod	d		19 40									20 40							21 40						
Porth	a		19 43									20 43							21 43						
	d		19 44									20 44							21 44						
Dinas Rhondda	d		19 48									20 48							21 48						
Tonypandy	d		19 50									20 50							21 50						
Llwynypia	d		19 52									20 52							21 52						
Ystrad Rhondda	a		19 55									20 55							21 55						
	d		19 59									20 59							21 59						
Ton Pentre	d		20 01									21 01							22 01						
Treorchy	d		20 04									21 04							22 04						
Ynyswen	d		20 07									21 07							22 07						
Treherbert	a		20 12									21 12							22 12						

When events are being held at the Principality Stadium, services are subject to alteration. Please check times before travelling.

For connections to Cardiff Bay please refer to Table T124

Table T130-R

Mondays to Fridays
16 December to 15 May

Bridgend, Barry Island, Barry, Penarth and Cardiff - Coryton, Rhymney, Pontypridd, Merthyr, Aberdare and Treherbert

		AW	AW	AW	AW		AW	AW	AW	AW	AW	AW	AW	AW	AW
Bridgend	d								21 42						22 42
Llantwit Major	d								21 56						22 57
Rhoose Cardiff Int Airport ✈	d								22 06						23 07
Barry Island	d				21 56								22 45		
Barry 3	d				22 00				22 15				22 49		23 16
Barry Docks	d				22 03				22 18				22 52		23 19
Cadoxton	d				22 06				22 21				22 55		23 22
Dinas Powys	d				22 10				22 25				22 59		23 26
Eastbrook	d				22 13				22 28				23 02		23 29
Cogan	d				22 15				22 30				23 04		23 32
Penarth	d	21 48					22 20					22 51		23 26	
Dingle Road	d	21 50					22 22					22 53		23 28	
Grangetown	d	21 54			22 19		22 26		22 34			22 57	23 08	23 32	23 36
Cardiff Central 7	a	22 00			22 25		22 33		22 40			23 03	23 14	23 39	23 43
	d	22 01	22 06	22 21	22 26			22 35	22 41	22 46	22 55	23 16	23 26		
Cardiff Queen Street 3	a	22 05	22 10	22 25	22 30			22 39	22 45	22 50		23 20	23 30		
	d	22 05	22 10	22 25	22 30			22 39	22 45	22 50		23 20	23 30		
Heath Low Level	d			22 30											
Ty Glas	d			22 33											
Birchgrove	d			22 34											
Rhiwbina	d			22 36											
Whitchurch (Cardiff)	d			22 38											
Coryton	a			22 43											
Heath High Level	d	22 10						22 44				23 25			
Llanishen	d	22 13						22 47				23 28			
Lisvane & Thornhill	d	22 15						22 49				23 30			
Caerphilly	d	22a23						22 56				23 36			
Aber	d							22 58				23 38			
Energlyn & Churchill Park	d							23 00				23 40			
Llanbradach	d							23 04				23 44			
Ystrad Mynach	d							23 09				23a50			
Hengoed	d							23 12							
Pengam	d							23 15							
Gilfach Fargoed	d							23 18							
Bargoed	a							23 23							
	d							23 23							
Brithdir	d							23 27							
Tir-phil	d							23 30							
Pontlottyn	d							23 34							
Rhymney 3	a							23 39							
Cathays	d		22 12		22 33				22 48	22 53			23 33		
Llandaf	d		22 17		22 37				22 52	22 57			23 37		
Ninian Park	d										22 59				
Waun-gron Park	d										23 02				
Fairwater	d										23 04				
Danescourt	d										23 06				
Radyr 3	a		22 20		22 41				22 55	23 00	23 13		23 41		
	d		22 20		22 41				22 55	23 00			23 41		
Taffs Well	d		22 24		22 45				22 59	23 04			23 45		
Trefforest Estate	d				22 49										
Trefforest	d		22 31		22 53				23 06	23 11			23 52		
Pontypridd 3	a		22 35		22 58				23 10	23 15			23 58		
	d		22 35		22 58				23 11	23 15					
Abercynon	d				23 05				23 18						
Penrhiwceiber	d								23 24						
Mountain Ash	a								23 28						
	d								23 28						
Fernhill	d								23 31						
Cwmbach	d								23 35						
Aberdare	a								23 43						
Quakers Yard	d				23 09										
Merthyr Vale	a				23 14										
	d				23 15										
Troed Y Rhiw	d				23 19										
Pentre-bach	d				23 22										
Merthyr Tydfil	a				23 30										
Trehafod	d		22 40							23 20					
Porth	a		22 43							23 23					
	d		22 44							23 24					
Dinas Rhondda	d		22 48							23 28					
Tonypandy	d		22 50							23 30					
Llwynypia	d		22 52							23 32					
Ystrad Rhondda	a		22 55							23 35					
	d		22 59							23 38					
Ton Pentre	d		23 01							23 40					
Treorchy	d		23 04							23 43					
Ynyswen	d		23 07							23 46					
Treherbert	a		23 12							23 51					

When events are being held at the Principality Stadium, services are subject to alteration. Please check times before travelling.

For connections to Cardiff Bay please refer to Table T124

Table T130-R

Saturdays
21 December to 16 May

Bridgend, Barry Island, Barry, Penarth and Cardiff - Coryton, Rhymney, Pontypridd, Merthyr, Aberdare and Treherbert

		AW	AW		AW	AW	AW	AW	AW	AW		AW	AW	AW	AW	AW	AW	AW	AW	AW		AW	AW	AW	AW
Bridgend	d													05 42											
Llantwit Major	d													05 56											
Rhoose Cardiff Int Airport ✈	d													06 06											
Barry Island	d		05 15						05 51								06 26							06 56	
Barry 3	d		05 19						05 55					06 15			06 30							07 00	
Barry Docks	d		05 22						05 58					06 18			06 33							07 03	
Cadoxton	d		05 25						06 01					06 21			06 36							07 06	
Dinas Powys	d		05 29						06 05					06 25			06 40							07 10	
Eastbrook	d		05 32						06 08					06 28			06 43							07 13	
Cogan	d		05 34						06 10					06 30			06 45							07 15	
Penarth	d							06 02							06 32							07 02			07 18
Dingle Road	d							06 04							06 34							07 04			07 20
Grangetown	d		05 38					06 08	06 14					06 34	06 38		06 49					07 08		07 20	07 24
Cardiff Central 7	a		05 44					06 14	06 20					06 40	06 45		06 55					07 14		07 26	07 30
	d	05 26	05 47	05 51		05 56	06 11	06 15	06 21	06 26		06 31	06 36	06 41	06 46	06 51	06 56	07 06	07 06	07 11		07 16	07 21	07 26	07 31
Cardiff Queen Street 3	a	05 30	05 51	05 55		06 00	06 15	06 20	06 25	06 30		06 35	06 40	06 45	06 50	06 55	07 00	07 10		07 15		07 20	07 26	07 30	07 35
	d	05 30	05 51	05 56		06 00	06 15	06 20	06 25	06 30		06 36	06 40	06 45	06 50	06 55	07 00	07 10		07 15		07 20	07 26	07 30	07 35
Heath Low Level	d			06 01					06 30							07 00							07 31		
Ty Glas	d			06 04					06 33							07 03							07 34		
Birchgrove	d			06 05					06 34							07 04							07 35		
Rhiwbina	d			06 07					06 36							07 06							07 37		
Whitchurch (Cardiff)	d			06 09					06 38							07 08							07 39		
Coryton	a			06 13					06 43							07 13							07 43		
Heath High Level	d		05 56					06 25							06 55							07 25			07 40
Llanishen	d		05 59					06 28							06 58							07 28			07 43
Lisvane & Thornhill	d		06 01					06 30							07 00							07 31			07 45
Caerphilly	d		06a08					06 36							07 06							07 37			07 51
Aber	d							06 38							07 08							07 39			07 53
Energlyn & Churchill Park	d																					07 42			
Llanbradach	d							06 42							07 12							07 46			07 57
Ystrad Mynach	d							06 47							07 17							07 52			08 02
Hengoed	d							06 50							07 20							07 55			08 05
Pengam	d							06 53							07 23							07 58			08 08
Gilfach Fargoed	d																								
Bargoed	a							07 01							07 31							08 06			08 14
	d																								08 14
Brithdir	d																								08 18
Tir-phil	d																								08 21
Pontlottyn	d																								08 25
Rhymney 3	a																								08 30
Cathays	d	05 33				06 03	06 18			06 33		06 38	06 43	06 48			07 03	07 12		07 18				07 33	
Llandaf	d	05 37				06 07	06 22			06 37			06 47	06 52			07 07	07 17		07 22				07 37	
Ninian Park	d																		07 10						
Waun-gron Park	d																		07 13						
Fairwater	d																		07 15						
Danescourt	d																		07 17						
Radyr 3	a	05 41				06 11	06 26			06 41		06 45	06 50	06 56			07 11	07 20	07 24	07 26				07 41	
	d	05 41				06 11	06 26			06 41		06 45	06 50	06 56			07 11	07 20		07 26				07 41	
Taffs Well	d	05 45				06 15	06 30			06 45		06a50	06 54	07 00			07 15	07 24		07 30				07 45	
Trefforest Estate	d	05 49				06 19				06 49							07 19							07 49	
Trefforest	d	05 53				06 23	06 37			06 53			07 01	07 07			07 23	07 31		07 37				07 53	
Pontypridd 3	a	05 57				06 28	06 41			06 58			07 05	07 11			07 28	07 35		07 41				07 58	
	d	06 00			06 12	06 28	06 42			06 58			07 05	07 12			07 28	07 35		07 42				07 58	
Abercynon	d	06 07			06 19	06 35	06 49			07 05				07 19			07 35			07 49				08 05	
Penrhiwceiber	d				06 24		06 55							07 25						07 55					
Mountain Ash	a				06 30		07 00							07 30						08 00					
	d				06 33		07 03							07 33						08 03					
Fernhill	d				06 36		07 06							07 36						08 06					
Cwmbach	d				06 40		07 10							07 40						08 10					
Aberdare	a				06 46		07 16							07 46						08 16					
Quakers Yard	d	06 11				06 39				07 09							07 39							08 09	
Merthyr Vale	a	06 16				06 44				07 14							07 44							08 14	
	d	06 17				06 47				07 17							07 47							08 17	
Troed Y Rhiw	d	06 21				06 51				07 21							07 51							08 21	
Pentre-bach	d	06 24				06 54				07 24							07 54							08 24	
Merthyr Tydfil	a	06 31				07 01				07 31							08 01							08 31	
Trehafod	d												07 10					07 40							
Porth	a												07 13					07 43							
	d												07 14					07 44							
Dinas Rhondda	d												07 18					07 48							
Tonypandy	d												07 20					07 50							
Llwynypia	d												07 22					07 52							
Ystrad Rhondda	a												07 25					07 55							
	d												07 29					07 59							
Ton Pentre	d												07 31					08 01							
Treorchy	d												07 34					08 04							
Ynyswen	d												07 37					08 07							
Treherbert	a												07 42					08 12							

When events are being held at the Principality Stadium, services are subject to alteration. Please check times before travelling.

For connections to Cardiff Bay please refer to Table T124

Table T130-R

Saturdays

21 December to 16 May

Bridgend, Barry Island, Barry, Penarth and Cardiff - Coryton, Rhymney, Pontypridd, Merthyr, Aberdare and Treherbert

		AW	AW	AW	AW	AW	AW	AW	AW	AW	AW	AW	AW	AW	AW	AW	AW	AW	AW	AW	AW	AW	AW
Bridgend	d			06 42														07 42					
Llantwit Major	d			06 56														07 56					
Rhoose Cardiff Int Airport ✈	d			07 06														08 06					
Barry Island	d						07 26				07 41			07 56							08 26		
Barry 3	d			07 15			07 30				07 45			08 00				08 15			08 30		
Barry Docks	d			07 18			07 33				07 48			08 03				08 18			08 33		
Cadoxton	d			07 21			07 36				07 51			08 06				08 21			08 36		
Dinas Powys	d			07 25			07 40				07 55			08 10				08 25			08 40		
Eastbrook	d			07 28			07 43				07 58			08 13				08 28			08 43		
Cogan	d			07 30			07 45				08 00			08 15				08 30			08 45		
Penarth	d				07 34			07 47				08 03			08 18				08 33			08 48	
Dingle Road	d				07 36			07 49				08 05			08 20				08 35			08 50	
Grangetown	d			07 34	07 40		07 49	07 53			08 05	08 09		08 21	08 24			08 34	08 39		08 49	08 54	
Cardiff Central 7	a			07 41	07 46		07 55	08 00			08 10	08 15		08 26	08 30			08 40	08 45		08 55	09 00	
	d	07 35	07 35	07 41	07 46	07 51	07 56	08 01	08 05	08 06	08 11	08 15	08 22	08 26	08 31	08 35	08 36	08 40	08 46	08 51	08 56	09 01	09 05
Cardiff Queen Street 3	a	07 39		07 45	07 50	07 55	08 00	08 05	08 09		08 15	08 19	08 26	08 30	08 35	08 39		08 44	08 50	08 55	09 00	09 05	09 09
	d	07 39		07 45	07 50	07 55	08 00	08 05	08 09		08 15	08 20	08 26	08 30	08 35	08 39		08 45	08 50	08 55	09 00	09 05	09 09
Heath Low Level	d					08 00							08 31							09 00			
Ty Glas	d					08 03							08 33							09 03			
Birchgrove	d					08 04							08 35							09 04			
Rhiwbina	d					08 06							08 37							09 06			
Whitchurch (Cardiff)	d					08 08							08 38							09 08			
Coryton	a					08 13							08 43							09 13			
Heath High Level	d				07 55			08 10				08 25			08 40				08 54			09 10	
Llanishen	d				07 58			08 13				08 28			08 43				08 57			09 13	
Lisvane & Thornhill	d				08 00			08 16				08 30			08 45				09 00			09 16	
Caerphilly	d				08 06			08 22				08 37			08 51				09 06			09 22	
Aber	d				08 08			08 24				08 39			08 53				09 08			09 24	
Energlyn & Churchill Park	d							08 27				08 41										09 27	
Llanbradach	d				08 12			08 31				08 45			08 57				09 12			09 31	
Ystrad Mynach	d				08 17			08 37				08 50			09 02				09 17			09 37	
Hengoed	d				08 20			08 40				08 53			09 05				09 20			09 40	
Pengam	d				08 23			08 44				08 56			09 08				09 23			09 44	
Gilfach Fargoed	d							08 47														09 47	
Bargoed	a				08 31			08 52				09 02			09 15				09 28			09 52	
	d											09 02											
Brithdir	d											09 05											
Tir-phil	d											09 08											
Pontlottyn	d											09 13											
Rhymney 3	a											09 18											
Cathays	d	07 42		07 48			08 03		08 12		08 18			08 33		08 42		08 48			09 03		09 12
Llandaf	d	07 46		07 52			08 07		08 16		08 22			08 37		08 46		08 52			09 07		09 16
Ninian Park	d		07 41							08 10							08 40						
Waun-gron Park	d		07 44							08 13							08 43						
Fairwater	d		07 46							08 15							08 45						
Danescourt	d		07 48							08 17							08 47						
Radyr 3	a	07 50	07 54	07 56			08 11		08 20	08 24	08 26			08 41		08 50	08 54	08 56			09 11		09 20
	d	07 50		07 56			08 11		08 20		08 26			08 41		08 50		08 56			09 11		09 20
Taffs Well	d	07 54		08 00			08 15		08 24		08 30			08 45		08 54		09 00			09 15		09 24
Trefforest Estate	d						08 19							08 49							09 19		
Trefforest	d	08 01		08 07			08 23		08 31		08 37			08 53		09 01		09 07			09 23		09 31
Pontypridd 3	a	08 05		08 11			08 28		08 35		08 41			08 58		09 05		09 11			09 28		09 35
	d	08 05		08 12			08 28		08 35		08 42			08 58		09 05		09 12			09 28		09 35
Abercynon	d			08 19			08 35				08 49			09 05				09 19			09 35		
Penrhiwceiber	d			08 25							08 55							09 25					
Mountain Ash	a			08 30							09 00							09 30					
	d			08 33							09 03							09 33					
Fernhill	d			08 36							09 06							09 36					
Cwmbach	d			08 40							09 10							09 40					
Aberdare	a			08 46							09 16							09 46					
Quakers Yard	d						08 39							09 09							09 39		
Merthyr Vale	a						08 44							09 14							09 44		
	d						08 47							09 17							09 47		
Troed Y Rhiw	d						08 51							09 21							09 51		
Pentre-bach	d						08 54							09 24							09 54		
Merthyr Tydfil	a						09 01							09 31							10 01		
Trehafod	d	08 10							08 40							09 10							09 40
Porth	a	08 13							08 43							09 13							09 43
	d	08 14							08 44							09 14							09 44
Dinas Rhondda	d	08 18							08 48							09 18							09 48
Tonypandy	d	08 20							08 50							09 20							09 50
Llwynypia	d	08 22							08 52							09 22							09 52
Ystrad Rhondda	a	08 25							08 55							09 25							09 55
	d	08 29							08 59							09 29							09 59
Ton Pentre	d	08 31							09 01							09 31							10 01
Treorchy	d	08 34							09 04							09 34							10 04
Ynyswen	d	08 37							09 07							09 37							10 07
Treherbert	a	08 42							09 12							09 42							10 12

When events are being held at the Principality Stadium, services are subject to alteration. Please check times before travelling.

For connections to Cardiff Bay please refer to Table T124

Table T130-R

Saturdays

21 December to 16 May

Bridgend, Barry Island, Barry, Penarth and Cardiff - Coryton, Rhymney, Pontypridd, Merthyr, Aberdare and Treherbert

		AW	AW	AW	AW	AW	AW	AW	AW	AW	AW	AW	AW	AW	AW	AW	AW	AW	AW	AW	AW	AW
Bridgend	d									08 42												
Llantwit Major	d									08 56												
Rhoose Cardiff Int Airport ✈	d									09 06												
Barry Island	d		08 41			08 56							09 27					09 41			09 56	
Barry 3	d		08 45			09 00				09 15			09 31					09 45			10 00	
Barry Docks	d		08 48			09 03				09 18			09 34					09 48			10 03	
Cadoxton	d		08 51			09 06				09 21			09 37					09 51			10 06	
Dinas Powys	d		08 55			09 10				09 25			09 41					09 55			10 10	
Eastbrook	d		08 58			09 13				09 28			09 44					09 58			10 13	
Cogan	d		09 00			09 15				09 30			09 46					10 00			10 15	
Penarth	d						09 18				09 33				09 48				10 03			10 18
Dingle Road	d						09 20				09 35				09 50				10 05			10 20
Grangetown	d		09 04			09 19	09 24			09 34	09 39		09 50		09 54			10 04	10 09		10 19	10 24
Cardiff Central 7	a		09 10			09 25	09 30			09 40	09 45		09 56		10 00			10 10	10 15		10 25	10 30
	d	09 05	09 11	09 14	09 21	09 26	09 31	09 35	09 36	09 41	09 46	09 51	09 56		10 01	10 05	10 06	10 11	10 16	10 21	10 26	10 31
Cardiff Queen Street 3	a		09 15	09 18	09 25	09 30	09 35	09 39		09 45	09 49	09 55	10 00		10 05	10 09		10 15	10 20	10 25	10 30	10 35
	d		09 15	09 20	09 25	09 30	09 35	09 39		09 45	09 50	09 55	10 00		10 05	10 09		10 15	10 20	10 25	10 30	10 35
Heath Low Level	d				09 30							10 00								10 30		
Ty Glas	d				09 33							10 03								10 33		
Birchgrove	d				09 34							10 04								10 34		
Rhiwbina	d				09 36							10 06								10 36		
Whitchurch (Cardiff)	d				09 38							10 08								10 38		
Coryton	a				09 43							10 13								10 43		
Heath High Level	d			09 25			09 40				09 55				10 10				10 25			10 40
Llanishen	d			09 28			09 43				09 58				10 13				10 28			10 43
Lisvane & Thornhill	d			09 30			09 45				10 00				10 16				10 30			10 45
Caerphilly	d			09 37			09 51				10 06				10 22				10 37			10 51
Aber	d			09 39			09 53				10 08				10 24				10 39			10 53
Energlyn & Churchill Park	d			09 41											10 27				10 41			
Llanbradach	d			09 45			09 57				10 12				10 31				10 45			10 57
Ystrad Mynach	d			09 50			10 02				10 17				10 37				10 50			11 02
Hengoed	d			09 53			10 05				10 20				10 40				10 53			11 05
Pengam	d			09 56			10 08				10 23				10 44				10 56			11 08
Gilfach Fargoed	d														10 47							
Bargoed	a			10 02			10 15				10 30				10 52				11 02			11 15
	d			10 02															11 02			
Brithdir	d			10 05															11 05			
Tir-phil	d			10 08															11 08			
Pontlottyn	d			10 13															11 13			
Rhymney 3	a			10 18															11 18			
Cathays	d		09 18			09 33		09 42		09 48			10 03			10 12		10 18			10 33	
Llandaf	d		09 22			09 37		09 46		09 52			10 07			10 16		10 22			10 37	
Ninian Park	d	09 10							09 40								10 10					
Waun-gron Park	d	09 13							09 43								10 13					
Fairwater	d	09 15							09 45								10 15					
Danescourt	d	09 17							09 47								10 17					
Radyr 3	a	09 24	09 26			09 41		09 50	09 54	09 56			10 11			10 20	10 24	10 26			10 41	
	d		09 26			09 41		09 50		09 56			10 11			10 20		10 26			10 41	
Taffs Well	d		09 30			09 45		09 54		10 00			10 15			10 24		10 30			10 45	
Trefforest Estate	d					09 49															10 49	
Trefforest	d		09 37			09 53		10 01		10 07			10 21			10 31		10 37			10 53	
Pontypridd 3	a		09 41			09 58		10 05		10 11			10 31			10 35		10 41			10 58	
	d		09 42			09 58		10 05		10 12				10 34		10 35		10 42			10 58	
Abercynon	d		09 49			10 05				10 19				10 40				10 49			11 05	
Penrhiwceiber	d		09 55							10 25								10 55				
Mountain Ash	a		10 00							10 30								11 00				
	d		10 03							10 33								11 03				
Fernhill	d		10 06							10 36								11 06				
Cwmbach	d		10 10							10 40								11 10				
Aberdare	a		10 16							10 46								11 16				
Quakers Yard	d					10 09								10 44							11 09	
Merthyr Vale	a					10 14								10 49							11 14	
	d					10 17								10 51							11 17	
Troed Y Rhiw	d					10 21								10 55							11 21	
Pentre-bach	d					10 24								10 58							11 24	
Merthyr Tydfil	a					10 31								11 06							11 31	
Trehafod	d							10 10								10 40						
Porth	a							10 13								10 43						
	d							10 14								10 44						
Dinas Rhondda	d							10 18								10 48						
Tonypandy	d							10 20								10 50						
Llwynypia	d							10 22								10 52						
Ystrad Rhondda	a							10 25								10 55						
	d							10 29								10 59						
Ton Pentre	d							10 31								11 01						
Treorchy	d							10 34								11 04						
Ynyswen	d							10 37								11 07						
Treherbert	a							10 42								11 12						

When events are being held at the Principality Stadium, services are subject to alteration. Please check times before travelling.

For connections to Cardiff Bay please refer to Table T124

Table T130-R

Saturdays

21 December to 16 May

Bridgend, Barry Island, Barry, Penarth and Cardiff - Coryton, Rhymney, Pontypridd, Merthyr, Aberdare and Treherbert

		AW	AW	AW	AW	AW	AW	AW	AW	AW	AW	AW	AW	AW	AW	AW	AW	AW	AW	AW	AW	AW	AW
Bridgend	d			09 42															10 42				
Llantwit Major	d			09 56															10 56				
Rhoose Cardiff Int Airport ✈	d			10 06															11 06				
Barry Island	d							10 26				10 41			10 56							11 26	
Barry [3]	d			10 15				10 30				10 45			11 00				11 15			11 30	
Barry Docks	d			10 18				10 33				10 48			11 03				11 18			11 33	
Cadoxton	d			10 21				10 36				10 51			11 06				11 21			11 36	
Dinas Powys	d			10 25				10 40				10 55			11 10				11 25			11 40	
Eastbrook	d			10 28				10 43				10 58			11 13				11 28			11 43	
Cogan	d			10 30				10 45				11 00			11 15				11 30			11 45	
Penarth	d				10 33					10 48			11 04			11 18				11 33			11 48
Dingle Road	d				10 35					10 50			11 06			11 20				11 35			11 50
Grangetown	d			10 34	10 40			10 49		10 54		11 04	11 10		11 19	11 24			11 34	11 39		11 49	11 54
Cardiff Central [7]	a			10 43	10 45			10 56		11 00		11 11	11 16		11 25	11 30			11 40	11 45		11 55	12 01
	d	10 35	10 36		10 46	10 51	10 52	10 57		11 01	11 07	11 11	11 16	11 21	11 26	11 31	11 35	11 36	11 41	11 46	11 51	11 56	12 01
Cardiff Queen Street [3]	a	10 39			10 50		10 56	11 01		11 05		11 15	11 20	11 25	11 30	11 35	11 39		11 45	11 50	11 55	12 00	12 05
	d	10 39			10 50		10 56	11 01		11 05		11 15	11 20	11 25	11 30	11 35	11 39		11 45	11 50	11 55	12 00	12 05
Heath Low Level	d						11 01							11 30							12 00		
Ty Glas	d						11 04							11 33							12 03		
Birchgrove	d						11 05							11 34							12 04		
Rhiwbina	d						11 07							11 36							12 06		
Whitchurch (Cardiff)	d						11 09							11 38							12 08		
Coryton	a						11 14							11 43							12 13		
Heath High Level	d				10 55					11 10			11 25			11 40				11 55			12 10
Llanishen	d				10 58					11 13			11 28			11 43				11 58			12 13
Lisvane & Thornhill	d				11 00					11 16			11 30			11 45				12 00			12 16
Caerphilly	d				11 06					11 22			11 37			11 51				12 06			12 22
Aber	d				11 08					11 24			11 39			11 53				12 08			12 24
Energlyn & Churchill Park	d									11 27			11 41										12 27
Llanbradach	d				11 12					11 31			11 45			11 57				12 12			12 31
Ystrad Mynach	d				11 17					11 37			11 50			12 02				12 17			12 37
Hengoed	d				11 20					11 40			11 53			12 05				12 20			12 40
Pengam	d				11 23					11 44			11 56			12 08				12 23			12 44
Gilfach Fargoed	d									11 47													12 47
Bargoed	a				11 30					11 52			12 02			12 15				12 30			12 52
	d												12 02										
Brithdir	d												12 05										
Tir-phil	d												12 08										
Pontlottyn	d												12 13										
Rhymney [3]	a												12 18										
Cathays	d	10 42						11 04				11 18			11 33		11 42		11 48			12 03	
Llandaf	d	10 46						11 08				11 22			11 37		11 46		11 52			12 07	
Ninian Park	d		10 41								11 11							11 41					
Waun-gron Park	d		10 44								11 14							11 44					
Fairwater	d		10 46								11 16							11 46					
Danescourt	d		10 48						←		11 18							11 48					
Radyr [3]	a	10 50	10 54			11 04		11 12	11 04		11 24	11 26			11 41		11 50	11 54	11 56			12 11	
	d	10 50				11 20		11 12	11 20			11 26			11 41		11 50		11 56			12 11	
Taffs Well	d	10 54				→		11 16	11 24			11 30			11 45		11 54		12 00			12 15	
Trefforest Estate	d							11 20							11 49							12 19	
Trefforest	d	11 01						11 24	11 31			11 37			11 53		12 01		12 07			12 23	
Pontypridd [3]	a	11 05						11 29	11 34			11 41			11 58		12 05		12 11			12 28	
	d	11 05						11 29	11 35			11 42			11 58		12 05		12 12			12 28	
Abercynon	d							11 36				11 49			12 05				12 20			12 35	
Penrhiwceiber	d											11 55							12 26				
Mountain Ash	a											12 00							12 31				
	d											12 03							12 33				
Fernhill	d											12 06							12 36				
Cwmbach	d											12 10							12 40				
Aberdare	a											12 16							12 46				
Quakers Yard	d							11 40							12 09							12 39	
Merthyr Vale	a							11 45							12 14							12 44	
	d							11 47							12 17							12 47	
Troed Y Rhiw	d							11 51							12 21							12 51	
Pentre-bach	d							11 54							12 24							12 54	
Merthyr Tydfil	a							12 01							12 31							13 01	
Trehafod	d	11 10							11 40								12 10						
Porth	a	11 13							11 43								12 13						
	d	11 14							11 44								12 14						
Dinas Rhondda	d	11 18							11 48								12 18						
Tonypandy	d	11 20							11 50								12 20						
Llwynypia	d	11 22							11 52								12 22						
Ystrad Rhondda	a	11 25							11 55								12 25						
	d	11 29							11 59								12 29						
Ton Pentre	d	11 31							12 01								12 31						
Treorchy	d	11 34							12 04								12 34						
Ynyswen	d	11 37							12 07								12 37						
Treherbert	a	11 42							12 12								12 42						

When events are being held at the Principality Stadium, services are subject to alteration. Please check times before travelling.

For connections to Cardiff Bay please refer to Table T124

Table T130-R

Saturdays

21 December to 16 May

Bridgend, Barry Island, Barry, Penarth and Cardiff - Coryton, Rhymney, Pontypridd, Merthyr, Aberdare and Treherbert

		AW	AW	AW	AW	AW	AW	AW	AW	AW	AW	AW	AW	AW	AW	AW	AW	AW	AW	AW	AW	AW
Bridgend	d										11 42											
Llantwit Major	d										11 56											
Rhoose Cardiff Int Airport ✈	d										12 06											
Barry Island	d			11 41			11 56							12 26				12 41			12 56	
Barry [3]	d			11 45			12 00				12 15			12 30				12 45			13 00	
Barry Docks	d			11 48			12 03				12 18			12 33				12 48			13 03	
Cadoxton	d			11 51			12 06				12 21			12 36				12 51			13 06	
Dinas Powys	d			11 55			12 10				12 25			12 40				12 55			13 10	
Eastbrook	d			11 58			12 13				12 28			12 43				12 58			13 13	
Cogan	d			12 00			12 15				12 30			12 45				13 00			13 15	
Penarth	d				12 03			12 18				12 33			12 48				13 03			13 18
Dingle Road	d				12 05			12 20				12 35			12 50				13 05			13 20
Grangetown	d			12 05	12 09		12 19	12 24			12 34	12 39		12 49	12 54			13 04	13 09		13 20	13 24
Cardiff Central [7]	a			12 10	12 15		12 25	12 30			12 40	12 45		12 55	13 00			13 10	13 16		13 25	13 30
	d	12 05	12 06	12 11	12 16	12 21	12 26	12 31	12 35	12 36	12 41	12 46	12 51	12 56	13 01	13 05	13 06	13 11	13 16	13 21	13 26	13 31
Cardiff Queen Street [3]	a	12 09		12 15	12 20	12 25	12 30	12 35	12 39		12 45	12 50	12 55	13 00	13 05	13 09		13 15	13 20	13 25	13 30	13 35
	d	12 09		12 15	12 20	12 25	12 30	12 35	12 39		12 45	12 50	12 55	13 00	13 05	13 09		13 15	13 20	13 25	13 30	13 35
Heath Low Level	d					12 30							13 00							13 30		
Ty Glas	d					12 33							13 03							13 33		
Birchgrove	d					12 34							13 04							13 34		
Rhiwbina	d					12 36							13 06							13 36		
Whitchurch (Cardiff)	d					12 38							13 08							13 38		
Coryton	a					12 44							13 13							13 43		
Heath High Level	d				12 25			12 40				12 55			13 10				13 25			13 40
Llanishen	d				12 28			12 43				12 58			13 13				13 28			13 43
Lisvane & Thornhill	d				12 30			12 45				13 00			13 16				13 30			13 45
Caerphilly	d				12 37			12 51				13 06			13 22				13 37			13 51
Aber	d				12 39			12 53				13 08			13 24				13 39			13 53
Energlyn & Churchill Park	d				12 41										13 27				13 41			
Llanbradach	d				12 45			12 57				13 12			13 31				13 45			13 57
Ystrad Mynach	d				12 50			13 02				13 17			13 37				13 50			14 02
Hengoed	d				12 53			13 05				13 20			13 40				13 53			14 05
Pengam	d				12 56			13 08				13 23			13 44				13 56			14 08
Gilfach Fargoed	d														13 47							
Bargoed	a				13 02			13 15				13 30			13 52				14 02			14 15
	d				13 02														14 02			
Brithdir	d				13 05														14 05			
Tir-phil	d				13 08														14 08			
Pontlottyn	d				13 13														14 13			
Rhymney [3]	a				13 18														14 18			
Cathays	d	12 12		12 18			12 33		12 42		12 48			13 03		13 12		13 18			13 33	
Llandaf	d	12 16		12 22			12 37		12 46		12 52			13 07		13 16		13 22			13 37	
Ninian Park	d		12 10							12 40							13 10					
Waun-gron Park	d		12 13							12 43							13 13					
Fairwater	d		12 15							12 45							13 15					
Danescourt	d		12 17							12 47							13 17					
Radyr [3]	a	12 20	12 24	12 25			12 41		12 50	12 54	12 56			13 11		13 20	13 24	13 26			13 41	
	d	12 20		12 25			12 41		12 50		12 56			13 11		13 20		13 26			13 41	
Taffs Well	d	12 24		12 29			12 45		12 54		13 00			13 15		13 24		13 30			13 45	
Trefforest Estate	d						12 49							13 19							13 49	
Trefforest	d	12 31		12 36			12 53		13 01		13 07			13 23		13 31		13 37			13 53	
Pontypridd [3]	a	12 35		12 41			12 58		13 05		13 11			13 28		13 35		13 41			13 58	
	d	12 35					12 58		13 05		13 12			13 28		13 35		13 42			13 58	
Abercynon	d						13 05				13 19			13 35				13 49			14 05	
Penrhiwceiber	d										13 25							13 55				
Mountain Ash	a										13 30							14 00				
	d										13 33							14 03				
Fernhill	d										13 36							14 06				
Cwmbach	d										13 40							14 10				
Aberdare	a										13 46							14 16				
Quakers Yard	d						13 09							13 39							14 09	
Merthyr Vale	a						13 14							13 44							14 14	
	d						13 17							13 47							14 17	
Troed Y Rhiw	d						13 21							13 51							14 21	
Pentre-bach	d						13 24							13 54							14 24	
Merthyr Tydfil	a						13 31							14 01							14 31	
Trehafod	d	12 40							13 10							13 40						
Porth	a	12 43							13 13							13 43						
	d	12 44							13 14							13 44						
Dinas Rhondda	d	12 48							13 18							13 48						
Tonypandy	d	12 50							13 20							13 50						
Llwynypia	d	12 52							13 22							13 52						
Ystrad Rhondda	a	12 55							13 25							13 55						
	d	12 59							13 29							13 59						
Ton Pentre	d	13 01							13 31							14 01						
Treorchy	d	13 04							13 34							14 04						
Ynyswen	d	13 07							13 37							14 07						
Treherbert	a	13 12							13 42							14 12						

When events are being held at the Principality Stadium, services are subject to alteration. Please check times before travelling.

For connections to Cardiff Bay please refer to Table T124

Table T130-R

Saturdays

21 December to 16 May

Bridgend, Barry Island, Barry, Penarth and Cardiff - Coryton, Rhymney, Pontypridd, Merthyr, Aberdare and Treherbert

Station		AW	AW	AW	AW	AW	AW	AW	AW	AW	AW	AW	AW	AW	AW	AW	AW	AW	AW	AW	AW	AW	AW
Bridgend	d			12 42														13 42					
Llantwit Major	d			12 56														13 56					
Rhoose Cardiff Int Airport ✈	d			13 06														14 06					
Barry Island	d						13 26				13 41			13 56							14 26		
Barry 3	d			13 15			13 31				13 45			14 00				14 15			14 30		
Barry Docks	d			13 18			13 34				13 48			14 03				14 18			14 33		
Cadoxton	d			13 21			13 37				13 51			14 06				14 21			14 36		
Dinas Powys	d			13 25			13 41				13 55			14 10				14 25			14 40		
Eastbrook	d			13 28			13 43				13 58			14 13				14 28			14 43		
Cogan	d			13 30			13 46				14 00			14 15				14 30			14 45		
Penarth	d				13 33			13 48				14 03			14 18				14 33				
Dingle Road	d				13 35			13 50				14 05			14 20				14 35				
Grangetown	d			13 34	13 39		13 50	13 54			14 04	14 09		14 20	14 24			14 34	14 39		14 49		
Cardiff Central 7	a			13 40	13 45		13 56	14 00			14 10	14 15		14 25	14 30			14 40	14 45		14 55		
	d	13 35	13 36	13 41	13 46	13 51	13 56	14 01	14 05	14 06	14 11	14 16	14 21	14 26	14 31	14 35	14 36	14 41	14 46	14 51	14 56	14 57	
Cardiff Queen Street 3	a	13 39		13 45	13 50	13 55	14 00	14 05	14 09		14 15	14 20	14 25	14 30	14 35	14 39		14 45	14 50	14 55	15 00		
	d	13 39		13 45	13 50	13 55	14 00	14 05	14 09		14 15	14 20	14 25	14 30	14 35	14 39		14 45	14 50	14 55	15 00		
Heath Low Level	d					14 00							14 30							15 00			
Ty Glas	d					14 03							14 33							15 03			
Birchgrove	d					14 04							14 34							15 04			
Rhiwbina	d					14 06							14 36							15 06			
Whitchurch (Cardiff)	d					14 08							14 38							15 08			
Coryton	a					14 13							14 43							15 13			
Heath High Level	d				13 55			14 10				14 25			14 40				14 55				
Llanishen	d				13 58			14 13				14 28			14 43				14 58				
Lisvane & Thornhill	d				14 00			14 16				14 30			14 45				15 00				
Caerphilly	d				14 06			14 22				14 37			14 51				15 06				
Aber	d				14 08			14 24				14 39			14 53				15 08				
Energlyn & Churchill Park	d							14 27				14 41											
Llanbradach	d				14 12			14 31				14 45			14 57				15 12				
Ystrad Mynach	d				14 17			14 37				14 50			15 02				15 17				
Hengoed	d				14 20			14 40				14 53			15 05				15 20				
Pengam	d				14 23			14 44				14 56			15 08				15 23				
Gilfach Fargoed	d							14 47															
Bargoed	a				14 30			14 52				15 02			15 15				15 30				
	d											15 02											
Brithdir	d											15 05											
Tir-phil	d											15 08											
Pontlottyn	d											15 13											
Rhymney 3	a											15 18											
Cathays	d	13 42		13 48			14 03		14 12		14 18			14 33		14 42		14 48			15 03		
Llandaf	d	13 46		13 52			14 07		14 16		14 22			14 37		14 46		14 52			15 07		
Ninian Park	d		13 40							14 10							14 40						
Waun-gron Park	d		13 43							14 13							14 43						
Fairwater	d		13 45							14 15							14 45						
Danescourt	d		13 47							14 17							14 47						←
Radyr 3	a	13 50	13 54	13 56			14 11		14 20	14 24	14 26			14 41		14 50	14 54	14 56			15 11	15 10	15 11
	d	13 50		13 56			14 11		14 20		14 26			14 41		14 50		14 56			15 11	15 20	15 11
Taffs Well	d	13 54		14 00			14 15		14 24		14 30			14 45		14 54		15 00			→	→	15 15
Trefforest Estate	d						14 19							14 49									15 19
Trefforest	d	14 01		14 07			14 23		14 31		14 37			14 53		15 01		15 07					15 23
Pontypridd 3	a	14 05		14 11			14 28		14 35		14 41			14 58		15 05		15 11					15 28
	d	14 05		14 12			14 28		14 35		14 42			14 58		15 05		15 12					15 28
Abercynon	d			14 19			14 35				14 49			15 05				15 19					15 35
Penrhiwceiber	d			14 25							14 55							15 25					
Mountain Ash	a			14 30							15 00							15 30					
	d			14 33							15 03							15 33					
Fernhill	d			14 36							15 06							15 36					
Cwmbach	d			14 40							15 10							15 40					
Aberdare	a			14 46							15 16							15 46					
Quakers Yard	d						14 39							15 09									15 39
Merthyr Vale	a						14 44							15 14									15 44
	d						14 47							15 17									15 47
Troed Y Rhiw	d						14 51							15 21									15 51
Pentre-bach	d						14 54							15 24									15 54
Merthyr Tydfil	a						15 01							15 31									16 01
Trehafod	d	14 10							14 40							15 10							
Porth	a	14 13							14 43							15 13							
	d	14 14							14 44							15 14							
Dinas Rhondda	d	14 18							14 48							15 18							
Tonypandy	d	14 20							14 50							15 20							
Llwynypia	d	14 22							14 52							15 22							
Ystrad Rhondda	a	14 25							14 55							15 25							
	d	14 29							14 59							15 29							
Ton Pentre	d	14 31							15 01							15 31							
Treorchy	d	14 34							15 04							15 34							
Ynyswen	d	14 37							15 07							15 37							
Treherbert	a	14 42							15 12							15 42							

When events are being held at the Principality Stadium, services are subject to alteration. Please check times before travelling.

For connections to Cardiff Bay please refer to Table T124

Table T130-R

Saturdays

21 December to 16 May

Bridgend, Barry Island, Barry, Penarth and Cardiff - Coryton, Rhymney, Pontypridd, Merthyr, Aberdare and Treherbert

Station		AW	AW	AW	AW	AW	AW	AW	AW	AW	AW	AW	AW	AW	AW	AW	AW	AW	AW	AW	AW	AW	AW
Bridgend	d											14 42											
Llantwit Major	d											14 56											
Rhoose Cardiff Int Airport ✈	d											15 06											
Barry Island	d				14 41			14 56							15 26				15 41			15 56	
Barry 3	d				14 45			15 00				15 15			15 30				15 45			16 00	
Barry Docks	d				14 48			15 03				15 18			15 33				15 48			16 03	
Cadoxton	d				14 51			15 06				15 21			15 36				15 51			16 06	
Dinas Powys	d				14 55			15 10				15 25			15 40				15 55			16 10	
Eastbrook	d				14 58			15 13				15 28			15 43				15 58			16 13	
Cogan	d				15 00			15 15				15 30			15 45				16 00			16 15	
Penarth	d		14 48			15 03			15 18				15 33			15 47				16 03			16 18
Dingle Road	d		14 50			15 05			15 20				15 35			15 49				16 05			16 20
Grangetown	d		14 54		15 04	15 09		15 19	15 24			15 34	15 39		15 49	15 53			16 04	16 09		16 19	16 24
Cardiff Central 7	a		15 00		15 10	15 15		15 25	15 30			15 40	15 45		15 55	15 59			16 10	16 15		16 25	16 30
	d		15 01	15 06	15 11	15 16	15 21	15 26	15 31	15 35	15 36	15 41	15 46	15 51	15 56	16 01	16 05	16 06	16 11	16 16	16 21	16 26	16 31
Cardiff Queen Street 3	a		15 05		15 15	15 20	15 25	15 30	15 35	15 39		15 45	15 50	15 55	16 00	16 05	16 09		16 15	16 20	16 25	16 30	16 35
	d		15 05		15 15	15 20	15 25	15 30	15 35	15 39		15 45	15 50	15 55	16 00	16 05	16 09		16 15	16 20	16 25	16 30	16 35
Heath Low Level	d						15 30							16 00							16 30		
Ty Glas	d						15 33							16 03							16 33		
Birchgrove	d						15 34							16 04							16 34		
Rhiwbina	d						15 36							16 06							16 36		
Whitchurch (Cardiff)	d						15 38							16 08							16 38		
Coryton	a						15 43							16 13							16 43		
Heath High Level	d		15 10			15 25			15 40				15 55			16 10				16 25			16 40
Llanishen	d		15 13			15 28			15 43				15 58			16 13				16 28			16 43
Lisvane & Thornhill	d		15 16			15 30			15 45				16 00			16 16				16 30			16 45
Caerphilly	d		15 22			15 37			15 51				16 06			16 22				16 37			16 51
Aber	d		15 24			15 39			15 53				16 08			16 24				16 39			16 53
Energlyn & Churchill Park	d		15 27			15 41										16 27				16 41			
Llanbradach	d		15 31			15 45			15 57				16 12			16 31				16 45			16 57
Ystrad Mynach	d		15 37			15 50			16 02				16 17			16 37				16 50			17 02
Hengoed	d		15 40			15 53			16 05				16 20			16 40				16 53			17 05
Pengam	d		15 44			15 56			16 08				16 23			16 44				16 56			17 08
Gilfach Fargoed	d		15 47													16 47							
Bargoed	a		15 53			16 02			16 13				16 30			16 52				17 02			17 15
	d					16 02														17 02			
Brithdir	d					16 05														17 05			
Tir-phil	d					16 08														17 08			
Pontlottyn	d					16 13														17 13			
Rhymney 3	a					16 18														17 20			
Cathays	d				15 18			15 33		15 42		15 48			16 03		16 12		16 18			16 33	
Llandaf	d				15 22			15 37		15 46		15 52			16 07		16 16		16 22			16 37	
Ninian Park	d			15 10							15 40							16 11					
Waun-gron Park	d			15 13							15 43							16 14					
Fairwater	d			15 15							15 45							16 16					
Danescourt	d	←		15 17							15 47							16 18					
Radyr 3	a	15 10		15 24	15 26			15 41		15 50	15 54	15 56			16 11		16 20	16 24	16 26			16 41	
	d	15 20			15 26			15 41		15 50		15 56			16 11		16 20		16 26			16 41	
Taffs Well	d	15 24			15 30			15 45		15 54		16 00			16 15		16 24		16 30			16 45	
Trefforest Estate	d							15 49							16 19							16 49	
Trefforest	d	15 31			15 37			15 53		16 01		16 07			16 23		16 31		16 37			16 53	
Pontypridd 3	a	15 34			15 41			15 58		16 05		16 11			16 28		16 35		16 41			16 58	
	d	15 35			15 42			15 58		16 05		16 12			16 28		16 35		16 42			16 58	
Abercynon	d				15 49			16 05				16 19			16 35				16 49			17 05	
Penrhiwceiber	d				15 55							16 25							16 55				
Mountain Ash	a				16 00							16 30							17 00				
	d				16 03							16 33							17 03				
Fernhill	d				16 06							16 36							17 06				
Cwmbach	d				16 10							16 40							17 10				
Aberdare	a				16 16							16 46							17 16				
Quakers Yard	d							16 09							16 39							17 09	
Merthyr Vale	a							16 14							16 44							17 14	
	d							16 17							16 47							17 17	
Troed Y Rhiw	d							16 21							16 51							17 21	
Pentre-bach	d							16 24							16 54							17 24	
Merthyr Tydfil	a							16 31							17 01							17 31	
Trehafod	d	15 40								16 10							16 40						
Porth	a	15 43								16 13							16 43						
	d	15 44								16 14							16 44						
Dinas Rhondda	d	15 48								16 18							16 48						
Tonypandy	d	15 50								16 20							16 50						
Llwynypia	d	15 52								16 22							16 52						
Ystrad Rhondda	a	15 55								16 25							16 55						
	d	15 59								16 29							16 59						
Ton Pentre	d	16 01								16 31							17 01						
Treorchy	d	16 04								16 34							17 04						
Ynyswen	d	16 07								16 37							17 07						
Treherbert	a	16 12								16 42							17 12						

When events are being held at the Principality Stadium, services are subject to alteration. Please check times before travelling.

For connections to Cardiff Bay please refer to Table T124

Table T130-R

Saturdays
21 December to 16 May

Bridgend, Barry Island, Barry, Penarth and Cardiff - Coryton, Rhymney, Pontypridd, Merthyr, Aberdare and Treherbert

Station		AW		AW	AW	AW	AW	AW	AW	AW	AW	AW		AW	AW	AW	AW	AW	AW	AW	AW	AW		AW	AW
Bridgend	d				15 42															16 42					
Llantwit Major	d				15 56															16 56					
Rhoose Cardiff Int Airport ✈	d				16 06															17 06					
Barry Island	d							16 26				16 41				16 56									17 26
Barry 3	d				16 15			16 30				16 45				17 00				17 15					17 30
Barry Docks	d				16 18			16 33				16 48				17 03				17 18					17 33
Cadoxton	d				16 21			16 36				16 51				17 06				17 21					17 36
Dinas Powys	d				16 25			16 40				16 55				17 10				17 25					17 40
Eastbrook	d				16 28			16 43				16 58				17 13				17 28					17 43
Cogan	d				16 30			16 45				17 00				17 15				17 30					17 45
Penarth	d					16 33								17 03			17 18				17 33				
Dingle Road	d					16 35								17 05			17 20				17 35				
Grangetown	d				16 34	16 39		16 49				17 04		17 09		17 19	17 24			17 34	17 39				17 49
Cardiff Central 7	a				16 40	16 45		16 55				17 10		17 15		17 25	17 30			17 40	17 46				17 55
	d	16 35		16 36	16 41	16 46	16 51	16 56	17 01	17 05	17 06	17 11		17 16	17 21	17 26	17 31	17 35	17 36	17 41		17 46		17 51	17 56
Cardiff Queen Street 3	a	16 39			16 45	16 50	16 55	17 00	17 05	17 09		17 15		17 20	17 25	17 30	17 35	17 39		17 45		17 50		17 55	18 00
	d	16 39			16 45	16 50	16 55	17 00	17 05	17 09		17 15		17 20	17 25	17 30	17 35	17 39		17 45		17 51		17 55	18 00
Heath Low Level	d						17 00								17 30									18 00	
Ty Glas	d						17 03								17 33									18 03	
Birchgrove	d						17 04								17 34									18 04	
Rhiwbina	d						17 06								17 36									18 06	
Whitchurch (Cardiff)	d						17 08								17 38									18 08	
Coryton	a						17 13								17 43									18 13	
Heath High Level	d					16 55			17 10					17 25			17 40					17 55			
Llanishen	d					16 58			17 13					17 28			17 43					17 59			
Lisvane & Thornhill	d					17 00			17 15					17 31			17 45					18 02			
Caerphilly	d					17 06			17 22					17 37			17 52					18 08			
Aber	d					17 08			17 24					17 39			17 54					18 11			
Energlyn & Churchill Park	d								17 26					17 41			17 56					18 14			
Llanbradach	d					17 12			17 30					17 45			18 00					18 18			
Ystrad Mynach	d					17 17			17 35					17 50			18 05					18 24			
Hengoed	d					17 20			17 38					17 53			18 08					18 27			
Pengam	d					17 23			17 41					17 56			18 11					18 31			
Gilfach Fargoed	d								17 44								18 14								
Bargoed	a					17 30			17 49					18 03			18 18					18 37			
	d								17 49								18 18					18 37			
Brithdir	d								17 53								18 22					18 41			
Tir-phil	d								17 56								18 25					18 44			
Pontlottyn	d								18 00								18 29					18 49			
Rhymney 3	a								18 06								18 35					18 56			
Cathays	d	16 42			16 48			17 03		17 12		17 18				17 33		17 42		17 48					18 03
Llandaf	d	16 46			16 52			17 07		17 16		17 22				17 37		17 46		17 52					18 07
Ninian Park	d			16 40							17 10								17 40						
Waun-gron Park	d			16 43							17 13								17 43						
Fairwater	d			16 45							17 15								17 45						
Danescourt	d			16 47							17 17								17 47						
Radyr 3	a	16 50		16 54	16 56			17 11		17 20	17 24	17 26				17 41		17 50	17 54	17 56					18 11
	d	16 50			16 56			17 11		17 20		17 26				17 41		17 50		17 56					18 11
Taffs Well	d	16 54			17 00			17 15		17 24		17 30				17 45		17 54		18 00					18 15
Trefforest Estate	d							17 19								17 49									18 19
Trefforest	d	17 01			17 07			17 23		17 31		17 37				17 53		18 01		18 07					18 23
Pontypridd 3	a	17 05			17 11			17 28		17 35		17 41				17 58		18 05		18 11					18 28
	d	17 05			17 12			17 28		17 35		17 42				17 58		18 05		18 12					18 28
Abercynon	d				17 19			17 35				17 49				18 05				18 19					18 35
Penrhiwceiber	d				17 25							17 55								18 25					
Mountain Ash	a				17 30							18 00								18 30					
	d				17 33							18 03								18 33					
Fernhill	d				17 36							18 06								18 36					
Cwmbach	d				17 40							18 10								18 40					
Aberdare	a				17 46							18 16								18 46					
Quakers Yard	d							17 39								18 09									18 39
Merthyr Vale	a							17 44								18 14									18 44
	d							17 47								18 17									18 47
Troed Y Rhiw	d							17 51								18 21									18 51
Pentre-bach	d							17 54								18 24									18 54
Merthyr Tydfil	a							18 01								18 31									19 01
Trehafod	d	17 10								17 40								18 10							
Porth	a	17 13								17 43								18 13							
	d	17 14								17 44								18 14							
Dinas Rhondda	d	17 18								17 48								18 18							
Tonypandy	d	17 20								17 50								18 20							
Llwynypia	d	17 22								17 52								18 22							
Ystrad Rhondda	a	17 25								17 55								18 25							
	d	17 29								17 59								18 29							
Ton Pentre	d	17 31								18 01								18 31							
Treorchy	d	17 34								18 04								18 34							
Ynyswen	d	17 37								18 07								18 37							
Treherbert	a	17 42								18 12								18 42							

When events are being held at the Principality Stadium, services are subject to alteration. Please check times before travelling.

For connections to Cardiff Bay please refer to Table T124

Table T130-R

Saturdays
21 December to 16 May

Bridgend, Barry Island, Barry, Penarth and Cardiff - Coryton, Rhymney, Pontypridd, Merthyr, Aberdare and Treherbert

Station		AW	AW	AW	AW	AW	AW	AW		AW	AW	AW	AW	AW	AW	AW	AW	AW		AW	AW	AW	AW	AW	AW
Bridgend	d												17 42											18 42	
Llantwit Major	d												17 56											18 56	
Rhoose Cardiff Int Airport ✈	d												18 06											19 06	
Barry Island	d				17 41			17 56								18 26				18 41	18 56				
Barry 3	d				17 45			18 00					18 15			18 31				18 45	19 00			19 15	
Barry Docks	d				17 48			18 03					18 18			18 34				18 48	19 03			19 18	
Cadoxton	d				17 51			18 06					18 21			18 37				18 51	19 06			19 21	
Dinas Powys	d				17 55			18 10					18 25			18 41				18 55	19 10			19 25	
Eastbrook	d				17 58			18 13					18 28			18 43				18 58	19 13			19 28	
Cogan	d				18 00			18 15					18 30			18 46				19 00	19 15			19 30	
Penarth	d	17 48				18 03				18 18				18 34			18 48					19 18			
Dingle Road	d	17 50				18 05				18 20				18 36			18 50					19 20			
Grangetown	d	17 54			18 04	18 09		18 19		18 24			18 34	18 40		18 50	18 54			19 04	19 19	19 24		19 34	
Cardiff Central 7	a	18 00			18 11	18 15		18 25		18 30			18 40	18 47		18 57	19 00			19 10	19 25	19 30		19 40	
	d	18 01	18 05	18 06	18 11	18 16	18 21	18 26		18 31	18 35	18 36	18 42		18 51		19 01	19 05		19 11	19 26	19 31	19 36	19 43	19 51
Cardiff Queen Street 3	a	18 05	18 09		18 15	18 20	18 25	18 30		18 35	18 39		18 46		18 55		19 05	19 09		19 15	19 30	19 35		19 47	19 55
	d	18 05	18 09		18 15	18 20	18 25	18 30		18 35	18 39		18 46		18 55		19 05	19 09		19 15	19 30	19 36		19 47	19 55
Heath Low Level	d						18 30								19 00										20 00
Ty Glas	d						18 33								19 03										20 03
Birchgrove	d						18 34								19 04										20 04
Rhiwbina	d						18 36								19 06										20 06
Whitchurch (Cardiff)	d						18 38								19 08										20 08
Coryton	a						18 43								19 13										20 13
Heath High Level	d	18 10				18 25				18 40							19 10					19 40			
Llanishen	d	18 13				18 28				18 43							19 13					19 43			
Lisvane & Thornhill	d	18 15				18 30				18 45							19 15					19 46			
Caerphilly	d	18 21				18 36				18 52							19a23					19 52			
Aber	d	18 23				18 38				18 54												19 54			
Energlyn & Churchill Park	d					18 41				18 56												19 57			
Llanbradach	d	18 27				18 44				19 00												20 00			
Ystrad Mynach	d	18 32				18a52				19 05												20 06			
Hengoed	d	18 35								19 08												20 08			
Pengam	d	18 38								19 11												20 12			
Gilfach Fargoed	d	18 41								19 14												20 15			
Bargoed	a	18 47								19 19												20 19			
	d									19 19												20 19			
Brithdir	d									19 23												20 23			
Tir-phil	d									19 26												20 26			
Pontlottyn	d									19 30												20 30			
Rhymney 3	a									19 36												20 35			
Cathays	d		18 12		18 18			18 33			18 42		18 49					19 12		19 18	19 33			19 50	
Llandaf	d		18 16		18 22			18 37			18 46		18 53					19 16		19 22	19 37			19 54	
Ninian Park	d			18 11								18 40											19 40		
Waun-gron Park	d			18 14								18 43											19 43		
Fairwater	d			18 16								18 45											19 45		
Danescourt	d			18 18								18 47											19 47		
Radyr 3	a		18 20	18 24	18 25			18 41			18 50	18 54	18 57					19 20		19 26	19 41		19 54	19 58	
	d		18 20		18 25			18 41			18 50		18 57					19 20		19 26	19 41			19 58	
Taffs Well	d		18 24		18 29			18 45			18 54		19 01					19 24		19 30	19 45			20 02	
Trefforest Estate	d							18 49													19 49				
Trefforest	d		18 31		18 36			18 53			19 01		19 08					19 31		19 37	19 53			20 09	
Pontypridd 3	a		18 35		18 41			18 58			19 05		19 12					19 35		19 41	19 58			20 13	
	d		18 35					18 58			19 05		19 13					19 35		19 42	19 58			20 13	
Abercynon	d							19 05					19 20							19 50	20 05			20 21	
Penrhiwceiber	d												19 25							19 56				20 27	
Mountain Ash	a												19 30							20 02				20 32	
	d												19 33							20 03				20 33	
Fernhill	d												19 36							20 06				20 36	
Cwmbach	d												19 40							20 10				20 40	
Aberdare	a												19 46							20 16				20 46	
Quakers Yard	d							19 09													20 09				
Merthyr Vale	a							19 14													20 14				
	d							19 17													20 15				
Troed Y Rhiw	d							19 21													20 19				
Pentre-bach	d							19 24													20 22				
Merthyr Tydfil	a							19 31													20 28				
Trehafod	d		18 40								19 10							19 40							
Porth	a		18 43								19 13							19 43							
	d		18 44								19 14							19 44							
Dinas Rhondda	d		18 48								19 18							19 48							
Tonypandy	d		18 50								19 20							19 50							
Llwynypia	d		18 52								19 22							19 52							
Ystrad Rhondda	a		18 55								19 25							19 55							
	d		18 59								19 29							19 59							
Ton Pentre	d		19 01								19 31							20 01							
Treorchy	d		19 04								19 34							20 04							
Ynyswen	d		19 07								19 37							20 07							
Treherbert	a		19 12								19 42							20 12							

When events are being held at the Principality Stadium, services are subject to alteration. Please check times before travelling.

For connections to Cardiff Bay please refer to Table T124

Table T130-R

Saturdays
21 December to 16 May

Bridgend, Barry Island, Barry, Penarth and Cardiff - Coryton, Rhymney, Pontypridd, Merthyr, Aberdare and Treherbert

		AW	AW	AW		AW	AW	AW	AW	AW	AW	AW	AW	AW		AW	AW	AW	AW	AW	AW	AW	AW	AW
Bridgend	d							19 42									20 42							21 42
Llantwit Major	d							19 56									20 56							21 56
Rhoose Cardiff Int Airport ✈	d							20 06									21 06							22 06
Barry Island	d	19 26		19 56								20 56									21 56			
Barry 3	d	19 30		20 00				20 15				21 00					21 15				22 00			22 15
Barry Docks	d	19 33		20 03				20 18				21 03					21 18				22 03			22 18
Cadoxton	d	19 36		20 06				20 21				21 06					21 21				22 06			22 21
Dinas Powys	d	19 40		20 10				20 25				21 10					21 25				22 10			22 25
Eastbrook	d	19 43		20 13				20 28				21 13					21 28				22 13			22 28
Cogan	d	19 45		20 15				20 30				21 15					21 30				22 15			22 30
Penarth	d		19 48			20 18				20 48						21 24		21 48					22 22	
Dingle Road	d		19 50			20 20				20 50						21 26		21 50					22 24	
Grangetown	d	19 49	19 54	20 19		20 24		20 34		20 54		21 19				21 30	21 34	21 54			22 19		22 28	22 34
Cardiff Central 7	a	19 55	20 00	20 25		20 30		20 40		21 00		21 26				21 38	21 40	22 00			22 25		22 34	22 40
	d	20 02	20 06	20 26		20 31	20 36	20 41	20 52	21 01	21 05	21 27	21 32	21 36			21 43	22 01	22 06	22 21	22 26	22 35	22 41	22 46
Cardiff Queen Street 3	a	20 06	20 10	20 30		20 35		20 45	20 56	21 05	21 09	21 31	21 36				21 47	22 05	22 10	22 25	22 30	22 39	22 45	22 50
	d	20 06	20 10	20 30		20 35		20 45	20 56	21 05	21 09	21 31	21 36				21 47	22 05	22 10	22 26	22 30	22 39	22 45	22 50
Heath Low Level	d								21 01											22 31				
Ty Glas	d								21 03											22 33				
Birchgrove	d								21 05											22 35				
Rhiwbina	d								21 07											22 37				
Whitchurch (Cardiff)	d								21 08											22 38				
Coryton	a								21 13											22 43				
Heath High Level	d	20 11				20 40				21 11			21 41					22 10				22 44		
Llanishen	d	20 14				20 43				21 14			21 44					22 13				22 47		
Lisvane & Thornhill	d	20 16				20 45				21 16			21 46					22 15				22 49		
Caerphilly	d	20a24				20 51				21 22			21 53					22a23				22 56		
Aber	d					20 53				21 24			21 55									22 58		
Energlyn & Churchill Park	d					20 55				21 26			21 57									23 00		
Llanbradach	d					20 59				21 30			22 01									23 04		
Ystrad Mynach	d					21 04				21a38			22 06									23 09		
Hengoed	d					21 07							22 09									23 12		
Pengam	d					21 10							22 12									23 15		
Gilfach Fargoed	d					21 13							22 15									23 18		
Bargoed	a					21 18							22 20									23 23		
	d					21 18							22 20									23 23		
Brithdir	d					21 22							22 24									23 27		
Tir-phil	d					21 25							22 27									23 30		
Pontlottyn	d					21 29							22 31									23 34		
Rhymney 3	a					21 33							22 34									23 37		
Cathays	d		20 13	20 33				20 48			21 12	21 34					21 50		22 12		22 33		22 48	22 53
Llandaf	d		20 17	20 37				20 52			21 16	21 38					21 54		22 17		22 37		22 52	22 57
Ninian Park	d						20 40							21 40										
Waun-gron Park	d						20 43							21 43										
Fairwater	d						20 45							21 45										
Danescourt	d						20 47							21 47										
Radyr 3	a		20 20	20 41			20 54	20 56			21 20	21 42		21 54			21 57		22 20		22 41		22 55	23 00
	d		20 20	20 41				20 56			21 20	21 42					21 58		22 20		22 41		22 55	23 00
Taffs Well	d		20 24	20 45				21 00			21 24	21 46					22 02		22 24		22 45		22 59	23 04
Trefforest Estate	d			20 49								21 50									22 49			
Trefforest	d		20 31	20 53				21 07			21 31	21 54					22 09		22 31		22 53		23 06	23 11
Pontypridd 3	a		20 35	20 58				21 11			21 35	21 59					22 13		22 35		22 58		23 10	23 15
	d		20 35	20 58				21 12			21 35	21 59					22 14		22 35		22 58		23 11	23 15
Abercynon	d			21 05				21 19				22 06					22 21				23 05		23 18	
Penrhiwceiber	d							21 25									22 27						23 24	
Mountain Ash	a							21 29									22 30						23 28	
	d							21 29									22 31						23 28	
Fernhill	d							21 32									22 34						23 31	
Cwmbach	d							21 36									22 38						23 35	
Aberdare	a							21 43									22 44						23 43	
Quakers Yard	d			21 09								22 10									23 09			
Merthyr Vale	a			21 14								22 15									23 14			
	d			21 15								22 16									23 15			
Troed Y Rhiw	d			21 19								22 20									23 19			
Pentre-bach	d			21 22								22 23									23 22			
Merthyr Tydfil	a			21 30								22 31									23 30			
Trehafod	d		20 40								21 40								22 40					23 20
Porth	a		20 43								21 43								22 43					23 23
	d		20 44								21 44								22 44					23 24
Dinas Rhondda	d		20 48								21 48								22 48					23 28
Tonypandy	d		20 50								21 50								22 50					23 30
Llwynypia	d		20 52								21 52								22 52					23 32
Ystrad Rhondda	a		20 55								21 55								22 55					23 35
	d		20 59								21 59								22 59					23 38
Ton Pentre	d		21 01								22 01								23 01					23 40
Treorchy	d		21 04								22 04								23 04					23 43
Ynyswen	d		21 07								22 07								23 07					23 46
Treherbert	a		21 12								22 12								23 12					23 52

When events are being held at the Principality Stadium, services are subject to alteration. Please check times before travelling.

For connections to Cardiff Bay please refer to Table T124

Table T130-R

Saturdays
21 December to 16 May

Bridgend, Barry Island, Barry, Penarth and Cardiff - Coryton, Rhymney, Pontypridd, Merthyr, Aberdare and Treherbert

		AW	AW	AW	AW	AW
Bridgend	d					22 42
Llantwit Major	d					22 56
Rhoose Cardiff Int Airport ✈	d					23 06
Barry Island	d			22 45		
Barry 3	d			22 49		23 15
Barry Docks	d			22 52		23 18
Cadoxton	d			22 55		23 21
Dinas Powys	d			22 59		23 25
Eastbrook	d			23 02		23 28
Cogan	d			23 04		23 32
Penarth	d		22 51		23 26	
Dingle Road	d		22 53		23 28	
Grangetown	d		22 57	23 08	23 32	23 36
Cardiff Central 7	a		23 03	23 14	23 38	23 40
	d	22 54	23 16	23 26		
Cardiff Queen Street 3	a		23 20	23 30		
	d		23 20	23 30		
Heath Low Level	d					
Ty Glas	d					
Birchgrove	d					
Rhiwbina	d					
Whitchurch (Cardiff)	d					
Coryton	a					
Heath High Level	d		23 25			
Llanishen	d		23 28			
Lisvane & Thornhill	d		23 30			
Caerphilly	d		23 36			
Aber	d		23 38			
Energlyn & Churchill Park	d		23 40			
Llanbradach	d		23 44			
Ystrad Mynach	d		23a52			
Hengoed	d					
Pengam	d					
Gilfach Fargoed	d					
Bargoed	a					
	d					
Brithdir	d					
Tir-phil	d					
Pontlottyn	d					
Rhymney 3	a					
Cathays	d			23 33		
Llandaf	d			23 37		
Ninian Park	d	22 58				
Waun-gron Park	d	23 01				
Fairwater	d	23 03				
Danescourt	d	23 05				
Radyr 3	a	23 12		23 41		
	d			23 41		
Taffs Well	d			23 45		
Trefforest Estate	d					
Trefforest	d			23 52		
Pontypridd 3	a			23 58		
	d					
Abercynon	d					
Penrhiwceiber	d					
Mountain Ash	a					
	d					
Fernhill	d					
Cwmbach	d					
Aberdare	a					
Quakers Yard	d					
Merthyr Vale	a					
	d					
Troed Y Rhiw	d					
Pentre-bach	d					
Merthyr Tydfil	a					
Trehafod	d					
Porth	a					
	d					
Dinas Rhondda	d					
Tonypandy	d					
Llwynypia	d					
Ystrad Rhondda	a					
	d					
Ton Pentre	d					
Treorchy	d					
Ynyswen	d					
Treherbert	a					

When events are being held at the Principality Stadium, services are subject to alteration. Please check times before travelling.

For connections to Cardiff Bay please refer to Table T124

Table T130-R

Sundays

15 December to 10 May

Bridgend, Barry Island, Barry, Penarth and Cardiff - Coryton, Rhymney, Pontypridd, Merthyr, Aberdare and Treherbert

		AW	AW	AW	AW	AW	AW	AW	AW	AW	AW	AW	AW	AW	AW	AW	AW	AW	AW	AW	AW	AW	AW
Bridgend	d											09 42											11 42
Llantwit Major	d											09 56											11 56
Rhoose Cardiff Int Airport ✈	d											10 06											12 06
Barry Island	d					08 56				09 56			10 26				10 56			11 26	11 56		
Barry 3	d					09 00				10 00		10 15	10 31				11 00			11 31	12 00		12 15
Barry Docks	d					09 03				10 03		10 18	10 34				11 03			11 34	12 03		12 18
Cadoxton	d					09 06				10 06		10 21	10 37				11 06			11 37	12 06		12 21
Dinas Powys	d					09 10				10 10		10 25	10 41				11 10			11 41	12 10		12 25
Eastbrook	d					09 13				10 13		10 28	10 43				11 13			11 43	12 13		12 28
Cogan	d					09 15				10 15		10 30	10 46				11 15			11 46	12 15		12 30
Penarth	d						09 33												11 32				
Dingle Road	d						09 35												11 34				
Grangetown	d					09 19	09 39			10 19		10 34	10 50				11 19		11 38	11 50	12 19		12 34
Cardiff Central 7	a					09 26	09 46			10 25		10 40	10 56				11 25		11 45	11 56	12 25		12 41
	d	08 26	09 00	09 05	09 35	09 41		10 00	10 05	10 26	10 35	10 41		11 00	11 05	11 35	11 41	12 00	12 05		12 26	12 35	
Cardiff Queen Street 3	a	08 30	09 04	09 09	09 39	09 45		10 04	10 09	10 30	10 39	10 45		11 04	11 09	11 39	11 45	12 04	12 09		12 30	12 39	
	d	08 31	09 04	09 09	09 39	09 46		10 04	10 09	10 30	10 39	10 46		11 04	11 09	11 39	11 46	12 04	12 09		12 30	12 39	
Heath Low Level	d																						
Ty Glas	d																						
Birchgrove	d																						
Rhiwbina	d																						
Whitchurch (Cardiff)	d																						
Coryton	a																						
Heath High Level	d			09 14	09 44				10 14		10 44				11 14	11 44			12 14			12 44	
Llanishen	d			09 17	09 47				10 17		10 47				11 17	11 47			12 17			12 47	
Lisvane & Thornhill	d			09 19	09 49				10 19		10 49				11 19	11 49			12 19			12 50	
Caerphilly	d			09 25	09a56				10 25		10a56				11 26	11a56			12 26			12a56	
Aber	d			09 27					10 27						11 28				12 28				
Energlyn & Churchill Park	d			09 29					10 29						11 30				12 30				
Llanbradach	d			09 33					10 33						11 33				12 34				
Ystrad Mynach	d			09 38					10 38						11 38				12 39				
Hengoed	d			09 41					10 41						11 41				12 42				
Pengam	d			09 44					10 44						11 44				12 45				
Gilfach Fargoed	d			09 47					10 47						11 47				12 48				
Bargoed	a			09 52					10 51						11 51				12 52				
	d			09 52					10 51						11 51				12 52				
Brithdir	d			09 56					10 55						11 55				12 56				
Tir-phil	d			09 59					10 58						11 58				12 59				
Pontlottyn	d			10 03					11 02						12 02				13 03				
Rhymney 3	a			10 08					11 08						12 06				13 08				
Cathays	d	08 33	09 07			09 48		10 07		10 33		10 48		11 07			11 48	12 07			12 33		
Llandaf	d	08 38	09 11			09 53		10 11		10 37		10 53		11 11			11 53	12 11			12 37		
Ninian Park	d																						
Waun-gron Park	d																						
Fairwater	d																						
Danescourt	d																						
Radyr 3	a	08 41	09 15			09 56		10 15		10 41		10 56		11 15			11 56	12 15			12 41		
	d	08 41	09 15			09 56		10 15		10 41		10 56		11 15			11 56	12 15			12 41		
Taffs Well	d	08 45	09 19			10 00		10 19		10 45		11 00		11 19			12 00	12 19			12 45		
Trefforest Estate	d																						
Trefforest	d	08 53	09 26			10 07		10 26		10 53		11 07		11 26			12 07	12 26			12 53		
Pontypridd 3	a	08 57	09 31			10 11		10 31		10 57		11 11		11 31			12 11	12 31			12 57		
	d	08 58	09 31			10 12		10 31		10 58		11 12		11 31			12 12	12 31			12 58		
Abercynon	d	09 05				10 19				11 05		11 19					12 19				13 05		
Penrhiwceiber	d					10 25						11 25					12 25						
Mountain Ash	a					10 29						11 29					12 29						
	d					10 30						11 30					12 30						
Fernhill	d					10 33						11 33					12 33						
Cwmbach	d					10 37						11 37					12 37						
Aberdare	a					10 43						11 43					12 43						
Quakers Yard	d	09 09								11 09											13 09		
Merthyr Vale	a	09 14								11 14											13 14		
	d	09 15								11 15											13 15		
Troed Y Rhiw	d	09 19								11 19											13 19		
Pentre-bach	d	09 22								11 22											13 22		
Merthyr Tydfil	a	09 30								11 30											13 30		
Trehafod	d		09 36					10 36						11 36				12 36					
Porth	a		09 39					10 39						11 39				12 39					
	d		09 40					10 40						11 40				12 40					
Dinas Rhondda	d		09 44					10 44						11 44				12 44					
Tonypandy	d		09 46					10 46						11 46				12 46					
Llwynypia	d		09 48					10 48						11 48				12 48					
Ystrad Rhondda	a		09 51					10 51						11 51				12 51					
	d		09 54					10 54						11 54				12 54					
Ton Pentre	d		09 56					10 56						11 56				12 56					
Treorchy	d		09 59					10 59						11 59				12 59					
Ynyswen	d		10 02					11 02						12 02				13 02					
Treherbert	a		10 07					11 07						12 07				13 07					

When events are being held at the Principality Stadium, services are subject to alteration. Please check times before travelling.

For connections to Cardiff Bay please refer to Table T124

Table T130-R

Sundays

15 December to 10 May

Bridgend, Barry Island, Barry, Penarth and Cardiff - Coryton, Rhymney, Pontypridd, Merthyr, Aberdare and Treherbert

		AW	AW	AW	AW	AW	AW	AW	AW	AW	AW	AW	AW	AW	AW	AW	AW	AW	AW	AW	AW	AW	AW
Bridgend	d											13 42											15 42
Llantwit Major	d											13 56											15 56
Rhoose Cardiff Int Airport ✈	d											14 06											16 06
Barry Island	d	12 26				12 56			13 25	13 56			14 26				14 56			15 26	15 56		
Barry 3	d	12 31				13 00			13 30	14 00		14 15	14 31				15 00			15 31	16 00		16 15
Barry Docks	d	12 34				13 03			13 33	14 03		14 18	14 34				15 03			15 34	16 03		16 18
Cadoxton	d	12 37				13 06			13 36	14 06		14 21	14 37				15 06			15 37	16 06		16 21
Dinas Powys	d	12 41				13 10			13 40	14 10		14 25	14 41				15 10			15 41	16 10		16 25
Eastbrook	d	12 43				13 13			13 43	14 13		14 28	14 43				15 13			15 43	16 13		16 28
Cogan	d	12 46				13 15			13 45	14 15		14 30	14 46				15 15			15 46	16 15		16 30
Penarth	d						13 33											15 32					
Dingle Road	d						13 35											15 34					
Grangetown	d	12 50				13 19	13 39		13 49	14 19		14 34	14 50				15 19	15 38		15 50	16 19		16 34
Cardiff Central 7	a	12 56				13 25	13 45		13 55	14 25		14 41	14 57				15 25	15 45		15 56	16 25		16 40
	d		13 00	13 05	13 35	13 41		14 00	14 05	14 26	14 35			15 00	15 05	15 35	15 41		16 00	16 05	16 28	16 35	16 41
Cardiff Queen Street 3	a		13 04	13 09	13 39	13 45		14 04	14 09	14 30	14 39			15 04	15 09	15 39	15 45		16 04	16 09	16 32	16 39	16 45
	d		13 04	13 09	13 39	13 46		14 04	14 09	14 30	14 39			15 04	15 09	15 39	15 46		16 04	16 09	16 32	16 39	16 46
Heath Low Level	d																						
Ty Glas	d																						
Birchgrove	d																						
Rhiwbina	d																						
Whitchurch (Cardiff)	d																						
Coryton	a																						
Heath High Level	d			13 14	13 44				14 14		14 44				15 14	15 44				16 14		16 44	
Llanishen	d			13 17	13 47				14 17		14 47				15 17	15 47				16 17		16 47	
Lisvane & Thornhill	d			13 19	13 49				14 19		14 50				15 19	15 49				16 19		16 50	
Caerphilly	d			13 26	13a56				14 26		14a56				15 26	15a56				16 26		16a56	
Aber	d			13 28					14 28						15 28					16 28			
Energlyn & Churchill Park	d			13 30					14 30						15 30					16 30			
Llanbradach	d			13 33					14 34						15 33					16 34			
Ystrad Mynach	d			13 38					14 39						15 38					16 39			
Hengoed	d			13 41					14 42						15 41					16 42			
Pengam	d			13 44					14 45						15 44					16 45			
Gilfach Fargoed	d			13 47					14 48						15 47					16 48			
Bargoed	a			13 51					14 52						15 51					16 52			
	d			13 51					14 52						15 51					16 52			
Brithdir	d			13 55					14 56						15 55					16 56			
Tir-phil	d			13 58					14 59						15 58					16 59			
Pontlottyn	d			14 02					15 03						16 02					17 03			
Rhymney 3	a			14 08					15 07						16 07					17 08			
Cathays	d		13 07			13 48		14 07		14 33				15 07			15 48		16 07		16 35		16 48
Llandaf	d		13 11			13 53		14 11		14 37				15 11			15 53		16 11		16 39		16 53
Ninian Park	d																						
Waun-gron Park	d																						
Fairwater	d																						
Danescourt	d																						
Radyr 3	a		13 15			13 56		14 15		14 41				15 15			15 56		16 15		16 43		16 56
	d		13 15			13 56		14 15		14 41				15 15			15 56		16 15		16 43		16 56
Taffs Well	d		13 19			14 00		14 19		14 45				15 19			16 00		16 19		16 47		17 00
Trefforest Estate	d																						
Trefforest	d		13 26			14 07		14 26		14 53				15 26			16 07		16 26		16 55		17 07
Pontypridd 3	a		13 31			14 11		14 31		14 57				15 31			16 11		16 31		16 59		17 11
	d		13 31			14 12		14 31		14 58				15 31			16 12		16 31		17 00		17 12
Abercynon	d					14 19				15 05							16 19				17 07		17 19
Penrhiwceiber	d					14 25											16 25						17 25
Mountain Ash	a					14 29											16 29						17 29
	d					14 30											16 30						17 30
Fernhill	d					14 33											16 33						17 33
Cwmbach	d					14 37											16 37						17 37
Aberdare	a					14 43											16 43						17 43
Quakers Yard	d									15 09											17 11		
Merthyr Vale	a									15 14											17 16		
	d									15 15											17 17		
Troed Y Rhiw	d									15 19											17 21		
Pentre-bach	d									15 22											17 24		
Merthyr Tydfil	a									15 30											17 31		
Trehafod	d		13 36					14 36						15 36					16 36				
Porth	a		13 39					14 39						15 39					16 39				
	d		13 40					14 40						15 40					16 40				
Dinas Rhondda	d		13 44					14 44						15 44					16 44				
Tonypandy	d		13 46					14 46						15 46					16 46				
Llwynypia	d		13 48					14 48						15 48					16 48				
Ystrad Rhondda	a		13 51					14 51						15 51					16 51				
	d		13 54					14 54						15 54					16 54				
Ton Pentre	d		13 56					14 56						15 56					16 56				
Treorchy	d		13 59					14 59						15 59					16 59				
Ynyswen	d		14 02					15 02						16 02					17 02				
Treherbert	a		14 07					15 07						16 07					17 07				

When events are being held at the Principality Stadium, services are subject to alteration. Please check times before travelling.

For connections to Cardiff Bay please refer to Table T124

Table T130-R

Sundays
15 December to 10 May

Bridgend, Barry Island, Barry, Penarth and Cardiff - Coryton, Rhymney, Pontypridd, Merthyr, Aberdare and Treherbert

Station		AW	AW	AW	AW	AW	AW	AW	AW	AW	AW	AW
Bridgend	d											17 42
Llantwit Major	d											17 56
Rhoose Cardiff Int Airport ✈	d											18 06
Barry Island	d	16 26				16 56			17 26	17 56		
Barry 3	d	16 31				17 00			17 31	18 00		18 15
Barry Docks	d	16 34				17 03			17 34	18 03		18 18
Cadoxton	d	16 37				17 06			17 37	18 06		18 21
Dinas Powys	d	16 41				17 10			17 41	18 10		18 25
Eastbrook	d	16 43				17 13			17 43	18 13		18 28
Cogan	d	16 46				17 15			17 46	18 15		18 30
Penarth	d							17 32				
Dingle Road	d							17 34				
Grangetown	d	16 50				17 19		17 38	17 50	18 19		18 34
Cardiff Central 7	a	16 56				17 25		17 44	17 56	18 25		18 40
	d		17 00	17 05	17 35	17 41	18 00	18 05		18 26	18 35	18 41
Cardiff Queen Street 3	a		17 04	17 09	17 39	17 45	18 04	18 09		18 30	18 39	18 45
	d		17 04	17 09	17 39	17 46	18 04	18 09		18 30	18 39	18 46
Heath Low Level	d											
Ty Glas	d											
Birchgrove	d											
Rhiwbina	d											
Whitchurch (Cardiff)	d											
Coryton	a											
Heath High Level	d			17 14	17 44			18 14			18 44	
Llanishen	d			17 17	17 47			18 17			18 47	
Lisvane & Thornhill	d			17 19	17 49			18 19			18 50	
Caerphilly	d			17 26	17a56			18 26			18a56	
Aber	d			17 28				18 28				
Energlyn & Churchill Park	d			17 30				18 30				
Llanbradach	d			17 33				18 34				
Ystrad Mynach	d			17 38				18 39				
Hengoed	d			17 41				18 42				
Pengam	d			17 44				18 45				
Gilfach Fargoed	d			17 47				18 48				
Bargoed	a			17 51				18 52				
	d			17 51				18 52				
Brithdir	d			17 55				18 56				
Tir-phil	d			17 58				18 59				
Pontlottyn	d			18 02				19 03				
Rhymney 3	a			18 07				19 08				
Cathays	d		17 07			17 48	18 07			18 33		18 48
Llandaf	d		17 11			17 53	18 11			18 37		18 53
Ninian Park	d											
Waun-gron Park	d											
Fairwater	d											
Danescourt	d											
Radyr 3	a		17 15			17 56	18 14			18 41		18 56
	d		17 15			17 56	18 15			18 41		18 56
Taffs Well	d		17 19			18 00	18 19			18 45		19 00
Trefforest Estate	d											
Trefforest	d		17 26			18 07	18 26			18 53		19 07
Pontypridd 3	a		17 31			18 11	18 31			18 57		19 11
	d		17 31			18 12	18 31			18 58		19 12
Abercynon	d					18 19				19 05		19 19
Penrhiwceiber	d					18 25						19 25
Mountain Ash	a					18 29						19 29
	d					18 30						19 30
Fernhill	d					18 33						19 33
Cwmbach	d					18 37						19 37
Aberdare	a					18 43						19 43
Quakers Yard	d									19 09		
Merthyr Vale	a									19 14		
	d									19 15		
Troed Y Rhiw	d									19 19		
Pentre-bach	d									19 22		
Merthyr Tydfil	a									19 30		
Trehafod	d		17 36				18 36					
Porth	a		17 39				18 39					
	d		17 40				18 40					
Dinas Rhondda	d		17 44				18 44					
Tonypandy	d		17 46				18 46					
Llwynypia	d		17 48				18 48					
Ystrad Rhondda	a		17 51				18 51					
	d		17 54				18 54					
Ton Pentre	d		17 56				18 56					
Treorchy	d		17 59				18 59					
Ynyswen	d		18 02				19 02					
Treherbert	a		18 07				19 07					

Station		AW	AW	AW	AW	AW	AW	AW	AW	AW	AW
Bridgend	d										
Llantwit Major	d										
Rhoose Cardiff Int Airport ✈	d										
Barry Island	d	18 26			18 56		19 26	19 26			19 56
Barry 3	d	18 31			19 00		19 31	19 31			20 00
Barry Docks	d	18 34			19 03		19 34	19 34			20 03
Cadoxton	d	18 37			19 06		19 37	19 37			20 06
Dinas Powys	d	18 41			19 10		19 41	19 41			20 10
Eastbrook	d	18 43			19 13		19 43	19 43			20 13
Cogan	d	18 46			19 15		19 46	19 46			20 15
Penarth	d					19 32					
Dingle Road	d					19 34					
Grangetown	d	18 50			19 19	19 38	19 50	19 50			20 19
Cardiff Central 7	a	18 56			19 25	19 46	19 55	19 55			20 25
	d		19 00	19 35	19 41		20 00		20 00	20 05	20 26
Cardiff Queen Street 3	a		19 04	19 39	19 45		20 04		20 04	20 09	20 30
	d		19 04	19 39	19 46		20 04		20 04	20 09	20 30
Heath Low Level	d										
Ty Glas	d										
Birchgrove	d										
Rhiwbina	d										
Whitchurch (Cardiff)	d										
Coryton	a										
Heath High Level	d			19 44						20 14	
Llanishen	d			19 47						20 17	
Lisvane & Thornhill	d			19 49						20 19	
Caerphilly	d			19a56						20 26	
Aber	d									20 28	
Energlyn & Churchill Park	d									20 30	
Llanbradach	d									20 34	
Ystrad Mynach	d									20 39	
Hengoed	d									20 42	
Pengam	d									20 45	
Gilfach Fargoed	d									20 48	
Bargoed	a									20 52	
	d									20 52	
Brithdir	d									20 56	
Tir-phil	d									20 59	
Pontlottyn	d									21 03	
Rhymney 3	a									21 07	
Cathays	d		19 07		19 48		20 07		20 07		20 33
Llandaf	d		19 11		19 53		20 11		20 11		20 37
Ninian Park	d										
Waun-gron Park	d										
Fairwater	d										
Danescourt	d										
Radyr 3	a		19 15		19 56		20 15		20 15		20 41
	d		19 15		19 56		20 15		20 15		20 41
Taffs Well	d		19 19		20 00		20 19		20 19		20 45
Trefforest Estate	d										
Trefforest	d		19 26		20 07		20 26		20 26		20 53
Pontypridd 3	a		19 31		20 11		20 31		20 31		20 58
	d		19 31		20 12		20 31		20 31		20 58
Abercynon	d				20 19						21 05
Penrhiwceiber	d				20 25						
Mountain Ash	a				20 29						
	d				20 30						
Fernhill	d				20 33						
Cwmbach	d				20 37						
Aberdare	a				20 43						
Quakers Yard	d										21 09
Merthyr Vale	a										21 14
	d										21 15
Troed Y Rhiw	d										21 19
Pentre-bach	d										21 22
Merthyr Tydfil	a										21 30
Trehafod	d		19 36				20 36		20 36		
Porth	a		19 39				20 39		20 39		
	d		19 40				20 40		20 40		
Dinas Rhondda	d		19 44				20 44		20 44		
Tonypandy	d		19 46				20 46		20 46		
Llwynypia	d		19 48				20 48		20 48		
Ystrad Rhondda	a		19 51				20 51		20 51		
	d		19 54				20 54		20 54		
Ton Pentre	d		19 56				20 56		20 56		
Treorchy	d		19 59				20 59		20 59		
Ynyswen	d		20 02				21 02		21 02		
Treherbert	a		20 07				21 07		21 07		

When events are being held at the Principality Stadium, services are subject to alteration. Please check times before travelling.

For connections to Cardiff Bay please refer to Table T124

NRT DECEMBER 19 EDITION

Table T130-R

Sundays
15 December to 10 May

Bridgend, Barry Island, Barry, Penarth and Cardiff - Coryton, Rhymney, Pontypridd, Merthyr, Aberdare and Treherbert

Station		AW	AW	AW	AW	AW	AW	AW	AW	AW
Bridgend	d	19 42							21 42	
Llantwit Major	d	19 56							21 56	
Rhoose Cardiff Int Airport ✈	d	20 06							22 06	
Barry Island	d			20 27		20 56	21 27	21 56		22 56
Barry 3	d	20 15		20 31		21 01	21 31	22 01	22 15	23 00
Barry Docks	d	20 18		20 34		21 04	21 34	22 04	22 18	23 03
Cadoxton	d	20 21		20 37		21 07	21 37	22 07	22 21	23 06
Dinas Powys	d	20 25		20 41		21 11	21 41	22 11	22 25	23 10
Eastbrook	d	20 28		20 44		21 13	21 44	22 13	22 28	23 13
Cogan	d	20 30		20 46		21 16	21 46	22 16	22 30	23 15
Penarth	d				20 52					
Dingle Road	d				20 54					
Grangetown	d	20 34		20 50	20 58	21 20	21 50	22 20	22 34	23 19
Cardiff Central 7	a	20 41		20 56	21 05	21 26	21 56	22 26	22 41	23 26
	d		21 00	21 00	21 16	22 06				
Cardiff Queen Street 3	a		21 04	21 04	21 20	22 10				
	d		21 04	21 04	21 20	22 10				
Heath Low Level	d									
Ty Glas	d									
Birchgrove	d									
Rhiwbina	d									
Whitchurch (Cardiff)	d									
Coryton	a									
Heath High Level	d				21 25					
Llanishen	d				21 28					
Lisvane & Thornhill	d				21 30					
Caerphilly	d				21 36					
Aber	d				21 38					
Energlyn & Churchill Park	d				21 40					
Llanbradach	d				21 44					
Ystrad Mynach	d				21 49					
Hengoed	d				21 52					
Pengam	d				21 55					
Gilfach Fargoed	d				21 58					
Bargoed	a				22 03					
	d				22 03					
Brithdir	d				22 07					
Tir-phil	d				22 10					
Pontlottyn	d				22 14					
Rhymney 3	a				22 19					
Cathays	d		21 07	21 07		22 13				
Llandaf	d		21 11	21 11		22 17				
Ninian Park	d									
Waun-gron Park	d									
Fairwater	d									
Danescourt	d									
Radyr 3	a		21 15	21 15		22 20				
	d		21 15	21 15		22 20				
Taffs Well	d		21 19	21 19		22 24				
Trefforest Estate	d									
Trefforest	d		21 26	21 26		22 31				
Pontypridd 3	a		21 31	21 31		22 36				
	d		21 31	21 31		22 36				
Abercynon	d									
Penrhiwceiber	d									
Mountain Ash	a									
	d									
Fernhill	d									
Cwmbach	d									
Aberdare	a									
Quakers Yard	d									
Merthyr Vale	a									
	d									
Troed Y Rhiw	d									
Pentre-bach	d									
Merthyr Tydfil	a									
Trehafod	d		21 36	21 36		22 41				
Porth	a		21 39	21 39		22 44				
	d		21 40	21 40		22 45				
Dinas Rhondda	d		21 44	21 44		22 49				
Tonypandy	d		21 46	21 46		22 51				
Llwynypia	d		21 48	21 48		22 53				
Ystrad Rhondda	a		21 51	21 51		22 56				
	d		21 54	21 54		22 59				
Ton Pentre	d		21 56	21 56		23 01				
Treorchy	d		21 59	21 59		23 04				
Ynyswen	d		22 02	22 02		23 07				
Treherbert	a		22 07	22 07		23 13				

When events are being held at the Principality Stadium, services are subject to alteration. Please check times before travelling.

For connections to Cardiff Bay please refer to Table T124

Table T131-F

Mondays to Fridays

16 December to 15 May

Manchester, Holyhead and Crewe - Cardiff

Miles	Miles	Station		AW MO ◇	AW MX ◇	AW ◇	AW	AW ◇ 🍴	AW ◇	AW ◇	AW ◇ 🍴	AW ◇	AW	AW	AW ◇ 🍴	AW ■1 ⊠	AW ◇	AW ◇ 🍴	AW ◇	AW	AW ◇	AW ◇	AW
0	—	**Manchester Piccadilly** 10 ⇌	d												06 30			07 30					
6	—	Stockport	d												06 39			07 39					
12	—	Wilmslow	d												06 47			07 47					
—	0	Holyhead	d									04 25				05 34					06 28		
—	25	Bangor (Gwynedd)	d									04 57				06 02					07 06		
—	—	Llandudno	d										05 53						06 41	07 08		07 45	08 02
—	40	Llandudno Junction	d									05 15	06a02			06 20			06 51	07a18	07 25	07 54	08a12
—	85	Chester	d									06 20				07 16			07 53		08 19	08a51	
—	97	Wrexham General	d									06 35				07 35					08 35		
—	102	Ruabon	d									06 42									08 42		
—	106	Chirk	d									06 48									08 49		
—	109	Gobowen	d									06 54									08 54		
31	—	**Crewe** 10	d					04 50			05 58			06 40	07 08		07 34	08 10	08a19				
35½	—	Nantwich	d					04 58			06 06			06 47	07 17		07 42						
40	—	Wrenbury	d								06x12						07x48						
44¾	—	Whitchurch (Shrops)	d					05 09			06 19			06 59			07 57						
49¼	—	Prees	d								06x25						08x02						
53	—	Wem	d	00 04				05 18			06 30			07 09			08 09						
56½	—	Yorton	d	00x09							06x35						08x13						
63¾	126	**Shrewsbury** 5	a	00 17				05 30			06 46	07 14		07 25	07 43	08 06	08 26	08 40			09 13		
—	—		d			04 46		05 31	05 56	06 10	06 48	07 17			07 43	08 10		08 40			09 15		
76½	—	Church Stretton	d			05 04		05 46	06 14	06 26	07 03				07 59						09 30		
83¾	—	Craven Arms 3	d			05a14		05 54	06 26	06 34	07 11				08 07						09 38		
91	154	Ludlow	d					06 02		06 43	07 18	07 43			08 15			09 06			09 45		
102	—	Leominster	d					06 12		06 54	07 29	07 53			08 25			09 17					
114½	177½	**Hereford** 7	a					06 31		07 10	07 45	08 10			08 42	08 56		09 33			10 10		
—	—		d		00 10		05 26	06 40		07 10	07 48	08 10			08 43	09 00		09 36			10 10		
138½	—	Abergavenny	d		00 34		05 51	07 03		07 34	08 12	08 33			09 07			09 58			10 33		
148	211	Pontypool and New Inn	d		00 44		06 02	07 14		07 45	08 22	08 43			09 18			10 10			10 43		
151	214	Cwmbran	d		00 49		06 07	07 19		07 50	08 28	08 48			09 24			10 14			10 48		
158	221	**Newport (South Wales)** 5	a		01 02		06 19	07 31		08 01	08 39	09 01			09 37	09 43		10 29			11 00		
169¾	232	**Cardiff Central** 7	a		01 23		06 35	07 49		08 18	08 56	09 15			09 57	09 58		10 45			11 16		
—	—	Swansea	a					08 52	10 02		09 56				10 56			11 38					

Station		AW ◇ 🍴	AW ◇ 🍴	AW ■ 🍴	AW ◇ 🍴	AW ◇ 🍴	AW ◇ 🍴	AW ◇	AW ◇ 🍴	AW	AW ◇ 🍴	AW	AW ◇ 🍴	AW ■ 🍴	AW ◇ 🍴	AW ■ 🍴	AW ◇ 🍴	AW	AW ■1 ⊠	AW	AW ◇	AW ■ 🍴	AW
Manchester Piccadilly 10 ⇌	d	08 31			09 31				10 31				11 31			12 31						13 31	
Stockport	d	08 39			09 39				10 39				11 39			12 39						13 39	
Wilmslow	d	08 47			09 47				10 47				11 47			12 47						13 47	
Holyhead	d					08 05								10 40					11 34				
Bangor (Gwynedd)	d					09 02								11 09					12 01				
Llandudno	d			08 30			09 45	10 08			10 44	11 13			11 44					12 47	13 09		14 08
Llandudno Junction	d			08 39		09 25	09 54	10a19			10 53	11a22		11 27	11 53				12 19	12a57	13a19		14a18
Chester	d			09 28		10 21	10a51				11a50			12 19	12a50				13 16				
Wrexham General	d			09 45		10 36								12 35					13 31				
Ruabon	d			09 52		10 43								12 42					13 39				
Chirk	d			09 58		10 49								12 48					13 46				
Gobowen	d			10 04		10 55								12 54					13 51				
Crewe 10	d	09 08	09 14		10 08				11 08	11 20			12 08			13 10		13 20				14 08	
Nantwich	d		09 22							11 28								13 28				14 17	
Wrenbury	d		09x29							11x35								13x35					
Whitchurch (Shrops)	d		09 37							11 43								13 43				14 28	
Prees	d		09x43							11x49								13x49					
Wem	d		09 49							11 55								13 55					
Yorton	d		09x55							12x01								14x01					
Shrewsbury 5	a	09 38	10 07	10 23	10 38	11 14			11 38	12 13			12 38	13 13		13 40		14 13	14 16			14 46	
	d	09 40	10 09	10 25	10 39	11 14			11 39				12 39	13 15		13 40	14 05		14 17			14 51	
Church Stretton	d		10 27		10 54				11 54					13 30			14 23					15 06	
Craven Arms 3	d		10 37			11 36								13 38			14 34					15 14	
Ludlow	d	10 06			11 08	11 43			12 08				13 05	13 46		14 06						15 21	
Leominster	d	10 16			11 18				12 18				13 15			14 17						15 32	
Hereford 7	a	10 32			11 35	12 07			12 35				13 32	14 10		14 32			15 07			15 50	
	d	10 34			11 35	12 09			12 35				13 32	14 11		14 34			15 09			15 51	
Abergavenny	d	10 57			11 58	12 32			12 58				13 55	14 34		14 57			15 32			16 14	
Pontypool and New Inn	d					12 42							14 05									16 23	
Cwmbran	d	11 10			12 11	12 47			13 11				14 10			15 09			15 45			16 28	
Newport (South Wales) 5	a	11 21		11 53	12 22	12 58			13 22				14 22	14 56		15 21			15 58			16 40	
Cardiff Central 7	a	11 36		12 06	12 38	13 15			13 36				14 39	15 11		15 42			16 15			16 57	
Swansea	a	12 40	14 20		13 40				14 29				15 32	16 15		16 39	18 14					18 10	

For connections from Liverpool Lime Street and Runcorn refer to Table T91. For connections to Bristol Temple Meads refer to Table T132

When events are being held at the Principality Stadium, services are subject to alteration. Please check times before travelling.

For other services between Shrewsbury and Chester refer to Table T75

For other stations served by AW trains from and to Cardiff between Chester and Holyhead refer to Table T81

For connections to Reading and London Paddington via Newport refer to Table T125

Table T131-F

Mondays to Fridays

16 December to 15 May

Manchester, Holyhead and Crewe - Cardiff

Station		AW ■ 🍴	AW	AW ◇ 🍴	AW ◇ 🍴	AW ■ 🍴	AW ◇ 🍴	AW ■	AW ◇	AW ■ 🍴	AW ◇	AW ◇ 🍴	AW ■ 🍴	AW ■1 ⊠	AW	AW FO ◇	AW FX ◇	AW ◇	AW ◇	AW FO ◇	AW FX ◇	AW ◇
Manchester Piccadilly 10 ⇌	d	14 31				15 31				16 31			17 31			18 31	18 31			19 31	19 31	
Stockport	d	14 39				15 39				16 39			17 39			18 39	18 39			19 40	19 40	
Wilmslow	d	14 47				15 47				16 47			17 49			18 47	18 47			19 47	19 47	
Holyhead	d						14 36							16 51								
Bangor (Gwynedd)	d						15 04							17 18								
Llandudno	d			14 40	15 08			16 06	16 20			17 07			18 08			18 44	19 05			19 35
Llandudno Junction	d			14 49	15 17		15 28	16 15	16a29			17 17		17 36	18a18			18 53	19a14			19 46
Chester	d			15a47	16a15		16 23	17a12				18a14		18 22				19a50				20 45
Wrexham General	d						16 37							18 37								
Ruabon	d						16 44							18 45								
Chirk	d						16 51							18 52								
Gobowen	d						16 56							18 57								
Crewe 10	d	15 08	15 22			16 08				17 09	17 20		18 09			19 08	19 08			20 10	20 10	21a07
Nantwich	d		15 30			16 17					17 28		18 18			19 17	19 17			20 18	20 18	
Wrenbury	d		15x37								17x35					19x23	19x23					
Whitchurch (Shrops)	d		15 45			16 28					17 43		18 29			19 29	19 29			20 29	20 29	
Prees	d		15x51								17x50					19x35	19x35					
Wem	d		15 57			16 36					17 56		18 37			19 40	19 40			20 37	20 37	
Yorton	d		16x03								18x01					19x45	19x45					
Shrewsbury 5	a	15 38	16 14			16 48	17 15			17 39	18 14		18 49	19 21		19 56	19 56			20 49	20 49	
	d	15 40				16 51	17 16			17 41	18 24		18 52	19 23		19 56	19 56			20 52	20 52	
Church Stretton	d					17 06	17 31			17 56	18 42		19 07			20 11	20 11			21 07	21 07	
Craven Arms 3	d					17 14	17 39			18 04	18 54		19 15			20 19	20 19			21 15	21 15	
Ludlow	d	16 06				17 21	17 46			18 11			19 22	19 51		20 27	20 27			21 22	21 22	
Leominster	d	16 16				17 32	17 57			18 22			19 33			20 37	20 37			21 33	21 33	
Hereford 7	a	16 32				17 50	18 13			18 38			19 49	20 15		20 54	20 54			21 49	21 49	
	d	16 33				17 51	18 14			18 39			19 51	20 15		20 54	20 54			21 54	21 54	
Abergavenny	d	16 56				18 14	18 37			19 02			20 14	20 38		21 22	21 22			22 17	22 17	
Pontypool and New Inn	d					18 24				19 12			20 24			21 32	21 32					
Cwmbran	d	17 09				18 29	18 49			19 17			20 29	20 52		21 37	21 37			22 29	22 29	
Newport (South Wales) 5	a	17 20				18 40	19 06			19 29			20 40	21 06		21 51	21 51			22 41	22 43	
Cardiff Central 7	a	17 37				18 54	19 20			19 45			20 55	21 24		22 08	22 08			23 00	23 07	
Swansea	a	18 41				20 07				20 41	22 23					23 10						

Station		AW	AW FO ◇	AW FX ◇	AW ◇	AW	AW ◇	AW ◇	AW ◇	AW
Manchester Piccadilly 10 ⇌	d		20 31				21 36		22 36	
Stockport	d		20 41				21 45		22 45	
Wilmslow	d		20 49				21 52		22 53	
Holyhead	d									
Bangor (Gwynedd)	d									
Llandudno	d	20 09			20 43	21 11				21 45
Llandudno Junction	d	20a19			20 52	21a22				21 55
Chester	d			20 55	21a49					23 01
Wrexham General	d									
Ruabon	d									
Chirk	d									
Gobowen	d									
Crewe 10	d		21 20	21 20			22 13		23 14	23a28
Nantwich	d		21 27	21 27			22 21		23 22	
Wrenbury	d		21x33	21x33			22x26		23x28	
Whitchurch (Shrops)	d		21 41	21 41			22 34		23 35	
Prees	d		21x47	21x47			22x39		23x41	
Wem	d		21 52	21 52			22 45		23 46	
Yorton	d		21x57	21x57			22x49		23x51	
Shrewsbury 5	a		22 07	22 08			23 02		00 04	
	d		22 08	22 08				23 09		
Church Stretton	d		22 24	22 24				23 25		
Craven Arms 3	d		22 33	22 33				23 33		
Ludlow	d		22 41	22 41				23 42		
Leominster	d		22 53	22 53				23 53		
Hereford 7	a		23 07	23 08				00 09		
	d		23 09	23 09				00 10		
Abergavenny	d		23 33	23 33				00 34		
Pontypool and New Inn	d		23 44	23 44				00 44		
Cwmbran	d		23 49	23 49				00 49		
Newport (South Wales) 5	a		00 01	00 02				01 02		
Cardiff Central 7	a		00 14	00 20				01 23		
Swansea	a									

For connections from Liverpool Lime Street and Runcorn refer to Table T91. For connections to Bristol Temple Meads refer to Table T132

When events are being held at the Principality Stadium, services are subject to alteration. Please check times before travelling.

For other services between Shrewsbury and Chester refer to Table T75

For other stations served by AW trains from and to Cardiff between Chester and Holyhead refer to Table T81

For connections to Reading and London Paddington via Newport refer to Table T125

Table T131-F

Saturdays

21 December to 16 May

Manchester, Holyhead and Crewe - Cardiff

		AW	AW	AW	AW	AW	AW	AW	AW	AW	AW	AW	AW	AW	AW	AW	AW	AW	AW	AW	AW	AW	AW
		◇	◇		◇ ⊼	◇	◇ ⊼	◇	◇ ⊼	◇			◇ ⊼	◇ ⊼	◇	◇		■ ⊼		◇ ⊼		◇ ⊼	◇ ⊼
Manchester Piccadilly 10	d								06 30				07 31					08 30				09 31	
Stockport	d								06 39				07 40					08 39				09 40	
Wilmslow	d								06 47				07 47					08 47				09 47	
Holyhead	d							04 25							06 35								08 20
Bangor (Gwynedd)	d							04 57							07 07								09 01
Llandudno	d									06 34	07 08					07 45	08 08			08 45	09 08		
Llandudno Junction	d							05 15		06 44	07a18				07 25	07 54	08a18			08 54	09a18		09 25
Chester	d							06 20		07a40					08 20	08a51				09a51			10 19
Wrexham General	d							06 35							08 35								10 34
Ruabon	d							06 42							08 42								10 41
Chirk	d							06 48							08 48								10 47
Gobowen	d							06 54							08 54								10 53
Crewe 10	d				04 54		05 55		07 09			07 20	08 08					09 09	09 20			10 08	
Nantwich	d				05 02		06 03		07 18			07 28	08 17						09 28				
Wrenbury	d						06x09					07x35							09x35				
Whitchurch (Shrops)	d				05 13		06 16		07 29			07 42	08 28						09 43				
Prees	d						06x22					07x48							09x49				
Wem	d				05 22		06 27		07 37			07 54							09 55				
Yorton	d						06x32					07x59							10x01				
Shrewsbury 5	a				05 35		06 43	07 13	07 50			08 08	08 47		09 13			09 39	10 12			10 38	11 12
	d		05 15		05 40	06 11	06 44	07 18	07 52				08 50	09 00	09 17			09 41				10 39	11 16
Church Stretton	d		05 33		05 55	06 27	06 59		08 07				09 05	09 19				09 56				10 54	
Craven Arms 3	d		05 47		06 03	06 35	07 07		08 15				09 13	09 29				10 04				11 02	
Ludlow	d				06 10	06 44	07 14	07 44	08 22				09 20		09 43			10 11				11 09	11 42
Leominster	d				06 21	06 55	07 25	07 54	08 33				09 31					10 22				11 20	
Hereford 7	a				06 37	07 11	07 42	08 11	08 50				09 49		10 07			10 38				11 36	12 07
	d	00 10		05 38	06 47	07 11	07 44	08 11	08 51				09 51		10 09			10 40				11 40	12 07
Abergavenny	d	00 34		06 03	07 10	07 35	08 07	08 34	09 14				10 14		10 32			11 03				12 03	12 30
Pontypool and New Inn	d	00 44		06 14	07 20	07 46	08 17	08 44							10 42								12 40
Cwmbran	d	00 49		06 19	07 25	07 51	08 22	08 49	09 26				10 26		10 47			11 15				12 15	12 45
Newport (South Wales) 5	a	01 02		06 32	07 37	08 02	08 39	09 05	09 39				10 38		11 01			11 28				12 28	12 57
Cardiff Central 7	a	01 23		06 53	07 54	08 17	08 53	09 21	09 59				11 03		11 17			11 54				12 56	13 14
Swansea	a		09 24		08 48		09 55		10 53				12 00	13 02				12 57				13 58	

		AW	AW	AW	AW	AW	AW	AW	AW	AW	AW	AW	AW	AW	AW	AW	AW	AW	AW	AW	AW	AW	AW
		■ ⊼		◇	■ ⊼		◇ ⊼		◇ ⊼	■ ⊼	◇ ⊼		■ ⊼	◇ ⊼	◇ ⊼		◇		■ ⊼	◇ ⊼		■ ⊼	
Manchester Piccadilly 10	d				10 31				11 31				12 31						13 31			14 31	
Stockport	d				10 40				11 39				12 39						13 39			14 39	
Wilmslow	d				10 47				11 47				12 47						13 47			14 47	
Holyhead	d									10 33										12 39			
Bangor (Gwynedd)	d									11 05										13 07			
Llandudno	d	09 45	10 10	10 22			10 44	11 08			11 44	12 08			12 40	12 46	13 08				14 08		
Llandudno Junction	d	09 54	10a20	10a33			10 53	11a18		11 23	11 53	12a18			12 53	12a56	13a19			13 25	14a18		
Chester	d	10a51					11a50			12 19	12a50				13a50					14 19			
Wrexham General	d									12 34										14 33			
Ruabon	d									12 41										14 40			
Chirk	d									12 47										14 47			
Gobowen	d									12 53										14 52			
Crewe 10	d				11 08	11 20			12 09				13 08					13 20	14 08			15 09	15 20
Nantwich	d					11 31			12 18									13 28	14 17				15 28
Wrenbury	d					11x38												13x35					15x35
Whitchurch (Shrops)	d					11 46			12 29									13 43	14 27				15 43
Prees	d					11x53												13x49					15x49
Wem	d					11 59												13 55					15 55
Yorton	d					12x04												14x01					16x01
Shrewsbury 5	a				11 39	12 15			12 47	13 12			13 38					14 13	14 46	15 11		15 40	16 13
	d				11 42				12 50	13 14			13 40	13 58					14 46	15 13		15 47	
Church Stretton	d				11 57				13 05	13 29				14 16					15 01			16 02	
Craven Arms 3	d				12 05				13 13	13 37				14 26					15 09			16 10	
Ludlow	d				12 12				13 20	13 44			14 06						15 17	15 39		16 17	
Leominster	d				12 23				13 31				14 16						15 27			16 28	
Hereford 7	a				12 39				13 50	14 09			14 33						15 44	16 03		16 44	
	d				12 41				13 51	14 10			14 33						15 46	16 04		16 47	
Abergavenny	d				13 04				14 14	14 33			14 56						16 09	16 27		17 10	
Pontypool and New Inn	d									14 43										16 37			
Cwmbran	d				13 16				14 26	14 48			15 09						16 21	16 42		17 22	
Newport (South Wales) 5	a				13 29				14 39	15 05			15 22						16 39	16 53		17 37	
Cardiff Central 7	a				13 54				14 55	15 24			15 37						16 57	17 09		17 55	
Swansea	a				14 56				15 57				16 35	18 02					18 07			19 03	

For connections from Liverpool Lime Street and Runcorn refer to Table T91. For connections to Bristol Temple Meads refer to Table T132

When events are being held at the Principality Stadium, services are subject to alteration. Please check times before travelling.

For other services between Shrewsbury and Chester refer to Table T75

For other stations served by AW trains from and to Cardiff between Chester and Holyhead refer to Table T81

For connections to Reading and London Paddington via Newport refer to Table T125

NRT DECEMBER 19 EDITION

Table T131-F

Saturdays

21 December to 16 May

Manchester, Holyhead and Crewe - Cardiff

		AW	AW	AW	AW	AW	AW	AW	AW	AW	AW	AW	AW	AW	AW	AW	AW	AW	AW	AW	AW	AW
		◇ ⊼		■ ⊼	◇ ⊼	◇ ⊼		◇	■ ⊼	◇ ⊼		◇		■ ⊼	◇ ⊼	◇ ⊼		◇	◇	◇		◇
Manchester Piccadilly 10	d			15 31					16 31					17 31				18 31				19 31
Stockport	d			15 39					16 39					17 39				18 39				19 40
Wilmslow	d			15 47					16 47					17 47				18 47				19 47
Holyhead	d				14 27										16 52							
Bangor (Gwynedd)	d				14 55										17 20							
Llandudno	d	14 42	15 08			15 44	16 07	16 20		16 44	17 08					17 44	18 08		18 44	19 03	19 13	
Llandudno Junction	d	14 51	15a18		15 18	15 53	16a17	16a31		16 53	17a18				17 38	17 53	18a18		18 53	19a11	19a22	
Chester	d	15a48			16 22	16a50				17a50					18 33	18a50			19a50			
Wrexham General	d				16 37										18 47							
Ruabon	d				16 44										18 54							
Chirk	d				16 50										19 01							
Gobowen	d				16 56										19 06							
Crewe 10	d			16 08					17 08				17 20	18 09				19 10				20 09
Nantwich	d			16 17					17 17				17 28	18 17				19 18				20 17
Wrenbury	d												17x35					19x24				
Whitchurch (Shrops)	d			16 27					17 27				17 43	18 28				19 31				20 28
Prees	d												17x49					19x37				
Wem	d												17 55					19 42				20 36
Yorton	d												18x01					19x47				
Shrewsbury 5	a			16 46	17 15				17 45				18 13	18 48	19 25			19 57				20 48
	d			16 46	17 16				17 46			17 57		18 54	19 26			19 58				20 48
Church Stretton	d			17 01					18 01			18 13		19 09	19 41			20 13				21 03
Craven Arms 3	d			17 09					18 09			18 24		19 17	19 49			20 21				21 11
Ludlow	d			17 17	17 42				18 16					19 24	19 56			20 28				21 19
Leominster	d			17 27					18 27					19 35				20 39				21 29
Hereford 7	a			17 45	18 06				18 44					19 51	20 21			20 55				21 46
	d			17 50	18 07				18 51					19 52	20 27			20 56				21 46
Abergavenny	d			18 13	18 30				19 14					20 15	20 50			21 19				22 09
Pontypool and New Inn	d				18 40									20 24				21 28				
Cwmbran	d			18 25	18 45				19 26					20 29	21 02			21 33				22 22
Newport (South Wales) 5	a			18 40	18 56				19 38					20 41	21 15			21 45				22 35
Cardiff Central 7	a			18 59	19 09				19 55					20 59	21 34			22 06				22 57
Swansea	a			20 07								22 04						23 08				

		AW	AW	AW	AW	AW	AW	AW	AW
		◇		◇		◇	◇	◇	
Manchester Piccadilly 10	d			20 30		21 33	22 35		
Stockport	d			20 39		21 43	22 45		
Wilmslow	d			20 47		21 53	22 53		
Holyhead	d								
Bangor (Gwynedd)	d								
Llandudno	d	19 42	20 08		20 43			21 45	
Llandudno Junction	d	19 51	20a17		20 52			21 55	
Chester	d	20a48			21a48			23 01	
Wrexham General	d								
Ruabon	d								
Chirk	d								
Gobowen	d								
Crewe 10	d			21 09		22 13	23 14	23a27	
Nantwich	d			21 17		22 21	23 22		
Wrenbury	d			21x23		22x26	23x28		
Whitchurch (Shrops)	d			21 30		22 34	23 35		
Prees	d			21x36		22x39	23x41		
Wem	d			21 41		22 45	23 46		
Yorton	d			21x46		22x49	23x51		
Shrewsbury 5	a			21 55		23 01	00 05		
	d			21 55					
Church Stretton	d			22 10					
Craven Arms 3	d			22 18					
Ludlow	d			22 26					
Leominster	d			22 37					
Hereford 7	a			22 53					
	d			22 55					23 15
Abergavenny	d			23 18					23 38
Pontypool and New Inn	d			23 28					
Cwmbran	d			23 33					23 50
Newport (South Wales) 5	a			23 49					00 03
Cardiff Central 7	a			00 12					00 22
Swansea	a								

For connections from Liverpool Lime Street and Runcorn refer to Table T91. For connections to Bristol Temple Meads refer to Table T132

When events are being held at the Principality Stadium, services are subject to alteration. Please check times before travelling.

For other services between Shrewsbury and Chester refer to Table T75

For other stations served by AW trains from and to Cardiff between Chester and Holyhead refer to Table T81

For connections to Reading and London Paddington via Newport refer to Table T125

Table T131-F

Manchester, Holyhead and Crewe - Cardiff

Sundays

15 December to 10 May

		AW	AW	AW	AW	AW	AW	AW	AW	AW	AW	AW	AW	AW	AW	AW	AW	AW	AW	AW	AW	AW	AW
		🚌	◇ 🛒		■ 🛒	◇	■ 🛒	◇			■ 🛒	■ 🛒			■ 🛒			◇	■ 🛒			■ 🛒	■ 🛒
Manchester Piccadilly 10 ⇌	d				09 30		10 31				11 30				12 32				13 30			14 30	14 30
Stockport	d				09 41		10 40				11 43				12 43				13 40			14 40	14 40
Wilmslow	d				09 49		10 48				11 52				12 50				13 48			14 48	14 48
Holyhead	d											10 20											
Bangor (Gwynedd)	d											10 59											
Llandudno	d					10 22			11 07				11 40	12 18			13 17	13 28		13 52	14 20		
Llandudno Junction	d					10a31			11a17			11 22	11a50	12a28			13a27	13a37		14a02	14a30		
Chester	d											12 29											
Wrexham General	d											12 44											
Ruabon	d											12 51											
Chirk	d											12 57											
Gobowen	d											13 03											
Crewe 10	d			09 21	10 14		11 11			11 25	12 13				13 13	13 21			14 10			15 11	15 11
Nantwich	d			09 29	10 22					11 33						13 29							
Wrenbury	d			09x36						11x41						13x36							
Whitchurch (Shrops)	d			09 44	10 34					11 48						13 44							
Prees	d			09x50						11x55						13x50							
Wem	d			09 56	10 44					12 01						13 56							
Yorton	d			10x02						12x06						14x02							
Shrewsbury 6	a			10 14	10 59		11 42			12 18	12 43	13 23			13 46	14 14			14 44			15 45	15 45
	d	07 50			11 06		11 48	12 04			12 45	13 23			13 50				14 45			15 48	15 48
Church Stretton	d	08 15			11 22			12 22				13 39							15 01				
Craven Arms 3	d	08 35			11 30			12 33				13 47							15 09				
Ludlow	d	08 55			11 39		12 16				13 14	13 55			14 18				15 18			16 18	16 18
Leominster	d	09 20			11 50		12 27				13 26	14 05			14 29				15 29			16 29	16 29
Hereford 7	a	09 50			12 08		12 43				13 41	14 22			14 45				15 46			16 45	16 45
	d		10 07		12 10		12 46				13 42	14 22			14 47				15 47			16 48	16 48
Abergavenny	d		10 31		12 34		13 09				14 05	14 45			15 10				16 11			17 13	17 13
Pontypool and New Inn	d		10 41				13 19					14 55							16 22				
Cwmbran	d		10 46		12 47		13 25				14 22	15 00			15 22				16 27			17 26	17 26
Newport (South Wales) 5	a		10 58		13 05		13 40				14 34	15 12			15 41				16 39			17 40	17 40
Cardiff Central 7	a		11 13		13 21		14 01				14 50	15 26			15 57				16 57			17 57	17 57
Swansea	a		12 12		14 20		15 07	16 03			15 48				17 03				18 08				19 01

		AW	AW	AW	AW	AW	AW	AW	AW	AW	AW	AW	AW	AW	AW	AW	AW	AW	AW	AW	AW
			◇		■ 🛒			■ 🛒			■ 🛒	■ 🛒			■		◇	◇	◇		◇
Manchester Piccadilly 10 ⇌	d				15 30			16 30			17 30				18 30			19 30	20 30		
Stockport	d				15 40			16 40			17 40				18 40			19 40	20 40		
Wilmslow	d				15 48			16 48			17 48				18 48			19 48	20 48		
Holyhead	d											16 25									
Bangor (Gwynedd)	d											17 04									
Llandudno	d			15 14		15 44	16 16			16 52			17 20	18 05			18 59				
Llandudno Junction	d			15a24		15a54	16a26			17a02		17 25	17a30	18a15			19a08				
Chester	d											18 25									
Wrexham General	d											18 41									
Ruabon	d											18 48									
Chirk	d											18 55									
Gobowen	d											19 00									
Crewe 10	d	15 18			16 13			17 13	17 26		18 13				19 13	19 18		20 10	21 11	21 45	23 30
Nantwich	d	15 26							17 34							19 27			21 18	21 53	23 38
Wrenbury	d	15x33							17x41							19x34			21x23	22x00	23x44
Whitchurch (Shrops)	d	15 41							17 49							19 42			21 32	22 08	23 52
Prees	d	15x47							17x55							19x48			21x37	22x14	23x58
Wem	d	15 53							18 01							19 54			21 44	22 20	00 04
Yorton	d	15x59							18x07							20x00			21x48	22x26	00x09
Shrewsbury 6	a	16 11			16 44			17 45	18 19		18 44	19 19			19 46	20 12		20 46	21 59	22 38	00 17
	d		16 20		16 44			17 46			18 44	19 22			19 46			20 49	22 04		
Church Stretton	d		16 39		17 00							19 38						21 05	22 20		
Craven Arms 3	d		16 49		17 08							19 46						21 13	22 29		
Ludlow	d				17 16			18 14			19 12	19 54			20 14			21 22	22 37		
Leominster	d				17 26			18 24				20 04			20 24			21 33	22 49		
Hereford 7	a				17 43			18 42			19 39	20 19			20 40			21 48	23 04		
	d				17 44			18 44			19 39	20 22			20 41			21 49	23 05		
Abergavenny	d				18 07			19 08			20 03	20 45			21 04			22 13	23 29		
Pontypool and New Inn	d				18 17							20 55						22 24	23 39		
Cwmbran	d				18 22			19 22			20 16	21 00			21 17			22 29	23 44		
Newport (South Wales) 5	a				18 34			19 36			20 28	21 13			21 27			22 40	23 56		
Cardiff Central 7	a				18 53			19 52			20 46	21 32			21 44			22 58	00 15		
Swansea	a		20 25		20 02			20 52			21 49				22 46			00 02			

For connections from Liverpool Lime Street and Runcorn refer to Table T91. For connections to Bristol Temple Meads refer to Table T132

When events are being held at the Principality Stadium, services are subject to alteration. Please check times before travelling.

For other services between Shrewsbury and Chester refer to Table T75

For other stations served by AW trains from and to Cardiff between Chester and Holyhead refer to Table T81

For connections to Reading and London Paddington via Newport refer to Table T125

Table T131-R

Cardiff - Crewe, Holyhead and Manchester

Mondays to Fridays

16 December to 15 May

Miles	Miles			AW	AW	AW	AW	AW	AW	AW	AW	AW	AW	AW	AW	AW	AW	AW	AW	AW	AW	AW	AW
				MO	MX	MX			MX	MO													
				◇	◇	◇			◇	◇	◇	◇	◇	◇	◇ 🛒	■1 ☒	◇ 🛒	◇ 🛒		■ 🛒	◇	◇ 🛒	◇ 🛒
—	—	Swansea	d																	06 38	06 04		07 49
0	0	**Cardiff Central** 7	d			00 30			04 35	04 35		05 12	05 38		06 45	07 02				07 50			08 50
11¾	11¾	**Newport (South Wales)** 5	d			00 50			04 53	04 54		05 31	05 58		06 59	07 16				08 05			09 05
18¾	18¾	Cwmbran	d			01 02			05 05	05 05		05 42	06 08		07 10	07 27				08 15			09 15
21¾	21¾	Pontypool and New Inn	d			01 08			05 11	05 11		05 48	06 14							08 21			
31¼	31¼	Abergavenny	d	00 05		01 19			05 22	05 22		05 57	06 23		07 23	07 41				08 30			09 28
55¼	55¼	**Hereford** 7	a	00 31		01 51			05 47	05 47		06 22	06 48		07 48	08 06				08 56			09 53
—	—		d						05 47	05 47		06 25	06 49		07 48	08 07				08 57			09 55
67¾	—	Leominster	d						06 00	06 00		06 38	07 02		08 01					09 10			10 08
78¾	78¾	Ludlow	d						06 11	06 11		06 49	07 13		08 12	08 28				09 21			10 19
86	86	Craven Arms 3	d						06 20	06 20		06 57	07 21	07 29	08 21					09 29	09 46		10 27
93¼	93¼	Church Stretton	d						06 29	06 29		07 08	07 30	07 42	08 30					09 38	09 59		10 36
106	106	**Shrewsbury** 6	a						06 44	06 44		07 25	07 45	07 58	08 45	08 59				09 54	10 15		10 51
			d		00 12		05 31		06 45	06 45		07 25	07 46	08 00	08 47	09 01				09 55	10 16	10 25	10 55
113¾	—	Yorton	d		00x21		05x40							08x09							10x26		
116¾	—	Wem	d		00 26		05 45		06 57	06 57			07 57	08 16							10 33		
120	—	Prees	d		00x31		05x50							08x20							10x38		
125	—	Whitchurch (Shrops)	d		00 38		05 57		07 05	07 05			08 06	08 28	09 04						10 46		11 12
129¾	—	Wrenbury	d		00x44		06x03							08x34							10x52		
134¼	—	Nantwich	d		00 51		06 09		07 15	07 15			08 15	08 41	09 14						10 59		11 21
138¾	—	**Crewe** 10	a		01 03		06 17		07 25	07 25			08 25	08 52	09 24					10 27	11 11		11 29
			d					06 27	07 27	07 27			08 28		09 29				09 42	10 30			11 30
—	123¾	Gobowen	a									07 42										10 42	
—	126¾	Chirk	a									07 48										10 48	
—	130¾	Ruabon	a									07 54										10 54	
—	135¾	Wrexham General	a									08 01				09 29						11 02	
—	147¾	Chester	a									08 20				09 48			10 03			11 21	
—	192¼	Llandudno Junction	a									09 16				10 31			10 59			12 18	
—	—	Llandudno	d								07 45	09a27					09 45	10 44	11a09				
—	207¾	Bangor (Gwynedd)	a													10 50						12 42	
—	232¾	Holyhead	a													11 20						13 21	
157¾	—	Wilmslow	a					06 44	07 47	07 47			08 47		09 49					10 48			11 49
163¾	—	Stockport	a					06 55	07 59	07 59			08 59		09 59					10 59			11 59
169¾	—	**Manchester Piccadilly** 10 ⇌	a					07 08	08 10	08 10	09 54		09 12		10 11		11 55	12 54		11 11			12 13

		AW	AW	AW	AW	AW	AW	AW	AW	AW	AW	AW	AW	AW	AW	AW	AW	AW	AW	AW	AW	AW	AW
		◇ 🛒	■ 🛒		◇ 🛒	◇ 🛒	■ 🛒	■1 ☒	◇ 🛒	■ 🛒		◇ 🛒	◇ 🛒	◇ 🛒	◇ 🛒	■ 🛒		◇ 🛒	◇ 🛒	■ 🛒	■ 🛒	■	■ 🛒
Swansea	d		08 53				09 55		09 30				11 55			12 56				13 55			14 55
Cardiff Central 7	d	09 22	10 05				10 51	11 24		11 56			12 49	13 22		14 05				14 49	15 22		15 49
Newport (South Wales) 5	d	09 36	10 19				11 05	11 39		12 09			13 03	13 37		14 19				15 03	15 37		16 03
Cwmbran	d	09 47	10 29				11 15	11 50		12 20			13 13	13 47		14 29				15 13	15 47		16 13
Pontypool and New Inn	d	09 52						11 56						13 53							15 53		16 18
Abergavenny	d	10 02	10 42				11 28	12 08		12 33			13 26	14 02		14 43				15 26	16 02		16 28
Hereford 7	a	10 27	11 07				11 53	12 32		12 59			13 51	14 27		15 07				15 51	16 27		16 53
	d	10 29	11 08				11 55	12 33		12 59			13 55	14 29		15 08				15 55	16 28		16 54
Leominster	d		11 21				12 08			13 12			14 08			15 21				16 08	16 41		17 07
Ludlow	d	10 50	11 32				12 19			13 23			14 19	14 50		15 32				16 19	16 52		17 18
Craven Arms 3	d	10 58					12 27		13 04	13 32			14 27	14 59						16 27	17 01		17 27
Church Stretton	d	11 07					12 36		13 17	13 41			14 36	15 08							17 10		17 36
Shrewsbury 6	a	11 22	11 59				12 51	13 22	13 33	13 57			14 51	15 24		15 59				16 49	17 24		17 51
	d	11 25	11 59	12 24		12 26	12 53	13 25		13 58	14 24	14 25	14 52	15 29		15 59	16 24		16 24	16 50	17 25		17 53
Yorton	d			12x34							14x34						16x34						
Wem	d			12 40							14 40						16 40			17 01			
Prees	d			12x45							14x45						16x45						
Whitchurch (Shrops)	d			12 52			13 10				14 52		15 09				16 52			17 10			18 10
Wrenbury	d			12x59							14x59						16x59						
Nantwich	d			13 05			13 19				15 05		15 18				17 05			17 19			18 20
Crewe 10	a		12 29	13 15			13 29			14 29	15 15		15 29			16 29	17 15			17 28			18 28
	d		12 30				13 30			14 30			15 30			16 30				17 30			18 30
Gobowen	a	11 42				12 43		13 42				14 42		15 46					16 42		17 42		
Chirk	a	11 47				12 49		13 48				14 48		15 51					16 48		17 48		
Ruabon	a	11 54				12 55		13 55				14 54		15 58					16 54		17 54		
Wrexham General	a	12 01				13 03		14 05				15 01		16 04					17 02		18 03		
Chester	a	12 20				13 21		14 23				15 20		16 24					17 22		18 22		
Llandudno Junction	a	13 13				14 14		15 20				16 14		17 16					18 21		19 18		
Llandudno	d				11 44										14 40			15 08				16 06	
Bangor (Gwynedd)	a	13 30				14 36		15 37				16 43		17 40					18 49		19 37		
Holyhead	a	14 14				15 17		16 06				17 15		18 21					19 17		20 20		
Wilmslow	a		12 49				13 49			14 49			15 49			16 49				17 49			18 49
Stockport	a		12 59				13 58			14 59			15 59			16 59				17 59			18 59
Manchester Piccadilly 10 ⇌	a		13 13		13 54		14 13			15 13			16 13		16 54	17 13		17 24		18 13		18 27	19 13

For connections from Bristol Temple Meads refer to Table T132. For connections to Runcorn and Liverpool Lime Street refer to Table T91

When events are being held at the Principality Stadium, services are subject to alteration. Please check times before travelling.

For other services between Shrewsbury and Chester refer to Table T75

For other stations served by AW trains from and to Cardiff between Chester and Holyhead refer to Table T81

For connections to Reading and London Paddington via Newport refer to Table T125

Table T131-R

Mondays to Fridays

16 December to 15 May

Cardiff - Crewe, Holyhead and Manchester

Station		AW	AW	AW	AW	AW	AW	AW	AW	AW	AW	AW	AW	AW	AW	AW	AW	AW	AW	AW	AW	AW
									FO	FX			FX	FO		MWO	TThO	FO			FX	FO
		■			■	■ 1		■	■	■												
			◇	◇			◇					◇	◇	◇	◇	◇	◇	◇	◇	◇	◇	◇
			🛒	🛒	🛒	⊠		🛒	🛒	🛒		🛒										
Swansea	d	15 05	14 35		15 55			16 55	17 05	17 05		17 50							18 27			
Cardiff Central 7	d	16 22			16 49	17 16		17 49	18 22	18 22		18 55	19 34	19 34		20 14	20 14	20 14		21 15	21 55	21 55
Newport (South Wales) 5	d	16 35			17 03	17 31		18 03	18 35	18 35		19 09	19 50	19 50		20 28	20 28	20 28		21 28	22 12	22 12
Cwmbran	d	16 46			17 13	17 42		18 13	18 46	18 46		19 19	20 00	20 00		20 38	20 38	20 38		21 40	22 23	22 23
Pontypool and New Inn	d				17 19	17 49		18 19				19 24	20 05	20 05		20 44	20 44	20 44			22 29	22 29
Abergavenny	d	16 59			17 28	18 00		18 28	18 59	18 59		19 34	20 15	20 15		20 53	20 53	20 53		21 53	22 39	22 39
Hereford 7	a	17 24			17 53	18 25		18 53	19 24	19 24		19 59	20 40	20 40		21 20	21 20	21 20		22 20	23 06	23 06
	d	17 25			17 57	18 25		18 55	19 25	19 25		19 59	20 41	20 42		21 20	21 20	21 20		22 20	23 10	23 10
Leominster	d				18 10			19 08				20 12	20 54	20 55		21 33	21 33	21 33		22 33	23 23	23 23
Ludlow	d				18 22			19 19	19 46	19 46		20 23	21 05	21 06		21 44	21 44	21 44		22 44	23 34	23 34
Craven Arms 3	d		18 00		18 31			19 27				20 32	21 14	21 14		21 52	21 52	21 52	22 20	22 53	23 44	23 44
Church Stretton	d		18 12		18 41			19 36				20 41	21 23	21 23		22 01	22 01	22 01	22 35	23 02	23 53	23 53
Shrewsbury 5	a	18 11	18 28		18 56	19 09		19 51	20 13	20 13		20 56	21 38	21 38		22 19	22 19	22 19	22 53	23 17	00 09	00 09
	d	18 13	18 29		18 57	19 09		19 52	20 15	20 15	20 32	20 57	21 41	21 44		22 20	22 20	22 20		23 18	00 12	00 14
Yorton	d		18x39								20x41					22x28	22x28	22x28		23x27	00x21	00x23
Wem	d		18 44								20 46					22 33	22 33	22 33		23 32	00 26	00 28
Prees	d		18x49								20x51					22x37	22x37	22x37		23x37	00x31	00x33
Whitchurch (Shrops)	d		18 57		19 14						20 58	21 14				22 45	22 45	22 45		23 44	00 38	00 40
Wrenbury	d		19x03								21x04					22x50	22x50	22x50		23x50	00x44	00x46
Nantwich	d		19 10		19 23						21 10	21 24				22 57	22 57	22 57		23 56	00 51	00 53
Crewe 10	a	18 44	19 21		19 33			20 23	20 45	20 46	21 19	21 33				23 07	23 07	23 07		00 06	01 03	01 05
	d	18 45			19 37			20 24		20 47		21 35				23 08	23 08	23 08		00 07		
Gobowen	a												21 58	22 01								
Chirk	a												22 03	22 07								
Ruabon	a												22 10	22 13								
Wrexham General	a					19 38							22 17	22 20								
Chester	a	19 05				19 58				21 07			22 37	22 41						00 26		
Llandudno Junction	a					20 51							23 51	23 51								
Llandudno	d			17 07			18 44								20 43							
Bangor (Gwynedd)	a					21 09							00 15	00 14								
Holyhead	a					21 41							00 43	00 43								
Wilmslow	a				19 57			20 42				21 52				23 26	23 26	23 26				
Stockport	a				20 07			20 53				22 01				23 34	23 35	23 35				
Manchester Piccadilly 10 ✈	a			19 24	20 19		20 56	21 07				22 15			22 55	23 48	23 49	23 50				

For connections from Bristol Temple Meads refer to Table T132. For connections to Runcorn and Liverpool Lime Street refer to Table T91

When events are being held at the Principality Stadium, services are subject to alteration. Please check times before travelling.

For other services between Shrewsbury and Chester refer to Table T75

For other stations served by AW trains from and to Cardiff between Chester and Holyhead refer to Table T81

For connections to Reading and London Paddington via Newport refer to Table T125

Table T131-R

Saturdays

21 December to 16 May

Cardiff - Crewe, Holyhead and Manchester

Station		AW	AW	AW	AW	AW	AW	AW	AW	AW	AW	AW	AW	AW	AW	AW	AW	AW	AW	AW	AW	AW	AW
												■					■		■	■	■		
		◇	◇			◇	◇	◇	◇		◇		◇	◇	◇	◇						◇	◇
												🛒		🛒	🛒	🛒	🛒		🛒	🛒	🛒	🛒	🛒
Swansea	d										04 31						06 49				07 47		
Cardiff Central 7	d		00 30			04 35	05 21		05 37					06 52	07 22		07 52				08 52	09 23	
Newport (South Wales) 5	d		00 46			04 52	05 34		05 52					07 06	07 37		08 06				09 06	09 38	
Cwmbran	d		00 56			05 03	05 45		06 02					07 16	07 47		08 16				09 16	09 48	
Pontypool and New Inn	d		01 02			05 09	05 50		06 08						07 53							09 54	
Abergavenny	d		01 13			05 18	06 00		06 17					07 29	08 02		08 29				09 29	10 03	
Hereford 7	a		01 40			05 43	06 25		06 42					07 54	08 29		08 54				09 54	10 27	
	d					05 46	06 26		06 46					07 55	08 30		08 56				09 55	10 30	
Leominster	d					05 59	06 39		07 00					08 08			09 09				10 08		
Ludlow	d					06 10	06 50		07 11					08 19	08 51		09 20				10 19	10 51	
Craven Arms 3	d					06 18	06 59		07 19		07 54			08 27	08 59						10 27	10 59	
Church Stretton	d					06 27	07 08		07 28		08 07			08 36	09 08						10 36	11 09	
Shrewsbury 5	a					06 42	07 23		07 43		08 24			08 52	09 24		09 47				10 51	11 24	
	d	00 14			05 44	06 45	07 25		07 45	07 58		08 25		08 52	09 26		09 49	10 18		10 25	10 52	11 25	
Yorton	d	00x23			05x54					08x08								10x28					
Wem	d	00 28			06 00	06 56			07 56	08 14								10 34					
Prees	d	00x33			06x05					08x19								10x39					
Whitchurch (Shrops)	d	00 40			06 12	07 05			08 05	08 26				09 09			10 06	10 47			11 09		
Wrenbury	d	00x46			06x19					08x33								10x53					
Nantwich	d	00 53			06 25	07 14			08 14	08 40				09 18			10 15	11 00			11 18		
Crewe 10	a	01 05			06 35	07 25			08 24	08 50				09 28			10 25	11 10			11 26		
	d			06 27		07 27			08 28					09 30			10 30				11 30		
Gobowen	a						07 42					08 42			09 43					10 43		11 42	
Chirk	a						07 47					08 48			09 48					10 48		11 47	
Ruabon	a						07 54					08 54			09 55					10 55		11 54	
Wrexham General	a						08 01					09 02			10 02					11 02		12 00	
Chester	a						08 20					09 21			10 20					11 22		12 19	
Llandudno Junction	a						09 14					10 19			11 13					12 16		13 16	
Llandudno	d							06 34					07 45			08 45			09 45				10 44
Bangor (Gwynedd)	a						09 37					10 37			11 37					12 33		13 33	
Holyhead	a						10 13					11 10			12 09					13 12		14 13	
Wilmslow	a			06 44		07 46			08 46					09 48			10 48				11 49		
Stockport	a			06 55		07 59			08 59					10 00			10 59				11 59		
Manchester Piccadilly 10 ✈	a			07 07		08 10		08 54	09 13				09 54	10 14		10 54	11 13		11 55		12 12		12 54

Station		AW	AW	AW	AW	AW	AW	AW	AW	AW	AW	AW	AW	AW	AW	AW	AW	AW	AW	AW	AW	AW
								■		■			■			■			■			■
		◇		◇	◇	◇	◇		◇			◇		◇	◇			◇		◇	◇	
		🛒		🛒	🛒	🛒	🛒	🛒	🛒	🛒		🛒	🛒	🛒	🛒	🛒		🛒	🛒	🛒	🛒	🛒
Swansea	d	08 54				09 54	09 15			10 55			12 00			12 53				14 00	13 12	
Cardiff Central 7	d	09 55				10 55		11 12		11 55			12 55	13 21		13 55				14 55		15 23
Newport (South Wales) 5	d	10 09				11 09		11 37		12 09			13 09	13 36		14 09				15 09		15 38
Cwmbran	d	10 19				11 19		11 47		12 19			13 19	13 47		14 19				15 19		15 48
Pontypool and New Inn	d							11 53						13 52								15 54
Abergavenny	d	10 32				11 32		12 02		12 32			13 32	14 02		14 32				15 32		16 03
Hereford 7	a	10 57				11 57		12 27		12 57			13 57	14 27		14 57				15 57		16 27
	d	10 58				11 58		12 28		12 58			14 00	14 27		14 58				15 59		16 29
Leominster	d	11 11				12 11				13 11			14 13			15 11				16 12		16 42
Ludlow	d	11 22				12 22		12 49		13 22			14 24	14 48		15 22				16 23		16 54
Craven Arms 3	d					12 30	12 40	12 57					14 32	14 57						16 31	16 43	
Church Stretton	d					12 39	12 53	13 06					14 42	15 06						16 40	16 56	17 08
Shrewsbury 5	a	11 49				12 54	13 10	13 21		13 49			14 56	15 25		15 49				16 55	17 12	17 22
	d	11 49	12 24		12 25	12 55		13 25		13 49	14 24	14 24	14 57	15 30		15 49	16 24		16 25	16 57		17 26
Yorton	d		12x34								14x34						16x34					
Wem	d		12 40								14 40						16 40					
Prees	d		12x45								14x45						16x45					
Whitchurch (Shrops)	d	12 06	12 52							14 06	14 52					16 06	16 52					
Wrenbury	d		12x59								14x59						16x59					
Nantwich	d	12 15	13 05							14 15	15 05					16 15	17 05					
Crewe 10	a	12 25	13 15			13 27				14 25	15 15		15 28			16 25	17 15			17 28		
	d	12 30				13 30				14 30			15 30			16 30				17 30		
Gobowen	a				12 43			13 42				14 42		15 47					16 42			17 43
Chirk	a				12 48			13 47				14 47		15 52					16 48			17 48
Ruabon	a				12 55			13 54				14 54		15 59					16 54			17 55
Wrexham General	a				13 01			14 01				15 01		16 05					17 02			18 02
Chester	a				13 20			14 20				15 21		16 24					17 19			18 20
Llandudno Junction	a				14 15			15 15				16 15		17 16					18 19			19 14
Llandudno	d			11 44					12 40						14 42			15 44				
Bangor (Gwynedd)	a				14 38			15 32				16 39		17 40					18 43			19 34
Holyhead	a				15 09			16 12				17 11		18 18					19 13			20 17
Wilmslow	a	12 48				13 48				14 48			15 47			16 48				17 48		
Stockport	a	12 59				13 59				15 00			16 00			17 00				18 00		
Manchester Piccadilly 10 ✈	a	13 13		13 54		14 14			14 54	15 15			16 15		16 54	17 14		17 54		18 15		

For connections from Bristol Temple Meads refer to Table T132. For connections to Runcorn and Liverpool Lime Street refer to Table T91

When events are being held at the Principality Stadium, services are subject to alteration. Please check times before travelling.

For other services between Shrewsbury and Chester refer to Table T75

For other stations served by AW trains from and to Cardiff between Chester and Holyhead refer to Table T81

For connections to Reading and London Paddington via Newport refer to Table T125

Table T131-R

Cardiff - Crewe, Holyhead and Manchester

Saturdays
21 December to 16 May

Station		AW ◇ 🛒	AW ■ 🛒	AW	AW ◇	AW ◇ 🛒	AW ◇	AW ■ 🛒	AW ■ 🛒	AW ◇	AW ■ 🛒
Swansea	d		14 55		15 08			15 55			16 55
Cardiff Central 7	d		15 55		16 15			16 55	17 23		17 55
Newport (South Wales) 5	d		16 09		16 30			17 09	17 36		18 09
Cwmbran	d		16 19		16 41			17 19	17 47		18 20
Pontypool and New Inn	d		16 24		16 46				17 52		18 25
Abergavenny	d		16 34		17a00			17 32	18 02		18 35
Hereford 7	a		16 59					17 57	18 26		19 00
	d		17 00					17 58	18 27		19 00
Leominster	d		17 13					18 11			19 13
Ludlow	d		17 24					18 22	18 48		19 24
Craven Arms 3	d							18 30	18 57		
Church Stretton	d							18 39	19 06		
Shrewsbury 5	a		17 51					18 54	19 21		19 51
	d		17 52	18 25			18 25	18 56	19 28		19 52
Yorton	d			18x35							
Wem	d			18 41							
Prees	d			18x46							
Whitchurch (Shrops)	d		18 08	18 53							20 09
Wrenbury	d			19x00							
Nantwich	d		18 18	19 06							20 18
Crewe 10	a		18 28	19 16				19 27			20 28
	d		18 30					19 30			20 30
Gobowen	a						18 43		19 45		
Chirk	a						18 48		19 50		
Ruabon	a						18 55		19 57		
Wrexham General	a						19 02		20 03		
Chester	a						19 22		20 24		
Llandudno Junction	a						20 22		21 26		
Llandudno	d	16 44				17 44				18 44	
Bangor (Gwynedd)	a						20 49		21 43		
Holyhead	a						21 28		22 24		
Wilmslow	a		18 48					19 48			20 47
Stockport	a		19 00					19 59			21 00
Manchester Piccadilly 10 ⛴	a	18 53	19 15			19 54		20 13		20 56	21 15

Station		AW	AW ◇	AW ◇ 🛒	AW ◇	AW ◇	AW ◇	AW ◇	AW ◇	AW ◇
Swansea	d			17 55		18 17			20 55	
Cardiff Central 7	d			18 50	19 34		20 12	20 55	21 54	
Newport (South Wales) 5	d			19 04	19 48		20 27	21 09	22 12	
Cwmbran	d			19 15	19 59		20 38	21 21	22 24	
Pontypool and New Inn	d			19 20	20 04		20 43		22 29	
Abergavenny	d			19 30	20 14		20 53	21 34	22 39	
Hereford 7	a			19 55	20 39		21 18	21 59	23 04	
	d			19 56	20 40		21 20	22 00		
Leominster	d			20 09	20 54		21 33	22 14		
Ludlow	d			20 20	21 05		21 44	22 25		
Craven Arms 3	d			20 29	21 13	21 40	21 54	22 33		
Church Stretton	d			20 38	21 22	21 52	22 03	22 42		
Shrewsbury 5	a			20 53	21 37	22 09	22 18	22 57		
	d	20 32		20 57	21 39		22 19	23 06		23 30
Yorton	d	20x41					22x27	23x15		23x39
Wem	d	20 46					22 32	23 20		23 44
Prees	d	20x51					22x36	23x25		23x49
Whitchurch (Shrops)	d	20 58					22 44	23 32		23 55
Wrenbury	d	21x04					22x49	23x38		00x01
Nantwich	d	21 10					22 55	23 44		00 07
Crewe 10	a	21 19		21 28			23 05	23 54		00 17
	d			21 30			23 06	23 57		
Gobowen	a				21 56					
Chirk	a				22 01					
Ruabon	a				22 08					
Wrexham General	a				22 15					
Chester	a				22 34			00 23		
Llandudno Junction	a				23 36					
Llandudno	d		19 42							
Bangor (Gwynedd)	a									
Holyhead	a									
Wilmslow	a			21 48			23 24			
Stockport	a			21 58			23 35			
Manchester Piccadilly 10 ⛴	a		21 55	22 13			23 49			

For connections from Bristol Temple Meads refer to Table T132. For connections to Runcorn and Liverpool Lime Street refer to Table T91

When events are being held at the Principality Stadium, services are subject to alteration. Please check times before travelling.

For other services between Shrewsbury and Chester refer to Table T75

For other stations served by AW trains from and to Cardiff between Chester and Holyhead refer to Table T81

For connections to Reading and London Paddington via Newport refer to Table T125

Table T131-R

Cardiff - Crewe, Holyhead and Manchester

Sundays
15 December to 10 May

Station		AW ◇ A	AW ◇	AW ◇	AW ◇	AW	AW ◇	AW ■	AW ■	AW	AW ◇ 🛒	AW
Swansea	d							08 22			10 30	
Cardiff Central 7	d						08 30	09 28	09 28		11 34	
Newport (South Wales) 5	d						08 52	09 47	09 47		11 50	
Cwmbran	d						09 03	09 59	09 59		12 06	
Pontypool and New Inn	d						09 09	10 05	10 05		12 12	
Abergavenny	d						09 18	10 15	10 15		12 23	
Hereford 7	a						09 45	10 43	10 43		12 51	
	d						09 47	10 45	10 45		12 52	
Leominster	d						10 01	10 58	10 58		13 05	
Ludlow	d						10 12	11 10	11 10		13 17	
Craven Arms 3	d						10 20					
Church Stretton	d						10 29					
Shrewsbury 5	a						10 46	11 41	11 41		13 47	
	d				09 55	10 22	10 48	11 44	11 44	12 24	13 49	14 22
Yorton	d					10x31				12x33		14x31
Wem	d					10 36				12 38		14 36
Prees	d					10x41				12x43		14x41
Whitchurch (Shrops)	d					10 48				12 50		14 48
Wrenbury	d	00x01				10x54				12x56		14x54
Nantwich	d	00 07				11 00				13 02		15 00
Crewe 10	a	00 17			10 26	11 10	11 23	12 24	12 24	13 12	14 26	15 10
	d		08 30	09 29	10 28		11 23	12 28	12 28		14 30	
Gobowen	a											
Chirk	a											
Ruabon	a											
Wrexham General	a											
Chester	a											
Llandudno Junction	a											
Llandudno	d											
Bangor (Gwynedd)	a											
Holyhead	a											
Wilmslow	a		08 49	09 50	10 47		11 42	12 48	12 48		14 50	
Stockport	a				11 00			13 00	13 00		15 02	
Manchester Piccadilly 10 ⛴	a		09 13	10 11	11 16		12 07	13 15	13 15		15 15	

Station		AW ◇ 🛒	AW ◇	AW ■ 🛒	AW ■ 🛒	AW	AW ■ 🛒	AW ■ 🛒	AW ■ 🛒	AW	AW ◇ 🛒	AW ■ 🛒
Swansea	d	11 34	11 11		12 49		13 43		14 56			15 31
Cardiff Central 7	d	12 36		13 25	13 51		14 54	15 17	15 56			16 40
Newport (South Wales) 5	d	12 50		13 39	14 05		15 08	15 32	16 14			16 55
Cwmbran	d	13 06		13 53	14 15		15 23	15 47	16 24			17 09
Pontypool and New Inn	d	13 11		13 59				15 52				17 15
Abergavenny	d	13 21		14 08	14 28		15 36	16 02	16 37			17 25
Hereford 7	a	13 47		14 35	14 54		16 02	16 29	17 03			17 50
	d	13 49		14 35	14 54		16 03	16 31	17 04			17 53
Leominster	d	14 03		14 48	15 07			16 44				18 06
Ludlow	d	14 14		14 59	15 18		16 24	16 55	17 26			18 17
Craven Arms 3	d	14 23	14 44	15 08				17 03				18 26
Church Stretton	d	14 33	14 57					17 12				18 35
Shrewsbury 5	a	14 50	15 13	15 29	15 53		16 52	17 27	17 53			18 50
	d	14 51		15 33	15 54	16 24	16 53	17 31	17 54	18 24	18 24	18 54
Yorton	d					16x33				18x33		
Wem	d					16 38				18 38		
Prees	d					16x43				18x43		
Whitchurch (Shrops)	d					16 50				18 50		
Wrenbury	d					16x56				18x56		
Nantwich	d					17 02				19 02		
Crewe 10	a	15 26			16 28	17 12	17 27		18 27	19 12		19 25
	d	15 28			16 30		17 30		18 31			19 31
Gobowen	a			15 50				17 48			18 42	
Chirk	a			15 56				17 54			18 47	
Ruabon	a			16 02				18 00			18 53	
Wrexham General	a			16 10				18 08			19 00	
Chester	a			16 29				18 26				
Llandudno Junction	a			17 31				19 24			20 30	
Llandudno	d											
Bangor (Gwynedd)	a			17 54				19 48			20 52	
Holyhead	a			18 38				20 18			21 26	
Wilmslow	a	15 48			16 49		17 49		18 49			19 49
Stockport	a	16 00			17 00		18 01		19 00			20 00
Manchester Piccadilly 10 ⛴	a	16 14			17 17		18 18		19 16			20 16

Station		AW ◇	AW ■ 🛒	AW	AW ■ 🛒	AW ◇	AW ◇	AW ◇	AW ◇
Swansea	d	15 36	16 52		17 37	18 40			22 10
Cardiff Central 7	d		17 54		18 40	19 40		21 10	23 20
Newport (South Wales) 5	d		18 09		18 55	19 56		21 24	23 39
Cwmbran	d		18 23		19 09	20 10		21 38	23 49
Pontypool and New Inn	d		18 29			20 16		21 44	23 55
Abergavenny	d		18 38		19 22	20 26		21 53	00 05
Hereford 7	a		19 03		19 48	20 53		22 19	00 31
	d		19 05		19 50	20 54		22 19	
Leominster	d		19 19		20 04	21 08		22 32	
Ludlow	d		19 30		20 15	21 19		22 43	
Craven Arms 3	d	19 00			20 23	21 29		22 52	
Church Stretton	d	19 13			20 32	21 38		23 01	
Shrewsbury 5	a	19 35	19 57		20 47	21 56		23 17	
	d		19 59	20 21	20 50		22 32	23 19	
Yorton	d			20x30				23x28	
Wem	d			20 35				23 33	
Prees	d			20x40				23x38	
Whitchurch (Shrops)	d			20 47				23 45	
Wrenbury	d			20x53				23x51	
Nantwich	d			20 59				23 57	
Crewe 10	a		20 30	21 09	21 22		23 04	00 07	
	d		20 32		21 31		23 08	00 10	
Gobowen	a								
Chirk	a								
Ruabon	a								
Wrexham General	a								
Chester	a						23 33	00 34	
Llandudno Junction	a								
Llandudno	d								
Bangor (Gwynedd)	a								
Holyhead	a								
Wilmslow	a		20 50		21 52				
Stockport	a		21 01		22 04				
Manchester Piccadilly 10 ⛴	a		21 15		22 19				

A not 15 December

Table T132-F

Mondays to Fridays

16 December to 15 May

Bath Spa - Bristol - Cardiff

Miles	Miles			AW	GW	AW	GW	AW	GW	XC	XC	AW	GW	AW	GW	XC	XC	GW	AW	XC	GW	GW	GW
				MX	MX	MX	MX	MX	MX	MO	MX												
				◇		◇	◇1 ⌶	◇	◇1 ⌶	◇1	◇1		◇	◇	◇	◇1 A ⌶	◇1		◇ ⌶	◇1	◇1 ⌶		◇1 ⌶
0	—	**Bath Spa 7**	d		00 03				01 01							06 10		06 28			06 46	07 00	07 09
1	—	Oldfield Park	d															06 31				07 03	
7	—	Keynsham	d															06 38				07 10	
11½	—	**Bristol Temple Meads 10**	a		00 15				01 12							06 23		06 48			06 58	07 17	07 22
—	—		d						01 22	05 20	05 20		05 54		06 27	06 32		06 53			07 07		
16	—	Filton Abbey Wood	d										06 01		06 37			07 04			07 15		
—	0	**Bristol Parkway 7**	a							05 29	05 29					06 40					07 18		
—	—		d				00 15			05 38	05 38										07 28		
17½	—	Patchway	d										06 06		06 42								
21	4¾	Pilning	d																				
28	11¾	Severn Tunnel Jn	d										06 17	06 30	06 53		06 57	07 17		07 31			
38	21¾	Newport (South Wales)	a				00 40		01s54	06 00	06 06		06 28	06 42	07 04		07 09	07 28		07 42	07 49		
—	—		d	00 02		00 14	00 43	01 03		06 08	06 08	06 22	06 29	06 43	07 05		07 10	07 29	07 33	07 44	07 52		
49¾	33½	**Cardiff Central 7**	a	00 20		00 34	00 58	01 23	02 13	06 21	06 21	06 35	06 42	06 57	07 20		07 22	07 42	07 49	08 00	08 03		

		AW	GW	GW	GW	GW	SW	GW	GW	AW	AW	GW	AW	GW	GW	GW	XC	GW	GW	GW	GW	AW	AW
		◇	◇		◇1 ⌶		◇1	◇	◇1 ⌶	◇ ⌶	◇	◇1 ⌶	◇	◇		◇1 ⌶	◇1 ⌶	◇1 B ⌶	■	◇	◇1 ⌶	◇ ⌶	■ ⊠
Bath Spa 7	d			07 14		07 25	07 37	07 50	07 57						08 10	08 24			08 30	08 45	08 56		
Oldfield Park	d			07 17		07 28	07 40	07 53							08 13				08 33	08 48			
Keynsham	d			07 24		07 35	07 47	08 00	08 06						08 20				08 40	08 57			
Bristol Temple Meads 10	a			07 34		07 43	07 55	08 08	08 13						08 28	08 36			08 48	09 05	09 10		
	d		07 27	07 38		07 53		08 17						08 22	08 37				08 56				
Filton Abbey Wood	d		07 38	07 46		08 01		08a27						08 36	08 46				09 04				
Bristol Parkway 7	a			07 53											08 50								
	d				08 04							08 33						09 03					
Patchway	d		07 43			08 09								08 40									
Pilning	d																						
Severn Tunnel Jn	d		07 54								08 38			08 51									
Newport (South Wales)	a		08 06		08 23	08 29					08 50	08 53		09 08				09 22	09 28				
	d	08 03	08 08		08 26	08 31				08 41	08 50	08 55	09 02	09 10			09 13	09 25	09 30			09 39	09 44
Cardiff Central 7	a	08 18	08 23		08 37	08 45				08 56	09 07	09 07	09 15	09 24			09 27	09 38	09 45			09 57	09 58

		AW	GW	GW	GW	GW	XC	GW	AW	GW	GW	AW	GW	AW	GW	GW	GW	XC	AW	GW	GW	GW
		◇	◇1 ⌶	◇		◇1 ⌶	◇1	◇1 ⌶	◇ ⌶	◇	◇1 ⌶		◇1 ⌶	◇	◇	◇	◇1 ⌶	◇1 ⌶	◇ ⌶	◇1 ⌶	◇	◇1 ⌶
Bath Spa 7	d				09 11	09 24				09 36	09 55					10 11	10 26				10 37	10 55
Oldfield Park	d				09 14											10 14						
Keynsham	d				09 21											10 21						
Bristol Temple Meads 10	a				09 29	09 36				09 51	10 07					10 29	10 37				10 51	11 07
	d			09 27	09 38					09 56					10 27	10 37					10 57	
Filton Abbey Wood	d			09 36	09 45					10 05					10 36	10 45					11 05	
Bristol Parkway 7	a				09 50											10 50						
	d		09 35					10 03					10 33							11 04		
Patchway	d			09 40											10 40							
Pilning	d																					
Severn Tunnel Jn	d	09 38		09 51											10 53							
Newport (South Wales)	a	09 50	09 54	10 02				10 21		10 33			10 51		11 04					11 24	11 30	
	d	09 51	09 57	10 04			10 12	10 24	10 30	10 34		10 38	10 53	11 00	11 06			11 12	11 22	11 26	11 31	
Cardiff Central 7	a	10 06	10 09	10 20			10 25	10 37	10 45	10 47		10 55	11 05	11 16	11 23			11 25	11 36	11 39	11 46	

		AW	AW	GW	GW	GW	GW	XC	AW	GW	GW	SW	GW	AW	AW	GW	GW	GW	GW	XC	AW	GW	GW
		◇	■ ⌶	◇1 ⌶	◇	◇	◇1 ⌶	◇1 ⌶	◇ ⌶	◇1 ✕	◇	◇1	◇1 ⌶	◇	◇ ⌶	◇1 ⌶	◇	◇ C ⌶	◇1 ⌶	◇1 ⌶	◇ ⌶	◇1 ⌶	◇
Bath Spa 7	d					11 07	11 24				11 37	11 47	11 55					12 11	12 24				12 37
Oldfield Park	d					11 10						11 50						12 14					
Keynsham	d					11 17						11 57						12 21					
Bristol Temple Meads 10	a					11 29	11 39				11 50	12 05	12 10					12 30	12 36				12 49
	d				11 20	11 37					11 56						12 23	12 38					12 57
Filton Abbey Wood	d				11 36	11 45					12 05						12 36	12 46					13 05
Bristol Parkway 7	a					11 49												12 50					
	d			11 34						12 03						12 33						13 04	
Patchway	d				11 40												12 40						
Pilning	d																						
Severn Tunnel Jn	d	11 33			11 51									12 39			12 52						
Newport (South Wales)	a	11 46		11 56	12 02					12 25	12 30			12 52		13 02	13 06					13 24	13 29
	d	11 49	11 54	11 59	12 04			12 10	12 23	12 27	12 32			12 53	13 00	13 05	13 07			13 14	13 23	13 27	13 31
Cardiff Central 7	a	12 15	12 06	12 11	12 22			12 22	12 38	12 39	12 44			13 07	13 15	13 17	13 27			13 26	13 36	13 39	13 43

A ⌶ from Bristol Temple Meads

B The Saint David

C ⌶ to Bristol Temple Meads

When events are being held at the Principality Stadium, services are subject to alteration. Please check times before travelling.

NRT DECEMBER 19 EDITION

Table T132-F

Mondays to Fridays

16 December to 15 May

Bath Spa - Bristol - Cardiff

		GW	GW	GW	GW	GW	XC	AW	GW	GW	GW	AW	AW	GW	GW	GW	GW	XC	AW	GW	GW	SW
		◇1 ⌶	◇1 ⌶	◇	◇	◇1 ⌶	◇1 ⌶	◇ ⌶	◇1 ⌶	◇	◇1 ⌶	◇	■ ⌶	◇1 ⌶	◇	◇	◇1 ⌶	◇1 ⌶	■ ⌶	◇1 ⌶	◇	◇1
Bath Spa 7	d	12 56			13 16	13 24				13 37	13 58					14 11	14 24				14 37	14 47
Oldfield Park	d				13 19											14 14						14 50
Keynsham	d				13 26											14 21						14 57
Bristol Temple Meads 10	a	13 10			13 35	13 40				13 51	14 12					14 29	14 36				14 49	15 05
	d			13 21	13 38					13 57					14 24	14 38					14 57	
Filton Abbey Wood	d			13 36	13 45					14 05					14 36	14 46					15 06	
Bristol Parkway 7	a				13 50											14 50						
	d		13 33						14 03					14 33						15 04		
Patchway	d			13 40											14 40							
Pilning	d																					
Severn Tunnel Jn.	d			13 51								14 39			14 51							
Newport (South Wales)	a		13 55	14 02					14 23	14 30		14 51		14 59	15 05					15 22	15 30	
	d		13 57	14 04			14 13	14 22	14 26	14 32		14 51	14 56	15 01	15 06			15 11	15 22	15 25	15 32	
Cardiff Central 7	a		14 09	14 21			14 25	14 39	14 39	14 46		15 07	15 11	15 17	15 22			15 23	15 42	15 36	15 44	

		GW	AW	GW	AW	GW	GW	GW	GW	XC	GW	GW	GW	AW	GW	GW	GW	GW	XC	AW	GW	GW	GW
		◇1 ⌶	◇	◇1 ⌶	■ ⊠	◇		◇	◇1 ⌶	◇1 ⌶	◇1 ⌶	◇	◇1 ⌶	■ ⌶	◇1 ⌶	◇		◇1 ⌶	◇1 ⌶	■ ⌶	◇1 ⌶		■
Bath Spa 7	d	14 55					15 01	15 11	15 24			15 37	15 55				16 11	16 25				16 30	16 37
Oldfield Park	d						15 04	15 14									16 14						
Keynsham	d						15 11	15 21									16 21					16 38	
Bristol Temple Meads 10	a	15 09					15 19	15 29	15 36			15 49	16 08				16 29	16 38				16 46	16 50
	d					15 20	15 30	15 38				15 56				16 26	16 38					17 06	16 57
Filton Abbey Wood	d					15 35	15a39	15 46				16 05				16 35	16 46					→	17 07
Bristol Parkway 7	a							15 50									16 50						
	d			15 33							16 05				16 33						17 04		
Patchway	d					15 40										16 40							
Pilning	d																						
Severn Tunnel Jn.	d		15 28			15 51										16 51							17 20
Newport (South Wales)	a		15 41	15 52		16 03					16 23	16 30			16 54	17 02					17 25		17 31
	d		15 42	15 54	16 00	16 06				16 14	16 25	16 31		16 41	16 55	17 04			17 13	17 22	17 27		17 32
Cardiff Central 7	a		15 55	16 07	16 15	16 22				16 29	16 35	16 44		16 57	17 07	17 18			17 25	17 37	17 39		17 45

		GW	GW	GW	AW	GW	GW	GW	GW	XC	GW	GW	GW	AW	GW	AW	GW	AW	GW	GW	GW	GW
			◇1 A ⌶	◇1 ⌶	◇	◇1 ⌶	◇	◇	◇1 ⌶	◇1	◇1 ⌶	■	◇1 ⌶	■ ⌶	◇1 ⌶	◇	◇1 ⌶	◇ ⌶	◇	◇1 ⌶		◇1 ⌶
Bath Spa 7	d			16 54				17 11	17 24			17 37	17 57							18 13	18 19	18 25
Oldfield Park	d							17 14													18 22	
Keynsham	d	←						17 21													18 29	
Bristol Temple Meads 10	a	16 46		17 06				17 29	17 36			17 50	18 08							18 27	18 37	18 41
	d	17 06					17 24	17 38				17 56							18 24		18 41	
Filton Abbey Wood	d	17 18					17 32	17 46				18 04							18 38		18 51	
Bristol Parkway 7	a	17 22						17 50													18 56	
	d		17 26			17 39					18 05				18 26		18 38					
Patchway	d						17 36												18 45			
Pilning	d																					
Severn Tunnel Jn.	d				17 40		17 47					18 21				18 40			18 57			
Newport (South Wales)	a		17 44		17 53	18 00	18 04				18 23	18 32			18 44	18 53	18 59		19 10			
	d		17 46		17 54	18 02	18 06			18 16	18 25	18 33		18 41	18 46	18 54	19 01	19 06	19 12			
Cardiff Central 7	a		17 57		18 11	18 14	18 21			18 29	18 37	18 46		18 54	18 57	19 08	19 15	19 20	19 26			

		XC	GW	AW	GW	GW	SW	GW	AW	GW	GW	GW	GW	GW	GW	XC	GW	GW	GW	AW	XC	AW	GW
		◇1	◇1 ⌶	■ ⌶	■	◇1 ⌶	◇1	◇1 B ⌶	◇	◇1 ⌶	◇		◇1 C ⌶	◇1 ⌶	◇	◇1	◇1 D ⌶	◇	◇1 ⌶	■ ⌶	◇1	◇	◇1 ⌶
Bath Spa 7	d				18 37	18 53	18 58					19 05	19 15	19 25	19 31			19 37	19 56				
Oldfield Park	d											19 08			19 34								
Keynsham	d											19 15			19 41								
Bristol Temple Meads 10	a				18 50	19 08	19 15					19 23	19 27	19 37	19 49			19 53	20 07				
	d				18 56						19 23	19 38						19 57			20 14		
Filton Abbey Wood	d				19 04						19 37	19 49						20 05			20 21		
Bristol Parkway 7	a											19 54											
	d		19 03					19 28		19 39							20 03						20 35
Patchway	d										19 45										20 25		
Pilning	d																						
Severn Tunnel Jn.	d				19 19				19 41		19 56							20 20			20 35	20 41	
Newport (South Wales)	a		19 21		19 32			19 46	19 54	19 57	20 07						20 24	20 31			20 46	20 54	20 57
	d	19 16	19 24	19 30	19 34			19 48	19 54	20 00	20 09					20 14	20 26	20 33		20 41	20 47	20 54	21 00
Cardiff Central 7	a	19 28	19 38	19 45	19 47			19 59	20 10	20 12	20 25					20 27	20 37	20 45		20 55	21 02	21 09	21 15

A The Capitals United

B The Red Dragon

C The Bristolian

D Y Cymro/The Welshman

When events are being held at the Principality Stadium, services are subject to alteration. Please check times before travelling.

Table T132-F

Bath Spa - Bristol - Cardiff

Mondays to Fridays

16 December to 15 May

		GW		GW	GW	GW	AW	XC	GW	GW	GW	AW		GW	GW	GW	XC FO	XC FX	GW FO	GW FX	GW FO	GW FX		SW	GW
Bath Spa	d			20 07	20 15	20 25				20 38	20 55				21 11	21 24					21 37	21 37		21 51	21 59
Oldfield Park	d			20 10											21 14										
Keynsham	d			20 17											21 21									21 59	
Bristol Temple Meads	a			20 25	20 30	20 37				20 50	21 07				21 29	21 37					21 51	21 51		22 06	22 12
	d	20 20		20 43						20 57				21 29	21 37						21 55	21 55			
Filton Abbey Wood	d	20 28		20 51						21 05				21 37	21 49						22 02	22 03			
Bristol Parkway	a			20 56											21 53										
	d								21 04										22 03	22 03					
Patchway	d	20 33												21 41							22 07	22 08			
Pilning	d																								
Severn Tunnel Jn.	d	20 45								21 20				21 53			22 05	22 05			22 20	22 19			
Newport (South Wales)	a	21 02							21 22	21 31				22 04			22 16	22 17	22 24	22 31	22 32	22 38			
	d	21 03					21 07	21 14	21 25	21 32		21 53		22 06			22 18	22 18	22 26	22 32	22 33	22 39			
Cardiff Central	a	21 29					21 24	21 27	21 40	21 45		22 08		22 20			22 30	22 36	22 39	22 48	22 46	22 58			

		AW FO	AW FX	GW FO	GW FX	GW FO	GW FX	GW FO		GW	GW FX	GW FO	GW FX	GW	GW	AW FO	AW FX	GW FO		GW FX
Bath Spa	d					22 18	22 18			22 25		22 38	22 38	23 11	23 25			23 56		23 57
Oldfield Park	d					22 21	22 21							23 14						
Keynsham	d					22 28	22 28							23 21						
Bristol Temple Meads	a					22 36	22 36			22 45		22 50	22 50	23 29	23 36			00 08		00 09
	d			22 34	22 34		22 45					22 57	22 57							
Filton Abbey Wood	d			22 42	22 42		22 53					23 04	23 04							
Bristol Parkway	a						22 58													
	d							23 02			23 02									
Patchway	d											23 09	23 09							
Pilning	d																			
Severn Tunnel Jn.	d			22 54	22 56							23 20	23 20			23 51	23 51			
Newport (South Wales)	a			23 11	23 13			23 21			23 27	23 31	23 37			00 07	00 13			
	d	22 41	22 44	23 13	23 15			23 24			23 30	23 33	23 39			00 07	00 14			
Cardiff Central	a	23 00	23 07	23 32	23 34			23 35			23 45	23 45	23 57			00 22	00 34			

Saturdays

21 December to 16 May

		AW	GW	AW	GW	AW	GW	AW	AW	GW		XC	GW	AW	GW	XC	AW	GW	GW	GW		SW	GW	GW	AW
Bath Spa	d		00 03				01 01												07 11			07 35		07 51	
Oldfield Park	d																		07 14			07 38			
Keynsham	d																		07 21			07 45			
Bristol Temple Meads	a		00 15				01 12												07 29			07 52		08 04	
	d						01 22			06 28			06 57		07 05			07 29	07 39				07 57		
Filton Abbey Wood	d									06 35			07 09		07 14			07 37	07 46				08 05		
Bristol Parkway	a														07 17				07 51						
	d				00 15										07 25					08 04					
Patchway	d									06 40								07 41							
Pilning	d																								
Severn Tunnel Jn.	d								06 30	06 51		06 55	07 21			07 37		07 52							
Newport (South Wales)	a				00 34		01s54		06 43	07 02		07 06	07 32		07 44	07 49		08 06		08 25			08 30		
	d	00 01		00 07	00 36	01 03		06 38	06 44	07 03		07 07	07 34	07 40	07 46	07 50	08 03	08 08		08 26			08 32		08 39
Cardiff Central	a	00 14		00 22	00 47	01 23	02 13	06 53	07 01	07 17		07 20	07 49	07 54	07 58	08 06	08 17	08 24		08 38			08 44		08 53

		AW	GW	GW	GW	AW		XC	GW	GW	GW	GW	AW	AW	GW	GW		GW	GW	XC	GW	GW A	GW	AW	AW
Bath Spa	d			08 13	08 23					08 34	08 47	08 54						09 09	09 23			09 39	09 49		
Oldfield Park	d			08 15								08 57						09 12							
Keynsham	d			08 22								09 04						09 19							
Bristol Temple Meads	a			08 31	08 37					08 47	09 00	09 13						09 27	09 37			09 52	10 04		
	d		08 25	08 39						08 57						09 29		09 39				09 57			
Filton Abbey Wood	d		08 33	08 46						09 06						09 38		09 46				10 06			
Bristol Parkway	a			08 51														09 51							
	d								09 04						09 38						10 04				
Patchway	d		08 37													09 45									
Pilning	d																								
Severn Tunnel Jn.	d	08 38	08 48											09 40		09 56									
Newport (South Wales)	a	08 51	08 58						09 23	09 29				09 53	09 57	10 07					10 24	10 30			
	d	08 52	09 00			09 05		09 10	09 26	09 31			09 41	09 53	09 59	10 08				10 15	10 25	10 32		10 43	10 47
Cardiff Central	a	09 07	09 15			09 21		09 23	09 39	09 44			09 59	10 14	10 12	10 23				10 29	10 40	10 45		10 57	11 03

A   ⌶ to Bristol Temple Meads

When events are being held at the Principality Stadium, services are subject to alteration. Please check times before travelling.

Table T132-F

Bath Spa - Bristol - Cardiff

Saturdays

21 December to 16 May

		GW	AW	GW	GW	GW	XC	GW		GW A	GW	AW	AW	GW	GW	GW	GW	XC		GW	GW A	GW	SW	AW	AW
Bath Spa	d				10 10	10 23				10 38	10 49					11 10	11 21				11 38	11 48	11 54		
Oldfield Park	d				10 13											11 13							11 57		
Keynsham	d				10 20											11 20							12 04		
Bristol Temple Meads	a				10 29	10 37				10 50	11 04					11 29	11 34				11 50	12 04	12 12		
	d			10 25	10 39					10 57					11 28	11 39					11 57				
Filton Abbey Wood	d			10 36	10 46					11 07					11 38	11 46					12 05				
Bristol Parkway	a				10 51											11 51									
	d	10 38						11 04						11 38						12 04					
Patchway	d			10 44											11 45										
Pilning	d																								
Severn Tunnel Jn.	d			10 55									11 33		11 56										12 38
Newport (South Wales)	a	10 57		11 06				11 23		11 30			11 47	11 57	12 07					12 23	12 30				12 52
	d	10 58	11 03	11 08			11 12	11 25		11 31		11 37	11 47	11 59	12 08			12 13		12 25	12 31			12 40	12 52
Cardiff Central	a	11 11	11 17	11 22			11 25	11 37		11 45		11 54	12 01	12 13	12 23			12 26		12 39	12 45			12 56	13 06

		AW	GW	GW		GW	GW	XC	GW	GW A	GW	AW	GW	GW		GW	GW	XC	GW	GW	GW	AW	AW	AW
Bath Spa	d					12 11	12 23			12 40	12 49					13 12	13 23			13 38	13 50			
Oldfield Park	d					12 14										13 14								
Keynsham	d					12 21										13 21								
Bristol Temple Meads	a					12 29	12 37			12 53	13 04					13 30	13 37			13 50	14 04			
	d			12 20		12 39				12 57				13 31		13 39				13 57				
Filton Abbey Wood	d			12 40		12 46				13 07				13 42		13 46				14 05				
Bristol Parkway	a					12 51										13 51								
	d		12 38						13 04				13 40						14 04					
Patchway	d			12 45										13 46										
Pilning	d																							
Severn Tunnel Jn.	d			12 56										13 57									14 38	
Newport (South Wales)	a		13 01	13 07					13 23	13 30			14 00	14 07					14 23	14 30			14 51	
	d	12 57	13 03	13 08				13 15	13 25	13 32		13 37	14 01	14 09				14 13	14 25	14 31		14 40	14 52	14 56
Cardiff Central	a	13 14	13 18	13 23				13 27	13 38	13 45		13 54	14 14	14 23				14 25	14 37	14 45		14 55	15 09	15 12

		GW	AW	GW	GW	GW	XC	AW	GW	GW		GW	SW	AW	GW	GW	GW	GW	XC	GW		GW	GW	AW	AW
Bath Spa	d				14 10	14 23				14 38		14 47	14 53				15 10	15 23				15 38	15 50		
Oldfield Park	d				14 13								14 56				15 13								
Keynsham	d				14 20								15 03				15 20								
Bristol Temple Meads	a				14 29	14 37				14 50		15 04	15 10				15 29	15 37				15 50	16 04		
	d			14 24	14 39					14 57						15 28	15 39					15 57			
Filton Abbey Wood	d			14 31	14 46					15 07						15 38	15 46					16 05			
Bristol Parkway	a				14 51												15 51								
	d	14 39							15 04						15 38					16 04					
Patchway	d			14 36												15 44									
Pilning	d																								
Severn Tunnel Jn.	d			14 47										15 23		15 55									
Newport (South Wales)	a	15 00		15 04					15 23	15 30				15 37	15 58	16 06				16 23		16 30			
	d	15 02	15 06	15 06			15 14	15 22	15 26	15 31				15 37	15 59	16 08			16 12	16 25		16 31		16 39	16 54
Cardiff Central	a	15 17	15 24	15 25			15 27	15 37	15 40	15 46				15 51	16 14	16 23			16 25	16 37		16 46		16 57	17 09

		GW	GW	GW	GW	XC		GW	GW	GW	AW	AW	GW	GW	GW	GW		XC	GW	GW	GW	AW	AW	AW	GW
Bath Spa	d			16 10	16 23				16 38	16 49					17 10	17 23				17 38	17 49				
Oldfield Park	d			16 13											17 13										
Keynsham	d			16 20											17 20										
Bristol Temple Meads	a			16 28	16 37				16 50	17 04					17 29	17 37				17 50	18 03				
	d		16 28	16 39					16 57					17 28	17 39					17 57					
Filton Abbey Wood	d		16 38	16 46					17 07					17 38	17 46					18 06					
Bristol Parkway	a			16 51											17 51										
	d	16 38						17 04					17 38						18 04						18 38
Patchway	d		16 45											17 45											
Pilning	d																								
Severn Tunnel Jn.	d		16 56						17 20			17 38		17 56						18 20		18 26			
Newport (South Wales)	a	16 57	17 07					17 23	17 31			17 51	17 58	18 07					18 23	18 31		18 38			19 00
	d	16 59	17 08			17 13		17 24	17 32		17 37	17 52	17 59	18 07				18 12	18 24	18 32		18 39	18 42	18 57	19 02
Cardiff Central	a	17 12	17 23			17 26		17 38	17 46		17 55	18 09	18 12	18 23				18 26	18 36	18 46		18 52	18 59	19 09	19 14

A   ⌶ to Bristol Temple Meads

When events are being held at the Principality Stadium, services are subject to alteration. Please check times before travelling.

Table T132-F

Bath Spa - Bristol - Cardiff

Saturdays
21 December to 16 May

		GW	GW	GW	XC	GW	GW	GW	SW	AW	AW	GW	XC	GW	GW	GW	GW	GW	GW	GW	AW	XC	GW
		◇		◇1 T	◇1	◇1 T	◇	◇1 T	◇1	■ T	◇	◇1 T	◇1	◇		◇1 T	◇1 T	◇	◇	◇1 T	■ T	◇1	◇
Bath Spa 7	d		18 10	18 25			18 38	18 47	18 53						19 10		19 22	19 29	19 38	19 49			20 12
Oldfield Park	d		18 13						18 56						19 13			19 32					20 15
Keynsham	d		18 20						19 03						19 20			19 39					20 22
Bristol Temple Meads 10	a		18 30	18 37			18 50	18 59	19 12						19 28		19 35	19 49	19 51	20 03			20 31
	d	18 32	18 39				18 57							19 25	19 39				19 57			20 14	
Filton Abbey Wood	d	18 40	18 46				19 06							19 40	19 46				20 05			20 21	
Bristol Parkway 7	a		18 51												19 51								
	d					19 04						19 40				20 04							
Patchway	d	18 45												19 47								20 25	
Pilning	d																						
Severn Tunnel Jn.	d	18 56					19 20				19 38			20 00					20 20			20 35	
Newport (South Wales)	a	19 06				19 23	19 31				19 51	19 59		20 11		20 23			20 31			20 46	
	d	19 07			19 12	19 24	19 32			19 38	19 52	20 01	20 08	20 13		20 25			20 33		20 41	20 47	
Cardiff Central 7	a	19 20			19 24	19 40	19 47			19 55	20 08	20 13	20 20	20 25		20 39			20 46		20 59	21 00	

		GW	AW	GW	XC	AW	GW	GW	GW	AW	GW	GW	GW	XC	GW	AW	GW	GW	SW	GW	GW	GW
		◇1 T	◇	◇1 T	◇1	◇ T	◇1 T	◇	◇1 T	◇	◇		◇1 T	◇1	◇1 T	◇	◇	◇1 T	◇1		◇	◇1 T
Bath Spa 7	d	20 22						20 38	20 48			21 11	21 22				21 38	21 47	21 53	22 19	22 38	22 52
Oldfield Park	d											21 14								22 22		
Keynsham	d											21 21							22 01	22 29		
Bristol Temple Meads 10	a	20 35						20 50	21 00			21 30	21 37				21 51	21 59	22 08	22 39	22 50	23 05
	d							20 57			21 29						22 00				22 55	
Filton Abbey Wood	d							21 06			21 36						22 08				23 02	
Bristol Parkway 7	a																					
	d			20 38			21 04								22 04							
Patchway	d										21 41						22 12				23 07	
Pilning	d																					
Severn Tunnel Jn.	d		20 39					21 20			21 52			22 06			22 23				23 18	
Newport (South Wales)	a		20 52	20 57			21 24	21 31			22 09			22 23	22 30		22 40				23 35	
	d		20 53	20 58	21 10	21 16	21 25	21 33		21 45	22 10			22 24	22 31	22 35	22 42				23 36	
Cardiff Central 7	a		21 07	21 10	21 22	21 34	21 37	21 46		22 06	22 31			22 43	22 47	22 57	23 00				23 55	

		GW	GW	AW	AW	GW
			◇1 T	◇	◇	◇1 T
Bath Spa 7	d	23 11				23 52
Oldfield Park	d	23 14				
Keynsham	d	23 21				
Bristol Temple Meads 10	a	23 30				00 05
	d					
Filton Abbey Wood	d					
Bristol Parkway 7	a					
	d		23 18			
Patchway	d					
Pilning	d					
Severn Tunnel Jn.	d				23 49	
Newport (South Wales)	a		23 44		00 12	
	d		23 46	23 50	00 12	
Cardiff Central 7	a		00 04	00 12	00 36	

Sundays
15 December to 10 May

		AW	AW	GW	GW	AW	AW	GW	GW	GW	GW	AW	GW	GW	GW	GW	GW	AW	XC	GW	GW	GW	GW
		A	◇ A	◇1 A T	◇	◇ T	◇	◇1 T	◇ B	◇ C	◇1 T	◇ T	◇	◇1 T	◇1 T	◇1 T	◇1 T	◇	◇1 T	◇1 T	◇1 T	■	◇1 T
Bath Spa 7	d			01 02					09 19	09 19	09 30		10 16	10 27	10 46		11 21					11 29	11 46
Oldfield Park	d								09 22	09 22			10 18									11 32	
Keynsham	d								09 29	09 29			10 26									11 39	
Bristol Temple Meads 10	a			01 15					09 39	09 39	09 47		10 36	10 41	11 00		11 38					11 48	12 00
	d				08 43				09 44	09 50			10 43									11 54	
Filton Abbey Wood	d				08 50				09 55	09 58			10 50									12 03	
Bristol Parkway 7	a																						
	d							09 53								10 57				11 37	11 58		
Patchway	d								09 59	10 02													
Pilning	d																						
Severn Tunnel Jn.	d				09 03		09 25		10 10	10 13			11 03					11 28				12 20	
Newport (South Wales)	a				09 20		09 44	10 10	10 21	10 24			11 13			11 18		11 41		11 58	12 18	12 32	
	d	00 04	00 12		09 21	09 33	09 45	10 10	10 23	10 26		10 59	11 14			11 18		11 42	11 54	11 59	12 18	12 33	
Cardiff Central 7	a	00 22	00 36		09 40	09 54	10 03	10 24	10 35	10 38		11 13	11 28			11 32		11 55	12 06	12 11	12 32	12 45	

A not 15 December **B** from 12 January **C** until 5 January

When events are being held at the Principality Stadium, services are subject to alteration. Please check times before travelling.

NRT DECEMBER 19 EDITION

Table T132-F

Bath Spa - Bristol - Cardiff

Sundays
15 December to 10 May

		SW	GW	GW	XC	GW	AW	GW	GW	GW	AW	GW	AW	GW	XC	GW	GW	GW	AW	GW	GW	GW
		◇1		◇1 T	◇1 T	◇1 T	■ T	◇1 T	◇	◇1 T	◇	◇1 T	■ T	◇1 T	◇1 T	◇1 T	◇	◇1 T	■ T	◇	◇1 T	◇1 T
Bath Spa 7	d	11 53	12 11	12 21						12 51		13 21					13 27	13 46			14 21	
Oldfield Park	d	11 56	12 14														13 30					
Keynsham	d	12 03	12 21														13 37					
Bristol Temple Meads 10	a	12 11	12 29	12 33						13 04		13 37					13 45	13 59			14 37	
	d								12 54								13 54			14 16		
Filton Abbey Wood	d								13 01								14 00			14 23		
Bristol Parkway 7	a																					
	d					12 36		12 58						13 37		13 58						14 36
Patchway	d																					
Pilning	d																					
Severn Tunnel Jn.	d								13 16		13 20						14 15			14 36		
Newport (South Wales)	a					12 57		13 18	13 27		13 33			13 54		14 18	14 26			14 47		14 56
	d				12 54	12 59	13 06	13 18	13 29		13 34		13 41	13 54	14 12	14 20	14 28		14 35	14 48		14 58
Cardiff Central 7	a				13 06	13 11	13 21	13 32	13 41		13 47		14 01	14 11	14 24	14 30	14 42		14 50	15 01		15 10

		XC	AW	GW	GW	GW	SW	AW	GW	AW	GW	XC	GW	GW	GW	AW	GW	GW	GW	GW	XC	AW	GW
		◇1 T	■ T	◇1 T	◇	◇1 T	◇1	◇	◇1 R	■ T	◇1 T	◇1 T	◇1 T	◇	◇1 T	■ T	◇	◇	◇1 T	◇1 T	◇1 T	◇	◇1 T
Bath Spa 7	d				14 27	14 46	14 55		15 21					15 25	15 46			16 11	16 21				
Oldfield Park	d				14 30		14 58							15 31				16 13					
Keynsham	d				14 38		15 05							15 38				16 21					
Bristol Temple Meads 10	a				14 47	14 59	15 13		15 38					15 46	15 59			16 29	16 37				
	d				14 54									15 57			16 13						
Filton Abbey Wood	d				15 01									16 05			16 20						
Bristol Parkway 7	a																						
	d			15 00							15 36		16 00							16 37			17 01
Patchway	d																						
Pilning	d																						
Severn Tunnel Jn.	d				15 17			15 20						16 18			16 33					17 09	
Newport (South Wales)	a			15 18	15 29			15 35			15 56		16 21	16 29			16 44			16 54		17 22	17 23
	d	15 08	15 13	15 18	15 29			15 35		15 42	15 58	16 12	16 22	16 30		16 40	16 45			16 54	17 08	17 23	17 23
Cardiff Central 7	a	15 21	15 26	15 32	15 42			15 49		15 57	16 10	16 25	16 32	16 44		16 57	16 58			17 10	17 20	17 37	17 38

		GW	GW	GW	AW	GW	XC	GW	GW	GW	GW	GW	AW	GW	XC	GW	GW	GW	GW	GW	AW	AW
		◇	◇1 T	◇1 T	■ T	◇1 R	◇1 T	◇1 T	■	◇1 T	◇	◇1 T	■ T	◇1 T	◇1	◇1 T	◇	◇1 T	◇	◇1 T	■ T	◇
Bath Spa 7	d	16 29	16 46	17 21					17 27	17 46	18 06	18 21					18 31	18 46	18 52	19 21		
Oldfield Park	d								17 31		18 08								18 56			
Keynsham	d								17 38		18 16								19 03			
Bristol Temple Meads 10	a	16 41	17 00	17 37					17 46	17 59	18 26	18 37					18 44	18 59	19 12	19 34		
	d	16 50							17 54								18 54					
Filton Abbey Wood	d	17 03							18 01								19 01					
Bristol Parkway 7	a																					
	d					17 37		17 59						18 37		18 58						
Patchway	d	17 07															19 06					
Pilning	d																					
Severn Tunnel Jn.	d	17 18							18 17								19 18					19 32
Newport (South Wales)	a	17 31				17 57		18 18	18 29					18 54		19 18	19 29					19 51
	d	17 32			17 40	17 58	18 08	18 18	18 30				18 37	18 54	19 08	19 19	19 31				19 36	19 51
Cardiff Central 7	a	17 45			17 57	18 10	18 20	18 32	18 43				18 53	19 10	19 21	19 33	19 43				19 52	20 09

		GW	XC	GW	GW	GW	GW	GW	AW	GW	XC	AW	GW	GW	SW	GW	GW	GW	AW	AW	GW	GW	GW
		◇1 R	◇1	◇	◇1 T	◇1 T	◇	◇1 T	■ T	◇1 T	◇1	■ T	◇	◇1 T	◇1	◇	◇1 R	◇1 T	■	◇	◇	◇1 T	◇1 T
Bath Spa 7	d			19 25	19 45		20 02	20 21					20 26	20 46	20 53	21 02		21 21			21 25	21 50	
Oldfield Park	d						20 04									21 05							
Keynsham	d						20 12								21 01	21 11							
Bristol Temple Meads 10	a			19 39	19 58		20 22	20 37					20 41	21 04	21 08	21 20		21 34			21 40	22 04	
	d			19 42									20 45								21 45		
Filton Abbey Wood	d			19 50									20 52								21 51		
Bristol Parkway 7	a																						
	d	19 36				19 58				20 39							21 02						22 05
Patchway	d																				21 56		
Pilning	d																						
Severn Tunnel Jn.	d			20 02									21 05							21 17	22 07		
Newport (South Wales)	a	19 56		20 13		20 18				20 59			21 18				21 19			21 33	22 18		22 21
	d	19 58	20 08	20 15		20 19			20 29	20 59	21 08	21 14	21 19				21 20		21 29	21 34	22 21		22 21
Cardiff Central 7	a	20 10	20 21	20 29		20 33			20 46	21 16	21 21	21 32	21 31				21 34		21 44	21 48	22 33		22 35

When events are being held at the Principality Stadium, services are subject to alteration. Please check times before travelling.

Table T132-F

Sundays
15 December to 10 May

Bath Spa - Bristol - Cardiff

		GW	GW	AW	GW	GW	GW	AW	GW	AW
			◇1 🛒	◇	◇	◇1 🛒	◇1 ⊓	◇	◇1 🛒	◇
Bath Spa 7	d	22 10	22 20		22 24	22 46			23 21	
Oldfield Park	d	22 13								
Keynsham	d	22 20								
Bristol Temple Meads 10	a	22 30	22 36		22 38	23 01			23 35	
	d				22 44					
Filton Abbey Wood	d				22 51					
Bristol Parkway 7	a									
	d						23 02			
Patchway	d									
Pilning	d									
Severn Tunnel Jn	d				23 04			23 15		
Newport (South Wales)	a				23 16		23 19	23 33		
	d			22 41	23 16		23 20	23 33		23 56
Cardiff Central 7	a			22 58	23 29		23 34	23 52		00 15

When events are being held at the Principality Stadium, services are subject to alteration. Please check times before travelling.

AVAILABLE FROM MP Middleton Press

Country Railway Routes
BATH
GREEN PARK
TO BRISTOL
Vic Mitchell and Keith Smith
MP Middleton Press

Table T132-R

Mondays to Fridays
16 December to 15 May

Cardiff - Bristol - Bath Spa

Miles	Miles			GW MX	AW MX	AW MX	AW MO	GW	GW	AW	GW	AW	GW	GW	GW	GW	GW	GW	AW	GW	GW	GW	GW
				◇	◇	◇	◇	◇	◇1 🛒	◇	◇1 🛒	◇	◇1 🛒	◇	◇1 🛒	◇1 🛒		◇1 🛒	◇	◇1 🛒	◇1 🛒	◇1 🛒	◇1 A 🛒
0	0	**Cardiff Central 7**	d		00 30	04 35	04 35		05 07	05 12		05 38						05 56	06 10	06 15	06 25		
11¾	11¾	Newport (South Wales)	a		00 48	04 52	04 53		05 24	05 30		05 55						06 06	06 23	06 26	06 35		
—	—		d						05 25									06 08	06 24	06 28	06 37		
21¾	21¾	Severn Tunnel Jn	d	00 05															06a34				
28¾	28¾	Pilning	d																				
32¼	32¼	Patchway	d	00 21																			
—	33½	**Bristol Parkway 7**	a						05 51									06 28		06 48	06 57		
—	—		d														06 12						
33¾	—	Filton Abbey Wood	d	00 25													06 16						
38¾	—	**Bristol Temple Meads 10**	a	00 39													06 30						
—	—		d					05 00			05 25		05 46	05 51	06 00	06 30	06 39					06 49	07 00
42¾	—	Keynsham	d											05 58			06 46						
48¾	—	Oldfield Park	d											06 05			06 53						
49¾	—	**Bath Spa 7**	a					05 12			05 36		05 57	06 07	06 12	06 41	06 55					07 01	07 11

		GW	XC	AW	GW	GW	GW	XC	GW	AW	AW	GW	GW	GW	GW	XC	AW	GW	GW	GW	SW	GW	GW
		◇	◇1	◇ 🛒	◇1 🛒	◇1 🛒		◇1	◇1 🛒	■ ⊠	◇	◇1 🛒	◇1 B 🛒	◇1 🛒	■	◇1	■ 🛒	◇1 🛒	◇	◇1 🛒	◇1	◇	◇1 🛒
Cardiff Central 7	d	06 30	06 38	06 45	06 53			06 57		07 02	07 06	07 13	07 24		07 28	07 45	07 50			07 55		08 00	
Newport (South Wales)	a	06 42	06 53	06 59	07 03			07 09		07 15	07 19	07 24	07 34		07 40	07 57	08 03			08 06		08 12	
	d	06 44	06 54		07 05			07 11			07 20	07 25	07 36		07 42					08 09		08 14	
Severn Tunnel Jn	d	06 54	07a04					07 21			07a30				07 52							08 24	
Pilning	d																						
Patchway	d	07 07						07 33														08 39	
Bristol Parkway 7	a				07 25							07 49	07 58							08 29			
	d																		08 22				
Filton Abbey Wood	d	07 12						07 37							08 07				08 26			08 44	
Bristol Temple Meads 10	a	07 20						07 48							08 16				08 34			08 52	
	d	07 24				07 28	07 38		07 49					08 00	08 19			08 30	08 41		08 49		09 00
Keynsham	d						07 45								08 27				08 49		08 56		
Oldfield Park	d						07 52								08 34				08 56		09 03		
Bath Spa 7	a	07 36				07 42	07 54		08 00					08 11	08 36			08 42	08 59		09 05		09 11

		GW	GW	GW	GW	XC	AW	GW	GW	GW	GW	AW	GW	AW	GW	XC	GW	GW	GW	GW	GW	AW
		◇1 C 🛒		◇	◇1 🛒	◇1	◇ 🛒	◇1 🛒	◇	◇	◇1 🛒	◇	◇1 D 🛒	◇ 🛒	◇	◇1 🛒	◇1 🛒		◇1 🛒	◇	◇1 🛒	■ 🛒
Cardiff Central 7	d	08 18		08 27	08 41	08 45	08 50			09 00		09 07	09 18	09 22	09 27	09 45			09 51	10 00		10 05
Newport (South Wales)	a	08 28		08 39	08 52	08 58	09 03			09 12		09 22	09 29	09 36	09 39	09 57			10 01	10 12		10 18
	d	08 30		08 41	08 53					09 14		09 22	09 31		09 41				10 03	10 14		
Severn Tunnel Jn	d			08 51						09 24		09a33			09 51					10 24		
Pilning	d																					
Patchway	d									09 39										10 39		
Bristol Parkway 7	a	08 54			09 14								09 54						10 24			
	d								09 19									10 16				
Filton Abbey Wood	d		08 51	09 07					09 23	09 43					10 06			10 20		10 43		
Bristol Temple Meads 10	a		08 59	09 19					09 33	09 51					10 14			10 29		10 51		
	d		09 04	09 23				09 30	09 45		10 00				10 23		10 30	10 47			11 00	
Keynsham	d		09 11						09 53									10 54				
Oldfield Park	d		09 18						10 00									11 01				
Bath Spa 7	a		09 20	09 35				09 41	10 02		10 11				10 35		10 41	11 04			11 11	

		AW	AW	GW	GW	GW	GW	GW	XC	AW	GW	GW	GW	AW	GW	XC	GW	GW	GW	AW	SW	GW	GW
		◇	◇	◇1 🛒	◇	◇1 🛒	◇	◇1 🛒	◇1	■ 🛒	◇	◇1 🛒	◇1 🛒	■ ⊠	◇	◇1 🛒	◇1 🛒	◇	◇1 🛒	■ 🛒	◇1 🛒	◇	◇1 🛒
Cardiff Central 7	d	10 09	10 13	10 18	10 30			10 41	10 45	10 51	11 00		11 18	11 24	11 30	11 45			11 51	11 56		12 00	
Newport (South Wales)	a	10 23	10 28	10 31	10 42			10 52	10 57	11 04	11 12		11 28	11 38	11 42	11 57			12 01	12 09		12 12	
	d	10 23		10 33	10 44			10 53			11 14		11 30		11 44				12 03			12 14	
Severn Tunnel Jn	d	10a33									11 24											12 24	
Pilning	d																						
Patchway	d										11 39											12 39	
Bristol Parkway 7	a			10 54				11 18					11 53						12 23				
	d						11 16											12 16					
Filton Abbey Wood	d				11 07		11 19				11 43				12 07			12 20				12 43	
Bristol Temple Meads 10	a				11 16		11 27				11 51				12 15			12 29				12 51	
	d				11 22	11 30	11 45					12 00			12 22		12 30	12 42			12 49		13 00
Keynsham	d						11 52											12 49			12 56		
Oldfield Park	d						11 59											12 56			13 03		
Bath Spa 7	a				11 34	11 41	12 02					12 11			12 34		12 41	12 59			13 05		13 11

A The Bristolian
B The Capitals United
C Y Cymro/The Welshman
D The Red Dragon

When events are being held at the Principality Stadium, services are subject to alteration. Please check times before travelling.

Table T132-R

Cardiff - Bristol - Bath Spa

Mondays to Fridays
16 December to 15 May

		AW	GW	GW	XC	AW	GW	GW	GW	GW	GW	AW	GW	AW	GW	XC	GW	GW	GW	GW	GW	AW	GW
		◇	◇1 🍴	◇	◇1 🍴	◇ 🍴	◇1 🍴		◇1 🍴	◇	◇1 🍴	◇	◇1 🍴	◇ 🍴	◇	◇1 🍴	◇1 🍴	◇	◇1 🍴	◇	◇1 🍴	■ 🍴	◇1 🍴
Cardiff Central 7	d	12 10	12 18	12 30	12 45	12 49			12 54	13 00		13 10	13 18	13 22	13 30	13 45			13 53	14 00		14 05	14 18
Newport (South Wales)	a	12 24	12 28	12 42	12 57	13 02			13 05	13 12		13 24	13 28	13 36	13 42	13 57			14 03	14 12		14 18	14 28
	d	12 24	12 30	12 44					13 07	13 14		13 25	13 30		13 44				14 05	14 14			14 30
Severn Tunnel Jn	d	12a35								13 24		13a35								14 24			
Pilning	d																						
Patchway	d									13 39										14 39			
Bristol Parkway 7	a		12 53						13 27				13 54						14 25				14 54
	d							13 16										14 13					
Filton Abbey Wood	d			13 07				13 20		13 44					14 07			14 17		14 44			
Bristol Temple Meads 10	a			13 15				13 28		13 52					14 16			14 29		14 52			
	d			13 22			13 30	13 45			14 00				14 22		14 30	14 45			15 00		
Keynsham	d							13 52										14 52					
Oldfield Park	d							13 59										14 59					
Bath Spa 7	a			13 34			13 41	14 02			14 11				14 34		14 41	15 02			15 11		

		GW	XC	AW	GW	GW	GW	GW	SW	AW	GW	AW	GW	GW	GW	XC	AW	GW	GW	GW	GW	GW	AW
		◇	◇1 🍴	■ 🍴	◇1 🍴		◇1 🍴	◇	◇1	◇	◇1 🍴	■ 🍴	◇1 🍴		◇	◇1 🍴	■ 🍴	◇1 🍴	◇	◇1 🍴	◇	◇1 🍴	◇
Cardiff Central 7	d	14 30	14 45	14 49			14 54	15 00		15 09	15 18	15 22			15 30	15 45	15 49			15 54	16 00		16 08
Newport (South Wales)	a	14 42	14 57	15 02			15 05	15 12		15 22	15 28	15 36			15 42	15 57	16 02			16 05	16 12		16 23
	d	14 44					15 07	15 14		15 23	15 30				15 44					16 07	16 14		16 24
Severn Tunnel Jn	d							15 24		15a33											16 24		16a34
Pilning	d																						
Patchway	d							15 36													16 39		
Bristol Parkway 7	a						15 27				15 54									16 27			
	d					15 16													16 14				
Filton Abbey Wood	d	15 07				15 20		15 41						16 03	16 07				16 18		16 43		
Bristol Temple Meads 10	a	15 15				15 29		15 49							16 15				16 28		16 51		
	d	15 22			15 30	15 44			15 50				16 00		16 22			16 30	16 45			17 00	
Keynsham	d					15 51			15 57					16 16					16 52				
Oldfield Park	d					15 58			16 04					16 22					16 59				
Bath Spa 7	a	15 34			15 41	16 00			16 07				16 12	16 25	16 34			16 41	17 01			17 11	

		GW	GW	AW	GW	XC	AW	GW	GW	GW	GW	GW	AW	AW	GW	GW	GW	XC	AW	GW	GW	GW
			◇1 A 🍴	■	■	◇1 🍴	■ 🍴	◇1 🍴	◇	◇1 🍴	◇	◇1 🍴	◇	■ ⊠		◇1 🍴	■	◇1 🍴	■ 🍴	◇1 🍴		◇1 🍴
Cardiff Central 7	d		16 18	16 22	16 27	16 45	16 49			16 54	17 00		17 07	17 16		17 20	17 30	17 45	17 49			17 54
Newport (South Wales)	a		16 28	16 35	16 39	16 57	17 01			17 05	17 12		17 20	17 31		17 32	17 42	17 57	18 02			18 05
	d		16 30		16 41					17 07	17 14		17 22			17 35	17 44					18 07
Severn Tunnel Jn	d				16 51						17 24		17a32				17 54					
Pilning	d																					
Patchway	d										17 36											
Bristol Parkway 7	a		16 54							17 27						17 55						18 27
	d	16 45							17 16						17 45						18 16	
Filton Abbey Wood	d	16 51			17 06				17 20		17 41				17 49		18 11				18 20	
Bristol Temple Meads 10	a	17 05			17 14				17 27		17 49				18 01		18 19				18 29	
	d	17 09			17 22			17 30	17 45			18 00			18 05		18 24			18 30	18 43	
Keynsham	d	17 16							17 52						18 12						18 50	
Oldfield Park	d	17 23							17 59						18 19						18 57	
Bath Spa 7	a	17 25			17 34			17 41	18 02			18 11			18 22		18 36			18 42	19 00	

		GW	GW	AW	GW	AW	GW	XC	GW	SW	GW	GW	AW	GW	GW	GW	GW	AW FX	AW FO	XC	GW	GW	GW
		◇	◇1 🍴	◇	◇1 🍴	■ 🍴	◇	◇1	◇1 🍴	◇1		◇1 🍴	◇ 🍴	◇	◇1 🍴	◇1 🍴	◇	◇	◇	◇1	◇	◇	◇1 🍴
Cardiff Central 7	d	18 00		18 07	18 18	18 22	18 30	18 45				18 50	18 55	19 00		19 18	19 30	19 34	19 34	19 49		20 00	
Newport (South Wales)	a	18 12		18 20	18 28	18 35	18 42	18 57				19 02	19 08	19 12		19 29	19 42	19 48	19 49	20 01		20 12	
	d	18 14		18 21	18 30		18 44					19 05		19 14		19 30	19 44			20 02		20 14	
Severn Tunnel Jn	d	18 24		18a31			18 54							19 24						20a13		20 24	
Pilning	d																						
Patchway	d	18 37												19 37								20 37	
Bristol Parkway 7	a				18 51							19 25				19 50							
	d										19 16										20 30		
Filton Abbey Wood	d	18 42					19 11				19 20			19 42			20 07				20 34	20 41	
Bristol Temple Meads 10	a	18 50					19 19				19 29			19 51			20 15				20 42	20 53	
	d		19 00				19 23		19 30	19 35	19 41				20 00		20 24				20 46		21 00
Keynsham	d									19 42	19 50										20 53		
Oldfield Park	d										19 57										21 00		
Bath Spa 7	a		19 11				19 35		19 41	19 49	20 00				20 11		20 36				21 02		21 11

A The Saint David

When events are being held at the Principality Stadium, services are subject to alteration. Please check times before travelling.

NRT DECEMBER 19 EDITION

Table T132-R

Cardiff - Bristol - Bath Spa

Mondays to Fridays
16 December to 15 May

		AW	GW	GW	GW	GW	XC	AW	AW	GW	GW	SW	XC	AW	GW	GW	GW FO	GW FX	GW FO	GW FX	GW FO	GW FX	GW
		◇	◇1 🍴	◇	◇	◇1 🍴	◇1	◇	◇	◇1 🍴	◇	◇1	◇1	◇	◇1 🍴		◇	◇	◇1 🍴	◇1 🍴	◇	◇	
Cardiff Central 7	d	20 14	20 21	20 30	21 00		21 05	21 09	21 15	21 20	21 30		21 45	21 55			22 00	22 00	22 19	22 18	22 30	22 30	
Newport (South Wales)	a	20 27	20 31	20 42	21 12		21 17	21 24	21 28	21 31	21 42		21 57	22 10			22 14	22 14	22 29	22 34	22 42	22 46	
	d		20 33	20 44	21 14			21 24		21 32	21 44						22 16	22 16	22 31	22 35	22 44	22 48	
Severn Tunnel Jn	d				21 24			21a35			21 54						22 29	22 33			22 54	23 05	
Pilning	d																						
Patchway	d				21 37												22 42	22 46			23 09	23 18	
Bristol Parkway 7	a		20 53							21 52									22 52	23 04			
	d																						
Filton Abbey Wood	d			21 07	21 41						22 12						22 46	22 50			23 13	23 22	
Bristol Temple Meads 10	a			21 15	21 50						22 23						23 01	23 01			23 23	23 35	
	d			21 23		22 00						22 25			22 40	22 53							23 45
Keynsham	d											22 32				23 00							23 52
Oldfield Park	d															23 07							23 59
Bath Spa 7	a			21 36		22 11						22 39			22 51	23 10							00 01

		AW FO	AW FX	GW FO	GW FX
		◇	◇	◇	◇
Cardiff Central 7	d	23 20	23 20	23 30	23 30
Newport (South Wales)	a	23 35	23 40	23 42	23 46
	d	23 35	23 40	23 44	23 48
Severn Tunnel Jn	d	23a49	23a58	23 54	00 05
Pilning	d				
Patchway	d			00 07	00 21
Bristol Parkway 7	a				
	d				
Filton Abbey Wood	d			00 11	00 25
Bristol Temple Meads 10	a			00 25	00 39
	d				
Keynsham	d				
Oldfield Park	d				
Bath Spa 7	a				

Saturdays
21 December to 16 May

		GW	AW	AW	GW	AW	GW	AW	GW	GW	GW	AW	GW	GW	GW	GW	GW	XC	GW	AW	GW	GW	XC
		◇	◇	◇	◇1 🍴	◇	◇1 🍴	◇	◇	◇1 🍴	◇1 🍴	◇	◇1 🍴		◇1 🍴	◇1 🍴	◇	◇1	◇1 🍴	◇ 🍴	◇1 🍴		◇1
Cardiff Central 7	d		00 30	04 35	05 14	05 21		05 37		05 44		06 10			06 20		06 29	06 38	06 48	06 52			07 00
Newport (South Wales)	a		00 45	04 51	05 24	05 34		05 51		05 54		06 25			06 30		06 41	06 52	06 58	07 05			07 12
	d				05 26					05 56		06 26			06 32		06 44	06 53	07 00				07 14
Severn Tunnel Jn	d											06a37					06 54	07a03					07 25
Pilning	d																						
Patchway	d	00 07																					07 36
Bristol Parkway 7	a				05 53					06 16					06 52				07 20				
	d													06 19									
Filton Abbey Wood	d	00 11												06 23			07 09						07 40
Bristol Temple Meads 10	a	00 25												06 31			07 17						07 52
	d						05 30		05 40		06 00		06 30	06 40		06 57	07 21				07 30	07 40	
Keynsham	d								05 47					06 47								07 47	
Oldfield Park	d								05 54					06 54								07 54	
Bath Spa 7	a						05 41		05 56		06 11		06 41	06 56		07 08	07 33				07 41	07 56	

		GW	AW	GW	AW	GW	GW	GW	GW	XC	AW	SW	GW	GW	GW	GW	GW	XC	AW	GW	GW	GW	GW
		◇1 🍴	◇	◇1 🍴	◇ 🍴	◇	◇1 🍴	◇	◇1 🍴	◇1	■ 🍴	◇1	◇	◇1 🍴	◇1 🍴	◇	◇1 🍴	◇1	■ 🍴	◇1 🍴	◇	◇	◇1 🍴
Cardiff Central 7	d		07 06	07 18	07 22	07 27			07 41	07 45	07 52		08 00		08 20	08 27	08 41	08 45	08 52			09 00	
Newport (South Wales)	a		07 21	07 28	07 36	07 39			07 55	07 59	08 05		08 12		08 30	08 39	08 53	08 57	09 05			09 12	
	d		07 22	07 32		07 41			07 56				08 14		08 32	08 41	08 55					09 14	
Severn Tunnel Jn	d		07a32			07 51							08 24			08 51						09 24	
Pilning	d												08 33										
Patchway	d												08 40									09 36	
Bristol Parkway 7	a			07 54					08 20						08 54		09 15						
	d							08 15													09 18		
Filton Abbey Wood	d					08 06		08 19					08 45			09 06					09 21	09 41	
Bristol Temple Meads 10	a					08 14		08 28					08 53			09 15					09 30	09 50	
	d	07 57				08 22	08 30	08 40				08 50		09 01		09 22				09 30	09 40		09 57
Keynsham	d							08 47				08 57									09 47		
Oldfield Park	d							08 54				09 04									09 54		
Bath Spa 7	a	08 08				08 34	08 42	08 56				09 06		09 12		09 34				09 41	09 56		10 08

When events are being held at the Principality Stadium, services are subject to alteration. Please check times before travelling.

Table T132-R

Saturdays

Cardiff - Bristol - Bath Spa

21 December to 16 May

		AW	GW	AW	GW	XC	GW	GW	GW	AW	GW	GW	AW	GW	AW	GW	GW	XC	AW	GW	GW	GW	GW
		◇	◇1 🛒	◇ 🛒	◇ A 🛒	◇1 🛒	◇1 🛒		◇1 🛒	◇ 🛒	◇	◇1 🛒	◇	◇1 🛒	◇	◇ A 🛒	◇1 🛒	◇1	◇ 🛒	◇1 🛒	◇	◇	◇1 🛒
Cardiff Central 7	d	09 04	09 19	09 23	09 28	09 45			09 50	09 55	10 00		10 07	10 19	10 23	10 30	10 41	10 45	10 55			11 00	
Newport (South Wales)	a	09 19	09 29	09 37	09 40	09 57			10 01	10 08	10 11		10 21	10 29	10 38	10 42	10 53	10 58	11 08			11 12	
	d	09 20	09 32		09 42				10 03		10 13		10 22	10 32		10 44	10 54					11 14	
Severn Tunnel Jn	d	09a30			09 52						10 23		10a32									11 24	
Pilning	d																						
Patchway	d										10 35											11 36	
Bristol Parkway 7	a		09 54						10 23					10 55			11 14						
	d							10 17													11 18		
Filton Abbey Wood	d				10 07			10 21			10 40					11 07					11 21	11 41	
Bristol Temple Meads 10	a				10 15			10 32			10 51					11 15					11 32	11 50	
	d				10 22		10 30	10 43				10 57				11 22				11 30	11 40		11 57
Keynsham	d							10 50													11 47		
Oldfield Park	d							10 57													11 54		
Bath Spa 7	a				10 34		10 41	10 59				11 08				11 34				11 41	11 56		12 08

		AW	GW	GW	GW	XC	AW	GW	GW	SW	GW	GW	AW	GW	GW	XC	GW	GW	GW	AW	GW	GW
		■ 🛒	◇1 🛒	◇ A 🛒	◇1 🛒	◇1 🛒	■ 🛒	◇1 🛒	◇	◇1 🛒	◇	◇1 🛒	◇	◇1 🛒	◇ A 🛒	◇1 🛒	◇1 🛒		◇1 🛒	■ 🛒	◇	◇1 🛒
Cardiff Central 7	d	11 12	11 19	11 30	11 41	11 45	11 55				12 00		12 07	12 20	12 27	12 45			12 49	12 55	13 00	
Newport (South Wales)	a	11 26	11 29	11 42	11 53	11 57	12 08				12 12		12 20	12 30	12 39	12 57			13 01	13 08	13 12	
	d		11 32	11 44	11 54						12 14		12 21	12 32	12 41				13 04		13 14	
Severn Tunnel Jn	d										12 24		12a31								13 24	
Pilning	d																					
Patchway	d										12 36										13 36	
Bristol Parkway 7	a		11 54		12 15									12 54					13 25			
	d								12 22									13 18				
Filton Abbey Wood	d			12 07					12 25		12 41				13 04			13 21			13 44	
Bristol Temple Meads 10	a			12 16					12 33		12 50				13 12			13 30			13 52	
	d			12 22				12 30	12 40	12 48		12 57			13 22		13 30	13 45				13 57
Keynsham	d								12 47	12 55								13 52				
Oldfield Park	d								12 54	13 02								13 59				
Bath Spa 7	a			12 34				12 41	12 56	13 04		13 10			13 34		13 41	14 01				14 08

		AW	GW	AW	GW	XC	GW	GW	GW	AW	GW	GW	AW	GW	GW	GW	XC	AW	GW	GW	SW	GW	GW
		◇	◇1 🛒	◇ 🛒	◇	◇1 🛒	◇1 🛒	◇	◇1 🛒	■ 🛒	◇	◇1 🛒	◇ 🛒	◇1 🛒	◇	◇1 🛒	◇1 🛒	◇ 🛒	◇1 🛒		◇1	◇	◇1 🛒
Cardiff Central 7	d	13 12	13 18	13 21	13 30	13 45			13 50	13 55	14 00		14 13	14 21	14 30	14 41	14 45	14 55				15 00	
Newport (South Wales)	a	13 27	13 30	13 35	13 42	13 58			14 01	14 08	14 12		14 28	14 31	14 42	14 53	14 57	15 08				15 11	
	d	13 27	13 32		13 44				14 03		14 14			14 33	14 44	14 54						15 13	
Severn Tunnel Jn	d	13a38									14 24											15 23	
Pilning	d										14 33												
Patchway	d										14 39											15 35	
Bristol Parkway 7	a		13 54						14 24					14 54		15 15							
	d							14 18												15 18			
Filton Abbey Wood	d				14 07			14 21			14 44				15 07					15 21		15 40	
Bristol Temple Meads 10	a				14 15			14 31			14 52				15 15					15 32		15 51	
	d				14 22		14 30	14 40				14 57			15 22				15 30	15 40	15 50		15 58
Keynsham	d							14 47												15 47	15 57		
Oldfield Park	d							14 54												15 53	16 04		
Bath Spa 7	a				14 34		14 41	14 56				15 08			15 34				15 41	15 56	16 06		16 12

		AW	GW	AW	GW	GW	XC	AW	GW	GW	GW	GW	AW	AW	GW	GW	XC	GW	GW	GW	AW	GW	GW
		◇	◇1 🛒	■ 🛒	◇	◇1 🛒	◇1 🛒	■ 🛒	◇1 🛒	◇	◇	◇1 🛒	◇	◇	◇1 🛒	◇	◇1 🛒	◇1 🛒	◇	◇1 🛒	■ 🛒	◇	◇1 🛒
Cardiff Central 7	d	15 07	15 19	15 23	15 30	15 41	15 45	15 55			16 00		16 06	16 15	16 22	16 27	16 45			16 51	16 55	17 00	
Newport (South Wales)	a	15 19	15 29	15 37	15 42	15 53	15 58	16 08			16 12		16 20	16 30	16 33	16 39	16 57			17 02	17 08	17 12	
	d	15 22	15 31		15 44	15 54					16 14		16 21		16 35	16 41				17 03		17 14	
Severn Tunnel Jn	d	15a32									16 24		16a31			16 51						17 24	
Pilning	d																						
Patchway	d										16 36											17 36	
Bristol Parkway 7	a		15 54			16 15									16 55					17 24			
	d									16 18									17 18				
Filton Abbey Wood	d				16 10					16 21	16 41					17 06			17 21			17 41	
Bristol Temple Meads 10	a				16 18					16 30	16 50					17 14			17 32			17 51	
	d				16 22				16 30	16 45		16 57				17 22		17 30	17 43				17 57
Keynsham	d									16 52									17 50				
Oldfield Park	d									16 59									17 57				
Bath Spa 7	a				16 34				16 41	17 01		17 08				17 34		17 41	17 59				18 08

A 🛒 from Bristol Temple Meads

When events are being held at the Principality Stadium, services are subject to alteration. Please check times before travelling.

Table T132-R

Saturdays

Cardiff - Bristol - Bath Spa

21 December to 16 May

		AW	GW	AW	GW	XC	GW	AW	GW	GW	GW	GW	AW	GW	GW	SW	XC	AW	GW	GW	GW	GW	GW
		◇	◇1 🛒	■ 🛒	◇	◇1 🛒	◇1 🛒	■ 🛒	◇1 🛒		◇	◇1 🛒	◇	◇1 🛒	◇	◇1	◇1	◇ 🛒		◇	◇1 🛒	◇1 🛒	◇
Cardiff Central 7	d	17 07	17 19	17 23	17 27	17 45	17 51	17 55			18 00		18 06	18 22	18 27		18 45	18 50		19 00		19 19	19 30
Newport (South Wales)	a	17 21	17 29	17 36	17 39	17 57	18 02	18 09			18 12		18 21	18 32	18 39		18 57	19 04		19 12		19 29	19 42
	d	17 21	17 31		17 41		18 03				18 14		18 21	18 34	18 41					19 14		19 32	19 44
Severn Tunnel Jn	d	17a31			17 51						18 24		18a32		18 51					19 24			
Pilning	d																						
Patchway	d										18 36									19 36			
Bristol Parkway 7	a		17 54				18 23							18 54								19 54	
	d									18 26									19 18				
Filton Abbey Wood	d				18 06					18 29	18 41				19 06				19 22	19 41			20 07
Bristol Temple Meads 10	a				18 14					18 38	18 50				19 14				19 35	19 50			20 15
	d				18 22				18 30	18 45		19 00			19 22	19 35			19 42		19 57		20 22
Keynsham	d									18 52						19 42			19 49				
Oldfield Park	d									18 59						19 49			19 56				
Bath Spa 7	a				18 34				18 41	19 01		19 11			19 34	19 51			19 58		20 08		20 34

		AW	GW	GW	GW	XC	AW	GW	GW	XC	AW	GW	GW	GW	AW	AW	GW	SW	GW	GW	GW	GW
		◇	◇	◇1 A	◇1 🛒	◇1	◇	◇1 🛒	◇	◇1	◇	◇1 🛒	◇	◇1 🛒	◇	◇		◇1	◇1 🛒	◇		◇
Cardiff Central 7	d	19 34		19 54		20 00	20 12	20 23	20 30	20 48	20 55		21 00		21 11	21 54				22 00		22 47
Newport (South Wales)	a	19 47		20 05		20 12	20 27	20 33	20 42	21 00	21 08		21 12		21 26	22 11				22 15		23 02
	d			20 07		20 13		20 35	20 44				21 14		21 27					22 15		23 02
Severn Tunnel Jn	d			20 18		20a24							21 24		21a37					22 35		
Pilning	d																					
Patchway	d			20 29									21 37							22 47		
Bristol Parkway 7	a							20 55														
	d		20 10																			
Filton Abbey Wood	d		20 15	20 34					21 07				21 41							22 51		
Bristol Temple Meads 10	a		20 27	20 47					21 16				21 49							23 02		23 42
	d		20 44		20 57				21 22			21 30		21 57			22 03	22 23	22 40		23 12	
Keynsham	d		20 51														22 10	22 30			23 19	
Oldfield Park	d		20 58														22 17				23 26	
Bath Spa 7	a		21 00		21 08				21 34			21 41		22 08			22 19	22 37	22 52		23 28	

		AW
		◇
Cardiff Central 7	d	23 18
Newport (South Wales)	a	23 35
	d	23 37
Severn Tunnel Jn	d	23a56
Pilning	d	
Patchway	d	
Bristol Parkway 7	a	
	d	
Filton Abbey Wood	d	
Bristol Temple Meads 10	a	
	d	
Keynsham	d	
Oldfield Park	d	
Bath Spa 7	a	

Sundays

15 December to 10 May

		GW	GW	GW	GW	GW	GW	AW	AW	GW	GW	GW	GW	GW	GW	AW	GW	GW	GW	GW	GW	AW	XC
		◇1 🛒	◇1 🛒	◇	◇1 🛒	◇1 🛒	◇	◇	◇	◇1 🛒	◇1 🛒	◇	◇1 🛒	◇ B	◇ C	■	◇1 🛒	◇1 🛒	◇1 🛒	◇	◇1 🛒	◇	◇1
Cardiff Central 7	d		07 50				08 10	08 23	08 30	08 50				09 13	09 20	09 28	09 35			10 13	10 20	10 30	10 45
Newport (South Wales)	a		08 05				08 27	08 40	08 49	09 05				09 29	09 36	09 47	09 51			10 25	10 29	10 45	10 57
	d		08 07				08 28	08 41		09 07				09 31	09 38		09 54			10 27	10 32	10 45	
Severn Tunnel Jn	d						08 46	08a59						09 48	09 48					10 37		10a58	
Pilning	d																						
Patchway	d																						
Bristol Parkway 7	a		08 32							09 32							10 19				10 54		
	d																						
Filton Abbey Wood	d						09 00							10 00	10 00					10 50			
Bristol Temple Meads 10	a						09 10													11 00			
	d	07 45		08 19	08 30	09 00	09 20				09 30	09 34	10 00					10 30	11 00	11 10			
Keynsham	d			08 26								09 41								11 16			
Oldfield Park	d			08 33								09 48								11 23			
Bath Spa 7	a	07 56		08 36	08 41	09 11	09 31				09 41	09 50	10 11	10 31	10 31			10 41	11 11	11 26			

A 1 from Patchway

B until 29 March

C from 5 April

When events are being held at the Principality Stadium, services are subject to alteration. Please check times before travelling.

Table T132-R

Sundays

15 December to 10 May

Cardiff - Bristol - Bath Spa

		GW		GW	GW	GW	GW	AW	XC	GW	GW	GW		SW	GW	GW	AW	AW	XC	GW	GW	GW		GW	GW
		◇1 🛒		◇1 🛒	◇1 🛒	■ ◇ A	◇1 🛒	◇ 🛒	◇1	◇1 🛒	◇1 🛒	◇1 🛒		◇1	◇	◇1 🛒	◇	◇ 🛒	◇1 🛒	◇1 🛒	◇1 🛒	◇1 🛒		◇	◇1 🛒
Cardiff Central 7	d	10 50				11 13	11 20	11 34	11 45	11 50					12 13	12 20	12 24	12 36	12 45	12 50				13 13	13 20
Newport (South Wales)	a	11 01				11 25	11 29	11 50	11 57	12 01					12 25	12 30	12 39	12 49	12 57	13 01				13 24	13 29
	d	11 03				11 27	11 32			12 03					12 26	12 32	12 39			13 04				13 26	13 32
Severn Tunnel Jn	d					11 37									12 36		12a52							13 37	
Pilning	d																								
Patchway	d														12 48										
Bristol Parkway 7	a	11 22					11 54			12 22						12 54				13 23					13 54
	d																								
Filton Abbey Wood	d					11 50									12 53									13 50	
Bristol Temple Meads 10	a					12 05									13 02									13 59	
	d			11 30	12 00	12 10					12 30	13 00		13 04	13 10						13 30	14 00		14 09	
Keynsham	d					12 17								13 11	13 17									14 17	
Oldfield Park	d					12 24								13 18	13 24									14 24	
Bath Spa 7	a			11 41	12 11	12 25					12 41	13 11		13 20	13 27						13 41	14 11		14 26	

		AW	GW	XC	AW	GW	GW	GW		GW	AW	XC	GW	AW	GW	GW	SW	GW		AW	GW	XC	GW	AW	GW
		■ 🛒	◇1 🛒	◇1 🛒	■ 🛒	◇1 🛒	◇1 🛒	◇		◇1 🛒	◇	◇1 🛒	◇1 🛒	■ 🛒	◇1 🛒	◇1 🛒	◇1	◇		■ 🛒	◇1 🛒	◇1 🛒	◇1 🛒	■ 🛒	◇1 🛒
Cardiff Central 7	d	13 25	13 41	13 45	13 51			14 13		14 20	14 25	14 45	14 50	14 54				15 13		15 17	15 20	15 45	15 50	15 56	
Newport (South Wales)	a	13 38	13 53	13 59	14 04			14 23		14 29	14 40	14 57	15 01	15 08				15 25		15 31	15 34	15 57	16 00	16 12	
	d		13 55					14 25		14 33	14 40		15 03					15 27			15 35		16 03		
Severn Tunnel Jn	d							14 33			14a52							15 37							
Pilning	d																								
Patchway	d																	15 49							
Bristol Parkway 7	a		14 18							14 54			15 23								15 54		16 22		
	d																								
Filton Abbey Wood	d							14 50										15 52							
Bristol Temple Meads 10	a							14 59										16 04							
	d					14 30	15 00	15 10							15 30	16 00	16 04	16 10							16 30
Keynsham	d							15 17									16 11	16 17							
Oldfield Park	d							15 23									16 18	16 24							
Bath Spa 7	a					14 41	15 11	15 27							15 41	16 11	16 20	16 25							16 41

		GW	GW	GW		AW	GW	GW	GW	AW	XC	GW	GW	GW		GW	GW	GW	XC	GW	AW	GW	GW	GW	
		◇1 🛒	◇	◇1		◇	◇1 🛒	◇	◇	■ 🛒	◇1 🛒	◇1 🛒	◇1 🛒	◇		◇1 🛒	◇1 🛒	◇	◇1 🛒	◇1 🛒	■ 🛒	◇1 🛒	◇	◇1 🛒	
Cardiff Central 7	d		16 13	16 20		16 25		16 36		16 40	16 45	16 50		17 13		17 20		17 40	17 45	17 50	17 54		18 12	18 20	
Newport (South Wales)	a		16 25	16 30		16 40		16 49		16 54	16 57	17 01		17 25		17 29		17 52	17 57	18 01	18 07		18 25	18 29	
	d		16 27	16 32		16 40		16 51				17 04		17 27		17 32		17 54		18 03			18 26	18 33	
Severn Tunnel Jn	d		16 37			16a52								17 37									18 37		
Pilning	d																								
Patchway	d																	18 15							
Bristol Parkway 7	a			16 54								17 23				17 54				18 24				18 54	
	d																								
Filton Abbey Wood	d		16 50					17 14						17 50				18 18					18 50		
Bristol Temple Meads 10	a		17 02					17 23						18 03				18 28					19 01		
	d	17 00	17 10				17 30	17 40	17 45				18 00	18 15			18 30	18 40				19 00	19 15		
Keynsham	d		17 17						17 52									18 47							
Oldfield Park	d		17 24						17 59									18 54							
Bath Spa 7	a	17 11	17 26				17 41	17 52	18 02				18 12	18 26			18 41	18 56				19 11	19 26		

		AW	AW	XC	GW	GW	GW	GW	AW	XC		GW	AW	GW	GW	GW	XC	AW	GW	GW		SW	GW	GW	GW
		◇	■ 🛒	◇1 🛒	◇1 🛒	◇1	◇	◇1 🛒	◇	◇1		◇1 🛒	◇	◇1 🛒		◇	◇1	◇	◇1 🛒	◇1 🛒		◇1	◇1 🛒	◇	
Cardiff Central 7	d	18 24	18 40	18 45			19 13	19 20	19 40	19 45		20 20	20 24			20 30	20 45	21 10	21 20					21 25	
Newport (South Wales)	a	18 39	18 53	18 57			19 25	19 29	19 55	19 58		20 29	20 39			20 42	20 58	21 23	21 30					21 37	
	d	18 39					19 27	19 33				20 32	20 39			20 44			21 32					21 39	
Severn Tunnel Jn	d	18a52					19 37						20a49			20 54								21 49	
Pilning	d																								
Patchway	d																							22 00	
Bristol Parkway 7	a							19 54				20 51							21 53						
	d																								
Filton Abbey Wood	d						19 51									21 09								22 04	
Bristol Temple Meads 10	a						20 06									21 18								22 21	
	d				19 30	20 01	20 15							20 30	20 48	21 25				21 30		21 35	22 20		22 25
Keynsham	d						20 22								20 55							21 42			22 32
Oldfield Park	d						20 29								21 02										22 39
Bath Spa 7	a				19 41	20 13	20 31							20 41	21 05	21 37				21 41		21 49	22 32		22 42

A ◇ from Bristol Temple Meads ■ to Bristol Temple Meads

When events are being held at the Principality Stadium, services are subject to alteration. Please check times before travelling.

Table T132-R

Sundays

15 December to 10 May

Cardiff - Bristol - Bath Spa

		GW		AW	GW	AW
		◇		◇	◇	◇
Cardiff Central 7	d	22 15		22 26	23 15	23 20
Newport (South Wales)	a	22 26		22 41	23 27	23 37
	d	22 28		22 41	23 29	
Severn Tunnel Jn	d	22 35		22a56		
Pilning	d					
Patchway	d	22 52				
Bristol Parkway 7	a					
	d					
Filton Abbey Wood	d	22 54				
Bristol Temple Meads 10	a	23 08			23 59	
	d	23 15				
Keynsham	d					
Oldfield Park	d					
Bath Spa 7	a	23 29				

When events are being held at the Principality Stadium, services are subject to alteration. Please check times before travelling.

Table T133-F

Mondays to Fridays
16 December to 15 May

Bristol - Avonmouth and Severn Beach

Miles			GW	GW	GW	GW	GW ◇	GW	GW	GW ◇	GW	GW	GW ◇	GW	GW	GW	GW	GW	GW	GW	GW	GW	GW
0	Bristol Temple Meads 10	d	05 12	05 37	05 46	06 18	06 27	06 53	07 01	07 27	07 45	07 57	08 17	08 32	08 45	09 11	09 45	10 00	10 36	10 45	11 11	11 45	12 02
1	Lawrence Hill	d	05 15	05 40	05 49	06 22	06 30	06 56	07 04	07 30	07 48	08 00	08 20	08 35	08 48	09 14	09 48	10 03		10 49	11 14	11 49	12 05
1½	Stapleton Road	d	05 17	05 42	05a51	06 24	06a32	06a58	07 06	07a32	07a50	08 02	08a22	08 37	08a50	09 16	09a50	10 05	10 39	10a51	11 16	11a51	12 07
2¾	Montpelier	d	05 20	05 45		06 30			07 09			08 05		08 40		09 19		10 08	10 43		11 19		12 10
3¼	Redland	d	05 22	05 47		06 32			07 11			08 07		08 42		09 21		10 10	10 45		11 21		12 12
4	Clifton Down	d	05 25	05 50		06 35			07 14			08 11		08 45		09 24		10 15	10 48		11 24		12 16
6	Sea Mills	d	05 29	05 54		06 39			07 18			08 15		08 49		09 28		10 19	10 52		11 28		12 20
7¼	Shirehampton	d	05 33	05 58		06 42			07 22			08 19		08 53		09 32		10 23	10 56		11 32		12 24
9	Avonmouth 2	d	05 37	06a01		06 46			07 26			08a22		08a56		09 36		10a26	10a59		11 37		12a27
10	St Andrews Road	d	05 40			06 50			07 30														
13½	Severn Beach	a	05 47			06 57			07 37							09 45					11 46		

		GW	GW	GW	GW	GW	GW	GW	GW	GW	GW	GW	GW	GW	GW	GW	GW	GW	GW ◇	GW	GW	GW ◇	GW
Bristol Temple Meads 10	d	12 36	12 45	13 11	13 45	14 00	14 35	14 45	15 11	15 45	16 00	16 04	16 36	16 45	17 06	17 12	17 45	18 03	18 24	18 45	18 50	19 23	19 28
Lawrence Hill	d		12 49	13 14	13 49	14 03		14 49	15 14	15 49	16 03	16 08	16 39	16 49	17 09	17 15	17 49	18 06	18 27	18 49	18 53	19 26	19 31
Stapleton Road	d	12 39	12a51	13 16	13a51	14 05	14 38	14a51	15 16	15a51	16 05	16a10	16 41	16a51	17a11	17 17	17a51	18 08	18a29	18a51	18 56	19a28	19 34
Montpelier	d	12 43		13 19		14 08	14 42		15 20		16 08		16 44			17 20		18 11			18 59		19 37
Redland	d	12 45		13 21		14 10	14 44		15 22		16 10		16 46			17 22		18 13			19 01		19 39
Clifton Down	d	12 48		13 24		14 15	14 48		15 25		16 16		16 49			17 25		18 17			19 08		19 42
Sea Mills	d	12 52		13 28		14 19	14 52		15 29		16 20		16 53			17 29		18 21			19 12		19 46
Shirehampton	d	12 56		13 32		14 23	14 56		15 32		16 24		16 57			17 33		18 24			19 16		19 50
Avonmouth 2	d	12a59		13 36		14a26	14a59		15 37		16a27		17a00			17 37		18 29			19a19		19a53
St Andrews Road	d			13 40					15 41							17 41		18 32					
Severn Beach	a			13 47					15 48							17 48		18 39					

		GW	GW	GW	GW	GW	GW
Bristol Temple Meads 10	d	19 38	20 28	20 45	21 37	21 45	22 19
Lawrence Hill	d	19 41	20 31	20 49	21 40	21 48	22 22
Stapleton Road	d	19a43	20 33	20a51	21a42	21 51	22 24
Montpelier	d		20 36			21 54	22 27
Redland	d		20 38			21 56	22 29
Clifton Down	d		20 41			21 59	22 33
Sea Mills	d		20 45			22 03	22 37
Shirehampton	d		20 49			22 07	22 41
Avonmouth 2	d		20 53			22a10	22 45
St Andrews Road	d		20 57				22 48
Severn Beach	a		21 04				22 55

Saturdays
21 December to 16 May

		GW	GW	GW ◇	GW	GW	GW	GW	GW	GW	GW	GW	GW	GW	GW	GW	GW	GW	GW	GW	GW	GW	GW
Bristol Temple Meads 10	d	06 03	06 37	06 57	07 12	07 43	08 02	08 38	08 45	09 12	09 45	10 02	10 38	10 45	11 12	11 45	12 02	12 38	12 45	13 12	13 47	14 02	14 38
Lawrence Hill	d	06 06	06 40	07 00	07 15	07 46	08 05	08 41	08 48	09 15	09 48	10 05	10 41	10 48	11 15	11 48	12 05	12 41	12 48	13 15	13 50	14 05	14 41
Stapleton Road	d	06 08	06 42	07a02	07 17	07a48	08 07	08 43	08a50	09 17	09a50	10 07	10 43	10a50	11 17	11a50	12 07	12 43	12a50	13 17	13a52	14 07	14 43
Montpelier	d	06 12	06 45		07 20		08 10	08 46		09 20		10 10	10 46		11 20		12 10	12 46		13 20		14 10	14 46
Redland	d	06 14	06 47		07 22		08 12	08 48		09 22		10 12	10 48		11 22		12 12	12 48		13 22		14 12	14 48
Clifton Down	d	06 17	06 50		07 25		08 18	08 51		09 25		10 16	10 51		11 25		12 16	12 51		13 25		14 16	14 51
Sea Mills	d	06 21	06 54		07 29		08 22	08 55		09 29		10 20	10 55		11 29		12 20	12 55		13 29		14 20	14 55
Shirehampton	d	06 24	06 58		07 33		08 25	08 59		09 33		10 23	10 59		11 33		12 23	12 59		13 33		14 23	14 59
Avonmouth 2	d	06a29	07a02		07 37		08a30	09a03		09 37		10a28	11a03		11 37		12a28	13a03		13 37		14a28	15a03
St Andrews Road	d				07 40					09 40					11 40					13 40			
Severn Beach	a				07 48					09 48					11 48					13 48			

		GW	GW	GW	GW	GW	GW	GW	GW	GW	GW	GW	GW ◇	GW	GW	GW	GW
Bristol Temple Meads 10	d	14 47	15 12	15 46	16 02	16 38	16 45	17 12	17 45	18 02	18 45	19 02	19 25	19 45	20 33	21 32	22 16
Lawrence Hill	d	14 50	15 15	15 50	16 05	16 41	16 49	17 15	17 49	18 05	18 48	19 05	19 29	19 48	20 36	21 35	22 19
Stapleton Road	d	14a52	15 17	15a52	16 07	16 43	16a51	17 17	17a51	18 07	18a50	19 07	19a31	19a50	20 38	21 37	22 21
Montpelier	d		15 20		16 10	16 46		17 20		18 10		19 10			20 41	21 40	22 24
Redland	d		15 22		16 12	16 48		17 22		18 12		19 12			20 43	21 42	22 26
Clifton Down	d		15 25		16 16	16 51		17 25		18 16		19 16			20 46	21 46	22 29
Sea Mills	d		15 29		16 20	16 55		17 29		18 20		19 20			20 50	21 50	22 33
Shirehampton	d		15 33		16 23	16 59		17 33		18 23		19 23			20 54	21 53	22 37
Avonmouth 2	d		15 37		16a28	17a03		17 37		18 27		19 27			20 58	21a58	22 41
St Andrews Road	d		15 40					17 40		18 31		19 31			21 01		22 44
Severn Beach	a		15 48					17 48		18 38		19 38			21 09		22 52

Sundays
15 December to 10 May

		GW	GW	GW	GW	GW		GW	GW	GW	GW	GW	GW
Bristol Temple Meads 10	d	09 01	09 47	10 58	12 22	13 23	and hourly until	16 23	17 23	17 57	18 55	19 53	20 53
Lawrence Hill	d	09 04	09 50	11 01	12 26	13 26		16 26	17 26	18 00	18 55	19 56	20 56
Stapleton Road	d	09 06	09 52	11 03	12 28	13 28		16 28	17 28	18 02	18 57	19 58	20 58
Montpelier	d	09 09	09 56	11 06	12 31	13 31		16 31	17 32	18 05	19 00	20 01	21 01
Redland	d	09 11	09 58	11 08	12 33	13 33		16 33	17 34	18 07	19 02	20 03	21 03
Clifton Down	d	09 14	10 01	11 12	12 36	13 36		16 36	17 36	18 10	19 08	20 06	21 07
Sea Mills	d	09 18	10 05	11 15	12 40	13 40		16 40	17 40	18 14	19 11	20 10	21 11
Shirehampton	d	09 22	10 09	11 19	12 44	13 44		16 44	17 44	18 18	19 16	20 14	21 14
Avonmouth 2	d	09 26	10 13	11 23	12 48	13 48		16 48	17 53	18 23	19 20	20a17	21a18
St Andrews Road	d	09 29	10 16	11 26	12 51	13 51		16 51	17 57	18 27	19 22		
Severn Beach	a	09 36	10 23	11 33	12 58	13 58		16 58	18 04	18 34	19 30		

Table T133-R

Mondays to Fridays
16 December to 15 May

Severn Beach and Avonmouth - Bristol

Miles			GW MX ◇	GW	GW	GW	GW	GW	GW	GW	GW	GW	GW	GW	GW	GW	GW	GW	GW	GW	GW	GW	GW
0	Severn Beach	d			05 53			07 14	07 47					09 51					11 52				
3½	St Andrews Road	d			05 59			07 20	07 53					09 57					11 58				
4½	Avonmouth 2	d			06 03	06 21		07 25	07 57	08 32		09 11		10 01	10 35		11 11		12 02	12 35		13 11	
6	Shirehampton	d			06 07	06 24		07 28	08 01	08 35		09 14		10 05	10 38		11 14		12 06	12 38		13 14	
7½	Sea Mills	d			06 11	06 28		07 32	08 05	08 39		09 18		10 09	10 42		11 18		12 10	12 42		13 18	
9½	Clifton Down	d			06 16	06 34		07 37	08 10	08 46		09 24		10 14	10 47		11 24		12 15	12 47		13 24	
10¼	Redland	d			06 18	06 36		07 40	08 12	08 48		09 26		10 17	10 50		11 26		12 17	12 50		13 26	
10¾	Montpelier	d			06 20	06 38		07 42	08 14	08 50		09 28		10 19	10 52		11 28		12 19	12 52		13 28	
12	Stapleton Road	d	00 31	06 22	06 27	06 44	07 11	07 47	08 20	08 56	09 19	09 35	10 20	10 25	10 57	11 20	11 34	12 18	12 25	12 57	13 19	13 34	14 19
12½	Lawrence Hill	d	00 34	06 24	06 30	06 47	07 14	07 49	08 22	08 58	09 21	09 37	10 22	10 27	10 59	11 22	11 36	12 20	12 28	12 59	13 21	13 36	14 21
13½	Bristol Temple Meads 10	a	00 39	06 30	06 33	06 50	07 17	07 53	08 25	09 01	09 25	09 41	10 26	10 32	11 03	11 26	11 39	12 25	12 32	13 03	13 25	13 39	14 25

		GW	GW	GW	GW	GW	GW	GW	GW	GW	GW	GW	GW	GW	GW	GW	GW	GW	GW ◇	GW ◇	GW	GW
Severn Beach	d	13 52					15 53							17 53	18 44						21 35	
St Andrews Road	d													17 59	18 50						21 41	
Avonmouth 2	d	14 01	14 35		15 11		16 02		16 36		17 12			18 03	18 54		19 28	20 07			21 45	
Shirehampton	d	14 05	14 38		15 14		16 06		16 39		17 15			18 07	18 58		19 31	20 10			21 49	
Sea Mills	d	14 09	14 42		15 18		16 10		16 43		17 19			18 11	19 02		19 35	20 14			21 53	
Clifton Down	d	14 14	14 48		15 24		16 15		16 50		17 25			18 16	19 07		19 42	20 20			21 59	
Redland	d	14 16	14 50		15 26		16 17		16 53		17 27			18 18	19 09		19 44	20 22			22 01	
Montpelier	d	14 18	14 52		15 28		16 19		16 55		17 29			18 20	19 11		19 46	20 24			22 03	
Stapleton Road	d	14 24	14 58	15 20	15 34	16 20	16 25	16 57	17 02	17 18	17 35	17 55	18 20	18 26	19 17	19 22	19 52	20 31	20 47	21 32	22 09	22 35
Lawrence Hill	d	14 27	15 00	15 22	15 36	16 22	16 28	16 59	17 04	17 20	17 37	17 58	18 22	18 29	19 19	19 24	19 54	20 34	20 50	21a34	22 11	22 37
Bristol Temple Meads 10	a	14 30	15 03	15 26	15 39	16 26	16 31	17 05	17 08	17 24	17 40	18 01	18 26	18 32	19 22	19 28	19 57	20 37	20 53		22 14	22 41

		GW	GW FO ◇	GW FX ◇	GW
Severn Beach	d				23 00
St Andrews Road	d				23 06
Avonmouth 2	d	22 20			23 10
Shirehampton	d	22 23			23 14
Sea Mills	d	22 27			23 18
Clifton Down	d	22 33			23 24
Redland	d	22 36			23 26
Montpelier	d	22 38			23 28
Stapleton Road	d	22 43	22 52	22 56	23 33
Lawrence Hill	d	22 45	22 54	22 58	23 35
Bristol Temple Meads 10	a	22 49	23 01	23 01	23 38

Saturdays
21 December to 16 May

		GW ◇	GW	GW	GW	GW	GW	GW	GW	GW	GW	GW	GW	GW	GW	GW	GW	GW	GW	GW	GW	GW	GW
Severn Beach	d						07 54					09 52					11 52					13 52	
St Andrews Road	d						08 00					09 58					11 58					13 58	
Avonmouth 2	d		06 37		07 12		08 04	08 38		09 12		10 02	10 38		11 12		12 02	12 38		13 12		14 02	14 38
Shirehampton	d		06 40		07 15		08 08	08 41		09 15		10 06	10 41		11 15		12 06	12 41		13 15		14 06	14 41
Sea Mills	d		06 44		07 19		08 12	08 45		09 19		10 10	10 45		11 19		12 10	12 45		13 19		14 10	14 45
Clifton Down	d		06 50		07 26		08 17	08 51		09 26		10 15	10 51		11 26		12 15	12 51		13 26		14 15	14 51
Redland	d		06 52		07 28		08 19	08 53		09 28		10 17	10 53		11 28		12 17	12 53		13 28		14 17	14 53
Montpelier	d		06 54		07 30		08 21	08 55		09 30		10 19	10 55		11 30		12 19	12 55		13 30		14 19	14 55
Stapleton Road	d	00 17	06 59	07 03	07 35	08 18	08 26	09 00	09 17	09 35	10 19	10 24	11 00	11 19	11 35	12 19	12 24	13 00	13 19	13 35	14 19	14 25	15 00
Lawrence Hill	d	00 20	07 01	07 06	07 37	08 20	08 28	09 02	09 20	09 37	10 21	10 26	11 02	11 21	11 37	12 21	12 26	13 02	13 21	13 37	14 21	14 27	15 02
Bristol Temple Meads 10	a	00 25	07 06	07 10	07 42	08 25	08 32	09 07	09 24	09 43	10 26	10 30	11 07	11 26	11 43	12 26	12 30	13 07	13 26	13 43	14 26	14 32	15 07

		GW	GW	GW	GW	GW	GW	GW	GW	GW	GW	GW	GW	GW ◇	GW	GW	GW
Severn Beach	d				15 52					17 52		18 52	19 42		21 22		22 55
St Andrews Road	d				15 58					17 58		18 58	19 48		21 28		23 01
Avonmouth 2	d		15 12		16 02	16 38		17 12		18 02		19 02	19 52		21 32	22 16	23 05
Shirehampton	d		15 15		16 06	16 41		17 15		18 06		19 06	19 56		21 36	22 19	23 09
Sea Mills	d		15 19		16 10	16 45		17 19		18 10		19 10	20 00		21 40	22 23	23 13
Clifton Down	d		15 26		16 15	16 51		17 26		18 15		19 15	20 05		21 45	22 29	23 18
Redland	d		15 28		16 17	16 53		17 28		18 17		19 17	20 07		21 47	22 31	23 20
Montpelier	d		15 30		16 19	16 55		17 30		18 19		19 19	20 09		21 49	22 33	23 22
Stapleton Road	d	15 19	15 35	16 19	16 24	17 00	17 19	17 35	18 19	18 24	19 17	19 24	20 14	20 20	21 54	22 38	23 27
Lawrence Hill	d	15 21	15 37	16 21	16 26	17 02	17 21	17 37	18 21	18 26	19 19	19 26	20 16	20 22	21 56	22 40	23 29
Bristol Temple Meads 10	a	15 26	15 43	16 26	16 30	17 07	17 26	17 43	18 26	18 30	19 25	19 30	20 21	20 27	22 00	22 46	23 34

Sundays
15 December to 10 May

		GW	GW	GW	GW		GW	GW	GW	GW	GW	GW
Severn Beach	d	09 39	10 28	11 55	13 12	and hourly until	17 12	18 12	18 43	19 42		
St Andrews Road	d	09 45	10 34	12 01	13 18		17 18	18 18	18 49	19 48		
Avonmouth 2	d	09 49	10 38	12 05	13 22		17 22	18 23	18 54	19 52	20 22	21 22
Shirehampton	d	09 52	10 42	12 09	13 26		17 26	18 26	18 57	19 56	20 25	21 25
Sea Mills	d	09 56	10 46	12 13	13 30		17 30	18 30	19 01	20 00	20 29	21 29
Clifton Down	d	10 01	10 51	12 18	13 36		17 36	18 36	19 06	20 06	20 34	21 34
Redland	d	10 03	10 53	12 21	13 39		17 39	18 39	19 09	20 09	20 37	21 37
Montpelier	d	10 05	10 55	12 23	13 41		17 41	18 41	19 11	20 11	20 39	21 39
Stapleton Road	d	10 10	11 00	12 27	13 45		17 45	18 45	19 15	20 15	20 44	21 43
Lawrence Hill	d	10 12	11 02	12 29	13 47		17 47	18 47	19 17	20 17	20 46	21 45
Bristol Temple Meads 10	a	10 15	11 05	12 33	13 52		17 52	18 51	19 20	20 22	20 49	21 51

Table T134-F

Mondays to Fridays

16 December to 15 May

Gloucester - Taunton

Miles	Station		GW MX	GW	GW	GW	GW	XC	GW	GW	GW		GW	XC	GW	XC	GW	GW	GW	XC	GW		GW	XC	GW
			◇		◇	■ 🍴		◇■	◇				◇	◇■	◇	◇■ 🍴	■		◇	◇■ 🍴	◇			◇■ 🍴	◇
—	Cardiff Central 7	d											06 30	06 57			07 28				08 00				08 27
0	**Gloucester 7**	d								06 04	06 26				07 00				07 46						
13	Cam & Dursley	d								06 16	06 39				07 16				08 00						
28	Yate	d								06 31	06 53				07 30				08 13						
34	**Bristol Parkway 7**	a								06 42	07 01				07 39				08 22						
—		d					06 12			06 43	07 02				07 40	07 55		08 13	08 22	08 27				08 55	
35¼	Filton Abbey Wood	d	00 25				06 16			06 47	07 05		07 12	07 37	07 43		08 07	08 17	08 26		08 44		08 51		09 07
38¼	Stapleton Road	d	00 31				06 22				07 11														
38¾	Lawrence Hill	d	00 34				06 24				07 14														
39½	**Bristol Temple Meads 10**	a	00 39				06 30			06 55	07 17		07 20	07 48	07 51	08 05	08 16	08 25	08 34	08 38	08 52		08 59	09 05	09 19
—		d		05 00	05 26	06 05		06 40	06 44	07 03	07 19				07 53	08 12		08 27		08 45	08 55				
40½	Bedminster	d								07 06	07 22				07 56			08 30							
41½	Parson Street	d								07 08	07 24				07 58			08 32							
47½	Nailsea & Backwell	d		05 11		06 15				07 16	07 32				08 06			08 40			09 04				
51¼	Yatton	d		05 17		06 21				07 21	07 37				08 11			08 45			09 10				
55½	Worle	d		05 23		06 27				07 28	07 43				08 17			08 51			09 16				
58½	Weston Milton	d		05 28						07 33	07 49				08 22			08 55							
59¾	**Weston-super-Mare**	a		05 31	05 45	06 34			07 04	07 37	07 52				08 26			09 00			09 22				
—		d		05 35	05 50				07 09	07 38					08 27						09 23				
67¼	Highbridge & Burnham	d		05 46	06 01				07 20	07 49					08 38						09 34				
73½	Bridgwater	d		05 53	06 09				07 27	07 57					08 46						09 42				
85¼	**Taunton**	a		06 06	06 20			07 10	07 38	08 09					08 58	08 42				09 16	09 53				

Station		GW	GW	XC	GW	XC	GW		GW	GW	XC	GW	GW	GW	XC	GW	GW		GW	XC	GW	XC	GW	GW	GW
			◇	◇■ 🍴	◇	◇■ 🍴	◇				◇■ 🍴	◇■ 🍴	◇■ 🍴	◇	◇■ 🍴	◇			◇	◇■ 🍴	◇	◇■ 🍴	◇		◇
Cardiff Central 7	d				09 00		09 27							10 00		10 30					11 00		11 30		
Gloucester 7	d		08 42							09 41									10 42						11 40
Cam & Dursley	d		08 55							09 54									10 54						11 53
Yate	d		09 08							10 07									11 07						12 06
Bristol Parkway 7	a		09 16							10 16									11 15						12 15
	d		09 19	09 30		10 00				10 16	10 22	10 26			10 59				11 16	11 21		11 59			12 16
Filton Abbey Wood	d	09 13	09 23		09 43		10 06		10 14	10 20				10 43		11 07	11 14		11 19		11 43		12 07	12 13	12 20
Stapleton Road	d	09 19							10 20								11 20							12 18	
Lawrence Hill	d	09 21							10 22								11 22							12 20	
Bristol Temple Meads 10	a	09 25	09 33	09 40	09 51	10 09	10 14		10 26	10 29	10 31	10 36		10 51	11 08	11 16	11 26		11 27	11 31	11 51	12 08	12 15	12 25	12 29
	d	09 27		09 45	09 55				10 27		10 45		10 49	10 55	11 15		11 27			11 45	11 55			12 27	
Bedminster	d	09 30							10 30								11 30							12 30	
Parson Street	d	09 33							10 33								11 33							12 33	
Nailsea & Backwell	d	09 40			10 04				10 40					11 04			11 40				12 04			12 40	
Yatton	d	09 46			10 10				10 46					11 10			11 46				12 10			12 46	
Worle	d	09 52			10 16				10 52					11 16			11 52				12 16			12 52	
Weston Milton	d	09 57							10 57								11 57							12 57	
Weston-super-Mare	a	10 00			10 22				11 00				11 07	11 22	11 33		12 00				12 22			13 00	
	d				10 23								11 09	11 23	11 40						12 23				
Highbridge & Burnham	d				10 34									11 34							12 34				
Bridgwater	d				10 42									11 42							12 42				
Taunton	a			10 17	10 55						11 17		11 28	11 55	11 59					12 17	12 55				

Station		XC	GW		XC	GW	GW	GW	XC	GW	GW	XC	GW		GW	GW	XC	GW	XC	GW	GW	GW	XC		GW
		◇■ 🍴	◇		◇■ 🍴	◇			◇■ 🍴	◇	◇■ 🍴	◇■ 🍴	◇			◇	◇■ 🍴	◇	◇■ 🍴	◇			◇■ 🍴		◇
Cardiff Central 7	d		12 00			12 30				13 00			13 30					14 00		14 30					15 00
Gloucester 7	d							12 42								13 37						14 41			
Cam & Dursley	d							12 54								13 50						14 54			
Yate	d							13 07								14 03						15 07			
Bristol Parkway 7	a							13 16								14 13						15 16			
	d	12 22			12 55			13 16	13 21		13 55	13 59				14 13	14 23		14 55			15 16	15 21		
Filton Abbey Wood	d		12 43			13 07	13 13	13 20		13 44			14 07		14 13	14 17		14 44		15 07	15 14	15 20			15 41
Stapleton Road	d						13 19								14 19						15 20				
Lawrence Hill	d						13 21								14 21						15 22				
Bristol Temple Meads 10	a	12 32	12 51		13 04	13 15	13 25	13 28	13 32	13 52	14 04	14 08	14 16		14 25	14 29	14 32	14 52	15 04	15 15	15 26	15 29	15 34		15 49
	d	12 45	12 55		13 10		13 27		13 45	13 55	14 07				14 27		14 45	14 54	15 09		15 27		15 45		15 51
Bedminster	d						13 30								14 30						15 30				15 54
Parson Street	d						13 33								14 33						15 33				15 56
Nailsea & Backwell	d		13 04				13 40			14 04					14 40			15 03			15 40				16 04
Yatton	d		13 10				13 46			14 10	14 20				14 46			15 09			15 46				16 09
Worle	d		13 16				13 52			14 16					14 52			15 15			15 52				16 15
Weston Milton	d						13 57								14 57						15 57				16 20
Weston-super-Mare	a		13 22				14 00			14 22	14 31				15 00			15 21			16 00				16 24
	d		13 24							14 23								15 24							16 26
Highbridge & Burnham	d		13 35							14 34								15 35							16 37
Bridgwater	d		13 43							14 42								15 43							16 44
Taunton	a	13 17	13 56		13 41				14 17	14 53							15 17	15 56	15 40				16 17		16 57

For connections from London Paddington refer to Table T125

For full services to Brighton, Portsmouth Harbour, Westbury and Weymouth refer to Table T123

NRT DECEMBER 19 EDITION

Table T134-F

Mondays to Fridays

16 December to 15 May

Gloucester - Taunton

Station		XC	GW	GW	GW		GW	XC	GW	GW	GW	XC	GW	GW	GW		GW	XC	GW	GW	XC	GW	GW	GW	GW
		◇■ 🍴	◇■ 🍴	◇			◇	◇■ 🍴	◇		◇■ 🍴	◇■ A 🍴	◇■ 🍴	■			◇	◇■ 🍴	◇		◇■ 🍴	◇■ 🍴	■		
Cardiff Central 7	d			15 30					16 00					16 27					17 00				17 30		
Gloucester 7	d						15 38										16 42								17 42
Cam & Dursley	d						15 51										16 54								17 54
Yate	d						16 05										17 07								18 07
Bristol Parkway 7	a						16 13										17 16								18 16
	d	15 57	16 01				16 14	16 23		16 45	16 55	16 59					17 16	17 23		17 45	17 59			18 10	18 16
Filton Abbey Wood	d			16 07	16 14		16 18		16 43	16 51				17 06	17 12		17 20		17 41	17 49			18 11	18 14	18 20
Stapleton Road	d				16 20					16 57					17 18					17 55				18 20	
Lawrence Hill	d				16 22					16 59			←		17 20					17 58				18 22	
Bristol Temple Meads 10	a	16 06	16 09	16 15	16 26		16 28	16 32	16 51	17 05	17 04	17 08	17 04	17 14	17 24		17 27	17 32	17 49	18 01	18 08		18 19	18 26	18 29
	d	16 09	16 13		16 27			16 45	16 53		17 16	17 11	17 16		17 27			17 45	17 53		18 11	18 16		18 27	
Bedminster	d				16 30				16 56		→				17 30				17 57					18 30	
Parson Street	d				16 33				16 58						17 33				18 00					18 33	
Nailsea & Backwell	d		16 23		16 40				17 06				17 26		17 40				18 07			18 26		18 40	
Yatton	d		16 28		16 46				17 11				17 32		17 46				18 13			18 32		18 46	
Worle	d		16 34		16 52				17 17				17 38		17 52				18 19			18 38		18 52	
Weston Milton	d				16 57				17 23						17 57				18 24					18 57	
Weston-super-Mare	a		16 41		17 00				17 26				17 44		18 00				18 28			18 44		19 00	
	d								17 30										18 29			18 46			
Highbridge & Burnham	d								17 41										18 40			18 56			
Bridgwater	d								17 48										18 48			19 04			
Taunton	a	16 42						17 17	18 01			17 42						18 17	19 02		18 44	19 15			

Station			XC	GW	XC	GW	GW	GW	GW	XC	GW		XC	GW	GW	GW	XC	GW	GW	GW	XC		GW	GW	GW
			◇■ 🍴	◇	◇■ 🍴	◇■ 🍴	◇			◇■ 🍴	◇		◇■ 🍴	◇■ 🍴	◇		◇■ A 🍴	◇■ 🍴	◇	◇	◇■ A 🍴		◇		◇
Cardiff Central 7	d			18 00			18 30				19 00				19 30					20 00			20 30		
Gloucester 7	d								18 42	19 08						19 42								20 42	
Cam & Dursley	d								18 54							19 54								20 54	
Yate	d								19 07							20 07								21 07	
Bristol Parkway 7	a								19 16	19 34						20 16								21 16	
	d		18 24		18 56			19 10	19 16	19 36			19 57			20 16	20 22	20 26	20 30		20 55			21 16	21 21
Filton Abbey Wood	d			18 42			19 11	19 15	19 20		19 42				20 07	20 20			20 34	20 41			21 07	21 20	21 25
Stapleton Road	d							19 22												20 47					21 32
Lawrence Hill	d							19 24												20 50					21a34
Bristol Temple Meads 10	a		18 33	18 50	19 05		19 19	19 28	19 29	19 45	19 51		20 07		20 15	20 28	20 31	20 35	20 42	20 53	21 04		21 15	21 28	
	d		18 45	18 55		19 14		19 29		19 47	19 53			20 15			20 37	20 43		20 55	21 08				
Bedminster	d			18 58				19 32			19 56									20 58					
Parson Street	d			19 00				19 35			19 58									21 00					
Nailsea & Backwell	d			19 08		19 24		19 42			20 06			20 25				20 53		21 08					
Yatton	d			19 13		19 29		19 48			20 11			20 31				20 58		21 13					
Worle	d			19 19		19 35		19 54			20 17			20 37				21 04		21 19					
Weston Milton	d			19 24		19 41		19 58			20 23			20 41						21 23					
Weston-super-Mare	a			19 28		19 44		20 02			20 26			20 45				21 11		21 28					
	d			19 29		19 46					20 30									21 32					
Highbridge & Burnham	d			19 40		19 56					20 41									21 43					
Bridgwater	d			19 48		20 04					20 48									21 50					
Taunton	a		19 18	19 59		20 15				20 18	21 01						21 07			22 04	21 44				

Station		XC	GW	XC	GW	GW	XC		GW FO	GW	GW FX	GW	GW FO	XC	GW FX	GW	GW		GW FO	GW FX
		◇■ A 🍴	◇	◇■	◇		◇■		◇		◇	◇	◇	◇■	◇	◇■ 🍴			◇	◇
Cardiff Central 7	d		21 00		21 30				22 00		22 00		22 30		22 30				23 30	23 30
Gloucester 7	d						22 05			22 11							23 17			
Cam & Dursley	d									22 23										
Yate	d									22 36										
Bristol Parkway 7	a						22 31			22 45							23 46			
	d	21 27		21 56		22 25	22 32			22 45				23 21			23 47			
Filton Abbey Wood	d		21 41		22 12	22 29			22 46	22 49	22 50		23 13		23 22		23 50		00 11	00 25
Stapleton Road	d					22 35			22 52		22 56								00 17	00 31
Lawrence Hill	d					22 37			22 54		22 58								00 20	00 34
Bristol Temple Meads 10	a	21 36	21 50	22 05	22 23	22 41	22 44		23 01	22 57	23 01		23 23	23 30	23 35		23 58		00 25	00 39
	d	21 44	21 55									23 05				23 47				
Bedminster	d		21 58									23 08								
Parson Street	d		22 00									23 10								
Nailsea & Backwell	d		22 08									23 18				23s56				
Yatton	d		22 13									23 23				00s02				
Worle	d		22 19									23 29				00s08				
Weston Milton	d		22 24									23 34								
Weston-super-Mare	a		22 28									23 38				00s16				
	d		22 29									23 39								
Highbridge & Burnham	d		22 40									23 50				00s27				
Bridgwater	d		22 47									23 57				00s34				
Taunton	a	22 14	23 00									00s08				00s45				

A 🍴 to Bristol Temple Meads

For connections from London Paddington refer to Table T125

For full services to Brighton, Portsmouth Harbour, Westbury and Weymouth refer to Table T123

Table T134-F

Gloucester - Taunton

Saturdays
21 December to 16 May

		GW	GW	XC	GW	GW		GW	GW	GW	GW	GW	GW	XC	GW	XC		GW	GW	GW	XC	GW	XC	GW	GW
		◇	◇	◇1				◇			◇		◇1 ⛾	◇1		◇1 ⛾		◇		◇	◇1 ⛾	◇	◇1 ⛾	◇	
Cardiff Central 7	d										06 29			07 00				07 27				08 00		08 27	
Gloucester 7	d									06 18					07 06					07 40					
Cam & Dursley	d									06 30					07 19					07 53					
Yate	d									06 43					07 33					08 06					
Bristol Parkway 7	a									06 52					07 41					08 14					
	d					06 19				06 55					07 42	07 55			08 09	08 15	08 25		08 55		09 09
Filton Abbey Wood	d	00 11				06 23				06 58	07 09			07 40	07 45			08 06	08 13	08 19		08 45		09 06	09 12
Stapleton Road	d	00 17								07 03									08 18						09 17
Lawrence Hill	d	00 20								07 06									08 20						09 20
Bristol Temple Meads 10	a	00 25				06 31				07 10	07 17			07 52	07 53	08 04		08 14	08 25	08 28	08 36	08 53	09 05	09 15	09 24
	d		05 27	06 07	06 16			06 42	06 48			07 22	07 42		07 55	08 10			08 27		08 45	08 56			09 27
Bedminster	d								06 52			07 25							08 30						09 30
Parson Street	d								06 56			07 28							08 33						09 33
Nailsea & Backwell	d				06 25				07 03			07 36			08 04				08 40			09 05			09 40
Yatton	d				06 31				07 08			07 41			08 10				08 46			09 11			09 46
Worle	d				06 37				07 14			07 47			08 16				08 52			09 17			09 52
Weston Milton	d								07 19			07 53							08 57						09 57
Weston-super-Mare	a		05 46		06 42			07 01	07 25			07 56			08 25				09 01			09 22			10 01
	d		05 50		06 49			07 07				07 58										09 23			
Highbridge & Burnham	d		06 01		07 00			07 18				08 09										09 34			
Bridgwater	d		06 08		07 07			07 26				08 17										09 42			
Taunton	a		06 20	07 13	07 19			07 38				08 30	08 14			08 41					09 18	09 54			

		GW		XC	GW	XC	GW	GW	GW	GW	XC	GW		XC	GW	GW	GW	XC	GW	XC	GW	GW		GW	XC
		◇		◇1 ⛾	◇	◇1 ⛾	◇1 ⛾	◇			◇1 ⛾	◇		◇1 ⛾	◇		◇	◇1 ⛾	◇	◇1 ⛾	◇			◇	◇1 ⛾
Cardiff Central 7	d				09 00			09 28				10 00			10 30				11 00		11 30				
Gloucester 7	d	08 42								09 41							10 42							11 46	
Cam & Dursley	d	08 55								09 54							10 55							11 59	
Yate	d	09 08								10 08							11 08							12 13	
Bristol Parkway 7	a	09 17								10 16							11 17							12 21	
	d	09 18		09 25		09 59			10 10	10 17	10 25			10 57		11 10	11 18	11 25		11 55		12 10		12 22	12 27
Filton Abbey Wood	d	09 21			09 41			10 07	10 14	10 21		10 40			11 07	11 14	11 21		11 41		12 07	12 14		12 25	
Stapleton Road	d								10 19							11 19						12 19			
Lawrence Hill	d								10 21							11 21						12 21			
Bristol Temple Meads 10	a	09 30		09 34	09 50	10 08		10 15	10 26	10 32	10 36	10 51		11 09	11 15	11 26	11 32	11 36	11 50	12 05	12 16	12 26		12 33	12 38
	d			09 45	09 55		10 09		10 27		10 45	10 56		11 12		11 27		11 45	11 55			12 27			12 45
Bedminster	d								10 30							11 30						12 30			
Parson Street	d								10 33							11 33						12 33			
Nailsea & Backwell	d				10 04				10 40			11 06				11 40			12 04			12 40			
Yatton	d				10 10				10 46			11 11				11 46			12 10			12 46			
Worle	d				10 16				10 52			11 17				11 52			12 16			12 52			
Weston Milton	d								10 57							11 57						12 57			
Weston-super-Mare	a				10 22		10 28		11 01			11 24		11 30		12 01			12 22			13 01			
	d				10 24							11 26		11 38					12 24						
Highbridge & Burnham	d				10 35							11 36							12 35						
Bridgwater	d				10 42							11 44							12 42						
Taunton	a			10 17	10 54						11 17	11 56		12 00				12 17	12 54						13 17

		GW	XC	GW	GW	GW	XC	GW		XC	GW	GW	GW	XC	GW	XC	GW	GW		GW	XC	GW	XC	GW	GW
		◇	◇1 ⛾	◇			◇1 ⛾	◇		◇1 ⛾	◇		◇	◇1 ⛾	◇	◇1 ⛾	◇				◇1 ⛾	◇	◇1 ⛾	◇	
Cardiff Central 7	d	12 00		12 27				13 00			13 30				14 00		14 30					15 00		15 30	
Gloucester 7	d					12 42							13 42							14 42					
Cam & Dursley	d					12 55							13 55							14 55					
Yate	d					13 08							14 08							15 08					
Bristol Parkway 7	a					13 17							14 17							15 17					
	d		12 55		13 10	13 18	13 25			14 00		14 10	14 18	14 25		14 58		15 10		15 18	15 25		16 00		16 10
Filton Abbey Wood	d	12 41		13 04	13 14	13 21		13 44			14 07	14 14	14 21		14 44		15 07	15 14		15 21		15 40		16 10	16 14
Stapleton Road	d				13 19							14 19						15 19							16 19
Lawrence Hill	d				13 21							14 21						15 21							16 21
Bristol Temple Meads 10	a	12 50	13 05	13 12	13 26	13 30	13 34	13 52		14 09	14 15	14 26	14 31	14 36	14 52	15 07	15 15	15 26		15 32	15 36	15 51	16 09	16 18	16 26
	d	12 55			13 27		13 46	13 56				14 27		14 46	14 55	15 10		15 27			15 45	15 56			16 27
Bedminster	d				13 30							14 30						15 30							16 30
Parson Street	d				13 33			14 00				14 33						15 33							16 33
Nailsea & Backwell	d	13 04			13 40			14 08				14 40			15 04			15 40				16 06			16 40
Yatton	d	13 10			13 46			14 13				14 46			15 10			15 46				16 11			16 46
Worle	d	13 16			13 52			14 19				14 52			15 16			15 52				16 17			16 52
Weston Milton	d				13 57							14 57						15 57							16 57
Weston-super-Mare	a	13 22			14 01			14 25				15 01			15 22			16 01				16 24			17 01
	d	13 24						14 26							15 27							16 26			
Highbridge & Burnham	d	13 35						14 37							15 38							16 36			
Bridgwater	d	13 42						14 45							15 45							16 44			
Taunton	a	13 54					14 17	14 56						15 17	15 57	15 41					16 15	16 56			

For connections from London Paddington refer to Table T125

For full services to Brighton, Portsmouth Harbour, Westbury and Weymouth refer to Table T123

Table T134-F

Gloucester - Taunton

Saturdays
21 December to 16 May

		GW	XC	GW	XC	GW	GW	GW	XC	GW		XC	GW	GW	GW	GW	XC	GW	XC	GW		GW	GW	GW	XC
		◇	◇1 ⛾	◇	◇1 ⛾	◇		◇	◇1 ⛾	◇		◇1 ⛾	◇1 ⛾	◇			◇1 ⛾	◇	◇1 ⛾	◇1 ⛾		◇			◇1 ⛾
Cardiff Central 7	d			16 00		16 27				17 00				17 27				18 00				18 27			
Gloucester 7	d	15 42						16 42								17 50								18 42	
Cam & Dursley	d	15 55						16 55								18 03								18 55	
Yate	d	16 08						17 08								18 16								19 08	
Bristol Parkway 7	a	16 17						17 17								18 25								19 17	
	d	16 18	16 25		16 55		17 10	17 18	17 25			17 55			18 10	18 26	18 31		18 55				19 08	19 18	19 25
Filton Abbey Wood	d	16 21		16 41		17 06	17 14	17 21		17 41				18 06	18 14	18 29		18 41				19 06	19 12	19 22	
Stapleton Road	d						17 19								18 19								19 17		
Lawrence Hill	d						17 21								18 21								19 19		
Bristol Temple Meads 10	a	16 30	16 34	16 50	17 04	17 14	17 26	17 32	17 35	17 51		18 04		18 14	18 26	18 38	18 42	18 50	19 05			19 14	19 25	19 35	19 36
	d		16 45	16 53	17 09		17 27		17 45	17 55			18 10		18 27		18 45	18 55		19 10					19 45
Bedminster	d						17 30								18 30			18 58							
Parson Street	d						17 33								18 33			19 01							
Nailsea & Backwell	d			17 03			17 40			18 04			18 21		18 40			19 09		19 21					
Yatton	d			17 08			17 46			18 10			18 26		18 46			19 14		19 26					
Worle	d			17 14			17 52			18 16			18 32		18 52			19 20		19 32					
Weston Milton	d						17 57								18 57			19 25							
Weston-super-Mare	a			17 21			18 01			18 22			18 38		19 01			19 28		19 40					
	d			17 22						18 24			18 39					19 30							
Highbridge & Burnham	d			17 34						18 35			18 50					19 41							
Bridgwater	d			17 41						18 42			18 57					19 48							
Taunton	a		17 17	17 53	17 39				18 17	18 54			19 08				19 17	20 00							20 16

		GW	GW	XC	GW	GW		GW	XC	GW	XC	GW	GW	XC	GW	GW		XC	GW	XC	GW				
		◇	◇1 ⛾	◇1 ⛾	◇	◇			◇1 ⛾	◇1 A	◇1 B ⛾	◇1 ⛾	◇	◇1 B ⛾	◇	◇1 ⛾		◇1		◇1 ⛾	◇				
Cardiff Central 7	d	19 00			19 30					19 54			20 30		21 00						22 00				
Gloucester 7	d							19 42											21 33	22 05					
Cam & Dursley	d							19 56											21 46						
Yate	d							20 09											21 59						
Bristol Parkway 7	a							20 18											22 07	22 31					
	d			20 00		20 10		20 19	20 25		20 55			21 25				22 00	22 08	22 32					
Filton Abbey Wood	d	19 41			20 07	20 15		20 22		20 34			21 07		21 41				22 12		22 51				
Stapleton Road	d					20 20																			
Lawrence Hill	d					20 22																			
Bristol Temple Meads 10	a	19 50		20 09	20 15	20 27		20 31	20 34	20 47	21 04		21 16	21 34	21 49			22 12	22 22	22 41	23 02				
	d	19 55	20 08						20 45		21 07	21 11		21 45	21 54	22 08									
Bedminster	d														21 57										
Parson Street	d														21 59										
Nailsea & Backwell	d	20 04	20 18									21 21			22 07	22s17									
Yatton	d	20 10	20 24									21 26			22 12	22s22									
Worle	d	20 16	20 30									21 32			22 18	22s28									
Weston Milton	d	20 21										21 36			22 23										
Weston-super-Mare	a	20 25	20 37									21 39			22 26	22s35									
	d	20 26	20 39									21 41			22 27										
Highbridge & Burnham	d	20 37	20 49									21 51			22 38	22s46									
Bridgwater	d	20 44	20 57									21 58			22 45	22s53									
Taunton	a	20 56	21 08						21 16		21 37	22 09		22 16	22 56	23 04									

Sundays
15 December to 10 May

		GW	GW	XC	GW	GW	XC	GW	GW	GW		GW	GW	XC	GW	GW	GW	XC	GW	GW		GW	XC	GW	GW
		◇	◇	◇1 ⛾		◇	◇1 ⛾	◇ C	◇ D	◇1 ⛾			◇1 ⛾	◇1 ⛾	◇		◇1 ⛾	◇1 ⛾	◇1 ⛾	1			◇1 ⛾	◇	◇1 ⛾
Cardiff Central 7	d					08 10		09 13	09 20						10 13					11 13				12 13	
Gloucester 7	d											09 30										11 38			
Cam & Dursley	d											09 44										11 52			
Yate	d											09 58										12 05			
Bristol Parkway 7	a											10 06										12 14			
	d											10 07		10 40				11 41				12 15	12 43		
Filton Abbey Wood	d					09 00		10a00	10a00			10 10			10 50					11 50		12 19		12 53	
Stapleton Road	d															11 00									
Lawrence Hill	d															11 02									
Bristol Temple Meads 10	a					09 10						10 20		10 49	11 00	11 05		11 50		12 05		12 27	12 52	13 02	
	d	07 26	08 28	08 44	09 00		09 48			09 57		10 25	10 44	10 58		11 10	11 41	11 55	12 01				12 55		13 11
Bedminster	d											10 28				11 13									
Parson Street	d											10 30				11 16									
Nailsea & Backwell	d		08 37		09 08							10 37				11 23			12 12						
Yatton	d	07 38	08 43		09 13							10 42				11 28			12 17						
Worle	d		08 49		09 19							10 49				11 35			12 23						
Weston Milton	d																								
Weston-super-Mare	a	07 48	08 55		09 28							10 54	11 03			11 41			12 33						
	d	07 49	09 01									10 55				11 42									
Highbridge & Burnham	d		09 12									11 06				11 53									
Bridgwater	d	08 05	09 19									11 13				12 00									
Taunton	a	08 17	09 31	09 14			10 18			10 29		11 25		11 29		12 12	12 16	12 26					13 26		13 45

A 1 from Filton Abbey Wood
B ⛾ to Bristol Temple Meads
C until 29 March
D from 5 April

For connections from London Paddington refer to Table T125

For full services to Brighton, Portsmouth Harbour, Westbury and Weymouth refer to Table T123

Table T134-F

Sundays

15 December to 10 May

Gloucester - Taunton

		GW		XC	GW	GW	XC	GW	GW	XC	GW	XC		GW	GW	XC	GW	XC	GW	GW	XC	GW		GW	GW
				◇1 ✠	◇	◇1 ✠	◇1 ✠		◇	◇1 ✠		◇1 ✠			◇	◇1 ✠		◇1 ✠	◇	◇1 ✠	◇1 ✠	◇			
Cardiff Central 7	d				13 13				14 13						15 13				16 13			16 36			
Gloucester 7	d										14 43														16 39
Cam & Dursley	d										14 56														16 53
Yate	d										15 09														17 06
Bristol Parkway 7	a										15 18														17 14
	d			13 25			14 25			14 57	15 19	15 24				15 57		16 25			16 58				17 14
Filton Abbey Wood	d				13 50				14 50		15 22				15 52				16 50			17 14			17 20
Stapleton Road	d																								
Lawrence Hill	d													←											
Bristol Temple Meads 10	a			13 34	13 59		14 34		14 59	15 06	15 30	15 36		15 30	16 04	16 09		16 34	17 02		17 07	17 23			17 29
	d	13 15		13 45		14 00	14 45	14 50			15 50	15 45		15 50		16 14	16 25	16 45		17 05				17 28	
Bedminster	d							14 53			→			15 53			16 28							17 31	
Parson Street	d							14 56						15 55			16 30							17 33	
Nailsea & Backwell	d	13 25				14 11		15 04						16 03			16 38			17 15				17 41	
Yatton	d	13 30				14 17		15 09						16 08			16 43			17 20				17 46	
Worle	d	13 36				14 23		15 15						16 14			16 49			17 26				17 52	
Weston Milton	d							15 20						16 19			16 54							17 57	
Weston-super-Mare	a	13 42				14 29		15 23						16 25			16 58			17 33				18 01	
	d	13 42						15 24						16 28						17 35					
Highbridge & Burnham	d	13 54						15 35						16 39						17 45					
Bridgwater	d	14 01						15 42						16 47						17 53					
Taunton	a	14 13		14 17			15 15	15 54				16 16		16 59		16 47		17 16		18 04					

		XC	GW	XC	GW	GW	XC	GW		GW	XC	GW	GW	GW	XC	GW	XC	GW		XC	GW	XC	GW	GW	XC
		◇1 ✠	◇	◇1 ✠	◇	◇	◇1 ✠	◇		◇1 ✠	◇1 ✠			◇1 ✠	◇1 ✠	◇1 ✠	◇1 A ✠	◇		◇1 A ✠		◇1	◇		◇1 A ✠
Cardiff Central 7	d		17 13			17 40		18 12										19 13					20 30		
Gloucester 7	d												18 36											20 39	
Cam & Dursley	d												18 49											20 54	
Yate	d												19 02											21 07	
Bristol Parkway 7	a												19 10											21 16	
	d	17 25		17 55			18 25				19 03		19 11		19 25		19 56			20 25		20 57		21 16	21 25
Filton Abbey Wood	d		17 50			18 18		18 50					19 14					19 51					21 09	21 20	
Stapleton Road	d											19 15													
Lawrence Hill	d											19 17													
Bristol Temple Meads 10	a	17 34	18 03	18 08		18 28	18 34	19 01			19 12	19 20	19 24		19 36		20 05	20 06		20 35		21 06	21 18	21 30	21 35
	d	17 45			18 25		18 45			19 05		19 25		19 38	19 45	20 05	20 16			20 45	20 55				21 45
Bedminster	d				18 28																20 58				
Parson Street	d				18 31																21 00				
Nailsea & Backwell	d				18 38					19 17		19 34				20 14					21 08				
Yatton	d				18 44					19 22		19 40				20 19					21 13				
Worle	d				18 50					19 30		19 45				20 24					21 19				
Weston Milton	d									19 35		19 49													
Weston-super-Mare	a				18 55					19 38		19 52				20 32	20 37				21 26				
	d				19 00							20 00					20 39				21 26				
Highbridge & Burnham	d				19 11							20 11									21 37				
Bridgwater	d				19 18							20 18									21 45				
Taunton	a	18 17			19 29		19 16					20 35		20 09	20 15		20 58			21 16	21 58				22 16

		GW	XC	GW		XC	XC	GW	GW	XC
		◇1 ✠	◇1	◇		◇1	◇1	◇		◇1
Cardiff Central 7	d			21 25				22 15		
Gloucester 7	d					22 05				
Cam & Dursley	d									
Yate	d									
Bristol Parkway 7	a					22 31				
	d		22 02			22 32	22 55			23 21
Filton Abbey Wood	d			22 04				22 54		
Stapleton Road	d									
Lawrence Hill	d									
Bristol Temple Meads 10	a		22 11	22 21		22 41	23 04	23 08		23 30
	d	22 05							23 10	
Bedminster	d								23 13	
Parson Street	d								23 15	
Nailsea & Backwell	d	22 16							23 23	
Yatton	d	22 21							23 28	
Worle	d	22 27							23 34	
Weston Milton	d	22 33							23 39	
Weston-super-Mare	a	22 36							23 43	
	d									
Highbridge & Burnham	d									
Bridgwater	d									
Taunton	a									

A ✠ to Bristol Temple Meads

For connections from London Paddington refer to Table T125

For full services to Brighton, Portsmouth Harbour, Westbury and Weymouth refer to Table T123

Table T134-R

Mondays to Fridays

16 December to 15 May

Taunton - Gloucester

Miles			GW MO	GW	XC	GW	GW	GW		XC	GW	XC	GW	GW	XC	GW	GW	GW		GW	XC	GW	GW	GW	GW
				◇1 ✠	◇1		◇			◇1	◇	◇1 ✠	◇1 A ✠		◇1 ✠	◇1 ✠	◇	◇1 ✠			◇1 ✠			◇1 ✠	
0	Taunton	d									05 15						06 09			06 38	06 51			06 55	
11¾	Bridgwater	d									05 27						06 20			06 49				07 06	
18	Highbridge & Burnham	d									05 35						06 27			06 56				07 13	
25¾	Weston-super-Mare	a									05 45						06 37			07 06				07 23	
—		d									05 47		06 20				06 39	06 48		07 10				07 24	
27	Weston Milton	d									05 50		06 24				06 42	06 52		07 13					
29½	Worle	d									05 54		06 28				06 46	06 56		07 17				07 30	
33½	Yatton	d	00 02								06 00		06 34				06 52	07 02		07 23				07 36	
37¾	Nailsea & Backwell	d	00 08								06 06		06 40				06 58	07 08		07 29				07 42	
43¾	Parson Street	d	00 16								06 14						07 06			07 36					
44½	Bedminster	d	00 19								06 17						07 09			07 39			←		
45½	Bristol Temple Meads 10	a	00 23								06 22		06 53				07 13	07 19		07 43	07 24		07 43	07 53	
—		d		04 53	05 20	05 46	05 54	06 10		06 24	06 27	06 32		06 53	07 00	07 07	07 27			07 45	07 34	07 38	07 45		07 53
46½	Lawrence Hill	d				05 49					06 30			06 56			07 30			→			07 48		
47	Stapleton Road	d				05 52					06 32			06 59			07 32						07 51		
50	Filton Abbey Wood	d				05 58	06 01	06 17			06 37			07 04		07 15	07 38					07 46	07 57		08 01
51¼	Bristol Parkway 7	a		05 02	05 29	06 02		06 21		06 34		06 40			07 08	07 18					07 42	07 53	08 01		
—		d			05 38			06 22		06 34						07 28						07 54			
57½	Yate	d						06 31														08 03			
72¼	Cam & Dursley	d						06 43														08 16			
85¼	Gloucester 7	a						07 00		07 04												08 31			
—	Cardiff Central 7	a			06 21		06 42				07 20			07 42		08 03	08 23								08 45

		XC	GW	GW		GW	XC	GW	GW	GW	GW	XC	GW	XC		GW	GW	GW	XC	GW	GW	XC	GW	GW	
		◇1 ✠	◇	◇		◇1 ✠	◇1 ✠			◇1 ✠	■	◇1 ✠	◇	◇1 ✠				◇	◇1 ✠	◇1 ✠	◇	◇1 ✠	◇		
Taunton	d			07 02		07 22	07 53					08 08	08 17	08 53							09 18	09 53			
Bridgwater	d			07 14		07 33							08 28								09 29				
Highbridge & Burnham	d			07 22		07 41							08 35								09 37				
Weston-super-Mare	a			07 32		07 50						08 36	08 45								09 47				
	d			07 39		07 54			08 10			08 38	08 46				09 10			09 44	09 49			10 10	
Weston Milton	d			07 43		07 58			08 13				08 49				09 13							10 13	
Worle	d			07 47		08 02			08 17				08 53				09 17			09 50	09 54			10 17	
Yatton	d			07 53		08 08			08 23				08 59				09 23			09 56	10 00			10 23	
Nailsea & Backwell	d			07 59		08 14			08 29				09 05				09 29			10 02	10 06			10 29	
Parson Street	d			08 07					08 38				09 13				09 36							10 36	
Bedminster	d			08 10					08 40				09 16				09 39							10 39	
Bristol Temple Meads 10	a			08 14		08 25	08 29		08 43			08 54	09 20	09 24			09 43			10 11	10 19	10 24		10 43	
	d	08 00	08 17	08 22			08 34	08 37	08 45	08 53	08 56	09 00	09 27	09 34		09 38	09 45	09 56	10 00	10 20	10 27	10 34	10 37	10 45	
Lawrence Hill	d		08 20						08 48								09 48							10 49	
Stapleton Road	d		08 22						08 51								09 51							10 51	
Filton Abbey Wood	d		08a27	08 36				08 46	08a56		09 04		09 36			09 45	09a56	10 05			10 36		10 45	10a56	
Bristol Parkway 7	a	08 08					08 42	08 50		09 02		09 08		09 42		09 50			10 08	10 32		10 42	10 50		
	d							08 51								09 50							10 50		
Yate	d							09 00								09 59							10 59		
Cam & Dursley	d							09 12								10 11							11 11		
Gloucester 7	a							09 31								10 29							11 29		
Cardiff Central 7	a			09 24							09 45		10 20					10 47			11 23				

		GW	GW	XC	GW	XC	GW	GW	GW	GW		XC	GW	XC	GW	GW	GW	XC	GW	XC		GW	GW	GW	GW
		◇1 ✠	◇	◇1 ✠	◇	◇1 ✠	◇		◇	◇		◇1 ✠	◇	◇1 ✠	◇		◇	◇1 ✠	◇	◇1 ✠		◇		◇	◇
Taunton	d				10 20	10 53				11 10		11 21		11 53					12 18	12 53					13 09
Bridgwater	d				10 31					11 21									12 29						13 20
Highbridge & Burnham	d				10 38					11 28									12 36						13 27
Weston-super-Mare	a				10 48					11 38									12 46						13 37
	d				10 49			11 10		11 42						12 10			12 49				13 10		13 47
Weston Milton	d							11 13								12 13							13 13		
Worle	d				10 54			11 17		11 47						12 17			12 54				13 17		13 52
Yatton	d				11 00			11 23		11 53						12 23			13 00				13 23		13 58
Nailsea & Backwell	d				11 06			11 29		11 59						12 29			13 06				13 29		14 04
Parson Street	d							11 36								12 36							13 37		
Bedminster	d							11 39					←			12 39							13 39		
Bristol Temple Meads 10	a				11 17	11 24		11 43		12 10		11 55	12 10	12 24		12 43			13 17	13 26			13 43		14 15
	d	10 53	10 57	11 00	11 20	11 34	11 37	11 45	11 56	12 23		12 00	12 23	12 35	12 38	12 45	12 57	13 00	13 21	13 34		13 38	13 45	13 57	14 24
Lawrence Hill	d							11 49		→						12 49							13 49		→
Stapleton Road	d							11 51								12 51							13 51		
Filton Abbey Wood	d		11 05		11 36		11 45	11a56	12 05				12 36		12 46	12a57	13 05		13 36			13 45	13a56	14 05	
Bristol Parkway 7	a	11 02		11 08		11 42	11 49					12 08		12 43	12 50			13 08		13 42		13 50			
	d						11 50								12 50							13 50			
Yate	d						11 58								12 59							13 59			
Cam & Dursley	d						12 10								13 12							14 11			
Gloucester 7	a						12 27								13 29							14 27			
Cardiff Central 7	a		11 46		12 22				12 44				13 27				13 43		14 21					14 46	

A The Bristolian

For connections to London Paddington refer to Table T125

For full services to Cardiff Central, Cheltenham Spa, Gloucester and Great Malvern refer to Table T123

Table T134-R

Mondays to Fridays

16 December to 15 May

Taunton - Gloucester

		XC	GW	GW	XC	GW	GW	GW	XC	GW	GW	GW	XC	GW	GW	GW	XC	GW	GW	XC	GW	GW
		◇1	◇1	◇	◇1	◇		◇	◇1	◇	◇1		◇1	◇		◇	◇1		◇	◇1		
		⌶	⌶		⌶				⌶		⌶		⌶				⌶			⌶		
Taunton	d	13 21	13 34		13 53					14 20			14 53				15 11		15 15	15 53		
Bridgwater	d									14 31									15 26			
Highbridge & Burnham	d									14 39									15 34			
Weston-super-Mare	a		13 54							14 49							15 33		15 44			
	d		14 02				14 10			14 49	15 03				15 11		15 34		15 49			16 10
Weston Milton	d						14 13								15 14							16 13
Worle	d						14 17			14 55					15 18				15 54			16 17
Yatton	d						14 23			15 01					15 24				16 00			16 23
Nailsea & Backwell	d						14 29			15 07					15 30				16 06			16 29
Parson Street	d						14 37								15 37							16 36
Bedminster	d			←			14 39								15 40							16 39
Bristol Temple Meads 10	a	13 54	14 19	14 15	14 26		14 43			15 18	15 21		15 26		15 44		15 56		16 17	16 24		16 43
	d	14 00	14 23	14 24	14 30	14 38	14 45	14 57	15 00	15 20	15 23	15 30	15 32	15 38	15 45	15 56	16 00	16 04	16 26	16 34	16 38	16 45
Lawrence Hill	d						14 49								15 49			16 08				16 49
Stapleton Road	d						14 51								15 51			16 11				16 51
Filton Abbey Wood	d			14 36		14 46	14a57	15 06		15 35		15a39		15 46	15a57	16 05		16 16	16 35		16 46	16a57
Bristol Parkway 7	a	14 08	14 31		14 38	14 50			15 08		15 32		15 41	15 50			16 08	16 21		16 42	16 50	
	d					14 51								15 51							16 51	
Yate	d					15 00								16 00							17 00	
Cam & Dursley	d					15 13								16 12							17 12	
Gloucester 7	a					15 30								16 29							17 33	
Cardiff Central 7	a			15 22				15 44		16 22						16 44			17 18			

		GW	GW	XC	GW	GW	GW	XC	GW	GW	GW	GW	XC	GW	GW	XC	GW	GW	GW	GW	XC	GW	XC
		■	◇	◇1		◇	◇1	◇1	◇		■	◇	◇1	◇1	◇	◇1			■	◇	◇1	◇	◇1
							A																
				⌶			⌶	⌶					⌶	⌶		⌶					⌶		⌶
Taunton	d		16 10	16 25				16 53				17 10	17 22			17 53				18 08	18 25		18 53
Bridgwater	d		16 21									17 21								18 19			
Highbridge & Burnham	d		16 28									17 28								18 26			
Weston-super-Mare	a		16 38									17 38								18 38			
	d		16 43				17 04			17 10		17 46		18 03				18 10		18 46			
Weston Milton	d		16 46							17 13		17 49						18 13		18 50			
Worle	d		16 50							17 17		17 53						18 17		18 54			
Yatton	d		16 56							17 23		17 59						18 23		19 00			
Nailsea & Backwell	d		17 02							17 29		18 05						18 29		19 06			
Parson Street	d		17 10							17 37		18 13						18 36		19 14			
Bedminster	d		17 13			←				17 39		18 16			←			18 39		19 17		←	
Bristol Temple Meads 10	a		17 17	16 57		17 17	17 23	17 28		17 43		18 20	17 56	18 21	18 20	18 25		18 43		19 21	18 56	19 21	19 26
	d	16 57	17 24	17 00	17 06	17 24	17 25	17 34	17 38	17 45	17 56	18 24	18 00	18 23	18 24	18 34	18 41	18 45	18 56	19 23	19 00	19 23	19 34
Lawrence Hill	d		→		17 09					17 49		→			18 27			18 49		→		19 26	
Stapleton Road	d				17 12					17 51					18 29			18 51				19 29	
Filton Abbey Wood	d	17 07			17 18	17 32			17 46	17 57	18 04				18 38		18 51	18 57	19 04			19 37	
Bristol Parkway 7	a			17 08	17 22		17 34	17 42	17 50	18 03			18 08	18 32		18 42	18 56	19 01			19 08		19 42
	d								17 51								18 56						
Yate	d								18 00								19 05						
Cam & Dursley	d								18 12								19 17						
Gloucester 7	a								18 30								19 33						
Cardiff Central 7	a	17 45				18 21					18 46				19 26				19 47			20 25	

		GW	GW	GW	XC	XC	GW	XC	GW	GW	GW	GW	GW	XC	GW	GW	GW	GW	GW	GW	GW	XC
																		FX	FO	FO	FX	
				◇	◇1	◇1	◇	◇1	◇		◇1	◇	◇	◇1	◇			◇1	◇1	◇	◇	◇1
								B														
								⌶			⌶							⌶	⌶			
Taunton	d						19 07	19 53			20 06		20 14	20 27				21 16	21 16			21 22
Bridgwater	d						19 20						20 25									
Highbridge & Burnham	d						19 30						20 33									
Weston-super-Mare	a						19 44				20 26		20 43									
	d		19 10				19 48			20 10	20 28		20 56									
Weston Milton	d		19 13							20 13												
Worle	d		19 18				19 54			20 17			21 02									
Yatton	d		19 24				20 00			20 23			21 08									
Nailsea & Backwell	d		19 30				20 06			20 29			21 14									
Parson Street	d		19 38							20 36												
Bedminster	d		19 40							20 39					←							
Bristol Temple Meads 10	a		19 44				20 18	20 24		20 43	20 45		21 25	20 59	21 25			21 49	21 50			21 53
	d	19 38	19 46	19 57	20 00	20 14	20 20	20 34	20 43	20 45		20 57	21 29	21 01	21 29	21 37	21 45			21 55	21 55	22 00
Lawrence Hill	d	19 41								20 49			→			21 40						
Stapleton Road	d	19 44								20 51						21 43						
Filton Abbey Wood	d	19 49	19 54	20 05		20 21	20 28		20 51	20 57		21 05			21 37	21 49	21 52			22 02	22 03	
Bristol Parkway 7	a	19 54	19 58		20 09			20 42	20 56	21 00				21 09		21 53	21 57					22 08
	d		19 58		20 10					21 01							21 58					
Yate	d		20 07							21 09							22 06					
Cam & Dursley	d		20 19							21 31							22 18					
Gloucester 7	a		20 34		20 38					21 47							22 34					
Cardiff Central 7	a			20 45		21 02	21 29					21 45			22 20					22 46	22 58	

A The Merchant Venturer

B ⌶ to Bristol Temple Meads

For connections to London Paddington refer to Table T125

For full services to Cardiff Central, Cheltenham Spa, Gloucester and Great Malvern refer to Table T123

Table T134-R

Mondays to Fridays

16 December to 15 May

Taunton - Gloucester

		GW	GW	GW	GW	GW	GW	GW	GW	GW	GW
			FO	FX		FX	FO	FO	FX		
		1	◇	◇	◇	◇		◇	◇	◇	
		⌶									
Taunton	d		21 28	21 28	21 44					22 20	22 43
Bridgwater	d		21 39	21 39							22 54
Highbridge & Burnham	d		21 46	21 46							23 01
Weston-super-Mare	a		21 56	21 56	22 06					22 42	23 11
	d	21 39	21 57	21 57	22 08					22 46	23 13
Weston Milton	d	21 43									23 16
Worle	d	21 47	22 02	22 02							23 20
Yatton	d	21 53	22 08	22 08							23 26
Nailsea & Backwell	d	21 59	22 14	22 14							23 32
Parson Street	d	22 06	22 22	22 22							23 39
Bedminster	d	22 09	22 25	22 25							23 42
Bristol Temple Meads 10	a	22 14	22 29	22 29	22 32					23 05	23 47
	d		22 34	22 34		22 45	22 46	22 57	22 57		
Lawrence Hill	d										
Stapleton Road	d										
Filton Abbey Wood	d		22 42	22 42		22 53	22 54	23 04	23 04		
Bristol Parkway 7	a					22 58	22 59				
	d					23 00	23 00				
Yate	d					23 08	23 09				
Cam & Dursley	d					23 20	23 21				
Gloucester 7	a					23 38	23 40				
Cardiff Central 7	a		23 32	23 34				23 45	23 57		

Saturdays

21 December to 16 May

		XC	GW	GW	GW	GW	XC	GW	GW	XC	GW	GW	GW	GW	XC	GW	GW	XC	GW	GW	GW	XC	GW
		◇1		◇	◇1	◇	◇1	◇1	◇	◇1			◇1	◇	◇1	◇1		◇1			◇1	◇1	◇
																A							
		⌶			⌶		⌶	⌶		⌶			⌶		⌶			⌶			⌶	⌶	
Taunton	d			05 18					06 17	06 53			06 57				07 38	07 53			07 57	08 10	
Bridgwater	d			05 29					06 28				07 08				07 49				08 08		
Highbridge & Burnham	d			05 36					06 35				07 15				07 56				08 15		
Weston-super-Mare	a			05 46					06 45				07 25				08 08				08 25		
	d			05 48	06 20				06 47				07 27			07 42	08 09				08 28		
Weston Milton	d			05 51					06 50							07 46	08 13						
Worle	d			05 56	06 26				06 54				07 33			07 51	08 17						
Yatton	d			06 02	06 32				07 00				07 39			07 57	08 23				08 37		
Nailsea & Backwell	d			06 09	06 38				07 06				07 45			08 03	08 29				08 43		
Parson Street	d			06 18					07 14							08 11	08 36						
Bedminster	d			06 21					07 16							08 14	08 39			←			
Bristol Temple Meads 10	a			06 25	06 49				07 20	07 24			07 54			08 17	08 43	08 24		08 43	08 55	08 45	
	d	06 15	06 20	06 28		06 57	07 00	07 05	07 29	07 34	07 39	07 43		07 57	08 00	08 25	08 45	08 34	08 39	08 45		09 00	08 57
Lawrence Hill	d					07 00						07 46					→			08 48		→	
Stapleton Road	d					07 03						07 49								08 51			
Filton Abbey Wood	d		06 27	06 35		07 09		07 14	07 37		07 46	07 55		08 05		08 33			08 46	08 58			09 06
Bristol Parkway 7	a	06 23	06 31				07 08	07 17		07 42	07 51	08 00			08 08			08 42	08 51	09 03			
	d	06 25	06 33					07 25			07 51								08 51				
Yate	d		06 42								08 00								09 00				
Cam & Dursley	d		06 54								08 12								09 12				
Gloucester 7	a	06 53	07 12								08 28								09 28				
Cardiff Central 7	a			07 17		07 49		07 58	08 24					08 44		09 15							09 44

		XC	GW	XC	GW	GW	GW	XC	GW	XC	GW	GW	GW	XC	GW	GW	XC	GW	GW	GW	GW	XC	GW
		◇1	◇	◇1			◇	◇1	◇	◇1	◇		◇	◇1	◇	◇1	◇1	◇		◇	◇	◇1	◇
		⌶		⌶				⌶		⌶				⌶		⌶	⌶					⌶	
Taunton	d			08 53					09 18	09 53					10 20		10 53				11 06	11 19	
Bridgwater	d								09 29						10 31						11 17		
Highbridge & Burnham	d								09 36						10 38						11 24		
Weston-super-Mare	a								09 46						10 48						11 34		
	d		08 48			09 10			09 48			10 10			10 49	11 03			11 10		11 39		
Weston Milton	d					09 13						10 13							11 13				
Worle	d		08 53			09 17			09 53			10 17			10 54				11 17		11 44		
Yatton	d		08 59			09 23			09 59			10 23			11 00				11 23		11 50		
Nailsea & Backwell	d		09 05			09 29			10 05			10 29			11 06				11 29		11 56		
Parson Street	d					09 36						10 36							11 37				
Bedminster	d	←				09 39						10 39							11 39				←
Bristol Temple Meads 10	a	08 45	09 16	09 24		09 43			10 16	10 24		10 43			11 17	11 21	11 25		11 43		12 07	11 51	12 07
	d	09 00	09 29	09 34	09 39	09 45	09 57	10 00	10 25	10 34	10 39	10 45	10 57	11 00	11 28		11 34	11 39	11 45	11 57	12 20	12 00	12 20
Lawrence Hill	d					09 48						10 48							11 48		→		
Stapleton Road	d					09 51						10 51							11 51				
Filton Abbey Wood	d		09 38		09 46	09 57	10 06		10 36		10 46	10 57	11 07		11 38			11 46	11 57	12 05			12 40
Bristol Parkway 7	a	09 08		09 42	09 51	10 02		10 08		10 42	10 51	11 02		11 08			11 42	11 51	12 02			12 08	
	d				09 51						10 51							11 51					
Yate	d				10 00						11 00							12 00					
Cam & Dursley	d				10 12						11 12							12 12					
Gloucester 7	a				10 30						11 28							12 29					
Cardiff Central 7	a		10 23				10 45		11 22				11 45		12 23					12 45			13 23

A 1 from Bristol Temple Meads

For connections to London Paddington refer to Table T125

For full services to Cardiff Central, Cheltenham Spa, Gloucester and Great Malvern refer to Table T123

Table T134-R

Saturdays
21 December to 16 May

Taunton - Gloucester

		XC	GW	GW	GW	XC	GW	XC		GW	GW	GW	GW	XC	GW	XC	GW	GW		GW	XC	GW	XC	GW	GW
		◇1 🛒	◇		◇	◇1 🛒	◇	◇1 🛒		◇		◇	◇	◇1 🛒	◇	◇1 🛒	◇			◇	◇1 🛒	◇	◇1 🛒	◇	
Taunton	d	11 53					12 18	12 53					13 10	13 20		13 53						14 20	14 53		
Bridgwater	d						12 29						13 21									14 31			
Highbridge & Burnham	d						12 36						13 28									14 38			
Weston-super-Mare	a						12 46						13 38									14 48			
	d			12 10			12 48				13 10		13 40					14 12				14 49			15 11
Weston Milton	d			12 13							13 13							14 15							15 14
Worle	d			12 17			12 54				13 17		13 47					14 19				14 54			15 18
Yatton	d			12 23			13 00				13 23		13 53					14 25				15 00			15 24
Nailsea & Backwell	d			12 29			13 06				13 29		13 59					14 31				15 06			15 30
Parson Street	d			12 36							13 37							14 38							15 38
Bedminster	d			12 39							13 39				←			14 41							15 40
Bristol Temple Meads 10	a	12 24		12 43			13 16	13 24			13 43		14 10	13 55	14 10	14 26		14 45				15 17	15 25		15 44
	d	12 35	12 39	12 45	12 57	13 00	13 31	13 35		13 39	13 47	13 57	14 24	14 00	14 24	14 34	14 39	14 47		14 57	15 00	15 28	15 34	15 39	15 46
Lawrence Hill	d			12 48							13 50		→					14 50							15 50
Stapleton Road	d			12 51							13 53							14 53							15 52
Filton Abbey Wood	d		12 46	12 57	13 07		13 42			13 46	13 58	14 05			14 31		14 46	14 59		15 07		15 38		15 46	15 58
Bristol Parkway 7	a	12 43	12 51	13 02		13 08		13 44		13 51	14 03			14 08		14 42	14 51	15 04			15 08		15 42	15 51	16 03
	d		12 51							13 51							14 51							15 51	
Yate	d		13 00							14 00							15 00							16 00	
Cam & Dursley	d		13 12							14 12							15 12							16 12	
Gloucester 7	a		13 28							14 30							15 28							16 28	
Cardiff Central 7	a				13 45		14 23					14 45			15 25					15 46		16 23			

		GW	XC	GW		XC	GW	GW	GW	XC	GW	XC	GW	GW		GW	XC	GW	XC	GW	GW	GW	XC	GW	
		◇	◇1 🛒	◇		◇1 🛒			◇	◇1 🛒	◇	◇1 🛒	◇			◇	◇1 🛒	◇	◇1 🛒			◇	◇1 🛒	◇	
Taunton	d		15 06	15 18		15 53					16 18	16 53					17 12	17 18	17 53					18 18	
Bridgwater	d			15 29							16 29							17 29						18 29	
Highbridge & Burnham	d			15 36							16 36							17 36						18 36	
Weston-super-Mare	a		15 26	15 46							16 46							17 46						18 47	
	d		15 27	15 48				16 11			16 48			17 10				17 48			18 10			18 48	
Weston Milton	d							16 14						17 13							18 13				
Worle	d			15 53				16 18			16 53			17 17				17 54			18 17			18 53	
Yatton	d			15 59				16 24			16 59			17 23				18 00			18 23			18 59	
Nailsea & Backwell	d			16 05				16 30			17 05			17 29				18 06			18 29			19 05	
Parson Street	d							16 37			17 14			17 37							18 37				
Bedminster	d							16 40						17 40							18 39				
Bristol Temple Meads 10	a		15 47	16 16		16 24		16 44			17 19	17 26		17 44			17 47	18 15	18 26		18 43			19 16	
	d	15 57	16 00	16 28		16 34	16 39	16 45	16 57	17 00	17 28	17 34	17 39	17 45		17 57	18 00	18 32	18 34	18 39	18 45	18 57	19 00	19 25	
Lawrence Hill	d							16 49						17 49							18 48			19 29	
Stapleton Road	d							16 52						17 51							18 51			19 32	
Filton Abbey Wood	d	16 05		16 38			16 46	16 58	17 07		17 38		17 46	17 57		18 06		18 40		18 46	18 59	19 06		19 40	
Bristol Parkway 7	a		16 08			16 42	16 51	17 03		17 08		17 42	17 51	18 03			18 08		18 42	18 51	19 04		19 08		
	d						16 51						17 51							18 51					
Yate	d						17 00						18 00							19 00					
Cam & Dursley	d						17 12						18 12							19 12					
Gloucester 7	a						17 28						18 30							19 28					
Cardiff Central 7	a	16 46		17 23					17 46		18 23					18 46		19 20				19 47		20 25	

		XC	GW	GW	GW	XC	GW	XC	GW	GW		GW	XC	GW	GW	GW	GW	GW	GW	GW		GW	GW	GW	
		◇1 🛒			◇	◇1		◇1	◇			1	◇1 A 🛒		◇1 🛒	◇	◇	◇1 🛒	◇				◇1 🛒	◇	
Taunton	d	18 53					19 10		19 30			19 37	19 53				20 17	21 20				21 25	21 40		
Bridgwater	d						19 21					19 48					20 28					21 36	21 51		
Highbridge & Burnham	d						19 28					19 55					20 35					21 43	21 58		
Weston-super-Mare	a						19 38		19 54			20 05					20 47					21 53	22 08		
	d			19 10			19 42		19 55			20 07			20 27		20 49					21 54	22 10		
Weston Milton	d			19 13								20 12					20 52					21 57			
Worle	d			19 17			19 48					20 17					20 56					22 01	22 16		
Yatton	d			19 23			19 54					20 23			20 37		21 02					22 07	22 22		
Nailsea & Backwell	d			19 29			20 00					20 29					21 08					22 13	22 28		
Parson Street	d			19 37													21 16					22 21			
Bedminster	d			19 39										←			21 19					22 24			
Bristol Temple Meads 10	a	19 29		19 43			20 12		20 16			20 42	20 24		20 50		21 22	21 50				22 29	22 37		
	d	19 32	19 39	19 45	19 57	20 00		20 14		20 39			20 30	20 39		20 57	21 29		22 00	22 06				22 55	
Lawrence Hill	d			19 48						→															
Stapleton Road	d			19 51																					
Filton Abbey Wood	d		19 46	19 57	20 05			20 21						20 46		21 06	21 36		22 08	22 14				23 02	
Bristol Parkway 7	a	19 40	19 51	20 02		20 08							20 38	20 50						22 17					
	d		19 51											20 51						22 19					
Yate	d		20 00											21 00						22 27					
Cam & Dursley	d		20 12											21 12						22 39					
Gloucester 7	a		20 29											21 32						22 55					
Cardiff Central 7	a				20 46			21 00								21 46	22 31		23 00					23 55	

A 🛒 to Bristol Temple Meads

For connections to London Paddington refer to Table T125

For full services to Cardiff Central, Cheltenham Spa, Gloucester and Great Malvern refer to Table T123

NRT DECEMBER 19 EDITION

Table T134-R

Sundays
15 December to 10 May

Taunton - Gloucester

		GW	GW	XC	GW	GW		GW	GW	GW	XC	GW	GW	XC	GW	GW		GW	GW	XC	GW	XC	XC	GW	GW
		◇	◇1 🛒	◇1 🛒		◇ A			◇ B	◇1 🛒	◇1 🛒	◇	◇	◇1 🛒		◇1 🛒		■		◇1 🛒	◇	◇1 🛒	◇1 🛒		◇1 🛒
Taunton	d							08 28					10 12	10 53					11 36	11 53		12 00	12 53		
Bridgwater	d							08 39					10 23						11 47						
Highbridge & Burnham	d							08 46					10 30						11 54						
Weston-super-Mare	a							08 56					10 40						12 04			12 20			
	d		08 26					08 59		09 55			10 43			11 32			12 09			12 22			13 25
Weston Milton	d							09 02					10 46						12 12						
Worle	d		08 32					09 06		10 01			10 50						12 16						13 31
Yatton	d		08 38					09 12		10 07			10 56						12 22						13 37
Nailsea & Backwell	d		08 44					09 18		10 13			11 02						12 28						13 43
Parson Street	d							09 27					11 10						12 37						
Bedminster	d							09 30					11 13						12 39						
Bristol Temple Meads 10	a		08 54					09 33		10 20			11 16	11 24		11 50			12 42	12 24		12 48	13 24		13 53
	d	08 43		09 15	09 20	09 44		09 47	09 50		10 29	10 43		11 29	11 38			11 54		12 29	12 54	13 00	13 29	13 38	
Lawrence Hill	d							09 50																	
Stapleton Road	d							09a52																	
Filton Abbey Wood	d	08 50			09 25	09 55			09 58			10 50			11 43			12 03			13 01			13 43	
Bristol Parkway 7	a			09 23	09 29						10 37			11 37	11 47					12 37		13 08	13 37	13 47	
	d			09 24	09 29										11 48									13 48	
Yate	d				09 39										11 58									13 59	
Cam & Dursley	d				09 51										12 11									14 11	
Gloucester 7	a			09 52	10 09										12 28									14 28	
Cardiff Central 7	a	09 40				10 35			10 38			11 28						12 45			13 41				

		GW		XC	GW	GW	XC	GW	XC	XC	GW	GW		GW	XC	GW	GW	XC	GW	XC	GW	GW		XC	GW
		◇		◇1 🛒	◇		◇1 🛒	◇	◇1 🛒	◇1 🛒		◇1 🛒		◇	◇1 🛒	◇		◇1 🛒	◇	◇1 🛒		◇1 🛒		◇1 🛒	
Taunton	d			13 26		13 37	13 53			14 53							15 19	15 53		16 00	16 08	16 16		16 53	
Bridgwater	d					13 48											15 30				16 19				
Highbridge & Burnham	d					13 55											15 37				16 27				
Weston-super-Mare	a					14 05											15 46			16 20	16 37				
	d					14 07						15 26					15 49			16 30	16 38				
Weston Milton	d					14 10											15 52				16 41				
Worle	d					14 17						15 32					15 56				16 45				
Yatton	d					14 23						15 38					16 02				16 51				
Nailsea & Backwell	d					14 29						15 44					16 08				16 57				
Parson Street	d					14 37															17 05				
Bedminster	d					14 40															17 07				
Bristol Temple Meads 10	a			13 57		14 44	14 26			15 24		15 54					16 20	16 26		16 47	17 12	16 53		17 26	
	d	13 54		14 00	14 16		14 29	14 54	15 00	15 29	15 38			15 57	16 00	16 13	16 23	16 29	16 50	17 00	17 23			17 29	17 38
Lawrence Hill	d																16 26				17 26				
Stapleton Road	d																16a28				17a28				
Filton Abbey Wood	d	14 00			14 23			15 01			15 43			16 05		16 20			17 03						17 43
Bristol Parkway 7	a			14 08			14 37		15 08	15 37	15 47				16 08			16 37		17 08				17 37	17 47
	d										15 48														17 47
Yate	d										15 59														17 58
Cam & Dursley	d										16 11														18 11
Gloucester 7	a										16 29														18 27
Cardiff Central 7	a	14 42			15 01			15 42						16 44		16 58			17 45						

		GW	GW	GW	XC	GW	XC	GW		GW	XC	GW	XC	GW	GW	XC	XC	GW		GW	GW	GW	GW	GW	XC	GW	GW	GW	GW	GW
		◇	■	◇1 🛒	◇1 🛒		◇1 🛒	◇			◇1 🛒	◇	◇1 🛒	◇	◇1 🛒	◇1 C 🛒	◇1 C 🛒			1	◇	◇1 🛒	◇		◇1	◇1 🛒		◇		
Taunton	d			17 03		17 19	17 53					18 38	18 53		18 58	19 24	19 53							20 54		21 42			22 17	
Bridgwater	d			17 15		17 29									19 08									21 05					22 28	
Highbridge & Burnham	d			17 22		17 36									19 15									21 12					22 35	
Weston-super-Mare	a			17 31		17 46									19 25									21 21					22 44	
	d	17 09		17 33		17 49				18 16					19 26					20 15		21 05		21 28					22 46	23 49
Weston Milton	d	17 12								18 19														21 31					22 49	23 52
Worle	d	17 17				17 54				18 24					19 32					20 21				21 35					22 53	23 56
Yatton	d	17 23		17 42		18 00				18 30					19 38					20 27				21 41					22 59	00 02
Nailsea & Backwell	d	17 29		17 48		18 06				18 36					19 44					20 33				21 47					23 05	00 08
Parson Street	d	17 37								18 43														21 54					23 13	00 16
Bedminster	d	17 39								18 46														21 57					23 15	00 19
Bristol Temple Meads 10	a	17 43		17 59		18 17	18 26			18 50		19 16	19 24		19 53	19 57	20 26			20 44		21 19		22 01		22 13			23 19	00 23
	d		17 54		18 00		18 29	18 54		18 55	19 00		19 31	19 42		20 00	20 29	20 37			20 45		21 45		22 10		22 30	22 44		
Lawrence Hill	d									18 55																				
Stapleton Road	d									18a57																				
Filton Abbey Wood	d		18 01					19 01						19 50				20 42			20 52		21 51				22 35	22 51		
Bristol Parkway 7	a				18 08		18 37				19 08		19 39			20 08	20 37	20 46							22 18		22 39			
	d																	20 46									22 39			
Yate	d																	20 57									22 49			
Cam & Dursley	d																	21 10									23 02			
Gloucester 7	a																	21 28									23 19			
Cardiff Central 7	a		18 43					19 43						20 29							21 31		22 33					23 29		

A from 12 January

B until 5 January

C 🛒 to Bristol Temple Meads

For connections to London Paddington refer to Table T125

For full services to Cardiff Central, Cheltenham Spa, Gloucester and Great Malvern refer to Table T123

Table T135-F

Mondays to Fridays

16 December to 15 May

London and Birmingham - Devon and Cornwall

Miles	Miles	Miles			GW MX ◇1 A ⊼	GW MX ◇ B	GW MX 1 C	GW MO 1 D	GW	GW	XC MO ◇1 ⊼	GW MX	GW MO	GW 1 ⊼	GW	XC MX ◇1 ⊼	GW MX	GW MO 1 A	GW ◇1 ⊼	GW	GW	GW ◇	GW
0	—	—	**London Paddington** 15 ⊖	d																			
18½	—	—	Slough 3	d																			
36	—	—	**Reading** 7	d			00u49	00u51															
41¼	—	—	Theale	d																			
49½	—	—	Thatcham	d																			
53	—	—	Newbury	d																			
61½	—	—	Hungerford	d																			
75¼	—	—	Pewsey	d																			
95½	—	—	Westbury 123	d																			
101¼	—	—	Frome 123	d																			
115¾	—	—	Castle Cary 123	d																			
—	0	—	**Birmingham New Street** 12	d																			
—	—	—	Cardiff Central 7	d																			
—	—	—	Newport (South Wales)	d																			
—	—	—	Swindon	d																			
—	87	—	Bristol Parkway 7	d																			
—	88¼	—	Filton Abbey Wood	d																			
—	—	—	Bath Spa 7	d																			
—	92½	—	**Bristol Temple Meads** 10	d																		05 26	
—	112¾	—	Weston-super-Mare	d																		05 50	
—	126½	—	Bridgwater	d																		06 09	
143	138½	—	Taunton	d			02 38															06 21	
157¾	—	—	Tiverton Parkway	d																		06 35	
173¾	—	—	**Exeter St Davids** 6	a			03 08	03 23														06 50	
—	—	—	Exmouth	d																			
—	—	—	Exeter Central	d																			
—	—	—	**Exeter St Davids** 6	d			04 11	04 36	04 58	05 30					05 58					06 27	06 31	06 54	
174¾	—	—	Exeter St Thomas	d					05 01						06 01						06 34	06 57	
182¼	—	—	Starcross	d					05 10						06 11						06 44	07 05	
184¼	—	—	Dawlish Warren	d					05 15						06 16						06 49	07 10	
185¾	—	—	Dawlish	d					05 19	05 45					06 20					06 40	06 53	07 14	
188¾	—	—	Teignmouth	d					05 24	05 50					06 25					06 45	06 58	07 19	
193¾	—	0	Newton Abbot	a			04 31	04 56	05 31	05 57					06 32					06 51	07 05	07 25	
—	—	—		d			04 32	04 57	05 31	05 58				06 20	06 34					06 54	07 06	07 26	
—	—	5¼	Torre	d					05 40	06 08					06 44						07 16		
—	—	6	Torquay	d					05 43	06 11				06 31	06 47						07 19		
—	—	8¾	Paignton	a					05 49	06 17				06 36	06 53						07 25		
202½	—	—	Totnes	d	00 05															07 07		07 39	
214	—	—	Ivybridge	d														←		07 22		07 55	
225¾	—	—	**Plymouth**	a	00 31		05s11	05s36										05s36		07 37		08 11	
—	—	—		d							06 00	06 00	06 17			06 22	06 41		07 14	07 41		08 17	
227	—	—	Devonport	d				→											07 18			08 21	
227½	—	—	Dockyard	d																			
228	—	—	Keyham	d																			
228¾	—	—	St Budeaux Ferry Road	d																			
230	—	—	Saltash	d									06 26				06 50		07 25	07 51		08 27	
235	—	—	St Germans	d									06 32				06 56		07 31	07 58		08 34	
240¼	—	—	Menheniot	d															07x39				
243¾	—	—	Liskeard 6	d			06s05				06 23	06 24	06 44			06 45	07 08	07s04	07 46	08 13		08 45	
252½	—	—	Bodmin Parkway	d			06s19				06 35	06 36	06 56			06 58	07 19	07s18	07 58	08 25		08 57	
256	—	—	Lostwithiel	d			06s26				06 40	06 42	07 01			07 04	07 24	07s25	08 03	08 30		09 02	
260¾	—	—	Par	d			06s34				06 46	06 49	07 08			07 11	07 31	07s34	08 10	08 37		09 09	09 21
—	—	—	Newquay	a																			10 13
265	—	—	St Austell	d			06s43				06 53	06 56	07 15			07 19	07 38	07s42	08 17	08 45		09 16	
279½	—	—	Truro	d			07s03				07 09	07 13	07 33			07 36	07 55	08s01	08 34	09 02		09 33	
288½	—	—	Redruth	d		00 09	07s17				07 20	07 30	07 45			07 48	08 07	08s15	08 45	09 14		09 45	
292	—	—	Camborne	d		00 15	07s24				07 27	07 37	07 51			07 54	08 13	08s23	08 52	09 20		09 51	
298	—	—	Hayle	d		00 23	07s34				07 35	07 46	07 59			08 03	08 21	08s32	09 00	09 28		09 59	
299½	—	—	St Erth	d		00 26	07s39				07 39	07 49	08 02			08 07	08 25	08s38	09 04	09 31		10 02	
305¾	—	—	**Penzance**	a		00 35	07 50				07 47	08 00	08 11			08 17	08 34	08 49	09 13	09 40		10 11	

A From London Paddington
B From Plymouth
C From London Paddington. The Night Riviera
D From London Paddington to Penzance

For connections from Heathrow Airport, Gatwick Airport and Oxford refer to Tables T148 and T116. Table T116 includes services to/from Bedwyn.

For the complete service between Westbury and Castle Cary refer to Table T123

Table T135-F

Mondays to Fridays

16 December to 15 May

London and Birmingham - Devon and Cornwall

		GW	GW ◇1 ⊼	GW A	XC ◇1	GW B	GW ◇	GW A	GW ◇	GW B	GW	GW ◇1 ⊼	GW	XC ◇1 ⊼	GW ◇	GW	GW ◇1 C ⊼	GW A	XC ◇1 D ⊼	GW B	GW A	GW ◇1 ⊼	GW B
London Paddington 15 ⊖	d											06 37					07 04					08 04	
Slough 3	d																						
Reading 7	d											07 03					07 29					08 29	
Theale	d																						
Thatcham	d																						
Newbury	d																07 44						
Hungerford	d																						
Pewsey	d																08 03						
Westbury 123	d																08 21						
Frome 123	d																						
Castle Cary 123	d																08 41						
Birmingham New Street 12	d													06 42					07 12				
Cardiff Central 7	d																						
Newport (South Wales)	d																						
Swindon	d																						
Bristol Parkway 7	d													07 55					08 27				
Filton Abbey Wood	d																						
Bath Spa 7	d																						
Bristol Temple Meads 10	d				06 40				06 44					08 12					08 45				
Weston-super-Mare	d								07 09														
Bridgwater	d								07 27														
Taunton	d				07 11				07 39			08 18		08 43			09 03		09 17			09 44	
Tiverton Parkway	d				07 23				07 53					08 55			09 16		09 30				
Exeter St Davids 6	a				07 37				08 08			08 40		09 09			09 29		09 44			10 07	
Exmouth	d	06 16		06 55				07 24			07 54		08 24					08 54			09 24		
Exeter Central	d	06 51		07 24				07 53			08 24		08 53					09 23			09 52		
Exeter St Davids 6	d	07 04	07 25	07 30	07 43			08 00	08 10		08 32	08 43	09 00	09 12		09 25	09 31	09 37	09 48		10 00	10 10	
Exeter St Thomas	d			07 33				08 03			08 35							09 40					
Starcross	d			07 43		←		08 13		←	08 44							09 49		←			
Dawlish Warren	d			07 54		07 54		08 25		08 25	08 55							10 00		10 00			
Dawlish	d	07 19	07 37	→		07 58		→		08 29	08 59		09 13			09 38	09 44	→		10 04	10 13		
Teignmouth	d	07 24	07 42			08 03				08 34	09 04		09 18			09 43	09 49			10 09	10 18		←
Newton Abbot	a	07 31	07 49		08 01	08 10			08 31	08 41	09 11		09 25	09 30		09 49	09 55		10 06	10 16	10 25	10 29	10 25
	d	07 37	07 50		08 02	08 10			08 33	08 41	09 11		09 25	09 35		09 50	09 57		10 07	10 17	10 39	10 31	10 39
Torre	d	07 45				08 21				08 50	09 20		09 34				10 06			10 25	→		10 47
Torquay	d	07 48				08 24				08 53	09 23		09 37	09 46			10 10			10 28			10 50
Paignton	a	07 54				08 30				08 59	09 29		09 43	09 54			10 15			10 34			10 56
Totnes	d		08 02		08 14				08 46							10 03			10 19			10 42	
Ivybridge	d		08 17						09 02							10 18							
Plymouth	a		08 31		08 40				09 16			09 34				10 32			10 45			11 08	
	d						08 47		09 21			09 46			10 17	10 40						11 17	
Devonport	d																						
Dockyard	d																						
Keyham	d																						
St Budeaux Ferry Road	d															10 47							
Saltash	d						08 56		09 30			09 55			10 28	10 52							
St Germans	d						09 02		09 37			10 02			10 34	10 59							
Menheniot	d																						
Liskeard 6	d						09 14		09 48			10 14			10 46	11 14						11 42	
Bodmin Parkway	d						09 26		10 00			10 26			10 58	11 25						11 54	
Lostwithiel	d						09 31		10 05			10 31			11 03	11 30							
Par	d						09 38		10 12						11 10	11 37						12 04	
Newquay	a																						
St Austell	d						09 45		10 19			10 43			11 17	11 44						12 12	
Truro	d						10 02		10 36			11 01			11 34	12 01						12 29	
Redruth	d						10 14		10 48			11 13			11 46	12 13						12 41	
Camborne	d						10 20		10 54			11 19			11 52	12 19						12 48	
Hayle	d						10 28		11 02			11 27			12 00	12 27							
St Erth	d						10 31		11 05			11 32			12 03	12 31						12 59	
Penzance	a						10 40		11 14			11 41			12 12	12 40						13 08	

A To Paignton
B From Exmouth
C The Devon Express
D From Derby

For connections from Heathrow Airport, Gatwick Airport and Oxford refer to Tables T148 and T116. Table T116 includes services to/from Bedwyn.

For the complete service between Westbury and Castle Cary refer to Table T123

Table T135-F

Mondays to Fridays

16 December to 15 May

London and Birmingham - Devon and Cornwall

		GW	GW	GW	XC	GW	GW	GW	GW	GW	XC	GW	GW	GW	GW	GW	XC	GW	GW	GW	XC	GW	GW
		◇	◇		◇1 A ✠		◇1 ✠				◇1 B ✠	◇1 ✠	◇1 C ✠	D	■ 1 E ✠	F	◇1 G ✠	◇	◇	D	◇1 H ✠	F	◇1 ✠
London Paddington 15 ⊖	d						09 04					09 02	09 37		10 04								10 35
Slough 3	d																						
Reading 7	d						09 29					09 27	10 02		10u29								11 01
Theale	d																						
Thatcham	d																						
Newbury	d												10 17										11 16
Hungerford	d																						
Pewsey	d												10 38										11 35
Westbury 123	d												10 56										11 54
Frome 123	d																						
Castle Cary 123	d												11 16										12 14
Birmingham New Street 12	d				08 12						09 12						09 42				10 12		
Cardiff Central 7	d		08 00																				
Newport (South Wales)	d		08 14																				
Swindon	d											09 59											
Bristol Parkway 7	d				09 30						10 22						10 59				11 21		
Filton Abbey Wood	d		08 44																				
Bath Spa 7	d											10 26											
Bristol Temple Meads 10	d		08 55		09 45						10 45	10 49					11 15				11 45		
Weston-super-Mare	d		09 23									11 09					11 40						
Bridgwater	d		09 42																				
Taunton	d		09 54		10 18		10 48				11 18	11 29	11 37		11 46		12 00				12 18		12 35
Tiverton Parkway	d		10 08		10 31		11 00				11 31		11 49		11 58		12 12				12 30		
Exeter St Davids 6	a		10 23		10 45		11 13				11 45	11 53	12 02		12 11		12 26				12 44		12 59
Exmouth	d			09 57		10 23				10 57				11 23						11 57			
Exeter Central	d			10 21		10 51				11 21				11 57						12 21			
Exeter St Davids 6	d		10 25	10 29	10 49	11 00	11 16		11 26	11 30	11 48		12 05	12 09	12 15		12 28			12 32	12 48		
Exeter St Thomas	d			10 32						11 33										12 35			
Starcross	d			10 41						11 42						←				12 46		←	
Dawlish Warren	d			10 46						11 47				12 26		12 26				12 59		12 59	
Dawlish	d			10 50		11 13				11 51			12 17	→		12 30	12 40			→		13 03	
Teignmouth	d			10 55		11 18				11 56			12 22			12 35	12 45					13 08	
Newton Abbot	a		10 45	11 02	11 08	11 25	11 35		11 46	12 03	12 07		12 29		12 34	12 42	12 51				13 06	13 16	
	d		10 46	11 05	11 09	11 26	11 36		11 47	12 05	12 08		12 30		12 35	12 43	12 52				13 08	13 16	
Torre	d			11 15		11 34				12 15			12 39			12 51						13 25	
Torquay	d			11 18		11 37				12 18			12 43			12 54	13 03					13 28	
Paignton	a			11 24		11 43				12 24			12 49			13 00	13 08					13 34	
Totnes	d		11 00		11 21		11 48		12 00		12 21				12 47						13 20		
Ivybridge	d		11 15						12 16														
Plymouth	a		11 29		11 48		12 14		12 30		12 47				13 11						13 46		
	d		11 46					12 17	12 47						13 20				13 46				
Devonport	d																						
Dockyard	d																						
Keyham	d																						
St Budeaux Ferry Road	d																						
Saltash	d		11 55					12 26	12 56										13 56				
St Germans	d		12 01					12 32	13 03										14 03				
Menheniot	d																		14x11				
Liskeard 6	d		12 13					12 44	13 14						13 44				14 17				
Bodmin Parkway	d		12 24					12 56	13 26						13 57				14 28				
Lostwithiel	d		12 29					13 01	13 31										14 33				
Par	d	12 13	12 36					13 08	13 38						14 07			14 15	14 40				
Newquay	a	13 05																15 07					
St Austell	d		12 43					13 15	13 45						14 14				14 47				
Truro	d		13 00					13 32	14 02						14 32				15 03				
Redruth	d		13 12					13 44	14 14						14 44				15 15				
Camborne	d		13 18					13 50	14 20						14 51				15 21				
Hayle	d		13 26					13 58	14 28										15 29				
St Erth	d		13 30					14 01	14 31						15 01				15 33				
Penzance	a		13 39					14 10	14 40						15 10				15 42				

A From Leeds
B From York
C The Torbay Express
D To Paignton
E The Cornish Riviera
F From Exmouth
G From Manchester Piccadilly
H From Newcastle

For connections from Heathrow Airport, Gatwick Airport and Oxford refer to Tables T148 and T116. Table T116 includes services to/from Bedwyn.

For the complete service between Westbury and Castle Cary refer to Table T123

Table T135-F

Mondays to Fridays

16 December to 15 May

London and Birmingham - Devon and Cornwall

		GW	GW	GW	GW	GW	XC	GW	XC	GW	GW	GW	GW	XC	GW	GW	GW	GW	GW	GW	XC	GW
			◇1 A ✠	◇	◇		◇1 B ✠		◇1 C ✠	■ 1 D ✕✠	◇			◇1 E ✠	◇	◇1 ✠		◇1 ✕	◇		◇1 F ✠	
London Paddington 15 ⊖	d		11 04							12 04						12 36		13 04				
Slough 3	d																					
Reading 7	d		11 29							12u29						13 01		13u29				
Theale	d																					
Thatcham	d																					
Newbury	d															13 16						
Hungerford	d																					
Pewsey	d															13 35						
Westbury 123	d															13 53						
Frome 123	d																					
Castle Cary 123	d															14 14						
Birmingham New Street 12	d						11 12		11 42					12 12							13 12	
Cardiff Central 7	d																		13 00			
Newport (South Wales)	d																		13 14			
Swindon	d																					
Bristol Parkway 7	d						12 22		12 55					13 21							14 23	
Filton Abbey Wood	d																		13 44			
Bath Spa 7	d																					
Bristol Temple Meads 10	d						12 45		13 10					13 45					13 55		14 45	
Weston-super-Mare	d																		14 23			
Bridgwater	d																		14 42			
Taunton	d		12 46				13 18		13 42	13 47				14 18		14 36		14 45	14 54		15 18	
Tiverton Parkway	d		12 58				13 31		13 54					14 31				14 58	15 08		15 31	
Exeter St Davids 6	a		13 12				13 45		14 08	14 12				14 45		14 59		15 12	15 23		15 45	
Exmouth	d	12 23				12 57		13 23				13 57					14 23			14 57		
Exeter Central	d	12 51				13 21		13 51				14 21					14 51			15 21		
Exeter St Davids 6	d	13 00	13 14		13 18	13 29	13 49	14 00		14 14		14 29		14 48			15 00	15 13	15 25	15 29	15 48	
Exeter St Thomas	d					13 32						14 32								15 32		
Starcross	d					13 41						14 40								15 41		
Dawlish Warren	d					13 46						14 45								15 46		
Dawlish	d	13 13				13 50		14 13				14 49					15 13			15 50		
Teignmouth	d	13 18				13 55		14 18				14 54					15 18			15 55		
Newton Abbot	a	13 25	13 33		13 38	14 02	14 08	14 25		14 33		15 01		15 07			15 25	15 32	15 45	16 02	16 07	
	d	13 26	13 34		13 39	14 04	14 09	14 26		14 34		15 04		15 08			15 26	15 34	15 46	16 03	16 08	
Torre	d	13 35				14 14		14 35				15 13					15 34			16 12		
Torquay	d	13 38				14 17		14 38				15 16					15 37			16 15		
Paignton	a	13 44				14 24		14 44				15 22					15 43			16 21		
Totnes	d		13 46		13 53		14 21			14 46				15 21				15 45	15 59		16 21	
Ivybridge	d				14 09														16 15			
Plymouth	a		14 12		14 23		14 48			15 10				15 47				16 12	16 29		16 47	
	d			14 17	14 46					15 19			15 46		15 55				16 47			17 00
Devonport	d														16 00							17 04
Dockyard	d														16x02							17x04
Keyham	d														16 06							17 08
St Budeaux Ferry Road	d														16 10							17 10
Saltash	d			14 26	14 55								15 55		16 15				16 56			17 15
St Germans	d			14 32	15 01								16 01		16 23				17 03			17 22
Menheniot	d														16x30							17x29
Liskeard 6	d			14 44	15 14					15 43			16 14		16 39				17 14			17a35
Bodmin Parkway	d			14 56	15 25					15 56			16 26		16 51				17 26			
Lostwithiel	d			15 01	15 30								16 31		16 57				17 31			
Par	d			15 08	15 37					16 06	16 15		16 38		17 05				17 38			
Newquay	a										17 07											
St Austell	d			15 15	15 44					16 13			16 45		17 13				17 45			
Truro	d			15 32	16 01					16 31			17 02		17 32				18 02			
Redruth	d			15 44	16 13					16 43			17 14		17 44				18 14			
Camborne	d			15 50	16 19					16 50			17 20		17 50				18 20			
Hayle	d			15 58	16 27								17 28		17 58				18 28			
St Erth	d			16 01	16 31					17 00			17 31		18 01				18 31			
Penzance	a			16 10	16 40					17 09			17 40		18 10				18 40			

A The Mayflower
B From Edinburgh
C From Manchester Piccadilly
D The Royal Duchy. ✕ to Taunton ✠ from Taunton
E From Glasgow Central
F From Dundee

For connections from Heathrow Airport, Gatwick Airport and Oxford refer to Tables T148 and T116. Table T116 includes services to/from Bedwyn.

For the complete service between Westbury and Castle Cary refer to Table T123

Table T135-F

Mondays to Fridays

16 December to 15 May

London and Birmingham - Devon and Cornwall

Station		GW	XC ◇1 A 🛒	GW ■ 1 🛒	GW ◇	GW ◇	GW B	XC ◇1 C 🛒	GW D	XC ◇1 A 🛒	GW B	GW ◇1 E 🛒	GW D	GW ◇1 🛒	GW	GW B	XC ◇1 F 🛒	GW D	GW B	XC ◇1 G 🛒	GW ◇1 🛒	GW D	GW
London Paddington 15 ⊖	d			14 04								15 04		14 36							16 04		
Slough 3	d																						
Reading 7	d			14u29								15 29		15 01							16 29		
Theale	d																						
Thatcham	d																						
Newbury	d													15 16									
Hungerford	d																						
Pewsey	d													15 35									
Westbury 123	d													15 58									
Frome 123	d																						
Castle Cary 123	d													16 18									
Birmingham New Street 12	d		13 42					14 12		14 42							15 12			15 42			
Cardiff Central 7	d																						
Newport (South Wales)	d																						
Swindon	d																						
Bristol Parkway 7	d		14 55					15 21		15 57							16 23			16 59			
Filton Abbey Wood	d																						
Bath Spa 7	d																						
Bristol Temple Meads 10	d		15 09					15 45		16 09							16 45			17 11			
Weston-super-Mare	d																						
Bridgwater	d																						
Taunton	d		15 41	15 46				16 18		16 43		16 48		16 54			17 18			17 43	17 50		
Tiverton Parkway	d		15 53	15 59				16 31		16 55		17 01					17 30			17 55	18 03		
Exeter St Davids 6	a		16 07	16 13				16 45		17 09		17 15		17 22			17 44			18 09	18 17		
Exmouth	d	15 23					15 55				16 23					16 55			17 24				17 54
Exeter Central	d	15 51					16 23				16 51					17 23			17 52				18 22
Exeter St Davids 6	d	15 57		16 14		16 22	16 34	16 47			16 58	17 16		17 28		17 32	17 46		18 00	18 11	18 20		18 29
Exeter St Thomas	d	16 00					16 37				17 01					17 35			18 03				18 32
Starcross	d	16 09					16 46		←		17 10					17 44		←	18 12			←	18 40
Dawlish Warren	d	16 14					16 58		16 58		17 15					17 57		17 57	18 34			18 34	18 45
Dawlish	d	16 18					→		17 02		17 19					→		18 01	→	18 23		18 38	18 49
Teignmouth	d	16 23							17 07		17 24		←					18 06		18 28		18 43	18 54
Newton Abbot	a	16 30		16 33		16 45		17 05	17 14		17 31	17 35	17 31	17 47			18 04	18 13		18 34	18 39	18 50	19 01
	d	16 30		16 35		16 46		17 07	17 15		17 40	17 37	17 40	17 48			18 06	18 13		18 35	18 41	18 50	19 03
Torre	d	16 39							17 23		→		17 48					18 22				18 59	19 13
Torquay	d	16 42							17 26				17 51					18 25		18 46		19 02	19 17
Paignton	a	16 48							17 32				17 57					18 31		18 51		19 08	19 24
Totnes	d			16 46		16 59		17 19				17 48		18 00			18 18				18 52		
Ivybridge	d					17 15								18 14							19 07		
Plymouth	a			17 12		17 29		17 45				18 13		18 28			18 44				19 20		
	d			17 20		17 46						18 21			18 31		18 51				19 33		
Devonport	d														18 34								
Dockyard	d														18x35								
Keyham	d														18 39								
St Budeaux Ferry Road	d														18 42								
Saltash	d			17 30		17 55									18 46						19 43		
St Germans	d			17 37		18 01									18 53						19 50		
Menheniot	d														19x00								
Liskeard 6	d			17 48		18 14						18 46			19 07		19 17				20 02		
Bodmin Parkway	d			18 02		18 26						18 58			19 20		19 30				20 14		
Lostwithiel	d			18 07		18 31									19 25								
Par	d			18 14	18 23	18 38						19 08			19 32		19 41				20 24		
Newquay	a				19 15																		
St Austell	d			18 22		18 45						19 16			19 39		19 48				20 31		
Truro	d			18 39		19 02						19 33			19 56		20 09				20 48		
Redruth	d			18 51		19 14						19 45			20 08		20 20				20 59		
Camborne	d			18 58		19 20						19 52			20 14		20 26				21 06		
Hayle	d			19 06		19 28									20 22								
St Erth	d			19 14		19 31						20 02			20 25		20 36				21 15		
Penzance	a			19 23		19 40						20 11			20 34		20 45				21 24		

A From Manchester Piccadilly
B To Paignton
C From Glasgow Central
D From Exmouth
E The Cornishman
F From Glasgow Central. 🛒 to Plymouth
G From Manchester Piccadilly. 🛒 to Bristol Temple Meads

For connections from Heathrow Airport, Gatwick Airport and Oxford refer to Tables T148 and T116. Table T116 includes services to/from Bedwyn.

For the complete service between Westbury and Castle Cary refer to Table T123

Table T135-F

Mondays to Fridays

16 December to 15 May

London and Birmingham - Devon and Cornwall

Station		GW ◇	XC ◇1 A 🛒	GW	GW FX ◇1 B 🛒	GW ◇1 C 🛒	XC ◇1 D 🛒	GW ◇1 🛒	XC ◇1 E 🛒	GW	GW F	GW ◇1 G 🛒	GW ■ 1 H ✕🛒	GW ◇1 I 🛒	GW ◇	GW ◇1 🛒	XC ◇1 J 🛒	GW G	GW ◇1 🛒	GW FX ■ 1 K ✕🛒	GW FO ■ 1 K ✕🛒	GW L
London Paddington 15 ⊖	d				16 38	16 38		17 04				17 37	18 04			18 07			18 37	19 04	19 04	
Slough 3	d																					
Reading 7	d				17 03	17 03		17 29				18 04	18 29			18 38			19 05	19 30	19u30	
Theale	d															18 46						
Thatcham	d															18 54						
Newbury	d				17 18	17 18						18 21	18 43			19 00			19 22	19 45	19 45	
Hungerford	d				17 28	17 28										19 11			19 32			
Pewsey	d				17 40	17 40		17 59				18 40				19 26			19 49			
Westbury 123	d				17 59	17 59						18 59				19 57			20 08			
Frome 123	d															20a07						
Castle Cary 123	d				18 19	18 19						19 19							20 28			
Birmingham New Street 12	d		16 12				16 42		17 12								18 12					
Cardiff Central 7	d														18 00							
Newport (South Wales)	d														18 14							
Swindon	d																					
Bristol Parkway 7	d		17 23				17 59		18 24								19 36					
Filton Abbey Wood	d														18 42							
Bath Spa 7	d																					
Bristol Temple Meads 10	d		17 45				18 11		18 45						18 55		19 47					
Weston-super-Mare	d														19 29							
Bridgwater	d														19 48							
Taunton	d		18 18		18 41	18 41	18 45	18 52	19 20			19 41	19 49		20 00		20 19		20 49	20 56	20 56	
Tiverton Parkway	d		18 30				18 59	19 04	19 32			19 53			20 14		20 32		21 02	21 08	21 08	
Exeter St Davids 6	a		18 44		19 04	19 04	19 13	19 18	19 46			20 08	20 11		20 29		20 47		21 16	21 21	21 21	
Exmouth	d			18 24						19 24												
Exeter Central	d			18 53						19 52				←								
Exeter St Davids 6	d		18 47	19 00		19 13		19 26	19 48	20 00		20 19	20 14	20 19	20 40		20 50	20 55	21 17	21 24	21 24	
Exeter St Thomas	d			19 03								→		20 22				20 58				
Starcross	d			19 12										20 31				21 07				
Dawlish Warren	d			19 25										20 36				21 12				
Dawlish	d			19 29						20 13				20 40				21 16				
Teignmouth	d			19 34						20 18				20 45				21 21				←
Newton Abbot	a		19 05	19 41				19 45	20 06	20 25			20 33	20 52	21 00		21 09	21 28	21 36	21 43	21 43	21 28
	d		19 07	19 41				19 46	20 08	20 25			20 35	20 56	21 01		21 10	21 47	21 38	21 44	21 44	21 47
Torre	d			19 50						20 34				21 05				→				21 55
Torquay	d			19 53						20 37				21 09								21 58
Paignton	a			19 59						20 43				21 16								22 04
Totnes	d		19 19					19 58	20 20				20 46		21 14		21 23			21 56	21 56	
Ivybridge	d														21 30							
Plymouth	a		19 45			20 05		20 23	20 46				21 12		21 44		21 51		22 13	22 22	22 23	
	d		19 51					20 32	20 52				21 20		21 47						22 38	
Devonport	d																					
Dockyard	d																					
Keyham	d																					
St Budeaux Ferry Road	d																					
Saltash	d							20 41							21 56						22 47	
St Germans	d							20 48							22 03						22 53	
Menheniot	d																					
Liskeard 6	d		20 14					21 01	21 15				21 45		22 14						23 05	
Bodmin Parkway	d		20 26					21 13	21 27				21 57		22 26						23 17	
Lostwithiel	d							21 18	21 32						22 31						23 22	
Par	d	20 28	20 36					21 24	21 38				22 07		22 38						23 29	
Newquay	a	21 20																				
St Austell	d		20 42					21 32	21 45				22 15		22 45						23 36	
Truro	d		20 59					21 49	22 01				22 32		23 02						23 54	
Redruth	d		21 10					22 01	22 12				22 44		23 14						00 06	
Camborne	d		21 16					22 07	22 19						23 20						00 13	
Hayle	d								22 27						23 28						00 21	
St Erth	d		21 26					22 17	22 31		22 49				23 31						00 24	
Penzance	a		21 35					22 26	22 39		22 59		23 07		23 40						00 34	

A From Aberdeen. 🛒 to Plymouth
B until 2 April
C FO until 27 March, from 3 April
D From Manchester Piccadilly
E From Glasgow Central. 🛒 to Plymouth
F From St Ives
G To Paignton
H The Golden Hind. ✕ to Taunton 🛒 from Taunton
I From London Paddington
J From Edinburgh
K The Armada. ✕ to Taunton 🛒 from Taunton
L From Exeter St Davids

For connections from Heathrow Airport, Gatwick Airport and Oxford refer to Tables T148 and T116. Table T116 includes services to/from Bedwyn.

For the complete service between Westbury and Castle Cary refer to Table T123

Table T135-F

Mondays to Fridays

16 December to 15 May

London and Birmingham - Devon and Cornwall

		XC	GW	GW	XC	GW	XC	GW	GW	GW	GW	GW	GW	GW	GW	GW
			FX									FX	FO	FX	FO	FX
		◇1	◇		◇1	◇1	◇1		◇1	◇	◇	◇1	◇1	■	■	■
		A			B		C							D	E	F
		⚒			⚒	⚒	⚒		⚒			⚒	⚒	🛏	🛏	🛏
London Paddington 15 ⊖	d					20 04			21 04			22 00	22 00	23 45	23 45	
Slough 3	d															
Reading 7	d					20 28			21 29			22 24	22 25	00u49	00u46	
Theale	d															
Thatcham	d															
Newbury	d								21 44							
Hungerford	d															
Pewsey	d					20 59			22 03							
Westbury 123	d					21 17			22 21							
Frome 123	d															
Castle Cary 123	d					21 37			22 41							
Birmingham New Street 12	d	19 12			19 42		20 12									
Cardiff Central 7	d									21 00						
Newport (South Wales)	d									21 14						
Swindon	d											22 57	22 57			
Bristol Parkway 7	d	20 22			20 55		21 27									
Filton Abbey Wood	d									21 41						
Bath Spa 7	d											23 25	23 25			
Bristol Temple Meads 10	d	20 37			21 08		21 44			21 55	23 05	23 47	23 47			
Weston-super-Mare	d									22 29	23 39	00s16	00s16			
Bridgwater	d									22 47	23 57	00s34	00s34			
Taunton	d	21 08			21 45	21 58	22 15		23 04	23 08	00s08	00s45	00s45	02 38	02 38	
Tiverton Parkway	d	21 20			21 57	22 11	22 27		23 17	23 22	00s24	00s58	00s58			
Exeter St Davids 6	a	21 34			22 11	22 25	22 41		23 31	23 37	00 40	01 13	01 13	03 08	03 08	
Exmouth	d															
Exeter Central	d															
Exeter St Davids 6	d	21 36		21 54	22 12	22 26	22 42	22 55	23 33					04 11	04 11	
Exeter St Thomas	d			21 57				22 58								
Starcross	d			22 06				23 07								
Dawlish Warren	d			22 11				23 12								
Dawlish	d			22 15		22 39		23 16								
Teignmouth	d			22 20		22 44		23 21								
Newton Abbot	a	21 54		22 27	22 31	22 50	23 01	23 28	23 52					04 31	04 31	
	d	21 55		22 28	22 32	22 52	23 02	23 28	23 53					04 32	04 33	
Torre	d			22 37				23 37								
Torquay	d			22 40				23 40								
Paignton	a			22 46				23 46								
Totnes	d	22 07			22 44	23 03	23 14		00 05							
Ivybridge	d					23 18										←
Plymouth	a	22 35			23 10	23 32	23 40		00 31					05s11	05s11	05s11
	d		22 38													
Devonport	d													→		
Dockyard	d															
Keyham	d															
St Budeaux Ferry Road	d															
Saltash	d		22 47													
St Germans	d		22 53													
Menheniot	d															
Liskeard 6	d		23 05												06s04	06s05
Bodmin Parkway	d		23 17												06s18	06s19
Lostwithiel	d		23 22												06s25	06s26
Par	d		23 29												06s33	06s34
Newquay	a															
St Austell	d		23 36												06s42	06s43
Truro	d		23 54												07s02	07s03
Redruth	d		00 09												07s17	07s17
Camborne	d		00 15												07s24	07s24
Hayle	d		00 23												07s34	07s34
St Erth	d		00 26												07s38	07s39
Penzance	a		00 35												07 50	07 50

A From Glasgow Central. ⚒ to Bristol Temple Meads
B From Manchester Piccadilly. ⚒ to Bristol Temple Meads
C From Edinburgh. ⚒ to Bristol Temple Meads
D To Penzance. The Night Riviera
E The Night Riviera
F From London Paddington. The Night Riviera

For connections from Heathrow Airport, Gatwick Airport and Oxford refer to Tables T148 and T116. Table T116 includes services to/from Bedwyn.

For the complete service between Westbury and Castle Cary refer to Table T123

NRT DECEMBER 19 EDITION

Table T135-F

Saturdays

21 December to 16 May

London and Birmingham - Devon and Cornwall

		GW	GW	GW	GW	GW	GW	GW	GW	GW	XC	GW	GW	GW	GW	GW	GW	GW	GW	XC	GW	GW	GW
			■	■			■																
		◇1	1								◇1				◇			1		◇1			
		A	B	C			D					E							F		G		F
		⚒	⚒	🛏			🛏				⚒												
London Paddington 15 ⊖	d																						
Slough 3	d																						
Reading 7	d			00u46																			
Theale	d																						
Thatcham	d																						
Newbury	d																						
Hungerford	d																						
Pewsey	d																						
Westbury 123	d																						
Frome 123	d																						
Castle Cary 123	d																						
Birmingham New Street 12	d																						
Cardiff Central 7	d																						
Newport (South Wales)	d																						
Swindon	d																						
Bristol Parkway 7	d																						
Filton Abbey Wood	d																						
Bath Spa 7	d																						
Bristol Temple Meads 10	d														05 27					06 07			
Weston-super-Mare	d														05 50								
Bridgwater	d														06 08								
Taunton	d			02 38											06 22					07 14			
Tiverton Parkway	d														06 36					07 26			
Exeter St Davids 6	a			03 08											06 51					07 40			
Exmouth	d																06 15		06 55				07 25
Exeter Central	d																06 44		07 26				07 54
Exeter St Davids 6	d			04 11	04 58				05 30	05 58			06 28	06 32	06 53		07 10	07 25	07 33	07 41			08 00
Exeter St Thomas	d				05 01					06 01				06 35	06 56				07 36				08 03
Starcross	d				05 10					06 10				06 44	07 04				07 45		←		08 12
Dawlish Warren	d				05 15					06 15				06 49	07 09				07 55		07 55		08 25
Dawlish	d				05 19				05 43	06 19			06 41	06 53	07 13		07 23	07 37	→		07 59		→
Teignmouth	d				05 24				05 48	06 24			06 46	06 58	07 18		07 28	07 42			08 04		
Newton Abbot	a			04 31	05 31				05 55	06 31			06 52	07 05	07 24		07 36	07 49		08 00	08 11		
	d			04 33	05 32				05 56	06 35			06 54	07 06	07 25		07 38	07 52		08 01	08 12		
Torre	d				05 40				06 05	06 43				07 15			07 46				08 20		
Torquay	d				05 43				06 08	06 46				07 18			07 49				08 23		
Paignton	a				05 51				06 16	06 54				07 26			07 57				08 31		
Totnes	d	00 05											07 07		07 38			08 04		08 13			
Ivybridge	d						←						07 23		07 54			08 19					
Plymouth	a	00 31		05s11			05s11						07 37		08 08			08 34		08 39			
	d					05 18					06 23		07 40		08 16							08 47	
Devonport	d			→											08 20								
Dockyard	d																						
Keyham	d																						
St Budeaux Ferry Road	d																						
Saltash	d												07 49		08 26							08 56	
St Germans	d												07 55		08 33							09 02	
Menheniot	d																						
Liskeard 6	d					05 42	06s04				06 46		08 07		08 44							09 14	
Bodmin Parkway	d					05 54	06s18				06 58		08 18		08 56							09 26	
Lostwithiel	d					05 59	06s25				07 03		08 23		09 01							09 31	
Par	d					06 10	06s33	06 52			07 09		08 30		09 08	09 25						09 38	
Newquay	a							07 45								10 18							
St Austell	d					06 17	06s42				07 16		08 37		09 15							09 45	
Truro	d					06 35	07s02				07 32		08 54		09 32							10 02	
Redruth	d		00 06			06 47	07s17				07 43		09 06		09 44							10 14	
Camborne	d		00 13			06 53	07s24				07 50		09 12		09 50							10 20	
Hayle	d		00 21			07 01	07s34				07 58		09 20		09 58							10 28	
St Erth	d		00 24			07 06	07s38				08 02	08 17	09 23		10 01							10 31	
Penzance	a		00 34			07 18	07 50				08 10	08 29	09 32		10 10							10 40	

A From London Paddington
B From London Paddington. The Armada
C From London Paddington to Penzance. The Night Riviera
D From London Paddington. The Night Riviera
E From St Ives
F To Paignton
G From Exmouth

For connections from Heathrow Airport, Gatwick Airport and Oxford refer to Tables T148 and T116. Table T116 includes services to/from Bedwyn.

For the complete service between Westbury and Castle Cary refer to Table T123

Saturdays

21 December to 16 May

London and Birmingham - Devon and Cornwall

		GW ◇	GW A	GW B	GW ◇■ 🍴	GW A		GW	XC ◇■ 🍴	GW	GW	GW	XC ◇■ C 🍴	GW B	GW ◇■ 🍴	GW A		GW ◇	GW ◇	GW	XC ◇■ D 🍴	GW	GW ◇■ 🍴	GW ◇■ 🍴	GW
London Paddington 15 ⊖	d														08 03								08 35	09 03	
Slough 3	d																								
Reading 7	d														08 28								09 00	09 28	
Theale	d																								
Thatcham	d																								
Newbury	d																						09 15		
Hungerford	d																								
Pewsey	d																						09 34		
Westbury 123	d																						09 53		
Frome 123	d																								
Castle Cary 123	d																						10 13		
Birmingham New Street 12	d								06 42				07 12								08 12				
Cardiff Central 7	d																		08 00						
Newport (South Wales)	d																		08 14						
Swindon	d																								
Bristol Parkway 7	d								07 55				08 25								09 25				
Filton Abbey Wood	d																		08 45						
Bath Spa 7	d																								
Bristol Temple Meads 10	d	06 42			07 42				08 10				08 45						08 56		09 45				
Weston-super-Mare	d	07 07																	09 23						
Bridgwater	d	07 26																	09 42						
Taunton	d	07 38			08 16				08 42				09 19		09 44				09 55		10 18		10 35	10 44	
Tiverton Parkway	d	07 52							08 54				09 32						10 09		10 31		10 47	10 57	
Exeter St Davids 6	a	08 07			08 39				09 08				09 47		10 08				10 24		10 45		11 02	11 11	
Exmouth	d			07 55				08 25				08 55		09 25						09 55		10 24			
Exeter Central	d			08 26				08 54				09 23		09 54						10 23		10 53			
Exeter St Davids 6	d	08 09		08 33	08 43			09 01	09 10		09 27	09 31	09 49	10 03	10 09				10 26	10 30	10 49	11 01		11 13	
Exeter St Thomas	d			08 36								09 34								10 33					
Starcross	d		←	08 45		←						09 43				←				10 42					
Dawlish Warren	d		08 25	08 56		08 56						09 48		10 21		10 21				10 47					
Dawlish	d		08 29	→		09 00		09 14			09 40	09 52		→		10 25				10 51		11 14			
Teignmouth	d		08 34			09 05		09 19			09 45	09 57				10 30				10 56		11 19			
Newton Abbot	a	08 31	08 41		09 02	09 12		09 26	09 31		09 51	10 04	10 08		10 28	10 37			10 46	11 03	11 08	11 26		11 32	
	d	08 32	08 42		09 03	09 13		09 27	09 33		09 52	10 05	10 09		10 30	10 38			10 47	11 05	11 09	11 27		11 34	
Torre	d		08 51			09 21		09 36				10 14				10 46				11 13		11 36			
Torquay	d		08 54			09 24		09 39	09 47			10 17				10 49				11 16		11 39			
Paignton	a		09 02			09 32		09 45	09 54			10 26				10 57				11 26		11 47			
Totnes	d	08 45									10 05		10 22		10 42				11 01		11 21			11 46	
Ivybridge	d	09 00									10 20								11 16						
Plymouth	a	09 14			09 38						10 34		10 48		11 08				11 30		11 48			12 13	
	d	09 17			09 46					10 13	10 44				11 18				11 47						12 20
Devonport	d									10 17															
Dockyard	d																								
Keyham	d																								
St Budeaux Ferry Road	d										10 50														
Saltash	d	09 26			09 55					10 23	10 55								11 56						12 29
St Germans	d	09 33								10 30	11 01								12 03						
Menheniot	d									10x37															
Liskeard 6	d	09 46			10 14					10 44	11 14				11 43				12 14						12 44
Bodmin Parkway	d	09 58			10 26					10 56	11 26				11 56				12 26						12 56
Lostwithiel	d	10 03								11 01	11 31								12 31						13 01
Par	d	10 10								11 08	11 38				12 06			12 12	12 38						13 08
Newquay	a																	13 05							
St Austell	d	10 17			10 41					11 15	11 45				12 14				12 45						13 15
Truro	d	10 34			11 00					11 32	12 02				12 31				13 02						13 32
Redruth	d	10 46			11 12					11 44	12 14				12 42				13 14						13 44
Camborne	d	10 52			11 19					11 50	12 20				12 49				13 20						13 50
Hayle	d	11 00			11 27					11 58	12 28								13 28						13 58
St Erth	d	11 03			11 32					12 01	12 31				13 00				13 31						14 01
Penzance	a	11 12			11 41					12 10	12 40				13 09				13 40						14 10

A From Exmouth
B To Paignton
C From Derby
D From Leeds

For connections from Heathrow Airport, Gatwick Airport and Oxford refer to Tables T148 and T116. Table T116 includes services to/from Bedwyn.

For the complete service between Westbury and Castle Cary refer to Table T123

Saturdays

21 December to 16 May

London and Birmingham - Devon and Cornwall

		GW		GW	XC ◇■ A 🍴	GW	GW ◇■ B 🍴	GW ◇	XC ◇■ C 🍴	GW	GW D	XC ◇■ E 🍴		GW F	GW ◇■ 🍴	GW	GW ◇■ 🍴	GW	GW	GW D	XC ◇■ G 🍴	GW F		GW D	GW ◇■ H 🍴
London Paddington 15 ⊖	d						10 02								10 35		11 02								12 02
Slough 3	d																								
Reading 7	d						10 28								11 00		11 28								12 28
Theale	d																								
Thatcham	d																								
Newbury	d														11 16										
Hungerford	d																								
Pewsey	d														11 35										
Westbury 123	d														11 53										
Frome 123	d																								
Castle Cary 123	d														12 13										
Birmingham New Street 12	d				09 12				09 42			10 12									11 12				
Cardiff Central 7	d																								
Newport (South Wales)	d																								
Swindon	d																								
Bristol Parkway 7	d				10 25				10 57			11 25									12 27				
Filton Abbey Wood	d																								
Bath Spa 7	d																								
Bristol Temple Meads 10	d				10 45				11 12			11 45									12 45				
Weston-super-Mare	d								11 38																
Bridgwater	d																								
Taunton	d				11 18		11 44		12 01			12 18			12 35		12 45				13 18				13 44
Tiverton Parkway	d				11 31		11 57		12 13			12 31					12 57				13 31				
Exeter St Davids 6	a				11 45		12 11		12 31			12 45			12 59		13 11				13 45				14 08
Exmouth	d			10 56		11 24					11 56					12 24				12 57				13 24	
Exeter Central	d			11 23		11 55					12 23					12 53				13 27				13 53	
Exeter St Davids 6	d	11 26		11 30	11 48	12 02	12 13		12 33		12 37	12 49				13 01	13 13		13 28	13 35	13 49			14 03	14 09
Exeter St Thomas	d			11 33							12 40									13 38					
Starcross	d			11 42							12 49			←						13 46		←			
Dawlish Warren	d			11 47							13 00			13 00					13 39	13 59		13 59		14 21	
Dawlish	d			11 51		12 15			12 45		→			13 04		13 14			13 43	→		14 03		→	
Teignmouth	d			11 56		12 20			12 50					13 09		13 19			13 48			14 08			
Newton Abbot	a	11 46		12 03	12 06	12 27	12 32		12 56			13 07		13 18		13 26	13 32		13 55		14 08	14 17			14 28
	d	11 48		12 05	12 07	12 27	12 34		12 57			13 09		13 19		13 27	13 34		13 56		14 09	14 18			14 30
Torre	d			12 13		12 36								13 27		13 36						14 26			
Torquay	d			12 16		12 39			13 08					13 30		13 39						14 29			
Paignton	a			12 26		12 47			13 14					13 36		13 47						14 35			
Totnes	d	12 01			12 19		12 46					13 21					13 46		14 08		14 21				14 42
Ivybridge	d	12 16																	14 24						
Plymouth	a	12 30			12 45		13 13					13 47					14 13		14 38		14 48				15 08
	d	12 47					13 20			13 46								14 20	14 47						15 20
Devonport	d																								
Dockyard	d																								
Keyham	d																								
St Budeaux Ferry Road	d																								
Saltash	d	12 56								13 55								14 29	14 56						
St Germans	d	13 03								14 01									15 03						
Menheniot	d																								
Liskeard 6	d	13 14					13 45			14 14								14 44	15 14						15 44
Bodmin Parkway	d	13 26					13 58			14 26								14 56	15 26						15 57
Lostwithiel	d	13 31								14 31								15 01	15 31						
Par	d	13 38					14 08	14 12		14 38								15 08	15 38						16 07
Newquay	a							15 05																	
St Austell	d	13 45					14 16			14 45								15 15	15 45						16 14
Truro	d	14 02					14 33			15 02								15 32	16 02						16 32
Redruth	d	14 14					14 45			15 14								15 44	16 14						16 44
Camborne	d	14 20					14 52			15 20								15 50	16 20						16 51
Hayle	d	14 28								15 28								15 58	16 28						
St Erth	d	14 31					15 02			15 31								16 01	16 31						17 01
Penzance	a	14 40					15 11			15 40								16 10	16 40						17 11

A From York
B The Cornish Riviera
C From Manchester Piccadilly
D To Paignton
E From Newcastle
F From Exmouth
G From Edinburgh
H The Royal Duchy

For connections from Heathrow Airport, Gatwick Airport and Oxford refer to Tables T148 and T116. Table T116 includes services to/from Bedwyn.

For the complete service between Westbury and Castle Cary refer to Table T123

Table T135-F

Saturdays

21 December to 16 May

London and Birmingham - Devon and Cornwall

		GW A	GW	GW ◇	GW	XC ◇1 B ✕	GW ◇1 ✕	GW	GW ◇1 ✕	GW ◇	GW	XC ◇1 C ✕	XC ◇1 D ✕	GW E	GW F	GW ◇1 ✕	GW A	GW ◇	GW	GW F	XC ◇1 B ✕	GW A	GW ◇1 ✕
London Paddington 15 ⊖	d						12 35		13 02							14 02							14 35
Slough 3	d																						
Reading 7	d						13 00		13 28							14 28							15 00
Theale	d																						
Thatcham	d																						
Newbury	d						13 15																15 15
Hungerford	d																						
Pewsey	d						13 34																15 34
Westbury 123	d						13 53																15 54
Frome 123	d																						
Castle Cary 123	d						14 13																16 14
Birmingham New Street 12	d					12 12						13 12	13 42								14 12		
Cardiff Central 7	d									13 00													
Newport (South Wales)	d									13 14													
Swindon	d																						
Bristol Parkway 7	d					13 25						14 25	14 58								15 25		
Filton Abbey Wood	d									13 44													
Bath Spa 7	d																						
Bristol Temple Meads 10	d					13 46				13 56		14 46	15 10								15 45		
Weston-super-Mare	d									14 26													
Bridgwater	d									14 45													
Taunton	d					14 18	14 34		14 49	14 57		15 18	15 42			15 47					16 16		16 35
Tiverton Parkway	d					14 31			15 02	15 11		15 31	15 54			16 00					16 29		
Exeter St Davids 6	a					14 45	14 59		15 16	15 26		15 45	16 08			16 14					16 43		16 59
Exmouth	d		13 56					14 24			14 56				15 24					15 55			
Exeter Central	d		14 23					14 53			15 24				15 53					16 24			
Exeter St Davids 6	d		14 30			14 49		15 01	15 17	15 28	15 32	15 51			16 03	16 15			16 27	16 34	16 46		17 01
Exeter St Thomas	d		14 33								15 35				16 06					16 37			
Starcross	d	←	14 42								15 44				16 15		←			16 46		←	
Dawlish Warren	d	14 21	14 47								15 49				16 27		16 27			16 57		16 57	
Dawlish	d	14 25	14 51					15 14			15 53				→		16 31			→		17 01	
Teignmouth	d	14 30	14 56					15 19			15 58						16 36					17 06	
Newton Abbot	a	14 37	15 03			15 08		15 26	15 36	15 50	16 05	16 14				16 34	16 43		16 47		17 04	17 13	17 20
	d	14 38	15 05			15 09		15 27	15 38	15 52	16 08	16 15				16 36	16 44		16 49		17 06	17 14	17 21
Torre	d	14 46	15 13					15 36			16 16						16 52					17 22	
Torquay	d	14 49	15 16					15 39			16 19						16 55					17 25	
Paignton	a	14 57	15 26					15 47			16 27						17 01					17 31	
Totnes	d					15 22			15 50	16 05		16 28				16 47			17 02		17 18		
Ivybridge	d									16 21									17 17				
Plymouth	a					15 48			16 16	16 35		16 54				17 14			17 31		17 44		17 56
	d				15 46				16 24	16 47						17 21			17 46				
Devonport	d																						
Dockyard	d																						
Keyham	d																						
St Budeaux Ferry Road	d																						
Saltash	d				15 55					16 56									17 55				
St Germans	d				16 01					17 03									18 01				
Menheniot	d				16x07																		
Liskeard 6	d				16 14				16 48	17 14						17 46			18 14				
Bodmin Parkway	d				16 26				17 01	17 26						17 59			18 26				
Lostwithiel	d				16 31					17 31									18 31				
Par	d			16 12	16 38					17 38						18 09		18 13	18 38				
Newquay	a			17 05														19 06					
St Austell	d				16 45				17 16	17 45						18 17			18 45				
Truro	d				17 02				17 33	18 02						18 34			19 02				
Redruth	d				17 14				17 44	18 14						18 46			19 14				
Camborne	d				17 20				17 51	18 20						18 52			19 20				
Hayle	d				17 28				18 00	18 28									19 28				
St Erth	d				17 31				18 04	18 31				18 41		19 03			19 31				
Penzance	a				17 40				18 14	18 40				18 52		19 13			19 40				

A From Exmouth
B From Glasgow Central
C From Dundee
D From Manchester Piccadilly
E From St Ives
F To Paignton

For connections from Heathrow Airport, Gatwick Airport and Oxford refer to Tables T148 and T116. Table T116 includes services to/from Bedwyn.

For the complete service between Westbury and Castle Cary refer to Table T123

Table T135-F

Saturdays

21 December to 16 May

London and Birmingham - Devon and Cornwall

		GW A	GW ◇1 ✕	GW B	GW	GW A	XC ◇1 C ✕	GW B	GW D	GW	GW ◇	GW A	XC ◇1 E ✕	GW ◇1 ✕	GW B	GW A	XC ◇1 F ✕	GW B	GW ◇1 G ✕	GW A	GW ◇1 ✕	GW B
London Paddington 15 ⊖	d		15 02											16 03					16 35		17 03	
Slough 3	d																					
Reading 7	d		15 28											16 28					17 00		17 28	
Theale	d																					
Thatcham	d																					
Newbury	d																		17 15			
Hungerford	d																					
Pewsey	d																		17 34			
Westbury 123	d																		17 52			
Frome 123	d																					
Castle Cary 123	d																		18 12			
Birmingham New Street 12	d						15 12						15 42				16 12					
Cardiff Central 7	d																					
Newport (South Wales)	d																					
Swindon	d																					
Bristol Parkway 7	d						16 25						16 55				17 25					
Filton Abbey Wood	d																					
Bath Spa 7	d																					
Bristol Temple Meads 10	d						16 45						17 09				17 45					
Weston-super-Mare	d																					
Bridgwater	d																					
Taunton	d		16 45				17 18						17 40	17 46			18 18		18 34		18 46	
Tiverton Parkway	d		16 58				17 31						17 52	17 59			18 31		18 46		18 58	
Exeter St Davids 6	a		17 12				17 45						18 07	18 13			18 45		19 00		19 12	
Exmouth	d	16 27				16 56						17 27				17 56				18 26		
Exeter Central	d	16 57				17 25						17 58				18 25				18 54		
Exeter St Davids 6	d	17 04	17 14			17 35	17 47		18 00			18 05	18 15	18 20		18 35	18 47		19 03	19 06	19 17	
Exeter St Thomas	d	17 07				17 38						18 08				18 38				19 09		
Starcross	d	17 15		←		17 47		←				18 16			←	18 46		←		19 17		←
Dawlish Warren	d	17 27		17 27		17 58		17 58	18 11			18 32			18 32	18 58		18 58		19 28		19 28
Dawlish	d	→		17 31		→		18 02	18 15			→	18 28		18 37	→		19 02		→		19 32
Teignmouth	d			17 36				18 07	18 20				18 33		18 42			19 07				19 37
Newton Abbot	a		17 34	17 43			18 06	18 14	18 27				18 39	18 44	18 51		19 05	19 14	19 22		19 36	19 45
	d		17 36	17 44			18 07	18 15	18 28				18 40	18 46	18 52		19 07	19 15	19 23		19 38	19 46
Torre	d			17 52				18 23							19 00			19 23	19 33			19 54
Torquay	d			17 55				18 26					18 51		19 03			19 26	19 37			19 57
Paignton	a			18 02				18 32					18 56		19 09			19 34	19 43			20 05
Totnes	d		17 48				18 20		18 40					18 57			19 19				19 50	
Ivybridge	d								18 56					19 12								
Plymouth	a		18 14				18 46		19 09					19 26			19 45				20 16	
	d		18 22		18 35		19 02			19 25							19 51				20 25	
Devonport	d				18 38																	
Dockyard	d				18x39																	
Keyham	d				18 43																	
St Budeaux Ferry Road	d				18 46																	
Saltash	d				18 50					19 34											20 35	
St Germans	d				18 57					19 40											20 42	
Menheniot	d				19x04																	
Liskeard 6	d		18 47		19 11		19 25			19 52							20 14				20 54	
Bodmin Parkway	d		18 59		19 24		19 38			20 04							20 26				21 07	
Lostwithiel	d				19 29					20 09							20 31					
Par	d		19 09		19 36		19 49			20 16	20 22						20 37				21 17	
Newquay	a										21 15											
St Austell	d		19 16		19 43		19 56			20 23							20 44				21 25	
Truro	d		19 33		20 00		20 15			20 40							21 00				21 42	
Redruth	d		19 45		20 12		20 27			20 52							21 11				21 54	
Camborne	d		19 51		20 18		20 33			20 58							21 18					
Hayle	d				20 26					21 06							21 26					
St Erth	d		20 02		20 29		20 43			21 09							21 30				22 08	
Penzance	a		20 12		20 38		20 53			21 18							21 39				22 18	

A To Paignton
B From Exmouth
C From Glasgow Central. ✕ to Plymouth
D not from 4 January until 11 January
E From Manchester Piccadilly
F From Aberdeen. ✕ to Plymouth
G The Torbay Express

For connections from Heathrow Airport, Gatwick Airport and Oxford refer to Tables T148 and T116. Table T116 includes services to/from Bedwyn.

For the complete service between Westbury and Castle Cary refer to Table T123

Table T135-F

Saturdays
21 December to 16 May

London and Birmingham - Devon and Cornwall

		GW	XC	GW	GW	GW	XC	GW	GW	GW	XC	GW	XC	GW	GW	XC	GW	GW
			◇1	◇1		◇	◇1	◇	◇1		◇1		◇1	◇1		◇1	◇	◇1
		A	B			C	D	E		F	G	H	I			J		
			⊼	⊼			⊼		⊼		⊼		⊼	⊼		⊼		⊼
London Paddington 15 ⊖	d			18 03					19 03					20 03				20 29
Slough 3	d																	
Reading 7	d			18 28					19 28					20 28				20 54
Theale	d																	
Thatcham	d																	
Newbury	d								19 44					20 44				
Hungerford	d																	
Pewsey	d								20 03					21 03				
Westbury 123	d								20 21					21 21				
Frome 123	d																	
Castle Cary 123	d								20 41					21 41				
Birmingham New Street 12	d		17 12				18 12				19 12		19 42			20 12		
Cardiff Central 7	d					18 00											21 00	
Newport (South Wales)	d					18 14											21 14	
Swindon	d																	21 22
Bristol Parkway 7	d		18 31				19 25				20 25		20 55			21 25		
Filton Abbey Wood	d					18 41											21 41	
Bath Spa 7	d																	21 47
Bristol Temple Meads 10	d		18 45			18 55	19 45				20 45		21 07			21 45	21 54	22 08
Weston-super-Mare	d					19 30											22 27	22s35
Bridgwater	d					19 48											22 45	22s53
Taunton	d		19 18	19 45		20 02	20 17		21 03		21 17		21 38	22 03		22 17	22 58	23 06
Tiverton Parkway	d		19 31	19 57		20 16	20 30		21 15		21 30		21 50	22 15		22 30	23 12	23 19
Exeter St Davids 6	a		19 45	20 10		20 31	20 44		21 29		21 44		22 04	22 29		22 44	23 29	23 33
Exmouth	d				19 25					20 58								
Exeter Central	d				19 54			←		21 28								
Exeter St Davids 6	d		19 46	20 13	20 16	20 50	20 46	20 50	21 31	21 35	21 46		22 05	22 32		22 49		
Exeter St Thomas	d				20 19	→				21 38								
Starcross	d				20 28					21 46		←						
Dawlish Warren	d				20 33					21 59		21 59						
Dawlish	d				20 37			21 03		→		22 03		22 44				
Teignmouth	d				20 42			21 08				22 08		22 49				
Newton Abbot	a		20 04	20 32	20 49		21 04	21 14	21 50		22 04	22 15	22 24	22 56		23 07		
	d		20 06	20 33	20 50		21 06	21 16	21 51		22 06	22 16	22 25	22 58	23 02	23 09		
Torre	d				20 59							22 24			23 10			
Torquay	d				21 02							22 27			23 13			
Paignton	a				21 10							22 35			23 20			
Totnes	d		20 18	20 45			21 18	21 29	22 03		22 18		22 37	23 10		23 21		
Ivybridge	d							21 44										
Plymouth	a		20 44	21 11			21 44	21 58	22 30		22 44		23 03	23 36		23 47		
	d		20 51	21 20														
Devonport	d																	
Dockyard	d																	
Keyham	d																	
St Budeaux Ferry Road	d																	
Saltash	d																	
St Germans	d																	
Menheniot	d																	
Liskeard 6	d		21 14	21 44														
Bodmin Parkway	d		21 26	21 57														
Lostwithiel	d																	
Par	d		21 36	22 07														
Newquay	a																	
St Austell	d		21 42	22 14														
Truro	d		21 59	22 32														
Redruth	d		22 10	22 44														
Camborne	d		22 16	22 51														
Hayle	d			23 00														
St Erth	d	22 18	22 31	23 04														
Penzance	a	22 30	22 39	23 14														

A From St Ives
B From Glasgow Central. ⊼ to Plymouth
C To Plymouth
D From Edinburgh
E From Cardiff Central
F To Paignton
G From Glasgow Central
H From Exmouth
I From Manchester Piccadilly. ⊼ to Bristol Temple Meads
J From Edinburgh. ⊼ to Bristol Temple Meads

For connections from Heathrow Airport, Gatwick Airport and Oxford refer to Tables T148 and T116. Table T116 includes services to/from Bedwyn.

For the complete service between Westbury and Castle Cary refer to Table T123

Table T135-F

Sundays
15 December to 10 May

London and Birmingham - Devon and Cornwall

		GW	GW	GW	GW	GW	GW	XC	GW	GW	GW	GW	GW	XC	GW	GW	GW	GW	GW	XC	GW	GW	GW
					◇			◇1		◇	◇1			◇1		◇1	◇1			◇1	◇1		◇1
				A		B	A		C		D		A		C					E	D		F
								⊼			⊼			⊼		⊼	⊼			⊼	⊼		⊼
London Paddington 15 ⊖	d										07 57					08 00	08 51				10 03		10 00
Slough 3	d																						
Reading 7	d										08 26					08 29	09 15				10 27		10 24
Theale	d																						
Thatcham	d																						
Newbury	d										08 41												
Hungerford	d																						
Pewsey	d										09 00												
Westbury 123	d										09 19						10 04						
Frome 123	d																						
Castle Cary 123	d										09 38						10 25						
Birmingham New Street 12	d																			09 30			
Cardiff Central 7	d																						
Newport (South Wales)	d																						
Swindon	d															09 05							10 56
Bristol Parkway 7	d																			10 40			
Filton Abbey Wood	d																						
Bath Spa 7	d															09 30							11 21
Bristol Temple Meads 10	d				07 26			08 44		08 28				09 48		09 57				10 58			11 41
Weston-super-Mare	d				07 49					09 01													
Bridgwater	d				08 05					09 19													
Taunton	d				08 17			09 15		09 32	09 58			10 19		10 30	10 43			11 32	11 40		12 17
Tiverton Parkway	d				08 32			09 27		09 47	10 11			10 31						11 45	11 52		
Exeter St Davids 6	a				08 47			09 41		10 02	10 27			10 45		10 53	11 09			11 59	12 08		12 41
Exmouth	d						08 55						09 55					10 57				11 57	
Exeter Central	d						09 23						10 21					11 22				12 20	
Exeter St Davids 6	d			08 37	08 48		09 32	09 42		10 05	10 27		10 33	10 46		10 55	11 10	11 30	11 44	12 01	12 09	12 29	12 42
Exeter St Thomas	d			08 39			09 34						10 36					11 32				12 31	
Starcross	d			08 48		←	09 43		←				10 44		←			11 41				12 40	
Dawlish Warren	d			09 02		09 02	09 52		09 52				10 55		10 55			11 46				12 45	
Dawlish	d			→	09 00	09 06	→		09 56	10 17			→		10 59	11 08		11 50				12 49	12 55
Teignmouth	d				09 04	09 11			10 01	10 21					11 04	11 13		11 55				12 54	13 00
Newton Abbot	a				09 13	09 18		10 01	10 08	10 29	10 48			11 05	11 11	11 19	11 30	12 02	12 07	12 19	12 29	13 01	13 06
	d				09 13	09 19		10 02	10 09	10 30	10 49			11 06	11 13	11 21	11 30	12 03	12 07	12 21	12 29	13 02	13 08
Torre	d					09 27			10 18						11 21			12 12				13 11	
Torquay	d					09 30			10 21						11 24			12 15				13 14	
Paignton	a					09 36			10 29						11 32			12 21				13 20	
Totnes	d				09 25			10 14		10 41	11 03			11 18			11 42		12 19	12 33	12 41		
Ivybridge	d				09 40					10 57									12 34				
Plymouth	a				09 54			10 40		11 10	11 30			11 44		11 56	12 10		12 48	12 59	13 10		13 43
	d	08 55			10 00					11 10	11 35									13 06	13 20		
Devonport	d	08 59																					
Dockyard	d																						
Keyham	d																						
St Budeaux Ferry Road	d	09 03																					
Saltash	d	09 07			10 08					11 21													
St Germans	d	09 14			10 14					11 27													
Menheniot	d				10x21																		
Liskeard 6	d	09 25			10 29					11 39	12 01									13 31	13 44		
Bodmin Parkway	d	09 37			10 40					11 50	12 13									13 43	13 57		
Lostwithiel	d	09 42			10 44					11 54													
Par	d	09 49	10 05		10 52					12 02	12 24	12 35								13 53	14 07		
Newquay	a		10 57									13 27											
St Austell	d	09 56			11 00					12 10	12 31									13 59	14 21		
Truro	d	10 12			11 16					12 26	12 48									14 16	14 38		
Redruth	d	10 24			11 28					12 38	13 01									14 27	14 50		
Camborne	d	10 30			11 34					12 44	13 07									14 33	14 57		
Hayle	d	10 38			11 42					12 52													
St Erth	d	10 41			11 45					12 56	13 20									14 43	15 08		
Penzance	a	10 50			11 54					13 05	13 29									14 52	15 17		

A To Paignton
B From Exeter St Davids
C From Exmouth
D ⊡ from Plymouth ⊼ to Plymouth
E ⊼ to Plymouth
F ⊡ from Exeter St Davids ⊼ to Exeter St Davids

For connections from Heathrow Airport, Gatwick Airport and Oxford refer to Tables T148 and T116. Table T116 includes services to/from Bedwyn.

For the complete service between Westbury and Castle Cary refer to Table T123

Table T135-F

Sundays

15 December to 10 May

London and Birmingham - Devon and Cornwall

		XC	GW	GW	GW	GW		GW	XC	GW	GW	GW	GW	XC	GW	GW		GW	GW	GW	GW	XC	GW	GW	XC
		◇1	◇1		◇1				◇1	◇1	◇	◇1		◇1		◇1			◇1			◇1	◇1		◇1
		A							A			B		C								D			E
		🍴	🍴		🍴				🍴	🍴		🍽		🍴		🍴			🍴			🍴	🍴		🍴
London Paddington 15 ⊖	d		10 36		11 03					12 03		11 29				12 36			13 03				14 03		
Slough 3	d																								
Reading 7	d		11 01		11 27					12 27		11 53				13 00			13 27				14 27		
Theale	d																								
Thatcham	d																								
Newbury	d		11 15													13 15									
Hungerford	d																								
Pewsey	d		11 34													13 34									
Westbury 123	d		11 52													13 52									
Frome 123	d																								
Castle Cary 123	d		12 12													14 12									
Birmingham New Street 12	d	10 30							11 30					12 12								13 12			14 12
Cardiff Central 7	d																								
Newport (South Wales)	d																								
Swindon	d											12 21													
Bristol Parkway 7	d	11 41							12 43					13 25								14 25			15 24
Filton Abbey Wood	d																								
Bath Spa 7	d											12 51													
Bristol Temple Meads 10	d	11 55							12 55			13 11		13 45								14 45			15 45
Weston-super-Mare	d																								
Bridgwater	d																								
Taunton	d	12 27	12 32		12 39				13 27	13 40		13 49		14 18		14 32			14 40			15 16	15 40		16 17
Tiverton Parkway	d	12 39			12 52				13 39	13 52				14 31					14 52			15 29	15 52		16 29
Exeter St Davids 6	a	12 54	12 59		13 08				13 54	14 08		14 18		14 45		14 59			15 08			15 43	16 08		16 44
Exmouth	d							12 57					13 57					14 23			14 57			15 56	
Exeter Central	d			12 48				13 20					14 20					14 52			15 20			16 20	
Exeter St Davids 6	d	12 55		12 59	13 09			13 28	13 55	14 09		14 20	14 28	14 47	14 56			15 00	15 09		15 28	15 44	16 09	16 28	16 45
Exeter St Thomas	d							13 31					14 31								15 30			16 31	
Starcross	d							13 39					14 39								15 39			16 39	
Dawlish Warren	d			13 11				13 44				14 31	14 44								15 44			16 44	
Dawlish	d			13 15				13 48				14 36	14 48					15 13			15 48			16 48	
Teignmouth	d			13 20				13 53				14 41	14 53					15 18			15 53			16 53	
Newton Abbot	a	13 15		13 27	13 30			14 00	14 14	14 30		14 47	15 00	15 06	15 16			15 25	15 30		16 00	16 03	16 30	17 00	17 04
	d	13 16		13 27	13 31			14 02	14 15	14 31		14 49	15 02	15 07	15 17			15 28	15 31		16 02	16 06	16 31	17 02	17 05
Torre	d			13 36				14 10					15 10					15 37			16 10			17 10	
Torquay	d			13 39				14 13				15 00	15 13					15 40			16 13			17 13	
Paignton	a			13 45				14 19				15 05	15 19					15 46			16 21			17 19	
Totnes	d	13 29			13 42				14 28	14 42				15 19	15 28				15 39			16 18	16 42		17 18
Ivybridge	d														15 44										
Plymouth	a	13 55			14 10				14 54	15 09				15 46	15 59				16 11			16 44	17 09		17 44
	d					14 30				15 15										16 20			17 15		
Devonport	d																								
Dockyard	d																								
Keyham	d																								
St Budeaux Ferry Road	d																								
Saltash	d					14 39														16 29					
St Germans	d					14 45														16 35					
Menheniot	d																								
Liskeard 6	d					14 57				15 39										16 47			17 40		
Bodmin Parkway	d					15 08				15 51										16 58			17 53		
Lostwithiel	d					15 13														17 03					
Par	d					15 20				16 02	16 15									17 10			18 03		
Newquay	a										17 08														
St Austell	d					15 27				16 09										17 17			18 10		
Truro	d					15 44				16 26										17 34			18 27		
Redruth	d					15 56				16 38										17 46			18 39		
Camborne	d					16 02				16 46										17 52			18 47		
Hayle	d					16 10														18 00					
St Erth	d					16 19				16 56										18 04			18 57		
Penzance	a					16 28				17 05										18 13			19 08		

A From Leeds
B 🍽 from Exeter St Davids 🍴 to Exeter St Davids
C From York
D From Newcastle
E From Edinburgh

For connections from Heathrow Airport, Gatwick Airport and Oxford refer to Tables T148 and T116. Table T116 includes services to/from Bedwyn.

For the complete service between Westbury and Castle Cary refer to Table T123

NRT DECEMBER 19 EDITION

Table T135-F

Sundays

15 December to 10 May

London and Birmingham - Devon and Cornwall

		GW		GW	GW	XC	GW	GW	GW	XC	GW	GW		GW	GW	XC	GW	GW	GW	XC	GW	GW		GW	GW
				◇1	◇1	◇1				◇1		◇1				◇1	◇1	◇1		◇1	◇	◇1		◇1	
						A		B		C						D				E					F
				🍴	🍴	🍴				🍴		🍴				🍴	🍴	🍴		🍴		🍴		🍴	
London Paddington 15 ⊖	d			14 36	15 03							16 03					16 36	17 03				18 03		18 00	
Slough 3	d																								
Reading 7	d			15 00	15 26							16 27					17 00	17 27				18 27		18 24	
Theale	d																								
Thatcham	d																								
Newbury	d			15 15													17 15								
Hungerford	d																								
Pewsey	d			15 34													17 34								
Westbury 123	d			15 52													17 51								
Frome 123	d																								
Castle Cary 123	d			16 12													18 12								
Birmingham New Street 12	d					14 42				15 12						16 12				17 12					
Cardiff Central 7	d																								
Newport (South Wales)	d																								
Swindon	d																							18 56	
Bristol Parkway 7	d					15 57				16 25						17 25				18 25					
Filton Abbey Wood	d																								
Bath Spa 7	d																							19 21	
Bristol Temple Meads 10	d					16 14				16 45						17 45				18 45	18 25			19 38	
Weston-super-Mare	d																				19 00				
Bridgwater	d																				19 18				
Taunton	d			16 32	16 39	16 48				17 17		17 40				18 19	18 32	18 40		19 17	19 31	19 40		20 10	
Tiverton Parkway	d				16 52	17 01				17 30		17 52				18 31		18 52		19 30	19 45	19 52			
Exeter St Davids 6	a			16 59	17 08	17 15				17 44		18 08				18 45	18 56	19 08		19 44	20 00	20 08		20 33	
Exmouth	d						16 54								17 57				19 00						19 57
Exeter Central	d						17 20								18 20				19 24						20 25
Exeter St Davids 6	d	16 56			17 09	17 17	17 28			17 47	17 56	18 09			18 28	18 48	18 59	19 09	19 31	19 49		20 09		20 35	20 39
Exeter St Thomas	d						17 31								18 31				19 33						20 41
Starcross	d						17 39								18 39				19 42						20 50
Dawlish Warren	d						17 44								18 44				19 47						20 58
Dawlish	d					17 29	17 48								18 48				19 51						→
Teignmouth	d					17 34	17 53								18 53				19 56						
Newton Abbot	a	17 16			17 30	17 40	18 00			18 05	18 16	18 30			19 00	19 06	19 17	19 30	20 03	20 07		20 29		20 54	
	d	17 17			17 31	17 41	18 02			18 07	18 17	18 31			19 02	19 08	19 18	19 30	20 03	20 09		20 29		20 55	
Torre	d						18 10								19 10				20 12						
Torquay	d					17 52	18 13								19 13				20 15						
Paignton	a					17 57	18 24								19 19				20 21						
Totnes	d	17 28			17 41					18 19	18 28	18 39				19 20	19 29	19 41		20 21		20 41		21 07	
Ivybridge	d	17 44									18 44						19 46								
Plymouth	a	17 58			18 11					18 45	18 59	19 09				19 46	20 00	20 09		20 47		21 09		21 33	
	d								18 20	18 51		19 15		19 39				20 15		20 51		21 15			
Devonport	d																								
Dockyard	d																								
Keyham	d																								
St Budeaux Ferry Road	d																								
Saltash	d								18 29					19 48											
St Germans	d								18 35					19 54											
Menheniot	d								18x43																
Liskeard 6	d								18 49	19 14		19 40		20 06				20 41		21 14		21 40			
Bodmin Parkway	d								19 01	19 26		19 53		20 17				20 54		21 26		21 53			
Lostwithiel	d								19 06					20 22											
Par	d								19 13	19 36		20 03		20 29				21 04		21 36		22 03			
Newquay	a																								
St Austell	d								19 23	19 42		20 10		20 37				21 11		21 42		22 10			
Truro	d								19 40	19 59		20 27		20 54				21 28		21 59		22 27			
Redruth	d								19 52	20 10		20 39		21 06				21 40		22 10		22 39			
Camborne	d								19 58	20 16		20 47		21 12				21 48		22 16		22 47			
Hayle	d								20 06					21 20											
St Erth	d							19 55	20 09	20 26		20 57		21 24				21 58		22 26		22 57			
Penzance	a							20 05	20 18	20 35		21 06		21 33				22 07		22 35		23 06			

A From Manchester Piccadilly
B From St Ives
C From Edinburgh. 🍴 to Plymouth
D From Edinburgh
E From Glasgow Central. 🍴 to Plymouth
F To Paignton

For connections from Heathrow Airport, Gatwick Airport and Oxford refer to Tables T148 and T116. Table T116 includes services to/from Bedwyn.

For the complete service between Westbury and Castle Cary refer to Table T123

Table T135-F

Sundays

15 December to 10 May

London and Birmingham - Devon and Cornwall

		XC	GW	GW	GW	XC	GW	XC	GW	GW	XC	GW	GW
		◇1 A ⌶	B	◇1 ⌶	◇1 ⌶	◇1 C ⌶		◇1 D ⌶		◇1 ⌶	◇1 E ⌶	◇1 ⌶	■ ⌶
London Paddington ⊖	d			18 36	19 03					20 03		21 03	23 50
Slough	d												
Reading	d			19 00	19 27					20 27		21 27	00u51
Theale	d												
Thatcham	d												
Newbury	d			19 15						20 42			
Hungerford	d												
Pewsey	d			19 34						21 01			
Westbury 123	d			19 51						21 20			
Frome 123	d												
Castle Cary 123	d			20 10						21 40			
Birmingham New Street	d	18 12				18 42		19 12			20 12		
Cardiff Central	d												
Newport (South Wales)	d												
Swindon	d												
Bristol Parkway	d	19 25				19 56		20 25			21 25		
Filton Abbey Wood	d												
Bath Spa	d												
Bristol Temple Meads	d	19 45				20 16		20 45			21 45		
Weston-super-Mare	d					20 39							
Bridgwater	d												
Taunton	d	20 17		20 32	20 42	21 00		21 17		22 03	22 17	22 41	
Tiverton Parkway	d	20 30			20 55	21 12		21 30		22 13	22 30	22 59	
Exeter St Davids	a	20 44		20 54	21 11	21 27		21 44		22 29	22 44	23 13	03 23
Exmouth	d						20 57		21 27				
Exeter Central	d						21 25		21 55				
Exeter St Davids	d	20 46		20 55	21 11	21 29	21 33	21 46	22 01	22 30	22 46		04 36
Exeter St Thomas	d								22 04				
Starcross	d		←						22 12				
Dawlish Warren	d		20 58						22 17				
Dawlish	d		21 02	21 10		21 41	21 46		22 21				
Teignmouth	d		21 07	21 15		21 46	21 51		22 26				
Newton Abbot	a	21 08	21 17	21 21	21 31	21 52	21 58	22 04	22 33	22 50	23 04		04 56
	d	21 09	21 18	21 21	21 32	21 53	21 59	22 06	22 35	22 50	23 06		04 57
Torre	d		21 26				22 07		22 43				
Torquay	d		21 29				22 10		22 46				
Paignton	a		21 35				22 16		22 52				
Totnes	d	21 22		21 33	21 43			22 18		23 02	23 18		
Ivybridge	d			21 49									
Plymouth	a	21 48		22 05	22 12	22 36		22 44		23 30	23 44		05s36
	d												
Devonport	d												
Dockyard	d												
Keyham	d												
St Budeaux Ferry Road	d												
Saltash	d												
St Germans	d												
Menheniot	d												
Liskeard	d												07s04
Bodmin Parkway	d												07s18
Lostwithiel	d												07s25
Par	d												07s34
Newquay	a												
St Austell	d												07s42
Truro	d												08s01
Redruth	d												08s15
Camborne	d												08s23
Hayle	d												08s32
St Erth	d												08s38
Penzance	a												08 49

A From Glasgow Central
B From Exmouth
C From Manchester Piccadilly. ⌶ to Bristol Temple Meads
D From Aberdeen. ⌶ to Bristol Temple Meads
E From Glasgow Central. ⌶ to Bristol Temple Meads

For connections from Heathrow Airport, Gatwick Airport and Oxford refer to Tables T148 and T116. Table T116 includes services to/from Bedwyn.

For the complete service between Westbury and Castle Cary refer to Table T123

Table T135-R

Mondays to Fridays

16 December to 15 May

Cornwall and Devon - Birmingham and London

Miles	Miles	Miles			GW MX	GW MO	GW MX	GW MX	GW	GW	GW	XC	GW	GW	GW	GW	GW	GW	GW	XC	GW	XC	GW
					A	■ B ⌶		■ B	◇1 ⌶	◇1 ⌶	◇1 ⌶	◇1 C ⌶	◇	◇1 D ⌶	E	◇1 F ⌶	◇1 G ⌶	A	E	◇1 H ⌶	A	◇1 I ⌶	◇1 J X⌶
0	—	—	**Penzance**	d																			04 58
5¾	—	—	St Erth	d																			
7¼	—	—	Hayle	d																			
13¼	—	—	Camborne	d																			
16¾	—	—	Redruth	d																			05 19
25¾	—	—	Truro	d																			05 32
40¼	—	—	St Austell	d																			05 48
—	—	—	Newquay	d																			
44¼	—	—	Par	d																			
49¼	—	—	Lostwithiel	d																			
52¾	—	—	Bodmin Parkway	d																			06 04
61¾	—	—	Liskeard	d																			06 17
65	—	—	Menheniot	d																			
70¼	—	—	St Germans	d																			
75¼	—	—	Saltash	d																			
76½	—	—	St Budeaux Ferry Road	d																			
77¼	—	—	Keyham	d																			
77¾	—	—	Dockyard	d																			
78¼	—	—	Devonport	d																			
79½	—	—	**Plymouth**	a																			06 44
—	—	—		d							04 51	05 25		05 34		05 47				06 27			06 52
90¼	—	—	Ivybridge	d										05 48									
102¾	—	—	Totnes	d				00 22				05 51		06 02						06 53			
—	—	0	Paignton	d			00 01								06 02				06 39			07 01	
—	—	2¼	Torquay	d			00 06								06 07				06 44			07 07	
—	—	3	Torre	d			00 09								06 10			←	06 47				
111½	—	8¼	Newton Abbot	a			00 17	00 34			05 25	06 02		06 13	06 18	06 21		06 18	06 55	07 04		07 15	07 26
—	—	—		d		00 01	00 18	00 36			05 27	06 04		06 15	06 34	06 23		06 34	06 56	07 06		07 17	07 28
116½	—	—	Teignmouth	d			00 25							06 22	→			06 41	07 03			07 24	
119¾	—	—	Dawlish	d			00 30							06 27				06 46	07 08		←	07 29	
121	—	—	Dawlish Warren	d														06 50	07 18		07 18		
123	—	—	Starcross	d														06 55	→		07 23		
130½	—	—	Exeter St Thomas	d	00 07		00 42											07 04			07 32		
131½	—	—	**Exeter St Davids**	a	00 11	00 23	00 47	01 00			05 45	06 23		06 38		06 42		07 08		07 25	07 37	07 41	07 46
—	—	—	Exeter Central	a														07 19			07 47		
—	—	—	Exmouth	a													←	07 49			08 19		
—	—	—	**Exeter St Davids**	d		00 59		01 01			05 47	06 25	06 33	06 51		06 45	06 51			07 27		07 42	07 49
148	—	—	Tiverton Parkway	d							06 02	06 38	06 48	→			07 05			07 41		07 56	
162¼	0	—	Taunton	d				01 40			06 15	06 51	07 02			07 09	07 18			07 53		08 08	08 13
—	11¾	—	Bridgwater	a									07 12										
—	25¾	—	Weston-super-Mare	a									07 32									08 36	
—	45½	—	**Bristol Temple Meads**	a								07 24	08 14							08 29		08 54	
—	—	—		d					05 10			07 34	08 22							08 34		09 00	
—	—	—	Bath Spa	a																			
—	—	—	Filton Abbey Wood	a									08 30										
—	51¼	—	Bristol Parkway	a								07 42								08 42		09 08	
—	—	—	Swindon	a																			
—	—	—	Newport (South Wales)	a									09 08										
—	—	—	Cardiff Central	a									09 24										
—	138¼	—	**Birmingham New Street**	a								08 56								09 58		10 23	
190	—	—	Castle Cary 123	d							06 41						07 39						
204	—	—	Frome 123	d						06 12													
209¾	—	—	Westbury 123	d					05 59	06 23	07 01						08 00						
230	—	—	Pewsey	d					06 16	06 41	07 19						08 17						
243¾	—	—	Hungerford	a					06 32	06 56	07 35												
252¼	—	—	Newbury	a					06 44	07 08	07 44						08 34						
255¾	—	—	Thatcham	a					06 49	07 14													
264½	—	—	Theale	a					06 57	07 22													
269¾	—	—	**Reading**	a		04s05		03s51	07 08	07 31	08 01					08 28	08 53						09 30
286¾	—	—	Slough	a																			
305¼	—	—	**London Paddington** ⊖	a		05 04		05 04	07 35	08 01	08 36					08 59	09 19						09 59

A From Paignton
B From Penzance. The Night Riviera
C To Edinburgh
D To London Paddington
E To Exmouth
F The Armada
G From Plymouth
H To Glasgow Central
I To Manchester Piccadilly. ⌶ from Newton Abbot
J The Golden Hind. X from Plymouth to Reading ⌶ to Plymouth ⌶ from Reading

For connections to Oxford, Gatwick Airport and Heathrow Airport refer to Tables T116 and T148

For connections from Swansea refer to Table T128

Table T135-R

Mondays to Fridays
16 December to 15 May

Cornwall and Devon - Birmingham and London

		GW	GW ◇1 ⊼	GW	GW A	XC ◇1 B ⊼	GW C	GW	GW	GW ◇1 ⊼	XC ◇1 D ⊼	GW A	GW ◇1 ⊼	GW C	GW ◇	GW E	GW	GW ◇1 ⊼	XC ◇1 F ⊼	GW ◇	GW	XC ◇1 G ⊼	GW
Penzance	d	05 21						05 40		06 04	06 30				06 40	06 58		07 10		07 52			
St Erth	d							05 48			06 38				06 48	07a06		07 19		08 00			
Hayle	d	05 31						05 52							06 52					08 04			
Camborne	d	05 41						06 01		06 20	06 48				07 01			07 30		08 13			
Redruth	d							06 07		06 27	06 54				07 07			07 37		08 19			
Truro	d	05a56						06 19		06 39	07 06				07 19			07 49		08 30			
St Austell	d							06 35		06 55	07 22				07 35			08 05		08 47			
Newquay	d																						
Par	d							06 42		07 02	07 28				07 42			08 12		08 53			
Lostwithiel	d							06 49		07 09					07 49			08 19		09 00			
Bodmin Parkway	d							06 54		07 16	07 39				07 54			08 26		09 06			
Liskeard 6	d							07 07		07 29	07 51				08 07			08 39		09 19			
Menheniot	d							07x11		07x34					08x11								
St Germans	d							07 22		07 43					08 22			08 50		09 29			
Saltash	d							07 29		07 51					08 29			08 58		09 36			
St Budeaux Ferry Road	d							07 33							08 34								
Keyham	d							07 35							08 37								
Dockyard	d							07x36							08x38								
Devonport	d							07 39		07 59					08 41								
Plymouth	a							07 44		08 05	08 18				08 45			09 09		09 46			
	d					07 27		07 45		08 12	08 25		08 35		08 47			09 15	09 27				
Ivybridge	d							08 00					08 49										
Totnes	d					07 53		08 14		08 39	08 51		09 03		09 13			09 42	09 53				
Paignton	d		07 10	07 20	07 37				08 15			08 53					09 17				09 50	10 14	10 23
Torquay	d		07 16	07 25	07 42				08 20			08 58					09 22				09 56	10 20	10 28
Torre	d		07 19	07 28	07 45				08 23			09 01					09 25				09 59		10 31
Newton Abbot	a		07 26	07 36	07 55	08 04		08 25	08 31	08 50	09 02	09 09	09 14		09 25		09 33	09 53	10 04		10 09	10 28	10 39
	d		07 33	07 38	07 56	08 06		08 26	08 32	08 51	09 03	09 10	09 16		09 26		09 34	09 54	10 06		10 12	10 29	10 40
Teignmouth	d		07 40	07 45	08 03			08 33	08 39			09 17	09 23				09 41				10 19	10 36	10 47
Dawlish	d		07 45	07 50	08 08		←	08 38	08 44			09 22	09 28	←			09 46				10 24	10 41	10 52
Dawlish Warren	d			07 54	08 19		08 19		08 48			09 32		09 32			09 50				10 28		
Starcross	d			07 59	→		08 24		08 53			→					09 54				10 33		
Exeter St Thomas	d			08 08			08 34		09 02								10 03				10 42		
Exeter St Davids 6	a		07 56	08 13		08 25	08 40	08 51	09 06	09 09	09 23		09 39	09 47	09 51		10 08	10 12	10 25		10 47	10 53	11 06
Exeter Central	a			08 19			08 47		09 19					09 54			10 18				10 53		11 18
Exmouth	a			08 49			09 19		09 49					10 17			10 47				11 17		11 47
Exeter St Davids 6	d		08 03			08 27				09 12	09 27		09 41		09 53			10 15	10 27			10 54	
Tiverton Parkway	d		08 18			08 41				09 26	09 41							10 29	10 41			11 08	
Taunton	d		08 31			08 53				09 39	09 53		10 04		10 20			10 42	10 53			11 21	
Bridgwater	a														10 30								
Weston-super-Mare	a														10 48								
Bristol Temple Meads 10	a					09 24					10 24				11 17				11 24			11 55	
	d					09 34					10 34				11 20				11 34			12 00	
Bath Spa 7	a														11 30								
Filton Abbey Wood	a																						
Bristol Parkway 7	a					09 42					10 42								11 42			12 08	
Swindon	a																						
Newport (South Wales)	a														12 02								
Cardiff Central 7	a														12 22								
Birmingham New Street 12	a					10 56					11 58								12 56			13 25	
Castle Cary 123	d		08 52										10 25										
Frome 123	d																						
Westbury 123	d		09 13										10 45										
Pewsey	d		09 30										11 01										
Hungerford	a																						
Newbury	a												11 19										
Thatcham	a																						
Theale	a																						
Reading 7	a		10 00							10 56			11 38					11 58					
Slough 3	a																						
London Paddington 15 ⊖	a		10 29							11 29			12 09					12 29					

A To Exmouth
B To Edinburgh
C From Paignton
D To Glasgow Central. ⊼ from Plymouth
E To St Ives
F To Aberdeen
G To Manchester Piccadilly

For connections to Oxford, Gatwick Airport and Heathrow Airport refer to Tables T116 and T148

For connections from Swansea refer to Table T128

Table T135-R

Mondays to Fridays
16 December to 15 May

Cornwall and Devon - Birmingham and London

		GW ◇1 ⊼	GW A	XC R ◇1 B ⊼	GW ◇1 C ⊼	GW D	GW ◇	GW	GW ◇1 E ⊼	XC ◇1 F ⊼	GW	GW ◇	GW	XC ◇1 G ⊼	GW	GW ◇1 ⊼	GW R 1 H ✕⊼	XC ◇1 I ⊼	GW ◇1 ⊼	GW	GW ◇	GW ◇	GW
Penzance	d	08 15		08 37			08 50		09 15	09 25	09 50						10 15				10 50	11 15	
St Erth	d	08 24		08 45			08 58		09 24	09 34	09 58						10 24				10 58	11 23	
Hayle	d						09 02			09 38	10 02										11 02	11 27	
Camborne	d	08 35		08 55			09 11		09 35	09 48	10 11						10 35				11 11	11 36	
Redruth	d	08 42		09 01			09 17		09 42	09 54	10 17						10 42				11 17	11 42	
Truro	d	08 54		09 13			09 29		09 54	10 07	10 29						10 54				11 29	11 54	
St Austell	d	09 10		09 29			09 46		10 10	10 24	10 46						11 10				11 46	12 10	
Newquay	d											10 23											
Par	d	09 17		09 35			09 52		10 17	10 31	10 52	11a12					11 17				11 52	12 17	
Lostwithiel	d						09 59			10 38	11 03										11 59	12 24	
Bodmin Parkway	d	09 29		09 46			10 05		10 29	10 44	11 09						11 29				12 05	12 29	
Liskeard 6	d	09 42		09 58			10 18		10 42	10 56	11 23						11 42				12 18	12 42	
Menheniot	d																						
St Germans	d						10 28				11 33										12 28	12 53	
Saltash	d						10 35				11 40										12 36	13 00	
St Budeaux Ferry Road	d																						
Keyham	d																						
Dockyard	d																						
Devonport	d																						
Plymouth	a	10 07		10 21			10 45		11 07	11 20	11 50						12 07				12 45	13 12	
	d	10 13		10 27			10 48		11 16	11 27				11 50			12 16	12 27			12 49		
Ivybridge	d						11 03														13 04		
Totnes	d	10 39		10 53			11 17		11 42	11 53				12 16			12 42	12 53			13 17		
Paignton	d		10 39		10 52			11 20					11 52		12 20					12 53			13 18
Torquay	d		10 44		10 59			11 25					11 57		12 25					12 58			13 23
Torre	d		10 47		11 02			11 28					12 00		12 28					13 01			13 26
Newton Abbot	a	10 50	10 55	11 04	11 10		11 29	11 36	11 53	12 05			12 10	12 27	12 36		12 53	13 05		13 11	13 29		13 35
	d	10 52	10 56	11 06	11 12		11 30	11 37	11 55	12 06			12 11	12 28	12 37		12 55	13 06		13 12	13 30		13 36
Teignmouth	d		11 03		11 19			11 44					12 18		12 44					13 19			13 43
Dawlish	d		11 08		11 24	←		11 49					12 23		12 49					13 24			13 48
Dawlish Warren	d		11 29			11 29							12 28							13 29			
Starcross	d		→			11 33							12 32							13 33			
Exeter St Thomas	d					11 42							12 41							13 42			
Exeter St Davids 6	a	11 10		11 25	11 36	11 47	11 52	12 03	12 13	12 25			12 46	12 50	13 04		13 13	13 25		13 47	13 51		14 04
Exeter Central	a					11 54		12 18					12 53		13 15					13 53			14 18
Exmouth	a					12 17		12 47					13 17		13 47					14 17			14 47
Exeter St Davids 6	d	11 15		11 27	11 38				12 15	12 27				12 52		13 06	13 15	13 27	13 40		13 53		
Tiverton Parkway	d	11 30		11 41					12 30	12 41				13 06		13 21	13 30	13 41					
Taunton	d	11 43		11 53	12 01				12 43	12 53				13 21		13 34	13 43	13 53	14 03		14 20		
Bridgwater	a																				14 31		
Weston-super-Mare	a															13 54					14 49		
Bristol Temple Meads 10	a			12 24						13 26				13 54		14 19		14 26			15 18		
	d			12 35						13 34				14 00		14 23		14 30			15 20		
Bath Spa 7	a																						
Filton Abbey Wood	a																				15 27		
Bristol Parkway 7	a			12 43						13 42				14 08		14 31		14 38					
Swindon	a																						
Newport (South Wales)	a																				16 03		
Cardiff Central 7	a																				16 22		
Birmingham New Street 12	a			13 56						14 56				15 23				15 56					
Castle Cary 123	d				12 21														14 24				
Frome 123	d																						
Westbury 123	d				12 48														14 47				
Pewsey	d				13 07														15 09				
Hungerford	a																						
Newbury	a				13 24														15 27				
Thatcham	a																						
Theale	a																						
Reading 7	a	12 59			13 41				14 02								14 59		15 43				
Slough 3	a																						
London Paddington 15 ⊖	a	13 29			14 09				14 27							15 45	15 29		16 11				

A To Exmouth
B To Glasgow Central. ⊼ ◇ from Plymouth R to Plymouth
C ⊼ from Newbury ⊼ to Newbury
D From Paignton
E The Cornish Riviera
F To Dundee
G To Manchester Piccadilly
H The Cornishman. ✕ from Plymouth to Reading ⊼ to Plymouth ⊼ from Reading
I To Glasgow Central

For connections to Oxford, Gatwick Airport and Heathrow Airport refer to Tables T116 and T148

For connections from Swansea refer to Table T128

Table T135-R

Mondays to Fridays

16 December to 15 May

Cornwall and Devon - Birmingham and London

		GW ◇[1] A ✕⌶	XC ◇[1] B ⌶	GW ◇	XC ◇[1] C ⌶	GW	GW ◇[1] D ⌶	GW	GW ◇[1] E ⌶	XC ◇[1] B ⌶	GW ◇[1] ⌶	GW	GW ◇	GW ◇	GW	XC ◇[1] C ⌶	GW	GW ◇[1] F ⌶	XC ◇[1] G ⌶	GW ◇	GW	XC ◇[1] C ⌶
Penzance	d			11 50					12 15				12 50		13 15					13 50		
St Erth	d			11 58					12 24				12 58		13 23					13 58		
Hayle	d			12 02									13 02		13 27					14 02		
Camborne	d			12 11					12 35				13 11		13 36					14 11		
Redruth	d			12 17					12 42				13 17		13 42					14 17		
Truro	d			12 29					12 54				13 29		13 54					14 29		
St Austell	d			12 46					13 10				13 46		14 10					14 46		
Newquay	d													13 10								
Par	d			12 52					13 17				13 52	13a59	14 17					14 52		
Lostwithiel	d			12 59									13 59		14 24					14 59		
Bodmin Parkway	d			13 05					13 29				14 05		14 29					15 05		
Liskeard [6]	d			13 18					13 42				14 18		14 42					15 18		
Menheniot	d			13x22																		
St Germans	d			13 32									14 28		14 53					15 28		
Saltash	d			13 39									14 35		15 00					15 36		
St Budeaux Ferry Road	d																					
Keyham	d																					
Dockyard	d																					
Devonport	d																					
Plymouth	a			13 50					14 09				14 45		15 09					15 45		
	d	13 13	13 27						14 15	14 27			14 48					15 14	15 27			
Ivybridge	d												15 03									
Totnes	d	13 39	13 53						14 42	14 53			15 16					15 40	15 53			
Paignton	d					13 53	14 12	14 20				14 52				15 15	15 24				15 53	
Torquay	d					13 58	14 18	14 25				14 58				15 21	15 29				15 58	
Torre	d					14 01		14 28				15 01					15 32				16 01	
Newton Abbot	a	13 50	14 05			14 11	14 26	14 36	14 53	15 04		15 11	15 28			15 29	15 40	15 51	16 05		16 09	
	d	13 52	14 06			14 12	14 28	14 37	14 54	15 06		15 12	15 29			15 34	15 41	15 53	16 06		16 10	
Teignmouth	d					14 19	14 35	14 44				15 19				15 41	15 48				16 17	
Dawlish	d					14 24	14 40	14 49				15 24				15 46	15 53				16 22	
Dawlish Warren	d					14 29						15 29									16 26	
Starcross	d					14 33						15 33									16 31	
Exeter St Thomas	d					14 42						15 42									16 40	
Exeter St Davids [6]	a	14 10	14 25			14 47	14 51	15 04	15 12	15 25		15 47	15 50			15 58	16 07	16 11	16 25		16 44	
Exeter Central	a					14 53		15 18				15 53					16 18				16 50	
Exmouth	a					15 17		15 47				16 17					16 47				17 19	
Exeter St Davids [6]	d	14 15	14 27		14 45		14 53		15 15	15 27	15 38					15 59		16 14	16 27			16 56
Tiverton Parkway	d	14 29	14 41		14 58		15 08		15 29	15 41						16 13		16 28	16 41			17 10
Taunton	d	14 42	14 53		15 11		15 20		15 42	15 53	16 02					16 25		16 41	16 53			17 22
Bridgwater	a																					
Weston-super-Mare	a				15 33																	
Bristol Temple Meads [10]	a		15 26		15 56					16 24						16 57			17 28			17 56
	d		15 32		16 00					16 34						17 00			17 34			18 00
Bath Spa [7]	a																					
Filton Abbey Wood	a																					
Bristol Parkway [7]	a		15 41		16 08					16 42						17 08			17 42			18 08
Swindon	a																					
Newport (South Wales)	a																					
Cardiff Central [7]	a																					
Birmingham New Street [12]	a		16 56		17 24					17 56						18 23			18 56			19 23
Castle Cary 123	d										16 23											
Frome 123	d																					
Westbury 123	d						15 58				16 46											
Pewsey	d										17 02											
Hungerford	a																					
Newbury	a										17 20											
Thatcham	a																					
Theale	a																					
Reading [7]	a	15 57					16 41		16 59		17 38							17 57				
Slough [3]	a																					
London Paddington [15] ⊖	a	16 29					17 12		17 29		18 09							18 24				

A ✕ to Reading ⌶ from Reading
B To Edinburgh
C To Manchester Piccadilly
D The Torbay Express
E The Royal Duchy
F The Mayflower
G To Leeds

For connections to Oxford, Gatwick Airport and Heathrow Airport refer to Tables T116 and T148

For connections from Swansea refer to Table T128

Table T135-R

Mondays to Fridays

16 December to 15 May

Cornwall and Devon - Birmingham and London

		GW	GW ◇[1] ⌶	GW A	XC ◇[1] B ⌶	GW C	GW	GW ◇[1] ⌶	GW ◇	GW	XC ◇[1] D ⌶	GW	GW A	XC ◇[1] B ⌶	GW C	GW ◇	GW	GW ◇[1] E ✕⌶	GW	XC ◇[1] F ⌶	GW ◇[1] ⌶	GW	GW ◇
Penzance	d		14 15				14 50			15 15						15 50		16 15					16 50
St Erth	d		14 24				14 58			15 23						15 58		16 24					16 58
Hayle	d						15 02			15 27						16 02							17 02
Camborne	d		14 35				15 11			15 36						16 11		16 35					17 11
Redruth	d		14 42				15 17			15 42						16 17		16 42					17 17
Truro	d		14 54				15 28			15 54						16 29		16 54					17 29
St Austell	d		15 10				15 45			16 10						16 46		17 10					17 46
Newquay	d								15 10														
Par	d		15 17				15 51		15a58	16 17						16 52		17 17					17 52
Lostwithiel	d						15 58			16 24						16 59							17 59
Bodmin Parkway	d		15 29				16 04			16 29						17 05		17 29					18 05
Liskeard [6]	d		15 43				16 17			16 42						17 18		17 42	17 58				18 18
Menheniot	d									16x46													
St Germans	d						16 27			16 57						17 28							18 28
Saltash	d						16 34			17 04						17 35			18 13				18 35
St Budeaux Ferry Road	d									17 08									18 17				
Keyham	d									17 10													
Dockyard	d									17x11													
Devonport	d									17 15													
Plymouth	a		16 07				16 44			17 19						17 45		18 07	18 25				18 45
	d		16 15		16 27			16 49						17 27		17 50		18 15		18 27			18 45
Ivybridge	d							17 03								18 05							19 00
Totnes	d		16 42		16 53			17 17						17 53		18 19		18 42		18 53			19 14
Paignton	d	16 12		16 40								17 19	17 39				18 20					18 52	
Torquay	d	16 17		16 45								17 24	17 44				18 25					18 57	
Torre	d	16 20		16 48								17 27	17 47				18 28					19 00	
Newton Abbot	a	16 28	16 53	16 56	17 04			17 28				17 35	17 55	18 05		18 31	18 40	18 53		19 04		19 09	19 25
	d	16 29	16 54	16 57	17 05			17 30				17 36	17 56	18 06		18 32	18 42	18 54		19 05		19 09	19 26
Teignmouth	d	16 36		17 04								17 43	18 03			18 39	18 49					19 16	
Dawlish	d	16 41		17 09		←						17 48	18 08		←	18 44	18 54					19 21	
Dawlish Warren	d	16 45		17 20		17 20						17 52	18 18		18 18	18 48						19 26	
Starcross	d	16 50		→		17 25						17 57	→		18 22							19 30	
Exeter St Thomas	d	16 59				17 34						18 06			18 32							19 39	
Exeter St Davids [6]	a	17 04	17 12		17 25	17 38		17 48				18 15		18 25	18 37	19 04	19 09	19 13		19 24		19 43	19 47
Exeter Central	a	17 18				17 44						18 21			18 49		19 17						
Exmouth	a	17 49				18 19						18 51			19 19		19 49						
Exeter St Davids [6]	d		17 15		17 27			17 51			17 59			18 27				19 15		19 27	19 39		19 48
Tiverton Parkway	d		17 29		17 40			18 05			18 13			18 41				19 30		19 41	19 53		
Taunton	d		17 42		17 53			18 18			18 25			18 53				19 43		19 53	20 06		20 14
Bridgwater	a																						20 25
Weston-super-Mare	a																				20 26		20 43
Bristol Temple Meads [10]	a				18 25						18 56			19 26						20 24	20 45		21 25
	d				18 34						19 00			19 34						20 34			21 29
Bath Spa [7]	a																						
Filton Abbey Wood	a																						21 36
Bristol Parkway [7]	a				18 42						19 08			19 42						20 42			
Swindon	a																						
Newport (South Wales)	a																						22 04
Cardiff Central [7]	a																						22 20
Birmingham New Street [12]	a				19 56						20 23			20 56						22 01			
Castle Cary 123	d							18 39															
Frome 123	d																						
Westbury 123	d							19 00															
Pewsey	d							19 17															
Hungerford	a																						
Newbury	a							19 34															
Thatcham	a																						
Theale	a																						
Reading [7]	a		18 57					19 52										20 58					
Slough [3]	a																						
London Paddington [15] ⊖	a		19 24					20 22										21 29					

A To Exmouth
B To Leeds
C From Paignton
D To Manchester Piccadilly
E ✕ from Plymouth to Reading ⌶ to Plymouth ⌶ from Reading
F ⌶ to Bristol Temple Meads

For connections to Oxford, Gatwick Airport and Heathrow Airport refer to Tables T116 and T148

For connections from Swansea refer to Table T128

Table T135-R

Mondays to Fridays

16 December to 15 May

Cornwall and Devon - Birmingham and London

		GW FX ◇1 A ⊼	GW ◇1 B ⊼	GW ◇	GW ◇	XC ◇1	GW	GW	GW C	GW FX ◇1 ⊼	GW FO ◇1 ⊼	XC ◇1	GW D	GW ◇ E	GW	GW ◇	GW	GW ◇	GW	GW 1 ⊼	GW ◇	GW F
Penzance	d				17 15					17 45	17 45				18 15	18 50					19 15	
St Erth	d				17 23					17 54	17 54				18 23	18 58					19 23	
Hayle	d				17 27					17 58	17 58				18 27	19 02					19 27	
Camborne	d				17 36					18 08	18 08				18 36	19 11					19 36	
Redruth	d				17 42					18 15	18 15				18 42	19 17					19 42	
Truro	d				17 54					18 26	18 26				18 54	19 29					19 54	20 10
St Austell	d				18 10					18 44	18 44				19 10	19 46					20 10	20 28
Newquay	d			17 19													19 22					
Par	d			18a08	18 17					18 51	18 51				19 17	19 52	20a10				20 17	20a34
Lostwithiel	d				18 24					18 58	18 58				19 24	19 59					20 24	
Bodmin Parkway	d				18 29					19 05	19 05				19 29	20 05					20 29	
Liskeard 6	d				18 42					19 18	19 18				19 42	20 18					20 42	
Menheniot	d																				20x46	
St Germans	d				18 53										19 53	20 34					20 56	
Saltash	d				19 01										20 01	20 42					21 03	
St Budeaux Ferry Road	d																				21 08	
Keyham	d																				21 10	
Dockyard	d																				21x11	
Devonport	d																				21 14	
Plymouth	a				19 10					19 42	19 42				20 11	20 51					21 19	
	d		18 57							19 48	19 48				20 20						21 32	
Ivybridge	d														20 35						21 47	
Totnes	d									20 15	20 15				20 48						22 00	
Paignton	d						19 20	19 50	20 03			20 18							21 12	21 36		
Torquay	d						19 25	19 55	20 08			20 24							21 17	21 42		
Torre	d						19 28	19 58	20 11				←						21 20	21 45		
Newton Abbot	a		19 31				19 36	20 06	20 19	20 26	20 26	20 32	20 19		21 00				21 29	21 52	22 12	
	d		19 33				19 37	20 07	20 38	20 27	20 27	20 33	20 38		21 02				21 35		22 14	
Teignmouth	d						19 44	20 14	→				20 45		21 09				21 42		22 21	
Dawlish	d						19 49	20 19					20 51		21 14				21 47		22 26	
Dawlish Warren	d							20 23					20 55		21 18				21 51		22 30	
Starcross	d							20 28					21 00						21 56		22 34	
Exeter St Thomas	d							20 37					21 09						22 05		22 42	
Exeter St Davids 6	a		19 53				20 04	20 41		20 45	20 45	20 52	21 13		21 29				22 09		22 47	
Exeter Central	a						20 20						21 20						22 18			
Exmouth	a						20 50						21 50						22 47			
Exeter St Davids 6	d	19 55	19 55			20 00				20 48	20 48	20 56		21 14				21 50				
Tiverton Parkway	d	20 08	20 08			20 15				21 03	21 03	21 09		21 29				22 06				
Taunton	d	20 21	20 21			20 27				21 16	21 16	21 22		21 44				22 20				
Bridgwater	a																					
Weston-super-Mare	a													22 06				22 42				
Bristol Temple Meads 10	a					20 59				21 49	21 50	21 53		22 32				23 05				
	d					21 01				22 00	22 00	22 00										
Bath Spa 7	a									22 11	22 11											
Filton Abbey Wood	a																					
Bristol Parkway 7	a					21 09						22 08										
Swindon	a									22 38	22 38											
Newport (South Wales)	a																					
Cardiff Central 7	a																					
Birmingham New Street 12	a					22 25						23 41										
Castle Cary 123	d	20 43	20 43																			
Frome 123	d																					
Westbury 123	d	21 06	21 06																			
Pewsey	d	21 23	21 23																			
Hungerford	a																					
Newbury	a	21 40	21 40																			
Thatcham	a																					
Theale	a																					
Reading 7	a	21 59	21 59							23 11	23 11											
Slough 3	a																					
London Paddington 15 ⊖	a	22 29	22 29							23 56	23 56											

A until 2 April
B FO until 27 March, from 3 April
C To Exmouth
D From Paignton
E From Exeter Central
F From Falmouth Docks

For connections to Oxford, Gatwick Airport and Heathrow Airport refer to Tables T116 and T148

For connections from Swansea refer to Table T128

Table T135-R

Mondays to Fridays

16 December to 15 May

Cornwall and Devon - Birmingham and London

		GW FX ◇	GW FO ◇1 ⊼	GW	GW A	GW	GW B	GW FO C	GW FX D	GW FO E	XC ◇1
Penzance	d	20 15	20 15					21 45	21 45		22 10
St Erth	d	20 23	20 23					21u55	21u55		22 18
Hayle	d	20 27	20 27								22 22
Camborne	d	20 36	20 36					22u08	22u08		22 30
Redruth	d	20 42	20 42					22u16	22u16		22 37
Truro	d	20 54	20 54					22u29	22u29		22 48
St Austell	d	21 10	21 10					22u47	22u47		23 04
Newquay	d			21 26							
Par	d	21 17	21 17	22a15				22u56	22u56		23 11
Lostwithiel	d	21 23	21 24								23 17
Bodmin Parkway	d	21 29	21 29					23u08	23u08		23 24
Liskeard 6	d	21 42	21 43					23u24	23u24		23 36
Menheniot	d										
St Germans	d	21 53	21 53								
Saltash	d	21 59	22 00								
St Budeaux Ferry Road	d										
Keyham	d						22 57				
Dockyard	d						22x58				
Devonport	d						23 01				
Plymouth	a	22 10	22 11				23 05				00 01
	d						23 15	23u54	23u54		
Ivybridge	d						23 30				
Totnes	d						23 44	00 22	00 22		
Paignton	d				22 20	23 20					
Torquay	d				22 25	23 25					
Torre	d				22 28	23 28					
Newton Abbot	a				22 37	23 36	23 56	00 34	00 34		
	d				22 37	23 37	23 57	00 36	00 36		
Teignmouth	d				22 44	23 44					
Dawlish	d				22 49	23 49					
Dawlish Warren	d				22 54	23 53					
Starcross	d				22 58	23 58					
Exeter St Thomas	d				23 09	00 07					
Exeter St Davids 6	a				23 14	00 11	00 20	00 58	01 00		
Exeter Central	a										
Exmouth	a									←	
Exeter St Davids 6	d							01 06	01 01	01 06	
Tiverton Parkway	d							→			
Taunton	d								01 40	01 42	
Bridgwater	a										
Weston-super-Mare	a										
Bristol Temple Meads 10	a										
	d										
Bath Spa 7	a										
Filton Abbey Wood	a										
Bristol Parkway 7	a										
Swindon	a										
Newport (South Wales)	a										
Cardiff Central 7	a										
Birmingham New Street 12	a										
Castle Cary 123	d										
Frome 123	d										
Westbury 123	d										
Pewsey	d										
Hungerford	a										
Newbury	a										
Thatcham	a										
Theale	a										
Reading 7	a								03s51	04s00	
Slough 3	a										
London Paddington 15 ⊖	a								05 04	05 07	

A from 10 January
B From Gunnislake
C To London Paddington. The Night Riviera
D The Night Riviera
E From Penzance. The Night Riviera

For connections to Oxford, Gatwick Airport and Heathrow Airport refer to Tables T116 and T148

For connections from Swansea refer to Table T128

Table T135-R

Saturdays

21 December to 16 May

Cornwall and Devon - Birmingham and London

Station		GW	GW	GW	GW	GW	XC	GW	GW	GW	XC	GW	XC	GW	GW	GW	XC	GW	GW	GW	GW	GW	XC
		A		B 🛏		◇	◇1 C ✕	D	◇1 ✕	A	◇1 E ✕		◇1 F ✕	◇1 ✕	◇1 ✕		◇1 C ✕				◇1 ✕	D	◇1 E ✕
Penzance	d				05 15														05 40		06 12		06 30
St Erth	d																		05 48				06 38
Hayle	d																		05 52				06 42
Camborne	d				05 32														06 01		06 29		06 50
Redruth	d				05 38														06 07		06 36		06 57
Truro	d				05a50														06 19		06 48		07 08
St Austell	d																		06 35		07 05		07 24
Newquay	d																						
Par	d																		06 42		07 12		07 31
Lostwithiel	d																		06 49				07 37
Bodmin Parkway	d																		06 55		07 24		07 44
Liskeard 6	d																		07 08		07 37		07 56
Menheniot	d																		07x12				
St Germans	d																		07 21		07 48		
Saltash	d																		07 28		07 55		
St Budeaux Ferry Road	d																		07 32				
Keyham	d																		07 34				
Dockyard	d																		07x35				
Devonport	d																		07 38				
Plymouth	a																		07 43		08 06		08 19
	d						05 27		05 52		06 23			06 52			07 24		07 46		08 12		08 27
Ivybridge	d																		08 01				
Totnes	d			00 22			05 53		06 19		06 49			07 19			07 50		08 14		08 39		08 53
Paignton	d		00 01					06 10				06 46	07 00			07 20		07 50		08 15		08 38	
Torquay	d		00 06					06 15				06 51	07 06			07 25		07 55		08 20		08 43	
Torre	d		00 09					06 18		←		06 54				07 28		07 58		08 23		08 46	
Newton Abbot	a		00 17	00 34			06 04	06 26	06 30	06 26	07 00	07 02	07 14	07 30		07 36	08 01	08 06	08 26	08 31	08 50	08 54	09 04
	d		00 18	00 36			06 06	06 35	06 31	06 35	07 02	07 06	07 19	07 31		07 38	08 03	08 07	08 27	08 33	08 52	08 56	09 06
Teignmouth	d		00 25					→		06 42		07 13	07 26			07 45		08 14	08 34	08 40		09 03	
Dawlish	d		00 30							06 47		07 18	07 31			07 50		08 19	08 39	08 45		09 08	
Dawlish Warren	d										06 52		07 22				07 54		08 23		08 49		09 18	
Starcross	d										06 56		07 26				07 59		08 28		08 54		→	
Exeter St Thomas	d	00 07	00 42							07 05		07 35				08 08		08 37		09 03			
Exeter St Davids 6	a	00 11	00 47	00 58			06 25		06 50	07 09	07 21	07 39	07 43	07 50		08 12	08 22	08 41	08 52	09 07	09 11		09 25
Exeter Central	a										07 21		07 47				08 21		08 48		09 18			
Exmouth	a										07 51		08 21				08 51		09 21		09 51			
Exeter St Davids 6	d			01 06		05 46	06 27		06 56		07 26		07 45	07 54	08 04		08 27				09 16		09 27
Tiverton Parkway	d					06 01	06 40		07 11		07 40		07 58	08 08	08 19		08 41				09 31		09 41
Taunton	d			01 42		06 17	06 53		07 28		07 53		08 10	08 22	08 32		08 53				09 44		09 53
Bridgwater	a					06 27																	
Weston-super-Mare	a					06 45																	
Bristol Temple Meads 10	a					07 20	07 24				08 24		08 45				09 24						10 24
	d					07 29	07 34				08 34		09 00				09 34						10 34
Bath Spa 7	a																						
Filton Abbey Wood	a					07 36																	
Bristol Parkway 7	a						07 42				08 42		09 08				09 42						10 42
Swindon	a																						
Newport (South Wales)	a					08 06																	
Cardiff Central 7	a					08 24																	
Birmingham New Street 12	a						08 56				09 56		10 25				10 56						11 56
Castle Cary 123	d								07 49					08 42									
Frome 123	d																						
Westbury 123	d								08 10						09 11								
Pewsey	d								08 27						09 28								
Hungerford	a																						
Newbury	a								08 45														
Thatcham	a																						
Theale	a																						
Reading 7	a			04s00					09 01					09 41	09 59						11 01		
Slough 3	a																						
London Paddington 15 ⊖	a			05 07					09 30					10 07	10 29						11 29		

A From Paignton
B From Penzance. The Night Riviera
C To Edinburgh
D To Exmouth
E To Glasgow Central
F To Manchester Piccadilly. ✕ from Newton Abbot

For connections to Oxford, Gatwick Airport and Heathrow Airport refer to Tables T116 and T148

For connections from Swansea refer to Table T128

Table T135-R

Saturdays

21 December to 16 May

Cornwall and Devon - Birmingham and London

Station		GW	GW	GW	GW	GW	GW	GW	XC	GW	GW	XC	GW	GW	XC	GW	GW	GW	GW	GW	GW	XC	GW
		A	◇1 B ✕	◇	C		◇1 ✕	◇	◇1 D ✕			◇1 E ✕		◇1 ✕	◇1 F ✕	C	◇1 ✕				◇1 G ✕	◇1 H ✕	
Penzance	d			06 40	06 50		07 08			07 38				08 15	08 33	08 41			08 50		09 15		
St Erth	d			06 48	06a58		07 18			07 48				08 24	08 43	08a49			08 58		09 24		
Hayle	d			06 52			07 22			07 51									09 02				
Camborne	d			07 01			07 32			08 01				08 35	08 53				09 11		09 35		
Redruth	d			07 07			07 39			08 07				08 42	08 59				09 17		09 42		
Truro	d			07 19			07 51			08 20				08 55	09 11				09 29		09 55		
St Austell	d			07 35			08 08			08 36				09 11	09 27				09 45		10 11		
Newquay	d								07 48																
Par	d			07 42			08 15	08a38		08 45				09 18	09 33				09 53		10 18		
Lostwithiel	d			07 49						08 52									10 00				
Bodmin Parkway	d			07 54			08 27			08 57				09 30	09 44				10 05		10 30		
Liskeard 6	d			08 07			08 40			09 10				09 43	09 56				10 18		10 43		
Menheniot	d			08x11																			
St Germans	d			08 20			08 51			09 21									10 29				
Saltash	d			08 29			08 58			09 29									10 36				
St Budeaux Ferry Road	d			08 33																			
Keyham	d			08 36																			
Dockyard	d			08x37																			
Devonport	d			08 39																			
Plymouth	a			08 45			09 09			09 38				10 08	10 19				10 45		11 07		
	d			08 47			09 15		09 27					10 14	10 27				10 50		11 14	11 27	
Ivybridge	d			09 02															11 05				
Totnes	d			09 15			09 42		09 53					10 42	10 53				11 18		11 41	11 53	
Paignton	d		08 55			09 22					09 50	10 12	10 20					10 55		11 20			11 54
Torquay	d		09 01			09 27					09 56	10 18	10 25					11 00		11 25			11 59
Torre	d		09 05			09 30					09 59		10 28					11 03		11 28			12 02
Newton Abbot	a		09 12	09 28		09 38	09 53		10 04		10 10	10 26	10 36	10 53	11 04			11 11	11 30	11 36	11 52	12 04	12 10
	d		09 14	09 29		09 39	09 54		10 06		10 12	10 27	10 38	10 54	11 06			11 12	11 31	11 38	11 54	12 06	12 12
Teignmouth	d		09 22			09 46					10 19	10 34	10 45					11 19		11 45			12 19
Dawlish	d	←	09 27			09 51					10 24	10 39	10 50					11 24		11 50			12 24
Dawlish Warren	d	09 18				09 55					10 28		10 54					11 29		11 54			12 28
Starcross	d	09 22									10 33							11 33					12 33
Exeter St Thomas	d	09 31									10 42							11 42					12 42
Exeter St Davids 6	a	09 35	09 39	09 52		10 08	10 13		10 25		10 46	10 52	11 07	11 13	11 25			11 47	11 54	12 07	12 13	12 25	12 47
Exeter Central	a	09 42				10 20					10 55		11 20					11 55		12 20			12 55
Exmouth	a	10 19				10 50					11 20		11 50					12 20		12 50			13 20
Exeter St Davids 6	d		09 42	09 53			10 15		10 27			10 53		11 15	11 27		11 43				12 15	12 27	
Tiverton Parkway	d						10 30		10 41			11 07		11 30	11 41						12 30	12 41	
Taunton	d		10 06	10 20			10 43		10 53			11 19		11 43	11 53		12 07				12 43	12 53	
Bridgwater	a			10 30																			
Weston-super-Mare	a			10 48																			
Bristol Temple Meads 10	a			11 17					11 25			11 51			12 24							13 24	
	d			11 28					11 34			12 00			12 35							13 35	
Bath Spa 7	a																						
Filton Abbey Wood	a			11 35																			
Bristol Parkway 7	a								11 42			12 08			12 43							13 44	
Swindon	a																						
Newport (South Wales)	a			12 07																			
Cardiff Central 7	a			12 23																			
Birmingham New Street 12	a								12 56			13 25			13 56							14 56	
Castle Cary 123	d		10 27														12 28						
Frome 123	d																						
Westbury 123	d		10 48														12 49						
Pewsey	d		11 06														13 07						
Hungerford	a																						
Newbury	a		11 23														13 24						
Thatcham	a																						
Theale	a																						
Reading 7	a		11 41				11 59							12 59			13 42				13 59		
Slough 3	a																						
London Paddington 15 ⊖	a		12 08				12 29							13 29			14 09				14 29		

A From Paignton
B The Torbay Express
C To St Ives
D To Aberdeen
E To Manchester Piccadilly
F To Glasgow Central. ✕ from Plymouth
G The Cornish Riviera
H To Dundee

For connections to Oxford, Gatwick Airport and Heathrow Airport refer to Tables T116 and T148

For connections from Swansea refer to Table T128

Table T135-R

Saturdays

21 December to 16 May

Cornwall and Devon - Birmingham and London

		XC ◇1 A ⚒	GW	GW ◇	GW	GW ◇1 ⚒	XC ◇1 B ⚒	GW ◇1 ⚒	GW	GW ◇	GW	GW	GW ◇1 ⚒	GW C	XC ◇1 D ⚒	GW	XC ◇1 A ⚒	GW E	GW	GW ◇1 F ⚒	XC ◇1 D ⚒	GW ◇1 ⚒
Penzance	d	09 43	09 55			10 15				10 50	11 15					11 48				12 15		
St Erth	d	09 51	10 03			10 24				10 58	11 23					11 56				12 24		
Hayle	d		10 07							11 02	11 27					12 00						
Camborne	d	10 01	10 16			10 35				11 11	11 36					12 09				12 35		
Redruth	d	10 08	10 22			10 42				11 17	11 42					12 15				12 42		
Truro	d	10 19	10 34			10 55				11 29	11 54					12 27				12 55		
St Austell	d	10 35	10 51			11 11				11 46	12 10					12 43				13 11		
Newquay	d			10 20																		
Par	d	10 42	10 57	11a10		11 19				11 52	12 17					12 50						
Lostwithiel	d	10 48	11 04							11 59	12 24					12 57						
Bodmin Parkway	d	10 55	11 10			11 31				12 05	12 29					13 02				13 28		
Liskeard [6]	d	11 14	11 23			11 44				12 18	12 42					13 15				13 41		
Menheniot	d																					
St Germans	d		11 33							12 28	12 53					13 26						
Saltash	d		11 40							12 36	13 00					13 33						
St Budeaux Ferry Road	d																					
Keyham	d																					
Dockyard	d																					
Devonport	d																					
Plymouth	a	11 39	11 50			12 08				12 45	13 09					13 43				14 07		
	d	11 50				12 15	12 27			12 48			13 15		13 27					14 15	14 27	
Ivybridge	d									13 03												
Totnes	d	12 16				12 42	12 53			13 17			13 42		13 53					14 42	14 53	
Paignton	d				12 20				12 55			13 20		13 41			13 57		14 20			
Torquay	d				12 25				13 00			13 25		13 46			14 03		14 25			
Torre	d				12 28				13 03			13 28		13 49					14 28			
Newton Abbot	a	12 27			12 36	12 53	13 05		13 11	13 28		13 36	13 53	13 57	14 04		14 12		14 36	14 53	15 04	
	d	12 28			12 38	12 54	13 06		13 13	13 30		13 38	13 54	13 59	14 06		14 13		14 38	14 54	15 06	
Teignmouth	d				12 45				13 20			13 45		14 06			14 20		14 45			
Dawlish	d				12 50				13 25			13 50		14 11			14 26	←	14 50			
Dawlish Warren	d				12 54				13 29					14 30				14 30				
Starcross	d								13 34					→				14 34				
Exeter St Thomas	d								13 43									14 43				
Exeter St Davids [6]	a	12 51			13 07	13 13	13 25		13 47	13 51		14 06	14 13		14 26		14 36	14 48	15 05	15 13	15 25	
Exeter Central	a				13 20				13 55			14 20						14 55	15 20			
Exmouth	a				13 50				14 20			14 50						15 20	15 50			
Exeter St Davids [6]	d	12 53				13 15	13 27	13 43		13 53			14 15		14 27		14 40			15 15	15 27	15 43
Tiverton Parkway	d	13 07				13 30	13 41						14 30		14 41		14 53			15 30	15 41	
Taunton	d	13 20				13 43	13 53	14 07		14 20			14 43		14 53		15 06			15 43	15 53	16 07
Bridgwater	a									14 30												
Weston-super-Mare	a									14 48							15 26					
Bristol Temple Meads [10]	a	13 55					14 26			15 17					15 25		15 47				16 24	
	d	14 00					14 34			15 28					15 34		16 00				16 34	
Bath Spa [7]	a																					
Filton Abbey Wood	a									15 35												
Bristol Parkway [7]	a	14 08					14 42								15 42		16 08				16 42	
Swindon	a																					
Newport (South Wales)	a									16 06												
Cardiff Central [7]	a									16 23												
Birmingham New Street [12]	a	15 25					15 56								16 56		17 25				17 56	
Castle Cary 123	d							14 28														16 28
Frome 123	d																					
Westbury 123	d							14 48														16 48
Pewsey	d							15 06														17 06
Hungerford	a																					
Newbury	a							15 23														17 23
Thatcham	a																					
Theale	a																					
Reading [7]	a					14 59		15 41					15 59							16 59		17 41
Slough [3]	a																					
London Paddington [15] ⊖	a					15 29		16 08					16 30							17 29		18 09

A To Manchester Piccadilly
B To Glasgow Central
C To Exmouth
D To Edinburgh
E From Paignton
F The Royal Duchy

For connections to Oxford, Gatwick Airport and Heathrow Airport refer to Tables T116 and T148

For connections from Swansea refer to Table T128

NRT DECEMBER 19 EDITION

Table T135-R

Saturdays

21 December to 16 May

Cornwall and Devon - Birmingham and London

		GW	GW	GW ◇	GW	GW	GW ◇1 ⚒	XC ◇1 A ⚒	GW	XC ◇1 B ⚒	GW	GW	GW ◇1 ⚒	XC ◇1 C ⚒	GW	GW ◇	GW	GW ◇1 ⚒	GW	GW	XC ◇1 C ⚒	GW	GW ◇
Penzance	d		12 50		13 15						13 50		14 15		14 50				15 15				15 50
St Erth	d		12 58		13 23						13 58		14 24		14 58				15 23				15 58
Hayle	d		13 02		13 27						14 02				15 02				15 27				16 02
Camborne	d		13 11		13 36						14 11		14 35		15 11				15 36				16 11
Redruth	d		13 17		13 42						14 17		14 42		15 17				15 42				16 17
Truro	d		13 29		13 54						14 29		14 55		15 29				15 53				16 29
St Austell	d		13 46		14 10						14 45		15 11		15 46				16 10				16 46
Newquay	d			13 10												15 10							
Par	d		13 52	14a00	14 17						14 52		15 18		15 52	16a00			16 16				16 52
Lostwithiel	d		13 59		14 24						14 59				15 59				16 23				16 59
Bodmin Parkway	d		14 05		14 29						15 04		15 30		16 05				16 29				17 05
Liskeard [6]	d		14 18		14 42						15 17		15 43		16 18				16 45				17 18
Menheniot	d																		16x49				
St Germans	d		14 28		14 53						15 28				16 28				16 57				17 28
Saltash	d		14 35		15 00						15 35				16 35				17 04				17 35
St Budeaux Ferry Road	d																		17 09				
Keyham	d																		17 11				
Dockyard	d																		17x12				
Devonport	d																		17 14				
Plymouth	a		14 45		15 09						15 44		16 08		16 45				17 22				17 45
	d		14 48				15 15	15 27			15 48		16 15	16 27				16 50			17 27		17 46
Ivybridge	d		15 03								16 03							17 04					18 01
Totnes	d		15 17				15 42	15 53			16 16		16 42	16 53				17 19			17 53		18 15
Paignton	d	14 55				15 20			15 50			16 18					16 52			17 18		17 50	
Torquay	d	15 00				15 25			15 55			16 23					16 57			17 23		17 55	
Torre	d	15 03				15 28			15 58			16 26					17 00			17 26		17 58	
Newton Abbot	a	15 11	15 29			15 36	15 53	16 05	16 06		16 28	16 34	16 53	17 05			17 08	17 30		17 34	18 05	18 06	18 26
	d	15 13	15 31			15 38	15 54	16 06	16 10		16 29	16 35	16 54	17 06			17 10	17 31		17 36	18 06	18 10	18 27
Teignmouth	d	15 20				15 45			16 17			16 42					17 17			17 43		18 17	18 34
Dawlish	d	15 25				15 50			16 22			16 47					17 22			17 48		18 22	18 39
Dawlish Warren	d	15 29							16 26			16 51					17 26			17 52		18 26	18 43
Starcross	d	15 34							16 31			16 56					17 31			17 57		18 31	
Exeter St Thomas	d	15 43							16 40			17 05					17 40			18 06		18 40	
Exeter St Davids [6]	a	15 47	15 53			16 07	16 13	16 25	16 45		16 50	17 09	17 13	17 25			17 45	17 50		18 10	18 25	18 44	18 54
Exeter Central	a	15 54				16 20			16 52			17 19					17 52			18 19		18 51	
Exmouth	a	16 20				16 52			17 22			17 52					18 22			18 50		19 21	
Exeter St Davids [6]	d						16 15	16 27		16 45			17 15	17 27				17 53			18 27		19 00
Tiverton Parkway	d						16 30	16 41		16 59			17 29	17 41				18 08			18 41		19 15
Taunton	d						16 43	16 53		17 12			17 43	17 53				18 23			18 53		19 30
Bridgwater	a																						
Weston-super-Mare	a																						19 54
Bristol Temple Meads [10]	a							17 26		17 47				18 26							19 29		20 16
	d							17 34		18 00				18 34							19 32		
Bath Spa [7]	a																						
Filton Abbey Wood	a																						
Bristol Parkway [7]	a							17 42		18 08				18 42							19 40		
Swindon	a																						
Newport (South Wales)	a																						
Cardiff Central [7]	a																						
Birmingham New Street [12]	a							18 56		19 25				19 56							20 52		
Castle Cary 123	d																	18 44					
Frome 123	d																						
Westbury 123	d																	19 06					
Pewsey	d																	19 23					
Hungerford	a																						
Newbury	a																	19 41					
Thatcham	a																						
Theale	a																						
Reading [7]	a						17 59						19 00					19 59					
Slough [3]	a																						
London Paddington [15] ⊖	a						18 30						19 29					20 27					

A To York
B To Manchester Piccadilly
C To Leeds

For connections to Oxford, Gatwick Airport and Heathrow Airport refer to Tables T116 and T148

For connections from Swansea refer to Table T128

Table T135-R

Saturdays
21 December to 16 May

Cornwall and Devon - Birmingham and London

		GW	GW	XC	GW	GW	GW	GW	GW	GW	GW	GW	GW	GW	GW	GW	GW	GW	GW	GW	XC	GW	GW
			◇1	◇1		◇					1	◇1									◇1		
				A											B								
			(trolley)	(trolley)								(trolley)											
Penzance	d		16 20			16 50		17 15				17 50		18 15	18 58		19 27				21 30		
St Erth	d		16 29			16 58		17 23				17 59		18 23	19a06		19 35				21 39		
Hayle	d					17 02		17 27				18 03		18 27			19 39						
Camborne	d		16 40			17 11		17 36				18 13		18 36			19 48				21 49		
Redruth	d		16 47			17 17		17 42				18 20		18 42			19 54				21 56		
Truro	d		17 00			17 29		17 54				18 32		18 54			20 06				22 08		
St Austell	d		17 16			17 46		18 10				18 48		19 10			20 22				22 25		
Newquay	d						17 10									19 08				21 17			
Par	d		17 23			17 52	18a00	18 17				18 55		19 17		19a59	20 29			22 12	22 32		
Lostwithiel	d					17 59		18 24				19 02		19 24			20 36			22 19			
Bodmin Parkway	d		17 35			18 05		18 29				19 09		19 29			20 42			22 25	22 43		
Liskeard [6]	d		17 48			18 18		18 42				19 22		19 42			20 58			22 38	22 55		
Menheniot	d																21x02			22x42			
St Germans	d					18 28		18 53						19 53			21 10			22 51			
Saltash	d					18 35		19 00						20 01			21 17			22 58			
St Budeaux Ferry Road	d																21 22			23 02			
Keyham	d																21 24			23 04			
Dockyard	d																21x26			23x05			
Devonport	d																21 28			23 08			
Plymouth	a		18 12			18 45		19 09				19 46		20 11			21 34			23 14	23 18		
	d		18 16	18 27		18 46						19 52		20 20					21 47				
Ivybridge	d					19 01								20 35					22 02				
Totnes	d		18 43	18 53		19 15						20 19		20 48					22 16				
Paignton	d	18 20			18 52				19 20	19 38	20 08		20 20					21 20				22 42	23 25
Torquay	d	18 25			18 57				19 25	19 43	20 14		20 25					21 25				22 47	23 30
Torre	d	18 28			19 00				19 28	19 46			20 28					21 28				22 50	23 33
Newton Abbot	a	18 36	18 54	19 04	19 08	19 27			19 36	19 54	20 25	20 30	20 38	21 01				21 36	22 28			22 59	23 41
	d	18 40	18 55	19 06	19 09	19 28			19 39	19 58		20 32	20 39	21 02				21 37	22 28				23 42
Teignmouth	d	18 47			19 16				19 46	20 05			20 46	21 09				21 44	22 35				23 49
Dawlish	d	18 52			19 21				19 51	20 10			20 51	21 14				21 49	22 40				23 54
Dawlish Warren	d				19 25				19 55	20 14			20 55					21 53	22 45				23 58
Starcross	d				19 30					20 19			20 59					21 58	22 49				00 02
Exeter St Thomas	d				19 39					20 28			21 08					22 07	22 58				00 11
Exeter St Davids [6]	a	19 06	19 14	19 25	19 43	19 48			20 08	20 32		20 51	21 13	21 28				22 11	23 04				00 15
Exeter Central	a	19 19							20 20				21 20					22 20					
Exmouth	a	19 50							20 50				21 50					22 50					
Exeter St Davids [6]	d		19 16	19 27		19 50						20 52											
Tiverton Parkway	d		19 31	19 41								21 07											
Taunton	d		19 45	19 53		20 17						21 20											
Bridgwater	a					20 27																	
Weston-super-Mare	a					20 47																	
Bristol Temple Meads [10]	a			20 24		21 22						21 50											
	d			20 30		21 29						21 57											
Bath Spa [7]	a											22 08											
Filton Abbey Wood	a					21 36																	
Bristol Parkway [7]	a			20 38																			
Swindon	a											22 35											
Newport (South Wales)	a					22 09																	
Cardiff Central [7]	a					22 31																	
Birmingham New Street [12]	a			21 51																			
Castle Cary 123	d		20 06																				
Frome 123	d																						
Westbury 123	d		20 27																				
Pewsey	d		20 45																				
Hungerford	a																						
Newbury	a																						
Thatcham	a																						
Theale	a																						
Reading [7]	a		21 18									23 10											
Slough [3]	a																						
London Paddington [15] ⊖	a		21 44									23 41											

A (trolley) to Bristol Temple Meads
B To St Ives

For connections to Oxford, Gatwick Airport and Heathrow Airport refer to Tables T116 and T148

For connections from Swansea refer to Table T128

Table T135-R

Sundays
15 December to 10 May

Cornwall and Devon - Birmingham and London

		GW	GW	GW	GW	GW	GW	XC	GW	GW	GW	GW	XC	GW	XC	GW	GW	XC	GW	XC	GW	GW	GW
				◇1	◇1	◇	◇1	◇1			◇1	◇1	◇1		◇1		◇1	◇1		◇1	◇1		◇
		A	B					C			D		E		F		D	G		F		H	
				(trolley)	(trolley)		(trolley)	(trolley)			(restaurant)	(trolley)	(trolley)		(trolley)		(restaurant)	(trolley)		(trolley)	(trolley)		
Penzance	d										08 15			08 50			09 18	09 30			10 18	10 27	
St Erth	d										08 23			08 58			09 26	09 38			10 26	10a35	
Hayle	d													09 02									
Camborne	d										08 35			09 11			09 38	09 48			10 38		
Redruth	d										08 41			09 17			09 44	09 55			10 44		
Truro	d										08 54			09 28			09 57	10 08			10 57		
St Austell	d										09 10			09 45			10 12	10 24			11 12		
Newquay	d																						11 05
Par	d										09 18			09 51			10 20	10 30			11 20		11a54
Lostwithiel	d													09 58									
Bodmin Parkway	d										09 29			10 04			10 32	10 41			11 32		
Liskeard [6]	d										09 42			10 17			10 46	10 55			11 46		
Menheniot	d													10x22									
St Germans	d													10 31									
Saltash	d													10 38									
St Budeaux Ferry Road	d																						
Keyham	d																						
Dockyard	d																						
Devonport	d																						
Plymouth	a										10 04			10 48			11 08	11 18			12 07		
	d				08 32		09 07	09 25		09 48	10 10		10 25				11 15	11 27		12 00	12 15		
Ivybridge	d									10 03													
Totnes	d				08 59		09 34	09 51		10 16	10 39		10 51				11 43	11 53			12 41		
Paignton	d								09 50			10 36			10 50	10 57			11 53				
Torquay	d								09 55			10 42			10 56	11 02			11 59				
Torre	d								09 58							11 05			12 02				
Newton Abbot	a				09 10		09 45	10 02	10 06	10 28	10 50	10 51	11 02		11 06	11 13	11 54	12 04	12 10	12 35	12 53		
	d				09 12		09 47	10 04	10 08	10 28	10 52	10 55	11 04		11 08	11 14	11 56	12 06	12 12	12 38	12 54		
Teignmouth	d				09 19				10 15			11 02			11 15	11 21			12 19				
Dawlish	d				09 24				10 20			11 07			11 20	11 26			12 24				
Dawlish Warren	d								10 25							11 31			12 29				
Starcross	d	00 02							10 29							11 35			12 33				
Exeter St Thomas	d	00 11							10 38							11 44			12 42				
Exeter St Davids [6]	a	00 15			09 36		10 06	10 23	10 42	10 52	11 11	11 19	11 24		11 32	11 47	12 15	12 25	12 48	12 57	13 13		
Exeter Central	a								10 52							11 54			12 53				
Exmouth	a								11 19							12 20			13 19				
Exeter St Davids [6]	d		07 59	08 34	09 38	09 42	10 08	10 27			11 13	11 21	11 27		11 34		12 16	12 27		13 00	13 15		
Tiverton Parkway	d		08 14	08 49		09 57	10 22	10 41			11 27		11 41		11 48		12 31	12 41		13 13	13 29		
Taunton	d		08 28	09 01	10 00	10 12	10 34	10 53			11 39	11 49	11 53		12 00		12 42	12 53		13 26	13 41		
Bridgwater	a		08 38			10 22																	
Weston-super-Mare	a		08 56			10 40									12 20								
Bristol Temple Meads [10]	a		09 33			11 16		11 24					12 24		12 48			13 24		13 57			
	d							11 29					12 29		13 00			13 29		14 00			
Bath Spa [7]	a																						
Filton Abbey Wood	a																						
Bristol Parkway [7]	a							11 37					12 37		13 08			13 37		14 08			
Swindon	a																						
Newport (South Wales)	a																						
Cardiff Central [7]	a																						
Birmingham New Street [12]	a							12 49					13 49		14 18			14 49		15 18			
Castle Cary 123	d			09 21	10 21							12 09											
Frome 123	d																						
Westbury 123	d			09 48	10 44		11 12					12 30											
Pewsey	d			10 05	11 01							12 47											
Hungerford	a																						
Newbury	a			10 23	11 18							13 05											
Thatcham	a																						
Theale	a																						
Reading [7]	a			10 40	11 35		11 56				12 55	13 22					13 58				14 57		
Slough [3]	a																						
London Paddington [15] ⊖	a			11 08	12 06		12 23				13 23	13 53					14 23				15 24		

A not 15 December. From Paignton
B To Severn Beach
C To Aberdeen
D (restaurant) from Plymouth (trolley) to Plymouth
E To Glasgow Central
F To Manchester Piccadilly
G To Edinburgh. (trolley) from Plymouth
H from 5 April. To St Ives

For connections to Oxford, Gatwick Airport and Heathrow Airport refer to Tables T116 and T148

For connections from Swansea refer to Table T128

Table T135-R

Sundays

15 December to 10 May

Cornwall and Devon - Birmingham and London

Station		XC ◇1 A 🍴	GW ◇1 🍴	GW	XC ◇1 B 🍴	GW	GW ◇1 🍴	GW C	XC ◇1 D 🍴	GW	GW	GW	GW ◇1 🍴	XC ◇1 D 🍴	XC ◇1 E 🍴	GW ◇1 🍴	GW	GW ◇1 🍴	GW	GW ◇1 🍴	GW ◇	GW F	XC ◇1 G 🍴
Penzance	d					11 10		11 40					12 13		12 35				13 08				
St Erth	d					11 18		11a48					12 21		12 43				13 19				
Hayle	d					11 22									12 47				13 22				
Camborne	d					11 31							12 33		12 55				13 32				
Redruth	d					11 37							12 39		13 02				13 38				
Truro	d					11 48							12 52		13 13				13 49				
St Austell	d					12 05							13 07		13 30				14 05				
Newquay	d																				14 20		
Par	d					12 11							13 15		13 36				14 12		15a09		
Lostwithiel	d					12 18									13 43				14 19				
Bodmin Parkway	d					12 24							13 27		13 50				14 24				
Liskeard 6	d					12 37							13 40		14 02				14 37				
Menheniot	d																						
St Germans	d					12 47													14 48				
Saltash	d					12 54													14 55				
St Budeaux Ferry Road	d																						
Keyham	d																						
Dockyard	d																						
Devonport	d																						
Plymouth	a					13 04							14 03		14 25				15 04				
	d	12 27			12 53		13 15		13 25		13 35		14 10	14 25	14 34			14 55		15 10			15 27
Ivybridge	d										13 52												
Totnes	d	12 53					13 41		13 51		14 05		14 38	14 51	15 00					15 36			15 53
Paignton	d			12 51						13 51		14 13					15 00					15 38	
Torquay	d			12 57						13 56		14 18					15 05					15 43	
Torre	d			13 00						13 59		14 21					15 08					15 46	
Newton Abbot	a	13 05		13 08	13 28		13 53		14 02	14 07	14 17	14 29	14 50	15 03	15 11		15 16	15 29		15 48		15 54	16 05
	d	13 06		13 11	13 30		13 54		14 04	14 08	14 19	14 31	14 51	15 04	15 13		15 17	15 29		15 49		15 55	16 06
Teignmouth	d			13 19						14 15	14 26	14 38					15 24					16 03	
Dawlish	d			13 24						14 20	14 31	14 43					15 29					16 08	
Dawlish Warren	d			13 29						14 25	14 35	14 48					15 34					16 18	
Starcross	d			13 33						14 29		14 52										→	
Exeter St Thomas	d			13 42						14 39		15 01											
Exeter St Davids 6	a	13 25		13 46	13 51		14 13		14 23	14 43	14 47	15 06	15 10	15 23	15 32		15 46	15 49		16 08			16 25
Exeter Central	a			13 53						14 49		15 18					15 52						
Exmouth	a			14 20						15 19		15 50					16 19						
Exeter St Davids 6	d	13 27	13 39		13 54		14 15		14 27				15 12	15 27	15 34	15 40		15 53		16 10			16 27
Tiverton Parkway	d	13 41					14 30		14 41				15 27	15 41	15 47					16 25			16 41
Taunton	d	13 53	14 03				14 42		14 53				15 40	15 53	16 00	16 03		16 16		16 37			16 53
Bridgwater	a																						
Weston-super-Mare	a														16 20								
Bristol Temple Meads 10	a	14 26			14 48				15 24					16 26	16 47			16 53					17 26
	d	14 29			15 00				15 29					16 29	17 00			17 00					17 29
Bath Spa 7	a																	17 11					
Filton Abbey Wood	a																						
Bristol Parkway 7	a	14 37			15 08				15 37					16 37	17 08								17 37
Swindon	a																	17 38					
Newport (South Wales)	a																						
Cardiff Central 7	a																						
Birmingham New Street 12	a	15 52			16 18				16 49					17 50	18 18								18 50
Castle Cary 123	d		14 24													16 24							
Frome 123	d																						
Westbury 123	d		14 45													16 45							
Pewsey	d		15 02													17 02							
Hungerford	a																						
Newbury	a		15 19													17 19							
Thatcham	a																						
Theale	a																						
Reading 7	a		15 36				15 58						16 56			17 36		18 11		17 53			
Slough 3	a																						
London Paddington 15 ⊖	a		16 06				16 24						17 21			18 06		18 38		18 23			

A To Glasgow Central
B To Manchester Piccadilly
C until 29 March. To St Ives
D To Edinburgh
E To Manchester Piccadilly. 🍴 from Plymouth
F To Exmouth
G To York

For connections to Oxford, Gatwick Airport and Heathrow Airport refer to Tables T116 and T148

For connections from Swansea refer to Table T128

Table T135-R

Sundays

15 December to 10 May

Cornwall and Devon - Birmingham and London

Station		GW A	GW ◇1 🍴	GW	GW	GW ◇1 🍴	XC ◇1 B 🍴	GW ◇1 🍴	GW	GW	GW ◇	GW ◇1 🍴	XC ◇1 C 🍴	GW	GW ◇1 🍴	XC ◇1 D 🍴	GW ◇1 🍴	XC ◇1 E 🍴	GW	GW	GW	GW
Penzance	d					14 18					15 04		15 35				16 18			17 15		
St Erth	d					14 26					15 13		15 43				16 26			17 23		
Hayle	d										15 16									17 27		
Camborne	d					14 38					15 26		15 53				16 38			17 36		
Redruth	d					14 44					15 32		15 59				16 44			17 42		
Truro	d					14 57					15 43		16 11				16 57			17 53		
St Austell	d					15 12					15 59		16 27				17 12			18 10		
Newquay	d																				17 55	
Par	d					15 20					16 06		16 33				17 20			18 16	18a44	
Lostwithiel	d										16 13									18 23		
Bodmin Parkway	d					15 32					16 18		16 44				17 32			18 29		
Liskeard 6	d					15 45					16 31		16 56				17 45			18 42		
Menheniot	d																					
St Germans	d										16 42									18 52		
Saltash	d										16 49									19 02		
St Budeaux Ferry Road	d																					
Keyham	d																					
Dockyard	d																					
Devonport	d																					
Plymouth	a					16 08					16 58		17 19				18 07			19 12		
	d			15 41		16 15	16 25			16 41	16 59	17 15	17 27		17 46		18 15	18 27		19 15		
Ivybridge	d			15 56						16 56	17 14									19 30		
Totnes	d			16 09		16 42	16 51			17 09	17 28	17 42	17 53		18 12		18 42	18 53		19 43		
Paignton	d		15 59		16 17				16 49					17 50		18 20			18 53			19 45
Torquay	d		16 05		16 22				16 55					17 56		18 26			18 59			19 50
Torre	d				16 25				16 58					17 59					19 02			19 53
Newton Abbot	a		16 13	16 21	16 33	16 53	17 03		17 07	17 21	17 39	17 53	18 04	18 07	18 24	18 34	18 53	19 05	19 10	19 55		20 01
	d		16 15	16 23	16 34	16 55	17 04		17 08	17 23	17 40	17 55	18 06	18 10	18 25	18 35	18 55	19 06	19 12	19 56		20 02
Teignmouth	d		16 22		16 41				17 16					18 17	18 32				19 19			20 10
Dawlish	d	←	16 27		16 46				17 21					18 22	18 37				19 24			20 15
Dawlish Warren	d	16 18			16 51				17 25					18 27					19 29			20 19
Starcross	d	16 22			16 55				17 29					18 31					19 33			20 23
Exeter St Thomas	d	16 31			17 04				17 39					18 40					19 42			20 33
Exeter St Davids 6	a	16 34	16 39	16 44	17 09	17 14	17 23		17 44	17 48	18 04	18 14	18 25	18 46	18 49	18 56	19 14	19 25	19 46	20 17		20 37
Exeter Central	a	16 46			17 18				17 54					18 52					19 53			20 53
Exmouth	a	17 19			17 49				18 20					19 24					20 23			21 23
Exeter St Davids 6	d		16 41			17 16	17 27	17 40			18 05	18 16	18 27		18 50	18 58	19 16	19 27				
Tiverton Parkway	d					17 30	17 41				18 21	18 30	18 41			19 11	19 30	19 41				
Taunton	d		17 03			17 42	17 53	18 03			18 38	18 42	18 53		19 13	19 24	19 42	19 53				
Bridgwater	a		17 14																			
Weston-super-Mare	a		17 31																			
Bristol Temple Meads 10	a		17 59				18 26				19 16		19 24			19 57		20 26				
	d		18 00				18 29						19 31			20 00		20 29				
Bath Spa 7	a		18 12																			
Filton Abbey Wood	a																					
Bristol Parkway 7	a						18 37						19 39			20 08		20 37				
Swindon	a		18 38																			
Newport (South Wales)	a																					
Cardiff Central 7	a																					
Birmingham New Street 12	a						19 50						20 54			21 18		21 50				
Castle Cary 123	d							18 24														
Frome 123	d																					
Westbury 123	d							18 47							19 54							
Pewsey	d							19 04														
Hungerford	a																					
Newbury	a							19 22														
Thatcham	a																					
Theale	a																					
Reading 7	a		19 10			18 58		19 38				19 58			20 40		20 58					
Slough 3	a																					
London Paddington 15 ⊖	a		19 38			19 24		20 07				20 25			21 10		21 23					

A From Paignton
B To Leeds
C To Leeds. 🍴 from Plymouth
D 🍴 to Bristol Temple Meads
E To Leeds. 🍴 to Bristol Temple Meads

For connections to Oxford, Gatwick Airport and Heathrow Airport refer to Tables T116 and T148

For connections from Swansea refer to Table T128

Table T135-R

Cornwall and Devon - Birmingham and London

Sundays

15 December to 10 May

		GW	GW	GW	GW	GW	GW	GW	GW	GW
		◇1 ✠	◇1 ✠							■ A ⇌ ✠
Penzance	d	17 50			19 00	20 26				21 15
St Erth	d	17 58			19 08	20 38				21u25
Hayle	d				19 12	20 42				
Camborne	d	18 10			19 21	20 51				21u39
Redruth	d	18 16			19 27	20 57				21u46
Truro	d	18 29			19 38	21 08				22u01
St Austell	d	18 45			19 55	21 25				22u19
Newquay	d									
Par	d	18 53			20 01	21 31				
Lostwithiel	d				20 08	21 38				
Bodmin Parkway	d	19 05			20 14	21 44				22u35
Liskeard ■	d	19 18			20 27	21 57				22u50
Menheniot	d				20x32					
St Germans	d				20 41	22 08				
Saltash	d				20 48	22 15				
St Budeaux Ferry Road	d									
Keyham	d									
Dockyard	d									
Devonport	d									
Plymouth	a	19 41			20 58	22 24				
	d	19 45	20 15		21 15					23u20
Ivybridge	d				21 30					
Totnes	d	20 15	20 42		21 44					23 48
Paignton	d			20 53			21 53	22 30	23 00	
Torquay	d			20 59			21 59	22 35	23 05	
Torre	d			21 02			22 02	22 38	23 08	
Newton Abbot	a	20 26	20 53	21 11	21 55		22 10	22 46	23 16	23 59
	d	20 28	20 54	21 12	21 56		22 12	22 49	23 18	00 01
Teignmouth	d			21 19	22 03		22 19	22 56	23 25	
Dawlish	d			21 24	22 08		22 24	23 01	23 30	
Dawlish Warren	d			21 29			22 29		23 35	
Starcross	d			21 33			22 33		23 39	
Exeter St Thomas	d			21 42			22 42		23 48	
Exeter St Davids ■	a	20 47	21 13	21 49	22 21		22 49	23 16	23 52	00 23
Exeter Central	a			21 56			22 56	23 23		
Exmouth	a			22 26			23 26	23 55		
Exeter St Davids ■	d	20 49	21 15							00 59
Tiverton Parkway	d	21 04	21 30							
Taunton	d	21 16	21 42							
Bridgwater	a									
Weston-super-Mare	a									
Bristol Temple Meads ■	a		22 13							
	d		22 20							
Bath Spa ■	a		22 32							
Filton Abbey Wood	a									
Bristol Parkway ■	a									
Swindon	a		22 59							
Newport (South Wales)	a									
Cardiff Central ■	a									
Birmingham New Street ■	a									
Castle Cary 123	d	21 37								
Frome 123	d									
Westbury 123	d	21 58								
Pewsey	d	22 15								
Hungerford	a									
Newbury	a	22 32								
Thatcham	a									
Theale	a									
Reading ■	a	22 49	23 34							04s05
Slough ■	a									
London Paddington ■ ⊖	a	23 35	00 12							05 04

A The Night Riviera

For connections to Oxford, Gatwick Airport and Heathrow Airport refer to Tables T116 and T148

For connections from Swansea refer to Table T128

Table T136-F

Exmouth - Exeter - Barnstaple

Mondays to Fridays

16 December to 15 May

Miles	Miles			GW MO	GW MX	GW	GW	SW	GW	GW	GW	SW	GW	GW	SW	GW	GW	GW	GW	SW	GW	GW	GW
				A				◇1 B	C		C	◇1 D	C		◇1 E	C	C		C	◇1 E	C		C
0	—	**Exmouth**	d		00 19				06 16		06 55		07 24			07 54	08 24		08 54		09 24		09 57
2	—	Lympstone Village	d	00 03	00 23				06 20		06 59		07 28			07 58	08 28		08 58		09 28		10 01
3	—	Lympstone Commando	d	00x04	00x24				06x21		07x01		07x30			08x00	08x30		09x00		09x29		
3½	—	Exton	d	00x06	00x26				06x23		07x02		07x31			08x01	08x31		09x01		09x31		
5	—	Topsham	d	00 11	00 31				06 28		07 08		07 37			08 07	08 37		09 07		09 36		10 08
—	—	Newcourt	d	00 15	00 35				06 32		07 11		07 40			08 10	08 40		09 10		09 40		10 11
7	—	Digby & Sowton	d	00 18	00 38				06 35		07 14		07 43			08 13	08 43		09 13		09 43		10 14
9	—	Polsloe Bridge	d	00 21	00 41				06 38		07 18		07 47			08 17	08 47		09 17		09 46		
10	—	St James' Park	d	00 24	00 44				06 45		07 20		07 50	08 01		08 20	08 50	09 11	09 20		09 49	10 11	
10½	—	**Exeter Central**	a	00 27	00 46				06 50		07 23		07 52	08 03		08 23	08 52	09 13	09 22		09 51	10 13	10 20
—	—		d	00 27	00 47			06 30	06 51		07 24	07 39	07 53	08 04	08 18	08 24	08 53	09 14	09 23	09 41	09 52	10 14	10 21
11¼	—	**Exeter St Davids** ■	a	00 31	00 50			06 33	06 54		07 27	07 42	07 56	08 07	08 22	08 28	08 56	09 17	09 26	09 44	09 55	10 17	10 24
—	—		d			05 22	06 12			07 10				08 10				09 19				10 19	
15½	—	Newton St Cyres	d																				
18¾	0	Crediton	d			05 32	06 22			07 19				08 28				09 33				10 31	
21¾	3½	Yeoford	d				06x29			07x26				08x34				09x39				10x37	
—	14¼	Sampford Courtenay	d																				
—	18	Okehampton	a																				
24½	—	Copplestone	d				06x34			07x32				08x39				09x45				10x43	
26¼	—	Morchard Road	d				06x38			07x34				08x42				09x47				10x45	
28¾	—	Lapford	d							07x39													
32½	—	Eggesford	d			05 54	06 51			07 54				09 01				10 04				11 01	
36½	—	Kings Nympton	d							08x00				09x07									
39¼	—	Portsmouth Arms	d							08x05													
43½	—	Umberleigh	d			06x08	07x05			08x11				09x17				10x17				11x14	
45¾	—	Chapelton	d							08x16													
50¼	—	**Barnstaple**	a			06 19	07 15			08 25				09 28				10 28				11 25	

		SW	GW	GW	GW	SW	GW	GW	GW	SW	GW	GW	GW	SW	GW	GW	GW	SW	GW	GW	GW	SW	GW
		◇1 F	C		C	◇1 F	C		C	◇1 F	C		C	◇1 F	C		C	◇1 F	C		C	◇1 F	C
Exmouth	d		10 23		10 57		11 23		11 57		12 23		12 57		13 23		13 57		14 23		14 57		15 23
Lympstone Village	d		10 27		11 01		11 27		12 01		12 27		13 01		13 27		14 01		14 27		15 01		15 27
Lympstone Commando	d		10x28				11x28				12x28				13x28				14x28				15x28
Exton	d		10x30				11x30				12x30				13x30				14x30				15x30
Topsham	d		10 35		11 07		11 35		12 08		12 35		13 07		13 35		14 07		14 35		15 07		15 35
Newcourt	d		10 39		11 11		11 39		12 11		12 39		13 11		13 39		14 11		14 39		15 11		15 39
Digby & Sowton	d		10 42		11 14		11 42		12 14		12 42		13 14		13 42		14 14		14 42		15 14		15 42
Polsloe Bridge	d		10 45				11 45				12 45				13 45				14 45				15 45
St James' Park	d		10 48	11 11			11 48	12 11			12 48	13 09			13 48	14 11			14 48	15 11			15 48
Exeter Central	a		10 50	11 13	11 20		11 50	12 13	12 20		12 50	13 11	13 20		13 50	14 13	14 20		14 50	15 13	15 20		15 50
	d	10 40	10 51	11 14	11 21	11 39	11 57	12 14	12 21	12 39	12 51	13 12	13 21	13 39	13 51	14 14	14 21	14 39	14 51	15 14	15 21	15 40	15 51
Exeter St Davids ■	a	10 43	10 54	11 17	11 24	11 43	12 00	12 17	12 24	12 43	12 54	13 15	13 24	13 43	13 54	14 17	14 24	14 43	14 54	15 17	15 24	15 43	15 54
	d			11 19				12 19				13 19				14 19				15 19			
Newton St Cyres	d																						
Crediton	d			11 31				12 33				13 32				14 32				15 32			
Yeoford	d			11x37				12x39				13x38				14x38				15x38			
Sampford Courtenay	d																						
Okehampton	a																						
Copplestone	d			11x43				12x45				13x44				14x44				15x44			
Morchard Road	d			11x45				12x47				13x46				14x46				15x46			
Lapford	d																						
Eggesford	d			12 01				13 04				14 01				15 03				16 01			
Kings Nympton	d											14x06											
Portsmouth Arms	d																						
Umberleigh	d			12x15				13x18				14x17				15x17				16x15			
Chapelton	d																						
Barnstaple	a			12 25				13 28				14 27				15 27				16 25			

		GW	GW	SW	GW	GW	GW	SW	SW	GW	GW	GW	SW	GW	GW	GW	SW	GW	GW	GW	SW	GW
			C	◇1 F	C		C	◇1 G ✠	◇1 F	C		C	◇1 F	C			◇1 F	C			◇1 F	◇ H
Exmouth	d		15 55		16 23		16 55			17 24		17 54		18 24		18 56		19 24		19 59		
Lympstone Village	d		15 59		16 27		16 59			17 28		17 58		18 28		19 00		19 28		20 03		
Lympstone Commando	d		16x00		16x28		17x00			17x29		17x59		18x29				19x29		20x04		
Exton	d		16x02		16x30		17x02			17x31		18x01		18x31				19x31		20x06		
Topsham	d		16 07		16 35		17 07			17 36		18 06		18 37		19 07		19 36		20 11		
Newcourt	d		16 11		16 39		17 11			17 40		18 10		18 41		19 11		19 40		20 15		
Digby & Sowton	d		16 14		16 42		17 14			17 43		18 13		18 44		19 14		19 43		20 18		
Polsloe Bridge	d		16 17		16 45		17 17			17 46		18 16		18 47				19 46		20 21		
St James' Park	d	16 09	16 20		16 48	17 10	17 20			17 49	18 12	18 19		18 50	19 14			19 49	20 18	20 24		
Exeter Central	a	16 11	16 22		16 50	17 12	17 22			17 51	18 14	18 21		18 52	19 16	19 25		19 51	20 20	20 26		
	d	16 13	16 23	16 39	16 51	17 14	17 23	17 29	17 39	17 52	18 15	18 22	18 40	18 53	19 17	19 28	19 41	19 52	20 21	20 28	20 39	21 01
Exeter St Davids ■	a	16 16	16 26	16 43	16 54	17 17	17 26	17 32	17 42	17 55	18 18	18 25	18 44	18 56	19 20	19 31	19 44	19 55	20 24	20 31	20 44	21 04
	d	16 18				17 19					18 20				19 22				20 26			
Newton St Cyres	d	16x23				17x24									19x27							
Crediton	d	16 30				17 31					18 35				19 39				20 37			
Yeoford	d	16x36				17x37					18x41				19x45				20x43			
Sampford Courtenay	d																					
Okehampton	a																					
Copplestone	d	16x42				17x43					18x46				19x51				20x48			
Morchard Road	d	16x44				17x45					18x49				19x53				20x51			
Lapford	d	16x49				17x50																
Eggesford	d	17 01				18 02					19 07				20 08				21 04			
Kings Nympton	d	17x06				18x08																
Portsmouth Arms	d					18x13																
Umberleigh	d	17x17				18x19					19x20				20x22				21x18			
Chapelton	d					18x24																
Barnstaple	a	17 27				18 33					19 31				20 32				21 28			

A From Exmouth
B From Axminster
C To Paignton
D From Gillingham (Dorset)
E From Salisbury
F From London Waterloo
G From Honiton
H To Bristol Temple Meads

For connections at Exeter St Davids refer to Table T135

Table T136-F

Mondays to Fridays
16 December to 15 May

Exmouth - Exeter - Barnstaple

		GW	GW	SW	GW	SW	GW	GW	SW
				◇1 A		◇1 A	FO		◇1 A
Exmouth	d		20 59		21 55			22 54	
Lympstone Village	d		21 03		21 59			22 58	
Lympstone Commando	d		21x04		22x00			22x59	
Exton	d		21x06		22x02			23x01	
Topsham	d		21 11		22 07			23 06	
Newcourt	d		21 15		22 11			23 10	
Digby & Sowton	d		21 18		22 14			23 13	
Polsloe Bridge	d		21 21		22 17			23 16	
St James' Park	d	21 15	21 24		22 20			23 19	
Exeter Central	a	21 17	21 26		22 22			23 21	
	d	21 18	21 28	21 40	22 23	22 41	22 48	23 22	23 42
Exeter St Davids	a	21 21	21 31	21 43	22 26	22 44	22 51	23 25	23 45
	d	21 24					22 52		
Newton St Cyres	d	21x29							
Crediton	d	21 36					23 03		
Yeoford	d	21x42					23x09		
Sampford Courtenay	d								
Okehampton	a								
Copplestone	d	21x48					23x15		
Morchard Road	d	21x50					23x17		
Lapford	d	21x55					23x22		
Eggesford	d	22 07					23 35		
Kings Nympton	d	22x12					23x41		
Portsmouth Arms	d								
Umberleigh	d	22x23					23x51		
Chapelton	d								
Barnstaple	a	22 33					00 02		

Saturdays
21 December to 16 May

		GW	GW	GW	SW	GW	GW	GW	SW	GW	GW	SW
					◇1 B	C		C	◇1 D	C		◇1 E
Exmouth	d	00 19				06 15		06 55		07 25		
Lympstone Village	d	00 23				06 19		06 59		07 29		
Lympstone Commando	d	00x24				06x20		07x00		07x30		
Exton	d	00x26				06x22		07x02		07x32		
Topsham	d	00 31				06 28		07 08		07 38		
Newcourt	d	00 35				06 32		07 12		07 41		
Digby & Sowton	d	00 38				06 35		07 15		07 44		
Polsloe Bridge	d	00 41				06 38		07 18		07 48		
St James' Park	d	00 44				06 41		07 21		07 50	08 10	
Exeter Central	a	00 46				06 43		07 23		07 53	08 12	
	d	00 47			06 28	06 44		07 26	07 39	07 54	08 13	08 19
Exeter St Davids	a	00 50			06 31	06 47		07 29	07 42	07 57	08 16	08 22
	d		05 24	06 16			07 13				08 18	
Newton St Cyres	d											
Crediton	d		05 34	06 26			07 25				08 32	
Yeoford	d		05x40	06x32			07x31				08x38	
Sampford Courtenay	d											
Okehampton	a											
Copplestone	d		05x46	06x38			07x36				08x43	
Morchard Road	d		05x48	06x40			07x39				08x46	
Lapford	d						07x44					
Eggesford	d		06 02	06 57			07 59				09 04	
Kings Nympton	d						08x04				09x09	
Portsmouth Arms	d						08x10					
Umberleigh	d		06x15	07x10			08x15				09x19	
Chapelton	d						08x20					
Barnstaple	a		06 28	07 23			08 30				09 31	

		GW	GW	GW	GW	SW	GW	GW	GW	SW	GW	GW
		C	C		C	◇1 E	C		C	◇1 A	C	
Exmouth	d	07 55	08 25		08 55		09 25		09 55		10 24	
Lympstone Village	d	07 59	08 29		08 59		09 29		09 59		10 28	
Lympstone Commando	d	08x00	08x30		09x00		09x30		10x00		10x29	
Exton	d	08x02	08x32		09x02		09x32				10x31	
Topsham	d	08 07	08 38		09 07		09 37		10 09		10 37	
Newcourt	d	08 11	08 42		09 11		09 41		10 12		10 40	
Digby & Sowton	d	08 14	08 45		09 14		09 44		10 15		10 43	
Polsloe Bridge	d	08 17	08 48		09 17		09 47				10 47	
St James' Park	d	08 20	08 51	09 12	09 20		09 51	10 11			10 49	11 11
Exeter Central	a	08 24	08 53	09 14	09 22		09 53	10 13	10 21		10 52	11 13
	d	08 26	08 54	09 15	09 23	09 41	09 54	10 14	10 23	10 39	10 53	11 14
Exeter St Davids	a	08 29	08 57	09 18	09 26	09 44	09 57	10 17	10 26	10 42	10 56	11 17
	d			09 20				10 19				11 19
Newton St Cyres	d											
Crediton	d			09 32				10 32				11 32
Yeoford	d			09x38				10x38				11x38
Sampford Courtenay	d											
Okehampton	a											
Copplestone	d			09x43				10x43				11x43
Morchard Road	d			09x46				10x46				11x46
Lapford	d											
Eggesford	d			10 01				11 01				12 01
Kings Nympton	d											
Portsmouth Arms	d											
Umberleigh	d			10x14				11x14				12x14
Chapelton	d											
Barnstaple	a			10 26				11 26				12 26

A From London Waterloo
B From Axminster
C To Paignton
D From Yeovil Junction
E From Salisbury

For connections at Exeter St Davids refer to Table T135

Table T136-F

Saturdays
21 December to 16 May

Exmouth - Exeter - Barnstaple

		GW	SW	GW	GW	GW	SW	GW	GW	GW	SW
		A	◇1 B	A		A	◇1 B	A		A	◇1 B
Exmouth	d	10 56		11 24		11 56		12 24		12 57	
Lympstone Village	d	11 00		11 28		12 00		12 28		13 01	
Lympstone Commando	d	11x01		11x29		12x01		12x29		13x02	
Exton	d			11x31				12x31			
Topsham	d	11 09		11 37		12 09		12 37		13 09	
Newcourt	d	11 12		11 40		12 12		12 40		13 12	
Digby & Sowton	d	11 15		11 43		12 15		12 43		13 15	
Polsloe Bridge	d			11 47				12 47			
St James' Park	d			11 49	12 11			12 49	13 11		
Exeter Central	a	11 21		11 52	12 13	12 21		12 52	13 13	13 21	
	d	11 23	11 39	11 55	12 14	12 23	12 39	12 53	13 14	13 27	13 39
Exeter St Davids	a	11 26	11 42	11 57	12 17	12 26	12 42	12 56	13 17	13 30	13 42
	d				12 19				13 19		
Newton St Cyres	d										
Crediton	d				12 32				13 32		
Yeoford	d				12x38				13x38		
Sampford Courtenay	d										
Okehampton	a										
Copplestone	d				12x43				13x43		
Morchard Road	d				12x46				13x46		
Lapford	d										
Eggesford	d				13 01				14 01		
Kings Nympton	d								14x07		
Portsmouth Arms	d										
Umberleigh	d				13x14				14x16		
Chapelton	d										
Barnstaple	a				13 26				14 29		

		GW	GW	GW	SW	GW	GW	GW	SW	GW	GW	GW
		A		A	◇1 B	A		A	◇1 B	A		A
Exmouth	d	13 24		13 56		14 24		14 56		15 24		15 55
Lympstone Village	d	13 28		14 00		14 28		15 00		15 28		15 59
Lympstone Commando	d	13x29		14x01		14x29		15x01		15x29		16x00
Exton	d	13x31				14x31				15x31		16x02
Topsham	d	13 37		14 09		14 37		15 09		15 37		16 08
Newcourt	d	13 40		14 12		14 40		15 12		15 40		16 11
Digby & Sowton	d	13 43		14 15		14 43		15 15		15 43		16 14
Polsloe Bridge	d	13 47				14 47				15 47		16 18
St James' Park	d	13 49	14 11			14 49	15 11			15 49	16 11	16 20
Exeter Central	a	13 52	14 13	14 21		14 52	15 13	15 21		15 52	16 13	16 23
	d	13 53	14 14	14 23	14 39	14 53	15 14	15 24	15 39	15 53	16 14	16 24
Exeter St Davids	a	13 56	14 17	14 26	14 42	14 56	15 17	15 27	15 42	15 56	16 17	16 27
	d		14 19				15 19				16 19	
Newton St Cyres	d											
Crediton	d		14 32				15 32				16 32	
Yeoford	d		14x38				15x38				16x38	
Sampford Courtenay	d											
Okehampton	a											
Copplestone	d		14x43				15x43				16x43	
Morchard Road	d		14x46				15x46				16x46	
Lapford	d										16x51	
Eggesford	d		15 01				16 06				17 05	
Kings Nympton	d										17x10	
Portsmouth Arms	d											
Umberleigh	d		15x14				16x19				17x20	
Chapelton	d											
Barnstaple	a		15 26				16 31				17 32	

		SW	GW	GW	GW	SW	GW	GW	GW	SW	GW	GW
		◇1 B	A		A	◇1 B	A		A	◇1 B	A	
Exmouth	d		16 27		16 56		17 27		17 56		18 26	
Lympstone Village	d		16 31		17 00		17 31		18 00		18 30	
Lympstone Commando	d		16x32		17x01		17x32		18x01		18x31	
Exton	d		16x34		17x03		17x34		18x03		18x33	
Topsham	d		16 39		17 09		17 41		18 09		18 38	
Newcourt	d		16 43		17 13		17 44		18 12		18 42	
Digby & Sowton	d		16 46		17 16		17 47		18 15		18 45	
Polsloe Bridge	d		16 49		17 19		17 51		18 19		18 48	
St James' Park	d		16 52	17 12	17 22		17 54	18 12	18 21		18 51	19 14
Exeter Central	a		16 54	17 15	17 24		17 56	18 15	18 24		18 53	19 16
	d	16 39	16 57	17 15	17 25	17 38	17 58	18 15	18 25	18 38	18 54	19 17
Exeter St Davids	a	16 42	17 00	17 19	17 28	17 42	18 01	18 19	18 28	18 42	18 57	19 20
	d			17 22				18 22				19 22
Newton St Cyres	d							18x27				19x27
Crediton	d			17 33				18 35				19 41
Yeoford	d			17x39				18x41				19x47
Sampford Courtenay	d											
Okehampton	a											
Copplestone	d			17x44				18x46				19x52
Morchard Road	d			17x47				18x49				19x55
Lapford	d			17x52								
Eggesford	d			18 07				19 13				20 09
Kings Nympton	d			18x13								
Portsmouth Arms	d			18x18								
Umberleigh	d			18x24				19x26				20x22
Chapelton	d			18x28								
Barnstaple	a			18 39				19 38				20 34

		GW	SW	GW	GW	GW	SW	GW	GW	SW	GW	SW
			◇1 B	A			◇1 B		A	◇1 B		◇1 B
Exmouth	d	18 56		19 25		19 58			20 58		21 54	
Lympstone Village	d	19 00		19 29		20 02			21 02		21 58	
Lympstone Commando	d	19x01		19x30		20x03			21x03		21x59	
Exton	d			19x32		20x05			21x05		22x01	
Topsham	d	19 11		19 38		20 10			21 10		22 07	
Newcourt	d	19 14		19 42		20 14			21 14		22 11	
Digby & Sowton	d	19 17		19 45		20 17			21 17		22 14	
Polsloe Bridge	d			19 48		20 20			21 20		22 17	
St James' Park	d			19 51	20 16	20 23		21 16	21 23		22 20	
Exeter Central	a	19 26		19 53	20 18	20 25		21 18	21 25		22 22	
	d	19 28	19 39	19 54	20 19	20 26	20 42	21 19	21 28	21 39	22 23	22 42
Exeter St Davids	a	19 32	19 42	19 57	20 22	20 31	20 45	21 22	21 31	21 42	22 26	22 45
	d				20 25			21 24				
Newton St Cyres	d							21x29				
Crediton	d				20 37			21 35				
Yeoford	d				20x43			21x41				
Sampford Courtenay	d											
Okehampton	a											
Copplestone	d				20x48			21x46				
Morchard Road	d				20x51			21x49				
Lapford	d							21x53				
Eggesford	d				21 06			22 06				
Kings Nympton	d							22x12				
Portsmouth Arms	d											
Umberleigh	d				21x19			22x21				
Chapelton	d											
Barnstaple	a				21 31			22 34				

		GW	GW
Exmouth	d	22 54	23 49
Lympstone Village	d	22 58	23 53
Lympstone Commando	d	22x59	23x54
Exton	d	23x01	23x56
Topsham	d	23 06	00 01
Newcourt	d	23 10	00 05
Digby & Sowton	d	23 13	00 08
Polsloe Bridge	d	23 16	00 11
St James' Park	d	23 19	00 14
Exeter Central	a	23 21	00 16
	d	23 22	00 17
Exeter St Davids	a	23 25	00 20
	d		
Newton St Cyres	d		
Crediton	d		
Yeoford	d		
Sampford Courtenay	d		
Okehampton	a		
Copplestone	d		
Morchard Road	d		
Lapford	d		
Eggesford	d		
Kings Nympton	d		
Portsmouth Arms	d		
Umberleigh	d		
Chapelton	d		
Barnstaple	a		

A To Paignton
B From London Waterloo

For connections at Exeter St Davids refer to Table T135

Table T136-F

Sundays
15 December to 10 May

Exmouth - Exeter - Barnstaple

		GW A	GW	SW ◇1 B	GW	GW C	GW	GW C	SW ◇1 D	GW	GW	GW C	SW ◇1 E	GW	GW	GW C	SW ◇1 E	GW C	GW	GW	GW C	SW ◇1 E	GW
Exmouth	d					08 55		09 55		10 23		10 57		11 23		11 57			12 25		12 57		13 24
Lympstone Village	d					08 59		09 59		10 27		11 01		11 27		12 01			12 29		13 01		13 28
Lympstone Commando	d					09x00		10x01		10x28				11x28					12x30				13x29
Exton	d					09x02		10x02		10x30				11x30					12x32				13x31
Topsham	d	00 01				09 07		10 06		10 35		11 10		11 35		12 08			12 37		13 07		13 36
Newcourt	d	00 05				09 11		10 10		10 39		11 13		11 39		12 11			12 41		13 11		13 40
Digby & Sowton	d	00 08				09 14		10 13		10 42		11 16		11 42		12 14			12 44		13 14		13 43
Polsloe Bridge	d	00 11				09 17		10 16		10 45				11 45					12 47				13 46
St James' Park	d	00 14			09 12	09 20	10 12	10 19		10 48	11 10			11 48	12 12				12 51	13 12			13 49
Exeter Central	a	00 16			09 14	09 23	10 14	10 21		10 51	11 12	11 22		11 51	12 14	12 20			12 53	13 14	13 20		13 52
	d	00 17		08 40	09 15	09 23	10 15	10 21	10 43	10 51	11 13	11 22	11 39	11 52	12 15	12 20	12 39	12 48	12 54	13 15	13 20	13 39	13 52
Exeter St Davids ■	a	00 20		08 43	09 18	09 29	10 18	10 25	10 46	10 56	11 16	11 26	11 42	11 56	12 18	12 24	12 42	12 51	12 58	13 18	13 26	13 42	13 56
	d		08 38		09 20		10 20				11 17				12 20					13 22			
Newton St Cyres	d				09x25										12x26								
Crediton	d		08 47		09 32		10 30				11 33				12 33					13 32			
Yeoford	d				09x39		10x37				11x40				12x40					13x39			
Sampford Courtenay	d																						
Okehampton	a																						
Copplestone	d				09x44		10x43				11x45				12x46					13x44			
Morchard Road	d				09x48		10x46				11x49				12x49					13x48			
Lapford	d				09x50										12x54								
Eggesford	d		09 10		10 03		11 05				12 06				13 04					14 06			
Kings Nympton	d				10x09										13x10								
Portsmouth Arms	d				10x14										13x16								
Umberleigh	d				10x22		11x19				12x21				13x22					14x21			
Chapelton	d				10x25										13x27								
Barnstaple	a		09 32		10 34		11 29				12 30				13 34					14 30			

		GW	GW C	SW ◇1 E	GW C	GW	GW C	SW ◇1 E	GW	GW	GW C	SW ◇1 E	GW	GW	GW C	SW ◇1 E	GW	GW	GW C	SW ◇1 E	GW	GW	GW C
Exmouth	d		13 57		14 23		14 57		15 23		15 56		16 24		16 54		17 23		17 57		18 25		19 00
Lympstone Village	d		14 01		14 27		15 01		15 27		16 00		16 28		16 58		17 27		18 01		18 29		19 04
Lympstone Commando	d				14x28				15x28				16x29				17x28				18x31		
Exton	d				14x30				15x30				16x31				17x30				18x33		
Topsham	d		14 07		14 35		15 07		15 35		16 07		16 36		17 07		17 35		18 07		18 38		19 10
Newcourt	d		14 11		14 39		15 11		15 39		16 11		16 40		17 11		17 39		18 11		18 41		19 15
Digby & Sowton	d		14 14		14 42		15 14		15 42		16 14		16 43		17 14		17 42		18 14		18 44		19 18
Polsloe Bridge	d				14 45				15 45				16 46				17 45				18 48		
St James' Park	d	14 12			14 48	15 12			15 48	16 12			16 49	17 12			17 48	18 12			18 50	19 12	
Exeter Central	a	14 14	14 20		14 50	15 14	15 20		15 51	16 14	16 20		16 52	17 14	17 20		17 51	18 14	18 20		18 53	19 14	19 24
	d	14 15	14 20	14 42	14 52	15 15	15 20	15 39	15 51	16 15	16 20	16 39	16 52	17 15	17 20	17 38	17 51	18 15	18 20	18 39	18 53	19 15	19 24
Exeter St Davids ■	a	14 18	14 24	14 45	14 55	15 18	15 24	15 42	15 55	16 18	16 24	16 42	16 57	17 18	17 24	17 41	17 55	18 18	18 24	18 42	18 57	19 18	19 28
	d	14 20				15 20				16 20				17 20				18 20				19 20	
Newton St Cyres	d									16x26													
Crediton	d	14 34				15 35				16 31				17 35				18 34				19 31	
Yeoford	d	14x41				15x42				16x38				17x42				18x41				19x38	
Sampford Courtenay	d																						
Okehampton	a																						
Copplestone	d	14x46				15x48				16x44				17x48				18x47				19x43	
Morchard Road	d	14x50				15 51				16x47				17x51				18x50				19x47	
Lapford	d									16x50													
Eggesford	d	15 08				16 06				17 08				18 09				19 04				20 04	
Kings Nympton	d									17x15													
Portsmouth Arms	d									17x20													
Umberleigh	d	15x23				16x21				17x27				18x24				19x19				20x19	
Chapelton	d									17x32													
Barnstaple	a	15 32				16 30				17 39				18 33				19 28				20 28	

		SW ◇1 E	GW	GW C	SW ◇1 E	GW C	SW ◇1 E	GW C	SW ◇1 E	GW	GW	GW
Exmouth	d			19 57		20 57		21 27		22 30	23 30	23 59
Lympstone Village	d			20 01		21 01		21 31		22 34	23 34	00 03
Lympstone Commando	d			20x02		21x02		21x32		22x35	23x35	00x04
Exton	d			20x04		21x04		21x34		22x37	23x37	00x06
Topsham	d			20 09		21 09		21 39		22 42	23 42	00 11
Newcourt	d			20 13		21 13		21 43		22 46	23 46	00 15
Digby & Sowton	d			20 16		21 16		21 46		22 49	23 49	00 18
Polsloe Bridge	d			20 19		21 19		21 49		22 52	23 52	00 21
St James' Park	d		20 09	20 22		21 22		21 52		22 55	23 55	00 24
Exeter Central	a		20 11	20 25		21 25		21 55		22 58	23 58	00 27
	d	19 39	20 12	20 25	20 40	21 25	21 39	21 55	22 41	22 58	23 58	00 27
Exeter St Davids ■	a	19 42	20 15	20 29	20 43	21 29	21 43	21 59	22 44	23 02	00 02	00 31
	d		20 17									
Newton St Cyres	d		20x23									
Crediton	d		20 30									
Yeoford	d		20x37									
Sampford Courtenay	d											
Okehampton	a											
Copplestone	d		20x43									
Morchard Road	d		20x46									
Lapford	d		20x49									
Eggesford	d		21 01									
Kings Nympton	d		21x06									
Portsmouth Arms	d		21x13									
Umberleigh	d		21x19									
Chapelton	d		21x24									
Barnstaple	a		21 31									

A not 15 December. From Exmouth
B From Salisbury
C To Paignton
D From Basingstoke
E From London Waterloo

For connections at Exeter St Davids refer to Table T135

Table T136-R

Mondays to Fridays
16 December to 15 May

Barnstaple - Exeter - Exmouth

Miles	Miles			GW MX A	SW ◇1 B	SW ◇1 B	GW	GW	SW ◇1 B	GW	GW C	SW ◇1 B	GW	GW C	GW C	SW ◇1 B	GW	GW C	GW C	SW ◇1 B	GW	GW C	GW C
0	—	**Barnstaple**	d										06 27				07 21				08 35		
4¼	—	Chapelton	d														07x27						
6¾	—	Umberleigh	d										06x35				07x31				08x43		
10¾	—	Portsmouth Arms	d														07x38						
13¾	—	Kings Nympton	d														07x43						
17½	—	Eggesford	d										06 52				07 53				09 01		
21½	—	Lapford	d														07x59				09x06		
23¾	—	Morchard Road	d										07x00				08x03				09x10		
25½	—	Copplestone	d										07x03				08x06				09x13		
—	0	Okehampton	d																				
—	3¾	Sampford Courtenay	d																				
28½	14½	Yeoford	d										07x08				08x12				09x18		
32	18	Crediton	d										07 19				08 21				09 29		
34¾	—	Newton St Cyres	d														08x24						
39	—	**Exeter St Davids ■**	a										07 31				08 34				09 41		
—			d		05 10	05 30	05 45	06 08	06 41	06 48	07 16	07 25	07 32	07 44	08 16	08 23	08 35	08 44	09 16	09 25	09 42	09 51	10 15
39¾	—	**Exeter Central**	a		05 13	05 33	05 48	06 11	06 44	06 51	07 19	07 28	07 35	07 47	08 19	08 26	08 38	08 47	09 19	09 28	09 45	09 54	10 18
—			d				05 49	06 12		06 52	07 20		07 37	07 48	08 20		08 40	08 48	09 20		09 46	09 55	10 19
40¼	—	St James' Park	d					06 14		06 54	07 22		07a39	07 50	08 22		08a42	08 50	09 22		09a48		10 21
41¼	—	Polsloe Bridge	d					06 17		06 57	07 25			07 53	08 25			08 53	09 25				10 24
43¼	—	Digby & Sowton	d				05 55	06 21		07 01	07 29			07 57	08 29			08 57	09 29			10 01	10 28
—	—	Newcourt	d				05 58	06 24		07 04	07 32			08 00	08 32			09 00	09 32			10 04	10 31
45¼	—	Topsham	d	00 01			06 02	06 28		07 08	07 37			08 07	08 37			09 07	09 37			10 08	10 35
46¾	—	Exton	d	00x03				06x30		07x10	07x39			08x09	08x39			09x09	09x39				10x37
47¼	—	Lympstone Commando	d	00x05				06x32		07x12	07x41			08x11	08x41			09x11	09x41				10x39
48¼	—	Lympstone Village	d	00 08			06 07	06 36		07 16	07 44			08 14	08 44			09 14	09 44			10 13	10 43
50¼	—	**Exmouth**	a	00 13			06 12	06 40		07 20	07 49			08 19	08 49			09 19	09 49			10 17	10 47

		SW ◇1 B	GW	GW C	GW C	SW ◇1 B	GW	GW C	GW C	SW ◇1 B	GW	GW C	GW C	SW ◇1 B	GW	GW C	GW C	SW ◇1 B	GW	GW C	GW C	SW ◇1 B	GW
Barnstaple	d		09 35				10 35				11 35				12 35				13 35				14 35
Chapelton	d																						
Umberleigh	d		09x43				10x43				11x43				12x43				13x43				14x43
Portsmouth Arms	d																						
Kings Nympton	d		09x53												12x54								
Eggesford	d		10 03				11 00				12 00				13 04				14 00				15 00
Lapford	d																						
Morchard Road	d		10x11				11x08				12x08				13x12				14x08				15x08
Copplestone	d		10x15				11x12				12x12				13x16				14x12				15x12
Okehampton	d																						
Sampford Courtenay	d																						
Yeoford	d		10x19				11x16				12x16				13x20				14x16				15x16
Crediton	d		10 29				11 29				12 28				13 29				14 29				15 29
Newton St Cyres	d																						
Exeter St Davids ■	a		10 41				11 41				12 40				13 41				14 41				15 41
	d	10 25	10 43	10 50	11 15	11 25	11 42	11 51	12 15	12 25	12 42	12 50	13 12	13 25	13 43	13 50	14 15	14 25	14 43	14 50	15 15	15 25	15 42
Exeter Central	a	10 28	10 46	10 53	11 18	11 28	11 45	11 54	12 18	12 28	12 45	12 53	13 15	13 28	13 46	13 53	14 18	14 28	14 46	14 53	15 18	15 28	15 45
	d		10 47	10 54	11 19		11 46	11 55	12 19		12 46	12 54	13 18		13 47	13 54	14 19		14 47	14 54	15 19		15 46
St James' Park	d		10a49		11 21		11a48		12 21		12a48		13 21		13a49		14 21		14a49		15 21		15a48
Polsloe Bridge	d				11 24				12 24				13 24				14 24				15 24		
Digby & Sowton	d			11 00	11 28			12 01	12 28			13 00	13 28			14 00	14 28			15 00	15 28		
Newcourt	d			11 03	11 31			12 04	12 31			13 03	13 31			14 03	14 31			15 03	15 31		
Topsham	d			11 07	11 35			12 08	12 35			13 07	13 35			14 07	14 35			15 07	15 35		
Exton	d				11x37				12x37				13x37				14x37				15x37		
Lympstone Commando	d				11x39				12x39				13x39				14x39				15x39		
Lympstone Village	d			11 12	11 43			12 13	12 43			13 12	13 43			14 12	14 43			15 12	15 43		
Exmouth	a			11 17	11 47			12 17	12 47			13 17	13 47			14 17	14 47			15 17	15 47		

		GW C	GW C	SW ◇1 B	SW ◇1 D	GW C	GW	GW C	SW ◇1 B	GW C	SW ◇1 E	GW	GW C	SW ◇1 B	GW C	GW	GW C	SW ◇1 B	GW	GW C	SW ◇1 B	GW
Barnstaple	d						15 35					16 31				17 33			18 38			19 42
Chapelton	d															17x38						
Umberleigh	d						15x43					16x39				17x43			18x46			19x50
Portsmouth Arms	d															17x49						
Kings Nympton	d											16x50							18x56			
Eggesford	d						16 00					17 03				18 03			19 07			20 07
Lapford	d															18x09			19x12			
Morchard Road	d						16x08					17x11				18x13			19x17			20x15
Copplestone	d						16x12					17x15				18x16			19x19			20x19
Okehampton	d																					
Sampford Courtenay	d																					
Yeoford	d						16x16					17x19				18x21			19x25			20x23
Crediton	d						16 39					17 39				18 37			19 40			20 37
Newton St Cyres	d															18x40						20 40
Exeter St Davids ■	a						16 51					17 51				18 50			19 52			20 51
	d	15 50	16 15	16 25	16 39	16 47	16 54	17 15	17 25	17 41	17 46	17 54	18 18	18 25	18 46	18 53	19 14	19 25	19 54	20 17	20 25	20 52
Exeter Central	a	15 53	16 18	16 28	16 42	16 50	16 57	17 18	17 28	17 44	17 49	17 57	18 21	18 28	18 49	18 56	19 17	19 28	19 57	20 20	20 28	20 55
	d	15 54	16 19			16 51	16 58	17 19		17 45		17 58	18 22		18 50	18 57	19 19		19 58	20 22		
St James' Park	d		16 21			16 53	17a00	17 21		17 47		18a00	18 24		18 52	18a59	19 22		20a00	20 24		
Polsloe Bridge	d		16 24			16 56		17 24		17 51			18 27		18 55		19 25			20 27		
Digby & Sowton	d	16 00	16 28			17 00		17 28		17 55			18 31		18 59		19 29			20 31		
Newcourt	d	16 03	16 31			17 03		17 31		17 58			18 34		19 02		19 32			20 34		
Topsham	d	16 07	16 35			17 07		17 36		18 06			18 38		19 07		19 37			20 38		
Exton	d		16x37			17x09		17x38		18x08			18x40		19x09		19x39			20x40		
Lympstone Commando	d		16x39			17x11		17x40		18x10			18x42		19x11		19x41			20x42		
Lympstone Village	d	16 12	16 43			17 15		17 44		18 14			18 46		19 15		19 44			20 45		
Exmouth	a	16 17	16 47			17 19		17 49		18 19			18 51		19 19		19 49			20 50		

A From Exeter St Davids
B To London Waterloo
C From Paignton
D To Honiton
E To Axminster

For connections at Exeter St Davids refer to Table T135

Table T136-R

Barnstaple - Exeter - Exmouth

Mondays to Fridays
16 December to 15 May

		GW	SW	GW	GW	GW	SW	GW	SW	GW	GW	GW
			■	FX	FO		■		■		FX	FO
		A	B			A	B		C			
Barnstaple	d			20 38	20 38			21 41			22 39	23 09
Chapelton	d											
Umberleigh	d			20x46	20x46			21x49			22x47	23x17
Portsmouth Arms	d											
Kings Nympton	d											
Eggesford	d			21 05	21 05			22 07			23 04	23 34
Lapford	d											
Morchard Road	d			21x13	21x13			22x15			23x12	23x42
Copplestone	d			21x17	21x17			22x19			23x16	23x46
Okehampton	d											
Sampford Courtenay	d											
Yeoford	d			21x21	21x21			22x23			23x20	23x50
Crediton	d			21 35	21 35			22 33			23 30	23 59
Newton St Cyres	d			21 38	21 38			22x36			23 33	00 03
Exeter St Davids ■	a			21 48	21 48			22 47			23 43	00 12
	d	21 17	21 25		21 50	22 15	22 25		23 27	23 40		
Exeter Central	a	21 20	21 28		21 53	22 18	22 28		23 30	23 43		
	d	21 22				22 19				23 44		
St James' Park	d	21 24				22 21				23 46		
Polsloe Bridge	d	21 27				22 24				23 49		
Digby & Sowton	d	21 31				22 28				23 53		
Newcourt	d	21 34				22 31				23 56		
Topsham	d	21 38				22 35				00 01		
Exton	d	21x40				22x37				00x03		
Lympstone Commando	d	21x42				22x39				00x05		
Lympstone Village	d	21 45				22 42				00 08		
Exmouth	a	21 50				22 47				00 13		

Saturdays
21 December to 16 May

		GW	GW	GW	SW	SW	GW	GW	SW	GW	GW	SW	GW	GW	GW	SW	GW	GW	GW	SW	GW	GW	GW
					◇■	◇■			◇■			◇■				◇■				◇■			
		D	E		F	F			F		A	F		A	A	F	A		A	F	A		A
Barnstaple	d			00 06									06 31					07 26				08 34	
Chapelton	d																	07x31					
Umberleigh	d												06x39					07x36				08x42	
Portsmouth Arms	d																	07x42					
Kings Nympton	d																	07x48				08x53	
Eggesford	d			00s28									06 56					07 58				09 03	
Lapford	d																	08x04				09 08	
Morchard Road	d												07x04					08x08				09x13	
Copplestone	d												07x08					08x11				09x15	
Okehampton	d																						
Sampford Courtenay	d																						
Yeoford	d												07x12					08x16				09x21	
Crediton	d			00s48									07 23					08 33				09 31	
Newton St Cyres	d		00 03															08x36					
Exeter St Davids ■	a		00 12	01 01									07 34					08 49				09 43	
	d				05 10	05 30	05 45	06 08	06 37	06 48	07 18	07 25	07 36	07 44	08 18	08 24	08 45	08 51	09 15	09 25	09 39	09 48	10 17
Exeter Central	a				05 13	05 33	05 48	06 11	06 40	06 51	07 21	07 28	07 39	07 47	08 21	08 27	08 48	08 54	09 18	09 28	09 42	09 51	10 20
	d						05 49	06 12		06 52	07 22		07 40	07 48	08 22		08 49	08 55	09 19		09 47	09 52	10 21
St James' Park	d							06 14		06 54	07 24		07a43	07 51	08 24		08 51	08a57	09 21		09 49	09a54	10 23
Polsloe Bridge	d							06 17		06 57	07 27			07 53	08 27		08 54		09 24		09 53		10 26
Digby & Sowton	d						05 55	06 21		07 01	07 31			07 57	08 31		08 58		09 28		09 57		10 30
Newcourt	d						05 58	06 24		07 04	07 34			08 00	08 34		09 01		09 31		10 00		10 33
Topsham	d	00 01					06 02	06 28		07 08	07 38			08 08	08 38		09 08		09 38		10 06		10 37
Exton	d	00x03						06x30		07x10	07x40			08x10	08x40		09x10		09x40		10x09		10x39
Lympstone Commando	d	00x05						06x32		07x12	07x42			08x12	08x42		09x12		09x42		10x10		10x41
Lympstone Village	d	00 08					06 07	06 35		07 15	07 45			08 15	08 45		09 15		09 45		10 13		10 45
Exmouth	a	00 13					06 12	06 41		07 21	07 51			08 21	08 51		09 21		09 51		10 19		10 50

		SW	GW	GW	GW	SW	GW	GW	GW	SW	GW	GW	GW	SW	GW	GW	GW	SW	GW	GW	GW	SW	GW
		◇■				◇■				◇■				◇■				◇■				◇■	
		F		A	A	F		A	A	F		A	A	F		A	A	F		A	A	F	
Barnstaple	d		09 35				10 35				11 35				12 32				13 35				14 35
Chapelton	d																						
Umberleigh	d		09x43				10x43				11x43				12x40				13x43				14x43
Portsmouth Arms	d																						
Kings Nympton	d														12x51								
Eggesford	d		10 00				11 00				12 00				13 01				14 00				15 00
Lapford	d																						
Morchard Road	d		10x08				11x08				12x08				13x09				14x08				15x08
Copplestone	d		10x12				11x12				12x12				13x13				14x12				15x12
Okehampton	d																						
Sampford Courtenay	d																						
Yeoford	d		10x16				11x16				12x16				13x17				14x16				15x16
Crediton	d		10 29				11 29				12 29				13 29				14 29				15 29
Newton St Cyres	d																						
Exeter St Davids ■	a		10 40				11 40				12 40				13 40				14 40				15 40
	d	10 25	10 42	10 52	11 17	11 25	11 42	11 52	12 17	12 25	12 42	12 52	13 17	13 25	13 42	13 52	14 17	14 25	14 42	14 52	15 17	15 25	15 42
Exeter Central	a	10 28	10 45	10 55	11 20	11 28	11 45	11 55	12 20	12 28	12 45	12 55	13 20	13 28	13 45	13 55	14 20	14 28	14 45	14 55	15 20	15 28	15 45
	d		10 46	10 56	11 21		11 46	11 56	12 21		12 46	12 56	13 21		13 46	13 56	14 21		14 46	14 56	15 21		15 46
St James' Park	d		10a50		11 23		11a50		12 23		12a50		13 23		13a50		14 23		14a50		15 23		15a50
Polsloe Bridge	d				11 26				12 26				13 26				14 26				15 26		
Digby & Sowton	d			11 02	11 30			12 02	12 30			13 02	13 30			14 02	14 30			15 02	15 30		
Newcourt	d			11 05	11 33			12 05	12 33			13 05	13 33			14 05	14 33			15 05	15 33		
Topsham	d			11 09	11 37			12 09	12 37			13 09	13 37			14 09	14 37			15 09	15 37		
Exton	d				11x39				12x39				13x39				14x39				15x39		
Lympstone Commando	d			11x11	11x41			12x11	12x41			13x11	13x41			14x11	14x41			15x11	15x41		
Lympstone Village	d			11 14	11 45			12 14	12 45			13 14	13 45			14 14	14 45			15 14	15 45		
Exmouth	a			11 20	11 50			12 20	12 50			13 20	13 50			14 20	14 50			15 20	15 50		

A From Paignton
B To Salisbury
C To Yeovil Junction
D From Exeter St Davids
E From Barnstaple
F To London Waterloo

Table T136-R

Barnstaple - Exeter - Exmouth

Saturdays
21 December to 16 May

		GW	GW	SW	GW	GW	GW	SW	GW	GW	GW	SW	GW	GW	GW	SW	GW	GW	SW	GW	GW	SW
				◇■				◇■				◇■				◇■			◇■			◇■
		A	A	B	A		A	B	A		A	B	A		A	B		A	B		A	C
Barnstaple	d					15 40				16 39				17 36			18 43			19 42		
Chapelton	d													17x41								
Umberleigh	d					15x48				16x47				17x46			18x51			19x50		
Portsmouth Arms	d																18x58					
Kings Nympton	d													17x56			19x02					
Eggesford	d					16 05				17 04				18 07			19 13			20 10		
Lapford	d													18x12			19x18					
Morchard Road	d					16x13				17x12				18x17			19x23			20x18		
Copplestone	d					16x17				17x16				18x19			19x25			20x22		
Okehampton	d																					
Sampford Courtenay	d																					
Yeoford	d					16x21				17x20				18x25			19x31			20x26		
Crediton	d					16 40				17 40				18 41			19 41			20 38		
Newton St Cyres	d													18x44						20x42		
Exeter St Davids ■	a					16 53				17 53				18 54			19 52			20 54		
	d	15 51	16 17	16 25	16 49	16 55	17 16	17 25	17 49	17 55	18 16	18 25	18 48	18 56	19 16	19 25	19 53	20 17	20 25	20 56	21 17	21 25
Exeter Central	a	15 54	16 20	16 28	16 52	16 58	17 19	17 28	17 52	17 58	18 19	18 28	18 51	18 59	19 19	19 28	19 56	20 20	20 28	20 59	21 20	21 28
	d	15 55	16 21		16 53	16 59	17 20		17 53	17 59	18 20		18 52	19 00	19 21		19 57	20 21		21 00	21 21	
St James' Park	d		16 23		16 55	17a01	17 22		17 55	18a01	18 22		18 54	19a02	19 23		20a00	20 23		21a04	21 23	
Polsloe Bridge	d		16 26		16 58		17 25		17 58		18 25		18 57		19 26			20 26			21 26	
Digby & Sowton	d	16 01	16 30		17 02		17 29		18 02		18 29		19 01		19 30			20 30			21 30	
Newcourt	d	16 04	16 33		17 05		17 32		18 05		18 32		19 04		19 33			20 33			21 33	
Topsham	d	16 09	16 39		17 09		17 39		18 09		18 38		19 08		19 37			20 37			21 37	
Exton	d		16x41		17x11		17x41		18x11		18x40		19x10		19x39			20x39			21x39	
Lympstone Commando	d	16x11	16x43		17x13		17x43		18x13		18x42		19x12		19x41			20x41			21x41	
Lympstone Village	d	16 14	16 47		17 17		17 47		18 17		18 46		19 16		19 45			20 45			21 45	
Exmouth	a	16 20	16 52		17 22		17 52		18 22		18 50		19 21		19 50			20 50			21 50	

		GW	GW	GW	SW	GW	GW
					◇■		
			A		C		
Barnstaple	d	20 40		21 40			22 38
Chapelton	d						
Umberleigh	d	20x48		21x48			22x46
Portsmouth Arms	d						
Kings Nympton	d						
Eggesford	d	21 05		22 08			23 03
Lapford	d						
Morchard Road	d	21x13		22x16			23x11
Copplestone	d	21x17		22x20			23x15
Okehampton	d						
Sampford Courtenay	d						
Yeoford	d	21x21		22x24			23x19
Crediton	d	21 37		22 34			23 29
Newton St Cyres	d			22x37			23x32
Exeter St Davids ■	a	21 50		22 48			23 43
	d		22 17		23 00	23 13	
Exeter Central	a		22 20		23 03	23 16	
	d		22 21			23 17	
St James' Park	d		22 23			23 19	
Polsloe Bridge	d		22 26			23 22	
Digby & Sowton	d		22 30			23 26	
Newcourt	d		22 33			23 29	
Topsham	d		22 37			23 33	
Exton	d		22x39			23x35	
Lympstone Commando	d		22x41			23x37	
Lympstone Village	d		22 45			23 41	
Exmouth	a		22 50			23 46	

Sundays
15 December to 10 May

		GW	SW	GW	SW	GW	GW	SW	GW	GW	GW	SW	GW	GW	GW	SW	GW	GW	GW	SW	GW	GW	GW
			◇■		◇■			◇■				◇■				◇■				◇■			
			B		B			B	A			B	A			B	A			B	A		
Barnstaple	d									09 36				10 38				11 33				12 37	
Chapelton	d																	11x38					
Umberleigh	d									09x44				10x46				11x43				12x45	
Portsmouth Arms	d																	11x49					
Kings Nympton	d																	11x55					
Eggesford	d									10 01				11 04				12 04				13 04	
Lapford	d									10x07								12x11					
Morchard Road	d									10x11				11x12				12x15				13x12	
Copplestone	d									10x14				11x15				12x18				13x15	
Okehampton	d																						
Sampford Courtenay	d																						
Yeoford	d									10x18				11x19				12x23				13x19	
Crediton	d									10 30				11 35				12 36				13 33	
Newton St Cyres	d									10x34								12x40				13x38	
Exeter St Davids ■	a									10 48				11 54				12 50				13 48	
	d	08 18	08 24	09 15	09 25	09 50	10 15	10 25	10 49	10 53	11 15	11 25	11 50	11 56	12 15	12 25	12 50	12 54	13 15	13 25	13 50	13 56	14 15
Exeter Central	a	08 21	08 27	09 18	09 28	09 53	10 18	10 28	10 52	10 56	11 18	11 28	11 54	11 59	12 18	12 28	12 53	12 57	13 18	13 28	13 53	13 59	14 18
	d	08 22		09 19		09 54	10 19		10 53	10 57	11 19		11 55	12 00	12 19		12 54	12 57	13 19		13 54	14 00	14 19
St James' Park	d	08 24		09 21			10 21			10a59	11 21			12a02	12 21			12a59	13 21			14a02	14 21
Polsloe Bridge	d	08 27		09 24			10 24				11 24				12 24				13 24				14 24
Digby & Sowton	d	08 31		09 28		10 00	10 28		10 59		11 28		12 01		12 28		13 00		13 28		14 00		14 28
Newcourt	d	08 34		09 31		10 03	10 31		11 02		11 31		12 04		12 31		13 03		13 31		14 03		14 31
Topsham	d	08 38		09 37		10 08	10 37		11 08		11 37		12 08		12 37		13 07		13 37		14 07		14 37
Exton	d	08x40		09x39			10x39				11x39		12x10		12x39		13x09		13x39		14x09		14x39
Lympstone Commando	d	08x42		09x41			10x41				11x41		12x12		12x41		13x11		13x41		14x11		14x41
Lympstone Village	d	08 45		09 44		10 13	10 44		11 13		11 44		12 15		12 44		13 14		13 44		14 14		14 44
Exmouth	a	08 51		09 50		10 18	10 50		11 19		11 50		12 20		12 50		13 19		13 50		14 20		14 50

A From Paignton
B To London Waterloo
C To Salisbury

For connections at Exeter St Davids refer to Table T135

Table T136-R

Sundays

15 December to 10 May

Barnstaple - Exeter - Exmouth

		SW ◇1 A	GW B	GW	GW B	SW ◇1 A	GW B	GW	GW	SW ◇1 A	GW B	GW
Barnstaple	d			13 39				14 35				15 38
Chapelton	d							14x41				
Umberleigh	d			13x47				14x45				15x46
Portsmouth Arms	d							14x51				15x53
Kings Nympton	d							14x57				
Eggesford	d			14 05				15 07				16 05
Lapford	d							15x13				
Morchard Road	d			14x12				15x17				16x13
Copplestone	d			14x16				15x20				16x16
Okehampton	d											
Sampford Courtenay	d											
Yeoford	d			14x20				15x25				16x21
Crediton	d			14 32				15 36				16 37
Newton St Cyres	d			14x36								
Exeter St Davids 6	a			14 49				15 52				16 49
	d	14 25	14 46	14 54	15 15	15 25	15 49	15 55	16 15	16 25	16 43	16 55
Exeter Central	a	14 28	14 49	14 57	15 18	15 28	15 52	15 58	16 18	16 28	16 46	16 58
	d		14 50	14 58	15 19		15 53	15 59	16 19		16 53	16 59
St James' Park	d		14 52	15a00	15 21			16a01	16 21			17a01
Polsloe Bridge	d		14 55		15 24				16 24			
Digby & Sowton	d		14 59		15 28		15 59		16 28		16 59	
Newcourt	d		15 02		15 31		16 02		16 31		17 02	
Topsham	d		15 07		15 37		16 06		16 37		17 06	
Exton	d		15x09		15x39		16x08		16x39		17x08	
Lympstone Commando	d		15x11		15x41		16x10		16x41		17x10	
Lympstone Village	d		15 14		15 44		16 14		16 44		17 13	
Exmouth	a		15 19		15 50		16 19		16 50		17 19	

		GW B	SW ◇1 A	GW B	GW	GW	SW ◇1 A	GW B	GW	SW ◇1 A	GW B	GW
Barnstaple	d				16 35				17 43			18 38
Chapelton	d				16x41							
Umberleigh	d				16x45				17x51			18x46
Portsmouth Arms	d				16x51							
Kings Nympton	d				16x57							
Eggesford	d				17 07				18 08			19 03
Lapford	d				17x13							
Morchard Road	d				17x17				18x16			19x11
Copplestone	d				17x20				18x19			19x14
Okehampton	d											
Sampford Courtenay	d											
Yeoford	d				17x25				18x24			19x19
Crediton	d				17 36				18 38			19 35
Newton St Cyres	d				17 40							
Exeter St Davids 6	a				17 49				18 53			19 53
	d	17 15	17 25	17 51	17 55	18 15	18 25	18 49	18 56	19 25	19 50	19 55
Exeter Central	a	17 18	17 28	17 54	17 58	18 18	18 28	18 52	18 59	19 28	19 53	19 58
	d	17 19		17 55	17 59	18 19		18 53	19 00		19 54	19 58
St James' Park	d	17 21			18a01	18 21		18 55	19a02		19 56	20a00
Polsloe Bridge	d	17 24				18 24		18 58			19 59	
Digby & Sowton	d	17 28		18 01		18 28		19 02			20 03	
Newcourt	d	17 31		18 04		18 31		19 05			20 06	
Topsham	d	17 37		18 08		18 37		19 11			20 10	
Exton	d	17x39		18x10		18x39		19x13			20x12	
Lympstone Commando	d	17x41		18x12		18x41		19x15			20x14	
Lympstone Village	d	17 44		18 16		18 44		19 20			20 18	
Exmouth	a	17 49		18 20		18 50		19 24			20 23	

		SW ◇1 A	GW	GW B	SW ◇1 C	GW	GW B	SW 1 C	GW	GW B	SW ◇1 D	GW B
Barnstaple	d		19 38			20 33			21 36			
Chapelton	d								21x42			
Umberleigh	d		19x46			20x41			21x46			
Portsmouth Arms	d								21x52			
Kings Nympton	d								21x58			
Eggesford	d		20 03			21 00			22 08			
Lapford	d								22x14			
Morchard Road	d		20x11			21x09			22x18			
Copplestone	d		20x14			21x12			22x21			
Okehampton	d											
Sampford Courtenay	d											
Yeoford	d		20x19			21x17			22x26			
Crediton	d		20 29			21 26			22 36			
Newton St Cyres	d								22 40			
Exeter St Davids 6	a		20 39			21 37			22 50			
	d	20 25		20 50	21 25		21 53	22 25		22 53	23 13	23 20
Exeter Central	a	20 28		20 53	21 28		21 56	22 28		22 56	23 16	23 23
	d			20 54			21 57			22 57		23 24
St James' Park	d			20 56			21 59			22 59		23 26
Polsloe Bridge	d			20 59			22 02			23 02		23 29
Digby & Sowton	d			21 03			22 06			23 06		23 33
Newcourt	d			21 06			22 09			23 09		23 36
Topsham	d			21 10			22 13			23 13		23 42
Exton	d			21x12			22x15			23x15		23x44
Lympstone Commando	d			21x14			22x17			23x17		23x46
Lympstone Village	d			21 18			22 20			23 21		23 49
Exmouth	a			21 23			22 26			23 26		23 55

A To London Waterloo
B From Paignton
C To Salisbury
D To Yeovil Junction

For connections at Exeter St Davids refer to Table T135

Table T139-F

Mondays to Fridays

16 December to 15 May

Plymouth - Gunnislake

Miles			GW	GW	GW ◇1 A 🚲	GW ◇ B	GW	GW	GW C	GW	GW	GW ◇ A	GW	GW D	GW	GW A	GW
0	**Plymouth**	d	04 58	06 33	07 14	08 17	08 22	10 22	10 40	12 24	14 24	15 55	16 34	17 00	18 25	18 31	21 30
1¼	Devonport	d		06 36	07a18	08a20	08 25	10 25		12 27	14 27	16 00	16 37	17 04	18 28	18 34	21 33
1½	Dockyard	d		06x38			08x27	10x27		12x29	14x29	16x02	16x39	17x04	18x30	18x35	21x35
2¼	Keyham	d		06 40			08 29	10 29		12 31	14 31	16 06	16 41	17 08	18 32	18 39	21 37
—	St Budeaux Ferry Road	a							10 46			16 09		17 09		18 41	
3	St Budeaux Victoria Road	d	05 05	06 43			08 32	10 32		12 34	14 34		16 44		18 35		21 40
7¼	Bere Ferrers	d		06 50			08 39	10 39		12 41	14 41		16 51		18 42		21 47
10	Bere Alston	a	05 17	06 56			08 45	10 45		12 47	14 47		16 57		18 48		21 53
—		d	05 19	06 59			08 48	10 48		12 50	14 50		17 00		18 51		21 56
11¾	Calstock	d	05 26	07 06			08 55	10 55		12 57	14 57		17 07		18 58		22 03
14½	**Gunnislake**	a	05 39	07 21			09 10	11 10		13 12	15 12		17 22		19 13		22 18

Saturdays

21 December to 16 May

		GW	GW ◇ B	GW	GW A	GW	GW C	GW	GW	GW	GW	GW A	GW
Plymouth	d	06 27	08 16	08 22	10 13	10 22	10 44	12 24	14 24	16 36	18 26	18 35	21 30
Devonport	d	06 30	08a19	08 25	10a16	10 25		12 27	14 27	16 39	18 29	18 38	21 33
Dockyard	d	06x31		08x26		10x26		12x28	14x28	16x40	18x30	18x39	21x34
Keyham	d	06 33		08 28		10 28		12 30	14 30	16 42	18 32	18 43	21 36
St Budeaux Ferry Road	a						10 50					18 45	
St Budeaux Victoria Road	d	06 38		08 33		10 33		12 35	14 35	16 47	18 37		21 41
Bere Ferrers	d	06 45		08 40		10 40		12 42	14 42	16 54	18 44		21 48
Bere Alston	a	06 51		08 46		10 46		12 48	14 48	17 00	18 50		21 54
	d	06 53		08 48		10 48		12 50	14 50	17 02	18 52		21 56
Calstock	d	07 00		08 55		10 55		12 57	14 57	17 09	18 59		22 03
Gunnislake	a	07 13		09 08		11 08		13 10	15 10	17 22	19 12		22 16

Sundays

15 December to 10 May

		GW A	GW	GW	GW	GW	GW
Plymouth	d	08 55	09 10	11 17	13 00	15 19	17 41
Devonport	d	08 59	09 13	11 20	13 03	15 22	17 44
Dockyard	d		09x14	11x21	13x04	15x23	17x45
Keyham	d		09 16	11 23	13 06	15 25	17 47
St Budeaux Ferry Road	a	09 02					
St Budeaux Victoria Road	d		09 20	11 27	13 10	15 29	17 51
Bere Ferrers	d		09 27	11 34	13 17	15 36	17 58
Bere Alston	a		09 34	11 41	13 24	15 43	18 05
	d		09 36	11 43	13 26	15 45	18 07
Calstock	d		09 43	11 50	13 33	15 52	18 14
Gunnislake	a		09 56	12 03	13 46	16 05	18 27

A To Penzance
B From Bristol Temple Meads to Penzance
C From Exeter St Davids to Penzance
D To Liskeard

For connections at Plymouth refer to Table T135

Table T139-R

Mondays to Fridays
16 December to 15 May

Gunnislake - Plymouth

Miles			GW	GW	GW	GW	GW	GW	GW	GW	GW	GW	GW	GW	GW	GW	GW
					◇■		◇									◇	
				A	B		C					D		E		A	F
					⌶												
0	**Gunnislake**	d	05 43			07 29		09 14	11 14	13 18	15 14		17 31		19 18		22 20
3	Calstock	d	05 55			07 41		09 26	11 26	13 30	15 26		17 43		19 30		22 32
4½	Bere Alston	a	06 01			07 47		09 32	11 32	13 36	15 32		17 49		19 36		22 38
—		d	06 04			07 50		09 35	11 35	13 39	15 35		17 52		19 39		22 41
7½	Bere Ferrers	d	06 09			07 55		09 40	11 40	13 44	15 40		17 57		19 44		22 46
11½	St Budeaux Victoria Road	d	06 17			08 03		09 48	11 48	13 52	15 48		18 05		19 52		22 54
—	St Budeaux Ferry Road	d		07 33			08 34					17 08		18 17		21 08	
12½	Keyham	d	06 20	07 35		08 06	08 37	09 51	11 51	13 55	15 51	17 10	18 08		19 55	21 10	22 57
13	Dockyard	d	06x22	07x36		08x08	08x38	09x53	11x53	13x57	15x53	17x11	18x10		19x57	21x11	22x58
13½	Devonport	d	06 24	07 39	07 59	08 10	08 41	09 55	11 55	13 59	15 55	17 15	18 12		19 59	21 14	23 01
14½	**Plymouth**	a	06 30	07 44	08 05	08 16	08 45	10 01	12 01	14 05	16 01	17 19	18 16	18 25	20 05	21 19	23 05

Saturdays
21 December to 16 May

		GW	GW	GW	GW	GW	GW	GW	GW	GW	GW	GW	GW	GW
				◇										
		A		C					D			D		G
Gunnislake	d		07 16		09 14	11 14	13 14	15 14		17 34	19 18		22 20	
Calstock	d		07 28		09 26	11 26	13 26	15 26		17 46	19 30		22 32	
Bere Alston	a		07 34		09 32	11 32	13 32	15 32		17 52	19 36		22 38	
	d		07 37		09 35	11 35	13 35	15 35		17 55	19 39		22 41	
Bere Ferrers	d		07 42		09 40	11 40	13 40	15 40		18 00	19 44		22 46	
St Budeaux Victoria Road	d		07 50		09 48	11 48	13 48	15 48		18 08	19 52		22 54	
St Budeaux Ferry Road	d	07 32		08 33					17 09			21 22		23 02
Keyham	d	07 34	07 53	08 36	09 51	11 51	13 51	15 51	17 11	18 11	19 55	21 24	22 57	23 04
Dockyard	d	07x35	07x54	08x37	09x52	11x52	13x52	15x52	17x12	18x12	19x56	21x26	22x58	23x05
Devonport	d	07 38	07 56	08 39	09 54	11 54	13 54	15 54	17 14	18 14	19 58	21 28	23 00	23 08
Plymouth	a	07 43	08 03	08 45	10 00	12 00	14 00	16 00	17 22	18 20	20 04	21 34	23 07	23 14

Sundays
15 December to 10 May

		GW	GW	GW	GW	GW
Gunnislake	d	10 10	12 07	13 58	16 09	18 35
Calstock	d	10 21	12 18	14 09	16 20	18 46
Bere Alston	a	10 28	12 25	14 16	16 27	18 53
	d	10 30	12 27	14 18	16 29	18 55
Bere Ferrers	d	10 35	12 32	14 23	16 34	19 00
St Budeaux Victoria Road	d	10 44	12 41	14 32	16 43	19 09
St Budeaux Ferry Road	d					
Keyham	d	10 46	12 43	14 34	16 45	19 11
Dockyard	d	10x48	12x45	14x36	16x47	19x13
Devonport	d	10 50	12 47	14 38	16 49	19 15
Plymouth	a	10 55	12 52	14 43	16 54	19 20

A From Penzance to Exeter St Davids
B From Penzance to London Paddington
C From Penzance to Cardiff Central
D From Penzance
E From Liskeard
F To Exeter St Davids
G From Newquay

For connections at Plymouth refer to Table T135

Table T140-F

Mondays to Fridays
16 December to 15 May

Liskeard - Looe

Miles			GW	GW	GW	GW	GW	GW	GW	GW	GW	GW	GW	GW	GW	GW	GW
0	**Liskeard** ■	d	05 57	07 13	08 30	09 36	10 36	11 36	12 36	13 36	14 36	15 40	16 44	17 46	18 49	19 49	21 05
2	Coombe Junction Halt	a			08 36							15 46					
—		d			08 39							15 49					
3¾	St Keyne Wishing Well Halt	d	06x09	07x25	08x46	09x48		11x48		13x48		15x56		17x58		20x01	21x17
5	Causeland	d	06x13	07x29	08x50	09x52		11x52		13x52		16x00		18x02		20x05	21x21
6½	Sandplace	d	06x16	07x32	08x53	09x55		11x55		13x55		16x03		18x05		20x08	21x24
8¾	**Looe**	a	06 26	07 42	09 03	10 05	11 04	12 05	13 04	14 05	15 04	16 13	17 12	18 15	19 17	20 18	21 34

Saturdays
21 December to 16 May

		GW	GW	GW	GW	GW	GW	GW	GW	GW	GW	GW	GW	GW	GW	GW
Liskeard ■	d	06 00	07 22	08 27	09 36	10 36	11 36	12 36	13 36	14 36	15 40	16 50	17 52	18 52	19 56	21 00
Coombe Junction Halt	a			08 33							15 46					
	d			08 36							15 49					
St Keyne Wishing Well Halt	d	06x12	07x34	08x42	09x48		11x48		13x48		15x55		18x04		20x08	21x12
Causeland	d	06x15	07x37	08x46	09x51		11x51		13x51		15x59		18x07		20x11	21x15
Sandplace	d	06x19	07x41	08x49	09x55		11x55		13x55		16x02		18x11		20x15	21x19
Looe	a	06 31	07 53	09 00	10 07	11 04	12 07	13 04	14 07	15 04	16 13	17 18	18 23	19 20	20 27	21 31

Sundays
15 December to 10 May

		GW	GW	GW	GW	GW	GW	GW	GW
		A	A	A	A	A	A	A	A
Liskeard ■	d	09 36	10 40	12 20	13 50	15 05	16 39	17 55	20 15
Coombe Junction Halt	a	⌇	⌇	⌇	⌇	⌇	⌇	⌇	⌇
	d	⌇	⌇	⌇	⌇	⌇	⌇	⌇	⌇
St Keyne Wishing Well Halt	d	09x49	10x53	12x33	14x03	15x18	16x52	18x08	20x28
Causeland	d	09x52	10x56	12x36	14x06	15x21	16x55	18x11	20x31
Sandplace	d	09x56	11x00	12x40	14x10	15x25	16x59	18x15	20x35
Looe	a	10 05	11 09	12 49	14 19	15 34	17 08	18 24	20 44

A from 5 April

For connections at Liskeard refer to Table T135

Table T140-R

Mondays to Fridays
16 December to 15 May

Looe - Liskeard

Miles			GW	GW	GW	GW	GW	GW	GW	GW	GW	GW	GW	GW	GW	GW	GW
0	**Looe**	d	06 34	07 54	09 05	10 08	11 06	12 08	13 06	14 08	15 06	16 16	17 14	18 17	19 19	20 29	21 36
2¼	Sandplace	d	06x39	07x59	09x10		11x11		13x11		15x11		17x19		19x24		21x41
3¾	Causeland	d	06x43	08x03	09x14		11x15		13x15		15x15		17x23		19x28		21x45
5	St Keyne Wishing Well Halt	d	06x46	08x06	09x17		11x18		13x18		15x18		17x26		19x31		21x48
6¾	Coombe Junction Halt	a		08 16							15 28						
—		d		08 19							15 31						
8¾	**Liskeard** ■	a	07 01	08 26	09 33	10 34	11 33	12 33	13 34	14 33	15 37	16 42	17 42	18 43	19 47	20 55	22 04

Saturdays
21 December to 16 May

		GW	GW	GW	GW	GW	GW	GW	GW	GW	GW	GW	GW	GW	GW	GW
Looe	d	06 32	07 55	09 02	10 08	11 05	12 08	13 05	14 08	15 05	16 14	17 20	18 24	19 22	20 28	21 38
Sandplace	d	06x36	07x59	09x06		11x09		13x09		15x09		17x24		19x26		21x42
Causeland	d	06x40	08x03	09x10		11x13		13x13		15x13		17x28		19x30		21x46
St Keyne Wishing Well Halt	d	06x44	08x07	09x14		11x17		13x17		15x17		17x32		19x34		21x50
Coombe Junction Halt	a			09 21						15 24						
	d			09 23						15 26						
Liskeard ■	a	07 02	08 23	09 35	10 34	11 33	12 32	13 35	14 32	15 37	16 38	17 48	18 48	19 50	20 52	22 08

Sundays
15 December to 10 May

		GW	GW	GW	GW	GW	GW	GW	GW
		A	A	A	A	A	A	A	A
Looe	d	10 08	11 12	12 55	14 22	15 45	17 11	18 30	20 50
Sandplace	d	10x13	11x17	13x00	14x27	15x50	17x16	18x35	20x55
Causeland	d	10x17	11x21	13x04	14x31	15x54	17x20	18x39	20x59
St Keyne Wishing Well Halt	d	10x21	11x25	13x08	14x35	15x58	17x24	18x43	21x03
Coombe Junction Halt	a	⌇	⌇	⌇	⌇	⌇	⌇	⌇	⌇
	d	⌇	⌇	⌇	⌇	⌇	⌇	⌇	⌇
Liskeard ■	a	10 36	11 40	13 23	14 50	16 13	17 39	18 58	21 18

A from 5 April

For connections at Liskeard refer to Table T135

Table T142-F

Par - Newquay

Mondays to Fridays
16 December to 15 May

Miles			GW	GW	GW	GW	GW	GW
				◇	◇	◇	◇	◇
0	**Par**	d	09 21	12 13	14 15	16 15	18 23	20 28
4¼	Luxulyan	d	09x31	12x23	14x25	16x25	18x33	20x38
6¼	Bugle	d	09x37	12x29	14x31	16x31	18x39	20x44
8¾	Roche	d	09x42	12x34	14x36	16x36	18x44	20x49
14½	St Columb Road	d	09x53	12x45	14x47	16x47	18x55	21x00
18¼	Quintrell Downs	d	10 01	12 53	14 55	16 55	19 03	21 08
20¾	**Newquay**	a	10 13	13 05	15 07	17 07	19 15	21 20

Saturdays
21 December to 16 May

		GW	GW	GW	GW	GW	GW	GW
				◇	◇	◇	◇	◇
Par	d	06 52	09 25	12 12	14 12	16 12	18 13	20 22
Luxulyan	d	07x02	09x35	12x22	14x22	16x22	18x23	20x32
Bugle	d	07x08	09x41	12x28	14x28	16x28	18x29	20x38
Roche	d	07x13	09x46	12x33	14x33	16x33	18x34	20x43
St Columb Road	d	07x24	09x57	12x44	14x44	16x44	18x45	20x54
Quintrell Downs	d	07 32	10 05	12 52	14 52	16 52	18 53	21 02
Newquay	a	07 45	10 18	13 05	15 05	17 05	19 06	21 15

Sundays
15 December to 10 May

		GW	GW	GW
				◇
Par	d	10 05	12 35	16 15
Luxulyan	d	10x16	12x46	16x26
Bugle	d	10x22	12x52	16x34
Roche	d	10x27	12x57	16x38
St Columb Road	d	10x38	13x08	16x50
Quintrell Downs	d	10 46	13 16	16 58
Newquay	a	10 57	13 27	17 08

For connections at Par refer to Table T135

Table T142-R

Newquay - Par

Mondays to Fridays
16 December to 15 May

Miles			GW	GW	GW	GW	GW	GW
			◇	◇	◇	◇		
0	**Newquay**	d	10 23	13 10	15 10	17 19	19 22	21 26
2½	Quintrell Downs	d	10 29	13 16	15 16	17 25	19 28	21 32
6½	St Columb Road	d	10x36	13x23	15x23	17x32	19x35	21x39
12	Roche	d	10x47	13x34	15x34	17x43	19x46	21x50
14½	Bugle	d	10x52	13x39	15x39	17x48	19x51	21x55
16½	Luxulyan	d	10x59	13x46	15x46	17x55	19x58	22x02
20¾	**Par**	a	11 12	13 59	15 58	18 08	20 10	22 15

Saturdays
21 December to 16 May

		GW	GW	GW	GW	GW	GW	GW
		◇	◇	◇	◇			
								A
Newquay	d	07 48	10 20	13 10	15 10	17 10	19 08	21 17
Quintrell Downs	d	07 54	10 26	13 16	15 16	17 16	19 14	21 23
St Columb Road	d	08x01	10x33	13x23	15x23	17x23	19x21	21x30
Roche	d	08x12	10x44	13x34	15x34	17x34	19x32	21x41
Bugle	d	08x17	10x49	13x39	15x39	17x39	19x37	21x46
Luxulyan	d	08x22	10x54	13x44	15x44	17x44	19x42	21x51
Par	a	08 38	11 10	14 00	16 00	18 00	19 59	22 06

Sundays
15 December to 10 May

		GW	GW	GW
		◇	◇	
Newquay	d	11 05	14 20	17 55
Quintrell Downs	d	11 11	14 26	18 01
St Columb Road	d	11x19	14x34	18x09
Roche	d	11x30	14x45	18x20
Bugle	d	11x35	14x50	18x25
Luxulyan	d	11x40	14x55	18x30
Par	a	11 54	15 09	18 44

A To Plymouth

For connections at Par refer to Table T135

Table T143-F

Truro - Falmouth

Mondays to Fridays
16 December to 15 May

Miles			GW	GW	GW	GW	GW	GW		GW	GW	GW	GW	GW	GW	GW	GW	GW	GW	GW	GW
0	**Truro**	d	06 04	06 30	07 01	07 44	08 15	08 45	and at the same minutes past each hour until	15 15	15 45	16 15	16 46	17 18	17 49	18 30	19 06	19 41	20 41	21 40	22 52
4¼	Perranwell	d	06 11	06 37	07 08	07 51	08 22			15 22		16 22	16 53	17 25	17 56	18 37	19 13	19 48	20 48	21 47	22 59
8¼	Penryn	d	06 18	06 45	07 15	07 58	08 29	08 59		15 29	15 59	16 29	17 00	17 32	18 03	18 44	19 20	19 55	20 55	21 54	23 06
10¼	Penmere	d	06 22	06 49	07 19	08 02	08 33	09 03		15 33	16 03	16 33	17 04	17 36	18 07	18 48	19 24	19 59	20 59	21 58	23 10
11¾	Falmouth Town	d	06 25	06 52	07 22	08 05	08 36	09 06		15 36	16 06	16 36	17 07	17 39	18 10	18 51	19 27	20 02	21 02	22 01	23 13
12¼	**Falmouth Docks**	a	06 28	06 55	07 25	08 08	08 39	09 09		15 39	16 09	16 39	17 10	17 42	18 13	18 54	19 30	20 05	21 05	22 04	23 16

Saturdays
21 December to 16 May

		GW	GW	GW	GW	GW	GW		GW	GW	GW	GW	GW	GW	GW	GW	GW	GW	GW	GW
Truro	d	06 03	06 30	07 10	07 41	08 12	08 43	and at the same minutes past each hour until	15 12	15 43	16 12	16 45	17 16	17 47	18 38	19 11	19 42	20 43	21 45	22 42
Perranwell	d	06 10	06 37	07 17	07 48	08 19			15 19		16 19	16 52	17 23	17 54	18 45	19 18	19 49	20 50	21 52	22 49
Penryn	d	06 17	06 44	07 24	07 55	08 26	08 56		15 26	15 56	16 26	16 59	17 30	18 01	18 52	19 25	19 56	20 57	21 59	22 56
Penmere	d	06 22	06 49	07 29	08 00	08 31	09 01		15 31	16 01	16 31	17 04	17 35	18 06	18 57	19 30	20 01	21 02	22 04	23 01
Falmouth Town	d	06 25	06 52	07 32	08 03	08 34	09 04		15 34	16 04	16 34	17 07	17 38	18 09	19 00	19 33	20 04	21 05	22 07	23 04
Falmouth Docks	a	06 27	06 54	07 34	08 05	08 36	09 06		15 36	16 06	16 36	17 09	17 40	18 11	19 02	19 35	20 06	21 07	22 09	23 06

Sundays
15 December to 10 May

		GW	GW	GW	GW	GW	GW	GW	GW	GW	GW	GW	GW
Truro	d	08 55	09 59	11 25	12 40	13 40	14 45	15 51	17 15	18 40	19 50	20 50	22 04
Perranwell	d	09 02	10 06	11 32	12 47	13 47	14 52	15 58	17 22	18 47	19 57	20 57	22 11
Penryn	d	09 09	10 13	11 39	12 54	13 54	14 59	16 05	17 29	18 54	20 04	21 04	22 18
Penmere	d	09 14	10 18	11 44	12 59	13 59	15 04	16 09	17 34	18 59	20 09	21 09	22 23
Falmouth Town	d	09 17	10 21	11 47	13 02	14 02	15 07	16 12	17 37	19 02	20 12	21 12	22 26
Falmouth Docks	a	09 19	10 23	11 49	13 04	14 04	15 09	16 15	17 39	19 04	20 14	21 14	22 28

For connections at Truro refer to Table T135

NRT DECEMBER 19 EDITION

Table T143-R

Falmouth - Truro

Mondays to Fridays
16 December to 15 May

Miles			GW	GW	GW	GW	GW	GW	GW	GW	GW	GW		GW	GW	GW	GW	GW	GW	GW	GW	GW
0	**Falmouth Docks**	d	06 31	07 01	07 44	08 15	08 45	09 15	09 45	10 15	10 45	11 15	and at the same minutes past each hour until	15 45	16 15	16 46	17 18	17 49	18 30	19 06	19 41	20 08
0½	Falmouth Town	d	06 34	07 04	07 47	08 18	08 48	09 18	09 48	10 18	10 48	11 18		15 48	16 18	16 49	17 21	17 52	18 33	19 09	19 44	20 11
2	Penmere	d	06 37	07 07	07 50	08 21	08 51	09 21	09 51	10 21	10 51	11 21		15 51	16 21	16 52	17 24	17 55	18 36	19 12	19 47	20 14
4	Penryn	d	06 44	07 14	07 57	08 28	08 59	09 28	09 59	10 28	10 59	11 28		15 59	16 28	16 59	17 31	18 02	18 43	19 24	19 54	20 19
8	Perranwell	d	06 51	07 21	08 04	08 35		09 35		10 35		11 35			16 35	17 06	17 38	18 09	18 50	19 31	20 01	20 26
12¼	**Truro**	a	06 59	07 29	08 12	08 43	09 13	09 42	10 13	10 42	11 13	11 43		16 13	16 43	17 14	17 46	18 17	18 57	19 38	20 08	20 33

		GW	GW	GW
Falmouth Docks	d	21 07	22 10	23 18
Falmouth Town	d	21 10	22 13	23 21
Penmere	d	21 13	22 16	23 24
Penryn	d	21 20	22 23	23 31
Perranwell	d	21 27	22 30	23 38
Truro	a	21 35	22 38	23 46

Saturdays
21 December to 16 May

		GW	GW	GW	GW	GW		GW	GW	GW	GW	GW	GW	GW	GW	GW	GW	GW	GW	GW
Falmouth Docks	d	06 30	07 10	07 41	08 12	08 42	and at the same minutes past each hour until	15 12	15 42	16 12	16 45	17 16	17 47	18 38	19 11	19 42	20 09	21 10	22 12	23 10
Falmouth Town	d	06 33	07 13	07 44	08 15	08 45		15 15	15 45	16 15	16 48	17 19	17 50	18 41	19 14	19 45	20 12	21 13	22 15	23 13
Penmere	d	06 36	07 16	07 47	08 18	08 48		15 18	15 48	16 18	16 51	17 22	17 53	18 44	19 17	19 48	20 15	21 16	22 18	23 16
Penryn	d	06 44	07 24	07 55	08 26	08 56		15 26	15 56	16 26	16 59	17 30	18 01	18 53	19 25	19 56	20 20	21 21	22 23	23 21
Perranwell	d	06 51	07 31	08 02	08 33			15 33		16 33	17 06	17 37	18 08	19 00	19 32	20 03	20 27	21 28	22 30	23 28
Truro	a	06 58	07 38	08 09	08 40	09 10		15 40	16 10	16 40	17 13	17 44	18 16	19 08	19 39	20 10	20 35	21 37	22 39	23 38

Sundays
15 December to 10 May

		GW	GW	GW	GW	GW	GW	GW	GW	GW	GW	GW	GW
Falmouth Docks	d	09 25	10 26	11 52	13 10	14 07	15 12	16 20	17 45	19 07	20 20	21 20	22 33
Falmouth Town	d	09 28	10 29	11 55	13 13	14 10	15 15	16 23	17 48	19 10	20 23	21 23	22 35
Penmere	d	09 31	10 32	11 58	13 16	14 13	15 18	16 26	17 51	19 13	20 26	21 26	22 38
Penryn	d	09 36	10 37	12 03	13 23	14 18	15 23	16 31	17 56	19 18	20 31	21 30	22 43
Perranwell	d	09 43	10 44	12 10	13 30	14 25	15 30	16 38	18 03	19 25	20 38	21 37	22 50
Truro	a	09 51	10 52	12 18	13 37	14 33	15 38	16 45	18 11	19 33	20 46	21 45	23 01

For connections at Truro refer to Table T135

Table T144-F

St Erth - St Ives

Mondays to Fridays

16 December to 15 May

Miles			GW	GW	GW	GW	GW	GW	GW	GW	GW	GW	GW	GW	GW	GW	GW	GW	GW	GW	GW	GW	GW
—	Penzance	d	06 58																				
0	**St Erth**	d	07 06	07 50	08 49	09 38	10 18	10 48	11 18	11 48	12 18	12 48	13 19	13 48	14 18	14 48	15 18	15 48	16 19	16 48	17 18	17 48	18 18
0¾	Lelant Saltings	d		07 52																			
1	Lelant	d	07x10	07x53	08x51		10x20				12x20				14x20		15x20			16x50		17x50	
3	Carbis Bay	d	07 15	07 59	08 57	09 45	10 26	10 55	11 25	11 55	12 26	12 55	13 26	13 55	14 26	14 55	15 26	15 55	16 26	16 56	17 25	17 56	18 25
4¼	**St Ives**	a	07 18	08 03	09 00	09 48	10 29	10 58	11 29	11 58	12 29	12 58	13 29	13 58	14 29	14 58	15 29	15 58	16 29	16 59	17 28	17 59	18 28

		GW	GW	GW	GW	GW	GW	GW
Penzance	d							
St Erth	d	18 48	19 20	19 50	20 19	20 48	21 23	22 22
Lelant Saltings	d							
Lelant	d	18x51		19x53		20x51		22x24
Carbis Bay	d	18 56	19 27	19 58	20 26	20 56	21 30	22 30
St Ives	a	19 01	19 30	20 01	20 29	21 00	21 33	22 33

Saturdays

21 December to 16 May

		GW	GW	GW	GW	GW	GW	GW	GW	GW	GW	GW	GW	GW	GW	GW	GW	GW	GW	GW	GW	GW	GW
Penzance	d	06 50		08 41																		18 58	
St Erth	d	06 59	07 49	08 50	09 50	10 21	10 52	11 22	11 52	12 22	12 52	13 22	13 52	14 21	14 52	15 22	15 52	16 22	16 52	17 22	18 08	19 07	20 05
Lelant Saltings	d		07 51																				
Lelant	d	07x01	07x52	08x52		10x23				12x24				14x23		15x24			16x54		18x10	19x09	20x07
Carbis Bay	d	07 07	07 58	08 58	09 57	10 29	10 59	11 29	11 59	12 30	12 59	13 29	13 59	14 29	14 59	15 30	15 59	16 29	17 00	17 29	18 16	19 15	20 13
St Ives	a	07 11	08 03	09 02	10 01	10 32	11 03	11 33	12 03	12 34	13 03	13 33	14 03	14 33	15 03	15 34	16 03	16 33	17 04	17 33	18 20	19 20	20 17

		GW	GW	GW
Penzance	d			
St Erth	d	20 36	21 14	21 47
Lelant Saltings	d			
Lelant	d		21x16	21x49
Carbis Bay	d	20 43	21 22	21 55
St Ives	a	20 47	21 26	21 59

Sundays

15 December to 10 May

		GW A	GW A	GW A	GW B	GW A	GW B	GW A	GW	GW	GW	GW	GW	GW	GW	GW	GW	GW	GW	GW
Penzance	d	10 27			11 40															
St Erth	d	10 36	11 13	11 48	11 50	12 18	12 30	12 48	13 18	13 47	14 15	14 44	15 18	15 48	16 18	16 48	17 28	18 01	18 28	19 18
Lelant Saltings	d					12 20	12 33													
Lelant	d	10x39		11x50	11x53						14x18					16x51				19x21
Carbis Bay	d	10 44	11 20	11 55	11 58	12 26	12 39	12 55	13 25	13 54	14 23	14 51	15 25	15 55	16 25	16 56	17 35	18 08	18 35	19 26
St Ives	a	10 48	11 24	11 59	12 03	12 30	12 42	12 58	13 28	13 57	14 26	14 54	15 28	15 58	16 28	16 59	17 38	18 12	18 38	19 30

A from 5 April

B until 29 March

For connections at St Erth refer to Table T135

NRT DECEMBER 19 EDITION

Table T144-R

St Ives - St Erth

Mondays to Fridays

16 December to 15 May

Miles			GW	GW	GW	GW	GW	GW	GW	GW	GW	GW	GW	GW	GW	GW	GW	GW	GW	GW	GW	GW	GW
0	**St Ives**	d	07 32	08 07	09 11	10 03	10 33	11 03	11 33	12 03	12 33	13 03	13 33	14 03	14 33	15 02	15 33	16 03	16 33	17 03	17 32	18 03	18 33
1¼	Carbis Bay	d	07 35	08 10	09 14	10 06	10 36	11 06	11 36	12 06	12 36	13 06	13 36	14 06	14 36	15 05	15 36	16 06	16 36	17 06	17 35	18 06	18 36
3¼	Lelant	d	07x40	08x15	09x19			11x10				13x10				15x09		16x12			17x39		18x41
3½	Lelant Saltings	d			09 21																		
4¼	**St Erth**	a	07 44	08 19	09 24	10 14	10 44	11 15	11 44	12 14	12 44	13 15	13 44	14 14	14 44	15 14	15 44	16 16	16 44	17 14	17 44	18 14	18 47
—	Penzance	a																					

		GW	GW	GW	GW	GW	GW	GW
St Ives	d	19 05	19 34	20 04	20 33	21 04	21 37	22 36
Carbis Bay	d	19 08	19 37	20 07	20 36	21 07	21 40	22 39
Lelant	d		19x42		20x41		21x45	22x44
Lelant Saltings	d							
St Erth	a	19 17	19 46	20 15	20 46	21 15	21 50	22 49
Penzance	a							22 59

Saturdays

21 December to 16 May

		GW	GW	GW	GW	GW	GW	GW	GW	GW	GW	GW	GW	GW	GW	GW	GW	GW	GW	GW	GW	GW	GW
St Ives	d	07 30	08 06	09 05	10 05	10 36	11 06	11 36	12 06	12 36	13 06	13 36	14 06	14 36	15 06	15 36	16 06	16 36	17 06	17 37	18 28	19 26	20 20
Carbis Bay	d	07 33	08 09	09 08	10 08	10 39	11 09	11 39	12 09	12 39	13 09	13 39	14 09	14 39	15 09	15 39	16 09	16 39	17 09	17 40	18 31	19 29	20 23
Lelant	d	07x37	08x13	09x12			11x13				13x13				15x13				17x14		18x35	19x33	
Lelant Saltings	d			09 14																			
St Erth	a	07 43	08 17	09 18	10 17	10 48	11 18	11 48	12 18	12 48	13 19	13 48	14 18	14 48	15 18	15 48	16 18	16 48	17 19	17 48	18 40	19 39	20 32
Penzance	a		08 29																		18 52		

		GW	GW	GW
St Ives	d	20 52	21 30	22 05
Carbis Bay	d	20 55	21 33	22 08
Lelant	d	20x59	21x37	22x12
Lelant Saltings	d			
St Erth	a	21 04	21 43	22 17
Penzance	a			22 30

Sundays

15 December to 10 May

		GW A	GW A	GW A	GW B	GW A	GW B	GW A	GW	GW	GW	GW	GW	GW	GW	GW	GW	GW	GW	GW
St Ives	d	10 53	11 26	12 03	12 05	12 33	12 44	13 03	13 33	14 00	14 29	14 57	15 33	16 03	16 33	17 03	17 41	18 14	18 41	19 41
Carbis Bay	d	10 56	11 29	12 06	12 08	12 36	12 47	13 06	13 36	14 03	14 33	15 00	15 36	16 06	16 36	17 07	17 44	18 18	18 45	19 44
Lelant	d	11x01		12x11	12x13						14x38					17x12				19x49
Lelant Saltings	d																			19 51
St Erth	a	11 05	11 37	12 15	12 17	12 44	12 55	13 14	13 44	14 11	14 41	15 08	15 44	16 14	16 44	17 15	17 52	18 26	18 52	19 54
Penzance	a																			20 05

A from 5 April

B until 29 March

For connections at St Erth refer to Table T135

Reading - Guildford, Redhill and Gatwick Airport

Mondays to Fridays
16 December to 15 May

Miles				GW MO	GW	GW	GW	GW	GW	GW	GW	GW	GW	GW	GW	GW	GW	GW	GW	GW	GW	GW	GW	GW
				1	1 🛒	1 🛒	1 🛒	1 🛒	1 🛒	1	1 🛒	1	1	1	1	1	1	1	1	1	1	1	1	1
0	**Reading 7**	149	d		04 31	05 32	05 54	06 05	06 32	07 04	07 58	08 18	08 35	08 58	09 33	09 50	10 30	10 55	11 59	12 53	13 51	14 57	15 26	16 00
6¾	Wokingham	149	d		04 40	05 41	06 05	06 16	06 42	07 13	08 08	08 29	08 45	09 08	09 43	09 59	10 40	11 04	12 08	13 02	14 00	15 06	15 38	16 10
10	Crowthorne		d				06 11	06 22		07 19	08 14	08 35		09 14		10 05		11 10	12 14	13 08	14 06	15 12	15 44	16 16
11½	Sandhurst		d				06 14	06 25		07 23	08 17	08 39		09 18		10 09		11 14	12 18	13 12	14 10	15 16	15 48	16 20
13½	Blackwater		d		04 49	05 49	06 18	06 29	06 51	07 27	08 21	08 43	08 54	09 21	09 52	10 13	10 49	11 18	12 22	13 16	14 14	15 20	15 52	16 23
15½	Farnborough North		d				06 23	06 34		07 32	08 26	08 48		09 26		10 18		11 23	12 27	13 21	14 19	15 25		16 28
17½	North Camp		d		04 56	05 55	06 28	06 38	06 57	07 36	08 30	08 52	09 01	09 31	09 58	10 22	10 56	11 27	12 31	13 25	14 23	15 29	15 58	16 33
19½	Ash 5	149	d				06 32	06 42		07 40	08 34	08 56		09 35		10 26		11 31	12 35	13 29	14 27	15 33		16 37
21½	Wanborough	149	d				06 37																	16 41
25¾	**Guildford**	149	a		05 08	06 06	06 44	06 51	07 09	07 49	08 43	09 05	09 12	09 44	10 10	10 35	11 08	11 40	12 44	13 38	14 36	15 42	16 10	16 48
—			d		05 10	06 08	06 44	06 53	07 10	07 52	08 46		09 14	09 45	10 11	10 37	11 10	11 42	12 45	13 40	14 38	15 44	16 11	16 50
27¾	Shalford		d				06 51	06a57		07 57	08 51			09 50		10 42		11 47	12 51	13 45	14 48	15 49		16 55
29¾	Chilworth		d				06 55			08 01	08 56			09 55				11 51		13 49		15 53		16 59
33½	Gomshall		d				07 02			08 08	09 02			10 02				11 58		13 56		16 00		17 06
38¼	Dorking West		d				07 09			08 16	09 10					10 54			13 04		15 01	16 07		17 13
39	Dorking Deepdene		d	00 17	05 27	06 24	07 12		07 28	08 18	09 12		09 32	10 10	10 29	10 57	11 27	12 06	13 07	14 04	15 05	16 10	16 29	17 16
41¾	Betchworth		d				07 17			08 23	09 18					11 02			13 12		15 10	16 15		17 21
44½	Reigate	186	d	00 27	05 37	06 32	07 24		07 41	08 32	09 24		09 41	10 19	10 38	11 08	11 35	12 16	13 19	14 14	15 17	16 21	16 38	17 27
46½	**Redhill**	186	a	00 31	05 41	06 36	07 28		07 46	08 38	09 28		09 45	10 23	10 42	11 14	11 40	12 22	13 23	14 18	15 23	16 26	16 42	17 33
52¼	**Gatwick Airport 10**	186	a	00 42	05 54	06 54			07 57	08 51			09 56		10 55		11 50						16 53	

			GW	GW	GW	GW	GW	XC	GW	GW	GW	GW	GW	GW FO
			1	1 🛒	1	1	1	◇1	1	1 🛒	1	1	1	1
Reading 7	149	d	16 31	16 47	16 58	17 18	18 03	18 17	18 28	19 01	20 02	21 20	22 29	23 34
Wokingham	149	d	16 41	16 59	17 10	17 29	18 12		18 38	19 10	20 11	21 29	22 38	
Crowthorne		d		17 05	17 16	17 35	18 18			19 16	20 17	21 35	22 44	23 50
Sandhurst		d		17 09	17 20	17 39	18 22			19 20	20 21	21 39	22 48	23 54
Blackwater		d	16 50	17 12	17 23	17 43	18 26		18 47	19 24	20 25	21 43	22 52	23 57
Farnborough North		d		17 17	17 28	17 48	18 31			19 29	20 30	21 48	22 57	00 02
North Camp		d	16 56	17 22	17 33	17 52	18 35		18 54	19 33	20 34	21 52	23 01	00 07
Ash 5	149	d		17 26	17 37		18 39			19 37	20 38	21 56	23 05	00 11
Wanborough	149	d			17 41									00 15
Guildford	149	a	17 08	17 35	17 48	18 04	18 48	18 51	19 05	19 46	20 47	22 05	23 14	00 22
		d	17 09	17 37	17 49	18 06	18 50		19 07	19 48	20 48	22 07	23 19	00 24
Shalford		d		17a41	17 54		18 55			19a53	20 54	22 12	23 24	
Chilworth		d			17 59		18 59				20 58		23 28	
Gomshall		d			18 06		19 06		19 19		21 05		23 35	
Dorking West		d			18 14		19 13				21 12		23 43	
Dorking Deepdene		d	17 27		18 17	18 23	19 16		19 27		21 15	22 26	23 45	00 41
Betchworth		d				18 29	19 21				21 20		23 50	
Reigate	186	d	17 36		18 26	18 35	19 27		19 36		21 26	22 36	23 56	00 51
Redhill	186	a	17 40		18 30	18 39	19 33		19 40		21 31	22 40	00 01	00 55
Gatwick Airport 10	186	a	17 51			18 50			19 51			22 52	00 14	01 06

Saturdays
21 December to 16 May

			GW	GW	GW	GW	GW	GW	GW	GW	GW	GW	GW	GW	GW	GW	GW	GW	GW	XC	GW	GW	GW	GW
			1	1	1	1	1	1	1	1	1	1	1	1	1	1	1	1	1	◇1	1	1	1	1
Reading 7	149	d		04 28	05 31	05 59	06 31	06 59	07 59	08 59	09 59	10 59	11 59	12 59	13 59	14 59	15 59	16 59	17 59	18 25	18 59	19 59	20 31	21 20
Wokingham	149	d		04 39	05 41	06 08	06 40	07 08	08 08	09 08	10 08	11 08	12 08	13 08	14 08	15 08	16 08	17 08	18 08		19 08	20 08	20 40	21 29
Crowthorne		d				06 14		07 14	08 14	09 14	10 14	11 14	12 14	13 14	14 14	15 14	16 14	17 14	18 14		19 14	20 14		21 35
Sandhurst		d				06 18		07 18	08 18	09 18	10 18	11 18	12 18	13 18	14 18	15 18	16 18	17 18	18 18		19 18	20 18		21 39
Blackwater		d		04 47	05 50	06 22	06 49	07 22	08 22	09 22	10 22	11 22	12 22	13 22	14 22	15 22	16 22	17 22	18 22		19 22	20 22	20 49	21 43
Farnborough North		d	00 02			06 27		07 27	08 27	09 27	10 27	11 27	12 27	13 27	14 27	15 27	16 27	17 27	18 27		19 27	20 27		21 48
North Camp		d	00 07	04 54	05 56	06 31	06 56	07 31	08 31	09 31	10 31	11 31	12 31	13 31	14 31	15 31	16 31	17 31	18 31		19 31	20 31	20 56	21 52
Ash 5	149	d	00 11			06 35		07 35	08 35	09 35	10 35	11 35	12 35	13 35	14 35	15 35	16 35	17 35	18 35		19 35	20 35		21 56
Wanborough	149	d	00 15																					
Guildford	149	a	00 22	05 05	06 08	06 44	07 07	07 44	08 44	09 44	10 44	11 44	12 44	13 44	14 44	15 44	16 44	17 44	18 44	19 01	19 44	20 44	21 08	22 05
		d	00 24	05 07	06 09	06 46	07 09	07 46	08 46	09 46	10 46	11 46	12 46	13 46	14 46	15 46	16 46	17 46	18 46		19 46	20 46	21 09	22 07
Shalford		d				06 51		07 51	08 51	09 51	10 51	11 51	12 51	13 51	14 52	15 51	16 51	17 51	18 51		19 51	20 51	21 14	22 12
Chilworth		d						07 55		09 55		11 55		13 55		15 55		17 55			19 55		21 19	
Gomshall		d						08 02		10 02		12 02		14 02		16 02		18 02			20 02		21 26	
Dorking West		d				07 04			09 04		11 04		13 04		15 05		17 04		19 04			21 04		22 25
Dorking Deepdene		d	00 41	05 25	06 27	07 07	07 27	08 10	09 07	10 10	11 07	12 10	13 07	14 10	15 08	16 10	17 07	18 10	19 07		20 10	21 07	21 34	22 28
Betchworth		d				07 12			09 12		11 12		13 12		15 13		17 12		19 12			21 12		22 33
Reigate	186	d	00 51	05 35	06 36	07 17	07 35	08 18	09 17	10 18	11 17	12 18	13 17	14 18	15 18	16 18	17 17	18 18	19 17		20 18	21 17	21 43	22 40
Redhill	186	a	00 55	05 39	06 40	07 23	07 39	08 24	09 23	10 24	11 23	12 24	13 23	14 24	15 24	16 24	17 23	18 24	19 23		20 24	21 23	21 47	22 44
Gatwick Airport 10	186	a	01 06	05 51	06 54		07 50																22 00	22 58

Reading - Guildford, Redhill and Gatwick Airport

Saturdays
21 December to 16 May

			GW	GW
			1	1
Reading 7	149	d	22 32	23 34
Wokingham	149	d	22 41	
Crowthorne		d	22 47	23 48
Sandhurst		d	22 51	23 52
Blackwater		d	22 55	23 55
Farnborough North		d	23 00	23 59
North Camp		d	23 04	00 05
Ash 5	149	d	23 08	00 09
Wanborough	149	d		00 13
Guildford	149	a	23 17	00 20
		d	23 20	00 22
Shalford		d	23 25	
Chilworth		d	23 29	
Gomshall		d	23 35	
Dorking West		d	23 44	
Dorking Deepdene		d	23 46	00 39
Betchworth		d	23 51	
Reigate	186	d	23 57	00 49
Redhill	186	a	00 02	00 53
Gatwick Airport 10	186	a	00 20	01 04

Sundays
15 December to 10 May

			GW	GW	GW	GW	GW	GW	GW	GW	GW	GW	GW	GW	GW	GW	GW	GW	GW	GW	GW	GW	GW	GW
			1 A	1	1	1	1	1	1	1	1	1	1	1	1	1	1	1	1	1	1	1	1	1
Reading 7	149	d		06 03	06 57	07 39	08 13	08 41	09 13	09 41	10 13	10 41	11 13	11 41	12 13	12 41	13 13	13 41	14 13	14 41	15 13	15 41	16 13	16 41
Wokingham	149	d		06 13	07 07	07 50	08 22	08 50	09 22	09 50	10 22	10 50	11 22	11 50	12 22	12 50	13 22	13 50	14 22	14 50	15 21	15 50	16 21	16 50
Crowthorne		d				07 56		08 56		09 56		10 56		11 56		12 56		13 56		14 56		15 56		16 56
Sandhurst		d				08 00		09 00		10 00		11 00		12 00		13 00		14 00		15 00		16 00		17 00
Blackwater		d		06 21	07 15	08 04	08 32	09 04	09 32	10 04	10 32	11 04	11 32	12 04	12 32	13 04	13 32	14 04	14 32	15 04	15 31	16 04	16 31	17 04
Farnborough North		d				08 08		09 09		10 09		11 09		12 09		13 09		14 09		15 09		16 09		17 09
North Camp		d	00 05	06 29	07 23	08 13	08 38	09 13	09 38	10 13	10 38	11 13	11 38	12 13	12 38	13 13	13 38	14 13	14 38	15 13	15 38	16 13	16 38	17 13
Ash 5	149	d	00 09			08 17		09 17		10 17		11 17		12 17		13 17		14 17		15 17		16 17		17 17
Wanborough	149	d	00 13																					
Guildford	149	a	00 20	06 40	07 34	08 26	08 50	09 26	09 50	10 26	10 50	11 26	11 50	12 26	12 50	13 26	13 50	14 26	14 49	15 26	15 49	16 26	16 50	17 26
		d	00 22	06 41	07 35	08 27	08 51	09 28	09 51	10 28	10 51	11 28	11 51	12 28	12 51	13 28	13 51	14 28	14 51	15 28	15 51	16 28	16 51	17 28
Shalford		d				08 32		09 33		10 33		11 33		12 33		13 33		14 33		15 33		16 33		17 33
Chilworth		d				08 37				10 37				12 37				14 37				16 37		
Gomshall		d				08 44				10 44				12 44				14 44				16 44		
Dorking West		d						09 47				11 47				13 46				15 47				17 47
Dorking Deepdene		d	00 39	07 00	07 54	08 52	09 08	09 50	10 08	10 52	11 08	11 50	12 08	12 52	13 08	13 49	14 08	14 52	15 08	15 50	16 08	16 52	17 08	17 50
Betchworth		d						09 55				11 55				13 54				15 55				17 55
Reigate	186	d	00 49	07 09	08 03	09 01	09 17	10 02	10 17	11 02	11 17	12 02	12 17	13 02	13 17	14 01	14 17	15 02	15 17	16 02	16 16	17 02	17 17	18 02
Redhill	186	a	00 53	07 13	08 07	09 05	09 24	10 06	10 24	11 06	11 24	12 06	12 24	13 06	13 24	14 05	14 24	15 06	15 24	16 06	16 24	17 06	17 24	18 06
Gatwick Airport 10	186	a	01 04	07 26	08 24		09 35		10 35		11 35		12 35		13 35		14 35		15 35		16 35		17 35	

			GW	GW	GW	GW	GW	GW	GW	XC	GW	GW
			1	1	1	1	1	1	1	◇1	1	1
Reading 7	149	d	17 13	17 41	18 13	18 41	19 13	20 14	21 13	22 14	22 18	23 13
Wokingham	149	d	17 21	17 50	18 21	18 50	19 21	20 22	21 21		22 27	23 22
Crowthorne		d		17 56		18 56		20 29	21 28			23 28
Sandhurst		d		18 00		19 00		20 33	21 32			23 32
Blackwater		d	17 31	18 04	18 31	19 04	19 31	20 35	21 36		22 36	23 36
Farnborough North		d		18 09		19 09		20 42	21 41			23 41
North Camp		d	17 38	18 13	18 38	19 13	19 38	20 45	21 45		22 43	23 45
Ash 5	149	d		18 17		19 17		20 50	21 49			23 49
Wanborough	149	d										
Guildford	149	a	17 49	18 26	18 50	19 26	19 50	20 58	21 58	22 41	22 54	23 58
		d	17 51	18 28	18 51	19 28	19 51	21 00	22 01		22 56	23 59
Shalford		d		18 33		19 33		21 05			23 01	
Chilworth		d		18 37				21 09			23 05	
Gomshall		d		18 44				21 16			23 12	
Dorking West		d				19 47		21 24			23 20	
Dorking Deepdene		d	18 08	18 52	19 08	19 50	20 08	21 25	22 21		23 21	00 17
Betchworth		d				19 55		21 31			23 27	
Reigate	186	d	18 17	19 02	19 17	20 02	20 17	21 37	22 29		23 33	00 27
Redhill	186	a	18 24	19 06	19 24	20 06	20 24	21 43	22 35		23 39	00 31
Gatwick Airport 10	186	a	18 35		19 35		20 35	21 58	22 47		23 57	00 42

A not 15 December

Table T148-R

Mondays to Fridays
16 December to 15 May

Gatwick Airport, Redhill and Guildford - Reading

Miles			GW MX 1	XC ◇1	GW 1	GW 1	GW 1	GW 1	GW 1	GW 1	GW 1	GW 1	GW 1	GW 1	GW 1	GW 1	GW	GW 1	GW 1	GW 1	GW 1	GW 1	GW 1
0	**Gatwick Airport 10**	186 d				07 03	08 02		09 02	10 00	10 59	12 00	13 00	14 00	15 00	16 00		18 00	19 00		19 58	21 00	23 18
5¾	**Redhill**	186 d			06 44	07 14	08 16		09 15	10 14	11 15	12 14	13 14	14 14	15 14	16 14		18 14	19 14		20 12	21 14	23 32
7¾	Reigate	186 d			06 48	07 18	08 21		09 19	10 19	11 20	12 19	13 19	14 19	15 19	16 19		18 19	19 19		20 17	21 19	23 37
10½	Betchworth	d																					
13¼	Dorking Deepdene	d			06 55	07 25	08 28		09 26	10 27	11 27	12 26	13 26	14 26	15 26	16 27		18 27	19 27		20 25	21 27	23 45
14	Dorking West	d																					
18½	Gomshall	d				07 33																	
22½	Chilworth	d																					
24½	Shalford	d															18 00			20 03			
26½	**Guildford**	a			07 14	07 46	08 46		09 42	10 44	11 44	12 43	13 43	14 44	15 44	16 44	18 04	18 43	19 43	20 07	20 42	21 43	00 01
—		d	00 03	06 01	07 15	07 48	08 48	09 09	09 44	10 45	11 46	12 45	13 45	14 45	15 45	16 45	18 06	18 45	19 44	20 09	20 44	21 45	00 03
30½	Wanborough	149 d						09 18															
32½	Ash 5	149 d			07 25	07 57		09 22									18 16			20 19			
34½	North Camp	d	00 16		07 29	08 01	09 00	09 27		10 58	11 59	12 58	13 58	14 58	15 58	16 58	18 20	19 01	19 58	20 23	20 56	21 58	00 16
36½	Farnborough North	d			07 33	08 05		09 31									18 24			20 27			
38½	Blackwater	d	00 22		07 38	08 10	09 07	09 35		11 04	12 05	13 04	14 04	15 04	16 04	17 04	18 29	19 07	20 04	20 32	21 03	22 04	00 22
40½	Sandhurst	d			07 42	08 13		09 39									18 33			20 36			
42½	Crowthorne	d			07 46	08 17		09 43									18 37			20 40			
45½	Wokingham	149 d	00 34		07 52	08 22	09 15	09 50	10 06	11 13	12 14	13 13	14 13	15 13	16 13	17 13	18 42	19 18	20 13	20 45	21 10	22 14	00 34
52½	**Reading 7**	149 a	00 48	06 33	08 01	08 32	09 25	09 59	10 15	11 22	12 23	13 22	14 22	15 22	16 22	17 22	18 51	19 30	20 23	20 56	21 21	22 26	00 48

Saturdays
21 December to 16 May

		GW 1	XC ◇1	GW 1	GW 1		GW 1	GW 1	GW 1	GW 1	GW 1
Gatwick Airport 10	186 d			05 55	07 00	and hourly until	18 00	19 00	20 00	21 00	23 18
Redhill	186 d			06 12	07 14		18 14	19 14	20 14	21 14	23 32
Reigate	186 d			06 17	07 19		18 19	19 19	20 19	21 19	23 37
Betchworth	d										
Dorking Deepdene	d			06 24	07 26		18 26	19 26	20 26	21 26	23 44
Dorking West	d										
Gomshall	d										
Chilworth	d										
Shalford	d										
Guildford	a			06 42	07 44		18 44	19 44	20 44	21 44	00 02
	d	00 03	06 09	06 43	07 45		18 45	19 45	20 45	21 45	00 03
Wanborough	149 d										
Ash 5	149 d										
North Camp	d	00 16		06 56	07 58		18 58	19 58	20 58	21 58	00 16
Farnborough North	d										
Blackwater	d	00 22		07 02	08 04		19 04	20 04	21 04	22 04	00 22
Sandhurst	d										
Crowthorne	d										
Wokingham	149 d	00 34		07 11	08 13		19 13	20 13	21 13	22 13	00 34
Reading 7	149 a	00 48	06 44	07 20	08 22		19 22	20 22	21 22	22 22	00 47

Sundays
15 December to 10 May

		GW 1 A	GW 1	GW 1	GW 1	GW 1	GW 1	GW 1	XC ◇1	GW 1	GW 1	GW 1	GW 1	GW 1		GW 1	GW 1	GW 1
Gatwick Airport 10	186 d		06 11	07 11	08 11	09 15	10 15	11 15		12 15	13 15	14 15	15 15	16 15	and hourly until	19 15	20 15	22 18
Redhill	186 d		06 23	07 23	08 26	09 30	10 29	11 29		12 29	13 29	14 29	15 29	16 29		19 29	20 29	22 34
Reigate	186 d		06 27	07 30	08 31	09 35	10 34	11 34		12 34	13 34	14 34	15 34	16 34		19 34	20 34	22 40
Betchworth	d																	
Dorking Deepdene	d		06 36	07 37	08 38	09 42	10 41	11 42		12 41	13 41	14 41	15 41	16 42		19 42	20 42	22 48
Dorking West	d																	
Gomshall	d																	
Chilworth	d																	
Shalford	d																	23 02
Guildford	a		06 55	07 54	08 56	10 00	10 59	12 00		12 59	14 00	14 59	16 00	17 00		20 00	21 00	23 07
	d	00 03	06 56	07 56	08 58	10 01	11 00	12 00	12 14	13 00	14 00	15 00	16 00	17 00		20 00	21 00	23 09
Wanborough	149 d																	
Ash 5	149 d			08 06														
North Camp	d	00 16	07 09	08 10	09 11	10 14	11 13	12 13		13 13	14 13	15 13	16 13	17 13		20 13	21 13	23 20
Farnborough North	d			08 14														
Blackwater	d	00 22	07 15	08 19	09 17	10 20	11 19	12 19		13 19	14 19	15 19	16 19	17 19		20 19	21 19	23 27
Sandhurst	d			08 23														
Crowthorne	d			08 27														
Wokingham	149 d	00 34	07 24	08 32	09 27	10 28	11 28	12 28		13 28	14 28	15 28	16 28	17 28		20 28	21 28	23 36
Reading 7	149 a	00 47	07 33	08 41	09 38	10 38	11 38	12 38	12 47	13 38	14 38	15 38	16 38	17 38		20 38	21 39	23 47

A not 15 December

Table T149-F

Mondays to Fridays
16 December to 15 May

London - Hounslow, Richmond, Kingston, Windsor, Weybridge, Ascot, Guildford and Reading

Miles	Miles	Miles			SW MX	SW MX	SW MO	SW MX	SW MX	SW MX 1	SW MX 1	SW MO	SW MX	SW MO	SW MX	SW MO	SW MO	SW MX	SW MX	SW MO	SW MX	SW	SW
0	—	0	**London Waterloo 15** ⊖	d																00 18	00 18		
1¼	—	1¼	Vauxhall ⊖	d														00 02		00 22	00 22		
2¾	—	2¾	Queenstown Rd.(Battersea)	d																00 25	00 25		
4	—	4	**Clapham Junction 10**	d														00 08	00 03	00 29	00 30		
4¾	—	4¾	Wandsworth Town	d															00 05	00 32	00 33		
5¾	—	5¾	Putney	d														00 12	00 08	00 35	00 36		
7	0	7	Barnes	d													00 03		00 12	00 38	00 39		
—	0½	—	Barnes Bridge	d															00 14				
—	1½	—	Chiswick	d															00 17				
—	2½	—	Kew Bridge	d															00 20				
—	3½	—	Brentford	d															00 23				
—	4¼	—	Syon Lane	d															00 25				
—	5	—	Isleworth	d															00 27				
—	6½	—	**Hounslow**	d					00 01										00 31				
8¼	—	8¼	Mortlake	d													00 05			00 40	00 41		
9	—	9	North Sheen	d													00 07			00 42	00 43		
9¾	—	9¾	**Richmond** ⊖	d											00 06		00 10	00 18		00 45	00 46		
10¾	—	10¾	St Margarets	d									00 01				00 12			00 47	00 48		
11¼	—	11¼	Twickenham	a									00 03		00 10		00 14	00 22		00 49	00 50		
—	—	—		d								00 03	00 04		00 10	00 12	00 15	00 22		00 50	00 51	04 52	
12¼	—	—	Strawberry Hill	d									00 08			00 15				00s53	00s54	04 55	
12½	—	—	Fulwell	a																			
13½	—	—	Teddington	a									00 11			00 18				00s56	00s57	04 58	
14¾	—	—	Hampton Wick	a									00 13			00 21				00s59	01s00	05 01	
15¼	—	—	**Kingston**	a									00 15			00 23				01 01	01 02	05 03	
—	—	12½	Whitton	d													00 18	00 25					
—	—	14¾	Feltham	d					00 06			00 09			00 16		00 22	00 29	00 36				
—	—	17½	Ashford (Surrey)	d		00 03			00 10								00 26	00 33	00 40				
0	—	19	**Staines**	d		00 07			00 14			00 15		00 22	00 23		00a30	00a37	00a47				05 23
2½	—	—	Wraysbury	d		00 11																	
3¾	—	—	Sunnymeads	d		00 14																	
4¾	—	—	Datchet	d		00 17																	
6¾	—	—	**Windsor & Eton Riverside**	a		00 21																	
—	—	21	Egham	d					00 19			00 20		00s26	00 27								05 27
0	—	23¼	Virginia Water	a					00 23			00 24		00s31	00 31								05 31
—	—	—		d				00 01	00 23			00 24			00 31								05 31
2½	—	—	Chertsey	d					00 29					00s36									
4	—	—	Addlestone	d					00 32					00s39									
5¾	—	—	**Weybridge**	a					00 36														
—	—	25¼	Longcross	d																			
—	—	27	Sunningdale	d				00 07				00 30			00 37								05 37
—	0	29	**Ascot 3**	d			00 05	00 13			00 23	00 35			00 42								05 43
—	3¼	—	Bagshot	d							00 29												
—	6½	—	Camberley	a							00 35												
—	8¾	—	Frimley	d						00 13	00 40												
—	12	—	Ash Vale	d						00 19	00 47												
—	14½	—	**Aldershot**	a						00 24	00s52												
—	—	—		d																			
—	17¼	—	Ash 5	d																			
—	19¼	—	Wanborough	d																			
—	23½	—	**Guildford**	a																			
—	—	31¼	Martins Heron	d			00 09	00 17				00 39			00 46								05 47
—	—	32¼	Bracknell	d			00 13	00 20				00 43			00 50								05 50
—	—	36¾	**Wokingham**	d			00 19	00 30				00 49			00 56								05 57
—	—	38¾	Winnersh	d			00 23	00 33				00 53											06 00
—	—	39¼	Winnersh Triangle	d	00 02		00 25	00 35				00 55											06 02
—	—	40½	Earley	d	00 05		00 27	00 38				00 57											06 05
—	—	43½	**Reading 7**	a	00 11		00 32	00 44				01 02			01 05								06 11

The xx15 and xx45 services from London Waterloo to Whitton continue to London Waterloo via Brentford

The xx03 and xx33 London Waterloo to Kingston services continue to London Waterloo via Wimbledon

The xx07 and xx37 services from London Waterloo to Whitton continue to London Waterloo via Richmond

For additional services between Wokingham and Reading refer to Table T148

Table T149-F

Mondays to Fridays

16 December to 15 May

London - Hounslow, Richmond, Kingston, Windsor, Weybridge, Ascot, Guildford and Reading

Station		SW	SW	SW	SW	SW	SW	SW 1	SW 1		SW 1	SW 1	SW	SW 1	SW 1	SW	SW	SW	SW		SW	SW	SW	SW	SW
London Waterloo 15 ⊖	d		05 05	05 10			05 33						05 50					05 52	05 58			06 03	06 15	06 20	
Vauxhall ⊖	d		05 09	05 14			05 37											05 56	06 02			06 07	06 19		
Queenstown Rd.(Battersea)	d		05 12	05 17			05 40											05 59				06 10	06 22		
Clapham Junction 10	d		05 15	05 20		05 32	05 43						05 58					06 02	06 08			06 13	06 25	06 28	
Wandsworth Town	d		05 18	05 23		05 35	05 46											06 05				06 16	06 28		
Putney	d		05 21	05 26		05 38	05 49											06 08	06 12			06 19	06 31		
Barnes	d		05 24	05 30		05 42	05 52											06 12				06 22	06 35		
Barnes Bridge	d			05 32		05 44												06 14							
Chiswick	d			05 35		05 47												06 17							
Kew Bridge	d			05 37		05 50												06 20							
Brentford	d			05 40		05 53												06 23							
Syon Lane	d			05 42		05 55												06 25							
Isleworth	d			05 44		05 57												06 27							
Hounslow	d			05a47		06 01												06 31							
Mortlake	d		05 26				05 54															06 24	06 37		
North Sheen	d		05 28				05 56															06 26	06 39		←
Richmond ⊖	d		05 31				05 59						06 06						06 18			06 29	06 42	06 36	06 42
St Margarets	d		05 33				06 01															06 31	→		06 44
Twickenham	a		05 35				06 03						06 10						06 21			06 33		06 40	06 46
	d		05 36		05 53		06 04						06 10			06 17			06 24			06 34		06 40	06 47
Strawberry Hill	d						06 07															06 37			
Fulwell	a																								
Teddington	a						06 10															06 40			
Hampton Wick	a						06 14															06 44			
Kingston	a						06 16															06 45			
Whitton	d		05 39		05 56											06a20			06 27		←				06a50
Feltham	d		05 43		06 00	06 06							06 16					06 38	06 31		06 38			06 46	
Ashford (Surrey)	d		05 47		06 04	06 10												→	06 35		06 42				
Staines	d	05 44	05 53		06 08	06 14							06 23						06 39		06 46			06 53	
Wraysbury	d				06 12														06 43						
Sunnymeads	d				06 15														06 46						
Datchet	d				06 18														06 49						
Windsor & Eton Riverside	a				06 22														06 56						
Egham	d	05 49	05 57			06 19							06 27								06 50			06 57	
Virginia Water	a	05 53	06 01			06 23							06 31								06 55			07 01	
	d	05 53	06 01			06 23							06 31								06 55			07 01	
Chertsey	d	05 59				06 29															07 00				
Addlestone	d	06 02				06 32															07 03				
Weybridge	a	06 07				06 37															07 08				
Longcross	d												06 35											07 05	
Sunningdale	d		06 07										06 38											07 08	
Ascot 3	d		06 13								06 18		06 43	06 48			06 54							07 13	
Bagshot	d										06 24			06 54											
Camberley	a										06 30			07 00											
Frimley	d										06 35			07 05											
Ash Vale	d										06 41			07 13											
Aldershot	a										06 47			07 18											
	d							06 08	06 38			07 09			07 40										
Ash 5	d							06 15	06 47			07 15			07 47										
Wanborough	d							06 19	06 50			07 19			07 50										
Guildford	a							06 26	06 57			07 26			07 57										
Martins Heron	d		06 17										06 47				06 58							07 17	
Bracknell	d		06 20										06 50				07 01							07 20	
Wokingham	d		06 27										06 57				07 10							07 27	
Winnersh	d		06 30										07 00											07 30	
Winnersh Triangle	d		06 32										07 02											07 32	
Earley	d		06 35										07 05											07 35	
Reading 7	a		06 41										07 11				07 18							07 41	

The xx15 and xx45 services from London Waterloo to Whitton continue to London Waterloo via Brentford

The xx03 and xx33 London Waterloo to Kingston services continue to London Waterloo via Wimbledon

The xx07 and xx37 services from London Waterloo to Whitton continue to London Waterloo via Richmond

For additional services between Wokingham and Reading refer to Table T148

Table T149-F

Mondays to Fridays

16 December to 15 May

London - Hounslow, Richmond, Kingston, Windsor, Weybridge, Ascot, Guildford and Reading

Station		SW 1	SW 1	SW	SW		SW	SW	SW	SW	SW	SW	SW	SW 1	SW 1		SW	SW	SW	SW	SW	SW	SW	SW	SW
London Waterloo 15 ⊖	d				06 22		06 28			06 33	06 45	06 50					06 52	06 58		07 03	07 07				07 15
Vauxhall ⊖	d				06 26		06 32			06 37	06 49						06 56	07 02		07 07					07 19
Queenstown Rd.(Battersea)	d				06 29					06 40	06 52						06 59			07 10					07 22
Clapham Junction 10	d				06 32		06 38			06 43	06 55	06 58					07 02	07 08		07 13	07 16				07 25
Wandsworth Town	d				06 35					06 46	06 58						07 05			07 16					07 28
Putney	d				06 38		06 42			06 49	07 01						07 08	07 12		07 19					07 31
Barnes	d				06 42					06 52	07 05						07 12			07 22					07 35
Barnes Bridge	d				06 44												07 14								
Chiswick	d				06 47												07 17								
Kew Bridge	d				06 50												07 20								
Brentford	d				06 53												07 23								
Syon Lane	d				06 55												07 25								
Isleworth	d				06 57												07 27								
Hounslow	d				07 01				06 48								07 31								
Mortlake	d									06 54	07 07									07 25					07 37
North Sheen	d									06 56	07 09		←							07 27			←		07 39
Richmond ⊖	d						06 48			06 59	07 12	07 06	07 12					07 18		07 29	07 24		07 29		07 42
St Margarets	d									07 01	→		07 14							→			07 32		→
Twickenham	a						06 51		06 56	07 03		07 10	07 16					07 21			07 28		07 34		
	d						06 52			07 04		07 10	07 17					07 22	07 26		07 29		07 34	07 38	
Strawberry Hill	d									07 07									07 30				07 38	07 46	
Fulwell	a																		07 32						
Teddington	a									07 10													07 41	07 49	
Hampton Wick	a									07 14													07 45	07 51	
Kingston	a									07 16													07 47	07 53	
Whitton	d						06 55	←					07a20					07 25				←			
Feltham	d				07 06		06 59	07 06				07 16					07 39	07 29			07 35	07 39			
Ashford (Surrey)	d				→		07 03	07 10									→	07 33			07 39	07 43			
Staines	d						07 07	07 14				07 23						07 37			07 43	07 47			
Wraysbury	d						07 11											07 41							
Sunnymeads	d						07 14											07 44							
Datchet	d						07 17											07 47							
Windsor & Eton Riverside	a						07 21											07 51							
Egham	d							07 19				07 27									07 47	07 51			
Virginia Water	a							07 23				07 31									07 53	07 56			
	d							07 23				07 31									07 53	07 56			
Chertsey	d							07 29														08 01			
Addlestone	d							07 32														08 04			
Weybridge	a							07 37														08 09			
Longcross	d											07 35													
Sunningdale	d											07 38									07 59				
Ascot 3	d	07 23		07 33								07 43		07 53							08 03				
Bagshot	d	07 29												07 59											
Camberley	a	07 35												08 05											
Frimley	d	07 43												08 13											
Ash Vale	d	07 49												08 19											
Aldershot	a	07 54												08 24											
	d		08 10												08 40										
Ash 5	d		08 17												08 47										
Wanborough	d		08 20												08 50										
Guildford	a		08 27												08 57										
Martins Heron	d			07 37								07 47									08 07				
Bracknell	d			07 40								07 50									08 10				
Wokingham	d			07 48								07 57									08 17				
Winnersh	d											08 00													
Winnersh Triangle	d											08 02													
Earley	d											08 05													
Reading 7	a			07 57								08 11									08 27				

The xx15 and xx45 services from London Waterloo to Whitton continue to London Waterloo via Brentford

The xx03 and xx33 London Waterloo to Kingston services continue to London Waterloo via Wimbledon

The xx07 and xx37 services from London Waterloo to Whitton continue to London Waterloo via Richmond

For additional services between Wokingham and Reading refer to Table T148

Table T149-F

Mondays to Fridays

16 December to 15 May

London - Hounslow, Richmond, Kingston, Windsor, Weybridge, Ascot, Guildford and Reading

		SW	SW	SW	SW	SW	SW	SW	SW	SW	SW	SW ■	SW	SW	SW	SW ■	SW ■	SW	SW	SW	SW	SW
London Waterloo [15] ⊖	d	07 20		07 22	07 28	07 33	07 34			07 41			07 45	07 50				07 52	07 58	08 03	08 07	
Vauxhall ⊖	d			07 26	07 32	07 37	07 39			07 45			07 49					07 56	08 02	08 07		
Queenstown Rd.(Battersea)	d			07 29		07 40				07 48			07 52					07 59		08 10		
Clapham Junction [10]	d	07 28		07 32	07 38	07 43	07 46			07 51	07 54		07 55	07 58				08 02	08 08	08 13	08 16	
Wandsworth Town	d			07 35		07 46				07 54			07 58					08 06		08 16		
Putney	d			07 38	07 42	07 49				07 57			08 01					08 09	08 12	08 19		
Barnes	d			07 42		07 52				08 00			08 05					08 12		08 23		
Barnes Bridge	d			07 44						08 02								08 14				
Chiswick	d			07 47						08 05								08 18				
Kew Bridge	d			07 50						08 08								08 20				
Brentford	d			07 53						08 11								08 23				
Syon Lane	d			07 55						08 13								08 25				
Isleworth	d			07 57						08 15								08 27				
Hounslow	d			08 01						08 27								08 31				
Mortlake	d					07 55							08 07							08 25		
North Sheen	d		←			07 57			←				08 09		←					08 27		
Richmond ⊖	d	07 36	07 42		07 48	07 59	07 54		07 59		08 02		08 12	08 06	08 12				08 18	08 30	08 25	
St Margarets	d		07 44			→			08 02				→		08 14					→		
Twickenham	a	07 40	07 46		07 52		07 58		08 04		08 07			08 10	08 16				08 22		08 28	
	d	07 41	07 47		07 52		07 58		08 04		08 07			08 10	08 17				08 22		08 29	
Strawberry Hill	d								08 08		08 16											
Fulwell	a																					
Teddington	a								08 11		08 19											
Hampton Wick	a								08 14		08 21											
Kingston	a								08 16		08 23											
Whitton	d		07a50		07 55			←		08a33					08a20				08 25			←
Feltham	d	07 47		08 09	07 59		08 04	08 09						08 16				08 39	08 29		08 35	08 39
Ashford (Surrey)	d			→	08 04		08 08	08 13										→	08 34		08 39	08 43
Staines	d	07 53			08 07		08 12	08 17						08 23					08 37		08 43	08 47
Wraysbury	d				08 12														08 42			
Sunnymeads	d				08 14														08 44			
Datchet	d				08 17														08 47			
Windsor & Eton Riverside	a				08 22														08 52			
Egham	d	07 58					08 17	08 21						08 27							08 47	08 51
Virginia Water	a	08 02						08 26						08 31							08 51	08 56
	d	08 02						08 26						08 31							08 51	08 56
Chertsey	d							08 31														09 01
Addlestone	d							08 34														09 04
Weybridge	a							08 39														09 09
Longcross	d	08 05												08 35							08 55	
Sunningdale	d	08 09												08 38							08 58	
Ascot [3]	d	08 13					08 27							08 43		08 53					09 03	
Bagshot	d						08 33									08 59						
Camberley	a						08 38									09 05						
Frimley	d						08 43									09 13						
Ash Vale	d						08 50									09 19						
Aldershot	a						08 54									09 25						
	d											09 10					09 40					
Ash [5]	d											09 17					09 47					
Wanborough	d											09 20					09 50					
Guildford	a											09 27					09 57					
Martins Heron	d	08 17												08 47							09 07	
Bracknell	d	08 21												08 50							09 10	
Wokingham	d	08 28												08 57							09 19	
Winnersh	d	08 32												09 00							09 22	
Winnersh Triangle	d	08 34												09 02							09 24	
Earley	d	08 36												09 05							09 27	
Reading [7]	a	08 42												09 11							09 33	

The xx15 and xx45 services from London Waterloo to Whitton continue to London Waterloo via Brentford

The xx03 and xx33 London Waterloo to Kingston services continue to London Waterloo via Wimbledon

The xx07 and xx37 services from London Waterloo to Whitton continue to London Waterloo via Richmond

For additional services between Wokingham and Reading refer to Table T148

Table T149-F

Mondays to Fridays

16 December to 15 May

London - Hounslow, Richmond, Kingston, Windsor, Weybridge, Ascot, Guildford and Reading

		SW	SW	SW	SW	SW	SW ■	SW ■	SW	SW	SW	SW	SW	SW	SW	SW	SW	SW	SW ■	SW ■	GW ■	SW	SW
London Waterloo [15] ⊖	d		08 10	08 15	08 20				08 22	08 28	08 33	08 37			08 40	08 45	08 50					08 52	08 58
Vauxhall ⊖	d		08 14	08 19					08 26	08 32	08 37				08 44	08 49						08 57	09 02
Queenstown Rd.(Battersea)	d		08 17	08 22					08 29		08 40				08 47	08 52						09 00	
Clapham Junction [10]	d		08 21	08 25	08 28				08 32	08 38	08 43	08 46			08 50	08 55	08 58					09 03	09 08
Wandsworth Town	d		08 23	08 28					08 35		08 46				08 53	08 58						09 06	
Putney	d		08 26	08 31					08 38	08 42	08 49				08 56	09 01						09 09	09 12
Barnes	d		08 30	08 35					08 42		08 53				08 59	09 05						09 12	
Barnes Bridge	d		08 32						08 44						09 01							09 14	
Chiswick	d		08 34						08 47						09 04							09 17	
Kew Bridge	d		08 37						08 50						09 06							09 20	
Brentford	d		08 40						08 53						09 09							09 23	
Syon Lane	d		08 42						08 55						09 11							09 25	
Isleworth	d		08 44						08 57						09 13							09 27	
Hounslow	d		08 48						09 01						09 18							09 31	
Mortlake	d			08 37							08 55					09 07							
North Sheen	d	←		08 39		←					08 57			←		09 09		←					
Richmond ⊖	d	08 30		08 42	08 36	08 42				08 48	09 00	08 55		09 00		09 12	09 06	09 12					09 18
St Margarets	d	08 32		→		08 44					→			09 02		→		09 14					
Twickenham	a	08 34			08 40	08 46				08 51		08 58		09 04			09 10	09 16					09 22
	d	08 35			08 40	08 47				08 52		08 59		09 05			09 10	09 17					09 22
Strawberry Hill	d	08 38												09 08									
Fulwell	a																						
Teddington	a	08 41												09 11									
Hampton Wick	a	08 44												09 14									
Kingston	a	08 46												09 16									
Whitton	d		08a53			08a50				08 55			←		09a25			09a20					09 25
Feltham	d				08 46				09 09	08 59		09 05	09 09				09 16					09 36	09 29
Ashford (Surrey)	d								→	09 03		09 09	09 13									→	09 34
Staines	d				08 53					09 07		09 13	09 17				09 23						09 37
Wraysbury	d									09 11													09 42
Sunnymeads	d									09 14													09 44
Datchet	d									09 17													09 47
Windsor & Eton Riverside	a									09 21													09 52
Egham	d				08 57							09 17	09 21				09 27						
Virginia Water	a				09 01							09 21	09 26				09 31						
	d				09 01							09 21	09 26				09 31						
Chertsey	d												09 31										
Addlestone	d												09 35										
Weybridge	a												09 42										
Longcross	d																09 35						
Sunningdale	d				09 08							09 27					09 38						
Ascot [3]	d				09 13		09 23					09 31					09 43		09 53				
Bagshot	d						09 29												09 59				
Camberley	a						09 35												10 05				
Frimley	d						09 43												10 13				
Ash Vale	d						09 49												10 19				
Aldershot	a						09 54												10 24				
	d							10 10												10 40			
Ash [5]	d							10 17												10 47			
Wanborough	d							10 20												10 50			
Guildford	a							10 27												10 57			
Martins Heron	d				09 17							09 35					09 47						
Bracknell	d				09 20							09 39					09 50						
Wokingham	d				09 27							09 46					09 57				10 06		
Winnersh	d				09 30												10 00						
Winnersh Triangle	d				09 32												10 02						
Earley	d				09 35												10 05						
Reading [7]	a				09 42							09 55					10 11				10 15		

The xx15 and xx45 services from London Waterloo to Whitton continue to London Waterloo via Brentford

The xx03 and xx33 London Waterloo to Kingston services continue to London Waterloo via Wimbledon

The xx07 and xx37 services from London Waterloo to Whitton continue to London Waterloo via Richmond

For additional services between Wokingham and Reading refer to Table T148

London - Hounslow, Richmond, Kingston, Windsor, Weybridge, Ascot, Guildford and Reading

Mondays to Fridays
16 December to 15 May

		SW	SW	SW	SW	SW	SW	SW ■	SW ■	SW	SW	SW	SW	SW	SW	SW	SW	SW ■	SW ■	SW	SW	SW
London Waterloo [15]	⊖ d		09 03	09 07	09 15	09 20				09 22	09 28		09 33	09 37	09 45	09 50				09 52	09 58	
Vauxhall	⊖ d		09 07	09 11	09 20					09 26	09 32		09 37	09 42	09 49					09 56	10 02	
Queenstown Rd.(Battersea)	d		09 10	09 14	09 23					09 29			09 40	09 44	09 52					09 59		
Clapham Junction [10]	d		09 13	09 17	09 26	09 28				09 32	09 38		09 43	09 47	09 55	09 58				10 02	10 08	
Wandsworth Town	d		09 16	09 20	09 28					09 35			09 46	09 50	09 58					10 05		
Putney	d		09 19	09 23	09 31					09 38	09 42		09 49	09 53	10 01					10 08	10 12	
Barnes	d		09 22	09 27	09 35					09 42			09 52	09 57	10 05					10 12		
Barnes Bridge	d			09 29						09 44				09 59						10 14		
Chiswick	d			09 32						09 47				10 02						10 17		
Kew Bridge	d			09 35						09 50				10 05						10 20		
Brentford	d			09 38						09 53				10 08						10 23		
Syon Lane	d			09 40						09 55				10 10						10 25		
Isleworth	d			09 42						09 57				10 12						10 27		
Hounslow	d			09 48						10 01				10 18						10 31		
Mortlake	d		09 24		09 37								09 54		10 07							
North Sheen	d		09 26		09 39		←						09 56		10 09		←					
Richmond	⊖ d		09 29		09 42	09 36	09 42				09 48		09 59		10 12	10 06	10 12				10 18	
St Margarets	d		09 31		→		09 44						10 01		→		10 14					
Twickenham	a		09 33			09 40	09 46				09 51		10 03			10 10	10 16				10 21	
	d		09 34			09 40	09 47				09 52		10 04			10 10	10 17				10 22	
Strawberry Hill	d		09 37										10 07									
Fulwell	a																					
Teddington	a		09 40										10 10									
Hampton Wick	a		09 44										10 14									
Kingston	a		09 46										10 16									
Whitton	d	←		09a53			09a50				09 55	←		10a26			10a20				10 25	←
Feltham	d	09 36				09 46				10 06	09 59	10 06				10 16				10 36	10 29	10 36
Ashford (Surrey)	d	09 40								→	10 03	10 10								→	10 33	10 40
Staines	d	09 44				09 53					10 07	10 14				10 23					10 37	10 44
Wraysbury	d										10 11										10 41	
Sunnymeads	d										10 14										10 44	
Datchet	d										10 17										10 47	
Windsor & Eton Riverside	a										10 22										10 52	
Egham	d	09 49				09 57						10 19				10 27						10 49
Virginia Water	a	09 53				10 01						10 23				10 31						10 53
	d	09 53				10 01						10 23				10 31						10 53
Chertsey	d	09 59										10 29										10 59
Addlestone	d	10 02										10 32										11 02
Weybridge	a	10 07										10 37										11 07
Longcross	d					10 05										10 35						
Sunningdale	d					10 08										10 38						
Ascot [3]	d					10 13		10 23								10 43		10 53				
Bagshot	d							10 29										10 59				
Camberley	a							10 35										11 05				
Frimley	d							10 43										11 13				
Ash Vale	d							10 49										11 19				
Aldershot	a							10 54										11 24				
	d								11 10										11 40			
Ash [5]	d								11 17										11 47			
Wanborough	d								11 20										11 50			
Guildford	a								11 27										11 57			
Martins Heron	d					10 17										10 47						
Bracknell	d					10 20										10 50						
Wokingham	d					10 27										10 57						
Winnersh	d					10 30										11 00						
Winnersh Triangle	d					10 32										11 02						
Earley	d					10 35										11 05						
Reading [7]	a					10 41										11 11						

The xx15 and xx45 services from London Waterloo to Whitton continue to London Waterloo via Brentford

The xx03 and xx33 London Waterloo to Kingston services continue to London Waterloo via Wimbledon

The xx07 and xx37 services from London Waterloo to Whitton continue to London Waterloo via Richmond

For additional services between Wokingham and Reading refer to Table T148

London - Hounslow, Richmond, Kingston, Windsor, Weybridge, Ascot, Guildford and Reading

Mondays to Fridays
16 December to 15 May

		SW	SW	SW	SW	SW	SW ■	SW ■	SW	SW	SW	SW	SW	SW	SW	SW	SW ■	SW ■	SW	SW	SW	SW	SW
London Waterloo [15]	⊖ d	10 03	10 07	10 15	10 20				10 22	10 28		10 33	10 37	10 45	10 50				10 52	10 58		11 03	11 07
Vauxhall	⊖ d	10 07	10 11	10 19					10 26	10 32		10 37	10 41	10 49					10 56	11 02		11 07	11 11
Queenstown Rd.(Battersea)	d	10 10	10 14	10 22					10 29			10 40	10 44	10 52					10 59			11 10	11 14
Clapham Junction [10]	d	10 13	10 17	10 25	10 28				10 32	10 38		10 43	10 47	10 55	10 58				11 02	11 08		11 13	11 17
Wandsworth Town	d	10 16	10 20	10 28					10 35			10 46	10 50	10 58					11 05			11 16	11 20
Putney	d	10 19	10 23	10 31					10 38	10 42		10 49	10 53	11 01					11 08	11 12		11 19	11 23
Barnes	d	10 22	10 27	10 35					10 42			10 52	10 57	11 05					11 12			11 22	11 27
Barnes Bridge	d		10 29						10 44				10 59						11 14				11 29
Chiswick	d		10 32						10 47				11 02						11 17				11 32
Kew Bridge	d		10 35						10 50				11 05						11 20				11 35
Brentford	d		10 38						10 53				11 08						11 23				11 38
Syon Lane	d		10 40						10 55				11 10						11 25				11 40
Isleworth	d		10 42						10 57				11 12						11 27				11 42
Hounslow	d		10 48						11 01				11 18						11 31				11 48
Mortlake	d	10 24		10 37								10 54		11 07								11 24	
North Sheen	d	10 26		10 39		←						10 56		11 09		←						11 26	
Richmond	⊖ d	10 29		10 42	10 36	10 42				10 48		10 59		11 12	11 06	11 12				11 18		11 29	
St Margarets	d	10 31		→		10 44						11 01		→		11 14						11 31	
Twickenham	a	10 33			10 40	10 46				10 51		11 03			11 10	11 16				11 21		11 33	
	d	10 34			10 40	10 47				10 52		11 04			11 10	11 17				11 22		11 34	
Strawberry Hill	d	10 37										11 07										11 37	
Fulwell	a																						
Teddington	a	10 40										11 10										11 40	
Hampton Wick	a	10 44										11 14										11 44	
Kingston	a	10 46										11 16										11 46	
Whitton	d		10a56			10a50				10 55	←		11a23			11a20				11 25	←		11a53
Feltham	d				10 46				11 06	10 59	11 06				11 16				11 36	11 29	11 36		
Ashford (Surrey)	d								→	11 03	11 10								→	11 33	11 40		
Staines	d				10 53					11 07	11 14				11 23					11 37	11 44		
Wraysbury	d									11 11										11 41			
Sunnymeads	d									11 14										11 44			
Datchet	d									11 17										11 47			
Windsor & Eton Riverside	a									11 22										11 51			
Egham	d				10 57						11 19				11 27						11 49		
Virginia Water	a				11 01						11 23				11 31						11 53		
	d				11 01						11 23				11 31						11 53		
Chertsey	d										11 29										11 59		
Addlestone	d										11 32										12 02		
Weybridge	a										11 37										12 07		
Longcross	d				11 05										11 35								
Sunningdale	d				11 08										11 38								
Ascot [3]	d				11 13		11 23								11 43		11 53						
Bagshot	d						11 29										11 59						
Camberley	a						11 35										12 05						
Frimley	d						11 43										12 13						
Ash Vale	d						11 49										12 19						
Aldershot	a						11 54										12 24						
	d							12 10										12 40					
Ash [5]	d							12 17										12 47					
Wanborough	d							12 20										12 50					
Guildford	a							12 27										12 57					
Martins Heron	d				11 17										11 47								
Bracknell	d				11 20										11 50								
Wokingham	d				11 27										11 57								
Winnersh	d				11 30										12 00								
Winnersh Triangle	d				11 32										12 02								
Earley	d				11 35										12 05								
Reading [7]	a				11 41										12 11								

The xx15 and xx45 services from London Waterloo to Whitton continue to London Waterloo via Brentford

The xx03 and xx33 London Waterloo to Kingston services continue to London Waterloo via Wimbledon

The xx07 and xx37 services from London Waterloo to Whitton continue to London Waterloo via Richmond

For additional services between Wokingham and Reading refer to Table T148

Table T149-F

Mondays to Fridays
16 December to 15 May

London - Hounslow, Richmond, Kingston, Windsor, Weybridge, Ascot, Guildford and Reading

		SW	SW	SW	SW 1	SW 1	SW	SW	SW	SW	SW	SW	SW	SW	SW 1	SW 1	SW	SW	SW	SW	SW	SW	SW
London Waterloo 15 ⊖	d	11 15	11 20				11 22	11 28		11 33	11 37	11 45	11 50				11 52	11 58		12 03	12 07	12 15	12 20
Vauxhall ⊖	d	11 19					11 26	11 32		11 37	11 41	11 49					11 56	12 02		12 07	12 11	12 19	
Queenstown Rd.(Battersea)	d	11 22					11 29			11 40	11 44	11 52					11 59			12 10	12 14	12 22	
Clapham Junction 10	d	11 25	11 28				11 32	11 38		11 43	11 47	11 55	11 58				12 02	12 08		12 13	12 17	12 25	12 28
Wandsworth Town	d	11 28					11 35			11 46	11 50	11 58					12 05			12 16	12 20	12 28	
Putney	d	11 31					11 38	11 42		11 49	11 53	12 01					12 08	12 12		12 19	12 23	12 31	
Barnes	d	11 35					11 42			11 52	11 57	12 05					12 12			12 22	12 27	12 35	
Barnes Bridge	d						11 44				11 59						12 14				12 29		
Chiswick	d						11 47				12 02						12 17				12 34		
Kew Bridge	d						11 50				12 05						12 20				12 37		
Brentford	d						11 53				12 08						12 23				12 40		
Syon Lane	d						11 55				12 10						12 25				12 42		
Isleworth	d						11 57				12 12						12 27				12 44		
Hounslow	d						12 01				12 18						12 31				12 48		
Mortlake	d	11 37								11 54		12 07								12 24		12 37	
North Sheen	d	11 39		←						11 56		12 09		←						12 26		12 39	
Richmond ⊖	d	11 42	11 36	11 42				11 48		11 59		12 12	12 06	12 12				12 18		12 29		12 42	12 36
St Margarets	d	→		11 44						12 01		→		12 14						12 31		→	
Twickenham	a		11 40	11 47				11 51		12 03			12 10	12 16				12 21		12 33			12 40
	d		11 40	11 47				11 52		12 04			12 10	12 17				12 22		12 34			12 40
Strawberry Hill	d									12 07										12 37			
Fulwell	a																						
Teddington	a									12 10										12 40			
Hampton Wick	a									12 14										12 44			
Kingston	a									12 16										12 46			
Whitton	d			11a50				11 55	←		12a23			12a20				12 25	←		12a53		
Feltham	d		11 46				12 06	11 59	12 06				12 16				12 36	12 29	12 36				12 46
Ashford (Surrey)	d						→	12 03	12 10								→	12 33	12 40				
Staines	d		11 53					12 07	12 14				12 23					12 37	12 44				12 53
Wraysbury	d							12 11										12 41					
Sunnymeads	d							12 14										12 44					
Datchet	d							12 17										12 47					
Windsor & Eton Riverside	a							12 21										12 51					
Egham	d		11 57						12 19				12 27						12 49				12 57
Virginia Water	a		12 01						12 23				12 31						12 53				13 01
	d		12 01						12 23				12 31						12 53				13 01
Chertsey	d								12 29										12 59				
Addlestone	d								12 32										13 02				
Weybridge	a								12 37										13 07				
Longcross	d		12 05										12 35										13 05
Sunningdale	d		12 08										12 38										13 08
Ascot 3	d		12 13		12 23								12 43		12 53								13 13
Bagshot	d				12 29										12 59								
Camberley	a				12 35										13 05								
Frimley	d				12 43										13 13								
Ash Vale	d				12 49										13 19								
Aldershot	a				12 54										13 24								
	d					13 10										13 40							
Ash 5	d					13 17										13 47							
Wanborough	d					13 20										13 50							
Guildford	a					13 27										13 57							
Martins Heron	d		12 17										12 47										13 17
Bracknell	d		12 20										12 50										13 20
Wokingham	d		12 27										12 57										13 27
Winnersh	d		12 30										13 00										13 30
Winnersh Triangle	d		12 32										13 02										13 32
Earley	d		12 35										13 05										13 35
Reading 7	a		12 41										13 11										13 41

The xx15 and xx45 services from London Waterloo to Whitton continue to London Waterloo via Brentford

The xx03 and xx33 London Waterloo to Kingston services continue to London Waterloo via Wimbledon

The xx07 and xx37 services from London Waterloo to Whitton continue to London Waterloo via Richmond

For additional services between Wokingham and Reading refer to Table T148

Table T149-F

Mondays to Fridays
16 December to 15 May

London - Hounslow, Richmond, Kingston, Windsor, Weybridge, Ascot, Guildford and Reading

		SW	SW 1	SW 1	SW	SW	SW	SW	SW	SW	SW	SW	SW 1	SW 1	SW	SW	SW	SW	SW	SW	SW	SW
London Waterloo 15 ⊖	d				12 22	12 28		12 33	12 37	12 45	12 50				12 52	12 58		13 03	13 07	13 15	13 20	
Vauxhall ⊖	d				12 26	12 32		12 37	12 41	12 49					12 56	13 02		13 07	13 11	13 19		
Queenstown Rd.(Battersea)	d				12 29			12 40	12 44	12 52					12 59			13 10	13 14	13 22		
Clapham Junction 10	d				12 32	12 38		12 43	12 47	12 55	12 58				13 02	13 08		13 13	13 17	13 25	13 28	
Wandsworth Town	d				12 35			12 46	12 50	12 58					13 05			13 16	13 20	13 28		
Putney	d				12 38	12 42		12 49	12 53	13 01					13 08	13 12		13 19	13 23	13 31		
Barnes	d				12 42			12 52	12 57	13 05					13 12			13 22	13 27	13 35		
Barnes Bridge	d				12 44				12 59						13 14				13 29			
Chiswick	d				12 47				13 02						13 17				13 32			
Kew Bridge	d				12 50				13 05						13 20				13 35			
Brentford	d				12 53				13 08						13 23				13 38			
Syon Lane	d				12 55				13 10						13 25				13 40			
Isleworth	d				12 57				13 12						13 27				13 42			
Hounslow	d				13 01				13 18						13 31				13 48			
Mortlake	d							12 54		13 07								13 24		13 37		
North Sheen	d	←						12 56		13 09		←						13 26		13 39		←
Richmond ⊖	d	12 42				12 48		12 59		13 12	13 06	13 12				13 18		13 29		13 42	13 36	13 42
St Margarets	d	12 44						13 01		→		13 14						13 31		→		13 44
Twickenham	a	12 46				12 51		13 03			13 10	13 16				13 21		13 33			13 40	13 46
	d	12 47				12 52		13 04			13 10	13 17				13 22		13 34			13 40	13 47
Strawberry Hill	d							13 07										13 37				
Fulwell	a																					
Teddington	a							13 10										13 40				
Hampton Wick	a							13 14										13 44				
Kingston	a							13 16										13 46				
Whitton	d	12a50				12 55	←		13a23			13a20				13 25	←		13a53			13a50
Feltham	d				13 06	12 59	13 06				13 16				13 36	13 29	13 36				13 46	
Ashford (Surrey)	d				→	13 03	13 10								→	13 33	13 40					
Staines	d					13 07	13 14				13 23					13 37	13 44				13 53	
Wraysbury	d					13 11										13 41						
Sunnymeads	d					13 14										13 44						
Datchet	d					13 17										13 47						
Windsor & Eton Riverside	a					13 22										13 51						
Egham	d						13 19				13 27						13 49				13 57	
Virginia Water	a						13 23				13 31						13 54				14 01	
	d						13 23				13 31						13 54				14 01	
Chertsey	d						13 29										14 00					
Addlestone	d						13 32										14 03					
Weybridge	a						13 37										14 07					
Longcross	d										13 35										14 05	
Sunningdale	d										13 38										14 08	
Ascot 3	d		13 23								13 43		13 53								14 13	
Bagshot	d		13 29										13 59									
Camberley	a		13 35										14 05									
Frimley	d		13 43										14 13									
Ash Vale	d		13 49										14 19									
Aldershot	a		13 54										14 24									
	d			14 10										14 40								
Ash 5	d			14 17										14 47								
Wanborough	d			14 20										14 50								
Guildford	a			14 27										14 57								
Martins Heron	d										13 47										14 17	
Bracknell	d										13 50										14 20	
Wokingham	d										13 57										14 27	
Winnersh	d										14 00										14 30	
Winnersh Triangle	d										14 02										14 32	
Earley	d										14 05										14 35	
Reading 7	a										14 11										14 41	

The xx15 and xx45 services from London Waterloo to Whitton continue to London Waterloo via Brentford

The xx03 and xx33 London Waterloo to Kingston services continue to London Waterloo via Wimbledon

The xx07 and xx37 services from London Waterloo to Whitton continue to London Waterloo via Richmond

For additional services between Wokingham and Reading refer to Table T148

Table T149-F

Mondays to Fridays
16 December to 15 May

London - Hounslow, Richmond, Kingston, Windsor, Weybridge, Ascot, Guildford and Reading

		SW 1	SW 1	SW	SW	SW	SW		SW	SW	SW	SW	SW 1	SW 1	SW	SW	SW		SW	SW	SW	SW	SW	SW 1	SW 1
London Waterloo 15 ⊖	d			13 22	13 28		13 33		13 37	13 45	13 50				13 52	13 58			14 03	14 07	14 15	14 20			
Vauxhall ⊖	d			13 26	13 32		13 37		13 41	13 49					13 56	14 02			14 07	14 11	14 19				
Queenstown Rd.(Battersea)	d			13 29			13 40		13 44	13 52					13 59				14 10	14 14	14 22				
Clapham Junction 10	d			13 32	13 38		13 43		13 47	13 55	13 58				14 02	14 08			14 13	14 17	14 25	14 28			
Wandsworth Town	d			13 35			13 46		13 50	13 58					14 05				14 16	14 20	14 28				
Putney	d			13 38	13 42		13 49		13 53	14 01					14 08	14 12			14 19	14 23	14 31				
Barnes	d			13 42			13 52		13 57	14 05					14 12				14 23	14 27	14 35				
Barnes Bridge	d			13 44					13 59						14 14					14 29					
Chiswick	d			13 47					14 02						14 17					14 32					
Kew Bridge	d			13 50					14 05						14 20					14 35					
Brentford	d			13 53					14 08						14 23					14 38					
Syon Lane	d			13 55					14 10						14 25					14 40					
Isleworth	d			13 57					14 12						14 27					14 42					
Hounslow	d			14 01					14 18						14 31					14 48					
Mortlake	d						13 54			14 07									14 25		14 37				
North Sheen	d						13 56			14 09		←							14 27		14 39		←		
Richmond ⊖	d				13 48		13 59			14 12	14 06	14 12				14 18			14 30		14 42	14 36	14 42		
St Margarets	d						14 01			→		14 14							14 32		→		14 44		
Twickenham	a				13 51		14 03				14 10	14 16				14 21			14 34			14 40	14 46		
	d				13 52		14 04				14 10	14 17				14 22			14 35			14 40	14 47		
Strawberry Hill	d						14 07												14 38						
Fulwell	a																								
Teddington	a						14 10												14 41						
Hampton Wick	a						14 14												14 45						
Kingston	a						14 16												14 47						
Whitton	d				13 55	←			14a23			14a20				14 25	←			14a53			14a50		
Feltham	d			14 06	13 59	14 06					14 16				14 36	14 29	14 36					14 46			
Ashford (Surrey)	d			→	14 03	14 10									→	14 33	14 40								
Staines	d				14 07	14 14					14 23					14 37	14 45					14 53			
Wraysbury	d				14 11											14 41									
Sunnymeads	d				14 14											14 44									
Datchet	d				14 17											14 47									
Windsor & Eton Riverside	a				14 21											14 51									
Egham	d					14 19					14 27						14 49					14 57			
Virginia Water	a					14 23					14 31						14 53					15 01			
	d					14 23					14 31						14 53					15 01			
Chertsey	d					14 29											14 59								
Addlestone	d					14 32											15 02								
Weybridge	a					14 37											15 07								
Longcross	d										14 35											15 05			
Sunningdale	d										14 38											15 08			
Ascot 3	d	14 23									14 43		14 53									15 13		15 23	
Bagshot	d	14 29											14 59											15 29	
Camberley	a	14 35											15 05											15 35	
Frimley	d	14 43											15 13											15 43	
Ash Vale	d	14 49											15 19											15 49	
Aldershot	a	14 54											15 24											15 54	
	d		15 10											15 40											16 10
Ash 5	d		15 17											15 47											16 17
Wanborough	d		15 20											15 50											16 20
Guildford	a		15 27											15 57											16 27
Martins Heron	d										14 47											15 17			
Bracknell	d										14 50											15 20			
Wokingham	d										14 57											15 27			
Winnersh	d										15 00											15 30			
Winnersh Triangle	d										15 02											15 32			
Earley	d										15 05											15 35			
Reading 7	a										15 11											15 41			

The xx15 and xx45 services from London Waterloo to Whitton continue to London Waterloo via Brentford

The xx03 and xx33 London Waterloo to Kingston services continue to London Waterloo via Wimbledon

The xx07 and xx37 services from London Waterloo to Whitton continue to London Waterloo via Richmond

For additional services between Wokingham and Reading refer to Table T148

Table T149-F

Mondays to Fridays
16 December to 15 May

London - Hounslow, Richmond, Kingston, Windsor, Weybridge, Ascot, Guildford and Reading

		SW	SW		SW	SW	SW	SW	SW	SW	SW 1	SW 1	SW		SW	SW	SW	SW	SW	SW	SW	SW	SW		SW 1
London Waterloo 15 ⊖	d	14 22	14 28			14 33	14 37	14 45	14 50				14 52		14 58	15 01	15 05			15 07	15 15	15 20			
Vauxhall ⊖	d	14 26	14 32			14 37	14 41	14 49					14 56		15 02	15 05	15 09			15 11	15 19				
Queenstown Rd.(Battersea)	d	14 29				14 40	14 44	14 52					14 59			15 08				15 14	15 22				
Clapham Junction 10	d	14 32	14 38			14 43	14 47	14 55	14 58				15 02		15 08	15 11	15 15			15 17	15 25	15 28			
Wandsworth Town	d	14 35				14 46	14 50	14 58					15 05			15 14				15 20	15 28				
Putney	d	14 38	14 42			14 49	14 53	15 01					15 08		15 12	15 17				15 23	15 31				
Barnes	d	14 42				14 52	14 57	15 05					15 12			15 22				15 27	15 35				
Barnes Bridge	d	14 44					14 59						15 14							15 29					
Chiswick	d	14 47					15 02						15 17							15 32					
Kew Bridge	d	14 50					15 05						15 20							15 35					
Brentford	d	14 53					15 08						15 23							15 38					
Syon Lane	d	14 55					15 10						15 25							15 40					
Isleworth	d	14 57					15 12						15 27							15 42					
Hounslow	d	15 01					15 18						15 31							15 48					
Mortlake	d					14 54		15 07								15 24					15 37				
North Sheen	d					14 56		15 09		←						15 26			←		15 39		←		
Richmond ⊖	d		14 48			14 59		15 12	15 06	15 12					15 18	15 29	15 23		15 29		15 42	15 36	15 42		
St Margarets	d					15 01		→		15 14						→			15 31		→		15 44		
Twickenham	a		14 51			15 03			15 10	15 16					15 21		15 27		15 33			15 40	15 46		
	d		14 52			15 04			15 10	15 17					15 22		15 27		15 34			15 40	15 47		
Strawberry Hill	d					15 07													15 37						
Fulwell	a																								
Teddington	a					15 10													15 40						
Hampton Wick	a					15 14													15 44						
Kingston	a					15 16													15 46						
Whitton	d		14 55		←		15a23			15a20					15 25			←		15a53			15a50		
Feltham	d	15 06	14 59		15 06				15 16				15 38		15 29		15 33	15 38				15 46			
Ashford (Surrey)	d	→	15 03		15 10								→		15 33		15 37	15 42							
Staines	d		15 07		15 14				15 23						15 37		15 41	15 46				15 53			
Wraysbury	d		15 11												15 41										
Sunnymeads	d		15 14												15 44										
Datchet	d		15 17												15 47										
Windsor & Eton Riverside	a		15 21												15 51										
Egham	d				15 19				15 27								15 46	15 50				15 57			
Virginia Water	a				15 23				15 31								15 50	15 55				16 01			
	d				15 23				15 31								15 50	15 55				16 01			
Chertsey	d				15 29													16 01							
Addlestone	d				15 32													16 04							
Weybridge	a				15 37													16 08							
Longcross	d																15 53								
Sunningdale	d								15 38								15 57					16 08			
Ascot 3	d								15 43		15 53						16 01					16 13			16 23
Bagshot	d										15 59														16 29
Camberley	a										16 05														16 35
Frimley	d										16 13														16 43
Ash Vale	d										16 19														16 49
Aldershot	a										16 24														16 54
	d											16 40													
Ash 5	d											16 47													
Wanborough	d											16 50													
Guildford	a											16 57													
Martins Heron	d								15 47								16 05					16 17			
Bracknell	d								15 50								16 09					16 20			
Wokingham	d								15 57								16 17					16 27			
Winnersh	d								16 00													16 30			
Winnersh Triangle	d								16 02													16 32			
Earley	d								16 05													16 35			
Reading 7	a								16 11								16 28					16 41			

The xx15 and xx45 services from London Waterloo to Whitton continue to London Waterloo via Brentford

The xx03 and xx33 London Waterloo to Kingston services continue to London Waterloo via Wimbledon

The xx07 and xx37 services from London Waterloo to Whitton continue to London Waterloo via Richmond

For additional services between Wokingham and Reading refer to Table T148

Table T149-F

Mondays to Fridays
16 December to 15 May

London - Hounslow, Richmond, Kingston, Windsor, Weybridge, Ascot, Guildford and Reading

Station		SW 1	SW	SW	SW	SW	SW	SW	SW		SW	SW	SW	SW 1	SW 1	SW	SW	SW	SW		SW	SW	SW	SW	SW
London Waterloo 15 ⊖	d		15 22	15 28	15 31	15 35			15 37		15 45	15 50				15 52	15 58	16 01	16 05				16 07	16 15	16 20
Vauxhall ⊖	d		15 26	15 32	15 35	15 39			15 41		15 49					15 56	16 02	16 05	16 09				16 12	16 19	
Queenstown Rd.(Battersea)	d		15 29		15 38				15 44		15 52					15 59		16 08					16 15	16 22	
Clapham Junction 10	d		15 32	15 38	15 41	15 45			15 47		15 55	15 58				16 02	16 08	16 11	16 15				16 18	16 25	16 28
Wandsworth Town	d		15 35		15 44				15 50		15 58					16 05		16 14					16 21	16 28	
Putney	d		15 38	15 42	15 47				15 53		16 01					16 08	16 12	16 17					16 24	16 31	
Barnes	d		15 42		15 52				15 57		16 05					16 12		16 22					16 27	16 35	
Barnes Bridge	d		15 44						15 59							16 14							16 29		
Chiswick	d		15 47						16 02							16 17							16 32		
Kew Bridge	d		15 50						16 05							16 20							16 34		
Brentford	d		15 53						16 08							16 23							16 37		
Syon Lane	d		15 55						16 10							16 25							16 39		
Isleworth	d		15 57						16 12							16 27							16 41		
Hounslow	d		16 01						16 18							16 31							16 48		
Mortlake	d				15 54						16 07							16 24						16 37	
North Sheen	d				15 56			←			16 09		←					16 26				←		16 39	
Richmond ⊖	d			15 48	15 59	15 53		15 59			16 12	16 06	16 12				16 18	16 29	16 23			16 29		16 42	16 36
St Margarets	d				→			16 01			→		16 14					→				16 31		→	
Twickenham	a			15 51		15 57		16 03				16 10	16 16				16 21		16 27			16 33			16 40
	d			15 52		15 57		16 04				16 10	16 17				16 22		16 27			16 34			16 40
Strawberry Hill	d							16 07														16 37			
Fulwell	a																								
Teddington	a							16 10														16 42			
Hampton Wick	a							16 14														16 46			
Kingston	a							16 16														16 48			
Whitton	d			15 55			←		16a23				16a20				16 25				←		16a52		
Feltham	d		16 08	15 59		16 03	16 08					16 16				16 38	16 29		16 33		16 38				16 46
Ashford (Surrey)	d		→	16 03		16 07	16 12									→	16 33		16 37		16 42				
Staines	d			16 07		16 11	16 16					16 23					16 37		16 41		16 46				16 53
Wraysbury	d			16 11													16 41								
Sunnymeads	d			16 14													16 44								
Datchet	d			16 17													16 47								
Windsor & Eton Riverside	a			16 21													16 51								
Egham	d					16 16	16 20					16 27							16 46		16 50				16 57
Virginia Water	a					16 20	16 25					16 31							16 50		16 55				17 01
	d					16 20	16 25					16 31							16 50		16 55				17 01
Chertsey	d						16 30														17 00				
Addlestone	d						16 33														17 03				
Weybridge	a						16 38														17 08				
Longcross	d					16 23													16 53						
Sunningdale	d					16 27						16 38							16 57						17 08
Ascot 3	d					16 31						16 43		16 53					17 01						17 13
Bagshot	d													16 59											
Camberley	a													17 05											
Frimley	d													17 13											
Ash Vale	d													17 19											
Aldershot	a													17 24											
	d	17 10													17 40										
Ash 3	d	17 17													17 47										
Wanborough	d	17 20													17 50										
Guildford	a	17 27													17 57										
Martins Heron	d					16 35						16 47							17 05						17 17
Bracknell	d					16 39						16 50							17 09						17 20
Wokingham	d					16 50						16 57							17 17						17 27
Winnersh	d											17 00													17 30
Winnersh Triangle	d											17 02													17 32
Earley	d											17 05													17 35
Reading 7	a					17 01						17 11							17 28						17 42

The xx15 and xx45 services from London Waterloo to Whitton continue to London Waterloo via Brentford

The xx03 and xx33 London Waterloo to Kingston services continue to London Waterloo via Wimbledon

The xx07 and xx37 services from London Waterloo to Whitton continue to London Waterloo via Richmond

For additional services between Wokingham and Reading refer to Table T148

Table T149-F

Mondays to Fridays
16 December to 15 May

London - Hounslow, Richmond, Kingston, Windsor, Weybridge, Ascot, Guildford and Reading

Station		SW	SW 1	SW 1	SW ◇		SW ◇	SW	SW	SW ◇	SW	SW	SW	SW	SW		SW ◇	SW ◇	SW 1	SW ◇	SW	SW	SW ◇	SW	SW
London Waterloo 15 ⊖	d				16 22		16 28	16 31	16 35			16 37	16 45	16 50			16 52	16 54		16 58	17 01	17 05			17 07
Vauxhall ⊖	d				16 26		16 32	16 35	16 39			16 42	16 49				16 56	16 59		17 02	17 05	17 09			17 13
Queenstown Rd.(Battersea)	d				16 29			16 38				16 45	16 52				16 59				17 08				17 16
Clapham Junction 10	d				16 32		16 38	16 41	16 45			16 48	16 55	16 58			17 02	17 05		17 08	17 11	17 15			17 19
Wandsworth Town	d				16 35			16 44				16 50	16 58				17 05				17 14				17 21
Putney	d				16 38		16 42	16 47				16 53	17 01				17 08			17 12	17 17				17 24
Barnes	d				16 42			16 52				16 56	17 05				17 12				17 22				17 27
Barnes Bridge	d				16 44							16 58					17 14								17 29
Chiswick	d				16 47							17 01					17 17								17 32
Kew Bridge	d				16 50							17 04					17 20								17 35
Brentford	d				16 53							17 07					17 23								17 38
Syon Lane	d				16 55							17 09					17 25								17 40
Isleworth	d				16 57							17 11					17 27								17 42
Hounslow	d				17 01							17 15					17 32	17 19							17 46
Mortlake	d							16 54					17 07								17 24				
North Sheen	d	←						16 56			←		17 09		←						17 26			←	
Richmond ⊖	d	16 42					16 48	16 59	16 53		16 59		17 12	17 06	17 12					17 18	17 29	17 23		17 29	
St Margarets	d	16 44						→			17 01		→		17 14						→			17 31	
Twickenham	a	16 46					16 51		16 57		17 03			17 10	17 16					17 21		17 27		17 33	
	d	16 47					16 52		16 57		17 04			17 10	17 17					17 22		17 27		17 34	
Strawberry Hill	d										17 07													17 37	
Fulwell	a																								
Teddington	a										17 12													17 42	
Hampton Wick	a										17 16													17 46	
Kingston	a										17 18													17 48	
Whitton	d	16a50					16 55			←		17a22		17 13	17a20					17 25			←		17a53
Feltham	d				17 08		16 59		17 03	17 08				17 18			17 38	17 25		17 29		17 33	17 38		
Ashford (Surrey)	d				→		17 03		17 07	17 12							→			17 33		17 37	17 42		
Staines	d						17 07		17 11	17 16				17 24				17 31		17 37		17 41	17 46		
Wraysbury	d						17 11													17 41					
Sunnymeads	d						17 14													17 44					
Datchet	d						17 17													17 47					
Windsor & Eton Riverside	a						17 23													17 53					
Egham	d								17 16	17 21				17 29				17 36				17 46	17 51		
Virginia Water	a								17 20	17 25				17 33				17 40				17 50	17 55		
	d								17 20	17 25				17 33				17 40				17 50	17 55		
Chertsey	d									17 31													18 01		
Addlestone	d									17 34													18 04		
Weybridge	a									17 40													18 10		
Longcross	d								17 23									17 44							
Sunningdale	d								17 27					17 38				17 47				17 55			
Ascot 3	d		17 23						17 31					17 43				17 53				18 00			
Bagshot	d		17 29															17 59							
Camberley	a		17 35															18 05							
Frimley	d		17 43															18 09							
Ash Vale	d		17 49															18 16							
Aldershot	a		17 54															18 21							
	d			18 10															18 40						
Ash 3	d			18 17															18 50						
Wanborough	d			18 20															18 54						
Guildford	a			18 27															19 01						
Martins Heron	d								17 35					17 47								18 04			
Bracknell	d								17 39					17 50								18 08			
Wokingham	d								17 48					17 57								18 19			
Winnersh	d													18 00											
Winnersh Triangle	d													18 02											
Earley	d													18 05											
Reading 7	a								18 00					18 12								18 33			

The xx15 and xx45 services from London Waterloo to Whitton continue to London Waterloo via Brentford

The xx03 and xx33 London Waterloo to Kingston services continue to London Waterloo via Wimbledon

The xx07 and xx37 services from London Waterloo to Whitton continue to London Waterloo via Richmond

For additional services between Wokingham and Reading refer to Table T148

Table T149-F

Mondays to Fridays
16 December to 15 May

London - Hounslow, Richmond, Kingston, Windsor, Weybridge, Ascot, Guildford and Reading

		SW	SW	SW	SW	SW 1	SW 1	SW ◇	SW ◇	SW ◇	SW	SW	SW ◇	SW	SW	SW	SW	SW	SW	SW ◇	SW ◇	SW 1
London Waterloo 15 ⊖	d	17 13	17 15	17 20				17 22	17 24	17 28	17 31	17 35			17 37	17 43	17 45	17 50		17 52	17 54	
Vauxhall ⊖	d	17 17	17 20					17 26	17 29	17 32	17 35	17 39			17 42	17 47	17 50			17 56	17 59	
Queenstown Rd.(Battersea)	d		17 23					17 29			17 38				17 45		17 53			17 59		
Clapham Junction 10	d	17 23	17 26	17 28				17 32	17 35	17 38	17 42	17 45			17 48	17 53	17 56	17 58		18 02	18 05	
Wandsworth Town	d		17 28					17 35			17 44				17 51		17 58			18 05		
Putney	d	17 27	17 31					17 38		17 42	17 47				17 54	17 57	18 01			18 08		
Barnes	d		17 35					17 42			17 52				17 57		18 05			18 12		
Barnes Bridge	d							17 44							17 59					18 14		
Chiswick	d							17 47							18 02					18 17		
Kew Bridge	d							17 50							18 05					18 20		
Brentford	d							17 53							18 08					18 23		
Syon Lane	d							17 56							18 10					18 25		
Isleworth	d							17 58							18 12					18 27		
Hounslow	d							18 02	17 50						18 16					18 32	18 19	
Mortlake	d		17 37								17 54						18 07					
North Sheen	d		17 39		←						17 56			←			18 09		←			
Richmond ⊖	d	17 33	17 42	17 37	17 42					17 48	17 59	17 53		17 59		18 03	18 12	18 07	18 12			
St Margarets	d		→		17 44						→			18 01			→		18 14			
Twickenham	a	17 37		17 40	17 46					17 51		17 57		18 03		18 07		18 10	18 16			
	d	17 37		17 41	17 47					17 52		17 57		18 04		18 07		18 11	18 17			
Strawberry Hill	d	17 41												18 07		18 11						
Fulwell	a															18 13						
Teddington	a	17 46												18 12								
Hampton Wick	a	17 54												18 16								
Kingston	a	17 56												18 18								
Whitton	d				17a50					17 55			←		18a23			18 14	18a20			
Feltham	d			17 47				18 08	17 56	17 59		18 03	18 08					18 18		18 38	18 25	
Ashford (Surrey)	d							→		18 03		18 07	18 12							→		
Staines	d			17 53					18 02	18 09		18 13	18 17					18 25			18 31	
Wraysbury	d									18 13												
Sunnymeads	d									18 15												
Datchet	d									18 18												
Windsor & Eton Riverside	a								18 15	18 25												
Egham	d			17 58								18 18	18 21					18 29			18 36	
Virginia Water	a			18 02								18 22	18 26					18 33			18 40	
	d			18 02								18 22	18 26					18 33			18 40	
Chertsey	d												18 31									
Addlestone	d												18 34									
Weybridge	a												18 40									
Longcross	d											18 25									18 44	
Sunningdale	d			18 09								18 29						18 38			18 47	
Ascot 3	d			18 13		18 23						18 33						18 43			18 53	
Bagshot	d					18 29															18 59	
Camberley	a					18 35															19 05	
Frimley	d					18 43															19 09	
Ash Vale	d					18 49															19 16	
Aldershot	a					18 54															19 21	
	d						19 10															19 42
Ash 5	d						19 18															19 49
Wanborough	d						19 20															19 52
Guildford	a						19 28															19 59
Martins Heron	d			18 17								18 37						18 47				
Bracknell	d			18 21								18 41						18 51				
Wokingham	d			18 27								18 47						18 57				
Winnersh	d			18 31														19 01				
Winnersh Triangle	d			18 33														19 03				
Earley	d			18 35														19 05				
Reading 7	a			18 42								18 58						19 12				

The xx15 and xx45 services from London Waterloo to Whitton continue to London Waterloo via Brentford

The xx03 and xx33 London Waterloo to Kingston services continue to London Waterloo via Wimbledon

The xx07 and xx37 services from London Waterloo to Whitton continue to London Waterloo via Richmond

For additional services between Wokingham and Reading refer to Table T148

Table T149-F

Mondays to Fridays
16 December to 15 May

London - Hounslow, Richmond, Kingston, Windsor, Weybridge, Ascot, Guildford and Reading

		SW ◇	SW	SW	SW ◇	SW	SW	SW	SW	SW	SW	SW 1	SW 1	SW ◇	SW ◇	SW ◇	SW	SW	SW ◇	SW	SW	SW	SW
London Waterloo 15 ⊖	d	17 58	18 01	18 05			18 07	18 12	18 15	18 20				18 22	18 24	18 28	18 31	18 35			18 37	18 43	18 45
Vauxhall ⊖	d	18 02	18 05	18 09			18 12	18 16	18 20					18 26	18 29	18 32	18 35	18 39			18 42	18 47	18 50
Queenstown Rd.(Battersea)	d		18 08				18 15		18 23					18 29			18 38				18 45		18 53
Clapham Junction 10	d	18 08	18 11	18 15			18 18	18 22	18 26	18 28				18 32	18 35	18 38	18 41	18 45			18 48	18 53	18 56
Wandsworth Town	d		18 14				18 21		18 28					18 35			18 44				18 51		18 59
Putney	d	18 12	18 17				18 24	18 26	18 31					18 38		18 42	18 47				18 54	18 57	19 02
Barnes	d		18 22				18 27		18 35					18 42			18 52				18 57		19 05
Barnes Bridge	d						18 29							18 45							18 59		
Chiswick	d						18 32							18 48							19 02		
Kew Bridge	d						18 35							18 50							19 05		
Brentford	d						18 38							18 54							19 08		
Syon Lane	d						18 40							18 56							19 10		
Isleworth	d						18 42							18 58							19 12		
Hounslow	d						18 46							19 02	18 49						19 16		
Mortlake	d		18 24						18 37								18 54						19 08
North Sheen	d		18 26			←			18 39		←						18 56			←			19 10
Richmond ⊖	d	18 18	18 29	18 23		18 29		18 33	18 42	18 37	18 42					18 48	18 59	18 53		18 59		19 03	19 12
St Margarets	d		→			18 31			→		18 44						→			19 01			→
Twickenham	a	18 21		18 27		18 33		18 37		18 40	18 46					18 51		18 57		19 03		19 07	
	d	18 22		18 27		18 34		18 37		18 41	18 47					18 52		18 57		19 04		19 07	
Strawberry Hill	d					18 37		18 41												19 07		19 11	
Fulwell	a							18 43														19 13	
Teddington	a					18 42														19 12			
Hampton Wick	a					18 46														19 16			
Kingston	a					18 48														19 18			
Whitton	d	18 25			←		18a53				18a50					18 55			←		19a23		
Feltham	d	18 29		18 33	18 38					18 47				19 08	18 55	18 59		19 03	19 08				
Ashford (Surrey)	d	18 33		18 37	18 42									→		19 03		19 07	19 12				
Staines	d	18 37		18 41	18 46					18 53					19 02	19 07		19 11	19 16				
Wraysbury	d	18 41														19 11							
Sunnymeads	d	18 44														19 14							
Datchet	d	18 47														19 17							
Windsor & Eton Riverside	a	18 53													19 15	19 23							
Egham	d			18 46	18 51					18 58								19 16	19 21				
Virginia Water	a			18 50	18 55					19 02								19 20	19 25				
	d			18 50	18 55					19 02								19 20	19 25				
Chertsey	d				19 01														19 31				
Addlestone	d				19 04														19 34				
Weybridge	a				19 10														19 42				
Longcross	d																	19 23					
Sunningdale	d			18 55						19 09								19 27					
Ascot 3	d			19 00						19 13		19 23						19 31					
Bagshot	d											19 29											
Camberley	a											19 35											
Frimley	d											19 43											
Ash Vale	d											19 49											
Aldershot	a											19 54											
	d												20 15										
Ash 5	d												20 25										
Wanborough	d												20 29										
Guildford	a												20 36										
Martins Heron	d			19 04						19 17								19 35					
Bracknell	d			19 07						19 21								19 39					
Wokingham	d			19 15						19 27								19 47					
Winnersh	d									19 31													
Winnersh Triangle	d									19 33													
Earley	d									19 35													
Reading 7	a			19 28						19 42								20 00					

The xx15 and xx45 services from London Waterloo to Whitton continue to London Waterloo via Brentford

The xx03 and xx33 London Waterloo to Kingston services continue to London Waterloo via Wimbledon

The xx07 and xx37 services from London Waterloo to Whitton continue to London Waterloo via Richmond

For additional services between Wokingham and Reading refer to Table T148

Table T149-F

Mondays to Fridays

16 December to 15 May

London - Hounslow, Richmond, Kingston, Windsor, Weybridge, Ascot, Guildford and Reading

		SW	SW		SW ◇	SW ◇	SW 1	SW ◇	SW	SW	SW ◇	SW	SW		SW	SW	SW	SW 1	SW 1	SW	SW	SW	SW		SW
London Waterloo 15 ⊖	d	18 50			18 52	18 54		18 58	19 01	19 05			19 07		19 15	19 20				19 22	19 28	19 31	19 35		
Vauxhall ⊖	d				18 56	18 59		19 02	19 05	19 09			19 12		19 19					19 26	19 32	19 36	19 39		
Queenstown Rd.(Battersea)	d				18 59				19 08				19 15		19 22					19 29		19 39			
Clapham Junction 10	d	18 59			19 04	19 05		19 08	19 11	19 15			19 18		19 25	19 28				19 32	19 38	19 42	19 45		
Wandsworth Town	d				19 07				19 14				19 21		19 28					19 35		19 44			
Putney	d				19 10			19 12	19 17				19 24		19 31					19 38	19 42	19 47			
Barnes	d				19 12				19 22				19 27		19 35					19 42		19 52			
Barnes Bridge	d				19 14								19 29							19 44					
Chiswick	d				19 17								19 32							19 47					
Kew Bridge	d				19 21								19 35							19 50					
Brentford	d				19 23								19 38							19 53					
Syon Lane	d				19 26								19 40							19 55					
Isleworth	d				19 28								19 42							19 57					
Hounslow	d				19 32	19 19							19 48							20 01					
Mortlake	d								19 24						19 37							19 54			
North Sheen	d		←						19 26			←			19 39		←					19 56			
Richmond ⊖	d	19 07	19 12					19 18	19 29	19 23		19 29			19 42	19 36	19 42				19 48	19 59	19 53		
St Margarets	d		19 15						→			19 31			→		19 44					→			
Twickenham	a	19 11	19 17					19 21		19 27		19 33				19 40	19 46				19 51		19 57		
	d	19 11	19 17					19 22		19 27		19 34				19 40	19 47				19 52		19 57		
Strawberry Hill	d											19 37													
Fulwell	a																								
Teddington	a											19 42													
Hampton Wick	a											19 46													
Kingston	a											19 48													
Whitton	d		19a20					19 25			←		19a53				19a50				19 55				←
Feltham	d	19 17			19 38	19 25		19 29		19 33	19 38					19 46				20 08	19 59		20 04		20 08
Ashford (Surrey)	d				→			19 33		19 37	19 42									→	20 03		20 08		20 12
Staines	d	19 24				19 31		19 37		19 41	19 46					19 53					20 07		20 12		20 16
Wraysbury	d							19 41													20 11				
Sunnymeads	d							19 44													20 14				
Datchet	d							19 47													20 17				
Windsor & Eton Riverside	a							19 53													20 21				
Egham	d	19 28				19 36				19 46	19 51					19 57							20 17		20 21
Virginia Water	a	19 32				19 40				19 50	19 55					20 01							20 21		20 25
	d	19 32				19 40				19 50	19 55					20 01							20 21		20 25
Chertsey	d										20 01														20 31
Addlestone	d										20 04														20 34
Weybridge	a										20 10														20 39
Longcross	d					19 44																	20 24		
Sunningdale	d	19 38				19 47				19 55						20 08							20 28		
Ascot 3	d	19 43				19 53				20 00						20 13		20 23					20 32		
Bagshot	d					19 59												20 29							
Camberley	a					20 05												20 35							
Frimley	d					20 09												20 43							
Ash Vale	d					20 18												20 49							
Aldershot	a					20 24												20 54							
	d						20 40												21 10						
Ash 5	d						20 47												21 17						
Wanborough	d						20 50												21 20						
Guildford	a						20 57												21 27						
Martins Heron	d	19 47								20 04						20 17							20 36		
Bracknell	d	19 50								20 07						20 20							20 40		
Wokingham	d	19 57								20 17						20 27							20 49		
Winnersh	d	20 00														20 30									
Winnersh Triangle	d	20 02														20 32									
Earley	d	20 05														20 35									
Reading 7	a	20 12								20 26						20 41							20 59		

The xx15 and xx45 services from London Waterloo to Whitton continue to London Waterloo via Brentford

The xx03 and xx33 London Waterloo to Kingston services continue to London Waterloo via Wimbledon

The xx07 and xx37 services from London Waterloo to Whitton continue to London Waterloo via Richmond

For additional services between Wokingham and Reading refer to Table T148

NRT DECEMBER 19 EDITION

Table T149-F

Mondays to Fridays

16 December to 15 May

London - Hounslow, Richmond, Kingston, Windsor, Weybridge, Ascot, Guildford and Reading

		SW	SW	SW	SW	SW	SW 1	SW 1	SW		SW	SW	SW	SW	SW	SW	SW	SW	SW		SW 1	SW 1	SW	SW	SW
London Waterloo 15 ⊖	d		19 37	19 45	19 50				19 52		19 58	20 01	20 05			20 07	20 15	20 20					20 22	20 28	
Vauxhall ⊖	d		19 43	19 49					19 56		20 02	20 06	20 09			20 11	20 19						20 26	20 32	
Queenstown Rd.(Battersea)	d		19 46	19 52					19 59			20 09				20 14	20 22						20 29		
Clapham Junction 10	d		19 49	19 55	19 58				20 02		20 08	20 13	20 16			20 17	20 25	20 28					20 32	20 38	
Wandsworth Town	d		19 51	19 58					20 05			20 16				20 20	20 28						20 35		
Putney	d		19 54	20 01					20 08		20 12	20 19				20 23	20 31						20 38	20 42	
Barnes	d		19 57	20 05					20 12			20 22				20 27	20 35						20 42		
Barnes Bridge	d		19 59						20 14							20 29							20 44		
Chiswick	d		20 02						20 17							20 32							20 47		
Kew Bridge	d		20 05						20 20							20 35							20 50		
Brentford	d		20 08						20 23							20 38							20 53		
Syon Lane	d		20 10						20 25							20 40							20 55		
Isleworth	d		20 12						20 27							20 42							20 57		
Hounslow	d		20 18						20 31							20 48							21 01		
Mortlake	d			20 07								20 25					20 37								
North Sheen	d	←		20 09		←						20 27			←		20 39		←						
Richmond ⊖	d	19 59		20 12	20 06	20 12					20 18	20 29	20 24		20 29		20 42	20 36	20 42					20 48	
St Margarets	d	20 01		→		20 14						→			20 32		→		20 44						
Twickenham	a	20 03			20 10	20 16					20 21		20 28		20 34			20 40	20 46					20 51	
	d	20 04			20 10	20 17					20 22		20 28		20 34			20 40	20 47					20 52	
Strawberry Hill	d	20 07													20 38										
Fulwell	a																								
Teddington	a	20 10													20 41										
Hampton Wick	a	20 14													20 44										
Kingston	a	20 16													20 46										
Whitton	d		20a23			20a20					20 25			←		20a53			20a50					20 55	←
Feltham	d				20 16				20 38		20 29		20 34	20 38				20 46					21 06	20 59	21 06
Ashford (Surrey)	d								→		20 33		20 38	20 42									→	21 03	21 10
Staines	d				20 23						20 37		20 42	20 46				20 53						21 07	21 14
Wraysbury	d										20 41													21 11	
Sunnymeads	d										20 44													21 14	
Datchet	d										20 47													21 17	
Windsor & Eton Riverside	a										20 51													21 21	
Egham	d				20 27								20 47	20 51				20 57							21 19
Virginia Water	a				20 31								20 51	20 55				21 01							21 23
	d				20 31								20 51	20 55				21 01							21 23
Chertsey	d													21 01											21 29
Addlestone	d													21 04											21 32
Weybridge	a													21 09											21 37
Longcross	d												20 54												
Sunningdale	d				20 38								20 58					21 08							
Ascot 3	d				20 43		20 53						21 02					21 13			21 23				
Bagshot	d						20 59														21 29				
Camberley	a						21 05														21 35				
Frimley	d						21 13														21 43				
Ash Vale	d						21 19														21 49				
Aldershot	a						21 24														21 54				
	d							21 40														22 10			
Ash 5	d							21 47														22 17			
Wanborough	d							21 50														22 20			
Guildford	a							21 57														22 27			
Martins Heron	d				20 47								21 06					21 17							
Bracknell	d				20 50								21 10					21 20							
Wokingham	d				20 57								21 16					21 27							
Winnersh	d				21 00													21 30							
Winnersh Triangle	d				21 02													21 32							
Earley	d				21 05													21 35							
Reading 7	a				21 11								21 27					21 41							

The xx15 and xx45 services from London Waterloo to Whitton continue to London Waterloo via Brentford

The xx03 and xx33 London Waterloo to Kingston services continue to London Waterloo via Wimbledon

The xx07 and xx37 services from London Waterloo to Whitton continue to London Waterloo via Richmond

For additional services between Wokingham and Reading refer to Table T148

Table T149-F

Mondays to Fridays

16 December to 15 May

London - Hounslow, Richmond, Kingston, Windsor, Weybridge, Ascot, Guildford and Reading

		SW	SW	SW	SW		SW	SW [1]	SW [1]	SW	SW	SW	SW	SW	SW		SW	SW	SW [1]	SW [1]	SW	SW	SW	SW	SW
London Waterloo [15] ⊖	d	20 33	20 37	20 45	20 50					20 52	20 58		21 03	21 07	21 15		21 20				21 22	21 28		21 33	21 37
Vauxhall ⊖	d	20 37	20 41	20 49						20 56	21 02		21 07	21 11	21 19						21 27	21 32		21 37	21 41
Queenstown Rd.(Battersea)	d	20 40	20 44	20 52						20 59			21 10	21 14	21 22						21 30			21 40	21 44
Clapham Junction [10]	d	20 43	20 47	20 55	20 58					21 02	21 08		21 13	21 17	21 25		21 28				21 33	21 38		21 43	21 47
Wandsworth Town	d	20 46	20 50	20 58						21 05			21 16	21 20	21 28						21 36			21 46	21 50
Putney	d	20 49	20 53	21 01						21 08	21 12		21 19	21 23	21 31						21 39	21 42		21 49	21 53
Barnes	d	20 52	20 57	21 05						21 12			21 22	21 27	21 35						21 42			21 52	21 57
Barnes Bridge	d		20 59							21 14				21 29							21 44				21 59
Chiswick	d		21 02							21 17				21 32							21 47				22 02
Kew Bridge	d		21 05							21 20				21 35							21 50				22 05
Brentford	d		21 08							21 23				21 38							21 53				22 08
Syon Lane	d		21 10							21 25				21 40							21 55				22 10
Isleworth	d		21 12							21 27				21 42							21 57				22 12
Hounslow	d		21 18							21 31				21 48							22 01				22 18
Mortlake	d	20 54		21 07									21 24		21 37									21 54	
North Sheen	d	20 56		21 09			←						21 26		21 39			←						21 56	
Richmond ⊖	d	20 59		21 12	21 06		21 12				21 18		21 29		21 42		21 36	21 42				21 48		21 59	
St Margarets	d	21 01		→			21 14						21 31		→			21 44						22 01	
Twickenham	a	21 03			21 10		21 16				21 21		21 33				21 40	21 47				21 51		22 03	
	d	21 04			21 10		21 17				21 22		21 34				21 40	21 47				21 52		22 04	
Strawberry Hill	d	21 07											21 37											22 07	
Fulwell	a																								
Teddington	a	21 10											21 40											22 10	
Hampton Wick	a	21 14											21 44											22 14	
Kingston	a	21 16											21 46											22 16	
Whitton	d		21a23				21a20				21 25	←		21a53				21a50				21 55	←		22a23
Feltham	d				21 16					21 36	21 29	21 36					21 46				22 06	21 59	22 06		
Ashford (Surrey)	d									→	21 33	21 40									→	22 03	22 10		
Staines	d				21 23						21 37	21 44					21 53					22 07	22 14		
Wraysbury	d										21 41											22 11			
Sunnymeads	d										21 44											22 14			
Datchet	d										21 47											22 17			
Windsor & Eton Riverside	a										21 51											22 21			
Egham	d				21 27							21 49					21 57						22 19		
Virginia Water	a				21 31							21 53					22 01						22 23		
	d				21 31							21 53					22 01						22 23		
Chertsey	d											21 59											22 29		
Addlestone	d											22 02											22 32		
Weybridge	a											22 07											22 37		
Longcross	d																								
Sunningdale	d				21 38												22 07								
Ascot [3]	d				21 43			21 53									22 13		22 23						
Bagshot	d							21 59											22 29						
Camberley	a							22 05											22 35						
Frimley	d							22 13											22 43						
Ash Vale	d							22 19											22 49						
Aldershot	a							22 24											22 54						
	d								22 40											23 10					
Ash [5]	d								22 47											23 17					
Wanborough	d								22 50											23 20					
Guildford	a								22 57											23 27					
Martins Heron	d				21 47												22 17								
Bracknell	d				21 50												22 20								
Wokingham	d				21 57												22 27								
Winnersh	d				22 00												22 30								
Winnersh Triangle	d				22 02												22 32								
Earley	d				22 05												22 35								
Reading [7]	a				22 11												22 41								

The xx15 and xx45 services from London Waterloo to Whitton continue to London Waterloo via Brentford

The xx03 and xx33 London Waterloo to Kingston services continue to London Waterloo via Wimbledon

The xx07 and xx37 services from London Waterloo to Whitton continue to London Waterloo via Richmond

For additional services between Wokingham and Reading refer to Table T148

Table T149-F

Mondays to Fridays

16 December to 15 May

London - Hounslow, Richmond, Kingston, Windsor, Weybridge, Ascot, Guildford and Reading

			SW	SW	SW	SW [1]	SW [1]	SW	SW	SW	SW		SW	SW [1]	SW	SW	SW	SW	SW	SW [1]	SW		SW	SW	SW
London Waterloo [15] ⊖	d		21 45	21 50				21 52	21 58		22 03		22 20		22 22	22 28		22 33	22 50		22 52		22 58		23 03
Vauxhall ⊖	d		21 49					21 56	22 02		22 07				22 26	22 32		22 37			22 56		23 02		23 07
Queenstown Rd.(Battersea)	d		21 52					21 59			22 10				22 29			22 40			22 59				23 10
Clapham Junction [10]	d		21 55	21 58				22 02	22 08		22 13		22 28		22 32	22 38		22 43	22 58		23 02		23 08		23 13
Wandsworth Town	d		21 58					22 05			22 16				22 35			22 46			23 05				23 16
Putney	d		22 01					22 08	22 12		22 19				22 38	22 42		22 49			23 08		23 12		23 19
Barnes	d		22 05					22 12			22 22				22 42			22 52			23 12				23 22
Barnes Bridge	d							22 14							22 44						23 14				
Chiswick	d							22 17							22 47						23 17				
Kew Bridge	d							22 20							22 50						23 20				
Brentford	d							22 23							22 53						23 23				
Syon Lane	d							22 25							22 55						23 25				
Isleworth	d							22 27							22 57						23 27				
Hounslow	d							22 31							23 01						23 31				
Mortlake	d		22 07								22 24							22 54							23 24
North Sheen	d		22 09		←						22 26							22 56							23 26
Richmond ⊖	d		22 12	22 06	22 12				22 18		22 29		22 36			22 48		22 59	23 06				23 18		23 29
St Margarets	d		→		22 14						22 31							23 01							23 31
Twickenham	a			22 10	22 16				22 21		22 33		22 40			22 51		23 03	23 10				23 21		23 33
	d			22 10					22 22		22 34		22 40			22 52		23 04	23 10				23 22		23 34
Strawberry Hill	d										22 37							23 07							23 37
Fulwell	a																								
Teddington	a										22 40							23 10							23 40
Hampton Wick	a										22 44							23 14							23 44
Kingston	a										22 46							23 16							23 46
Whitton	d								22 25	←						22 55	←						23 25	←	
Feltham	d			22 16				22 36	22 29	22 36			22 46		23 06	22 59	23 06		23 16		23 36		23 29	23 36	
Ashford (Surrey)	d							→	22 33	22 40					→	23 03	23 10				→		23 33	23 40	
Staines	d			22 23					22 37	22 44			22 53			23 07	23 14		23 23				23 37	23 44	
Wraysbury	d								22 41							23 11							23 41		
Sunnymeads	d								22 44							23 14							23 44		
Datchet	d								22 47							23 17							23 47		
Windsor & Eton Riverside	a								22 51							23 21							23 51		
Egham	d			22 28						22 49			22 57				23 19		23 27					23 49	
Virginia Water	a			22 32						22 53			23 01				23 23		23 31					23 53	
	d			22 32						22 53			23 01				23 23		23 31					23 53	
Chertsey	d									22 59							23 29							23 59	
Addlestone	d									23 02							23 32							00a02	
Weybridge	a									23 07							23 37								
Longcross	d																								
Sunningdale	d			22 37									23 07						23 37						
Ascot [3]	d			22 43		22 53							23 13	23 23					23 43	23 53					
Bagshot	d					22 59								23 29						23 59					
Camberley	a					23 05								23 35						00 05					
Frimley	d					23 13								23 43						00 13					
Ash Vale	d					23 19								23 49						00 19					
Aldershot	a					23 24								23 54						00 24					
	d						23 40																		
Ash [5]	d						23 47																		
Wanborough	d						23 50																		
Guildford	a						23 57																		
Martins Heron	d			22 47									23 17						23 47						
Bracknell	d			22 50									23 20						23 50						
Wokingham	d			22 57									23 27						23 57						
Winnersh	d			23 00									23 30						23 59						
Winnersh Triangle	d			23 02									23 32						00 02						
Earley	d			23 07									23 35						00 05						
Reading [7]	a			23 16									23 41						00 11						

The xx15 and xx45 services from London Waterloo to Whitton continue to London Waterloo via Brentford

The xx03 and xx33 London Waterloo to Kingston services continue to London Waterloo via Wimbledon

The xx07 and xx37 services from London Waterloo to Whitton continue to London Waterloo via Richmond

For additional services between Wokingham and Reading refer to Table T148

Table T149-F

Mondays to Fridays

16 December to 15 May

London - Hounslow, Richmond, Kingston, Windsor, Weybridge, Ascot, Guildford and Reading

Station		SW	SW	SW	SW	SW	SW		SW	SW	SW
London Waterloo 15 ⊖	d	23 20	23 22	23 28		23 33	23 50		23 52	23 58	
Vauxhall ⊖	d		23 26	23 32		23 37			23 57	00 02	
Queenstown Rd.(Battersea)	d		23 29			23 40			23 59		
Clapham Junction 10	d	23 28	23 32	23 38		23 43	23 58		00 03	00 08	
Wandsworth Town	d		23 35			23 46			00 05		
Putney	d		23 38	23 42		23 49			00 08	00 12	
Barnes	d		23 42			23 52			00 12		
Barnes Bridge	d		23 44						00 14		
Chiswick	d		23 47						00 17		
Kew Bridge	d		23 50						00 20		
Brentford	d		23 53						00 23		
Syon Lane	d		23 55						00 25		
Isleworth	d		23 57						00 27		
Hounslow	d		00 01						00 31		
Mortlake	d					23 54					
North Sheen	d					23 56					
Richmond ⊖	d	23 36		23 48		23 59	00 06			00 18	
St Margarets	d					00 01					
Twickenham	a	23 40		23 51		00 03	00 10			00 22	
	d	23 40		23 52		00 04	00 10			00 22	
Strawberry Hill	d					00 08					
Fulwell	a										
Teddington	a					00 11					
Hampton Wick	a					00 13					
Kingston	a					00 15					
Whitton	d			23 55	←					00 25	←
Feltham	d	23 46	00 06	23 59	00 06		00 16		00 36	00 29	00 36
Ashford (Surrey)	d		→	00 03	00 10				→	00 33	00 40
Staines	d	23 53		00 07	00 14		00 23			00a37	00a47
Wraysbury	d			00 11							
Sunnymeads	d			00 14							
Datchet	d			00 17							
Windsor & Eton Riverside	a			00 21							
Egham	d	23 57			00 19		00 27				
Virginia Water	a	00 01			00 23		00 31				
	d	00 01			00 23		00 31				
Chertsey	d				00 29						
Addlestone	d				00 32						
Weybridge	a				00 36						
Longcross	d										
Sunningdale	d	00 07					00 37				
Ascot 3	d	00 13					00 42				
Bagshot	d										
Camberley	a										
Frimley	d										
Ash Vale	d										
Aldershot	a										
	d										
Ash 5	d										
Wanborough	d										
Guildford	a										
Martins Heron	d	00 17					00 46				
Bracknell	d	00 20					00 50				
Wokingham	d	00 30					00 56				
Winnersh	d	00 33									
Winnersh Triangle	d	00 35									
Earley	d	00 38									
Reading 7	a	00 44					01 05				

The xx15 and xx45 services from London Waterloo to Whitton continue to London Waterloo via Brentford

The xx03 and xx33 London Waterloo to Kingston services continue to London Waterloo via Wimbledon

The xx07 and xx37 services from London Waterloo to Whitton continue to London Waterloo via Richmond

For additional services between Wokingham and Reading refer to Table T148

Table T149-F

Saturdays

21 December to 16 May

London - Hounslow, Richmond, Kingston, Windsor, Weybridge, Ascot, Guildford and Reading

Station		SW	SW	SW	SW	SW	SW	SW	SW	SW 1		SW	SW 1	SW	SW	SW	SW	SW	SW	SW		SW	SW	SW 1	SW 1
London Waterloo 15 ⊖	d											00 18					05 05					05 33	05 50		
Vauxhall ⊖	d							00 02				00 22					05 09					05 37			
Queenstown Rd.(Battersea)	d											00 25					05 12					05 40			
Clapham Junction 10	d							00 08	00 03			00 30					05 15			05 32		05 43	05 58		
Wandsworth Town	d								00 05			00 33					05 18			05 35		05 46			
Putney	d							00 12	00 08			00 36					05 21			05 38		05 49			
Barnes	d								00 12			00 39					05 24			05 42		05 52			
Barnes Bridge	d								00 14											05 44					
Chiswick	d								00 17											05 47					
Kew Bridge	d								00 20											05 50					
Brentford	d								00 23											05 53					
Syon Lane	d								00 25											05 55					
Isleworth	d								00 27											05 57					
Hounslow	d					00 01			00 31											06 01					
Mortlake	d											00 41					05 26					05 54			
North Sheen	d											00 43					05 28					05 56			
Richmond ⊖	d						00 06	00 18				00 46					05 31					05 59	06 06		
St Margarets	d	00 01										00 48					05 33					06 01			
Twickenham	a	00 03					00 10	00 22				00 50					05 35					06 03	06 10		
	d	00 04					00 10	00 22				00 51		04 52			05 36	05 39	05 53			06 04	06 10		
Strawberry Hill	d	00 08										00s54		04 55								06 07			
Fulwell	a																								
Teddington	a	00 11										00s57		04 58								06 10			
Hampton Wick	a	00 13										01s00		05 01								06 14			
Kingston	a	00 15										01 02		05 03								06 16			
Whitton	d							00 25									05 39	05a42	05 56						
Feltham	d					00 06	00 16	00 29	00 36								05 43		06 00	06 06			06 16		
Ashford (Surrey)	d				00 03	00 10		00 33	00 40								05 47		06 04	06 10					
Staines	d				00 07	00 14	00 23	00a37	00a47						05 23	05 44	05 53		06 08	06 14			06 23		
Wraysbury	d				00 11														06 12						
Sunnymeads	d				00 14														06 15						
Datchet	d				00 17														06 18						
Windsor & Eton Riverside	a				00 21														06 22						
Egham	d					00 19	00 27								05 27	05 49	05 57			06 19			06 27		
Virginia Water	a					00 23	00 31								05 31	05 53	06 01			06 23			06 31		
	d			00 01		00 23	00 31								05 31	05 53	06 01			06 23			06 31		
Chertsey	d					00 29										05 59				06 29					
Addlestone	d					00 32										06 02				06 32					
Weybridge	a					00 36										06 07				06 37					
Longcross	d																						06 35		
Sunningdale	d			00 07			00 37								05 38		06 07						06 38		
Ascot 3	d			00 13			00 42						00 45		05 43		06 13						06 43		
Bagshot	d												00 51												
Camberley	a												00 57												
Frimley	d									00 13			01 01												
Ash Vale	d									00 19			01 08												
Aldershot	a									00 24			01s13												
	d																							06 10	06 40
Ash 5	d																							06 17	06 46
Wanborough	d																							06 20	06 50
Guildford	a																							06 27	06 57
Martins Heron	d			00 17			00 46								05 47		06 17						06 47		
Bracknell	d			00 20			00 50								05 50		06 20						06 50		
Wokingham	d			00 30			00 56								05 57		06 27						06 57		
Winnersh	d			00 33											06 00		06 30						07 00		
Winnersh Triangle	d		00 02	00 35											06 02		06 32						07 02		
Earley	d		00 05	00 38											06 05		06 35						07 05		
Reading 7	a		00 11	00 44			01 05								06 11		06 41						07 11		

The xx15 and xx45 services from London Waterloo to Whitton continue to London Waterloo via Brentford

The xx03 and xx33 London Waterloo to Kingston services continue to London Waterloo via Wimbledon

The xx07 and xx37 services from London Waterloo to Whitton continue to London Waterloo via Richmond

For additional services between Wokingham and Reading refer to Table T148

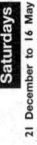

Table T149-F

Saturdays

21 December to 16 May

London - Hounslow, Richmond, Kingston, Windsor, Weybridge, Ascot, Guildford and Reading

		SW 1	SW 1	SW 1	SW	SW	SW	SW	SW	SW 1	SW 1	SW	SW	SW	SW	SW	SW 1	SW 1	SW	SW	SW	SW	SW
London Waterloo 15 ⊖	d				05 52	05 58		06 03	06 20			06 22	06 28		06 33	06 50			06 52	06 58		07 03	07 07
Vauxhall ⊖	d				05 56	06 02		06 07				06 26	06 32		06 37				06 56	07 02		07 07	07 11
Queenstown Rd.(Battersea)	d				05 59			06 10				06 29			06 40				06 59			07 10	07 14
Clapham Junction 10	d				06 02	06 08		06 13	06 28			06 32	06 38		06 43	06 58			07 02	07 08		07 13	07 17
Wandsworth Town	d				06 05			06 16				06 35			06 46				07 05			07 16	07 20
Putney	d				06 08	06 12		06 19				06 38	06 42		06 49				07 08	07 12		07 19	07 23
Barnes	d				06 12			06 22				06 42			06 52				07 12			07 22	07 27
Barnes Bridge	d				06 14							06 44							07 14				07 29
Chiswick	d				06 17							06 47							07 17				07 32
Kew Bridge	d				06 20							06 50							07 20				07 35
Brentford	d				06 23							06 53							07 23				07 38
Syon Lane	d				06 25							06 55							07 25				07 40
Isleworth	d				06 27							06 57							07 27				07 42
Hounslow	d				06 31							07 01							07 31				07 48
Mortlake	d							06 24							06 54							07 24	
North Sheen	d							06 26							06 56							07 26	
Richmond ⊖	d					06 18		06 29	06 36				06 48		06 59	07 06				07 18		07 29	
St Margarets	d							06 31							07 01							07 31	
Twickenham	a					06 21		06 33	06 40				06 51		07 03	07 10				07 21		07 33	
	d					06 22		06 34	06 40				06 52		07 04	07 10				07 22		07 34	
Strawberry Hill	d							06 37							07 07							07 37	
Fulwell	a																						
Teddington	a							06 40							07 10							07 40	
Hampton Wick	a							06 44							07 14							07 44	
Kingston	a							06 46							07 16							07 46	
Whitton	d					06 25	←						06 55	←						07 25	←		07a53
Feltham	d				06 38	06 29	06 38		06 46			07 06	06 59	07 06		07 16			07 36	07 29	07 36		
Ashford (Surrey)	d				→	06 33	06 42					→	07 03	07 10					→	07 33	07 40		
Staines	d					06 37	06 46		06 53				07 07	07 14		07 23				07 37	07 44		
Wraysbury	d					06 41							07 11							07 41			
Sunnymeads	d					06 44							07 14							07 44			
Datchet	d					06 47							07 17							07 47			
Windsor & Eton Riverside	a					06 51							07 21							07 51			
Egham	d						06 50		06 57					07 19		07 27					07 49		
Virginia Water	a						06 55		07 01					07 23		07 31					07 53		
	d						06 55		07 01					07 23		07 31					07 53		
Chertsey	d						07 00							07 29							07 59		
Addlestone	d						07 03							07 32							08 02		
Weybridge	a						07 08							07 37							08 07		
Longcross	d								07 05							07 35							
Sunningdale	d								07 08							07 38							
Ascot 3	d		06 53						07 13	07 23						07 43	07 53						
Bagshot	d		06 59							07 29							07 59						
Camberley	a		07 05							07 35							08 05						
Frimley	d		07 13							07 43							08 13						
Ash Vale	d		07 19							07 49							08 19						
Aldershot	a		07 24							07 54							08 24						
	d	07 10		07 40							08 10							08 40					
Ash 5	d	07 17		07 47							08 17							08 47					
Wanborough	d	07 20		07 50							08 20							08 50					
Guildford	a	07 27		07 57							08 27							08 57					
Martins Heron	d								07 17							07 47							
Bracknell	d								07 20							07 50							
Wokingham	d								07 27							07 57							
Winnersh	d								07 30							08 00							
Winnersh Triangle	d								07 32							08 02							
Earley	d								07 35							08 05							
Reading 7	a								07 41							08 11							

The xx15 and xx45 services from London Waterloo to Whitton continue to London Waterloo via Brentford

The xx03 and xx33 London Waterloo to Kingston services continue to London Waterloo via Wimbledon

The xx07 and xx37 services from London Waterloo to Whitton continue to London Waterloo via Richmond

For additional services between Wokingham and Reading refer to Table T148

Table T149-F

Saturdays

21 December to 16 May

London - Hounslow, Richmond, Kingston, Windsor, Weybridge, Ascot, Guildford and Reading

		SW	SW	SW	SW 1	SW 1	SW	SW	SW	SW	SW	SW	SW	SW	SW 1	SW 1	SW	SW	SW	SW	SW	SW
London Waterloo 15 ⊖	d	07 15	07 20				07 22	07 28		07 33	07 37	07 45	07 50				07 52	07 58		08 03	08 07	08 15
Vauxhall ⊖	d	07 19					07 26	07 32		07 37	07 41	07 49					07 56	08 02		08 07	08 11	08 19
Queenstown Rd.(Battersea)	d	07 22					07 29			07 40	07 44	07 52					07 59			08 10	08 14	08 22
Clapham Junction 10	d	07 25	07 28				07 32	07 38		07 43	07 47	07 55	07 58				08 02	08 08		08 13	08 17	08 25
Wandsworth Town	d	07 28					07 35			07 46	07 50	07 58					08 05			08 16	08 20	08 28
Putney	d	07 31					07 38	07 42		07 49	07 53	08 01					08 08	08 12		08 19	08 23	08 31
Barnes	d	07 35					07 42			07 52	07 57	08 05					08 12			08 22	08 27	08 35
Barnes Bridge	d						07 44				07 59						08 14				08 29	
Chiswick	d						07 47				08 02						08 17				08 32	
Kew Bridge	d						07 50				08 05						08 20				08 35	
Brentford	d						07 53				08 08						08 23				08 38	
Syon Lane	d						07 55				08 10						08 25				08 40	
Isleworth	d						07 57				08 12						08 27				08 42	
Hounslow	d						08 01				08 18						08 31				08 48	
Mortlake	d	07 37								07 54		08 07								08 24		08 37
North Sheen	d	07 39		←						07 56		08 09		←						08 26		08 39
Richmond ⊖	d	07 42	07 36	07 42				07 48		07 59		08 12	08 06	08 12				08 18		08 29		08 42
St Margarets	d	→		07 44						08 01		→		08 14						08 31		→
Twickenham	a		07 40	07 46				07 51		08 03			08 10	08 16				08 21		08 33		
	d		07 40	07 47				07 52		08 04			08 10	08 17				08 22		08 34		
Strawberry Hill	d									08 07										08 37		
Fulwell	a																					
Teddington	a									08 10										08 40		
Hampton Wick	a									08 14										08 44		
Kingston	a									08 16										08 46		
Whitton	d			07a50				07 55	←		08a23			08a20				08 25	←		08a53	
Feltham	d		07 46				08 06	07 59	08 06				08 16				08 36	08 29	08 36			
Ashford (Surrey)	d						→	08 03	08 10								→	08 33	08 40			
Staines	d		07 53					08 07	08 14				08 23					08 37	08 44			
Wraysbury	d							08 11										08 41				
Sunnymeads	d							08 14										08 44				
Datchet	d							08 17										08 47				
Windsor & Eton Riverside	a							08 21										08 51				
Egham	d		07 57						08 19				08 27						08 49			
Virginia Water	a		08 01						08 23				08 31						08 53			
	d		08 01						08 23				08 31						08 53			
Chertsey	d								08 29										08 59			
Addlestone	d								08 32										09 02			
Weybridge	a								08 37										09 07			
Longcross	d		08 05										08 35									
Sunningdale	d		08 08										08 38									
Ascot 3	d		08 13		08 23								08 43		08 53							
Bagshot	d				08 29										08 59							
Camberley	a				08 35										09 05							
Frimley	d				08 43										09 13							
Ash Vale	d				08 49										09 19							
Aldershot	a				08 54										09 24							
	d					09 10										09 40						
Ash 5	d					09 17										09 47						
Wanborough	d					09 20										09 50						
Guildford	a					09 27										09 57						
Martins Heron	d		08 17										08 47									
Bracknell	d		08 20										08 50									
Wokingham	d		08 27										08 57									
Winnersh	d		08 30										09 00									
Winnersh Triangle	d		08 32										09 02									
Earley	d		08 35										09 05									
Reading 7	a		08 41										09 11									

The xx15 and xx45 services from London Waterloo to Whitton continue to London Waterloo via Brentford

The xx03 and xx33 London Waterloo to Kingston services continue to London Waterloo via Wimbledon

The xx07 and xx37 services from London Waterloo to Whitton continue to London Waterloo via Richmond

For additional services between Wokingham and Reading refer to Table T148

Table T149-F

Saturdays

21 December to 16 May

London - Hounslow, Richmond, Kingston, Windsor, Weybridge, Ascot, Guildford and Reading

		SW	SW	SW 1	SW 1	SW	SW	SW	SW	SW	SW	SW	SW	SW 1	SW 1	SW	SW	SW	SW	SW	SW	SW	SW
London Waterloo 15 ⊖	d	08 20				08 22	08 28		08 33	08 37	08 45	08 50				08 52	08 58		09 03	09 07	09 15	09 20	
Vauxhall ⊖	d					08 26	08 32		08 37	08 41	08 49					08 56	09 02		09 07	09 11	09 19		
Queenstown Rd.(Battersea)	d					08 29			08 40	08 44	08 52					08 59			09 10	09 14	09 22		
Clapham Junction 10	d	08 28				08 32	08 38		08 43	08 47	08 55	08 58				09 02	09 08		09 13	09 17	09 25	09 28	
Wandsworth Town	d					08 35			08 46	08 50	08 58					09 05			09 16	09 20	09 28		
Putney	d					08 38	08 42		08 49	08 53	09 01					09 08	09 12		09 19	09 23	09 31		
Barnes	d					08 42			08 52	08 57	09 05					09 12			09 22	09 27	09 35		
Barnes Bridge	d					08 44				08 59						09 14				09 29			
Chiswick	d					08 47				09 02						09 17				09 32			
Kew Bridge	d					08 50				09 05						09 20				09 35			
Brentford	d					08 53				09 08						09 23				09 38			
Syon Lane	d					08 55				09 10						09 25				09 40			
Isleworth	d					08 57				09 12						09 27				09 42			
Hounslow	d					09 01				09 18						09 31				09 48			
Mortlake	d								08 54		09 07								09 24		09 37		
North Sheen	d		←						08 56		09 09		←						09 26		09 39		←
Richmond ⊖	d	08 36	08 42				08 48		08 59		09 12	09 06	09 12				09 18		09 29		09 42	09 36	09 42
St Margarets	d		08 44						09 01		→		09 14						09 31		→		09 44
Twickenham	a	08 40	08 46				08 51		09 03			09 10	09 16				09 21		09 33			09 40	09 46
	d	08 40	08 47				08 52		09 04			09 10	09 17				09 22		09 34			09 40	09 47
Strawberry Hill	d								09 07										09 37				
Fulwell	a																						
Teddington	a								09 10										09 40				
Hampton Wick	a								09 14										09 44				
Kingston	a								09 16										09 46				
Whitton	d		08a50				08 55	←		09a23			09a20				09 25	←		09a53			09a50
Feltham	d	08 46				09 06	08 59	09 06				09 16				09 36	09 29	09 36				09 46	
Ashford (Surrey)	d					→	09 03	09 10								→	09 33	09 40					
Staines	d	08 53					09 07	09 14				09 23					09 37	09 44				09 53	
Wraysbury	d						09 11										09 41						
Sunnymeads	d						09 14										09 44						
Datchet	d						09 17										09 47						
Windsor & Eton Riverside	a						09 21										09 51						
Egham	d	08 57						09 19				09 27						09 49				09 57	
Virginia Water	a	09 01						09 23				09 31						09 53				10 01	
	d	09 01						09 23				09 31						09 53				10 01	
Chertsey	d							09 29										09 59					
Addlestone	d							09 32										10 02					
Weybridge	a							09 37										10 07					
Longcross	d	09 05										09 35										10 05	
Sunningdale	d	09 08										09 38										10 08	
Ascot 3	d	09 13		09 23								09 43		09 53								10 13	
Bagshot	d			09 29										09 59									
Camberley	a			09 35										10 05									
Frimley	d			09 43										10 13									
Ash Vale	d			09 49										10 19									
Aldershot	a			09 54										10 24									
	d				10 10										10 40								
Ash 5	d				10 17										10 47								
Wanborough	d				10 20										10 50								
Guildford	a				10 27										10 57								
Martins Heron	d	09 17										09 47										10 17	
Bracknell	d	09 20										09 50										10 20	
Wokingham	d	09 27										09 57										10 27	
Winnersh	d	09 30										10 00										10 30	
Winnersh Triangle	d	09 32										10 02										10 32	
Earley	d	09 35										10 05										10 35	
Reading 7	a	09 41										10 11										10 41	

The xx15 and xx45 services from London Waterloo to Whitton continue to London Waterloo via Brentford

The xx03 and xx33 London Waterloo to Kingston services continue to London Waterloo via Wimbledon

The xx07 and xx37 services from London Waterloo to Whitton continue to London Waterloo via Richmond

For additional services between Wokingham and Reading refer to Table T148

NRT DECEMBER 19 EDITION

Table T149-F

Saturdays

21 December to 16 May

London - Hounslow, Richmond, Kingston, Windsor, Weybridge, Ascot, Guildford and Reading

		SW 1	SW 1	SW	SW	SW	SW	SW	SW	SW	SW	SW 1	SW 1	SW	SW	SW	SW	SW	SW	SW	SW	SW 1
London Waterloo 15 ⊖	d			09 22	09 28		09 33	09 37	09 45	09 50				09 52	09 58		10 03	10 07	10 15	10 20		
Vauxhall ⊖	d			09 26	09 32		09 37	09 41	09 49					09 56	10 02		10 07	10 11	10 19			
Queenstown Rd.(Battersea)	d			09 29			09 40	09 44	09 52					09 59			10 10	10 14	10 22			
Clapham Junction 10	d			09 32	09 38		09 43	09 47	09 55	09 58				10 02	10 08		10 13	10 17	10 25	10 28		
Wandsworth Town	d			09 35			09 46	09 50	09 58					10 05			10 16	10 20	10 28			
Putney	d			09 38	09 42		09 49	09 53	10 01					10 08	10 12		10 19	10 23	10 31			
Barnes	d			09 42			09 52	09 57	10 05					10 12			10 22	10 27	10 35			
Barnes Bridge	d			09 44				09 59						10 14				10 29				
Chiswick	d			09 47				10 02						10 17				10 32				
Kew Bridge	d			09 50				10 05						10 20				10 35				
Brentford	d			09 53				10 08						10 23				10 38				
Syon Lane	d			09 55				10 10						10 25				10 40				
Isleworth	d			09 57				10 12						10 27				10 42				
Hounslow	d			10 01				10 18						10 31				10 48				
Mortlake	d						09 54		10 07								10 24		10 37			
North Sheen	d						09 56		10 09		←						10 26		10 39		←	
Richmond ⊖	d				09 48		09 59		10 12	10 06	10 12				10 18		10 29		10 42	10 36	10 42	
St Margarets	d						10 01		→		10 14						10 31		→		10 44	
Twickenham	a				09 51		10 03			10 10	10 16				10 21		10 33			10 40	10 46	
	d				09 52		10 04			10 10	10 17				10 22		10 34			10 40	10 47	
Strawberry Hill	d						10 07										10 37					
Fulwell	a																					
Teddington	a						10 10										10 40					
Hampton Wick	a						10 14										10 44					
Kingston	a						10 16										10 46					
Whitton	d				09 55	←		10a23			10a20				10 25	←		10a53			10a50	
Feltham	d			10 06	09 59	10 06				10 16				10 36	10 29	10 36				10 46		
Ashford (Surrey)	d			→	10 03	10 10								→	10 33	10 40						
Staines	d				10 07	10 14				10 23					10 37	10 44				10 53		
Wraysbury	d				10 11										10 41							
Sunnymeads	d				10 14										10 44							
Datchet	d				10 17										10 47							
Windsor & Eton Riverside	a				10 21										10 51							
Egham	d					10 19				10 27						10 49				10 57		
Virginia Water	a					10 23				10 31						10 53				11 01		
	d					10 23				10 31						10 53				11 01		
Chertsey	d					10 29										10 59						
Addlestone	d					10 32										11 02						
Weybridge	a					10 37										11 07						
Longcross	d									10 35										11 05		
Sunningdale	d									10 38										11 08		
Ascot 3	d	10 23								10 43		10 53								11 13		11 23
Bagshot	d	10 29										10 59										11 29
Camberley	a	10 35										11 05										11 35
Frimley	d	10 43										11 13										11 43
Ash Vale	d	10 49										11 19										11 49
Aldershot	a	10 54										11 24										11 54
	d		11 10										11 40									
Ash 5	d		11 17										11 47									
Wanborough	d		11 20										11 50									
Guildford	a		11 27										11 57									
Martins Heron	d									10 47										11 17		
Bracknell	d									10 50										11 20		
Wokingham	d									10 57										11 27		
Winnersh	d									11 00										11 30		
Winnersh Triangle	d									11 02										11 32		
Earley	d									11 05										11 35		
Reading 7	a									11 11										11 41		

The xx15 and xx45 services from London Waterloo to Whitton continue to London Waterloo via Brentford

The xx03 and xx33 London Waterloo to Kingston services continue to London Waterloo via Wimbledon

The xx07 and xx37 services from London Waterloo to Whitton continue to London Waterloo via Richmond

For additional services between Wokingham and Reading refer to Table T148

Table T149-F

Saturdays

21 December to 16 May

London - Hounslow, Richmond, Kingston, Windsor, Weybridge, Ascot, Guildford and Reading

		SW ■1	SW	SW	SW	SW	SW	SW	SW	SW		SW ■1	SW ■1	SW	SW	SW	SW	SW	SW	SW		SW	SW ■1	SW ■1	SW
London Waterloo 15 ⊖	d		10 22	10 28		10 33	10 37	10 45	10 50					10 52	10 58		11 03	11 07	11 15	11 20					11 22
Vauxhall ⊖	d		10 26	10 32		10 37	10 41	10 49						10 56	11 02		11 07	11 11	11 19						11 26
Queenstown Rd.(Battersea)	d		10 29			10 40	10 44	10 52						10 59			11 10	11 14	11 22						11 29
Clapham Junction 10	d		10 32	10 38		10 43	10 47	10 55	10 58					11 02	11 08		11 13	11 17	11 25	11 28					11 32
Wandsworth Town	d		10 35			10 46	10 50	10 58						11 05			11 16	11 20	11 28						11 35
Putney	d		10 38	10 42		10 49	10 53	11 01						11 08	11 12		11 19	11 23	11 31						11 38
Barnes	d		10 42			10 52	10 57	11 05						11 12			11 22	11 27	11 35						11 42
Barnes Bridge	d		10 44				10 59							11 14				11 29							11 44
Chiswick	d		10 47				11 02							11 17				11 32							11 47
Kew Bridge	d		10 50				11 05							11 20				11 35							11 50
Brentford	d		10 53				11 08							11 23				11 38							11 53
Syon Lane	d		10 55				11 10							11 25				11 40							11 55
Isleworth	d		10 57				11 12							11 27				11 42							11 57
Hounslow	d		11 01				11 18							11 31				11 48							12 01
Mortlake	d					10 54		11 07									11 24		11 37						
North Sheen	d					10 56		11 09		←							11 26		11 39			←			
Richmond ⊖	d			10 48		10 59		11 12	11 06	11 12					11 18		11 29		11 42	11 36		11 42			
St Margarets	d					11 01		→		11 14							11 31		→			11 44			
Twickenham	a			10 51		11 03			11 10	11 16					11 21		11 33			11 40		11 46			
	d			10 52		11 04			11 10	11 17					11 22		11 34			11 40		11 47			
Strawberry Hill	d					11 07											11 37								
Fulwell	a																								
Teddington	a					11 10											11 40								
Hampton Wick	a					11 14											11 44								
Kingston	a					11 16											11 46								
Whitton	d			10 55	←		11a23			11a20					11 25	←		11a53				11a50			
Feltham	d		11 06	10 59	11 06				11 16					11 36	11 29	11 36				11 46					12 06
Ashford (Surrey)	d		→	11 03	11 10									→	11 33	11 40									→
Staines	d			11 07	11 14				11 23						11 37	11 44				11 53					
Wraysbury	d			11 11											11 41										
Sunnymeads	d			11 14											11 44										
Datchet	d			11 17											11 47										
Windsor & Eton Riverside	a			11 21											11 51										
Egham	d				11 19				11 27							11 49				11 57					
Virginia Water	a				11 23				11 31							11 53				12 01					
	d				11 23				11 31							11 53				12 01					
Chertsey	d				11 29											11 59									
Addlestone	d				11 32											12 02									
Weybridge	a				11 37											12 07									
Longcross	d								11 35											12 05					
Sunningdale	d								11 38											12 08					
Ascot 3	d								11 43			11 53								12 13			12 23		
Bagshot	d											11 59											12 29		
Camberley	a											12 05											12 35		
Frimley	d											12 13											12 43		
Ash Vale	d											12 19											12 49		
Aldershot	a											12 24											12 54		
	d	12 10											12 40											13 10	
Ash 5	d	12 17											12 47											13 17	
Wanborough	d	12 20											12 51											13 20	
Guildford	a	12 27											12 58											13 27	
Martins Heron	d								11 47											12 17					
Bracknell	d								11 50											12 20					
Wokingham	d								11 57											12 27					
Winnersh	d								12 00											12 30					
Winnersh Triangle	d								12 02											12 32					
Earley	d								12 05											12 35					
Reading 7	a								12 11											12 41					

The xx15 and xx45 services from London Waterloo to Whitton continue to London Waterloo via Brentford

The xx03 and xx33 London Waterloo to Kingston services continue to London Waterloo via Wimbledon

The xx07 and xx37 services from London Waterloo to Whitton continue to London Waterloo via Richmond

For additional services between Wokingham and Reading refer to Table T148

Table T149-F

Saturdays

21 December to 16 May

London - Hounslow, Richmond, Kingston, Windsor, Weybridge, Ascot, Guildford and Reading

		SW	SW	SW	SW	SW		SW	SW	SW ■1	SW ■1	SW	SW	SW	SW	SW		SW	SW	SW	SW ■1	SW ■1	SW	SW	SW
London Waterloo 15 ⊖	d	11 28		11 33	11 37	11 45		11 50				11 52	11 58		12 03	12 07		12 15	12 20				12 22	12 28	
Vauxhall ⊖	d	11 32		11 37	11 41	11 49						11 56	12 02		12 07	12 11		12 19					12 26	12 32	
Queenstown Rd.(Battersea)	d			11 40	11 44	11 52						11 59			12 10	12 14		12 22					12 29		
Clapham Junction 10	d	11 38		11 43	11 47	11 55		11 58				12 02	12 08		12 13	12 17		12 25	12 28				12 32	12 38	
Wandsworth Town	d			11 46	11 50	11 58						12 05			12 16	12 20		12 28					12 35		
Putney	d	11 42		11 49	11 53	12 01						12 08	12 12		12 19	12 23		12 31					12 38	12 42	
Barnes	d			11 52	11 57	12 05						12 12			12 22	12 27		12 35					12 42		
Barnes Bridge	d				11 59							12 14				12 29							12 44		
Chiswick	d				12 02							12 17				12 32							12 47		
Kew Bridge	d				12 05							12 20				12 35							12 50		
Brentford	d				12 08							12 23				12 38							12 53		
Syon Lane	d				12 10							12 25				12 40							12 55		
Isleworth	d				12 12							12 27				12 42							12 57		
Hounslow	d				12 18							12 31				12 48							13 01		
Mortlake	d			11 54		12 07									12 24			12 37							
North Sheen	d			11 56		12 09			←						12 26			12 39		←					
Richmond ⊖	d	11 48		11 59		12 12		12 06	12 12				12 18		12 29			12 42	12 36	12 42				12 48	
St Margarets	d			12 01		→			12 14						12 31			→		12 44					
Twickenham	a	11 51		12 03				12 10	12 16				12 21		12 33				12 40	12 46				12 51	
	d	11 52		12 04				12 10	12 17				12 22		12 34				12 40	12 47				12 52	
Strawberry Hill	d			12 07											12 37										
Fulwell	a																								
Teddington	a			12 10											12 40										
Hampton Wick	a			12 14											12 44										
Kingston	a			12 16											12 46										
Whitton	d	11 55	←		12a23				12a20				12 25	←		12a53				12a50				12 55	←
Feltham	d	11 59	12 06					12 16				12 36	12 29	12 36					12 46				13 06	12 59	13 06
Ashford (Surrey)	d	12 03	12 10									→	12 33	12 40									→	13 03	13 10
Staines	d	12 07	12 14					12 23					12 37	12 44					12 53					13 07	13 14
Wraysbury	d	12 11											12 41											13 11	
Sunnymeads	d	12 14											12 44											13 14	
Datchet	d	12 17											12 47											13 17	
Windsor & Eton Riverside	a	12 21											12 51											13 21	
Egham	d		12 19					12 27						12 49					12 57						13 19
Virginia Water	a		12 23					12 31						12 53					13 01						13 23
	d		12 23					12 31						12 53					13 01						13 23
Chertsey	d		12 29											12 59											13 29
Addlestone	d		12 32											13 02											13 32
Weybridge	a		12 37											13 07											13 37
Longcross	d							12 35											13 05						
Sunningdale	d							12 38											13 08						
Ascot 3	d							12 43		12 53									13 13		13 23				
Bagshot	d									12 59											13 29				
Camberley	a									13 05											13 35				
Frimley	d									13 13											13 43				
Ash Vale	d									13 19											13 49				
Aldershot	a									13 24											13 54				
	d										13 40											14 10			
Ash 5	d										13 47											14 17			
Wanborough	d										13 50											14 20			
Guildford	a										13 57											14 27			
Martins Heron	d							12 47											13 17						
Bracknell	d							12 50											13 20						
Wokingham	d							12 57											13 27						
Winnersh	d							13 00											13 30						
Winnersh Triangle	d							13 02											13 32						
Earley	d							13 05											13 35						
Reading 7	a							13 11											13 41						

The xx15 and xx45 services from London Waterloo to Whitton continue to London Waterloo via Brentford

The xx03 and xx33 London Waterloo to Kingston services continue to London Waterloo via Wimbledon

The xx07 and xx37 services from London Waterloo to Whitton continue to London Waterloo via Richmond

For additional services between Wokingham and Reading refer to Table T148

Table T149-F

Saturdays
21 December to 16 May

London - Hounslow, Richmond, Kingston, Windsor, Weybridge, Ascot, Guildford and Reading

		SW		SW	SW	SW	SW	SW 1	SW 1	SW	SW	SW		SW	SW	SW	SW	SW	SW 1	SW 1	SW	SW		SW	SW
London Waterloo 15	⊖ d	12 33		12 37	12 45	12 50				12 52	12 58			13 03	13 07	13 15	13 20				13 22	13 28			13 33
Vauxhall	⊖ d	12 37		12 41	12 49					12 56	13 02			13 07	13 11	13 19					13 26	13 32			13 37
Queenstown Rd.(Battersea)	d	12 40		12 44	12 52					12 59				13 10	13 14	13 22					13 29				13 40
Clapham Junction 10	d	12 43		12 47	12 55	12 58				13 02	13 08			13 13	13 17	13 25	13 28				13 32	13 38			13 43
Wandsworth Town	d	12 46		12 50	12 58					13 05				13 16	13 20	13 28					13 35				13 46
Putney	d	12 49		12 53	13 01					13 08	13 12			13 19	13 23	13 31					13 38	13 42			13 49
Barnes	d	12 52		12 57	13 05					13 12				13 22	13 27	13 35					13 42				13 52
Barnes Bridge	d			12 59						13 14					13 29						13 44				
Chiswick	d			13 02						13 17					13 32						13 47				
Kew Bridge	d			13 05						13 20					13 35						13 50				
Brentford	d			13 08						13 23					13 38						13 53				
Syon Lane	d			13 10						13 25					13 40						13 55				
Isleworth	d			13 12						13 27					13 42						13 57				
Hounslow	d			13 18						13 31					13 48						14 01				
Mortlake	d	12 54			13 07									13 24		13 37									13 54
North Sheen	d	12 56			13 09		←							13 26		13 39		←							13 56
Richmond	⊖ d	12 59			13 12	13 06	13 12				13 18			13 29		13 42	13 36	13 42				13 48			13 59
St Margarets	d	13 01			→		13 14							13 31		→		13 44							14 01
Twickenham	a	13 03				13 10	13 16				13 21			13 33			13 40	13 46				13 51			14 03
	d	13 04				13 10	13 17				13 22			13 34			13 40	13 47				13 52			14 04
Strawberry Hill	d	13 07												13 37											14 07
Fulwell	a																								
Teddington	a	13 10												13 40											14 10
Hampton Wick	a	13 14												13 44											14 14
Kingston	a	13 16												13 46											14 16
Whitton	d			13a23			13a20				13 25	←			13a53			13a50				13 55		←	
Feltham	d					13 16				13 36	13 29	13 36					13 46				14 06	13 59		14 06	
Ashford (Surrey)	d									→	13 33	13 40									→	14 03		14 10	
Staines	d					13 23					13 37	13 44					13 53					14 07		14 14	
Wraysbury	d										13 41											14 11			
Sunnymeads	d										13 44											14 14			
Datchet	d										13 47											14 17			
Windsor & Eton Riverside	a										13 51											14 21			
Egham	d					13 27						13 49					13 57							14 19	
Virginia Water	a					13 31						13 53					14 01							14 23	
	d					13 31						13 53					14 01							14 23	
Chertsey	d											13 59												14 29	
Addlestone	d											14 02												14 32	
Weybridge	a											14 07												14 37	
Longcross	d					13 35											14 05								
Sunningdale	d					13 38											14 08								
Ascot 3	d					13 43		13 53									14 13		14 23						
Bagshot	d							13 59											14 29						
Camberley	a							14 05											14 35						
Frimley	d							14 13											14 43						
Ash Vale	d							14 19											14 49						
Aldershot	a							14 24											14 54						
	d								14 40											15 10					
Ash 5	d								14 47											15 17					
Wanborough	d								14 50											15 20					
Guildford	a								14 57											15 27					
Martins Heron	d					13 47											14 17								
Bracknell	d					13 50											14 20								
Wokingham	d					13 57											14 27								
Winnersh	d					14 00											14 30								
Winnersh Triangle	d					14 02											14 32								
Earley	d					14 05											14 35								
Reading 7	a					14 11											14 41								

The xx15 and xx45 services from London Waterloo to Whitton continue to London Waterloo via Brentford

The xx03 and xx33 London Waterloo to Kingston services continue to London Waterloo via Wimbledon

The xx07 and xx37 services from London Waterloo to Whitton continue to London Waterloo via Richmond

For additional services between Wokingham and Reading refer to Table T148

Table T149-F

Saturdays
21 December to 16 May

London - Hounslow, Richmond, Kingston, Windsor, Weybridge, Ascot, Guildford and Reading

		SW	SW	SW	SW	SW 1	SW 1	SW		SW	SW	SW	SW	SW	SW	SW	SW 1	SW 1		SW	SW	SW	SW	SW	SW
London Waterloo 15	⊖ d	13 37	13 45	13 50				13 52		13 58		14 03	14 07	14 15	14 20					14 22	14 28		14 33	14 37	14 45
Vauxhall	⊖ d	13 41	13 49					13 56		14 02		14 07	14 11	14 19						14 26	14 32		14 37	14 41	14 49
Queenstown Rd.(Battersea)	d	13 44	13 52					13 59				14 10	14 14	14 22						14 29			14 40	14 44	14 52
Clapham Junction 10	d	13 47	13 55	13 58				14 02		14 08		14 13	14 17	14 25	14 28					14 32	14 38		14 43	14 47	14 55
Wandsworth Town	d	13 50	13 58					14 05				14 16	14 20	14 28						14 35			14 46	14 50	14 58
Putney	d	13 53	14 01					14 08		14 12		14 19	14 23	14 31						14 38	14 42		14 49	14 53	15 01
Barnes	d	13 57	14 05					14 12				14 22	14 27	14 35						14 42			14 52	14 57	15 05
Barnes Bridge	d	13 59						14 14					14 29							14 44				14 59	
Chiswick	d	14 02						14 17					14 32							14 47				15 02	
Kew Bridge	d	14 05						14 20					14 35							14 50				15 05	
Brentford	d	14 08						14 23					14 38							14 53				15 08	
Syon Lane	d	14 10						14 25					14 40							14 55				15 10	
Isleworth	d	14 12						14 27					14 42							14 57				15 12	
Hounslow	d	14 18						14 31					14 48							15 01				15 18	
Mortlake	d		14 07									14 24		14 37									14 54		15 07
North Sheen	d		14 09		←							14 26		14 39		←							14 56		15 09
Richmond	⊖ d		14 12	14 06	14 12					14 18		14 29		14 42	14 36	14 42					14 48		14 59		15 12
St Margarets	d		→		14 14							14 31		→		14 44							15 01		→
Twickenham	a			14 10	14 16					14 21		14 33			14 40	14 46					14 51		15 03		
	d			14 10	14 17					14 22		14 34			14 40	14 47					14 52		15 04		
Strawberry Hill	d											14 37											15 07		
Fulwell	a																								
Teddington	a											14 40											15 10		
Hampton Wick	a											14 44											15 14		
Kingston	a											14 46											15 16		
Whitton	d	14a23			14a20					14 25	←		14a53			14a50					14 55	←		15a23	
Feltham	d			14 16				14 36		14 29	14 36				14 46					15 06	14 59	15 06			
Ashford (Surrey)	d							→		14 33	14 40									→	15 03	15 10			
Staines	d			14 23						14 37	14 44				14 53						15 07	15 14			
Wraysbury	d									14 41											15 11				
Sunnymeads	d									14 44											15 14				
Datchet	d									14 47											15 17				
Windsor & Eton Riverside	a									14 51											15 21				
Egham	d			14 27							14 49				14 57							15 19			
Virginia Water	a			14 31							14 53				15 01							15 23			
	d			14 31							14 53				15 01							15 23			
Chertsey	d										14 59											15 29			
Addlestone	d										15 02											15 32			
Weybridge	a										15 07											15 37			
Longcross	d			14 35											15 05										
Sunningdale	d			14 38											15 08										
Ascot 3	d			14 43		14 53									15 13		15 23								
Bagshot	d					14 59											15 29								
Camberley	a					15 05											15 35								
Frimley	d					15 13											15 43								
Ash Vale	d					15 19											15 49								
Aldershot	a					15 24											15 54								
	d						15 40											16 10							
Ash 5	d						15 47											16 17							
Wanborough	d						15 50											16 20							
Guildford	a						15 57											16 27							
Martins Heron	d			14 47											15 17										
Bracknell	d			14 50											15 20										
Wokingham	d			14 57											15 27										
Winnersh	d			15 00											15 30										
Winnersh Triangle	d			15 02											15 32										
Earley	d			15 05											15 35										
Reading 7	a			15 11											15 41										

The xx15 and xx45 services from London Waterloo to Whitton continue to London Waterloo via Brentford

The xx03 and xx33 London Waterloo to Kingston services continue to London Waterloo via Wimbledon

The xx07 and xx37 services from London Waterloo to Whitton continue to London Waterloo via Richmond

For additional services between Wokingham and Reading refer to Table T148

Table T149-F

Saturdays

21 December to 16 May

London - Hounslow, Richmond, Kingston, Windsor, Weybridge, Ascot, Guildford and Reading

		SW	SW	SW ■1		SW ■1	SW	SW	SW	SW	SW	SW	SW	SW		SW ■1	SW ■1	SW	SW	SW	SW	SW	SW	SW
London Waterloo ■15 ⊖	d	14 50					14 52	14 58		15 03	15 07	15 15	15 20					15 22	15 28		15 33	15 37	15 45	15 50
Vauxhall ⊖	d						14 56	15 02		15 07	15 11	15 19						15 26	15 32		15 37	15 41	15 49	
Queenstown Rd.(Battersea)	d						14 59			15 10	15 14	15 22						15 29			15 40	15 44	15 52	
Clapham Junction ■10	d	14 58					15 02	15 08		15 13	15 17	15 25	15 28					15 32	15 38		15 43	15 47	15 55	15 58
Wandsworth Town	d						15 05			15 16	15 20	15 28						15 35			15 46	15 50	15 58	
Putney	d						15 08	15 12		15 19	15 23	15 31						15 38	15 42		15 49	15 53	16 01	
Barnes	d						15 12			15 22	15 27	15 35						15 42			15 52	15 57	16 05	
Barnes Bridge	d						15 14				15 29							15 44				15 59		
Chiswick	d						15 17				15 32							15 47				16 02		
Kew Bridge	d						15 20				15 35							15 50				16 05		
Brentford	d						15 23				15 38							15 53				16 08		
Syon Lane	d						15 25				15 40							15 55				16 10		
Isleworth	d						15 27				15 42							15 57				16 12		
Hounslow	d						15 31				15 48							16 01				16 18		
Mortlake	d									15 24		15 37									15 54		16 07	
North Sheen	d		←							15 26		15 39		←							15 56		16 09	
Richmond ⊖	d	15 06	15 12					15 18		15 29		15 42	15 36	15 42					15 48		15 59		16 12	16 06
St Margarets	d		15 14							15 31		→		15 44							16 01		→	
Twickenham	a	15 10	15 16					15 21		15 33			15 40	15 46					15 51		16 03			16 10
	d	15 10	15 17					15 22		15 34			15 40	15 47					15 52		16 04			16 10
Strawberry Hill	d									15 37											16 07			
Fulwell	a																							
Teddington	a									15 40											16 10			
Hampton Wick	a									15 44											16 14			
Kingston	a									15 46											16 16			
Whitton	d		15a20					15 25	←		15a53			15a50					15 55	←		16a23		
Feltham	d	15 16					15 36	15 29	15 36				15 46					16 06	15 59	16 06				16 16
Ashford (Surrey)	d						→	15 33	15 40									→	16 03	16 10				
Staines	d	15 23						15 37	15 44				15 53						16 07	16 14				16 23
Wraysbury	d							15 41											16 11					
Sunnymeads	d							15 44											16 14					
Datchet	d							15 47											16 17					
Windsor & Eton Riverside	a							15 51											16 21					
Egham	d	15 27							15 49				15 57							16 19				16 27
Virginia Water	a	15 31							15 53				16 01							16 23				16 31
	d	15 31							15 53				16 01							16 23				16 31
Chertsey	d								15 59											16 29				
Addlestone	d								16 02											16 32				
Weybridge	a								16 07											16 37				
Longcross	d	15 35											16 05											16 35
Sunningdale	d	15 38											16 08											16 38
Ascot ■3	d	15 43		15 53									16 13			16 23								16 43
Bagshot	d			15 59												16 29								
Camberley	a			16 05												16 35								
Frimley	d			16 13												16 43								
Ash Vale	d			16 19												16 49								
Aldershot	a			16 24												16 54								
	d					16 40											17 10							
Ash ■5	d					16 47											17 17							
Wanborough	d					16 50											17 20							
Guildford	a					16 57											17 27							
Martins Heron	d	15 47											16 17											16 47
Bracknell	d	15 50											16 20											16 50
Wokingham	d	15 57											16 27											16 57
Winnersh	d	16 00											16 30											17 00
Winnersh Triangle	d	16 02											16 32											17 02
Earley	d	16 05											16 35											17 05
Reading ■7	a	16 11											16 41											17 11

The xx15 and xx45 services from London Waterloo to Whitton continue to London Waterloo via Brentford

The xx03 and xx33 London Waterloo to Kingston services continue to London Waterloo via Wimbledon

The xx07 and xx37 services from London Waterloo to Whitton continue to London Waterloo via Richmond

For additional services between Wokingham and Reading refer to Table T148

Table T149-F

Saturdays

21 December to 16 May

London - Hounslow, Richmond, Kingston, Windsor, Weybridge, Ascot, Guildford and Reading

		SW	SW ■1	SW ■1	SW	SW	SW	SW	SW	SW		SW	SW	SW ■1	SW ■1	SW	SW	SW	SW	SW		SW	SW	SW	SW ■1
London Waterloo ■15 ⊖	d				15 52	15 58		16 03	16 07	16 15		16 20				16 22	16 28		16 33	16 37		16 45	16 50		
Vauxhall ⊖	d				15 56	16 02		16 07	16 11	16 19						16 26	16 32		16 37	16 41		16 49			
Queenstown Rd.(Battersea)	d				15 59			16 10	16 14	16 22						16 29			16 40	16 44		16 52			
Clapham Junction ■10	d				16 02	16 08		16 13	16 17	16 25		16 28				16 32	16 38		16 43	16 47		16 55	16 58		
Wandsworth Town	d				16 05			16 16	16 20	16 28						16 35			16 46	16 50		16 58			
Putney	d				16 08	16 12		16 19	16 23	16 31						16 38	16 42		16 49	16 53		17 01			
Barnes	d				16 12			16 22	16 27	16 35						16 42			16 52	16 57		17 05			
Barnes Bridge	d				16 14				16 29							16 44				16 59					
Chiswick	d				16 17				16 32							16 47				17 02					
Kew Bridge	d				16 20				16 35							16 50				17 05					
Brentford	d				16 23				16 38							16 53				17 08					
Syon Lane	d				16 25				16 40							16 55				17 10					
Isleworth	d				16 27				16 42							16 57				17 12					
Hounslow	d				16 31				16 48							17 01				17 18					
Mortlake	d							16 24		16 37									16 54			17 07			
North Sheen	d	←						16 26		16 39			←						16 56			17 09		←	
Richmond ⊖	d	16 12				16 18		16 29		16 42		16 36	16 42				16 48		16 59			17 12	17 06	17 12	
St Margarets	d	16 14						16 31		→			16 44						17 01			→		17 14	
Twickenham	a	16 16				16 21		16 33				16 40	16 46				16 51		17 03				17 10	17 16	
	d	16 17				16 22		16 34				16 40	16 47				16 52		17 04				17 10	17 17	
Strawberry Hill	d							16 37											17 07						
Fulwell	a																								
Teddington	a							16 40											17 10						
Hampton Wick	a							16 44											17 14						
Kingston	a							16 46											17 16						
Whitton	d	16a20				16 25	←		16a53				16a50				16 55	←		17a23				17a20	
Feltham	d				16 36	16 29	16 36					16 46				17 06	16 59	17 06					17 16		
Ashford (Surrey)	d				→	16 33	16 40									→	17 03	17 10							
Staines	d					16 37	16 44					16 53					17 07	17 14					17 23		
Wraysbury	d					16 41											17 11								
Sunnymeads	d					16 44											17 14								
Datchet	d					16 47											17 17								
Windsor & Eton Riverside	a					16 51											17 21								
Egham	d						16 49					16 57						17 19					17 27		
Virginia Water	a						16 53					17 01						17 23					17 31		
	d						16 53					17 01						17 23					17 31		
Chertsey	d						16 59											17 29							
Addlestone	d						17 02											17 32							
Weybridge	a						17 07											17 37							
Longcross	d											17 05											17 35		
Sunningdale	d											17 08											17 38		
Ascot ■3	d		16 53									17 13		17 23									17 43		17 53
Bagshot	d		16 59											17 29											17 59
Camberley	a		17 05											17 35											18 05
Frimley	d		17 13											17 43											18 13
Ash Vale	d		17 19											17 49											18 19
Aldershot	a		17 24											17 54											18 24
	d			17 40											18 10										
Ash ■5	d			17 47											18 17										
Wanborough	d			17 50											18 20										
Guildford	a			17 57											18 27										
Martins Heron	d											17 17											17 47		
Bracknell	d											17 20											17 50		
Wokingham	d											17 27											17 57		
Winnersh	d											17 30											18 00		
Winnersh Triangle	d											17 32											18 02		
Earley	d											17 35											18 05		
Reading ■7	a											17 41											18 11		

The xx15 and xx45 services from London Waterloo to Whitton continue to London Waterloo via Brentford

The xx03 and xx33 London Waterloo to Kingston services continue to London Waterloo via Wimbledon

The xx07 and xx37 services from London Waterloo to Whitton continue to London Waterloo via Richmond

For additional services between Wokingham and Reading refer to Table T148

Table T149-F

Saturdays

21 December to 16 May

London - Hounslow, Richmond, Kingston, Windsor, Weybridge, Ascot, Guildford and Reading

Station		SW 1	SW	SW	SW	SW		SW	SW	SW	SW	SW 1	SW 1	SW	SW	SW		SW	SW	SW	SW	SW	SW 1	SW 1	SW
London Waterloo 15 ⊖	d		16 52	16 58		17 03		17 07	17 15	17 20				17 22	17 28			17 33	17 37	17 45	17 50				17 52
Vauxhall ⊖	d		16 56	17 02		17 07		17 11	17 19					17 26	17 32			17 37	17 41	17 49					17 56
Queenstown Rd.(Battersea)	d		16 59			17 10		17 14	17 22					17 29				17 40	17 44	17 52					17 59
Clapham Junction 10	d		17 02	17 08		17 13		17 17	17 25	17 28				17 32	17 38			17 43	17 47	17 55	17 58				18 02
Wandsworth Town	d		17 05			17 16		17 20	17 28					17 35				17 46	17 50	17 58					18 05
Putney	d		17 08	17 12		17 19		17 23	17 31					17 38	17 42			17 49	17 53	18 01					18 08
Barnes	d		17 12			17 22		17 27	17 35					17 42				17 52	17 57	18 05					18 12
Barnes Bridge	d		17 14					17 29						17 44					17 59						18 14
Chiswick	d		17 17					17 32						17 47					18 02						18 17
Kew Bridge	d		17 20					17 35						17 50					18 05						18 20
Brentford	d		17 23					17 38						17 53					18 08						18 23
Syon Lane	d		17 25					17 40						17 55					18 10						18 25
Isleworth	d		17 27					17 42						17 57					18 12						18 27
Hounslow	d		17 31					17 48						18 01					18 18						18 31
Mortlake	d					17 24			17 37									17 54		18 07					
North Sheen	d					17 26			17 39		←							17 56		18 09		←			
Richmond ⊖	d			17 18		17 29			17 42	17 36	17 42				17 48			17 59		18 12	18 06	18 12			
St Margarets	d					17 31			→		17 44							18 01		→		18 14			
Twickenham	a			17 21		17 33				17 40	17 46				17 51			18 03			18 10	18 16			
	d			17 22		17 34				17 40	17 47				17 52			18 04			18 10	18 17			
Strawberry Hill	d					17 37												18 07							
Fulwell	a																								
Teddington	a					17 40												18 10							
Hampton Wick	a					17 44												18 14							
Kingston	a					17 46												18 16							
Whitton	d			17 25	←			17a53			17a50				17 55	←			18a23			18a20			
Feltham	d		17 36	17 29	17 36					17 46				18 06	17 59	18 06					18 16				18 36
Ashford (Surrey)	d		→	17 33	17 40									→	18 03	18 10									→
Staines	d			17 37	17 44					17 53					18 07	18 14					18 23				
Wraysbury	d			17 41											18 11										
Sunnymeads	d			17 44											18 14										
Datchet	d			17 47											18 17										
Windsor & Eton Riverside	a			17 51											18 21										
Egham	d				17 49					17 57						18 19					18 27				
Virginia Water	a				17 53					18 01						18 23					18 31				
	d				17 53					18 01						18 23					18 31				
Chertsey	d				17 59											18 29									
Addlestone	d				18 02											18 32									
Weybridge	a				18 07											18 37									
Longcross	d									18 05											18 35				
Sunningdale	d									18 08											18 38				
Ascot 3	d									18 13		18 23									18 43		18 53		
Bagshot	d											18 29											18 59		
Camberley	a											18 35											19 05		
Frimley	d											18 43											19 13		
Ash Vale	d											18 49											19 19		
Aldershot	a											18 54											19 24		
	d	18 40											19 10											19 40	
Ash 5	d	18 47											19 17											19 47	
Wanborough	d	18 50											19 20											19 50	
Guildford	a	18 57											19 27											19 57	
Martins Heron	d									18 17											18 47				
Bracknell	d									18 20											18 50				
Wokingham	d									18 27											18 57				
Winnersh	d									18 30											19 00				
Winnersh Triangle	d									18 32											19 02				
Earley	d									18 35											19 05				
Reading 7	a									18 41											19 11				

The xx15 and xx45 services from London Waterloo to Whitton continue to London Waterloo via Brentford

The xx03 and xx33 London Waterloo to Kingston services continue to London Waterloo via Wimbledon

The xx07 and xx37 services from London Waterloo to Whitton continue to London Waterloo via Richmond

For additional services between Wokingham and Reading refer to Table T148

NRT DECEMBER 19 EDITION

Table T149-F

Saturdays

21 December to 16 May

London - Hounslow, Richmond, Kingston, Windsor, Weybridge, Ascot, Guildford and Reading

Station		SW		SW	SW	SW	SW	SW	SW	SW 1	SW 1	SW		SW	SW	SW	SW	SW	SW	SW	SW 1	SW 1		SW	SW
London Waterloo 15 ⊖	d	17 58			18 03	18 07	18 15	18 20				18 22		18 28		18 33	18 37	18 45	18 50					18 52	18 58
Vauxhall ⊖	d	18 02			18 07	18 11	18 19					18 26		18 32		18 37	18 41	18 49						18 56	19 02
Queenstown Rd.(Battersea)	d				18 10	18 14	18 22					18 29				18 40	18 44	18 52						18 59	
Clapham Junction 10	d	18 08			18 13	18 17	18 25	18 28				18 32		18 38		18 43	18 47	18 55	18 58					19 02	19 08
Wandsworth Town	d				18 16	18 20	18 28					18 35				18 46	18 50	18 58						19 05	
Putney	d	18 12			18 19	18 23	18 31					18 38		18 42		18 49	18 53	19 01						19 08	19 12
Barnes	d				18 22	18 27	18 35					18 42				18 52	18 57	19 05						19 12	
Barnes Bridge	d					18 29						18 44					18 59							19 14	
Chiswick	d					18 32						18 47					19 02							19 17	
Kew Bridge	d					18 35						18 50					19 05							19 20	
Brentford	d					18 38						18 53					19 08							19 23	
Syon Lane	d					18 40						18 55					19 10							19 25	
Isleworth	d					18 42						18 57					19 12							19 27	
Hounslow	d					18 48						19 01					19 18							19 31	
Mortlake	d				18 24		18 37									18 54		19 07							
North Sheen	d				18 26		18 39		←							18 56		19 09		←					
Richmond ⊖	d	18 18			18 29		18 42	18 36	18 42					18 48		18 59		19 12	19 06	19 12					19 18
St Margarets	d				18 31		→		18 44							19 01		→		19 14					
Twickenham	a	18 21			18 33			18 40	18 46					18 51		19 03			19 10	19 16					19 21
	d	18 22			18 34			18 40	18 47					18 52		19 04			19 10	19 17					19 22
Strawberry Hill	d				18 37											19 07									
Fulwell	a																								
Teddington	a				18 40											19 10									
Hampton Wick	a				18 44											19 14									
Kingston	a				18 46											19 16									
Whitton	d	18 25		←		18a53			18a50					18 55	←		19a23			19a20					19 25
Feltham	d	18 29		18 36				18 46				19 06		18 59	19 06				19 16					19 36	19 29
Ashford (Surrey)	d	18 33		18 40								→		19 03	19 10									→	19 33
Staines	d	18 37		18 44				18 53						19 07	19 14				19 23						19 37
Wraysbury	d	18 41												19 11											19 41
Sunnymeads	d	18 44												19 14											19 44
Datchet	d	18 47												19 17											19 47
Windsor & Eton Riverside	a	18 51												19 21											19 51
Egham	d			18 49				18 57							19 19				19 27						
Virginia Water	a			18 53				19 01							19 23				19 31						
	d			18 53				19 01							19 23				19 31						
Chertsey	d			18 59											19 29										
Addlestone	d			19 02											19 32										
Weybridge	a			19 07											19 37										
Longcross	d							19 05											19 35						
Sunningdale	d							19 08											19 38						
Ascot 3	d							19 13		19 23									19 43		19 53				
Bagshot	d									19 29											19 59				
Camberley	a									19 35											20 05				
Frimley	d									19 43											20 13				
Ash Vale	d									19 49											20 19				
Aldershot	a									19 54											20 24				
	d										20 10											20 40			
Ash 5	d										20 17											20 47			
Wanborough	d										20 20											20 50			
Guildford	a										20 27											20 57			
Martins Heron	d							19 17											19 47						
Bracknell	d							19 20											19 50						
Wokingham	d							19 27											19 57						
Winnersh	d							19 30											20 00						
Winnersh Triangle	d							19 32											20 02						
Earley	d							19 35											20 05						
Reading 7	a							19 41											20 11						

The xx15 and xx45 services from London Waterloo to Whitton continue to London Waterloo via Brentford

The xx03 and xx33 London Waterloo to Kingston services continue to London Waterloo via Wimbledon

The xx07 and xx37 services from London Waterloo to Whitton continue to London Waterloo via Richmond

For additional services between Wokingham and Reading refer to Table T148

Table T149-F

Saturdays

21 December to 16 May

London - Hounslow, Richmond, Kingston, Windsor, Weybridge, Ascot, Guildford and Reading

		SW	SW	SW	SW	SW	SW	SW 1		SW 1	SW	SW	SW	SW	SW	SW	SW	SW		SW 1	SW 1	SW	SW	SW	SW
London Waterloo [15] ⊖	d		19 03	19 07	19 15	19 20					19 22	19 28		19 33	19 37	19 45	19 50					19 52	19 58		20 03
Vauxhall ⊖	d		19 07	19 11	19 19						19 26	19 32		19 37	19 41	19 49						19 56	20 02		20 07
Queenstown Rd.(Battersea)	d		19 10	19 14	19 22						19 29			19 40	19 44	19 52						19 59			20 10
Clapham Junction [10]	d		19 13	19 17	19 25	19 28					19 32	19 38		19 44	19 47	19 55	19 58					20 02	20 09		20 13
Wandsworth Town	d		19 16	19 20	19 28						19 35			19 47	19 50	19 58						20 05			20 16
Putney	d		19 19	19 23	19 31						19 38	19 42		19 50	19 53	20 01						20 08	20 13		20 19
Barnes	d		19 22	19 27	19 35						19 42			19 53	19 57	20 05						20 12			20 22
Barnes Bridge	d			19 29							19 44				19 59							20 14			
Chiswick	d			19 32							19 47				20 02							20 17			
Kew Bridge	d			19 35							19 50				20 05							20 20			
Brentford	d			19 38							19 53				20 08							20 23			
Syon Lane	d			19 40							19 55				20 10							20 25			
Isleworth	d			19 42							19 57				20 12							20 27			
Hounslow	d			19 48							20 01				20 18							20 31			
Mortlake	d		19 24		19 37									19 55		20 07									20 24
North Sheen	d		19 26		19 39		←							19 57		20 09		←							20 26
Richmond ⊖	d		19 29		19 42	19 36	19 42					19 48		20 00		20 12	20 06	20 12					20 19		20 29
St Margarets	d		19 31		→		19 44							20 02		→		20 14							20 31
Twickenham	a		19 33			19 40	19 46					19 51		20 04			20 10	20 16					20 22		20 33
	d		19 34			19 40	19 47					19 52		20 05			20 10	20 17					20 23		20 34
Strawberry Hill	d		19 37											20 08											20 37
Fulwell	a																								
Teddington	a		19 40											20 11											20 40
Hampton Wick	a		19 44											20 15											20 44
Kingston	a		19 46											20 17											20 46
Whitton	d	←		19a53			19a50					19 55	←		20a23			20a20					20 26	←	
Feltham	d	19 36				19 46					20 06	19 59	20 06				20 16					20 36	20 30	20 36	
Ashford (Surrey)	d	19 40									→	20 03	20 10									→	20 34	20 40	
Staines	d	19 44				19 53						20 07	20 14				20 23						20 38	20 44	
Wraysbury	d											20 11											20 42		
Sunnymeads	d											20 14											20 45		
Datchet	d											20 17											20 48		
Windsor & Eton Riverside	a											20 21											20 52		
Egham	d	19 49				19 57							20 19				20 27							20 49	
Virginia Water	a	19 53				20 01							20 23				20 31							20 53	
	d	19 53				20 01							20 23				20 31							20 53	
Chertsey	d	19 59											20 29											20 59	
Addlestone	d	20 02											20 32											21 02	
Weybridge	a	20 07											20 37											21 07	
Longcross	d					20 05											20 35								
Sunningdale	d					20 08											20 38								
Ascot [3]	d					20 13		20 23									20 43			20 53					
Bagshot	d							20 29												20 59					
Camberley	a							20 35												21 05					
Frimley	d							20 43												21 13					
Ash Vale	d							20 49												21 19					
Aldershot	a							20 54												21 24					
	d									21 10											21 40				
Ash [5]	d									21 17											21 47				
Wanborough	d									21 20											21 50				
Guildford	a									21 27											21 57				
Martins Heron	d					20 17											20 47								
Bracknell	d					20 20											20 50								
Wokingham	d					20 27											20 57								
Winnersh	d					20 30											21 00								
Winnersh Triangle	d					20 32											21 02								
Earley	d					20 35											21 05								
Reading [7]	a					20 41											21 11								

The xx15 and xx45 services from London Waterloo to Whitton continue to London Waterloo via Brentford

The xx03 and xx33 London Waterloo to Kingston services continue to London Waterloo via Wimbledon

The xx07 and xx37 services from London Waterloo to Whitton continue to London Waterloo via Richmond

For additional services between Wokingham and Reading refer to Table T148

Table T149-F

Saturdays

21 December to 16 May

London - Hounslow, Richmond, Kingston, Windsor, Weybridge, Ascot, Guildford and Reading

		SW	SW	SW		SW	SW 1	SW 1	SW	SW	SW	SW	SW	SW		SW	SW	SW 1	SW 1	SW	SW	SW	SW	SW	
London Waterloo [15] ⊖	d	20 07	20 15	20 20					20 22	20 28		20 33	20 37	20 45		20 50				20 52	20 58		21 03	21 07	
Vauxhall ⊖	d	20 11	20 19						20 26	20 32		20 37	20 41	20 49						20 56	21 02		21 07	21 11	
Queenstown Rd.(Battersea)	d	20 14	20 22						20 29			20 40	20 44	20 52						20 59			21 10	21 14	
Clapham Junction [10]	d	20 17	20 26	20 28					20 32	20 38		20 43	20 47	20 55		20 58				21 02	21 08		21 13	21 17	
Wandsworth Town	d	20 20	20 29						20 35			20 46	20 50	20 58						21 05			21 16	21 20	
Putney	d	20 23	20 32						20 38	20 42		20 49	20 53	21 01						21 08	21 12		21 19	21 23	
Barnes	d	20 27	20 35						20 42			20 52	20 57	21 05						21 12			21 22	21 27	
Barnes Bridge	d	20 29							20 44				20 59							21 14				21 29	
Chiswick	d	20 32							20 47				21 02							21 17				21 32	
Kew Bridge	d	20 35							20 50				21 05							21 20				21 35	
Brentford	d	20 38							20 53				21 08							21 23				21 38	
Syon Lane	d	20 40							20 55				21 10							21 25				21 40	
Isleworth	d	20 42							20 57				21 12							21 27				21 42	
Hounslow	d	20 48							21 01				21 18							21 31				21 48	
Mortlake	d		20 37									20 54		21 07									21 24		
North Sheen	d		20 39			←						20 56		21 09			←						21 26		
Richmond ⊖	d		20 42	20 36		20 42				20 48		20 59		21 12		21 06	21 12				21 18		21 29		
St Margarets	d		→			20 44						21 01		→			21 14						21 31		
Twickenham	a			20 40		20 46				20 51		21 03				21 10	21 16				21 21		21 33		
	d			20 40		20 47				20 52		21 04				21 10	21 17				21 22		21 34		
Strawberry Hill	d											21 07											21 37		
Fulwell	a																								
Teddington	a											21 10											21 40		
Hampton Wick	a											21 14											21 44		
Kingston	a											21 16											21 46		
Whitton	d	20a53				20a50				20 55	←		21a23				21a20				21 25	←		21a53	
Feltham	d			20 46					21 06	20 59	21 06					21 16				21 36	21 29	21 36			
Ashford (Surrey)	d								→	21 03	21 10									→	21 33	21 40			
Staines	d			20 53						21 07	21 14					21 23					21 37	21 44			
Wraysbury	d									21 11											21 41				
Sunnymeads	d									21 14											21 44				
Datchet	d									21 17											21 47				
Windsor & Eton Riverside	a									21 21											21 51				
Egham	d			20 57							21 19					21 27						21 49			
Virginia Water	a			21 01							21 23					21 31						21 53			
	d			21 01							21 23					21 31						21 53			
Chertsey	d										21 29											21 59			
Addlestone	d										21 32											22 02			
Weybridge	a										21 37											22 07			
Longcross	d			21 05																					
Sunningdale	d			21 08												21 37									
Ascot [3]	d			21 13			21 23									21 43		21 53							
Bagshot	d						21 29											21 59							
Camberley	a						21 35											22 05							
Frimley	d						21 43											22 13							
Ash Vale	d						21 49											22 19							
Aldershot	a						21 54											22 24							
	d							22 10											22 40						
Ash [5]	d							22 17											22 47						
Wanborough	d							22 20											22 50						
Guildford	a							22 27											22 57						
Martins Heron	d			21 17												21 47									
Bracknell	d			21 20												21 50									
Wokingham	d			21 27												21 57									
Winnersh	d			21 30												22 00									
Winnersh Triangle	d			21 32												22 02									
Earley	d			21 35												22 05									
Reading [7]	a			21 41												22 11									

The xx15 and xx45 services from London Waterloo to Whitton continue to London Waterloo via Brentford

The xx03 and xx33 London Waterloo to Kingston services continue to London Waterloo via Wimbledon

The xx07 and xx37 services from London Waterloo to Whitton continue to London Waterloo via Richmond

For additional services between Wokingham and Reading refer to Table T148

Table T149-F

Saturdays
21 December to 16 May

London - Hounslow, Richmond, Kingston, Windsor, Weybridge, Ascot, Guildford and Reading

		SW	SW	SW	SW 1	SW 1	SW	SW	SW	SW	SW	SW	SW	SW	SW 1	SW	SW	SW	SW	SW	SW 1	SW	SW
London Waterloo 15 ⊖	d	21 15	21 20				21 22	21 28		21 33	21 37	21 45	21 50			21 52	21 58		22 03	22 20		22 22	22 28
Vauxhall ⊖	d	21 19					21 26	21 32		21 37	21 41	21 49				21 56	22 02		22 07			22 26	22 32
Queenstown Rd.(Battersea)	d	21 22					21 29			21 40	21 44	21 52				21 59			22 10			22 29	
Clapham Junction 10	d	21 25	21 28				21 32	21 38		21 43	21 47	21 55	21 58			22 02	22 08		22 13	22 28		22 32	22 38
Wandsworth Town	d	21 28					21 35			21 46	21 50	21 58				22 05			22 16			22 35	
Putney	d	21 31					21 38	21 42		21 49	21 53	22 01				22 08	22 12		22 19			22 38	22 42
Barnes	d	21 35					21 42			21 52	21 57	22 05				22 12			22 22			22 42	
Barnes Bridge	d						21 44				21 59					22 14						22 44	
Chiswick	d						21 47				22 02					22 17						22 47	
Kew Bridge	d						21 50				22 05					22 20						22 50	
Brentford	d						21 53				22 08					22 23						22 53	
Syon Lane	d						21 55				22 10					22 25						22 55	
Isleworth	d						21 57				22 12					22 27						22 57	
Hounslow	d						22 01				22 18					22 31						23 01	
Mortlake	d	21 37								21 54		22 07							22 24				
North Sheen	d	21 39		←						21 56		22 09		←					22 26				
Richmond ⊖	d	21 42	21 36	21 42				21 48		21 59		22 12	22 06	22 12			22 18		22 29	22 36			22 48
St Margarets	d	→		21 44						22 01		→		22 14					22 31				
Twickenham	a		21 40	21 46				21 51		22 03			22 10	22 16			22 21		22 33	22 40			22 51
	d		21 40	21 47				21 52		22 04			22 10				22 22		22 34	22 40			22 52
Strawberry Hill	d									22 07									22 37				
Fulwell	a																						
Teddington	a									22 10									22 40				
Hampton Wick	a									22 14									22 44				
Kingston	a									22 16									22 46				
Whitton	d			21a50				21 55	←		22a23						22 25	←					22 55
Feltham	d		21 46				22 06	21 59	22 06				22 16			22 36	22 29	22 36		22 46		23 06	22 59
Ashford (Surrey)	d						→	22 03	22 10							→	22 33	22 40				→	23 03
Staines	d		21 53					22 07	22 14				22 23				22 37	22 44		22 53			23 07
Wraysbury	d							22 11									22 41						23 11
Sunnymeads	d							22 14									22 44						23 14
Datchet	d							22 17									22 47						23 17
Windsor & Eton Riverside	a							22 21									22 51						23 21
Egham	d		21 57						22 19				22 27					22 49		22 57			
Virginia Water	a		22 01						22 23				22 31					22 53		23 01			
	d		22 01						22 23				22 31					22 53		23 01			
Chertsey	d								22 29									22 59					
Addlestone	d								22 32									23 02					
Weybridge	a								22 37									23 07					
Longcross	d																						
Sunningdale	d		22 07										22 37							23 07			
Ascot 3	d		22 13		22 23								22 43		22 53					23 13	23 23		
Bagshot	d				22 29										22 59						23 29		
Camberley	a				22 35										23 05						23 35		
Frimley	d				22 43										23 13						23 43		
Ash Vale	d				22 49										23 19						23 49		
Aldershot	a				22 54										23 24						23 54		
	d					23 10																	
Ash 5	d					23 17																	
Wanborough	d					23 20																	
Guildford	a					23 27																	
Martins Heron	d		22 17										22 47							23 17			
Bracknell	d		22 20										22 50							23 20			
Wokingham	d		22 27										22 57							23 27			
Winnersh	d		22 30										23 00							23 30			
Winnersh Triangle	d		22 32										23 02							23 32			
Earley	d		22 35										23 05							23 35			
Reading 7	a		22 41										23 11							23 41			

The xx15 and xx45 services from London Waterloo to Whitton continue to London Waterloo via Brentford

The xx03 and xx33 London Waterloo to Kingston services continue to London Waterloo via Wimbledon

The xx07 and xx37 services from London Waterloo to Whitton continue to London Waterloo via Richmond

For additional services between Wokingham and Reading refer to Table T148

Table T149-F

Saturdays
21 December to 16 May

London - Hounslow, Richmond, Kingston, Windsor, Weybridge, Ascot, Guildford and Reading

		SW	SW	SW	SW 1	SW	SW	SW	SW	SW	SW	SW	SW	SW	SW	SW	SW	SW
London Waterloo 15 ⊖	d		22 33	22 50		22 52	22 58		23 03	23 20	23 22	23 28		23 33	23 50	23 52	23 58	
Vauxhall ⊖	d		22 37			22 56	23 02		23 07		23 26	23 32		23 37		23 56	00 02	
Queenstown Rd.(Battersea)	d		22 40			22 59			23 10		23 29			23 40		23 59		
Clapham Junction 10	d		22 43	22 58		23 02	23 08		23 13	23 28	23 32	23 38		23 43	23 58	00 02	00 08	
Wandsworth Town	d		22 46			23 05			23 16		23 35			23 46		00 05		
Putney	d		22 49			23 08	23 12		23 19		23 38	23 42		23 49		00 08	00 12	
Barnes	d		22 52			23 12			23 22		23 42			23 52		00 12		
Barnes Bridge	d					23 14					23 44					00 14		
Chiswick	d					23 17					23 47					00 17		
Kew Bridge	d					23 20					23 50					00 20		
Brentford	d					23 23					23 53					00 23		
Syon Lane	d					23 25					23 55					00 25		
Isleworth	d					23 27					23 57					00 27		
Hounslow	d					23 31					00 01					00 31		
Mortlake	d		22 54						23 24					23 54				
North Sheen	d		22 56						23 26					23 56				
Richmond ⊖	d		22 59	23 06			23 18		23 29	23 36		23 48		23 59	00 06		00 18	
St Margarets	d		23 01						23 31					00 01				
Twickenham	a		23 03	23 10			23 21		23 33	23 40		23 51		00 03	00 10		00 22	
	d		23 04	23 10			23 22		23 34	23 40		23 52		00 04	00 10		00 22	
Strawberry Hill	d		23 07						23 37					00 09				
Fulwell	a																	
Teddington	a		23 10						23 41					00 12				
Hampton Wick	a		23 14						23 44					00 14				
Kingston	a		23 16						23 46					00 16				
Whitton	d	←					23 25	←				23 55	←				00 25	←
Feltham	d	23 06		23 16		23 36	23 29	23 36		23 46	00 06	23 59	00 06		00 16	00 36	00 29	00 36
Ashford (Surrey)	d	23 10				→	23 33	23 40			→	00 03	00 10			→	00 33	00 40
Staines	d	23 14		23 23			23 37	23 44		23 53		00 07	00 14		00 23		00a37	00a47
Wraysbury	d						23 41					00 11						
Sunnymeads	d						23 44					00 14						
Datchet	d						23 47					00 17						
Windsor & Eton Riverside	a						23 51					00 21						
Egham	d	23 19		23 27				23 49		23 57			00 19		00 27			
Virginia Water	a	23 23		23 31				23 53		00 01			00 23		00 31			
	d	23 23		23 31				23 53		00 01			00 23		00 31			
Chertsey	d	23 29						23 59					00 29					
Addlestone	d	23 32						00a02					00 32					
Weybridge	a	23 37											00 36					
Longcross	d																	
Sunningdale	d			23 37						00 07					00 37			
Ascot 3	d			23 43	23 53					00 13					00 42			
Bagshot	d				23 59													
Camberley	a				00 05													
Frimley	d				00 13													
Ash Vale	d				00 19													
Aldershot	a				00 24													
	d																	
Ash 5	d																	
Wanborough	d																	
Guildford	a																	
Martins Heron	d			23 47						00 17					00 46			
Bracknell	d			23 50						00 20					00 49			
Wokingham	d			23 57						00 30					00 56			
Winnersh	d			23 59						00 33								
Winnersh Triangle	d			00 02						00 35								
Earley	d			00 05						00 38								
Reading 7	a			00 11						00 44					01 04			

The xx15 and xx45 services from London Waterloo to Whitton continue to London Waterloo via Brentford

The xx03 and xx33 London Waterloo to Kingston services continue to London Waterloo via Wimbledon

The xx07 and xx37 services from London Waterloo to Whitton continue to London Waterloo via Richmond

For additional services between Wokingham and Reading refer to Table T148

Table T149-F

Sundays

15 December to 10 May

London - Hounslow, Richmond, Kingston, Windsor, Weybridge, Ascot, Guildford and Reading

		SW	SW	SW	SW	SW	SW	SW	SW	SW		SW	SW	SW	SW	SW	SW	SW	SW	SW		SW	SW	SW	SW
		A	A	A	A	A	A	A	A	1 A			1									1	1		
London Waterloo 15 ⊖	d											00 18		06 14			06 44		07 09	07 14				07 39	07 44
Vauxhall ⊖	d							00 02				00 22		06 18			06 48		07 13	07 18				07 43	07 48
Queenstown Rd.(Battersea)	d											00 28		06 21			06 51			07 21					07 51
Clapham Junction 10	d							00 08	00 02			00 31		06 24			06 54		07 19	07 24				07 49	07 54
Wandsworth Town	d								00 05			00 34		06 27			06 57			07 27					07 57
Putney	d							00 12	00 08			00 37		06 30			07 00		07 23	07 30				07 53	08 00
Barnes	d								00 12			00 40		06 33			07 03			07 33					08 03
Barnes Bridge	d								00 14																
Chiswick	d								00 17																
Kew Bridge	d								00 20																
Brentford	d								00 23																
Syon Lane	d								00 25																
Isleworth	d								00 27																
Hounslow	d					00 01			00 31																
Mortlake	d											00 42		06 35			07 05			07 35					08 05
North Sheen	d											00 44		06 37			07 07			07 37					08 07
Richmond ⊖	d						00 06	00 18				00 47		06 40			07 10		07 29	07 40				07 59	08 10
St Margarets	d	00 01										00 49		06 42			07 12			07 42					08 12
Twickenham	a	00 03					00 10	00 22				00 51		06 44			07 14		07 32	07 44				08 02	08 14
	d	00 04					00 10	00 22				00 52		06 45			07 15		07 33	07 45				08 03	08 15
Strawberry Hill	d	00 09										00s55		06 49						07 49					
Fulwell	a																								
Teddington	a	00 12										00s58		06 52						07 52					
Hampton Wick	a	00 14										01s01		06 57						07 57					
Kingston	a	00 16										01 03		06 59						07 59					
Whitton	d							00 25									07 18								08 18
Feltham	d					00 06	00 16	00 29	00 36								07 22		07 39					08 09	08 22
Ashford (Surrey)	d				00 03	00 10		00 33	00 40								07 26								08 26
Staines	d				00 07	00 14	00 23	00a37	00a47						06 32	07 15	07 30	07 40	07 45					08 15	08 30
Wraysbury	d				00 11												07 34								08 34
Sunnymeads	d				00 14												07 37								08 37
Datchet	d				00 17												07 40								08 40
Windsor & Eton Riverside	a				00 21												07 44								08 44
Egham	d					00 19	00 27								06 36	07 20		07 45	07 50					08 20	
Virginia Water	a					00 23	00 31								06 41	07 24		07 49	07 54					08 24	
	d			00 01		00 23	00 31								06 41	07 24		07 49	07 54					08 24	
Chertsey	d					00 29									06 46			07 55							
Addlestone	d					00 32									06 49			07a58							
Weybridge	a					00 36									06 53										
Longcross	d															07 27								08 27	
Sunningdale	d			00 07			00 37									07 30			08 00					08 30	
Ascot 3	d			00 13			00 42						00 46			07 35			08 05				08 13	08 35	
Bagshot	d												00 52										08 19		
Camberley	a												00 58										08 25		
Frimley	d									00 13			01 02										08 29		
Ash Vale	d									00 19			01 09										08 36		
Aldershot	a									00 24			01s14										08 41		
	d																					07 48	08 48		
Ash 5	d																					07 55	08 55		
Wanborough	d																					07 59	08 59		
Guildford	a																					08 06	09 06		
Martins Heron	d			00 17			00 46									07 39			08 09					08 39	
Bracknell	d			00 20			00 49									07 43			08 13					08 43	
Wokingham	d			00 30			00 56									07 49			08 19					08 49	
Winnersh	d			00 33												07 53			08 23					08 53	
Winnersh Triangle	d		00 02	00 35												07 55			08 25					08 55	
Earley	d		00 05	00 38												07 57			08 27					08 57	
Reading 7	a		00 11	00 44			01 04									08 02			08 32					09 02	

A not 15 December

For additional services between Wokingham and Reading refer to Table T148

Table T149-F

Sundays

15 December to 10 May

London - Hounslow, Richmond, Kingston, Windsor, Weybridge, Ascot, Guildford and Reading

		SW	SW	SW	SW	SW		SW	SW	SW	SW	SW	SW	SW	SW	SW		SW	SW	SW	SW	SW	SW	SW	SW
				1								1								1					
London Waterloo 15 ⊖	d	07 50	08 09		08 14	08 25		08 39	08 44	08 50	09 09		09 14	09 25	09 39	09 44		09 50	10 09		10 14	10 25	10 39	10 44	10 50
Vauxhall ⊖	d	07 54	08 13		08 18	08 29		08 43	08 48	08 54	09 13		09 18	09 29	09 43	09 48		09 54	10 13		10 18	10 29	10 43	10 48	10 54
Queenstown Rd.(Battersea)	d	07 57			08 21				08 51	08 57			09 21			09 51		09 57			10 21			10 51	10 57
Clapham Junction 10	d	08 00	08 19		08 24	08 35		08 49	08 54	09 00	09 19		09 24	09 35	09 49	09 54		10 00	10 19		10 24	10 35	10 49	10 54	11 00
Wandsworth Town	d	08 03			08 27				08 57	09 03			09 27			09 57		10 03			10 27			10 57	11 03
Putney	d	08 06	08 23		08 30	08 39		08 53	09 00	09 06	09 23		09 30	09 39	09 53	10 00		10 06	10 23		10 30	10 39	10 53	11 00	11 06
Barnes	d	08 09			08 33				09 03	09 09			09 33			10 03		10 09			10 33			11 03	11 09
Barnes Bridge	d	08 11								09 11								10 11							11 11
Chiswick	d	08 13								09 13								10 13							11 13
Kew Bridge	d	08 16								09 16								10 16							11 16
Brentford	d	08 19								09 19								10 19							11 19
Syon Lane	d	08 21								09 21								10 21							11 21
Isleworth	d	08 23								09 23								10 23							11 23
Hounslow	d	08 26								09 26								10 26							11 26
Mortlake	d				08 35				09 05				09 35			10 05					10 35			11 05	
North Sheen	d				08 37				09 07				09 37			10 07					10 37			11 07	
Richmond ⊖	d		08 29		08 40	08 45		08 59	09 10		09 29		09 40	09 45	09 59	10 10			10 29		10 40	10 45	10 59	11 10	
St Margarets	d				08 42				09 12				09 42			10 12					10 42			11 12	
Twickenham	a		08 32		08 44	08 48		09 02	09 14		09 32		09 44	09 48	10 02	10 14			10 32		10 44	10 48	11 02	11 14	
	d		08 33		08 45	08 49		09 03	09 15		09 33		09 45	09 49	10 03	10 15			10 33		10 45	10 49	11 03	11 15	
Strawberry Hill	d				08 49								09 49								10 49				
Fulwell	a																								
Teddington	a				08 52								09 52								10 52				
Hampton Wick	a				08 57								09 57								10 57				
Kingston	a				08 59								09 59								10 59				
Whitton	d					08 52			09 18					09 52		10 18						10 52		11 18	
Feltham	d	08 32	08 39			08 56		09 09	09 22	09 32	09 39			09 56	10 09	10 22		10 32	10 39			10 56	11 09	11 22	11 32
Ashford (Surrey)	d	08 36				09 00			09 26	09 36				10 00		10 26		10 36				11 00		11 26	11 36
Staines	d	08 40	08 45			09 04		09 15	09 30	09 40	09 45			10 04	10 15	10 30		10 40	10 45			11 04	11 15	11 30	11 40
Wraysbury	d								09 34							10 34								11 35	
Sunnymeads	d								09 37							10 37								11 38	
Datchet	d					09 12			09 40					10 12		10 40						11 12		11 42	
Windsor & Eton Riverside	a					09 16			09 44					10 16		10 44						11 16		11 46	
Egham	d	08 45	08 50					09 20		09 45	09 50				10 20			10 45	10 50				11 20		11 45
Virginia Water	a	08 49	08 54					09 24		09 49	09 54				10 24			10 49	10 54				11 24		11 49
	d	08 49	08 54					09 24		09 49	09 54				10 24			10 49	10 54				11 24		11 49
Chertsey	d	08 55								09 55								10 55							11 55
Addlestone	d	08a58								09a58								10a58							11a58
Weybridge	a																								
Longcross	d							09 27							10 27								11 27		
Sunningdale	d		09 00					09 30			10 00				10 30				11 00				11 30		
Ascot 3	d		09 05	09 13				09 35			10 05	10 13			10 35				11 05	11 13			11 35		
Bagshot	d			09 19								10 19								11 19					
Camberley	a			09 25								10 25								11 25					
Frimley	d			09 29								10 29								11 29					
Ash Vale	d			09 36								10 36								11 36					
Aldershot	a			09 41								10 41								11 41					
	d			09 48								10 48								11 48					
Ash 5	d			09 55								10 55								11 55					
Wanborough	d			09 59								10 59								11 59					
Guildford	a			10 06								11 06								12 06					
Martins Heron	d		09 09					09 39			10 09				10 39				11 09				11 39		
Bracknell	d		09 13					09 43			10 13				10 43				11 13				11 43		
Wokingham	d		09 19					09 49			10 19				10 49				11 19				11 49		
Winnersh	d		09 23					09 53			10 23				10 53				11 23				11 53		
Winnersh Triangle	d		09 25					09 55			10 25				10 55				11 25				11 55		
Earley	d		09 27					09 57			10 27				10 57				11 27				11 57		
Reading 7	a		09 32					10 02			10 32				11 02				11 32				12 02		

For additional services between Wokingham and Reading refer to Table T148

Table T149-F

Sundays

15 December to 10 May

London - Hounslow, Richmond, Kingston, Windsor, Weybridge, Ascot, Guildford and Reading

		SW	SW [1]	SW	SW	SW	SW	SW	SW	SW [1]	SW	SW	SW	SW	SW	SW	SW	SW [1]	SW	SW	SW	SW
London Waterloo [15] ⊖	d	11 09		11 14	11 25	11 39	11 44	11 50	12 09		12 14	12 25		12 39	12 44	12 50	13 09		13 14	13 25		13 39
Vauxhall ⊖	d	11 13		11 18	11 29	11 43	11 48	11 54	12 13		12 18	12 29		12 43	12 48	12 54	13 13		13 18	13 29		13 43
Queenstown Rd.(Battersea)	d			11 22			11 51	11 57			12 21				12 51	12 57			13 21			
Clapham Junction [10]	d	11 19		11 25	11 35	11 49	11 54	12 00	12 19		12 24	12 35		12 49	12 54	13 00	13 19		13 24	13 35		13 49
Wandsworth Town	d			11 28			11 57	12 03			12 27				12 57	13 03			13 27			
Putney	d	11 23		11 31	11 39	11 53	12 00	12 06	12 23		12 30	12 39		12 53	13 00	13 06	13 23		13 30	13 39		13 53
Barnes	d			11 34			12 03	12 09			12 33				13 03	13 09			13 33			
Barnes Bridge	d							12 11								13 11						
Chiswick	d							12 13								13 13						
Kew Bridge	d							12 16								13 16						
Brentford	d							12 19								13 19						
Syon Lane	d							12 21								13 21						
Isleworth	d							12 23								13 23						
Hounslow	d							12 26								13 26						
Mortlake	d			11 36			12 05				12 35				13 05				13 35			
North Sheen	d			11 38			12 07				12 37				13 07				13 37			
Richmond ⊖	d	11 29		11 41	11 45	11 59	12 10		12 29		12 40	12 45		12 59	13 10		13 29		13 40	13 45		13 59
St Margarets	d			11 43			12 12				12 42				13 12				13 42			
Twickenham	a	11 32		11 45	11 48	12 02	12 14		12 32		12 44	12 48		13 02	13 14		13 32		13 44	13 48		14 02
	d	11 33		11 45	11 49	12 03	12 15		12 33		12 45	12 49	12 56	13 03	13 15		13 33		13 45	13 49	13 56	14 03
Strawberry Hill	d			11 49							12 49								13 49			
Fulwell	a																					
Teddington	a			11 53							12 53								13 52			
Hampton Wick	a			11 57							12 57								13 57			
Kingston	a			11 59							12 59								13 59			
Whitton	d				11 52		12 18					12 52	12a59		13 18					13 52	13a59	
Feltham	d	11 39			11 56	12 09	12 22	12 32	12 39			12 56		13 09	13 22	13 32	13 39			13 56		14 09
Ashford (Surrey)	d				12 00		12 26	12 36				13 00			13 26	13 36				14 00		
Staines	d	11 45			12 04	12 15	12 30	12 40	12 45			13 04		13 15	13 30	13 40	13 45			14 04		14 15
Wraysbury	d						12 34								13 34							
Sunnymeads	d						12 37								13 37							
Datchet	d				12 12		12 40					13 12			13 40					14 12		
Windsor & Eton Riverside	a				12 16		12 44					13 16			13 44					14 16		
Egham	d	11 50				12 20		12 45	12 50					13 20		13 45	13 50					14 20
Virginia Water	a	11 54				12 24		12 49	12 54					13 24		13 49	13 54					14 24
	d	11 54				12 24		12 49	12 54					13 24		13 49	13 54					14 24
Chertsey	d							12 55								13 55						
Addlestone	d							12a58								13a58						
Weybridge	a																					
Longcross	d					12 27								13 27								14 27
Sunningdale	d	12 00				12 30			13 00					13 30			14 00					14 30
Ascot [3]	d	12 05	12 13			12 35			13 05	13 13				13 35			14 05	14 13				14 35
Bagshot	d		12 19							13 19								14 19				
Camberley	a		12 25							13 25								14 25				
Frimley	d		12 29							13 29								14 29				
Ash Vale	d		12 36							13 36								14 36				
Aldershot	a		12 41							13 41								14 41				
	d		12 48							13 48								14 48				
Ash [5]	d		12 55							13 55								14 55				
Wanborough	d		12 59							13 59								14 59				
Guildford	a		13 06							14 06								15 06				
Martins Heron	d	12 09				12 39			13 09					13 39			14 09					14 39
Bracknell	d	12 13				12 43			13 13					13 43			14 13					14 43
Wokingham	d	12 19				12 49			13 19					13 49			14 19					14 49
Winnersh	d	12 23				12 53			13 23					13 53			14 23					14 53
Winnersh Triangle	d	12 25				12 55			13 25					13 55			14 25					14 55
Earley	d	12 27				12 57			13 27					13 57			14 27					14 57
Reading [7]	a	12 32				13 02			13 32					14 05			14 32					15 02

For additional services between Wokingham and Reading refer to Table T148

Table T149-F

Sundays

15 December to 10 May

London - Hounslow, Richmond, Kingston, Windsor, Weybridge, Ascot, Guildford and Reading

		SW	SW	SW	SW [1]	SW	SW	SW	SW	SW	SW		SW	SW	SW	SW [1]	SW	SW	SW	SW	SW	SW	SW
London Waterloo [15] ⊖	d	13 44	13 50	14 09		14 14	14 20	14 25		14 39			17 44	17 50	18 09		18 14	18 20	18 25		18 39		18 44
Vauxhall ⊖	d	13 48	13 54	14 13		14 18	14 24	14 29		14 43			17 48	17 54	18 13		18 18	18 24	18 29		18 43		18 48
Queenstown Rd.(Battersea)	d	13 51	13 57			14 21	14 27						17 51	17 57			18 21	18 27					18 51
Clapham Junction [10]	d	13 54	14 00	14 19		14 24	14 30	14 35		14 49			17 54	18 00	18 19		18 24	18 30	18 35		18 49		18 54
Wandsworth Town	d	13 57	14 03			14 27	14 33						17 57	18 03			18 27	18 33					18 57
Putney	d	14 00	14 06	14 23		14 30	14 36	14 39		14 53	←		18 00	18 06	18 23		18 30	18 36	18 39		18 53	←	19 00
Barnes	d	14 03	14 09			14 33	14 39				14 39		18 03	18 09			18 33	18 39				18 39	19 03
Barnes Bridge	d		14 11				→				14 41			18 11				→				18 41	
Chiswick	d		14 13								14 44			18 13								18 44	
Kew Bridge	d		14 16								14 46			18 16								18 46	
Brentford	d		14 19								14 49			18 19								18 49	
Syon Lane	d		14 21								14 51			18 21								18 51	
Isleworth	d		14 23								14 53			18 23								18 53	
Hounslow	d		14 26								14 57			18 26								18 57	
Mortlake	d	14 05				14 35							18 05				18 35						19 05
North Sheen	d	14 07				14 37							18 07				18 37						19 07
Richmond ⊖	d	14 10		14 29		14 40		14 45		14 59			18 10		18 29		18 40		18 45		18 59		19 10
St Margarets	d	14 12				14 42							18 12				18 42						19 12
Twickenham	a	14 14		14 32		14 44		14 49		15 02	15 04		18 14		18 32		18 44		18 49		19 02	19 04	19 14
	d	14 15		14 33		14 45		14 49	14 56	15 03	15 11		18 15		18 33		18 45		18 49	18 56	19 03	19 11	19 15
Strawberry Hill	d					14 49					15 14						18 49					19 14	
Fulwell	a																						
Teddington	a					14 52					15 17						18 52					19 17	
Hampton Wick	a					14 57					15 20						18 57					19 20	
Kingston	a					14 59					15 22	and at the same minutes past each hour until					18 59					19 22	
Whitton	d	14 18						14 52	14a59				18 18						18 52	18a59			19 18
Feltham	d	14 22	14 32	14 39				14 57		15 09			18 22	18 32	18 39				18 57		19 09		19 22
Ashford (Surrey)	d	14 26	14 36					15 01					18 26	18 36					19 01				19 26
Staines	d	14 30	14 40	14 45				15 05		15 15			18 30	18 40	18 45				19 05		19 15		19 30
Wraysbury	d	14 34											18 34										19 34
Sunnymeads	d	14 37											18 37										19 37
Datchet	d	14 40						15 12					18 40						19 12				19 40
Windsor & Eton Riverside	a	14 44						15 17					18 44						19 17				19 44
Egham	d		14 45	14 50						15 20				18 45	18 50						19 20		
Virginia Water	a		14 49	14 54						15 24				18 49	18 54						19 24		
	d		14 49	14 54						15 24				18 49	18 54						19 24		
Chertsey	d		14 55											18 55									
Addlestone	d		14a58											18a58									
Weybridge	a																						
Longcross	d									15 27											19 27		
Sunningdale	d			15 00						15 30					19 00						19 30		
Ascot [3]	d			15 05	15 13					15 35					19 05	19 13					19 35		
Bagshot	d				15 19											19 19							
Camberley	a				15 25											19 25							
Frimley	d				15 29											19 29							
Ash Vale	d				15 36											19 36							
Aldershot	a				15 41											19 41							
	d				15 48											19 48							
Ash [5]	d				15 55											19 55							
Wanborough	d				15 59											19 59							
Guildford	a				16 06											20 06							
Martins Heron	d			15 09						15 39					19 09						19 39		
Bracknell	d			15 13						15 43					19 13						19 43		
Wokingham	d			15 19						15 49					19 19						19 49		
Winnersh	d			15 23						15 53					19 23						19 53		
Winnersh Triangle	d			15 25						15 55					19 25						19 55		
Earley	d			15 27						15 57					19 27						19 57		
Reading [7]	a			15 32						16 02					19 32						20 02		

For additional services between Wokingham and Reading refer to Table T148

Table T149-F

Sundays

15 December to 10 May

London - Hounslow, Richmond, Kingston, Windsor, Weybridge, Ascot, Guildford and Reading

		SW	SW	SW 1	SW	SW	SW	SW	SW	SW	SW	SW
London Waterloo 15 ⊖	d	18 50	19 09		19 14	19 20	19 25		19 39		19 44	19 50
Vauxhall ⊖	d	18 54	19 13		19 18	19 24	19 29		19 43		19 48	19 54
Queenstown Rd.(Battersea)	d	18 57			19 21	19 27					19 51	19 57
Clapham Junction 10	d	19 00	19 19		19 24	19 30	19 35		19 49		19 54	20 00
Wandsworth Town	d	19 03			19 27	19 33					19 57	20 03
Putney	d	19 06	19 23		19 30	19 36	19 39		19 53	←	20 00	20 06
Barnes	d	19 09			19 33	19 39				19 39	20 03	20 09
Barnes Bridge	d	19 11				→				19 41		20 11
Chiswick	d	19 13								19 44		20 13
Kew Bridge	d	19 16								19 46		20 16
Brentford	d	19 19								19 49		20 19
Syon Lane	d	19 21								19 51		20 21
Isleworth	d	19 23								19 53		20 23
Hounslow	d	19 26								19 57		20 26
Mortlake	d				19 35						20 05	
North Sheen	d				19 37						20 07	
Richmond ⊖	d		19 29		19 40		19 45		19 59		20 10	
St Margarets	d				19 42						20 12	
Twickenham	a		19 32		19 44		19 49		20 02	20 04	20 14	
	d		19 33		19 45		19 49	19 56	20 03	20 11	20 15	
Strawberry Hill	d				19 49					20 14		
Fulwell	a											
Teddington	a				19 52					20 17		
Hampton Wick	a				19 57					20 20		
Kingston	a				19 59					20 22		
Whitton	d						19 52	19a59			20 18	
Feltham	d	19 32	19 39				19 57		20 09		20 22	20 32
Ashford (Surrey)	d	19 36					20 01				20 26	20 36
Staines	d	19 41	19 45				20 05		20 15		20 30	20 40
Wraysbury	d										20 34	
Sunnymeads	d										20 37	
Datchet	d						20 12				20 40	
Windsor & Eton Riverside	a						20 17				20 44	
Egham	d	19 45	19 50						20 20			20 45
Virginia Water	a	19 49	19 54						20 24			20 49
	d	19 49	19 54						20 24			20 49
Chertsey	d	19 55										20 55
Addlestone	d	19a58										20a58
Weybridge	a											
Longcross	d								20 27			
Sunningdale	d		20 00						20 30			
Ascot 8	d		20 05	20 13					20 35			
Bagshot	d			20 19								
Camberley	a			20 25								
Frimley	d			20 29								
Ash Vale	d			20 36								
Aldershot	a			20 41								
	d			20 48								
Ash 5	d			20 57								
Wanborough	d			21 00								
Guildford	a			21 07								
Martins Heron	d		20 09						20 39			
Bracknell	d		20 13						20 43			
Wokingham	d		20 19						20 49			
Winnersh	d		20 23						20 53			
Winnersh Triangle	d		20 25						20 55			
Earley	d		20 27						20 57			
Reading 7	a		20 32						21 02			

		SW	SW 1	SW	SW	SW	SW	SW	SW	SW	SW	SW
London Waterloo 15 ⊖	d	20 09		20 14	20 20	20 25		20 39		20 44	20 50	21 09
Vauxhall ⊖	d	20 13		20 18	20 24	20 29		20 43		20 48	20 54	21 13
Queenstown Rd.(Battersea)	d			20 21	20 27					20 51	20 57	
Clapham Junction 10	d	20 19		20 24	20 30	20 35		20 49		20 54	21 00	21 19
Wandsworth Town	d			20 27	20 33					20 57	21 03	
Putney	d	20 23		20 30	20 36	20 39		20 53	←	21 00	21 06	21 23
Barnes	d			20 33	20 39				20 39	21 03	21 09	
Barnes Bridge	d				→				20 41		21 11	
Chiswick	d								20 44		21 13	
Kew Bridge	d								20 46		21 16	
Brentford	d								20 49		21 19	
Syon Lane	d								20 51		21 21	
Isleworth	d								20 53		21 23	
Hounslow	d								20 57		21 26	
Mortlake	d			20 35						21 05		
North Sheen	d			20 37						21 07		
Richmond ⊖	d	20 29		20 40		20 45		20 59		21 10		21 29
St Margarets	d			20 42						21 12		
Twickenham	a	20 32		20 44		20 49		21 02	21 04	21 14		21 32
	d	20 33		20 45		20 49	20 56	21 03	21 11	21 15		21 33
Strawberry Hill	d			20 49					21 14			
Fulwell	a											
Teddington	a			20 52					21 17			
Hampton Wick	a			20 57					21 20			
Kingston	a			20 59					21 22			
Whitton	d					20 52	20a59			21 18		
Feltham	d	20 39				20 57		21 09		21 22	21 32	21 39
Ashford (Surrey)	d					21 01				21 26	21 36	
Staines	d	20 45				21 05		21 15		21 30	21 40	21 45
Wraysbury	d									21 34		
Sunnymeads	d									21 37		
Datchet	d					21 12				21 40		
Windsor & Eton Riverside	a					21 17				21 44		
Egham	d	20 50						21 20			21 45	21 50
Virginia Water	a	20 54						21 24			21 49	21 54
	d	20 54						21 24			21 49	21 54
Chertsey	d										21 55	
Addlestone	d										21a58	
Weybridge	a											
Longcross	d							21 27				
Sunningdale	d	21 00						21 30				22 00
Ascot 8	d	21 05	21 13					21 35				22 05
Bagshot	d		21 19									
Camberley	a		21 25									
Frimley	d		21 29									
Ash Vale	d		21 36									
Aldershot	a		21 41									
	d		21 48									
Ash 5	d		21 55									
Wanborough	d		21 59									
Guildford	a		22 06									
Martins Heron	d	21 09						21 39				22 09
Bracknell	d	21 13						21 43				22 13
Wokingham	d	21 19						21 49				22 19
Winnersh	d	21 23						21 53				22 23
Winnersh Triangle	d	21 25						21 55				22 25
Earley	d	21 27						21 57				22 27
Reading 7	a	21 32						22 02				22 32

For additional services between Wokingham and Reading refer to Table T148

Table T149-F

Sundays

15 December to 10 May

London - Hounslow, Richmond, Kingston, Windsor, Weybridge, Ascot, Guildford and Reading

		SW 1	SW	SW	SW	SW	SW	SW	SW	SW	SW 1	SW	SW
London Waterloo 15 ⊖	d		21 14		21 20	21 39		21 44	21 50	22 09		22 14	
Vauxhall ⊖	d		21 18		21 24	21 43		21 48	21 54	22 13		22 18	
Queenstown Rd.(Battersea)	d		21 21		21 27			21 51	21 57			22 21	
Clapham Junction 10	d		21 24		21 30	21 49		21 54	22 00	22 19		22 24	
Wandsworth Town	d		21 27		21 33			21 57	22 03			22 27	
Putney	d		21 30		21 36	21 53	←	22 00	22 06	22 23		22 30	
Barnes	d		21 33		21 39		21 39	22 03	22 09			22 33	
Barnes Bridge	d				→		21 41		22 11				
Chiswick	d						21 44		22 13				
Kew Bridge	d						21 46		22 16				
Brentford	d						21 49		22 19				
Syon Lane	d						21 51		22 21				
Isleworth	d						21 53		22 23				
Hounslow	d						21 57		22 26				
Mortlake	d		21 35					22 05				22 35	
North Sheen	d		21 37					22 07				22 37	
Richmond ⊖	d		21 40			21 59		22 10		22 29		22 40	
St Margarets	d		21 42					22 12				22 42	
Twickenham	a		21 44			22 02	22 04	22 14		22 32		22 44	
	d		21 45	21 56		22 03	22 11	22 15		22 33		22 45	22 56
Strawberry Hill	d		21 49				22 14					22 49	
Fulwell	a												
Teddington	a		21 52				22 17					22 52	
Hampton Wick	a		21 57				22 20					22 57	
Kingston	a		21 59				22 22					22 59	
Whitton	d			21a59				22 18					22a59
Feltham	d					22 09		22 22	22 32	22 39			
Ashford (Surrey)	d							22 26	22 36				
Staines	d					22 15		22 30	22 40	22 45			
Wraysbury	d							22 34					
Sunnymeads	d							22 37					
Datchet	d							22 40					
Windsor & Eton Riverside	a							22 44					
Egham	d					22 20			22 45	22 50			
Virginia Water	a					22 24			22 49	22 54			
	d					22 24			22 49	22 54			
Chertsey	d								22 55				
Addlestone	d								22a58				
Weybridge	a												
Longcross	d												
Sunningdale	d					22 30				23 00			
Ascot 8	d	22 13				22 35				23 05	23 13		
Bagshot	d	22 19									23 19		
Camberley	a	22 25									23 25		
Frimley	d	22 29									23 29		
Ash Vale	d	22 36									23 36		
Aldershot	a	22 41									23 41		
	d	22 48											
Ash 5	d	22 55											
Wanborough	d	22 58											
Guildford	a	23 06											
Martins Heron	d					22 39				23 09			
Bracknell	d					22 43				23 13			
Wokingham	d					22 49				23 19			
Winnersh	d					22 53				23 23			
Winnersh Triangle	d					22 55				23 25			
Earley	d					22 57				23 27			
Reading 7	a					23 02				23 32			

		SW	SW	SW	SW	SW	SW	SW	SW	SW	SW	SW
London Waterloo 15 ⊖	d	22 20	22 39		22 44	22 50	23 09	23 14	23 20	23 39		23 44
Vauxhall ⊖	d	22 24	22 43		22 48	22 54	23 13	23 18	23 24	23 43		23 48
Queenstown Rd.(Battersea)	d	22 27			22 51	22 57		23 21	23 27			23 51
Clapham Junction 10	d	22 30	22 49		22 54	23 00	23 19	23 24	23 30	23 49		23 54
Wandsworth Town	d	22 33			22 57	23 03		23 27	23 33			23 57
Putney	d	22 36	22 53	←	23 00	23 06	23 23	23 30	23 36	23 53	←	23 59
Barnes	d	22 39		22 39	23 03	23 09		23 33	23 39		23 39	00 03
Barnes Bridge	d	→		22 41		23 11			→		23 41	
Chiswick	d			22 44		23 13					23 44	
Kew Bridge	d			22 46		23 16					23 46	
Brentford	d			22 49		23 19					23 49	
Syon Lane	d			22 51		23 21					23 51	
Isleworth	d			22 53		23 23					23 53	
Hounslow	d			22 57		23 26					23 58	
Mortlake	d				23 05			23 35				00 05
North Sheen	d				23 07			23 37				00 07
Richmond ⊖	d		22 59		23 10		23 29	23 40		23 59		00 10
St Margarets	d				23 12			23 42				00 12
Twickenham	a		23 02	23 04	23 14		23 32	23 44		00 02	00 05	00 14
	d		23 03	23 11	23 15		23 33	23 45		00 03	00 12	00 15
Strawberry Hill	d			23 14				23 48			00 15	
Fulwell	a											
Teddington	a			23 17				23 51			00 18	
Hampton Wick	a			23 20				23 54			00 21	
Kingston	a			23 22				23 56			00 23	
Whitton	d				23 18							00 18
Feltham	d		23 09		23 22	23 32	23 39			00 09		00 22
Ashford (Surrey)	d				23 26	23 36						00 26
Staines	d		23 15		23 30	23 40	23 45			00 15		00a30
Wraysbury	d				23 34							
Sunnymeads	d				23 37							
Datchet	d				23 40							
Windsor & Eton Riverside	a				23 44							
Egham	d		23 20			23 45	23 50			00 20		
Virginia Water	a		23 24			23 49	23 54			00 24		
	d		23 24			23 49	23 54			00 24		
Chertsey	d					23 55						
Addlestone	d					23a58						
Weybridge	a											
Longcross	d											
Sunningdale	d		23 30				23 59			00 30		
Ascot 8	d		23 35				00 05			00 35		
Bagshot	d											
Camberley	a											
Frimley	d											
Ash Vale	d											
Aldershot	a											
	d											
Ash 5	d											
Wanborough	d											
Guildford	a											
Martins Heron	d		23 39				00 09			00 39		
Bracknell	d		23 43				00 13			00 43		
Wokingham	d		23 49				00 19			00 49		
Winnersh	d		23 53				00 23			00 53		
Winnersh Triangle	d		23 55				00 25			00 55		
Earley	d		23 57				00 27			00 57		
Reading 7	a		00 02				00 32			01 02		

For additional services between Wokingham and Reading refer to Table T148

Table T149-R

Mondays to Fridays

16 December to 15 May

Reading, Guildford, Ascot, Weybridge, Windsor, Kingston, Richmond and Hounslow - London

Miles	Miles	Miles	Miles			SW MO	SW MX	SW MO	SW MX [1]	SW MX	SW MO	SW MX	SW MX	SW		SW	SW	SW	SW	SW	SW	SW	SW ◇	SW ◇
—	—	0	—	**Reading** [7]	d																			
—	—	3	—	Earley	d																			
—	—	4¼	—	Winnersh Triangle	d																			
—	—	4¾	—	Winnersh	d																			
—	—	6¾	—	**Wokingham**	d				00 02															
—	—	11¼	—	Bracknell	d				00 08															
—	—	12¼	—	Martins Heron	d				00 11															
—	0	—	—	**Guildford**	d																			
—	4¼	—	—	Wanborough	d																			
—	6¼	—	—	Ash [5]	d																			
—	9	—	—	**Aldershot**	a																			
—	—	—	—		d																			
—	11½	—	—	Ash Vale	d																			
—	14¾	—	—	Frimley	d																			
—	17	—	—	Camberley	a																			
—	—	—	—		d																			
—	20¼	—	—	Bagshot	d																			
—	23½	14½	—	**Ascot** [3]	d				00a17											05 34				
—	—	16½	—	Sunningdale	d															05 37				
—	—	18¼	—	Longcross	d																			
0	—	—	—	**Weybridge**	d																			
1¾	—	—	—	Addlestone	d																		05 39	
3¼	—	—	—	Chertsey	d																		05 42	
11	—	5¾	—	Virginia Water	a															05 43			05 47	
—	—	—	—		d															05 43			05 54	
—	—	22½	—	Egham	d															05 47			05 57	
—	—	—	0	**Windsor & Eton Riverside**	d																			05 53
—	—	—	2	Datchet	d																			05 56
—	—	—	3	Sunnymeads	d																			05 59
—	—	—	4¼	Wraysbury	d																			06 02
—	—	24½	6¾	**Staines**	d											04 53			05 37	05 53			06 03	06 08
—	—	26	—	Ashford (Surrey)	d											04 56			05 40				06 06	06 11
—	—	28¾	—	Feltham	d								00 05			05 01			05 45	05 59			06 11	06 16
—	—	31	—	Whitton	d			00 02								05 05			05 49					06 20
0	—	—	—	**Kingston**	d									01 17								05 59		
0½	—	—	—	Hampton Wick	d									01s22								06 01		
1¾	—	—	—	Teddington	d									01s25								06 05		
2¾	—	—	—	Fulwell	d													05 36						
3	—	—	—	Strawberry Hill	d					00 03				01a28				05 38				06 08		
4	—	32¼	—	Twickenham	a			00 05		00 06			00 10			05 08		05 42	05 52	06 04		06 12		06 23
—	—	—	—		d								00 11			05 08		05 43	05 53	06 06		06 13		06 23
4½	—	32¾	—	St Margarets	d											05 10		05 45				06 15		
5½	—	33¾	—	**Richmond** ⊖	d								00 15			05 14		05 49	05 58	06 11		06 19		06 28
6¼	—	34½	—	North Sheen	d											05 16		05 51				06 21		
7	—	35¼	—	Mortlake	d											05 18		05 53				06 23		
—	0	—	—	**Hounslow**	d												05 31				06 01		06 16	
—	—	—	—	Isleworth	d												05 34				06 04		06 19	
—	2¼	—	—	Syon Lane	d												05 36				06 06		06 21	
—	3	—	—	Brentford	d												05 39				06 09		06 24	
—	4	—	—	Kew Bridge	d												05 41				06 11		06 26	
—	5	—	—	Chiswick	d												05 44				06 14		06 29	
—	6	—	—	Barnes Bridge	d							00 01					05 46				06 16		06 31	
8¼	6½	36½	—	Barnes	d							00 04				05 21	05 49	05 56			06 19	06 26	06 34	
9½	—	37¾	—	Putney	d						00 05	00 07				05 24	05 52	05 59	06 04	06 18	06 22	06 29	06 37	06 34
10½	—	38¾	—	Wandsworth Town	d		00 02					00 10				05 27	05 55	06 02			06 25	06 32	↪	
11¼	—	39½	—	Clapham Junction [10]	d	00 02	00 05				00 09	00 13	00 24			05 30	05 58	06 05	06 09	06 22	06 28	06 35		06 39
12½	—	41¼	—	Queenstown Rd.(Battersea)	d	00 05	00 08					00 16				05 33	06 01	06 08			06 31	06 38		
14	—	42¼	—	Vauxhall ⊖	d	00 08	00 12				00 15	00 20				05 37	06 05	06 12	06 15	06 28	06 35	06 42		06 45
15¼	—	43½	—	**London Waterloo** [15] ⊖	a	00 14	00 16				00 19	00 24	00 38			05 41	06 09	06 16	06 19	06 37	06 41	06 46		06 49

Table T149-R

Mondays to Fridays

16 December to 15 May

Reading, Guildford, Ascot, Weybridge, Windsor, Kingston, Richmond and Hounslow - London

		SW ◇	SW	SW	SW	SW	SW	SW [1]	SW ◇	SW		SW	SW	SW ◇	SW	SW	SW	SW	SW	SW ◇		SW ◇	SW	SW	SW
Reading [7]	d				05 41		05 52								06 11			06 23							
Earley	d				05 46										06 16										
Winnersh Triangle	d				05 48										06 18										
Winnersh	d				05 50										06 20										
Wokingham	d				05 55		06 01								06 25			06 32							
Bracknell	d				06 02		06 08								06 32			06 38							
Martins Heron	d				06 05		06 11								06 35			06 41							
Guildford	d																								
Wanborough	d																								
Ash [5]	d																								
Aldershot	a																								
	d							05 58																	
Ash Vale	d							06 02																	
Frimley	d							06 10																	
Camberley	a							06 14																	
	d							06 18																	
Bagshot	d							06 23																	
Ascot [3]	d				06 10		06 16	06a30							06 40			06 46							
Sunningdale	d				06 13		06 20								06 43			06 50							
Longcross	d														06 46										
Weybridge	d													06 32											
Addlestone	d													06 36											
Chertsey	d													06 39											
Virginia Water	a				06 19		06 25							06 44	06 49			06 55							
	d				06 19		06 25							06 45	06 49			06 55							
Egham	d				06 23		06 29							06 48	06 53			06 59							
Windsor & Eton Riverside	d								06 23											06 53			07 02		
Datchet	d								06 26											06 56					
Sunnymeads	d								06 29											06 59					
Wraysbury	d								06 32											07 02					
Staines	d			06 24	06 29		06 34		06 38					06 54	06 59			07 04		07 08			07 12		
Ashford (Surrey)	d			06 27					06 41					06 57						07 11			07 15		
Feltham	d			06 32	06 35		06 42		06 46					07 02	07 05			07 12		07 16			07 20		
Whitton	d		06 20						06 50			06 50	06 53							07 20					07 20
Kingston	d					06 29											06 59								
Hampton Wick	d					06 31											07 01								
Teddington	d					06 35											07 05								
Fulwell	d																		07 12						
Strawberry Hill	d					06 38											07 08		07 14					←	
Twickenham	a				06 40	06 42	06 47		06 53				06 56		07 10		07 12	07 17	07 18	07 23				07 18	
	d				06 41	06 43	06 48		06 53				06 58		07 11		07 13	07 18	07 27	07 23				07 27	
St Margarets	d					06 45							07 00				07 15		↪					07 29	
Richmond ⊖	d				06 45	06 49	06 54		06 58				07 04		07 15		07 19	07 24		07 28				07 32	
North Sheen	d					06 51							07 06				07 21							07 34	
Mortlake	d					06 53							07 08				07 23							07 37	
Hounslow	d		06 31	06 44								06 59		07 14									07 25		07 29
Isleworth	d		06 34	06 47								07 02		07 17											07 32
Syon Lane	d		06 36	06 50								07 05		07 20											07 35
Brentford	d		06 39	06 53								07 08		07 23									07 31		07 38
Kew Bridge	d		06 41	06 55								07 10		07 25											07 40
Chiswick	d		06 44	06 58								07 13		07 28											07 43
Barnes Bridge	d		06 46	07 01						←		07 16		07 31		←						←			07 46
Barnes	d	←	06 49	07 04		06 56				07 04		07 19	07 11	07 34		07 19	07 26					07 34		07 40	07 49
Putney	d	06 37	06 52	→	06 52	06 59			07 04	07 07		→	07 14	→	07 22	07 22	07 29			07 34		07 37		07 43	07 52
Wandsworth Town	d	06 40	06 55			07 02				07 10			07 17			07 25	07 32					07 40		07 46	07 55
Clapham Junction [10]	d	06 43	06 58		06 56	07 05	07 03		07 09	07 13			07 20		07 26	07 28	07 35	07 33		07 39		07 43	07 42	07 49	07 58
Queenstown Rd.(Battersea)	d	06 46	07 01			07 08				07 16			07 23			07 31	07 38					07 47		07 52	08 01
Vauxhall ⊖	d	06 50	07 05			07 12	07 08		07 15	07 20			07 27			07 35	07 42	07 38		07 45		07 51	07 48	07 56	08 05
London Waterloo [15] ⊖	a	06 56	07 13		07 07	07 18	07 16		07 21	07 27			07 34		07 37	07 42	07 48	07 46		07 51		07 57	07 58	08 04	08 11

Table T149-R

Mondays to Fridays

16 December to 15 May

Reading, Guildford, Ascot, Weybridge, Windsor, Kingston, Richmond and Hounslow - London

Station		SW	SW	SW	SW	SW		SW	SW	SW	SW	SW	SW	SW	SW	SW		SW	SW	SW	SW	SW	SW	SW	SW
		◇	1	◇						◇	◇			◇	1					◇			◇	◇	
Reading 7	d				06 41			06 54								07 11					07 23				
Earley	d				06 46											07 16									
Winnersh Triangle	d				06 48											07 18									
Winnersh	d				06 50											07 20									
Wokingham	d				06 55			07 03								07 25					07 32				
Bracknell	d				07 02			07 09								07 32					07 38				
Martins Heron	d				07 05			07 12								07 35					07 41				
Guildford	d		06 23												06 53										
Wanborough	d		06 29												06 59										
Ash 3	d		06 33												07 03										
Aldershot	a		06 40												07 10										
	d	06 26												06 57											
Ash Vale	d	06 30												07 02											
Frimley	d	06 40												07 11											
Camberley	a	06 44												07 15											
	d	06 47												07 17											
Bagshot	d	06 52												07 22											
Ascot 3	d	06 59			07 10			07 17						07 29		07 40					07 46				
Sunningdale	d	07 02			07 13			07 21						07 32		07 43					07 50				
Longcross	d	07 05												07 35											
Weybridge	d			07 02																07 33					
Addlestone	d			07 06																07 37					
Chertsey	d			07 09																07 40					
Virginia Water	a	07 09		07 14	07 19			07 26						07 39						07 45	07 55				
	d	07 09		07 15	07 19			07 26						07 39						07 50	07 55				
Egham	d	07 12		07 18	07 23			07 29						07 42		07 50				07 54	07 58				
Windsor & Eton Riverside	d									07 23													07 53		
Datchet	d									07 26													07 56		
Sunnymeads	d									07 29													07 59		
Wraysbury	d									07 32													08 02		
Staines	d	07 18		07 24	07 29			07 35		07 38				07 48		07 56				07 59	08 04		08 08		
Ashford (Surrey)	d	07 21		07 27						07 41				07 51						08 02			08 11		
Feltham	d	07 26		07 32	07 36			07 42		07 46				07 56		08 02				08 07	08 11		08 16		
Whitton	d	07 30								07 50			07 50	08 00									08 20		
Kingston	d					07 29													07 59						
Hampton Wick	d					07 31													08 01						
Teddington	d					07 35													08 05						
Fulwell	d								07 42													08 12			
Strawberry Hill	d					07 38			07 44			←							08 08			08 14			←
Twickenham	a	07 33			07 41	07 42		07 47	07 48	07 53		07 48		08 03		08 09			08 12		08 16	08 18	08 23		08 18
	d	07 33			07 41	07 43		07 48	07 57	07 54		07 57		08 03		08 09			08 13		08 17	08 27	08 24		08 27
St Margarets	d					07 45			→			07 59							08 15			→			08 29
Richmond ⊖	d	07 38			07 46	07 49		07 54		07 58		08 02		08 08		08 14			08 19		08 23		08 28		08 32
North Sheen	d					07 51						08 04							08 21						08 34
Mortlake	d					07 53						08 07							08 23						08 37
Hounslow	d			07 44									07 59					08 10		08 14					
Isleworth	d			07 47									08 02							08 17					
Syon Lane	d			07 50									08 05							08 20					
Brentford	d			07 53									08 08					08 16		08 23					
Kew Bridge	d			07 55									08 10							08 25					
Chiswick	d			07 58									08 13							08 28					
Barnes Bridge	d			08 01							←		08 16							08 31					
Barnes	d			08 04		07 56					08 04	08 10	08 19						08 26	08 34				←	08 40
Putney	d			→		07 59				08 05	08 07	08 13	08 22						08 29	08 37			08 35	08 37	08 43
Wandsworth Town	d					08 02					08 10	08 16	08 25						08 32	→				08 40	08 46
Clapham Junction 10	d	07 47			07 54	08 05		08 03		08 09	08 13	08 19	08 28	08 17		08 22		08 26	08 35		08 33		08 39	08 43	08 49
Queenstown Rd.(Battersea)	d					08 08					08 16	08 22	08 31						08 38					08 46	08 52
Vauxhall ⊖	d	07 53				08 12		08 09		08 15	08 20	08 26	08 35	08 23				08 32	08 42		08 38		08 45	08 50	08 56
London Waterloo 15 ⊖	a	08 00			08 06	08 18		08 16		08 21	08 28	08 34	08 42	08 29		08 36		08 39	08 49		08 46		08 51	08 58	09 04

Table T149-R

Mondays to Fridays

16 December to 15 May

Reading, Guildford, Ascot, Weybridge, Windsor, Kingston, Richmond and Hounslow - London

Station		SW		SW	SW	SW	SW	SW	SW	SW	SW	SW		SW	SW	SW	SW	SW	SW	SW	SW	SW		SW	SW
				◇	1						◇			1	1	◇	◇							◇	
Reading 7	d						07 41					07 53								08 11					08 24
Earley	d						07 46													08 16					
Winnersh Triangle	d						07 48													08 18					
Winnersh	d						07 51													08 20					
Wokingham	d						07 55					08 02								08 25					08 33
Bracknell	d						08 02					08 08								08 31					08 40
Martins Heron	d						08 05					08 11								08 34					08 43
Guildford	d				07 23										07 53										
Wanborough	d				07 29										07 59										
Ash 3	d				07 33										08 03										
Aldershot	a				07 40										08 10										
	d			07 27										08 00											
Ash Vale	d			07 31										08 04											
Frimley	d			07 40										08 10											
Camberley	a			07 44										08 14											
	d			07 47										08 18											
Bagshot	d			07 52										08 23											
Ascot 3	d			07 59			08 09					08 16		08a30						08 39					08 47
Sunningdale	d			08 02			08 13					08 19								08 42					08 51
Longcross	d			08 05																08 45					
Weybridge	d										08 03													08 33	
Addlestone	d										08 07													08 37	
Chertsey	d										08 11													08 40	
Virginia Water	a			08 09							08 16	08 24												08 45	08 56
	d			08 09							08 20	08 25												08 52	08 56
Egham	d			08 12			08 20				08 24	08 29								08 51				08 55	09 00
Windsor & Eton Riverside	d															08 23									
Datchet	d															08 26									
Sunnymeads	d															08 29									
Wraysbury	d															08 32									
Staines	d			08 18			08 25				08 29	08 34				08 38				08 56				09 01	09 05
Ashford (Surrey)	d			08 21							08 32					08 41								09 04	
Feltham	d			08 26			08 32				08 37	08 42				08 46				09 03				09 09	09 13
Whitton	d	08 20		08 30		08 33										08 50		08 50	08 53						
Kingston	d									08 29												08 59			
Hampton Wick	d									08 31												09 01			
Teddington	d									08 35												09 05			
Fulwell	d																								
Strawberry Hill	d									08 38												09 08			
Twickenham	a			08 33		08 36	08 39			08 42		08 47				08 53			08 56	09 10		09 12			09 18
	d			08 33		08 37	08 40			08 43		08 48				08 53			08 58	09 11		09 13			09 19
St Margarets	d									08 45									09 00			09 15			
Richmond ⊖	d			08 38		08 42	08 45			08 49		08 54				08 58			09 04	09 15		09 19			09 24
North Sheen	d									08 51									09 06			09 21			
Mortlake	d									08 53									09 08			09 23			
Hounslow	d	08 29						08 40			08 44							09 01						09 14	
Isleworth	d	08 32									08 47							09 04						09 17	
Syon Lane	d	08 34									08 49							09 06						09 19	
Brentford	d	08 37						08 46			08 52							09 09						09 22	
Kew Bridge	d	08 40									08 55							09 11						09 25	
Chiswick	d	08 43									08 58							09 14						09 28	
Barnes Bridge	d	08 46									09 01							09 16			←			09 31	
Barnes	d	08 49							←	08 56	09 04						←	09 19	09 11		09 19	09 26		09 34	
Putney	d	08 52				08 48			08 52	08 59	09 07					09 04	09 07	→	09 14		09 22	09 29		09 37	
Wandsworth Town	d	→				08 51			08 55	09 02	→						09 10		09 17		09 25	09 32		→	
Clapham Junction 10	d			08 47		08 55	08 54	08 57	08 58	09 05		09 03				09 09	09 13		09 20	09 24	09 28	09 35			09 33
Queenstown Rd.(Battersea)	d								09 02	09 08							09 16		09 23		09 31	09 38			
Vauxhall ⊖	d			08 53		09 01		09 05	09 05	09 12		09 09				09 15	09 20		09 27		09 35	09 42			09 38
London Waterloo 15 ⊖	a			09 00		09 07	09 06	09 13	09 15	09 19		09 18				09 21	09 29		09 34	09 39	09 43	09 51			09 45

Table T149-R

Mondays to Fridays
16 December to 15 May

Reading, Guildford, Ascot, Weybridge, Windsor, Kingston, Richmond and Hounslow - London

		SW 1	SW 1	SW	SW	SW ◇	SW ◇	SW		SW	SW	SW 1	SW 1	SW	SW	SW	SW	SW		SW	SW	SW	SW	SW	SW
Reading 7	d									08 42												09 12			
Earley	d									08 47												09 17			
Winnersh Triangle	d									08 49												09 19			
Winnersh	d									08 51												09 21			
Wokingham	d									08 56												09 26			
Bracknell	d									09 02												09 32			
Martins Heron	d									09 05												09 35			
Guildford	d		08 23										08 53												
Wanborough	d		08 29										08 59												
Ash 5	d		08 33										09 03												
Aldershot	a		08 40										09 10												
	d	08 30										09 00													
Ash Vale	d	08 34										09 04													
Frimley	d	08 40										09 10													
Camberley	a	08 44										09 14													
	d	08 48										09 18													
Bagshot	d	08 53										09 23													
Ascot 8	d	09a00								09 10		09a30										09 40			
Sunningdale	d									09 13												09 43			
Longcross	d									09 16												09 46			
Weybridge	d			09 03														09 33							
Addlestone	d			09 07														09 37							
Chertsey	d			09 10											←			09 40							←
Virginia Water	a			09 15						09 20					09 15			09 45				09 50			09 45
	d			09 24						09 20					09 24			09 54				09 50			09 54
Egham	d			→						09 23					09 27			→				09 53			09 57
Windsor & Eton Riverside	d					08 53										09 23									
Datchet	d					08 56										09 26									
Sunnymeads	d					08 59										09 29									
Wraysbury	d					09 02										09 32									
Staines	d					09 10				09 29					09 33	09 38						09 59			10 03
Ashford (Surrey)	d					09 13									09 36	09 41									10 06
Feltham	d					09 18				09 35					09 41	09 46						10 05			10 11
Whitton	d				09 20	09 22		09 25								09 50				09 50	09 53				
Kingston	d													09 29										09 59	
Hampton Wick	d													09 31										10 01	
Teddington	d													09 35										10 05	
Fulwell	d																								
Strawberry Hill	d													09 38										10 08	
Twickenham	a					09 25		09 28		09 40				09 42		09 53					09 56	10 10		10 12	
	d					09 25		09 29		09 41				09 43		09 53					09 58	10 11		10 13	
St Margarets	d							09 31						09 45							10 00			10 15	
Richmond ⊖	d					09 30		09 35		09 45				09 49		09 58					10 04	10 15		10 19	
North Sheen	d							09 37						09 51							10 06			10 21	
Mortlake	d							09 39						09 53							10 08			10 23	
Hounslow	d				09 31										09 46					10 01					10 16
Isleworth	d				09 34										09 49					10 04					10 19
Syon Lane	d				09 36										09 51					10 06					10 21
Brentford	d				09 39										09 54					10 09					10 24
Kew Bridge	d				09 41										09 56					10 11					10 26
Chiswick	d				09 44										09 59					10 14					10 29
Barnes Bridge	d				09 46						←				10 01					10 16			←		10 31
Barnes	d				09 49		←	09 42			09 49			09 56	10 04		←			10 19	10 11		10 19	10 26	10 34
Putney	d				→	09 36	09 37	09 45			09 52			09 59	10 07	10 04	10 07			→	10 14		10 22	10 29	10 37
Wandsworth Town	d						09 40	09 48			09 55			10 02	→		10 10				10 17		10 25	10 32	→
Clapham Junction 10	d					09 41	09 43	09 51		09 54	09 58			10 05		10 09	10 13				10 20	10 24	10 28	10 35	
Queenstown Rd.(Battersea)	d						09 46	09 54			10 01			10 08			10 16				10 23		10 31	10 38	
Vauxhall ⊖	d					09 46	09 50	09 58			10 05			10 12		10 15	10 20				10 27		10 35	10 42	
London Waterloo 15 ⊖	a					09 53	09 58	10 02		10 04	10 12			10 19		10 19	10 26				10 32	10 34	10 41	10 46	

NRT DECEMBER 19 EDITION

Table T149-R

Mondays to Fridays
16 December to 15 May

Reading, Guildford, Ascot, Weybridge, Windsor, Kingston, Richmond and Hounslow - London

		SW	SW	SW		SW 1	SW 1	SW	SW	SW	SW	SW	SW	SW		SW	SW	SW	SW 1	SW 1	SW	SW	SW	SW	
Reading 7	d		09 25								09 42						09 56							10 12	
Earley	d		09 30								09 47						10 01							10 17	
Winnersh Triangle	d		09 32								09 49						10 03							10 19	
Winnersh	d		09 34								09 51						10 05							10 21	
Wokingham	d		09 39								09 56						10 10							10 26	
Bracknell	d		09 47								10 02						10 17							10 32	
Martins Heron	d		09 50								10 05						10 20							10 35	
Guildford	d						09 23													09 53					
Wanborough	d						09 29													09 59					
Ash 5	d						09 33													10 03					
Aldershot	a						09 40													10 10					
	d					09 30													10 00						
Ash Vale	d					09 34													10 04						
Frimley	d					09 40													10 10						
Camberley	a					09 44													10 14						
	d					09 48													10 18						
Bagshot	d					09 53													10 23						
Ascot 8	d		09 55			10a00					10 10						10 25		10a30					10 40	
Sunningdale	d		09 58								10 13						10 28							10 43	
Longcross	d										10 16													10 46	
Weybridge	d							10 03													10 33				
Addlestone	d							10 07													10 37				
Chertsey	d							10 10						←							10 40				
Virginia Water	a		10 03					10 15			10 20			10 15			10 33				10 45			10 50	
	d		10 03					10 24			10 20			10 24			10 33				10 54			10 50	
Egham	d		10 06					→			10 23			10 27			10 36				→			10 53	
Windsor & Eton Riverside	d	09 53														10 23									
Datchet	d	09 56														10 26									
Sunnymeads	d	09 59														10 29									
Wraysbury	d	10 02														10 32									
Staines	d	10 08	10 14								10 29			10 33		10 38	10 42							10 59	
Ashford (Surrey)	d	10 11												10 36		10 41									
Feltham	d	10 16	10 20								10 35			10 41		10 46	10 49							11 05	
Whitton	d	10 20							10 20	10 26						10 50						10 50	10 56		
Kingston	d												10 30												
Hampton Wick	d												10 32												
Teddington	d												10 35												
Fulwell	d																								
Strawberry Hill	d												10 38												
Twickenham	a	10 23	10 26							10 28	10 40		10 42			10 53	10 55						10 58	11 10	
	d	10 23	10 27							10 28	10 41		10 43			10 53	10 56						10 58	11 11	
St Margarets	d									10 30			10 45										11 00		
Richmond ⊖	d	10 28	10 31							10 34	10 45		10 49			10 58	11 01						11 04	11 15	
North Sheen	d									10 36			10 51										11 07		
Mortlake	d									10 38			10 53										11 08		
Hounslow	d								10 31					10 46								11 01			
Isleworth	d								10 34					10 49								11 04			
Syon Lane	d								10 36					10 51								11 06			
Brentford	d								10 39					10 54								11 09			
Kew Bridge	d								10 41					10 56								11 11			
Chiswick	d								10 44					10 59								11 14			
Barnes Bridge	d								10 46			←		11 01								11 16			
Barnes	d			←					10 49	10 41		10 49	10 56	11 04				←				11 19	11 11		
Putney	d	10 34		10 37					→	10 44		10 52	10 59	11 07		11 04		11 07				→	11 15		
Wandsworth Town	d			10 40						10 47		10 55	11 02	→				11 10					11 17		
Clapham Junction 10	d	10 39	10 42	10 43						10 50	10 54	10 58	11 05			11 09	11 12	11 14					11 21	11 24	
Queenstown Rd.(Battersea)	d			10 47						10 53		11 01	11 08					11 17					11 23		
Vauxhall ⊖	d	10 45		10 50						10 57		11 05	11 12			11 15		11 21					11 28		
London Waterloo 15 ⊖	a	10 49	10 50	10 56						11 02	11 04	11 11	11 16			11 19	11 26	11 28					11 32	11 34	

Table T149-R

Mondays to Fridays

16 December to 15 May

Reading, Guildford, Ascot, Weybridge, Windsor, Kingston, Richmond and Hounslow - London

		SW	SW [1]	SW [1]	SW	SW	SW	SW	SW	SW	SW	SW	SW	SW [1]	SW [1]	SW	SW	SW	SW	SW	SW	SW	SW
Reading [7]	d											10 42											11 12
Earley	d											10 47											11 17
Winnersh Triangle	d											10 49											11 19
Winnersh	d											10 51											11 21
Wokingham	d											10 56											11 26
Bracknell	d											11 02											11 32
Martins Heron	d											11 05											11 35
Guildford	d			10 23											10 53								
Wanborough	d			10 29											10 59								
Ash [5]	d			10 33											11 03								
Aldershot	a			10 40											11 10								
	d		10 30											11 00									
Ash Vale	d		10 34											11 04									
Frimley	d		10 40											11 10									
Camberley	a		10 44											11 14									
	d		10 48											11 18									
Bagshot	d		10 53											11 23									
Ascot [3]	d		11a00									11 10		11a30									11 40
Sunningdale	d											11 13											11 43
Longcross	d											11 16											11 46
Weybridge	d								11 03											11 33			
Addlestone	d								11 07											11 37			
Chertsey	d					←			11 10								←			11 40			
Virginia Water	a					10 45			11 15			11 20					11 15			11 45			11 50
	d					10 54			11 24			11 20					11 24			11 54			11 50
Egham	d					10 57			→			11 23					11 27			→			11 53
Windsor & Eton Riverside	d						10 53											11 23					
Datchet	d						10 56											11 26					
Sunnymeads	d						10 59											11 29					
Wraysbury	d						11 02											11 32					
Staines	d					11 03	11 08					11 29					11 33	11 38					11 59
Ashford (Surrey)	d					11 06	11 11										11 36	11 41					
Feltham	d					11 11	11 16					11 35					11 41	11 46					12 05
Whitton	d						11 20			11 20	11 23							11 50			11 50	11 53	
Kingston	d				10 59											11 29							
Hampton Wick	d				11 01											11 31							
Teddington	d				11 05											11 35							
Fulwell	d																						
Strawberry Hill	d				11 08											11 38							
Twickenham	a				11 12		11 23				11 26	11 40				11 42		11 53				11 56	12 10
	d				11 13		11 23				11 28	11 41				11 43		11 53				11 58	12 11
St Margarets	d				11 15						11 30					11 45						12 00	
Richmond ⊖	d				11 19		11 28				11 34	11 45				11 49		11 58				12 04	12 15
North Sheen	d				11 21						11 36					11 51						12 06	
Mortlake	d				11 23						11 38					11 53						12 08	
Hounslow	d					11 16				11 31							11 46				12 01		
Isleworth	d					11 19				11 34							11 49				12 04		
Syon Lane	d					11 21				11 36							11 51				12 06		
Brentford	d					11 24				11 39							11 54				12 09		
Kew Bridge	d					11 26				11 41							11 56				12 11		
Chiswick	d					11 29				11 44							11 59				12 14		
Barnes Bridge	d	←				11 31				11 46			←				12 01				12 16		
Barnes	d	11 19			11 26	11 34		←		11 49	11 41		11 49			11 56	12 04		←		12 19	12 11	
Putney	d	11 22			11 29	11 37	11 34	11 37		→	11 44		11 52			11 59	12 07	12 04	12 07		→	12 14	
Wandsworth Town	d	11 25			11 32	→		11 40			11 47		11 55			12 02	→		12 10			12 17	
Clapham Junction [10]	d	11 28			11 35		11 39	11 43			11 50	11 54	11 58			12 05		12 09	12 14			12 21	12 24
Queenstown Rd.(Battersea)	d	11 31			11 38			11 46			11 53		12 01			12 08			12 17			12 24	
Vauxhall ⊖	d	11 35			11 42		11 45	11 50			11 57		12 05			12 12		12 15	12 21			12 27	
London Waterloo [15] ⊖	a	11 41			11 46		11 49	11 56			12 02	12 04	12 11			12 16		12 19	12 26			12 32	12 34

Table T149-R

Mondays to Fridays

16 December to 15 May

Reading, Guildford, Ascot, Weybridge, Windsor, Kingston, Richmond and Hounslow - London

		SW	SW [1]	SW [1]	SW	SW	SW	SW	SW	SW	SW	SW	SW	SW [1]	SW [1]	SW	SW	SW	SW	SW	SW	SW	SW
Reading [7]	d											11 42											12 12
Earley	d											11 47											12 17
Winnersh Triangle	d											11 49											12 19
Winnersh	d											11 51											12 21
Wokingham	d											11 56											12 26
Bracknell	d											12 02											12 32
Martins Heron	d											12 05											12 35
Guildford	d			11 23											11 53								
Wanborough	d			11 29											11 59								
Ash [5]	d			11 33											12 03								
Aldershot	a			11 40											12 10								
	d		11 30											12 00									
Ash Vale	d		11 34											12 04									
Frimley	d		11 40											12 10									
Camberley	a		11 44											12 14									
	d		11 48											12 18									
Bagshot	d		11 53											12 23									
Ascot [3]	d		12a00									12 10		12a30									12 40
Sunningdale	d											12 13											12 43
Longcross	d											12 16											12 46
Weybridge	d								12 03											12 33			
Addlestone	d								12 07											12 37			
Chertsey	d					←			12 10								←			12 40			
Virginia Water	a					11 45			12 15			12 20					12 15			12 45			12 50
	d					11 54			12 24			12 20					12 24			12 54			12 50
Egham	d					11 57			→			12 23					12 27			→			12 53
Windsor & Eton Riverside	d						11 53											12 23					
Datchet	d						11 56											12 26					
Sunnymeads	d						11 59											12 29					
Wraysbury	d						12 02											12 32					
Staines	d					12 03	12 08					12 29					12 33	12 38					12 59
Ashford (Surrey)	d					12 06	12 11										12 36	12 41					
Feltham	d					12 11	12 16					12 35					12 41	12 46					13 05
Whitton	d						12 20			12 20	12 23							12 50			12 50	12 53	
Kingston	d				11 59											12 29							
Hampton Wick	d				12 01											12 31							
Teddington	d				12 05											12 35							
Fulwell	d																						
Strawberry Hill	d				12 08											12 38							
Twickenham	a				12 12		12 23				12 26	12 40				12 42		12 53				12 56	13 10
	d				12 13		12 23				12 28	12 41				12 43		12 53				12 58	13 11
St Margarets	d				12 15						12 30					12 45						13 00	
Richmond ⊖	d				12 19		12 28				12 34	12 45				12 49		12 58				13 04	13 15
North Sheen	d				12 21						12 36					12 51						13 06	
Mortlake	d				12 23						12 38					12 53						13 08	
Hounslow	d					12 16				12 31							12 46				13 01		
Isleworth	d					12 19				12 34							12 49				13 04		
Syon Lane	d					12 21				12 36							12 51				13 06		
Brentford	d					12 24				12 39							12 54				13 09		
Kew Bridge	d					12 26				12 41							12 56				13 11		
Chiswick	d					12 29				12 44							12 59				13 14		
Barnes Bridge	d	←				12 31				12 46			←				13 01				13 16		
Barnes	d	12 19			12 26	12 34		←		12 49	12 41		12 49			12 56	13 04		←		13 19	13 11	
Putney	d	12 22			12 29	12 37	12 34	12 37		→	12 44		12 52			12 59	13 07	13 04	13 07		→	13 14	
Wandsworth Town	d	12 25			12 32	→		12 40			12 47		12 55			13 02	→		13 10			13 17	
Clapham Junction [10]	d	12 28			12 35		12 39	12 43			12 50	12 54	12 58			13 05		13 09	13 13			13 20	13 24
Queenstown Rd.(Battersea)	d	12 31			12 38			12 46			12 53		13 01			13 08			13 16			13 23	
Vauxhall ⊖	d	12 35			12 42		12 45	12 50			12 57		13 05			13 12		13 15	13 20			13 27	
London Waterloo [15] ⊖	a	12 41			12 46		12 49	12 56			13 02	13 04	13 12			13 16		13 19	13 26			13 32	13 34

Table T149-R

Mondays to Fridays
16 December to 15 May

Reading, Guildford, Ascot, Weybridge, Windsor, Kingston, Richmond and Hounslow - London

		SW		SW 1	SW 1	SW	SW	SW	SW	SW	SW	SW		SW	SW	SW 1	SW 1	SW	SW	SW	SW	SW		SW	SW
Reading 7	d													12 42											
Earley	d													12 47											
Winnersh Triangle	d													12 49											
Winnersh	d													12 51											
Wokingham	d													12 56											
Bracknell	d													13 02											
Martins Heron	d													13 05											
Guildford	d				12 23												12 53								
Wanborough	d				12 29												12 59								
Ash 5	d				12 33												13 03								
Aldershot	a				12 40												13 10								
	d			12 30												13 00									
Ash Vale	d			12 34												13 04									
Frimley	d			12 40												13 10									
Camberley	a			12 44												13 14									
	d			12 48												13 18									
Bagshot	d			12 53												13 23									
Ascot 3	d			13a00										13 10		13a30									
Sunningdale	d													13 13											
Longcross	d													13 16											
Weybridge	d									13 03												13 33			
Addlestone	d									13 07												13 37			
Chertsey	d						←			13 10									←			13 40			
Virginia Water	a						12 45			13 15				13 20					13 15			13 45			
	d						12 54			13 24				13 20					13 24			13 54			
Egham	d						12 57			→				13 23					13 27			→			
Windsor & Eton Riverside	d							12 53												13 23					
Datchet	d							12 56												13 26					
Sunnymeads	d							12 59												13 29					
Wraysbury	d							13 02												13 32					
Staines	d						13 03	13 08						13 29					13 33	13 38					
Ashford (Surrey)	d						13 06	13 11											13 36	13 41					
Feltham	d						13 11	13 16						13 35					13 41	13 46					
Whitton	d							13 20			13 20	13 23								13 50				13 50	13 53
Kingston	d					12 59												13 29							
Hampton Wick	d					13 01												13 31							
Teddington	d					13 05												13 35							
Fulwell	d																								
Strawberry Hill	d					13 08												13 38							
Twickenham	a					13 12		13 23				13 26		13 40				13 42		13 53					13 56
	d					13 13		13 23				13 28		13 41				13 43		13 53					13 58
St Margarets	d					13 15						13 30						13 45							14 00
Richmond ⊖	d					13 19		13 28				13 34		13 45				13 49		13 58					14 04
North Sheen	d					13 21						13 36						13 51							14 06
Mortlake	d					13 23						13 38						13 53							14 08
Hounslow	d						13 16				13 31								13 46					14 01	
Isleworth	d						13 19				13 34								13 49					14 04	
Syon Lane	d						13 21				13 36								13 51					14 06	
Brentford	d						13 24				13 39								13 54					14 09	
Kew Bridge	d						13 26				13 41								13 56					14 11	
Chiswick	d						13 29				13 44								13 59					14 14	
Barnes Bridge	d	←					13 31				13 46				←				14 01					14 16	
Barnes	d	13 19				13 26	13 34		←		13 49	13 41			13 49			13 56	14 04		←			14 19	14 11
Putney	d	13 22				13 29	13 37	13 34	13 37		→	13 44			13 52			13 59	14 07	14 04	14 07			→	14 14
Wandsworth Town	d	13 25				13 32	→		13 40			13 47			13 55			14 02	→		14 10				14 17
Clapham Junction 10	d	13 28				13 35		13 39	13 44			13 50		13 54	14 00			14 05		14 09	14 14				14 20
Queenstown Rd.(Battersea)	d	13 31				13 38			13 47			13 53			14 03			14 08			14 17				14 23
Vauxhall ⊖	d	13 35				13 42		13 45	13 51			13 57			14 07			14 12		14 15	14 21				14 27
London Waterloo 15 ⊖	a	13 42				13 46		13 49	13 56			14 02		14 04	14 11			14 16		14 19	14 26				14 32

Table T149-R

Mondays to Fridays
16 December to 15 May

Reading, Guildford, Ascot, Weybridge, Windsor, Kingston, Richmond and Hounslow - London

		SW	SW	SW 1	SW 1	SW	SW	SW		SW	SW	SW	SW	SW	SW	SW 1	SW 1	SW		SW	SW	SW	SW	SW	SW
Reading 7	d	13 12												13 42											
Earley	d	13 17												13 47											
Winnersh Triangle	d	13 19												13 49											
Winnersh	d	13 21												13 51											
Wokingham	d	13 26												13 56											
Bracknell	d	13 32												14 02											
Martins Heron	d	13 35												14 05											
Guildford	d				13 23												13 53								
Wanborough	d				13 29												13 59								
Ash 5	d				13 33												14 03								
Aldershot	a				13 40												14 10								
	d			13 30												14 00									
Ash Vale	d			13 34												14 04									
Frimley	d			13 40												14 10									
Camberley	a			13 44												14 14									
	d			13 48												14 18									
Bagshot	d			13 53												14 23									
Ascot 3	d	13 40		14a00										14 10		14a30									
Sunningdale	d	13 43												14 13											
Longcross	d	13 46												14 16											
Weybridge	d										14 03												14 33		
Addlestone	d										14 07												14 37		
Chertsey	d						←				14 10									←			14 40		
Virginia Water	a	13 50					13 45				14 15			14 20						14 15			14 45		
	d	13 50					13 54				14 24			14 20						14 24			14 54		
Egham	d	13 53					13 57				→			14 23						14 27			→		
Windsor & Eton Riverside	d							13 53													14 23				
Datchet	d							13 56													14 26				
Sunnymeads	d							13 59													14 29				
Wraysbury	d							14 02													14 32				
Staines	d	13 59					14 03	14 08						14 29						14 33	14 38				
Ashford (Surrey)	d						14 06	14 11												14 36	14 41				
Feltham	d	14 05					14 11	14 16						14 35						14 41	14 46				
Whitton	d							14 20				14 20	14 23								14 50			14 50	14 53
Kingston	d					13 59												14 29							
Hampton Wick	d					14 01												14 31							
Teddington	d					14 05												14 35							
Fulwell	d																								
Strawberry Hill	d					14 08												14 38							
Twickenham	a	14 10				14 12		14 23					14 26	14 40				14 42			14 53				14 56
	d	14 11				14 13		14 23					14 28	14 41				14 43			14 53				14 58
St Margarets	d					14 15							14 30					14 45							15 00
Richmond ⊖	d	14 15				14 19		14 28					14 34	14 45				14 49			14 58				15 04
North Sheen	d					14 21							14 36					14 51							15 06
Mortlake	d					14 23							14 38					14 53							15 08
Hounslow	d						14 16					14 31								14 46				15 01	
Isleworth	d						14 19					14 34								14 49				15 04	
Syon Lane	d						14 21					14 36								14 51				15 06	
Brentford	d						14 24					14 39								14 54				15 09	
Kew Bridge	d						14 26					14 41								14 56				15 11	
Chiswick	d						14 29					14 44								14 59				15 14	
Barnes Bridge	d		←				14 31					14 46			←					15 01				15 16	
Barnes	d		14 19			14 26	14 34			←		14 49	14 41		14 49			14 56		15 04		←		15 19	15 11
Putney	d		14 22			14 29	14 37	14 34		14 37		→	14 44		14 52			14 59		15 07	15 04	15 07		→	15 14
Wandsworth Town	d		14 25			14 32	→			14 40			14 47		14 55			15 02		→		15 10			15 17
Clapham Junction 10	d	14 24	14 28			14 35		14 39		14 43			14 50	14 54	14 58			15 05			15 09	15 13			15 20
Queenstown Rd.(Battersea)	d		14 31			14 38				14 46			14 53		15 01			15 08				15 16			15 23
Vauxhall ⊖	d		14 35			14 42		14 45		14 50			14 57		15 05			15 12			15 15	15 20			15 27
London Waterloo 15 ⊖	a	14 34	14 41			14 46		14 49		14 56			15 05	15 07	15 11			15 16			15 19	15 26			15 35

Table T149-R

Mondays to Fridays
16 December to 15 May

Reading, Guildford, Ascot, Weybridge, Windsor, Kingston, Richmond and Hounslow - London

		SW	SW	SW 1	SW 1	SW	SW	SW	SW	SW	SW	SW	SW	SW	SW 1	SW 1	SW	SW	SW	SW	SW	SW
Reading 7	d	14 12											14 42									
Earley	d	14 17											14 47									
Winnersh Triangle	d	14 19											14 49									
Winnersh	d	14 21											14 51									
Wokingham	d	14 26											14 56									
Bracknell	d	14 32											15 02									
Martins Heron	d	14 35											15 05									
Guildford	d				14 23											14 53						
Wanborough	d				14 29											14 59						
Ash 5	d				14 33											15 03						
Aldershot	a				14 40											15 10						
	d			14 30											15 00							
Ash Vale	d			14 34											15 04							
Frimley	d			14 40											15 10							
Camberley	a			14 44											15 14							
	d			14 48											15 18							
Bagshot	d			14 53											15 23							
Ascot 3	d	14 40		15a00									15 10		15a30							
Sunningdale	d	14 43											15 13									
Longcross	d	14 46											15 16									
Weybridge	d									15 03											15 33	
Addlestone	d									15 07											15 37	
Chertsey	d						←			15 10								←			15 40	
Virginia Water	a	14 50					14 45			15 15			15 20					15 15			15 45	
	d	14 50					14 54			15 24			15 20					15 24			15 54	
Egham	d	14 54					14 57			→			15 23					15 27			→	
Windsor & Eton Riverside	d							14 53											15 23			
Datchet	d							14 56											15 26			
Sunnymeads	d							14 59											15 29			
Wraysbury	d							15 02											15 32			
Staines	d	14 59					15 03	15 08					15 29					15 33	15 38			
Ashford (Surrey)	d						15 06	15 11										15 36	15 41			
Feltham	d	15 05					15 11	15 16					15 35					15 41	15 46			
Whitton	d							15 20			15 20	15 23							15 50			15 50
Kingston	d					14 59											15 29					
Hampton Wick	d					15 01											15 31					
Teddington	d					15 05											15 35					
Fulwell	d																					
Strawberry Hill	d					15 08											15 38					
Twickenham	a	15 10				15 12		15 23				15 26	15 40				15 42		15 53			
	d	15 11				15 13		15 23				15 28	15 41				15 43		15 53			
St Margarets	d					15 15						15 30					15 45					
Richmond ⊖	d	15 15				15 19		15 28				15 34	15 45				15 49		15 58			
North Sheen	d					15 21						15 36					15 51					
Mortlake	d					15 23						15 38					15 53					
Hounslow	d						15 16				15 31							15 46				16 01
Isleworth	d						15 19				15 34							15 49				16 04
Syon Lane	d						15 21				15 36							15 51				16 06
Brentford	d						15 24				15 39							15 54				16 09
Kew Bridge	d						15 26				15 41							15 56				16 11
Chiswick	d						15 29				15 44							15 59				16 14
Barnes Bridge	d		←				15 31				15 46			←				16 01				16 16
Barnes	d		15 19			15 26	15 34		←		15 49	15 41		15 49			15 56	16 04		←		16 19
Putney	d		15 22			15 29	15 37	15 34	15 37		→	15 44		15 52			15 59	16 07	16 04	16 07		→
Wandsworth Town	d		15 25			15 32	→		15 40			15 47		15 55			16 02	→		16 10		
Clapham Junction 10	d	15 24	15 28			15 35		15 39	15 43			15 50	15 54	15 58			16 05		16 09	16 13		
Queenstown Rd.(Battersea)	d		15 31			15 38			15 46			15 53		16 01			16 08			16 16		
Vauxhall ⊖	d		15 35			15 42		15 45	15 50			15 57		16 05			16 12		16 15	16 20		
London Waterloo 15 ⊖	a	15 37	15 42			15 47		15 50	15 56			16 05	16 07	16 11			16 16		16 19	16 26		

Table T149-R

Mondays to Fridays
16 December to 15 May

Reading, Guildford, Ascot, Weybridge, Windsor, Kingston, Richmond and Hounslow - London

		SW	SW	SW	SW 1	SW 1	SW	SW	SW	SW	SW	SW	SW	SW	SW	SW 1	SW 1	SW	SW	SW	SW	SW	SW
Reading 7	d		15 12											15 42									
Earley	d		15 17											15 47									
Winnersh Triangle	d		15 19											15 49									
Winnersh	d		15 21											15 51									
Wokingham	d		15 26											15 56									
Bracknell	d		15 32											16 02									
Martins Heron	d		15 35											16 05									
Guildford	d					15 23											15 53						
Wanborough	d					15 29											15 59						
Ash 5	d					15 33											16 03						
Aldershot	a					15 40											16 10						
	d				15 30											16 00							
Ash Vale	d				15 34											16 04							
Frimley	d				15 40											16 10							
Camberley	a				15 44											16 14							
	d				15 48											16 18							
Bagshot	d				15 53											16 23							
Ascot 3	d		15 40		16a00									16 10		16a30							
Sunningdale	d		15 43											16 13									
Longcross	d		15 46											16 16									
Weybridge	d										16 03											16 33	
Addlestone	d										16 07											16 41	
Chertsey	d							←			16 10								←			16 44	
Virginia Water	a		15 50					15 45			16 15			16 20					16 15			16 49	
	d		15 50					15 54			16 24			16 20					16 24			16 54	
Egham	d		15 53					15 57			→			16 24					16 27			→	
Windsor & Eton Riverside	d								15 53											16 23			
Datchet	d								15 56											16 26			
Sunnymeads	d								15 59											16 29			
Wraysbury	d								16 02											16 32			
Staines	d		15 59					16 03	16 08					16 29					16 33	16 38			
Ashford (Surrey)	d							16 06	16 11										16 36	16 41			
Feltham	d		16 05					16 11	16 16					16 35					16 41	16 46			
Whitton	d	15 53							16 20			16 20	16 23							16 50			16 50
Kingston	d						15 59											16 29					
Hampton Wick	d						16 01											16 31					
Teddington	d						16 05											16 35					
Fulwell	d																						
Strawberry Hill	d						16 08											16 38					
Twickenham	a	15 56	16 10				16 12		16 23				16 26	16 40				16 42		16 53			
	d	15 58	16 11				16 13		16 23				16 28	16 41				16 43		16 53			
St Margarets	d	16 00					16 15						16 30					16 45					
Richmond ⊖	d	16 04	16 15				16 19		16 28				16 34	16 45				16 49		16 58			
North Sheen	d	16 06					16 21						16 36					16 51					
Mortlake	d	16 08					16 23						16 38					16 53					
Hounslow	d							16 16				16 31							16 46				17 01
Isleworth	d							16 19				16 34							16 49				17 04
Syon Lane	d							16 21				16 36							16 51				17 06
Brentford	d							16 24				16 39							16 54				17 09
Kew Bridge	d							16 26				16 41							16 56				17 11
Chiswick	d							16 29				16 44							16 59				17 14
Barnes Bridge	d			←				16 31				16 46			←				17 01				17 16
Barnes	d	16 11		16 19			16 26	16 34		←		16 49	16 41		16 49			16 56	17 04		←		17 19
Putney	d	16 14		16 22			16 29	16 37	16 34	16 37		→	16 44		16 52			16 59	17 07	17 04	17 07		→
Wandsworth Town	d	16 17		16 25			16 32	→		16 40			16 47		16 55			17 02	→		17 10		
Clapham Junction 10	d	16 20	16 24	16 28			16 35		16 39	16 43			16 50	16 54	16 58			17 05		17 09	17 13		
Queenstown Rd.(Battersea)	d	16 23		16 31			16 38			16 46			16 53		17 01			17 08			17 16		
Vauxhall ⊖	d	16 27		16 35			16 42		16 45	16 50			16 57		17 05			17 12		17 15	17 20		
London Waterloo 15 ⊖	a	16 35	16 37	16 41			16 46		16 49	16 56			17 05	17 07	17 11			17 16		17 19	17 27		

Table T149-R

Mondays to Fridays

16 December to 15 May

Reading, Guildford, Ascot, Weybridge, Windsor, Kingston, Richmond and Hounslow - London

		SW	SW	SW	SW	SW	SW	SW	SW	SW	SW	SW	SW	SW	SW	SW	SW	SW	SW	SW	SW	SW	SW
									◇	1	1											◇	1
Reading 7	d		16 12						16 23							16 41						16 50	
Earley	d		16 17						16 28							16 46						16 55	
Winnersh Triangle	d		16 19						16 30							16 48						16 58	
Winnersh	d		16 21						16 32							16 50						17 00	
Wokingham	d		16 26						16 37							16 55						17 04	
Bracknell	d		16 32						16 43							17 02						17 15	
Martins Heron	d		16 35						16 46							17 05						17 18	
Guildford	d										16 23												
Wanborough	d										16 29												
Ash 5	d										16 33												
Aldershot	a										16 40												
	d									16 30													17 00
Ash Vale	d									16 34													17 04
Frimley	d									16 40													17 10
Camberley	a									16 44													17 14
	d									16 48													17 18
Bagshot	d									16 53													17 23
Ascot 3	d		16 40						16 55	17a00						17 10						17 25	17a30
Sunningdale	d		16 43						16 58							17 13						17 28	
Longcross	d		16 46													17 16							
Weybridge	d											17 03											
Addlestone	d											17 07											
Chertsey	d					←						17 10							←				
Virginia Water	a		16 50			16 49			17 03			17 15				17 20			17 15			17 33	
	d		16 50			16 54			17 03			17 24				17 20			17 24			17 33	
Egham	d		16 53			16 57			17 06			→				17 23			17 27			17 37	
Windsor & Eton Riverside	d						16 53													17 23			
Datchet	d						16 56													17 26			
Sunnymeads	d						16 59													17 29			
Wraysbury	d						17 02													17 32			
Staines	d		16 59			17 03	17 08		17 14							17 29			17 33	17 38		17 44	
Ashford (Surrey)	d					17 06	17 11												17 36	17 41			
Feltham	d		17 05			17 11	17 16		17 20							17 35			17 41	17 46		17 51	
Whitton	d	16 52					17 20						17 20	17 22						17 50			
Kingston	d				16 59													17 29					
Hampton Wick	d				17 01													17 31					
Teddington	d				17 05													17 35					
Fulwell	d																						
Strawberry Hill	d				17 08										17 31			17 38					
Twickenham	a	16 56	17 10		17 12		17 23							17 25	17 34	17 40		17 42		17 53			
	d	16 58	17 11		17 13		17 23							17 27	17 35	17 41		17 43		17 53			
St Margarets	d	17 00			17 15									17 29				17 45					
Richmond ⊖	d	17 03	17 15		17 19		17 28							17 33	17 40	17 45		17 49		17 58			
North Sheen	d	17 05			17 21									17 35				17 51					
Mortlake	d	17 08			17 23									17 37				17 53					
Hounslow	d					17 16			17 26				17 31						17 46			17 56	
Isleworth	d					17 19							17 34						17 49				
Syon Lane	d					17 21							17 36						17 51				
Brentford	d					17 24			17 31				17 39						17 54			18 02	
Kew Bridge	d					17 26							17 41						17 56				
Chiswick	d					17 29							17 44						17 59				
Barnes Bridge	d			←		17 31							17 46				←		18 01				
Barnes	d	17 11		17 19	17 26	17 34		←					17 49	17 40			17 49	17 56	18 04		←		
Putney	d	17 14		17 22	17 29	17 37	17 34	17 37	17 39				→	17 43			17 52	17 59	18 07	18 04	18 07	18 09	
Wandsworth Town	d	17 17		17 25	17 32	→		17 40						17 46			17 55	18 02	→		18 10		
Clapham Junction 10	d	17 22	17 24	17 28	17 35		17 39	17 43	17 44					17 52	17 50	17 54	17 58	18 05		18 09	18 13	18 14	
Queenstown Rd.(Battersea)	d	17 25		17 31	17 38			17 46						17 55			18 01	18 08			18 16		
Vauxhall ⊖	d	17 28		17 35	17 42		17 45	17 50						17 58			18 05	18 12		18 15	18 20		
London Waterloo 15 ⊖	a	17 37	17 37	17 41	17 46		17 49	17 56	17 56					18 05	17 59	18 07	18 11	18 19		18 19	18 26	18 26	

NRT DECEMBER 19 EDITION

Table T149-R

Mondays to Fridays

16 December to 15 May

Reading, Guildford, Ascot, Weybridge, Windsor, Kingston, Richmond and Hounslow - London

		SW	SW	SW	SW	SW	SW	SW	SW	SW	SW	SW	SW	SW	SW	SW	SW	SW	SW	SW	SW	SW
		1											◇	1	1							
Reading 7	d						17 12						17 23						17 42			
Earley	d						17 17						17 28						17 47			
Winnersh Triangle	d						17 19						17 30						17 49			
Winnersh	d						17 21						17 32						17 51			
Wokingham	d						17 26						17 37						17 56			
Bracknell	d						17 32						17 43						18 02			
Martins Heron	d						17 35						17 46						18 05			
Guildford	d	16 53													17 23							
Wanborough	d	16 59													17 29							
Ash 5	d	17 03													17 33							
Aldershot	a	17 10													17 40							
	d													17 30								
Ash Vale	d													17 34								
Frimley	d													17 40								
Camberley	a													17 44								
	d													17 48								
Bagshot	d													17 53								
Ascot 3	d						17 40						17 55	18a00					18 10			
Sunningdale	d						17 43						17 58						18 13			
Longcross	d						17 46												18 16			
Weybridge	d		17 37													18 07						
Addlestone	d		17 41													18 11						
Chertsey	d		17 44							←						18 14						←
Virginia Water	a		17 49				17 50			17 49			18 03			18 19			18 20			18 19
	d		17 54				17 50			17 54			18 03			18 24			18 20			18 24
Egham	d		→				17 53			17 57			18 06			→			18 23			18 27
Windsor & Eton Riverside	d										17 53											
Datchet	d										17 56											
Sunnymeads	d										17 59											
Wraysbury	d										18 02											
Staines	d						17 59			18 03	18 08		18 14						18 29			18 33
Ashford (Surrey)	d									18 06	18 11											18 36
Feltham	d						18 05			18 11	18 16		18 20						18 35			18 41
Whitton	d				17 50	17 53					18 20						18 20	18 23				
Kingston	d								17 59												18 29	
Hampton Wick	d								18 01												18 31	
Teddington	d								18 05												18 35	
Fulwell	d																					
Strawberry Hill	d					17 59			18 08												18 38	
Twickenham	a				17 56	18 02	18 10		18 12		18 23							18 26	18 40		18 42	
	d				17 58	18 03	18 11		18 13		18 23							18 28	18 41		18 43	
St Margarets	d				18 00	18 05			18 15									18 30			18 45	
Richmond ⊖	d				18 04	18 08	18 15		18 19		18 28							18 34	18 45		18 49	
North Sheen	d				18 06	18 10			18 21									18 36			18 51	
Mortlake	d				18 08	18 13			18 23									18 38			18 53	
Hounslow	d			18 01						18 16			18 26				18 31					18 46
Isleworth	d			18 04						18 19							18 34					18 49
Syon Lane	d			18 06						18 21							18 36					18 51
Brentford	d			18 09						18 24			18 31				18 39					18 54
Kew Bridge	d			18 11						18 26							18 41					18 56
Chiswick	d			18 14						18 29							18 44					18 59
Barnes Bridge	d			18 16				←		18 31							18 46			←		19 01
Barnes	d			18 19	18 11	18 16		18 19	18 26	18 34		←					18 49	18 41		18 49	18 56	19 04
Putney	d			→	18 14	18 19		18 22	18 29	18 37	18 34	18 37	18 39				→	18 44		18 52	18 59	19 07
Wandsworth Town	d				18 17			18 25	18 32	→		18 40						18 47		18 55	19 02	→
Clapham Junction 10	d				18 22	18 24	18 27	18 28	18 35		18 39	18 43	18 44					18 52	18 54	18 58	19 05	
Queenstown Rd.(Battersea)	d				18 25			18 31	18 38			18 46						18 55		19 01	19 08	
Vauxhall ⊖	d				18 29	18 30		18 36	18 42		18 45	18 50						18 58		19 05	19 12	
London Waterloo 15 ⊖	a				18 35	18 35	18 37	18 41	18 49		18 49	18 56	18 56					19 03	19 05	19 11	19 16	

Table T149-R

Mondays to Fridays
16 December to 15 May

Reading, Guildford, Ascot, Weybridge, Windsor, Kingston, Richmond and Hounslow - London

		SW	SW	SW ◇	SW 1	SW 1	SW	SW	SW	SW	SW	SW	SW ◇	SW 1	SW 1	SW	SW	SW	SW	SW	SW	SW	SW	SW	SW
Reading 7	d			17 55						18 12		18 25										18 42	
Earley	d			18 00						18 17												18 47	
Winnersh Triangle	d			18 02						18 19												18 49	
Winnersh	d			18 04						18 21												18 51	
Wokingham	d			18 09						18 26		18 34										18 56	
Bracknell	d			18 16						18 32		18 41										19 02	
Martins Heron	d			18 19						18 35		18 44										19 05	
Guildford	d					17 53								18 23									
Wanborough	d					17 59								18 29									
Ash 5	d					18 03								18 33									
Aldershot	a					18 12								18 44									
	d				18 00								18 30										
Ash Vale	d				18 04								18 34										
Frimley	d				18 10								18 40										
Camberley	a				18 14								18 44										
	d				18 18								18 48										
Bagshot	d				18 23								18 53										
Ascot 3	d			18 25	18a30					18 40		18a48	19a02									19 10	
Sunningdale	d			18 28						18 43												19 13	
Longcross	d									18 46												19 16	
Weybridge	d						18 37												19 07				
Addlestone	d						18 41												19 11				
Chertsey	d						18 44									←			19 14				
Virginia Water	a			18 33			18 49			18 50						18 49			19 19			19 20	
	d			18 33			18 54			18 50						18 54			19 24			19 20	
Egham	d			18 37			→			18 53						18 57			→			19 23	
Windsor & Eton Riverside	d	18 23															18 53						
Datchet	d	18 26															18 56						
Sunnymeads	d	18 29															18 59						
Wraysbury	d	18 32															19 02						
Staines	d	18 38		18 44						18 59						19 03	19 08					19 29	
Ashford (Surrey)	d	18 41														19 06	19 11						
Feltham	d	18 46		18 50						19 05						19 11	19 16					19 35	
Whitton	d	18 50						18 50	18 53								19 20			19 20	19 23		
Kingston	d														18 59								
Hampton Wick	d														19 01								
Teddington	d														19 05								
Fulwell	d																						
Strawberry Hill	d														19 08								
Twickenham	a	18 53							18 56	19 10					19 12		19 23				19 26	19 40	
	d	18 53							18 58	19 11					19 13		19 23				19 28	19 41	
St Margarets	d								19 00						19 15						19 30		
Richmond ⊖	d	18 58							19 04	19 15					19 19		19 28				19 34	19 45	
North Sheen	d								19 06						19 21						19 36		
Mortlake	d								19 08						19 23						19 38		
Hounslow	d			18 56				19 01								19 16				19 31			
Isleworth	d							19 04								19 19				19 34			
Syon Lane	d							19 06								19 21				19 36			
Brentford	d			19 01				19 09								19 24				19 39			
Kew Bridge	d							19 11								19 26				19 41			
Chiswick	d							19 14								19 29				19 44			
Barnes Bridge	d							19 16			←					19 31				19 46			←
Barnes	d		←					19 19	19 12		19 19				19 26	19 34		←		19 49	19 41		19 49
Putney	d	19 04	19 07	19 09				→	19 15		19 22				19 29	19 37	19 34	19 37		→	19 44		19 52
Wandsworth Town	d		19 10						19 18		19 25				19 32	→		19 40			19 47		19 55
Clapham Junction 10	d	19 09	19 13	19 14					19 21	19 25	19 28				19 35		19 39	19 43			19 50	19 54	19 58
Queenstown Rd.(Battersea)	d		19 16						19 24		19 31				19 38			19 46			19 53		20 01
Vauxhall ⊖	d	19 15	19 20						19 28		19 35				19 42			19 50			19 57		20 05
London Waterloo 15 ⊖	a	19 19	19 26	19 26					19 36	19 37	19 41				19 46		19 49	19 56			20 05	20 07	20 11

Table T149-R

Mondays to Fridays
16 December to 15 May

Reading, Guildford, Ascot, Weybridge, Windsor, Kingston, Richmond and Hounslow - London

		SW	SW	SW	SW	SW	SW 1	SW 1	SW	SW	SW	SW	SW	SW ◇	SW 1	SW 1	SW	SW	SW	SW	SW	SW
Reading 7	d					18 52						19 12		19 23								
Earley	d					18 57						19 17		19 28								
Winnersh Triangle	d					18 59						19 19		19 30								
Winnersh	d					19 01						19 21		19 32								
Wokingham	d					19 06						19 26		19 37								
Bracknell	d					19 12						19 32		19 43								
Martins Heron	d					19 15						19 35		19 46								
Guildford	d							18 53								19 23						
Wanborough	d							18 59								19 29						
Ash 5	d							19 03								19 33						
Aldershot	a							19 14								19 40						
	d						19 00								19 30							
Ash Vale	d						19 04								19 34							
Frimley	d						19 10								19 40							
Camberley	a						19 14								19 44							
	d						19 18								19 48							
Bagshot	d						19 23								19 53							
Ascot 3	d					19 20	19a30					19 40		19a50	20a02							
Sunningdale	d					19 23						19 43										
Longcross	d											19 46										
Weybridge	d								19 37												20 05	
Addlestone	d								19 41												20 09	
Chertsey	d		←						19 44									←			20 12	
Virginia Water	a		19 19			19 28			19 49			19 50						19 49			20 17	
	d		19 24			19 28			19 54			19 50						19 54			20 24	
Egham	d		19 27			19 31			→			19 53						19 57			→	
Windsor & Eton Riverside	d			19 23															19 53			
Datchet	d			19 26															19 56			
Sunnymeads	d			19 29															19 59			
Wraysbury	d			19 32															20 02			
Staines	d		19 33	19 38		19a41						19 59						20 03	20 08			
Ashford (Surrey)	d		19 36	19 41														20 06	20 11			
Feltham	d		19 41	19 46								20 05						20 11	20 16			
Whitton	d			19 50						19 50	19 53								20 20			20 20
Kingston	d	19 29															19 59					
Hampton Wick	d	19 31															20 01					
Teddington	d	19 35															20 05					
Fulwell	d																					
Strawberry Hill	d	19 38															20 08					
Twickenham	a	19 42		19 53							19 56	20 10					20 12		20 23			
	d	19 43		19 53							19 58	20 11					20 13		20 23			
St Margarets	d	19 45									20 00						20 15					
Richmond ⊖	d	19 49		19 58							20 04	20 15					20 19		20 28			
North Sheen	d	19 51									20 06						20 21					
Mortlake	d	19 53									20 08						20 23					
Hounslow	d		19 46							20 01								20 16				20 31
Isleworth	d		19 49							20 04								20 19				20 34
Syon Lane	d		19 51							20 06								20 21				20 36
Brentford	d		19 54							20 09								20 24				20 39
Kew Bridge	d		19 56							20 11								20 26				20 41
Chiswick	d		19 59							20 14								20 29				20 44
Barnes Bridge	d		20 01							20 16			←					20 31				20 46
Barnes	d	19 56	20 04		←					20 19	20 11		20 19				20 26	20 34		←		20 49
Putney	d	19 59	20 07	20 04	20 07					→	20 14		20 22				20 29	20 37	20 34	20 37		→
Wandsworth Town	d	20 02	→		20 10						20 17		20 25				20 32	→		20 40		
Clapham Junction 10	d	20 05		20 09	20 13						20 20	20 24	20 28				20 35		20 39	20 43		
Queenstown Rd.(Battersea)	d	20 08			20 16						20 23		20 31				20 38			20 46		
Vauxhall ⊖	d	20 12		20 15	20 20						20 27		20 35				20 42		20 45	20 50		
London Waterloo 15 ⊖	a	20 16		20 19	20 26						20 32	20 34	20 41				20 46		20 49	20 56		

Table T149-R

Mondays to Fridays

16 December to 15 May

Reading, Guildford, Ascot, Weybridge, Windsor, Kingston, Richmond and Hounslow - London

Station		SW	SW	SW	SW 1	SW 1	SW	SW	SW	SW		SW	SW	SW	SW	SW	SW 1	SW 1	SW	SW		SW	SW	SW	SW
Reading 7	d		19 42												20 12										
Earley	d		19 47												20 17										
Winnersh Triangle	d		19 49												20 19										
Winnersh	d		19 51												20 21										
Wokingham	d		19 56												20 26										
Bracknell	d		20 02												20 32										
Martins Heron	d		20 05												20 35										
Guildford	d					19 53												20 23							
Wanborough	d					19 59												20 29							
Ash 5	d					20 03												20 33							
Aldershot	a					20 10												20 40							
	d				20 00												20 30								
Ash Vale	d				20 04												20 34								
Frimley	d				20 10												20 40								
Camberley	a				20 14												20 44								
	d				20 18												20 48								
Bagshot	d				20 23												20 53								
Ascot 3	d		20 10		20a30										20 40		21a00								
Sunningdale	d		20 13												20 43										
Longcross	d		20 16												20 46										
Weybridge	d											20 33												21 03	
Addlestone	d											20 37												21 07	
Chertsey	d							←				20 40								←				21 10	
Virginia Water	a		20 20					20 17				20 45			20 50					20 45				21 15	
	d		20 20					20 24				20 54			20 50					20 54				21 24	
Egham	d		20 23					20 27				→			20 53					20 57				→	
Windsor & Eton Riverside	d								20 23													20 53			
Datchet	d								20 26													20 56			
Sunnymeads	d								20 29													20 59			
Wraysbury	d								20 32													21 02			
Staines	d		20 29					20 33	20 38						20 59					21 03		21 08			
Ashford (Surrey)	d							20 36	20 41											21 06		21 11			
Feltham	d		20 35					20 41	20 46						21 05					21 11		21 16			
Whitton	d	20 23							20 50				20 50	20 53								21 20			21 20
Kingston	d						20 29												20 59						
Hampton Wick	d						20 31												21 01						
Teddington	d						20 35												21 05						
Fulwell	d																								
Strawberry Hill	d						20 38												21 08						
Twickenham	a	20 26	20 40				20 42		20 53					20 56	21 10				21 12			21 23			
	d	20 28	20 41				20 43		20 53					20 58	21 11				21 13			21 23			
St Margarets	d	20 30					20 45							21 00					21 15						
Richmond ⊖	d	20 34	20 45				20 49		20 58					21 04	21 15				21 19			21 28			
North Sheen	d	20 36					20 51							21 06					21 21						
Mortlake	d	20 38					20 53							21 08					21 23						
Hounslow	d							20 46					21 01							21 16					21 31
Isleworth	d							20 49					21 04							21 19					21 34
Syon Lane	d							20 51					21 06							21 21					21 36
Brentford	d							20 54					21 09							21 24					21 39
Kew Bridge	d							20 56					21 11							21 26					21 41
Chiswick	d							20 59					21 14							21 29					21 44
Barnes Bridge	d			←				21 01					21 16			←				21 31					21 46
Barnes	d	20 41		20 49			20 56	21 04		←			21 19	21 11		21 19			21 26	21 34			←		21 49
Putney	d	20 44		20 52			20 59	21 07	21 04	21 07			→	21 14		21 22			21 29	21 37		21 34	21 37		→
Wandsworth Town	d	20 47		20 55			21 02	→		21 10				21 17		21 25			21 32	→			21 40		
Clapham Junction 10	d	20 50	20 54	20 58			21 05		21 09	21 13				21 20	21 24	21 28			21 35			21 39	21 43		
Queenstown Rd.(Battersea)	d	20 53		21 01			21 08			21 16				21 23		21 31			21 38				21 46		
Vauxhall ⊖	d	20 57		21 05			21 12		21 15	21 20				21 27		21 35			21 42			21 45	21 50		
London Waterloo 15 ⊖	a	21 02	21 04	21 11			21 16		21 19	21 26				21 32	21 34	21 41			21 46			21 49	21 56		

Table T149-R

Mondays to Fridays

16 December to 15 May

Reading, Guildford, Ascot, Weybridge, Windsor, Kingston, Richmond and Hounslow - London

Station		SW	SW	SW	SW 1	SW 1		SW	SW	SW	SW	SW	SW	SW	SW	SW		SW 1	SW 1	SW	SW	SW	SW	SW	SW
Reading 7	d		20 42												21 12										
Earley	d		20 47												21 17										
Winnersh Triangle	d		20 49												21 19										
Winnersh	d		20 51												21 21										
Wokingham	d		20 56												21 26										
Bracknell	d		21 02												21 32										
Martins Heron	d		21 05												21 35										
Guildford	d					20 53													21 23						
Wanborough	d					20 59													21 29						
Ash 5	d					21 03													21 33						
Aldershot	a					21 10													21 40						
	d				21 00													21 30							
Ash Vale	d				21 04													21 34							
Frimley	d				21 10													21 40							
Camberley	a				21 14													21 44							
	d				21 18													21 48							
Bagshot	d				21 23													21 53							
Ascot 3	d		21 10		21a30										21 40			22a00							
Sunningdale	d		21 13												21 43										
Longcross	d		21 16																						
Weybridge	d											21 33													22 03
Addlestone	d											21 37													22 07
Chertsey	d								←			21 40									←				22 10
Virginia Water	a		21 20						21 15			21 45			21 49						21 45				22 15
	d		21 20						21 24			21 54			21 49						21 54				22 24
Egham	d		21 23						21 27			→			21 53						21 57				→
Windsor & Eton Riverside	d									21 23												21 53			
Datchet	d									21 26												21 56			
Sunnymeads	d									21 29												21 59			
Wraysbury	d									21 32												22 02			
Staines	d		21 29						21 33	21 38					21 59						22 03	22 08			
Ashford (Surrey)	d								21 36	21 41											22 06	22 11			
Feltham	d		21 35						21 41	21 46					22 05						22 11	22 16			
Whitton	d	21 23								21 50			21 50	21 53								22 20		22 23	
Kingston	d							21 29												21 59					
Hampton Wick	d							21 31												22 01					
Teddington	d							21 35												22 05					
Fulwell	d																								
Strawberry Hill	d							21 38												22 08					
Twickenham	a	21 26	21 40					21 42		21 53				21 56	22 10					22 12		22 23		22 26	
	d	21 28	21 41					21 43		21 53				21 58	22 11					22 13		22 23		22 28	
St Margarets	d	21 30						21 45						22 00						22 15				22 30	
Richmond ⊖	d	21 34	21 45					21 49		21 58				22 04	22 15					22 19		22 28		22 34	
North Sheen	d	21 36						21 51						22 06						22 21				22 36	
Mortlake	d	21 38						21 53						22 08						22 23				22 38	
Hounslow	d								21 46				22 01								22 16				
Isleworth	d								21 49				22 04								22 19				
Syon Lane	d								21 51				22 06								22 21				
Brentford	d								21 54				22 09								22 24				
Kew Bridge	d								21 56				22 11								22 26				
Chiswick	d								21 59				22 14								22 29				
Barnes Bridge	d			←					22 01				22 16			←					22 31				
Barnes	d	21 41		21 49				21 56	22 04		←		22 19	22 11		22 19				22 26	22 34		←	22 41	
Putney	d	21 44		21 52				21 59	22 07	22 04	22 07		→	22 14		22 22				22 29	22 37	22 34	22 37	22 44	
Wandsworth Town	d	21 47		21 55				22 02	→		22 10			22 17		22 25				22 32	→		22 40	22 47	
Clapham Junction 10	d	21 50	21 54	21 58				22 05		22 09	22 13			22 20	22 24	22 28				22 35		22 39	22 43	22 50	
Queenstown Rd.(Battersea)	d	21 53		22 01				22 08			22 16			22 23		22 31				22 38			22 46	22 53	
Vauxhall ⊖	d	21 57		22 05				22 12		22 15	22 20			22 27		22 35				22 42		22 45	22 50	22 57	
London Waterloo 15 ⊖	a	22 02	22 04	22 11				22 16		22 19	22 26			22 32	22 35	22 42				22 46		22 49	22 56	23 02	

Table T149-R

Mondays to Fridays

16 December to 15 May

Reading, Guildford, Ascot, Weybridge, Windsor, Kingston, Richmond and Hounslow - London

		SW	SW 1	SW 1	SW	SW	SW	SW	SW	SW	SW 1	SW 1	SW FX	SW FO	SW	SW	SW	SW	SW	SW 1	SW 1	SW
Reading 7	d	21 42								22 12									22 42			
Earley	d	21 47								22 17									22 47			
Winnersh Triangle	d	21 49								22 19									22 49			
Winnersh	d	21 51								22 21									22 51			
Wokingham	d	21 56								22 26									22 56			
Bracknell	d	22 02								22 32									23 02			
Martins Heron	d	22 05								22 35									23 05			
Guildford	d			21 53								22 23									22 53	
Wanborough	d			21 59								22 29									22 59	
Ash 5	d			22 03								22 33									23 03	
Aldershot	a			22 10								22 40									23 10	
	d		22 00								22 30									23 00		
Ash Vale	d		22 04								22 34									23 04		
Frimley	d		22 10								22 40									23 10		
Camberley	a		22 14								22 44									23 14		
	d		22 18								22 48									23 18		
Bagshot	d		22 23								22 53									23 23		
Ascot 3	d	22 10	22a30							22 40	23a00								23 10	23a30		
Sunningdale	d	22 13								22 43									23 13			
Longcross	d																					
Weybridge	d								22 33									23 03				
Addlestone	d								22 37									23 07				
Chertsey	d					←			22 40						←			23 10				
Virginia Water	a	22 19				22 15			22 45	22 49					22 45			23 15	23 19			
	d	22 19				22 24			22 54	22 49					22 54			23 24	23 19			
Egham	d	22 23				22 27			→	22 53					22 57			→	23 23			
Windsor & Eton Riverside	d						22 23									22 53						
Datchet	d						22 26									22 56						
Sunnymeads	d						22 29									22 59						
Wraysbury	d						22 32									23 02						
Staines	d	22 29				22 33	22 38			22 59					23 03	23 08			23 29			
Ashford (Surrey)	d					22 36	22 41								23 06	23 11						
Feltham	d	22 35				22 41	22 46			23 05					23 11	23 16			23 35			
Whitton	d						22 50									23 20						
Kingston	d				22 29								22 59	22 59								23 29
Hampton Wick	d				22 31								23 01	23 01								23 31
Teddington	d				22 35								23 05	23 05								23 35
Fulwell	d																					
Strawberry Hill	d				22 38								23 08	23 08								23 38
Twickenham	a	22 40			22 42		22 53			23 10			23 12	23 12		23 23			23 40			23 42
	d	22 41			22 43		22 53			23 11			23 13	23 13		23 23			23 41			23 43
St Margarets	d				22 45								23 15	23 15								23 45
Richmond ⊖	d	22 45			22 49		22 58			23 15			23 19	23 19		23 28			23 45			23 49
North Sheen	d				22 51								23 21	23 21								23 51
Mortlake	d				22 53								23 23	23 23								23 53
Hounslow	d					22 46									23 16							
Isleworth	d					22 49									23 19							
Syon Lane	d					22 51									23 21							
Brentford	d					22 54									23 24							
Kew Bridge	d					22 56									23 26							
Chiswick	d					22 59									23 29							
Barnes Bridge	d					23 01									23 31							
Barnes	d				22 56	23 04		←					23 26	23 26	23 34		←					23 56
Putney	d				22 59	23 07	23 04	23 07					23 29	23 29	23 37	23 34	23 37					23 59
Wandsworth Town	d				23 02	→		23 10					23 32	23 32	→		23 40					00 02
Clapham Junction 10	d	22 54			23 05		23 09	23 13		23 24			23 35	23 35		23 39	23 43		23 54			00 05
Queenstown Rd.(Battersea)	d				23 08			23 16					23 38	23 38			23 46					00 08
Vauxhall ⊖	d				23 12		23 15	23 20					23 42	23 42		23 45	23 50					00 12
London Waterloo 15 ⊖	a	23 04			23 17		23 20	23 25		23 34			23 46	23 47		23 49	23 56		00 04			00 16

Table T149-R

Mondays to Fridays

16 December to 15 May

Reading, Guildford, Ascot, Weybridge, Windsor, Kingston, Richmond and Hounslow - London

		SW	SW	SW	SW	SW	SW	SW 1	SW 1	SW 1
Reading 7	d					23 12				23 52
Earley	d					23 17				
Winnersh Triangle	d					23 19				
Winnersh	d					23 21				
Wokingham	d					23 26				00 02
Bracknell	d					23 32				00 08
Martins Heron	d					23 35				00 11
Guildford	d								23 33	
Wanborough	d								23 39	
Ash 5	d								23 43	
Aldershot	a								23 52	
	d							23 30		
Ash Vale	d							23 34		
Frimley	d							23 40		
Camberley	a							23 44		
	d							23 48		
Bagshot	d							23 53		
Ascot 3	d					23 40		00a01		00a17
Sunningdale	d					23 43				
Longcross	d									
Weybridge	d				23 33					
Addlestone	d				23 37					
Chertsey	d	←			23 40		←			
Virginia Water	a	23 15			23 45	23 49	23 45			
	d	23 24			23 54	23 49	23 54			
Egham	d	23 27			→	23 53	23 57			
Windsor & Eton Riverside	d		23 28							
Datchet	d		23 31							
Sunnymeads	d		23 34							
Wraysbury	d		23 37							
Staines	d	23 33	23a42			23 59	00a02			
Ashford (Surrey)	d	23 36								
Feltham	d	23 41				00 05				
Whitton	d									
Kingston	d			23 55						
Hampton Wick	d			23 57						
Teddington	d			23 59						
Fulwell	d									
Strawberry Hill	d			00 03						
Twickenham	a			00 06		00 10				
	d					00 11				
St Margarets	d									
Richmond ⊖	d					00 15				
North Sheen	d									
Mortlake	d									
Hounslow	d	23 46								
Isleworth	d	23 49								
Syon Lane	d	23 51								
Brentford	d	23 54								
Kew Bridge	d	23 56								
Chiswick	d	23 59								
Barnes Bridge	d	00 01								
Barnes	d	00 04								
Putney	d	00 07								
Wandsworth Town	d	00 10								
Clapham Junction 10	d	00 13				00 24				
Queenstown Rd.(Battersea)	d	00 16								
Vauxhall ⊖	d	00 20								
London Waterloo 15 ⊖	a	00 24				00 38				

Table T149-R

Saturdays

21 December to 16 May

Reading, Guildford, Ascot, Weybridge, Windsor, Kingston, Richmond and Hounslow - London

		SW	SW	SW 1	SW	SW	SW	SW	SW	SW		SW	SW	SW	SW	SW	SW	SW	SW 1	SW		SW	SW	SW	SW
Reading 7	d																	05 42							
Earley	d																	05 47							
Winnersh Triangle	d																	05 49							
Winnersh	d																	05 51							
Wokingham	d			00 02														05 56							
Bracknell	d			00 08														06 02							
Martins Heron	d			00 11														06 05							
Guildford	d																								
Wanborough	d																								
Ash 5	d																								
Aldershot	a																								
	d																		06 00						
Ash Vale	d																		06 04						
Frimley	d																		06 10						
Camberley	a																		06 14						
	d																		06 18						
Bagshot	d																		06 23						
Ascot 3	d			00a17														06 10	06a30						
Sunningdale	d																	06 13							
Longcross	d																								
Weybridge	d																								06 33
Addlestone	d														05 39										06 37
Chertsey	d														05 42										06 40
Virginia Water	a														05 47			06 20							06 45
	d														05 54			06 20							06 54
Egham	d														05 57			06 24							→
Windsor & Eton Riverside	d															05 53							06 23		
Datchet	d															05 56							06 26		
Sunnymeads	d															05 59							06 29		
Wraysbury	d															06 02							06 32		
Staines	d							04 58				05 37			06 03	06 08		06 29				06 33	06 38		
Ashford (Surrey)	d							05 01				05 40			06 06	06 11						06 36	06 41		
Feltham	d					00 05		05 06				05 45			06 11	06 16		06 35				06 41	06 46		
Whitton	d							05 10		05 42		05 49				06 20							06 50		
Kingston	d						01 17							05 59						06 29					
Hampton Wick	d						01s19							06 01						06 31					
Teddington	d						01s22							06 05						06 35					
Fulwell	d																								
Strawberry Hill	d				00 03		01a32		05 38					06 08						06 38					
Twickenham	a				00 06	00 10		05 13	05 41			05 52		06 12		06 23		06 40		06 42			06 53		
	d					00 11		05 13	05 43			05 53		06 13		06 23		06 41		06 43			06 53		
St Margarets	d							05 15	05 45					06 15						06 45					
Richmond ⊖	d					00 15		05 19	05 49			05 58		06 19		06 28		06 45		06 49			06 58		
North Sheen	d							05 21	05 51					06 21						06 51					
Mortlake	d							05 23	05 53					06 23						06 53					
Hounslow	d									05 47					06 16							06 46			
Isleworth	d									05 50					06 19							06 49			
Syon Lane	d									05 52					06 21							06 51			
Brentford	d									05 54					06 24							06 54			
Kew Bridge	d									05 57					06 26							06 56			
Chiswick	d									05 59					06 29							06 59			
Barnes Bridge	d		00 01							06 02					06 31							07 01			
Barnes	d		00 04					05 26	05 56	06 05			←	06 26	06 34		←			06 56		07 04		←	
Putney	d		00 07					05 29	05 59	06 08		06 04	06 08	06 29	06 37	06 34	06 37			06 59		07 07	07 04	07 07	
Wandsworth Town	d	00 02	00 10					05 32	06 02	→			06 11	06 32	→		06 40			07 02		→		07 10	
Clapham Junction 10	d	00 05	00 13			00 24		05 35	06 05			06 09	06 14	06 35		06 39	06 43	06 54		07 05			07 09	07 13	
Queenstown Rd.(Battersea)	d	00 08	00 16					05 38	06 08				06 17	06 38			06 46			07 08				07 16	
Vauxhall ⊖	d	00 12	00 20					05 42	06 12			06 15	06 20	06 42		06 45	06 50			07 12			07 15	07 20	
London Waterloo 15 ⊖	a	00 16	00 24			00 38		05 46	06 16			06 19	06 26	06 46		06 49	06 56	07 04		07 19			07 19	07 26	

NRT DECEMBER 19 EDITION

Table T149-R

Saturdays

21 December to 16 May

Reading, Guildford, Ascot, Weybridge, Windsor, Kingston, Richmond and Hounslow - London

		SW	SW 1	SW 1	SW	SW		SW	SW	SW	SW	SW 1	SW 1	SW	SW	SW		SW	SW	SW	SW	SW	SW	SW	SW 1
Reading 7	d	06 12									06 42												07 12		
Earley	d	06 17									06 47												07 17		
Winnersh Triangle	d	06 19									06 49												07 19		
Winnersh	d	06 21									06 51												07 21		
Wokingham	d	06 26									06 56												07 26		
Bracknell	d	06 32									07 02												07 32		
Martins Heron	d	06 35									07 05												07 35		
Guildford	d			06 23									06 53												
Wanborough	d			06 29									06 59												
Ash 5	d			06 33									07 03												
Aldershot	a			06 40									07 10												
	d		06 30									07 00													07 30
Ash Vale	d		06 34									07 04													07 34
Frimley	d		06 40									07 10													07 40
Camberley	a		06 44									07 14													07 44
	d		06 48									07 18													07 48
Bagshot	d		06 53									07 23													07 53
Ascot 3	d	06 40	07a00								07 10	07a30											07 40		08a00
Sunningdale	d	06 43									07 13												07 43		
Longcross	d	06 46									07 16												07 46		
Weybridge	d									07 03										07 33					
Addlestone	d									07 07										07 37					
Chertsey	d					←				07 10						←				07 40					
Virginia Water	a	06 50				06 45				07 15	07 20					07 15				07 45			07 50		
	d	06 50				06 54				07 24	07 20					07 24				07 54			07 50		
Egham	d	06 54				06 57				→	07 24					07 27				→			07 54		
Windsor & Eton Riverside	d							06 53										07 23							
Datchet	d							06 56										07 26							
Sunnymeads	d							06 59										07 29							
Wraysbury	d							07 02										07 32							
Staines	d	06 59				07 03		07 08			07 29					07 33		07 38					07 59		
Ashford (Surrey)	d					07 06		07 11								07 36		07 41							
Feltham	d	07 05				07 11		07 16			07 35					07 41		07 46					08 05		
Whitton	d							07 20										07 50			07 50	07 53			
Kingston	d				06 59										07 29										
Hampton Wick	d				07 01										07 31										
Teddington	d				07 05										07 35										
Fulwell	d																								
Strawberry Hill	d				07 08										07 38										
Twickenham	a	07 10			07 12			07 23			07 40				07 42			07 53				07 56	08 10		
	d	07 11			07 13			07 23			07 41				07 43			07 53				07 58	08 11		
St Margarets	d				07 15										07 45							08 00			
Richmond ⊖	d	07 15			07 19			07 28			07 45				07 49			07 58				08 04	08 15		
North Sheen	d				07 21										07 51							08 06			
Mortlake	d				07 23										07 53							08 08			
Hounslow	d					07 16								07 31		07 46					08 01				
Isleworth	d					07 19								07 34		07 49					08 04				
Syon Lane	d					07 21								07 36		07 51					08 06				
Brentford	d					07 24								07 39		07 54					08 09				
Kew Bridge	d					07 26								07 41		07 56					08 11				
Chiswick	d					07 29								07 44		07 59					08 14				
Barnes Bridge	d					07 31								07 46		08 01					08 16			←	
Barnes	d				07 26	07 34			←					07 49	07 56	08 04			←		08 19	08 11		08 19	
Putney	d				07 29	07 37		07 34	07 37					07 52	07 59	08 07		08 04	08 07		→	08 14		08 22	
Wandsworth Town	d				07 32	→			07 40					07 55	08 02	→			08 10			08 17		08 25	
Clapham Junction 10	d	07 24			07 35			07 39	07 43		07 54			07 58	08 05			08 09	08 13			08 20	08 24	08 28	
Queenstown Rd.(Battersea)	d				07 38				07 46					08 01	08 08				08 16			08 23		08 31	
Vauxhall ⊖	d				07 42			07 45	07 50					08 05	08 12			08 15	08 20			08 27		08 35	
London Waterloo 15 ⊖	a	07 34			07 46			07 49	07 56		08 04			08 11	08 16			08 19	08 26			08 32	08 36	08 41	

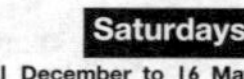

Table T149-R

Saturdays

21 December to 16 May

Reading, Guildford, Ascot, Weybridge, Windsor, Kingston, Richmond and Hounslow - London

		SW 1		SW	SW	SW	SW	SW	SW	SW	SW	SW		SW 1	SW 1	SW	SW	SW	SW	SW	SW	SW		SW	SW
Reading 7	d										07 42													08 12	
Earley	d										07 47													08 17	
Winnersh Triangle	d										07 49													08 19	
Winnersh	d										07 51													08 21	
Wokingham	d										07 56													08 26	
Bracknell	d										08 02													08 32	
Martins Heron	d										08 05													08 35	
Guildford	d	07 23													07 53										
Wanborough	d	07 29													07 59										
Ash 5	d	07 33													08 03										
Aldershot	a	07 40													08 10										
	d													08 00											
Ash Vale	d													08 04											
Frimley	d													08 10											
Camberley	a													08 14											
	d													08 18											
Bagshot	d													08 23											
Ascot 3	d										08 10			08a30										08 40	
Sunningdale	d										08 13													08 43	
Longcross	d										08 16													08 46	
Weybridge	d							08 03												08 33					
Addlestone	d							08 07												08 37					
Chertsey	d				←			08 10									←			08 40					
Virginia Water	a				07 45			08 15			08 20						08 15			08 45				08 50	
	d				07 54			08 24			08 20						08 24			08 54				08 50	
Egham	d				07 57			→			08 24						08 27			→				08 54	
Windsor & Eton Riverside	d					07 53												08 23							
Datchet	d					07 56												08 26							
Sunnymeads	d					07 59												08 29							
Wraysbury	d					08 02												08 32							
Staines	d				08 03	08 08					08 29						08 33	08 38						08 59	
Ashford (Surrey)	d				08 06	08 11											08 36	08 41							
Feltham	d				08 11	08 16					08 35						08 41	08 46						09 05	
Whitton	d					08 20			08 20	08 23								08 50			08 50	08 53			
Kingston	d			07 59												08 29									
Hampton Wick	d			08 01												08 31									
Teddington	d			08 05												08 35									
Fulwell	d																								
Strawberry Hill	d			08 08												08 38									
Twickenham	a			08 12		08 23				08 26	08 40					08 42		08 53				08 56		09 10	
	d			08 13		08 23				08 28	08 41					08 43		08 53				08 58		09 11	
St Margarets	d			08 15						08 30						08 45						09 00			
Richmond ⊖	d			08 19		08 28				08 34	08 45					08 49		08 58				09 04		09 15	
North Sheen	d			08 21						08 36						08 51						09 06			
Mortlake	d			08 23						08 38						08 53						09 08			
Hounslow	d				08 16				08 31								08 46				09 01				
Isleworth	d				08 19				08 34								08 49				09 04				
Syon Lane	d				08 21				08 36								08 51				09 06				
Brentford	d				08 24				08 39								08 54				09 09				
Kew Bridge	d				08 26				08 41								08 56				09 11				
Chiswick	d				08 29				08 44								08 59				09 14				
Barnes Bridge	d				08 31				08 46			←					09 01				09 16				←
Barnes	d			08 26	08 34		←		08 49	08 41		08 49				08 56	09 04		←		09 19	09 11			09 19
Putney	d			08 29	08 37	08 34	08 37		→	08 44		08 52				08 59	09 07	09 04	09 07		→	09 14			09 22
Wandsworth Town	d			08 32	→		08 40			08 47		08 55				09 02	→		09 10			09 17			09 25
Clapham Junction 10	d			08 35		08 39	08 43			08 50	08 54	08 58				09 05		09 09	09 13			09 20		09 24	09 28
Queenstown Rd.(Battersea)	d			08 38			08 46			08 53		09 01				09 08			09 16			09 23			09 31
Vauxhall ⊖	d			08 42		08 45	08 50			08 57		09 05				09 12		09 15	09 20			09 27			09 35
London Waterloo 15 ⊖	a			08 46		08 49	08 56			09 02	09 06	09 11				09 16		09 19	09 26			09 32		09 37	09 41

Table T149-R

Saturdays

21 December to 16 May

Reading, Guildford, Ascot, Weybridge, Windsor, Kingston, Richmond and Hounslow - London

		SW 1	SW 1	SW	SW	SW	SW	SW		SW	SW	SW	SW	SW 1	SW 1	SW	SW	SW		SW	SW	SW	SW	SW	SW
Reading 7	d											08 42												09 12	
Earley	d											08 47												09 17	
Winnersh Triangle	d											08 49												09 19	
Winnersh	d											08 51												09 21	
Wokingham	d											08 56												09 26	
Bracknell	d											09 02												09 32	
Martins Heron	d											09 05												09 35	
Guildford	d		08 23												08 53										
Wanborough	d		08 29												08 59										
Ash 5	d		08 33												09 03										
Aldershot	a		08 40												09 10										
	d	08 30												09 00											
Ash Vale	d	08 34												09 04											
Frimley	d	08 40												09 10											
Camberley	a	08 44												09 14											
	d	08 48												09 18											
Bagshot	d	08 53												09 23											
Ascot 3	d	09a00										09 10		09a30										09 40	
Sunningdale	d											09 13												09 43	
Longcross	d											09 16												09 46	
Weybridge	d							09 03													09 33				
Addlestone	d							09 07													09 37				
Chertsey	d				←			09 10									←				09 40				
Virginia Water	a				08 45			09 15				09 20					09 15				09 45			09 50	
	d				08 54			09 24				09 20					09 24				09 54			09 50	
Egham	d				08 57			→				09 24					09 27				→			09 54	
Windsor & Eton Riverside	d					08 53												09 23							
Datchet	d					08 56												09 26							
Sunnymeads	d					08 59												09 29							
Wraysbury	d					09 02												09 32							
Staines	d				09 03	09 08						09 29					09 33	09 38						09 59	
Ashford (Surrey)	d				09 06	09 11											09 36	09 41							
Feltham	d				09 11	09 16						09 35					09 41	09 46						10 05	
Whitton	d					09 20				09 20	09 23							09 50				09 50	09 53		
Kingston	d			08 59												09 29									
Hampton Wick	d			09 01												09 31									
Teddington	d			09 05												09 35									
Fulwell	d																								
Strawberry Hill	d			09 08												09 38									
Twickenham	a			09 12		09 23					09 26	09 40				09 42		09 53					09 56	10 10	
	d			09 13		09 23					09 28	09 41				09 43		09 53					09 58	10 11	
St Margarets	d			09 15							09 30					09 45							10 00		
Richmond ⊖	d			09 19		09 28					09 34	09 45				09 49		09 58					10 04	10 15	
North Sheen	d			09 21							09 36					09 51							10 06		
Mortlake	d			09 23							09 38					09 53							10 08		
Hounslow	d				09 16					09 31							09 46					10 01			
Isleworth	d				09 19					09 34							09 49					10 04			
Syon Lane	d				09 21					09 36							09 51					10 06			
Brentford	d				09 24					09 39							09 54					10 09			
Kew Bridge	d				09 26					09 41							09 56					10 11			
Chiswick	d				09 29					09 44							09 59					10 14			
Barnes Bridge	d				09 31					09 46			←				10 01					10 16			←
Barnes	d			09 26	09 34		←			09 49	09 41		09 49			09 56	10 04			←		10 19	10 11		10 19
Putney	d			09 29	09 37	09 34	09 37			→	09 44		09 52			09 59	10 07	10 04		10 07		→	10 14		10 22
Wandsworth Town	d			09 32	→		09 40				09 47		09 55			10 02	→			10 10			10 17		10 25
Clapham Junction 10	d			09 35		09 39	09 43				09 50	09 54	09 58			10 05		10 09		10 13			10 20	10 24	10 28
Queenstown Rd.(Battersea)	d			09 38			09 46				09 53		10 01			10 08				10 16			10 23		10 31
Vauxhall ⊖	d			09 42		09 45	09 50				09 57		10 05			10 12		10 15		10 20			10 27		10 35
London Waterloo 15 ⊖	a			09 47		09 49	09 56				10 02	10 04	10 11			10 16		10 19		10 26			10 32	10 34	10 41

Table T149-R

Saturdays

21 December to 16 May

Reading, Guildford, Ascot, Weybridge, Windsor, Kingston, Richmond and Hounslow - London

		SW ■1	SW ■1	SW	SW	SW	SW	SW	SW	SW	SW	SW	SW ■1	SW ■1	SW	SW	SW	SW	SW	SW	SW	SW
Reading ■7	d										09 42											10 12
Earley	d										09 47											10 17
Winnersh Triangle	d										09 49											10 19
Winnersh	d										09 51											10 21
Wokingham	d										09 56											10 26
Bracknell	d										10 02											10 32
Martins Heron	d										10 05											10 35
Guildford	d		09 23											09 53								
Wanborough	d		09 29											09 59								
Ash ■5	d		09 33											10 03								
Aldershot	a		09 40											10 10								
	d	09 30											10 00									
Ash Vale	d	09 34											10 04									
Frimley	d	09 40											10 10									
Camberley	a	09 44											10 14									
	d	09 48											10 18									
Bagshot	d	09 53											10 23									
Ascot ■3	d	10a00									10 10		10a30									10 40
Sunningdale	d										10 13											10 43
Longcross	d										10 16											10 46
Weybridge	d							10 03											10 33			
Addlestone	d							10 07											10 37			
Chertsey	d				←			10 10								←			10 40			
Virginia Water	a				09 45			10 15			10 20					10 15			10 45			10 50
	d				09 54			10 24			10 20					10 24			10 54			10 50
Egham	d				09 57			→			10 24					10 27			→			10 54
Windsor & Eton Riverside	d					09 53											10 23					
Datchet	d					09 56											10 26					
Sunnymeads	d					09 59											10 29					
Wraysbury	d					10 02											10 32					
Staines	d				10 03	10 08					10 29					10 33	10 38					10 59
Ashford (Surrey)	d				10 06	10 11										10 36	10 41					
Feltham	d				10 11	10 16					10 35					10 41	10 46					11 05
Whitton	d					10 20			10 20	10 23							10 50			10 50	10 53	
Kingston	d			09 59											10 29							
Hampton Wick	d			10 01											10 31							
Teddington	d			10 05											10 35							
Fulwell	d																					
Strawberry Hill	d			10 08											10 38							
Twickenham	a			10 12		10 23				10 26	10 40				10 42		10 53				10 56	11 10
	d			10 13		10 23				10 28	10 41				10 43		10 53				10 58	11 11
St Margarets	d			10 15						10 30					10 45						11 00	
Richmond ⊖	d			10 19		10 28				10 34	10 45				10 49		10 58				11 04	11 15
North Sheen	d			10 21						10 36					10 51						11 06	
Mortlake	d			10 23						10 38					10 53						11 08	
Hounslow	d				10 16				10 31							10 46				11 01		
Isleworth	d				10 19				10 34							10 49				11 04		
Syon Lane	d				10 21				10 36							10 51				11 06		
Brentford	d				10 24				10 39							10 54				11 09		
Kew Bridge	d				10 26				10 41							10 56				11 11		
Chiswick	d				10 29				10 44							10 59				11 14		
Barnes Bridge	d				10 31				10 46			←				11 01				11 16		
Barnes	d			10 26	10 34		←		10 49	10 41		10 49			10 56	11 04		←		11 19	11 11	
Putney	d			10 29	10 37	10 34	10 37		→	10 44		10 52			10 59	11 07	11 04	11 07		→	11 14	
Wandsworth Town	d			10 32	→		10 40			10 47		10 55			11 02	→		11 10			11 17	
Clapham Junction ■10	d			10 35		10 39	10 43			10 50	10 54	10 58			11 05		11 09	11 13			11 20	11 24
Queenstown Rd.(Battersea)	d			10 38			10 46			10 53		11 01			11 08			11 16			11 23	
Vauxhall ⊖	d			10 42		10 45	10 50			10 57		11 05			11 12		11 15	11 20			11 27	
London Waterloo ■15 ⊖	a			10 46		10 49	10 56			11 02	11 04	11 11			11 16		11 19	11 26			11 32	11 34

Table T149-R

Saturdays

21 December to 16 May

Reading, Guildford, Ascot, Weybridge, Windsor, Kingston, Richmond and Hounslow - London

		SW	SW ■1	SW ■1	SW	SW	SW	SW	SW	SW	SW	SW	SW	SW ■1	SW ■1	SW	SW	SW	SW	SW	SW	SW	SW
Reading ■7	d											10 42											11 12
Earley	d											10 47											11 17
Winnersh Triangle	d											10 49											11 19
Winnersh	d											10 51											11 21
Wokingham	d											10 56											11 26
Bracknell	d											11 02											11 32
Martins Heron	d											11 05											11 35
Guildford	d			10 23											10 53								
Wanborough	d			10 29											10 59								
Ash ■5	d			10 33											11 03								
Aldershot	a			10 40											11 10								
	d		10 30											11 00									
Ash Vale	d		10 34											11 04									
Frimley	d		10 40											11 10									
Camberley	a		10 44											11 14									
	d		10 48											11 18									
Bagshot	d		10 53											11 23									
Ascot ■3	d		11a00									11 10		11a30									11 40
Sunningdale	d											11 13											11 43
Longcross	d											11 16											11 46
Weybridge	d								11 03											11 33			
Addlestone	d								11 07											11 37			
Chertsey	d					←			11 10								←			11 40			
Virginia Water	a					10 45			11 15			11 20					11 15			11 45			11 50
	d					10 54			11 24			11 20					11 24			11 54			11 50
Egham	d					10 57			→			11 24					11 27			→			11 54
Windsor & Eton Riverside	d						10 53											11 23					
Datchet	d						10 56											11 26					
Sunnymeads	d						10 59											11 29					
Wraysbury	d						11 02											11 32					
Staines	d					11 03	11 08					11 29					11 33	11 38					11 59
Ashford (Surrey)	d					11 06	11 11										11 36	11 41					
Feltham	d					11 11	11 16					11 35					11 41	11 46					12 05
Whitton	d						11 20			11 20	11 23							11 50			11 50	11 53	
Kingston	d				10 59											11 29							
Hampton Wick	d				11 01											11 31							
Teddington	d				11 05											11 35							
Fulwell	d																						
Strawberry Hill	d				11 08											11 38							
Twickenham	a				11 12		11 23				11 26	11 40				11 42		11 53				11 56	12 10
	d				11 13		11 23				11 28	11 41				11 43		11 53				11 58	12 11
St Margarets	d				11 15						11 30					11 45						12 00	
Richmond ⊖	d				11 19		11 28				11 34	11 45				11 49		11 58				12 04	12 15
North Sheen	d				11 21						11 36					11 51						12 06	
Mortlake	d				11 23						11 38					11 53						12 08	
Hounslow	d					11 16				11 31							11 46				12 01		
Isleworth	d					11 19				11 34							11 49				12 04		
Syon Lane	d					11 21				11 36							11 51				12 06		
Brentford	d					11 24				11 39							11 54				12 09		
Kew Bridge	d					11 26				11 41							11 56				12 11		
Chiswick	d					11 29				11 44							11 59				12 14		
Barnes Bridge	d	←				11 31				11 46			←				12 01				12 16		
Barnes	d	11 19			11 26	11 34		←		11 49	11 41		11 49			11 56	12 04		←		12 19	12 11	
Putney	d	11 22			11 29	11 37	11 34	11 37		→	11 44		11 52			11 59	12 07	12 04	12 07		→	12 14	
Wandsworth Town	d	11 25			11 32	→		11 40			11 47		11 55			12 02	→		12 10			12 17	
Clapham Junction ■10	d	11 28			11 35		11 39	11 43			11 50	11 54	11 58			12 05		12 09	12 13			12 20	12 24
Queenstown Rd.(Battersea)	d	11 31			11 38			11 46			11 53		12 01			12 08			12 16			12 23	
Vauxhall ⊖	d	11 35			11 42		11 45	11 50			11 57		12 05			12 12		12 15	12 20			12 27	
London Waterloo ■15 ⊖	a	11 41			11 46		11 49	11 56			12 02	12 04	12 11			12 16		12 19	12 26			12 32	12 34

Table T149-R

Saturdays

21 December to 16 May

Reading, Guildford, Ascot, Weybridge, Windsor, Kingston, Richmond and Hounslow - London

		SW	SW 1	SW 1	SW	SW	SW	SW	SW	SW	SW	SW	SW	SW 1	SW 1	SW	SW	SW	SW	SW	SW	SW	SW
Reading 7	d											11 42											12 12
Earley	d											11 47											12 17
Winnersh Triangle	d											11 49											12 19
Winnersh	d											11 51											12 21
Wokingham	d											11 56											12 26
Bracknell	d											12 02											12 32
Martins Heron	d											12 05											12 35
Guildford	d			11 23											11 53								
Wanborough	d			11 29											11 59								
Ash 5	d			11 33											12 03								
Aldershot	a			11 40											12 10								
	d		11 30											12 00									
Ash Vale	d		11 34											12 04									
Frimley	d		11 40											12 10									
Camberley	a		11 44											12 14									
	d		11 48											12 18									
Bagshot	d		11 53											12 23									
Ascot 3	d		12a00									12 10		12a30									12 40
Sunningdale	d											12 13											12 43
Longcross	d											12 16											12 46
Weybridge	d								12 03											12 33			
Addlestone	d								12 07											12 37			
Chertsey	d					←			12 10								←			12 40			
Virginia Water	a					11 45			12 15			12 20					12 15			12 45			12 50
	d					11 54			12 24			12 20					12 24			12 54			12 50
Egham	d					11 57			→			12 24					12 27			→			12 54
Windsor & Eton Riverside	d						11 53											12 23					
Datchet	d						11 56											12 26					
Sunnymeads	d						11 59											12 29					
Wraysbury	d						12 02											12 32					
Staines	d					12 03	12 08					12 29					12 33	12 38					12 59
Ashford (Surrey)	d					12 06	12 11										12 36	12 41					
Feltham	d					12 11	12 16					12 35					12 41	12 46					13 05
Whitton	d						12 20			12 20	12 23							12 50			12 50	12 53	
Kingston	d				11 59											12 29							
Hampton Wick	d				12 01											12 31							
Teddington	d				12 05											12 35							
Fulwell	d																						
Strawberry Hill	d				12 08											12 38							
Twickenham	a				12 12		12 23				12 26	12 40				12 42		12 53				12 56	13 10
	d				12 13		12 23				12 28	12 41				12 43		12 53				12 58	13 11
St Margarets	d				12 15						12 30					12 45						13 00	
Richmond ⊖	d				12 19		12 28				12 34	12 45				12 49		12 58				13 04	13 15
North Sheen	d				12 21						12 36					12 51						13 06	
Mortlake	d				12 23						12 38					12 53						13 08	
Hounslow	d					12 16				12 31							12 46				13 01		
Isleworth	d					12 19				12 34							12 49				13 04		
Syon Lane	d					12 21				12 36							12 51				13 06		
Brentford	d					12 24				12 39							12 54				13 09		
Kew Bridge	d					12 26				12 41							12 56				13 11		
Chiswick	d					12 29				12 44							12 59				13 14		
Barnes Bridge	d	←				12 31				12 46			←				13 01				13 16		
Barnes	d	12 19			12 26	12 34		←		12 49	12 41		12 49			12 56	13 04		←		13 19	13 11	
Putney	d	12 22			12 29	12 37	12 34	12 37		→	12 44		12 52			12 59	13 07	13 04	13 07		→	13 14	
Wandsworth Town	d	12 25			12 32	→		12 40			12 47		12 55			13 02	→		13 10			13 17	
Clapham Junction 10	d	12 28			12 35		12 39	12 43			12 50	12 54	12 59			13 05		13 09	13 13			13 20	13 24
Queenstown Rd.(Battersea)	d	12 31			12 38			12 46			12 53		13 02			13 08			13 16			13 23	
Vauxhall ⊖	d	12 35			12 42		12 45	12 50			12 57		13 05			13 12		13 15	13 20			13 27	
London Waterloo 15 ⊖	a	12 41			12 46		12 49	12 56			13 02	13 04	13 11			13 16		13 19	13 26			13 32	13 34

Table T149-R

Saturdays

21 December to 16 May

Reading, Guildford, Ascot, Weybridge, Windsor, Kingston, Richmond and Hounslow - London

		SW	SW 1	SW 1	SW	SW	SW	SW	SW	SW	SW	SW	SW	SW 1	SW 1	SW	SW	SW	SW	SW	SW	SW
Reading 7	d											12 42										
Earley	d											12 47										
Winnersh Triangle	d											12 49										
Winnersh	d											12 51										
Wokingham	d											12 56										
Bracknell	d											13 02										
Martins Heron	d											13 05										
Guildford	d			12 23											12 53							
Wanborough	d			12 29											12 59							
Ash 5	d			12 33											13 03							
Aldershot	a			12 40											13 10							
	d		12 30											13 00								
Ash Vale	d		12 34											13 04								
Frimley	d		12 40											13 10								
Camberley	a		12 44											13 14								
	d		12 48											13 18								
Bagshot	d		12 53											13 23								
Ascot 3	d		13a00									13 10		13a30								
Sunningdale	d											13 13										
Longcross	d											13 16										
Weybridge	d								13 03											13 33		
Addlestone	d								13 07											13 37		
Chertsey	d					←			13 10								←			13 40		
Virginia Water	a					12 45			13 15			13 20					13 15			13 45		
	d					12 54			13 24			13 20					13 24			13 54		
Egham	d					12 57			→			13 24					13 27			→		
Windsor & Eton Riverside	d						12 53											13 23				
Datchet	d						12 56											13 26				
Sunnymeads	d						12 59											13 29				
Wraysbury	d						13 02											13 32				
Staines	d					13 03	13 08					13 29					13 33	13 38				
Ashford (Surrey)	d					13 06	13 11										13 36	13 41				
Feltham	d					13 11	13 16					13 35					13 41	13 46				
Whitton	d						13 20			13 20	13 23							13 50			13 50	13 53
Kingston	d				12 59											13 29						
Hampton Wick	d				13 01											13 31						
Teddington	d				13 05											13 35						
Fulwell	d																					
Strawberry Hill	d				13 08											13 38						
Twickenham	a				13 12		13 23				13 26	13 40				13 42		13 53				13 56
	d				13 13		13 23				13 28	13 41				13 43		13 53				13 58
St Margarets	d				13 15						13 30					13 45						14 00
Richmond ⊖	d				13 19		13 28				13 34	13 45				13 49		13 58				14 04
North Sheen	d				13 21						13 36					13 51						14 06
Mortlake	d				13 23						13 38					13 53						14 08
Hounslow	d					13 16				13 31							13 46				14 01	
Isleworth	d					13 19				13 34							13 49				14 04	
Syon Lane	d					13 21				13 36							13 51				14 06	
Brentford	d					13 24				13 39							13 54				14 09	
Kew Bridge	d					13 26				13 41							13 56				14 11	
Chiswick	d					13 29				13 44							13 59				14 14	
Barnes Bridge	d	←				13 31				13 46			←				14 01				14 16	
Barnes	d	13 19			13 26	13 34		←		13 49	13 41		13 49			13 56	14 04		←		14 19	14 11
Putney	d	13 22			13 29	13 37	13 34	13 37		→	13 44		13 52			13 59	14 07	14 04	14 07		→	14 14
Wandsworth Town	d	13 25			13 32	→		13 40			13 47		13 55			14 02	→		14 10			14 17
Clapham Junction 10	d	13 28			13 35		13 39	13 43			13 50	13 54	13 58			14 05		14 09	14 13			14 20
Queenstown Rd.(Battersea)	d	13 31			13 38			13 46			13 53		14 01			14 08			14 16			14 23
Vauxhall ⊖	d	13 35			13 42		13 45	13 50			13 57		14 05			14 12		14 15	14 20			14 27
London Waterloo 15 ⊖	a	13 41			13 46		13 49	13 56			14 02	14 04	14 11			14 16		14 19	14 26			14 32

Table T149-R

Saturdays

21 December to 16 May

Reading, Guildford, Ascot, Weybridge, Windsor, Kingston, Richmond and Hounslow - London

		SW	SW	SW	SW	SW	SW	SW		SW	SW	SW	SW	SW	SW	SW	SW	SW		SW	SW	SW	SW	SW	SW
				1	1											1	1								
Reading 7	d	13 12												13 42											
Earley	d	13 17												13 47											
Winnersh Triangle	d	13 19												13 49											
Winnersh	d	13 21												13 51											
Wokingham	d	13 26												13 56											
Bracknell	d	13 32												14 02											
Martins Heron	d	13 35												14 05											
Guildford	d				13 23												13 53								
Wanborough	d				13 29												13 59								
Ash 5	d				13 33												14 03								
Aldershot	a				13 40												14 10								
	d			13 30												14 00									
Ash Vale	d			13 34												14 04									
Frimley	d			13 40												14 10									
Camberley	a			13 44												14 14									
	d			13 48												14 18									
Bagshot	d			13 53												14 23									
Ascot 3	d	13 40		14a00										14 10		14a30									
Sunningdale	d	13 43												14 13											
Longcross	d	13 46												14 16											
Weybridge	d										14 03												14 33		
Addlestone	d										14 07												14 37		
Chertsey	d						←				14 10									←			14 40		
Virginia Water	a	13 50					13 45				14 15			14 20						14 15			14 45		
	d	13 50					13 54				14 24			14 20						14 24			14 54		
Egham	d	13 54					13 57				→			14 24						14 27			→		
Windsor & Eton Riverside	d							13 53													14 23				
Datchet	d							13 56													14 26				
Sunnymeads	d							13 59													14 29				
Wraysbury	d							14 02													14 32				
Staines	d	13 59					14 03	14 08						14 29						14 33	14 38				
Ashford (Surrey)	d						14 06	14 11												14 36	14 41				
Feltham	d	14 05					14 11	14 16						14 35						14 41	14 46				
Whitton	d							14 20				14 20	14 23								14 50			14 50	14 53
Kingston	d					13 59												14 29							
Hampton Wick	d					14 01												14 31							
Teddington	d					14 05												14 35							
Fulwell	d																								
Strawberry Hill	d					14 08												14 38							
Twickenham	a	14 10				14 12		14 23					14 26	14 40				14 42			14 53				14 56
	d	14 11				14 13		14 23					14 28	14 41				14 43			14 53				14 58
St Margarets	d					14 15							14 30					14 45							15 00
Richmond ⊖	d	14 15				14 19		14 28					14 34	14 45				14 49			14 58				15 04
North Sheen	d					14 21							14 36					14 51							15 06
Mortlake	d					14 23							14 38					14 53							15 08
Hounslow	d						14 16					14 31								14 46				15 01	
Isleworth	d						14 19					14 34								14 49				15 04	
Syon Lane	d						14 21					14 36								14 51				15 06	
Brentford	d						14 24					14 39								14 54				15 09	
Kew Bridge	d						14 26					14 41								14 56				15 11	
Chiswick	d						14 29					14 44								14 59				15 14	
Barnes Bridge	d		←				14 31					14 46			←					15 01				15 16	
Barnes	d		14 19			14 26	14 34			←		14 49	14 41		14 49			14 56		15 04		←		15 19	15 11
Putney	d		14 22			14 29	14 37	14 34		14 37		→	14 44		14 52			14 59		15 07	15 04	15 07		→	15 14
Wandsworth Town	d		14 25			14 32	→			14 40			14 47		14 55			15 02		→		15 10			15 17
Clapham Junction 10	d	14 24	14 28			14 35		14 39		14 43			14 50	14 54	14 58			15 05			15 09	15 13			15 20
Queenstown Rd.(Battersea)	d		14 31			14 38				14 46			14 53		15 01			15 08				15 16			15 23
Vauxhall ⊖	d		14 35			14 42		14 45		14 50			14 57		15 05			15 12			15 15	15 20			15 27
London Waterloo 15 ⊖	a	14 34	14 41			14 46		14 49		14 56			15 02	15 04	15 11			15 16			15 19	15 26			15 32

NRT DECEMBER 19 EDITION

Table T149-R

Saturdays

21 December to 16 May

Reading, Guildford, Ascot, Weybridge, Windsor, Kingston, Richmond and Hounslow - London

		SW	SW	SW		SW	SW	SW	SW	SW	SW	SW	SW	SW		SW	SW	SW	SW	SW	SW	SW	SW	SW
				1		1											1	1						
Reading 7	d	14 12												14 42										
Earley	d	14 17												14 47										
Winnersh Triangle	d	14 19												14 49										
Winnersh	d	14 21												14 51										
Wokingham	d	14 26												14 56										
Bracknell	d	14 32												15 02										
Martins Heron	d	14 35												15 05										
Guildford	d					14 23												14 53						
Wanborough	d					14 29												14 59						
Ash 5	d					14 33												15 03						
Aldershot	a					14 40												15 10						
	d			14 30													15 00							
Ash Vale	d			14 34													15 04							
Frimley	d			14 40													15 10							
Camberley	a			14 44													15 14							
	d			14 48													15 18							
Bagshot	d			14 53													15 23							
Ascot 3	d	14 40		15a00										15 10			15a30							
Sunningdale	d	14 43												15 13										
Longcross	d	14 46												15 16										
Weybridge	d										15 03												15 33	
Addlestone	d										15 07												15 37	
Chertsey	d							←			15 10									←			15 40	
Virginia Water	a	14 50						14 45			15 15			15 20						15 15			15 45	
	d	14 50						14 54			15 24			15 20						15 24			15 54	
Egham	d	14 54						14 57			→			15 24						15 27			→	
Windsor & Eton Riverside	d								14 53												15 23			
Datchet	d								14 56												15 26			
Sunnymeads	d								14 59												15 29			
Wraysbury	d								15 02												15 32			
Staines	d	14 59						15 03	15 08					15 29						15 33	15 38			
Ashford (Surrey)	d							15 06	15 11											15 36	15 41			
Feltham	d	15 05						15 11	15 16					15 35						15 41	15 46			
Whitton	d								15 20			15 20	15 23								15 50			15 50
Kingston	d						14 59												15 29					
Hampton Wick	d						15 01												15 31					
Teddington	d						15 05												15 35					
Fulwell	d																							
Strawberry Hill	d						15 08												15 38					
Twickenham	a	15 10					15 12		15 23				15 26	15 40					15 42		15 53			
	d	15 11					15 13		15 23				15 28	15 41					15 43		15 53			
St Margarets	d						15 15						15 30						15 45					
Richmond ⊖	d	15 15					15 19		15 28				15 34	15 45					15 49		15 58			
North Sheen	d						15 21						15 36						15 51					
Mortlake	d						15 23						15 38						15 53					
Hounslow	d							15 16				15 31								15 46				16 01
Isleworth	d							15 19				15 34								15 49				16 04
Syon Lane	d							15 21				15 36								15 51				16 06
Brentford	d							15 24				15 39								15 54				16 09
Kew Bridge	d							15 26				15 41								15 56				16 11
Chiswick	d							15 29				15 44								15 59				16 14
Barnes Bridge	d		←					15 31				15 46				←				16 01				16 16
Barnes	d		15 19				15 26	15 34		←		15 49	15 41			15 49			15 56	16 04		←		16 19
Putney	d		15 22				15 29	15 37	15 34	15 37		→	15 44			15 52			15 59	16 07	16 04	16 07		→
Wandsworth Town	d		15 25				15 32	→		15 40			15 47			15 55			16 02	→		16 10		
Clapham Junction 10	d	15 24	15 28				15 35		15 39	15 43			15 50	15 54		15 58			16 05		16 09	16 13		
Queenstown Rd.(Battersea)	d		15 31				15 38			15 46			15 53			16 01			16 08			16 16		
Vauxhall ⊖	d		15 35				15 42		15 45	15 50			15 57			16 05			16 12		16 15	16 20		
London Waterloo 15 ⊖	a	15 34	15 41				15 46		15 49	15 56			16 02	16 04		16 11			16 16		16 19	16 26		

Table T149-R

Saturdays

21 December to 16 May

Reading, Guildford, Ascot, Weybridge, Windsor, Kingston, Richmond and Hounslow - London

		SW	SW	SW	SW	SW	SW	SW	SW	SW		SW	SW	SW	SW	SW	SW	SW	SW	SW		SW	SW	SW	SW
					1	1											1	1							
Reading 7	d		15 12												15 42										
Earley	d		15 17												15 47										
Winnersh Triangle	d		15 19												15 49										
Winnersh	d		15 21												15 51										
Wokingham	d		15 26												15 56										
Bracknell	d		15 32												16 02										
Martins Heron	d		15 35												16 05										
Guildford	d					15 23												15 53							
Wanborough	d					15 29												15 59							
Ash 5	d					15 33												16 03							
Aldershot	a					15 40												16 10							
	d				15 30												16 00								
Ash Vale	d				15 34												16 04								
Frimley	d				15 40												16 10								
Camberley	a				15 44												16 14								
	d				15 48												16 18								
Bagshot	d				15 53												16 23								
Ascot 3	d		15 40		16a00										16 10		16a30								
Sunningdale	d		15 43												16 13										
Longcross	d		15 46												16 16										
Weybridge	d											16 03												16 33	
Addlestone	d											16 07												16 37	
Chertsey	d							←				16 10								←				16 40	
Virginia Water	a		15 50					15 45				16 15			16 20					16 15				16 45	
	d		15 50					15 54				16 24			16 20					16 24				16 54	
Egham	d		15 54					15 57				→			16 24					16 27				→	
Windsor & Eton Riverside	d								15 53													16 23			
Datchet	d								15 56													16 26			
Sunnymeads	d								15 59													16 29			
Wraysbury	d								16 02													16 32			
Staines	d		15 59					16 03	16 08						16 29					16 33		16 38			
Ashford (Surrey)	d							16 06	16 11											16 36		16 41			
Feltham	d		16 05					16 11	16 16						16 35					16 41		16 46			
Whitton	d	15 53							16 20				16 20	16 23								16 50			16 50
Kingston	d						15 59												16 29						
Hampton Wick	d						16 01												16 31						
Teddington	d						16 05												16 35						
Fulwell	d																								
Strawberry Hill	d						16 08												16 38						
Twickenham	a	15 56	16 10				16 12		16 23					16 26	16 40				16 42			16 53			
	d	15 58	16 11				16 13		16 23					16 28	16 41				16 43			16 53			
St Margarets	d	16 00					16 15							16 30					16 45						
Richmond ⊖	d	16 04	16 15				16 19		16 28					16 34	16 45				16 49			16 58			
North Sheen	d	16 06					16 21							16 36					16 51						
Mortlake	d	16 08					16 23							16 38					16 53						
Hounslow	d							16 16					16 31							16 46					17 01
Isleworth	d							16 19					16 34							16 49					17 04
Syon Lane	d							16 21					16 36							16 51					17 06
Brentford	d							16 24					16 39							16 54					17 09
Kew Bridge	d							16 26					16 41							16 56					17 11
Chiswick	d							16 29					16 44							16 59					17 14
Barnes Bridge	d			←				16 31					16 46			←				17 01					17 16
Barnes	d	16 11		16 19			16 26	16 34		←			16 49	16 41		16 49			16 56	17 04			←		17 19
Putney	d	16 14		16 22			16 29	16 37	16 34	16 37			→	16 44		16 52			16 59	17 07		17 04	17 07		→
Wandsworth Town	d	16 17		16 25			16 32	→		16 40				16 47		16 55			17 02	→			17 10		
Clapham Junction 10	d	16 20	16 24	16 28			16 35		16 39	16 43				16 50	16 54	16 58			17 05			17 09	17 13		
Queenstown Rd.(Battersea)	d	16 23		16 31			16 38			16 46				16 53		17 01			17 08				17 16		
Vauxhall ⊖	d	16 27		16 35			16 42		16 45	16 50				16 57		17 05			17 12			17 15	17 20		
London Waterloo 15 ⊖	a	16 32	16 34	16 41			16 46		16 49	16 56				17 02	17 04	17 11			17 16			17 19	17 26		

Table T149-R

Saturdays

21 December to 16 May

Reading, Guildford, Ascot, Weybridge, Windsor, Kingston, Richmond and Hounslow - London

		SW	SW	SW	SW	SW		SW	SW	SW	SW	SW	SW	SW	SW	SW		SW	SW	SW	SW	SW	SW	SW	SW
					1	1												1	1						
Reading 7	d		16 12												16 42										
Earley	d		16 17												16 47										
Winnersh Triangle	d		16 19												16 49										
Winnersh	d		16 21												16 51										
Wokingham	d		16 26												16 56										
Bracknell	d		16 32												17 02										
Martins Heron	d		16 35												17 05										
Guildford	d					16 23													16 53						
Wanborough	d					16 29													16 59						
Ash 5	d					16 33													17 03						
Aldershot	a					16 40													17 10						
	d				16 30													17 00							
Ash Vale	d				16 34													17 04							
Frimley	d				16 40													17 10							
Camberley	a				16 44													17 14							
	d				16 48													17 18							
Bagshot	d				16 53													17 23							
Ascot 3	d		16 40		17a00										17 10			17a30							
Sunningdale	d		16 43												17 13										
Longcross	d		16 46												17 16										
Weybridge	d											17 03												17 33	
Addlestone	d											17 07												17 37	
Chertsey	d								←			17 10									←			17 40	
Virginia Water	a		16 50						16 45			17 15			17 20						17 15			17 45	
	d		16 50						16 54			17 24			17 20						17 24			17 54	
Egham	d		16 54						16 57			→			17 24						17 27			→	
Windsor & Eton Riverside	d									16 53												17 23			
Datchet	d									16 56												17 26			
Sunnymeads	d									16 59												17 29			
Wraysbury	d									17 02												17 32			
Staines	d		16 59						17 03	17 08					17 29						17 33	17 38			
Ashford (Surrey)	d								17 06	17 11											17 36	17 41			
Feltham	d		17 05						17 11	17 16					17 35						17 41	17 46			
Whitton	d	16 53								17 20			17 20	17 23								17 50			17 50
Kingston	d							16 59												17 29					
Hampton Wick	d							17 01												17 31					
Teddington	d							17 05												17 35					
Fulwell	d																								
Strawberry Hill	d							17 08												17 38					
Twickenham	a	16 56	17 10					17 12		17 23				17 26	17 40					17 42		17 53			
	d	16 58	17 11					17 13		17 23				17 28	17 41					17 43		17 53			
St Margarets	d	17 00						17 15						17 30						17 45					
Richmond ⊖	d	17 04	17 15					17 19		17 28				17 34	17 45					17 49		17 58			
North Sheen	d	17 06						17 21						17 36						17 51					
Mortlake	d	17 08						17 23						17 38						17 53					
Hounslow	d								17 16				17 31								17 46				18 01
Isleworth	d								17 19				17 34								17 49				18 04
Syon Lane	d								17 21				17 36								17 51				18 06
Brentford	d								17 24				17 39								17 54				18 09
Kew Bridge	d								17 26				17 41								17 56				18 11
Chiswick	d								17 29				17 44								17 59				18 14
Barnes Bridge	d			←					17 31				17 46			←					18 01				18 16
Barnes	d	17 11		17 19				17 26	17 34		←		17 49	17 41		17 49				17 56	18 04		←		18 19
Putney	d	17 14		17 22				17 29	17 37	17 34	17 37		→	17 44		17 52				17 59	18 07	18 04	18 07		→
Wandsworth Town	d	17 17		17 25				17 32	→		17 40			17 47		17 55				18 02	→		18 10		
Clapham Junction 10	d	17 20	17 24	17 28				17 35		17 39	17 43			17 50	17 54	17 58				18 05		18 09	18 13		
Queenstown Rd.(Battersea)	d	17 23		17 31				17 38			17 46			17 53		18 01				18 08			18 16		
Vauxhall ⊖	d	17 27		17 35				17 42		17 45	17 50			17 57		18 05				18 12		18 15	18 20		
London Waterloo 15 ⊖	a	17 32	17 34	17 41				17 46		17 49	17 56			18 02	18 04	18 11				18 16		18 19	18 26		

Table T149-R

Saturdays

21 December to 16 May

Reading, Guildford, Ascot, Weybridge, Windsor, Kingston, Richmond and Hounslow - London

		SW		SW	SW	SW ■1	SW ■1	SW	SW	SW	SW	SW		SW	SW	SW	SW	SW ■1	SW ■1	SW	SW	SW		SW	SW
Reading [7]	d			17 12												17 42									
Earley	d			17 17												17 47									
Winnersh Triangle	d			17 19												17 49									
Winnersh	d			17 21												17 51									
Wokingham	d			17 26												17 56									
Bracknell	d			17 32												18 02									
Martins Heron	d			17 35												18 05									
Guildford	d						17 23												17 53						
Wanborough	d						17 29												17 59						
Ash [5]	d						17 33												18 03						
Aldershot	a						17 40												18 10						
	d					17 30												18 00							
Ash Vale	d					17 34												18 04							
Frimley	d					17 40												18 10							
Camberley	a					17 44												18 14							
	d					17 48												18 18							
Bagshot	d					17 53												18 23							
Ascot [3]	d			17 40		18a00										18 10		18a30							
Sunningdale	d			17 43												18 13									
Longcross	d			17 46												18 16									
Weybridge	d											18 03													18 33
Addlestone	d											18 07													18 37
Chertsey	d								←			18 10									←				18 40
Virginia Water	a			17 50					17 45			18 15				18 20					18 15				18 45
	d			17 50					17 54			18 24				18 20					18 24				18 54
Egham	d			17 54					17 57			→				18 24					18 27				→
Windsor & Eton Riverside	d									17 53												18 23			
Datchet	d									17 56												18 26			
Sunnymeads	d									17 59												18 29			
Wraysbury	d									18 02												18 32			
Staines	d			17 59					18 03	18 08						18 29					18 33	18 38			
Ashford (Surrey)	d								18 06	18 11											18 36	18 41			
Feltham	d			18 05					18 11	18 16						18 35					18 41	18 46			
Whitton	d	17 53								18 20				18 20	18 23							18 50			
Kingston	d							17 59												18 29					
Hampton Wick	d							18 01												18 31					
Teddington	d							18 05												18 35					
Fulwell	d																								
Strawberry Hill	d							18 08												18 38					
Twickenham	a	17 56		18 10				18 12		18 23					18 26	18 40				18 42		18 53			
	d	17 58		18 11				18 13		18 23					18 28	18 41				18 43		18 53			
St Margarets	d	18 00						18 15							18 30					18 45					
Richmond ⊖	d	18 04		18 15				18 19		18 28					18 34	18 45				18 49		18 58			
North Sheen	d	18 06						18 21							18 36					18 51					
Mortlake	d	18 08						18 23							18 38					18 53					
Hounslow	d								18 16					18 31							18 46				
Isleworth	d								18 19					18 34							18 49				
Syon Lane	d								18 21					18 36							18 51				
Brentford	d								18 24					18 39							18 54				
Kew Bridge	d								18 26					18 41							18 56				
Chiswick	d								18 29					18 44							18 59				
Barnes Bridge	d				←				18 31					18 46			←				19 01				
Barnes	d	18 11			18 19			18 26	18 34		←			18 49	18 41		18 49			18 56	19 04			←	
Putney	d	18 14			18 22			18 29	18 37	18 34	18 37			→	18 44		18 52			18 59	19 07	19 04		19 07	
Wandsworth Town	d	18 17			18 25			18 32	→		18 40				18 47		18 55			19 02	→			19 10	
Clapham Junction [10]	d	18 20		18 24	18 28			18 35		18 39	18 43				18 50	18 54	18 58			19 05		19 09		19 13	
Queenstown Rd.(Battersea)	d	18 23			18 31			18 38			18 46				18 53		19 01			19 08				19 16	
Vauxhall ⊖	d	18 27			18 35			18 42		18 45	18 50				18 57		19 05			19 12		19 15		19 20	
London Waterloo [15] ⊖	a	18 32		18 34	18 41			18 46		18 49	18 56				19 02	19 04	19 11			19 16		19 19		19 26	

Table T149-R

Saturdays

21 December to 16 May

Reading, Guildford, Ascot, Weybridge, Windsor, Kingston, Richmond and Hounslow - London

		SW	SW	SW	SW	SW ■1	SW ■1	SW		SW	SW	SW	SW	SW	SW	SW	SW	SW ■1		SW ■1	SW	SW	SW	SW	SW
Reading [7]	d			18 12												18 42									
Earley	d			18 17												18 47									
Winnersh Triangle	d			18 19												18 49									
Winnersh	d			18 21												18 51									
Wokingham	d			18 26												18 56									
Bracknell	d			18 32												19 02									
Martins Heron	d			18 35												19 05									
Guildford	d						18 23													18 53					
Wanborough	d						18 29													18 59					
Ash [5]	d						18 33													19 03					
Aldershot	a						18 40													19 10					
	d					18 30												19 00							
Ash Vale	d					18 34												19 04							
Frimley	d					18 40												19 10							
Camberley	a					18 44												19 14							
	d					18 48												19 18							
Bagshot	d					18 53												19 23							
Ascot [3]	d			18 40		19a00										19 10		19a30							
Sunningdale	d			18 43												19 13									
Longcross	d			18 46												19 16									
Weybridge	d												19 03												19 33
Addlestone	d												19 07												19 37
Chertsey	d									←			19 10									←			19 40
Virginia Water	a			18 50						18 45			19 15			19 20						19 15			19 45
	d			18 50						18 54			19 24			19 20						19 24			19 54
Egham	d			18 54						18 57			→			19 24						19 27			→
Windsor & Eton Riverside	d										18 53												19 23		
Datchet	d										18 56												19 26		
Sunnymeads	d										18 59												19 29		
Wraysbury	d										19 02												19 32		
Staines	d			18 59						19 03	19 08					19 29						19 33	19 38		
Ashford (Surrey)	d									19 06	19 11											19 36	19 41		
Feltham	d			19 05						19 11	19 16					19 35						19 41	19 46		
Whitton	d	18 50	18 53								19 20			19 20	19 23								19 50		
Kingston	d							18 59													19 29				
Hampton Wick	d							19 01													19 31				
Teddington	d							19 05													19 35				
Fulwell	d																								
Strawberry Hill	d							19 08													19 38				
Twickenham	a		18 56	19 10				19 12			19 23				19 26	19 40					19 42		19 53		
	d		18 58	19 11				19 13			19 23				19 28	19 41					19 43		19 53		
St Margarets	d		19 00					19 15							19 30						19 45				
Richmond ⊖	d		19 04	19 15				19 19			19 28				19 34	19 45					19 49		19 58		
North Sheen	d		19 06					19 21							19 36						19 51				
Mortlake	d		19 08					19 23							19 38						19 53				
Hounslow	d	19 01								19 16				19 31								19 46			
Isleworth	d	19 04								19 19				19 34								19 49			
Syon Lane	d	19 06								19 21				19 36								19 51			
Brentford	d	19 09								19 24				19 39								19 54			
Kew Bridge	d	19 11								19 26				19 41								19 56			
Chiswick	d	19 14								19 29				19 44								19 59			
Barnes Bridge	d	19 16			←					19 31				19 46			←					20 01			
Barnes	d	19 19	19 11		19 19			19 26		19 34		←		19 49	19 41		19 49				19 56	20 04		←	
Putney	d	→	19 14		19 22			19 29		19 37	19 34	19 37		→	19 44		19 52				19 59	20 07	20 04	20 07	
Wandsworth Town	d		19 17		19 25			19 32		→		19 40			19 47		19 55				20 02	→		20 10	
Clapham Junction [10]	d		19 20	19 24	19 29			19 35			19 39	19 43			19 50	19 54	19 58				20 05		20 09	20 13	
Queenstown Rd.(Battersea)	d		19 23		19 32			19 38				19 46			19 53		20 01				20 08			20 16	
Vauxhall ⊖	d		19 27		19 36			19 42			19 45	19 50			19 57		20 05				20 12		20 15	20 20	
London Waterloo [15] ⊖	a		19 32	19 34	19 41			19 46			19 49	19 56			20 02	20 04	20 11				20 16		20 19	20 26	

Table T149-R

Saturdays
21 December to 16 May

Reading, Guildford, Ascot, Weybridge, Windsor, Kingston, Richmond and Hounslow - London

		SW	SW	SW		SW	SW 1	SW 1	SW	SW	SW	SW	SW	SW		SW	SW	SW	SW 1	SW 1	SW	SW	SW	SW
Reading 7	d			19 12													19 42							
Earley	d			19 17													19 47							
Winnersh Triangle	d			19 19													19 49							
Winnersh	d			19 21													19 51							
Wokingham	d			19 26													19 56							
Bracknell	d			19 32													20 02							
Martins Heron	d			19 35													20 05							
Guildford	d							19 23												19 53				
Wanborough	d							19 29												19 59				
Ash 5	d							19 33												20 03				
Aldershot	a							19 40												20 10				
	d						19 30												20 00					
Ash Vale	d						19 34												20 04					
Frimley	d						19 40												20 10					
Camberley	a						19 44												20 14					
	d						19 48												20 18					
Bagshot	d						19 53												20 23					
Ascot 3	d			19 40			20a00										20 10		20a30					
Sunningdale	d			19 43													20 13							
Longcross	d			19 46													20 16							
Weybridge	d												20 03											
Addlestone	d												20 07											
Chertsey	d									←			20 10									←		
Virginia Water	a			19 50						19 45			20 15				20 20					20 15		
	d			19 50						19 54			20 24				20 20					20 24		
Egham	d			19 54						19 57			→				20 24					20 27		
Windsor & Eton Riverside	d										19 53												20 23	
Datchet	d										19 56												20 26	
Sunnymeads	d										19 59												20 29	
Wraysbury	d										20 02												20 32	
Staines	d			19 59						20 03	20 08						20 29					20 33	20 38	
Ashford (Surrey)	d									20 06	20 11											20 36	20 41	
Feltham	d			20 05						20 11	20 16						20 35					20 41	20 46	
Whitton	d	19 50	19 53								20 20			20 20		20 23							20 50	
Kingston	d								19 59												20 29			
Hampton Wick	d								20 01												20 31			
Teddington	d								20 05												20 35			
Fulwell	d																							
Strawberry Hill	d								20 08												20 38			
Twickenham	a		19 56	20 10					20 12		20 23					20 26	20 40				20 42		20 53	
	d		19 58	20 11					20 13		20 23					20 28	20 41				20 43		20 53	
St Margarets	d		20 00						20 15							20 30					20 45			
Richmond ⊖	d		20 04	20 15					20 19		20 28					20 34	20 45				20 49		20 58	
North Sheen	d		20 06						20 21							20 36					20 51			
Mortlake	d		20 08						20 23							20 38					20 53			
Hounslow	d	20 01								20 16				20 31								20 46		
Isleworth	d	20 04								20 19				20 34								20 49		
Syon Lane	d	20 06								20 21				20 36								20 51		
Brentford	d	20 09								20 24				20 39								20 54		
Kew Bridge	d	20 11								20 26				20 41								20 56		
Chiswick	d	20 14								20 29				20 44								20 59		
Barnes Bridge	d	20 16				←				20 31				20 46				←				21 01		
Barnes	d	20 19	20 11			20 19			20 26	20 34		←		20 49		20 41		20 49			20 56	21 04		←
Putney	d	→	20 14			20 22			20 29	20 37	20 34	20 37		→		20 44		20 52			20 59	21 07	21 04	21 07
Wandsworth Town	d		20 17			20 25			20 32	→		20 40				20 47		20 55			21 02	→		21 10
Clapham Junction 10	d		20 20	20 24		20 28			20 35		20 39	20 43				20 50	20 54	20 58			21 05		21 09	21 13
Queenstown Rd.(Battersea)	d		20 23			20 31			20 38			20 46				20 53		21 01			21 08			21 16
Vauxhall ⊖	d		20 27			20 35			20 42		20 45	20 50				20 57		21 05			21 12		21 15	21 20
London Waterloo 15 ⊖	a		20 32	20 34		20 41			20 46		20 49	20 56				21 02	21 04	21 11			21 16		21 19	21 26

Table T149-R

Saturdays
21 December to 16 May

Reading, Guildford, Ascot, Weybridge, Windsor, Kingston, Richmond and Hounslow - London

		SW	SW	SW	SW	SW	SW 1	SW 1	SW	SW		SW	SW	SW	SW	SW	SW	SW	SW 1	SW 1		SW	SW	SW	SW
Reading 7	d				20 12												20 42								
Earley	d				20 17												20 47								
Winnersh Triangle	d				20 19												20 49								
Winnersh	d				20 21												20 51								
Wokingham	d				20 26												20 56								
Bracknell	d				20 32												21 02								
Martins Heron	d				20 35												21 05								
Guildford	d							20 23												20 53					
Wanborough	d							20 29												20 59					
Ash 5	d							20 33												21 03					
Aldershot	a							20 40												21 10					
	d						20 30												21 00						
Ash Vale	d						20 34												21 04						
Frimley	d						20 40												21 10						
Camberley	a						20 44												21 14						
	d						20 48												21 18						
Bagshot	d						20 53												21 23						
Ascot 3	d				20 40		21a00										21 10		21a30						
Sunningdale	d				20 43												21 13								
Longcross	d				20 46												21 16								
Weybridge	d	20 33												21 03											
Addlestone	d	20 37												21 07											
Chertsey	d	20 40								←				21 10									←		
Virginia Water	a	20 45			20 50					20 45				21 15			21 20						21 15		
	d	20 54			20 50					20 54				21 24			21 20						21 24		
Egham	d	→			20 54					20 57				→			21 24						21 27		
Windsor & Eton Riverside	d											20 53												21 23	
Datchet	d											20 56												21 26	
Sunnymeads	d											20 59												21 29	
Wraysbury	d											21 02												21 32	
Staines	d				20 59					21 03		21 08					21 29						21 33	21 38	
Ashford (Surrey)	d									21 06		21 11											21 36	21 41	
Feltham	d				21 05					21 11		21 16					21 35						21 41	21 46	
Whitton	d		20 50	20 53								21 20			21 20	21 23								21 50	
Kingston	d								20 59													21 29			
Hampton Wick	d								21 01													21 31			
Teddington	d								21 05													21 35			
Fulwell	d																								
Strawberry Hill	d								21 08													21 38			
Twickenham	a			20 56	21 10				21 12			21 23				21 26	21 40					21 42		21 53	
	d			20 58	21 11				21 13			21 23				21 28	21 41					21 43		21 53	
St Margarets	d			21 00					21 15							21 30						21 45			
Richmond ⊖	d			21 04	21 15				21 19			21 28				21 34	21 45					21 49		21 58	
North Sheen	d			21 06					21 21							21 36						21 51			
Mortlake	d			21 08					21 23							21 38						21 53			
Hounslow	d		21 01							21 16					21 31								21 46		
Isleworth	d		21 04							21 19					21 34								21 49		
Syon Lane	d		21 06							21 21					21 36								21 51		
Brentford	d		21 09							21 24					21 39								21 54		
Kew Bridge	d		21 11							21 26					21 41								21 56		
Chiswick	d		21 14							21 29					21 44								21 59		
Barnes Bridge	d		21 16			←				21 31					21 46			←					22 01		
Barnes	d		21 19	21 11		21 19			21 26	21 34			←		21 49	21 41		21 49				21 56	22 04		←
Putney	d		→	21 14		21 22			21 29	21 37		21 34	21 37		→	21 44		21 52				21 59	22 07	22 04	22 07
Wandsworth Town	d			21 17		21 25			21 32	→			21 40			21 47		21 55				22 02	→		22 10
Clapham Junction 10	d			21 20	21 24	21 28			21 35			21 39	21 43			21 50	21 54	21 58				22 05		22 09	22 13
Queenstown Rd.(Battersea)	d			21 23		21 31			21 38				21 46			21 53		22 01				22 08			22 16
Vauxhall ⊖	d			21 27		21 35			21 42			21 45	21 50			21 57		22 05				22 12		22 15	22 20
London Waterloo 15 ⊖	a			21 32	21 34	21 41			21 46			21 49	21 56			22 02	22 04	22 11				22 16		22 19	22 26

Table T149-R

Saturdays

21 December to 16 May

Reading, Guildford, Ascot, Weybridge, Windsor, Kingston, Richmond and Hounslow - London

		SW	SW	SW	SW	SW		SW 1	SW 1	SW	SW	SW	SW	SW	SW	SW		SW 1	SW 1	SW	SW	SW	SW	SW	SW
Reading 7	d				21 12											21 42									22 12
Earley	d				21 17											21 47									22 17
Winnersh Triangle	d				21 19											21 49									22 19
Winnersh	d				21 21											21 51									22 21
Wokingham	d				21 26											21 56									22 26
Bracknell	d				21 32											22 02									22 32
Martins Heron	d				21 35											22 05									22 35
Guildford	d								21 23										21 53						
Wanborough	d								21 29										21 59						
Ash 8	d								21 33										22 03						
Aldershot	a								21 40										22 10						
	d							21 30										22 00							
Ash Vale	d							21 34										22 04							
Frimley	d							21 40										22 10							
Camberley	a							21 44										22 14							
	d							21 48										22 18							
Bagshot	d							21 53										22 23							
Ascot 8	d				21 40			22a00								22 10		22a30							22 40
Sunningdale	d				21 43											22 13									22 43
Longcross	d																								
Weybridge	d	21 33													22 03									22 33	
Addlestone	d	21 37													22 07									22 37	
Chertsey	d	21 40									←				22 10						←			22 40	
Virginia Water	a	21 45			21 49						21 45				22 15	22 19					22 15			22 45	22 49
	d	21 54			21 49						21 54				22 24	22 19					22 24			22 54	22 49
Egham	d	→			21 53						21 57				→	22 23					22 27			→	22 53
Windsor & Eton Riverside	d											21 53										22 23			
Datchet	d											21 56										22 26			
Sunnymeads	d											21 59										22 29			
Wraysbury	d											22 02										22 32			
Staines	d				21 59						22 03	22 08				22 29					22 33	22 38			22 59
Ashford (Surrey)	d										22 06	22 11									22 36	22 41			
Feltham	d				22 05						22 11	22 16				22 35					22 41	22 46			23 05
Whitton	d		21 50	21 53								22 20		22 23								22 50			
Kingston	d									21 59										22 29					
Hampton Wick	d									22 01										22 31					
Teddington	d									22 05										22 35					
Fulwell	d																								
Strawberry Hill	d									22 08										22 38					
Twickenham	a			21 56	22 10					22 12		22 23		22 26		22 40				22 42		22 53			23 10
	d			21 58	22 11					22 13		22 23		22 28		22 41				22 43		22 53			23 11
St Margarets	d			22 00						22 15				22 30						22 45					
Richmond ⊖	d			22 04	22 15					22 19		22 28		22 34		22 45				22 49		22 58			23 15
North Sheen	d			22 06						22 21				22 36						22 51					
Mortlake	d			22 08						22 23				22 38						22 53					
Hounslow	d		22 01								22 16										22 46				
Isleworth	d		22 04								22 19										22 49				
Syon Lane	d		22 06								22 21										22 51				
Brentford	d		22 09								22 24										22 54				
Kew Bridge	d		22 11								22 26										22 56				
Chiswick	d		22 14								22 29										22 59				
Barnes Bridge	d		22 16			←					22 31										23 01				
Barnes	d		22 19	22 11		22 19				22 26	22 34		←	22 41						22 56	23 04		←		
Putney	d		→	22 14		22 22				22 29	22 37	22 34	22 37	22 44						22 59	23 07	23 04	23 07		
Wandsworth Town	d			22 17		22 25				22 32	→		22 40	22 47						23 02	→		23 10		
Clapham Junction 10	d			22 20	22 24	22 28				22 35		22 39	22 43	22 50		22 54				23 05		23 09	23 13		23 24
Queenstown Rd.(Battersea)	d			22 23		22 31				22 38			22 46	22 53						23 08			23 16		
Vauxhall ⊖	d			22 27		22 35				22 42		22 45	22 50	22 57						23 12		23 15	23 20		
London Waterloo 15 ⊖	a			22 32	22 34	22 41				22 46		22 49	22 56	23 02		23 04				23 16		23 19	23 26		23 34

Table T149-R

Saturdays

21 December to 16 May

Reading, Guildford, Ascot, Weybridge, Windsor, Kingston, Richmond and Hounslow - London

		SW 1		SW 1	SW	SW	SW	SW	SW	SW	SW	SW 1		SW 1	SW	SW	SW	SW	SW	SW	SW 1	SW			
Reading 7	d									22 42									23 12						
Earley	d									22 47									23 17						
Winnersh Triangle	d									22 49									23 19						
Winnersh	d									22 51									23 21						
Wokingham	d									22 56									23 26						
Bracknell	d									23 02									23 32						
Martins Heron	d									23 05									23 35						
Guildford	d			22 23										22 53								23 30			
Wanborough	d			22 29										22 59								23 36			
Ash 8	d			22 33										23 03								23 40			
Aldershot	a			22 40										23 10								23 47			
	d	22 30										23 00									23 30				
Ash Vale	d	22 34										23 04									23 34				
Frimley	d	22 40										23 10									23 40				
Camberley	a	22 44										23 14									23 44				
	d	22 48										23 18									23 48				
Bagshot	d	22 53										23 23									23 53				
Ascot 8	d	23a00								23 10		23a30							23 40		00a01				
Sunningdale	d									23 13									23 43						
Longcross	d																								
Weybridge	d								23 03									23 33							
Addlestone	d								23 07									23 37							
Chertsey	d					←			23 10		←							23 40		←					
Virginia Water	a					22 45			23 15	23 19	23 15							23 45	23 49	23 45					
	d					22 54			23 24	23 19	23 24							23 54	23 49	23 54					
Egham	d					22 57			→	23 23	23 27							→	23 53	23 57					
Windsor & Eton Riverside	d						22 53								23 28										
Datchet	d						22 56								23 31										
Sunnymeads	d						22 59								23 34										
Wraysbury	d						23 02								23 37										
Staines	d					23 03	23 08			23 29	23a32				23a42				23 59	00a02					
Ashford (Surrey)	d					23 06	23 11																		
Feltham	d					23 11	23 16			23 35									00 05						
Whitton	d						23 20																		
Kingston	d				22 59											23 29	23 55								
Hampton Wick	d				23 01											23 31	23 57								
Teddington	d				23 05											23 35	23 59								
Fulwell	d																								
Strawberry Hill	d				23 08											23 38	00 03								
Twickenham	a				23 12		23 23			23 40						23 42	00 06		00 10						
	d				23 13		23 23			23 41						23 43			00 11						
St Margarets	d				23 15											23 45									
Richmond ⊖	d				23 19		23 28			23 45						23 49			00 15						
North Sheen	d				23 21											23 51									
Mortlake	d				23 23											23 53									
Hounslow	d					23 16																			
Isleworth	d					23 19																			
Syon Lane	d					23 21																			
Brentford	d					23 24																			
Kew Bridge	d					23 26																			
Chiswick	d					23 29																			
Barnes Bridge	d					23 31																			
Barnes	d				23 26	23 34		←								23 56									
Putney	d				23 29	23 37	23 34	23 37								23 59									
Wandsworth Town	d				23 32	→		23 40								00 02									
Clapham Junction 10	d				23 35		23 39	23 43		23 54						00 06			00 24						
Queenstown Rd.(Battersea)	d				23 38			23 46								00 09									
Vauxhall ⊖	d				23 42		23 45	23 50								00 12									
London Waterloo 15 ⊖	a				23 46		23 49	23 56		00 02						00 17			00 37						

Table T149-R

Sundays
15 December to 10 May

Reading, Guildford, Ascot, Weybridge, Windsor, Kingston, Richmond and Hounslow - London

		SW	SW	SW	SW	SW	SW	SW	SW	SW	SW	SW	SW	SW	SW	SW	SW	SW	SW	SW	SW	SW	SW
		A	A	A							■							■					
Reading 7	d														07 54		08 24				08 54		
Earley	d														07 59		08 29				08 59		
Winnersh Triangle	d														08 01		08 31				09 01		
Winnersh	d														08 03		08 33				09 03		
Wokingham	d														08 08		08 38				09 08		
Bracknell	d														08 14		08 44				09 14		
Martins Heron	d														08 17		08 47				09 17		
Guildford	d										07 17							08 17					
Wanborough	d										07 23							08 23					
Ash 8	d										07 27							08 27					
Aldershot	a										07 34							08 34					
	d										07 40							08 40					
Ash Vale	d										07 45							08 45					
Frimley	d										07 51							08 51					
Camberley	a										07 55							08 55					
	d										07 55							08 55					
Bagshot	d										08 01							09 01					
Ascot 3	d									07 22	08a07				08 22		08 52	09a07			09 22		
Sunningdale	d									07 25					08 25		08 55				09 25		
Longcross	d									07 28					08 28						09 28		
Weybridge	d								07 00														
Addlestone	d								07 04					08 04						09 04			
Chertsey	d								07 07					08 07						09 07			
Virginia Water	a								07 12	07 31				08 12	08 31		09 01			09 12	09 31		
	d								07 12	07 31				08 12	08 31		09 01			09 12	09 31		
Egham	d								07 16	07 36				08 16	08 36		09 06			09 16	09 36		
Windsor & Eton Riverside	d							07 01					08 01						09 01			09 34	
Datchet	d							07 04					08 04						09 04			09 37	
Sunnymeads	d							07 07					08 07						09 07				
Wraysbury	d							07 10					08 10						09 10				
Staines	d							07 16	07 21	07 41			08 16	08 21	08 41		09 11		09 16	09 21	09 41	09 45	
Ashford (Surrey)	d							07 19	07 24				08 19	08 24					09 19	09 24		09 48	
Feltham	d			00 05				07 24	07 29	07 47			08 24	08 29	08 47		09 17		09 24	09 29	09 47	09 53	
Whitton	d							07 28					08 28						09 28			09 57	
Kingston	d				01 17	02 11	06 49					07 49				08 49							09 49
Hampton Wick	d				01s22	02s13	06 51					07 51				08 51							09 51
Teddington	d				01s25	02s15	06 56					07 56				08 56							09 56
Fulwell	d																						
Strawberry Hill	d		00 03		01a37	02s18	06 59					07 59				08 59							09 59
Twickenham	a		00 06	00 10		02 22	07 02	07 31		07 52		08 02	08 31		08 52	09 02	09 22		09 31		09 52	10 00	10 02
	d			00 11			07 03	07 32		07 53		08 03	08 32		08 53	09 03	09 23		09 32		09 53	10 01	10 03
St Margarets	d						07 05	07 34				08 05	08 34			09 05			09 34				10 05
Richmond ⊖	d			00 15			07 09	07 37		07 57		08 09	08 37		08 57	09 09	09 27		09 37		09 57	10 05	10 09
North Sheen	d						07 11	07 39				08 11	08 39			09 11			09 39				10 11
Mortlake	d						07 13	07 42				08 13	08 42			09 13			09 42				10 13
Hounslow	d								07 35					08 35						09 35			
Isleworth	d								07 38					08 38						09 38			
Syon Lane	d								07 40					08 40						09 40			
Brentford	d								07 42					08 42						09 42			
Kew Bridge	d								07 45					08 45						09 45			
Chiswick	d								07 47					08 47						09 47			
Barnes Bridge	d								07 50					08 50						09 50			
Barnes	d						07 16	07 45	07 53			08 16	08 45	08 53		09 16			09 45	09 53			10 16
Putney	d						07 19	07 48	07 56	08 04		08 19	08 48	08 56	09 04	09 19	09 34		09 48	09 56	10 04	10 14	10 19
Wandsworth Town	d	00 02					07 22	07 51	07 59			08 22	08 51	08 59		09 22			09 51	09 59			10 22
Clapham Junction 10	d	00 06		00 24			07 25	07 54	08 02	08 08		08 25	08 54	09 02	09 08	09 25	09 38		09 54	10 02	10 08	10 18	10 25
Queenstown Rd.(Battersea)	d	00 09					07 28	07 57	08 05			08 28	08 57	09 05		09 28			09 57	10 05			10 28
Vauxhall ⊖	d	00 12					07 32	08 00	08 08	08 14		08 32	09 00	09 08	09 14	09 32	09 44		10 00	10 08	10 14	10 24	10 32
London Waterloo 15 ⊖	a	00 17		00 37			07 36	08 06	08 13	08 22		08 36	09 06	09 13	09 20	09 36	09 50		10 05	10 13	10 20	10 29	10 36

A not 15 December

Table T149-R

Sundays
15 December to 10 May

Reading, Guildford, Ascot, Weybridge, Windsor, Kingston, Richmond and Hounslow - London

		SW	SW	SW	SW	SW	SW	SW	SW	SW	SW	SW	SW	SW	SW	SW	SW	SW	SW	SW	SW	SW	SW
			■							■							■						
Reading 7	d	09 24				09 54			10 24				10 54			11 24					11 54		
Earley	d	09 29				09 59			10 29				10 59			11 29					11 59		
Winnersh Triangle	d	09 31				10 01			10 31				11 01			11 31					12 01		
Winnersh	d	09 33				10 03			10 33				11 03			11 33					12 03		
Wokingham	d	09 38				10 08			10 38				11 08			11 38					12 08		
Bracknell	d	09 44				10 14			10 44				11 14			11 44					12 14		
Martins Heron	d	09 47				10 17			10 47				11 17			11 47					12 17		
Guildford	d		09 17							10 17							11 17						
Wanborough	d		09 23							10 23							11 23						
Ash 8	d		09 27							10 27							11 27						
Aldershot	a		09 34							10 34							11 34						
	d		09 40							10 40							11 40						
Ash Vale	d		09 45							10 45							11 45						
Frimley	d		09 51							10 51							11 51						
Camberley	a		09 55							10 55							11 55						
	d		09 55							10 55							11 55						
Bagshot	d		10 01							11 01							12 01						
Ascot 3	d	09 52	10a07			10 22			10 52	11a07			11 22			11 52	12a07				12 22		
Sunningdale	d	09 55				10 25			10 55				11 25			11 55					12 25		
Longcross	d					10 28							11 28								12 28		
Weybridge	d																						
Addlestone	d				10 04							11 04							12 04				
Chertsey	d				10 07							11 07							12 07				
Virginia Water	a	10 01			10 12	10 31			11 01			11 12	11 31			12 01			12 12		12 31		
	d	10 01			10 12	10 31			11 01			11 12	11 31			12 01			12 12		12 31		
Egham	d	10 05			10 16	10 35			11 05			11 16	11 35			12 05			12 16		12 35		
Windsor & Eton Riverside	d			10 01			10 34				11 01			11 34				12 01					12 34
Datchet	d			10 04			10 37				11 04			11 37				12 04					12 37
Sunnymeads	d			10 07							11 07							12 07					
Wraysbury	d			10 10							11 10							12 10					
Staines	d	10 11		10 16	10 21	10 41	10 45		11 11		11 16	11 21	11 41	11 45		12 11		12 16	12 21		12 41		12 45
Ashford (Surrey)	d			10 19	10 24		10 48				11 19	11 24		11 48				12 19	12 24				12 48
Feltham	d	10 17		10 24	10 29	10 47	10 53		11 17		11 24	11 29	11 47	11 53		12 17		12 24	12 29		12 47		12 53
Whitton	d			10 28			10 57				11 28			11 57				12 28					12 57
Kingston	d							10 49							11 49					12 35			
Hampton Wick	d							10 51							11 51					12 37			
Teddington	d							10 56							11 56					12 40			
Fulwell	d																						
Strawberry Hill	d							10 59							11 59					12 43		←	
Twickenham	a	10 22		10 31		10 52	11 00	11 02	11 22		11 31		11 52	12 00	12 02	12 22		12 31		12 46	12 52	12 46	13 00
	d	10 23		10 32		10 53	11 01	11 03	11 23		11 32		11 53	12 01	12 03	12 23		12 32		12 56	12 53	12 56	13 01
St Margarets	d			10 34				11 05			11 34				12 05			12 34		→			
Richmond ⊖	d	10 27		10 37		10 57	11 05	11 09	11 27		11 37		11 57	12 05	12 09	12 27		12 37			12 57		13 05
North Sheen	d			10 39				11 11			11 39				12 11			12 39					
Mortlake	d			10 42				11 13			11 42				12 13			12 42					
Hounslow	d				10 35							11 35							12 35			13 05	
Isleworth	d				10 38							11 38							12 38			13 08	
Syon Lane	d				10 40							11 40							12 40			13 10	
Brentford	d				10 42							11 42							12 42			13 12	
Kew Bridge	d				10 45							11 45							12 45			13 15	
Chiswick	d				10 47							11 47							12 47			13 17	
Barnes Bridge	d				10 50							11 50							12 50			13 20	
Barnes	d			10 45	10 53			11 16			11 45	11 53			12 16			12 45	12 53			13 23	
Putney	d	10 34		10 48	10 56	11 04	11 14	11 19	11 34		11 48	11 56	12 04	12 14	12 19	12 34		12 48	12 56		13 04	→	13 14
Wandsworth Town	d			10 51	10 59			11 22			11 51	11 59			12 22			12 51	12 59				
Clapham Junction 10	d	10 38		10 53	11 02	11 08	11 18	11 25	11 38		11 53	12 02	12 08	12 18	12 25	12 38		12 53	13 02		13 08		13 18
Queenstown Rd.(Battersea)	d			10 57	11 05			11 28			11 57	12 05			12 28			12 57	13 05				
Vauxhall ⊖	d	10 44		11 00	11 08	11 14	11 24	11 32	11 44		12 00	12 08	12 14	12 24	12 32	12 44		13 00	13 08		13 14		13 24
London Waterloo 15 ⊖	a	10 50		11 05	11 13	11 20	11 29	11 36	11 50		12 05	12 13	12 18	12 29	12 36	12 48		13 05	13 13		13 18		13 29

Table T149-R

Sundays

15 December to 10 May

Reading, Guildford, Ascot, Weybridge, Windsor, Kingston, Richmond and Hounslow - London

		SW		SW	SW	SW 1	SW	SW	SW	SW	SW	SW		SW	SW	SW	SW 1	SW	SW	SW	SW	SW		SW	SW
Reading 7	d				12 24					12 54						13 24					13 54				
Earley	d				12 29					12 59						13 29					13 59				
Winnersh Triangle	d				12 31					13 01						13 31					14 01				
Winnersh	d				12 33					13 03						13 33					14 03				
Wokingham	d				12 38					13 08						13 38					14 08				
Bracknell	d				12 44					13 14						13 44					14 14				
Martins Heron	d				12 47					13 17						13 47					14 17				
Guildford	d					12 17											13 17								
Wanborough	d					12 23											13 23								
Ash 5	d					12 27											13 27								
Aldershot	a					12 35											13 34								
	d					12 40											13 40								
Ash Vale	d					12 45											13 45								
Frimley	d					12 51											13 51								
Camberley	a					12 55											13 55								
	d					12 55											13 55								
Bagshot	d					13 01											14 01								
Ascot 3	d				12 52	13a07				13 22						13 52	14a07				14 22				
Sunningdale	d				12 55					13 25						13 55					14 25				
Longcross	d									13 28											14 28				
Weybridge	d																								
Addlestone	d							13 04											14 04						
Chertsey	d							13 07											14 07						
Virginia Water	a				13 01			13 12		13 31						14 01			14 12		14 31				
	d				13 01			13 12		13 31						14 01			14 12		14 31				
Egham	d				13 05			13 16		13 35						14 05			14 16		14 35				
Windsor & Eton Riverside	d						13 01					13 34						14 01						14 34	
Datchet	d						13 04					13 37						14 04						14 37	
Sunnymeads	d						13 07											14 07							
Wraysbury	d						13 10											14 10							
Staines	d				13 11		13 16	13 21		13 41		13 45				14 11		14 16	14 21		14 41			14 45	
Ashford (Surrey)	d						13 19	13 24				13 48						14 19	14 24					14 48	
Feltham	d				13 17		13 24	13 29		13 47		13 53				14 17		14 24	14 29		14 47			14 53	
Whitton	d						13 28					13 57						14 28						14 57	
Kingston	d	12 49							13 35					13 49						14 35					14 49
Hampton Wick	d	12 51							13 37					13 51						14 37					14 51
Teddington	d	12 56							13 40					13 56						14 40					14 56
Fulwell	d																								
Strawberry Hill	d	12 59							13 43		←			13 59						14 43		←			14 59
Twickenham	a	13 02			13 22		13 31		13 46	13 52	13 46	14 00		14 02		14 22		14 31		14 46	14 52	14 46		15 00	15 02
	d	13 03			13 23		13 32		13 56	13 53	13 56	14 01		14 03		14 23		14 32		14 56	14 53	14 56		15 01	15 03
St Margarets	d	13 05					13 34		→					14 05				14 34		→					15 05
Richmond ⊖	d	13 09			13 27		13 37			13 57		14 05		14 08		14 27		14 37			14 57			15 05	15 09
North Sheen	d	13 11					13 39							14 10				14 39							15 11
Mortlake	d	13 13					13 42							14 13				14 42							15 13
Hounslow	d							13 35			14 05								14 35			15 05			
Isleworth	d							13 38			14 08								14 38			15 08			
Syon Lane	d							13 40			14 10								14 40			15 10			
Brentford	d							13 42			14 12								14 42			15 12			
Kew Bridge	d							13 45			14 15								14 45			15 15			
Chiswick	d							13 47			14 17								14 47			15 17			
Barnes Bridge	d			←				13 50			14 20				←				14 50			15 20			
Barnes	d	13 16		13 23			13 45	13 53			14 23			14 16	14 23			14 45	14 53			15 23			15 16
Putney	d	13 19		13 26	13 34		13 48	13 56		14 04	→	14 14		14 19	14 26	14 34		14 48	14 56		15 04	→		15 14	15 19
Wandsworth Town	d	13 22		13 29			13 51	13 59						14 22	14 29			14 51	14 59						15 22
Clapham Junction 10	d	13 25		13 32	13 38		13 54	14 02		14 08		14 18		14 25	14 32	14 39		14 54	15 02		15 08			15 18	15 25
Queenstown Rd.(Battersea)	d	13 28		13 35			13 57	14 05						14 28	14 35			14 57	15 05						15 28
Vauxhall ⊖	d	13 32		13 38	13 44		14 00	14 08		14 14		14 24		14 32	14 38	14 45		15 00	15 08		15 14			15 24	15 32
London Waterloo 15 ⊖	a	13 36		13 43	13 48		14 05	14 13		14 23		14 29		14 41	14 43	14 54		15 05	15 13		15 18			15 29	15 36

Table T149-R

Sundays

15 December to 10 May

Reading, Guildford, Ascot, Weybridge, Windsor, Kingston, Richmond and Hounslow - London

		SW	SW	SW	SW 1	SW	SW	SW		SW	SW	SW	SW	SW	SW	SW	SW 1	SW		SW	SW	SW	SW	SW	SW
Reading 7	d			14 24						14 54						15 24						15 5			
Earley	d			14 29						14 59						15 29						15 5			
Winnersh Triangle	d			14 31						15 01						15 31						16 0			
Winnersh	d			14 33						15 03						15 33						16 0			
Wokingham	d			14 38						15 08						15 38						16 0			
Bracknell	d			14 44						15 14						15 44						16 1			
Martins Heron	d			14 47						15 17						15 47						16 1			
Guildford	d				14 17												15 17								
Wanborough	d				14 23												15 23								
Ash 5	d				14 27												15 27								
Aldershot	a				14 34												15 34								
	d				14 40												15 40								
Ash Vale	d				14 45												15 45								
Frimley	d				14 51												15 51								
Camberley	a				14 55												15 55								
	d				14 55												15 55								
Bagshot	d				15 01												16 01								
Ascot 3	d			14 52	15a07					15 22						15 52	16a07					16 2			
Sunningdale	d			14 55						15 25						15 55						16 2			
Longcross	d									15 28												16 2			
Weybridge	d																								
Addlestone	d						15 04													16 04					
Chertsey	d						15 07													16 07					
Virginia Water	a			15 01			15 12			15 31						16 01				16 12		16 3			
	d			15 01			15 12			15 31						16 01				16 12		16 3			
Egham	d			15 05			15 16			15 35						16 05				16 16		16 3			
Windsor & Eton Riverside	d					15 01						15 34						16 01						16 34	
Datchet	d					15 04						15 37						16 04						16 37	
Sunnymeads	d					15 07												16 07							
Wraysbury	d					15 10												16 10							
Staines	d			15 11		15 16	15 21			15 41		15 45				16 11		16 16		16 21		16 4		16 45	
Ashford (Surrey)	d					15 19	15 24					15 48						16 19		16 24				16 48	
Feltham	d			15 17		15 24	15 29			15 47		15 53				16 17		16 24		16 29		16 4		16 53	
Whitton	d		15 01			15 28						15 57			16 01			16 28						16 57	
Kingston	d							15 35					15 49								16 35				16 49
Hampton Wick	d							15 37					15 51								16 37				16 51
Teddington	d							15 40					15 56								16 40				16 56
Fulwell	d																								
Strawberry Hill	d							15 43			←		15 59								16 43		←		16 59
Twickenham	a		15 04	15 22		15 31		15 46		15 52	15 46	16 00	16 02		16 04	16 22		16 31			16 46	16 5	16 46	17 00	17 02
	d			15 23		15 32		15 56		15 53	15 56	16 01	16 03			16 23		16 32			16 56	16 5	16 56	17 01	17 03
St Margarets	d					15 34		→					16 05					16 34			→				17 05
Richmond ⊖	d			15 27		15 37				15 57		16 05	16 09			16 27		16 37				16 5		17 05	17 09
North Sheen	d					15 39							16 11					16 39							17 11
Mortlake	d					15 42							16 13					16 42							17 13
Hounslow	d						15 35				16 05									16 35			17 05		
Isleworth	d						15 38				16 08									16 38			17 08		
Syon Lane	d						15 40				16 10									16 40			17 10		
Brentford	d						15 42				16 12									16 42			17 12		
Kew Bridge	d						15 45				16 15									16 45			17 15		
Chiswick	d						15 47				16 17									16 47			17 17		
Barnes Bridge	d	←					15 50				16 20			←						16 50			17 20		
Barnes	d	15 23				15 45	15 53				16 23		16 16	16 23				16 45		16 53			17 23		17 16
Putney	d	15 26		15 34		15 48	15 56			16 04	→	16 14	16 19	16 26		16 34		16 48		16 56		17 0	→	17 14	17 19
Wandsworth Town	d	15 29				15 51	15 59						16 22	16 29				16 51		16 59					17 22
Clapham Junction 10	d	15 32		15 38		15 54	16 02			16 08		16 18	16 25	16 32		16 38		16 54		17 02		17 0		17 18	17 25
Queenstown Rd.(Battersea)	d	15 35				15 57	16 05						16 28	16 35				16 57		17 05					17 28
Vauxhall ⊖	d	15 38		15 44		16 00	16 08			16 14		16 24	16 32	16 38		16 44		17 00		17 08		17 1		17 24	17 32
London Waterloo 15 ⊖	a	15 43		15 48		16 05	16 13			16 18		16 29	16 36	16 43		16 48		17 05		17 13		17 1		17 29	17 36

Table T149-R

Sundays

15 December to 10 May

Reading, Guildford, Ascot, Weybridge, Windsor, Kingston, Richmond and Hounslow - London

		SW	SW	SW		SW ■1	SW	SW	SW	SW	SW	SW	SW	SW	SW	SW	SW ■1	SW	SW	SW	SW	
Reading ■7	d			16 24						16 54						17 24					17 54	
Earley	d			16 29						16 59						17 29					17 59	
Winnersh Triangle	d			16 31						17 01						17 31					18 01	
Winnersh	d			16 33						17 03						17 33					18 03	
Wokingham	d			16 38						17 08						17 38					18 08	
Bracknell	d			16 44						17 14						17 44					18 14	
Martins Heron	d			16 47						17 17						17 47					18 17	
Guildford	d					16 17											17 17					
Wanborough	d					16 23											17 23					
Ash ■5	d					16 27											17 27					
Aldershot	a					16 34											17 34					
	d					16 40											17 40					
Ash Vale	d					16 45											17 45					
Frimley	d					16 51											17 51					
Camberley	a					16 55											17 55					
	d					16 55											17 55					
Bagshot	d					17 01											18 01					
Ascot ■3	d			16 52		17a07				17 22						17 52	18a07				18 22	
Sunningdale	d			16 55						17 25						17 55					18 25	
Longcross	d									17 28											18 28	
Weybridge	d																					
Addlestone	d							17 04											18 04			
Chertsey	d							17 07											18 07			
Virginia Water	a			17 01				17 12		17 31						18 01			18 12		18 31	
	d			17 01				17 12		17 31						18 01			18 12		18 31	
Egham	d			17 05				17 16		17 36						18 05			18 16		18 35	and at the same minutes past each hour until
Windsor & Eton Riverside	d						17 01					17 34						18 01				
Datchet	d						17 04					17 37						18 04				
Sunnymeads	d						17 07											18 07				
Wraysbury	d						17 10											18 10				
Staines	d			17 11			17 16	17 21		17 41		17 45				18 11		18 16	18 21		18 41	
Ashford (Surrey)	d						17 19	17 24				17 48						18 19	18 24			
Feltham	d			17 17			17 24	17 29		17 47		17 53				18 17		18 24	18 29		18 47	
Whitton	d		17 01				17 28					17 57			18 01			18 28				
Kingston	d								17 35				17 49							18 35		
Hampton Wick	d								17 37				17 51							18 37		
Teddington	d								17 40				17 56							18 40		
Fulwell	d																					
Strawberry Hill	d								17 43		←		17 59							18 43		
Twickenham	a		17 04	17 22			17 31		17 46	17 52	17 46	18 00	18 02		18 04	18 22		18 31		18 46	18 52	
	d			17 23			17 32		17 56	17 53	17 56	18 01	18 03			18 23		18 32		18 56	18 53	
St Margarets	d						17 34		→				18 05					18 34		→		
Richmond ⊖	d			17 27			17 37			17 57		18 05	18 09			18 27		18 37			18 57	
North Sheen	d						17 39						18 11					18 39				
Mortlake	d						17 42						18 13					18 42				
Hounslow	d							17 35			18 05								18 35			
Isleworth	d							17 38			18 08								18 38			
Syon Lane	d							17 40			18 10								18 40			
Brentford	d							17 42			18 12								18 42			
Kew Bridge	d							17 45			18 15								18 45			
Chiswick	d							17 47			18 17								18 47			
Barnes Bridge	d	←						17 50			18 20			←					18 50			
Barnes	d	17 23					17 45	17 53			18 23		18 16	18 23				18 45	18 53			
Putney	d	17 26		17 34			17 48	17 56		18 04	→	18 14	18 19	18 26		18 34		18 48	18 56		19 04	
Wandsworth Town	d	17 29					17 51	17 59					18 22	18 29				18 51	18 59			
Clapham Junction ■10	d	17 32		17 38			17 54	18 02		18 08		18 18	18 25	18 32		18 38		18 54	19 02		19 08	
Queenstown Rd.(Battersea)	d	17 35					17 57	18 05					18 28	18 35				18 57	19 05			
Vauxhall ⊖	d	17 38		17 44			18 00	18 08		18 14		18 24	18 32	18 38		18 44		19 00	19 08		19 14	
London Waterloo ■15 ⊖	a	17 43		17 48			18 05	18 13		18 18		18 29	18 36	18 43		18 48		19 05	19 13		19 18	

Table T149-R

Sundays

15 December to 10 May

Reading, Guildford, Ascot, Weybridge, Windsor, Kingston, Richmond and Hounslow - London

		SW	SW	SW	SW	SW	SW	SW ■1	SW	SW	SW	SW		SW	SW	SW	SW	SW	SW	SW ■1	SW	SW		SW	SW
Reading ■7	d						20 24					20 54							21 24						21 54
Earley	d						20 29					20 59							21 29						21 59
Winnersh Triangle	d						20 31					21 01							21 31						22 01
Winnersh	d						20 33					21 03							21 33						22 03
Wokingham	d						20 38					21 08							21 38						22 08
Bracknell	d						20 44					21 14							21 44						22 14
Martins Heron	d						20 47					21 17							21 47						22 17
Guildford	d							20 17												21 17					
Wanborough	d							20 23												21 23					
Ash ■5	d							20 27												21 27					
Aldershot	a							20 34												21 34					
	d							20 40												21 40					
Ash Vale	d							20 45												21 45					
Frimley	d							20 51												21 51					
Camberley	a							20 55												21 55					
	d							20 55												21 55					
Bagshot	d							21 01												22 01					
Ascot ■3	d						20 52	21a07				21 22							21 52	22a07					22 22
Sunningdale	d						20 55					21 25							21 55						22 25
Longcross	d											21 28													
Weybridge	d																								
Addlestone	d									21 04												22 04			
Chertsey	d									21 07												22 07			
Virginia Water	a						21 01			21 12		21 31							22 01			22 12			22 31
	d						21 01			21 12		21 31							22 01			22 12			22 31
Egham	d						21 05			21 16		21 35							22 05			22 16			22 35
Windsor & Eton Riverside	d		20 34						21 01						21 34						22 01				
Datchet	d		20 37						21 04						21 37						22 04				
Sunnymeads	d								21 07												22 07				
Wraysbury	d								21 10												22 10				
Staines	d		20 45				21 11		21 16	21 21		21 41			21a45				22 11		22 16	22 21			22 41
Ashford (Surrey)	d		20 48						21 19	21 24											22 19	22 24			
Feltham	d		20 53				21 17		21 24	21 29		21 47							22 17		22 24	22 29			22 47
Whitton	d		20 57			21 01			21 28									22 01			22 28				
Kingston	d			20 49							21 35					21 49								22 35	
Hampton Wick	d			20 51							21 37					21 51								22 37	
Teddington	d			20 56							21 40					21 56								22 40	
Fulwell	d																								
Strawberry Hill	d	←		20 59							21 43			←		21 59								22 43	
Twickenham	a	20 46	21 00	21 02		21 04	21 22		21 31		21 46	21 52		21 46		22 02		22 04	22 22		22 31			22 46	22 52
	d	20 56	21 01	21 03			21 23		21 32		21 56	21 53		21 56		22 03			22 23		22 32			22 56	22 53
St Margarets	d			21 05					21 34		→					22 05					22 34			→	
Richmond ⊖	d		21 05	21 09			21 27		21 37			21 57				22 09			22 27		22 37				22 57
North Sheen	d			21 11					21 39							22 11					22 39				
Mortlake	d			21 13					21 42							22 13					22 42				
Hounslow	d	21 05								21 35				22 05								22 35			
Isleworth	d	21 08								21 38				22 08								22 38			
Syon Lane	d	21 10								21 40				22 10								22 40			
Brentford	d	21 12								21 42				22 12								22 42			
Kew Bridge	d	21 15								21 45				22 15								22 45			
Chiswick	d	21 17								21 47				22 17								22 47			
Barnes Bridge	d	21 20			←					21 50				22 20			←					22 50			
Barnes	d	21 23		21 16	21 23				21 45	21 53				22 23		22 16	22 23				22 45	22 53			
Putney	d	→	21 14	21 19	21 26		21 34		21 48	21 56		22 04		→		22 19	22 26		22 34		22 48	22 56			23 04
Wandsworth Town	d			21 22	21 29				21 51	21 59						22 22	22 29				22 51	22 59			
Clapham Junction ■10	d		21 18	21 25	21 32		21 38		21 54	22 02		22 08				22 25	22 32		22 38		22 54	23 02			23 08
Queenstown Rd.(Battersea)	d			21 28	21 35				21 57	22 05						22 28	22 35				22 57	23 05			
Vauxhall ⊖	d		21 24	21 32	21 38		21 44		22 00	22 08		22 14				22 32	22 38		22 44		23 00	23 08			23 14
London Waterloo ■15 ⊖	a		21 29	21 36	21 43		21 48		22 05	22 13		22 18				22 36	22 43		22 48		23 05	23 13			23 18

Table T149-R

Sundays
15 December to 10 May

Reading, Guildford, Ascot, Weybridge, Windsor, Kingston, Richmond and Hounslow - London

Station		SW	SW	SW	SW	SW	SW 1	SW		SW	SW 1	SW	SW	SW
Reading 7	d					22 24							22 54	
Earley	d					22 29							22 59	
Winnersh Triangle	d					22 31							23 01	
Winnersh	d					22 33							23 03	
Wokingham	d					22 38							23 08	
Bracknell	d					22 44							23 14	
Martins Heron	d					22 47							23 17	
Guildford	d						22 17				23 17			
Wanborough	d						22 23				23 23			
Ash 3	d						22 27				23 27			
Aldershot	a						22 34				23 34			
	d						22 40							
Ash Vale	d						22 45							
Frimley	d						22 51							
Camberley	a						22 55							
	d						22 55							
Bagshot	d						23 01							
Ascot 3	d					22 52	23a07						23 22	
Sunningdale	d					22 55							23 25	
Longcross	d													
Weybridge	d													
Addlestone	d									23 04				
Chertsey	d									23 07				
Virginia Water	a					23 01				23 12			23 31	
	d					23 01				23 12			23 31	
Egham	d					23 05				23 16			23 35	
Windsor & Eton Riverside	d							23 01						
Datchet	d							23 04						
Sunnymeads	d							23 07						
Wraysbury	d							23 10						
Staines	d					23 11		23 16		23 21			23 41	
Ashford (Surrey)	d							23 19		23 24				
Feltham	d					23 17		23 24		23 29			23 47	
Whitton	d				23 01			23 28						
Kingston	d		22 49									23 35		23 47
Hampton Wick	d		22 51									23 37		23 49
Teddington	d		22 56									23 40		23 51
Fulwell	d													
Strawberry Hill	d	←	22 59									23 43		23a54
Twickenham	a	22 46	23 02		23 04	23 22		23 31				23 46	23 52	
	d	22 56	23 03			23 23		23 32					23 54	
St Margarets	d		23 05					23 34						
Richmond ⊖	d		23 09			23 27		23 37					23 58	
North Sheen	d		23 11					23 39						
Mortlake	d		23 13					23 42						
Hounslow	d	23 05								23 35				
Isleworth	d	23 08								23 38				
Syon Lane	d	23 10								23 40				
Brentford	d	23 12								23 42				
Kew Bridge	d	23 15								23 45				
Chiswick	d	23 17								23 47				
Barnes Bridge	d	23 20		←						23 50				
Barnes	d	23 23	23 16	23 23				23 45		23 53				
Putney	d	→	23 19	23 26		23 34		23 48		23 56			00 05	
Wandsworth Town	d		23 22	23 29				23 51		23 59				
Clapham Junction 10	d		23 25	23 32		23 38		23 54		00 02			00 09	
Queenstown Rd.(Battersea)	d		23 28	23 35				23 57		00 05				
Vauxhall ⊖	d		23 32	23 38		23 44		23 59		00 08			00 15	
London Waterloo 15 ⊖	a		23 36	23 43		23 48		00 05		00 14			00 19	

Table T152-F

Mondays to Fridays
16 December to 15 May

London - Chessington South, Dorking, Guildford, Shepperton and Hampton Court

Miles	Miles	Miles	Miles	Miles	Station		SW MO A	SN MO B	SW MO A	SW MX A	SW MX A	SW MX A	SW MX A	SW MO	SW MX		SW MX	SW MX C	SW MO	SW MX	SW ◇1 D	SW	SW ◇1 E	SW	SW
0	—	—	—	0	**London Waterloo** 15 ⊖	d								00 01	00 09		00 15	00 27	00 42	00 42	05 00	05 12	05 20		05 39
1¼	—	—	—	1¼	Vauxhall ⊖	d							00 01	00 04	00 13		00 19	00 31	00 46	00 46	05 04	05 16	05 24		05 43
4	—	—	—	4	**Clapham Junction** 10	d							00 06	00 09	00 20		00 26	00 37	00 51	00 51	05 11	05 21	05 29		05 48
5½	—	—	—	5½	Earlsfield	d					00 02		00 09	00 12	00 24		00 29	00s41			05 14	05 24	05 32		05 51
7¼	—	—	—	7¼	**Wimbledon** 6 ⊖ 🚋	d					00 06		00 13	00 16	00 28		00 33	00 45	01 05	01 05	05 18	05 28	05 36	05 49	05 55
8¾	—	0	0	8¾	Raynes Park 6	d						00 01	00 16	00 19			00 36	00 48	01 08	01 08		05 31			05 58
—	—	1	1	—	Motspur Park	d						00 04					00 39								06 01
—	—	—	2½	—	Malden Manor	d																			
—	—	—	3½	—	Tolworth	d																			
—	—	—	4½	—	Chessington North	d																			
—	—	—	5¼	—	**Chessington South**	a																			
—	—	2	—	—	Worcester Park	d						00 07					00 42								06 04
—	—	3¼	—	—	Stoneleigh	d	00 01					00 10					00 45								06 07
—	—	4¼	—	—	Ewell West	d	00 03					00 12					00 47								06 09
—	—	5½	—	—	**Epsom** 3 182	a	00 07					00 16					00 51								06 13
—	—	—	—	—		d						00 19													06 13
—	—	7½	—	—	Ashtead 182	d						00 23													06 17
—	0	9¼	—	—	Leatherhead 182	d		00 02				00 26													06 21
—	—	12½	—	—	Box Hill & Westhumble 182	d		00 07																	
—	—	13¼	—	—	**Dorking** 4 182	a		00 09																	
9¾	—	—	—	9¾	New Malden 6	d							00 19	00 22				00 50	01 11	01 11		05 34			
—	—	—	—	11¼	Norbiton	d							00 22						01 14	01 14		05 37			
—	—	—	—	12	Kingston	a							00 25						01 17	01 17		05 40			
—	—	—	—	—		d							00 25						01 17	01 17		05 40			
—	—	—	—	12½	Hampton Wick	d							00 27						01s22	01s22		05 42			
—	—	—	—	13¾	Teddington	d							00 30						01s25	01s25		05 45			
—	—	—	—	—	Strawberry Hill	a													01 28	01 31					
—	—	—	—	14¾	Fulwell	d							00 34									05 49			
—	—	—	—	16½	Hampton	d							00 38									05 53			
—	—	—	—	18¼	Kempton Park	d							00 41												
—	—	—	—	18¾	Sunbury	d							00 43									05 57			
—	—	—	—	19¼	Upper Halliford	d							00 45									05 59			
—	—	—	—	20¾	**Shepperton**	a							00 50									06 04			
11	—	—	—	—	Berrylands	d								00 25				00s53							
12	—	—	0	—	**Surbiton** 6	d				00 05	00 14			00 31	00 35			00s56			05 26		05 44	05 57	
—	—	—	2	—	Thames Ditton	d				00 09															
—	—	—	3	—	**Hampton Court**	a				00 12															
14	—	—	—	—	Hinchley Wood	d					00 18			00 35										06 01	
15¼	—	—	—	—	Claygate	d					00 20			00 38										06 04	
17	—	—	—	—	Oxshott	d					00 24			00 41										06 07	
19	—	—	—	—	Cobham & Stoke D'abernon	d					00 27			00 45										06 11	
—	2½	—	—	—	Bookham	d						00 32													06 26
21¼	4¼	—	—	—	Effingham Junction 6	d					00 32	00 36		00 49										06 15	06 30
22¼	—	—	—	—	Horsley	d					00 34	00 39		00 52										06 18	
25½	—	—	—	—	Clandon	d					00 39	00 44		00 57										06 23	
28¾	—	—	—	—	London Road (Guildford)	d			00 03		00 44	00 49		01 02										06 28	06 39
30	—	—	—	—	**Guildford**	a			00 07		00 50	00 53		01 06	01 08						06 00		06 18	06 32	06 43

A From London Waterloo
B From London Victoria
C To Woking
D To Portsmouth Harbour
E To Haslemere

The xx27 and xx57 London Waterloo to Strawberry Hill services continue to London Waterloo via Richmond

Table T152-F

Mondays to Fridays
16 December to 15 May

London - Chessington South, Dorking, Guildford, Shepperton and Hampton Court

		SW A	SW	SW B	SW B	SW	SW	SW	SW	SN C	SW	SW	SW B	SW	SW	SW	SW	SW	SW	SW	SW	SW B
London Waterloo 15 ⊖	d	05 50				06 03	06 06	06 12	06 16		06 20	06 24	06 27	06 33	06 36	06 39		06 42	06 47	06 50	06 54	06 57
Vauxhall ⊖	d	05 54				06 07	06 10	06 16	06 20		06 24	06 28	06 31	06 37	06 40	06 43		06 46	06 51	06 54	06 58	07 01
Clapham Junction 10	d	05 59				06 12	06 15	06 21	06 25		06 29	06 33	06 36	06 42	06 45	06 48		06 51	06 56	06 59	07 03	07 06
Earlsfield	d	06 02				06 15	06 18	06 24	06 28		06 32	06 36	06 39	06 45	06 48	06 51		06 54	06 59	07 02	07 06	07 09
Wimbledon 6 ⊖	d	06 06	06 10		06 13	06 19	06 22	06 28	06 33		06 36	06 40	06 43	06 49	06 52	06 55		06 58	07 03	07 06	07 10	07 13
Raynes Park 6	d		06 13		06 16		06 25	06 31	06 36			06 43	06 46		06 55	06 58		07 01	07 06		07 13	07 16
Motspur Park	d		06 16						06 39			06 46				07 01			07 09		07 16	
Malden Manor	d		06 20						06 43										07 13			
Tolworth	d		06 22						06 45										07 15			
Chessington North	d		06 25						06 48										07 18			
Chessington South	a		06 28						06 52										07 23			
Worcester Park	d											06 49				07 04					07 19	
Stoneleigh	d											06 52				07 07					07 22	
Ewell West	d											06 54				07 09					07 24	
Epsom 3 182	a											06 58				07 13					07 28	
	d									06 39		06 58				07 13					07 28	
Ashtead 182	d											07 02				07 17					07 32	
Leatherhead 182	d									06 45		07 06				07 21					07 36	
Box Hill & Westhumble 182	d											07 11									07 41	
Dorking 4 182	a											07 13									07 43	
New Malden 6	d				06 19		06 28	06 34					06 49		06 58			07 04				07 19
Norbiton	d				06 22			06 37					06 52					07 07				07 22
Kingston	a				06 25			06 40					06 55					07 10				07 25
	d			05 59	06 29			06 40					06 59					07 10				07 29
Hampton Wick	d			06 01	06 31			06 42					07 01					07 12				07 31
Teddington	d			06 05	06 35			06 45					07 05					07 15				07 35
Strawberry Hill	a			06 08	06 38								07 08									07 38
Fulwell	d							06 49									07 07	07 19				
Hampton	d							06 53									07 10	07 23				
Kempton Park	d																07 14					
Sunbury	d							06 57									07 15	07 27				
Upper Halliford	d							06 59									07 17	07 29				
Shepperton	a							07 05									07 23	07 35				
Berrylands	d						06 30								07 00							
Surbiton 6	d	06a13				06 27	06 35				06 44			06 57	07 05					07 14		
Thames Ditton	d						06 39								07 09							
Hampton Court	a						06 42								07 12							
Hinchley Wood	d					06 31								07 01								
Claygate	d					06 34								07 04								
Oxshott	d					06 37								07 07								
Cobham & Stoke D'abernon	d					06 41								07 11								
Bookham	d									06 50						07 26						
Effingham Junction 6	d					06 45				06 54				07 15		07a30						
Horsley	d					06 48								07 18								
Clandon	d					06 53								07 23								
London Road (Guildford)	d					06 58								07 28								
Guildford	a					07 04				07 06	07 19			07 34						07 47		

A To Woking B To London Waterloo C From London Bridge

The xx27 and xx57 London Waterloo to Strawberry Hill services continue to London Waterloo via Richmond

Table T152-F

Mondays to Fridays
16 December to 15 May

London - Chessington South, Dorking, Guildford, Shepperton and Hampton Court

		SW	SW	SW	SW A	SW	SW	SW B	SW	SW C	SW	SW	SW	SW	SW C	SW	SW	SW	SW C	SW	SW	SW	SW
London Waterloo 15 ⊖	d	07 03	07 06	07 09		07 12	07 17	07 20	07 24	07 27	07 33	07 36	07 39	07 42		07 47	07 50	07 54	07 57	08 03	08 06	08 09	08 12
Vauxhall ⊖	d	07 07	07 10	07 13		07 16	07 21	07 24	07 28	07 31	07 37	07 40	07 43	07 46		07 51	07 54	07 58	08 01	08 07	08 10	08 13	08 16
Clapham Junction 10	d	07 12	07 15	07 18		07 21	07 26	07 29	07 33	07 36	07 42	07 45	07 48	07 51	07 54	07 56	07 59	08 03	08 06	08 12	08 15	08 18	08 21
Earlsfield	d	07 15	07 18	07 21		07 24	07 29	07 32	07 36	07 39	07 45	07 48	07 51	07 54		07 59	08 02	08 06	08 09	08 15	08 18	08 21	08 24
Wimbledon 6 ⊖	d	07 19	07 22	07 25		07 28	07 33	07 36	07 40	07 43	07 49	07 52	07 55	07 58		08 03	08 06	08 10	08 13	08 19	08 22	08 25	08 28
Raynes Park 6	d		07 25	07 28		07 31	07 36		07 43	07 46		07 55	07 58	08 01		08 06		08 13	08 16		08 25	08 28	08 31
Motspur Park	d			07 31			07 39		07 46				08 01			08 09		08 16				08 31	
Malden Manor	d						07 43									08 13							
Tolworth	d						07 45									08 15							
Chessington North	d						07 48									08 18							
Chessington South	a						07 53									08 24							
Worcester Park	d			07 34					07 49				08 04					08 19				08 34	
Stoneleigh	d			07 37					07 52				08 07					08 22				08 37	
Ewell West	d			07 39					07 54				08 10					08 24				08 39	
Epsom 3 182	a			07 47					07 59				08 14					08 28				08 43	
	d			07 47					07 59				08 17					08 28				08 47	
Ashtead 182	d			07 51					08 02				08 21					08 32				08 51	
Leatherhead 182	d			07 55					08 06				08 25					08 36				08 55	
Box Hill & Westhumble 182	d								08 11									08 41					
Dorking 4 182	a								08 14									08 43					
New Malden 6	d		07 28			07 34				07 49		07 58		08 04					08 19		08 28		08 34
Norbiton	d					07 37				07 52				08 07					08 22				08 37
Kingston	a					07 40				07 55				08 10	08 23				08 25				08 40
	d					07 40				07 59				08 10					08 29				08 40
Hampton Wick	d					07 42				08 01				08 12					08 31				08 42
Teddington	d					07 45				08 05				08 15					08 35				08 45
Strawberry Hill	a									08 08									08 38				
Fulwell	d				07 32	07 49								08 19									08 49
Hampton	d				07 35	07 53								08 23									08 53
Kempton Park	d				07 39	07 56								08 26									08 56
Sunbury	d				07 40	07 58								08 28									08 58
Upper Halliford	d				07 42	08 00								08 30									09 00
Shepperton	a				07 48	08 05								08 35									09 05
Berrylands	d		07 30									08 00									08 30		
Surbiton 6	d	07 27	07 35					07a43			07 57	08 05					08 14			08 27	08 35		
Thames Ditton	d		07 39									08 09									08 39		
Hampton Court	a		07 42									08 12									08 42		
Hinchley Wood	d	07 31									08 01									08 31			
Claygate	d	07 34									08 04									08 34			
Oxshott	d	07 37									08 07									08 37			
Cobham & Stoke D'abernon	d	07 41									08 11									08 41			
Bookham	d			08 00									08 30									09 00	
Effingham Junction 6	d	07 45		08 04							08 15		08 34							08 45		09 04	
Horsley	d	07 48		08 07							08 18		08 37							08 48		09 07	
Clandon	d	07 53		08 12							08 23		08 42							08 53		09 12	
London Road (Guildford)	d	07 58		08 17							08 28		08 47							08 58		09 17	
Guildford	a	08 04		08 21							08 34		08 51				08 50			09 04		09 21	

A From Twickenham B To Woking C To London Waterloo

The xx27 and xx57 London Waterloo to Strawberry Hill services continue to London Waterloo via Richmond

Table T152-F

Mondays to Fridays

16 December to 15 May

London - Chessington South, Dorking, Guildford, Shepperton and Hampton Court

		SW	SW A	SW	SW B	SW	SW	SW	SW	SW	SW A	SW	SW B	SW	SW	SW	SW	SW	SW A	SW	SW B	SW
London Waterloo 15 ⊖	d	08 17	08 20	08 24	08 27	08 33	08 36	08 39	08 42	08 47	08 50	08 54	08 57	09 03	09 06	09 09	09 12	09 17	09 20	09 24	09 27	09 33
Vauxhall ⊖	d	08 21	08 24	08 28	08 31	08 37	08 40	08 43	08 46	08 51	08 54	08 58	09 01	09 07	09 10	09 13	09 16	09 21	09 24	09 28	09 31	09 37
Clapham Junction 10	d	08 26	08 29	08 33	08 36	08 42	08 45	08 48	08 51	08 56	08 59	09 03	09 06	09 12	09 15	09 18	09 21	09 26	09 29	09 33	09 36	09 42
Earlsfield	d	08 29	08 32	08 36	08 39	08 45	08 48	08 51	08 54	08 59	09 02	09 06	09 09	09 15	09 18	09 21	09 24	09 29	09 32	09 36	09 39	09 45
Wimbledon 6 ⊖	d	08 33	08 36	08 40	08 43	08 49	08 52	08 55	08 58	09 03	09 06	09 10	09 13	09 19	09 22	09 25	09 28	09 33	09 36	09 40	09 43	09 49
Raynes Park 6	d	08 36		08 43	08 46		08 55	08 58	09 01	09 06		09 13	09 16		09 25	09 28	09 31	09 36		09 43	09 46	
Motspur Park	d	08 39		08 46				09 01		09 09		09 16				09 31		09 39		09 46		
Malden Manor	d	08 43								09 13								09 43				
Tolworth	d	08 45								09 15								09 45				
Chessington North	d	08 48								09 18								09 48				
Chessington South	a	08 53								09 23								09 53				
Worcester Park	d			08 49				09 04				09 19				09 34				09 49		
Stoneleigh	d			08 52				09 07				09 22				09 37				09 52		
Ewell West	d			08 54				09 09				09 24				09 39				09 54		
Epsom 3 182	a			08 58				09 17				09 28				09 43				09 58		
	d			08 58				09 17				09 28				09 43				09 58		
Ashtead 182	d			09 02				09 21				09 32				09 47				10 02		
Leatherhead 182	d			09 06				09 25				09 36				09 51				10 06		
Box Hill & Westhumble 182	d			09 11								09 41								10 11		
Dorking 4 182	a			09 13								09 43								10 13		
New Malden 6	d				08 49		08 58		09 04				09 19		09 28		09 34				09 49	
Norbiton	d				08 52				09 07				09 22				09 37				09 52	
Kingston	a				08 55				09 10				09 25				09 40				09 55	
	d				08 59				09 10				09 29				09 40				09 59	
Hampton Wick	d				09 01				09 12				09 31				09 42				10 01	
Teddington	d				09 05				09 15				09 35				09 45				10 05	
Strawberry Hill	a				09 08								09 38								10 08	
Fulwell	d								09 19								09 49					
Hampton	d								09 23								09 53					
Kempton Park	d								09 26								09 56					
Sunbury	d								09 28								09 58					
Upper Halliford	d								09 30								10 00					
Shepperton	a								09 35								10 05					
Berrylands	d						09 00								09 30							
Surbiton 6	d		08a43			08 57	09 05				09a13			09 27	09 35				09a43			09 57
Thames Ditton	d						09 09								09 39							
Hampton Court	a						09 12								09 42							
Hinchley Wood	d					09 01								09 31								10 01
Claygate	d					09 04								09 34								10 04
Oxshott	d					09 07								09 37								10 07
Cobham & Stoke D'abernon	d					09 11								09 41								10 11
Bookham	d							09 30								09 56						
Effingham Junction 6	d					09 15		09 34						09 45		10 00						10 15
Horsley	d					09 18		09 37						09 48		10 03						10 18
Clandon	d					09 23		09 42						09 53		10 08						10 23
London Road (Guildford)	d					09 28		09 47						09 58		10 13						10 28
Guildford	a					09 35		09 51						10 04		10 17						10 34

A To Woking

B To London Waterloo

The xx27 and xx57 London Waterloo to Strawberry Hill services continue to London Waterloo via Richmond

Table T152-F

Mondays to Fridays

16 December to 15 May

London - Chessington South, Dorking, Guildford, Shepperton and Hampton Court

		SW	SW	SW	SW	SW A	SW	SW B	SW	SW	SW	SW	SW	SW A	SW	SW B	SW	SW	SW	SW	SW	SW A	SW
London Waterloo 15 ⊖	d	09 36	09 39	09 41	09 47	09 50	09 54	09 58	10 03	10 06	10 09	10 12	10 17	10 20	10 24	10 27	10 33	10 36	10 39	10 42	10 47	10 50	10 54
Vauxhall ⊖	d	09 40	09 43	09 46	09 51	09 54	09 58	10 03	10 07	10 10	10 13	10 16	10 21	10 24	10 28	10 31	10 37	10 40	10 43	10 46	10 51	10 54	10 58
Clapham Junction 10	d	09 45	09 48	09 51	09 56	09 59	10 03	10 08	10 12	10 15	10 18	10 21	10 26	10 29	10 33	10 36	10 42	10 45	10 48	10 51	10 56	10 59	11 03
Earlsfield	d	09 48	09 51	09 54	09 59	10 02	10 06	10 12	10 15	10 18	10 21	10 24	10 29	10 32	10 36	10 39	10 45	10 48	10 51	10 54	10 59	11 02	11 06
Wimbledon 6 ⊖	d	09 52	09 55	09 58	10 03	10 06	10 10	10 17	10 19	10 22	10 25	10 28	10 33	10 36	10 40	10 43	10 49	10 52	10 55	10 58	11 03	11 06	11 10
Raynes Park 6	d	09 55	09 58	10 01	10 06		10 13	10 19		10 25	10 28	10 31	10 36		10 43	10 46		10 55	10 58	11 01	11 06		11 13
Motspur Park	d		10 01		10 09		10 16				10 31		10 39		10 46				11 01		11 09		11 16
Malden Manor	d				10 13								10 43								11 13		
Tolworth	d				10 15								10 45								11 15		
Chessington North	d				10 18								10 48								11 18		
Chessington South	a				10 21								10 53								11 23		
Worcester Park	d		10 04				10 19				10 34				10 49				11 04				11 19
Stoneleigh	d		10 07				10 22				10 37				10 52				11 07				11 22
Ewell West	d		10 09				10 24				10 39				10 54				11 09				11 24
Epsom 3 182	a		10 13				10 28				10 43				10 58				11 13				11 28
	d		10 13				10 28				10 43				10 58				11 13				11 28
Ashtead 182	d		10 17				10 32				10 47				11 02				11 17				11 32
Leatherhead 182	d		10 21				10 36				10 51				11 06				11 21				11 36
Box Hill & Westhumble 182	d						10 41								11 11								11 41
Dorking 4 182	a						10 43								11 13								11 43
New Malden 6	d	09 58		10 04				10 21		10 28		10 34				10 49		10 58		11 04			
Norbiton	d			10 07				10 25				10 37				10 52				11 07			
Kingston	a			10 10				10 27				10 40				10 55				11 10			
	d			10 10				10 30				10 40				10 59				11 10			
Hampton Wick	d			10 12				10 32				10 42				11 01				11 12			
Teddington	d			10 15				10 35				10 45				11 05				11 15			
Strawberry Hill	a							10 38								11 08							
Fulwell	d			10 19								10 49								11 19			
Hampton	d			10 23								10 53								11 23			
Kempton Park	d			10 26								10 56								11 26			
Sunbury	d			10 28								10 58								11 28			
Upper Halliford	d			10 30								11 00								11 30			
Shepperton	a			10 35								11 05								11 35			
Berrylands	d	10 00								10 30								11 00					
Surbiton 6	d	10 05				10a13			10 27	10 35				10a43			10 57	11 05				11a13	
Thames Ditton	d	10 09								10 39								11 09					
Hampton Court	a	10 12								10 42								11 12					
Hinchley Wood	d								10 31								11 01						
Claygate	d								10 34								11 04						
Oxshott	d								10 37								11 07						
Cobham & Stoke D'abernon	d								10 41								11 11						
Bookham	d		10 26								10 56								11 26				
Effingham Junction 6	d		10 30						10 45		11 00						11 15		11 30				
Horsley	d		10 33						10 48		11 03						11 18		11 33				
Clandon	d		10 38						10 53		11 08						11 23		11 38				
London Road (Guildford)	d		10 43						10 58		11 13						11 28		11 43				
Guildford	a		10 47						11 05		11 17						11 34		11 51				

A To Woking

B To London Waterloo

The xx27 and xx57 London Waterloo to Strawberry Hill services continue to London Waterloo via Richmond

Table T152-F

Mondays to Fridays

16 December to 15 May

London - Chessington South, Dorking, Guildford, Shepperton and Hampton Court

		SW A	SW	SW	SW	SW	SW	SW B	SW	SW A	SW	SW	SW	SW	SW	SW B	SW	SW A	SW	SW	SW	SW	SW
London Waterloo [15] ⊖	d	10 57	11 03	11 06	11 09	11 12	11 17	11 20	11 24	11 27	11 33	11 36	11 39	11 42	11 47	11 50	11 54	11 57	12 03	12 06	12 09	12 12	12 17
Vauxhall ⊖	d	11 01	11 07	11 10	11 13	11 16	11 21	11 24	11 28	11 31	11 37	11 40	11 43	11 46	11 51	11 54	11 58	12 01	12 07	12 10	12 13	12 16	12 21
Clapham Junction [10]	d	11 06	11 12	11 15	11 18	11 21	11 26	11 29	11 33	11 36	11 42	11 45	11 48	11 51	11 56	11 59	12 03	12 06	12 12	12 15	12 18	12 21	12 26
Earlsfield	d	11 09	11 15	11 18	11 21	11 24	11 29	11 32	11 36	11 39	11 45	11 48	11 51	11 54	11 59	12 02	12 06	12 09	12 15	12 18	12 21	12 24	12 29
Wimbledon [6] ⊖	d	11 13	11 19	11 22	11 25	11 28	11 33	11 36	11 40	11 43	11 49	11 52	11 55	11 58	12 03	12 06	12 10	12 13	12 19	12 22	12 25	12 28	12 33
Raynes Park [6]	d	11 16		11 25	11 28	11 31	11 36		11 43	11 46		11 55	11 58	12 01	12 06		12 13	12 16		12 25	12 28	12 31	12 36
Motspur Park	d				11 31		11 39		11 46				12 01		12 09		12 16				12 31		12 39
Malden Manor	d						11 43								12 13								12 43
Tolworth	d						11 45								12 15								12 45
Chessington North	d						11 48								12 18								12 48
Chessington South	a						11 53								12 23								12 53
Worcester Park	d				11 34				11 49				12 04				12 19				12 34		
Stoneleigh	d				11 37				11 52				12 07				12 22				12 37		
Ewell West	d				11 39				11 54				12 09				12 24				12 39		
Epsom [3] 182	a				11 43				11 58				12 12				12 28				12 43		
	d				11 43				11 58				12 13				12 28				12 43		
Ashtead 182	d				11 47				12 02				12 17				12 32				12 47		
Leatherhead 182	d				11 51				12 06				12 21				12 36				12 51		
Box Hill & Westhumble 182	d								12 11								12 41						
Dorking [4] 182	a								12 13								12 43						
New Malden [6]	d	11 19		11 28		11 34				11 49		11 58		12 04				12 19		12 28		12 34	
Norbiton	d	11 22				11 37				11 52				12 07				12 22				12 37	
Kingston	a	11 25				11 40				11 55				12 09				12 25				12 40	
	d	11 29				11 40				11 59				12 10				12 29				12 40	
Hampton Wick	d	11 31				11 42				12 01				12 12				12 31				12 42	
Teddington	d	11 35				11 45				12 05				12 15				12 35				12 45	
Strawberry Hill	a	11 38								12 08								12 38					
Fulwell	d					11 49								12 19								12 49	
Hampton	d					11 53								12 23								12 53	
Kempton Park	d					11 56								12 26								12 56	
Sunbury	d					11 58								12 28								12 58	
Upper Halliford	d					12 00								12 30								13 00	
Shepperton	a					12 05								12 36								13 05	
Berrylands	d			11 30								12 00								12 30			
Surbiton [6]	d		11 27	11 35				11a43			11 57	12 05				12a13			12 27	12 35			
Thames Ditton	d			11 39								12 09								12 39			
Hampton Court	a			11 42								12 12								12 42			
Hinchley Wood	d		11 31								12 01								12 31				
Claygate	d		11 34								12 04								12 34				
Oxshott	d		11 37								12 07								12 37				
Cobham & Stoke D'abernon	d		11 41								12 11								12 41				
Bookham	d				11 56								12 26								12 56		
Effingham Junction [6]	d		11 45		12 00						12 15		12 30						12 45		13 00		
Horsley	d		11 48		12 03						12 18		12 33						12 48		13 03		
Clandon	d		11 53		12 08						12 23		12 38						12 53		13 08		
London Road (Guildford)	d		11 58		12 13						12 28		12 43						12 58		13 13		
Guildford	a		12 02		12 17						12 34		12 47						13 04		13 17		

A To London Waterloo

B To Woking

The xx27 and xx57 London Waterloo to Strawberry Hill services continue to London Waterloo via Richmond

Table T152-F

Mondays to Fridays

16 December to 15 May

London - Chessington South, Dorking, Guildford, Shepperton and Hampton Court

		SW A	SW	SW B	SW	SW	SW	SW	SW	SW A	SW	SW B	SW	SW	SW	SW	SW	SW A	SW	SW B	SW	SW
London Waterloo [15] ⊖	d	12 20	12 24	12 27	12 33	12 36	12 39	12 42	12 47	12 50	12 54	12 57	13 03	13 06	13 09	13 12	13 17	13 20	13 24	13 27	13 33	13 36
Vauxhall ⊖	d	12 24	12 28	12 31	12 37	12 40	12 43	12 46	12 51	12 54	12 58	13 01	13 07	13 10	13 13	13 16	13 21	13 24	13 28	13 31	13 37	13 40
Clapham Junction [10]	d	12 29	12 33	12 36	12 42	12 45	12 48	12 51	12 56	12 59	13 03	13 06	13 12	13 15	13 18	13 21	13 26	13 29	13 33	13 36	13 42	13 45
Earlsfield	d	12 32	12 36	12 39	12 45	12 48	12 51	12 54	12 59	13 02	13 06	13 09	13 15	13 18	13 21	13 24	13 29	13 32	13 36	13 39	13 45	13 48
Wimbledon [6] ⊖	d	12 36	12 40	12 43	12 49	12 52	12 55	12 58	13 03	13 06	13 10	13 13	13 19	13 22	13 25	13 28	13 33	13 36	13 40	13 43	13 49	13 52
Raynes Park [6]	d		12 43	12 46		12 55	12 58	13 01	13 06		13 13	13 16		13 25	13 28	13 31	13 36		13 43	13 46		13 55
Motspur Park	d		12 46				13 01		13 09		13 16				13 31		13 39		13 46			
Malden Manor	d								13 13								13 43					
Tolworth	d								13 15								13 45					
Chessington North	d								13 18								13 48					
Chessington South	a								13 23								13 53					
Worcester Park	d		12 49				13 04				13 19				13 34				13 49			
Stoneleigh	d		12 52				13 07				13 22				13 37				13 52			
Ewell West	d		12 54				13 09				13 24				13 39				13 54			
Epsom [3] 182	a		12 58				13 13				13 28				13 43				13 59			
	d		12 58				13 13				13 28				13 43				14 00			
Ashtead 182	d		13 02				13 17				13 32				13 47				14 04			
Leatherhead 182	d		13 06				13 21				13 36				13 51				14 07			
Box Hill & Westhumble 182	d		13 11								13 41								14 12			
Dorking [4] 182	a		13 13								13 43								14 15			
New Malden [6]	d			12 49		12 58		13 04				13 19		13 28		13 34				13 49		13 58
Norbiton	d			12 52				13 07				13 22				13 37				13 52		
Kingston	a			12 55				13 10				13 25				13 40				13 55		
	d			12 59				13 10				13 29				13 40				13 59		
Hampton Wick	d			13 01				13 12				13 31				13 42				14 01		
Teddington	d			13 05				13 15				13 35				13 45				14 05		
Strawberry Hill	a			13 08								13 38								14 08		
Fulwell	d							13 19								13 49						
Hampton	d							13 23								13 53						
Kempton Park	d							13 26								13 56						
Sunbury	d							13 28								13 58						
Upper Halliford	d							13 30								14 00						
Shepperton	a							13 35								14 05						
Berrylands	d					13 00								13 30								14 00
Surbiton [6]	d	12a43			12 57	13 05				13a13			13 27	13 35				13a43			13 57	14 05
Thames Ditton	d					13 09								13 39								14 09
Hampton Court	a					13 12								13 42								14 12
Hinchley Wood	d				13 01								13 31								14 01	
Claygate	d				13 04								13 34								14 04	
Oxshott	d				13 07								13 37								14 07	
Cobham & Stoke D'abernon	d				13 11								13 41								14 11	
Bookham	d						13 26								13 56							
Effingham Junction [6]	d				13 15		13 30						13 45		14 00						14 15	
Horsley	d				13 18		13 33						13 48		14 03						14 18	
Clandon	d				13 23		13 38						13 53		14 08						14 23	
London Road (Guildford)	d				13 28		13 43						13 58		14 13						14 28	
Guildford	a				13 34		13 47						14 04		14 17						14 34	

A To Woking

B To London Waterloo

The xx27 and xx57 London Waterloo to Strawberry Hill services continue to London Waterloo via Richmond

Table T152-F

Mondays to Fridays
16 December to 15 May

London - Chessington South, Dorking, Guildford, Shepperton and Hampton Court

Station		SW	SW	SW	SW A	SW	SW B	SW	SW	SW	SW	SW	SW A	SW	SW B	SW	SW	SW	SW	SW	SW A	SW	SW B
London Waterloo [15] ⊖	d	13 39	13 42	13 47	13 50	13 54	13 57	14 03	14 06	14 09	14 12	14 17	14 20	14 24	14 27	14 33	14 36	14 39	14 42	14 47	14 50	14 54	14 57
Vauxhall ⊖	d	13 43	13 46	13 51	13 54	13 58	14 01	14 07	14 10	14 13	14 16	14 21	14 24	14 28	14 31	14 37	14 40	14 43	14 46	14 51	14 54	14 58	15 01
Clapham Junction [10]	d	13 48	13 51	13 56	13 59	14 03	14 06	14 12	14 15	14 18	14 21	14 26	14 29	14 33	14 36	14 42	14 45	14 48	14 51	14 56	14 59	15 03	15 06
Earlsfield	d	13 51	13 54	13 59	14 02	14 06	14 09	14 15	14 18	14 21	14 24	14 29	14 32	14 36	14 39	14 45	14 48	14 51	14 54	14 59	15 02	15 06	15 09
Wimbledon [6] ⊖ 🚋	d	13 55	13 58	14 03	14 06	14 10	14 13	14 19	14 22	14 25	14 28	14 33	14 36	14 40	14 43	14 49	14 52	14 55	14 58	15 03	15 06	15 10	15 13
Raynes Park [6]	d	13 58	14 01	14 06		14 13	14 16		14 25	14 28	14 31	14 36		14 43	14 46		14 55	14 58	15 01	15 06		15 13	15 16
Motspur Park	d	14 01		14 09		14 16				14 31		14 39		14 46				15 01		15 09		15 16	
Malden Manor	d			14 13								14 43								15 13			
Tolworth	d			14 15								14 45								15 15			
Chessington North	d			14 18								14 48								15 18			
Chessington South	a			14 23								14 53								15 23			
Worcester Park	d	14 04				14 19				14 34				14 49				15 04				15 19	
Stoneleigh	d	14 07				14 22				14 37				14 52				15 07				15 22	
Ewell West	d	14 09				14 24				14 39				14 54				15 09				15 24	
Epsom [3] 182	a	14 13				14 28				14 43				14 58				15 13				15 28	
	d	14 13				14 28				14 43				14 58				15 13				15 28	
Ashtead 182	d	14 17				14 32				14 47				15 02				15 17				15 32	
Leatherhead 182	d	14 21				14 36				14 51				15 06				15 21				15 36	
Box Hill & Westhumble 182	d					14 41								15 11								15 41	
Dorking [4] 182	a					14 43								15 13								15 43	
New Malden [6]	d		14 04				14 19		14 28		14 34				14 49		14 58		15 04				15 19
Norbiton	d		14 07				14 22				14 37				14 52				15 07				15 22
Kingston	a		14 10				14 25				14 40				14 55				15 10				15 25
	d		14 10				14 29				14 40				14 59				15 10				15 29
Hampton Wick	d		14 12				14 31				14 42				15 01				15 12				15 31
Teddington	d		14 15				14 35				14 45				15 05				15 15				15 35
Strawberry Hill	a						14 38								15 08								15 38
Fulwell	d		14 19								14 49								15 19				
Hampton	d		14 23								14 53								15 23				
Kempton Park	d		14 26								14 56								15 26				
Sunbury	d		14 28								14 58								15 28				
Upper Halliford	d		14 30								15 00								15 30				
Shepperton	a		14 35								15 05								15 35				
Berrylands	d								14 30								15 00						
Surbiton [6]	d				14a13			14 27	14 35				14a43			14 57	15 05				15a13		
Thames Ditton	d								14 39								15 09						
Hampton Court	a								14 42								15 12						
Hinchley Wood	d							14 31								15 01							
Claygate	d							14 34								15 04							
Oxshott	d							14 37								15 07							
Cobham & Stoke D'abernon	d							14 41								15 11							
Bookham	d	14 26								14 56								15 26					
Effingham Junction [6]	d	14 30						14 45		15 00						15 15		15 30					
Horsley	d	14 33						14 48		15 03						15 18		15 33					
Clandon	d	14 38						14 53		15 08						15 23		15 38					
London Road (Guildford)	d	14 43						14 58		15 13						15 28		15 43					
Guildford	a	14 47						15 04		15 17						15 34		15 47					

A To Woking
B To London Waterloo

The xx27 and xx57 London Waterloo to Strawberry Hill services continue to London Waterloo via Richmond

NRT DECEMBER 19 EDITION

Table T152-F

Mondays to Fridays
16 December to 15 May

London - Chessington South, Dorking, Guildford, Shepperton and Hampton Court

Station		SW	SW	SW	SW	SW	SW A	SW	SW B	SW	SW	SW	SW	SW	SW A	SW	SW B	SW	SW	SW	SW	SW
London Waterloo [15] ⊖	d	15 03	15 06	15 09	15 12	15 17	15 20	15 24	15 27	15 33	15 36	15 39	15 42	15 47	15 50	15 54	15 57	16 03	16 06	16 09	16 12	16 17
Vauxhall ⊖	d	15 07	15 10	15 13	15 16	15 21	15 24	15 28	15 31	15 37	15 40	15 43	15 46	15 51	15 54	15 58	16 01	16 07	16 10	16 13	16 16	16 21
Clapham Junction [10]	d	15 12	15 15	15 18	15 21	15 26	15 29	15 33	15 36	15 42	15 45	15 48	15 51	15 56	15 59	16 03	16 06	16 12	16 15	16 18	16 21	16 26
Earlsfield	d	15 15	15 18	15 21	15 24	15 29	15 32	15 36	15 39	15 45	15 48	15 51	15 54	15 59	16 02	16 06	16 09	16 15	16 18	16 21	16 24	16 29
Wimbledon [6] ⊖ 🚋	d	15 19	15 22	15 25	15 28	15 33	15 36	15 40	15 43	15 49	15 52	15 55	15 58	16 03	16 06	16 10	16 13	16 19	16 22	16 25	16 28	16 33
Raynes Park [6]	d		15 25	15 28	15 31	15 36		15 43	15 46		15 55	15 58	16 01	16 06		16 13	16 16		16 25	16 28	16 31	16 36
Motspur Park	d			15 31		15 39		15 46				16 01		16 09		16 16				16 31		16 39
Malden Manor	d					15 43								16 13								16 43
Tolworth	d					15 45								16 15								16 45
Chessington North	d					15 48								16 18								16 48
Chessington South	a					15 53								16 23								16 53
Worcester Park	d			15 34				15 49				16 04				16 19				16 34		
Stoneleigh	d			15 37				15 52				16 07				16 22				16 37		
Ewell West	d			15 39				15 54				16 09				16 24				16 39		
Epsom [3] 182	a			15 43				15 58				16 13				16 28				16 43		
	d			15 43				15 58				16 13				16 28				16 43		
Ashtead 182	d			15 47				16 02				16 17				16 32				16 47		
Leatherhead 182	d			15 51				16 06				16 21				16 36				16 51		
Box Hill & Westhumble 182	d							16 11								16 41						
Dorking [4] 182	a							16 13								16 43						
New Malden [6]	d		15 28		15 34				15 49		15 58		16 04				16 19		16 28		16 34	
Norbiton	d				15 37				15 52				16 07				16 22				16 37	
Kingston	a				15 40				15 55				16 10				16 25				16 40	
	d				15 40				15 59				16 10				16 29				16 40	
Hampton Wick	d				15 42				16 01				16 12				16 31				16 42	
Teddington	d				15 45				16 05				16 15				16 35				16 45	
Strawberry Hill	a								16 08								16 38					
Fulwell	d				15 49								16 19								16 49	
Hampton	d				15 53								16 23								16 53	
Kempton Park	d				15 56								16 26								16 56	
Sunbury	d				15 58								16 28								16 58	
Upper Halliford	d				16 00								16 30								17 00	
Shepperton	a				16 05								16 35								17 05	
Berrylands	d		15 30								16 00								16 30			
Surbiton [6]	d	15 27	15 35				15a43			15 57	16 05				16a13			16 27	16 35			
Thames Ditton	d		15 39								16 09								16 39			
Hampton Court	a		15 42								16 12								16 44			
Hinchley Wood	d	15 31								16 01								16 31				
Claygate	d	15 34								16 04								16 34				
Oxshott	d	15 37								16 07								16 37				
Cobham & Stoke D'abernon	d	15 41								16 11								16 41				
Bookham	d			15 56								16 26								16 56		
Effingham Junction [6]	d	15 45		16 00						16 15		16 30						16 45		17 00		
Horsley	d	15 48		16 03						16 18		16 33						16 48		17 03		
Clandon	d	15 53		16 08						16 23		16 38						16 53		17 08		
London Road (Guildford)	d	15 58		16 13						16 28		16 43						16 58		17 13		
Guildford	a	16 04		16 17						16 34		16 47						17 04		17 19		

A To Woking
B To London Waterloo

The xx27 and xx57 London Waterloo to Strawberry Hill services continue to London Waterloo via Richmond

Table T152-F

Mondays to Fridays
16 December to 15 May

London - Chessington South, Dorking, Guildford, Shepperton and Hampton Court

		SW	SW	SW	SW	SW	SW	SW	SW	SW	SW	SW	SW	SW	SW	SW	SW	SW	SW	SW	SW	SW	SW
		◇ A		B						◇ A		B	◇1						◇ A		B		◇1
London Waterloo [15] ⊖	d	16 20	16 24	16 27	16 33	16 36	16 39	16 42	16 47	16 50	16 54	16 57	17 02	17 03	17 06	17 09	17 12	17 17	17 20	17 24	17 27	17 31	17 32
Vauxhall ⊖	d	16 24	16 28	16 31	16 37	16 40	16 43	16 46	16 51	16 54	16 58	17 01		17 07	17 10	17 13	17 16	17 21	17 24	17 28	17 31	17 35	
Clapham Junction [10]	d	16 29	16 33	16 36	16 42	16 45	16 48	16 51	16 56	16 59	17 03	17 06		17 12	17 15	17 18	17 21	17 26	17 29	17 33	17 36	17 40	
Earlsfield	d	16 32	16 36	16 39	16 45	16 48	16 51	16 54	16 59	17 02	17 06	17 09		17 15	17 18	17 21	17 24	17 29	17 32	17 36	17 39	17 43	
Wimbledon [6] ⊖	d	16 36	16 40	16 43	16 49	16 52	16 55	16 58	17 03	17 06	17 10	17 13		17 19	17 22	17 25	17 28	17 33	17 36	17 40	17 43	17 47	
Raynes Park [6]	d		16 43	16 46		16 55	16 58	17 01	17 06		17 13	17 16			17 25	17 28	17 31	17 36		17 43	17 46	17 50	
Motspur Park	d		16 46				17 01		17 09		17 16					17 31		17 39				17 54	
Malden Manor	d								17 13									17 43					
Tolworth	d								17 15									17 45					
Chessington North	d								17 18									17 48					
Chessington South	a								17 23									17 53					
Worcester Park	d		16 49				17 04				17 19					17 34				17 47		17 57	
Stoneleigh	d		16 52				17 07				17 22					17 37						18 00	
Ewell West	d		16 54				17 09				17 24					17 39						18 03	
Epsom [3] 182	a		16 58				17 13				17 28					17 43				17 57		18 08	
	d		16 58				17 17				17 28					17 47				17 57			
Ashtead 182	d		17 02				17 21				17 32					17 51				18 01			
Leatherhead 182	d		17 06				17 24				17 36					17 55				18 05			
Box Hill & Westhumble 182	d		17 11								17 41									18 10			
Dorking [4] 182	a		17 13								17 43									18 15			
New Malden [6]	d			16 49		16 58		17 04				17 19			17 28		17 34				17 49		
Norbiton	d			16 52				17 07				17 22					17 37				17 52		
Kingston	a			16 55				17 10				17 25					17 40				17 55		
	d			16 59				17 10				17 29					17 40				17 59		
Hampton Wick	d			17 01				17 12				17 31					17 42				18 01		
Teddington	d			17 05				17 15				17 35					17 45				18 05		
Strawberry Hill	a			17 08								17 38									18 08		
Fulwell	d							17 19									17 49						
Hampton	d							17 23									17 53						
Kempton Park	d							17 26									17 56						
Sunbury	d							17 28									17 58						
Upper Halliford	d							17 30									18 00						
Shepperton	a							17 35									18 06						
Berrylands	d					17 00									17 30								
Surbiton [6]	d	16a43			16 57	17 05				17a13			17 18	17 27	17 35				17a43				17 48
Thames Ditton	d					17 09									17 39								
Hampton Court	a					17 14									17 44								
Hinchley Wood	d				17 01									17 35									
Claygate	d				17 04									17 37									
Oxshott	d				17 07									17 41									
Cobham & Stoke D'abernon	d				17 11									17 45									
Bookham	d						17 30									18 00							
Effingham Junction [6]	d				17 15		17 42							17 49		18 12							
Horsley	d				17 18		17 45							17 52									
Clandon	d				17 23		17 50							17 57									
London Road (Guildford)	d				17 28		17 55							18 02		18 21							
Guildford	a				17 34		18 01						17 57	18 08		18 25							18 29

A To Woking
B To London Waterloo

The xx27 and xx57 London Waterloo to Strawberry Hill services continue to London Waterloo via Richmond

Table T152-F

Mondays to Fridays
16 December to 15 May

London - Chessington South, Dorking, Guildford, Shepperton and Hampton Court

		SW	SW	SN	SW	SW	SW	SW	SW	SW	SW	SW	SW	SW	SW	SW	SW	SW	SW	SW	SW	SW	SW
				A					◇ B		C		◇1 D							◇ B		C	
London Waterloo [15] ⊖	d	17 33	17 36		17 39	17 43	17 42	17 47	17 50	17 54	17 57	18 01	18 02	18 03	18 06	18 09	18 12	18 12	18 16	18 20	18 24	18 27	18 31
Vauxhall ⊖	d	17 38	17 41		17 44	17 47	17 47	17 51	17 54	17 58	18 01	18 05		18 08	18 11	18 14	18 16	18 17	18 21	18 24	18 28	18 31	18 35
Clapham Junction [10]	d	17 43	17 46		17 49	17 53	17 52	17 56	17 59	18 03	18 06	18 10		18 13	18 16	18 19	18 22	18 22	18 26	18 29	18 33	18 36	18 40
Earlsfield	d	17 46	17 49		17 52		17 55	17 59	18 02	18 06	18 09	18 13		18 16	18 19	18 22		18 25	18 29	18 32	18 36	18 39	18 43
Wimbledon [6] ⊖	d	17 50	17 53		17 56		17 59	18 03	18 06	18 10	18 13	18 17		18 20	18 23	18 26		18 29	18 33	18 36	18 40	18 43	18 47
Raynes Park [6]	d		17 56		17 59		18 02	18 06		18 13	18 16	18 20			18 26	18 29		18 32	18 36		18 43	18 46	18 50
Motspur Park	d				18 02			18 09				18 23				18 32			18 39				18 53
Malden Manor	d							18 13											18 43				
Tolworth	d							18 15											18 45				
Chessington North	d							18 18											18 48				
Chessington South	a							18 23											18 53				
Worcester Park	d				18 05					18 17		18 26				18 35					18 47		18 56
Stoneleigh	d				18 08							18 29				18 38							18 59
Ewell West	d				18 11							18 32				18 40							19 02
Epsom [3] 182	a				18 19					18 27		18 38				18 50					18 57		19 08
	d			18 10	18 19					18 27						18 53					18 57		
Ashtead 182	d			18 15	18 23					18 31						18 57					19 01		
Leatherhead 182	d			18 19	18 27					18 35						19 00					19 05		
Box Hill & Westhumble 182	d									18 40											19 10		
Dorking [4] 182	a									18 45											19 13		
New Malden [6]	d		17 59				18 05				18 19				18 29			18 35				18 49	
Norbiton	d						18 08				18 22							18 38				18 52	
Kingston	a						18 11				18 25							18 41				18 55	
	d						18 11				18 29							18 41				18 59	
Hampton Wick	d						18 13				18 31							18 43				19 01	
Teddington	d						18 16				18 35							18 46				19 05	
Strawberry Hill	a					18 11					18 38						18 41					19 08	
Fulwell	d					18 13	18 20										18 43	18 50					
Hampton	d					18 17	18 24										18 47	18 54					
Kempton Park	d						18 27											18 57					
Sunbury	d					18 21	18 29										18 51	18 59					
Upper Halliford	d					18 23	18 31										18 53	19 01					
Shepperton	a					18 28	18 40										18 58	19 10					
Berrylands	d		18 01												18 31								
Surbiton [6]	d	17 58	18 06						18a13				18a17	18 28	18 36					18a43			
Thames Ditton	d		18 10												18 40								
Hampton Court	a		18 15												18 45								
Hinchley Wood	d	18 05												18 35									
Claygate	d	18 08												18 38									
Oxshott	d	18 11												18 41									
Cobham & Stoke D'abernon	d	18 15												18 45									
Bookham	d			18 24	18 32											19 06							
Effingham Junction [6]	d	18 20		18 28	18a43									18 50		19 10							
Horsley	d	18 22		18 30										18 52		19 12							
Clandon	d	18 27		18 35										18 57		19 17							
London Road (Guildford)	d	18 32		18 40										19 02		19 22							
Guildford	a	18 40		18 44										19 08		19 28							

A From London Bridge
B To Woking
C To London Waterloo
D To Farnham

The xx27 and xx57 London Waterloo to Strawberry Hill services continue to London Waterloo via Richmond

Table T152-F

Mondays to Fridays

16 December to 15 May

London - Chessington South, Dorking, Guildford, Shepperton and Hampton Court

		SW	SW	SW	SW	SW	SW	SW ◇ A	SW	SW	SW B	SW 1 C	SW	SW	SW	SN D	SW	SW	SW	SW A	SW	SW
London Waterloo 15 ⊖	d	18 33	18 36	18 40	18 43	18 42	18 47	18 50	18 53	18 54	18 57	19 01	19 02	19 03	19 06		19 09	19 12	19 17	19 20	19 23	19 24
Vauxhall ⊖	d	18 38	18 41	18 44	18 47	18 47	18 51	18 54		18 58	19 01	19 05		19 08	19 11		19 14	19 17	19 21	19 24		19 28
Clapham Junction 10	d	18 43	18 46	18 49	18 53	18 52	18 56	18 59		19 03	19 06	19 10		19 13	19 16		19 19	19 22	19 26	19 29		19 33
Earlsfield	d	18 46	18 49	18 52		18 55	18 59	19 02		19 06	19 09	19 13		19 16	19 19		19 22	19 25	19 29	19 32		19 36
Wimbledon 6 ⊖	d	18 50	18 53	18 56		18 59	19 03	19 06		19 10	19 13	19 17		19 20	19 23		19 26	19 29	19 33	19 36		19 40
Raynes Park 6	d		18 56	18 59		19 02	19 06			19 13	19 16	19 20			19 26		19 29	19 32	19 36			19 43
Motspur Park	d			19 02			19 09					19 23					19 32		19 39			19 46
Malden Manor	d						19 13												19 43			
Tolworth	d						19 15												19 45			
Chessington North	d						19 18												19 48			
Chessington South	a						19 23												19 53			
Worcester Park	d			19 05						19 17		19 26					19 35					19 49
Stoneleigh	d			19 08								19 29					19 38					19 52
Ewell West	d			19 10								19 32					19 40					19 54
Epsom 3 182	a			19 19						19 30		19 38					19 48					19 58
	d			19 20						19 31						19 40	19 50					19 58
Ashtead 182	d			19 24						19 35						19 45	19 54					20 02
Leatherhead 182	d			19 28						19 38						19 49	19 57					20 06
Box Hill & Westhumble 182	d									19 43												20 11
Dorking 4 182	a									19 46												20 13
New Malden 6	d		18 59			19 05					19 19				19 29			19 35				
Norbiton	d					19 08					19 22							19 38				
Kingston	a					19 11					19 25							19 41				
	d					19 11					19 29							19 41				
Hampton Wick	d					19 13					19 31							19 43				
Teddington	d					19 16					19 35							19 46				
Strawberry Hill	a				19 11						19 38											
Fulwell	d				19 13	19 20												19 50				
Hampton	d				19 17	19 24												19 54				
Kempton Park	d					19 27												19 57				
Sunbury	d				19 21	19 29												19 59				
Upper Halliford	d				19 23	19 31												20 01				
Shepperton	a				19 28	19 39												20 05				
Berrylands	d		19 01												19 31							
Surbiton 6	d	18 58	19 06					19a13	19 09				19a17	19 28	19 36					19a43	19 40	
Thames Ditton	d		19 10												19 40						19 45	
Hampton Court	a		19 15												19 43						19 47	
Hinchley Wood	d	19 02							19 13					19 32								
Claygate	d	19 05							19 16					19 35								
Oxshott	d	19 08							19 19					19 38								
Cobham & Stoke D'abernon	d	19 12							19 23					19 42								
Bookham	d			19 34												19 54	20 03					
Effingham Junction 6	d	19 16		19 39					19 27					19 46		19 58	20 07					
Horsley	d	19 19		19 41					19 30					19 48		20 00	20 09					
Clandon	d	19 24		19 46					19 35					19 53		20 05	20 14					
London Road (Guildford)	d	19 29		19 51					19 40					19 58		20 10	20 19					
Guildford	a	19 35		19 57					19 46					20 03		20 15	20 24					

A To Woking
B To London Waterloo
C To Farnham
D From London Bridge

The xx27 and xx57 London Waterloo to Strawberry Hill services continue to London Waterloo via Richmond

Table T152-F

Mondays to Fridays

16 December to 15 May

London - Chessington South, Dorking, Guildford, Shepperton and Hampton Court

		SW A	SW	SW	SW	SW	SW	SW B	SW	SW A	SW	SW	SW	SW	SW	SW B	SW	SW A	SW	SW	SW	SW	SW
London Waterloo 15 ⊖	d	19 27	19 33	19 36	19 38	19 42	19 47	19 50	19 54	19 57	20 03	20 06	20 09	20 12	20 17	20 20	20 24	20 27	20 33	20 36	20 39	20 42	20 47
Vauxhall ⊖	d	19 31	19 37	19 40	19 43	19 46	19 51	19 54	19 58	20 01	20 07	20 10	20 13	20 16	20 21	20 24	20 28	20 31	20 37	20 40	20 43	20 46	20 51
Clapham Junction 10	d	19 36	19 42	19 45	19 48	19 51	19 56	19 59	20 03	20 06	20 12	20 15	20 18	20 21	20 26	20 29	20 33	20 36	20 42	20 45	20 48	20 51	20 56
Earlsfield	d	19 39	19 45	19 48	19 51	19 54	19 59	20 02	20 06	20 09	20 15	20 18	20 21	20 24	20 29	20 32	20 36	20 39	20 45	20 48	20 51	20 54	20 59
Wimbledon 6 ⊖	d	19 43	19 49	19 52	19 55	19 58	20 03	20 06	20 10	20 13	20 19	20 22	20 25	20 28	20 33	20 36	20 40	20 43	20 49	20 52	20 55	20 58	21 03
Raynes Park 6	d	19 46		19 55	19 58	20 01	20 06		20 13	20 16		20 25	20 28	20 31	20 36		20 43	20 46		20 55	20 58	21 01	21 06
Motspur Park	d				20 01		20 09		20 16				20 31		20 39		20 46				21 01		21 09
Malden Manor	d						20 13								20 43								21 13
Tolworth	d						20 15								20 45								21 15
Chessington North	d						20 18								20 48								21 18
Chessington South	a						20 23								20 53								21 23
Worcester Park	d				20 04				20 19				20 34				20 49				21 04		
Stoneleigh	d				20 07				20 22				20 37				20 52				21 07		
Ewell West	d				20 09				20 24				20 39				20 54				21 09		
Epsom 3 182	a				20 13				20 28				20 43				20 58				21 13		
	d				20 13				20 28				20 43				20 58				21 13		
Ashtead 182	d				20 17				20 32				20 47				21 02				21 17		
Leatherhead 182	d				20 21				20 36				20 51				21 06				21 21		
Box Hill & Westhumble 182	d								20 41								21 11						
Dorking 4 182	a								20 43								21 13						
New Malden 6	d	19 49		19 58		20 04				20 19		20 28		20 34				20 49		20 58		21 04	
Norbiton	d	19 52				20 07				20 22				20 37				20 52				21 07	
Kingston	a	19 55				20 10				20 25				20 40				20 55				21 10	
	d	19 59				20 10				20 29				20 40				20 59				21 10	
Hampton Wick	d	20 01				20 12				20 31				20 42				21 01				21 12	
Teddington	d	20 05				20 15				20 35				20 45				21 05				21 15	
Strawberry Hill	a	20 08								20 38								21 08					
Fulwell	d					20 19								20 49								21 19	
Hampton	d					20 23								20 53								21 23	
Kempton Park	d					20 26								20 56								21 26	
Sunbury	d					20 28								20 58								21 28	
Upper Halliford	d					20 30								21 00								21 30	
Shepperton	a					20 35								21 05								21 35	
Berrylands	d			20 00								20 30								21 00			
Surbiton 6	d		19 57	20 05				20a13			20 27	20 35				20a43			20 57	21 05			
Thames Ditton	d			20 09								20 39								21 09			
Hampton Court	a			20 12								20 42								21 12			
Hinchley Wood	d		20 01								20 31								21 01				
Claygate	d		20 04								20 34								21 04				
Oxshott	d		20 07								20 37								21 07				
Cobham & Stoke D'abernon	d		20 11								20 41								21 11				
Bookham	d				20 26								20 56								21 26		
Effingham Junction 6	d		20 15		20 30						20 45		21 00						21 15		21 30		
Horsley	d		20 18		20 33						20 48		21 03						21 18		21 33		
Clandon	d		20 23		20 38						20 53		21 08						21 23		21 38		
London Road (Guildford)	d		20 28		20 43						20 58		21 13						21 28		21 43		
Guildford	a		20 34		20 47						21 04		21 17						21 34		21 47		

A To London Waterloo
B To Woking

The xx27 and xx57 London Waterloo to Strawberry Hill services continue to London Waterloo via Richmond

Table T152-F

Mondays to Fridays
16 December to 15 May

London - Chessington South, Dorking, Guildford, Shepperton and Hampton Court

		SW A	SW	SW B	SW	SW	SW	SW	SW	SW A	SW	SW B	SW	SW	SW	SW	SW	SW A	SW	SW B	SW	SW
London Waterloo 15 ⊖	d	20 50	20 54	20 57	21 03	21 06	21 09	21 12	21 17	21 20	21 24	21 27	21 33	21 36	21 39	21 42	21 47	21 50	21 54	21 57	22 03	22 06
Vauxhall ⊖	d	20 54	20 58	21 01	21 07	21 10	21 13	21 16	21 21	21 24	21 28	21 31	21 37	21 40	21 43	21 46	21 51	21 54	21 58	22 01	22 07	22 10
Clapham Junction 10	d	20 59	21 03	21 06	21 12	21 15	21 18	21 21	21 26	21 29	21 33	21 36	21 42	21 45	21 48	21 51	21 56	21 59	22 03	22 06	22 12	22 15
Earlsfield	d	21 02	21 06	21 09	21 15	21 18	21 21	21 24	21 29	21 32	21 36	21 39	21 45	21 48	21 51	21 54	21 59	22 02	22 06	22 09	22 15	22 18
Wimbledon 6 ⊖	d	21 06	21 10	21 13	21 19	21 22	21 25	21 28	21 33	21 36	21 40	21 43	21 49	21 52	21 55	21 58	22 03	22 06	22 10	22 13	22 19	22 22
Raynes Park 6	d		21 13	21 16		21 25	21 28	21 31	21 36		21 43	21 46		21 55	21 58	22 01	22 06		22 13	22 16		22 25
Motspur Park	d		21 16				21 31		21 39		21 46				22 01		22 09		22 16			
Malden Manor	d								21 43								22 13					
Tolworth	d								21 45								22 15					
Chessington North	d								21 48								22 18					
Chessington South	a								21 53								22 23					
Worcester Park	d		21 19				21 34				21 49				22 04				22 19			
Stoneleigh	d		21 22				21 37				21 52				22 07				22 22			
Ewell West	d		21 24				21 39				21 54				22 09				22 24			
Epsom 3 182	a		21 28				21 43				21 58				22 13				22 28			
	d		21 28				21 43				21 58				22 13							
Ashtead 182	d		21 32				21 47				22 02				22 17							
Leatherhead 182	d		21 36				21 51				22 06				22 21							
Box Hill & Westhumble 182	d		21 41								22 11											
Dorking 4 182	a		21 43								22 13											
New Malden 6	d			21 19		21 28		21 34				21 49		21 58		22 04				22 19		22 28
Norbiton	d			21 22				21 37				21 52				22 07				22 22		
Kingston	a			21 25				21 40				21 55				22 10				22 25		
	d			21 29				21 40				21 59				22 10				22 29		
Hampton Wick	d			21 31				21 42				22 01				22 12				22 31		
Teddington	d			21 35				21 45				22 05				22 15				22 35		
Strawberry Hill	a			21 38								22 08								22 38		
Fulwell	d							21 49								22 19						
Hampton	d							21 53								22 23						
Kempton Park	d							21 56								22 26						
Sunbury	d							21 58								22 28						
Upper Halliford	d							22 00								22 30						
Shepperton	a							22 05								22 35						
Berrylands	d					21 30								22 00								22 30
Surbiton 6	d	21a13			21 27	21 35				21a43			21 57	22 05				22a13			22 27	22 35
Thames Ditton	d					21 39								22 09								22 39
Hampton Court	a					21 42								22 12								22 42
Hinchley Wood	d				21 31								22 01								22 31	
Claygate	d				21 34								22 04								22 34	
Oxshott	d				21 37								22 07								22 37	
Cobham & Stoke D'abernon	d				21 41								22 11								22 41	
Bookham	d						21 56								22 26							
Effingham Junction 6	d				21 45		22 00						22 15		22 30						22 45	
Horsley	d				21 48		22 03						22 18		22 33						22 48	
Clandon	d				21 53		22 08						22 23		22 38						22 53	
London Road (Guildford)	d				21 58		22 13						22 28		22 43						22 58	
Guildford	a				22 04		22 17						22 34		22 47						23 04	

A To Woking
B To London Waterloo

The xx27 and xx57 London Waterloo to Strawberry Hill services continue to London Waterloo via Richmond

Table T152-F

Mondays to Fridays
16 December to 15 May

London - Chessington South, Dorking, Guildford, Shepperton and Hampton Court

		SW	SW	SW	SW A	SW B	SW	SW	SW	SW	SW A	SW B	SW	SW	SW	SW	SW	SW A	SW C	SW	SW	SW	SW
London Waterloo 15 ⊖	d	22 09	22 12	22 17	22 20	22 27	22 33	22 36	22 39	22 42	22 50	22 57	23 00	23 03	23 06	23 09	23 12	23 20	23 27	23 36	23 42	23 50	23 57
Vauxhall ⊖	d	22 13	22 16	22 21	22 24	22 31	22 37	22 40	22 43	22 46	22 54	23 01	23 04	23 07	23 10	23 13	23 16	23 24	23 31	23 40	23 46	23 54	00 01
Clapham Junction 10	d	22 18	22 21	22 26	22 29	22 36	22 42	22 45	22 48	22 51	22 59	23 06	23 09	23 12	23 15	23 18	23 21	23 29	23 36	23 45	23 51	23 59	00 06
Earlsfield	d	22 21	22 24	22 29	22 32	22 39	22 45	22 48	22 51	22 54	23 02	23 09	23 12	23 15	23 18	23 21	23 24	23 32	23 39	23 48	23 54	00 02	00 09
Wimbledon 6 ⊖	d	22 25	22 28	22 33	22 36	22 43	22 49	22 52	22 55	22 58	23 06	23 13	23 16	23 19	23 22	23 25	23 28	23 36	23 43	23 52	23 58	00 06	00 13
Raynes Park 6	d	22 28	22 31	22 36		22 46		22 55	22 58	23 01		23 16	23 19		23 25	23 28	23 31		23 46	23 55	00 01		00 16
Motspur Park	d	22 31		22 39					23 01				23 22			23 31					00 04		
Malden Manor	d			22 43									23 26										
Tolworth	d			22 45									23 28										
Chessington North	d			22 48									23 31										
Chessington South	a			22 53									23 36										
Worcester Park	d	22 34							23 04							23 34					00 07		
Stoneleigh	d	22 37							23 07							23 37					00 10		
Ewell West	d	22 39							23 09							23 39					00 12		
Epsom 3 182	a	22 43							23 13							23 43					00 16		
	d	22 43							23 13							23 43					00 19		
Ashtead 182	d	22 47							23 17							23 47					00 23		
Leatherhead 182	d	22 51							23 21							23 51					00 26		
Box Hill & Westhumble 182	d	22 56														23 56							
Dorking 4 182	a	22 58														23 58							
New Malden 6	d		22 34			22 49		22 58		23 04		23 19			23 28		23 34		23 49	23 58			00 19
Norbiton	d		22 37			22 52				23 07		23 22					23 37		23 52				00 22
Kingston	a		22 40			22 55				23 10		23 25					23 40		23 55				00 25
	d		22 40			22 59				23 10		23 29					23 40		23 55				00 25
Hampton Wick	d		22 42			23 01				23 12		23 31					23 42		23 57				00 27
Teddington	d		22 45			23 05				23 15		23 35					23 45		23 59				00 30
Strawberry Hill	a					23 08						23 38							00 03				
Fulwell	d		22 49							23 19							23 49						00 34
Hampton	d		22 53							23 23							23 53						00 38
Kempton Park	d		22 56							23 26							23 56						00 41
Sunbury	d		22 58							23 28							23 58						00 43
Upper Halliford	d		23 00							23 30							23 59						00 45
Shepperton	a		23 05							23 35							00 05						00 50
Berrylands	d							23 00							23 30					23 59			
Surbiton 6	d				22a43		22 57	23 05			23a13			23 27	23 35			23a44		00 05		00 14	
Thames Ditton	d							23 09							23 39					00 09			
Hampton Court	a							23 12							23 42					00 12			
Hinchley Wood	d						23 01							23 31								00 18	
Claygate	d						23 04							23 34								00 20	
Oxshott	d						23 07							23 37								00 24	
Cobham & Stoke D'abernon	d						23 11							23 41								00 27	
Bookham	d								23 26												00 32		
Effingham Junction 6	d						23 15		23 30					23 45							00 36	00 32	
Horsley	d						23 18		23 33					23 48							00 39	00 34	
Clandon	d						23 23		23 38					23 53							00 44	00 39	
London Road (Guildford)	d						23 28		23 43					23 58							00 49	00 44	
Guildford	a						23 34		23 47					00 04							00 53	00 50	

A To Woking
B To London Waterloo
C To Twickenham

The xx27 and xx57 London Waterloo to Strawberry Hill services continue to London Waterloo via Richmond

Table T152-F

Saturdays

21 December to 16 May

London - Chessington South, Dorking, Guildford, Shepperton and Hampton Court

			SW	SW	SW	SW	SW	SW	SW	SW	SW ■	SW	SW ◇■	SW	SW	SW	SW	SW	SW	SW	SW	SW	SW	SW
			A	A	A	A			B		C		D	B	E	E				B	E			
London Waterloo 15	⊖	d					00 09	00 15	00 27	00 42	05 00	05 12	05 20	05 50			06 06	06 12	06 17	06 20	06 27	06 33	06 36	06 39
Vauxhall	⊖	d				00 01	00 13	00 19	00 31	00 46	05 04	05 16	05 24	05 54			06 10	06 16	06 21	06 24	06 31	06 37	06 40	06 43
Clapham Junction 10		d				00 06	00 20	00 26	00 37	00 51	05 11	05 21	05 29	05 59			06 15	06 21	06 26	06 29	06 36	06 42	06 45	06 48
Earlsfield		d		00 02		00 09	00 23	00 29	00s41		05 14	05 24	05 32	06 02			06 18	06 24	06 29	06 32	06 39	06 45	06 48	06 51
Wimbledon 6	⊖ ⛴	d		00 06		00 13	00 27	00 33	00 45	01 05	05 18	05 28	05 36	06 06		06 13	06 22	06 28	06 33	06 36	06 43	06 49	06 52	06 55
Raynes Park 6		d			00 01	00 16		00 36	00 48	01 08		05 31				06 16	06 25	06 31	06 36		06 46		06 55	06 58
Motspur Park		d			00 04			00 39											06 39					07 01
Malden Manor		d																	06 43					
Tolworth		d																	06 45					
Chessington North		d																	06 48					
Chessington South		a																	06 51					
Worcester Park		d			00 07			00 42																07 04
Stoneleigh		d			00 10			00 45																07 07
Ewell West		d			00 12			00 47																07 09
Epsom 3	182	a			00 16			00 51																07 13
		d			00 19																			07 13
Ashtead	182	d			00 23																			07 17
Leatherhead	182	d			00 26																			07 21
Box Hill & Westhumble	182	d																						
Dorking 4	182	a																						
New Malden 6		d				00 19			00 50	01 11		05 34				06 19	06 28	06 34			06 49		06 58	
Norbiton		d				00 22				01 14		05 37				06 22		06 37			06 52			
Kingston		a				00 25				01 17		05 40				06 25		06 40			06 55			
		d				00 25				01 17		05 40			05 59	06 29		06 40			06 59			
Hampton Wick		d				00 27				01s19		05 42			06 01	06 31		06 42			07 01			
Teddington		d				00 30				01s22		05 45			06 05	06 35		06 45			07 05			
Strawberry Hill		a								01 32					06 08	06 38					07 08			
Fulwell		d				00 34						05 49						06 49						
Hampton		d				00 38						05 53						06 53						
Kempton Park		d				00 41						05 56						06 56						
Sunbury		d				00 43						05 58						06 58						
Upper Halliford		d				00 45						06 00						07 00						
Shepperton		a				00 50						06 03						07 03						
Berrylands		d							00s53								06 30						07 00	
Surbiton 6		d	00 05	00 14			00 35		00s56		05 26		05 44	06a13			06 35			06a43		06 57	07 05	
Thames Ditton		d	00 09														06 39						07 09	
Hampton Court		a	00 12														06 42						07 12	
Hinchley Wood		d		00 18																		07 01		
Claygate		d		00 20																		07 04		
Oxshott		d		00 24																		07 07		
Cobham & Stoke D'abernon		d		00 27																		07 11		
Bookham		d			00 32																			07 26
Effingham Junction 6		d		00 32	00 36																	07 15		07 30
Horsley		d		00 34	00 39																	07 18		07 33
Clandon		d		00 39	00 44																	07 23		07 38
London Road (Guildford)		d		00 44	00 49																	07 28		07 43
Guildford		a		00 50	00 53		01 07				06 00		06 23									07 32		07 47

A From London Waterloo
B To Woking
C To Haslemere
D To Portsmouth Harbour
E To London Waterloo

NRT DECEMBER 19 EDITION

Table T152-F

Saturdays

21 December to 16 May

London - Chessington South, Dorking, Guildford, Shepperton and Hampton Court

			SW	SW	SW	SW	SW	SW	SW	SW	SW	SW	SW	SW	SW	SW	SW	SW	SW	SW	SW	SW	SW	SW
					A	B						A		B						A		B		
London Waterloo 15	⊖	d	06 42	06 47	06 50	06 57	07 03	07 06	07 09	07 12	07 17	07 20	07 24	07 27	07 33	07 36	07 39	07 42	07 47	07 50	07 54	07 57	08 03	08 06
Vauxhall	⊖	d	06 46	06 51	06 54	07 01	07 07	07 10	07 13	07 16	07 21	07 24	07 28	07 31	07 37	07 40	07 43	07 46	07 51	07 54	07 58	08 01	08 07	08 10
Clapham Junction 10		d	06 51	06 56	06 59	07 06	07 12	07 15	07 18	07 21	07 26	07 29	07 33	07 36	07 42	07 45	07 48	07 51	07 56	07 59	08 03	08 06	08 12	08 15
Earlsfield		d	06 54	06 59	07 02	07 09	07 15	07 18	07 21	07 24	07 29	07 32	07 36	07 39	07 45	07 48	07 51	07 54	07 59	08 02	08 06	08 09	08 15	08 18
Wimbledon 6	⊖ ⛴	d	06 58	07 03	07 06	07 13	07 19	07 22	07 25	07 28	07 33	07 36	07 40	07 43	07 49	07 52	07 55	07 58	08 03	08 06	08 10	08 13	08 19	08 22
Raynes Park 6		d	07 01	07 06		07 16		07 25	07 28	07 31	07 36		07 43	07 46		07 55	07 58	08 01	08 06		08 13	08 16		08 25
Motspur Park		d		07 09					07 31		07 39		07 46				08 01		08 09		08 16			
Malden Manor		d		07 13							07 43								08 13					
Tolworth		d		07 15							07 45								08 15					
Chessington North		d		07 18							07 48								08 18					
Chessington South		a		07 21							07 51								08 21					
Worcester Park		d							07 34				07 49				08 04				08 19			
Stoneleigh		d							07 37				07 52				08 07				08 22			
Ewell West		d							07 39				07 54				08 09				08 24			
Epsom 3	182	a							07 43				07 58				08 13				08 28			
		d							07 43				07 58				08 13				08 28			
Ashtead	182	d							07 47				08 02				08 17				08 32			
Leatherhead	182	d							07 51				08 06				08 21				08 36			
Box Hill & Westhumble	182	d											08 11								08 41			
Dorking 4	182	a											08 13								08 43			
New Malden 6		d	07 04			07 19		07 28		07 34				07 49		07 58		08 04				08 19		08 28
Norbiton		d	07 07			07 22				07 37				07 52				08 07				08 22		
Kingston		a	07 10			07 25				07 40				07 55				08 10				08 25		
		d	07 10			07 29				07 40				07 59				08 10				08 29		
Hampton Wick		d	07 12			07 31				07 42				08 01				08 12				08 31		
Teddington		d	07 15			07 35				07 45				08 05				08 15				08 35		
Strawberry Hill		a				07 38								08 08								08 38		
Fulwell		d	07 19							07 49								08 19						
Hampton		d	07 23							07 53								08 23						
Kempton Park		d	07 26							07 56								08 26						
Sunbury		d	07 28							07 58								08 28						
Upper Halliford		d	07 30							08 00								08 30						
Shepperton		a	07 33							08 03								08 33						
Berrylands		d						07 30								08 00								08 30
Surbiton 6		d			07a13		07 27	07 35				07a43			07 57	08 05				08a13			08 27	08 35
Thames Ditton		d						07 39								08 09								08 39
Hampton Court		a						07 42								08 12								08 42
Hinchley Wood		d					07 31								08 01								08 31	
Claygate		d					07 34								08 04								08 34	
Oxshott		d					07 37								08 07								08 37	
Cobham & Stoke D'abernon		d					07 41								08 11								08 41	
Bookham		d							07 56								08 26							
Effingham Junction 6		d					07 45		08 00						08 15		08 30						08 45	
Horsley		d					07 48		08 03						08 18		08 33						08 48	
Clandon		d					07 53		08 08						08 23		08 38						08 53	
London Road (Guildford)		d					07 58		08 13						08 28		08 43						08 58	
Guildford		a					08 02		08 17						08 32		08 47						09 02	

A To Woking
B To London Waterloo

Table T152-F

Saturdays

21 December to 16 May

London - Chessington South, Dorking, Guildford, Shepperton and Hampton Court

Station		SW	SW	SW	SW A	SW	SW B	SW	SW	SW	SW	SW	SW A	SW	SW B	SW	SW	SW	SW	SW	SW A	SW
London Waterloo 15 ⊖	d	08 09	08 12	08 17	08 20	08 24	08 27	08 33	08 36	08 39	08 42	08 47	08 50	08 54	08 57	09 03	09 06	09 09	09 12	09 17	09 20	09 24
Vauxhall ⊖	d	08 13	08 16	08 21	08 24	08 28	08 31	08 37	08 40	08 43	08 46	08 51	08 54	08 58	09 01	09 07	09 10	09 13	09 16	09 21	09 24	09 28
Clapham Junction 10	d	08 18	08 21	08 26	08 29	08 33	08 36	08 42	08 45	08 48	08 51	08 56	08 59	09 03	09 06	09 12	09 15	09 18	09 21	09 26	09 29	09 33
Earlsfield	d	08 21	08 24	08 29	08 32	08 36	08 39	08 45	08 48	08 51	08 54	08 59	09 02	09 06	09 09	09 15	09 18	09 21	09 24	09 29	09 32	09 36
Wimbledon 6 ⊖ ⛴	d	08 25	08 28	08 33	08 36	08 40	08 43	08 49	08 52	08 55	08 58	09 03	09 06	09 10	09 13	09 19	09 22	09 25	09 28	09 33	09 36	09 40
Raynes Park 6	d	08 28	08 31	08 36		08 43	08 46		08 55	08 58	09 01	09 06		09 13	09 16		09 25	09 28	09 31	09 36		09 43
Motspur Park	d	08 31		08 39		08 46				09 01		09 09		09 16				09 31		09 39		09 46
Malden Manor	d			08 43								09 13								09 43		
Tolworth	d			08 45								09 15								09 45		
Chessington North	d			08 48								09 18								09 48		
Chessington South	a			08 51								09 21								09 51		
Worcester Park	d	08 34				08 49				09 04				09 19				09 34				09 49
Stoneleigh	d	08 37				08 52				09 07				09 22				09 37				09 52
Ewell West	d	08 39				08 54				09 09				09 24				09 39				09 54
Epsom 3 182	a	08 43				08 58				09 13				09 28				09 43				09 58
	d	08 43				08 58				09 13				09 28				09 43				09 58
Ashtead 182	d	08 47				09 02				09 17				09 32				09 47				10 02
Leatherhead 182	d	08 51				09 06				09 21				09 36				09 51				10 06
Box Hill & Westhumble 182	d					09 11								09 41								10 11
Dorking 4 182	a					09 13								09 43								10 13
New Malden 6	d		08 34				08 49		08 58		09 04				09 19		09 28		09 34			
Norbiton	d		08 37				08 52				09 07				09 22				09 37			
Kingston	a		08 40				08 55				09 10				09 25				09 40			
	d		08 40				08 59				09 10				09 29				09 40			
Hampton Wick	d		08 42				09 01				09 12				09 31				09 42			
Teddington	d		08 45				09 05				09 15				09 35				09 45			
Strawberry Hill	a						09 08								09 38							
Fulwell	d		08 49								09 19								09 49			
Hampton	d		08 53								09 23								09 53			
Kempton Park	d		08 56								09 26								09 56			
Sunbury	d		08 58								09 28								09 58			
Upper Halliford	d		09 00								09 30								10 00			
Shepperton	a		09 03								09 33								10 03			
Berrylands	d								09 00								09 30					
Surbiton 6	d				08a43			08 57	09 05				09a13			09 27	09 35				09a43	
Thames Ditton	d								09 09								09 39					
Hampton Court	a								09 12								09 42					
Hinchley Wood	d							09 01								09 31						
Claygate	d							09 04								09 34						
Oxshott	d							09 07								09 37						
Cobham & Stoke D'abernon	d							09 11								09 41						
Bookham	d	08 56								09 26								09 56				
Effingham Junction 6	d	09 00						09 15		09 30						09 45		10 00				
Horsley	d	09 03						09 18		09 33						09 48		10 03				
Clandon	d	09 08						09 23		09 38						09 53		10 08				
London Road (Guildford)	d	09 13						09 28		09 43						09 58		10 13				
Guildford	a	09 17						09 32		09 47						10 02		10 17				

A To Woking

B To London Waterloo

Table T152-F

Saturdays

21 December to 16 May

London - Chessington South, Dorking, Guildford, Shepperton and Hampton Court

Station		SW A	SW	SW	SW	SW	SW	SW B	SW	SW A	SW	SW	SW	SW	SW	SW B	SW	SW A	SW	SW	SW	SW	SW
London Waterloo 15 ⊖	d	09 27	09 33	09 36	09 39	09 42	09 47	09 50	09 54	09 57	10 03	10 06	10 09	10 12	10 17	10 20	10 24	10 27	10 33	10 36	10 39	10 42	10 47
Vauxhall ⊖	d	09 31	09 37	09 40	09 43	09 46	09 51	09 54	09 58	10 01	10 07	10 10	10 13	10 16	10 21	10 24	10 28	10 31	10 37	10 40	10 43	10 46	10 51
Clapham Junction 10	d	09 36	09 42	09 45	09 48	09 51	09 56	09 59	10 03	10 06	10 12	10 15	10 18	10 21	10 26	10 29	10 33	10 36	10 42	10 45	10 48	10 51	10 56
Earlsfield	d	09 39	09 45	09 48	09 51	09 54	09 59	10 02	10 06	10 09	10 15	10 18	10 21	10 24	10 29	10 32	10 36	10 39	10 45	10 48	10 51	10 54	10 59
Wimbledon 6 ⊖ ⛴	d	09 43	09 49	09 52	09 55	09 58	10 03	10 06	10 10	10 13	10 19	10 22	10 25	10 28	10 33	10 36	10 40	10 43	10 49	10 52	10 55	10 58	11 03
Raynes Park 6	d	09 46		09 55	09 58	10 01	10 06		10 13	10 16		10 25	10 28	10 31	10 36		10 43	10 46		10 55	10 58	11 01	11 06
Motspur Park	d				10 01		10 09		10 16				10 31		10 39		10 46				11 01		11 09
Malden Manor	d						10 13								10 43								11 13
Tolworth	d						10 15								10 45								11 15
Chessington North	d						10 18								10 48								11 18
Chessington South	a						10 21								10 51								11 21
Worcester Park	d				10 04				10 19				10 34				10 49				11 04		
Stoneleigh	d				10 07				10 22				10 37				10 52				11 07		
Ewell West	d				10 09				10 24				10 39				10 54				11 09		
Epsom 3 182	a				10 13				10 28				10 43				10 58				11 13		
	d				10 13				10 28				10 43				10 58				11 13		
Ashtead 182	d				10 17				10 32				10 47				11 02				11 17		
Leatherhead 182	d				10 21				10 36				10 51				11 06				11 21		
Box Hill & Westhumble 182	d								10 41								11 11						
Dorking 4 182	a								10 43								11 13						
New Malden 6	d	09 49		09 58		10 04				10 19		10 28		10 34				10 49		10 58		11 04	
Norbiton	d	09 52				10 07				10 22				10 37				10 52				11 07	
Kingston	a	09 55				10 10				10 25				10 40				10 55				11 10	
	d	09 59				10 10				10 29				10 40				10 59				11 10	
Hampton Wick	d	10 01				10 12				10 31				10 42				11 01				11 12	
Teddington	d	10 05				10 15				10 35				10 45				11 05				11 15	
Strawberry Hill	a	10 08								10 38								11 08					
Fulwell	d					10 19								10 49								11 19	
Hampton	d					10 23								10 53								11 23	
Kempton Park	d					10 26								10 56								11 26	
Sunbury	d					10 28								10 58								11 28	
Upper Halliford	d					10 30								11 00								11 30	
Shepperton	a					10 33								11 03								11 33	
Berrylands	d			10 00								10 30								11 00			
Surbiton 6	d		09 57	10 05				10a13			10 27	10 35				10a43			10 57	11 05			
Thames Ditton	d			10 09								10 39								11 09			
Hampton Court	a			10 12								10 42								11 12			
Hinchley Wood	d		10 01								10 31								11 01				
Claygate	d		10 04								10 34								11 04				
Oxshott	d		10 07								10 37								11 07				
Cobham & Stoke D'abernon	d		10 11								10 41								11 11				
Bookham	d				10 26								10 56								11 26		
Effingham Junction 6	d		10 15		10 30						10 45		11 00						11 15		11 30		
Horsley	d		10 18		10 33						10 48		11 03						11 18		11 33		
Clandon	d		10 23		10 38						10 53		11 08						11 23		11 38		
London Road (Guildford)	d		10 28		10 43						10 58		11 13						11 28		11 43		
Guildford	a		10 32		10 47						11 02		11 17						11 32		11 47		

A To London Waterloo

B To Woking

Table T152-F

Saturdays

21 December to 16 May

London - Chessington South, Dorking, Guildford, Shepperton and Hampton Court

Station		SW A	SW	SW B	SW	SW	SW	SW	SW	SW A	SW	SW B	SW	SW	SW	SW	SW	SW A	SW	SW B	SW	SW
London Waterloo 15 ⊖	d	10 50	10 54	10 57	11 03	11 06	11 09	11 12	11 17	11 20	11 24	11 27	11 33	11 36	11 39	11 42	11 47	11 50	11 54	11 57	12 03	12 06
Vauxhall ⊖	d	10 54	10 58	11 01	11 07	11 10	11 13	11 16	11 21	11 24	11 28	11 31	11 37	11 40	11 43	11 46	11 51	11 54	11 58	12 01	12 07	12 10
Clapham Junction 10	d	10 59	11 03	11 06	11 12	11 15	11 18	11 21	11 26	11 29	11 33	11 36	11 42	11 45	11 48	11 51	11 56	11 59	12 03	12 06	12 12	12 15
Earlsfield	d	11 02	11 06	11 09	11 15	11 18	11 21	11 24	11 29	11 32	11 36	11 39	11 45	11 48	11 51	11 54	11 59	12 02	12 06	12 09	12 15	12 18
Wimbledon 6 ⊖	d	11 06	11 10	11 13	11 19	11 22	11 25	11 28	11 33	11 36	11 40	11 43	11 49	11 52	11 55	11 58	12 03	12 06	12 10	12 13	12 19	12 22
Raynes Park 6	d		11 13	11 16		11 25	11 28	11 31	11 36		11 43	11 46		11 55	11 58	12 01	12 06		12 13	12 16		12 25
Motspur Park	d		11 16				11 31		11 39		11 46				12 01		12 09		12 16			
Malden Manor	d								11 43								12 13					
Tolworth	d								11 45								12 15					
Chessington North	d								11 48								12 18					
Chessington South	a								11 51								12 21					
Worcester Park	d		11 19				11 34				11 49				12 04				12 19			
Stoneleigh	d		11 22				11 37				11 52				12 07				12 22			
Ewell West	d		11 24				11 39				11 54				12 09				12 24			
Epsom 3 182	a		11 28				11 43				11 58				12 13				12 28			
	d		11 28				11 43				11 58				12 13				12 28			
Ashtead 182	d		11 32				11 47				12 02				12 17				12 32			
Leatherhead 182	d		11 36				11 51				12 06				12 21				12 36			
Box Hill & Westhumble 182	d		11 41								12 11								12 41			
Dorking 4 182	a		11 43								12 13								12 43			
New Malden 6	d			11 19		11 28		11 34				11 49		11 58		12 04				12 19		12 28
Norbiton	d			11 22				11 37				11 52				12 07				12 22		
Kingston	a			11 25				11 40				11 55				12 10				12 25		
	d			11 29				11 40				11 59				12 10				12 29		
Hampton Wick	d			11 31				11 42				12 01				12 12				12 31		
Teddington	d			11 35				11 45				12 05				12 15				12 35		
Strawberry Hill	a			11 38								12 08								12 38		
Fulwell	d							11 49								12 19						
Hampton	d							11 53								12 23						
Kempton Park	d							11 56								12 26						
Sunbury	d							11 58								12 28						
Upper Halliford	d							12 00								12 30						
Shepperton	a							12 03								12 33						
Berrylands	d					11 30								12 00								12 30
Surbiton 6	d	11a13			11 27	11 35				11a43			11 57	12 05				12a13			12 27	12 35
Thames Ditton	d					11 39								12 09								12 39
Hampton Court	a					11 42								12 12								12 42
Hinchley Wood	d				11 31								12 01								12 31	
Claygate	d				11 34								12 04								12 34	
Oxshott	d				11 37								12 07								12 37	
Cobham & Stoke D'abernon	d				11 41								12 11								12 41	
Bookham	d						11 56								12 26							
Effingham Junction 6	d				11 45		12 00						12 15		12 30						12 45	
Horsley	d				11 48		12 03						12 18		12 33						12 48	
Clandon	d				11 53		12 08						12 23		12 38						12 53	
London Road (Guildford)	d				11 58		12 13						12 28		12 43						12 58	
Guildford	a				12 02		12 17						12 32		12 47						13 02	

A To Woking

B To London Waterloo

Table T152-F

Saturdays

21 December to 16 May

London - Chessington South, Dorking, Guildford, Shepperton and Hampton Court

Station		SW	SW	SW	SW A	SW	SW B	SW	SW	SW	SW	SW	SW A	SW	SW B	SW	SW	SW	SW	SW	SW A	SW	SW B
London Waterloo 15 ⊖	d	12 09	12 12	12 17	12 20	12 24	12 27	12 33	12 36	12 39	12 42	12 47	12 50	12 54	12 57	13 03	13 06	13 09	13 12	13 17	13 20	13 24	13 27
Vauxhall ⊖	d	12 13	12 16	12 21	12 24	12 28	12 31	12 37	12 40	12 43	12 46	12 51	12 54	12 58	13 01	13 07	13 10	13 13	13 16	13 21	13 24	13 28	13 31
Clapham Junction 10	d	12 18	12 21	12 26	12 29	12 33	12 36	12 42	12 45	12 48	12 51	12 56	12 59	13 03	13 06	13 12	13 15	13 18	13 21	13 26	13 29	13 33	13 36
Earlsfield	d	12 21	12 24	12 29	12 32	12 36	12 39	12 45	12 48	12 51	12 54	12 59	13 02	13 06	13 09	13 15	13 18	13 21	13 24	13 29	13 32	13 36	13 39
Wimbledon 6 ⊖	d	12 25	12 28	12 33	12 36	12 40	12 43	12 49	12 52	12 55	12 58	13 03	13 06	13 10	13 13	13 19	13 22	13 25	13 28	13 33	13 36	13 40	13 43
Raynes Park 6	d	12 28	12 31	12 36		12 43	12 46		12 55	12 58	13 01	13 06		13 13	13 16		13 25	13 28	13 31	13 36		13 43	13 46
Motspur Park	d	12 31		12 39		12 46				13 01		13 09		13 16				13 31		13 39		13 46	
Malden Manor	d			12 43								13 13								13 43			
Tolworth	d			12 45								13 15								13 45			
Chessington North	d			12 48								13 18								13 48			
Chessington South	a			12 51								13 21								13 51			
Worcester Park	d	12 34				12 49				13 04				13 19				13 34				13 49	
Stoneleigh	d	12 37				12 52				13 07				13 22				13 37				13 52	
Ewell West	d	12 39				12 54				13 09				13 24				13 39				13 54	
Epsom 3 182	a	12 43				12 58				13 13				13 28				13 43				13 58	
	d	12 43				12 58				13 13				13 28				13 43				13 58	
Ashtead 182	d	12 47				13 02				13 17				13 32				13 47				14 02	
Leatherhead 182	d	12 51				13 06				13 21				13 36				13 51				14 06	
Box Hill & Westhumble 182	d					13 11								13 41								14 11	
Dorking 4 182	a					13 13								13 43								14 13	
New Malden 6	d		12 34				12 49		12 58		13 04				13 19		13 28		13 34				13 49
Norbiton	d		12 37				12 52				13 07				13 22				13 37				13 52
Kingston	a		12 40				12 55				13 10				13 25				13 40				13 55
	d		12 40				12 59				13 10				13 29				13 40				13 59
Hampton Wick	d		12 42				13 01				13 12				13 31				13 42				14 01
Teddington	d		12 45				13 05				13 15				13 35				13 45				14 05
Strawberry Hill	a						13 08								13 38								14 08
Fulwell	d		12 49								13 19								13 49				
Hampton	d		12 53								13 23								13 53				
Kempton Park	d		12 56								13 26								13 56				
Sunbury	d		12 58								13 28								13 58				
Upper Halliford	d		13 00								13 30								14 00				
Shepperton	a		13 03								13 33								14 03				
Berrylands	d								13 00								13 30						
Surbiton 6	d				12a43			12 57	13 05				13a13			13 27	13 35				13a43		
Thames Ditton	d								13 09								13 39						
Hampton Court	a								13 12								13 42						
Hinchley Wood	d							13 01								13 31							
Claygate	d							13 04								13 34							
Oxshott	d							13 07								13 37							
Cobham & Stoke D'abernon	d							13 11								13 41							
Bookham	d	12 56								13 26								13 56					
Effingham Junction 6	d	13 00						13 15		13 30						13 45		14 00					
Horsley	d	13 03						13 18		13 33						13 48		14 03					
Clandon	d	13 08						13 23		13 38						13 53		14 08					
London Road (Guildford)	d	13 13						13 28		13 43						13 58		14 13					
Guildford	a	13 17						13 32		13 47						14 02		14 17					

A To Woking

B To London Waterloo

Table T152-F

London - Chessington South, Dorking, Guildford, Shepperton and Hampton Court

		SW	SW	SW	SW	SW	SW A	SW	SW B	SW	SW	SW	SW	SW	SW A	SW	SW B	SW	SW	SW	SW	SW	SW A
London Waterloo 15 ⊖	d	13 33	13 36	13 39	13 42	13 47	13 50	13 54	13 57	14 03	14 06	14 09	14 12	14 17	14 20	14 24	14 27	14 33	14 36	14 39	14 42	14 47	14 50
Vauxhall ⊖	d	13 37	13 40	13 43	13 46	13 51	13 54	13 58	14 01	14 07	14 10	14 13	14 16	14 21	14 24	14 28	14 31	14 37	14 40	14 43	14 46	14 51	14 54
Clapham Junction 10	d	13 42	13 45	13 48	13 51	13 56	13 59	14 03	14 06	14 12	14 15	14 18	14 21	14 26	14 29	14 33	14 36	14 42	14 45	14 48	14 51	14 56	14 59
Earlsfield	d	13 45	13 48	13 51	13 54	13 59	14 02	14 06	14 09	14 15	14 18	14 21	14 24	14 29	14 32	14 36	14 39	14 45	14 48	14 51	14 54	14 59	15 02
Wimbledon 6 ⊖	d	13 49	13 52	13 55	13 58	14 03	14 06	14 10	14 13	14 19	14 22	14 25	14 28	14 33	14 36	14 40	14 43	14 49	14 52	14 55	14 58	15 03	15 06
Raynes Park 6	d		13 55	13 58	14 01	14 06		14 13	14 16		14 25	14 28	14 31	14 36		14 43	14 46		14 55	14 58	15 01	15 06	
Motspur Park	d			14 01		14 09		14 16				14 31		14 39		14 46				15 01		15 09	
Malden Manor	d					14 13								14 43								15 13	
Tolworth	d					14 15								14 45								15 15	
Chessington North	d					14 18								14 48								15 18	
Chessington South	a					14 21								14 51								15 21	
Worcester Park	d			14 04				14 19				14 34				14 49				15 04			
Stoneleigh	d			14 07				14 22				14 37				14 52				15 07			
Ewell West	d			14 09				14 24				14 39				14 54				15 09			
Epsom 3 182	a			14 13				14 27				14 43				14 58				15 13			
	d			14 13				14 28				14 43				14 58				15 13			
Ashtead 182	d			14 17				14 32				14 47				15 02				15 17			
Leatherhead 182	d			14 21				14 36				14 51				15 06				15 21			
Box Hill & Westhumble 182	d							14 41								15 11							
Dorking 4 182	a							14 45								15 13							
New Malden 6	d		13 58		14 04				14 19		14 28		14 34				14 49		14 58		15 04		
Norbiton	d				14 07				14 22				14 37				14 52				15 07		
Kingston	a				14 10				14 25				14 40				14 55				15 10		
	d				14 10				14 29				14 40				14 59				15 10		
Hampton Wick	d				14 12				14 31				14 42				15 01				15 12		
Teddington	d				14 15				14 35				14 45				15 05				15 15		
Strawberry Hill	a								14 38								15 08						
Fulwell	d				14 19								14 49								15 19		
Hampton	d				14 23								14 53								15 23		
Kempton Park	d				14 26								14 56								15 26		
Sunbury	d				14 28								14 58								15 28		
Upper Halliford	d				14 30								15 00								15 30		
Shepperton	a				14 33								15 03								15 33		
Berrylands	d		14 00								14 30								15 00				
Surbiton 6	d	13 57	14 05				14a13			14 27	14 35				14a43			14 57	15 05				15a13
Thames Ditton	d		14 09								14 39								15 09				
Hampton Court	a		14 12								14 42								15 12				
Hinchley Wood	d	14 01								14 31								15 01					
Claygate	d	14 04								14 34								15 04					
Oxshott	d	14 07								14 37								15 07					
Cobham & Stoke D'abernon	d	14 11								14 41								15 11					
Bookham	d			14 26								14 56								15 26			
Effingham Junction 6	d	14 15		14 30						14 45		15 00						15 15		15 30			
Horsley	d	14 18		14 33						14 48		15 03						15 18		15 33			
Clandon	d	14 23		14 38						14 53		15 08						15 23		15 38			
London Road (Guildford)	d	14 28		14 43						14 58		15 13						15 28		15 43			
Guildford	a	14 32		14 47						15 02		15 17						15 32		15 47			

A To Woking
B To London Waterloo

Table T152-F

London - Chessington South, Dorking, Guildford, Shepperton and Hampton Court

		SW	SW A	SW	SW	SW	SW	SW	SW B	SW	SW A	SW	SW	SW	SW	SW	SW B	SW	SW A	SW	SW	SW
London Waterloo 15 ⊖	d	14 54	14 57	15 03	15 06	15 09	15 12	15 17	15 20	15 24	15 27	15 33	15 36	15 39	15 42	15 47	15 50	15 54	15 57	16 03	16 06	16 09
Vauxhall ⊖	d	14 58	15 01	15 07	15 10	15 13	15 16	15 21	15 24	15 28	15 31	15 37	15 40	15 43	15 46	15 51	15 54	15 58	16 01	16 07	16 10	16 13
Clapham Junction 10	d	15 03	15 06	15 12	15 15	15 18	15 21	15 26	15 29	15 33	15 36	15 42	15 45	15 48	15 51	15 56	15 59	16 03	16 06	16 12	16 15	16 18
Earlsfield	d	15 06	15 09	15 15	15 18	15 21	15 24	15 29	15 32	15 36	15 39	15 45	15 48	15 51	15 54	15 59	16 02	16 06	16 09	16 15	16 18	16 21
Wimbledon 6 ⊖	d	15 10	15 13	15 19	15 22	15 25	15 28	15 33	15 36	15 40	15 43	15 49	15 52	15 55	15 58	16 03	16 06	16 10	16 13	16 19	16 22	16 25
Raynes Park 6	d	15 13	15 16		15 25	15 28	15 31	15 36		15 43	15 46		15 55	15 58	16 01	16 06		16 13	16 16		16 25	16 28
Motspur Park	d	15 16				15 31		15 39		15 46				16 01		16 09		16 16				16 31
Malden Manor	d							15 43								16 13						
Tolworth	d							15 45								16 15						
Chessington North	d							15 48								16 18						
Chessington South	a							15 51								16 21						
Worcester Park	d	15 19				15 34				15 49				16 04				16 19				16 34
Stoneleigh	d	15 22				15 37				15 52				16 07				16 22				16 37
Ewell West	d	15 24				15 39				15 54				16 09				16 24				16 39
Epsom 3 182	a	15 28				15 43				15 58				16 13				16 28				16 43
	d	15 28				15 43				15 58				16 13				16 28				16 43
Ashtead 182	d	15 32				15 47				16 02				16 17				16 32				16 47
Leatherhead 182	d	15 36				15 51				16 06				16 21				16 36				16 51
Box Hill & Westhumble 182	d	15 41								16 11								16 41				
Dorking 4 182	a	15 43								16 13								16 43				
New Malden 6	d		15 19		15 28		15 34				15 49		15 58		16 04				16 19		16 28	
Norbiton	d		15 22				15 37				15 52				16 07				16 22			
Kingston	a		15 25				15 40				15 55				16 10				16 25			
	d		15 29				15 40				15 59				16 10				16 29			
Hampton Wick	d		15 31				15 42				16 01				16 12				16 31			
Teddington	d		15 35				15 45				16 05				16 15				16 35			
Strawberry Hill	a		15 38								16 08								16 38			
Fulwell	d						15 49								16 19							
Hampton	d						15 53								16 23							
Kempton Park	d						15 56								16 26							
Sunbury	d						15 58								16 28							
Upper Halliford	d						16 00								16 30							
Shepperton	a						16 03								16 33							
Berrylands	d				15 30								16 00								16 30	
Surbiton 6	d			15 27	15 35				15a43			15 57	16 05				16a13			16 27	16 35	
Thames Ditton	d				15 39								16 09								16 39	
Hampton Court	a				15 42								16 12								16 42	
Hinchley Wood	d			15 31								16 01								16 31		
Claygate	d			15 34								16 04								16 34		
Oxshott	d			15 37								16 07								16 37		
Cobham & Stoke D'abernon	d			15 41								16 11								16 41		
Bookham	d					15 56								16 26								16 56
Effingham Junction 6	d			15 45		16 00						16 15		16 30						16 45		17 00
Horsley	d			15 48		16 03						16 18		16 33						16 48		17 03
Clandon	d			15 53		16 08						16 23		16 38						16 53		17 08
London Road (Guildford)	d			15 58		16 13						16 28		16 43						16 58		17 13
Guildford	a			16 02		16 17						16 32		16 47						17 02		17 17

A To London Waterloo
B To Woking

Table T152-F

Saturdays
21 December to 16 May

London - Chessington South, Dorking, Guildford, Shepperton and Hampton Court

Station		SW	SW	SW A	SW	SW B	SW	SW	SW	SW	SW	SW A	SW	SW B	SW	SW	SW	SW	SW	SW A	SW	SW B	SW
London Waterloo 15 ⊖	d	16 12	16 17	16 20	16 24	16 27	16 33	16 36	16 39	16 42	16 47	16 50	16 54	16 57	17 03	17 06	17 09	17 12	17 17	17 20	17 24	17 27	17 33
Vauxhall ⊖	d	16 16	16 21	16 24	16 28	16 31	16 37	16 40	16 43	16 46	16 51	16 54	16 58	17 01	17 07	17 10	17 13	17 16	17 21	17 24	17 28	17 31	17 37
Clapham Junction 10	d	16 21	16 26	16 29	16 33	16 36	16 42	16 45	16 48	16 51	16 56	16 59	17 03	17 06	17 12	17 15	17 18	17 21	17 26	17 29	17 33	17 36	17 42
Earlsfield	d	16 24	16 29	16 32	16 36	16 39	16 45	16 48	16 51	16 54	16 59	17 02	17 06	17 09	17 15	17 18	17 21	17 24	17 29	17 32	17 36	17 39	17 45
Wimbledon 6 ⊖	d	16 28	16 33	16 36	16 40	16 43	16 49	16 52	16 55	16 58	17 03	17 06	17 10	17 13	17 19	17 22	17 25	17 28	17 33	17 36	17 40	17 43	17 49
Raynes Park 6	d	16 31	16 36		16 43	16 46		16 55	16 58	17 01	17 06		17 13	17 16		17 25	17 28	17 31	17 36		17 43	17 46	
Motspur Park	d		16 39		16 46				17 01		17 09		17 16				17 31		17 39		17 46		
Malden Manor	d		16 43								17 13								17 43				
Tolworth	d		16 45								17 15								17 45				
Chessington North	d		16 48								17 18								17 48				
Chessington South	a		16 51								17 21								17 51				
Worcester Park	d				16 49				17 04				17 19				17 34				17 49		
Stoneleigh	d				16 52				17 07				17 22				17 37				17 52		
Ewell West	d				16 54				17 09				17 24				17 39				17 54		
Epsom 3	182 a				16 58				17 13				17 28				17 43				17 58		
	d				16 58				17 13				17 28				17 43				17 58		
Ashtead	182 d				17 02				17 17				17 32				17 47				18 02		
Leatherhead	182 d				17 06				17 21				17 36				17 51				18 06		
Box Hill & Westhumble	182 d				17 11								17 41								18 11		
Dorking 4	182 a				17 13								17 43								18 13		
New Malden 6	d	16 34				16 49		16 58		17 04				17 19		17 28		17 34				17 49	
Norbiton	d	16 37				16 52				17 07				17 22				17 37				17 52	
Kingston	a	16 40				16 55				17 10				17 25				17 40				17 55	
	d	16 40				16 59				17 10				17 29				17 40				17 59	
Hampton Wick	d	16 42				17 01				17 12				17 31				17 42				18 01	
Teddington	d	16 45				17 05				17 15				17 35				17 45				18 05	
Strawberry Hill	a					17 08								17 38								18 08	
Fulwell	d	16 49								17 19								17 49					
Hampton	d	16 53								17 23								17 53					
Kempton Park	d	16 56								17 26								17 56					
Sunbury	d	16 58								17 28								17 58					
Upper Halliford	d	17 00								17 30								18 00					
Shepperton	a	17 03								17 33								18 03					
Berrylands	d							17 00								17 30							
Surbiton 6	d			16a43			16 57	17 05				17a13			17 27	17 35				17a43			17 57
Thames Ditton	d							17 09								17 39							
Hampton Court	a							17 12								17 42							
Hinchley Wood	d						17 01								17 31								18 01
Claygate	d						17 04								17 34								18 04
Oxshott	d						17 07								17 37								18 07
Cobham & Stoke D'abernon	d						17 11								17 41								18 11
Bookham	d								17 26								17 56						
Effingham Junction 6	d						17 15		17 30						17 45		18 00						18 15
Horsley	d						17 18		17 33						17 48		18 03						18 18
Clandon	d						17 23		17 38						17 53		18 08						18 23
London Road (Guildford)	d						17 28		17 43						17 58		18 13						18 28
Guildford	a						17 32		17 47						18 02		18 17						18 32

A To Woking
B To London Waterloo

Table T152-F

Saturdays
21 December to 16 May

London - Chessington South, Dorking, Guildford, Shepperton and Hampton Court

Station		SW	SW	SW	SW	SW A	SW	SW B	SW	SW	SW	SW	SW	SW A	SW	SW B	SW	SW	SW	SW	SW	SW A
London Waterloo 15 ⊖	d	17 36	17 39	17 42	17 47	17 50	17 54	17 57	18 03	18 06	18 09	18 12	18 17	18 20	18 24	18 27	18 33	18 36	18 39	18 42	18 47	18 50
Vauxhall ⊖	d	17 40	17 43	17 46	17 51	17 54	17 58	18 01	18 07	18 10	18 13	18 16	18 21	18 24	18 28	18 31	18 37	18 40	18 43	18 46	18 51	18 54
Clapham Junction 10	d	17 45	17 48	17 51	17 56	17 59	18 03	18 06	18 12	18 15	18 18	18 21	18 26	18 29	18 33	18 36	18 42	18 45	18 48	18 51	18 56	18 59
Earlsfield	d	17 48	17 51	17 54	17 59	18 02	18 06	18 09	18 15	18 18	18 21	18 24	18 29	18 32	18 36	18 39	18 45	18 48	18 51	18 54	18 59	19 02
Wimbledon 6 ⊖	d	17 52	17 55	17 58	18 03	18 06	18 10	18 13	18 19	18 22	18 25	18 28	18 33	18 36	18 40	18 43	18 49	18 52	18 55	18 58	19 03	19 06
Raynes Park 6	d	17 55	17 58	18 01	18 06		18 13	18 16		18 25	18 28	18 31	18 36		18 43	18 46		18 55	18 58	19 01	19 06	
Motspur Park	d		18 01		18 09		18 16				18 31		18 39		18 46				19 01		19 09	
Malden Manor	d				18 13								18 43								19 13	
Tolworth	d				18 15								18 45								19 15	
Chessington North	d				18 18								18 48								19 18	
Chessington South	a				18 21								18 51								19 21	
Worcester Park	d		18 04				18 19				18 34				18 49				19 04			
Stoneleigh	d		18 07				18 22				18 37				18 52				19 07			
Ewell West	d		18 09				18 24				18 39				18 54				19 09			
Epsom 3	182 a		18 13				18 29				18 43				18 58				19 13			
	d		18 13				18 30				18 43				18 58				19 13			
Ashtead	182 d		18 17				18 34				18 47				19 02				19 17			
Leatherhead	182 d		18 21				18 37				18 51				19 06				19 21			
Box Hill & Westhumble	182 d						18 42								19 11							
Dorking 4	182 a						18 45								19 13							
New Malden 6	d	17 58		18 04				18 19		18 28		18 34				18 49		18 58		19 04		
Norbiton	d			18 07				18 22				18 37				18 52				19 07		
Kingston	a			18 10				18 25				18 40				18 55				19 10		
	d			18 10				18 29				18 40				18 59				19 10		
Hampton Wick	d			18 12				18 31				18 42				19 01				19 12		
Teddington	d			18 15				18 35				18 45				19 05				19 15		
Strawberry Hill	a							18 38								19 08						
Fulwell	d			18 19								18 49								19 19		
Hampton	d			18 23								18 53								19 23		
Kempton Park	d			18 26								18 56								19 26		
Sunbury	d			18 28								18 58								19 28		
Upper Halliford	d			18 30								19 00								19 30		
Shepperton	a			18 33								19 03								19 33		
Berrylands	d	18 00								18 30								19 00				
Surbiton 6	d	18 05				18a13			18 27	18 35				18a43			18 57	19 05				19a13
Thames Ditton	d	18 09								18 39								19 09				
Hampton Court	a	18 12								18 42								19 12				
Hinchley Wood	d								18 31								19 01					
Claygate	d								18 34								19 04					
Oxshott	d								18 37								19 07					
Cobham & Stoke D'abernon	d								18 41								19 11					
Bookham	d		18 26								18 56								19 26			
Effingham Junction 6	d		18 30						18 45		19 00						19 15		19 30			
Horsley	d		18 33						18 48		19 03						19 18		19 33			
Clandon	d		18 38						18 53		19 08						19 23		19 38			
London Road (Guildford)	d		18 43						18 58		19 13						19 28		19 43			
Guildford	a		18 47						19 02		19 17						19 32		19 47			

A To Woking
B To London Waterloo

Table T152-F

Saturdays

21 December to 16 May

London - Chessington South, Dorking, Guildford, Shepperton and Hampton Court

Station		SW	SW A	SW	SW	SW	SW	SW	SW B	SW	SW A	SW	SW	SW	SW	SW	SW B	SW	SW A	SW	SW	SW	SW
London Waterloo 15 ⊖	d	18 54	18 57	19 03	19 06	19 09	19 12	19 17	19 20	19 24	19 27	19 33	19 36	19 39	19 42	19 47	19 50	19 54	19 57	20 03	20 06	20 09	20 12
Vauxhall ⊖	d	18 58	19 01	19 07	19 10	19 13	19 16	19 21	19 24	19 28	19 31	19 37	19 40	19 43	19 46	19 51	19 54	19 58	20 01	20 07	20 10	20 13	20 16
Clapham Junction 10	d	19 03	19 06	19 12	19 15	19 18	19 21	19 26	19 29	19 33	19 36	19 42	19 45	19 48	19 51	19 56	19 59	20 03	20 06	20 12	20 15	20 18	20 21
Earlsfield	d	19 06	19 09	19 15	19 18	19 21	19 24	19 29	19 32	19 36	19 39	19 45	19 48	19 51	19 54	19 59	20 02	20 06	20 09	20 15	20 18	20 21	20 24
Wimbledon 6 ⊖ ⛴	d	19 10	19 13	19 19	19 22	19 25	19 28	19 33	19 36	19 40	19 43	19 49	19 52	19 55	19 58	20 03	20 06	20 10	20 13	20 19	20 22	20 25	20 28
Raynes Park 6	d	19 13	19 16		19 25	19 28	19 31	19 36		19 43	19 46		19 55	19 58	20 01	20 06		20 13	20 16		20 25	20 28	20 31
Motspur Park	d	19 16				19 31		19 39		19 46				20 01		20 09		20 16				20 31	
Malden Manor	d							19 43								20 13							
Tolworth	d							19 45								20 15							
Chessington North	d							19 48								20 18							
Chessington South	a							19 51								20 21							
Worcester Park	d	19 19				19 34				19 49				20 04				20 19				20 34	
Stoneleigh	d	19 22				19 37				19 52				20 07				20 22				20 37	
Ewell West	d	19 24				19 39				19 54				20 09				20 24				20 39	
Epsom 3 182	a	19 28				19 43				19 58				20 13				20 28				20 43	
	d	19 28				19 43				19 58				20 13				20 28				20 43	
Ashtead 182	d	19 32				19 47				20 02				20 17				20 32				20 47	
Leatherhead 182	d	19 36				19 51				20 06				20 21				20 36				20 51	
Box Hill & Westhumble 182	d	19 41								20 11								20 41					
Dorking 4 182	a	19 43								20 13								20 43					
New Malden 6	d		19 19		19 28		19 34				19 49		19 58		20 04				20 19		20 28		20 34
Norbiton	d		19 22				19 37				19 52				20 07				20 22				20 37
Kingston	a		19 25				19 40				19 55				20 10				20 25				20 40
	d		19 29				19 40				19 59				20 10				20 29				20 40
Hampton Wick	d		19 31				19 42				20 01				20 12				20 31				20 42
Teddington	d		19 35				19 45				20 05				20 15				20 35				20 45
Strawberry Hill	a		19 38								20 08								20 38				
Fulwell	d						19 49								20 19								20 49
Hampton	d						19 53								20 23								20 53
Kempton Park	d						19 56								20 26								20 56
Sunbury	d						19 58								20 28								20 58
Upper Halliford	d						20 00								20 30								21 00
Shepperton	a						20 03								20 33								21 03
Berrylands	d				19 30								20 00								20 30		
Surbiton 6	d			19 27	19 35				19a43			19 57	20 05				20a13			20 27	20 35		
Thames Ditton	d				19 39								20 09								20 39		
Hampton Court	a				19 42								20 12								20 42		
Hinchley Wood	d			19 31								20 01								20 31			
Claygate	d			19 34								20 04								20 34			
Oxshott	d			19 37								20 07								20 37			
Cobham & Stoke D'abernon	d			19 41								20 11								20 41			
Bookham	d					19 56								20 26								20 56	
Effingham Junction 6	d			19 45		20 00						20 15		20 30						20 45		21 00	
Horsley	d			19 48		20 03						20 18		20 33						20 48		21 03	
Clandon	d			19 53		20 08						20 23		20 38						20 53		21 08	
London Road (Guildford)	d			19 58		20 13						20 28		20 43						20 58		21 13	
Guildford	a			20 02		20 17						20 32		20 47						21 02		21 17	

A To London Waterloo

B To Woking

Table T152-F

Saturdays

21 December to 16 May

London - Chessington South, Dorking, Guildford, Shepperton and Hampton Court

Station		SW	SW A	SW	SW B	SW	SW	SW	SW	SW	SW A	SW	SW B	SW	SW	SW	SW	SW	SW A	SW	SW B	SW	SW
London Waterloo 15 ⊖	d	20 17	20 20	20 24	20 27	20 33	20 36	20 39	20 42	20 47	20 50	20 54	20 57	21 03	21 06	21 09	21 12	21 17	21 20	21 24	21 27	21 33	21 36
Vauxhall ⊖	d	20 21	20 24	20 28	20 31	20 37	20 40	20 43	20 46	20 51	20 54	20 58	21 01	21 07	21 10	21 13	21 16	21 21	21 24	21 28	21 31	21 37	21 40
Clapham Junction 10	d	20 26	20 29	20 33	20 36	20 42	20 45	20 48	20 51	20 56	20 59	21 03	21 06	21 12	21 15	21 18	21 21	21 26	21 29	21 33	21 36	21 42	21 45
Earlsfield	d	20 29	20 32	20 36	20 39	20 45	20 48	20 51	20 54	20 59	21 02	21 06	21 09	21 15	21 18	21 21	21 24	21 29	21 32	21 36	21 39	21 45	21 48
Wimbledon 6 ⊖ ⛴	d	20 33	20 36	20 40	20 43	20 49	20 52	20 55	20 58	21 03	21 06	21 10	21 13	21 19	21 22	21 25	21 28	21 33	21 36	21 40	21 43	21 49	21 52
Raynes Park 6	d	20 36		20 43	20 46		20 55	20 58	21 01	21 06		21 13	21 16		21 25	21 28	21 31	21 36		21 43	21 46		21 55
Motspur Park	d	20 39		20 46				21 01		21 09		21 16				21 31		21 39		21 46			
Malden Manor	d	20 43								21 13								21 43					
Tolworth	d	20 45								21 15								21 45					
Chessington North	d	20 48								21 18								21 48					
Chessington South	a	20 51								21 21								21 51					
Worcester Park	d			20 49				21 04				21 19				21 34				21 49			
Stoneleigh	d			20 52				21 07				21 22				21 37				21 52			
Ewell West	d			20 54				21 09				21 24				21 39				21 54			
Epsom 3 182	a			20 58				21 13				21 28				21 43				21 58			
	d			20 58				21 13				21 28				21 43				21 58			
Ashtead 182	d			21 02				21 17				21 32				21 47				22 02			
Leatherhead 182	d			21 06				21 21				21 36				21 51				22 06			
Box Hill & Westhumble 182	d			21 11								21 41								22 11			
Dorking 4 182	a			21 13								21 43								22 13			
New Malden 6	d				20 49		20 58		21 04				21 19		21 28		21 34				21 49		21 58
Norbiton	d				20 52				21 07				21 22				21 37				21 52		
Kingston	a				20 55				21 10				21 25				21 40				21 55		
	d				20 59				21 10				21 29				21 40				21 59		
Hampton Wick	d				21 01				21 12				21 31				21 42				22 01		
Teddington	d				21 05				21 15				21 35				21 45				22 05		
Strawberry Hill	a				21 08								21 38								22 08		
Fulwell	d								21 19								21 49						
Hampton	d								21 23								21 53						
Kempton Park	d								21 26								21 56						
Sunbury	d								21 28								21 58						
Upper Halliford	d								21 30								22 00						
Shepperton	a								21 33								22 03						
Berrylands	d						21 00								21 30								22 00
Surbiton 6	d		20a43			20 57	21 05				21a13			21 27	21 35				21a43			21 57	22 05
Thames Ditton	d						21 09								21 39								22 09
Hampton Court	a						21 12								21 42								22 12
Hinchley Wood	d					21 01								21 31								22 01	
Claygate	d					21 04								21 34								22 04	
Oxshott	d					21 07								21 37								22 07	
Cobham & Stoke D'abernon	d					21 11								21 41								22 11	
Bookham	d							21 26								21 56							
Effingham Junction 6	d					21 15		21 30						21 45		22 00						22 15	
Horsley	d					21 18		21 33						21 48		22 03						22 18	
Clandon	d					21 23		21 38						21 53		22 08						22 23	
London Road (Guildford)	d					21 28		21 43						21 58		22 13						22 28	
Guildford	a					21 32		21 47						22 02		22 17						22 32	

A To Woking

B To London Waterloo

Table T152-F

Saturdays
21 December to 16 May

London - Chessington South, Dorking, Guildford, Shepperton and Hampton Court

Station		SW	SW	SW	SW A	SW	SW B	SW	SW	SW	SW	SW	SW A	SW B	SW	SW	SW	SW	SW A	SW B	SW	SW
London Waterloo	d	21 39	21 42	21 47	21 50	21 54	21 57	22 03	22 06	22 09	22 12	22 17	22 20	22 27	22 33	22 36	22 39	22 42	22 50	22 57	23 00	23 03
Vauxhall	d	21 43	21 46	21 51	21 54	21 58	22 01	22 07	22 10	22 13	22 16	22 21	22 24	22 31	22 37	22 40	22 43	22 46	22 54	23 01	23 04	23 07
Clapham Junction	d	21 48	21 51	21 56	21 59	22 03	22 06	22 12	22 15	22 18	22 21	22 26	22 29	22 36	22 42	22 45	22 48	22 51	22 59	23 06	23 09	23 12
Earlsfield	d	21 51	21 54	21 59	22 02	22 06	22 09	22 15	22 18	22 21	22 24	22 29	22 32	22 39	22 45	22 48	22 51	22 54	23 02	23 09	23 12	23 15
Wimbledon	d	21 55	21 58	22 03	22 06	22 10	22 13	22 19	22 22	22 25	22 28	22 33	22 36	22 43	22 49	22 52	22 55	22 58	23 06	23 13	23 16	23 19
Raynes Park	d	21 58	22 01	22 06		22 13	22 16		22 25	22 28	22 31	22 36		22 46		22 55	22 58	23 01		23 16	23 19	
Motspur Park	d	22 01		22 09		22 16				22 31		22 39					23 01				23 22	
Malden Manor	d			22 13								22 43									23 26	
Tolworth	d			22 15								22 45									23 28	
Chessington North	d			22 18								22 48									23 31	
Chessington South	a			22 21								22 51									23 33	
Worcester Park	d	22 04				22 19				22 34							23 04					
Stoneleigh	d	22 07				22 22				22 37							23 07					
Ewell West	d	22 09				22 24				22 39							23 09					
Epsom 182	a	22 13				22 28				22 43							23 13					
	d	22 13								22 43							23 13					
Ashtead 182	d	22 17								22 47							23 17					
Leatherhead 182	d	22 21								22 51							23 21					
Box Hill & Westhumble 182	d									22 56												
Dorking 182	a									22 58												
New Malden	d		22 04				22 19		22 28		22 34			22 49		22 58		23 04		23 19		
Norbiton	d		22 07				22 22				22 37			22 52				23 07		23 22		
Kingston	a		22 10				22 25				22 40			22 55				23 10		23 25		
	d		22 10				22 29				22 40			22 59				23 10		23 29		
Hampton Wick	d		22 12				22 31				22 42			23 01				23 12		23 31		
Teddington	d		22 15				22 35				22 45			23 05				23 15		23 35		
Strawberry Hill	a						22 38							23 08						23 38		
Fulwell	d		22 19								22 49							23 19				
Hampton	d		22 23								22 53							23 23				
Kempton Park	d		22 26								22 56							23 26				
Sunbury	d		22 28								22 58							23 28				
Upper Halliford	d		22 30								23 00							23 30				
Shepperton	a		22 33								23 03							23 33				
Berrylands	d								22 30							23 00						
Surbiton	d				22a13			22 27	22 35				22a43		22 57	23 04			23a13			23 27
Thames Ditton	d								22 39							23 09						
Hampton Court	a								22 45							23 12						
Hinchley Wood	d							22 31							23 01							23 31
Claygate	d							22 34							23 04							23 34
Oxshott	d							22 37							23 07							23 37
Cobham & Stoke D'abernon	d							22 41							23 11							23 41
Bookham	d	22 26															23 26					
Effingham Junction	d	22 30						22 45							23 15		23 30					23 45
Horsley	d	22 33						22 48							23 18		23 33					23 48
Clandon	d	22 38						22 53							23 23		23 38					23 53
London Road (Guildford)	d	22 43						22 58							23 28		23 43					23 58
Guildford	a	22 49						23 02							23 32		23 47					00 02

A To Woking
B To London Waterloo

Table T152-F

Saturdays
21 December to 16 May

London - Chessington South, Dorking, Guildford, Shepperton and Hampton Court

Station		SW	SW	SW	SW A	SW B	SW	SW	SW	SW
London Waterloo	d	23 06	23 09	23 12	23 20	23 27	23 36	23 42	23 50	23 57
Vauxhall	d	23 10	23 13	23 16	23 24	23 31	23 40	23 46	23 54	00 01
Clapham Junction	d	23 15	23 18	23 21	23 29	23 36	23 45	23 51	23 59	00 06
Earlsfield	d	23 18	23 21	23 24	23 32	23 39	23 48	23 54	00 02	00 09
Wimbledon	d	23 22	23 25	23 28	23 36	23 43	23 52	23 58	00 06	00 13
Raynes Park	d	23 25	23 28	23 31		23 46	23 55	00 01		00 16
Motspur Park	d		23 31					00 04		
Malden Manor	d									
Tolworth	d									
Chessington North	d									
Chessington South	a									
Worcester Park	d		23 34					00 07		
Stoneleigh	d		23 37					00 10		
Ewell West	d		23 39					00 12		
Epsom 182	a		23 43					00 16		
	d		23 43					00 19		
Ashtead 182	d		23 47					00 23		
Leatherhead 182	d		23 51					00 26		
Box Hill & Westhumble 182	d		23 56							
Dorking 182	a		23 58							
New Malden	d	23 28		23 34		23 49	23 58			00 19
Norbiton	d			23 37		23 52				00 22
Kingston	a			23 40		23 55				00 25
	d			23 40		23 55				00 25
Hampton Wick	d			23 42		23 57				00 27
Teddington	d			23 45		23 59				00 30
Strawberry Hill	a					00 03				
Fulwell	d			23 49						00 34
Hampton	d			23 53						00 38
Kempton Park	d			23 56						00 41
Sunbury	d			23 58						00 43
Upper Halliford	d			23 59						00 45
Shepperton	a			00 03						00 48
Berrylands	d	23 30					23 59			
Surbiton	d	23 35			23a44		00 05		00 14	
Thames Ditton	d	23 39					00 09			
Hampton Court	a	23 42					00 12			
Hinchley Wood	d								00 18	
Claygate	d								00 20	
Oxshott	d								00 24	
Cobham & Stoke D'abernon	d								00 27	
Bookham	d							00 32		
Effingham Junction	d							00 36	00 32	
Horsley	d							00 39	00 34	
Clandon	d							00 44	00 39	
London Road (Guildford)	d							00 49	00 44	
Guildford	a							00 53	00 51	

A To Woking
B To Twickenham

Table T152-F

Sundays
15 December to 10 May

London - Chessington South, Dorking, Guildford, Shepperton and Hampton Court

Station			SW A	SW A	SW A	SW A	SW	SW	SW B	SW	SW C		SW D	SW	SW	SW	SW	SW	SW D	SW	SW		SW	SW	SW	SW
London Waterloo 15	⊖	d					00 09	00 15	00 27	00 42	01 42		06 20		06 57			07 10	07 18		07 27			07 40	07 48	07 57
Vauxhall	⊖	d				00 01	00 13	00 19	00 31	00 46	01 46		06 24		07 01			07 14	07 22		07 31			07 44	07 52	08 01
Clapham Junction 10		d				00 06	00 20	00 26	00 38	00 53	01 53		06 29		07 06			07 19	07 27		07 36			07 49	07 57	08 06
Earlsfield		d		00 02		00 09	00 23	00 29	00s41						07 09			07 22	07 30		07 39			07 52	08 00	08 09
Wimbledon 6	⊖ ⇌	d		00 06		00 13	00 27	00 33	00 45	01 05	01 59		06 36	06 48	07 13	07 16	07 20	07 26	07 34	07 38	07 43		07 48	07 56	08 04	08 13
Raynes Park 6		d			00 01	00 16		00 36	00 48	01 08	02 02		06 39	06 52	07 17		07 23		07 38	07 40	07 47		07 52		08 07	08 17
Motspur Park		d			00 04			00 39						06 55			07 26			07 43			07 55			
Malden Manor		d																		07 47						
Tolworth		d																		07 49						
Chessington North		d																		07 52						
Chessington South		a																		07 56						
Worcester Park		d			00 07			00 42						06 58			07 29						07 58			
Stoneleigh		d			00 10			00 45						07 01			07 32						08 01			
Ewell West		d			00 12			00 47						07 03			07 34						08 03			
Epsom 3	182	a			00 16			00 51						07 07			07 38						08 07			
		d			00 19																		08 08			
Ashtead	182	d			00 23																		08 12			
Leatherhead	182	d			00 26																		08 16			
Box Hill & Westhumble	182	d																								
Dorking 4	182	a																								
New Malden 6		d				00 19			00 51	01 11	02 04		06 42		07 19				07 40		07 49				08 11	08 19
Norbiton		d				00 22				01 14	02 08		06 45						07 44						08 13	
Kingston		a				00 25				01 17	02 10		06 48						07 46						08 16	
		d				00 25				01 17	02 11		06 49						07 49						08 16	
Hampton Wick		d				00 27				01s22	02s13		06 51						07 51						08 18	
Teddington		d				00 30				01s25	02s15		06 56						07 56						08 22	
Strawberry Hill		a								01 37	02s18		06 59						07 59							
Fulwell		d				00 34																			08 25	
Hampton		d				00 38																			08 30	
Kempton Park		d				00 41																			08 32	
Sunbury		d				00 43																			08 35	
Upper Halliford		d				00 45																			08 37	
Shepperton		a				00 48																			08 40	
Berrylands		d							00s53						07 22						07 52					08 22
Surbiton 6		d	00 05	00 14			00 35		00s57						07 26	07 32		07 35			07 56			08 05		08 26
Thames Ditton		d	00 09												07 30						08 00					08 30
Hampton Court		a	00 12												07 33						08 03					08 33
Hinchley Wood		d		00 18												07 36										
Claygate		d		00 20												07 39										
Oxshott		d		00 24												07 42										
Cobham & Stoke D'abernon		d		00 27												07 46										
Bookham		d			00 32																		08 22			
Effingham Junction 6		d		00 32	00 36											07 50							08 26			
Horsley		d		00 34	00 39											07 53							08 28			
Clandon		d		00 39	00 44											07 58							08 33			
London Road (Guildford)		d		00 44	00 49											08 03							08 38			
Guildford		a		00 51	00 53		01 07									08 07		08 14					08 42	08 40		

A not 15 December. From London Waterloo
B To Woking
C To Twickenham
D To London Waterloo

Table T152-F

Sundays
15 December to 10 May

London - Chessington South, Dorking, Guildford, Shepperton and Hampton Court

Station			SW	SW	SW	SW	SW A		SW	SW	SW	SW	SW	SW	SW	SW	SW		SW	SW A	SW	SW	SW	SW	SW	SW
London Waterloo 15	⊖	d			08 02	08 10	08 18		08 21	08 27	08 33	08 40	08 48	08 51	08 57	09 02			09 10	09 18	09 21	09 27	09 32	09 40	09 48	09 51
Vauxhall	⊖	d			08 06	08 14	08 22		08 25	08 31	08 37	08 44	08 52	08 55	09 01	09 06			09 14	09 22	09 25	09 31	09 36	09 44	09 52	09 55
Clapham Junction 10		d			08 11	08 19	08 27		08 30	08 36	08 41	08 49	08 57	09 00	09 06	09 11			09 19	09 27	09 30	09 36	09 41	09 49	09 57	10 00
Earlsfield		d			08 14	08 22	08 30		08 33	08 39	08 44	08 52	09 00	09 03	09 09	09 14			09 22	09 30	09 33	09 39	09 44	09 52	10 00	10 03
Wimbledon 6	⊖ ⇌	d	08 02	08 08	08 18	08 26	08 34		08 37	08 43	08 48	08 56	09 04	09 07	09 13	09 18			09 26	09 34	09 37	09 43	09 48	09 56	10 04	10 07
Raynes Park 6		d	08 05	08 10	08 22		08 38		08 41	08 47	08 53		09 07	09 11	09 16	09 22				09 37	09 40	09 46	09 52		10 07	10 10
Motspur Park		d		08 13	08 26				08 44		08 56			09 14		09 25					09 43		09 55			10 13
Malden Manor		d		08 17					08 47					09 17							09 47					10 17
Tolworth		d		08 19					08 50					09 20							09 49					10 19
Chessington North		d		08 22					08 53					09 23							09 52					10 22
Chessington South		a		08 26					08 56					09 26							09 55					10 25
Worcester Park		d			08 27						08 58					09 28							09 58			
Stoneleigh		d			08 30						09 01					09 31							10 01			
Ewell West		d			08 34						09 04					09 33							10 03			
Epsom 3	182	a			08 36						09 07					09 37							10 07			
		d			08 38						09 08					09 38							10 08			
Ashtead	182	d			08 42						09 12					09 42							10 12			
Leatherhead	182	d			08 46						09 16					09 46							10 16			
Box Hill & Westhumble	182	d			08 51											09 51										
Dorking 4	182	a			08 53											09 53										
New Malden 6		d	08 08				08 40			08 49			09 10		09 19					09 40		09 49			10 10	
Norbiton		d					08 44						09 13							09 43					10 13	
Kingston		a					08 46						09 15							09 46					10 16	
		d					08 49						09 16							09 49					10 16	
Hampton Wick		d					08 51						09 18							09 51					10 18	
Teddington		d					08 56						09 21							09 56					10 21	
Strawberry Hill		a					08 59													09 59						
Fulwell		d											09 25												10 25	
Hampton		d											09 29												10 29	
Kempton Park		d											09 32												10 32	
Sunbury		d											09 34												10 34	
Upper Halliford		d											09 36												10 36	
Shepperton		a											09 40												10 39	
Berrylands		d	08 10							08 52					09 21							09 51				
Surbiton 6		d	08 32			08 35				08 56		09 05			09 25		09 32		09 36			09 55		10 05		
Thames Ditton		d								09 00					09 30							10 00				
Hampton Court		a								09 03					09 33							10 03				
Hinchley Wood		d	08 36														09 36									
Claygate		d	08 39														09 39									
Oxshott		d	08 42														09 42									
Cobham & Stoke D'abernon		d	08 46														09 46									
Bookham		d									09 22												10 22			
Effingham Junction 6		d	08 50								09 26						09 50						10 26			
Horsley		d	08 53								09 28						09 53						10 28			
Clandon		d	08 58								09 33						09 58						10 33			
London Road (Guildford)		d	09 03								09 38						10 03						10 38			
Guildford		a	09 07			09 09					09 42	09 48					10 07		10 09				10 45	10 46		

A To London Waterloo

Table T152-F

Sundays
15 December to 10 May

London - Chessington South, Dorking, Guildford, Shepperton and Hampton Court

Station		SW		SW	SW	SW	SW A	SW	SW	SW	SW	SW		SW	SW	SW	SW	SW	SW A	SW	SW	SW		SW	SW
London Waterloo 15 ⊖	d	09 57			10 02	10 10	10 18	10 21	10 27	10 32	10 40	10 48		10 51	10 57		11 02	11 10	11 18	11 21	11 27	11 32		11 40	11 48
Vauxhall ⊖	d	10 01			10 06	10 14	10 22	10 25	10 31	10 36	10 44	10 52		10 55	11 01		11 06	11 14	11 22	11 25	11 31	11 36		11 44	11 52
Clapham Junction 10	d	10 06			10 11	10 19	10 27	10 30	10 36	10 41	10 49	10 57		11 00	11 06		11 12	11 19	11 27	11 30	11 36	11 42		11 49	11 57
Earlsfield	d	10 09			10 14	10 22	10 30	10 33	10 39	10 44	10 52	11 00		11 03	11 10		11 15	11 22	11 30	11 33	11 39	11 45		11 52	12 00
Wimbledon 6 ⊖	d	10 13		10 17	10 18	10 26	10 34	10 37	10 43	10 48	10 56	11 04		11 07	11 14	11 14	11 19	11 26	11 34	11 37	11 43	11 49		11 56	12 04
Raynes Park 6	d	10 16			10 22		10 37	10 40	10 46	10 52		11 07		11 10	11 17		11 23		11 37	11 40	11 46	11 52			12 07
Motspur Park	d				10 25			10 43		10 55				11 13			11 26			11 43		11 55			
Malden Manor	d							10 47						11 17						11 47					
Tolworth	d							10 49						11 19						11 49					
Chessington North	d							10 52						11 22						11 52					
Chessington South	a							10 55						11 25						11 55					
Worcester Park	d				10 28					10 58							11 28					11 58			
Stoneleigh	d				10 31					11 01							11 31					12 01			
Ewell West	d				10 33					11 03							11 34					12 03			
Epsom 3 182	a				10 37					11 07							11 37					12 07			
	d				10 38					11 08							11 38					12 08			
Ashtead 182	d				10 42					11 12							11 42					12 12			
Leatherhead 182	d				10 46					11 16							11 46					12 16			
Box Hill & Westhumble 182	d				10 51												11 51								
Dorking 4 182	a				10 53												11 53								
New Malden 6	d	10 19					10 40		10 49			11 10			11 20				11 40		11 49				12 10
Norbiton	d						10 43					11 13							11 43						12 13
Kingston	a						10 46					11 16							11 46						12 16
	d						10 49					11 16							11 49						12 16
Hampton Wick	d						10 51					11 18							11 51						12 18
Teddington	d						10 56					11 21							11 56						12 21
Strawberry Hill	a						10 59												11 59						
Fulwell	d											11 25													12 25
Hampton	d											11 29													12 29
Kempton Park	d											11 32													12 32
Sunbury	d											11 34													12 34
Upper Halliford	d											11 36													12 36
Shepperton	a											11 39													12 39
Berrylands	d	10 21							10 51						11 23						11 51				
Surbiton 6	d	10 25		10 32		10 35			10 55		11 05				11 27	11 32		11 35			11 55			12 05	
Thames Ditton	d	10 30							11 00						11 31						12 00				
Hampton Court	a	10 33							11 03						11 34						12 03				
Hinchley Wood	d			10 36												11 36									
Claygate	d			10 39												11 39									
Oxshott	d			10 42												11 42									
Cobham & Stoke D'abernon	d			10 46												11 46									
Bookham	d									11 22												12 22			
Effingham Junction 6	d			10 50						11 26						11 50						12 26			
Horsley	d			10 53						11 28						11 53						12 28			
Clandon	d			10 58						11 33						11 58						12 33			
London Road (Guildford)	d			11 03						11 38						12 03						12 38			
Guildford	a			11 07		11 14				11 42	11 46					12 07		12 14				12 42		12 46	

A To London Waterloo

Table T152-F

Sundays
15 December to 10 May

London - Chessington South, Dorking, Guildford, Shepperton and Hampton Court

Station		SW	SW	SW	SW	SW	SW A	SW A		SW	SW	SW	SW	SW	SW	SW	SW	SW		SW	SW A	SW A	SW	SW	SW
London Waterloo 15 ⊖	d	11 51	11 57	12 02		12 10		12 18		12 21	12 27	12 32	12 40	12 48	12 51	12 57	13 00	13 02		13 10		13 18	13 21	13 27	13 32
Vauxhall ⊖	d	11 55	12 01	12 06		12 14		12 22		12 25	12 31	12 36	12 44	12 52	12 55	13 01	13 04	13 06		13 14		13 22	13 25	13 31	13 36
Clapham Junction 10	d	12 00	12 06	12 11		12 19		12 27		12 30	12 36	12 42	12 49	12 57	13 00	13 06	13 09	13 11		13 19		13 27	13 30	13 36	13 41
Earlsfield	d	12 03	12 10	12 15		12 22		12 30		12 33	12 39	12 45	12 52	13 00	13 03	13 09	13 12	13 14		13 22		13 30	13 33	13 39	13 44
Wimbledon 6 ⊖	d	12 07	12 14	12 19	12 19	12 26		12 34		12 37	12 43	12 49	12 56	13 04	13 07	13 13	13 16	13 18		13 26		13 34	13 37	13 43	13 48
Raynes Park 6	d	12 10	12 17	12 23				12 37		12 40	12 46	12 52		13 07	13 10	13 16		13 22				13 37	13 40	13 46	13 52
Motspur Park	d	12 13		12 26						12 43		12 55			13 13			13 25					13 43		13 55
Malden Manor	d	12 17								12 47					13 17								13 47		
Tolworth	d	12 19								12 49					13 19								13 49		
Chessington North	d	12 22								12 52					13 22								13 52		
Chessington South	a	12 25								12 55					13 25								13 55		
Worcester Park	d			12 28								12 58						13 28							13 58
Stoneleigh	d			12 31								13 01						13 31							14 01
Ewell West	d			12 34								13 03						13 33							14 03
Epsom 3 182	a			12 37								13 07						13 37							14 07
	d			12 38								13 08						13 38							14 08
Ashtead 182	d			12 42								13 12						13 42							14 12
Leatherhead 182	d			12 46								13 16						13 46							14 16
Box Hill & Westhumble 182	d			12 51														13 51							
Dorking 4 182	a			12 53														13 53							
New Malden 6	d		12 19					12 40			12 49			13 10		13 19						13 40		13 49	
Norbiton	d							12 43						13 13								13 43			
Kingston	a							12 46						13 16								13 46			
	d						12 35	12 49						13 16							13 35	13 49			
Hampton Wick	d						12 37	12 51						13 18							13 37	13 51			
Teddington	d						12 40	12 56						13 21							13 40	13 56			
Strawberry Hill	a						12 43	12 59													13 43	13 59			
Fulwell	d													13 25											
Hampton	d													13 29											
Kempton Park	d													13 32											
Sunbury	d													13 34											
Upper Halliford	d													13 36											
Shepperton	a													13 39											
Berrylands	d		12 21								12 51					13 21								13 51	
Surbiton 6	d		12 25		12 32	12 35					12 55		13 05			13 25	13 32			13 35				13 55	
Thames Ditton	d		12 30								13 00					13 30								14 00	
Hampton Court	a		12 33								13 03					13 33								14 03	
Hinchley Wood	d				12 36												13 36								
Claygate	d				12 39												13 39								
Oxshott	d				12 42												13 42								
Cobham & Stoke D'abernon	d				12 46												13 46								
Bookham	d											13 22													14 22
Effingham Junction 6	d				12 50							13 26					13 50								14 26
Horsley	d				12 53							13 28					13 53								14 28
Clandon	d				12 58							13 33					13 58								14 33
London Road (Guildford)	d				13 03							13 38					14 03								14 38
Guildford	a				13 07	13 14						13 42	13 46				14 07			14 14					14 42

A To London Waterloo

Table T152-F

Sundays

15 December to 10 May

London - Chessington South, Dorking, Guildford, Shepperton and Hampton Court

		SW	SW	SW		SW	SW	SW	SW	SW A	SW A	SW	SW	SW		SW	SW	SW	SW	SW	SW	SW	SW A	SW A
London Waterloo 15 ⊖	d	13 40	13 48	13 51		13 57	14 00	14 02	14 10		14 18	14 21	14 27	14 32		14 40	14 48	14 51	14 57	15 00	15 02	15 10		15 18
Vauxhall ⊖	d	13 44	13 52	13 55		14 01	14 04	14 06	14 14		14 22	14 25	14 31	14 36		14 44	14 52	14 55	15 01	15 04	15 06	15 14		15 22
Clapham Junction 10	d	13 49	13 57	14 00		14 06	14 09	14 11	14 19		14 27	14 30	14 36	14 41		14 49	14 57	15 00	15 06	15 09	15 11	15 19		15 27
Earlsfield	d	13 52	14 00	14 03		14 09	14 12	14 14	14 22		14 30	14 33	14 39	14 44		14 52	15 00	15 03	15 09	15 12	15 14	15 22		15 30
Wimbledon 6 ⊖ ⇌	d	13 56	14 04	14 07		14 13	14 16	14 18	14 26		14 34	14 37	14 43	14 48		14 56	15 04	15 07	15 13	15 16	15 18	15 26		15 34
Raynes Park 6	d		14 07	14 10		14 16		14 22			14 37	14 40	14 46	14 52			15 07	15 10	15 16		15 22			15 37
Motspur Park	d			14 13				14 25				14 43		14 55				15 13			15 25			
Malden Manor	d			14 17								14 47						15 17						
Tolworth	d			14 19								14 49						15 19						
Chessington North	d			14 22								14 52						15 22						
Chessington South	a			14 25								14 55						15 25						
Worcester Park	d							14 28						14 58							15 28			
Stoneleigh	d							14 31						15 01							15 31			
Ewell West	d							14 33						15 03							15 33			
Epsom 3 182	a							14 37						15 07							15 37			
	d							14 38						15 08							15 38			
Ashtead 182	d							14 42						15 12							15 42			
Leatherhead 182	d							14 46						15 16							15 46			
Box Hill & Westhumble 182	d							14 51													15 51			
Dorking 4 182	a							14 53													15 53			
New Malden 6	d		14 10			14 19					14 40		14 49				15 10		15 19					15 40
Norbiton	d		14 13								14 43						15 13							15 43
Kingston	a		14 16								14 46						15 16							15 46
	d		14 16							14 35	14 49						15 16						15 35	15 49
Hampton Wick	d		14 18							14 37	14 51						15 18						15 37	15 51
Teddington	d		14 21							14 40	14 56						15 21						15 40	15 56
Strawberry Hill	a									14 43	14 59												15 43	15 59
Fulwell	d		14 25														15 25							
Hampton	d		14 29														15 29							
Kempton Park	d		14 32														15 32							
Sunbury	d		14 34														15 34							
Upper Halliford	d		14 36														15 36							
Shepperton	a		14 39														15 39							
Berrylands	d					14 21							14 51						15 21					
Surbiton 6	d	14 05				14 25	14 32		14 35				14 55			15 05			15 25	15 32		15 35		
Thames Ditton	d					14 30							15 00						15 30					
Hampton Court	a					14 33							15 03						15 33					
Hinchley Wood	d						14 36													15 36				
Claygate	d						14 39													15 39				
Oxshott	d						14 42													15 42				
Cobham & Stoke D'abernon	d						14 46													15 46				
Bookham	d													15 22										
Effingham Junction 6	d						14 50							15 26						15 50				
Horsley	d						14 53							15 28						15 53				
Clandon	d						14 58							15 33						15 58				
London Road (Guildford)	d						15 03							15 38						16 03				
Guildford	a	14 46					15 07		15 14					15 42		15 46				16 07		16 14		

A To London Waterloo

Table T152-F

Sundays

15 December to 10 May

London - Chessington South, Dorking, Guildford, Shepperton and Hampton Court

		SW	SW	SW	SW	SW	SW	SW	SW	SW		SW	SW A	SW A	SW	SW	SW	SW	SW	SW		SW	SW	SW	SW
London Waterloo 15 ⊖	d	15 21	15 27	15 32	15 40	15 48	15 51	15 57	16 00	16 02		16 10		16 18	16 21	16 27	16 32	16 40	16 48	16 51		16 57	17 00	17 02	17 10
Vauxhall ⊖	d	15 25	15 31	15 36	15 44	15 52	15 55	16 01	16 04	16 06		16 14		16 22	16 25	16 31	16 36	16 44	16 52	16 55		17 01	17 04	17 06	17 14
Clapham Junction 10	d	15 30	15 36	15 41	15 49	15 57	16 00	16 06	16 09	16 11		16 19		16 27	16 30	16 36	16 41	16 49	16 57	17 00		17 06	17 09	17 11	17 19
Earlsfield	d	15 33	15 39	15 44	15 52	16 00	16 03	16 09	16 12	16 14		16 22		16 30	16 33	16 39	16 44	16 52	17 00	17 03		17 09	17 12	17 14	17 22
Wimbledon 6 ⊖ ⇌	d	15 37	15 43	15 48	15 56	16 04	16 07	16 13	16 16	16 18		16 26		16 34	16 37	16 43	16 48	16 56	17 04	17 07		17 13	17 16	17 18	17 26
Raynes Park 6	d	15 40	15 46	15 52		16 07	16 10	16 16		16 22				16 37	16 40	16 46	16 52		17 07	17 10		17 16		17 22	
Motspur Park	d	15 43		15 55			16 13			16 25					16 43		16 55			17 13				17 25	
Malden Manor	d	15 47					16 17								16 47					17 17					
Tolworth	d	15 49					16 19								16 49					17 19					
Chessington North	d	15 52					16 22								16 52					17 22					
Chessington South	a	15 55					16 25								16 55					17 25					
Worcester Park	d			15 58						16 28							16 58							17 28	
Stoneleigh	d			16 01						16 31							17 01							17 31	
Ewell West	d			16 03						16 33							17 03							17 33	
Epsom 3 182	a			16 07						16 37							17 07							17 37	
	d			16 08						16 38							17 08							17 38	
Ashtead 182	d			16 12						16 42							17 12							17 42	
Leatherhead 182	d			16 16						16 46							17 16							17 46	
Box Hill & Westhumble 182	d									16 51														17 51	
Dorking 4 182	a									16 53														17 53	
New Malden 6	d		15 49			16 10		16 19						16 40		16 49			17 10			17 19			
Norbiton	d					16 13								16 43					17 13						
Kingston	a					16 16								16 46					17 16						
	d					16 16							16 35	16 49					17 16						
Hampton Wick	d					16 18							16 37	16 51					17 18						
Teddington	d					16 21							16 40	16 56					17 21						
Strawberry Hill	a												16 43	16 59											
Fulwell	d					16 25													17 25						
Hampton	d					16 29													17 29						
Kempton Park	d					16 32													17 32						
Sunbury	d					16 34													17 34						
Upper Halliford	d					16 36													17 36						
Shepperton	a					16 39													17 39						
Berrylands	d		15 51					16 21								16 51						17 21			
Surbiton 6	d		15 55		16 05			16 25	16 32			16 35				16 55		17 05				17 25	17 32		17 35
Thames Ditton	d		16 00					16 30								17 00						17 30			
Hampton Court	a		16 03					16 33								17 03						17 33			
Hinchley Wood	d								16 36														17 36		
Claygate	d								16 39														17 39		
Oxshott	d								16 42														17 42		
Cobham & Stoke D'abernon	d								16 46														17 46		
Bookham	d			16 22													17 22								
Effingham Junction 6	d			16 26					16 50								17 26						17 50		
Horsley	d			16 28					16 53								17 28						17 53		
Clandon	d			16 33					16 58								17 33						17 58		
London Road (Guildford)	d			16 38					17 03								17 38						18 03		
Guildford	a			16 42	16 46				17 07			17 14					17 42	17 46					18 07		18 14

A To London Waterloo

Table T152-F

Sundays

15 December to 10 May

London - Chessington South, Dorking, Guildford, Shepperton and Hampton Court

Station	SW A	SW A	SW	SW	SW	SW	SW	SW	SW	SW	SW	SW	SW A	SW A	SW	SW	SW	SW	SW	SW	SW	SW
London Waterloo 15 ⊖ d		17 18	17 21	17 27	17 32	17 40	17 48	17 51	17 57	18 00	18 02	18 10		18 18	18 21	18 27	18 32	18 40	18 48	18 51	18 57	19 00
Vauxhall ⊖ d		17 22	17 25	17 31	17 36	17 44	17 52	17 55	18 01	18 04	18 06	18 14		18 22	18 25	18 31	18 36	18 44	18 52	18 55	19 01	19 04
Clapham Junction 10 d		17 27	17 30	17 36	17 41	17 49	17 57	18 00	18 06	18 09	18 11	18 19		18 27	18 30	18 36	18 41	18 49	18 57	19 00	19 06	19 09
Earlsfield d		17 30	17 33	17 39	17 44	17 52	18 00	18 03	18 09	18 12	18 14	18 22		18 30	18 33	18 39	18 44	18 52	19 00	19 03	19 09	19 12
Wimbledon 6 ⊖ d		17 34	17 37	17 43	17 48	17 56	18 04	18 07	18 13	18 16	18 18	18 26		18 34	18 37	18 43	18 48	18 56	19 04	19 07	19 13	19 16
Raynes Park 6 d		17 37	17 40	17 46	17 52		18 07	18 10	18 16		18 22			18 37	18 40	18 46	18 52		19 07	19 10	19 16	
Motspur Park d			17 43		17 55			18 13			18 25				18 43		18 55			19 13		
Malden Manor d			17 47					18 17							18 47					19 17		
Tolworth d			17 49					18 19							18 49					19 19		
Chessington North d			17 52					18 22							18 52					19 22		
Chessington South a			17 55					18 25							18 55					19 25		
Worcester Park d					17 58						18 28						18 58					
Stoneleigh d					18 01						18 31						19 01					
Ewell West d					18 03						18 33						19 03					
Epsom 3 182 a					18 07						18 37						19 07					
d					18 08						18 38						19 08					
Ashtead 182 d					18 12						18 42						19 12					
Leatherhead 182 d					18 16						18 46						19 16					
Box Hill & Westhumble 182 d											18 51											
Dorking 4 182 a											18 53											
New Malden 6 d		17 40		17 49			18 10		18 19					18 40		18 49			19 10		19 19	
Norbiton d		17 43					18 13							18 43					19 13			
Kingston a		17 46					18 16							18 46					19 16			
d	17 35	17 49					18 16						18 35	18 49					19 16			
Hampton Wick d	17 37	17 51					18 18						18 37	18 51					19 18			
Teddington d	17 40	17 56					18 21						18 40	18 56					19 21			
Strawberry Hill a	17 43	17 59											18 43	18 59								
Fulwell d							18 25												19 25			
Hampton d							18 29												19 29			
Kempton Park d							18 32												19 32			
Sunbury d							18 34												19 34			
Upper Halliford d							18 36												19 36			
Shepperton a							18 39												19 39			
Berrylands d				17 51					18 21							18 51					19 21	
Surbiton 6 d				17 55		18 05			18 25	18 32		18 35				18 55		19 05			19 25	19 32
Thames Ditton d				18 00					18 30							19 00					19 30	
Hampton Court a				18 03					18 33							19 03					19 33	
Hinchley Wood d										18 36												19 36
Claygate d										18 39												19 39
Oxshott d										18 42												19 42
Cobham & Stoke D'abernon d										18 46												19 46
Bookham d					18 22												19 22					
Effingham Junction 6 d					18 26					18 50							19 26					19 50
Horsley d					18 28					18 53							19 28					19 53
Clandon d					18 33					18 58							19 33					19 58
London Road (Guildford) d					18 38					19 03							19 38					20 03
Guildford a					18 42	18 46				19 07		19 14					19 42	19 46				20 07

A To London Waterloo

Table T152-F

Sundays

15 December to 10 May

London - Chessington South, Dorking, Guildford, Shepperton and Hampton Court

Station	SW	SW	SW A	SW A	SW	SW	SW	SW	SW	SW	SW	SW	SW	SW A	SW A	SW	SW	SW	SW	SW	SW
London Waterloo 15 ⊖ d	19 02	19 10		19 18	19 21	19 27	19 32	19 40	19 48	19 57	20 00	20 02	20 10		20 18	20 21	20 27	20 32	20 40	20 48	20 57
Vauxhall ⊖ d	19 06	19 14		19 22	19 25	19 31	19 36	19 44	19 52	20 01	20 04	20 06	20 14		20 22	20 25	20 31	20 36	20 44	20 52	21 01
Clapham Junction 10 d	19 11	19 19		19 27	19 30	19 36	19 41	19 49	19 57	20 06	20 09	20 11	20 19		20 27	20 30	20 36	20 41	20 49	20 57	21 06
Earlsfield d	19 14	19 22		19 30	19 33	19 39	19 44	19 52	20 00	20 09	20 12	20 14	20 22		20 30	20 33	20 39	20 44	20 52	21 00	21 09
Wimbledon 6 ⊖ d	19 18	19 26		19 34	19 37	19 43	19 48	19 56	20 04	20 13	20 16	20 18	20 26		20 34	20 37	20 43	20 48	20 56	21 04	21 13
Raynes Park 6 d	19 22			19 37	19 40	19 46	19 52		20 07	20 16		20 22			20 37	20 40	20 46	20 52		21 07	21 16
Motspur Park d	19 25				19 43		19 55					20 25				20 43		20 55			
Malden Manor d					19 47											20 47					
Tolworth d					19 49											20 49					
Chessington North d					19 52											20 52					
Chessington South a					19 55											20 55					
Worcester Park d	19 28						19 58					20 28						20 58			
Stoneleigh d	19 31						20 01					20 31						21 01			
Ewell West d	19 33						20 03					20 33						21 03			
Epsom 3 182 a	19 37						20 07					20 37						21 07			
d	19 38						20 08					20 38						21 08			
Ashtead 182 d	19 42						20 12					20 42						21 12			
Leatherhead 182 d	19 46						20 16					20 46						21 16			
Box Hill & Westhumble 182 d	19 51											20 51									
Dorking 4 182 a	19 53											20 53									
New Malden 6 d				19 40		19 49			20 10	20 19					20 40		20 49			21 10	21 19
Norbiton d				19 43					20 13						20 43					21 13	
Kingston a				19 46					20 16						20 46					21 16	
d			19 35	19 49					20 16					20 35	20 49					21 16	
Hampton Wick d			19 37	19 51					20 18					20 37	20 51					21 18	
Teddington d			19 40	19 56					20 21					20 40	20 56					21 21	
Strawberry Hill a			19 43	19 59										20 43	20 59						
Fulwell d									20 25											21 25	
Hampton d									20 29											21 29	
Kempton Park d									20 32											21 32	
Sunbury d									20 34											21 34	
Upper Halliford d									20 36											21 36	
Shepperton a									20 39											21 41	
Berrylands d						19 51				20 21							20 51				21 21
Surbiton 6 d		19 35				19 55		20 05		20 25	20 32		20 35				20 55		21 05		21 25
Thames Ditton d						20 00				20 30							21 00				21 30
Hampton Court a						20 03				20 33							21 03				21 33
Hinchley Wood d											20 36										
Claygate d											20 39										
Oxshott d											20 42										
Cobham & Stoke D'abernon d											20 46										
Bookham d							20 22											21 22			
Effingham Junction 6 d							20 26				20 50							21 26			
Horsley d							20 28				20 53							21 28			
Clandon d							20 33				20 58							21 33			
London Road (Guildford) d							20 38				21 03							21 38			
Guildford a		20 14					20 42	20 46			21 07		21 14					21 42	21 46		

A To London Waterloo

Table T152-F

Sundays

15 December to 10 May

London - Chessington South, Dorking, Guildford, Shepperton and Hampton Court

		SW	SW	SW	SW A	SW A	SW	SW	SW	SW	SW	SW	SW	SW	SW A	SW A	SW	SW	SW	SW	SW	SW	SW
London Waterloo [15] ⊖	d	21 00	21 02	21 10		21 18	21 21	21 32	21 40	21 48	21 57	22 00	22 02	22 10		22 18	22 21	22 32	22 40	22 48	22 51	22 57	23 00
Vauxhall ⊖	d	21 04	21 06	21 14		21 22	21 25	21 36	21 44	21 52	22 01	22 04	22 06	22 14		22 22	22 25	22 36	22 44	22 52	22 55	23 01	23 04
Clapham Junction [10]	d	21 09	21 11	21 19		21 27	21 30	21 41	21 49	21 57	22 06	22 09	22 11	22 19		22 27	22 30	22 41	22 49	22 57	23 00	23 06	23 09
Earlsfield	d	21 12	21 14	21 22		21 30	21 33	21 44	21 52	22 00	22 09	22 12	22 14	22 22		22 30	22 33	22 44	22 52	23 00	23 03	23 09	23 12
Wimbledon [6] ⊖	d	21 16	21 18	21 26		21 34	21 37	21 48	21 56	22 04	22 13	22 16	22 18	22 26		22 34	22 37	22 48	22 56	23 04	23 07	23 13	23 16
Raynes Park [6]	d		21 22			21 37	21 40	21 52		22 07	22 16		22 22			22 37	22 40	22 52		23 07	23 10	23 16	
Motspur Park	d		21 25				21 43	21 55					22 25				22 43	22 55			23 13		
Malden Manor	d						21 47										22 47				23 17		
Tolworth	d						21 49										22 49				23 19		
Chessington North	d						21 52										22 52				23 22		
Chessington South	a						21 55										22 55				23 25		
Worcester Park	d		21 28					21 58					22 28					22 58					
Stoneleigh	d		21 31					22 01					22 31					23 01					
Ewell West	d		21 33					22 03					22 33					23 03					
Epsom [3] 182	a		21 37					22 07					22 37					23 07					
	d		21 38					22 08					22 38					23 08					
Ashtead 182	d		21 42					22 12					22 42					23 12					
Leatherhead 182	d		21 46					22 16					22 46					23 16					
Box Hill & Westhumble 182	d		21 51										22 51										
Dorking [4] 182	a		21 53										22 53										
New Malden [6]	d					21 40				22 10	22 19					22 40				23 10		23 19	
Norbiton	d					21 43				22 13						22 43				23 13			
Kingston	a					21 46				22 16						22 46				23 16			
	d				21 35	21 49				22 16					22 35	22 49				23 16			
Hampton Wick	d				21 37	21 51				22 18					22 37	22 51				23 18			
Teddington	d				21 40	21 56				22 21					22 40	22 56				23 21			
Strawberry Hill	a				21 43	21 59									22 43	22 59							
Fulwell	d									22 25										23 25			
Hampton	d									22 29										23 29			
Kempton Park	d									22 32										23 32			
Sunbury	d									22 34										23 34			
Upper Halliford	d									22 36										23 36			
Shepperton	a									22 39										23 39			
Berrylands	d										22 21											23 21	
Surbiton [6]	d	21 32		21 35					22 05		22 25	22 32		22 35					23 05			23 25	23 32
Thames Ditton	d										22 30											23 30	
Hampton Court	a										22 33											23 33	
Hinchley Wood	d	21 36										22 36											23 36
Claygate	d	21 39										22 39											23 39
Oxshott	d	21 42										22 42											23 42
Cobham & Stoke D'abernon	d	21 46										22 46											23 46
Bookham	d							22 22										23 22					
Effingham Junction [6]	d	21 50						22 26				22 50						23 26					23 50
Horsley	d	21 53						22 28				22 53						23 28					23 53
Clandon	d	21 58						22 33				22 58						23 33					23 58
London Road (Guildford)	d	22 03						22 38				23 03						23 38					00 03
Guildford	a	22 07		22 14				22 42	22 46			23 07		23 13				23 42	23 46				00 07

A To London Waterloo

Table T152-F

Sundays

15 December to 10 May

London - Chessington South, Dorking, Guildford, Shepperton and Hampton Court

		SW	SW	SW A	SW	SW
London Waterloo [15] ⊖	d	23 02	23 10		23 18	23 32
Vauxhall ⊖	d	23 06	23 14		23 22	23 36
Clapham Junction [10]	d	23 11	23 19		23 27	23 41
Earlsfield	d	23 14	23 22		23 30	23 44
Wimbledon [6] ⊖	d	23 18	23 26		23 34	23 48
Raynes Park [6]	d	23 22			23 37	23 52
Motspur Park	d	23 25				23 55
Malden Manor	d					
Tolworth	d					
Chessington North	d					
Chessington South	a					
Worcester Park	d	23 28				23 58
Stoneleigh	d	23 31				00 01
Ewell West	d	23 33				00 03
Epsom [3] 182	a	23 37				00 07
	d					
Ashtead 182	d					
Leatherhead 182	d					
Box Hill & Westhumble 182	d					
Dorking [4] 182	a					
New Malden [6]	d				23 40	
Norbiton	d				23 43	
Kingston	a				23 46	
	d			23 35	23 47	
Hampton Wick	d			23 37	23 49	
Teddington	d			23 40	23 51	
Strawberry Hill	a			23 43	23 54	
Fulwell	d					
Hampton	d					
Kempton Park	d					
Sunbury	d					
Upper Halliford	d					
Shepperton	a					
Berrylands	d					
Surbiton [6]	d		23 35			
Thames Ditton	d					
Hampton Court	a					
Hinchley Wood	d					
Claygate	d					
Oxshott	d					
Cobham & Stoke D'abernon	d					
Bookham	d					
Effingham Junction [6]	d					
Horsley	d					
Clandon	d					
London Road (Guildford)	d					
Guildford	a		00 19			

A To Twickenham

Table T152-R

Mondays to Fridays

16 December to 15 May

Hampton Court, Shepperton, Guildford, Dorking and Chessington South - London

Miles	Miles	Miles	Miles	Miles			SW MO A	SW MX B	SW MX C	SW MX D	SW MX ◇■ E	SW MX A	SW MX D	SW MO D	SW	SW F	SW	SW	SW	SW ◇	SW	SW	SW	SW D
0	—	—	—	—	**Guildford**	d									04 20			04 58			05 14		05 37		
1¼	—	—	—	—	London Road (Guildford)	d												05 02					05 41		
4½	—	—	—	—	Clandon	d												05 07					05 46		
7¾	—	—	—	—	Horsley	d												05 11					05 50		
8¾	0	—	—	—	Effingham Junction [6]	d												05 15					05 53		
—	1¾	—	—	—	Bookham	d												05 18							
11	—	—	—	—	Cobham & Stoke d'Abernon	d																	05 57		
13	—	—	—	—	Oxshott	d																	06 00		
14¾	—	—	—	—	Claygate	d																	06 03		
16	—	—	—	—	Hinchley Wood	d																	06 06		
—	—	—	0	—	**Hampton Court**	d																05 54			
—	—	—	1	—	Thames Ditton	d						00 02										05 56			
18	—	—	3	—	**Surbiton** [6]	d					00 08	00 12			04 54						05 56	06 02	06 11		
19	—	—	—	—	Berrylands	d						00 14										06 04			
—	—	—	—	0	**Shepperton**	d													05 23						
—	—	—	—	1½	Upper Halliford	d													05 26						
—	—	—	—	2	Sunbury	d													05 28						
—	—	—	—	2½	Kempton Park	d																			
—	—	—	—	4¼	Hampton	d													05 33						
—	—	—	—	6	Fulwell	d													05 36						
—	—	—	0	—	Strawberry Hill	d							00 08	00 15			04 55		05 38						06 07
—	—	—	1¼	7	Teddington	d							00 11	00 18			04 59			05 44					06 11
—	—	—	—	8¼	Hampton Wick	d							00 13	00 21			05 01			05 46					06 14
—	—	—	—	8¾	Kingston	a							00 15	00 23			05 03			05 48					06 16
—	—	—	—	—		d											05 04			05 49					06 19
—	—	—	—	9½	Norbiton	d											05 06			05 51					06 21
20	—	—	—	11	New Malden [6]	d						00 17					05 10			05 55		06 07			06 25
—	—	0	—	—	**Dorking** [4]	182 d																		05 46	
—	—	0¾	—	—	Box Hill & Westhumble	182 d																		05 49	
—	4½	4	—	—	Leatherhead	182 d												05 23						05 55	
—	—	5¾	—	—	Ashtead	182 d												05 27						05 58	
—	—	7¾	—	—	**Epsom** [3]	182 a												05 31						06 03	
—	—	—	—	—		d												05 33						06 04	
—	—	9	—	—	Ewell West	d												05 36						06 07	
—	—	10	—	—	Stoneleigh	d												05 39						06 10	
—	—	11¼	—	—	Worcester Park	d												05 42						06 13	
—	0	—	—	—	**Chessington South**	d																			
—	0¾	—	—	—	Chessington North	d																			
—	1¾	—	—	—	Tolworth	d																			
—	2¾	—	—	—	Malden Manor	d																			
—	3¾	12¼	—	—	Motspur Park	d												05 45						06 16	
21¼	5¼	13¼	—	12	Raynes Park [6]	d	00 01					00 20					05 13	05 49		05 58		06 10		06 19	06 28
22¾	6¾	14¾	—	13½	**Wimbledon** [6]	⊖ ⛴ d	00a04				00 16	00a23			05 02		05 17	05 53		06 02	06 05	06 14	06 20	06 23	06 32
24½	8½	16½	—	15¼	Earlsfield	d											05 21	05 58		06 05	06 08	06 17	06 24	06 27	06 35
26	10	18	—	16¾	**Clapham Junction** [10]	d				00 05	00 23				05 09		05 25	06 02	06 05	06 09	06 12	06 21	06 28	06 31	06 39
28¾	12¾	20¾	—	19½	Vauxhall	⊖ d		00 02	00 05	00 12							05 31	06 07	06 12	06 14	06 17	06 26	06 33	06 36	06 44
30	14	22	—	20¾	**London Waterloo** [15]	⊖ a		00 09	00 11	00 16	00 33				05 18		05 35	06 11	06 16	06 19	06 22	06 31	06 37	06 40	06 49

A From Hampton Court
B From Shepperton
C From Guildford
D From London Waterloo
E From Portsmouth Harbour
F From Twickenham

Table T152-R

Mondays to Fridays

16 December to 15 May

Hampton Court, Shepperton, Guildford, Dorking and Chessington South - London

		SW ◇ A	SW	SW	SW	SW	SW	SW	SW B	SW ◇ A	SW	SW	SW	SW	SW	SW C	SN D	SW	SW B	SW	SW	SW
Guildford	d					05 58	06 04							06 28	06 34		06 39					
London Road (Guildford)	d					06 02	06 08							06 32	06 38		06 42					
Clandon	d					06 07	06 13							06 37	06 43		06 47					
Horsley	d					06 11	06 17							06 41	06 47		06 52					
Effingham Junction [6]	d					06 15	06 21							06 46	06 51		06 55					
Bookham	d					06 18								06 49			06 59					
Cobham & Stoke d'Abernon	d						06 25								06 54							
Oxshott	d						06 28								06 58							
Claygate	d						06 31								07 01							
Hinchley Wood	d						06 34								07 04							
Hampton Court	d			06 23								06 53										
Thames Ditton	d			06 25								06 55										
Surbiton [6]	d	06 28		06 31			06 41			06 57		07 01			07 11	07 15						
Berrylands	d			06 34								07 03										
Shepperton	d				06 10								06 40									
Upper Halliford	d				06 13								06 43									
Sunbury	d				06 15								06 45									
Kempton Park	d																					
Hampton	d				06 19								06 49									
Fulwell	d				06 22								06 52									
Strawberry Hill	d								06 37										07 07			
Teddington	d				06 27				06 41				06 57						07 11		07 19	
Hampton Wick	d				06 29				06 44				06 59						07 14		07 21	
Kingston	a				06 31				06 45				07 01						07 16		07 23	
	d				06 32				06 48				07 02						07 18		07 25	
Norbiton	d				06 34				06 50				07 04						07 20		07 27	
New Malden [6]	d			06 37	06 40				06 55			07 06	07 09						07 25		07 31	
Dorking [4]	182 d										06 31									07 01		
Box Hill & Westhumble	182 d										06 33									07 04		
Leatherhead	182 d					06 23					06 38			06 54			07 05			07 09		
Ashtead	182 d					06 27					06 42			06 57			07 09			07 12		
Epsom [3]	182 a					06 31					06 46			07 02			07 13			07 17		
	d		06 18			06 33					06 47			07 03						07 17		07 21
Ewell West	d		06 21			06 36					06 51			07 06								07 24
Stoneleigh	d		06 24			06 39					06 53			07 09								07 27
Worcester Park	d		06 28			06 42					06 57			07 12						07 24		07 30
Chessington South	d							06 38										07 08				
Chessington North	d							06 40										07 10				
Tolworth	d							06 43										07 13				
Malden Manor	d							06 45										07 15				
Motspur Park	d		06 31			06 45		06 50			07 00			07 14				07 20				07 33
Raynes Park [6]	d		06 35	06 40	06 43	06 49		06 54	06 58		07 04	07 09	07 12	07 18		07 21		07 24	07 28	07 31	07 34	07 37
Wimbledon [6]	⊖ ⛴ d	06 35	06 39	06 44	06 47	06 53	06 50	06 58	07 02	07 05	07 08	07 13	07 16	07 22	07 19	07 25		07 28	07 32	07 35	07 38	07 41
Earlsfield	d	06 39	06 42	06 48	06 51	06 57	06 54	07 02	07 06	07 09	07 12	07 17	07 20	07 26	07 23	07 29		07 32	07 36	07 39	07 42	07 45
Clapham Junction [10]	d	06 43	06 46	06 52	06 55	07 01	06 58	07 06	07 10	07 13	07 16	07 21	07 24	07 30	07 27			07 36	07 40	07 43	07 46	07 49
Vauxhall	⊖ d	06 48	06 51	06 57	07 00	07 06	07 03	07 11	07 15	07 18	07 21	07 26	07 29	07 35	07 32			07 41	07 45	07 48	07 51	07 54
London Waterloo [15]	⊖ a	06 52	06 56	07 03	07 06	07 12	07 09	07 18	07 21	07 24	07 27	07 33	07 35	07 41	07 39	07 43		07 47	07 51	07 55	07 57	08 02

A From Woking
B From London Waterloo
C From Esher
D To London Bridge

Table T152-R

Mondays to Fridays

16 December to 15 May

Hampton Court, Shepperton, Guildford, Dorking and Chessington South - London

		SW	SW	SW	SW	SW	SN		SW	SW	SW	SW	SW	SW	SW	SW	SW		SW	SW	SW	SW	SW	SW	SW
							A				B			C								B			D
Guildford	d				06 58	07 03	07 12		07 16											07 35					
London Road (Guildford)	d				07 02	07 07	07 15		07 20											07 39					
Clandon	d				07 07	07 12			07 25											07 44					
Horsley	d				07 11	07 17			07 29											07 48					
Effingham Junction 6	d				07 16	07 21	07 25		07 33										07 46	07 52					
Bookham	d				07 19		07 29												07 49						
Cobham & Stoke d'Abernon	d					07 24			07 36											07 55					
Oxshott	d					07 28			07 40											07 59					
Claygate	d					07 31			07 43											08 02					
Hinchley Wood	d					07 34			07 46											08 05					
Hampton Court	d		07 23													07 53									
Thames Ditton	d		07 25													07 55									
Surbiton 6	d		07 31			07 41			07 53							08 01				08 11					
Berrylands	d		07 33													08 03									
Shepperton	d	07 00		07 11									07 30				07 41							08 00	
Upper Halliford	d	07 03		07 14									07 33				07 44							08 03	
Sunbury	d	07 05		07 16									07 35				07 46							08 05	
Kempton Park	d																								
Hampton	d	07 09		07 20									07 39				07 50							08 09	
Fulwell	d	07 12		07 23									07 42				07 53							08 12	
Strawberry Hill	d	07 14									07 38		07 44	07 46								08 08		08 14	08 16
Teddington	d			07 28							07 42			07 49			07 58					08 11			08 19
Hampton Wick	d			07 30							07 45			07 51			08 00					08 14			08 21
Kingston	a			07 32							07 47			07 53			08 02					08 16			08 23
	d			07 33							07 48			07 55			08 03					08 18			08 25
Norbiton	d			07 35							07 50			07 57			08 05					08 20			08 27
New Malden 6	d		07 37	07 40		07 45					07 55			08 01		08 06	08 10			08 15		08 25			08 31
Dorking 4	182 d											07 31											08 01		
Box Hill & Westhumble	182 d											07 34											08 04		
Leatherhead	182 d				07 24		07 35					07 39							07 55				08 09		
Ashtead	182 d				07 27		07 39					07 42							07 58				08 12		
Epsom 3	182 a				07 32		07 43					07 47							08 03				08 17		
	d				07 34							07 47			07 51				08 03				08 17		
Ewell West	d				07 37										07 54				08 07						
Stoneleigh	d				07 40										07 57				08 09						
Worcester Park	d				07 43							07 54			08 00				08 13				08 24		
Chessington South	d									07 38											08 08				
Chessington North	d									07 40											08 10				
Tolworth	d									07 43											08 13				
Malden Manor	d									07 45											08 15				
Motspur Park	d				07 46					07 50					08 03				08 16		08 20				
Raynes Park 6	d		07 40	07 43	07 50					07 54	07 58	08 01		08 04	08 07	08 10	08 13		08 20		08 24	08 28	08 31		08 34
Wimbledon 6 ⊖	d		07 44	07 47	07 54	07 50				07 58	08 02	08 05		08 08	08 11	08 14	08 17		08 24	08 20	08 28	08 32	08 35		08 38
Earlsfield	d		07 48	07 51	07 58	07 54				08 02	08 06	08 09		08 12	08 15	08 18	08 21		08 28	08 24	08 32	08 36	08 39		08 42
Clapham Junction 10	d	07 49	07 52	07 55	08 02	07 58				08 06	08 10	08 13	08 19	08 16	08 19	08 22	08 25		08 32	08 28	08 36	08 40	08 43	08 49	08 46
Vauxhall ⊖	d	07 56	07 57	08 00	08 07	08 03				08 11	08 15	08 18	08 26	08 21	08 24	08 27	08 30		08 37	08 33	08 41	08 45	08 48	08 56	08 51
London Waterloo 15 ⊖	a	08 04	08 04	08 06	08 13	08 10			08 13	08 18	08 21	08 24	08 34	08 27	08 32	08 34	08 36		08 43	08 41	08 48	08 51	08 54	09 04	08 57

A To London Bridge
B From London Waterloo
C From Twickenham
D From Clapham Junction

Table T152-R

Mondays to Fridays

16 December to 15 May

Hampton Court, Shepperton, Guildford, Dorking and Chessington South - London

		SW	SW		SW	SW	SW	SW	SW	SW	SW	SW	SW		SW	SW	SW	SW	SW	SW	SW	SW	SW		SW
									A	◇									A	◇					
Guildford	d					07 58	08 07			08 22						08 34				08 46					08 58
London Road (Guildford)	d					08 02	08 11									08 38									09 02
Clandon	d					08 07	08 16									08 43									09 07
Horsley	d					08 11	08 20									08 47									09 11
Effingham Junction 6	d					08 16	08 24								08 46	08 51									09 15
Bookham	d					08 19									08 49										09 18
Cobham & Stoke d'Abernon	d						08 27									08 54									
Oxshott	d						08 31									08 58									
Claygate	d						08 34									09 01									
Hinchley Wood	d						08 37									09 04									
Hampton Court	d		08 23									08 53										09 23			
Thames Ditton	d		08 25									08 55										09 25			
Surbiton 6	d		08 31				08 42			08 57		09 01				09 11				09 27		09 31			
Berrylands	d		08 33									09 03										09 33			
Shepperton	d				08 11								08 41										09 11		
Upper Halliford	d				08 14								08 44										09 14		
Sunbury	d				08 16								08 46										09 16		
Kempton Park	d																						09 18		
Hampton	d				08 20								08 50										09 21		
Fulwell	d				08 23								08 53										09 24		
Strawberry Hill	d								08 38										09 08						
Teddington	d				08 28				08 41				08 58						09 11				09 29		
Hampton Wick	d				08 30				08 44				09 00						09 14				09 31		
Kingston	a				08 32				08 46				09 02						09 16				09 33		
	d				08 33				08 48				09 03						09 18				09 34		
Norbiton	d				08 35				08 50				09 05						09 20				09 36		
New Malden 6	d		08 36		08 40				08 55			09 06	09 10						09 25			09 36	09 40		
Dorking 4	182 d										08 31										09 01				
Box Hill & Westhumble	182 d										08 34										09 04				
Leatherhead	182 d					08 24					08 39				08 54						09 09				09 23
Ashtead	182 d					08 27					08 42				08 57						09 12				09 27
Epsom 3	182 a					08 32					08 47				09 02						09 17				09 31
	d	08 21				08 34					08 47				09 04						09 17				09 34
Ewell West	d	08 24				08 37					08 51				09 07						09 21				09 37
Stoneleigh	d	08 27				08 40					08 53				09 10						09 23				09 40
Worcester Park	d	08 30				08 43					08 57				09 13						09 27				09 43
Chessington South	d							08 38										09 08							
Chessington North	d							08 40										09 10							
Tolworth	d							08 43										09 13							
Malden Manor	d							08 45										09 15							
Motspur Park	d	08 33				08 46		08 50			09 00				09 15			09 20			09 30				09 45
Raynes Park 6	d	08 37	08 40		08 43	08 50		08 54	08 58		09 04	09 10	09 13		09 19		09 22	09 24	09 28		09 34	09 40	09 43		09 49
Wimbledon 6 ⊖	d	08 41	08 44		08 47	08 54		08 58	09 02	09 05	09 08	09 14	09 17		09 23	09 20	09 26	09 29	09 32	09 35	09 38	09 44	09 47		09 53
Earlsfield	d	08 45	08 48		08 51	08 58		09 02	09 06	09 09	09 12	09 18	09 21		09 27	09 24	09 30	09 32	09 36	09 39	09 42	09 47	09 50		09 57
Clapham Junction 10	d	08 49	08 52		08 55	09 02		09 06	09 10	09 13	09 16	09 22	09 25		09 31	09 28		09 36	09 40	09 43	09 46	09 51	09 54		10 01
Vauxhall ⊖	d	08 54	08 57		09 00	09 07		09 11	09 15	09 18	09 21	09 27	09 30		09 36	09 33		09 41	09 45	09 48	09 51	09 56	09 59		10 06
London Waterloo 15 ⊖	a	09 02	09 04		09 06	09 13	09 01	09 18	09 21	09 24	09 27	09 33	09 36		09 42	09 39	09 46	09 48	09 51	09 54	09 57	10 02	10 04		10 10

A From London Waterloo

Table T152-R

Mondays to Fridays
16 December to 15 May

Hampton Court, Shepperton, Guildford, Dorking and Chessington South - London

		SW	SW	SW A	SW B	SW	SW	SW	SW	SW	SW	SW A	SW B	SW	SW	SW	SW	SW	SW	SW A	SW B	SW	SW
Guildford	d	09 07							09 28	09 37							09 58	10 07					
London Road (Guildford)	d	09 11							09 32	09 41							10 02	10 11					
Clandon	d	09 16							09 37	09 46							10 07	10 16					
Horsley	d	09 20							09 41	09 50							10 11	10 20					
Effingham Junction 6	d	09 23							09 45	09 53							10 15	10 23					
Bookham	d								09 48								10 18						
Cobham & Stoke d'Abernon	d	09 27								09 57								10 27					
Oxshott	d	09 30								10 00								10 30					
Claygate	d	09 33								10 03								10 33					
Hinchley Wood	d	09 36								10 06								10 36					
Hampton Court	d						09 54								10 24								10 54
Thames Ditton	d						09 56								10 26								10 56
Surbiton 6	d	09 41			09 57		10 02			10 11			10 27		10 32			10 41			10 57		11 02
Berrylands	d						10 04								10 34								11 04
Shepperton	d							09 41								10 11							
Upper Halliford	d							09 44								10 14							
Sunbury	d							09 46								10 16							
Kempton Park	d							09 48								10 18							
Hampton	d							09 51								10 21							
Fulwell	d							09 54								10 24							
Strawberry Hill	d			09 37								10 07								10 37			
Teddington	d			09 41				09 59				10 11				10 29				10 41			
Hampton Wick	d			09 44				10 01				10 14				10 31				10 44			
Kingston	a			09 46				10 03				10 16				10 33				10 46			
	d			09 48				10 04				10 18				10 34				10 48			
Norbiton	d			09 50				10 06				10 20				10 36				10 50			
New Malden 6	d			09 55			10 07	10 10				10 25			10 37	10 40				10 55			11 07
Dorking 4	182 d					09 32								10 02								10 32	
Box Hill & Westhumble	182 d					09 35								10 05								10 35	
Leatherhead	182 d					09 40			09 53					10 10			10 23					10 40	
Ashtead	182 d					09 43			09 57					10 13			10 27					10 43	
Epsom 3	182 a					09 48			10 01					10 18			10 31					10 48	
	d					09 49			10 04					10 19			10 34					10 49	
Ewell West	d					09 52			10 07					10 22			10 37					10 52	
Stoneleigh	d					09 55			10 10					10 25			10 40					10 55	
Worcester Park	d					09 58			10 13					10 28			10 43					10 58	
Chessington South	d		09 38								10 08								10 38				
Chessington North	d		09 40								10 10								10 40				
Tolworth	d		09 43								10 13								10 43				
Malden Manor	d		09 45								10 15								10 45				
Motspur Park	d		09 49			10 00			10 15		10 19			10 30			10 45		10 49			11 00	
Raynes Park 6	d		09 53	09 58		10 04	10 10	10 13	10 19		10 23	10 28		10 34	10 40	10 43	10 49		10 53	10 58		11 04	11 10
Wimbledon 6 ⊖ ⛴	d	09 50	09 57	10 02	10 05	10 08	10 14	10 17	10 23	10 20	10 27	10 32	10 35	10 38	10 44	10 47	10 53	10 50	10 57	11 02	11 05	11 08	11 14
Earlsfield	d	09 54	10 01	10 05	10 08	10 12	10 17	10 20	10 27	10 24	10 31	10 35	10 38	10 42	10 47	10 50	10 57	10 54	11 01	11 05	11 08	11 12	11 17
Clapham Junction 10	d	09 58	10 05	10 09	10 12	10 16	10 21	10 24	10 31	10 28	10 35	10 39	10 42	10 46	10 51	10 54	11 01	10 58	11 05	11 09	11 12	11 16	11 21
Vauxhall ⊖	d	10 03	10 10	10 14	10 17	10 21	10 26	10 29	10 36	10 33	10 40	10 44	10 47	10 51	10 56	10 59	11 06	11 03	11 10	11 14	11 17	11 21	11 26
London Waterloo 15 ⊖	a	10 07	10 16	10 19	10 22	10 25	10 31	10 34	10 40	10 37	10 46	10 49	10 52	10 55	11 01	11 04	11 10	11 07	11 16	11 19	11 22	11 25	11 31

A From London Waterloo
B From Woking

Table T152-R

Mondays to Fridays
16 December to 15 May

Hampton Court, Shepperton, Guildford, Dorking and Chessington South - London

		SW	SW	SW	SW	SW A	SW B	SW	SW	SW	SW	SW	SW	SW A	SW B	SW	SW	SW	SW	SW	SW	SW A	SW B
Guildford	d		10 28	10 37							10 58	11 07							11 28	11 37			
London Road (Guildford)	d		10 32	10 41							11 02	11 11							11 32	11 41			
Clandon	d		10 37	10 46							11 07	11 16							11 37	11 46			
Horsley	d		10 41	10 50							11 11	11 20							11 41	11 50			
Effingham Junction 6	d		10 45	10 53							11 15	11 23							11 45	11 53			
Bookham	d		10 48								11 18								11 48				
Cobham & Stoke d'Abernon	d			10 57								11 27								11 57			
Oxshott	d			11 00								11 30								12 00			
Claygate	d			11 03								11 33								12 03			
Hinchley Wood	d			11 06								11 36								12 06			
Hampton Court	d								11 24								11 54						
Thames Ditton	d								11 26								11 56						
Surbiton 6	d			11 11			11 27		11 32			11 41			11 57		12 02			12 11			12 27
Berrylands	d								11 34								12 04						
Shepperton	d	10 41								11 11								11 41					
Upper Halliford	d	10 44								11 14								11 44					
Sunbury	d	10 46								11 16								11 46					
Kempton Park	d	10 48								11 18								11 48					
Hampton	d	10 51								11 21								11 51					
Fulwell	d	10 54								11 24								11 54					
Strawberry Hill	d					11 07								11 37								12 07	
Teddington	d	10 59				11 11				11 29				11 41				11 59				12 11	
Hampton Wick	d	11 01				11 14				11 31				11 44				12 01				12 14	
Kingston	a	11 03				11 16				11 33				11 46				12 03				12 16	
	d	11 04				11 18				11 34				11 48				12 04				12 18	
Norbiton	d	11 06				11 20				11 36				11 50				12 06				12 20	
New Malden 6	d	11 10				11 25			11 37	11 40				11 55			12 07	12 10				12 25	
Dorking 4	182 d							11 02								11 32							
Box Hill & Westhumble	182 d							11 05								11 35							
Leatherhead	182 d		10 53					11 10			11 23					11 40			11 53				
Ashtead	182 d		10 57					11 13			11 27					11 43			11 57				
Epsom 3	182 a		11 01					11 18			11 31					11 48			12 01				
	d		11 04					11 19			11 34					11 49			12 04				
Ewell West	d		11 07					11 22			11 37					11 52			12 07				
Stoneleigh	d		11 10					11 25			11 40					11 55			12 10				
Worcester Park	d		11 13					11 28			11 43					11 58			12 13				
Chessington South	d				11 08								11 38								12 08		
Chessington North	d				11 10								11 40								12 10		
Tolworth	d				11 13								11 43								12 13		
Malden Manor	d				11 15								11 45								12 15		
Motspur Park	d		11 15		11 19			11 30			11 45		11 49			12 00			12 15		12 19		
Raynes Park 6	d	11 13	11 19		11 23	11 28		11 34	11 40	11 43	11 49		11 53	11 58		12 04	12 10	12 13	12 19		12 23	12 28	
Wimbledon 6 ⊖ ⛴	d	11 17	11 23	11 20	11 27	11 32	11 35	11 38	11 44	11 47	11 53	11 50	11 57	12 02	12 05	12 08	12 14	12 16	12 23	12 20	12 27	12 32	12 35
Earlsfield	d	11 20	11 27	11 24	11 31	11 35	11 38	11 42	11 47	11 50	11 57	11 54	12 01	12 05	12 08	12 12	12 17	12 20	12 27	12 24	12 31	12 35	12 38
Clapham Junction 10	d	11 24	11 31	11 28	11 35	11 39	11 42	11 46	11 51	11 54	12 01	11 58	12 05	12 09	12 12	12 16	12 21	12 24	12 31	12 28	12 35	12 39	12 42
Vauxhall ⊖	d	11 29	11 36	11 33	11 40	11 44	11 47	11 51	11 56	11 59	12 06	12 03	12 10	12 14	12 17	12 21	12 26	12 29	12 36	12 33	12 40	12 44	12 47
London Waterloo 15 ⊖	a	11 34	11 40	11 37	11 46	11 49	11 52	11 55	12 01	12 04	12 10	12 07	12 16	12 19	12 22	12 25	12 31	12 34	12 40	12 37	12 46	12 49	12 52

A From London Waterloo
B From Woking

Table T152-R

Mondays to Fridays

16 December to 15 May

Hampton Court, Shepperton, Guildford, Dorking and Chessington South - London

		SW	SW	SW	SW	SW	SW	SW A	SW B	SW	SW	SW	SW	SW	SW	SW A	SW B	SW	SW	SW	SW	SW
Guildford	d				11 58	12 07							12 28	12 37							12 58	13 07
London Road (Guildford)	d				12 02	12 11							12 32	12 41							13 02	13 11
Clandon	d				12 07	12 16							12 37	12 46							13 07	13 16
Horsley	d				12 11	12 20							12 41	12 50							13 11	13 20
Effingham Junction 6	d				12 15	12 23							12 45	12 53							13 15	13 23
Bookham	d				12 18								12 48								13 18	
Cobham & Stoke d'Abernon	d					12 27								12 57								13 27
Oxshott	d					12 30								13 00								13 30
Claygate	d					12 33								13 03								13 33
Hinchley Wood	d					12 36								13 06								13 36
Hampton Court	d		12 24								12 54								13 24			
Thames Ditton	d		12 26								12 56								13 26			
Surbiton 6	d		12 32			12 41			12 57		13 02			13 11			13 27		13 32			13 41
Berrylands	d		12 34								13 04								13 34			
Shepperton	d			12 11								12 41								13 11		
Upper Halliford	d			12 14								12 44								13 14		
Sunbury	d			12 16								12 46								13 16		
Kempton Park	d			12 18								12 48								13 18		
Hampton	d			12 21								12 51								13 21		
Fulwell	d			12 24								12 54								13 24		
Strawberry Hill	d							12 37								13 07						
Teddington	d			12 29				12 41				12 59				13 11				13 29		
Hampton Wick	d			12 31				12 44				13 01				13 14				13 31		
Kingston	a			12 33				12 46				13 03				13 16				13 33		
	d			12 34				12 48				13 04				13 18				13 34		
Norbiton	d			12 36				12 50				13 06				13 20				13 36		
New Malden 6	d		12 37	12 40				12 55			13 07	13 10				13 25			13 37	13 40		
Dorking 4	182 d	12 02								12 32								13 02				
Box Hill & Westhumble	182 d	12 05								12 35								13 05				
Leatherhead	182 d	12 10			12 23					12 40			12 53					13 10			13 23	
Ashtead	182 d	12 13			12 27					12 43			12 57					13 13			13 27	
Epsom 3	182 a	12 18			12 31					12 48			13 01					13 18			13 31	
	d	12 19			12 34					12 49			13 04					13 19			13 34	
Ewell West	d	12 22			12 37					12 52			13 07					13 22			13 37	
Stoneleigh	d	12 25			12 40					12 55			13 10					13 25			13 40	
Worcester Park	d	12 28			12 43					12 58			13 13					13 28			13 43	
Chessington South	d						12 38								13 08							
Chessington North	d						12 40								13 10							
Tolworth	d						12 43								13 13							
Malden Manor	d						12 45								13 15							
Motspur Park	d	12 30			12 45		12 49			13 00			13 15		13 19			13 30			13 45	
Raynes Park 6	d	12 34	12 40	12 43	12 49		12 53	12 58		13 04	13 10	13 13	13 19		13 23	13 28		13 34	13 40	13 43	13 49	
Wimbledon 6 ⊖ ⛴	d	12 38	12 44	12 47	12 53	12 50	12 57	13 02	13 05	13 08	13 14	13 17	13 23	13 20	13 27	13 32	13 35	13 38	13 44	13 47	13 53	13 50
Earlsfield	d	12 42	12 47	12 50	12 57	12 54	13 01	13 05	13 08	13 12	13 17	13 20	13 27	13 24	13 31	13 35	13 38	13 42	13 47	13 50	13 57	13 54
Clapham Junction 10	d	12 46	12 51	12 54	13 01	12 58	13 05	13 09	13 12	13 16	13 21	13 24	13 31	13 28	13 35	13 39	13 42	13 46	13 51	13 54	14 01	13 58
Vauxhall ⊖	d	12 51	12 56	12 59	13 06	13 03	13 10	13 14	13 17	13 21	13 26	13 29	13 36	13 33	13 40	13 44	13 47	13 51	13 56	13 59	14 06	14 03
London Waterloo 15 ⊖	a	12 55	13 01	13 04	13 10	13 07	13 16	13 19	13 22	13 25	13 31	13 34	13 40	13 37	13 46	13 49	13 52	13 55	14 01	14 04	14 10	14 07

A From London Waterloo B From Woking

Table T152-R

Mondays to Fridays

16 December to 15 May

Hampton Court, Shepperton, Guildford, Dorking and Chessington South - London

		SW	SW A	SW B	SW	SW	SW	SW	SW	SW	SW A	SW B	SW	SW	SW	SW	SW	SW	SW A	SW B	SW	SW	SW
Guildford	d							13 28	13 37							13 58	14 07						
London Road (Guildford)	d							13 32	13 41							14 02	14 11						
Clandon	d							13 37	13 46							14 07	14 16						
Horsley	d							13 41	13 50							14 11	14 20						
Effingham Junction 6	d							13 45	13 53							14 15	14 23						
Bookham	d							13 48								14 18							
Cobham & Stoke d'Abernon	d								13 57								14 27						
Oxshott	d								14 00								14 30						
Claygate	d								14 03								14 33						
Hinchley Wood	d								14 06								14 36						
Hampton Court	d					13 54								14 24								14 54	
Thames Ditton	d					13 56								14 26								14 56	
Surbiton 6	d			13 57		14 02			14 11			14 27		14 32			14 41			14 57		15 02	
Berrylands	d					14 04								14 34								15 04	
Shepperton	d						13 41								14 11								14 41
Upper Halliford	d						13 44								14 14								14 44
Sunbury	d						13 46								14 16								14 46
Kempton Park	d						13 48								14 18								14 48
Hampton	d						13 51								14 21								14 51
Fulwell	d						13 54								14 24								14 54
Strawberry Hill	d		13 37								14 07								14 38				
Teddington	d		13 41				13 59				14 11				14 29				14 42				14 59
Hampton Wick	d		13 44				14 01				14 14				14 31				14 45				15 01
Kingston	a		13 46				14 03				14 16				14 33				14 47				15 03
	d		13 48				14 04				14 18				14 34				14 48				15 04
Norbiton	d		13 50				14 06				14 20				14 36				14 50				15 06
New Malden 6	d		13 55			14 07	14 10				14 25			14 37	14 40				14 55			15 07	15 10
Dorking 4	182 d				13 32								14 02								14 32		
Box Hill & Westhumble	182 d				13 35								14 05								14 35		
Leatherhead	182 d				13 40			13 53					14 10			14 23					14 40		
Ashtead	182 d				13 43			13 57					14 13			14 27					14 43		
Epsom 3	182 a				13 48			14 01					14 18			14 31					14 48		
	d				13 49			14 04					14 19			14 34					14 49		
Ewell West	d				13 52			14 07					14 22			14 37					14 52		
Stoneleigh	d				13 55			14 10					14 25			14 40					14 55		
Worcester Park	d				13 58			14 13					14 28			14 43					14 58		
Chessington South	d	13 38								14 08								14 38					
Chessington North	d	13 40								14 10								14 40					
Tolworth	d	13 43								14 13								14 43					
Malden Manor	d	13 45								14 15								14 45					
Motspur Park	d	13 49			14 00			14 15		14 19			14 30			14 45		14 49			15 00		
Raynes Park 6	d	13 53	13 58		14 04	14 10	14 13	14 19		14 23	14 28		14 34	14 40	14 43	14 49		14 53	14 58		15 04	15 10	15 13
Wimbledon 6 ⊖ ⛴	d	13 57	14 02	14 05	14 08	14 14	14 17	14 23	14 20	14 27	14 32	14 35	14 38	14 44	14 47	14 53	14 50	14 57	15 02	15 05	15 08	15 14	15 17
Earlsfield	d	14 01	14 05	14 08	14 12	14 17	14 20	14 27	14 24	14 31	14 35	14 38	14 42	14 47	14 50	14 57	14 54	15 01	15 05	15 08	15 12	15 17	15 20
Clapham Junction 10	d	14 05	14 09	14 12	14 16	14 21	14 24	14 31	14 28	14 35	14 39	14 42	14 46	14 51	14 54	15 01	14 58	15 05	15 09	15 12	15 16	15 21	15 24
Vauxhall ⊖	d	14 10	14 14	14 17	14 21	14 26	14 29	14 36	14 33	14 40	14 44	14 47	14 51	14 56	14 59	15 06	15 03	15 10	15 14	15 17	15 21	15 26	15 29
London Waterloo 15 ⊖	a	14 16	14 19	14 22	14 25	14 31	14 34	14 40	14 37	14 46	14 49	14 52	14 55	15 01	15 04	15 10	15 07	15 16	15 19	15 22	15 25	15 31	15 34

A From London Waterloo B From Woking

Table T152-R

Mondays to Fridays

16 December to 15 May

Hampton Court, Shepperton, Guildford, Dorking and Chessington South - London

		SW	SW		SW	SW A	SW B	SW	SW	SW	SW	SW	SW		SW A	SW B	SW	SW	SW	SW	SW	SW	SW A		SW B
Guildford	d	14 28	14 37								14 58	15 07								15 28	15 37				
London Road (Guildford)	d	14 32	14 41								15 02	15 11								15 32	15 41				
Clandon	d	14 37	14 46								15 07	15 16								15 37	15 46				
Horsley	d	14 41	14 50								15 11	15 20								15 41	15 50				
Effingham Junction [6]	d	14 45	14 53								15 15	15 23								15 45	15 53				
Bookham	d	14 48									15 18									15 48					
Cobham & Stoke d'Abernon	d		14 57									15 27									15 57				
Oxshott	d		15 00									15 30									16 00				
Claygate	d		15 03									15 33									16 03				
Hinchley Wood	d		15 06									15 36									16 06				
Hampton Court	d								15 24									15 54							
Thames Ditton	d								15 26									15 56							
Surbiton [6]	d		15 11				15 27		15 32			15 41				15 57		16 02			16 11				16 27
Berrylands	d								15 34									16 04							
Shepperton	d									15 11									15 41						
Upper Halliford	d									15 14									15 44						
Sunbury	d									15 16									15 46						
Kempton Park	d									15 18									15 48						
Hampton	d									15 21									15 51						
Fulwell	d									15 24									15 54						
Strawberry Hill	d					15 07									15 37								16 07		
Teddington	d					15 11				15 29					15 41				15 59				16 11		
Hampton Wick	d					15 14				15 31					15 44				16 01				16 14		
Kingston	a					15 16				15 33					15 46				16 03				16 16		
	d					15 18				15 34					15 48				16 04				16 18		
Norbiton	d					15 20				15 36					15 50				16 06				16 20		
New Malden [6]	d					15 25			15 37	15 40					15 55			16 07	16 10				16 25		
Dorking [4]	182 d							15 02									15 32								
Box Hill & Westhumble	182 d							15 05									15 35								
Leatherhead	182 d	14 53						15 10			15 23						15 40			15 53					
Ashtead	182 d	14 57						15 13			15 27						15 43			15 57					
Epsom [3]	182 a	15 01						15 18			15 31						15 48			16 01					
	d	15 04						15 19			15 34						15 49			16 04					
Ewell West	d	15 07						15 22			15 37						15 52			16 07					
Stoneleigh	d	15 10						15 25			15 40						15 55			16 10					
Worcester Park	d	15 13						15 28			15 43						15 58			16 13					
Chessington South	d				15 08								15 38									16 08			
Chessington North	d				15 10								15 40									16 10			
Tolworth	d				15 13								15 43									16 13			
Malden Manor	d				15 15								15 45									16 15			
Motspur Park	d	15 15			15 19			15 30			15 45		15 49				16 00			16 15		16 19			
Raynes Park [6]	d	15 19			15 23	15 28		15 34	15 40	15 43	15 49		15 53		15 58		16 04	16 10	16 13	16 19		16 23	16 28		
Wimbledon [6] ⊖	d	15 23	15 20		15 27	15 32	15 35	15 38	15 44	15 47	15 53	15 50	15 57		16 02	16 05	16 08	16 14	16 17	16 23	16 20	16 27	16 32		16 35
Earlsfield	d	15 27	15 24		15 31	15 35	15 38	15 42	15 47	15 50	15 57	15 54	16 01		16 05	16 08	16 12	16 17	16 20	16 27	16 24	16 31	16 35		16 38
Clapham Junction [10]	d	15 31	15 28		15 35	15 39	15 42	15 46	15 51	15 54	16 01	15 58	16 05		16 09	16 12	16 16	16 21	16 24	16 31	16 28	16 35	16 39		16 42
Vauxhall ⊖	d	15 36	15 33		15 40	15 44	15 47	15 51	15 56	15 59	16 06	16 03	16 10		16 14	16 17	16 21	16 26	16 29	16 36	16 33	16 40	16 44		16 47
London Waterloo [15] ⊖	a	15 40	15 37		15 46	15 49	15 52	15 55	16 01	16 04	16 10	16 07	16 16		16 19	16 22	16 25	16 31	16 34	16 40	16 37	16 46	16 49		16 52

A From London Waterloo **B** From Woking

Table T152-R

Mondays to Fridays

16 December to 15 May

Hampton Court, Shepperton, Guildford, Dorking and Chessington South - London

		SW	SW	SW	SW	SW	SW	SW A	SW B		SW	SW	SW	SW	SW	SW	SW A	SW B	SW		SW	SW	SW	SW	SW
Guildford	d				15 58	16 07								16 28	16 37								16 58	17 07	
London Road (Guildford)	d				16 02	16 11								16 32	16 41								17 02	17 11	
Clandon	d				16 07	16 16								16 37	16 46								17 07	17 16	
Horsley	d				16 11	16 20								16 41	16 50								17 11	17 20	
Effingham Junction [6]	d				16 15	16 23								16 45	16 53								17 15	17 23	
Bookham	d				16 18									16 48									17 18		
Cobham & Stoke d'Abernon	d					16 27									16 57									17 27	
Oxshott	d					16 30									17 00									17 30	
Claygate	d					16 33									17 03									17 33	
Hinchley Wood	d					16 36									17 06									17 36	
Hampton Court	d		16 24									16 54									17 24				
Thames Ditton	d		16 26									16 56									17 26				
Surbiton [6]	d		16 32			16 41			16 57			17 01			17 11			17 26			17 31			17 41	
Berrylands	d		16 34									17 04									17 34				
Shepperton	d			16 11									16 41									17 11			
Upper Halliford	d			16 14									16 44									17 14			
Sunbury	d			16 16									16 46									17 16			
Kempton Park	d			16 18									16 48									17 18			
Hampton	d			16 21									16 51									17 21			
Fulwell	d			16 24									16 54									17 24			
Strawberry Hill	d							16 37									17 07								
Teddington	d			16 29				16 43					16 59				17 13					17 29			
Hampton Wick	d			16 31				16 46					17 01				17 16					17 31			
Kingston	a			16 33				16 48					17 03				17 18					17 33			
	d			16 34				16 48					17 04				17 18					17 34			
Norbiton	d			16 36				16 50					17 06				17 20					17 36			
New Malden [6]	d		16 37	16 40				16 55				17 07	17 10				17 25				17 37	17 40			
Dorking [4]	182 d	16 02									16 32								17 02						
Box Hill & Westhumble	182 d	16 05									16 35								17 05						
Leatherhead	182 d	16 10			16 23						16 40			16 53					17 10				17 23		
Ashtead	182 d	16 13			16 27						16 43			16 57					17 13				17 27		
Epsom [3]	182 a	16 18			16 31						16 48			17 01					17 18				17 31		
	d	16 19			16 34						16 49			17 04					17 19				17 34		
Ewell West	d	16 22			16 37						16 52			17 07					17 22				17 37		
Stoneleigh	d	16 25			16 40						16 55			17 10					17 25				17 40		
Worcester Park	d	16 28			16 43						16 58			17 13					17 28				17 43		
Chessington South	d						16 38									17 08									17 38
Chessington North	d						16 40									17 10									17 40
Tolworth	d						16 43									17 13									17 43
Malden Manor	d						16 45									17 15									17 45
Motspur Park	d	16 30			16 45		16 49				17 00			17 15		17 19			17 30				17 45		17 49
Raynes Park [6]	d	16 34	16 40	16 43	16 49		16 53	16 58			17 04	17 09	17 13	17 19		17 23	17 28		17 34		17 39	17 43	17 49		17 53
Wimbledon [6] ⊖	d	16 38	16 44	16 47	16 53	16 50	16 57	17 02	17 05		17 08	17 13	17 17	17 23	17 20	17 27	17 32	17 35	17 38		17 43	17 47	17 53	17 50	17 58
Earlsfield	d	16 42	16 47	16 50	16 57	16 54	17 01	17 05	17 08		17 12	17 17	17 20	17 27	17 24	17 31	17 35	17 38	17 42		17 47	17 50	17 57	17 54	18 01
Clapham Junction [10]	d	16 46	16 51	16 54	17 01	16 58	17 05	17 09	17 12		17 16	17 21	17 24	17 31	17 28	17 35	17 39	17 42	17 46		17 51	17 54	18 01	17 58	18 05
Vauxhall ⊖	d	16 51	16 56	16 59	17 06	17 03	17 10	17 14	17 17		17 21	17 26	17 29	17 36	17 33	17 40	17 44	17 47	17 51		17 56	17 59	18 06	18 03	18 10
London Waterloo [15] ⊖	a	16 55	17 01	17 04	17 10	17 07	17 16	17 19	17 22		17 25	17 30	17 35	17 40	17 37	17 47	17 49	17 52	17 55		18 00	18 04	18 10	18 07	18 16

A From London Waterloo **B** From Woking

Table T152-R

Mondays to Fridays

16 December to 15 May

Hampton Court, Shepperton, Guildford, Dorking and Chessington South - London

		SW A	SW B	SW	SW A	SW	SW	SW	SW	SW	SW A	SW B	SW	SW	SW	SW	SW	SW	SW A	SW B	SW	SW	SW
Guildford	d							17 28	17 37							17 56	18 07						
London Road (Guildford)	d							17 32	17 41							18 00	18 11						
Clandon	d							17 37	17 46							18 05	18 16						
Horsley	d							17 41	17 50							18 09	18 20						
Effingham Junction 6	d							17 45	17 53							18 15	18 23						
Bookham	d							17 48								18 18							
Cobham & Stoke d'Abernon	d								17 57								18 27						
Oxshott	d								18 00								18 30						
Claygate	d								18 03								18 33						
Hinchley Wood	d								18 06								18 36						
Hampton Court	d					17 54								18 24								18 54	
Thames Ditton	d					17 56								18 26								18 56	
Surbiton 6	d		17 56			18 01			18 11			18 26		18 31			18 41			18 56		19 02	
Berrylands	d					18 04								18 34								19 04	
Shepperton	d						17 41								18 11								18 36
Upper Halliford	d						17 44								18 14								18 39
Sunbury	d						17 46								18 16								18 41
Kempton Park	d						17 48								18 18								18 43
Hampton	d						17 51								18 21								18 51
Fulwell	d						17 54								18 24								18 54
Strawberry Hill	d	17 37			17 41						18 07								18 37				
Teddington	d	17 43			17 52		17 59				18 13				18 29				18 43				18 59
Hampton Wick	d	17 46			17 54		18 01				18 16				18 31				18 46				19 01
Kingston	a	17 48			17 56		18 03				18 18				18 33				18 48				19 03
	d	17 48			17 58		18 04				18 18				18 34				18 48				19 04
Norbiton	d	17 50			18 00		18 06				18 20				18 36				18 50				19 06
New Malden 6	d	17 55			18 04	18 07	18 10				18 25			18 37	18 40				18 55			19 07	19 10
Dorking 4	182 d			17 32									17 53								18 32		
Box Hill & Westhumble	182 d			17 35									17 56								18 35		
Leatherhead	182 d			17 40				17 53					18 01			18 23					18 40		
Ashtead	182 d			17 43				17 57					18 04			18 27					18 43		
Epsom 3	182 a			17 48				18 01					18 09			18 31					18 48		
	d			17 48				18 04					18 19			18 34					18 49		
Ewell West	d			17 52				18 07					18 22			18 37					18 52		
Stoneleigh	d			17 54				18 10					18 25			18 40					18 55		
Worcester Park	d			17 57				18 13					18 28			18 43					18 58		
Chessington South	d									18 08								18 38					
Chessington North	d									18 10								18 40					
Tolworth	d									18 13								18 43					
Malden Manor	d									18 15								18 45					
Motspur Park	d			18 00				18 15		18 19			18 30			18 45		18 49			19 00		
Raynes Park 6	d	17 57		18 03	18 06	18 09	18 13	18 19		18 22	18 28		18 34	18 39	18 43	18 49		18 53	18 58		19 04	19 10	19 13
Wimbledon 6 ⊖ ⇌	d	18 01	18 04	18 07	18 10	18 13	18 17	18 23	18 20	18 26	18 32	18 35	18 38	18 43	18 47	18 53	18 50	18 57	19 02	19 05	19 08	19 14	19 17
Earlsfield	d	18 05	18 08	18 11	18 14	18 17	18 20	18 27	18 24	18 30	18 35	18 38	18 42	18 47	18 50	18 57	18 54	19 01	19 05	19 08	19 12	19 17	19 20
Clapham Junction 10	d	18 09	18 12	18 15	18 18	18 21	18 24	18 31	18 28	18 34	18 39	18 42	18 46	18 51	18 54	19 01	18 58	19 05	19 09	19 12	19 16	19 21	19 24
Vauxhall ⊖	d	18 14	18 17	18 20	18 23	18 26	18 29	18 36	18 33	18 39	18 44	18 47	18 51	18 56	18 59	19 06	19 03	19 10	19 14	19 17	19 21	19 26	19 29
London Waterloo 15 ⊖	a	18 19	18 21	18 24	18 27	18 30	18 34	18 41	18 39	18 45	18 49	18 53	18 55	19 00	19 04	19 11	19 09	19 15	19 19	19 24	19 26	19 31	19 34

A From London Waterloo B From Woking

Table T152-R

Mondays to Fridays

16 December to 15 May

Hampton Court, Shepperton, Guildford, Dorking and Chessington South - London

		SW	SW	SW	SW A	SW B	SW	SW	SW	SW	SN C	SW	SW	SW A	SW B	SW	SW	SW	SW	SW	SW	SW A
Guildford	d	18 28	18 35								19 02	19 07							19 28	19 37		
London Road (Guildford)	d	18 32	18 39								19 06	19 11							19 32	19 41		
Clandon	d	18 37	18 44								19 11	19 16							19 37	19 46		
Horsley	d	18 41	18 48								19 16	19 20							19 41	19 50		
Effingham Junction 6	d	18 45	18 51							19 12	19 19	19 23							19 45	19 53		
Bookham	d	18 48								19 18	19 23								19 48			
Cobham & Stoke d'Abernon	d		18 55									19 27								19 57		
Oxshott	d		18 58									19 30								20 00		
Claygate	d		19 01									19 33								20 03		
Hinchley Wood	d		19 04									19 36								20 06		
Hampton Court	d							19 24									19 54					
Thames Ditton	d							19 26									19 56					
Surbiton 6	d		19 11			19 27		19 32				19 41			19 57		20 02			20 11		
Berrylands	d							19 34									20 04					
Shepperton	d								19 06									19 36				
Upper Halliford	d								19 09									19 39				
Sunbury	d								19 11									19 41				
Kempton Park	d								19 13									19 43				
Hampton	d								19 21									19 51				
Fulwell	d								19 24									19 54				
Strawberry Hill	d				19 07									19 37								20 07
Teddington	d				19 13				19 29					19 43				19 59				20 12
Hampton Wick	d				19 16				19 31					19 46				20 01				20 14
Kingston	a				19 18				19 33					19 48				20 03				20 16
	d				19 18				19 34					19 48				20 04				20 18
Norbiton	d				19 20				19 36					19 50				20 06				20 20
New Malden 6	d				19 25			19 37	19 40					19 55			20 07	20 10				20 25
Dorking 4	182 d						19 03									19 32						
Box Hill & Westhumble	182 d						19 05									19 35						
Leatherhead	182 d	18 55					19 10			19 23	19 29					19 40			19 53			
Ashtead	182 d	18 58					19 14			19 27	19 34					19 43			19 57			
Epsom 3	182 a	19 03					19 18			19 31	19 41					19 48			20 01			
	d	19 04					19 19			19 34						19 49			20 04			
Ewell West	d	19 07					19 22			19 37						19 52			20 07			
Stoneleigh	d	19 10					19 25			19 40						19 55			20 10			
Worcester Park	d	19 13					19 28			19 43						19 58			20 13			
Chessington South	d			19 08									19 38								20 08	
Chessington North	d			19 10									19 40								20 10	
Tolworth	d			19 13									19 43								20 13	
Malden Manor	d			19 15									19 45								20 15	
Motspur Park	d	19 15		19 20			19 30			19 45			19 49			20 00			20 15		20 19	
Raynes Park 6	d	19 19		19 23	19 28		19 34	19 40	19 43	19 49			19 53	19 58		20 04	20 10	20 13	20 19		20 23	20 28
Wimbledon 6 ⊖ ⇌	d	19 23	19 20	19 27	19 32	19 35	19 38	19 44	19 47	19 53		19 50	19 57	20 02	20 05	20 08	20 14	20 17	20 23	20 20	20 27	20 32
Earlsfield	d	19 27	19 24	19 31	19 35	19 39	19 42	19 47	19 50	19 57		19 54	20 01	20 05	20 08	20 12	20 17	20 20	20 27	20 24	20 31	20 35
Clapham Junction 10	d	19 31	19 28	19 35	19 39	19 42	19 46	19 51	19 54	20 01		19 58	20 05	20 09	20 12	20 16	20 21	20 24	20 31	20 28	20 35	20 39
Vauxhall ⊖	d	19 36	19 33	19 40	19 44	19 47	19 51	19 56	19 59	20 06		20 03	20 10	20 14	20 17	20 21	20 26	20 29	20 36	20 33	20 40	20 44
London Waterloo 15 ⊖	a	19 41	19 37	19 46	19 49	19 52	19 55	20 01	20 04	20 10		20 07	20 16	20 19	20 22	20 25	20 31	20 34	20 40	20 37	20 46	20 49

A From London Waterloo B From Woking C To London Bridge

Table T152-R

Mondays to Fridays

16 December to 15 May

Hampton Court, Shepperton, Guildford, Dorking and Chessington South - London

		SW A	SW	SW	SW	SW	SW	SW	SW B	SW A	SW	SW	SW	SW	SW	SW	SW B	SW A	SW	SW	SW	SW	SW
Guildford	d					19 58	20 07							20 28	20 37							20 58	21 07
London Road (Guildford)	d					20 02	20 11							20 32	20 41							21 02	21 11
Clandon	d					20 07	20 16							20 37	20 46							21 07	21 16
Horsley	d					20 11	20 20							20 41	20 50							21 11	21 20
Effingham Junction 6	d					20 15	20 23							20 45	20 53							21 15	21 23
Bookham	d					20 18								20 48								21 18	
Cobham & Stoke d'Abernon	d						20 27								20 57								21 27
Oxshott	d						20 30								21 00								21 30
Claygate	d						20 33								21 03								21 33
Hinchley Wood	d						20 36								21 06								21 36
Hampton Court	d			20 24								20 54								21 24			
Thames Ditton	d			20 26								20 56								21 26			
Surbiton 6	d	20 26		20 32			20 41			20 57		21 02			21 11			21 27		21 32			21 41
Berrylands	d			20 34								21 04								21 34			
Shepperton	d				20 11								20 41								21 11		
Upper Halliford	d				20 14								20 44								21 14		
Sunbury	d				20 16								20 46								21 16		
Kempton Park	d				20 18								20 48								21 18		
Hampton	d				20 21								20 51								21 21		
Fulwell	d				20 24								20 54								21 24		
Strawberry Hill	d								20 38								21 07						
Teddington	d				20 29				20 41				20 59				21 11				21 29		
Hampton Wick	d				20 31				20 44				21 01				21 14				21 31		
Kingston	a				20 33				20 46				21 03				21 16				21 33		
	d				20 34				20 48				21 04				21 18				21 34		
Norbiton	d				20 36				20 50				21 06				21 20				21 36		
New Malden 6	d			20 37	20 40				20 55			21 07	21 10				21 25			21 37	21 40		
Dorking 4 182	d		20 02								20 32								21 02				
Box Hill & Westhumble 182	d		20 05								20 35								21 05				
Leatherhead 182	d		20 10			20 23					20 40			20 55					21 10			21 23	
Ashtead 182	d		20 13			20 27					20 43			20 59					21 12			21 27	
Epsom 3 182	a		20 18			20 31					20 48			21 03					21 18			21 31	
	d		20 19			20 34					20 49			21 04					21 19			21 34	
Ewell West	d		20 22			20 37					20 52			21 07					21 22			21 37	
Stoneleigh	d		20 25			20 40					20 55			21 10					21 25			21 40	
Worcester Park	d		20 28			20 43					20 58			21 13					21 28			21 43	
Chessington South	d							20 38								21 08							
Chessington North	d							20 40								21 10							
Tolworth	d							20 43								21 13							
Malden Manor	d							20 45								21 15							
Motspur Park	d		20 30			20 45		20 49			21 00			21 15		21 19			21 30			21 45	
Raynes Park 6	d		20 34	20 40	20 43	20 49		20 53	20 58		21 04	21 10	21 13	21 20		21 23	21 28		21 34	21 40	21 43	21 49	
Wimbledon 6 ⊖ ⛴	d	20 35	20 38	20 44	20 47	20 53	20 50	20 57	21 02	21 05	21 08	21 14	21 17	21 24	21 21	21 27	21 32	21 35	21 38	21 44	21 47	21 53	21 50
Earlsfield	d	20 39	20 42	20 47	20 50	20 57	20 54	21 01	21 05	21 08	21 12	21 17	21 20	21 28	21 25	21 31	21 35	21 38	21 42	21 47	21 50	21 57	21 54
Clapham Junction 10	d	20 42	20 46	20 51	20 54	21 01	20 58	21 05	21 09	21 12	21 16	21 21	21 24	21 32	21 29	21 35	21 39	21 42	21 46	21 51	21 54	22 01	21 58
Vauxhall ⊖	d	20 47	20 51	20 56	20 59	21 06	21 03	21 10	21 14	21 17	21 21	21 26	21 29	21 37	21 34	21 40	21 44	21 47	21 51	21 56	21 59	22 06	22 03
London Waterloo 15 ⊖	a	20 52	20 55	21 01	21 04	21 10	21 07	21 16	21 19	21 22	21 25	21 31	21 34	21 41	21 38	21 46	21 49	21 52	21 55	22 01	22 04	22 10	22 07

A From Woking   B From London Waterloo

Table T152-R

Mondays to Fridays

16 December to 15 May

Hampton Court, Shepperton, Guildford, Dorking and Chessington South - London

		SW	SW A	SW B	SW	SW	SW	SW	SW	SW	SW A	SW B	SW	SW	SW	SW	SW	SW	SW A	SW B	SW	SW
Guildford	d							21 28	21 37							21 58	22 07					
London Road (Guildford)	d							21 32	21 41							22 02	22 11					
Clandon	d							21 37	21 46							22 07	22 16					
Horsley	d							21 41	21 50							22 11	22 20					
Effingham Junction 6	d							21 45	21 53							22 15	22 23					
Bookham	d							21 48								22 18						
Cobham & Stoke d'Abernon	d								21 57								22 27					
Oxshott	d								22 00								22 30					
Claygate	d								22 03								22 33					
Hinchley Wood	d								22 06								22 36					
Hampton Court	d					21 54								22 24								22 54
Thames Ditton	d					21 56								22 26								22 56
Surbiton 6	d			21 57		22 02			22 11			22 27		22 32			22 41			22 57		23 02
Berrylands	d					22 04								22 34								23 04
Shepperton	d						21 41								22 11							
Upper Halliford	d						21 44								22 14							
Sunbury	d						21 46								22 16							
Kempton Park	d						21 48								22 18							
Hampton	d						21 51								22 21							
Fulwell	d						21 54								22 24							
Strawberry Hill	d		21 37								22 07								22 37			
Teddington	d		21 41				21 59				22 11				22 29				22 41			
Hampton Wick	d		21 44				22 01				22 14				22 31				22 44			
Kingston	a		21 46				22 03				22 16				22 33				22 46			
	d		21 48				22 04				22 18				22 34				22 48			
Norbiton	d		21 50				22 06				22 20				22 36				22 50			
New Malden 6	d		21 55			22 07	22 10				22 25			22 37	22 40				22 55			23 07
Dorking 4 182	d				21 32								22 02								22 32	
Box Hill & Westhumble 182	d				21 35								22 05								22 35	
Leatherhead 182	d				21 40			21 53					22 10			22 23					22 40	
Ashtead 182	d				21 43			21 57					22 12			22 27					22 43	
Epsom 3 182	a				21 48			22 01					22 18			22 31					22 48	
	d				21 49			22 04					22 19			22 34					22 49	
Ewell West	d				21 52			22 07					22 22			22 37					22 52	
Stoneleigh	d				21 55			22 10					22 25			22 40					22 55	
Worcester Park	d				21 58			22 13					22 28			22 43					22 58	
Chessington South	d	21 38								22 08								22 38				
Chessington North	d	21 40								22 10								22 40				
Tolworth	d	21 43								22 13								22 43				
Malden Manor	d	21 45								22 15								22 45				
Motspur Park	d	21 49			22 00			22 15		22 19			22 30			22 45		22 49			23 00	
Raynes Park 6	d	21 54	21 58		22 04	22 10	22 13	22 19		22 23	22 28		22 34	22 40	22 43	22 49		22 53	22 58		23 04	23 10
Wimbledon 6 ⊖ ⛴	d	21 57	22 02	22 05	22 08	22 14	22 17	22 23	22 20	22a27	22 32	22 35	22 38	22 44	22 47	22 53	22 50	22 57	23 02	23 05	23 08	23 14
Earlsfield	d	22 01	22 05	22 08	22 12	22 17	22 20	22 27	22 24		22 35	22 38	22 42	22 47	22 50	22 57	22 54	23 01	23 05	23 08	23 11	23 17
Clapham Junction 10	d	22 05	22 09	22 12	22 16	22 21	22 24	22 31	22 28		22 39	22 42	22 46	22 51	22 54	23 01	22 58	23 05	23 09	23 12	23 15	23 21
Vauxhall ⊖	d	22 10	22 14	22 17	22 21	22 26	22 29	22 36	22 33		22 44	22 47	22 51	22 56	22 59	23 06	23 03	23 10	23 14	23 17	23 20	23 26
London Waterloo 15 ⊖	a	22 16	22 19	22 22	22 25	22 32	22 34	22 40	22 39		22 49	22 54	22 56	23 03	23 06	23 12	23 09	23 16	23 19	23 26	23 28	23 31

A From London Waterloo   B From Woking

Table T152-R

Mondays to Fridays
16 December to 15 May

Hampton Court, Shepperton, Guildford, Dorking and Chessington South - London

		SW	SW	SW	SW A	SW FO B	SW FX B	SW FO	SW FX	SW	SW	SW	SW	SW FX A	SW FO A	SW ◇1 C	SW
Guildford	d		22 37					22 46	22 46			23 07				23 39	
London Road (Guildford)	d		22 41					22 50	22 50			23 11					
Clandon	d		22 46					22 55	22 55			23 16					
Horsley	d		22 50					22 59	22 59			23 20					
Effingham Junction [6]	d		22 53					23 03	23 03			23 23					
Bookham	d							23 06	23 06								
Cobham & Stoke d'Abernon	d		22 57									23 27					
Oxshott	d		23 00									23 30					
Claygate	d		23 03									23 33					
Hinchley Wood	d		23 06									23 36					
Hampton Court	d									23 24							23 59
Thames Ditton	d									23 26							00 02
Surbiton [6]	d		23 11			23 27	23 27			23 32		23 41				00 08	00 12
Berrylands	d									23 34		23 43					00 14
Shepperton	d	22 41									23 11						
Upper Halliford	d	22 44									23 14						
Sunbury	d	22 46									23 16						
Kempton Park	d	22 48									23 18						
Hampton	d	22 51									23 21						
Fulwell	d	22 54									23 24						
Strawberry Hill	d				23 07									23 37	23 37		
Teddington	d	22 59			23 11						23 29			23 41	23 41		
Hampton Wick	d	23 01			23 14						23 31			23 44	23 44		
Kingston	a	23 03			23 16						23 33			23 46	23 46		
	d	23 04			23 18						23 34			23 49	23 49		
Norbiton	d	23 06			23 20						23 36			23 51	23 51		
New Malden [6]	d	23 10			23 25					23 37	23 41	23 46		23 55	23 55		00 17
Dorking [4] 182	d																
Box Hill & Westhumble 182	d																
Leatherhead 182	d							23 11	23 11								
Ashtead 182	d							23 14	23 14								
Epsom [3] 182	a							23 19	23 19								
	d							23 19	23 19								
Ewell West	d							23 22	23 22								
Stoneleigh	d							23 25	23 25								
Worcester Park	d							23 28	23 28								
Chessington South	d			23 08									23 40				
Chessington North	d			23 10									23 42				
Tolworth	d			23 13									23 44				
Malden Manor	d			23 15									23 47				
Motspur Park	d			23 19				23 30	23 30				23 50				
Raynes Park [6]	d	23 13		23 23	23 28			23 34	23 34	23 40	23 43	23 49	23 54	23 58	23 58		00 20
Wimbledon [6] ⊖	d	23 17	23 20	23a27	23 32	23 36	23 36	23 38	23 38	23a44	23 50	23 53	23a57	00 02	00 02	00 16	00a23
Earlsfield	d	23 20	23 24		23 36	23 39	23 39	23 42	23 42		23 53	23 56		00 05	00 05		
Clapham Junction [10]	d	23 25	23 28		23 40	23 43	23 43	23 46	23 46		23 57	23 59		00 09	00 09	00 23	
Vauxhall ⊖	d	23 30	23 33		23 45	23 48	23 48	23 51	23 51		00 02	00 05		00 14	00 14		
London Waterloo [15] ⊖	a	23 34	23 37		23 49	23 56	23 57	23 58	23 59		00 09	00 11		00 20	00 22	00 33	

A From London Waterloo
B From Woking
C From Portsmouth Harbour

Table T152-R

Saturdays
21 December to 16 May

Hampton Court, Shepperton, Guildford, Dorking and Chessington South - London

		SW A	SW B	SW C	SW ◇1 D	SW E	SW C	SW	SW F	SW	SW	SW	SW	SW	SW C	SW G	SW	SW	SW	SW	SW C	SW G	SW
Guildford	d							04 25				05 14											
London Road (Guildford)	d																						
Clandon	d																						
Horsley	d																						
Effingham Junction [6]	d																						
Bookham	d																						
Cobham & Stoke d'Abernon	d																						
Oxshott	d																						
Claygate	d																						
Hinchley Wood	d																						
Hampton Court	d												05 54				06 24						06 54
Thames Ditton	d					00 02							05 56				06 26						06 56
Surbiton [6]	d				00 08	00 12		04 54				05 56	06 02			06 26	06 32					06 57	07 02
Berrylands	d					00 14							06 04				06 34						07 04
Shepperton	d																	06 11					
Upper Halliford	d																	06 14					
Sunbury	d																	06 16					
Kempton Park	d																	06 18					
Hampton	d																	06 21					
Fulwell	d																	06 24					
Strawberry Hill	d						00 08		04 55						06 07						06 37		
Teddington	d						00 11		04 59		05 44				06 11			06 29			06 41		
Hampton Wick	d						00 13		05 01		05 46				06 14			06 31			06 44		
Kingston	a						00 15		05 03		05 48				06 16			06 33			06 46		
	d								05 04		05 49				06 18			06 34			06 48		
Norbiton	d								05 06		05 51				06 20			06 36			06 50		
New Malden [6]	d					00 17			05 10		05 55		06 07		06 25		06 37	06 40			06 55		07 07
Dorking [4] 182	d																						
Box Hill & Westhumble 182	d																						
Leatherhead 182	d																						
Ashtead 182	d																						
Epsom [3] 182	a																						
	d									05 34				06 04					06 34				
Ewell West	d									05 37				06 07					06 37				
Stoneleigh	d									05 40				06 10					06 40				
Worcester Park	d									05 43				06 13					06 43				
Chessington South	d																			06 38			
Chessington North	d																			06 40			
Tolworth	d																			06 43			
Malden Manor	d																			06 45			
Motspur Park	d									05 45				06 15					06 45	06 49			
Raynes Park [6]	d					00 20			05 13	05 49	05 58		06 10	06 19	06 28		06 40	06 43	06 49	06 53	06 58		07 10
Wimbledon [6] ⊖	d				00 16	00a23		05 02	05 17	05 53	06 02	06 05	06 14	06 23	06 32	06 35	06 44	06 47	06 53	06 57	07 02	07 05	07 14
Earlsfield	d								05 21	05 58	06 05	06 08	06 17	06 27	06 35	06 38	06 47	06 50	06 57	07 01	07 05	07 08	07 17
Clapham Junction [10]	d			00 05	00 23			05 09	05 25	06 02	06 09	06 12	06 21	06 31	06 39	06 42	06 51	06 54	07 01	07 05	07 09	07 12	07 21
Vauxhall ⊖	d	00 02	00 05	00 12					05 30	06 07	06 14	06 17	06 26	06 36	06 44	06 47	06 56	06 59	07 06	07 10	07 14	07 17	07 26
London Waterloo [15] ⊖	a	00 09	00 11	00 16	00 33			05 18	05 35	06 11	06 19	06 22	06 31	06 40	06 49	06 54	07 01	07 05	07 10	07 16	07 19	07 22	07 31

A From Shepperton
B From Guildford
C From London Waterloo
D From Portsmouth Harbour
E From Hampton Court
F From Twickenham
G From Woking

Table T152-R

Saturdays

21 December to 16 May

Hampton Court, Shepperton, Guildford, Dorking and Chessington South - London

		SW	SW	SW	SW	SW A		SW B	SW	SW	SW	SW	SW	SW A	SW B	SW		SW	SW	SW	SW	SW A	SW B	SW	SW
Guildford	d		06 28	06 37							06 58	07 07							07 28	07 37					
London Road (Guildford)	d		06 32	06 41							07 02	07 11							07 32	07 41					
Clandon	d		06 37	06 46							07 07	07 16							07 37	07 46					
Horsley	d		06 41	06 50							07 11	07 20							07 41	07 50					
Effingham Junction 6	d		06 45	06 53							07 15	07 23							07 45	07 53					
Bookham	d		06 48								07 18								07 48						
Cobham & Stoke d'Abernon	d			06 57								07 27								07 57					
Oxshott	d			07 00								07 30								08 00					
Claygate	d			07 03								07 33								08 03					
Hinchley Wood	d			07 06								07 36								08 06					
Hampton Court	d								07 24							07 54									08 24
Thames Ditton	d								07 26							07 56									08 26
Surbiton 6	d			07 11				07 27	07 32			07 41			07 57	08 02				08 11			08 27		08 32
Berrylands	d								07 34							08 04									08 34
Shepperton	d	06 41								07 11								07 41							
Upper Halliford	d	06 44								07 14								07 44							
Sunbury	d	06 46								07 16								07 46							
Kempton Park	d	06 48								07 18								07 48							
Hampton	d	06 51								07 21								07 51							
Fulwell	d	06 54								07 24								07 54							
Strawberry Hill	d					07 07								07 37								08 07			
Teddington	d	06 59				07 11				07 29				07 41				07 59				08 11			
Hampton Wick	d	07 01				07 14				07 31				07 44				08 01				08 14			
Kingston	a	07 03				07 16				07 33				07 46				08 03				08 16			
	d	07 04				07 18				07 34				07 48				08 04				08 18			
Norbiton	d	07 06				07 20				07 36				07 50				08 06				08 20			
New Malden 6	d	07 10				07 25			07 37	07 40				07 55		08 07		08 10				08 25			08 37
Dorking 4	182 d																							08 02	
Box Hill & Westhumble	182 d																							08 05	
Leatherhead	182 d		06 55								07 23								07 53					08 10	
Ashtead	182 d		06 59								07 27								07 57					08 13	
Epsom 3	182 a		07 04								07 31								08 01					08 18	
	d		07 04								07 34								08 04					08 19	
Ewell West	d		07 08								07 37								08 07					08 22	
Stoneleigh	d		07 10								07 40								08 10					08 25	
Worcester Park	d		07 13								07 43								08 13					08 28	
Chessington South	d				07 08								07 38								08 08				
Chessington North	d				07 10								07 40								08 10				
Tolworth	d				07 13								07 43								08 13				
Malden Manor	d				07 15								07 45								08 15				
Motspur Park	d		07 16		07 19						07 45		07 49						08 15		08 19			08 30	
Raynes Park 6	d	07 13	07 19		07 23	07 28			07 40	07 43	07 49		07 53	07 58		08 10		08 13	08 19		08 23	08 28		08 34	08 40
Wimbledon 6 ⊖	d	07 17	07 23	07 20	07 27	07 32		07 35	07 44	07 47	07 53	07 50	07 57	08 02	08 05	08 14		08 17	08 23	08 20	08 27	08 32	08 35	08 38	08 44
Earlsfield	d	07 20	07 27	07 24	07 31	07 35		07 38	07 47	07 50	07 57	07 54	08 01	08 05	08 08	08 17		08 20	08 27	08 24	08 31	08 35	08 38	08 42	08 47
Clapham Junction 10	d	07 24	07 31	07 28	07 35	07 39		07 42	07 51	07 54	08 01	07 58	08 05	08 09	08 12	08 21		08 24	08 31	08 28	08 35	08 39	08 42	08 46	08 51
Vauxhall ⊖	d	07 29	07 36	07 33	07 40	07 44		07 47	07 56	07 59	08 06	08 03	08 10	08 14	08 17	08 26		08 29	08 36	08 33	08 40	08 44	08 47	08 51	08 56
London Waterloo 15 ⊖	a	07 35	07 40	07 37	07 46	07 49		07 52	08 01	08 05	08 10	08 07	08 16	08 19	08 22	08 31		08 35	08 40	08 37	08 46	08 49	08 52	08 55	09 01

A From London Waterloo   B From Woking

Table T152-R

Saturdays

21 December to 16 May

Hampton Court, Shepperton, Guildford, Dorking and Chessington South - London

		SW		SW	SW	SW	SW A	SW B	SW	SW	SW	SW		SW	SW	SW A	SW B	SW	SW	SW	SW	SW		SW	SW A
Guildford	d			07 58	08 07							08 28		08 37							08 58	09 07			
London Road (Guildford)	d			08 02	08 11							08 32		08 41							09 02	09 11			
Clandon	d			08 07	08 16							08 37		08 46							09 07	09 16			
Horsley	d			08 11	08 20							08 41		08 50							09 11	09 20			
Effingham Junction 6	d			08 15	08 23							08 45		08 53							09 15	09 23			
Bookham	d			08 18								08 48									09 18				
Cobham & Stoke d'Abernon	d				08 27									08 57								09 27			
Oxshott	d				08 30									09 00								09 30			
Claygate	d				08 33									09 03								09 33			
Hinchley Wood	d				08 36									09 06								09 36			
Hampton Court	d									08 54									09 24						
Thames Ditton	d									08 56									09 26						
Surbiton 6	d				08 41			08 57		09 02				09 11			09 27		09 32			09 41			
Berrylands	d									09 04									09 34						
Shepperton	d	08 11									08 41									09 11					
Upper Halliford	d	08 14									08 44									09 14					
Sunbury	d	08 16									08 46									09 16					
Kempton Park	d	08 18									08 48									09 18					
Hampton	d	08 21									08 51									09 21					
Fulwell	d	08 24									08 54									09 24					
Strawberry Hill	d						08 37									09 07									09 37
Teddington	d	08 29					08 41				08 59					09 11				09 29					09 41
Hampton Wick	d	08 31					08 44				09 01					09 14				09 31					09 44
Kingston	a	08 33					08 46				09 03					09 16				09 33					09 46
	d	08 34					08 48				09 04					09 18				09 34					09 48
Norbiton	d	08 36					08 50				09 06					09 20				09 36					09 50
New Malden 6	d	08 40					08 55			09 07	09 10					09 25			09 37	09 40					09 55
Dorking 4	182 d								08 32									09 02							
Box Hill & Westhumble	182 d								08 35									09 05							
Leatherhead	182 d			08 23					08 40			08 53						09 10			09 23				
Ashtead	182 d			08 27					08 43			08 57						09 13			09 27				
Epsom 3	182 a			08 31					08 48			09 01						09 18			09 31				
	d			08 34					08 49			09 04						09 19			09 34				
Ewell West	d			08 37					08 52			09 07						09 22			09 37				
Stoneleigh	d			08 40					08 55			09 10						09 25			09 40				
Worcester Park	d			08 43					08 58			09 13						09 28			09 43				
Chessington South	d					08 38									09 08									09 38	
Chessington North	d					08 40									09 10									09 40	
Tolworth	d					08 43									09 13									09 43	
Malden Manor	d					08 45									09 15									09 45	
Motspur Park	d			08 45		08 49			09 00			09 15			09 19			09 30			09 45			09 49	
Raynes Park 6	d	08 43		08 49		08 53	08 58		09 04	09 10	09 13	09 19			09 23	09 28		09 34	09 40	09 43	09 49			09 53	09 58
Wimbledon 6 ⊖	d	08 47		08 53	08 50	08 57	09 02	09 05	09 08	09 14	09 17	09 23		09 20	09 27	09 32	09 35	09 38	09 44	09 47	09 53	09 50		09 57	10 02
Earlsfield	d	08 50		08 57	08 54	09 01	09 05	09 08	09 12	09 17	09 20	09 27		09 24	09 31	09 35	09 38	09 42	09 47	09 50	09 57	09 54		10 01	10 05
Clapham Junction 10	d	08 54		09 01	08 58	09 05	09 09	09 12	09 16	09 21	09 24	09 31		09 28	09 35	09 39	09 42	09 46	09 51	09 54	10 01	09 58		10 05	10 09
Vauxhall ⊖	d	08 59		09 06	09 03	09 10	09 14	09 17	09 21	09 26	09 29	09 36		09 33	09 40	09 44	09 47	09 51	09 56	09 59	10 06	10 03		10 10	10 14
London Waterloo 15 ⊖	a	09 05		09 10	09 07	09 16	09 19	09 22	09 25	09 31	09 35	09 40		09 37	09 46	09 49	09 52	09 55	10 01	10 05	10 10	10 07		10 16	10 19

A From London Waterloo   B From Woking

Table T152-R

Saturdays

21 December to 16 May

Hampton Court, Shepperton, Guildford, Dorking and Chessington South - London

		SW A	SW	SW	SW	SW	SW	SW		SW B	SW A	SW	SW	SW	SW	SW	SW	SW B		SW A	SW	SW	SW	SW	SW
Guildford	d					09 28	09 37								09 58	10 07								10 28	10 37
London Road (Guildford)	d					09 32	09 41								10 02	10 11								10 32	10 41
Clandon	d					09 37	09 46								10 07	10 16								10 37	10 46
Horsley	d					09 41	09 50								10 11	10 20								10 41	10 50
Effingham Junction 6	d					09 45	09 53								10 15	10 23								10 45	10 53
Bookham	d					09 48									10 18									10 48	
Cobham & Stoke d'Abernon	d						09 57									10 27									10 57
Oxshott	d						10 00									10 30									11 00
Claygate	d						10 03									10 33									11 03
Hinchley Wood	d						10 06									10 36									11 06
Hampton Court	d			09 54									10 24									10 54			
Thames Ditton	d			09 56									10 26									10 56			
Surbiton 6	d	09 57		10 02			10 11				10 27		10 32			10 41				10 57		11 02			11 11
Berrylands	d			10 04									10 34									11 04			
Shepperton	d				09 41									10 11									10 41		
Upper Halliford	d				09 44									10 14									10 44		
Sunbury	d				09 46									10 16									10 46		
Kempton Park	d				09 48									10 18									10 48		
Hampton	d				09 51									10 21									10 51		
Fulwell	d				09 54									10 24									10 54		
Strawberry Hill	d									10 07								10 37							
Teddington	d				09 59					10 11				10 29				10 41					10 59		
Hampton Wick	d				10 01					10 14				10 31				10 44					11 01		
Kingston	a				10 03					10 16				10 33				10 46					11 03		
	d				10 04					10 18				10 34				10 48					11 04		
Norbiton	d				10 06					10 20				10 36				10 50					11 06		
New Malden 6	d			10 07	10 10					10 25			10 37	10 40				10 55				11 07	11 10		
Dorking 4	182 d		09 32									10 02									10 32				
Box Hill & Westhumble	182 d		09 35									10 05									10 35				
Leatherhead	182 d		09 40			09 53						10 10			10 23						10 40			10 53	
Ashtead	182 d		09 43			09 57						10 13			10 27						10 43			10 57	
Epsom 3	182 a		09 48			10 01						10 18			10 31						10 48			11 01	
	d		09 49			10 04						10 19			10 34						10 49			11 04	
Ewell West	d		09 52			10 07						10 22			10 37						10 52			11 07	
Stoneleigh	d		09 55			10 10						10 25			10 40						10 55			11 10	
Worcester Park	d		09 58			10 13						10 28			10 43						10 58			11 13	
Chessington South	d							10 08									10 38								
Chessington North	d							10 10									10 40								
Tolworth	d							10 13									10 43								
Malden Manor	d							10 15									10 45								
Motspur Park	d		10 00			10 15		10 19				10 30			10 45		10 49				11 00			11 15	
Raynes Park 6	d		10 04	10 10	10 13	10 19		10 23		10 28		10 34	10 40	10 43	10 49		10 53	10 58			11 04	11 10	11 13	11 19	
Wimbledon 6 ⊖ ⛴	d	10 05	10 08	10 14	10 17	10 23	10 20	10 27		10 32	10 35	10 38	10 44	10 47	10 53	10 50	10 57	11 02		11 05	11 08	11 14	11 17	11 23	11 20
Earlsfield	d	10 08	10 12	10 17	10 20	10 27	10 24	10 31		10 35	10 38	10 42	10 47	10 50	10 57	10 54	11 01	11 05		11 08	11 12	11 17	11 20	11 27	11 24
Clapham Junction 10	d	10 12	10 16	10 21	10 24	10 31	10 28	10 35		10 39	10 42	10 46	10 51	10 54	11 01	10 58	11 05	11 09		11 12	11 16	11 21	11 24	11 31	11 28
Vauxhall ⊖	d	10 17	10 21	10 26	10 29	10 36	10 33	10 40		10 44	10 47	10 51	10 56	10 59	11 06	11 03	11 10	11 14		11 17	11 21	11 26	11 29	11 36	11 33
London Waterloo 15 ⊖	a	10 22	10 25	10 31	10 35	10 40	10 37	10 46		10 49	10 52	10 55	11 01	11 05	11 10	11 07	11 16	11 19		11 22	11 25	11 31	11 35	11 40	11 37

A From Woking

B From London Waterloo

Table T152-R

Saturdays

21 December to 16 May

Hampton Court, Shepperton, Guildford, Dorking and Chessington South - London

		SW	SW A	SW B		SW	SW	SW	SW	SW	SW	SW A	SW B	SW		SW	SW	SW	SW	SW	SW A	SW B	SW	SW
Guildford	d								10 58	11 07								11 28	11 37					
London Road (Guildford)	d								11 02	11 11								11 32	11 41					
Clandon	d								11 07	11 16								11 37	11 46					
Horsley	d								11 11	11 20								11 41	11 50					
Effingham Junction 6	d								11 15	11 23								11 45	11 53					
Bookham	d								11 18									11 48						
Cobham & Stoke d'Abernon	d									11 27									11 57					
Oxshott	d									11 30									12 00					
Claygate	d									11 33									12 03					
Hinchley Wood	d									11 36									12 06					
Hampton Court	d						11 24									11 54								12 24
Thames Ditton	d						11 26									11 56								12 26
Surbiton 6	d			11 27			11 32			11 41			11 57			12 02			12 11			12 27		12 32
Berrylands	d						11 34									12 04								12 34
Shepperton	d							11 11									11 41							
Upper Halliford	d							11 14									11 44							
Sunbury	d							11 16									11 46							
Kempton Park	d							11 18									11 48							
Hampton	d							11 21									11 51							
Fulwell	d							11 24									11 54							
Strawberry Hill	d		11 07									11 37									12 07			
Teddington	d		11 11					11 29				11 41					11 59				12 11			
Hampton Wick	d		11 14					11 31				11 44					12 01				12 14			
Kingston	a		11 16					11 33				11 46					12 03				12 16			
	d		11 18					11 34				11 48					12 04				12 18			
Norbiton	d		11 20					11 36				11 50					12 06				12 20			
New Malden 6	d		11 25				11 37	11 40				11 55				12 07	12 10				12 25			12 37
Dorking 4	182 d					11 02								11 32									12 02	
Box Hill & Westhumble	182 d					11 05								11 35									12 05	
Leatherhead	182 d					11 10			11 23					11 40				11 53					12 10	
Ashtead	182 d					11 13			11 27					11 43				11 57					12 13	
Epsom 3	182 a					11 18			11 31					11 48				12 01					12 18	
	d					11 19			11 34					11 49				12 04					12 19	
Ewell West	d					11 22			11 37					11 52				12 07					12 22	
Stoneleigh	d					11 25			11 40					11 55				12 10					12 25	
Worcester Park	d					11 28			11 43					11 58				12 13					12 28	
Chessington South	d	11 08									11 38									12 08				
Chessington North	d	11 10									11 40									12 10				
Tolworth	d	11 13									11 43									12 13				
Malden Manor	d	11 15									11 45									12 15				
Motspur Park	d	11 19				11 30			11 45		11 49			12 00				12 15		12 19			12 30	
Raynes Park 6	d	11 23	11 28			11 34	11 40	11 43	11 49		11 53	11 58		12 04		12 10	12 13	12 19		12 23	12 28		12 34	12 40
Wimbledon 6 ⊖ ⛴	d	11 27	11 32	11 35		11 38	11 44	11 47	11 53	11 50	11 57	12 02	12 05	12 08		12 14	12 17	12 23	12 20	12 27	12 32	12 35	12 38	12 44
Earlsfield	d	11 31	11 35	11 38		11 42	11 47	11 50	11 57	11 54	12 01	12 05	12 08	12 12		12 17	12 20	12 27	12 24	12 31	12 35	12 38	12 42	12 47
Clapham Junction 10	d	11 35	11 39	11 42		11 46	11 51	11 54	12 01	11 58	12 05	12 09	12 12	12 16		12 21	12 24	12 31	12 28	12 35	12 39	12 42	12 46	12 51
Vauxhall ⊖	d	11 40	11 44	11 47		11 51	11 56	11 59	12 06	12 03	12 10	12 14	12 17	12 21		12 26	12 29	12 36	12 33	12 40	12 44	12 47	12 51	12 56
London Waterloo 15 ⊖	a	11 46	11 49	11 52		11 55	12 01	12 05	12 10	12 07	12 16	12 19	12 22	12 25		12 31	12 35	12 40	12 37	12 46	12 49	12 52	12 55	13 01

A From London Waterloo

B From Woking

Table T152-R

Saturdays

21 December to 16 May

Hampton Court, Shepperton, Guildford, Dorking and Chessington South - London

		SW	SW	SW	SW	SW A	SW B	SW	SW	SW		SW	SW	SW	SW A	SW B	SW	SW	SW	SW		SW	SW	SW A	SW B
Guildford	d		11 58	12 07								12 28	12 37							12 58		13 07			
London Road (Guildford)	d		12 02	12 11								12 32	12 41							13 02		13 11			
Clandon	d		12 07	12 16								12 37	12 46							13 07		13 16			
Horsley	d		12 11	12 20								12 41	12 50							13 11		13 20			
Effingham Junction 6	d		12 15	12 23								12 45	12 53							13 15		13 23			
Bookham	d		12 18									12 48								13 18					
Cobham & Stoke d'Abernon	d			12 27									12 57									13 27			
Oxshott	d			12 30									13 00									13 30			
Claygate	d			12 33									13 03									13 33			
Hinchley Wood	d			12 36									13 06									13 36			
Hampton Court	d								12 54									13 24							
Thames Ditton	d								12 56									13 26							
Surbiton 6	d			12 41			12 57		13 02				13 11			13 27		13 32				13 41			13 57
Berrylands	d								13 04									13 34							
Shepperton	d	12 11								12 41									13 11						
Upper Halliford	d	12 14								12 44									13 14						
Sunbury	d	12 16								12 46									13 16						
Kempton Park	d	12 18								12 48									13 18						
Hampton	d	12 21								12 51									13 21						
Fulwell	d	12 24								12 54									13 24						
Strawberry Hill	d					12 37									13 07									13 37	
Teddington	d	12 29				12 41				12 59					13 11				13 29					13 41	
Hampton Wick	d	12 31				12 44				13 01					13 14				13 31					13 44	
Kingston	a	12 33				12 46				13 03					13 16				13 33					13 46	
	d	12 34				12 48				13 04					13 18				13 34					13 48	
Norbiton	d	12 36				12 50				13 06					13 20				13 36					13 50	
New Malden 6	d	12 40				12 55			13 07	13 10					13 25			13 37	13 40					13 55	
Dorking 4	182 d							12 32									13 02								
Box Hill & Westhumble	182 d							12 35									13 05								
Leatherhead	182 d		12 23					12 40				12 53					13 10			13 23					
Ashtead	182 d		12 27					12 43				12 57					13 13			13 27					
Epsom 3	182 a		12 31					12 48				13 01					13 18			13 31					
	d		12 34					12 49				13 04					13 19			13 34					
Ewell West	d		12 37					12 52				13 07					13 22			13 37					
Stoneleigh	d		12 40					12 55				13 10					13 25			13 40					
Worcester Park	d		12 43					12 58				13 13					13 28			13 43					
Chessington South	d				12 38									13 08									13 38		
Chessington North	d				12 40									13 10									13 40		
Tolworth	d				12 43									13 13									13 43		
Malden Manor	d				12 45									13 15									13 45		
Motspur Park	d		12 45		12 49			13 00				13 15		13 19			13 30			13 45			13 49		
Raynes Park 6	d	12 43	12 49		12 53	12 58		13 04	13 10	13 13		13 19		13 23	13 28		13 34	13 40	13 43	13 49			13 53	13 58	
Wimbledon 6 ⊖ ⛴	d	12 47	12 53	12 50	12 57	13 02	13 05	13 08	13 14	13 17		13 23	13 20	13 27	13 32	13 35	13 38	13 44	13 47	13 53		13 50	13 57	14 02	14 05
Earlsfield	d	12 50	12 57	12 54	13 01	13 05	13 08	13 12	13 17	13 20		13 27	13 24	13 31	13 35	13 38	13 42	13 47	13 50	13 57		13 54	14 01	14 05	14 08
Clapham Junction 10	d	12 54	13 01	12 58	13 05	13 09	13 12	13 16	13 21	13 24		13 31	13 28	13 35	13 39	13 42	13 46	13 51	13 54	14 01		13 58	14 05	14 09	14 12
Vauxhall ⊖	d	12 59	13 06	13 03	13 10	13 14	13 17	13 21	13 26	13 29		13 36	13 33	13 40	13 44	13 47	13 51	13 56	13 59	14 06		14 03	14 10	14 14	14 17
London Waterloo 15 ⊖	a	13 05	13 10	13 07	13 16	13 19	13 22	13 25	13 31	13 35		13 40	13 37	13 46	13 49	13 52	13 55	14 01	14 05	14 10		14 07	14 16	14 19	14 22

A From London Waterloo **B** From Woking

NRT DECEMBER 19 EDITION

Table T152-R

Saturdays

21 December to 16 May

Hampton Court, Shepperton, Guildford, Dorking and Chessington South - London

		SW	SW	SW	SW	SW		SW	SW A	SW B	SW	SW	SW	SW	SW	SW		SW A	SW B	SW	SW	SW	SW	SW	SW
Guildford	d				13 28	13 37								13 58	14 07								14 28	14 37	
London Road (Guildford)	d				13 32	13 41								14 02	14 11								14 32	14 41	
Clandon	d				13 37	13 46								14 07	14 16								14 37	14 46	
Horsley	d				13 41	13 50								14 11	14 20								14 41	14 50	
Effingham Junction 6	d				13 45	13 53								14 15	14 23								14 45	14 53	
Bookham	d				13 48									14 18									14 48		
Cobham & Stoke d'Abernon	d					13 57									14 27									14 57	
Oxshott	d					14 00									14 30									15 00	
Claygate	d					14 03									14 33									15 03	
Hinchley Wood	d					14 06									14 36									15 06	
Hampton Court	d		13 54									14 24									14 54				
Thames Ditton	d		13 56									14 26									14 56				
Surbiton 6	d		14 02			14 11				14 27		14 32			14 41				14 57		15 02			15 11	
Berrylands	d		14 04									14 34									15 04				
Shepperton	d			13 41									14 11									14 41			
Upper Halliford	d			13 44									14 14									14 44			
Sunbury	d			13 46									14 16									14 46			
Kempton Park	d			13 48									14 18									14 48			
Hampton	d			13 51									14 21									14 51			
Fulwell	d			13 54									14 24									14 54			
Strawberry Hill	d								14 07									14 37							
Teddington	d			13 59					14 11				14 29					14 41				14 59			
Hampton Wick	d			14 01					14 14				14 31					14 44				15 01			
Kingston	a			14 03					14 16				14 33					14 46				15 03			
	d			14 04					14 18				14 34					14 48				15 04			
Norbiton	d			14 06					14 20				14 36					14 50				15 06			
New Malden 6	d		14 07	14 10					14 25			14 37	14 40					14 55			15 07	15 10			
Dorking 4	182 d	13 32									14 02									14 32					
Box Hill & Westhumble	182 d	13 35									14 05									14 35					
Leatherhead	182 d	13 40			13 53						14 10			14 23						14 40			14 53		
Ashtead	182 d	13 43			13 57						14 13			14 27						14 43			14 57		
Epsom 3	182 a	13 48			14 01						14 18			14 31						14 48			15 01		
	d	13 49			14 04						14 19			14 34						14 49			15 04		
Ewell West	d	13 52			14 07						14 22			14 37						14 52			15 07		
Stoneleigh	d	13 55			14 10						14 25			14 40						14 55			15 10		
Worcester Park	d	13 58			14 13						14 28			14 43						14 58			15 13		
Chessington South	d							14 08								14 38									15 08
Chessington North	d							14 10								14 40									15 10
Tolworth	d							14 13								14 43									15 13
Malden Manor	d							14 15								14 45									15 15
Motspur Park	d	14 00			14 15			14 19			14 30			14 45		14 49				15 00			15 15		15 19
Raynes Park 6	d	14 04	14 10	14 13	14 19			14 23	14 28		14 34	14 40	14 43	14 49		14 53		14 58		15 04	15 10	15 13	15 19		15 23
Wimbledon 6 ⊖ ⛴	d	14 08	14 14	14 17	14 23	14 20		14 27	14 32	14 35	14 38	14 44	14 47	14 53	14 50	14 57		15 02	15 05	15 08	15 14	15 17	15 23	15 20	15 27
Earlsfield	d	14 12	14 17	14 20	14 27	14 24		14 31	14 35	14 38	14 42	14 47	14 50	14 57	14 54	15 01		15 05	15 08	15 12	15 17	15 20	15 27	15 24	15 31
Clapham Junction 10	d	14 16	14 21	14 24	14 31	14 28		14 35	14 39	14 42	14 46	14 51	14 54	15 01	14 58	15 05		15 09	15 12	15 16	15 21	15 24	15 31	15 28	15 35
Vauxhall ⊖	d	14 21	14 26	14 29	14 36	14 33		14 40	14 44	14 47	14 51	14 56	14 59	15 06	15 03	15 10		15 14	15 17	15 21	15 26	15 29	15 36	15 33	15 40
London Waterloo 15 ⊖	a	14 25	14 31	14 35	14 40	14 37		14 46	14 49	14 52	14 55	15 01	15 05	15 10	15 07	15 16		15 19	15 22	15 25	15 31	15 35	15 40	15 37	15 46

A From London Waterloo **B** From Woking

Table T152-R

Saturdays

21 December to 16 May

Hampton Court, Shepperton, Guildford, Dorking and Chessington South - London

		SW A	SW B	SW	SW	SW	SW	SW	SW	SW A	SW B	SW	SW	SW	SW	SW	SW	SW A	SW B	SW	SW	SW
Guildford	d						14 58	15 07							15 28	15 37						
London Road (Guildford)	d						15 02	15 11							15 32	15 41						
Clandon	d						15 07	15 16							15 37	15 46						
Horsley	d						15 11	15 20							15 41	15 50						
Effingham Junction 6	d						15 15	15 23							15 45	15 53						
Bookham	d						15 18								15 48							
Cobham & Stoke d'Abernon	d							15 27								15 57						
Oxshott	d							15 30								16 00						
Claygate	d							15 33								16 03						
Hinchley Wood	d							15 36								16 06						
Hampton Court	d				15 24								15 54								16 24	
Thames Ditton	d				15 26								15 56								16 26	
Surbiton 6	d		15 27		15 32			15 41			15 57		16 02			16 11			16 27		16 32	
Berrylands	d				15 34								16 04								16 34	
Shepperton	d					15 11								15 41								16 11
Upper Halliford	d					15 14								15 44								16 14
Sunbury	d					15 16								15 46								16 16
Kempton Park	d					15 18								15 48								16 18
Hampton	d					15 21								15 51								16 21
Fulwell	d					15 24								15 54								16 24
Strawberry Hill	d	15 07								15 37								16 07				
Teddington	d	15 11				15 29				15 41				15 59				16 11				16 29
Hampton Wick	d	15 14				15 31				15 44				16 01				16 14				16 31
Kingston	a	15 16				15 33				15 46				16 03				16 16				16 33
	d	15 18				15 34				15 48				16 04				16 18				16 34
Norbiton	d	15 20				15 36				15 50				16 06				16 20				16 36
New Malden 6	d	15 25			15 37	15 40				15 55			16 07	16 10				16 25			16 37	16 40
Dorking 4	182 d			15 02								15 32								16 02		
Box Hill & Westhumble	182 d			15 05								15 35								16 05		
Leatherhead	182 d			15 10			15 23					15 40			15 53					16 10		
Ashtead	182 d			15 13			15 27					15 43			15 57					16 13		
Epsom 3	182 a			15 18			15 31					15 48			16 01					16 18		
	d			15 19			15 34					15 49			16 04					16 19		
Ewell West	d			15 22			15 37					15 52			16 07					16 22		
Stoneleigh	d			15 25			15 40					15 55			16 10					16 25		
Worcester Park	d			15 28			15 43					15 58			16 13					16 28		
Chessington South	d								15 38								16 08					
Chessington North	d								15 40								16 10					
Tolworth	d								15 43								16 13					
Malden Manor	d								15 45								16 15					
Motspur Park	d			15 30			15 45		15 49			16 00			16 15		16 19			16 30		
Raynes Park 6	d	15 28		15 34	15 40	15 43	15 49		15 53	15 58		16 04	16 10	16 13	16 19		16 23	16 28		16 34	16 40	16 43
Wimbledon 6 ⊖	d	15 32	15 35	15 38	15 44	15 47	15 53	15 50	15 57	16 02	16 05	16 08	16 14	16 17	16 23	16 20	16 27	16 32	16 35	16 38	16 44	16 47
Earlsfield	d	15 35	15 38	15 42	15 47	15 50	15 57	15 54	16 01	16 05	16 08	16 12	16 17	16 20	16 27	16 24	16 31	16 35	16 38	16 42	16 47	16 50
Clapham Junction 10	d	15 39	15 42	15 46	15 51	15 54	16 01	15 58	16 05	16 09	16 12	16 16	16 21	16 24	16 31	16 28	16 35	16 39	16 42	16 46	16 51	16 54
Vauxhall ⊖	d	15 44	15 47	15 51	15 56	15 59	16 06	16 03	16 10	16 14	16 17	16 21	16 26	16 29	16 36	16 33	16 40	16 44	16 47	16 51	16 56	16 59
London Waterloo 15 ⊖	a	15 49	15 52	15 55	16 01	16 05	16 10	16 07	16 16	16 19	16 22	16 25	16 31	16 35	16 40	16 37	16 46	16 49	16 52	16 55	17 01	17 05

A From London Waterloo B From Woking

Table T152-R

Saturdays

21 December to 16 May

Hampton Court, Shepperton, Guildford, Dorking and Chessington South - London

		SW	SW	SW	SW A	SW B	SW	SW	SW	SW	SW	SW	SW A	SW B	SW	SW	SW	SW	SW	SW	SW A	SW B	SW
Guildford	d	15 58	16 07							16 28	16 37							16 58	17 07				
London Road (Guildford)	d	16 02	16 11							16 32	16 41							17 02	17 11				
Clandon	d	16 07	16 16							16 37	16 46							17 07	17 16				
Horsley	d	16 11	16 20							16 41	16 50							17 11	17 20				
Effingham Junction 6	d	16 15	16 23							16 45	16 53							17 15	17 23				
Bookham	d	16 18								16 48								17 18					
Cobham & Stoke d'Abernon	d		16 27								16 57								17 27				
Oxshott	d		16 30								17 00								17 30				
Claygate	d		16 33								17 03								17 33				
Hinchley Wood	d		16 36								17 06								17 36				
Hampton Court	d							16 54								17 24							
Thames Ditton	d							16 56								17 26							
Surbiton 6	d		16 41			16 57		17 02			17 11			17 27		17 32			17 41			17 57	
Berrylands	d							17 04								17 34							
Shepperton	d								16 41								17 11						
Upper Halliford	d								16 44								17 14						
Sunbury	d								16 46								17 16						
Kempton Park	d								16 48								17 18						
Hampton	d								16 51								17 21						
Fulwell	d								16 54								17 24						
Strawberry Hill	d				16 37								17 07								17 37		
Teddington	d				16 41				16 59				17 11				17 29				17 41		
Hampton Wick	d				16 44				17 01				17 14				17 31				17 44		
Kingston	a				16 46				17 03				17 16				17 33				17 46		
	d				16 48				17 04				17 18				17 34				17 48		
Norbiton	d				16 50				17 06				17 20				17 36				17 50		
New Malden 6	d				16 55			17 07	17 10				17 25			17 37	17 40				17 55		
Dorking 4	182 d						16 32								17 02								17 32
Box Hill & Westhumble	182 d						16 35								17 05								17 35
Leatherhead	182 d	16 23					16 40			16 53					17 10			17 23					17 40
Ashtead	182 d	16 27					16 43			16 57					17 13			17 27					17 43
Epsom 3	182 a	16 31					16 48			17 01					17 18			17 31					17 48
	d	16 34					16 49			17 04					17 19			17 34					17 49
Ewell West	d	16 37					16 52			17 07					17 22			17 37					17 52
Stoneleigh	d	16 40					16 55			17 10					17 25			17 40					17 55
Worcester Park	d	16 43					16 58			17 13					17 28			17 43					17 58
Chessington South	d			16 38								17 08								17 38			
Chessington North	d			16 40								17 10								17 40			
Tolworth	d			16 43								17 13								17 43			
Malden Manor	d			16 45								17 15								17 45			
Motspur Park	d	16 45		16 49			17 00			17 15		17 19			17 30			17 45		17 49			18 00
Raynes Park 6	d	16 49		16 53	16 58		17 04	17 10	17 13	17 19		17 23	17 28		17 34	17 40	17 43	17 49		17 53	17 58		18 04
Wimbledon 6 ⊖	d	16 53	16 50	16 57	17 02	17 05	17 08	17 14	17 17	17 23	17 20	17 27	17 32	17 35	17 38	17 44	17 47	17 53	17 50	17 57	18 02	18 05	18 08
Earlsfield	d	16 57	16 54	17 01	17 05	17 08	17 12	17 17	17 20	17 27	17 24	17 31	17 35	17 38	17 42	17 47	17 50	17 57	17 54	18 01	18 05	18 08	18 12
Clapham Junction 10	d	17 01	16 58	17 05	17 09	17 12	17 16	17 21	17 24	17 31	17 28	17 35	17 39	17 42	17 46	17 51	17 54	18 01	17 58	18 05	18 09	18 12	18 16
Vauxhall ⊖	d	17 06	17 03	17 10	17 14	17 17	17 21	17 26	17 29	17 36	17 33	17 40	17 44	17 47	17 51	17 56	17 59	18 06	18 03	18 10	18 14	18 17	18 21
London Waterloo 15 ⊖	a	17 10	17 07	17 16	17 19	17 22	17 25	17 31	17 35	17 40	17 37	17 46	17 49	17 52	17 55	18 01	18 05	18 10	18 07	18 16	18 19	18 22	18 25

A From London Waterloo B From Woking

Table T152-R

Saturdays

21 December to 16 May

Hampton Court, Shepperton, Guildford, Dorking and Chessington South - London

		SW	SW	SW	SW	SW	SW A	SW B	SW	SW	SW	SW	SW	SW	SW A	SW B	SW	SW	SW	SW	SW	SW
Guildford	d			17 28	17 37							17 58	18 07							18 28	18 37	
London Road (Guildford)	d			17 32	17 41							18 02	18 11							18 32	18 41	
Clandon	d			17 37	17 46							18 07	18 16							18 37	18 46	
Horsley	d			17 41	17 50							18 11	18 20							18 41	18 50	
Effingham Junction 6	d			17 45	17 53							18 15	18 23							18 45	18 53	
Bookham	d			17 48								18 18								18 48		
Cobham & Stoke d'Abernon	d				17 57								18 27								18 57	
Oxshott	d				18 00								18 30								19 00	
Claygate	d				18 03								18 33								19 03	
Hinchley Wood	d				18 06								18 36								19 06	
Hampton Court	d	17 54								18 24								18 54				
Thames Ditton	d	17 56								18 26								18 56				
Surbiton 6	d	18 02			18 11			18 27		18 32			18 41			18 57		19 02			19 11	
Berrylands	d	18 04								18 34								19 04				
Shepperton	d		17 41								18 11								18 41			
Upper Halliford	d		17 44								18 14								18 44			
Sunbury	d		17 46								18 16								18 46			
Kempton Park	d		17 48								18 18								18 48			
Hampton	d		17 51								18 21								18 51			
Fulwell	d		17 54								18 24								18 54			
Strawberry Hill	d						18 07								18 37							
Teddington	d		17 59				18 11				18 29				18 41				18 59			
Hampton Wick	d		18 01				18 14				18 31				18 44				19 01			
Kingston	a		18 03				18 16				18 33				18 46				19 03			
	d		18 04				18 18				18 34				18 48				19 04			
Norbiton	d		18 06				18 20				18 36				18 50				19 06			
New Malden 6	d	18 07	18 10				18 25			18 37	18 40				18 55			19 07	19 10			
Dorking 4	182 d								18 02								18 32					
Box Hill & Westhumble	182 d								18 05								18 35					
Leatherhead	182 d			17 53					18 10			18 23					18 40			18 53		
Ashtead	182 d			17 57					18 13			18 27					18 43			18 57		
Epsom 3	182 a			18 01					18 18			18 31					18 48			19 01		
	d			18 04					18 19			18 34					18 49			19 04		
Ewell West	d			18 07					18 22			18 37					18 52			19 07		
Stoneleigh	d			18 10					18 25			18 40					18 55			19 10		
Worcester Park	d			18 13					18 28			18 43					18 58			19 13		
Chessington South	d					18 08								18 38								19 08
Chessington North	d					18 10								18 40								19 10
Tolworth	d					18 13								18 43								19 13
Malden Manor	d					18 15								18 45								19 15
Motspur Park	d			18 15		18 19			18 30			18 45		18 49			19 00			19 15		19 19
Raynes Park 6	d	18 10	18 13	18 19		18 23	18 28		18 34	18 40	18 43	18 49		18 53	18 58		19 04	19 10	19 13	19 19		19 23
Wimbledon 6 ⊖	d	18 14	18 17	18 23	18 20	18 27	18 32	18 35	18 38	18 44	18 47	18 53	18 50	18 57	19 02	19 05	19 08	19 14	19 17	19 23	19 20	19 27
Earlsfield	d	18 17	18 20	18 27	18 24	18 31	18 35	18 38	18 42	18 47	18 50	18 57	18 54	19 01	19 05	19 08	19 12	19 17	19 20	19 27	19 24	19 31
Clapham Junction 10	d	18 21	18 24	18 31	18 28	18 35	18 39	18 42	18 46	18 51	18 54	19 01	18 58	19 05	19 09	19 12	19 16	19 21	19 24	19 31	19 28	19 35
Vauxhall ⊖	d	18 26	18 29	18 36	18 33	18 40	18 44	18 47	18 51	18 56	18 59	19 06	19 03	19 10	19 14	19 17	19 21	19 26	19 29	19 36	19 33	19 40
London Waterloo 15 ⊖	a	18 31	18 35	18 40	18 37	18 46	18 49	18 52	18 55	19 01	19 05	19 10	19 07	19 16	19 19	19 22	19 25	19 31	19 35	19 40	19 37	19 46

A From London Waterloo B From Woking

Table T152-R

Saturdays

21 December to 16 May

Hampton Court, Shepperton, Guildford, Dorking and Chessington South - London

		SW A	SW B	SW	SW	SW	SW	SW	SW	SW A	SW B	SW	SW	SW	SW	SW	SW	SW A	SW B	SW	SW	SW	SW
Guildford	d						18 58	19 07							19 28	19 37							19 58
London Road (Guildford)	d						19 02	19 11							19 32	19 41							20 02
Clandon	d						19 07	19 16							19 37	19 46							20 07
Horsley	d						19 11	19 20							19 41	19 50							20 11
Effingham Junction 6	d						19 15	19 23							19 45	19 53							20 15
Bookham	d						19 18								19 48								20 18
Cobham & Stoke d'Abernon	d							19 27								19 57							
Oxshott	d							19 30								20 00							
Claygate	d							19 33								20 03							
Hinchley Wood	d							19 36								20 06							
Hampton Court	d				19 24								19 54								20 24		
Thames Ditton	d				19 26								19 56								20 26		
Surbiton 6	d		19 27		19 32			19 41			19 57		20 02			20 11			20 27		20 32		
Berrylands	d				19 34								20 04								20 34		
Shepperton	d					19 11								19 41								20 11	
Upper Halliford	d					19 14								19 44								20 14	
Sunbury	d					19 16								19 46								20 16	
Kempton Park	d					19 18								19 48								20 18	
Hampton	d					19 21								19 51								20 21	
Fulwell	d					19 24								19 54								20 24	
Strawberry Hill	d	19 07								19 37								20 08					
Teddington	d	19 11				19 29				19 41				19 59				20 12				20 29	
Hampton Wick	d	19 14				19 31				19 44				20 01				20 15				20 31	
Kingston	a	19 16				19 33				19 46				20 03				20 17				20 33	
	d	19 18				19 34				19 48				20 04				20 18				20 34	
Norbiton	d	19 20				19 36				19 50				20 06				20 20				20 36	
New Malden 6	d	19 25			19 37	19 40				19 55			20 07	20 10				20 25			20 37	20 40	
Dorking 4	182 d			19 02								19 32								20 02			
Box Hill & Westhumble	182 d			19 05								19 35								20 05			
Leatherhead	182 d			19 10			19 23					19 40			19 53					20 10			20 23
Ashtead	182 d			19 13			19 27					19 43			19 57					20 13			20 27
Epsom 3	182 a			19 18			19 31					19 48			20 01					20 18			20 31
	d			19 19			19 34					19 49			20 04					20 19			20 34
Ewell West	d			19 22			19 37					19 52			20 07					20 22			20 37
Stoneleigh	d			19 25			19 40					19 55			20 10					20 25			20 40
Worcester Park	d			19 28			19 43					19 58			20 13					20 28			20 43
Chessington South	d								19 38								20 08						
Chessington North	d								19 40								20 10						
Tolworth	d								19 43								20 13						
Malden Manor	d								19 45								20 15						
Motspur Park	d			19 30			19 45		19 49			20 00			20 15		20 19			20 30			20 45
Raynes Park 6	d	19 28		19 34	19 40	19 43	19 49		19 53	19 58		20 04	20 10	20 13	20 19		20 23	20 28		20 34	20 40	20 43	20 49
Wimbledon 6 ⊖	d	19 32	19 35	19 38	19 44	19 47	19 53	19 50	19 57	20 02	20 05	20 08	20 14	20 17	20 23	20 20	20 27	20 32	20 35	20 38	20 44	20 47	20 53
Earlsfield	d	19 35	19 38	19 42	19 47	19 50	19 57	19 54	20 01	20 05	20 08	20 12	20 17	20 20	20 27	20 24	20 31	20 35	20 38	20 42	20 47	20 50	20 57
Clapham Junction 10	d	19 39	19 42	19 46	19 51	19 54	20 01	19 58	20 05	20 09	20 12	20 16	20 21	20 24	20 31	20 28	20 35	20 39	20 42	20 46	20 51	20 54	21 01
Vauxhall ⊖	d	19 44	19 47	19 51	19 56	19 59	20 06	20 03	20 10	20 14	20 17	20 21	20 26	20 29	20 36	20 33	20 40	20 44	20 47	20 51	20 56	20 59	21 06
London Waterloo 15 ⊖	a	19 49	19 52	19 55	20 01	20 05	20 10	20 07	20 16	20 19	20 22	20 25	20 31	20 35	20 40	20 37	20 46	20 49	20 52	20 55	21 01	21 05	21 10

A From London Waterloo B From Woking

Table T152-R

Saturdays

21 December to 16 May

Hampton Court, Shepperton, Guildford, Dorking and Chessington South - London

		SW	SW	SW A	SW B	SW	SW	SW	SW	SW	SW	SW A	SW B	SW	SW	SW	SW	SW	SW	SW A	SW B	SW	SW
Guildford	d	20 07							20 28	20 37							20 58	21 07					
London Road (Guildford)	d	20 11							20 32	20 41							21 02	21 11					
Clandon	d	20 16							20 37	20 46							21 07	21 16					
Horsley	d	20 20							20 41	20 50							21 11	21 20					
Effingham Junction 6	d	20 23							20 45	20 53							21 15	21 23					
Bookham	d								20 48								21 18						
Cobham & Stoke d'Abernon	d	20 27								20 57								21 27					
Oxshott	d	20 30								21 00								21 30					
Claygate	d	20 33								21 03								21 33					
Hinchley Wood	d	20 36								21 06								21 36					
Hampton Court	d						20 54								21 24								21 54
Thames Ditton	d						20 56								21 26								21 56
Surbiton 6	d	20 41			20 57		21 02			21 11			21 27		21 32			21 41			21 57		22 02
Berrylands	d						21 04								21 34								22 04
Shepperton	d							20 41								21 11							
Upper Halliford	d							20 44								21 14							
Sunbury	d							20 46								21 16							
Kempton Park	d							20 48								21 18							
Hampton	d							20 51								21 21							
Fulwell	d							20 54								21 24							
Strawberry Hill	d			20 37								21 07								21 37			
Teddington	d			20 41				20 59				21 11				21 29				21 41			
Hampton Wick	d			20 44				21 01				21 14				21 31				21 44			
Kingston	a			20 46				21 03				21 16				21 33				21 46			
	d			20 48				21 04				21 18				21 34				21 48			
Norbiton	d			20 50				21 06				21 20				21 36				21 50			
New Malden 6	d			20 55			21 07	21 10				21 25			21 37	21 40				21 55			22 07
Dorking 4 182	d					20 32								21 02								21 32	
Box Hill & Westhumble 182	d					20 35								21 05								21 35	
Leatherhead 182	d					20 40			20 53					21 10			21 23					21 40	
Ashtead 182	d					20 43			20 57					21 12			21 27					21 43	
Epsom 3 182	a					20 48			21 01					21 18			21 31					21 48	
	d					20 49			21 04					21 19			21 34					21 49	
Ewell West	d					20 52			21 07					21 22			21 37					21 52	
Stoneleigh	d					20 55			21 10					21 25			21 40					21 55	
Worcester Park	d					20 58			21 13					21 28			21 43					21 58	
Chessington South	d		20 38								21 08								21 38				
Chessington North	d		20 40								21 10								21 40				
Tolworth	d		20 43								21 13								21 43				
Malden Manor	d		20 45								21 15								21 45				
Motspur Park	d		20 49			21 00			21 15		21 19			21 30			21 45		21 49			22 00	
Raynes Park 6	d		20 53	20 58		21 04	21 10	21 13	21 19		21 23	21 28		21 34	21 40	21 43	21 49		21 53	21 58		22 04	22 10
Wimbledon 6 ⊖ ⇌	d	20 50	20 57	21 02	21 05	21 08	21 14	21 17	21 23	21 20	21 27	21 32	21 35	21 38	21 44	21 47	21 53	21 50	21 57	22 02	22 05	22 08	22 14
Earlsfield	d	20 54	21 01	21 05	21 08	21 12	21 17	21 20	21 27	21 24	21 31	21 35	21 38	21 42	21 47	21 50	21 57	21 54	22 01	22 05	22 08	22 12	22 17
Clapham Junction 10	d	20 58	21 05	21 09	21 12	21 16	21 21	21 24	21 31	21 28	21 35	21 39	21 42	21 46	21 51	21 54	22 01	21 58	22 05	22 09	22 12	22 16	22 21
Vauxhall ⊖	d	21 03	21 10	21 14	21 17	21 21	21 26	21 29	21 36	21 33	21 40	21 44	21 47	21 51	21 56	21 59	22 06	22 03	22 10	22 14	22 17	22 21	22 26
London Waterloo 15 ⊖	a	21 07	21 16	21 19	21 22	21 25	21 31	21 35	21 40	21 37	21 46	21 49	21 52	21 55	22 01	22 05	22 10	22 07	22 16	22 19	22 22	22 25	22 31

A From London Waterloo B From Woking

Table T152-R

Saturdays

21 December to 16 May

Hampton Court, Shepperton, Guildford, Dorking and Chessington South - London

		SW	SW	SW	SW	SW A	SW B	SW	SW	SW	SW	SW	SW	SW A	SW B	SW	SW	SW	SW	SW	SW A	SW B
Guildford	d		21 28	21 37							21 58	22 07							22 37			
London Road (Guildford)	d		21 32	21 41							22 02	22 11							22 41			
Clandon	d		21 37	21 46							22 07	22 16							22 46			
Horsley	d		21 41	21 50							22 11	22 20							22 50			
Effingham Junction 6	d		21 45	21 53							22 15	22 23							22 53			
Bookham	d		21 48								22 18											
Cobham & Stoke d'Abernon	d			21 57								22 27							22 57			
Oxshott	d			22 00								22 30							23 00			
Claygate	d			22 03								22 33							23 03			
Hinchley Wood	d			22 06								22 36							23 06			
Hampton Court	d								22 24								22 54					
Thames Ditton	d								22 26								22 56					
Surbiton 6	d			22 11			22 27		22 32			22 41			22 57		23 02		23 11			23 27
Berrylands	d								22 34								23 04					
Shepperton	d	21 41								22 11								22 41				
Upper Halliford	d	21 44								22 14								22 44				
Sunbury	d	21 46								22 16								22 46				
Kempton Park	d	21 48								22 18								22 48				
Hampton	d	21 51								22 21								22 51				
Fulwell	d	21 54								22 24								22 54				
Strawberry Hill	d					22 07								22 37							23 07	
Teddington	d	21 59				22 11				22 29				22 41				22 59			23 11	
Hampton Wick	d	22 01				22 14				22 31				22 44				23 01			23 14	
Kingston	a	22 03				22 16				22 33				22 46				23 03			23 16	
	d	22 04				22 18				22 34				22 48				23 04			23 18	
Norbiton	d	22 06				22 20				22 36				22 50				23 06			23 20	
New Malden 6	d	22 10				22 25			22 37	22 40				22 55			23 07	23 10			23 25	
Dorking 4 182	d							22 02								22 32						
Box Hill & Westhumble 182	d							22 05								22 35						
Leatherhead 182	d		21 53					22 10			22 23					22 40						
Ashtead 182	d		21 57					22 12			22 27					22 43						
Epsom 3 182	a		22 01					22 18			22 31					22 48						
	d		22 04					22 19			22 34					22 49						
Ewell West	d		22 07					22 22			22 37					22 52						
Stoneleigh	d		22 10					22 25			22 40					22 55						
Worcester Park	d		22 13					22 28			22 43					22 58						
Chessington South	d				22 08								22 38							23 08		
Chessington North	d				22 10								22 40							23 10		
Tolworth	d				22 13								22 43							23 13		
Malden Manor	d				22 15								22 45							23 15		
Motspur Park	d		22 15		22 19			22 30			22 45		22 49			23 00				23 19		
Raynes Park 6	d	22 13	22 19		22 23	22 28		22 34	22 40	22 43	22 49		22 53	22 58		23 04	23 10	23 13		23 23	23 28	
Wimbledon 6 ⊖ ⇌	d	22 17	22 23	22 20	22a27	22 32	22 35	22 38	22 44	22 47	22 53	22 50	22 57	23 02	23 05	23 08	23 14	23 17	23 20	23a26	23 32	23 35
Earlsfield	d	22 20	22 27	22 24		22 35	22 38	22 42	22 47	22 50	22 57	22 54	23 01	23 05	23 08	23 12	23 17	23 20	23 24		23 35	23 38
Clapham Junction 10	d	22 24	22 31	22 28		22 39	22 42	22 46	22 51	22 54	23 01	22 58	23 05	23 09	23 12	23 16	23 21	23 24	23 28		23 39	23 42
Vauxhall ⊖	d	22 29	22 36	22 33		22 44	22 47	22 51	22 56	22 59	23 06	23 03	23 10	23 14	23 17	23 21	23 26	23 29	23 33		23 44	23 47
London Waterloo 15 ⊖	a	22 35	22 41	22 39		22 49	22 53	22 55	23 01	23 05	23 11	23 07	23 16	23 19	23 24	23 28	23 31	23 35	23 37		23 49	23 54

A From London Waterloo B From Woking

Table T152-R

Saturdays
21 December to 16 May

Hampton Court, Shepperton, Guildford, Dorking and Chessington South - London

		SW	SW	SW	SW	SW	SW	SW		SW
								◇1		
							A	B		
Guildford	d	22 46			23 07			23 39		
London Road (Guildford)	d	22 50			23 11					
Clandon	d	22 55			23 16					
Horsley	d	22 59			23 20					
Effingham Junction 6	d	23 03			23 23					
Bookham	d	23 06								
Cobham & Stoke d'Abernon	d				23 27					
Oxshott	d				23 30					
Claygate	d				23 33					
Hinchley Wood	d				23 36					
Hampton Court	d		23 24							23 59
Thames Ditton	d		23 26							00 02
Surbiton 6	d		23 32		23 41			00 08		00 12
Berrylands	d		23 34		23 43					00 14
Shepperton	d			23 11						
Upper Halliford	d			23 14						
Sunbury	d			23 16						
Kempton Park	d			23 18						
Hampton	d			23 21						
Fulwell	d			23 24						
Strawberry Hill	d						23 37			
Teddington	d			23 29			23 41			
Hampton Wick	d			23 31			23 44			
Kingston	a			23 33			23 46			
	d			23 34			23 48			
Norbiton	d			23 36			23 50			
New Malden 6	d		23 37	23 40	23 46		23 55			00 17
Dorking 4	182 d									
Box Hill & Westhumble	182 d									
Leatherhead	182 d	23 11								
Ashtead	182 d	23 14								
Epsom 3	182 a	23 19								
	d	23 19								
Ewell West	d	23 22								
Stoneleigh	d	23 25								
Worcester Park	d	23 28								
Chessington South	d					23 40				
Chessington North	d					23 42				
Tolworth	d					23 44				
Malden Manor	d					23 47				
Motspur Park	d	23 30				23 50				
Raynes Park 6	d	23 34	23 40	23 43	23 49	23 54	23 58			00 20
Wimbledon 6 ⊖ ⛴	d	23 38	23a44	23 49	23 53	23a57	00 02	00 16		00a23
Earlsfield	d	23 42		23 53	23 56		00 05			
Clapham Junction 10	d	23 46		23 57	23 59		00 09	00 23		
Vauxhall ⊖	d	23 51		00 02	00 05		00 15			
London Waterloo 15 ⊖	a	23 59		00 09	00 14		00 22	00 32		

A From London Waterloo
B From Portsmouth Harbour

NRT DECEMBER 19 EDITION

Table T152-R

Sundays
15 December to 10 May

Hampton Court, Shepperton, Guildford, Dorking and Chessington South - London

		SW	SW	SW	SW	SW	SW	SW	SW	SW		SW	SW	SW	SW	SW	SW	SW	SW	SW		SW	SW	SW	SW
					◇1													1							
		A	B	C	D	E	C	F	G								G	H							
Guildford	d									06 57					07 24					07 50			07 57		
London Road (Guildford)	d																			07 54					
Clandon	d																			07 59					
Horsley	d																			08 03					
Effingham Junction 6	d																			08 06					
Bookham	d																								
Cobham & Stoke d'Abernon	d																			08 10					
Oxshott	d																			08 13					
Claygate	d																			08 16					
Hinchley Wood	d																			08 19					
Hampton Court	d													07 35					08 05						
Thames Ditton	d					00 02								07 37					08 07						
Surbiton 6	d				00 08	00 12		07 00		07 30				07 43	08 00			08 10	08 13	08a23			08 30		
Berrylands	d					00 14								07 45					08 15						
Shepperton	d												07 11												08 11
Upper Halliford	d												07 14												08 14
Sunbury	d												07 16												08 16
Kempton Park	d												07 18												08 18
Hampton	d												07 21												08 21
Fulwell	d												07 24												08 24
Strawberry Hill	d						00 09		06 49								07 49								
Teddington	d						00 12		06 55				07 29				07 55								08 29
Hampton Wick	d						00 14		06 57				07 31				07 57								08 31
Kingston	a						00 16		06 59				07 33				07 59								08 33
	d								07 04				07 34				08 04								08 34
Norbiton	d								07 06				07 36				08 06								08 36
New Malden 6	d					00 17			07 10				07 40	07 48			08 10		08 18						08 40
Dorking 4	182 d																								
Box Hill & Westhumble	182 d																								
Leatherhead	182 d																								
Ashtead	182 d																								
Epsom 3	182 a																								
	d											07 23				07 53								08 23	
Ewell West	d											07 26				07 56								08 26	
Stoneleigh	d											07 29				07 59								08 29	
Worcester Park	d											07 32				08 02								08 32	
Chessington South	d																					08 10			
Chessington North	d																					08 12			
Tolworth	d																					08 14			
Malden Manor	d																					08 17			
Motspur Park	d											07 34				08 04						08 20		08 34	
Raynes Park 6	d					00 20			07 13			07 38	07 43	07 51		08 08	08 13		08 21			08 24		08 38	08 43
Wimbledon 6 ⊖ ⛴	d				00 16	00a23		07 08	07 20	07 38		07 42	07 47	07 55	08 07	08 12	08 17	08 20	08 26			08 29	08 37	08 42	08 47
Earlsfield	d							07 12	07 24	07 42		07 46	07 51	07 59	08 11	08 17	08 21		08 30			08 33	08 41	08 46	08 51
Clapham Junction 10	d			00 06	00 23			07 16	07 29	07 46		07 51	07 57	08 03	08 17	08 22	08 27	08 29	08 36			08 39	08 45	08 50	08 57
Vauxhall ⊖	d	00 02	00 05	00 12				07 21	07 34	07 51		07 56	08 02	08 08	08 22	08 27	08 32		08 41			08 44	08 50	08 55	09 02
London Waterloo 15 ⊖	a	00 09	00 14	00 17	00 32			07 27	07 40	07 57		08 02	08 08	08 15	08 28	08 36	08 38	08 39	08 47			08 50	08 57	09 02	09 08

A not 15 December. From Shepperton
B not 15 December. From Guildford
C not 15 December. From London Waterloo
D not 15 December. From Portsmouth Harbour
E not 15 December. From Hampton Court
F From Woking
G From London Waterloo
H From Farnham

Table T152-R

Sundays

15 December to 10 May

Hampton Court, Shepperton, Guildford, Dorking and Chessington South - London

Station		SW	SW	SW	SW	SW A	SW	SW	SW	SW	SW	SW	SW	SW	SW	SW	SW A	SW	SW	SW	SW	SW	SW
Guildford	d			08 20	08 24				08 50	08 57					09 20	09 24				09 50	09 57		
London Road (Guildford)	d			08 24					08 54						09 24					09 54			
Clandon	d			08 29					08 59						09 29					09 59			
Horsley	d			08 33					09 03						09 33					10 03			
Effingham Junction 6	d			08 36					09 06						09 36					10 06			
Bookham	d			08 39											09 39								
Cobham & Stoke d'Abernon	d								09 10											10 10			
Oxshott	d								09 13											10 13			
Claygate	d								09 16											10 16			
Hinchley Wood	d								09 19											10 19			
Hampton Court	d	08 35					09 05						09 35					10 05					
Thames Ditton	d	08 37					09 07						09 37					10 07					
Surbiton 6	d	08 43			09 00		09 13		09 24	09 30			09 43			10 00		10 13		10 24	10 30		
Berrylands	d	08 45					09 15						09 45					10 15					
Shepperton	d											09 11											10 11
Upper Halliford	d											09 14											10 14
Sunbury	d											09 16											10 16
Kempton Park	d											09 18											10 18
Hampton	d											09 21											10 21
Fulwell	d											09 24											10 24
Strawberry Hill	d					08 49											09 49						
Teddington	d					08 55						09 29					09 55						10 29
Hampton Wick	d					08 57						09 31					09 57						10 31
Kingston	a					08 59						09 33					09 59						10 33
	d					09 04						09 34					10 04						10 34
Norbiton	d					09 06						09 36					10 06						10 36
New Malden 6	d	08 48				09 10	09 18					09 40	09 48				10 10	10 18					10 40
Dorking 4	182 d										09 07											10 07	
Box Hill & Westhumble	182 d										09 10											10 10	
Leatherhead	182 d			08 45							09 15				09 45							10 15	
Ashtead	182 d			08 48							09 18				09 48							10 18	
Epsom 3	182 a			08 53							09 23				09 53							10 23	
	d			08 53							09 23				09 53							10 23	
Ewell West	d			08 57							09 27				09 57							10 27	
Stoneleigh	d			08 59							09 29				09 59							10 29	
Worcester Park	d			09 02							09 32				10 02							10 32	
Chessington South	d		08 40					09 10						09 40					10 10				
Chessington North	d		08 42					09 12						09 42					10 12				
Tolworth	d		08 44					09 14						09 44					10 14				
Malden Manor	d		08 47					09 17						09 47					10 17				
Motspur Park	d		08 50	09 05				09 20			09 35			09 50	10 05				10 20			10 35	
Raynes Park 6	d	08 51	08 54	09 08		09 13	09 21	09 24			09 38	09 43	09 51	09 54	10 08		10 13	10 21	10 24			10 38	10 43
Wimbledon 6 ⊖ ⛴	d	08 55	08 58	09 12	09 07	09 17	09 25	09 28	09a31	09 38	09 44	09 48	09 56	09 59	10 13	10 08	10 17	10 25	10 28	10a33	10 38	10 42	10 47
Earlsfield	d	08 59	09 02	09 16	09 11	09 21	09 29	09 32		09 41	09 48	09 52	09 59	10 02	10 17	10 12	10 20	10 28	10 31		10 41	10 46	10 50
Clapham Junction 10	d	09 03	09 09	09 20	09 15	09 25	09 34	09 37		09 48	09 52	09 56	10 06	10 10	10 23	10 16	10 26	10 32	10 36		10 46	10 50	10 54
Vauxhall ⊖	d	09 08	09 14	09 25	09 20	09 30	09 39	09 42		09 53	09 57	10 01	10 11	10 15	10 28	10 21	10 32	10 37	10 41		10 51	10 55	10 59
London Waterloo 15 ⊖	a	09 16	09 21	09 32	09 27	09 36	09 46	09 48		09 59	10 03	10 07	10 17	10 21	10 34	10 27	10 36	10 42	10 45		10 55	10 59	11 04

A From London Waterloo

Table T152-R

Sundays

15 December to 10 May

Hampton Court, Shepperton, Guildford, Dorking and Chessington South - London

Station		SW	SW	SW	SW	SW A	SW	SW	SW	SW	SW	SW	SW	SW	SW	SW	SW A	SW	SW	SW	SW
Guildford	d			10 20	10 24				10 50	10 57					11 20	11 24				11 50	11 57
London Road (Guildford)	d			10 24					10 54						11 24					11 54	
Clandon	d			10 29					10 59						11 29					11 59	
Horsley	d			10 33					11 03						11 33					12 03	
Effingham Junction 6	d			10 36					11 06						11 36					12 06	
Bookham	d			10 39											11 39						
Cobham & Stoke d'Abernon	d								11 10											12 10	
Oxshott	d								11 13											12 13	
Claygate	d								11 16											12 16	
Hinchley Wood	d								11 19											12 19	
Hampton Court	d	10 35					11 05						11 35					12 05			
Thames Ditton	d	10 37					11 07						11 37					12 07			
Surbiton 6	d	10 43			11 00		11 13		11 24	11 30			11 43			12 00		12 13		12 24	12 30
Berrylands	d	10 45					11 15						11 45					12 15			
Shepperton	d											11 11									
Upper Halliford	d											11 14									
Sunbury	d											11 16									
Kempton Park	d											11 18									
Hampton	d											11 21									
Fulwell	d											11 24									
Strawberry Hill	d					10 49											11 49				
Teddington	d					10 55						11 29					11 55				
Hampton Wick	d					10 57						11 31					11 57				
Kingston	a					10 59						11 33					11 59				
	d					11 04						11 34					12 04				
Norbiton	d					11 06						11 36					12 06				
New Malden 6	d	10 48				11 10	11 18					11 40	11 48				12 10	12 18			
Dorking 4	182 d										11 07										
Box Hill & Westhumble	182 d										11 10										
Leatherhead	182 d			10 45							11 15				11 45						
Ashtead	182 d			10 48							11 18				11 48						
Epsom 3	182 a			10 53							11 23				11 53						
	d			10 53							11 23				11 53						
Ewell West	d			10 57							11 27				11 57						
Stoneleigh	d			10 59							11 29				11 59						
Worcester Park	d			11 02							11 32				12 02						
Chessington South	d		10 40					11 10						11 40					12 10		
Chessington North	d		10 42					11 12						11 42					12 12		
Tolworth	d		10 44					11 14						11 44					12 14		
Malden Manor	d		10 47					11 17						11 47					12 17		
Motspur Park	d		10 50	11 05				11 20			11 35			11 50	12 05				12 20		
Raynes Park 6	d	10 51	10 54	11 08		11 13	11 21	11 24			11 38	11 43	11 51	11 54	12 08		12 13	12 21	12 24		
Wimbledon 6 ⊖ ⛴	d	10 55	10 58	11 12	11 08	11 17	11 25	11 28	11a33	11 38	11 42	11 47	11 55	11 58	12 12	12 08	12 17	12 25	12 28	12 31	12 38
Earlsfield	d	10 58	11 01	11 16	11 11	11 20	11 28	11 31		11 41	11 46	11 50	11 58	12 01	12 16	12 11	12 20	12 28	12 31	12 35	12 41
Clapham Junction 10	d	11 02	11 05	11 20	11 16	11 24	11 32	11 35		11 46	11 50	11 54	12 02	12 05	12 20	12 16	12 24	12 32	12 35	12 40	12 46
Vauxhall ⊖	d	11 07	11 13	11 25	11 21	11 32	11 37	11 40		11 51	11 55	11 59	12 07	12 13	12 25	12 21	12 29	12 37	12 40	12 45	12 51
London Waterloo 15 ⊖	a	11 12	11 17	11 29	11 26	11 36	11 42	11 45		11 55	11 59	12 09	12 17	12 22	12 29	12 26	12 34	12 47	12 50	12 49	12 55

A From London Waterloo

Table T152-R

Sundays

15 December to 10 May

Hampton Court, Shepperton, Guildford, Dorking and Chessington South - London

	SW	SW	SW	SW	SW	SW	SW A	SW	SW	SW	SW		SW	SW	SW	SW	SW	SW	SW A	SW	SW	SW	SW
Guildford d					12 20	12 24				12 50	12 57						14 20	14 24				14 50	14 57
London Road (Guildford) d					12 24					12 54							14 24					14 54	
Clandon d					12 29					12 59							14 29					14 59	
Horsley d					12 33					13 03							14 33					15 03	
Effingham Junction d					12 36					13 06							14 36					15 06	
Bookham d					12 39												14 39						
Cobham & Stoke d'Abernon d										13 10												15 10	
Oxshott d										13 13												15 13	
Claygate d										13 16												15 16	
Hinchley Wood d										13 19												15 19	
Hampton Court d			12 35					13 05							14 35					15 05			
Thames Ditton d			12 37					13 07							14 37					15 07			
Surbiton d			12 43			13 00		13 13		13 24	13 30				14 43			15 00		15 13		15 24	15 30
Berrylands d			12 45					13 15							14 45					15 15			
Shepperton d		12 11												14 11									
Upper Halliford d		12 14												14 14									
Sunbury d		12 16												14 16									
Kempton Park d		12 18												14 18									
Hampton d		12 21												14 21									
Fulwell d		12 24										and at the same minutes past each hour until		14 24									
Strawberry Hill d							12 49												14 49				
Teddington d		12 29					12 55							14 29					14 55				
Hampton Wick d		12 31					12 57							14 31					14 57				
Kingston a		12 33					12 59							14 33					14 59				
d		12 34					13 04							14 34					15 04				
Norbiton d		12 36					13 06							14 36					15 06				
New Malden d		12 40	12 48				13 10	13 18						14 40	14 48				15 10	15 18			
Dorking 182 d	12 07												14 07										
Box Hill & Westhumble 182 d	12 10												14 10										
Leatherhead 182 d	12 15				12 45								14 15				14 45						
Ashtead 182 d	12 18				12 48								14 18				14 48						
Epsom 182 a	12 23				12 53								14 23				14 53						
d	12 23				12 53								14 23				14 53						
Ewell West d	12 27				12 57								14 27				14 57						
Stoneleigh d	12 29				12 59								14 29				14 59						
Worcester Park d	12 32				13 02								14 32				15 02						
Chessington South d				12 40					13 10							14 40					15 10		
Chessington North d				12 42					13 12							14 42					15 12		
Tolworth d				12 44					13 14							14 44					15 14		
Malden Manor d				12 47					13 17							14 47					15 17		
Motspur Park d	12 35			12 50	13 05				13 20				14 35			14 50	15 05				15 20		
Raynes Park d	12 38	12 43	12 51	12 54	13 08		13 13	13 21	13 24				14 38	14 43	14 51	14 54	15 08		15 13	15 21	15 24		
Wimbledon ⊖ d	12 42	12 47	12 55	12 58	13 12	13 08	13 17	13 25	13 28	13 31	13 38		14 42	14 47	14 55	14 58	15 12	15 08	15 17	15 25	15 28	15 31	15 38
Earlsfield d	12 46	12 50	12 58	13 01	13 16	13 11	13 20	13 28	13 31	13 35	13 41		14 46	14 50	14 58	15 01	15 16	15 11	15 20	15 28	15 31	15 35	15 41
Clapham Junction d	12 50	12 54	13 02	13 05	13 20	13 15	13 24	13 32	13 35	13 39	13 45		14 50	14 54	15 02	15 05	15 20	15 15	15 24	15 32	15 35	15 39	15 45
Vauxhall ⊖ d	12 55	12 59	13 07	13 10	13 25	13 20	13 29	13 37	13 40	13 44	13 50		14 55	14 59	15 07	15 10	15 25	15 20	15 29	15 37	15 40	15 44	15 50
London Waterloo ⊖ a	12 59	13 04	13 12	13 15	13 29	13 25	13 34	13 42	13 45	13 48	13 55		14 59	15 04	15 12	15 15	15 29	15 25	15 34	15 42	15 45	15 48	15 55

A From London Waterloo

Table T152-R

Sundays

15 December to 10 May

Hampton Court, Shepperton, Guildford, Dorking and Chessington South - London

	SW	SW A	SW	SW	SW	SW	SW	SW A	SW	SW	SW	SW	SW	SW A	SW	SW	SW	SW	SW	SW A	SW
Guildford d						15 20	15 24				15 50	15 57						16 20	16 24		
London Road (Guildford) d						15 24					15 54							16 24			
Clandon d						15 29					15 59							16 29			
Horsley d						15 33					16 03							16 33			
Effingham Junction d						15 36					16 06							16 36			
Bookham d						15 39												16 39			
Cobham & Stoke d'Abernon d											16 10										
Oxshott d											16 13										
Claygate d											16 16										
Hinchley Wood d											16 19										
Hampton Court d				15 35					16 05							16 35					17 05
Thames Ditton d				15 37					16 07							16 37					17 07
Surbiton d				15 43			16 00		16 13		16 24	16 30				16 43			17 00		17 13
Berrylands d				15 45					16 15							16 45					17 15
Shepperton d			15 11												16 11						
Upper Halliford d			15 14												16 14						
Sunbury d			15 16												16 16						
Kempton Park d			15 18												16 18						
Hampton d			15 21												16 21						
Fulwell d			15 24												16 24						
Strawberry Hill d		15 14						15 49						16 14						16 49	
Teddington d		15 17	15 29					15 55						16 17	16 29					16 55	
Hampton Wick d		15 20	15 31					15 57						16 20	16 31					16 57	
Kingston a		15 22	15 33					15 59						16 22	16 33					16 59	
d			15 34					16 04							16 34					17 04	
Norbiton d			15 36					16 06							16 36					17 06	
New Malden d			15 40	15 48				16 10	16 18						16 40	16 48				17 10	17 18
Dorking 182 d	15 07												16 07								
Box Hill & Westhumble 182 d	15 10												16 10								
Leatherhead 182 d	15 15					15 45							16 15					16 45			
Ashtead 182 d	15 18					15 48							16 18					16 48			
Epsom 182 a	15 23					15 53							16 23					16 53			
d	15 23					15 53							16 23					16 53			
Ewell West d	15 27					15 57							16 27					16 57			
Stoneleigh d	15 29					15 59							16 29					16 59			
Worcester Park d	15 32					16 02							16 32					17 02			
Chessington South d					15 40					16 10							16 40				
Chessington North d					15 42					16 12							16 42				
Tolworth d					15 44					16 14							16 44				
Malden Manor d					15 47					16 17							16 47				
Motspur Park d	15 35				15 50	16 05				16 20			16 35				16 50	17 05			
Raynes Park d	15 38		15 43	15 51	15 54	16 08		16 13	16 21	16 24			16 38		16 43	16 51	16 54	17 08		17 13	17 21
Wimbledon ⊖ d	15 42		15 47	15 55	15 58	16 12	16 08	16 17	16 25	16 28	16 31	16 38	16 42		16 47	16 55	16 58	17 12	17 08	17 17	17 25
Earlsfield d	15 46		15 50	15 58	16 01	16 16	16 11	16 20	16 28	16 31	16 35	16 41	16 46		16 50	16 58	17 01	17 16	17 11	17 20	17 28
Clapham Junction d	15 50		15 54	16 02	16 05	16 20	16 15	16 24	16 32	16 35	16 39	16 45	16 50		16 54	17 02	17 05	17 20	17 15	17 24	17 32
Vauxhall ⊖ d	15 55		15 59	16 07	16 10	16 25	16 20	16 29	16 37	16 40	16 44	16 50	16 55		16 59	17 07	17 10	17 25	17 20	17 29	17 37
London Waterloo ⊖ a	15 59		16 04	16 12	16 15	16 29	16 25	16 34	16 42	16 45	16 48	16 55	16 59		17 04	17 12	17 15	17 29	17 25	17 34	17 42

A From London Waterloo

Table T152-R

Sundays

15 December to 10 May

Hampton Court, Shepperton, Guildford, Dorking and Chessington South - London

		SW	SW	SW	SW	SW A	SW		SW	SW	SW	SW	SW A	SW	SW	SW	SW		SW	SW A	SW	SW	SW	SW	SW
Guildford	d		16 50	16 57							17 20	17 24				17 50	17 57							18 20	18 24
London Road (Guildford)	d		16 54								17 24					17 54								18 24	
Clandon	d		16 59								17 29					17 59								18 29	
Horsley	d		17 03								17 33					18 03								18 33	
Effingham Junction 6	d		17 06								17 36					18 06								18 36	
Bookham	d										17 39													18 39	
Cobham & Stoke d'Abernon	d		17 10													18 10									
Oxshott	d		17 13													18 13									
Claygate	d		17 16													18 16									
Hinchley Wood	d		17 19													18 19									
Hampton Court	d								17 35					18 05								18 35			
Thames Ditton	d								17 37					18 07								18 37			
Surbiton 6	d		17 24	17 30					17 43			18 00		18 13		18 24	18 30					18 43			19 00
Berrylands	d								17 45					18 15								18 45			
Shepperton	d						17 11														18 11				
Upper Halliford	d						17 14														18 14				
Sunbury	d						17 16														18 16				
Kempton Park	d						17 18														18 18				
Hampton	d						17 21														18 21				
Fulwell	d						17 24														18 24				
Strawberry Hill	d					17 14							17 49							18 14					
Teddington	d					17 17	17 29						17 55							18 17	18 29				
Hampton Wick	d					17 20	17 31						17 57							18 20	18 31				
Kingston	a					17 22	17 33						17 59							18 22	18 33				
	d						17 34						18 04								18 34				
Norbiton	d						17 36						18 06								18 36				
New Malden 6	d						17 40		17 48				18 10	18 18							18 40	18 48			
Dorking 4 182	d				17 07														18 07						
Box Hill & Westhumble 182	d				17 10														18 10						
Leatherhead 182	d				17 15						17 45								18 15					18 45	
Ashtead 182	d				17 18						17 48								18 18					18 48	
Epsom 3 182	a				17 23						17 53								18 23					18 53	
	d				17 23						17 53								18 23					18 53	
Ewell West	d				17 27						17 57								18 27					18 57	
Stoneleigh	d				17 29						17 59								18 29					18 59	
Worcester Park	d				17 32						18 02								18 32					19 02	
Chessington South	d	17 10								17 40					18 10								18 40		
Chessington North	d	17 12								17 42					18 12								18 42		
Tolworth	d	17 14								17 44					18 14								18 44		
Malden Manor	d	17 17								17 47					18 17								18 47		
Motspur Park	d	17 20			17 35					17 50	18 05				18 20				18 35				18 50	19 05	
Raynes Park 6	d	17 24			17 38		17 43		17 51	17 54	18 08		18 13	18 21	18 24				18 38		18 43	18 51	18 54	19 08	
Wimbledon 6 ⊖	d	17 28	17 31	17 38	17 42		17 47		17 55	17 58	18 12	18 08	18 17	18 25	18 28	18 31	18 38		18 42		18 47	18 55	18 58	19 12	19 08
Earlsfield	d	17 31	17 35	17 41	17 46		17 50		17 58	18 01	18 16	18 11	18 20	18 28	18 31	18 35	18 41		18 46		18 50	18 58	19 01	19 16	19 11
Clapham Junction 10	d	17 35	17 39	17 45	17 50		17 54		18 02	18 05	18 20	18 15	18 24	18 32	18 35	18 39	18 45		18 50		18 54	19 02	19 05	19 20	19 15
Vauxhall ⊖	d	17 40	17 44	17 50	17 55		17 59		18 07	18 10	18 25	18 20	18 29	18 37	18 40	18 44	18 50		18 55		18 59	19 07	19 10	19 25	19 20
London Waterloo 15 ⊖	a	17 45	17 48	17 55	17 59		18 04		18 12	18 15	18 29	18 25	18 34	18 42	18 45	18 48	18 55		18 59		19 04	19 12	19 15	19 29	19 25

A From London Waterloo

Table T152-R

Sundays

15 December to 10 May

Hampton Court, Shepperton, Guildford, Dorking and Chessington South - London

		SW A	SW		SW	SW	SW	SW	SW A	SW	SW	SW	SW		SW	SW A	SW	SW	SW	SW	SW	SW A	SW		SW
Guildford	d					18 50	18 57						19 20		19 24				19 50	19 57					
London Road (Guildford)	d					18 54							19 24						19 54						
Clandon	d					18 59							19 29						19 59						
Horsley	d					19 03							19 33						20 03						
Effingham Junction 6	d					19 06							19 36						20 06						
Bookham	d												19 39												
Cobham & Stoke d'Abernon	d					19 10													20 10						
Oxshott	d					19 13													20 13						
Claygate	d					19 16													20 16						
Hinchley Wood	d					19 19													20 19						
Hampton Court	d		19 05								19 35						20 05								20 35
Thames Ditton	d		19 07								19 37						20 07								20 37
Surbiton 6	d		19 13			19 24	19 30				19 43				20 00		20 13		20 24	20 30					20 43
Berrylands	d		19 15								19 45						20 15								20 45
Shepperton	d									19 11													20 11		
Upper Halliford	d									19 14													20 14		
Sunbury	d									19 16													20 16		
Kempton Park	d									19 18													20 18		
Hampton	d									19 21													20 21		
Fulwell	d									19 24													20 24		
Strawberry Hill	d	18 49							19 14							19 49						20 14			
Teddington	d	18 55							19 17	19 29						19 55						20 17	20 29		
Hampton Wick	d	18 57							19 20	19 31						19 57						20 20	20 31		
Kingston	a	18 59							19 22	19 33						19 59						20 22	20 33		
	d	19 04								19 34						20 04							20 34		
Norbiton	d	19 06								19 36						20 06							20 36		
New Malden 6	d	19 10	19 18							19 40	19 48					20 10	20 18						20 40		20 48
Dorking 4 182	d							19 07													20 07				
Box Hill & Westhumble 182	d							19 10													20 10				
Leatherhead 182	d							19 15					19 45								20 15				
Ashtead 182	d							19 18					19 48								20 18				
Epsom 3 182	a							19 23					19 53								20 23				
	d							19 23					19 53								20 23				
Ewell West	d							19 27					19 57								20 27				
Stoneleigh	d							19 29					19 59								20 29				
Worcester Park	d							19 32					20 02								20 32				
Chessington South	d				19 10							19 40						20 10							
Chessington North	d				19 12							19 42						20 12							
Tolworth	d				19 14							19 44						20 14							
Malden Manor	d				19 17							19 47						20 17							
Motspur Park	d				19 20			19 35				19 50	20 05					20 20			20 35				
Raynes Park 6	d	19 13	19 21		19 24			19 38		19 43	19 51	19 54	20 08			20 13	20 21	20 24			20 38		20 43		20 51
Wimbledon 6 ⊖	d	19 17	19 25		19 28	19 31	19 38	19 42		19 47	19 55	19 58	20 12		20 08	20 17	20 25	20 28	20 31	20 38	20 42		20 47		20 55
Earlsfield	d	19 20	19 28		19 31	19 35	19 41	19 46		19 50	19 58	20 01	20 16		20 11	20 20	20 28	20 31	20 35	20 41	20 46		20 50		20 58
Clapham Junction 10	d	19 24	19 32		19 35	19 39	19 45	19 50		19 54	20 02	20 05	20 20		20 15	20 24	20 32	20 35	20 39	20 45	20 50		20 54		21 02
Vauxhall ⊖	d	19 29	19 37		19 40	19 44	19 50	19 55		19 59	20 07	20 10	20 25		20 20	20 29	20 37	20 40	20 44	20 50	20 55		20 59		21 07
London Waterloo 15 ⊖	a	19 34	19 42		19 45	19 48	19 55	20 00		20 04	20 12	20 15	20 29		20 25	20 34	20 42	20 45	20 48	20 55	21 01		21 04		21 13

A From London Waterloo

Table T152-R

Sundays

15 December to 10 May

Hampton Court, Shepperton, Guildford, Dorking and Chessington South - London

Station		SW	SW	SW A	SW	SW	SW	SW	SW		SW A	SW	SW	SW	SW	SW A	SW	SW	SW		SW	SW	SW A	SW	SW
Guildford	d	20 20	20 24				20 50	20 57						21 20	21 24				21 50		21 57				22 20
London Road (Guildford)	d	20 24					20 54							21 24					21 54						22 24
Clandon	d	20 29					20 59							21 29					21 59						22 29
Horsley	d	20 33					21 03							21 33					22 03						22 33
Effingham Junction [6]	d	20 36					21 06							21 36					22 06						22 36
Bookham	d	20 39												21 39											22 39
Cobham & Stoke d'Abernon	d						21 10												22 10						
Oxshott	d						21 13												22 13						
Claygate	d						21 16												22 16						
Hinchley Wood	d						21 19												22 19						
Hampton Court	d				21 05								21 35				22 05								
Thames Ditton	d				21 07								21 37				22 07								
Surbiton [6]	d		21 00		21 13		21 24	21 30					21 43		22 00		22 13		22 24		22 30				
Berrylands	d				21 15								21 45				22 15								
Shepperton	d											21 11												22 11	
Upper Halliford	d											21 14												22 14	
Sunbury	d											21 16												22 16	
Kempton Park	d											21 18												22 18	
Hampton	d											21 21												22 21	
Fulwell	d											21 24												22 24	
Strawberry Hill	d			20 49							21 14					21 49							22 14		
Teddington	d			20 55							21 17	21 29				21 55							22 17	22 29	
Hampton Wick	d			20 57							21 20	21 31				21 57							22 20	22 31	
Kingston	a			20 59							21 22	21 33				21 59							22 22	22 33	
	d			21 04								21 34				22 04								22 34	
Norbiton	d			21 06								21 36				22 06								22 36	
New Malden [6]	d			21 10	21 18							21 40	21 48			22 10	22 18							22 40	
Dorking [4]	182 d								21 07													22 07			
Box Hill & Westhumble	182 d								21 10													22 10			
Leatherhead	182 d	20 45							21 15					21 45								22 15			22 45
Ashtead	182 d	20 48							21 18					21 48								22 18			22 48
Epsom [3]	182 a	20 53							21 23					21 53								22 23			22 53
	d	20 53							21 23					21 53								22 23			22 53
Ewell West	d	20 57							21 27					21 57								22 27			22 57
Stoneleigh	d	20 59							21 29					21 59								22 29			22 59
Worcester Park	d	21 02							21 32					22 02								22 32			23 02
Chessington South	d					21 10												22 10							
Chessington North	d					21 12												22 12							
Tolworth	d					21 14												22 14							
Malden Manor	d					21 17												22 17							
Motspur Park	d	21 05				21 20			21 35					22 05				22 20				22 35			23 05
Raynes Park [6]	d	21 08		21 13	21 21	21 24			21 38			21 43	21 51	22 08		22 13	22 21	22 24				22 38		22 43	23 08
Wimbledon [6] ⊖	d	21 12	21 08	21 17	21 25	21 28	21 31	21 38	21 42			21 47	21 55	22 12	22 08	22 17	22 25	22 28	22 31		22 38	22 42		22 47	23 12
Earlsfield	d	21 16	21 11	21 20	21 28	21 31	21 35	21 41	21 46			21 50	21 58	22 16	22 11	22 20	22 28	22 31	22 35		22 41	22 46		22 50	23 16
Clapham Junction [10]	d	21 20	21 15	21 24	21 32	21 35	21 39	21 45	21 50			21 54	22 02	22 20	22 15	22 24	22 32	22 35	22 39		22 45	22 50		22 54	23 20
Vauxhall ⊖	d	21 25	21 20	21 29	21 37	21 40	21 44	21 50	21 55			21 59	22 07	22 25	22 20	22 29	22 37	22 40	22 44		22 50	22 55		22 59	23 25
London Waterloo [15] ⊖	a	21 29	21 25	21 36	21 42	21 45	21 48	21 55	22 00			22 04	22 12	22 29	22 25	22 36	22 43	22 45	22 48		22 55	23 00		23 06	23 29

A From London Waterloo

Table T152-R

Sundays

15 December to 10 May

Hampton Court, Shepperton, Guildford, Dorking and Chessington South - London

Station		SW	SW A	SW	SW		SW	SW	SW	SW A	SW	SW	SW	SW A
Guildford	d	22 24					22 50	22 57						
London Road (Guildford)	d						22 54							
Clandon	d						22 59							
Horsley	d						23 03							
Effingham Junction [6]	d						23 06							
Bookham	d													
Cobham & Stoke d'Abernon	d						23 10							
Oxshott	d						23 13							
Claygate	d						23 16							
Hinchley Wood	d						23 19							
Hampton Court	d			23 05									23 45	
Thames Ditton	d			23 07									23 47	
Surbiton [6]	d	23 00		23 13			23 24	23 30					23 53	
Berrylands	d			23 15									23 55	
Shepperton	d										23 11			
Upper Halliford	d										23 14			
Sunbury	d										23 16			
Kempton Park	d										23 18			
Hampton	d										23 21			
Fulwell	d										23 24			
Strawberry Hill	d		22 49							23 14				23 48
Teddington	d		22 55							23 17	23 29			23 51
Hampton Wick	d		22 57							23 20	23 31			23 54
Kingston	a		22 59							23 22	23 33			23 56
	d		23 04								23 34			
Norbiton	d		23 06								23 36			
New Malden [6]	d		23 10	23 18							23 40		23 58	
Dorking [4]	182 d								23 07					
Box Hill & Westhumble	182 d								23 10					
Leatherhead	182 d								23 15					
Ashtead	182 d								23 18					
Epsom [3]	182 a								23 23					
	d								23 23					
Ewell West	d								23 27					
Stoneleigh	d								23 29					
Worcester Park	d								23 32					
Chessington South	d				23 10							23 40		
Chessington North	d				23 12							23 42		
Tolworth	d				23 14							23 44		
Malden Manor	d				23 17							23 47		
Motspur Park	d				23 20				23 35			23 50		
Raynes Park [6]	d		23 13	23 21	23 24				23 38		23 43	23 54	00 01	
Wimbledon [6] ⊖	d	23 08	23 17	23 25	23 28		23 31	23 38	23 42		23 47	23a59	00a04	
Earlsfield	d	23 11	23 20	23 28	23 31		23 35	23 41	23 46		23 50			
Clapham Junction [10]	d	23 15	23 24	23 32	23 35		23 39	23 45	23 50		23 54			
Vauxhall ⊖	d	23 20	23 29	23 37	23 40		23 44	23 50	23 55		23 59			
London Waterloo [15] ⊖	a	23 25	23 35	23 42	23 45		23 48	23 55	00 01		00 04			

A From London Waterloo

Table T155-F

Mondays to Fridays

16 December to 15 May

London - Woking, Guildford, Alton and Basingstoke

Miles	Miles	Miles			SW MX 1	SW MO 1	SW MO 1	SW MX 1	SW MX 1	SW MO ◇1	SW MX ◇1	SW MO	SW MX ◇1	SW MX	SW MO 1	SW MO	SW MX ◇1	SW MX	SW MX 1	SW MO 1	SW MX 1	SW MO 1	SW MX ◇1
0	—	—	**London Waterloo** 15 ⊖	d																			00 05
1¼	—	—	Vauxhall ⊖	d																			
4	—	—	Clapham Junction 10	d																			00u12
5½	—	—	Earlsfield	d																			
7¼	—	—	Wimbledon 6 ⊖	d																			00u18
12	—	—	**Surbiton** 6	d																00 05	00 06		
14½	—	—	Esher	d																00 09			
16	—	—	Hersham	d																00 12			
17	—	—	Walton-on-Thames	d																00 15	00 13		
19	—	—	Weybridge	d																00 18	00 17		
20½	—	—	Byfleet & New Haw	d												00 02		00 06		00 21			
21¾	—	—	West Byfleet	d										00 03		00 05		00 09		00 24	00 22	←	
24½	0	—	**Woking**	a										00 08		00 11		00 15		00 30	00 26	00 30	00 35
—	—	—		d					00 01	00 02	00 03	00 05	00 07		00 08		00 13			00 33	00 28	00 33	00 37
—	2½	—	Worplesdon	d													00 18			→			
—	6	—	**Guildford**	a						00 10		00 19					00 24						
28	—	0	Brookwood	d				00 03	00 07												00 34	00 39	
—	—	4½	Ash Vale	d		00 03			00 15										00 19			00 47	
—	—	7	**Aldershot**	a		00 07			00 19										00 24			00 51	
—	—	—		d		00 08			00 20										00 24			00 52	
—	—	10	**Farnham**	a		00 13			00 25										00 30			00 57	
—	—	—		d		00 14			00 26														
—	—	14	Bentley	d	00 03	00 24			00 33														
—	—	18¾	**Alton**	a	00 10	00 31			00 40														
33¼	—	—	Farnborough (Main)	d				00 11			00 14				00 19						00 41		
36½	—	—	Fleet	d			00 04	00 16			00 20				00 25						00 47		
40	—	—	Winchfield	d			00 10	00 22													00s52		
42¼	—	—	Hook	d			00 14	00 26													00s57		
47¾	—	—	**Basingstoke**	a			00 21	00 35			00 33		00 28		00 39						01 06		00 55

		SW MX 1	SW MX 1	SW MX	SW MX	SW MO ◇1	SW ◇1	SW ◇1	SW ◇1	SW ◇1	SW 1	SW ◇1	SW ◇1	SW 1	SW 1	SW 1	SW	SW 1	SW ◇1	SW ◇1	SW ◇1	SW	SW ◇1
London Waterloo 15 ⊖	d			00 09	00 27	00 50	01 05	05 00	05 20	05 30			05 45				05 50		06 12	06 15		06 20	06 30
Vauxhall ⊖	d			00 13	00 31		01 09	05 04	05 24								05 54					06 24	
Clapham Junction 10	d			00 20	00 37	00 57	01 15	05 11	05 29	05u37			05 52				05 59		06u19	06u22		06 29	06u37
Earlsfield	d			00 24	00s41			05 14	05 32								06 02					06 32	
Wimbledon 6 ⊖	d			00 28	00 45		01s27	05 18	05 36	05 43							06 06					06 36	
Surbiton 6	d			00 35	00s56		01s35	05 26	05 44								06 14		06 30			06 44	
Esher	d			00s39				05 30	05 48								06 18					06 48	
Hersham	d			00s42				05 33	05 51								06 21					06 51	
Walton-on-Thames	d			00s45				05 37	05 54								06 24		06 37			06 54	
Weybridge	d			00s48				05 41	05 57								06 27		06 41			06 57	
Byfleet & New Haw	d			00s51				05 44	06 00								06 30					07 00	
West Byfleet	d			00s54	01s07			05 47	06 04			←					06 33				←	07 03	
Woking	a			00 59	01 12	01 16	01 48	05 51	06 09	05 59		06 09	06 12				06 38		06 49	06 42	06 49	07 07	06 56
	d		00 40	01 00		01 18	01 49	05 53	06 10	06 01	06 02	06 10	06 13	06 19		06 30			06 51	06 43	06 51	07 10	06 57
Worplesdon	d								→				06 18						→	06 48		→	
Guildford	a			01 08		01s26		06 00				06 18	06 24							06 54			
Brookwood	d		00 46								06 08			06 25		06 36					06 57		
Ash Vale	d	00 47	00 54								06 16					06 45							
Aldershot	a	00s52	00 58								06 20					06 50							
	d		00 59								06 21				06 41	06 51		07 11					
Farnham	a	00 58	01 04								06 26				06 46	06 56		07 16					
	d		01 05								06 27					06 57							
Bentley	d		01s11								06 33					07 03							
Alton	a		01 18								06 40					07 11							
Farnborough (Main)	d						01s58							06 33							07 05		
Fleet	d						02s04							06 38							07 10		
Winchfield	d													06 44							07 16		
Hook	d													06 48							07 20		
Basingstoke	a						02s16			06 20				06 58							07 28		07 16

		SW 1	SW ◇1	SW	SW 1	SW ◇1	SW ◇1	SW 1	SW ◇1	SW	SW 1	SW ◇1	SW 1	SW ◇1	SW ◇1 trolley	SW	SW 1	SW 1	SW ◇1	SW 1	SW	SW 1	SW 1
London Waterloo 15 ⊖	d		06 35			06 42	06 45	06 50		06 50	06 53	07 00		07 03	07 10			07 12	07 15		07 20	07 23	07 27
Vauxhall ⊖	d									06 54											07 24		
Clapham Junction 10	d		06u42			06u49	06u52			06 59	07u00			07u10	07u17			07u20	07u23		07 29	07u30	
Earlsfield	d									07 02											07 32		
Wimbledon 6 ⊖	d									07 06						←					07 36		
Surbiton 6	d					07 00				07 14	07 11					07 14		07 30			07 44	07 41	
Esher	d									→						07 18					→		
Hersham	d															07 21							
Walton-on-Thames	d					07 07										07 24		07 37					
Weybridge	d					07 11										07 27		07 41					
Byfleet & New Haw	d															07 30							
West Byfleet	d			←					←		07 21		←			07 33				←		07 51	
Woking	a		07 01	07 07		07 18	07 12	07 14	07 18		07 26	07 24	07 26	07 29	07 35	07 37		07 48	07 43	07 48		08 00	07 53
	d	06 58	07 02	07 10		07 19	07 13		07 19		07 30	07 25	07 30	07 30	07 39	07 39		07 49	07 43	07 49		08 02	
Worplesdon	d					→	07 18				→							→	07 48			→	
Guildford	a			07 19			07 24					07 32				07 47			07 54				
Brookwood	d	07 06							07 25				07 36							07 55			
Ash Vale	d	07 17											07 44										
Aldershot	a	07 22											07 49										
	d	07 23			07 41								07 50				08 11						
Farnham	a	07 28			07 46								07 55				08 16						
	d	07 29											07 56										
Bentley	d	07 35											08 02										
Alton	a	07 42											08 10										
Farnborough (Main)	d								07 33											08 03			
Fleet	d								07 38											08 08			
Winchfield	d								07 44											08 14			
Hook	d								07 48											08 18			
Basingstoke	a		07 22						07 56					07 48	07 58					08 26			

Table T155-F

Mondays to Fridays

16 December to 15 May

London - Woking, Guildford, Alton and Basingstoke

		SW ◇1 trolley	SW 1	SW	SW ◇1 trolley	SW 1	SW	SW 1	SW ◇1 trolley	SW 1	SW ◇1	SW ◇1 trolley	SW 1	SW	SW 1	SW ◇1 trolley	SW 1	SW ◇1 trolley	SW ◇1	SW	SW 1	SW 1
London Waterloo 15 ⊖	d	07 30		07 34	07 35				07 39	07 42	07 45	07 50		07 50	07 53	08 00		08 05	08 08			08 12
Vauxhall ⊖	d			07 39										07 54								
Clapham Junction 10	d			07 46					07u45		07u52	07u57		07 59	08u00			08u12				08u19
Earlsfield	d													08 02								
Wimbledon 6 ⊖	d						←							08 06						←		
Surbiton 6	d						07 44			08 00				08 14	08 11					08 14		08 30
Esher	d						07 48							→						08 18		
Hersham	d						07 51													08 21		
Walton-on-Thames	d						07 54			08 07										08 24		08 37
Weybridge	d						07 57			08 11										08 27		08 41
Byfleet & New Haw	d						08 00													08 30		
West Byfleet	d					←	08 03						←		08 21		←			08 33		
Woking	a	07 55			07 58	08 00	08 08			08 18	08 11	08 16	08 18		08 30	08 24	08 30		08 33	08 37		08 48
	d	07 55			08 00	08 02				08 19	08 13	08 17	08 19		08 31	08 25	08 31		08 34	08 39		08 49
Worplesdon	d									→	08 18				→							→
Guildford	a	08 04									08 24					08 33				08 50		
Brookwood	d					08 08							08 25				08 37					
Ash Vale	d			08 50		08 16		←									08 45					
Aldershot	a			08 54		08 20											08 49					
	d		08 41			08 21		08 41									08 50				09 11	
Farnham	a		→			08 26		08 46									08 55				09 16	
	d					08 27											08 56					
Bentley	d					08 33											09 02					
Alton	a					08 40											09 10					
Farnborough (Main)	d								08 13				08 33						08 45			
Fleet	d								08 19				08 38									
Winchfield	d												08 44									
Hook	d												08 48									
Basingstoke	a				08 19				08 32			08 36	08 58					08 47	08 58			

		SW ◇1	SW ◇1 trolley	SW 1	SW	SW 1	SW ◇1 trolley	SW ◇1 trolley	SW 1	SW	SW ◇1	SW 1	SW 1	SW ◇1	SW ◇1 trolley	SW 1	SW	SW 1	SW ◇1 trolley	SW 1	SW ◇1 trolley	SW ◇1	SW
London Waterloo 15 ⊖	d	08 15	08 20		08 20	08 24	08 30	08 35			08 39		08 42	08 45	08 50		08 50	08 53	09 00		09 05	09 09	
Vauxhall ⊖	d				08 24												08 54						
Clapham Junction 10	d	08u22	08u28		08 29						08u46			08u53			08 59	09u00			09u12		
Earlsfield	d				08 32												09 02						
Wimbledon 6 ⊖	d				08 36					←							09 06						←
Surbiton 6	d				08 44	08 41				08 44			09 00				09 14	09 11					09 14
Esher	d				→					08 48							→						09 18
Hersham	d									08 51													09 21
Walton-on-Thames	d									08 54			09 07										09 24
Weybridge	d									08 57			09 11										09 27
Byfleet & New Haw	d									09 00													09 30
West Byfleet	d			←		08 51			←	09 03						←		09 21		←			09 33
Woking	a	08 43	08 46	08 48		09 00	08 54	08 58	09 00	09 08			09 18	09 12	09 15	09 18		09 28	09 24	09 28		09 33	09 38
	d	08 43	08 46	08 49		09 00	08 55		09 00				09 19	09 13	09 16	09 19		09 30	09 25	09 30		09 34	
Worplesdon	d	08 48				→							→	09 18				→					
Guildford	a	08 54					09 02							09 24					09 32				
Brookwood	d			08 55					09 06							09 25				09 36			
Ash Vale	d								09 14											09 44			
Aldershot	a								09 19											09 49			
	d								09 20			09 41								09 50			
Farnham	a								09 25			09 46								09 55			
	d								09 26											09 56			
Bentley	d																			10 02			
Alton	a								09 38											10 10			
Farnborough (Main)	d			09 03							09 13					09 33						09 46	
Fleet	d			09 08							09 19					09 38							
Winchfield	d			09 14												09 44							
Hook	d			09 18												09 48							
Basingstoke	a		09 05	09 28							09 32				09 36	09 58					09 47	09 59	

		SW 1	SW 1	SW ◇1	SW ◇1 trolley	SW 1	SW	SW 1	SW ◇1 trolley	SW ◇1 trolley	SW 1	SW	SW ◇1	SW 1	SW 1	SW ◇1	SW ◇1 trolley	SW 1	SW	SW 1	SW ◇1 trolley	SW 1
London Waterloo 15 ⊖	d		09 12	09 15	09 20		09 20	09 24	09 30	09 35			09 39		09 42	09 45	09 50		09 50	09 53	10 00	
Vauxhall ⊖	d						09 24												09 54			
Clapham Junction 10	d		09u19	09u22	09u27		09 29						09u46			09u52	09u57		09 59	10u00		
Earlsfield	d						09 32												10 02			
Wimbledon 6 ⊖	d						09 36					←							10 06			
Surbiton 6	d		09 30				09 44	09 41				09 44			10 00				10 14	10 11		
Esher	d						→					09 48							→			
Hersham	d											09 51										
Walton-on-Thames	d		09 37									09 54			10 07							
Weybridge	d		09 41									09 57			10 11							
Byfleet & New Haw	d											10 00										
West Byfleet	d					←		09 51			←	10 03						←		10 21		←
Woking	a		09 48	09 42	09 45	09 48		09 59	09 54	09 58	09 59	10 08			10 18	10 12	10 15	10 18		10 29	10 24	10 29
	d		09 49	09 43	09 46	09 49		10 00	09 55		10 00				10 19	10 13	10 16	10 19		10 30	10 25	10 30
Worplesdon	d		→					→							→	10 18				→		
Guildford	a			09 50					10 02							10 24					10 32	
Brookwood	d					09 55					10 06							10 25				10 36
Ash Vale	d										10 14											10 44
Aldershot	a										10 19											10 49
	d	10 11									10 20			10 41								10 50
Farnham	a	10 16									10 25			10 46								10 55
	d										10 26											10 56
Bentley	d																					11 02
Alton	a										10 37											11 10
Farnborough (Main)	d					10 03							10 13					10 33				
Fleet	d					10 08							10 19					10 38				
Winchfield	d					10 14												10 44				
Hook	d					10 18												10 48				
Basingstoke	a				10 05	10 28							10 31				10 36	10 58				

Table T155-F

Mondays to Fridays

16 December to 15 May

London - Woking, Guildford, Alton and Basingstoke

		SW ◇1 ⊼	SW ◇1	SW	SW 1	SW 1	SW ◇1	SW ◇1 ⊼	SW 1		SW	SW 1	SW ◇1 ⊼	SW ◇1 ⊼	SW 1	SW	SW ◇1	SW 1	SW 1		SW ◇1	SW ◇1 ⊼	SW 1	SW	SW 1
London Waterloo 15 ⊖	d	10 05	10 09			10 12	10 15	10 20			10 20	10 23	10 30	10 35			10 39		10 42		10 45	10 50		10 50	10 53
Vauxhall ⊖	d										10 24													10 54	
Clapham Junction 10	d	10u12				10u19	10u22	10u27			10 29	10u30					10u46				10u52	10u57		10 59	11u00
Earlsfield	d										10 32													11 02	
Wimbledon 6 ⊖	d			←							10 36					←								11 06	
Surbiton 6	d			10 14		10 30					10 44	10 41				10 44			11 00					11 14	11 11
Esher	d			10 18							→					10 48								→	
Hersham	d			10 21												10 51									
Walton-on-Thames	d			10 24		10 37										10 54			11 07						
Weybridge	d			10 27		10 41										10 57			11 11						
Byfleet & New Haw	d			10 30												11 00									
West Byfleet	d			10 33					←			10 51			←	11 03							←		11 21
Woking	a		10 33	10 38		10 49	10 41	10 45	10 49			10 59	10 54	10 58	10 59	11 08			11 19		11 12	11 15	11 19		11 29
	d		10 34			10 49	10 43	10 46	10 49			11 00	10 55		11 00				11 20		11 13	11 16	11 20		11 30
Worplesdon	d					→						→							→		11 18				→
Guildford	a						10 50						11 02								11 24				
Brookwood	d								10 56						11 06								11 26		
Ash Vale	d														11 14										
Aldershot	a														11 19										
	d				11 11										11 20			11 41							
Farnham	a				11 16										11 25			11 46							
	d														11 26										
Bentley	d																								
Alton	a														11 37										
Farnborough (Main)	d		10 45						11 04								11 13						11 34		
Fleet	d								11 09								11 19						11 39		
Winchfield	d								11 15														11 45		
Hook	d								11 18														11 49		
Basingstoke	a	10 48	10 58					11 05	11 28								11 31					11 36	11 58		

		SW ◇1 ⊼	SW 1	SW ◇1 ⊼	SW ◇1		SW	SW 1	SW 1	SW ◇1	SW ◇1 ⊼	SW 1	SW	SW 1	SW ◇1 ⊼		SW ◇1 ⊼	SW 1	SW	SW ◇1	SW 1	SW 1	SW ◇1	SW ◇1 ⊼	SW 1
London Waterloo 15 ⊖	d	11 00		11 05	11 09				11 12	11 15	11 20		11 20	11 23	11 30		11 35			11 39		11 42	11 45	11 50	
Vauxhall ⊖	d												11 24												
Clapham Junction 10	d			11u12					11u19	11u22	11u27		11 29	11u30						11u46			11u52	11u57	
Earlsfield	d												11 32												
Wimbledon 6 ⊖	d						←						11 36						←						
Surbiton 6	d						11 14		11 30				11 44	11 41					11 44			12 00			
Esher	d						11 18						→						11 48						
Hersham	d						11 21												11 51						
Walton-on-Thames	d						11 24		11 37										11 54			12 07			
Weybridge	d						11 27		11 41										11 57			12 11			
Byfleet & New Haw	d						11 30												12 00						
West Byfleet	d		←				11 33					←		11 51				←	12 03						←
Woking	a	11 24	11 29		11 33		11 38		11 48	11 41	11 45	11 48		11 59	11 54		11 58	11 59	12 08			12 18	12 12	12 15	12 18
	d	11 25	11 30		11 34				11 49	11 43	11 46	11 49		12 00	11 55			12 00				12 19	12 13	12 16	12 19
Worplesdon	d								→					→								→	12 18		
Guildford	a	11 32								11 50					12 02								12 24		
Brookwood	d		11 36									11 55						12 06							12 25
Ash Vale	d		11 44															12 14							
Aldershot	a		11 49															12 19							
	d		11 50					12 11										12 20			12 41				
Farnham	a		11 55					12 16										12 25			12 46				
	d		11 56															12 26							
Bentley	d		12 02																						
Alton	a		12 10															12 37							
Farnborough (Main)	d				11 45							12 03								12 13					12 33
Fleet	d											12 08								12 19					12 38
Winchfield	d											12 14													12 44
Hook	d											12 18													12 48
Basingstoke	a			11 48	11 58						12 05	12 28								12 31				12 35	12 58

			SW	SW 1	SW ◇1 ⊼	SW 1	SW ◇1 ⊼	SW ◇1	SW	SW 1	SW 1		SW ◇1	SW ◇1 ⊼	SW 1	SW	SW 1	SW ◇1 ⊼	SW ◇1 ⊼	SW 1	SW		SW ◇1	SW 1	SW 1
London Waterloo 15 ⊖	d		11 50	11 53	12 00		12 05	12 09			12 12		12 15	12 20		12 20	12 23	12 30	12 35				12 39		12 42
Vauxhall ⊖	d		11 54													12 24									
Clapham Junction 10	d		11 59	12u00			12u12				12u19		12u22	12u27		12 29	12u30						12u46		
Earlsfield	d		12 02													12 32									
Wimbledon 6 ⊖	d		12 06						←							12 36					←				
Surbiton 6	d		12 14	12 11					12 14		12 30					12 44	12 41				12 44				13 00
Esher	d		→						12 18							→					12 48				
Hersham	d								12 21												12 51				
Walton-on-Thames	d								12 24		12 37										12 54				13 07
Weybridge	d								12 27		12 41										12 57				13 11
Byfleet & New Haw	d								12 30												13 00				
West Byfleet	d			12 21		←			12 33						←		12 51			←	13 03				
Woking	a			12 29	12 24	12 29		12 33	12 38		12 48		12 41	12 45	12 48		12 59	12 54	12 58	12 59	13 08				13 18
	d			12 30	12 25	12 30		12 34			12 49		12 43	12 46	12 49		13 00	12 55		13 00					13 19
Worplesdon	d			→							→						→								→
Guildford	a				12 32								12 50					13 02							
Brookwood	d					12 36									12 55					13 06					
Ash Vale	d					12 44														13 14					
Aldershot	a					12 49														13 19					
	d					12 50				13 11										13 20				13 41	
Farnham	a					12 55				13 16										13 25				13 46	
	d					12 56														13 26					
Bentley	d					13 02																			
Alton	a					13 10														13 37					
Farnborough (Main)	d							12 45							13 03								13 13		
Fleet	d														13 08								13 19		
Winchfield	d														13 14										
Hook	d														13 18										
Basingstoke	a						12 47	12 58						13 05	13 28								13 31		

Table T155-F

Mondays to Fridays

16 December to 15 May

London - Woking, Guildford, Alton and Basingstoke

		SW ◇1	SW ◇1 ⊼	SW 1	SW	SW 1	SW ◇1 ⊼		SW 1	SW ◇1 ⊼	SW ◇1	SW	SW 1	SW 1	SW ◇1	SW ◇1 ⊼	SW 1		SW	SW 1	SW ◇1 ⊼	SW ◇1 ⊼	SW 1	SW	SW ◇1
London Waterloo 15 ⊖	d	12 45	12 50		12 50	12 53	13 00			13 05	13 09			13 12	13 15	13 20			13 20	13 23	13 30	13 35			13 39
Vauxhall ⊖	d				12 54														13 24						
Clapham Junction 10	d	12u52	12u57		12 59	13u00				13u12				13u19	13u22	13u27			13 29	13u30					13u46
Earlsfield	d				13 02														13 32						
Wimbledon 6 ⊖	d				13 06							←							13 36					←	
Surbiton 6	d				13 14	13 11						13 14		13 30					13 44	13 41				13 44	
Esher	d				→							13 18							→					13 48	
Hersham	d											13 21												13 51	
Walton-on-Thames	d											13 24		13 37										13 54	
Weybridge	d											13 27		13 41										13 57	
Byfleet & New Haw	d											13 30												14 00	
West Byfleet	d			←		13 21			←			13 33					←			13 51			←	14 03	
Woking	a	13 12	13 15	13 18		13 29	13 24		13 29		13 33	13 38		13 48	13 41	13 45	13 48			13 59	13 54	13 58	13 59	14 08	
	d	13 13	13 16	13 19		13 30	13 25		13 30		13 34			13 49	13 43	13 46	13 49			14 00	13 55		14 00		
Worplesdon	d	13 18				→								→						→					
Guildford	a	13 24					13 32								13 50						14 02				
Brookwood	d			13 25					13 36								13 55						14 06		
Ash Vale	d								13 44														14 14		
Aldershot	a								13 49														14 19		
	d								13 50				14 11										14 20		
Farnham	a								13 55				14 16										14 25		
	d								13 56														14 26		
Bentley	d								14 02																
Alton	a								14 11														14 37		
Farnborough (Main)	d			13 33							13 45						14 03								14 13
Fleet	d			13 38													14 08								14 19
Winchfield	d			13 44													14 14								
Hook	d			13 48													14 18								
Basingstoke	a		13 36	13 58						13 47	13 58					14 05	14 28								14 31

		SW 1	SW 1		SW ◇1	SW ◇1 ⊼	SW 1	SW	SW 1	SW ◇1 ⊼	SW 1	SW ◇1 ⊼	SW ◇1		SW	SW 1	SW 1	SW ◇1	SW ◇1 ⊼	SW 1	SW	SW 1	SW ◇1 ⊼		SW ◇1 ⊼
London Waterloo 15 ⊖	d		13 42		13 45	13 50		13 50	13 53	14 00		14 05	14 09				14 12	14 15	14 20		14 20	14 23	14 30		14 35
Vauxhall ⊖	d							13 54													14 24				
Clapham Junction 10	d				13u52	13u57		13 59	14u00			14u12					14u19	14u22	14u27		14 29	14u30			
Earlsfield	d							14 02													14 32				
Wimbledon 6 ⊖	d							14 06							←						14 36				
Surbiton 6	d		14 00					14 14	14 11						14 14		14 30				14 44	14 41			
Esher	d							→							14 18						→				
Hersham	d														14 21										
Walton-on-Thames	d		14 07												14 24		14 37								
Weybridge	d		14 11												14 27		14 41								
Byfleet & New Haw	d														14 30										
West Byfleet	d						←		14 21		←				14 33					←		14 51			
Woking	a		14 19		14 12	14 15	14 19		14 29	14 24	14 29		14 33		14 38		14 48	14 42	14 45	14 48		14 59	14 54		14 58
	d		14 20		14 13	14 16	14 20		14 30	14 25	14 30		14 34				14 49	14 43	14 46	14 49		15 00	14 55		
Worplesdon	d		→		14 18				→								→					→			
Guildford	a				14 24					14 32								14 50					15 02		
Brookwood	d						14 26				14 36									14 55					
Ash Vale	d										14 44														
Aldershot	a										14 49														
	d	14 41									14 50					15 11									
Farnham	a	14 46									14 55					15 16									
	d										14 56														
Bentley	d										15 02														
Alton	a										15 10														
Farnborough (Main)	d						14 34						14 45							15 03					
Fleet	d						14 39													15 08					
Winchfield	d						14 45													15 14					
Hook	d						14 49													15 18					
Basingstoke	a					14 36	14 58					14 48	14 58						15 05	15 28					

		SW 1	SW	SW ◇1	SW 1	SW 1	SW ◇1	SW ◇1 ⊼	SW 1		SW	SW 1	SW ◇1 ⊼	SW 1	SW ◇1 ⊼	SW ◇1	SW	SW 1	SW ◇1		SW ◇1	SW ◇1 ⊼	SW ◇1	SW	SW 1
London Waterloo 15 ⊖	d			14 39		14 42	14 45	14 50			14 50	14 53	15 00		15 05	15 09			15 12		15 15	15 20		15 20	15 23
Vauxhall ⊖	d										14 54													15 24	
Clapham Junction 10	d			14u46			14u52	14u57			14 59	15u00			15u12				15 19		15u22	15u27		15 29	15u30
Earlsfield	d										15 02													15 32	
Wimbledon 6 ⊖	d		←								15 06						←							15 36	
Surbiton 6	d		14 44			15 00					15 14	15 11					15 14		15 30					15 44	15 41
Esher	d		14 48								→						15 18							→	
Hersham	d		14 51														15 21								
Walton-on-Thames	d		14 54			15 07											15 24		15 37						
Weybridge	d		14 57			15 11											15 27		15 41						
Byfleet & New Haw	d		15 00														15 30								
West Byfleet	d	←	15 03						←			15 21		←			15 33						←		15 51
Woking	a	14 59	15 08			15 18	15 12	15 15	15 18			15 29	15 24	15 29		15 33	15 38		15 48		15 42	15 45	15 48		15 59
	d	15 00				15 19	15 13	15 16	15 19			15 30	15 25	15 30		15 34			15 49		15 43	15 46	15 49		16 00
Worplesdon	d					→	15 18					→							→						→
Guildford	a						15 24						15 32								15 50				
Brookwood	d	15 06							15 25					15 36									15 55		
Ash Vale	d	15 14												15 44											
Aldershot	a	15 19												15 49											
	d	15 20			15 41									15 50				16 11							
Farnham	a	15 25			15 46									15 55				16 16							
	d	15 26												15 56											
Bentley	d													16 02											
Alton	a	15 37												16 10											
Farnborough (Main)	d			15 13					15 33							15 45							16 03		
Fleet	d			15 19					15 38														16 08		
Winchfield	d								15 44														16 14		
Hook	d								15 48														16 18		
Basingstoke	a			15 31				15 36	15 58						15 47	15 58						16 05	16 28		

Table T155-F

Mondays to Fridays
16 December to 15 May

London - Woking, Guildford, Alton and Basingstoke

		SW ◇1 ⚒	SW ◇1 ⚒	SW 1	SW	SW ◇1	SW 1	SW 1	SW ◇1	SW ◇1 ⚒	SW 1	SW	SW 1	SW ◇1 ⚒	SW 1	SW ◇1 ⚒	SW ◇1	SW	SW 1	SW ◇1	SW ◇1	SW ◇1 ⚒	SW ◇1
London Waterloo 15 ⊖	d	15 30	15 35			15 39		15 42	15 45	15 50		15 50	15 53	16 00		16 05	16 09			16 12	16 15	16 20	
Vauxhall ⊖	d											15 54											
Clapham Junction 10	d					15u46			15u52	15u57		15 59	16u00			16u12				16u19	16u22	16u27	
Earlsfield	d											16 02											
Wimbledon 6 ⊖	d				←							16 06						←					
Surbiton 6	d				15 44			16 00				16 14	16 11					16 14		16 30			
Esher	d				15 48							→						16 18					
Hersham	d				15 51													16 21					
Walton-on-Thames	d				15 54			16 07										16 24		16 37			
Weybridge	d				15 57			16 11										16 27		16 41			
Byfleet & New Haw	d				16 00													16 30					
West Byfleet	d			←	16 03						←		16 21		←			16 33					←
Woking	a	15 54	15 58	15 59	16 08			16 17	16 12	16 15	16 17		16 29	16 24	16 29		16 33	16 38		16 48	16 42		16 48
	d	15 55		16 00				16 18	16 13	16 16	16 18		16 30	16 25	16 30		16 34			16 50	16 43	16u46	16 50
Worplesdon	d							→	16 18				→							→	16 48		
Guildford	a	16 02							16 23					16 33							16 54		
Brookwood	d			16 06							16 25				16 36								16 55
Ash Vale	d			16 14											16 44								
Aldershot	a			16 19											16 49								
	d			16 20			16 41								16 50				17 11				
Farnham	a			16 25			16 46								16 55				17 16				
	d			16 26											16 56								
Bentley	d														17 02								
Alton	a			16 37											17 10								
Farnborough (Main)	d					16 13					16 33						16 45						17 03
Fleet	d					16 19					16 38												17 08
Winchfield	d										16 44												17 14
Hook	d										16 48												17 18
Basingstoke	a					16 31				16 36	16 58					16 47	16 58					17 05	17 30

		SW ◇	SW ◇1	SW ◇1 ⚒	SW ◇1	SW ◇	SW ◇1	SW 1	SW ◇1	SW ◇1	SW ◇1 ⚒	SW ◇1	SW ◇	SW ◇	SW ◇1	SW ◇1 ⚒	SW ◇1	SW ◇1	SW ◇1	SW ◇1	SW ◇1	SW ◇1
London Waterloo 15 ⊖	d	16 20	16 25	16 30			16 39		16 42	16 45	16 50		16 50	16 54	16 55	17 00		17 02	17 09	17 11	17 15	17 18
Vauxhall ⊖	d	16 24											16 54	16 59								
Clapham Junction 10	d	16 29					16u46			16u52	16u57		16 59	17 05	17u02							
Earlsfield	d	16 32											17 02									
Wimbledon 6 ⊖	d	16 36				←							17 06									
Surbiton 6	d	16 44	16 41			16 44			17 00				17 14					17 18				
Esher	d	→				16 48							17 18					17 22				
Hersham	d					16 51							17 21					17 25				
Walton-on-Thames	d					16 54			17 07				17 24					17 29				
Weybridge	d					16 57			17 11				17 27					17 33				
Byfleet & New Haw	d					17 00							17 30					17 36				
West Byfleet	d		16 51		←	17 03						←	17 33		17 21		←	17 39				
Woking	a		16 59	16 55	16 59	17 11			17 19	17 12		17 19	17 40		17 29	17 24	17 29	17 46	17 32	17 35		17 42
	d		17 00	16 55	17 00				17 20	17 13	17u16	17 20			17 30	17 25	17 30	17 47	17 34	17 37		17 43
Worplesdon	d		→						→	17 18					→			→				17 48
Guildford	a			17 03						17 24						17 33					17 50	17 53
Brookwood	d				17 06							17 26					17 36			17 43		
Ash Vale	d				17 14									18 16			17 44					
Aldershot	a				17 19									→			17 49					
	d				17 20			17 41									17 50					
Farnham	a				17 25			17 46									17 55					
	d				17 26												17 56					
Bentley	d				17 32												18 02					
Alton	a				17 39												18 09					
Farnborough (Main)	d						17 13					17 34								17 51		
Fleet	d						17 19					17 39								17 56		
Winchfield	d											17 45								18 02		
Hook	d											17 49								18 06		
Basingstoke	a						17 31				17 36	18 00							17 52	18 16		

		SW ◇1 ⚒	SW ◇1	SW ◇	SW ◇1	SW ◇1	SW ◇1	SW ◇1 ⚒	SW ◇	SW 1	SW ◇	SW ◇1	SW ◇1	SW ◇1	SW ◇1	SW ◇1	SW ◇1	SW ◇1 ⚒	SW ◇	SW ◇1	SW ◇	SW ◇1	SW ◇1
London Waterloo 15 ⊖	d	17 20		17 20	17 23	17 25		17 30				17 32	17 39	17 41	17 45	17 48		17 50	17 50	17 53	17 54	17 55	
Vauxhall ⊖	d			17 24															17 54		17 59		
Clapham Junction 10	d			17 29															17 59		18 05		
Earlsfield	d			17 32															18 02				
Wimbledon 6 ⊖	d			17 36					←										18 06				
Surbiton 6	d			17 44	17 39				17 44			17 48							18 14	18 09			
Esher	d			→					17 48			17 52							→				
Hersham	d								17 51			17 55											
Walton-on-Thames	d								17 54			17 59											
Weybridge	d								17 57			18 03											
Byfleet & New Haw	d								18 00			18 06											
West Byfleet	d		←				←		18 03			18 09					←			18 19			←
Woking	a		17 46		17 51	17 50	17 51		18 10			18 14	18 02			18 11	18 14			18 23		18 20	18 23
	d	17u46	17 47		17 52	17 51	17 52	17u55				18 16	18 04			18 13	18 16			18 25		18 21	18 25
Worplesdon	d				→			18 00				→					18 21			→			
Guildford	a		17 57					18 09							18 20		18 29						
Brookwood	d						18 00				←			18 11								18 27	
Ash Vale	d					18 03					18 16										19 16	18 35	
Aldershot	a					18 08					18 21										→	18 40	
	d					18 09				18 13	18 25											18 41	
Farnham	a					18 14				18 20	18 32											18 46	
	d					18 15																18 47	
Bentley	d					18 24																18 53	
Alton	a					18 31																19 01	
Farnborough (Main)	d						18 08							18 19									18 39
Fleet	d						18 13							18 24									18 44
Winchfield	d						18 19							18 30									18 50
Hook	d						18 23							18 34									18 54
Basingstoke	a	18 05					18 32						18 22	18 45		18 31		18 37					19 03

Table T155-F

Mondays to Fridays
16 December to 15 May

London - Woking, Guildford, Alton and Basingstoke

		SW ◇	SW ◇1 ⚒	SW 1	SW ◇1	SW ◇1	SW ◇1	SW ◇1	SW ◇1	SW ◇1 ⚒	SW ◇1	SW ◇	SW ◇1	SW ◇1	SW ◇1	SW ◇1 ⚒	SW ◇	SW 1	SW ◇	SW 1	SW ◇1	SW ◇1
London Waterloo 15 ⊖	d		18 00		18 02	18 09	18 12	18 15	18 17	18 20		18 20	18 23	18 25		18 30					18 32	18 39
Vauxhall ⊖	d											18 24										
Clapham Junction 10	d								18u24	18u27		18 29		18u33								18u46
Earlsfield	d											18 32										
Wimbledon 6 ⊖	d	←										18 36					←					
Surbiton 6	d	18 14			18 18							18 44	18 40				18 44				18 48	
Esher	d	18 18			18 22							→					18 48				18 52	
Hersham	d	18 21			18 25												18 51				18 55	
Walton-on-Thames	d	18 24			18 29												18 54				18 59	
Weybridge	d	18 27			18 33												18 57				19 03	
Byfleet & New Haw	d	18 30			18 36												19 00				19 06	
West Byfleet	d	18 33			18 39						←				←		19 03				19 09	
Woking	a	18 41			18 47	18 32			18 43		18 47		18 52	18 51	18 52	18 55	19 16				19 18	19 05
	d				18 48	18 34			18 44	18u46	18 48		18 53	18 52	18 53	18 55					19 20	19 06
Worplesdon	d				→				18 49				→								→	
Guildford	a		18 31					18 50	18 54							19 03						
Brookwood	d						18 41								19 02				←			
Ash Vale	d													19 04					19 16			
Aldershot	a										19 04			19 09					19 21			
	d			18 45							19 05			19 10				19 15	19 21	19 41		
Farnham	a			18 51							19 12			19 16				19 22	19 30	19 46		
	d													19 17								
Bentley	d													19 24								
Alton	a													19 31								
Farnborough (Main)	d						18 48								19 10							
Fleet	d						18 54								19 15							
Winchfield	d						18 59								19 21							
Hook	d						19 04								19 25							
Basingstoke	a					18 53	19 18			19 05					19 34							19 28

		SW ◇1	SW ◇1	SW ◇1	SW ◇1 ⚒	SW ◇1	SW ◇	SW ◇	SW ◇1	SW ◇1 ⚒	SW 1	SW ◇1 ⚒	SW ◇1	SW 1	SW ◇1	SW ◇1 ⚒	SW 1	SW	SW 1	SW 1	SW ◇1 ⚒	SW ◇1 ⚒	SW 1
London Waterloo 15 ⊖	d	18 41	18 45	18 48	18 50		18 50	18 54	18 55	19 00	19 02	19 05	19 09	19 11	19 15	19 20		19 20		19 25	19 30	19 35	
Vauxhall ⊖	d						18 54	18 59										19 24					
Clapham Junction 10	d						18 59	19 05	19u02			19u12		19u18	19u22	19u27		19 29		19u33			
Earlsfield	d						19 02											19 32					
Wimbledon 6 ⊖	d						19 06											19 36					
Surbiton 6	d						19 14				19 18							19 44					
Esher	d						19 18				19 22							19 48					
Hersham	d						19 21				19 25							19 51					
Walton-on-Thames	d						19 24				19 29							19 54					
Weybridge	d						19 27				19 33							19 57					
Byfleet & New Haw	d						19 30				19 36							20 00					
West Byfleet	d					←	19 33		19 20		19 39						←	20 03		19 51			←
Woking	a		19 10	19 12		19 18	19 41		19 24		19 48		19 33	19 37	19 42		19 48	20 08		19 59	19 54	19 58	19 59
	d		19 11	19 14	19u19	19 20			19 25		19 50		19 34	19 38	19 43	19u46	19 50			20 00	19 55		20 00
Worplesdon	d		19 16								→				19 48					→			
Guildford	a		19 22							19 32					19 54						20 03		
Brookwood	d	19 13							19 32					19 45									20 06
Ash Vale	d							20 18	19 39														20 14
Aldershot	a							→	19 44								20 05						20 19
	d								19 45								20 06		20 11				20 19
Farnham	a								19 51								20 13		20 17				20 25
	d								19 53														20 25
Bentley	d								19 59														20 32
Alton	a								20 07														20 39
Farnborough (Main)	d	19 20				19 31							19 45	19 52									
Fleet	d	19 26				19 37								19 58									
Winchfield	d	19 31				19 42								20 03									
Hook	d	19 36				19 47								20 08									
Basingstoke	a	19 45		19 33	19 38	20 00						19 47	19 58	20 15		20 06							

		SW ◇	SW ◇1	SW 1	SW 1	SW ◇1	SW ◇1	SW ◇1 ⚒	SW 1	SW	SW 1	SW ◇1 ⚒	SW 1	SW ◇1 ⚒	SW ◇1	SW	SW 1	SW 1	SW ◇1	SW ◇1 ⚒	SW 1	SW	SW 1
London Waterloo 15 ⊖	d		19 39		19 42	19 45	19 48	19 50		19 50	19 53	20 00		20 05	20 09			20 12	20 15	20 20		20 20	20 23
Vauxhall ⊖	d									19 54												20 24	
Clapham Junction 10	d		19u46			19u52				19 59	20u00			20u12				20u19	20u22	20u27		20 29	20u30
Earlsfield	d									20 02												20 32	
Wimbledon 6 ⊖	d									20 06						←						20 36	
Surbiton 6	d				20 00					20 14	20 11					20 14		20 30				20 44	20 41
Esher	d									→						20 18						→	
Hersham	d															20 21							
Walton-on-Thames	d				20 07											20 24		20 37					
Weybridge	d				20 11											20 27		20 41					
Byfleet & New Haw	d															20 30							
West Byfleet	d								←		20 21		←			20 33					←		20 51
Woking	a				20 18	20 12			20 18		20 29	20 24	20 29		20 33	20 38		20 48	20 42	20 45	20 48		20 59
	d				20 19	20 13		20u16	20 19		20 30	20 25	20 30		20 34			20 49	20 43	20 46	20 49		21 00
Worplesdon	d				→	20 18					→							→					→
Guildford	a					20 24						20 33							20 50				
Brookwood	d	←							20 25				20 36								20 55		
Ash Vale	d	20 18											20 44										
Aldershot	a	20 24											20 49										
	d	20 24		20 41									20 50				21 11						
Farnham	a	20 32		20 48									20 55				21 16						
	d												20 56										
Bentley	d												21 02										
Alton	a												21 10										
Farnborough (Main)	d		20 13						20 33						20 45						21 03		
Fleet	d		20 19						20 38												21 08		
Winchfield	d								20 44												21 14		
Hook	d								20 48												21 18		
Basingstoke	a		20 30				20 31	20 36	20 58					20 47	20 58					21 05	21 28		

Table T155-F

Mondays to Fridays
16 December to 15 May

London - Woking, Guildford, Alton and Basingstoke

		SW ◇1 ⊼	SW ◇1 ⊼	SW 1	SW	SW ◇1	SW 1	SW 1	SW ◇1	SW ◇1 ⊼		SW 1	SW	SW 1	SW ◇1 ⊼	SW 1	SW ◇1 ⊼	SW ◇1	SW	SW 1		SW 1	SW 1	SW ◇1 ⊼
London Waterloo [15] ⊖ d		20 30	20 35			20 39		20 42	20 45	20 50			20 50	20 53	21 00		21 05	21 09				21 12	21 15	21 20
Vauxhall ⊖ d													20 54											
Clapham Junction [10] d						20u46			20u52	20u57			20 59	21u00			21u12					21u19	21u22	21u27
Earlsfield d													21 02											
Wimbledon [6] ⊖ d					←								21 06						←					
Surbiton [6] d					20 44			21 00					21 14	21 11					21 14			21 30		
Esher d					20 48								→						21 18					
Hersham d					20 51														21 21					
Walton-on-Thames d					20 54			21 07											21 24			21 37		
Weybridge d					20 57			21 11											21 27			21 41		
Byfleet & New Haw d					21 00														21 30					
West Byfleet d				←	21 03							←		21 21		←			21 33					
Woking a		20 54	20 58	20 59	21 08			21 18	21 12	21 15		21 18		21 29	21 24	21 29		21 33	21 38			21 48	21 42	21 45
d		20 55		21 00				21 19	21 13	21 16		21 19		21 30	21 25	21 30		21 34				21 49	21 43	21 46
Worplesdon d								→	21 18					→								→		
Guildford a		21 03							21 24						21 33								21 51	
Brookwood d				21 06								21 25				21 36								
Ash Vale d				21 14												21 44								
Aldershot a				21 19												21 49								
d				21 20			21 41									21 50				22 11				
Farnham a				21 25			21 46									21 55				22 16				
d				21 26												21 56								
Bentley d				21 32												22 02								
Alton a				21 39												22 09								
Farnborough (Main) d						21 13						21 33						21 45						
Fleet d						21 19						21 38												
Winchfield d												21 44												
Hook d												21 48												
Basingstoke a						21 31				21 35		21 58					21 47	21 58						22 05

	SW 1	SW	SW 1	SW ◇1	SW ◇1 ⊼	SW 1		SW	SW ◇1	SW 1	SW 1	SW ◇1	SW ◇1	SW 1	SW	SW 1		SW ◇1	SW 1	SW ◇1 ⊼	SW ◇1	SW	SW 1	SW 1
London Waterloo [15] ⊖ d		21 20	21 23	21 30	21 35				21 39		21 42	21 45	21 50		21 50	21 53		22 00		22 05	22 08			22 12
Vauxhall ⊖ d		21 24													21 54									
Clapham Junction [10] d		21 29	21u30						21u46			21u52	21u57		21 59	22u00				22u12				22u19
Earlsfield d		21 32													22 02									
Wimbledon [6] ⊖ d		21 36						←							22 06							←		
Surbiton [6] d		21 44	21 41					21 44			22 00				22 14	22 11						22 14		22 30
Esher d		→						21 48							→							22 18		
Hersham d								21 51														22 21		
Walton-on-Thames d								21 54			22 07											22 24		22 37
Weybridge d								21 57			22 11											22 27		22 41
Byfleet & New Haw d								22 00														22 30		
West Byfleet d	←		21 51			←		22 03						←		22 21			←			22 33		
Woking a	21 48		21 59	21 54	21 58	21 59		22 08			22 18	22 12	22 15	22 18		22 29		22 24	22 29		22 33	22 38		22 47
d	21 49		22 00	21 55		22 00					22 19	22 13	22 16	22 19		22 30		22 25	22 30		22 34			22 49
Worplesdon d			→								→	22 18				→								→
Guildford a				22 03								22 24						22 33						
Brookwood d	21 55					22 06								22 25					22 36					
Ash Vale d						22 14													22 44					
Aldershot a						22 19													22 49					
d						22 20				22 41									22 50				23 11	
Farnham a						22 25				22 46									22 55				23 16	
d						22 26													22 56					
Bentley d						22 32													23 02					
Alton a						22 39													23 09					
Farnborough (Main) d	22 03								22 13					22 33							22 45			
Fleet d	22 08								22 19					22 38										
Winchfield d	22 14													22 44										
Hook d	22 18													22 48										
Basingstoke a	22 28								22 31				22 35	22 58						22 47	22 58			

	SW 1	SW 1 ⊼		SW 1	SW	SW 1	SW ◇1	SW ◇1 ⊼	SW 1	SW	SW ◇1	SW 1		SW ◇1	SW ◇1	SW 1	SW	SW	SW 1	SW ◇1	SW 1	SW ◇1		SW
London Waterloo [15] ⊖ d	22 15	22 20			22 20	22 23	22 30	22 35			22 39	22 42		22 45	22 50		22 50	22 52	22 53	23 00		23 05		
Vauxhall ⊖ d					22 24												22 54	22 56						
Clapham Junction [10] d	22u22	22u27			22 29	22u30					22u46	22u49		22u52	22u57		22 59	23 02	23u00	23u07		23u12		
Earlsfield d					22 32												23 02							
Wimbledon [6] ⊖ d					22 36					←							23 06							←
Surbiton [6] d					22 44	22 41				22 44		23 00					23 14		23 11					23 14
Esher d					→					22 48							→							23 18
Hersham d										22 51														23 21
Walton-on-Thames d										22 54		23 07												23 24
Weybridge d										22 57		23 11												23 27
Byfleet & New Haw d										23 00								00 06						23 30
West Byfleet d				←		22 51			←	23 03						←		→	23 21		←			23 33
Woking a	22 42	22 45		22 47		22 59	22 54	22 58	22 59	23 08		23 18		23 12	23 15	23 18			23 29	23 26	23 29	23 31		23 39
d	22 43	22 46		22 49		23 00	22 55		23 00			23 19		23 13	23 16	23 19			23 31	23 27	23 31	23 33		
Worplesdon d						→						→		23 18					→					
Guildford a	22 51						23 03							23 24						23 35				
Brookwood d				22 55					23 06							23 25					23 36			
Ash Vale d									23 14												23 44			
Aldershot a									23 19												23 49			
d									23 20												23 50			
Farnham a									23 25												23 55			
d									23 26												23 56			
Bentley d									23 33												00 03			
Alton a									23 41												00 10			
Farnborough (Main) d				23 02							23 16					23 33								
Fleet d				23 08							23 21					23 38								
Winchfield d				23 13												23 44								
Hook d				23 18												23 48								
Basingstoke a		23 05		23 28							23 33				23 37	23 57						23 51		

Table T155-F

Mondays to Fridays
16 December to 15 May

London - Woking, Guildford, Alton and Basingstoke

	SW 1	SW 1	SW ◇1	SW	SW 1	SW ◇1	SW 1	SW 1		SW ◇1	SW ◇1	SW	SW ◇1	SW	SW 1
London Waterloo [15] ⊖ d		23 12	23 15	23 20	23 23	23 30				23 35	23 40		23 45		23 48
Vauxhall ⊖ d				23 24											
Clapham Junction [10] d		23u19	23u22	23 29	23u30					23u42	23u47		23u52		23u55
Earlsfield d				23 32											
Wimbledon [6] ⊖ d				23 36								←			
Surbiton [6] d		23 38		23 44	23 41							23 44			00 06
Esher d				→								23 48			
Hersham d												23 51			
Walton-on-Thames d		23 45										23 54			00 13
Weybridge d		23 49										23 57		←	00 17
Byfleet & New Haw d												23 59		00 06	
West Byfleet d					23 55		←	←				00 03		00 09	00 22
Woking a		23 55	23 41		23 59	23 53	23 55	23 59		00 01	00 06	00 08	00 11	00 15	00 26
d		23 57	23 43		00 01	23 55	23 57	00 01		00 03	00 07		00 13		00 28
Worplesdon d		→			→								00 18		
Guildford a			23 50			00 02							00 24		
Brookwood d							00 03	00 07							00 34
Ash Vale d								00 15							
Aldershot a								00 19							
d	23 58							00 20							
Farnham a	00 03							00 25							
d								00 26							
Bentley d								00 33							
Alton a								00 40							
Farnborough (Main) d							00 11			00 14					00 41
Fleet d							00 16			00 20					00 47
Winchfield d							00 22								00s52
Hook d							00 26								00s57
Basingstoke a							00 35			00 33	00 28				01 06

Saturdays
21 December to 16 May

	SW 1	SW 1	SW 1	SW ◇1	SW ◇1	SW	SW ◇1	SW	SW 1		SW ◇1	SW 1	SW 1	SW	SW	SW ◇1	SW 1	SW 1	SW ◇1		SW ◇1	SW 1	SW ◇1	SW 1
London Waterloo [15] ⊖ d											00 05			00 09	00 27	01 05		05 00	05 20		05 30			
Vauxhall ⊖ d														00 13	00 31	01 09		05 04	05 24					
Clapham Junction [10] d											00u12			00 20	00 37	01 15		05 11	05 29		05u37			
Earlsfield d														00 23	00s41			05 14	05 32					
Wimbledon [6] ⊖ d											00u18			00 27	00 45	01s20		05 18	05 36		05 43			
Surbiton [6] d									00 06					00 35	00s56	01s28		05 26	05 44					
Esher d														00s39				05 30	05 48					
Hersham d														00s42				05 33	05 52					
Walton-on-Thames d									00 13					00s44				05 37	05 55					
Weybridge d									00 17					00s48				05 41	05 58					
Byfleet & New Haw d								00 06						00s51				05 44	06 01					
West Byfleet d						00 03		00 09	00 22					00s54	01s07			05 47	06 04				←	
Woking a						00 08		00 15	00 26		00 35			00 58	01 12	01 41		05 51	06 10		05 59		06 10	
d			00 01	00 03	00 07		00 13		00 28		00 37		00 40	01 00		01 42		05 53	06 13		06 01	06 03	06 13	06 19
Worplesdon d							00 18												→				06 18	
Guildford a							00 24							01 07				06 00					06 23	
Brookwood d		00 03	00 07						00 34				00 46									06 10		06 25
Ash Vale d			00 15									00 19	00 54				01 08					06 18		
Aldershot a			00 19									00 24	00 58				01s13					06 23		
d			00 20									00 24	00 59									06 23		
Farnham a			00 25									00 30	01 04				01 19					06 28		
d			00 26										01 05									06 28		
Bentley d	00 03		00 33										01s11									06 35		
Alton a	00 10		00 40										01 18									06 43		
Farnborough (Main) d		00 11		00 14					00 41							01s51								06 33
Fleet d		00 16		00 20					00 47							01s57								06 38
Winchfield d		00 22							00s52															06 43
Hook d		00 26							00s57															06 48
Basingstoke a		00 35		00 33	00 28				01 06		00 55					02s09					06 20			06 58

Table T155-F

London - Woking, Guildford, Alton and Basingstoke

Saturdays

21 December to 16 May

		SW		SW	SW	SW	SW	SW	SW	SW	SW	SW		SW	SW	SW	SW	SW	SW	SW	SW	SW		SW	SW
		1		1		1	1	1	1	1		◇1		1	◇1	1	◇1	◇1	◇1		1	◇1 ⊼			1
London Waterloo 15 ⊖	d				05 50		06 12	06 15			06 20	06 30			06 35		06 42	06 45		06 50	06 54	07 10			
Vauxhall ⊖	d				05 54						06 24									06 54					
Clapham Junction 10	d				05 59		06u19	06u22			06 29	06u37			06u42		06u49	06u52		06 59	07u01	07u17			
Earlsfield	d				06 02						06 32									07 02					
Wimbledon 8 ⊖	d				06 06						06 36									07 06				←	
Surbiton 8	d				06 14		06 30				06 44						07 00			07 14	07 12			07 14	
Esher	d				06 18						06 48									→				07 18	
Hersham	d				06 21						06 51													07 21	
Walton-on-Thames	d				06 24		06 37				06 54						07 07							07 24	
Weybridge	d				06 27		06 41				06 57						07 11							07 27	
Byfleet & New Haw	d				06 30						07 00													07 30	
West Byfleet	d				06 33				←		07 03			←					←		07 22			07 33	
Woking	a				06 38		06 48	06 42	06 48		07 08	06 56			07 00		07 18	07 12	07 18		07 26	07 35		07 38	
	d			06 30			06 49	06 43	06 49	07 00		06 57		07 00	07 01		07 19	07 13	07 19		07 30	07 36			
Worplesdon	d						→			→							→	07 18							
Guildford	a							06 50										07 23							
Brookwood	d			06 36					06 55					07 06					07 25		07 36				
Ash Vale	d			06 44										07 14							07 44				
Aldershot	a			06 49										07 19							07 49				
	d	06 41		06 50		07 11								07 20		07 41					07 50				08 11
Farnham	a	06 46		06 55		07 16								07 25		07 46					07 55				08 16
	d			06 56										07 26							07 56				
Bentley	d			07 02										07 32							08 02				
Alton	a			07 10										07 40							08 10				
Farnborough (Main)	d								07 03										07 33						
Fleet	d								07 08										07 38						
Winchfield	d								07 14										07 44						
Hook	d								07 18										07 48						
Basingstoke	a								07 28			07 16			07 22				07 58			07 58			

		SW	SW	SW	SW	SW	SW	SW		SW	SW	SW	SW	SW	SW	SW	SW	SW		SW	SW	SW	SW	SW	SW
		1	1	1		1	◇1	◇1		1		◇1	1	1	◇1	◇1 ⊼	1			1	◇1	1	◇1	◇1	
London Waterloo 15 ⊖	d	07 12	07 15		07 20	07 24	07 30	07 35				07 39		07 42	07 45	07 50		07 50		07 54	08 00		08 05	08 09	
Vauxhall ⊖	d				07 24													07 54							
Clapham Junction 10	d	07u20	07u23		07 29	07u31						07u46			07u52	07u57		07 59		08u01			08u12		
Earlsfield	d				07 32													08 02							
Wimbledon 8 ⊖	d				07 36						←							08 06							←
Surbiton 8	d	07 30			07 44	07 42					07 44			08 00				08 14		08 12					08 14
Esher	d				→						07 48							→							08 18
Hersham	d										07 51														08 21
Walton-on-Thames	d	07 37									07 54			08 07											08 24
Weybridge	d	07 41									07 57			08 11											08 27
Byfleet & New Haw	d										08 00														08 30
West Byfleet	d			←		07 52				←	08 03						←			08 22		←			08 33
Woking	a	07 48	07 42	07 48		07 59	07 54	07 58		07 59	08 08			08 18	08 12	08 15	08 18			08 29	08 24	08 29		08 33	08 38
	d	07 49	07 43	07 49		08 00	07 55	08 00		08 00				08 19	08 13	08 16	08 19			08 30	08 25	08 30		08 34	
Worplesdon	d	→				→								→	08 18					→					
Guildford	a		07 51				08 02								08 24						08 32				
Brookwood	d			07 55						08 06							08 25					08 36			
Ash Vale	d									08 14												08 44			
Aldershot	a									08 19												08 49			
	d									08 20			08 41									08 50			
Farnham	a									08 25			08 46									08 55			
	d									08 26												08 56			
Bentley	d									08 32												09 02			
Alton	a									08 39												09 10			
Farnborough (Main)	d			08 03								08 13					08 33							08 45	
Fleet	d			08 08								08 19					08 38								
Winchfield	d			08 14													08 44								
Hook	d			08 18													08 48								
Basingstoke	a			08 28				08 20				08 31				08 36	08 58						08 47	08 58	

		SW	SW	SW		SW	SW	SW	SW	SW	SW	SW	SW	SW		SW	SW	SW	SW	SW	SW	SW	SW	SW
		1	1	1		◇1 ⊼	1		1	◇1	◇1 ⊼	1		◇1		1	1	◇1	◇1 ⊼	1		1	◇1 ⊼	1
London Waterloo 15 ⊖	d		08 12	08 15		08 20		08 20	08 24	08 30	08 35			08 39			08 42	08 45	08 50		08 50	08 54	09 00	
Vauxhall ⊖	d							08 24													08 54			
Clapham Junction 10	d		08u19	08u22		08u27		08 29	08u31					08u46				08u52	08u57		08 59	09u01		
Earlsfield	d							08 32													09 02			
Wimbledon 8 ⊖	d							08 36					←								09 06			
Surbiton 8	d		08 30					08 44	08 42				08 44				09 00				09 14	09 12		
Esher	d							→					08 48								→			
Hersham	d												08 51											
Walton-on-Thames	d		08 37										08 54				09 07							
Weybridge	d		08 41										08 57				09 11							
Byfleet & New Haw	d												09 00											
West Byfleet	d						←		08 52			←	09 03							←		09 22		←
Woking	a		08 48	08 42		08 45	08 48		08 59	08 54	08 58	08 59	09 08				09 18	09 12	09 15	09 18		09 29	09 24	09 29
	d		08 49	08 43		08 46	08 49		09 00	08 55		09 00					09 19	09 13	09 16	09 19		09 30	09 25	09 30
Worplesdon	d		→						→								→	09 18				→		
Guildford	a			08 50						09 02								09 24					09 32	
Brookwood	d						08 55					09 06								09 25				09 36
Ash Vale	d											09 14												09 44
Aldershot	a											09 19												09 49
	d	09 11										09 20				09 41								09 50
Farnham	a	09 16										09 25				09 46								09 55
	d											09 26												09 56
Bentley	d																							10 02
Alton	a											09 37												10 10
Farnborough (Main)	d						09 03							09 13						09 33				
Fleet	d						09 08							09 19						09 38				
Winchfield	d						09 14													09 44				
Hook	d						09 18													09 48				
Basingstoke	a					09 05	09 28							09 32					09 36	09 58				

Table T155-F

London - Woking, Guildford, Alton and Basingstoke

Saturdays

21 December to 16 May

		SW	SW	SW	SW	SW	SW	SW	SW	SW		SW	SW	SW	SW	SW	SW	SW	SW	SW		SW	SW	SW	SW
		◇1	◇1		1	1	1	◇1 ⊼	1			1	◇1 ⊼	◇1 ⊼	1		◇1	1	1	◇1		◇1 ⊼	1		1
London Waterloo 15 ⊖	d	09 05	09 09			09 12	09 15	09 20		09 20		09 24	09 30	09 35			09 39		09 42	09 45		09 50		09 50	09 54
Vauxhall ⊖	d									09 24														09 54	
Clapham Junction 10	d	09u12				09u19	09u22	09u27		09 29		09u31					09u46			09u52		09u57		09 59	10u01
Earlsfield	d									09 32														10 02	
Wimbledon 8 ⊖	d			←						09 36						←								10 06	
Surbiton 8	d			09 14		09 30				09 44		09 42				09 44			10 00					10 14	10 12
Esher	d			09 18						→						09 48								→	
Hersham	d			09 21												09 51									
Walton-on-Thames	d			09 24		09 37										09 54			10 07						
Weybridge	d			09 27		09 41										09 57			10 11						
Byfleet & New Haw	d			09 30												10 00									
West Byfleet	d			09 33					←			09 52			←	10 03							←		10 22
Woking	a		09 33	09 38		09 48	09 42	09 45	09 48			09 59	09 54	09 58	09 59	10 08			10 18	10 12		10 15	10 18		10 29
	d		09 34			09 49	09 43	09 46	09 49			10 00	09 55		10 00				10 19	10 13		10 16	10 19		10 30
Worplesdon	d					→						→							→	10 18					→
Guildford	a						09 50						10 02							10 24					
Brookwood	d								09 55						10 06								10 25		
Ash Vale	d														10 14										
Aldershot	a														10 19										
	d				10 11										10 20			10 41							
Farnham	a				10 16										10 25			10 46							
	d														10 26										
Bentley	d																								
Alton	a														10 37										
Farnborough (Main)	d		09 45						10 03								10 13						10 33		
Fleet	d								10 08								10 19						10 38		
Winchfield	d								10 14														10 44		
Hook	d								10 18														10 48		
Basingstoke	a	09 47	09 58					10 05	10 28								10 31					10 36	10 58		

		SW	SW	SW	SW	SW		SW	SW	SW	SW	SW	SW	SW	SW	SW		SW	SW	SW	SW	SW	SW	SW	SW
		◇1 ⊼	1	◇1	◇1			1	1	1	◇1 ⊼	1		1	◇1 ⊼	◇1 ⊼		1		◇1	1	1	◇1	◇1 ⊼	1
London Waterloo 15 ⊖	d	10 00		10 05	10 09				10 12	10 15	10 20		10 20	10 24	10 30	10 35				10 39		10 42	10 45	10 50	
Vauxhall ⊖	d												10 24												
Clapham Junction 10	d			10u12					10u19	10u22	10u27		10 29	10u31						10u46			10u52	10u57	
Earlsfield	d												10 32												
Wimbledon 8 ⊖	d					←							10 36						←						
Surbiton 8	d					10 14			10 30				10 44	10 42					10 44			11 00			
Esher	d					10 18							→						10 48						
Hersham	d					10 21													10 51						
Walton-on-Thames	d					10 24			10 37										10 54			11 07			
Weybridge	d					10 27			10 41										10 57			11 11			
Byfleet & New Haw	d					10 30													11 00						
West Byfleet	d		←			10 33						←		10 52				←	11 03						←
Woking	a	10 24	10 29		10 33	10 38			10 48	10 42	10 45	10 48		10 59	10 54	10 58		10 59	11 08			11 18	11 12	11 15	11 18
	d	10 25	10 30		10 34				10 49	10 43	10 46	10 49		11 00	10 55			11 00				11 19	11 13	11 16	11 19
Worplesdon	d								→					→								→	11 18		
Guildford	a	10 32								10 50					11 02								11 24		
Brookwood	d		10 36									10 55						11 06							11 25
Ash Vale	d		10 44															11 14							
Aldershot	a		10 49															11 19							
	d		10 50					11 11										11 20			11 41				
Farnham	a		10 55					11 16										11 25			11 46				
	d		10 56															11 26							
Bentley	d		11 02																						
Alton	a		11 10															11 37							
Farnborough (Main)	d				10 45							11 03								11 13					11 33
Fleet	d											11 08								11 19					11 38
Winchfield	d											11 14													11 44
Hook	d											11 18													11 48
Basingstoke	a			10 47	10 58						11 05	11 28								11 31				11 36	11 58

		SW		SW	SW	SW	SW	SW	SW	SW	SW	SW		SW	SW	SW	SW	SW	SW	SW	SW	SW		SW	SW
				1	◇1 ⊼	1	◇1 ⊼	◇1		1	1	1		◇1 ⊼	1		1	◇1 ⊼	◇1 ⊼	1		◇1		1	1
London Waterloo 15 ⊖	d	10 50		10 54	11 00		11 05	11 09			11 12	11 15		11 20		11 20	11 24	11 30	11 35			11 39			11 42
Vauxhall ⊖	d	10 54														11 24									
Clapham Junction 10	d	10 59		11u01			11u12				11u19	11u22		11u27		11 29	11u31					11u46			
Earlsfield	d	11 02														11 32									
Wimbledon 8 ⊖	d	11 06							←							11 36					←				
Surbiton 8	d	11 14		11 12					11 14		11 30					11 44	11 42				11 44				12 00
Esher	d	→							11 18							→					11 48				
Hersham	d								11 21												11 51				
Walton-on-Thames	d								11 24		11 37										11 54				12 07
Weybridge	d								11 27		11 41										11 57				12 11
Byfleet & New Haw	d								11 30												12 00				
West Byfleet	d			11 22		←			11 33						←		11 52			←	12 03				
Woking	a			11 29	11 24	11 29		11 33	11 38		11 48	11 42		11 45	11 48		11 59	11 54	11 58	11 59	12 08				12 18
	d			11 30	11 25	11 30		11 34			11 49	11 43		11 46	11 49		12 00	11 55		12 00					12 19
Worplesdon	d			→							→						→								→
Guildford	a				11 32							11 50						12 02							
Brookwood	d					11 36									11 55					12 06					
Ash Vale	d					11 44														12 14					
Aldershot	a					11 49														12 19					
	d					11 50				12 11										12 20				12 41	
Farnham	a					11 55				12 16										12 25				12 46	
	d					11 56														12 26					
Bentley	d					12 02																			
Alton	a					12 10														12 37					
Farnborough (Main)	d							11 45							12 03							12 13			
Fleet	d														12 08							12 19			
Winchfield	d														12 14										
Hook	d														12 18										
Basingstoke	a						11 47	11 58						12 05	12 28							12 31			

Table T155-F

Saturdays
21 December to 16 May

London - Woking, Guildford, Alton and Basingstoke

		SW	SW	SW	SW	SW	SW	SW		SW	SW	SW	SW	SW	SW	SW	SW	SW		SW	SW	SW	SW	SW	SW
		◇1	◇1	1		1	◇1	1		◇1	◇1		1	1	1	◇1	1			1	◇1	◇1	1		◇1
			(trolley)				(trolley)			(trolley)						(trolley)					(trolley)	(trolley)			
London Waterloo 15 ⊖	d	11 45	11 50		11 50	11 54	12 00			12 05	12 09			12 12	12 15	12 20		12 20		12 24	12 30	12 35			12 39
Vauxhall ⊖	d				11 54													12 24							
Clapham Junction 10	d	11u52	11u57		11 59	12u01				12u12				12u19	12u22	12u27		12 29		12u31					12u46
Earlsfield	d				12 02													12 32							
Wimbledon 6 ⊖	d				12 06							←						12 36						←	
Surbiton 6	d				12 14	12 12						12 14		12 30				12 44		12 42				12 44	
Esher	d				→							12 18						→						12 48	
Hersham	d											12 21												12 51	
Walton-on-Thames	d											12 24		12 37										12 54	
Weybridge	d											12 27		12 41										12 57	
Byfleet & New Haw	d											12 30												13 00	
West Byfleet	d			←		12 22		←				12 33					←			12 52			←	13 03	
Woking	a	12 12	12 15	12 18		12 29	12 24	12 29			12 33	12 38		12 48	12 42	12 45	12 48			12 59	12 54	12 58	12 59	13 08	
	d	12 13	12 16	12 19		12 30	12 25	12 30			12 34			12 49	12 43	12 46	12 49			13 00	12 55		13 00		
Worplesdon	d	12 18				→								→						→					
Guildford	a	12 24					12 32								12 50						13 02				
Brookwood	d			12 25				12 36									12 55						13 06		
Ash Vale	d							12 44															13 14		
Aldershot	a							12 49															13 19		
	d							12 50					13 11										13 20		
Farnham	a							12 55					13 16										13 25		
	d							12 56															13 26		
Bentley	d							13 02																	
Alton	a							13 10															13 37		
Farnborough (Main)	d			12 33							12 45						13 03								13 13
Fleet	d			12 38													13 08								13 19
Winchfield	d			12 44													13 14								
Hook	d			12 48													13 18								
Basingstoke	a		12 36	12 58						12 47	12 58					13 05	13 28								13 31

		SW	SW	SW		SW	SW	SW	SW	SW	SW	SW	SW	SW		SW	SW	SW	SW	SW	SW	SW	SW	SW	
		1	1	◇1		◇1	1		1	◇1	1	◇1	◇1			1	1	1	◇1	1		1	◇1	◇1	
						(trolley)				(trolley)		(trolley)							(trolley)				(trolley)	(trolley)	
London Waterloo 15 ⊖	d		12 42	12 45		12 50		12 50	12 54	13 00		13 05	13 09				13 12	13 15	13 20		13 20	13 24	13 30	13 35	
Vauxhall ⊖	d							12 54													13 24				
Clapham Junction 10	d			12u52		12u57		12 59	13u01			13u12					13u19	13u22	13u27		13 29	13u31			
Earlsfield	d							13 02													13 32				
Wimbledon 6 ⊖	d							13 06						←							13 36				
Surbiton 6	d		13 00					13 14	13 12					13 14			13 30				13 44	13 42			
Esher	d							→						13 18							→				
Hersham	d													13 21											
Walton-on-Thames	d		13 07											13 24			13 37								
Weybridge	d		13 11											13 27			13 41								
Byfleet & New Haw	d													13 30											
West Byfleet	d						←		13 22		←			13 33						←		13 52			
Woking	a		13 18	13 12		13 15	13 18		13 29	13 24	13 29		13 33	13 38			13 49	13 42	13 45	13 49		13 59	13 54	13 58	
	d		13 19	13 13		13 16	13 19		13 30	13 25	13 30		13 34				13 50	13 43	13 46	13 50		14 00	13 55		
Worplesdon	d		→	13 18					→								→					→			
Guildford	a			13 24						13 32								13 50					14 02		
Brookwood	d						13 25				13 36									13 56					
Ash Vale	d										13 44														
Aldershot	a										13 49														
	d	13 41									13 50					14 11									
Farnham	a	13 46									13 55					14 16									
	d										13 56														
Bentley	d										14 02														
Alton	a										14 10														
Farnborough (Main)	d						13 33						13 45							14 04					
Fleet	d						13 38													14 09					
Winchfield	d						13 44													14 15					
Hook	d						13 48													14 19					
Basingstoke	a					13 36	13 58					13 47	13 58						14 05	14 28					

		SW	SW	SW	SW	SW	SW	SW	SW	SW		SW	SW	SW	SW	SW	SW	SW	SW	SW		SW	SW	SW	SW
		1		◇1	1	1	◇1	◇1	1			1	◇1	1	◇1	◇1		1	1	1		◇1	1		1
								(trolley)					(trolley)		(trolley)							(trolley)			
London Waterloo 15 ⊖	d			13 39		13 42	13 45	13 50		13 50		13 54	14 00		14 05	14 09			14 12	14 15		14 20		14 20	14 24
Vauxhall ⊖	d									13 54														14 24	
Clapham Junction 10	d			13u46			13u52	13u57		13 59		14u01			14u11				14u19	14u22		14u27		14 29	14u31
Earlsfield	d									14 02														14 32	
Wimbledon 6 ⊖	d		←							14 06							←							14 36	
Surbiton 6	d		13 44			14 00				14 14		14 12					14 14		14 30					14 44	14 42
Esher	d		13 48							→							14 18							→	
Hersham	d		13 51														14 21								
Walton-on-Thames	d		13 54			14 07											14 24		14 37						
Weybridge	d		13 57			14 11											14 27		14 41						
Byfleet & New Haw	d		14 00														14 30								
West Byfleet	d	←	14 03						←			14 22		←			14 33						←		14 52
Woking	a	13 59	14 08			14 18	14 12	14 15	14 18			14 29	14 24	14 29		14 33	14 38		14 48	14 42		14 45	14 48		14 59
	d	14 00				14 19	14 13	14 16	14 19			14 30	14 25	14 30		14 34			14 49	14 43		14 46	14 49		15 00
Worplesdon	d					→	14 18					→							→						→
Guildford	a						14 24						14 32							14 50					
Brookwood	d	14 06							14 25					14 36									14 55		
Ash Vale	d	14 14												14 44											
Aldershot	a	14 19												14 49											
	d	14 20			14 41									14 50				15 11							
Farnham	a	14 25			14 46									14 55				15 16							
	d	14 26												14 56											
Bentley	d													15 02											
Alton	a	14 37												15 10											
Farnborough (Main)	d			14 13					14 33							14 45							15 03		
Fleet	d			14 19					14 38														15 08		
Winchfield	d								14 44														15 14		
Hook	d								14 48														15 18		
Basingstoke	a			14 31				14 36	14 58						14 47	14 58						15 05	15 28		

Table T155-F

Saturdays
21 December to 16 May

London - Woking, Guildford, Alton and Basingstoke

		SW	SW	SW	SW	SW		SW	SW	SW	SW	SW	SW	SW	SW	SW		SW	SW	SW	SW	SW	SW	SW	SW
		◇1	◇1	1		◇1		1	1	◇1	◇1	1		1	◇1	1		◇1	◇1		1	1	1	◇1	1
		(trolley)	(trolley)								(trolley)				(trolley)			(trolley)						(trolley)	
London Waterloo 15 ⊖	d	14 30	14 35			14 39			14 42	14 45	14 50		14 50	14 54	15 00			15 05	15 09			15 12	15 15	15 20	
Vauxhall ⊖	d												14 54												
Clapham Junction 10	d					14u46				14u52	14u57		14 59	15u01				15u12				15u19	15u22	15u27	
Earlsfield	d												15 02												
Wimbledon 6 ⊖	d				←								15 06							←					
Surbiton 6	d				14 44				15 00				15 14	15 12						15 14		15 30			
Esher	d				14 48								→							15 18					
Hersham	d				14 51															15 21					
Walton-on-Thames	d				14 54				15 07											15 24		15 37			
Weybridge	d				14 57				15 11											15 27		15 41			
Byfleet & New Haw	d				15 00															15 30					
West Byfleet	d			←	15 03							←		15 22		←				15 33					←
Woking	a	14 54	14 58	14 59	15 08				15 18	15 12	15 15	15 18		15 29	15 24	15 29			15 33	15 38		15 48	15 42	15 45	15 48
	d	14 55		15 00					15 19	15 13	15 16	15 19		15 30	15 25	15 30			15 34			15 49	15 43	15 46	15 49
Worplesdon	d								→	15 18				→								→			
Guildford	a	15 02								15 24					15 32								15 50		
Brookwood	d			15 06								15 25				15 36									15 55
Ash Vale	d			15 14												15 44									
Aldershot	a			15 19												15 49									
	d			15 20				15 41								15 50					16 11				
Farnham	a			15 25				15 46								15 55					16 16				
	d			15 26												15 56									
Bentley	d															16 02									
Alton	a			15 37												16 10									
Farnborough (Main)	d					15 13						15 33							15 45						16 03
Fleet	d					15 19						15 38													16 08
Winchfield	d											15 44													16 14
Hook	d											15 48													16 18
Basingstoke	a					15 31					15 36	15 58						15 47	15 58					16 05	16 28

		SW		SW	SW	SW	SW	SW	SW	SW	SW	SW		SW	SW	SW	SW	SW	SW	SW	SW	SW		SW	SW
				1	◇1	◇1	1		◇1	1	1	◇1		◇1	1		1	◇1	1	◇1	◇1			1	1
					(trolley)	(trolley)								(trolley)				(trolley)		(trolley)					
London Waterloo 15 ⊖	d	15 20		15 24	15 30	15 35			15 39		15 42	15 45		15 50		15 50	15 54	16 00		16 05	16 09				16 12
Vauxhall ⊖	d	15 24														15 54									
Clapham Junction 10	d	15 29		15u31					15u46			15u52		15u57		15 59	16u01			16u12					16u19
Earlsfield	d	15 32														16 02									
Wimbledon 6 ⊖	d	15 36						←								16 06						←			
Surbiton 6	d	15 44		15 42				15 44			16 00					16 14	16 12					16 14			16 30
Esher	d	→						15 48								→						16 18			
Hersham	d							15 51														16 21			
Walton-on-Thames	d							15 54			16 07											16 24			16 37
Weybridge	d							15 57			16 11											16 27			16 41
Byfleet & New Haw	d							16 00														16 30			
West Byfleet	d			15 52			←	16 03							←		16 22		←			16 33			
Woking	a			15 59	15 54	15 58	15 59	16 08			16 19	16 12		16 15	16 19		16 29	16 24	16 29		16 33	16 38			16 48
	d			16 00	15 55		16 00				16 20	16 13		16 16	16 20		16 30	16 25	16 30		16 34				16 49
Worplesdon	d			→							→	16 18					→								→
Guildford	a				16 02							16 24						16 32							
Brookwood	d						16 06								16 26				16 36						
Ash Vale	d						16 14												16 44						
Aldershot	a						16 19												16 49						
	d						16 20			16 41									16 50					17 11	
Farnham	a						16 25			16 46									16 55					17 16	
	d						16 26												16 56						
Bentley	d																		17 02						
Alton	a						16 37												17 10						
Farnborough (Main)	d								16 13						16 34						16 45				
Fleet	d								16 19						16 39										
Winchfield	d														16 45										
Hook	d														16 49										
Basingstoke	a								16 31					16 36	16 58					16 47	16 58				

		SW	SW	SW	SW	SW	SW	SW		SW	SW	SW	SW	SW	SW	SW	SW	SW		SW	SW	SW	SW	SW	SW
		1	◇1	1		1	◇1	◇1		1		◇1	1	1	◇1	◇1	1			1	◇1	1	◇1	◇1	
			(trolley)				(trolley)	(trolley)								(trolley)					(trolley)		(cup)		
London Waterloo 15 ⊖	d	16 15	16 20		16 20	16 24	16 30	16 35				16 39		16 42	16 45	16 50		16 50		16 54	17 00		17 05	17 09	
Vauxhall ⊖	d				16 24													16 54							
Clapham Junction 10	d	16u22	16u27		16 29	16u31						16u46			16u52	16u57		16 59		17u01			17u12		
Earlsfield	d				16 32													17 02							
Wimbledon 6 ⊖	d				16 36						←							17 06							←
Surbiton 6	d				16 44	16 42					16 44			17 00				17 14		17 12					17 14
Esher	d				→						16 48							→							17 18
Hersham	d										16 51														17 21
Walton-on-Thames	d										16 54			17 07											17 24
Weybridge	d										16 57			17 11											17 27
Byfleet & New Haw	d										17 00														17 30
West Byfleet	d			←		16 52				←	17 03						←			17 22		←			17 33
Woking	a	16 42	16 45	16 48		16 59	16 54	16 58		16 59	17 08			17 18	17 12	17 15	17 18			17 29	17 24	17 29		17 33	17 38
	d	16 43	16 46	16 49		17 00	16 55			17 00				17 19	17 13	17 16	17 19			17 30	17 25	17 30		17 34	
Worplesdon	d					→								→	17 18					→					
Guildford	a	16 50					17 02								17 24						17 32				
Brookwood	d			16 55						17 06							17 25					17 36			
Ash Vale	d									17 14												17 44			
Aldershot	a									17 19												17 49			
	d									17 20			17 41									17 50			
Farnham	a									17 25			17 46									17 55			
	d									17 26												17 56			
Bentley	d									17 32												18 02			
Alton	a									17 39												18 10			
Farnborough (Main)	d			17 03								17 13					17 33							17 45	
Fleet	d			17 08								17 19					17 38								
Winchfield	d			17 14													17 44								
Hook	d			17 18													17 48								
Basingstoke	a		17 05	17 28								17 31				17 36	17 58						17 48	17 58	

Table T155-F

London - Woking, Guildford, Alton and Basingstoke

Saturdays
21 December to 16 May

		SW 1	SW 1	SW 1	SW ◇1 ⊼	SW 1	SW	SW 1	SW ◇1 ⊼	SW ◇1 ⊼	SW 1	SW	SW ◇1	SW 1	SW 1	SW ◇1	SW ◇1 ⊼	SW 1	SW	SW 1	SW ◇1 ⊼	SW 1
London Waterloo 15 ⊖	d		17 12	17 15	17 20		17 20	17 24	17 30	17 35			17 39		17 42	17 45	17 50		17 50	17 54	18 00	
Vauxhall ⊖	d						17 24												17 54			
Clapham Junction 10	d		17u19	17u22	17u27		17 29	17u31					17u46			17u52	17u57		17 59	18u01		
Earlsfield	d						17 32												18 02			
Wimbledon 6 ⊖	d						17 36					←							18 06			
Surbiton 6	d		17 30				17 44	17 42				17 44			18 00				18 14	18 12		
Esher	d						→					17 48							→			
Hersham	d											17 51										
Walton-on-Thames	d		17 37									17 54			18 07							
Weybridge	d		17 41									17 57			18 11							
Byfleet & New Haw	d											18 00										
West Byfleet	d					←		17 52			←	18 03						←		18 22		←
Woking	a		17 48	17 42	17 45	17 48		17 59	17 54	17 58	17 59	18 08			18 18	18 12	18 15	18 18		18 29	18 24	18 29
	d		17 49	17 43	17 46	17 49		18 00	17 55		18 00				18 19	18 13	18 16	18 19		18 30	18 25	18 30
Worplesdon	d		→					→							→	18 18				→		
Guildford	a			17 50					18 02							18 24					18 32	
Brookwood	d					17 55					18 06							18 25				18 36
Ash Vale	d										18 14											18 44
Aldershot	a										18 19											18 49
	d	18 11									18 20			18 41								18 50
Farnham	a	18 16									18 25			18 46								18 55
	d										18 26											18 56
Bentley	d										18 32											19 02
Alton	a										18 39											19 10
Farnborough (Main)	d					18 03							18 13					18 33				
Fleet	d					18 08							18 19					18 38				
Winchfield	d					18 14												18 44				
Hook	d					18 18												18 48				
Basingstoke	a				18 05	18 28							18 31				18 36	18 58				

		SW ◇1 ⊼	SW ◇1	SW	SW 1	SW 1	SW 1	SW ◇1 ⊼	SW 1	SW	SW 1	SW ◇1 ⊼	SW ◇1 ⊼	SW 1	SW	SW ◇1	SW 1	SW 1	SW ◇1	SW ◇1 ⊼	SW 1	SW	SW 1
London Waterloo 15 ⊖	d	18 05	18 09			18 12	18 15	18 20		18 20	18 24	18 30	18 35			18 39		18 42	18 45	18 50		18 50	18 54
Vauxhall ⊖	d									18 24												18 54	
Clapham Junction 10	d	18u12				18u19	18u22	18u27		18 29	18u31					18u46			18u52	18u57		18 59	19u01
Earlsfield	d									18 32												19 02	
Wimbledon 6 ⊖	d			←						18 36					←							19 06	
Surbiton 6	d			18 14		18 30				18 44	18 42				18 44			19 00				19 14	19 12
Esher	d			18 18						→					18 48							→	
Hersham	d			18 21											18 51								
Walton-on-Thames	d			18 24		18 37									18 54			19 07					
Weybridge	d			18 27		18 41									18 57			19 11					
Byfleet & New Haw	d			18 30											19 00								
West Byfleet	d			18 33					←		18 52			←	19 03						←		19 22
Woking	a		18 33	18 38		18 48	18 42	18 45	18 48		18 59	18 54	18 58	18 59	19 08			19 18	19 12	19 15	19 18		19 29
	d		18 34			18 49	18 43	18 46	18 49		19 00	18 55		19 00				19 19	19 13	19 16	19 19		19 30
Worplesdon	d					→					→							→	19 18				→
Guildford	a						18 50					19 02							19 24				
Brookwood	d								18 55					19 06							19 25		
Ash Vale	d													19 14									
Aldershot	a													19 19									
	d				19 11									19 20			19 41						
Farnham	a				19 16									19 25			19 46						
	d													19 26									
Bentley	d													19 32									
Alton	a													19 39									
Farnborough (Main)	d		18 45						19 03							19 13					19 33		
Fleet	d								19 08							19 19					19 38		
Winchfield	d								19 14												19 44		
Hook	d								19 18												19 48		
Basingstoke	a	18 48	18 58					19 05	19 28							19 31				19 36	19 58		

		SW ◇1 ⊼	SW 1	SW ◇1 ⊼	SW ◇1	SW	SW 1	SW 1	SW 1	SW ◇1 ⊼	SW 1	SW	SW 1	SW ◇1 ⊼	SW ◇1 ⊼	SW 1	SW	SW ◇1	SW 1	SW 1	SW ◇1	SW ◇1 ⊼	SW 1
London Waterloo 15 ⊖	d	19 00		19 05	19 09			19 12	19 15	19 20		19 20	19 24	19 30	19 35			19 39		19 42	19 45	19 50	
Vauxhall ⊖	d											19 24											
Clapham Junction 10	d			19u12				19u19	19u22	19u27		19 29	19u31					19u46			19u52	19u57	
Earlsfield	d											19 32											
Wimbledon 6 ⊖	d					←						19 36					←						
Surbiton 6	d					19 14		19 30				19 44	19 42				19 44			20 00			
Esher	d					19 18						→					19 48						
Hersham	d					19 21											19 51						
Walton-on-Thames	d					19 24		19 37									19 54			20 07			
Weybridge	d					19 27		19 41									19 57			20 11			
Byfleet & New Haw	d					19 30											20 00						
West Byfleet	d		←			19 33					←		19 52			←	20 03						←
Woking	a	19 24	19 29		19 33	19 38		19 48	19 42	19 45	19 48		19 59	19 54	19 58	19 59	20 08			20 18	20 12	20 15	20 18
	d	19 25	19 30		19 34			19 49	19 43	19 46	19 49		20 00	19 55		20 00				20 19	20 13	20 16	20 19
Worplesdon	d							→					→							→	20 18		
Guildford	a	19 32							19 50					20 02							20 24		
Brookwood	d		19 36								19 55					20 06							20 25
Ash Vale	d		19 44													20 14							
Aldershot	a		19 49													20 19							
	d		19 50				20 11									20 20			20 41				
Farnham	a		19 55				20 16									20 25			20 46				
	d		19 56													20 26							
Bentley	d		20 02													20 32							
Alton	a		20 10													20 39							
Farnborough (Main)	d				19 45						20 03							20 13					20 33
Fleet	d										20 08							20 19					20 38
Winchfield	d										20 14												20 44
Hook	d										20 18												20 48
Basingstoke	a			19 47	19 58					20 05	20 28							20 31				20 36	20 58

Table T155-F

London - Woking, Guildford, Alton and Basingstoke

Saturdays
21 December to 16 May

		SW	SW 1	SW ◇1	SW 1	SW ◇1 ⊼	SW ◇1	SW	SW 1	SW 1	SW 1	SW ◇1 ⊼	SW 1	SW	SW 1	SW ◇1	SW 1	SW ◇1 ⊼	SW	SW ◇1	SW 1	SW ◇1
London Waterloo 15 ⊖	d	19 50	19 54	20 00		20 05	20 09			20 12	20 15	20 20		20 20	20 24	20 30		20 35		20 39		20 42
Vauxhall ⊖	d	19 54												20 24								
Clapham Junction 10	d	19 59	20u01			20u12				20u19	20u22	20u27		20 29	20u31					20u46		
Earlsfield	d	20 02												20 32								
Wimbledon 6 ⊖	d	20 06						←						20 36					←			
Surbiton 6	d	20 14	20 12					20 14		20 30				20 44	20 42				20 44			21 00
Esher	d	→						20 18						→					20 48			
Hersham	d							20 21											20 51			
Walton-on-Thames	d							20 24		20 37									20 54			21 07
Weybridge	d							20 27		20 41									20 57			21 11
Byfleet & New Haw	d							20 30											21 00			
West Byfleet	d		20 22		←			20 33					←		20 52		←		21 03			
Woking	a		20 29	20 24	20 29		20 33	20 38		20 48	20 41	20 45	20 48		20 59	20 54	20 59	20 59	21 08			21 18
	d		20 30	20 25	20 30		20 34			20 49	20 43	20 46	20 49		21 00	20 55	21 00					21 19
Worplesdon	d		→							→					→							→
Guildford	a			20 32							20 50					21 02						
Brookwood	d				20 36								20 55				21 06					
Ash Vale	d				20 44												21 14					
Aldershot	a				20 49												21 19					
	d				20 50				21 11								21 20				21 41	
Farnham	a				20 55				21 16								21 25				21 46	
	d				20 56												21 26					
Bentley	d				21 02												21 32					
Alton	a				21 10												21 39					
Farnborough (Main)	d						20 45						21 03							21 13		
Fleet	d												21 08							21 19		
Winchfield	d												21 14									
Hook	d												21 18									
Basingstoke	a					20 47	20 58					21 05	21 28							21 32		

		SW ◇1	SW ◇1 ⊼	SW ◇1	SW	SW 1	SW ◇1	SW 1	SW ◇1 ⊼	SW	SW 1	SW 1	SW 1	SW ◇1 ⊼	SW 1	SW	SW 1	SW ◇1	SW ◇1 ⊼	SW 1	SW	SW ◇1	SW 1
London Waterloo 15 ⊖	d	20 45	20 50		20 50	20 54	21 00		21 05			21 12	21 15	21 20		21 20	21 24	21 30	21 35			21 39	
Vauxhall ⊖	d				20 54											21 24							
Clapham Junction 10	d	20u52	20u57		20 59	21u01			21u12			21u19	21u22	21u27		21 29	21u31					21u46	
Earlsfield	d				21 02											21 32							
Wimbledon 6 ⊖	d				21 06					←						21 36					←		
Surbiton 6	d				21 14	21 12				21 14		21 30				21 44	21 42				21 44		
Esher	d				→					21 18						→					21 48		
Hersham	d									21 21											21 51		
Walton-on-Thames	d									21 24		21 37									21 54		
Weybridge	d									21 27		21 41									21 57		
Byfleet & New Haw	d									21 30											22 00		
West Byfleet	d			←		21 22		←		21 33					←		21 52			←	22 03		
Woking	a	21 12	21 15	21 18		21 29	21 24	21 29	21 31	21 38		21 48	21 41	21 45	21 48		21 59	21 54	21 58	21 59	22 08		
	d	21 13	21 16	21 19		21 30	21 25	21 30	21 32			21 49	21 43	21 46	21 49		22 00	21 55		22 00			
Worplesdon	d	21 18				→						→					→						
Guildford	a	21 24					21 32						21 50					22 02					
Brookwood	d			21 25				21 36							21 55					22 06			
Ash Vale	d							21 44												22 14			
Aldershot	a							21 49												22 19			
	d							21 50			22 11									22 20			22 41
Farnham	a							21 55			22 16									22 25			22 46
	d							21 56												22 26			
Bentley	d							22 02												22 32			
Alton	a							22 10												22 39			
Farnborough (Main)	d			21 33											22 03							22 13	
Fleet	d			21 38											22 08							22 19	
Winchfield	d			21 44											22 14								
Hook	d			21 48											22 18								
Basingstoke	a		21 36	21 58					21 50					22 05	22 25							22 31	

		SW ◇1	SW ◇1	SW ◇1	SW ◇1	SW	SW 1	SW ◇1	SW 1	SW ◇1 ⊼	SW	SW 1	SW 1	SW ◇1 ⊼	SW 1	SW	SW 1	SW ◇1	SW ◇1 ⊼	SW 1	SW	SW ◇1
London Waterloo 15 ⊖	d	21 42	21 45	21 50		21 50	21 54	22 00		22 05			22 12	22 20		22 20	22 24	22 30	22 35			22 39
Vauxhall ⊖	d					21 54										22 24						
Clapham Junction 10	d		21u52	21u57		21 59	22u01			22u12			22u19	22u27		22 29	22u31					22u46
Earlsfield	d					22 02										22 32						
Wimbledon 6 ⊖	d					22 06					←					22 36					←	
Surbiton 6	d	22 00				22 14	22 12				22 14		22 30			22 44	22 42				22 44	
Esher	d					→					22 18					→					22 48	
Hersham	d										22 21										22 51	
Walton-on-Thames	d	22 07									22 24		22 37								22 54	
Weybridge	d	22 11									22 27		22 41								22 57	
Byfleet & New Haw	d										22 30										23 00	
West Byfleet	d				←		22 22		←		22 33				←		22 52			←	23 03	
Woking	a	22 18	22 12	22 15	22 18		22 29	22 24	22 29	22 31	22 38		22 48	22 45	22 48		22 59	22 54	22 58	22 59	23 08	
	d	22 19	22 13	22 16	22 19		22 30	22 25	22 30	22 32			22 49	22 46	22 49		23 00	22 55		23 00		
Worplesdon	d	→	22 18				→						→				→					
Guildford	a		22 24					22 32										23 02				
Brookwood	d				22 25				22 36						22 55					23 06		
Ash Vale	d								22 44											23 14		
Aldershot	a								22 49											23 19		
	d								22 50			23 11								23 20		
Farnham	a								22 55			23 16								23 25		
	d								22 56											23 26		
Bentley	d								23 02											23 33		
Alton	a								23 10											23 40		
Farnborough (Main)	d				22 33										23 03							23 16
Fleet	d				22 38										23 08							23 21
Winchfield	d				22 44										23 14							
Hook	d				22 48										23 18							
Basingstoke	a			22 36	22 58					22 50				23 05	23 25							23 34

Table T155-F

Saturdays
21 December to 16 May

London - Woking, Guildford, Alton and Basingstoke

		SW 1	SW ◇1	SW 1	SW	SW	SW 1	SW ◇1	SW 1	SW ◇1	SW	SW	SW 1	SW ◇1	SW 1	SW	SW 1	SW ◇1	SW ◇1	SW	SW ◇1	SW	SW 1
London Waterloo 15 ⊖	d	22 42	22 45		22 50	22 52	22 54	23 00		23 05			23 12	23 15		23 20	23 24	23 35	23 40		23 45		23 48
Vauxhall ⊖	d				22 54	22 56										23 24							
Clapham Junction 10	d	22u49	22u52		22 59	23 02	23u01	23u07		23u12			23u19	23u22		23 29	23u31	23u42	23u47		23u52		23u55
Earlsfield	d				23 02											23 32							
Wimbledon 6 ⊖	d				23 06						←					23 36				←			
Surbiton 6	d	23 00			23 14		23 12				23 14		23 38			23 44	23 42			23 44			00 06
Esher	d				→						23 18					→				23 48			
Hersham	d										23 21									23 51			
Walton-on-Thames	d	23 07									23 24		23 45							23 54			00 13
Weybridge	d	23 11									23 27		23 49							23 57		←	00 17
Byfleet & New Haw	d					00 06					23 30									23 59		00 06	
West Byfleet	d			←		→	23 22		←		23 33				←		23 55			00 03		00 09	00 22
Woking	a	23 18	23 12	23 18			23 29	23 26	23 29	23 31	23 39		23 55	23 42	23 55		23 59	00 01	00 06	00 09	00 11	00 15	00 26
	d	23 19	23 13	23 19			23 30	23 27	23 30	23 32			23 57	23 44	23 57		00 01	00 03	00 08		00 13		00 28
Worplesdon	d	→	23 18				→						→								00 18		
Guildford	a		23 23					23 34						23 51							00 24		
Brookwood	d			23 25					23 35						00 03		00 07						00 34
Ash Vale	d								23 44								00 15						
Aldershot	a								23 49								00 19						
	d								23 50			23 58					00 20						
Farnham	a								23 55			00 03					00 25						
	d								23 58								00 26						
Bentley	d								00 04								00 33						
Alton	a								00 11								00 40						
Farnborough (Main)	d			23 33											00 10			00 14					00 41
Fleet	d			23 38											00 16			00 20					00 47
Winchfield	d			23 44											00 21								00s52
Hook	d			23 48											00 26								00s57
Basingstoke	a			23 55						23 50					00 33			00 33	00 27				01 06

Sundays
15 December to 10 May

		SW 1 A	SW 1 A	SW 1 A	SW ◇1 A	SW ◇1 A	SW A	SW ◇1 A	SW A	SW 1 A	SW ◇1	SW 1	SW	SW	SW ◇1	SW 1	SW 1	SW 1	SW 1	SW	SW	SW	SW
London Waterloo 15 ⊖	d										00 05		00 09	00 27	01 05					07 10		07 40	07 50
Vauxhall ⊖	d												00 13	00 31	01 09					07 14		07 44	07 54
Clapham Junction 10	d										00u12		00 20	00 38	01 15					07 19		07 49	08 00
Earlsfield	d												00 23	00s41						07 22		07 52	
Wimbledon 6 ⊖	d										00u18		00 27	00 45	01s27					07 26		07 56	
Surbiton 6	d									00 06			00 35	00s57	01s35					07 35		08 05	
Esher	d												00s39							07 39		08 09	
Hersham	d												00s42							07 42		08 12	
Walton-on-Thames	d									00 13			00s44							07 45		08 15	
Weybridge	d									00 17			00s48							07 49		08 19	
Byfleet & New Haw	d								00 06				00s51							07 51	08 02	08 21	09 02
West Byfleet	d						00 03		00 09	00 22			00s54	01s07						07 54	08 05	08 24	→
Woking	a						00 09		00 15	00 26	00 35		00 58	01 12	01 48					07 59	08 11	08 29	
	d			00 01	00 03	00 08		00 13		00 28	00 37	00 40	01 00		01 49		07 32	07 46	07 49	08 05		08 30	
Worplesdon	d							00 18														→	
Guildford	a							00 24					01 07				07 40			08 14			
Brookwood	d	00 03		00 07						00 34		00 45						07 51	07 55				
Ash Vale	d			00 15								00 53				01 09			08 03				
Aldershot	a			00 19								00 58				01s14			08 07				
	d			00 20								00 58							08 08				
Farnham	a			00 25								01 04				01 20			08 13				
	d			00 26								01 04							08 14				
Bentley	d		00 04	00 33								01s10							08 24				
Alton	a		00 11	00 40								01 18							08 31				
Farnborough (Main)	d	00 10			00 14					00 41					01s58			07 59					
Fleet	d	00 16			00 20					00 47					02s04			08 04					
Winchfield	d	00 21								00s52								08 10					
Hook	d	00 26								00s57								08 14					
Basingstoke	a	00 33			00 33	00 27				01 06	00 55				02s16			08 21					

A not 15 December

NRT DECEMBER 19 EDITION

Table T155-F

Sundays
15 December to 10 May

London - Woking, Guildford, Alton and Basingstoke

		SW ◇1	SW	SW ◇1	SW 1		SW	SW ◇1 A 🛒	SW	SW ◇1	SW ◇1	SW	SW	SW	SW ◇1	SW ◇1	SW	SW 1		SW	SW ◇1 🛒	SW
London Waterloo 15 ⊖	d	07 51		08 00	08 07		08 10	08 15		08 30	08 35		08 40	08 50	08 54	09 00		09 07		09 10	09 15	
Vauxhall ⊖	d						08 14						08 44	08 54						09 14		
Clapham Junction 10	d	08u01		08u09	08 15		08 19	08u23		08u39	08u45		08 49	09 00	09u03	09u09		09 15		09 19	09u22	
Earlsfield	d						08 22						08 52							09 22		
Wimbledon 6 ⊖	d				08 22		08 26						08 56					09 22		09 26		
Surbiton 6	d				08 30		08 35						09 05					09 30		09 36		
Esher	d						08 39						09 09							09 39		
Hersham	d						08 42						09 12							09 42		
Walton-on-Thames	d						08 45						09 15							09 45		
Weybridge	d						08 49					←	09 19							09 49		
Byfleet & New Haw	d						08 51					09 02	09 21	10 02						09 51		
West Byfleet	d		←				08 54		←			09 05	09 24	→			←			09 54		←
Woking	a	08 27	08 29	08 34	08 42		08 59	08 46	08 59	09 03	09 08	09 11	09 29		09 27	09 34	09 29	09 42		10 00	09 47	10 00
	d	08 28	08 30	08 35	08 46	08 49	09 01	08 47	09 01	09 04	09 09		09 38		09 28	09 35	09 38	09 46	09 49	10 01	09 47	10 01
Worplesdon	d		08 34				→						→				09 42			→		
Guildford	a		08 40	08 43					09 09	09 12						09 43	09 48					10 09
Brookwood	d				08 51	08 55												09 51	09 55			
Ash Vale	d					09 03													10 03			
Aldershot	a					09 07													10 07			
	d					09 08													10 08			
Farnham	a					09 13													10 13			
	d					09 14													10 14			
Bentley	d					09 24													10 24			
Alton	a					09 31													10 31			
Farnborough (Main)	d				08 59													09 59				
Fleet	d				09 04													10 04				
Winchfield	d				09 10													10 10				
Hook	d				09 14													10 14				
Basingstoke	a	08 46			09 21			09 06			09 28				09 46			10 24			10 07	

		SW ◇1	SW ◇1 🛒	SW	SW	SW	SW ◇1	SW ◇1	SW	SW 1		SW	SW ◇1 🛒	SW ◇1	SW	SW ◇1 🛒	SW	SW	SW	SW ◇1	SW ◇1	SW
London Waterloo 15 ⊖	d	09 30	09 35		09 40	09 50	09 54	10 00		10 07		10 10	10 15	10 30		10 35		10 40	10 50	10 54	11 00	
Vauxhall ⊖	d				09 44	09 54						10 14						10 44	10 54			
Clapham Junction 10	d	09u39	09u45		09 49	10 00	10u03	10u09		10 15		10 19	10u22	10u39		10u45		10 49	11 00	11u03	11u09	
Earlsfield	d				09 52							10 22						10 52				
Wimbledon 6 ⊖	d				09 56					10 22		10 26						10 56				
Surbiton 6	d				10 05					10 30		10 35						11 05				
Esher	d				10 09							10 39						11 09				
Hersham	d				10 12							10 42						11 12				
Walton-on-Thames	d				10 15							10 45						11 15				
Weybridge	d			←	10 19							10 49					←	11 19				
Byfleet & New Haw	d			10 02	10 21	11 02						10 51					11 02	11 21	12 02			
West Byfleet	d			10 05	10 24	→			←			10 54			←		11 05	11 24	→			←
Woking	a	10 03	10 08	10 11	10 29		10 26	10 31	10 29	10 42		10 59	10 45	11 01	10 59	11 07	11 11	11 29		11 26	11 32	11 29
	d	10 04	10 09		10 35		10 28	10 32	10 35	10 46	10 49	11 05	10 46	11 02	11 05	11 08		11 35		11 28	11 33	11 35
Worplesdon	d				→				10 39			→						→				11 39
Guildford	a	10 13						10 40	10 46					11 10	11 14						11 41	11 46
Brookwood	d									10 51	10 55											
Ash Vale	d										11 03											
Aldershot	a										11 07											
	d										11 08											
Farnham	a										11 13											
	d										11 14											
Bentley	d										11 24											
Alton	a										11 31											
Farnborough (Main)	d									10 59												
Fleet	d									11 04												
Winchfield	d									11 10												
Hook	d									11 14												
Basingstoke	a		10 28				10 46			11 21			11 05			11 26				11 46		

A 🛒 from Woking

Table T155-F

Sundays

15 December to 10 May

London - Woking, Guildford, Alton and Basingstoke

		SW 1		SW	SW ◇1 🍴	SW ◇1 🍴	SW	SW ◇1 🍴	SW	SW	SW	SW ◇1 🍴	SW ◇1	SW	SW 1		SW	SW ◇1 🍴	SW ◇1 🍴	SW	SW ◇1 🍴	SW
London Waterloo 15 ⊖	d	11 07		11 10	11 15	11 30		11 35		11 40	11 50	11 54	12 00		12 07		12 10	12 15	12 30		12 35	
Vauxhall ⊖	d			11 14						11 44	11 54						12 14					
Clapham Junction 10	d	11 16		11 19	11u22	11u39		11u45		11 49	12 00	12u03	12u09		12 16		12 19	12u22	12u39		12u45	
Earlsfield	d			11 22						11 52							12 22					
Wimbledon 6 ⊖	d	11 23		11 26						11 56					12 23		12 26					
Surbiton 6	d	11 30		11 35						12 05					12 30		12 35					
Esher	d			11 39						12 09							12 39					
Hersham	d			11 42						12 12							12 42					
Walton-on-Thames	d			11 45						12 15							12 45					
Weybridge	d			11 49					←	12 19							12 49					←
Byfleet & New Haw	d			11 51					12 02	12 21	13 02						12 51					13 02
West Byfleet	d			11 54			←		12 05	12 24	→			←			12 54			←		13 05
Woking	a	11 42		11 59	11 45	12 01	11 59	12 07	12 11	12 29		12 26	12 32	12 29	12 42		12 59	12 45	13 01	12 59	13 07	13 11
	d	11 46	11 49	12 05	11 46	12 02	12 05	12 08		12 35		12 28	12 33	12 35	12 46	12 49	13 05	12 46	13 02	13 05	13 08	
Worplesdon	d			→						→				12 39			→					
Guildford	a					12 10	12 14						12 41	12 46					13 10	13 14		
Brookwood	d	11 51	11 55												12 51	12 55						
Ash Vale	d		12 03													13 03						
Aldershot	a		12 07													13 07						
	d		12 08													13 08						
Farnham	a		12 13													13 13						
	d		12 14													13 14						
Bentley	d		12 24													13 24						
Alton	a		12 31													13 31						
Farnborough (Main)	d	11 59													12 59							
Fleet	d	12 04													13 04							
Winchfield	d	12 10													13 10							
Hook	d	12 14													13 14							
Basingstoke	a	12 21			12 05			12 26				12 46			13 21			13 05			13 26	

		SW	SW	SW ◇1 🍴	SW ◇1	SW	SW 1		SW	SW ◇1 🍴	SW ◇1 🍴	SW	SW ◇1 🍴	SW	SW	SW	SW ◇1 🍴	SW ◇1	SW	SW 1		SW	SW ◇1 🍴
London Waterloo 15 ⊖	d	12 40	12 50	12 54	13 00		13 07		13 10	13 15	13 30		13 35		13 40	13 50	13 54	14 00		14 07		14 10	14 15
Vauxhall ⊖	d	12 44	12 54						13 14						13 44	13 54						14 14	
Clapham Junction 10	d	12 49	13 00	13u03	13u09		13 15		13 19	13u22	13u39		13u42		13 49	14 00	14u03	14u09		14 15		14 19	14u22
Earlsfield	d	12 52							13 22						13 52							14 22	
Wimbledon 6 ⊖	d	12 56					13 22		13 26						13 56					14 22		14 26	
Surbiton 6	d	13 05					13 30		13 35						14 05					14 30		14 35	
Esher	d	13 09							13 39						14 09							14 39	
Hersham	d	13 12							13 42						14 12							14 42	
Walton-on-Thames	d	13 15							13 45						14 15							14 45	
Weybridge	d	13 19							13 49					←	14 19							14 49	
Byfleet & New Haw	d	13 21	14 02						13 51					14 02	14 21	15 02						14 51	
West Byfleet	d	13 24	→			←			13 54			←		14 05	14 24	→			←			14 54	
Woking	a	13 29		13 26	13 31	13 29	13 42		13 59	13 45	14 01	13 59	14 06	14 11	14 29		14 26	14 31	14 29	14 42		14 59	14 45
	d	13 35		13 28	13 32	13 35	13 46	13 49	14 05	13 46	14 02	14 05	14 07		14 35		14 28	14 32	14 35	14 46	14 49	15 05	14 46
Worplesdon	d	→				13 39			→						→				14 39			→	
Guildford	a				13 40	13 46					14 10	14 14						14 40	14 46				
Brookwood	d						13 51	13 55												14 51	14 55		
Ash Vale	d							14 03													15 03		
Aldershot	a							14 07													15 07		
	d							14 08													15 08		
Farnham	a							14 13													15 13		
	d							14 14													15 14		
Bentley	d							14 24													15 24		
Alton	a							14 31													15 31		
Farnborough (Main)	d						13 59													14 59			
Fleet	d						14 04													15 04			
Winchfield	d						14 10													15 10			
Hook	d						14 14													15 14			
Basingstoke	a			13 46			14 21			14 05			14 26				14 46			15 21			15 05

Table T155-F

Sundays

15 December to 10 May

London - Woking, Guildford, Alton and Basingstoke

		SW ◇1 🍴	SW	SW ◇1 🍴	SW	SW	SW	SW ◇1 🍴	SW ◇1	SW	SW 1		SW	SW ◇1 🍴	SW ◇1 🍴	SW	SW ◇1 🍴	SW	SW 1		SW	SW ◇1	SW
London Waterloo 15 ⊖	d	14 30		14 35		14 40	14 50	14 54	15 00		15 07		15 10	15 20	15 30		15 35		15 37		15 40	15 50	15 50
Vauxhall ⊖	d					14 44	14 54						15 14								15 44		15 54
Clapham Junction 10	d	14u39		14u42		14 49	15 00	15u03	15u09		15 15		15 19	15u27	15u39		15u42		15 46		15 49	15u58	16 00
Earlsfield	d					14 52							15 22								15 52		
Wimbledon 6 ⊖	d					14 56					15 22		15 26						15 53		15 56		
Surbiton 6	d					15 05					15 30		15 35						16 02		16 05		
Esher	d					15 09							15 39								16 09		
Hersham	d					15 12							15 42								16 12		
Walton-on-Thames	d					15 15							15 45						16 09		16 15		
Weybridge	d				←	15 19							15 49					←	16 13		16 19		
Byfleet & New Haw	d				15 02	15 21	16 02						15 51					16 02			16 21		17 02
West Byfleet	d		←		15 05	15 24	→			←			15 54			←		16 05			16 24		→
Woking	a	15 01	14 59	15 06	15 11	15 29		15 26	15 31	15 29	15 42		15 59	15 45	16 01	15 59	16 06	16 11	16 19		16 29	16 19	
	d	15 02	15 05	15 07		15 35		15 28	15 32	15 35	15 46	15 49	16 05	15 46	16 02	16 05	16 07		16 23	16 26	16 35	16 21	
Worplesdon	d					→				15 39			→								→		
Guildford	a	15 10	15 14						15 40	15 46					16 10	16 14							
Brookwood	d										15 51	15 55							16 28	16 32			
Ash Vale	d											16 03								16 41			
Aldershot	a											16 07								16 45			
	d											16 08								16 46			
Farnham	a											16 13								16 51			
	d											16 14								16 55			
Bentley	d											16 24											
Alton	a											16 31								17 06			
Farnborough (Main)	d										15 59								16 36			16 32	
Fleet	d										16 04								16 42				
Winchfield	d										16 10												
Hook	d										16 14												
Basingstoke	a			15 26				15 46			16 21			16 05			16 26		16 54			16 46	

		SW ◇1	SW	SW ◇1 🍴	SW 1		SW	SW ◇1 🍴	SW ◇1 🍴	SW	SW ◇1 🍴	SW	SW 1		SW	SW ◇1	SW	SW ◇1	SW	SW ◇1 🍴	SW 1		SW
London Waterloo 15 ⊖	d	16 00		16 05	16 07		16 10	16 20	16 30		16 35		16 37		16 40	16 50	16 50	17 00		17 05	17 07		17 10
Vauxhall ⊖	d						16 14								16 44		16 54						17 14
Clapham Junction 10	d	16u09		16u12	16 16		16 19	16u27	16u39		16u42		16 46		16 49	16u58	17 00	17u09		17u12	17 16		17 19
Earlsfield	d						16 22								16 52								17 22
Wimbledon 6 ⊖	d				16 22		16 26						16 53		16 56						17 22		17 26
Surbiton 6	d				16 30		16 35						17 02		17 05						17 30		17 35
Esher	d						16 39								17 09								17 39
Hersham	d						16 42								17 12								17 42
Walton-on-Thames	d						16 45						17 09		17 15								17 45
Weybridge	d						16 49					←	17 13		17 19								17 49
Byfleet & New Haw	d						16 51					17 02			17 21		18 02						17 51
West Byfleet	d		←				16 54			←		17 05			17 24		→		←				17 54
Woking	a	16 31	16 29	16 35	16 42		16 59	16 45	17 01	16 59	17 06	17 11	17 19		17 29	17 19		17 31	17 29	17 35	17 42		17 59
	d	16 32	16 35	16 37	16 46	16 49	17 05	16 46	17 02	17 05	17 07		17 23	17 26	17 35	17 21		17 32	17 35	17 37	17 46	17 49	18 05
Worplesdon	d		16 39				→								→				17 39				→
Guildford	a	16 40	16 46						17 10	17 14								17 40	17 46				
Brookwood	d				16 51	16 55							17 28	17 32							17 51	17 55	
Ash Vale	d					17 03								17 41								18 03	
Aldershot	a					17 07								17 45								18 07	
	d					17 08								17 46								18 08	
Farnham	a					17 13								17 51								18 13	
	d					17 14								17 55								18 14	
Bentley	d					17 24																18 24	
Alton	a					17 31								18 06								18 31	
Farnborough (Main)	d				16 59								17 36			17 32					17 59		
Fleet	d				17 04								17 42								18 04		
Winchfield	d				17 10																18 10		
Hook	d				17 14																18 14		
Basingstoke	a			16 56	17 21			17 05			17 26		17 54			17 46				17 56	18 21		

Table T155-F

Sundays

15 December to 10 May

London - Woking, Guildford, Alton and Basingstoke

		SW ◇1 ✠	SW ◇1 ✠	SW	SW ◇1 ✠	SW	SW 1		SW	SW ◇1	SW ◇1	SW	SW ◇1	SW	SW ◇1 ✠	SW 1		SW	SW ◇1 ✠	SW ◇1 ✠	SW	SW ◇1 ✠	SW
London Waterloo 15 ⊖	d	17 20	17 30		17 35		17 37		17 40	17 45	17 50	17 50	18 00		18 05	18 07		18 10	18 20	18 30		18 35	
Vauxhall ⊖	d								17 44			17 54						18 14					
Clapham Junction 10	d	17u27	17u39		17u42		17 46		17 49	17u53	17u58	18 00	18u09		18u12	18 16		18 19	18u27	18u39		18u42	
Earlsfield	d								17 52									18 22					
Wimbledon 6 ⊖	d						17 53		17 56							18 22		18 26					
Surbiton 6	d						18 02		18 05							18 30		18 35					
Esher	d								18 09									18 39					
Hersham	d								18 12									18 42					
Walton-on-Thames	d						18 09		18 15									18 45					
Weybridge	d					←	18 13		18 19									18 49					←
Byfleet & New Haw	d					18 02			18 21			19 02						18 51					19 02
West Byfleet	d			←		18 05			18 24			→		←				18 54			←		19 05
Woking	a	17 45	18 01	17 59	18 06	18 15	18 19		18 29	18 12	18 19		18 31	18 29	18 35	18 42		18 59	18 45	19 01	18 59	19 06	19 15
	d	17 46	18 02	18 05	18 07		18 23	18 26	18 35	18 13	18 21		18 32	18 35	18 37	18 46	18 49	19 05	18 46	19 02	19 05	19 07	
Worplesdon	d								→					18 39				→					
Guildford	a		18 10	18 14									18 40	18 46						19 10	19 14		
Brookwood	d						18 28	18 32								18 51	18 55						
Ash Vale	d							18 41									19 03						
Aldershot	a							18 45									19 07						
	d							18 46									19 08						
Farnham	a							18 51									19 13						
	d							18 55									19 14						
Bentley	d																19 24						
Alton	a							19 06									19 31						
Farnborough (Main)	d						18 36				18 32					18 59							
Fleet	d						18 42									19 04							
Winchfield	d															19 10							
Hook	d															19 14							
Basingstoke	a	18 05			18 26		18 54			18 33	18 46				18 56	19 21			19 05			19 26	

		SW 1		SW	SW ◇1	SW ◇1	SW	SW ◇	SW ◇1	SW	SW ◇1 ✠	SW 1		SW	SW ◇1 ✠	SW ◇1 ✠	SW	SW ◇1 ✠	SW	SW 1		SW	SW ◇1
London Waterloo 15 ⊖	d	18 37		18 40	18 45	18 50	18 50	18 55	19 00		19 05	19 07		19 10	19 20	19 30		19 35		19 37		19 40	19 45
Vauxhall ⊖	d			18 44			18 54							19 14								19 44	
Clapham Junction 10	d	18 46		18 49	18u53	18u58	19 00	19u02	19u09		19u12	19 16		19 19	19u27	19u39		19u42		19 46		19 49	19u53
Earlsfield	d			18 52										19 22								19 52	
Wimbledon 6 ⊖	d	18 53		18 56								19 22		19 26						19 53		19 56	
Surbiton 6	d	19 02		19 05								19 30		19 35						20 02		20 05	
Esher	d			19 09										19 39								20 09	
Hersham	d			19 12										19 42								20 12	
Walton-on-Thames	d	19 09		19 15										19 45						20 09		20 15	
Weybridge	d	19 13		19 19										19 49					←	20 13		20 19	
Byfleet & New Haw	d			19 21			20 02							19 51					20 02			20 21	
West Byfleet	d			19 24			→			←				19 54			←		20 05			20 24	
Woking	a	19 19		19 29	19 12	19 19			19 31	19 29	19 35	19 42		19 59	19 45	20 01	19 59	20 06	20 15	20 19		20 29	20 12
	d	19 23	19 26	19 35	19 13	19 21			19 32	19 35	19 37	19 46	19 49	20 05	19 46	20 02	20 05	20 07		20 23	20 26	20 35	20 13
Worplesdon	d			→						19 39				→								→	
Guildford	a							19 33	19 40	19 46						20 10	20 14						
Brookwood	d	19 28	19 32									19 51	19 55							20 28	20 32		
Ash Vale	d		19 41										20 03								20 41		
Aldershot	a		19 45										20 07								20 45		
	d		19 46										20 08								20 46		
Farnham	a		19 51										20 13								20 51		
	d		19 55										20 14								20 55		
Bentley	d												20 24										
Alton	a		20 06										20 31								21 06		
Farnborough (Main)	d	19 36				19 32						19 59								20 36			
Fleet	d	19 42										20 04								20 42			
Winchfield	d											20 10											
Hook	d											20 14											
Basingstoke	a	19 54			19 33	19 46					19 56	20 21			20 05			20 26		20 54			20 33

Table T155-F

Sundays

15 December to 10 May

London - Woking, Guildford, Alton and Basingstoke

		SW ◇1	SW	SW ◇1	SW ◇1	SW	SW ◇1 ✠	SW 1		SW	SW ◇1 ✠	SW ◇1 ✠	SW	SW ◇1 ✠	SW	SW 1		SW	SW ◇1	SW ◇1	SW	SW ◇1	SW ◇1
London Waterloo 15 ⊖	d	19 50	19 50	19 55	20 00		20 05	20 07		20 10	20 20	20 30		20 35		20 37		20 40	20 45	20 50	20 50	20 55	21 00
Vauxhall ⊖	d		19 54							20 14								20 44			20 54		
Clapham Junction 10	d	19u58	20 00	20u02	20u09		20u12	20 16		20 19	20u27	20u39		20u42		20 46		20 49	20u53	20u58	21 00	21u02	21u09
Earlsfield	d									20 22								20 52					
Wimbledon 6 ⊖	d							20 22		20 26						20 53		20 56					
Surbiton 6	d							20 30		20 35						21 02		21 05					
Esher	d									20 39								21 09					
Hersham	d									20 42								21 12					
Walton-on-Thames	d									20 45						21 09		21 15					
Weybridge	d									20 49					←	21 13		21 19					
Byfleet & New Haw	d		21 02							20 51					21 02			21 21			22 02		
West Byfleet	d		→			←				20 54			←		21 05			21 24			→		
Woking	a	20 19			20 31	20 29	20 35	20 42		20 59	20 45	21 01	20 59	21 06	21 15	21 19		21 29	21 12	21 19			21 31
	d	20 21			20 32	20 35	20 37	20 46	20 49	21 05	20 46	21 02	21 05	21 07		21 23	21 26	21 35	21 13	21 21			21 32
Worplesdon	d					20 39				→								→					
Guildford	a			20 33	20 40	20 46						21 10	21 14									21 33	21 40
Brookwood	d							20 51	20 55							21 28	21 32						
Ash Vale	d								21 03								21 41						
Aldershot	a								21 07								21 45						
	d								21 08								21 46						
Farnham	a								21 13								21 51						
	d								21 14								21 55						
Bentley	d								21 24														
Alton	a								21 31								22 06						
Farnborough (Main)	d	20 32						20 59								21 36				21 32			
Fleet	d							21 04								21 42							
Winchfield	d							21 10															
Hook	d							21 14															
Basingstoke	a	20 46					20 56	21 21			21 05			21 26		21 54			21 33	21 46			

		SW	SW ◇1	SW 1		SW	SW ◇1 ✠	SW ◇1	SW	SW ◇1 ✠	SW	SW 1		SW	SW ◇1 ✠	SW	SW ◇1	SW	SW ◇1	SW 1		SW	SW 1 ✠
London Waterloo 15 ⊖	d		21 05	21 07		21 10	21 20	21 30		21 35		21 37		21 40	21 50	21 50	22 00		22 05	22 07		22 10	22 20
Vauxhall ⊖	d					21 14								21 44		21 54						22 14	
Clapham Junction 10	d		21u12	21 16		21 19	21u27	21u39		21u42		21 46		21 49	21u58	22 00	22u09		22u12	22 16		22 19	22u27
Earlsfield	d					21 22								21 52								22 22	
Wimbledon 6 ⊖	d			21 22		21 26						21 53		21 56						22 22		22 26	
Surbiton 6	d			21 30		21 35						22 02		22 05						22 30		22 35	
Esher	d					21 39								22 09								22 39	
Hersham	d					21 42								22 12								22 42	
Walton-on-Thames	d					21 45						22 09		22 15								22 45	
Weybridge	d					21 49					←	22 13		22 19								22 49	
Byfleet & New Haw	d					21 51					22 02			22 21		23 02						22 51	
West Byfleet	d	←				21 54			←		22 05			22 24		→		←				22 54	
Woking	a	21 29	21 35	21 42		21 59	21 45	22 01	21 59	22 06	22 11	22 19		22 29	22 19		22 31	22 29	22 35	22 42		22 59	22 45
	d	21 35	21 37	21 46	21 49	22 05	21 46	22 02	22 05	22 07		22 23	22 26	22 35	22 21		22 32	22 35	22 37	22 46	22 49	23 05	22 46
Worplesdon	d	21 39				→								→				22 39				→	
Guildford	a	21 46						22 10	22 14								22 40	22 46					
Brookwood	d			21 51	21 55							22 28	22 32							22 51	22 55		
Ash Vale	d				22 03								22 41								23 03		
Aldershot	a				22 07								22 45								23 07		
	d				22 08								22 46								23 08		
Farnham	a				22 13								22 51								23 13		
	d				22 14								22 55								23 14		
Bentley	d				22 24																23 24		
Alton	a				22 31								23 06								23 31		
Farnborough (Main)	d			21 59								22 36			22 32					22 59			
Fleet	d			22 04								22 42								23 04			
Winchfield	d			22 10																23 10			
Hook	d			22 14																23 14			
Basingstoke	a		21 56	22 21			22 05			22 26		22 54			22 46				22 56	23 22			23 05

Table T155-F

Sundays
15 December to 10 May

London - Woking, Guildford, Alton and Basingstoke

		SW	SW	SW	SW	SW	SW		SW	SW	SW	SW	SW	SW	SW		SW	SW	SW	SW	SW	SW
		◇1		◇1 ⅄		1	1			◇1 ⅄		◇1		◇1	1			◇1		1		1
London Waterloo 15 ⊖	d	22 30		22 35			22 37		22 40	22 50	22 50	23 00		23 05	23 07		23 10	23 30		23 35		23 40
Vauxhall ⊖	d								22 44		22 54						23 14					23 44
Clapham Junction 10	d	22u39		22u42			22 46		22 49	22u58	23 00	23u09		23u12	23 16		23 19	23u39		23u44		23 49
Earlsfield	d								22 52								23 22					23 52
Wimbledon 6 ⊖	d						22 53		22 56						23 22		23 26					23 56
Surbiton 6	d						23 02		23 05						23 30		23 35					00 05
Esher	d								23 09								23 39					00 09
Hersham	d								23 12								23 42					00 12
Walton-on-Thames	d						23 09		23 15								23 45					00 15
Weybridge	d				←		23 13		23 19								23 49				←	00 18
Byfleet & New Haw	d				23 02				23 21		00 02						23 51				00 02	00 21
West Byfleet	d		←		23 05				23 24		→		←				23 54		←		00 05	00 24
Woking	a	23 01	22 59	23 06	23 11		23 19		23 29	23 19		23 31	23 29	23 35	23 42		23 59	00 01	23 59	00 07	00 11	00 30
	d	23 02	23 05	23 07			23 23	23 26	23 35	23 21		23 32	23 35	23 37	23 46	23 49	00 05	00 02	00 05	00 08		00 33
Worplesdon	d								→				23 39				→					
Guildford	a	23 10	23 13									23 40	23 46					00 10	00 19			
Brookwood	d						23 28	23 32							23 51	23 55						00 39
Ash Vale	d					23 36		23 41								00 03						00 47
Aldershot	a					23 41		23 45								00 07						00 51
	d					23 42		23 49								00 08						00 52
Farnham	a					23 47		23 54								00 13						00 57
	d							23 55								00 14						
Bentley	d															00 24						
Alton	a							00 06								00 31						
Farnborough (Main)	d						23 36			23 32					23 59					00 19		
Fleet	d						23 42								00 04					00 25		
Winchfield	d														00 10							
Hook	d														00 14							
Basingstoke	a			23 26			23 53			23 46				23 56	00 21					00 39		

AVAILABLE FROM MP Middleton Press

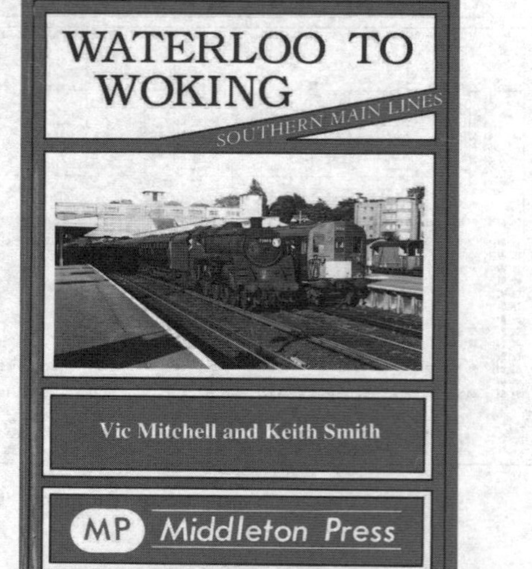

Table T155-R

Mondays to Fridays
16 December to 15 May

Basingstoke, Alton, Guildford and Woking - Waterloo

Miles	Miles	Miles			SW MO	SW MO	SW MX	SW	SW	SW	SW	SW	SW	SW	SW	SW	SW	SW	SW	SW	SW	SW	SW
					◇1	1	◇1		◇	◇	◇1	◇		◇1	◇	◇1	◇1	◇1 ⅄	◇1	◇	◇	◇1	◇1
0	—	—	**Basingstoke**	d							04 54					05 39	05 50	05 54	06 03				
5½	—	—	Hook	d							05 01						05 57						
7¾	—	—	Winchfield	d							05 05						06 01						
11¼	—	—	Fleet	d			00 01				05 10					05 50	06 06						
14½	—	—	Farnborough (Main)	d			00 06				05 16					05 56	06 12						
—	0	—	**Alton**	d																		05 42	
—	4¾	—	Bentley	d																		05 49	
—	8¾	—	Farnham	a																		05 55	
—	—	—		d																		05 56	
—	11¾	—	**Aldershot**	d																		06 02	
—	14¾	—	Ash Vale	d																		06 07	
19¾	18¾	—	Brookwood	d			00 13				05 23						06 19					06 14	
—	—	0	**Guildford**	d		00 05		04 20		05 14				05 50									
—	—	3½	Worplesdon	d						05 19		←		05 55									←
23½	—	6	**Woking**	a		00 13	00 18	04 28		05 24	05 28	05 24		06 00		06 05	06 24	06 12				06 19	06 24
—	—	—		d	00 04		00 20	04 30	05 27	05 32	05 29	05 32	05 43	06 01	06 04	06 06	06 26	06 14				06 20	06 26
26	—	—	West Byfleet	d			00 25		05 32	→		05 36	05 47		06 08		→					06 25	
27¼	—	—	Byfleet & New Haw	d					05 35			05 39			06 11								
28¾	—	—	Weybridge	d			00 29					05 42	05 51		06 14								
30¾	—	—	Walton-on-Thames	d			00 33					05 46	05 55		06 18								
31¾	—	—	Hersham	d								05 48			06 20								
33¼	—	—	Esher	d								05 51			06 23					←			
35¾	—	—	**Surbiton** 6	a			00 39	04 54			05 40	05 55	06 01		06 27					06 27		06 35	06 40
40½	—	—	Wimbledon 6 ⊖	a			00 47	05 01			05 48	06 04			→					06 35			06 47
42¼	—	—	Earlsfield	a								06 08								06 39	←		
43¾	—	—	Clapham Junction 10	a	00 23		00 53	05 08	06 43		06 00	06 12		06 20		06 25		06 33	06 37	06 42	06 43	06 48	06 54
46½	—	—	Vauxhall ⊖	a					→		06 07	06 17								06 47	06 49		
47¾	—	—	**London Waterloo** 15 ⊖	a	00 33		01 04	05 18			06 12	06 22	06 20	06 30		06 34		06 41	06 46	06 52	06 56	06 56	07 04

		SW	SW	SW	SW	SW	SW	SW	SW	SW	SW	SW	SW	SW	SW	SW	SW	SW	SW	SW	SW	SW	SW
		◇1	◇	1	◇1		◇1 ⅄	◇	◇1	◇1 ⅄	◇1	◇	◇1 ⅄	◇1		1	◇1	◇1	1	1	◇1 ⅄	◇1	◇1
Basingstoke	d								06 23	06 27			06 36							06 43	06 51		06 54
Hook	d								06 30														07 01
Winchfield	d								06 34														07 05
Fleet	d								06 40											06 54			07 10
Farnborough (Main)	d								06 45											07 00			07 16
Alton	d										06 12												
Bentley	d										06 19												
Farnham	a										06 24												
	d			06 02				06 19			06 26								06 32				
Aldershot	d			06 08				06 26			06 32								06 38				
Ash Vale	d							06 30			06 37												
Brookwood	d								06 52		06 44												07 23
Guildford	d	06 16		06a26	06 27		06 34										06 52		06a57			07 07	
Worplesdon	d	06 21												←			06 58						
Woking	a	06 26			06 35		06 41		06 57	06 45	06 49		06 54	06 57			07 03			07 10			07 28
	d	06 27	06 32		06 37	06 41	06 43		06 59	06 47	06 50		06 55	06 59		07 01	07 04	07 07		07 11			07 29
West Byfleet	d		06 36			06 46			→							07 06		07 13					→
Byfleet & New Haw	d		06 39			06 49												07 16					
Weybridge	d		06 42			06 52										07 10		07 20					
Walton-on-Thames	d		06 46			06 56										07 15		07 24					
Hersham	d		06 49			06 59										07 18		07 28					
Esher	d		06 52			07 02									07 10	07 21		07 31					
Surbiton 6	a		06 56			07 06									07 14	07 25		07 35					
Wimbledon 6 ⊖	a		07 04												07 24								
Earlsfield	a		07 08									←			07 28								
Clapham Junction 10	a		07 12		06 58		07 02	07 46		07 06	07 10	07 12	07 14				07 23						
Vauxhall ⊖	a		→					→				07 17											
London Waterloo 15 ⊖	a	06 51			07 08	07 26	07 12			07 18	07 20	07 24	07 24	07 28	07 43	07 43	07 34	07 59		07 38	07 36	07 40	

		SW	SW	SW	SW	SW	SW	SW	SW	SW	SW	SW	SW	SW	SW	SW	SW	SW	SW	SW	SW	SW
		◇1	◇	◇	◇1	◇1 ⅄	◇1	1	◇1	◇1	◇1	◇1 ⅄	◇1	◇1	◇1	◇	◇1	◇1	◇1	◇1 ⅄	◇1 ⅄	1
Basingstoke	d	07 00							07 06		07 14								07 24	07 30		
Hook	d								07 13										07 31			
Winchfield	d								07 17										07 35			
Fleet	d								07 22										07 40			
Farnborough (Main)	d								07 28										07 46			
Alton	d				06 44												07 14					
Bentley	d				06 51												07 21					
Farnham	a				06 56												07 26					
	d			06 51	06 58			07 02								07 20	07 28					07 34
Aldershot	d			06 57	07 04			07 09								07 27	07 34					07 40
Ash Vale	d			07 02	07 09											07 31	07 39					
Brookwood	d				07 16												07 46		07 53			
Guildford	d					07 18		07a26				07 28	07 37					07 45			07 54	07a57
Worplesdon	d						←					07 34						07 51				
Woking	a	07 18			07 21	07 25	07 28				07 32	07 39					07 51	07 56	07 58			
	d	07 19			07 23	07 27	07 29			07 32	07 34	07 41			07 47		07 52	07 57	08 00			
West Byfleet	d									07 37				07 46	07 54							
Byfleet & New Haw	d													07 49	07 57							
Weybridge	d									07 41				07 52	08 01							
Walton-on-Thames	d									07 46				07 57	08 06							
Hersham	d									07 49				08 00	08 09							
Esher	d									07 52				08 03	08 13							
Surbiton 6	a									07 56				08 07	08 18							
Wimbledon 6 ⊖	a																					
Earlsfield	a		←																			
Clapham Junction 10	a		07 46	08 16												08 46						
Vauxhall ⊖	a		07 52	08 22												08 52						
London Waterloo 15 ⊖	a	07 46	08 00	08 29	07 51	07 53	07 59		08 06	08 20	08 01	08 08	08 11	08 26	08 36	09 00	08 22	08 24	08 29	08 14	08 31	

Table T155-R

Mondays to Fridays

16 December to 15 May

Basingstoke, Alton, Guildford and Woking - Waterloo

Station		SW ◇1	SW 1	SW ◇1	SW ◇1	SW ◇1	SW ◇1	SW ◇	SW ◇1	SW ◇1 🛒		SW ◇1	SW ◇1 🛒	SW ◇1	SW ◇	SW 1	SW ◇1	SW ◇1	SW ◇1	SW ◇1		SW ◇1	SW ◇1	SW ◇1	SW ◇1 🛒
Basingstoke	d			07 36	07 47				07 52	07 59							08 05	08 16					08 21	08 25	08 29
Hook	d			07 43					07 59								08 12						08 28		
Winchfield	d			07 47					08 04								08 16						08 33		
Fleet	d			07 52					08 09								08 22						08 38		
Farnborough (Main)	d			07 58					08 15								08 28						08 44		
Alton	d											07 44													
Bentley	d											07 51													
Farnham	a											07 56													
	d		07 39									07 58				08 04									
Aldershot	d		07 46									08 04				08 10									
Ash Vale	d		07 50									08 09													
Brookwood	d		07 57						08 23			08 16											08 51		
Guildford	d						08 02						08 19		08 22	08a27				08 34					
Worplesdon	d					←	08 08							←					←	08 40					
Woking	a		08 03	08 08	08 05	08 08	08 13		08 28	08 18		08 21	08 26	08 28	08 30		08 38	08 34	08 38	08 45			08 56		08 48
	d	08 02	08 05	08 09	08 06	08 09	08 14	08 17	08 30	08 19		08 24	08 28	08 30	08 32		08 39	08 36	08 39	08 46		08 47	08 58		08 50
West Byfleet	d	08 06	08 16	→				08 26	→						08 36		→					08 53	→		
Byfleet & New Haw	d		08 19					08 29							08 39							08 57			
Weybridge	d	08 11	08 22					08 32							08 43							09 01			
Walton-on-Thames	d	08 15	08 27					08 36							08 47							09 06			
Hersham	d	08 17	08 30					08 39							08 49							09 09			
Esher	d	08 21	08 33					08 43							08 52							09 13			
Surbiton 6	a	08 25	08 37					08 47							08 56							09 17			
Wimbledon 6 ⊖	a														→							→			
Earlsfield	a																								
Clapham Junction 10	a																			09 05					
Vauxhall ⊖	a																								
London Waterloo 15 ⊖	a	08 44	08 59		08 36	08 38	08 41	09 06		08 46		08 52	08 54	08 59				09 06	09 10	09 18				09 10	09 21

Station		SW ◇1	SW ◇	SW ◇1 🛒	SW ◇1	SW ◇1		SW ◇	SW ◇1 🛒	SW 1	SW ◇1	SW ◇1	SW 1	SW ◇1 🛒	SW ◇	SW 1		SW ◇1 🛒	SW ◇1 🛒	SW 1	SW 1	SW 1	SW	SW ◇1	SW ◇1
Basingstoke	d			08 35							08 43		08 54	08 59										09 16	
Hook	d												09 01												
Winchfield	d												09 05												
Fleet	d										08 54		09 10											09 27	
Farnborough (Main)	d										09 00		09 16											09 32	
Alton	d	08 14														08 44									
Bentley	d	08 21														08 51									
Farnham	a	08 26														08 56									
	d	08 28								08 34						08 58						09 04			
Aldershot	d	08 34								08 40						09 04						09 10			
Ash Vale	d	08 39														09 09									
Brookwood	d	08 46											09 23			09 16									
Guildford	d							08 46	08 53	08a57		09 04							09 19			09a27			09 34
Worplesdon	d				←			08 51				09 10									←				09 40
Woking	a	08 51		08 53	08 56			08 59				09 14	09 28	09 18		09 21			09 27		09 28			09 41	09 44
	d	08 52		08 56	08 58			09 02				09 15	09 29	09 19		09 22		09 24	09 28		09 29		09 33	09 43	09 45
West Byfleet	d							09 06					→			09 27							09 37		
Byfleet & New Haw	d							09 09															09 40		
Weybridge	d							09 13													09 36		09 43		
Walton-on-Thames	d							09 17													09 40		09 47		
Hersham	d							09 19															09 49		
Esher	d		←			←		09 22							←					←			09 52		
Surbiton 6	a		08 56		09 09	09 17		09 26							09 26	09 37				09 37	09 46		09 56		
Wimbledon 6 ⊖	a		09 04					→							09 34	→							→		
Earlsfield	a		09 08												09 38										
Clapham Junction 10	a		09 12	09 15							09 26	09 34		09 38	09 42			09 43		09 50	09 57				10 04
Vauxhall ⊖	a		09 17												09 47										
London Waterloo 15 ⊖	a	09 21	09 24	09 25	09 30	09 40			09 30		09 37	09 45		09 51	09 54			09 53	09 55	09 59	10 05			10 08	10 15

Station		SW 1		SW ◇1 🛒	SW	SW 1	SW ◇1 🛒	SW 1	SW ◇1 🛒	SW	SW 1	SW ◇1 🛒		SW ◇1	SW 1	SW ◇1 🛒	SW ◇1 🛒	SW	SW 1	SW ◇1 🛒	SW 1	SW 1		SW	SW ◇1
Basingstoke	d	09 24		09 30			09 36					09 43			09 54	09 57									10 17
Hook	d	09 31													10 01										
Winchfield	d	09 35													10 05										
Fleet	d	09 40										09 54			10 10										
Farnborough (Main)	d	09 46										10 00			10 16										10 30
Alton	d					09 14													09 44						
Bentley	d					09 21													09 51						
Farnham	a					09 26													09 56						
	d					09 28					09 34								09 58			10 04			
Aldershot	d					09 34					09 40								10 04			10 10			
Ash Vale	d					09 39													10 09						
Brookwood	d	09 53				09 46									10 23				10 16						
Guildford	d								09 49		09a57			10 04						10 19		10a27			
Worplesdon	d							←													←				
Woking	a	09 58		09 48		09 51	09 54	09 58	09 59					10 11	10 28	10 15			10 21	10 26	10 28				10 39
	d	09 59		09 50		09 52	09 56	09 59	10 00	10 03				10 12	10 29	10 17	10 21		10 22	10 27	10 29			10 33	10 41
West Byfleet	d	→				09 57				10 07					→				10 27					10 37	
Byfleet & New Haw	d									10 10														10 40	
Weybridge	d							10 06		10 13											10 36			10 43	
Walton-on-Thames	d							10 10		10 17											10 40			10 47	
Hersham	d									10 19														10 49	
Esher	d				←					10 22								←						10 52	
Surbiton 6	a				09 56	10 07		10 16		10 26								10 26	10 37		10 46			10 56	
Wimbledon 6 ⊖	a				10 04					→								10 34						→	
Earlsfield	a				10 08													10 38							
Clapham Junction 10	a			10 09	10 12		10 15					10 25		10 31		10 36		10 42	10 49		10 57				
Vauxhall ⊖	a				10 17													10 47							
London Waterloo 15 ⊖	a			10 19	10 22	10 27	10 23	10 36	10 29			10 34		10 40		10 49	10 49	10 52	10 58	10 52	11 05				11 08

Table T155-R

Mondays to Fridays

16 December to 15 May

Basingstoke, Alton, Guildford and Woking - Waterloo

Station		SW ◇1	SW 1	SW ◇1 🛒	SW ◇1 🛒	SW	SW 1	SW ◇1 🛒		SW 1	SW ◇1	SW 1	SW	SW ◇1	SW 1	SW ◇1 🛒	SW ◇1 🛒	SW		SW 1	SW ◇1 🛒	SW 1	SW 1	SW	SW ◇1
Basingstoke	d		10 24	10 30	10 35						10 43				10 54	10 57									11 17
Hook	d		10 31												11 01										
Winchfield	d		10 35												11 05										
Fleet	d		10 40								10 54				11 10										
Farnborough (Main)	d		10 46								11 00				11 16										11 30
Alton	d						10 14													10 44					
Bentley	d						10 21													10 51					
Farnham	a						10 26													10 56					
	d						10 28			10 34										10 58			11 04		
Aldershot	d						10 34			10 40										11 04			11 10		
Ash Vale	d						10 39													11 09					
Brookwood	d		10 53				10 46								11 23					11 16					
Guildford	d	10 34						10 49		10a57				11 04							11 19		11a27		
Worplesdon	d	10 40										←										←			
Woking	a	10 44	10 58	10 48			10 51	10 56				10 58		11 11	11 28	11 15				11 21	11 26	11 28			11 39
	d	10 45	10 59	10 50			10 52	10 57				10 59	11 03	11 12	11 29	11 17	11 21			11 22	11 27	11 29		11 33	11 41
West Byfleet	d		→				10 57						11 07		→					11 27				11 37	
Byfleet & New Haw	d												11 10											11 40	
Weybridge	d											11 06	11 13									11 36		11 43	
Walton-on-Thames	d											11 10	11 17									11 40		11 47	
Hersham	d												11 19											11 49	
Esher	d					←							11 22					←						11 52	
Surbiton 6	a					10 56	11 07					11 16	11 26					11 26		11 37		11 46		11 56	
Wimbledon 6 ⊖	a					11 04							→					11 34						→	
Earlsfield	a					11 08												11 38							
Clapham Junction 10	a	11 04			11 11	11 12	11 21				11 25			11 32		11 36		11 42		11 49		11 57			
Vauxhall ⊖	a					11 17												11 47							
London Waterloo 15 ⊖	a	11 13		11 19	11 19	11 22	11 29	11 24			11 34	11 36		11 43		11 49	11 49	11 52		11 58	11 51	12 06			12 08

Station		SW ◇1	SW 1	SW ◇1 🛒		SW ◇1 🛒	SW	SW 1	SW ◇1 🛒	SW 1	SW ◇1	SW 1	SW	SW ◇1		SW 1	SW ◇1 🛒	SW ◇1 🛒	SW	SW 1	SW ◇1 🛒	SW 1	SW 1	SW	
Basingstoke	d		11 24	11 30		11 35					11 43					11 54	11 57								
Hook	d		11 31													12 01									
Winchfield	d		11 35													12 05									
Fleet	d		11 40								11 54					12 10									
Farnborough (Main)	d		11 46								12 00					12 16									
Alton	d							11 15												11 44					
Bentley	d																			11 51					
Farnham	a							11 25												11 56					
	d							11 28		11 34										11 58			12 04		
Aldershot	d							11 34		11 40										12 04			12 10		
Ash Vale	d							11 39												12 09					
Brookwood	d		11 53					11 46								12 23				12 16					
Guildford	d	11 34							11 49	11a57				12 04							12 19		12a27		
Worplesdon	d	11 40										←										←			
Woking	a	11 44	11 58	11 48				11 51	11 56			11 58		12 11		12 28	12 15			12 21	12 26	12 28			
	d	11 45	11 59	11 50				11 52	11 57			11 59	12 03	12 12		12 29	12 17	12 21		12 22	12 27	12 29		12 33	
West Byfleet	d		→					11 57					12 07			→				12 27				12 37	
Byfleet & New Haw	d												12 10											12 40	
Weybridge	d											12 06	12 13									12 36		12 43	
Walton-on-Thames	d											12 10	12 17									12 40		12 47	
Hersham	d												12 19											12 49	
Esher	d						←						12 22						←					12 52	
Surbiton 6	a						11 56	12 07				12 16	12 26						12 26	12 37		12 46		12 56	
Wimbledon 6 ⊖	a						12 04						→						12 34					→	
Earlsfield	a						12 08												12 38						
Clapham Junction 10	a	12 04				12 11	12 12	12 19			12 25			12 32			12 36		12 42	12 49		12 57			
Vauxhall ⊖	a						12 17												12 47						
London Waterloo 15 ⊖	a	12 15		12 19		12 20	12 22	12 28	12 22		12 34	12 38		12 45			12 49	12 49	12 52	12 58	12 51	13 05			

Station		SW ◇1	SW ◇1	SW 1	SW ◇1 🛒	SW ◇1 🛒	SW	SW 1	SW ◇1 🛒	SW 1		SW ◇1	SW 1	SW	SW ◇1	SW 1	SW ◇1 🛒	SW ◇1 🛒	SW	SW 1		SW ◇1 🛒	SW 1	SW 1	SW
Basingstoke	d	12 17		12 24	12 30	12 35						12 43				12 54	12 57								
Hook	d			12 31												13 01									
Winchfield	d			12 35												13 05									
Fleet	d			12 40								12 54				13 10									
Farnborough (Main)	d	12 30		12 46								13 00				13 16									
Alton	d							12 15												12 44					
Bentley	d																			12 51					
Farnham	a							12 25												12 56					
	d							12 28		12 34										12 58				13 04	
Aldershot	d							12 34		12 40										13 04				13 10	
Ash Vale	d							12 39												13 09					
Brookwood	d			12 53				12 46								13 23				13 16					
Guildford	d		12 34						12 49	12a57					13 04							13 19		13a27	
Worplesdon	d		12 40										←										←		
Woking	a	12 40	12 44	12 58	12 48			12 51	12 56				12 58		13 11	13 28	13 15			13 21		13 26	13 28		
	d	12 41	12 45	12 59	12 50			12 52	12 57				12 59	13 03	13 12	13 29	13 17	13 21		13 22		13 27	13 29		13 33
West Byfleet	d			→				12 57						13 07		→				13 27					13 37
Byfleet & New Haw	d													13 10											13 40
Weybridge	d												13 06	13 13									13 36		13 43
Walton-on-Thames	d												13 10	13 17									13 40		13 47
Hersham	d													13 19											13 49
Esher	d						←							13 22					←						13 52
Surbiton 6	a						12 56	13 07					13 16	13 26					13 26	13 37			13 46		13 56
Wimbledon 6 ⊖	a						13 04							→					13 34						→
Earlsfield	a						13 08												13 38						
Clapham Junction 10	a		13 04			13 11	13 12	13 19				13 25			13 32		13 36		13 42	13 49			13 57		
Vauxhall ⊖	a						13 17												13 47						
London Waterloo 15 ⊖	a	13 08	13 13		13 19	13 20	13 22	13 28	13 22			13 34	13 36		13 41		13 49	13 49	13 52	13 58		13 51	14 08		

Table T155-R

Mondays to Fridays

16 December to 15 May

Basingstoke, Alton, Guildford and Woking - Waterloo

		SW ◇1	SW ◇1	SW 1	SW ◇1 🍴	SW ◇1 🍴		SW	SW 1	SW ◇1 🍴	SW 1	SW ◇1	SW 1	SW	SW ◇1	SW 1		SW ◇1 🍴	SW ◇1 🍴	SW	SW 1	SW ◇1 🍴	SW 1	SW 1	SW
Basingstoke	d	13 17		13 24	13 30	13 35						13 43				13 54		13 57							
Hook	d			13 31												14 01									
Winchfield	d			13 35												14 05									
Fleet	d			13 40								13 54				14 10									
Farnborough (Main)	d	13 30		13 46								14 00				14 16									
Alton	d								13 15												13 44				
Bentley	d																				13 51				
Farnham	a								13 25												13 56				
	d								13 28		13 34										13 58			14 04	
Aldershot	d								13 34		13 40										14 04			14 10	
Ash Vale	d								13 39												14 09				
Brookwood	d			13 53					13 46							14 23					14 16				
Guildford	d		13 34							13 49	13a57				14 04							14 19		14a27	
Worplesdon	d		13 40										←										←		
Woking	a	13 39	13 44	13 58	13 48				13 51	13 56			13 58		14 11	14 28		14 15			14 21	14 26	14 28		
	d	13 41	13 45	13 59	13 50				13 52	13 57			13 59	14 03	14 12	14 29		14 17	14 21		14 22	14 27	14 29		14 33
West Byfleet	d			→					13 57					14 07		→					14 27				14 37
Byfleet & New Haw	d													14 10											14 40
Weybridge	d												14 06	14 13									14 36		14 43
Walton-on-Thames	d												14 10	14 17									14 40		14 47
Hersham	d													14 19											14 49
Esher	d							←						14 22						←					14 52
Surbiton [6]	a							13 56	14 07				14 16	14 26						14 26	14 37		14 46		14 56
Wimbledon [6] ⊖	a							14 04						→						14 34					→
Earlsfield	a							14 08												14 38					
Clapham Junction [10]	a		14 04			14 11		14 12	14 19			14 25			14 32			14 36		14 42	14 49		14 57		
Vauxhall ⊖	a							14 17												14 47					
London Waterloo [15] ⊖	a	14 08	14 14		14 19	14 20		14 22	14 28	14 22		14 34	14 36		14 40			14 49	14 49	14 52	14 58	14 57	15 06		

		SW ◇1		SW ◇1	SW 1	SW ◇1 🍴	SW ◇1 🍴	SW	SW 1	SW ◇1 🍴	SW 1	SW ◇1		SW 1	SW	SW ◇1	SW 1	SW ◇1 🍴	SW ◇1 🍴	SW	SW 1	SW ◇1 🍴		SW 1	SW 1
Basingstoke	d	14 17			14 24	14 30	14 35					14 43					14 54	14 57							
Hook	d				14 31												15 01								
Winchfield	d				14 35												15 05								
Fleet	d				14 40							14 54					15 10								
Farnborough (Main)	d	14 30			14 46							15 00					15 16								
Alton	d								14 15												14 44				
Bentley	d																				14 51				
Farnham	a								14 25												14 56				
	d								14 28		14 34										14 58				15 04
Aldershot	d								14 34		14 40										15 04				15 10
Ash Vale	d								14 39												15 09				
Brookwood	d				14 53				14 46								15 23				15 16				
Guildford	d			14 34						14 49	14a57					15 04						15 19			15a27
Worplesdon	d			14 40										←										←	
Woking	a	14 39		14 44	14 58	14 48			14 51	14 56				14 58		15 11	15 28	15 15			15 21	15 26		15 28	
	d	14 41		14 45	14 59	14 50			14 52	14 57				14 59	15 03	15 12	15 29	15 17	15 21		15 22	15 27		15 29	
West Byfleet	d				→				14 57						15 07		→				15 27				
Byfleet & New Haw	d														15 10										
Weybridge	d													15 06	15 13									15 36	
Walton-on-Thames	d													15 10	15 17									15 40	
Hersham	d														15 19										
Esher	d							←							15 22					←					
Surbiton [6]	a							14 56	15 07					15 16	15 26					15 26	15 37			15 46	
Wimbledon [6] ⊖	a							15 04							→					15 34					
Earlsfield	a							15 08												15 38					
Clapham Junction [10]	a			15 04			15 11	15 12	15 19			15 25				15 32		15 36		15 42	15 49			15 57	
Vauxhall ⊖	a							15 17												15 47					
London Waterloo [15] ⊖	a	15 08		15 13		15 19	15 20	15 22	15 28	15 22		15 34		15 38		15 40		15 49	15 49	15 52	15 58	15 51		16 06	

		SW	SW ◇1	SW ◇1	SW 1	SW ◇1 🍴	SW ◇1 🍴	SW		SW 1	SW ◇1 🍴	SW 1	SW ◇1	SW 1	SW	SW ◇1	SW 1	SW ◇1 🍴		SW ◇1 🍴	SW	SW 1	SW ◇1 🍴	SW 1	SW 1
Basingstoke	d		15 17		15 24	15 30	15 35						15 43				15 54	15 57							
Hook	d				15 31												16 01								
Winchfield	d				15 35												16 05								
Fleet	d				15 40								15 54				16 10								
Farnborough (Main)	d		15 30		15 46								16 00				16 16								
Alton	d									15 15												15 44			
Bentley	d																					15 51			
Farnham	a									15 25												15 56			
	d									15 28		15 34										15 58			16 04
Aldershot	d									15 34		15 40										16 04			16 10
Ash Vale	d									15 39												16 09			
Brookwood	d				15 53					15 46							16 23					16 16			
Guildford	d			15 34							15 49	15a57				16 01							16 19		16a27
Worplesdon	d			15 40										←		16 07								←	
Woking	a		15 39	15 44	15 58	15 48				15 51	15 56			15 58		16 11	16 28	16 15				16 21	16 27	16 28	
	d	15 33	15 41	15 45	15 59	15 50				15 52	15 57			15 59	16 03	16 12	16 29	16 17		16 21		16 22	16 27	16 29	
West Byfleet	d	15 37			→					15 57					16 07		→					16 27			
Byfleet & New Haw	d	15 40													16 10										
Weybridge	d	15 43												16 06	16 13									16 36	
Walton-on-Thames	d	15 47												16 10	16 17									16 40	
Hersham	d	15 49													16 19										
Esher	d	15 52						←							16 22						←				
Surbiton [6]	a	15 56						15 56		16 07				16 16	16 26						16 26	16 37		16 46	
Wimbledon [6] ⊖	a	→						16 04							→						16 34				
Earlsfield	a							16 08													16 38				
Clapham Junction [10]	a			16 04			16 11	16 12					16 25			16 32		16 36			16 42	16 50		16 57	
Vauxhall ⊖	a							16 17													16 47				
London Waterloo [15] ⊖	a		16 09	16 13		16 19	16 19	16 22		16 24	16 22		16 34	16 38		16 45		16 49		16 49	16 52	16 59	16 54	17 08	

Table T155-R

Mondays to Fridays

16 December to 15 May

Basingstoke, Alton, Guildford and Woking - Waterloo

		SW	SW ◇1	SW ◇1		SW 1	SW ◇1 🍴	SW ◇1 🍴	SW	SW 1	SW ◇1	SW 1	SW ◇1	SW 1		SW	SW ◇1 🍴	SW 1	SW ◇1 🍴	SW	SW ◇1 🍴	SW 1	SW ◇1 🍴	SW 1	
Basingstoke	d		16 17			16 24	16 30	16 35					16 43					16 54	16 57						
Hook	d					16 31												17 01							
Winchfield	d					16 35												17 05							
Fleet	d					16 40							16 54					17 10							
Farnborough (Main)	d		16 30			16 46							17 00					17 16							
Alton	d									16 15												16 44			
Bentley	d																					16 51			
Farnham	a									16 25												16 56			
	d									16 28		16 34										16 58			
Aldershot	d									16 34		16 40										17 04			
Ash Vale	d									16 39												17 09			
Brookwood	d					16 53				16 46								17 23				17 16			
Guildford	d			16 34							16 49	16a57					17 01						17 19		
Worplesdon	d			16 40										←			17 07							←	
Woking	a		16 39	16 44		16 58	16 48			16 51	16 56			16 58			17 11	17 28	17 15			17 21	17 26	17 28	
	d	16 33	16 41	16 45		16 59	16 50			16 52	16 57			16 59		17 02	17 12	17 29	17 17		17 21	17 22	17 27	17 29	
West Byfleet	d	16 37				→				16 57						17 06		→				17 27			
Byfleet & New Haw	d	16 40														17 09									
Weybridge	d	16 43												17 06		17 12								17 36	
Walton-on-Thames	d	16 47												17 10		17 16								17 40	
Hersham	d	16 49														17 18									
Esher	d	16 52							←							17 21				←					
Surbiton [6]	a	16 56							16 56	17 07				17 16		17 25				17 25		17 37		17 46	
Wimbledon [6] ⊖	a	→							17 05							→				17 35					
Earlsfield	a								17 08											17 38					
Clapham Junction [10]	a			17 04				17 11	17 12				17 25				17 33		17 37	17 42		17 50		17 57	
Vauxhall ⊖	a								17 17											17 47					
London Waterloo [15] ⊖	a		17 08	17 17			17 19	17 24	17 22	17 29	17 29		17 36	17 38			17 44		17 56	17 52	17 55	17 59	17 57	18 08	

		SW 1	SW	SW ◇1	SW ◇1	SW 1	SW ◇1 🍴	SW ◇1 🍴	SW	SW 1		SW ◇1	SW 1	SW ◇1	SW 1	SW	SW ◇1 🍴	SW 1	SW ◇1 🍴	SW		SW ◇1 🍴	SW 1	SW ◇1 🍴	SW 1
Basingstoke	d			17 17		17 24	17 30	17 35						17 43				17 54	17 56						
Hook	d					17 31												18 01							
Winchfield	d					17 35												18 05							
Fleet	d					17 40								17 54				18 10							
Farnborough (Main)	d			17 30		17 46								18 00				18 16							
Alton	d									17 14													17 44		
Bentley	d									17 21													17 51		
Farnham	a									17 26													17 56		
	d	17 04								17 28			17 34										17 58		
Aldershot	d	17 10								17 34			17 40										18 04		
Ash Vale	d									17 39													18 09		
Brookwood	d					17 53				17 46								18 23					18 16		
Guildford	d	17a27			17 34							17 49	17a57				18 01							18 23	
Worplesdon	d				17 40										←		18 07								←
Woking	a			17 39	17 44	17 58	17 48			17 51		17 58			17 58		18 11	18 28	18 14				18 21		18 28
	d		17 32	17 41	17 45	17 59	17 50			17 52		17 59			17 59	18 02	18 12	18 29	18 16			18 21	18 22		18 29
West Byfleet	d		17 36			→				17 57						18 06		→					18 27		
Byfleet & New Haw	d		17 39													18 09									
Weybridge	d		17 42												18 06	18 12									18 36
Walton-on-Thames	d		17 46												18 10	18 16									18 40
Hersham	d		17 48													18 18									
Esher	d		17 51						←							18 21				←					
Surbiton [6]	a		17 55						17 55	18 07					18 16	18 25				18 25			18 37		18 46
Wimbledon [6] ⊖	a		→						18 04							→				18 34					
Earlsfield	a								18 08											18 38					
Clapham Junction [10]	a				18 04			18 11	18 11	18 21				18 25			18 32		18 36	18 42			18 49		18 58
Vauxhall ⊖	a								18 16											18 47					
London Waterloo [15] ⊖	a			18 12	18 14		18 22	18 19	18 21	18 29		18 27		18 38	18 40		18 43		18 49	18 53		18 53	18 59	18 59	19 06

		SW 1	SW	SW ◇1	SW ◇1	SW 1		SW ◇1 🍴	SW ◇1 🍴	SW	SW 1	SW ◇1	SW 1	SW	SW ◇1 🍴	SW 1		SW ◇1	SW ◇1	SW 1	SW ◇1 🍴	SW	SW 1	SW ◇1 🍴	SW ◇1 🍴
Basingstoke	d			18 17		18 24		18 30	18 35			18 39						18 43		18 54	19 01				
Hook	d					18 31														19 01					
Winchfield	d					18 35														19 05					
Fleet	d					18 40												18 54		19 10					
Farnborough (Main)	d			18 30		18 46												19 00		19 16					
Alton	d										18 14												18 35		
Bentley	d										18 23												18 42		
Farnham	a										18 27												18 47		
	d	18 04									18 28					18 34							18 58		
Aldershot	d	18 10									18 34					18 40							19 04		
Ash Vale	d										18 39												19 09		
Brookwood	d					18 53					18 46									19 23			19 16		
Guildford	d	18a27			18 34										18 53	19a01			19 01						19 23
Worplesdon	d				18 40								←						19 07						
Woking	a			18 40	18 44	18 58		18 48			18 52	18 57	18 58		19 03				19 14	19 28	19 20		19 21		
	d		18 32	18 41	18 45	18 59		18 50			18 52	18 59	18 59	19 02	19 04				19 15	19 29	19 21		19 22	19 26	
West Byfleet	d		18 36			→					18 57			19 06						→			19 27		
Byfleet & New Haw	d		18 39											19 09											
Weybridge	d		18 42										19 06	19 12											
Walton-on-Thames	d		18 46										19 10	19 16											
Hersham	d		18 48											19 18											
Esher	d		18 51							←				19 21								←			
Surbiton [6]	a		18 55							18 55	19 07		19 16	19 25								19 25	19 37		
Wimbledon [6] ⊖	a		→							19 05				→								19 35			
Earlsfield	a									19 08												19 39			
Clapham Junction [10]	a				19 04				19 11	19 11								19 26	19 34		19 40	19 41	19 49		
Vauxhall ⊖	a									19 16												19 46			
London Waterloo [15] ⊖	a			19 08	19 15			19 19	19 19	19 24	19 26	19 24	19 36		19 29			19 34	19 43		19 52	19 52	19 57	19 52	19 59

Table T155-R

Mondays to Fridays
16 December to 15 May

Basingstoke, Alton, Guildford and Woking - Waterloo

		SW		SW	SW	SW	SW	SW	SW	SW	SW	SW		SW	SW	SW	SW	SW	SW	SW	SW	SW		SW	SW
		■		■		◇■	◇■	■	◇■ ⌘	◇■ ⌘		■		◇■ ⌘	■	◇■	■		◇■		■	◇■ ⌘		◇■	■
Basingstoke	d					19 17		19 24	19 30	19 35						19 43									19 54
Hook	d							19 31																	20 01
Winchfield	d							19 35																	20 05
Fleet	d							19 40								19 54									20 10
Farnborough (Main)	d					19 31		19 46								20 00									20 16
Alton	d											19 08									19 38				
Bentley	d																				19 45				
Farnham	a											19 18									19 52				
	d			19 04								19 28			19 36						19 58				
Aldershot	d			19 10								19 34			19 42						20 04				
Ash Vale	d											19 39									20 09				
Brookwood	d							19 53				19 46									20 16				20 23
Guildford	d			19a28			19 34							19 49	19a59				20 04					20 19	
Worplesdon	d	←					19 40										←								
Woking	a	19 28				19 41	19 44	19 58	19 48			19 51		19 56			19 58		20 11		20 21			20 26	20 28
	d	19 29			19 33	19 41	19 45	19 59	19 50			19 52		19 57			19 59	20 02	20 12		20 22	20 23		20 27	20 29
West Byfleet	d				19 37			→				19 57						20 06			20 27				
Byfleet & New Haw	d				19 40													20 09							
Weybridge	d	19 36			19 43												20 06	20 12							20 36
Walton-on-Thames	d	19 40			19 47												20 10	20 16							20 40
Hersham	d				19 49													20 18							
Esher	d				19 52						←							20 21		←					
Surbiton ■	a	19 47			19 56						19 56	20 07					20 16	20 25		20 25	20 37				20 46
Wimbledon ■ ⊖	a				→						20 04							→		20 35					→
Earlsfield	a										20 08									20 39					
Clapham Junction ■10	a	19 58					20 05			20 11	20 12	20 19				20 27			20 33	20 41	20 49				
Vauxhall ⊖	a										20 17									20 46					
London Waterloo ■15 ⊖	a	20 07				20 09	20 14		20 19	20 21	20 22	20 28		20 27		20 35	20 39		20 42	20 52	20 58	20 49		20 51	

		SW	SW	SW	SW	SW	SW	SW		SW	SW	SW	SW	SW	SW	SW	SW	SW		SW	SW	SW	SW	SW	SW
		◇■ ⌘	■		◇■	◇■	■	■		◇■	◇■ ⌘		■	◇■	■	■	◇■			◇■	■	◇■ ⌘	◇■ ⌘		■
Basingstoke	d	20 10			20 17			20 24		20 30	20 35						20 43				20 54	20 59			
Hook	d							20 31													21 01				
Winchfield	d							20 35													21 05				
Fleet	d							20 40									20 54				21 10				
Farnborough (Main)	d				20 30			20 46									21 00				21 16				
Alton	d												20 15												20 44
Bentley	d																								20 51
Farnham	a												20 25												20 56
	d						20 09						20 28			20 34									20 58
Aldershot	d						20 15						20 34			20 40									21 04
Ash Vale	d												20 39												21 09
Brookwood	d							20 53					20 46								21 23				21 16
Guildford	d					20 34	20a36							20 49		20a57				21 04					
Worplesdon	d					20 40									←										
Woking	a	20 30			20 39	20 44		20 58		20 48			20 51	20 58	20 58					21 11	21 28	21 17			21 21
	d	20 31		20 33	20 41	20 45		20 59		20 50			20 52	20 59	20 59			21 03		21 12	21 29	21 18	21 22		21 22
West Byfleet	d			20 37				→					20 57					21 07			→				21 27
Byfleet & New Haw	d			20 40														21 10							
Weybridge	d			20 43											21 06			21 13							
Walton-on-Thames	d			20 47											21 10			21 17							
Hersham	d			20 49														21 19							
Esher	d		←	20 52								←						21 22						←	
Surbiton ■	a		20 46	20 56								20 56	21 07		21 16			21 26						21 26	21 37
Wimbledon ■ ⊖	a			→								21 04						→						21 34	
Earlsfield	a											21 08												21 38	
Clapham Junction ■10	a	20 53	20 59			21 06				21 10	21 11	21 12	21 23				21 27			21 34		21 38		21 42	21 50
Vauxhall ⊖	a											21 17												21 47	
London Waterloo ■15 ⊖	a	21 02	21 08		21 10	21 19				21 19	21 27	21 22	21 34	21 29	21 38		21 38			21 42		21 49	21 51	21 52	21 58

		SW	SW	SW		SW	SW	SW	SW	SW	SW	SW	SW	SW		SW	SW	SW	SW	SW	SW	SW	SW	SW
		◇■	■	■			◇■	◇■	◇■		■	◇■	◇■	■		◇■	■		◇■	■	■	◇■		■
Basingstoke	d							21 24	21 30			21 35							21 43		21 54	22 00		
Hook	d							21 31													22 01			
Winchfield	d							21 35													22 05			
Fleet	d							21 40											21 54		22 10			
Farnborough (Main)	d							21 46											22 00		22 16			
Alton	d										21 15													21 44
Bentley	d																							21 51
Farnham	a										21 25													21 56
	d			21 04							21 28						21 34							21 58
Aldershot	d			21 10							21 34						21 40							22 04
Ash Vale	d										21 39													22 09
Brookwood	d							21 53			21 46										22 23			22 16
Guildford	d	21 19		21a27			21 34						21 49				21a57			22 04				
Worplesdon	d		←				21 40									←								
Woking	a	21 26	21 28				21 44	21 58	21 48		21 51	21 53	21 57			21 58			22 09	22 14	22 28	22 19		22 21
	d	21 27	21 29			21 33	21 45	21 59	21 50		21 52	21 54	21 58			21 59		22 03	22 10	22 15	22 29	22 20		22 22
West Byfleet	d					21 37		→			21 57							22 07			→			22 27
Byfleet & New Haw	d					21 40												22 10						
Weybridge	d		21 36			21 43										22 06		22 13						
Walton-on-Thames	d		21 40			21 47										22 10		22 17						
Hersham	d					21 49												22 19						
Esher	d					21 52				←				←				22 22					←	
Surbiton ■	a		21 46			21 56				21 56	22 07			22 07		22 16		22 26					22 26	22 37
Wimbledon ■ ⊖	a					→				22 04	→							→					22 34	
Earlsfield	a									22 08													22 38	
Clapham Junction ■10	a		21 57				22 04		22 09	22 12		22 13		22 20					22 29	22 34		22 39	22 42	22 49
Vauxhall ⊖	a									22 17													22 47	
London Waterloo ■15 ⊖	a	21 53	22 05				22 13		22 19	22 22		22 21	22 27	22 29		22 34			22 41	22 43		22 49	22 54	22 58

NRT DECEMBER 19 EDITION

Table T155-R

Mondays to Fridays
16 December to 15 May

Basingstoke, Alton, Guildford and Woking - Waterloo

		SW	SW	SW	SW	SW	SW	SW	SW	SW		SW	SW	SW	SW	SW FO	SW FX	SW	SW FO	SW FX		SW FO	SW FX	SW FX	SW FO
		◇■	◇■	■	■		◇■		■	■		◇■	◇■	■	◇■			◇■				■	■	■	■
Basingstoke	d											22 24	22 36					22 43						22 54	22 54
Hook	d											22 31												23 01	23 01
Winchfield	d											22 35												23 05	23 05
Fleet	d											22 40						22 54						23 10	23 10
Farnborough (Main)	d											22 46						23 00						23 16	23 16
Alton	d								22 15													22 44	22 44		
Bentley	d																					22 51	22 51		
Farnham	a								22 25													22 56	22 56		
	d				22 04				22 28	22 34												22 58	22 58		
Aldershot	d				22 10				22 34	22 40												23 04	23 04		
Ash Vale	d								22 39													23 09	23 09		
Brookwood	d								22 46			22 53										23 16	23 16	23 23	23 23
Guildford	d		22 19		22a27		22 34			22a57															
Worplesdon	d			←			22 40								←										
Woking	a		22 26	22 28			22 44		22 51			22 58	22 54		22 58			23 09				23 21	23 21	23 28	23 28
	d	22 23	22 27	22 29		22 33	22 45		22 52			22 59	22 55		22 59	23 03	23 03	23 10				23 22	23 22	23 33	23 33
West Byfleet	d					22 37			22 57			→				23 07	23 07					23 27	23 27	→	→
Byfleet & New Haw	d					22 40										23 10	23 10								
Weybridge	d			22 36		22 43									23 06	23 13	23 13								
Walton-on-Thames	d			22 40		22 47									23 10	23 17	23 17								
Hersham	d					22 49										23 19	23 19								
Esher	d					22 52		←						←		23 22	23 22		←	←					
Surbiton ■	a			22 46		22 56		22 56	23 07					23 07	23 16	23 26	23 26		23 26	23 26		23 37	23 37		
Wimbledon ■ ⊖	a					→		23 04	→							→	→		23 35	23 35		→	→		
Earlsfield	a							23 08											23 39	23 39					
Clapham Junction ■10	a			22 58			23 04	23 12					23 14	23 19				23 30	23 43	23 43					
Vauxhall ⊖	a							23 17											23 48	23 48					
London Waterloo ■15 ⊖	a	22 49	22 51	23 06			23 14	23 26					23 26	23 28	23 34			23 40	23 56	23 57					

		SW	SW FO	SW FX	SW FX	SW FO		SW FO	SW FX	SW FX	SW FO	SW	SW	SW	SW	SW		SW	SW
		◇■	■	■	■	■		◇■	◇■	■	■		■	◇■	■	■		◇■	■
Basingstoke	d	23 07						23 13	23 13									23 44	
Hook	d																	23 51	
Winchfield	d																	23 55	
Fleet	d																	00 01	
Farnborough (Main)	d																	00 06	
Alton	d														23 15				23 48
Bentley	d																		23 55
Farnham	a														23 26				00 09
	d												23 04		23 28	23 34			
Aldershot	d												23 10		23 34	23 40			
Ash Vale	d														23 39				
Brookwood	d														23 46			00 13	
Guildford	d											23 15	23a27	23 39		23a57			
Worplesdon	d				←	←								23 45					
Woking	a	23 26			23 28	23 28		23 31	23 31			23 36		23 49	23 51			00 18	
	d	23 27			23 33	23 33		23 33	23 33					23 56				00 20	
West Byfleet	d				23 37	23 37												00 25	
Byfleet & New Haw	d				23 40	23 40													
Weybridge	d				23 43	23 43												00 29	
Walton-on-Thames	d				23 47	23 47												00 33	
Hersham	d				23 49	23 49													
Esher	d		←	←	23 52	23 52				←	←								
Surbiton ■	a		23 37	23 37	23 57	23 57				23 57	23 57			00 08				00 39	
Wimbledon ■ ⊖	a				→	→				00 07	00 07			00 16				00 47	
Earlsfield	a																		
Clapham Junction ■10	a	23 47	23 50	23 50				23 54	23 54	00 21	00 21			00 22				00 53	
Vauxhall ⊖	a									00 30	00 31								
London Waterloo ■15 ⊖	a	23 55	00 02	00 05				00 04	00 07	00 36	00 36			00 33				01 04	

Table T155-R

Basingstoke, Alton, Guildford and Woking - Waterloo

Saturdays

21 December to 16 May

		SW ◇[1]	SW	SW	SW	SW [1]		SW	SW	SW ◇[1]	SW [1]	SW ◇[1]	SW ◇[1] 🍴	SW	SW	SW ◇[1]		SW	SW ◇[1]	SW ◇[1]	SW ◇[1] 🍴	SW	SW [1]	SW ◇[1]	SW [1]
Basingstoke	d					04 54						05 54	05 59							06 24	06 30				
Hook	d					05 01						06 01								06 31					
Winchfield	d					05 05						06 05								06 35					
Fleet	d	00 01				05 10						06 10								06 40					
Farnborough (Main)	d	00 06				05 16						06 16								06 46					
Alton	d																						06 14		
Bentley	d																						06 21		
Farnham	a																						06 26		
	d										06 04												06 28		06 34
Aldershot	d										06 10												06 34		06 40
Ash Vale	d																						06 39		
Brookwood	d	00 13				05 23						06 23								06 53			06 46		
Guildford	d		04 25		05 14					06 04	06a27								06 34						06a57
Worplesdon	d				05 19			←								←			06 40					←	
Woking	a	00 18	04 33		05 24	05 28		05 24		06 11		06 28	06 18			06 28			06 44	06 58	06 48		06 51	06 58	
	d	00 20	04 35	05 27	05 32	05 29		05 32	06 02	06 12		06 29	06 19			06 29		06 33	06 45	06 59	06 50		06 52	06 59	
West Byfleet	d	00 25		05 32	→			05 36	06 06			→						06 37		→			06 57		
Byfleet & New Haw	d			05 35				05 39	06 09									06 40							
Weybridge	d	00 29						05 42	06 12							06 36		06 43						07 06	
Walton-on-Thames	d	00 33						05 46	06 16							06 40		06 47						07 10	
Hersham	d							05 48	06 18									06 49							
Esher	d							05 51	06 21					←				06 52				←			
Surbiton [6]	a	00 39	04 54			05 40		05 55	06 25					06 25		06 46		06 56				06 56	07 07	07 16	
Wimbledon [6]	⊖ a	00 47	05 01			05 48		06 04	→					06 34				→				07 04			
Earlsfield	a							06 08						06 38	←							07 08			
Clapham Junction [10]	a	00 53	05 08	06 43		06 00		06 12		06 31			06 38	06 42	06 43	06 57			07 04			07 12	07 18		
Vauxhall	⊖ a			→		06 07		06 17						06 47	06 49							07 17			
London Waterloo [15]	⊖ a	01 04	05 18			06 12		06 22		06 40			06 49	06 54	06 56	07 05			07 13		07 19	07 22	07 27	07 35	

		SW ◇[1]		SW	SW [1]	SW [1]	SW ◇[1] 🍴	SW	SW [1]	SW ◇[1] 🍴	SW ◇[1]	SW [1]		SW [1]	SW	SW ◇[1]	SW ◇[1]	SW ◇[1] 🍴	SW	SW [1]	SW ◇[1] 🍴	SW ◇[1]		SW [1]	SW ◇[1]
Basingstoke	d	06 40				06 54	06 57			07 08							07 24	07 30							07 43
Hook	d					07 01											07 31								
Winchfield	d					07 05											07 35								
Fleet	d					07 10											07 40								07 54
Farnborough (Main)	d					07 16											07 46								08 00
Alton	d								06 44											07 14					
Bentley	d								06 51											07 21					
Farnham	a								06 56											07 26					
	d								06 58					07 04						07 28				07 34	
Aldershot	d								07 04					07 10						07 34				07 40	
Ash Vale	d								07 09											07 39					
Brookwood	d					07 23			07 16								07 53			07 46					
Guildford	d				07 04						07 19			07a27		07 34					07 49			07a57	
Worplesdon	d											←				07 40						←			
Woking	a	06 58			07 11	07 28	07 16		07 21	07 26		07 28				07 44	07 58	07 48		07 51	07 56	07 58			
	d	07 00		07 03	07 12	07 29	07 17		07 22	07 27		07 29			07 33	07 45	07 59	07 50		07 52	07 57	07 59			
West Byfleet	d			07 07		→			07 27						07 37		→			07 57					
Byfleet & New Haw	d			07 10											07 40										
Weybridge	d			07 13								07 36			07 43							08 06			
Walton-on-Thames	d			07 17								07 40			07 47							08 10			
Hersham	d			07 19											07 49										
Esher	d			07 22				←							07 52				←						
Surbiton [6]	a			07 26				07 26	07 37			07 46			07 56				07 56	08 07		08 16			
Wimbledon [6]	⊖ a			→				07 34							→				08 04						
Earlsfield	a							07 38											08 08						
Clapham Junction [10]	a				07 31		07 38	07 42	07 49			07 57				08 04			08 12	08 19					08 27
Vauxhall	⊖ a							07 47											08 17						
London Waterloo [15]	⊖ a	07 29			07 40		07 49	07 52	07 59	07 52	08 03	08 06				08 13		08 19	08 22	08 28	08 23	08 37			08 38

		SW	SW [1]	SW [1]	SW ◇[1] 🍴	SW	SW [1]	SW ◇[1] 🍴		SW ◇[1] 🍴	SW [1]	SW [1]	SW	SW ◇[1]	SW ◇[1]	SW ◇[1]	SW ◇[1] 🍴	SW ◇[1]		SW	SW [1]	SW ◇[1] 🍴	SW [1]	SW ◇[1]	SW ◇[1]
Basingstoke	d			07 54	07 57									08 17		08 24	08 30	08 35						08 43	
Hook	d			08 01												08 31									
Winchfield	d			08 05												08 35									
Fleet	d			08 10												08 40								08 54	
Farnborough (Main)	d			08 16										08 30		08 46								09 00	
Alton	d						07 44														08 14				
Bentley	d						07 51														08 21				
Farnham	a						07 56														08 26				
	d						07 58					08 04									08 28		08 34		
Aldershot	d						08 04					08 10									08 34		08 40		
Ash Vale	d						08 09														08 39				
Brookwood	d			08 23			08 16									08 53					08 46				
Guildford	d		08 04							08 19		08a27			08 34							08 49	08a57		
Worplesdon	d										←				08 40										←
Woking	a		08 11	08 28	08 15		08 21			08 26	08 28			08 39	08 44	08 58	08 48				08 51	08 56			08 58
	d	08 03	08 12	08 29	08 17		08 22	08 23		08 27	08 29		08 33	08 41	08 45	08 59	08 50				08 52	08 57			08 59
West Byfleet	d	08 07		→			08 27						08 37			→					08 57				
Byfleet & New Haw	d	08 10											08 40												
Weybridge	d	08 13									08 36		08 43												09 06
Walton-on-Thames	d	08 17									08 40		08 47												09 10
Hersham	d	08 19											08 49												
Esher	d	08 22				←							08 52							←					
Surbiton [6]	a	08 26				08 26	08 37				08 46		08 56							08 56	09 07				09 16
Wimbledon [6]	⊖ a	→				08 34							→							09 04					
Earlsfield	a					08 38														09 08					
Clapham Junction [10]	a		08 33		08 37	08 42	08 49				08 57				09 04			09 11		09 12	09 19			09 25	
Vauxhall	⊖ a					08 47														09 17					
London Waterloo [15]	⊖ a		08 42		08 49	08 52	08 58	08 49		08 52	09 09			09 09	09 13		09 19	09 19		09 22	09 28	09 25		09 34	09 38

		SW	SW [1]	SW [1]		SW ◇[1] 🍴	SW ◇[1] 🍴	SW	SW [1]	SW ◇[1] 🍴	SW [1]	SW [1]	SW	SW ◇[1]		SW ◇[1]	SW [1]	SW ◇[1] 🍴	SW ◇[1] 🍴	SW	SW [1]	SW ◇[1] 🍴	SW [1]	SW ◇[1]	
Basingstoke	d			08 54		08 57								09 17			09 24	09 30	09 36					09 43	
Hook	d			09 01													09 31								
Winchfield	d			09 05													09 35								
Fleet	d			09 10													09 40							09 54	
Farnborough (Main)	d			09 16										09 30			09 46							10 00	
Alton	d								08 44												09 14				
Bentley	d								08 51												09 21				
Farnham	a								08 56												09 26				
	d								08 58			09 04									09 28		09 34		
Aldershot	d								09 04			09 10									09 34		09 40		
Ash Vale	d								09 09												09 39				
Brookwood	d			09 23					09 16								09 53				09 46				
Guildford	d		09 04							09 19		09a27				09 34						09 49	09a57		
Worplesdon	d										←					09 40									
Woking	a		09 11	09 28		09 15			09 21	09 26	09 28			09 39		09 44	09 58	09 48			09 51	09 56			
	d	09 03	09 12	09 29		09 17	09 21		09 22	09 27	09 29		09 33	09 41		09 45	09 59	09 50			09 52	09 57			
West Byfleet	d	09 07		→					09 27				09 37				→				09 57				
Byfleet & New Haw	d	09 10											09 40												
Weybridge	d	09 13									09 36		09 43												
Walton-on-Thames	d	09 17									09 40		09 47												
Hersham	d	09 19											09 49												
Esher	d	09 22						←					09 52							←					
Surbiton [6]	a	09 26						09 26	09 37		09 46		09 56							09 56	10 07				
Wimbledon [6]	⊖ a	→						09 34					→							10 04					
Earlsfield	a							09 38												10 08					
Clapham Junction [10]	a		09 31			09 36		09 42	09 49		09 57					10 04			10 11	10 12	10 19			10 25	
Vauxhall	⊖ a							09 47												10 17					
London Waterloo [15]	⊖ a		09 43			09 49	09 49	09 52	09 58	09 52	10 08			10 08		10 13		10 19	10 19	10 22	10 28	10 23		10 34	

		SW [1]	SW	SW [1]	SW [1]	SW ◇[1] 🍴	SW ◇[1] 🍴	SW	SW [1]	SW ◇[1] 🍴		SW [1]	SW [1]	SW	SW ◇[1]	SW ◇[1]	SW [1]	SW ◇[1] 🍴	SW ◇[1] 🍴	SW		SW [1]	SW ◇[1] 🍴	SW [1]	SW ◇[1]
Basingstoke	d				09 54	09 57									10 17		10 24	10 30	10 35						10 43
Hook	d				10 01												10 31								
Winchfield	d				10 05												10 35								
Fleet	d				10 10												10 40								10 54
Farnborough (Main)	d				10 16										10 30		10 46								11 00
Alton	d								09 44													10 14			
Bentley	d								09 51													10 21			
Farnham	a								09 56													10 26			
	d								09 58				10 04									10 28		10 34	
Aldershot	d								10 04				10 10									10 34		10 40	
Ash Vale	d								10 09													10 39			
Brookwood	d				10 23				10 16								10 53					10 46			
Guildford	d			10 04						10 19			10a27			10 34							10 49	10a57	
Worplesdon	d	←										←				10 40									
Woking	a	09 58		10 11	10 28	10 15			10 21	10 26		10 28			10 39	10 44	10 58	10 48				10 51	10 56		
	d	09 59	10 03	10 12	10 29	10 17	10 21		10 22	10 27		10 29		10 33	10 41	10 45	10 59	10 50				10 52	10 57		
West Byfleet	d		10 07		→				10 27					10 37			→					10 57			
Byfleet & New Haw	d		10 10											10 40											
Weybridge	d	10 06	10 13									10 36		10 43											
Walton-on-Thames	d	10 10	10 17									10 40		10 47											
Hersham	d		10 19											10 49											
Esher	d		10 22					←						10 52						←					
Surbiton [6]	a	10 16	10 26					10 26	10 37			10 46		10 56						10 56		11 07			
Wimbledon [6]	⊖ a		→					10 34						→						11 04					
Earlsfield	a							10 38												11 08					
Clapham Junction [10]	a			10 31		10 36		10 42	10 49			10 57				11 04			11 11	11 12		11 19			11 26
Vauxhall	⊖ a							10 47												11 17					
London Waterloo [15]	⊖ a	10 36		10 43		10 49	10 49	10 52	10 58	10 52		11 05			11 08	11 13		11 19	11 19	11 22		11 28	11 22		11 34

		SW [1]	SW	SW [1]	SW [1]	SW ◇[1] 🍴		SW ◇[1] 🍴	SW	SW [1]	SW ◇[1] 🍴	SW [1]	SW [1]	SW	SW ◇[1]	SW ◇[1]		SW [1]	SW ◇[1] 🍴	SW ◇[1] 🍴	SW	SW [1]	SW ◇[1] 🍴	SW [1]	SW ◇[1]
Basingstoke	d				10 54	10 57									11 17			11 24	11 30	11 35					11 43
Hook	d				11 01													11 31							
Winchfield	d				11 05													11 35							
Fleet	d				11 10													11 40							11 54
Farnborough (Main)	d				11 16										11 30			11 46							12 00
Alton	d									10 44												11 15			
Bentley	d									10 51															
Farnham	a									10 56												11 25			
	d									10 58			11 04									11 28		11 34	
Aldershot	d									11 04			11 10									11 34		11 40	
Ash Vale	d									11 09												11 39			
Brookwood	d				11 23					11 16								11 53				11 46			
Guildford	d			11 04							11 19		11a27			11 34							11 49	11a57	
Worplesdon	d	←										←				11 40									
Woking	a	10 58		11 11	11 28	11 15				11 21	11 26	11 28			11 40	11 44		11 58	11 48			11 51	11 56		
	d	10 59	11 03	11 12	11 29	11 17		11 21		11 22	11 27	11 29		11 33	11 41	11 45		11 59	11 50			11 52	11 57		
West Byfleet	d		11 07		→					11 27				11 37				→				11 57			
Byfleet & New Haw	d		11 10											11 40											
Weybridge	d	11 06	11 13									11 36		11 43											
Walton-on-Thames	d	11 10	11 17									11 40		11 47											
Hersham	d		11 19											11 49											
Esher	d		11 22						←					11 52							←				
Surbiton [6]	a	11 16	11 26						11 26	11 37		11 46		11 56							11 56	12 07			
Wimbledon [6]	⊖ a		→						11 34					→							12 04				
Earlsfield	a								11 38												12 08				
Clapham Junction [10]	a			11 32		11 36			11 42	11 49		11 57				12 04				12 11	12 12	12 19			12 25
Vauxhall	⊖ a								11 47												12 17				
London Waterloo [15]	⊖ a	11 36		11 43		11 48		11 49	11 52	11 58	11 52	12 08			12 12	12 14			12 19	12 21	12 22	12 28	12 24		12 34

Table T155-R

Saturdays
21 December to 16 May

Basingstoke, Alton, Guildford and Woking - Waterloo

		SW 1		SW	SW 1	SW 1	SW ◇1 🛒	SW ◇1 🛒	SW	SW 1	SW ◇1 🛒	SW 1		SW 1	SW	SW ◇1	SW ◇1	SW 1	SW ◇1 🛒	SW ◇1 🛒	SW	SW 1		SW ◇1 🛒	SW 1
Basingstoke	d					11 54	11 57									12 17		12 24	12 30	12 35					
Hook	d					12 01												12 31							
Winchfield	d					12 05												12 35							
Fleet	d					12 10												12 40							
Farnborough (Main)	d					12 16										12 30		12 46							
Alton	d									11 44												12 15			
Bentley	d									11 51															
Farnham	a									11 56												12 25			
	d									11 58				12 04								12 28			12 34
Aldershot	d									12 04				12 10								12 34			12 40
Ash Vale	d									12 09												12 39			
Brookwood	d					12 23				12 16								12 53				12 46			
Guildford	d				12 04						12 19			12a27			12 34							12 49	12a58
Worplesdon	d	←										←					12 40								
Woking	a	11 58			12 11	12 28	12 15			12 21	12 26	12 28				12 39	12 44	12 58	12 48			12 51		12 56	
	d	11 59		12 03	12 12	12 29	12 17	12 21		12 22	12 27	12 29			12 33	12 41	12 45	12 59	12 50			12 52		12 57	
West Byfleet	d			12 07		→				12 27					12 37			→				12 57			
Byfleet & New Haw	d			12 10											12 40										
Weybridge	d	12 06		12 13								12 36			12 43										
Walton-on-Thames	d	12 10		12 17								12 40			12 47										
Hersham	d			12 19											12 49										
Esher	d			12 22					←						12 52						←				
Surbiton 6	a	12 16		12 26					12 26	12 37		12 46			12 56						12 56	13 07			
Wimbledon 6 ⊖	a			→					12 34						→						13 04				
Earlsfield	a								12 38												13 08				
Clapham Junction 10	a				12 31		12 36		12 42	12 49		12 57					13 04			13 11	13 12	13 19			
Vauxhall ⊖	a								12 47												13 17				
London Waterloo 15 ⊖	a	12 38			12 43		12 49	12 51	12 52	12 58	12 53	13 08				13 11	13 13		13 19	13 21	13 22	13 29		13 27	

		SW ◇1	SW 1	SW	SW 1	SW 1	SW ◇1 🛒	SW ◇1 🛒		SW	SW 1	SW ◇1 🛒	SW 1	SW 1	SW	SW ◇1	SW ◇1	SW 1		SW ◇1 🛒	SW ◇1 🛒	SW	SW 1	SW ◇1 🛒	SW 1
Basingstoke	d	12 43				12 54	12 57									13 17		13 24		13 30	13 35				
Hook	d					13 01												13 31							
Winchfield	d					13 05												13 35							
Fleet	d	12 54				13 10												13 40							
Farnborough (Main)	d	13 00				13 16										13 30		13 46							
Alton	d										12 44												13 15		
Bentley	d										12 51														
Farnham	a										12 56												13 25		
	d										12 58			13 04									13 28		13 34
Aldershot	d										13 04			13 10									13 34		13 40
Ash Vale	d										13 09												13 39		
Brookwood	d					13 23					13 16							13 53					13 46		
Guildford	d				13 04							13 19		13a27			13 34							13 49	13a57
Worplesdon	d		←										←				13 40								
Woking	a		12 58		13 11	13 28	13 15				13 21	13 26	13 28			13 39	13 44	13 58		13 48			13 51	13 56	
	d		12 59	13 03	13 12	13 29	13 17	13 21			13 22	13 27	13 29		13 33	13 41	13 45	13 59		13 50			13 52	13 57	
West Byfleet	d			13 07		→					13 27				13 37			→					13 57		
Byfleet & New Haw	d			13 10											13 40										
Weybridge	d		13 06	13 13									13 36		13 43										
Walton-on-Thames	d		13 10	13 17									13 40		13 47										
Hersham	d			13 19											13 49										
Esher	d			13 22						←					13 52							←			
Surbiton 6	a		13 16	13 26						13 26	13 37		13 46		13 56							13 56	14 07		
Wimbledon 6 ⊖	a			→						13 34					→							14 04			
Earlsfield	a									13 38												14 08			
Clapham Junction 10	a	13 25			13 31		13 36			13 42	13 49		13 57				14 04				14 11	14 12	14 19		
Vauxhall ⊖	a									13 47												14 17			
London Waterloo 15 ⊖	a	13 34	13 38		13 43		13 49	13 51		13 52	13 58	13 53	14 09			14 11	14 13			14 19	14 21	14 22	14 29	14 24	

		SW ◇1	SW 1	SW		SW 1	SW 1	SW ◇1 🛒	SW ◇1 🛒	SW	SW 1	SW ◇1 🛒	SW 1	SW 1		SW	SW ◇1	SW ◇1	SW 1	SW ◇1 🛒	SW ◇1 🛒	SW	SW 1	SW ◇1 🛒	
Basingstoke	d	13 43					13 54	13 57									14 17		14 24	14 30	14 35				
Hook	d						14 01												14 31						
Winchfield	d						14 05												14 35						
Fleet	d	13 54					14 10												14 40						
Farnborough (Main)	d	14 00					14 16										14 30		14 46						
Alton	d										13 44												14 15		
Bentley	d										13 51														
Farnham	a										13 56												14 25		
	d										13 58			14 04									14 28		
Aldershot	d										14 04			14 10									14 34		
Ash Vale	d										14 09												14 39		
Brookwood	d						14 23				14 16								14 53				14 46		
Guildford	d					14 04						14 19		14a27				14 34						14 49	
Worplesdon	d		←										←					14 40							
Woking	a		13 58			14 11	14 28	14 15			14 21	14 26	14 28				14 39	14 44	14 58	14 48			14 51	14 56	
	d		13 59	14 03		14 12	14 29	14 17	14 21		14 22	14 27	14 29			14 33	14 41	14 45	14 59	14 50			14 52	14 57	
West Byfleet	d			14 07			→				14 27					14 37			→				14 57		
Byfleet & New Haw	d			14 10												14 40									
Weybridge	d		14 06	14 13									14 36			14 43									
Walton-on-Thames	d		14 10	14 17									14 40			14 47									
Hersham	d			14 19												14 49									
Esher	d			14 22						←						14 52						←			
Surbiton 6	a		14 16	14 26						14 26	14 37		14 46			14 56						14 56	15 07		
Wimbledon 6 ⊖	a			→						14 34						→						15 04			
Earlsfield	a									14 38												15 08			
Clapham Junction 10	a	14 25				14 31		14 36		14 42	14 49		14 57					15 04			15 11	15 12	15 19		
Vauxhall ⊖	a									14 47												15 17			
London Waterloo 15 ⊖	a	14 34	14 38			14 44		14 49	14 51	14 52	14 58	14 56	15 05				15 11	15 14		15 19	15 21	15 22	15 29	15 27	

Table T155-R

Saturdays
21 December to 16 May

Basingstoke, Alton, Guildford and Woking - Waterloo

		SW 1	SW ◇1	SW 1	SW	SW 1	SW 1	SW ◇1 🛒	SW ◇1 🛒	SW		SW 1	SW ◇1 🛒	SW 1	SW 1	SW	SW ◇1	SW ◇1	SW 1	SW ◇1 🛒		SW ◇1 🛒	SW	SW 1	SW ◇1 🛒
Basingstoke	d		14 43				14 54	14 57									15 17		15 24	15 30		15 35			
Hook	d						15 01												15 31						
Winchfield	d						15 05												15 35						
Fleet	d		14 54				15 10												15 40						
Farnborough (Main)	d		15 00				15 16										15 30		15 46						
Alton	d											14 44												15 15	
Bentley	d											14 51													
Farnham	a											14 56												15 25	
	d	14 34										14 58			15 04									15 28	
Aldershot	d	14 40										15 04			15 10									15 34	
Ash Vale	d											15 09												15 39	
Brookwood	d						15 23					15 16							15 53					15 46	
Guildford	d	14a57				15 04							15 19		15a27			15 34							15 49
Worplesdon	d			←										←				15 40							
Woking	a			14 58		15 11	15 28	15 15				15 21	15 26	15 28			15 39	15 44	15 58	15 48				15 51	15 56
	d			14 59	15 03	15 12	15 29	15 17	15 21			15 22	15 27	15 29		15 33	15 41	15 45	15 59	15 50				15 52	15 57
West Byfleet	d				15 07		→					15 27				15 37			→					15 57	
Byfleet & New Haw	d				15 10											15 40									
Weybridge	d			15 06	15 13									15 36		15 43									
Walton-on-Thames	d			15 10	15 17									15 40		15 47									
Hersham	d				15 19											15 49									
Esher	d				15 22					←						15 52							←		
Surbiton 6	a			15 16	15 26					15 26		15 37		15 46		15 56							15 56	16 07	
Wimbledon 6 ⊖	a				→					15 34						→							16 04		
Earlsfield	a									15 38													16 08		
Clapham Junction 10	a		15 25			15 31		15 36		15 42		15 49		15 57				16 04				16 11	16 12	16 19	
Vauxhall ⊖	a									15 47													16 17		
London Waterloo 15 ⊖	a		15 34	15 38		15 44		15 49	15 51	15 52		15 58	15 56	16 05			16 11	16 14		16 19		16 21	16 22	16 28	16 24

		SW 1	SW ◇1	SW 1	SW	SW 1		SW 1	SW ◇1 🛒	SW ◇1 🛒	SW	SW 1	SW ◇1 🛒	SW 1	SW 1	SW		SW ◇1	SW ◇1	SW 1	SW ◇1 🛒	SW ◇1 🛒	SW	SW 1	SW ◇1 🛒
Basingstoke	d		15 43					15 54	15 57									16 17		16 24	16 30	16 35			
Hook	d							16 01												16 31					
Winchfield	d							16 05												16 35					
Fleet	d		15 54					16 10												16 40					
Farnborough (Main)	d		16 00					16 16										16 30		16 46					
Alton	d											15 44												16 15	
Bentley	d											15 51													
Farnham	a											15 56												16 25	
	d	15 34										15 58			16 04									16 28	
Aldershot	d	15 40										16 04			16 10									16 34	
Ash Vale	d											16 09												16 39	
Brookwood	d							16 23				16 16								16 53				16 46	
Guildford	d	15a57				16 04							16 19		16a27				16 34						16 49
Worplesdon	d			←										←					16 40						
Woking	a			15 58		16 11		16 28	16 15			16 21	16 26	16 28				16 39	16 44	16 58	16 48			16 51	16 56
	d			15 59	16 03	16 12		16 29	16 17	16 21		16 22	16 27	16 29		16 33		16 41	16 45	16 59	16 50			16 52	16 57
West Byfleet	d				16 07			→				16 27				16 37				→				16 57	
Byfleet & New Haw	d				16 10											16 40									
Weybridge	d			16 06	16 13									16 36		16 43									
Walton-on-Thames	d			16 10	16 17									16 40		16 47									
Hersham	d				16 19											16 49									
Esher	d				16 22						←					16 52							←		
Surbiton 6	a			16 16	16 26						16 26	16 37		16 46		16 56							16 56	17 07	
Wimbledon 6 ⊖	a				→						16 34					→							17 04		
Earlsfield	a										16 38												17 08		
Clapham Junction 10	a		16 25			16 31			16 36		16 42	16 49		16 57					17 04			17 11	17 12	17 19	
Vauxhall ⊖	a										16 47												17 17		
London Waterloo 15 ⊖	a		16 34	16 36		16 40			16 49	16 49	16 52	16 58	16 52	17 06				17 09	17 13		17 19	17 19	17 22	17 28	17 22

		SW 1		SW ◇1	SW 1	SW	SW 1	SW 1	SW ◇1 🛒	SW ◇1 🛒	SW	SW 1		SW ◇1 🛒	SW 1	SW 1	SW	SW ◇1	SW ◇1	SW 1	SW ◇1 🛒	SW ◇1 🛒		SW	SW 1
Basingstoke	d			16 43				16 54	16 57									17 17		17 24	17 30	17 35			
Hook	d							17 01												17 31					
Winchfield	d							17 05												17 35					
Fleet	d			16 54				17 10												17 40					
Farnborough (Main)	d			17 00				17 16										17 30		17 46					
Alton	d											16 44													17 15
Bentley	d											16 51													
Farnham	a											16 56													17 25
	d	16 34										16 58				17 04									17 28
Aldershot	d	16 40										17 04				17 10									17 34
Ash Vale	d											17 09													17 39
Brookwood	d							17 23				17 16								17 53					17 46
Guildford	d	16a57					17 04							17 19		17a27			17 34						
Worplesdon	d				←										←				17 40						
Woking	a				16 58		17 11	17 28	17 15			17 21		17 26	17 28			17 39	17 44	17 58	17 48				17 51
	d				16 59	17 03	17 12	17 29	17 17	17 21		17 22		17 27	17 29		17 33	17 41	17 45	17 59	17 50				17 52
West Byfleet	d					17 07		→				17 27					17 37			→					17 57
Byfleet & New Haw	d					17 10											17 40								
Weybridge	d				17 06	17 13									17 36		17 43								
Walton-on-Thames	d				17 10	17 17									17 40		17 47								
Hersham	d					17 19											17 49								
Esher	d					17 22					←						17 52							←	
Surbiton 6	a				17 16	17 26					17 26	17 37			17 46		17 56							17 56	18 07
Wimbledon 6 ⊖	a					→					17 34						→							18 04	
Earlsfield	a										17 38													18 08	
Clapham Junction 10	a			17 25			17 31		17 36		17 42	17 49			17 57				18 04			18 11		18 12	18 19
Vauxhall ⊖	a										17 47													18 17	
London Waterloo 15 ⊖	a			17 34	17 36		17 40		17 45	17 49	17 52	17 58		17 52	18 05			18 08	18 13		18 19	18 19		18 22	18 28

Table T155-R

Saturdays

21 December to 16 May

Basingstoke, Alton, Guildford and Woking - Waterloo

	SW ◇1 🍴	SW 1	SW ◇1	SW 1	SW	SW 1	SW 1		SW ◇1 🍴	SW ◇1 🍴	SW	SW 1	SW ◇1	SW 1	SW 1	SW	SW ◇1		SW ◇1	SW 1	SW ◇1 🍴	SW ◇1 🍴	SW	SW 1
Basingstoke d			17 43				17 54		17 57								18 17			18 24	18 30	18 35		
Hook d							18 01													18 31				
Winchfield d							18 05													18 35				
Fleet d			17 54				18 10													18 40				
Farnborough (Main) d			18 00				18 16										18 30			18 46				
Alton d												17 44												18 15
Bentley d												17 51												
Farnham a												17 56												18 25
d		17 34										17 58			18 04									18 28
Aldershot d		17 40										18 04			18 10									18 34
Ash Vale d												18 09												18 39
Brookwood d							18 23					18 16								18 53				18 46
Guildford d	17 49	17a57				18 04							18 19		18a27				18 34					
Worplesdon d				←										←					18 40					
Woking a	17 56			17 58		18 11	18 28		18 15			18 21	18 26	18 28			18 39		18 44	18 58	18 48			18 51
d	17 57			17 59	18 03	18 12	18 29		18 17	18 21		18 22	18 27	18 29		18 33	18 41		18 45	18 59	18 50			18 52
West Byfleet d					18 07		→					18 27				18 37				→				18 57
Byfleet & New Haw d					18 10											18 40								
Weybridge d				18 06	18 13									18 36		18 43								
Walton-on-Thames d				18 10	18 17									18 40		18 47								
Hersham d					18 19											18 49								
Esher d					18 22						←					18 52							←	
Surbiton 6 a				18 16	18 26						18 26	18 37		18 46		18 56							18 56	19 07
Wimbledon 6 ⊖ a					→						18 34					→							19 04	
Earlsfield a											18 38												19 08	
Clapham Junction 10 a			18 25			18 31			18 36		18 42	18 49		18 57					19 04			19 11	19 12	19 19
Vauxhall ⊖ a											18 47												19 17	
London Waterloo 15 ⊖ a	18 22		18 34	18 37		18 43			18 49	18 49	18 52	18 58	18 52	19 05			19 08		19 13		19 19	19 19	19 22	19 28

	SW ◇1 🍴	SW 1	SW ◇1		SW 1	SW	SW 1	SW 1	SW ◇1 🍴	SW ◇1 🍴	SW	SW 1	SW ◇1		SW 1	SW 1	SW	SW ◇1	SW ◇1	SW 1	SW ◇1	SW ◇1	SW	
Basingstoke d			18 43					18 54	18 57									19 17		19 24	19 30	19 35		
Hook d								19 01												19 31				
Winchfield d								19 05												19 35				
Fleet d			18 54					19 10												19 40				
Farnborough (Main) d			19 00					19 16										19 30		19 46				
Alton d												18 44												
Bentley d												18 51												
Farnham a												18 56												
d		18 34										18 58				19 04								
Aldershot d		18 40										19 04				19 10								
Ash Vale d												19 09												
Brookwood d								19 23				19 16								19 53				
Guildford d	18 49	18a57					19 04						19 19			19a27			19 34					
Worplesdon d					←										←				19 40					
Woking a	18 56				18 58		19 11	19 28	19 15			19 21	19 26		19 28			19 39	19 44	19 58	19 48			
d	18 57				18 59	19 03	19 12	19 29	19 17	19 21		19 22	19 27		19 29		19 33	19 41	19 45	19 59	19 50			
West Byfleet d						19 07		→				19 27					19 37			→				
Byfleet & New Haw d						19 10											19 40							
Weybridge d					19 06	19 13									19 36		19 43							
Walton-on-Thames d					19 10	19 17									19 40		19 47							
Hersham d						19 19											19 49							
Esher d						19 22					←						19 52						←	
Surbiton 6 a					19 16	19 26					19 26	19 37			19 46		19 56						19 56	
Wimbledon 6 ⊖ a						→					19 34						→						20 04	
Earlsfield a											19 38												20 08	
Clapham Junction 10 a			19 25				19 31		19 36		19 42	19 49			19 57				20 04			20 11	20 12	
Vauxhall ⊖ a											19 47												20 17	
London Waterloo 15 ⊖ a	19 22		19 34		19 37		19 40		19 49	19 49	19 52	19 58	19 52		20 05			20 09	20 13		20 19	20 19	20 22	

	SW 1	SW ◇1	SW 1	SW ◇1	SW 1	SW	SW 1	SW 1	SW ◇1 🍴		SW ◇1 🍴	SW	SW 1	SW ◇1	SW 1	SW 1	SW	SW ◇1	SW ◇1		SW 1	SW ◇1	SW ◇1 🍴	SW
Basingstoke d				19 43				19 54	19 57									20 17			20 24	20 30	20 35	
Hook d								20 01													20 31			
Winchfield d								20 05													20 35			
Fleet d				19 54				20 10													20 40			
Farnborough (Main) d				20 00				20 16										20 30			20 46			
Alton d	19 15												19 44											
Bentley d													19 51											
Farnham a	19 25												19 56											
d	19 28		19 34										19 58			20 04								
Aldershot d	19 34		19 40										20 04			20 10								
Ash Vale d	19 39												20 09											
Brookwood d	19 46							20 23					20 16								20 53			
Guildford d		19 49	19a57				20 04							20 19		20a27			20 34					
Worplesdon d					←										←				20 40					
Woking a	19 51	19 56			19 58		20 11	20 28	20 15				20 21	20 26	20 28			20 39	20 44		20 58	20 48		
d	19 52	19 57			19 59	20 03	20 12	20 29	20 17		20 21		20 22	20 27	20 29		20 33	20 41	20 45		20 59	20 50		
West Byfleet d	19 57					20 07		→					20 27				20 37				→			
Byfleet & New Haw d						20 10											20 40							
Weybridge d					20 06	20 13									20 36		20 43							
Walton-on-Thames d					20 10	20 17									20 40		20 47							
Hersham d						20 19											20 49							
Esher d						20 22						←					20 52							←
Surbiton 6 a	20 07				20 16	20 26						20 26	20 37		20 46		20 56							20 56
Wimbledon 6 ⊖ a						→						20 34					→							21 04
Earlsfield a												20 38												21 08
Clapham Junction 10 a	20 19			20 25			20 31		20 36			20 42	20 49		20 57				21 04				21 11	21 12
Vauxhall ⊖ a												20 47												21 17
London Waterloo 15 ⊖ a	20 28	20 22		20 34	20 37		20 40		20 49		20 51	20 52	20 58	20 53	21 06			21 10	21 13			21 19	21 19	21 22

Table T155-R

Saturdays

21 December to 16 May

Basingstoke, Alton, Guildford and Woking - Waterloo

	SW 1	SW ◇1	SW 1	SW ◇1	SW 1		SW	SW 1	SW ◇1 🍴	SW	SW 1	SW ◇1	SW 1	SW 1	SW		SW ◇1 🍴	SW 1	SW ◇1	SW	SW 1	SW ◇1	SW ◇1 🍴	SW ◇1
Basingstoke d				20 43										20 54			21 11					21 24	21 35	
Hook d														21 01								21 31		
Winchfield d														21 05								21 35		
Fleet d				20 54										21 10								21 40		
Farnborough (Main) d				21 00										21 16								21 46		
Alton d	20 15										20 44										21 15			
Bentley d											20 51													
Farnham a	20 25										20 56										21 25			
d	20 28		20 34								20 58		21 04								21 28			
Aldershot d	20 34		20 40								21 04		21 10								21 34			
Ash Vale d	20 39										21 09										21 39			
Brookwood d	20 46										21 16			21 23							21 46	21 53		
Guildford d		20 49	20a57					21 04				21 19	21a27						21 34					21 49
Worplesdon d					←														21 40					
Woking a	20 51	20 56			20 58			21 11			21 21	21 26		21 28			21 30		21 45		21 51	21 58	21 53	21 57
d	20 52	20 57			20 59		21 03	21 12	21 21		21 22	21 27		21 29	21 33		21 36		21 46		21 52	21 59	21 54	21 58
West Byfleet d	20 57						21 07				21 27				21 37						21 57	→		
Byfleet & New Haw d							21 10								21 40									
Weybridge d					21 06		21 13							21 36	21 43									
Walton-on-Thames d					21 10		21 17							21 40	21 47									
Hersham d							21 19								21 49									
Esher d							21 22			←					21 52			←		←				
Surbiton 6 a	21 07				21 16		21 26			21 26	21 37			21 46	21 56			21 46		21 56	22 07			
Wimbledon 6 ⊖ a							→			21 34				→	→					22 04	→			
Earlsfield a										21 38										22 08				
Clapham Junction 10 a	21 19			21 25				21 31		21 42	21 49						21 55	21 59	22 05	22 12			22 13	
Vauxhall ⊖ a										21 47										22 17				
London Waterloo 15 ⊖ a	21 28	21 22		21 36	21 39			21 40	21 49	21 52	21 58	21 52					22 04	22 08	22 16	22 22			22 21	22 24

	SW 1		SW ◇1	SW 1	SW	SW ◇1	SW 1	SW ◇1	SW	SW 1	SW 1		SW 1	SW ◇1	SW 1	SW 1	SW	SW ◇1	SW	SW 1	SW 1		SW ◇1	SW ◇1
Basingstoke d						21 43							21 54	22 09									22 24	22 35
Hook d													22 01										22 31	
Winchfield d													22 05										22 35	
Fleet d						21 54							22 10										22 40	
Farnborough (Main) d						22 00							22 16										22 46	
Alton d										21 44										22 15				
Bentley d										21 51														
Farnham a										21 56										22 25				
d				21 34						21 58	22 04									22 28	22 34			
Aldershot d				21 40						22 04	22 10									22 34	22 40			
Ash Vale d										22 09										22 39				
Brookwood d										22 16			22 23							22 46			22 53	
Guildford d				21a57			22 04				22a27							22 34			22a57			
Worplesdon d			←													←		22 40						
Woking a			21 58			22 09	22 11			22 21			22 28	22 27		22 28		22 44		22 51			22 58	22 53
d			21 59		22 03	22 10	22 13	22 21		22 22			22 29	22 29		22 29	22 33	22 45		22 52			22 59	22 54
West Byfleet d					22 07					22 27			→				22 37			22 57			→	
Byfleet & New Haw d					22 10												22 40							
Weybridge d			22 06		22 13											22 36	22 43							
Walton-on-Thames d			22 10		22 17											22 40	22 47							
Hersham d					22 19												22 49							
Esher d	←				22 22				←						←		22 52		←					
Surbiton 6 a	22 07		22 16		22 27				22 27	22 37					22 37	22 46	22 56		22 56	23 07				
Wimbledon 6 ⊖ a					→				22 34	→							→		23 04	→				
Earlsfield a									22 38										23 08					
Clapham Junction 10 a	22 19					22 29	22 33		22 42					22 48	22 52	22 57		23 04	23 12					23 13
Vauxhall ⊖ a									22 47										23 17					
London Waterloo 15 ⊖ a	22 28		22 34			22 38	22 45	22 49	22 53					22 57	23 01	23 09		23 13	23 24					23 21

	SW 1	SW ◇1	SW	SW ◇1	SW	SW 1	SW 1		SW 1	SW 1	SW ◇1	SW 1	SW 1	SW ◇1	SW 1	SW ◇1	SW 1		SW ◇1	SW 1				
Basingstoke d				22 43						22 54	23 09			23 14					23 43					
Hook d										23 01									23 51					
Winchfield d										23 05									23 55					
Fleet d				22 54						23 10									00 01					
Farnborough (Main) d				23 00						23 16									00 06					
Alton d							22 44										23 15			23 46				
Bentley d							22 51													23 53				
Farnham a							22 56										23 25			23 58				
d							22 58		23 04								23 28							
Aldershot d							23 04		23 10								23 34							
Ash Vale d							23 09										23 39							
Brookwood d							23 16			23 23							23 46		00 13					
Guildford d						23 04			23a27							23 39								
Worplesdon d		←											←			23 45								
Woking a		22 58		23 09		23 11	23 21			23 28	23 27		23 28	23 32		23 50	23 51		00 18					
d		22 59	23 03	23 10			23 22			23 33	23 29		23 33	23 34		23 56			00 20					
West Byfleet d			23 07				23 27			→			23 37						00 25					
Byfleet & New Haw d			23 10										23 40											
Weybridge d		23 06	23 13										23 43						00 29					
Walton-on-Thames d		23 10	23 17										23 47						00 33					
Hersham d			23 19										23 49											
Esher d	←		23 22		←							←	23 52		←									
Surbiton 6 a	23 07	23 16	23 26		23 26		23 37					23 37	23 57		23 57	00 07			00 39					
Wimbledon 6 ⊖ a			→		23 34		→						→		00 06	00 16			00 47					
Earlsfield a					23 38																			
Clapham Junction 10 a	23 20			23 29	23 42						23 48	23 52		23 56	00 21	00 22			00 53					
Vauxhall ⊖ a					23 47										00 27									
London Waterloo 15 ⊖ a	23 30	23 32		23 39	23 54						23 57	00 01		00 08	00 34	00 32			01 04					

Table T155-R

Sundays
15 December to 10 May

Basingstoke, Alton, Guildford and Woking - Waterloo

	SW ◇1 A	SW	SW	SW	SW ◇1 ⌶	SW	SW	SW 1	SW 1	SW ◇1	SW	SW ◇1	SW	SW 1	SW ◇1 ⌶	SW	SW	SW ◇1	SW	SW	SW 1	SW 1
Basingstoke d					07 20			07 16		07 44					08 10						08 16	
Hook d								07 23													08 23	
Winchfield d								07 27													08 27	
Fleet d	00 01							07 32													08 32	
Farnborough (Main) d	00 06							07 38													08 38	
Alton d																						08 15
Bentley d																						08 23
Farnham a																						08 28
d									07 30													08 30
Aldershot d									07 36					07 48								08 36
Ash Vale d									07 41													08 41
Brookwood d	00 13							07 45	07 48												08 45	08 48
Guildford d			06 57	07 24							07 57	08 05		08a06			08 24	08 35				
Worplesdon d				07 30													08 30					
Woking a	00 18		07 05	07 34	07 39			07 50	07 54	08 02	08 05	08 13			08 28		08 34	08 42			08 50	08 54
d	00 20	06 36	07 06	07 36	07 40		07 52		07 58	08 04	08 06	08 15			08 30		08 36	08 45		08 52		08 58
West Byfleet d	00 25	06 40	07 10	07 40			07 56				08 10						08 40			08 56		
Byfleet & New Haw d		06 43	07 13	07 43			08 00				08 13						08 43			09 00		
Weybridge d	00 29	06 46	07 16	07 46							08 16						08 46					
Walton-on-Thames d	00 33	06 50	07 20	07 50							08 20						08 50					
Hersham d		06 52	07 22	07 52							08 22						08 52					
Esher d		06 55	07 25	07 55							08 25		←				08 55		←			
Surbiton 6 a	00 39	06 59	07 29	07 59					08 09		08 30		08 30				08 59		08 59			09 09
Wimbledon 6 ⊖ a	00 47	07 07	07 37	08 06					08 20		→		08 36				→		09 06			09 19
Earlsfield a		07 12	07 42	08 11		←							08 41			←			09 11			
Clapham Junction 10 a	00 53	07 15	07 45	08 16	08 05	08 16	09 01		08 27	08 31		08 39	08 44		08 57	09 01		09 06	09 14	10 01		09 26
Vauxhall ⊖ a		07 20	07 50	→		08 21	→						08 50			09 08			09 20	→		
London Waterloo 15 ⊖ a	01 04	07 27	07 57		08 21	08 28			08 39	08 43		08 50	08 57		09 10	09 13		09 16	09 27			09 39

	SW ◇1	SW	SW ◇1	SW ◇1 ⌶	SW	SW	SW	SW ◇1	SW	SW	SW 1	SW 1	SW ◇1	SW	SW ◇1	SW ◇1 ⌶	SW ◇1 ⌶	SW	SW	SW	SW ◇1 ⌶	SW
Basingstoke d	08 44			09 04							09 16		09 44			10 00	10 04					
Hook d											09 23											
Winchfield d											09 27											
Fleet d											09 32											
Farnborough (Main) d											09 38											
Alton d												09 15										
Bentley d												09 23										
Farnham a												09 28										
d												09 30										
Aldershot d												09 36										
Ash Vale d												09 41										
Brookwood d											09 45	09 48										
Guildford d		08 57	09 05				09 24	09 35						09 57	10 05					10 24	10 35	
Worplesdon d							09 30													10 30		
Woking a	09 02	09 05	09 15	09 23			09 34	09 42			09 50	09 54	10 02	10 05	10 15	10 19	10 23			10 34	10 42	
d	09 04	09 06	09 15	09 24			09 36	09 45		09 52		09 58	10 04	10 06	10 15	10 20	10 24			10 36	10 45	
West Byfleet d		09 10					09 40			09 56				10 10						10 40		
Byfleet & New Haw d		09 13					09 43			10 00				10 13						10 43		
Weybridge d		09 16					09 46							10 16						10 46		
Walton-on-Thames d		09 20					09 50							10 20						10 50		
Hersham d		09 22					09 52							10 22						10 52		
Esher d		09 25			←		09 55		←					10 25				←		10 55		←
Surbiton 6 a		09 29			09 29		09 59		09 59			10 09		10 29				10 29		10 59		10 59
Wimbledon 6 ⊖ a		→			09 37		→		10 08			10 17		→				10 37		→		11 07
Earlsfield a					09 41	←			10 12									10 41	←			11 11
Clapham Junction 10 a	09 30		09 38	09 44	09 47	10 01		10 05	10 15	11 01		10 23	10 27		10 35	10 39	10 43	10 45	11 01		11 04	11 16
Vauxhall ⊖ a					09 52	10 08			10 20	→								10 50	11 08			11 21
London Waterloo 15 ⊖ a	09 41		09 49	09 56	09 59	10 13		10 16	10 27			10 34	10 39		10 46	10 50	10 55	10 55	11 13		11 14	11 26

A not 15 December

Table T155-R

Sundays
15 December to 10 May

Basingstoke, Alton, Guildford and Woking - Waterloo

	SW	SW 1	SW 1	SW ◇1 ⌶	SW	SW ◇1	SW ◇1 ⌶	SW ◇1 ⌶	SW	SW	SW	SW ◇1 ⌶	SW	SW	SW 1	SW 1	SW ◇1 ⌶	SW	SW ◇1	SW ◇1 ⌶	SW ◇1 ⌶	SW
Basingstoke d		10 16		10 44			11 00	11 04							11 16		11 44			12 00	12 04	
Hook d		10 23													11 23							
Winchfield d		10 27													11 27							
Fleet d		10 32													11 32							
Farnborough (Main) d		10 38													11 38							
Alton d			10 15													11 15						
Bentley d			10 23													11 23						
Farnham a			10 28													11 28						
d			10 30													11 30						
Aldershot d			10 36													11 36						
Ash Vale d			10 41													11 41						
Brookwood d		10 45	10 48												11 45	11 48						
Guildford d					10 57	11 05					11 24	11 35						11 57	12 05			
Worplesdon d											11 30											
Woking a		10 50	10 54	11 02	11 05	11 14	11 18	11 23			11 34	11 42			11 50	11 54	12 02	12 05	12 13	12 18	12 23	
d	10 52		10 58	11 04	11 06	11 15	11 20	11 24			11 36	11 45		11 52		11 58	12 04	12 06	12 15	12 20	12 24	
West Byfleet d	10 56				11 10						11 40			11 56				12 10				
Byfleet & New Haw d	11 00				11 13						11 43			12 00				12 13				
Weybridge d					11 16						11 46							12 16				
Walton-on-Thames d					11 20						11 50							12 20				
Hersham d					11 22						11 52							12 22				
Esher d					11 25				←		11 55		←					12 25				←
Surbiton 6 a			11 09		11 29				11 29		11 59		11 59			12 09		12 29				12 29
Wimbledon 6 ⊖ a			11 17		→				11 37		→		12 07			12 17		→				12 37
Earlsfield a									11 41	←			12 11									12 41
Clapham Junction 10 a	12 01		11 23	11 26		11 34	11 39	11 43	11 45	12 01		12 04	12 16	13 01		12 23	12 27		12 34	12 39	12 43	12 45
Vauxhall ⊖ a	→								11 50	12 08			12 21	→								12 50
London Waterloo 15 ⊖ a			11 34	11 39		11 44	11 50	11 55	11 55	12 13		12 14	12 26			12 34	12 37		12 43	12 49	12 54	12 55

	SW	SW	SW ◇1 ⌶	SW	SW	SW 1	SW 1	SW ◇1 ⌶	SW	SW ◇1	SW ◇1 ⌶	SW ◇1 ⌶	SW	SW	SW	SW ◇1 ⌶	SW	SW	SW 1	SW 1	SW ◇1 ⌶
Basingstoke d						12 16		12 44			13 00	13 04							13 16		13 44
Hook d						12 23													13 23		
Winchfield d						12 27													13 27		
Fleet d						12 32													13 32		
Farnborough (Main) d						12 38													13 38		
Alton d							12 15													13 15	
Bentley d							12 23													13 23	
Farnham a							12 28													13 28	
d							12 30													13 30	
Aldershot d							12 36													13 36	
Ash Vale d							12 41													13 41	
Brookwood d						12 45	12 48												13 45	13 48	
Guildford d		12 24	12 35						12 57	13 05					13 24	13 35					
Worplesdon d		12 30													13 30						
Woking a		12 34	12 42			12 50	12 54	13 02	13 05	13 14	13 18	13 23			13 34	13 42			13 50	13 54	14 02
d		12 36	12 45		12 52		12 58	13 04	13 06	13 15	13 20	13 24			13 36	13 45		13 52		13 58	14 04
West Byfleet d		12 40			12 56				13 10						13 40			13 56			
Byfleet & New Haw d		12 43			13 00				13 13						13 43			14 00			
Weybridge d		12 46							13 16						13 46						
Walton-on-Thames d		12 50							13 20						13 50						
Hersham d		12 52							13 22						13 52						
Esher d		12 55		←					13 25				←		13 55		←				
Surbiton 6 a		12 59		12 59			13 09		13 29				13 29		13 59		13 59			14 09	
Wimbledon 6 ⊖ a		→		13 07			13 17		→				13 37		→		14 07			14 17	
Earlsfield a	←			13 11									13 41	←			14 11				
Clapham Junction 10 a	13 01		13 04	13 15	14 01		13 23	13 27		13 34	13 39	13 43	13 45	14 01		14 04	14 15	15 01		14 23	14 27
Vauxhall ⊖ a	13 08			13 20	→								13 50	14 08			14 20	→			
London Waterloo 15 ⊖ a	13 13		13 14	13 25			13 34	13 37		13 44	13 49	13 54	13 55	14 13		14 14	14 25			14 34	14 37

	SW	SW ◇1	SW ◇1 ⌶	SW ◇1 ⌶	SW	SW 1	SW 1	SW	SW	SW ◇1 ⌶	SW	SW	SW 1	SW 1	SW ◇1 ⌶	SW	SW ◇1	SW ◇1 ⌶	SW ◇1 ⌶	SW	SW 1	SW 1
Basingstoke d			14 00	14 04		13 50							14 16		14 44			15 00	15 04		14 50	
Hook d													14 23									
Winchfield d													14 27									
Fleet d						14 02							14 32								15 02	
Farnborough (Main) d						14 08							14 38								15 08	
Alton d							13 45							14 15								14 45
Bentley d														14 23								
Farnham a							13 55							14 28								14 55
d							14 00							14 30								15 00
Aldershot d							14 06							14 36								15 06
Ash Vale d							14 11							14 41								15 11
Brookwood d						14 15	14 18						14 45	14 48							15 15	15 18
Guildford d	13 57	14 05							14 24	14 35						14 57	15 05					
Worplesdon d									14 30													
Woking a	14 05	14 13	14 18	14 23		14 20	14 24		14 34	14 42			14 50	14 54	15 02	15 05	15 13	15 18	15 23		15 20	15 24
d	14 06	14 15	14 20	14 24			14 28		14 36	14 45		14 52		14 58	15 04	15 06	15 15	15 20	15 24			15 28
West Byfleet d	14 10								14 40			14 56				15 10						
Byfleet & New Haw d	14 13								14 43			15 00				15 13						
Weybridge d	14 16						14 34		14 46							15 16						15 34
Walton-on-Thames d	14 20						14 38		14 50							15 20						15 38
Hersham d	14 22								14 52							15 22						
Esher d	14 25								14 55		←					15 25						
Surbiton 6 a	14 29						14 45		14 59		14 59			15 09		15 29						15 45
Wimbledon 6 ⊖ a	14 37						14 52		→		15 07			15 17		15 37						15 52
Earlsfield a	14 41				←			←			15 11					15 41				←		
Clapham Junction 10 a	14 45	14 34	14 39	14 43	14 45		14 58	15 01		15 04	15 15	16 01		15 23	15 27	15 45	15 34	15 39	15 43	15 45		15 58
Vauxhall ⊖ a	→				14 50			15 08			15 20	→				→				15 50		
London Waterloo 15 ⊖ a		14 44	14 49	14 54	14 55		15 09	15 13		15 14	15 25			15 34	15 37		15 44	15 49	15 54	15 55		16 09

Table T155-R

Sundays

15 December to 10 May

Basingstoke, Alton, Guildford and Woking - Waterloo

		SW	SW	SW ◇1 ⚲	SW	SW	SW 1	SW 1	SW ◇1 ⚲	SW	SW ◇1	SW ◇1 ⚲	SW ◇1 ⚲	SW	SW 1	SW 1	SW	SW	SW ◇1 ⚲	SW	SW ◇1	SW
Basingstoke	d						15 16		15 44			16 00	16 04		15 50						16 35	
Hook	d						15 23															
Winchfield	d						15 27															
Fleet	d						15 32								16 02							
Farnborough (Main)	d						15 38								16 08							
Alton	d							15 15								15 45						
Bentley	d							15 23														
Farnham	a							15 28								15 55						
	d							15 30								16 00						
Aldershot	d							15 36								16 06						
Ash Vale	d							15 41								16 11						
Brookwood	d						15 45	15 48							16 15	16 18						
Guildford	d		15 24	15 35						15 57	16 05							16 24	16 35			
Worplesdon	d		15 30															16 30				
Woking	a		15 34	15 44			15 50	15 54	16 02	16 05	16 13	16 18	16 23		16 20	16 24		16 34	16 42		16 53	
	d		15 36	15 45		15 52	15 58		16 04	16 06	16 15	16 20	16 24		16 28			16 36	16 45	16 52	16 55	
West Byfleet	d		15 40			15 56				16 10								16 40		16 56		
Byfleet & New Haw	d		15 43			16 00				16 13								16 43		17 00		
Weybridge	d		15 46							16 16					16 34			16 46				
Walton-on-Thames	d		15 50							16 20					16 38			16 50				
Hersham	d		15 52							16 22								16 52				
Esher	d		15 55		←					16 25								16 55				
Surbiton 6	a		15 59		15 59		16 09			16 29					16 45			16 59				
Wimbledon 6 ⊖	a		→		16 07		16 17			16 37					16 52			17 07				
Earlsfield	a	←			16 11					16 41				←			←	17 11				←
Clapham Junction 10	a	16 01		16 04	16 15	17 01	16 23		16 27	16 45	16 34	16 39	16 43	16 45	16 58		17 01	17 15	17 04	18 01	17 14	17 15
Vauxhall ⊖	a	16 08			16 20	→				→				16 50			17 08	→		→		17 20
London Waterloo 15 ⊖	a	16 13		16 14	16 25		16 34		16 37		16 44	16 49	16 54	16 55	17 09		17 13		17 14		17 24	17 25

		SW 1	SW 1	SW	SW ◇1 ⚲	SW ◇1	SW ◇1 ⚲	SW ◇1 ⚲	SW	SW ◇1 ⚲	SW 1	SW 1	SW	SW	SW ◇1 ⚲	SW	SW ◇1	SW ◇1 ⚲	SW	SW 1	SW 1	SW
Basingstoke	d	16 16			16 44		17 00	17 04			16 50						17 27	17 35		17 16		
Hook	d	16 23																		17 23		
Winchfield	d	16 27																		17 27		
Fleet	d	16 32									17 02									17 32		
Farnborough (Main)	d	16 38			16 58						17 08									17 38		
Alton	d		16 15									16 45									17 15	
Bentley	d		16 23																		17 23	
Farnham	a		16 28									16 55									17 28	
	d		16 30									17 00									17 30	
Aldershot	d		16 36									17 06									17 36	
Ash Vale	d		16 41									17 11									17 41	
Brookwood	d	16 45	16 48								17 15	17 18								17 45	17 48	
Guildford	d			16 57		17 05				17 17				17 24	17 35							17 57
Worplesdon	d													17 30								
Woking	a	16 50	16 54	17 05	17 07	17 13	17 18	17 23			17 20	17 24		17 34	17 42			17 53		17 50	17 54	18 05
	d	16 58		17 06	17 09	17 15	17 20	17 24			17 28			17 36	17 45	17 52		17 55		17 58		18 06
West Byfleet	d			17 10										17 40		17 56						18 10
Byfleet & New Haw	d			17 13										17 43		18 00						18 13
Weybridge	d			17 16							17 34			17 46								18 16
Walton-on-Thames	d			17 20							17 38			17 50								18 20
Hersham	d			17 22										17 52								18 22
Esher	d			17 25										17 55								18 25
Surbiton 6	a	17 09		17 29							17 45			17 59						18 09		18 29
Wimbledon 6 ⊖	a	17 17		17 37							17 52			18 07						18 17		18 37
Earlsfield	a			17 41					←				←	18 11					←			18 41
Clapham Junction 10	a	17 23		17 45	17 28	17 34	17 39	17 43	17 45	17 47	17 58		18 01	18 15	18 06	19 01	18 10	18 14	18 15	18 23		18 45
Vauxhall ⊖	a			→					17 50				18 08	→		→			18 20			→
London Waterloo 15 ⊖	a	17 34			17 39	17 44	17 49	17 54	17 55	17 57	18 09		18 13		18 17		18 19	18 25	18 25	18 34		

		SW ◇1 ⚲	SW ◇1	SW ◇1 ⚲	SW ◇1 ⚲	SW	SW ◇1 ⚲	SW 1	SW 1	SW	SW	SW ◇1 ⚲	SW	SW ◇1	SW	SW ◇1	SW 1	SW 1	SW	SW ◇1	SW ◇1	SW ◇1 ⚲	SW ◇1 ⚲
Basingstoke	d	17 44		18 00	18 04			17 50						18 27		18 35	18 16			18 44		19 00	19 04
Hook	d																18 23						
Winchfield	d																18 27						
Fleet	d							18 02									18 32						
Farnborough (Main)	d	17 58						18 08									18 38			18 58			
Alton	d								17 45									18 15					
Bentley	d																	18 23					
Farnham	a								17 55									18 28					
	d								18 00									18 30					
Aldershot	d								18 06									18 36					
Ash Vale	d								18 11									18 41					
Brookwood	d							18 15	18 18								18 45	18 48					
Guildford	d		18 05				18 17				18 24	18 35							18 57		19 05		
Worplesdon	d										18 30												
Woking	a	18 07	18 13	18 18	18 23			18 20	18 24		18 34	18 42				18 53	18 50	18 54	19 05	19 07	19 13	19 18	19 23
	d	18 09	18 15	18 20	18 24			18 28			18 36	18 45	18 52			18 55	18 58		19 06	19 09	19 15	19 20	19 24
West Byfleet	d										18 40		18 56						19 10				
Byfleet & New Haw	d										18 43		19 00						19 13				
Weybridge	d							18 34			18 46								19 16				
Walton-on-Thames	d							18 38			18 50								19 20				
Hersham	d										18 52								19 22				
Esher	d										18 55								19 25				
Surbiton 6	a							18 45			18 59						19 09		19 29				
Wimbledon 6 ⊖	a							18 53			19 07						19 17		19 37				
Earlsfield	a					←				←	19 11				←				19 41				
Clapham Junction 10	a	18 28	18 34	18 39	18 43	18 45	18 47	18 59		19 01	19 15	19 04	20 01	19 10	19 15	19 15	19 23		19 45	19 28	19 34	19 39	19 43
Vauxhall ⊖	a					18 50				19 08	→		→		19 20				→				
London Waterloo 15 ⊖	a	18 39	18 44	18 49	18 54	18 55	18 57	19 10		19 13		19 14		19 19	19 25	19 25	19 34			19 39	19 44	19 49	19 54

Table T155-R

Sundays

15 December to 10 May

Basingstoke, Alton, Guildford and Woking - Waterloo

		SW	SW ◇1 ⚲	SW 1	SW 1	SW	SW	SW ◇1 ⚲	SW	SW ◇1	SW ◇1	SW	SW 1	SW 1	SW	SW ◇1	SW ◇1	SW ◇1 ⚲	SW ◇1 A ⚲	SW	SW 1	SW 1	SW
Basingstoke	d			18 50						19 27	19 35		19 16			19 44		20 00	20 04		19 50		
Hook	d												19 23										
Winchfield	d												19 27										
Fleet	d			19 02									19 32								20 02		
Farnborough (Main)	d			19 08									19 38			19 58					20 08		
Alton	d				18 45									19 15								19 45	
Bentley	d													19 23									
Farnham	a				18 55									19 28								19 55	
	d				19 00									19 30								20 00	
Aldershot	d				19 06									19 36								20 06	
Ash Vale	d				19 11									19 41								20 11	
Brookwood	d			19 15	19 18								19 45	19 48							20 15	20 18	
Guildford	d		19 17				19 24	19 35							19 57		20 05						
Worplesdon	d						19 30																
Woking	a			19 20	19 24		19 34	19 42			19 53		19 50	19 54	20 05	20 08	20 13	20 18	20 23		20 20	20 24	
	d			19 28			19 36	19 45	19 52		19 55		19 58		20 06	20 09	20 15	20 20	20 24		20 28		
West Byfleet	d						19 40		19 56						20 10								
Byfleet & New Haw	d						19 43		20 00						20 13								
Weybridge	d			19 34			19 46								20 16						20 34		
Walton-on-Thames	d			19 38			19 50								20 20						20 38		
Hersham	d						19 52								20 22								
Esher	d						19 55								20 25								
Surbiton 6	a			19 45			19 59						20 09		20 29						20 45		
Wimbledon 6 ⊖	a			19 53			20 07						20 17		20 37						20 53		
Earlsfield	a	←				←	20 11					←			20 41					←			←
Clapham Junction 10	a	19 45	19 47	19 59		20 01	20 15	20 06	21 01	20 10	20 14	20 15	20 23		20 45	20 28	20 34	20 39	20 43	20 45	20 59		21 01
Vauxhall ⊖	a	19 50				20 08	→		→			20 20			→					20 50			21 08
London Waterloo 15 ⊖	a	19 55	19 57	20 10		20 13		20 17		20 19	20 24	20 25	20 34			20 40	20 44	20 49	20 54	20 55	21 11		21 13

		SW	SW ◇1	SW	SW ◇1	SW	SW 1	SW 1	SW	SW ◇1	SW ◇1	SW ◇1 ⚲	SW ◇1 ⚲	SW	SW 1	SW 1	SW	SW	SW ◇1	SW	SW ◇1	SW
Basingstoke	d				20 35		20 16			20 44		21 00	21 04		20 50						21 35	
Hook	d						20 23															
Winchfield	d						20 27															
Fleet	d						20 32								21 02							
Farnborough (Main)	d						20 38			20 58					21 08							
Alton	d							20 15								20 45						
Bentley	d							20 23														
Farnham	a							20 28								20 55						
	d							20 30								21 00						
Aldershot	d							20 36								21 06						
Ash Vale	d							20 41								21 11						
Brookwood	d						20 45	20 48							21 15	21 18						
Guildford	d	20 24	20 35						20 57		21 05							21 24	21 35			
Worplesdon	d	20 30																21 30				
Woking	a	20 34	20 42		20 53		20 50	20 54	21 05	21 08	21 13	21 18	21 23		21 20	21 24		21 34	21 42		21 53	
	d	20 36	20 45	20 52	20 55		20 58		21 06	21 09	21 15	21 20	21 24		21 28			21 36	21 45	21 52	21 55	
West Byfleet	d	20 40		20 56					21 10									21 40		21 56		
Byfleet & New Haw	d	20 43		21 00					21 13									21 43		22 00		
Weybridge	d	20 46							21 16						21 34			21 46				
Walton-on-Thames	d	20 50							21 20						21 38			21 50				
Hersham	d	20 52							21 22									21 52				
Esher	d	20 55							21 25									21 55				
Surbiton 6	a	20 59					21 09		21 29						21 45			22 00				
Wimbledon 6 ⊖	a	21 07					21 17		21 37						21 53			22 07				
Earlsfield	a	21 11				←			21 41					←			←	22 11				←
Clapham Junction 10	a	21 15	21 04	22 01	21 14	21 15	21 23		21 45	21 28	21 34	21 39	21 43	21 45	21 59		22 01	22 15	22 04	23 01	22 14	22 15
Vauxhall ⊖	a	→		→		21 20			→					21 50			22 08	→		→		22 20
London Waterloo 15 ⊖	a		21 14		21 24	21 25	21 34			21 39	21 44	21 49	21 54	21 55	22 10		22 13		22 14		22 24	22 25

		SW 1	SW 1	SW	SW ◇1	SW ◇1	SW ◇1	SW	SW 1	SW 1	SW	SW	SW ◇1	SW	SW ◇1	SW	SW 1	SW 1	SW	SW ◇1	SW ◇1	SW	SW 1
Basingstoke	d	21 16			21 44		22 04		21 50						22 35		22 16			22 44			
Hook	d	21 23															22 23						
Winchfield	d	21 27															22 27						
Fleet	d	21 32							22 02								22 32						
Farnborough (Main)	d	21 38			21 58				22 08								22 38			22 58			
Alton	d		21 15							21 45								22 15					22 45
Bentley	d		21 23															22 23					
Farnham	a		21 28							21 55								22 28					22 55
	d		21 30							22 00								22 30					23 00
Aldershot	d		21 36							22 06								22 36					23 06
Ash Vale	d		21 41							22 11								22 41					23 11
Brookwood	d	21 45	21 48						22 15	22 18							22 45	22 48					23 18
Guildford	d			21 57		22 05						22 24	22 35						22 57		23 05		
Worplesdon	d											22 30											
Woking	a	21 50	21 54	22 05	22 08	22 13	22 23		22 21	22 24		22 34	22 42		22 54		22 50	22 54	23 05	23 08	23 14		23 24
	d	21 58		22 06	22 09	22 15	22 24		22 28			22 36	22 45	22 52	22 55		22 58		23 06	23 09	23 15		23 28
West Byfleet	d			22 10								22 40		22 56					23 10				
Byfleet & New Haw	d			22 13								22 43		23 00					23 13				
Weybridge	d			22 16					22 34			22 46							23 16				23 34
Walton-on-Thames	d			22 20					22 38			22 50							23 20				23 38
Hersham	d			22 22								22 52							23 22				
Esher	d			22 25								22 55							23 25			←	
Surbiton 6	a	22 09		22 29					22 45			22 59					23 09		23 29			23 29	23 45
Wimbledon 6 ⊖	a	22 17		22 37					22 53			23 07					23 17		→			23 37	→
Earlsfield	a			22 41				←			←	23 11				←						23 41	
Clapham Junction 10	a	22 23		22 45	22 28	22 34	22 43	22 45	22 59		23 01	23 15	23 04	00 01	23 14	23 15	23 23			23 28	23 34	23 45	
Vauxhall ⊖	a			→				22 50			23 08	→		→		23 20						23 50	
London Waterloo 15 ⊖	a	22 34			22 39	22 44	22 54	22 55	23 10		23 13		23 14		23 24	23 25	23 33			23 39	23 44	23 55	

A ⚲ to Woking

Table T155-R

Sundays
15 December to 10 May

Basingstoke, Alton, Guildford and Woking - Waterloo

Station		SW ◇1	SW 1	SW	SW ◇1	SW 1	SW 1	SW ◇1
Basingstoke	d	23 10				23 16		23 44
Hook	d					23 23		
Winchfield	d					23 27		
Fleet	d					23 32		
Farnborough (Main)	d					23 38		
Alton	d						23 15	
Bentley	d						23 23	
Farnham	a						23 28	
	d						23 30	
Aldershot	d						23 36	
Ash Vale	d						23 41	
Brookwood	d					23 45	23 48	
Guildford	d				23 35			
Worplesdon	d							
Woking	a	23 28			23 42	23 50	23 54	00 02
	d	23 30			23 45			00 04
West Byfleet	d							
Byfleet & New Haw	d							
Weybridge	d							
Walton-on-Thames	d							
Hersham	d							
Esher	d		←					
Surbiton 5	a		23 45					
Wimbledon 5 ⊖	a		23 54					
Earlsfield	a			←				
Clapham Junction 10	a	23 49	23 59	00 01	00 04			00 23
Vauxhall ⊖	a			00 08				
London Waterloo 15 ⊖	a	23 58	00 10	00 14	00 14			00 33

AVAILABLE FROM MP Middleton Press

NRT DECEMBER 19 EDITION

Table T156-F

Mondays to Fridays
16 December to 15 May

London - Guildford, Haslemere and Portsmouth

Miles	Station		SW MX ◇1	SW MX ◇1	SW MO ◇1	SW MX ◇1	SW MX ◇1	SW MX ◇1	SW MO ◇1	SW MX ◇1	SW MO ◇1	SW 1	SW ◇1	SW ◇1	SW ◇1	SW ◇1	SW ◇1	SW ◇1	SW ◇1	SW ◇1	SW ◇1 🚲	SW ◇1	SW ◇1
0	**London Waterloo** 15 ⊖	d									00 50		05 00	05 20	05 45	06 15	06 45	07 00		07 15	07 30		07 45
—	Clapham Junction	d									00 57		05 11	05 29	05 52	06u22	06u52			07u23			07u52
24½	**Woking**	a									01 16		05 51	06 09	06 12	06 42	07 12	07 24		07 43	07 55		08 11
—		d							00 02	00 13	01 18		05 53	06 10	06 13	06 43	07 13	07 25		07 43	07 55		08 13
26¾	Worplesdon	d								00 18					06 18	06 48	07 18			07 48			08 18
30¼	**Guildford**	a							00 10	00 24	01s26		06 00	06 18	06 24	06 54	07 24	07 32		07 54	08 04		08 24
—		d					00 04		00 12	00 27		05 09	06 03	06 20	06 30	06 56	07 25	07 33		07 55	08 04		08 25
33½	Farncombe	d								00 33			06 09	06 26	06 36	07 02	07 31			08 01			08 31
34¾	Godalming	d				00 01	00 10		00 18	00 36			06 12	06 29	06 39	07 05	07 34	07 40		08 04	08 12		08 34
36¼	Milford (Surrey)	d				00s05				00s40			06 16		06 43	07 09	07 38			08 08			08 38
38½	Witley	d				00s10		←		00s44			06 20		06 47	07 14	07 43		←	08 13		←	08 43
43	**Haslemere** 4	a				00 17	00 21	00 17	00 29	00 51		05 23	06 27	06 41	06 54	07 20	07 49	07 53	07 49	08 19	08 23	08 19	08 50
—		d			00 07	00 26	00 22	00 26	00 29	00 51		05 24	06 28		06 55	07 21	07 57	07 54	07 57	08 30	08 24	08 30	08 57
46½	Liphook	d		00 03	00 12	→		00s31		00s56		05 29	06 33		07 00	07 26	→		08 02	→		08 35	→
51½	Liss	d		00 09	00 18			00s37		01s02		05 35	06 39		07 06	07 32			08 08			08 41	
55	Petersfield	d	00 05	00 15	00 23		00 33	00 42	00 40	01 08		05 45	06 45		07 11	07 38		08 05	08 14		08 35	08 46	
63¼	Rowlands Castle	d		00 24	00 33			00s52		01s17		05 55	06 54		07 21	07 47			08 23			08 56	
66½	**Havant**	a	00 18	00 29	00 38		00 45	00 57	00 53	01 22	02s00	06 00	06 59		07 26	07 52		08 19	08 28		08 50	09 01	
—		d	00 18	00 30	00 39		00 46	00 57	00 53	01 23		06 00	07 00		07 27	07 53		08 19	08 29		08 50	09 01	
67¼	Bedhampton	a		00 33	00 41			01s00		01s25		06 03	07 02		07 30	07 55			08 31			09 04	
70½	Hilsea	a		00 38				01s05		01s31		06 08	07 08		07 38	08 01			08 37			09 09	
72¾	Fratton	a	00 27	00 42	00 49		00 54	01 09	01 02	01s35	02s10	06 12	07 12		07 42	08 05		08 28	08 41		08 59	09 13	
73¾	**Portsmouth & Southsea**	a	00 31	00 46	00 53		00 58	01 13	01 05	01 39	02s14	06 16	07 16		07 46	08 08		08 31	08 45		09 03	09 17	
74½	**Portsmouth Harbour** ⛴	a	00 35		00 58		01 03		01 09		02 19	06 20	07 21		07 51	08 13		08 36	08 50		09 08	09 22	

Station		SW ◇1 🚲	SW ◇1	SW ◇1	SW ◇1 🚲	SW ◇1	SW ◇1 🚲	SW ◇1	SW ◇1	SW ◇1 🚲	SW ◇1	SW ◇1 🚲	SW ◇1	SW ◇1	SW ◇1 🚲	SW ◇1	SW ◇1 🚲	SW ◇1	SW ◇1	SW ◇1 🚲	SW ◇1	SW ◇1 🚲	SW ◇1
London Waterloo 15 ⊖	d	08 00		08 15	08 30	08 45	09 00		09 15	09 30	09 45	10 00		10 15	10 30	10 45	11 00		11 15	11 30	11 45	12 00	
Clapham Junction	d			08u22		08u53			09u22		09u52			10u22		10u52			11u22		11u52		
Woking	a	08 24		08 43	08 54	09 12	09 24		09 42	09 54	10 12	10 24		10 41	10 54	11 12	11 24		11 41	11 54	12 12	12 24	
	d	08 25		08 43	08 55	09 13	09 25		09 43	09 55	10 13	10 25		10 43	10 55	11 13	11 25		11 43	11 55	12 13	12 25	
Worplesdon	d			08 48		09 18					10 18					11 18					12 18		
Guildford	a	08 33		08 54	09 02	09 24	09 32		09 50	10 02	10 24	10 32		10 50	11 02	11 24	11 32		11 50	12 02	12 24	12 32	
	d	08 33		08 55	09 03	09 25	09 33		09 52	10 03	10 25	10 33		10 52	11 03	11 25	11 33		11 52	12 03	12 25	12 33	
Farncombe	d			09 01		09 31			09 58		10 31			10 58		11 31			11 58		12 31		
Godalming	d	08 40		09 04	09 10	09 34	09 40		10 01	10 10	10 34	10 40		11 01	11 10	11 34	11 40		12 01	12 10	12 34	12 40	
Milford (Surrey)	d			09 08					10 05					11 05					12 05				
Witley	d		←	09 13				←	10 09				←	11 09				←	12 09				←
Haslemere 4	a	08 53	08 50	09 20	09 24	09 45	09 50	09 45	10 16	10 20	10 45	10 50	10 45	11 16	11 21	11 45	11 50	11 45	12 16	12 20	12 45	12 50	12 45
	d	08 54	08 57		09 24	09 56	09 51	09 56		10 21	10 56	10 51	10 56		11 21	11 56	11 51	11 56		12 21	12 56	12 51	12 56
Liphook	d		09 02			→		10 01			→		11 01			→		12 01			→		13 01
Liss	d		09 08					10 07					11 07					12 07					13 07
Petersfield	d	09 05	09 14		09 35		10 02	10 12		10 32		11 02	11 12		11 32		12 02	12 12		12 32		13 02	13 12
Rowlands Castle	d		09 23					10 22					11 22					12 22					13 22
Havant	a	09 18	09 28		09 51		10 17	10 27		10 45		11 17	11 27		11 45		12 17	12 27		12 45		13 17	13 27
	d	09 19	09 29		09 51		10 17	10 28		10 45		11 17	11 28		11 45		12 17	12 28		12 45		13 17	13 28
Bedhampton	a		09 31					10 30					11 30					12 30					13 30
Hilsea	a		09 37					10 36					11 36					12 36					13 36
Fratton	a	09 27	09 41		10 00		10 26	10 40		10 54		11 26	11 40		11 54		12 26	12 40		12 54		13 26	13 40
Portsmouth & Southsea	a	09 31	09 45		10 03		10 29	10 45		10 57		11 29	11 45		11 57		12 29	12 45		12 57		13 29	13 45
Portsmouth Harbour ⛴	a	09 36			10 08		10 34			11 02		11 34			12 02		12 34			13 02		13 34	

Station		SW ◇1	SW ◇1 🚲	SW ◇1	SW ◇1 🚲	SW ◇1	SW ◇1	SW ◇1 🚲	SW ◇1	SW ◇1 🚲	SW ◇1	SW ◇1	SW ◇1 🚲	SW ◇1	SW ◇1 🚲	SW ◇1	SW ◇1	SW ◇1 🚲	SW ◇1	SW ◇1	SW ◇1 🚲	SW ◇1
London Waterloo 15 ⊖	d	12 15	12 30	12 45	13 00		13 15	13 30	13 45	14 00		14 15	14 30	14 45	15 00		15 15	15 30		15 45	16 00	
Clapham Junction	d	12u22		12u52			13u22		13u52			14u22		14u52			15u22			15u52		
Woking	a	12 41	12 54	13 12	13 24		13 41	13 54	14 12	14 24		14 42	14 54	15 12	15 24		15 42	15 54		16 12	16 24	
	d	12 43	12 55	13 13	13 25		13 43	13 55	14 13	14 25		14 43	14 55	15 13	15 25		15 43	15 55		16 13	16 25	
Worplesdon	d			13 18					14 18					15 18						16 18		
Guildford	a	12 50	13 02	13 24	13 32		13 50	14 02	14 24	14 32		14 50	15 02	15 24	15 32		15 50	16 02		16 23	16 33	
	d	12 52	13 03	13 25	13 33		13 52	14 03	14 25	14 33		14 52	15 03	15 25	15 33		15 52	16 03		16 25	16 34	
Farncombe	d	12 58		13 31			13 58		14 31			14 58		15 31			15 58			16 31		
Godalming	d	13 01	13 10	13 34	13 40		14 01	14 10	14 34	14 40		15 01	15 10	15 34	15 40		16 01	16 10		16 34	16 42	
Milford (Surrey)	d	13 05					14 05					15 05					16 05			16 38		
Witley	d	13 09				←	14 09				←	15 09				←	16 09		←	16 42		←
Haslemere 4	a	13 16	13 21	13 45	13 50	13 45	14 16	14 20	14 45	14 50	14 45	15 16	15 20	15 45	15 50	15 45	16 16	16 20	16 16	16 49	16 53	16 49
	d		13 21	13 56	13 51	13 56		14 21	14 56	14 51	14 56		15 21	15 56	15 51	15 56	16 26	16 21	16 26	16 57	16 53	16 57
Liphook	d			→		14 01			→		15 01			→		16 01	→		16 31	→		17 02
Liss	d					14 07					15 07					16 07			16 37			17 08
Petersfield	d		13 32		14 02	14 12		14 39		15 02	15 12		15 32		16 02	16 12		16 32	16 42		17 04	17 13
Rowlands Castle	d					14 22					15 22					16 22			16 52			17 23
Havant	a		13 45		14 17	14 27		14 52		15 15	15 27		15 45		16 17	16 27		16 45	16 58		17 17	17 28
	d		13 45		14 17	14 28		14 52		15 17	15 28		15 45		16 17	16 28		16 45	16 59		17 17	17 28
Bedhampton	a					14 30					15 30					16 30			17 02			17 31
Hilsea	a					14 36					15 36					16 36			17 07			17 36
Fratton	a		13 54		14 26	14 40		15 01		15 26	15 40		15 54		16 26	16 40		16 54	17 11		17 26	17 40
Portsmouth & Southsea	a		13 57		14 29	14 45		15 04		15 29	15 45		15 57		16 29	16 44		16 57	17 15		17 29	17 44
Portsmouth Harbour ⛴	a		14 02		14 34			15 08		15 34			16 02		16 36	16 50		17 02	17 22		17 34	17 48

Table T156-F

London - Guildford, Haslemere and Portsmouth

Mondays to Fridays
16 December to 15 May

Station	SW ◇1	SW ◇1 ⫪	SW ◇1	SW ◇1	SW ◇1 ⫪	SW ◇1	SW ◇1	SW ◇1	SW ◇1 ⫪	SW ◇1	SW ◇1 ⫪
London Waterloo 15 ⊖ d	16 15	16 30		16 45	17 00		17 15	17 18	17 30	17 45	18 00
Clapham Junction d	16u22			16u52							
Woking a	16 42	16 55		17 12	17 24			17 42			
d	16 43	16 55		17 13	17 25			17 43	17u55		
Worplesdon d	16 48			17 18				17 48	18 00		
Guildford a	16 54	17 03		17 24	17 33		17 50	17 53	18 09	18 20	18 31
d	16 55	17 04		17 25	17 34		17 53	17 56	18 10	18 22	18 33
Farncombe d	17 01			17 31				18 03		18 28	
Godalming d	17 04	17 12		17 34	17 42			18 06	18 16	18 31	18 40
Milford (Surrey) d	17 08			17 38				18 10		18 35	
Witley d	17 13		←	17 43		←		18 14		18 39	
Haslemere 4 a	17 20	17 23	17 20	17 50	17 53	17 50	18 08	18 23	18 27	18 48	18 50
d	17 29	17 24	17 29	17 59	17 54	17 59	18 09		18 28	18 55	18 51
Liphook d	→		17 34	→		18 04	18 14			→	
Liss d			17 40			18 10	18 21				
Petersfield d		17 36	17 45		18 06	18 16	18 27		18 40		19 03
Rowlands Castle d			17 55			18 25	18 37				
Havant a		17 49	18 01		18 18	18 30	18 43		18 52		19 17
d		17 50	18 02		18 19	18 31	18 43		18 53		19 17
Bedhampton a			18 04			18 33	18 46				
Hilsea a			18 10			18 39	18 51				
Fratton a		17 59	18 14		18 27	18 43	18 56		19 02		19 26
Portsmouth & Southsea a		18 03	18 17		18 31	18 47	19 03		19 05		19 30
Portsmouth Harbour ⛴ a		18 09	18 24		18 38	18 51			19 12		19 36

Station	SW ◇1	SW ◇1	SW ◇1	SW ◇1 ⫪	SW ◇1	SW ◇1 ⫪	SW ◇1	SW ◇1	SW ◇1 ⫪	SW ◇1	SW ◇1
London Waterloo 15 ⊖ d		18 15	18 17	18 30	18 45	19 00		19 15	19 30		19 45
Clapham Junction d			18u24					19u22			19u52
Woking a			18 43	18 55	19 10			19 42	19 54		20 12
d			18 44	18 55	19 11			19 43	19 55		20 13
Worplesdon d			18 49		19 16			19 48			20 18
Guildford a		18 50	18 54	19 03	19 22	19 32		19 54	20 03		20 24
d		18 52	18 56	19 05	19 23	19 34		19 55	20 04		20 25
Farncombe d			19 02		19 29			20 01			20 31
Godalming d		18 59	19 05	19 12	19 32	19 41		20 04	20 12		20 34
Milford (Surrey) d			19 09		19 36			20 08			20 38
Witley d	←		19 13		19 41		←	20 13		←	20 43
Haslemere 4 a	18 48	19 10	19 22	19 24	19 48	19 51	19 48	20 20	20 23	20 20	20 50
d	18 55	19 10		19 25	19 56	19 52	19 56	20 28	20 24	20 28	20 58
Liphook d	19 00	19 15			→		20 01	→		20 33	→
Liss d	19 06	19 22					20 07			20 39	
Petersfield d	19 12	19 28		19 37		20 04	20 13		20 36	20 44	
Rowlands Castle d	19 21	19 38					20 22			20 54	
Havant a	19 28	19 43		19 52		20 17	20 27		20 51	20 59	
d		19 43		19 52		20 17	20 28		20 51	20 59	
Bedhampton a		19 46					20 31			21 02	
Hilsea a		19 51					20 36				
Fratton a		19 55		20 01		20 26	20 40		21 00		
Portsmouth & Southsea a		20 03		20 05		20 30	20 46		21 04		
Portsmouth Harbour ⛴ a				20 11		20 34			21 08		

Station	SW ◇1 ⫪	SW ◇1	SW ◇1	SW ◇1 ⫪	SW ◇1	SW ◇1 ⫪	SW ◇1	SW 1	SW ◇1	SW ◇1	SW ◇1
London Waterloo 15 ⊖ d	20 00		20 15	20 30	20 45	21 00		21 15	21 30	21 45	22 00
Clapham Junction d			20u22		20u52			21u22		21u52	
Woking a	20 24		20 42	20 54	21 12	21 24		21 42	21 54	22 12	22 24
d	20 25		20 43	20 55	21 13	21 25		21 43	21 55	22 13	22 25
Worplesdon d					21 18					22 18	
Guildford a	20 33		20 50	21 03	21 24	21 33		21 51	22 03	22 24	22 33
d	20 34		20 52	21 04	21 25	21 34		21 52	22 04	22 25	22 34
Farncombe d	20 40		20 58		21 31	21 40		21 58		22 31	22 40
Godalming d	20 43		21 01	21 11	21 34	21 43		22 01	22 11	22 34	22 43
Milford (Surrey) d			21 05		21 38			22 05		22 38	
Witley d		←	21 09		21 43		←	22 09		22 43	
Haslemere 4 a	20 54	20 50	21 16	21 22	21 50	21 54	21 50	22 16	22 22	22 50	22 54
d	20 55	20 58		21 23	21 58	21 55	21 58		22 23	22 58	22 55
Liphook d		21 03			→		22 03			→	
Liss d		21 09					22 09				
Petersfield d	21 06	21 15		21 34		22 06	22 15		22 34		23 06
Rowlands Castle d		21 24					22 24				
Havant a	21 18	21 29		21 46		22 18	22 31		22 46		23 18
d	21 19	21 30		21 47		22 19	22 31		22 48		23 19
Bedhampton a		21 32					22 34				
Hilsea a		21 39					22 39				
Fratton a	21 27	21 43		21 55		22 27	22 43		22 59		23 27
Portsmouth & Southsea a	21 31	21 47		21 59		22 31	22 47		23 04		23 31
Portsmouth Harbour ⛴ a	21 36			22 03		22 36	22 51		23 08		23 36

Station	SW ◇1	SW 1	SW ◇1	SW ◇1	SW ◇1	SW ◇1	SW ◇1	SW ◇1	SW ◇1	SW ◇1
London Waterloo 15 ⊖ d		22 15	22 30	22 45	23 00		23 15	23 30		23 45
Clapham Junction d		22u22		22u52	23u07		23u22			23u52
Woking a		22 42	22 54	23 12	23 26		23 41	23 53		00 11
d		22 43	22 55	23 13	23 27		23 43	23 55		00 13
Worplesdon d				23 18						00 18
Guildford a		22 51	23 03	23 24	23 35		23 50	00 02		00 24
d		22 52	23 04	23 25	23 36		23 52	00 04		00 27
Farncombe d		22 58		23 31			23 58			00 33
Godalming d		23 01	23 11	23 34	23 43		00 01	00 10		00 36
Milford (Surrey) d		23 05		23 38			00s05			00s40
Witley d	←	23 09		23 43		←	00s10		←	00s44
Haslemere 4 a	22 50	23 16	23 22	23 50	23 53	23 50	00 17	00 21	00 17	00 51
d	22 58		23 23	23 58	23 54	23 58	00 26	00 22	00 26	00 51
Liphook d	23 03			→		00 03	→		00s31	00s56
Liss d	23 09					00 09			00s37	01s02
Petersfield d	23 15		23 34		00 05	00 15		00 33	00 42	01 08
Rowlands Castle d	23 24					00 24			00s52	01s17
Havant a	23 29		23 49		00 18	00 29		00 45	00 57	01 22
d	23 30		23 50		00 18	00 30		00 46	00 57	01 23
Bedhampton a	23 33					00 33			01s00	01s25
Hilsea a	23 38					00 38			01s05	01s31
Fratton a	23 42		23 58		00 27	00 42		00 54	01 09	01s35
Portsmouth & Southsea a	23 47		00 02		00 31	00 46		00 58	01 13	01 39
Portsmouth Harbour ⛴ a			00 06		00 35			01 03		

Saturdays
21 December to 16 May

Station	SW ◇1	SW ◇1	SW ◇1	SW ◇1	SW ◇1	SW ◇1	SW 1	SW 1	SW ◇1	SW 1	SW ◇1
London Waterloo 15 ⊖ d								05 00	05 20	06 15	06 45
Clapham Junction d								05 11	05 29	06u22	06u52
Woking a								05 51	06 10	06 42	07 12
d						00 13		05 53	06 13	06 43	07 13
Worplesdon d						00 18			06 18		07 18
Guildford a						00 24		06 00	06 23	06 50	07 23
d				00 04		00 27	05 15	06 02	06 25	06 52	07 25
Farncombe d						00 33		06 08	06 31	06 58	07 31
Godalming d			00 01	00 10		00 36		06 11	06 34	07 01	07 34
Milford (Surrey) d			00s05			00s40		06 15		07 05	
Witley d			00s10		←	00s44		06 19		07 09	
Haslemere 4 a			00 17	00 21	00 17	00 51	05 29	06 26	06 44	07 16	07 44
d			00 26	00 22	00 26	00 51	05 30		06 45		07 45
Liphook d		00 03	→		00s31	00s56	05 35		06 50		07 50
Liss d		00 09			00s37	01s02	05 41		06 56		07 56
Petersfield d	00 05	00 15		00 33	00 42	01 08	05 46		07 02		08 01
Rowlands Castle d		00 24			00s52	01s17	05 56		07 11		08 11
Havant a	00 18	00 29		00 45	00 57	01 22	06 01		07 22		08 17
d	00 18	00 30		00 46	00 57	01 23	06 02		07 22		08 17
Bedhampton a		00 33			01s00	01s25	06 04		07 25		08 20
Hilsea a		00 38			01s05	01s31	06 10		07 30		08 25
Fratton a	00 27	00 42		00 54	01 09	01s35	06 14		07 34		08 29
Portsmouth & Southsea a	00 31	00 46		00 58	01 13	01 39	06 17		07 37		08 33
Portsmouth Harbour ⛴ a	00 35			01 03			06 22		07 43		08 38

Station	SW ◇1	SW ◇1	SW ◇1	SW ◇1	SW ◇1	SW 1	SW ◇1	SW ◇1	SW ◇1 ⫪	SW ◇1	SW 1
London Waterloo 15 ⊖ d	07 15	07 30	07 45	08 00		08 15	08 30	08 45	09 00		09 15
Clapham Junction d	07u23		07u52			08u22		08u52			09u22
Woking a	07 42	07 54	08 12	08 24		08 42	08 54	09 12	09 24		09 42
d	07 43	07 55	08 13	08 25		08 43	08 55	09 13	09 25		09 43
Worplesdon d			08 18					09 18			
Guildford a	07 51	08 02	08 24	08 32		08 50	09 02	09 24	09 32		09 50
d	07 52	08 03	08 25	08 33		08 52	09 03	09 25	09 33		09 52
Farncombe d	07 58		08 31			08 58		09 31			09 58
Godalming d	08 01	08 10	08 34	08 40		09 01	09 10	09 34	09 40		10 01
Milford (Surrey) d	08 05					09 05					10 05
Witley d	08 09				←	09 09				←	10 09
Haslemere 4 a	08 16	08 21	08 45	08 50	08 45	09 16	09 21	09 45	09 50	09 45	10 16
d		08 21	08 56	08 51	08 56		09 21	09 56	09 51	09 56	
Liphook d			→		09 01			→		10 01	
Liss d					09 07					10 07	
Petersfield d		08 32		09 02	09 12		09 32		10 02	10 12	
Rowlands Castle d					09 22					10 22	
Havant a		08 45		09 17	09 27		09 45		10 17	10 27	
d		08 45		09 17	09 28		09 45		10 17	10 28	
Bedhampton a					09 30					10 30	
Hilsea a					09 36					10 36	
Fratton a		08 54		09 26	09 40		09 54		10 26	10 40	
Portsmouth & Southsea a		08 57		09 29	09 44		09 57		10 30	10 44	
Portsmouth Harbour ⛴ a		09 02		09 34			10 02		10 34		

Table T156-F

London - Guildford, Haslemere and Portsmouth

Saturdays
21 December to 16 May

Station	SW ◇1 ⫪	SW ◇1	SW ◇1 ⫪	SW ◇1	SW 1	SW ◇1 ⫪	SW ◇1	SW ◇1 ⫪	
London Waterloo 15 ⊖ d	09 30	09 45	10 00		10 15	10 30	10 45	11 00	
Clapham Junction d		09u52			10u22		10u52		
Woking a	09 54	10 12	10 24		10 42	10 54	11 12	11 24	
d	09 55	10 13	10 25		10 43	10 55	11 13	11 25	
Worplesdon d		10 18					11 18		
Guildford a	10 02	10 24	10 32		10 50	11 02	11 24	11 32	
d	10 03	10 25	10 33		10 52	11 03	11 25	11 33	
Farncombe d		10 31			10 58		11 31		
Godalming d	10 10	10 34	10 40		11 01	11 10	11 34	11 40	
Milford (Surrey) d					11 05				
Witley d				←	11 09				
Haslemere 4 a	10 21	10 45	10 50	10 45	11 16	11 21	11 45	11 50	and at the same minutes past each hour until
d	10 21	10 56	10 51	10 56		11 21	11 56	11 51	
Liphook d		→		11 01			→		
Liss d				11 07					
Petersfield d	10 32		11 02	11 12		11 32		12 02	
Rowlands Castle d				11 22					
Havant a	10 45		11 17	11 27		11 45		12 17	
d	10 45		11 17	11 28		11 45		12 17	
Bedhampton a				11 30					
Hilsea a				11 36					
Fratton a	10 54		11 26	11 40		11 54		12 26	
Portsmouth & Southsea a	10 57		11 30	11 44		11 57		12 29	
Portsmouth Harbour ⛴ a	11 02		11 34			12 02		12 34	

Station	SW ◇1	SW 1	SW ◇1 ⫪	SW ◇1	SW ◇1 ⫪	SW ◇1	SW 1	SW ◇1 ⫪	SW ◇1	SW ◇1 ⫪	SW ◇1	SW 1	SW ◇1 ⫪
London Waterloo 15 ⊖ d		17 15	17 30	17 45	18 00		18 15	18 30	18 45	19 00		19 15	19 30
Clapham Junction d		17u22		17u52			18u22		18u52			19u22	
Woking a		17 42	17 54	18 12	18 24		18 42	18 54	19 12	19 24		19 42	19 54
d		17 43	17 55	18 13	18 25		18 43	18 55	19 13	19 25		19 43	19 55
Worplesdon d				18 18					19 18				
Guildford a		17 50	18 02	18 24	18 32		18 50	19 02	19 24	19 32		19 50	20 02
d		17 52	18 03	18 25	18 33		18 52	19 03	19 25	19 33		19 52	20 03
Farncombe d		17 58		18 31			18 58		19 31			19 58	
Godalming d		18 01	18 10	18 34	18 40		19 01	19 10	19 34	19 40		20 01	20 10
Milford (Surrey) d		18 05					19 05					20 05	
Witley d	←	18 09				←	19 09				←	20 09	
Haslemere 4 a	17 45	18 16	18 21	18 45	18 50	18 45	19 16	19 20	19 45	19 50	19 45	20 16	20 21
d	17 56		18 21	18 56	18 51	18 56		19 21	19 56	19 51	19 56		20 21
Liphook d	18 01			→		19 01			→		20 01		
Liss d	18 07					19 07					20 07		
Petersfield d	18 12		18 32		19 02	19 12		19 32		20 02	20 12		20 32
Rowlands Castle d	18 22					19 22					20 22		
Havant a	18 27		18 45		19 17	19 27		19 45		20 17	20 27		20 45
d	18 28		18 45		19 17	19 28		19 45		20 17	20 28		20 45
Bedhampton a	18 30					19 30					20 30		
Hilsea a	18 36					19 36					20 36		
Fratton a	18 40		18 54		19 26	19 40		19 54		20 26	20 40		20 54
Portsmouth & Southsea a	18 44		18 57		19 29	19 44		19 57		20 29	20 44		20 57
Portsmouth Harbour ⛴ a			19 02		19 34			20 02		20 33			21 02

Station	SW ◇1	SW ◇1	SW ◇1	SW 1	SW ◇1	SW ◇1	SW ◇1	SW ◇1	SW 1	SW ◇1
London Waterloo 15 ⊖ d	19 45	20 00		20 15	20 30	20 45	21 00		21 15	21 30
Clapham Junction d	19u52			20u22		20u52			21u22	
Woking a	20 12	20 24		20 41	20 54	21 12	21 24		21 41	21 54
d	20 13	20 25		20 43	20 55	21 13	21 25		21 43	21 55
Worplesdon d	20 18					21 18				
Guildford a	20 24	20 32		20 50	21 02	21 24	21 32		21 50	22 02
d	20 25	20 33		20 52	21 03	21 25	21 33		21 52	22 03
Farncombe d	20 31			20 58		21 31	21 39		21 58	
Godalming d	20 34	20 40		21 01	21 10	21 34	21 43		22 01	22 10
Milford (Surrey) d				21 05					22 05	
Witley d			←	21 09				←	22 09	
Haslemere 4 a	20 45	20 50	20 45	21 16	21 21	21 45	21 53	21 45	22 17	22 20
d	20 56	20 51	20 56		21 21	21 57	21 54	21 57		22 21
Liphook d	→		21 01			→		22 02		
Liss d			21 07					22 08		
Petersfield d		21 02	21 12		21 32		22 05	22 13		22 32
Rowlands Castle d			21 22					22 23		
Havant a		21 15	21 27		21 45		22 18	22 31		22 45
d		21 15	21 27		21 45		22 18	22 31		22 45
Bedhampton a			21 30					22 34		
Hilsea a			21 35					22 40		
Fratton a		21 24	21 39		21 54		22 27	22 44		22 54
Portsmouth & Southsea a		21 27	21 44		21 57		22 30	22 48		22 57
Portsmouth Harbour ⛴ a		21 32			22 02		22 36	22 53		23 04

Station	SW ◇1	SW ◇1	SW ◇1	SW ◇1	SW ◇1	SW ◇1	SW ◇1	SW ◇1	SW ◇1
London Waterloo 15 ⊖ d	21 45	22 00		22 30	22 45	23 00		23 15	23 45
Clapham Junction d	21u52				22u52	23u07		23u22	23u52
Woking a	22 12	22 24		22 54	23 12	23 26		23 42	00 11
d	22 13	22 25		22 55	23 13	23 27		23 44	00 13
Worplesdon d	22 18				23 18				00 18
Guildford a	22 24	22 32		23 02	23 23	23 34		23 51	00 24
d	22 25	22 33		23 03	23 25	23 36		23 53	00 25
Farncombe d	22 31	22 39		23 09	23 31			23 59	00 31
Godalming d	22 34	22 43		23 13	23 34	23 43		00 01	00 34
Milford (Surrey) d	22 38				23 38				00s38
Witley d	22 43		←		23 42		←		00s43
Haslemere 4 a	22 50	22 53	22 50	23 23	23 49	23 53	23 49	00 12	00 49
d	22 59	22 54	22 59	23 24	23 58	23 54	23 58	00 13	00 50
Liphook d	→		23 04		→		00 03		00s55
Liss d			23 10				00 09		01s01
Petersfield d		23 05	23 15	23 35		00 05	00 15	00 24	01 06
Rowlands Castle d			23 25				00 24		01s16
Havant a		23 18	23 30	23 48		00 18	00 29	00 36	01 21
d		23 18	23 31	23 48		00 18	00 30	00 37	01 21
Bedhampton a			23 33				00 33		01s24
Hilsea a			23 40				00 38		01s29
Fratton a		23 27	23 44	23 57		00 27	00 42	00 45	01s33
Portsmouth & Southsea a		23 30	23 48	00 01		00 30	00 46	00 49	01 37
Portsmouth Harbour ⛴ a		23 36	23 53	00 05		00 35		00 54	

Sundays
15 December to 10 May

Station	SW ◇1 A	SW ◇1 A	SW ◇1 A	SW ◇1 A	SW 1	SW ◇1	SW ◇1	SW ◇1	SW ◇1
London Waterloo 15 ⊖ d						08 00	08 30	09 00	09 30
Clapham Junction d						08u09	08u39	09u09	09u39
Woking a						08 34	09 03	09 34	10 03
d				00 13	07 32	08 35	09 04	09 35	10 04
Worplesdon d				00 18					
Guildford a				00 24	07 40	08 43	09 12	09 43	10 13
d				00 25	07 42	08 45	09 14	09 45	10 14
Farncombe d				00 31	07 48	08 53		09 53	
Godalming d			00 01	00 34	07 51	08 56	09 21	09 56	10 21
Milford (Surrey) d				00s38	07 55	09 00		10 00	
Witley d				00s43	07 59	09 04		10 04	
Haslemere 4 a			00 12	00 49	08 06	09 11	09 32	10 11	10 32
d			00 13	00 50	08 07	09 12	09 32	10 12	10 32
Liphook d		00 03		00s55	08 12	09 17		10 17	
Liss d		00 09		01s01	08 18	09 23		10 23	
Petersfield d	00 05	00 15	00 24	01 06	08 23	09 28	09 43	10 28	10 43
Rowlands Castle d		00 24		01s16	08 33	09 38		10 38	
Havant a	00 18	00 29	00 36	01 21	08 38	09 43	09 56	10 43	10 56
d	00 18	00 30	00 37	01 21	08 39	09 44	09 56	10 44	10 56
Bedhampton a		00 33		01s24	08 41	09 46		10 46	
Hilsea a		00 38		01s29					
Fratton a	00 27	00 42	00 45	01s33	08 49	09 54	10 05	10 54	11 05
Portsmouth & Southsea a	00 30	00 46	00 49	01 37	08 53	09 58	10 08	10 58	11 08
Portsmouth Harbour ⛴ a	00 35		00 54		08 57	10 04	10 13	11 04	11 13

Station	SW ◇1	SW ◇1	SW ◇1	SW ◇1 ⫪	SW ◇1	SW ◇1 ⫪	SW ◇1	SW ◇1 ⫪		SW ◇1	SW ◇1 ⫪	SW ◇1
London Waterloo 15 ⊖ d	10 00	10 30	11 00	11 30	12 00	12 30	13 00	13 30		16 00	16 30	17 00
Clapham Junction d	10u09	10u39	11u09	11u39	12u09	12u39	13u09	13u39		16u09	16u39	17u09
Woking a	10 31	11 01	11 32	12 01	12 32	13 01	13 31	14 01		16 31	17 01	17 31
d	10 32	11 02	11 33	12 02	12 33	13 02	13 32	14 02		16 32	17 02	17 32
Worplesdon d												
Guildford a	10 40	11 10	11 41	12 10	12 41	13 10	13 40	14 10		16 40	17 10	17 40
d	10 42	11 12	11 42	12 12	12 42	13 12	13 42	14 12		16 42	17 12	17 42
Farncombe d	10 48		11 48		12 48		13 48			16 48		17 48
Godalming d	10 51	11 18	11 51	12 18	12 51	13 18	13 51	14 18		16 51	17 18	17 51
Milford (Surrey) d	10 55		11 55		12 55		13 55			16 55		17 55
Witley d	10 59		11 59		12 59		13 59			16 59		17 59
Haslemere 4 a	11 06	11 29	12 06	12 29	13 06	13 29	14 06	14 29	and at the same minutes past each hour until	17 06	17 29	18 06
d	11 07	11 30	12 07	12 30	13 07	13 30	14 07	14 30		17 07	17 30	18 07
Liphook d	11 12		12 12		13 12		14 12			17 12		18 12
Liss d	11 18		12 18		13 18		14 18			17 18		18 18
Petersfield d	11 23	11 41	12 23	12 41	13 23	13 41	14 23	14 41		17 23	17 41	18 23
Rowlands Castle d	11 33		12 33		13 33		14 33			17 33		18 33
Havant a	11 40	11 53	12 40	12 53	13 40	13 53	14 40	14 53		17 40	17 53	18 40
d	11 41	11 54	12 41	12 54	13 41	13 54	14 41	14 54		17 41	17 54	18 41
Bedhampton a	11 43		12 43		13 43		14 43			17 43		18 43
Hilsea a												
Fratton a	11 51	12 02	12 51	13 02	13 51	14 03	14 51	15 02		17 51	18 02	18 51
Portsmouth & Southsea a	11 55	12 07	12 56	13 07	13 55	14 07	14 55	15 07		17 55	18 07	18 55
Portsmouth Harbour ⛴ a	12 00	12 11	13 00	13 11	14 00	14 11	15 00	15 11		18 00	18 11	19 00

A not 15 December

Table T156-F

Sundays

15 December to 10 May

London - Guildford, Haslemere and Portsmouth

		SW ◇1 trolley	SW ◇1	SW ◇1 trolley	SW ◇	SW ◇1	SW ◇1 trolley	SW ◇1	SW ◇1	SW ◇1 trolley	SW ◇1	SW ◇1	SW ◇1	SW ◇1	SW ◇1	SW ◇1	SW ◇1
London Waterloo 15 ⊖	d	17 30	18 00	18 30	18 55	19 00	19 30	19 55	20 00	20 30	20 55	21 00	21 30	22 00	22 30	23 00	23 30
Clapham Junction	d	17u39	18u09	18u39	19u02	19u09	19u39	20u02	20u09	20u39	21u02	21u09	21u39	22u09	22u39	23u09	23u39
Woking	a	18 01	18 31	19 01		19 31	20 01		20 31	21 01		21 31	22 01	22 31	23 01	23 31	00 01
	d	18 02	18 32	19 02		19 32	20 02		20 32	21 02		21 32	22 02	22 32	23 02	23 32	00 02
Worplesdon	d																
Guildford	a	18 10	18 40	19 10	19 33	19 40	20 10	20 33	20 40	21 10	21 33	21 40	22 10	22 40	23 10	23 40	00 10
	d	18 12	18 42	19 12	19 34	19 42	20 12	20 34	20 42	21 12	21 34	21 42	22 12	22 42	23 12	23 42	00 12
Farncombe	d		18 48			19 48			20 48			21 48		22 48		23 48	
Godalming	d	18 18	18 51	19 18		19 51	20 18		20 51	21 18		21 51	22 18	22 51	23 18	23 51	00 18
Milford (Surrey)	d		18 55			19 55			20 55			21 55		22 55		23 55	
Witley	d		18 59			19 59			20 59			21 59		22 59		23 59	
Haslemere 4	a	18 29	19 06	19 29		20 06	20 29		21 06	21 29		22 06	22 29	23 06	23 29	00 06	00 29
	d	18 30	19 07	19 30		20 07	20 30		21 07	21 30		22 07	22 30	23 07	23 30	00 07	00 29
Liphook	d		19 12			20 12			21 12			22 12		23 12		00 12	
Liss	d		19 18			20 18			21 18			22 18		23 18		00 18	
Petersfield	d	18 41	19 23	19 41		20 23	20 41		21 23	21 41		22 23	22 41	23 23	23 41	00 23	00 40
Rowlands Castle	d		19 33			20 33			21 33			22 33		23 33		00 33	
Havant	a	18 53	19 40	19 53	20 07	20 40	20 53	21 07	21 40	21 53	22 07	22 40	22 53	23 42	23 53	00 38	00 53
	d	18 54	19 41	19 54	20 08	20 41	20 54	21 08	21 41	21 54	22 08	22 41	22 54	23 43	23 54	00 39	00 53
Bedhampton	a		19 43			20 43			21 43			22 43		23 45		00 41	
Hilsea	a																
Fratton	a	19 02	19 51	20 02	20 16	20 51	21 02	21 16	21 51	22 03	22 16	22 51	23 02	23 53	00 02	00 49	01 02
Portsmouth & Southsea	a	19 06	19 54	20 07	20 22	20 55	21 07	21 22	21 55	22 07	22 22	22 56	23 07	23 57	00 06	00 53	01 05
Portsmouth Harbour ⛴	a	19 11	19 58	20 11		21 00	21 13		22 00	22 11		23 00	23 11	00 01	00 10	00 58	01 09

Table T156-R

Mondays to Fridays

16 December to 15 May

Portsmouth, Haslemere and Guildford - London

Miles			SW MO 1	SW MX 1	SW ◇1	SW ◇1	SW ◇1	SW ◇1 trolley	SW ◇1	SW ◇1	SW ◇1 trolley	SW ◇1 trolley	SW ◇1	SW ◇1	SW ◇1 trolley	SW ◇1	SW ◇1	SW ◇1 trolley	SW ◇1	SW ◇1	SW ◇1 trolley	SW ◇1	SW ◇1 trolley
0	**Portsmouth Harbour** ⛴	d			04 25	05 12		05 19		05 50	06 15				06 43			07 14		07 31	07 45		08 15
0¾	**Portsmouth & Southsea**	d			04 30	05 17		05 24		05 55	06 20				06 48		06 58	07 18		07 36	07 50		08 20
1¾	Fratton	d			04 34	05 21		05 28		05 59	06 24				06 52		07 03	07 22		07 40	07 54		08 24
4	Hilsea	d			04 38			05 32		06 03				06 40			07 07			07 44			
7¼	Bedhampton	d			04 43			05 37		06 08				06 45			07 12			07 49			
8	**Havant**	a			04 45	05 29		05 39		06 10	06 34			06 47	07 00		07 15	07 31		07 51	08 03		08 32
—		d			04 46	05 30		05 40		06 11	06 34	06 40		06 48	07 01	07 10	07 16	07 32		07 52	08 04		08 34
11¼	Rowlands Castle	d			04 52			05 46		06 16				06 54			07 22			07 57			
19½	Petersfield	d			05 03	05 44		05 57	06 11	06 28	06 48	06 54		07 06	07 15	07 24	07 34	07 47		08 09	08 18		08 48
23	Liss	d		00 02	05 08			06 02	06 16	06 34				07 11	07 21		07 39			08 14			
27¾	Liphook	d		00 09	05 15			06 09	06 23	06 41				07 19	07 28		07 47		←	08 22		←	
31½	**Haslemere** 4	a		00 15	05 20	05 57		06 14	06 28	06 47	07 02	07 07		07 24	07 34	07 37	07 53	07 59	07 53	08 28	08 31	08 28	09 01
—		d		00 15	05 21	05 58	06 02	06 16	06 29	06 48	07 02	07 08	07 12	07 25	07 35	07 39	08 09	08 01	08 09	08 39	08 32	08 39	09 02
36	Witley	d		00 21	05 27		06 08		06 35				07 18			07 45	→		08 15	→		08 45	
38¾	Milford (Surrey)	d		00 25	05 31		06 13		06 39				07 23			07 49			08 19			08 49	
40	Godalming	d		00 29	05 35	06 08	06 17	06 26	06 43	06 58		07 18	07 27	07 35	07 45	07 53		08 11	08 24		08 42	08 54	09 12
41	Farncombe	d		00 32	05 38		06 20		06 46	07 01		07 22	07 31	07 39		07 56			08 27			08 57	
44½	**Guildford**	a		00 37	05 48	06 15	06 25	06 32	06 51	07 06	07 16	07 27	07 36	07 44	07 51	08 01		08 17	08 32		08 49	09 02	09 18
—		d	00 05		05 50	06 16	06 27	06 34	06 52	07 07	07 18	07 28	07 37	07 45	07 54	08 02		08 19	08 34		08 53	09 04	09 19
47¾	Worplesdon	d			05 55	06 21			06 58			07 34		07 51		08 08			08 40			09 10	
50½	**Woking**	a	00 13		06 00	06 26	06 35	06 41	07 03		07 25	07 39		07 56		08 13		08 26	08 45			09 14	09 27
—		d			06 01	06 27	06 37	06 43	07 04		07 27	07 41		07 57		08 14		08 28	08 46			09 15	09 28
—	Clapham Junction	a			06 20		06 58	07 02	07 23										09 05			09 34	
74½	**London Waterloo** 15 ⊖	a			06 30	06 51	07 08	07 12	07 34	07 40	07 53	08 08	08 11	08 24	08 31	08 41		08 54	09 18		09 30	09 45	09 55

		SW ◇1	SW ◇1 trolley	SW ◇1	SW ◇1 trolley	SW ◇1	SW ◇1 trolley	SW ◇1	SW ◇1 trolley	SW ◇1	SW ◇1 trolley	SW ◇1	SW ◇1 trolley	SW ◇1	SW ◇1 trolley	SW ◇1	SW ◇1 trolley	SW ◇1	SW ◇1 trolley	SW ◇1	SW ◇1 trolley	SW ◇1
Portsmouth Harbour ⛴	d	08 19	08 45		09 15	09 19	09 45		10 15		10 45		11 15		11 45		12 15		12 45		13 15	
Portsmouth & Southsea	d	08 24	08 50		09 20	09 24	09 50		10 20	10 24	10 50		11 20	11 24	11 50		12 20	12 24	12 50		13 20	13 24
Fratton	d	08 28	08 54		09 24	09 28	09 54		10 24	10 28	10 54		11 24	11 28	11 54		12 24	12 28	12 54		13 24	13 28
Hilsea	d	08 32				09 32				10 32				11 32				12 32				13 32
Bedhampton	d	08 37				09 37				10 37				11 37				12 37				13 37
Havant	a	08 39	09 02		09 33	09 39	10 03		10 32	10 39	11 03		11 32	11 39	12 03		12 32	12 39	13 03		13 32	13 39
	d	08 40	09 04		09 34	09 40	10 04		10 34	10 40	11 04		11 34	11 40	12 04		12 34	12 40	13 04		13 34	13 40
Rowlands Castle	d	08 46				09 46				10 46				11 46				12 46				13 46
Petersfield	d	08 57	09 18		09 48	09 57	10 18		10 48	10 57	11 18		11 48	11 57	12 18		12 48	12 57	13 18		13 48	13 57
Liss	d	09 02				10 02				11 02				12 02				13 02				14 02
Liphook	d	09 09				10 09				11 09				12 09				13 09				14 09
Haslemere 4	a	09 15	09 31		10 00	10 15	10 31		11 00	11 15	11 31		12 00	12 15	12 31		13 00	13 15	13 31		14 00	14 15
	d	09 15	09 32	09 40	10 02	10 15	10 32	10 40	11 02	11 15	11 32	11 40	12 02	12 15	12 32	12 40	13 02	13 15	13 32	13 40	14 02	14 15
Witley	d			09 46				10 46				11 46				12 46				13 46		
Milford (Surrey)	d			09 50				10 50				11 50				12 50				13 50		
Godalming	d	09 25	09 42	09 54	10 12	10 25	10 42	10 54	11 12	11 25	11 42	11 54	12 12	12 25	12 42	12 54	13 12	13 25	13 42	13 54	14 12	14 25
Farncombe	d	09 28		09 57		10 28		10 57		11 28		11 57		12 28		12 57		13 28		13 57		14 28
Guildford	a	09 33	09 48	10 02	10 18	10 33	10 48	11 02	11 18	11 33	11 48	12 02	12 18	12 33	12 48	13 02	13 18	13 33	13 48	14 02	14 18	14 33
	d	09 34	09 49	10 04	10 19	10 34	10 49	11 04	11 19	11 34	11 49	12 04	12 19	12 34	12 49	13 04	13 19	13 34	13 49	14 04	14 19	14 34
Worplesdon	d	09 40				10 40				11 40				12 40				13 40				14 40
Woking	a	09 44	09 59	10 11	10 26	10 44	10 56	11 11	11 26	11 44	11 56	12 11	12 26	12 44	12 56	13 11	13 26	13 44	13 56	14 11	14 26	14 44
	d	09 45	10 00	10 12	10 27	10 45	10 57	11 12	11 27	11 45	11 57	12 12	12 27	12 45	12 57	13 12	13 27	13 45	13 57	14 12	14 27	14 45
Clapham Junction	a	10 04		10 31		11 04		11 32		12 04		12 32		13 04		13 32		14 04		14 32		15 04
London Waterloo 15 ⊖	a	10 15	10 29	10 40	10 52	11 13	11 24	11 43	11 51	12 15	12 22	12 45	12 51	13 13	13 22	13 41	13 51	14 14	14 22	14 40	14 57	15 13

		SW ◇1 trolley	SW ◇1	SW ◇1 trolley	SW ◇1	SW ◇1 trolley	SW ◇1	SW ◇1 trolley	SW ◇1	SW ◇1	SW ◇1 trolley	SW ◇1 trolley	SW ◇1	SW ◇1	SW ◇1 trolley	SW ◇1 trolley	SW ◇1	SW ◇1 trolley	SW ◇1	SW ◇1 trolley	SW ◇1	SW ◇1 trolley	SW ◇1
Portsmouth Harbour ⛴	d	13 45		14 15		14 45		15 15			15 45	16 15			16 45	17 15	17 19	17 45		18 15	18 19	18 45	
Portsmouth & Southsea	d	13 50		14 20	14 24	14 50		15 20	15 24		15 50	16 20	16 24		16 50	17 19	17 24	17 50		18 20	18 24	18 50	
Fratton	d	13 54		14 24	14 28	14 54		15 24	15 28		15 54	16 24	16 28		16 54	17 24	17 28	17 54		18 24	18 28	18 54	
Hilsea	d				14 32				15 32				16 32				17 32				18 32		
Bedhampton	d				14 37				15 37				16 37				17 37				18 37		
Havant	a	14 03		14 32	14 39	15 03		15 32	15 39		16 03	16 32	16 39		17 03	17 33	17 39	18 03		18 33	18 39	19 02	
	d	14 04		14 34	14 40	15 04		15 34	15 40	15 52	16 04	16 34	16 40	17 00	17 04	17 34	17 40	18 04		18 34	18 40	19 04	
Rowlands Castle	d				14 46				15 46				16 46				17 46				18 46		
Petersfield	d	14 18		14 48	14 57	15 18		15 48	15 57	16 07	16 18	16 48	16 57	17 14	17 18	17 48	17 57	18 18		18 48	18 57	19 18	
Liss	d				15 02				16 02		16 23		17 02		17 23		18 02				19 02		
Liphook	d				15 09				16 09		16 30		17 09		17 30		18 09				19 09		
Haslemere 4	a	14 31		15 00	15 15	15 31		16 00	16 15	16 20	16 35	17 00	17 15	17 27	17 35	18 01	18 15	18 31		19 00	19 14	19 31	
	d	14 32	14 40	15 02	15 15	15 32	15 37	16 02	16 15	16 25	16 37	17 02	17 15	17 32	17 37	18 02	18 15	18 32	18 37	19 02	19 15	19 32	19 40
Witley	d		14 46				15 43			16 31	16 43				17 43				18 43				19 46
Milford (Surrey)	d		14 50				15 47			16 35	16 47				17 47				18 47				19 50
Godalming	d	14 42	14 54	15 12	15 25	15 42	15 51	16 12	16 25	16 40	16 51	17 12	17 25	17 42	17 51	18 12	18 25	18 42	18 51	19 12	19 25	19 42	19 54
Farncombe	d		14 57		15 28		15 54		16 28	16 43	16 54		17 28		17 54		18 28		18 54		19 28		19 57
Guildford	a	14 48	15 02	15 18	15 33	15 48	15 59	16 18	16 33	16 48	16 59	17 18	17 33	17 48	17 59	18 19	18 33	18 48	19 00	19 18	19 33	19 48	20 02
	d	14 49	15 04	15 19	15 34	15 49	16 01	16 19	16 34	16 49	17 01	17 19	17 34	17 49	18 01	18 23	18 34	18 53	19 01	19 23	19 34	19 49	20 04
Worplesdon	d				15 40		16 07		16 40		17 07		17 40		18 07		18 40		19 07		19 40		
Woking	a	14 56	15 11	15 26	15 44	15 56	16 11	16 27	16 44	16 56	17 11	17 26	17 44	17 58	18 11		18 44	19 03	19 14		19 44	19 56	20 11
	d	14 57	15 12	15 27	15 45	15 57	16 12	16 27	16 45	16 57	17 12	17 27	17 45	17 59	18 12		18 45	19 04	19 15		19 45	19 57	20 12
Clapham Junction	a		15 32		16 04		16 32		17 04		17 33		18 04		18 32		19 04		19 34		20 05		20 33
London Waterloo 15 ⊖	a	15 22	15 40	15 51	16 13	16 22	16 45	16 54	17 17	17 29	17 44	17 57	18 14	18 27	18 43	18 59	19 15	19 29	19 43	19 59	20 14	20 27	20 42

Table T156-R

Mondays to Fridays
16 December to 15 May

Portsmouth, Haslemere and Guildford - London

		SW	SW	SW	SW	SW	SW	SW	SW	SW	SW	SW	SW	SW
		◇1	◇1	◇1	◇1	◇1	◇1	◇1	1	◇1	◇1	1	◇1	1
Portsmouth Harbour ⛴	d	19 15	19 19	19 45		20 15		20 45		21 15			22 19	23 19
Portsmouth & Southsea	d	19 20	19 24	19 50		20 20	20 24	20 50		21 20	21 24		22 24	23 24
Fratton	d	19 24	19 28	19 54		20 24	20 28	20 54		21 24	21 28		22 28	23 28
Hilsea	d		19 32				20 32				21 32		22 32	23 32
Bedhampton	d		19 37				20 37				21 37		22 38	23 37
Havant	a	19 33	19 39	20 03		20 32	20 39	21 02		21 32	21 39		22 40	23 39
	d	19 34	19 40	20 04		20 34	20 40	21 04		21 34	21 40		22 40	23 40
Rowlands Castle	d		19 46				20 46				21 46		22 46	23 46
Petersfield	d	19 48	19 57	20 18		20 48	20 57	21 18		21 48	21 57		22 57	23 57
Liss	d		20 02				21 02				22 02		23 02	00 02
Liphook	d		20 09				21 09				22 09		23 09	00 09
Haslemere 4	a	20 01	20 15	20 31		21 01	21 15	21 31		22 01	22 15		23 15	00 15
	d	20 02	20 15	20 32	20 40	21 02	21 15	21 32	21 40	22 02	22 15	22 40	23 15	00 15
Witley	d				20 46				21 46			22 46	23 21	00 21
Milford (Surrey)	d				20 50				21 50			22 50	23 25	00 25
Godalming	d	20 12	20 25	20 42	20 54	21 12	21 25	21 42	21 54	22 12	22 25	22 54	23 29	00 29
Farncombe	d		20 28		20 57		21 28		21 57		22 28	22 57	23 32	00 32
Guildford	a	20 18	20 33	20 48	21 02	21 18	21 33	21 48	22 02	22 18	22 33	23 05	23 37	00 37
	d	20 19	20 34	20 49	21 04	21 19	21 34	21 49	22 04	22 19	22 34		23 39	
Worplesdon	d		20 40				21 40				22 40		23 45	
Woking	a	20 26	20 44	20 58	21 11	21 26	21 44	21 57	22 14	22 26	22 44		23 49	
	d	20 27	20 45	20 59	21 12	21 27	21 45	21 58	22 15	22 27	22 45		23 56	
Clapham Junction	a		21 06		21 34		22 04		22 34		23 04		00 22	
London Waterloo 15 ⊖	a	20 51	21 19	21 29	21 42	21 53	22 13	22 27	22 43	22 51	23 14		00 33	

Saturdays
21 December to 16 May

		SW	SW	SW	SW	SW	SW	SW	SW	SW	SW	SW	SW	SW	SW	SW	SW	SW	SW	SW	SW	SW	SW
		1	◇1	◇1	1	1	◇1	◇1	◇1 🛒	1	◇1 🛒	◇1	◇1 🛒	1	◇1 🛒	◇1	◇1 🛒	1	◇1 🛒	◇1	◇1 🛒	1	◇1 🛒
Portsmouth Harbour ⛴	d		04 43	05 19		05 40	06 15		06 45		07 15		07 45		08 15		08 45		09 15		09 45		10 15
Portsmouth & Southsea	d		04 48	05 24		05 44	06 20	06 24	06 50		07 20	07 24	07 50		08 20	08 24	08 50		09 20	09 24	09 50		10 20
Fratton	d		04 52	05 28		05a47	06 24	06 28	06 54		07 24	07 28	07 54		08 24	08 28	08 54		09 24	09 28	09 54		10 24
Hilsea	d		04 56	05 32				06 32				07 32				08 32				09 32			
Bedhampton	d		05 01	05 37				06 37				07 37				08 37				09 37			
Havant	a		05 03	05 39			06 32	06 39	07 03		07 32	07 40	08 03		08 32	08 39	09 03		09 32	09 39	10 03		10 32
	d		05 04	05 40			06 34	06 40	07 04		07 34	07 40	08 04		08 34	08 40	09 04		09 34	09 40	10 04		10 34
Rowlands Castle	d		05 09	05 46				06 46				07 46				08 46				09 46			
Petersfield	d		05 20	05 57			06 48	06 57	07 18		07 48	07 57	08 18		08 48	08 57	09 18		09 48	09 57	10 18		10 48
Liss	d	00 02	05 25	06 02				07 02				08 02				09 02				10 02			
Liphook	d	00 09	05 32	06 09				07 09				08 09				09 09				10 09			
Haslemere 4	a	00 15	05 39	06 14			07 00	07 15	07 31		08 00	08 15	08 31		09 00	09 15	09 31		10 00	10 15	10 31		11 00
	d	00 15	05 40	06 15	06 40		07 02	07 15	07 32	07 40	08 02	08 15	08 32	08 40	09 02	09 15	09 32	09 40	10 02	10 15	10 32	10 40	11 02
Witley	d	00 21	05 46		06 46					07 46				08 46				09 46				10 46	
Milford (Surrey)	d	00 25	05 50		06 50					07 50				08 50				09 50				10 50	
Godalming	d	00 29	05 54	06 25	06 54		07 12	07 25	07 42	07 54	08 12	08 25	08 42	08 54	09 12	09 25	09 42	09 54	10 12	10 25	10 42	10 54	11 12
Farncombe	d	00 32	05 57	06 28	06 57			07 28		07 57		08 28		08 57		09 28		09 57		10 28		10 57	
Guildford	a	00 37	06 02	06 33	07 02		07 18	07 33	07 48	08 02	08 18	08 33	08 48	09 02	09 18	09 33	09 48	10 02	10 18	10 33	10 48	11 02	11 18
	d		06 04	06 34	07 04		07 19	07 34	07 49	08 04	08 19	08 34	08 49	09 04	09 19	09 34	09 49	10 04	10 19	10 34	10 49	11 04	11 19
Worplesdon	d			06 40				07 40				08 40				09 40				10 40			
Woking	a		06 11	06 44	07 11			07 44	07 56	08 11	08 26	08 44	08 56	09 11	09 26	09 44	09 56	10 11	10 26	10 44	10 56	11 11	11 26
	d		06 12	06 45	07 12			07 45	07 57	08 12	08 27	08 45	08 57	09 12	09 27	09 45	09 57	10 12	10 27	10 45	10 57	11 12	11 27
Clapham Junction	a		06 31	07 04	07 31			08 04		08 33		09 04		09 31		10 04		10 31		11 04		11 32	
London Waterloo 15 ⊖	a		06 40	07 13	07 40		08 03	08 13	08 23	08 42	08 52	09 13	09 25	09 43	09 52	10 13	10 23	10 43	10 52	11 13	11 22	11 43	11 52

		SW	SW	SW	SW	SW	SW	SW	SW	SW	SW	SW	SW	SW	SW	SW	SW	SW	SW	SW	SW	SW	SW
		◇1	◇1 🛒	1	◇1 🛒	◇1	◇1 🛒	1	◇1 🛒	◇1	◇1 🛒	1	◇1 🛒	◇1	◇1 🛒	1	◇1 🛒	◇1	◇1 🛒	1	◇1 🛒	◇1	◇1 🛒
Portsmouth Harbour ⛴	d		10 45		11 15		11 45		12 15		12 45		13 15		13 45		14 15		14 45		15 15		15 45
Portsmouth & Southsea	d	10 24	10 50		11 20	11 24	11 50		12 20	12 24	12 50		13 20	13 24	13 50		14 20	14 24	14 50		15 20	15 24	15 50
Fratton	d	10 28	10 54		11 24	11 28	11 54		12 24	12 28	12 54		13 24	13 28	13 54		14 24	14 28	14 54		15 24	15 28	15 54
Hilsea	d	10 32				11 32				12 32				13 32				14 32				15 32	
Bedhampton	d	10 37				11 37				12 37				13 37				14 37				15 37	
Havant	a	10 39	11 03		11 32	11 39	12 03		12 32	12 39	13 03		13 32	13 39	14 03		14 32	14 39	15 03		15 32	15 39	16 03
	d	10 40	11 04		11 34	11 40	12 04		12 34	12 40	13 04		13 34	13 40	14 04		14 34	14 40	15 04		15 34	15 40	16 04
Rowlands Castle	d	10 46				11 46				12 46				13 46				14 46				15 46	
Petersfield	d	10 57	11 18		11 48	11 57	12 18		12 48	12 57	13 18		13 48	13 57	14 18		14 48	14 57	15 18		15 48	15 57	16 18
Liss	d	11 02				12 02				13 02				14 02				15 02				16 02	
Liphook	d	11 09				12 09				13 09				14 09				15 09				16 09	
Haslemere 4	a	11 15	11 31		12 00	12 15	12 31		13 00	13 15	13 31		14 00	14 15	14 31		15 00	15 15	15 31		16 00	16 15	16 31
	d	11 15	11 32	11 40	12 02	12 15	12 32	12 40	13 02	13 15	13 32	13 40	14 02	14 15	14 32	14 40	15 02	15 15	15 32	15 40	16 02	16 15	16 32
Witley	d			11 46				12 46				13 46				14 46				15 46			
Milford (Surrey)	d			11 50				12 50				13 50				14 50				15 50			
Godalming	d	11 25	11 42	11 54	12 12	12 25	12 42	12 54	13 12	13 25	13 42	13 54	14 12	14 25	14 42	14 54	15 12	15 25	15 42	15 54	16 12	16 25	16 42
Farncombe	d	11 28		11 57		12 28		12 57		13 28		13 57		14 28		14 57		15 28		15 57		16 28	
Guildford	a	11 33	11 48	12 02	12 18	12 33	12 48	13 02	13 18	13 33	13 48	14 02	14 18	14 33	14 48	15 02	15 18	15 33	15 48	16 02	16 18	16 33	16 48
	d	11 34	11 49	12 04	12 19	12 34	12 49	13 04	13 19	13 34	13 49	14 04	14 19	14 34	14 49	15 04	15 19	15 34	15 49	16 04	16 19	16 34	16 49
Worplesdon	d	11 40				12 40				13 40				14 40				15 40				16 40	
Woking	a	11 44	11 56	12 11	12 26	12 44	12 56	13 11	13 26	13 44	13 56	14 11	14 26	14 44	14 56	15 11	15 26	15 44	15 56	16 11	16 26	16 44	16 56
	d	11 45	11 57	12 12	12 27	12 45	12 57	13 12	13 27	13 45	13 57	14 12	14 27	14 45	14 57	15 12	15 27	15 45	15 57	16 12	16 27	16 45	16 57
Clapham Junction	a	12 04		12 31		13 04		13 31		14 04		14 31		15 04		15 31		16 04		16 31		17 04	
London Waterloo 15 ⊖	a	12 14	12 24	12 43	12 53	13 13	13 27	13 43	13 53	14 13	14 24	14 44	14 56	15 14	15 27	15 44	15 56	16 14	16 24	16 40	16 52	17 13	17 22

Table T156-R

Saturdays
21 December to 16 May

Portsmouth, Haslemere and Guildford - London

		SW	SW	SW	SW	SW	SW	SW	SW	SW	SW	SW	SW	SW	SW	SW	SW	SW	SW	SW	SW	SW
		1	◇1 🛒	◇1	◇1 🛒	1	◇1	◇1	◇1 🛒	1	◇1	◇1	◇1	1	◇1	◇1	◇1	1	◇1	◇1	◇1	1
Portsmouth Harbour ⛴	d		16 15		16 45		17 15		17 45		18 15		18 45		19 15		19 45		20 15		20 45	
Portsmouth & Southsea	d		16 20	16 24	16 50		17 20	17 24	17 50		18 20	18 24	18 50		19 20	19 24	19 50		20 20	20 24	20 48	
Fratton	d		16 24	16 28	16 54		17 24	17 28	17 54		18 24	18 28	18 54		19 24	19 28	19 54		20 24	20 28	20 52	
Hilsea	d			16 32				17 32				18 32				19 32				20 32		
Bedhampton	d			16 37				17 37				18 37				19 37				20 37		
Havant	a		16 32	16 39	17 03		17 32	17 39	18 04		18 32	18 39	19 03		19 32	19 39	20 03		20 32	20 39	21 03	
	d		16 34	16 40	17 04		17 34	17 40	18 04		18 34	18 40	19 04		19 34	19 40	20 04		20 34	20 40	21 04	
Rowlands Castle	d			16 46				17 46				18 46				19 46				20 46		
Petersfield	d		16 48	16 57	17 18		17 48	17 57	18 18		18 48	18 57	19 18		19 48	19 57	20 18		20 48	20 57	21 18	
Liss	d			17 02				18 02				19 02				20 02				21 02		
Liphook	d			17 09				18 09				19 09				20 09				21 09		
Haslemere 4	a		17 00	17 15	17 31		18 00	18 15	18 32		19 00	19 15	19 31		20 00	20 15	20 31		21 00	21 15	21 31	
	d	16 40	17 02	17 15	17 32	17 40	18 02	18 15	18 32	18 40	19 02	19 15	19 32	19 40	20 02	20 15	20 32	20 40	21 02	21 15	21 32	21 40
Witley	d	16 46				17 46				18 46				19 46				20 46				21 46
Milford (Surrey)	d	16 50				17 50				18 50				19 50				20 50				21 50
Godalming	d	16 54	17 12	17 25	17 42	17 54	18 12	18 25	18 42	18 54	19 12	19 25	19 42	19 54	20 12	20 25	20 42	20 54	21 12	21 25	21 42	21 54
Farncombe	d	16 57		17 28		17 57		18 28		18 57		19 28		19 57		20 28		20 57		21 28		21 57
Guildford	a	17 02	17 18	17 33	17 48	18 02	18 18	18 33	18 48	19 02	19 18	19 33	19 48	20 02	20 18	20 33	20 48	21 02	21 18	21 33	21 48	22 02
	d	17 04	17 19	17 34	17 49	18 04	18 19	18 34	18 49	19 04	19 19	19 34	19 49	20 04	20 19	20 34	20 49	21 04	21 19	21 34	21 49	22 04
Worplesdon	d			17 40				18 40				19 40				20 40				21 40		
Woking	a	17 11	17 26	17 44	17 56	18 11	18 26	18 44	18 56	19 11	19 26	19 44	19 56	20 11	20 26	20 44	20 56	21 11	21 26	21 45	21 57	22 11
	d	17 12	17 27	17 45	17 57	18 12	18 27	18 45	18 57	19 12	19 27	19 45	19 57	20 12	20 27	20 45	20 57	21 12	21 27	21 46	21 58	22 13
Clapham Junction	a	17 31		18 04		18 31		19 04		19 31		20 04		20 31		21 04		21 31		22 05		22 33
London Waterloo 15 ⊖	a	17 40	17 52	18 13	18 22	18 43	18 52	19 13	19 22	19 40	19 52	20 13	20 22	20 40	20 53	21 13	21 22	21 40	21 52	22 16	22 24	22 45

		SW	SW	SW	SW
		◇1	1	◇1	1
Portsmouth Harbour ⛴	d	21 19		22 19	23 19
Portsmouth & Southsea	d	21 24		22 24	23 24
Fratton	d	21 28		22 28	23 28
Hilsea	d	21 32		22 32	23 32
Bedhampton	d	21 37		22 38	23 37
Havant	a	21 39		22 40	23 39
	d	21 40		22 40	23 40
Rowlands Castle	d	21 46		22 46	23 46
Petersfield	d	21 57		22 57	23 57
Liss	d	22 02		23 02	00 02
Liphook	d	22 09		23 09	00 09
Haslemere 4	a	22 15		23 15	00 14
	d	22 15	22 40	23 15	00 15
Witley	d		22 46	23 21	00 21
Milford (Surrey)	d		22 50	23 25	00 25
Godalming	d	22 25	22 54	23 29	00 29
Farncombe	d	22 28	22 57	23 32	00 32
Guildford	a	22 33	23 02	23 37	00 37
	d	22 34	23 04	23 39	
Worplesdon	d	22 40		23 45	
Woking	a	22 44	23 11	23 50	
	d	22 45		23 56	
Clapham Junction	a	23 04		00 22	
London Waterloo 15 ⊖	a	23 13		00 32	

Sundays
15 December to 10 May

		SW	SW	SW	SW	SW	SW	SW	SW	SW	SW	SW	SW	SW	SW	SW	SW	SW	SW	SW	SW	SW	SW
		1 A	◇1	◇1	◇1	◇1	◇1	◇1 🛒	◇1	◇1 🛒	◇1	◇1 🛒	◇1	◇1 🛒	◇1	◇1 🛒	◇1	◇1 🛒	◇1	◇1 🛒	◇1	◇1 🛒	◇1 🛒
Portsmouth Harbour ⛴	d		06 48	07 32	07 48	08 32	08 48	09 32	09 48	10 32	10 48	11 32	11 48	12 32	12 48	13 32	13 48	14 32	14 48	15 32	15 48		16 32
Portsmouth & Southsea	d		06 53	07 37	07 53	08 37	08 53	09 37	09 53	10 37	10 53	11 37	11 53	12 37	12 53	13 37	13 53	14 37	14 53	15 37	15 53	16 26	16 37
Fratton	d		06 57	07 41	07 57	08 41	08 57	09 41	09 57	10 41	10 57	11 41	11 57	12 41	12 57	13 41	13 57	14 41	14 57	15 41	15 57	16 31	16 41
Hilsea	d																						
Bedhampton	d		07 04		08 04		09 04		10 04		11 04		12 04		13 04		14 04		15 04		16 04		
Havant	a		07 07	07 49	08 07	08 49	09 07	09 50	10 07	10 49	11 07	11 49	12 07	12 50	13 07	13 49	14 07	14 49	15 07	15 49	16 07	16 39	16 49
	d		07 07	07 50	08 07	08 50	09 07	09 50	10 07	10 50	11 07	11 50	12 07	12 50	13 07	13 50	14 07	14 50	15 07	15 50	16 07	16 40	16 50
Rowlands Castle	d		07 13		08 13		09 13		10 13		11 13		12 13		13 13		14 13		15 13		16 13		
Petersfield	d		07 24	08 04	08 24	09 04	09 24	10 04	10 24	11 04	11 24	12 04	12 24	13 04	13 24	14 04	14 24	15 04	15 24	16 04	16 24		17 04
Liss	d	00 02	07 29		08 29		09 29		10 29		11 29		12 29		13 29		14 29		15 29		16 29		
Liphook	d	00 09	07 36		08 36		09 36		10 36		11 36		12 36		13 36		14 36		15 36		16 36		
Haslemere 4	a	00 14	07 41	08 16	08 41	09 16	09 41	10 17	10 41	11 16	11 41	12 16	12 41	13 17	13 41	14 16	14 41	15 16	15 41	16 16	16 41		17 16
	d	00 15	07 42	08 17	08 42	09 17	09 42	10 17	10 42	11 17	11 42	12 17	12 42	13 17	13 42	14 17	14 42	15 17	15 42	16 17	16 42		17 17
Witley	d	00 21	07 48		08 48		09 48		10 48		11 48		12 48		13 48		14 48		15 48		16 48		
Milford (Surrey)	d	00 25	07 52		08 52		09 52		10 52		11 52		12 52		13 52		14 52		15 52		16 52		
Godalming	d	00 29	07 56	08 27	08 56	09 27	09 56	10 27	10 56	11 27	11 56	12 27	12 56	13 27	13 56	14 27	14 56	15 27	15 56	16 27	16 56		17 27
Farncombe	d	00 32	07 59		08 59		09 59		10 59		11 59		12 59		13 59		14 59		15 59		16 59		
Guildford	a	00 37	08 04	08 33	09 04	09 33	10 04	10 33	11 04	11 33	12 04	12 33	13 04	13 33	14 04	14 33	15 04	15 33	16 04	16 33	17 04	17 15	17 33
	d		08 05	08 35	09 05	09 35	10 05	10 35	11 05	11 35	12 05	12 35	13 05	13 35	14 05	14 35	15 05	15 35	16 05	16 35	17 05	17 17	17 35
Worplesdon	d																						
Woking	a		08 13	08 42	09 15	09 42	10 15	10 42	11 14	11 42	12 13	12 42	13 14	13 42	14 13	14 42	15 13	15 44	16 13	16 42	17 13		17 42
	d		08 15	08 45	09 15	09 45	10 15	10 45	11 15	11 45	12 15	12 45	13 15	13 45	14 15	14 45	15 15	15 45	16 15	16 45	17 15		17 45
Clapham Junction	a		08 39	09 06	09 38	10 05	10 35	11 04	11 34	12 04	12 34	13 04	13 34	14 04	14 34	15 04	15 34	16 04	16 34	17 04	17 34	17 47	18 06
London Waterloo 15 ⊖	a		08 50	09 16	09 49	10 16	10 46	11 14	11 44	12 14	12 43	13 14	13 44	14 14	14 44	15 14	15 44	16 14	16 44	17 14	17 44	17 57	18 17

A not 15 December

Table T156-R

Sundays
15 December to 10 May

Portsmouth, Haslemere and Guildford - London

		SW ◇■1	SW ◇■1 ⊼	SW ◇■1 ⊼	SW ◇■1	SW ◇■1 ⊼	SW ◇■1 ⊼	SW ◇■1	SW ◇■1	SW ◇■1	SW ◇■1	SW ◇■1	SW ◇■1	SW ◇■1	SW ◇■1	SW ■1
Portsmouth Harbour ⛴	d	16 48		17 32	17 48		18 32	18 48	19 32	19 48	20 32	20 48	21 32	21 48	22 32	22 48
Portsmouth & Southsea	d	16 53	17 26	17 37	17 53	18 26	18 37	18 53	19 37	19 53	20 37	20 53	21 37	21 53	22 37	22 52
Fratton	d	16 57	17 31	17 41	17 57	18 31	18 41	18 57	19 41	19 57	20 41	20 57	21 41	21 57	22 41	22 56
Hilsea	d															
Bedhampton	d	17 04			18 04			19 04		20 05		21 04		22 04		23 03
Havant	a	17 07	17 39	17 49	18 07	18 39	18 49	19 07	19 49	20 07	20 49	21 07	21 49	22 07	22 49	23 06
	d	17 07	17 40	17 50	18 07	18 40	18 50	19 07	19 50	20 08	20 50	21 07	21 50	22 07	22 50	23 07
Rowlands Castle	d	17 13			18 13			19 13		20 13		21 13		22 13		23 13
Petersfield	d	17 24		18 04	18 24		19 04	19 24	20 04	20 24	21 04	21 24	22 04	22 24	23 04	23 24
Liss	d	17 29			18 29			19 29		20 29		21 29		22 29		23 29
Liphook	d	17 36			18 36			19 36		20 36		21 36		22 36		23 36
Haslemere 4	a	17 41		18 16	18 41		19 16	19 41	20 16	20 41	21 16	21 41	22 16	22 41	23 16	23 41
	d	17 42		18 17	18 42		19 17	19 42	20 17	20 42	21 17	21 42	22 17	22 42	23 17	23 42
Witley	d	17 48			18 48			19 48		20 48		21 48		22 48		23 48
Milford (Surrey)	d	17 52			18 52			19 52		20 52		21 52		22 52		23 52
Godalming	d	17 56		18 27	18 56		19 27	19 56	20 27	20 56	21 27	21 56	22 27	22 56	23 27	23 56
Farncombe	d	17 59			18 59			19 59		20 59		21 59		22 59		23 59
Guildford	a	18 04	18 15	18 33	19 04	19 15	19 33	20 04	20 33	21 04	21 33	22 04	22 33	23 04	23 33	00 04
	d	18 05	18 17	18 35	19 05	19 17	19 35	20 05	20 35	21 05	21 35	22 05	22 35	23 05	23 35	00 05
Worplesdon	d															
Woking	a	18 13		18 42	19 13		19 42	20 13	20 42	21 13	21 42	22 13	22 42	23 14	23 42	00 13
	d	18 15		18 45	19 15		19 45	20 15	20 45	21 15	21 45	22 15	22 45	23 15	23 45	
Clapham Junction	a	18 34	18 47	19 04	19 34	19 47	20 06	20 34	21 04	21 34	22 04	22 34	23 04	23 34	00 04	
London Waterloo 15 ⊖	a	18 44	18 57	19 14	19 44	19 57	20 17	20 44	21 14	21 44	22 14	22 44	23 14	23 44	00 14	

AVAILABLE FROM MP Middleton Press

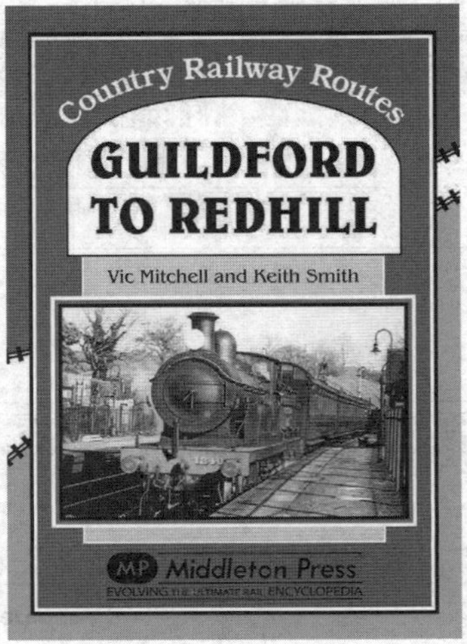

NRT DECEMBER 19 EDITION

Table T157-F

Mondays to Fridays
16 December to 15 May

Havant - Portsmouth Harbour
(Complete service)

		SW MX ◇■1	SW MO ◇■1	SW MO ◇■1 ⊼	SW MX ◇■1	SW MX ◇■1	SW MX ◇■1	SW MO ◇■1	SW MX ◇■1	SW MO ◇■1		SW MX ◇■1	SW MX ◇■1	SW ■1	SN	SN	SW ■1	SN	SW ■1	SN		SW ■1	SW ◇■1	SW ■1	SN
Havant	d					00 18	00 30	00 39	00 46	00 53		00 57	01 23	04 40	05 21	05 40	06 00	06 07		06 35			07 00		07 11
Bedhampton	d						00 33	00 41				01s00	01s25	04 43			06 03			06 37			07 03		
Hilsea	d			00 03	00 04		00 38					01s05	01s31	04 48			06 08		06 34	06 43		07 03	07 08	07 13	
Fratton	d		00 03	00 07	00 08	00 28	00 43	00 50	00 55	01 02		01 10	01s35	04 52	05 30	05 49	06 13	06 16	06 41	06 48		07 08	07 13	07 18	07 21
Portsmouth & Southsea	a		00 06	00 10	00 11	00 31	00 46	00 53	00 58	01 05		01 13	01 39	04 55	05 33	05 52	06 16	06 20	06 44	06 51		07 11	07 16	07 21	07 25
	d	00 03	00 07	00 11	00 13	00 32		00 54	00 59	01 06				04 56	05 34	05 52	06 17	06 20	06 46	06 52		07 12	07 17	07 22	
Portsmouth Harbour ⛴	a	00 06	00 10	00 14	00 16	00 35		00 58	01 03	01 09				04 59	05 37	05 56	06 20	06 24	06 49	06 57		07 17	07 21	07 27	

		GW ◇	SW ■1	SW ◇■1	SN	SN		SW ◇■1	SW ■1	SN	SW ■1	GW ◇	SW ◇■1	SW ◇■1	SN	SW ■1		SN	SW ◇■1 ⊼	SW ◇■1	SW ◇■1	SN	SW ◇■1 ⊼	SW ■1	SW ◇■1
Havant	d			07 27	07 32	07 49		07 53		08 03			08 19	08 29	08 34			08 47	08 50		09 01	09 10	09 19		09 29
Bedhampton	d			07 30	07 35	07 52		07 56						08 32	08 36						09 04				09 32
Hilsea	d		07 35	07 38	07 40	07 57		08 01	08 04		08 06			08 37	08 41	08 45				09 05	09 09			09 33	09 37
Fratton	d	07 27	07 40	07 43	07 45	08 01		08 05	08 08	08 13	08 11	08 18	08 28	08 42	08 46	08 50		08 56	09 00	09 09	09 14	09 19	09 28	09 37	09 41
Portsmouth & Southsea	a	07 30	07 43	07 46	07 48	08 05		08 08	08 13	08 16	08 18	08 21	08 31	08 45	08 49	08 53		08 59	09 03	09 12	09 17	09 23	09 31	09 44	09 45
	d	07 33	07 43	07 47				08 10	08 14	08 16		08 22	08 33	08 46		08 55		09 00	09 05	09 14	09 18		09 33		
Portsmouth Harbour ⛴	a	07 38	07 48	07 51				08 13	08 18	08 22		08 26	08 36	08 50		08 58		09 04	09 08	09 18	09 22		09 36		

		SN		GW ◇	SN ■1	SW ◇■1 ⊼	SW ◇■1	SN	SW ◇■1 ⊼	SW ■1	SW ◇■1	GW ■		SN	SW ◇■1 ⊼	SN ■1	SW ◇■1	SN	SW ◇■1 ⊼	SW ■1	SW ◇■1	GW ◇		SN	SW ◇■1 ⊼
Havant	d	09 34			09 48	09 51		10 10	10 17		10 28			10 34	10 45	10 49		11 06	11 17		11 28			11 34	11 45
Bedhampton	d	09 36									10 31			10 36							11 31			11 36	
Hilsea	d	09 42					10 03			10 33	10 36			10 42			11 03			11 33	11 36			11 42	
Fratton	d	09 47		09 49	09 57	10 00	10 08	10 19	10 26	10 37	10 40	10 44		10 47	10 54	10 58	11 08	11 15	11 26	11 37	11 40	11 44		11 47	11 54
Portsmouth & Southsea	a	09 50		09 52	10 00	10 03	10 11	10 23	10 29	10 44	10 45	10 47		10 50	10 57	11 01	11 11	11 18	11 29	11 44	11 45	11 47		11 50	11 57
	d			09 53	10 00	10 05	10 12		10 31			10 48			10 59	11 02	11 12	11 18	11 31			11 48			11 59
Portsmouth Harbour ⛴	a			09 56	10 04	10 08	10 20		10 34			10 51			11 02	11 05	11 20	11 22	11 34			11 51			12 02

		SN ■1	SW ◇■1	SN	SW ◇■1 ⊼	SW ■1	SW ◇■1	GW ◇		SN	SW ◇■1 ⊼	SN ■1	SW ◇■1	SN	SW ◇■1 ⊼	SW ■1	SW ◇■1	GW ◇		SN	SW ◇■1 ⊼	SN ■1	SW ◇■1	SN	SW ◇■1 ⊼
Havant	d	11 49		12 06	12 17		12 28			12 34	12 45	12 49		13 06	13 17		13 28			13 34	13 45	13 49		14 06	14 17
Bedhampton	d						12 31			12 36							13 31			13 37					
Hilsea	d		12 03			12 33	12 36			12 42			13 03			13 33	13 36			13 42			14 03		
Fratton	d	11 58	12 08	12 15	12 26	12 37	12 40	12 44		12 47	12 54	12 58	13 08	13 15	13 26	13 37	13 40	13 43		13 47	13 54	13 58	14 08	14 15	14 26
Portsmouth & Southsea	a	12 01	12 11	12 18	12 29	12 44	12 45	12 47		12 50	12 57	13 01	13 11	13 18	13 29	13 44	13 45	13 46		13 50	13 57	14 01	14 11	14 18	14 29
	d	12 02	12 12	12 18	12 31			12 48			12 59	13 02	13 12	13 18	13 31			13 47			13 59	14 02	14 12	14 18	14 31
Portsmouth Harbour ⛴	a	12 05	12 20	12 22	12 34			12 51			13 02	13 05	13 20	13 22	13 34			13 50			14 02	14 05	14 20	14 22	14 34

		SW ■1	SW ◇■1	GW ◇		SN	SN ■1	SW ◇■1 ⊼	SW ◇■1	SN	SW ◇■1 ⊼	SW ■1	SW ◇■1	GW ◇		SN	SW ◇■1 ⊼	SN ■1	SW ◇■1	SN	SW ◇■1 ⊼	SW ■1	SW ◇■1	GW ◇	
Havant	d		14 28			14 34	14 49	14 52		15 06	15 17		15 28			15 34	15 45	15 49		16 10	16 17		16 28		
Bedhampton	d		14 31			14 36							15 31			15 36							16 31		
Hilsea	d	14 33	14 36			14 42			15 03			15 33	15 36			15 42			16 03			16 33	16 36		
Fratton	d	14 37	14 40	14 43		14 47	14 58	15 01	15 08	15 15	15 26	15 37	15 40	15 43		15 47	15 54	15 58	16 09	16 19	16 26	16 37	16 40	16 44	
Portsmouth & Southsea	a	14 44	14 45	14 46		14 50	15 01	15 04	15 11	15 18	15 29	15 42	15 45	15 46		15 50	15 57	16 01	16 13	16 23	16 29	16 40	16 44	16 48	
	d			14 47			15 02	15 05	15 12	15 18	15 31	15 43		15 47			15 59	16 02	16 14		16 31	16 41	16 45	16 49	
Portsmouth Harbour ⛴	a			14 50			15 05	15 08	15 20	15 22	15 34	15 48		15 50			16 02	16 05	16 20		16 36	16 44	16 50	16 52	

		SN	SW ◇■1 ⊼	SN ■1	SW ◇■1	SW ◇■1	SN	SW ◇■1 ⊼	SW ◇■1	SW ■1		SW ◇■1	GW ◇	SN	SW ◇■1 ⊼	SN ■1	SW ◇■1	SW ◇■1	SN	SW ◇■1 ⊼		SW ■1	SW ◇■1	SW ◇■1	GW ◇
Havant	d	16 34	16 45	16 49		16 59	17 09	17 17				17 28		17 34	17 50	17 54		18 02	18 14	18 19				18 31	
Bedhampton	d	16 36				17 02						17 31		17 36				18 05						18 34	
Hilsea	d	16 42			17 03	17 07				17 33		17 36		17 42			18 03	18 10				18 33		18 39	
Fratton	d	16 47	16 54	16 58	17 08	17 12	17 19	17 26	17 31	17 37		17 41	17 44	17 47	18 00	18 03	18 08	18 14	18 24	18 28		18 37	18 40	18 43	18 46
Portsmouth & Southsea	a	16 50	16 57	17 01	17 11	17 15	17 23	17 29	17 34	17 44		17 44	17 48	17 50	18 03	18 08	18 11	18 17	18 28	18 31		18 44	18 44	18 47	18 50
	d		16 59	17 02	17 12	17 17		17 31	17 36			17 45	17 49		18 04		18 13	18 19		18 33			18 45	18 48	18 51
Portsmouth Harbour ⛴	a		17 02	17 05	17 20	17 22		17 34	17 39			17 48	17 52		18 09		18 20	18 24		18 38			18 50	18 51	18 54

		SN	SN ■1	SW ◇■1	SW ◇■1 ⊼	SW ◇■1		SN	SW ◇■1 ⊼	SW ◇■1	SW ■1	GW ■	SN	SN ■1	SW ◇■1	SW ◇■1 ⊼		SW ◇■1	SN	SW ◇■1 ⊼	SW ■1	SW ◇■1	GW ■	SN	SN ■1
Havant	d	18 34	18 49	18 43	18 53			19 11	19 17				19 34	19 49	19 43	19 52			20 10	20 17		20 28		20 35	20 48
Bedhampton	d	18 37		18 46									19 36		19 46							20 31		20 38	
Hilsea	d	18 44		18 52		19 05				19 28	19 33		19 42		19 51			20 03			20 33	20 36		20 44	
Fratton	d	18 48	18 58	18 57	19 02	19 09		19 20	19 27	19 33	19 37	19 44	19 47	19 58	19 57	20 02		20 08	20 19	20 27	20 37	20 41	20 43	20 48	20 57
Portsmouth & Southsea	a	18 53	19 01	19 03	19 05	19 12		19 23	19 30	19 36	19 44	19 47	19 50	20 01	20 03	20 05		20 12	20 23	20 30	20 42	20 46	20 46	20 53	21 00
	d		19 02		19 06	19 14			19 31	19 38		19 48		20 02		20 06		20 14		20 31			20 47		21 00
Portsmouth Harbour ⛴	a		19 05		19 12	19 20			19 36	19 43		19 51		20 05		20 11		20 20		20 34			20 50		21 04

Table T157-F

Havant - Portsmouth Harbour

(Complete service)

Mondays to Fridays
16 December to 15 May

Station		SW ◇1 ⊼	SW ◇1	SN	SW ◇1 ⊼	SW 1	GW ◇	SW ◇1	SW ◇1 ⊼	SN 1	SW ◇1	SN	SW ◇1 ⊼	SW 1	SW ◇1	GW ◇	SW ◇1	SN 1	SW ◇1	SN	SW ◇1	SW 1	SW ◇1
Havant	d	20 51		21 11	21 19			21 30	21 47	21 50		22 11	22 19		22 31		22 48	22 53		23 11	23 19		23 30
Bedhampton	d							21 33							22 34								23 33
Hilsea	d		21 03			21 33		21 39			22 04			22 33	22 39				23 06			23 33	23 38
Fratton	d	21 01	21 08	21 20	21 28	21 37	21 40	21 44	21 56	22 00	22 08	22 20	22 28	22 37	22 44	22 57	23 00	23 04	23 13	23 20	23 28	23 37	23 43
Portsmouth & Southsea	a	21 04	21 11	21 23	21 31	21 40	21 43	21 47	21 59	22 03	22 11	22 23	22 31	22 44	22 47	23 00	23 04	23 07	23 16	23 23	23 31	23 44	23 47
	d	21 05	21 13		21 33	21 41	21 44		22 00	22 03	22 13	22 23	22 33		22 48	23 01	23 04	23 09	23 18	23 24	23 33		
Portsmouth Harbour	a	21 08	21 18		21 36	21 44	21 49		22 03	22 07	22 16	22 27	22 36		22 51	23 04	23 08	23 12	23 22	23 28	23 36		

Station		GW ◇	SN 1	SW ◇1
Havant	d		23 37	23 50
Bedhampton	d			
Hilsea	d			
Fratton	d	23 45	23 49	23 59
Portsmouth & Southsea	a	23 48	23 52	00 02
	d	23 49		00 03
Portsmouth Harbour	a	23 53		00 06

Saturdays
21 December to 16 May

Station		SW ◇1	SW ◇1	SW ◇1	SW ◇1	SW ◇1	SW ◇1	SW ◇1	SW 1	SN	SN 1	SW 1	SN	SW 1	SN	SN 1	SW 1	SN	SW ◇1	SW 1	GW	SN	SN 1
Havant	d			00 18	00 30	00 46	00 57	01 23	04 40	05 34	05 49	06 02	06 06		06 34	06 49		07 06	07 22			07 34	07 49
Bedhampton	d				00 33		01s00	01s25	04 43	05 36		06 05			06 36				07 25			07 36	
Hilsea	d		00 04		00 38		01s05	01s31	04 48	05 42		06 10		06 37	06 42		07 03		07 30	07 33		07 42	
Fratton	d		00 08	00 28	00 43	00 55	01 10	01s35	04 52	05 47	05 58	06 14	06 18	06 43	06 47	06 58	07 08	07 15	07 34	07 37	07 43	07 47	07 58
Portsmouth & Southsea	a		00 11	00 31	00 46	00 58	01 13	01 39	04 55	05 50	06 01	06 17	06 21	06 46	06 50	07 01	07 11	07 18	07 37	07 42	07 46	07 50	08 01
	d	00 03	00 13	00 32		00 59			04 57		06 02	06 18	06 22			07 01	07 12	07 18	07 39		07 46		08 01
Portsmouth Harbour	a	00 06	00 16	00 35		01 03			05 00		06 05	06 22	06 25			07 05	07 16	07 22	07 43		07 50		08 05

Station		SW 1	SN	SW ◇1	SW 1	GW ◇	SN	SW ◇1	SN 1	SW ◇1	SN	SW ◇1	SW 1	SW ◇1	GW ◇	SN	SW ◇1	SN 1	SW ◇1	SN	SW ◇1 ⊼	SW 1	SW ◇1
Havant	d		08 06	08 17			08 34	08 45	08 49		09 06	09 17		09 28		09 34	09 45	09 49		10 09	10 17		10 28
Bedhampton	d			08 20			08 36							09 31		09 36							10 31
Hilsea	d	08 03		08 25	08 33		08 42			09 04			09 33	09 36		09 42			10 03			10 33	10 36
Fratton	d	08 08	08 17	08 30	08 37	08 41	08 47	08 54	08 58	09 09	09 15	09 26	09 37	09 40	09 43	09 47	09 54	09 58	10 08	10 18	10 27	10 37	10 40
Portsmouth & Southsea	a	08 11	08 20	08 33	08 42	08 45	08 50	08 57	09 01	09 12	09 18	09 29	09 42	09 44	09 46	09 50	09 57	10 01	10 11	10 21	10 30	10 42	10 44
	d	08 12	08 20	08 34		08 46		08 58	09 01	09 13	09 18	09 31			09 47		09 58	10 01	10 12	10 22	10 31		
Portsmouth Harbour	a	08 18	08 24	08 38		08 49		09 02	09 05	09 18	09 22	09 34			09 51		10 02	10 05	10 18	10 25	10 34		

Station		GW ◇	SN	SW ◇1 ⊼	SN 1	SW ◇1	SN	SW ◇1 ⊼	SW 1	SW ◇1	GW ◇	SN	SW ◇1 ⊼	SN 1	SW ◇1	SN	SW ◇1 ⊼	SW 1	SW ◇1	GW ◇ ⊼	SN	SW ◇1 ⊼
Havant	d		10 34	10 45	10 49		11 06	11 17		11 28		11 34	11 45	11 49		12 06	12 17		12 28		12 34	12 45
Bedhampton	d		10 36							11 31		11 36							12 31		12 36	
Hilsea	d		10 42			11 03			11 33	11 36		11 42			12 03			12 33	12 36		12 42	
Fratton	d	10 43	10 47	10 54	10 58	11 08	11 15	11 27	11 37	11 40	11 43	11 47	11 54	11 58	12 08	12 15	12 26	12 37	12 40	12 43	12 47	12 54
Portsmouth & Southsea	a	10 46	10 50	10 57	11 01	11 11	11 18	11 30	11 42	11 44	11 46	11 50	11 57	12 01	12 11	12 18	12 29	12 42	12 44	12 46	12 50	12 57
	d	10 47		10 58	11 01	11 12	11 18	11 31			11 47		11 58	12 01	12 12	12 18	12 31			12 47		12 58
Portsmouth Harbour	a	10 50		11 02	11 05	11 18	11 22	11 34			11 50		12 02	12 05	12 18	12 22	12 34			12 50		13 02

Station		SN 1	SW ◇1	SN	SW ◇1 ⊼	SW 1	SW ◇1	GW ◇ ⊼	SN	SW ◇1 ⊼	SN 1	SW ◇1	SN	SW ◇1 ⊼	SW 1	SW ◇1	GW ◇ ⊼	SN	SW ◇1 ⊼	SN 1	SW ◇1	SN	SW ◇1 ⊼
Havant	d	12 49		13 06	13 17		13 28		13 34	13 45	13 49		14 06	14 17		14 28		14 34	14 45	14 49		15 06	15 17
Bedhampton	d						13 31		13 36							14 31		14 36					
Hilsea	d		13 03			13 33	13 36		13 42			14 03			14 33	14 36		14 42			15 03		
Fratton	d	12 58	13 08	13 15	13 26	13 37	13 40	13 43	13 47	13 54	13 58	14 08	14 15	14 26	14 37	14 40	14 43	14 47	14 54	14 58	15 08	15 15	15 26
Portsmouth & Southsea	a	13 01	13 11	13 18	13 29	13 42	13 44	13 46	13 50	13 57	14 01	14 11	14 18	14 29	14 42	14 44	14 46	14 50	14 57	15 01	15 11	15 18	15 29
	d	13 01	13 12	13 18	13 31			13 47		13 58	14 01	14 12	14 18	14 31			14 47		14 58	15 01	15 12	15 18	15 31
Portsmouth Harbour	a	13 05	13 18	13 22	13 34			13 50		14 02	14 05	14 18	14 22	14 34			14 50		15 02	15 05	15 18	15 22	15 34

Station		SW 1	SW ◇1	GW ◇ ⊼	SN	SW ◇1 ⊼	SN 1	SW ◇1	SN	SW ◇1 ⊼	SW 1	SW ◇1	GW ◇	SN	SW ◇1 ⊼	SN 1	SW ◇1	SN	SW ◇1 ⊼	SW 1	SW ◇1	GW ◇
Havant	d		15 28		15 34	15 45	15 49		16 06	16 17		16 28		16 34	16 45	16 49		17 06	17 17		17 28	
Bedhampton	d		15 31		15 36							16 31		16 36							17 31	
Hilsea	d	15 33	15 36		15 42			16 03			16 33	16 36		16 42			17 03			17 33	17 36	
Fratton	d	15 37	15 40	15 43	15 47	15 54	15 58	16 08	16 15	16 26	16 37	16 40	16 43	16 47	16 54	16 58	17 08	17 15	17 26	17 37	17 40	17 43
Portsmouth & Southsea	a	15 42	15 44	15 46	15 50	15 57	16 01	16 11	16 18	16 29	16 40	16 44	16 46	16 50	16 57	17 01	17 11	17 18	17 29	17 42	17 44	17 46
	d			15 47		15 58	16 01	16 12	16 18	16 31	16 41		16 47		16 58	17 01	17 12	17 18	17 31			17 47
Portsmouth Harbour	a			15 50		16 02	16 05	16 18	16 22	16 34	16 44		16 50		17 02	17 05	17 18	17 22	17 34			17 50

Station		SN	SW ◇1 ⊼	SN 1	SW ◇1	SN	SW ◇1 ⊼	SW 1	SW ◇1	GW ◇	SN	SW ◇1 ⊼	SN 1	SW ◇1	SN	SW ◇1 ⊼	SW 1	SW ◇1	GW ◇	SN	SW ◇1 ⊼	SN 1	SW ◇1
Havant	d	17 34	17 45	17 49		18 09	18 17		18 28		18 34	18 45	18 49		19 06	19 17		19 28		19 34	19 45	19 49	
Bedhampton	d	17 36							18 31		18 36							19 31		19 36			
Hilsea	d	17 42			18 03			18 33	18 36		18 42			19 03			19 33	19 36		19 42			20 03
Fratton	d	17 47	17 54	17 58	18 08	18 18	18 26	18 37	18 40	18 43	18 47	18 54	18 58	19 08	19 15	19 26	19 37	19 40	19 43	19 47	19 54	19 58	20 08
Portsmouth & Southsea	a	17 50	17 57	18 01	18 11	18 21	18 29	18 42	18 44	18 46	18 50	18 57	19 01	19 11	19 18	19 29	19 42	19 44	19 46	19 50	19 57	20 01	20 11
	d		17 58	18 01	18 12	18 22	18 31			18 47		18 58	19 01	19 12	19 18	19 31			19 47		19 58	20 01	20 12
Portsmouth Harbour	a		18 02	18 05	18 18	18 25	18 34			18 50		19 02	19 05	19 18	19 22	19 34			19 50		20 02	20 05	20 18

Table T157-F

Havant - Portsmouth Harbour

(Complete service)

Saturdays
21 December to 16 May

Station		SN	SW ◇1 ⊼	SW 1	SW ◇1	GW ◇	SN	SW ◇1 ⊼	SN 1	SW ◇1	SN	SW ◇1	SW 1	SW ◇1	GW ◇	SW ◇1	SN 1	SW ◇1	SN	SW ◇1	SW 1	GW ◇
Havant	d	20 06	20 17		20 28		20 34	20 45	20 49		21 06	21 15		21 27		21 45	21 49		22 06	22 18		
Bedhampton	d				20 31		20 36							21 30								
Hilsea	d			20 33	20 36		20 43			21 03			21 33	21 35				22 03			22 33	
Fratton	d	20 15	20 26	20 37	20 40	20 42	20 48	20 54	20 58	21 08	21 15	21 24	21 37	21 40	21 43	21 54	21 58	22 08	22 15	22 27	22 37	22 42
Portsmouth & Southsea	a	20 18	20 29	20 42	20 44	20 45	20 52	20 57	21 01	21 10	21 18	21 27	21 40	21 44	21 46	21 57	22 01	22 11	22 18	22 30	22 40	22 45
	d	20 18	20 30			20 46		20 58	21 01	21 11	21 18	21 29	21 41		21 47	21 58	22 01	22 12	22 18	22 32	22 41	22 46
Portsmouth Harbour	a	20 22	20 33			20 49		21 02	21 05	21 16	21 22	21 32	21 45		21 50	22 02	22 05	22 18	22 22	22 36	22 45	22 50

Station		SW ◇1	SN	SW ◇1	SW ◇1	SN	SW ◇1	SW 1	GW ◇	SW ◇1	SN 1	SW ◇1
Havant	d	22 31	22 39	22 45		23 06	23 18			23 31	23 37	23 48
Bedhampton	d	22 34								23 34		
Hilsea	d	22 40			23 05			23 33		23 40		
Fratton	d	22 45	22 49	22 54	23 10	23 15	23 27	23 37	23 42	23 45	23 48	23 57
Portsmouth & Southsea	a	22 48	22 52	22 57	23 13	23 18	23 30	23 40	23 45	23 48	23 51	00 01
	d	22 49	22 53	22 58	23 13	23 18	23 32		23 46	23 49		00 02
Portsmouth Harbour	a	22 53	22 56	23 04	23 18	23 22	23 36		23 49	23 53		00 05

Sundays
15 December to 10 May

Station		SW ◇1 A	SW ◇1 A	SW ◇1 A	SW ◇1 A	SW ◇1 A	SW ◇1 A	SN	SW 1	SW 1	SN	SW 1	SW 1	SN	SW ◇1	SN	SW 1	SW ◇1	SN	SW ◇1	SW 1	SW 1	SN 1
Havant	d			00 18	00 30	00 37	01 21	07 15			08 16		08 39	08 50		09 19		09 44	09 51	09 56			10 37
Bedhampton	d				00 33		01s24						08 41	08 52				09 46	09 53				
Hilsea	d		00 03		00 38		01s29		07 24	08 00		08 26			09 00		09 30				10 00	10 24	
Fratton	d		00 07	00 27	00 43	00 46	01s33	07 24	07 29	08 04	08 25	08 30	08 50	09 00	09 05	09 28	09 34	09 55	10 01	10 05	10 10	10 29	10 47
Portsmouth & Southsea	a		00 10	00 30	00 46	00 49	01 37	07 27	07 32	08 07	08 28	08 33	08 53	09 03	09 08	09 31	09 37	09 58	10 04	10 08	10 13	10 32	10 52
	d	00 02	00 12	00 32		00 50		07 27		08 08	08 29		08 54	09 04	09 10	09 32		09 59	10 05	10 09	10 14		10 53
Portsmouth Harbour	a	00 05	00 15	00 35		00 54		07 31		08 11	08 32		08 57	09 07	09 20	09 35		10 04	10 08	10 13	10 20		10 56

Station		SW ◇1	SN	SW ◇1	SW 1	SW 1	GW ◇	SN 1	SW ◇1	SN	SW ◇1	SW 1	SW 1	GW ◇	SN 1	SW ◇1	SN	SW ◇1 ⊼	SW 1	SW 1	SN 1	SW ◇1	SN
Havant	d	10 44	10 50	10 56				11 37	11 41	11 50	11 54				12 37	12 41	12 50	12 54			13 37	13 41	13 50
Bedhampton	d	10 46	10 52						11 43	11 52						12 43	12 52					13 43	13 52
Hilsea	d				11 00	11 24						12 00	12 25						13 00	13 25			
Fratton	d	10 55	11 00	11 05	11 10	11 29	11 41	11 47	11 52	12 00	12 03	12 10	12 34	12 41	12 48	12 52	13 00	13 03	13 10	13 30	13 46	13 52	14 00
Portsmouth & Southsea	a	10 58	11 03	11 08	11 13	11 32	11 44	11 50	11 55	12 03	12 07	12 13	12 37	12 44	12 52	12 56	13 03	13 07	13 13	13 33	13 49	13 55	14 03
	d	10 59	11 04	11 09	11 14		11 45	11 52	11 56	12 04	12 08	12 14		12 45	12 53	12 57	13 04	13 08	13 14		13 50	13 56	14 04
Portsmouth Harbour	a	11 04	11 07	11 13	11 20		11 51	11 55	12 00	12 07	12 11	12 20		12 51	12 56	13 00	13 07	13 11	13 20		13 53	14 00	14 07

Station		SW ◇1 ⊼	SW 1	SW 1	GW ◇	SN 1	SW ◇1	SN	SW ◇1 ⊼	SW 1	SW 1	SN 1	SW ◇1	SN	SW ◇1 ⊼	SW 1	SW 1	GW ◇	SN 1	SW ◇1	SW ◇1 ⊼	SW 1
Havant	d	13 54				14 37	14 41	14 50	14 54			15 37	15 41	15 50	15 54				16 37	16 41	16 54	
Bedhampton	d						14 43	14 52					15 43	15 52						16 43		
Hilsea	d		14 00	14 26						15 00	15 26					16 00	16 26					16 59
Fratton	d	14 04	14 10	14 30	14 41	14 48	14 52	15 00	15 03	15 10	15 30	15 46	15 52	16 00	16 03	16 10	16 30	16 42	16 48	16 52	17 03	17 10
Portsmouth & Southsea	a	14 07	14 13	14 33	14 44	14 51	14 55	15 03	15 07	15 13	15 33	15 49	15 55	16 03	16 07	16 13	16 33	16 45	16 51	16 55	17 07	17 13
	d	14 08	14 14		14 45	14 52	14 56	15 04	15 08	15 14		15 50	15 56	16 04	16 08	16 14		16 45	16 52	16 56	17 08	17 14
Portsmouth Harbour	a	14 11	14 20		14 51	14 56	15 00	15 07	15 11	15 20		15 53	16 00	16 07	16 11	16 20		16 51	16 55	17 00	17 11	17 20

Station		SW 1	GW ◇	SN 1	SW ◇1	SN	SW ◇1 ⊼	SW ◇1	SW 1	GW ◇	SN 1	SW ◇1	SW ◇1 ⊼	SW ◇1	SW 1	GW ◇	SN 1	SW ◇1	SN	SW ◇1 ⊼	SW ◇1	SW ◇	SW 1
Havant	d			17 37	17 41	17 50	17 54				18 37	18 41	18 54				19 37	19 41	19 50	19 54		20 08	
Bedhampton	d				17 43	17 52						18 43						19 43	19 52				
Hilsea	d	17 26						18 00	18 26					19 00	19 26						20 00		20 25
Fratton	d	17 30	17 41	17 47	17 52	18 00	18 03	18 10	18 30	18 41	18 48	18 52	19 03	19 10	19 30	19 41	19 48	19 51	20 00	20 03	20 10	20 17	20 30
Portsmouth & Southsea	a	17 33	17 44	17 50	17 55	18 03	18 07	18 13	18 33	18 44	18 51	18 55	19 06	19 13	19 33	19 44	19 51	19 54	20 03	20 07	20 13	20 22	20 33
	d		17 45	17 51	17 56	18 04	18 08	18 14		18 45	18 52	18 56	19 08	19 14		19 45	19 52	19 55	20 04	20 08	20 14		
Portsmouth Harbour	a		17 51	17 54	18 00	18 07	18 11	18 20		18 53	18 55	19 00	19 11	19 20		19 51	19 55	19 58	20 07	20 11	20 20		

Station		GW ◇	SN 1	SW ◇1	SN	SW ◇1 ⊼	SW ◇1	GW ◇	SW ◇1	SW 1	GW ◇	SN 1	SW ◇1	SN	SW ◇1 ⊼	SW ◇1	SW ◇1	SW 1	GW ◇	SN 1	SW ◇1	GW
Havant	d		20 37	20 41	20 50	20 54			21 08			21 37	21 41	21 50	21 54		22 08			22 37	22 41	22 46
Bedhampton	d			20 43	20 52								21 43	21 52							22 43	
Hilsea	d						21 00			21 25						22 00		22 26				
Fratton	d	20 41	20 48	20 52	21 00	21 03	21 10	21 13	21 17	21 30	21 41	21 46	21 52	22 00	22 04	22 10	22 17	22 30	22 40	22 48	22 52	22 59
Portsmouth & Southsea	a	20 44	20 51	20 55	21 03	21 07	21 13	21 17	21 22	21 33	21 43	21 49	21 55	22 03	22 07	22 13	22 22	22 33	22 44	22 52	22 56	23 02
	d	20 45	20 52	20 56	21 04	21 08	21 14	21 17			21 44	21 50	21 56	22 04	22 08	22 14			22 44	22 53	22 57	23 03
Portsmouth Harbour	a	20 50	20 55	21 00	21 07	21 13	21 20	21 22			21 48	21 54	22 00	22 07	22 11	22 20			22 51	22 56	23 00	23 07

A not 15 December

Table T157-F

Sundays

15 December to 10 May

Havant - Portsmouth Harbour
(Complete service)

		SW		SW	SN	SN	SW	GW	SW	SW
		◇1		◇1		1	1	◇	◇1	◇1
Havant	d	22 54			22 58	23 17			23 43	23 54
Bedhampton	d				23 01				23 45	
Hilsea	d			23 00			23 28			
Fratton	d	23 03		23 08	23 12	23 26	23 33	23 43	23 54	00 03
Portsmouth & Southsea	a	23 07		23 11	23 15	23 29	23 36	23 46	23 57	00 06
	d	23 08		23 12	23 16	23 30		23 47	23 58	00 07
Portsmouth Harbour ⛴	a	23 11		23 15	23 20	23 33		23 50	00 01	00 10

Table T157-R

Mondays to Fridays

16 December to 15 May

Portsmouth Harbour - Havant
(Complete service)

		SW	SW	SW	SW	SW		SN	SW	SW	SN	GW	SN	SW	SW	SW		SN	SW	SW	SW	GW	SW	SN	GW
		◇1	◇1	1	◇1	◇1 🛒		1	◇1	◇1	1	■		◇1 🛒	1	◇1			◇1 🛒	◇1	◇1		◇1 🛒		◇
Portsmouth Harbour ⛴	d	04 25	05 00		05 12	05 19		05 28	05 43	05 50	05 57	06 01	06 12	06 15		06 23		06 32	06 43	06 50		07 09	07 14	07 18	07 21
Portsmouth & Southsea	a	04 28	05 03		05 15	05 22		05 31	05 46	05 53	06 00	06 04	06 15	06 18		06 26		06 35	06 46	06 53		07 12	07 17	07 21	07 24
	d	04 30	05 05	05 13	05 17	05 24		05 32	05 48	05 55	06 01	06 05	06 16	06 20	06 23	06 28		06 36	06 48	06 55	06 58	07 13	07 18	07 22	07 25
Fratton	d	04 34	05 09	05 17	05 21	05 28		05 36	05 52	05 59	06 05	06a08	06 20	06 24	06 27	06 32		06 40	06 52	06 59	07 03	07 17	07 22	07 26	07a29
Hilsea	d	04 38	05a13	05a21		05 32		05 40	05a56	06 03			06 24		06a31	06a36				07a03	07 07			07 30	
Bedhampton	d	04 43				05 37		05 45		06 08			06 29								07 12			07 35	
Havant	a	04 45			05 29	05 39		05 47		06 10	06 14		06 31	06 34				06 50	07 00		07 15	07 25	07 31	07 38	

		SW		SN	SW	SW	SW	SW	SN	SW	SN	SW		SW	GW	SN	SW	SW	SN	SW	SN	SW		SW	GW
		◇1			◇1	1	◇1 🛒	◇1		◇1	1	◇1 🛒		◇1	◇		1	◇1 🛒		◇1	1	◇1 🛒		◇1	◇
Portsmouth Harbour ⛴	d	07 24			07 31	07 35	07 45	07 54		08 05		08 15		08 19	08 23	08 29		08 45		08 59	09 11	09 15		09 19	09 23
Portsmouth & Southsea	a	07 27			07 34	07 38	07 48	07 57		08 08		08 18		08 22	08 26	08 32		08 48		09 02	09 14	09 18		09 22	09 26
	d	07 28		07 33	07 36	07 39	07 50	07 58	08 01	08 09	08 14	08 20		08 24	08 27	08 33	08 38	08 50	08 57	09 04	09 15	09 20		09 24	09 27
Fratton	d	07 32		07 37	07 40	07 43	07 54	08 02	08 05	08 13	08 18	08 24		08 28	08a31	08 37	08 42	08 54	09 01	09 08	09 19	09 24		09 28	09a31
Hilsea	d	07a36			07 44	07a47		08a06	08 09	08a17				08 32			08a46		09 05	09a12				09 32	
Bedhampton	d				07 49						08 25			08 37					09 12					09 37	
Havant	a			07 45	07 51		08 03		08 15		08 28	08 32		08 39		08 45		09 02	09 14		09 27	09 33		09 39	

		SN	SW	SW	SN	SW	SN	SW		SW	GW	SN	SW	SW	SN	SW	SN	SW		SW	GW	SN	SW	SW	SN
			1	◇1 🛒		◇1	1	◇1 🛒		◇1	◇		1	◇1 🛒		◇1	1	◇1 🛒		◇1	◇		1	◇1 🛒	
Portsmouth Harbour ⛴	d		09 33	09 45		09 59	10 11	10 15			10 23			10 45		10 59	11 11	11 15			11 23	11 29		11 45	
Portsmouth & Southsea	a		09 36	09 48		10 02	10 14	10 18			10 26			10 48		11 02	11 14	11 18			11 26	11 32		11 48	
	d	09 33	09 38	09 50	09 57	10 04	10 15	10 20		10 24	10 27	10 33	10 38	10 50	10 57	11 04	11 15	11 20		11 24	11 27	11 33	11 38	11 50	11 57
Fratton	d	09 37	09 42	09 54	10 01	10 08	10 19	10 24		10 28	10a31	10 37	10 42	10 54	11 01	11 08	11 19	11 24		11 28	11a31	11 37	11 42	11 54	12 01
Hilsea	d		09a46		10 05	10a12				10 32			10a46		11 05	11a12				11 32			11a46		12 05
Bedhampton	d				10 11					10 37					11 10					11 37					12 10
Havant	a	09 45		10 03	10 14		10 27	10 32		10 39		10 45		11 03	11 13		11 27	11 32		11 39		11 45		12 03	12 13

Table T157-R

Mondays to Fridays

16 December to 15 May

Portsmouth Harbour - Havant
(Complete service)

		SW	SN	SW		SW	GW	SN	SW	SW	SN	SW	SN	SW		SW	GW	SN	SW	SW	SN	SW	SN	SW	
		◇1	1	◇1 🛒		◇1	◇		1	◇1 🛒		◇1	1	◇1 🛒		◇1	◇		1	◇1 🛒		◇1	1	◇1 🛒	
Portsmouth Harbour ⛴	d	11 59	12 11	12 15			12 23	12 29		12 45		12 59	13 11	13 15			13 23	13 29		13 45		13 59	14 11	14 15	
Portsmouth & Southsea	a	12 02	12 14	12 18			12 26	12 32		12 48		13 02	13 14	13 18			13 26	13 32		13 48		14 02	14 14	14 18	
	d	12 04	12 15	12 20		12 24	12 27	12 33	12 38	12 50	12 57	13 04	13 15	13 20		13 24	13 27	13 33	13 38	13 50	13 57	14 04	14 15	14 20	
Fratton	d	12 08	12 19	12 24		12 28	12a31	12 37	12 42	12 54	13 01	13 08	13 19	13 24		13 28	13a31	13 37	13 42	13 54	14 01	14 08	14 19	14 24	
Hilsea	d	12a12				12 32			12a46		13 05	13a12				13 32			13a46		14 05	14a12			
Bedhampton	d					12 37					13 11					13 37					14 10				
Havant	a		12 27	12 32		12 39		12 45		13 03	13 13		13 27	13 32		13 39		13 45		14 03	14 13		14 27	14 32	

		SW	GW	SN	SW	SW	SN	SW	SN	SW		SW	GW	SN	SW	SW	SN	SW	SN	SW		SW	GW	SN	SW
		◇1	■		1	◇1 🛒		◇1	1	◇1 🛒		◇1	■		1	◇1 🛒		◇1	1	◇1 🛒		◇1	■		1
Portsmouth Harbour ⛴	d		14 23	14 29		14 45		14 59	15 11	15 15			15 23	15 29		15 45		15 59	16 11	16 15			16 23		16 33
Portsmouth & Southsea	a		14 26	14 32		14 48		15 02	15 14	15 18			15 26	15 32		15 48		16 02	16 14	16 18			16 26		16 36
	d	14 24	14 27	14 33	14 38	14 50	14 57	15 04	15 15	15 20		15 24	15 27	15 33	15 38	15 50	15 57	16 04	16 15	16 20		16 24	16 27	16 33	16 38
Fratton	d	14 28	14a31	14 37	14 42	14 54	15 01	15 08	15 19	15 24		15 28	15a31	15 37	15 42	15 54	16 01	16 08	16 19	16 24		16 28	16a31	16 37	16 42
Hilsea	d	14 32			14a46		15 05	15a12				15 32			15a46		16 05	16a12				16 32			16a46
Bedhampton	d	14 37					15 13					15 37					16 10					16 37			
Havant	a	14 39		14 45		15 03	15 16		15 27	15 32		15 39		15 45		16 03	16 13		16 27	16 32		16 39		16 45	

		SW	SN	SW	SN	SW		SW	GW	SN	SW	SW	SW	SN	SW	SN		SW	SW	GW	SN	SW	SW	SN	SW
		◇1 🛒		◇1	1	◇1 🛒		◇1	◇		1	◇1 🛒	1		◇1	1		◇1 🛒	◇1	◇		1	◇1 🛒		◇1
Portsmouth Harbour ⛴	d	16 45		16 59	17 11	17 15		17 19	17 23		17 33	17 45	17 49		17 59			18 15	18 19	18 24			18 45		18 59
Portsmouth & Southsea	a	16 48		17 02	17 14	17 18		17 23	17 26		17 36	17 48	17 53		18 02			18 18	18 22	18 27			18 48		19 02
	d	16 50	16 57	17 04	17 15	17 19		17 24	17 27	17 33	17 38	17 50	17 54	17 57	18 04	18 15		18 20	18 24	18 29	18 33	18 38	18 50	18 57	19 04
Fratton	d	16 54	17 01	17 08	17 19	17 24		17 28	17a31	17 37	17 42	17 54	17 58	18 02	18 08	18 19		18 24	18 28	18a32	18 37	18 42	18 54	19 01	19 08
Hilsea	d		17 05	17a12				17 32			17a46		18a02	18 06	18a12				18 32			18a46		19 05	19a12
Bedhampton	d		17 10					17 37						18 11					18 37					19 10	
Havant	a	17 03	17 13		17 27	17 33		17 39		17 45		18 03		18 13		18 27		18 33	18 39		18 46		19 02	19 13	

		SN		SW	SW	GW	SN	SW	SW	SN	SW	SN		SW	SW	GW	SN	SW	SW	SN	SW	SN		SW	SW
		1		◇1	◇1	◇		1	◇1		◇1	1		◇1	◇1	◇		1	◇1		◇1	1		◇1	◇1
Portsmouth Harbour ⛴	d	19 11		19 15	19 19	19 23			19 45		19 59	20 11		20 15		20 23			20 45		20 59	21 11		21 15	
Portsmouth & Southsea	a	19 14		19 18	19 23	19 26			19 48		20 02	20 14		20 18		20 26			20 48		21 02	21 14		21 18	
	d	19 15		19 20	19 24	19 27	19 33	19 38	19 50	19 57	20 04	20 15		20 20	20 24	20 27	20 33	20 38	20 50	20 57	21 04	21 15		21 20	21 24
Fratton	d	19 19		19 24	19 28	19a31	19 37	19 42	19 54	20 01	20 08	20 19		20 24	20 28	20a31	20 37	20 42	20 54	21 01	21 08	21 19		21 24	21 28
Hilsea	d				19 32			19a46		20 05	20a12				20 32			20a46		21 05	21a12				21 32
Bedhampton	d				19 37					20 10					20 37					21 11					21 37
Havant	a	19 27		19 33	19 39		19 45		20 03	20 13		20 27		20 32	20 39		20 45		21 02	21 14		21 29		21 32	21 39

		GW	SN	SW	SW	SN	SW	SW		SN	SN	SW	SW
				1	1		◇1	1				1	1
Portsmouth Harbour ⛴	d	21 23			21 54	22 15	22 19	22 33		22 40	23 16	23 19	23 24
Portsmouth & Southsea	a	21 26			21 57	22 18	22 22	22 37		22 43	23 19	23 22	23 28
	d	21 27	21 33	21 38	21 59	22 19	22 24	22 38		22 44	23 20	23 24	23 29
Fratton	d	21a31	21 37	21 42	22 03	22 23	22 28	22 42		22 48	23 24	23 28	23 33
Hilsea	d			21a46	22a07	22 27	22 32	22a46		22 52	23 28	23 32	23a37
Bedhampton	d					22 32	22 38			22 57	23 33	23 37	
Havant	a		21 46			22 34	22 40			22 59	23 35	23 39	

Table T157-R

Portsmouth Harbour - Havant

(Complete service)

Saturdays

21 December to 16 May

		SW	SN	SW	SW	SW		SW	SN	GW	SN	SW	SW	SN	SW	SW		GW	SN	SW	SN	SW	SW	GW	SN
		◇■	■	■	◇■	■		◇■		◇	■	◇■	◇■		■	◇■ 🍴				◇■	■	◇■ 🍴	◇■	◇ 🍴	
Portsmouth Harbour ⛴	d	04 43			05 19	05 40		05 48		06 08	06 11	06 15		06 29		06 45		06 50		06 59	07 11	07 15		07 23	07 29
Portsmouth & Southsea	a	04 46			05 22	05 43		05 51		06 11	06 15	06 18		06 32		06 48		06 53		07 02	07 14	07 18		07 26	07 32
	d	04 48	04 55	05 16	05 24	05 44		05 53	05 57	06 12	06 15	06 20	06 24	06 33	06 38	06 50		06 54	06 57	07 04	07 15	07 20	07 24	07 27	07 33
Fratton	d	04 52	04 59	05 20	05 28	05a47		05 57	06 01	06a15	06 19	06 24	06 28	06 37	06 42	06 54		06 58	07 02	07 08	07 19	07 24	07 28	07a31	07 37
Hilsea	d	04 56		05a24	05 32			06a01	06 05				06 32		06a46				07 06	07a12			07 32		
Bedhampton	d	05 01			05 37				06 10				06 37						07 11				07 37		
Havant	a	05 03	05 07		05 39				06 13		06 27	06 32	06 39	06 45		07 03		07 07	07 14		07 27	07 32	07 40		07 45

		SW		SW	SN	SW	SN	SW	SW	GW	SN	SW		SW	SN	SW	SN	SW	SW	GW	SN	SW		SW	SN
		■		◇■ 🍴		◇■	■	◇■ 🍴	◇■	◇ 🍴		■		◇■ 🍴		◇■	■	◇■ 🍴	◇■	◇ 🍴		■		◇■ 🍴	
Portsmouth Harbour ⛴	d			07 45		07 59	08 11	08 15		08 23	08 29			08 45		08 59	09 11	09 15		09 23	09 29			09 45	
Portsmouth & Southsea	a			07 48		08 02	08 14	08 18		08 26	08 32			08 48		09 02	09 14	09 18		09 26	09 32			09 48	
	d	07 38		07 50	07 57	08 04	08 15	08 20	08 24	08 27	08 33	08 38		08 50	08 57	09 04	09 15	09 20	09 24	09 27	09 33	09 38		09 50	09 57
Fratton	d	07 42		07 54	08 01	08 08	08 19	08 24	08 28	08a31	08 37	08 42		08 54	09 01	09 08	09 19	09 24	09 28	09a31	09 37	09 42		09 54	10 01
Hilsea	d	07a46			08 05	08a12			08 32			08a46			09 05	09a12			09 32			09a46			10 05
Bedhampton	d				08 10				08 37						09 10				09 37						10 10
Havant	a			08 03	08 13		08 27	08 32	08 39		08 45			09 03	09 13		09 27	09 32	09 39		09 45			10 03	10 13

		SW	SN	SW	SW	GW	SN	SW		SW	SN	SW	SN	SW	SW	GW	SN	SW		SW	SN	SW	SN	SW	SW
		◇■	■	◇■ 🍴	◇■	◇ 🍴		■		◇■ 🍴		◇■	■	◇■ 🍴	◇■	◇		■		◇■ 🍴		◇■	■	◇■ 🍴	◇■
Portsmouth Harbour ⛴	d	09 59	10 11	10 15		10 23	10 29			10 45		10 59	11 11	11 15		11 23	11 29			11 45		11 59	12 11	12 15	
Portsmouth & Southsea	a	10 02	10 14	10 18		10 26	10 32			10 48		11 02	11 14	11 18		11 26	11 32			11 48		12 02	12 14	12 18	
	d	10 04	10 15	10 20	10 24	10 27	10 33	10 38		10 50	10 57	11 04	11 15	11 20	11 24	11 27	11 33	11 38		11 50	11 57	12 04	12 15	12 20	12 24
Fratton	d	10 08	10 19	10 24	10 28	10a31	10 37	10 42		10 54	11 01	11 08	11 19	11 24	11 28	11a31	11 37	11 42		11 54	12 01	12 08	12 19	12 24	12 28
Hilsea	d	10a12			10 32			10a46			11 05	11a12			11 32			11a46			12 05	12a12			12 32
Bedhampton	d				10 37						11 10				11 37						12 10				12 37
Havant	a		10 27	10 32	10 39		10 45			11 03	11 13		11 27	11 32	11 39		11 45			12 03	12 13		12 27	12 32	12 39

		GW	SN	SW		SW	SN	SW	SN	SW	SW	GW	SN	SW		SW	SN	SW	SN	SW	SW	GW	SN	SW	
		◇		■		◇■ 🍴		◇■	■	◇■ 🍴	◇■	◇		■		◇■ 🍴		◇■	■	◇■ 🍴	◇■	◇		■	
Portsmouth Harbour ⛴	d	12 23	12 29			12 45		12 59	13 11	13 15		13 23	13 29			13 45		13 59	14 11	14 15		14 23	14 29		
Portsmouth & Southsea	a	12 26	12 32			12 48		13 02	13 14	13 18		13 26	13 32			13 48		14 02	14 14	14 18		14 26	14 32		
	d	12 27	12 33	12 38		12 50	12 57	13 04	13 15	13 20	13 24	13 27	13 33	13 38		13 50	13 57	14 04	14 15	14 20	14 24	14 27	14 33	14 38	
Fratton	d	12a31	12 37	12 42		12 54	13 01	13 08	13 19	13 24	13 28	13a31	13 37	13 42		13 54	14 01	14 08	14 19	14 24	14 28	14a31	14 37	14 42	
Hilsea	d			12a46			13 05	13a12			13 32			13a46			14 05	14a12			14 32			14a46	
Bedhampton	d						13 10				13 37						14 10				14 37				
Havant	a		12 45			13 03	13 13		13 27	13 32	13 39		13 45			14 03	14 13		14 27	14 32	14 39		14 45		

		SW	SN	SW	SN	SW	SW	GW	SN	SW		SW	SN	SW	SN	SW	SW	GW	SN	SW		SW	SN	SW	SN
		◇■ 🍴		◇■	■	◇■ 🍴	◇■	◇		■		◇■ 🍴		◇■	■	◇■ 🍴	◇■	◇		■		◇■ 🍴		◇■	■
Portsmouth Harbour ⛴	d	14 45		14 59	15 11	15 15		15 23	15 29			15 45		15 59	16 11	16 15		16 23	16 29			16 45		16 59	17 11
Portsmouth & Southsea	a	14 48		15 02	15 14	15 18		15 26	15 32			15 48		16 02	16 14	16 18		16 26	16 32			16 48		17 02	17 14
	d	14 50	14 57	15 04	15 15	15 20	15 24	15 27	15 33	15 38		15 50	15 57	16 04	16 15	16 20	16 24	16 27	16 33	16 38		16 50	16 57	17 04	17 15
Fratton	d	14 54	15 01	15 08	15 19	15 24	15 28	15a31	15 37	15 42		15 54	16 01	16 08	16 19	16 24	16 28	16a31	16 37	16 42		16 54	17 01	17 08	17 19
Hilsea	d		15 05	15a12			15 32			15a46			16 05	16a12			16 32			16a46			17 05	17a12	
Bedhampton	d		15 14				15 37						16 10				16 37						17 10		
Havant	a	15 03	15 16		15 27	15 32	15 39		15 45			16 03	16 13		16 27	16 32	16 39		16 45			17 03	17 13		17 27

		SW	SW	GW	SN	SW		SW	SN	SW	SN	SW	SW	GW	SN	SW		SW	SN	SW	SN	SW	SW	GW	SN
		◇■	◇■	◇		■		◇■ 🍴		◇■	■	◇■	◇■	◇		■		◇■		◇■	■	◇■	◇■	◇	
Portsmouth Harbour ⛴	d	17 15		17 23	17 29	17 33		17 45		17 59	18 11	18 15		18 23	18 29			18 45		18 59	19 11	19 15		19 23	19 29
Portsmouth & Southsea	a	17 18		17 26	17 32	17 36		17 48		18 02	18 14	18 18		18 26	18 32			18 48		19 02	19 14	19 18		19 26	19 32
	d	17 20	17 24	17 27	17 33	17 38		17 50	17 57	18 04	18 15	18 20	18 24	18 27	18 33	18 38		18 50	18 57	19 04	19 15	19 20	19 24	19 27	19 33
Fratton	d	17 24	17 28	17a31	17 37	17 42		17 54	18 01	18 08	18 19	18 24	18 28	18a31	18 37	18 42		18 54	19 01	19 08	19 19	19 24	19 28	19a31	19 37
Hilsea	d		17 32			17a46			18 05	18a12			18 32			18a46			19 05	19a12			19 32		
Bedhampton	d		17 37						18 10				18 37						19 10				19 37		
Havant	a	17 32	17 39		17 45			18 04	18 13		18 27	18 32	18 39		18 45			19 03	19 13		19 27	19 32	19 39		19 45

		SW		SW	SN	SW	SN	SW	SW	GW	SN	SW		SW	SN	SW	SN	SW	GW	SW	SN	SW		SN	SW
		■		◇■		◇■	■	◇■	◇■	◇		■		◇■		◇■	■	◇■	■	■		■			◇■
Portsmouth Harbour ⛴	d			19 45		19 59	20 11	20 15		20 23	20 29			20 45		20 59	21 11	21 19	21 23		21 40	21 54		22 15	22 19
Portsmouth & Southsea	a			19 48		20 02	20 14	20 18		20 26	20 32			20 48		21 02	21 14	21 22	21 26		21 43	21 57		22 18	22 22
	d	19 38		19 50	19 57	20 04	20 15	20 20	20 24	20 27	20 33	20 38		20 48	20 57	21 04	21 15	21 24	21 27	21 38	21 44	21 59		22 19	22 24
Fratton	d	19 42		19 54	20 01	20 08	20 19	20 24	20 28	20a31	20 37	20 42		20 52	21 01	21 08	21 19	21 28	21a30	21 42	21 48	22 03		22 23	22 28
Hilsea	d	19a46			20 05	20a12			20 32			20a46			21 05	21a12		21 32		21a46	21 52	22a07		22 27	22 32
Bedhampton	d				20 10				20 37						21 10			21 37			21 57			22 32	22 38
Havant	a			20 03	20 13		20 27	20 32	20 39		20 45			21 03	21 13		21 27	21 39			21 59			22 35	22 40

		SW	SN	SN	SW	SW
		■			■	■
Portsmouth Harbour ⛴	d	22 33	22 40	23 15	23 19	23 24
Portsmouth & Southsea	a	22 36	22 43	23 18	23 22	23 27
	d	22 38	22 44	23 19	23 24	23 28
Fratton	d	22 42	22 48	23 23	23 28	23 32
Hilsea	d	22a46	22 52	23 27	23 32	23a36
Bedhampton	d		22 57	23 32	23 37	
Havant	a		22 59	23 34	23 39	

Table T157-R

Portsmouth Harbour - Havant

(Complete service)

Sundays

15 December to 10 May

		SW	SW	SN	SW	SW		SW	SW	SN	SN	SW	SW	SW	SW	SN		GW	SN	SW	SW	SW	SW	SN	SN
		■	◇■		◇■	◇■		■	◇■	■		◇■	◇■	■	◇■	■		■		◇■ 🍴	◇■ 🍴	■	◇■	■	
Portsmouth Harbour ⛴	d	06 37	06 48	07 14	07 17	07 32			07 48	08 01	08 14	08 17	08 32		08 48	09 01		09 08	09 14	09 17	09 32		09 48	10 01	10 14
Portsmouth & Southsea	a	06 40	06 51	07 17	07 20	07 35			07 51	08 04	08 17	08 20	08 35		08 51	09 04		09 11	09 17	09 20	09 35		09 51	10 04	10 17
	d	06 42	06 53	07 18	07 22	07 37		07 42	07 53	08 05	08 18	08 22	08 37	08 42	08 53	09 05		09 12	09 18	09 22	09 37	09 42	09 53	10 05	10 18
Fratton	d	06 46	06 57	07 22	07 26	07 41		07 46	07 57	08 09	08 22	08 26	08 41	08 46	08 57	09 09		09a15	09 22	09 26	09 41	09 46	09 57	10 09	10 22
Hilsea	d	06a50			07a30			07a50				08a30		08a50						09a30		09a50			
Bedhampton	d		07 04	07 30					08 04		08 30				09 04				09 30				10 04		10 30
Havant	a		07 07	07 33		07 49			08 07	08 17	08 33		08 49		09 07	09 17			09 33		09 50		10 07	10 17	10 33

		SW		SW	SW	SW	SN	GW	SN	SW	SW	SW		SW	SN	SN	SW	SW	SW	SW	SN	GW		SN	SW
		◇■ 🍴		◇■ 🍴	■	◇■	■	◇		◇■ 🍴	◇■ 🍴	■		◇■	■		◇■ 🍴	◇■ 🍴	■	◇■	■	◇			◇■ 🍴
Portsmouth Harbour ⛴	d	10 17		10 32		10 48	11 01	11 08	11 14	11 17	11 32			11 48	12 01	12 13	12 17	12 32		12 48	13 01	13 08		13 14	13 17
Portsmouth & Southsea	a	10 20		10 35		10 51	11 04	11 11	11 17	11 20	11 35			11 51	12 04	12 16	12 20	12 35		12 51	13 04	13 11		13 17	13 20
	d	10 22		10 37	10 42	10 53	11 05	11 12	11 18	11 22	11 37	11 42		11 53	12 05	12 17	12 22	12 37	12 42	12 53	13 05	13 12		13 18	13 22
Fratton	d	10 26		10 41	10 46	10 57	11 09	11a15	11 22	11 26	11 41	11 46		11 57	12 09	12 21	12 26	12 41	12 46	12 57	13 09	13a15		13 22	13 26
Hilsea	d	10a30			10a50					11a30		11a50					12a30		12a50						13a30
Bedhampton	d					11 04			11 30					12 04		12 29				13 04				13 30	
Havant	a			10 49		11 07	11 17		11 33		11 49			12 07	12 17	12 32		12 50		13 07	13 17			13 33	

		SW	SW	SW	SN	GW	SN	SW		SW	SW	SW	SN	GW	SN	SW	SW	SW		SW	SN	GW	SN	SW	SW
		◇■ 🍴	■	◇■	■	◇		◇■ 🍴		◇■ 🍴	■	◇■	■	■		◇■ 🍴	◇■ 🍴	■		◇■	■	◇		◇■ 🍴	◇■ 🍴
Portsmouth Harbour ⛴	d	13 32		13 48	14 01	14 08	14 14	14 17		14 32		14 48	15 01	15 08	15 14	15 17	15 32			15 48	16 01	16 08	16 14	16 17	
Portsmouth & Southsea	a	13 35		13 51	14 04	14 11	14 17	14 20		14 35		14 51	15 04	15 11	15 17	15 20	15 35			15 51	16 04	16 11	16 17	16 20	
	d	13 37	13 42	13 53	14 05	14 12	14 18	14 22		14 37	14 42	14 53	15 05	15 12	15 18	15 22	15 37	15 42		15 53	16 05	16 12	16 18	16 22	16 26
Fratton	d	13 41	13 46	13 57	14 09	14a15	14 22	14 26		14 41	14 46	14 57	15 09	15a15	15 22	15 26	15 41	15 46		15 57	16 09	16a15	16 22	16 26	16 31
Hilsea	d		13a50					14a30			14a50					15a30		15a50						16a30	
Bedhampton	d			14 04			14 30					15 04			15 30					16 04			16 30		
Havant	a	13 49		14 07	14 17		14 33			14 49		15 07	15 17		15 33		15 49			16 07	16 17		16 33		16 39

		SW	SW	SW		SN	GW	SW	SW	SW	SW	SW	SN	GW		SN	SW	SW	SW	SW	SW	SN	GW	SW	
		◇■ 🍴	■	◇■		■	◇	◇■	◇■ 🍴	◇■ 🍴	■	◇■	■	◇			◇■	◇■ 🍴	◇■ 🍴	■	◇■	■	◇	◇■	
Portsmouth Harbour ⛴	d	16 32		16 48		17 01	17 08	17 17		17 32		17 48	18 01	18 08		18 14	18 17		18 32		18 48	19 01	19 08	19 17	
Portsmouth & Southsea	a	16 35		16 51		17 04	17 11	17 20		17 35		17 51	18 04	18 11		18 17	18 20		18 35		18 51	19 04	19 11	19 20	
	d	16 37	16 42	16 53		17 05	17 12	17 22	17 26	17 37	17 42	17 53	18 05	18 12		18 18	18 22	18 26	18 37	18 42	18 53	19 05	19 12	19 22	
Fratton	d	16 41	16 46	16 57		17 09	17a15	17 26	17 31	17 41	17 46	17 57	18 09	18a15		18 22	18 26	18 31	18 41	18 46	18 57	19 09	19a15	19 26	
Hilsea	d		16a50					17a30			17a50						18a30			18a50				19a30	
Bedhampton	d			17 04								18 04				18 30					19 04				
Havant	a	16 49		17 07		17 17			17 39	17 49		18 07	18 17			18 33		18 39	18 49		19 07	19 17			

		SW	SW	SW	SN	GW	SN	SW	SW	SW		SW	SN	SN	SW	SW	SW	SW	SN	GW		SN	SW	SW	SW
		◇■	■	◇■	■	◇		◇■	◇■	■		◇■	■		◇■	◇■	■	◇■					■	◇■	■
Portsmouth Harbour ⛴	d	19 32		19 48	20 01	20 08	20 14	20 17	20 32			20 48	21 01	21 14	21 17	21 32		21 48	22 01	22 05		22 14	22 17	22 32	
Portsmouth & Southsea	a	19 35		19 51	20 04	20 11	20 17	20 20	20 35			20 51	21 04	21 17	21 20	21 35		21 52	22 04	22 11		22 17	22 21	22 35	
	d	19 37	19 42	19 53	20 05	20 12	20 18	20 22	20 37	20 42		20 53	21 05	21 18	21 22	21 37	21 42	21 53	22 05	22 12		22 18	22 22	22 37	22 42
Fratton	d	19 41	19 46	19 57	20 09	20a15	20 22	20 26	20 41	20 46		20 57	21 09	21 22	21 26	21 41	21 46	21 57	22 09	22a15		22 22	22 26	22 41	22 46
Hilsea	d		19a50					20a30		20a50					21a30		21a50						22a30		22a50
Bedhampton	d			20 05			20 30					21 04		21 30				22 04							
Havant	a	19 49		20 07	20 17		20 33		20 49			21 07	21 17	21 33		21 49		22 07	22 17			22 30		22 49	

		SW	SN	SW
		■		■
Portsmouth Harbour ⛴	d	22 48	23 01	23 17
Portsmouth & Southsea	a	22 51	23 04	23 20
	d	22 52	23 05	23 22
Fratton	d	22 56	23 09	23 26
Hilsea	d			23a30
Bedhampton	d	23 03		
Havant	a	23 06	23 18	

Table T158-F

Mondays to Fridays

16 December to 15 May

London - Basingstoke, Southampton, Romsey, Bournemouth and Weymouth

Miles	Miles	Miles			SW	SW	SW	SW	SW	SW	SW	SW	SW	SW	SW	SW	SW	SW	SW	SW	SW	SW	SW
					MX	MX	MO	MO	MX	MO	MX	MO	MX	MX	MO	MX	MO	MO	MX	MX	MX	MX	MO
					◇1 (trolley)	◇1	◇1	◇1	◇1 (trolley)	◇1 (trolley)	◇1	1	1	1	◇1 (trolley)	◇1	◇1	◇1 (trolley)	◇1	◇1	1	◇1	◇1
0	—	—	**London Waterloo 15** ⊖	d																		00 05	00 50
4	—	—	**Clapham Junction 10**	d																		00u12	00 57
24¼	—	—	**Woking**	d																00 03	00 28	00 37	01 18
33¼	—	—	Farnborough (Main)	d										00 11						00 14	00 41		
36½	—	—	Fleet	d								00 04		00 16						00 20	00 47		
—	—	—	Reading 7	d																			
47¾	—	—	**Basingstoke**	a								00 21		00 35						00 33	01 06	00 55	
—	—	—		d																00 35		00 56	
58	—	—	Micheldever	d												00 03							
66½	—	—	**Winchester**	d											00 07	00 13	00 14			00 51		01 13	
69¾	—	—	Shawford	d											00 12								
—	0	0	**Romsey**	d																			
—	—	5¼	Chandlers Ford	d														←					
73½	0	7¼	Eastleigh 3	a											00 17	00 22	00 23	00 17		00 59		01 21	
—	—	—		d							00 02				00 30	00 23	00 24	00 30	00 30	01 00		01 22	
—	4½	—	Hedge End	d											↦			00s36	00s36				
—	5½	—	Botley	d														00s39	00s39				
—	11	—	Fareham	d														00s47	00s47				
—	14¼	—	Portchester	d														00s53	00s53				
—	16¾	—	Cosham	d														00s57	00s57				
—	18¼	—	Hilsea	a																			
—	20½	—	Fratton	a														01s05	01s05				02s10
—	21½	—	**Portsmouth & Southsea**	a														01s08	01 09				02s14
—	22¼	—	**Portsmouth Harbour** ⛴	a														01 12					02 19
75	—	—	**Southampton Airport Pkwy** ✈	d							00 06					00 28	00 28			01 05		01 26	
75¾	—	—	Swaythling	d																			
77¼	—	—	St Denys	d												00s32	00s32						
79¼	—	—	**Southampton Central** ⛴	a							00 13					00 37	00 37			01 12		01 35	
—	—	—		d						00 03						00 38	00 40					01 37	
80¼	—	—	Millbrook (Hants)	d																			
82	0	—	Redbridge	d																			
—	6	—	**Romsey**	d																			
—	9¾	—	Mottisfont & Dunbridge	d									00 04										
—	13½	—	Dean	d									00 09										
—	22½	—	**Salisbury**	a									00 24										
82½	—	—	Totton	d												00s43	00s45					01s42	
85½	—	—	Ashurst New Forest	d																			
88	—	—	Beaulieu Road	d																			
92¾	—	—	**Brockenhurst 3**	a						00 16						00s54	00s56					01s53	
—	—	—		d					00 05	00 17													
95½	—	—	Sway	d																			
98½	—	—	New Milton	d				00 04		00 24						01s02	01s04					02s00	
101	—	—	Hinton Admiral	d	00 02			00 08															
104¼	—	—	Christchurch	d	00 07			00 13								01s09	01s11					02s07	
106¼	—	—	Pokesdown	d	00 11			00 17								01s13	01s15					02s11	
108	—	—	**Bournemouth**	a	00 15			00 21	00 21	00 34						01 17	01 19					02 15	
—	—	—		d	00 16			00 22	00 22	00 37						01 18	01 20						
110¾	—	—	Branksome	d	00 21			00 27	00 27	00 43						01s23	01s25						
112	—	—	Parkstone (Dorset)	d	00 24			00 30	00 30	00 46						01s26	01s28						
113¾	—	—	**Poole 4**	a	00 28			00 34	00 35	00 51						01 30	01 32						
—	—	—		d																			
116	—	—	Hamworthy	d																			
118¾	—	—	Holton Heath	d																			
120¾	—	—	Wareham	d			00 03																
125¾	—	—	Wool	d			00 10																
130¼	—	—	Moreton (Dorset)	d		00 04	00 16																
135¾	—	—	**Dorchester South**	d		00 12	00 24																
—	—	—	Dorchester West	d																			
140½	—	—	Upwey	d		00 18	00 31																
142¾	—	—	**Weymouth**	a		00 23	00 36																

For services from Brockenhurst - Lymington refer to Table T159

Table T158-F

Mondays to Fridays

16 December to 15 May

London - Basingstoke, Southampton, Romsey, Bournemouth and Weymouth

		SW	SW	SW	SW	SW	SW	SW	SW	GW	SW	SW	SW	SW	SW	SW	XC	SW	SW	SW	SW	SW	SW
		MO	MX																				
		◇1	◇1	1	1	1	1	1	1	◇	◇1	◇1	1	1	1	1	◇1 (trolley)	◇1	◇1	1	◇1	◇1	◇1
London Waterloo 15 ⊖	d	01 05	01 05								05 30							06 12	06 30			06 42	07 03
Clapham Junction 10	d	01 15	01 15								05u37							06u19	06u37			06u49	07u10
Woking	d	01 49	01 49								06 01					06 19		06 51	06 57			07 19	07 30
Farnborough (Main)	d	01s58	01s58													06 33		07 05				07 33	
Fleet	d	02s04	02s04													06 38		07 10				07 38	
Reading 7	d																				←		
Basingstoke	a	02s16	02s16								06 20					06 58		07 28	07 16		07 28	07 56	07 48
	d						05 40				06 21			06 44		07 00		07 30	07 18		07 30	08 00	07 50
Micheldever	d						05 50									07 10		↦			07 41	↦	
Winchester	d	02s33	02s33				05 59		06 18		06 38			07 00		07 19			07 35		07 50		08 06
Shawford	d								06 23					07 05							07 55		
Romsey	d							05 58							07 07					07 13			
Chandlers Ford	d							06 06							07 14								
Eastleigh 3	a	02s42	02s42				06 07	06 11	06 28		06 47			07 12	07 20	07 27			07 44	07 49	08 00		
	d			06 01			06 08	06 12	06 30		06 48		07 02	07 13	07 21	07 28			07 45	07 50	08 02		
Hedge End	d			06 07					06 36				07 08			07 34							
Botley	d			06 11					06 40				07 12			07 38							
Fareham	d			06 19					06 48				07 21			07 47							
Portchester	d			06 24					06 53				07 26			07 52							
Cosham	d			06 29					06 58				07 30			07 57							
Hilsea	a			06 34					07 03				07 35			08 04							
Fratton	a			06 40					07 07				07 39			08 08							
Portsmouth & Southsea	a			06 44					07 11				07 43			08 13							
Portsmouth Harbour ⛴	a			06 49					07 17				07 48			08 18							
Southampton Airport Pkwy ✈	d	02s46	02s46				06 13	06 16			06 53			07 17	07 26				07 49		08 06		08 15
Swaythling	d						06 15	06 18						07 20	07 29						08 09		
St Denys	d	02s51	02s51				06 18	06 21						07 24	07 32						08 12		
Southampton Central ⛴	a	02 56	02 57				06 25	06 29			07 00			07 29	07 37				07 57		08 17		08 25
	d						06 26	06 31			07 02	07 19		07 30	07 38		07 56		07 59		08 18		08 27
Millbrook (Hants)	d							06 33				07 21			07 41						08 21		
Redbridge	d							06 37				07 25			07 45						08 24		
Romsey	d							06 45							07 53					08a03			
Mottisfont & Dunbridge	d							06 50							07 58								
Dean	d							06 55							08 03								
Salisbury	a							07 08							08 16								
Totton	d						06 32				07 07	07 28		07 36					08 04		08 27		08 33
Ashurst New Forest	d						06 36					07 32							08 09		08 32		
Beaulieu Road	d											07 37							08 13				
Brockenhurst 3	a						06 44				07 18	07 43		07 49			08 09		08 19		08 40		08 45
	d					06 15	06 45				07 18	07 44		08 00			08 10		08 20		08 41		08 46
Sway	d					06 20	06 49				07 23	07 48							08 24				08 51
New Milton	d					06 25	06 54				07 28	07 53							08 29				08 56
Hinton Admiral	d					06 29	06 58				07 32	07 57							08 33				09 00
Christchurch	d					06 34	07 03				07 37	08 02							08 38				09 05
Pokesdown	d					06 37	07 07				07 40	08 06							08 42				09 08
Bournemouth	a					06 41	07 11				07 44	08 10		08 15			08 24		08 46		08 55		09 12
	d				06 11	06 44	07 12				07 46	08 11							08 47		08 57		09 14
Branksome	d				06 16	06 49	07 17				07 51	08 16							08 52		09a02		09 19
Parkstone (Dorset)	d				06 19	06 52	07 20				07 54	08 19							08 55				09 22
Poole 4	a				06 23	06 55	07 24				07 57	08 23							08 59				09 25
	d				06 24	06 57	07 25				07 58	08 24							09 00				09 26
Hamworthy	d				06 29	07 02	07 30				08 03	08 29							09 05				09 31
Holton Heath	d				06 33	07 06	07 34				08 07	08 33											09 35
Wareham	d				06 38	07 11	07 39				08 12	08 38							09 12				09 40
Wool	d				06 44	07 17	07 45				08 19	08 44							09 19				09 47
Moreton (Dorset)	d				06 50	07 23	07 51				08 25	08 50							09 25				09 53
Dorchester South	d				06 58	07 31	07 59				08 33	08 58							09 33				10 01
Dorchester West	d									08 07													
Upwey	d				07 05	07 38	08 06			08 14	08 39	09 05							09 39				10 07
Weymouth	a				07 09	07 42	08 10			08 19	08 44	09 09							09 44				10 12

For services from Brockenhurst - Lymington refer to Table T159

Table T158-F

Mondays to Fridays
16 December to 15 May

London - Basingstoke, Southampton, Romsey, Bournemouth and Weymouth

		SW	SW ◇1	XC ◇1 ⚒	SW ◇1 A ⚒	SW B	SW	GW ◇	SW ◇1 ⚒	XC ◇1 ⚒	SW ◇1 A ⚒	SW ◇1 ⚒	SW 1	SW ◇1	XC ◇1 ⚒	SW ◇1 A ⚒	SW ◇1 ⚒	GW	SN 1	SW 1	SW ◇1	SW ◇1 A ⚒	SW ◇1	SW 1
London Waterloo 15 ⊖	d				07 35				07 39		08 05			08 08		08 35					08 39	09 05		
Clapham Junction 10	d								07u45		08u12										08u46	09u12		
Woking	d				08 00									08 34		09 00								
Farnborough (Main)	d								08 13					08 45							09 13			
Fleet	d								08 19												09 19			
Reading 7	d		←	07 52						08 19					08 48			08 55						
Basingstoke	a		07 56	08 11	08 19				08 32	08 41	08 47			08 58	09 10			09 16			09 32	09 47		
	d		08 00	08 12	08 20				08 33	08 42	08 49			09 00	09 12						09 33	09 49		
Micheldever	d		08 10											09 10										
Winchester	d		08 19	08 27	08 37				08 50	08 58	09 05			09 19	09 27	09 33					09 49	10 05		
Shawford	d		08 24						08 54												09 54			
Romsey	d	08 07					08 13						09 07							09 14				10 07
Chandlers Ford	d	08 14											09 14											10 14
Eastleigh 3	a	08 20	08 30		08 46		08 49		09 00				09 20	09 27						09 49	09 59			10 20
	d	08 21	08 30		08 47		08 50		09 01				09 21	09 28					09 43	09 50	10 04			10 21
Hedge End	d		08 36											09 34										
Botley	d		08 40											09 38										
Fareham	d		08 49											09 48										
Portchester	d		08 54											09 53										
Cosham	d		08 59											09 58					10a03					
Hilsea	a		09 05											10 03										
Fratton	a		09 09											10 07										
Portsmouth & Southsea	a		09 12											10 11										
Portsmouth Harbour ⛴	a		09 18											10 20										
Southampton Airport Pkwy ✈	d	08 25		08 36	08 51				09 05	09 10	09 14		09 25		09 36	09 42					10 08	10 14		10 25
Swaythling	d	08 27											09 27											10 27
St Denys	d	08 30										←	09 30										←	10 30
Southampton Central ⛴	a	08 35		08 42	08 58				09 12	09 17	09 22	09 12	09 35		09 43	09 50					10 17	10 22	10 17	10 35
	d	08 37		08 45	09 00	09 05			09 30		09 25	09 30	09 37		09 45	09 51					10 30	10 24	10 30	10 45
Millbrook (Hants)	d	08 40							→				09 40								→			10 48
Redbridge	d	08 43											09 43											10 51
Romsey	d	08 51					09a03						09 54							10a03				10 59
Mottisfont & Dunbridge	d	08 56											09 59											11 04
Dean	d	09 02											10 04											11 10
Salisbury	a	09 15											10 17											11 22
Totton	d					09 11						09 35											10 35	
Ashurst New Forest	d											09 40											10 40	
Beaulieu Road	d																←						10 44	
Brockenhurst 3	a			09 00	09 13	09 21					09 38	09 49			09 58	10 04	09 49					10 37	10 51	
	d			09 01	09 14	09 22					09 39	10 16			09 59	10 05	10 16					10 38	11 16	
Sway	d					09 26						→					10 21						→	
New Milton	d					09 31					09 46						10 26					10 45		
Hinton Admiral	d					09 35											10 30							
Christchurch	d					09 40					09 53						10 35					10 52		
Pokesdown	d					09 44					09 57						10 38					10 56		
Bournemouth	a			09 16	09 28	09 48					10 01				10 13	10 20	10 42					11 00		
	d				09 33	09 49					10 04					10 24	10 44					11 04		
Branksome	d				09 38	09 54										10 29	10 49							
Parkstone (Dorset)	d				09 41	09 57										10 32	10 52							
Poole 4	a				09 44	10 01					10 13					10 36	10 55					11 13		
	d				09 45						10 14					10 37						11 14		
Hamworthy	d				09 50						10 19					10 42						11 19		
Holton Heath	d										10 23											11 23		
Wareham	d				09 57						10 28					10 49						11 28		
Wool	d										10 35											11 35		
Moreton (Dorset)	d										10 41											11 41		
Dorchester South	d				10 13						10 54					11 05						11 49		
Dorchester West	d							10 48																
Upwey	d							10 56			11 02											11 55		
Weymouth	a				10 23			11 01			11 06					11 16						12 02		

A ⚒ to Bournemouth
B From Portsmouth Harbour

For services from Brockenhurst - Lymington refer to Table T159

Table T158-F

Mondays to Fridays
16 December to 15 May

London - Basingstoke, Southampton, Romsey, Bournemouth and Weymouth

		SW ◇1	XC ◇1 ⚒	SW 1	GW ◇	SW ◇1 A ⚒	SW ◇1	SW ◇1	XC ◇1 ⚒	SW ◇1 A ⚒	SW ◇1	SW 1	SW ◇1	XC 1 ⚒	SW ◇1 A ⚒	SW ◇1	SN 1	SW 1	SW ◇1	SW ◇1 A ⚒	SW ◇1	SW 1
London Waterloo 15 ⊖	d	09 09				09 35		09 39		10 05			10 09		10 35				10 39	11 05		
Clapham Junction 10	d							09u46		10u12									10u46	11u12		
Woking	d	09 34				10 00							10 34		11 00							
Farnborough (Main)	d	09 46						10 13					10 45						11 13			
Fleet	d							10 19											11 19			
Reading 7	d		09 49						10 19					10 50								
Basingstoke	a	09 59	10 09					10 31	10 42	10 48			10 58	11 09					11 31	11 48		
	d	10 00	10 12					10 33	10 44	10 49			11 00	11 12					11 33	11 49		
Micheldever	d	10 11											11 10									
Winchester	d	10 20	10 27			10 33		10 49	10 59	11 05			11 19	11 27	11 33				11 49	12 05		
Shawford	d							10 54											11 54			
Romsey	d			10 20								11 07						11 20				12 07
Chandlers Ford	d											11 14										12 14
Eastleigh 3	a	10 27		10 49				10 59				11 20	11 27					11 49	11 59			12 20
	d	10 28		10 50				11 00				11 21	11 28				11 41	11 50	12 00			12 21
Hedge End	d	10 36											11 34									
Botley	d	10 39											11 38									
Fareham	d	10 48											11 48									
Portchester	d	10 53											11 53									
Cosham	d	10 58											11 58				12a02					
Hilsea	a	11 03											12 03									
Fratton	a	11 07											12 07									
Portsmouth & Southsea	a	11 11											12 11									
Portsmouth Harbour ⛴	a	11 20											12 20									
Southampton Airport Pkwy ✈	d		10 36			10 42		11 05	11 09	11 14		11 25		11 36	11 42				12 05	12 14		12 25
Swaythling	d											11 27										12 27
St Denys	d										←	11 30									←	12 30
Southampton Central ⛴	a		10 43			10 49		11 12	11 17	11 22	11 12	11 36		11 43	11 49				12 12	12 21	12 12	12 36
	d		10 45			10 51		11 30		11 24	11 30	11 37		11 45	11 51				12 30	12 24	12 30	12 37
Millbrook (Hants)	d							→				11 40							→			12 40
Redbridge	d											11 43										12 43
Romsey	d			11a03								11 51						12a03				12 51
Mottisfont & Dunbridge	d											11 56										12 56
Dean	d											12 02										13 02
Salisbury	a											12 15										13 15
Totton	d										11 35										12 35	
Ashurst New Forest	d										11 40										12 40	
Beaulieu Road	d						←				11 44					←						
Brockenhurst 3	a		10 58			11 04	10 51			11 37	11 51			11 58	12 04	11 51				12 37	12 51	
	d		10 59			11 05	11 16			11 38	12 16			11 59	12 05	12 16				12 38	13 16	
Sway	d						11 21				→					12 21					→	
New Milton	d						11 26			11 45						12 26				12 45		
Hinton Admiral	d						11 30									12 30						
Christchurch	d						11 35			11 52						12 35				12 52		
Pokesdown	d						11 38			11 56						12 38				12 56		
Bournemouth	a		11 13			11 20	11 42			12 00				12 13	12 20	12 42				13 00		
	d					11 24	11 44			12 04					12 24	12 44				13 04		
Branksome	d					11 29	11 49								12 29	12 49						
Parkstone (Dorset)	d					11 32	11 52								12 32	12 52						
Poole 4	a					11 36	11 55			12 13					12 36	12 55				13 13		
	d					11 37				12 14					12 37					13 14		
Hamworthy	d					11 42				12 19					12 42					13 19		
Holton Heath	d									12 23										13 23		
Wareham	d					11 49				12 28					12 49					13 28		
Wool	d									12 35										13 35		
Moreton (Dorset)	d									12 41										13 41		
Dorchester South	d					12 05				12 49					13 05					13 49		
Dorchester West	d				11 53																	
Upwey	d				12 01					12 55										13 55		
Weymouth	a				12 06	12 15				13 02					13 15					14 02		

A ⚒ to Bournemouth

For services from Brockenhurst - Lymington refer to Table T159

Table T158-F

Mondays to Fridays

16 December to 15 May

London - Basingstoke, Southampton, Romsey, Bournemouth and Weymouth

		SW	XC	SW	GW	SW	SW	SW	XC	SW	SW	SW	SW	XC	SW	SW	SW	SW	SW	SW	SW	SW	XC
		◇1	◇1	1	◇	◇1	◇1	◇1	◇1	◇1	◇1	1	◇1	◇1	◇1	◇1	1	◇1	◇1	◇1	1	◇1	◇1
			☕			A ☕			☕	A ☕				☕	A ☕				A ☕				☕
London Waterloo 15 ⊖	d	11 09				11 35		11 39		12 05			12 09		12 35			12 39	13 05			13 09	
Clapham Junction 10	d							11u46		12u12								12u46	13u12				
Woking	d	11 34				12 00							12 34		13 00							13 34	
Farnborough (Main)	d	11 45						12 13					12 45					13 13				13 45	
Fleet	d							12 19										13 19					
Reading 7	d		11 49						12 19					12 50									13 49
Basingstoke	a	11 58	12 10					12 31	12 42	12 47			12 58	13 09				13 31	13 47			13 58	14 10
	d	12 00	12 12					12 33	12 44	12 49			13 00	13 12				13 33	13 49			14 00	14 12
Micheldever	d	12 10											13 10									14 10	
Winchester	d	12 19	12 27			12 33		12 49	12 59	13 05			13 19	13 27	13 33			13 49	14 05			14 19	14 27
Shawford	d							12 54										13 54					
Romsey	d			12 20								13 07					13 20				14 07		
Chandlers Ford	d											13 14									14 14		
Eastleigh 8	a	12 27		12 49				12 59				13 20	13 27				13 49	13 59			14 20	14 27	
	d	12 28		12 50				13 00				13 21	13 28				13 50	14 00			14 21	14 28	
Hedge End	d	12 34											13 34									14 34	
Botley	d	12 38											13 38									14 38	
Fareham	d	12 48											13 48									14 48	
Portchester	d	12 53											13 53									14 53	
Cosham	d	12 58											13 58									14 58	
Hilsea	a	13 03											14 03									15 03	
Fratton	a	13 07											14 07									15 07	
Portsmouth & Southsea	a	13 11											14 11									15 11	
Portsmouth Harbour ⛴	a	13 20											14 20									15 20	
Southampton Airport Pkwy ✈	d		12 36			12 42		13 05	13 10	13 14		13 25		13 36	13 42			14 05	14 14		14 25		14 35
Swaythling	d											13 27									14 27		
St Denys	d										←	13 30								←	14 30		
Southampton Central ⛴	a		12 43			12 49		13 12	13 18	13 22	13 12	13 36		13 42	13 49			14 12	14 22	14 12	14 35		14 42
	d		12 45			12 51		13 30		13 24	13 30	13 37		13 45	13 51			14 30	14 24	14 30	14 37		14 44
Millbrook (Hants)	d							→				13 40						→			14 40		
Redbridge	d											13 43									14 43		
Romsey	d			13a03								13 51					14a03				14 51		
Mottisfont & Dunbridge	d											13 56									14 56		
Dean	d											14 02									15 02		
Salisbury	a											14 15									15 15		
Totton	d										13 35									14 35			
Ashurst New Forest	d										13 40									14 40			
Beaulieu Road	d						←				13 44					←							
Brockenhurst 3	a		12 58			13 04	12 51			13 37	13 51			13 58	14 04	13 51			14 37	14 51			14 57
	d		12 59			13 05	13 16			13 38	14 16			13 59	14 05	14 16			14 38	15 16			14 58
Sway	d						13 21				→					14 21				→			
New Milton	d						13 26			13 45						14 26			14 45				
Hinton Admiral	d						13 30									14 30							
Christchurch	d						13 35			13 52						14 35			14 52				
Pokesdown	d						13 38			13 56						14 38			14 56				
Bournemouth	a		13 13			13 20	13 42			14 00				14 13	14 20	14 42			15 00				15 12
	d					13 24	13 44			14 04					14 24	14 44			15 04				
Branksome	d					13 29	13 49								14 29	14 49							
Parkstone (Dorset)	d					13 32	13 52								14 32	14 52							
Poole 4	a					13 36	13 55			14 13					14 36	14 55			15 13				
	d					13 37				14 14					14 37				15 14				
Hamworthy	d					13 42				14 19					14 42				15 19				
Holton Heath	d									14 23									15 23				
Wareham	d					13 49				14 28					14 49				15 28				
Wool	d									14 35									15 35				
Moreton (Dorset)	d									14 41									15 41				
Dorchester South	d					14 05				14 49					15 05				15 49				
Dorchester West	d				13 53																		
Upwey	d				14 01					14 55									15 55				
Weymouth	a				14 06	14 15				15 02					15 15				16 02				

A ☕ to Bournemouth

For services from Brockenhurst - Lymington refer to Table T159

Table T158-F

Mondays to Fridays

16 December to 15 May

London - Basingstoke, Southampton, Romsey, Bournemouth and Weymouth

		SW	SW	SW	SW	XC	SW	SW	SW	SW	XC	SW	GW	SW	SW	SW	SW	SW	SW	SW	XC	SW
		◇1	◇1	1	◇1	◇1	◇1	◇1	1	◇1	◇1	1	◇	◇1	◇1	◇1	◇1	◇1	1	◇1	◇1	◇1
		A ☕				☕	A ☕				☕			A ☕			A ☕				☕	
London Waterloo 15 ⊖	d	13 35			13 39		14 05			14 09				14 35		14 39	15 05			15 09		15 12
Clapham Junction 10	d				13u46		14u12									14u46	15u12					15 19
Woking	d	14 00								14 34				15 00						15 34		15 49
Farnborough (Main)	d				14 13					14 45						15 13				15 45		16 03
Fleet	d				14 19											15 19						16 08
Reading 7	d					14 19					14 49										15 49	
Basingstoke	a				14 31	14 41	14 48			14 58	15 10					15 31	15 47			15 58	16 10	16 28
	d				14 33	14 44	14 49			15 00	15 12					15 33	15 49			16 00	16 12	16 29
Micheldever	d									15 10										16 10		→
Winchester	d	14 33			14 49	14 59	15 05			15 19	15 27			15 33		15 49	16 05			16 19	16 27	
Shawford	d				14 54											15 54						
Romsey	d			14 13					15 07			15 20							16 07			
Chandlers Ford	d								15 14										16 14			
Eastleigh 8	a			14 49	14 59				15 20	15 27		15 49				15 59			16 20	16 27		
	d			14 50	15 00				15 21	15 28		15 50				16 00			16 21	16 28		
Hedge End	d									15 34										16 34		
Botley	d									15 38										16 38		
Fareham	d									15 48										16 48		
Portchester	d									15 53										16 53		
Cosham	d									15 58										16 58		
Hilsea	a									16 03										17 03		
Fratton	a									16 07										17 07		
Portsmouth & Southsea	a									16 13										17 11		
Portsmouth Harbour ⛴	a									16 20										17 20		
Southampton Airport Pkwy ✈	d	14 42			15 05	15 09	15 14		15 25		15 36			15 42		16 05	16 14		16 25		16 36	
Swaythling	d								15 27										16 27			
St Denys	d							←	15 30									←	16 30			
Southampton Central ⛴	a	14 49			15 12	15 17	15 22	15 12	15 36		15 42			15 49		16 15	16 22	16 15	16 36		16 43	
	d	14 51			15 30		15 24	15 30	15 37		15 45			15 51		16 30	16 24	16 30	16 37		16 45	
Millbrook (Hants)	d				→				15 40							→			16 40			
Redbridge	d								15 43										16 43			
Romsey	d			15a03					15 51			16a03							16 51			
Mottisfont & Dunbridge	d								15 56										16 56			
Dean	d								16 02										17 02			
Salisbury	a								16 15										17 15			
Totton	d							15 35										16 35				
Ashurst New Forest	d							15 40										16 40				
Beaulieu Road	d		←					15 44							←			16 44				
Brockenhurst 3	a	15 04	14 51				15 37	15 51			15 58			16 04	15 51		16 37	16 51			16 58	
	d	15 05	15 16				15 38	16 28			15 59			16 05	16 28		16 38				16 59	
Sway	d		15 21					→							16 33		16 43					
New Milton	d		15 26				15 45								16 38		16 48					
Hinton Admiral	d		15 30												16 42		16 52					
Christchurch	d		15 35				15 52								16 47		16 57					
Pokesdown	d		15 38				15 56								16 50		17 00					
Bournemouth	a	15 20	15 42				16 00				16 13			16 20	16 54		17 04				17 14	
	d	15 24	15 44				16 04							16 24	16 56		17 09					
Branksome	d	15 29	15 49											16 29	17 01							
Parkstone (Dorset)	d	15 32	15 52											16 32	17 04							
Poole 4	a	15 36	15 55				16 13							16 36	17 07		17 18					
	d	15 37					16 14							16 37			17 19					
Hamworthy	d	15 42					16 19							16 42			17 24					
Holton Heath	d						16 23										17 28					
Wareham	d	15 49					16 28							16 49			17 33					
Wool	d						16 35							16 55			17 39					
Moreton (Dorset)	d						16 41										17 45					
Dorchester South	d	16 05					16 49							17 06			17 53					
Dorchester West	d												16 53									
Upwey	d						16 55						17 01				18 00					
Weymouth	a	16 15					17 02						17 06	17 15			18 06					

A ☕ to Bournemouth

For services from Brockenhurst - Lymington refer to Table T159

Table T158-F

Mondays to Fridays

16 December to 15 May

London - Basingstoke, Southampton, Romsey, Bournemouth and Weymouth

		SW ◇1 A ⚒		SW 1	SW 1	SW ◇1	GW ◇	SW ◇1	XC ◇1 ⚒	SW ◇1 A ⚒	SW ◇1	SW	SW ◇1	XC ◇1 ⚒	SW ◇1 A ⚒		GW	SW	SW	SW ◇1	SW ◇1 A ⚒		SW 1
London Waterloo 15 ⊖	d	15 35						15 39		16 05			16 09		16 35					16 39	17 05		
Clapham Junction 10	d							15u46		16u12										16u46			
Woking	d	16 00											16 34		17u00								
Farnborough (Main)	d							16 13					16 45							17 13			
Fleet	d							16 19												17 19			
Reading 7	d					←			16 19					16 52			16 55						
Basingstoke	a					16 28		16 31	16 42	16 47			16 58	17 10			17 22			17 31			
	d					16 29		16 33	16 44	16 49			17 00	17 12					17 24	17 32			
Micheldever	d												17 10						17 34				
Winchester	d	16 33		16 38		16 45		16 50	16 59	17 05			17 19	17 27	17 33				17 44	17 52	18 00		
Shawford	d			16 43				16 55											17 49	17 56			
Romsey	d				16 20							17 07						17 20					18 07
Chandlers Ford	d											17 14											18 14
Eastleigh 8	a			16 48	16 49	16 53		17 00				17 20	17 27					17 49	17 54	18 02			18 20
	d			16 49	16 50	16 55		17 01				17 21	17 28					17 50	17 55	18 02			18 21
Hedge End	d					17 01							17 34							18 08			
Botley	d					17 05							17 38							18 12			
Fareham	d					17 13							17 48							18 23			
Portchester	d					17 18							17 53							18 28			
Cosham	d					17 23							17 58							18 33			
Hilsea	a												18 03										
Fratton	a					17 30							18 07							18 40			
Portsmouth & Southsea	a					17 34							18 11							18 44			
Portsmouth Harbour ⛴	a					17 39							18 20							18 50			
Southampton Airport Pkwy ✈	d	16 42		16 54				17 06	17 09	17 14		17 25		17 36	17 42				18 00		18 10		18 25
Swaythling	d			16 56								17 27							18 02				18 27
St Denys	d			16 59							←	17 30							18 05				18 30
Southampton Central ⛴	a	16 49		17 04				17 13	17 17	17 21	17 13	17 36		17 42	17 49				18 10		18 17		18 36
	d	16 53	16 56	17 06				17 30		17 24	17 30	17 37		17 45	17 53	17 56					18 21	18 24	18 40
Millbrook (Hants)	d							→				17 40											18 48
Redbridge	d			17 10								17 43											18 52
Romsey	d				17a03							17 51						18a03					19 01
Mottisfont & Dunbridge	d											17 56											19 06
Dean	d											18 02											19 11
Salisbury	a											18 15											19 24
Totton	d		17 02	17 13							17 35					18 02						18 29	
Ashurst New Forest	d		17 06								17 40					18 06						18 34	
Beaulieu Road	d										17 44												
Brockenhurst 3	a	17 08	17 14	17 24						17 37	17 51			17 58	18 07	18 14						18 42	
	d	17 09	17 15	17 25						17 38				17 59	18 08	18 15						18 43	
Sway	d		17 19							17 43						18 19						18 47	
New Milton	d		17 24	17 32						17 48						18 24						18 52	
Hinton Admiral	d		17 28							17 52						18 28						18 56	
Christchurch	d		17 33	17 39						17 57						18 33						19 01	
Pokesdown	d		17 37							18 00						18 37						19 05	
Bournemouth	a	17 24	17 41	17 48						18 04				18 14	18 24	18 41					18 48	19 09	
	d	17 25	17 42							18 09					18 25						18 50	19 10	
Branksome	d	17 30	17 47												18 30						18 55	19 15	
Parkstone (Dorset)	d	17 33	17 50												18 33						18 58	19 18	
Poole 4	a	17 37	17 54							18 18					18 37						19 02	19 24	
	d	17 38								18 19					18 38						19 03		
Hamworthy	d	17 43								18 24					18 43						19 08		
Holton Heath	d									18 28											19 12		
Wareham	d	17 50								18 33					18 50						19 17		
Wool	d	17 56								18 39					18 56						19 23		
Moreton (Dorset)	d									18 46											19 29		
Dorchester South	d	18 09								18 54					19 09						19 37		
Dorchester West	d						18 47																
Upwey	d						18 55			19 00											19 44		
Weymouth	a	18 18					19 00			19 08					19 25						19 50		

A ⚒ to Bournemouth

For services from Brockenhurst - Lymington refer to Table T159

Table T158-F

Mondays to Fridays

16 December to 15 May

London - Basingstoke, Southampton, Romsey, Bournemouth and Weymouth

		SW ◇1	XC ◇1 ⚒	SW 1	GW ◇	SW ◇1 A ⚒		SW ◇1	SW ◇1	SW ◇1 A ⚒	SW ◇1 ⚒	SW 1	SW 1	SW ◇1	XC ◇1 ⚒	SW ◇1 A ⚒		SW 1	SW ◇1	SW ◇1	SW ◇1 A ⚒	SW ◇1	SW 1
London Waterloo 15 ⊖	d	17 09				17 35		17 39	17 48	18 05				18 09		18 35			18 39	18 48	19 05		
Clapham Junction 10	d																		18u46		19u12		
Woking	d	17 34						18 04	18 13					18 34					19 06	19 14			
Farnborough (Main)	d																						
Fleet	d																						
Reading 7	d		17 52												18 52								
Basingstoke	a	17 52	18 09					18 22	18 31					18 53	19 09				19 28	19 33	19 47		
	d	17 54	18 11					18 24	18 33					18 55	19 11				19 30	19 34	19 49		
Micheldever	d	18 04						18 34						19 05						19 45			
Winchester	d	18 14	18 26			18 30		18 44	18 50	19 00		19 05		19 14	19 26	19 31			19 46	19 55	20 05		
Shawford	d	18 18						18 49				19 09		19 19					19 51				
Romsey	d			18 20									19 07					19 20					20 07
Chandlers Ford	d												19 14										20 14
Eastleigh 8	a	18 24		18 49				18 54	18 58			19 15	19 20	19 25				19 50	19 56	20 04			20 20
	d	18 25		18 50				18 55	18 59			19 16	19 21	19 29				19 50	20 01	20 05			20 21
Hedge End	d	18 31						19 01						19 35					20 07				
Botley	d	18 36						19 05						19 39					20 18				
Fareham	d	18 45						19 14						19 48					20a27				
Portchester	d	18 50						19 19						19 53									
Cosham	d	18 55						19 24						19 58									
Hilsea	a	19 05						19 28						20 03									
Fratton	a	19 09						19 32						20 07									
Portsmouth & Southsea	a	19 12						19 36						20 12									
Portsmouth Harbour ⛴	a	19 20						19 43						20 20									
Southampton Airport Pkwy ✈	d		18 35			18 39			19 03	19 09		19 20	19 25		19 34	19 40				20 09	20 14		20 25
Swaythling	d								19 06			19 23	19 27										20 27
St Denys	d								19 09			19 26	19 30										20 30
Southampton Central ⛴	a		18 43			18 46			19 17	19 18		19 33	19 35		19 41	19 47				20 16	20 21		20 36
	d		18 45			18 51	18 54			19 21	19 24		19 37		19 43	19 51	19 54			20 18	20 25	20 28	20 37
Millbrook (Hants)	d												19 40										20 40
Redbridge	d												19 43										20 43
Romsey	d			19a04									19 51					20a03					20 51
Mottisfont & Dunbridge	d												19 56										20 56
Dean	d												20 02										21 02
Salisbury	a												20 15										21 15
Totton	d						18 59				19 29						19 59					20 33	
Ashurst New Forest	d						19 04				19 34						20 04					20 38	
Beaulieu Road	d																						
Brockenhurst 3	a		18 58				19 12				19 42				19 57		20 12			20 31	20 40	20 46	
	d		18 59				19 13				19 43				19 58		20 13			20 35	20 42	20 46	
Sway	d						19 17				19 47						20 19					20 51	
New Milton	d						19 22				19 52						20 24			20 42		20 56	
Hinton Admiral	d						19 26				19 56						20 28					21 00	
Christchurch	d						19 31				20 01						20 33					21 05	
Pokesdown	d						19 35				20 05						20 37					21 08	
Bournemouth	a		19 13			19 21	19 39			19 48	20 09				20 12	20 20	20 41			20 52	20 57	21 12	
	d					19 22	19 40			19 50	20 10					20 22	20 42			20 54	21 01	21 14	
Branksome	d					19 27	19 45			19 55	20 15					20 27	20 47				21 06	21 19	
Parkstone (Dorset)	d					19 30	19 48			19 58	20 18					20 30	20 50				21 09	21 22	
Poole 4	a					19 34	19 54			20 02	20 24					20 34	20 56			21 08	21 12	21 25	
	d					19 35				20 03						20 35					21 13		
Hamworthy	d					19 40				20 08						20 40					21 18		
Holton Heath	d									20 12													
Wareham	d					19 47				20 17						20 47					21 26		
Wool	d					19 53				20 23						20 53					21 33		
Moreton (Dorset)	d									20 29											21 39		
Dorchester South	d					20 04				20 37						21 04					21 47		
Dorchester West	d				19 54																		
Upwey	d				20 01					20 44											21 53		
Weymouth	a				20 06	20 15				20 50						21 15					21 59		

A ⚒ to Bournemouth

For services from Brockenhurst - Lymington refer to Table T159

Table T158-F

Mondays to Fridays
16 December to 15 May

London - Basingstoke, Southampton, Romsey, Bournemouth and Weymouth

		SW	XC	SW	SW	SW	SW	GW	SW	SW	SW	SW	SW	XC	SW	SW	SW	SW	GW	SW	SW	SW
		◇1	◇1	◇1	◇1	1	◇1	◇	◇1	◇1	◇1	1	◇1	◇1	◇1	◇1	1	◇1		◇1	1	◇1
				A											A							
			🛒	🛒	🛒					🛒					🛒					🛒		
London Waterloo 15 ⊖	d	19 09		19 35			19 39		19 48	20 05			20 09		20 35			20 39		21 05		21 09
Clapham Junction 10	d						19u46			20u12								20u46		21u12		
Woking	d	19 34		20 00									20 34		21 00							21 34
Farnborough (Main)	d	19 45					20 13						20 45					21 13				21 45
Fleet	d						20 19											21 19				
Reading 7	d		19 49											20 49								
Basingstoke	a	19 58	20 09				20 30		20 31	20 47			20 58	21 09				21 31		21 47		21 58
	d	20 00	20 12				20 31		20 33	20 49			21 00	21 11				21 33		21 49		22 00
Micheldever	d	20 10							20 45				21 10					21 43				22 10
Winchester	d	20 19	20 27	20 33			20 48		20 54	21 05			21 19	21 26	21 33			21 52		22 05		22 19
Shawford	d	20 24					20 52						21 24					21 57				22 24
Romsey	d					20 20						21 07					21 20				22 07	
Chandlers Ford	d											21 14									22 14	
Eastleigh 3	a	20 29				20 49	20 58		21 02			21 20	21 30				21 49	22 02		22 13	22 21	22 30
	d	20 30				20 50	20 59		21 03			21 21	21 31				21 50	22 03	22 09	22 14	22 22	22 33
Hedge End	d	20 36					21 05						21 37									22 39
Botley	d	20 40					21 09						21 41									22 43
Fareham	d	20 49					21a20						21 49									22 51
Portchester	d	20 54											21 54									22 56
Cosham	d	20 59											21 59									23 01
Hilsea	a	21 03											22 04									23 06
Fratton	a	21 07											22 08									23 10
Portsmouth & Southsea	a	21 11											22 11									23 16
Portsmouth Harbour ⛴	a	21 18											22 16									23 22
Southampton Airport Pkwy ✈	d		20 36	20 42					21 07	21 15		21 25		21 35	21 42			22 08	22 13	22 18	22 26	
Swaythling	d											21 27									22 28	
St Denys	d								21 11		←	21 30									22 31	
Southampton Central ⛴	a		20 43	20 49					21 17	21 24	21 17	21 35		21 41	21 49			22 17	22 20	22 25	22 36	
	d		20 45	20 51					21 30	21 25	21 30	21 37		21 43	21 51				22 22	22 27	22 38	
Millbrook (Hants)	d								→			21 40									22 40	
Redbridge	d											21 43									22 44	
Romsey	d					21a03						21 51					22a03		22 35		22 52	
Mottisfont & Dunbridge	d											21 56									22 57	
Dean	d											22 02									23 02	
Salisbury	a											22 15							22 53		23 15	
Totton	d			20 56						21 31	21 36									22 32		
Ashurst New Forest	d										21 41									22 37		
Beaulieu Road	d										21 45					←						
Brockenhurst 3	a		21 00	21 07						21 41	21 52			21 57	22 04	21 52				22 45		
	d		21 01	21 08	21 16					21 42	22 16			21 59	22 05	22 16				22 47		
Sway	d				21 21					21 47	→					22 21				22 52		
New Milton	d				21 26					21 52						22 26				22 57		
Hinton Admiral	d				21 30					21 56						22 30				23 01		
Christchurch	d				21 35					22 01						22 35				23 06		
Pokesdown	d				21 38					22 04						22 38				23 10		
Bournemouth	a		21 15	21 23	21 42					22 08				22 15	22 20	22 42				23 14		
	d			21 27	21 44					22 10					22 24	22 44				23 16		
Branksome	d			21 32	21 49					22 15					22 29	22 49				23 21		
Parkstone (Dorset)	d			21 35	21 52					22 18					22 32	22 52				23 25		
Poole 4	a			21 38	21 55					22 22					22 36	22 55				23 29		
	d			21 39											22 37							
Hamworthy	d			21 44											22 42							
Holton Heath	d																					
Wareham	d			21 51											22 49							
Wool	d			21 58											22 55							
Moreton (Dorset)	d			22 04											23 01							
Dorchester South	d			22 12											23 09							
Dorchester West	d							22 49														
Upwey	d			22 18				22 56							23 16							
Weymouth	a			22 23				23 01							23 20							

A 🛒 to Bournemouth

For services from Brockenhurst - Lymington refer to Table T159

Table T158-F

Mondays to Fridays
16 December to 15 May

London - Basingstoke, Southampton, Romsey, Bournemouth and Weymouth

		XC	SW	SW	SW	SW	XC	SW	SW	SW	XC	SW	SW	SW	SW	SW
		◇1	◇1	◇1	1	◇1	◇1	◇1	1	◇1	◇1	◇1	1	◇1	◇1	◇1
			A													
			🛒	🛒				🛒				🛒				
London Waterloo 15 ⊖	d		21 35			21 39		22 05		22 08		22 35		22 39	23 05	23 35
Clapham Junction 10	d					21u46		22u12						22u46	23u12	23u42
Woking	d		22 00							22 34		23 00			23 33	00 03
Farnborough (Main)	d					22 13				22 45				23 16		00 14
Fleet	d					22 19								23 21		00 20
Reading 7	d	21 52					22 23				22 49					
Basingstoke	a	22 09				22 31	22 41	22 47		22 58	23 07			23 33	23 51	00 33
	d	22 10				22 33	22 44	22 49		23 00	23 09			23 34	23 53	00 35
Micheldever	d					22 43				23 10					00 03	
Winchester	d	22 25	22 33			22 52	22 59	23 05		23 19	23 26	23 33		23 51	00 13	00 51
Shawford	d					22 57				23 24				23 55		
Romsey	d				22 20				23 11				23 08			
Chandlers Ford	d								23 18							
Eastleigh 3	a				22 49	23 02		23 14	23 24	23 30			23 37	00 01	00 22	00 59
	d				22 50	23 03		23 15	23 24	23 31			23 38	00 02	00 23	01 00
Hedge End	d									23 37						
Botley	d									23 41						
Fareham	d									23 49						
Portchester	d									23 54						
Cosham	d									23 59						
Hilsea	a									00 04						
Fratton	a									00 08						
Portsmouth & Southsea	a									00 11						
Portsmouth Harbour ⛴	a									00 16						
Southampton Airport Pkwy ✈	d	22 34	22 42			23 08	23 12	23 20	23 28		23 37	23 42		00 06	00 28	01 05
Swaythling	d								23 31							
St Denys	d								23 34						00s32	
Southampton Central ⛴	a	22 41	22 50			23 17	23 20	23 29	23 39		23 43	23 49		00 13	00 37	01 12
	d	22 43	22 51					23 30	23 42			23 51			00 38	
Millbrook (Hants)	d								23 44							
Redbridge	d								23 48							
Romsey	d				23a04				23 59				23a50			
Mottisfont & Dunbridge	d								00 04							
Dean	d								00 09							
Salisbury	a								00 24							
Totton	d							23 36							00s43	
Ashurst New Forest	d							23 40								
Beaulieu Road	d															
Brockenhurst 3	a	22 58	23 05					23 48				00 04			00s54	
	d	22 59	23 06	23 16				23 49				00 05				
Sway	d			23 21				23 54								
New Milton	d			23 26				23 58							01s02	
Hinton Admiral	d			23 30				00 02								
Christchurch	d			23 35				00 07							01s09	
Pokesdown	d			23 38				00 11							01s13	
Bournemouth	a	23 17	23 22	23 42				00 15				00 21			01 17	
	d		23 27	23 44				00 16				00 22			01 18	
Branksome	d		23 32	23 49				00 21				00 27			01s23	
Parkstone (Dorset)	d		23 35	23 52				00 24				00 30			01s26	
Poole 4	a		23 38	23 55				00 28				00 35			01 30	
	d		23 40													
Hamworthy	d		23 45													
Holton Heath	d															
Wareham	d		23 51													
Wool	d		23 58													
Moreton (Dorset)	d		00 04													
Dorchester South	d		00 12													
Dorchester West	d															
Upwey	d		00 18													
Weymouth	a		00 23													

A 🛒 to Bournemouth

For services from Brockenhurst - Lymington refer to Table T159

Table T158-F

Saturdays

21 December to 16 May

London - Basingstoke, Southampton, Romsey, Bournemouth and Weymouth

		SW	SW	SW	SW	SW	SW	SW	SW	SW	SW	SW	SW	SW	SW	SW	SW	SW	SW	SW	SW	GW	SW
		◇1 ╤	◇1	◇1	1	◇1 ╤	◇1	◇1	1	◇1	1	◇1	◇1	1	◇1	1	◇1	1	1	1	1		◇1
London Waterloo 15 ⊖	d											00 05	01 05										05 30
Clapham Junction 10	d											00u12	01 15										05u37
Woking	d									00 03	00 28	00 37	01 42										06 01
Farnborough (Main)	d								00 11	00 14	00 41		01s51										
Fleet	d								00 16	00 20	00 47		01s57										
Reading 7	d																						
Basingstoke	a								00 35	00 33	01 06	00 55	02s09										06 20
	d									00 35		00 56		05 10									06 21
Micheldever	d						00 03																06 31
Winchester	d						00 13			00 51		01 13	02s26	05 26									06 41
Shawford	d																						
Romsey	d																	05 58			06 09		
Chandlers Ford	d																	06 06					
Eastleigh 8	a						00 22			00 59		01 21	02s35	05 34				06 12			06 49		06 50
	d		00 02				00 23	00 30		01 00		01 22		05 35				06 13	06 24	06 28	06 50		06 51
Hedge End	d							00s36												06 34			
Botley	d							00s39												06 38			
Fareham	d							00s47												06 46			
Portchester	d							00s53												06 51			
Cosham	d							00s57												06 56			
Hilsea	a																			07 03			
Fratton	a							01s05												07 07			
Portsmouth & Southsea	a							01 09												07 11			
Portsmouth Harbour ⛴	a																			07 16			
Southampton Airport Pkwy ✈	d		00 06				00 28			01 05		01 26	02s39	05 40				06 18	06 28				06 56
Swaythling	d																	06 20					
St Denys	d						00s32						02s44	05 44				06 23					
Southampton Central ⛴	a		00 13				00 37			01 12		01 35	02 49	05 49				06 28	06 35				07 03
	d						00 38					01 37					06 21	06 30					07 05
Millbrook (Hants)	d																	06 32					
Redbridge	d																	06 36					
Romsey	d																	06 44			07a03		
Mottisfont & Dunbridge	d				00 04													06 49					
Dean	d				00 09													06 54					
Salisbury	a				00 24													07 07					
Totton	d						00s43					01s42					06 26						07 10
Ashurst New Forest	d																06 31						
Beaulieu Road	d																						
Brockenhurst 3	a						00s54					01s53					06 39						07 21
	d					00 05										06 15	06 40						07 22
Sway	d															06 20	06 44						07 26
New Milton	d						01s02					02s00				06 25	06 49						07 31
Hinton Admiral	d	00 02														06 29	06 53						07 35
Christchurch	d	00 07					01s09					02s07				06 34	06 58						07 40
Pokesdown	d	00 11					01s13					02s11				06 37	07 02						07 44
Bournemouth	a	00 15				00 21	01 17					02 15				06 41	07 06						07 48
	d	00 16				00 22	01 18								06 11	06 44	07 11						07 49
Branksome	d	00 21				00 27	01s23								06 16	06 49	07 16						07 54
Parkstone (Dorset)	d	00 24				00 30	01s26								06 19	06 52	07 19						07 57
Poole 4	a	00 28				00 35	01 30								06 23	06 55	07 23						08 01
	d														06 24	06 57	07 24						08 02
Hamworthy	d														06 29	07 02	07 29						08 07
Holton Heath	d														06 33	07 06	07 33						
Wareham	d														06 38	07 11	07 38						08 13
Wool	d														06 44	07 17	07 44						08 20
Moreton (Dorset)	d			00 04											06 50	07 23	07 50						08 26
Dorchester South	d			00 12											06 58	07 31	07 58						08 34
Dorchester West	d																					08 04	
Upwey	d			00 18											07 05	07 38	08 05					08 12	08 41
Weymouth	a			00 23											07 09	07 42	08 09					08 18	08 45

For services from Brockenhurst - Lymington refer to Table T159

Table T158-F

Saturdays

21 December to 16 May

London - Basingstoke, Southampton, Romsey, Bournemouth and Weymouth

		SW	SW	SW	SW	SW	SW	SW	SW	XC	SW	SW	GW	SW	XC	SW	SW	SW	SW	XC	SW	SW	SW
		◇1	1	1	◇1	1	◇1	1	◇1	◇1 ╤	◇1	1	◇	◇1	◇1 ╤	◇1	◇1	1	◇1	◇1 ╤	◇1 A ╤	◇1	1
London Waterloo 15 ⊖	d				06 30				06 42		07 35			07 39		08 05			08 09		08 35		
Clapham Junction 10	d				06u37				06u49					07u46		08u12							
Woking	d			06 19	06 57				07 19		08 00								08 34		09 00		
Farnborough (Main)	d			06 33					07 33					08 13					08 45				
Fleet	d			06 38					07 38					08 19									
Reading 7	d									07 49					08 19					08 49			
Basingstoke	a			06 58	07 16				07 58	08 08	08 20			08 31	08 40	08 47			08 58	09 11			
	d			07 00	07 18				08 00	08 12	08 21			08 33	08 44	08 49			09 00	09 12			
Micheldever	d			07 10					08 10										09 10				
Winchester	d			07 19	07 34				08 19	08 27	08 38			08 49	08 59	09 05			09 19	09 27	09 33		
Shawford	d			07 24					08 24					08 54									
Romsey	d		07 07			07 13		08 07				08 13						09 07					09 20
Chandlers Ford	d		07 14					08 14										09 14					
Eastleigh 8	a		07 20	07 29	07 42	07 49		08 20	08 30		08 46	08 49		08 59				09 20	09 27				09 49
	d		07 21	07 30	07 43	07 50		08 21	08 31		08 47	08 50		09 00				09 21	09 28				09 50
Hedge End	d			07 36					08 37										09 34				
Botley	d			07 40					08 41										09 38				
Fareham	d			07 48					08 49										09 48				
Portchester	d			07 53					08 54										09 53				
Cosham	d			07 58					08 59										09 58				
Hilsea	a			08 03					09 04										10 03				
Fratton	a			08 07					09 08										10 07				
Portsmouth & Southsea	a			08 11					09 12										10 11				
Portsmouth Harbour ⛴	a			08 18					09 18										10 18				
Southampton Airport Pkwy ✈	d		07 25		07 48			08 25		08 36	08 51			09 05	09 09	09 14		09 25		09 36	09 42		
Swaythling	d		07 27					08 27										09 27					
St Denys	d		07 30					08 30									←	09 30					
Southampton Central ⛴	a		07 35		07 56			08 36		08 43	08 58			09 12	09 17	09 22	09 12	09 36		09 42	09 49		
	d	07 21	07 37		08 00		08 17	08 37		08 45	09 00			09 30		09 24	09 30	09 37		09 45	09 51		
Millbrook (Hants)	d		07 40					08 40						→				09 40					
Redbridge	d		07 43					08 43										09 43					
Romsey	d		07 51			08a03		08 51				09a03						09 51					10a03
Mottisfont & Dunbridge	d		07 56					08 56										09 56					
Dean	d		08 02					09 02										10 02					
Salisbury	a		08 15					09 15										10 15					
Totton	d	07 26			08 05		08 22				09 05						09 35						
Ashurst New Forest	d	07 31					08 27										09 40						
Beaulieu Road	d						08 31										09 44					←	
Brockenhurst 3	a	07 39			08 16		08 37			08 58	09 16					09 37	09 51			09 58	10 05	09 51	
	d	07 40			08 17		08 38			08 59	09 17					09 38	10 16			09 59	10 06	10 16	
Sway	d	07 44			08 21		08 42				09 21						→					10 21	
New Milton	d	07 49			08 26		08 47				09 26					09 45						10 26	
Hinton Admiral	d	07 53			08 30		08 51				09 30											10 30	
Christchurch	d	07 58			08 35		08 56				09 35					09 52						10 35	
Pokesdown	d	08 02			08 39		09 00				09 39					09 56						10 38	
Bournemouth	a	08 06			08 43		09 04			09 13	09 43					10 00				10 13	10 21	10 42	
	d	08 11			08 44		09 09				09 44					10 04					10 25	10 44	
Branksome	d	08 16			08 49		09 14				09 49										10 30	10 49	
Parkstone (Dorset)	d	08 19			08 52		09 17				09 52										10 33	10 52	
Poole 4	a	08 23			08 56		09 21				09 56					10 13					10 36	10 55	
	d	08 24			08 57		09 22				09 57					10 14					10 37		
Hamworthy	d	08 29			09 02		09 27				10 02					10 19					10 42		
Holton Heath	d	08 33					09 31									10 23							
Wareham	d	08 38			09 09		09 35				10 09					10 28					10 49		
Wool	d	08 44			09 15		09 42									10 35							
Moreton (Dorset)	d	08 50			09 21		09 48									10 41							
Dorchester South	d	08 58			09 29		09 56				10 27					10 51					11 05		
Dorchester West	d												10 44										
Upwey	d	09 05			09 36		10 02						10 52			10 57							
Weymouth	a	09 09			09 40		10 07				10 35		10 58			11 02					11 14		

A ╤ to Bournemouth

For services from Brockenhurst - Lymington refer to Table T159

Table T158-F

Saturdays

21 December to 16 May

London - Basingstoke, Southampton, Romsey, Bournemouth and Weymouth

		SW	SW	SW	SW	SW	XC	SW	GW	SW	SW	SW	XC	SW	SW	SW	SW	XC	SW	SW	SW	SW
		◇1	◇1	◇1	1	◇1	◇1 🍴	1	◇	◇1 A 🍴	◇1	◇1	◇1 🍴	◇1	◇1	1	◇1	◇1 🍴	◇1 A 🍴	◇1	1	◇1
London Waterloo 15 ⊖	d	08 39	09 05			09 09				09 35		09 39		10 05			10 09		10 35			10 39
Clapham Junction 10	d	08u46	09u12									09u46		10u12								10u46
Woking	d					09 34				10 00							10 34		11 00			
Farnborough (Main)	d	09 13				09 45						10 13					10 45					11 13
Fleet	d	09 19										10 19										11 19
Reading 7	d						09 49						10 19					10 49				
Basingstoke	a	09 32	09 47			09 58	10 09					10 31	10 40	10 47			10 58	11 10				11 31
	d	09 33	09 49			10 00	10 11					10 33	10 42	10 49			11 00	11 11				11 33
Micheldever	d					10 10											11 10					
Winchester	d	09 49	10 05			10 19	10 26			10 33		10 49	10 57	11 05			11 19	11 29	11 33			11 49
Shawford	d	09 54										10 54										11 54
Romsey	d				10 07			10 20								11 07					11 20	
Chandlers Ford	d				10 14											11 14						
Eastleigh 8	a	09 59			10 20	10 27		10 49				10 59				11 20	11 27				11 49	11 59
	d	10 00			10 21	10 28		10 50				11 00				11 21	11 28				11 50	12 00
Hedge End	d					10 34											11 34					
Botley	d					10 38											11 38					
Fareham	d					10 48											11 48					
Portchester	d					10 53											11 53					
Cosham	d					10 58											11 58					
Hilsea	a					11 03											12 03					
Fratton	a					11 07											12 07					
Portsmouth & Southsea	a					11 11											12 11					
Portsmouth Harbour ⛴	a					11 18											12 18					
Southampton Airport Pkwy ✈	d	10 05	10 14		10 25		10 36			10 42		11 05	11 10	11 14		11 25		11 38	11 42			12 05
Swaythling	d				10 27											11 27						
St Denys	d			←	10 30										←	11 30						
Southampton Central ⛴	a	10 12	10 22	10 12	10 36		10 43			10 49		11 12	11 17	11 22	11 12	11 36		11 44	11 50			12 12
	d	10 30	10 24	10 30	10 37		10 45			10 51		11 30		11 24	11 30	11 37		11 46	11 51			12 30
Millbrook (Hants)	d	→			10 40							→				11 40						→
Redbridge	d				10 43											11 43						
Romsey	d				10 59			11a03								11 51					12a03	
Mottisfont & Dunbridge	d				11 04											11 56						
Dean	d				11 10											12 02						
Salisbury	a				11 22											12 15						
Totton	d			10 35											11 35							
Ashurst New Forest	d			10 40											11 40							
Beaulieu Road	d										←				11 44					←		
Brockenhurst 3	a		10 37	10 51			10 58			11 04	10 51			11 37	11 51			11 59	12 04	11 51		
	d		10 38	11 16			10 59			11 05	11 16			11 38	12 16			12 00	12 05	12 16		
Sway	d			→							11 21				→					12 21		
New Milton	d		10 45								11 26			11 45						12 26		
Hinton Admiral	d										11 30									12 30		
Christchurch	d		10 52								11 35			11 52						12 35		
Pokesdown	d		10 56								11 38			11 56						12 38		
Bournemouth	a		11 00				11 13			11 20	11 42			12 00				12 14	12 20	12 42		
	d		11 04							11 24	11 44			12 04					12 24	12 44		
Branksome	d									11 29	11 49								12 29	12 49		
Parkstone (Dorset)	d									11 32	11 52								12 32	12 52		
Poole 4	a		11 13							11 36	11 55			12 13					12 36	12 55		
	d		11 14							11 37				12 14					12 37			
Hamworthy	d		11 19							11 42				12 19					12 42			
Holton Heath	d		11 23											12 23								
Wareham	d		11 28							11 49				12 28					12 49			
Wool	d		11 35											12 35								
Moreton (Dorset)	d		11 41											12 41								
Dorchester South	d		11 49							12 05				12 49					13 05			
Dorchester West	d								11 53													
Upwey	d		11 55						12 01					12 55								
Weymouth	a		12 00						12 07	12 13				13 00					13 13			

A 🍴 to Bournemouth

For services from Brockenhurst - Lymington refer to Table T159

NRT DECEMBER 19 EDITION

Table T158-F

Saturdays

21 December to 16 May

London - Basingstoke, Southampton, Romsey, Bournemouth and Weymouth

		SW	SW	SW	SW	XC	SW	GW	SW	SW	SW	XC	SW	SW	SW	SW	XC	SW	SW	SW	SW	SW	SW
		◇1 A 🍴	◇1	1	◇1	◇1 🍴	1	◇	◇1 A 🍴	◇1	◇1	◇1 🍴	◇1 A 🍴	◇1	1	◇1	◇1 🍴	1	◇1	◇1 A 🍴	◇1	◇1	◇1 A 🍴
London Waterloo 15 ⊖	d	11 05			11 09				11 35		11 39		12 05			12 09				12 35		12 39	13 05
Clapham Junction 10	d	11u12									11u46		12u12									12u46	13u12
Woking	d				11 34				12 00							12 34				13 00			
Farnborough (Main)	d				11 45						12 13					12 45						13 13	
Fleet	d										12 19											13 19	
Reading 7	d					11 49						12 19					12 49						
Basingstoke	a	11 47			11 58	12 09					12 31	12 40	12 47			12 58	13 09					13 31	13 47
	d	11 49			12 00	12 11					12 33	12 42	12 49			13 00	13 11					13 33	13 49
Micheldever	d				12 10											13 10							
Winchester	d	12 05			12 19	12 26			12 33		12 49	12 57	13 05			13 19	13 26			13 33		13 49	14 05
Shawford	d										12 54											13 54	
Romsey	d			12 07			12 20								13 07			13 20					
Chandlers Ford	d			12 14											13 14								
Eastleigh 8	a			12 20	12 27		12 49				12 59				13 20	13 27		13 49				13 59	
	d			12 21	12 28		12 50				13 00				13 21	13 28		13 50				14 00	
Hedge End	d				12 34											13 34							
Botley	d				12 38											13 38							
Fareham	d				12 48											13 48							
Portchester	d				12 53											13 53							
Cosham	d				12 58											13 58							
Hilsea	a				13 03											14 03							
Fratton	a				13 07											14 07							
Portsmouth & Southsea	a				13 11											14 11							
Portsmouth Harbour ⛴	a				13 18											14 18							
Southampton Airport Pkwy ✈	d	12 14		12 25		12 34			12 42		13 05	13 09	13 14		13 25		13 34			13 42		14 05	14 14
Swaythling	d			12 27											13 27								
St Denys	d		←	12 30										←	13 30								
Southampton Central ⛴	a	12 22	12 12	12 36		12 41			12 49		13 12	13 16	13 22	13 12	13 36		13 41			13 49		14 12	14 22
	d	12 24	12 30	12 37		12 45			12 51		13 30		13 24	13 30	13 37		13 44			13 51		14 30	14 24
Millbrook (Hants)	d			12 40							→				13 40							→	
Redbridge	d			12 43											13 43								
Romsey	d			12 51			13a03								13 51			14a03					
Mottisfont & Dunbridge	d			12 56											13 56								
Dean	d			13 02											14 02								
Salisbury	a			13 15											14 15								
Totton	d		12 35											13 35									
Ashurst New Forest	d		12 40											13 40									
Beaulieu Road	d									←				13 44							←		
Brockenhurst 3	a	12 37	12 51			12 58			13 04	12 51			13 37	13 51			13 57			14 04	13 51		14 37
	d	12 38	13 16			12 59			13 05	13 16			13 38	14 16			13 58			14 05	14 16		14 38
Sway	d		→							13 21				→							14 21		
New Milton	d	12 45								13 26			13 45								14 26		14 45
Hinton Admiral	d									13 30											14 30		
Christchurch	d	12 52								13 35			13 52								14 35		14 52
Pokesdown	d	12 56								13 38			13 56								14 38		14 56
Bournemouth	a	13 00				13 13			13 20	13 42			14 00				14 12			14 20	14 42		15 00
	d	13 04							13 24	13 44			14 04							14 24	14 44		15 04
Branksome	d								13 29	13 49										14 29	14 49		
Parkstone (Dorset)	d								13 32	13 52										14 32	14 52		
Poole 4	a	13 13							13 36	13 55			14 13							14 36	14 55		15 13
	d	13 14							13 37				14 14							14 37			15 14
Hamworthy	d	13 19							13 42				14 19							14 42			15 19
Holton Heath	d	13 23											14 23										15 23
Wareham	d	13 28							13 49				14 28							14 49			15 28
Wool	d	13 35											14 35										15 35
Moreton (Dorset)	d	13 41											14 41										15 41
Dorchester South	d	13 49							14 05				14 49							15 05			15 49
Dorchester West	d							13 53											14 54				
Upwey	d	13 55						14 01					14 55						15 01				15 55
Weymouth	a	14 00						14 07	14 14				15 00						15 06	15 13			16 00

A 🍴 to Bournemouth

For services from Brockenhurst - Lymington refer to Table T159

Table T158-F

Saturdays
21 December to 16 May

London - Basingstoke, Southampton, Romsey, Bournemouth and Weymouth

		SW ◇1	SW 1	SW ◇1	XC ◇1 (buffet)	SW ◇1 A (buffet)	SW ◇1	SN 1	SW 1	SW ◇1	XC ◇1 (buffet)	SW ◇1 (buffet)	SW ◇1	SW 1	SW ◇1	XC ◇1 (buffet)	SW 1	GW ◇	SW ◇1 A (buffet)	SW ◇1	SW ◇1	SW ◇1 A (buffet)
London Waterloo 15 ⊖	d			13 09		13 35				13 39		14 05			14 09				14 35		14 39	15 05
Clapham Junction 10	d									13u46		14u11									14u46	15u12
Woking	d			13 34		14 00									14 34				15 00			
Farnborough (Main)	d			13 45						14 13					14 45						15 13	
Fleet	d									14 19											15 19	
Reading 7	d				13 49						14 19					14 49						
Basingstoke	a			13 58	14 09					14 31	14 40	14 47			14 58	15 09					15 31	15 47
	d			14 00	14 11					14 33	14 44	14 49			15 00	15 12					15 33	15 49
Micheldever	d			14 10											15 10							
Winchester	d			14 19	14 26	14 33				14 49	14 59	15 05			15 19	15 27			15 33		15 49	16 05
Shawford	d									14 54											15 54	
Romsey	d		14 07						14 13					15 07			15 20					
Chandlers Ford	d		14 14											15 14								
Eastleigh 3	a		14 20	14 27					14 49	14 59				15 20	15 27		15 49				15 59	
	d		14 21	14 28				14 41	14 50	15 00				15 21	15 28		15 50				16 00	
Hedge End	d			14 34											15 34							
Botley	d			14 38											15 38							
Fareham	d			14 48				15a00							15 48							
Portchester	d			14 53											15 53							
Cosham	d			14 58											15 58							
Hilsea	a			15 03											16 03							
Fratton	a			15 07											16 07							
Portsmouth & Southsea	a			15 11											16 11							
Portsmouth Harbour ⛴	a			15 18											16 18							
Southampton Airport Pkwy ✈	d		14 25		14 34	14 42				15 05	15 09	15 14		15 25		15 36			15 42		16 05	16 14
Swaythling	d		14 27											15 27								
St Denys	d	←	14 30										←	15 30								
Southampton Central ⛴	a	14 12	14 35		14 43	14 49				15 12	15 17	15 22	15 12	15 36		15 42			15 49		16 12	16 22
	d	14 30	14 37		14 45	14 51				15 30		15 24	15 30	15 37		15 45			15 51		16 30	16 24
Millbrook (Hants)	d		14 40							→				15 40							→	
Redbridge	d		14 43											15 43								
Romsey	d		14 51						15a03					15 51			16a03					
Mottisfont & Dunbridge	d		14 56											15 56								
Dean	d		15 02											16 02								
Salisbury	a		15 15											16 15								
Totton	d	14 35											15 35									
Ashurst New Forest	d	14 40											15 40									
Beaulieu Road	d						←						15 44							←		
Brockenhurst 3	a	14 51			14 58	15 04	14 51					15 37	15 51			15 58			16 05	15 51		16 37
	d	15 16			14 59	15 05	15 16					15 38	16 16			15 59			16 06	16 16		16 38
Sway	d	→					15 21						→							16 21		
New Milton	d						15 26					15 45								16 26		16 45
Hinton Admiral	d						15 30													16 30		
Christchurch	d						15 35					15 52								16 35		16 52
Pokesdown	d						15 38					15 56								16 38		16 56
Bournemouth	a				15 13	15 20	15 42					16 00				16 13			16 20	16 42		17 00
	d					15 24	15 44					16 04							16 24	16 44		17 04
Branksome	d					15 29	15 49												16 29	16 49		
Parkstone (Dorset)	d					15 32	15 52												16 32	16 52		
Poole 4	a					15 36	15 55					16 13							16 36	16 55		17 13
	d					15 37						16 14							16 37			17 14
Hamworthy	d					15 42						16 19							16 42			17 19
Holton Heath	d											16 23										17 23
Wareham	d					15 49						16 28							16 49			17 28
Wool	d											16 35										17 35
Moreton (Dorset)	d											16 41										17 41
Dorchester South	d					16 05						16 49							17 05			17 49
Dorchester West	d																	16 54				
Upwey	d											16 56						17 02				17 55
Weymouth	a					16 13						17 00						17 08	17 16			18 00

A (buffet) to Bournemouth

For services from Brockenhurst - Lymington refer to Table T159

Table T158-F

Saturdays
21 December to 16 May

London - Basingstoke, Southampton, Romsey, Bournemouth and Weymouth

		SW ◇1	SW 1	SW ◇1	XC ◇1 (buffet)	SW ◇1 A (buffet)	SW ◇1	SW 1	SW ◇1	XC ◇1 (buffet)	SW ◇1 A (buffet)	SW ◇1	SW 1	SW ◇1	XC ◇1 (buffet)	SW 1	GW ◇	SW ◇1 A (buffet)	SW ◇1	SW ◇1	SW ◇1 B (restaurant)	SW ◇1	SW 1
London Waterloo 15 ⊖	d			15 09		15 35			15 39		16 05			16 09				16 35		16 39	17 05		
Clapham Junction 10	d								15u46		16u12									16u46	17u12		
Woking	d			15 34		16 00								16 34				17 00					
Farnborough (Main)	d			15 45					16 13					16 45						17 13			
Fleet	d								16 19											17 19			
Reading 7	d				15 49					16 19					16 49								
Basingstoke	a			15 58	16 09				16 31	16 40	16 47			16 58	17 09					17 31	17 48		
	d			16 00	16 12				16 33	16 44	16 49			17 00	17 12					17 33	17 49		
Micheldever	d			16 10										17 10									
Winchester	d			16 19	16 27	16 33			16 49	16 59	17 05			17 19	17 27			17 33		17 49	18 05		
Shawford	d								16 54											17 54			
Romsey	d		16 07					16 20					17 07			17 20							18 07
Chandlers Ford	d		16 14										17 14										18 14
Eastleigh 3	a		16 20	16 27				16 49	16 59				17 20	17 27		17 49				17 59			18 20
	d		16 21	16 28				16 50	17 00				17 21	17 28		17 50				18 00			18 21
Hedge End	d			16 34										17 34									
Botley	d			16 38										17 38									
Fareham	d			16 48										17 48									
Portchester	d			16 53										17 53									
Cosham	d			16 58										17 58									
Hilsea	a			17 03										18 03									
Fratton	a			17 07										18 07									
Portsmouth & Southsea	a			17 11										18 11									
Portsmouth Harbour ⛴	a			17 18										18 18									
Southampton Airport Pkwy ✈	d		16 25		16 36	16 42			17 05	17 09	17 14		17 25		17 36			17 42		18 05	18 14		18 25
Swaythling	d		16 27										17 27										18 27
St Denys	d	←	16 30									←	17 30									←	18 30
Southampton Central ⛴	a	16 12	16 36		16 42	16 49			17 12	17 17	17 22	17 12	17 36		17 42			17 49		18 12	18 22	18 12	18 36
	d	16 30	16 37		16 45	16 51			17 30		17 24	17 30	17 37		17 45			17 51		18 30	18 24	18 30	18 37
Millbrook (Hants)	d		16 40						→				17 40							→			18 40
Redbridge	d		16 43										17 43										18 43
Romsey	d		16 51					17a03					17 51			18a03							19 01
Mottisfont & Dunbridge	d		16 56										17 56										19 06
Dean	d		17 02										18 02										19 11
Salisbury	a		17 15										18 15										19 24
Totton	d	16 35										17 35										18 35	
Ashurst New Forest	d	16 40										17 40										18 40	
Beaulieu Road	d						←					17 44							←				
Brockenhurst 3	a	16 51			16 58	17 04	16 51				17 37	17 51			17 58			18 04	17 51		18 37	18 51	
	d	17 16			16 59	17 05	17 16				17 38	18 16			17 59			18 05	18 16		18 38	19 16	
Sway	d	→					17 21					→							18 21			→	
New Milton	d						17 26				17 45								18 26		18 45		
Hinton Admiral	d						17 30												18 30				
Christchurch	d						17 35				17 52								18 35		18 52		
Pokesdown	d						17 38				17 56								18 38		18 56		
Bournemouth	a				17 13	17 20	17 42				18 00				18 13			18 20	18 42		19 00		
	d					17 24	17 44				18 04							18 24	18 44		19 04		
Branksome	d					17 29	17 49											18 29	18 49				
Parkstone (Dorset)	d					17 32	17 52											18 32	18 52				
Poole 4	a					17 36	17 55				18 13							18 36	18 55		19 13		
	d					17 37					18 14							18 37			19 14		
Hamworthy	d					17 42					18 19							18 42			19 19		
Holton Heath	d										18 23										19 23		
Wareham	d					17 49					18 28							18 49			19 28		
Wool	d										18 35										19 35		
Moreton (Dorset)	d										18 41										19 41		
Dorchester South	d					18 05					18 49							19 05			19 49		
Dorchester West	d																18 53						
Upwey	d										18 55						19 01				19 55		
Weymouth	a					18 13					19 00						19 08	19 13			20 00		

A (buffet) to Bournemouth
B (restaurant) to Bournemouth

For services from Brockenhurst - Lymington refer to Table T159

Table T158-F

Saturdays
21 December to 16 May

London - Basingstoke, Southampton, Romsey, Bournemouth and Weymouth

		SW	XC	SW	GW	SW	SW	SW	SW	SW	SW	SW	XC	SW	SW	SW	SW	SW	SW	SW	SW	XC	SW
		◇1	◇1	1	◇	◇1	◇1	◇1	◇1	◇1	1	◇1	◇1	◇1	◇1	1	◇1	◇1	◇1	1	◇1	◇1	◇1
						A			A					A				A					A
			[catering]			[catering]			[catering]				[catering]	[catering]				[catering]				[catering]	[catering]
London Waterloo 15 ⊖	d	17 09				17 35		17 39	18 05			18 09		18 35			18 39	19 05			19 09		19 35
Clapham Junction 10	d							17u46	18u12								18u46	19u12					
Woking	d	17 34				18 00						18 34		19 00							19 34		20 00
Farnborough (Main)	d	17 45						18 13				18 45					19 13				19 45		
Fleet	d							18 19									19 19						
Reading 7	d		17 49										18 49									19 49	
Basingstoke	a	17 58	18 09					18 31	18 48			18 58	19 09				19 31	19 47			19 58	20 09	
	d	18 00	18 11					18 33	18 49			19 00	19 12				19 33	19 49			20 00	20 12	
Micheldever	d	18 10										19 10									20 10		
Winchester	d	18 19	18 26			18 33		18 49	19 05			19 19	19 27	19 33			19 49	20 05			20 19	20 27	20 33
Shawford	d							18 54									19 54						
Romsey	d			18 20							19 07					19 20				20 07			
Chandlers Ford	d										19 14									20 14			
Eastleigh 3	a	18 27		18 49				18 59			19 20	19 27				19 49	19 59			20 20	20 27		
	d	18 28		18 50				19 00			19 21	19 28				19 50	20 00			20 21	20 28		
Hedge End	d	18 34										19 34									20 34		
Botley	d	18 38										19 38									20 38		
Fareham	d	18 48										19 48									20 48		
Portchester	d	18 53										19 53									20 53		
Cosham	d	18 58										19 58									20 58		
Hilsea	a	19 03										20 03									21 03		
Fratton	a	19 07										20 07									21 07		
Portsmouth & Southsea	a	19 11										20 11									21 10		
Portsmouth Harbour ⛴	a	19 18										20 18									21 16		
Southampton Airport Pkwy ✈	d		18 34			18 42		19 05	19 14		19 25		19 36	19 42			20 05	20 14		20 25		20 36	20 42
Swaythling	d										19 27									20 27			
St Denys	d									←	19 30								←	20 30			
Southampton Central ⛴	a		18 41			18 50		19 12	19 21	19 12	19 36		19 42	19 49			20 14	20 21	20 14	20 36		20 42	20 49
	d		18 42			18 51		19 30	19 24	19 30	19 37		19 44	19 51			20 30	20 24	20 30	20 37		20 45	20 51
Millbrook (Hants)	d							→			19 40						→			20 40			
Redbridge	d										19 43									20 43			
Romsey	d			19a04							19 51					20a03				20 51			
Mottisfont & Dunbridge	d										19 56									20 56			
Dean	d										20 02									21 02			
Salisbury	a										20 15									21 15			
Totton	d									19 35									20 35				
Ashurst New Forest	d									19 40									20 40				
Beaulieu Road	d						←			19 44					←								
Brockenhurst 3	a		18 57			19 04	18 51		19 37	19 51			19 57	20 04	19 51			20 37	20 51			20 58	21 04
	d		18 58			19 05	19 16		19 38	20 16			19 58	20 05	20 16			20 38	21 16			20 59	21 05
Sway	d						19 21			→					20 21				→				
New Milton	d						19 26		19 45						20 26			20 45					
Hinton Admiral	d						19 30								20 30								
Christchurch	d						19 35		19 52						20 35			20 52					
Pokesdown	d						19 38		19 56						20 38			20 56					
Bournemouth	a		19 13			19 20	19 42		20 00				20 12	20 20	20 42			21 00				21 13	21 20
	d					19 24	19 44		20 04					20 24	20 44			21 04					21 24
Branksome	d					19 29	19 49							20 29	20 49								21 29
Parkstone (Dorset)	d					19 32	19 52							20 32	20 52								21 32
Poole 4	a					19 36	19 55		20 13					20 36	20 55			21 13					21 36
	d					19 37			20 14					20 37				21 14					21 37
Hamworthy	d					19 42			20 19					20 42				21 19					21 42
Holton Heath	d								20 23														
Wareham	d					19 49			20 28					20 49				21 26					21 49
Wool	d								20 35									21 33					21 55
Moreton (Dorset)	d								20 41									21 39					22 01
Dorchester South	d					20 05			20 49					21 05				21 49					22 09
Dorchester West	d				19 53																		
Upwey	d				20 02				20 55									21 56					22 16
Weymouth	a				20 09	20 14			21 00					21 13				22 00					22 20

A [catering] to Bournemouth

For services from Brockenhurst - Lymington refer to Table T159

NRT DECEMBER 19 EDITION

Table T158-F

Saturdays
21 December to 16 May

London - Basingstoke, Southampton, Romsey, Bournemouth and Weymouth

		SW	SW	SW	SW	SW	SW	XC	SW	GW	SW	SW	GW	SW	SW	SW	SW	XC	SW	SW	SW	XC
		◇1	1	◇1	◇1	1	◇1	◇1	1	◇	◇1	◇1	1	◇1	◇1	1	◇1	◇1	◇1	1	◇1	◇1
											A								A			
					[catering]						[catering]				[catering]				[catering]			
London Waterloo 15 ⊖	d			19 39	20 05		20 09				20 35	20 39		20 42	21 05				21 35		21 39	
Clapham Junction 10	d			19u46	20u12							20u46			21u12						21u46	
Woking	d						20 34				21 00			21 19	21 32				22 00			
Farnborough (Main)	d			20 13			20 45					21 13		21 33							22 13	
Fleet	d			20 19								21 19		21 38							22 19	
Reading 7	d							20 49									←	21 49				22 19
Basingstoke	a			20 31	20 47		20 58	21 09				21 32		21 58	21 50		21 58	22 10			22 31	22 41
	d			20 33	20 49		21 00	21 12				21 33		22 00	21 51		22 00	22 12			22 33	22 44
Micheldever	d						21 10					21 43		→			22 10				22 43	
Winchester	d			20 49	21 05		21 19	21 27			21 33	21 52			22 08		22 19	22 27	22 33		22 53	22 59
Shawford	d			20 54								21 57									22 57	
Romsey	d		20 20			21 07			21 20							22 07				22 20		
Chandlers Ford	d					21 14										22 14						
Eastleigh 3	a		20 49	20 59		21 20	21 27		21 49			22 02			22 16	22 20	22 27			22 49	23 03	
	d		20 50	21 00		21 21	21 28		21 50			22 03	22 09		22 16	22 22	22 28			22 50	23 04	
Hedge End	d						21 34										22 34					
Botley	d						21 38										22 38					
Fareham	d						21 48										22 50					
Portchester	d						21 53										22 55					
Cosham	d						21 58										23 00					
Hilsea	a						22 03										23 04					
Fratton	a						22 07										23 09					
Portsmouth & Southsea	a						22 11										23 13					
Portsmouth Harbour ⛴	a						22 18										23 18					
Southampton Airport Pkwy ✈	d			21 05	21 14	21 25		21 36			21 42	22 08	22 13		22 20	22 26		22 36	22 42		23 08	23 12
Swaythling	d					21 27										22 28						
St Denys	d					21 30										22 31						
Southampton Central ⛴	a			21 12	21 22	21 36		21 43			21 49	22 17	22 23		22 27	22 36		22 42	22 49		23 17	23 20
	d				21 24	21 37		21 45			21 51		22 24		22 29	22 38		22 45	22 51			
Millbrook (Hants)	d					21 40										22 40						
Redbridge	d					21 43										22 44						
Romsey	d		21a03			21 51			22a03				22 36			22 52				23a03		
Mottisfont & Dunbridge	d					21 56										22 57						
Dean	d					22 02										23 02						
Salisbury	a					22 15							22 55			23 15						
Totton	d				21 29										22 34							
Ashurst New Forest	d				21 34										22 39							
Beaulieu Road	d	←																				
Brockenhurst 3	a	20 51			21 42			21 58			22 04				22 47			22 58	23 04			
	d	21 16			21 43			21 59			22 05				22 48			23 00	23 05			
Sway	d	21 20			21 48										22 53							
New Milton	d	21 25			21 53										22 58							
Hinton Admiral	d	21 29			21 57										23 02							
Christchurch	d	21 34			22 02										23 07							
Pokesdown	d	21 38			22 06										23 11							
Bournemouth	a	21 42			22 10			22 15			22 20				23 15			23 19	23 24			
	d	21 43			22 12						22 24				23 17				23 27			
Branksome	d	21 48			22 17						22 29				23 22				23 32			
Parkstone (Dorset)	d	21 51			22 21						22 32				23 26				23 35			
Poole 4	a	21 55			22 26						22 36				23 30				23 39			
	d										22 37								23 40			
Hamworthy	d										22 42								23 45			
Holton Heath	d																					
Wareham	d										22 49								23 51			
Wool	d										22 55								23 58			
Moreton (Dorset)	d										23 01								00 04			
Dorchester South	d										23 09								00 12			
Dorchester West	d									22 52												
Upwey	d									23 00	23 16								00 18			
Weymouth	a									23 08	23 20								00 23			

A [catering] to Bournemouth

For services from Brockenhurst - Lymington refer to Table T159

Table T158-F

Saturdays
21 December to 16 May

London - Basingstoke, Southampton, Romsey, Bournemouth and Weymouth

		SW	SW	SW	SW	XC	SW	SW	SW	SW	SW
		◇1	◇1 ⊼	1	◇1	◇1	◇1 ⊼	1	◇1	◇1	◇1
London Waterloo 15 ⊖	d	21 42	22 05				22 35		22 39	23 05	23 35
Clapham Junction 10	d		22u12						22u46	23u12	23u42
Woking	d	22 19	22 32				23 00			23 32	00 03
Farnborough (Main)	d	22 33							23 16		00 14
Fleet	d	22 38							23 21		00 20
Reading 7	d				←	22 52					
Basingstoke	a	22 58	22 50		22 58	23 09			23 34	23 50	00 33
	d	23 00	22 52		23 00	23 12			23 36	23 52	00 35
Micheldever	d	→			23 10					00 02	
Winchester	d		23 08		23 19	23 27	23 33		23 52	00 11	00 51
Shawford	d								23 57		
Romsey	d			23 11				23 08			
Chandlers Ford	d			23 18							
Eastleigh 3	a		23 16	23 24	23 27			23 37	00 02	00 19	00 59
	d		23 17	23 24	23 28			23 38	00 03	00 20	01 00
Hedge End	d				23 34						
Botley	d				23 38						
Fareham	d				23 48						
Portchester	d				23 53						
Cosham	d				23 58						
Hilsea	a				00 03						
Fratton	a				00 07						
Portsmouth & Southsea	a				00 10						
Portsmouth Harbour ⛴	a				00 15						
Southampton Airport Pkwy ✈	d		23 22	23 28		23 36	23 42		00 08	00 24	01 05
Swaythling	d			23 31							
St Denys	d			23 34						00s28	
Southampton Central ⛴	a		23 29	23 39		23 43	23 49		00 18	00 33	01 12
	d		23 30	23 42			23 51			00 35	
Millbrook (Hants)	d			23 44							
Redbridge	d			23 48							
Romsey	d			23 57				23a50			
Mottisfont & Dunbridge	d			00 02							
Dean	d			00 08							
Salisbury	a			00 21							
Totton	d		23 36							00s40	
Ashurst New Forest	d		23 40								
Beaulieu Road	d										
Brockenhurst 3	a		23 48				00 04			00s51	
	d		23 49				00 05				
Sway	d		23 54								
New Milton	d		23 58							00s59	
Hinton Admiral	d		00 02								
Christchurch	d		00 07							01s06	
Pokesdown	d		00 11							01s10	
Bournemouth	a		00 15				00 21			01 14	
	d		00 16				00 22			01 15	
Branksome	d		00 21				00 27			01s20	
Parkstone (Dorset)	d		00 24				00 30			01s23	
Poole 4	a		00 30				00 35			01 27	
	d										
Hamworthy	d										
Holton Heath	d										
Wareham	d										
Wool	d										
Moreton (Dorset)	d										
Dorchester South	d										
Dorchester West	d										
Upwey	d										
Weymouth	a										

For services from Brockenhurst - Lymington refer to Table T159

Table T158-F

Sundays
15 December to 10 May

London - Basingstoke, Southampton, Romsey, Bournemouth and Weymouth

		SW	SW	SW	SW	SW	SW	SW	SW	SW	SW	SW	SW	SW	SW	SW		SW	SW	SW	SW		GW
		◇1	1	◇1	◇1	◇1	◇1	◇1	1	◇1	1	◇1	◇1	1	◇1	◇1		◇1	1	1	◇1		◇
		A ⊼	A	A	A	A ⊼	A		A	A	A												
London Waterloo 15 ⊖	d											00 05	01 05								07 51		
Clapham Junction 10	d											00u12	01 15								08u01		
Woking	d									00 03	00 28	00 37	01 49								08 28		
Farnborough (Main)	d								00 10	00 14	00 41		01s58										
Fleet	d								00 16	00 20	00 47		02s04										
Reading 7	d																						
Basingstoke	a								00 33	00 33	01 06	00 55	02s16								08 46		
	d									00 35		00 56				07 48					08 48		
Micheldever	d						00 02									07 58					08 58		
Winchester	d						00 11			00 51		01 13	02s33			08 07					09 08		
Shawford	d															08 12					09 12		
Romsey	d																		08 35	08 39			
Chandlers Ford	d																		08 42				
Eastleigh 3	a						00 19			00 59		01 21	02s42			08 17			08 47	09 13	09 18		
	d			00 03			00 20	00 30		01 00		01 22				08 21	08 24		08 54	09 15	09 22	09 26	
Hedge End	d							00s36									08 30					09 32	
Botley	d							00s39									08 34					09 36	
Fareham	d							00s47						07 44			08 42					09 45	
Portchester	d							00s53						07 49			08 47					09 50	
Cosham	d							00s57						07 54			08 52					09 55	
Hilsea	a													08 00			09 00					10 00	
Fratton	a							01s05						08 04			09 04					10 09	
Portsmouth & Southsea	a							01 08						08 07			09 08					10 13	
Portsmouth Harbour ⛴	a													08 11			09 20					10 20	
Southampton Airport Pkwy ✈	d			00 08			00 24			01 05		01 26	02s46			08 25			08 58		09 27		
Swaythling	d																		09 01				
St Denys	d						00s28						02s51						09 04				
Southampton Central ⛴	a			00 18			00 33			01 12		01 35	02 56			08 32			09 09		09 34		
	d						00 35					01 37				08 34		09 03	09 10		09 35		
Millbrook (Hants)	d																		09 13				
Redbridge	d																		09 16				
Romsey	d																		09 24	09a28			
Mottisfont & Dunbridge	d		00 02																09 29				
Dean	d		00 08																09 35				
Salisbury	a		00 21																09 48				
Totton	d						00s40					01s42				08 39					09 41		
Ashurst New Forest	d															08 44					09 45		
Beaulieu Road	d															08 48					09 50		
Brockenhurst 3	a						00s51					01s53				08 54		09 16			09 56		
	d					00 05										08 55		09 17			09 57		
Sway	d															09 00					10 01		
New Milton	d						00s59					02s00				09 05		09 24			10 06		
Hinton Admiral	d	00 02														09 09					10 10		
Christchurch	d	00 07					01s06					02s07				09 14					10 15		
Pokesdown	d	00 11					01s10					02s11				09 17					10 19		
Bournemouth	a	00 15				00 21	01 14					02 15				09 21		09 34			10 23		
	d	00 16				00 22	01 15								08 39	09 25		09 39			10 24		
Branksome	d	00 21				00 27	01s20								08 44			09 44					
Parkstone (Dorset)	d	00 24				00 30	01s23								08 47			09 47					
Poole 4	a	00 30				00 35	01 27								08 50	09 34		09 50			10 33		
	d														08 51			09 51					
Hamworthy	d														08 56			09 56					
Holton Heath	d																						
Wareham	d														09 03			10 03					
Wool	d														09 10			10 10					
Moreton (Dorset)	d				00 04										09 16			10 16					
Dorchester South	d				00 12										09 24			10 24					
Dorchester West	d																						10 29
Upwey	d				00 18										09 31			10 31					10 37
Weymouth	a				00 23										09 35			10 35					10 42

A not 15 December

For services from Brockenhurst - Lymington refer to Table T159

Table T158-F

Sundays
15 December to 10 May

London - Basingstoke, Southampton, Romsey, Bournemouth and Weymouth

		SW	SW	SW	SW		XC	GW	SW	SW	SW	SW		XC	SW	SW	SW	SW		XC	SW	SW	SW
		◇1	1	1	◇1		◇1 🛒	◇	◇1 🛒	1	1	◇1		◇1 🛒	◇1 A 🛒	1	1	◇1		◇1 🛒	◇1 A 🛒	1	1
London Waterloo 15 ⊖	d	08 35			08 54				09 35			09 54			10 35			10 54			11 35		
Clapham Junction 10	d	08u45			09u03				09u45			10u03			10u45			11u03			11u45		
Woking	d	09 09			09 28				10 09			10 28			11 08			11 28			12 08		
Farnborough (Main)	d																						
Fleet	d																						
Reading 7	d						09 52							10 52						11 52			
Basingstoke	a	09 28			09 46		10 10		10 28			10 46		11 09	11 26			11 46		12 09	12 26		
	d	09 29			09 48		10 12		10 29			10 48		11 11	11 28			11 48		12 11	12 28		
Micheldever	d				09 58							10 58						11 58					
Winchester	d	09 46			10 08		10 27		10 46			11 08		11 26	11 44			12 08		12 27	12 44		
Shawford	d				10 12							11 12						12 12					
Romsey	d		09 35	09 32						10 35	10 32					11 35	11 32					12 35	12 32
Chandlers Ford	d		09 42							10 42						11 42						12 42	
Eastleigh 8	a		09 48	10 13	10 18					10 48	11 13	11 18				11 48	12 13	12 18				12 48	13 13
	d		09 54	10 15	10 22	10 26				10 54	11 15	11 22	11 26			11 54	12 15	12 22	12 26			12 54	13 15
Hedge End	d					10 32							11 32						12 32				
Botley	d					10 36							11 36						12 36				
Fareham	d					10 45							11 45						12 45				
Portchester	d					10 50							11 50						12 50				
Cosham	d					10 55							11 55						12 55				
Hilsea	a					11 00							12 00						13 00				
Fratton	a					11 09							12 09						13 09				
Portsmouth & Southsea	a					11 13							12 13						13 13				
Portsmouth Harbour ⛴	a					11 20							12 20						13 20				
Southampton Airport Pkwy ✈	d	09 55	09 58		10 27		10 36		10 55	10 58		11 27		11 34	11 53	11 58		12 27		12 35	12 53	12 58	
Swaythling	d		10 01							11 01						12 01						13 01	
St Denys	d		10 04							11 04						12 04						13 04	
Southampton Central ⛴	a	10 02	10 09		10 34		10 42		11 02	11 09		11 34		11 43	12 00	12 09		12 34		12 43	13 00	13 09	
	d	10 03	10 10		10 35		10 50		11 03	11 10		11 35		11 49	12 03	12 10		12 35		12 49	13 03	13 10	
Millbrook (Hants)	d		10 13							11 13						12 13						13 13	
Redbridge	d		10 16							11 16						12 16						13 16	
Romsey	d		10 24	10a28						11 24	11a28					12 24	12a28					13 24	13a28
Mottisfont & Dunbridge	d		10 29							11 29						12 29						13 29	
Dean	d		10 35							11 35						12 35						13 35	
Salisbury	a		10 48							11 48						12 48						13 48	
Totton	d				10 41							11 41						12 41					
Ashurst New Forest	d				10 45							11 45						12 45					
Beaulieu Road	d				10 50							11 50						12 50					
Brockenhurst 3	a	10 17			10 56		11 07		11 17			11 56		12 07	12 16			12 56		13 07	13 16		
	d	10 17			10 57		11 12		11 17			11 57		12 08	12 17			12 57		13 11	13 17		
Sway	d				11 01							12 01						13 01					
New Milton	d	10 24			11 06				11 24			12 06			12 24			13 06			13 24		
Hinton Admiral	d				11 10							12 10						13 10					
Christchurch	d				11 15							12 15						13 15					
Pokesdown	d				11 19							12 19						13 19					
Bournemouth	a	10 34			11 23		11 26		11 34			12 23		12 26	12 34			13 23		13 26	13 34		
	d	10 39			11 24				11 39			12 24			12 39			13 24			13 39		
Branksome	d	10 44							11 44						12 44						13 44		
Parkstone (Dorset)	d	10 47							11 47						12 47						13 47		
Poole 4	a	10 50			11 33				11 50			12 33			12 50			13 33			13 50		
	d	10 51							11 51						12 51						13 51		
Hamworthy	d	10 56							11 56						12 56						13 56		
Holton Heath	d																						
Wareham	d	11 03							12 03						13 03						14 03		
Wool	d	11 10							12 10						13 10						14 10		
Moreton (Dorset)	d	11 16							12 16						13 16						14 16		
Dorchester South	d	11 24							12 24						13 24						14 24		
Dorchester West	d							11 41															
Upwey	d	11 31						11 49	12 31						13 31						14 31		
Weymouth	a	11 35						11 54	12 35						13 35						14 35		

A 🛒 to Bournemouth

For services from Brockenhurst - Lymington refer to Table T159

NRT DECEMBER 19 EDITION

Table T158-F

Sundays
15 December to 10 May

London - Basingstoke, Southampton, Romsey, Bournemouth and Weymouth

		SW		XC	SW	SW	SW	SW		XC	GW	SW	SW	SW	SW		XC	SW	SW	SW	SW	
		◇1 🛒		◇1 🛒	◇1 A 🛒	1	1	◇1 🛒		◇1 🛒	◇	◇1 A 🛒	1	1	◇1 🛒		◇1 🛒	◇1 A 🛒	1	1	◇1 🛒	
London Waterloo 15 ⊖	d	11 54			12 35			12 54				13 35			13 54			14 35			14 54	
Clapham Junction 10	d	12u03			12u45			13u03				13u42			14u03			14u42			15u03	
Woking	d	12 28			13 08			13 28				14 07			14 28			15 07			15 28	
Farnborough (Main)	d																					
Fleet	d																					
Reading 7	d			12 52						13 52							14 52					
Basingstoke	a	12 46		13 09	13 26			13 46		14 09		14 26			14 46		15 09	15 26			15 46	
	d	12 48		13 11	13 28			13 48		14 11		14 28			14 48		15 11	15 28			15 48	
Micheldever	d	12 58						13 58							14 58						15 58	
Winchester	d	13 08		13 27	13 44			14 08		14 27		14 44			15 08		15 27	15 44			16 08	
Shawford	d	13 12						14 12							15 12						16 12	
Romsey	d					13 35	13 32						14 35	14 32					15 35	15 32		
Chandlers Ford	d					13 42							14 42						15 42			
Eastleigh 8	a	13 18				13 48	14 13	14 18					14 48	15 13	15 18				15 48	16 13	16 18	
	d	13 22	13 26			13 54	14 15	14 22	14 26				14 54	15 15	15 22	15 26			15 54	16 15	16 22	16 26
Hedge End	d		13 32						14 32							15 32						16 32
Botley	d		13 36						14 36							15 36						16 36
Fareham	d		13 45						14 45							15 45						16 45
Portchester	d		13 50						14 50							15 50						16 50
Cosham	d		13 55						14 55							15 55						16 55
Hilsea	a		14 00						15 00							16 00						16 59
Fratton	a		14 09						15 09							16 09						17 08
Portsmouth & Southsea	a		14 13						15 13							16 13						17 13
Portsmouth Harbour ⛴	a		14 20						15 20							16 20						17 20
Southampton Airport Pkwy ✈	d	13 27		13 35	13 53	13 58		14 27		14 35		14 53	14 58		15 27		15 35	15 53	15 58		16 27	
Swaythling	d					14 01							15 01						16 01			
St Denys	d					14 04							15 04						16 04			
Southampton Central ⛴	a	13 34		13 43	14 00	14 09		14 34		14 43		15 00	15 09		15 34		15 43	16 00	16 09		16 34	
	d	13 35		13 49	14 03	14 10		14 35		14 49		15 03	15 10		15 35		15 49	16 03	16 10		16 35	
Millbrook (Hants)	d					14 13							15 13						16 13			
Redbridge	d					14 16							15 16						16 16			
Romsey	d					14 24	14a28						15 24	15a28					16 24	16a28		
Mottisfont & Dunbridge	d					14 29							15 29						16 29			
Dean	d					14 35							15 35						16 35			
Salisbury	a					14 48							15 48						16 48			
Totton	d	13 41						14 41							15 41						16 41	
Ashurst New Forest	d	13 45						14 45							15 45						16 45	
Beaulieu Road	d	13 50						14 50							15 50						16 50	
Brockenhurst 3	a	13 56		14 07	14 16			14 56		15 07		15 16			15 56		16 07	16 16			16 56	
	d	13 57		14 11	14 17			14 57		15 11		15 17			15 57		16 11	16 17			16 57	
Sway	d	14 01						15 01							16 01						17 01	
New Milton	d	14 06			14 24			15 06				15 24			16 06			16 24			17 06	
Hinton Admiral	d	14 10						15 10							16 10						17 10	
Christchurch	d	14 15						15 15							16 15						17 15	
Pokesdown	d	14 19						15 19							16 19						17 19	
Bournemouth	a	14 23		14 26	14 34			15 23		15 26		15 34			16 23		16 26	16 34			17 23	
	d	14 24			14 39			15 24				15 39			16 24			16 39			17 24	
Branksome	d				14 44							15 44						16 44				
Parkstone (Dorset)	d				14 47							15 47						16 47				
Poole 4	a	14 33			14 50			15 33				15 50			16 33			16 50			17 33	
	d				14 51							15 51						16 51				
Hamworthy	d				14 56							15 56						16 56				
Holton Heath	d																					
Wareham	d				15 03							16 03						17 03				
Wool	d				15 10							16 10						17 10				
Moreton (Dorset)	d				15 16							16 16						17 16				
Dorchester South	d				15 24							16 24						17 24				
Dorchester West	d										15 36											
Upwey	d				15 31						15 44	16 31						17 31				
Weymouth	a				15 35						15 49	16 35						17 35				

A 🛒 to Bournemouth

For services from Brockenhurst - Lymington refer to Table T159

Table T158-F

London - Basingstoke, Southampton, Romsey, Bournemouth and Weymouth

Sundays

15 December to 10 May

		XC ◇1 ✠	SW ◇1 A ✠	SW 1	SW 1	SW ◇1	SW ◇1 ✠	SW ◇1	XC ◇1 ✠	SW ◇1 A ✠	SW 1	SW 1	GW ◇	SW ◇1	SW ◇1 ✠	SW ◇1	XC ◇1 ✠	SW ◇1 A ✠	SW 1	SW 1	SW ◇1	SW ◇1 ✠	SW ◇1
London Waterloo 15 ⊖	d		15 35			15 50	16 05			16 35				16 50	17 05			17 35			17 50	18 05	
Clapham Junction 10	d		15u42			15u58	16u12			16u42				16u58	17u12			17u42			17u58	18u12	
Woking	d		16 07			16 21	16 37			17 07				17 21	17 37			18 07			18 21	18 37	
Farnborough (Main)	d					16 32								17 32							18 32		
Fleet	d																						
Reading 7	d	15 52							16 52								17 52						
Basingstoke	a	16 09	16 26			16 46	16 56		17 09	17 26				17 46	17 56		18 09	18 26			18 46	18 56	
	d	16 12	16 28			16 47	16 57		17 10	17 28				17 47	17 57		18 10	18 28			18 47	18 57	
Micheldever	d					16 57								17 57							18 57		
Winchester	d	16 27	16 44			17 07	17 14		17 25	17 44				18 07	18 14		18 25	18 44			19 07	19 14	
Shawford	d					17 12								18 12							19 12		
Romsey	d			16 35	16 32						17 35	17 32							18 35	18 32			
Chandlers Ford	d			16 42				←			17 42					←			18 42				←
Eastleigh 3	a			16 48	17 15	17 17	17 22	17 17			17 48	18 13		18 17	18 22	18 17			18 48	19 15	19 17	19 22	19 17
	d			16 54	17 16	17 26	17 23	17 26			17 54	18 15		18 26	18 23	18 26			18 54	19 16	19 26	19 23	19 26
Hedge End	d					→		17 32						→		18 32					→		19 32
Botley	d							17 36								18 36							19 36
Fareham	d							17 45								18 45							19 45
Portchester	d							17 50								18 50							19 50
Cosham	d							17 55								18 55							19 55
Hilsea	a							18 00								19 00							20 00
Fratton	a							18 09								19 09							20 09
Portsmouth & Southsea	a							18 13								19 13							20 13
Portsmouth Harbour ⛴	a							18 20								19 20							20 20
Southampton Airport Pkwy ✈	d	16 36	16 53	16 58			17 27		17 34	17 53	17 58				18 27		18 34	18 53	18 58			19 27	
Swaythling	d			17 01							18 01								19 01				
St Denys	d			17 04							18 04								19 04				
Southampton Central ⛴	a	16 42	17 00	17 09			17 34		17 42	18 00	18 09				18 34		18 42	19 00	19 09			19 34	
	d	16 49	17 03	17 10			17 36		17 49	18 03	18 10				18 36		18 49	19 03	19 10			19 36	
Millbrook (Hants)	d			17 13							18 13								19 13				
Redbridge	d			17 16							18 16								19 16				
Romsey	d			17 24	17a28						18 24	18a28							19 24	19a28			
Mottisfont & Dunbridge	d			17 29							18 29								19 29				
Dean	d			17 35							18 35								19 35				
Salisbury	a			17 48							18 48								19 48				
Totton	d						17 41								18 41							19 41	
Ashurst New Forest	d						17 46								18 46							19 46	
Beaulieu Road	d						17 50								18 50							19 50	
Brockenhurst 3	a	17 06	17 16				17 56		18 06	18 16					18 56		19 06	19 16				19 56	
	d	17 11	17 17				17 57		18 11	18 17					18 57		19 11	19 17				19 57	
Sway	d						18 01								19 01							20 01	
New Milton	d		17 24				18 06			18 24					19 06			19 24				20 06	
Hinton Admiral	d						18 10								19 10							20 10	
Christchurch	d						18 15								19 15							20 15	
Pokesdown	d						18 19								19 19							20 19	
Bournemouth	a	17 26	17 34				18 23		18 26	18 34					19 23		19 26	19 34				20 23	
	d		17 39				18 24			18 39					19 24			19 39				20 24	
Branksome	d		17 44							18 44								19 44					
Parkstone (Dorset)	d		17 47							18 47								19 47					
Poole 4	a		17 50				18 33			18 50					19 33			19 50				20 33	
	d		17 51							18 51								19 51					
Hamworthy	d		17 56							18 56								19 56					
Holton Heath	d																						
Wareham	d		18 03							19 03								20 03					
Wool	d		18 10							19 10								20 10					
Moreton (Dorset)	d		18 16							19 16								20 16					
Dorchester South	d		18 24							19 24								20 24					
Dorchester West	d												19 48										
Upwey	d		18 31							19 31			19 56					20 31					
Weymouth	a		18 35							19 35			20 04					20 36					

A ✠ to Bournemouth

For services from Brockenhurst - Lymington refer to Table T159

Table T158-F

London - Basingstoke, Southampton, Romsey, Bournemouth and Weymouth

Sundays

15 December to 10 May

		XC ◇1 ✠	SW ◇1 A ✠	SW 1	SW 1	SW ◇1	SW ◇1 ✠	SW ◇1	XC ◇1 ✠	SW ◇1 A ✠	SW 1	SW 1	GW	SW ◇1	SW ◇1 ✠	SW ◇1	XC ◇1	SW ◇1 A ✠	SW 1	SW 1	SW ◇1	SW ◇1	SW ◇1
London Waterloo 15 ⊖	d		18 35			18 50	19 05			19 35				19 50	20 05			20 35			20 50	21 05	
Clapham Junction 10	d		18u42			18u58	19u12			19u42				19u58	20u12			20u42			20u58	21u12	
Woking	d		19 07			19 21	19 37			20 07				20 21	20 37			21 07			21 21	21 37	
Farnborough (Main)	d					19 32								20 32							21 32		
Fleet	d																						
Reading 7	d	18 52							19 52								20 52						
Basingstoke	a	19 09	19 26			19 46	19 56		20 09	20 26				20 46	20 56		21 09	21 26			21 46	21 56	
	d	19 10	19 28			19 47	19 57		20 10	20 28				20 47	20 57		21 11	21 28			21 47	21 57	
Micheldever	d					19 57								20 57							21 57		
Winchester	d	19 25	19 44			20 07	20 14		20 25	20 44				21 07	21 14		21 27	21 44			22 07	22 14	
Shawford	d					20 12								21 12							22 12		
Romsey	d			19 35	19 32						20 35	20 32							21 35	21 32			
Chandlers Ford	d			19 42				←			20 42					←			21 42				←
Eastleigh 3	a			19 48	20 13	20 17	20 22	20 17			20 48	21 13		21 17	21 22	21 17			21 48	22 13	22 17	22 22	22 17
	d			19 54	20 15	20 26	20 23	20 26			20 54	21 15		21 26	21 23	21 26			21 54	22 15	22 26	22 23	22 26
Hedge End	d					→		20 32						→		21 32					→		22 32
Botley	d							20 36								21 36							22 36
Fareham	d							20 45								21 45							22 45
Portchester	d							20 50								21 50							22 50
Cosham	d							20 55								21 55							22 55
Hilsea	a							21 00								22 00							23 00
Fratton	a							21 09								22 09							23 08
Portsmouth & Southsea	a							21 13								22 13							23 11
Portsmouth Harbour ⛴	a							21 20								22 20							23 15
Southampton Airport Pkwy ✈	d	19 34	19 53	19 58			20 27		20 34	20 53	20 58				21 27		21 35	21 53	21 58			22 27	
Swaythling	d			20 01							21 01								22 01				
St Denys	d			20 04							21 04								22 04				
Southampton Central ⛴	a	19 42	20 01	20 09			20 34		20 42	21 00	21 09				21 34		21 43	22 00	22 09			22 34	
	d	19 49	20 03	20 10			20 36		20 49	21 03	21 10				21 36		21 49	22 03	22 10			22 36	
Millbrook (Hants)	d			20 13							21 13								22 13				
Redbridge	d			20 16							21 16								22 16				
Romsey	d			20 24	20a28						21 24	21a28							22a24	22a31			
Mottisfont & Dunbridge	d			20 29							21 29												
Dean	d			20 35							21 35												
Salisbury	a			20 48							21 48												
Totton	d						20 41								21 41							22 41	
Ashurst New Forest	d						20 46								21 46							22 46	
Beaulieu Road	d						20 50								21 50								
Brockenhurst 3	a	20 06	20 16				20 56		21 06	21 16					21 56		22 07	22 16				22 54	
	d	20 11	20 17				20 57		21 11	21 17					21 57		22 11	22 17				22 57	
Sway	d						21 01								22 01							23 01	
New Milton	d		20 24				21 06			21 24					22 06			22 24				23 06	
Hinton Admiral	d						21 10								22 10							23 10	
Christchurch	d						21 15								22 15							23 15	
Pokesdown	d						21 19								22 19							23 19	
Bournemouth	a	20 26	20 34				21 23		21 26	21 34					22 23		22 26	22 34				23 23	
	d		20 39				21 24			21 39					22 24			22 39				23 24	
Branksome	d		20 44							21 44								22 44					
Parkstone (Dorset)	d		20 47							21 47								22 47					
Poole 4	a		20 50				21 33			21 50					22 33			22 50				23 33	
	d		20 51							21 51								22 51					
Hamworthy	d		20 56							21 56								22 56					
Holton Heath	d																						
Wareham	d		21 03							22 03								23 03					
Wool	d		21 10							22 10								23 10					
Moreton (Dorset)	d		21 16							22 16								23 16					
Dorchester South	d		21 24							22 24								23 24					
Dorchester West	d												22 53										
Upwey	d		21 31							22 31			23 01					23 31					
Weymouth	a		21 36							22 36			23 06					23 36					

A ✠ to Bournemouth

For services from Brockenhurst - Lymington refer to Table T159

Table T158-F

Sundays
15 December to 10 May

London - Basingstoke, Southampton, Romsey, Bournemouth and Weymouth

		XC	SW	SW	SW	SW	SW	SW	SW	SW	SW	SW
		◇1	◇1	1	◇1	1	◇1	◇1	◇1	◇1	◇1	◇1
			A									
			🛒		🛒			🛒	🛒	🛒		🛒
London Waterloo 15 ⊖	d		21 35		21 50		22 05		22 35	22 50	23 05	
Clapham Junction 10	d		21u42		21u58		22u12		22u42	22u58	23u12	
Woking	d		22 07		22 21		22 37		23 07	23 21	23 37	
Farnborough (Main)	d				22 32					23 32		
Fleet	d											
Reading 7	d	21 52										
Basingstoke	a	22 09	22 26		22 46		22 56		23 26	23 46	23 56	
	d	22 11	22 28		22 47		22 57		23 28	23 47	23 57	
Micheldever	d				22 57					23 57		
Winchester	d	22 26	22 44		23 07		23 14		23 44	00 07	00 14	
Shawford	d				23 12					00 12		
Romsey	d			22 35		22 28						
Chandlers Ford	d			22 42				←				←
Eastleigh 3	a			22 48	23 18	23 19	23 22	23 18		00 17	00 23	00 17
	d			22 54	23 26	23 22	23 23	23 26		00 30	00 24	00 30
Hedge End	d				→			23 32		→		00s36
Botley	d							23 36				00s39
Fareham	d							23 45				00s47
Portchester	d							23 50				00s53
Cosham	d							23 55				00s57
Hilsea	a							00 02				
Fratton	a							00 07				01s05
Portsmouth & Southsea	a							00 10				01s08
Portsmouth Harbour ⛴	a							00 14				01 12
Southampton Airport Pkwy ✈	d	22 34	22 53	22 58			23 27		23 53		00 28	
Swaythling	d			23 01								
St Denys	d			23 04							00s32	
Southampton Central ⛴	a	22 43	23 00	23 09			23 34		00 01		00 37	
	d		23 03	23 10			23 36		00 03		00 40	
Millbrook (Hants)	d			23 13								
Redbridge	d			23 16								
Romsey	d			23 24		23a35						
Mottisfont & Dunbridge	d			23 29								
Dean	d			23 35								
Salisbury	a			23 51								
Totton	d						23 41				00s45	
Ashurst New Forest	d						23 46					
Beaulieu Road	d											
Brockenhurst 3	a		23 16				23 54		00 16		00s56	
	d		23 17				23 55		00 17			
Sway	d						23 59					
New Milton	d		23 24				00 04		00 24		01s04	
Hinton Admiral	d						00 08					
Christchurch	d						00 13				01s11	
Pokesdown	d						00 17				01s15	
Bournemouth	a		23 34				00 21		00 34		01 19	
	d		23 39				00 22		00 37		01 20	
Branksome	d		23 44				00 27		00 43		01s25	
Parkstone (Dorset)	d		23 47				00 30		00 46		01s28	
Poole 4	a		23 50				00 34		00 51		01 32	
	d		23 51									
Hamworthy	d		23 56									
Holton Heath	d											
Wareham	d		00 03									
Wool	d		00 10									
Moreton (Dorset)	d		00 16									
Dorchester South	d		00 24									
Dorchester West	d											
Upwey	d		00 31									
Weymouth	a		00 36									

A 🛒 to Bournemouth

For services from Brockenhurst - Lymington refer to Table T159

Table T158-R

Mondays to Fridays
16 December to 15 May

Weymouth, Bournemouth, Romsey, Southampton and Basingstoke - London

Miles	Miles	Miles			SW	SW	SW	SW	XC	SW	SW	GW	GW	SW	SW	SW	SW	XC	SW	SW	SW	SW	SW
					MX	MX	MX																
					◇1	1	◇1	◇1	◇1	◇1	◇1		◇	1	1	◇1	1	◇1	◇1	1	◇1	◇1	1
																🛒					🛒		
0	—	—	**Weymouth**	d									05 28										
2¼	—	—	Upwey	d									05 33										
—	—	—	Dorchester West	a									05 40										
7	—	—	**Dorchester South**	d																			
12½	—	—	Moreton (Dorset)	d																			
17	—	—	Wool	d																			
22	—	—	Wareham	d																			
24	—	—	Holton Heath	d																			
26¾	—	—	Hamworthy	d																			
29	—	—	**Poole** 4	a																			
—	—	—		d												05 00				05 26	05 45		
30¾	—	—	Parkstone (Dorset)	d												05 04				05 30			
32	—	—	Branksome	d												05 07				05 33			
34¾	—	—	**Bournemouth**	a												05 12				05 38	05 54		
—	—	—		d												05 15				05 40	05 57		
36½	—	—	Pokesdown	d												05 19				05 44			
38½	—	—	Christchurch	d												05 23				05 48			
41¾	—	—	Hinton Admiral	d																05 53			
44¼	—	—	New Milton	d												05 30				05 57			
47¼	—	—	Sway	d																06 02			
50	—	—	**Brockenhurst** 3	a												05 37				06 07	06 12		
—	—	—		d												05 38					06 14		
54¾	—	—	Beaulieu Road	d																			
57¼	—	—	Ashurst New Forest	d																			
60¼	—	—	Totton	d												05 49	06 14						
—	0	—	**Salisbury**	d										05 35									
—	9	—	Dean	d										05 47									
—	12¾	—	Mottisfont & Dunbridge	d										05 53									
—	16½	—	**Romsey**	d										05 58									
60¾	22½	—	Redbridge	d													06 16						
62½	—	—	Millbrook (Hants)	d													06 20						←
63½	—	—	**Southampton Central** ⛴	a												05 54	06 25				06 27		06 25
—	—	—		d				04 52	05 15	05 20					05 40	05 55	06 33	06 16			06 30		06 33
65½	—	—	St Denys	d			00 04	04 57							05 45		→						06 39
67	—	—	Swaythling	d			00 07	05 00							05 48								06 42
67¾	—	—	**Southampton Airport Pkwy** ✈	d			00 10	05 03	05 22	05 28					05 51	06 03		06 23	06 28		06 38		06 45
—	0	—	**Portsmouth Harbour** ⛴	d							05 00											05 43	
—	0¾	—	**Portsmouth & Southsea**	d							05 05											05 48	
—	1¾	—	Fratton	d							05 09											05 52	
—	4	—	Hilsea	d							05 13											05 56	
—	5½	—	Cosham	d							05 19											06 03	
—	8	—	Portchester	d							05 23											06 08	
—	11¼	—	Fareham	d							05 29											06 19	
—	16¾	—	Botley	d							05 37											06 28	
—	17¾	—	Hedge End	d		00 05					05 41											06 33	
69¼	22¼	0	Eastleigh 3	a		00 13	00 14	05 06		05 31	05 47				05 55	06 07			06 31			06 42	06 48
—	—	—		d		00 19		05 07		05 32	05 49					06 08			06 32			06 43	06 50
—	24¼	2	Chandlers Ford	d										06 06									06 55
—	29½	7¼	**Romsey**	a										06 44									07 03
73	—	—	Shawford	d				05 13			05 56											06 49	
76¼	—	—	**Winchester**	d		00a28		05 19	05 31	05 42	06 02					06 18		06 32	06 42		06 48	06 55	
84¾	—	—	Micheldever	d				05 27		05 51	06 10											07 03	
95	—	—	**Basingstoke**	a				05 38	05 46	06 01	06 20					06 35		06 47	06 59			07 13	
—	—	—		d				05 39	05 49	06 03	06 23	06 31				06 36		06 49	07 00			07 14	
—	—	—	Reading 7	a					06 05			06 56						07 06					
106¼	—	—	Fleet	d	00 01			05 50			06 40												
109½	—	—	Farnborough (Main)	d	00 06			05 56			06 45												
118½	—	—	**Woking**	a	00 18			06 05			06 57					06 54			07 18			07 32	
138¾	—	—	**Clapham Junction** 10	a	00 53			06 25		06 37						07 14							
142¾	—	—	**London Waterloo** 15 ⊖	a	01 04			06 34		06 46	07 28					07 24			07 46		07 48	08 01	

For services from Brockenhurst - Lymington refer to Table T159

Table T158-R

Mondays to Fridays
16 December to 15 May

Weymouth, Bournemouth, Romsey, Southampton and Basingstoke - London

		SW	SW	SW	SW	SW	SW	SW	XC	SW	SW	SW	SW	SW	SW	XC	SW	SW	GW	SW	XC	SW	SW
		◇[1]	◇[1]	◇[1] ⊥	◇[1] ⊥	◇[1]	[1]	◇[1]	◇[1] ⊥	◇[1]	◇[1] ⊥	◇[1] A ⊥	◇[1]	[1]	◇[1]	◇[1]	◇[1] ⊥	◇[1] A ⊥	◇	◇[1]	◇[1] ⊥		◇[1] ⊥
Weymouth	d											05 55						06 25	06 44				
Upwey	d											05 59						06 29	06 49				
Dorchester West	a																		06 56				
Dorchester South	d											06 07						06 37					
Moreton (Dorset)	d											06 14						06 44					
Wool	d											06 20						06 50					
Wareham	d											06 27						06 57					
Holton Heath	d											06 31											
Hamworthy	d											06 36						07 04					
Poole [4]	a											06 40						07 08					
	d				06 11							06 41					06 50	07 11					07 20
Parkstone (Dorset)	d				06 15							06 45					06 54	07 15					07 24
Branksome	d				06 18							06 49					06 57	07 19					07 27
Bournemouth	a				06 23							06 54					07 02	07 24					07 32
	d			06 04	06 26				06 30		06 34	06 56			07 00		07 04	07 26			07 30		07 34
Pokesdown	d			06 08							06 38						07 08						07 38
Christchurch	d			06 12							06 42				07 06		07 12						07 42
Hinton Admiral	d			06 17							06 47						07 17						07 47
New Milton	d			06 21							06 51				07 13		07 21						07 51
Sway	d			06 26							06 56						07 26						07 56
Brockenhurst [3]	a			06 31					06 45		07 01				07 21		07 31				07 47		08 01
	d			06 33					06 46		07 03				07 22		07 33				07 48		08 03
Beaulieu Road	d																						08 08
Ashurst New Forest	d			06 41							07 11						07 41						08 12
Totton	d			06 46							07 16						07 46						08 17
Salisbury	d													06 50									
Dean	d													07 02									
Mottisfont & Dunbridge	d													07 08									
Romsey	d						07 07							07 13								08 07	
Redbridge	d													07 23									
Millbrook (Hants)	d													07 26									
Southampton Central	a			06 51	06 55				07 01		07 21	07 25		07 30	07 36		07 51	07 55			08 03		08 23
	d		06 43	07 00				07 10	07 14		07 30			07 35	07 37	07 56	08 00				08 12		08 48
St Denys	d		06 48											07 40	07 43								→
Swaythling	d		06 51											07 43	07 46								
Southampton Airport Pkwy	d	06 51	06 55	07 08				07 18	07 22		07 38			07 46	07 50	08 03	08 08				08 19		
Portsmouth Harbour	d					06 23							06 50							07 24			
Portsmouth & Southsea	d					06 28							06 55							07 28			
Fratton	d					06 32							06 59							07 32			
Hilsea	d					06 36							07 03							07 36			
Cosham	d					06 42							07 08							07 42			
Portchester	d					06 46							07 13							07 46			
Fareham	d					06 53							07 20							07 52			
Botley	d					07 01							07 28							08 01			
Hedge End	d					07 05							07 32							08 05			
Eastleigh [3]	a	06 54	06 58			07 11	07 20	07 21					07 38	07 49	07 53					08 12		08 20	
	d	06 55	06 59			07 13	07 21	07 30					07 43	07 50	07 54					08 13		08 21	
Chandlers Ford	d													07 55									
Romsey	a						07 52							08 03								08 51	
Shawford	d		07 05					07 36		←			07 49		08 00					08 20			
Winchester	d	07 05	07 11	07 18		07 22		07 42	07 31	07 42	07 48		07 55		08 06	08 12	08 18			08 26	08 31		
Micheldever	d					07 31		→					08 03										
Basingstoke	a		07 27			07 41			07 46	08 00			08 14		08 23	08 26	08 34			08 42	08 47		
	d		07 36			07 47			07 51	08 05			08 16		08 25	08 28	08 35			08 43	08 49		
Reading [7]	a								08 09							08 44					09 05		
Fleet	d		07 52							08 22										08 54			
Farnborough (Main)	d		07 58							08 28										09 00			
Woking	a		08 08			08 05				08 38			08 34				08 53						
Clapham Junction [10]	a																09 15			09 26			
London Waterloo [15] ⊖	a	08 04	08 38	08 16		08 36				09 10	08 50		09 06		09 10		09 25			09 37			

A ⊥ from Bournemouth

For services from Brockenhurst - Lymington refer to Table T159

Table T158-R

Mondays to Fridays
16 December to 15 May

Weymouth, Bournemouth, Romsey, Southampton and Basingstoke - London

		SW	SW	SW	SW	SW	SW	SW	SW	XC	SW	SN	SW	SW	SW	XC	SW	SW	SW	GW	XC	SW	SW
			◇[1] A ⊥	◇[1]		◇[1] ⊥	◇[1] ⊥	◇[1] ⊥	[1]	[1] ⊥	[1]	[1]	◇[1] A ⊥	◇[1]	[1]	◇[1] ⊥	◇[1]	◇[1] A ⊥	◇[1]	◇	◇[1] ⊥	◇[1] A ⊥	[1]
Weymouth	d		06 55						07 25				07 55					08 20		08 49		09 03	
Upwey	d		06 59						07 29				07 59					08 24		08 54			
Dorchester West	a																			09 01			
Dorchester South	d		07 07						07 37				08 07					08 33				09 13	
Moreton (Dorset)	d		07 14						07 44				08 14					08 39					
Wool	d		07 20						07 50				08 20					08 45					
Wareham	d		07 27						07 57				08 27					08 53				09 28	
Holton Heath	d		07 31						08 01				08 30					08 56					
Hamworthy	d		07 36						08 06				08 35					09 01				09 35	
Poole [4]	a		07 40						08 10				08 40					09 06				09 39	
	d		07 41				07 55		08 11				08 41				08 50	09 07				09 40	
Parkstone (Dorset)	d		07 45				07 59		08 15				08 45				08 54					09 44	
Branksome	d		07 49				08 02		08 19				08 48				08 57					09 48	
Bournemouth	a		07 54				08 07		08 24				08 54				09 02	09 17				09 54	
	d		07 59				08 10		08 25	08 45			08 59				09 05	09 22			09 45	09 59	
Pokesdown	d						08 14		08 29								09 09	09 26					
Christchurch	d						08 18		08 33								09 13	09 30					
Hinton Admiral	d						08 24		08 38								09 18						
New Milton	d						08 29		08 42								09 22	09 37					
Sway	d						08 34		08 47								09 27						
Brockenhurst [3]	a		08 14				08 39		08 52	08 59			09 14				09 32	09 44			09 59	10 14	
	d		08 15				08 41			09 00			09 15				09 33	09 45			10 00	10 15	
Beaulieu Road	d																09 38						
Ashurst New Forest	d						08 48										09 42						
Totton	d						08 53										09 47						
Salisbury	d	07 50													08 50								
Dean	d	08 02													09 02								
Mottisfont & Dunbridge	d	08 08													09 08								
Romsey	d	08 13									09 07				09 14								10 07
Redbridge	d	08 21													09 21								
Millbrook (Hants)	d	08 25			←	←									09 25								
Southampton Central	a	08 27	08 28		08 27	08 23	08 58			09 13			09 28		09 28		09 53	09 58			10 13	10 28	
	d	08 35	08 30		08 35	08 48	09 00			09 17		09 26	09 30		09 35	09 47	09 55	10 00			10 17	10 30	
St Denys	d	→			08 40	08 53									09 40								
Swaythling	d				08 43	08 56									09 43								
Southampton Airport Pkwy	d		08 38		08 46	08 59	09 08			09 24		09 34	09 38		09 46	09 54	10 03	10 08			10 24	10 38	
Portsmouth Harbour	d			07 54										08 59									
Portsmouth & Southsea	d			07 58										09 04									
Fratton	d			08 02										09 08									
Hilsea	d			08 06										09 12									
Cosham	d			08 12										09 17									
Portchester	d			08 16										09 22									
Fareham	d			08 22										09 28									
Botley	d			08 31										09 35									
Hedge End	d			08 35										09 40									
Eastleigh [3]	a			08 42	08 49	09 03					09 20	09 38		09 46	09 49		10 06						10 20
	d			08 43	08 50	09 14					09 21			09 47	09 50		10 14						10 21
Chandlers Ford	d				08 55										09 55								
Romsey	a				09 03						09 53				10 03								10 59
Shawford	d			08 49		09 19		←									10 19		←				
Winchester	d		08 48	08 55		09 25	09 18	09 25		09 33			09 48	09 56		10 03	10 25	10 18	10 25		10 33	10 48	
Micheldever	d			09 03		→								10 06			→						
Basingstoke	a			09 14			09 35	09 41		09 47				10 15		10 18		10 34	10 41		10 47		
	d			09 16			09 36	09 43		09 49				10 17		10 20		10 35	10 43		10 49		
Reading [7]	a									10 06						10 37					11 06		
Fleet	d			09 27				09 54											10 54				
Farnborough (Main)	d			09 32				10 00						10 30					11 00				
Woking	a		09 22	09 41			09 54						10 20	10 39								11 19	
Clapham Junction [10]	a		09 43				10 15	10 25										11 11	11 25				
London Waterloo [15] ⊖	a		09 53	10 08			10 23	10 34					10 49	11 08				11 19	11 34			11 49	

A ⊥ from Bournemouth

For services from Brockenhurst - Lymington refer to Table T159

Table T158-R

Mondays to Fridays
16 December to 15 May

Weymouth, Bournemouth, Romsey, Southampton and Basingstoke - London

		SW	SW	SW	SW	SW	XC	SW	SN	SW	SW	SW	XC	SW	SW	SW	XC	SW	GW	SW	SW	SW
		◇1	1	◇1	◇1 A 🛒	◇1	◇1 🛒	1	1	◇1 A 🛒	◇1	1	1 🛒	◇1	◇1 A 🛒	◇1	◇1 🛒	◇1 A 🛒	◇	1	◇1	1
Weymouth	d				09 20					10 03					10 20			11 03	11 11			
Upwey	d				09 24										10 24				11 16			
Dorchester West	a																		11 23			
Dorchester South	d				09 33					10 13					10 33			11 13				
Moreton (Dorset)	d				09 39										10 39							
Wool	d				09 45										10 45							
Wareham	d				09 53					10 28					10 53			11 28				
Holton Heath	d				09 56										10 56							
Hamworthy	d				10 01					10 35					11 01			11 35				
Poole 4	a				10 06					10 39					11 06			11 39				
	d			09 50	10 07					10 40				10 50	11 07			11 40				
Parkstone (Dorset)	d			09 54						10 44				10 54				11 44				
Branksome	d			09 57						10 48				10 57				11 48				
Bournemouth	a			10 02	10 17					10 54				11 02	11 17			11 54				
	d			10 05	10 22		10 45			10 59				11 05	11 22		11 45	11 59				
Pokesdown	d			10 09	10 26									11 09	11 26							
Christchurch	d			10 13	10 30									11 13	11 30							
Hinton Admiral	d			10 18										11 18								
New Milton	d			10 22	10 37									11 22	11 37							
Sway	d			10 27										11 27								
Brockenhurst 3	a			10 32	10 44		10 59			11 14				11 32	11 44		11 59	12 14				
	d			10 33	10 45		11 00			11 15				11 33	11 45		12 00	12 15				
Beaulieu Road	d													11 38								
Ashurst New Forest	d			10 40										11 42								
Totton	d			10 45										11 47								
Salisbury	d		09 56									10 56										11 56
Dean	d		10 08									11 08										12 09
Mottisfont & Dunbridge	d		10 14									11 14										12 14
Romsey	d		10 20					11 07				11 20								12 07		12 20
Redbridge	d		10 27									11 27										12 27
Millbrook (Hants)	d		10 31									11 31										12 31
Southampton Central ⛴	a		10 34	10 53	10 58		11 13			11 28		11 34		11 53	11 58		12 12	12 28				12 34
	d		10 35	10 55	11 00		11 17		11 26	11 30		11 35	11 47	11 55	12 00		12 17	12 30				12 35
St Denys	d		10 40									11 40										12 40
Swaythling	d		10 43									11 43										12 43
Southampton Airport Pkwy ✈	d		10 46	11 03	11 08		11 24		11 34	11 38		11 46	11 54	12 03	12 08		12 24	12 38				12 46
Portsmouth Harbour ⛴	d	09 59									10 59										11 59	
Portsmouth & Southsea	d	10 04									11 04										12 04	
Fratton	d	10 08									11 08										12 08	
Hilsea	d	10 12									11 12										12 12	
Cosham	d	10 17									11 17										12 17	
Portchester	d	10 22									11 22										12 22	
Fareham	d	10 28									11 28										12 28	
Botley	d	10 35									11 35										12 35	
Hedge End	d	10 40									11 40										12 40	
Eastleigh 3	a	10 46	10 49	11 06				11 20	11 38		11 47	11 49		12 06						12 20	12 46	12 49
	d	10 47	10 50	11 14				11 21			11 47	11 50		12 14						12 21	12 47	12 50
Chandlers Ford	d		10 55									11 55										12 55
Romsey	a		11 03					11 51				12 03								12 51		13 03
Shawford	d			11 19		←								12 19		←						
Winchester	d	10 56		11 25	11 18	11 25	11 33			11 48	11 56		12 03	12 25	12 18	12 25	12 33	12 48			12 56	
Micheldever	d	11 05		→							12 05			→							13 05	
Basingstoke	a	11 15			11 34	11 41	11 47				12 15		12 17		12 34	12 41	12 47				13 15	
	d	11 17			11 35	11 43	11 49				12 17		12 19		12 35	12 43	12 49				13 17	
Reading 7	a						12 06						12 36				13 07					
Fleet	d					11 54										12 54						
Farnborough (Main)	d	11 30				12 00					12 30					13 00					13 30	
Woking	a	11 39								12 19	12 40							13 20			13 39	
Clapham Junction 10	a				12 11	12 25									13 11	13 25						
London Waterloo 15 ⊖	a	12 08			12 20	12 34				12 49	13 08				13 20	13 34		13 49			14 08	

A 🛒 from Bournemouth

For services from Brockenhurst - Lymington refer to Table T159

Table T158-R

Mondays to Fridays
16 December to 15 May

Weymouth, Bournemouth, Romsey, Southampton and Basingstoke - London

		SW	SW	SW	XC	SW	SW	SW	SW	XC	SW	SW	SW	XC	SW	GW	SW	SW	SW	SW	SW	SW	XC
		◇1	◇1 A 🛒	◇1	◇1 🛒	◇1 A 🛒	1	◇1	1	◇1 🛒	◇1	◇1 A 🛒	◇1	◇1 🛒	◇1 A 🛒	◇	1	◇1	1	◇1	◇1 A 🛒	◇1	◇1 🛒
Weymouth	d		11 20			12 03						12 20			13 03	13 12					13 20		
Upwey	d		11 24									12 24				13 17					13 24		
Dorchester West	a															13 24							
Dorchester South	d		11 33			12 13						12 33			13 13						13 33		
Moreton (Dorset)	d											12 39									13 39		
Wool	d		11 45									12 45									13 45		
Wareham	d		11 53			12 28						12 53			13 28						13 53		
Holton Heath	d		11 56									12 56									13 56		
Hamworthy	d		12 01			12 35						13 01			13 35						14 01		
Poole 4	a		12 06			12 39						13 06			13 39						14 06		
	d	11 50	12 07			12 40					12 50	13 07			13 40					13 50	14 07		
Parkstone (Dorset)	d	11 54				12 44					12 54				13 44					13 54			
Branksome	d	11 57				12 48					12 57				13 48					13 57			
Bournemouth	a	12 02	12 17			12 54					13 02	13 17			13 54					14 02	14 17		
	d	12 05	12 22		12 45	12 59					13 05	13 22		13 45	13 59					14 05	14 22		14 45
Pokesdown	d	12 09	12 26								13 09	13 26								14 09	14 26		
Christchurch	d	12 13	12 30								13 13	13 30								14 13	14 30		
Hinton Admiral	d	12 18									13 18									14 18			
New Milton	d	12 22	12 37								13 22	13 37								14 22	14 37		
Sway	d	12 27									13 27									14 27			
Brockenhurst 3	a	12 32	12 44		12 59	13 14					13 32	13 44		13 59	14 14					14 32	14 44		14 59
	d	12 33	12 45		13 00	13 15					13 33	13 45		14 00	14 15					14 33	14 45		15 00
Beaulieu Road	d										13 38												
Ashurst New Forest	d	12 40									13 42									14 40			
Totton	d	12 45									13 47									14 45			
Salisbury	d								12 56										13 50				
Dean	d								13 08										14 02				
Mottisfont & Dunbridge	d								13 14										14 08				
Romsey	d						13 07		13 20								14 07		14 13				
Redbridge	d								13 27										14 21				
Millbrook (Hants)	d								13 31										14 24				
Southampton Central ⛴	a	12 52	12 58		13 13	13 28			13 34		13 53	13 58		14 13	14 28				14 30	14 53	14 58		15 13
	d	12 55	13 00		13 16	13 30			13 35	13 47	13 55	14 00		14 15	14 30				14 36	14 55	15 00		15 17
St Denys	d								13 40										14 40				
Swaythling	d								13 43										14 43				
Southampton Airport Pkwy ✈	d	13 03	13 08		13 23	13 38			13 46	13 54	14 03	14 08		14 22	14 38				14 46	15 03	15 08		15 24
Portsmouth Harbour ⛴	d							12 59										13 59					
Portsmouth & Southsea	d							13 04										14 04					
Fratton	d							13 08										14 08					
Hilsea	d							13 12										14 12					
Cosham	d							13 17										14 17					
Portchester	d							13 22										14 22					
Fareham	d							13 28										14 28					
Botley	d							13 35										14 35					
Hedge End	d							13 40										14 40					
Eastleigh 3	a	13 06					13 20	13 46	13 49		14 06						14 20	14 46	14 49	15 09			
	d	13 14					13 21	13 47	13 50		14 14						14 21	14 47	14 50	15 14			
Chandlers Ford	d								13 55										14 55				
Romsey	a						13 51		14 03								14 51		15 03				
Shawford	d	13 19		←							14 19		←							15 19		←	
Winchester	d	13 25	13 18	13 25	13 32	13 48		13 56		14 03	14 25	14 18	14 25	14 31	14 48			14 56		15 25	15 18	15 25	15 33
Micheldever	d	→						14 05			→							15 05		→			
Basingstoke	a		13 34	13 42	13 46			14 15		14 17		14 34	14 41	14 45				15 15			15 34	15 41	15 47
	d		13 35	13 43	13 49			14 17		14 19		14 35	14 43	14 49				15 17			15 35	15 43	15 49
Reading 7	a				14 06					14 36				15 06									16 09
Fleet	d			13 54									14 54									15 54	
Farnborough (Main)	d			14 00				14 30					15 00					15 30				16 00	
Woking	a					14 20		14 39							15 19			15 39					
Clapham Junction 10	a		14 11	14 25								15 11	15 25								16 11	16 25	
London Waterloo 15 ⊖	a		14 20	14 34		14 49		15 08				15 20	15 34		15 49			16 09			16 19	16 34	

A 🛒 from Bournemouth

For services from Brockenhurst - Lymington refer to Table T159

Table T158-R

Mondays to Fridays
16 December to 15 May

Weymouth, Bournemouth, Romsey, Southampton and Basingstoke - London

		SW ◇1 A 🛒	SW 1	SW ◇1	SW 1	XC ◇1 🛒	SW ◇1	SW ◇1 A 🛒	SW ◇1	GW ◇	XC ◇1 🛒	SW ◇1 A 🛒	SW 1	SW ◇1	GW	SW 1	SW ◇1	SW ◇1 A 🛒	SW ◇1	XC ◇1 🛒	SW ◇1 A 🛒	SW
Weymouth	d	14 03						14 20		14 55		15 03						15 20			16 03	
Upwey	d							14 24		15 00								15 24				
Dorchester West	a									15 07												
Dorchester South	d	14 13						14 33				15 13						15 33			16 13	
Moreton (Dorset)	d							14 39										15 39				
Wool	d							14 45										15 45				
Wareham	d	14 28						14 53				15 28						15 53			16 28	
Holton Heath	d							14 56										15 56				
Hamworthy	d	14 35						15 01				15 35						16 01			16 35	
Poole 4	a	14 39						15 06				15 39						16 06			16 39	
	d	14 40					14 50	15 07				15 40					15 50	16 07			16 40	
Parkstone (Dorset)	d	14 44					14 54					15 44					15 54				16 44	
Branksome	d	14 48					14 57					15 48					15 57				16 48	
Bournemouth	a	14 54					15 02	15 17				15 54					16 02	16 17			16 54	
	d	14 59					15 05	15 22			15 45	15 59					16 05	16 22		16 45	16 59	
Pokesdown	d						15 09	15 26									16 09	16 26				
Christchurch	d						15 13	15 30									16 13	16 30				
Hinton Admiral	d						15 18										16 18					
New Milton	d						15 22	15 37									16 22	16 37				
Sway	d						15 27										16 27					
Brockenhurst 3	a	15 14					15 32	15 44			15 59	16 14					16 32	16 44		16 59	17 14	
	d	15 15					15 33	15 45			16 00	16 15					16 33	16 45		17 00	17 15	
Beaulieu Road	d																					
Ashurst New Forest	d						15 40										16 40					
Totton	d						15 45										16 45					
Salisbury	d				14 56											15 56						
Dean	d				15 08											16 08						
Mottisfont & Dunbridge	d				15 14											16 14						
Romsey	d		15 07		15 20								16 07			16 20						17 07
Redbridge	d				15 27											16 27						
Millbrook (Hants)	d				15 31											16 31						
Southampton Central ⛴	a	15 28			15 34		15 53	15 58			16 13	16 28				16 34	16 51	16 58		17 13	17 28	
	d	15 30			15 35	15 46	15 55	16 00			16 17	16 30				16 35	16 52	17 00		17 17	17 30	
St Denys	d				15 40											16 40	16 57					
Swaythling	d				15 43											16 43	17 00					
Southampton Airport Pkwy ✈	d	15 38			15 46	15 53	16 03	16 08			16 24	16 38				16 46	17 04	17 08		17 24	17 38	
Portsmouth Harbour ⛴	d			14 59										15 59								
Portsmouth & Southsea	d			15 04										16 04								
Fratton	d			15 08										16 08								
Hilsea	d			15 12										16 12								
Cosham	d			15 17										16 17								
Portchester	d			15 22										16 22								
Fareham	d			15 28										16 28								
Botley	d			15 35										16 35								
Hedge End	d			15 40										16 40								
Eastleigh 3	a		15 20	15 46	15 49		16 08						16 20	16 46		16 49	17 07					17 20
	d		15 21	15 47	15 50		16 14						16 21	16 47		16 50	17 14					17 21
Chandlers Ford	d				15 55											16 55						
Romsey	a		15 51		16 03								16 51			17 03						17 51
Shawford	d						16 19		←								17 19		←			
Winchester	d	15 48		15 56		16 02	16 25	16 18	16 25		16 33	16 48		16 56			17 25	17 18	17 25	17 33	17 48	
Micheldever	d			16 05			→							17 05			→					
Basingstoke	a			16 15		16 17		16 34	16 41		16 47			17 15				17 34	17 42	17 47		
	d			16 17		16 19		16 35	16 43		16 49			17 17	17 32			17 35	17 43	17 49		
Reading 7	a					16 38					17 05				17 55					18 07		
Fleet	d								16 54										17 54			
Farnborough (Main)	d			16 30					17 00					17 30					18 00			
Woking	a	16 19		16 39								17 20		17 39							18 19	
Clapham Junction 10	a							17 11	17 25									18 11	18 25			
London Waterloo 15 ⊖	a	16 49		17 08				17 24	17 36			17 55		18 12				18 19	18 38		18 53	

A 🛒 from Bournemouth

For services from Brockenhurst - Lymington refer to Table T159

Table T158-R

Mondays to Fridays
16 December to 15 May

Weymouth, Bournemouth, Romsey, Southampton and Basingstoke - London

		SW ◇1	SW	SW 1	XC ◇1 🛒	SW ◇1	SW ◇1 A 🛒	SW ◇1	XC ◇1 🛒	SW 1	SW 1	SW ◇1 A 🛒	SW 1	GW	SW ◇1	SW 1	SW ◇1	SW ◇1 A 🛒	SW ◇1	GW ◇	XC ◇1 🛒	SW ◇1 A 🛒	SW 1
Weymouth	d						16 20					17 03						17 17		17 23		18 03	
Upwey	d						16 24											17 21		17 28			
Dorchester West	a																			17 35			
Dorchester South	d						16 33					17 13						17 32				18 13	
Moreton (Dorset)	d						16 39																
Wool	d						16 45											17 45					
Wareham	d						16 53					17 28						17 53				18 28	
Holton Heath	d						16 56											17 56					
Hamworthy	d						17 01					17 35						18 01				18 35	
Poole 4	a						17 06					17 39						18 06				18 39	
	d					16 50	17 07					17 40					17 50	18 07				18 40	
Parkstone (Dorset)	d					16 54						17 44					17 54					18 44	
Branksome	d					16 57						17 48					17 57					18 48	
Bournemouth	a					17 03	17 18					17 54					18 02	18 17				18 54	
	d					17 05	17 22		17 45			17 59					18 05	18 22			18 45	18 59	
Pokesdown	d					17 09	17 26										18 09	18 26					
Christchurch	d					17 13	17 30										18 13	18 30					
Hinton Admiral	d					17 18											18 18						
New Milton	d					17 22	17 37										18 22	18 37					
Sway	d					17 27											18 27						
Brockenhurst 3	a					17 32	17 44		17 59			18 14					18 32	18 44			18 59	19 14	
	d			17 20		17 33	17 45		18 00			18 15					18 33	18 45			19 00	19 15	
Beaulieu Road	d			17 25													18 38						
Ashurst New Forest	d			17 29		17 40											18 42						
Totton	d			17 34		17 45											18 47						
Salisbury	d		16 56													17 56							
Dean	d		17 08													18 08							
Mottisfont & Dunbridge	d		17 14													18 14							
Romsey	d		17 20							18 07						18 20							19 07
Redbridge	d		17 27													18 27							
Millbrook (Hants)	d		17 31													18 31							
Southampton Central ⛴	a		17 34	17 41		17 53	17 58		18 13			18 28				18 34	18 53	18 58			19 13	19 28	
	d		17 35	17 44	17 47	17 55	18 00		18 15		18 17	18 30				18 35	18 55	19 00			19 17	19 30	
St Denys	d		17 40	17 49							18 22					18 40							
Swaythling	d		17 43								18 25					18 43							
Southampton Airport Pkwy ✈	d		17 46		17 54	18 03	18 08		18 22		18 28	18 38				18 46	19 03	19 08			19 24	19 38	
Portsmouth Harbour ⛴	d	16 59											17 49		17 59								
Portsmouth & Southsea	d	17 04											17 54		18 04								
Fratton	d	17 08											17 58		18 08								
Hilsea	d	17 12											18 02		18 12								
Cosham	d	17 17											18 09		18 17								
Portchester	d	17 22											18 13		18 22								
Fareham	d	17 28		18a17									18 21		18 28								
Botley	d	17 35											18 29		18 35								
Hedge End	d	17 40											18 33		18 40								
Eastleigh 3	a	17 46	17 49			18 06				18 20	18 32		18 39		18 46	18 49	19 06						19 20
	d	17 47	17 50			18 12				18 21	18 33				18 47	18 50	19 14						19 21
Chandlers Ford	d		17 55													18 55							
Romsey	a		18 03							19 00						19 04							19 51
Shawford	d					18 17		←									19 19		←				
Winchester	d	17 56			18 03	18 23	18 18	18 23	18 31		18a41	18 48			18 56		19 25	19 18	19 25		19 33	19 48	
Micheldever	d	18 05				→									19 05		→						
Basingstoke	a	18 15			18 17		18 34	18 41	18 47						19 15			19 34	19 41		19 47		
	d	18 17			18 19		18 35	18 43	18 49					18 53	19 17			19 35	19 43		19 49		
Reading 7	a				18 38				19 06					19 11							20 06		
Fleet	d							18 54											19 54				
Farnborough (Main)	d	18 30						19 00							19 31				20 00				
Woking	a	18 40										19 25			19 41							20 21	
Clapham Junction 10	a						19 11	19 26										20 11	20 27				
London Waterloo 15 ⊖	a	19 08					19 19	19 34				19 52			20 09			20 21	20 35			20 49	

A 🛒 from Bournemouth

For services from Brockenhurst - Lymington refer to Table T159

Table T158-R

Mondays to Fridays
16 December to 15 May

Weymouth, Bournemouth, Romsey, Southampton and Basingstoke - London

		SW	SW	SW	SW	SW	XC	SW	SW	SW	SW	SW	SW	SW	SW	SW	SW	SW	SW	SW	SW	GW	GW
		◇1	1	◇1	◇1	◇1	◇1	◇1	1	◇1	1	◇1	◇1	◇1	◇1	1	◇1	1	◇1	◇1	◇1	◇	◇
					A			A															
Weymouth	d				18 20			19 03					19 20		19 59					20 07		20 15	
Upwey	d				18 24								19 24							20 11		20 20	
Dorchester West	a																					20 27	
Dorchester South	d				18 33			19 13					19 37		20 11					20 21			
Moreton (Dorset)	d				18 39								19 43							20 28			
Wool	d				18 45								19 49							20 34			
Wareham	d				18 53			19 28					19 57		20 28					20 42			
Holton Heath	d				18 56																		
Hamworthy	d				19 01			19 35					20 03		20 35					20 48			
Poole 4	a				19 06			19 39					20 08		20 39					20 53			
	d			18 50	19 07			19 40				19 50	20 09		20 40					20 54			
Parkstone (Dorset)	d			18 54				19 44				19 54			20 44					20 58			
Branksome	d			18 57				19 48				19 57			20 48					21 01			
Bournemouth	a			19 02	19 17			19 54				20 02	20 18		20 54					21 07			
	d			19 05	19 22		19 45	19 59				20 05	20 22		20 59					21 12			
Pokesdown	d			19 09	19 26							20 09	20 26							21 16			
Christchurch	d			19 13	19 30							20 13	20 30							21 20			
Hinton Admiral	d			19 18								20 18								21 25			
New Milton	d			19 22	19 37							20 22	20 37							21 29			
Sway	d			19 27								20 27								21 34			
Brockenhurst 3	a			19 32	19 44		19 59	20 14				20 32	20 44		21 14					21 39			
	d			19 33	19 45		20 00	20 15				20 33	20 45		21 15					21 40			
Beaulieu Road	d											20 38											
Ashurst New Forest	d			19 41								20 42								21 47			
Totton	d			19 46								20 47								21 52			
Salisbury	d		18 56								19 56							20 56					21 33
Dean	d		19 08								20 08							21 08					
Mottisfont & Dunbridge	d		19 14								20 14							21 14					
Romsey	d		19 20						20 07		20 20					21 07		21 20					21 52
Redbridge	d		19 27								20 27							21 27					
Millbrook (Hants)	d		19 31								20 31							21 31					
Southampton Central	a		19 34	19 51	19 58		20 13	20 28			20 34	20 53	20 58		21 28			21 34		21 57			22 02
	d		19 35	19 55	20 00		20 17	20 30			20 35	20 55	21 00		21 30			21 35	21 55	22 00			22 07
St Denys	d		19 40								20 40							21 40					
Swaythling	d		19 43								20 43							21 43					
Southampton Airport Pkwy	d		19 46	20 03	20 08		20 24	20 38			20 46	21 03	21 08		21 38			21 46	22 03	22 08			22 14
Portsmouth Harbour	d	18 59								19 59							20 59						
Portsmouth & Southsea	d	19 04								20 04							21 04						
Fratton	d	19 08								20 08							21 08						
Hilsea	d	19 12								20 12							21 12						
Cosham	d	19 17								20 17							21 17						
Portchester	d	19 22								20 22							21 22						
Fareham	d	19 28								20 28							21 28						
Botley	d	19 35								20 35							21 35						
Hedge End	d	19 40								20 40							21 40						
Eastleigh 3	a	19 46	19 50	20 06					20 20	20 46	20 49	21 06				21 20	21 46	21 49	22 06				22 19
	d	19 47	19 50	20 14					20 21	20 47	20 50	21 12				21 21	21 47	21 50	22 14				
Chandlers Ford	d		19 56								20 55							21 55					
Romsey	a		20 03						20 51		21 03					21 51		22 03					
Shawford	d			20 19		←				20 53		21 18		←					22 20		←		
Winchester	d	19 56		20 25	20 18	20 25	20 33	20 48		20 59		21 24	21 18	21 24	21 48		21 56		22 26	22 18	22 26		
Micheldever	d	20 05		→						21 07		→					22 05		→				
Basingstoke	a	20 15			20 34	20 41	20 47			21 21			21 34	21 41			22 15			22 34	22 42		
	d	20 17			20 35	20 43	20 49			21 24			21 35	21 43			22 24			22 36	22 43		
Reading 7	a						21 07																
Fleet	d					20 54				21 40				21 54			22 40				22 54		
Farnborough (Main)	d	20 30				21 00				21 46				22 00			22 46				23 00		
Woking	a	20 39						21 21		21 58			21 53	22 09	22 23		22 58			22 54	23 09		
Clapham Junction 10	a				21 11	21 27							22 13	22 29						23 14	23 30		
London Waterloo 15 ⊖	a	21 10			21 27	21 38		21 51		22 34			22 21	22 41	22 49		23 34			23 26	23 40		

A from Bournemouth

For services from Brockenhurst - Lymington refer to Table T159

NRT DECEMBER 19 EDITION

Table T158-R

Mondays to Fridays
16 December to 15 May

Weymouth, Bournemouth, Romsey, Southampton and Basingstoke - London

		SW	SW	SW	SW	SW	SW	SW	SW	SW	SW	SW
				FO	FX							
		1	1	◇1	◇1	1	◇1	1	1	1	◇1	1
Weymouth	d						21 10				22 10	23 10
Upwey	d						21 14				22 14	23 14
Dorchester West	a											
Dorchester South	d						21 22				22 22	23 22
Moreton (Dorset)	d						21 28				22 28	23 28
Wool	d						21 34				22 34	23 34
Wareham	d						21 42				22 42	23 42
Holton Heath	d											
Hamworthy	d						21 48				22 48	23 48
Poole 4	a						21 53				22 53	23 53
	d						21 54				22 54	23 54
Parkstone (Dorset)	d						21 58				22 58	
Branksome	d						22 01				23 01	
Bournemouth	a						22 07				23 07	00 03
	d						22 12				23 12	
Pokesdown	d						22 16				23 16	
Christchurch	d						22 20				23 20	
Hinton Admiral	d						22 25				23 25	
New Milton	d						22 29				23 29	
Sway	d						22 34				23 34	
Brockenhurst 3	a						22 39				23 39	
	d						22 40				23 40	
Beaulieu Road	d											
Ashurst New Forest	d						22 47				23 47	
Totton	d						22 52				23 52	
Salisbury	d					21 56			22 45			
Dean	d					22 08			22 57			
Mottisfont & Dunbridge	d					22 14			23 03			
Romsey	d	22 07				22 20		23 11	23 08			
Redbridge	d					22 27			23 16			
Millbrook (Hants)	d					22 31			23 19			
Southampton Central	a					22 34	22 57		23 22		23 57	
	d			22 30	22 30	22 35	23 00		23 23		23 59	
St Denys	d					22 40			23 28		00 04	
Swaythling	d					22 43			23 31		00 07	
Southampton Airport Pkwy	d			22 38	22 38	22 46	23 08		23 34		00 10	
Portsmouth Harbour	d		21 54							23 24		
Portsmouth & Southsea	d		21 59							23 29		
Fratton	d		22 03							23 33		
Hilsea	d		22 07							23 37		
Cosham	d		22 12							23 42		
Portchester	d		22 17							23 47		
Fareham	d		22 23							23 53		
Botley	d		22 31							23 59		
Hedge End	d		22 35							00 05		
Eastleigh 3	a	22 21	22 41	22 41	22 41	22 49	23 11	23 24	23 37	00 13	00 14	
	d	22 22		22 46	22 46	22 50	23 12	23 24	23 38	00 19		
Chandlers Ford	d					22 55			23 43			
Romsey	a	22 51				23 04		23 58	23 50			
Shawford	d						23 18					
Winchester	d			22 55	22 55		23 24			00a28		
Micheldever	d						23 33					
Basingstoke	a			23 11	23 11		23 43					
	d			23 13	23 13		23 44					
Reading 7	a											
Fleet	d						00 01					
Farnborough (Main)	d						00 06					
Woking	a			23 31	23 31		00 18					
Clapham Junction 10	a			23 54	23 54		00 53					
London Waterloo 15 ⊖	a			00 04	00 07		01 04					

For services from Brockenhurst - Lymington refer to Table T159

Table T158-R

Saturdays

21 December to 16 May

Weymouth, Bournemouth, Romsey, Southampton and Basingstoke - London

		SW	SW	SW	XC	SW	SW	SW	SW	SW	SW	SW	XC	SW	SW	SW	SW	XC	SW	XC	SW	SW	SW
		◇1	1	◇1	◇1	◇1	1	◇1	1	1	◇1	1	◇1	◇1	◇1	1	◇1	◇1	◇1	◇1	◇1	1	◇1
															⚒					⚒	A ⚒		
Weymouth	d																				05 42		
Upwey	d																						
Dorchester West	a																						
Dorchester South	d																				05 52		
Moreton (Dorset)	d																						
Wool	d																				06 02		
Wareham	d																				06 10		
Holton Heath	d																				06 13		
Hamworthy	d																				06 18		
Poole 4	a																				06 23		
	d														05 26						06 24		
Parkstone (Dorset)	d														05 30						06 28		
Branksome	d														05 34						06 31		
Bournemouth	a														05 40						06 37		
	d														05 42			06 25		06 38	06 42		
Pokesdown	d														05 46						06 46		
Christchurch	d														05 50						06 50		
Hinton Admiral	d														05 55						06 55		
New Milton	d														06 00						07 00		
Sway	d														06 05						07 05		
Brockenhurst 3	a														06 10			06 39		06 52	07 10		
	d														06 11			06 40		06 53	07 11		
Beaulieu Road	d																						
Ashurst New Forest	d														06 18						07 18		
Totton	d														06 23						07 23		
Salisbury	d								05 35														
Dean	d								05 47														
Mottisfont & Dunbridge	d								05 53														
Romsey	d								05 58	06 09												07 07	
Redbridge	d									06 16													
Millbrook (Hants)	d									06 20						←							
Southampton Central ⛴	a									06 23					06 29	06 23		06 52		07 08	07 28		
	d				05 09	05 12		05 30		06 35	06 00		06 20		06 30	06 35		06 54	07 00	07 11	07 30		
St Denys	d			00 04				05 35		→						06 40							
Swaythling	d			00 07				05 38								06 43							
Southampton Airport Pkwy ✈	d			00 10	05 16	05 20		05 41			06 08		06 27		06 38	06 46		07 01	07 08	07 18	07 38		
Portsmouth Harbour ⛴	d											05 40		05 48									06 59
Portsmouth & Southsea	d											05 44		05 53									07 04
Fratton	d											05 48		05 57									07 08
Hilsea	d													06 01									07 12
Cosham	d						05 09					05 56		06 06									07 17
Portchester	d						05 14							06 11									07 22
Fareham	d						05 20					06 04		06 17									07 28
Botley	d						05 27							06 24									07 35
Hedge End	d		00 05				05 32							06 29									07 40
Eastleigh 3	a		00 13	00 14		05 23	05 39	05 45			06 11	06 17		06 37	06 41	06 49			07 11			07 20	07 46
	d		00 19			05 24		05 46			06 13			06 47	06 42	06 50			07 13			07 21	07 47
Chandlers Ford	d								06 06							06 55							
Romsey	a								06 43							07 03						07 51	
Shawford	d							05 52						06 53			←		07 18				
Winchester	d		00a28		05 25	05 34		06 00			06 23		06 36	07 00	06 51		07 00	07 10	07 24	07 29	07 48		07 56
Micheldever	d							06 08						→			07 08						08 05
Basingstoke	a				05 39	05 50		06 18			06 39		06 50		07 07		07 19	07 24	07 40	07 44			08 15
	d				05 40	05 54		06 24			06 40		06 51		07 08		07 24	07 26	07 43	07 51			08 17
Reading 7	a				06 00								07 08					07 41		08 08			
Fleet	d	00 01				06 10		06 40									07 40		07 54				
Farnborough (Main)	d	00 06				06 16		06 46									07 46		08 00				08 30
Woking	a	00 18				06 28		06 58			06 58				07 26		07 58				08 21		08 39
Clapham Junction 10	a	00 53				06 57													08 27				
London Waterloo 15 ⊖	a	01 04				07 05		07 35			07 29				07 52		08 37		08 38		08 49		09 09

A ⚒ from Bournemouth

For services from Brockenhurst - Lymington refer to Table T159

Table T158-R

Saturdays

21 December to 16 May

Weymouth, Bournemouth, Romsey, Southampton and Basingstoke - London

		SW	XC	SW	SW	SW	GW	XC	SW	SW	SW	SW	SW	SW	SW	XC	SW	SW	SW	SW	XC	SW	SW
		1	◇1	◇1	◇1	◇1	◇	◇1	◇1	1	◇1	1	◇1	◇1	◇1	◇1	◇1	1	◇1	1	◇1	◇1	◇1
								⚒	A ⚒					A ⚒		⚒	A ⚒				⚒		A ⚒
Weymouth	d				06 20		06 40		06 55					07 20			08 03						08 20
Upwey	d				06 24		06 45		06 59					07 24									08 24
Dorchester West	a						06 52																
Dorchester South	d				06 33				07 07					07 33			08 13						08 33
Moreton (Dorset)	d				06 39				07 14					07 39									08 39
Wool	d				06 45				07 20					07 45									08 45
Wareham	d				06 53				07 27					07 53			08 28						08 53
Holton Heath	d				06 56				07 31					07 56									08 56
Hamworthy	d				07 01				07 36					08 01			08 35						09 01
Poole 4	a				07 06				07 40					08 06			08 39						09 06
	d			06 50	07 07				07 41				07 50	08 07			08 40					08 50	09 07
Parkstone (Dorset)	d			06 54					07 45				07 54				08 44					08 54	
Branksome	d			06 57					07 49				07 57				08 48					08 57	
Bournemouth	a			07 02	07 17				07 54				08 02	08 17			08 54					09 03	09 17
	d			07 05	07 22			07 47	07 59				08 05	08 22		08 47	08 59					09 05	09 22
Pokesdown	d			07 09	07 26								08 09	08 26								09 09	09 26
Christchurch	d			07 13	07 30								08 13	08 30								09 13	09 30
Hinton Admiral	d			07 18									08 18									09 18	
New Milton	d			07 22	07 37								08 22	08 37								09 22	09 37
Sway	d			07 27									08 27									09 27	
Brockenhurst 3	a			07 32	07 44			08 01	08 14				08 32	08 44		09 01	09 14					09 32	09 44
	d			07 33	07 44			08 02	08 15				08 33	08 45		09 02	09 15					09 33	09 45
Beaulieu Road	d																					09 38	
Ashurst New Forest	d			07 40									08 40									09 42	
Totton	d			07 45									08 45									09 47	
Salisbury	d	06 50										07 50								08 56			
Dean	d	07 02										08 02								09 08			
Mottisfont & Dunbridge	d	07 08										08 08								09 14			
Romsey	d	07 13								08 07		08 13						09 07		09 20			
Redbridge	d	07 21										08 21								09 27			
Millbrook (Hants)	d	07 24										08 24								09 31			
Southampton Central ⛴	a	07 31		07 52	07 58			08 15	08 28			08 28	08 52	08 58		09 15	09 28			09 34		09 53	09 58
	d	07 35	07 49	07 55	08 00			08 20	08 30			08 35	08 55	09 00		09 18	09 30			09 35	09 47	09 55	10 00
St Denys	d	07 40										08 40								09 40			
Swaythling	d	07 43										08 43								09 43			
Southampton Airport Pkwy ✈	d	07 46	07 56	08 03	08 08			08 27	08 38			08 46	09 03	09 08		09 25	09 38			09 46	09 54	10 03	10 08
Portsmouth Harbour ⛴	d										07 59								08 59				
Portsmouth & Southsea	d										08 04								09 04				
Fratton	d										08 08								09 08				
Hilsea	d										08 12								09 12				
Cosham	d										08 17								09 17				
Portchester	d										08 22								09 22				
Fareham	d										08 28								09 28				
Botley	d										08 35								09 35				
Hedge End	d										08 40								09 40				
Eastleigh 3	a	07 49		08 06						08 20	08 46	08 49	09 06					09 20	09 46	09 49		10 06	
	d	07 50		08 14						08 21	08 47	08 50	09 14					09 21	09 47	09 50		10 14	
Chandlers Ford	d	07 55										08 55								09 55			
Romsey	a	08 03								08 51		09 03						09 51		10 03			
Shawford	d			08 19		←							09 19		←							10 19	
Winchester	d		08 05	08 25	08 18	08 25		08 36	08 48		08 56		09 25	09 18	09 25	09 34	09 48		09 56		10 03	10 25	10 18
Micheldever	d			→							09 05		→						10 05			→	
Basingstoke	a		08 19		08 34	08 41		08 50			09 15			09 35	09 41	09 50			10 15		10 17		10 34
	d		08 20		08 35	08 43		08 51			09 17			09 36	09 43	09 51			10 17		10 20		10 35
Reading 7	a		08 37					09 09								10 08					10 37		
Fleet	d					08 54									09 54								
Farnborough (Main)	d					09 00					09 30				10 00				10 30				
Woking	a								09 19		09 39						10 19		10 39				
Clapham Junction 10	a				09 11	09 25								10 11	10 25								11 11
London Waterloo 15 ⊖	a				09 19	09 34			09 49		10 08			10 19	10 34		10 49		11 08				11 19

A ⚒ from Bournemouth

For services from Brockenhurst - Lymington refer to Table T159

Table T158-R

Saturdays

21 December to 16 May

Weymouth, Bournemouth, Romsey, Southampton and Basingstoke - London

		SW ◇1	GW ◇	XC ◇1 🛒	SW ◇1 A 🛒	SW 1	SW ◇1	SW 1	SW ◇1	SW ◇1 A 🛒	SW ◇1	XC ◇1 🛒	SW ◇1 A 🛒	SW 1	SW ◇1	SW 1	XC ◇1 🛒	SW ◇1	SW ◇1 A 🛒	SW ◇1	XC ◇1 🛒	SW ◇1 A 🛒
Weymouth	d		08 47		09 03					09 20			10 03						10 20			11 03
Upwey	d		08 52							09 24									10 24			
Dorchester West	a		09 00																			
Dorchester South	d				09 13					09 33			10 13						10 33			11 13
Moreton (Dorset)	d									09 39									10 39			
Wool	d									09 45									10 45			
Wareham	d				09 28					09 53			10 28						10 53			11 28
Holton Heath	d									09 56									10 56			
Hamworthy	d				09 35					10 01			10 35						11 01			11 35
Poole 4	a				09 39					10 06			10 39						11 06			11 39
	d				09 40				09 50	10 07			10 40					10 50	11 07			11 40
Parkstone (Dorset)	d				09 44				09 54				10 44					10 54				11 44
Branksome	d				09 48				09 57				10 48					10 57				11 48
Bournemouth	a				09 54				10 02	10 17			10 54					11 02	11 17			11 54
	d			09 47	09 59				10 05	10 22		10 47	10 59					11 05	11 22		11 47	11 59
Pokesdown	d								10 09	10 26								11 09	11 26			
Christchurch	d								10 13	10 30								11 13	11 30			
Hinton Admiral	d								10 18									11 18				
New Milton	d								10 22	10 37								11 22	11 37			
Sway	d								10 27									11 27				
Brockenhurst 3	a			10 01	10 14				10 32	10 44		11 01	11 14					11 32	11 44		12 01	12 14
	d			10 02	10 15				10 33	10 45		11 02	11 15					11 33	11 45		12 02	12 15
Beaulieu Road	d																	11 38				
Ashurst New Forest	d								10 40									11 42				
Totton	d								10 45									11 47				
Salisbury	d							09 56								10 56						
Dean	d							10 08								11 08						
Mottisfont & Dunbridge	d							10 14								11 14						
Romsey	d					10 07		10 20						11 07		11 20						
Redbridge	d							10 27								11 27						
Millbrook (Hants)	d							10 31								11 31						
Southampton Central ⛴	a			10 15	10 28			10 34	10 53	10 58		11 15	11 28			11 34		11 53	11 58		12 15	12 28
	d			10 17	10 30			10 35	10 55	11 00		11 20	11 30			11 35	11 47	11 55	12 00		12 20	12 30
St Denys	d							10 40								11 40						
Swaythling	d							10 43								11 43						
Southampton Airport Pkwy ✈	d			10 24	10 38			10 46	11 03	11 08		11 27	11 38			11 46	11 54	12 03	12 08		12 27	12 38
Portsmouth Harbour ⛴	d						09 59								10 59							
Portsmouth & Southsea	d						10 04								11 04							
Fratton	d						10 08								11 08							
Hilsea	d						10 12								11 12							
Cosham	d						10 17								11 17							
Portchester	d						10 22								11 22							
Fareham	d						10 28								11 28							
Botley	d						10 35								11 35							
Hedge End	d						10 40								11 40							
Eastleigh 3	a					10 20	10 46	10 49	11 06					11 20	11 46	11 49		12 06				
	d					10 21	10 47	10 50	11 14					11 21	11 47	11 50		12 14				
Chandlers Ford	d							10 55								11 55						
Romsey	a					10 59		11 03						11 51		12 03						
Shawford	d	←							11 19		←							12 19		←		
Winchester	d	10 25		10 33	10 48		10 56		11 25	11 18	11 25	11 36	11 48		11 56		12 03	12 25	12 18	12 25	12 36	12 48
Micheldever	d						11 05		→						12 05			→				
Basingstoke	a	10 41		10 50			11 15			11 34	11 41	11 50			12 15		12 17		12 34	12 41	12 50	
	d	10 43		10 51			11 17			11 35	11 43	11 51			12 17		12 20		12 35	12 43	12 51	
Reading 7	a			11 09								12 08					12 37				13 09	
Fleet	d	10 54									11 54									12 54		
Farnborough (Main)	d	11 00					11 30				12 00				12 30					13 00		
Woking	a				11 19		11 40						12 19		12 39							13 19
Clapham Junction 10	a	11 26								12 11	12 25								13 11	13 25		
London Waterloo 15 ⊖	a	11 34			11 49		12 12			12 21	12 34		12 51		13 11				13 21	13 34		13 51

A 🛒 from Bournemouth

For services from Brockenhurst - Lymington refer to Table T159

NRT DECEMBER 19 EDITION

Table T158-R

Saturdays

21 December to 16 May

Weymouth, Bournemouth, Romsey, Southampton and Basingstoke - London

		GW ◇	SW 1	SW ◇1	SW 1	SW ◇1	SW ◇1 A 🛒	SW ◇1	XC ◇1 🛒	SW ◇1 A 🛒	SW ◇1	SW 1	SW ◇1	SW 1	XC ◇1 🛒	SW ◇1	SW ◇1 A 🛒	SW ◇1	XC ◇1 🛒	SW 1	SN 1	SW ◇1 A 🛒	GW ◇
Weymouth	d	11 10					11 22			12 03	12 10						12 20					13 03	13 10
Upwey	d	11 15					11 27				12 15						12 24						13 15
Dorchester West	a	11 23									12 22												13 23
Dorchester South	d						11 35			12 13							12 33					13 13	
Moreton (Dorset)	d						11 41										12 39						
Wool	d						11 47										12 45						
Wareham	d						11 54			12 28							12 53					13 28	
Holton Heath	d						11 58										12 56						
Hamworthy	d						12 03			12 35							13 01					13 35	
Poole 4	a						12 07			12 39							13 06					13 39	
	d					11 50	12 08			12 40						12 50	13 07					13 40	
Parkstone (Dorset)	d					11 54				12 44						12 54						13 44	
Branksome	d					11 57				12 48						12 57						13 48	
Bournemouth	a					12 02	12 17			12 54						13 02	13 17					13 54	
	d					12 05	12 22		12 47	12 59						13 05	13 22		13 47			13 59	
Pokesdown	d					12 09	12 26									13 09	13 26						
Christchurch	d					12 13	12 30									13 13	13 30						
Hinton Admiral	d					12 18										13 18							
New Milton	d					12 22	12 37									13 22	13 37						
Sway	d					12 27										13 27							
Brockenhurst 3	a					12 32	12 44		13 01	13 14						13 32	13 44		14 01			14 14	
	d					12 33	12 45		13 02	13 15						13 33	13 45		14 02			14 15	
Beaulieu Road	d															13 38							
Ashurst New Forest	d					12 40										13 42							
Totton	d					12 45										13 47							
Salisbury	d				11 56									12 56									
Dean	d				12 08									13 08									
Mottisfont & Dunbridge	d				12 14									13 14									
Romsey	d		12 07		12 20							13 07		13 20						14 07			
Redbridge	d				12 27									13 27									
Millbrook (Hants)	d				12 31									13 31									
Southampton Central ⛴	a				12 34	12 51	12 58		13 15	13 28				13 34		13 53	13 58		14 15			14 28	
	d				12 35	12 55	13 00		13 20	13 30				13 35	13 47	13 55	14 00		14 20		14 26	14 30	
St Denys	d				12 40									13 40									
Swaythling	d				12 43									13 43									
Southampton Airport Pkwy ✈	d				12 46	13 03	13 08		13 27	13 38				13 46	13 54	14 03	14 08		14 27		14 34	14 38	
Portsmouth Harbour ⛴	d			11 59									12 59										
Portsmouth & Southsea	d			12 04									13 04										
Fratton	d			12 08									13 08										
Hilsea	d			12 12									13 12										
Cosham	d			12 17									13 17										
Portchester	d			12 22									13 22										
Fareham	d			12 28									13 28										
Botley	d			12 35									13 35										
Hedge End	d			12 40									13 40										
Eastleigh 3	a		12 20	12 46	12 49	13 06						13 20	13 46	13 49		14 06				14 20	14 37		
	d		12 21	12 47	12 50	13 14						13 21	13 47	13 50		14 14				14 21			
Chandlers Ford	d				12 55									13 55									
Romsey	a		12 51		13 03							13 51		14 03						14 51			
Shawford	d					13 19		←								14 19		←					
Winchester	d			12 56		13 25	13 18	13 25	13 36	13 48			13 56		14 03	14 25	14 18	14 25	14 36			14 48	
Micheldever	d			13 05		→							14 05			→							
Basingstoke	a			13 15			13 34	13 41	13 50				14 15		14 17		14 34	14 41	14 50				
	d			13 17			13 35	13 43	13 51				14 17		14 20		14 35	14 43	14 51				
Reading 7	a								14 08						14 37				15 09				
Fleet	d							13 54										14 54					
Farnborough (Main)	d			13 30				14 00					14 30					15 00					
Woking	a			13 39						14 19			14 39									15 19	
Clapham Junction 10	a						14 11	14 25									15 11	15 25					
London Waterloo 15 ⊖	a			14 11			14 21	14 34		14 51			15 11				15 21	15 34				15 51	

A 🛒 from Bournemouth

For services from Brockenhurst - Lymington refer to Table T159

Table T158-R

Saturdays

21 December to 16 May

Weymouth, Bournemouth, Romsey, Southampton and Basingstoke - London

		SW	SW	SW	SW	SW	XC	SW	SW	SW	SW	XC	SW	SW	SW	GW	XC	SW	SW	SW	SW	SW
		◇1	1	◇1	◇1	◇1	◇1	◇1	1	◇1	1	◇1	◇1	◇1	◇1	◇	◇1	◇1	1	◇1	1	◇1
					A ⌶		⌶	A ⌶				⌶		A ⌶			⌶	A ⌶				
Weymouth	d				13 20			14 03						14 20		14 55		15 03				
Upwey	d				13 24									14 24		15 00						
Dorchester West	a															15 08						
Dorchester South	d				13 33			14 13						14 33				15 13				
Moreton (Dorset)	d				13 39									14 39								
Wool	d				13 45									14 45								
Wareham	d				13 53			14 28						14 53				15 28				
Holton Heath	d				13 56									14 56								
Hamworthy	d				14 01			14 35						15 01				15 35				
Poole 4	a				14 06			14 39						15 06				15 39				
	d			13 50	14 07			14 40					14 50	15 07				15 40				15 50
Parkstone (Dorset)	d			13 54				14 44					14 54					15 44				15 54
Branksome	d			13 57				14 48					14 57					15 48				15 57
Bournemouth	a			14 02	14 17			14 54					15 02	15 17				15 54				16 02
	d			14 05	14 22		14 47	14 59					15 05	15 22			15 47	15 59				16 05
Pokesdown	d			14 09	14 26								15 09	15 26								16 09
Christchurch	d			14 13	14 30								15 13	15 30								16 13
Hinton Admiral	d			14 18									15 18									16 18
New Milton	d			14 22	14 37								15 22	15 37								16 22
Sway	d			14 27									15 27									16 27
Brockenhurst 3	a			14 32	14 44		15 01	15 14					15 32	15 44			16 01	16 14				16 32
	d			14 33	14 45		15 02	15 15					15 33	15 45			16 02	16 15				16 33
Beaulieu Road	d												15 38									
Ashurst New Forest	d			14 40									15 42									16 40
Totton	d			14 45									15 47									16 45
Salisbury	d		13 50								14 56										15 56	
Dean	d		14 02								15 08										16 08	
Mottisfont & Dunbridge	d		14 08								15 14										16 14	
Romsey	d		14 13						15 07		15 20								16 07		16 20	
Redbridge	d		14 21								15 27										16 27	
Millbrook (Hants)	d		14 24								15 31										16 31	
Southampton Central ⛴	a		14 28	14 51	14 58		15 15	15 28			15 34		15 53	15 58			16 15	16 28			16 34	16 51
	d		14 35	14 55	15 00		15 20	15 30			15 35	15 47	15 55	16 00			16 20	16 30			16 35	16 55
St Denys	d		14 40								15 40										16 40	
Swaythling	d		14 43								15 43										16 43	
Southampton Airport Pkwy ✈	d		14 46	15 03	15 08		15 27	15 38			15 46	15 54	16 03	16 08			16 27	16 38			16 46	17 03
Portsmouth Harbour ⛴	d	13 59								14 59										15 59		
Portsmouth & Southsea	d	14 04								15 04										16 04		
Fratton	d	14 08								15 08										16 08		
Hilsea	d	14 12								15 12										16 12		
Cosham	d	14 17								15 17										16 17		
Portchester	d	14 22								15 22										16 22		
Fareham	d	14 28								15 28										16 28		
Botley	d	14 35								15 35										16 35		
Hedge End	d	14 40								15 40										16 40		
Eastleigh 3	a	14 46	14 49	15 06					15 20	15 46	15 49		16 06						16 20	16 46	16 49	17 06
	d	14 47	14 50	15 14					15 21	15 47	15 50		16 14						16 21	16 47	16 50	17 14
Chandlers Ford	d		14 55								15 55										16 55	
Romsey	a		15 03						15 51		16 03								16 51		17 03	
Shawford	d			15 19		←							16 20		←							17 19
Winchester	d	14 56		15 25	15 18	15 25	15 36	15 48		15 56		16 03	16 26	16 18	16 26		16 36	16 48		16 56		17 25
Micheldever	d	15 05		→						16 05			→							17 05		→
Basingstoke	a	15 15			15 34	15 41	15 50			16 15		16 17		16 34	16 42		16 50			17 15		
	d	15 17			15 35	15 43	15 51			16 17		16 20		16 35	16 43		16 51			17 17		
Reading 7	a						16 08					16 37					17 09					
Fleet	d					15 54									16 54							
Farnborough (Main)	d	15 30				16 00				16 30					17 00					17 30		
Woking	a	15 39						16 19		16 39								17 19		17 39		
Clapham Junction 10	a				16 11	16 25								17 11	17 25							
London Waterloo 15 ⊖	a	16 11			16 21	16 34		16 49		17 09				17 19	17 34			17 49		18 08		

A ⌶ from Bournemouth

For services from Brockenhurst - Lymington refer to Table T159

Table T158-R

Saturdays

21 December to 16 May

Weymouth, Bournemouth, Romsey, Southampton and Basingstoke - London

		SW	SW	XC	SW	SW	SW	SW	SW	XC	SW	SW	SW	SW	XC	SW	SW	SW	SW	SW	SW	SW	GW
		◇1	◇1	◇1	◇1	1	◇1	1	1	◇1	1	◇1	◇1	◇1	◇1	◇1	1	◇1	1	◇1	◇1	◇1	◇
		A ⌶		⌶	A ⌶					⌶			A ⌶		⌶	A ⌶							
Weymouth	d	15 20			16 03								16 20			17 03					17 20		17 28
Upwey	d	15 24											16 24								17 24		17 33
Dorchester West	a																						17 41
Dorchester South	d	15 33			16 13								16 33			17 13					17 33		
Moreton (Dorset)	d	15 39											16 39								17 39		
Wool	d	15 45											16 45								17 45		
Wareham	d	15 53			16 28								16 53			17 28					17 53		
Holton Heath	d	15 56											16 56								17 56		
Hamworthy	d	16 01			16 35								17 01			17 35					18 01		
Poole 4	a	16 06			16 39								17 06			17 39					18 06		
	d	16 07			16 40							16 50	17 07			17 40				17 50	18 07		
Parkstone (Dorset)	d				16 44							16 54				17 44				17 54			
Branksome	d				16 48							16 57				17 48				17 57			
Bournemouth	a	16 17			16 54							17 02	17 17			17 54				18 02	18 17		
	d	16 22		16 47	16 59							17 05	17 22		17 47	17 59				18 05	18 22		
Pokesdown	d	16 26										17 09	17 26							18 09	18 26		
Christchurch	d	16 30										17 13	17 30							18 13	18 30		
Hinton Admiral	d											17 18								18 18			
New Milton	d	16 37										17 22	17 37							18 22	18 37		
Sway	d											17 27								18 27			
Brockenhurst 3	a	16 44		17 01	17 14							17 32	17 44		18 01	18 14				18 32	18 44		
	d	16 45		17 02	17 15							17 33	17 45		18 02	18 15				18 33	18 45		
Beaulieu Road	d											17 38											
Ashurst New Forest	d											17 42								18 40			
Totton	d											17 47								18 45			
Salisbury	d							16 56											17 56				
Dean	d							17 08											18 08				
Mottisfont & Dunbridge	d							17 14											18 14				
Romsey	d					17 07		17 20									18 07		18 20				
Redbridge	d							17 27											18 27				
Millbrook (Hants)	d							17 31											18 31				
Southampton Central ⛴	a	16 58		17 15	17 28			17 34				17 53	17 58		18 16	18 28			18 34	18 51	18 58		
	d	17 00		17 20	17 30			17 35	17 39	17 47		17 55	18 00		18 20	18 30			18 35	18 55	19 00		
St Denys	d							17 40	17 44										18 40				
Swaythling	d							17 43	17 47										18 43				
Southampton Airport Pkwy ✈	d	17 08		17 27	17 38			17 46	17 50	17 54		18 03	18 08		18 27	18 38			18 46	19 03	19 08		
Portsmouth Harbour ⛴	d						16 59											17 59					
Portsmouth & Southsea	d						17 04											18 04					
Fratton	d						17 08											18 08					
Hilsea	d						17 12											18 12					
Cosham	d						17 17											18 17					
Portchester	d						17 22											18 22					
Fareham	d						17 28											18 28					
Botley	d						17 35											18 35					
Hedge End	d						17 40											18 40					
Eastleigh 3	a					17 20	17 46	17 49	17 54			18 06					18 20	18 46	18 49	19 06			
	d					17 21	17 47	17 50	17 59			18 14					18 21	18 47	18 50	19 14			
Chandlers Ford	d							17 55											18 55				
Romsey	a					17 51		18 03									19 00		19 04				
Shawford	d		←						18 04		←	18 19		←						19 19		←	
Winchester	d	17 18	17 25	17 36	17 48		17 56		18 10	18 03	18 10	18 25	18 18	18 25	18 36	18 48		18 56		19 25	19 18	19 25	
Micheldever	d						18 05		→		18 19	→						19 05		→			
Basingstoke	a	17 34	17 41	17 50			18 15			18 17	18 29		18 34	18 41	18 50			19 15			19 34	19 41	
	d	17 35	17 43	17 51			18 17			18 20			18 35	18 43	18 51			19 17			19 35	19 43	
Reading 7	a			18 07						18 37					19 08								
Fleet	d		17 54											18 54								19 54	
Farnborough (Main)	d		18 00				18 30							19 00				19 30				20 00	
Woking	a				18 19		18 39									19 19		19 39					
Clapham Junction 10	a	18 11	18 25										19 11	19 25							20 11	20 25	
London Waterloo 15 ⊖	a	18 19	18 34		18 49		19 08						19 19	19 34		19 49		20 09			20 19	20 34	

A ⌶ from Bournemouth

For services from Brockenhurst - Lymington refer to Table T159

Table T158-R

Saturdays
21 December to 16 May

Weymouth, Bournemouth, Romsey, Southampton and Basingstoke - London

		XC	SW	SW	SW	SW	SW	SW	SW	XC	SW	SW	SW	SW	SW	SW	SW	SW	SW	SW	SW	SW	SW
		◇1	◇1	1	◇1	1	◇1	◇1	◇1	◇1	◇1	1	◇1	1	◇1	◇1	◇1	◇1	1	◇1	1	◇1	◇1
			A					A			A					A							
		✠	✠					✠			✠					✠							
Weymouth	d		18 03					18 20			19 03					19 20							20 10
Upwey	d							18 24								19 24							20 14
Dorchester West	a																						
Dorchester South	d		18 13					18 33			19 13					19 33							20 22
Moreton (Dorset)	d							18 39								19 39							20 28
Wool	d							18 45								19 45							20 34
Wareham	d		18 28					18 53			19 28					19 53							20 42
Holton Heath	d							18 56								19 56							
Hamworthy	d		18 35					19 01			19 35					20 01							20 48
Poole 4	a		18 39					19 06			19 39					20 06							20 53
	d		18 40				18 50	19 07			19 40				19 50	20 07							20 54
Parkstone (Dorset)	d		18 44				18 54				19 44				19 54								20 58
Branksome	d		18 48				18 57				19 48				19 57								21 01
Bournemouth	a		18 54				19 02	19 17			19 54				20 02	20 17							21 07
	d	18 47	18 59				19 05	19 22		19 47	19 59				20 05	20 22		20 59					21 12
Pokesdown	d						19 09	19 26							20 09	20 26							21 16
Christchurch	d						19 13	19 30							20 13	20 30							21 20
Hinton Admiral	d						19 18								20 18								21 25
New Milton	d						19 22	19 37							20 22	20 37							21 29
Sway	d						19 27								20 27								21 34
Brockenhurst 3	a	19 01	19 14				19 32	19 44		20 01	20 14				20 32	20 44		21 14					21 39
	d	19 02	19 15				19 33	19 45		20 02	20 15				20 33	20 45		21 15					21 40
Beaulieu Road	d														20 38								
Ashurst New Forest	d						19 40								20 42								21 47
Totton	d						19 45								20 47								21 52
Salisbury	d					18 56								19 56							20 56		
Dean	d					19 08								20 08							21 08		
Mottisfont & Dunbridge	d					19 14								20 14							21 14		
Romsey	d			19 07		19 20						20 07		20 20					21 07		21 20		
Redbridge	d					19 27								20 27							21 27		
Millbrook (Hants)	d					19 31								20 31							21 31		
Southampton Central ⛴	a	19 15	19 28			19 34	19 51	19 58		20 15	20 28			20 34	20 53	20 58		21 28			21 34		21 57
	d	19 20	19 30			19 35	19 55	20 00		20 20	20 30			20 35	20 55	21 00		21 30			21 35	21 55	22 00
St Denys	d					19 40								20 40							21 40		
Swaythling	d					19 43								20 43							21 43		
Southampton Airport Pkwy ✈	d	19 27	19 38			19 46	20 03	20 08		20 27	20 38			20 46	21 03	21 08		21 38			21 46	22 03	22 08
Portsmouth Harbour ⛴	d				18 59								19 59							20 59			
Portsmouth & Southsea	d				19 04								20 04							21 04			
Fratton	d				19 08								20 08							21 08			
Hilsea	d				19 12								20 12							21 12			
Cosham	d				19 17								20 17							21 17			
Portchester	d				19 22								20 22							21 22			
Fareham	d				19 28								20 28							21 28			
Botley	d				19 35								20 35							21 35			
Hedge End	d				19 40								20 40							21 40			
Eastleigh 3	a			19 20	19 46	19 49	20 06					20 20	20 46	20 49	21 06				21 20	21 46	21 49	22 06	
	d			19 21	19 47	19 50	20 14					20 21	20 47	20 50	21 14				21 21	21 47	21 50	22 14	
Chandlers Ford	d					19 55								20 55							21 55		
Romsey	a			19 51		20 03						20 51		21 03					21 51		22 03		
Shawford	d						20 19		←						21 19		←					22 19	
Winchester	d	19 36	19 48		19 56		20 25	20 18	20 25	20 36	20 48		20 56		21 25	21 18	21 25	21 48		21 56		22 25	22 18
Micheldever	d				20 05		→						21 05		→					22 05		→	
Basingstoke	a	19 50			20 15			20 34	20 41	20 50			21 17			21 34	21 41			22 15			22 34
	d	19 51			20 17			20 35	20 43	20 51			21 24			21 35	21 43			22 24			22 35
Reading 7	a	20 08								21 08													
Fleet	d								20 54				21 40				21 54			22 40			
Farnborough (Main)	d				20 30				21 00				21 46				22 00			22 46			
Woking	a		20 20		20 39						21 20		21 58			21 53	22 09	22 19		22 58			22 53
Clapham Junction 10	a							21 11	21 25							22 13	22 29						23 13
London Waterloo 15 ⊖	a		20 51		21 10			21 19	21 36		21 49		22 34			22 21	22 38	22 49		23 32			23 21

A ✠ from Bournemouth

For services from Brockenhurst - Lymington refer to Table T159

NRT DECEMBER 19 EDITION

Table T158-R

Saturdays
21 December to 16 May

Weymouth, Bournemouth, Romsey, Southampton and Basingstoke - London

		SW	GW	SW	SW	SW	SW	SW	SW	SW	SW	SW	SW
		◇1		1	1	◇1	1	◇1	1	1	1	1	◇1
Weymouth	d		20 20					21 10				22 10	23 10
Upwey	d		20 25					21 14				22 14	23 14
Dorchester West	a		20 33										
Dorchester South	d							21 22				22 22	23 22
Moreton (Dorset)	d							21 28				22 28	23 28
Wool	d							21 34				22 34	23 34
Wareham	d							21 42				22 42	23 42
Holton Heath	d												
Hamworthy	d							21 48				22 48	23 48
Poole 4	a							21 53				22 53	23 53
	d							21 54				22 54	23 54
Parkstone (Dorset)	d							21 58				22 58	
Branksome	d							22 01				23 01	
Bournemouth	a							22 07				23 07	00 03
	d							22 12				23 12	
Pokesdown	d							22 16				23 16	
Christchurch	d							22 20				23 20	
Hinton Admiral	d							22 25				23 25	
New Milton	d							22 29				23 29	
Sway	d							22 34				23 34	
Brockenhurst 3	a							22 39				23 39	
	d							22 40				23 40	
Beaulieu Road	d												
Ashurst New Forest	d							22 47				23 47	
Totton	d							22 52				23 52	
Salisbury	d						21 56			22 45			
Dean	d						22 08			22 57			
Mottisfont & Dunbridge	d						22 14			23 03			
Romsey	d			22 07			22 20		23 11	23 08			
Redbridge	d						22 27			23 16			
Millbrook (Hants)	d						22 31			23 19			
Southampton Central ⛴	a						22 34	22 57		23 22		23 57	
	d					22 30	22 35	23 00		23 23		23 59	
St Denys	d						22 40			23 28		00 04	
Swaythling	d						22 43			23 31		00 07	
Southampton Airport Pkwy ✈	d					22 38	22 46	23 08		23 34		00 10	
Portsmouth Harbour ⛴	d				21 54						23 24		
Portsmouth & Southsea	d				21 59						23 28		
Fratton	d				22 03						23 32		
Hilsea	d				22 07						23 36		
Cosham	d				22 12						23 42		
Portchester	d				22 17						23 47		
Fareham	d				22 23						23 53		
Botley	d				22 30						23 59		
Hedge End	d				22 35						00 05		
Eastleigh 3	a			22 20	22 41	22 42	22 49	23 11	23 24	23 37	00 11	00 14	
	d			22 22		22 47	22 50	23 12	23 24	23 38	00 21		
Chandlers Ford	d						22 55			23 43			
Romsey	a			22 51			23 03		23 57	23 50			
Shawford	d	←						23 19					
Winchester	d	22 25				22 56		23 25			00a31		
Micheldever	d							23 33					
Basingstoke	a	22 41				23 12		23 43					
	d	22 43				23 14		23 43					
Reading 7	a												
Fleet	d	22 54						00 01					
Farnborough (Main)	d	23 00						00 06					
Woking	a	23 09				23 32		00 18					
Clapham Junction 10	a	23 29				23 56		00 53					
London Waterloo 15 ⊖	a	23 39				00 08		01 04					

For services from Brockenhurst - Lymington refer to Table T159

Table T158-R

Sundays
15 December to 10 May

Weymouth, Bournemouth, Romsey, Southampton and Basingstoke - London

Station		SW ◇1 A	SW 1 A	SW 1 A	SW ◇1	SW ◇1	SW ◇1 B ⌶	SW 1	SW 1	SW ◇1	SW ◇1	SW 1	XC ◇1 ⌶	SW ◇1 C ⌶	GW ◇ D	SW 1	SW 1	SW ◇1 ⌶	SW ◇1 E ⌶	SW 1	XC ◇1 ⌶	SW ◇1 C ⌶	SW 1
Weymouth	d													07 48	08 07							08 48	
Upwey	d													07 52								08 52	
Dorchester West	a														08 18								
Dorchester South	d													08 00								09 00	
Moreton (Dorset)	d													08 07								09 07	
Wool	d													08 13								09 13	
Wareham	d													08 20								09 20	
Holton Heath	d																						
Hamworthy	d													08 27								09 27	
Poole 4	a													08 31								09 31	
	d						06 50				07 50			08 32					08 55			09 32	
Parkstone (Dorset)	d						06 54				07 54			08 36								09 36	
Branksome	d						06 57				07 57			08 40								09 40	
Bournemouth	a						07 02				08 02			08 46					09 04			09 47	
	d						07 06				08 06			08 50					09 06		09 40	09 51	
Pokesdown	d						07 10				08 10								09 10				
Christchurch	d						07 14				08 14								09 14				
Hinton Admiral	d						07 19				08 19								09 19				
New Milton	d						07 23				08 23			09 01					09 23			10 02	
Sway	d						07 28				08 28								09 28				
Brockenhurst 3	a						07 33				08 33			09 08					09 33		09 54	10 09	
	d						07 34				08 34			09 09					09 34		09 55	10 10	
Beaulieu Road	d										08 39								09 39				
Ashurst New Forest	d						07 43				08 43								09 43				
Totton	d						07 48				08 48								09 48				
Salisbury	d							08 08	08 20							09 08							10 08
Dean	d							08 20								09 20							10 20
Mottisfont & Dunbridge	d							08 26								09 26							10 26
Romsey	d							08 35	08 39							09 32	09 35						10 32
Redbridge	d								08 46							09 39							10 39
Millbrook (Hants)	d								08 50			←				09 43				←			10 43
Southampton Central ⛴	a						07 53		08 52		08 53	08 52		09 23		09 45			09 53	09 45	10 07	10 23	10 45
	d				06 55		07 55		08 59		08 55	08 59	09 20	09 25		09 59			09 55	09 59	10 20	10 25	10 59
St Denys	d			00 04					→			09 04				→				10 04			→
Swaythling	d			00 07								09 07								10 07			
Southampton Airport Pkwy ✈	d			00 10	07 03		08 03				09 03	09 10	09 27	09 33					10 03	10 10	10 27	10 33	
Portsmouth Harbour ⛴	d					07 17				08 17								09 17					
Portsmouth & Southsea	d					07 22				08 22								09 22					
Fratton	d					07 26				08 26								09 26					
Hilsea	d					07 30				08 30								09 30					
Cosham	d					07 35				08 35								09 35					
Portchester	d					07 40				08 40								09 40					
Fareham	d					07 46				08 46								09 46					
Botley	d					07 54				08 54								09 54					
Hedge End	d		00 05			07 58				08 58								09 58					
Eastleigh 8	a		00 11	00 14	07 07	08 04	08 07			09 04	09 07	09 13					09 48	10 04	10 07	10 13			
	d		00 21		07 11	08 11				09 11		09 15					09 54	10 11		10 15			
Chandlers Ford	d							08 42				09 20								10 20			
Romsey	a							09 24				09 28					10 24			10 28			
Shawford	d				07 17	08 17				09 17								10 17					
Winchester	d		00a31		07 23	08 23				09 23			09 36	09 42				10 23			10 36	10 42	
Micheldever	d				07 32	08 32				09 32								10 32					
Basingstoke	a				07 42	08 42				09 42			09 50	09 58				10 42			10 50	10 58	
	d				07 44	08 44				09 44			09 51	10 00				10 44			10 51	11 00	
Reading 7	a												10 08								11 10		
Fleet	d	00 01																					
Farnborough (Main)	d	00 06																					
Woking	a	00 18			08 02	09 02				10 02				10 19				11 02				11 18	
Clapham Junction 10	a	00 53			08 31	09 30				10 27				10 39				11 26				11 39	
London Waterloo 15 ⊖	a	01 04			08 43	09 41				10 39				10 50				11 39				11 50	

A not 15 December
B ⌶ to Eastleigh
C ⌶ from Bournemouth
D from 5 April
E ⌶ from Eastleigh

For services from Brockenhurst - Lymington refer to Table T159

Table T158-R

Sundays
15 December to 10 May

Weymouth, Bournemouth, Romsey, Southampton and Basingstoke - London

Station		SW 1	SW ◇1 ⌶	SW ◇1 A ⌶	SW 1	XC ◇1 ⌶	SW ◇1 A ⌶	SW 1	SW 1	SW ◇1 ⌶	SW ◇1 B ⌶	SW 1	XC ◇1 ⌶	SW ◇1 A ⌶	GW ◇	SW 1	SW 1	SW ◇1 ⌶	SW ◇1 A ⌶	SW 1	XC ◇1 ⌶	SW ◇1 A ⌶	SW 1
Weymouth	d						09 48							10 48	11 00							11 48	
Upwey	d						09 52							10 52	11 05							11 52	
Dorchester West	a														11 12								
Dorchester South	d						10 00							11 00								12 00	
Moreton (Dorset)	d						10 07							11 07								12 07	
Wool	d						10 13							11 13								12 13	
Wareham	d						10 20							11 20								12 20	
Holton Heath	d																						
Hamworthy	d						10 27							11 27								12 27	
Poole 4	a						10 31							11 31								12 31	
	d			09 55			10 32				10 55			11 32					11 55			12 32	
Parkstone (Dorset)	d						10 36							11 36								12 36	
Branksome	d						10 40							11 40								12 40	
Bournemouth	a			10 04			10 46				11 04			11 46					12 04			12 46	
	d			10 06		10 40	10 50				11 06		11 40	11 50					12 06		12 40	12 50	
Pokesdown	d			10 10							11 10								12 10				
Christchurch	d			10 14							11 14								12 14				
Hinton Admiral	d			10 19							11 19								12 19				
New Milton	d			10 23			11 01				11 23			12 01					12 23			13 01	
Sway	d			10 28							11 28								12 28				
Brockenhurst 3	a			10 33		10 54	11 08				11 33		11 54	12 08					12 33		12 54	13 08	
	d			10 34		10 55	11 09				11 34		11 55	12 09					12 34		12 55	13 09	
Beaulieu Road	d			10 39							11 39								12 39				
Ashurst New Forest	d			10 43							11 43								12 43				
Totton	d			10 48							11 48								12 48				
Salisbury	d							11 08								12 08							13 08
Dean	d							11 20								12 20							13 20
Mottisfont & Dunbridge	d							11 26								12 26							13 26
Romsey	d	10 35						11 32	11 35							12 32	12 35						13 32
Redbridge	d							11 39								12 39							13 39
Millbrook (Hants)	d				←			11 43				←				12 43				←			13 43
Southampton Central ⛴	a			10 53	10 45	11 07	11 23	11 45			11 53	11 45	12 07	12 23		12 45			12 53	12 45	13 07	13 23	13 45
	d			10 55	10 59	11 20	11 25	11 59			11 55	11 59	12 20	12 25		12 59			12 55	12 59	13 20	13 25	13 59
St Denys	d				11 04			→				12 04				→				13 04			→
Swaythling	d				11 07							12 07								13 07			
Southampton Airport Pkwy ✈	d			11 03	11 10	11 27	11 33				12 03	12 10	12 27	12 33					13 03	13 10	13 27	13 33	
Portsmouth Harbour ⛴	d		10 17							11 17								12 17					
Portsmouth & Southsea	d		10 22							11 22								12 22					
Fratton	d		10 26							11 26								12 26					
Hilsea	d		10 30							11 30								12 30					
Cosham	d		10 35							11 35								12 35					
Portchester	d		10 40							11 40								12 40					
Fareham	d		10 46							11 46								12 46					
Botley	d		10 54							11 54								12 54					
Hedge End	d		10 58							11 58								12 58					
Eastleigh 8	a	10 48	11 04	11 07	11 13				11 48	12 04	12 07	12 13					12 48	13 04	13 07	13 13			
	d	10 54	11 11		11 15				11 54	12 11		12 15					12 54	13 11		13 15			
Chandlers Ford	d				11 20							12 20								13 20			
Romsey	a	11 24			11 28				12 24			12 28					13 24			13 28			
Shawford	d		11 17							12 17								13 17					
Winchester	d		11 23			11 36	11 42			12 23			12 36	12 42				13 23			13 36	13 42	
Micheldever	d		11 32							12 32								13 32					
Basingstoke	a		11 42			11 50	11 58			12 42			12 50	12 58				13 42			13 50	13 58	
	d		11 44			11 51	12 00			12 44			12 51	13 00				13 44			13 51	14 00	
Reading 7	a					12 07							13 09								14 07		
Fleet	d																						
Farnborough (Main)	d																						
Woking	a		12 02				12 18			13 02				13 18				14 02				14 18	
Clapham Junction 10	a		12 27				12 39			13 27				13 39				14 27				14 39	
London Waterloo 15 ⊖	a		12 37				12 49			13 37				13 49				14 37				14 49	

A ⌶ from Bournemouth
B ⌶ from Eastleigh

For services from Brockenhurst - Lymington refer to Table T159

Table T158-R

Sundays

15 December to 10 May

Weymouth, Bournemouth, Romsey, Southampton and Basingstoke - London

		SW ■	SW ◇■ ⚒	SW ◇■ A ⚒	SW ■	XC ◇■ ⚒	SW ◇■ B ⚒	SW ■	SW ■	SW ◇■ ⚒	SW ◇■ A ⚒	SW ■	XC ◇■ ⚒	SW ◇■ B ⚒	GW ◇	SW ■	SW ■	SW ◇■ ⚒	SW ◇■	SW ■	SW ◇■ ⚒	XC ◇■ ⚒
Weymouth	d						12 48							13 48	14 08							
Upwey	d						12 52							13 52	14 13							
Dorchester West	a														14 20							
Dorchester South	d						13 00							14 00								
Moreton (Dorset)	d						13 07							14 07								
Wool	d						13 13							14 13								
Wareham	d						13 20							14 20								
Holton Heath	d																					
Hamworthy	d						13 27							14 27								
Poole 4	a						13 31							14 31								
	d			12 55			13 32				13 55			14 32					14 55			
Parkstone (Dorset)	d						13 36							14 36								
Branksome	d						13 40							14 40								
Bournemouth	a			13 04			13 46				14 04			14 46					15 04			
	d			13 06		13 40	13 50				14 06		14 40	14 50					15 06			15 40
Pokesdown	d			13 10							14 10								15 10			
Christchurch	d			13 14							14 14								15 14			
Hinton Admiral	d			13 19							14 19								15 19			
New Milton	d			13 23			14 01				14 23			15 01					15 23			
Sway	d			13 28							14 28								15 28			
Brockenhurst 3	a			13 33		13 54	14 08				14 33		14 54	15 08					15 33			15 54
	d			13 34		13 55	14 09				14 34		14 55	15 09					15 34			15 55
Beaulieu Road	d			13 39							14 39								15 39			
Ashurst New Forest	d			13 43							14 43								15 43			
Totton	d			13 48							14 48								15 48			
Salisbury	d							14 08								15 08						
Dean	d							14 20								15 20						
Mottisfont & Dunbridge	d							14 26								15 26						
Romsey	d	13 35						14 32	14 35							15 32	15 35					
Redbridge	d							14 39								15 39						
Millbrook (Hants)	d				←			14 43				←				15 43				←		
Southampton Central ⛴	a			13 53	13 45	14 07	14 23	14 45			14 53	14 45	15 07	15 23		15 45			15 53	15 45		16 08
	d			13 55	13 59	14 20	14 25	14 59			14 55	14 59	15 20	15 25		15 59			15 55	15 59		16 20
St Denys	d				14 04			→				15 04				→				16 04		
Swaythling	d				14 07							15 07								16 07		
Southampton Airport Pkwy ✈	d			14 03	14 10	14 27	14 33				15 03	15 10	15 27	15 33					16 03	16 10		16 27
Portsmouth Harbour ⛴	d		13 17							14 17								15 17				
Portsmouth & Southsea	d		13 22							14 22								15 22				
Fratton	d		13 26							14 26								15 26				
Hilsea	d		13 30							14 30								15 30				
Cosham	d		13 35							14 35								15 35				
Portchester	d		13 40							14 40								15 40				
Fareham	d		13 46							14 46								15 46				
Botley	d		13 54							14 54								15 54				
Hedge End	d		13 58							14 58								15 58				
Eastleigh 3	a	13 48	14 04	14 07	14 13				14 48	15 04	15 07	15 13					15 48	16 04	16 06	16 13		
	d	13 54		14 11	14 15				14 54		15 11	15 15					15 54	16 11	16 07	16 15		
Chandlers Ford	d				14 20							15 20								16 20		
Romsey	a	14 24			14 28				15 24			15 28					16 24			16 28		
Shawford	d			14 17							15 17							16 17			←	
Winchester	d			14 23		14 36	14 42				15 23		15 36	15 42				16 23	16 17		16 23	16 36
Micheldever	d			14 32							15 32							→			16 32	
Basingstoke	a			14 42		14 50	14 58				15 42		15 50	15 58					16 33		16 42	16 50
	d			14 44		14 51	15 00				15 44		15 51	16 00					16 35		16 44	16 51
Reading 7	a					15 10							16 07									17 09
Fleet	d																					
Farnborough (Main)	d																				16 58	
Woking	a			15 02			15 18				16 02			16 18					16 53		17 07	
Clapham Junction 10	a			15 27			15 39				16 27			16 39					17 14		17 28	
London Waterloo 15 ⊖	a			15 37			15 49				16 37			16 49					17 24		17 39	

A ⚒ from Eastleigh B ⚒ from Bournemouth

For services from Brockenhurst - Lymington refer to Table T159

Table T158-R

Sundays

15 December to 10 May

Weymouth, Bournemouth, Romsey, Southampton and Basingstoke - London

		SW ◇■ A ⚒	SW ■	SW ■	SW ◇■ ⚒	SW ◇■ ⚒	SW ■	SW ◇■	SW ◇■ ⚒	XC ◇■ ⚒	SW ◇■ A ⚒	GW ◇	SW ■	SW ■	SW ◇■	SW ◇■	SW ■	SW ◇■	XC ◇■ ⚒	SW ◇■ A ⚒	SW ■	SW ■	SW ◇■
Weymouth	d	14 48									15 48	16 10								16 48			
Upwey	d	14 52									15 52	16 15								16 52			
Dorchester West	a											16 22											
Dorchester South	d	15 00									16 00									17 00			
Moreton (Dorset)	d	15 07									16 07									17 07			
Wool	d	15 13									16 13									17 13			
Wareham	d	15 20									16 20									17 20			
Holton Heath	d																						
Hamworthy	d	15 27									16 27									17 27			
Poole 4	a	15 31									16 31									17 31			
	d	15 32				15 55		16 18			16 32					16 55				17 32			
Parkstone (Dorset)	d	15 36									16 36									17 36			
Branksome	d	15 40									16 40									17 40			
Bournemouth	a	15 46				16 04		16 28			16 46					17 04				17 46			
	d	15 50				16 06		16 31		16 40	16 50					17 06			17 40	17 50			
Pokesdown	d					16 10										17 10							
Christchurch	d					16 14										17 14							
Hinton Admiral	d					16 19										17 19							
New Milton	d	16 01				16 23					17 01					17 23				18 01			
Sway	d					16 28										17 28							
Brockenhurst 3	a	16 08				16 33				16 54	17 08					17 33			17 54	18 08			
	d	16 09				16 34				16 55	17 09					17 34			17 55	18 09			
Beaulieu Road	d					16 39										17 39							
Ashurst New Forest	d					16 43										17 43							
Totton	d					16 48										17 48							
Salisbury	d		16 08										17 08								18 08		
Dean	d		16 20										17 20								18 20		
Mottisfont & Dunbridge	d		16 26										17 26								18 26		
Romsey	d		16 32	16 35									17 32	17 35							18 32	18 35	
Redbridge	d		16 39										17 39								18 39		
Millbrook (Hants)	d		16 43				←						17 43				←				18 43		
Southampton Central ⛴	a	16 23	16 45			16 53	16 45	16 58		17 08	17 23		17 45			17 53	17 45		18 09	18 23	18 45		
	d	16 25	16 57			16 55	16 57	17 00		17 20	17 25		17 59			17 55	17 59		18 20	18 25	18 57		
St Denys	d		→				17 06						→				18 04				→		
Swaythling	d						17 09										18 07						
Southampton Airport Pkwy ✈	d	16 33				17 03	17 12			17 27	17 33					18 03	18 10		18 27	18 33			
Portsmouth Harbour ⛴	d				16 17										17 17								18 17
Portsmouth & Southsea	d				16 22										17 22								18 22
Fratton	d				16 26										17 26								18 26
Hilsea	d				16 30										17 30								18 30
Cosham	d				16 35										17 35								18 35
Portchester	d				16 40										17 40								18 40
Fareham	d				16 46										17 46								18 46
Botley	d				16 54										17 54								18 54
Hedge End	d				16 58										17 58								18 58
Eastleigh 3	a			16 48	17 04	17 06	17 15							17 48	18 04	18 06	18 13					18 48	19 04
	d			16 54	17 11	17 07	17 16							17 54	18 11	18 07	18 15					18 54	19 11
Chandlers Ford	d						17 21										18 20						
Romsey	a			17 24			17 28							18 24			18 28					19 24	
Shawford	d				17 17				←						18 17			←					19 17
Winchester	d	16 42			17 23	17 17			17 23	17 36	17 42				18 23	18 17		18 23	18 36	18 42			19 23
Micheldever	d				→				17 32						→			18 32					→
Basingstoke	a	16 58				17 33			17 42	17 50	17 58					18 33		18 42	18 50	18 58			
	d	17 00				17 35			17 44	17 51	18 00					18 35		18 44	18 51	19 00			
Reading 7	a									18 07									19 09				
Fleet	d																						
Farnborough (Main)	d								17 58									18 58					
Woking	a	17 18				17 53			18 07		18 18					18 53		19 07		19 18			
Clapham Junction 10	a	17 39				18 14		18 02	18 28		18 39					19 15		19 28		19 39			
London Waterloo 15 ⊖	a	17 49				18 25		18 13	18 39		18 49					19 25		19 39		19 49			

A ⚒ from Bournemouth

For services from Brockenhurst - Lymington refer to Table T159

Table T158-R

Sundays

15 December to 10 May

Weymouth, Bournemouth, Romsey, Southampton and Basingstoke - London

		SW	SW	SW	SW	XC	SW	GW	SW	SW	SW	SW	SW	SW	XC	SW	SW	SW	SW	SW	SW	SW	SW
		◇1	1	◇1	◇1	◇1	◇1	◇	1	1	◇1	◇1	1	◇1	◇1	◇1	1	1	◇1	◇1	1	◇1	1
						⊼	A ⊼									A ⊼							
Weymouth	d						17 48	17 56								18 48							
Upwey	d						17 52	18 01								18 52							
Dorchester West	a							18 08															
Dorchester South	d						18 00									19 00							
Moreton (Dorset)	d						18 07									19 07							
Wool	d						18 13									19 13							
Wareham	d						18 20									19 20							
Holton Heath	d																						
Hamworthy	d						18 27									19 27							
Poole 4	a						18 31									19 31							
	d	17 55		18 18			18 32					18 55				19 32				19 55			
Parkstone (Dorset)	d						18 36									19 36							
Branksome	d						18 40									19 40							
Bournemouth	a	18 04		18 28			18 46					19 04				19 46				20 04			
	d	18 06		18 31		18 40	18 50					19 06			19 40	19 50				20 06			
Pokesdown	d	18 10										19 10								20 10			
Christchurch	d	18 14										19 14								20 14			
Hinton Admiral	d	18 19										19 19								20 19			
New Milton	d	18 23					19 01					19 23				20 01				20 23			
Sway	d	18 28										19 28								20 28			
Brockenhurst 3	a	18 33				18 54	19 08					19 33			19 54	20 08				20 33			
	d	18 34				18 55	19 09					19 34			19 55	20 09				20 34			
Beaulieu Road	d	18 39										19 39								20 39			
Ashurst New Forest	d	18 43										19 43								20 43			
Totton	d	18 48										19 48								20 48			
Salisbury	d								19 08								20 08						21 08
Dean	d								19 20								20 20						21 20
Mottisfont & Dunbridge	d								19 26								20 26						21 26
Romsey	d								19 32	19 35							20 32	20 35					21 32
Redbridge	d								19 39								20 39						21 39
Millbrook (Hants)	d		←						19 43				←				20 43				←		21 43
Southampton Central ⛴	a	18 53	18 45	18 58		19 07	19 23		19 45			19 53	19 45		20 07	20 23	20 45			20 53	20 45		21 45
	d	18 55	18 57	19 00		19 20	19 25		19 59			19 55	19 59		20 20	20 25	20 59			20 55	20 59		21 59
St Denys	d		19 06						→				20 04				→				21 04		→
Swaythling	d		19 09										20 07								21 07		
Southampton Airport Pkwy ✈	d	19 03	19 12			19 27	19 33					20 03	20 10		20 27	20 33				21 03	21 10		
Portsmouth Harbour ⛴	d										19 17								20 17				
Portsmouth & Southsea	d										19 22								20 22				
Fratton	d										19 26								20 26				
Hilsea	d										19 30								20 30				
Cosham	d										19 35								20 35				
Portchester	d										19 40								20 40				
Fareham	d										19 46								20 46				
Botley	d										19 54								20 54				
Hedge End	d										19 58								20 58				
Eastleigh 3	a	19 06	19 15							19 48	20 04	20 06	20 13					20 48	21 05	21 06	21 13		
	d	19 07	19 16							19 54	20 11	20 07	20 15					20 54	21 11	21 07	21 15		
Chandlers Ford	d		19 21										20 20								21 20		
Romsey	a		19 28							20 24			20 28					21 24			21 28		
Shawford	d				←						20 17			←					21 17			←	
Winchester	d	19 17			19 23	19 36	19 42				20 23	20 17		20 23	20 36	20 42			21 23	21 17		21 23	
Micheldever	d				19 32						→			20 32					→			21 32	
Basingstoke	a	19 33			19 42	19 50	19 58					20 33		20 42	20 50	20 58				21 33		21 42	
	d	19 35			19 44	19 51	20 00					20 35		20 44	20 51	21 00				21 35		21 44	
Reading 7	a					20 07									21 07								
Fleet	d																						
Farnborough (Main)	d				19 58									20 58								21 58	
Woking	a	19 53			20 08		20 18					20 53		21 08		21 18				21 53		22 08	
Clapham Junction 10	a	20 14		20 02	20 28		20 39					21 14		21 28		21 39				22 14		22 28	
London Waterloo 15 ⊖	a	20 24		20 13	20 40		20 49					21 24		21 39		21 49				22 24		22 39	

A ⊼ from Bournemouth

For services from Brockenhurst - Lymington refer to Table T159

Table T158-R

Sundays

15 December to 10 May

Weymouth, Bournemouth, Romsey, Southampton and Basingstoke - London

		SW	SW	SW	SW	SW	GW	SW	SW	SW	SW	SW	SW	SW	SW
		1	◇1	◇1	1	◇1		1	1	1	◇1	1	◇1	1	1
Weymouth	d			19 58			20 09				20 58		21 58	22 58	
Upwey	d			20 02			20 14				21 02		22 02	23 02	
Dorchester West	a						20 21								
Dorchester South	d			20 10							21 10		22 10	23 10	
Moreton (Dorset)	d			20 17							21 17		22 17	23 17	
Wool	d			20 23							21 23		22 23	23 23	
Wareham	d			20 30							21 30		22 30	23 30	
Holton Heath	d														
Hamworthy	d			20 37							21 37		22 37	23 37	
Poole 4	a			20 42							21 42		22 42	23 41	
	d			20 50							21 50		22 50	23 50	
Parkstone (Dorset)	d			20 54							21 54		22 54	23 54	
Branksome	d			20 57							21 57		22 57	23 57	
Bournemouth	a			21 03							22 03		23 03	00 03	
	d			21 06							22 08		23 08		
Pokesdown	d			21 10							22 12		23 12		
Christchurch	d			21 14							22 16		23 16		
Hinton Admiral	d			21 19							22 21		23 21		
New Milton	d			21 23							22 25		23 25		
Sway	d			21 28							22 30		23 30		
Brockenhurst 3	a			21 33							22 35		23 35		
	d			21 34							22 36		23 36		
Beaulieu Road	d			21 39											
Ashurst New Forest	d			21 43							22 43		23 43		
Totton	d			21 48							22 48		23 48		
Salisbury	d														
Dean	d														
Mottisfont & Dunbridge	d														
Romsey	d	21 35						22 28	22 35						
Redbridge	d							22 35							
Millbrook (Hants)	d				←			22 39				←			
Southampton Central ⛴	a			21 53	21 45			22 41			22 53	22 41	23 54		
	d			21 55	21 59			23 05			22 55	23 05			
St Denys	d				22 04			→				23 10			
Swaythling	d				22 07							23 13			
Southampton Airport Pkwy ✈	d			22 03	22 10						23 03	23 16			
Portsmouth Harbour ⛴	d		21 17							22 17					23 17
Portsmouth & Southsea	d		21 22							22 22					23 22
Fratton	d		21 26							22 26					23 26
Hilsea	d		21 30							22 30					23 30
Cosham	d		21 35							22 35					23 35
Portchester	d		21 40							22 40					23 40
Fareham	d		21 46							22 46					23 46
Botley	d		21 54							22 54					23 54
Hedge End	d		21 58							22 58					23 58
Eastleigh 3	a	21 48	22 05	22 06	22 13				22 48	23 05	23 09	23 19			00 05
	d	21 54	22 11	22 07	22 15				22 54		23 11	23 22			
Chandlers Ford	d				22 20							23 27			
Romsey	a	22 24			22 31				23 23			23 35			
Shawford	d		22 18			←					23 17				
Winchester	d		22 23	22 17		22 23					23 23				
Micheldever	d		→			22 32					23 32				
Basingstoke	a			22 34		22 42					23 42				
	d			22 35		22 44					23 44				
Reading 7	a														
Fleet	d														
Farnborough (Main)	d					22 58									
Woking	a			22 54		23 08					00 02				
Clapham Junction 10	a			23 14		23 28					00 23				
London Waterloo 15 ⊖	a			23 24		23 39					00 33				

For services from Brockenhurst - Lymington refer to Table T159

Table T159-F

Mondays to Fridays
16 December to 15 May

Brockenhurst - Lymington - Yarmouth (Isle of Wight)

		SW 1		SW 1	SW 1		SW 1	SW 1		SW 1
Brockenhurst 3	d	05 59	and every 30 minutes until	09 29	10 12	and every 30 minutes until	18 12	18 48	and every 30 minutes until	22 18
Lymington Town	d	06 07		09 37	10 20		18 20	18 56		22 26
Lymington Pier ⛴	a	06 10		09 40	10 23		18 23	18 59		22 29
	d									
Yarmouth (I.O.W.) ⛴	a									

Saturdays
21 December to 16 May

		SW 1		SW 1	SW 1	SW 1
Brockenhurst 3	d	06 12	and every 30 minutes until	21 12	21 48	22 18
Lymington Town	d	06 20		21 20	21 56	22 26
Lymington Pier ⛴	a	06 22		21 22	21 58	22 28
	d					
Yarmouth (I.O.W.) ⛴	a					

Sundays
15 December to 10 May

		SW 1		SW 1
Brockenhurst 3	d	08 59	and every 30 minutes until	21 59
Lymington Town	d	09 07		22 07
Lymington Pier ⛴	a	09 09		22 09
	d			
Yarmouth (I.O.W.) ⛴	a			

For connections from Brockenhurst refer to Table T158

Table T159-R

Mondays to Fridays
16 December to 15 May

Yarmouth (Isle of Wight) - Lymington - Brockenhurst

		SW 1		SW 1	SW 1		SW 1	SW 1		SW 1	SW 1
Yarmouth (I.O.W.) ⛴	d		and every 30 minutes until			and every 30 minutes until			and every 30 minutes until		
Lymington Pier ⛴	a										
	d	06 14		09 44	10 27		18 27	19 03		22 03	22 36
Lymington Town	d	06 16		09 46	10 29		18 29	19 05		22 05	22 38
Brockenhurst 3	a	06 25		09 55	10 38		18 38	19 14		22 14	22 47

Saturdays
21 December to 16 May

		SW 1		SW 1	SW 1	SW 1
Yarmouth (I.O.W.) ⛴	d		and every 30 minutes until			
Lymington Pier ⛴	a					
	d	06 27		21 27	22 03	22 36
Lymington Town	d	06 29		21 29	22 05	22 38
Brockenhurst 3	a	06 37		21 37	22 13	22 46

Sundays
15 December to 10 May

		SW 1		SW 1
Yarmouth (I.O.W.) ⛴	d		and every 30 minutes until	
Lymington Pier ⛴	a			
	d	09 14		22 14
Lymington Town	d	09 16		22 16
Brockenhurst 3	a	09 24		22 24

For connections from Brockenhurst refer to Table T158

Table T160-F

Mondays to Fridays
16 December to 15 May

London - Salisbury - Yeovil and Exeter

Miles			SW MX	SW MX	SW MX	SW MO	SW MO	SW	SW	SW	GW	SW	SW	SW	SW	SW	SW	SW	SW		SW	SW	SW
			◇1	◇1	◇1	1	◇1	◇1	◇1	◇1		◇1	◇1	◇1	◇1	◇1	◇1	◇1	◇1		◇1	◇1	◇1
			A	A	A	A	A				B				C ⚒	D ⚒	C ⚒	⚒	C ⚒		⚒	C ⚒	⚒
0	**London Waterloo** 15 ⊖	d												06 35	07 10	07 50	08 20	08 50	09 20		09 50	10 20	10 50
4	Clapham Junction 10	d												06u42	07u17	07u57	08u28		09u27		09u57	10u27	10u57
24½	Woking	d			00 07	00 08								07 02	07 39	08 17	08 46	09 16	09 46		10 16	10 46	11 16
47¾	**Basingstoke**	d			00 29	00 41								07 24	08 00	08 38	09 07	09 38	10 07		10 38	11 07	11 38
55½	Overton	d			00s37	00s49								07 32	08 08	08 46		09 46			10 46		11 46
59¼	Whitchurch (Hants)	d			00s42	00s54								07 37	08 13	08 51		09 51			10 51		11 51
66½	Andover	d	00 01		00 51	01 03								07 46	08 22	09 00	09 24	10 00	10 24		11 00	11 24	12 00
72¾	Grateley	d	00 08		00s58	01s10								07 53	08 29	09 07		10 07			11 07		12 07
83¾	**Salisbury** 123	a	00 21		01 11	01 22								08 05	08 43	09 20	09 43	10 20	10 42		11 19	11 43	12 20
—																							
—		d								06 07	06 10	06 40	07 38	08 08	08 47	09 24	09 47		10 47	10 52	11 23	11 47	
—	Warminster 123	d									06 29	07 02				09 44				11 12			
—	Westbury 123	d									06 41	07 11				09 56				11 21			
—	Trowbridge 123	d									06 47	07 17								11 27			
—	Bradford-on-Avon 123	d									06 53	07 23								11 33			
—	Bath Spa 7 123	a									07 13	07 36								11 45			
—	Bristol Temple Meads 10 123	a									07 34	07 55								12 05			
—	Frome	d														10 05							
—	Bruton	d														10 17							
—	Castle Cary	d														10 22							
—	Yeovil Pen Mill	a														10 36							
—		d																					
96¼	Tisbury	d								06 29			07 57	08 27	09 06		10 06		11 06		11 38	12 06	
105¼	Gillingham (Dorset)	a								06 39			08 07	08 37	09 16		10 16		11 16		11 48	12 16	
—		d							05 51	06 42			08 11		09 17		10 17		11 17		11 52	12 17	
112¼	Templecombe	d							05 58	06 50			08 19		09 25		10 25		11 25		11 59	12 25	
118¼	Sherborne	d							06 06	06 57			08 26		09 32		10 32		11 32		12 07	12 32	
122¾	Yeovil Junction	a							06 11	07 03			08 32		09 38		10 38		11 38		12 12	12 38	
—		d							06 15	07 07			08 39		09 42		10 39		11 39		12 19	12 39	
—	Yeovil Pen Mill	a																			12 24		
—		d																					
131¾	Crewkerne	d							06 24	07 16			08 49		09 51		10 49		11 49			12 49	
144¾	Axminster	a							06 43	07 36			09 02		10 04		11 02		12 02			13 02	
—		d		00 05			00 09	05 52	06 57	07 37			09 03		10 05		11 03		12 03			13 03	
155	Honiton	a		00s17			00s20	06 03	07 08	07 48			09 15		10 16		11 15		12 15			13 15	
—		d						06 04	07 12	07 52			09 16		10 17		11 16		12 16			13 16	
159½	Feniton	d					00s26	06 10	07 18	07 58			09 21		10 23				12 21				
163¼	Whimple	d					00s31	06 15	07 23	08 03			09 26				11 24					13 24	
—	Cranbrook	d		00s29			00s36	06 20	07 28	08 08			09 31		10 30		11 28		12 29			13 28	
169	Pinhoe	d		00s33			00s40	06 24	07 32	08 13			09 35				11 32		12 33			13 32	
171¾	**Exeter Central**	a						06 28	07 37	08 17			09 39		10 39		11 37		12 37			13 37	
172¾	**Exeter St Davids** 6	a		00 42			00 47	06 33	07 42	08 22			09 44		10 43		11 43		12 43			13 43	

A From London Waterloo
B To Gloucester
C ⚒ to Axminster
D ⚒ to Salisbury

For alternative services from London Waterloo to Woking and Basingstoke, refer to Table T155

For services between Salisbury and Bristol Temple Meads, refer to Table T123

Table T160-F

Mondays to Fridays

16 December to 15 May

London - Salisbury - Yeovil and Exeter

		SW ◇1 A ✠	SW ◇1 B ✠	SW ◇1 A ✠		SW ◇1 ✠	SW ◇1 A ✠	SW ◇1 B ✠	SW ◇1 ✠	SW ◇1 A ✠	SW ◇1 ✠	SW ◇1 A ✠	SW ◇1 B ✠	SW ◇1 A ✠		SW ◇1 C ✠	SW ◇1 A ✠	SW ◇1 B ✠	SW ◇1 B ✠	SW ◇1	SW ◇1 ✠
London Waterloo 15 ⊖	d	11 20	11 50	12 20		12 50	13 20	13 50		14 20	14 50	15 20	15 50	16 20		16 50	17 20	17 50	18 20		18 50
Clapham Junction 10	d	11u27	11u57	12u27		12u57	13u27	13u57		14u27	14u57	15u27	15u57	16u27		16u57			18u27		
Woking	d	11 46	12 16	12 46		13 16	13 46	14 16		14 46	15 16	15 46	16 16	16u46		17u16	17u46		18u46		19u19
Basingstoke	d	12 07	12 38	13 07		13 38	14 07	14 38		15 07	15 38	16 07	16 38	17 07		17 38	18 07	18 38	19 07		19 39
Overton	d		12 46			13 46		14 46			15 46		16 46	17 16		17 46	18 16	18 47	19 16		19 47
Whitchurch (Hants)	d		12 51			13 51		14 51			15 51		16 51	17 21		17 51	18 21	18 52	19 21		19 52
Andover	d	12 24	13 00	13 24		14 00	14 24	15 00		15 24	16 00	16 24	17 00	17 30		18 00	18 30	19 00	19 30		20 01
Grateley	d		13 07			14 07		15 07			16 07		17 07	17 38		18 07	18 38	19 08	19 38		20 08
Salisbury 123	a	12 43	13 20	13 43		14 20	14 43	15 20		15 43	16 20	16 44	17 20	17 50		18 20	18 50	19 20	19 50		20 20
	d	12 47	13 24	13 47	13 52	14 24	14 47	15 23		15 47		16 47	17 23	17 54	18 01	18 23	18 54	19 26	19 54	19 58	20 24
Warminster 123	d				14 12	14 44									18 21					20 18	
Westbury 123	d				14 21	14 55									18 30					20 34	
Trowbridge 123	d				14 27										18 36						
Bradford-on-Avon 123	d				14 33										18 42						
Bath Spa 7 123	a				14 45										18 56						
Bristol Temple Meads 10 123	a				15 05										19 15						
Frome	d					15 04														20 43	
Bruton	d					15 16														20 55	
Castle Cary	d					15 22														20a59	
Yeovil Pen Mill	a					15 33															
	d																				
Tisbury	d	13 06	13 38	14 06			15 06	15 37		16 06		17 06	17 37	18 08		18 37	19 08	19 40	20 09		20 38
Gillingham (Dorset)	a	13 16	13 48	14 16			15 16	15 47		16 16		17 16	17 47	18 17		18 47	19 18	19 51	20 19		20 48
	d	13 17	13 52	14 17			15 17	15 52		16 17		17 17	17 52	18 18		18 52	19 19	19 56	20 20		20 51
Templecombe	d	13 25	13 59	14 25			15 25	15 59		16 25		17 25	18 00	18 26		18 59	19 26	20 03	20 27		20 59
Sherborne	d	13 32	14 07	14 32			15 32	16 07		16 32		17 32	18 07	18 33		19 07	19 34	20 11	20 35		21 06
Yeovil Junction	a	13 38	14 12	14 38			15 38	16 12		16 38		17 38	18 13	18 39		19 12	19 40	20 16	20 40		21 12
	d	13 39	14 18	14 39			15 39	16 20		16 39		17 39		18 40		19 17	19 41	20 21	20 42		21 17
Yeovil Pen Mill	a		14 25					16 28								19 25		20 28			21 24
	d																				
Crewkerne	d	13 49		14 49			15 49			16 49		17 49		18 50			19 50		20 51		
Axminster	a	14 02		15 02			16 02			17 02		18 02		19 03			20 03		21 04		
	d	14 03		15 03			16 03			17 03		18 03		19 04			20 04		21 05		
Honiton	a	14 15		15 14			16 15			17 15		18 14		19 17			20 16		21 16		
	d	14 16		15 15			16 16		17 07	17 16		18 16		19 18			20 17		21 17		
Feniton	d	14 21		15 21						17 21				19 23					21 23		
Whimple	d			15 26			16 24					18 25					20 25				
Cranbrook	d	14 29		15 30			16 29			17 29		18 30		19 31			20 29		21 30		
Pinhoe	d	14 33		15 34			16 33			17 33		18 34		19 35			20 33		21 34		
Exeter Central	a	14 37		15 39			16 37		17 28	17 37		18 38		19 39			20 38		21 39		
Exeter St Davids 6	a	14 43		15 43			16 43		17 32	17 42		18 44		19 44			20 44		21 43		

		SW ◇1 B ✠		SW ◇1 ✠	SW ◇1 B ✠	SW ◇1 ✠	SW ◇1 B ✠	SW ◇1 ✠	SW 1 ✠	SW ◇1	SW FX ◇1	SW FO ◇1
London Waterloo 15 ⊖	d	19 20		19 50	20 20	20 50	21 20	21 50	22 20	22 50	23 40	23 40
Clapham Junction 10	d	19u27			20u27	20u57	21u27	21u57	22u27	22u57	23u47	23u47
Woking	d	19u46		20u16	20 46	21 16	21 46	22 16	22 46	23 16	00 07	00 07
Basingstoke	d	20 07		20 38	21 07	21 37	22 07	22 37	23 06	23 38	00 29	00 29
Overton	d	20 16		20 46	21 15	21 46		22 46		23 47	00s37	00s37
Whitchurch (Hants)	d	20 21		20 51	21 20	21 51		22 51		23 53	00s42	00s42
Andover	d	20 30		21 00	21 29	22 00	22 24	23 00	23 23	00 01	00 51	00 51
Grateley	d	20 38		21 07	21 36	22 07		23 07		00 08	00s58	00s58
Salisbury 123	a	20 50		21 20	21 48	22 20	22 41	23 21	23 40	00 21	01 11	01 11
	d	20 54	20 57		21 53		22 48		23 43			01 14
Warminster 123	d		21 17									
Westbury 123	d		21 25									
Trowbridge 123	d		21 31									
Bradford-on-Avon 123	d		21 37									
Bath Spa 7 123	a		21 50									
Bristol Temple Meads 10 123	a		22 06									
Frome	d											
Bruton	d											
Castle Cary	d											
Yeovil Pen Mill	a											
	d											
Tisbury	d	21 08			22 08		23 07		00s01			01s27
Gillingham (Dorset)	a	21 18			22 17		23 17		00s12			01s37
	d	21 19			22 18		23 18					
Templecombe	d	21 26			22 26		23 25		00s20			01s45
Sherborne	d	21 34			22 33		23 33		00s27			01s53
Yeovil Junction	a				22 39		23 38		00 33			01 59
	d				22 40		23 39					
Yeovil Pen Mill	a											
	d											
Crewkerne	d	21 52			22 50		23 49					
Axminster	a	22 05			23 03		00 03					
	d	22 06			23 05		00 05					
Honiton	a	22 17			23 16		00s17					
	d	22 18			23 17							
Feniton	d				23 22							
Whimple	d	22 26			23 27							
Cranbrook	d	22 31			23 32		00s29					
Pinhoe	d	22 35			23 36		00s33					
Exeter Central	a	22 39			23 40							
Exeter St Davids 6	a	22 44			23 45		00 42					

A ✠ to Axminster
B ✠ to Salisbury
C To Westbury, ✠ to Salisbury

For alternative services from London Waterloo to Woking and Basingstoke, refer to Table T155

For services between Salisbury and Bristol Temple Meads, refer to Table T123

Table T160-F

Saturdays

21 December to 16 May

London - Salisbury - Yeovil and Exeter

		SW ◇1 A	SW ◇1 A	SW ◇1 A	SW ◇1	GW B	SW ◇1	SW ◇1	SW ◇1	SW ◇1	SW ◇1 C	SW ◇1 D ✠	SW ◇1 ✠	SW ◇1 D ✠	SW ◇1 E ✠	SW ◇1 D ✠		SW ◇1 ✠	SW ◇1 D ✠	SW ◇1 ✠	SW ◇1 D ✠	SW ◇1 ✠
London Waterloo 15 ⊖	d										06 35	07 10	07 50	08 20	08 50	09 20		09 50	10 20	10 50	11 20	11 50
Clapham Junction 10	d										06u42	07u17	07u57	08u27	08u57	09u27		09u57	10u27	10u57	11u27	11u57
Woking	d			00 07							07 01	07 36	08 16	08 46	09 16	09 46		10 16	10 46	11 16	11 46	12 16
Basingstoke	d			00 29							07 23	07 59	08 38	09 06	09 38	10 07		10 38	11 09	11 38	12 07	12 38
Overton	d			00s37							07 31	08 08	08 46		09 46			10 46		11 46		12 46
Whitchurch (Hants)	d			00s42							07 36	08 13	08 51		09 51			10 51		11 51		12 51
Andover	d	00 01		00 51							07 45	08 21	09 00	09 24	10 00	10 24		11 00	11 26	12 00	12 24	13 00
Grateley	d	00 08		00s58							07 52	08 29	09 07		10 07			11 07		12 07		13 07
Salisbury 123	a	00 21		01 11							08 05	08 42	09 20	09 42	10 20	10 42		11 20	11 42	12 20	12 42	13 20
	d			01 14		06 08		06 15	06 40	07 47	08 13	08 47		09 47	10 26	10 47	10 52		11 47		12 47	
Warminster 123	d					06 28			07 00						10 46		11 12					
Westbury 123	d					06 41			07 09						10 57		11 21					
Trowbridge 123	d					06 47			07 15								11 27					
Bradford-on-Avon 123	d					06 53			07 21								11 33					
Bath Spa 7 123	a					07 10			07 33								11 52					
Bristol Temple Meads 10 123	a					07 29			07 52								12 12					
Frome	d														11a06							
Bruton	d																					
Castle Cary	d																					
Yeovil Pen Mill	a																					
	d																					
Tisbury	d			01s27				06 29		08 01	08 32	09 06		10 06		11 06			12 06		13 06	
Gillingham (Dorset)	a			01s37				06 39		08 11	08 42	09 16		10 16		11 16			12 16		13 16	
	d							06 42		08 14	09 00	09 17		10 17		11 17			12 17		13 17	
Templecombe	d			01s45				06 50		08 22	09 07	09 25		10 25		11 25			12 25		13 25	
Sherborne	d			01s53				06 57		08 29	09 15	09 32		10 32		11 32			12 32		13 32	
Yeovil Junction	a			01 59				07 03		08 35	09 20	09 38		10 38		11 38			12 38		13 38	
	d						06 15	07 07		08 39	09 35	09 39		10 39		11 39			12 39		13 39	
Yeovil Pen Mill	a										09 45											
	d																					
Crewkerne	d						06 24	07 16		08 49		09 49		10 49		11 49			12 49		13 49	
Axminster	a						06 43	07 36		09 02		10 02		11 02		12 02			13 02		14 02	
	d		00 05		05 52		06 57	07 38		09 03		10 03		11 03		12 03			13 03		14 03	
Honiton	a		00s17		06 03		07 08	07 49		09 15		10 15		11 15		12 15			13 15		14 15	
	d				06 04		07 12	07 54		09 16		10 16		11 16		12 16			13 16		14 16	
Feniton	d				06 09		07 18	08 00		09 21		10 21				12 21					14 21	
Whimple	d				06 14		07 23	08 05		09 26				11 24					13 24			
Cranbrook	d		00s29		06 19		07 28	08 09		09 31		10 29		11 28		12 29			13 28		14 29	
Pinhoe	d		00s33		06 23		07 32	08 13		09 35		10 33		11 32		12 33			13 32		14 33	
Exeter Central	a				06 27		07 37	08 18		09 39		10 37		11 37		12 37			13 37		14 37	
Exeter St Davids 6	a		00 42		06 31		07 42	08 22		09 44		10 42		11 42		12 42			13 42		14 42	

		SW ◇1 D ✠		SW ◇1 ✠	SW ◇1 D ✠	SW ◇1 ✠	SW ◇1 D ✠	SW ◇1 ✠	SW ◇1 D ✠	SW ◇1 ✠	SW ◇1 D ✠		SW ◇1 ✠	SW ◇1 D ✠	SW ◇1 E ✠	SW ◇1 E ✠	SW ◇1 ✠	SW ◇1 E ✠		SW ◇1 ✠	SW ◇1 E ✠	SW ◇1 ✠	SW ◇1 E ✠	SW ◇1	SW ◇1 ✠	SW ◇1
London Waterloo 15 ⊖	d	12 20		12 50	13 20	13 50	14 20	14 50	15 20	15 50	16 20		16 50	17 20	17 50	18 20	18 50	19 20		19 50	20 20	20 50	21 20	21 50	22 20	23 40
Clapham Junction 10	d	12u27		12u57	13u27	13u57	14u27	14u57	15u27	15u57	16u27		16u57	17u27	17u57	18u27	18u57	19u27		19u57	20u27	20u57	21u27	21u57	22u27	23u47
Woking	d	12 46		13 16	13 46	14 16	14 46	15 16	15 46	16 16	16 46		17 16	17 46	18 16	18 46	19 16	19 46		20 16	20 46	21 16	21 46	22 16	22 46	00 08
Basingstoke	d	13 07		13 38	14 07	14 38	15 07	15 38	16 07	16 38	17 07		17 38	18 07	18 38	19 07	19 38	20 07		20 38	21 07	21 38	22 07	22 38	23 07	00 28
Overton	d			13 46		14 46		15 46		16 46			17 46		18 46		19 46			20 46		21 46		22 46	23 15	00s37
Whitchurch (Hants)	d			13 51		14 51		15 51		16 51			17 51		18 51		19 51			20 51		21 51		22 51	23 20	00s42
Andover	d	13 24		14 00	14 24	15 00	15 24	16 00	16 24	17 00	17 24		18 00	18 24	19 00	19 24	20 00	20 24		21 00	21 24	22 00	22 24	23 00	23 29	00 50
Grateley	d			14 07		15 07		16 07		17 07			18 07		19 07		20 07			21 07		22 07		23 07	23 36	00s58
Salisbury 123	a	13 42		14 20	14 42	15 20	15 42	16 20	16 42	17 20	17 42		18 20	18 43	19 20	19 43	20 20	20 45		21 20	21 44	22 20	22 44	23 20	23 48	01 10
	d	13 47	13 52		14 47		15 47		16 47		17 47	17 56		18 47	19 27	19 47		20 47	20 57		21 48		22 55			
Warminster 123	d		14 12									18 16			19 46				21 17							
Westbury 123	d		14 21									18 25			19 58				21 25							
Trowbridge 123	d		14 27									18 31							21 31							
Bradford-on-Avon 123	d		14 33									18 37							21 37							
Bath Spa 7 123	a		14 51									18 52							21 52							
Bristol Temple Meads 10 123	a		15 10									19 12							22 08							
Frome	d														20 07											
Bruton	d														20 19											
Castle Cary	d														20 24											
Yeovil Pen Mill	a														20 38											
	d														20 39											
Tisbury	d	14 06			15 06		16 06		17 06		18 06			19 08		20 06		21 06			22 06		23s08			
Gillingham (Dorset)	a	14 16			15 16		16 16		17 16		18 16			19 18		20 16		21 16			22 17		23s19			
	d	14 17			15 17		16 17		17 17		18 17			19 19		20 17		21 17			22 17					
Templecombe	d	14 25			15 25		16 25		17 25		18 25			19 26		20 25		21 25			22 25		23s27			
Sherborne	d	14 32			15 32		16 32		17 32		18 32			19 34		20 32		21 32			22 32		23s34			
Yeovil Junction	a	14 38			15 38		16 38		17 38		18 38			19 39	20 45	20 38		21 38			22 38		23 40			
	d	14 39			15 39		16 39		17 39		18 39			19 41		20 39		21 39			22 39					
Yeovil Pen Mill	a																									
	d																									
Crewkerne	d	14 49			15 49		16 49		17 49		18 49			19 50		20 49		21 49			22 49					
Axminster	a	15 02			16 02		17 02		18 02		19 02			20 03		21 02		22 02			23 02					
	d	15 03			16 03		17 03		18 03		19 03			20 05		21 03		22 03			23 03					
Honiton	a	15 15			16 15		17 15		18 16		19 15			20 16		21 16		22 16			23 15					
	d	15 16			16 16		17 16		18 16		19 16			20 16		21 17		22 17								
Feniton	d				16 21				18 21					20 23				22 22								
Whimple	d	15 24					17 24				19 24					21 25		22 27								
Cranbrook	d	15 28			16 29		17 28		18 29		19 28			20 30		21 29		22 32								
Pinhoe	d	15 32			16 33		17 32				19 32					21 33		22 36								
Exeter Central	a	15 37			16 37		17 37		18 37		19 37			20 41		21 38		22 40								
Exeter St Davids 6	a	15 42			16 42		17 42		18 42		19 42			20 45		21 42		22 45								

A From London Waterloo
B To Gloucester
C To Weymouth
D ✠ to Axminster
E ✠ to Salisbury

For alternative services from London Waterloo to Woking and Basingstoke, refer to Table T155

For services between Salisbury and Bristol Temple Meads, refer to Table T123

Table T160-F

Sundays
15 December to 10 May

London - Salisbury - Yeovil and Exeter

	SW ◇1 A	SW ◇1	SW ◇1	SW ◇1 B ✠	SW ◇1 C	SW ◇1 D ✠		SW ◇1 C	SW ◇1 D ✠	SW ◇1 C	SW ◇1 D ✠	SW ◇1 C	SW ◇1 D ✠		SW ◇1 C	SW ◇1 D ✠	SW ◇1 C	SW ◇1 D ✠	SW ◇1 C	SW ◇1 D ✠	SW ◇1 C	SW ◇1 D ✠
London Waterloo 15 ⊖ d				08 15		09 15			10 15		11 15		12 15			13 15		14 15		15 20		16 20
Clapham Junction 10 d				08u23		09u22			10u22		11u22		12u22			13u22		14u22		15u27		16u27
Woking d	00∫08			08 47		09 47			10 46		11 46		12 46			13 46		14 46		15 46		16 46
Basingstoke d	00∫28		08 03	09 08	09 33	10 08		10 33	11 07	11 31	12 07	12 31	13 07		13 31	14 07	14 31	15 07	15 31	16 07	16 31	17 07
Overton d	00s37		08 11		09 41			10 41		11 39		12 39			13 40		14 39		15 39		16 39	
Whitchurch (Hants) d	00s42		08 16		09 46			10 46		11 45		12 44			13 45		14 44		15 44		16 44	
Andover d	00∫50		08 25	09 25	09 55	10 25		10 55	11 24	11 53	12 24	12 53	13 24		13 53	14 24	14 53	15 24	15 53	16 24	16 53	17 24
Grateley d	00s58		08 32		10 02			11 02		12 00		13 00			14 01		15 00		16 00		17 00	
Salisbury 123 a	01∫10		08 45	09 42	10 18	10 42		11 18	11 42	12 14	12 42	13 14	13 42		14 14	14 42	15 14	15 42	16 14	16 42	17 14	17 42
d		06 54	08 47	09 47		10 47	10 55		11 47		12 47		13 47	13 55	14 19	14 47		15 47	16 14	16 47	17 16	17 47
Warminster 123 d							11 15							14 15							17 36	
Westbury 123 d							11 24							14 24							17 48	
Trowbridge 123 d							11 30							14 30								
Bradford-on-Avon 123 d							11 36							14 36								
Bath Spa 7 123 a							11 52							14 54								
Bristol Temple Meads 10 123 a							12 11							15 13								
Frome d																					17a57	
Bruton d																						
Castle Cary d																						
Yeovil Pen Mill a																						
Tisbury d		07 06	09 06	10 07		11 06			12 06		13 06		14 06		14 33	15 06		16 06	16 33	17 06		18 06
Gillingham (Dorset) a		07 16	09 16	10 17		11 16			12 16		13 16		14 16		14 43	15 16		16 16	16 43	17 16		18 16
d		07 17	09 17	10 18		11 17			12 17		13 17		14 17		14 51	15 17		16 17		17 17		18 17
Templecombe d		07 25	09 25	10 25		11 25			12 25		13 25		14 25		14 58	15 25		16 25		17 25		18 25
Sherborne d		07 32	09 32	10 33		11 32			12 32		13 32		14 32		15 06	15 32		16 32		17 32		18 32
Yeovil Junction a		07 38	09 38	10 38		11 38			12 38		13 38		14 38		15 11	15 38		16 38		17 38		18 38
d		07 39	09 39	10 39		11 39			12 39		13 39		14 39		15 16	15 39		16 39		17 39		18 39
Yeovil Pen Mill a															15 21							
d																						
Crewkerne d		07 49	09 49	10 49		11 49			12 49		13 49		14 49			15 49		16 49		17 49		18 49
Axminster a		08 02	10 02	11 02		12 02			13 02		14 02		15 02			16 02		17 02		18 02		19 02
d		08 03	10 03	11 03		12 03			13 03		14 03		15 03			16 03		17 03		18 03		19 03
Honiton a		08 15	10 15	11 15		12 15			13 15		14 15		15 15			16 15		17 15		18 15		19 15
d		08 16	10 16	11 16		12 16			13 16		14 16		15 16			16 16		17 16		18 16		19 16
Feniton d		08 21	10 21			12 21					14 21					16 21				18 21		
Whimple d		08 26	10 26	11 24					13 24				15 24					17 24				19 24
Cranbrook d		08 31	10 31	11 28		12 29			13 28		14 29		15 28			16 29		17 28		18 29		19 28
Pinhoe d		08 35	10 35	11 32		12 33			13 32		14 33		15 32			16 33		17 32		18 33		19 32
Exeter Central a		08 39	10 39	11 37		12 37			13 37		14 37		15 37			16 37		17 37		18 37		19 37
Exeter St Davids 6 a		08 43	10 46	11 42		12 42			13 42		14 45		15 42			16 42		17 41		18 42		19 42

	SW ◇1 C	SW ◇1 D ✠	SW ◇1	SW ◇1 D ✠		SW ◇1	SW ◇1 E ✠	SW ◇1	SW ◇1 E ✠	SW ◇1	SW ◇1 E ✠	SW 1 ✠	SW 1
London Waterloo 15 ⊖ d		17 20	17 45	18 20		18 45	19 20	19 45	20 20	20 45	21 20	22 20	23 35
Clapham Junction 10 d		17u27	17u53	18u27		18u53	19u27	19u53	20u27	20u53	21u27	22u27	23u44
Woking d		17 46	18 13	18 46		19 13	19 46	20 13	20 46	21 13	21 46	22 46	00 08
Basingstoke d	17 31	18 07	18 34	19 07		19 34	20 07	20 34	21 07	21 34	22 07	23 07	00 41
Overton d	17 39		18 43			19 43		20 43		21 43		23 15	00s49
Whitchurch (Hants) d	17 44		18 48			19 48		20 48		21 48		23 20	00s54
Andover d	17 53	18 24	18 56	19 24		19 56	20 24	20 56	21 24	21 56	22 24	23 29	01 03
Grateley d	18 00		19 04			20 04		21 04		22 04		23 36	01s10
Salisbury 123 a	18 14	18 42	19 17	19 42		20 17	20 42	21 17	21 42	22 17	22 42	23 48	01 22
d		18 47	19 21	19 47	19 55		20 47		21 47		22 47	23 53	
Warminster 123 d			19 41		20 15								
Westbury 123 d			19 55		20 23								
Trowbridge 123 d					20 29								
Bradford-on-Avon 123 d					20 35								
Bath Spa 7 123 a					20 52								
Bristol Temple Meads 10 123 a					21 08								
Frome d			20 05										
Bruton d			20 16										
Castle Cary d			20 21										
Yeovil Pen Mill a			20 36										
Tisbury d		19 06		20 06			21 06		22 06		23 06	00s06	
Gillingham (Dorset) a		19 16		20 16			21 16		22 16		23 16	00s17	
d		19 17		20 17			21 17		22 17		23 17		
Templecombe d		19 25		20 25			21 25		22 25		23 25	00s25	
Sherborne d		19 32		20 32			21 32		22 32		23 32	00s32	
Yeovil Junction a		19 38		20 38			21 38		22 38		23 38	00 38	
d		19 40		20 39			21 39				23 39		
Yeovil Pen Mill a													
d													
Crewkerne d		19 50		20 49			21 49				23 49		
Axminster a		20 03		21 02			22 02				00 08		
d		20 04		21 03			22 03				00 09		
Honiton a		20 16		21 15			22 15				00s20		
d		20 17		21 16			22 16						
Feniton d		20 22					22 21				00s26		
Whimple d				21 24			22 27				00s31		
Cranbrook d		20 30		21 28			22 31				00s36		
Pinhoe d		20 34		21 32			22 35				00s40		
Exeter Central a		20 38		21 37			22 40						
Exeter St Davids 6 a		20 43		21 43			22 44				00 47		

A not 15 December. From London Waterloo
B ✠ from Woking to Axminster
C From Reading
D ✠ to Axminster
E ✠ to Salisbury

For alternative services from London Waterloo to Woking and Basingstoke, refer to Table T155

For services between Salisbury and Bristol Temple Meads, refer to Table T123

Table T160-R

Mondays to Fridays
16 December to 15 May

Yeovil and Exeter - Salisbury - London

Miles		SW ◇1 ✠	SW ◇1 ✠	GW	SW ◇1 A ✠	SW ◇1 A ✠	SW ◇1 A ✠	SW ◇1 B ✠	SW ◇1 A ✠	SW ◇1 A ✠	SW ◇1 B ✠	SW ◇1 B ✠	SW ◇1 A ✠	SW ◇1 A ✠	SW ◇1 B ✠	SW ◇1 A ✠	SW ◇1 B ✠	SW ◇1 ✠	SW ◇1 A ✠	SW ◇1 B ✠	SW ◇1 A ✠	SW ◇1 B ✠
0	**Exeter St Davids** 6 d						05 10	05 30			06 41	07 25			08 23		09 25			10 25		11 25
0¾	**Exeter Central** d						05 14	05 34			06 45	07 30			08 27		09 30			10 30		11 30
3½	Pinhoe d						05 19	05 39			06 50	07 34			08 32		09 34			10 34		11 34
—	Cranbrook d						05 23	05 43			06 54	07 39			08 36		09 39			10 39		11 39
9¼	Whimple d						05 28	05 48			06 59				08 41		09 44					11 44
13	Feniton d						05 34	05 54			07 05				08 47					10 47		
17½	Honiton a						05 40	06 00			07 11	07 51			08 53		09 54			10 53		11 54
—	d						05 41	06 20			07 12	07 52			08 55		09 55			10 55		11 55
27¾	Axminster a						05 51	06 30			07 22	08 02			09 05		10 05			11 05		12 05
—	d						05 52	06 31			07 23	08 03			09 06		10 06			11 06		12 06
40¾	Crewkerne d						06 05	06 44			07 36	08 16			09 19		10 19			11 19		12 19
—	Yeovil Pen Mill a																					
—	d					05 41			07 11													
49¾	Yeovil Junction a					05 46	06 14	06 52	07 16		07 45	08 25			09 27		10 27			11 27		12 27
—	d				05 14	05 50	06 20	06 53	07 20		07 50	08 29			09 29	09 53	10 29			11 29	11 53	12 29
54¼	Sherborne d				05 20	05 56	06 26	07 00	07 26		07 56	08 35			09 35	09 59	10 35			11 35	11 59	12 35
60¼	Templecombe d				05 28	06 04	06 34	07 07	07 34		08 04	08 43			09 43	10 07	10 43			11 43	12 07	12 43
67¾	Gillingham (Dorset) a				05 35	06 11	06 41	07 14	07 41		08 11	08 50			09 50	10 14	10 50			11 50	12 14	12 50
—	d				05 36	06 12	06 42	07 15	07 42		08 12	08 51	09 18		09 51	10 18	10 51			11 51	12 18	12 51
76¼	Tisbury d				05 46	06 24	06 52	07 26	07 52		08 22	09 01	09 28		10 01	10 28	11 01			12 01	12 28	13 01
—	Yeovil Pen Mill a																					
—	d									06 55									10 45			
—	Castle Cary d									07 10									11 04			
—	Bruton d									07 15									11 09			
—	Frome d									07 27									11 21			
—	Bristol Temple Meads 10 123 d													08 49								
—	Bath Spa 7 123 d													09 07								
—	Bradford-on-Avon 123 d													09 24								
—	Trowbridge 123 d													09 29								
—	Westbury 123 d			05 24						07 40				09 40					11 36			
—	Warminster 123 d			05 32						07 48				09 48					11 48			
88¾	**Salisbury** 123 a			05 51	06 01	06 39	07 07	07 40	08 06	08 10	08 37	09 16	09 43	10 09	10 16	10 43	11 16		12 09	12 17	12 43	13 17
—	d	05 10	05 43		06 06	06 45	07 15	07 45		08 15	08 47	09 21	09 47		10 21	10 47	11 21	11 47		12 21	12 47	13 21
99¾	Grateley d	05 22	05 55		06 19	06 57	07 27	07 57		08 27	08 59		09 59			10 59		11 59			12 59	
106	Andover d	05 30	06 03		06 26	07 05	07 35	08 05		08 35	09 06	09 38	10 06		10 38	11 06	11 38	12 06		12 38	13 06	13 38
113¾	Whitchurch (Hants) d	05 38	06 11		06 35	07 13	07 43	08 13		08 43	09 14		10 14			11 14		12 14			13 14	
117	Overton d	05 44	06 17		06 41	07 19	07 49	08 19		08 49	09 20		10 20			11 20		12 20			13 20	
124¾	**Basingstoke** a	05 53	06 26		06 49	07 28	07 58	08 28		08 58	09 28	09 55	10 28		10 55	11 28	11 55	12 28		12 55	13 28	13 56
148¼	Woking a	06 12	06 45				08 18	08 48		09 18	09 48	10 15	10 48		11 15	11 48	12 15	12 48		13 15	13 48	14 15
168¼	Clapham Junction 10 a	06 33	07 06							09 38	10 09	10 36			11 36		12 36			13 36		14 36
172½	**London Waterloo** 15 ⊖ a	06 41	07 18		07 36	08 14	08 46	09 21		09 51	10 19	10 49	11 19		11 49	12 19	12 49	13 19		13 49	14 19	14 49

	SW ◇1 ✠	SW ◇1 ✠	SW ◇1 B ✠	SW ◇1 A ✠	SW ◇1 B ✠	SW ◇1 ✠	SW ◇1 A ✠	SW ◇1 B ✠	SW ◇1 A ✠	SW ◇1 A ✠	SW ◇1 B ✠	SW ◇1 ✠	SW ◇1 A ✠	SW ◇1 B ✠	SW ◇1 ✠	SW ◇1 B ✠	SW ◇1	SW ◇1	SW ◇1 B ✠	SW ◇1	SW ◇1	SW ◇1 C
Exeter St Davids 6 d			12 25		13 25			14 25			15 25			16 25		17 25		17 46	18 25		19 25	
Exeter Central d			12 30		13 30			14 30			15 30			16 30		17 30		17 50	18 30		19 30	
Pinhoe d			12 34		13 34			14 34			15 34			16 34		17 34		17 55	18 35		19 34	
Cranbrook d			12 39		13 39			14 39			15 39			16 39		17 39		18 00	18 39		19 39	
Whimple d					13 44						15 44							18 05	18 44		19 44	
Feniton d			12 47					14 47						16 47		17 47		18 10	18 49			
Honiton a			12 53		13 54			14 53			15 54			16 53		17 54		18 17	18 55		19 54	
d			12 55		13 55			14 55			15 55			16 55		17 55		18 19	18 56		19 55	
Axminster a			13 05		14 05			15 05			16 05			17 05		18 05		18 29	19 06		20 05	
d			13 06		14 06			15 06			16 06			17 06		18 06			19 07		20 06	
Crewkerne d			13 19		14 19			15 19			16 19			17 19		18 19			19 20		20 19	
Yeovil Pen Mill a																						
d				13 44					15 44													
Yeovil Junction a			13 27	13 49	14 27			15 27	15 49		16 28			17 27		18 27			19 29		20 27	
d			13 29	13 53	14 29		14 50	15 29	15 53		16 29		16 46	17 29		18 29			19 30		20 29	
Sherborne d			13 35	13 59	14 35			15 35	15 59		16 35			17 35		18 35			19 36		20 35	
Templecombe d			13 43	14 07	14 43			15 43	16 07		16 43			17 43		18 43			19 44		20 43	
Gillingham (Dorset) a			13 50	14 14	14 50			15 50	16 14		16 50			17 50		18 50			19 51		20 50	
d			13 51	14 18	14 51			15 51	16 18		16 51			17 51		18 51			19 52		20 51	
Tisbury d			14 01	14 28	15 01			16 01	16 28		17 01			18 01		19 01			20 02		21 01	
Yeovil Pen Mill a							14 55						16 51									
d							15 02						16 53									
Castle Cary d							15 14						17 07									
Bruton d							15 19						17 12									
Frome d							15 31						17 24									
Bristol Temple Meads 10 123 d		12 49								15 50										19 35		
Bath Spa 7 123 d		13 07								16 08										19 51		
Bradford-on-Avon 123 d		13 23								16 25										20 02		
Trowbridge 123 d		13 30								16 31										20 08		
Westbury 123 d		13 40					15 42			16 40			17 45							20 16		
Warminster 123 d		13 48					15 50			16 48			17 54							20 24		
Salisbury 123 a		14 10	14 17	14 43	15 16		16 12	16 16	16 43	17 08	17 16		18 17	18 21		19 22			20 21	20 44	21 21	
d	13 47		14 21	14 47	15 21	15 47		16 21	16 47		17 20	17 47		18 26	18 47	19 24	19 47		20 23	20 47	21 25	21 49
Grateley d	13 59			14 59		15 59			16 59			17 59			18 59		19 59			20 59		22 01
Andover d	14 06		14 38	15 06	15 38	16 06		16 38	17 06		17 37	18 06		18 43	19 06	19 47	20 06		20 41	21 06	21 42	22 08
Whitchurch (Hants) d	14 14			15 14		16 14			17 14			18 14			19 14		20 14			21 14		22 16
Overton d	14 20			15 20		16 20			17 20			18 20			19 20		20 20			21 20		22 22
Basingstoke a	14 28		14 55	15 28	15 55	16 28		16 55	17 28		17 54	18 28		19 00	19 28	20 08	20 28		20 58	21 28	21 59	22 31
Woking a	14 48		15 15	15 48	16 15	16 48		17 15	17 48		18 14	18 48		19 20	19 48	20 30	20 48		21 17	21 48	22 19	
Clapham Junction 10 a			15 36		16 36			17 37			18 36			19 40		20 53	21 10		21 38	22 09	22 39	
London Waterloo 15 ⊖ a	15 19		15 49	16 19	16 49	17 19		17 56	18 22		18 49	19 19		19 52	20 19	21 02	21 19		21 49	22 19	22 49	

A ✠ from Salisbury
B ✠ from Axminster
C To Reading

Table T160-R

Yeovil and Exeter - Salisbury - London

Mondays to Fridays
16 December to 15 May

		SW	SW	SW	SW	SW	SW
		◇1	◇1	1	◇1	1	1
Exeter St Davids [6]	d	20 25		21 25		22 25	23 27
Exeter Central	d	20 30		21 30		22 30	23 31
Pinhoe	d	20 34		21 34		22 35	23s36
Cranbrook	d	20 39		21 39		22 39	23s40
Whimple	d			21 44		22 44	23s45
Feniton	d	20 47		21 49		22 50	23s51
Honiton	a	20 54		21 56		22 56	23s57
	d	20 55		21 57		22 57	
Axminster	a	21 05		22 07		23 07	00s08
	d	21 06		22 08		23 08	
Crewkerne	d	21 19		22 21		23 21	00s21
Yeovil Pen Mill	a						
	d						
Yeovil Junction	a	21 27		22 29		23 29	00 30
	d	21 29		22 30		23 31	
Sherborne	d	21 35		22 36			
Templecombe	d	21 43		22 44			
Gillingham (Dorset)	a	21 50		22 51			
	d	21 51		22 52			
Tisbury	d	22 01		23 03			
Yeovil Pen Mill	a						
	d						
Castle Cary	d		21 41				
Bruton	d		21 46				
Frome	d		21 58				
Bristol Temple Meads [10] 123	d				22 25		
Bath Spa [7] 123	d				22 41		
Bradford-on-Avon 123	d				22 52		
Trowbridge 123	d				22 58		
Westbury 123	d		22 18		23 07		
Warminster 123	d		22 26		23 14		
Salisbury 123	a	22 21	22 46	23 17	23 37	00 14	
	d	22 25					
Grateley	d	22 37					
Andover	d	22 44					
Whitchurch (Hants)	d	22 52					
Overton	d	22 58					
Basingstoke	a	23 06					
Woking	a	23 26					
Clapham Junction [10]	a	23 47					
London Waterloo [15] ⊖	a	23 55					

Saturdays
21 December to 16 May

		SW	SW	GW	SW	SW	SW	SW	SW	SW	SW	SW	SW	SW	SW	SW	SW	SW	SW	SW	SW	SW	SW
		◇1	◇1		◇1	◇1	◇1	◇1	◇1	◇1	◇1	◇1	◇1	◇1	◇1	◇1	◇1	◇1	◇1	◇1	◇1	◇1	◇1
							A	B			B	B		A	B		B			B		B	
		⊥	⊥		⊥	⊥	⊥	⊥	⊥		⊥	⊥	⊥	⊥	⊥	⊥	⊥	⊥		⊥	⊥	⊥	⊥
Exeter St Davids [6]	d						05 10	05 30			06 37	07 25			08 24		09 25			10 25		11 25	
Exeter Central	d						05 14	05 34			06 41	07 30			08 28		09 30			10 30		11 30	
Pinhoe	d						05 19	05 39			06 47	07 34			08 33		09 34			10 34		11 34	
Cranbrook	d						05 23	05 43			06 51	07 39			08 37		09 40			10 39		11 39	
Whimple	d						05 28	05 48			06 57	07 44			08 42		09 45					11 44	
Feniton	d						05 34	05 54			07 05				08 47					10 47			
Honiton	a						05 40	06 00			07 11	07 53			08 54		09 54			10 53		11 54	
	d						05 41	06 20			07 13	07 55			08 55		09 55			10 55		11 55	
Axminster	a						05 51	06 30			07 23	08 05			09 05		10 05			11 05		12 05	
	d						05 52	06 31			07 24	08 06			09 06		10 06			11 06		12 06	
Crewkerne	d						06 05	06 44			07 37	08 19			09 19		10 19			11 19		12 19	
Yeovil Pen Mill	a																						
	d																						
Yeovil Junction	a						06 14	06 52			07 45	08 27			09 27		10 27			11 27		12 27	
	d						06 20	06 53			07 53	08 29			09 29	09 53	10 29			11 29		12 29	
Sherborne	d						06 26	07 00			07 59	08 35			09 35	09 59	10 35			11 35		12 35	
Templecombe	d						06 34	07 07			08 07	08 43			09 43	10 07	10 43			11 43		12 43	
Gillingham (Dorset)	a						06 41	07 14			08 14	08 50			09 50	10 14	10 50			11 50		12 50	
	d						06 42	07 17			08 17	08 51			09 51	10 17	10 51			11 51		12 51	
Tisbury	d						06 52	07 27			08 27	09 01			10 01	10 27	11 01			12 01		13 01	
Yeovil Pen Mill	a																						
	d																						
Castle Cary	d									07 36													
Bruton	d									07 41													
Frome	d									07 54									11 30				
Bristol Temple Meads [10] 123	d													08 50									
Bath Spa [7] 123	d													09 08									
Bradford-on-Avon 123	d													09 22									
Trowbridge 123	d													09 28									
Westbury 123	d			05 24						08 10				09 40					11 43				
Warminster 123	d			05 32						08 18				09 48					11 50				
Salisbury 123	a			05 53			07 07	07 42		08 37	08 42	09 16		10 09	10 16	10 42	11 16		12 11	12 16		13 16	
	d	05 15	05 47		06 21	06 47	07 21	07 47	08 21		08 47	09 21	09 47	10 21		10 47	11 21	11 47		12 21	12 47	13 21	13 47
Grateley	d	05 27	05 59			06 59		07 59			08 59		09 59			10 59		11 59			12 59		13 59
Andover	d	05 35	06 06		06 38	07 06	07 38	08 06	08 38		09 06	09 38	10 06	10 38		11 06	11 38	12 06		12 38	13 06	13 38	14 06
Whitchurch (Hants)	d	05 43	06 14			07 14		08 14			09 14		10 14			11 14		12 14			13 14		14 14
Overton	d	05 49	06 20			07 20		08 20			09 20		10 20			11 20		12 20			13 20		14 20
Basingstoke	a	05 58	06 28		06 55	07 28	07 55	08 28	08 55		09 28	09 55	10 28	10 55		11 28	11 55	12 28		12 55	13 28	13 55	14 28
Woking	a	06 18	06 48		07 16	07 48	08 15	08 48	09 15		09 48	10 15	10 48	11 15		11 48	12 15	12 48		13 15	13 48	14 15	14 48
Clapham Junction [10]	a	06 38			07 38		08 37		09 36			10 36		11 36			12 36			13 36		14 36	
London Waterloo [15] ⊖	a	06 49	07 19		07 49	08 19	08 49	09 19	09 49		10 19	10 49	11 19	11 48		12 19	12 49	13 19		13 49	14 19	14 49	15 19

A ⊥ from Salisbury
B ⊥ from Axminster

For alternative services from Woking and Basingstoke to London Waterloo, refer to Table T155

For services between Bristol Temple Meads and Salisbury, refer to Table T123

Table T160-R

Yeovil and Exeter - Salisbury - London

Saturdays
21 December to 16 May

		SW	SW	SW	SW	SW	SW	SW	SW	SW	SW	SW	SW	SW	SW	SW	SW	SW	SW	SW	SW	SW
		◇1	◇1	◇1	◇1	◇1	◇1	◇1	◇1	◇1	◇1	◇1	◇1	◇1	◇1	◇1	◇1	◇1	◇1	◇1	◇1	◇1
			A		A		A		B	A		A	C	A		A						
		⊥	⊥	⊥	⊥	⊥	⊥	⊥	⊥	⊥	⊥	⊥	⊥	⊥		⊥						
Exeter St Davids [6]	d		12 25		13 25		14 25			15 25		16 25		17 25		18 25		19 25	20 25	21 25		23 00
Exeter Central	d		12 30		13 30		14 30			15 30		16 30		17 30		18 30		19 30	20 30	21 30		23 04
Pinhoe	d		12 34		13 34		14 34			15 34		16 34		17 34		18 34		19 34	20 34	21 34		23s09
Cranbrook	d		12 39		13 39		14 39			15 39		16 39		17 39		18 39		19 39	20 39	21 39		23s13
Whimple	d				13 44					15 44				17 44				19 44	20 44	21 44		23s18
Feniton	d		12 47				14 47					16 47		17 49		18 47			20 49	21 49		23s24
Honiton	a		12 54		13 54		14 53			15 54		16 53		17 55		18 53		19 54	20 55	21 55		23s30
	d		12 55		13 55		14 55			15 55		16 55		17 56		18 55		19 55	20 56	21 56		
Axminster	a		13 05		14 05		15 05			16 05		17 05		18 06		19 05		20 05	21 06	22 06		23s42
	d		13 06		14 06		15 06			16 06		17 06		18 07		19 06		20 06	21 07	22 07		
Crewkerne	d		13 19		14 19		15 19			16 19		17 19		18 20		19 19		20 19	21 20	22 20		23s55
Yeovil Pen Mill	a																					
	d												17 39									
Yeovil Junction	a		13 27		14 27		15 27			16 27		17 27	17 44	18 29		19 27		20 27	21 29	22 29		00s04
	d		13 29		14 29		15 29			16 29		17 29	17 53	18 30		19 29		20 29	21 30	22 30		
Sherborne	d		13 35		14 35		15 35			16 35		17 35	17 59	18 37		19 35		20 35	21 36	22 36		
Templecombe	d		13 43		14 43		15 43			16 43		17 43	18 07	18 44		19 43		20 43	21 44	22 44		
Gillingham (Dorset)	a		13 50		14 50		15 50			16 50		17 50	18 14	18 51		19 50		20 50	21 51	22 51		
	d		13 51		14 51		15 51			16 51		17 51	18 17	18 52		19 51		20 51	21 52	22 52		
Tisbury	d		14 01		15 01		16 01			17 01		18 01	18 27	19 03		20 01		21 01	22 02	23 02		
Yeovil Pen Mill	a																					
	d																					
Castle Cary	d																					
Bruton	d																					
Frome	d																					
Bristol Temple Meads [10] 123	d	12 48							15 50								19 35				22 23	
Bath Spa [7] 123	d	13 06							16 08								19 54				22 39	
Bradford-on-Avon 123	d	13 20							16 25								20 10				22 50	
Trowbridge 123	d	13 27							16 31								20 17				22 56	
Westbury 123	d	13 38							16 40								20 24				23 05	
Warminster 123	d	13 46							16 48								20 32				23 12	
Salisbury 123	a	14 07	14 16		15 16		16 16		17 09	17 16		18 16	18 41	19 18		20 16	20 51	21 16	22 17	23 23	23 33	00 41
	d		14 21	14 47	15 21	15 47	16 21	16 47		17 21	17 47	18 21	18 47	19 21	19 47	20 26	20 53	21 26	22 26			
Grateley	d			14 59		15 59		16 59			17 59		18 59		19 59	20 38		21 38	22 38			
Andover	d		14 38	15 06	15 38	16 06	16 38	17 06		17 38	18 06	18 38	19 06	19 38	20 06	20 45	21 12	21 45	22 45			
Whitchurch (Hants)	d			15 14		16 14		17 14			18 14		19 14		20 14	20 53		21 53	22 53			
Overton	d			15 20		16 20		17 20			18 20		19 20		20 20	20 59		21 59	22 59			
Basingstoke	a		14 55	15 28	15 55	16 28	16 55	17 28		17 55	18 28	18 55	19 28	19 55	20 28	21 08	21 28	22 07	23 07			
Woking	a		15 15	15 48	16 15	16 48	17 15	17 48		18 15	18 48	19 15	19 48	20 15	20 48	21 30		22 27	23 27			
Clapham Junction [10]	a		15 36		16 36		17 36			18 36		19 36		20 36		21 55		22 48	23 48			
London Waterloo [15] ⊖	a		15 49	16 19	16 49	17 19	17 45	18 19		18 49	19 19	19 49	20 19	20 49	21 19	22 04		22 57	23 57			

A ⊥ from Axminster
B ⊥ from Salisbury
C From Weymouth. ⊥ from Salisbury to Basingstoke

For alternative services from Woking and Basingstoke to London Waterloo, refer to Table T155

For services between Bristol Temple Meads and Salisbury, refer to Table T123

Table T160-R

Yeovil and Exeter - Salisbury - London

Sundays
15 December to 10 May

		SW	SW	SW	SW	SW	SW	SW	SW	SW	SW	SW	SW	SW	SW	SW	SW	SW	SW	SW	SW	SW	SW
		◇1	◇1	◇1	◇1	◇1	◇1	◇1	◇1	◇1	◇1	◇1	◇1	◇1	◇1	◇1	◇1	◇1	◇1	◇1	◇1	◇1	◇1
		⚯	⚯	A	B ⚯	A	B ⚯	A	B ⚯	A		C ⚯	A	D ⚯	A	D ⚯	A	D ⚯		A	D ⚯	A	D ⚯
Exeter St Davids 6	d								08 24			09 25		10 25		11 25		12 25			13 25		14 25
Exeter Central	d								08 28			09 30		10 30		11 30		12 30			13 30		14 30
Pinhoe	d								08 35			09 34		10 34		11 34		12 34			13 34		14 34
Cranbrook	d								08 40			09 39		10 39		11 39		12 39			13 39		14 39
Whimple	d											09 44				11 44					13 44		
Feniton	d								08 48					10 47				12 47					14 47
Honiton	a								08 55			09 53		10 53		11 53		12 53			13 53		14 53
	d								08 56			09 55		10 55		11 55		12 55			13 55		14 55
Axminster	a								09 06			10 05		11 05		12 05		13 05			14 05		15 05
	d								09 07			10 06		11 06		12 06		13 06			14 06		15 06
Crewkerne	d								09 20			10 19		11 19		12 19		13 19			14 19		15 19
Yeovil Pen Mill	a																						
	d																						
Yeovil Junction	a								09 28			10 27		11 27		12 27		13 27			14 27		15 27
	d				07 29		08 29		09 30		09 50	10 29		11 29		12 29		13 29			14 29		15 29
Sherborne	d				07 35		08 35		09 36			10 35		11 35		12 35		13 35			14 35		15 35
Templecombe	d				07 43		08 43		09 44			10 43		11 43		12 43		13 43			14 43		15 43
Gillingham (Dorset)	a				07 50		08 50		09 51			10 50		11 50		12 50		13 50			14 50		15 50
	d				07 51		08 51		09 52			10 51		11 51		12 51		13 51			14 51		15 51
Tisbury	d				08 01		09 01		10 02			11 01		12 01		13 01		14 01			15 01		16 01
Yeovil Pen Mill	a										09 55												
	d										09 57												
Castle Cary	d										10 12												
Bruton	d										10 17												
Frome	d										10 30												
Bristol Temple Meads 10 123	d																		13 04				
Bath Spa 7 123	d																		13 22				
Bradford-on-Avon 123	d																		13 34				
Trowbridge 123	d																		13 40				
Westbury 123	d										10 43								13 50				
Warminster 123	d										10 51								13 58				
Salisbury 123	a				08 16		09 16		10 17		11 12	11 16		12 16		13 16		14 16	14 19		15 16		16 16
	d	06 45	07 27	07 52	08 27	08 44	09 27	09 44	10 27	10 44		11 27	11 44	12 27	12 44	13 27	13 44	14 27		14 44	15 27	15 44	16 27
Grateley	d		07 39			08 56		09 56		10 56			11 56		12 56		13 56			14 56		15 56	
Andover	d	07 02	07 46	08 09	08 45	09 03	09 45	10 03	10 45	11 03		11 45	12 03	12 45	13 03	13 45	14 03	14 45		15 03	15 45	16 03	16 45
Whitchurch (Hants)	d		07 54			09 11		10 11		11 11			12 11		13 11		14 11			15 11		16 11	
Overton	d		08 00			09 17		10 17		11 17			12 17		13 17		14 17			15 17		16 17	
Basingstoke	a	07 19	08 08	08 26	09 02	09 26	10 03	10 26	11 03	11 26		12 03	12 26	13 03	13 26	14 03	14 26	15 03		15 26	16 03	16 26	17 03
Woking	a	07 39	08 28		09 23		10 23		11 23			12 23		13 23		14 23		15 23			16 23		17 23
Clapham Junction 10	a	08 05	08 57		09 44		10 43		11 43			12 43		13 43		14 43		15 43			16 43		17 43
London Waterloo 15 ⊖	a	08 21	09 10		09 56		10 55		11 55			12 54		13 54		14 54		15 54			16 54		17 54

		SW	SW	SW	SW	SW	SW	SW	SW	SW	SW	SW	SW	SW	SW	SW
		◇1	◇1	◇1	◇1	◇1	◇1	◇1	◇1	◇1	◇1	◇1	◇1	◇1	1	◇1
			D ⚯	B ⚯		D ⚯		E ⚯		D ⚯						
Exeter St Davids 6	d		15 25			16 25		17 25		18 25	19 25	20 25		21 25	22 25	23 13
Exeter Central	d		15 30			16 30		17 30		18 30	19 30	20 30		21 30	22 30	23 18
Pinhoe	d		15 34			16 34		17 34		18 34	19 34	20 34		21 34	22 36	23s23
Cranbrook	d		15 39			16 39		17 39		18 39	19 39	20 39		21 39	22 40	23s28
Whimple	d		15 44					17 44			19 44	20 44		21 44	22 45	
Feniton	d					16 47				18 47		20 49		21 49	22 50	
Honiton	a		15 53			16 53		17 53		18 53	19 53	20 55		21 55	22 57	23s40
	d		15 55			16 55		17 55		18 55	19 55	20 56		21 56	22 58	
Axminster	a		16 05			17 05		18 05		19 05	20 05	21 06		22 06	23 08	23s52
	d		16 06			17 06		18 06		19 06	20 06	21 07		22 07	23 09	
Crewkerne	d		16 19			17 19		18 19		19 19	20 19	21 20		22 20	23 22	00s08
Yeovil Pen Mill	a															
	d	15 43														
Yeovil Junction	a	15 48	16 27			17 27		18 27		19 27	20 27	21 29		22 29	23 31	00 17
	d	15 53	16 29			17 29		18 29		19 29	20 29	21 30		22 30	23 33	
Sherborne	d	15 59	16 35			17 35		18 35		19 35	20 35	21 36		22 36		
Templecombe	d	16 07	16 43			17 43		18 43		19 43	20 43	21 44		22 44		
Gillingham (Dorset)	a	16 14	16 50			17 50		18 50		19 50	20 50	21 51		22 51		
	d	16 17	16 51		17 17	17 51		18 51		19 51	20 51	21 52		22 52		
Tisbury	d	16 28	17 01		17 28	18 01		19 01		20 01	21 01	22 02		23 02		
Yeovil Pen Mill	a															
	d															
Castle Cary	d															
Bruton	d															
Frome	d								18 33							
Bristol Temple Meads 10 123	d			16 04									21 35			
Bath Spa 7 123	d			16 22									21 51			
Bradford-on-Avon 123	d			16 34									22 02			
Trowbridge 123	d			16 40									22 08			
Westbury 123	d			16 50					18 50				22 17			
Warminster 123	d			16 58					18 58				22 24			
Salisbury 123	a	16 42	17 16	17 19	17 42	18 16		19 16	19 19	20 16	21 16	22 16	22 45	23 17	00 20	
	d	16 44	17 27		17 44	18 27	18 44	19 27		20 21	21 21	22 27				
Grateley	d	16 56			17 56		18 56			20 33	21 33	22 39				
Andover	d	17 03	17 45		18 03	18 45	19 03	19 45		20 40	21 40	22 46				
Whitchurch (Hants)	d	17 11			18 11		19 11			20 48	21 48	22 54				
Overton	d	17 17			18 17		19 17			20 54	21 54	23 00				
Basingstoke	a	17 26	18 03		18 26	19 03	19 26	20 03		21 03	22 03	23 08				
Woking	a		18 23			19 23		20 23		21 23	22 23	23 28				
Clapham Junction 10	a	18 10	18 43		19 10	19 43	20 10	20 43		21 43	22 43	23 49				
London Waterloo 15 ⊖	a	18 19	18 54		19 19	19 54	20 19	20 54		21 54	22 54	23 58				

A To Reading
B ⚯ from Salisbury
C ⚯ from Yeovil Junction
D ⚯ from Axminster
E ⚯ from Axminster to Woking

For alternative services from Woking and Basingstoke to London Waterloo, refer to Table T155

For services between Bristol Temple Meads and Salisbury, refer to Table T123

Table T165-F

Portsmouth and Chichester - Fareham and Southampton

Mondays to Fridays
16 December to 15 May

Miles	Miles			SW	SN	SW	SN	SW	GW	SN	SW	SW	SN	SW	SN	GW	SW	SN	SW	SN	SW	SW	GW
				◇1	1	1	1	◇1		1	1	◇1	1	◇1	1	◇	◇1	1	1	1	◇1	◇1	◇
				A	B		C	A	D	B		A	E	A	F	D	A	E		G	A	H	D
0	—	Portsmouth Harbour	d	05 00				05 43	06 01			06 23		06 50		07 21	07 24		07 35		07 54	08 05	08 23
0¾	—	Portsmouth & Southsea	d	05 05		05 13		05 48	06 05		06 23	06 28		06 55		07 25	07 28		07 39		07 58	08 09	08 27
1¾	—	Fratton	d	05 09		05 17		05 52	06 09		06 27	06 32		06 59		07 29	07 32		07 43		08 02	08 13	08 31
4	—	Hilsea	d	05 13		05 21		05 56			06 31	06 36		07 03			07 36		07 47		08 06	08 17	
—	0	Chichester 4	d		05 07		05 23			06 11			06 27		07 06			07 27		07 44			
—	8¾	Havant	d		05 17		05 34			06 22			06 42		07 20			07 39		08 00			
5½	12¾	**Cosham**	d	05 19	05 24	05 28	05 42	06 03	06 16	06 30	06 36	06 42	06 50	07 08	07 27	07 37	07 42	07 46	07 53	08 08	08 12	08 23	08 39
8	—	**Portchester**	d	05 23	05 28	05 33	05 46	06 08			06 41	06 46	06 54	07 13	07 31		07 46		07 57	08 12	08 16	08 28	
11¼	—	**Fareham**	a	05 28	05 33	05 38	05 51	06 13	06 24	06 38	06 46	06 51	06 59	07 18	07 36	07 44	07 51	07 56	08 02	08 17	08 21	08 33	08 46
—	—		d		05 34	05 40	05 52		06 25	06 38	06 47		07 00		07 37	07 45		07 57	08 03	08 18		08 35	08 47
15	—	**Swanwick**	d		05 40	05 46	05 58			06 44	06 53		07 06		07 43			08 03	08 10	08 24		08 42	
17	—	**Bursledon**	d			05 50					06 57								08 13	08 27			
18¼	—	**Hamble**	d			05 53					07 00								08 17	08 30			
19	—	**Netley**	d		05 46	05 55	06 04				07 02				07 49				08 19	08 32		08 48	
20¾	—	**Sholing**	d			05 59					07 06								08 23	08 36			
21½	—	**Woolston**	d		05 50	06 01	06 08				07 08				07 54				08 25	08 38		08 52	
23¼	—	**Bitterne**	d			06 05					07 12								08 28	08 41			
23¾	—	St Denys	d			06 08					07 15								08 31	08 45		08 58	
25¾	—	Southampton Central	a		06 00	06 13	06 18		06 45	07 02	07 21		07 25		08 03	08 07		08 20	08 38	08 52		09 03	09 07

		SN	SW	SW	SN	GW	SN	SW	GW	SW	SN	GW	SN	SW	SW	SN	GW	SN	SW	SW	SN	GW	SN
		1	1	◇1	1	◇	1	1	◇	◇1	1	◇	1	1	◇1	1	◇	1	1	◇1	1	◇	1
		E		A	G	D	E		I	A	G	D	E		A	G	D	E		A	G	D	E
Portsmouth Harbour	d			08 59		09 23		09 33		09 59		10 23			10 59		11 23			11 59		12 23	
Portsmouth & Southsea	d		08 38	09 04		09 27		09 38		10 04		10 27		10 38	11 04		11 27		11 38	12 04		12 27	
Fratton	d		08 42	09 08		09 31		09 42		10 08		10 31		10 42	11 08		11 31		11 42	12 08		12 31	
Hilsea	d		08 46	09 12				09 46		10 12				10 46	11 12				11 46	12 12			
Chichester 4	d	08 27			09 07		09 27		09 46		10 07		10 27			11 07		11 27			12 07		12 27
Havant	d	08 39			09 23		09 40		09 57		10 21		10 39			11 21		11 39			12 21		12 39
Cosham	d	08 46	08 51	09 17	09 30	09 39	09 47	09 51	10 05	10 17	10 29	10 39	10 46	10 51	11 17	11 29	11 39	11 46	11 51	12 17	12 29	12 39	12 46
Portchester	d		08 56	09 22	09 34			09 56		10 22	10 33			10 56	11 22	11 33			11 56	12 22	12 33		
Fareham	a	08 54	09 01	09 27	09 39	09 46	09 55	10 01	10 12	10 27	10 38	10 46	10 54	11 01	11 27	11 38	11 46	11 54	12 01	12 27	12 38	12 46	12 56
	d	08 54	09 03		09 40	09 47	09 55	10 02	10 15		10 39	10 47	10 55	11 03		11 39	11 47	11 55	12 03		12 39	12 47	12 57
Swanwick	d	09 00	09 09		09 46		10 01	10 08			10 45		11 01	11 09		11 45		12 01	12 09		12 45		13 03
Bursledon	d		09 13					10 12						11 13					12 13				
Hamble	d		09 16					10 15						11 16					12 16				
Netley	d		09 18					10 17						11 18					12 18				
Sholing	d		09 22					10 21						11 22					12 22				
Woolston	d		09 24					10 23						11 24					12 24				
Bitterne	d		09 28					10 27						11 28					12 28				
St Denys	d		09 31					10 30						11 31					12 31				
Southampton Central	a	09 20	09 38		10 05	10 07	10 19	10 38	10 40		11 03	11 07	11 19	11 38		12 02	12 07	12 19	12 38		13 03	13 07	13 20

		SW	SW	SN	GW	SN	SW	SW	SN	GW	SN	SW	SW	SN	GW	SN	SW	SW	SN	GW	SN	SW
		1	◇1	1	◇	1	1	◇1	1		1	1	◇1	1		1	1	◇1	1		1	1
			A	G	D	E		A	G	D	E		A	G	D	E		A	G	D	E	
Portsmouth Harbour	d		12 59		13 23			13 59		14 23			14 59		15 23			15 59		16 23		16 33
Portsmouth & Southsea	d	12 38	13 04		13 27		13 38	14 04		14 27		14 38	15 04		15 27		15 38	16 04		16 27		16 38
Fratton	d	12 42	13 08		13 31		13 42	14 08		14 31		14 42	15 08		15 31		15 42	16 08		16 31		16 42
Hilsea	d	12 46	13 12				13 46	14 12				14 46	15 12				15 46	16 12				16 46
Chichester 4	d			13 07		13 27			14 07		14 27			15 07		15 27			16 07		16 27	
Havant	d			13 22		13 39			14 21		14 39			15 21		15 39			16 21		16 39	
Cosham	d	12 51	13 17	13 29	13 39	13 46	13 51	14 17	14 29	14 39	14 46	14 51	15 17	15 29	15 39	15 46	15 51	16 17	16 29	16 39	16 46	16 51
Portchester	d	12 56	13 22	13 33			13 56	14 22	14 33			14 56	15 22	15 33			15 56	16 22	16 33			16 56
Fareham	a	13 01	13 27	13 38	13 46	13 54	14 01	14 27	14 38	14 46	14 54	15 01	15 27	15 38	15 46	15 54	16 01	16 27	16 38	16 46	16 54	17 01
	d	13 03		13 40	13 47	13 55	14 03		14 39	14 47	14 55	15 03		15 39	15 47	15 55	16 03		16 39	16 47	16 55	17 03
Swanwick	d	13 09		13 46		14 01	14 09		14 45		15 01	15 09		15 45		16 01	16 09		16 45		17 01	17 09
Bursledon	d	13 13					14 13					15 13					16 13					17 13
Hamble	d	13 16					14 16					15 16					16 16					17 16
Netley	d	13 18					14 18					15 18					16 18					17 18
Sholing	d	13 22					14 22					15 22					16 22					17 22
Woolston	d	13 24					14 24					15 24					16 24					17 24
Bitterne	d	13 28					14 28					15 28					16 28					17 28
St Denys	d	13 31					14 31					15 31					16 31					17 31
Southampton Central	a	13 38		14 03	14 07	14 19	14 39		15 03	15 07	15 19	15 38		16 03	16 07	16 20	16 38		17 02	17 07	17 19	17 38

A To London Waterloo
B From Barnham
C From Littlehampton
D To Cardiff Central
E From Brighton
F From Gatwick Airport
G From London Victoria
H To Poole
I From Brighton to Great Malvern

Table T165-F

Portsmouth and Chichester - Fareham and Southampton

Mondays to Fridays
16 December to 15 May

		SW ◇1 A	SN 1 B	GW ◇ C	SN 1 D	SW 1	GW ◇ E	SW 1 F	SW ◇1 A	SN 1 B	GW ◇ C	SN 1 D	SW 1	SW ◇1 A	SN 1 B	GW ◇ C	SN 1 D	SW 1	SW ◇1 A	SN 1 B	GW ◇ C	SN 1 D	SW 1
Portsmouth Harbour	d	16 59		17 23		17 33		17 49	17 59		18 24			18 59		19 23			19 59		20 23		
Portsmouth & Southsea	d	17 04		17 27		17 38		17 54	18 04		18 29		18 38	19 04		19 27		19 38	20 04		20 27		20 38
Fratton	d	17 08		17 31		17 42		17 58	18 08		18 33		18 42	19 08		19 31		19 42	20 08		20 31		20 42
Hilsea	d	17 12				17 46		18 02	18 12				18 46	19 12				19 46	20 12				20 46
Chichester 4	d		17 07		17 27		17 47			18 07		18 27			19 07		19 28			20 07		20 28	
Havant	d		17 21		17 39		17 58			18 22		18 40			19 21		19 40			20 21		20 40	
Cosham	d	17 17	17 29	17 39	17 46	17 51	18 04	18 09	18 17	18 30	18 40	18 47	18 51	19 17	19 29	19 39	19 47	19 51	20 17	20 29		20 47	20 51
Portchester	d	17 22	17 33			17 56		18 13	18 22	18 34			18 56	19 22	19 33			19 56	20 22	20 33			20 56
Fareham	a	17 27	17 38	17 46	17 54	18 01	18 12	18 18	18 27	18 39	18 48	18 54	19 01	19 27	19 38	19 46	19 54	20 01	20 27	20 38	20 44	20 54	21 01
	d		17 39	17 47	17 55	18 03	18 13			18 40	18 49	18 55	19 03		19 39	19 47	19 55	20 03		20 39	20 45	20 55	21 03
Swanwick	d		17 45		18 01	18 09				18 46		19 01	19 09		19 45		20 01	20 09		20 45		21 01	21 09
Bursledon	d					18 13							19 13					20 13					21 13
Hamble	d					18 16							19 16					20 16					21 16
Netley	d		17 51			18 18							19 18					20 18					21 18
Sholing	d					18 22							19 22					20 22					21 22
Woolston	d		17 55			18 24							19 24					20 24					21 24
Bitterne	d					18 28							19 28					20 28					21 28
St Denys	d		18 00			18 31							19 31					20 31					21 31
Southampton Central	a		18 05	18 08	18 19	18 38	18 41			19 03	19 09	19 20	19 38		20 03	20 07	20 19	20 38		21 03	21 06	21 20	21 38

		SW ◇1 G	SW ◇1 A	GW ◇ H	SN 1 B	SN 1 D	SW 1	SW 1 F	SN 1 B	SW 1	SW 1 I
Portsmouth Harbour	d		20 59	21 23				21 54		22 33	23 24
Portsmouth & Southsea	d		21 04	21 27			21 38	21 59		22 38	23 29
Fratton	d		21 08	21 31			21 42	22 03		22 42	23 33
Hilsea	d		21 12				21 46	22 07		22 46	23 37
Chichester 4	d				21 11	21 27			22 07		
Havant	d	20 59			21 34	21 39			22 28		
Cosham	d	21 08	21 17		21 41	21 46	21 51	22 12	22 35	22 51	23 42
Portchester	d	21 13	21 22		21 45		21 56	22 17	22 39	22 56	23 47
Fareham	a	21 18	21 27	21 44	21 50	21 55	22 01	22 22	22 44	23 01	23 52
	d	21 19		21 47	21 51	21 56	22 03		22 44	23 03	
Swanwick	d	21 26			21 57	22 02	22 09		22 50	23 09	
Bursledon	d						22 13			23 13	
Hamble	d						22 16			23 16	
Netley	d	21 31					22 18			23 18	
Sholing	d						22 22			23 22	
Woolston	d	21 36			22 05		22 24			23 24	
Bitterne	d						22 28			23 28	
St Denys	d				22 10		22 31			23 31	
Southampton Central	a	21 45		22 20	22 15	22 23	22 38		23 08	23 36	

Saturdays
21 December to 16 May

		SW 1 F	SN 1 J	SW 1	SN 1 J	SW 1	SW ◇1 A	GW ◇ C	SN 1 D	SN 1 D	SW 1	SW ◇1 A	SN 1 K	GW ◇ C	SN 1 D	SW 1	SW ◇1 A	SN 1 B	GW ◇ C	SN 1 D	SW 1	SW ◇1 A	SN 1 B
Portsmouth Harbour	d					05 40	05 48	06 08				06 59		07 23			07 59		08 23			08 59	
Portsmouth & Southsea	d			05 16		05 44	05 53	06 12			06 38	07 04		07 27		07 38	08 04		08 27		08 38	09 04	
Fratton	d			05 20		05 48	05 57	06 16			06 42	07 08		07 31		07 42	08 08		08 31		08 42	09 08	
Hilsea	d			05 24			06 01				06 46	07 12				07 46	08 12				08 46	09 12	
Chichester 4	d		05 08		05 27				06 09	06 27			07 05		07 27			08 07		08 27			09 07
Havant	d		05 20		05 39				06 21	06 39			07 19		07 39			08 21		08 39			09 21
Cosham	d	05 09	05 27	05 31	05 46	05 56	06 06	06 23	06 28	06 46	06 51	07 17	07 27	07 39	07 46	07 51	08 17	08 29	08 39	08 46	08 51	09 17	09 29
Portchester	d	05 14		05 35			06 11				06 56	07 22	07 31			07 56	08 22	08 33			08 56	09 22	09 33
Fareham	a	05 19	05 35	05 41	05 54	06 03	06 16	06 31	06 36	06 54	07 01	07 27	07 36	07 46	07 54	08 01	08 27	08 38	08 46	08 54	09 01	09 27	09 38
	d		05 36	05 42	05 55	06 04		06 32	06 37	06 55	07 03		07 37	07 47	07 55	08 03		08 39	08 47	08 55	09 03		09 39
Swanwick	d		05 42	05 49	06 01				06 43	07 01	07 09		07 43		08 01	08 09		08 45		09 01	09 09		09 45
Bursledon	d			05 52							07 13					08 13					09 13		
Hamble	d			05 56							07 16					08 16					09 16		
Netley	d			05 58							07 18		07 49			08 18					09 18		
Sholing	d			06 02							07 22					08 22					09 22		
Woolston	d			06 04							07 24		07 54			08 24					09 24		
Bitterne	d			06 07							07 28					08 28					09 28		
St Denys	d			06 10							07 31					08 31					09 31		
Southampton Central	a		06 01	06 15	06 19	06 35		06 53	07 00	07 18	07 38		08 03	08 08	08 19	08 38		09 03	09 08	09 19	09 38		10 03

A To London Waterloo
B From London Victoria
C To Cardiff Central
D From Brighton
E From Brighton to Bristol Parkway
F To Eastleigh
G From London Waterloo
H To Bristol Temple Meads
I To Winchester
J From Barnham
K From Gatwick Airport

Table T165-F

Saturdays
21 December to 16 May

Portsmouth and Chichester - Fareham and Southampton

		GW ◇ A	SN 1 B	SW 1	GW ◇ C	SW ◇1 D	SN 1 E	GW ◇ A	SN 1 B	SW 1	SW ◇1 D	SN 1 E	GW ◇ A	SN 1 B	SW 1	SW ◇1 D	SN 1 E	GW ◇ A	SN 1 B	SW 1	SW ◇1 D	SN 1 E
Portsmouth Harbour	d	09 23				09 59		10 23			10 59		11 23			11 59		12 23			12 59	
Portsmouth & Southsea	d	09 27		09 38		10 04		10 27		10 38	11 04		11 27		11 38	12 04		12 27		12 38	13 04	
Fratton	d	09 31		09 42		10 08		10 31		10 42	11 08		11 31		11 42	12 08		12 31		12 42	13 08	
Hilsea	d			09 46		10 12				10 46	11 12				11 46	12 12				12 46	13 12	
Chichester 4	d		09 27		09 51		10 07		10 27			11 07		11 27			12 07		12 27			13 07
Havant	d		09 39		10 03		10 21		10 39			11 21		11 39			12 21		12 39			13 21
Cosham	d	09 39	09 46	09 51	10 11	10 17	10 29	10 39	10 46	10 51	11 17	11 29	11 39	11 46	11 51	12 17	12 29	12 39	12 46	12 51	13 17	13 29
Portchester	d			09 56		10 22	10 33			10 56	11 22	11 33			11 56	12 22	12 33			12 56	13 22	13 33
Fareham	a	09 46	09 54	10 01	10 19	10 27	10 38	10 46	10 54	11 01	11 27	11 38	11 46	11 54	12 01	12 27	12 38	12 46	12 54	13 01	13 27	13 38
	d	09 47	09 55	10 03	10 20		10 39	10 47	10 55	11 03		11 39	11 47	11 55	12 03		12 39	12 47	12 55	13 03		13 39
Swanwick	d		10 01	10 09			10 45		11 01	11 09		11 45		12 01	12 09		12 45		13 01	13 09		13 45
Bursledon	d			10 13						11 13					12 13					13 13		
Hamble	d			10 16						11 16					12 16					13 16		
Netley	d			10 18						11 18					12 18					13 18		
Sholing	d			10 22						11 22					12 22					13 22		
Woolston	d			10 24						11 24					12 24					13 24		
Bitterne	d			10 28						11 28					12 28					13 28		
St Denys	d			10 31						11 31					12 31					13 31		
Southampton Central	a	10 08	10 19	10 38	10 41		11 03	11 08	11 19	11 38		12 03	12 08	12 19	12 38		13 03	13 08	13 19	13 38		14 03

		GW ◇ A	SN 1 B	SW 1	SW ◇1 D	SN 1 E	GW ◇ A	SN 1 B	SW 1	SW ◇1 D	SN 1 E	GW ◇ A	SN 1 B	SW 1	SW ◇1 D	SN 1 E	GW ◇ A	SN 1 B	SW 1	SW ◇1 D	SN 1 E	GW ◇ A	SN 1 B
Portsmouth Harbour	d	13 23			13 59		14 23			14 59		15 23			15 59		16 23			16 59		17 23	
Portsmouth & Southsea	d	13 27		13 38	14 04		14 27		14 38	15 04		15 27		15 38	16 04		16 27		16 38	17 04		17 27	
Fratton	d	13 31		13 42	14 08		14 31		14 42	15 08		15 31		15 42	16 08		16 31		16 42	17 08		17 31	
Hilsea	d			13 46	14 12				14 46	15 12				15 46	16 12				16 46	17 12			
Chichester 4	d		13 27			14 07		14 27			15 07		15 27			16 07		16 27			17 07		17 27
Havant	d		13 39			14 21		14 39			15 21		15 39			16 21		16 39			17 21		17 39
Cosham	d	13 39	13 46	13 51	14 17	14 29	14 39	14 46	14 51	15 17	15 29	15 39	15 46	15 51	16 17	16 29	16 39	16 46	16 51	17 17	17 29	17 39	17 46
Portchester	d			13 56	14 22	14 33			14 56	15 22	15 33			15 56	16 22	16 33			16 56	17 22	17 33		
Fareham	a	13 46	13 54	14 01	14 27	14 38	14 46	14 54	15 01	15 27	15 38	15 46	15 54	16 01	16 27	16 38	16 46	16 54	17 01	17 27	17 38	17 46	17 54
	d	13 47	13 55	14 03		14 39	14 47	14 55	15 03		15 39	15 47	15 55	16 03		16 39	16 47	16 55	17 03		17 39	17 47	17 55
Swanwick	d		14 01	14 09		14 45		15 01	15 09		15 45		16 01	16 09		16 45		17 01	17 09		17 45		18 01
Bursledon	d			14 13					15 13					16 13					17 13				
Hamble	d			14 16					15 16					16 16					17 16				
Netley	d			14 18					15 18					16 18					17 18				
Sholing	d			14 22					15 22					16 22					17 22				
Woolston	d			14 24					15 24					16 24					17 24				
Bitterne	d			14 28					15 28					16 28					17 28				
St Denys	d			14 31					15 31					16 31					17 31				
Southampton Central	a	14 08	14 19	14 38		15 03	15 08	15 19	15 38		16 03	16 08	16 19	16 38		17 03	17 08	17 19	17 38		18 03	18 08	18 20

		SW 1	GW ◇ F	SW ◇1 D	SN 1 E	GW ◇ A	SN 1 B	SW 1	SW ◇1 D	SN 1 E	GW ◇ A	SN 1 B	SW 1	SW ◇1 D	SN 1 E	GW ◇ A	SN 1 B	SW 1	SW ◇1 D	GW 1 G	SN 1 E	SN 1 B
Portsmouth Harbour	d	17 33		17 59		18 23			18 59		19 23			19 59		20 23			20 59	21 23		
Portsmouth & Southsea	d	17 38		18 04		18 27		18 38	19 04		19 27		19 38	20 04		20 27		20 38	21 04	21 27		
Fratton	d	17 42		18 08		18 31		18 42	19 08		19 31		19 42	20 08		20 31		20 42	21 08	21 31		
Hilsea	d	17 46		18 12				18 46	19 12				19 46	20 12				20 46	21 12			
Chichester 4	d		17 50		18 07		18 27			19 07		19 27			20 07		20 27				21 11	21 27
Havant	d		18 05		18 21		18 39			19 21		19 39			20 21		20 39				21 32	21 39
Cosham	d	17 51	18 12	18 17	18 29	18 39	18 46	18 51	19 17	19 29	19 39	19 46	19 51	20 17	20 29		20 46	20 51	21 17		21 40	21 46
Portchester	d	17 56		18 22	18 33			18 56	19 22	19 33			19 56	20 22	20 33			20 56	21 22		21 44	
Fareham	a	18 01	18 20	18 27	18 38	18 46	18 54	19 01	19 27	19 38	19 46	19 54	20 01	20 27	20 38	20 45	20 54	21 01	21 27	21 44	21 49	21 55
	d	18 03	18 21		18 39	18 47	18 55	19 03		19 39	19 47	19 55	20 03		20 39	20 47	20 55	21 03		21 45	21 50	21 57
Swanwick	d	18 09			18 45		19 01	19 09		19 45		20 01	20 09		20 45		21 01	21 09			21 56	22 03
Bursledon	d	18 13						19 13					20 13					21 13				
Hamble	d	18 16						19 16					20 16					21 16				
Netley	d	18 18						19 18					20 18					21 18				
Sholing	d	18 22						19 22					20 22					21 22				
Woolston	d	18 24						19 24					20 24					21 24			22 05	
Bitterne	d	18 28						19 28					20 28					21 28				
St Denys	d	18 31						19 31					20 31					21 31			22 09	
Southampton Central	a	18 38	18 43		19 03	19 08	19 19	19 38		20 03	20 08	20 19	20 38		21 03	21 10	21 19	21 38		22 23	22 14	22 20

		SW 1	SW 1 H	SN 1 E	SW 1	SW 1 I
Portsmouth Harbour	d		21 54		22 33	23 24
Portsmouth & Southsea	d	21 38	21 59		22 38	23 28
Fratton	d	21 42	22 03		22 42	23 32
Hilsea	d	21 46	22 07		22 46	23 36
Chichester 4	d			22 07		
Havant	d			22 28		
Cosham	d	21 51	22 12	22 35	22 51	23 42
Portchester	d	21 56	22 17	22 39	22 56	23 47
Fareham	a	22 01	22 22	22 44	23 01	23 52
	d	22 03		22 45	23 03	
Swanwick	d	22 09		22 51	23 09	
Bursledon	d	22 13			23 13	
Hamble	d	22 16			23 16	
Netley	d	22 18			23 18	
Sholing	d	22 22			23 22	
Woolston	d	22 24			23 24	
Bitterne	d	22 28			23 28	
St Denys	d	22 31			23 31	
Southampton Central	a	22 38		23 08	23 36	

A To Cardiff Central
B From Brighton
C From Brighton to Great Malvern
D To London Waterloo
E From London Victoria
F From Brighton to Bristol Temple Meads
G To Westbury
H To Eastleigh
I To Winchester

Table T165-F

Sundays
15 December to 10 May

Portsmouth and Chichester - Fareham and Southampton

		SW ■	SW ◇■ A	SW ■	SN B	SW ◇■ A	SW ■	SN ■ C	GW D	SW ◇■ A	SW ■	SN ■ C	SW ◇■ A	SW ■	SN ■ C	GW ◇ D	SW ◇■ A	SW ■	SN ■ C	GW ◇ E	SW ◇■ A	SW ■	SN ■ C
Portsmouth Harbour	d	06 37	07 17			08 17			09 08	09 17			10 17			11 08	11 17				12 17		
Portsmouth & Southsea	d	06 42	07 22	07 42		08 22	08 42		09 12	09 22	09 42		10 22	10 42		11 12	11 22	11 42			12 22	12 42	
Fratton	d	06 46	07 26	07 46		08 26	08 46		09 16	09 26	09 46		10 26	10 46		11 15	11 26	11 46			12 26	12 46	
Hilsea	d	06 50	07 30	07 50		08 30	08 50			09 30	09 50		10 30	10 50			11 30	11 50			12 30	12 50	
Chichester ■	d				07 57			08 59				09 59			10 59				11 59	12 04			12 59
Havant	d				08 10			09 11				10 11			11 11				12 11	12 15			13 11
Cosham	d	06 55	07 35	07 55	08 17	08 35	08 55	09 18	09 23	09 35	09 55	10 18	10 35	10 55	11 18	11 23	11 35	11 55	12 18	12 25	12 35	12 55	13 18
Portchester	d	07 00	07 40	08 00		08 40	09 00			09 40	10 00		10 40	11 00			11 40	12 00			12 40	13 00	
Fareham	a	07 05	07 45	08 05	08 25	08 45	09 05	09 25	09 31	09 45	10 05	10 25	10 45	11 05	11 25	11 31	11 45	12 05	12 25	12 33	12 45	13 05	13 25
	d	07 06		08 06	08 26		09 06	09 26	09 32		10 06	10 26		11 06	11 26	11 32		12 06	12 26	12 34		13 06	13 26
Swanwick	d	07 12		08 12	08 32		09 12	09 33			10 12	10 33		11 12	11 33			12 12	12 33			13 12	13 33
Bursledon	d	07 16		08 16			09 16				10 16			11 16				12 16				13 16	
Hamble	d	07 19		08 19			09 19				10 19			11 19				12 19				13 19	
Netley	d	07 21		08 21			09 21				10 21			11 21				12 21				13 21	
Sholing	d	07 25		08 25			09 25				10 25			11 25				12 25				13 25	
Woolston	d	07 27		08 27			09 27				10 27			11 27				12 27				13 27	
Bitterne	d	07 31		08 31			09 31				10 31			11 31				12 31				13 31	
St Denys	d	07 34		08 34			09 34				10 34			11 34				12 34				13 34	
Southampton Central	a	07 40		08 40	08 50		09 40	09 50	09 54		10 40	10 50		11 40	11 50	11 55		12 40	12 50	12 55		13 40	13 50

		GW ◇ D	SW ◇■ A	SW ■	SN ■ C	GW ◇ D	SW ◇■ A	SW ■	SN ■ C	GW D	SW ◇■ A	SW ■	SN ■ C	GW ◇ D	SW ◇■ A	GW ◇ F	SW ■	SN ■ C	GW ◇ D	SW ◇■ A	SW ■	SN ■ C	GW ◇ D
Portsmouth Harbour	d	13 08	13 17			14 08	14 17			15 08	15 17			16 08	16 17				17 08	17 17			18 08
Portsmouth & Southsea	d	13 12	13 22	13 42		14 12	14 22	14 42		15 12	15 22	15 42		16 12	16 22		16 42		17 12	17 22	17 42		18 12
Fratton	d	13 16	13 26	13 46		14 16	14 26	14 46		15 16	15 26	15 46		16 16	16 26		16 46		17 16	17 26	17 46		18 16
Hilsea	d		13 30	13 50			14 30	14 50			15 30	15 50			16 30		16 50			17 30	17 50		
Chichester ■	d				13 59				14 59				15 59			16 35		16 59				17 59	
Havant	d				14 11				15 11				16 11			16 44		17 11				18 11	
Cosham	d	13 23	13 35	13 55	14 18	14 23	14 35	14 55	15 18	15 23	15 35	15 55	16 18	16 23	16 35	16 51	16 55	17 18	17 23	17 35	17 55	18 18	18 23
Portchester	d		13 40	14 00			14 40	15 00			15 40	16 00			16 40		17 00			17 40	18 00		
Fareham	a	13 31	13 45	14 05	14 25	14 31	14 45	15 05	15 25	15 31	15 45	16 05	16 25	16 31	16 45	16 59	17 05	17 25	17 31	17 45	18 05	18 25	18 31
	d	13 32		14 06	14 26	14 32		15 06	15 26	15 32		16 06	16 26	16 32		16 59	17 06	17 26	17 32		18 06	18 26	18 32
Swanwick	d			14 12	14 33			15 12	15 33			16 12	16 33				17 12	17 33			18 12	18 33	
Bursledon	d			14 16				15 16				16 16					17 16				18 16		
Hamble	d			14 19				15 19				16 19					17 19				18 19		
Netley	d			14 21				15 21				16 21					17 21				18 21		
Sholing	d			14 25				15 25				16 25					17 25				18 25		
Woolston	d			14 27				15 27				16 27					17 27				18 27		
Bitterne	d			14 31				15 31				16 31					17 31				18 31		
St Denys	d			14 34				15 34				16 34					17 34				18 34		
Southampton Central	a	13 55		14 40	14 50	14 55		15 40	15 50	15 55		16 40	16 50	16 55		17 20	17 44	17 50	17 55		18 40	18 50	18 55

		SW ◇■ A	GW ◇ F	SW ■	SN ■ C	GW ◇ D	SW ◇■ A	SW ■	SN ■ C	GW ◇ D	SW ◇■ A	SW ■	SN ■ C	SW ◇■ A	SW ■	SN ■ C	GW G	SW ■ H	SW ■	SW ■ H
Portsmouth Harbour	d	18 17				19 08	19 17			20 08	20 17			21 17			22 05	22 17		23 17
Portsmouth & Southsea	d	18 22		18 42		19 12	19 22	19 42		20 12	20 22	20 42		21 22	21 42		22 12	22 22	22 42	23 22
Fratton	d	18 26		18 46		19 16	19 26	19 46		20 16	20 26	20 46		21 26	21 46		22 16	22 26	22 46	23 26
Hilsea	d	18 30		18 50			19 30	19 50			20 30	20 50		21 30	21 50			22 30	22 50	23 30
Chichester ■	d		18 35		18 59				19 59				20 59			21 59				
Havant	d		18 50		19 11				20 11				21 12			22 11				
Cosham	d	18 35	18 57	19 00	19 18	19 23	19 35	19 55	20 18		20 35	20 55	21 19	21 35	21 55	22 18		22 35	22 55	23 35
Portchester	d	18 40		19 05			19 40	20 00			20 40	21 00		21 40	22 00			22 40	23 00	23 40
Fareham	a	18 45	19 04	19 10	19 25	19 31	19 45	20 05	20 25	20 31	20 45	21 05	21 26	21 45	22 05	22 25	22 31	22 45	23 05	23 45
	d		19 05	19 11	19 26	19 32		20 06	20 26	20 32		21 06	21 27		22 06	22 26	22 32		23 06	
Swanwick	d			19 17	19 33			20 12	20 33			21 12	21 34		22 12	22 33			23 12	
Bursledon	d			19 21				20 16				21 16			22 16				23 16	
Hamble	d			19 24				20 19				21 19			22 19				23 19	
Netley	d			19 26				20 21				21 21			22 21				23 21	
Sholing	d			19 30				20 25				21 25			22 25				23 25	
Woolston	d			19 32				20 27				21 27			22 27				23 27	
Bitterne	d			19 36				20 31				21 31			22 31				23 31	
St Denys	d			19 39				20 34				21 34			22 34				23 34	
Southampton Central	a		19 26	19 44	19 50	19 55		20 40	20 50	20 55		21 40	21 51		22 40	22 50	22 55		23 40	

A To London Waterloo
B From Littlehampton
C From Brighton
D To Cardiff Central
E From Brighton to Cardiff Central
F From Brighton to Bristol Temple Meads
G To Westbury
H To Eastleigh

NRT DECEMBER 19 EDITION

Table T165-R

Mondays to Fridays
16 December to 15 May

Southampton and Fareham - Chichester and Portsmouth

Miles	Miles			SN ■ A	SW ■ B	SN ■ C	SW ■ D	SW ■	SN ■ E	GW ◇ F	SW ■ B	SN ■ E	SW ■ G	SW ■	SN ■ A	GW ◇ F	SW ■	SN ■ E	SW ◇■ H	SN ■ A	SW ■	GW ◇ I	SN ■ E
0	—	Southampton Central	d	05 46		06 08		06 23	06 36	06 49		07 12		07 17	07 33	07 41	07 52	08 09		08 28	08 44	09 05	09 13
2	—	St Denys	d					06 29						07 23			07 58	08 15			08 49		
2½	—	Bitterne	d					06 32						07 25			08 00				08 52		
4¼	—	Woolston	d	05 56		06 17		06 35	06 46					07 29			08 04				08 55		
5	—	Sholing	d					06 38						07 31			08 06				08 58		
6¾	—	Netley	d					06 42						07 35			08 11				09 02		
7½	—	Hamble	d					06 44						07 37			08 13				09 04		
8¾	—	Bursledon	d					06 47						07 40			08 16				09 07		
10¼	—	Swanwick	d	06 04		06 27		06 51	06 57			07 31		07 44	07 51		08 20	08 28		08 48	09 11		09 32
14½	—	Fareham	a	06 10		06 34		06 57	07 03	07 11		07 37		07 51	07 57	08 02	08 27	08 34		08 55	09 17	09 33	09 38
—	—		d	06 11	06 19	06 36	06 48	06 58	07 04	07 12	07 21	07 38	07 47	07 52	07 57	08 03	08 28	08 35	08 49	08 56	09 18	09 34	09 39
17¾	—	Portchester	d	06 16	06 24	06 41	06 53	07 03	07 09		07 26	07 43	07 52	07 57			08 33	08 40	08 54		09 23		09 44
20¼	0	Cosham	d	06 21	06 29	06 46	06 58	07 08	07 13	07 20	07 30	07 47	07 57	08 02	08 06	08 11	08 38	08 44	08 59	09 04	09 28	09 42	09 48
—	4	Havant	a	06 27		06 53			07 19			07 55			08 12			08 51		09 10			09 54
—	12¾	Chichester ■	a	06 43		07 08			07 37			08 09			08 23			09 06		09 22			10 08
21¾	—	Hilsea	a		06 34		07 03	07 13			07 35		08 04	08 06			08 45		09 05		09 33		
24	—	Fratton	a		06 40		07 07	07 17		07 26	07 39		08 08	08 10		08 18	08 49		09 09		09 37	09 49	
25	—	Portsmouth & Southsea	a		06 44		07 11	07 21		07 30	07 43		08 13	08 18		08 21	08 53		09 12		09 44	09 52	
25¾	—	Portsmouth Harbour	a		06 49		07 17	07 27		07 38	07 48		08 18			08 26	08 58		09 18			09 56	

		SW ◇■ H	SN ■ A	SW ■	GW I	SN ■ E	SW ◇■ H	SN ■ A	SW ■	GW ◇ I	SN ■ E	SW ◇■ H	SN ■ A	SW ■	GW ◇ I	SN ■ E	SW ◇■ H	SN ■ A	SW ■	GW ◇ I	SN ■ E	SW ◇■ H	SN ■ A
Southampton Central	d		09 26	09 44	10 07	10 13		10 28	10 44	11 06	11 13		11 26	11 44	12 06	12 13		12 28	12 44	13 06	13 13		13 28
St Denys	d			09 49					10 49					11 49					12 49				
Bitterne	d			09 52					10 52					11 52					12 52				
Woolston	d			09 55					10 55					11 55					12 55				
Sholing	d			09 58					10 58					11 58					12 58				
Netley	d			10 02					11 02					12 02					13 02				
Hamble	d			10 04					11 04					12 04					13 04				
Bursledon	d			10 07					11 07					12 07					13 07				
Swanwick	d			10 11		10 32		10 46	11 11		11 32			12 11		12 32		12 46	13 11		13 32		13 46
Fareham	a			10 17	10 28	10 38		10 52	11 17	11 28	11 38			12 17	12 28	12 38		12 52	13 17	13 27	13 38		13 52
	d	09 48		10 18	10 29	10 39	10 48	10 53	11 18	11 29	11 39	11 48		12 18	12 29	12 39	12 48	12 53	13 18	13 28	13 39	13 48	13 53
Portchester	d	09 53		10 23		10 44	10 53		11 23		11 44	11 53		12 23		12 44	12 53		13 23		13 44	13 53	
Cosham	d	09 58	10 04	10 28	10 37	10 48	10 58	11 02	11 28	11 37	11 48	11 58	12 02	12 28	12 37	12 48	12 58	13 02	13 28	13 36	13 48	13 58	14 02
Havant	a		10 10			10 54		11 09			11 54		12 09			12 54		13 09			13 54		14 09
Chichester ■	a		10 22			11 08		11 21			12 08		12 21			13 08		13 21			14 08		14 21
Hilsea	a	10 03		10 33			11 03		11 33			12 03		12 33			13 03		13 33			14 03	
Fratton	a	10 07		10 37	10 43		11 07		11 37	11 43		12 07		12 37	12 43		13 07		13 37	13 42		14 07	
Portsmouth & Southsea	a	10 11		10 44	10 47		11 11		11 44	11 47		12 11		12 44	12 47		13 11		13 44	13 46		14 11	
Portsmouth Harbour	a	10 20			10 51		11 20			11 51		12 20			12 51		13 20			13 50		14 20	

		SW ■	GW ◇ I	SN ■ E	SW ◇■ H	SN ■ A	GW ◇ J	SW ■	GW ◇ I	SN ■ E	SW ◇■ H	SN ■ A	SW ■	GW ◇ I	SN ■ K	SW ◇■ L	SW ◇■ H	SN ■ A	SW ◇■ H	SW ■	GW ◇ I	SN ■ E
Southampton Central	d	13 44	14 06	14 13		14 28	14 34	14 44	15 05	15 13		15 28	15 44	16 06	16 12			16 28		16 44	17 06	17 14
St Denys	d	13 49						14 49					15 49							16 49		
Bitterne	d	13 52						14 52					15 52							16 52		
Woolston	d	13 55						14 55					15 55							16 55		
Sholing	d	13 58						14 58					15 58							16 58		
Netley	d	14 02						15 02					16 02							17 02		
Hamble	d	14 04						15 04					16 04							17 04		
Bursledon	d	14 07						15 07					16 07							17 07		
Swanwick	d	14 11		14 33		14 46		15 11		15 32		15 46	16 11		16 32			16 46		17 11		17 32
Fareham	a	14 17	14 27	14 39		14 52	14 56	15 17	15 27	15 38		15 52	16 17	16 27	16 38			16 52		17 17	17 27	17 38
	d	14 18	14 28	14 40	14 48	14 53	14 57	15 18	15 28	15 39	15 48	15 53	16 18	16 28	16 39	16 44	16 48	16 53	17 13	17 18	17 28	17 39
Portchester	d	14 23		14 45	14 53			15 23		15 44	15 53		16 23		16 44		16 53		17 18	17 23		17 44
Cosham	d	14 28	14 36	14 49	14 58	15 01	15 05	15 28	15 36	15 49	15 58	16 02	16 28	16 36	16 48	16 52	16 58	17 02	17 23	17 28	17 36	17 48
Havant	a			14 55		15 07	15 11			15 55		16 09			16 54	16 58		17 09				17 54
Chichester ■	a			15 09		15 18	15 25			16 09		16 21			17 08			17 21				18 08
Hilsea	a	14 33			15 03			15 33			16 03		16 33				17 03			17 33		
Fratton	a	14 37	14 42		15 07			15 37	15 42		16 07		16 37	16 42			17 07		17 30	17 37	17 43	
Portsmouth & Southsea	a	14 44	14 46		15 11			15 42	15 46		16 13		16 40	16 48			17 11		17 34	17 44	17 48	
Portsmouth Harbour	a		14 50		15 20			15 48	15 50		16 20		16 44	16 52			17 20		17 39		17 52	

A To Brighton
B From Eastleigh
C To London Bridge
D From Winchester
E To London Victoria
F From Bristol Temple Meads
G From Woking
H From London Waterloo
I From Cardiff Central
J From Great Malvern to Brighton
K To Horsham
L To London Waterloo

Table T165-R

Mondays to Fridays
16 December to 15 May

Southampton and Fareham - Chichester and Portsmouth

		SW ◇1 A	SN 1 B	SW 1 C	SW ◇1 A	GW ◇ D	SN 1 E	SW ◇1 A	SN 1 B	SW ◇1 A	SW 1	GW ■ D	SN 1 E	SW ◇1 A	SN 1 B	SW 1	GW ■ D	SN 1 E	SW ◇1 A	SN 1 B	SW 1	GW ◇ D
Southampton Central	d		17 28	17 44		18 06	18 13		18 28		18 44	19 07	19 12		19 28	19 44	20 05	20 13		20 28	20 44	21 04
St Denys	d			17 49							18 49					19 49					20 49	
Bitterne	d			17 52							18 52					19 52					20 52	
Woolston	d			17 55							18 55					19 55					20 55	
Sholing	d			17 58							18 58					19 58					20 58	
Netley	d			18 02							19 02					20 02					21 02	
Hamble	d			18 04							19 04					20 04					21 04	
Bursledon	d			18 07							19 07					20 07					21 07	
Swanwick	d		17 46	18 11			18 32		18 46		19 11		19 32		19 46	20 11		20 32		20 46	21 11	
Fareham	a		17 52	18 17		18 27	18 38		18 52		19 17	19 28	19 38		19 52	20 17	20 28	20 38		20 53	21 17	21 25
	d	17 48	17 53	18 18	18 23	18 28	18 39	18 45	18 53	19 14	19 18	19 29	19 39	19 48	19 53	20 18	20 29	20 39	20 49	20 54	21 18	21 26
Portchester	d	17 53		18 23	18 28		18 44	18 50		19 19	19 23		19 44	19 53		20 23		20 44	20 54		21 23	
Cosham	d	17 58	18 02	18 28	18 33	18 36	18 48	18 55	19 02	19 24	19 28	19 37	19 48	19 58	20 02	20 28		20 48	20 59	21 02	21 28	
Havant	a		18 09				18 54		19 09				19 54		20 09			20 54		21 09		
Chichester 4	a		18 21				19 08		19 21				20 08		20 21			21 08		21 21		
Hilsea	a	18 03		18 33				19 05		19 28	19 33			20 03		20 33			21 03		21 33	
Fratton	a	18 07		18 37	18 40	18 45		19 09		19 32	19 37	19 43		20 07		20 37	20 43		21 07		21 37	21 40
Portsmouth & Southsea	a	18 11		18 44	18 44	18 50		19 12		19 36	19 44	19 47		20 12		20 42	20 46		21 11		21 40	21 43
Portsmouth Harbour	a	18 20			18 50	18 54		19 20		19 43		19 51		20 20			20 50		21 18		21 44	21 49

		SN 1 B	SW ◇1 A	SN 1 F	SW 1	GW ◇ D	SN G	SW ◇1 A	SN 1 G	SW 1	GW ◇ D	SN H	SW ◇1 A
Southampton Central	d	21 13		21 32	21 44	22 07	22 21		22 33	22 44	23 08	23 12	
St Denys	d				21 49					22 49		23 22	
Bitterne	d				21 52					22 52			
Woolston	d				21 55					22 55			
Sholing	d				21 58					22 58			
Netley	d				22 02					23 02			
Hamble	d				22 04					23 04			
Bursledon	d				22 07					23 07			
Swanwick	d	21 33		21 52	22 11		22 40		22 51	23 11			
Fareham	a	21 39		21 59	22 17	22 43	22 46		22 57	23 17	23 31	23 38	
	d	21 40	21 49	22 00	22 18	22 44	22 47	22 51	22 57	23 18	23 32	23 38	23 49
Portchester	d	21 45	21 54	22 05	22 23		22 52	22 56		23 23			23 54
Cosham	d	21 49	21 59	22 09	22 28		22 56	23 01	23 06	23 28		23 47	23 59
Havant	a	21 55		22 15			23 03		23 12			23 53	
Chichester 4	a	22 06		22 35			23 17		23 22			00 05	
Hilsea	a		22 04		22 33			23 06		23 32			00 04
Fratton	a		22 08		22 37	22 57		23 10		23 37	23 45		00 08
Portsmouth & Southsea	a		22 11		22 44	23 00		23 16		23 44	23 48		00 11
Portsmouth Harbour	a		22 16			23 04		23 22			23 53		00 16

Saturdays
21 December to 16 May

		SW 1	SN 1 E	SW 1 I	SN 1 B	SW 1	GW J	SN 1 E	SW 1 K	SN 1 B	SW 1	GW ◇ L	SN 1 E	SW ◇1 A	SN 1 B	SW 1	GW ◇ D	SN 1 E	SW ◇1 A	SN 1 B	SW 1	GW ◇ D	SN 1 E
Southampton Central	d	05 44	06 13		06 25	06 44	07 06	07 13		07 28	07 44	08 02	08 13		08 28	08 44	09 05	09 13		09 28	09 44	10 05	10 13
St Denys	d	05 49				06 49					07 49					08 49					09 49		
Bitterne	d	05 52				06 52					07 52					08 52					09 52		
Woolston	d	05 55				06 55					07 55					08 55					09 55		
Sholing	d	05 58				06 58					07 58					08 58					09 58		
Netley	d	06 02				07 02					08 02					09 02					10 02		
Hamble	d	06 04				07 04					08 04					09 04					10 04		
Bursledon	d	06 07				07 07					08 07					09 07					10 07		
Swanwick	d	06 11	06 32		06 43	07 11		07 30		07 46	08 11		08 30		08 46	09 11		09 32		09 46	10 11		10 32
Fareham	a	06 20	06 38		06 49	07 17	07 27	07 36		07 52	08 17	08 24	08 36		08 53	09 17	09 27	09 38		09 52	10 17	10 27	10 38
	d	06 21	06 39	06 46	06 52	07 18	07 28	07 37	07 48	07 53	08 18	08 25	08 37	08 49	08 54	09 18	09 28	09 39	09 48	09 53	10 18	10 28	10 39
Portchester	d	06 26	06 44	06 51		07 23		07 42	07 53		08 23		08 42	08 54		09 23		09 44	09 53		10 23		10 44
Cosham	d	06 31	06 48	06 56	07 00	07 28	07 36	07 46	07 58	08 02	08 28	08 33	08 46	08 59	09 03	09 28	09 36	09 48	09 58	10 02	10 28	10 36	10 48
Havant	a		06 54		07 10			07 52		08 09			08 52		09 09			09 54		10 09			10 54
Chichester 4	a		07 08		07 23			08 06		08 21			09 06		09 21			10 08		10 21			11 08
Hilsea	a	06 37		07 03		07 33			08 03		08 33			09 04		09 33			10 03		10 33		
Fratton	a	06 42		07 07		07 37	07 42		08 07		08 37	08 40		09 08		09 37	09 43		10 07		10 37	10 42	
Portsmouth & Southsea	a	06 46		07 11		07 42	07 46		08 11		08 42	08 45		09 12		09 42	09 46		10 11		10 42	10 46	
Portsmouth Harbour	a			07 16			07 50		08 18			08 49		09 18			09 51		10 18			10 50	

A From London Waterloo
B To Brighton
C From Brockenhurst
D From Cardiff Central
E To London Victoria
F To Gatwick Airport
G To Littlehampton
H To Barnham
I From Eastleigh
J From Westbury
K From Woking
L From Bristol Temple Meads

Table T165-R

Saturdays
21 December to 16 May

Southampton and Fareham - Chichester and Portsmouth

		SW ◇1 A	SN 1 B	SW 1	GW ◇ C	SN 1 D	SW ◇1 A	SN 1 B	SW 1	GW ◇ C 🛒	SN 1 D	SW ◇1 A	SN 1 B	SW 1	GW ◇ C 🛒	SN 1 D	SW ◇1 A	SN 1 B	SW 1	GW ◇ C 🛒	SN 1 D	SW ◇1 A
Southampton Central	d		10 28	10 44	11 05	11 13		11 28	11 44	12 05	12 13		12 28	12 44	13 05	13 13		13 28	13 44	14 05	14 13	
St Denys	d			10 49					11 49					12 49					13 49			
Bitterne	d			10 52					11 52					12 52					13 52			
Woolston	d			10 55					11 55					12 55					13 55			
Sholing	d			10 58					11 58					12 58					13 58			
Netley	d			11 02					12 02					13 02					14 02			
Hamble	d			11 04					12 04					13 04					14 04			
Bursledon	d			11 07					12 07					13 07					14 07			
Swanwick	d		10 46	11 11		11 32		11 46	12 11		12 32		12 46	13 11		13 32		13 46	14 11		14 32	
Fareham	a		10 52	11 17	11 27	11 38		11 52	12 17	12 27	12 38		12 52	13 17	13 27	13 38		13 52	14 17	14 27	14 38	
	d	10 48	10 53	11 18	11 28	11 39	11 48	11 53	12 18	12 28	12 39	12 48	12 53	13 18	13 28	13 39	13 48	13 53	14 18	14 28	14 39	14 48
Portchester	d	10 53		11 23		11 44	11 53		12 23		12 44	12 53		13 23		13 44	13 53		14 23		14 44	14 53
Cosham	d	10 58	11 02	11 28	11 36	11 48	11 58	12 02	12 28	12 36	12 48	12 58	13 02	13 28	13 36	13 48	13 58	14 02	14 28	14 36	14 48	14 58
Havant	a		11 09			11 54		12 09			12 54		13 09			13 54		14 09			14 54	
Chichester 4	a		11 21			12 08		12 21			13 08		13 21			14 08		14 21			15 08	
Hilsea	a	11 03		11 33			12 03		12 33			13 03		13 33			14 03		14 33			15 03
Fratton	a	11 07		11 37	11 42		12 07		12 37	12 42		13 07		13 37	13 42		14 07		14 37	14 42		15 07
Portsmouth & Southsea	a	11 11		11 42	11 46		12 11		12 42	12 46		13 11		13 42	13 46		14 11		14 42	14 46		15 11
Portsmouth Harbour	a	11 18			11 50		12 18			12 50		13 18			13 50		14 18			14 50		15 18

		SN 1 B	GW ◇ E	SN 1 F	SW 1	GW ◇ C 🛒	SN 1 D	SW ◇1 A	SN 1 B	SW 1	GW ◇ C	SN 1 D	SW ◇1 A	SN 1 B	SW 1	GW ◇ C	SN 1 D	SW ◇1 A	SN 1 B	SW 1	GW ◇ C	SN 1 D	SW ◇1 A
Southampton Central	d	14 26	14 34		14 44	15 05	15 13		15 28	15 43	16 05	16 13		16 28	16 44	17 05	17 13		17 28	17 44	18 05	18 13	
St Denys	d				14 49					15 49					16 49					17 49			
Bitterne	d				14 52					15 52					16 52					17 52			
Woolston	d				14 55					15 55					16 55					17 55			
Sholing	d				14 58					15 58					16 58					17 58			
Netley	d				15 02					16 02					17 02					18 02			
Hamble	d				15 04					16 04					17 04					18 04			
Bursledon	d				15 07					16 07					17 07					18 07			
Swanwick	d			←	15 11		15 32		15 46	16 11		16 32		16 46	17 11		17 32		17 46	18 11		18 32	
Fareham	a	15 00	14 55	15 00	15 17	15 27	15 38		15 52	16 17	16 27	16 38		16 52	17 17	17 27	17 38		17 52	18 17	18 27	18 38	
	d	15 00	14 56	15 00	15 18	15 28	15 39	15 48	15 53	16 18	16 28	16 39	16 48	16 53	17 18	17 28	17 39	17 48	17 53	18 18	18 28	18 39	18 48
Portchester	d	→			15 23		15 44	15 53		16 23		16 44	16 53		17 23		17 44	17 53		18 23		18 44	18 53
Cosham	d		15 04		15 28	15 36	15 48	15 58	16 02	16 28	16 36	16 48	16 58	17 02	17 28	17 36	17 48	17 58	18 02	18 28	18 36	18 48	18 58
Havant	a		15 10	15 13			15 54		16 09			16 54		17 09			17 54		18 09			18 54	
Chichester 4	a		15 21	15 24			16 08		16 21			17 08		17 21			18 08		18 21			19 08	
Hilsea	a				15 33			16 03		16 33			17 03		17 33			18 03		18 33			19 03
Fratton	a				15 37	15 42		16 07		16 37	16 42		17 07		17 37	17 42		18 07		18 37	18 42		19 07
Portsmouth & Southsea	a				15 42	15 46		16 11		16 40	16 46		17 11		17 42	17 46		18 11		18 42	18 46		19 11
Portsmouth Harbour	a					15 50		16 18		16 44	16 50		17 18			17 50		18 18			18 50		19 18

		SN 1 B	SW 1	GW ◇ C	SN 1 D	SW ◇1 A	SN 1 B	SW 1	GW ◇ C	SN 1 D	SW ◇1 A	SN 1 B	SW 1	GW ◇ C	SN 1 B	SW ◇1 A	SN 1 G	SW 1	GW ◇ C	SN H	SW ◇1 A	SN 1 H
Southampton Central	d	18 28	18 44	19 05	19 13		19 28	19 44	20 05	20 13		20 28	20 44	21 05	21 13		21 32	21 44	22 05	22 21		22 26
St Denys	d		18 49					19 49					20 49					21 49				
Bitterne	d		18 52					19 52					20 52					21 52				
Woolston	d		18 55					19 55					20 55					21 55				
Sholing	d		18 58					19 58					20 58					21 58				
Netley	d		19 02					20 02					21 02					22 02				
Hamble	d		19 04					20 04					21 04					22 04				
Bursledon	d		19 07					20 07					21 07					22 07				
Swanwick	d	18 46	19 11		19 32		19 46	20 11		20 32		20 46	21 11		21 33		21 51	22 11		22 38		22 46
Fareham	a	18 52	19 17	19 27	19 38		19 52	20 17	20 27	20 38		20 52	21 17	21 27	21 39		21 57	22 17	22 26	22 44		22 53
	d	18 53	19 18	19 28	19 39	19 48	19 53	20 18	20 28	20 39	20 48	20 53	21 18	21 28	21 40	21 48	21 58	22 18	22 27	22 45	22 50	22 54
Portchester	d		19 23		19 44	19 53		20 23		20 44	20 53		21 23		21 45	21 53	22 03	22 23		22 50	22 55	
Cosham	d	19 02	19 28	19 36	19 48	19 58	20 02	20 28		20 48	20 58	21 02	21 28		21 49	21 58	22 07	22 28		22 55	23 00	23 03
Havant	a	19 09			19 54		20 09			20 54		21 09			21 55		22 13			23 04		23 09
Chichester 4	a	19 21			20 08		20 21			21 08		21 21			22 06		22 33			23 18		23 21
Hilsea	a		19 33			20 03		20 33			21 03		21 33			22 03		22 33			23 04	
Fratton	a		19 37	19 42		20 07		20 37	20 42		21 07		21 37	21 42		22 07		22 37	22 41		23 09	
Portsmouth & Southsea	a		19 42	19 46		20 11		20 42	20 45		21 10		21 40	21 46		22 11		22 40	22 45		23 13	
Portsmouth Harbour	a			19 50		20 18			20 49		21 16		21 45	21 50		22 18		22 45	22 50		23 18	

		SW 1	GW ◇ C	SN H	SW ◇1 A
Southampton Central	d	22 44	23 06	23 16	
St Denys	d	22 49		23 22	
Bitterne	d	22 52			
Woolston	d	22 55			
Sholing	d	22 58			
Netley	d	23 02			
Hamble	d	23 04			
Bursledon	d	23 07			
Swanwick	d	23 11			
Fareham	a	23 17	23 27	23 38	
	d	23 18	23 28	23 38	23 48
Portchester	d	23 23			23 53
Cosham	d	23 28		23 47	23 58
Havant	a			23 53	
Chichester 4	a			00 05	
Hilsea	a	23 33			00 03
Fratton	a	23 37	23 41		00 07
Portsmouth & Southsea	a	23 40	23 45		00 10
Portsmouth Harbour	a		23 49		00 15

A From London Waterloo
B To Brighton
C From Cardiff Central
D To London Victoria
E From Great Malvern to Brighton
F From Southampton Central to Brighton
G To Gatwick Airport
H To Littlehampton

Table T165-R

Sundays

15 December to 10 May

Southampton and Fareham - Chichester and Portsmouth

		SW ■	SW ■	SN ■ A	SW ■	SW ◇■ B	SN ■ A	GW C	SW ■	SW ■ D		SN ■ A	SW ■	SW ■ D	SN ■ A	SW ■	GW ◇ E	SW ■ D	SN ■ A	SW ■		GW ◇ E	SW ■ D	SN ■ A	SW ■
Southampton Central	d	06 35		07 30	07 35		08 21	08 31	08 35			09 30	09 35		10 30	10 35	11 04		11 30	11 35		12 04		12 30	12 35
St Denys	d	06 41			07 41				08 41				09 41			10 41				11 41					12 41
Bitterne	d	06 43			07 43				08 43				09 43			10 43				11 43					12 43
Woolston	d	06 47			07 47				08 47				09 47			10 47				11 47					12 47
Sholing	d	06 49			07 49				08 49				09 49			10 49				11 49					12 49
Netley	d	06 53			07 53				08 53				09 53			10 53				11 53					12 53
Hamble	d	06 55			07 55				08 55				09 55			10 55				11 55					12 55
Bursledon	d	06 58			07 58				08 58				09 58			10 58				11 58					12 58
Swanwick	d	07 02		07 47	08 02		08 40		09 02			09 47	10 02		10 47	11 02			11 47	12 02				12 47	13 02
Fareham	a	07 09		07 53	08 09		08 46	08 53	09 09			09 53	10 09		10 53	11 09	11 26		11 53	12 09		12 26		12 53	13 09
	d	07 10	07 44	07 54	08 10	08 42	08 47	08 54	09 10	09 45		09 54	10 10	10 45	10 54	11 10	11 26	11 45	11 54	12 10		12 26	12 45	12 54	13 10
Portchester	d	07 15	07 49		08 15	08 47			09 15	09 50			10 15	10 50		11 15		11 50		12 15			12 50		13 15
Cosham	d	07 20	07 54	08 03	08 20	08 52	08 56	09 02	09 20	09 55		10 03	10 20	10 55	11 03	11 20	11 34	11 55	12 03	12 20		12 34	12 55	13 03	13 20
Havant	a			08 10			09 02	09 13				10 10			11 10				12 10					13 10	
Chichester ■	a			08 22			09 14	09 24				10 22			11 22				12 22					13 22	
Hilsea	a	07 24	08 00		08 26	09 00			09 30	10 00			10 24	11 00		11 24		12 00		12 25			13 00		13 25
Fratton	a	07 28	08 04		08 30	09 04			09 34	10 09			10 28	11 09		11 28	11 40	12 09		12 33		12 40	13 09		13 29
Portsmouth & Southsea	a	07 32	08 07		08 33	09 08			09 37	10 13			10 32	11 13		11 32	11 44	12 13		12 37		12 44	13 13		13 33
Portsmouth Harbour	a		08 11			09 20				10 20				11 20			11 51	12 20				12 51	13 20		

		GW ◇ F	SW ■ D	SN ■ A	SW ■	GW ◇ E		SW ■ D	SN ■ A	SW ■	GW ◇ F	SW ■ D	SN ■ A	SW ■	GW ◇ E	SW ■ D		SN ■ A	SW ■	GW ◇ E	SW ◇■ D	SN ■ A	SW ■	GW ◇ E	SW ◇■ D
Southampton Central	d	13 04		13 30	13 35	14 04			14 30	14 35	15 06		15 30	15 35	16 05			16 30	16 35	17 04		17 30	17 35	18 04	
St Denys	d				13 41					14 41				15 41					16 41				17 41		
Bitterne	d				13 43					14 43				15 43					16 43				17 43		
Woolston	d				13 47					14 47				15 47					16 47				17 47		
Sholing	d				13 49					14 49				15 49					16 49				17 49		
Netley	d				13 53					14 53				15 53					16 53				17 53		
Hamble	d				13 55					14 55				15 55					16 55				17 55		
Bursledon	d				13 58					14 58				15 58					16 58				17 58		
Swanwick	d			13 47	14 02				14 47	15 02			15 47	16 02				16 47	17 02			17 47	18 02		
Fareham	a	13 29		13 53	14 09	14 26			14 53	15 09	15 27		15 53	16 09	16 27			16 53	17 09	17 26		17 53	18 09	18 26	
	d	13 30	13 45	13 54	14 10	14 26		14 45	14 54	15 10	15 28	15 45	15 54	16 10	16 27	16 45		16 54	17 10	17 26	17 45	17 54	18 10	18 26	18 45
Portchester	d		13 50		14 15			14 50		15 15		15 50		16 15		16 50			17 15		17 50		18 15		18 50
Cosham	d	13 38	13 55	14 03	14 20	14 34		14 55	15 03	15 20	15 36	15 55	16 03	16 20	16 35	16 55		17 03	17 20	17 34	17 55	18 03	18 20	18 34	18 55
Havant	a	13 45		14 10					15 10		15 42		16 10					17 10				18 10			
Chichester ■	a	13 57		14 22					15 22		15 57		16 22					17 22				18 22			
Hilsea	a		14 00		14 26			15 00		15 26		16 00		16 26		16 59			17 26		18 00		18 26		19 00
Fratton	a		14 09		14 30	14 40		15 09		15 30		16 09		16 30	16 40	17 08			17 30	17 40	18 09		18 30	18 40	19 09
Portsmouth & Southsea	a		14 13		14 33	14 44		15 13		15 33		16 13		16 33	16 45	17 13			17 33	17 44	18 13		18 33	18 44	19 13
Portsmouth Harbour	a		14 20			14 51		15 20				16 20			16 51	17 20				17 51	18 20			18 53	19 20

		SN ■ A		SW ■	GW ◇ E	SW ◇■ D	SN ■ A	GW ◇ F	SW ■	GW ◇ E	SW ◇■ D	SN ■ A		GW ◇ E	SW ■	GW ◇ E	SW ◇■ D	SN ■ A	SW ■	GW ◇ E	SW ◇■ D	SN G		SW ■	SN G
Southampton Central	d	18 30		18 35	19 04		19 23	19 28	19 35	20 04		20 28		20 33	20 35	21 04		21 30	21 35	22 03		22 30		22 35	22 58
St Denys	d			18 41					19 41						20 41				21 41					22 41	
Bitterne	d			18 43					19 43						20 43				21 43					22 43	
Woolston	d			18 47					19 47						20 47				21 47					22 47	
Sholing	d			18 49					19 49						20 49				21 49					22 49	
Netley	d			18 53					19 53						20 53				21 53					22 53	
Hamble	d			18 55					19 55						20 55				21 55					22 55	
Bursledon	d			18 58					19 58						20 58				21 58					22 58	
Swanwick	d	18 47		19 02			19 41		20 02			20 46			21 02			21 47	22 02			22 47		23 02	23 15
Fareham	a	18 53		19 09	19 24		19 48	19 53	20 09	20 24		20 52		20 58	21 09	21 24		21 53	22 09	22 26		22 53		23 09	23 21
	d	18 54		19 10	19 26	19 45	19 49	19 54	20 10	20 26	20 45	20 53		20 59	21 10	21 26	21 45	21 54	22 10	22 27	22 45	22 54		23 10	23 22
Portchester	d			19 15		19 50			20 15		20 50				21 15		21 50		22 15		22 50			23 15	
Cosham	d	19 03		19 20	19 34	19 55	19 57	20 02	20 20		20 55	21 03			21 20		21 55	22 03	22 20		22 55	23 04		23 20	23 31
Havant	a	19 10					20 03	20 10				21 10						22 10				23 11			23 38
Chichester ■	a	19 22					20 15	20 21				21 22						22 22				23 22			23 50
Hilsea	a			19 26		20 00			20 25		21 00				21 25		22 00		22 26		23 00			23 28	
Fratton	a			19 30	19 40	20 09			20 29	20 40	21 09			21 12	21 29	21 40	22 09		22 30	22 39	23 08			23 32	
Portsmouth & Southsea	a			19 33	19 44	20 13			20 33	20 44	21 13			21 17	21 33	21 43	22 13		22 33	22 44	23 11			23 36	
Portsmouth Harbour	a				19 51	20 20				20 50	21 20			21 22		21 48	22 20			22 51	23 15				

		GW ◇ E	SW ◇■ D H
Southampton Central	d	23 08	
St Denys	d		
Bitterne	d		
Woolston	d		
Sholing	d		
Netley	d		
Hamble	d		
Bursledon	d		
Swanwick	d		
Fareham	a	23 29	
	d	23 30	23 45
Portchester	d		23 50
Cosham	d		23 55
Havant	a		
Chichester ■	a		
Hilsea	a		00 02
Fratton	a	23 43	00 07
Portsmouth & Southsea	a	23 46	00 10
Portsmouth Harbour	a	23 50	00 14

A To Brighton
B From Basingstoke
C From Romsey to Brighton
D From London Waterloo
E From Cardiff Central
F From Cardiff Central to Brighton
G To Littlehampton

Table T167-F

Mondays to Fridays

16 December to 15 May

Ryde - Shanklin (Isle of Wight)

Miles			IL	IL	IL	IL	IL	IL	IL	IL	IL		IL	IL	IL	IL	IL	IL	IL	IL	IL		IL	IL	IL
0	**Ryde Pier Head**	d	05 49	06 07	06 49	07 07	07 49	08 07	08 49	09 07	09 49		10 07	10 49	11 07	11 49	12 07	12 49	13 07	13 49	14 07		14 49	15 07	15 49
0½	**Ryde Esplanade**	d	05 51	06 09	06 52	07 09	07 52	08 09	08 52	09 09	09 52		10 09	10 52	11 09	11 52	12 09	12 52	13 09	13 52	14 09		14 52	15 09	15 52
1¼	Ryde St Johns Road	d	05 55	06 13	06 55	07 13	07 55	08 13	08 55	09 13	09 55		10 13	10 55	11 13	11 55	12 13	12 55	13 13	13 55	14 13		14 55	15 13	15 55
2¼	Smallbrook Junction §	d												10 58		11 58	12 15	12 58	13 15				14 58	15 15	15 58
4¾	Brading	d	06 02	06 20	07 03	07 20	08 03	08 20	09 03	09 20	10 03		10 20	11 03	11 20	12 03	12 20	13 03	13 20	14 03	14 20		15 03	15 20	16 03
6½	Sandown	d	06 07	06 25	07 07	07 25	08 07	08 25	09 07	09 25	10 07		10 25	11 07	11 25	12 07	12 25	13 07	13 25	14 07	14 25		15 07	15 25	16 07
7¼	Lake	d	06 09	06 27	07 10	07 27	08 10	08 27	09 10	09 27	10 10		10 27	11 10	11 27	12 10	12 27	13 10	13 27	14 10	14 27		15 10	15 27	16 10
8½	**Shanklin**	a	06 12	06 30	07 13	07 30	08 13	08 30	09 13	09 30	10 13		10 30	11 13	11 30	12 13	12 30	13 13	13 30	14 13	14 30		15 13	15 30	16 13

		IL	IL	IL	IL	IL	IL		IL	IL	IL	IL	IL	IL
Ryde Pier Head	d	16 07	16 49	17 07	17 49	18 07	18 49		19 07	19 49	20 07	20 49	21 49	23 15
Ryde Esplanade	d	16 09	16 52	17 09	17 52	18 09	18 52		19 09	19 52	20 09	20 51	21 51	23 17
Ryde St Johns Road	d	16 13	16 55	17 13	17 55	18 13	18 55		19 13	19 55	20 13	20 55	21 55	23a21
Smallbrook Junction §	d	16 15												
Brading	d	16 20	17 03	17 20	18 03	18 20	19 03		19 20	20 03	20 20	21 01	22 01	
Sandown	d	16 25	17 07	17 25	18 07	18 25	19 07		19 25	20 07	20 25	21 05	22 05	
Lake	d	16 27	17 10	17 27	18 10	18 27	19 10		19 27	20 10	20 27	21 08	22 08	
Shanklin	a	16 30	17 13	17 30	18 13	18 30	19 13		19 30	20 13	20 30	21 11	22 11	

Saturdays

21 December to 16 May

		IL	IL	IL	IL	IL	IL	IL	IL	IL		IL	IL	IL	IL	IL	IL	IL	IL	IL		IL	IL	IL	IL
Ryde Pier Head	d	05 49	06 07	06 49	07 07	07 49	08 07	08 49	09 07	09 49		10 07	10 49	11 07	11 49	12 07	12 49	13 07	13 49	14 07		14 49	15 07	15 49	16 07
Ryde Esplanade	d	05 51	06 09	06 52	07 09	07 52	08 09	08 52	09 09	09 52		10 09	10 52	11 09	11 52	12 09	12 52	13 09	13 52	14 09		14 52	15 09	15 52	16 09
Ryde St Johns Road	d	05 55	06 13	06 55	07 13	07 55	08 13	08 55	09 13	09 55		10 13	10 55	11 13	11 55	12 13	12 55	13 13	13 55	14 13		14 55	15 13	15 55	16 13
Smallbrook Junction §	d												10 58		11 58	12 15	12 58	13 15				14 58	15 15	15 58	16 15
Brading	d	06 02	06 20	07 03	07 20	08 03	08 20	09 03	09 20	10 03		10 20	11 03	11 20	12 03	12 20	13 03	13 20	14 03	14 20		15 03	15 20	16 03	16 20
Sandown	d	06 07	06 25	07 07	07 25	08 07	08 25	09 07	09 25	10 07		10 25	11 07	11 25	12 07	12 25	13 07	13 25	14 07	14 25		15 07	15 25	16 07	16 25
Lake	d	06 09	06 27	07 10	07 27	08 10	08 27	09 10	09 27	10 10		10 27	11 10	11 27	12 10	12 27	13 10	13 27	14 10	14 27		15 10	15 27	16 10	16 27
Shanklin	a	06 12	06 30	07 13	07 30	08 13	08 30	09 13	09 30	10 13		10 30	11 13	11 30	12 13	12 30	13 13	13 30	14 13	14 30		15 13	15 30	16 13	16 30

		IL	IL	IL	IL	IL		IL	IL	IL	IL	IL	IL
Ryde Pier Head	d	16 49	17 07	17 49	18 07	18 49		19 07	19 49	20 07	20 49	21 49	23 15
Ryde Esplanade	d	16 52	17 09	17 52	18 09	18 52		19 09	19 52	20 09	20 51	21 51	23 17
Ryde St Johns Road	d	16 55	17 13	17 55	18 13	18 55		19 13	19 55	20 13	20 55	21 55	23a21
Smallbrook Junction §	d												
Brading	d	17 03	17 20	18 03	18 20	19 03		19 20	20 03	20 20	21 01	22 01	
Sandown	d	17 07	17 25	18 07	18 25	19 07		19 25	20 07	20 25	21 05	22 05	
Lake	d	17 10	17 27	18 10	18 27	19 10		19 27	20 10	20 27	21 08	22 08	
Shanklin	a	17 13	17 30	18 13	18 30	19 13		19 30	20 13	20 30	21 11	22 11	

Sundays

15 December to 10 May

		IL	IL	IL	IL	IL	IL	IL	IL	IL		IL	IL	IL	IL	IL	IL	IL	IL	IL		IL	IL	IL	IL
Ryde Pier Head	d	06 49	07 49		08 49	09 07	09 49	10 07	10 49	11 07		11 49	12 07	12 49	13 07	13 49	14 07	14 49	15 07	15 49		16 07	16 49	17 07	17 49
Ryde Esplanade	d	06 52	07 52		08 52	09 09	09 52	10 09	10 52	11 09		11 52	12 09	12 52	13 09	13 52	14 09	14 52	15 09	15 52		16 09	16 52	17 09	17 52
Ryde St Johns Road	d	06 55	07 55	08 13	08 55	09 13	09 55	10 13	10 55	11 13		11 55	12 13	12 55	13 13	13 55	14 13	14 55	15 13	15 55		16 13	16 55	17 13	17 55
Smallbrook Junction §	d								10 58			11 58	12 15	12 58	13 15			14 58	15 15	15 58		16 15			
Brading	d	07 03	08 03	08 20	09 03	09 20	10 03	10 20	11 03	11 20		12 03	12 20	13 03	13 20	14 03	14 20	15 03	15 20	16 03		16 20	17 03	17 20	18 03
Sandown	d	07 07	08 07	08 25	09 07	09 25	10 07	10 25	11 07	11 25		12 07	12 25	13 07	13 25	14 07	14 25	15 07	15 25	16 07		16 25	17 07	17 25	18 07
Lake	d	07 10	08 10	08 27	09 10	09 27	10 10	10 27	11 10	11 27		12 10	12 27	13 10	13 27	14 10	14 27	15 10	15 27	16 10		16 27	17 10	17 27	18 10
Shanklin	a	07 13	08 13	08 30	09 13	09 30	10 13	10 30	11 13	11 30		12 13	12 30	13 13	13 30	14 13	14 30	15 13	15 30	16 13		16 30	17 13	17 30	18 13

		IL	IL	IL	IL	IL		IL	IL	IL
Ryde Pier Head	d	18 07	18 49	19 07	19 49	20 07		20 49	21 49	23 15
Ryde Esplanade	d	18 09	18 52	19 09	19 52	20 09		20 51	21 51	23 17
Ryde St Johns Road	d	18 13	18 55	19 13	19 55	20a13		20 55	21 55	23a21
Smallbrook Junction §	d									
Brading	d	18 20	19 03	19 20	20 03			21 01	22 01	
Sandown	d	18 25	19 07	19 25	20 07			21 05	22 05	
Lake	d	18 27	19 10	19 27	20 10			21 08	22 08	
Shanklin	a	18 30	19 13	19 30	20 13			21 11	22 11	

§ Smallbrook Jn. is only open for access to the I.O.W Steam Railway. For days of operation please enquire locally.

Table T167-R

Mondays to Fridays

16 December to 15 May

Shanklin - Ryde (Isle of Wight)

Miles			IL	IL	IL	IL	IL	IL	IL	IL	IL	IL	IL	IL	IL	IL	IL	IL	IL	IL	IL	IL	IL
0	**Shanklin**	d			06 18	06 38	07 18	07 38	08 18	08 38	09 18	09 38	10 18	10 38	11 18	11 38	12 18	12 38	13 18	13 38	14 18	14 38	15 18
1¾	Lake	d			06 21	06 41	07 21	07 41	08 21	08 41	09 21	09 41	10 21	10 41	11 21	11 41	12 21	12 41	13 21	13 41	14 21	14 41	15 21
2	Sandown	d			06 24	06 44	07 24	07 44	08 24	08 44	09 24	09 44	10 24	10 44	11 24	11 44	12 24	12 44	13 24	13 44	14 24	14 44	15 24
3¾	Brading	d			06 28	06 48	07 28	07 48	08 28	08 48	09 28	09 48	10 28	10 48	11 28	11 48	12 28	12 48	13 28	13 48	14 28	14 48	15 28
6¼	Smallbrook Junction §	d												10 53		11 53	12 33	12 53	13 33			14 53	15 33
7¼	Ryde St Johns Road	d	05 35	05 56	06 35	06 55	07 35	07 55	08 35	08 55	09 35	09 55	10 35	10 55	11 35	11 55	12 35	12 55	13 35	13 55	14 35	14 55	15 35
8¼	**Ryde Esplanade**	d	05 40	06 00	06 40	07 00	07 40	08 00	08 40	09 00	09 40	10 00	10 40	11 00	11 40	12 00	12 40	13 00	13 40	14 00	14 40	15 00	15 40
8½	**Ryde Pier Head**	a	05 42	06 02	06 42	07 02	07 42	08 02	08 42	09 02	09 42	10 02	10 42	11 02	11 42	12 02	12 42	13 02	13 42	14 02	14 42	15 02	15 42

		IL	IL	IL	IL	IL	IL	IL	IL	IL	IL	IL	IL	IL
Shanklin	d	15 38	16 18	16 38	17 18	17 38	18 18	18 38	19 18	19 38	20 18	20 38	21 18	22 38
Lake	d	15 41	16 21	16 41	17 21	17 41	18 21	18 41	19 21	19 41	20 21	20 41	21 21	22 41
Sandown	d	15 44	16 24	16 44	17 24	17 44	18 24	18 44	19 24	19 44	20 24	20 44	21 24	22 44
Brading	d	15 48	16 28	16 48	17 28	17 48	18 28	18 48	19 28	19 48	20 28	20 48	21 28	22 48
Smallbrook Junction §	d	15 53	16 33											
Ryde St Johns Road	d	15 55	16 35	16 55	17 35	17 55	18 35	18 55	19 35	19 55	20 34	20a54	21 34	22 54
Ryde Esplanade	d	16 00	16 40	17 00	17 40	18 00	18 40	19 00	19 40	20 00	20 38		21 38	22 58
Ryde Pier Head	a	16 02	16 42	17 02	17 42	18 02	18 42	19 02	19 42	20 02	20 41		21 41	23 00

Saturdays

21 December to 16 May

		IL	IL	IL	IL	IL	IL	IL	IL	IL	IL	IL	IL	IL	IL	IL	IL	IL	IL	IL	IL	IL	IL
Shanklin	d			06 18	06 38	07 18	07 38	08 18	08 38	09 18	09 38	10 18	10 38	11 18	11 38	12 18	12 38	13 18	13 38	14 18	14 38	15 18	15 38
Lake	d			06 21	06 41	07 21	07 41	08 21	08 41	09 21	09 41	10 21	10 41	11 21	11 41	12 21	12 41	13 21	13 41	14 21	14 41	15 21	15 41
Sandown	d			06 24	06 44	07 24	07 44	08 24	08 44	09 24	09 44	10 24	10 44	11 24	11 44	12 24	12 44	13 24	13 44	14 24	14 44	15 24	15 44
Brading	d			06 28	06 48	07 28	07 48	08 28	08 48	09 28	09 48	10 28	10 48	11 28	11 48	12 28	12 48	13 28	13 48	14 28	14 48	15 28	15 48
Smallbrook Junction §	d												10 53		11 53	12 33	12 53	13 33			14 53	15 33	15 53
Ryde St Johns Road	d	05 35	05 56	06 35	06 55	07 35	07 55	08 35	08 55	09 35	09 55	10 35	10 55	11 35	11 55	12 35	12 55	13 35	13 55	14 35	14 55	15 35	15 55
Ryde Esplanade	d	05 40	06 00	06 40	07 00	07 40	08 00	08 40	09 00	09 40	10 00	10 40	11 00	11 40	12 00	12 40	13 00	13 40	14 00	14 40	15 00	15 40	16 00
Ryde Pier Head	a	05 42	06 02	06 42	07 02	07 42	08 02	08 42	09 02	09 42	10 02	10 42	11 02	11 42	12 02	12 42	13 02	13 42	14 02	14 42	15 02	15 42	16 02

		IL	IL	IL	IL	IL	IL	IL	IL	IL	IL	IL	IL
Shanklin	d	16 18	16 38	17 18	17 38	18 18	18 38	19 18	19 38	20 18	20 38	21 18	22 38
Lake	d	16 21	16 41	17 21	17 41	18 21	18 41	19 21	19 41	20 21	20 41	21 21	22 41
Sandown	d	16 24	16 44	17 24	17 44	18 24	18 44	19 24	19 44	20 24	20 44	21 24	22 44
Brading	d	16 28	16 48	17 28	17 48	18 28	18 48	19 28	19 48	20 28	20 48	21 28	22 48
Smallbrook Junction §	d	16 33											
Ryde St Johns Road	d	16 35	16 55	17 35	17 55	18 35	18 55	19 35	19 55	20 34	20a54	21 34	22 54
Ryde Esplanade	d	16 40	17 00	17 40	18 00	18 40	19 00	19 40	20 00	20 38		21 38	22 58
Ryde Pier Head	a	16 42	17 02	17 42	18 02	18 42	19 02	19 42	20 02	20 41		21 41	23 00

Sundays

15 December to 10 May

		IL	IL	IL	IL	IL	IL	IL	IL	IL	IL	IL	IL	IL	IL	IL	IL	IL	IL	IL	IL	IL	IL
Shanklin	d		07 18	08 18	08 38	09 18	09 38	10 18	10 38	11 18	11 38	12 18	12 38	13 18	13 38	14 18	14 38	15 18	15 38	16 18	16 38	17 18	17 38
Lake	d		07 21	08 21	08 41	09 21	09 41	10 21	10 41	11 21	11 41	12 21	12 41	13 21	13 41	14 21	14 41	15 21	15 41	16 21	16 41	17 21	17 41
Sandown	d		07 24	08 24	08 44	09 24	09 44	10 24	10 44	11 24	11 44	12 24	12 44	13 24	13 44	14 24	14 44	15 24	15 44	16 24	16 44	17 24	17 44
Brading	d		07 28	08 28	08 48	09 28	09 48	10 28	10 48	11 28	11 48	12 28	12 48	13 28	13 48	14 28	14 48	15 28	15 48	16 28	16 48	17 28	17 48
Smallbrook Junction §	d								10 53		11 53	12 33	12 53	13 33			14 53	15 33	15 53	16 33			
Ryde St Johns Road	d	06 35	07 35	08 35	08 55	09 35	09 55	10 35	10 55	11 35	11 55	12 35	12 55	13 35	13 55	14 35	14 55	15 35	15 55	16 35	16 55	17 35	17 55
Ryde Esplanade	d	06 40	07 40	08 40	09 00	09 40	10 00	10 40	11 00	11 40	12 00	12 40	13 00	13 40	14 00	14 40	15 00	15 40	16 00	16 40	17 00	17 40	18 00
Ryde Pier Head	a	06 42	07 42	08 42	09 02	09 42	10 02	10 42	11 02	11 42	12 02	12 42	13 02	13 42	14 02	14 42	15 02	15 42	16 02	16 42	17 02	17 42	18 02

		IL	IL	IL	IL	IL	IL	IL
Shanklin	d	18 18	18 38	19 18	19 38	20 18	21 18	22 38
Lake	d	18 21	18 41	19 21	19 41	20 21	21 21	22 41
Sandown	d	18 24	18 44	19 24	19 44	20 24	21 24	22 44
Brading	d	18 28	18 48	19 28	19 48	20 28	21 28	22 48
Smallbrook Junction §	d							
Ryde St Johns Road	d	18 35	18 55	19 35	19 55	20 34	21 34	22 54
Ryde Esplanade	d	18 40	19 00	19 40	20 00	20 38	21 38	22 58
Ryde Pier Head	a	18 42	19 02	19 42	20 02	20 41	21 41	23 00

§ Smallbrook Jn. is only open for access to the I.O.W Steam Railway. For days of operation please enquire locally.

Table T167A

Reproduced courtesy of *European Rail Timetable Ltd.*

PORTSMOUTH - RYDE - SHANKLIN

2nd class IL

Through fares including ferry travel are available. Allow 10 minutes for connections between trains and ferries. Operator: Wightlink ✆ 0333 999 7333. www.wightlink.co.uk

Portsmouth Harbour - Ryde Pierhead: 0515Ⓐ, 0615⚒, 0715 and hourly until 1815, 1920, 2020, 2120, 2245.

Ryde Pierhead - Portsmouth Harbour. Journey time: ± 22 minutes. 0547Ⓐ, 0647⚒, 0747 and hourly until 2147, 2310.

Additional services operate on Ⓐ and on public holidays.

Ryde Pierhead - Shanklin: Trains call at **Sandown** 18 minutes later. *14 km*

⚒: 0549, 0607, 0649, 0707, 0749, 0807, 0849, 0907, 0949, 1007, 1049*, 1107, 1149*, 1207*, 1249*, 1307*, 1349, 1407, 1449*, 1507*, 1549*, 1607*, 1649, 1707, 1749, 1807, 1849, 1907, 1949, 2007, 2049, 2149.

⑦: 0649, 0749, 0849, 0907, 0949, 1007, 1049*, 1107, 1149*, 1207, 1249*, 1307*, 1349, 1407, 1449*, 1507*, 1549*, 1607*, 1649, 1707, 1749, 1807, 1849, 1907, 1949, 2049, 2149.

Shanklin - Ryde Pierhead: Trains call at **Sandown** 6 minutes later. Journey time: ± 24 minutes

⚒: 0618, 0638, 0718, 0738, 0818, 0838, 0918, 0938, 1018, 1038*, 1118, 1138*, 1218*, 1238*, 1318*, 1338, 1418, 1438*, 1518*, 1538*, 1618*, 1638, 1718, 1738, 1818, 1838, 1918, 1938, 2018, 2118, 2238.

⑦: 0718, 0818, 0838, 0918, 0938, 1018, 1038, 1118, 1138, 1218*, 1318*, 1338, 1418, 1438*, 1518*, 1538*, 1618*, 1638, 1718, 1738, 1818, 1918, 1938, 2018, 2118, 2238.

* – Also calls at Smallbrook Junction (connection with **Isle of Wight Steam Railway**, see note △) 9 minutes from Ryde / 15 minutes from Shanklin, when Steam Railway is operating.

△ – **Isle of Wight Steam Railway** (Smallbrook Junction - Wootton: *9 km*). ✆ 01983 882204. www.iwsteamrailway.co.uk

Table T170-F

Mondays to Fridays

16 December to 15 May

London Victoria - Battersea Park, Wandsworth Common, Balham, Streatham Common, Norbury, Thornton Heath & Selhurst-Croydon

Miles	Miles	Miles	Miles			SN MX A	SN MO A	SN MX A	SN MO B	SN MX C	SN MO	SN MX	SN [1] D	SN E	SN F	SN F	SN	SN E	SN	SN	SN	SN [1] G	SN F
0	0	—	—	**London Victoria**	d						00 12	00 13	04 35	05 41		06 00	06 06	06 11	06 16		06 20		06 30
1¼	1¼	—	—	**Battersea Park**	d				00 01		00 16	00 17				06 04	06 10		06 20		06 24		06 34
—	—	—	0	Shepherd's Bush	d																	06 21	
—	—	—	0¾	Kensington (Olympia)	d																	06 24	
—	—	—	1¼	West Brompton	d																	06 27	
—	—	—	2½	Imperial Wharf	d																	06 29	
2¾	2¾	—	4	Clapham Junction	a				00 05		00 20	00 21	04 42	05 48		06 08	06 14	06 18	06 24		06 28	06 34	06 38
—	—	—	—	Clapham Junction	d			00 04	00 06		00 20	00 21	04 42	05 48		06 09	06 14	06 18	06 24		06 28	06 35	06 39
4	4	—	5¾	**Wandsworth Common**	d			00 07	00 09		00 23	00 24				06 12	06 17		06 27		06 31		06 42
4½	4½	—	6	**Balham**	d		00 02	00 10	00a11		00 26	00 27		05 53		06 15	06 20	06 23	06 30		06 34	06 41	06 45
—	—	0	—	London Bridge	d				00a50											06 14	07a18		
6¾	6¾	8¼	7¾	**Streatham Common**	d		00 06			00 26	00 31	00 32				06 20			06 35	06 42		06 46	06 50
7½	7½	9	8½	**Norbury**	d	00 01	00 09			00 28	00 33	00 34				06 22			06 37	06 44		06 48	06 52
8¾	8¾	10¼	10	**Thornton Heath**	d	00 04	00 12			00 31	00 36	00 37				06 25			06 40	06 47		06 51	06 55
9¾	9½	11	10¾	**Selhurst**	d	00 07	00a14			00a34	00 39	00 40	04 54		05 56	06 29			06 44	06a50		06 55	06 58
—	10¾	—	11¾	East Croydon	a						00 43	00 44	04 57									06 59	
—	13¾	—	—	Purley	a								05 04										
10½	—	12¼	—	West Croydon	a	00 13									06 00	06 33	06 52		06 49				07 03
15	—	—	—	Sutton	a	00 26								06 13	06 19	06 46		06 43	07 03				07 16

		SN	SN E	SN	SN	SN	SN F	SN	SN E	SN	SN	SN	SN [1] G	SN F	SN	SN E	SN	SN	SN	SN [1] G	SN F	SN	SN E
London Victoria	d	06 36	06 41	06 46		06 50	07 00	07 06	07 11	07 16		07 20		07 30	07 36	07 41	07 46		07 50		08 00	08 06	08 11
Battersea Park	d	06 40		06 50		06 54	07 04	07 10		07 20		07 24		07 34	07 40		07 50		07 54		08 04	08 10	
Shepherd's Bush	d												07 22							07 50			
Kensington (Olympia)	d												07 25							07 52			
West Brompton	d												07 28							07 55			
Imperial Wharf	d												07 30							07 57			
Clapham Junction	a	06 44	06 48	06 54		06 58	07 08	07 14	07 18	07 24		07 28	07 35	07 38	07 44	07 48	07 54		07 58	08 04	08 08	08 14	08 18
Clapham Junction	d	06 44	06 48	06 54		06 58	07 09	07 14	07 18	07 24		07 28	07 35	07 39	07 44	07 48	07 54		07 58	08 05	08 09	08 14	08 18
Wandsworth Common	d	06 47		06 57		07 01	07 12	07 17		07 27		07 31	07 39	07 42	07 47		07 57		08 01		08 12	08 17	
Balham	d	06 50	06 53	07 00		07 04	07 15	07 20	07 23	07 30		07 35	07 42	07 45	07 50	07 53	08 00		08 04	08 11	08 15	08 20	08 23
London Bridge	d				06 44	07a48					07 14	08a18						07 44	08a48				
Streatham Common	d			07 05	07 12		07 20			07 35	07 42		07 46	07 50			08 05	08 12		08 16	08 20		
Norbury	d			07 07	07 14		07 22			07 37	07 44		07 49	07 53			08 07	08 14		08 18	08 22		
Thornton Heath	d			07 10	07 17		07 25			07 40	07 47		07 52	07 56			08 10	08 18		08 21	08 25		
Selhurst	d			07 14	07a20		07 28			07 44	07a50		07 56	07 59			08 14	08a20		08 26	08 29		
East Croydon	a												08 01							08 31			
Purley	a																						
West Croydon	a	07 22		07 19			07 33	07 52		07 49				08 04	08 22		08 19				08 33	08 52	
Sutton	a		07 13	07 33			07 46		07 43	08 03				08 17		08 13	08 33				08 46		08 43

		SN	SN	SN [1] H	SN	SN [1] I	SN F	SN	SN E	SN	SN	SN	SN	SN F	SN	SN E	SN	SN	SN	SN [1] I	SN F	SN	SN E
London Victoria	d	08 16			08 20		08 30	08 36	08 41	08 46		08 50	08 57	09 00	09 07	09 11	09 16		09 20		09 30	09 36	09 41
Battersea Park	d	08 20			08 24		08 34	08 40		08 50		08 54		09 04	09 12		09 20		09 24		09 34	09 40	
Shepherd's Bush	d			08 11																09 22			
Kensington (Olympia)	d			08 14																09 25			
West Brompton	d			08 17																09 28			
Imperial Wharf	d			08 19		←														09 30			
Clapham Junction	a	08 24		08 25	08 28	08 25	08 38	08 44	08 48	08 54		08 58	09 05	09 08	09 15	09 18	09 24		09 28	09 35	09 38	09 44	09 48
Clapham Junction	d	08 24		→	08 28	08 35	08 39	08 44	08 48	08 54		08 58	09 06	09 09	09 16	09 19	09 24		09 28	09 35	09 39	09 45	09 48
Wandsworth Common	d	08 27			08 31		08 42	08 47		08 57		09 01		09 12	09 19		09 27		09 31		09 42	09 48	
Balham	d	08 30			08 34	08 41	08 45	08 50	08 53	09 00		09 04	09 11	09 15	09 21	09 24	09 30		09 34	09 41	09 45	09 50	09 53
London Bridge	d		08 14		09a18						08 44	09a48						09 14	10a17				
Streatham Common	d	08 35	08 42			08 46	08 50			09 05	09 12		09 16	09 20			09 35	09 42		09 46	09 49		
Norbury	d	08 37	08 44			08 48	08 52			09 07	09 14		09 18	09 22			09 37	09 44		09 48	09 52		
Thornton Heath	d	08 40	08 47			08 51	08 55			09 10	09 17		09 21	09 25			09 40	09 47		09 51	09 55		
Selhurst	d	08 44	08a50			08 55	08 58			09 14	09a20		09 25	09 28			09 44	09a50		09 55	09 58		
East Croydon	a					09 01							09 30							10 00			
Purley	a																						
West Croydon	a	08 48					09 03	09 22		09 18				09 33	09 52		09 48				10 03	10 22	
Sutton	a	09 03					09 16		09 13	09 33				09 46		09 43	10 03				10 16		10 13

A – From London Victoria
B – From London Victoria to Norwood Junction
C – From London Bridge
D – To Gatwick Airport
E – To Epsom
F – To Epsom Downs
G – From Watford Junction
H – From Milton Keynes Central to East Croydon
I – From Milton Keynes Central

For faster services between London Victoria, Clapham Junction and East Croydon, refer to Table T175

For other Shepherd's Bush connecting trains, refer to Table T176

Table T170-F

Mondays to Fridays
16 December to 15 May

London Victoria - Battersea Park, Wandsworth Common, Balham, Streatham Common, Norbury, Thornton Heath & Selhurst-Croydon

		SN	SN	SN	SN	SN	SN	SN	SN	SN	SN	SN	SN	SN	SN	SN	SN	SN	SN	SN	SN	SN	SN
			A		B		C		A		1 D	B		C		A		B		C		A	
London Victoria 15	⊖ d	09 46		09 50	10 00	10 06	10 11	10 16		10 20		10 30	10 36	10 41	10 46		10 50	11 00	11 06	11 11	11 16		11 20
Battersea Park	d	09 50		09 54	10 04	10 10		10 20		10 24		10 34	10 40		10 50		10 54	11 04	11 10		11 20		11 24
Shepherd's Bush	⊖ d										10 22												
Kensington (Olympia)	⊖ d										10 25												
West Brompton	⊖ d										10 28												
Imperial Wharf	d										10 30												
Clapham Junction 10	a	09 54		09 58	10 08	10 14	10 18	10 24		10 28	10 35	10 38	10 44	10 48	10 54		10 58	11 08	11 14	11 18	11 24		11 28
Clapham Junction	d	09 54		09 58	10 09	10 14	10 18	10 24		10 28	10 35	10 39	10 44	10 48	10 54		10 58	11 09	11 14	11 18	11 24		11 28
Wandsworth Common	d	09 57		10 01	10 12	10 17		10 27		10 31		10 42	10 47		10 57		11 01	11 12	11 17		11 27		11 31
Balham 4	⊖ d	10 00		10 04	10 15	10 20	10 23	10 30		10 34	10 41	10 45	10 50	10 53	11 00		11 04	11 15	11 20	11 23	11 30		11 34
London Bridge	d		09 44	10a47					10 14	11a17						10 44	11a47					11 14	12a17
Streatham Common 4	d	10 05	10 12		10 20			10 35	10 42		10 46	10 50			11 05	11 12		11 20			11 35	11 42	
Norbury	d	10 07	10 14		10 22			10 37	10 44		10 48	10 52			11 07	11 14		11 22			11 37	11 44	
Thornton Heath	d	10 10	10 17		10 25			10 40	10 47		10 51	10 55			11 10	11 17		11 25			11 40	11 47	
Selhurst 4	d	10 14	10 21		10 28			10 45	10 51		10 55	10 58			11 13	11 21		11 28			11 45	11 51	
East Croydon	a		10 24						10 54		10 59					11 24						11 54	
Purley	a		10 31						11 01							11 31						12 01	
West Croydon 4	a	10 18			10 33	10 57		10 50				11 03	11 21		11 18			11 33	11 57		11 50		
Sutton 4	a	10 33			10 46		10 43	11 03				11 16		11 13	11 33			11 46		11 43	12 03		

		SN	SN	SN	SN	SN	SN	SN	SN	SN	SN	SN	SN	SN	SN MW FO	SN MW FO	SN TThO	SN MW FO	SN TThO	SN	SN MW FO	SN TThO
		1 D	B		C		A		B		C		A		1 D	B	B			C		
London Victoria 15	⊖ d		11 30	11 36	11 41	11 46		11 50	12 00	12 06	12 11	12 16		12 20		12 30	12 30	12 36	12 36	12 41	12 46	12 46
Battersea Park	d		11 34	11 40		11 50		11 54	12 04	12 10		12 20		12 24		12 34	12 34	12 40	12 40		12 50	12 50
Shepherd's Bush	⊖ d	11 22													12 22							
Kensington (Olympia)	⊖ d	11 25													12 25							
West Brompton	⊖ d	11 28													12 28							
Imperial Wharf	d	11 30													12 30							
Clapham Junction 10	a	11 35	11 38	11 44	11 48	11 54		11 58	12 08	12 14	12 18	12 24		12 28	12 35	12 38	12 42	12 44	12 45	12 48	12 54	12 54
Clapham Junction	d	11 35	11 39	11 45	11 48	11 54		11 58	12 09	12 14	12 18	12 24		12 28	12 35	12 39	12 42	12 44	12 45	12 48	12 54	12 54
Wandsworth Common	d		11 42	11 48		11 57		12 01	12 12	12 17		12 27		12 31		12 42	12 45	12 47	12 48		12 57	12 57
Balham 4	⊖ d	11 41	11 45	11 50	11 53	12 00		12 04	12 15	12 20	12 23	12 30		12 34	12 41	12 45	12 48	12 50	12 51	12 54	13 00	13 00
London Bridge	d						11 44	12a47					12 14	13a17								
Streatham Common 4	d	11 46	11 50			12 05	12 12		12 20			12 35	12 42		12 46	12 50	12 53				13 05	13 05
Norbury	d	11 48	11 52			12 07	12 14		12 22			12 37	12 44		12 48	12 52	12 55				13 07	13 07
Thornton Heath	d	11 51	11 55			12 10	12 17		12 25			12 40	12 47		12 51	12 55	12 58				13 10	13 10
Selhurst 4	d	11 55	11 58			12 13	12 21		12 28			12 45	12 51		12 55	12 58	13 04				13 13	13 15
East Croydon	a	11 59					12 24						12 54		12 59							
Purley	a						12 31						13 01									
West Croydon 4	a		12 03	12 21		12 18			12 33	12 57		12 50				13 03	13 11	13 21	13 27		13 18	13 19
Sutton 4	a		12 16		12 13	12 33			12 46		12 43	13 03				13 16	13 24			13 13	13 33	13 33

		SN	SN	SN	SN	SN	SN	SN	SN	SN	SN	SN	SN	SN	SN	SN	SN	SN	SN	SN	SN	SN	SN
		A		B		C		A		1 D	B		C		A		B		C		A		1 D
London Victoria 15	⊖ d		12 50	13 00	13 06	13 11	13 16		13 20		13 30	13 36	13 41	13 46		13 50	14 00	14 06	14 11	14 16		14 20	
Battersea Park	d		12 54	13 04	13 10		13 20		13 24		13 34	13 40		13 50		13 54	14 04	14 10		14 20		14 24	
Shepherd's Bush	⊖ d									13 22													14 22
Kensington (Olympia)	⊖ d									13 25													14 25
West Brompton	⊖ d									13 28													14 28
Imperial Wharf	d									13 30													14 30
Clapham Junction 10	a		12 58	13 08	13 14	13 18	13 24		13 28	13 35	13 38	13 44	13 48	13 54		13 58	14 08	14 14	14 18	14 24		14 28	14 35
Clapham Junction	d		12 58	13 09	13 14	13 18	13 24		13 28	13 35	13 39	13 44	13 48	13 54		13 58	14 09	14 14	14 18	14 24		14 28	14 35
Wandsworth Common	d		13 01	13 12	13 17		13 27		13 31		13 42	13 47		13 57		14 01	14 12	14 17		14 27		14 31	
Balham 4	⊖ d		13 04	13 15	13 20	13 23	13 30		13 34	13 41	13 45	13 50	13 53	14 00		14 04	14 15	14 20	14 23	14 30		14 34	14 41
London Bridge	d	12 44	13a47					13 14	14a17						13 44	14a47					14 14	15a17	
Streatham Common 4	d	13 12		13 20			13 35	13 42		13 46	13 50			14 05	14 12		14 20			14 35	14 42		14 46
Norbury	d	13 14		13 22			13 37	13 44		13 48	13 52			14 07	14 14		14 22			14 37	14 44		14 48
Thornton Heath	d	13 17		13 25			13 40	13 47		13 51	13 55			14 10	14 17		14 25			14 40	14 47		14 51
Selhurst 4	d	13 21		13 28			13 45	13 51		13 55	13 58			14 13	14 21		14 28			14 45	14 51		14 55
East Croydon	a	13 24						13 54		13 59					14 24						14 54		14 59
Purley	a	13 31						14 01							14 31						15 01		
West Croydon 4	a			13 33	13 57		13 50				14 03	14 21		14 18			14 33	14 57		14 50			
Sutton 4	a			13 46		13 43	14 03				14 16		14 13	14 33			14 46		14 43	15 06			

A To Caterham
B To Epsom Downs
C To Epsom
D From Milton Keynes Central

For faster services between London Victoria, Clapham Junction and East Croydon, refer to Table T175

For other Shepherd's Bush connecting trains, refer to Table T176

NRT DECEMBER 19 EDITION

Table T170-F

Mondays to Fridays
16 December to 15 May

London Victoria - Battersea Park, Wandsworth Common, Balham, Streatham Common, Norbury, Thornton Heath & Selhurst-Croydon

		SN	SN	SN	SN	SN	SN	SN	SN	SN	SN	SN	SN	SN	SN	SN	SN	SN	SN	SN	SN	SN
		A		B		C		A		B		C		1 D	A		B		C		1	A
London Victoria 15	⊖ d	14 30	14 36	14 41	14 46		14 50	15 00	15 06	15 11	15 16		15 20		15 30	15 36	15 41	15 46		15 50		16 00
Battersea Park	d	14 34	14 40		14 50		14 54	15 04	15 10		15 20		15 24		15 34	15 40		15 50		15 54		16 04
Shepherd's Bush	⊖ d													15 22							15 49	
Kensington (Olympia)	⊖ d													15 25							15 52	
West Brompton	⊖ d													15 28							15 55	
Imperial Wharf	d													15 30							15 57	
Clapham Junction 10	a	14 38	14 44	14 48	14 54		14 58	15 08	15 14	15 18	15 24		15 28	15 35	15 38	15 44	15 48	15 54		15 58	16 02	16 08
Clapham Junction	d	14 39	14 44	14 48	14 54		14 58	15 09	15 14	15 18	15 24		15 28	15 35	15 39	15 44	15 48	15 54		15 58	16 05	16 09
Wandsworth Common	d	14 42	14 47		14 57		15 01	15 12	15 17		15 27		15 31		15 42	15 47		15 57		16 01		16 12
Balham 4	⊖ d	14 45	14 50	14 53	15 00		15 04	15 15	15 20	15 23	15 30		15 34	15 41	15 45	15 50	15 53	16 00		16 04	16 11	16 15
London Bridge	d					14 44	15a47					15 14	16a18						15 44	16a48		
Streatham Common 4	d	14 50			15 05	15 12		15 20			15 35	15 42		15 46	15 50			16 05	16 12		16 16	16 20
Norbury	d	14 52			15 07	15 14		15 22			15 37	15 44		15 48	15 52			16 07	16 14		16 18	16 22
Thornton Heath	d	14 55			15 10	15 17		15 25			15 40	15 47		15 51	15 55			16 10	16 17		16 21	16 25
Selhurst 4	d	14 58			15 13	15 21		15 28			15 45	15 51		15 55	15 58			16 13	16 21		16 25	16 28
East Croydon	a					15 24						15 54		16 00					16 24		16 34	
Purley	a					15 31						16 01							16 31			
West Croydon 4	a	15 03	15 21		15 18			15 33	15 57		15 50				16 03	16 21		16 18				16 33
Sutton 4	a	15 16		15 13	15 33			15 46		15 43	16 03				16 16		16 13	16 33				16 46

		SN	SN	SN	SN	SN	SN	SN	SN	SN	SN	SN	SN	SN	SN	SN	SN	SN	SN	SN	SN	SN	SN
			B				1 D	A		B				1 E	A		B				1 D	A	
London Victoria 15	⊖ d	16 06	16 12	16 16		16 20		16 30	16 36	16 41	16 46		16 50		17 00	17 06	17 11	17 16		17 20		17 30	17 36
Battersea Park	d	16 10		16 20		16 24		16 34	16 40		16 50		16 54		17 04	17 10		17 20		17 24		17 34	17 40
Shepherd's Bush	⊖ d						16 22							16 46							17 22		
Kensington (Olympia)	⊖ d						16 25							16 49							17 25		
West Brompton	⊖ d						16 28							16 52							17 28		
Imperial Wharf	d						16 30							16 55							17 30		
Clapham Junction 10	a	16 14	16 19	16 24		16 28	16 35	16 38	16 44	16 48	16 54		16 58	17 01	17 08	17 14	17 18	17 24		17 28	17 35	17 38	17 44
Clapham Junction	d	16 14	16 19	16 24		16 28	16 35	16 39	16 44	16 48	16 54		16 58	17 05	17 09	17 14	17 18	17 24		17 28	17 35	17 39	17 44
Wandsworth Common	d	16 17		16 27		16 31		16 42	16 47		16 57		17 01		17 12	17 17		17 27		17 31		17 42	17 47
Balham 4	⊖ d	16 20	16 24	16 30		16 34	16 41	16 45	16 50	16 53	17 00		17 04	17 11	17 15	17 20	17 23	17 30		17 34	17 41	17 45	17 50
London Bridge	d				16 14	17a18						16 44	17a48						17 14	18a18			
Streatham Common 4	d			16 35	16 42		16 46	16 50			17 05	17 12		17 16	17 20			17 35	17 42		17 46	17 50	
Norbury	d			16 37	16 44		16 48	16 52			17 07	17 14		17 18	17 22			17 37	17 44		17 48	17 52	
Thornton Heath	d			16 40	16 47		16 51	16 55			17 10	17 17		17 21	17 25			17 40	17 47		17 51	17 55	
Selhurst 4	d			16 44	16a50		16 55	16 58			17 14	17a20		17 25	17 28			17 44	17a50		17 55	17 58	
East Croydon	a						17 00							17 30							18 00		
Purley	a																						
West Croydon 4	a	16 52		16 49				17 03	17 22		17 19				17 33	17 52		17 49				18 03	18 22
Sutton 4	a		16 43	17 03				17 16		17 13	17 33				17 46		17 43	18 03				18 16	

		SN	SN	SN	SN	SN	SN	SN	SN	SN	SN	SN	SN	SN	SN	SN	SN	SN	SN	SN	SN	SN
		B				1	A		B				1 D	A		B				A		B
London Victoria 15	⊖ d	17 41	17 46		17 50		18 00	18 06	18 11	18 16		18 20		18 30	18 36	18 41	18 46		18 50	19 00	19 06	19 11
Battersea Park	d		17 50		17 54		18 04	18 10		18 20		18 24		18 34	18 40		18 50		18 54	19 04	19 10	
Shepherd's Bush	⊖ d					17 49							18 22									
Kensington (Olympia)	⊖ d					17 52							18 24									
West Brompton	⊖ d					17 55							18 27									
Imperial Wharf	d					17 57							18 30									
Clapham Junction 10	a	17 48	17 54		17 58	18 02	18 08	18 14	18 18	18 24		18 28	18 35	18 38	18 44	18 48	18 54		18 58	19 08	19 14	19 18
Clapham Junction	d	17 48	17 54		17 58	18 05	18 09	18 14	18 18	18 24		18 28	18 35	18 39	18 44	18 48	18 54		18 58	19 09	19 14	19 18
Wandsworth Common	d		17 57		18 01		18 12	18 17		18 27		18 31		18 42	18 47		18 57		19 01	19 12	19 17	
Balham 4	⊖ d	17 53	18 00		18 04	18 11	18 15	18 20	18 23	18 30		18 34	18 41	18 45	18 50	18 53	19 00		19 04	19 15	19 20	19 23
London Bridge	d			17 44	18a48						18 14	19a18						18 44	19a48			
Streatham Common 4	d		18 05	18 12		18 16	18 20			18 35	18 42		18 46	18 50			19 05	19 12		19 20		
Norbury	d		18 07	18 14		18 18	18 22			18 37	18 44		18 48	18 52			19 07	19 14		19 22		
Thornton Heath	d		18 10	18 17		18 21	18 25			18 40	18 47		18 51	18 55			19 10	19 17		19 25		
Selhurst 4	d		18 14	18a20		18 26	18 28			18 44	18a50		18 55	18 58			19 13	19a20		19 28		
East Croydon	a					18 31							19 01									
Purley	a																					
West Croydon 4	a		18 19				18 33	18 52		18 49				19 03	19 21		19 18			19 33	19 51	
Sutton 4	a	18 13	18 33				18 46		18 43	19 03				19 16		19 13	19 33			19 46		19 43

A To Epsom Downs
B To Epsom
C To Caterham
D From Milton Keynes Central
E From Watford Junction

For faster services between London Victoria, Clapham Junction and East Croydon, refer to Table T175

For other Shepherd's Bush connecting trains, refer to Table T176

Table T170-F

Mondays to Fridays
16 December to 15 May

London Victoria - Battersea Park, Wandsworth Common, Balham, Streatham Common, Norbury, Thornton Heath & Selhurst-Croydon

	SN	SN	SN	SN	SN	SN	SN	SN	SN	SN	SN	SN	SN	SN	SN	SN	SN	SN	SN	SN	SN	SN
		A		1 B	C		D		A		C		D		A		1 B	C		D		A
London Victoria 15 ⊖ d	19 16		19 20		19 30	19 36	19 41	19 46		19 50	20 00	20 06	20 11	20 16		20 20		20 30	20 36	20 41	20 46	
Battersea Park d	19 20		19 24		19 34	19 40		19 50		19 54	20 04	20 10		20 20		20 24		20 34	20 40		20 50	
Shepherd's Bush ⊖ d				19 22													20 22					
Kensington (Olympia) ⊖ d				19 25													20 25					
West Brompton ⊖ d				19 28													20 28					
Imperial Wharf d				19 30													20 30					
Clapham Junction 10 a	19 24		19 28	19 35	19 38	19 44	19 48	19 54		19 58	20 08	20 14	20 18	20 24		20 28	20 35	20 38	20 44	20 48	20 54	
Clapham Junction d	19 24		19 28	19 35	19 39	19 44	19 48	19 54		19 58	20 09	20 14	20 18	20 24		20 28	20 35	20 39	20 45	20 48	20 54	
Wandsworth Common d	19 27		19 31		19 42	19 47		19 57		20 01	20 12	20 17		20 27		20 31		20 42	20 48		20 57	
Balham 4 ⊖ d	19 30		19 34	19 41	19 45	19 50	19 53	20 00		20 04	20 15	20 20	20 23	20 30		20 34	20 41	20 45	20 51	20 53	21 00	
London Bridge d		19 14	20a20						19 44	20a48					20 14	21a17						20 44
Streatham Common 4 d	19 35	19 42		19 46	19 50			20 05	20 12		20 20			20 35	20 42		20 46	20 50			21 05	21 12
Norbury d	19 37	19 44		19 48	19 52			20 07	20 14		20 22			20 37	20 44		20 48	20 52			21 07	21 14
Thornton Heath d	19 40	19 47		19 51	19 55			20 10	20 17		20 25			20 40	20 47		20 51	20 55			21 10	21 17
Selhurst 4 d	19 43	19 51		19 55	19 58			20 13	20 21		20 30			20 45	20 50		20 55	20 58			21 13	21 20
East Croydon a		19 54		19 59					20 24						20 53		20 59					21 24
Purley a		20 01							20 31						21 01							21 32
West Croydon 4 a	19 48				20 03	20 21		20 18			20 34	20 57		20 50				21 03	21 21		21 18	
Sutton 4 a	20 03				20 16		20 13	20 33			20 47		20 43	21 03				21 16		21 13	21 33	

	SN	SN	SN	SN	SN	SN	SN	SN	SN	SN	SN	SN	SN	SN	SN	SN	SN	SN	SN	SN	SN
		C		D		A		C		D		A		C		D		A		1 B	C
London Victoria 15 ⊖ d	20 50	21 00	21 06	21 11	21 16		21 20	21 30	21 36	21 41	21 47		21 50	22 00	22 06	22 11	22 16		22 20		22 30
Battersea Park d	20 54	21 04	21 10		21 20		21 24	21 34	21 40		21 51		21 54	22 04	22 10		22 20		22 24		22 34
Shepherd's Bush ⊖ d																				22 19	
Kensington (Olympia) ⊖ d																				22 21	
West Brompton ⊖ d																				22 24	
Imperial Wharf d																				22 27	
Clapham Junction 10 a	20 58	21 08	21 14	21 18	21 24		21 28	21 42	21 45	21 48	21 55		21 58	22 08	22 14	22 18	22 24		22 28	22 31	22 38
Clapham Junction d	20 58	21 09	21 14	21 18	21 24		21 28	21 42	21 45	21 48	21 56		21 59	22 09	22 14	22 18	22 24		22 28	22 35	22 39
Wandsworth Common d	21 01	21 12	21 17		21 27		21 31	21 45	21 48		21 59		22 02	22 12	22 17		22 27		22 31		22 42
Balham 4 ⊖ d	21 04	21 15	21 20	21 23	21 30		21 34	21 48	21 51	21 54	22 01		22 04	22 15	22 20	22 23	22 30		22 34	22 41	22 45
London Bridge d	21a47					21 14	22a17					21 44	22a47					22 14	23a17		
Streatham Common 4 d		21 20			21 35	21 42		21 53			22 05	22 12		22 20			22 35	22 42		22 46	22 50
Norbury d		21 22			21 37	21 44		21 55			22 08	22 14		22 22			22 37	22 44		22 48	22 52
Thornton Heath d		21 25			21 40	21 47		21 58			22 12	22 17		22 25			22 40	22 47		22 51	22 55
Selhurst 4 d		21 28			21 43	21 51		22 04			22 15	22 21		22 28			22 43	22 51		22 55	22 58
East Croydon a						21 54						22 24						22 54		22 59	
Purley a						22 01						22 31						23 01			
West Croydon 4 a		21 33	21 51		21 48			22 11	22 27		22 19			22 33	22 51		22 48				23 03
Sutton 4 a		21 46		21 43	22 03			22 24		22 13	22 33			22 46		22 43	23 03				23 16

	SN	SN	SN	SN	SN	SN	SN	SN	SN	SN	SN	SN	SN	SN	SN	SN
		D				C		D				E				
London Victoria 15 ⊖ d	22 36	22 41	22 46		22 50	23 00	23 06	23 11	23 16		23 20	23 25	23 32	23 40		23 56
Battersea Park d	22 40		22 50		22 54	23 04	23 10		23 20		23 24			23 44		
Shepherd's Bush ⊖ d																
Kensington (Olympia) ⊖ d																
West Brompton ⊖ d																
Imperial Wharf d																
Clapham Junction 10 a	22 44	22 48	22 54		22 58	23 08	23 14	23 18	23 24		23 28	23 32	23 39	23 48		00 03
Clapham Junction d	22 45	22 48	22 54		22 58	23 09	23 14	23 18	23 24		23 28	23 32	23 40	23 48		00 04
Wandsworth Common d	22 48		22 57		23 01	23 12	23 17		23 27		23 31			23 51		00 07
Balham 4 ⊖ d	22 50	22 53	23 00		23 04	23 15	23 20	23 23	23 30		23 34	23 37	23 44	23 54		00 10
London Bridge d				22 44	23a47					23 14	00a16				23 54	00a50
Streatham Common 4 d			23 05	23 12		23 20			23 35	23 42				23 59	00 26	
Norbury d			23 07	23 14		23 22			23 37	23 44				00 01	00 28	
Thornton Heath d			23 10	23 17		23 25			23 40	23 47				00 04	00 31	
Selhurst 4 d			23 13	23a20		23 28			23 43	23a50				00 07	00a34	
East Croydon a																
Purley a																
West Croydon 4 a	23 21		23 18			23 33	23 52		23 48				00 16	00 13		
Sutton 4 a		23 13	23 33			23 46		23 43	00 03			23 58		00 26		

A To Caterham
B From Milton Keynes Central
C To Epsom Downs
D To Epsom
E To Horsham

For faster services between London Victoria, Clapham Junction and East Croydon, refer to Table T175

For other Shepherd's Bush connecting trains, refer to Table T176

Table T170-F

Saturdays
21 December to 16 May

London Victoria - Battersea Park, Wandsworth Common, Balham, Streatham Common, Norbury, Thornton Heath & Selhurst-Croydon

	SN	SN	SN	SN	SN	SN	SN	SN	SN	SN	SN	SN	SN	SN	SN	SN	SN	SN	SN	SN	SN	SN
	A	A	B	C	D	E	B			1 F	1 F	1 G	H	E	I		1 J	H		E		I
London Victoria 15 ⊖ d			00 10		00 13	00 20	00 25	00 30		01 10	05 08	05 20	06 00	06 11		06 20		06 30	06 36	06 41	06 46	
Battersea Park d			00 14		00 17		00 29	00 34					06 04			06 24		06 34	06 40		06 50	
Shepherd's Bush ⊖ d																	06 19					
Kensington (Olympia) ⊖ d																	06 22					
West Brompton ⊖ d																	06 25					
Imperial Wharf d																	06 28					
Clapham Junction 10 a			00 18		00 21	00 27	00 33	00 38		01 17	05 15	05 27	06 08	06 18		06 28	06 32	06 38	06 44	06 48	06 54	
Clapham Junction d		00 04	00 18		00 21	00 27	00 33	00 39		01 17	05 16	05 28	06 09	06 18		06 28	06 35	06 39	06 44	06 48	06 54	
Wandsworth Common d		00 07	00 21		00 24		00 36	00 42					06 12			06 31		06 42	06 47		06 57	
Balham 4 ⊖ d		00 10	00a24		00 27	00 33	00a39	00 45					06 15	06 23		06 34	06 41	06 45	06 50	06 53	07 00	
London Bridge d		00a50							00 25						06 14	07a14						06 44
Streatham Common 4 d				00 26	00 32			00 52	00 55				06 20		06 42		06 46	06 50			07 05	07 12
Norbury d	00 01			00 28	00 34			00 54	00 57				06 22		06 44		06 48	06 52			07 07	07 14
Thornton Heath d	00 04			00 31	00 37			00 57	01 00				06 25		06 47		06 51	06 55			07 10	07 17
Selhurst 4 d	00 07			00a34	00 40			01 00	01a03	01 29	05 27	05 40	06 28		06 51		06 55	06 58			07 13	07 21
East Croydon a					00 44					01 32	05 31	05 44			06 54		06 59					07 24
Purley a										01 38	05 37				07 01							07 31
West Croydon 4 a	00 13							01 05					06 35					07 03	07 22		07 18	
Sutton 4 a	00 26					00 53		01 18					06 48	06 43				07 16		07 13	07 33	

	SN	SN	SN	SN	SN	SN	SN	SN	SN	SN	SN	SN	SN	SN	SN	SN	SN	SN	SN	SN	SN	SN
		H		E		I		1 J	H		E		I		H		E		I		1 K	H
London Victoria 15 ⊖ d	06 50	07 00	07 06	07 11	07 16		07 20		07 30	07 36	07 41	07 46		07 50	08 00	08 06	08 11	08 16		08 20		08 30
Battersea Park d	06 54	07 04	07 10		07 20		07 24		07 34	07 40		07 50		07 54	08 04	08 10		08 20		08 24		08 34
Shepherd's Bush ⊖ d								07 21													08 19	
Kensington (Olympia) ⊖ d								07 24													08 22	
West Brompton ⊖ d								07 27													08 25	
Imperial Wharf d								07 29													08 28	
Clapham Junction 10 a	06 58	07 08	07 14	07 18	07 24		07 28	07 34	07 38	07 44	07 48	07 54		07 58	08 08	08 14	08 18	08 24		08 28	08 32	08 38
Clapham Junction d	06 58	07 09	07 14	07 18	07 24		07 28	07 35	07 39	07 44	07 48	07 54		07 58	08 09	08 14	08 18	08 24		08 28	08 35	08 39
Wandsworth Common d	07 01	07 12	07 17		07 27		07 31		07 42	07 47		07 57		08 01	08 12	08 17		08 27		08 31		08 42
Balham 4 ⊖ d	07 04	07 15	07 20	07 23	07 30		07 34	07 41	07 45	07 50	07 53	08 00		08 04	08 15	08 20	08 23	08 30		08 34	08 41	08 45
London Bridge d	07a44					07 14	08a14						07 44	08a44					08 14	09a14		
Streatham Common 4 d		07 21			07 35	07 42		07 46	07 50			08 05	08 12		08 21			08 35	08 42		08 46	08 50
Norbury d		07 23			07 37	07 44		07 48	07 52			08 07	08 14		08 23			08 37	08 44		08 48	08 52
Thornton Heath d		07 26			07 40	07 47		07 51	07 55			08 10	08 17		08 26			08 40	08 47		08 51	08 55
Selhurst 4 d		07 29			07 45	07 51		07 55	07 58			08 13	08 21		08 29			08 45	08 51		08 55	08 58
East Croydon a						07 54		07 59					08 24						08 54		08 59	
Purley a						08 01							08 31						09 01			
West Croydon 4 a		07 34	07 57		07 50				08 03	08 21		08 18			08 33	08 57		08 50				09 03
Sutton 4 a		07 46		07 43	08 03				08 16		08 13	08 33			08 46		08 43	09 03				09 16

	SN	SN	SN	SN	SN	SN		SN	SN	SN	SN	SN	SN	SN	SN	SN	SN	SN	SN	SN	SN	SN
		E		I		H			E		I		1 K	H		E		I		H		E
London Victoria 15 ⊖ d	08 36	08 41	08 46		08 50	09 00	and at the same minutes past each hour until	13 06	13 11	13 16		13 20		13 30	13 36	13 41	13 46		13 50	14 00	14 06	14 11
Battersea Park d	08 40		08 50		08 54	09 04		13 10		13 20		13 24		13 34	13 40		13 50		13 54	14 04	14 10	
Shepherd's Bush ⊖ d													13 19									
Kensington (Olympia) ⊖ d													13 22									
West Brompton ⊖ d													13 25									
Imperial Wharf d													13 28									
Clapham Junction 10 a	08 44	08 48	08 54		08 58	09 08		13 14	13 18	13 24		13 28	13 32	13 38	13 44	13 48	13 54		13 58	14 08	14 14	14 18
Clapham Junction d	08 44	08 48	08 54		08 58	09 09		13 14	13 18	13 24		13 28	13 35	13 39	13 44	13 48	13 54		13 58	14 09	14 14	14 18
Wandsworth Common d	08 47		08 57		09 01	09 12		13 17		13 27		13 31		13 42	13 47		13 57		14 01	14 12	14 17	
Balham 4 ⊖ d	08 50	08 53	09 00		09 04	09 15		13 20	13 23	13 30		13 34	13 41	13 45	13 50	13 53	14 00		14 04	14 15	14 20	14 23
London Bridge d				08 44	09a44						13 14	14a14						13 44	14a44			
Streatham Common 4 d			09 05	09 12		09 21				13 35	13 42		13 46	13 50			14 05	14 12		14 21		
Norbury d			09 07	09 14		09 23				13 37	13 44		13 48	13 52			14 07	14 14		14 23		
Thornton Heath d			09 10	09 17		09 26				13 40	13 47		13 51	13 55			14 10	14 17		14 26		
Selhurst 4 d			09 13	09 21		09 29				13 45	13 51		13 55	13 58			14 13	14 21		14 29		
East Croydon a				09 24							13 54		13 59					14 24				
Purley a				09 31							14 01							14 31				
West Croydon 4 a	09 21		09 18			09 34		13 57		13 50				14 03	14 21		14 18			14 34	14 57	
Sutton 4 a		09 13	09 33			09 46			13 43	14 03				14 16		14 13	14 33			14 46		14 43

A From London Victoria
B To Norwood Junction
C From London Bridge
D not 16 May
E To Epsom
F To Brighton
G To East Grinstead
H To Epsom Downs
I To Caterham
J From Watford Junction
K From Milton Keynes Central

For faster services between London Victoria, Clapham Junction and East Croydon, refer to Table T175

For other Shepherd's Bush connecting trains, refer to Table T176

Table T170-F

Saturdays

21 December to 16 May

London Victoria - Battersea Park, Wandsworth Common, Balham, Streatham Common, Norbury, Thornton Heath & Selhurst-Croydon

		SN	SN A	SN	SN 1 B	SN C	SN	SN D	SN	SN A	SN	SN C	SN	SN D	SN		SN A	SN	SN 1 B	SN C	SN	SN D	SN
London Victoria 15 ⊖	d	14 16		14 20		14 30	14 36	14 41	14 46		14 50	15 00	15 06	15 11	15 16			19 20		19 30	19 36	19 41	19 46
Battersea Park	d	14 20		14 24		14 34	14 40		14 50		14 54	15 04	15 10		15 20			19 24		19 34	19 40		19 50
Shepherd's Bush ⊖	d				14 19														19 19				
Kensington (Olympia) ⊖	d				14 22														19 22				
West Brompton ⊖	d				14 25														19 25				
Imperial Wharf	d				14 28											and at the same minutes past each hour until			19 28				
Clapham Junction 10	a	14 24		14 28	14 32	14 38	14 44	14 48	14 54		14 58	15 08	15 14	15 18	15 24			19 28	19 32	19 38	19 44	19 48	19 54
Clapham Junction	d	14 24		14 28	14 35	14 39	14 44	14 48	14 54		14 58	15 09	15 14	15 18	15 24			19 28	19 35	19 39	19 44	19 48	19 54
Wandsworth Common	d	14 27		14 31		14 42	14 47		14 57		15 01	15 12	15 17		15 27			19 31		19 42	19 47		19 57
Balham 4 ⊖	d	14 30		14 34	14 41	14 45	14 50	14 53	15 00		15 04	15 15	15 20	15 23	15 30			19 34	19 41	19 45	19 50	19 53	20 00
London Bridge	d		14 14	15a14						14 44	15a44						19 14	20a14					
Streatham Common 4	d	14 35	14 42		14 46	14 50			15 05	15 12		15 21			15 35		19 42		19 46	19 50			20 05
Norbury	d	14 37	14 44		14 48	14 52			15 07	15 14		15 23			15 37		19 44		19 48	19 52			20 07
Thornton Heath	d	14 40	14 47		14 51	14 55			15 10	15 17		15 26			15 40		19 47		19 51	19 55			20 10
Selhurst 4	d	14 45	14 51		14 55	14 58			15 13	15 21		15 29			15 45		19 51		19 55	19 58			20 13
East Croydon	a		14 54		14 59					15 24							19 54		19 59				
Purley	a		15 01							15 31							20 01						
West Croydon 4	a	14 50				15 03	15 21		15 18			15 34	15 57		15 50					20 03	20 21		20 18
Sutton 4	a	15 06				15 16		15 13	15 33			15 46		15 43	16 03					20 16		20 13	20 33

		SN A	SN	SN C	SN	SN D	SN	SN A	SN	SN 1 B	SN C	SN	SN D	SN	SN A	SN	SN C	SN	SN D	SN	SN A	SN	SN 1 E
London Victoria 15 ⊖	d		19 50	20 00	20 06	20 11	20 16		20 20		20 30	20 36	20 41	20 46		20 50	21 00	21 06	21 11	21 16		21 20	
Battersea Park	d		19 54	20 04	20 10		20 20		20 24		20 34	20 40		20 50		20 54	21 04	21 10		21 20		21 24	
Shepherd's Bush ⊖	d									20 20													21 16
Kensington (Olympia) ⊖	d									20 22													21 20
West Brompton ⊖	d									20 25													21 23
Imperial Wharf	d									20 28													21 26
Clapham Junction 10	a		19 58	20 08	20 14	20 18	20 24		20 28	20 33	20 38	20 44	20 48	20 54		20 58	21 08	21 14	21 18	21 24		21 28	21 30
Clapham Junction	d		19 58	20 09	20 14	20 18	20 24		20 28	20 35	20 39	20 44	20 48	20 54		20 58	21 09	21 14	21 18	21 24		21 28	21 35
Wandsworth Common	d		20 01	20 12	20 17		20 27		20 31		20 42	20 47		20 57		21 01	21 12	21 17		21 27		21 31	
Balham 4 ⊖	d		20 04	20 15	20 20	20 23	20 30		20 34	20 41	20 45	20 50	20 53	21 00		21 04	21 15	21 20	21 23	21 30		21 34	21 41
London Bridge	d	19 44	20a44					20 14	21a14						20 44	21a44					21 14	22a20	
Streatham Common 4	d	20 12		20 21			20 35	20 42		20 46	20 50			21 05	21 12		21 21			21 35	21 42		21 46
Norbury	d	20 14		20 23			20 37	20 44		20 48	20 52			21 07	21 14		21 23			21 37	21 44		21 48
Thornton Heath	d	20 17		20 26			20 40	20 47		20 51	20 55			21 10	21 17		21 26			21 40	21 47		21 51
Selhurst 4	d	20 21		20 29			20 45	20 51		20 55	20 58			21 13	21 21		21 29			21 45	21 51		21 55
East Croydon	a	20 24						20 54		20 59					21 24						21 54		21 59
Purley	a	20 31						21 01							21 31						22 01		
West Croydon 4	a			20 34	20 57		20 50				21 03	21 21		21 18			21 34	21 57		21 50			
Sutton 4	a			20 46		20 43	21 03				21 16		21 13	21 33			21 46		21 43	22 03			

		SN C	SN	SN D	SN	SN A	SN	SN C	SN	SN D	SN	SN A	SN	SN 1 E	SN C	SN	SN D	SN	SN	SN	SN C	SN
London Victoria 15 ⊖	d	21 30	21 36	21 41	21 46		21 50	22 00	22 06	22 11	22 16		22 20		22 30	22 36	22 41	22 46		22 50	23 00	23 06
Battersea Park	d	21 34	21 40		21 50		21 54	22 04	22 10		22 20		22 24		22 34	22 40		22 50		22 54	23 04	23 10
Shepherd's Bush ⊖	d													22 15								
Kensington (Olympia) ⊖	d													22 23								
West Brompton ⊖	d													22 26								
Imperial Wharf	d													22 29								
Clapham Junction 10	a	21 38	21 44	21 48	21 54		21 58	22 08	22 14	22 18	22 24		22 28	22 33	22 38	22 44	22 48	22 54		22 58	23 08	23 14
Clapham Junction	d	21 39	21 44	21 48	21 54		21 58	22 08	22 14	22 18	22 24		22 28	22 35	22 39	22 44	22 49	22 54		22 58	23 09	23 14
Wandsworth Common	d	21 42	21 47		21 57		22 01	22 11	22 17		22 27		22 31		22 42	22 47		22 57		23 01	23 12	23 17
Balham 4 ⊖	d	21 45	21 50	21 53	22 00		22 04	22 14	22 20	22 23	22 30		22 34	22 41	22 45	22 50	22 53	23 00		23 04	23 15	23 20
London Bridge	d					21 44	22a45					22 14	23a15						22 45	23a44		
Streatham Common 4	d	21 50			22 05	22 12		22 21			22 35	22 42		22 46	22 50			23 05	23 17		23 20	
Norbury	d	21 52			22 07	22 14		22 23			22 37	22 44		22 48	22 52			23 07	23 19		23 23	
Thornton Heath	d	21 55			22 10	22 17		22 26			22 40	22 47		22 51	22 55			23 10	23 22		23 26	
Selhurst 4	d	21 58			22 13	22 21		22 29			22 45	22 51		22 55	22 58			23 13	23a25		23 29	
East Croydon	a					22 24						22 54		22 59								
Purley	a					22 31						23 01										
West Croydon 4	a	22 03	22 21		22 18			22 34	22 57		22 50				23 03	23 21		23 18			23 34	23 51
Sutton 4	a	22 16		22 13	22 33			22 46		22 43	23 03				23 16		23 13	23 33			23 46	

A To Caterham
B From Milton Keynes Central
C To Epsom Downs
D To Epsom
E From Watford Junction

For faster services between London Victoria, Clapham Junction and East Croydon, refer to Table T175

For other Shepherd's Bush connecting trains, refer to Table T176

Table T170-F

Saturdays

21 December to 16 May

London Victoria - Battersea Park, Wandsworth Common, Balham, Streatham Common, Norbury, Thornton Heath & Selhurst-Croydon

		SN A	SN	SN	SN	SN	SN	SN A	SN	SN
London Victoria 15 ⊖	d	23 11	23 16		23 20	23 32	23 40	23 45		23 56
Battersea Park	d		23 20		23 24		23 44			
Shepherd's Bush ⊖	d									
Kensington (Olympia) ⊖	d									
West Brompton ⊖	d									
Imperial Wharf	d									
Clapham Junction 10	a	23 18	23 24		23 28	23 39	23 48	23 52		00 03
Clapham Junction	d	23 18	23 24		23 28	23 39	23 48	23 53		00 04
Wandsworth Common	d		23 27		23 31		23 51			00 07
Balham 4 ⊖	d	23 23	23 30		23 34	23 44	23 54	23 57		00 10
London Bridge	d			23 14	00a16				23 55	00a49
Streatham Common 4	d		23 35	23 42			23 59		00 27	
Norbury	d		23 37	23 44			00 01		00 29	
Thornton Heath	d		23 40	23 47			00 04		00 32	
Selhurst 4	d		23 43	23a50			00 07		00a35	
East Croydon	a									
Purley	a									
West Croydon 4	a		23 48			00 18	00 14			
Sutton 4	a	23 43	00 03				00 27	00 17		

Sundays

15 December to 10 May

		SN B	SN B	SN C	SN D	SN	SN C	SN	SN	SN C	SN 1 E	SN F	SN	SN 1 E	SN F	SN	SN	SN 1 G	SN	SN H	SN F	SN	SN
London Victoria 15 ⊖	d			00 10		00 15	00 25	00 30		00 40	01 08	06 40	06 45	07 02	07 10	07 16	07 21	07 32		07 34	07 40	07 46	07 51
Battersea Park	d			00 14		00 19	00 29	00 34		00 44			06 49			07 20	07 25			07 38		07 50	07 55
Shepherd's Bush ⊖	d																						
Kensington (Olympia) ⊖	d																						
West Brompton ⊖	d																						
Imperial Wharf	d																						
Clapham Junction 10	a			00 18		00 23	00 33	00 38		00 48	01 17	06 47	06 53	07 10	07 17	07 24	07 29	07 39		07 42	07 47	07 54	07 59
Clapham Junction	d		00 04	00 18		00 23	00 33	00 39		00 48	01 17	06 47	06 53	07 10	07 17	07 24	07 30	07 40		07 43	07 47	07 54	08 00
Wandsworth Common	d		00 07	00 21		00 26	00 36	00 42		00 51			06 56			07 27	07 33			07 46		07 57	08 03
Balham 4 ⊖	d		00 10	00a24		00 29	00a39	00 45		00a54		06 53	07 00		07 23	07 31	07 36			07 49	07 53	08 01	08 06
London Bridge	d		00a49						00 25										07 16				
Streatham Common 4	d				00 27	00 35		00 52	00 55				07 04			07 35			07 49	07 54		08 05	
Norbury	d	00 01			00 29	00 37		00 54	00 57				07 07			07 37			07 51	07 56		08 07	
Thornton Heath	d	00 04			00 32	00 40		00 57	01 00				07 10			07 40			07 54	07 59		08 10	
Selhurst 4	d	00 07			00a35	00 43		01 00	01a03		01 29		07 13	07 22		07 43		07 51	07 57	08 02		08 13	
East Croydon	a					00 47					01 32			07 26				07 56	08 00				
Purley	a										01 38			07 32									
West Croydon 4	a	00 14						01 05					07 19			07 48	08 10			08 07		08 19	08 40
Sutton 4	a	00 27						01 17				07 12	07 32		07 42	08 01				08 20	08 12	08 32	

		SN 1 E	SN	SN H	SN F	SN	SN	SN	SN H	SN	SN	SN A	SN	SN H	SN	SN	SN A	SN	SN H	SN	SN	SN A	SN
London Victoria 15 ⊖	d	08 02		08 04	08 10	08 16		08 21	08 34	08 46		08 52	08 56	09 02	09 16		09 22	09 26	09 32	09 46		09 52	09 56
Battersea Park	d			08 08		08 20		08 25	08 38	08 50			09 00	09 06	09 20			09 30	09 36	09 50			10 00
Shepherd's Bush ⊖	d																						
Kensington (Olympia) ⊖	d																						
West Brompton ⊖	d																						
Imperial Wharf	d																						
Clapham Junction 10	a	08 09		08 13	08 17	08 24		08 29	08 42	08 54		08 58	09 04	09 10	09 24		09 28	09 34	09 40	09 54		09 58	10 04
Clapham Junction	d	08 10		08 14	08 17	08 24		08 30	08 43	08 54		08 58	09 04	09 10	09 24		09 28	09 34	09 40	09 54		09 58	10 04
Wandsworth Common	d			08 17		08 27		08 33	08 46	08 57			09 07	09 13	09 27			09 37	09 43	09 57			10 07
Balham 4 ⊖	d			08 20	08 23	08 31		08 36	08 49	09 00		09 03	09 10	09 16	09 30		09 33	09 40	09 46	10 00		10 03	10 10
London Bridge	d		07 46				08 16				08 47					09 16					09 49		
Streatham Common 4	d		08 19	08 24		08 35	08 46		08 54	09 05	09 16			09 21	09 35	09 46			09 51	10 05	10 17		
Norbury	d		08 21	08 26		08 37	08 49		08 56	09 07	09 19			09 23	09 37	09 49			09 53	10 07	10 20		
Thornton Heath	d		08 24	08 29		08 40	08 52		08 59	09 10	09 22			09 26	09 40	09 52			09 56	10 10	10 23		
Selhurst 4	d	08 21	08 27	08 32		08 43	08 56		09 02	09 13	09 26			09 30	09 43	09 56			10 00	10 13	10 26		
East Croydon	a	08 26	08 30				08 59				09 29					09 59					10 29		
Purley	a	08 32																					
West Croydon 4	a			08 37		08 49		09 05	09 09	09 19			09 38	09 34	09 49			10 08	10 04	10 19			10 38
Sutton 4	a			08 49	08 42	09 02			09 21	09 32		09 23		09 47	10 02		09 53		10 17	10 32		10 23	

A To Epsom
B not 15 December. From London Victoria
C To Norwood Junction
D not 15 December. From London Bridge
E To Brighton
F To Dorking
G To Bognor Regis
H To Epsom Downs

For faster services between London Victoria, Clapham Junction and East Croydon, refer to Table T175

For other Shepherd's Bush connecting trains, refer to Table T176

Table T170-F

Sundays
15 December to 10 May

London Victoria - Battersea Park, Wandsworth Common, Balham, Streatham Common, Norbury, Thornton Heath & Selhurst-Croydon

		SN A	SN	SN		SN B	SN	SN A	SN	SN	SN B	SN	SN A	SN	SN	SN B	SN	SN A	SN	SN	SN B	SN	SN
London Victoria 15 ⊖	d	10 02	10 16			20 22	20 26	20 32	20 46		20 52	20 56	21 02	21 16		21 22	21 26	21 32	21 46		21 52	21 56	22 02
Battersea Park	d	10 06	10 20				20 30	20 36	20 50			21 00	21 06	21 20			21 30	21 36	21 50			22 00	22 06
Shepherd's Bush ⊖	d																						
Kensington (Olympia) ⊖	d																						
West Brompton ⊖	d																						
Imperial Wharf	d				and at the same minutes past each hour until																		
Clapham Junction 10	a	10 10	10 24			20 28	20 34	20 40	20 54		20 58	21 04	21 10	21 24		21 28	21 34	21 40	21 54		21 58	22 04	22 10
Clapham Junction	d	10 10	10 24			20 28	20 34	20 40	20 54		20 58	21 04	21 10	21 24		21 28	21 34	21 40	21 54		21 58	22 04	22 10
Wandsworth Common	d	10 13	10 27				20 37	20 43	20 57			21 07	21 13	21 27			21 37	21 43	21 57			22 07	22 13
Balham 4 ⊖	d	10 16	10 30			20 33	20 40	20 46	21 00		21 03	21 10	21 16	21 30		21 33	21 40	21 46	22 00		22 03	22 10	22 16
London Bridge	d			10 19						20 49					21 19					21 49			
Streatham Common 4	d	10 21	10 35	10 47				20 51	21 05	21 17			21 21	21 35	21 47			21 51	22 05	22 17			22 24
Norbury	d	10 23	10 37	10 50				20 53	21 07	21 20			21 23	21 37	21 50			21 53	22 07	22 20			22 27
Thornton Heath	d	10 26	10 40	10 53				20 56	21 10	21 23			21 26	21 40	21 53			21 56	22 10	22 23			22 30
Selhurst 4	d	10 30	10 43	10 56				21 00	21 13	21 26			21 30	21 43	21 56			22 00	22 13	22 26			22 33
East Croydon	a			10 59						21 29					21 59					22 29			
Purley	a																						
West Croydon 4	a	10 34	10 49				21 08	21 04	21 19			21 38	21 34	21 49			22 08	22 04	22 19			22 36	22 39
Sutton 4	a	10 47	11 02			20 53		21 17	21 32		21 23		21 47	22 02		21 53		22 17	22 32		22 23		22 52

		SN	SN	SN B	SN	SN	SN	SN	SN B	SN	SN	SN	SN B	SN	SN ■ C	SN	SN	SN	SN D
London Victoria 15 ⊖	d	22 16		22 22	22 26	22 32	22 46		22 52	22 56	23 02	23 16	23 22	23 26	23 32		23 34	23 46	23 56
Battersea Park	d	22 20			22 30	22 36	22 50			23 00	23 06	23 20		23 30			23 38	23 50	00 01
Shepherd's Bush ⊖	d																		
Kensington (Olympia) ⊖	d																		
West Brompton ⊖	d																		
Imperial Wharf	d																		
Clapham Junction 10	a	22 24		22 28	22 34	22 40	22 54		22 58	23 04	23 10	23 24	23 29	23 34	23 39		23 42	23 54	00 05
Clapham Junction	d	22 24		22 28	22 34	22 40	22 54		22 58	23 04	23 10	23 24	23 29	23 34	23 40		23 43	23 55	00 06
Wandsworth Common	d	22 27			22 37	22 43	22 57			23 07	23 13	23 27		23 37			23 46	23 58	00 09
Balham 4 ⊖	d	22 30		22 33	22 40	22 46	23 00		23 03	23 10	23 16	23 31	23 35	23 40			23 49	00 02	00a11
London Bridge	d		22 19					22 49								23 17			
Streatham Common 4	d	22 35	22 47			22 51	23 07	23 17			23 21	23 36				23 49	23 53	00 06	
Norbury	d	22 37	22 50			22 53	23 09	23 20			23 23	23 38				23 51	23 56	00 09	
Thornton Heath	d	22 40	22 53			22 56	23 12	23 23			23 26	23 41				23 54	23 59	00 12	
Selhurst 4	d	22 43	22 56			23 00	23 15	23 26			23a29	23 44			23 51	23 59	00a01	00a14	
East Croydon	a		22 59					23 29							23 56	00 02			
Purley	a														00 02				
West Croydon 4	a	22 49			23 08	23 04	23 21			23 38		23 49		00 08					
Sutton 4	a	23 02		22 53		23 17	23 34		23 23			00 02	23 54						

A To Epsom Downs
B To Epsom
C To Brighton
D To Norwood Junction

For faster services between London Victoria, Clapham Junction and East Croydon, refer to Table T175

For other Shepherd's Bush connecting trains, refer to Table T176

Table T170-R

Mondays to Fridays
16 December to 15 May

Croydon-Selhurst, Thornton Heath, Norbury, Streatham Common, Balham, Wandsworth Common & Battersea Park - London Victoria

Miles	Miles	Miles	Miles			SN MO A	SN MO B	SN MO ■ C	SN	SN ■ D	SN	SN E	SN	SN	SN E	SN F	SN ■ G	SN H	SN ■ D	SN I	SN ■ J	SN	SN E
0	—	—	—	Sutton 4	d											05 51				06 12			
4½	—	—	0	West Croydon 4	d											06 06							
—	0	—	—	Purley	d																		
3	—	0	—	East Croydon	d												06 09						
5½	4¼	1	1¼	**Selhurst** 4	d						05 28		05 40	06 01		06 11	06 12	←	06 16			06 25	
—	5	1	2	**Thornton Heath**	d						05 30		05 43	06 03		06 13		06 13	06 19			06 28	
2¾	6	3	3½	**Norbury**	d						05 33		05 46	06 06		→		06 16	06 22			06 31	
8½	7	4	4	**Streatham Common** 4	d						05 35		05 49	06 09				06 19	06 25			06 36	
—	—	—	10½	London Bridge	a						06 01			06 36								07 06	
10½	9	6	—	**Balham** 4 ⊖	d		00 06		05 03	05 27		05 40	05 55		06 10			06 25	06 29	06 33			06 40
11	9½	6½	—	**Wandsworth Common**	d	00 01	00 08		05 05			05 42	05 57		06 12			06 27			←		06 42
12½	10¾	8	—	Clapham Junction	a	00 05	00 12		05 08	05 31		05 46	06 01		06 16		06 20	06 31	06 35	06 37	06 35		06 46
—	—	—	—	Clapham Junction 10	d	00 05	00 13	00 16	05 09	05 32		05 46	06 01		06 16		06 20	06 31	06 40	06 38	06 40		06 46
—	—	9¾	—	Imperial Wharf	a					05 37									→		06 45		
—	—	10¼	—	West Brompton ⊖	a					05 40											06 47		
—	—	11¼	—	Kensington (Olympia) ⊖	a					05 43											06 50		
—	—	11¾	—	Shepherd's Bush ⊖	a					05 46											06 53		
13¾	12¼	—	—	**Battersea Park**	d	00 09	00 16		05 12			05 50	06 05		06 20			06 35					06 50
15	13½	—	—	London Victoria 15 ⊖	a	00 13	00 21	00 23	05 17			05 54	06 09		06 24		06 27	06 40		06 45			06 54

		SN	SN	SN	SN I	SN K	SN	SN F	SN	SN A	SN L	SN ■ D	SN I	SN ■ M	SN	SN	SN K	SN F	SN	SN A	SN L	SN ■ N	SN I
Sutton 4	d			06 16	06 42				06 41		06 51		07 12			07 00			07 11		07 21		07 42
West Croydon 4	d		06 21	06 34				06 52	06 56		07 04					07 18		07 22	07 26		07 34		
Purley	d																						
East Croydon	d											07 10										07 40	
Selhurst 4	d	06 31		06 40			06 56		07 01		07 10	07 16			07 20	07 26			07 31		07 40	07 46	
Thornton Heath	d	06 33		06 43			06 58		07 03		07 13	07 19			07 23	07 28			07 33		07 43	07 49	
Norbury	d	06 36		06 46			07 01		07 06		07 16	07 22			07 27	07 31			07 36		07 46	07 52	
Streatham Common 4	d	06 39		06 49			07 06		07 09		07 19	07 25			07 31	07 36			07 39		07 49	07 55	
London Bridge	a						07 36			←						08 06				←			
Balham 4 ⊖	d	06 44	06 51	06 55	07 03	07 10		07 21	07 14	07 21	07 25	07 29	07 32		07 36		07 40	07 51	07 44	07 51	07 55	07 59	08 02
Wandsworth Common	d	06 46	06 53	06 57		07 12		→	07 16	07 23	07 27			←	07 38		07 42	→	07 46	07 53	07 57		
Clapham Junction	a	06 50	06 57	07 01	07 07	07 16			07 20	07 27	07 31	07 35	07 37	07 35	07 41		07 46		07 50	07 57	08 01	08 05	08 07
Clapham Junction 10	d	06 50	06 57	07 01	07 08	07 16			07 20	07 27	07 31	07 39	07 38	07 39	07 42		07 46		07 50	07 57	08 01	08 18	08 08
Imperial Wharf	a											→		07 44								→	
West Brompton ⊖	a													07 47									
Kensington (Olympia) ⊖	a													07 50									
Shepherd's Bush ⊖	a													07 53									
Battersea Park	d	06 54	07 01	07 05		07 20			07 24	07 31	07 35				07 45		07 50		07 54	08 01	08 05		
London Victoria 15 ⊖	a	06 58	07 05	07 09	07 15	07 24			07 28	07 35	07 39		07 46		07 50		07 54		07 59	08 05	08 09		08 16

		SN	SN	SN K	SN ■ O	SN F	SN	SN A	SN L	SN ■ D	SN I	SN ■ M	SN	SN	SN K	SN F	SN	SN A	SN L	SN ■	SN	SN I	SN K
Sutton 4	d		07 30				07 41		07 51		08 12			08 00			08 11		08 21		08 30	08 42	
West Croydon 4	d		07 48			07 52	07 56		08 04					08 18		08 22	08 26		08 34		08 48		
Purley	d																						
East Croydon	d									08 11										08 40			
Selhurst 4	d	07 50	07 56				08 01		08 10	08 16			08 20	08 26			08 31		08 40	08 46	08 56		
Thornton Heath	d	07 53	07 58				08 03		08 13	08 19			08 23	08 28			08 34		08 43	08 49	08 58		
Norbury	d	07 57	08 01				08 06		08 16	08 22			08 27	08 31			08 37		08 46	08 52	09 01		
Streatham Common 4	d	08 01	08 06				08 09		08 19	08 25			08 31	08 36			08 40		08 49	08 55	09 06		
London Bridge	a		08 36					←						09 06				←			09 36		
Balham 4 ⊖	d	08 05		08 10		08 21	08 14	08 21	08 25	08 29	08 32		08 35		08 40	08 51	08 45	08 51	08 55	08 59		09 03	09 10
Wandsworth Common	d	08 07		08 12	←	→	08 16	08 23	08 27			←	08 37		08 42	→	08 47	08 54	08 57				09 12
Clapham Junction	a	08 11		08 16	08 05		08 20	08 27	08 31	08 35	08 37	08 35	08 41		08 46		08 51	08 57	09 01	09 05		09 07	09 16
Clapham Junction 10	d	08 11		08 16	08 18		08 20	08 27	08 31	08 40	08 38	08 40	08 41		08 46		08 53	08 58	09 01	09 06		09 09	09 16
Imperial Wharf	a				08 22					→		08 44								09 10			
West Brompton ⊖	a				08 25							08 47								09 13			
Kensington (Olympia) ⊖	a				08 28							08 50								09 16			
Shepherd's Bush ⊖	a				08 31							08 53								09 19			
Battersea Park	d	08 15		08 20			08 24	08 31	08 35				08 45		08 50		08 57	09 02	09 05				09 20
London Victoria 15 ⊖	a	08 19		08 24			08 30	08 35	08 40		08 45		08 50		08 54		09 04	09 08	09 10			09 19	09 24

A From West Croydon
B From Dorking
C From East Grinstead
D To Milton Keynes Central
E From Norwood Junction
F To London Victoria
G From Eastbourne
H From Sutton (Surrey)
I From Epsom
J From Selhurst to Milton Keynes Central
K From London Bridge
L From Epsom Downs
M From East Croydon to Milton Keynes Central
N To Watford Junction
O From East Croydon to Watford Junction

For faster services between London Victoria, Clapham Junction and East Croydon, refer to Table T175

For other Shepherd's Bush connecting trains, refer to Table T176

Table T170-R

Mondays to Fridays
16 December to 15 May

Croydon-Selhurst, Thornton Heath, Norbury, Streatham Common, Balham, Wandsworth Common & Battersea Park - London Victoria

		SN	SN	SN	SN	SN 1	SN	SN 1	SN	SN	SN	SN	SN	SN	SN	SN	SN	SN	SN	SN	SN	SN 1	SN
		A		B	C	D	E	F	G	H	A		B	C	E	H	G	A		B	C	D	E
Sutton	d		08 41		08 51		09 12					09 11		09 21	09 42				09 41		09 51		10 12
West Croydon	d	08 52	08 56		09 04						09 21	09 26		09 34				09 51	09 56		10 04		
Purley	d								09 15								09 45						
East Croydon	d					09 10			09 21								09 51					10 10	
Selhurst	d		09 01		09 10	09 16			09 27			09 31		09 40			09 56		10 01		10 10	10 16	
Thornton Heath	d		09 03		09 13	09 19			09 29			09 33		09 43			09 58		10 03		10 13	10 19	
Norbury	d		09 06		09 16	09 22			09 32			09 36		09 46			10 01		10 06		10 16	10 22	
Streatham Common	d		09 09		09 19	09 25			09 36			09 39		09 49			10 06		10 09		10 19	10 25	
London Bridge	a			←					10 06				←				10 36			←			
Balham	d	09 21	09 14	09 21	09 25	09 29	09 33			09 40	09 51	09 44	09 51	09 55	10 03	10 10		10 21	10 14	10 21	10 25	10 29	10 33
Wandsworth Common	d	→	09 16	09 23	09 27			←		09 42	→	09 46	09 53	09 57		10 12		→	10 16	10 23	10 27		
Clapham Junction	a		09 20	09 27	09 31	09 35	09 37	09 35		09 46		09 50	09 57	10 01	10 07	10 16			10 20	10 27	10 31	10 35	10 37
Clapham Junction	d		09 20	09 27	09 31	09 39	09 38	09 39		09 46		09 50	09 57	10 01	10 08	10 16			10 20	10 27	10 31	10 41	10 38
Imperial Wharf	a					→		09 43														→	
West Brompton	a							09 46															
Kensington (Olympia)	a							09 50															
Shepherd's Bush	a							09 53															
Battersea Park	d		09 24	09 31	09 35					09 50		09 54	10 01	10 05		10 20			10 24	10 31	10 36		
London Victoria	a		09 30	09 35	09 40		09 45			09 54		09 58	10 05	10 09	10 15	10 24			10 28	10 35	10 40		10 45

		SN 1	SN	SN	SN	SN	SN	SN	SN	SN	SN	SN	SN	SN	SN	SN 1	SN	SN 1	SN	SN	SN	SN
		F	G	H	A		B	C	E	H	G	A		B	C	D	E	F	G	H	A	
Sutton	d					10 11		10 21	10 42				10 41		10 51		11 12					11 11
West Croydon	d				10 21	10 26		10 34				10 51	10 56		11 04						11 21	11 26
Purley	d		10 15								10 45								11 15			
East Croydon	d		10 22								10 52					11 10			11 22			
Selhurst	d		10 26			10 31		10 40			10 56		11 01		11 10	11 16			11 26			11 31
Thornton Heath	d		10 28			10 33		10 43			10 58		11 03		11 13	11 19			11 28			11 33
Norbury	d		10 31			10 36		10 46			11 01		11 06		11 16	11 22			11 31			11 36
Streatham Common	d		10 36			10 39		10 49			11 06		11 09		11 19	11 25			11 36			11 39
London Bridge	a		11 06				←				11 36			←					12 06			
Balham	d			10 40	10 51	10 44	10 51	10 55	11 03	11 10		11 21	11 14	11 21	11 25	11 29	11 33			11 40	11 51	11 44
Wandsworth Common	d	←		10 42	→	10 46	10 53	10 57		11 12		→	11 16	11 23	11 27			←		11 42	→	11 46
Clapham Junction	a	10 35		10 46		10 50	10 57	11 01	11 07	11 16			11 20	11 27	11 31	11 35	11 37	11 35		11 46		11 50
Clapham Junction	d	10 41		10 46		10 50	10 57	11 01	11 08	11 16			11 20	11 27	11 31	11 39	11 38	11 39		11 46		11 50
Imperial Wharf	a	10 45														→		11 43				
West Brompton	a	10 48																11 46				
Kensington (Olympia)	a	10 51																11 50				
Shepherd's Bush	a	10 54																11 53				
Battersea Park	d			10 50		10 54	11 01	11 05		11 20			11 24	11 31	11 35					11 50		11 54
London Victoria	a			10 54		10 58	11 05	11 09	11 15	11 24			11 28	11 35	11 39		11 45			11 54		11 58

		SN	SN	SN	SN	SN	SN	SN	SN	SN	SN 1	SN	SN 1	SN	SN	SN	SN	SN	SN	SN	SN	SN	SN
		B	C	E	H	G	A		B	C	D	E	F	G	H	A		B	C	E	H	G	A
Sutton	d		11 21	11 42				11 41		11 51		12 12					12 11		12 21	12 42			
West Croydon	d		11 34				11 51	11 56		12 04						12 21	12 26		12 34				12 51
Purley	d					11 45								12 15								12 45	
East Croydon	d					11 52					12 10			12 22								12 52	
Selhurst	d		11 40			11 56		12 01		12 10	12 16			12 26			12 31		12 40			12 56	
Thornton Heath	d		11 43			11 58		12 03		12 13	12 19			12 28			12 33		12 43			12 58	
Norbury	d		11 46			12 01		12 06		12 16	12 22			12 31			12 36		12 46			13 01	
Streatham Common	d		11 49			12 06		12 09		12 19	12 25			12 36			12 39		12 49			13 06	
London Bridge	a	←				12 36			←					13 06				←				13 36	
Balham	d	11 51	11 55	12 03	12 10		12 21	12 14	12 21	12 25	12 29	12 33			12 40	12 51	12 44	12 51	12 55	13 03	13 10		13 21
Wandsworth Common	d	11 53	11 57		12 12		→	12 16	12 23	12 27			←		12 42	→	12 46	12 53	12 57		13 12		→
Clapham Junction	a	11 57	12 01	12 07	12 16			12 20	12 27	12 31	12 35	12 37	12 35		12 46		12 50	12 57	13 01	13 07	13 16		
Clapham Junction	d	11 57	12 01	12 08	12 16			12 20	12 27	12 31	12 39	12 38	12 39		12 46		12 50	12 57	13 01	13 08	13 16		
Imperial Wharf	a										→		12 45										
West Brompton	a												12 48										
Kensington (Olympia)	a												12 51										
Shepherd's Bush	a												12 53										
Battersea Park	d	12 01	12 05		12 20			12 24	12 31	12 35					12 50		12 54	13 01	13 05		13 20		
London Victoria	a	12 05	12 09	12 15	12 24			12 28	12 35	12 39		12 45			12 54		12 58	13 05	13 09	13 15	13 24		

A To London Victoria
B From West Croydon
C From Epsom Downs
D To Milton Keynes Central
E From Epsom
F From East Croydon to Milton Keynes Central
G From Caterham
H From London Bridge

For faster services between London Victoria, Clapham Junction and East Croydon, refer to Table T175

For other Shepherd's Bush connecting trains, refer to Table T176

Table T170-R

Mondays to Fridays
16 December to 15 May

Croydon-Selhurst, Thornton Heath, Norbury, Streatham Common, Balham, Wandsworth Common & Battersea Park - London Victoria

		SN	SN	SN TThO	SN MWFO	SN MWFO 1	SN TThO 1	SN	SN MWFO 1	SN TThO 1	SN	SN	SN	SN	SN	SN	SN	SN	SN	SN	SN	SN
			A	B	B	C	C	D	E	F	G	H	I		A	B	D	H	G	I		A
Sutton	d	12 41		12 50	12 51			13 12						13 11		13 21	13 42				13 41	
West Croydon	d	12 56		13 04	13 04								13 21	13 26		13 34				13 51	13 56	
Purley	d										13 15								13 45			
East Croydon	d					13 10					13 22								13 52			
Selhurst	d	13 01		13 09	13 10	13 16	13 18				13 26			13 31		13 40			13 56		14 01	
Thornton Heath	d	13 03		13 13	13 13	13 19	13 20				13 28			13 33		13 43			13 58		14 03	
Norbury	d	13 06		13 16	13 16	13 22	13 23				13 31			13 36		13 46			14 01		14 06	
Streatham Common	d	13 09		13 19	13 19	13 25	13 26				13 36			13 39		13 49			14 06		14 09	
London Bridge	a		←								14 06				←				14 36			←
Balham	d	13 14	13 21	13 25	13 25	13 29	13 30	13 33				13 40	13 51	13 44	13 51	13 55	14 03	14 10		14 21	14 14	14 21
Wandsworth Common	d	13 16	13 23	13 27	13 27				←	←		13 42	→	13 46	13 53	13 57		14 12		→	14 16	14 23
Clapham Junction	a	13 20	13 27	13 31	13 31	13 35	13 35	13 37	13 35	13 35		13 46		13 50	13 57	14 01	14 07	14 16			14 20	14 27
Clapham Junction	d	13 20	13 27	13 31	13 31	13 39	13 39	13 38	13 39	13 39		13 46		13 50	13 57	14 01	14 08	14 16			14 20	14 27
Imperial Wharf	a					→	→		13 43	13 43												
West Brompton	a								13 46	13 46												
Kensington (Olympia)	a								13 50	13 50												
Shepherd's Bush	a								13 53	13 53												
Battersea Park	d	13 24	13 31	13 35	13 35							13 50		13 54	14 01	14 05		14 20			14 24	14 31
London Victoria	a	13 28	13 35	13 39	13 39			13 45				13 54		13 58	14 05	14 09	14 15	14 24			14 28	14 35

		SN	SN 1	SN	SN 1	SN	SN	SN	SN	SN	SN	SN 1	SN	SN 1	SN	SN	SN	SN	SN	SN	SN 1	SN	SN 1
		B	C	D	E	G	H	I		A	B	J	D	K	G	H	I		A	B	C	D	E
Sutton	d	13 51		14 12					14 11		14 21		14 42					14 41		14 51		15 12	
West Croydon	d	14 04						14 21	14 26		14 34						14 51	14 56		15 04			
Purley	d					14 15									14 45								
East Croydon	d		14 10			14 22									14 52						15 10		
Selhurst	d	14 10	14 16			14 26			14 31		14 40	14 46			14 56			15 01		15 10	15 16		
Thornton Heath	d	14 13	14 19			14 28			14 33		14 43	14 49			14 58			15 03		15 13	15 19		
Norbury	d	14 16	14 22			14 31			14 36		14 46	14 52			15 01			15 06		15 16	15 22		
Streatham Common	d	14 19	14 25			14 36			14 39		14 49	14 55			15 06			15 09		15 19	15 25		
London Bridge	a					15 06				←					15 36				←				
Balham	d	14 25	14 29	14 33			14 40	14 51	14 44	14 51	14 55	14 59	15 03			15 10	15 21	15 14	15 21	15 25	15 29	15 33	
Wandsworth Common	d	14 27			←		14 42	→	14 46	14 53	14 57			←		15 12	→	15 16	15 23	15 27			←
Clapham Junction	a	14 31	14 35	14 37	14 35		14 46		14 50	14 57	15 01	15 05	15 07	15 05		15 16		15 20	15 27	15 31	15 35	15 37	15 35
Clapham Junction	d	14 31	14 40	14 38	14 40		14 46		14 50	14 57	15 01	15 10	15 08	15 10		15 16		15 20	15 27	15 31	15 39	15 38	15 39
Imperial Wharf	a		→		14 44							→		15 14							→		15 44
West Brompton	a				14 47									15 17									15 47
Kensington (Olympia)	a				14 51									15 21									15 50
Shepherd's Bush	a				14 54									15 23									15 53
Battersea Park	d	14 35					14 50		14 54	15 01	15 05					15 20		15 24	15 31	15 35			
London Victoria	a	14 39		14 45			14 54		14 58	15 05	15 09		15 15			15 24		15 28	15 35	15 39		15 45	

		SN	SN	SN	SN	SN	SN	SN 1	SN	SN	SN	SN	SN	SN	SN	SN 1	SN	SN 1	SN	SN	SN	SN
		G	H	I		A	B	L	D	H	G	I		A	B	C	D	E	G	H	I	
Sutton	d				15 12		15 21		15 42				15 41		15 51		16 12					16 11
West Croydon	d			15 21	15 26		15 34					15 51	15 56		16 04						16 21	16 26
Purley	d	15 15									15 45								16 15			
East Croydon	d	15 22						15 43			15 51					16 10			16 21			
Selhurst	d	15 26			15 31		15 40	15 46			15 56		16 01		16 10	16 16			16 26			16 31
Thornton Heath	d	15 28			15 33		15 43	15 49			15 58		16 03		16 13	16 19			16 28			16 33
Norbury	d	15 31			15 36		15 46	15 52			16 01		16 06		16 16	16 22			16 31			16 36
Streatham Common	d	15 36			15 39		15 49	15 55			16 06		16 09		16 19	16 25			16 36			16 39
London Bridge	a	16 06				←					16 36			←					17 06			
Balham	d		15 40	15 51	15 44	15 51	15 55	16 00	16 03	16 10		16 21	16 14	16 21	16 25	16 29	16 33			16 40	16 51	16 44
Wandsworth Common	d		15 42	→	15 46	15 53	15 57			16 12		→	16 16	16 23	16 27			←		16 42	→	16 46
Clapham Junction	a		15 46		15 50	15 57	16 01	16 04	16 07	16 16			16 20	16 27	16 31	16 35	16 37	16 35		16 46		16 50
Clapham Junction	d		15 46		15 50	15 57	16 01	16 04	16 08	16 16			16 20	16 27	16 31	16 39	16 38	16 39		16 46		16 50
Imperial Wharf	a															→		16 44				
West Brompton	a																	16 47				
Kensington (Olympia)	a																	16 50				
Shepherd's Bush	a																	16 53				
Battersea Park	d		15 50		15 54	16 01	16 05			16 20			16 24	16 31	16 35					16 50		16 54
London Victoria	a		15 54		15 58	16 05	16 11	16 13	16 15	16 24			16 28	16 35	16 39		16 45			16 54		16 58

A From West Croydon
B From Epsom Downs
C To Milton Keynes Central
D From Epsom
E From East Croydon to Milton Keynes Central
F From Selhurst to Milton Keynes Central
G From Caterham
H From London Bridge
I To London Victoria
J To Shepherd's Bush
K From Selhurst
L From South Croydon

For faster services between London Victoria, Clapham Junction and East Croydon, refer to Table T175

For other Shepherd's Bush connecting trains, refer to Table T176

Table T170-R

Mondays to Fridays
16 December to 15 May

Croydon-Selhurst, Thornton Heath, Norbury, Streatham Common, Balham, Wandsworth Common & Battersea Park - London Victoria

	SN A	SN B	SN 1 C	SN D	SN 1 E	SN F	SN G	SN H	SN	SN A	SN B	SN 1 I	SN D	SN 1 J	SN F	SN G	SN H	SN	SN A	SN B	SN 1	SN D
Sutton 4 d		16 21		16 42					16 41		16 51		17 12					17 11		17 21		17 42
West Croydon 4 d		16 34						16 51	16 56		17 04						17 22	17 26		17 34		
Purley d						16 45									17 15							
East Croydon d			16 40			16 51						17 10			17 21						17 40	
Selhurst 4 d		16 40	16 46			16 56			17 01		17 10	17 16			17 26			17 31		17 40	17 46	
Thornton Heath d		16 43	16 49			16 58			17 03		17 13	17 19			17 28			17 33		17 43	17 49	
Norbury d		16 46	16 52			17 01			17 06		17 16	17 22			17 31			17 36		17 46	17 52	
Streatham Common 4 d		16 49	16 55			17 06			17 09		17 19	17 25			17 36			17 39		17 49	17 55	
London Bridge a	←					17 36				←					18 06				←			
Balham 4 d	16 51	16 55	16 59	17 03			17 12	17 21	17 14	17 21	17 25	17 30	17 33			17 40	17 51	17 44	17 51	17 55	17 59	18 03
Wandsworth Common d	16 53	16 57			←		17 14	→	17 16	17 23	17 27			←		17 42	→	17 46	17 53	17 57		
Clapham Junction a	16 57	17 01	17 05	17 07	17 05		17 17		17 20	17 27	17 31	17 35	17 37	17 35		17 46		17 50	17 57	18 01	18 04	18 07
Clapham Junction 10 d	16 57	17 01	17 09	17 08	17 09		17 18		17 20	17 27	17 31	17 39	17 38	17 39		17 46		17 50	17 57	18 01	18 05	18 08
Imperial Wharf a			→		17 13							→		17 44								
West Brompton a					17 16									17 47								
Kensington (Olympia) a					17 19									17 50								
Shepherd's Bush a					17 22									17 53								
Battersea Park d	17 01	17 05					17 21		17 24	17 31	17 35					17 50		17 54	18 01	18 05		
London Victoria 15 a	17 05	17 09		17 15			17 26		17 28	17 35	17 39		17 45			17 54		17 58	18 05	18 09	18 14	18 19

	SN G	SN F	SN H	SN	SN A	SN B	SN 1 I	SN	SN D	SN 1 J	SN G	SN H	SN	SN A	SN B	SN	SN D	SN G	SN H	SN	SN A
Sutton 4 d				17 41		17 51		18 00	18 12				18 11		18 21	18 30	18 42			18 41	
West Croydon 4 d			17 52	17 56		18 04		18 18				18 22	18 26		18 34	18 48			18 52	18 56	
Purley d		17 45																			
East Croydon d		17 51					18 10														
Selhurst 4 d		17 56		18 01		18 10	18 16	18 26					18 31		18 40	18 56				19 01	
Thornton Heath d		17 58		18 03		18 13	18 19	18 28					18 33		18 43	18 58				19 03	
Norbury d		18 01		18 06		18 16	18 22	18 31					18 36		18 46	19 01				19 06	
Streatham Common 4 d		18 06		18 09		18 19	18 25	18 36					18 39		18 49	19 06				19 09	
London Bridge a		18 36			←			19 06						←		19 36					←
Balham 4 d	18 10		18 21	18 14	18 21	18 25	18 29		18 33		18 40	18 51	18 44	18 51	18 55		19 03	19 10	19 21	19 14	19 21
Wandsworth Common d	18 12		→	18 16	18 23	18 27				←	18 42	→	18 46	18 53	18 57			19 12	→	19 16	19 23
Clapham Junction a	18 16			18 20	18 27	18 31	18 35		18 37	18 35	18 46		18 50	18 57	19 01		19 07	19 16		19 20	19 27
Clapham Junction 10 d	18 16			18 20	18 27	18 31	18 39		18 38	18 39	18 46		18 50	18 57	19 01		19 08	19 16		19 20	19 27
Imperial Wharf a							→			18 44											
West Brompton a										18 47											
Kensington (Olympia) a										18 50											
Shepherd's Bush a										18 53											
Battersea Park d	18 20			18 24	18 31	18 35					18 50		18 54	19 01	19 05			19 20		19 24	19 31
London Victoria 15 a	18 24			18 30	18 36	18 39			18 45		18 54		19 00	19 05	19 09		19 15	19 24		19 28	19 35

	SN B	SN 1 I	SN	SN D	SN 1 J	SN G	SN H	SN	SN A	SN B	SN D	SN G	SN	SN H	SN	SN A	SN B	SN 1 I	SN D	SN G	SN	SN H
Sutton 4 d	18 51		19 00	19 12				19 11		19 21	19 42				19 41		19 51		20 12			
West Croydon 4 d	19 04		19 18				19 22	19 26		19 34				19 52	19 56		20 04					20 21
Purley d																						
East Croydon d		19 10																20 10				
Selhurst 4 d	19 10	19 16	19 26					19 31		19 40			19 56		20 01		20 10	20 16			20 29	
Thornton Heath d	19 13	19 19	19 28					19 33		19 43			19 58		20 03		20 13	20 19			20 31	
Norbury d	19 16	19 22	19 31					19 36		19 46			20 01		20 06		20 16	20 22			20 34	
Streatham Common 4 d	19 19	19 25	19 36					19 39		19 49			20 06		20 09		20 19	20 25			20 37	
London Bridge a			20 07						←				20 36			←					21 06	
Balham 4 d	19 25	19 29		19 33		19 40	19 51	19 44	19 51	19 55	20 03	20 10		20 21	20 14	20 21	20 25	20 29	20 33	20 40		20 51
Wandsworth Common d	19 27				←	19 42	→	19 46	19 53	19 57		20 12		→	20 16	20 23	20 27			20 42		→
Clapham Junction a	19 31	19 35		19 37	19 35	19 46		19 50	19 57	20 01	20 07	20 16			20 20	20 27	20 31	20 35	20 37	20 46		
Clapham Junction 10 d	19 31	19 40		19 38	19 40	19 46		19 50	19 57	20 01	20 08	20 16			20 20	20 27	20 31	20 36	20 38	20 46		
Imperial Wharf a		→			19 44													20 40				
West Brompton a					19 47													20 43				
Kensington (Olympia) a					19 51													20 47				
Shepherd's Bush a					19 54													20 50				
Battersea Park d	19 35					19 50		19 54	20 01	20 05		20 20			20 24	20 31	20 35			20 50		
London Victoria 15 a	19 39			19 45		19 54		19 58	20 05	20 09	20 17	20 24			20 30	20 35	20 39		20 45	20 54		

A From West Croydon
B From Epsom Downs
C To Shepherd's Bush
D From Epsom
E From East Croydon
F From Caterham
G From London Bridge
H To London Victoria
I To Milton Keynes Central
J From East Croydon to Milton Keynes Central

For faster services between London Victoria, Clapham Junction and East Croydon, refer to Table T175

For other Shepherd's Bush connecting trains, refer to Table T176

Table T170-R

Mondays to Fridays
16 December to 15 May

Croydon-Selhurst, Thornton Heath, Norbury, Streatham Common, Balham, Wandsworth Common & Battersea Park - London Victoria

	SN	SN A	SN B	SN C	SN D	SN E	SN F	SN	SN A	SN B	SN 1 G	SN C	SN D	SN E	SN F	SN	SN A	SN B	SN C	SN D	SN E	SN F
Sutton 4 d	20 11		20 21	20 42				20 41		20 51		21 12				21 11		21 21	21 42			
West Croydon 4 d	20 26		20 34				20 51	20 56		21 04					21 22	21 26		21 34				21 51
Purley d						20 45								21 15							21 45	
East Croydon d						20 54					21 10			21 24							21 52	
Selhurst 4 d	20 32		20 40			20 58		21 01		21 10	21 16			21 28		21 31		21 40			21 56	
Thornton Heath d	20 34		20 43			21 00		21 03		21 13	21 19			21 30		21 34		21 43			21 58	
Norbury d	20 37		20 46			21 03		21 06		21 16	21 22			21 33		21 37		21 46			22 01	
Streatham Common 4 d	20 40		20 49			21 06		21 09		21 19	21 25			21 37		21 40		21 49			22 07	
London Bridge a		←				21 36			←					22 06			←				22 36	
Balham 4 d	20 44	20 51	20 55	21 03	21 10		21 21	21 14	21 21	21 25	21 29	21 33	21 40		21 51	21 44	21 51	21 55	22 03	22 10		22 21
Wandsworth Common d	20 46	20 53	20 57		21 12		→	21 16	21 23	21 27			21 42		→	21 46	21 53	21 57		22 12		→
Clapham Junction a	20 50	20 57	21 01	21 07	21 16			21 20	21 27	21 31	21 35	21 37	21 46			21 50	21 57	22 01	22 07	22 16		
Clapham Junction 10 d	20 50	20 57	21 01	21 08	21 16			21 20	21 27	21 31	21 36	21 39	21 46			21 50	21 57	22 01	22 08	22 16		
Imperial Wharf a											21 40											
West Brompton a											21 43											
Kensington (Olympia) a											21 47											
Shepherd's Bush a											21 50											
Battersea Park d	20 54	21 01	21 05		21 20			21 24	21 31	21 35			21 50			21 54	22 01	22 05		22 20		
London Victoria 15 a	20 58	21 07	21 09	21 15	21 24			21 28	21 35	21 39		21 46	21 54			21 58	22 05	22 09	22 16	22 24		

	SN	SN A	SN B	SN 1 G	SN C	SN D	SN E	SN F	SN	SN A	SN B	SN C	SN D	SN E	SN F	SN	SN A	SN B	SN C	SN D	SN FX B	SN FO B
Sutton 4 d	21 41		21 50		22 12				22 11		22 21	22 42				22 41		22 51	23 12		23 15	23 15
West Croydon 4 d	21 56		22 04					22 21	22 26		22 34				22 51	22 56		23 04			23 28	23 28
Purley d							22 15							22 45								
East Croydon d							22 22							22 52								
Selhurst 4 d	22 01		22 09	22 17			22 26		22 31		22 40			22 56		23 01		23 10			23 35	23 35
Thornton Heath d	22 03		22 13	22 19			22 28		22 33		22 43			22 58		23 03		23 13			23 38	23 38
Norbury d	22 06		22 16	22 22			22 31		22 36		22 46			23 01		23 06		23 16			23 41	23 41
Streatham Common 4 d	22 10		22 19	22 25			22 36		22 39		22 49			23 06		23 09		23 19			23 44	23 44
London Bridge a		←					23 06			←				23 36			←					
Balham 4 d	22 15	22 21	22 25	22 30	22 33	22 40		22 51	22 44	22 51	22 55	23 03	23 10		23 21	23 14	23 21	23 25	23 33	23 37	23 48	23 48
Wandsworth Common d	22 17	22 23	22 27			22 42		→	22 46	22 53	22 57		23 12		→	23 16	23 23	23 27			23 50	23 50
Clapham Junction a	22 20	22 27	22 31	22 35	22 37	22 46			22 50	22 57	23 01	23 07	23 16			23 20	23 27	23 31	23 37	23 41	23 54	23 54
Clapham Junction 10 d	22 21	22 27	22 31	22 36	22 38	22 46			22 50	22 57	23 01	23 08	23 16			23 20	23 27	23 31	23 38	23 42	23 54	23 54
Imperial Wharf a				22 40																		
West Brompton a				22 43																		
Kensington (Olympia) a				22 47																		
Shepherd's Bush a				22 50																		
Battersea Park d	22 24	22 31	22 35			22 50			22 54	23 01	23 05		23 20			23 24	23 31	23 35			23 58	23 58
London Victoria 15 a	22 29	22 37	22 39		22 45	22 55			23 01	23 05	23 09	23 15	23 24			23 28	23 37	23 39	23 47	23 50	00 03	00 05

Saturdays
21 December to 16 May

	SN	SN 1 H	SN 1 I	SN J	SN	SN 1 H	SN J	SN	SN	SN	SN	SN C	SN D	SN	SN F	SN	SN A	SN	SN 1 H	SN C	SN 1 K	SN E
Sutton 4 d											06 21	06 42				06 41		06 51		07 12		
West Croydon 4 d										06 21	06 34				06 51	06 56		07 04				
Purley d			05 24																			07 15
East Croydon d			05 30			06 10													07 10			07 23
Selhurst 4 d			05 33		06 10	06 16		06 26	06 32		06 40			06 56		07 01		07 10	07 16			07 27
Thornton Heath d			05 36		06 13	06 19		06 28	06 34		06 43			06 58		07 03		07 13	07 19			07 29
Norbury d			05 39		06 16	06 22		06 31	06 37		06 46			07 01		07 06		07 16	07 22			07 32
Streatham Common 4 d			05 41		06 19	06 25		06 36	06 40		06 49			07 06		07 09		07 19	07 25			07 36
London Bridge a								07 07						07 37			←					08 07
Balham 4 d		05 33	05 46	06 10	06 25	06 29	06 40		06 44	06 51	06 55	07 03	07 10		07 21	07 14	07 21	07 25	07 29	07 33		
Wandsworth Common d				06 12	06 27		06 42		06 46	06 53	06 57		07 12		→	07 16	07 23	07 27			←	
Clapham Junction a		05 37	05 50	06 16	06 31	06 35	06 46		06 50	06 57	07 01	07 07	07 16			07 20	07 27	07 31	07 35	07 37	07 35	
Clapham Junction 10 d	05 02	05 39	05 51	06 16	06 31	06 40	06 46		06 50	06 57	07 01	07 08	07 16			07 20	07 27	07 31	07 40	07 38	07 40	
Imperial Wharf a		05 43				06 44													→		07 44	
West Brompton a		05 46				06 47															07 47	
Kensington (Olympia) a		05 49				06 51															07 51	
Shepherd's Bush a		05 52				06 54															07 54	
Battersea Park d	05 06		05 54	06 20	06 35		06 50		06 54	07 01	07 05		07 20			07 24	07 31	07 35				
London Victoria 15 a	05 11		05 59	06 24	06 39		06 54		06 58	07 05	07 09	07 15	07 24			07 28	07 35	07 39		07 45		

A From West Croydon
B From Epsom Downs
C From Epsom
D From London Bridge
E From Caterham
F To London Victoria
G To Watford Junction
H To Milton Keynes Central
I From Brighton
J From Norwood Junction
K From East Croydon to Milton Keynes Central

For faster services between London Victoria, Clapham Junction and East Croydon, refer to Table T175

For other Shepherd's Bush connecting trains, refer to Table T176

Table T170-R

Saturdays

21 December to 16 May

Croydon-Selhurst, Thornton Heath, Norbury, Streatham Common, Balham, Wandsworth Common & Battersea Park - London Victoria

		SN	SN	SN	SN	SN	SN	SN	SN	SN	SN	SN	SN	SN 1	SN	SN 1	SN	SN	SN	SN	SN	SN
		A	B		C	D	E	A	F	B		C	D	G	E	H	F	A	B		C	D
Sutton 4	d			07 11		07 21	07 42				07 41		07 51		08 12					08 11		08 21
West Croydon 4	d		07 21	07 26		07 34				07 51	07 56		08 04						08 21	08 26		08 34
Purley	d								07 45								08 15					
East Croydon	d								07 53					08 10			08 23					
Selhurst 4	d			07 31		07 40			07 57		08 01		08 10	08 16			08 27			08 31		08 40
Thornton Heath	d			07 33		07 43			07 59		08 03		08 13	08 19			08 29			08 33		08 43
Norbury	d			07 36		07 46			08 02		08 06		08 16	08 22			08 32			08 36		08 46
Streatham Common 4	d			07 39		07 49			08 06		08 09		08 19	08 25			08 36			08 39		08 49
London Bridge	a				←				08 37			←					09 07				←	
Balham 4	d	07 40	07 51	07 44	07 51	07 55	08 03	08 10		08 21	08 14	08 21	08 25	08 29	08 33			08 40	08 51	08 44	08 51	08 55
Wandsworth Common	d	07 42	→	07 46	07 53	07 57		08 12		→	08 16	08 23	08 27			←		08 42	→	08 46	08 53	08 57
Clapham Junction	a	07 46		07 50	07 57	08 01	08 07	08 16			08 20	08 27	08 31	08 35	08 37	08 35		08 46		08 50	08 57	09 01
Clapham Junction 10	d	07 46		07 50	07 57	08 01	08 08	08 16			08 20	08 27	08 31	08 40	08 38	08 40		08 46		08 50	08 57	09 01
Imperial Wharf	a													→		08 45						
West Brompton	a															08 47						
Kensington (Olympia)	a															08 51						
Shepherd's Bush	a															08 54						
Battersea Park	d	07 50		07 54	08 01	08 05		08 20			08 24	08 31	08 35					08 50		08 54	09 01	09 05
London Victoria 15	a	07 54		07 58	08 05	08 09	08 15	08 24			08 28	08 35	08 39		08 45			08 54		08 58	09 05	09 09

		SN	SN	SN	SN	SN	SN	SN	SN 1	SN	SN 1	SN	SN	SN	SN	SN	SN	SN	SN	SN	SN	SN	SN	SN
		E	A	F	B		C	D	G	E	H	F	A	B		C	D	E	A	F	B		C	D
Sutton 4	d	08 42				08 41		08 51		09 12					09 11		09 21	09 42				09 41		09 51
West Croydon 4	d				08 51	08 56		09 04						09 22	09 26		09 35				09 51	09 56		10 04
Purley	d			08 45								09 15								09 45				
East Croydon	d			08 53					09 10			09 23								09 53				
Selhurst 4	d			08 57		09 01		09 10	09 16			09 27			09 31		09 40			09 57		10 01		10 10
Thornton Heath	d			08 59		09 03		09 13	09 19			09 29			09 33		09 43			09 59		10 03		10 13
Norbury	d			09 02		09 06		09 16	09 22			09 32			09 36		09 46			10 02		10 06		10 16
Streatham Common 4	d			09 06		09 09		09 19	09 25			09 36			09 39		09 49			10 06		10 09		10 19
London Bridge	a			09 37			←					10 07				←				10 37			←	
Balham 4	d	09 03	09 10		09 21	09 14	09 21	09 25	09 29	09 33			09 40	09 51	09 44	09 51	09 55	10 03	10 10		10 21	10 14	10 21	10 25
Wandsworth Common	d		09 12		→	09 16	09 23	09 27			←		09 42	→	09 46	09 53	09 57		10 12		→	10 16	10 23	10 27
Clapham Junction	a	09 07	09 16			09 20	09 27	09 31	09 35	09 37	09 35		09 46		09 50	09 57	10 01	10 07	10 16			10 20	10 27	10 31
Clapham Junction 10	d	09 08	09 16			09 20	09 27	09 31	09 40	09 38	09 40		09 46		09 50	09 57	10 01	10 08	10 16			10 20	10 27	10 31
Imperial Wharf	a								→		09 44													
West Brompton	a										09 47													
Kensington (Olympia)	a										09 51													
Shepherd's Bush	a										09 54													
Battersea Park	d		09 20			09 24	09 31	09 35					09 50		09 54	10 01	10 05		10 20			10 24	10 31	10 35
London Victoria 15	a	09 15	09 24			09 28	09 35	09 39		09 45			09 54		09 58	10 05	10 09	10 15	10 24			10 28	10 35	10 39

		SN 1	SN	SN 1	SN	SN	SN	SN	SN	SN		SN	SN	SN	SN	SN	SN	SN	SN 1	SN	SN 1	SN	SN	SN
		G	E	H	F	A	B		C	D		E	A	F	B		C	D	G	E	H	F	A	B
Sutton 4	d		10 12					10 11		10 21		13 42				13 41		13 51		14 12				
West Croydon 4	d						10 21	10 26		10 34					13 51	13 56		14 04						14 21
Purley	d				10 15									13 45								14 15		
East Croydon	d	10 10			10 23									13 53					14 10			14 23		
Selhurst 4	d	10 16			10 27			10 31		10 40	and at the same minutes past each hour until			13 57		14 01		14 10	14 16			14 27		
Thornton Heath	d	10 19			10 29			10 33		10 43				13 59		14 03		14 13	14 19			14 29		
Norbury	d	10 22			10 32			10 36		10 46				14 02		14 06		14 16	14 22			14 32		
Streatham Common 4	d	10 25			10 36			10 39		10 49				14 06		14 09		14 19	14 25			14 36		
London Bridge	a				11 07				←					14 37			←					15 07		
Balham 4	d	10 29	10 33			10 40	10 51	10 44	10 51	10 55		14 03	14 10		14 21	14 14	14 21	14 25	14 29	14 33			14 40	14 51
Wandsworth Common	d			←		10 42	→	10 46	10 53	10 57			14 12		→	14 16	14 23	14 27			←		14 42	→
Clapham Junction	a	10 35	10 37	10 35		10 46		10 50	10 57	11 01		14 07	14 16			14 20	14 27	14 31	14 35	14 37	14 35		14 46	
Clapham Junction 10	d	10 40	10 38	10 40		10 46		10 50	10 57	11 01		14 08	14 16			14 20	14 27	14 31	14 40	14 38	14 40		14 46	
Imperial Wharf	a	→		10 44															→		14 44			
West Brompton	a			10 47																	14 47			
Kensington (Olympia)	a			10 51																	14 51			
Shepherd's Bush	a			10 54																	14 54			
Battersea Park	d					10 50		10 54	11 01	11 05			14 20			14 24	14 31	14 35					14 50	
London Victoria 15	a		10 45			10 54		10 58	11 05	11 09		14 15	14 24			14 28	14 35	14 39		14 45			14 54	

A From London Bridge
B To London Victoria
C From West Croydon
D From Epsom Downs
E From Epsom
F From Caterham
G To Milton Keynes Central
H From East Croydon to Milton Keynes Central

For faster services between London Victoria, Clapham Junction and East Croydon, refer to Table T175

For other Shepherd's Bush connecting trains, refer to Table T176

Table T170-R

Saturdays

21 December to 16 May

Croydon-Selhurst, Thornton Heath, Norbury, Streatham Common, Balham, Wandsworth Common & Battersea Park - London Victoria

		SN	SN	SN	SN	SN	SN	SN	SN	SN	SN	SN 1	SN	SN 1	SN	SN	SN	SN	SN	SN	SN	SN	SN
			A	B	C	D	E	F		A	B	G	C	H	E	D	F		A	B	C	D	E
Sutton 4	d	14 11		14 21	14 42				14 41		14 51		15 12					15 12		15 21	15 42		
West Croydon 4	d	14 26		14 34				14 51	14 56		15 04						15 21	15 26		15 34			
Purley	d						14 45								15 15								15 45
East Croydon	d						14 53					15 10			15 23								15 53
Selhurst 4	d	14 31		14 40			14 57		15 01		15 10	15 16			15 27			15 31		15 40			15 57
Thornton Heath	d	14 33		14 43			14 59		15 03		15 13	15 19			15 29			15 33		15 43			15 59
Norbury	d	14 36		14 46			15 02		15 06		15 16	15 22			15 32			15 36		15 46			16 02
Streatham Common 4	d	14 39		14 49			15 06		15 09		15 19	15 25			15 36			15 39		15 49			16 06
London Bridge	a		←				15 37			←					16 07				←				16 37
Balham 4	d	14 44	14 51	14 55	15 03	15 10		15 21	15 14	15 21	15 25	15 29	15 33			15 40	15 51	15 44	15 51	15 55	16 03	16 10	
Wandsworth Common	d	14 46	14 53	14 57		15 12		→	15 16	15 23	15 27			←		15 42	→	15 46	15 53	15 57		16 12	
Clapham Junction	a	14 50	14 57	15 01	15 07	15 16			15 20	15 27	15 31	15 35	15 37	15 35		15 46		15 50	15 57	16 01	16 07	16 16	
Clapham Junction 10	d	14 50	14 57	15 01	15 08	15 16			15 20	15 27	15 31	15 40	15 38	15 40		15 46		15 50	15 57	16 01	16 08	16 16	
Imperial Wharf	a											→		15 44									
West Brompton	a													15 47									
Kensington (Olympia)	a													15 51									
Shepherd's Bush	a													15 54									
Battersea Park	d	14 54	15 01	15 05		15 20			15 24	15 31	15 35					15 50		15 54	16 01	16 05		16 20	
London Victoria 15	a	14 58	15 05	15 09	15 15	15 24			15 28	15 35	15 39		15 45			15 54		15 58	16 05	16 09	16 15	16 24	

		SN	SN	SN	SN	SN 1	SN	SN 1	SN	SN	SN	SN	SN	SN	SN	SN	SN	SN	SN	SN	SN	SN 1	SN
		F		A	B	G	C	H	E	D	F		A	B	C	D	E	F		A	B	G	C
Sutton 4	d		15 41		15 51		16 12					16 11		16 21	16 42				16 41		16 51		17 12
West Croydon 4	d	15 51	15 56		16 04						16 21	16 26		16 34				16 52	16 56		17 04		
Purley	d								16 15								16 45						
East Croydon	d					16 10			16 23								16 53					17 10	
Selhurst 4	d		16 01		16 10	16 16			16 27			16 31		16 40			16 57		17 01		17 10	17 16	
Thornton Heath	d		16 03		16 13	16 19			16 29			16 33		16 43			16 59		17 03		17 13	17 19	
Norbury	d		16 06		16 16	16 22			16 32			16 36		16 46			17 02		17 06		17 16	17 22	
Streatham Common 4	d		16 09		16 19	16 25			16 36			16 39		16 49			17 06		17 09		17 19	17 25	
London Bridge	a			←					17 07				←				17 37			←			
Balham 4	d	16 21	16 14	16 21	16 25	16 29	16 33			16 40	16 51	16 44	16 51	16 55	17 03	17 10		17 21	17 14	17 21	17 25	17 29	17 33
Wandsworth Common	d	→	16 16	16 23	16 27			←		16 42	→	16 46	16 53	16 57		17 12		→	17 16	17 23	17 27		
Clapham Junction	a		16 20	16 27	16 31	16 35	16 37	16 35		16 46		16 50	16 57	17 01	17 07	17 16			17 20	17 27	17 31	17 35	17 37
Clapham Junction 10	d		16 20	16 27	16 31	16 40	16 38	16 40		16 46		16 50	16 57	17 01	17 08	17 16			17 20	17 27	17 31	17 40	17 38
Imperial Wharf	a					→		16 44														→	
West Brompton	a							16 47															
Kensington (Olympia)	a							16 51															
Shepherd's Bush	a							16 54															
Battersea Park	d		16 24	16 31	16 35					16 50		16 54	17 01	17 05		17 20			17 24	17 31	17 35		
London Victoria 15	a		16 28	16 35	16 39		16 45			16 54		16 58	17 05	17 09	17 15	17 24			17 28	17 35	17 39		17 45

		SN 1	SN	SN	SN	SN	SN	SN	SN	SN	SN	SN	SN	SN	SN	SN 1	SN	SN 1	SN	SN	SN	SN
		H	E	D	F		A	B	C	D	E	F		A	B	I	C	J	E	D	F	
Sutton 4	d					17 11		17 21	17 42				17 41		17 51		18 12					18 11
West Croydon 4	d				17 21	17 26		17 34				17 51	17 56		18 04						18 21	18 26
Purley	d		17 15								17 45								18 15			
East Croydon	d		17 23								17 53					18 09			18 23			
Selhurst 4	d		17 27			17 31		17 40			17 57		18 01		18 10	18 16			18 27			18 31
Thornton Heath	d		17 29			17 33		17 43			17 59		18 03		18 13	18 19			18 29			18 33
Norbury	d		17 32			17 36		17 46			18 02		18 06		18 16	18 22			18 32			18 36
Streatham Common 4	d		17 36			17 39		17 49			18 06		18 09		18 19	18 25			18 36			18 39
London Bridge	a		18 07				←				18 37			←					19 07			
Balham 4	d			17 40	17 51	17 44	17 51	17 55	18 03	18 10		18 21	18 14	18 21	18 25	18 29	18 33			18 40	18 51	18 44
Wandsworth Common	d	←		17 42	→	17 46	17 53	17 57		18 12		→	18 16	18 23	18 27			←		18 42	→	18 46
Clapham Junction	a	17 35		17 46		17 50	17 57	18 01	18 07	18 16			18 20	18 27	18 31	18 35	18 37	18 35		18 46		18 50
Clapham Junction 10	d	17 40		17 46		17 50	17 57	18 01	18 08	18 16			18 20	18 27	18 31	18 40	18 38	18 40		18 46		18 50
Imperial Wharf	a	17 44														→		18 44				
West Brompton	a	17 47																18 47				
Kensington (Olympia)	a	17 51																18 51				
Shepherd's Bush	a	17 54																18 54				
Battersea Park	d			17 50		17 54	18 01	18 05		18 20			18 24	18 31	18 35					18 50		18 54
London Victoria 15	a			17 54		17 58	18 05	18 09	18 15	18 24			18 28	18 35	18 39		18 45			18 54		18 58

A From West Croydon
B From Epsom Downs
C From Epsom
D From London Bridge
E From Caterham
F To London Victoria
G To Milton Keynes Central
H From East Croydon to Milton Keynes Central
I To Watford Junction
J From East Croydon to Watford Junction

For faster services between London Victoria, Clapham Junction and East Croydon, refer to Table T175

For other Shepherd's Bush connecting trains, refer to Table T176

Table T170-R

Saturdays
21 December to 16 May

Croydon-Selhurst, Thornton Heath, Norbury, Streatham Common, Balham, Wandsworth Common & Battersea Park - London Victoria

	SN A	SN B	SN C	SN D	SN E	SN F	SN	SN A	SN B	SN ■1 G	SN C	SN D	SN E	SN F	SN	SN A	SN B	SN C	SN D	SN E	SN F
Sutton ■4 d		18 21	18 42				18 41		18 51		19 12				19 11		19 21	19 42			
West Croydon ■4 d		18 34				18 51	18 56		19 04					19 21	19 26		19 34				19 51
Purley d					18 45								19 15							19 45	
East Croydon d					18 53					19 10			19 23							19 54	
Selhurst ■4 d		18 40			18 57		19 01		19 10	19 16			19 27		19 31		19 40			19 58	
Thornton Heath d		18 43			18 59		19 03		19 13	19 19			19 29		19 33		19 43			20 00	
Norbury d		18 46			19 02		19 06		19 16	19 22			19 32		19 36		19 46			20 03	
Streatham Common ■4 d		18 49			19 06		19 09		19 19	19 25			19 36		19 39		19 49			20 06	
London Bridge a	←				19 37			←					20 07			←				20 37	
Balham ■4 ⊖ d	18 51	18 55	19 03	19 10		19 21	19 14	19 21	19 25	19 29	19 33	19 40		19 51	19 44	19 51	19 55	20 03	20 10		20 21
Wandsworth Common d	18 53	18 57		19 12		→	19 16	19 23	19 27			19 42		→	19 46	19 53	19 57		20 12		→
Clapham Junction a	18 57	19 01	19 07	19 16			19 20	19 27	19 31	19 35	19 37	19 46			19 50	19 57	20 01	20 07	20 16		
Clapham Junction ■10 d	18 57	19 01	19 08	19 16			19 20	19 27	19 31	19 36	19 38	19 46			19 50	19 57	20 01	20 08	20 16		
Imperial Wharf a										19 40											
West Brompton ⊖ a										19 43											
Kensington (Olympia) ⊖ a										19 47											
Shepherd's Bush ⊖ a										19 50											
Battersea Park d	19 01	19 05		19 20			19 24	19 31	19 35			19 50			19 54	20 01	20 05		20 20		
London Victoria ■15 ⊖ a	19 05	19 09	19 15	19 24			19 28	19 35	19 39		19 45	19 54			19 58	20 05	20 09	20 15	20 24		

	SN	SN A	SN B	SN ■1 G	SN C	SN D	SN E	SN F	SN	SN ■1 H	SN A	SN B	SN C	SN D	SN E	SN F	SN	SN A	SN B	SN ■1 G	SN C	SN ■1 H
Sutton ■4 d	19 41		19 51		20 12				20 11			20 21	20 42				20 41		20 51		21 12	
West Croydon ■4 d	19 56		20 04					20 21	20 26			20 34				20 51	20 56		21 04			
Purley d							20 15								20 45							
East Croydon d				20 10			20 23								20 53					21 10		
Selhurst ■4 d	20 01		20 10	20 16			20 27		20 31			20 40			20 57		21 01		21 10	21 16		
Thornton Heath d	20 03		20 13	20 19			20 29		20 33			20 43			20 59		21 03		21 13	21 19		
Norbury d	20 06		20 16	20 22			20 32		20 36			20 46			21 02		21 06		21 16	21 22		
Streatham Common ■4 d	20 09		20 19	20 25			20 36		20 39			20 49			21 06		21 09		21 19	21 25		
London Bridge a		←					21 07				←				21 37			←				
Balham ■4 ⊖ d	20 14	20 21	20 25	20 29	20 33	20 40		20 51	20 44		20 51	20 55	21 03	21 10		21 21	21 14	21 21	21 25	21 29	21 33	
Wandsworth Common d	20 16	20 23	20 27			20 42		→	20 46	←	20 53	20 57		21 12		→	21 16	21 23	21 27			←
Clapham Junction a	20 20	20 27	20 31	20 35	20 37	20 46			20 50	20 35	20 57	21 01	21 07	21 16			21 20	21 27	21 31	21 35	21 37	21 35
Clapham Junction ■10 d	20 20	20 27	20 31	20 51	20 38	20 46			20 50	20 51	20 57	21 01	21 08	21 16			21 20	21 27	21 31	21 39	21 38	21 39
Imperial Wharf a				→						20 56										→		21 43
West Brompton ⊖ a										20 59												21 46
Kensington (Olympia) ⊖ a										21 02												21 50
Shepherd's Bush ⊖ a										21 05												21 53
Battersea Park d	20 24	20 31	20 35			20 50			20 54		21 01	21 05		21 20			21 24	21 31	21 35			
London Victoria ■15 ⊖ a	20 28	20 35	20 39		20 45	20 54			20 58		21 05	21 09	21 15	21 24			21 28	21 35	21 39		21 45	

	SN E	SN D	SN F	SN	SN A	SN B	SN C	SN D	SN E	SN F	SN	SN A	SN B	SN ■1 G	SN C	SN ■1 H	SN E	SN D	SN F	SN	SN A	SN B
Sutton ■4 d				21 11		21 21	21 42				21 41		21 51		22 12					22 11		22 21
West Croydon ■4 d			21 22	21 26		21 35				21 51	21 56		22 04						22 21	22 26		22 34
Purley d	21 15								21 45								22 15					
East Croydon d	21 23								21 53					22 10			22 23					
Selhurst ■4 d	21 27			21 31		21 40			21 57		22 01		22 10	22 16			22 27			22 31		22 40
Thornton Heath d	21 29			21 33		21 43			21 59		22 03		22 13	22 19			22 29			22 33		22 43
Norbury d	21 32			21 36		21 46			22 02		22 06		22 16	22 22			22 32			22 36		22 46
Streatham Common ■4 d	21 36			21 39		21 49			22 06		22 09		22 19	22 25			22 36			22 39		22 49
London Bridge a	22 07				←				22 37			←					23 07				←	
Balham ■4 ⊖ d		21 40	21 51	21 44	21 51	21 55	22 03	22 10		22 21	22 14	22 21	22 25	22 29	22 33			22 40	22 51	22 44	22 51	22 55
Wandsworth Common d		21 42	→	21 46	21 53	21 57		22 12		→	22 16	22 23	22 27			←		22 42	→	22 46	22 53	22 57
Clapham Junction a		21 46		21 50	21 57	22 01	22 07	22 16			22 20	22 27	22 31	22 35	22 37	22 35		22 46		22 50	22 57	23 01
Clapham Junction ■10 d		21 46		21 50	21 57	22 01	22 08	22 16			22 20	22 27	22 31	22 39	22 38	22 39		22 46		22 50	22 57	23 01
Imperial Wharf a														→		22 43						
West Brompton ⊖ a																22 46						
Kensington (Olympia) ⊖ a																22 50						
Shepherd's Bush ⊖ a																22 53						
Battersea Park d		21 50		21 54	22 01	22 05		22 20			22 24	22 31	22 35					22 50		22 54	23 01	23 05
London Victoria ■15 ⊖ a		21 54		21 58	22 05	22 09	22 15	22 24			22 30	22 35	22 39		22 45			22 54		23 00	23 05	23 09

A From West Croydon
B From Epsom Downs
C From Epsom
D From London Bridge
E From Caterham
F To London Victoria
G To Watford Junction
H From East Croydon to Watford Junction

For faster services between London Victoria, Clapham Junction and East Croydon, refer to Table T175

For other Shepherd's Bush connecting trains, refer to Table T176

Table T170-R

Saturdays
21 December to 16 May

Croydon-Selhurst, Thornton Heath, Norbury, Streatham Common, Balham, Wandsworth Common & Battersea Park - London Victoria

	SN A	SN B	SN C	SN D	SN	SN E	SN F	SN A	SN B	SN C	SN	SN F
Sutton ■4 d	22 42				22 41		22 51	23 12				23 21
West Croydon ■4 d				22 51	22 56		23 04				23 21	23 34
Purley d			22 45							23 15		
East Croydon d			22 53							23 23		
Selhurst ■4 d			22 57		23 01		23 12			23 27		23 42
Thornton Heath d			22 59		23 03		23 15			23 29		23 44
Norbury d			23 02		23 06		23 18			23 32		23 47
Streatham Common ■4 d			23 06		23 09		23 21			23 36		23 50
London Bridge a			23 37			←				00 06		
Balham ■4 ⊖ d	23 03	23 10		23 21	23 14	23 21	23 25	23 33	23 40		23 51	23 56
Wandsworth Common d		23 12		→	23 16	23 23	23 27		23 42		23 53	23 58
Clapham Junction a	23 07	23 16			23 20	23 27	23 31	23 37	23 46		23 57	00 01
Clapham Junction ■10 d	23 08	23 16			23 20	23 27	23 31	23 39	23 46		23 57	00 02
Imperial Wharf a												
West Brompton ⊖ a												
Kensington (Olympia) ⊖ a												
Shepherd's Bush ⊖ a												
Battersea Park d		23 20			23 24	23 31	23 35		23 50		00 01	00 05
London Victoria ■15 ⊖ a	23 15	23 24			23 30	23 35	23 39	23 48	23 54		00 05	00 09

Sundays
15 December to 10 May

	SN G	SN H	SN I	SN ■1 J	SN	SN	SN D	SN A	SN E	SN A	SN	SN	SN	SN	SN K	SN	SN	SN	SN	SN K	SN	SN
Sutton ■4 d								06 53		07 14		07 09			07 44		07 39			08 14		08 09
West Croydon ■4 d							06 59	07 07				07 23		07 31			07 53		08 03			08 22
Purley d				05 23																		
East Croydon d				05 30		06 44					07 14					07 44					08 14	
Selhurst ■4 d				05 33	06 27	06 47		07 12			07 17	07 28	07 41			07 47	07 58	08 11			08 17	08 28
Thornton Heath d				05 36	06 30	06 49		07 14			07 19	07 30	07 43			07 49	08 00	08 13			08 19	08 30
Norbury d				05 39	06 33	06 52		07 17			07 22	07 33	07 46			07 52	08 03	08 16			08 22	08 33
Streatham Common ■4 d				05 42	06 36	06 55		07 20			07 25	07 36	07 49			07 55	08 06	08 19			08 25	08 36
London Bridge a						07 22			←		07 52					08 22					08 53	
Balham ■4 ⊖ d			00 10	05 47	06 41		07 28	07 25	07 28	07 35		07 41	07 54	07 59	08 05		08 11	08 24	08 29	08 35		08 41
Wandsworth Common d			00 12		06 43		→	07 27	07 30			07 43	07 56	08 01			08 13	08 26	08 31			08 43
Clapham Junction a			00 16	05 51	06 47			07 30	07 34	07 40		07 46	08 00	08 04	08 10		08 16	08 30	08 35	08 41		08 46
Clapham Junction ■10 d		00 02	00 16	05 51	06 47			07 31	07 34	07 41		07 47	08 01	08 05	08 11		08 17	08 32	08 35	08 42		08 47
Imperial Wharf a																						
West Brompton ⊖ a																						
Kensington (Olympia) ⊖ a																						
Shepherd's Bush ⊖ a																						
Battersea Park d	00 01	00 05	00 20	05 55	06 51			07 34	07 38			07 50	08 05	08 08			08 20	08 36	08 39			08 50
London Victoria ■15 ⊖ a	00 05	00 09	00 24	05 59	06 55			07 39	07 42	07 48		07 55	08 09	08 13	08 19		08 25	08 40	08 43	08 49		08 55

	SN A	SN	SN	SN	SN	SN A	SN D	SN F	SN E	SN	SN	SN A	SN D	SN F	SN E	SN		SN	SN A	SN D	SN F	SN E	SN
Sutton ■4 d	08 26				08 39	08 56		08 51			09 09	09 26		09 21			and at the same minutes past each hour until	11 39	11 56		11 51		
West Croydon ■4 d			08 33		08 52		09 01	09 04			09 22		09 31	09 34				11 52		12 01	12 04		
Purley d																							
East Croydon d				08 44						09 14						09 44							12 14
Selhurst ■4 d		08 41		08 47	08 57			09 11		09 17	09 27			09 41		09 47		11 57			12 11		12 17
Thornton Heath d		08 43		08 49	08 59			09 13		09 19	09 29			09 43		09 49		11 59			12 13		12 19
Norbury d		08 46		08 52	09 02			09 16		09 22	09 32			09 46		09 52		12 02			12 16		12 22
Streatham Common ■4 d		08 49		08 55	09 05			09 19		09 25	09 35			09 49		09 55		12 05			12 19		12 25
London Bridge a				09 23					←	09 52					←	10 22						←	12 52
Balham ■4 ⊖ d	08 49	08 54	08 58		09 10	09 17	09 28	09 24	09 28		09 40	09 47	09 58	09 54	09 58			12 10	12 17	12 28	12 24	12 28	
Wandsworth Common d		08 56	09 00		09 12		→	09 26	09 30		09 42		→	09 56	10 00			12 12		→	12 26	12 30	
Clapham Junction a	08 53	09 00	09 03		09 16	09 21		09 30	09 33		09 46	09 51		10 00	10 03			12 16	12 21		12 30	12 33	
Clapham Junction ■10 d	08 53	09 01	09 04		09 17	09 22		09 31	09 34		09 47	09 52		10 01	10 04			12 17	12 22		12 31	12 34	
Imperial Wharf a																							
West Brompton ⊖ a																							
Kensington (Olympia) ⊖ a																							
Shepherd's Bush ⊖ a																							
Battersea Park d		09 04	09 07		09 20			09 34	09 37		09 50			10 04	10 07			12 20			12 34	12 37	
London Victoria ■15 ⊖ a	09 00	09 09	09 12		09 25	09 29		09 39	09 42		09 55	09 59		10 09	10 12			12 25	12 29		12 39	12 42	

A From Epsom
B From London Bridge
C From Caterham
D To London Victoria
E From West Croydon
F From Epsom Downs
G not 15 December. From West Croydon
H not 15 December. From Epsom Downs
I not 15 December. From London Bridge
J From Brighton
K From Dorking

For faster services between London Victoria, Clapham Junction and East Croydon, refer to Table T175

For other Shepherd's Bush connecting trains, refer to Table T176

Table T170-R

Sundays
15 December to 10 May

Croydon-Selhurst, Thornton Heath, Norbury, Streatham Common, Balham, Wandsworth Common & Battersea Park - London Victoria

Station		SN	SN A	SN B	SN C	SN D	SN	SN	SN A	SN B	SN C	SN D	SN	SN	SN A	SN B	SN C	SN D	SN	SN	SN A	SN B	SN C
Sutton	d	12 09	12 26		12 21			12 39	12 56		12 51			13 09	13 26		13 21			13 39	13 56		13 51
West Croydon	d	12 22		12 31	12 34			12 52		13 01	13 04			13 22		13 31	13 34			13 52		14 01	14 04
Purley	d																						
East Croydon	d						12 44						13 14						13 44				
Selhurst	d	12 27			12 41		12 47	12 57			13 11		13 17	13 27			13 41		13 47	13 57			14 11
Thornton Heath	d	12 29			12 43		12 49	12 59			13 14		13 19	13 29			13 43		13 49	13 59			14 13
Norbury	d	12 32			12 46		12 52	13 02			13 17		13 22	13 32			13 46		13 52	14 02			14 16
Streatham Common	d	12 35			12 49		12 55	13 05			13 19		13 25	13 35			13 49		13 55	14 05			14 19
London Bridge	a					←	13 22					←	13 52					←	14 22				
Balham	d	12 40	12 47	12 58	12 54	12 58		13 10	13 17	13 28	13 24	13 28		13 40	13 47	13 58	13 54	13 58		14 10	14 17	14 28	14 24
Wandsworth Common	d	12 42		→	12 56	13 00		13 12		→	13 26	13 30		13 42		→	13 56	14 00		14 12		→	14 26
Clapham Junction	a	12 46	12 51		13 00	13 03		13 16	13 21		13 30	13 33		13 46	13 51		14 00	14 03		14 16	14 21		14 30
Clapham Junction	d	12 47	12 52		13 01	13 04		13 17	13 22		13 31	13 34		13 47	13 52		14 01	14 04		14 17	14 22		14 31
Imperial Wharf	a																						
West Brompton	a																						
Kensington (Olympia)	a																						
Shepherd's Bush	a																						
Battersea Park	d	12 50			13 04	13 07		13 20			13 34	13 37		13 50			14 04	14 07		14 20			14 34
London Victoria	a	12 55	12 59		13 09	13 12		13 25	13 29		13 39	13 42		13 55	13 59		14 09	14 12		14 25	14 29		14 39

Station		SN D	SN	SN	SN A	SN B	SN C	SN D	SN	SN	SN A	SN B	SN C	SN D	SN	SN	SN A	SN B	SN C	SN D	SN	SN
Sutton	d			14 09	14 26		14 21			14 39	14 56		14 51			15 09	15 26		15 21			15 39
West Croydon	d			14 22		14 31	14 34			14 52		15 01	15 04			15 22		15 31	15 34			15 52
Purley	d																					
East Croydon	d		14 14						14 44						15 14						15 44	
Selhurst	d		14 17	14 27			14 41		14 47	14 57			15 11		15 17	15 27			15 41		15 47	15 57
Thornton Heath	d		14 19	14 29			14 43		14 49	14 59			15 13		15 19	15 29			15 43		15 49	15 59
Norbury	d		14 22	14 32			14 46		14 52	15 02			15 16		15 22	15 32			15 46		15 52	16 02
Streatham Common	d		14 25	14 35			14 49		14 55	15 05			15 19		15 25	15 35			15 49		15 55	16 05
London Bridge	a	←	14 52					←	15 22					←	15 52					←	16 22	
Balham	d	14 28		14 40	14 47	14 58	14 54	14 58		15 10	15 17	15 28	15 24	15 28		15 40	15 47	15 58	15 54	15 58		16 10
Wandsworth Common	d	14 30		14 42		→	14 56	15 00		15 12		→	15 26	15 30		15 42		→	15 56	16 00		16 12
Clapham Junction	a	14 33		14 46	14 51		15 00	15 03		15 16	15 21		15 30	15 33		15 46	15 51		16 00	16 03		16 16
Clapham Junction	d	14 34		14 47	14 52		15 01	15 04		15 17	15 22		15 31	15 34		15 47	15 52		16 01	16 04		16 17
Imperial Wharf	a																					
West Brompton	a																					
Kensington (Olympia)	a																					
Shepherd's Bush	a																					
Battersea Park	d	14 37		14 50			15 04	15 07		15 20			15 34	15 37		15 50			16 04	16 07		16 20
London Victoria	a	14 42		14 55	14 59		15 09	15 12		15 25	15 29		15 39	15 42		15 55	15 59		16 09	16 12		16 25

Station		SN A	SN B	SN C	SN D	SN	SN	SN A	SN B	SN C	SN D	SN	SN	SN A	SN B	SN C	SN D	SN	SN	SN A	SN B	SN C	SN D
Sutton	d	15 56		15 51			16 09	16 26		16 21			16 39	16 56		16 51			17 09	17 26		17 21	
West Croydon	d		16 01	16 04			16 22		16 31	16 34			16 52		17 01	17 04			17 22		17 31	17 34	
Purley	d																						
East Croydon	d					16 14						16 44						17 14					
Selhurst	d			16 11		16 17	16 27			16 41		16 47	16 57			17 11		17 17	17 27			17 41	
Thornton Heath	d			16 14		16 19	16 29			16 43		16 49	16 59			17 14		17 19	17 29			17 43	
Norbury	d			16 17		16 22	16 32			16 46		16 52	17 02			17 17		17 22	17 32			17 46	
Streatham Common	d			16 19		16 25	16 35			16 49		16 55	17 05			17 19		17 25	17 35			17 49	
London Bridge	a				←	16 52					←	17 22					←	17 52					←
Balham	d	16 17	16 28	16 24	16 28		16 40	16 47	16 58	16 54	16 58		17 10	17 17	17 28	17 24	17 28		17 40	17 47	17 58	17 54	17 58
Wandsworth Common	d		→	16 26	16 30		16 42		→	16 56	17 00		17 12		→	17 26	17 30		17 42		→	17 56	18 00
Clapham Junction	a	16 21		16 30	16 33		16 46	16 51		17 00	17 03		17 16	17 21		17 30	17 33		17 46	17 51		18 00	18 03
Clapham Junction	d	16 22		16 31	16 34		16 47	16 52		17 01	17 04		17 17	17 22		17 31	17 34		17 47	17 52		18 01	18 04
Imperial Wharf	a																						
West Brompton	a																						
Kensington (Olympia)	a																						
Shepherd's Bush	a																						
Battersea Park	d			16 34	16 37		16 50			17 04	17 07		17 20			17 34	17 37		17 50			18 04	18 07
London Victoria	a	16 29		16 39	16 42		16 55	16 59		17 09	17 12		17 25	17 29		17 39	17 42		17 55	17 59		18 09	18 12

Station		SN	SN	SN A	SN B	SN C	SN D	SN	SN	SN A	SN B	SN C	SN D	SN	SN	SN A	SN B	SN C	SN D	SN	SN	SN A	SN B
Sutton	d		17 39	17 56		17 51			18 09	18 28		18 21			18 39	18 56		18 51			19 09	19 26	
West Croydon	d		17 52		18 01	18 04			18 22		18 31	18 34			18 52		19 01	19 04			19 22		19 31
Purley	d																						
East Croydon	d	17 44						18 14						18 44						19 14			
Selhurst	d	17 47	17 57			18 11		18 17	18 27			18 41		18 47	18 57			19 11		19 17	19 27		
Thornton Heath	d	17 49	17 59			18 13		18 19	18 29			18 43		18 49	18 59			19 13		19 19	19 29		
Norbury	d	17 52	18 02			18 16		18 22	18 32			18 46		18 52	19 02			19 16		19 22	19 32		
Streatham Common	d	17 55	18 05			18 19		18 25	18 35			18 49		18 55	19 05			19 19		19 25	19 35		
London Bridge	a	18 22					←	18 52					←	19 22					←	19 52			
Balham	d		18 10	18 17	18 28	18 24	18 28		18 40	18 47	18 58	18 54	18 58		19 10	19 17	19 28	19 24	19 28		19 40	19 47	19 58
Wandsworth Common	d		18 12		→	18 26	18 30		18 42		→	18 56	19 00		19 12		→	19 26	19 30		19 42		→
Clapham Junction	a		18 16	18 21		18 30	18 33		18 46	18 51		19 00	19 03		19 16	19 21		19 30	19 33		19 46	19 51	
Clapham Junction	d		18 17	18 22		18 31	18 34		18 47	18 52		19 01	19 04		19 17	19 22		19 31	19 34		19 47	19 52	
Imperial Wharf	a																						
West Brompton	a																						
Kensington (Olympia)	a																						
Shepherd's Bush	a																						
Battersea Park	d		18 20			18 34	18 37		18 50			19 04	19 07		19 20			19 34	19 37		19 50		
London Victoria	a		18 25	18 29		18 39	18 42		18 55	18 59		19 09	19 12		19 25	19 29		19 39	19 42		19 55	19 59	

A From Epsom
B To London Victoria
C From Epsom Downs
D From West Croydon

NRT DECEMBER 19 EDITION

Table T170-R

Sundays
15 December to 10 May

Croydon-Selhurst, Thornton Heath, Norbury, Streatham Common, Balham, Wandsworth Common & Battersea Park - London Victoria

Station		SN A	SN B	SN	SN	SN C	SN D	SN A	SN B	SN	SN	SN C	SN D	SN A	SN B	SN	SN	SN C	SN D	SN A	SN B	SN
Sutton	d	19 21			19 39	19 56		19 51			20 09	20 26		20 21			20 39	20 56		20 51		
West Croydon	d	19 34			19 52		20 01	20 04			20 22		20 31	20 34			20 52		21 01	21 04		
Purley	d																					
East Croydon	d			19 44						20 14						20 44						21 14
Selhurst	d	19 41		19 47	19 57			20 11		20 17	20 27			20 41		20 47	20 57			21 11		21 17
Thornton Heath	d	19 43		19 49	19 59			20 13		20 19	20 29			20 43		20 49	20 59			21 13		21 19
Norbury	d	19 46		19 52	20 02			20 16		20 22	20 32			20 46		20 52	21 02			21 16		21 22
Streatham Common	d	19 49		19 55	20 05			20 19		20 25	20 35			20 49		20 55	21 05			21 19		21 25
London Bridge	a		←	20 22					←	20 52					←	21 22					←	21 52
Balham	d	19 54	19 58		20 10	20 17	20 28	20 24	20 28		20 40	20 47	20 58	20 54	20 58		21 10	21 17	21 28	21 24	21 28	
Wandsworth Common	d	19 56	20 00		20 12		→	20 26	20 30		20 42		→	20 56	21 00		21 12		→	21 26	21 30	
Clapham Junction	a	20 00	20 03		20 16	20 21		20 30	20 33		20 46	20 51		21 00	21 03		21 16	21 21		21 30	21 33	
Clapham Junction	d	20 01	20 04		20 17	20 22		20 31	20 34		20 47	20 52		21 01	21 04		21 17	21 22		21 31	21 34	
Imperial Wharf	a																					
West Brompton	a																					
Kensington (Olympia)	a																					
Shepherd's Bush	a																					
Battersea Park	d	20 04	20 07		20 20			20 34	20 37		20 50			21 04	21 07		21 20			21 34	21 37	
London Victoria	a	20 09	20 12		20 25	20 29		20 39	20 42		20 55	20 59		21 09	21 12		21 25	21 29		21 39	21 42	

Station		SN	SN C	SN D	SN A	SN B	SN	SN	SN C	SN D	SN A	SN B	SN	SN	SN C	SN D	SN A	SN B	SN	SN	SN C	SN D	SN A
Sutton	d	21 09	21 26		21 21			21 39	21 56		21 51			22 09	22 26		22 21			22 39	22 56		22 51
West Croydon	d	21 22		21 31	21 34			21 52		22 01	22 04			22 22		22 31	22 34			22 52		23 01	23 04
Purley	d																						
East Croydon	d						21 44						22 14						22 42				
Selhurst	d	21 27			21 41		21 47	21 57			22 11		22 17	22 27			22 41		22 47	22 57			23 11
Thornton Heath	d	21 29			21 43		21 49	21 59			22 13		22 19	22 29			22 43		22 49	22 59			23 13
Norbury	d	21 32			21 46		21 52	22 02			22 16		22 22	22 32			22 46		22 52	23 02			23 16
Streatham Common	d	21 35			21 49		21 55	22 05			22 19		22 25	22 35			22 50		22 56	23 05			23 19
London Bridge	a					←	22 22					←	22 52					←	23 23				
Balham	d	21 40	21 47	21 58	21 54	21 58		22 10	22 17	22 28	22 24	22 28		22 40	22 47	22 58	22 55	22 58		23 10	23 17	23 28	23 24
Wandsworth Common	d	21 42		→	21 56	22 00		22 12		→	22 26	22 30		22 42		→	22 57	23 00		23 12		→	23 26
Clapham Junction	a	21 46	21 51		22 00	22 03		22 16	22 21		22 30	22 33		22 46	22 51		23 00	23 03		23 16	23 21		23 30
Clapham Junction	d	21 47	21 52		22 01	22 04		22 17	22 22		22 31	22 34		22 47	22 52		23 01	23 04		23 17	23 22		23 31
Imperial Wharf	a																						
West Brompton	a																						
Kensington (Olympia)	a																						
Shepherd's Bush	a																						
Battersea Park	d	21 50			22 04	22 07		22 20			22 34	22 37		22 50			23 04	23 07		23 20			23 34
London Victoria	a	21 55	21 59		22 09	22 12		22 25	22 29		22 39	22 42		22 55	22 59		23 09	23 12		23 25	23 30		23 39

Station		SN B	SN	SN	SN E	SN 1 F
Sutton	d		23 09		23 46	
West Croydon	d		23 22	23 31		
Purley	d					
East Croydon	d					23 55
Selhurst	d		23 27			23 59
Thornton Heath	d		23 29			
Norbury	d		23 32			
Streatham Common	d		23 35			
London Bridge	a	←				
Balham	d	23 28	23 40	23 58	00 06	
Wandsworth Common	d	23 30	23 42	00 01	00 08	
Clapham Junction	a	23 33	23 46	00 05	00 12	00 15
Clapham Junction	d	23 34	23 47	00 05	00 13	00 16
Imperial Wharf	a					
West Brompton	a					
Kensington (Olympia)	a					
Shepherd's Bush	a					
Battersea Park	d	23 37	23 50	00 09	00 16	
London Victoria	a	23 43	23 55	00 13	00 21	00 23

A From Epsom Downs
B From West Croydon
C From Epsom
D To London Victoria
E From Dorking
F From East Grinstead

For faster services between London Victoria, Clapham Junction and East Croydon, refer to Table T175

For other Shepherd's Bush connecting trains, refer to Table T176

Table T171-F

Mondays to Fridays
16 December to 15 May

London Victoria - Streatham Hill, West Norwood, Gipsy Hill and Crystal Palace - Norwood Junction & Croydon

Miles	Miles	Station		SN MO	SN MX	SN MO	SN MX	SN MX	SN	SN	SN	SN		SN	SN	SN	SN	SN	SN	SN	SN	SN		SN	SN
0	—	London Victoria 15 ⊖	d									06 06		06 20		06 36	06 50		07 06	07 20		07 36		07 50	
1¼	—	Battersea Park 4	d			00 01						06 10		06 24		06 40	06 54		07 10	07 24		07 40		07 54	
—	—	Clapham Junction 10	d			00 06	00 04					06 14		06 28		06 44	06 58		07 14	07 28		07 44		07 58	
4	—	Wandsworth Common	d			00 09	00 07					06 17		06 31		06 47	07 01		07 17	07 31		07 47		08 01	
5	—	Balham 4 ⊖	d			00 12	00 10					06 20		06 34		06 50	07 04		07 20	07 35		07 50		08 04	
6	—	**Streatham Hill**	d			00 16	00 15		05 39	06 09		06 25		06 39		06 55	07 09		07 25	07 39		07 55		08 09	
—	0	London Bridge	d					00 01			06 01				06 31			07 01			07 31				08 01
7¼	6¾	**West Norwood 4**	d			00 19	00 18	00 24	05 42	06 12	06 24	06 28		06 42	06 54	06 58	07 12	07 24	07 28	07 42	07 54	07 58		08 12	08 24
8¼	7¾	**Gipsy Hill**	d			00 22	00 21	00 27	05 45	06 15	06 27	06 31		06 45	06 57	07 01	07 15	07 27	07 31	07 45	07 57	08 01		08 15	08 27
9	8½	**Crystal Palace 4**	a			00 26	00 27	00 31	05 51	06 21	06 31	06 35		06 51	07 01	07 05	07 21	07 31	07 35	07 51	08 01	08 05		08 21	08 31
—	—	Crystal Palace	d			00 26	00 28		05 52	06 22		06 38		06 52		07 08	07 22		07 38	07 52		08 08		08 22	
—	—	Sydenham	a				00 32		05 56	06 26				06 56			07 26			07 56				08 26	
—	—	Forest Hill	a				00 35		05 58	06 28				06 58			07 28			07 58				08 28	
—	—	Honor Oak Park	a				00 37		06 01	06 31				07 01			07 31			08 01				08 31	
—	—	Brockley	a				00 40		06 03	06 33				07 03			07 33			08 03				08 33	
—	—	New Cross Gate	a				00 42		06 05	06 35				07 05			07 35			08 05				08 35	
—	—	London Bridge	a				00 50		06 18	06 48				07 18			07 48			08 18				08 48	
—	—	Norwood Junction 2	a			00 31						06 42				07 12			07 42			08 12			
			d	00 01	00 10							06 46				07 16			07 46			08 16			
12¼	—	West Croydon	a	00 08	00 16							06 52				07 22			07 52			08 22			
16¾	—	Sutton	a																						

Station		SN	SN	SN	SN	SN	SN	SN		SN	SN	SN	SN	SN	SN	SN	SN	SN		SN	SN	SN	SN	SN	SN
London Victoria 15 ⊖	d	08 06	08 20		08 36	08 50		09 07		09 20		09 36	09 50		10 06	10 20		10 36		10 50		11 06	11 20		11 36
Battersea Park 4	d	08 10	08 24		08 40	08 54		09 12		09 24		09 40	09 54		10 10	10 24		10 40		10 54		11 10	11 24		11 40
Clapham Junction 10	d	08 14	08 28		08 44	08 58		09 16		09 28		09 45	09 58		10 14	10 28		10 44		10 58		11 14	11 28		11 45
Wandsworth Common	d	08 17	08 31		08 47	09 01		09 19		09 31		09 48	10 01		10 17	10 31		10 47		11 01		11 17	11 31		11 48
Balham 4 ⊖	d	08 20	08 34		08 50	09 04		09 21		09 34		09 50	10 04		10 20	10 34		10 50		11 04		11 20	11 34		11 50
Streatham Hill	d	08 25	08 39		08 55	09 09		09 25		09 39		09 55	10 09		10 25	10 39		10 55		11 09		11 25	11 39		11 55
London Bridge	d			08 31			09 01				09 31			10 01			10 31				11 01			11 31	
West Norwood 4	d	08 28	08 42	08 54	08 58	09 12	09 24	09 29		09 42	09 54	09 58	10 12	10 24	10 28	10 42	10 54	10 58		11 12	11 24	11 28	11 42	11 54	11 58
Gipsy Hill	d	08 31	08 45	08 57	09 01	09 15	09 27	09 32		09 45	09 57	10 01	10 15	10 27	10 31	10 45	10 57	11 01		11 15	11 27	11 31	11 45	11 57	12 01
Crystal Palace 4	a	08 35	08 51	09 01	09 05	09 21	09 31	09 35		09 51	10 01	10 05	10 21	10 31	10 35	10 51	11 01	11 05		11 21	11 31	11 35	11 51	12 01	12 05
Crystal Palace	d	08 38	08 52		09 08	09 22		09 38		09 52		10 08	10 22		10 38	10 52		11 08		11 22		11 38	11 52		12 08
Sydenham	a		08 56			09 26				09 56			10 26			10 56				11 26			11 56		
Forest Hill	a		08 58			09 28				09 58			10 28			10 58				11 28			11 58		
Honor Oak Park	a		09 01			09 31				10 01			10 31			11 01				11 31			12 01		
Brockley	a		09 03			09 33				10 03			10 33			11 03				11 33			12 03		
New Cross Gate	a		09 05			09 35				10 05			10 35			11 05				11 35			12 05		
London Bridge	a		09 18			09 48				10 17			10 47			11 17				11 47			12 17		
Norwood Junction 2	a	08 42			09 12			09 42				10 12			10 42			11 12				11 42			12 12
	d	08 46			09 16			09 46				10 16			10 51			11 15				11 51			12 15
West Croydon	a	08 52			09 22			09 52				10 22			10 57			11 21				11 57			12 21
Sutton	a																								

Station		SN	SN	SN		SN	SN	SN MWFO	SN TThO	SN	SN	SN	SN	SN		SN	SN	SN	SN	SN	SN	SN	SN	SN	
London Victoria 15 ⊖	d	11 50		12 06		12 20		12 36	12 36	12 50		13 06	13 20			13 36	13 50		14 06	14 20		14 36	14 50		
Battersea Park 4	d	11 54		12 10		12 24		12 40	12 40	12 54		13 10	13 24			13 40	13 54		14 10	14 24		14 40	14 54		
Clapham Junction 10	d	11 58		12 14		12 28		12 44	12 45	12 58		13 14	13 28			13 44	13 58		14 14	14 28		14 44	14 58		
Wandsworth Common	d	12 01		12 17		12 31		12 47	12 48	13 01		13 17	13 31			13 47	14 01		14 17	14 31		14 47	15 01		
Balham 4 ⊖	d	12 04		12 20		12 34		12 50	12 51	13 04		13 20	13 34			13 50	14 04		14 20	14 34		14 50	15 04		
Streatham Hill	d	12 09		12 25		12 39		12 55	12 56	13 09		13 25	13 39			13 55	14 09		14 25	14 39		14 55	15 09		
London Bridge	d		12 01				12 31				13 01			13 31				14 01			14 31			15 01	
West Norwood 4	d	12 12	12 24	12 28		12 42	12 54	12 58	12 59	13 12	13 24	13 28	13 42	13 54		13 58	14 12	14 24	14 28	14 42	14 54	14 58	15 12	15 24	
Gipsy Hill	d	12 15	12 27	12 31		12 45	12 57	13 01	13 02	13 15	13 27	13 31	13 45	13 57		14 01	14 15	14 27	14 31	14 45	14 57	15 01	15 15	15 27	
Crystal Palace 4	a	12 21	12 31	12 35		12 51	13 01	13 05	13 06	13 21	13 31	13 35	13 51	14 01		14 05	14 21	14 31	14 35	14 51	15 01	15 05	15 21	15 31	
Crystal Palace	d	12 22		12 38		12 52		13 08	13 09	13 22		13 38	13 52			14 08	14 22		14 38	14 52		15 08	15 22		
Sydenham	a	12 26				12 56				13 26			13 56				14 26			14 56			15 26		
Forest Hill	a	12 28				12 58				13 28			13 58				14 28			14 58			15 28		
Honor Oak Park	a	12 31				13 01				13 31			14 01				14 31			15 01			15 31		
Brockley	a	12 33				13 03				13 33			14 03				14 33			15 03			15 33		
New Cross Gate	a	12 35				13 05				13 35			14 05				14 35			15 05			15 35		
London Bridge	a	12 47				13 17				13 47			14 17				14 47			15 17			15 47		
Norwood Junction 2	a			12 42				13 12	13 13			13 42				14 12			14 43			15 12			
	d			12 51				13 15	13 22			13 51				14 15			14 51			15 15			
West Croydon	a			12 57				13 21	13 27			13 57				14 21			14 57			15 21			
Sutton	a																								

For complete service between London Victoria and Balham, refer to Table T170

For faster services between London Victoria, Clapham Junction and East Croydon, refer to Table T175

For Shepherd's Bush connecting trains, refer to Table T176

Table T171-F

Mondays to Fridays
16 December to 15 May

London Victoria - Streatham Hill, West Norwood, Gipsy Hill and Crystal Palace - Norwood Junction & Croydon

Station		SN	SN	SN	SN	SN		SN	SN	SN	SN	SN	SN	SN	SN	SN		SN	SN	SN	SN	SN	SN	SN	SN
London Victoria 15 ⊖	d	15 06	15 20		15 36	15 50				16 06	16 20		16 36	16 50		17 06		17 20		17 36	17 50		18 06	18 20	
Battersea Park 4	d	15 10	15 24		15 40	15 54				16 10	16 24		16 40	16 54		17 10		17 24		17 40	17 54		18 10	18 24	
Clapham Junction 10	d	15 14	15 28		15 44	15 58				16 14	16 28		16 44	16 58		17 14		17 28		17 44	17 58		18 14	18 28	
Wandsworth Common	d	15 17	15 31		15 47	16 01				16 17	16 31		16 47	17 01		17 17		17 31		17 47	18 01		18 17	18 31	
Balham 4 ⊖	d	15 20	15 34		15 50	16 04				16 20	16 34		16 50	17 04		17 20		17 34		17 50	18 04		18 20	18 34	
Streatham Hill	d	15 25	15 39		15 55	16 09			16 17	16 25	16 39		16 55	17 09		17 25		17 39		17 55	18 09		18 25	18 39	
London Bridge	d			15 31				16 01	16a45			16 31			17 01				17 31			18 01			18 31
West Norwood 4	d	15 28	15 42	15 54	15 58	16 12		16 24		16 28	16 42	16 54	16 58	17 12	17 24	17 28		17 42	17 54	17 58	18 12	18 24	18 28	18 42	18 54
Gipsy Hill	d	15 31	15 45	15 57	16 01	16 15		16 27		16 31	16 45	16 57	17 01	17 15	17 27	17 31		17 45	17 57	18 01	18 15	18 27	18 31	18 45	18 57
Crystal Palace 4	a	15 35	15 51	16 01	16 05	16 21		16 31		16 35	16 51	17 01	17 05	17 21	17 31	17 35		17 51	18 01	18 05	18 21	18 31	18 35	18 51	19 01
Crystal Palace	d	15 38	15 52		16 08	16 22				16 38	16 52		17 08	17 22		17 38		17 52		18 08	18 22		18 38	18 52	
Sydenham	a		15 56			16 26					16 56			17 26				17 56			18 26			18 56	
Forest Hill	a		15 58			16 28					16 58			17 28				17 58			18 28			18 58	
Honor Oak Park	a		16 01			16 31					17 01			17 31				18 01			18 31			19 01	
Brockley	a		16 03			16 33					17 03			17 33				18 03			18 33			19 03	
New Cross Gate	a		16 05			16 35					17 05			17 35				18 05			18 35			19 05	
London Bridge	a		16 18			16 48					17 18			17 48				18 18			18 48			19 18	
Norwood Junction 2	a	15 42			16 12					16 42			17 12			17 42				18 12			18 42		
	d	15 51			16 15					16 46			17 16			17 46				18 16			18 46		
West Croydon	a	15 57			16 21					16 52			17 22			17 52				18 22			18 52		
Sutton	a																								

Station		SN		SN	SN	SN	SN	SN	SN	SN	SN	SN		SN	SN	SN	SN	SN	SN	SN	SN	SN		SN	SN
London Victoria 15 ⊖	d	18 36		18 50		19 06	19 20		19 36	19 50		20 06		20 20		20 36	20 50		21 06	21 20		21 36		21 50	
Battersea Park 4	d	18 40		18 54		19 10	19 24		19 40	19 54		20 10		20 24		20 40	20 54		21 10	21 24		21 40		21 54	
Clapham Junction 10	d	18 44		18 58		19 14	19 28		19 44	19 58		20 14		20 28		20 45	20 58		21 14	21 28		21 45		21 59	
Wandsworth Common	d	18 47		19 01		19 17	19 31		19 47	20 01		20 17		20 31		20 48	21 01		21 17	21 31		21 48		22 02	
Balham 4 ⊖	d	18 50		19 04		19 20	19 34		19 50	20 04		20 20		20 34		20 51	21 04		21 20	21 34		21 51		22 04	
Streatham Hill	d	18 55		19 09		19 25	19 39		19 55	20 09		20 25		20 39		20 55	21 09		21 25	21 39		21 56		22 09	
London Bridge	d				19 01			19 31			20 01				20 31			21 01			21 31				22 01
West Norwood 4	d	18 58		19 12	19 24	19 28	19 42	19 54	19 58	20 12	20 24	20 28		20 42	20 54	20 58	21 12	21 24	21 28	21 43	21 54	21 59		22 13	22 24
Gipsy Hill	d	19 01		19 15	19 27	19 31	19 45	19 57	20 01	20 15	20 27	20 31		20 45	20 57	21 01	21 15	21 27	21 31	21 46	21 57	22 02		22 16	22 27
Crystal Palace 4	a	19 05		19 21	19 31	19 35	19 51	20 01	20 05	20 21	20 31	20 35		20 51	21 01	21 05	21 21	21 31	21 35	21 51	22 01	22 06		22 21	22 31
Crystal Palace	d	19 08		19 22		19 38	19 52		20 08	20 22		20 38		20 52		21 08	21 22		21 38	21 52		22 09		22 22	
Sydenham	a			19 26			19 56			20 26				20 56			21 26			21 56				22 26	
Forest Hill	a			19 28			19 58			20 28				20 58			21 28			21 58				22 28	
Honor Oak Park	a			19 31			20 01			20 31				21 01			21 31			22 01				22 31	
Brockley	a			19 33			20 03			20 33				21 03			21 33			22 03				22 33	
New Cross Gate	a			19 35			20 05			20 35				21 05			21 35			22 05				22 35	
London Bridge	a			19 48			20 20			20 48				21 17			21 47			22 17				22 47	
Norwood Junction 2	a	19 12				19 42			20 12			20 42				21 12			21 42			22 13			
	d	19 15				19 45			20 15			20 51				21 15			21 45			22 22			
West Croydon	a	19 21				19 51			20 21			20 57				21 21			21 51			22 27			
Sutton	a																								

Station		SN	SN	SN	SN	SN	SN	SN		SN	SN	SN	SN
London Victoria 15 ⊖	d	22 06	22 20		22 36	22 50		23 06		23 20	23 32		23 56
Battersea Park 4	d	22 10	22 24		22 40	22 54		23 10		23 24			
Clapham Junction 10	d	22 14	22 28		22 45	22 58		23 14		23 28	23 40		00 04
Wandsworth Common	d	22 17	22 31		22 48	23 01		23 17		23 31			00 07
Balham 4 ⊖	d	22 20	22 34		22 50	23 04		23 20		23 34	23 44		00 10
Streatham Hill	d	22 25	22 39		22 55	23 09		23 25		23 39	23 48		00 15
London Bridge	d			22 31			23 01					23 31	
West Norwood 4	d	22 28	22 42	22 54	22 58	23 12	23 24	23 28		23 42	23 51	23 54	00 18
Gipsy Hill	d	22 31	22 45	22 57	23 01	23 15	23 27	23 31		23 45	23 54	23 57	00 21
Crystal Palace 4	a	22 35	22 51	23 01	23 05	23 21	23 31	23 36		23 49	23 58	00 01	00 27
Crystal Palace	d	22 38	22 52		23 08	23 22		23 38		23 53	23 58		00 28
Sydenham	a		22 56			23 26				23 57			00 32
Forest Hill	a		22 58			23 28				00 01			00 35
Honor Oak Park	a		23 01			23 31				00 04			00 37
Brockley	a		23 03			23 33				00 06			00 40
New Cross Gate	a		23 05			23 35				00 08			00 42
London Bridge	a		23 17			23 47				00 16			00 50
Norwood Junction 2	a	22 42			23 12			23 42			00 03		
	d	22 45			23 15			23 46			00 10		
West Croydon	a	22 51			23 21			23 52			00 16		
Sutton	a												

For complete service between London Victoria and Balham, refer to Table T170

For faster services between London Victoria, Clapham Junction and East Croydon, refer to Table T175

For Shepherd's Bush connecting trains, refer to Table T176

Table T171-F

Saturdays
21 December to 16 May

London Victoria - Streatham Hill, West Norwood, Gipsy Hill and Crystal Palace - Norwood Junction & Croydon

		SN	SN A	SN	SN	SN	SN	SN	SN	SN	SN	SN	SN	SN	SN	SN	SN	and at the same minutes past each hour until	SN	SN	SN	SN
London Victoria 15 ⊖	d				00 10	00 25				06 20	06 36	06 50		07 06	07 20		07 36		12 50		13 06	13 20
Battersea Park 4	d				00 14	00 29				06 24	06 40	06 54		07 10	07 24		07 40		12 54		13 10	13 24
Clapham Junction 10	d	00 04			00 18	00 33				06 28	06 44	06 58		07 14	07 28		07 44		12 58		13 14	13 28
Wandsworth Common	d	00 07			00 21	00 36				06 31	06 47	07 01		07 17	07 31		07 47		13 01		13 17	13 31
Balham 4 ⊖	d	00 10			00 24	00 39				06 34	06 50	07 04		07 20	07 34		07 50		13 04		13 20	13 34
Streatham Hill	d	00 15			00 29	00 44		05 39	06 09	06 39	06 55	07 09		07 25	07 39		07 55		13 09		13 25	13 39
London Bridge	d		00 01				00 31						07 02			07 32				13 02		
West Norwood 4	d	00 18	00 24		00 32	00 47	00 54	05 42	06 12	06 42	06 58	07 12	07 24	07 28	07 42	07 54	07 58		13 12	13 24	13 28	13 42
Gipsy Hill	d	00 21	00 27		00 35	00 50	00 57	05 45	06 15	06 45	07 01	07 15	07 27	07 31	07 45	07 57	08 01		13 15	13 27	13 31	13 45
Crystal Palace 4	a	00 27	00 31		00 39	00 54	01 01	05 49	06 19	06 51	07 05	07 21	07 31	07 35	07 51	08 01	08 05		13 21	13 31	13 35	13 51
Crystal Palace	d	00 28			00 40	00 55	01 04	05 52	06 22	06 52	07 08	07 22		07 38	07 52		08 08		13 22		13 38	13 52
Sydenham	a	00 32						05 56	06 26	06 56		07 26			07 56				13 26			13 56
Forest Hill	a	00 35						05 58	06 28	06 58		07 28			07 58				13 28			13 58
Honor Oak Park	a	00 37						06 01	06 31	07 01		07 31			08 01				13 31			14 01
Brockley	a	00 40						06 03	06 33	07 03		07 33			08 03				13 33			14 03
New Cross Gate	a	00 42						06 05	06 35	07 05		07 35			08 05				13 35			14 05
London Bridge	a	00 50						06 18	06 44	07 14		07 44			08 14				13 44			14 14
Norwood Junction 2	a				00 46	01 02	01 10				07 12			07 42			08 12				13 42	
	d			00 10							07 15			07 51			08 15				13 51	
West Croydon	a			00 16							07 22			07 57			08 21				13 57	
Sutton	a																					

		SN	SN	SN	SN	SN	SN	SN	SN	SN	SN	SN	and at the same minutes past each hour until	SN	SN	SN	SN	SN	SN	SN	SN	SN
London Victoria 15 ⊖	d		13 36	13 50		14 06	14 20		14 36	14 50		15 06		18 20		18 36	18 50		19 06	19 20		19 36
Battersea Park 4	d		13 40	13 54		14 10	14 24		14 40	14 54		15 10		18 24		18 40	18 54		19 10	19 24		19 40
Clapham Junction 10	d		13 44	13 58		14 14	14 28		14 44	14 58		15 14		18 28		18 44	18 58		19 14	19 28		19 44
Wandsworth Common	d		13 47	14 01		14 17	14 31		14 47	15 01		15 17		18 31		18 47	19 01		19 17	19 31		19 47
Balham 4 ⊖	d		13 50	14 04		14 20	14 34		14 50	15 04		15 20		18 34		18 50	19 04		19 20	19 34		19 50
Streatham Hill	d		13 55	14 09		14 25	14 39		14 55	15 09		15 25		18 39		18 55	19 09		19 25	19 39		19 55
London Bridge	d	13 32			14 02			14 32			15 02				18 32			19 02			19 32	
West Norwood 4	d	13 54	13 58	14 12	14 24	14 28	14 42	14 54	14 58	15 12	15 24	15 28		18 42	18 54	18 58	19 12	19 24	19 28	19 42	19 54	19 58
Gipsy Hill	d	13 57	14 01	14 15	14 27	14 31	14 45	14 57	15 01	15 15	15 27	15 31		18 45	18 57	19 01	19 15	19 27	19 31	19 45	19 57	20 01
Crystal Palace 4	a	14 01	14 05	14 21	14 31	14 35	14 51	15 01	15 05	15 21	15 31	15 35		18 51	19 01	19 05	19 21	19 31	19 35	19 51	20 01	20 05
Crystal Palace	d		14 08	14 22		14 38	14 52		15 08	15 22		15 38		18 52		19 08	19 22		19 38	19 52		20 08
Sydenham	a			14 26			14 56			15 26				18 56			19 26			19 56		
Forest Hill	a			14 28			14 58			15 28				18 58			19 28			19 58		
Honor Oak Park	a			14 31			15 01			15 31				19 01			19 31			20 01		
Brockley	a			14 33			15 03			15 33				19 03			19 33			20 03		
New Cross Gate	a			14 35			15 05			15 35				19 05			19 35			20 05		
London Bridge	a			14 44			15 14			15 44				19 14			19 44			20 14		
Norwood Junction 2	a		14 12			14 45			15 12			15 42				19 12			19 42			20 12
	d		14 15			14 51			15 15			15 51				19 15			19 51			20 13
West Croydon	a		14 21			14 57			15 21			15 57				19 21			19 57			20 21
Sutton	a																					

		SN	SN	SN	SN	SN	SN	SN	SN	SN	SN	SN	SN	SN	SN	SN	SN	SN	SN	SN	SN	SN	SN
London Victoria 15 ⊖	d	19 50		20 06	20 20		20 36	20 50		21 06	21 20		21 36	21 50		22 06	22 20		22 36	22 50		23 06	23 20
Battersea Park 4	d	19 54		20 10	20 24		20 40	20 54		21 10	21 24		21 40	21 54		22 10	22 24		22 40	22 54		23 10	23 24
Clapham Junction 10	d	19 58		20 14	20 28		20 44	20 58		21 14	21 28		21 44	21 58		22 14	22 28		22 44	22 58		23 14	23 28
Wandsworth Common	d	20 01		20 17	20 31		20 47	21 01		21 17	21 31		21 47	22 01		22 17	22 31		22 47	23 01		23 17	23 31
Balham 4 ⊖	d	20 04		20 20	20 34		20 50	21 04		21 20	21 34		21 50	22 04		22 20	22 34		22 50	23 04		23 20	23 34
Streatham Hill	d	20 09		20 25	20 39		20 55	21 09		21 25	21 39		21 55	22 09		22 25	22 39		22 55	23 09		23 25	23 39
London Bridge	d		20 02			20 32			21 02			21 32			22 02			22 32			23 02		
West Norwood 4	d	20 12	20 24	20 28	20 42	20 54	20 58	21 12	21 24	21 28	21 42	21 54	21 58	22 12	22 24	22 31	22 42	22 54	22 58	23 12	23 24	23 28	23 42
Gipsy Hill	d	20 15	20 27	20 31	20 45	20 57	21 01	21 15	21 27	21 31	21 45	21 57	22 01	22 15	22 27	22 34	22 45	22 57	23 01	23 15	23 27	23 31	23 45
Crystal Palace 4	a	20 21	20 31	20 35	20 51	21 01	21 05	21 21	21 31	21 35	21 51	22 01	22 05	22 21	22 31	22 37	22 51	23 01	23 05	23 21	23 31	23 37	23 51
Crystal Palace	d	20 22		20 38	20 52		21 08	21 22		21 38	21 52		22 08	22 22		22 38	22 52		23 08	23 22	23 34	23 38	23 53
Sydenham	a	20 26			20 56			21 26			21 56			22 26			22 56			23 26			23 58
Forest Hill	a	20 28			20 58			21 28			21 58			22 28			22 58			23 28			00 01
Honor Oak Park	a	20 31			21 01			21 31			22 01			22 31			23 01			23 31			00 04
Brockley	a	20 33			21 03			21 33			22 03			22 33			23 03			23 33			00 06
New Cross Gate	a	20 35			21 05			21 35			22 05			22 35			23 05			23 35			00 08
London Bridge	a	20 44			21 14			21 44			22 20			22 45			23 15			23 44			00 16
Norwood Junction 2	a			20 42			21 12			21 42			22 12			22 42			23 12		23 39	23 43	
	d			20 51			21 15			21 51			22 15			22 51			23 15			23 45	
West Croydon	a			20 57			21 21			21 57			22 21			22 57			23 21			23 51	
Sutton	a																						

A not 16 May

For complete service between London Victoria and Balham, refer to Table T170

For faster services between London Victoria, Clapham Junction and East Croydon, refer to Table T175

For Shepherd's Bush connecting trains, refer to Table T176

NRT DECEMBER 19 EDITION

Table T171-F

Saturdays
21 December to 16 May

London Victoria - Streatham Hill, West Norwood, Gipsy Hill and Crystal Palace - Norwood Junction & Croydon

		SN	SN	SN
London Victoria 15 ⊖	d	23 32		23 56
Battersea Park 4	d			
Clapham Junction 10	d	23 39		00 04
Wandsworth Common	d			00 07
Balham 4 ⊖	d	23 44		00 10
Streatham Hill	d	23 48		00 15
London Bridge	d		23 32	
West Norwood 4	d	23 52	23 55	00 18
Gipsy Hill	d	23 55	23 58	00 21
Crystal Palace 4	a	23 58	00 02	00 25
Crystal Palace	d	23 59	00 04	00 27
Sydenham	a			00 31
Forest Hill	a			00 34
Honor Oak Park	a			00 37
Brockley	a			00 39
New Cross Gate	a			00 41
London Bridge	a			00 49
Norwood Junction 2	a	00 04	00 09	
	d	00 06		
West Croydon	a	00 18		
Sutton	a			

Sundays
15 December to 10 May

		SN A	SN A	SN A	SN	SN	SN	SN	SN	SN	SN	SN	SN	SN	SN	SN	SN	SN	and at the same minutes past each hour until	SN	SN	SN	SN
London Victoria 15 ⊖	d					00 10	00 25		00 40	07 21		07 51		08 21		08 56		09 26			20 56		21 26
Battersea Park 4	d					00 14	00 29		00 44	07 25		07 55		08 25		09 00		09 30			21 00		21 30
Clapham Junction 10	d			00 04		00 18	00 33		00 48	07 30		08 00		08 30		09 04		09 34			21 04		21 34
Wandsworth Common	d			00 07		00 21	00 36		00 51	07 33		08 03		08 33		09 07		09 37			21 07		21 37
Balham 4 ⊖	d			00 10		00 24	00 39		00 54	07 36		08 06		08 36		09 10		09 40			21 10		21 40
Streatham Hill	d			00 15		00 29	00 44		00 59	07 43		08 13		08 43		09 14		09 44			21 14		21 44
London Bridge	d				00 01			00 31			07 35		08 03		08 35		09 05			20 35		21 05	
West Norwood 4	d			00 18	00 24	00 32	00 47	00 54	01 02	07 48	07 58	08 18	08 28	08 47	08 58	09 18	09 28	09 48		20 58	21 18	21 28	21 48
Gipsy Hill	d			00 21	00 27	00 35	00 50	00 57	01 05	07 51	08 01	08 21	08 31	08 50	09 01	09 21	09 31	09 51		21 01	21 21	21 31	21 51
Crystal Palace 4	a			00 25	00 31	00 39	00 54	01 01	01 09	07 54	08 05	08 24	08 35	08 53	09 05	09 24	09 35	09 54		21 05	21 24	21 35	21 54
Crystal Palace	d		00 04	00 27	00 34	00 40	00 55	01 04	01 10	07 55		08 25		08 54		09 25		09 55			21 25		21 55
Sydenham	a			00 31																			
Forest Hill	a			00 34																			
Honor Oak Park	a			00 37																			
Brockley	a			00 39																			
New Cross Gate	a			00 41																			
London Bridge	a			00 49																			
Norwood Junction 2	a		00 09		00 39	00 47	01 02	01 10	01 15	07 59		08 29		08 58		09 29		09 59			21 29		21 59
	d	00 06								08 04		08 34		08 59		09 31		10 01			21 31		22 01
West Croydon	a	00 18								08 10		08 40		09 05		09 38		10 08			21 38		22 08
Sutton	a																						

		SN	SN	SN	SN	SN	SN	SN	SN	SN
London Victoria 15 ⊖	d		21 56		22 26		22 56		23 26	23 56
Battersea Park 4	d		22 00		22 30		23 00		23 30	00 01
Clapham Junction 10	d		22 04		22 34		23 04		23 34	00 06
Wandsworth Common	d		22 07		22 37		23 07		23 37	00 09
Balham 4 ⊖	d		22 10		22 40		23 10		23 40	00 12
Streatham Hill	d		22 14		22 44		23 14		23 44	00 16
London Bridge	d	21 35		22 05		22 35		23 05		
West Norwood 4	d	21 58	22 18	22 28	22 48	22 58	23 18	23 28	23 48	00 19
Gipsy Hill	d	22 01	22 21	22 31	22 51	23 01	23 21	23 31	23 51	00 22
Crystal Palace 4	a	22 05	22 24	22 35	22 54	23 05	23 24	23 35	23 54	00 26
Crystal Palace	d		22 25		22 55	23 06	23 25	23 36	23 55	00 26
Sydenham	a									
Forest Hill	a									
Honor Oak Park	a									
Brockley	a									
New Cross Gate	a									
London Bridge	a									
Norwood Junction 2	a		22 29		22 59	23 11	23 29	23 40	23 59	00 31
	d		22 30		23 01		23 31		00 01	
West Croydon	a		22 36		23 08		23 38		00 08	
Sutton	a									

A not 15 December

For complete service between London Victoria and Balham, refer to Table T170

For faster services between London Victoria, Clapham Junction and East Croydon, refer to Table T175

For Shepherd's Bush connecting trains, refer to Table T176

Table T171-R

Mondays to Fridays

16 December to 15 May

Croydon & Norwood Junction- Crystal Palace, Gipsy Hill, West Norwood and Streatham Hill - London Victoria

Miles	Miles			SN MX	SN	SN	SN	SN	SN	SN	SN	SN	SN	SN	SN	SN	SN	SN	SN	SN	SN	SN	SN
0	—	Sutton	d																				
4½	—	West Croydon	d							06 21			06 52			07 22			07 52			08 22	
—	—	Norwood Junction	a							06 27			06 58			07 28			07 58			08 28	
—	—		d		05 21		05 49		06 19	06 28			06 59			07 28			07 58			08 28	
—	—	London Bridge	d									06 28			06 58			07 28			07 58		
—	—	New Cross Gate	d	00 04								06 34			07 04			07 34			08 04		
—	—	Brockley	d	00 07								06 37			07 07			07 37			08 07		
—	—	Honor Oak Park	d	00 09								06 39			07 09			07 39			08 09		
—	—	Forest Hill	d	00 12								06 42			07 12			07 42			08 12		
—	—	Sydenham	d	00 15								06 45			07 15			07 45			08 15		
7¾	0	Crystal Palace	a	00 20	05 25		05 55		06 26	06 33		06 50	07 04		07 20	07 33		07 50	08 03		08 20	08 33	
—	—	**Crystal Palace**	d	00 20	05 26	05 53	05 56	06 23	06 26	06 37	06 53	06 56	07 07	07 23	07 26	07 37	07 53	07 56	08 07	08 23	08 26	08 37	08 53
8½	0¾	**Gipsy Hill**	a	00 23	05 29	05 55	05 59	06 25	06 29	06 39	06 55	06 59	07 09	07 25	07 29	07 39	07 55	07 59	08 09	08 25	08 29	08 39	08 55
9½	1¾	**West Norwood**	a	00 26	05 32	05 58	06 02	06 28	06 32	06 42	06 58	07 02	07 12	07 28	07 32	07 42	07 58	08 02	08 12	08 28	08 32	08 42	08 58
—	8½	London Bridge	a			06 21		06 51			07 21			07 51			08 21			08 51			09 21
10¾	—	**Streatham Hill**	a	00 30	05 36		06 06		06 36	06 46		07 06	07 16		07 36	07 46		08 06	08 16		08 36	08 46	
11¾	—	Balham ⊖	a		05 40		06 10		06 40	06 51		07 10	07 21		07 40	07 51		08 10	08 21		08 40	08 51	
12¾	—	Wandsworth Common	a		05 42		06 12		06 42	06 53		07 12	07 23		07 42	07 53		08 12	08 23		08 42	08 53	
14	—	Clapham Junction	a		05 46		06 16		06 46	06 57		07 16	07 27		07 46	07 57		08 16	08 27		08 46	08 57	
15½	—	Battersea Park	a		05 50		06 20		06 50	07 01		07 20	07 31		07 50	08 01		08 20	08 31		08 50	09 01	
16¾	—	London Victoria ⊖	a		05 54		06 24		06 54	07 05		07 24	07 35		07 54	08 05		08 24	08 35		08 54	09 08	

		SN	SN	SN	SN	SN	SN	SN	SN	SN	SN	SN	SN	SN	SN	SN	SN	SN	SN	SN	SN	SN	SN
Sutton	d																						
West Croydon	d		08 52			09 21			09 51			10 21			10 51			11 21			11 51		
Norwood Junction	a		08 58			09 27			09 57			10 27			10 57			11 27			11 57		
	d		08 58			09 28			09 58			10 28			10 58			11 28			11 58		
London Bridge	d	08 28			08 58			09 28			09 58			10 28			10 58			11 28			11 58
New Cross Gate	d	08 34			09 04			09 34			10 04			10 34			11 04			11 34			12 04
Brockley	d	08 37			09 07			09 37			10 07			10 37			11 07			11 37			12 07
Honor Oak Park	d	08 39			09 09			09 39			10 09			10 39			11 09			11 39			12 09
Forest Hill	d	08 42			09 12			09 42			10 12			10 42			11 12			11 42			12 12
Sydenham	d	08 45			09 15			09 45			10 15			10 45			11 15			11 45			12 15
Crystal Palace	a	08 50	09 03		09 20	09 33		09 50	10 03		10 20	10 33		10 50	11 03		11 20	11 33		11 50	12 03		12 20
Crystal Palace	d	08 56	09 07	09 23	09 26	09 37	09 53	09 56	10 07	10 23	10 26	10 37	10 53	10 56	11 07	11 23	11 26	11 37	11 53	11 56	12 07	12 23	12 26
Gipsy Hill	a	08 59	09 09	09 25	09 29	09 39	09 55	09 59	10 09	10 25	10 29	10 39	10 55	10 59	11 09	11 25	11 29	11 39	11 55	11 59	12 09	12 25	12 29
West Norwood	a	09 02	09 12	09 28	09 32	09 42	09 58	10 02	10 12	10 28	10 32	10 42	10 58	11 02	11 12	11 28	11 32	11 42	11 58	12 02	12 12	12 28	12 32
London Bridge	a			09 51			10 21			10 51			11 21			11 51			12 21			12 51	
Streatham Hill	a	09 06	09 16		09 36	09 46		10 06	10 16		10 36	10 46		11 06	11 16		11 36	11 46		12 06	12 16		12 36
Balham ⊖	a	09 10	09 21		09 40	09 51		10 10	10 21		10 40	10 51		11 10	11 21		11 40	11 51		12 10	12 21		12 40
Wandsworth Common	a	09 12	09 23		09 42	09 53		10 12	10 23		10 42	10 53		11 12	11 23		11 42	11 53		12 12	12 23		12 42
Clapham Junction	a	09 16	09 27		09 46	09 57		10 16	10 27		10 46	10 57		11 16	11 27		11 46	11 57		12 16	12 27		12 46
Battersea Park	a	09 20	09 31		09 50	10 01		10 20	10 31		10 50	11 01		11 20	11 31		11 50	12 01		12 20	12 31		12 50
London Victoria ⊖	a	09 24	09 35		09 54	10 05		10 24	10 35		10 54	11 05		11 24	11 35		11 54	12 05		12 24	12 35		12 54

		SN	SN	SN	SN	SN	SN	SN	SN	SN	SN	SN	SN	SN	SN	SN	SN	SN	SN	SN	SN	SN
Sutton	d																					
West Croydon	d	12 21			12 51			13 21			13 51			14 21			14 51			15 21		
Norwood Junction	a	12 27			12 57			13 27			13 57			14 28			14 57			15 27		
	d	12 28			12 58			13 28			13 58			14 28			14 58			15 28		
London Bridge	d			12 28			12 58			13 28			13 58			14 28			14 58			15 28
New Cross Gate	d			12 34			13 04			13 34			14 04			14 34			15 04			15 34
Brockley	d			12 37			13 07			13 37			14 07			14 37			15 07			15 37
Honor Oak Park	d			12 39			13 09			13 39			14 09			14 39			15 09			15 39
Forest Hill	d			12 42			13 12			13 42			14 12			14 42			15 12			15 42
Sydenham	d			12 45			13 15			13 45			14 15			14 45			15 15			15 45
Crystal Palace	a	12 33		12 50	13 03		13 20	13 33		13 50	14 03		14 20	14 33		14 50	15 03		15 20	15 33		15 50
Crystal Palace	d	12 37	12 53	12 56	13 07	13 23	13 26	13 37	13 53	13 56	14 07	14 23	14 26	14 37	14 53	14 56	15 07	15 23	15 26	15 37	15 53	15 56
Gipsy Hill	a	12 39	12 55	12 59	13 09	13 25	13 29	13 39	13 55	13 59	14 09	14 25	14 29	14 39	14 55	14 59	15 09	15 25	15 29	15 39	15 55	15 59
West Norwood	a	12 42	12 58	13 02	13 12	13 28	13 32	13 42	13 58	14 02	14 12	14 28	14 32	14 42	14 58	15 02	15 12	15 28	15 32	15 42	15 58	16 02
London Bridge	a		13 21			13 51			14 21			14 51			15 21			15 51			16 21	
Streatham Hill	a	12 46		13 06	13 16		13 36	13 46		14 06	14 16		14 36	14 46		15 06	15 16		15 36	15 46		16 06
Balham ⊖	a	12 51		13 10	13 21		13 40	13 51		14 10	14 21		14 40	14 51		15 10	15 21		15 40	15 51		16 10
Wandsworth Common	a	12 53		13 12	13 23		13 42	13 53		14 12	14 23		14 42	14 53		15 12	15 23		15 42	15 53		16 12
Clapham Junction	a	12 57		13 16	13 27		13 46	13 57		14 16	14 27		14 46	14 57		15 16	15 27		15 46	15 57		16 16
Battersea Park	a	13 01		13 20	13 31		13 50	14 01		14 20	14 31		14 50	15 01		15 20	15 31		15 50	16 01		16 20
London Victoria ⊖	a	13 05		13 24	13 35		13 54	14 05		14 24	14 35		14 54	15 05		15 24	15 35		15 54	16 05		16 24

For complete service between London Victoria and Balham, refer to Table T170

For faster services between London Victoria, Clapham Junction and East Croydon, refer to Table T175

For Shepherd's Bush connecting trains, refer to Table T176

Table T171-R

Mondays to Fridays

16 December to 15 May

Croydon & Norwood Junction- Crystal Palace, Gipsy Hill, West Norwood and Streatham Hill - London Victoria

		SN	SN	SN	SN	SN	SN	SN	SN	SN	SN	SN	SN	SN	SN	SN	SN	SN	SN	SN	SN	SN
Sutton	d																					
West Croydon	d	15 51			16 21			16 51			17 22			17 52			18 22			18 52		
Norwood Junction	a	15 57			16 27			16 57			17 28			17 58			18 28			18 58		
	d	15 58			16 28			16 58			17 29			17 59			18 28			18 58		
London Bridge	d			15 58			16 28			16 58			17 28			17 58			18 28			18 58
New Cross Gate	d			16 04			16 34			17 04			17 34			18 04			18 34			19 04
Brockley	d			16 07			16 37			17 07			17 37			18 07			18 37			19 07
Honor Oak Park	d			16 09			16 39			17 09			17 39			18 09			18 39			19 09
Forest Hill	d			16 12			16 42			17 12			17 42			18 12			18 42			19 12
Sydenham	d			16 15			16 45			17 15			17 45			18 15			18 45			19 15
Crystal Palace	a	16 03		16 20	16 33		16 50	17 03		17 20	17 34		17 50	18 04		18 20	18 33		18 50	19 03		19 20
Crystal Palace	d	16 07	16 23	16 26	16 37	16 53	16 56	17 07	17 23	17 26	17 37	17 53	17 56	18 07	18 23	18 26	18 37	18 53	18 56	19 07	19 23	19 26
Gipsy Hill	a	16 09	16 25	16 29	16 39	16 55	16 59	17 09	17 25	17 29	17 39	17 55	17 59	18 09	18 25	18 29	18 39	18 55	18 59	19 09	19 25	19 29
West Norwood	a	16 12	16 28	16 32	16 42	16 58	17 02	17 12	17 28	17 32	17 42	17 58	18 02	18 12	18 28	18 32	18 42	18 58	19 02	19 12	19 28	19 32
London Bridge	a		16 51			17 21			17 51			18 21			18 51			19 21			19 51	
Streatham Hill	a	16 16		16 36	16 46		17 06	17 16		17 36	17 46		18 06	18 16		18 36	18 46		19 06	19 16		19 36
Balham ⊖	a	16 21		16 40	16 51		17 11	17 21		17 40	17 51		18 10	18 21		18 40	18 51		19 10	19 21		19 40
Wandsworth Common	a	16 23		16 42	16 53		17 14	17 23		17 42	17 53		18 12	18 23		18 42	18 53		19 12	19 23		19 42
Clapham Junction	a	16 27		16 46	16 57		17 17	17 27		17 46	17 57		18 16	18 27		18 46	18 57		19 16	19 27		19 46
Battersea Park	a	16 31		16 50	17 01		17 21	17 31		17 50	18 01		18 20	18 31		18 50	19 01		19 20	19 31		19 50
London Victoria ⊖	a	16 35		16 54	17 05		17 26	17 35		17 54	18 05		18 24	18 36		18 54	19 05		19 24	19 35		19 54

		SN	SN	SN	SN	SN	SN	SN	SN	SN	SN	SN	SN	SN	SN	SN	SN	SN	SN	SN	SN	SN	SN
Sutton	d																						
West Croydon	d	19 22			19 52			20 21			20 51			21 22			21 51			22 21			22 51
Norwood Junction	a	19 28			19 58			20 27			20 58			21 28			21 57			22 27			22 57
	d	19 28			19 58			20 28			20 59			21 28			21 58			22 28			22 58
London Bridge	d			19 28			19 58			20 28			20 58			21 28			21 58			22 28	
New Cross Gate	d			19 34			20 04			20 34			21 04			21 34			22 04			22 34	
Brockley	d			19 37			20 07			20 37			21 07			21 37			22 07			22 37	
Honor Oak Park	d			19 39			20 09			20 39			21 09			21 39			22 09			22 39	
Forest Hill	d			19 42			20 12			20 42			21 12			21 42			22 12			22 42	
Sydenham	d			19 45			20 15			20 45			21 15			21 45			22 15			22 45	
Crystal Palace	a	19 33		19 50	20 03		20 20	20 33		20 50	21 03		21 20	21 33		21 50	22 03		22 20	22 33		22 50	23 03
Crystal Palace	d	19 37	19 53	19 56	20 07	20 23	20 26	20 37	20 53	20 56	21 07	21 23	21 26	21 37	21 53	21 56	22 07	22 23	22 26	22 37	22 53	22 56	23 07
Gipsy Hill	a	19 39	19 55	19 59	20 09	20 25	20 29	20 39	20 55	20 59	21 09	21 25	21 29	21 39	21 55	21 59	22 09	22 25	22 29	22 39	22 55	22 59	23 09
West Norwood	a	19 42	19 58	20 02	20 12	20 28	20 32	20 42	20 58	21 02	21 12	21 28	21 32	21 42	21 58	22 02	22 12	22 28	22 32	22 42	22 58	23 02	23 12
London Bridge	a		20 22			20 51			21 21			21 51			22 21			22 51			23 21		
Streatham Hill	a	19 46		20 06	20 16		20 36	20 46		21 06	21 16		21 36	21 46		22 06	22 16		22 36	22 46		23 06	23 16
Balham ⊖	a	19 51		20 10	20 21		20 40	20 51		21 10	21 21		21 40	21 51		22 10	22 21		22 40	22 51		23 10	23 21
Wandsworth Common	a	19 53		20 12	20 23		20 42	20 53		21 12	21 23		21 42	21 53		22 12	22 23		22 42	22 53		23 12	23 23
Clapham Junction	a	19 57		20 16	20 27		20 46	20 57		21 16	21 27		21 46	21 57		22 16	22 27		22 46	22 57		23 16	23 27
Battersea Park	a	20 01		20 20	20 31		20 50	21 01		21 20	21 31		21 50	22 01		22 20	22 31		22 50	23 01		23 20	23 31
London Victoria ⊖	a	20 05		20 24	20 35		20 54	21 07		21 24	21 35		21 54	22 05		22 24	22 37		22 55	23 05		23 24	23 37

		SN	SN	SN	SN
Sutton	d				
West Croydon	d				
Norwood Junction	a				
	d				
London Bridge	d	22 58		23 28	23 58
New Cross Gate	d	23 04		23 34	00 04
Brockley	d	23 07		23 37	00 07
Honor Oak Park	d	23 09		23 39	00 09
Forest Hill	d	23 12		23 42	00 12
Sydenham	d	23 15		23 45	00 15
Crystal Palace	a	23 20		23 50	00 20
Crystal Palace	d	23 20	23 24	23 50	00 20
Gipsy Hill	a	23 23	23 26	23 53	00 23
West Norwood	a	23 26	23 29	23 56	00 26
London Bridge	a		23 52		
Streatham Hill	a	23 30		00 01	00 30
Balham ⊖	a	23 37			
Wandsworth Common	a				
Clapham Junction	a	23 41			
Battersea Park	a				
London Victoria ⊖	a	23 50			

For complete service between London Victoria and Balham, refer to Table T170

For faster services between London Victoria, Clapham Junction and East Croydon, refer to Table T175

For Shepherd's Bush connecting trains, refer to Table T176

Table T171-R

Saturdays
21 December to 16 May

Croydon & Norwood Junction- Crystal Palace, Gipsy Hill, West Norwood and Streatham Hill - London Victoria

Station		SN	SN	SN	SN	SN		SN	SN	SN	SN	SN	SN	SN	SN	SN		SN	SN	SN	SN	SN	SN	SN	SN
Sutton	d																								
West Croydon	d				06 21				06 51			07 21			07 51				08 21			08 51			09 22
Norwood Junction	a				06 27				06 57			07 27			07 57				08 27			08 57			09 28
	d		05 50	06 20	06 28	06 48			06 58	07 18		07 28			07 58				08 28			08 58			09 28
London Bridge	d							06 28			06 58			07 28				07 58			08 28			08 58	
New Cross Gate	d	00 04						06 35			07 05			07 35				08 05			08 35			09 05	
Brockley	d	00 07						06 37			07 07			07 37				08 07			08 37			09 07	
Honor Oak Park	d	00 09						06 40			07 10			07 40				08 10			08 40			09 10	
Forest Hill	d	00 12						06 42			07 12			07 42				08 12			08 42			09 12	
Sydenham	d	00 15						06 46			07 16			07 46				08 16			08 46			09 16	
Crystal Palace	a	00 20	05 55	06 24	06 33	06 52		06 50	07 03	07 22	07 20	07 33		07 50	08 03			08 20	08 33		08 50	09 03		09 20	09 33
Crystal Palace	d	00 20	05 56	06 26	06 37	06 53		06 56	07 07	07 23	07 26	07 37	07 53	07 56	08 07	08 23		08 26	08 37	08 53	08 56	09 07	09 23	09 26	09 37
Gipsy Hill	a	00 23	05 58	06 28	06 39	06 55		06 59	07 09	07 25	07 29	07 39	07 55	07 59	08 09	08 25		08 29	08 39	08 55	08 59	09 09	09 25	09 29	09 39
West Norwood	a	00 26	06 01	06 31	06 42	06 58		07 02	07 12	07 28	07 32	07 42	07 58	08 02	08 12	08 28		08 32	08 42	08 58	09 02	09 12	09 28	09 32	09 42
London Bridge	a					07 21				07 51			08 21			08 51				09 21			09 51		
Streatham Hill	a	00 30	06 06	06 35	06 46			07 06	07 16		07 36	07 46		08 06	08 16			08 36	08 46		09 06	09 16		09 36	09 46
Balham	a		06 10	06 40	06 51			07 10	07 21		07 40	07 51		08 10	08 21			08 40	08 51		09 10	09 21		09 40	09 51
Wandsworth Common	a		06 12	06 42	06 53			07 12	07 23		07 42	07 53		08 12	08 23			08 42	08 53		09 12	09 23		09 42	09 53
Clapham Junction	a		06 16	06 46	06 57			07 16	07 27		07 46	07 57		08 16	08 27			08 46	08 57		09 16	09 27		09 46	09 57
Battersea Park	a		06 20	06 50	07 01			07 20	07 31		07 50	08 01		08 20	08 31			08 50	09 01		09 20	09 31		09 50	10 01
London Victoria	a		06 24	06 54	07 05			07 24	07 35		07 54	08 05		08 24	08 35			08 54	09 05		09 24	09 35		09 54	10 05

Station		SN		SN	SN	SN	SN	SN	SN	SN	SN	SN	SN	SN	SN	SN	and at the same minutes past each hour until	SN	SN	SN	SN	SN	SN	
Sutton	d																							
West Croydon	d				09 51			10 21			10 51			11 21				15 51			16 21			
Norwood Junction	a				09 57			10 27			10 57			11 27				15 57			16 27			
	d				09 58			10 28			10 58			11 28				15 58			16 28			
London Bridge	d			09 28			09 58			10 28			10 58			11 28				15 58			16 28	
New Cross Gate	d			09 35			10 05			10 34			11 05			11 35				16 05			16 35	
Brockley	d			09 37			10 07			10 36			11 07			11 37				16 07			16 37	
Honor Oak Park	d			09 40			10 10			10 39			11 10			11 40				16 10			16 40	
Forest Hill	d			09 42			10 12			10 41			11 12			11 42				16 12			16 42	
Sydenham	d			09 46			10 16			10 45			11 16			11 46				16 16			16 46	
Crystal Palace	a			09 50	10 03		10 20	10 33		10 49	11 03		11 20	11 33		11 50		16 03		16 20	16 33		16 50	
Crystal Palace	d	09 53		09 56	10 07	10 23	10 26	10 37	10 53	10 56	11 07	11 23	11 26	11 37	11 53	11 56		16 07	16 23	16 26	16 37	16 53	16 56	
Gipsy Hill	a	09 55		09 59	10 09	10 25	10 29	10 39	10 55	10 59	11 09	11 25	11 29	11 39	11 55	11 59		16 09	16 25	16 29	16 39	16 55	16 59	
West Norwood	a	09 58		10 02	10 12	10 28	10 32	10 42	10 58	11 02	11 12	11 28	11 32	11 42	11 58	12 02		16 12	16 28	16 32	16 42	16 58	17 02	
London Bridge	a	10 21				10 51			11 21			11 51			12 21				16 51			17 21		
Streatham Hill	a			10 06	10 16		10 36	10 46		11 06	11 16		11 36	11 46		12 06		16 16		16 36	16 46		17 06	
Balham	a			10 10	10 21		10 40	10 51		11 10	11 21		11 40	11 51		12 10		16 21		16 40	16 51		17 10	
Wandsworth Common	a			10 12	10 23		10 42	10 53		11 12	11 23		11 42	11 53		12 12		16 23		16 42	16 53		17 12	
Clapham Junction	a			10 16	10 27		10 46	10 57		11 16	11 27		11 46	11 57		12 16		16 27		16 46	16 57		17 16	
Battersea Park	a			10 20	10 31		10 50	11 01		11 20	11 31		11 50	12 01		12 20		16 31		16 50	17 01		17 20	
London Victoria	a			10 24	10 35		10 54	11 05		11 24	11 35		11 54	12 05		12 24		16 35		16 54	17 05		17 24	

Station		SN	SN	SN	SN	SN	SN	SN	and at the same minutes past each hour until	SN	SN	SN	SN	SN	SN		SN	SN	SN	SN	SN	SN	SN	SN
Sutton	d																							
West Croydon	d	16 52			17 21			17 51				20 21			20 51				21 22			21 51		
Norwood Junction	a	16 58			17 27			17 57				20 27			20 57				21 28			21 57		
	d	16 59			17 28			17 58				20 28			20 58				21 28			21 58		
London Bridge	d			16 58			17 28				19 58			20 28				20 58			21 28			21 58
New Cross Gate	d			17 05			17 35				20 05			20 35				21 05			21 35			22 05
Brockley	d			17 07			17 37				20 07			20 37				21 07			21 37			22 07
Honor Oak Park	d			17 10			17 40				20 10			20 40				21 10			21 40			22 10
Forest Hill	d			17 12			17 42				20 12			20 42				21 12			21 42			22 12
Sydenham	d			17 16			17 46				20 16			20 46				21 16			21 46			22 16
Crystal Palace	a	17 04		17 20	17 33		17 50	18 03			20 20	20 33		20 50	21 03			21 20	21 33		21 50	22 03		22 20
Crystal Palace	d	17 07	17 23	17 26	17 37	17 53	17 56	18 07		20 23	20 26	20 37	20 53	20 56	21 07		21 23	21 26	21 37	21 53	21 56	22 07	22 23	22 26
Gipsy Hill	a	17 09	17 25	17 29	17 39	17 55	17 59	18 09		20 25	20 29	20 39	20 55	20 59	21 09		21 25	21 29	21 39	21 55	21 59	22 09	22 25	22 29
West Norwood	a	17 12	17 28	17 32	17 42	17 58	18 02	18 12		20 28	20 32	20 42	20 58	21 02	21 12		21 28	21 32	21 42	21 58	22 02	22 12	22 28	22 32
London Bridge	a		17 51			18 21				20 51			21 21				21 51			22 22			22 52	
Streatham Hill	a	17 16		17 36	17 46		18 06	18 16			20 36	20 46		21 06	21 16			21 36	21 46		22 06	22 16		22 36
Balham	a	17 21		17 40	17 51		18 10	18 21			20 40	20 51		21 10	21 21			21 40	21 51		22 10	22 21		22 40
Wandsworth Common	a	17 23		17 42	17 53		18 12	18 23			20 42	20 53		21 12	21 23			21 42	21 53		22 12	22 23		22 42
Clapham Junction	a	17 27		17 46	17 57		18 16	18 27			20 46	20 57		21 16	21 27			21 46	21 57		22 16	22 27		22 46
Battersea Park	a	17 31		17 50	18 01		18 20	18 31			20 50	21 01		21 20	21 31			21 50	22 01		22 20	22 31		22 50
London Victoria	a	17 35		17 54	18 05		18 24	18 35			20 54	21 05		21 24	21 35			21 54	22 05		22 24	22 35		22 54

For complete service between London Victoria and Balham, refer to Table T170

For faster services between London Victoria, Clapham Junction and East Croydon, refer to Table T175

For Shepherd's Bush connecting trains, refer to Table T176

Table T171-R

Saturdays
21 December to 16 May

Croydon & Norwood Junction- Crystal Palace, Gipsy Hill, West Norwood and Streatham Hill - London Victoria

Station		SN		SN	SN	SN	SN	SN	SN	SN	SN
Sutton	d										
West Croydon	d	22 21				22 51			23 21		
Norwood Junction	a	22 27				22 57			23 27		
	d	22 28				22 58			23 28		
London Bridge	d				22 28			22 58		23 28	23 58
New Cross Gate	d				22 35			23 05		23 35	00 05
Brockley	d				22 37			23 07		23 37	00 07
Honor Oak Park	d				22 40			23 10		23 40	00 10
Forest Hill	d				22 42			23 12		23 42	00 12
Sydenham	d				22 46			23 16		23 46	00 16
Crystal Palace	a	22 33			22 50	23 03		23 20	23 33	23 50	00 20
Crystal Palace	d	22 37		22 53	22 56	23 07	23 23	23 26	23 37	23 56	00 21
Gipsy Hill	a	22 39		22 55	22 59	23 09	23 25	23 29	23 39	23 59	00 23
West Norwood	a	22 42		22 58	23 02	23 12	23 28	23 32	23 42	00 02	00 26
London Bridge	a			23 23			23 51				
Streatham Hill	a	22 46			23 06	23 16		23 36	23 46	00 06	00 30
Balham	a	22 51			23 10	23 21		23 40	23 51	00 10	
Wandsworth Common	a	22 53			23 12	23 23		23 42	23 53	00 12	
Clapham Junction	a	22 57			23 16	23 27		23 46	23 57	00 16	
Battersea Park	a	23 01			23 20	23 31		23 50	00 01	00 20	
London Victoria	a	23 05			23 24	23 35		23 54	00 05	00 24	

Sundays
15 December to 10 May

Station		SN A	SN	SN	SN	SN	SN	SN	SN	SN	SN	SN	SN	SN	and at the same minutes past each hour until	SN	SN	SN	SN		SN	SN	SN	SN
Sutton	d																							
West Croydon	d			06 59		07 31		08 03		08 33		09 01		09 31			22 01		22 31			23 01		23 31
Norwood Junction	a			07 07		07 38		08 09		08 39		09 08		09 38			22 08		22 38			23 08		23 38
	d			07 09		07 38		08 09		08 39		09 09		09 39			22 09		22 39			23 09		23 39
London Bridge	d																							
New Cross Gate	d	00 05																						
Brockley	d	00 07																						
Honor Oak Park	d	00 10																						
Forest Hill	d	00 12																						
Sydenham	d	00 16																						
Crystal Palace	a	00 20		07 14		07 43		08 14		08 44		09 14		09 44			22 14		22 44			23 14		23 44
Crystal Palace	d	00 21	07 11	07 14	07 41	07 43	08 11	08 14	08 41	08 44	09 11	09 14	09 41	09 44		22 11	22 14	22 41	22 44		23 11	23 14	23 41	23 44
Gipsy Hill	a	00 23	07 13	07 17	07 43	07 46	08 13	08 17	08 43	08 47	09 13	09 17	09 43	09 47		22 13	22 17	22 43	22 47		23 13	23 17	23 43	23 47
West Norwood	a	00 26	07 16	07 20	07 46	07 49	08 16	08 20	08 46	08 50	09 16	09 20	09 46	09 50		22 16	22 20	22 46	22 50		23 16	23 20	23 46	23 50
London Bridge	a		07 39		08 09		08 43		09 09		09 39		10 09			22 39		23 09			23 39		00 09	
Streatham Hill	a	00 30		07 24		07 53		08 24		08 54		09 24		09 54			22 24		22 54			23 24		23 54
Balham	a			07 28		07 58		08 29		08 57		09 27		09 57			22 27		22 57			23 27		23 58
Wandsworth Common	a			07 30		08 01		08 31		09 00		09 30		10 00			22 30		23 00			23 30		00 01
Clapham Junction	a			07 34		08 04		08 35		09 03		09 33		10 03			22 33		23 03			23 33		00 05
Battersea Park	a			07 38		08 08		08 39		09 07		09 37		10 07			22 37		23 07			23 37		00 09
London Victoria	a			07 42		08 13		08 43		09 12		09 42		10 12			22 42		23 12			23 43		00 13

A not 15 December

For complete service between London Victoria and Balham, refer to Table T170

For faster services between London Victoria, Clapham Junction and East Croydon, refer to Table T175

For Shepherd's Bush connecting trains, refer to Table T176

Table T172-F

London via Wallington - Epsom Downs

Mondays to Fridays

16 December to 15 May

Miles	Miles	Station		SN MX	SN	SN	SN	SN	SN	SN	SN	SN		SN	SN	SN	SN	SN	SN	SN	SN	SN		SN	SN
—	—	London Victoria 15 ⊖	d					06 00		06 16	06 30				06 46	07 00		07 16	07 30			07 46		08 00	
—	—	Clapham Junction 10	d					06 09		06 24	06 39				06 54	07 09		07 24	07 39			07 54		08 09	
4¾	—	Balham 4 ⊖	d					06 15		06 30	06 45				07 00	07 15		07 30	07 45			08 00		08 15	
—	0	London Bridge	d				05 55		06 10			06 40		06 55			07 10			07 40	07 55				08 25
—	8¾	Norwood Junction	d				06 09		06 36			07 06		07 09			07 36			08 06	08 09				08 39
10¾	10½	West Croydon	d	00 14	05 53	06 04	06 15	06 34	06 42	06 49	07 04	07 12		07 16	07 19	07 34	07 42	07 49	08 05	08 12	08 16	08 19		08 34	08 45
11¾	11½	**Waddon**	d	00 16	05 55	06 07	06 18	06 36		06 52	07 06			07 18	07 22	07 36		07 52	08 07		08 18	08 22		08 36	08 48
13¼	13	**Wallington**	d	00 20	05 59	06 11	06 22	06 40	06 47	06 56	07 10	07 17		07 22	07 26	07 40	07 47	07 56	08 11	08 17	08 22	08 26		08 40	08 52
14¼	14	**Carshalton Beeches**	d	00 22	06 02	06 13	06 24	06 43		06 58	07 13			07 24	07 28	07 43		07 58	08 14		08 24	08 28		08 43	08 54
15¼	15	Sutton 4	a	00 26	06 05	06 19	06 28	06 46	06 52	07 03	07 16	07 22		07 28	07 33	07 46	07 52	08 03	08 17	08 22	08 28	08 33		08 46	08 58
—	—	Sutton	d			06 20		06 49			07 19					07 49			08 19					08 49	
16¼	—	**Belmont**	d			06 23		06 52			07 22					07 52			08 22					08 52	
17¾	—	**Banstead**	d			06 27		06 56			07 26					07 56			08 26					08 56	
19	—	**Epsom Downs**	a			06 30		06 59			07 29					07 59			08 29					08 59	

Station		SN	SN	SN	SN	SN	SN	SN		SN	SN	SN	SN	SN	SN	SN	SN	SN		SN	SN	SN	SN	SN	SN
London Victoria 15 ⊖	d	08 16	08 30		08 46	09 00		09 16		09 30		09 46	10 00		10 16	10 30		10 46		11 00		11 16	11 30		11 46
Clapham Junction 10	d	08 24	08 39		08 54	09 09		09 24		09 39		09 54	10 09		10 24	10 39		10 54		11 09		11 24	11 39		11 54
Balham 4 ⊖	d	08 30	08 45		09 00	09 15		09 30		09 45		10 00	10 15		10 30	10 45		11 00		11 15		11 30	11 45		12 00
London Bridge	d			08 55			09 25				09 55			10 25			10 55				11 25			11 55	
Norwood Junction	d			09 09			09 39				10 09			10 39			11 09				11 39			12 09	
West Croydon	d	08 49	09 04	09 15	09 19	09 34	09 45	09 49		10 04	10 15	10 19	10 34	10 45	10 50	11 04	11 15	11 19		11 34	11 45	11 50	12 04	12 15	12 18
Waddon	d	08 52	09 06	09 18	09 22	09 36	09 48	09 52		10 06	10 18	10 22	10 36	10 48	10 53	11 06	11 18	11 21		11 36	11 48	11 53	12 06	12 18	12 21
Wallington	d	08 56	09 10	09 22	09 26	09 40	09 52	09 56		10 10	10 22	10 26	10 40	10 52	10 57	11 10	11 22	11 25		11 40	11 52	11 57	12 10	12 22	12 25
Carshalton Beeches	d	08 58	09 13	09 24	09 28	09 43	09 54	09 58		10 13	10 24	10 28	10 43	10 54	11 00	11 13	11 24	11 28		11 43	11 54	12 00	12 13	12 24	12 28
Sutton 4	a	09 03	09 16	09 28	09 33	09 46	09 58	10 03		10 16	10 28	10 33	10 46	10 58	11 03	11 16	11 28	11 33		11 46	11 58	12 03	12 16	12 28	12 33
Sutton	d		09 19			09 49				10 19			10 49			11 19				11 49			12 19		
Belmont	d		09 22			09 52				10 22			10 52			11 22				11 52			12 22		
Banstead	d		09 26			09 56				10 26			10 56			11 26				11 56			12 26		
Epsom Downs	a		09 29			09 59				10 29			10 59			11 29				11 59			12 29		

Station		SN	SN	SN		SN MW FO	SN TThO	SN	SN MW FO	SN TThO	SN	SN	SN	SN		SN	SN	SN	SN	SN	SN	SN	SN	SN	
London Victoria 15 ⊖	d	12 00		12 16		12 30	12 30		12 46	12 46	13 00		13 16	13 30			13 46	14 00		14 16	14 30		14 46	15 00	
Clapham Junction 10	d	12 09		12 24		12 39	12 42		12 54	12 54	13 09		13 24	13 39			13 54	14 09		14 24	14 39		14 54	15 09	
Balham 4 ⊖	d	12 15		12 30		12 45	12 48		13 00	13 00	13 15		13 30	13 45			14 00	14 15		14 30	14 45		15 00	15 15	
London Bridge	d		12 25					12 55				13 25				13 55			14 25			14 55			
Norwood Junction	d		12 39					13 09				13 39				14 09			14 39			15 09			
West Croydon	d	12 34	12 45	12 50		13 04	13 12	13 15	13 18	13 20	13 34	13 45	13 50	14 04		14 15	14 18	14 34	14 45	14 50	15 04	15 15	15 18	15 34	
Waddon	d	12 36	12 48	12 53		13 06	13 14	13 18	13 21	13 23	13 36	13 48	13 53	14 06		14 18	14 21	14 36	14 48	14 54	15 06	15 18	15 21	15 36	
Wallington	d	12 40	12 52	12 57		13 10	13 18	13 22	13 25	13 27	13 40	13 52	13 57	14 10		14 22	14 25	14 40	14 52	14 58	15 10	15 22	15 25	15 40	
Carshalton Beeches	d	12 43	12 54	13 00		13 13	13 21	13 24	13 28	13 29	13 43	13 54	14 00	14 13		14 24	14 28	14 43	14 54	15 01	15 13	15 24	15 28	15 43	
Sutton 4	a	12 46	12 58	13 03		13 16	13 24	13 28	13 33	13 33	13 46	13 58	14 03	14 16		14 28	14 33	14 46	14 58	15 06	15 16	15 28	15 33	15 46	
Sutton	d	12 49				13 19	13 25				13 49			14 19				14 49			15 19			15 49	
Belmont	d	12 52				13 22	13 28				13 52			14 22				14 52			15 22			15 52	
Banstead	d	12 56				13 26	13 32				13 56			14 26				14 56			15 26			15 56	
Epsom Downs	a	12 59				13 29	13 35				13 59			14 29				14 59			15 29			15 59	

Station		SN	SN	SN	SN	SN	SN	SN	SN	SN		SN	SN	SN	SN	SN	SN	SN	SN	SN		SN	SN	SN	SN
London Victoria 15 ⊖	d		15 16	15 30		15 46	16 00			16 16		16 30			16 46	17 00			17 16	17 30				17 46	18 00
Clapham Junction 10	d		15 24	15 39		15 54	16 09			16 24		16 39			16 54	17 09			17 24	17 39				17 54	18 09
Balham 4 ⊖	d		15 30	15 45		16 00	16 15			16 30		16 45			17 00	17 15			17 30	17 45				18 00	18 15
London Bridge	d	15 25			15 55			16 10	16 25				16 40	16 55			17 10	17 25				17 40	17 55		
Norwood Junction	d	15 39			16 09			16 36	16 39				17 06	17 09			17 36	17 39				18 06	18 09		
West Croydon	d	15 45	15 50	16 04	16 15	16 18	16 34	16 42	16 46	16 49		17 04	17 12	17 16	17 19	17 34	17 42	17 46	17 49	18 04		18 12	18 16	18 19	18 34
Waddon	d	15 48	15 53	16 06	16 18	16 21	16 36		16 48	16 52		17 06		17 18	17 22	17 36		17 48	17 52	18 06			18 18	18 22	18 36
Wallington	d	15 52	15 57	16 10	16 22	16 25	16 40	16 47	16 52	16 56		17 10	17 17	17 22	17 26	17 40	17 47	17 52	17 56	18 10		18 17	18 22	18 26	18 40
Carshalton Beeches	d	15 54	16 00	16 13	16 24	16 28	16 43		16 54	16 58		17 13		17 24	17 28	17 43		17 54	17 58	18 13			18 24	18 28	18 43
Sutton 4	a	15 58	16 03	16 16	16 28	16 33	16 46	16 52	16 58	17 03		17 16	17 22	17 28	17 33	17 46	17 52	17 59	18 03	18 16		18 22	18 29	18 33	18 46
Sutton	d			16 19			16 49					17 19				17 49				18 19					18 49
Belmont	d			16 22			16 52					17 22				17 52				18 22					18 52
Banstead	d			16 26			16 56					17 26				17 56				18 26					18 56
Epsom Downs	a			16 29			16 59					17 29				17 59				18 29					18 59

Station		SN	SN	SN	SN	SN		SN	SN	SN	SN	SN	SN	SN	SN	SN		SN	SN	SN	SN	SN	SN	SN	SN
London Victoria 15 ⊖	d			18 16	18 30			18 46	19 00		19 16	19 30		19 46	20 00			20 16	20 30		20 46	21 00		21 16	21 30
Clapham Junction 10	d			18 24	18 39			18 54	19 09		19 24	19 39		19 54	20 09			20 24	20 39		20 54	21 09		21 24	21 42
Balham 4 ⊖	d			18 30	18 45			19 00	19 15		19 30	19 45		20 00	20 15			20 30	20 45		21 00	21 15		21 30	21 48
London Bridge	d	18 10	18 25			18 55				19 25			19 55			20 25				20 55			21 25		
Norwood Junction	d	18 36	18 39			19 09				19 39			20 09			20 39				21 09			21 39		
West Croydon	d	18 42	18 46	18 49	19 04	19 15		19 18	19 34	19 45	19 48	20 04	20 15	20 18	20 35	20 45		20 50	21 04	21 15	21 18	21 34	21 45	21 48	22 12
Waddon	d		18 48	18 52	19 06	19 18		19 21	19 36	19 48	19 51	20 06	20 18	20 21	20 37	20 48		20 53	21 06	21 18	21 21	21 36	21 48	21 51	22 14
Wallington	d	18 47	18 52	18 56	19 10	19 22		19 25	19 40	19 52	19 55	20 10	20 22	20 25	20 41	20 52		20 57	21 10	21 22	21 25	21 40	21 52	21 55	22 18
Carshalton Beeches	d		18 54	18 58	19 13	19 24		19 28	19 43	19 54	19 58	20 13	20 24	20 28	20 44	20 54		21 00	21 13	21 24	21 28	21 43	21 54	21 58	22 21
Sutton 4	a	18 52	18 59	19 03	19 16	19 29		19 33	19 46	19 58	20 03	20 16	20 28	20 33	20 47	20 58		21 03	21 16	21 28	21 33	21 46	21 58	22 03	22 24
Sutton	d				19 19				19 49			20 19			20 49				21 19			21 49			22 25
Belmont	d				19 22				19 52			20 22			20 52				21 22			21 52			22 28
Banstead	d				19 26				19 56			20 26			20 56				21 26			21 56			22 32
Epsom Downs	a				19 29				19 59			20 29			20 59				21 29			21 59			22 35

Station		SN		SN	SN	SN	SN	SN	SN	SN	SN	SN		SN
London Victoria 15 ⊖	d			21 47	22 00		22 16	22 30		22 46	23 00	23 16		23 40
Clapham Junction 10	d			21 56	22 09		22 24	22 39		22 54	23 09	23 24		23 48
Balham 4 ⊖	d			22 01	22 15		22 30	22 45		23 00	23 15	23 30		23 54
London Bridge	d	21 55				22 25			22 55					
Norwood Junction	d	22 09				22 39			23 09					
West Croydon	d	22 15		22 20	22 34	22 45	22 48	23 04	23 15	23 18	23 34	23 49		00 14
Waddon	d	22 18		22 23	22 36	22 48	22 51	23 06	23 18	23 21	23 36	23 52		00 16
Wallington	d	22 22		22 27	22 40	22 52	22 55	23 10	23 22	23 25	23 40	23 56		00 20
Carshalton Beeches	d	22 24		22 29	22 43	22 54	22 58	23 13	23 24	23 28	23 43	23 58		00 22
Sutton 4	a	22 28		22 33	22 46	22 58	23 03	23 16	23 28	23 33	23 46	00 03		00 26
Sutton	d				22 49			23 19			23 49			
Belmont	d				22 52			23 22			23 52			
Banstead	d				22 56			23 26			23 56			
Epsom Downs	a				22 59			23 29			23 59			

Table T172-F

London via Wallington - Epsom Downs

Saturdays

21 December to 16 May

Station		SN	SN	SN	SN	SN	SN	SN	SN	SN	SN	SN	SN		SN	SN	SN	SN	SN	SN		SN	SN	SN
London Victoria 15 ⊖	d		00 30	06 00	06 30		06 46	07 00		07 16	07 30		07 46		13 00		13 16	13 30		13 46		14 00		14 16
Clapham Junction 10	d		00 39	06 09	06 39		06 54	07 09		07 24	07 39		07 54		13 09		13 24	13 39		13 54		14 09		14 24
Balham 4 ⊖	d		00 45	06 15	06 45		07 00	07 15		07 30	07 45		08 00		13 15		13 30	13 45		14 00		14 15		14 30
London Bridge	d					06 55			07 25			07 55				13 25			13 55				14 25	
Norwood Junction	d					07 09			07 39			08 09				13 39			14 09				14 39	
West Croydon	d	00 14	01 06	06 35	07 04	07 15	07 19	07 34	07 45	07 50	08 04	08 15	08 18	and at the same minutes past each hour until	13 34	13 45	13 50	14 04	14 15	14 18		14 34	14 45	14 51
Waddon	d	00 16	01 08	06 38	07 06	07 18	07 22	07 37	07 48	07 53	08 06	08 18	08 21		13 37	13 48	13 53	14 06	14 18	14 21		14 37	14 48	14 55
Wallington	d	00 20	01 12	06 42	07 10	07 22	07 26	07 40	07 52	07 57	08 10	08 22	08 25		13 40	13 52	13 57	14 10	14 22	14 25		14 40	14 52	15 00
Carshalton Beeches	d	00 22	01 15	06 44	07 13	07 24	07 29	07 43	07 54	08 00	08 13	08 24	08 28		13 43	13 54	14 00	14 13	14 24	14 28		14 43	14 54	15 03
Sutton 4	a	00 26	01 18	06 48	07 16	07 28	07 33	07 46	07 58	08 03	08 16	08 28	08 33		13 46	13 58	14 03	14 16	14 28	14 33		14 46	14 58	15 06
Sutton	d			06 49	07 19			07 49			08 19				13 49			14 19				14 49		
Belmont	d			06 52	07 22			07 52			08 22				13 52			14 22				14 53		
Banstead	d			06 56	07 26			07 56			08 26				13 56			14 26				14 56		
Epsom Downs	a			06 59	07 29			07 59			08 29				13 59			14 29				15 00		

Station		SN	SN	SN	SN	SN	SN	SN		SN	SN	SN	SN	SN	SN		SN	SN	SN	SN	SN	SN	SN	SN
London Victoria 15 ⊖	d	14 30		14 46	15 00		15 16	15 30			20 46	21 00		21 16	21 30			21 46	22 00		22 16	22 30		22 46
Clapham Junction 10	d	14 39		14 54	15 09		15 24	15 39			20 54	21 09		21 24	21 39			21 54	22 08		22 24	22 39		22 54
Balham 4 ⊖	d	14 45		15 00	15 15		15 30	15 45			21 00	21 15		21 30	21 45			22 00	22 14		22 30	22 45		23 00
London Bridge	d		14 55			15 25				20 55			21 25				21 55			22 25			22 55	
Norwood Junction	d		15 09			15 39				21 09			21 39				22 09			22 39			23 09	
West Croydon	d	15 04	15 15	15 18	15 34	15 45	15 50	16 04	and at the same minutes past each hour until	21 15	21 18	21 34	21 45	21 50	22 04		22 15	22 18	22 34	22 45	22 50	23 04	23 15	23 18
Waddon	d	15 06	15 18	15 21	15 37	15 48	15 53	16 06		21 18	21 21	21 37	21 48	21 53	22 06		22 18	22 21	22 37	22 48	22 53	23 06	23 18	23 21
Wallington	d	15 10	15 22	15 25	15 40	15 52	15 57	16 10		21 22	21 25	21 40	21 52	21 57	22 10		22 22	22 25	22 40	22 52	22 57	23 10	23 22	23 25
Carshalton Beeches	d	15 13	15 24	15 28	15 43	15 54	16 00	16 13		21 24	21 28	21 43	21 54	22 00	22 13		22 24	22 28	22 43	22 54	23 00	23 13	23 24	23 28
Sutton 4	a	15 16	15 28	15 33	15 46	15 58	16 03	16 16		21 28	21 33	21 46	21 58	22 03	22 16		22 28	22 33	22 46	22 58	23 03	23 16	23 28	23 33
Sutton	d	15 24			15 49			16 19				21 49			22 19				22 49			23 19		
Belmont	d	15 27			15 52			16 22				21 52			22 22				22 52			23 22		
Banstead	d	15 31			15 56			16 26				21 56			22 26				22 56			23 26		
Epsom Downs	a	15 34			15 59			16 29				21 59			22 29				22 59			23 29		

Station		SN		SN	SN
London Victoria 15 ⊖	d	23 00		23 16	23 40
Clapham Junction 10	d	23 09		23 24	23 48
Balham 4 ⊖	d	23 15		23 30	23 54
London Bridge	d				
Norwood Junction	d				
West Croydon	d	23 34		23 48	00 14
Waddon	d	23 37		23 51	00 17
Wallington	d	23 40		23 55	00 21
Carshalton Beeches	d	23 43		23 58	00 23
Sutton 4	a	23 46		00 03	00 27
Sutton	d	23 49			
Belmont	d	23 52			
Banstead	d	23 56			
Epsom Downs	a	23 59			

Sundays

15 December to 10 May

Station		SN A	SN	SN	SN	SN	SN	SN	SN	SN	SN	SN	SN	SN		SN	SN	SN	SN		SN	SN
London Victoria 15 ⊖	d		00 30	06 45	07 16	07 34	07 46	08 04	08 16	08 34	08 46	09 02	09 16	09 32		13 46	14 02	14 16	14 32		14 46	15 02
Clapham Junction 10	d		00 39	06 53	07 24	07 43	07 54	08 14	08 24	08 43	08 54	09 10	09 24	09 40		13 54	14 10	14 24	14 40		14 54	15 10
Balham 4 ⊖	d		00 45	07 00	07 31	07 49	08 01	08 20	08 31	08 49	09 00	09 16	09 30	09 46		14 00	14 16	14 30	14 46		15 00	15 16
London Bridge	d																					
Norwood Junction	d																					
West Croydon	d	00 14	01 05	07 20	07 49	08 07	08 19	08 37	08 49	09 09	09 20	09 35	09 50	10 05	and at the same minutes past each hour until	14 20	14 35	14 50	15 05		15 20	15 35
Waddon	d	00 17	01 08	07 22	07 51	08 10	08 22	08 40	08 52	09 12	09 22	09 37	09 52	10 07		14 22	14 37	14 52	15 07		15 22	15 37
Wallington	d	00 21	01 11	07 26	07 55	08 14	08 26	08 43	08 56	09 15	09 26	09 41	09 56	10 11		14 26	14 41	14 56	15 11		15 26	15 41
Carshalton Beeches	d	00 23	01 14	07 29	07 58	08 16	08 28	08 46	08 58	09 18	09 29	09 44	09 59	10 14		14 29	14 44	14 59	15 14		15 29	15 44
Sutton 4	a	00 27	01 17	07 32	08 01	08 20	08 32	08 49	09 02	09 21	09 32	09 47	10 02	10 17		14 32	14 47	15 02	15 17		15 32	15 47
Sutton	d					08 21		08 50		09 22		09 50		10 20			14 50		15 20			15 54
Belmont	d					08 24		08 53		09 25		09 53		10 23			14 53		15 23			15 57
Banstead	d					08 28		08 57		09 29		09 57		10 27			14 57		15 27			16 01
Epsom Downs	a					08 31		09 00		09 32		10 00		10 30			15 00		15 30			16 04

Station		SN	SN	SN	SN		SN	SN	SN	SN		SN	SN	SN	SN	SN	SN	SN	SN
London Victoria 15 ⊖	d	15 16	15 32	15 46	16 02		20 16	20 32	20 46	21 02		21 16	21 32	21 46	22 02	22 16	22 32	22 46	23 16
Clapham Junction 10	d	15 24	15 40	15 54	16 10		20 24	20 40	20 54	21 10		21 24	21 40	21 54	22 10	22 24	22 40	22 54	23 24
Balham 4 ⊖	d	15 30	15 46	16 00	16 16		20 30	20 46	21 00	21 16		21 30	21 46	22 00	22 16	22 30	22 46	23 00	23 31
London Bridge	d																		
Norwood Junction	d																		
West Croydon	d	15 50	16 05	16 20	16 35	and at the same minutes past each hour until	20 50	21 05	21 20	21 35		21 50	22 05	22 20	22 40	22 49	23 05	23 22	23 49
Waddon	d	15 52	16 07	16 22	16 37		20 52	21 07	21 22	21 37		21 52	22 07	22 22	22 42	22 52	23 07	23 24	23 52
Wallington	d	15 56	16 11	16 26	16 41		20 56	21 11	21 26	21 41		21 56	22 11	22 26	22 46	22 56	23 11	23 28	23 56
Carshalton Beeches	d	15 59	16 14	16 29	16 44		20 59	21 14	21 29	21 44		21 59	22 14	22 29	22 49	22 58	23 14	23 31	23 58
Sutton 4	a	16 02	16 17	16 32	16 47		21 02	21 17	21 32	21 47		22 02	22 17	22 32	22 52	23 02	23 17	23 34	00 02
Sutton	d		16 20		16 50			21 20		21 50			22 20						
Belmont	d		16 23		16 53			21 23		21 53			22 23						
Banstead	d		16 27		16 57			21 27		21 57			22 27						
Epsom Downs	a		16 30		17 00			21 30		22 00			22 30						

A not 15 December

Table T172-R

Mondays to Fridays

16 December to 15 May

Epsom Downs via Wallington - London

Miles	Miles			SN	SN	SN	SN	SN	SN	SN		SN	SN	SN	SN	SN	SN	SN	SN	SN		SN	SN	SN	SN
0	—	**Epsom Downs**	d							06 39					07 09				07 39					08 09	
1¼	—	**Banstead**	d							06 42					07 12				07 42					08 12	
2¾	—	**Belmont**	d							06 45					07 15				07 45					08 15	
—	—	Sutton	a							06 48					07 18				07 48					08 18	
3	0	Sutton 4	d	05 42	05 51	05 56	06 16	06 26	06 41	06 51		06 56	07 00	07 11	07 21	07 26	07 30	07 41	07 51	07 56		08 00	08 11	08 21	08 26
4¾	1	**Carshalton Beeches**	d	05 45	05 54	05 59	06 19	06 29	06 44	06 54		06 59		07 14	07 24	07 29		07 44	07 54	07 59		08 04	08 14	08 24	08 29
5	2	**Wallington**	d	05 48	05 57	06 02	06 22	06 32	06 47	06 57		07 02	07 07	07 17	07 27	07 32	07 37	07 47	07 57	08 02		08 07	08 17	08 27	08 32
7¼	3½	**Waddon**	d	05 51	06 00	06 05	06 25	06 35	06 50	07 00		07 05		07 20	07 30	07 35		07 50	08 00	08 05		08 10	08 21	08 30	08 35
8½	4½	West Croydon	a	05 55	06 05	06 09	06 32	06 39	06 55	07 04		07 09	07 12	07 25	07 34	07 39	07 42	07 55	08 04	08 09		08 15	08 24	08 34	08 39
—	6¾	Norwood Junction	a	06 02		06 15		06 45				07 15				07 45				08 15					08 45
—	15	London Bridge	a	06 31		06 28		06 58				07 28	08 06			07 58	08 36			08 28		09 06			08 58
14½	—	Balham	d		06 25		06 55		07 14	07 25				07 44	07 55			08 14	08 25				08 45	08 55	
16¼	—	Clapham Junction	d		06 31		07 01		07 20	07 31				07 50	08 01			08 20	08 31				08 53	09 01	
19	—	London Victoria 15 ⊖	a		06 40		07 09		07 28	07 39				07 59	08 09			08 30	08 40				09 04	09 10	

		SN	SN	SN	SN	SN		SN	SN	SN	SN	SN	SN	SN	SN	SN		SN	SN	SN	SN	SN	SN	SN	SN
Epsom Downs	d			08 39				09 09			09 39			10 09				10 39			11 09			11 39	
Banstead	d			08 42				09 12			09 42			10 12				10 42			11 12			11 42	
Belmont	d			08 45				09 15			09 45			10 15				10 45			11 15			11 45	
Sutton	a			08 48				09 18			09 48			10 18				10 48			11 18			11 48	
Sutton 4	d	08 30	08 41	08 51	08 56	09 11		09 21	09 26	09 41	09 51	09 56	10 11	10 21	10 26	10 41		10 51	10 56	11 11	11 21	11 26	11 41	11 51	11 56
Carshalton Beeches	d		08 44	08 54	08 59	09 14		09 24	09 29	09 44	09 54	09 59	10 14	10 24	10 29	10 44		10 54	10 59	11 14	11 24	11 29	11 44	11 54	11 59
Wallington	d	08 37	08 47	08 57	09 02	09 17		09 27	09 32	09 47	09 57	10 02	10 17	10 27	10 32	10 47		10 57	11 02	11 17	11 27	11 32	11 47	11 57	12 02
Waddon	d		08 50	09 00	09 05	09 20		09 30	09 35	09 50	10 00	10 05	10 20	10 30	10 35	10 50		11 00	11 05	11 20	11 30	11 35	11 50	12 00	12 05
West Croydon	a	08 42	08 55	09 04	09 09	09 25		09 34	09 39	09 55	10 04	10 09	10 25	10 34	10 39	10 55		11 04	11 09	11 25	11 34	11 39	11 55	12 04	12 09
Norwood Junction	a				09 15				09 45			10 15			10 45				11 15			11 45			12 15
London Bridge	a	09 36			09 28				09 58			10 28			10 58				11 28			11 58			12 28
Balham	d		09 14	09 25		09 44		09 55		10 14	10 25		10 44	10 55		11 14		11 25		11 44	11 55		12 14	12 25	
Clapham Junction	d		09 20	09 31		09 50		10 01		10 20	10 31		10 50	11 01		11 20		11 31		11 50	12 01		12 20	12 31	
London Victoria 15 ⊖	a		09 30	09 40		09 58		10 09		10 28	10 40		10 58	11 09		11 28		11 39		11 58	12 09		12 28	12 39	

		SN		SN	SN	SN	SN TThO	SN MW FO	SN	SN	SN	SN		SN	SN MW FO	SN TThO	SN	SN	SN	SN	SN	SN		SN	SN
Epsom Downs	d			12 09			12 39	12 39			13 09				13 39	13 41			14 09			14 39			
Banstead	d			12 12			12 42	12 42			13 12				13 42	13 44			14 12			14 42			
Belmont	d			12 15			12 45	12 45			13 15				13 45	13 47			14 15			14 45			
Sutton	a			12 18			12 48	12 48			13 18				13 48	13 50			14 18			14 48			
Sutton 4	d	12 11		12 21	12 26	12 41	12 50	12 51	12 56	13 11	13 21	13 26		13 41	13 51	13 51	13 56	14 11	14 21	14 26	14 41	14 51		14 56	15 12
Carshalton Beeches	d	12 14		12 24	12 29	12 44	12 53	12 54	12 59	13 14	13 24	13 29		13 44	13 54	13 54	13 59	14 14	14 24	14 29	14 44	14 54		14 59	15 15
Wallington	d	12 17		12 27	12 32	12 47	12 56	12 57	13 02	13 17	13 27	13 32		13 47	13 57	13 57	14 02	14 17	14 27	14 32	14 47	14 57		15 02	15 18
Waddon	d	12 20		12 30	12 35	12 50	12 59	13 00	13 05	13 20	13 30	13 35		13 50	14 00	14 00	14 05	14 20	14 30	14 35	14 50	15 00		15 05	15 21
West Croydon	a	12 25		12 34	12 39	12 55	13 03	13 04	13 09	13 25	13 34	13 39		13 55	14 04	14 04	14 09	14 25	14 34	14 39	14 55	15 04		15 09	15 25
Norwood Junction	a				12 45				13 15			13 45					14 15			14 45				15 15	
London Bridge	a				12 58				13 28			13 58					14 28			14 58				15 28	
Balham	d	12 44		12 55		13 14	13 25	13 25		13 44	13 55			14 14	14 25	14 25		14 44	14 55		15 14	15 25			15 44
Clapham Junction	d	12 50		13 01		13 20	13 31	13 31		13 50	14 01			14 20	14 31	14 31		14 50	15 01		15 20	15 31			15 50
London Victoria 15 ⊖	a	12 58		13 09		13 28	13 39	13 39		13 58	14 09			14 28	14 39	14 39		14 58	15 09		15 28	15 39			15 58

		SN	SN	SN	SN	SN	SN	SN		SN	SN	SN	SN	SN	SN	SN	SN	SN		SN	SN	SN	SN	SN	SN
Epsom Downs	d	15 09			15 41			16 09				16 39			17 09			17 39				18 09			
Banstead	d	15 12			15 44			16 12				16 42			17 12			17 42				18 12			
Belmont	d	15 15			15 47			16 15				16 45			17 15			17 45				18 15			
Sutton	a	15 18			15 50			16 18				16 48			17 18			17 48				18 18			
Sutton 4	d	15 21	15 26	15 41	15 51	15 56	16 11	16 21		16 26	16 41	16 51	16 56	17 11	17 21	17 26	17 41	17 51		18 00	18 11	18 21	18 26	18 30	18 41
Carshalton Beeches	d	15 24	15 29	15 44	15 54	15 59	16 14	16 24		16 29	16 44	16 54	16 59	17 14	17 24	17 29	17 44	17 54			18 14	18 24	18 29		18 44
Wallington	d	15 27	15 32	15 47	15 57	16 02	16 17	16 27		16 32	16 47	16 57	17 02	17 17	17 27	17 32	17 47	17 57		18 07	18 17	18 27	18 32	18 37	18 47
Waddon	d	15 30	15 35	15 50	16 00	16 05	16 20	16 30		16 35	16 50	17 00	17 05	17 20	17 30	17 35	17 50	18 00			18 20	18 30	18 35		18 50
West Croydon	a	15 34	15 39	15 55	16 04	16 09	16 25	16 34		16 39	16 55	17 04	17 09	17 25	17 34	17 39	17 55	18 04		18 12	18 25	18 34	18 39	18 42	18 55
Norwood Junction	a		15 45			16 15				16 45			17 15			17 45							18 45		
London Bridge	a		15 58			16 28				16 58			17 28			17 58				19 06			18 58	19 36	
Balham	d	15 55		16 14	16 25		16 44	16 55			17 14	17 25		17 44	17 55		18 14	18 25			18 44	18 55			19 14
Clapham Junction	d	16 01		16 20	16 31		16 50	17 01			17 20	17 31		17 50	18 01		18 20	18 31			18 50	19 01			19 20
London Victoria 15 ⊖	a	16 11		16 28	16 39		16 58	17 09			17 28	17 39		17 58	18 09		18 30	18 39			19 00	19 09			19 28

		SN	SN	SN		SN	SN	SN	SN	SN	SN	SN	SN	SN		SN	SN	SN	SN	SN	SN	SN	SN	SN	
Epsom Downs	d	18 39				19 09			19 39			20 09				20 39			21 09			21 39			
Banstead	d	18 42				19 12			19 42			20 12				20 42			21 12			21 42			
Belmont	d	18 45				19 15			19 45			20 15				20 45			21 15			21 45			
Sutton	a	18 48				19 18			19 48			20 18				20 48			21 18			21 48			
Sutton 4	d	18 51	19 00	19 11		19 21	19 26	19 41	19 51	19 56	20 11	20 21	20 26	20 41		20 51	20 56	21 11	21 21	21 26	21 41	21 50	21 56	22 11	
Carshalton Beeches	d	18 54		19 14		19 24	19 29	19 44	19 54	19 59	20 14	20 24	20 29	20 44		20 54	20 59	21 14	21 24	21 29	21 44	21 53	21 59	22 14	
Wallington	d	18 57	19 07	19 17		19 27	19 32	19 47	19 57	20 02	20 17	20 27	20 32	20 47		20 57	21 02	21 17	21 27	21 32	21 47	21 56	22 02	22 17	
Waddon	d	19 00		19 20		19 30	19 35	19 50	20 00	20 05	20 20	20 30	20 35	20 50		21 00	21 05	21 20	21 30	21 35	21 50	22 00	22 05	22 20	
West Croydon	a	19 04	19 12	19 25		19 34	19 39	19 55	20 04	20 09	20 25	20 34	20 39	20 55		21 04	21 09	21 25	21 34	21 39	21 55	22 03	22 09	22 25	
Norwood Junction	a						19 45			20 15			20 45				21 15			21 45			22 15		
London Bridge	a		20 07				19 58			20 28			20 58				21 28			21 58			22 28		
Balham	d	19 25		19 44		19 55		20 14	20 25		20 44	20 55		21 14		21 25		21 44	21 55		22 15	22 25		22 44	
Clapham Junction	d	19 31		19 50		20 01		20 20	20 31		20 50	21 01		21 20		21 31		21 50	22 01		22 21	22 31		22 50	
London Victoria 15 ⊖	a	19 39		19 58		20 09		20 30	20 39		20 58	21 09		21 28		21 39		21 58	22 09		22 29	22 39		23 01	

		SN	SN	SN	SN	SN	SN FX	SN FO		SN
Epsom Downs	d	22 09			22 41		23 05	23 05		23 37
Banstead	d	22 12			22 44		23 08	23 08		23 40
Belmont	d	22 15			22 47		23 11	23 11		23 43
Sutton	a	22 18			22 50		23 14	23 14		23 46
Sutton 4	d	22 21	22 26	22 41	22 51	22 56	23 15	23 15	23 26	23 49
Carshalton Beeches	d	22 24	22 29	22 44	22 54	22 59	23 18	23 18	23 29	23 52
Wallington	d	22 27	22 32	22 47	22 57	23 02	23 21	23 21	23 32	23 55
Waddon	d	22 30	22 35	22 50	23 00	23 05	23 24	23 24	23 35	23 58
West Croydon	a	22 34	22 39	22 55	23 04	23 09	23 27	23 27	23 39	00 02
Norwood Junction	a		22 45			23 15				
London Bridge	a		22 58			23 28				
Balham	d	22 55		23 14	23 25		23 48	23 48		
Clapham Junction	d	23 01		23 20	23 31		23 54	23 54		
London Victoria 15 ⊖	a	23 09		23 28	23 39		00 03	00 05		

Table T172-R

Saturdays

21 December to 16 May

Epsom Downs via Wallington - London

		SN	SN	SN	SN	SN	SN	SN	SN	SN		SN	SN	SN	SN	SN	SN	SN	SN	SN	SN	SN	SN		
Epsom Downs	d						07 09			07 39				08 09			08 39			09 09			09 39		
Banstead	d						07 12			07 42				08 12			08 42			09 12			09 42		
Belmont	d						07 15			07 45				08 15			08 45			09 15			09 45		
Sutton	a						07 18			07 48				08 18			08 48			09 18			09 48		
Sutton 4	d	06 21	06 41	06 51	06 56	07 11	07 21	07 26	07 41	07 51		07 56	08 11	08 21	08 26	08 41	08 51	08 55	09 11	09 21	09 26	09 41	09 51		
Carshalton Beeches	d	06 24	06 44	06 54	06 59	07 14	07 24	07 29	07 44	07 54		07 59	08 14	08 24	08 29	08 44	08 54	08 59	09 14	09 24	09 29	09 44	09 54		
Wallington	d	06 27	06 47	06 57	07 02	07 17	07 27	07 32	07 47	07 57		08 02	08 17	08 27	08 32	08 47	08 57	09 02	09 17	09 27	09 32	09 47	09 57		
Waddon	d	06 30	06 50	07 00	07 05	07 20	07 30	07 35	07 50	08 00		08 05	08 20	08 30	08 35	08 50	09 00	09 05	09 20	09 30	09 35	09 50	10 00		
West Croydon	a	06 34	06 55	07 04	07 09	07 25	07 34	07 39	07 55	08 04		08 09	08 25	08 34	08 39	08 55	09 04	09 09	09 25	09 34	09 39	09 55	10 04		
Norwood Junction	a				07 15			07 45				08 15			08 45			09 15			09 45				
London Bridge	a				07 28			07 58				08 28			08 58			09 28			09 58				
Balham	d	06 55	07 14	07 25		07 44	07 55		08 14	08 25			08 44	08 55		09 14	09 25		09 44	09 55		10 14	10 25		
Clapham Junction	d	07 01	07 20	07 31		07 50	08 01		08 20	08 31			08 50	09 01		09 20	09 31		09 50	10 01		10 20	10 31		
London Victoria 15 ⊖	a	07 09	07 28	07 39		07 58	08 09		08 28	08 39			08 58	09 09		09 28	09 39		09 58	10 09		10 28	10 39		

		SN		SN	SN	SN	SN	SN	SN		SN	SN	SN	SN	SN	SN	SN	SN	SN		SN	SN	SN	SN
Epsom Downs	d				14 09			14 39				15 09			15 41			16 09				16 39		
Banstead	d				14 12			14 42				15 12			15 44			16 12				16 42		
Belmont	d				14 15			14 45				15 15			15 47			16 15				16 45		
Sutton	a		and at		14 18			14 48				15 18			15 50			16 18				16 48		
Sutton 4	d	09 56	the same	14 11	14 21	14 26	14 41	14 51	14 56		15 12	15 21	15 26	15 41	15 51	15 56	16 11	16 21	16 26		16 41	16 51	16 56	17 11
Carshalton Beeches	d	09 59	minutes	14 14	14 24	14 29	14 44	14 54	14 59		15 15	15 24	15 29	15 44	15 54	15 59	16 14	16 24	16 29		16 44	16 54	16 59	17 14
Wallington	d	10 02	past	14 17	14 27	14 32	14 47	14 57	15 02		15 18	15 27	15 32	15 47	15 57	16 02	16 17	16 27	16 32		16 47	16 57	17 02	17 17
Waddon	d	10 05	each	14 20	14 30	14 35	14 50	15 00	15 05		15 21	15 30	15 35	15 50	16 00	16 05	16 20	16 30	16 35		16 50	17 00	17 05	17 20
West Croydon	a	10 09	hour until	14 25	14 34	14 39	14 55	15 04	15 09		15 25	15 34	15 39	15 55	16 04	16 09	16 25	16 34	16 39		16 55	17 04	17 09	17 25
Norwood Junction	a	10 15				14 45			15 15				15 45			16 15			16 45				17 15	
London Bridge	a	10 28				14 58			15 28				15 58			16 28			16 58				17 28	
Balham	d			14 44	14 55		15 14	15 25			15 44	15 55		16 14	16 25		16 44	16 55			17 14	17 25		17 44
Clapham Junction	d			14 50	15 01		15 20	15 31			15 50	16 01		16 20	16 31		16 50	17 01			17 20	17 31		17 50
London Victoria 15 ⊖	a			14 58	15 09		15 28	15 39			15 58	16 09		16 28	16 39		16 58	17 09			17 28	17 39		17 58

		SN	SN	SN	SN	SN		SN	SN	SN	SN	SN	SN	SN	SN	SN		SN	SN	SN	SN	SN	SN	SN	SN
Epsom Downs	d	17 09			17 39				18 09			18 39			19 09				19 39			20 09			20 39
Banstead	d	17 12			17 42				18 12			18 42			19 12				19 42			20 12			20 42
Belmont	d	17 15			17 45				18 15			18 45			19 15				19 45			20 15			20 45
Sutton	a	17 18			17 48				18 18			18 48			19 18				19 48			20 18			20 48
Sutton 4	d	17 21	17 26	17 41	17 51	17 56		18 11	18 21	18 26	18 41	18 51	18 55	19 11	19 21	19 26		19 41	19 51	19 56	20 11	20 21	20 26	20 41	20 51
Carshalton Beeches	d	17 24	17 29	17 44	17 54	17 59		18 14	18 24	18 29	18 44	18 54	18 59	19 14	19 24	19 29		19 44	19 54	19 59	20 14	20 24	20 29	20 44	20 54
Wallington	d	17 27	17 32	17 47	17 57	18 02		18 17	18 27	18 32	18 47	18 57	19 02	19 17	19 27	19 32		19 47	19 57	20 02	20 17	20 27	20 32	20 47	20 57
Waddon	d	17 30	17 35	17 50	18 00	18 05		18 20	18 30	18 35	18 50	19 00	19 05	19 20	19 30	19 35		19 50	20 00	20 05	20 20	20 30	20 35	20 50	21 00
West Croydon	a	17 34	17 39	17 55	18 04	18 09		18 25	18 34	18 39	18 55	19 04	19 09	19 25	19 34	19 39		19 55	20 04	20 09	20 25	20 34	20 39	20 55	21 04
Norwood Junction	a		17 45			18 15				18 45			19 15			19 45				20 15			20 45		
London Bridge	a		17 58			18 28				18 58			19 28			19 58				20 28			20 58		
Balham	d	17 55		18 14	18 25			18 44	18 55		19 14	19 25		19 44	19 55			20 14	20 25		20 44	20 55		21 14	21 25
Clapham Junction	d	18 01		18 20	18 31			18 50	19 01		19 20	19 31		19 50	20 01			20 20	20 31		20 50	21 01		21 20	21 31
London Victoria 15 ⊖	a	18 09		18 28	18 39			18 58	19 09		19 28	19 39		19 58	20 09			20 28	20 39		20 58	21 09		21 28	21 39

		SN		SN	SN	SN	SN	SN	SN	SN	SN	SN		SN	SN	SN	SN	SN	SN
Epsom Downs	d				21 09			21 39			22 09				22 39		23 09		23 39
Banstead	d				21 12			21 42			22 12				22 42		23 12		23 42
Belmont	d				21 15			21 45			22 15				22 45		23 15		23 45
Sutton	a				21 18			21 48			22 18				22 48		23 18		23 48
Sutton 4	d	20 56		21 11	21 21	21 26	21 41	21 51	21 56	22 11	22 21	22 26		22 41	22 51	22 56	23 21	23 32	23 51
Carshalton Beeches	d	20 59		21 14	21 24	21 29	21 44	21 54	21 59	22 14	22 24	22 29		22 44	22 54	22 59	23 24	23 35	23 54
Wallington	d	21 02		21 17	21 27	21 32	21 47	21 57	22 02	22 17	22 27	22 32		22 47	22 57	23 02	23 27	23 37	23 57
Waddon	d	21 05		21 20	21 30	21 35	21 50	22 00	22 05	22 20	22 30	22 35		22 50	23 00	23 05	23 30	23 40	00 01
West Croydon	a	21 09		21 25	21 34	21 39	21 55	22 04	22 09	22 25	22 34	22 39		22 55	23 04	23 09	23 34	23 45	00 05
Norwood Junction	a	21 15				21 45			22 15			22 45				23 15			
London Bridge	a	21 28				21 58			22 28			22 58				23 28			
Balham	d			21 44	21 55		22 14	22 25		22 44	22 55			23 14	23 25		23 56		
Clapham Junction	d			21 50	22 01		22 20	22 31		22 50	23 01			23 20	23 31		00 02		
London Victoria 15 ⊖	a			21 58	22 09		22 30	22 39		23 00	23 09			23 30	23 39		00 09		

Sundays

15 December to 10 May

		SN A	SN A	SN A	SN	SN	SN	SN	SN	SN	SN	SN		SN	SN	SN	SN		SN	SN	SN	SN
Epsom Downs	d									08 39		09 09			14 39		15 09		15 39			16 11
Banstead	d									08 42		09 12			14 42		15 12		15 42			16 14
Belmont	d									08 45		09 15			14 45		15 15		15 45			16 17
Sutton	a									08 48		09 18	and at		14 48		15 18		15 48			16 20
Sutton 4	d			00 03	06 53	07 09	07 39	08 09	08 39	08 51	09 09	09 21	the same	14 39	14 51	15 09	15 21		15 39	15 51	16 09	16 21
Carshalton Beeches	d			00 06	06 56	07 12	07 42	08 12	08 42	08 54	09 12	09 24	minutes	14 42	14 54	15 12	15 24		15 42	15 54	16 12	16 24
Wallington	d			00 08	06 59	07 15	07 45	08 15	08 45	08 57	09 15	09 27	past	14 45	14 57	15 15	15 27		15 45	15 57	16 15	16 27
Waddon	d	00 01		00 11	07 02	07 18	07 48	08 18	08 48	09 00	09 18	09 30	each	14 48	15 00	15 18	15 30		15 48	16 00	16 18	16 30
West Croydon	a	00 05		00 15	07 06	07 21	07 51	08 21	08 51	09 04	09 21	09 34	hour until	14 51	15 04	15 21	15 34		15 51	16 04	16 21	16 34
Norwood Junction	a																					
London Bridge	a																					
Balham	d				07 25	07 41	08 11	08 41	09 10	09 24	09 40	09 54		15 10	15 24	15 40	15 54		16 10	16 24	16 40	16 54
Clapham Junction	d		00 02		07 31	07 47	08 17	08 47	09 17	09 31	09 47	10 01		15 17	15 31	15 47	16 01		16 17	16 31	16 47	17 01
London Victoria 15 ⊖	a		00 09		07 39	07 55	08 25	08 55	09 25	09 39	09 55	10 09		15 25	15 39	15 55	16 09		16 25	16 39	16 55	17 09

A not 15 December

Table T172-R

Sundays

15 December to 10 May

Epsom Downs via Wallington - London

		SN	SN	SN	SN		SN	SN	SN	SN	SN	SN	SN	SN	SN	SN	SN
Epsom Downs	d		16 39		17 09			20 39		21 09		21 39		22 09		22 39	
Banstead	d		16 42		17 12			20 42		21 12		21 42		22 12		22 42	
Belmont	d		16 45		17 15			20 45		21 15		21 45		22 15		22 45	
Sutton	a		16 48		17 18	and at		20 48		21 18		21 48		22 18		22 48	
Sutton ■	d	16 39	16 51	17 09	17 21	the same	20 39	20 51	21 09	21 21	21 39	21 51	22 09	22 21	22 39	22 51	23 09
Carshalton Beeches	d	16 42	16 54	17 12	17 24	minutes	20 42	20 54	21 12	21 24	21 42	21 54	22 12	22 24	22 42	22 54	23 12
Wallington	d	16 45	16 57	17 15	17 27	past	20 45	20 57	21 15	21 27	21 45	21 57	22 15	22 27	22 45	22 57	23 15
Waddon	d	16 48	17 00	17 18	17 30	each	20 48	21 00	21 18	21 30	21 48	22 00	22 18	22 30	22 48	23 00	23 18
West Croydon	a	16 51	17 04	17 21	17 34	hour until	20 51	21 04	21 21	21 34	21 51	22 04	22 21	22 34	22 51	23 04	23 21
Norwood Junction	a																
London Bridge	a																
Balham	d	17 10	17 24	17 40	17 54		21 10	21 24	21 40	21 54	22 10	22 24	22 40	22 55	23 10	23 24	23 40
Clapham Junction	d	17 17	17 31	17 47	18 01		21 17	21 31	21 47	22 01	22 17	22 31	22 47	23 01	23 17	23 31	23 47
London Victoria ■ ⊖	a	17 25	17 39	17 55	18 09		21 25	21 39	21 55	22 09	22 25	22 39	22 55	23 09	23 25	23 39	23 55

AVAILABLE FROM MP Middleton Press

Table T173-F

Mondays to Fridays

16 December to 15 May

London Bridge - South Bermondsey, Queens Road Peckham, Peckham Rye, East Dulwich, North Dulwich, Tulse Hill and Streatham

Miles	Miles	Miles	Miles			TL MX A	SN MX B	SN MX	TL A	TL C	SN	TL A	SN	TL D		SN	SN	TL A	SN	TL A	SN	SN	TL E	SN
0	0	—	—	London Bridge ■ ⊖	d			00 01			05 39		06 01			06 08	06 14		06 31		06 38	06 44		07 01
1¾	1¾	—	—	**South Bermondsey**	d			00 05			05 44		06 05			06 14	06 19		06 35		06 44	06 49		07 05
2¾	2¾	—	—	Queens Rd Peckham	d		00 02	00 08			05 47		06 08			06 17	06 22		06 38		06 47	06 52		07 08
3½	3½	—	—	Peckham Rye ■	d		00 06	00 11			05 50		06 11			06 20	06 25		06 41		06 50	06 55		07 11
4¼	4¼	—	—	**East Dulwich**	d		00 09	00 14			05 53		06 14			06 23	06 28		06 44		06 53	06 58		07 14
4¾	4¾	—	—	**North Dulwich**	d		00 11	00 17			05 55		06 17			06 25	06 30		06 47		06 55	07 00		07 17
—	—	0	0	St Pancras International	d				05 12	05 27		05 42		05 57				06 12		06 27			06 42	
—	—	1¼	1¼	Farringdon	d				05 17	05 32		05 47		06 02				06 17		06 32			06 47	
—	—	1½	1½	City Thameslink	d				05 19	05 34		05 49		06 04				06 19		06 34			06 49	
—	—	2	2	London Blackfriars	d				05 21	05 36		05 51		06 06				06 21		06 36			06 51	
—	—	3¼	3¼	Elephant & Castle	d				05 25	05 40		05 55		06 10				06 25		06 40			06 55	
—	—	5	5	Loughborough Jn.	d	00 02			05 30	05 45		06 00		06 15				06 30		06 45			07 00	
—	—	6	6	Herne Hill	d	00 06			05 35	05 50		06 05		06 20				06 35		06 50			07 05	
6	6	7	7	**Tulse Hill**	d	00 11	00 18	00 21	05 40	05 56	05 59	06 10	06 21	06 26		06 29	06 34	06 40	06 51	06 56	06 59	07 04	07 10	07 21
—	6¾	—	—	West Norwood	a			00 24					06 24						06 54					07 24
—	7¾	—	—	Gipsy Hill	a			00 27					06 27						06 57					07 27
—	8½	—	—	Crystal Palace	a			00 31					06 31						07 01					07 31
—	10	—	—	**Birkbeck**	a								06 35						07 05					07 35
—	11½	—	—	Beckenham Junction	a								06 39						07 09					07 39
7½	—	8½	8½	**Streatham**	d	00 14	00 22		05 44	06 00	06 04	06 14		06 30		06 34	06 38	06 44		07 00	07 04	07 08	07 14	
8	—	—	—	Streatham Common	a		00 25										06 41					07 11		
9	—	—	—	Norbury	a		00 28										06 44					07 14		
10¼	—	—	—	Thornton Heath	a		00 31										06 47					07 17		
11	—	—	—	Selhurst	a		00 34										06 50					07 20		
12	—	—	—	East Croydon	a																			
—	—	10	—	Tooting	a	00 18			05 48		06 08	06 18				06 38		06 48			07 08		07 18	
—	—	11½	—	Haydons Road	a	00 22			05 52		06 12	06 22				06 42		06 52			07 12		07 22	
—	—	12¼	—	Wimbledon	a	00 24			05 54		06 14	06 24				06 44		06 54			07 14		07 24	
—	—	—	10¼	Mitcham Eastfields	a					06 04				06 34						07 04				
—	—	—	11¼	Mitcham Junction	a					06 07				06 37						07 07				
—	—	—	12½	Hackbridge	a					06 10				06 40						07 10				
—	—	—	13¾	Carshalton	a					06 13				06 43						07 13				
—	—	—	14½	Sutton	a	00 44			06 14	06 17	06 34	06 44		06 47		07 04		07 14		07 17	07 34		07 44	

		TL E	SN	SN	TL E	SN	TL E	SN	SN	TL E		SN	TL E	SN	TL E	SN	TL E	SN	TL E	SN		TL E	SN
London Bridge ■ ⊖	d		07 07	07 14		07 31		07 37	07 44			08 01		08 14		08 31		08 44		09 01			09 14
South Bermondsey	d		07 14	07 19		07 35		07 44	07 49			08 05		08 19		08 35		08 49		09 05			09 19
Queens Rd Peckham	d		07 17	07 22		07 38		07 47	07 52			08 08		08 22		08 38		08 52		09 08			09 22
Peckham Rye ■	d		07 20	07 25		07 41		07 50	07 55			08 11		08 25		08 41		08 55		09 11			09 25
East Dulwich	d		07 23	07 28		07 44		07 53	07 58			08 14		08 28		08 44		08 58		09 14			09 28
North Dulwich	d		07 25	07 30		07 47		07 55	08 00			08 17		08 30		08 47		09 00		09 17			09 30
St Pancras International	d	06 57			07 12		07 27			07 42			07 57		08 12		08 27		08 42			08 57	
Farringdon	d	07 02			07 17		07 32			07 47			08 02		08 17		08 32		08 47			09 02	
City Thameslink	d	07 04			07 19		07 34			07 49			08 04		08 19		08 34		08 49			09 04	
London Blackfriars	d	07 06			07 21		07 36			07 51			08 06		08 21		08 36		08 51			09 06	
Elephant & Castle	d	07 10			07 25		07 40			07 55			08 10		08 25		08 40		08 55			09 10	
Loughborough Jn	d	07 15			07 30		07 45			08 00			08 15		08 30		08 45		09 00			09 15	
Herne Hill	d	07 20			07 35		07 50			08 05			08 20		08 35		08 50		09 05			09 20	
Tulse Hill	d	07 26	07 29	07 34	07 40	07 51	07 56	07 59	08 04	08 10		08 21	08 27	08 34	08 40	08 51	08 57	09 04	09 10	09 21		09 27	09 34
West Norwood	a					07 54						08 24				08 54				09 24			
Gipsy Hill	a					07 57						08 27				08 57				09 27			
Crystal Palace	a					08 01						08 31				09 01				09 31			
Birkbeck	a					08 05						08 35				09 05				09 35			
Beckenham Junction	a					08 09						08 39				09 09				09 39			
Streatham	d	07 30	07 34	07 38	07 44		08 00	08 04	08 08	08 14			08 30	08 38	08 44		09 00	09 08	09 14			09 30	09 38
Streatham Common	a			07 41					08 11					08 41				09 11					09 41
Norbury	a			07 44					08 14					08 44				09 14					09 44
Thornton Heath	a			07 47					08 17					08 47				09 17					09 47
Selhurst	a			07 50					08 20					08 50				09 20					09 50
East Croydon	a																						
Tooting	a		07 38		07 48			08 08		08 18					08 48				09 18				
Haydons Road	a		07 42		07 52			08 12		08 22					08 52				09 22				
Wimbledon	a		07 44		07 54			08 14		08 24					08 54				09 24				
Mitcham Eastfields	a	07 34					08 04						08 34				09 04					09 34	
Mitcham Junction	a	07 37					08 07						08 37				09 07					09 37	
Hackbridge	a	07 40					08 10						08 40				09 10					09 40	
Carshalton	a	07 43					08 13						08 43				09 13					09 43	
Sutton	a	07 47	08 04		08 14		08 17	08 34		08 44			08 47		09 14		09 17		09 44			09 47	

A From Luton
B From London Bridge
C From West Hampstead Thameslink
D From Kentish Town
E From St Albans City

Table T173-F

Mondays to Fridays

16 December to 15 May

London Bridge - South Bermondsey, Queens Road Peckham, Peckham Rye, East Dulwich, North Dulwich, Tulse Hill and Streatham

		TL A	SN	TL A	SN B	TL A	SN	TL A	SN B		TL A	SN	TL A	SN B	TL A	SN	TL A	SN B	TL A	SN	TL A	SN B	TL A
London Bridge 4 ⊖	d		09 31		09 44		10 01		10 14			13 31		13 44		14 01		14 14		14 31		14 44	
South Bermondsey	d		09 35		09 49		10 05		10 19			13 35		13 49		14 05		14 19		14 35		14 49	
Queens Rd Peckham	d		09 38		09 52		10 08		10 22			13 38		13 52		14 08		14 22		14 38		14 52	
Peckham Rye 4	d		09 41		09 55		10 11		10 25			13 41		13 55		14 11		14 25		14 41		14 55	
East Dulwich	d		09 44		09 58		10 14		10 28			13 44		13 58		14 14		14 28		14 44		14 58	
North Dulwich	d		09 47		10 00		10 17		10 30			13 47		14 00		14 17		14 30		14 47		15 00	
St Pancras International	d	09 12		09 27		09 42		09 57			13 12		13 27		13 42		13 57		14 12		14 27		14 42
Farringdon	d	09 17		09 32		09 47		10 02			13 17		13 32		13 47		14 02		14 17		14 32		14 47
City Thameslink	d	09 19		09 34		09 49		10 04			13 19		13 34		13 49		14 04		14 19		14 34		14 49
London Blackfriars	d	09 21		09 36		09 51		10 06			13 21		13 36		13 51		14 06		14 21		14 36		14 51
Elephant & Castle	d	09 25		09 40		09 55		10 10			13 25		13 40		13 55		14 10		14 25		14 40		14 55
Loughborough Jn	d	09 30		09 45		10 00		10 15		and at	13 30		13 45		14 00		14 15		14 30		14 45		15 00
Herne Hill	d	09 35		09 50		10 05		10 20		the same	13 35		13 50		14 05		14 20		14 35		14 50		15 05
Tulse Hill	d	09 40	09 51	09 56	10 04	10 10	10 21	10 26	10 34	minutes	13 40	13 51	13 56	14 04	14 10	14 21	14 26	14 34	14 39	14 51	14 56	15 04	15 10
West Norwood	a		09 54				10 24			past		13 54				14 24				14 54			
Gipsy Hill	a		09 57				10 27			each		13 57				14 27				14 57			
Crystal Palace	a		10 01				10 31			hour until		14 01				14 31				15 01			
Birkbeck	a		10 05				10 35					14 05				14 35				15 05			
Beckenham Junction	a		10 09				10 39					14 09				14 39				15 09			
Streatham	d	09 44		10 00	10 08	10 14		10 30	10 38		13 44		14 00	14 08	14 14		14 30	14 38	14 42		15 00	15 08	15 14
Streatham Common	a				10 11				10 41					14 11				14 41				15 11	
Norbury	a				10 14				10 44					14 14				14 44				15 14	
Thornton Heath	a				10 17				10 47					14 17				14 47				15 17	
Selhurst	a				10 20				10 50					14 20				14 50				15 20	
East Croydon	a				10 24				10 54					14 24				14 54				15 24	
Tooting	a	09 48				10 18					13 48				14 18				14 46				15 18
Haydons Road	a	09 52				10 22					13 52				14 22				14 50				15 22
Wimbledon	a	09 54				10 24					13 54				14 24				14 52				15 24
Mitcham Eastfields	a			10 04				10 34					14 04				14 34				15 04		
Mitcham Junction	a			10 07				10 37					14 07				14 37				15 07		
Hackbridge	a			10 10				10 40					14 10				14 40				15 10		
Carshalton	a			10 13				10 43					14 13				14 43				15 13		
Sutton	a	10 14		10 17		10 44		10 47			14 14		14 17		14 44		14 47		15 14		15 17		15 44

		SN	TL A	SN B	TL A	SN	TL A	SN B	TL A	SN	TL A	SN	TL A	SN	TL A	SN	TL A	SN	SN	TL A	SN	TL A	SN
London Bridge 4 ⊖	d	15 01		15 14		15 31		15 44		16 01		16 14		16 31		16 44		16 52	17 01		17 14		17 22
South Bermondsey	d	15 05		15 19		15 35		15 49		16 05		16 19		16 35		16 49		16 59	17 05		17 19		17 29
Queens Rd Peckham	d	15 08		15 22		15 38		15 52		16 08		16 22		16 38		16 52		17 02	17 08		17 22		17 32
Peckham Rye 4	d	15 11		15 25		15 41		15 55		16 11		16 25		16 41		16 55		17 05	17 11		17 25		17 35
East Dulwich	d	15 14		15 28		15 44		15 58		16 14		16 28		16 44		16 58		17 08	17 14		17 28		17 38
North Dulwich	d	15 17		15 30		15 47		16 00		16 17		16 30		16 47		17 00		17 10	17 17		17 30		17 40
St Pancras International	d		14 57		15 12		15 27		15 42		15 57		16 12		16 27		16 42			16 57		17 12	
Farringdon	d		15 02		15 17		15 32		15 47		16 02		16 17		16 32		16 47			17 02		17 17	
City Thameslink	d		15 04		15 19		15 34		15 49		16 04		16 19		16 34		16 49			17 04		17 19	
London Blackfriars	d		15 06		15 21		15 36		15 51		16 06		16 21		16 36		16 51			17 06		17 21	
Elephant & Castle	d		15 10		15 25		15 40		15 55		16 10		16 25		16 40		16 55			17 10		17 25	
Loughborough Jn	d		15 15		15 30		15 45		16 00		16 15		16 30		16 45		17 00			17 15		17 30	
Herne Hill	d		15 20		15 35		15 50		16 05		16 20		16 35		16 50		17 05			17 20		17 35	
Tulse Hill	d	15 21	15 26	15 34	15 40	15 51	15 56	16 04	16 10	16 21	16 26	16 34	16 40	16 51	16 56	17 04	17 10	17 16	17 21	17 26	17 34	17 40	17 46
West Norwood	a	15 24				15 54				16 24				16 54					17 24				
Gipsy Hill	a	15 27				15 57				16 27				16 57					17 27				
Crystal Palace	a	15 31				16 01				16 31				17 01					17 31				
Birkbeck	a	15 35				16 05				16 35				17 05					17 35				
Beckenham Junction	a	15 39				16 09				16 39				17 09					17 39				
Streatham	d		15 30	15 38	15 44		16 00	16 08	16 14		16 30	16 38	16 44		17 00	17 08	17 14	17 20		17 30	17 38	17 44	17 50
Streatham Common	a			15 41				16 11				16 41				17 11					17 41		
Norbury	a			15 44				16 14				16 44				17 14					17 44		
Thornton Heath	a			15 47				16 17				16 47				17 17					17 47		
Selhurst	a			15 50				16 20				16 50				17 20					17 50		
East Croydon	a			15 54				16 24															
Tooting	a				15 48				16 18				16 48				17 18					17 48	
Haydons Road	a				15 52				16 22				16 52				17 22					17 52	
Wimbledon	a				15 54				16 24				16 54				17 24					17 54	
Mitcham Eastfields	a		15 34				16 04				16 34				17 04			17 24		17 34			17 54
Mitcham Junction	a		15 37				16 07				16 37				17 07			17 27		17 37			17 57
Hackbridge	a		15 40				16 10				16 40				17 10			17 30		17 40			18 00
Carshalton	a		15 43				16 13				16 43				17 13			17 33		17 43			18 03
Sutton	a		15 47		16 14		16 17		16 44		16 47		17 14		17 17		17 44	17 37		17 47		18 14	18 07

A From St Albans City **B** To Caterham

Table T173-F

Mondays to Fridays

16 December to 15 May

London Bridge - South Bermondsey, Queens Road Peckham, Peckham Rye, East Dulwich, North Dulwich, Tulse Hill and Streatham

		SN	TL A	SN	TL A	SN	SN	TL A	SN	TL A	SN	SN	TL A	SN	TL A	SN	TL A	SN B	TL A	SN	TL A	SN B
London Bridge 4 ⊖	d	17 31		17 44		17 52	18 01		18 14		18 22	18 31		18 44		19 01		19 14		19 31		19 44
South Bermondsey	d	17 35		17 49		17 59	18 05		18 19		18 29	18 35		18 49		19 05		19 19		19 35		19 49
Queens Rd Peckham	d	17 38		17 52		18 02	18 08		18 22		18 32	18 38		18 52		19 08		19 22		19 38		19 52
Peckham Rye 4	d	17 41		17 55		18 05	18 11		18 25		18 35	18 41		18 55		19 11		19 25		19 41		19 55
East Dulwich	d	17 44		17 58		18 08	18 14		18 28		18 38	18 44		18 58		19 14		19 28		19 44		19 58
North Dulwich	d	17 47		18 00		18 10	18 17		18 30		18 40	18 47		19 00		19 17		19 30		19 47		20 00
St Pancras International	d		17 27		17 42			17 57		18 12			18 27		18 42		18 57		19 12		19 27	
Farringdon	d		17 32		17 47			18 02		18 17			18 32		18 47		19 02		19 17		19 32	
City Thameslink	d		17 34		17 49			18 04		18 19			18 34		18 49		19 04		19 19		19 34	
London Blackfriars	d		17 36		17 51			18 06		18 21			18 36		18 51		19 06		19 21		19 36	
Elephant & Castle	d		17 40		17 55			18 10		18 25			18 40		18 55		19 10		19 25		19 40	
Loughborough Jn	d		17 45		18 00			18 15		18 30			18 45		19 00		19 15		19 30		19 45	
Herne Hill	d		17 50		18 05			18 20		18 35			18 50		19 05		19 20		19 35		19 50	
Tulse Hill	d	17 51	17 56	18 04	18 10	18 16	18 21	18 26	18 34	18 40	18 46	18 51	18 56	19 04	19 10	19 21	19 26	19 34	19 40	19 51	19 56	20 04
West Norwood	a	17 54					18 24					18 54				19 24				19 54		
Gipsy Hill	a	17 57					18 27					18 57				19 27				19 57		
Crystal Palace	a	18 01					18 31					19 01				19 31				20 01		
Birkbeck	a	18 05					18 35					19 05				19 35				20 05		
Beckenham Junction	a	18 09					18 39					19 09				19 39				20 09		
Streatham	d		18 00	18 08	18 14	18 20		18 30	18 38	18 44	18 50		19 00	19 08	19 14		19 30	19 38	19 44		20 00	20 08
Streatham Common	a			18 11					18 41					19 11				19 41				20 11
Norbury	a			18 14					18 44					19 14				19 44				20 14
Thornton Heath	a			18 17					18 47					19 17				19 47				20 17
Selhurst	a			18 20					18 50					19 20				19 50				20 20
East Croydon	a																	19 54				20 24
Tooting	a				18 18					18 48					19 18				19 48			
Haydons Road	a				18 22					18 52					19 22				19 52			
Wimbledon	a				18 24					18 54					19 24				19 54			
Mitcham Eastfields	a		18 04			18 24		18 34			18 54		19 04				19 34				20 04	
Mitcham Junction	a		18 07			18 27		18 37			18 57		19 07				19 37				20 07	
Hackbridge	a		18 10			18 30		18 40			19 00		19 10				19 40				20 10	
Carshalton	a		18 13			18 33		18 43			19 03		19 13				19 43				20 13	
Sutton	a		18 17		18 44	18 37		18 47		19 14	19 07		19 17		19 44		19 47		20 14		20 17	

		TL A	SN	TL A	SN B	TL A	SN	TL A	SN B	TL A	SN	TL A	SN B	TL A	SN	TL A	SN B	TL A	SN	TL A	SN B	TL A	SN
London Bridge 4 ⊖	d		20 01		20 14		20 31		20 44		21 01		21 14		21 31		21 44		22 01		22 14		22 31
South Bermondsey	d		20 05		20 19		20 35		20 49		21 05		21 19		21 35		21 49		22 05		22 19		22 35
Queens Rd Peckham	d		20 08		20 22		20 38		20 52		21 08		21 22		21 38		21 53		22 08		22 22		22 38
Peckham Rye 4	d		20 11		20 25		20 41		20 55		21 11		21 25		21 41		21 56		22 11		22 25		22 41
East Dulwich	d		20 14		20 28		20 44		20 58		21 14		21 28		21 44		21 59		22 14		22 28		22 44
North Dulwich	d		20 17		20 30		20 47		21 00		21 17		21 30		21 47		22 01		22 17		22 30		22 47
St Pancras International	d	19 42		19 57		20 12		20 27		20 42		20 57		21 12		21 27		21 42		21 57		22 12	
Farringdon	d	19 47		20 02		20 17		20 32		20 47		21 02		21 17		21 32		21 47		22 02		22 17	
City Thameslink	d	19 49		20 04		20 19		20 34		20 49		21 04		21 19		21 34		21 49		22 04		22 19	
London Blackfriars	d	19 51		20 06		20 21		20 36		20 51		21 06		21 21		21 36		21 51		22 06		22 21	
Elephant & Castle	d	19 55		20 10		20 25		20 40		20 55		21 10		21 25		21 40		21 55		22 10		22 25	
Loughborough Jn	d	20 00		20 15		20 30		20 45		21 00		21 15		21 30		21 45		22 00		22 15		22 30	
Herne Hill	d	20 05		20 20		20 35		20 50		21 05		21 20		21 35		21 50		22 05		22 20		22 35	
Tulse Hill	d	20 10	20 21	20 26	20 34	20 40	20 51	20 56	21 04	21 10	21 21	21 26	21 34	21 41	21 51	21 56	22 04	22 10	22 21	22 26	22 34	22 40	22 51
West Norwood	a		20 24				20 54				21 24				21 54				22 24				22 54
Gipsy Hill	a		20 27				20 57				21 27				21 57				22 27				22 57
Crystal Palace	a		20 31				21 01				21 31				22 01				22 31				23 01
Birkbeck	a		20 35				21 05				21 35				22 05				22 35				23 05
Beckenham Junction	a		20 39				21 09				21 39				22 09				22 39				23 09
Streatham	d	20 14		20 30	20 38	20 44		21 00	21 08	21 14		21 30	21 38	21 44		22 00	22 08	22 14		22 30	22 38	22 44	
Streatham Common	a				20 41				21 11				21 41				22 11				22 41		
Norbury	a				20 44				21 14				21 44				22 14				22 44		
Thornton Heath	a				20 47				21 17				21 47				22 17				22 47		
Selhurst	a				20 50				21 20				21 50				22 20				22 50		
East Croydon	a				20 53				21 24				21 54				22 24				22 54		
Tooting	a	20 18				20 48				21 18				21 48				22 18				22 48	
Haydons Road	a	20 22				20 52				21 22				21 52				22 22				22 52	
Wimbledon	a	20 24				20 54				21 24				21 54				22 24				22 54	
Mitcham Eastfields	a			20 34				21 04				21 34				22 04				22 34			
Mitcham Junction	a			20 37				21 07				21 37				22 07				22 37			
Hackbridge	a			20 40				21 10				21 40				22 10				22 40			
Carshalton	a			20 43				21 13				21 43				22 13				22 43			
Sutton	a	20 44		20 47		21 14		21 17		21 44		21 47		22 14		22 17		22 44		22 47		23 14	

A From St Albans City **B** To Caterham

Table T173-F

Mondays to Fridays

16 December to 15 May

London Bridge - South Bermondsey, Queens Road Peckham, Peckham Rye, East Dulwich, North Dulwich, Tulse Hill and Streatham

		TL A	SN	TL A	SN	TL A	SN	TL A	SN	TL B	SN
London Bridge 4 ⊖	d		22 44		23 01		23 14		23 31		23 54
South Bermondsey	d		22 49		23 05		23 19		23 35		23 59
Queens Rd Peckham	d		22 52		23 08		23 22		23 38		00 02
Peckham Rye 4	d		22 55		23 11		23 25		23 41		00 06
East Dulwich	d		22 58		23 14		23 28		23 44		00 09
North Dulwich	d		23 00		23 17		23 30		23 47		00 11
St Pancras International	d	22 27		22 42		22 57		23 12		23 44	
Farringdon	d	22 32		22 47		23 02		23 17		23 49	
City Thameslink	d	22 34		22 49							
London Blackfriars	d	22 36		22 51		23 06		23 21		23 53	
Elephant & Castle	d	22 40		22 55		23 10		23 25		23 57	
Loughborough Jn	d	22 45		23 00		23 15		23 30		00 02	
Herne Hill	d	22 50		23 05		23 20		23 35		00 06	
Tulse Hill	d	22 56	23 04	23 10	23 21	23 26	23 34	23 40	23 51	00 11	00 18
West Norwood	a				23 24				23 54		
Gipsy Hill	a				23 27				23 57		
Crystal Palace	a				23 31				00 01		
Birkbeck	a										
Beckenham Junction	a										
Streatham	d	23 00	23 08	23 14		23 30	23 38	23 44		00 14	00 22
Streatham Common	a		23 11				23 41				00 25
Norbury	a		23 14				23 44				00 28
Thornton Heath	a		23 17				23 47				00 31
Selhurst	a		23 20				23 50				00 34
East Croydon	a										
Tooting	a			23 18				23 48		00 18	
Haydons Road	a			23 22				23 52		00 22	
Wimbledon	a			23 24				23 54		00 24	
Mitcham Eastfields	a	23 04				23 34					
Mitcham Junction	a	23 07				23 37					
Hackbridge	a	23 10				23 40					
Carshalton	a	23 13				23 43					
Sutton	a	23 17		23 44		23 47		00 14		00 44	

Saturdays

21 December to 16 May

		TL B	SN C	SN D	SN	SN E	TL B	TL F	TL B	TL F	SN G	TL B	TL B	SN G	TL A	SN	TL A	SN G	TL H	SN	TL A	SN G	TL A
London Bridge 4 ⊖	d			00 01	00 25	00 31					06 14			06 44		07 02		07 14		07 32		07 44	
South Bermondsey	d			00 05	00 29	00 35					06 19			06 49		07 06		07 19		07 36		07 49	
Queens Rd Peckham	d		00 02	00 08	00 33	00 38					06 22			06 52		07 09		07 22		07 39		07 52	
Peckham Rye 4	d		00 06	00 11	00 37	00 41					06 25			06 55		07 12		07 25		07 42		07 55	
East Dulwich	d		00 09	00 14	00 41	00 44					06 28			06 58		07 15		07 28		07 45		07 58	
North Dulwich	d		00 11	00 17	00 43	00 47					06 30			07 00		07 17		07 30		07 47		08 00	
St Pancras International	d						05 12	05 27	05 42	05 57		06 12	06 27		06 42		06 57		07 12		07 27		07 42
Farringdon	d						05 17	05 32	05 47	06 02		06 17	06 32		06 47		07 02		07 17		07 32		07 47
City Thameslink	d																						
London Blackfriars	d						05 21	05 36	05 51	06 06		06 21	06 36		06 51		07 06		07 21		07 36		07 51
Elephant & Castle	d						05 25	05 40	05 55	06 10		06 25	06 40		06 55		07 10		07 25		07 40		07 55
Loughborough Jn	d	00 02					05 30	05 45	06 00	06 15		06 30	06 45		07 00		07 15		07 30		07 45		08 00
Herne Hill	d	00 06					05 35	05 50	06 05	06 20		06 35	06 50		07 05		07 20		07 35		07 50		08 05
Tulse Hill	d	00 11	00 18	00 21	00 47	00 51	05 40	05 56	06 10	06 26	06 34	06 40	06 56	07 04	07 10	07 21	07 26	07 34	07 40	07 51	07 56	08 04	08 10
West Norwood	a			00 24		00 54										07 24				07 54			
Gipsy Hill	a			00 27		00 57										07 27				07 57			
Crystal Palace	a			00 31		01 01										07 31				08 01			
Birkbeck	a															07 35				08 05			
Beckenham Junction	a															07 39				08 09			
Streatham	d	00 14	00 22		00 51		05 44	06 00	06 14	06 30	06 38	06 44	07 00	07 08	07 14		07 30	07 38	07 44		08 00	08 08	08 14
Streatham Common	a		00 25		00 54						06 41			07 11				07 41				08 11	
Norbury	a		00 28		00 57						06 44			07 14				07 44				08 14	
Thornton Heath	a		00 31		01 00						06 47			07 17				07 47				08 17	
Selhurst	a		00 34		01 03						06 50			07 20				07 50				08 20	
East Croydon	a										06 54			07 24				07 54				08 24	
Tooting	a	00 18					05 48		06 18			06 48			07 18				07 48				08 18
Haydons Road	a	00 22					05 52		06 22			06 52			07 22				07 52				08 22
Wimbledon	a	00 24					05 54		06 24			06 54			07 24				07 54				08 24
Mitcham Eastfields	a							06 04		06 34			07 04				07 34				08 04		
Mitcham Junction	a							06 07		06 37			07 07				07 37				08 07		
Hackbridge	a							06 10		06 40			07 10				07 40				08 10		
Carshalton	a							06 13		06 43			07 13				07 43				08 13		
Sutton	a	00 44					06 14	06 17	06 44	06 47		07 14	07 17		07 44		07 47		08 14		08 17		08 44

A From St Albans City
B From Luton
C From London Bridge
D not 16 May
E To Norwood Junction
F From West Hampstead Thameslink
G To Caterham
H From Bedford

Table T173-F

Saturdays

21 December to 16 May

London Bridge - South Bermondsey, Queens Road Peckham, Peckham Rye, East Dulwich, North Dulwich, Tulse Hill and Streatham

		SN	TL A	SN B	TL A	SN	TL A	SN B	TL A	SN	TL A	SN B	TL A	SN	TL A	SN B	TL A		SN	TL A	SN B	TL A	SN
London Bridge 4 ⊖	d	08 02		08 14		08 32		08 44		09 02		09 14		09 32		09 44			20 02		20 14		20 32
South Bermondsey	d	08 06		08 19		08 36		08 49		09 06		09 19		09 36		09 49			20 06		20 19		20 36
Queens Rd Peckham	d	08 09		08 22		08 39		08 52		09 09		09 22		09 39		09 52			20 09		20 22		20 39
Peckham Rye 4	d	08 12		08 25		08 42		08 55		09 12		09 25		09 42		09 55			20 12		20 25		20 42
East Dulwich	d	08 15		08 28		08 45		08 58		09 15		09 28		09 45		09 58			20 15		20 28		20 45
North Dulwich	d	08 17		08 30		08 47		09 00		09 17		09 30		09 47		10 00			20 17		20 30		20 47
St Pancras International	d		07 57		08 12		08 27		08 42		08 57		09 12		09 27		09 42			19 57		20 12	
Farringdon	d		08 02		08 17		08 32		08 47		09 02		09 17		09 32		09 47			20 02		20 17	
City Thameslink	d										09 04		09 19		09 34		09 49			20 04		20 19	
London Blackfriars	d		08 06		08 21		08 36		08 51		09 06		09 21		09 36		09 51			20 06		20 21	
Elephant & Castle	d		08 10		08 25		08 40		08 55		09 10		09 25		09 40		09 55			20 10		20 25	
Loughborough Jn	d		08 15		08 30		08 45		09 00		09 15		09 30		09 45		10 00			20 15		20 30	
Herne Hill	d		08 20		08 35		08 50		09 05		09 20		09 35		09 50		10 05	and at		20 20		20 35	
Tulse Hill	d	08 21	08 26	08 34	08 40	08 51	08 56	09 04	09 10	09 21	09 26	09 34	09 40	09 51	09 56	10 04	10 10	the same	20 21	20 26	20 34	20 40	20 51
West Norwood	a	08 24				08 54				09 24				09 54				minutes	20 24				20 54
Gipsy Hill	a	08 27				08 57				09 27				09 57				past	20 27				20 57
Crystal Palace	a	08 31				09 01				09 31				10 01				each	20 31				21 01
Birkbeck	a	08 35				09 05				09 35				10 05				hour until	20 35				21 05
Beckenham Junction	a	08 39				09 09				09 39				10 09					20 39				21 09
Streatham	d		08 30	08 38	08 44		09 00	09 08	09 14		09 30	09 38	09 44		10 00	10 08	10 14			20 30	20 38	20 44	
Streatham Common	a			08 41				09 11				09 41				10 11					20 41		
Norbury	a			08 44				09 14				09 44				10 14					20 44		
Thornton Heath	a			08 47				09 17				09 47				10 17					20 47		
Selhurst	a			08 50				09 20				09 50				10 20					20 50		
East Croydon	a			08 54				09 24				09 54				10 24					20 54		
Tooting	a				08 48				09 18				09 48				10 18					20 48	
Haydons Road	a				08 52				09 22				09 52				10 22					20 52	
Wimbledon	a				08 54				09 24				09 54				10 24					20 54	
Mitcham Eastfields	a		08 34				09 04				09 34				10 04					20 34			
Mitcham Junction	a		08 37				09 07				09 37				10 07					20 37			
Hackbridge	a		08 40				09 10				09 40				10 10					20 40			
Carshalton	a		08 43				09 13				09 43				10 13					20 43			
Sutton	a		08 47		09 14		09 17		09 44		09 47		10 14		10 17		10 44			20 47		21 14	

		TL A	SN B	TL A	SN	TL A	SN B	TL A	SN	TL A	SN B	TL A	SN	TL A	SN B	TL A	SN	TL A	SN	TL A	SN C	TL A
London Bridge 4 ⊖	d		20 44		21 02		21 14		21 32		21 44		22 02		22 14		22 32		22 45		23 02	
South Bermondsey	d		20 49		21 06		21 19		21 36		21 49		22 06		22 19		22 36		22 49		23 06	
Queens Rd Peckham	d		20 52		21 09		21 22		21 39		21 52		22 09		22 22		22 39		22 52		23 09	
Peckham Rye 4	d		20 55		21 12		21 25		21 42		21 55		22 12		22 25		22 42		22 56		23 12	
East Dulwich	d		20 58		21 15		21 28		21 45		21 58		22 15		22 28		22 45		22 59		23 15	
North Dulwich	d		21 00		21 17		21 30		21 47		22 00		22 17		22 30		22 47		23 01		23 17	
St Pancras International	d	20 27		20 42		20 57		21 12		21 27		21 42		21 57		22 12		22 27		22 42		22 57
Farringdon	d	20 32		20 47		21 02		21 17		21 32		21 47		22 02		22 17		22 32		22 47		23 02
City Thameslink	d	20 34		20 49																		
London Blackfriars	d	20 36		20 51		21 06		21 21		21 36		21 51		22 06		22 21		22 36		22 51		23 06
Elephant & Castle	d	20 40		20 55		21 10		21 25		21 40		21 55		22 10		22 25		22 40		22 55		23 10
Loughborough Jn	d	20 45		21 00		21 15		21 30		21 45		22 00		22 15		22 30		22 45		23 00		23 15
Herne Hill	d	20 50		21 05		21 20		21 35		21 50		22 05		22 20		22 35		22 50		23 05		23 20
Tulse Hill	d	20 56	21 04	21 10	21 21	21 26	21 34	21 40	21 51	21 56	22 04	22 10	22 21	22 26	22 34	22 40	22 51	22 56	23 05	23 10	23 21	23 26
West Norwood	a				21 24				21 54				22 24				22 54				23 24	
Gipsy Hill	a				21 27				21 57				22 27				22 57				23 27	
Crystal Palace	a				21 31				22 01				22 31				23 01				23 31	
Birkbeck	a				21 35				22 05				22 35				23 05					
Beckenham Junction	a				21 39				22 09				22 39				23 09					
Streatham	d	21 00	21 08	21 14		21 30	21 38	21 44		22 00	22 08	22 14		22 30	22 38	22 44		23 00	23 11	23 14		23 30
Streatham Common	a		21 11				21 41				22 11				22 41				23 16			
Norbury	a		21 14				21 44				22 14				22 44				23 19			
Thornton Heath	a		21 17				21 47				22 17				22 47				23 22			
Selhurst	a		21 20				21 50				22 20				22 50				23 25			
East Croydon	a		21 24				21 54				22 24				22 54							
Tooting	a			21 18				21 48				22 18				22 48				23 18		
Haydons Road	a			21 22				21 52				22 22				22 52				23 22		
Wimbledon	a			21 24				21 54				22 24				22 54				23 24		
Mitcham Eastfields	a	21 04				21 34				22 04				22 34				23 04				23 34
Mitcham Junction	a	21 07				21 37				22 07				22 37				23 07				23 37
Hackbridge	a	21 10				21 40				22 10				22 40				23 10				23 40
Carshalton	a	21 13				21 43				22 13				22 43				23 13				23 43
Sutton	a	21 17		21 44		21 47		22 14		22 17		22 44		22 47		23 14		23 17		23 44		23 47

A From St Albans City
B To Caterham
C To Norwood Junction

Table T173-F

Saturdays
21 December to 16 May

London Bridge - South Bermondsey, Queens Road Peckham, Peckham Rye, East Dulwich, North Dulwich, Tulse Hill and Streatham

		SN	TL A	SN B	TL C	SN
London Bridge ⊖	d	23 14		23 32		23 55
South Bermondsey	d	23 19		23 36		23 59
Queens Rd Peckham	d	23 22		23 39		00 02
Peckham Rye	d	23 25		23 42		00 06
East Dulwich	d	23 28		23 45		00 09
North Dulwich	d	23 30		23 47		00 11
St Pancras International	d		23 12		23 44	
Farringdon	d		23 17		23 49	
City Thameslink	d					
London Blackfriars	d		23 21		23 53	
Elephant & Castle	d		23 25		23 57	
Loughborough Jn	d		23 30		00 02	
Herne Hill	d		23 35		00 06	
Tulse Hill	d	23 34	23 40	23 51	00 11	00 17
West Norwood	a			23 55		
Gipsy Hill	a			23 58		
Crystal Palace	a			00 02		
Birkbeck	a					
Beckenham Junction	a					
Streatham	d	23 38	23 44		00 14	00 21
Streatham Common	a	23 41				00 26
Norbury	a	23 44				00 29
Thornton Heath	a	23 47				00 32
Selhurst	a	23 50				00 35
East Croydon	a					
Tooting	a		23 48		00 18	
Haydons Road	a		23 52		00 22	
Wimbledon	a		23 54		00 24	
Mitcham Eastfields	a					
Mitcham Junction	a					
Hackbridge	a					
Carshalton	a					
Sutton	a		00 14		00 44	

Sundays
15 December to 10 May

		TL D	SN E	SN B	SN	SN B	SN	SN	SN	SN	SN	TL	SN	SN	TL	SN	SN	TL	SN	TL C	SN	TL	SN
London Bridge ⊖	d			00 01	00 25	00 31	07 16	07 35	07 46	08 03	08 16	08 30	08 35	08 47	09 00	09 05	09 16		09 35		09 49		10 05
South Bermondsey	d			00 05	00 29	00 35	07 24	07 39	07 54	08 09	08 24		08 39	08 54		09 09	09 24		09 39		09 55		10 09
Queens Rd Peckham	d		00 02	00 08	00 34	00 38	07 27	07 42	07 57	08 12	08 27		08 42	08 57		09 12	09 27		09 42		09 58		10 12
Peckham Rye	d		00 06	00 11	00 37	00 41	07 31	07 45	08 01	08 15	08 30		08 45	09 00		09 15	09 30		09 45		10 01		10 15
East Dulwich	d		00 09	00 14	00 41	00 44	07 34	07 48	08 04	08 18	08 33		08 48	09 03		09 18	09 33		09 48		10 04		10 18
North Dulwich	d		00 11	00 17	00 43	00 47	07 37	07 51	08 07	08 21	08 35		08 51	09 05		09 21	09 35		09 51		10 06		10 21
St Pancras International	d																			09 38			
Farringdon	d																			09 42			
City Thameslink	d																						
London Blackfriars	d																	09 30		09 47		10 00	
Elephant & Castle	d																	09 34		09 51		10 04	
Loughborough Jn	d	00 02																09 39		09 56		10 09	
Herne Hill	d	00 06																09 44		10 00		10 14	
Tulse Hill	d	00 11	00 17	00 21	00 47	00 51	07 42	07 55	08 12	08 25	08 39	08 46	08 55	09 09	09 16	09 25	09 39	09 48	09 55	10 04	10 10	10 18	10 25
West Norwood	a			00 24		00 54		07 58		08 28			08 58			09 28			09 58				10 28
Gipsy Hill	a			00 27		00 57		08 01		08 31			09 01			09 31			10 01				10 31
Crystal Palace	a			00 31		01 01		08 05		08 35			09 05			09 35			10 05				10 35
Birkbeck	a																						
Beckenham Junction	a																						
Streatham	d	00 14	00 21		00 51		07 46		08 16		08 43	08 50		09 13	09 20		09 43	09 52		10 08	10 14	10 22	
Streatham Common	a		00 26		00 54		07 49		08 19		08 46			09 16			09 46				10 17		
Norbury	a		00 29		00 57		07 51		08 21		08 49			09 19			09 49				10 20		
Thornton Heath	a		00 32		01 00		07 54		08 24		08 52			09 22			09 52				10 23		
Selhurst	a		00 35		01 03		07 57		08 27		08 54			09 24			09 54				10 25		
East Croydon	a						08 00		08 30		08 59			09 29			09 59				10 29		
Tooting	a	00 18																		10 12			
Haydons Road	a	00 22																		10 16			
Wimbledon	a	00 24																		10 18			
Mitcham Eastfields	a											08 53			09 23			09 55				10 25	
Mitcham Junction	a											08 56			09 26			09 58				10 28	
Hackbridge	a											08 59			09 29			10 01				10 31	
Carshalton	a											09 02			09 32			10 04				10 34	
Sutton	a	00 44										09 05			09 35			10 07		10 38		10 37	

A From St Albans City
B To Norwood Junction
C From Luton
D not 15 December. From Luton
E not 15 December. From London Bridge

Table T173-F

Sundays
15 December to 10 May

London Bridge - South Bermondsey, Queens Road Peckham, Peckham Rye, East Dulwich, North Dulwich, Tulse Hill and Streatham

		TL A	SN	TL	SN	TL A	SN	TL	SN	TL A	SN	TL	SN	TL A	SN	TL	SN	TL A	SN	TL	SN	TL A	SN
London Bridge ⊖	d		10 19		10 35		10 49		11 05		11 19		11 35		11 49		12 05		12 19		12 35		12 49
South Bermondsey	d		10 25		10 39		10 55		11 09		11 25		11 39		11 55		12 09		12 25		12 39		12 55
Queens Rd Peckham	d		10 28		10 42		10 58		11 12		11 28		11 42		11 58		12 12		12 28		12 42		12 58
Peckham Rye	d		10 31		10 45		11 01		11 15		11 31		11 45		12 01		12 15		12 31		12 45		13 01
East Dulwich	d		10 34		10 48		11 04		11 18		11 34		11 48		12 04		12 18		12 34		12 48		13 04
North Dulwich	d		10 36		10 51		11 06		11 21		11 36		11 51		12 06		12 21		12 36		12 51		13 06
St Pancras International	d	10 08				10 38				11 08				11 38				12 08		12 21		12 38	
Farringdon	d	10 12				10 42				11 12				11 42				12 12		12 25		12 42	
City Thameslink	d																						
London Blackfriars	d	10 17		10 30		10 47		11 00		11 17		11 30		11 47		12 00		12 17		12 30		12 47	
Elephant & Castle	d	10 21		10 34		10 51		11 04		11 21		11 34		11 51		12 04		12 21		12 34		12 51	
Loughborough Jn	d	10 26		10 39		10 56		11 09		11 26		11 39		11 56		12 09		12 26		12 39		12 56	
Herne Hill	d	10 30		10 44		11 00		11 14		11 30		11 44		12 00		12 14		12 30		12 44		13 00	
Tulse Hill	d	10 34	10 40	10 48	10 55	11 04	11 10	11 18	11 25	11 34	11 40	11 48	11 55	12 04	12 10	12 18	12 25	12 34	12 40	12 48	12 55	13 04	13 10
West Norwood	a				10 58				11 28				11 58				12 28				12 58		
Gipsy Hill	a				11 01				11 31				12 01				12 31				13 01		
Crystal Palace	a				11 05				11 35				12 05				12 35				13 05		
Birkbeck	a																						
Beckenham Junction	a																						
Streatham	d	10 38	10 44	10 52		11 08	11 14	11 22		11 38	11 44	11 52		12 08	12 14	12 22		12 38	12 44	12 52		13 08	13 14
Streatham Common	a		10 47				11 17				11 47				12 17				12 47				13 17
Norbury	a		10 50				11 20				11 50				12 20				12 50				13 20
Thornton Heath	a		10 53				11 23				11 53				12 23				12 53				13 23
Selhurst	a		10 55				11 25				11 55				12 25				12 55				13 25
East Croydon	a		10 59				11 29				11 59				12 29				12 59				13 29
Tooting	a	10 42				11 12				11 42				12 12				12 42				13 12	
Haydons Road	a	10 46				11 16				11 46				12 16				12 46				13 16	
Wimbledon	a	10 48				11 18				11 48				12 18				12 48				13 18	
Mitcham Eastfields	a			10 55				11 25				11 55				12 25				12 55			
Mitcham Junction	a			10 58				11 28				11 58				12 28				12 58			
Hackbridge	a			11 01				11 31				12 01				12 31				13 01			
Carshalton	a			11 04				11 34				12 04				12 34				13 04			
Sutton	a	11 08		11 07		11 38		11 37		12 08		12 07		12 38		12 37		13 08		13 07		13 38	

		TL A		SN	TL A	SN	TL B	SN	TL A	SN	TL B	SN	TL A	SN	TL B	SN	TL A	SN	SN	SN	SN C	SN	SN C	SN
London Bridge ⊖	d			20 05		20 19		20 35		20 49		21 05		21 19		21 35		21 49	22 05	22 19	22 35	22 49	23 05	23 17
South Bermondsey	d			20 09		20 25		20 39		20 55		21 09		21 25		21 39		21 55	22 09	22 25	22 39	22 55	23 09	23 24
Queens Rd Peckham	d			20 12		20 28		20 42		20 58		21 12		21 28		21 42		21 58	22 12	22 28	22 42	22 58	23 12	23 27
Peckham Rye	d			20 15		20 31		20 45		21 01		21 15		21 31		21 45		22 01	22 15	22 31	22 45	23 01	23 15	23 31
East Dulwich	d			20 18		20 34		20 48		21 04		21 18		21 34		21 48		22 04	22 18	22 34	22 48	23 04	23 18	23 34
North Dulwich	d			20 21		20 36		20 51		21 06		21 21		21 36		21 51		22 06	22 21	22 36	22 51	23 06	23 21	23 37
St Pancras International	d	12 51			20 08		20 21		20 38		20 51		21 08		21 21		21 38							
Farringdon	d	12 55			20 12		20 25		20 42		20 55		21 12		21 25		21 42							
City Thameslink	d																							
London Blackfriars	d	13 00			20 17		20 30		20 47		21 00		21 17		21 30		21 47							
Elephant & Castle	d	13 04			20 21		20 34		20 51		21 04		21 21		21 34		21 51							
Loughborough Jn	d	13 09			20 26		20 39		20 56		21 09		21 26		21 39		21 56							
Herne Hill	d	13 14	and at		20 30		20 44		21 00		21 14		21 30		21 44		22 00							
Tulse Hill	d	13 18	the same	20 25	20 34	20 40	20 48	20 55	21 04	21 10	21 18	21 25	21 34	21 40	21 48	21 55	22 04	22 10	22 25	22 40	22 55	23 10	23 25	23 42
West Norwood	a		minutes	20 28				20 58				21 28				21 58			22 28		22 58		23 28	
Gipsy Hill	a		past	20 31				21 01				21 31				22 01			22 31		23 01		23 31	
Crystal Palace	a		each	20 35				21 05				21 35				22 05			22 35		23 05		23 35	
Birkbeck	a		hour until																					
Beckenham Junction	a																							
Streatham	d	13 22			20 38	20 44	20 52		21 08	21 14	21 22		21 38	21 44	21 52		22 08	22 14		22 44		23 14		23 46
Streatham Common	a					20 47				21 17				21 47				22 17		22 47		23 17		23 49
Norbury	a					20 50				21 20				21 50				22 20		22 50		23 20		23 51
Thornton Heath	a					20 53				21 23				21 53				22 23		22 53		23 23		23 54
Selhurst	a					20 55				21 25				21 55				22 25		22 55		23 25		23 57
East Croydon	a					20 59				21 29				21 59				22 29		22 59		23 29		00 02
Tooting	a				20 42				21 12				21 42				22 12							
Haydons Road	a				20 46				21 16				21 46				22 16							
Wimbledon	a				20 48				21 18				21 48				22 18							
Mitcham Eastfields	a	13 25					20 55				21 25				21 55									
Mitcham Junction	a	13 28					20 58				21 28				21 58									
Hackbridge	a	13 31					21 01				21 31				22 01									
Carshalton	a	13 34					21 04				21 34				22 04									
Sutton	a	13 37			21 08		21 07		21 38		21 37		22 08		22 07		22 38							

A From Luton
B From St Albans City
C To Norwood Junction

Table T173-R

Mondays to Fridays
16 December to 15 May

Tulse Hill, Streatham, North Dulwich, East Dulwich, Peckham Rye, Queens Road Peckham and South Bermondsey - London Bridge

Miles	Miles	Miles	Miles			SN MO A	SN	SN	TL B	SN	TL B	SN	TL B	SN	TL B	SN	SN	TL B	SN	TL B	SN	SN	TL B
—	—	—	0	Sutton	d				05 46		05 49		06 16		06 19	06 36		06 46		06 49	07 06		07 16
—	—	—	1¼	Carshalton	d				05 49				06 19			06 39		06 49			07 09		07 19
—	—	—	2¼	Hackbridge	d				05 52				06 22			06 42		06 52			07 12		07 22
—	—	—	3¼	Mitcham Junction	d				05 55				06 25			06 45		06 55			07 15		07 25
—	—	—	4½	Mitcham Eastfields	d				05 58				06 28			06 48		06 58			07 18		07 28
—	—	0	—	Wimbledon	d						06 07				06 37					07 07			
—	—	0¾	—	Haydons Road	d						06 10				06 40					07 10			
—	—	2	—	Tooting	d						06 13				06 43					07 13			
0	—	—	—	East Croydon	d																		
1	—	—	—	Selhurst	d		05 28			06 01				06 25					06 56				
2	—	—	—	Thornton Heath	d		05 30			06 03				06 28					06 58				
3	—	—	—	Norbury	d		05 33			06 06				06 31					07 01				
4	—	—	—	Streatham Common	d		05 35			06 09				06 36					07 06				
4½	—	3½	6¼	**Streatham**	d		05 39		06 03	06 13	06 18		06 33	06 43	06 48	06 53		07 03	07 13	07 18	07 23		07 33
—	0	—	—	Beckenham Junction	d												06 45					07 15	
—	1½	—	—	**Birkbeck**	d												06 48					07 18	
—	3	—	—	Crystal Palace	d			05 53				06 23					06 53					07 23	
—	3¾	—	—	Gipsy Hill	d			05 55				06 25					06 55					07 25	
—	4¼	—	—	West Norwood	d			05 58				06 28					06 58					07 28	
6	5½	5	7¾	**Tulse Hill**	d		05 43	06 02	06 08	06 17	06 23	06 32	06 38	06 47	06 53	06 57	07 02	07 08	07 17	07 23	07 27	07 32	07 38
—	—	6	8¾	Herne Hill	a				06 11		06 26		06 41		06 56			07 11		07 26			07 41
—	—	7	9¾	Loughborough Jn	a				06 15		06 30		06 45		07 00			07 15		07 30			07 45
—	—	9	11¾	Elephant & Castle	a				06 19		06 34		06 49		07 04			07 19		07 34			07 49
—	—	10¼	13	London Blackfriars ■ ⊖	a				06 24		06 39		06 54		07 09			07 24		07 39			07 54
—	—	10¾	13¾	City Thameslink	a				06 26		06 41		06 56		07 11			07 26		07 41			07 56
—	—	11½	14	Farringdon	a				06 28		06 43		06 58		07 13			07 28		07 43			07 58
—	—	12¼	15¾	St Pancras International	a				06 33		06 48		07 03		07 18			07 33		07 48			08 03
7½	6¾	—	—	**North Dulwich**	d		05 46	06 06		06 21		06 36		06 51		07 00	07 06		07 21		07 30	07 36	
8	7¼	—	—	**East Dulwich**	d		05 49	06 08		06 23		06 38		06 53		07 02	07 08		07 23		07 32	07 38	
8¾	8	—	—	Peckham Rye ■	d		05 52	06 11		06 26		06 41		06 56		07 06	07 11		07 26		07 36	07 41	
9½	8¾	—	—	Queens Rd Peckham	d	00 01	05 54	06 13		06 28		06 43		06 58		07 08	07 13		07 28		07 38	07 43	
10½	9¾	—	—	**South Bermondsey**	d	00 04	05 56	06 16		06 31		06 46		07 01		07 10	07 16		07 31		07 40	07 46	
12¼	11½	—	—	London Bridge ■ ⊖	a	00 09	06 01	06 21		06 36		06 51		07 06		07 15	07 21		07 36		07 45	07 51	

		SN	TL B	SN	SN	TL B	SN	TL B	SN	SN	TL B	SN	TL B	SN	SN	TL B	SN	TL B	SN	TL B	SN C	TL B	SN
Sutton	d	07 00	07 19	07 36		07 46	07 30	07 49	08 06		08 16	08 00	08 19	08 36		08 46	08 30	08 49		09 16		09 19	
Carshalton	d			07 39		07 49			08 09		08 19			08 39		08 49				09 19			
Hackbridge	d			07 42		07 52			08 12		08 22			08 42		08 52				09 22			
Mitcham Junction	d			07 45		07 55			08 15		08 25			08 45		08 55				09 25			
Mitcham Eastfields	d			07 49		07 58			08 19		08 28			08 49		08 58				09 28			
Wimbledon	d		07 37					08 07					08 37					09 07				09 37	
Haydons Road	d		07 40					08 10					08 40					09 10				09 40	
Tooting	d		07 43					08 13					08 43					09 13				09 43	
East Croydon	d																				09 21		
Selhurst	d	07 26					07 56					08 26					08 56				09 27		
Thornton Heath	d	07 28					07 58					08 28					08 58				09 29		
Norbury	d	07 31					08 01					08 31					09 01				09 32		
Streatham Common	d	07 36					08 06					08 36					09 06				09 36		
Streatham	d	07 43	07 48	07 53		08 03	08 13	08 18	08 23		08 33	08 43	08 48	08 53		09 03	09 13	09 18		09 33	09 43	09 48	
Beckenham Junction	d				07 45					08 15					08 45				09 15				09 45
Birkbeck	d				07 48					08 18					08 48				09 18				09 48
Crystal Palace	d				07 53					08 23					08 53				09 23				09 53
Gipsy Hill	d				07 55					08 25					08 55				09 25				09 55
West Norwood	d				07 58					08 28					08 58				09 28				09 58
Tulse Hill	d	07 47	07 53	07 57	08 02	08 08	08 17	08 23	08 27	08 32	08 38	08 47	08 53	08 57	09 02	09 08	09 17	09 23	09 32	09 38	09 47	09 53	10 02
Herne Hill	a		07 56			08 11		08 26			08 41		08 56			09 11		09 26		09 41		09 56	
Loughborough Jn	a		08 00			08 15		08 30			08 45		09 00			09 15		09 30		09 45		10 00	
Elephant & Castle	a		08 04			08 19		08 34			08 49		09 04			09 19		09 34		09 49		10 04	
London Blackfriars ■ ⊖	a		08 09			08 24		08 39			08 54		09 09			09 24		09 39		09 54		10 09	
City Thameslink	a		08 11			08 26		08 41			08 56		09 11			09 26		09 41		09 56		10 11	
Farringdon	a		08 13			08 28		08 43			08 58		09 13			09 28		09 43		09 58		10 13	
St Pancras International	a		08 18			08 33		08 48			09 03		09 18			09 33		09 48		10 03		10 18	
North Dulwich	d	07 51		08 00	08 06		08 21		08 30	08 36		08 51		09 00	09 06		09 21		09 36		09 51		10 06
East Dulwich	d	07 53		08 02	08 08		08 23		08 32	08 38		08 53		09 02	09 08		09 23		09 38		09 53		10 08
Peckham Rye ■	d	07 56		08 06	08 11		08 26		08 36	08 41		08 56		09 06	09 11		09 26		09 41		09 56		10 11
Queens Rd Peckham	d	07 58		08 08	08 13		08 28		08 38	08 43		08 58		09 08	09 13		09 28		09 43		09 58		10 13
South Bermondsey	d	08 01		08 10	08 16		08 31		08 40	08 46		09 01		09 10	09 16		09 31		09 46		10 01		10 16
London Bridge ■ ⊖	a	08 06		08 15	08 21		08 36		08 47	08 51		09 06		09 17	09 21		09 36		09 51		10 06		10 21

A From Crystal Palace **B** To St Albans City **C** From Caterham

Table T173-R

Mondays to Fridays
16 December to 15 May

Tulse Hill, Streatham, North Dulwich, East Dulwich, Peckham Rye, Queens Road Peckham and South Bermondsey - London Bridge

		TL A	SN B	TL A	SN	TL A	SN B	TL A	SN	TL A	SN B		TL A	SN	TL A	SN B	TL A	SN	TL A	SN B	TL A	SN	TL A
Sutton	d	09 46		09 49		10 16		10 19		10 46			12 49		13 16		13 19		13 46		13 49		14 16
Carshalton	d	09 49				10 19				10 49					13 19				13 49				14 19
Hackbridge	d	09 52				10 22				10 52					13 22				13 52				14 22
Mitcham Junction	d	09 55				10 25				10 55					13 25				13 55				14 25
Mitcham Eastfields	d	09 58				10 28				10 58					13 28				13 58				14 28
Wimbledon	d			10 07				10 37					13 07				13 37				14 07		
Haydons Road	d			10 10				10 40					13 10				13 40				14 10		
Tooting	d			10 13				10 43					13 13				13 43				14 13		
East Croydon	d		09 51				10 22				10 52					13 22				13 52			
Selhurst	d		09 56				10 26				10 56					13 26				13 56			
Thornton Heath	d		09 58				10 28				10 58					13 28				13 58			
Norbury	d		10 01				10 31				11 01					13 31				14 01			
Streatham Common	d		10 06				10 36				11 06					13 36				14 06			
Streatham	d	10 03	10 13	10 18		10 33	10 43	10 48		11 03	11 13	and at the same minutes past each hour until	13 18		13 33	13 43	13 48		14 03	14 13	14 18		14 33
Beckenham Junction	d				10 15				10 45					13 15				13 45				14 15	
Birkbeck	d				10 18				10 48					13 18				13 48				14 18	
Crystal Palace	d				10 23				10 53					13 23				13 53				14 23	
Gipsy Hill	d				10 25				10 55					13 25				13 55				14 25	
West Norwood	d				10 28				10 58					13 28				13 58				14 28	
Tulse Hill	d	10 08	10 17	10 23	10 32	10 38	10 47	10 53	11 02	11 08	11 17		13 23	13 32	13 38	13 47	13 53	14 02	14 08	14 17	14 23	14 32	14 38
Herne Hill	a	10 11		10 26		10 41		10 56		11 11			13 26		13 41		13 56		14 11		14 26		14 41
Loughborough Jn	a	10 15		10 30		10 45		11 00		11 15			13 30		13 45		14 00		14 15		14 30		14 45
Elephant & Castle	a	10 19		10 34		10 49		11 04		11 19			13 34		13 49		14 04		14 19		14 34		14 49
London Blackfriars ■ ⊖	a	10 24		10 39		10 54		11 09		11 24			13 39		13 54		14 09		14 24		14 39		14 54
City Thameslink	a	10 26		10 41		10 56		11 11		11 26			13 41		13 56		14 11		14 26		14 41		14 56
Farringdon	a	10 28		10 43		10 58		11 13		11 28			13 43		13 58		14 13		14 28		14 43		14 58
St Pancras International	a	10 33		10 48		11 03		11 18		11 33			13 48		14 03		14 18		14 33		14 48		15 03
North Dulwich	d		10 21		10 36		10 51		11 06		11 21			13 36		13 51		14 06		14 21		14 36	
East Dulwich	d		10 23		10 38		10 53		11 08		11 23			13 38		13 53		14 08		14 23		14 38	
Peckham Rye ■	d		10 26		10 41		10 56		11 11		11 26			13 41		13 56		14 11		14 26		14 41	
Queens Rd Peckham	d		10 28		10 43		10 58		11 13		11 28			13 43		13 58		14 13		14 28		14 43	
South Bermondsey	d		10 31		10 46		11 01		11 16		11 31			13 46		14 01		14 16		14 31		14 46	
London Bridge ■ ⊖	a		10 36		10 51		11 06		11 21		11 36			13 51		14 06		14 21		14 36		14 51	

		SN B	TL A	SN	TL A	SN B	TL A	SN	TL A	SN B	TL A	SN	TL A	SN B	TL A	SN C	SN	TL A	SN B	TL A	SN	TL A	SN B
Sutton	d		14 18		14 46		14 49		15 16		15 19		15 46		15 49			16 16		16 19		16 46	
Carshalton	d				14 49				15 19				15 49					16 19				16 49	
Hackbridge	d				14 52				15 22				15 52					16 22				16 52	
Mitcham Junction	d				14 55				15 25				15 55					16 25				16 55	
Mitcham Eastfields	d				14 58				15 28				15 58					16 28				16 58	
Wimbledon	d		14 36				15 07				15 37				16 07					16 37			
Haydons Road	d		14 38				15 10				15 40				16 10					16 40			
Tooting	d		14 41				15 13				15 43				16 13					16 43			
East Croydon	d	14 22				14 52				15 22				15 51					16 21				16 51
Selhurst	d	14 26				14 56				15 26				15 56					16 26				16 56
Thornton Heath	d	14 28				14 58				15 28				15 58					16 28				16 58
Norbury	d	14 31				15 01				15 31				16 01					16 31				17 01
Streatham Common	d	14 36				15 06				15 36				16 06					16 36				17 06
Streatham	d	14 43	14 46		15 03	15 13	15 18		15 33	15 43	15 48		16 03	16 13	16 18			16 33	16 43	16 48		17 03	17 13
Beckenham Junction	d			14 45				15 15				15 45					16 15				16 45		
Birkbeck	d			14 48				15 18				15 48					16 18				16 48		
Crystal Palace	d			14 53				15 23				15 53					16 23				16 53		
Gipsy Hill	d			14 55				15 25				15 55					16 25				16 55		
West Norwood	d			14 58				15 28				15 58					16 28				16 58		
Tulse Hill	d	14 47	14 53	15 02	15 08	15 17	15 23	15 32	15 38	15 47	15 53	16 02	16 08	16 17	16 23	16 25	16 32	16 38	16 47	16 53	17 02	17 08	17 17
Herne Hill	a		14 56		15 11		15 26		15 41		15 56		16 11		16 26			16 41		16 56		17 11	
Loughborough Jn	a		15 00		15 15		15 30		15 45		16 00		16 15		16 30			16 45		17 00		17 15	
Elephant & Castle	a		15 04		15 19		15 34		15 49		16 04		16 19		16 34			16 49		17 04		17 19	
London Blackfriars ■ ⊖	a		15 09		15 24		15 39		15 54		16 09		16 24		16 39			16 54		17 09		17 24	
City Thameslink	a		15 11		15 26		15 41		15 56		16 11		16 26		16 41			16 56		17 11		17 26	
Farringdon	a		15 13		15 28		15 43		15 58		16 13		16 28		16 43			16 58		17 13		17 28	
St Pancras International	a		15 18		15 33		15 48		16 03		16 18		16 33		16 48			17 03		17 18		17 33	
North Dulwich	d	14 51		15 06		15 21		15 36		15 51		16 06		16 21		16 28	16 36		16 51		17 06		17 21
East Dulwich	d	14 53		15 08		15 23		15 38		15 53		16 08		16 23		16 30	16 38		16 53		17 08		17 23
Peckham Rye ■	d	14 56		15 11		15 26		15 41		15 56		16 11		16 26		16 35	16 41		16 56		17 11		17 26
Queens Rd Peckham	d	14 58		15 13		15 28		15 43		15 58		16 13		16 28		16 37	16 43		16 58		17 13		17 28
South Bermondsey	d	15 01		15 16		15 31		15 46		16 01		16 16		16 31		16 40	16 46		17 01		17 16		17 31
London Bridge ■ ⊖	a	15 06		15 21		15 36		15 51		16 06		16 21		16 36		16 45	16 51		17 06		17 21		17 36

A To St Albans City **B** From Caterham **C** From Streatham Hill

Table T173-R

Mondays to Fridays
16 December to 15 May

Tulse Hill, Streatham, North Dulwich, East Dulwich, Peckham Rye, Queens Road Peckham and South Bermondsey - London Bridge

		TL A	SN		TL A	SN B	TL A	SN	TL A	SN	SN B	TL A	SN		TL A	SN	SN	TL A	SN	TL A	SN	SN	TL A		SN
Sutton	d	16 49			17 16		17 19		17 46	17 38		17 49			18 16	18 08	18 00	18 19		18 46	18 38	18 30	18 49		
Carshalton	d				17 19				17 49						18 19					18 49					
Hackbridge	d				17 22				17 52						18 22					18 52					
Mitcham Junction	d				17 25				17 55						18 25					18 55					
Mitcham Eastfields	d				17 28				17 58						18 28					18 58					
Wimbledon	d	17 07					17 37			17 59		18 07				18 29		18 37			18 59		19 07		
Haydons Road	d	17 10					17 40			18 01		18 10				18 31		18 40			19 01		19 10		
Tooting	d	17 13					17 43			18 05		18 13				18 35		18 43			19 05		19 13		
East Croydon	d					17 21					17 51														
Selhurst	d					17 26					17 56						18 26					18 56			
Thornton Heath	d					17 28					17 58						18 28					18 58			
Norbury	d					17 31					18 01						18 31					19 01			
Streatham Common	d					17 36					18 06						18 36					19 06			
Streatham	d	17 18			17 33	17 43	17 48		18 03	18 10	18 13	18 18			18 33	18 40	18 43	18 48		19 03	19 10	19 13	19 18		
Beckenham Junction	d		17 15					17 45					18 15						18 45						19 15
Birkbeck	d		17 18					17 48					18 18						18 48						19 18
Crystal Palace	d		17 23					17 53					18 23						18 53						19 23
Gipsy Hill	d		17 25					17 55					18 25						18 55						19 25
West Norwood	d		17 28					17 58					18 28						18 58						19 28
Tulse Hill	d	17 23	17 32		17 38	17 47	17 53	18 02	18 08	18 14	18 17	18 23	18 32		18 38	18 44	18 47	18 53	19 02	19 08	19 14	19 17	19 23		19 32
Herne Hill	a	17 26			17 41		17 56		18 11			18 26			18 41			18 56		19 11			19 26		
Loughborough Jn	a	17 30			17 45		18 00		18 15			18 30			18 45			19 00		19 15			19 30		
Elephant & Castle	a	17 34			17 49		18 04		18 19			18 34			18 49			19 04		19 19			19 34		
London Blackfriars 3 ⊖	a	17 39			17 54		18 09		18 24			18 39			18 54			19 09		19 24			19 39		
City Thameslink	a	17 41			17 56		18 11		18 26			18 41			18 56			19 11		19 26			19 41		
Farringdon	a	17 43			17 58		18 13		18 28			18 43			18 58			19 13		19 28			19 43		
St Pancras International	a	17 48			18 03		18 18		18 33			18 48			19 03			19 18		19 33			19 48		
North Dulwich	d		17 36			17 51		18 06		18 18	18 21		18 36			18 47	18 51		19 06		19 17	19 21			19 36
East Dulwich	d		17 38			17 53		18 08		18 20	18 23		18 38			18 49	18 53		19 08		19 19	19 23			19 38
Peckham Rye 4	d		17 41			17 56		18 11		18 23	18 26		18 41			18 53	18 56		19 11		19 23	19 26			19 41
Queens Rd Peckham	d		17 43			17 58		18 13		18 25	18 28		18 43			18 55	18 58		19 13		19 25	19 28			19 43
South Bermondsey	d		17 46			18 01		18 16		18 28	18 31		18 46			18 58	19 01		19 16		19 28	19 31			19 46
London Bridge 4 ⊖	a		17 51			18 06		18 21		18 33	18 36		18 51			19 03	19 06		19 21		19 33	19 36			19 51

		TL A	SN	SN	TL A	SN	TL A	SN	TL A		SN	TL A	SN	TL A	SN	TL A	SN B	TL A	SN		TL A	SN B	TL C	SN	TL C
Sutton	d	19 16	19 08	19 00	19 19		19 46		19 49			20 16		20 21		20 46		20 49			21 16		21 19		21 46
Carshalton	d	19 19					19 49					20 19				20 49					21 19				21 49
Hackbridge	d	19 22					19 52					20 22				20 52					21 22				21 52
Mitcham Junction	d	19 25					19 55					20 25				20 55					21 25				21 55
Mitcham Eastfields	d	19 28					19 58					20 28				20 58					21 28				21 58
Wimbledon	d		19 29		19 37				20 07					20 43				21 07					21 37		
Haydons Road	d		19 31		19 40				20 10					20 46				21 10					21 40		
Tooting	d		19 35		19 43				20 13					20 49				21 13					21 43		
East Croydon	d																20 54					21 24			
Selhurst	d			19 26				19 56					20 29				20 58					21 28			
Thornton Heath	d			19 28				19 58					20 31				21 00					21 30			
Norbury	d			19 31				20 01					20 34				21 03					21 33			
Streatham Common	d			19 36				20 06					20 37				21 06					21 37			
Streatham	d	19 33	19 40	19 43	19 48		20 03	20 13	20 18			20 33	20 43	20 54		21 03	21 13	21 18			21 33	21 43	21 48		22 03
Beckenham Junction	d					19 45					20 15				20 45				21 15					21 45	
Birkbeck	d					19 48					20 18				20 48				21 18					21 48	
Crystal Palace	d					19 53					20 23				20 53				21 23					21 53	
Gipsy Hill	d					19 55					20 25				20 55				21 25					21 55	
West Norwood	d					19 58					20 28				20 58				21 28					21 58	
Tulse Hill	d	19 38	19 44	19 47	19 53	20 02	20 08	20 17	20 23		20 32	20 38	20 47	20 59	21 02	21 08	21 17	21 23	21 32		21 38	21 47	21 53	22 02	22 08
Herne Hill	a	19 41			19 56		20 11		20 26			20 41		21 02		21 11		21 26			21 41		21 56		22 11
Loughborough Jn	a	19 45			20 00		20 15		20 30			20 45		21 07		21 15		21 30			21 45		22 00		22 15
Elephant & Castle	a	19 49			20 04		20 19		20 34			20 49		21 11		21 19		21 34			21 49		22 04		22 19
London Blackfriars 3 ⊖	a	19 54			20 09		20 24		20 39			20 54		21 16		21 24		21 39			21 54		22 09		22 24
City Thameslink	a	19 56			20 11		20 26		20 41			20 56		21 18		21 26		21 41			21 56		22 11		22 26
Farringdon	a	19 58			20 13		20 28		20 43			20 58		21 21		21 28		21 43			21 58		22 13		22 28
St Pancras International	a	20 03			20 18		20 33		20 48			21 03		21 25		21 33		21 48			22 03		22 18		22 33
North Dulwich	d		19 47	19 51		20 06		20 21			20 36		20 51		21 06		21 21		21 36			21 51		22 06	
East Dulwich	d		19 49	19 53		20 08		20 23			20 38		20 53		21 08		21 23		21 38			21 53		22 08	
Peckham Rye 4	d		19 53	19 56		20 11		20 26			20 41		20 56		21 11		21 26		21 41			21 56		22 11	
Queens Rd Peckham	d		19 55	19 58		20 13		20 28			20 43		20 58		21 13		21 28		21 43			21 58		22 13	
South Bermondsey	d		19 58	20 01		20 16		20 31			20 46		21 01		21 16		21 31		21 46			22 01		22 16	
London Bridge 4 ⊖	a		20 03	20 07		20 22		20 36			20 51		21 06		21 21		21 36		21 51			22 06		22 21	

A To St Albans City
B From Caterham
C To Bedford

Table T173-R

Mondays to Fridays
16 December to 15 May

Tulse Hill, Streatham, North Dulwich, East Dulwich, Peckham Rye, Queens Road Peckham and South Bermondsey - London Bridge

		SN A	TL B	SN	TL B		SN A	TL B	SN	TL B	SN A	TL B	SN	TL B	TL B
Sutton	d		21 49		22 18			22 19		22 48		22 49		23 18	23 19
Carshalton	d				22 21					22 51				23 21	
Hackbridge	d				22 24					22 54				23 24	
Mitcham Junction	d				22 27					22 57				23 27	
Mitcham Eastfields	d				22 30					23 00				23 30	
Wimbledon	d		22 07					22 41				23 11			23 37
Haydons Road	d		22 10					22 44				23 14			23 40
Tooting	d		22 13					22 47				23 17			23 43
East Croydon	d	21 52					22 22				22 52				
Selhurst	d	21 56					22 26				22 56				
Thornton Heath	d	21 58					22 28				22 58				
Norbury	d	22 01					22 31				23 01				
Streatham Common	d	22 07					22 36				23 06				
Streatham	d	22 13	22 18		22 35		22 43	22 52		23 05	23 13	23 22		23 35	23 48
Beckenham Junction	d			22 15					22 45				23 15		
Birkbeck	d			22 18					22 48				23 18		
Crystal Palace	d			22 23					22 53				23 24		
Gipsy Hill	d			22 25					22 55				23 26		
West Norwood	d			22 28					22 58				23 29		
Tulse Hill	d	22 17	22 23	22 32	22 40		22 47	22 57	23 02	23 10	23 17	23 27	23 33	23 40	23 53
Herne Hill	a		22 26		22 43			23 00		23 13		23 30		23 43	23 56
Loughborough Jn	a		22 30		22 47			23 07		23 17		23 37		23 47	
Elephant & Castle	a		22 34		22 51			23 11		23 21		23 41		23 51	00 03
London Blackfriars 3 ⊖	a		22 39		22 56			23 16		23 26		23 46		00 01	00 08
City Thameslink	a		22 41												
Farringdon	a		22 43		23 03			23 21		23 33		23 53		00 06	00 13
St Pancras International	a		22 48		23 08			23 25		23 37		23 57		00 10	00 17
North Dulwich	d	22 21		22 36			22 51		23 06		23 21		23 37		
East Dulwich	d	22 23		22 38			22 53		23 08		23 23		23 39		
Peckham Rye 4	d	22 26		22 41			22 56		23 11		23 26		23 42		
Queens Rd Peckham	d	22 28		22 43			22 58		23 13		23 28		23 44		
South Bermondsey	d	22 31		22 46			23 01		23 16		23 31		23 47		
London Bridge 4 ⊖	a	22 36		22 51			23 06		23 21		23 36		23 52		

Saturdays
21 December to 16 May

		TL C	TL C	TL C	SN	TL C	SN D	TL C	SN	TL C		SN D	TL C	SN A	TL C	SN	TL C	SN A	TL C	SN		TL C
Sutton	d	05 46	05 49	06 16		06 19		06 46		06 49			07 16		07 19		07 46		07 49			08 16
Carshalton	d	05 49		06 19				06 49					07 19				07 49					08 19
Hackbridge	d	05 52		06 22				06 52					07 22				07 52					08 22
Mitcham Junction	d	05 55		06 25				06 55					07 25				07 55					08 25
Mitcham Eastfields	d	05 58		06 28				06 58					07 28				07 58					08 28
Wimbledon	d		06 07			06 37				07 07					07 37				08 07			
Haydons Road	d		06 10			06 40				07 10					07 40				08 10			
Tooting	d		06 13			06 43				07 13					07 43				08 13			
East Croydon	d													07 23				07 53				
Selhurst	d				06 26				06 56					07 27				07 57				
Thornton Heath	d				06 28				06 58					07 29				07 59				
Norbury	d				06 31				07 01					07 32				08 02				
Streatham Common	d				06 36				07 06					07 36				08 06				
Streatham	d	06 03	06 18	06 33	06 43	06 48		07 03	07 13	07 18			07 33	07 43	07 48		08 03	08 13	08 18			08 33
Beckenham Junction	d															07 45				08 15		
Birkbeck	d															07 48				08 18		
Crystal Palace	d						06 53					07 23				07 53				08 23		
Gipsy Hill	d						06 55					07 25				07 55				08 25		
West Norwood	d						06 58					07 28				07 58				08 28		
Tulse Hill	d	06 08	06 23	06 38	06 47	06 53	07 02	07 08	07 17	07 23		07 32	07 38	07 47	07 53	08 02	08 08	08 17	08 23	08 32		08 38
Herne Hill	a	06 11	06 26	06 41		06 56		07 11		07 26			07 41		07 56		08 11		08 26			08 41
Loughborough Jn	a	06 15	06 30	06 45		07 00		07 15		07 30			07 45		08 00		08 15		08 30			08 45
Elephant & Castle	a	06 19	06 34	06 49		07 04		07 19		07 34			07 49		08 04		08 19		08 34			08 49
London Blackfriars 3 ⊖	a	06 24	06 39	06 54		07 09		07 24		07 39			07 54		08 09		08 24		08 39			08 54
City Thameslink	a																					
Farringdon	a	06 28	06 43	06 58		07 13		07 28		07 43			07 58		08 13		08 28		08 43			08 58
St Pancras International	a	06 33	06 48	07 03		07 18		07 33		07 48			08 03		08 18		08 33		08 48			09 03
North Dulwich	d				06 51		07 06		07 21			07 36		07 51		08 06		08 21		08 36		
East Dulwich	d				06 53		07 08		07 23			07 38		07 53		08 08		08 23		08 38		
Peckham Rye 4	d				06 56		07 11		07 26			07 41		07 56		08 11		08 26		08 41		
Queens Rd Peckham	d				06 58		07 13		07 28			07 43		07 58		08 13		08 28		08 43		
South Bermondsey	d				07 01		07 16		07 31			07 46		08 01		08 16		08 31		08 46		
London Bridge 4 ⊖	a				07 07		07 21		07 37			07 51		08 07		08 21		08 37		08 51		

A From Caterham
B To Bedford
C To St Albans City
D From Norwood Junction

Table T173-R

Saturdays
21 December to 16 May

Tulse Hill, Streatham, North Dulwich, East Dulwich, Peckham Rye, Queens Road Peckham and South Bermondsey - London Bridge

		SN A	TL B	SN	TL B	SN A	TL B	SN	TL B		SN A	TL B	SN	TL B	SN A	TL B	SN	TL B	SN A	TL B	SN	TL B	SN A
Sutton	d		08 19		08 46		08 49		09 16			18 19		18 46		18 49		19 16		19 19		19 46	
Carshalton	d				08 49				09 19					18 49				19 19				19 49	
Hackbridge	d				08 52				09 22					18 52				19 22				19 52	
Mitcham Junction	d				08 55				09 25					18 55				19 25				19 55	
Mitcham Eastfields	d				08 58				09 28					18 58				19 28				19 58	
Wimbledon	d		08 37				09 07					18 37				19 07				19 37			
Haydons Road	d		08 40				09 10					18 40				19 10				19 40			
Tooting	d		08 43				09 13					18 43				19 13				19 43			
East Croydon	d	08 23				08 53					18 23				18 53				19 23				19 54
Selhurst	d	08 27				08 57					18 27				18 57				19 27				19 58
Thornton Heath	d	08 29				08 59					18 29				18 59				19 29				20 00
Norbury	d	08 32				09 02				and at	18 32				19 02				19 32				20 03
Streatham Common	d	08 36				09 06				the same	18 36				19 06				19 36				20 06
Streatham	d	08 43	08 48		09 03	09 13	09 18		09 33	minutes	18 43	18 48		19 03	19 13	19 18		19 33	19 43	19 48		20 03	20 13
Beckenham Junction	d			08 45				09 15		past			18 45				19 15				19 45		
Birkbeck	d			08 48				09 18		each			18 48				19 18				19 48		
Crystal Palace	d			08 53				09 23		hour until			18 53				19 23				19 53		
Gipsy Hill	d			08 55				09 25					18 55				19 25				19 55		
West Norwood	d			08 58				09 28					18 58				19 28				19 58		
Tulse Hill	d	08 47	08 53	09 02	09 08	09 17	09 23	09 32	09 38		18 47	18 53	19 02	19 08	19 17	19 23	19 32	19 38	19 47	19 53	20 02	20 08	20 17
Herne Hill	a		08 56		09 11		09 26		09 41			18 56		19 11		19 26		19 41		19 56		20 11	
Loughborough Jn	a		09 00		09 15		09 30		09 45			19 00		19 15		19 30		19 45		20 00		20 15	
Elephant & Castle	a		09 04		09 19		09 34		09 49			19 04		19 19		19 34		19 49		20 04		20 19	
London Blackfriars 3 ⊖	a		09 09		09 24		09 39		09 54			19 09		19 24		19 39		19 54		20 09		20 24	
City Thameslink	a		09 11		09 26		09 41		09 56			19 11		19 26		19 41		19 56		20 11		20 26	
Farringdon	a		09 13		09 28		09 43		09 58			19 13		19 28		19 43		19 58		20 13		20 28	
St Pancras International	a		09 18		09 33		09 48		10 03			19 18		19 33		19 48		20 03		20 18		20 33	
North Dulwich	d	08 51		09 06		09 21		09 36			18 51		19 06		19 21		19 36		19 51		20 06		20 21
East Dulwich	d	08 53		09 08		09 23		09 38			18 53		19 08		19 23		19 38		19 53		20 08		20 23
Peckham Rye 4	d	08 56		09 11		09 26		09 41			18 56		19 11		19 26		19 41		19 56		20 11		20 26
Queens Rd Peckham	d	08 58		09 13		09 28		09 43			18 58		19 13		19 28		19 43		19 58		20 13		20 28
South Bermondsey	d	09 01		09 16		09 31		09 46			19 01		19 16		19 31		19 46		20 01		20 16		20 31
London Bridge 4 ⊖	a	09 07		09 21		09 37		09 51			19 07		19 21		19 37		19 51		20 07		20 21		20 37

		TL B	SN	TL B	SN A	TL B	SN	TL B	SN A	TL B	SN	TL B	SN A	TL C	SN	TL C	SN A	TL C	SN	TL C	SN A	TL C	SN
Sutton	d	19 49		20 16		20 19		20 46		20 49		21 16		21 19		21 46		21 49		22 18		22 19	
Carshalton	d			20 19				20 49				21 19				21 49				22 21			
Hackbridge	d			20 22				20 52				21 22				21 52				22 24			
Mitcham Junction	d			20 25				20 55				21 25				21 55				22 27			
Mitcham Eastfields	d			20 28				20 58				21 28				21 58				22 30			
Wimbledon	d	20 07				20 37				21 07				21 37				22 07				22 41	
Haydons Road	d	20 10				20 40				21 10				21 40				22 10				22 44	
Tooting	d	20 13				20 43				21 13				21 43				22 13				22 47	
East Croydon	d				20 23				20 53				21 23				21 53				22 23		
Selhurst	d				20 27				20 57				21 27				21 57				22 27		
Thornton Heath	d				20 29				20 59				21 29				21 59				22 29		
Norbury	d				20 32				21 02				21 32				22 02				22 32		
Streatham Common	d				20 36				21 06				21 36				22 06				22 36		
Streatham	d	20 18		20 33	20 43	20 48		21 03	21 13	21 18		21 33	21 43	21 48		22 03	22 13	22 18		22 35	22 43	22 52	
Beckenham Junction	d		20 15				20 45				21 15				21 45				22 15				22 45
Birkbeck	d		20 18				20 48				21 18				21 48				22 18				22 48
Crystal Palace	d		20 23				20 53				21 23				21 53				22 23				22 53
Gipsy Hill	d		20 25				20 55				21 25				21 55				22 25				22 55
West Norwood	d		20 28				20 58				21 28				21 58				22 28				22 58
Tulse Hill	d	20 23	20 32	20 38	20 47	20 53	21 02	21 08	21 17	21 23	21 32	21 38	21 47	21 53	22 02	22 08	22 17	22 23	22 32	22 40	22 47	22 57	23 02
Herne Hill	a	20 26		20 41		20 56		21 11		21 26		21 41		21 56		22 11		22 26		22 43		23 00	
Loughborough Jn	a	20 30		20 45		21 00		21 15		21 30		21 45		22 00		22 15		22 30		22 47		23 07	
Elephant & Castle	a	20 34		20 49		21 04		21 19		21 34		21 49		22 04		22 19		22 34		22 51		23 11	
London Blackfriars 3 ⊖	a	20 39		20 54		21 09		21 24		21 39		21 54		22 09		22 24		22 39		22 59		23 16	
City Thameslink	a	20 41		20 56																			
Farringdon	a	20 43		20 58		21 13		21 28		21 43		21 58		22 13		22 28		22 43		23 03		23 21	
St Pancras International	a	20 48		21 03		21 18		21 33		21 48		22 03		22 18		22 33		22 48		23 08		23 25	
North Dulwich	d		20 36		20 51		21 06		21 21		21 36		21 51		22 06		22 21		22 36		22 51		23 06
East Dulwich	d		20 38		20 53		21 08		21 23		21 38		21 53		22 08		22 23		22 38		22 53		23 08
Peckham Rye 4	d		20 41		20 56		21 11		21 26		21 41		21 56		22 11		22 26		22 41		22 56		23 11
Queens Rd Peckham	d		20 43		20 58		21 13		21 28		21 43		21 58		22 13		22 28		22 43		22 58		23 13
South Bermondsey	d		20 46		21 01		21 16		21 31		21 46		22 01		22 16		22 31		22 46		23 01		23 16
London Bridge 4 ⊖	a		20 51		21 07		21 21		21 37		21 51		22 07		22 22		22 37		22 52		23 07		23 23

A From Caterham
B To St Albans City
C To Bedford

Table T173-R

Saturdays
21 December to 16 May

Tulse Hill, Streatham, North Dulwich, East Dulwich, Peckham Rye, Queens Road Peckham and South Bermondsey - London Bridge

		TL A	SN B	TL A	SN	TL A	SN B	TL A
Sutton	d	22 48		22 49		23 18		23 19
Carshalton	d	22 51				23 21		
Hackbridge	d	22 54				23 24		
Mitcham Junction	d	22 57				23 27		
Mitcham Eastfields	d	23 00				23 30		
Wimbledon	d			23 11				23 37
Haydons Road	d			23 14				23 40
Tooting	d			23 17				23 43
East Croydon	d		22 53				23 23	
Selhurst	d		22 57				23 27	
Thornton Heath	d		22 59				23 29	
Norbury	d		23 02				23 32	
Streatham Common	d		23 06				23 36	
Streatham	d	23 05	23 12	23 22		23 35	23 43	23 48
Beckenham Junction	d				23 15			
Birkbeck	d				23 18			
Crystal Palace	d				23 23			
Gipsy Hill	d				23 25			
West Norwood	d				23 28			
Tulse Hill	d	23 10	23 17	23 27	23 32	23 40	23 47	23 53
Herne Hill	a	23 13		23 30		23 43		23 56
Loughborough Jn	a	23 17		23 37		23 47		
Elephant & Castle	a	23 21		23 41		23 51		00 03
London Blackfriars 3 ⊖	a	23 26		23 46		00 01		00 08
City Thameslink	a							
Farringdon	a	23 31		23 53		00 06		00 13
St Pancras International	a	23 35		23 57		00 10		00 17
North Dulwich	d		23 21		23 36		23 51	
East Dulwich	d		23 23		23 38		23 53	
Peckham Rye 4	d		23 26		23 41		23 56	
Queens Rd Peckham	d		23 28		23 43		23 58	
South Bermondsey	d		23 31		23 46		00 02	
London Bridge 4 ⊖	a		23 37		23 51		00 06	

Sundays
15 December to 10 May

		SN C	SN	SN	SN	SN	SN	SN	SN	SN	SN	SN	SN	TL D	SN	SN	TL D	SN	SN	TL D	SN	TL	SN
Sutton	d													09 09			09 39			10 09		10 40	
Carshalton	d																					10 43	
Hackbridge	d																					10 45	
Mitcham Junction	d																					10 48	
Mitcham Eastfields	d																					10 51	
Wimbledon	d													09 27			09 57			10 27			
Haydons Road	d													09 29			09 59			10 29			
Tooting	d													09 32			10 02			10 32			
East Croydon	d		06 44		07 14		07 44		08 14		08 44		09 14			09 44			10 14				10 44
Selhurst	d		06 47		07 17		07 47		08 17		08 47		09 17			09 47			10 17				10 47
Thornton Heath	d		06 49		07 19		07 49		08 19		08 49		09 19			09 49			10 19				10 49
Norbury	d		06 52		07 22		07 52		08 22		08 52		09 22			09 52			10 22				10 52
Streatham Common	d		06 55		07 25		07 55		08 25		08 55		09 25			09 55			10 25				10 55
Streatham	d		06 59		07 29		07 59		08 29		08 59		09 29	09 37		09 59	10 07		10 29	10 37		10 55	10 59
Beckenham Junction	d																						
Birkbeck	d																						
Crystal Palace	d			07 11		07 41		08 11		08 41		09 11			09 41			10 11			10 41		
Gipsy Hill	d			07 13		07 43		08 13		08 43		09 13			09 43			10 13			10 43		
West Norwood	d			07 16		07 46		08 16		08 46		09 16			09 46			10 16			10 46		
Tulse Hill	d		07 03	07 20	07 33	07 50	08 03	08 20	08 33	08 50	09 03	09 20	09 33	09 41	09 50	10 03	10 11	10 20	10 33	10 41	10 50	10 59	11 03
Herne Hill	a													09 45			10 15			10 45		11 03	
Loughborough Jn	a													09 48			10 18			10 48		11 06	
Elephant & Castle	a													09 52			10 22			10 52		11 10	
London Blackfriars 3 ⊖	a													09 57			10 27			10 57		11 15	
City Thameslink	a																						
Farringdon	a													10 02			10 32			11 02			
St Pancras International	a													10 06			10 36			11 06			
North Dulwich	d		07 06	07 23	07 36	07 53	08 06	08 23	08 36	08 53	09 06	09 23	09 36		09 53	10 06		10 23	10 36		10 53		11 06
East Dulwich	d		07 08	07 25	07 38	07 55	08 08	08 25	08 38	08 55	09 08	09 25	09 38		09 55	10 08		10 25	10 38		10 55		11 08
Peckham Rye 4	d		07 11	07 29	07 42	07 59	08 11	08 29	08 41	08 59	09 11	09 29	09 41		09 59	10 11		10 29	10 41		10 59		11 11
Queens Rd Peckham	d		07 13	07 31	07 44	08 01	08 13	08 31	08 43	09 01	09 13	09 31	09 43		10 01	10 13		10 31	10 43		11 01		11 13
South Bermondsey	d	00 02	07 17	07 33	07 47	08 03	08 17	08 33	08 47	09 03	09 17	09 33	09 47		10 03	10 17		10 33	10 47		11 03		11 17
London Bridge 4 ⊖	a	00 06	07 22	07 39	07 52	08 09	08 22	08 43	08 53	09 09	09 23	09 39	09 52		10 09	10 22		10 39	10 52		11 09		11 22

A To Bedford
B From Caterham
C not 15 December. From Caterham
D To Luton

Table T173-R

Sundays
15 December to 10 May

Tulse Hill, Streatham, North Dulwich, East Dulwich, Peckham Rye, Queens Road Peckham and South Bermondsey - London Bridge

	TL A	SN	TL	SN	TL B	SN	TL A	SN	TL B	SN	TL A		SN	TL B	SN	TL A	SN	TL B	SN	TL A	SN	TL C
Sutton d	10 39		11 10		11 09		11 40		11 39		12 10			20 09		20 40		20 39		21 10		21 09
Carshalton d			11 13				11 43				12 13					20 43				21 13		
Hackbridge d			11 15				11 45				12 15					20 45				21 15		
Mitcham Junction d			11 18				11 48				12 18					20 48				21 18		
Mitcham Eastfields d			11 21				11 51				12 21					20 51				21 21		
Wimbledon d	10 57				11 27				11 57					20 27				20 57				21 27
Haydons Road d	10 59				11 29				11 59					20 29				20 59				21 29
Tooting d	11 02				11 32				12 02					20 32				21 02				21 32
East Croydon d				11 14				11 44					20 14				20 44				21 14	
Selhurst d				11 17				11 47					20 17				20 47				21 17	
Thornton Heath d				11 19				11 49					20 19				20 49				21 19	
Norbury d				11 22				11 52					20 22				20 52				21 22	
Streatham Common d				11 25				11 55				and at the same minutes past each hour until	20 25				20 55				21 25	
Streatham d	11 07		11 25	11 29	11 37		11 55	11 59	12 07		12 25		20 29	20 37		20 55	20 59	21 07		21 25	21 29	21 37
Beckenham Junction d																						
Birkbeck d																						
Crystal Palace d		11 11				11 41				12 11					20 41				21 11			
Gipsy Hill d		11 13				11 43				12 13					20 43				21 13			
West Norwood d		11 16				11 46				12 16					20 46				21 16			
Tulse Hill d	11 11	11 20	11 29	11 33	11 41	11 50	11 59	12 03	12 11	12 20	12 29		20 33	20 41	20 50	20 59	21 03	21 11	21 20	21 29	21 33	21 41
Herne Hill a	11 15		11 33		11 45		12 03		12 15		12 33			20 45		21 03		21 15		21 33		21 45
Loughborough Jn a	11 18		11 36		11 48		12 06		12 18		12 36			20 48		21 06		21 18		21 36		21 48
Elephant & Castle a	11 22		11 40		11 52		12 10		12 22		12 40			20 52		21 10		21 22		21 40		21 52
London Blackfriars 3 ⊖ a	11 27		11 45		11 57		12 15		12 27		12 45			20 57		21 15		21 27		21 45		21 57
City Thameslink a																						
Farringdon a	11 32				12 02		12 20		12 32		12 50			21 02		21 20		21 32		21 50		22 02
St Pancras International a	11 36				12 06		12 24		12 36		12 54			21 06		21 24		21 36		21 54		22 06
North Dulwich d		11 23		11 36		11 53		12 06		12 23			20 36		20 53		21 06		21 23		21 36	
East Dulwich d		11 25		11 38		11 55		12 08		12 25			20 38		20 55		21 08		21 25		21 38	
Peckham Rye 4 d		11 29		11 41		11 59		12 11		12 29			20 41		20 59		21 11		21 29		21 41	
Queens Rd Peckham d		11 31		11 43		12 01		12 13		12 31			20 43		21 01		21 13		21 31		21 43	
South Bermondsey d		11 33		11 47		12 03		12 17		12 33			20 47		21 03		21 17		21 33		21 47	
London Bridge 4 ⊖ a		11 39		11 52		12 09		12 22		12 39			20 52		21 09		21 22		21 39		21 52	

	SN	TL D	SN	TL A	SN	TL	SN		TL C	SN	TL C	SN	SN	SN
Sutton d		21 40		21 39		22 10			22 09		22 40			
Carshalton d		21 43				22 13					22 43			
Hackbridge d		21 45				22 15					22 45			
Mitcham Junction d		21 48				22 18					22 48			
Mitcham Eastfields d		21 51				22 21					22 51			
Wimbledon d				21 57					22 27					
Haydons Road d				21 59					22 29					
Tooting d				22 02					22 32					
East Croydon d			21 44				22 14					22 42		
Selhurst d			21 47				22 17					22 47		
Thornton Heath d			21 49				22 19					22 49		
Norbury d			21 52				22 22					22 52		
Streatham Common d			21 55				22 25					22 56		
Streatham d		21 55	21 59	22 07		22 25	22 29		22 37		22 55	22 59		
Beckenham Junction d														
Birkbeck d														
Crystal Palace d	21 41				22 11					22 41			23 11	23 41
Gipsy Hill d	21 43				22 13					22 43			23 13	23 43
West Norwood d	21 46				22 16					22 46			23 16	23 46
Tulse Hill d	21 50	21 59	22 03	22 11	22 20	22 29	22 33		22 41	22 50	22 59	23 03	23 20	23 50
Herne Hill a		22 03		22 15		22 33			22 45		23 03			
Loughborough Jn a		22 06		22 18		22 36			22 48		23 06			
Elephant & Castle a		22 10		22 22		22 40			22 52		23 10			
London Blackfriars 3 ⊖ a		22 15		22 27		22 45			22 57		23 15			
City Thameslink a														
Farringdon a		22 20		22 32					23 02		23 20			
St Pancras International a		22 24		22 36					23 06		23 24			
North Dulwich d	21 53		22 06		22 23		22 36			22 53		23 06	23 23	23 53
East Dulwich d	21 55		22 08		22 25		22 38			22 55		23 08	23 25	23 55
Peckham Rye 4 d	21 59		22 11		22 29		22 41			22 59		23 12	23 29	23 59
Queens Rd Peckham d	22 01		22 13		22 31		22 43			23 01		23 14	23 31	00 01
South Bermondsey d	22 03		22 17		22 33		22 47			23 03		23 18	23 33	00 04
London Bridge 4 ⊖ a	22 09		22 22		22 39		22 52			23 09		23 23	23 39	00 09

A To Luton
B To St Albans City
C To Bedford
D To West Hampstead Thameslink

NRT DECEMBER 19 EDITION

Table T175-F

Mondays to Fridays
16 December to 15 May

London - Norwood Junction and East Croydon - Summary of Fast Trains

Summary of Fast Trains

	SN MX 1	TL MO 1	TL MX 1	SN 1	SN MX	SN MX	SN MO	SN MX	TL 1		SN MX	TL MO 1	TL MX 1	TL 1	TL 1		TL 1	SN 1	TL		TL 1	SN 1	SN
London Victoria 15 ⊖ d	00 02			00 08			00 12	00 13								and every 30 minutes until		04 35				05 20	
Clapham Junction 10 d	00 09			00 15			00 20	00 21										04 42				05 29	
St Pancras International d									00 21			00 51	00 52	01 32	02 32		04 02		04 32		04 52		
Farringdon 3 ⊖ d									00 26												04 56		
City Thameslink 3 d																					04 58		
London Blackfriars 3 ⊖ d		00 01	00 02						00 31			01 01	01 02	01 40	02 40		04 10		04 40		05 01		
London Bridge 4 ⊖ d					00 10	00 17					00 35												05 34
Norwood Junction 2 a					00 34	00 30					00 59												05 58
East Croydon a	00 23	00 27	00 27	00 30	00 38	00 34	00 43	00 44	00 57		01 13	01 27	01 28	02 06	03 06		04 36	04 57	05 06		05 27	05 41	06 02

	TL 1	SN 1	TL 1	SN 1	SN 1	SN 1		TL 1	TL 1	SN	SN 1	TL 1	SN 1	TL 1	SN	SN 1		TL 1	TL 1	SN 1	SN	SN 1	SN 1	TL 1
London Victoria 15 ⊖ d		05 32		05 39	05 50	05 54				06 02			06 09			06 20					06 32		06 36	
Clapham Junction 10 d		05 42		05 46	05 57	06 01				06 09			06 16			06 27				06 35	06 39		06 43	
St Pancras International d	05 20							05 45	05 50			05 55		06 00				06 15	06 20					06 25
Farringdon 3 ⊖ d	05 24							05 49	05 54			05 59		06 04				06 19	06 24					06 29
City Thameslink 3 d	05 26							05 51	05 56			06 01		06 06				06 21	06 26					06 31
London Blackfriars 3 ⊖ d	05 29							05 54	05 59			06 04		06 09				06 24	06 29					06 34
London Bridge 4 ⊖ d	05 35		05 37					06 00	06 05		06 07	06 11		06 15	06 17			06 30	06 35			06 37		06 41
Norwood Junction 2 a			05 50					06 12										06 42						
East Croydon a	05 48	05 51	05 54	05 55	06 09	06 10		06 16	06 18	06 19	06 21	06 24	06 26	06 28	06 31	06 39		06 46	06 48	06 59	06 49	06 51	06 52	06 54

	SN 1	TL 1		SN	SN 1	TL 1	SN 1	TL 1	TL 1	SN	SN 1	SN 1		TL 1	SN 1	TL 1	SN 1	SN	TL 1	SN 1	TL 1	TL 1		SN 1
London Victoria 15 ⊖ d	06 39				06 46		06 50			07 02		07 06			07 09		07 16			07 20				
Clapham Junction 10 d	06 46				06 53		06 57			07 09		07 13			07 16		07 23			07 27				07 35
St Pancras International d		06 30				06 35		06 45	06 50					06 55		07 00			07 10		07 15	07 20		
Farringdon 3 ⊖ d		06 34				06 39		06 49	06 54					06 59		07 04			07 14		07 19	07 24		
City Thameslink 3 d		06 36				06 41		06 51	06 56					07 01		07 06			07 16		07 21	07 26		
London Blackfriars 3 ⊖ d		06 39				06 44		06 54	06 59					07 04		07 09			07 19		07 24	07 29		
London Bridge 4 ⊖ d		06 45		06 47		06 51		07 00	07 05		07 07			07 11		07 15		07 17	07 25		07 30	07 35		
Norwood Junction 2 a						07 02		07 12													07 42			
East Croydon a	06 56	06 59		07 01	07 02	07 06	07 09	07 16	07 18	07 19	07 21	07 22		07 24	07 27	07 29	07 32	07 32	07 38	07 39	07 46	07 48		08 01

	SN	SN 1	TL 1	SN 1	TL 1	SN 1	SN	TL 1		SN 1	SN 1	TL 1	TL 1	SN 1	SN	SN 1	SN 1	SN		TL 1	SN 1	TL 1	SN 1	SN
London Victoria 15 ⊖ d	07 32	07 36		07 39		07 46				07 50	07 55				08 01		08 06				08 09		08 16	
Clapham Junction 10 d	07 39	07 43		07 46		07 53				07 57	08 02			08 05	08 08		08 13				08 16		08 23	
St Pancras International d			07 25		07 30			07 40				07 45	07 50							07 55		08 00		
Farringdon 3 ⊖ d			07 29		07 34			07 44				07 49	07 54							07 59		08 04		
City Thameslink 3 d			07 31		07 36			07 46				07 51	07 56							08 01		08 06		
London Blackfriars 3 ⊖ d			07 34		07 39			07 49				07 54	07 59							08 04		08 09		
London Bridge 4 ⊖ d			07 41		07 45		07 47	07 55				08 00	08 05			08 07		08 10		08 11		08 15		08 17
Norwood Junction 2 a												08 12						08 36						
East Croydon a	07 49	07 52	07 54	07 57	08 00	08 03	08 03	08 08		08 09	08 11	08 16	08 18	08 31	08 19	08 21	08 22	08 42		08 24	08 27	08 29	08 33	08 33

	TL 1	TL 1	SN 1	SN 1		TL 1	TL 1	SN 1	SN 1	SN 1	SN	TL 1	SN 1	TL 1		SN 1	SN	TL 1	TL 1	SN 1	SN 1	TL 1	TL 1	SN 1
London Victoria 15 ⊖ d			08 20	08 25						08 36			08 39			08 46				08 50	08 55			
Clapham Junction 10 d			08 27	08 32					08 35	08 43			08 46			08 53				08 57	09 02			
St Pancras International d	08 05	08 10				08 15	08 20					08 25		08 30				08 35	08 40			08 45	08 50	
Farringdon 3 ⊖ d	08 09	08 14				08 19	08 24					08 29		08 34				08 39	08 44			08 49	08 54	
City Thameslink 3 d	08 11	08 16				08 21	08 26					08 31		08 36				08 41	08 46			08 51	08 56	
London Blackfriars 3 ⊖ d	08 14	08 19				08 24	08 29					08 34		08 39				08 44	08 49			08 54	08 59	
London Bridge 4 ⊖ d	08 21	08 25				08 30	08 35	08 37			08 40	08 41		08 45			08 47	08 51	08 55			09 00	09 05	09 07
Norwood Junction 2 a	08 32					08 42					09 06							09 02						
East Croydon a	08 36	08 38	08 39	08 41		08 46	08 48	08 51	09 01	08 52	09 12	08 54	08 57	08 58		09 02	09 03	09 06	09 08	09 09	09 11	09 14	09 18	09 21

		SN	SN 1	SN	TL 1	SN 1	TL 1	SN 1	SN	TL 1		TL 1	SN 1	SN 1	TL 1	TL 1	SN 1	SN 1	SN 1	SN		SN	TL 1	SN 1
London Victoria 15 ⊖ d		08 57	09 06			09 09		09 16					09 20	09 25				09 36	09 39					09 46
Clapham Junction 10 d		09 06	09 13			09 16		09 23					09 27	09 32			09 35	09 43	09 46					09 53
St Pancras International d					08 55		09 00			09 05		09 10			09 15	09 20							09 30	
Farringdon 3 ⊖ d					08 59		09 04			09 09		09 14			09 19	09 24							09 34	
City Thameslink 3 d					09 01		09 06			09 11		09 16			09 21	09 26							09 36	
London Blackfriars 3 ⊖ d					09 04		09 09			09 14		09 19			09 24	09 29							09 39	
London Bridge 4 ⊖ d				09 10	09 11		09 15		09 17	09 21		09 25			09 30	09 35				09 40		09 44	09 45	
Norwood Junction 2 a				09 36						09 32										10 06				
East Croydon a		09 30	09 22	09 42	09 24	09 26	09 28	09 32	09 32	09 36		09 38	09 39	09 41	09 44	09 48	10 00	09 52	09 56	10 13		10 24	09 58	10 02

	SN	TL 1	TL 1	SN 1	SN 1	TL 1		TL 1	SN 1	SN 1	SN 1	SN	SN	TL 1	SN	SN 1		TL 1	TL 1	SN 1	SN 1	TL 1	TL 1	SN 1
London Victoria 15 ⊖ d				09 50	09 55					10 06	10 09					10 16				10 20	10 25			
Clapham Junction 10 d				09 57	10 02					10 13	10 16					10 23				10 27	10 32			10 35
St Pancras International d		09 35	09 40			09 45		09 50						10 00				10 05				10 15	10 20	
Farringdon 3 ⊖ d		09 39	09 44			09 49		09 54						10 04				10 09				10 19	10 24	
City Thameslink 3 d		09 41	09 46			09 51		09 56						10 06				10 11				10 21	10 26	
London Blackfriars 3 ⊖ d		09 44	09 49			09 54		09 59						10 09				10 14				10 24	10 29	
London Bridge 4 ⊖ d	09 47	09 51	09 55			10 00		10 05	10 07			10 10	10 14	10 15	10 17			10 21	10 22			10 30	10 35	
Norwood Junction 2 a		10 02										10 36						10 32						
East Croydon a	10 02	10 06	10 08	10 09	10 11	10 14		10 18	10 21	10 22	10 26	10 43	10 54	10 28	10 31	10 32		10 36	10 38	10 39	10 41	10 44	10 48	10 59

London - Norwood Junction and East Croydon - Summary of Fast Trains

Summary of Fast Trains

	SN 1	SN 1	SN	SN	TL 1	SN	SN 1	TL 1		SN 1	SN 1	TL 1	TL 1	SN 1	SN 1	SN 1	SN	SN		TL 1	SN	SN 1	TL 1	SN 1
London Victoria 15 ⊖ d	10 36	10 39					10 46			10 50	10 55				11 06	11 09						11 16		11 20
Clapham Junction 10 d	10 43	10 46					10 53			10 57	11 02				11 13	11 16						11 23		11 27
St Pancras International d					10 30			10 35				10 45	10 50							11 00			11 05	
Farringdon 3 ⊖ d					10 34			10 39				10 49	10 54							11 04			11 09	
City Thameslink 3 d					10 36			10 41				10 51	10 56							11 06			11 11	
London Blackfriars 3 ⊖ d					10 39			10 44				10 54	10 59							11 09			11 14	
London Bridge 4 ⊖ d			10 40	10 44	10 45	10 47		10 51				11 00	11 05	11 07			11 10	11 14		11 15	11 17		11 21	
Norwood Junction 2 a			11 06					11 02									11 36						11 32	
East Croydon a	10 52	10 56	11 13	11 24	10 58	11 01	11 02	11 06		11 09	11 11	11 14	11 18	11 21	11 22	11 26	11 43	11 54		11 28	11 31	11 32	11 36	11 39

	SN 1	TL 1	TL 1	SN 1		SN 1	SN 1	SN	SN	TL 1	SN	SN 1	TL 1	SN 1		SN 1	TL 1	TL 1	SN 1	SN 1	SN 1	SN	SN	TL 1
London Victoria 15 ⊖ d	11 25					11 36	11 39					11 46		11 50		11 55				12 06	12 09			
Clapham Junction 10 d	11 32			11 35		11 43	11 46					11 53		11 57		12 02				12 13	12 16			
St Pancras International d		11 15	11 20							11 30			11 35				11 45	11 50						12 00
Farringdon 3 ⊖ d		11 19	11 24							11 34			11 39				11 49	11 54						12 04
City Thameslink 3 d		11 21	11 26							11 36			11 41				11 51	11 56						12 06
London Blackfriars 3 ⊖ d		11 24	11 29							11 39			11 44				11 54	11 59						12 09
London Bridge 4 ⊖ d		11 30	11 35					11 40	11 44	11 45	11 47		11 51				12 00	12 05	12 07			12 10	12 14	12 15
Norwood Junction 2 a								12 07					12 02									12 36		
East Croydon a	11 41	11 44	11 48	11 59		11 52	11 56	12 13	12 24	11 58	12 01	12 02	12 06	12 09		12 11	12 14	12 18	12 21	12 22	12 26	12 43	12 54	12 28

		SN	SN 1	TL 1	SN 1	SN 1	TL 1	TL 1	SN MW FO 1	SN 1		SN 1	SN	SN	TL 1	SN	SN 1	TL 1	SN 1	SN 1		TL 1	TL 1	SN 1
London Victoria 15 ⊖ d			12 16		12 20	12 25				12 36		12 39					12 46		12 50	12 55				
Clapham Junction 10 d			12 23		12 27	12 32			12 35	12 43		12 46					12 53		12 57	13 02				
St Pancras International d				12 05			12 15	12 20							12 30			12 35				12 45	12 50	
Farringdon 3 ⊖ d				12 09			12 19	12 24							12 34			12 39				12 49	12 54	
City Thameslink 3 d				12 11			12 21	12 26							12 36			12 41				12 51	12 56	
London Blackfriars 3 ⊖ d				12 14			12 24	12 29							12 39			12 44				12 54	12 59	
London Bridge 4 ⊖ d		12 17		12 21			12 30	12 35					12 40	12 44	12 45	12 47		12 51				13 00	13 05	13 07
Norwood Junction 2 a				12 32									13 06					13 02						
East Croydon a		12 31	12 32	12 36	12 39	12 41	12 44	12 48	12 59	12 52		12 56	13 13	13 24	12 58	13 01	13 02	13 06	13 09	13 11		13 14	13 18	13 21

	SN 1	SN 1	SN	SN	TL 1	SN		SN 1	TL 1	SN 1	SN 1	TL 1	TL 1	SN 1	SN 1	SN 1		SN	SN	TL 1	SN	SN 1	TL 1	SN 1
London Victoria 15 ⊖ d	13 06	13 09						13 16		13 20	13 25				13 36	13 39						13 46		13 50
Clapham Junction 10 d	13 13	13 16						13 23		13 27	13 32			13 35	13 43	13 46						13 53		13 57
St Pancras International d					13 00				13 05			13 15	13 20							13 30			13 35	
Farringdon 3 ⊖ d					13 04				13 09			13 19	13 24							13 34			13 39	
City Thameslink 3 d					13 06				13 11			13 21	13 26							13 36			13 41	
London Blackfriars 3 ⊖ d					13 09				13 14			13 24	13 29							13 39			13 44	
London Bridge 4 ⊖ d			13 10	13 14	13 15	13 17			13 21			13 30	13 35					13 40	13 44	13 45	13 47		13 51	
Norwood Junction 2 a			13 36						13 32									14 06					14 02	
East Croydon a	13 22	13 26	13 43	13 54	13 28	13 31		13 32	13 36	13 39	13 41	13 44	13 48	13 59	13 52	13 56		14 13	14 24	13 58	14 01	14 02	14 06	14 09

	SN 1	TL 1		TL 1	SN 1	SN 1	SN 1	SN	SN	TL 1	SN	SN 1		TL 1	SN 1	SN 1	TL 1	TL 1	SN 1	SN 1	SN 1	SN		SN
London Victoria 15 ⊖ d	13 55					14 06	14 09					14 16			14 20	14 25				14 36	14 39			
Clapham Junction 10 d	14 02					14 13	14 16					14 23			14 27	14 32			14 35	14 43	14 46			
St Pancras International d		13 45		13 50						14 00				14 05			14 15	14 20						
Farringdon 3 ⊖ d		13 49		13 54						14 04				14 09			14 19	14 24						
City Thameslink 3 d		13 51		13 56						14 06				14 11			14 21	14 26						
London Blackfriars 3 ⊖ d		13 54		13 59						14 09				14 14			14 24	14 29						
London Bridge 4 ⊖ d		14 00		14 05	14 07			14 10	14 14	14 15	14 17			14 21			14 30	14 35				14 40		14 44
Norwood Junction 2 a								14 36						14 32								15 06		
East Croydon a	14 11	14 14		14 18	14 21	14 22	14 26	14 43	14 54	14 28	14 31	14 32		14 36	14 39	14 41	14 44	14 48	14 59	14 53	14 56	15 13		15 24

	TL 1	SN	SN 1	TL 1	SN 1	SN 1	TL 1	TL 1		SN 1	SN 1	SN 1	SN	SN	TL 1	SN	SN 1	TL 1		SN 1	SN 1	TL 1	TL 1	SN 1
London Victoria 15 ⊖ d			14 46		14 50	14 55					15 06	15 09					15 16			15 20	15 25			
Clapham Junction 10 d			14 53		14 57	15 02					15 13	15 16					15 23			15 27	15 32			15 35
St Pancras International d	14 30			14 35			14 45	14 50							15 00			15 05				15 15	15 20	
Farringdon 3 ⊖ d	14 34			14 39			14 49	14 54							15 04			15 09				15 19	15 24	
City Thameslink 3 d	14 36			14 41			14 51	14 56							15 06			15 11				15 21	15 26	
London Blackfriars 3 ⊖ d	14 39			14 44			14 54	14 59							15 09			15 14				15 24	15 29	
London Bridge 4 ⊖ d	14 45	14 47		14 51			15 00	15 05		15 07			15 10	15 14	15 15	15 17		15 21				15 30	15 35	
Norwood Junction 2 a				15 02									15 36					15 32						
East Croydon a	14 58	15 01	15 02	15 06	15 09	15 11	15 14	15 18		15 21	15 22	15 26	15 43	15 54	15 28	15 31	15 32	15 36		15 39	15 41	15 44	15 48	16 00

	SN 1	SN 1	SN	SN		TL 1	SN 1	SN	TL 1	SN 1	SN 1	TL 1	TL 1	SN 1		SN 1	SN 1	SN 1	TL 1	SN 1	SN	TL 1	SN 1	SN 1
London Victoria 15 ⊖ d	15 36	15 39					15 46			15 50	15 55						16 06	16 09		16 16			16 20	16 25
Clapham Junction 10 d	15 43	15 46					15 53			15 57	16 02					16 05	16 13	16 16		16 23			16 27	16 32
St Pancras International d						15 30			15 35			15 45	15 50						16 00			16 05		
Farringdon 3 ⊖ d						15 34			15 39			15 49	15 54						16 04			16 09		
City Thameslink 3 d						15 36			15 41			15 51	15 56						16 06			16 11		
London Blackfriars 3 ⊖ d						15 39			15 44			15 54	15 59						16 09			16 14		
London Bridge 4 ⊖ d			15 40	15 44		15 45		15 47	15 51			16 00	16 05	16 07					16 15		16 17	16 21		
Norwood Junction 2 a			16 06						16 02													16 32		
East Croydon a	15 52	15 56	16 13	16 24		15 58	16 02	16 02	16 06	16 09	16 11	16 14	16 19	16 21		16 34	16 23	16 26	16 29	16 32	16 32	16 36	16 39	16 41

Table T175-F

Mondays to Fridays

16 December to 15 May

London - Norwood Junction and East Croydon - Summary of Fast Trains

Summary of Fast Trains

	TL 1	TL 1	SN 1	SN	SN 1	SN 1		TL 1	SN 1	TL 1	SN 1	SN	TL 1	TL 1	SN 1	SN 1		TL 1	SN 1	TL 1	SN 1	SN	SN 1	SN 1
London Victoria 15 ⊖ d				16 31		16 36			16 39		16 45				16 50	16 54						17 02		17 06
Clapham Junction 10 d			16 35	16 38		16 43			16 46		16 52				16 57	17 02					17 05	17 09		17 13
St Pancras International d	16 15	16 20						16 25		16 30			16 35	16 40				16 45		16 50				
Farringdon 3 ⊖ d	16 19	16 24						16 29		16 34			16 39	16 44				16 49		16 54				
City Thameslink 3 d	16 21	16 26						16 31		16 36			16 41	16 46				16 51		16 56				
London Blackfriars 3 ⊖ d	16 24	16 29						16 34		16 39			16 44	16 49				16 54		16 59				
London Bridge 4 ⊖ d	16 30	16 35			16 37			16 41		16 45		16 47	16 51	16 55				17 00	17 02	17 05			17 07	
Norwood Junction 2 a													17 02											
East Croydon a	16 44	16 49	17 00	16 49	16 51	16 52		16 54	16 56	16 59	17 01	17 02	17 06	17 08	17 09	17 11		17 14	17 16	17 19	17 30	17 19	17 21	17 22

	TL 1	SN 1		TL 1	SN 1	SN	TL 1	SN 1	SN 1	TL 1	SN 1	TL 1		SN 1	SN	SN 1	SN 1	TL 1	SN 1	TL 1	SN 1	SN		TL 1
London Victoria 15 ⊖ d		17 09			17 15			17 20	17 24						17 32		17 36		17 39		17 45			
Clapham Junction 10 d		17 16			17 22			17 28	17 32					17 35	17 39		17 43		17 46		17 52			
St Pancras International d	16 55			17 00			17 05			17 15		17 20						17 25		17 30				17 35
Farringdon 3 ⊖ d	16 59			17 04			17 09			17 19		17 24						17 29		17 34				17 39
City Thameslink 3 d	17 01			17 06			17 11			17 21		17 26						17 31		17 36				17 41
London Blackfriars 3 ⊖ d	17 04			17 09			17 14			17 24		17 29						17 34		17 39				17 44
London Bridge 4 ⊖ d	17 11			17 15		17 17	17 21			17 30	17 32	17 35				17 37		17 41		17 45		17 47		17 51
Norwood Junction 2 a							17 32																	18 02
East Croydon a	17 24	17 26		17 29	17 31	17 32	17 36	17 39	17 41	17 45	17 46	17 49		18 00	17 49	17 51	17 52	17 54	17 56	17 59	18 01	18 02		18 06

	TL 1	SN 1	SN 1	TL 1	SN 1	TL 1	SN 1	SN		SN 1	SN 1	TL 1	SN 1	TL 1	SN 1	SN	TL 1	SN 1		SN 1	TL 1	SN 1	TL 1	SN 1
London Victoria 15 ⊖ d		17 50	17 54					18 02			18 06		18 09		18 15			18 20		18 24				
Clapham Junction 10 d		17 58	18 02				18 05	18 09			18 13		18 16		18 22			18 27		18 32				18 35
St Pancras International d	17 40			17 45		17 50						17 55		18 00			18 05				18 15		18 20	
Farringdon 3 ⊖ d	17 44			17 49		17 54						17 59		18 04			18 09				18 19		18 24	
City Thameslink 3 d	17 46			17 51		17 56						18 01		18 06			18 11				18 21		18 26	
London Blackfriars 3 ⊖ d	17 49			17 54		17 59						18 04		18 09			18 14				18 24		18 29	
London Bridge 4 ⊖ d	17 55			18 00	18 03	18 05				18 07		18 11		18 15		18 17	18 21				18 30	18 32	18 35	
Norwood Junction 2 a																	18 32							
East Croydon a	18 08	18 09	18 11	18 14	18 16	18 19	18 31	18 19		18 21	18 22	18 24	18 27	18 29	18 31	18 33	18 36	18 39		18 41	18 44	18 46	18 49	19 01

	SN	SN 1	TL 1	SN 1		SN	TL 1	SN 1	SN	TL 1	SN 1	SN 1	TL 1	TL 1		SN 1	SN 1	SN	TL 1	SN 1	SN	TL 1	SN 1	SN
London Victoria 15 ⊖ d	18 32	18 36		18 39				18 45			18 50	18 54					19 06			19 09			19 16	
Clapham Junction 10 d	18 39	18 43		18 46				18 52			18 57	19 02					19 13			19 16			19 23	
St Pancras International d			18 25				18 30			18 35			18 45	18 50					18 55			19 00		
Farringdon 3 ⊖ d			18 29				18 34			18 39			18 49	18 54					18 59			19 04		
City Thameslink 3 d			18 31				18 36			18 41			18 51	18 56					19 01			19 06		
London Blackfriars 3 ⊖ d			18 34				18 39			18 44			18 54	18 59					19 04			19 09		
London Bridge 4 ⊖ d			18 41			18 41	18 45		18 47	18 51			19 00	19 05		19 07		19 10	19 11		19 14	19 15		19 17
Norwood Junction 2 a						19 06				19 02								19 36						
East Croydon a	18 49	18 52	18 54	18 57		19 13	18 59	19 01	19 03	19 06	19 09	19 11	19 14	19 19		19 21	19 22	19 43	19 24	19 27	19 54	19 29	19 32	19 32

		TL 1	SN 1	SN 1	TL 1	TL 1	SN 1	SN 1	SN 1	SN		SN	TL 1	SN 1	SN	TL 1	SN 1	SN 1	TL 1	TL 1		SN 1	SN 1	SN 1
London Victoria 15 ⊖ d			19 20	19 25				19 36	19 39					19 46			19 50	19 55					20 06	20 09
Clapham Junction 10 d			19 27	19 32			19 35	19 43	19 46					19 53			19 57	20 02					20 13	20 16
St Pancras International d		19 05			19 15	19 20							19 30			19 35			19 45	19 50				
Farringdon 3 ⊖ d		19 09			19 19	19 24							19 34			19 39			19 49	19 54				
City Thameslink 3 d		19 11			19 21	19 26							19 36			19 41			19 51	19 56				
London Blackfriars 3 ⊖ d		19 14			19 24	19 29							19 39			19 44			19 54	19 59				
London Bridge 4 ⊖ d		19 21			19 30	19 35				19 40		19 44	19 45		19 47	19 51			20 00	20 05		20 07		
Norwood Junction 2 a		19 32								20 06						20 02								
East Croydon a		19 36	19 39	19 41	19 44	19 48	19 59	19 52	19 57	20 13		20 24	19 58	20 02	20 02	20 06	20 09	20 11	20 14	20 18		20 21	20 22	20 26

	SN	SN	TL 1	SN	SN 1	TL 1		TL 1	SN 1	SN 1	TL 1	TL 1	SN 1	SN 1	SN 1	SN 1		SN	SN	SN	TL 1	TL 1	SN 1	SN 1
London Victoria 15 ⊖ d					20 16				20 20	20 25				20 36	20 39	20 46							20 50	20 55
Clapham Junction 10 d					20 23				20 27	20 32			20 35	20 43	20 46	20 53							20 57	21 02
St Pancras International d			20 00			20 05					20 15	20 20									20 35			
Farringdon 3 ⊖ d			20 04			20 09					20 19	20 24									20 39			
City Thameslink 3 d			20 06			20 11					20 21	20 26									20 41			
London Blackfriars 3 ⊖ d			20 09			20 14					20 24	20 29									20 44			
London Bridge 4 ⊖ d	20 12	20 14	20 15	20 17		20 21		20 22			20 30	20 35						20 40	20 44	20 47	20 51	20 52		
Norwood Junction 2 a	20 36					20 32												21 06			21 02			
East Croydon a	20 43	20 53	20 28	20 31	20 32	20 36		20 38	20 39	20 41	20 44	20 48	20 59	20 52	20 57	21 02		21 13	21 24	21 02	21 06	21 08	21 09	21 11

	TL 1	TL 1		SN 1	SN 1	SN 1	SN	SN	TL 1	SN	SN 1	TL 1		TL 1	SN 1	SN 1	TL 1	TL 1	SN 1	SN 1	SN	SN		SN
London Victoria 15 ⊖ d					21 06	21 09					21 16				21 20	21 25			21 36	21 39				
Clapham Junction 10 d					21 13	21 16					21 23				21 27	21 32			21 43	21 46				
St Pancras International d	20 45	20 50							21 00			21 05					21 15	21 20						
Farringdon 3 ⊖ d	20 49	20 54							21 04			21 09					21 19	21 24						
City Thameslink 3 d	20 51	20 56							21 06			21 11					21 21	21 26						
London Blackfriars 3 ⊖ d	20 54	20 59							21 09			21 14					21 24	21 29						
London Bridge 4 ⊖ d	21 00	21 05		21 07			21 10	21 14	21 15	21 17		21 21		21 22			21 30	21 35			21 40	21 44		21 47
Norwood Junction 2 a							21 36					21 32									22 06			
East Croydon a	21 14	21 21		21 21	21 24	21 27	21 43	21 54	21 28	21 31	21 32	21 36		21 38	21 39	21 41	21 44	21 48	21 52	21 57	22 13	22 24		22 01

Table T175-F

Mondays to Fridays
16 December to 15 May

London - Norwood Junction and East Croydon - Summary of Fast Trains

Summary of Fast Trains

		SN 1	TL 1	SN 1	SN 1		TL 1	TL 1	SN 1	SN 1	SN 1	SN	SN	TL 1	SN		SN 1	TL 1	SN 1	SN 1	TL 1	TL 1	SN 1	SN 1	SN 1
London Victoria 15 ⊖	d	21 46		21 50	21 55					22 06	22 09						22 16		22 20	22 25				22 36	22 39
Clapham Junction 10	d	21 53		21 57	22 02					22 13	22 16						22 23		22 27	22 32			22 35	22 43	22 46
St Pancras International	d		21 35				21 45	21 50						22 00				22 05			22 15	22 20			
Farringdon 3 ⊖	d		21 39				21 49	21 54						22 04				22 09			22 19	22 24			
City Thameslink 3	d		21 41				21 51	21 56						22 06				22 11			22 21	22 26			
London Blackfriars 3 ⊖	d		21 44				21 54	21 59						22 09				22 14			22 24	22 29			
London Bridge 4 ⊖	d		21 51				22 00	22 05	22 07			22 10	22 14	22 15	22 17			22 21			22 30	22 35			
Norwood Junction 2	a		22 02									22 36						22 32							
East Croydon	a	22 02	22 06	22 09	22 11		22 14	22 18	22 21	22 22	22 26	22 43	22 54	22 28	22 31		22 32	22 36	22 39	22 41	22 44	22 48	22 59	22 52	22 56

			SN	SN	SN 1	TL 1	SN 1	SN 1	TL 1	TL 1	SN 1		SN 1	SN 1	SN	TL 1	SN	SN 1	TL 1	SN 1	SN 1		TL 1	TL 1	SN 1
London Victoria 15 ⊖	d				22 46		22 52	22 56					23 06	23 09				23 16		23 22	23 25				23 36
Clapham Junction 10	d				22 53		23 00	23 03					23 13	23 16				23 23		23 29	23 32				23 43
St Pancras International	d					22 35			22 45	22 50						23 00			23 05				23 15	23 22	
Farringdon 3 ⊖	d					22 39			22 49	22 54						23 04			23 10				23 19	23 27	
City Thameslink 3	d					22 41			22 51	22 56															
London Blackfriars 3 ⊖	d					22 44			22 54	22 59						23 09			23 14				23 24	23 31	
London Bridge 4 ⊖	d		22 40	22 47		22 51			23 00	23 05	23 07				23 10	23 15	23 17		23 21				23 30	23 37	
Norwood Junction 2	a		23 06			23 02									23 36				23 32						
East Croydon	a		23 13	23 01	23 02	23 06	23 10	23 12	23 15	23 18	23 21		23 22	23 26	23 47	23 28	23 31	23 32	23 36	23 39	23 41		23 44	23 50	23 58

		SN	SN	SN 1	TL 1
London Victoria 15 ⊖	d			23 53	
Clapham Junction 10	d			23 59	
St Pancras International	d				23 51
Farringdon 3 ⊖	d				23 56
City Thameslink 3	d				
London Blackfriars 3 ⊖	d				00 02
London Bridge 4 ⊖	d	23 40	23 47		
Norwood Junction 2	a	00 06			
East Croydon	a	00 10	00 01	00 14	00 27

Saturdays
21 December to 16 May

		SN 1	TL 1	SN 1	SN	SN	SN	TL 1	SN	TL 1		SN 1	TL 1	SN 1	TL 1	SN 1	TL 1	TL 1	SN 1	TL 1		TL 1	TL 1	SN 1	SN 1
		A		A	A		A		A																
London Victoria 15 ⊖	d	00 02		00 08			00 13					01 10		02 10		03 10			04 10					05 08	05 20
Clapham Junction 10	d	00 09		00 15			00 21					01 17		02 17		03 17			04 17					05 16	05 28
St Pancras International	d							00 21		00 52			01 32		02 32		03 02	03 32		04 02		04 32	04 51		
Farringdon 3 ⊖	d							00 26															04 56		
City Thameslink 3	d																								
London Blackfriars 3 ⊖	d		00 02					00 31		01 02			01 40		02 40		03 10	03 40		04 10		04 40	05 01		
London Bridge 4 ⊖	d				00 10	00 17			00 35																
Norwood Junction 2	a				00 34	00 30			00 59																
East Croydon	a	00 23	00 27	00 30	00 38	00 34	00 44	00 57	01 13	01 28		01 32	02 06	02 32	03 06	03 32	03 36	04 06	04 31	04 36		05 06	05 27	05 31	05 44

		TL 1	SN 1	TL 1	TL 1	SN 1		SN 1	SN 1	SN	SN	TL 1	SN	SN 1	TL 1	TL 1		SN 1	SN 1	SN 1	SN	SN	SN	SN 1	SN 1
London Victoria 15 ⊖	d		05 39					06 06	06 09					06 20					06 36	06 39				06 50	06 55
Clapham Junction 10	d		05 46					06 13	06 16					06 27				06 35	06 43	06 46				06 57	07 02
St Pancras International	d	05 20		05 45	05 50							06 00			06 15	06 20									
Farringdon 3 ⊖	d	05 24		05 49	05 54							06 04			06 19	06 24									
City Thameslink 3	d																								
London Blackfriars 3 ⊖	d	05 29		05 54	05 59							06 09			06 24	06 29									
London Bridge 4 ⊖	d	05 35		06 00	06 05	06 07				06 11	06 14	06 15	06 17		06 30	06 35					06 40	06 44	06 47		
Norwood Junction 2	a									06 37											07 06				
East Croydon	a	05 48	05 56	06 14	06 18	06 21		06 22	06 26	06 43	06 54	06 28	06 32	06 39	06 44	06 48		06 59	06 52	06 56	07 13	07 24	07 01	07 09	07 11

		TL 1		TL 1	SN 1	SN 1	SN 1	SN	SN	TL 1	SN	TL 1		SN 1	SN 1	TL 1	TL 1	SN 1	SN 1	SN 1	SN	SN		SN	SN 1
London Victoria 15 ⊖	d					07 06	07 09							07 20	07 25				07 36	07 39					07 46
Clapham Junction 10	d					07 13	07 16							07 27	07 32			07 35	07 43	07 46					07 53
St Pancras International	d	06 45		06 50						07 00		07 05				07 15	07 20								
Farringdon 3 ⊖	d	06 49		06 54						07 04		07 09				07 19	07 24								
City Thameslink 3	d																								
London Blackfriars 3 ⊖	d	06 54		06 59						07 09		07 14				07 24	07 29								
London Bridge 4 ⊖	d	07 00		07 05	07 07			07 10	07 14	07 15	07 17	07 21				07 30	07 35				07 40	07 44		07 47	
Norwood Junction 2	a							07 36				07 32									08 06				
East Croydon	a	07 14		07 18	07 21	07 22	07 26	07 43	07 54	07 28	07 31	07 36		07 39	07 41	07 44	07 48	07 59	07 52	07 56	08 13	08 24		08 01	08 02

		TL 1	SN 1	SN 1	TL 1	TL 1	SN 1	SN 1		SN 1	SN	SN	TL 1	SN	SN 1	TL 1	SN 1	SN 1		TL 1	TL 1	SN 1	SN 1	SN 1	SN
London Victoria 15 ⊖	d		07 50	07 55				08 06		08 09					08 16		08 20	08 25					08 36	08 39	
Clapham Junction 10	d		07 57	08 02				08 13		08 16					08 23		08 27	08 32				08 35	08 43	08 46	
St Pancras International	d	07 35			07 45	07 50							08 00			08 05				08 15	08 20				
Farringdon 3 ⊖	d	07 39			07 49	07 54							08 04			08 09				08 19	08 24				
City Thameslink 3	d																								
London Blackfriars 3 ⊖	d	07 44			07 54	07 59							08 09			08 14				08 24	08 29				
London Bridge 4 ⊖	d	07 51			08 00	08 05	08 07				08 10	08 14	08 15	08 17		08 21				08 30	08 35				08 40
Norwood Junction 2	a	08 02									08 36					08 32									09 06
East Croydon	a	08 06	08 09	08 11	08 14	08 18	08 21	08 22		08 26	08 43	08 54	08 28	08 31	08 32	08 36	08 39	08 41		08 44	08 48	08 59	08 52	08 56	09 13

A not 16 May

Table T175-F

Saturdays
21 December to 16 May

London - Norwood Junction and East Croydon - Summary of Fast Trains

Summary of Fast Trains

			SN	SN	SN 1	TL 1	SN 1	SN 1	TL 1	TL 1	SN 1	SN 1	SN 1	SN	SN	TL 1	SN	SN 1	TL 1	SN 1	SN 1	TL 1	TL 1	SN 1	SN 1
London Victoria 15 ⊖	d				08 46		08 50	08 55				09 06	09 09					09 16		09 20	09 25				09 36
Clapham Junction 10	d				08 53		08 57	09 02				09 13	09 16					09 23		09 27	09 32			09 35	09 43
St Pancras International	d					08 35			08 45	08 50						09 00			09 05			09 15	09 20		
Farringdon 3 ⊖	d					08 39			08 49	08 54						09 04			09 09			09 19	09 24		
City Thameslink 3	d															09 06			09 11			09 21	09 26		
London Blackfriars 3 ⊖	d					08 44			08 54	08 59						09 09			09 14			09 24	09 29		
London Bridge 4 ⊖	d		08 44	08 47		08 51			09 00	09 05	09 07			09 10	09 14	09 15	09 17		09 21			09 30	09 35		
Norwood Junction 2	a					09 02								09 36					09 32						
East Croydon	a		09 24	09 01	09 02	09 06	09 09	09 11	09 14	09 18	09 21	09 22	09 26	09 43	09 54	09 28	09 31	09 32	09 36	09 39	09 41	09 44	09 48	09 59	09 52

		SN 1	SN	SN	SN	SN 1	TL 1	SN 1	SN 1	TL 1	TL 1		SN 1	SN 1	SN 1	SN	SN	TL 1	SN	SN 1	TL 1	SN 1	SN 1	TL 1
London Victoria 15 ⊖	d	09 39				09 46		09 50	09 55			and at		19 06	19 09					19 16		19 20	19 25	
Clapham Junction 10	d	09 46				09 53		09 57	10 02			the same		19 13	19 16					19 23		19 27	19 32	
St Pancras International	d						09 35			09 45	09 50	minutes						19 00			19 05			19 15
Farringdon 3 ⊖	d						09 39			09 49	09 54	past						19 04			19 09			19 19
City Thameslink 3	d						09 41			09 51	09 56	each						19 06			19 11			19 21
London Blackfriars 3 ⊖	d						09 44			09 54	09 59	hour until						19 09			19 14			19 24
London Bridge 4 ⊖	d		09 40	09 44	09 47		09 51			10 00	10 05		19 07			19 10	19 14	19 15	19 17		19 21			19 30
Norwood Junction 2	a		10 06				10 02									19 36					19 32			
East Croydon	a	09 56	10 13	10 24	10 01	10 02	10 06	10 09	10 11	10 14	10 18		19 21	19 22	19 26	19 43	19 54	19 28	19 31	19 32	19 36	19 39	19 41	19 44

		TL 1	SN 1	SN 1	SN 1	SN	SN	SN	SN 1	TL 1	SN 1	SN 1	TL 1	TL 1		SN 1	SN 1	SN 1	SN	SN	TL 1	SN	SN 1	TL 1
London Victoria 15 ⊖	d			19 36	19 39				19 46		19 50	19 55					20 06	20 09					20 16	
Clapham Junction 10	d		19 35	19 43	19 46				19 53		19 57	20 02					20 13	20 16					20 23	
St Pancras International	d	19 20								19 35			19 45	19 50							20 00			20 05
Farringdon 3 ⊖	d	19 24								19 39			19 49	19 54							20 04			20 09
City Thameslink 3	d	19 26								19 41			19 51	19 56							20 06			20 11
London Blackfriars 3 ⊖	d	19 29								19 44			19 54	19 59							20 09			20 14
London Bridge 4 ⊖	d	19 35				19 40	19 44	19 47		19 51			20 00	20 05		20 07			20 10	20 14	20 15	20 17		20 21
Norwood Junction 2	a					20 06				20 02									20 36					20 32
East Croydon	a	19 48	19 59	19 52	19 56	20 13	20 24	20 01	20 02	20 06	20 09	20 11	20 14	20 18		20 21	20 22	20 26	20 43	20 54	20 28	20 31	20 32	20 36

		SN 1	SN 1	TL 1	TL 1	SN 1	SN 1	SN 1	SN	SN		SN	SN 1	TL 1	SN 1	SN 1	TL 1	TL 1	SN 1	SN 1		SN 1	SN	SN	TL 1
London Victoria 15 ⊖	d	20 20	20 25				20 36	20 39					20 46		20 50	20 55				21 06		21 09			
Clapham Junction 10	d	20 27	20 32			20 35	20 43	20 46					20 53		20 57	21 02				21 13		21 16			
St Pancras International	d			20 15	20 20									20 35			20 45	20 50							21 00
Farringdon 3 ⊖	d			20 19	20 24									20 39			20 49	20 54							21 04
City Thameslink 3	d			20 21	20 26									20 41			20 51	20 56							
London Blackfriars 3 ⊖	d			20 24	20 29									20 44			20 54	20 59							21 09
London Bridge 4 ⊖	d			20 30	20 35				20 40	20 44		20 47		20 51			21 00	21 05	21 07				21 10	21 14	21 15
Norwood Junction 2	a								21 06					21 02									21 36		
East Croydon	a	20 39	20 41	20 44	20 48	20 59	20 52	20 57	21 13	21 24		21 01	21 02	21 06	21 09	21 11	21 14	21 18	21 21	21 22		21 26	21 43	21 54	21 28

		SN	SN 1	TL 1	SN 1	SN 1		TL 1	TL 1	SN 1	SN 1	SN 1	SN	SN	SN	SN 1		TL 1	SN 1	SN 1	TL 1	TL 1	SN 1	SN 1	SN 1
London Victoria 15 ⊖	d		21 16		21 20	21 25					21 36	21 39				21 46			21 50	21 55				22 06	22 09
Clapham Junction 10	d		21 23		21 27	21 32				21 35	21 43	21 46				21 53			21 57	22 02				22 13	22 16
St Pancras International	d			21 05				21 15	21 20									21 35			21 45	21 50			
Farringdon 3 ⊖	d			21 09				21 19	21 24									21 39			21 49	21 54			
City Thameslink 3	d																								
London Blackfriars 3 ⊖	d			21 14				21 24	21 29									21 44			21 54	21 59			
London Bridge 4 ⊖	d	21 17		21 21				21 30	21 35				21 40	21 44	21 47			21 51			22 00	22 05	22 07		
Norwood Junction 2	a			21 32									22 06					22 02							
East Croydon	a	21 31	21 32	21 36	21 39	21 41		21 44	21 48	21 59	21 52	21 56	22 13	22 24	22 01	22 02		22 06	22 09	22 11	22 14	22 18	22 21	22 22	22 26

		SN		SN	TL 1	SN	SN 1	TL 1	SN 1	SN 1	TL 1	TL 1		SN 1	SN 1	SN 1	SN	SN	SN 1	TL 1	SN 1	SN 1		TL 1	TL 1
London Victoria 15 ⊖	d						22 16		22 20	22 25					22 36	22 39			22 46		22 50	22 55			
Clapham Junction 10	d						22 23		22 27	22 32				22 35	22 43	22 46			22 53		22 57	23 02			
St Pancras International	d				22 00			22 05			22 15	22 20								22 35				22 45	22 50
Farringdon 3 ⊖	d				22 04			22 09			22 19	22 24								22 39				22 49	22 54
City Thameslink 3	d																								
London Blackfriars 3 ⊖	d				22 09			22 14			22 24	22 29								22 44				22 54	22 59
London Bridge 4 ⊖	d	22 10		22 14	22 15	22 17		22 21			22 30	22 35					22 40	22 47		22 51				23 00	23 05
Norwood Junction 2	a	22 36						22 32									23 06			23 02					
East Croydon	a	22 43		22 54	22 28	22 31	22 32	22 36	22 39	22 41	22 44	22 48		22 59	22 52	22 56	23 13	23 01	23 02	23 06	23 09	23 11		23 14	23 18

		SN 1	SN 1	SN 1	SN	TL 1	SN	SN 1		TL 1	SN 1	SN 1	TL 1	TL 1	SN 1	SN	SN	SN 1		TL 1
London Victoria 15 ⊖	d		23 06	23 09				23 16			23 20	23 25			23 36			23 53		
Clapham Junction 10	d		23 13	23 16				23 23			23 27	23 32			23 43			23 59		
St Pancras International	d					23 00				23 05			23 15	23 22						23 51
Farringdon 3 ⊖	d					23 04				23 10			23 19	23 27						23 56
City Thameslink 3	d																			
London Blackfriars 3 ⊖	d					23 09				23 14			23 24	23 31						00 01
London Bridge 4 ⊖	d	23 07			23 10	23 15	23 17			23 21			23 30	23 37		23 40	23 47			
Norwood Junction 2	a				23 36					23 32						00 08				
East Croydon	a	23 21	23 22	23 26	23 47	23 28	23 31	23 32		23 36	23 39	23 41	23 44	23 50	23 58	00 17	00 01	00 14		00 27

Table T175-F

Sundays

15 December to 10 May

London - Norwood Junction and East Croydon - Summary of Fast Trains

Summary of Fast Trains

	SN ■	TL ■ A	SN ■	SN	SN		TL ■ A	SN	TL ■ A	SN ■	SN ■	SN ■	SN ■	SN ■	SN ■		SN ■	TL ■	SN ■	SN	TL ■	SN	TL ■	SN ■
London Victoria 15 ⊖ d	00 02		00 08		00 15					01 08	02 08	03 08	04 10	05 02	05 45		06 32		07 02					07 32
Clapham Junction 10 d	00 09		00 15		00 23					01 17	02 17	03 17	04 17	05 10	05 53		06 40		07 10					07 40
St Pancras International d							00 21		00 51															
Farringdon 3 ⊖ d							00 26																	
City Thameslink 3 d																								
London Blackfriars 3 ⊖ d		00 01					00 31		01 01															
London Bridge 4 ⊖ d				00 17				00 35										07 11		07 16	07 19	07 31	07 41	
Norwood Junction 2 a				00 30				00 59													07 31	07 56		
East Croydon a	00 23	00 27	00 31	00 34	00 47		00 57	01 13	01 27	01 32	02 32	03 31	04 31	05 23	06 08		06 53	07 24	07 26	08 00	07 35	08 02	07 54	07 56

	SN ■		SN	SN	TL ■	SN ■	SN	TL ■	SN ■	SN ■	SN		TL ■	SN ■	SN ■	SN ■	SN	SN	SN	TL ■	SN ■		SN	TL ■
London Victoria 15 ⊖ d	07 43					08 02			08 14	08 32				08 46	08 51	08 55	09 05				09 16			
Clapham Junction 10 d	07 51					08 10			08 21	08 40				08 53	08 58	09 02	09 12				09 23			
St Pancras International d																								
Farringdon 3 ⊖ d																								
City Thameslink 3 d																								
London Blackfriars 3 ⊖ d																								
London Bridge 4 ⊖ d			07 46	08 01	08 11		08 16	08 19			08 24		08 41					08 47	08 54	09 11			09 16	09 19
Norwood Junction 2 a				08 26				08 31			08 49								09 19					09 31
East Croydon a	08 08		08 30	08 32	08 24	08 26	08 59	08 35	08 39	08 51	08 55		08 54	09 02	09 08	09 11	09 23	09 29	09 25	09 24	09 32		09 59	09 37

	SN ■	SN ■	SN	TL ■	SN ■	TL ■	SN ■		SN	TL ■	SN ■	SN	TL ■	SN ■	SN	TL ■	SN ■		SN	TL ■	SN ■	SN	TL ■	SN ■
London Victoria 15 ⊖ d	09 21	09 25			09 33		09 46				09 51			09 55	10 05		10 16				10 21			10 25
Clapham Junction 10 d	09 28	09 32			09 40		09 53				09 58			10 02	10 12		10 23				10 28			10 32
St Pancras International d						09 26				09 35			09 41			09 56							10 11	
Farringdon 3 ⊖ d						09 30				09 39			09 45			10 00							10 15	
City Thameslink 3 d																								
London Blackfriars 3 ⊖ d						09 35				09 44			09 50			10 05							10 20	
London Bridge 4 ⊖ d			09 24	09 27		09 41			09 49	09 51		09 54	09 56			10 11			10 19	10 21		10 24	10 26	
Norwood Junction 2 a			09 49							10 03		10 19								10 33		10 49		
East Croydon a	09 38	09 41	09 55	09 41	09 49	09 54	10 02		10 29	10 07	10 08	10 25	10 10	10 11	10 23	10 24	10 32		10 59	10 37	10 38	10 55	10 40	10 41

	SN ■	TL ■	SN ■		SN	TL ■	SN ■	SN	TL ■	SN ■	SN	TL ■	SN ■		SN	TL ■	SN ■	SN	TL ■	SN ■	SN ■	TL ■	SN ■	
London Victoria 15 ⊖ d	10 33		10 46				10 51			10 55	11 05		11 16				11 21			11 25	11 33		11 46	
Clapham Junction 10 d	10 40		10 53				10 58			11 02	11 12		11 23				11 28			11 32	11 40		11 53	
St Pancras International d		10 26				10 35			10 41			10 56							11 11			11 26		
Farringdon 3 ⊖ d		10 30				10 39			10 45			11 00							11 15			11 30		
City Thameslink 3 d																								
London Blackfriars 3 ⊖ d		10 35				10 44			10 50			11 05							11 20			11 35		
London Bridge 4 ⊖ d		10 41			10 49	10 51		10 54	10 56			11 11			11 19	11 21		11 24	11 26			11 41		
Norwood Junction 2 a						11 03		11 19								11 33		11 49						
East Croydon a	10 49	10 54	11 02		11 29	11 07	11 08	11 25	11 10	11 11	11 23	11 24	11 32		11 59	11 37	11 38	11 55	11 40	11 41	11 49	11 54	12 02	

	SN	TL ■	SN ■	SN	TL ■	SN ■	SN	TL ■	SN ■		SN	TL ■	SN ■	SN	TL ■	SN ■	SN ■	TL ■	SN ■		SN	TL ■	SN	TL ■
London Victoria 15 ⊖ d			11 51			11 55	12 05		12 16				12 21			12 25	12 33		12 46					
Clapham Junction 10 d			11 58			12 02	12 12		12 23				12 28			12 32	12 40		12 53					
St Pancras International d		11 35			11 41			11 56							12 11			12 26				12 35		12 41
Farringdon 3 ⊖ d		11 39			11 45			12 00							12 15			12 30				12 39		12 45
City Thameslink 3 d																								
London Blackfriars 3 ⊖ d		11 44			11 50			12 05							12 20			12 35				12 44		12 50
London Bridge 4 ⊖ d	11 49	11 51		11 54	11 56			12 11			12 19	12 21		12 24	12 26			12 41			12 49	12 51	12 54	12 56
Norwood Junction 2 a		12 03		12 20								12 33		12 50								13 03	13 20	
East Croydon a	12 29	12 07	12 08	12 25	12 10	12 11	12 23	12 24	12 32		12 59	12 37	12 38	12 55	12 40	12 41	12 49	12 54	13 02		13 29	13 07	13 25	13 10

	SN ■	SN ■	SN	TL ■	SN ■		SN	TL ■	SN ■	SN	TL ■	SN ■	SN ■	TL ■	SN ■		SN	TL ■	SN ■	SN	TL ■	SN ■	SN	TL ■
London Victoria 15 ⊖ d	12 51	12 55	13 05		13 16				13 21			13 25	13 33		13 46				13 51			13 55	14 05	
Clapham Junction 10 d	12 58	13 02	13 12		13 23				13 28			13 32	13 40		13 53				13 58			14 02	14 12	
St Pancras International d				12 56							13 11			13 26				13 35			13 41			13 56
Farringdon 3 ⊖ d				13 00							13 15			13 30				13 39			13 45			14 00
City Thameslink 3 d																								
London Blackfriars 3 ⊖ d				13 05							13 20			13 35				13 44			13 50			14 05
London Bridge 4 ⊖ d				13 11			13 19	13 21		13 24	13 26			13 41			13 49	13 51		13 54	13 56			14 11
Norwood Junction 2 a								13 33		13 50								14 03		14 20				
East Croydon a	13 11	13 12	13 23	13 24	13 32		13 59	13 37	13 38	13 55	13 40	13 41	13 49	13 54	14 02		14 29	14 07	14 08	14 25	14 10	14 11	14 23	14 24

	SN ■		SN	TL ■	SN ■	SN	TL ■	SN ■	SN ■	TL ■	SN ■		SN	TL ■	SN ■	SN	TL ■	SN ■	SN	TL ■	SN ■		SN	TL ■
London Victoria 15 ⊖ d	14 16				14 21			14 25	14 33		14 46				14 51			14 55	15 05		15 16			
Clapham Junction 10 d	14 23				14 28			14 32	14 40		14 53				14 58			15 02	15 12		15 23			
St Pancras International d							14 11			14 26				14 35			14 41			14 56				
Farringdon 3 ⊖ d							14 15			14 30				14 39			14 45			15 00				
City Thameslink 3 d																								
London Blackfriars 3 ⊖ d							14 20			14 35				14 44			14 50			15 05				
London Bridge 4 ⊖ d			14 19	14 21		14 24	14 26			14 41			14 49	14 51		14 54	14 56			15 11			15 19	15 21
Norwood Junction 2 a				14 33		14 50								15 03		15 20								15 33
East Croydon a	14 32		14 59	14 37	14 38	14 55	14 40	14 41	14 49	14 54	15 02		15 29	15 07	15 08	15 25	15 10	15 11	15 23	15 24	15 32		15 59	15 37

A not 15 December

Table T175-F

Sundays

15 December to 10 May

London - Norwood Junction and East Croydon - Summary of Fast Trains

Summary of Fast Trains

	SN ■	SN	TL ■		SN ■	SN ■	TL ■	SN ■	SN	TL ■	SN	TL ■	SN ■		SN ■	SN	TL ■	SN ■	SN	TL ■	SN ■	SN	TL ■	
London Victoria 15 ⊖ d	15 21				15 25	15 33		15 46					15 51		15 55	16 05		16 16			16 21			
Clapham Junction 10 d	15 28				15 32	15 40		15 53					15 58		16 02	16 12		16 23			16 28			
St Pancras International d			15 11				15 26			15 35		15 41					15 56						16 11	
Farringdon 3 ⊖ d			15 15				15 30			15 39		15 45					16 00						16 15	
City Thameslink 3 d																								
London Blackfriars 3 ⊖ d			15 20				15 35			15 44		15 50					16 05						16 20	
London Bridge 4 ⊖ d		15 24	15 26				15 41		15 49	15 51	15 54	15 56					16 11		16 19	16 21		16 24	16 26	
Norwood Junction 2 a		15 50								16 03	16 20									16 33		16 50		
East Croydon a	15 38	15 55	15 40		15 41	15 49	15 54	16 02	16 29	16 07	16 25	16 10	16 11		16 12	16 23	16 24	16 32	16 59	16 37	16 38	16 55	16 40	

	SN ■	SN ■	TL ■	SN ■	SN	TL ■	SN	TL ■	SN ■		SN ■	SN	TL ■	SN ■	SN	TL ■	SN ■	SN	TL ■	SN ■	SN ■	TL ■	SN ■	SN
London Victoria 15 ⊖ d	16 25	16 33		16 46					16 51		16 55	17 05		17 16			17 21			17 25	17 33		17 46	
Clapham Junction 10 d	16 32	16 40		16 53					16 58		17 02	17 12		17 23			17 28			17 32	17 40		17 53	
St Pancras International d			16 26			16 35		16 41					16 56						17 11			17 26		
Farringdon 3 ⊖ d			16 30			16 39		16 45					17 00						17 15			17 30		
City Thameslink 3 d																								
London Blackfriars 3 ⊖ d			16 35			16 44		16 50					17 05						17 20			17 35		
London Bridge 4 ⊖ d			16 41		16 49	16 51	16 54	16 56					17 11		17 19	17 21		17 24	17 26			17 41		17 49
Norwood Junction 2 a						17 03	17 20									17 33		17 50						
East Croydon a	16 41	16 49	16 54	17 02	17 29	17 07	17 25	17 10	17 11		17 12	17 23	17 24	17 32	17 59	17 37	17 38	17 55	17 40	17 41	17 49	17 54	18 02	18 29

	TL ■	SN ■	SN	TL ■	SN ■		SN	TL ■	SN ■	SN	TL ■	SN ■	SN	TL ■	SN ■	SN ■	TL ■	SN ■	SN	TL ■	SN ■	SN	TL ■
London Victoria 15 ⊖ d		17 51			17 55	and at the same minutes past each hour until	21 05		21 16			21 21			21 25	21 33		21 46			21 51		
Clapham Junction 10 d		17 58			18 02		21 12		21 23			21 28			21 32	21 40		21 53			21 58		
St Pancras International d	17 35			17 41				20 56						21 11			21 26			21 35			21 41
Farringdon 3 ⊖ d	17 39			17 45				21 00						21 15			21 30			21 39			21 45
City Thameslink 3 d																							
London Blackfriars 3 ⊖ d	17 44			17 50				21 05						21 20			21 35			21 44			21 50
London Bridge 4 ⊖ d	17 51		17 54	17 56				21 11		21 19	21 21		21 24	21 26			21 41		21 49	21 51		21 54	21 56
Norwood Junction 2 a	18 03		18 20								21 33		21 50							22 03		22 20	
East Croydon a	18 07	18 08	18 25	18 10	18 11		21 23	21 24	21 32	21 59	21 37	21 38	21 55	21 40	21 41	21 49	21 54	22 02	22 29	22 07	22 08	22 25	22 10

	SN ■		SN	TL ■	SN ■	SN	TL ■	SN ■	SN	TL ■	SN ■		SN ■	TL ■	SN ■	SN	TL ■	SN ■	SN ■	SN	TL ■		SN ■	SN
London Victoria 15 ⊖ d	21 55		22 05		22 16			22 21			22 25		22 33		22 46			22 51	23 05				23 16	
Clapham Junction 10 d	22 02		22 13		22 23			22 28			22 32		22 40		22 53			22 58	23 12				23 23	
St Pancras International d				21 56						22 11				22 26			22 35				22 56			
Farringdon 3 ⊖ d				22 00						22 15				22 30			22 39				23 00			
City Thameslink 3 d																								
London Blackfriars 3 ⊖ d				22 05						22 20				22 35			22 44				23 05			
London Bridge 4 ⊖ d				22 11		22 19	22 21		22 24	22 26				22 41		22 49	22 51			22 54	23 11			23 17
Norwood Junction 2 a							22 33		22 50								23 03			23 20				
East Croydon a	22 11		22 23	22 24	22 32	22 59	22 37	22 38	22 55	22 40	22 41		22 49	22 54	23 02	23 29	23 07	23 08	23 22	23 25	23 24		23 32	00 02

	SN	TL ■	SN ■	TL ■	SN	TL ■
London Victoria 15 ⊖ d			23 32			
Clapham Junction 10 d			23 40			
St Pancras International d		23 26				23 51
Farringdon 3 ⊖ d		23 30				23 56
City Thameslink 3 d						
London Blackfriars 3 ⊖ d		23 35				00 01
London Bridge 4 ⊖ d	23 31	23 41		23 45	23 50	
Norwood Junction 2 a	23 57				00 15	
East Croydon a	00 02	23 54	23 56	23 59	00 19	00 27

Table T175-R

Mondays to Fridays

16 December to 15 May

East Croydon and Norwood Junction - London - Summary of Fast Trains

	SN MO 1	TL MX 1	TL MO 1	SN MX 1	TL MX 1	TL MX 1	TL MO 1	TL 1	TL 1		TL 1	TL 1	TL 1	SN	TL 1	SN 1	SN 1	TL 1	TL 1	SN	SN 1
East Croydon d	00 06	00 09	00 10	00 17	00 23	00 40	00 40	01 10	02 10	and every 30 minutes until	04 10	04 40	05 10	05 20	05 40	05 53	06 00	06 01	06 03	06 08	06 09
Norwood Junction 2 d														05 25					06 08		
London Bridge 4 a													05 24	05 50	05 54			06 15	06 20	06 23	
London Blackfriars 3 a		00 36	00 36		00 49	01 06	01 06	01 36	02 36		04 36	05 06	05 31		06 01			06 21	06 26		
City Thameslink 3 a												05 08	05 33		06 03			06 23	06 28		
Farringdon 3 a		00 41										05 10	05 35		06 05			06 26	06 31		
St Pancras International a		00 45	00 45		00 59	01 13	01 15	01 43	02 43		04 43	05 15	05 40		06 10			06 30	06 35		
Clapham Junction 10 a	00 18			00 33												06 02	06 11				06 20
London Victoria 15 a	00 27			00 41												06 12	06 18				06 27

	SN 1	TL 1	SN	TL ◇1	SN 1	TL 1	SN	TL 1	TL 1	SN 1	SN 1	TL 1	SN 1	TL 1	SN	SN 1	TL 1	SN 1	SN 1	SN	TL 1	TL 1
East Croydon d	06 15	06 16	06 18	06 21	06 24	06 25	06 28	06 31	06 31	06 34	06 38	06 41	06 45	06 46	06 48	06 49	06 51	06 53	06 57	06 58	07 01	07 01
Norwood Junction 2 d									06 37													07 07
London Bridge 4 a		06 30	06 34	06 34		06 40		06 45	06 50		06 53	06 53		07 00	07 04		07 05		07 13		07 15	07 20
London Blackfriars 3 a		06 36		06 41		06 46		06 51	06 56			07 01		07 06			07 11				07 21	07 26
City Thameslink 3 a		06 38		06 43		06 48		06 53	06 58			07 03		07 08			07 13				07 23	07 28
Farringdon 3 a		06 41		06 46		06 51		06 56	07 01			07 06		07 11			07 16				07 26	07 31
St Pancras International a		06 45		06 50		06 55		07 00	07 05			07 10		07 15			07 20				07 30	07 35
Clapham Junction 10 a	06 25				06 33		06 39			06 44			06 55			06 58		07 02		07 10		
London Victoria 15 a	06 32				06 42		06 49			06 52			07 03			07 05		07 12		07 19		

	SN 1	TL 1	SN 1	SN 1	TL 1	SN	SN 1	TL 1	SN 1	TL 1	SN 1	SN	TL 1	TL 1	SN 1	SN 1	SN 1	TL 1	SN 1	SN 1	TL 1	SN
East Croydon d	07 04	07 10	07 10	07 15	07 16	07 18	07 19	07 21	07 24	07 25	07 27	07 28	07 31	07 31	07 34	07 38	07 38	07 40	07 40	07 45	07 46	07 48
Norwood Junction 2 d														07 37								
London Bridge 4 a		07 23			07 30	07 34		07 34		07 40	07 43		07 45	07 50			07 53	07 53			08 00	08 04
London Blackfriars 3 a		07 31			07 36			07 41		07 46			07 51	07 56				08 01			08 06	
City Thameslink 3 a		07 33			07 38			07 43		07 48			07 53	07 58				08 03			08 08	
Farringdon 3 a		07 36			07 41			07 46		07 51			07 56	08 01				08 06			08 11	
St Pancras International a		07 40			07 45			07 50		07 55			08 00	08 05				08 10			08 15	
Clapham Junction 10 a	07 14		07 35	07 25			07 28		07 33			07 40			07 44	07 47			08 05	07 57		
London Victoria 15 a	07 22			07 32			07 35		07 40			07 49			07 52	07 54				08 06		

	SN 1	SN 1	TL 1	SN 1	SN	TL 1	TL 1	SN 1	SN 1	SN 1	TL 1	SN 1	SN 1	TL 1	SN	SN 1	TL 1	SN 1	TL 1	SN 1	SN
East Croydon d	07 52	07 55	07 55	07 57	07 58	08 01	08 01	08 04	08 08	08 08	08 10	08 11	08 15	08 16	08 18	08 20	08 21	08 24	08 25	08 27	08 28
Norwood Junction 2 d							08 07														
London Bridge 4 a			08 10	08 13		08 15	08 20			08 23	08 23			08 30	08 34		08 34		08 40	08 43	
London Blackfriars 3 a			08 16			08 21	08 26				08 31			08 36			08 41		08 46		
City Thameslink 3 a			08 18			08 23	08 28				08 33			08 38			08 43		08 48		
Farringdon 3 a			08 21			08 26	08 31				08 36			08 41			08 46		08 51		
St Pancras International a			08 25			08 30	08 35				08 40			08 45			08 50		08 55		
Clapham Junction 10 a	08 01	08 04			08 10			08 14	08 17			08 35	08 27			08 30		08 33			08 40
London Victoria 15 a	08 09	08 12			08 19			08 22	08 24				08 35			08 37		08 40			08 49

	TL 1	TL 1	SN 1	SN 1	SN 1	SN 1	SN 1	TL 1	SN	SN 1	TL 1	SN 1	TL 1	SN	TL 1	TL 1	SN 1	SN 1	SN 1	SN 1	SN 1	TL 1
East Croydon d	08 31	08 31	08 34	08 38	08 38	08 40	08 45	08 46	08 48	08 50	08 51	08 54	08 55	08 58	09 01	09 01	09 04	09 08	09 09	09 10	09 15	09 16
Norwood Junction 2 d		08 37														09 07						
London Bridge 4 a	08 45	08 50			08 53			09 00	09 04		09 04		09 10		09 15	09 20		09 23				09 30
London Blackfriars 3 a	08 51	08 56						09 06			09 11		09 16		09 21	09 26						09 36
City Thameslink 3 a	08 53	08 58						09 08			09 13		09 18		09 23	09 28						09 38
Farringdon 3 a	08 56	09 01						09 11			09 16		09 21		09 26	09 31						09 41
St Pancras International a	09 00	09 05						09 15			09 20		09 25		09 30	09 35						09 45
Clapham Junction 10 a			08 44	08 47		09 05	08 57			09 00		09 03		09 10			09 14		09 18	09 35	09 25	
London Victoria 15 a			08 52	08 54			09 05			09 08		09 10		09 19			09 24		09 26		09 32	

	SN	SN 1	TL 1	SN	SN 1	TL 1	TL 1	TL 1	SN 1	SN 1	SN 1	TL 1	SN 1	SN	TL 1	SN	SN 1	TL 1	SN 1	TL 1	TL 1
East Croydon d	09 18	09 19	09 21	09 21	09 24	09 25	09 31	09 31	09 34	09 38	09 43	09 45	09 45	09 48	09 51	09 51	09 54	09 54	10 00	10 01	10 03
Norwood Junction 2 d								09 37													10 08
London Bridge 4 a	09 34		09 34	10 06		09 40	09 45	09 50		09 53		10 00		10 04	10 04	10 36		10 11		10 15	10 20
London Blackfriars 3 a			09 41			09 46	09 51	09 56				10 06			10 11					10 21	10 26
City Thameslink 3 a			09 43			09 48	09 53	09 58				10 08			10 13					10 23	10 28
Farringdon 3 a			09 46			09 51	09 56	10 01				10 11			10 16					10 26	10 31
St Pancras International a			09 50			09 55	10 00	10 05				10 15			10 20					10 30	10 35
Clapham Junction 10 a		09 28			09 33				09 44		09 52		09 55				10 03		10 10		
London Victoria 15 a		09 35			09 40				09 52		09 59		10 02				10 11		10 18		

	SN 1	SN 1	TL 1	SN 1	SN	SN 1	TL 1	SN	SN 1	SN 1	TL 1	TL 1	SN 1	SN 1	TL 1	SN 1	SN	SN 1	TL 1	SN	SN 1	SN
East Croydon d	10 10	10 12	10 15	10 15	10 18	10 19	10 21	10 22	10 24	10 30	10 32	10 33	10 38	10 42	10 45	10 45	10 48	10 49	10 51	10 52	10 54	10 57
Norwood Junction 2 d												10 38										11 03
London Bridge 4 a			10 30		10 34		10 34	11 06			10 45	10 50	10 53		11 00		11 04		11 04	11 36		11 31
London Blackfriars 3 a			10 36				10 41				10 51	10 56			11 06				11 11			
City Thameslink 3 a			10 38				10 43				10 53	10 58			11 08				11 13			
Farringdon 3 a			10 41				10 46				10 56	11 01			11 11				11 16			
St Pancras International a			10 45				10 50				11 00	11 05			11 15				11 20			
Clapham Junction 10 a	10 35	10 21		10 25		10 28			10 33	10 40				10 51		10 55		10 58			11 03	
London Victoria 15 a		10 29		10 35		10 39			10 41	10 48				10 59		11 02		11 05			11 11	

NRT DECEMBER 19 EDITION

Table T175-R

Mondays to Fridays

16 December to 15 May

East Croydon and Norwood Junction - London - Summary of Fast Trains

	SN 1	TL 1	TL 1	SN 1	SN 1	TL 1	SN 1	SN	SN 1	TL 1	SN	SN 1	SN	SN 1	TL 1	TL 1	SN 1	SN 1	TL 1	SN 1	SN
East Croydon d	11 00	11 01	11 03	11 10	11 12	11 15	11 15	11 18	11 19	11 21	11 22	11 24	11 27	11 30	11 31	11 33	11 38	11 42	11 45	11 45	11 48
Norwood Junction 2 d			11 08										11 33			11 38					
London Bridge 4 a		11 15	11 20			11 30		11 34		11 34	12 06		12 01		11 45	11 50	11 53		12 00		12 04
London Blackfriars 3 a		11 21	11 26			11 36				11 41					11 51	11 56			12 06		
City Thameslink 3 a		11 23	11 28			11 38				11 43					11 53	11 58			12 08		
Farringdon 3 a		11 26	11 31			11 41				11 46					11 56	12 01			12 11		
St Pancras International a		11 30	11 35			11 45				11 50					12 00	12 05			12 15		
Clapham Junction 10 a	11 10			11 35	11 21		11 25		11 28			11 33		11 40				11 51		11 55	
London Victoria 15 a	11 18				11 29		11 32		11 35			11 41		11 48				11 59		12 02	

	SN 1	TL 1	SN	SN 1	SN	SN 1	TL 1	TL 1	SN 1	SN 1	TL 1	SN 1	SN	SN 1	TL 1	SN	SN 1	SN	SN 1	TL 1	TL 1	SN 1
East Croydon d	11 49	11 51	11 52	11 54	11 57	12 00	12 01	12 03	12 10	12 12	12 15	12 15	12 18	12 19	12 21	12 22	12 24	12 27	12 30	12 31	12 33	12 38
Norwood Junction 2 d					12 03			12 08										12 33			12 38	
London Bridge 4 a		12 04	12 36		12 31		12 15	12 20			12 30		12 34		12 34	13 06		13 01		12 45	12 50	12 53
London Blackfriars 3 a		12 11					12 21	12 26			12 36				12 41					12 51	12 56	
City Thameslink 3 a		12 13					12 23	12 28			12 38				12 43					12 53	12 58	
Farringdon 3 a		12 16					12 26	12 31			12 41				12 46					12 56	13 01	
St Pancras International a		12 20					12 30	12 35			12 45				12 50					13 00	13 05	
Clapham Junction 10 a	11 58			12 03		12 10			12 35	12 22		12 25		12 28			12 33		12 40			
London Victoria 15 a	12 05			12 11		12 18				12 29		12 32		12 35			12 41		12 48			

	SN 1	TL 1	SN 1	SN	SN 1	TL 1	SN	SN 1	SN	SN 1	TL 1	TL 1	SN MW FO 1	SN 1	TL 1	SN 1	SN	SN 1	TL 1	SN	SN 1
East Croydon d	12 42	12 45	12 45	12 48	12 49	12 51	12 52	12 54	12 57	13 00	13 01	13 03	13 10	13 12	13 15	13 15	13 18	13 19	13 21	13 22	13 24
Norwood Junction 2 d									13 03			13 08									
London Bridge 4 a		13 00		13 04		13 04	13 36		13 31		13 15	13 20			13 30		13 34		13 34	14 06	
London Blackfriars 3 a		13 06				13 11					13 21	13 26			13 36				13 41		
City Thameslink 3 a		13 08				13 13					13 23	13 28			13 38				13 43		
Farringdon 3 a		13 11				13 16					13 26	13 31			13 41				13 46		
St Pancras International a		13 15				13 20					13 30	13 35			13 45				13 50		
Clapham Junction 10 a	12 51		12 55		12 58			13 03		13 10			13 35	13 21		13 25		13 28			13 33
London Victoria 15 a	12 59		13 02		13 05			13 11		13 18				13 29		13 32		13 35			13 41

	SN	SN 1	TL 1	TL 1	SN 1	SN 1	TL 1	SN 1	SN	SN 1	TL 1	SN	SN 1	SN	SN 1	TL 1	TL 1	SN 1	SN 1	TL 1	SN 1	SN
East Croydon d	13 27	13 30	13 31	13 33	13 39	13 42	13 45	13 45	13 48	13 49	13 51	13 52	13 54	13 57	14 00	14 01	14 03	14 10	14 12	14 15	14 15	14 18
Norwood Junction 2 d	13 33			13 38										14 03			14 08					
London Bridge 4 a	14 01		13 45	13 50	13 55		14 00		14 04		14 04	14 36		14 31		14 15	14 20			14 30		14 34
London Blackfriars 3 a			13 51	13 56			14 06				14 11					14 21	14 26			14 36		
City Thameslink 3 a			13 53	13 58			14 08				14 13					14 23	14 28			14 38		
Farringdon 3 a			13 56	14 01			14 11				14 16					14 26	14 31			14 41		
St Pancras International a			14 00	14 05			14 15				14 20					14 30	14 35			14 45		
Clapham Junction 10 a		13 40				13 51		13 55		13 58			14 03		14 10			14 35	14 21		14 25	
London Victoria 15 a		13 48				13 59		14 02		14 05			14 11		14 18				14 29		14 32	

	SN 1	TL 1	SN	SN 1	SN	SN 1	TL 1	TL 1	SN 1	SN 1	TL 1	SN 1	SN	SN 1	TL 1	SN	SN 1	SN	SN 1	TL 1	TL 1	SN 1
East Croydon d	14 19	14 21	14 22	14 24	14 27	14 30	14 31	14 33	14 38	14 42	14 45	14 45	14 48	14 49	14 51	14 52	14 54	14 57	15 00	15 01	15 03	15 10
Norwood Junction 2 d					14 33			14 38										15 03			15 08	
London Bridge 4 a		14 34	15 06		15 01		14 45	14 50	14 53		15 00		15 04		15 04	15 36		15 31		15 15	15 20	
London Blackfriars 3 a		14 41					14 51	14 56			15 06				15 11					15 21	15 26	
City Thameslink 3 a		14 43					14 53	14 58			15 08				15 13					15 23	15 28	
Farringdon 3 a		14 46					14 56	15 01			15 11				15 16					15 26	15 31	
St Pancras International a		14 50					15 00	15 05			15 15				15 20					15 30	15 35	
Clapham Junction 10 a	14 28			14 33		14 40				14 51		14 55		14 58			15 03		15 10			15 35
London Victoria 15 a	14 35			14 41		14 48				14 59		15 02		15 05			15 11		15 18			

	SN 1	TL 1	SN 1	SN	SN 1	TL 1	SN	SN 1	SN	SN 1	TL 1	TL 1	SN 1	SN 1	SN 1	TL 1	SN 1	SN	SN 1	TL 1	SN
East Croydon d	15 12	15 15	15 15	15 18	15 19	15 21	15 22	15 24	15 27	15 30	15 31	15 33	15 38	15 42	15 43	15 45	15 46	15 48	15 49	15 51	15 51
Norwood Junction 2 d									15 33			15 38									
London Bridge 4 a		15 30		15 34		15 34	16 06		16 01		15 45	15 50	15 53			16 00		16 04		16 04	16 36
London Blackfriars 3 a		15 36				15 41					15 51	15 56				16 06				16 11	
City Thameslink 3 a		15 38				15 43					15 53	15 58				16 08				16 13	
Farringdon 3 a		15 41				15 46					15 56	16 01				16 11				16 16	
St Pancras International a		15 45				15 50					16 00	16 05				16 15				16 20	
Clapham Junction 10 a	15 21		15 25		15 28			15 33		15 40				15 51	16 04		15 56		15 59		
London Victoria 15 a	15 29		15 32		15 35			15 41		15 49				16 00	→		16 03		16 09		

	SN 1	SN 1	TL 1	SN	SN 1	TL 1	TL 1	SN 1	SN 1	TL 1	SN 1	SN	SN 1	TL 1	SN	SN 1	TL 1	SN	SN 1	TL 1	TL 1	SN 1
East Croydon d	15 54		15 54	15 57	16 00	16 01	16 03	16 10	16 12	16 15	16 15	16 18	16 19	16 21	16 21	16 24	16 24	16 27	16 30	16 31	16 33	16 38
Norwood Junction 2 d				16 04			16 08											16 34			16 38	
London Bridge 4 a			16 10	16 31		16 15	16 20			16 30		16 34		16 34	17 06		16 40	17 01		16 45	16 50	16 54
London Blackfriars 3 a			16 16			16 21	16 26			16 36				16 41			16 46			16 51	16 56	
City Thameslink 3 a			16 18			16 23	16 28			16 38				16 43			16 48			16 53	16 58	
Farringdon 3 a			16 21			16 26	16 31			16 41				16 46			16 51			16 56	17 01	
St Pancras International a		←	16 25			16 30	16 35			16 45				16 50			16 55			17 00	17 05	
Clapham Junction 10 a	16 03	16 04			16 11			16 35	16 21		16 25		16 28			16 33			16 41			
London Victoria 15 a	16 11	16 13			16 19				16 29		16 32		16 35			16 41			16 48			

Table T175-R

East Croydon and Norwood Junction - London - Summary of Fast Trains

Mondays to Fridays

16 December to 15 May

	TL 1	SN 1	SN 1	TL 1	SN 1	SN	SN 1	TL 1	SN	TL 1	SN 1	SN	SN 1	TL 1	TL 1	TL 1	SN 1	SN 1	TL 1	SN 1	SN 1	SN
East Croydon d	16 40	16 40	16 42	16 45	16 45	16 48	16 49	16 51	16 51	16 54	16 56	16 57	17 00	17 01	17 03	17 10	17 10	17 12	17 15	17 15	17 18	17 18
Norwood Junction 2 d												17 04			17 08							
London Bridge 4 ⊖ a	16 54			17 00		17 04		17 04	17 36	17 10		17 31		17 15	17 20	17 23			17 30			17 34
London Blackfriars 3 ⊖ a	17 01			17 06				17 11		17 16				17 21	17 26	17 31			17 36			
City Thameslink 3 a	17 03			17 08				17 13		17 18				17 23	17 28	17 33			17 38			
Farringdon 3 ⊖ a	17 06			17 11				17 16		17 21				17 26	17 31	17 36			17 41			
St Pancras International a	17 10			17 15				17 20		17 25				17 30	17 35	17 40			17 45			
Clapham Junction 10 a		17 05	16 51		16 55		16 58				17 05		17 13				17 35	17 21		17 25	17 28	
London Victoria 15 ⊖ a			16 59		17 02		17 10				17 13		17 21					17 30		17 34	17 35	

	TL 1	SN	SN 1	TL 1	SN 1	TL 1	TL 1	SN 1	TL 1	SN 1	SN 1	TL 1	SN 1	SN 1	SN	TL 1	SN	SN 1	SN 1	TL 1	SN 1	TL 1
East Croydon d	17 21	17 21	17 24	17 25	17 30	17 31	17 33	17 38	17 40	17 40	17 42	17 45	17 45	17 48	17 48	17 51	17 51	17 54		17 55	18 00	18 01
Norwood Junction 2 d							17 38															
London Bridge 4 ⊖ a	17 34	18 06		17 40		17 45	17 50	17 54	17 53			18 00			18 04	18 04	18 36			18 10		18 15
London Blackfriars 3 ⊖ a	17 41			17 46		17 51	17 56		18 01			18 06				18 11				18 16		18 21
City Thameslink 3 a	17 43			17 48		17 53	17 58		18 03			18 08				18 13				18 18		18 23
Farringdon 3 ⊖ a	17 46			17 51		17 56	18 01		18 06			18 11				18 16				18 21		18 26
St Pancras International a	17 50			17 55		18 00	18 05		18 10			18 15				18 20			←	18 25		18 30
Clapham Junction 10 a			17 33		17 40					18 04	17 51		17 55	17 58				18 03	18 04		18 10	
London Victoria 15 ⊖ a			17 41		17 50					→	17 59		18 02	18 05				18 12	18 14		18 18	

	TL 1	SN 1	SN 1	TL 1	SN 1	SN 1	SN	TL 1	SN 1	TL 1	SN 1	TL 1	TL 1	SN 1	SN 1	TL 1	SN 1	SN 1	SN	TL 1	SN 1
East Croydon d	18 03	18 10	18 12	18 15	18 15	18 18	18 18	18 21	18 24	18 25	18 30	18 31	18 33	18 38	18 42	18 45	18 45	18 48	18 48	18 51	18 54
Norwood Junction 2 d	18 08												18 38								
London Bridge 4 ⊖ a	18 20			18 30			18 34	18 34		18 40		18 45	18 50	18 53		19 00			19 04	19 04	
London Blackfriars 3 ⊖ a	18 26			18 36				18 41		18 46		18 51	18 56			19 06				19 11	
City Thameslink 3 a	18 28			18 38				18 43		18 48		18 53	18 58			19 08				19 13	
Farringdon 3 ⊖ a	18 31			18 41				18 46		18 51		18 56	19 01			19 11				19 16	
St Pancras International a	18 35			18 45				18 50		18 55		19 00	19 05			19 15				19 20	
Clapham Junction 10 a		18 35	18 21		18 25	18 28			18 34		18 40				18 51		18 55	18 58			19 03
London Victoria 15 ⊖ a			18 29		18 32	18 35			18 42		18 48				18 59		19 03	19 05			19 11

	TL 1	SN 1	TL 1	TL 1	SN 1	SN 1	SN 1	TL 1	SN 1	SN 1	SN	TL 1	TL 1	SN 1	SN 1	TL 1	TL 1	SN 1	SN 1	TL 1	SN 1	SN
East Croydon d	18 55	19 00	19 01	19 03	19 08	19 10	19 12	19 15	19 15	19 18	19 18	19 21	19 25	19 26	19 30	19 31	19 33	19 38	19 42	19 45	19 45	19 48
Norwood Junction 2 d				19 08													19 38					
London Bridge 4 ⊖ a	19 10		19 15	19 20	19 23			19 30			19 34	19 34	19 40			19 45	19 50	19 53		20 00		20 05
London Blackfriars 3 ⊖ a	19 16		19 21	19 26				19 36				19 41	19 46			19 51	19 56			20 06		
City Thameslink 3 a	19 18		19 23	19 28				19 38				19 43	19 48			19 53	19 58			20 08		
Farringdon 3 ⊖ a	19 21		19 26	19 31				19 41				19 46	19 51			19 56	20 01			20 11		
St Pancras International a	19 25		19 30	19 35				19 45				19 50	19 55			20 00	20 05			20 15		
Clapham Junction 10 a		19 10				19 35	19 21		19 25	19 28				19 35	19 41				19 51		19 55	
London Victoria 15 ⊖ a		19 18					19 29		19 32	19 35				19 43	19 49				19 59		20 02	

	SN 1	TL 1	TL 1	SN 1	SN	SN 1	TL 1	TL 1	SN 1	SN 1	SN 1	TL 1	SN 1	SN	SN 1	TL 1	TL 1	SN 1	SN	SN 1	TL 1
East Croydon d	19 49	19 51	19 52	19 54	19 57	20 00	20 01	20 03	20 08	20 10	20 12	20 15	20 15	20 18	20 19	20 21	20 24	20 26	20 28	20 30	20 33
Norwood Junction 2 d					20 03			20 08											20 33		20 38
London Bridge 4 ⊖ a		20 04	20 12		20 31		20 15	20 20	20 23			20 30		20 34		20 34	20 41		21 01		20 50
London Blackfriars 3 ⊖ a		20 11					20 21	20 26				20 36				20 41					20 56
City Thameslink 3 a		20 13					20 23	20 28				20 38				20 43					20 58
Farringdon 3 ⊖ a		20 16					20 26	20 31				20 41				20 46					21 01
St Pancras International a		20 20					20 30	20 35				20 45				20 50					21 05
Clapham Junction 10 a	19 58			20 04		20 10				20 35	20 21		20 25		20 28			20 35		20 41	
London Victoria 15 ⊖ a	20 05			20 11		20 19					20 30		20 32		20 35			20 43		20 49	

	SN 1	SN 1	TL 1	SN 1	SN	SN 1	TL 1	TL 1	SN 1	SN	SN	SN 1	TL 1	TL 1	SN 1	SN 1	TL 1	SN 1	SN	SN 1	TL 1	SN 1
East Croydon d	20 38	20 43	20 45	20 45	20 48	20 49	20 51	20 52	20 54	20 54	20 57	21 00	21 01	21 03	21 10	21 12	21 15	21 15	21 18	21 19	21 21	21 24
Norwood Junction 2 d											21 03			21 08								
London Bridge 4 ⊖ a	20 54		21 00		21 04		21 04	21 11		21 36	21 31		21 15	21 20			21 30		21 34		21 34	
London Blackfriars 3 ⊖ a			21 06				21 11						21 21	21 26			21 36				21 41	
City Thameslink 3 a			21 08				21 13						21 23	21 28			21 38				21 43	
Farringdon 3 ⊖ a			21 11				21 16						21 26	21 31			21 41				21 46	
St Pancras International a			21 15				21 20						21 30	21 35			21 45				21 50	
Clapham Junction 10 a		20 52		20 58		21 01			21 06			21 12			21 35	21 21		21 25		21 28		21 33
London Victoria 15 ⊖ a		20 59		21 05		21 08			21 13			21 19				21 29		21 32		21 35		21 41

	SN	SN	SN 1	TL 1	SN 1	SN 1	TL 1	SN 1	SN	SN 1	TL 1	SN	SN 1	SN	SN 1	TL 1	TL 1	SN 1	TL 1	SN 1	SN	SN 1
East Croydon d	21 24	21 27	21 30	21 33	21 39	21 42	21 45	21 45	21 48	21 49	21 51	21 52	21 54	21 57	22 00	22 01	22 03	22 12	22 15	22 15	22 18	22 19
Norwood Junction 2 d		21 33		21 38										22 03			22 08					
London Bridge 4 ⊖ a	22 06	22 01		21 50	21 55		22 00		22 04		22 04	22 36		22 31		22 15	22 20		22 30		22 34	
London Blackfriars 3 ⊖ a				21 56			22 06				22 11					22 21	22 26		22 36			
City Thameslink 3 a				21 58			22 08				22 13					22 23	22 28		22 38			
Farringdon 3 ⊖ a				22 01			22 11				22 16					22 26	22 31		22 41			
St Pancras International a				22 05			22 15				22 20					22 30	22 35		22 45			
Clapham Junction 10 a			21 40			21 51		21 55		21 58			22 03		22 10			22 21		22 25		22 28
London Victoria 15 ⊖ a			21 49			21 59		22 02		22 05			22 11		22 18			22 29		22 35		22 37

	TL 1	SN	SN 1	SN	SN 1	SN 1	SN 1	TL 1	SN 1	SN	SN 1	TL 1	SN	SN 1	SN	SN 1	TL 1	SN 1	TL 1	SN 1	SN	SN 1
East Croydon d	22 21	22 22	22 24	22 27	22 30	22 38	22 43	22 45	22 45	22 48	22 49	22 51	22 52	22 54	22 57	23 00	23 01	23 12	23 15	23 15	23 18	23 19
Norwood Junction 2 d				22 33											23 03							
London Bridge 4 ⊖ a	22 34	23 06		23 01		22 53		23 00		23 04		23 04	23 36		23 31		23 15		23 30		23 34	
London Blackfriars 3 ⊖ a	22 41							23 06				23 11					23 21		23 36			
City Thameslink 3 a	22 43																					
Farringdon 3 ⊖ a	22 46							23 11				23 16					23 26		23 41			
St Pancras International a	22 50							23 15				23 20					23 30		23 45			
Clapham Junction 10 a			22 33		22 40		22 52		22 55		22 58			23 03		23 11		23 21		23 25		23 28
London Victoria 15 ⊖ a			22 42		22 49		23 00		23 02		23 05			23 12		23 19		23 30		23 32		23 35

	TL 1	SN 1	SN 1	SN 1	SN 1	TL 1
East Croydon d	23 21	23 30	23 38	23 42	23 45	23 53
Norwood Junction 2 d						
London Bridge 4 ⊖ a	23 34		23 53			
London Blackfriars 3 ⊖ a	23 41					00 18
City Thameslink 3 a						
Farringdon 3 ⊖ a	23 46					00 26
St Pancras International a	23 50					00 30
Clapham Junction 10 a		23 44		23 57	23 59	
London Victoria 15 ⊖ a		23 52		00 05	00 08	

Saturdays

21 December to 16 May

	TL 1	SN 1	TL 1	TL 1	TL 1	TL 1	SN 1	TL 1	TL 1	SN 1	TL 1	TL 1	SN 1	TL 1	TL 1	SN 1	TL 1	SN 1	TL 1	TL 1	SN 1	TL 1
East Croydon d	00 09	00 16	00 23	00 40	01 10	02 10	02 36	02 40	03 10	03 36	03 40	04 10	04 36	04 40	05 10	05 30	05 39	06 00	06 01	06 03	06 10	06 15
Norwood Junction 2 d																				06 08		
London Bridge 4 ⊖ a															05 25		05 54		06 15	06 20		06 30
London Blackfriars 3 ⊖ a	00 36		00 49	01 06	01 36	02 36		03 06	03 36		04 06	04 36		05 06	05 31		06 01		06 21	06 26		06 36
City Thameslink 3 a																						
Farringdon 3 ⊖ a	00 41													05 10	05 36		06 06		06 26	06 31		06 41
St Pancras International a	00 45		00 59	01 13	01 43	02 43		03 13	03 43		04 13	04 43		05 15	05 40		06 10		06 30	06 35		06 45
Clapham Junction 10 a		00 33					02 50			03 50			04 50			05 50		06 10			06 35	
London Victoria 15 ⊖ a		00 41					02 58			03 58			04 58			05 59		06 18				

	SN 1	TL 1	SN 1	TL 1	SN 1	TL 1	SN	SN 1	TL 1	SN 1	SN 1	TL 1	TL 1	SN 1	SN 1	TL 1	SN 1	SN	SN 1	TL 1	SN	SN 1
East Croydon d	06 19	06 21	06 24	06 33	06 42	06 45	06 48	06 49	06 51	06 54	07 00	07 01	07 03	07 10	07 12	07 15	07 15	07 18	07 19	07 21	07 23	07 24
Norwood Junction 2 d				06 38									07 08									
London Bridge 4 ⊖ a		06 34		06 50		07 00	07 05		07 04			07 15	07 20			07 30		07 35		07 34	08 07	
London Blackfriars 3 ⊖ a		06 41		06 56		07 06			07 11			07 21	07 26			07 36				07 41		
City Thameslink 3 a																						
Farringdon 3 ⊖ a		06 46		07 01		07 11			07 16			07 26	07 31			07 41				07 46		
St Pancras International a		06 50		07 05		07 15			07 20			07 30	07 35			07 45				07 50		
Clapham Junction 10 a	06 28		06 33		06 51			06 58		07 03	07 10			07 35	07 21		07 25		07 28			07 33
London Victoria 15 ⊖ a	06 35		06 41		06 59			07 05		07 11	07 18				07 29		07 32		07 35			07 41

	SN	SN 1	TL 1	SN 1	SN 1	TL 1	SN 1	SN	SN 1	TL 1	SN	SN 1	SN	SN 1	TL 1	TL 1	SN 1	SN 1	TL 1	SN 1	SN
East Croydon d	07 27	07 30	07 33	07 37	07 42	07 45	07 45	07 48	07 49	07 51	07 53	07 54	07 57	08 00	08 01	08 03	08 10	08 12	08 15	08 15	08 18
Norwood Junction 2 d	07 33		07 38										08 03			08 08					
London Bridge 4 ⊖ a	08 01		07 50	07 53		08 00		08 05		08 04	08 37		08 31		08 15	08 20			08 30		08 35
London Blackfriars 3 ⊖ a			07 56			08 06				08 11					08 21	08 26			08 36		
City Thameslink 3 a																					
Farringdon 3 ⊖ a			08 01			08 11				08 16					08 26	08 31			08 41		
St Pancras International a			08 05			08 15				08 20					08 30	08 35			08 45		
Clapham Junction 10 a		07 40			07 51		07 55		07 58			08 03		08 10			08 35	08 21		08 25	
London Victoria 15 ⊖ a		07 48			07 59		08 02		08 05			08 11		08 18				08 29		08 32	

	SN 1	TL 1	SN	SN 1	SN	SN 1	TL 1	SN 1	SN 1	TL 1	SN 1	SN	SN 1	TL 1	SN	SN 1	SN	SN 1	TL 1	TL 1	SN 1	SN 1	TL 1	SN 1
East Croydon d	08 19	08 21	08 23	08 24	08 27	08 30	08 33	08 37	08 42	08 45	08 45	08 48	08 49	08 51	08 53	08 54	08 57	09 00	09 01	09 03	09 10	09 12	09 15	09 15
Norwood Junction 2 d					08 33		08 38										09 03			09 08				
London Bridge 4 ⊖ a		08 34	09 07		09 01		08 50	08 53		09 00		09 05		09 04	09 37		09 31		09 15	09 20			09 30	
London Blackfriars 3 ⊖ a		08 41					08 56			09 06				09 11					09 21	09 26			09 36	
City Thameslink 3 a										09 08				09 13					09 23	09 28			09 38	
Farringdon 3 ⊖ a		08 46					09 01			09 11				09 16					09 26	09 31			09 41	
St Pancras International a		08 50					09 05			09 15				09 20					09 30	09 35			09 45	
Clapham Junction 10 a	08 28			08 33		08 40			08 51		08 55		08 58			09 03		09 10			09 35	09 21		09 25
London Victoria 15 ⊖ a	08 35			08 41		08 48			08 59		09 02		09 05			09 11		09 18				09 29		09 32

	SN	SN 1	TL 1	SN	SN 1	SN	SN 1	TL 1		SN 1	SN 1	TL 1	SN 1	SN	SN 1	TL 1	SN	SN 1	SN	SN 1	TL 1	TL 1	SN 1
East Croydon d	09 18	09 19	09 21	09 23	09 24	09 27	09 30	09 33	and at the same minutes past each hour until	12 37	12 42	12 45	12 45	12 48	12 49	12 51	12 53	12 54	12 57	13 00	13 01	13 03	13 10
Norwood Junction 2 d						09 33		09 38											13 03			13 08	
London Bridge 4 ⊖ a	09 35		09 34	10 07		10 01		09 50		12 53		13 00		13 05		13 04	13 37		13 31		13 15	13 20	
London Blackfriars 3 ⊖ a			09 41					09 56				13 06				13 11					13 21	13 26	
City Thameslink 3 a			09 43					09 58				13 08				13 13					13 23	13 28	
Farringdon 3 ⊖ a			09 46					10 01				13 11				13 16					13 26	13 31	
St Pancras International a			09 50					10 05				13 15				13 20					13 30	13 35	
Clapham Junction 10 a		09 28			09 33		09 40				12 51		12 55		12 58			13 03		13 10			13 35
London Victoria 15 ⊖ a		09 35			09 41		09 48				12 59		13 02		13 05			13 11		13 18			

Table T175-R

Saturdays

21 December to 16 May

East Croydon and Norwood Junction - London - Summary of Fast Trains

		SN 1	TL 1	SN 1	SN	SN 1	TL 1	SN	SN	SN	SN 1	TL 1		SN 1	SN 1	TL 1	SN 1	SN	SN 1	TL 1	SN	SN 1		SN	SN 1
East Croydon	d	13 12	13 15	13 15	13 18	13 19	13 21	13 23	13 24	13 27	13 30	13 33		13 37	13 42	13 45	13 45	13 48	13 49	13 51	13 53	13 54		13 57	14 00
Norwood Junction 2	d									13 33		13 38												14 03	
London Bridge 4	a		13 30		13 35		13 34	14 07		14 01		13 50		13 53		14 00		14 05		14 04	14 37			14 31	
London Blackfriars 3	a		13 36				13 41					13 56				14 06				14 11					
City Thameslink 3	a		13 38				13 43					13 58				14 08				14 13					
Farringdon 3	a		13 41				13 46					14 01				14 11				14 16					
St Pancras International	a		13 45				13 50					14 05				14 15				14 20					
Clapham Junction 10	a	13 21		13 25		13 28			13 33		13 40				13 51		13 55		13 58			14 03			14 10
London Victoria 15	a	13 29		13 32		13 35			13 41		13 48				13 59		14 02		14 05			14 11			14 18

		TL 1	TL 1	SN 1	SN 1	TL 1	SN 1	SN		SN 1	TL 1	SN	SN 1	SN	SN 1	TL 1	SN 1	SN 1		TL 1	SN 1	SN	SN 1	TL 1	SN
East Croydon	d	14 01	14 03	14 10	14 12	14 15	14 15	14 18		14 19	14 21	14 23	14 24	14 27	14 30	14 33	14 37	14 42		14 45	14 45	14 48	14 49	14 51	14 53
Norwood Junction 2	d		14 08											14 33		14 38									
London Bridge 4	a	14 15	14 20			14 30		14 35			14 34	15 07		15 01		14 50	14 53			15 00		15 05		15 04	15 37
London Blackfriars 3	a	14 21	14 26			14 36					14 41					14 56				15 06				15 11	
City Thameslink 3	a	14 23	14 28			14 38					14 43					14 58				15 08				15 13	
Farringdon 3	a	14 26	14 31			14 41					14 46					15 01				15 11				15 16	
St Pancras International	a	14 30	14 35			14 45					14 50					15 05				15 15				15 20	
Clapham Junction 10	a			14 35	14 21		14 25			14 28			14 33		14 40			14 51			14 55		14 58		
London Victoria 15	a				14 30		14 32			14 36			14 41		14 48			14 59			15 02		15 05		

		SN 1	SN	SN 1		TL 1	TL 1	SN 1	SN 1	TL 1	SN 1	SN	SN 1	TL 1		SN	SN 1	SN	SN 1	TL 1	SN 1	SN 1	TL 1	SN 1	
East Croydon	d	14 54	14 57	15 00		15 01	15 03	15 10	15 12	15 15	15 15	15 18	15 19	15 21		15 23	15 24	15 27	15 30	15 33	15 37	15 42	15 45	15 45	
Norwood Junction 2	d		15 03				15 08											15 33		15 38					
London Bridge 4	a		15 31			15 15	15 20			15 30		15 35		15 34		16 07		16 01		15 50	15 53		16 00		
London Blackfriars 3	a					15 21	15 26			15 36				15 41						15 56			16 06		
City Thameslink 3	a					15 23	15 28			15 38				15 43						15 58			16 08		
Farringdon 3	a					15 26	15 31			15 41				15 46						16 01			16 11		
St Pancras International	a					15 30	15 35			15 45				15 50						16 05			16 15		
Clapham Junction 10	a	15 03		15 10				15 35	15 21		15 25		15 28				15 33		15 40			15 51		15 55	
London Victoria 15	a	15 11		15 18					15 29		15 32		15 35				15 41		15 48			15 59		16 02	

		SN	SN 1	TL 1	SN	SN 1	SN	SN 1	TL 1	TL 1		SN 1	SN 1	TL 1	SN 1	SN	SN 1	TL 1	SN	SN 1		SN	SN 1	TL 1	SN 1
East Croydon	d	15 48	15 49	15 51	15 53	15 54	15 57	16 00	16 01	16 03		16 10	16 12	16 15	16 15	16 18	16 19	16 21	16 23	16 24		16 27	16 30	16 33	16 37
Norwood Junction 2	d						16 03			16 08												16 33		16 38	
London Bridge 4	a	16 05		16 04	16 37		16 31		16 15	16 20				16 30		16 35		16 34	17 07			17 01		16 50	16 53
London Blackfriars 3	a			16 11					16 21	16 26				16 36				16 41						16 56	
City Thameslink 3	a			16 13					16 23	16 28				16 38				16 43						16 58	
Farringdon 3	a			16 16					16 26	16 31				16 41				16 46						17 01	
St Pancras International	a			16 20					16 30	16 35				16 45				16 50						17 05	
Clapham Junction 10	a		15 58			16 03		16 10				16 35	16 21		16 25		16 28			16 33			16 40		
London Victoria 15	a		16 05			16 11		16 18					16 29		16 32		16 35			16 41			16 48		

		SN 1	TL 1	SN 1	SN	SN 1		TL 1	SN	SN 1	SN	SN 1	TL 1	TL 1	SN 1	SN 1		TL 1	SN 1	SN	SN 1	TL 1	SN	SN 1	SN
East Croydon	d	16 42	16 45	16 45	16 48	16 49		16 51	16 53	16 56	16 57	17 00	17 01	17 03	17 10	17 12		17 15	17 15	17 18	17 19	17 21	17 23	17 24	17 27
Norwood Junction 2	d										17 03			17 08											17 33
London Bridge 4	a		17 00		17 05			17 04	17 37		17 31		17 15	17 20				17 30		17 35		17 34	18 07		18 01
London Blackfriars 3	a		17 06					17 11					17 21	17 26				17 36				17 41			
City Thameslink 3	a		17 08					17 13					17 23	17 28				17 38				17 43			
Farringdon 3	a		17 11					17 16					17 26	17 31				17 41				17 46			
St Pancras International	a		17 15					17 20					17 30	17 35				17 45				17 50			
Clapham Junction 10	a	16 51		16 55		16 58				17 05		17 11			17 35	17 21			17 25		17 28			17 33	
London Victoria 15	a	16 59		17 02		17 05				17 13		17 19				17 29			17 32		17 35			17 41	

		SN 1		TL 1	SN 1	SN 1	TL 1	SN 1	SN	SN 1	TL 1	SN		SN 1	SN	SN 1	TL 1	TL 1	SN 1	SN 1	TL 1	SN 1		SN	SN 1
East Croydon	d	17 30		17 33	17 37	17 42	17 45	17 45	17 48	17 49	17 51	17 53		17 54	17 57	18 00	18 01	18 03	18 09	18 12	18 15	18 15		18 18	18 19
Norwood Junction 2	d			17 38											18 03			18 08							
London Bridge 4	a			17 50	17 53		18 00		18 05		18 04	18 37			18 31		18 15	18 20			18 30			18 35	
London Blackfriars 3	a			17 56			18 06				18 11						18 21	18 26			18 36				
City Thameslink 3	a			17 58			18 08				18 13						18 23	18 28			18 38				
Farringdon 3	a			18 01			18 11				18 16						18 26	18 31			18 41				
St Pancras International	a			18 05			18 15				18 20						18 30	18 35			18 45				
Clapham Junction 10	a	17 40				17 51		17 55		17 58				18 03		18 10			18 35	18 21		18 25			18 28
London Victoria 15	a	17 48				17 59		18 02		18 05				18 11		18 18				18 29		18 32			18 35

		TL 1	SN	SN 1	SN	SN 1	TL 1	SN 1		SN 1	TL 1	SN 1	SN	SN 1	TL 1	SN	SN 1	SN		SN 1	TL 1	TL 1	SN 1	SN 1	TL 1
East Croydon	d	18 21	18 23	18 24	18 27	18 30	18 33	18 37		18 42	18 45	18 45	18 48	18 49	18 51	18 53	18 54	18 57		19 00	19 01	19 03	19 10	19 12	19 15
Norwood Junction 2	d				18 33		18 38											19 03				19 08			
London Bridge 4	a	18 34	19 07		19 01		18 50	18 53			19 00		19 05		19 04	19 37		19 31			19 15	19 20			19 30
London Blackfriars 3	a	18 41					18 56				19 06				19 11						19 21	19 26			19 36
City Thameslink 3	a	18 43					18 58				19 08				19 13						19 23	19 28			19 38
Farringdon 3	a	18 46					19 01				19 11				19 16						19 26	19 31			19 41
St Pancras International	a	18 50					19 05				19 15				19 20						19 30	19 35			19 45
Clapham Junction 10	a			18 33		18 40				18 51		18 55		18 58			19 03			19 10			19 35	19 21	
London Victoria 15	a			18 41		18 48				18 59		19 02		19 05			19 11			19 18				19 29	

Table T175-R

Saturdays

21 December to 16 May

East Croydon and Norwood Junction - London - Summary of Fast Trains

		SN 1	SN	SN 1	TL 1	SN	SN 1	SN	SN 1	TL 1		SN 1	SN 1	TL 1	SN 1	SN	SN 1	TL 1	SN 1	SN		SN	SN 1	TL 1	TL 1
East Croydon	d	19 15	19 18	19 19	19 21	19 23	19 24	19 27	19 30	19 33		19 37	19 42	19 45	19 45	19 48	19 49	19 51	19 54	19 54		19 57	20 00	20 01	20 03
Norwood Junction 2	d							19 33		19 38												20 03			20 08
London Bridge 4	a		19 35		19 34	20 07		20 01		19 50		19 53		20 00		20 05		20 04		20 37		20 31		20 15	20 20
London Blackfriars 3	a				19 41					19 56				20 06				20 11						20 21	20 26
City Thameslink 3	a				19 43					19 58				20 08				20 13						20 23	20 28
Farringdon 3	a				19 46					20 01				20 11				20 16						20 26	20 31
St Pancras International	a				19 50					20 05				20 15				20 20						20 30	20 35
Clapham Junction 10	a	19 25		19 28			19 33		19 40				19 51		19 55		19 58		20 03				20 10		
London Victoria 15	a	19 32		19 35			19 41		19 48				19 59		20 02		20 05		20 11				20 18		

		SN 1	SN 1	TL 1	SN 1	SN		SN 1	TL 1	SN	SN 1	SN	SN 1	TL 1	SN 1	SN 1		TL 1	SN 1	SN	SN 1	TL 1	SN	SN 1	SN
East Croydon	d	20 10	20 12	20 15	20 15	20 18		20 19	20 21	20 23	20 24	20 27	20 30	20 33	20 37	20 42		20 45	20 45	20 48	20 49	20 51	20 53	20 54	20 57
Norwood Junction 2	d											20 33		20 38											21 03
London Bridge 4	a			20 30		20 35			20 34	21 07		21 01		20 50	20 53			21 00		21 05		21 04	21 37		21 31
London Blackfriars 3	a			20 36					20 41					20 56				21 06				21 11			
City Thameslink 3	a			20 38					20 43					20 58											
Farringdon 3	a			20 41					20 46					21 01				21 11				21 16			
St Pancras International	a			20 45					20 50					21 05				21 15				21 20			
Clapham Junction 10	a	20 35	20 21		20 25			20 28			20 33		20 40			20 51			20 55		20 58			21 03	
London Victoria 15	a		20 29		20 32			20 35			20 41		20 48			20 59			21 02		21 05			21 11	

		SN 1		TL 1	TL 1	SN 1	SN 1	TL 1	SN 1	SN	SN 1	TL 1		SN	SN 1	SN	SN 1	TL 1	SN 1	SN 1	TL 1	SN 1		SN	SN 1
East Croydon	d	21 00		21 01	21 03	21 10	21 12	21 15	21 15	21 18	21 19	21 21		21 23	21 24	21 27	21 30	21 33	21 37	21 42	21 45	21 45		21 48	21 49
Norwood Junction 2	d				21 08											21 33		21 38							
London Bridge 4	a			21 15	21 20			21 30		21 35		21 34		22 07		22 01		21 50	21 53		22 00			22 05	
London Blackfriars 3	a			21 21	21 26			21 36				21 41						21 56			22 06				
City Thameslink 3	a																								
Farringdon 3	a			21 26	21 31			21 41				21 46						22 01			22 11				
St Pancras International	a			21 30	21 35			21 45				21 50						22 05			22 15				
Clapham Junction 10	a	21 10				21 35	21 21		21 25		21 28				21 33		21 40			21 51		21 55			21 58
London Victoria 15	a	21 18					21 29		21 32		21 35				21 41		21 48			21 59		22 02			22 05

		TL 1	SN	SN 1	SN	SN 1	TL 1	TL 1		SN 1	SN 1	SN 1	TL 1	SN	SN 1	TL 1	SN	SN 1		SN	SN 1	SN 1	SN 1	SN 1	TL 1
East Croydon	d	21 51	21 53	21 54	21 57	22 00	22 01	22 03		22 10	22 12	22 15	22 16	22 18	22 19	22 21	22 23	22 24		22 27	22 30	22 37	22 43	22 45	22 46
Norwood Junction 2	d				22 03			22 08												22 33					
London Bridge 4	a	22 04	22 37		22 31		22 15	22 20					22 30	22 35		22 34	23 07			23 01		22 54			23 00
London Blackfriars 3	a	22 11					22 21	22 26					22 36			22 41									23 06
City Thameslink 3	a																								
Farringdon 3	a	22 16					22 26	22 31					22 41			22 46									23 11
St Pancras International	a	22 20					22 30	22 35					22 45			22 50									23 15
Clapham Junction 10	a			22 03		22 10				22 35	22 21	22 25			22 28			22 33			22 40		22 52	22 55	
London Victoria 15	a			22 11		22 18					22 28	22 32			22 35			22 41			22 48		23 00	23 02	

		SN	SN 1	TL 1		SN	SN 1	SN	SN 1	TL 1	SN 1	TL 1	SN 1	SN		SN 1	TL 1	SN	SN 1	SN 1	SN 1	SN	TL 1		
East Croydon	d	22 48	22 49	22 51		22 53	22 54	22 57	23 00	23 01	23 12	23 15	23 15	23 18		23 19	23 21	23 23	23 30	23 38	23 45	23 48	23 53		
Norwood Junction 2	d							23 03														23 53			
London Bridge 4	a	23 05		23 04		23 37		23 31		23 15		23 30		23 35			23 34	00 06		23 53		00 06			
London Blackfriars 3	a			23 11						23 21		23 36					23 41						00 19		
City Thameslink 3	a																								
Farringdon 3	a			23 16						23 26		23 41					23 46						00 26		
St Pancras International	a			23 20						23 30		23 45					23 50						00 30		
Clapham Junction 10	a		22 58				23 04		23 10		23 21		23 25			23 28			23 41		00 04				
London Victoria 15	a		23 05				23 11		23 18		23 29		23 32			23 35			23 50		00 12				

Sundays

15 December to 10 May

		TL 1 A	SN 1 A	TL 1 A	TL 1 A	TL 1	SN 1	SN 1	SN 1	SN 1		TL 1	TL 1	SN	SN 1	TL 1	SN	SN 1	SN	TL 1		TL 1	SN	SN 1	SN
East Croydon	d	00 10	00 16	00 23	00 40	01 10	02 36	03 37	04 36	05 30		06 34	06 41	06 44	06 51	07 10	07 14	07 23	07 29	07 32		07 40	07 44	07 51	07 59
Norwood Junction 2	d											06 38							07 35	07 36					08 06
London Bridge 4	a											06 52	06 56	07 22		07 25	07 52		08 05	07 50		07 55	08 22		08 36
London Blackfriars 3	a	00 36		00 49	01 06	01 36																			
City Thameslink 3	a																								
Farringdon 3	a	00 41																							
St Pancras International	a	00 45		00 59	01 15	01 43																			
Clapham Junction 10	a		00 33				02 49	03 50	04 49	05 51					07 05			07 37						08 07	
London Victoria 15	a		00 41				02 58	03 58	04 58	05 59					07 15			07 46						08 17	

		TL 1	SN	SN 1	SN	TL 1		TL 1	SN	SN 1	SN 1	SN 1	SN	TL 1	TL 1	SN 1		SN	SN 1	TL 1	SN 1	SN	SN	TL 1	TL 1
East Croydon	d	08 10	08 14	08 23	08 29	08 32		08 40	08 44	08 46	08 51	08 59	08 59	09 02	09 07	09 11		09 14	09 15	09 18	09 21	09 30	09 31	09 34	09 37
Norwood Junction 2	d				08 35	08 36							09 05		09 12								09 35		09 42
London Bridge 4	a	08 25	08 53		09 02	08 50		08 55	09 23				09 32	09 17	09 24			09 52		09 32			10 02	09 48	09 57
London Blackfriars 3	a														09 30					09 38				09 54	
City Thameslink 3	a																								
Farringdon 3	a														09 35					09 43				09 59	
St Pancras International	a														09 39					09 47				10 03	
Clapham Junction 10	a			08 38						08 55	09 02	09 08				09 20			09 24		09 32	09 39			
London Victoria 15	a			08 46						09 02	09 09	09 15				09 28			09 32		09 39	09 47			

A not 15 December

Table T175-R

Sundays
15 December to 10 May

East Croydon and Norwood Junction - London - Summary of Fast Trains

		SN 1	SN	SN 1	TL 1	SN 1	SN	SN 1		TL 1	TL 1	SN 1	SN	SN 1	TL 1	SN 1	SN	SN		TL 1	TL 1	SN 1	SN	SN 1	TL 1
East Croydon	d	09 41	09 44	09 45	09 48	09 51	10 01	10 04		10 04	10 07	10 11	10 14	10 15	10 18	10 21	10 30	10 31		10 34	10 37	10 41	10 44	10 45	10 48
Norwood Junction 2	d						10 05				10 12							10 35			10 42				
London Bridge 4	a		10 22		10 02		10 32			10 18	10 24		10 52		10 32			11 02		10 48	10 58		11 22		11 02
London Blackfriars 3	a				10 08					10 24	10 30				10 38					10 54					11 08
City Thameslink 3	a																								
Farringdon 3	a				10 13					10 29	10 35				10 43					10 59					11 13
St Pancras International	a				10 17					10 33	10 39				10 47					11 03					11 17
Clapham Junction 10	a	09 50		09 54		10 02		10 14				10 20		10 24		10 32	10 39					10 50		10 54	
London Victoria 15	a	09 58		10 02		10 09		10 21				10 28		10 32		10 39	10 47					10 58		11 02	

		SN 1	SN	SN 1		TL 1	TL 1	SN 1	SN	SN 1	TL 1	SN 1	SN	SN		TL 1	TL 1	SN 1	SN	SN 1	TL 1	SN 1	SN	SN 1	
East Croydon	d	10 51	11 01	11 04		11 04	11 07	11 11	11 14	11 15	11 18	11 21	11 30	11 31		11 34	11 37	11 40	11 44	11 45	11 48	11 51	12 01	12 04	
Norwood Junction 2	d		11 05				11 12							11 35			11 42						12 05		
London Bridge 4	a		11 32			11 18	11 24		11 52		11 32			12 02		11 48	11 57		12 22		12 02		12 32		
London Blackfriars 3	a					11 24	11 30				11 38					11 54					12 08				
City Thameslink 3	a																								
Farringdon 3	a					11 29	11 35				11 43					11 59					12 13				
St Pancras International	a					11 33	11 39				11 47					12 03					12 17				
Clapham Junction 10	a	11 02		11 14				11 20		11 24		11 32	11 39					11 50		11 54		12 02		12 14	
London Victoria 15	a	11 09		11 21				11 28		11 32		11 39	11 47					11 58		12 02		12 09		12 21	

		TL 1	TL 1	SN 1	SN	SN 1	TL 1	SN 1	SN	SN		TL 1	TL 1	SN 1	SN	SN 1	TL 1	SN 1	SN	TL 1		SN 1	TL 1	SN 1	SN
East Croydon	d	12 04	12 07	12 11	12 14	12 15	12 18	12 21	12 30	12 31		12 34	12 37	12 41	12 44	12 45	12 48	12 51	13 01	13 04		13 06	13 07	13 11	13 14
Norwood Junction 2	d		12 12							12 35			12 42						13 05				13 12		
London Bridge 4	a	12 18	12 24		12 52		12 32			13 02		12 48	12 57		13 22		13 02		13 32	13 18			13 24		13 52
London Blackfriars 3	a	12 24	12 30				12 38					12 54					13 08			13 24			13 30		
City Thameslink 3	a																								
Farringdon 3	a	12 29	12 35				12 45					12 59					13 13			13 29			13 35		
St Pancras International	a	12 33	12 39				12 49					13 03					13 17			13 33			13 39		
Clapham Junction 10	a			12 20		12 24		12 32	12 39					12 50		12 54		13 02				13 16		13 22	
London Victoria 15	a			12 28		12 32		12 39	12 47					12 58		13 02		13 09				13 23		13 30	

		SN 1	TL 1	SN 1	SN	SN		TL 1	TL 1	SN 1	SN	SN 1	TL 1	SN 1	SN	SN 1		TL 1	TL 1	SN 1	SN	SN 1	TL 1	SN 1	SN
East Croydon	d	13 15	13 18	13 21	13 30	13 31		13 34	13 37	13 41	13 44	13 45	13 48	13 51	14 01	14 04		14 04	14 07	14 11	14 14	14 15	14 18	14 21	14 30
Norwood Junction 2	d					13 35			13 42						14 05				14 12						
London Bridge 4	a		13 32			14 02		13 48	13 57		14 22		14 02		14 32			14 18	14 24		14 52		14 32		
London Blackfriars 3	a		13 38					13 54					14 08					14 24	14 30				14 38		
City Thameslink 3	a																								
Farringdon 3	a		13 43					13 59					14 13					14 29	14 35				14 43		
St Pancras International	a		13 47					14 03					14 17					14 33	14 39				14 47		
Clapham Junction 10	a	13 25		13 32	13 39					13 50		13 54		14 02		14 14				14 20		14 24		14 32	14 39
London Victoria 15	a	13 32		13 39	13 47					13 58		14 02		14 09		14 21				14 28		14 32		14 39	14 47

		SN		TL 1	TL 1	SN 1	SN	SN 1	TL 1	SN 1	SN	SN 1		TL 1	TL 1	SN 1	SN	SN 1	TL 1	SN 1	SN	SN		TL 1	TL 1
East Croydon	d	14 31		14 34	14 37	14 41	14 44	14 45	14 48	14 51	15 01	15 04		15 04	15 07	15 11	15 14	15 15	15 18	15 21	15 30	15 31		15 34	15 37
Norwood Junction 2	d	14 35			14 42						15 05				15 12							15 35			15 42
London Bridge 4	a	15 02		14 48	14 57		15 22		15 02		15 32			15 18	15 24		15 52		15 32			16 02		15 48	15 57
London Blackfriars 3	a			14 54					15 08					15 24	15 30				15 38					15 54	
City Thameslink 3	a																								
Farringdon 3	a			14 59					15 13					15 29	15 35				15 43					15 59	
St Pancras International	a			15 03					15 17					15 33	15 39				15 47					16 03	
Clapham Junction 10	a					14 50		14 54		15 02		15 14				15 20		15 24		15 32	15 39				
London Victoria 15	a					14 58		15 02		15 09		15 21				15 28		15 32		15 39	15 47				

		SN 1	SN	SN 1	TL 1	SN 1	SN	TL 1		SN 1	TL 1	SN 1	SN	SN 1	TL 1	SN 1	SN	SN		TL 1	TL 1	SN 1	SN	SN 1	TL 1
East Croydon	d	15 41	15 44	15 45	15 48	15 51	16 01	16 04		16 06	16 07	16 11	16 14	16 15	16 18	16 21	16 30	16 31		16 34	16 37	16 41	16 44	16 45	16 48
Norwood Junction 2	d						16 05				16 12							16 35			16 42				
London Bridge 4	a		16 22		16 02		16 32	16 18			16 24		16 52		16 32			17 02		16 48	16 57		17 22		17 02
London Blackfriars 3	a				16 08			16 24			16 30				16 38					16 54					17 08
City Thameslink 3	a																								
Farringdon 3	a				16 13			16 29			16 35				16 43					16 59					17 13
St Pancras International	a				16 17			16 33			16 39				16 47					17 03					17 17
Clapham Junction 10	a	15 50		15 54		16 02				16 16		16 22		16 25		16 32	16 39					16 50		16 54	
London Victoria 15	a	15 58		16 02		16 09				16 23		16 30		16 32		16 39	16 47					16 58		17 02	

		SN 1	SN	TL 1		SN 1	TL 1	SN 1	SN	SN 1	TL 1	SN 1	SN	SN	TL 1	TL 1	SN 1	SN	SN 1	TL 1	SN 1	SN	SN 1	TL 1	TL 1
East Croydon	d	16 51	17 01	17 04		17 06	17 07	17 11	17 14	17 15	17 18	17 21	17 30	17 31	17 34	17 37	17 41	17 44	17 45	17 48	17 51	18 01	18 04	18 04	18 07
Norwood Junction 2	d		17 05				17 12							17 35		17 42						18 05			18 12
London Bridge 4	a		17 32	17 18			17 24		17 52		17 32			18 02	17 48	17 57		18 22		18 02		18 32		18 18	18 24
London Blackfriars 3	a			17 24			17 30				17 38				17 54					18 08				18 24	18 30
City Thameslink 3	a																								
Farringdon 3	a			17 29			17 35				17 43				17 59					18 13				18 29	18 35
St Pancras International	a			17 33			17 39				17 47				18 03					18 17				18 33	18 39
Clapham Junction 10	a	17 02				17 16		17 22		17 25		17 32	17 39				17 50		17 54		18 02		18 14		
London Victoria 15	a	17 09				17 23		17 30		17 32		17 39	17 47				17 58		18 02		18 09		18 21		

Table T175-R

Sundays
15 December to 10 May

East Croydon and Norwood Junction - London - Summary of Fast Trains

		SN 1	SN	SN 1		TL 1	SN 1	SN	SN	TL 1	TL 1	SN 1	SN	SN 1	TL 1	SN 1	SN	SN 1	TL 1	TL 1	SN 1	SN	SN 1
East Croydon	d	18 11	18 14	18 15	and at the same minutes past each hour until	21 18	21 21	21 30	21 31	21 34	21 37	21 41	21 44	21 45	21 48	21 51	22 01	22 04	22 04	22 07	22 11	22 14	22 15
Norwood Junction 2	d								21 35		21 42						22 05			22 12			
London Bridge 4	a		18 52			21 32			22 02	21 48	21 57		22 22		22 02		22 32		22 18	22 24		22 52	
London Blackfriars 3	a					21 38				21 54					22 08				22 24	22 30			
City Thameslink 3	a																						
Farringdon 3	a					21 43				21 59					22 13				22 29	22 35			
St Pancras International	a					21 47				22 03					22 17				22 33	22 39			
Clapham Junction 10	a	18 20		18 24			21 32	21 39				21 50		21 54		22 02		22 14			22 20		22 24
London Victoria 15	a	18 28		18 32			21 39	21 47				21 58		22 02		22 09		22 21			22 28		22 32

		SN 1	SN	SN	TL 1	SN	SN 1	TL 1	SN 1	SN		SN 1	TL 1	TL 1	SN 1	SN 1	SN	TL 1	SN 1	SN 1
East Croydon	d	22 21	22 30	22 31	22 34	22 42	22 45	22 47	22 51	23 01		23 04	23 04	23 12	23 15	23 21	23 31	23 40	23 52	23 55
Norwood Junction 2	d			22 35				22 52		23 05				23 17			23 35			
London Bridge 4	a			23 02	22 48	23 23		23 05		23 32			23 18	23 30			00 03			
London Blackfriars 3	a				22 54								23 24					00 06		
City Thameslink 3	a																			
Farringdon 3	a				22 59								23 31					00 10		
St Pancras International	a				23 03								23 35					00 15		
Clapham Junction 10	a	22 32	22 39				22 54		23 02			23 14			23 24	23 32			00 08	00 15
London Victoria 15	a	22 39	22 47				23 02		23 09			23 21			23 31	23 39			00 17	00 23

AVAILABLE FROM MP Middleton Press

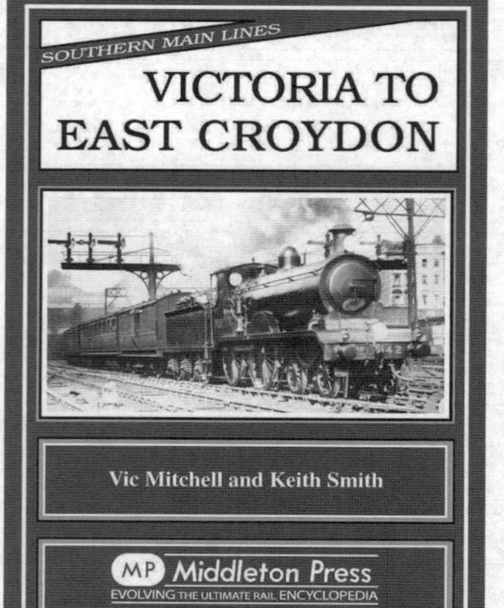

Table T176-F

Mondays to Fridays
16 December to 15 May

East Croydon, Balham and Clapham Junction-Imperial Wharf, West Brompton, Kensington Olympia and Shepherd's Bush - Willesden Junction, Stratford/Watford Junction, Milton Keynes

Miles	Miles			SN	SN	SN	LO	LO	SN	LO	LO	SN		LO	LO	LO	LO	LO	SN	LO	LO	LO		SN	LO
				1	1	1			1			1							1					1	
0	—	East Croydon	d																07 10					07 40	
1	—	Selhurst 4	d									06 16							07 16					07 46	
1¾	—	Thornton Heath	d									06 19							07 19					07 49	
3	—	Norbury	d									06 22							07 22					07 52	
4	—	Streatham Common 4	d									06 25							07 25					07 55	
5¼	—	Balham 4 ⊖	d		05 27							06 29							07 29					07 59	
6½	—	Wandsworth Common	d																						
7¾	—	Clapham Junction 10	a		05 31							06 35							07 35					08 05	
—	—		d	05 03	05 32	05 53	06 00	06 12	06 20	06 26	06 36	06 40		06 50	07 02	07 14	07 26	07 36	07 39	07 48	08 01	08 14		08 18	08 27
8¾	—	**Imperial Wharf**	d	05 07	05 37	05 58	06 04	06 16	06 24	06 30	06 40	06 45		06 54	07 06	07 18	07 30	07 40	07 44	07 53	08 05	08 18		08 22	08 31
9½	—	**West Brompton** ⊖	d	05 10	05 40	06 01	06 07	06 19	06 27	06 33	06 43	06 47		06 57	07 09	07 21	07 33	07 43	07 47	07 56	08 09	08 21		08 25	08 34
11½	—	**Kensington (Olympia)** ⊖	d	05 14	05 44	06 05	06 10	06 22	06 31	06 36	06 46	06 51		07 00	07 12	07 24	07 36	07 46	07 51	08 00	08 12	08 24		08 29	08 37
12¼	0	**Shepherd's Bush** ⊖	d	05 17	05 47	06 08	06 12	06 24	06 34	06 38	06 49	06 54		07 02	07 14	07 26	07 38	07 48	07 53	08 02	08 14	08 26		08 31	08 40
—	1½	Willesden Jn. High Level ⊖	a				06 21	06 34		06 46	06 58			07 10	07 22	07 34	07 46	07 56		08 10	08 22	08 34			08 46
—	4	West Hampstead ⊖	a				06 30	06 43		06 55	07 07			07 20	07 33	07 43	07 55	08 07		08 19	08 31	08 43			08 55
—	6	Gospel Oak	a				06 37	06 49		07 01	07 14			07 27	07 40	07 49	08 01	08 14		08 25	08 37	08 50			09 02
—	8¾	Highbury & Islington ⊖	a				06 47	07 01		07 14	07 23			07 36	07 49	07 59	08 13	08 24		08 36	08 47	09 02			09 11
—	13½	Stratford ⊖	a				07 04	07 17		07 30	07 40			07 54	08 06	08 19	08 31	08 41		08 53	09 06	09 19			09 31
17	—	Wembley Central ⊖	a		06 00	06 25			06 47			07 07							08 08					08 47	
20½	—	Harrow & Wealdstone ⊖	a	05 33	06 06	06 31						07 12							08 12					08 52	
25	—	Watford Junction	a	05 40	06 13	06 38			06 57			07 18							08 19					09 00	
32	—	Hemel Hempstead	a		06 21							07 26							08 27						
35½	—	Berkhamsted	a		06 26							07 31							08 31						
39¼	—	Tring	a		06 33							07 38							08 37						
47¾	—	Leighton Buzzard	a		06 41							07 46							08 46						
54¼	—	Bletchley	a		06 48							07 53							08 53						
57¼	—	Milton Keynes Central 10	a		06 55							08 02							09 00						

		LO	SN	LO	LO	SN	LO	LO		SN	LO	LO	LO	LO	SN	LO	LO	LO		LO	SN	LO	LO	LO	LO
			1			1				1					1						1				
East Croydon	d		08 11			08 40				09 10					10 10						11 10				
Selhurst 4	d		08 16			08 46				09 16					10 16						11 16				
Thornton Heath	d		08 19			08 49				09 19					10 19						11 19				
Norbury	d		08 22			08 52				09 22					10 22						11 22				
Streatham Common 4	d		08 25			08 55				09 25					10 25						11 25				
Balham 4 ⊖	d		08 29			08 59				09 29					10 29						11 29				
Wandsworth Common	d																								
Clapham Junction 10	a		08 35			09 05				09 35					10 35						11 35				
	d	08 36	08 40	08 50	09 02	09 06	09 14	09 29		09 39	09 48	10 01	10 17	10 30	10 41	10 48	11 02	11 17		11 32	11 39	11 47	12 02	12 17	12 32
Imperial Wharf	d	08 40	08 44	08 54	09 06	09 10	09 18	09 33		09 44	09 52	10 05	10 21	10 34	10 45	10 52	11 06	11 21		11 36	11 44	11 51	12 06	12 21	12 36
West Brompton ⊖	d	08 43	08 47	08 57	09 09	09 13	09 21	09 36		09 47	09 55	10 08	10 24	10 37	10 48	10 55	11 09	11 24		11 39	11 47	11 54	12 09	12 24	12 39
Kensington (Olympia) ⊖	d	08 46	08 51	09 00	09 12	09 17	09 24	09 39		09 50	09 58	10 11	10 27	10 42	10 51	10 58	11 12	11 27		11 42	11 50	11 57	12 12	12 27	12 42
Shepherd's Bush ⊖	d	08 48	08 53	09 02	09 14	09a19	09 26	09 41		09 53	10 00	10 13	10 29	10 44	10 54	11 00	11 14	11 29		11 44	11 53	11 59	12 14	12 29	12 44
Willesden Jn. High Level ⊖	a	08 56		09 10	09 22		09 34	09 49			10 07	10 23	10 38	10 52		11 08	11 21	11 39		11 52		12 07	12 23	12 36	12 52
West Hampstead ⊖	a	09 07		09 20	09 33		09 43	09 58			10 16	10 32	10 47	11 01		11 17	11 31	11 48		12 01		12 16	12 32	12 45	13 01
Gospel Oak	a	09 14		09 27	09 40		09 49	10 06			10 22	10 41	10 54	11 07		11 23	11 37	11 57		12 07		12 22	12 39	12 51	13 08
Highbury & Islington ⊖	a	09 24		09 36	09 49		10 00	10 16			10 34	10 51	11 03	11 19		11 35	11 49	12 06		12 19		12 34	12 50	13 03	13 19
Stratford ⊖	a	09 41		09 55	10 07		10 18	10 33			10 52	11 07	11 21	11 34		11 52	12 06	12 22		12 36		12 51	13 06	13 21	13 36
Wembley Central ⊖	a		09 08							10 08					11 09						12 09				
Harrow & Wealdstone ⊖	a		09 12							10 12					11 13						12 13				
Watford Junction	a		09 20							10 19					11 20						12 20				
Hemel Hempstead	a		09 28							10 27					11 28						12 28				
Berkhamsted	a		09 33							10 31					11 32						12 32				
Tring	a		09 40							10 38					11 38						12 38				
Leighton Buzzard	a		09 48							10 46					11 46						12 46				
Bletchley	a		09 55							10 55					11 53						12 53				
Milton Keynes Central 10	a		10 01							11 01					11 59						13 00				

For other Norbury line connections, refer to Table T170

For other Stratford line connecting trains, refer to Table T59

NRT DECEMBER 19 EDITION

Table T176-F

Mondays to Fridays
16 December to 15 May

East Croydon, Balham and Clapham Junction-Imperial Wharf, West Brompton, Kensington Olympia and Shepherd's Bush - Willesden Junction, Stratford/Watford Junction, Milton Keynes

		SN	LO	LO	LO	LO	SN	SN	LO	LO		LO	LO	LO	SN	LO	LO	SN	LO	SN		LO	LO	SN	LO
							MWFO	TThO																	
		1					1	1							1			1		1				1	
East Croydon	d	12 10					13 10								14 10									15 10	
Selhurst 4	d	12 16					13 16	13 18							14 16			14 46						15 16	
Thornton Heath	d	12 19					13 19	13 20							14 19			14 49						15 19	
Norbury	d	12 22					13 22	13 23							14 22			14 52						15 22	
Streatham Common 4	d	12 25					13 25	13 26							14 25			14 55						15 25	
Balham 4 ⊖	d	12 29					13 29	13 30							14 29			14 59						15 29	
Wandsworth Common	d																								
Clapham Junction 10	a	12 35					13 35	13 35							14 35			15 05						15 35	
	d	12 39	12 47	13 02	13 17	13 32	13 39	13 39	13 47	14 02		14 15	14 26	14 36	14 40	14 50	15 02	15 10	15 15	15 22		15 26	15 36	15 39	15 50
Imperial Wharf	d	12 45	12 51	13 06	13 21	13 36	13 44	13 44	13 51	14 06		14 19	14 30	14 40	14 45	14 54	15 06	15 15	15 19	15 26		15 30	15 40	15 44	15 54
West Brompton ⊖	d	12 48	12 54	13 09	13 24	13 39	13 47	13 47	13 54	14 09		14 22	14 33	14 43	14 48	14 57	15 09	15 18	15 22	15 29		15 33	15 43	15 47	15 57
Kensington (Olympia) ⊖	d	12 51	12 57	13 12	13 27	13 42	13 50	13 50	13 57	14 12		14 25	14 36	14 46	14 51	15 00	15 12	15 21	15 25	15 32		15 36	15 46	15 51	16 00
Shepherd's Bush ⊖	d	12 53	12 59	13 14	13 29	13 44	13 53	13 53	13 59	14 14		14 27	14 38	14 48	14 54	15 02	15 14	15a23	15 28	15 34		15 38	15 48	15 53	16 02
Willesden Jn. High Level ⊖	a		13 06	13 21	13 37	13 52			14 06	14 21		14 35	14 45	14 56		15 09	15 22		15 34			15 46	15 56		16 09
West Hampstead ⊖	a		13 15	13 30	13 46	14 01			14 15	14 30		14 44	14 54	15 07		15 19	15 31		15 43			15 55	16 05		16 19
Gospel Oak	a		13 22	13 36	13 52	14 07			14 22	14 37		14 50	15 00	15 13		15 25	15 37		15 51			16 02	16 11		16 25
Highbury & Islington ⊖	a		13 34	13 48	14 04	14 19			14 32	14 47		15 00	15 10	15 23		15 36	15 48		16 02			16 12	16 22		16 36
Stratford ⊖	a		13 51	14 06	14 21	14 36			14 51	15 06		15 19	15 30	15 40		15 56	16 06		16 19			16 30	16 40		16 56
Wembley Central ⊖	a	13 09					14 09	14 09							15 09					15 51				16 08	
Harrow & Wealdstone ⊖	a	13 13					14 13	14 13							15 13					15 56				16 12	
Watford Junction	a	13 20					14 20	14 20							15 20					16 04				16 19	
Hemel Hempstead	a	13 28					14 28	14 28							15 28									16 27	
Berkhamsted	a	13 33					14 32	14 32							15 32									16 31	
Tring	a	13 39					14 38	14 38							15 38									16 37	
Leighton Buzzard	a	13 47					14 46	14 46							15 46									16 46	
Bletchley	a	13 54					14 53	14 53							15 54									16 53	
Milton Keynes Central 10	a	14 00					14 59	14 59							16 00									17 00	

		LO	LO	LO	LO	SN		LO	LO	SN	LO	LO	LO	SN	LO	LO		LO	LO	LO	SN	LO	LO	LO	LO
						1				1				1							1				
East Croydon	d					16 10				16 40				17 10							18 10				
Selhurst 4	d					16 16				16 46				17 16							18 16				
Thornton Heath	d					16 19				16 49				17 19							18 19				
Norbury	d					16 22				16 52				17 22							18 22				
Streatham Common 4	d					16 25				16 55				17 25							18 25				
Balham 4 ⊖	d					16 29				16 59				17 30							18 29				
Wandsworth Common	d																								
Clapham Junction 10	a					16 35				17 05				17 35							18 35				
	d	16 02	16 14	16 26	16 36	16 39		16 50	17 03	17 09	17 14	17 26	17 36	17 39	17 50	18 02		18 14	18 26	18 36	18 39	18 50	19 02	19 14	19 27
Imperial Wharf	d	16 06	16 18	16 30	16 40	16 44		16 54	17 07	17 13	17 18	17 30	17 40	17 44	17 54	18 06		18 18	18 31	18 40	18 44	18 54	19 06	19 18	19 31
West Brompton ⊖	d	16 09	16 21	16 33	16 43	16 47		16 57	17 11	17 16	17 21	17 33	17 43	17 47	17 57	18 09		18 21	18 34	18 43	18 47	18 57	19 09	19 21	19 34
Kensington (Olympia) ⊖	d	16 12	16 24	16 36	16 46	16 51		17 00	17 14	17 20	17 24	17 36	17 46	17 51	18 00	18 12		18 24	18 37	18 46	18 51	19 00	19 12	19 24	19 37
Shepherd's Bush ⊖	d	16 15	16 26	16 38	16 48	16 53		17 02	17 17	17a22	17 27	17 38	17 48	17 53	18 02	18 14		18 26	18 40	18 48	18 53	19 02	19 15	19 26	19 39
Willesden Jn. High Level ⊖	a	16 23	16 34	16 46	16 56			17 10	17 24		17 34	17 46	17 56		18 10	18 22		18 34	18 47	18 56		19 10	19 22	19 34	19 47
West Hampstead ⊖	a	16 32	16 44	16 55	17 05			17 19	17 33		17 43	17 55	18 06		18 19	18 31		18 43	18 56	19 05		19 19	19 31	19 44	19 56
Gospel Oak	a	16 38	16 50	17 01	17 11			17 25	17 40		17 49	18 02	18 12		18 25	18 37		18 49	19 03	19 12		19 25	19 37	19 50	20 03
Highbury & Islington ⊖	a	16 49	17 00	17 12	17 22			17 35	17 50		18 00	18 12	18 23		18 36	18 48		19 00	19 12	19 21		19 36	19 47	20 00	20 13
Stratford ⊖	a	17 06	17 18	17 30	17 40			17 56	18 08		18 19	18 31	18 41		18 56	19 07		19 19	19 31	19 41		19 56	20 06	20 18	20 31
Wembley Central ⊖	a					17 07								18 09							19 09				
Harrow & Wealdstone ⊖	a					17 12								18 13							19 13				
Watford Junction	a					17 18								18 20							19 20				
Hemel Hempstead	a					17 28								18 28							19 28				
Berkhamsted	a					17 33								18 32							19 32				
Tring	a					17 39								18 38							19 38				
Leighton Buzzard	a					17 47								18 47							19 47				
Bletchley	a					17 54								18 54							19 55				
Milton Keynes Central 10	a					18 01								19 00							20 04				

For other Norbury line connections, refer to Table T170

For other Stratford line connecting trains, refer to Table T59

Table T176-F

Mondays to Fridays
16 December to 15 May

East Croydon, Balham and Clapham Junction-Imperial Wharf, West Brompton, Kensington Olympia and Shepherd's Bush - Willesden Junction, Stratford/Watford Junction, Milton Keynes

		LO	SN 1	LO	LO	LO	LO	SN 1		LO	LO	LO	LO	SN 1	LO	LO	LO	LO		SN 1	LO	LO	LO	LO	LO
East Croydon	d		19 10					20 10						21 10											
Selhurst 4	d		19 16					20 16						21 16						22 17					
Thornton Heath	d		19 19					20 19						21 19						22 19					
Norbury	d		19 22					20 22						21 22						22 22					
Streatham Common 4	d		19 25					20 25						21 25						22 25					
Balham 4 ⊖	d		19 29					20 29						21 29						22 30					
Wandsworth Common	d																								
Clapham Junction 10	a		19 35					20 35						21 35						22 35					
	d	19 36	19 40	19 50	20 02	20 14	20 28	20 36		20 44	21 00	21 17	21 30	21 36	21 44	21 59	22 14	22 29		22 36	22 44	23 00	23 15	23 30	23 45
Imperial Wharf	d	19 40	19 45	19 54	20 06	20 18	20 32	20 41		20 48	21 04	21 22	21 35	21 41	21 48	22 03	22 18	22 33		22 41	22 48	23 04	23 19	23 34	23 51
West Brompton ⊖	d	19 43	19 48	19 57	20 09	20 21	20 35	20 44		20 51	21 07	21 26	21 38	21 44	21 51	22 06	22 21	22 36		22 44	22 51	23 07	23 22	23 37	23 54
Kensington (Olympia) ⊖	d	19 46	19 51	20 00	20 12	20 24	20 38	20 47		20 54	21 10	21 29	21 42	21 47	21 54	22 10	22 24	22 39		22 48	22 54	23 10	23 25	23 40	23 57
Shepherd's Bush ⊖	d	19 48	19 54	20 02	20 14	20 26	20 40	20 50		20 56	21 12	21 31	21 44	21 50	21 56	22 12	22 26	22 41		22 51	22 56	23 13	23 27	23 42	23 59
Willesden Jn. High Level ⊖	a	19 57		20 11	20 23	20 34	20 48			21 04	21 19	21 38	21 51		22 05	22 24	22 34	22 49			23 03	23 21	23 36	23 51	00 06
West Hampstead ⊖	a	20 06		20 20	20 32	20 44	20 57			21 13	21 28	21 47	22 00		22 16	22 33	22 43	22 58			23 12				
Gospel Oak	a	20 13		20 26	20 39	20 51	21 03			21 19	21 34	21 54	22 07		22 23	22 39	22 50	23 04			23 18				
Highbury & Islington ⊖	a	20 22		20 36	20 50	21 02	21 15			21 31	21 44	22 03	22 18		22 33	22 49	23 01	23 16			23 34				
Stratford ⊖	a	20 40		20 54	21 06	21 18	21 32			21 48	22 04	22 21	22 34		22 49	23 05	23 18	23 33			23 50				
Wembley Central ⊖	a		20 08					21 08																	
Harrow & Wealdstone ⊖	a		20 12					21 12						22 16						23 23					
Watford Junction	a		20 19					21 19						22 23						23 34					
Hemel Hempstead	a		20 27					21 27																	
Berkhamsted	a		20 31					21 31																	
Tring	a		20 38					21 38																	
Leighton Buzzard	a		20 47					21 48																	
Bletchley	a		20 54					21 55																	
Milton Keynes Central 10	a		21 00					22 02																	

Saturdays
21 December to 16 May

		SN 1	SN 1	LO	LO	SN 1	LO	LO	SN 1	LO		LO	LO	LO	SN 1	LO	LO	LO	LO	SN 1		LO	LO	LO	LO
East Croydon	d								06 10						07 10					08 10					
Selhurst 4	d								06 16						07 16					08 16					
Thornton Heath	d								06 19						07 19					08 19					
Norbury	d								06 22						07 22					08 22					
Streatham Common 4	d								06 25						07 25					08 25					
Balham 4 ⊖	d		05 33						06 29						07 29					08 29					
Wandsworth Common	d																								
Clapham Junction 10	a		05 37						06 35						07 35					08 35					
	d	05 09	05 39	05 50	06 02	06 09	06 17	06 32	06 40	06 47		07 02	07 17	07 32	07 40	07 47	08 02	08 17	08 32	08 40		08 47	09 02	09 17	09 32
Imperial Wharf	d	05 13	05 43	05 54	06 06	06 14	06 21	06 36	06 45	06 51		07 06	07 21	07 36	07 45	07 51	08 06	08 21	08 36	08 45		08 51	09 06	09 21	09 36
West Brompton ⊖	d	05 16	05 46	05 57	06 09	06 17	06 24	06 39	06 48	06 54		07 09	07 24	07 39	07 48	07 54	08 09	08 24	08 39	08 48		08 54	09 09	09 24	09 39
Kensington (Olympia) ⊖	d	05 20	05 50	06 00	06 12	06 20	06 27	06 42	06 51	06 57		07 12	07 27	07 42	07 51	07 57	08 12	08 27	08 42	08 51		08 57	09 12	09 27	09 42
Shepherd's Bush ⊖	d	05 23	05 53	06 02	06 14	06 23	06 29	06 44	06 54	06 59		07 14	07 29	07 44	07 54	07 59	08 14	08 29	08 44	08 54		08 59	09 14	09 29	09 44
Willesden Jn. High Level ⊖	a			06 11	06 22		06 37	06 52		07 07		07 22	07 37	07 52		08 07	08 22	08 37	08 52			09 07	09 22	09 37	09 52
West Hampstead ⊖	a				06 31		06 46	07 01		07 16		07 31	07 46	08 01		08 16	08 31	08 46	09 01			09 16	09 31	09 46	10 01
Gospel Oak	a				06 37		06 52	07 07		07 22		07 37	07 52	08 07		08 22	08 37	08 52	09 07			09 22	09 37	09 52	10 07
Highbury & Islington ⊖	a				06 49		07 04	07 18		07 34		07 49	08 05	08 19		08 34	08 48	09 04	09 19			09 34	09 50	10 04	10 19
Stratford ⊖	a				07 06		07 21	07 36		07 51		08 06	08 21	08 36		08 51	09 06	09 21	09 36			09 51	10 06	10 21	10 36
Wembley Central ⊖	a		06 07			06 38			07 09						08 09					09 09					
Harrow & Wealdstone ⊖	a	05 41	06 12			06 43			07 13						08 13					09 13					
Watford Junction	a	05 47	06 18			06 50			07 20						08 20					09 20					
Hemel Hempstead	a		06 26						07 28						08 28					09 28					
Berkhamsted	a		06 31						07 32						08 32					09 32					
Tring	a		06 37						07 38						08 38					09 38					
Leighton Buzzard	a		06 45						07 46						08 46					09 48					
Bletchley	a		06 53						07 53						08 53					09 55					
Milton Keynes Central 10	a		06 59						07 59						08 59					10 01					

For other Norbury line connections, refer to Table T170

For other Stratford line connecting trains, refer to Table T59

Table T176-F

Saturdays
21 December to 16 May

East Croydon, Balham and Clapham Junction-Imperial Wharf, West Brompton, Kensington Olympia and Shepherd's Bush - Willesden Junction, Stratford/Watford Junction, Milton Keynes

		SN 1		LO	LO	LO	LO	SN 1	LO	LO	LO	LO		SN 1	LO	LO	LO	LO	SN 1	LO	LO	LO		LO	SN 1
East Croydon	d	09 10						10 10						11 10					12 10						13 10
Selhurst 4	d	09 16						10 16						11 16					12 16						13 16
Thornton Heath	d	09 19						10 19						11 19					12 19						13 19
Norbury	d	09 22						10 22						11 22					12 22						13 22
Streatham Common 4	d	09 25						10 25						11 25					12 25						13 25
Balham 4 ⊖	d	09 29						10 29						11 29					12 29						13 29
Wandsworth Common	d																								
Clapham Junction 10	a	09 35						10 35						11 35					12 35						13 35
	d	09 40		09 47	10 02	10 17	10 32	10 40	10 47	11 02	11 17	11 32		11 40	11 47	12 02	12 17	12 32	12 40	12 47	13 02	13 17		13 32	13 40
Imperial Wharf	d	09 45		09 51	10 06	10 21	10 36	10 45	10 51	11 06	11 21	11 36		11 45	11 51	12 06	12 21	12 36	12 45	12 51	13 06	13 21		13 36	13 45
West Brompton ⊖	d	09 48		09 54	10 09	10 24	10 39	10 48	10 54	11 09	11 24	11 39		11 48	11 54	12 09	12 24	12 39	12 48	12 54	13 09	13 24		13 39	13 48
Kensington (Olympia) ⊖	d	09 51		09 57	10 12	10 27	10 42	10 51	10 57	11 12	11 27	11 42		11 51	11 57	12 12	12 27	12 42	12 51	12 57	13 12	13 27		13 42	13 51
Shepherd's Bush ⊖	d	09 54		09 59	10 14	10 29	10 44	10 54	10 59	11 14	11 29	11 44		11 54	11 59	12 14	12 29	12 44	12 54	12 59	13 15	13 29		13 44	13 54
Willesden Jn. High Level ⊖	a			10 07	10 22	10 37	10 52		11 07	11 22	11 36	11 53			12 07	12 22	12 37	12 52		13 06	13 22	13 37		13 51	
West Hampstead ⊖	a			10 16	10 31	10 46	11 01		11 16	11 31	11 45	12 02			12 16	12 31	12 46	13 01		13 15	13 31	13 46		14 01	
Gospel Oak	a			10 22	10 37	10 52	11 07		11 23	11 37	11 51	12 08			12 22	12 37	12 52	13 07		13 21	13 37	13 52		14 07	
Highbury & Islington ⊖	a			10 34	10 49	11 04	11 19		11 35	11 49	12 04	12 19			12 34	12 49	13 04	13 19		13 34	13 49	14 02		14 19	
Stratford ⊖	a			10 51	11 06	11 21	11 36		11 51	12 06	12 21	12 36			12 51	13 06	13 21	13 36		13 51	14 06	14 21		14 36	
Wembley Central ⊖	a	10 09						11 09						12 09					13 09						14 09
Harrow & Wealdstone ⊖	a	10 13						11 13						12 13					13 13						14 13
Watford Junction	a	10 20						11 20						12 20					13 20						14 20
Hemel Hempstead	a	10 28						11 28						12 28					13 28						14 28
Berkhamsted	a	10 32						11 32						12 32					13 32						14 32
Tring	a	10 38						11 38						12 38					13 38						14 38
Leighton Buzzard	a	10 46						11 46						12 46					13 47						14 46
Bletchley	a	10 54						11 54						12 54					13 54						14 54
Milton Keynes Central 10	a	11 00						12 00						13 00					14 00						15 00

		LO	LO	LO	LO	SN 1	LO	LO		LO	LO	SN 1	LO	LO	LO	LO	SN 1	LO		LO	LO	LO	SN 1	LO	LO
East Croydon	d					14 10						15 10					16 10						17 10		
Selhurst 4	d					14 16						15 16					16 16						17 16		
Thornton Heath	d					14 19						15 19					16 19						17 19		
Norbury	d					14 22						15 22					16 22						17 22		
Streatham Common 4	d					14 25						15 25					16 25						17 25		
Balham 4 ⊖	d					14 29						15 29					16 29						17 29		
Wandsworth Common	d																								
Clapham Junction 10	a					14 35						15 35					16 35						17 35		
	d	13 47	14 03	14 17	14 32	14 40	14 47	15 02		15 17	15 32	15 40	15 47	16 02	16 17	16 32	16 40	16 47		17 02	17 17	17 32	17 40	17 47	18 02
Imperial Wharf	d	13 51	14 07	14 21	14 36	14 45	14 51	15 06		15 21	15 36	15 45	15 51	16 06	16 21	16 36	16 45	16 51		17 06	17 21	17 36	17 45	17 51	18 06
West Brompton ⊖	d	13 54	14 10	14 24	14 39	14 48	14 54	15 09		15 24	15 39	15 48	15 54	16 09	16 24	16 39	16 48	16 54		17 09	17 24	17 39	17 48	17 54	18 09
Kensington (Olympia) ⊖	d	13 57	14 13	14 27	14 42	14 51	14 57	15 12		15 27	15 42	15 51	15 57	16 12	16 27	16 42	16 51	16 57		17 12	17 27	17 42	17 51	17 57	18 12
Shepherd's Bush ⊖	d	13 59	14 16	14 29	14 44	14 54	14 59	15 14		15 29	15 44	15 54	15 59	16 14	16 29	16 44	16 54	16 59		17 14	17 29	17 44	17 54	17 59	18 14
Willesden Jn. High Level ⊖	a	14 06	14 22	14 37	14 52		15 07	15 22		15 37	15 52		16 07	16 22	16 37	16 52		17 07		17 22	17 37	17 51		18 06	18 22
West Hampstead ⊖	a	14 15	14 31	14 46	15 01		15 16	15 31		15 46	16 01		16 16	16 31	16 46	17 01		17 16		17 31	17 46	18 00		18 15	18 31
Gospel Oak	a	14 21	14 37	14 52	15 07		15 22	15 37		15 52	16 07		16 22	16 37	16 52	17 07		17 22		17 37	17 52	18 06		18 21	18 38
Highbury & Islington ⊖	a	14 31	14 49	15 04	15 19		15 34	15 49		16 04	16 19		16 32	16 49	17 02	17 19		17 34		17 49	18 04	18 16		18 31	18 49
Stratford ⊖	a	14 51	15 07	15 21	15 36		15 51	16 06		16 21	16 36		16 51	17 06	17 21	17 36		17 51		18 06	18 22	18 37		18 52	19 07
Wembley Central ⊖	a					15 09						16 09					17 09						18 09		
Harrow & Wealdstone ⊖	a					15 13						16 13					17 13						18 13		
Watford Junction	a					15 20						16 20					17 20						18 20		
Hemel Hempstead	a					15 28						16 28					17 28						18 28		
Berkhamsted	a					15 32						16 32					17 32						18 32		
Tring	a					15 38						16 38					17 38						18 38		
Leighton Buzzard	a					15 46						16 46					17 46						18 46		
Bletchley	a					15 54						16 54					17 53						18 55		
Milton Keynes Central 10	a					16 01						17 00					17 59						19 01		

For other Norbury line connections, refer to Table T170

For other Stratford line connecting trains, refer to Table T59

Table T176-F

Saturdays
21 December to 16 May

East Croydon, Balham and Clapham Junction-Imperial Wharf, West Brompton, Kensington Olympia and Shepherd's Bush - Willesden Junction, Stratford/Watford Junction, Milton Keynes

		LO	LO	SN 1	LO	LO	LO	LO	SN 1	LO	LO	LO	LO	LO	SN 1	LO	LO	LO	SN 1	LO	LO	LO	LO
East Croydon	d			18 09					19 10						20 10				21 10				
Selhurst 4	d			18 16					19 16						20 16				21 16				
Thornton Heath	d			18 19					19 19						20 19				21 19				
Norbury	d			18 22					19 22						20 22				21 22				
Streatham Common 4	d			18 25					19 25						20 25				21 25				
Balham 4 ⊖	d			18 29					19 29						20 29				21 29				
Wandsworth Common	d																						
Clapham Junction 10	a			18 35					19 35						20 35				21 35				
	d	18 17	18 32	18 40	18 47	19 02	19 17	19 32	19 36	19 47	20 02	20 17	20 32	20 47	20 51	21 02	21 17	21 33	21 39	21 47	22 02	22 17	22 32
Imperial Wharf	d	18 21	18 36	18 45	18 51	19 06	19 21	19 36	19 41	19 51	20 06	20 21	20 36	20 51	20 56	21 06	21 21	21 37	21 44	21 51	22 06	22 21	22 36
West Brompton ⊖	d	18 24	18 39	18 48	18 54	19 09	19 24	19 39	19 44	19 54	20 09	20 24	20 39	20 54	20 59	21 09	21 24	21 40	21 47	21 54	22 09	22 24	22 39
Kensington (Olympia) ⊖	d	18 27	18 42	18 51	18 57	19 12	19 27	19 43	19 47	19 57	20 12	20 27	20 42	20 57	21 03	21 12	21 27	21 43	21 50	21 57	22 12	22 27	22 42
Shepherd's Bush ⊖	d	18 29	18 44	18 54	18 59	19 14	19 29	19 45	19 50	19 59	20 14	20 29	20 44	20 59	21 06	21 14	21 29	21 45	21 53	21 59	22 14	22 29	22 44
Willesden Jn. High Level ⊖	a	18 37	18 52		19 07	19 22	19 37	19 52		20 07	20 22	20 37	20 52	21 07		21 22	21 37	21 52		22 07	22 22	22 39	22 52
West Hampstead ⊖	a	18 46	19 01		19 16	19 31	19 46	20 01		20 16	20 31	20 46	21 01	21 16		21 31	21 46	22 01		22 16	22 31		23 01
Gospel Oak	a	18 52	19 07		19 22	19 39	19 52	20 07		20 22	20 38	20 52	21 07	21 22		21 37	21 52	22 08		22 22	22 37		23 07
Highbury & Islington ⊖	a	19 04	19 19		19 34	19 49	20 04	20 19		20 34	20 49	21 04	21 19	21 34		21 49	22 04	22 19		22 34	22 49		23 19
Stratford ⊖	a	19 22	19 37		19 51	20 06	20 21	20 36		20 51	21 06	21 21	21 36	21 51		22 06	22 21	22 37		22 51	23 06		23 36
Wembley Central ⊖	a			19 08											21 21				22 11				
Harrow & Wealdstone ⊖	a			19 13					20 07						21 26				22 16				
Watford Junction	a			19 20					20 14						21 33				22 24				
Hemel Hempstead	a																						
Berkhamsted	a																						
Tring	a																						
Leighton Buzzard	a																						
Bletchley	a																						
Milton Keynes Central 10	a																						

		SN 1	LO	LO	LO	LO	LO
East Croydon	d	22 10					
Selhurst 4	d	22 16					
Thornton Heath	d	22 19					
Norbury	d	22 22					
Streatham Common 4	d	22 25					
Balham 4 ⊖	d	22 29					
Wandsworth Common	d						
Clapham Junction 10	a	22 35					
	d	22 39	22 47	23 02	23 17	23 32	23 47
Imperial Wharf	d	22 44	22 51	23 06	23 21	23 36	23 51
West Brompton ⊖	d	22 47	22 54	23 09	23 24	23 39	23 54
Kensington (Olympia) ⊖	d	22 50	22 57	23 12	23 27	23 42	23 57
Shepherd's Bush ⊖	d	22 53	22 59	23 14	23 29	23 44	23 59
Willesden Jn. High Level ⊖	a		23 08	23 21	23 38	23 55	00 09
West Hampstead ⊖	a			23 30			
Gospel Oak	a			23 36			
Highbury & Islington ⊖	a			23 48			
Stratford ⊖	a			00 06			
Wembley Central ⊖	a	23 07					
Harrow & Wealdstone ⊖	a	23 11					
Watford Junction	a	23 18					
Hemel Hempstead	a						
Berkhamsted	a						
Tring	a						
Leighton Buzzard	a						
Bletchley	a						
Milton Keynes Central 10	a						

For other Norbury line connections, refer to Table T170

For other Stratford line connecting trains, refer to Table T59

NRT DECEMBER 19 EDITION

Table T176-F

Sundays
15 December to 10 May

East Croydon, Balham and Clapham Junction-Imperial Wharf, West Brompton, Kensington Olympia and Shepherd's Bush - Willesden Junction, Stratford/Watford Junction, Milton Keynes

		SN	SN	SN	LO	LO	LO	SN	LO	LO	LO	LO	LO	SN	LO	LO	LO	LO	SN	LO	LO	LO	SN
East Croydon	d																						
Selhurst 4	d																						
Thornton Heath	d																						
Norbury	d																						
Streatham Common 4	d																						
Balham 4 ⊖	d																						
Wandsworth Common	d																						
Clapham Junction 10	a																						
	d	07 31	08 15	08 20	08 31	08 51	09 01	09 13	09 21	09 31	09 50	10 01	10 13	10 17	10 29	10 44	10 59	11 12	11 16	11 29	11 44	11 59	12 05
Imperial Wharf	d	07 35	08 19	08 24	08 35	08 55	09 05	09 17	09 25	09 35	09 54	10 05	10 17	10 21	10 33	10 48	11 03	11 16	11 20	11 33	11 48	12 03	12 09
West Brompton ⊖	d	07 38	08 22	08 27	08 38	08 58	09 08	09 20	09 28	09 38	09 57	10 08	10 20	10 24	10 36	10 51	11 06	11 19	11 23	11 36	11 51	12 06	12 12
Kensington (Olympia) ⊖	d	07 42	08 26	08 31	08 41	09 01	09 11	09 24	09 31	09 41	10 00	10 11	10 23	10 28	10 39	10 54	11 09	11 22	11 27	11 39	11 54	12 09	12 16
Shepherd's Bush ⊖	d	07a44	08 29	08a33	08 43	09 03	09 13	09 27	09 33	09 43	10 02	10 13	10 25	10 31	10 41	10 56	11 11	11 24	11 30	11 41	11 56	12 11	12 19
Willesden Jn. High Level ⊖	a				08 52	09 10	09 22		09 41	09 51	10 10	10 21	10 33		10 50	11 05	11 20	11 33		11 50	12 05	12 20	
West Hampstead ⊖	a					09 19			09 50	10 00	10 19	10 30	10 42		10 59	11 14	11 29	11 42		11 59	12 14	12 29	
Gospel Oak	a					09 25			09 57	10 07	10 25	10 36	10 48		11 05	11 20	11 35	11 48		12 05	12 20	12 35	
Highbury & Islington ⊖	a					09 37			10 06	10 17	10 36	10 48	11 00		11 17	11 32	11 47	12 00		12 17	12 32	12 47	
Stratford ⊖	a					09 55			10 25	10 35	10 54	11 05	11 17		11 33	11 49	12 04	12 17		12 33	12 48	13 03	
Wembley Central ⊖	a																						
Harrow & Wealdstone ⊖	a		08 47					09 45						10 47					11 48				12 35
Watford Junction	a		08 55					09 55						10 59					11 57				12 43
Hemel Hempstead	a																						
Berkhamsted	a																						
Tring	a																						
Leighton Buzzard	a																						
Bletchley	a																						
Milton Keynes Central 10	a																						

		LO	LO	LO	LO	SN	LO	LO	LO	LO	SN	LO	LO	LO	LO	SN	LO	LO	LO	LO	SN	LO
East Croydon	d																					
Selhurst 4	d																					
Thornton Heath	d																					
Norbury	d																					
Streatham Common 4	d																					
Balham 4 ⊖	d																					
Wandsworth Common	d																					
Clapham Junction 10	a																					
	d	12 14	12 29	12 44	12 59	13 05	13 14	13 29	13 43	13 59	14 05	14 14	14 29	14 44	14 59	15 05	15 14	15 29	15 44	15 59	16 05	16 14
Imperial Wharf	d	12 18	12 33	12 48	13 03	13 09	13 18	13 33	13 47	14 03	14 09	14 18	14 33	14 49	15 03	15 09	15 18	15 33	15 48	16 03	16 09	16 19
West Brompton ⊖	d	12 21	12 36	12 51	13 06	13 12	13 21	13 36	13 50	14 06	14 12	14 21	14 36	14 52	15 06	15 12	15 21	15 36	15 51	16 06	16 12	16 22
Kensington (Olympia) ⊖	d	12 24	12 39	12 54	13 09	13 16	13 24	13 39	13 53	14 09	14 16	14 24	14 39	14 55	15 09	15 16	15 24	15 39	15 54	16 09	16 16	16 25
Shepherd's Bush ⊖	d	12 26	12 41	12 56	13 11	13 19	13 26	13 41	13 55	14 11	14 19	14 26	14 41	14 58	15 11	15 19	15 26	15 41	15 56	16 11	16 19	16 28
Willesden Jn. High Level ⊖	a	12 35	12 50	13 05	13 20		13 35	13 50	14 03	14 20		14 35	14 50	15 07	15 20		15 35	15 50	16 05	16 20		16 37
West Hampstead ⊖	a	12 44	12 59	13 14	13 29		13 44	13 59	14 13	14 29		14 44	14 59	15 16	15 29		15 44	15 59	16 14	16 29		16 46
Gospel Oak	a	12 50	13 05	13 20	13 35		13 50	14 05	14 19	14 35		14 50	15 05	15 22	15 35		15 50	16 05	16 20	16 35		16 52
Highbury & Islington ⊖	a	13 02	13 17	13 32	13 47		14 02	14 17	14 31	14 47		15 02	15 17	15 34	15 47		16 02	16 17	16 32	16 47		17 03
Stratford ⊖	a	13 18	13 33	13 48	14 03		14 18	14 33	14 47	15 03		15 18	15 33	15 49	16 03		16 18	16 33	16 48	17 03		17 18
Wembley Central ⊖	a																					
Harrow & Wealdstone ⊖	a					13 35					14 35					15 35					16 35	
Watford Junction	a					13 43					14 43					15 43					16 43	
Hemel Hempstead	a																					
Berkhamsted	a																					
Tring	a																					
Leighton Buzzard	a																					
Bletchley	a																					
Milton Keynes Central 10	a																					

		LO	LO	LO	SN	LO	LO	LO	LO	SN	LO	LO	LO	LO	SN	LO	LO	LO	LO	SN	LO	LO	LO
East Croydon	d																						
Selhurst 4	d																						
Thornton Heath	d																						
Norbury	d																						
Streatham Common 4	d																						
Balham 4 ⊖	d																						
Wandsworth Common	d																						
Clapham Junction 10	a																						
	d	16 29	16 44	16 59	17 05	17 14	17 29	17 44	17 59	18 05	18 14	18 29	18 44	18 59	19 05	19 14	19 29	19 44	19 59	20 05	20 14	20 29	20 44
Imperial Wharf	d	16 33	16 48	17 03	17 09	17 18	17 33	17 48	18 03	18 09	18 18	18 33	18 48	19 03	19 09	19 18	19 33	19 48	20 03	20 09	20 18	20 33	20 48
West Brompton ⊖	d	16 36	16 51	17 06	17 12	17 21	17 36	17 51	18 06	18 12	18 21	18 36	18 51	19 06	19 12	19 21	19 36	19 51	20 06	20 12	20 21	20 36	20 51
Kensington (Olympia) ⊖	d	16 39	16 54	17 09	17 16	17 24	17 39	17 54	18 09	18 16	18 24	18 39	18 54	19 09	19 16	19 24	19 39	19 54	20 09	20 16	20 24	20 39	20 54
Shepherd's Bush ⊖	d	16 41	16 56	17 11	17 19	17 26	17 41	17 56	18 11	18 19	18 26	18 41	18 56	19 11	19 19	19 26	19 41	19 56	20 11	20 19	20 26	20 41	20 56
Willesden Jn. High Level ⊖	a	16 50	17 05	17 20		17 35	17 50	18 05	18 20		18 35	18 50	19 05	19 20		19 35	19 50	20 05	20 20		20 35	20 50	21 05
West Hampstead ⊖	a	16 59	17 14	17 29		17 44	17 59	18 14	18 29		18 44	18 59	19 14	19 29		19 44	19 59	20 14	20 29			20 59	
Gospel Oak	a	17 05	17 20	17 35		17 50	18 05	18 20	18 35		18 50	19 05	19 20	19 35		19 50	20 05	20 20	20 35			21 05	
Highbury & Islington ⊖	a	17 17	17 32	17 47		18 02	18 17	18 32	18 47		19 02	19 17	19 32	19 47		20 02	20 17	20 32	20 47			21 17	
Stratford ⊖	a	17 33	17 48	18 03		18 18	18 33	18 48	19 03		19 18	19 33	19 48	20 03		20 18	20 33	20 48	21 03			21 33	
Wembley Central ⊖	a																						
Harrow & Wealdstone ⊖	a				17 35					18 35					19 35					20 35			
Watford Junction	a				17 43					18 43					19 43					20 43			
Hemel Hempstead	a																						
Berkhamsted	a																						
Tring	a																						
Leighton Buzzard	a																						
Bletchley	a																						
Milton Keynes Central 10	a																						

Table T176-F

Sundays

15 December to 10 May

East Croydon, Balham and Clapham Junction-Imperial Wharf, West Brompton, Kensington Olympia and Shepherd's Bush - Willesden Junction, Stratford/Watford Junction, Milton Keynes

		LO	LO	SN	LO	LO	LO	LO	SN	LO	LO	LO	LO	LO	LO
East Croydon	d														
Selhurst [4]	d														
Thornton Heath	d														
Norbury	d														
Streatham Common [4]	d														
Balham [4] ⊖	d														
Wandsworth Common	d														
Clapham Junction [10]	a														
	d	20 59	21 14	21 19	21 29	21 44	22 00	22 15	22 19	22 31	22 46	23 01	23 16	23 31	23 46
Imperial Wharf	d	21 03	21 18	21 23	21 33	21 48	22 04	22 19	22 23	22 35	22 50	23 05	23 20	23 35	23 50
West Brompton ⊖	d	21 06	21 21	21 26	21 36	21 51	22 07	22 22	22 26	22 38	22 53	23 08	23 23	23 38	23 53
Kensington (Olympia) ⊖	d	21 09	21 24	21 30	21 39	21 54	22 10	22 25	22 30	22 41	22 56	23 11	23 26	23 41	23 56
Shepherd's Bush ⊖	d	21 11	21 26	21 33	21 41	21 56	22 12	22 27	22 33	22 43	22 58	23 13	23 28	23 43	23 58
Willesden Jn. High Level ⊖	a	21 20	21 35		21 50	22 05	22 21	22 37		22 52	23 07	23 22	23 37	23 52	00 05
West Hampstead ⊖	a	21 29			21 59		22 30								
Gospel Oak	a	21 37			22 05		22 36								
Highbury & Islington ⊖	a	21 47			22 17		22 48								
Stratford ⊖	a	22 03			22 33		23 04								
Wembley Central ⊖	a														
Harrow & Wealdstone ⊖	a			21 50					22 49						
Watford Junction	a			22 00					22 58						
Hemel Hempstead	a														
Berkhamsted	a														
Tring	a														
Leighton Buzzard	a														
Bletchley	a														
Milton Keynes Central [10]	a														

For other Norbury line connections, refer to Table T170

For other Stratford line connecting trains, refer to Table T59

Table T176-R

Mondays to Fridays

16 December to 15 May

Milton Keynes, Watford Junction/Stratford, Willesden Junction-Shepherd's Bush, Kensington Olympia, West Brompton and Imperial Wharf-Clapham Junction, Balham and East Croydon

Miles	Miles			LO MO	LO MO	SN MX [1]	LO MX	LO	LO	SN [1]	LO	LO	LO	LO	LO	SN [1]	LO	LO	SN [1]	LO	LO	SN [1]	LO
0	—	Milton Keynes Central [10]	d																			07 01	
3	—	Bletchley	d																			07 06	
9½	—	Leighton Buzzard	d																			07 13	
18	—	Tring	d																			07 21	
21¾	—	Berkhamsted	d																			07 26	
25¼	—	Hemel Hempstead	d																			07 30	
32¼	—	Watford Junction	d							05 54						06 53			07 24			07 38	
36¾	—	Harrow & Wealdstone ⊖	d							06 00						07 00			07 31			07 45	
40¼	—	Wembley Central ⊖	d							06 05						07 05			07 36			07 50	
—	0	Stratford [7] ⊖	d										06 07	06 17	06 28		06 39	06 53		07 05	07 18		07 30
—	4¾	Highbury & Islington ⊖	d										06 21	06 31	06 42		06 54	07 08		07 20	07 33		07 45
—	7½	Gospel Oak	d										06 31	06 43	06 52		07 06	07 19		07 31	07 43		07 55
—	9½	West Hampstead ⊖	d										06 37	06 49	06 58		07 12	07 25		07 37	07 49		08 02
—	12	Willesden Jn. High Level ⊖	d				00 01	05 58	06 10		06 23	06 35	06 47	06 59	07 08		07 22	07 35		07 47	07 59		08 11
44½	13½	**Shepherd's Bush** ⊖	d		00 05	00 06	00 09	06 05	06 16	06 21	06 30	06 41	06 53	07 05	07 17	07 22	07 29	07 42	07 50	07 54	08 06	08 11	08 17
45½	—	**Kensington (Olympia)** ⊖	d		00 07	00 08	00 11	06 07	06 18	06 24	06 32	06 43	06 55	07 07	07 19	07 25	07 31	07 44	07 52	07 56	08 09	08 14	08 19
47½	—	**West Brompton** ⊖	d		00 10	00 10	00 14	06 10	06 21	06 27	06 35	06 46	06 58	07 10	07 22	07 28	07 34	07 46	07 55	07 59	08 11	08 17	08 22
48½	—	**Imperial Wharf**	d	00 01	00 13	00 13	00 17	06 13	06 24	06 29	06 38	06 49	07 01	07 13	07 25	07 30	07 37	07 49	07 57	08 02	08 14	08 19	08 25
49½	—	Clapham Junction [10]	a	00 08	00 20	00 17	00 22	06 19	06 31	06 34	06 44	06 56	07 09	07 19	07 30	07 35	07 44	07 55	08 04	08 10	08 23	08 25	08 32
—	—		d							06 35						07 35			08 05			08 35	
50¾	—	Wandsworth Common	a													07 38							
51½	—	Balham [4] ⊖	a							06 40						07 41			08 10			08 40	
53¼	—	Streatham Common [4]	a							06 45						07 46			08 15			08 45	
54¼	—	Norbury	a							06 48						07 49			08 18			08 48	
55½	—	Thornton Heath	a							06 51						07 52			08 21			08 51	
56¼	—	Selhurst [4]	a							06 54						07 54			08 24			08 54	
57¼	—	East Croydon	a							06 59						08 01			08 31			09 01	

		LO	LO	LO	LO	LO	SN [1]	LO	LO	SN [1]	LO	SN [1]	LO	LO	SN [1]	LO	LO	LO	LO	SN [1]	LO	LO	LO
Milton Keynes Central [10]	d						08 12								09 12					10 12			
Bletchley	d						08 17								09 17					10 17			
Leighton Buzzard	d						08 24								09 24					10 24			
Tring	d						08 34								09 34					10 34			
Berkhamsted	d						08 38								09 38					10 38			
Hemel Hempstead	d						08 43								09 43					10 43			
Watford Junction	d						08 52			09 14					09 52					10 52			
Harrow & Wealdstone ⊖	d						08 59			09 23					09 59					10 59			
Wembley Central ⊖	d						09 04			09 28					10 04					11 04			
Stratford [7] ⊖	d	07 41	07 54	08 06	08 17	08 28		08 42	08 53		09 06		09 15	09 28		09 41	09 53	10 08	10 23		10 39	10 53	11 08
Highbury & Islington ⊖	d	07 56	08 09	08 21	08 32	08 43		08 57	09 07		09 19		09 31	09 44		09 56	10 07	10 24	10 37		10 54	11 07	11 22
Gospel Oak	d	08 07	08 19	08 31	08 43	08 53		09 06	09 20		09 33		09 41	09 54		10 05	10 17	10 35	10 49		11 03	11 19	11 34
West Hampstead ⊖	d	08 13	08 25	08 37	08 49	08 59		09 12	09 26		09 39		09 48	10 01		10 11	10 23	10 41	10 56		11 09	11 26	11 40
Willesden Jn. High Level ⊖	d	08 23	08 35	08 47	08 59	09 09		09 22	09 35		09 48		09 57	10 11		10 20	10 33	10 50	11 05		11 19	11 35	11 50
Shepherd's Bush ⊖	d	08 30	08 43	08 54	09 06	09 17	09 22	09 29	09 41	09 46	09 56	10 01	10 05	10 18	10 22	10 27	10 42	10 56	11 11	11 22	11 26	11 41	11 56
Kensington (Olympia) ⊖	d	08 32	08 45	08 56	09 08	09 19	09 25	09 31	09 43	09 49	09 58	10 03	10 07	10 20	10 25	10 29	10 44	10 58	11 13	11 25	11 29	11 43	11 58
West Brompton ⊖	d	08 34	08 47	08 58	09 10	09 22	09 28	09 33	09 46	09 52	10 01	10 05	10 10	10 22	10 28	10 32	10 47	11 01	11 16	11 28	11 32	11 46	12 01
Imperial Wharf	d	08 37	08 50	09 01	09 13	09 25	09 30	09 36	09 49	09 54	10 04	10 08	10 13	10 25	10 30	10 35	10 50	11 04	11 19	11 30	11 35	11 49	12 04
Clapham Junction [10]	a	08 46	08 56	09 08	09 19	09 33	09 35	09 44	09 55	10 00	10 11	10 12	10 20	10 33	10 35	10 43	10 58	11 10	11 25	11 35	11 41	11 55	12 10
	d						09 35								10 35					11 35			
Wandsworth Common	a																						
Balham [4] ⊖	a						09 40								10 40					11 40			
Streatham Common [4]	a						09 45								10 45					11 45			
Norbury	a						09 48								10 48					11 48			
Thornton Heath	a						09 51								10 51					11 51			
Selhurst [4]	a						09 54								10 54					11 54			
East Croydon	a						10 00								10 59					11 59			

For other Norbury line connections, refer to Table T170

For other Stratford line connecting trains, refer to Table T59

Table T176-R

Mondays to Fridays
16 December to 15 May

Milton Keynes, Watford Junction/Stratford, Willesden Junction-Shepherd's Bush, Kensington Olympia, West Brompton and Imperial Wharf-Clapham Junction, Balham and East Croydon

		LO	SN TThO [1]	SN MWFO [1]	LO	LO	LO	LO	SN [1]	LO	LO	LO	LO	SN [1]	LO	LO	LO	LO	SN [1]	LO	LO	SN [1]	LO
Milton Keynes Central [10]	d		11 12	11 12					12 12					13 12					14 12				
Bletchley	d		11 17	11 17					12 17					13 17					14 17				
Leighton Buzzard	d		11 24	11 24					12 24					13 24					14 24				
Tring	d		11 34	11 34					12 34					13 34					14 34				
Berkhamsted	d		11 38	11 38					12 38					13 38					14 39				
Hemel Hempstead	d		11 43	11 43					12 43					13 43					14 44				
Watford Junction	d		11 52	11 52					12 52					13 52					14 52				
Harrow & Wealdstone ⊖	d		11 59	11 59					12 59					13 59					15 00				
Wembley Central ⊖	d		12 03	12 03					13 04					14 04					15 04				
Stratford [7] ⊖	d	11 23			11 38	11 53	12 08	12 23		12 38	12 53	13 08	13 23		13 39	13 53	14 07	14 23		14 38	14 53		15 05
Highbury & Islington ⊖	d	11 37			11 52	12 07	12 22	12 37		12 52	13 07	13 22	13 37		13 55	14 07	14 21	14 37		14 52	15 07		15 19
Gospel Oak	d	11 49			12 02	12 17	12 34	12 49		13 05	13 19	13 34	13 49		14 05	14 19	14 33	14 50		15 04	15 20		15 32
West Hampstead ⊖	d	11 55			12 08	12 23	12 40	12 55		13 12	13 25	13 40	13 55		14 11	14 26	14 39	14 56		15 11	15 26		15 39
Willesden Jn. High Level ⊖	d	12 05			12 17	12 32	12 49	13 05		13 21	13 34	13 50	14 04		14 21	14 35	14 49	15 05		15 21	15 35		15 48
Shepherd's Bush ⊖	d	12 11	12 22	12 22	12 27	12 41	12 55	13 11	13 22	13 27	13 41	13 56	14 11	14 22	14 28	14 41	14 56	15 12	15 22	15 27	15 43	15 49	15 54
Kensington (Olympia) ⊖	d	12 13	12 25	12 25	12 29	12 43	12 57	13 13	13 25	13 29	13 43	13 58	14 13	14 25	14 30	14 43	14 58	15 14	15 25	15 30	15 45	15 52	15 56
West Brompton ⊖	d	12 16	12 28	12 28	12 32	12 46	13 00	13 16	13 28	13 32	13 46	14 01	14 16	14 28	14 32	14 46	15 01	15 16	15 28	15 33	15 47	15 55	15 59
Imperial Wharf	d	12 19	12 30	12 30	12 35	12 49	13 03	13 19	13 30	13 35	13 49	14 04	14 19	14 30	14 35	14 49	15 04	15 19	15 30	15 36	15 50	15 57	16 02
Clapham Junction [10]	a	12 25	12 35	12 35	12 40	12 55	13 10	13 25	13 35	13 40	13 55	14 10	14 25	14 35	14 41	14 55	15 09	15 28	15 35	15 43	15 58	16 02	16 07
	d			12 35					13 35					14 35					15 35			16 05	
Wandsworth Common	a																						
Balham [4] ⊖	a			12 40					13 40					14 40					15 40			16 10	
Streatham Common [4]	a			12 45					13 45					14 45					15 45			16 15	
Norbury	a			12 48					13 48					14 48					15 48			16 18	
Thornton Heath	a			12 51					13 51					14 51					15 51			16 21	
Selhurst [4]	a			12 54					13 54					14 54					15 54			16 24	
East Croydon	a			12 59					13 59					14 59					16 00			16 34	

		LO	LO	SN [1]	LO	LO	SN [1]	LO	LO	LO	SN [1]	LO	LO	SN [1]	LO	LO	LO	SN [1]	LO	LO	LO	LO
Milton Keynes Central [10]	d			15 12							16 12							17 12				
Bletchley	d			15 17							16 17							17 17				
Leighton Buzzard	d			15 24							16 24							17 24				
Tring	d			15 34							16 34							17 34				
Berkhamsted	d			15 38							16 38							17 38				
Hemel Hempstead	d			15 43							16 43							17 43				
Watford Junction	d			15 52			16 12				16 52							17 52				
Harrow & Wealdstone ⊖	d			15 59			16 20				17 00							18 00				
Wembley Central ⊖	d			16 04			16 25				17 05							18 05				
Stratford [7] ⊖	d	15 20	15 29		15 42	15 55		16 05	16 19	16 29		16 41	16 53		17 06	17 17	17 31		17 41	17 53	18 08	18 19
Highbury & Islington ⊖	d	15 34	15 43		15 56	16 10		16 19	16 34	16 44		16 56	17 08		17 21	17 32	17 46		17 56	18 08	18 23	18 34
Gospel Oak	d	15 45	15 54		16 07	16 19		16 30	16 43	16 55		17 07	17 19		17 31	17 41	17 55		18 07	18 19	18 33	18 43
West Hampstead ⊖	d	15 52	16 01		16 14	16 25		16 36	16 49	17 01		17 13	17 25		17 37	17 47	18 01		18 13	18 25	18 39	18 49
Willesden Jn. High Level ⊖	d	16 01	16 10		16 23	16 35		16 47	16 59	17 11		17 23	17 35		17 47	17 59	18 11		18 23	18 34	18 48	18 58
Shepherd's Bush ⊖	d	16 07	16 17	16 22	16 29	16 41	16 46	16 54	17 06	17 17	17 22	17 30	17 42	17 49	17 54	18 06	18 17	18 22	18 30	18 42	18 55	19 06
Kensington (Olympia) ⊖	d	16 09	16 19	16 25	16 31	16 43	16 49	16 56	17 08	17 19	17 25	17 32	17 44	17 52	17 56	18 08	18 19	18 24	18 32	18 44	18 57	19 08
West Brompton ⊖	d	16 12	16 22	16 28	16 34	16 46	16 52	16 59	17 10	17 22	17 28	17 34	17 46	17 55	17 59	18 10	18 22	18 27	18 34	18 46	18 59	19 10
Imperial Wharf	d	16 15	16 25	16 30	16 37	16 49	16 55	17 02	17 13	17 25	17 30	17 37	17 49	17 57	18 02	18 13	18 25	18 30	18 37	18 49	19 02	19 13
Clapham Junction [10]	a	16 22	16 31	16 35	16 44	16 57	17 01	17 10	17 21	17 31	17 35	17 43	17 58	18 02	18 11	18 22	18 33	18 35	18 46	18 58	19 10	19 21
	d			16 35			17 05				17 35			18 05				18 35				
Wandsworth Common	a																					
Balham [4] ⊖	a			16 40			17 10				17 40			18 10				18 40				
Streatham Common [4]	a			16 45			17 15				17 45			18 15				18 45				
Norbury	a			16 48			17 18				17 48			18 18				18 48				
Thornton Heath	a			16 51			17 21				17 51			18 21				18 51				
Selhurst [4]	a			16 54			17 24				17 54			18 24				18 54				
East Croydon	a			17 00			17 30				18 00			18 31				19 01				

For other Norbury line connections, refer to Table T170

For other Stratford line connecting trains, refer to Table T59

NRT DECEMBER 19 EDITION

Table T176-R

Mondays to Fridays
16 December to 15 May

Milton Keynes, Watford Junction/Stratford, Willesden Junction-Shepherd's Bush, Kensington Olympia, West Brompton and Imperial Wharf-Clapham Junction, Balham and East Croydon

		LO	SN [1]	LO	LO	LO	LO	LO	SN MO [1]	SN MX [1]	LO	LO	LO	LO	SN [1]	LO	LO	LO	LO	SN [1]	LO	LO	LO
Milton Keynes Central [10]	d		18 12						19 16	19 16					20 12					21 12			
Bletchley	d		18 18						19 21	19 21					20 19					21 17			
Leighton Buzzard	d		18 25						19 28	19 28					20 26					21 24			
Tring	d		18 35						19 36	19 37					20 35					21 34			
Berkhamsted	d		18 39						19 41	19 41					20 40					21 38			
Hemel Hempstead	d		18 44						19 45	19 46					20 44					21 43			
Watford Junction	d		18 52						19 54	19 54					20 52					21 52			
Harrow & Wealdstone ⊖	d		18 59						20 02	20 02					20 59					22 00			
Wembley Central ⊖	d		19 05						20 06	20 06					21 04								
Stratford [7] ⊖	d	18 29		18 41	18 53	19 05	19 17	19 29			19 42	19 53	20 05	20 20		20 35	20 46	21 07	21 19		21 34	21 49	22 04
Highbury & Islington ⊖	d	18 44		18 56	19 07	19 19	19 31	19 43			19 56	20 07	20 19	20 35		20 50	21 00	21 21	21 33		21 48	22 03	22 18
Gospel Oak	d	18 55		19 07	19 17	19 30	19 43	19 55			20 07	20 19	20 30	20 45		21 00	21 12	21 31	21 43		22 00	22 15	22 30
West Hampstead ⊖	d	19 01		19 13	19 23	19 36	19 50	20 01			20 13	20 26	20 36	20 51		21 06	21 18	21 38	21 51		22 06	22 21	22 36
Willesden Jn. High Level ⊖	d	19 11		19 23	19 32	19 47	19 59	20 11			20 22	20 35	20 45	21 01		21 16	21 27	21 48	22 01		22 16	22 31	22 46
Shepherd's Bush ⊖	d	19 17	19 22	19 30	19 41	19 53	20 05	20 17	20 22	20 22	20 29	20 41	20 53	21 07	21 19	21 23	21 36	21 55	22 07	22 19	22 23	22 37	22 52
Kensington (Olympia) ⊖	d	19 19	19 25	19 32	19 43	19 55	20 07	20 19	20 25	20 25	20 31	20 43	20 55	21 09	21 21	21 26	21 38	21 57	22 09	22 21	22 25	22 39	22 54
West Brompton ⊖	d	19 22	19 28	19 34	19 46	19 58	20 10	20 22	20 28	20 28	20 34	20 46	20 57	21 12	21 24	21 29	21 41	21 59	22 12	22 24	22 28	22 42	22 57
Imperial Wharf	d	19 25	19 30	19 37	19 50	20 01	20 13	20 25	20 30	20 30	20 37	20 49	21 01	21 15	21 27	21 32	21 45	22 02	22 15	22 27	22 31	22 45	23 00
Clapham Junction [10]	a	19 34	19 35	19 43	19 58	20 07	20 19	20 31	20 35	20 35	20 44	20 55	21 07	21 22	21 32	21 37	21 51	22 09	22 21	22 31	22 36	22 51	23 06
	d		19 35						20 35	20 35										22 35			
Wandsworth Common	a																						
Balham [4] ⊖	a		19 40						20 40	20 40										22 40			
Streatham Common [4]	a		19 45						20 45	20 45										22 45			
Norbury	a		19 48						20 48	20 48										22 48			
Thornton Heath	a		19 51						20 51	20 51										22 51			
Selhurst [4]	a		19 54						20 54	20 54										22 54			
East Croydon	a		19 59						20 59	20 59										22 59			

		SN [1]	LO	SN [1]	LO	LO	LO	SN [1]
Milton Keynes Central [10]	d			22 10				
Bletchley	d			22 15				
Leighton Buzzard	d			22 22				
Tring	d			22 34				
Berkhamsted	d			22 38				
Hemel Hempstead	d			22 43				
Watford Junction	d	22 28		22 53				23 42
Harrow & Wealdstone ⊖	d	22 34		23 00				23 48
Wembley Central ⊖	d							
Stratford [7] ⊖	d		22 14		22 36			
Highbury & Islington ⊖	d		22 28		22 50			
Gospel Oak	d		22 40		23 04			
West Hampstead ⊖	d		22 46		23 10			
Willesden Jn. High Level ⊖	d		23 00		23 19	23 30	23 44	
Shepherd's Bush ⊖	d	22 57	23 07	23 22	23 26	23 36	23 52	00 06
Kensington (Olympia) ⊖	d	23 00	23 09	23 24	23 28	23 38	23 54	00 08
West Brompton ⊖	d	23 03	23 12	23 27	23 31	23 41	23 56	00 10
Imperial Wharf	d	23 05	23 15	23 29	23 34	23 44	23 59	00 13
Clapham Junction [10]	a	23 10	23 21	23 34	23 41	23 51	00 05	00 17
	d							
Wandsworth Common	a							
Balham [4] ⊖	a							
Streatham Common [4]	a							
Norbury	a							
Thornton Heath	a							
Selhurst [4]	a							
East Croydon	a							

For other Norbury line connections, refer to Table T170

For other Stratford line connecting trains, refer to Table T59

Table T176-R

Saturdays

21 December to 16 May

Milton Keynes, Watford Junction/Stratford, Willesden Junction-Shepherd's Bush, Kensington Olympia, West Brompton and Imperial Wharf-Clapham Junction, Balham and East Croydon

		SN [1]	LO	LO	SN [1]	LO		LO	LO	LO	SN [1]	LO	LO	LO	LO	SN [1]		LO	LO	LO	LO	SN [1]	LO	LO	LO
Milton Keynes Central [10]	d															07 13						08 13			
Bletchley	d															07 18						08 18			
Leighton Buzzard	d															07 25						08 25			
Tring	d															07 34						08 34			
Berkhamsted	d															07 38						08 38			
Hemel Hempstead	d															07 43						08 43			
Watford Junction	d				05 52						06 55					07 52						08 52			
Harrow & Wealdstone ⊖	d				05 58						07 01					07 59						08 59			
Wembley Central ⊖	d				06 03						07 06					08 04						09 04			
Stratford [7] ⊖	d							05 55	06 08	06 23		06 38	06 53	07 08	07 23			07 38	07 53	08 08	08 23		08 38	08 53	09 08
Highbury & Islington ⊖	d							06 09	06 22	06 38		06 53	07 07	07 22	07 37			07 53	08 07	08 22	08 38		08 52	09 07	09 22
Gospel Oak	d							06 21	06 34	06 49		07 04	07 19	07 34	07 49			08 03	08 19	08 34	08 49		09 04	09 19	09 34
West Hampstead ⊖	d							06 27	06 40	06 55		07 10	07 25	07 40	07 55			08 09	08 25	08 40	08 55		09 10	09 25	09 40
Willesden Jn. High Level ⊖	d		00 01	06 05		06 20		06 37	06 50	07 05		07 20	07 35	07 50	08 05			08 20	08 35	08 50	09 05		09 20	09 35	09 50
Shepherd's Bush ⊖	d	00 06	00 09	06 11	06 19	06 26		06 43	06 56	07 11	07 21	07 26	07 41	07 56	08 11	08 19		08 27	08 41	08 56	09 11	09 19	09 26	09 41	09 56
Kensington (Olympia) ⊖	d	00 08	00 11	06 13	06 22	06 28		06 45	06 58	07 13	07 24	07 28	07 43	07 58	08 13	08 22		08 29	08 43	08 58	09 13	09 22	09 28	09 43	09 58
West Brompton ⊖	d	00 10	00 14	06 16	06 25	06 31		06 48	07 01	07 16	07 27	07 31	07 46	08 01	08 16	08 25		08 31	08 46	09 01	09 16	09 25	09 31	09 46	10 01
Imperial Wharf	d	00 13	00 17	06 19	06 28	06 34		06 51	07 04	07 19	07 29	07 34	07 49	08 04	08 19	08 28		08 34	08 49	09 04	09 19	09 28	09 34	09 49	10 04
Clapham Junction [10]	a	00 17	00 22	06 26	06 32	06 41		06 57	07 10	07 25	07 34	07 40	07 55	08 10	08 25	08 32		08 40	08 55	09 10	09 25	09 32	09 40	09 55	10 10
	d				06 35						07 35					08 35						09 35			
Wandsworth Common	a																								
Balham [4] ⊖	a				06 40						07 40					08 40						09 40			
Streatham Common [4]	a				06 45						07 45					08 45						09 45			
Norbury	a				06 48						07 48					08 48						09 48			
Thornton Heath	a				06 51						07 51					08 51						09 51			
Selhurst [4]	a				06 54						07 54					08 54						09 54			
East Croydon	a				06 59						07 59					08 59						09 59			

		LO		SN [1]	LO	LO	LO	LO	SN [1]	LO	LO	LO		LO	SN [1]	LO	LO	LO	LO	SN [1]	LO	LO		LO	LO
Milton Keynes Central [10]	d			09 12					10 12						11 12					12 12					
Bletchley	d			09 17					10 17						11 17					12 17					
Leighton Buzzard	d			09 24					10 24						11 24					12 24					
Tring	d			09 34					10 34						11 34					12 34					
Berkhamsted	d			09 38					10 38						11 38					12 38					
Hemel Hempstead	d			09 43					10 43						11 43					12 43					
Watford Junction	d			09 52					10 52						11 52					12 52					
Harrow & Wealdstone ⊖	d			09 59					10 59						11 59					12 59					
Wembley Central ⊖	d			10 04					11 04						12 04					13 04					
Stratford [7] ⊖	d	09 23			09 38	09 53	10 08	10 23		10 38	10 53	11 08		11 23		11 38	11 53	12 08	12 23		12 38	12 53		13 07	13 23
Highbury & Islington ⊖	d	09 37			09 52	10 08	10 22	10 37		10 53	11 07	11 22		11 37		11 52	12 07	12 23	12 37		12 53	13 07		13 21	13 37
Gospel Oak	d	09 49			10 04	10 21	10 34	10 49		11 04	11 19	11 34		11 49		12 04	12 19	12 35	12 49		13 04	13 19		13 33	13 49
West Hampstead ⊖	d	09 55			10 10	10 27	10 40	10 55		11 10	11 26	11 40		11 55		12 10	12 25	12 41	12 55		13 10	13 25		13 39	13 55
Willesden Jn. High Level ⊖	d	10 04			10 20	10 36	10 50	11 05		11 20	11 35	11 50		12 05		12 20	12 35	12 51	13 05		13 20	13 35		13 49	14 05
Shepherd's Bush ⊖	d	10 11		10 19	10 26	10 42	10 56	11 11	11 19	11 26	11 41	11 56		12 11	12 19	12 26	12 41	12 57	13 11	13 19	13 26	13 41		13 56	14 11
Kensington (Olympia) ⊖	d	10 13		10 22	10 28	10 44	10 58	11 13	11 22	11 28	11 43	11 58		12 13	12 22	12 28	12 43	12 59	13 13	13 22	13 28	13 43		13 58	14 13
West Brompton ⊖	d	10 16		10 25	10 31	10 47	11 01	11 16	11 25	11 31	11 46	12 01		12 16	12 25	12 31	12 46	13 02	13 16	13 25	13 31	13 46		14 01	14 16
Imperial Wharf	d	10 19		10 28	10 34	10 50	11 04	11 19	11 28	11 34	11 49	12 04		12 19	12 28	12 34	12 49	13 05	13 19	13 28	13 34	13 49		14 04	14 19
Clapham Junction [10]	a	10 25		10 32	10 40	10 55	11 10	11 25	11 32	11 40	11 55	12 10		12 25	12 32	12 40	12 55	13 13	13 25	13 32	13 40	13 55		14 12	14 25
	d			10 35					11 35						12 35					13 35					
Wandsworth Common	a																								
Balham [4] ⊖	a			10 40					11 40						12 40					13 40					
Streatham Common [4]	a			10 45					11 45						12 45					13 45					
Norbury	a			10 48					11 48						12 48					13 48					
Thornton Heath	a			10 51					11 51						12 51					13 51					
Selhurst [4]	a			10 54					11 54						12 54					13 54					
East Croydon	a			10 59					11 59						12 59					13 59					

For other Norbury line connections, refer to Table T170

For other Stratford line connecting trains, refer to Table T59

Table T176-R

Saturdays

21 December to 16 May

Milton Keynes, Watford Junction/Stratford, Willesden Junction-Shepherd's Bush, Kensington Olympia, West Brompton and Imperial Wharf-Clapham Junction, Balham and East Croydon

		SN [1]	LO		LO	SN [1]	LO		LO		SN [1]	LO		LO	SN [1]	LO	LO	LO	LO		SN [1]	LO
Milton Keynes Central [10]	d	13 12				14 12					15 12				16 12						17 12	
Bletchley	d	13 17				14 17					15 17				16 17						17 17	
Leighton Buzzard	d	13 24				14 24					15 24				16 24						17 24	
Tring	d	13 34				14 34					15 34				16 34						17 34	
Berkhamsted	d	13 38				14 38					15 38				16 38						17 38	
Hemel Hempstead	d	13 43				14 43					15 43				16 43						17 43	
Watford Junction	d	13 52				14 52					15 52				16 52						17 52	
Harrow & Wealdstone ⊖	d	13 59				14 59					15 59				16 59						17 59	
Wembley Central ⊖	d	14 04				15 04					16 04				17 04						18 04	
Stratford [7] ⊖	d		13 38	and every 15 minutes until	14 23		14 38	and every 15 minutes until	15 23			15 38	and every 15 minutes until	16 23		16 38	16 53	17 08	17 23			17 38
Highbury & Islington ⊖	d		13 52		14 37		14 52		15 37			15 52		16 37		16 52	17 07	17 22	17 37			17 52
Gospel Oak	d		14 04		14 49		15 04		15 49			16 04		16 49		17 04	17 19	17 34	17 49			18 04
West Hampstead ⊖	d		14 10		14 55		15 10		15 55			16 10		16 55		17 10	17 25	17 40	17 55			18 10
Willesden Jn. High Level ⊖	d		14 20		15 05		15 20		16 05			16 20		17 05		17 20	17 35	17 50	18 05			18 20
Shepherd's Bush ⊖	d	14 19	14 26		15 11	15 19	15 26		16 11		16 19	16 26		17 11	17 19	17 26	17 41	17 56	18 11		18 19	18 26
Kensington (Olympia) ⊖	d	14 22	14 28		15 13	15 22	15 28		16 13		16 22	16 28		17 13	17 22	17 28	17 43	17 58	18 13		18 22	18 28
West Brompton ⊖	d	14 25	14 31		15 16	15 25	15 31		16 16		16 25	16 31		17 16	17 25	17 31	17 46	18 01	18 16		18 25	18 31
Imperial Wharf	d	14 28	14 34		15 19	15 28	15 34		16 19		16 28	16 34		17 19	17 28	17 34	17 49	18 04	18 19		18 28	18 34
Clapham Junction [10]	a	14 32	14 40		15 25	15 32	15 40		16 25		16 32	16 40		17 25	17 32	17 40	17 55	18 13	18 28		18 32	18 43
	d	14 35				15 35					16 35				17 35						18 35	
Wandsworth Common	a																					
Balham [4] ⊖	a	14 40				15 40					16 40				17 40						18 40	
Streatham Common [4]	a	14 45				15 45					16 45				17 45						18 45	
Norbury	a	14 48				15 48					16 48				17 48						18 48	
Thornton Heath	a	14 51				15 51					16 51				17 51						18 51	
Selhurst [4]	a	14 54				15 54					16 54				17 54						18 54	
East Croydon	a	14 59				15 59					16 59				17 59						18 59	

		LO	LO	LO	SN [1]	LO	LO	LO		SN [1]	LO	SN [1]	LO		LO	SN [1]	LO	LO		LO	LO	SN [1]	LO	LO
Milton Keynes Central [10]	d				18 12							19 13												
Bletchley	d				18 17							19 18												
Leighton Buzzard	d				18 24							19 25												
Tring	d				18 34							19 34												
Berkhamsted	d				18 38							19 38												
Hemel Hempstead	d				18 43							19 43												
Watford Junction	d				18 51					19 31		19 51				20 43						21 46		
Harrow & Wealdstone ⊖	d				18 59					19 37		20 00				20 49						21 52		
Wembley Central ⊖	d				19 03					19 42		20 04				20 54						21 57		
Stratford [7] ⊖	d	17 53	18 08	18 23		18 38	18 53	19 08			19 23		19 38	and every 15 minutes until	20 23		20 38	20 53		21 08	21 23		21 38	21 53
Highbury & Islington ⊖	d	18 07	18 22	18 37		18 52	19 07	19 22			19 37		19 52		20 37		20 52	21 07		21 22	21 37		21 52	22 07
Gospel Oak	d	18 19	18 34	18 49		19 04	19 19	19 32			19 49		20 04		20 49		21 04	21 18		21 34	21 49		22 04	22 19
West Hampstead ⊖	d	18 25	18 40	18 55		19 10	19 25	19 38			19 55		20 10		20 55		21 10	21 24		21 40	21 55		22 10	22 25
Willesden Jn. High Level ⊖	d	18 35	18 50	19 05		19 20	19 35	19 50			20 05		20 20		21 05		21 20	21 35		21 50	22 05		22 20	22 35
Shepherd's Bush ⊖	d	18 41	18 56	19 11	19 19	19 26	19 41	19 56		20 01	20 11	20 20	20 26		21 11	21 16	21 26	21 41		21 57	22 11	22 15	22 26	22 41
Kensington (Olympia) ⊖	d	18 43	18 58	19 13	19 22	19 28	19 43	19 58		20 03	20 13	20 22	20 28		21 13	21 20	21 28	21 43		21 59	22 13	22 23	22 28	22 43
West Brompton ⊖	d	18 46	19 01	19 16	19 25	19 31	19 46	20 01		20 06	20 16	20 25	20 31		21 16	21 23	21 31	21 46		22 01	22 16	22 26	22 31	22 46
Imperial Wharf	d	18 49	19 04	19 19	19 28	19 34	19 49	20 04		20 09	20 19	20 28	20 34		21 19	21 26	21 34	21 49		22 04	22 19	22 29	22 34	22 49
Clapham Junction [10]	a	18 58	19 10	19 25	19 32	19 40	19 55	20 10		20 13	20 25	20 33	20 40		21 25	21 30	21 40	21 55		22 10	22 25	22 33	22 40	22 55
	d				19 35							20 35				21 35						22 35		
Wandsworth Common	a																							
Balham [4] ⊖	a				19 40							20 40				21 40						22 40		
Streatham Common [4]	a				19 45							20 45				21 45						22 45		
Norbury	a				19 48							20 48				21 48						22 48		
Thornton Heath	a				19 51							20 51				21 51						22 51		
Selhurst [4]	a				19 54							20 54				21 54						22 54		
East Croydon	a				19 59							20 59				21 59						22 59		

For other Norbury line connections, refer to Table T170

For other Stratford line connecting trains, refer to Table T59

Table T176-R

Saturdays
21 December to 16 May

Milton Keynes, Watford Junction/Stratford, Willesden Junction-Shepherd's Bush, Kensington Olympia, West Brompton and Imperial Wharf-Clapham Junction, Balham and East Croydon

		LO	LO	SN 1	LO	LO	SN 1	LO
Milton Keynes Central 10	d							
Bletchley	d							
Leighton Buzzard	d							
Tring	d							
Berkhamsted	d							
Hemel Hempstead	d							
Watford Junction	d			22 53			23 26	
Harrow & Wealdstone ⊖	d			22 59			23 32	
Wembley Central ⊖	d			23 04			23 37	
Stratford 7 ⊖	d	22 08			22 38			23 08
Highbury & Islington ⊖	d	22 22			22 52			23 22
Gospel Oak	d	22 34			23 04			23 34
West Hampstead ⊖	d	22 40			23 11			23 40
Willesden Jn. High Level ⊖	d	22 50	23 05		23 20	23 35		23 50
Shepherd's Bush ⊖	d	22 56	23 11	23 22	23 26	23 41	23 52	23 56
Kensington (Olympia) ⊖	d	22 58	23 13	23 24	23 28	23 43	23 54	23 58
West Brompton ⊖	d	23 01	23 16	23 27	23 31	23 46	23 57	00 02
Imperial Wharf	d	23 04	23 19	23 29	23 34	23 49	00 01	00 05
Clapham Junction 10	a	23 10	23 26	23 34	23 40	23 56	00 06	00 10
	d							
Wandsworth Common	a							
Balham 4 ⊖	a							
Streatham Common 4	a							
Norbury	a							
Thornton Heath	a							
Selhurst 4	a							
East Croydon	a							

Sundays
15 December to 10 May

		SN 1 A	LO A	LO	SN	LO	SN	LO	LO	LO	LO	SN	LO	LO	LO	LO	SN	LO		LO	SN
Milton Keynes Central 10	d																				
Bletchley	d																				
Leighton Buzzard	d																				
Tring	d																				
Berkhamsted	d																				
Hemel Hempstead	d																				
Watford Junction	d											09 17					10 17				11 22
Harrow & Wealdstone ⊖	d											09 23					10 23				11 28
Wembley Central ⊖	d																				
Stratford 7 ⊖	d												09 05		09 35	09 50		10 05	and	10 50	
Highbury & Islington ⊖	d												09 19		09 49	10 04		10 19	every 15	11 04	
Gospel Oak	d												09 31		10 01	10 16		10 31	minutes	11 16	
West Hampstead ⊖	d												09 37		10 07	10 22		10 37	until	11 22	
Willesden Jn. High Level ⊖	d			00 05		08 35		08 47	09 05	09 20	09 32		09 48	10 02	10 17	10 32		10 47		11 32	
Shepherd's Bush ⊖	d			00 11	07 57	08 41	08 48	08 53	09 11	09 26	09 38	09 44	09 54	10 08	10 23	10 38	10 44	10 53		11 38	11 47
Kensington (Olympia) ⊖	d			00 13	08 00	08 43	08 51	08 55	09 13	09 28	09 40	09 47	09 56	10 10	10 25	10 40	10 47	10 55		11 40	11 50
West Brompton ⊖	d		00 02	00 16	08 02	08 46	08 54	08 58	09 16	09 31	09 43	09 50	09 59	10 13	10 28	10 43	10 50	10 58		11 43	11 53
Imperial Wharf	d	00 01	00 05	00 19	08 05	08 49	08 56	09 01	09 19	09 34	09 46	09 52	10 02	10 16	10 31	10 46	10 52	11 01		11 46	11 55
Clapham Junction 10	a	00 06	00 10	00 26	08 09	08 56	09 01	09 08	09 26	09 41	09 53	09 57	10 09	10 24	10 39	10 54	10 57	11 09		11 54	12 00
	d																				
Wandsworth Common	a																				
Balham 4 ⊖	a																				
Streatham Common 4	a																				
Norbury	a																				
Thornton Heath	a																				
Selhurst 4	a																				
East Croydon	a																				

A not 15 December

For other Norbury line connections, refer to Table T170

For other Stratford line connecting trains, refer to Table T59

Table T176-R

Sundays
15 December to 10 May

Milton Keynes, Watford Junction/Stratford, Willesden Junction-Shepherd's Bush, Kensington Olympia, West Brompton and Imperial Wharf-Clapham Junction, Balham and East Croydon

		LO	LO	LO	LO	SN		LO	LO	LO	LO	SN	LO		LO	SN	LO	LO	LO	LO
Milton Keynes Central 10	d																			
Bletchley	d																			
Leighton Buzzard	d																			
Tring	d																			
Berkhamsted	d																			
Hemel Hempstead	d																			
Watford Junction	d					12 23						16 23				17 23				
Harrow & Wealdstone ⊖	d					12 29						16 29				17 29				
Wembley Central ⊖	d																			
Stratford 7 ⊖	d	11 05	11 20	11 35	11 50		and at	15 05	15 20	15 35	15 50		16 05		16 50		17 05	17 20	17 35	17 50
Highbury & Islington ⊖	d	11 19	11 34	11 49	12 04		the same	15 19	15 34	15 49	16 04		16 19	and	17 04		17 19	17 34	17 49	18 04
Gospel Oak	d	11 31	11 46	12 01	12 16		minutes	15 31	15 46	16 01	16 16		16 31	every 15	17 16		17 31	17 46	18 01	18 16
West Hampstead ⊖	d	11 37	11 52	12 07	12 22		past	15 37	15 52	16 07	16 22		16 37	minutes	17 22		17 37	17 52	18 07	18 22
Willesden Jn. High Level ⊖	d	11 47	12 02	12 17	12 32		each	15 47	16 02	16 17	16 32		16 47	until	17 32		17 47	18 02	18 17	18 32
Shepherd's Bush ⊖	d	11 53	12 08	12 23	12 38	12 48	hour until	15 53	16 08	16 23	16 38	16 48	16 53		17 38	17 48	17 53	18 08	18 23	18 38
Kensington (Olympia) ⊖	d	11 55	12 10	12 25	12 40	12 51		15 55	16 10	16 25	16 40	16 51	16 55		17 40	17 51	17 55	18 10	18 25	18 40
West Brompton ⊖	d	11 58	12 13	12 28	12 43	12 53		15 58	16 13	16 28	16 43	16 53	16 58		17 43	17 53	17 58	18 13	18 28	18 43
Imperial Wharf	d	12 01	12 16	12 31	12 46	12 56		16 01	16 16	16 31	16 46	16 56	17 01		17 46	17 56	18 01	18 16	18 31	18 46
Clapham Junction 10	a	12 09	12 24	12 39	12 54	13 00		16 09	16 24	16 39	16 54	17 00	17 10		17 55	18 00	18 10	18 24	18 39	18 54
	d																			
Wandsworth Common	a																			
Balham 4 ⊖	a																			
Streatham Common 4	a																			
Norbury	a																			
Thornton Heath	a																			
Selhurst 4	a																			
East Croydon	a																			

		SN	LO		LO	SN	LO	LO	LO	LO	SN	LO		LO	SN	LO	LO	LO	LO	SN	LO
Milton Keynes Central 10	d																				
Bletchley	d																				
Leighton Buzzard	d																				
Tring	d																				
Berkhamsted	d																				
Hemel Hempstead	d																				
Watford Junction	d	18 23				19 23					20 23				21 17					22 18	
Harrow & Wealdstone ⊖	d	18 29				19 29					20 29				21 24					22 24	
Wembley Central ⊖	d																				
Stratford 7 ⊖	d		18 05		18 50		19 05	19 20	19 35	19 50		20 05		20 50		21 05		21 35			22 05
Highbury & Islington ⊖	d		18 19	and	19 04		19 19	19 34	19 49	20 04		20 19	and	21 04		21 19		21 49			22 19
Gospel Oak	d		18 31	every 15	19 16		19 31	19 45	20 01	20 16		20 31	every 15	21 16		21 30		22 01			22 31
West Hampstead ⊖	d		18 37	minutes	19 22		19 37	19 51	20 07	20 22		20 37	minutes	21 22		21 36		22 07			22 37
Willesden Jn. High Level ⊖	d		18 47	until	19 32		19 47	20 01	20 17	20 32		20 47	until	21 32		21 46	22 02	22 17	22 32		22 47
Shepherd's Bush ⊖	d	18 48	18 53		19 38	19 48	19 53	20 08	20 24	20 38	20 48	20 53		21 38	21 43	21 53	22 08	22 24	22 38	22 45	22 53
Kensington (Olympia) ⊖	d	18 51	18 55		19 40	19 51	19 55	20 10	20 26	20 40	20 51	20 55		21 40	21 45	21 55	22 10	22 26	22 40	22 47	22 55
West Brompton ⊖	d	18 53	18 58		19 43	19 53	19 58	20 13	20 29	20 43	20 53	20 58		21 43	21 47	21 58	22 13	22 29	22 43	22 50	22 58
Imperial Wharf	d	18 56	19 01		19 46	19 56	20 01	20 16	20 32	20 46	20 56	21 01		21 46	21 50	22 01	22 16	22 32	22 46	22 53	23 01
Clapham Junction 10	a	19 00	19 09		19 54	20 00	20 09	20 24	20 39	20 54	21 00	21 09		21 54	21 54	22 09	22 23	22 39	22 53	22 57	23 09
	d																				
Wandsworth Common	a																				
Balham 4 ⊖	a																				
Streatham Common 4	a																				
Norbury	a																				
Thornton Heath	a																				
Selhurst 4	a																				
East Croydon	a																				

		LO	LO	LO	SN	LO	LO
Milton Keynes Central 10	d						
Bletchley	d						
Leighton Buzzard	d						
Tring	d						
Berkhamsted	d						
Hemel Hempstead	d						
Watford Junction	d				23 17		
Harrow & Wealdstone ⊖	d				23 23		
Wembley Central ⊖	d						
Stratford 7 ⊖	d						
Highbury & Islington ⊖	d						
Gospel Oak	d						
West Hampstead ⊖	d						
Willesden Jn. High Level ⊖	d	23 02	23 17	23 32		23 47	23 59
Shepherd's Bush ⊖	d	23 08	23 23	23 38	23 45	23 53	00 05
Kensington (Olympia) ⊖	d	23 10	23 25	23 40	23 47	23 55	00 07
West Brompton ⊖	d	23 13	23 28	23 43	23 50	23 58	00 10
Imperial Wharf	d	23 16	23 31	23 46	23 53	00 01	00 13
Clapham Junction 10	a	23 23	23 38	23 53	23 57	00 08	00 20
	d						
Wandsworth Common	a						
Balham 4 ⊖	a						
Streatham Common 4	a						
Norbury	a						
Thornton Heath	a						
Selhurst 4	a						
East Croydon	a						

Table T177-F

Mondays to Fridays

16 December to 15 May

London Bridge-New Cross Gate,Brockley, Honor Oak Park, Forest Hill, Sydenham, Crystal Palace, Penge West, Anerley-Norwood Junction and Croydon

Miles	Miles	Miles	Miles			LO MX A	SN MX B	LO MO A	LO MX A	SN MO C	LO MX D	SN MX E	LO MX A	SN MX	SN MX	SN F	LO	LO	LO	LO	LO	SN G	LO
0	—	—	0	London Bridge ④ ⊖	d									00 10	00 35	05 34						06 10	
—	—	0	—	Highbury & Islington	d														05 32	05 40	05 47		05 55
—	—	0½	—	Canonbury	d														05 34	05 42	05 49		05 57
—	0	1½	—	Dalston Junction	d														05 37	05 45	05 52		06 00
—	0½	2	—	Haggerston	d														05 39	05 47	05 54		06 02
—	1	2½	—	Hoxton	d														05 41	05 49	05 56		06 04
—	1¾	3¼	—	Shoreditch High Street	d														05 43	05 52	05 58		06 07
—	2¼	3¾	—	Whitechapel	d														05 46	05 54	06 01		06 09
—	3	4½	—	Shadwell	d														05 48	05 56	06 03		06 11
—	3½	5	—	Wapping	d														05 50	05 58	06 05		06 13
—	4	5½	—	Rotherhithe	d														05 51	06 00	06 06		06 15
—	4¼	5¾	—	Canada Water	d								00 02						05 53	06 02	06 08		06 17
—	4½	6	—	Surrey Quays	d								00 04						05 55	06 04	06 10		06 19
2¾	5¾	7¼	2¾	New Cross Gate ④	d						00 01	00 04	00 08	00 16	00 41	05 40	05 45	05 53	06 00	06 08	06 15	06 18	06 23
3¾	6½	8	3¾	**Brockley**	d						00 02	00 07	00 11	00 19	00 44	05 43	05 47	05 55	06 02	06 11	06 17	06 20	06 26
4¾	7½	9	4¾	**Honor Oak Park**	d					00 02	00 05	00 09	00 13	00 21	00 46	05 45	05 50	05 58	06 05	06 13	06 20	06 23	06 28
5½	8½	10	5½	**Forest Hill ④**	d				00 01	00 04	00 07	00 12	00 16	00 24	00 49	05 48	05 52	06 00	06 07	06 16	06 22	06 25	06 31
6¼	9¼	10¾	6¼	**Sydenham**	d			00 01	00 04	00 08	00 11	00 15	00 19	00 27	00 52	05 51	05 56	06 04	06 11	06 19	06 26	06 29	06 34
—	—	12	7½	**Crystal Palace ④**	a				00 09			00 20	00 24					06 11		06 24			06 39
7	10	—	—	**Penge West**	d		00 01	00 03		00 10	00 13			00 29	00 54	05 53	05 58		06 13		06 28	06 31	
7½	10½	—	—	**Anerley**	d	00 01	00 03	00 05		00 12	00 15			00 31	00 56	05 55	06 00		06 15		06 30	06 33	
8¾	11½	—	—	Norwood Junction ②	a	00 03	00 06	00 08		00 15	00 17			00 34	00 59	05 58	06 03		06 18		06 33	06 36	
—	—	—	—	Norwood Junction	d	00 03		00 08			00 18						06 03		06 18		06 33	06 36	
—	13¼	—	—	West Croydon ④ 🚋	a	00 13		00 16			00 29						06 12		06 28		06 39	06 42	
—	—	—	—	Norwood Junction	d		00 06			00 16				00 35	01 08	05 58							
10¼	—	—	—	East Croydon 🚋	a		00 10			00 19				00 38	01 13	06 02							
13¼	—	—	—	Purley	a					00 28						06 11							

		LO	SN H	LO	LO	SN G	LO	LO	SN H	LO	LO	SN G	LO	LO	SN H	LO	LO	SN G	LO	LO	SN H	LO	LO
London Bridge ④ ⊖	d		06 28			06 40			06 58			07 10			07 28			07 40			07 58		
Highbury & Islington	d	06 02		06 10	06 17		06 25	06 32		06 40	06 47		06 55	07 02		07 10	07 17		07 25	07 32		07 40	07 47
Canonbury	d	06 04		06 12	06 19		06 27	06 34		06 42	06 49		06 57	07 04		07 12	07 19		07 27	07 34		07 42	07 49
Dalston Junction	d	06 07		06 15	06 22		06 30	06 37		06 45	06 52		07 00	07 07		07 15	07 22		07 30	07 37		07 45	07 52
Haggerston	d	06 09		06 17	06 24		06 32	06 39		06 47	06 54		07 02	07 09		07 17	07 24		07 32	07 39		07 47	07 54
Hoxton	d	06 11		06 19	06 26		06 34	06 41		06 49	06 56		07 04	07 11		07 19	07 26		07 34	07 41		07 49	07 56
Shoreditch High Street	d	06 13		06 22	06 28		06 37	06 43		06 52	06 58		07 07	07 13		07 22	07 28		07 37	07 43		07 52	07 58
Whitechapel	d	06 16		06 24	06 31		06 39	06 46		06 54	07 01		07 09	07 16		07 24	07 31		07 39	07 46		07 54	08 01
Shadwell	d	06 18		06 26	06 33		06 41	06 48		06 56	07 03		07 11	07 18		07 26	07 33		07 41	07 48		07 56	08 03
Wapping	d	06 20		06 28	06 35		06 43	06 50		06 58	07 05		07 13	07 20		07 28	07 35		07 43	07 50		07 58	08 05
Rotherhithe	d	06 21		06 30	06 36		06 45	06 51		07 00	07 06		07 15	07 21		07 30	07 36		07 45	07 51		08 00	08 06
Canada Water	d	06 23		06 32	06 38		06 47	06 53		07 02	07 08		07 17	07 23		07 32	07 38		07 47	07 53		08 02	08 08
Surrey Quays	d	06 25		06 34	06 40		06 49	06 55		07 04	07 10		07 19	07 25		07 34	07 40		07 49	07 55		08 04	08 10
New Cross Gate ④	d	06 30	06 34	06 38	06 45	06 48	06 53	07 00	07 04	07 08	07 15	07 18	07 23	07 30	07 34	07 38	07 45	07 48	07 53	08 00	08 04	08 08	08 15
Brockley	d	06 32	06 37	06 41	06 47	06 50	06 56	07 02	07 07	07 11	07 17	07 20	07 26	07 32	07 37	07 41	07 47	07 50	07 56	08 02	08 07	08 11	08 17
Honor Oak Park	d	06 35	06 39	06 43	06 50	06 53	06 58	07 05	07 09	07 13	07 20	07 23	07 28	07 35	07 39	07 43	07 50	07 53	07 58	08 05	08 09	08 13	08 20
Forest Hill ④	d	06 37	06 42	06 46	06 52	06 55	07 01	07 07	07 12	07 16	07 22	07 25	07 31	07 37	07 42	07 46	07 52	07 55	08 01	08 07	08 12	08 16	08 22
Sydenham	d	06 41	06 45	06 49	06 56	06 59	07 04	07 11	07 15	07 19	07 26	07 29	07 34	07 41	07 45	07 49	07 56	07 59	08 04	08 11	08 15	08 19	08 26
Crystal Palace ④	a		06 50	06 54			07 09		07 20	07 24			07 39		07 50	07 54			08 09		08 20	08 24	
Penge West	d	06 43			06 58	07 01		07 13			07 28	07 31		07 43			07 58	08 01		08 13			08 28
Anerley	d	06 45			07 00	07 03		07 15			07 30	07 33		07 45			08 00	08 03		08 15			08 30
Norwood Junction ②	a	06 48			07 03	07 06		07 18			07 33	07 36		07 48			08 03	08 06		08 18			08 33
Norwood Junction	d	06 48			07 03	07 06		07 18			07 33	07 36		07 48			08 03	08 06		08 18			08 33
West Croydon ④ 🚋	a	06 58			07 09	07 12		07 28			07 39	07 42		07 58			08 09	08 12		08 28			08 39
Norwood Junction	d																						
East Croydon 🚋	a																						
Purley	a																						

A From Highbury and Islington Ell
B From London Bridge
C From London Bridge to Caterham
D From Dalston Junction Stn Ell
E From London Bridge to Streatham Hill
F To Caterham
G To Sutton (Surrey)
H To London Victoria

For full service between Highbury & Islington and Surrey Quays, refer to Table T178

For Sutton connections at West Croydon, refer to Table T172

Table T177-F

Mondays to Fridays

16 December to 15 May

London Bridge-New Cross Gate,Brockley, Honor Oak Park, Forest Hill, Sydenham, Crystal Palace, Penge West, Anerley-Norwood Junction and Croydon

		SN A	LO	LO	SN B	LO	LO	LO	LO	SN B	LO	LO	SN A	LO	LO	SN B	LO	LO	SN C	LO	LO	SN B
London Bridge ④ ⊖	d	08 10			08 28					08 58			09 10			09 28			09 40			09 58
Highbury & Islington	d		07 55	08 02		08 10	08 17	08 25	08 32		08 40	08 47		08 55	09 02		09 10	09 17		09 25	09 32	
Canonbury	d		07 57	08 04		08 12	08 19	08 27	08 34		08 42	08 49		08 57	09 04		09 12	09 19		09 27	09 34	
Dalston Junction	d		08 00	08 07		08 15	08 22	08 30	08 37		08 46	08 52		09 00	09 08		09 16	09 22		09 30	09 37	
Haggerston	d		08 02	08 09		08 17	08 24	08 32	08 39		08 47	08 54		09 02	09 09		09 17	09 24		09 32	09 39	
Hoxton	d		08 04	08 11		08 19	08 26	08 34	08 41		08 49	08 56		09 04	09 11		09 19	09 26		09 34	09 41	
Shoreditch High Street	d		08 07	08 13		08 22	08 28	08 37	08 43		08 52	08 58		09 07	09 13		09 22	09 28		09 37	09 43	
Whitechapel	d		08 09	08 16		08 24	08 31	08 39	08 46		08 54	09 01		09 09	09 16		09 24	09 31		09 39	09 46	
Shadwell	d		08 11	08 18		08 26	08 33	08 41	08 48		08 56	09 03		09 11	09 18		09 26	09 33		09 41	09 48	
Wapping	d		08 13	08 20		08 28	08 35	08 43	08 50		08 58	09 05		09 13	09 20		09 28	09 35		09 43	09 50	
Rotherhithe	d		08 15	08 21		08 30	08 36	08 45	08 51		09 00	09 06		09 15	09 21		09 30	09 36		09 45	09 51	
Canada Water	d		08 17	08 23		08 32	08 38	08 47	08 53		09 02	09 08		09 17	09 23		09 32	09 38		09 47	09 53	
Surrey Quays	d		08 19	08 25		08 34	08 40	08 49	08 55		09 04	09 10		09 19	09 25		09 34	09 40		09 49	09 55	
New Cross Gate ④	d	08 18	08 23	08 30	08 34	08 38	08 45	08 53	09 00	09 04	09 08	09 15	09 18	09 23	09 30	09 34	09 38	09 45	09 48	09 53	10 00	10 04
Brockley	d	08 20	08 26	08 32	08 37	08 41	08 47	08 56	09 02	09 07	09 11	09 17	09 20	09 26	09 32	09 37	09 41	09 47	09 50	09 56	10 02	10 07
Honor Oak Park	d	08 23	08 28	08 35	08 39	08 43	08 50	08 58	09 05	09 09	09 13	09 20	09 23	09 28	09 35	09 39	09 43	09 50	09 53	09 58	10 05	10 09
Forest Hill ④	d	08 25	08 31	08 37	08 42	08 46	08 52	09 01	09 07	09 12	09 16	09 22	09 25	09 31	09 37	09 42	09 46	09 52	09 55	10 01	10 07	10 12
Sydenham	d	08 29	08 34	08 41	08 45	08 49	08 56	09 04	09 11	09 15	09 19	09 26	09 29	09 34	09 41	09 45	09 49	09 56	09 59	10 04	10 11	10 15
Crystal Palace ④	a		08 39		08 50	08 54		09 09		09 20	09 24			09 39		09 50	09 54			10 09		10 20
Penge West	d	08 31		08 43			08 58		09 13			09 28	09 31		09 43			09 58	10 01		10 13	
Anerley	d	08 33		08 45			09 00		09 15			09 30	09 33		09 45			10 00	10 03		10 15	
Norwood Junction ②	a	08 36		08 48			09 03		09 18			09 33	09 36		09 48			10 03	10 06		10 18	
Norwood Junction	d			08 48			09 03		09 18			09 33			09 48			10 03			10 18	
West Croydon ④ 🚋	a			08 58			09 09		09 28			09 43			09 59			10 13			10 28	
Norwood Junction	d	08 39											09 39						10 09			
East Croydon 🚋	a	08 42											09 42						10 13			
Purley	a	08 50											09 54						10 24			

		LO	LO	SN C	LO	LO	SN B	LO	LO	SN C	LO	LO	SN B	LO	LO	SN C	LO	LO	SN B	LO	LO	SN C	LO
London Bridge ④ ⊖	d			10 10			10 28			10 40			10 58			11 10			11 28			11 40	
Highbury & Islington	d	09 40	09 47		09 55	10 02		10 10	10 17		10 25	10 32		10 40	10 47		10 55	11 02		11 10	11 17		11 25
Canonbury	d	09 42	09 49		09 57	10 04		10 12	10 19		10 27	10 34		10 42	10 49		10 57	11 04		11 12	11 19		11 27
Dalston Junction	d	09 45	09 52		10 00	10 07		10 15	10 22		10 30	10 37		10 45	10 52		11 00	11 07		11 15	11 22		11 30
Haggerston	d	09 47	09 54		10 02	10 09		10 17	10 24		10 32	10 39		10 47	10 54		11 02	11 09		11 17	11 24		11 32
Hoxton	d	09 49	09 56		10 04	10 11		10 19	10 26		10 34	10 41		10 49	10 56		11 04	11 11		11 19	11 26		11 34
Shoreditch High Street	d	09 52	09 58		10 07	10 13		10 22	10 28		10 37	10 43		10 52	10 58		11 07	11 13		11 22	11 28		11 37
Whitechapel	d	09 54	10 01		10 09	10 16		10 24	10 31		10 39	10 46		10 54	11 01		11 09	11 16		11 24	11 31		11 39
Shadwell	d	09 56	10 03		10 11	10 18		10 26	10 33		10 41	10 48		10 56	11 03		11 11	11 18		11 26	11 33		11 41
Wapping	d	09 58	10 05		10 13	10 20		10 28	10 35		10 43	10 50		10 58	11 05		11 13	11 20		11 28	11 35		11 43
Rotherhithe	d	10 00	10 06		10 15	10 21		10 30	10 36		10 45	10 51		11 00	11 06		11 15	11 21		11 30	11 36		11 45
Canada Water	d	10 02	10 08		10 17	10 23		10 32	10 38		10 47	10 53		11 02	11 08		11 17	11 23		11 32	11 38		11 47
Surrey Quays	d	10 04	10 10		10 19	10 25		10 34	10 40		10 49	10 55		11 04	11 10		11 19	11 25		11 34	11 40		11 49
New Cross Gate ④	d	10 08	10 15	10 18	10 23	10 30	10 34	10 38	10 45	10 48	10 53	11 00	11 04	11 08	11 15	11 18	11 23	11 30	11 34	11 38	11 45	11 48	11 53
Brockley	d	10 11	10 17	10 20	10 26	10 32	10 37	10 41	10 47	10 50	10 56	11 02	11 07	11 11	11 17	11 20	11 26	11 32	11 37	11 41	11 47	11 51	11 56
Honor Oak Park	d	10 13	10 20	10 23	10 28	10 35	10 39	10 43	10 50	10 53	10 58	11 05	11 09	11 13	11 20	11 23	11 28	11 35	11 39	11 43	11 50	11 53	11 58
Forest Hill ④	d	10 16	10 22	10 25	10 31	10 37	10 42	10 46	10 52	10 55	11 01	11 07	11 12	11 16	11 22	11 25	11 31	11 37	11 42	11 46	11 52	11 56	12 01
Sydenham	d	10 19	10 26	10 29	10 34	10 41	10 45	10 49	10 56	10 59	11 04	11 11	11 15	11 19	11 26	11 29	11 34	11 41	11 45	11 49	11 56	11 59	12 04
Crystal Palace ④	a	10 24			10 39		10 50	10 54			11 09		11 20	11 24			11 39		11 50	11 54			12 09
Penge West	d		10 28	10 31		10 43			10 58	11 01		11 13			11 28	11 31		11 43			11 58	12 01	
Anerley	d		10 30	10 33		10 45			11 00	11 03		11 15			11 30	11 33		11 45			12 00	12 03	
Norwood Junction ②	a		10 33	10 36		10 48			11 03	11 06		11 18			11 33	11 36		11 48			12 03	12 07	
Norwood Junction	d		10 33			10 48			11 03			11 18			11 33			11 48			12 03		
West Croydon ④ 🚋	a		10 43			10 58			11 09			11 28			11 39			11 54			12 09		
Norwood Junction	d			10 39						11 09						11 39						12 09	
East Croydon 🚋	a			10 43						11 13						11 43						12 13	
Purley	a			10 54						11 24						11 54						12 24	

A To Caterham
B To London Victoria
C To Coulsdon Town

For full service between Highbury & Islington and Surrey Quays, refer to Table T178

For Sutton connections at West Croydon, refer to Table T172

Table T177-F

Mondays to Fridays
16 December to 15 May

London Bridge-New Cross Gate,Brockley, Honor Oak Park, Forest Hill, Sydenham, Crystal Palace, Penge West, Anerley-Norwood Junction and Croydon

	LO	SN A	LO	LO	SN B	LO	LO	SN A	LO	LO	SN B	LO	LO	SN A	LO	LO	SN B	LO	LO	SN A	LO	LO
London Bridge [4] ⊖ d		11 58			12 10			12 28			12 40			12 58			13 10			13 28		
Highbury & Islington d	11 32		11 40	11 47		11 55	12 02		12 10	12 17		12 25	12 32		12 40	12 47		12 55	13 02		13 10	13 17
Canonbury d	11 34		11 42	11 49		11 57	12 04		12 12	12 19		12 27	12 34		12 42	12 49		12 57	13 04		13 12	13 19
Dalston Junction d	11 37		11 45	11 52		12 00	12 07		12 15	12 22		12 30	12 37		12 45	12 52		13 00	13 07		13 15	13 22
Haggerston d	11 39		11 47	11 54		12 02	12 09		12 17	12 24		12 32	12 39		12 47	12 54		13 02	13 09		13 17	13 24
Hoxton d	11 41		11 49	11 56		12 04	12 11		12 19	12 26		12 34	12 41		12 49	12 56		13 04	13 11		13 19	13 26
Shoreditch High Street d	11 43		11 52	11 58		12 07	12 13		12 22	12 28		12 37	12 43		12 52	12 58		13 07	13 13		13 22	13 28
Whitechapel d	11 46		11 54	12 01		12 09	12 16		12 24	12 31		12 39	12 46		12 54	13 01		13 09	13 16		13 24	13 31
Shadwell d	11 48		11 56	12 03		12 11	12 18		12 26	12 33		12 41	12 48		12 56	13 03		13 11	13 18		13 26	13 33
Wapping d	11 50		11 58	12 05		12 13	12 20		12 28	12 35		12 43	12 50		12 58	13 05		13 13	13 20		13 28	13 35
Rotherhithe d	11 51		12 00	12 06		12 15	12 21		12 30	12 36		12 45	12 51		13 00	13 06		13 15	13 21		13 30	13 36
Canada Water d	11 53		12 02	12 08		12 17	12 23		12 32	12 38		12 47	12 53		13 02	13 08		13 17	13 23		13 32	13 38
Surrey Quays d	11 55		12 04	12 10		12 19	12 25		12 34	12 40		12 49	12 55		13 04	13 10		13 19	13 25		13 34	13 40
New Cross Gate [4] d	12 00	12 04	12 08	12 15	12 18	12 23	12 30	12 34	12 38	12 45	12 48	12 53	13 00	13 04	13 08	13 15	13 18	13 23	13 30	13 34	13 38	13 45
Brockley d	12 02	12 07	12 11	12 17	12 20	12 26	12 32	12 37	12 41	12 47	12 50	12 56	13 02	13 07	13 11	13 17	13 20	13 26	13 32	13 37	13 41	13 47
Honor Oak Park d	12 05	12 09	12 13	12 20	12 23	12 28	12 35	12 39	12 43	12 50	12 53	12 58	13 05	13 09	13 13	13 20	13 23	13 28	13 35	13 39	13 43	13 50
Forest Hill [4] d	12 07	12 12	12 16	12 22	12 25	12 31	12 37	12 42	12 46	12 52	12 55	13 01	13 07	13 12	13 16	13 22	13 25	13 31	13 37	13 42	13 46	13 52
Sydenham d	12 11	12 15	12 19	12 26	12 29	12 34	12 41	12 45	12 49	12 56	12 59	13 04	13 11	13 15	13 19	13 26	13 29	13 34	13 41	13 45	13 49	13 56
Crystal Palace [4] a		12 20	12 24			12 39		12 50	12 54			13 09		13 20	13 24			13 39		13 50	13 54	
Penge West d	12 13			12 28	12 31		12 43			12 58	13 01		13 13			13 28	13 31		13 43			13 58
Anerley d	12 15			12 30	12 33		12 45			13 00	13 03		13 15			13 30	13 33		13 45			14 00
Norwood Junction [2] a	12 18			12 33	12 36		12 48			13 03	13 06		13 18			13 33	13 36		13 48			14 03
Norwood Junction d	12 18			12 33			12 48			13 03			13 18			13 33			13 48			14 03
West Croydon [4] ⇌ a	12 24			12 39			12 54			13 09			13 24			13 39			13 54			14 09
Norwood Junction d					12 39						13 09						13 39					
East Croydon ⇌ a					12 43						13 13						13 43					
Purley a					12 54						13 24						13 54					

	SN B	LO	LO	SN A	LO	LO	SN B	LO	LO	SN A	LO	LO	SN B	LO	LO	SN A	LO	LO	SN B	LO	LO	SN A
London Bridge [4] ⊖ d	13 40			13 58			14 10			14 28			14 40			14 58			15 10			15 28
Highbury & Islington d		13 25	13 32		13 40	13 47		13 55	14 02		14 10	14 17		14 25	14 32		14 40	14 47		14 55	15 02	
Canonbury d		13 27	13 34		13 42	13 49		13 57	14 04		14 12	14 19		14 27	14 34		14 42	14 49		14 57	15 04	
Dalston Junction d		13 30	13 37		13 45	13 52		14 00	14 07		14 15	14 22		14 30	14 37		14 45	14 52		15 00	15 07	
Haggerston d		13 32	13 39		13 47	13 54		14 02	14 09		14 17	14 24		14 32	14 39		14 47	14 54		15 02	15 09	
Hoxton d		13 34	13 41		13 49	13 56		14 04	14 11		14 19	14 26		14 34	14 41		14 49	14 56		15 04	15 11	
Shoreditch High Street d		13 37	13 43		13 52	13 58		14 07	14 13		14 22	14 28		14 37	14 43		14 52	14 58		15 07	15 13	
Whitechapel d		13 39	13 46		13 54	14 01		14 09	14 16		14 24	14 31		14 39	14 46		14 54	15 01		15 09	15 16	
Shadwell d		13 41	13 48		13 56	14 03		14 11	14 18		14 26	14 33		14 41	14 48		14 56	15 03		15 11	15 18	
Wapping d		13 43	13 50		13 58	14 05		14 13	14 20		14 28	14 35		14 43	14 50		14 58	15 05		15 13	15 20	
Rotherhithe d		13 45	13 51		14 00	14 06		14 15	14 21		14 30	14 36		14 45	14 51		15 00	15 06		15 15	15 21	
Canada Water d		13 47	13 53		14 02	14 08		14 17	14 23		14 32	14 38		14 47	14 53		15 02	15 08		15 17	15 23	
Surrey Quays d		13 49	13 55		14 04	14 10		14 19	14 25		14 34	14 40		14 49	14 55		15 04	15 10		15 19	15 25	
New Cross Gate [4] d	13 48	13 53	14 00	14 04	14 08	14 15	14 18	14 23	14 30	14 34	14 38	14 45	14 48	14 53	15 00	15 04	15 08	15 15	15 18	15 23	15 30	15 34
Brockley d	13 50	13 56	14 02	14 07	14 11	14 17	14 20	14 26	14 32	14 37	14 41	14 47	14 50	14 56	15 02	15 07	15 11	15 17	15 20	15 26	15 32	15 37
Honor Oak Park d	13 53	13 58	14 05	14 09	14 13	14 20	14 23	14 28	14 35	14 39	14 43	14 50	14 53	14 58	15 05	15 09	15 13	15 20	15 23	15 28	15 35	15 39
Forest Hill [4] d	13 55	14 01	14 07	14 12	14 16	14 22	14 25	14 31	14 37	14 42	14 46	14 52	14 55	15 01	15 07	15 12	15 16	15 22	15 25	15 31	15 37	15 42
Sydenham d	13 59	14 04	14 11	14 15	14 19	14 26	14 29	14 34	14 41	14 45	14 49	14 56	14 59	15 04	15 11	15 15	15 19	15 26	15 29	15 34	15 41	15 45
Crystal Palace [4] a		14 09		14 20	14 24			14 39		14 50	14 54			15 09		15 20	15 24			15 39		15 50
Penge West d	14 01		14 13			14 28	14 31		14 43			14 58	15 01		15 13			15 28	15 31		15 43	
Anerley d	14 03		14 15			14 30	14 33		14 45			15 00	15 03		15 15			15 30	15 33		15 45	
Norwood Junction [2] a	14 06		14 18			14 33	14 36		14 48			15 03	15 06		15 18			15 33	15 36		15 48	
Norwood Junction d			14 18			14 33			14 48			15 03			15 18			15 33			15 48	
West Croydon [4] ⇌ a			14 25			14 39			14 54			15 09			15 24			15 39			15 54	
Norwood Junction d	14 09						14 39						15 09						15 39			
East Croydon ⇌ a	14 13						14 43						15 13						15 43			
Purley a	14 24						14 54						15 24						15 54			

A To London Victoria

B To Coulsdon Town

For full service between Highbury & Islington and Surrey Quays, refer to Table T178

For Sutton connections at West Croydon, refer to Table T172

NRT DECEMBER 19 EDITION

Table T177-F

Mondays to Fridays
16 December to 15 May

London Bridge-New Cross Gate,Brockley, Honor Oak Park, Forest Hill, Sydenham, Crystal Palace, Penge West, Anerley-Norwood Junction and Croydon

	LO	LO	SN A	LO	LO	SN B	LO	LO	SN C	LO	LO	SN B	LO	LO	SN C	LO	LO	SN B	LO	LO	SN C	LO
London Bridge [4] ⊖ d			15 40			15 58			16 10			16 28			16 40			16 58			17 10	
Highbury & Islington d	15 10	15 17		15 25	15 32		15 40	15 47		15 55	16 02		16 10	16 17		16 25	16 32		16 40	16 47		16 55
Canonbury d	15 12	15 19		15 27	15 34		15 42	15 49		15 57	16 04		16 12	16 19		16 27	16 34		16 42	16 49		16 57
Dalston Junction d	15 15	15 22		15 30	15 37		15 45	15 52		16 00	16 07		16 15	16 22		16 30	16 37		16 45	16 52		17 00
Haggerston d	15 17	15 24		15 32	15 39		15 47	15 54		16 02	16 09		16 17	16 24		16 32	16 39		16 47	16 54		17 02
Hoxton d	15 19	15 26		15 34	15 41		15 49	15 56		16 04	16 11		16 19	16 26		16 34	16 41		16 49	16 56		17 04
Shoreditch High Street d	15 22	15 28		15 37	15 43		15 52	15 58		16 07	16 13		16 22	16 28		16 37	16 43		16 52	16 58		17 07
Whitechapel d	15 24	15 31		15 39	15 46		15 54	16 01		16 09	16 16		16 24	16 31		16 39	16 46		16 54	17 01		17 09
Shadwell d	15 26	15 33		15 41	15 48		15 56	16 03		16 11	16 18		16 26	16 33		16 41	16 48		16 56	17 03		17 11
Wapping d	15 28	15 35		15 43	15 50		15 58	16 05		16 13	16 20		16 28	16 35		16 43	16 50		16 58	17 05		17 13
Rotherhithe d	15 30	15 36		15 45	15 51		16 00	16 06		16 15	16 21		16 30	16 36		16 45	16 51		17 00	17 06		17 15
Canada Water d	15 32	15 38		15 47	15 53		16 02	16 08		16 17	16 23		16 32	16 38		16 47	16 53		17 02	17 08		17 17
Surrey Quays d	15 34	15 40		15 49	15 55		16 04	16 10		16 19	16 25		16 34	16 40		16 49	16 55		17 04	17 10		17 19
New Cross Gate [4] d	15 38	15 45	15 48	15 53	16 00	16 04	16 08	16 15	16 18	16 23	16 30	16 34	16 38	16 45	16 48	16 53	17 00	17 04	17 08	17 15	17 18	17 23
Brockley d	15 41	15 47	15 50	15 56	16 02	16 07	16 11	16 17	16 20	16 26	16 32	16 37	16 41	16 47	16 50	16 56	17 02	17 07	17 11	17 17	17 20	17 26
Honor Oak Park d	15 43	15 50	15 53	15 58	16 05	16 09	16 13	16 20	16 23	16 28	16 35	16 39	16 43	16 50	16 53	16 58	17 05	17 09	17 13	17 20	17 23	17 28
Forest Hill [4] d	15 46	15 52	15 55	16 01	16 07	16 12	16 16	16 22	16 25	16 31	16 37	16 42	16 46	16 52	16 55	17 01	17 07	17 12	17 16	17 22	17 25	17 31
Sydenham d	15 49	15 56	15 59	16 04	16 11	16 15	16 19	16 26	16 29	16 34	16 41	16 45	16 49	16 56	16 59	17 04	17 11	17 15	17 19	17 26	17 29	17 34
Crystal Palace [4] a	15 54			16 09		16 20	16 24			16 39		16 50	16 54			17 09		17 20	17 24			17 39
Penge West d		15 58	16 01		16 13			16 28	16 31		16 43			16 58	17 01		17 13			17 28	17 31	
Anerley d		16 00	16 03		16 15			16 30	16 33		16 45			17 00	17 03		17 15			17 30	17 33	
Norwood Junction [2] a		16 03	16 06		16 18			16 33	16 36		16 48			17 03	17 06		17 18			17 33	17 36	
Norwood Junction d		16 03			16 18			16 33	16 36		16 48			17 03	17 06		17 18			17 33	17 36	
West Croydon [4] ⇌ a		16 09			16 28			16 43	16 42		16 58			17 13	17 12		17 28			17 43	17 42	
Norwood Junction d			16 09																			
East Croydon ⇌ a			16 13																			
Purley a			16 24																			

	LO	SN B	LO	LO	SN C	LO	LO	SN B	LO	LO	SN C	LO	LO	SN B	LO	LO	SN A	LO	LO	SN B	LO
London Bridge [4] ⊖ d		17 28			17 40			17 58			18 10			18 28			18 41			18 58	
Highbury & Islington d	17 02		17 10	17 17		17 25	17 32		17 40	17 47		17 55	18 02		18 10	18 17		18 25	18 32		18 40
Canonbury d	17 04		17 12	17 19		17 27	17 34		17 42	17 49		17 57	18 04		18 12	18 19		18 27	18 34		18 42
Dalston Junction d	17 07		17 15	17 22		17 30	17 37		17 45	17 52		18 00	18 07		18 15	18 22		18 30	18 37		18 45
Haggerston d	17 09		17 17	17 24		17 32	17 39		17 47	17 54		18 02	18 09		18 17	18 24		18 32	18 39		18 47
Hoxton d	17 11		17 19	17 26		17 34	17 41		17 49	17 56		18 04	18 11		18 19	18 26		18 34	18 41		18 49
Shoreditch High Street d	17 13		17 22	17 28		17 37	17 43		17 52	17 58		18 07	18 13		18 22	18 28		18 37	18 43		18 52
Whitechapel d	17 16		17 24	17 31		17 39	17 46		17 54	18 01		18 09	18 16		18 24	18 31		18 39	18 46		18 54
Shadwell d	17 18		17 26	17 33		17 41	17 48		17 56	18 03		18 11	18 18		18 26	18 33		18 41	18 48		18 56
Wapping d	17 20		17 28	17 35		17 43	17 50		17 58	18 05		18 13	18 20		18 28	18 35		18 43	18 50		18 58
Rotherhithe d	17 21		17 30	17 36		17 45	17 51		18 00	18 06		18 15	18 21		18 30	18 36		18 45	18 51		19 00
Canada Water d	17 23		17 32	17 38		17 47	17 53		18 02	18 08		18 17	18 23		18 32	18 38		18 47	18 53		19 02
Surrey Quays d	17 25		17 34	17 40		17 49	17 55		18 04	18 10		18 19	18 25		18 34	18 40		18 49	18 55		19 04
New Cross Gate [4] d	17 30	17 34	17 38	17 45	17 48	17 53	18 00	18 04	18 08	18 15	18 18	18 23	18 30	18 34	18 38	18 45	18 48	18 53	19 00	19 04	19 08
Brockley d	17 32	17 37	17 41	17 47	17 50	17 56	18 02	18 07	18 11	18 17	18 20	18 26	18 32	18 37	18 41	18 47	18 50	18 56	19 02	19 07	19 11
Honor Oak Park d	17 35	17 39	17 43	17 50	17 53	17 58	18 05	18 09	18 13	18 20	18 23	18 28	18 35	18 39	18 43	18 50	18 53	18 58	19 05	19 09	19 13
Forest Hill [4] d	17 37	17 42	17 46	17 52	17 55	18 01	18 07	18 12	18 16	18 22	18 25	18 31	18 37	18 42	18 46	18 52	18 55	19 01	19 07	19 12	19 16
Sydenham d	17 41	17 45	17 49	17 56	17 59	18 04	18 11	18 15	18 19	18 26	18 29	18 34	18 41	18 45	18 49	18 56	18 59	19 04	19 11	19 15	19 19
Crystal Palace [4] a		17 50	17 54			18 09		18 20	18 24			18 39		18 50	18 54			19 09		19 20	19 24
Penge West d	17 43			17 58	18 01		18 13			18 28	18 31		18 43			18 58	19 01		19 13		
Anerley d	17 45			18 00	18 03		18 15			18 30	18 33		18 45			19 00	19 03		19 15		
Norwood Junction [2] a	17 48			18 03	18 06		18 18			18 33	18 36		18 48			19 03	19 06		19 18		
Norwood Junction d	17 48			18 03	18 06		18 18			18 33	18 36		18 48			19 03			19 18		
West Croydon [4] ⇌ a	17 58			18 13	18 12		18 28			18 43	18 42		18 58			19 13			19 28		
Norwood Junction d																	19 09				
East Croydon ⇌ a																	19 13				
Purley a																	19 22				

A To Coulsdon Town

B To London Victoria

C To Sutton (Surrey)

For full service between Highbury & Islington and Surrey Quays, refer to Table T178

For Sutton connections at West Croydon, refer to Table T172

Table T177-F

Mondays to Fridays

16 December to 15 May

London Bridge-New Cross Gate, Brockley, Honor Oak Park, Forest Hill, Sydenham, Crystal Palace, Penge West, Anerley-Norwood Junction and Croydon

Station		LO	SN A	LO	LO	SN B		LO	LO	SN A	LO	LO	SN B	LO	LO	SN A		LO	LO	SN B	LO	LO	SN A	LO	LO
London Bridge ■ ⊖	d		19 10			19 28				19 40			19 58			20 12				20 28			20 40		
Highbury & Islington	d	18 47		18 55	19 02			19 10	19 17		19 25	19 32		19 40	19 47			19 55	20 02		20 10	20 17		20 25	20 32
Canonbury	d	18 49		18 57	19 04			19 12	19 19		19 27	19 34		19 42	19 49			19 57	20 04		20 12	20 19		20 27	20 34
Dalston Junction	d	18 52		19 00	19 07			19 15	19 22		19 30	19 37		19 45	19 52			20 00	20 07		20 15	20 22		20 30	20 37
Haggerston	d	18 54		19 02	19 09			19 17	19 24		19 32	19 39		19 47	19 54			20 02	20 09		20 17	20 24		20 32	20 39
Hoxton	d	18 56		19 04	19 11			19 19	19 26		19 34	19 41		19 49	19 56			20 04	20 11		20 19	20 26		20 34	20 41
Shoreditch High Street	d	18 58		19 07	19 13			19 22	19 28		19 37	19 43		19 52	19 58			20 07	20 13		20 22	20 28		20 37	20 43
Whitechapel	d	19 01		19 09	19 16			19 24	19 31		19 39	19 46		19 54	20 01			20 09	20 16		20 24	20 31		20 39	20 46
Shadwell	d	19 03		19 11	19 18			19 26	19 33		19 41	19 48		19 56	20 03			20 11	20 18		20 26	20 33		20 41	20 48
Wapping	d	19 05		19 13	19 20			19 28	19 35		19 43	19 50		19 58	20 05			20 13	20 20		20 28	20 35		20 43	20 50
Rotherhithe	d	19 06		19 15	19 21			19 30	19 36		19 45	19 51		20 00	20 06			20 15	20 21		20 30	20 36		20 45	20 51
Canada Water	d	19 08		19 17	19 23			19 32	19 38		19 47	19 53		20 02	20 08			20 17	20 23		20 32	20 38		20 47	20 53
Surrey Quays	d	19 10		19 19	19 25			19 34	19 40		19 49	19 55		20 04	20 10			20 19	20 25		20 34	20 40		20 49	20 55
New Cross Gate ■	d	19 15	19 18	19 23	19 30	19 34		19 38	19 45	19 48	19 53	20 00	20 04	20 08	20 15	20 18		20 23	20 30	20 34	20 38	20 45	20 48	20 53	21 00
Brockley	d	19 17	19 20	19 26	19 32	19 37		19 41	19 47	19 50	19 56	20 02	20 07	20 11	20 17	20 21		20 26	20 32	20 37	20 41	20 47	20 50	20 56	21 02
Honor Oak Park	d	19 20	19 23	19 28	19 35	19 39		19 43	19 50	19 53	19 58	20 05	20 09	20 13	20 20	20 23		20 28	20 35	20 39	20 43	20 50	20 53	20 58	21 05
Forest Hill ■	d	19 22	19 25	19 31	19 37	19 42		19 46	19 52	19 55	20 01	20 07	20 12	20 16	20 22	20 26		20 31	20 37	20 42	20 46	20 52	20 55	21 01	21 07
Sydenham	d	19 26	19 29	19 34	19 41	19 45		19 49	19 56	19 59	20 04	20 11	20 15	20 19	20 26	20 29		20 34	20 41	20 45	20 49	20 56	20 59	21 04	21 11
Crystal Palace ■	a			19 39		19 50		19 54			20 09		20 20	20 24				20 39		20 50	20 54			21 09	
Penge West	d	19 28	19 31		19 43				19 58	20 01		20 13			20 28	20 31			20 43			20 58	21 01		21 13
Anerley	d	19 30	19 33		19 45				20 00	20 03		20 15			20 30	20 33			20 45			21 00	21 03		21 15
Norwood Junction ■	a	19 33	19 36		19 48				20 03	20 06		20 18			20 33	20 36			20 48			21 03	21 06		21 18
Norwood Junction	d	19 33			19 48				20 03			20 18			20 33				20 48			21 03			21 18
West Croydon ■	a	19 43			19 59				20 13			20 28			20 43				20 58			21 09			21 24
Norwood Junction	d		19 39							20 09						20 39							21 09		
East Croydon	a		19 43							20 13						20 43							21 13		
Purley	a		19 54							20 25						20 54							21 25		

Station		SN B		LO	LO	SN A	LO	LO	SN B	LO	LO	SN A		LO	LO	SN B	LO	LO	SN A	LO	LO	SN B		LO	LO
London Bridge ■ ⊖	d	20 58				21 10			21 28			21 40				21 58			22 10			22 28			
Highbury & Islington	d			20 40	20 47		20 55	21 02		21 10	21 17			21 25	21 32		21 40	21 47		21 55	22 02			22 10	22 17
Canonbury	d			20 42	20 49		20 57	21 04		21 12	21 19			21 27	21 34		21 42	21 49		21 57	22 04			22 12	22 19
Dalston Junction	d			20 45	20 52		21 00	21 07		21 15	21 22			21 30	21 37		21 45	21 52		22 00	22 07			22 15	22 22
Haggerston	d			20 47	20 54		21 02	21 09		21 17	21 24			21 32	21 39		21 47	21 54		22 02	22 09			22 17	22 24
Hoxton	d			20 49	20 56		21 04	21 11		21 19	21 26			21 34	21 41		21 49	21 56		22 04	22 11			22 19	22 26
Shoreditch High Street	d			20 52	20 58		21 07	21 13		21 22	21 28			21 37	21 43		21 52	21 58		22 07	22 13			22 22	22 28
Whitechapel	d			20 54	21 01		21 09	21 16		21 24	21 31			21 39	21 46		21 54	22 01		22 09	22 16			22 24	22 31
Shadwell	d			20 56	21 03		21 11	21 18		21 26	21 33			21 41	21 48		21 56	22 03		22 11	22 18			22 26	22 33
Wapping	d			20 58	21 05		21 13	21 20		21 28	21 35			21 43	21 50		21 58	22 05		22 13	22 20			22 28	22 35
Rotherhithe	d			21 00	21 06		21 15	21 21		21 30	21 36			21 45	21 51		22 00	22 06		22 15	22 21			22 30	22 36
Canada Water	d			21 02	21 08		21 17	21 23		21 32	21 38			21 47	21 53		22 02	22 08		22 17	22 23			22 32	22 38
Surrey Quays	d			21 04	21 10		21 19	21 25		21 34	21 40			21 49	21 55		22 04	22 10		22 19	22 25			22 34	22 40
New Cross Gate ■	d	21 04		21 08	21 15	21 18	21 23	21 30	21 34	21 38	21 45	21 48		21 53	22 00	22 04	22 08	22 15	22 18	22 23	22 30	22 34		22 38	22 45
Brockley	d	21 07		21 11	21 17	21 20	21 26	21 32	21 37	21 41	21 47	21 50		21 56	22 02	22 07	22 11	22 17	22 20	22 26	22 32	22 37		22 41	22 47
Honor Oak Park	d	21 09		21 13	21 20	21 23	21 28	21 35	21 39	21 43	21 50	21 53		21 58	22 05	22 09	22 13	22 20	22 23	22 28	22 35	22 39		22 43	22 50
Forest Hill ■	d	21 12		21 16	21 22	21 25	21 31	21 37	21 42	21 46	21 52	21 55		22 01	22 07	22 12	22 16	22 22	22 25	22 31	22 37	22 42		22 46	22 52
Sydenham	d	21 15		21 19	21 26	21 29	21 34	21 41	21 45	21 49	21 56	21 59		22 04	22 11	22 15	22 19	22 26	22 29	22 34	22 41	22 45		22 49	22 56
Crystal Palace ■	a	21 20		21 24			21 39		21 50	21 54				22 09		22 20	22 24			22 39		22 50		22 54	
Penge West	d				21 28	21 31		21 43			21 58	22 01			22 13			22 28	22 31		22 43				22 58
Anerley	d				21 30	21 33		21 45			22 00	22 03			22 15			22 30	22 33		22 45				23 00
Norwood Junction ■	a				21 33	21 36		21 48			22 03	22 06			22 18			22 33	22 36		22 48				23 03
Norwood Junction	d				21 33			21 48			22 03				22 18			22 33			22 48				23 03
West Croydon ■	a				21 39			21 54			22 09				22 24			22 39			22 54				23 09
Norwood Junction	d					21 39						22 09							22 39						
East Croydon	a					21 43						22 13							22 43						
Purley	a					21 54						22 24							22 53						

A To Coulsdon Town

B To London Victoria

For full service between Highbury & Islington and Surrey Quays, refer to Table T178

For Sutton connections at West Croydon, refer to Table T172

Table T177-F

Mondays to Fridays

16 December to 15 May

London Bridge-New Cross Gate, Brockley, Honor Oak Park, Forest Hill, Sydenham, Crystal Palace, Penge West, Anerley-Norwood Junction and Croydon

Station		SN A	LO	LO	SN B	LO	LO	SN	LO		LO	SN C	LO	LO	SN	LO	LO	SN C	LO
London Bridge ■ ⊖	d	22 40			22 58			23 10				23 28			23 40			23 58	
Highbury & Islington	d		22 25	22 32		22 40	22 47		22 55		23 02		23 10	23 17		23 25			23 40
Canonbury	d		22 27	22 34		22 42	22 49		22 57		23 04		23 12	23 19		23 27			23 42
Dalston Junction	d		22 30	22 37		22 45	22 52		23 00		23 07		23 15	23 22		23 30	23 38		23 45
Haggerston	d		22 32	22 39		22 47	22 54		23 02		23 09		23 17	23 24		23 32	23 39		23 47
Hoxton	d		22 34	22 41		22 49	22 56		23 04		23 11		23 19	23 26		23 34	23 41		23 49
Shoreditch High Street	d		22 37	22 43		22 52	22 58		23 07		23 13		23 22	23 28		23 37	23 43		23 52
Whitechapel	d		22 39	22 46		22 54	23 01		23 09		23 16		23 24	23 31		23 39	23 46		23 54
Shadwell	d		22 41	22 48		22 56	23 03		23 11		23 18		23 26	23 33		23 41	23 48		23 56
Wapping	d		22 43	22 50		22 58	23 05		23 13		23 20		23 28	23 35		23 43	23 50		23 58
Rotherhithe	d		22 45	22 51		23 00	23 06		23 15		23 21		23 30	23 36		23 45	23 51		23 59
Canada Water	d		22 47	22 53		23 02	23 08		23 17		23 23		23 32	23 38		23 47	23 53		00 02
Surrey Quays	d		22 49	22 55		23 04	23 10		23 19		23 25		23 34	23 40		23 49	23 55		00 04
New Cross Gate ■	d	22 48	22 53	23 00	23 04	23 08	23 15	23 18	23 23		23 30	23 34	23 38	23 45	23 48	23 53	00 01	00 04	00 08
Brockley	d	22 50	22 56	23 02	23 07	23 11	23 17	23 20	23 26		23 32	23 37	23 41	23 47	23 50	23 56	00 02	00 07	00 11
Honor Oak Park	d	22 53	22 58	23 05	23 09	23 13	23 20	23 23	23 28		23 35	23 39	23 43	23 50	23 53	23 58	00 05	00 09	00 13
Forest Hill ■	d	22 55	23 01	23 07	23 12	23 16	23 22	23 25	23 31		23 37	23 42	23 46	23 52	23 55	00 01	00 07	00 12	00 16
Sydenham	d	22 59	23 04	23 11	23 15	23 19	23 26	23 29	23 34		23 41	23 45	23 49	23 56	23 59	00 04	00 11	00 15	00 19
Crystal Palace ■	a		23 09		23 20	23 24			23 39			23 50	23 54			00 09		00 20	00 24
Penge West	d	23 01		23 13			23 28	23 31			23 43			23 58	00 01		00 13		
Anerley	d	23 03		23 15			23 30	23 33			23 45			00 01	00 03		00 15		
Norwood Junction ■	a	23 06		23 18			23 33	23 36			23 47			00 03	00 06		00 17		
Norwood Junction	d			23 18			23 33				23 48			00 03			00 18		
West Croydon ■	a			23 24			23 39				23 58			00 13			00 29		
Norwood Junction	d	23 09						23 39							00 06				
East Croydon	a	23 13						23 47							00 10				
Purley	a	23 24																	

Saturdays

21 December to 16 May

Station		LO D	LO D	SN E	LO F	SN G	LO D	SN H	SN H	LO		LO	LO	LO	SN A	LO	LO	SN B	LO	LO		SN A	LO	LO	SN B
London Bridge ■ ⊖	d							00 10	00 35						06 11			06 28				06 40			06 58
Highbury & Islington	d									05 25			05 40	05 47		05 55	06 02		06 10	06 17			06 25	06 32	
Canonbury	d									05 27			05 42	05 49		05 57	06 04		06 12	06 19			06 27	06 34	
Dalston Junction	d									05 30		05 37	05 45	05 52		06 00	06 07		06 15	06 22			06 30	06 37	
Haggerston	d									05 32		05 39	05 47	05 54		06 02	06 09		06 17	06 24			06 32	06 39	
Hoxton	d									05 34		05 41	05 49	05 56		06 04	06 11		06 19	06 26			06 34	06 41	
Shoreditch High Street	d									05 37		05 43	05 52	05 58		06 07	06 13		06 22	06 28			06 37	06 43	
Whitechapel	d									05 39		05 46	05 54	06 01		06 09	06 16		06 24	06 31			06 39	06 46	
Shadwell	d									05 41		05 48	05 56	06 03		06 11	06 18		06 26	06 33			06 41	06 48	
Wapping	d									05 43		05 50	05 58	06 05		06 13	06 20		06 28	06 35			06 43	06 50	
Rotherhithe	d									05 45		05 51	06 00	06 06		06 15	06 21		06 30	06 36			06 45	06 51	
Canada Water	d						00 02			05 47		05 53	06 02	06 08		06 17	06 23		06 32	06 38			06 47	06 53	
Surrey Quays	d						00 04			05 49		05 55	06 04	06 10		06 19	06 25		06 34	06 40			06 49	06 55	
New Cross Gate ■	d				00 01	00 04	00 08	00 16	00 41	05 53		06 00	06 08	06 15	06 18	06 23	06 30	06 35	06 38	06 45		06 48	06 53	07 00	07 05
Brockley	d				00 02	00 07	00 11	00 19	00 44	05 56		06 02	06 11	06 17	06 21	06 26	06 32	06 37	06 41	06 47		06 50	06 56	07 02	07 07
Honor Oak Park	d				00 05	00 09	00 13	00 21	00 46	05 58		06 05	06 13	06 20	06 23	06 28	06 35	06 40	06 43	06 50		06 53	06 58	07 05	07 10
Forest Hill ■	d		00 01		00 07	00 12	00 16	00 24	00 49	06 01		06 07	06 16	06 22	06 26	06 31	06 37	06 42	06 46	06 52		06 55	07 01	07 07	07 12
Sydenham	d		00 04		00 11	00 15	00 19	00 27	00 52	06 04		06 11	06 19	06 26	06 29	06 34	06 41	06 46	06 49	06 56		06 59	07 04	07 11	07 16
Crystal Palace ■	a		00 09			00 20	00 24			06 08			06 23			06 38		06 50	06 53				07 08		07 20
Penge West	d			00 01	00 13			00 29	00 54			06 13		06 28	06 31		06 43			06 58		07 01		07 13	
Anerley	d	00 01		00 03	00 15			00 31	00 56			06 15		06 30	06 33		06 45			07 00		07 03		07 15	
Norwood Junction ■	a	00 03		00 06	00 17			00 34	00 59			06 18		06 33	06 37		06 48			07 03		07 06		07 18	
Norwood Junction	d	00 03			00 18							06 18		06 33			06 48			07 03				07 18	
West Croydon ■	a	00 13			00 29							06 24		06 39			06 54			07 09				07 25	
Norwood Junction	d			00 06				00 35	01 08						06 39							07 09			
East Croydon	a			00 10				00 38	01 13						06 43							07 13			
Purley	a														06 54							07 24			

A To Coulsdon Town

B To London Victoria

C To Streatham Hill

D From Highbury and Islington Ell

E From London Bridge

F From Dalston Junction Stn Ell

G From London Bridge to Streatham Hill

H not 16 May

For full service between Highbury & Islington and Surrey Quays, refer to Table T178

For Sutton connections at West Croydon, refer to Table T172

Table T177-F

Saturdays
21 December to 16 May

London Bridge-New Cross Gate,Brockley, Honor Oak Park, Forest Hill, Sydenham, Crystal Palace, Penge West, Anerley-Norwood Junction and Croydon

	LO		LO	SN A	LO	LO	SN B	LO	LO	SN A	LO		LO	SN B	LO	LO	SN A	LO	LO	SN B	LO		LO	SN A
London Bridge ⊖ d				07 10			07 28			07 40				07 58			08 10			08 28				08 40
Highbury & Islington d	06 40		06 47		06 55	07 02		07 10	07 17		07 25		07 32		07 40	07 47		07 55	08 02		08 10		08 17	
Canonbury d	06 42		06 49		06 57	07 04		07 12	07 19		07 27		07 34		07 42	07 49		07 57	08 04		08 12		08 19	
Dalston Junction d	06 45		06 52		07 00	07 07		07 15	07 22		07 30		07 37		07 45	07 52		08 00	08 07		08 15		08 22	
Haggerston d	06 47		06 54		07 02	07 09		07 17	07 24		07 32		07 39		07 47	07 54		08 02	08 09		08 17		08 24	
Hoxton d	06 49		06 56		07 04	07 11		07 19	07 26		07 34		07 41		07 49	07 56		08 04	08 11		08 19		08 26	
Shoreditch High Street d	06 52		06 58		07 07	07 13		07 22	07 28		07 37		07 43		07 52	07 58		08 07	08 13		08 22		08 28	
Whitechapel d	06 54		07 01		07 09	07 16		07 24	07 31		07 39		07 46		07 54	08 01		08 09	08 16		08 24		08 31	
Shadwell d	06 56		07 03		07 11	07 18		07 26	07 33		07 41		07 48		07 56	08 03		08 11	08 18		08 26		08 33	
Wapping d	06 58		07 05		07 13	07 20		07 28	07 35		07 43		07 50		07 58	08 05		08 13	08 20		08 28		08 35	
Rotherhithe d	07 00		07 06		07 15	07 21		07 30	07 36		07 45		07 51		08 00	08 06		08 15	08 21		08 30		08 36	
Canada Water d	07 02		07 08		07 17	07 23		07 32	07 38		07 47		07 53		08 02	08 08		08 17	08 23		08 32		08 38	
Surrey Quays d	07 04		07 10		07 19	07 25		07 34	07 40		07 49		07 55		08 04	08 10		08 19	08 25		08 34		08 40	
New Cross Gate d	07 08		07 15	07 18	07 23	07 30	07 35	07 38	07 45	07 48	07 53		08 00	08 05	08 08	08 15	08 18	08 23	08 30	08 35	08 38		08 45	08 48
Brockley d	07 11		07 17	07 21	07 26	07 32	07 37	07 41	07 47	07 51	07 56		08 02	08 07	08 11	08 17	08 21	08 26	08 32	08 37	08 41		08 47	08 51
Honor Oak Park d	07 13		07 20	07 23	07 28	07 35	07 40	07 43	07 50	07 53	07 58		08 05	08 10	08 13	08 20	08 23	08 28	08 35	08 40	08 43		08 50	08 53
Forest Hill d	07 16		07 22	07 26	07 31	07 37	07 42	07 46	07 52	07 56	08 01		08 07	08 12	08 16	08 22	08 26	08 31	08 37	08 42	08 46		08 52	08 56
Sydenham d	07 19		07 26	07 29	07 34	07 41	07 46	07 49	07 56	07 59	08 04		08 11	08 16	08 19	08 26	08 29	08 34	08 41	08 46	08 49		08 56	08 59
Crystal Palace a	07 23				07 38		07 50	07 53			08 08			08 20	08 23			08 39		08 50	08 54			
Penge West d			07 28	07 31		07 43			07 58	08 01			08 13			08 28	08 31		08 43				08 58	09 01
Anerley d			07 30	07 33		07 45			08 00	08 03			08 15			08 30	08 33		08 45				09 00	09 03
Norwood Junction a			07 33	07 36		07 48			08 03	08 06			08 18			08 33	08 36		08 48				09 03	09 06
Norwood Junction d			07 33			07 48			08 03				08 18			08 33			08 48				09 03	
West Croydon a			07 39			07 54			08 09				08 24			08 39			08 58				09 13	
Norwood Junction d				07 39						08 09							08 39							09 09
East Croydon a				07 43						08 13							08 43							09 13
Purley a				07 54						08 24							08 54							09 24

	LO	LO	SN B	LO	LO	SN A	LO		LO	SN B	LO	LO	SN A	LO	LO	SN B	LO		LO	SN A	LO	LO	SN B	LO
London Bridge ⊖ d			08 58			09 10				09 28			09 40			09 58				10 10			10 28	
Highbury & Islington d	08 25	08 32		08 40	08 47		08 55		09 02		09 10	09 17		09 25	09 32		09 40		09 47		09 55	10 02		10 10
Canonbury d	08 27	08 34		08 42	08 49		08 57		09 04		09 12	09 19		09 27	09 34		09 42		09 49		09 57	10 04		10 12
Dalston Junction d	08 30	08 37		08 45	08 52		09 00		09 07		09 15	09 22		09 30	09 37		09 45		09 52		10 00	10 07		10 15
Haggerston d	08 32	08 39		08 47	08 54		09 02		09 09		09 17	09 24		09 32	09 39		09 47		09 54		10 02	10 09		10 17
Hoxton d	08 34	08 41		08 49	08 56		09 04		09 11		09 19	09 26		09 34	09 41		09 49		09 56		10 04	10 11		10 19
Shoreditch High Street d	08 37	08 43		08 52	08 58		09 07		09 13		09 22	09 28		09 37	09 43		09 52		09 58		10 07	10 13		10 22
Whitechapel d	08 39	08 46		08 54	09 01		09 09		09 16		09 24	09 31		09 39	09 46		09 54		10 01		10 09	10 16		10 24
Shadwell d	08 41	08 48		08 56	09 03		09 11		09 18		09 26	09 33		09 41	09 48		09 56		10 03		10 11	10 18		10 26
Wapping d	08 43	08 50		08 58	09 05		09 13		09 20		09 28	09 35		09 43	09 50		09 58		10 05		10 13	10 20		10 28
Rotherhithe d	08 45	08 51		09 00	09 06		09 15		09 21		09 30	09 36		09 45	09 51		10 00		10 06		10 15	10 21		10 30
Canada Water d	08 47	08 53		09 02	09 08		09 17		09 23		09 32	09 38		09 47	09 53		10 02		10 08		10 17	10 23		10 32
Surrey Quays d	08 49	08 55		09 04	09 10		09 19		09 25		09 34	09 40		09 49	09 55		10 04		10 10		10 19	10 25		10 34
New Cross Gate d	08 53	09 00	09 05	09 08	09 15	09 18	09 23		09 30	09 35	09 38	09 45	09 48	09 53	10 00	10 05	10 08		10 15	10 18	10 23	10 30	10 34	10 38
Brockley d	08 56	09 02	09 07	09 11	09 17	09 21	09 26		09 32	09 37	09 41	09 47	09 51	09 56	10 02	10 07	10 11		10 17	10 21	10 26	10 32	10 36	10 41
Honor Oak Park d	08 58	09 05	09 10	09 13	09 20	09 23	09 28		09 35	09 40	09 43	09 50	09 53	09 58	10 05	10 10	10 13		10 20	10 23	10 28	10 35	10 39	10 43
Forest Hill d	09 01	09 07	09 12	09 16	09 22	09 26	09 31		09 37	09 42	09 46	09 52	09 56	10 01	10 07	10 12	10 16		10 22	10 26	10 31	10 37	10 41	10 46
Sydenham d	09 04	09 11	09 16	09 19	09 26	09 29	09 34		09 41	09 46	09 49	09 56	09 59	10 04	10 11	10 16	10 19		10 26	10 29	10 34	10 41	10 45	10 49
Crystal Palace a	09 09		09 20	09 24			09 38			09 50	09 53			10 08		10 20	10 23				10 38		10 49	10 53
Penge West d		09 13			09 28	09 31			09 43			09 58	10 01		10 13				10 28	10 31		10 43		
Anerley d		09 15			09 30	09 33			09 45			10 00	10 03		10 15				10 30	10 33		10 45		
Norwood Junction a		09 18			09 33	09 36			09 48			10 03	10 06		10 18				10 33	10 36		10 48		
Norwood Junction d		09 18			09 33				09 48			10 03			10 18				10 33			10 48		
West Croydon a		09 28			09 43				09 58			10 13			10 28				10 43			10 54		
Norwood Junction d						09 39							10 09							10 39				
East Croydon a						09 43							10 13							10 43				
Purley a						09 54							10 24							10 54				

A To Coulsdon Town
B To London Victoria

For full service between Highbury & Islington and Surrey Quays, refer to Table T178

For Sutton connections at West Croydon, refer to Table T172

Table T177-F

Saturdays
21 December to 16 May

London Bridge-New Cross Gate,Brockley, Honor Oak Park, Forest Hill, Sydenham, Crystal Palace, Penge West, Anerley-Norwood Junction and Croydon

	LO	SN A	LO	LO	SN B	LO	LO	SN A	LO		LO	SN B	LO	LO	SN A	LO	LO	SN B	LO		LO	SN A	LO	LO
London Bridge ⊖ d		10 40			10 58			11 10				11 28			11 40			11 58				12 10		
Highbury & Islington d	10 17		10 25	10 32		10 40	10 47		10 55		11 02		11 10	11 17		11 25	11 32		11 40		11 47		11 55	12 02
Canonbury d	10 19		10 27	10 34		10 42	10 49		10 57		11 04		11 12	11 19		11 27	11 34		11 42		11 49		11 57	12 04
Dalston Junction d	10 22		10 30	10 37		10 45	10 52		11 00		11 07		11 15	11 22		11 30	11 37		11 45		11 52		12 00	12 07
Haggerston d	10 24		10 32	10 39		10 47	10 54		11 02		11 09		11 17	11 24		11 32	11 39		11 47		11 54		12 02	12 09
Hoxton d	10 26		10 34	10 41		10 49	10 56		11 04		11 11		11 19	11 26		11 34	11 41		11 49		11 56		12 04	12 11
Shoreditch High Street d	10 28		10 37	10 43		10 52	10 58		11 07		11 13		11 22	11 28		11 37	11 43		11 52		11 58		12 07	12 13
Whitechapel d	10 31		10 39	10 46		10 54	11 01		11 09		11 16		11 24	11 31		11 39	11 46		11 54		12 01		12 09	12 16
Shadwell d	10 33		10 41	10 48		10 56	11 03		11 11		11 18		11 26	11 33		11 41	11 48		11 56		12 03		12 11	12 18
Wapping d	10 35		10 43	10 50		10 58	11 05		11 13		11 20		11 28	11 35		11 43	11 50		11 58		12 05		12 13	12 20
Rotherhithe d	10 36		10 45	10 51		11 00	11 06		11 15		11 21		11 30	11 36		11 45	11 51		12 00		12 06		12 15	12 21
Canada Water d	10 38		10 47	10 53		11 02	11 08		11 17		11 23		11 32	11 38		11 47	11 53		12 02		12 08		12 17	12 23
Surrey Quays d	10 40		10 49	10 55		11 04	11 10		11 19		11 25		11 34	11 40		11 49	11 55		12 04		12 10		12 19	12 25
New Cross Gate d	10 45	10 48	10 53	11 00	11 05	11 08	11 15	11 18	11 23		11 30	11 35	11 38	11 45	11 48	11 53	12 00	12 05	12 08		12 15	12 18	12 23	12 30
Brockley d	10 47	10 51	10 56	11 02	11 07	11 11	11 17	11 21	11 26		11 32	11 37	11 41	11 47	11 51	11 56	12 02	12 07	12 11		12 17	12 21	12 26	12 32
Honor Oak Park d	10 50	10 53	10 58	11 05	11 10	11 13	11 20	11 23	11 28		11 35	11 40	11 43	11 50	11 53	11 58	12 05	12 10	12 13		12 20	12 23	12 28	12 35
Forest Hill d	10 52	10 56	11 01	11 07	11 12	11 16	11 22	11 26	11 31		11 37	11 42	11 46	11 52	11 56	12 01	12 07	12 12	12 16		12 22	12 26	12 31	12 37
Sydenham d	10 56	10 59	11 04	11 11	11 16	11 19	11 26	11 29	11 34		11 41	11 46	11 49	11 56	11 59	12 04	12 11	12 16	12 19		12 26	12 29	12 34	12 41
Crystal Palace a			11 08		11 20	11 23			11 38			11 50	11 53			12 08		12 20	12 23				12 38	
Penge West d	10 58	11 01		11 13			11 28	11 31			11 43			11 58	12 01		12 13				12 28	12 31		12 43
Anerley d	11 00	11 03		11 15			11 30	11 33			11 45			12 00	12 03		12 15				12 30	12 33		12 45
Norwood Junction a	11 03	11 06		11 18			11 33	11 36			11 48			12 03	12 06		12 18				12 33	12 36		12 48
Norwood Junction d	11 03			11 18			11 33				11 48			12 03			12 18				12 33			12 48
West Croydon a	11 09			11 24			11 39				11 54			12 09			12 24				12 39			12 54
Norwood Junction d		11 09						11 39							12 09							12 39		
East Croydon a		11 13						11 43							12 13							12 43		
Purley a		11 24						11 54							12 24							12 54		

	SN B	LO	LO	SN A	LO		LO	SN B	LO	LO	SN A	LO	LO	SN B	LO		LO	SN A	LO	LO	SN B	LO	LO	SN A
London Bridge ⊖ d	12 28			12 40				12 58			13 10			13 28				13 40			13 58			14 10
Highbury & Islington d		12 10	12 17		12 25		12 32		12 40	12 47		12 55	13 02		13 10		13 17		13 25	13 32		13 40	13 47	
Canonbury d		12 12	12 19		12 27		12 34		12 42	12 49		12 57	13 04		13 12		13 19		13 27	13 34		13 42	13 49	
Dalston Junction d		12 15	12 22		12 30		12 37		12 45	12 52		13 00	13 07		13 15		13 22		13 30	13 37		13 45	13 52	
Haggerston d		12 17	12 24		12 32		12 39		12 47	12 54		13 02	13 09		13 17		13 24		13 32	13 39		13 47	13 54	
Hoxton d		12 19	12 26		12 34		12 41		12 49	12 56		13 04	13 11		13 19		13 26		13 34	13 41		13 49	13 56	
Shoreditch High Street d		12 22	12 28		12 37		12 43		12 52	12 58		13 07	13 13		13 22		13 28		13 37	13 43		13 52	13 58	
Whitechapel d		12 24	12 31		12 39		12 46		12 54	13 01		13 09	13 16		13 24		13 31		13 39	13 46		13 54	14 01	
Shadwell d		12 26	12 33		12 41		12 48		12 56	13 03		13 11	13 18		13 26		13 33		13 41	13 48		13 56	14 03	
Wapping d		12 28	12 35		12 43		12 50		12 58	13 05		13 13	13 20		13 28		13 35		13 43	13 50		13 58	14 05	
Rotherhithe d		12 30	12 36		12 45		12 51		13 00	13 06		13 15	13 21		13 30		13 36		13 45	13 51		14 00	14 06	
Canada Water d		12 32	12 38		12 47		12 53		13 02	13 08		13 17	13 23		13 32		13 38		13 47	13 53		14 02	14 08	
Surrey Quays d		12 34	12 40		12 49		12 55		13 04	13 10		13 19	13 25		13 34		13 40		13 49	13 55		14 04	14 10	
New Cross Gate d	12 35	12 38	12 45	12 48	12 53		13 00	13 05	13 08	13 15	13 18	13 23	13 30	13 35	13 38		13 45	13 48	13 53	14 00	14 05	14 08	14 15	14 18
Brockley d	12 37	12 41	12 47	12 51	12 56		13 02	13 07	13 11	13 17	13 21	13 26	13 32	13 37	13 41		13 47	13 51	13 56	14 02	14 07	14 11	14 17	14 21
Honor Oak Park d	12 40	12 43	12 50	12 53	12 58		13 05	13 10	13 13	13 20	13 23	13 28	13 35	13 40	13 43		13 50	13 53	13 58	14 05	14 10	14 13	14 20	14 23
Forest Hill d	12 42	12 46	12 52	12 56	13 01		13 07	13 12	13 16	13 22	13 26	13 31	13 37	13 42	13 46		13 52	13 56	14 01	14 07	14 12	14 16	14 22	14 26
Sydenham d	12 46	12 49	12 56	12 59	13 04		13 11	13 16	13 19	13 26	13 29	13 34	13 41	13 46	13 49		13 56	13 59	14 04	14 11	14 16	14 19	14 26	14 29
Crystal Palace a	12 50	12 53			13 08			13 20	13 23			13 38		13 50	13 53				14 08		14 20	14 23		
Penge West d			12 58	13 01			13 13			13 28	13 31		13 43				13 58	14 01		14 13			14 28	14 31
Anerley d			13 00	13 03			13 15			13 30	13 33		13 45				14 00	14 03		14 15			14 30	14 33
Norwood Junction a			13 03	13 06			13 18			13 33	13 36		13 48				14 03	14 06		14 18			14 33	14 36
Norwood Junction d			13 03				13 18			13 33			13 48				14 03			14 18			14 33	
West Croydon a			13 09				13 24			13 39			13 54				14 09			14 24			14 39	
Norwood Junction d				13 09							13 39							14 09						14 38
East Croydon a				13 13							13 43							14 13						14 43
Purley a				13 24							13 54							14 24						14 54

A To Coulsdon Town
B To London Victoria

For full service between Highbury & Islington and Surrey Quays, refer to Table T178

For Sutton connections at West Croydon, refer to Table T172

Table T177-F

Saturdays

21 December to 16 May

London Bridge-New Cross Gate,Brockley, Honor Oak Park, Forest Hill, Sydenham, Crystal Palace, Penge West, Anerley-Norwood Junction and Croydon

		LO	LO	SN A	LO	LO	SN B	LO	LO	SN A	LO	LO	SN B	LO	LO	SN A	LO	LO	SN B	LO	LO	SN A	LO
London Bridge 4 ⊖	d			14 28			14 40			14 58			15 10			15 28			15 40			15 58	
Highbury & Islington	d	13 55	14 02		14 10	14 17		14 25	14 32		14 40	14 47		14 55	15 02		15 10	15 17		15 25	15 32		15 40
Canonbury	d	13 57	14 04		14 12	14 19		14 27	14 34		14 42	14 49		14 57	15 04		15 12	15 19		15 27	15 34		15 42
Dalston Junction	d	14 00	14 07		14 15	14 22		14 30	14 37		14 45	14 52		15 00	15 07		15 15	15 22		15 30	15 37		15 45
Haggerston	d	14 02	14 09		14 17	14 24		14 32	14 39		14 47	14 54		15 02	15 09		15 17	15 24		15 32	15 39		15 47
Hoxton	d	14 04	14 11		14 19	14 26		14 34	14 41		14 49	14 56		15 04	15 11		15 19	15 26		15 34	15 41		15 49
Shoreditch High Street	d	14 07	14 13		14 22	14 28		14 37	14 43		14 52	14 58		15 07	15 13		15 22	15 28		15 37	15 43		15 52
Whitechapel	d	14 09	14 16		14 24	14 31		14 39	14 46		14 54	15 01		15 09	15 16		15 24	15 31		15 39	15 46		15 54
Shadwell	d	14 11	14 18		14 26	14 33		14 41	14 48		14 56	15 03		15 11	15 18		15 26	15 33		15 41	15 48		15 56
Wapping	d	14 13	14 20		14 28	14 35		14 43	14 50		14 58	15 05		15 13	15 20		15 28	15 35		15 43	15 50		15 58
Rotherhithe	d	14 15	14 21		14 30	14 36		14 45	14 51		15 00	15 06		15 15	15 21		15 30	15 36		15 45	15 51		16 00
Canada Water	d	14 17	14 23		14 32	14 38		14 47	14 53		15 02	15 08		15 17	15 23		15 32	15 38		15 47	15 53		16 02
Surrey Quays	d	14 19	14 25		14 34	14 40		14 49	14 55		15 04	15 10		15 19	15 25		15 34	15 40		15 49	15 55		16 04
New Cross Gate 4	d	14 23	14 30	14 35	14 38	14 45	14 48	14 53	15 00	15 05	15 08	15 15	15 18	15 23	15 30	15 35	15 38	15 45	15 48	15 53	16 00	16 05	16 08
Brockley	d	14 26	14 32	14 37	14 41	14 47	14 51	14 56	15 02	15 07	15 11	15 17	15 21	15 26	15 32	15 37	15 41	15 47	15 51	15 56	16 02	16 07	16 11
Honor Oak Park	d	14 28	14 35	14 40	14 43	14 50	14 53	14 58	15 05	15 10	15 13	15 20	15 23	15 28	15 35	15 40	15 43	15 50	15 53	15 58	16 05	16 10	16 13
Forest Hill 4	d	14 31	14 37	14 42	14 46	14 52	14 56	15 01	15 07	15 12	15 16	15 22	15 26	15 31	15 37	15 42	15 46	15 52	15 56	16 01	16 07	16 12	16 16
Sydenham	d	14 34	14 41	14 46	14 49	14 56	14 59	15 04	15 11	15 16	15 19	15 26	15 29	15 34	15 41	15 46	15 49	15 56	15 59	16 04	16 11	16 16	16 19
Crystal Palace 4	a	14 38		14 50	14 53			15 08		15 20	15 23			15 38		15 50	15 53			16 08		16 20	16 23
Penge West	d		14 43			14 58	15 01		15 13			15 28	15 31		15 43			15 58	16 01		16 13		
Anerley	d		14 45			15 00	15 03		15 15			15 30	15 33		15 45			16 00	16 03		16 15		
Norwood Junction 2	a		14 48			15 03	15 06		15 18			15 33	15 36		15 48			16 03	16 06		16 18		
Norwood Junction	d		14 48			15 03			15 18			15 33			15 48			16 03			16 18		
West Croydon 4	a		14 54			15 09			15 24			15 39			15 58			16 13			16 28		
Norwood Junction	d						15 09						15 39						16 09				
East Croydon	a						15 13						15 43						16 13				
Purley	a						15 24						15 54						16 24				

		LO		SN B	LO	LO	SN A	LO	LO	SN B	LO	LO	SN A	LO	LO	SN B	LO	LO	SN A	LO	LO	SN B	LO
London Bridge 4 ⊖	d			19 10			19 28			19 40			19 58			20 10			20 28			20 40	
Highbury & Islington	d	15 47			18 55	19 02		19 10	19 17		19 25	19 32		19 40	19 47		19 55	20 02		20 10	20 17		20 25
Canonbury	d	15 49			18 57	19 04		19 12	19 19		19 27	19 34		19 42	19 49		19 57	20 04		20 12	20 19		20 27
Dalston Junction	d	15 52			19 00	19 07		19 15	19 22		19 30	19 37		19 45	19 52		20 00	20 07		20 15	20 22		20 30
Haggerston	d	15 54			19 02	19 09		19 17	19 24		19 32	19 39		19 47	19 54		20 02	20 09		20 17	20 24		20 32
Hoxton	d	15 56			19 04	19 11		19 19	19 26		19 34	19 41		19 49	19 56		20 04	20 11		20 19	20 26		20 34
Shoreditch High Street	d	15 58			19 07	19 13		19 22	19 28		19 37	19 43		19 52	19 58		20 07	20 13		20 22	20 28		20 37
Whitechapel	d	16 01			19 09	19 16		19 24	19 31		19 39	19 46		19 54	20 01		20 09	20 16		20 24	20 31		20 39
Shadwell	d	16 03			19 11	19 18		19 26	19 33		19 41	19 48		19 56	20 03		20 11	20 18		20 26	20 33		20 41
Wapping	d	16 05	and at the same minutes past each hour until		19 13	19 20		19 28	19 35		19 43	19 50		19 58	20 05		20 13	20 20		20 28	20 35		20 43
Rotherhithe	d	16 06			19 15	19 21		19 30	19 36		19 45	19 51		20 00	20 06		20 15	20 21		20 30	20 36		20 45
Canada Water	d	16 08			19 17	19 23		19 32	19 38		19 47	19 53		20 02	20 08		20 17	20 23		20 32	20 38		20 47
Surrey Quays	d	16 10			19 19	19 25		19 34	19 40		19 49	19 55		20 04	20 10		20 19	20 25		20 34	20 40		20 49
New Cross Gate 4	d	16 15		19 18	19 23	19 30	19 35	19 38	19 45	19 48	19 53	20 00	20 05	20 08	20 15	20 18	20 23	20 30	20 35	20 38	20 45	20 48	20 53
Brockley	d	16 17		19 21	19 26	19 32	19 37	19 41	19 47	19 51	19 56	20 02	20 07	20 11	20 17	20 21	20 26	20 32	20 37	20 41	20 47	20 51	20 56
Honor Oak Park	d	16 20		19 23	19 28	19 35	19 40	19 43	19 50	19 53	19 58	20 05	20 10	20 13	20 20	20 23	20 28	20 35	20 40	20 43	20 50	20 53	20 58
Forest Hill 4	d	16 22		19 26	19 31	19 37	19 42	19 46	19 52	19 56	20 01	20 07	20 12	20 16	20 22	20 26	20 31	20 37	20 42	20 46	20 52	20 56	21 01
Sydenham	d	16 26		19 29	19 34	19 41	19 46	19 49	19 56	19 59	20 04	20 11	20 16	20 19	20 26	20 29	20 34	20 41	20 46	20 49	20 56	20 59	21 04
Crystal Palace 4	a				19 38		19 50	19 53			20 08		20 20	20 23			20 38		20 50	20 53			21 08
Penge West	d	16 28		19 31		19 43			19 58	20 01		20 13			20 28	20 31		20 43			20 58	21 01	
Anerley	d	16 30		19 33		19 45			20 00	20 03		20 15			20 30	20 33		20 45			21 00	21 03	
Norwood Junction 2	a	16 33		19 36		19 48			20 03	20 06		20 18			20 33	20 36		20 48			21 03	21 06	
Norwood Junction	d	16 33				19 48			20 03			20 18			20 33			20 48			21 03		
West Croydon 4	a	16 43				19 58			20 13			20 28			20 43			20 58			21 13		
Norwood Junction	d			19 39						20 09						20 39						21 09	
East Croydon	a			19 43						20 13						20 43						21 13	
Purley	a			19 54						20 24						20 54						21 24	

A To London Victoria

B To Coulsdon Town

For full service between Highbury & Islington and Surrey Quays, refer to Table T178

For Sutton connections at West Croydon, refer to Table T172

Table T177-F

Saturdays

21 December to 16 May

London Bridge-New Cross Gate,Brockley, Honor Oak Park, Forest Hill, Sydenham, Crystal Palace, Penge West, Anerley-Norwood Junction and Croydon

		LO	SN A	LO	LO	SN B	LO	LO	SN A	LO	LO	SN B	LO	LO	SN A	LO	LO	SN B	LO	LO	SN A	LO	LO
London Bridge 4 ⊖	d		20 58			21 10			21 28			21 40			21 58			22 10			22 28		
Highbury & Islington	d	20 32		20 40	20 47		20 55	21 02		21 10	21 17		21 25	21 32		21 40	21 47		21 55	22 02		22 10	22 17
Canonbury	d	20 34		20 42	20 49		20 57	21 04		21 12	21 19		21 27	21 34		21 42	21 49		21 57	22 04		22 12	22 19
Dalston Junction	d	20 37		20 45	20 52		21 00	21 07		21 15	21 22		21 30	21 37		21 45	21 52		22 00	22 07		22 15	22 22
Haggerston	d	20 39		20 47	20 54		21 02	21 09		21 17	21 24		21 32	21 39		21 47	21 54		22 02	22 09		22 17	22 24
Hoxton	d	20 41		20 49	20 56		21 04	21 11		21 19	21 26		21 34	21 41		21 49	21 56		22 04	22 11		22 19	22 26
Shoreditch High Street	d	20 43		20 52	20 58		21 07	21 13		21 22	21 28		21 37	21 43		21 52	21 58		22 07	22 13		22 22	22 28
Whitechapel	d	20 46		20 54	21 01		21 09	21 16		21 24	21 31		21 39	21 46		21 54	22 01		22 09	22 16		22 24	22 31
Shadwell	d	20 48		20 56	21 03		21 11	21 18		21 26	21 33		21 41	21 48		21 56	22 03		22 11	22 18		22 26	22 33
Wapping	d	20 50		20 58	21 05		21 13	21 20		21 28	21 35		21 43	21 50		21 58	22 05		22 13	22 20		22 28	22 35
Rotherhithe	d	20 51		21 00	21 06		21 15	21 21		21 30	21 36		21 45	21 51		22 00	22 06		22 15	22 21		22 30	22 36
Canada Water	d	20 53		21 02	21 08		21 17	21 23		21 32	21 38		21 47	21 53		22 02	22 08		22 17	22 23		22 32	22 38
Surrey Quays	d	20 55		21 04	21 10		21 19	21 25		21 34	21 40		21 49	21 55		22 04	22 10		22 19	22 25		22 34	22 40
New Cross Gate 4	d	21 00	21 05	21 08	21 15	21 18	21 23	21 30	21 35	21 38	21 45	21 48	21 53	22 00	22 05	22 08	22 15	22 18	22 23	22 30	22 35	22 38	22 45
Brockley	d	21 02	21 07	21 11	21 17	21 21	21 26	21 32	21 37	21 41	21 47	21 51	21 56	22 02	22 07	22 11	22 17	22 21	22 26	22 32	22 37	22 41	22 47
Honor Oak Park	d	21 05	21 10	21 13	21 20	21 23	21 28	21 35	21 40	21 43	21 50	21 53	21 58	22 05	22 10	22 13	22 20	22 23	22 28	22 35	22 40	22 43	22 50
Forest Hill 4	d	21 07	21 12	21 16	21 22	21 26	21 31	21 37	21 42	21 46	21 52	21 56	22 01	22 07	22 12	22 16	22 22	22 26	22 31	22 37	22 42	22 46	22 52
Sydenham	d	21 11	21 16	21 19	21 26	21 29	21 34	21 41	21 46	21 49	21 56	21 59	22 04	22 11	22 16	22 19	22 26	22 29	22 34	22 41	22 46	22 49	22 56
Crystal Palace 4	a		21 20	21 23			21 38		21 50	21 53			22 08		22 20	22 23			22 38		22 50	22 53	
Penge West	d	21 13			21 28	21 31		21 43			21 58	22 01		22 13			22 28	22 31		22 43			22 58
Anerley	d	21 15			21 30	21 33		21 45			22 00	22 03		22 15			22 30	22 33		22 45			23 00
Norwood Junction 2	a	21 18			21 33	21 36		21 48			22 03	22 06		22 18			22 33	22 36		22 48			23 03
Norwood Junction	d	21 18			21 33			21 48			22 03			22 18			22 33			22 48			23 03
West Croydon 4	a	21 24			21 39			21 54			22 09			22 24			22 39			22 54			23 13
Norwood Junction	d					21 39						22 09						22 39					
East Croydon	a					21 43						22 13						22 43					
Purley	a					21 54						22 24						22 54					

		SN B	LO	LO	SN A	LO	LO	SN	LO	LO	SN A	LO	LO	SN	LO	LO	SN C	LO
London Bridge 4 ⊖	d	22 40			22 58			23 10			23 28			23 40			23 58	
Highbury & Islington	d		22 25	22 32		22 40	22 47		22 55	23 02		23 10	23 17		23 25	23 32		23 40
Canonbury	d		22 27	22 34		22 42	22 49		22 57	23 04		23 12	23 19		23 27	23 34		23 42
Dalston Junction	d		22 30	22 37		22 45	22 52		23 00	23 07		23 15	23 22		23 30	23 37		23 45
Haggerston	d		22 32	22 39		22 47	22 54		23 02	23 09		23 17	23 24		23 32	23 39		23 47
Hoxton	d		22 34	22 41		22 49	22 56		23 04	23 11		23 19	23 26		23 34	23 41		23 49
Shoreditch High Street	d		22 37	22 43		22 52	22 58		23 07	23 13		23 22	23 28		23 37	23 43		23 52
Whitechapel	d		22 39	22 46		22 54	23 01		23 09	23 16		23 24	23 31		23 39	23 46		23 54
Shadwell	d		22 41	22 48		22 56	23 03		23 11	23 18		23 26	23 33		23 41	23 48		23 56
Wapping	d		22 43	22 50		22 58	23 05		23 13	23 20		23 28	23 35		23 43	23 50		23 58
Rotherhithe	d		22 45	22 51		23 00	23 06		23 15	23 21		23 30	23 36		23 45	23 51		23 59
Canada Water	d		22 47	22 53		23 02	23 08		23 17	23 23		23 32	23 38		23 47	23 53		00 02
Surrey Quays	d		22 49	22 55		23 04	23 10		23 19	23 25		23 34	23 40		23 49	23 55		00 04
New Cross Gate 4	d	22 48	22 53	23 00	23 05	23 08	23 15	23 18	23 23	23 30	23 35	23 38	23 45	23 48	23 53	00 01	00 05	00 08
Brockley	d	22 51	22 56	23 02	23 07	23 11	23 17	23 20	23 26	23 32	23 37	23 41	23 47	23 50	23 56	00 03	00 07	00 11
Honor Oak Park	d	22 53	22 58	23 05	23 10	23 13	23 20	23 23	23 28	23 35	23 40	23 43	23 50	23 53	23 58	00 06	00 10	00 13
Forest Hill 4	d	22 56	23 01	23 07	23 12	23 16	23 22	23 25	23 31	23 37	23 42	23 46	23 52	23 55	00 01	00 08	00 12	00 16
Sydenham	d	22 59	23 04	23 11	23 16	23 19	23 26	23 29	23 34	23 41	23 46	23 49	23 56	23 59	00 04	00 11	00 16	00 19
Crystal Palace 4	a		23 08		23 20	23 23			23 38		23 50	23 53			00 08		00 20	00 23
Penge West	d	23 01		23 13			23 28	23 31		23 43			23 58	00 01		00 13		
Anerley	d	23 03		23 15			23 30	23 33		23 45			00 01	00 05		00 15		
Norwood Junction 2	a	23 06		23 18			23 33	23 36		23 48			00 03	00 08		00 18		
Norwood Junction	d			23 18			23 33			23 48			00 03			00 19		
West Croydon 4	a			23 28			23 43			23 58			00 13			00 28		
Norwood Junction	d	23 09						23 39						00 09				
East Croydon	a	23 13						23 47						00 17				
Purley	a	23 24																

A To London Victoria

B To Coulsdon Town

C To Streatham Hill

For full service between Highbury & Islington and Surrey Quays, refer to Table T178

For Sutton connections at West Croydon, refer to Table T172

Table T177-F

Sundays
15 December to 10 May

London Bridge-New Cross Gate,Brockley, Honor Oak Park, Forest Hill, Sydenham, Crystal Palace, Penge West, Anerley-Norwood Junction and Croydon

Station		LO A	LO A	SN B	LO A	SN C		LO A	SN	SN	LO	LO	LO	SN D	SN	LO		LO	SN D	SN	LO	SN D	LO	SN	LO
London Bridge 4 ⊖	d								00 20	00 35				07 31	07 38				08 01	08 08		08 24		08 38	
Highbury & Islington	d										06 35	06 51				07 21					07 51		08 07		08 21
Canonbury	d										06 37	06 53				07 23					07 53		08 09		08 23
Dalston Junction	d										06 40	06 56	07 12			07 26		07 42			07 56		08 12		08 26
Haggerston	d										06 42	06 57	07 13			07 27		07 43			07 57		08 13		08 27
Hoxton	d										06 44	06 59	07 15			07 29		07 45			07 59		08 15		08 29
Shoreditch High Street	d										06 46	07 02	07 18			07 32		07 48			08 02		08 18		08 32
Whitechapel	d										06 49	07 04	07 20			07 34		07 50			08 04		08 20		08 34
Shadwell	d										06 51	07 06	07 22			07 36		07 52			08 06		08 22		08 36
Wapping	d										06 53	07 08	07 24			07 38		07 54			08 08		08 24		08 38
Rotherhithe	d										06 54	07 10	07 26			07 40		07 56			08 10		08 26		08 40
Canada Water	d							00 02			06 56	07 12	07 28			07 42		07 58			08 12		08 28		08 42
Surrey Quays	d							00 04			06 58	07 14	07 30			07 44		08 00			08 14		08 30		08 44
New Cross Gate 4	d				00 01	00 05		00 08	00 26	00 41	07 04	07 18	07 34	07 38	07 44	07 48		08 04	08 08	08 14	08 18	08 30	08 34	08 44	08 48
Brockley	d				00 03	00 07		00 11	00 29	00 44	07 07	07 21	07 37	07 40	07 47	07 51		08 07	08 10	08 17	08 21	08 33	08 37	08 47	08 51
Honor Oak Park	d				00 06	00 10		00 13	00 31	00 46	07 09	07 23	07 39	07 43	07 49	07 53		08 09	08 13	08 19	08 23	08 35	08 39	08 49	08 53
Forest Hill 4	d		00 01		00 08	00 12		00 16	00 34	00 49	07 12	07 26	07 42	07 45	07 52	07 56		08 12	08 15	08 22	08 26	08 38	08 42	08 52	08 56
Sydenham	d		00 04		00 11	00 16		00 19	00 37	00 52	07 15	07 29	07 45	07 49	07 55	07 59		08 15	08 19	08 25	08 29	08 41	08 45	08 55	08 59
Crystal Palace 4	a		00 08			00 20		00 23				07 34			08 00	08 04				08 30	08 34			09 00	09 04
Penge West	d			00 01	00 13				00 39	00 54	07 17		07 47	07 51				08 17	08 21			08 43	08 47		
Anerley	d	00 01		00 05	00 15				00 41	00 56	07 19		07 49	07 53				08 19	08 23			08 45	08 49		
Norwood Junction 2	a	00 03		00 08	00 18				00 44	00 59	07 22		07 52	07 56				08 22	08 26			08 49	08 52		
Norwood Junction	d	00 03			00 19				00 45		07 22		07 52					08 22					08 52		
West Croydon 4	a	00 13			00 28				00 50		07 27		07 58					08 28					08 59		
Norwood Junction	d			00 09						01 08				07 56					08 26			08 52			
East Croydon	a			00 17						01 13				08 02					08 32			08 55			
Purley	a													08 11					08 41			09 04			

Station		SN D		LO	SN	LO	SN D	LO	SN	LO	SN D	LO		SN	LO	SN D	LO	SN	LO	SN D	LO	SN		LO	SN D
London Bridge 4 ⊖	d	08 54			09 08		09 24		09 38		09 54			10 08		10 24		10 38		10 54		11 08			11 24
Highbury & Islington	d			08 37		08 51		09 07		09 21		09 37			09 51		10 07		10 21		10 37			10 51	
Canonbury	d			08 39		08 53		09 09		09 23		09 39			09 53		10 09		10 23		10 39			10 53	
Dalston Junction	d			08 42		08 56		09 12		09 26		09 42			09 56		10 12		10 26		10 42			10 56	
Haggerston	d			08 43		08 57		09 13		09 27		09 43			09 57		10 13		10 27		10 43			10 57	
Hoxton	d			08 45		08 59		09 15		09 29		09 45			09 59		10 15		10 29		10 45			10 59	
Shoreditch High Street	d			08 48		09 02		09 18		09 32		09 48			10 02		10 18		10 32		10 48			11 02	
Whitechapel	d			08 50		09 04		09 20		09 34		09 50			10 04		10 20		10 34		10 50			11 04	
Shadwell	d			08 52		09 06		09 22		09 36		09 52			10 06		10 22		10 36		10 52			11 06	
Wapping	d			08 54		09 08		09 24		09 38		09 54			10 08		10 24		10 38		10 54			11 08	
Rotherhithe	d			08 56		09 10		09 26		09 40		09 56			10 10		10 26		10 40		10 56			11 10	
Canada Water	d			08 58		09 12		09 28		09 42		09 58			10 12		10 28		10 42		10 58			11 12	
Surrey Quays	d			09 00		09 14		09 30		09 44		10 00			10 14		10 30		10 44		11 00			11 14	
New Cross Gate 4	d	09 00		09 04	09 14	09 18	09 30	09 34	09 44	09 48	10 00	10 04		10 14	10 18	10 30	10 34	10 44	10 48	11 00	11 04	11 14		11 18	11 30
Brockley	d	09 03		09 07	09 17	09 21	09 33	09 37	09 47	09 51	10 03	10 07		10 17	10 21	10 33	10 37	10 47	10 51	11 03	11 07	11 17		11 21	11 33
Honor Oak Park	d	09 05		09 09	09 19	09 23	09 35	09 39	09 49	09 53	10 05	10 09		10 19	10 23	10 35	10 39	10 49	10 53	11 05	11 09	11 19		11 23	11 35
Forest Hill 4	d	09 08		09 12	09 22	09 26	09 38	09 42	09 52	09 56	10 08	10 12		10 22	10 26	10 38	10 42	10 52	10 56	11 08	11 12	11 22		11 26	11 38
Sydenham	d	09 11		09 15	09 25	09 29	09 41	09 45	09 55	09 59	10 11	10 15		10 25	10 29	10 41	10 45	10 55	10 59	11 11	11 15	11 25		11 29	11 41
Crystal Palace 4	a				09 30	09 34			10 00	10 04				10 30	10 34			11 00	11 04			11 30		11 34	
Penge West	d	09 13		09 17			09 43	09 47			10 13	10 17				10 43	10 47			11 13	11 17				11 43
Anerley	d	09 15		09 19			09 45	09 49			10 15	10 19				10 45	10 49			11 15	11 19				11 45
Norwood Junction 2	a	09 19		09 22			09 49	09 52			10 19	10 22				10 49	10 52			11 19	11 22				11 49
Norwood Junction	d			09 22				09 52				10 22					10 52				11 22				
West Croydon 4	a			09 29				09 59				10 29					10 59				11 29				
Norwood Junction	d	09 22					09 52				10 22					10 52				11 22					11 52
East Croydon	a	09 25					09 55				10 25					10 55				11 25					11 55
Purley	a	09 34					10 04				10 34					11 04				11 34					12 04

A not 15 December. From Highbury and Islington EII
B not 15 December. From London Bridge
C not 15 December. From London Bridge to Streatham Hill
D To Caterham

For full service between Highbury & Islington and Surrey Quays, refer to Table T178

For Sutton connections at West Croydon, refer to Table T172

Table T177-F

Sundays
15 December to 10 May

London Bridge-New Cross Gate,Brockley, Honor Oak Park, Forest Hill, Sydenham, Crystal Palace, Penge West, Anerley-Norwood Junction and Croydon

Station		LO	SN	LO		SN A	LO	LO	SN	LO	LO	SN A	LO	LO		SN	LO	LO	SN A	LO	LO	SN	LO	LO	
London Bridge 4 ⊖	d		11 38			11 54			12 08			12 24				12 38			12 54			13 08			
Highbury & Islington	d	11 07		11 21			11 37			11 53			12 08					12 28			12 43			12 58	
Canonbury	d	11 09		11 23			11 39			11 55			12 10					12 30			12 45			13 00	
Dalston Junction	d	11 12		11 26			11 42	11 48		11 58	12 03		12 13	12 18			12 28	12 33		12 43	12 48		12 58	13 03	
Haggerston	d	11 13		11 27			11 43	11 49		11 59	12 04		12 14	12 19			12 29	12 34		12 44	12 49		12 59	13 04	
Hoxton	d	11 15		11 29			11 45	11 51		12 01	12 06		12 16	12 21			12 31	12 36		12 46	12 51		13 01	13 06	
Shoreditch High Street	d	11 18		11 32			11 48	11 54		12 04	12 09		12 19	12 24			12 34	12 39		12 49	12 54		13 04	13 09	
Whitechapel	d	11 20		11 34			11 50	11 56		12 06	12 11		12 21	12 26			12 36	12 41		12 51	12 56		13 06	13 11	
Shadwell	d	11 22		11 36			11 52	11 58		12 08	12 13		12 23	12 28			12 38	12 43		12 53	12 58		13 08	13 13	
Wapping	d	11 24		11 38			11 54	12 00		12 10	12 15		12 25	12 30			12 40	12 45		12 55	13 00		13 10	13 15	
Rotherhithe	d	11 26		11 40			11 56	12 02		12 12	12 17		12 27	12 32			12 42	12 47		12 57	13 02		13 12	13 17	
Canada Water	d	11 28		11 42			11 58	12 04		12 14	12 19		12 29	12 34			12 44	12 49		12 59	13 04		13 14	13 19	
Surrey Quays	d	11 30		11 44			12 00	12 06		12 16	12 21		12 31	12 36			12 46	12 51		13 01	13 06		13 16	13 21	
New Cross Gate 4	d	11 34	11 44	11 48		12 00	12 04	12 10	12 14	12 20	12 25	12 30	12 35	12 40		12 44	12 50	12 55	13 00	13 05	13 10	13 14	13 20	13 25	
Brockley	d	11 37	11 47	11 51		12 03	12 07	12 13	12 17	12 23	12 28	12 33	12 38	12 43		12 47	12 53	12 58	13 03	13 08	13 13	13 17	13 23	13 28	
Honor Oak Park	d	11 39	11 49	11 53		12 05	12 09	12 15	12 19	12 25	12 30	12 35	12 40	12 45		12 49	12 55	13 00	13 05	13 10	13 15	13 19	13 25	13 30	
Forest Hill 4	d	11 42	11 52	11 56		12 08	12 12	12 18	12 22	12 28	12 33	12 38	12 43	12 48		12 52	12 58	13 03	13 08	13 13	13 18	13 22	13 28	13 33	
Sydenham	d	11 45	11 55	11 59		12 11	12 15	12 21	12 25	12 31	12 36	12 41	12 46	12 51		12 55	13 01	13 06	13 11	13 16	13 21	13 25	13 31	13 36	
Crystal Palace 4	a		12 00	12 04				12 25	12 30		12 40			12 55		13 00		13 11			13 26	13 30		13 41	
Penge West	d	11 47				12 14	12 17			12 33		12 44	12 48				13 03		13 14	13 18			13 33		
Anerley	d	11 49				12 16	12 19			12 35		12 46	12 50				13 05		13 16	13 20			13 35		
Norwood Junction 2	a	11 52				12 20	12 22			12 38		12 50	12 53				13 08		13 20	13 23			13 38		
Norwood Junction	d	11 52					12 22			12 38			12 53				13 08			13 23			13 38		
West Croydon 4	a	11 59					12 29			12 45			13 00				13 14			13 30			13 44		
Norwood Junction	d					12 22						12 52							13 22						
East Croydon	a					12 25						12 55							13 25						
Purley	a					12 34						13 04							13 34						

Station		SN A	LO	LO	SN	LO	LO	SN A	LO	LO		SN	LO	LO	SN A	LO	LO	SN	LO	LO		SN A	LO	LO	SN
London Bridge 4 ⊖	d	13 24			13 38			13 54				14 08			14 24			14 38				14 54			15 08
Highbury & Islington	d			13 13			13 28			13 43				13 58			14 13			14 28				14 43	
Canonbury	d			13 15			13 30			13 45				14 00			14 15			14 30				14 45	
Dalston Junction	d		13 13	13 18		13 28	13 33		13 43	13 48			13 58	14 03		14 13	14 18		14 28	14 33			14 43	14 48	
Haggerston	d		13 14	13 19		13 29	13 34		13 44	13 49			13 59	14 04		14 14	14 19		14 29	14 34			14 44	14 49	
Hoxton	d		13 16	13 21		13 31	13 36		13 46	13 51			14 01	14 06		14 16	14 21		14 31	14 36			14 46	14 51	
Shoreditch High Street	d		13 19	13 24		13 34	13 39		13 49	13 54			14 04	14 09		14 19	14 24		14 34	14 39			14 49	14 54	
Whitechapel	d		13 21	13 26		13 36	13 41		13 51	13 56			14 06	14 11		14 21	14 26		14 36	14 41			14 51	14 56	
Shadwell	d		13 23	13 28		13 38	13 43		13 53	13 58			14 08	14 13		14 23	14 28		14 38	14 43			14 53	14 58	
Wapping	d		13 25	13 30		13 40	13 45		13 55	14 00			14 10	14 15		14 25	14 30		14 40	14 45			14 55	15 00	
Rotherhithe	d		13 27	13 32		13 42	13 47		13 57	14 02			14 12	14 17		14 27	14 32		14 42	14 47			14 57	15 02	
Canada Water	d		13 29	13 34		13 44	13 49		13 59	14 04			14 14	14 19		14 29	14 34		14 44	14 49			14 59	15 04	
Surrey Quays	d		13 31	13 36		13 46	13 51		14 01	14 06			14 16	14 21		14 31	14 36		14 46	14 51			15 01	15 06	
New Cross Gate 4	d	13 30	13 35	13 40	13 44	13 50	13 55	14 00	14 05	14 10		14 14	14 20	14 25	14 30	14 35	14 40	14 44	14 50	14 55		15 00	15 05	15 10	15 14
Brockley	d	13 33	13 38	13 43	13 47	13 53	13 58	14 03	14 08	14 13		14 17	14 23	14 28	14 33	14 38	14 43	14 47	14 53	14 58		15 03	15 08	15 13	15 17
Honor Oak Park	d	13 35	13 40	13 45	13 49	13 55	14 00	14 05	14 10	14 15		14 19	14 25	14 30	14 35	14 40	14 45	14 49	14 55	15 00		15 05	15 10	15 15	15 19
Forest Hill 4	d	13 38	13 43	13 48	13 52	13 58	14 03	14 08	14 13	14 18		14 22	14 28	14 33	14 38	14 43	14 48	14 52	14 58	15 03		15 08	15 13	15 18	15 22
Sydenham	d	13 41	13 46	13 51	13 55	14 01	14 06	14 11	14 16	14 21		14 25	14 31	14 36	14 41	14 46	14 51	14 55	15 01	15 06		15 11	15 16	15 21	15 25
Crystal Palace 4	a			13 56	14 00		14 11			14 26		14 30		14 41			14 56	15 00		15 11				15 26	15 30
Penge West	d	13 44	13 48			14 03		14 14	14 18				14 33		14 44	14 48			15 03			15 14	15 18		
Anerley	d	13 46	13 50			14 05		14 16	14 20				14 35		14 46	14 50			15 05			15 16	15 20		
Norwood Junction 2	a	13 50	13 53			14 08		14 20	14 23				14 38		14 50	14 53			15 08			15 20	15 23		
Norwood Junction	d		13 53			14 08			14 23				14 38			14 53			15 08				15 23		
West Croydon 4	a		13 59			14 14			14 29				14 44			14 59			15 14				15 29		
Norwood Junction	d	13 52						14 22							14 52							15 22			
East Croydon	a	13 55						14 25							14 55							15 25			
Purley	a	14 04						14 34							15 04							15 34			

A To Caterham

For full service between Highbury & Islington and Surrey Quays, refer to Table T178

For Sutton connections at West Croydon, refer to Table T172

Table T177-F

Sundays

15 December to 10 May

London Bridge-New Cross Gate,Brockley, Honor Oak Park, Forest Hill, Sydenham, Crystal Palace, Penge West, Anerley-Norwood Junction and Croydon

		LO		LO	SN A	LO	LO	SN	LO	LO	SN A	LO		LO	SN	LO	LO	SN A	LO	LO	SN	LO		LO	SN A
London Bridge 4 ⊖	d				15 24			15 38			15 54				16 08			16 24			16 38				16 54
Highbury & Islington	d			14 58			15 13			15 28				15 43			15 58			16 13				16 28	
Canonbury	d			15 00			15 15			15 30				15 45			16 00			16 15				16 30	
Dalston Junction	d	14 58		15 03		15 13	15 18		15 28	15 33		15 43		15 48		15 58	16 03		16 13	16 18		16 28		16 33	
Haggerston	d	14 59		15 04		15 14	15 19		15 29	15 34		15 44		15 49		15 59	16 04		16 14	16 19		16 29		16 34	
Hoxton	d	15 01		15 06		15 16	15 21		15 31	15 36		15 46		15 51		16 01	16 06		16 16	16 21		16 31		16 36	
Shoreditch High Street	d	15 04		15 09		15 19	15 24		15 34	15 39		15 49		15 54		16 04	16 09		16 19	16 24		16 34		16 39	
Whitechapel	d	15 06		15 11		15 21	15 26		15 36	15 41		15 51		15 56		16 06	16 11		16 21	16 26		16 36		16 41	
Shadwell	d	15 08		15 13		15 23	15 28		15 38	15 43		15 53		15 58		16 08	16 13		16 23	16 28		16 38		16 43	
Wapping	d	15 10		15 15		15 25	15 30		15 40	15 45		15 55		16 00		16 10	16 15		16 25	16 30		16 40		16 45	
Rotherhithe	d	15 12		15 17		15 27	15 32		15 42	15 47		15 57		16 02		16 12	16 17		16 27	16 32		16 42		16 47	
Canada Water	d	15 14		15 19		15 29	15 34		15 44	15 49		15 59		16 04		16 14	16 19		16 29	16 34		16 44		16 49	
Surrey Quays	d	15 16		15 21		15 31	15 36		15 46	15 51		16 01		16 06		16 16	16 21		16 31	16 36		16 46		16 51	
New Cross Gate 4	d	15 20		15 25	15 30	15 35	15 40	15 44	15 50	15 55	16 00	16 05		16 10	16 14	16 20	16 25	16 30	16 35	16 40	16 44	16 50		16 55	17 00
Brockley	d	15 23		15 28	15 33	15 38	15 43	15 47	15 53	15 58	16 03	16 08		16 13	16 17	16 23	16 28	16 33	16 38	16 43	16 47	16 53		16 58	17 03
Honor Oak Park	d	15 25		15 30	15 35	15 40	15 45	15 49	15 55	16 00	16 05	16 10		16 15	16 19	16 25	16 30	16 35	16 40	16 45	16 49	16 55		17 00	17 05
Forest Hill 4	d	15 28		15 33	15 38	15 43	15 48	15 52	15 58	16 03	16 08	16 13		16 18	16 22	16 28	16 33	16 38	16 43	16 48	16 52	16 58		17 03	17 08
Sydenham	d	15 31		15 36	15 41	15 46	15 51	15 55	16 01	16 06	16 11	16 16		16 21	16 25	16 31	16 36	16 41	16 46	16 51	16 55	17 01		17 06	17 11
Crystal Palace 4	a			15 41			15 56	16 00		16 11				16 26	16 30		16 41			16 56	17 00			17 11	
Penge West	d	15 33			15 44	15 48			16 03		16 14	16 18				16 33		16 44	16 48			17 03			17 14
Anerley	d	15 35			15 46	15 50			16 05		16 16	16 20				16 35		16 46	16 50			17 05			17 16
Norwood Junction 2	a	15 38			15 50	15 53			16 08		16 20	16 23				16 38		16 50	16 53			17 08			17 20
Norwood Junction	d	15 38				15 53			16 08			16 23				16 38			16 53			17 08			
West Croydon 4	a	15 44				15 59			16 14			16 29				16 44			16 59			17 15			
Norwood Junction	d				15 52						16 22							16 52							17 22
East Croydon	a				15 55						16 25							16 55							17 25
Purley	a				16 04						16 34							17 04							17 34

		LO	LO	SN	LO	LO	SN A	LO		LO	SN	LO	LO	SN A	LO	LO	SN	LO		LO	SN A	LO	LO	SN	LO
London Bridge 4 ⊖	d			17 08			17 24				17 38			17 54			18 08				18 24			18 38	
Highbury & Islington	d		16 43			16 58				17 13			17 28			17 43				17 58			18 13		
Canonbury	d		16 45			17 00				17 15			17 30			17 45				18 00			18 15		
Dalston Junction	d	16 43	16 48		16 58	17 03		17 13		17 18		17 28	17 33		17 43	17 48		17 58		18 03		18 13	18 18		18 28
Haggerston	d	16 44	16 49		16 59	17 04		17 14		17 19		17 29	17 34		17 44	17 49		17 59		18 04		18 14	18 19		18 29
Hoxton	d	16 46	16 51		17 01	17 06		17 16		17 21		17 31	17 36		17 46	17 51		18 01		18 06		18 16	18 21		18 31
Shoreditch High Street	d	16 49	16 54		17 04	17 09		17 19		17 24		17 34	17 39		17 49	17 54		18 04		18 09		18 19	18 24		18 34
Whitechapel	d	16 51	16 56		17 06	17 11		17 21		17 26		17 36	17 41		17 51	17 56		18 06		18 11		18 21	18 26		18 36
Shadwell	d	16 53	16 58		17 08	17 13		17 23		17 28		17 38	17 43		17 53	17 58		18 08		18 13		18 23	18 28		18 38
Wapping	d	16 55	17 00		17 10	17 15		17 25		17 30		17 40	17 45		17 55	18 00		18 10		18 15		18 25	18 30		18 40
Rotherhithe	d	16 57	17 02		17 12	17 17		17 27		17 32		17 42	17 47		17 57	18 02		18 12		18 17		18 27	18 32		18 42
Canada Water	d	16 59	17 04		17 14	17 19		17 29		17 34		17 44	17 49		17 59	18 04		18 14		18 19		18 29	18 34		18 44
Surrey Quays	d	17 01	17 06		17 16	17 21		17 31		17 36		17 46	17 51		18 01	18 06		18 16		18 21		18 31	18 36		18 46
New Cross Gate 4	d	17 05	17 10	17 14	17 20	17 25	17 30	17 35		17 40	17 44	17 50	17 55	18 00	18 05	18 10	18 14	18 20		18 25	18 30	18 35	18 40	18 44	18 50
Brockley	d	17 08	17 13	17 17	17 23	17 28	17 33	17 38		17 43	17 47	17 53	17 58	18 03	18 08	18 13	18 17	18 23		18 28	18 33	18 38	18 43	18 47	18 53
Honor Oak Park	d	17 10	17 15	17 19	17 25	17 30	17 35	17 40		17 45	17 49	17 55	18 00	18 05	18 10	18 15	18 19	18 25		18 30	18 35	18 40	18 45	18 49	18 55
Forest Hill 4	d	17 13	17 18	17 22	17 28	17 33	17 38	17 43		17 48	17 52	17 58	18 03	18 08	18 13	18 18	18 22	18 28		18 33	18 38	18 43	18 48	18 52	18 58
Sydenham	d	17 16	17 21	17 25	17 31	17 36	17 41	17 46		17 51	17 55	18 01	18 06	18 11	18 16	18 21	18 25	18 31		18 36	18 41	18 46	18 51	18 55	19 01
Crystal Palace 4	a		17 26	17 30		17 41				17 56	18 00		18 11			18 26	18 30			18 41			18 56	19 00	
Penge West	d	17 18			17 33		17 44	17 48				18 03		18 14	18 18			18 33			18 44	18 48			19 03
Anerley	d	17 20			17 35		17 46	17 50				18 05		18 16	18 20			18 35			18 46	18 50			19 05
Norwood Junction 2	a	17 23			17 38		17 50	17 53				18 08		18 20	18 23			18 38			18 50	18 53			19 08
Norwood Junction	d	17 23			17 38			17 53				18 08			18 23			18 38				18 53			19 08
West Croydon 4	a	17 30			17 45			18 00				18 15			18 30			18 45				19 00			19 15
Norwood Junction	d						17 51							18 22							18 52				
East Croydon	a						17 55							18 25							18 55				
Purley	a						18 04							18 34							19 04				

A To Caterham

For full service between Highbury & Islington and Surrey Quays, refer to Table T178

For Sutton connections at West Croydon, refer to Table T172

Table T177-F

Sundays

15 December to 10 May

London Bridge-New Cross Gate,Brockley, Honor Oak Park, Forest Hill, Sydenham, Crystal Palace, Penge West, Anerley-Norwood Junction and Croydon

		LO	SN A	LO	LO	SN	LO	LO	SN A	LO	LO	SN	LO		LO	SN A	LO	LO	SN	LO	LO	SN A	LO	LO
London Bridge 4 ⊖	d		18 54			19 08			19 24			19 38		and at the same minutes past each hour until		21 54			22 08			22 24		
Highbury & Islington	d	18 28			18 43			18 58			19 13				21 28			21 43			21 58			22 13
Canonbury	d	18 30			18 45			19 00			19 15				21 30			21 45			22 00			22 15
Dalston Junction	d	18 33		18 43	18 48		18 58	19 03		19 13	19 18		19 28		21 33		21 43	21 48		21 58	22 03		22 13	22 18
Haggerston	d	18 34		18 44	18 49		18 59	19 04		19 14	19 19		19 29		21 34		21 44	21 49		21 59	22 04		22 14	22 19
Hoxton	d	18 36		18 46	18 51		19 01	19 06		19 16	19 21		19 31		21 36		21 46	21 51		22 01	22 06		22 16	22 21
Shoreditch High Street	d	18 39		18 49	18 54		19 04	19 09		19 19	19 24		19 34		21 39		21 49	21 54		22 04	22 09		22 19	22 24
Whitechapel	d	18 41		18 51	18 56		19 06	19 11		19 21	19 26		19 36		21 41		21 51	21 56		22 06	22 11		22 21	22 26
Shadwell	d	18 43		18 53	18 58		19 08	19 13		19 23	19 28		19 38		21 43		21 53	21 58		22 08	22 13		22 23	22 28
Wapping	d	18 45		18 55	19 00		19 10	19 15		19 25	19 30		19 40		21 45		21 55	22 00		22 10	22 15		22 25	22 30
Rotherhithe	d	18 47		18 57	19 02		19 12	19 17		19 27	19 32		19 42		21 47		21 57	22 02		22 12	22 17		22 27	22 32
Canada Water	d	18 49		18 59	19 04		19 14	19 19		19 29	19 34		19 44		21 49		21 59	22 04		22 14	22 19		22 29	22 34
Surrey Quays	d	18 51		19 01	19 06		19 16	19 21		19 31	19 36		19 46		21 51		22 01	22 06		22 16	22 21		22 31	22 36
New Cross Gate 4	d	18 55	19 00	19 05	19 10	19 14	19 20	19 25	19 30	19 35	19 40	19 44	19 50		21 55	22 00	22 05	22 10	22 14	22 20	22 25	22 30	22 35	22 40
Brockley	d	18 58	19 03	19 08	19 13	19 17	19 23	19 28	19 33	19 38	19 43	19 47	19 53		21 58	22 03	22 08	22 13	22 17	22 23	22 28	22 33	22 38	22 43
Honor Oak Park	d	19 00	19 05	19 10	19 15	19 19	19 25	19 30	19 35	19 40	19 45	19 49	19 55		22 00	22 05	22 10	22 15	22 19	22 25	22 30	22 35	22 40	22 45
Forest Hill 4	d	19 03	19 08	19 13	19 18	19 22	19 28	19 33	19 38	19 43	19 48	19 52	19 58		22 03	22 08	22 13	22 18	22 22	22 28	22 33	22 38	22 43	22 48
Sydenham	d	19 06	19 11	19 16	19 21	19 25	19 31	19 36	19 41	19 46	19 51	19 55	20 01		22 06	22 11	22 16	22 21	22 25	22 31	22 36	22 41	22 46	22 51
Crystal Palace 4	a	19 11			19 26	19 30		19 41			19 56	20 00			22 11			22 26	22 30		22 41			22 56
Penge West	d		19 14	19 18			19 33		19 44	19 48			20 03			22 14	22 18			22 33		22 44	22 48	
Anerley	d		19 16	19 20			19 35		19 46	19 50			20 05			22 16	22 20			22 35		22 46	22 50	
Norwood Junction 2	a		19 20	19 23			19 38		19 50	19 53			20 08			22 20	22 23			22 38		22 50	22 53	
Norwood Junction	d			19 23			19 38			19 53			20 08				22 23			22 38			22 53	
West Croydon 4	a			19 29			19 44			19 59			20 14				22 29			22 44			22 59	
Norwood Junction	d		19 22						19 52							22 22						22 52		
East Croydon	a		19 25						19 55							22 25						22 55		
Purley	a		19 34						20 04							22 34						23 04		

		SN	LO		SN B	LO	LO	SN	LO	LO	SN A	LO	LO		SN A
London Bridge 4 ⊖	d	22 38			22 54			23 11			23 31				23 50
Highbury & Islington	d						22 43					23 13	23 23		
Canonbury	d						22 45					23 15	23 25		
Dalston Junction	d		22 28			22 43	22 48		22 58	23 13		23 18	23 28		
Haggerston	d		22 29			22 44	22 49		22 59	23 14		23 19	23 29		
Hoxton	d		22 31			22 46	22 51		23 01	23 16		23 21	23 31		
Shoreditch High Street	d		22 34			22 49	22 54		23 04	23 19		23 24	23 34		
Whitechapel	d		22 36			22 51	22 56		23 06	23 21		23 26	23 36		
Shadwell	d		22 38			22 53	22 58		23 08	23 23		23 28	23 38		
Wapping	d		22 40			22 55	23 00		23 10	23 25		23 30	23 40		
Rotherhithe	d		22 42			22 57	23 02		23 12	23 27		23 32	23 42		
Canada Water	d		22 44			22 59	23 04		23 14	23 29		23 34	23 44		
Surrey Quays	d		22 46			23 01	23 06		23 16	23 31		23 36	23 46		
New Cross Gate 4	d	22 44	22 50		23 00	23 05	23 10	23 17	23 20	23 35	23 39	23 42	23 50		23 57
Brockley	d	22 47	22 53		23 03	23 08	23 13	23 19	23 23	23 38	23 41	23 45	23 53		23 59
Honor Oak Park	d	22 49	22 55		23 05	23 10	23 15	23 22	23 25	23 40	23 44	23 47	23 55		00 02
Forest Hill 4	d	22 52	22 58		23 08	23 13	23 18	23 24	23 28	23 43	23 46	23 50	23 58		00 04
Sydenham	d	22 55	23 01		23 11	23 16	23 21	23 28	23 31	23 46	23 50	23 53	00 01		00 08
Crystal Palace 4	a	23 00					23 26	23 33				23 57			
Penge West	d		23 03		23 14	23 18			23 33	23 48	23 52		00 03		00 10
Anerley	d		23 05		23 16	23 20			23 35	23 50	23 54		00 05		00 12
Norwood Junction 2	a		23 08		23 20	23 23			23 38	23 53	23 57		00 08		00 15
Norwood Junction	d		23 08			23 23			23 38	23 53			00 08		
West Croydon 4	a		23 14			23 29			23 45	23 59			00 16		
Norwood Junction	d				23 22						23 58				00 16
East Croydon	a				23 25						00 02				00 19
Purley	a				23 34						00 11				00 28

A To Caterham

B To Tattenham Corner

For full service between Highbury & Islington and Surrey Quays, refer to Table T178

For Sutton connections at West Croydon, refer to Table T172

Table T177-R

Mondays to Fridays
16 December to 15 May

Croydon and Norwood Junction-Anerley, Penge West, Crystal Palace, Sydenham, Forest Hill, Honor Oak Park, Brockley, New Cross Gate-London Bridge

Miles	Miles	Miles	Miles	Station		LO MX A	LO MX B	LO MX A	SN MX C	SN MX C	SN	LO	LO	LO	SN D	LO	LO	SN E	LO	LO	SN D	LO	LO
0	—	—	—	Purley	d						05 11												
3	—	—	—	East Croydon	d						05 20												
4¾	—	—	—	Norwood Junction [2]	a						05 24												
—	0	—	—	West Croydon [4]	d								05 31			05 46		05 57	06 01			06 16	
—	1¾	—	—	Norwood Junction	a								05 36			05 51		06 02	06 06			06 21	
—	—	—	—	Norwood Junction	d						05 25		05 37			05 52		06 03	06 07			06 22	
6	3	—	—	**Anerley**	d						05 28		05 40			05 55		06 06	06 10			06 25	
6¼	3¾	—	—	**Penge West**	d						05 29		05 41			05 56		06 08	06 11			06 26	
—	—	0	0	**Crystal Palace [4]**	d					00 28		05 32		05 47	05 52		06 02			06 17	06 22		06 32
7	4	1¼	1¼	**Sydenham**	d					00 32	05 32	05 36	05 44	05 51	05 56	05 59	06 06	06 11	06 14	06 21	06 26	06 29	06 36
7¾	4¾	2	2	**Forest Hill [4]**	d				00 01	00 35	05 35	05 39	05 47	05 54	05 58	06 02	06 09	06 13	06 17	06 24	06 28	06 32	06 39
8¾	5¾	3	3	**Honor Oak Park**	d				00 04	00 37	05 37	05 41	05 49	05 56	06 01	06 04	06 11	06 16	06 19	06 26	06 31	06 34	06 41
9¾	6¾	4	4	**Brockley**	d			00 01	00 06	00 40	05 40	05 44	05 52	05 59	06 03	06 07	06 14	06 18	06 22	06 29	06 33	06 37	06 44
—	7½	4¾	4¾	New Cross Gate	d			00 03	00 09	00 42	05 42	05 46	05 54	06 01	06 06	06 09	06 16	06 21	06 24	06 31	06 36	06 39	06 46
—	8¾	6	—	Surrey Quays	d			00 09				05 50	05 57	06 05		06 12	06 20		06 27	06 35		06 42	06 50
—	9¼	6½	—	Canada Water	d			00 11				05 52	05 59	06 07		06 14	06 22		06 29	06 37		06 44	06 52
—	9½	6¾	—	Rotherhithe	d		00 01	00 12				05 54	06 01	06 08		06 16	06 23		06 31	06 38		06 46	06 53
—	9¾	7	—	Wapping	d		00 02	00 14				05 55	06 02	06 10		06 17	06 25		06 32	06 40		06 47	06 55
—	10¼	7½	—	Shadwell	d		00 04	00 16				05 57	06 04	06 12		06 19	06 27		06 34	06 42		06 49	06 57
—	11	8	—	Whitechapel	d		00 07	00 18				06 00	06 07	06 14		06 22	06 29		06 37	06 44		06 52	06 59
—	11¾	8¾	—	Shoreditch High Street	d	00 02	00 09	00 21				06 02	06 09	06 17		06 24	06 32		06 39	06 47		06 54	07 02
—	12½	9½	—	Hoxton	d	00 04	00 11	00 23				06 04	06 11	06 19		06 26	06 34		06 41	06 49		06 56	07 04
—	13	10	—	Haggerston	d	00 06	00 13	00 25				06 06	06 13	06 21		06 28	06 36		06 43	06 51		06 58	07 06
—	13½	10½	—	Dalston Junction	a	00 08	00 15	00 27				06 08	06 15	06 23		06 30	06 38		06 45	06 53		07 00	07 08
—	—	11½	—	Canonbury	a	00 11	00 18	00 30				06 11	06 18	06 26		06 33	06 41		06 48	06 56		07 03	07 11
—	—	12	—	Highbury & Islington	a	00 15	00 25	00 32				06 15	06 23	06 30		06 38	06 45		06 53	07 00		07 08	07 15
12½	—	—	7½	London Bridge [4] ⊖	a				00 16	00 50	05 50				06 18			06 31			06 48		

Station		SN	LO	LO	SN C	LO	LO	SN	LO	LO	SN C	LO	LO	SN	LO	LO	SN C	LO	SN	LO	SN	LO	LO
Purley	d																						
East Croydon	d																						
Norwood Junction [2]	a																						
West Croydon [4]	d		06 31			06 46			07 01			07 15			07 31			07 46				08 01	
Norwood Junction	a		06 36			06 51			07 06			07 20			07 37			07 51				08 07	
Norwood Junction	d	06 34	06 37			06 52		07 04	07 07			07 22		07 34	07 37			07 52			08 04	08 07	
Anerley	d	06 37	06 40			06 55		07 07	07 10			07 25		07 37	07 40			07 55			08 07	08 10	
Penge West	d	06 38	06 41			06 56		07 08	07 11			07 26		07 38	07 41			07 56			08 08	08 11	
Crystal Palace [4]	d			06 47	06 52		07 02			07 17	07 22		07 32			07 47	07 52		07 59	08 03			08 17
Sydenham	d	06 41	06 44	06 51	06 56	06 59	07 06	07 11	07 14	07 21	07 26	07 29	07 36	07 41	07 44	07 51	07 56	07 59	08 03	08 06	08 11	08 14	08 21
Forest Hill [4]	d	06 43	06 47	06 54	06 58	07 02	07 09	07 13	07 17	07 24	07 28	07 32	07 39	07 43	07 47	07 54	07 58	08 02	08 06	08 09	08 13	08 17	08 24
Honor Oak Park	d	06 46	06 49	06 56	07 01	07 04	07 11	07 16	07 19	07 26	07 31	07 34	07 41	07 46	07 49	07 56	08 01	08 04	08 08	08 11	08 16	08 19	08 26
Brockley	d	06 48	06 52	06 59	07 03	07 07	07 14	07 18	07 22	07 29	07 33	07 37	07 44	07 48	07 52	07 59	08 03	08 07	08 11	08 14	08 18	08 22	08 29
New Cross Gate	d	06 51	06 54	07 01	07 06	07 09	07 16	07 21	07 24	07 31	07 36	07 39	07 46	07 51	07 54	08 01	08 06	08 09	08 14	08 16	08 21	08 24	08 31
Surrey Quays	d		06 57	07 05		07 12	07 20		07 27	07 35		07 42	07 50		07 57	08 05		08 12		08 20		08 27	08 35
Canada Water	d		06 59	07 07		07 14	07 22		07 29	07 37		07 44	07 52		07 59	08 07		08 14		08 22		08 29	08 37
Rotherhithe	d		07 01	07 08		07 16	07 23		07 31	07 38		07 46	07 53		08 01	08 08		08 16		08 23		08 31	08 38
Wapping	d		07 02	07 10		07 17	07 25		07 32	07 40		07 47	07 55		08 02	08 10		08 17		08 25		08 32	08 40
Shadwell	d		07 04	07 12		07 19	07 27		07 34	07 42		07 49	07 57		08 04	08 12		08 19		08 27		08 34	08 42
Whitechapel	d		07 07	07 14		07 22	07 29		07 37	07 44		07 52	07 59		08 07	08 14		08 22		08 29		08 37	08 44
Shoreditch High Street	d		07 09	07 17		07 24	07 32		07 39	07 47		07 54	08 02		08 09	08 17		08 24		08 32		08 39	08 47
Hoxton	d		07 11	07 19		07 26	07 34		07 41	07 49		07 56	08 04		08 11	08 19		08 26		08 34		08 41	08 49
Haggerston	d		07 13	07 21		07 28	07 36		07 43	07 51		07 58	08 06		08 13	08 21		08 28		08 36		08 43	08 51
Dalston Junction	a		07 15	07 23		07 30	07 38		07 46	07 53		08 01	08 08		08 16	08 23		08 31		08 39		08 46	08 53
Canonbury	a		07 18	07 26		07 33	07 41		07 48	07 56		08 03	08 11		08 18	08 26		08 33		08 41		08 48	08 56
Highbury & Islington	a		07 23	07 30		07 38	07 45		07 55	08 00		08 09	08 17		08 25	08 32		08 40		08 47		08 55	09 02
London Bridge [4] ⊖	a	07 01			07 18			07 31			07 48			08 01			08 18		08 25		08 31		

A From Crystal Palace
B From West Croydon
C From London Victoria
D From Streatham Hill
E From Epsom

For full service between Highbury & Islington and Surrey Quays, refer to Table T178

For Sutton connections at West Croydon, refer to Table T172

NRT DECEMBER 19 EDITION

Table T177-R

Mondays to Fridays
16 December to 15 May

Croydon and Norwood Junction-Anerley, Penge West, Crystal Palace, Sydenham, Forest Hill, Honor Oak Park, Brockley, New Cross Gate-London Bridge

Station		SN A	LO	SN	LO	SN	LO	LO	SN A	LO	LO	SN	LO	LO	SN A	LO	LO	SN	LO	LO	SN A	LO
Purley	d																					
East Croydon	d																					
Norwood Junction [2]	a																					
West Croydon [4]	d		08 15				08 31			08 45			09 01			09 16			09 31			09 46
Norwood Junction	a		08 21				08 37			08 50			09 06			09 21			09 36			09 51
Norwood Junction	d		08 22			08 34	08 37			08 52		09 04	09 07			09 22		09 34	09 37			09 52
Anerley	d		08 25			08 37	08 40			08 55		09 07	09 10			09 25		09 37	09 40			09 55
Penge West	d		08 26			08 38	08 41			08 56		09 08	09 11			09 26		09 39	09 41			09 56
Crystal Palace [4]	d	08 22		08 29	08 33			08 47	08 52		09 02			09 17	09 22		09 32			09 47	09 52	
Sydenham	d	08 26	08 29	08 33	08 36	08 41	08 44	08 51	08 56	08 59	09 06	09 11	09 14	09 21	09 26	09 29	09 36	09 41	09 44	09 51	09 56	09 59
Forest Hill [4]	d	08 28	08 32	08 36	08 39	08 43	08 47	08 54	08 58	09 02	09 09	09 13	09 17	09 24	09 28	09 32	09 39	09 44	09 47	09 54	09 58	10 02
Honor Oak Park	d	08 31	08 34	08 38	08 41	08 46	08 49	08 56	09 01	09 04	09 11	09 16	09 19	09 26	09 31	09 34	09 41	09 46	09 49	09 56	10 01	10 04
Brockley	d	08 33	08 37	08 41	08 44	08 48	08 52	08 59	09 03	09 07	09 14	09 18	09 22	09 29	09 33	09 37	09 44	09 49	09 52	09 59	10 03	10 07
New Cross Gate	d	08 36	08 39	08 44	08 46	08 51	08 54	09 01	09 06	09 09	09 16	09 21	09 24	09 31	09 36	09 39	09 46	09 52	09 54	10 01	10 06	10 09
Surrey Quays	d		08 42		08 50		08 57	09 05		09 12	09 20		09 27	09 35		09 42	09 50		09 57	10 05		10 12
Canada Water	d		08 44		08 52		08 59	09 07		09 14	09 22		09 29	09 37		09 44	09 52		09 59	10 07		10 14
Rotherhithe	d		08 46		08 53		09 01	09 08		09 16	09 23		09 31	09 38		09 46	09 53		10 01	10 08		10 16
Wapping	d		08 47		08 55		09 02	09 10		09 17	09 25		09 32	09 40		09 47	09 55		10 02	10 10		10 17
Shadwell	d		08 49		08 57		09 04	09 12		09 19	09 27		09 34	09 42		09 49	09 57		10 04	10 12		10 19
Whitechapel	d		08 52		08 59		09 07	09 14		09 22	09 29		09 37	09 44		09 52	09 59		10 07	10 14		10 22
Shoreditch High Street	d		08 54		09 02		09 09	09 17		09 24	09 32		09 39	09 47		09 54	10 02		10 09	10 17		10 24
Hoxton	d		08 56		09 04		09 11	09 19		09 26	09 34		09 41	09 49		09 56	10 04		10 11	10 19		10 26
Haggerston	d		08 58		09 06		09 13	09 21		09 28	09 36		09 43	09 51		09 58	10 06		10 13	10 21		10 28
Dalston Junction	a		09 01		09 09		09 16	09 23		09 31	09 38		09 45	09 53		10 00	10 08		10 15	10 23		10 30
Canonbury	a		09 03		09 11		09 18	09 26		09 33	09 41		09 48	09 56		10 03	10 11		10 18	10 26		10 33
Highbury & Islington	a		09 09		09 17		09 25	09 32		09 39	09 47		09 55	10 00		10 08	10 15		10 25	10 30		10 40
London Bridge [4] ⊖	a	08 48		08 56		09 01			09 18			09 31			09 48			10 01			10 17	

Station		LO	SN	LO	LO	SN A	LO	LO	SN	LO	LO	SN A	LO	LO	SN B	LO	LO	SN A	LO	LO	SN B	LO	LO
Purley	d														10 48						11 18		
East Croydon	d														10 57						11 27		
Norwood Junction [2]	a														11 02						11 32		
West Croydon [4]	d			10 01			10 15			10 31			10 46			11 01			11 16			11 31	
Norwood Junction	a			10 06			10 20			10 36			10 52			11 06			11 21			11 36	
Norwood Junction	d		10 03	10 07			10 21		10 33	10 37			10 52		11 03	11 07			11 22		11 33	11 37	
Anerley	d		10 06	10 10			10 24		10 36	10 40			10 55		11 06	11 10			11 25		11 36	11 40	
Penge West	d		10 07	10 11			10 25		10 37	10 41			10 56		11 08	11 11			11 26		11 38	11 41	
Crystal Palace [4]	d	10 02			10 17	10 22		10 32			10 47	10 52		11 02			11 17	11 22		11 32			11 47
Sydenham	d	10 06	10 10	10 14	10 21	10 26	10 28	10 36	10 40	10 44	10 51	10 56	10 59	11 06	11 11	11 14	11 21	11 26	11 29	11 36	11 41	11 44	11 51
Forest Hill [4]	d	10 09	10 13	10 17	10 24	10 28	10 32	10 39	10 43	10 47	10 54	10 58	11 02	11 09	11 13	11 17	11 24	11 28	11 32	11 39	11 43	11 47	11 54
Honor Oak Park	d	10 11	10 15	10 19	10 26	10 31	10 34	10 41	10 45	10 49	10 56	11 01	11 04	11 11	11 16	11 19	11 26	11 31	11 34	11 41	11 46	11 49	11 56
Brockley	d	10 14	10 18	10 22	10 29	10 33	10 37	10 44	10 48	10 52	10 59	11 03	11 07	11 14	11 18	11 22	11 29	11 33	11 37	11 44	11 48	11 52	11 59
New Cross Gate	d	10 16	10 20	10 24	10 31	10 36	10 39	10 46	10 50	10 54	11 01	11 06	11 09	11 16	11 21	11 24	11 31	11 36	11 39	11 46	11 51	11 54	12 01
Surrey Quays	d	10 20		10 27	10 35		10 42	10 50		10 57	11 05		11 12	11 20		11 27	11 35		11 42	11 50		11 57	12 05
Canada Water	d	10 22		10 29	10 37		10 44	10 52		10 59	11 07		11 14	11 22		11 29	11 37		11 44	11 52		11 59	12 07
Rotherhithe	d	10 23		10 31	10 38		10 46	10 53		11 01	11 08		11 16	11 23		11 31	11 38		11 46	11 53		12 01	12 08
Wapping	d	10 25		10 32	10 40		10 47	10 55		11 02	11 10		11 17	11 25		11 32	11 40		11 47	11 55		12 02	12 10
Shadwell	d	10 27		10 34	10 42		10 49	10 57		11 04	11 12		11 19	11 27		11 34	11 42		11 49	11 57		12 04	12 12
Whitechapel	d	10 29		10 37	10 44		10 52	10 59		11 07	11 14		11 22	11 29		11 37	11 44		11 52	11 59		12 07	12 14
Shoreditch High Street	d	10 32		10 39	10 47		10 54	11 02		11 09	11 17		11 24	11 32		11 39	11 47		11 54	12 02		12 09	12 17
Hoxton	d	10 34		10 41	10 49		10 56	11 04		11 11	11 19		11 26	11 34		11 41	11 49		11 56	12 04		12 11	12 19
Haggerston	d	10 36		10 43	10 51		10 58	11 06		11 13	11 21		11 28	11 36		11 43	11 51		11 58	12 06		12 13	12 21
Dalston Junction	a	10 38		10 45	10 53		11 00	11 08		11 15	11 23		11 30	11 38		11 45	11 53		12 00	12 08		12 15	12 23
Canonbury	a	10 41		10 48	10 56		11 03	11 11		11 18	11 26		11 33	11 41		11 48	11 56		12 03	12 11		12 18	12 26
Highbury & Islington	a	10 45		10 55	11 00		11 09	11 15		11 23	11 30		11 38	11 45		11 55	12 00		12 08	12 15		12 25	12 30
London Bridge [4] ⊖	a		10 31			10 47			11 01			11 17			11 31			11 47			12 01		

A From London Victoria
B From Coulsdon Town

For full service between Highbury & Islington and Surrey Quays, refer to Table T178

For Sutton connections at West Croydon, refer to Table T172

Croydon and Norwood Junction-Anerley, Penge West, Crystal Palace, Sydenham, Forest Hill, Honor Oak Park, Brockley, New Cross Gate-London Bridge

		SN A	LO	LO	SN B	LO	LO	SN A	LO	LO		SN B	LO	LO	SN A	LO	LO	SN B	LO	LO		SN A	LO	LO	SN B
Purley	d				11 48							12 18						12 48							13 18
East Croydon	d				11 57							12 27						12 57							13 27
Norwood Junction 2	a				12 02							12 32						13 02							13 32
West Croydon 4	d		11 46			12 01			12 16				12 31			12 46			13 01				13 16		
Norwood Junction	a		11 52			12 06			12 21				12 36			12 52			13 06				13 21		
Norwood Junction	d		11 52		12 03	12 07			12 22			12 33	12 37			12 52		13 03	13 07				13 22		13 33
Anerley	d		11 55		12 06	12 10			12 25			12 36	12 40			12 55		13 06	13 10				13 25		13 36
Penge West	d		11 56		12 08	12 11			12 26			12 38	12 41			12 56		13 08	13 11				13 26		13 38
Crystal Palace 4	d	11 52		12 02			12 17	12 22		12 32				12 47	12 52		13 02			13 17		13 22		13 32	
Sydenham	d	11 56	11 59	12 06	12 11	12 14	12 21	12 26	12 29	12 36		12 41	12 44	12 51	12 56	12 59	13 06	13 11	13 14	13 21		13 26	13 29	13 36	13 41
Forest Hill 4	d	11 58	12 02	12 09	12 13	12 17	12 24	12 28	12 32	12 39		12 43	12 47	12 54	12 58	13 02	13 09	13 13	13 17	13 24		13 28	13 32	13 39	13 43
Honor Oak Park	d	12 01	12 04	12 11	12 16	12 19	12 26	12 31	12 34	12 41		12 46	12 49	12 56	13 01	13 04	13 11	13 16	13 19	13 26		13 31	13 34	13 41	13 46
Brockley	d	12 03	12 07	12 14	12 18	12 22	12 29	12 33	12 37	12 44		12 48	12 52	12 59	13 03	13 07	13 14	13 18	13 22	13 29		13 33	13 37	13 44	13 48
New Cross Gate	d	12 06	12 09	12 16	12 21	12 24	12 31	12 36	12 39	12 46		12 51	12 54	13 01	13 06	13 09	13 16	13 21	13 24	13 31		13 36	13 39	13 46	13 51
Surrey Quays	d		12 12	12 20		12 27	12 35		12 42	12 50			12 57	13 05		13 12	13 20		13 27	13 35			13 42	13 50	
Canada Water	d		12 14	12 22		12 29	12 37		12 44	12 52			12 59	13 07		13 14	13 22		13 29	13 37			13 44	13 52	
Rotherhithe	d		12 16	12 23		12 31	12 38		12 46	12 53			13 01	13 08		13 16	13 23		13 31	13 38			13 46	13 53	
Wapping	d		12 17	12 25		12 32	12 40		12 47	12 55			13 02	13 10		13 17	13 25		13 32	13 40			13 47	13 55	
Shadwell	d		12 19	12 27		12 34	12 42		12 49	12 57			13 04	13 12		13 19	13 27		13 34	13 42			13 49	13 57	
Whitechapel	d		12 22	12 29		12 37	12 44		12 52	12 59			13 07	13 14		13 22	13 29		13 37	13 44			13 52	13 59	
Shoreditch High Street	d		12 24	12 32		12 39	12 47		12 54	13 02			13 09	13 17		13 24	13 32		13 39	13 47			13 54	14 02	
Hoxton	d		12 26	12 34		12 41	12 49		12 56	13 04			13 11	13 19		13 26	13 34		13 41	13 49			13 56	14 04	
Haggerston	d		12 28	12 36		12 43	12 51		12 58	13 06			13 13	13 21		13 28	13 36		13 43	13 51			13 58	14 06	
Dalston Junction	a		12 30	12 38		12 45	12 53		13 00	13 08			13 15	13 23		13 30	13 38		13 45	13 53			14 00	14 08	
Canonbury	a		12 33	12 41		12 48	12 56		13 03	13 11			13 18	13 26		13 33	13 41		13 48	13 56			14 03	14 11	
Highbury & Islington	a		12 38	12 45		12 53	13 00		13 08	13 15			13 23	13 30		13 38	13 45		13 53	14 00			14 08	14 15	
London Bridge 4 ⊖	a	12 17			12 31			12 47				13 01			13 17			13 31				13 47			14 01

		LO	LO	SN A	LO	LO		SN B	LO	LO	SN A	LO	LO	SN B	LO	LO		SN A	LO	LO	SN B	LO	LO	SN A	LO
Purley	d							13 48						14 18							14 48				
East Croydon	d							13 57						14 27							14 57				
Norwood Junction 2	a							14 02						14 32							15 02				
West Croydon 4	d	13 31			13 46				14 01			14 16			14 31				14 46			15 01			15 16
Norwood Junction	a	13 36			13 52				14 06			14 21			14 36				14 52			15 06			15 21
Norwood Junction	d	13 37			13 52			14 03	14 07			14 22		14 33	14 37				14 52		15 03	15 07			15 22
Anerley	d	13 40			13 55			14 06	14 10			14 25		14 36	14 40				14 55		15 06	15 10			15 25
Penge West	d	13 41			13 56			14 08	14 11			14 26		14 38	14 41				14 56		15 08	15 11			15 26
Crystal Palace 4	d		13 47	13 52		14 02				14 17	14 22		14 32			14 47		14 52		15 02			15 17	15 22	
Sydenham	d	13 44	13 51	13 56	13 59	14 06		14 11	14 14	14 21	14 26	14 29	14 36	14 41	14 44	14 51		14 56	14 59	15 06	15 11	15 14	15 21	15 26	15 29
Forest Hill 4	d	13 47	13 54	13 58	14 02	14 09		14 13	14 17	14 24	14 28	14 32	14 39	14 43	14 47	14 54		14 58	15 02	15 09	15 13	15 17	15 24	15 28	15 32
Honor Oak Park	d	13 49	13 56	14 01	14 04	14 11		14 16	14 19	14 26	14 31	14 34	14 41	14 46	14 49	14 56		15 01	15 04	15 11	15 16	15 19	15 26	15 31	15 34
Brockley	d	13 52	13 59	14 03	14 07	14 14		14 18	14 22	14 29	14 33	14 37	14 44	14 48	14 52	14 59		15 03	15 07	15 14	15 18	15 22	15 29	15 33	15 37
New Cross Gate	d	13 54	14 01	14 06	14 09	14 16		14 21	14 24	14 31	14 36	14 39	14 46	14 51	14 54	15 01		15 06	15 09	15 16	15 21	15 24	15 31	15 36	15 39
Surrey Quays	d	13 57	14 05		14 12	14 20			14 27	14 35		14 42	14 50		14 57	15 05			15 12	15 20		15 27	15 35		15 42
Canada Water	d	13 59	14 07		14 14	14 22			14 29	14 37		14 44	14 52		14 59	15 07			15 14	15 22		15 29	15 37		15 44
Rotherhithe	d	14 01	14 08		14 16	14 23			14 31	14 38		14 46	14 53		15 01	15 08			15 16	15 23		15 31	15 38		15 46
Wapping	d	14 02	14 10		14 17	14 25			14 32	14 40		14 47	14 55		15 02	15 10			15 17	15 25		15 32	15 40		15 47
Shadwell	d	14 04	14 12		14 19	14 27			14 34	14 42		14 49	14 57		15 04	15 12			15 19	15 27		15 34	15 42		15 49
Whitechapel	d	14 07	14 14		14 22	14 29			14 37	14 44		14 52	14 59		15 07	15 14			15 22	15 29		15 37	15 44		15 52
Shoreditch High Street	d	14 09	14 17		14 24	14 32			14 39	14 47		14 54	15 02		15 09	15 17			15 24	15 32		15 39	15 47		15 54
Hoxton	d	14 11	14 19		14 26	14 34			14 41	14 49		14 56	15 04		15 11	15 19			15 26	15 34		15 41	15 49		15 56
Haggerston	d	14 13	14 21		14 28	14 36			14 43	14 51		14 58	15 06		15 13	15 21			15 28	15 36		15 43	15 51		15 58
Dalston Junction	a	14 15	14 23		14 30	14 38			14 45	14 53		15 00	15 08		15 15	15 23			15 30	15 38		15 45	15 53		16 00
Canonbury	a	14 18	14 26		14 33	14 41			14 48	14 56		15 03	15 11		15 18	15 26			15 33	15 41		15 48	15 56		16 03
Highbury & Islington	a	14 23	14 30		14 38	14 45			14 53	15 00		15 08	15 15		15 23	15 30			15 38	15 45		15 53	16 00		16 08
London Bridge 4 ⊖	a			14 17				14 31			14 47			15 01				15 17			15 31			15 47	

A From London Victoria   B From Coulsdon Town

For full service between Highbury & Islington and Surrey Quays, refer to Table T178

For Sutton connections at West Croydon, refer to Table T172

Croydon and Norwood Junction-Anerley, Penge West, Crystal Palace, Sydenham, Forest Hill, Honor Oak Park, Brockley, New Cross Gate-London Bridge

		LO	SN A	LO	LO	SN B	LO	LO		SN A	LO	LO	SN B	LO	LO	SN A	LO	LO		SN B	LO	LO	SN A	LO	LO
Purley	d		15 18							15 50						16 20							16 50		
East Croydon	d		15 27							15 57						16 27							16 57		
Norwood Junction 2	a		15 32							16 03						16 33							17 03		
West Croydon 4	d			15 31			15 46				16 01			16 16			16 31				16 46			17 01	
Norwood Junction	a			15 36			15 52				16 06			16 21			16 36				16 51			17 06	
Norwood Junction	d		15 33	15 37			15 52			16 04	16 07			16 22		16 34	16 37				16 52		17 04	17 07	
Anerley	d		15 36	15 40			15 55			16 07	16 10			16 25		16 37	16 40				16 55		17 07	17 10	
Penge West	d		15 38	15 41			15 56			16 08	16 11			16 26		16 38	16 41				16 56		17 08	17 11	
Crystal Palace 4	d	15 32			15 47	15 52		16 02				16 17	16 22		16 32			16 47		16 52		17 02			17 17
Sydenham	d	15 36	15 41	15 44	15 51	15 56	15 59	16 06		16 11	16 14	16 21	16 26	16 29	16 36	16 41	16 44	16 51		16 56	16 59	17 06	17 11	17 14	17 21
Forest Hill 4	d	15 39	15 43	15 47	15 54	15 58	16 02	16 09		16 14	16 17	16 24	16 28	16 32	16 39	16 44	16 47	16 54		16 58	17 02	17 09	17 14	17 17	17 24
Honor Oak Park	d	15 41	15 46	15 49	15 56	16 01	16 04	16 11		16 16	16 19	16 26	16 31	16 34	16 41	16 46	16 49	16 56		17 01	17 04	17 11	17 16	17 19	17 26
Brockley	d	15 44	15 48	15 52	15 59	16 03	16 07	16 14		16 19	16 22	16 29	16 33	16 37	16 44	16 49	16 52	16 59		17 03	17 07	17 14	17 19	17 22	17 29
New Cross Gate	d	15 46	15 51	15 54	16 01	16 06	16 09	16 16		16 22	16 24	16 31	16 36	16 39	16 46	16 52	16 54	17 01		17 06	17 09	17 16	17 22	17 24	17 31
Surrey Quays	d	15 50		15 57	16 05		16 12	16 20			16 27	16 35		16 42	16 50		16 57	17 05			17 12	17 20		17 27	17 35
Canada Water	d	15 52		15 59	16 07		16 14	16 22			16 29	16 37		16 44	16 52		16 59	17 07			17 14	17 22		17 29	17 37
Rotherhithe	d	15 53		16 01	16 08		16 16	16 23			16 31	16 38		16 46	16 53		17 01	17 08			17 16	17 23		17 31	17 38
Wapping	d	15 55		16 02	16 10		16 17	16 25			16 32	16 40		16 47	16 55		17 02	17 10			17 17	17 25		17 32	17 40
Shadwell	d	15 57		16 04	16 12		16 19	16 27			16 34	16 42		16 49	16 57		17 04	17 12			17 19	17 27		17 34	17 42
Whitechapel	d	15 59		16 07	16 14		16 22	16 29			16 37	16 44		16 52	16 59		17 07	17 14			17 22	17 29		17 37	17 44
Shoreditch High Street	d	16 02		16 09	16 17		16 24	16 32			16 39	16 47		16 54	17 02		17 09	17 17			17 24	17 32		17 39	17 47
Hoxton	d	16 04		16 11	16 19		16 26	16 34			16 41	16 49		16 56	17 04		17 11	17 19			17 26	17 34		17 41	17 49
Haggerston	d	16 06		16 13	16 21		16 28	16 36			16 43	16 51		16 58	17 06		17 13	17 21			17 28	17 36		17 43	17 51
Dalston Junction	a	16 08		16 15	16 23		16 30	16 38			16 46	16 53		17 00	17 08		17 16	17 23			17 30	17 38		17 46	17 53
Canonbury	a	16 11		16 18	16 26		16 33	16 41			16 48	16 56		17 03	17 11		17 18	17 26			17 33	17 41		17 48	17 56
Highbury & Islington	a	16 15		16 23	16 30		16 40	16 45			16 55	17 00		17 10	17 15		17 25	17 30			17 40	17 45		17 55	18 00
London Bridge 4 ⊖	a		16 01			16 18				16 31			16 48			17 01				17 18			17 31		

		SN B	LO	LO		SN	LO	LO	SN B	LO	LO	SN	LO	LO		SN B	LO	LO	SN	LO	LO	SN B	LO	LO	
Purley	d																								
East Croydon	d																								
Norwood Junction 2	a																								
West Croydon 4	d		17 16				17 31			17 46			18 01				18 16			18 31			18 46		
Norwood Junction	a		17 21				17 36			17 51			18 06				18 21			18 36			18 51		
Norwood Junction	d		17 22			17 34	17 37			17 52		18 04	18 07				18 22		18 34	18 37			18 52		
Anerley	d		17 25			17 37	17 40			17 55		18 07	18 10				18 25		18 37	18 40			18 55		
Penge West	d		17 26			17 38	17 41			17 56		18 08	18 11				18 26		18 38	18 41			18 56		
Crystal Palace 4	d	17 22		17 32				17 47	17 52		18 02			18 17		18 22		18 32			18 47	18 52		19 02	
Sydenham	d	17 26	17 29	17 36		17 41	17 44	17 51	17 56	17 59	18 06	18 11	18 14	18 21		18 26	18 29	18 36	18 41	18 44	18 51	18 56	18 59	19 06	
Forest Hill 4	d	17 28	17 32	17 39		17 43	17 47	17 54	17 58	18 02	18 09	18 13	18 17	18 24		18 28	18 32	18 39	18 43	18 47	18 54	18 58	19 02	19 09	
Honor Oak Park	d	17 31	17 34	17 41		17 46	17 49	17 56	18 01	18 04	18 11	18 16	18 19	18 26		18 31	18 34	18 41	18 46	18 49	18 56	19 01	19 04	19 11	
Brockley	d	17 33	17 37	17 44		17 48	17 52	17 59	18 03	18 07	18 14	18 18	18 22	18 29		18 33	18 37	18 44	18 48	18 52	18 59	19 03	19 07	19 14	
New Cross Gate	d	17 36	17 39	17 46		17 51	17 54	18 01	18 06	18 09	18 16	18 21	18 24	18 31		18 36	18 39	18 46	18 51	18 54	19 01	19 06	19 09	19 16	
Surrey Quays	d		17 42	17 50			17 57	18 05		18 12	18 20		18 27	18 35			18 42	18 50		18 57	19 05		19 12	19 20	
Canada Water	d		17 44	17 52			17 59	18 07		18 14	18 22		18 29	18 37			18 44	18 52		18 59	19 07		19 14	19 22	
Rotherhithe	d		17 46	17 53			18 01	18 08		18 16	18 23		18 31	18 38			18 46	18 53		19 01	19 08		19 16	19 23	
Wapping	d		17 47	17 55			18 02	18 10		18 17	18 25		18 32	18 40			18 47	18 55		19 02	19 10		19 17	19 25	
Shadwell	d		17 49	17 57			18 04	18 12		18 19	18 27		18 34	18 42			18 49	18 57		19 04	19 12		19 19	19 27	
Whitechapel	d		17 52	17 59			18 07	18 14		18 22	18 29		18 37	18 44			18 52	18 59		19 07	19 14		19 22	19 29	
Shoreditch High Street	d		17 54	18 02			18 09	18 17		18 24	18 32		18 39	18 47			18 54	19 02		19 09	19 17		19 24	19 32	
Hoxton	d		17 56	18 04			18 11	18 19		18 26	18 34		18 41	18 49			18 56	19 04		19 11	19 19		19 26	19 34	
Haggerston	d		17 58	18 06			18 13	18 21		18 28	18 36		18 43	18 51			18 58	19 06		19 13	19 21		19 28	19 36	
Dalston Junction	a		18 00	18 08			18 15	18 23		18 30	18 38		18 45	18 53			19 00	19 08		19 15	19 23		19 30	19 38	
Canonbury	a		18 03	18 11			18 18	18 26		18 33	18 41		18 48	18 56			19 03	19 11		19 18	19 26		19 33	19 41	
Highbury & Islington	a		18 08	18 15			18 25	18 30		18 40	18 45		18 55	19 00			19 10	19 15		19 25	19 30		19 40	19 45	
London Bridge 4 ⊖	a	17 48				18 01			18 18			18 31				18 48			19 01			19 18			

A From Coulsdon Town   B From London Victoria

For full service between Highbury & Islington and Surrey Quays, refer to Table T178

For Sutton connections at West Croydon, refer to Table T172

Table T177-R

Mondays to Fridays

16 December to 15 May

Croydon and Norwood Junction-Anerley, Penge West, Crystal Palace, Sydenham, Forest Hill, Honor Oak Park, Brockley, New Cross Gate-London Bridge

		SN	LO	LO	SN A	LO		LO	SN	LO	LO	SN A	LO	LO	SN B	LO		LO	SN A	LO	LO	SN B	LO	LO	SN A
Purley	d														19 48							20 19			
East Croydon	d														19 57							20 28			
Norwood Junction 2	a														20 02							20 32			
West Croydon 4	d		19 01			19 16				19 31			19 46			20 01				20 16			20 31		
Norwood Junction	a		19 06			19 21				19 36			19 51			20 06				20 21			20 36		
Norwood Junction	d	19 04	19 07			19 22			19 34	19 37			19 52		20 03	20 07				20 22		20 33	20 37		
Anerley	d	19 07	19 10			19 25			19 37	19 40			19 55		20 06	20 10				20 25		20 36	20 40		
Penge West	d	19 08	19 11			19 26			19 38	19 41			19 56		20 08	20 11				20 26		20 38	20 41		
Crystal Palace 4	d			19 17	19 22			19 32			19 47	19 52		20 02				20 17	20 22		20 32			20 47	20 52
Sydenham	d	19 11	19 14	19 21	19 26	19 29		19 36	19 41	19 44	19 51	19 56	19 59	20 06	20 11	20 14		20 21	20 26	20 29	20 36	20 41	20 44	20 51	20 56
Forest Hill 4	d	19 13	19 17	19 24	19 28	19 32		19 39	19 43	19 47	19 54	19 58	20 02	20 09	20 13	20 17		20 24	20 28	20 32	20 39	20 43	20 47	20 54	20 58
Honor Oak Park	d	19 16	19 19	19 26	19 31	19 34		19 41	19 46	19 49	19 56	20 01	20 04	20 11	20 16	20 19		20 26	20 31	20 34	20 41	20 46	20 49	20 56	21 01
Brockley	d	19 18	19 22	19 29	19 33	19 37		19 44	19 48	19 52	19 59	20 03	20 07	20 14	20 18	20 22		20 29	20 33	20 37	20 44	20 48	20 52	20 59	21 03
New Cross Gate	d	19 21	19 24	19 31	19 36	19 39		19 46	19 51	19 54	20 01	20 06	20 09	20 16	20 21	20 24		20 31	20 36	20 39	20 46	20 51	20 54	21 01	21 06
Surrey Quays	d		19 27	19 35		19 42		19 50		19 57	20 05		20 12	20 20		20 27		20 35		20 42	20 50		20 57	21 05	
Canada Water	d		19 29	19 37		19 44		19 52		19 59	20 07		20 14	20 22		20 29		20 37		20 44	20 52		20 59	21 07	
Rotherhithe	d		19 31	19 38		19 46		19 53		20 01	20 08		20 16	20 23		20 31		20 38		20 46	20 53		21 01	21 08	
Wapping	d		19 32	19 40		19 47		19 55		20 02	20 10		20 17	20 25		20 32		20 40		20 47	20 55		21 02	21 10	
Shadwell	d		19 34	19 42		19 49		19 57		20 04	20 12		20 19	20 27		20 34		20 42		20 49	20 57		21 04	21 12	
Whitechapel	d		19 37	19 44		19 52		19 59		20 07	20 14		20 22	20 29		20 37		20 44		20 52	20 59		21 07	21 14	
Shoreditch High Street	d		19 39	19 47		19 54		20 02		20 09	20 17		20 24	20 32		20 39		20 47		20 54	21 02		21 09	21 17	
Hoxton	d		19 41	19 49		19 56		20 04		20 11	20 19		20 26	20 34		20 41		20 49		20 56	21 04		21 11	21 19	
Haggerston	d		19 43	19 51		19 58		20 06		20 13	20 21		20 28	20 36		20 43		20 51		20 58	21 06		21 13	21 21	
Dalston Junction	a		19 45	19 53		20 00		20 08		20 15	20 23		20 30	20 38		20 45		20 53		21 00	21 08		21 15	21 23	
Canonbury	a		19 48	19 56		20 03		20 11		20 18	20 26		20 33	20 41		20 48		20 56		21 03	21 11		21 18	21 26	
Highbury & Islington	a		19 55	20 00		20 10		20 15		20 25	20 30		20 40	20 45		20 53		21 00		21 08	21 15		21 23	21 30	
London Bridge 4 ⊖	a	19 31			19 48				20 01			20 20			20 31				20 48			21 01			21 17

		LO		LO	SN B	LO	LO	SN A	LO	LO	SN B	LO		LO	SN A	LO	LO	SN B	LO	LO	SN A	LO		LO	SN B
Purley	d				20 48						21 18							21 48							22 18
East Croydon	d				20 57						21 27							21 57							22 27
Norwood Junction 2	a				21 02						21 32							22 02							22 32
West Croydon 4	d	20 46				21 01			21 16			21 31				21 46			22 01			22 16			
Norwood Junction	a	20 52				21 06			21 21			21 36				21 51			22 06			22 21			
Norwood Junction	d	20 52			21 03	21 07			21 22		21 33	21 37				21 52		22 03	22 07			22 22			22 33
Anerley	d	20 55			21 06	21 10			21 25		21 36	21 40				21 55		22 06	22 10			22 25			22 36
Penge West	d	20 57			21 08	21 11			21 26		21 38	21 41				21 56		22 08	22 11			22 26			22 38
Crystal Palace 4	d			21 02			21 17	21 22		21 32				21 47	21 52		22 02			22 17	22 22			22 32	
Sydenham	d	20 59		21 06	21 11	21 14	21 21	21 26	21 29	21 36	21 41	21 44		21 51	21 56	21 59	22 06	22 11	22 14	22 21	22 26	22 29		22 36	22 41
Forest Hill 4	d	21 02		21 09	21 13	21 17	21 24	21 28	21 32	21 39	21 43	21 47		21 54	21 58	22 02	22 09	22 13	22 17	22 24	22 28	22 32		22 39	22 43
Honor Oak Park	d	21 04		21 11	21 16	21 19	21 26	21 31	21 34	21 41	21 46	21 49		21 56	22 01	22 04	22 11	22 16	22 19	22 26	22 31	22 34		22 41	22 46
Brockley	d	21 07		21 14	21 18	21 22	21 29	21 33	21 37	21 44	21 48	21 52		21 59	22 03	22 07	22 14	22 18	22 22	22 29	22 33	22 37		22 44	22 48
New Cross Gate	d	21 09		21 16	21 21	21 24	21 31	21 36	21 39	21 46	21 51	21 54		22 01	22 06	22 09	22 16	22 21	22 24	22 31	22 36	22 39		22 46	22 51
Surrey Quays	d	21 12		21 20		21 27	21 35		21 42	21 50		21 57		22 05		22 12	22 20		22 27	22 35		22 42		22 50	
Canada Water	d	21 14		21 22		21 29	21 37		21 44	21 52		21 59		22 07		22 14	22 22		22 29	22 37		22 44		22 52	
Rotherhithe	d	21 16		21 23		21 31	21 38		21 46	21 53		22 01		22 08		22 16	22 23		22 31	22 38		22 46		22 53	
Wapping	d	21 17		21 25		21 32	21 40		21 47	21 55		22 02		22 10		22 17	22 25		22 32	22 40		22 47		22 55	
Shadwell	d	21 19		21 27		21 34	21 42		21 49	21 57		22 04		22 12		22 19	22 27		22 34	22 42		22 49		22 57	
Whitechapel	d	21 22		21 29		21 37	21 44		21 52	21 59		22 07		22 14		22 22	22 29		22 37	22 44		22 52		22 59	
Shoreditch High Street	d	21 24		21 32		21 39	21 47		21 54	22 02		22 09		22 17		22 24	22 32		22 39	22 47		22 54		23 02	
Hoxton	d	21 26		21 34		21 41	21 49		21 56	22 04		22 11		22 19		22 26	22 34		22 41	22 49		22 56		23 04	
Haggerston	d	21 28		21 36		21 43	21 51		21 58	22 06		22 13		22 21		22 28	22 36		22 43	22 51		22 58		23 06	
Dalston Junction	a	21 30		21 38		21 45	21 53		22 00	22 08		22 15		22 23		22 30	22 38		22 45	22 53		23 00		23 08	
Canonbury	a	21 33		21 41		21 48	21 56		22 03	22 11		22 18		22 26		22 33	22 41		22 48	22 56		23 03		23 11	
Highbury & Islington	a	21 38		21 45		21 53	22 00		22 08	22 15		22 23		22 30		22 38	22 45		22 55	23 00		23 10		23 15	
London Bridge 4 ⊖	a				21 31			21 47			22 01				22 17			22 31			22 47				23 01

A From London Victoria B From Coulsdon Town

For full service between Highbury & Islington and Surrey Quays, refer to Table T178

For Sutton connections at West Croydon, refer to Table T172

Table T177-R

Mondays to Fridays

16 December to 15 May

Croydon and Norwood Junction-Anerley, Penge West, Crystal Palace, Sydenham, Forest Hill, Honor Oak Park, Brockley, New Cross Gate-London Bridge

		LO	LO		SN A	LO	LO	SN B	LO	LO	SN A	LO	LO		LO	LO	SN A
Purley	d							22 48									
East Croydon	d							22 57									
Norwood Junction 2	a							23 02									
West Croydon 4	d	22 31				22 46			23 01			23 16			23 31		
Norwood Junction	a	22 36				22 51			23 06			23 21			23 36		
Norwood Junction	d	22 37				22 52		23 03	23 07			23 22			23 37		
Anerley	d	22 40				22 55		23 06	23 10			23 25			23 40		
Penge West	d	22 41				22 56		23 08	23 11			23 26			23 41		
Crystal Palace 4	d		22 47		22 52		23 02			23 17	23 22		23 32			23 50	23 53
Sydenham	d	22 44	22 51		22 56	22 59	23 06	23 11	23 14	23 21	23 26	23 29	23 36		23 44	23 54	23 58
Forest Hill 4	d	22 47	22 54		22 58	23 02	23 09	23 13	23 17	23 24	23 28	23 32	23 39		23 47	23 56	00 01
Honor Oak Park	d	22 49	22 56		23 01	23 04	23 11	23 16	23 19	23 26	23 31	23 34	23 41		23 49	23 59	00 04
Brockley	d	22 52	22 59		23 03	23 07	23 14	23 18	23 22	23 29	23 33	23 37	23 44		23 52	00 01	00 06
New Cross Gate	d	22 54	23 01		23 06	23 09	23 16	23 21	23 24	23 31	23 36	23 39	23 46		23 54	00 03	00 09
Surrey Quays	d	22 57	23 05			23 12	23 20		23 27	23 35		23 42	23 50		23 57	00 09	
Canada Water	d	22 59	23 07			23 14	23 22		23 29	23 37		23 44	23 52		23 59	00 11	
Rotherhithe	d	23 01	23 08			23 16	23 23		23 31	23 38		23 46	23 53		00 01	00 12	
Wapping	d	23 02	23 10			23 17	23 25		23 32	23 40		23 47	23 55		00 02	00 14	
Shadwell	d	23 04	23 12			23 19	23 27		23 34	23 42		23 49	23 57		00 04	00 16	
Whitechapel	d	23 07	23 14			23 22	23 29		23 37	23 44		23 52	23 59		00 07	00 18	
Shoreditch High Street	d	23 09	23 17			23 24	23 32		23 39	23 47		23 54	00 02		00 09	00 21	
Hoxton	d	23 11	23 19			23 26	23 34		23 41	23 49		23 56	00 04		00 11	00 23	
Haggerston	d	23 13	23 21			23 28	23 36		23 43	23 51		23 58	00 06		00 13	00 25	
Dalston Junction	a	23 15	23 23			23 32	23 38		23 45	23 53		00 01	00 08		00 15	00 27	
Canonbury	a	23 18	23 26				23 41		23 50	23 56		00 03	00 11		00 18	00 30	
Highbury & Islington	a	23 25	23 30				23 45		23 55	23 59		00 10	00 15		00 25	00 32	
London Bridge 4 ⊖	a				23 17			23 31			23 47						00 16

Saturdays

21 December to 16 May

		LO C	LO D	LO C	SN A	LO	SN A	LO	LO	LO		SN E	LO	LO	LO	LO	SN E	LO	LO	SN		LO	LO	SN A	LO
Purley	d																								
East Croydon	d																								
Norwood Junction 2	a																								
West Croydon 4	d								05 31				05 46		06 01			06 16				06 31			06 46
Norwood Junction	a								05 36				05 51		06 06			06 21				06 36			06 51
Norwood Junction	d								05 37				05 52		06 07			06 22		06 33		06 37			06 52
Anerley	d								05 40				05 55		06 10			06 25		06 36		06 40			06 55
Penge West	d								05 41				05 56		06 11			06 26		06 38		06 41			06 56
Crystal Palace 4	d					00 04	00 28	05 32		05 47		05 52		06 02		06 17	06 22		06 32				06 47	06 52	
Sydenham	d					00 08	00 32	05 36	05 44	05 51		05 56	05 59	06 06	06 14	06 21	06 26	06 29	06 36	06 41		06 44	06 51	06 56	06 59
Forest Hill 4	d				00 01	00 11	00 35	05 39	05 47	05 54		05 58	06 02	06 09	06 17	06 24	06 28	06 32	06 39	06 43		06 47	06 54	06 58	07 02
Honor Oak Park	d				00 04	00 13	00 37	05 41	05 49	05 56		06 01	06 04	06 11	06 19	06 26	06 31	06 34	06 41	06 46		06 49	06 56	07 01	07 04
Brockley	d			00 01	00 06	00 16	00 40	05 44	05 52	05 59		06 03	06 07	06 14	06 22	06 29	06 33	06 37	06 44	06 48		06 52	06 59	07 03	07 07
New Cross Gate	d			00 03	00 09	00 18	00 42	05 46	05 54	06 01		06 06	06 09	06 16	06 24	06 31	06 36	06 39	06 46	06 51		06 54	07 01	07 06	07 09
Surrey Quays	d			00 09		00 22		05 50	05 57	06 05			06 12	06 20	06 27	06 35		06 42	06 50			06 57	07 05		07 12
Canada Water	d			00 11		00 24		05 52	05 59	06 07			06 14	06 22	06 29	06 37		06 44	06 52			06 59	07 07		07 14
Rotherhithe	d		00 01	00 12		00 25		05 53	06 01	06 08			06 16	06 23	06 31	06 38		06 46	06 53			07 01	07 08		07 16
Wapping	d		00 02	00 14		00 27		05 55	06 02	06 10			06 17	06 25	06 32	06 40		06 47	06 55			07 02	07 10		07 17
Shadwell	d		00 04	00 16		00 29		05 57	06 04	06 12			06 19	06 27	06 34	06 42		06 49	06 57			07 04	07 12		07 19
Whitechapel	d		00 07	00 18		00 31		05 59	06 07	06 14			06 22	06 29	06 37	06 44		06 52	06 59			07 07	07 14		07 22
Shoreditch High Street	d	00 02	00 09	00 21		00 34		06 02	06 09	06 17			06 24	06 32	06 39	06 47		06 54	07 02			07 09	07 17		07 24
Hoxton	d	00 04	00 11	00 23		00 36		06 04	06 11	06 19			06 26	06 34	06 41	06 49		06 56	07 04			07 11	07 19		07 26
Haggerston	d	00 06	00 13	00 25		00 38		06 06	06 13	06 21			06 28	06 36	06 43	06 51		06 58	07 06			07 13	07 21		07 28
Dalston Junction	a	00 08	00 15	00 27		00 40		06 08	06 15	06 23			06 30	06 38	06 45	06 53		07 00	07 08			07 15	07 23		07 30
Canonbury	a	00 11	00 18	00 30		00 43		06 11	06 18	06 26			06 33	06 41	06 48	06 56		07 03	07 11			07 18	07 26		07 33
Highbury & Islington	a	00 15	00 25	00 32		00 47		06 15	06 23	06 30			06 38	06 45	06 53	07 00		07 10	07 15			07 25	07 30		07 40
London Bridge 4 ⊖	a				00 16		00 50					06 18					06 44			07 01				07 14	

A From London Victoria
B From Coulsdon Town
C From Crystal Palace
D From West Croydon
E From Streatham Hill

For full service between Highbury & Islington and Surrey Quays, refer to Table T178

For Sutton connections at West Croydon, refer to Table T172

Table T177-R

Saturdays
21 December to 16 May

Croydon and Norwood Junction-Anerley, Penge West, Crystal Palace, Sydenham, Forest Hill, Honor Oak Park, Brockley, New Cross Gate-London Bridge

		LO		SN	LO	LO	SN A	LO	LO	SN B	LO	LO		SN A	LO	LO	SN B	LO	LO	SN A	LO	LO		SN B	LO
Purley	d									07 18							07 48							08 18	
East Croydon	d									07 27							07 57							08 27	
Norwood Junction	a									07 32							08 02							08 32	
West Croydon	d				07 01			07 16			07 31				07 46			08 01			08 16				08 31
Norwood Junction	a				07 06			07 21			07 36				07 52			08 06			08 21				08 36
Norwood Junction	d			07 03	07 07			07 22		07 33	07 37				07 52		08 03	08 07			08 22			08 33	08 37
Anerley	d			07 06	07 10			07 25		07 36	07 40				07 55		08 06	08 10			08 25			08 36	08 40
Penge West	d			07 08	07 11			07 26		07 38	07 41				07 57		08 08	08 11			08 26			08 38	08 41
Crystal Palace	d	07 02				07 17	07 22		07 32			07 47		07 52		08 02			08 17	08 22		08 32			
Sydenham	d	07 06		07 11	07 14	07 21	07 26	07 29	07 36	07 41	07 44	07 51		07 56	07 59	08 06	08 11	08 14	08 21	08 26	08 29	08 36		08 41	08 44
Forest Hill	d	07 09		07 13	07 17	07 24	07 28	07 32	07 39	07 43	07 47	07 54		07 58	08 02	08 09	08 13	08 17	08 24	08 28	08 32	08 39		08 43	08 47
Honor Oak Park	d	07 11		07 16	07 19	07 26	07 31	07 34	07 41	07 46	07 49	07 56		08 01	08 04	08 11	08 16	08 19	08 26	08 31	08 34	08 41		08 46	08 49
Brockley	d	07 14		07 18	07 22	07 29	07 33	07 37	07 44	07 48	07 52	07 59		08 03	08 07	08 14	08 18	08 22	08 29	08 33	08 37	08 44		08 48	08 52
New Cross Gate	d	07 16		07 21	07 24	07 31	07 36	07 39	07 46	07 51	07 54	08 01		08 06	08 09	08 16	08 21	08 24	08 31	08 36	08 39	08 46		08 51	08 54
Surrey Quays	d	07 20			07 27	07 35		07 42	07 50		07 57	08 05			08 12	08 20		08 27	08 35		08 42	08 50			08 57
Canada Water	d	07 22			07 29	07 37		07 44	07 52		07 59	08 07			08 14	08 22		08 29	08 37		08 44	08 52			08 59
Rotherhithe	d	07 23			07 31	07 38		07 46	07 53		08 01	08 08			08 16	08 23		08 31	08 38		08 46	08 53			09 01
Wapping	d	07 25			07 32	07 40		07 47	07 55		08 02	08 10			08 17	08 25		08 32	08 40		08 47	08 55			09 02
Shadwell	d	07 27			07 34	07 42		07 49	07 57		08 04	08 12			08 19	08 27		08 34	08 42		08 49	08 57			09 04
Whitechapel	d	07 29			07 37	07 44		07 52	07 59		08 07	08 14			08 22	08 29		08 37	08 44		08 52	08 59			09 07
Shoreditch High Street	d	07 32			07 39	07 47		07 54	08 02		08 09	08 17			08 24	08 32		08 39	08 47		08 54	09 02			09 09
Hoxton	d	07 34			07 41	07 49		07 56	08 04		08 11	08 19			08 26	08 34		08 41	08 49		08 56	09 04			09 11
Haggerston	d	07 36			07 43	07 51		07 58	08 06		08 13	08 21			08 28	08 36		08 43	08 51		08 58	09 06			09 13
Dalston Junction	a	07 38			07 45	07 53		08 00	08 08		08 15	08 23			08 30	08 38		08 45	08 53		09 00	09 08			09 15
Canonbury	a	07 41			07 48	07 56		08 03	08 11		08 18	08 26			08 33	08 41		08 48	08 56		09 03	09 11			09 18
Highbury & Islington	a	07 45			07 55	08 00		08 10	08 15		08 25	08 30			08 40	08 47		08 55	09 02		09 10	09 17			09 25
London Bridge ⊖	a			07 31			07 44			08 01				08 14			08 31			08 44				09 01	

		LO	SN A	LO	LO	SN B	LO	LO		SN A	LO	LO	SN B	LO	LO	SN A	LO	LO		SN B	LO	LO	SN A	LO	LO
Purley	d					08 48							09 18							09 48					
East Croydon	d					08 57							09 27							09 57					
Norwood Junction	a					09 02							09 32							10 02					
West Croydon	d			08 46			09 01				09 16			09 31			09 46				10 01			10 16	
Norwood Junction	a			08 52			09 06				09 21			09 36			09 52				10 06			10 21	
Norwood Junction	d			08 52		09 03	09 07				09 22		09 33	09 37			09 52			10 03	10 07			10 22	
Anerley	d			08 55		09 06	09 10				09 25		09 36	09 40			09 55			10 06	10 10			10 25	
Penge West	d			08 57		09 08	09 11				09 26		09 38	09 41			09 57			10 08	10 11			10 26	
Crystal Palace	d	08 47	08 52		09 02			09 17		09 22		09 32			09 47	09 52		10 02				10 17	10 22		10 32
Sydenham	d	08 51	08 56	08 59	09 06	09 11	09 14	09 21		09 26	09 29	09 36	09 41	09 44	09 51	09 56	09 59	10 06		10 11	10 14	10 21	10 26	10 29	10 36
Forest Hill	d	08 54	08 58	09 02	09 09	09 13	09 17	09 24		09 28	09 32	09 39	09 43	09 47	09 54	09 58	10 02	10 09		10 13	10 17	10 24	10 28	10 32	10 39
Honor Oak Park	d	08 56	09 01	09 04	09 11	09 16	09 19	09 26		09 31	09 34	09 41	09 46	09 49	09 56	10 01	10 04	10 11		10 16	10 19	10 26	10 31	10 34	10 41
Brockley	d	08 59	09 03	09 07	09 14	09 18	09 22	09 29		09 33	09 37	09 44	09 48	09 52	09 59	10 03	10 07	10 14		10 18	10 22	10 29	10 33	10 37	10 44
New Cross Gate	d	09 01	09 06	09 09	09 16	09 21	09 24	09 31		09 36	09 39	09 46	09 51	09 54	10 01	10 06	10 09	10 16		10 21	10 24	10 31	10 36	10 39	10 46
Surrey Quays	d	09 05		09 12	09 20		09 27	09 35			09 42	09 50		09 57	10 05		10 12	10 20			10 27	10 35		10 42	10 50
Canada Water	d	09 07		09 14	09 22		09 29	09 37			09 44	09 52		09 59	10 07		10 14	10 22			10 29	10 37		10 44	10 52
Rotherhithe	d	09 08		09 16	09 23		09 31	09 38			09 46	09 53		10 01	10 08		10 16	10 23			10 31	10 38		10 46	10 53
Wapping	d	09 10		09 17	09 25		09 32	09 40			09 47	09 55		10 02	10 10		10 17	10 25			10 32	10 40		10 47	10 55
Shadwell	d	09 12		09 19	09 27		09 34	09 42			09 49	09 57		10 04	10 12		10 19	10 27			10 34	10 42		10 49	10 57
Whitechapel	d	09 14		09 22	09 29		09 37	09 44			09 52	09 59		10 07	10 14		10 22	10 29			10 37	10 44		10 52	10 59
Shoreditch High Street	d	09 17		09 24	09 32		09 39	09 47			09 54	10 02		10 09	10 17		10 24	10 32			10 39	10 47		10 54	11 02
Hoxton	d	09 19		09 26	09 34		09 41	09 49			09 56	10 04		10 11	10 19		10 26	10 34			10 41	10 49		10 56	11 04
Haggerston	d	09 21		09 28	09 36		09 43	09 51			09 58	10 06		10 13	10 21		10 28	10 36			10 43	10 51		10 58	11 06
Dalston Junction	a	09 23		09 30	09 38		09 45	09 53			10 00	10 08		10 15	10 23		10 30	10 38			10 45	10 53		11 00	11 08
Canonbury	a	09 26		09 33	09 41		09 48	09 56			10 03	10 11		10 18	10 26		10 33	10 41			10 48	10 56		11 03	11 11
Highbury & Islington	a	09 30		09 40	09 45		09 55	10 00			10 10	10 15		10 25	10 30		10 40	10 45			10 55	11 00		11 08	11 15
London Bridge ⊖	a		09 14			09 31				09 44			10 01			10 14				10 31			10 44		

A From London Victoria   B From Coulsdon Town

For full service between Highbury & Islington and Surrey Quays, refer to Table T178

For Sutton connections at West Croydon, refer to Table T172

Table T177-R

Saturdays
21 December to 16 May

Croydon and Norwood Junction-Anerley, Penge West, Crystal Palace, Sydenham, Forest Hill, Honor Oak Park, Brockley, New Cross Gate-London Bridge

		SN A	LO	LO	SN B	LO	LO	SN A	LO	LO		SN B	LO	LO	SN A	LO	LO	SN B	LO	LO		SN A	LO	LO	SN B
Purley	d	10 18						10 48							11 18							11 48			
East Croydon	d	10 27						10 57							11 27							11 57			
Norwood Junction	a	10 32						11 02							11 32							12 02			
West Croydon	d		10 31			10 46			11 01				11 16			11 31			11 46				12 01		
Norwood Junction	a		10 36			10 52			11 06				11 21			11 36			11 52				12 06		
Norwood Junction	d	10 33	10 37			10 52		11 03	11 07				11 22		11 33	11 37			11 52			12 03	12 07		
Anerley	d	10 36	10 40			10 55		11 06	11 10				11 25		11 36	11 40			11 55			12 06	12 10		
Penge West	d	10 38	10 41			10 57		11 08	11 11				11 26		11 38	11 41			11 57			12 08	12 11		
Crystal Palace	d			10 47	10 52		11 02			11 17		11 22		11 32			11 47	11 52		12 02				12 17	12 22
Sydenham	d	10 41	10 44	10 51	10 56	10 59	11 06	11 11	11 14	11 21		11 26	11 29	11 36	11 41	11 44	11 51	11 56	11 59	12 06		12 11	12 14	12 21	12 26
Forest Hill	d	10 43	10 47	10 54	10 58	11 02	11 09	11 13	11 17	11 24		11 28	11 32	11 39	11 43	11 47	11 54	11 58	12 02	12 09		12 13	12 17	12 24	12 28
Honor Oak Park	d	10 46	10 49	10 56	11 01	11 04	11 11	11 16	11 19	11 26		11 31	11 34	11 41	11 46	11 49	11 56	12 01	12 04	12 11		12 16	12 19	12 26	12 31
Brockley	d	10 48	10 52	10 59	11 03	11 07	11 14	11 18	11 22	11 29		11 33	11 37	11 44	11 48	11 52	11 59	12 03	12 07	12 14		12 18	12 22	12 29	12 33
New Cross Gate	d	10 51	10 54	11 01	11 06	11 09	11 16	11 21	11 24	11 31		11 36	11 39	11 46	11 51	11 54	12 01	12 06	12 09	12 16		12 21	12 24	12 31	12 36
Surrey Quays	d		10 57	11 05		11 12	11 20		11 27	11 35			11 42	11 50		11 57	12 05		12 12	12 20			12 27	12 35	
Canada Water	d		10 59	11 07		11 14	11 22		11 29	11 37			11 44	11 52		11 59	12 07		12 14	12 22			12 29	12 37	
Rotherhithe	d		11 01	11 08		11 16	11 23		11 31	11 38			11 46	11 53		12 01	12 08		12 16	12 23			12 31	12 38	
Wapping	d		11 02	11 10		11 17	11 25		11 32	11 40			11 47	11 55		12 02	12 10		12 17	12 25			12 32	12 40	
Shadwell	d		11 04	11 12		11 19	11 27		11 34	11 42			11 49	11 57		12 04	12 12		12 19	12 27			12 34	12 42	
Whitechapel	d		11 07	11 14		11 22	11 29		11 37	11 44			11 52	11 59		12 07	12 14		12 22	12 29			12 37	12 44	
Shoreditch High Street	d		11 09	11 17		11 24	11 32		11 39	11 47			11 54	12 02		12 09	12 17		12 24	12 32			12 39	12 47	
Hoxton	d		11 11	11 19		11 26	11 34		11 41	11 49			11 56	12 04		12 11	12 19		12 26	12 34			12 41	12 49	
Haggerston	d		11 13	11 21		11 28	11 36		11 43	11 51			11 58	12 06		12 13	12 21		12 28	12 36			12 43	12 51	
Dalston Junction	a		11 15	11 23		11 30	11 38		11 45	11 53			12 00	12 08		12 15	12 23		12 30	12 38			12 45	12 53	
Canonbury	a		11 18	11 26		11 33	11 41		11 48	11 56			12 03	12 11		12 18	12 26		12 33	12 41			12 48	12 56	
Highbury & Islington	a		11 23	11 30		11 38	11 45		11 53	12 00			12 08	12 15		12 23	12 30		12 38	12 45			12 53	13 00	
London Bridge ⊖	a	11 01			11 14			11 31				11 44			12 01			12 14				12 31			12 44

		LO	LO	SN A	LO	LO		SN B	LO	LO	SN A	LO	LO	SN B	LO	LO		SN A	LO	LO	SN B	LO	LO	SN A	LO
Purley	d			12 18							12 48							13 18						13 48	
East Croydon	d			12 27							12 57							13 27						13 57	
Norwood Junction	a			12 32							13 02							13 32						14 02	
West Croydon	d	12 16			12 31				12 46			13 01			13 16				13 31			13 46			14 01
Norwood Junction	a	12 21			12 36				12 52			13 06			13 21				13 36			13 52			14 06
Norwood Junction	d	12 22		12 33	12 37				12 52		13 03	13 07			13 22			13 33	13 37			13 52		14 03	14 07
Anerley	d	12 25		12 36	12 40				12 55		13 06	13 10			13 25			13 36	13 40			13 55		14 06	14 10
Penge West	d	12 26		12 38	12 41				12 57		13 08	13 11			13 26			13 38	13 41			13 57		14 08	14 11
Crystal Palace	d		12 32			12 47		12 52		13 02			13 17	13 22		13 32				13 47	13 52		14 02		
Sydenham	d	12 29	12 36	12 41	12 44	12 51		12 56	12 59	13 06	13 11	13 14	13 21	13 26	13 29	13 36		13 41	13 44	13 51	13 56	13 59	14 06	14 11	14 14
Forest Hill	d	12 32	12 39	12 43	12 47	12 54		12 58	13 02	13 09	13 13	13 17	13 24	13 28	13 32	13 39		13 43	13 47	13 54	13 58	14 02	14 09	14 13	14 17
Honor Oak Park	d	12 34	12 41	12 46	12 49	12 56		13 01	13 04	13 11	13 16	13 19	13 26	13 31	13 34	13 41		13 46	13 49	13 56	14 01	14 04	14 11	14 16	14 19
Brockley	d	12 37	12 44	12 48	12 52	12 59		13 03	13 07	13 14	13 18	13 22	13 29	13 33	13 37	13 44		13 48	13 52	13 59	14 03	14 07	14 14	14 18	14 22
New Cross Gate	d	12 39	12 46	12 51	12 54	13 01		13 06	13 09	13 16	13 21	13 24	13 31	13 36	13 39	13 46		13 51	13 54	14 01	14 06	14 09	14 16	14 21	14 24
Surrey Quays	d	12 42	12 50		12 57	13 05			13 12	13 20		13 27	13 35		13 42	13 50			13 57	14 05		14 12	14 20		14 27
Canada Water	d	12 44	12 52		12 59	13 07			13 14	13 22		13 29	13 37		13 44	13 52			13 59	14 07		14 14	14 22		14 29
Rotherhithe	d	12 46	12 53		13 01	13 08			13 16	13 23		13 31	13 38		13 46	13 53			14 01	14 08		14 16	14 23		14 31
Wapping	d	12 47	12 55		13 02	13 10			13 17	13 25		13 32	13 40		13 47	13 55			14 02	14 10		14 17	14 25		14 32
Shadwell	d	12 49	12 57		13 04	13 12			13 19	13 27		13 34	13 42		13 49	13 57			14 04	14 12		14 19	14 27		14 34
Whitechapel	d	12 52	12 59		13 07	13 14			13 22	13 29		13 37	13 44		13 52	13 59			14 07	14 14		14 22	14 29		14 37
Shoreditch High Street	d	12 54	13 02		13 09	13 17			13 24	13 32		13 39	13 47		13 54	14 02			14 09	14 17		14 24	14 32		14 39
Hoxton	d	12 56	13 04		13 11	13 19			13 26	13 34		13 41	13 49		13 56	14 04			14 11	14 19		14 26	14 34		14 41
Haggerston	d	12 58	13 06		13 13	13 21			13 28	13 36		13 43	13 51		13 58	14 06			14 13	14 21		14 28	14 36		14 43
Dalston Junction	a	13 00	13 08		13 15	13 23			13 30	13 38		13 45	13 53		14 00	14 08			14 15	14 23		14 30	14 38		14 45
Canonbury	a	13 03	13 11		13 18	13 26			13 33	13 41		13 48	13 56		14 03	14 11			14 18	14 26		14 33	14 41		14 48
Highbury & Islington	a	13 08	13 15		13 23	13 30			13 38	13 45		13 53	14 00		14 08	14 15			14 23	14 30		14 38	14 45		14 53
London Bridge ⊖	a			13 01				13 14			13 31			13 44				14 01			14 14			14 31	

A From Coulsdon Town   B From London Victoria

For full service between Highbury & Islington and Surrey Quays, refer to Table T178

For Sutton connections at West Croydon, refer to Table T172

Table T177-R

Saturdays

21 December to 16 May

Croydon and Norwood Junction-Anerley, Penge West, Crystal Palace, Sydenham, Forest Hill, Honor Oak Park, Brockley, New Cross Gate-London Bridge

Station		LO	SN A	LO	LO	SN B	LO	LO		SN A	LO	LO	SN B	LO	LO	SN A	LO	LO		SN B	LO	LO	SN A	LO	LO
Purley	d					14 18							14 48							15 18					
East Croydon	d					14 27							14 57							15 27					
Norwood Junction 2	a					14 32							15 02							15 32					
West Croydon 4	d			14 16			14 31				14 46			15 01			15 16				15 31			15 46	
Norwood Junction	a			14 21			14 36				14 52			15 06			15 21				15 36			15 52	
Norwood Junction	d			14 22		14 33	14 37				14 52		15 03	15 07			15 22			15 33	15 37			15 52	
Anerley	d			14 25		14 36	14 40				14 55		15 06	15 10			15 25			15 36	15 40			15 55	
Penge West	d			14 26		14 38	14 41				14 57		15 08	15 11			15 26			15 38	15 41			15 57	
Crystal Palace 4	d	14 17	14 22		14 32			14 47		14 52		15 02			15 17	15 22		15 32				15 47	15 52		16 02
Sydenham	d	14 21	14 26	14 29	14 36	14 41	14 44	14 51		14 56	14 59	15 06	15 11	15 14	15 21	15 26	15 29	15 36		15 41	15 44	15 51	15 56	15 59	16 06
Forest Hill 4	d	14 24	14 28	14 32	14 39	14 43	14 47	14 54		14 58	15 02	15 09	15 13	15 17	15 24	15 28	15 32	15 39		15 43	15 47	15 54	15 58	16 02	16 09
Honor Oak Park	d	14 26	14 31	14 34	14 41	14 46	14 49	14 56		15 01	15 04	15 11	15 16	15 19	15 26	15 31	15 34	15 41		15 46	15 49	15 56	16 01	16 04	16 11
Brockley	d	14 29	14 33	14 37	14 44	14 48	14 52	14 59		15 03	15 07	15 14	15 18	15 22	15 29	15 33	15 37	15 44		15 48	15 52	15 59	16 03	16 07	16 14
New Cross Gate	d	14 31	14 36	14 39	14 46	14 51	14 54	15 01		15 06	15 09	15 16	15 21	15 24	15 31	15 36	15 39	15 46		15 51	15 54	16 01	16 06	16 09	16 16
Surrey Quays	d	14 35		14 42	14 50		14 57	15 05			15 12	15 20		15 27	15 35		15 42	15 50			15 57	16 05		16 12	16 20
Canada Water	d	14 37		14 44	14 52		14 59	15 07			15 14	15 22		15 29	15 37		15 44	15 52			15 59	16 07		16 14	16 22
Rotherhithe	d	14 38		14 46	14 53		15 01	15 08			15 16	15 23		15 31	15 38		15 46	15 53			16 01	16 08		16 16	16 23
Wapping	d	14 40		14 47	14 55		15 02	15 10			15 17	15 25		15 32	15 40		15 47	15 55			16 02	16 10		16 17	16 25
Shadwell	d	14 42		14 49	14 57		15 04	15 12			15 19	15 27		15 34	15 42		15 49	15 57			16 04	16 12		16 19	16 27
Whitechapel	d	14 44		14 52	14 59		15 07	15 14			15 22	15 29		15 37	15 44		15 52	15 59			16 07	16 14		16 22	16 29
Shoreditch High Street	d	14 47		14 54	15 02		15 09	15 17			15 24	15 32		15 39	15 47		15 54	16 02			16 09	16 17		16 24	16 32
Hoxton	d	14 49		14 56	15 04		15 11	15 19			15 26	15 34		15 41	15 49		15 56	16 04			16 11	16 19		16 26	16 34
Haggerston	d	14 51		14 58	15 06		15 13	15 21			15 28	15 36		15 43	15 51		15 58	16 06			16 13	16 21		16 28	16 36
Dalston Junction	a	14 53		15 00	15 08		15 15	15 23			15 30	15 38		15 45	15 53		16 00	16 08			16 15	16 23		16 30	16 38
Canonbury	a	14 56		15 03	15 11		15 18	15 26			15 33	15 41		15 48	15 56		16 03	16 11			16 18	16 26		16 33	16 41
Highbury & Islington	a	15 00		15 08	15 15		15 23	15 30			15 38	15 45		15 53	16 00		16 10	16 15			16 25	16 30		16 40	16 45
London Bridge 4 ⊖	a		14 44			15 01				15 14			15 31			15 44				16 01			16 14		

Station		SN B	LO	LO		SN A	LO	LO	SN B	LO	LO	SN A	LO	LO		SN B	LO	LO	SN A	LO	LO	SN B	LO	LO	
Purley	d	15 48							16 18							16 48						17 18			
East Croydon	d	15 57							16 27							16 57						17 27			
Norwood Junction 2	a	16 02							16 32							17 02						17 32			
West Croydon 4	d		16 01				16 16			16 31			16 46				17 01			17 16			17 31		
Norwood Junction	a		16 06				16 21			16 36			16 52				17 06			17 21			17 36		
Norwood Junction	d	16 03	16 07				16 22		16 33	16 37			16 52			17 03	17 07			17 22		17 33	17 37		
Anerley	d	16 06	16 10				16 25		16 36	16 40			16 55			17 06	17 10			17 25		17 36	17 40		
Penge West	d	16 08	16 11				16 26		16 38	16 41			16 57			17 08	17 11			17 26		17 38	17 41		
Crystal Palace 4	d			16 17		16 22		16 32			16 47	16 52		17 02				17 17	17 22		17 32			17 47	
Sydenham	d	16 11	16 14	16 21		16 26	16 29	16 36	16 41	16 44	16 51	16 56	16 59	17 06		17 11	17 14	17 21	17 26	17 29	17 36	17 41	17 44	17 51	
Forest Hill 4	d	16 13	16 17	16 24		16 28	16 32	16 39	16 43	16 47	16 54	16 58	17 02	17 09		17 13	17 17	17 24	17 28	17 32	17 39	17 43	17 47	17 54	
Honor Oak Park	d	16 16	16 19	16 26		16 31	16 34	16 41	16 46	16 49	16 56	17 01	17 04	17 11		17 16	17 19	17 26	17 31	17 34	17 41	17 46	17 49	17 56	
Brockley	d	16 18	16 22	16 29		16 33	16 37	16 44	16 48	16 52	16 59	17 03	17 07	17 14		17 18	17 22	17 29	17 33	17 37	17 44	17 48	17 52	17 59	
New Cross Gate	d	16 21	16 24	16 31		16 36	16 39	16 46	16 51	16 54	17 01	17 06	17 09	17 16		17 21	17 24	17 31	17 36	17 39	17 46	17 51	17 54	18 01	
Surrey Quays	d		16 27	16 35			16 42	16 50		16 57	17 05		17 12	17 20			17 27	17 35		17 42	17 50		17 57	18 05	
Canada Water	d		16 29	16 37			16 44	16 52		16 59	17 07		17 14	17 22			17 29	17 37		17 44	17 52		17 59	18 07	
Rotherhithe	d		16 31	16 38			16 46	16 53		17 01	17 08		17 16	17 23			17 31	17 38		17 46	17 53		18 01	18 08	
Wapping	d		16 32	16 40			16 47	16 55		17 02	17 10		17 17	17 25			17 32	17 40		17 47	17 55		18 02	18 10	
Shadwell	d		16 34	16 42			16 49	16 57		17 04	17 12		17 19	17 27			17 34	17 42		17 49	17 57		18 04	18 12	
Whitechapel	d		16 37	16 44			16 52	16 59		17 07	17 14		17 22	17 29			17 37	17 44		17 52	17 59		18 07	18 14	
Shoreditch High Street	d		16 39	16 47			16 54	17 02		17 09	17 17		17 24	17 32			17 39	17 47		17 54	18 02		18 09	18 17	
Hoxton	d		16 41	16 49			16 56	17 04		17 11	17 19		17 26	17 34			17 41	17 49		17 56	18 04		18 11	18 19	
Haggerston	d		16 43	16 51			16 58	17 06		17 13	17 21		17 28	17 36			17 43	17 51		17 58	18 06		18 13	18 21	
Dalston Junction	a		16 45	16 53			17 00	17 08		17 15	17 23		17 30	17 38			17 45	17 53		18 00	18 08		18 15	18 23	
Canonbury	a		16 48	16 56			17 03	17 11		17 18	17 26		17 33	17 41			17 48	17 56		18 03	18 11		18 18	18 26	
Highbury & Islington	a		16 55	17 00			17 10	17 15		17 25	17 30		17 40	17 45			17 55	18 00		18 10	18 15		18 25	18 30	
London Bridge 4 ⊖	a	16 31				16 44			17 01			17 14				17 31			17 44			18 01			

A From London Victoria

B From Coulsdon Town

For full service between Highbury & Islington and Surrey Quays, refer to Table T178

For Sutton connections at West Croydon, refer to Table T172

NRT DECEMBER 19 EDITION

Table T177-R

Saturdays

21 December to 16 May

Croydon and Norwood Junction-Anerley, Penge West, Crystal Palace, Sydenham, Forest Hill, Honor Oak Park, Brockley, New Cross Gate-London Bridge

Station		SN A	LO	LO	SN B	LO		LO	SN A	LO	LO	SN B	LO	LO	SN A	LO		LO	SN B	LO	LO	SN A	LO	LO	SN B
Purley	d				17 48							18 18							18 48						19 18
East Croydon	d				17 57							18 27							18 57						19 27
Norwood Junction 2	a				18 02							18 32							19 02						19 32
West Croydon 4	d		17 46			18 01				18 16			18 31			18 46				19 01			19 16		
Norwood Junction	a		17 52			18 06				18 21			18 36			18 52				19 06			19 21		
Norwood Junction	d		17 52		18 03	18 07				18 22		18 33	18 37			18 52			19 03	19 07			19 22		19 33
Anerley	d		17 55		18 06	18 10				18 25		18 36	18 40			18 55			19 06	19 10			19 25		19 36
Penge West	d		17 57		18 08	18 11				18 26		18 38	18 41			18 57			19 08	19 11			19 26		19 38
Crystal Palace 4	d	17 52		18 02				18 17	18 22		18 32			18 47	18 52			19 02			19 17	19 22		19 32	
Sydenham	d	17 56	17 59	18 06	18 11	18 14		18 21	18 26	18 29	18 36	18 41	18 44	18 51	18 56	18 59		19 06	19 11	19 14	19 21	19 26	19 29	19 36	19 41
Forest Hill 4	d	17 58	18 02	18 09	18 13	18 17		18 24	18 28	18 32	18 39	18 43	18 47	18 54	18 58	19 02		19 09	19 13	19 17	19 24	19 28	19 32	19 39	19 43
Honor Oak Park	d	18 01	18 04	18 11	18 16	18 19		18 26	18 31	18 34	18 41	18 46	18 49	18 56	19 01	19 04		19 11	19 16	19 19	19 26	19 31	19 34	19 41	19 46
Brockley	d	18 03	18 07	18 14	18 18	18 22		18 29	18 33	18 37	18 44	18 48	18 52	18 59	19 03	19 07		19 14	19 18	19 22	19 29	19 33	19 37	19 44	19 48
New Cross Gate	d	18 06	18 09	18 16	18 21	18 24		18 31	18 36	18 39	18 46	18 51	18 54	19 01	19 06	19 09		19 16	19 21	19 24	19 31	19 36	19 39	19 46	19 51
Surrey Quays	d		18 12	18 20		18 27		18 35		18 42	18 50		18 57	19 05		19 12		19 20		19 27	19 35		19 42	19 50	
Canada Water	d		18 14	18 22		18 29		18 37		18 44	18 52		18 59	19 07		19 14		19 22		19 29	19 37		19 44	19 52	
Rotherhithe	d		18 16	18 23		18 31		18 38		18 46	18 53		19 01	19 08		19 16		19 23		19 31	19 38		19 46	19 53	
Wapping	d		18 17	18 25		18 32		18 40		18 47	18 55		19 02	19 10		19 17		19 25		19 32	19 40		19 47	19 55	
Shadwell	d		18 19	18 27		18 34		18 42		18 49	18 57		19 04	19 12		19 19		19 27		19 34	19 42		19 49	19 57	
Whitechapel	d		18 22	18 29		18 37		18 44		18 52	18 59		19 07	19 14		19 22		19 29		19 37	19 44		19 52	19 59	
Shoreditch High Street	d		18 24	18 32		18 39		18 47		18 54	19 02		19 09	19 17		19 24		19 32		19 39	19 47		19 54	20 02	
Hoxton	d		18 26	18 34		18 41		18 49		18 56	19 04		19 11	19 19		19 26		19 34		19 41	19 49		19 56	20 04	
Haggerston	d		18 28	18 36		18 43		18 51		18 58	19 06		19 13	19 21		19 28		19 36		19 43	19 51		19 58	20 06	
Dalston Junction	a		18 30	18 38		18 45		18 53		19 00	19 08		19 15	19 23		19 30		19 38		19 45	19 53		20 00	20 08	
Canonbury	a		18 33	18 41		18 48		18 56		19 03	19 11		19 18	19 26		19 33		19 41		19 48	19 56		20 03	20 11	
Highbury & Islington	a		18 40	18 45		18 55		19 00		19 10	19 15		19 25	19 30		19 40		19 45		19 53	20 00		20 08	20 15	
London Bridge 4 ⊖	a	18 14			18 31				18 44			19 01			19 14				19 31			19 44			20 01

Station		LO		LO	SN A	LO	LO	SN B	LO	LO	SN A	LO		LO	SN B	LO	LO	SN A	LO	LO	SN B	LO		LO	SN A
Purley	d							19 48							20 18						20 48				
East Croydon	d							19 57							20 27						20 57				
Norwood Junction 2	a							20 02							20 32						21 02				
West Croydon 4	d	19 31				19 46			20 01			20 16				20 31			20 46			21 01			
Norwood Junction	a	19 36				19 52			20 06			20 21				20 36			20 52			21 06			
Norwood Junction	d	19 37				19 52		20 03	20 07			20 22			20 33	20 37			20 52		21 03	21 07			
Anerley	d	19 40				19 55		20 06	20 10			20 25			20 36	20 40			20 55		21 06	21 10			
Penge West	d	19 41				19 57		20 08	20 11			20 26			20 38	20 41			20 57		21 08	21 11			
Crystal Palace 4	d			19 47	19 52		20 02			20 17	20 22			20 32			20 47	20 52		21 02				21 17	21 22
Sydenham	d	19 44		19 51	19 56	19 59	20 06	20 11	20 14	20 21	20 26	20 29		20 36	20 41	20 44	20 51	20 56	20 59	21 06	21 11	21 14		21 21	21 26
Forest Hill 4	d	19 47		19 54	19 58	20 02	20 09	20 13	20 17	20 24	20 28	20 32		20 39	20 43	20 47	20 54	20 58	21 02	21 09	21 13	21 17		21 24	21 28
Honor Oak Park	d	19 49		19 56	20 01	20 04	20 11	20 16	20 19	20 26	20 31	20 34		20 41	20 46	20 49	20 56	21 01	21 04	21 11	21 16	21 19		21 26	21 31
Brockley	d	19 52		19 59	20 03	20 07	20 14	20 18	20 22	20 29	20 33	20 37		20 44	20 48	20 52	20 59	21 03	21 07	21 14	21 18	21 22		21 29	21 33
New Cross Gate	d	19 54		20 01	20 06	20 09	20 16	20 21	20 24	20 31	20 36	20 39		20 46	20 51	20 54	21 01	21 06	21 09	21 16	21 21	21 24		21 31	21 36
Surrey Quays	d	19 57		20 05		20 12	20 20		20 27	20 35		20 42		20 50		20 57	21 05		21 12	21 20		21 27		21 35	
Canada Water	d	19 59		20 07		20 14	20 22		20 29	20 37		20 44		20 52		20 59	21 07		21 14	21 22		21 29		21 37	
Rotherhithe	d	20 01		20 08		20 16	20 23		20 31	20 38		20 46		20 53		21 01	21 08		21 16	21 23		21 31		21 38	
Wapping	d	20 02		20 10		20 17	20 25		20 32	20 40		20 47		20 55		21 02	21 10		21 17	21 25		21 32		21 40	
Shadwell	d	20 04		20 12		20 19	20 27		20 34	20 42		20 49		20 57		21 04	21 12		21 19	21 27		21 34		21 42	
Whitechapel	d	20 07		20 14		20 22	20 29		20 37	20 44		20 52		20 59		21 07	21 14		21 22	21 29		21 37		21 44	
Shoreditch High Street	d	20 09		20 17		20 24	20 32		20 39	20 47		20 54		21 02		21 09	21 17		21 24	21 32		21 39		21 47	
Hoxton	d	20 11		20 19		20 26	20 34		20 41	20 49		20 56		21 04		21 11	21 19		21 26	21 34		21 41		21 49	
Haggerston	d	20 13		20 21		20 28	20 36		20 43	20 51		20 58		21 06		21 13	21 21		21 28	21 36		21 43		21 51	
Dalston Junction	a	20 15		20 23		20 30	20 38		20 45	20 53		21 00		21 08		21 15	21 23		21 30	21 38		21 45		21 53	
Canonbury	a	20 18		20 26		20 33	20 41		20 48	20 56		21 03		21 11		21 18	21 26		21 33	21 41		21 48		21 56	
Highbury & Islington	a	20 23		20 30		20 38	20 45		20 53	21 00		21 08		21 15		21 23	21 30		21 38	21 45		21 53		22 00	
London Bridge 4 ⊖	a				20 14			20 31			20 44				21 01			21 14			21 31				21 44

A From London Victoria

B From Coulsdon Town

For full service between Highbury & Islington and Surrey Quays, refer to Table T178

For Sutton connections at West Croydon, refer to Table T172

Table T177-R

Saturdays

21 December to 16 May

Croydon and Norwood Junction-Anerley, Penge West, Crystal Palace, Sydenham, Forest Hill, Honor Oak Park, Brockley, New Cross Gate-London Bridge

		LO	LO	SN A	LO	LO	SN B	LO	LO	SN A	LO	LO
Purley	d			21 18						21 48		
East Croydon	d			21 27						21 57		
Norwood Junction	a			21 32						22 02		
West Croydon	d	21 16			21 31			21 46			22 01	
Norwood Junction	a	21 21			21 36			21 52			22 06	
Norwood Junction	d	21 22		21 33	21 37			21 52		22 03	22 07	
Anerley	d	21 25		21 36	21 40			21 55		22 06	22 10	
Penge West	d	21 26		21 38	21 41			21 57		22 08	22 11	
Crystal Palace	d		21 32			21 47	21 52		22 02			22 17
Sydenham	d	21 29	21 36	21 41	21 44	21 51	21 56	21 59	22 06	22 11	22 14	22 21
Forest Hill	d	21 32	21 39	21 43	21 47	21 54	21 58	22 02	22 09	22 13	22 17	22 24
Honor Oak Park	d	21 34	21 41	21 46	21 49	21 56	22 01	22 04	22 11	22 16	22 19	22 26
Brockley	d	21 37	21 44	21 48	21 52	21 59	22 03	22 07	22 14	22 18	22 22	22 29
New Cross Gate	d	21 39	21 46	21 51	21 54	22 01	22 06	22 09	22 16	22 21	22 24	22 31
Surrey Quays	d	21 42	21 50		21 57	22 05		22 12	22 20		22 27	22 35
Canada Water	d	21 44	21 52		21 59	22 07		22 14	22 22		22 29	22 37
Rotherhithe	d	21 46	21 53		22 01	22 08		22 16	22 23		22 31	22 38
Wapping	d	21 47	21 55		22 02	22 10		22 17	22 25		22 32	22 40
Shadwell	d	21 49	21 57		22 04	22 12		22 19	22 27		22 34	22 42
Whitechapel	d	21 52	21 59		22 07	22 14		22 22	22 29		22 37	22 44
Shoreditch High Street	d	21 54	22 02		22 09	22 17		22 24	22 32		22 39	22 47
Hoxton	d	21 56	22 04		22 11	22 19		22 26	22 34		22 41	22 49
Haggerston	d	21 58	22 06		22 13	22 21		22 28	22 36		22 43	22 51
Dalston Junction	a	22 00	22 08		22 15	22 23		22 30	22 38		22 45	22 53
Canonbury	a	22 03	22 11		22 18	22 26		22 33	22 41		22 48	22 56
Highbury & Islington	a	22 08	22 15		22 23	22 30		22 38	22 45		22 53	23 00
London Bridge	a			22 01			22 20			22 31		

		SN B	LO	LO	SN A	LO	LO	SN B	LO	LO	SN A
Purley	d				22 18						22 48
East Croydon	d				22 27						22 57
Norwood Junction	a				22 32						23 02
West Croydon	d		22 16			22 31			22 46		
Norwood Junction	a		22 21			22 36			22 51		
Norwood Junction	d		22 22		22 33	22 37			22 52		23 03
Anerley	d		22 25		22 36	22 40			22 55		23 06
Penge West	d		22 26		22 38	22 41			22 56		23 08
Crystal Palace	d	22 22		22 32			22 47	22 52		23 02	
Sydenham	d	22 26	22 29	22 36	22 41	22 44	22 51	22 56	22 59	23 06	23 11
Forest Hill	d	22 28	22 32	22 39	22 43	22 47	22 54	22 58	23 02	23 09	23 13
Honor Oak Park	d	22 31	22 34	22 41	22 46	22 49	22 56	23 01	23 04	23 11	23 16
Brockley	d	22 33	22 37	22 44	22 48	22 52	22 59	23 03	23 07	23 14	23 18
New Cross Gate	d	22 36	22 39	22 46	22 51	22 54	23 01	23 06	23 09	23 16	23 21
Surrey Quays	d		22 42	22 50		22 57	23 05		23 12	23 20	
Canada Water	d		22 44	22 52		22 59	23 07		23 14	23 22	
Rotherhithe	d		22 46	22 53		23 01	23 08		23 16	23 23	
Wapping	d		22 47	22 55		23 02	23 10		23 17	23 25	
Shadwell	d		22 49	22 57		23 04	23 12		23 19	23 27	
Whitechapel	d		22 52	22 59		23 07	23 14		23 22	23 29	
Shoreditch High Street	d		22 54	23 02		23 09	23 17		23 24	23 32	
Hoxton	d		22 56	23 04		23 11	23 19		23 26	23 34	
Haggerston	d		22 58	23 06		23 13	23 21		23 28	23 36	
Dalston Junction	a		23 00	23 08		23 15	23 23		23 34	23 38	
Canonbury	a		23 03	23 11		23 18	23 26			23 41	
Highbury & Islington	a		23 10	23 15		23 25	23 30			23 45	
London Bridge	a	22 45			23 01			23 15			23 31

		LO	LO	SN B	LO	LO	LO	LO	SN B
Purley	d								
East Croydon	d								
Norwood Junction	a								
West Croydon	d	23 01			23 16		23 31		
Norwood Junction	a	23 06			23 21		23 36		
Norwood Junction	d	23 07			23 22		23 37		
Anerley	d	23 10			23 25		23 40		
Penge West	d	23 11			23 26		23 41		
Crystal Palace	d		23 17	23 22		23 32		23 50	23 53
Sydenham	d	23 14	23 21	23 26	23 29	23 36	23 44	23 54	23 58
Forest Hill	d	23 17	23 24	23 28	23 32	23 39	23 47	23 56	00 01
Honor Oak Park	d	23 19	23 26	23 31	23 34	23 41	23 49	23 59	00 04
Brockley	d	23 22	23 29	23 33	23 37	23 44	23 52	00 01	00 06
New Cross Gate	d	23 24	23 31	23 36	23 39	23 46	23 54	00 03	00 09
Surrey Quays	d	23 27	23 35		23 42	23 50	23 57	00 09	
Canada Water	d	23 29	23 37		23 44	23 52	23 59	00 11	
Rotherhithe	d	23 31	23 38		23 46	23 53	00 01	00 12	
Wapping	d	23 32	23 40		23 47	23 55	00 02	00 14	
Shadwell	d	23 34	23 42		23 49	23 57	00 04	00 16	
Whitechapel	d	23 37	23 44		23 52	23 59	00 07	00 18	
Shoreditch High Street	d	23 39	23 47		23 54	00 02	00 09	00 21	
Hoxton	d	23 41	23 49		23 56	00 04	00 11	00 23	
Haggerston	d	23 43	23 51		23 58	00 06	00 13	00 25	
Dalston Junction	a	23 45	23 53		00 01	00 08	00 15	00 27	
Canonbury	a	23 50	23 56		00 03	00 11	00 18	00 30	
Highbury & Islington	a	23 58	23 59		00 10	00 15	00 25	00 32	
London Bridge	a			23 44					00 16

A From Coulsdon Town

B From London Victoria

For full service between Highbury & Islington and Surrey Quays, refer to Table T178

For Sutton connections at West Croydon, refer to Table T172

Table T177-R

Sundays

15 December to 10 May

Croydon and Norwood Junction-Anerley, Penge West, Crystal Palace, Sydenham, Forest Hill, Honor Oak Park, Brockley, New Cross Gate-London Bridge

		LO A	LO B	LO A	SN C	LO	SN C	LO	LO	LO	LO	LO
Purley	d											
East Croydon	d											
Norwood Junction	a											
West Croydon	d								06 43		07 12	
Norwood Junction	a								06 48		07 18	
Norwood Junction	d								06 48		07 18	
Anerley	d								06 51		07 21	
Penge West	d								06 53		07 23	
Crystal Palace	d					00 04	00 27	06 36		07 07		07 37
Sydenham	d					00 08	00 32	06 40	06 55	07 11	07 25	07 41
Forest Hill	d				00 01	00 11	00 34	06 42	06 58	07 13	07 28	07 43
Honor Oak Park	d				00 04	00 13	00 37	06 45	07 00	07 16	07 30	07 46
Brockley	d			00 01	00 06	00 16	00 39	06 47	07 03	07 18	07 33	07 48
New Cross Gate	d			00 03	00 09	00 18	00 42	06 49	07 05	07 20	07 35	07 50
Surrey Quays	d			00 09		00 22		06 53	07 08	07 24	07 38	07 54
Canada Water	d			00 11		00 24		06 55	07 10	07 26	07 40	07 56
Rotherhithe	d		00 01	00 12		00 25		06 56	07 12	07 27	07 42	07 57
Wapping	d		00 02	00 14		00 27		06 58	07 13	07 29	07 43	07 59
Shadwell	d		00 04	00 16		00 29		07 00	07 15	07 31	07 45	08 01
Whitechapel	d		00 07	00 18		00 31		07 02	07 18	07 33	07 48	08 03
Shoreditch High Street	d	00 02	00 09	00 21		00 34		07 04	07 20	07 35	07 50	08 05
Hoxton	d	00 04	00 11	00 23		00 36		07 06	07 22	07 37	07 52	08 07
Haggerston	d	00 06	00 13	00 25		00 38		07 08	07 24	07 39	07 54	08 09
Dalston Junction	a	00 08	00 15	00 27		00 40		07 10	07 26	07 41	07 56	08 11
Canonbury	a	00 11	00 18	00 30		00 43		07 13	07 29	07 44	07 59	08 14
Highbury & Islington	a	00 15	00 25	00 32		00 46		07 19	07 34	07 50	08 03	08 20
London Bridge	a				00 16		00 49					

		SN D	LO	SN	LO	SN D	LO	SN	LO	SN E	LO	SN
Purley	d	07 20				07 50				08 20		
East Croydon	d	07 29				07 59				08 29		
Norwood Junction	a	07 33				08 05				08 33		
West Croydon	d		07 47				08 12				08 42	
Norwood Junction	a		07 52				08 18				08 48	
Norwood Junction	d	07 35	07 52			08 06	08 18			08 35	08 48	
Anerley	d	07 39	07 55			08 09	08 21			08 39	08 51	
Penge West	d	07 41	07 57			08 11	08 23			08 41	08 53	
Crystal Palace	d			07 58	08 07			08 24	08 37			08 54
Sydenham	d	07 45	07 59	08 03	08 11	08 15	08 25	08 29	08 41	08 45	08 55	08 59
Forest Hill	d	07 48	08 02	08 05	08 13	08 18	08 28	08 31	08 43	08 48	08 58	09 01
Honor Oak Park	d	07 50	08 04	08 08	08 16	08 20	08 30	08 34	08 46	08 50	09 00	09 04
Brockley	d	07 53	08 07	08 10	08 18	08 23	08 33	08 36	08 48	08 53	09 03	09 06
New Cross Gate	d	07 55	08 09	08 13	08 20	08 25	08 35	08 39	08 50	08 55	09 05	09 09
Surrey Quays	d		08 12		08 24		08 38		08 54		09 08	
Canada Water	d		08 14		08 26		08 40		08 56		09 10	
Rotherhithe	d		08 16		08 27		08 42		08 57		09 12	
Wapping	d		08 17		08 29		08 43		08 59		09 13	
Shadwell	d		08 19		08 31		08 45		09 01		09 15	
Whitechapel	d		08 22		08 33		08 48		09 03		09 18	
Shoreditch High Street	d		08 24		08 35		08 50		09 05		09 20	
Hoxton	d		08 26		08 37		08 52		09 07		09 22	
Haggerston	d		08 28		08 39		08 54		09 09		09 24	
Dalston Junction	a		08 30		08 41		08 56		09 11		09 26	
Canonbury	a		08 33		08 44		08 59		09 14		09 29	
Highbury & Islington	a		08 38		08 50		09 03		09 20		09 33	
London Bridge	a	08 05		08 20		08 36		08 46		09 02		09 16

		LO	SN E	LO	SN	LO	SN E	LO	SN	LO	SN E	LO
Purley	d		08 50				09 20				09 50	
East Croydon	d		08 59				09 31				10 01	
Norwood Junction	a		09 03				09 35				10 05	
West Croydon	d			09 13				09 42				10 12
Norwood Junction	a			09 18				09 48				10 18
Norwood Junction	d		09 05	09 18			09 35	09 48			10 05	10 18
Anerley	d		09 09	09 21			09 39	09 51			10 09	10 21
Penge West	d		09 11	09 23			09 41	09 53			10 11	10 23
Crystal Palace	d	09 07			09 24	09 37			09 54	10 07		
Sydenham	d	09 11	09 15	09 25	09 29	09 41	09 45	09 55	09 59	10 11	10 15	10 25
Forest Hill	d	09 13	09 18	09 28	09 31	09 43	09 48	09 58	10 01	10 13	10 18	10 28
Honor Oak Park	d	09 16	09 20	09 30	09 34	09 46	09 50	10 00	10 04	10 16	10 20	10 30
Brockley	d	09 18	09 23	09 33	09 36	09 48	09 53	10 03	10 06	10 18	10 23	10 33
New Cross Gate	d	09 20	09 25	09 35	09 39	09 50	09 55	10 05	10 09	10 20	10 25	10 35
Surrey Quays	d	09 24		09 38		09 54		10 08		10 24		10 38
Canada Water	d	09 26		09 40		09 56		10 10		10 26		10 40
Rotherhithe	d	09 27		09 42		09 57		10 12		10 27		10 42
Wapping	d	09 29		09 43		09 59		10 13		10 29		10 43
Shadwell	d	09 31		09 45		10 01		10 15		10 31		10 45
Whitechapel	d	09 33		09 48		10 03		10 18		10 33		10 48
Shoreditch High Street	d	09 35		09 50		10 05		10 20		10 35		10 50
Hoxton	d	09 37		09 52		10 07		10 22		10 37		10 52
Haggerston	d	09 39		09 54		10 09		10 24		10 39		10 54
Dalston Junction	a	09 41		09 56		10 11		10 26		10 41		10 56
Canonbury	a	09 44		09 59		10 14		10 29		10 44		10 59
Highbury & Islington	a	09 50		10 04		10 20		10 33		10 50		11 03
London Bridge	a		09 32		09 46		10 02		10 16		10 32	

		SN	LO	SN E	LO	SN	LO	SN E	LO	SN	LO
Purley	d			10 20				10 50			
East Croydon	d			10 31				11 01			
Norwood Junction	a			10 35				11 05			
West Croydon	d				10 42				11 12		
Norwood Junction	a				10 48				11 18		
Norwood Junction	d			10 35	10 48			11 05	11 18		
Anerley	d			10 39	10 51			11 09	11 21		
Penge West	d			10 41	10 53			11 11	11 23		
Crystal Palace	d	10 24	10 37			10 54	11 07			11 24	11 37
Sydenham	d	10 29	10 41	10 45	10 55	10 59	11 11	11 15	11 25	11 29	11 41
Forest Hill	d	10 31	10 43	10 48	10 58	11 01	11 13	11 18	11 28	11 31	11 43
Honor Oak Park	d	10 34	10 46	10 50	11 00	11 04	11 16	11 20	11 30	11 34	11 46
Brockley	d	10 36	10 48	10 53	11 03	11 06	11 18	11 23	11 33	11 36	11 48
New Cross Gate	d	10 39	10 50	10 55	11 05	11 09	11 20	11 25	11 35	11 39	11 50
Surrey Quays	d		10 54		11 08		11 24		11 38		11 54
Canada Water	d		10 56		11 10		11 26		11 40		11 56
Rotherhithe	d		10 57		11 12		11 27		11 42		11 57
Wapping	d		10 59		11 13		11 29		11 43		11 59
Shadwell	d		11 01		11 15		11 31		11 45		12 01
Whitechapel	d		11 03		11 18		11 33		11 48		12 03
Shoreditch High Street	d		11 05		11 20		11 35		11 50		12 05
Hoxton	d		11 07		11 22		11 37		11 52		12 07
Haggerston	d		11 09		11 24		11 39		11 54		12 09
Dalston Junction	a		11 11		11 26		11 41		11 57		12 11
Canonbury	a		11 14		11 29		11 44				12 14
Highbury & Islington	a		11 20		11 33		11 50				12 20
London Bridge	a	10 46		11 02		11 16		11 32		11 46	

A not 15 December. From Crystal Palace

B not 15 December. From West Croydon

C not 15 December. From London Victoria

D From Caterham

E From Tattenham Corner

For full service between Highbury & Islington and Surrey Quays, refer to Table T178

For Sutton connections at West Croydon, refer to Table T172

Table T177-R

Sundays

15 December to 10 May

Croydon and Norwood Junction-Anerley, Penge West, Crystal Palace, Sydenham, Forest Hill, Honor Oak Park, Brockley, New Cross Gate-London Bridge

		SN A	LO	SN		LO	SN A	LO	LO	SN	LO	SN A	LO	LO		SN	LO	LO	SN A	LO	LO	SN	LO	LO	
Purley	d	11 20					11 50					12 20							12 50						
East Croydon	d	11 31					12 01					12 31							13 01						
Norwood Junction	a	11 35					12 05					12 35							13 05						
West Croydon	d		11 42						12 12					12 42				12 57			13 12			13 27	
Norwood Junction	a		11 47						12 17					12 47				13 02			13 17			13 32	
Norwood Junction	d	11 35	11 47				12 05		12 17			12 35		12 47				13 02	13 05		13 17			13 32	
Anerley	d	11 39	11 50				12 09		12 20			12 39		12 50				13 05	13 09		13 20			13 35	
Penge West	d	11 41	11 52				12 11		12 22			12 41		12 52				13 07	13 11		13 22			13 37	
Crystal Palace	d			11 54		12 07		12 16		12 24	12 31		12 46			12 54	13 01			13 16		13 24	13 31		
Sydenham	d	11 45	11 54	11 59		12 11	12 15	12 20	12 24	12 29	12 35	12 44	12 50	12 54		12 59	13 05	13 09	13 14	13 20	13 24	13 29	13 35	13 39	
Forest Hill	d	11 48	11 57	12 01		12 13	12 18	12 22	12 27	12 31	12 37	12 46	12 52	12 57		13 01	13 07	13 12	13 16	13 22	13 27	13 31	13 37	13 42	
Honor Oak Park	d	11 50	11 59	12 04		12 16	12 20	12 25	12 29	12 34	12 40	12 49	12 55	12 59		13 04	13 10	13 14	13 19	13 25	13 29	13 34	13 40	13 44	
Brockley	d	11 53	12 02	12 06		12 18	12 23	12 27	12 32	12 36	12 42	12 51	12 57	13 02		13 06	13 12	13 17	13 21	13 27	13 32	13 36	13 42	13 47	
New Cross Gate	d	11 55	12 04	12 09		12 20	12 25	12 29	12 34	12 39	12 44	12 54	12 59	13 04		13 09	13 14	13 19	13 24	13 29	13 34	13 39	13 44	13 49	
Surrey Quays	d		12 07			12 24		12 35	12 37		12 48		13 03	13 07			13 18	13 22		13 33	13 37		13 48	13 52	
Canada Water	d		12 09			12 26		12 37	12 39		12 50		13 05	13 09			13 20	13 24		13 35	13 39		13 50	13 54	
Rotherhithe	d		12 11			12 27		12 39	12 41		12 51		13 06	13 11			13 21	13 26		13 36	13 41		13 51	13 56	
Wapping	d		12 12			12 29		12 40	12 42		12 53		13 08	13 12			13 23	13 27		13 38	13 42		13 53	13 57	
Shadwell	d		12 14			12 31		12 42	12 44		12 55		13 10	13 14			13 25	13 29		13 40	13 44		13 55	13 59	
Whitechapel	d		12 17			12 33		12 45	12 47		12 57		13 12	13 17			13 27	13 32		13 42	13 47		13 57	14 02	
Shoreditch High Street	d		12 19			12 35		12 47	12 49		12 59		13 14	13 19			13 29	13 34		13 44	13 49		13 59	14 04	
Hoxton	d		12 21			12 37		12 49	12 51		13 01		13 16	13 21			13 31	13 36		13 46	13 51		14 01	14 06	
Haggerston	d		12 23			12 39		12 51	12 53		13 03		13 18	13 23			13 33	13 38		13 48	13 53		14 03	14 08	
Dalston Junction	a		12 26			12 41		12 55	12 57		13 05		13 20	13 27			13 35	13 42		13 50	13 57		14 05	14 12	
Canonbury	a		12 29			12 44					13 08		13 23				13 38			13 53			14 08		
Highbury & Islington	a		12 33			12 50					13 16		13 29				13 44			13 59			14 14		
London Bridge ⊖	a	12 02		12 16			12 32			12 46		13 02				13 16			13 32			13 46			

		SN A	LO	LO	SN	LO	LO	SN A	LO	LO		SN	LO	LO	SN A	LO	LO	SN	LO	LO		SN A	LO	LO	SN
Purley	d	13 20						13 50							14 20							14 50			
East Croydon	d	13 31						14 01							14 31							15 01			
Norwood Junction	a	13 35						14 05							14 35							15 05			
West Croydon	d			13 42			13 57			14 12				14 27			14 42			14 57				15 12	
Norwood Junction	a			13 47			14 02			14 17				14 32			14 47			15 02				15 17	
Norwood Junction	d	13 35		13 47			14 02	14 05		14 17				14 32	14 35		14 47			15 02		15 05		15 17	
Anerley	d	13 39		13 50			14 05	14 09		14 20				14 35	14 39		14 50			15 05		15 09		15 20	
Penge West	d	13 41		13 52			14 07	14 11		14 22				14 37	14 41		14 52			15 07		15 11		15 22	
Crystal Palace	d		13 46		13 54	14 01			14 16			14 24	14 31			14 46		14 54	15 01				15 16		15 24
Sydenham	d	13 44	13 50	13 54	13 59	14 05	14 09	14 14	14 20	14 24		14 29	14 35	14 39	14 44	14 50	14 54	14 59	15 05	15 09		15 14	15 20	15 24	15 29
Forest Hill	d	13 46	13 52	13 57	14 01	14 07	14 12	14 16	14 22	14 27		14 31	14 37	14 42	14 46	14 52	14 57	15 01	15 07	15 12		15 16	15 22	15 27	15 31
Honor Oak Park	d	13 49	13 55	13 59	14 04	14 10	14 14	14 19	14 25	14 29		14 34	14 40	14 44	14 49	14 55	14 59	15 04	15 10	15 14		15 19	15 25	15 29	15 34
Brockley	d	13 51	13 57	14 02	14 06	14 12	14 17	14 21	14 27	14 32		14 36	14 42	14 47	14 51	14 57	15 02	15 06	15 12	15 17		15 21	15 27	15 32	15 36
New Cross Gate	d	13 54	13 59	14 04	14 09	14 14	14 19	14 24	14 29	14 34		14 39	14 44	14 49	14 54	14 59	15 04	15 09	15 14	15 19		15 24	15 29	15 34	15 39
Surrey Quays	d		14 03	14 07		14 18	14 22		14 33	14 37			14 48	14 52		15 03	15 07		15 18	15 22			15 33	15 37	
Canada Water	d		14 05	14 09		14 20	14 24		14 35	14 39			14 50	14 54		15 05	15 09		15 20	15 24			15 35	15 39	
Rotherhithe	d		14 06	14 11		14 21	14 26		14 36	14 41			14 51	14 56		15 06	15 11		15 21	15 26			15 36	15 41	
Wapping	d		14 08	14 12		14 23	14 27		14 38	14 42			14 53	14 57		15 08	15 12		15 23	15 27			15 38	15 42	
Shadwell	d		14 10	14 14		14 25	14 29		14 40	14 44			14 55	14 59		15 10	15 14		15 25	15 29			15 40	15 44	
Whitechapel	d		14 12	14 17		14 27	14 32		14 42	14 47			14 57	15 02		15 12	15 17		15 27	15 32			15 42	15 47	
Shoreditch High Street	d		14 14	14 19		14 29	14 34		14 44	14 49			14 59	15 04		15 14	15 19		15 29	15 34			15 44	15 49	
Hoxton	d		14 16	14 21		14 31	14 36		14 46	14 51			15 01	15 06		15 16	15 21		15 31	15 36			15 46	15 51	
Haggerston	d		14 18	14 23		14 33	14 38		14 48	14 53			15 03	15 08		15 18	15 23		15 33	15 38			15 48	15 53	
Dalston Junction	a		14 20	14 27		14 35	14 42		14 50	14 57			15 05	15 12		15 20	15 27		15 35	15 42			15 50	15 57	
Canonbury	a		14 23			14 38			14 53				15 08			15 23			15 38				15 53		
Highbury & Islington	a		14 29			14 44			14 59				15 14			15 29			15 44				15 59		
London Bridge ⊖	a	14 02			14 16			14 32				14 46			15 02			15 16				15 32			15 46

A From Tattenham Corner

For full service between Highbury & Islington and Surrey Quays, refer to Table T178

For Sutton connections at West Croydon, refer to Table T172

Table T177-R

Sundays

15 December to 10 May

Croydon and Norwood Junction-Anerley, Penge West, Crystal Palace, Sydenham, Forest Hill, Honor Oak Park, Brockley, New Cross Gate-London Bridge

		LO		LO	SN A	LO	LO	SN	LO	LO	SN A	LO		LO	SN	LO	LO	SN A	LO	LO	SN	LO		LO	SN A
Purley	d				15 20						15 50							16 20							16 50
East Croydon	d				15 31						16 01							16 31							17 01
Norwood Junction	a				15 35						16 05							16 35							17 05
West Croydon	d			15 27			15 42			15 57				16 12			16 27			16 42				16 57	
Norwood Junction	a			15 32			15 47			16 02				16 17			16 32			16 47				17 02	
Norwood Junction	d			15 32	15 35		15 47			16 02	16 05			16 17			16 32	16 35		16 47				17 02	17 05
Anerley	d			15 35	15 39		15 50			16 05	16 09			16 20			16 35	16 39		16 50				17 05	17 09
Penge West	d			15 37	15 41		15 52			16 07	16 11			16 22			16 37	16 41		16 52				17 07	17 11
Crystal Palace	d	15 31				15 46		15 54	16 01			16 16			16 24	16 31			16 46		16 54	17 01			
Sydenham	d	15 35		15 39	15 44	15 50	15 54	15 59	16 05	16 09	16 14	16 20		16 24	16 29	16 35	16 39	16 44	16 50	16 54	16 59	17 05		17 09	17 14
Forest Hill	d	15 37		15 42	15 46	15 52	15 57	16 01	16 07	16 12	16 16	16 22		16 27	16 31	16 37	16 42	16 46	16 52	16 57	17 01	17 07		17 12	17 16
Honor Oak Park	d	15 40		15 44	15 49	15 55	15 59	16 04	16 10	16 14	16 19	16 25		16 29	16 34	16 40	16 44	16 49	16 55	16 59	17 04	17 10		17 14	17 19
Brockley	d	15 42		15 47	15 51	15 57	16 02	16 06	16 12	16 17	16 21	16 27		16 32	16 36	16 42	16 47	16 51	16 57	17 02	17 06	17 12		17 17	17 21
New Cross Gate	d	15 44		15 49	15 54	15 59	16 04	16 09	16 14	16 19	16 24	16 29		16 34	16 39	16 44	16 49	16 54	16 59	17 04	17 09	17 14		17 19	17 24
Surrey Quays	d	15 48		15 52		16 03	16 07		16 18	16 22		16 33		16 37		16 48	16 52		17 03	17 07		17 18		17 22	
Canada Water	d	15 50		15 54		16 05	16 09		16 20	16 24		16 35		16 39		16 50	16 54		17 05	17 09		17 20		17 24	
Rotherhithe	d	15 51		15 56		16 06	16 11		16 21	16 26		16 36		16 41		16 51	16 56		17 06	17 11		17 21		17 26	
Wapping	d	15 53		15 57		16 08	16 12		16 23	16 27		16 38		16 42		16 53	16 57		17 08	17 12		17 23		17 27	
Shadwell	d	15 55		15 59		16 10	16 14		16 25	16 29		16 40		16 44		16 55	16 59		17 10	17 14		17 25		17 29	
Whitechapel	d	15 57		16 02		16 12	16 17		16 27	16 32		16 42		16 47		16 57	17 02		17 12	17 17		17 27		17 32	
Shoreditch High Street	d	15 59		16 04		16 14	16 19		16 29	16 34		16 44		16 49		16 59	17 04		17 14	17 19		17 29		17 34	
Hoxton	d	16 01		16 06		16 16	16 21		16 31	16 36		16 46		16 51		17 01	17 06		17 16	17 21		17 31		17 36	
Haggerston	d	16 03		16 08		16 18	16 23		16 33	16 38		16 48		16 53		17 03	17 08		17 18	17 23		17 33		17 38	
Dalston Junction	a	16 05		16 12		16 20	16 27		16 35	16 42		16 50		16 57		17 05	17 12		17 20	17 27		17 35		17 42	
Canonbury	a	16 08				16 23			16 38			16 53				17 08			17 23			17 38			
Highbury & Islington	a	16 14				16 29			16 44			16 59				17 14			17 29			17 44			
London Bridge ⊖	a				16 02			16 16			16 32				16 46			17 02			17 16				17 32

		LO	LO	SN	LO	LO	SN A	LO		LO	SN	LO	LO	SN A	LO	LO	SN	LO		LO	SN A	LO	LO	SN	LO
Purley	d						17 20							17 50							18 20				
East Croydon	d						17 31							18 01							18 31				
Norwood Junction	a						17 35							18 05							18 35				
West Croydon	d		17 12			17 27				17 42			17 57			18 12				18 27			18 42		
Norwood Junction	a		17 17			17 32				17 47			18 02			18 17				18 32			18 47		
Norwood Junction	d		17 17			17 32	17 35			17 47			18 02	18 05		18 17				18 32	18 35		18 47		
Anerley	d		17 20			17 35	17 39			17 50			18 05	18 09		18 20				18 35	18 39		18 50		
Penge West	d		17 22			17 37	17 41			17 52			18 07	18 11		18 22				18 37	18 41		18 52		
Crystal Palace	d	17 16		17 24	17 31			17 46			17 54	18 01			18 16		18 24	18 31				18 46		18 54	19 01
Sydenham	d	17 20	17 24	17 29	17 35	17 39	17 44	17 50		17 54	17 59	18 05	18 09	18 14	18 20	18 24	18 29	18 35		18 39	18 44	18 50	18 54	18 59	19 05
Forest Hill	d	17 22	17 27	17 31	17 37	17 42	17 46	17 52		17 57	18 01	18 07	18 12	18 16	18 22	18 27	18 31	18 37		18 42	18 46	18 52	18 57	19 01	19 07
Honor Oak Park	d	17 25	17 29	17 34	17 40	17 44	17 49	17 55		17 59	18 04	18 10	18 14	18 19	18 25	18 29	18 34	18 40		18 44	18 49	18 55	18 59	19 04	19 10
Brockley	d	17 27	17 32	17 36	17 42	17 47	17 51	17 57		18 02	18 06	18 12	18 17	18 21	18 27	18 32	18 36	18 42		18 47	18 51	18 57	19 02	19 06	19 12
New Cross Gate	d	17 29	17 34	17 39	17 44	17 49	17 54	17 59		18 04	18 09	18 14	18 19	18 24	18 29	18 34	18 39	18 44		18 49	18 54	18 59	19 04	19 09	19 14
Surrey Quays	d	17 33	17 37		17 48	17 52		18 03		18 07		18 18	18 22		18 33	18 37		18 48		18 52		19 03	19 07		19 18
Canada Water	d	17 35	17 39		17 50	17 54		18 05		18 09		18 20	18 24		18 35	18 39		18 50		18 54		19 05	19 09		19 20
Rotherhithe	d	17 36	17 41		17 51	17 56		18 06		18 11		18 21	18 26		18 36	18 41		18 51		18 56		19 06	19 11		19 21
Wapping	d	17 38	17 42		17 53	17 57		18 08		18 12		18 23	18 27		18 38	18 42		18 53		18 57		19 08	19 12		19 23
Shadwell	d	17 40	17 44		17 55	17 59		18 10		18 14		18 25	18 29		18 40	18 44		18 55		18 59		19 10	19 14		19 25
Whitechapel	d	17 42	17 47		17 57	18 02		18 12		18 17		18 27	18 32		18 42	18 47		18 57		19 02		19 12	19 17		19 27
Shoreditch High Street	d	17 44	17 49		17 59	18 04		18 14		18 19		18 29	18 34		18 44	18 49		18 59		19 04		19 14	19 19		19 29
Hoxton	d	17 46	17 51		18 01	18 06		18 16		18 21		18 31	18 36		18 46	18 51		19 01		19 06		19 16	19 21		19 31
Haggerston	d	17 48	17 53		18 03	18 08		18 18		18 23		18 33	18 38		18 48	18 53		19 03		19 08		19 18	19 23		19 33
Dalston Junction	a	17 50	17 57		18 05	18 12		18 20		18 27		18 35	18 42		18 50	18 57		19 05		19 12		19 20	19 27		19 35
Canonbury	a	17 53			18 08			18 23				18 38			18 53			19 08				19 23			19 38
Highbury & Islington	a	17 59			18 14			18 29				18 44			18 59			19 14				19 29			19 44
London Bridge ⊖	a			17 46			18 02				18 16			18 32			18 46				19 02			19 16	

A From Tattenham Corner

For full service between Highbury & Islington and Surrey Quays, refer to Table T178

For Sutton connections at West Croydon, refer to Table T172

Table T177-R

Sundays

15 December to 10 May

Croydon and Norwood Junction-Anerley, Penge West, Crystal Palace, Sydenham, Forest Hill, Honor Oak Park, Brockley, New Cross Gate-London Bridge

		LO	SN A	LO	LO	SN	LO	LO	SN A	LO		LO	SN	LO	LO	SN A	LO	LO	SN	LO		LO	SN A	LO	LO
Purley	d		18 50						19 20							19 50							20 20		
East Croydon	d		19 01						19 31							20 01							20 31		
Norwood Junction 2	a		19 05						19 35							20 05							20 35		
West Croydon 4	d	18 57			19 12			19 27				19 42			19 57			20 12				20 27			20 42
Norwood Junction	a	19 02			19 17			19 32				19 47			20 02			20 17				20 32			20 47
Norwood Junction	d	19 02	19 05		19 17			19 32	19 35			19 47			20 02	20 05		20 17				20 32	20 35		20 47
Anerley	d	19 05	19 09		19 20			19 35	19 39			19 50			20 05	20 09		20 20				20 35	20 39		20 50
Penge West	d	19 07	19 11		19 22			19 37	19 41			19 52			20 07	20 11		20 22				20 37	20 41		20 52
Crystal Palace 4	d			19 16		19 24	19 31			19 46			19 54	20 01			20 16		20 24	20 31				20 46	
Sydenham	d	19 09	19 14	19 20	19 24	19 29	19 35	19 39	19 44	19 50		19 54	19 59	20 05	20 09	20 14	20 20	20 24	20 29	20 35		20 39	20 44	20 50	20 54
Forest Hill 4	d	19 12	19 16	19 22	19 27	19 31	19 37	19 42	19 46	19 52		19 57	20 01	20 07	20 12	20 16	20 22	20 27	20 31	20 37		20 42	20 46	20 52	20 57
Honor Oak Park	d	19 14	19 19	19 25	19 29	19 34	19 40	19 44	19 49	19 55		19 59	20 04	20 10	20 14	20 19	20 25	20 29	20 34	20 40		20 44	20 49	20 55	20 59
Brockley	d	19 17	19 21	19 27	19 32	19 36	19 42	19 47	19 51	19 57		20 02	20 06	20 12	20 17	20 21	20 27	20 32	20 36	20 42		20 47	20 51	20 57	21 02
New Cross Gate	d	19 19	19 24	19 29	19 34	19 39	19 44	19 49	19 54	19 59		20 04	20 09	20 14	20 19	20 24	20 29	20 34	20 39	20 44		20 49	20 54	20 59	21 04
Surrey Quays	d	19 22		19 33	19 37		19 48	19 52		20 03		20 07		20 18	20 22		20 33	20 37		20 48		20 52		21 03	21 07
Canada Water	d	19 24		19 35	19 39		19 50	19 54		20 05		20 09		20 20	20 24		20 35	20 39		20 50		20 54		21 05	21 09
Rotherhithe	d	19 26		19 36	19 41		19 51	19 56		20 06		20 11		20 21	20 26		20 36	20 41		20 51		20 56		21 06	21 11
Wapping	d	19 27		19 38	19 42		19 53	19 57		20 08		20 12		20 23	20 27		20 38	20 42		20 53		20 57		21 08	21 12
Shadwell	d	19 29		19 40	19 44		19 55	19 59		20 10		20 14		20 25	20 29		20 40	20 44		20 55		20 59		21 10	21 14
Whitechapel	d	19 32		19 42	19 47		19 57	20 02		20 12		20 17		20 27	20 32		20 42	20 47		20 57		21 02		21 12	21 17
Shoreditch High Street	d	19 34		19 44	19 49		19 59	20 04		20 14		20 19		20 29	20 34		20 44	20 49		20 59		21 04		21 14	21 19
Hoxton	d	19 36		19 46	19 51		20 01	20 06		20 16		20 21		20 31	20 36		20 46	20 51		21 01		21 06		21 16	21 21
Haggerston	d	19 38		19 48	19 53		20 03	20 08		20 18		20 23		20 33	20 38		20 48	20 53		21 03		21 08		21 18	21 23
Dalston Junction	a	19 42		19 50	19 57		20 05	20 12		20 20		20 27		20 35	20 42		20 50	20 57		21 05		21 12		21 20	21 27
Canonbury	a			19 53			20 08			20 23				20 38			20 53			21 08				21 23	
Highbury & Islington	a			19 59			20 14			20 29				20 44			20 59			21 14				21 29	
London Bridge 4 ⊖	a		19 32			19 46			20 02				20 16			20 32			20 46				21 02		

		SN	LO	LO	SN A	LO		LO	SN	LO	LO	SN A	LO	LO	SN	LO		LO	SN A	LO	LO	SN	LO	SN A	LO
Purley	d				20 50							21 20							21 50					22 20	
East Croydon	d				21 01							21 31							22 01					22 31	
Norwood Junction 2	a				21 05							21 35							22 05					22 35	
West Croydon 4	d			20 57				21 12			21 27			21 42				21 57			22 12		22 27		
Norwood Junction	a			21 02				21 17			21 32			21 47				22 02			22 17		22 32		
Norwood Junction	d			21 02	21 05			21 17			21 32	21 35		21 47				22 02	22 05		22 17		22 32	22 35	
Anerley	d			21 05	21 09			21 20			21 35	21 39		21 50				22 05	22 09		22 20		22 35	22 39	
Penge West	d			21 07	21 11			21 22			21 37	21 41		21 52				22 07	22 11		22 22		22 37	22 41	
Crystal Palace 4	d	20 54	21 01			21 16			21 24	21 31			21 46		21 54	22 01				22 16		22 24			22 46
Sydenham	d	20 59	21 05	21 09	21 14	21 20		21 24	21 29	21 35	21 39	21 44	21 50	21 54	21 59	22 05		22 09	22 14	22 20	22 24	22 29	22 39	22 44	22 50
Forest Hill 4	d	21 01	21 07	21 12	21 16	21 22		21 27	21 31	21 37	21 42	21 46	21 52	21 57	22 01	22 07		22 12	22 16	22 22	22 27	22 31	22 42	22 46	22 52
Honor Oak Park	d	21 04	21 10	21 14	21 19	21 25		21 29	21 34	21 40	21 44	21 49	21 55	21 59	22 04	22 10		22 14	22 19	22 25	22 29	22 34	22 44	22 49	22 55
Brockley	d	21 06	21 12	21 17	21 21	21 27		21 32	21 36	21 42	21 47	21 51	21 57	22 02	22 06	22 12		22 17	22 21	22 27	22 32	22 36	22 47	22 51	22 57
New Cross Gate	d	21 09	21 14	21 19	21 24	21 29		21 34	21 39	21 44	21 49	21 54	21 59	22 04	22 09	22 14		22 19	22 24	22 29	22 34	22 39	22 49	22 54	22 59
Surrey Quays	d		21 18	21 22		21 33		21 37		21 48	21 52		22 03	22 07		22 18		22 22		22 33	22 37		22 52		23 03
Canada Water	d		21 20	21 24		21 35		21 39		21 50	21 54		22 05	22 09		22 20		22 24		22 35	22 39		22 54		23 05
Rotherhithe	d		21 21	21 26		21 36		21 41		21 51	21 56		22 06	22 11		22 21		22 26		22 36	22 41		22 56		23 06
Wapping	d		21 23	21 27		21 38		21 42		21 53	21 57		22 08	22 12		22 23		22 27		22 38	22 42		22 57		23 08
Shadwell	d		21 25	21 29		21 40		21 44		21 55	21 59		22 10	22 14		22 25		22 29		22 40	22 44		22 59		23 10
Whitechapel	d		21 27	21 32		21 42		21 47		21 57	22 02		22 12	22 17		22 27		22 32		22 42	22 47		23 02		23 12
Shoreditch High Street	d		21 29	21 34		21 44		21 49		21 59	22 04		22 14	22 19		22 29		22 34		22 44	22 49		23 04		23 14
Hoxton	d		21 31	21 36		21 46		21 51		22 01	22 06		22 16	22 21		22 31		22 36		22 46	22 51		23 06		23 16
Haggerston	d		21 33	21 38		21 48		21 53		22 03	22 08		22 18	22 23		22 33		22 38		22 48	22 53		23 08		23 18
Dalston Junction	a		21 35	21 42		21 50		21 57		22 05	22 12		22 20	22 27		22 35		22 42		22 50	22 57		23 12		23 20
Canonbury	a		21 38			21 53				22 08			22 23			22 38				22 53					23 23
Highbury & Islington	a		21 44			21 59				22 14			22 29			22 44				22 59					23 29
London Bridge 4 ⊖	a	21 16			21 32				21 46			22 02			22 16				22 32			22 46		23 02	

A From Tattenham Corner

For full service between Highbury & Islington and Surrey Quays, refer to Table T178

For Sutton connections at West Croydon, refer to Table T172

Table T177-R

Sundays

15 December to 10 May

Croydon and Norwood Junction-Anerley, Penge West, Crystal Palace, Sydenham, Forest Hill, Honor Oak Park, Brockley, New Cross Gate-London Bridge

		LO	SN	LO	SN A		LO	SN A
Purley	d				22 50			23 20
East Croydon	d				23 01			23 31
Norwood Junction 2	a				23 05			23 35
West Croydon 4	d	22 42		22 57				
Norwood Junction	a	22 47		23 02				
Norwood Junction	d	22 47		23 02	23 05			23 35
Anerley	d	22 50		23 05	23 09			23 39
Penge West	d	22 52		23 07	23 11			23 41
Crystal Palace 4	d		22 54				23 16	
Sydenham	d	22 54	22 59	23 09	23 14		23 20	23 44
Forest Hill 4	d	22 57	23 01	23 12	23 16		23 22	23 46
Honor Oak Park	d	22 59	23 04	23 14	23 19		23 25	23 49
Brockley	d	23 02	23 06	23 17	23 21		23 27	23 51
New Cross Gate	d	23 04	23 09	23 19	23 25		23 29	23 54
Surrey Quays	d	23 07		23 22			23 33	
Canada Water	d	23 09		23 24			23 35	
Rotherhithe	d	23 11		23 26			23 36	
Wapping	d	23 12		23 27			23 38	
Shadwell	d	23 14		23 29			23 40	
Whitechapel	d	23 17		23 32			23 42	
Shoreditch High Street	d	23 19		23 34			23 44	
Hoxton	d	23 21		23 36			23 46	
Haggerston	d	23 23		23 38			23 48	
Dalston Junction	a	23 27		23 42			23 50	
Canonbury	a						23 53	
Highbury & Islington	a						23 59	
London Bridge 4 ⊖	a		23 16		23 32			00 03

A From Tattenham Corner

For full service between Highbury & Islington and Surrey Quays, refer to Table T178

For Sutton connections at West Croydon, refer to Table T172

Table T178-F

Mondays to Fridays

16 December to 15 May

Highbury & Islington - New Cross, Crystal Palace, West Croydon and Clapham Junction

Miles	Miles	Miles	Miles	Station		LO MX A	LO MO A	LO MX A	LO MX B	LO MX B	LO MX A	LO MX A	LO MX B	LO MX A		LO MX	LO MX	LO	LO	LO	LO	LO	LO	LO	
0	0	—	—	Highbury & Islington	d											00 01	00 10	05 32		05 40		05 47	05 55	06 02	
0½	0½	—	—	Canonbury	d											00 03	00 12	05 34		05 42		05 49	05 57	06 04	
1½	1½	0	0	**Dalston Junction**	d											00 06	00 15	05 37	05 42	05 45	05 49	05 52	06 00	06 07	
2	2	0½	0½	**Haggerston**	d											00 08	00 17	05 39	05 44	05 47	05 51	05 54	06 02	06 09	
2½	2½	1	1	**Hoxton**	d											00 10	00 19	05 41	05 46	05 49	05 53	05 56	06 04	06 11	
3¼	3¼	1¾	1¾	**Shoreditch High Street**	d									00 01		00 13	00 21	05 43	05 48	05 52	05 55	05 58	06 07	06 13	
3¾	3¾	2¼	2¼	**Whitechapel**	d									00 04		00 15	00 24	05 46	05 51	05 54	05 58	06 01	06 09	06 16	
4½	4½	3	3	**Shadwell**	d									00 06		00 17	00 26	05 48	05 53	05 56	06 00	06 03	06 11	06 18	
5	5	3½	3½	**Wapping**	d								00 02	00 08		00 19	00 28	05 50	05 55	05 58	06 02	06 05	06 13	06 20	
5½	5½	4	4	**Rotherhithe**	d								00 03	00 09		00 21	00 29	05 51	05 56	06 00	06 03	06 06	06 15	06 21	
5¾	5¾	4¼	4¼	**Canada Water**	d							00 02	00 05	00 11		00 23	00 31	05 53	05 58	06 02	06 05	06 08	06 17	06 23	
6	6	4½	4½	**Surrey Quays**	d					00 01		00 04	00 07	00 13		00 25	00 33	05 55	06 00	06 04	06 07	06 10	06 19	06 25	
—	—	—	5¼	New Cross	a					00 04									06 04						
—	7¼	5¾	—	New Cross Gate 4	d				00 01			00 08		00a20			00a40	06 00		06 08		06 15	06 23	06 30	
—	8	6½	—	Brockley	d				00 02			00 11						06 02		06 11		06 17	06 26	06 32	
—	9	7½	—	Honor Oak Park	d				00 05			00 13						06 05		06 13		06 20	06 28	06 35	
—	10	8½	—	Forest Hill 4	d			00 01	00 07			00 16						06 07		06 16		06 22	06 31	06 37	
—	11¾	9	—	Sydenham	d		00 01	00 04	00 11			00 19						06 11		06 19		06 26	06 34	06 41	
—	12	—	—	Crystal Palace 4	a			00 09				00 24								06 24			06 39		
—	—	10	—	Penge West	d		00 03		00 13									06 13				06 28		06 43	
—	—	10½	—	Anerley	d	00 01	00 05		00 15									06 15				06 30		06 45	
—	—	11½	—	Norwood Junction 2	d	00 03	00 08		00 18									06 18				06 33		06 48	
—	—	13¼	—	West Croydon 4	a	00 13	00 16		00 29									06 28				06 39		06 58	
7½	—	—	—	Queens Rd Peckham	d								00 14			00 29					06 12				
8	—	—	—	Peckham Rye 4	d						00 02		00 18			00 33					06 15				
9	—	—	—	Denmark Hill 4	d						00 06		00 22			00 37					06 18				
11	—	—	—	**Clapham High Street** ⊖	d						00 10		00 26			00 41					06 23				
11¼	—	—	—	**Wandsworth Road**	d						00 12		00 28			00 43					06 24				
12¾	—	—	—	Clapham Junction	a						00 20		00 35			00 51					06 34				

Station		LO	LO	LO	LO	LO	LO	LO	LO	LO		LO	LO	LO	LO	LO	LO	LO	LO	LO		LO	LO	LO	LO
Highbury & Islington	d		06 10		06 17		06 25		06 32			06 40		06 47		06 55		07 02		07 10			07 17		07 25
Canonbury	d		06 12		06 19		06 27		06 34			06 42		06 49		06 57		07 04		07 12			07 19		07 27
Dalston Junction	d	06 12	06 15	06 19	06 22	06 27	06 30	06 34	06 37	06 42		06 45	06 49	06 52	06 57	07 00	07 04	07 07	07 12	07 15		07 19	07 22	07 27	07 30
Haggerston	d	06 14	06 17	06 21	06 24	06 29	06 32	06 36	06 39	06 44		06 47	06 51	06 54	06 59	07 02	07 06	07 09	07 14	07 17		07 21	07 24	07 29	07 32
Hoxton	d	06 16	06 19	06 23	06 26	06 31	06 34	06 38	06 41	06 46		06 49	06 53	06 56	07 01	07 04	07 08	07 11	07 16	07 19		07 23	07 26	07 31	07 34
Shoreditch High Street	d	06 18	06 22	06 25	06 28	06 33	06 37	06 40	06 43	06 48		06 52	06 55	06 58	07 03	07 07	07 10	07 13	07 18	07 22		07 25	07 28	07 33	07 37
Whitechapel	d	06 21	06 24	06 28	06 31	06 36	06 39	06 43	06 46	06 51		06 54	06 58	07 01	07 06	07 09	07 13	07 16	07 21	07 24		07 28	07 31	07 36	07 39
Shadwell	d	06 23	06 26	06 30	06 33	06 38	06 41	06 45	06 48	06 53		06 56	07 00	07 03	07 08	07 11	07 15	07 18	07 23	07 26		07 30	07 33	07 38	07 41
Wapping	d	06 25	06 28	06 32	06 35	06 40	06 43	06 47	06 50	06 55		06 58	07 02	07 05	07 10	07 13	07 17	07 20	07 25	07 28		07 32	07 35	07 40	07 43
Rotherhithe	d	06 26	06 30	06 33	06 36	06 41	06 45	06 48	06 51	06 56		07 00	07 03	07 06	07 11	07 15	07 18	07 21	07 26	07 30		07 33	07 36	07 41	07 45
Canada Water	d	06 28	06 32	06 35	06 38	06 43	06 47	06 50	06 53	06 58		07 02	07 05	07 08	07 13	07 17	07 20	07 23	07 28	07 32		07 35	07 38	07 43	07 47
Surrey Quays	d	06 30	06 34	06 37	06 40	06 45	06 49	06 52	06 55	07 00		07 04	07 07	07 10	07 15	07 19	07 22	07 25	07 30	07 34		07 37	07 40	07 45	07 49
New Cross	a	06 34				06 49				07 04					07 19				07 34					07 49	
New Cross Gate 4	d		06 38		06 45		06 53		07 00			07 08		07 15		07 23		07 30		07 38			07 45		07 53
Brockley	d		06 41		06 47		06 56		07 02			07 11		07 17		07 26		07 32		07 41			07 47		07 56
Honor Oak Park	d		06 43		06 50		06 58		07 05			07 13		07 20		07 28		07 35		07 43			07 50		07 58
Forest Hill 4	d		06 46		06 52		07 01		07 07			07 16		07 22		07 31		07 37		07 46			07 52		08 01
Sydenham	d		06 49		06 56		07 04		07 11			07 19		07 26		07 34		07 41		07 49			07 56		08 04
Crystal Palace 4	a		06 54				07 09					07 24				07 39				07 54					08 09
Penge West	d				06 58				07 13					07 28				07 43					07 58		
Anerley	d				07 00				07 15					07 30				07 45					08 00		
Norwood Junction 2	d				07 03				07 18					07 33				07 48					08 03		
West Croydon 4	a				07 09				07 28					07 39				07 58					08 09		
Queens Rd Peckham	d			06 42				06 57					07 12				07 27					07 42			
Peckham Rye 4	d			06 45				07 00					07 15				07 30					07 45			
Denmark Hill 4	d			06 48				07 03					07 18				07 33					07 48			
Clapham High Street ⊖	d			06 53				07 08					07 23				07 38					07 53			
Wandsworth Road	d			06 54				07 09					07 24				07 39					07 54			
Clapham Junction	a			07 09				07 19					07 34				07 49					08 04			

Station		LO	LO	LO	LO	LO		LO	LO	LO	LO	LO	LO	LO	LO	LO		LO	LO	LO	LO	LO	LO	LO	LO
Highbury & Islington	d		07 32		07 40			07 47		07 55		08 02		08 10		08 17			08 25		08 32		08 40		08 47
Canonbury	d		07 34		07 42			07 49		07 57		08 04		08 12		08 19			08 27		08 34		08 42		08 49
Dalston Junction	d	07 34	07 37	07 42	07 45	07 49		07 52	07 57	08 00	08 04	08 07	08 12	08 15	08 19	08 22		08 27	08 30	08 34	08 37	08 43	08 46	08 49	08 52
Haggerston	d	07 36	07 39	07 44	07 47	07 51		07 54	07 59	08 02	08 06	08 09	08 14	08 17	08 21	08 24		08 29	08 32	08 36	08 39	08 44	08 47	08 51	08 54
Hoxton	d	07 38	07 41	07 46	07 49	07 53		07 56	08 01	08 04	08 08	08 11	08 16	08 19	08 23	08 26		08 31	08 34	08 38	08 41	08 46	08 49	08 53	08 56
Shoreditch High Street	d	07 40	07 43	07 48	07 52	07 55		07 58	08 03	08 07	08 10	08 13	08 18	08 22	08 25	08 28		08 33	08 37	08 40	08 43	08 48	08 52	08 55	08 58
Whitechapel	d	07 43	07 46	07 51	07 54	07 58		08 01	08 06	08 09	08 13	08 16	08 21	08 24	08 28	08 31		08 36	08 39	08 43	08 46	08 51	08 54	08 58	09 01
Shadwell	d	07 45	07 48	07 53	07 56	08 00		08 03	08 08	08 11	08 15	08 18	08 23	08 26	08 30	08 33		08 38	08 41	08 45	08 48	08 53	08 56	09 00	09 03
Wapping	d	07 47	07 50	07 55	07 58	08 02		08 05	08 10	08 13	08 17	08 20	08 25	08 28	08 32	08 35		08 40	08 43	08 47	08 50	08 55	08 58	09 02	09 05
Rotherhithe	d	07 48	07 51	07 56	08 00	08 03		08 06	08 11	08 15	08 18	08 21	08 26	08 30	08 33	08 36		08 41	08 45	08 48	08 51	08 56	09 00	09 03	09 06
Canada Water	d	07 50	07 53	07 58	08 02	08 05		08 08	08 13	08 17	08 20	08 23	08 28	08 32	08 35	08 38		08 43	08 47	08 50	08 53	08 58	09 02	09 05	09 08
Surrey Quays	d	07 52	07 55	08 00	08 04	08 07		08 10	08 15	08 19	08 22	08 25	08 30	08 34	08 37	08 40		08 45	08 49	08 52	08 55	09 00	09 04	09 07	09 10
New Cross	a			08 04					08 19				08 34					08 49				09 05			
New Cross Gate 4	d		08 00		08 08			08 15		08 23		08 30		08 38		08 45			08 53		09 00		09 08		09 15
Brockley	d		08 02		08 11			08 17		08 26		08 32		08 41		08 47			08 56		09 02		09 11		09 17
Honor Oak Park	d		08 05		08 13			08 20		08 28		08 35		08 43		08 50			08 58		09 05		09 13		09 20
Forest Hill 4	d		08 07		08 16			08 22		08 31		08 37		08 46		08 52			09 01		09 07		09 16		09 22
Sydenham	d		08 11		08 19			08 26		08 34		08 41		08 49		08 56			09 04		09 11		09 19		09 26
Crystal Palace 4	a				08 24					08 39				08 54					09 09				09 24		
Penge West	d		08 13					08 28				08 43				08 58					09 13				09 28
Anerley	d		08 15					08 30				08 45				09 00					09 15				09 30
Norwood Junction 2	d		08 18					08 33				08 48				09 03					09 18				09 33
West Croydon 4	a		08 28					08 39				08 58				09 09					09 28				09 43
Queens Rd Peckham	d	07 57				08 12					08 27				08 44					08 59				09 12	
Peckham Rye 4	d	08 00				08 14					08 30				08 48					09 03				09 15	
Denmark Hill 4	d	08 03				08 17					08 33				08 52					09 07				09 18	
Clapham High Street ⊖	d	08 08				08 22					08 38				08 56					09 11				09 23	
Wandsworth Road	d	08 09				08 23					08 39				08 58					09 13				09 24	
Clapham Junction	a	08 24				08 39					08 49				09 09					09 24				09 34	

A From Highbury and Islington ELL

B From Dalston Junction Stn ELL

Table T178-F

Mondays to Fridays

16 December to 15 May

Highbury & Islington - New Cross, Crystal Palace, West Croydon and Clapham Junction

Station		LO		LO	LO	LO	LO	LO	LO	LO	LO	LO		LO	LO	LO	LO	LO	LO	LO	LO	LO		LO	LO
Highbury & Islington	d			08 55		09 02		09 10		09 17		09 25			09 32		09 40		09 47		09 55			10 02	
Canonbury	d			08 57		09 04		09 12		09 19		09 27			09 34		09 42		09 49		09 57			10 04	
Dalston Junction	d	08 57		09 00	09 04	09 08	09 13	09 16	09 19	09 22	09 27	09 30		09 34	09 37	09 42	09 45	09 49	09 52	09 57	10 00	10 04		10 07	10 12
Haggerston	d	08 59		09 02	09 06	09 09	09 14	09 17	09 21	09 24	09 29	09 32		09 36	09 39	09 44	09 47	09 51	09 54	09 59	10 02	10 06		10 09	10 14
Hoxton	d	09 01		09 04	09 08	09 11	09 16	09 19	09 23	09 26	09 31	09 34		09 38	09 41	09 46	09 49	09 53	09 56	10 01	10 04	10 08		10 11	10 16
Shoreditch High Street	d	09 03		09 07	09 10	09 13	09 18	09 22	09 25	09 28	09 33	09 37		09 40	09 43	09 48	09 52	09 55	09 58	10 03	10 07	10 10		10 13	10 18
Whitechapel	d	09 06		09 09	09 13	09 16	09 21	09 24	09 28	09 31	09 36	09 39		09 43	09 46	09 51	09 54	09 58	10 01	10 06	10 09	10 13		10 16	10 21
Shadwell	d	09 08		09 11	09 15	09 18	09 23	09 26	09 30	09 33	09 38	09 41		09 45	09 48	09 53	09 56	10 00	10 03	10 08	10 11	10 15		10 18	10 23
Wapping	d	09 10		09 13	09 17	09 20	09 25	09 28	09 32	09 35	09 40	09 43		09 47	09 50	09 55	09 58	10 02	10 05	10 10	10 13	10 17		10 20	10 25
Rotherhithe	d	09 11		09 15	09 18	09 21	09 26	09 30	09 33	09 36	09 41	09 45		09 48	09 51	09 56	10 00	10 03	10 06	10 11	10 15	10 18		10 21	10 26
Canada Water	d	09 13		09 17	09 20	09 23	09 28	09 32	09 35	09 38	09 43	09 47		09 50	09 53	09 58	10 02	10 05	10 08	10 13	10 17	10 20		10 23	10 28
Surrey Quays	d	09 15		09 19	09 22	09 25	09 30	09 34	09 37	09 40	09 45	09 49		09 52	09 55	10 00	10 04	10 07	10 10	10 15	10 19	10 22		10 25	10 30
New Cross	a	09 19					09 35				09 49					10 04				10 19					10 34
New Cross Gate 4	d			09 23		09 30		09 38		09 45		09 53			10 00		10 08		10 15		10 23			10 30	
Brockley	d			09 26		09 32		09 41		09 47		09 56			10 02		10 11		10 17		10 26			10 32	
Honor Oak Park	d			09 28		09 35		09 43		09 50		09 58			10 05		10 13		10 20		10 28			10 35	
Forest Hill 4	d			09 31		09 37		09 46		09 52		10 01			10 07		10 16		10 22		10 31			10 37	
Sydenham	d			09 34		09 41		09 49		09 56		10 04			10 11		10 19		10 26		10 34			10 41	
Crystal Palace 4	a			09 39				09 54				10 09					10 24				10 39				
Penge West	d					09 43				09 58					10 13				10 28					10 43	
Anerley	d					09 45				10 00					10 15				10 30					10 45	
Norwood Junction 2	d					09 48				10 03					10 18				10 33					10 48	
West Croydon 4	a					09 59				10 13					10 28				10 43					10 58	
Queens Rd Peckham	d				09 29				09 44					09 59				10 14				10 29			
Peckham Rye 4	d				09 33				09 48					10 03				10 18				10 33			
Denmark Hill 4	d				09 37				09 52					10 07				10 22				10 37			
Clapham High Street ⊖	d				09 41				09 56					10 11				10 26				10 41			
Wandsworth Road	d				09 43				09 58					10 13				10 28				10 43			
Clapham Junction	a				09 50				10 05					10 19				10 35				10 50			

Station		LO	LO	LO	LO	LO	LO	LO		LO	LO	LO	LO	LO	LO	LO	LO	LO		LO	LO	LO	LO	LO	LO
Highbury & Islington	d	10 10		10 17		10 25		10 32			10 40		10 47		10 55		11 02			11 10		11 17		11 25	
Canonbury	d	10 12		10 19		10 27		10 34			10 42		10 49		10 57		11 04			11 12		11 19		11 27	
Dalston Junction	d	10 15	10 19	10 22	10 27	10 30	10 34	10 37		10 42	10 45	10 49	10 52	10 57	11 00	11 04	11 07	11 12		11 15	11 19	11 22	11 27	11 30	11 34
Haggerston	d	10 17	10 21	10 24	10 29	10 32	10 36	10 39		10 44	10 47	10 51	10 54	10 59	11 02	11 06	11 09	11 14		11 17	11 21	11 24	11 29	11 32	11 36
Hoxton	d	10 19	10 23	10 26	10 31	10 34	10 38	10 41		10 46	10 49	10 53	10 56	11 01	11 04	11 08	11 11	11 16		11 19	11 23	11 26	11 31	11 34	11 38
Shoreditch High Street	d	10 22	10 25	10 28	10 33	10 37	10 40	10 43		10 48	10 52	10 55	10 58	11 03	11 07	11 10	11 13	11 18		11 22	11 25	11 28	11 33	11 37	11 40
Whitechapel	d	10 24	10 28	10 31	10 36	10 39	10 43	10 46		10 51	10 54	10 58	11 01	11 06	11 09	11 13	11 16	11 21		11 24	11 28	11 31	11 36	11 39	11 43
Shadwell	d	10 26	10 30	10 33	10 38	10 41	10 45	10 48		10 53	10 56	11 00	11 03	11 08	11 11	11 15	11 18	11 23		11 26	11 30	11 33	11 38	11 41	11 45
Wapping	d	10 28	10 32	10 35	10 40	10 43	10 47	10 50		10 55	10 58	11 02	11 05	11 10	11 13	11 17	11 20	11 25		11 28	11 32	11 35	11 40	11 43	11 47
Rotherhithe	d	10 30	10 33	10 36	10 41	10 45	10 48	10 51		10 56	11 00	11 03	11 06	11 11	11 15	11 18	11 21	11 26		11 30	11 33	11 36	11 41	11 45	11 48
Canada Water	d	10 32	10 35	10 38	10 43	10 47	10 50	10 53		10 58	11 02	11 05	11 08	11 13	11 17	11 20	11 23	11 28		11 32	11 35	11 38	11 43	11 47	11 50
Surrey Quays	d	10 34	10 37	10 40	10 45	10 49	10 52	10 55		11 00	11 04	11 07	11 10	11 15	11 19	11 22	11 25	11 30		11 34	11 37	11 40	11 45	11 49	11 52
New Cross	a				10 49					11 04				11 19				11 34					11 49		
New Cross Gate 4	d	10 38		10 45		10 53		11 00			11 08		11 15		11 23		11 30			11 38		11 45		11 53	
Brockley	d	10 41		10 47		10 56		11 02			11 11		11 17		11 26		11 32			11 41		11 47		11 56	
Honor Oak Park	d	10 43		10 50		10 58		11 05			11 13		11 20		11 28		11 35			11 43		11 50		11 58	
Forest Hill 4	d	10 46		10 52		11 01		11 07			11 16		11 22		11 31		11 37			11 46		11 52		12 01	
Sydenham	d	10 49		10 56		11 04		11 11			11 19		11 26		11 34		11 41			11 49		11 56		12 04	
Crystal Palace 4	a	10 54				11 09					11 24				11 39					11 54				12 09	
Penge West	d			10 58				11 13					11 28				11 43					11 58			
Anerley	d			11 00				11 15					11 30				11 45					12 00			
Norwood Junction 2	d			11 03				11 18					11 33				11 48					12 03			
West Croydon 4	a			11 09				11 28					11 39				11 54					12 09			
Queens Rd Peckham	d		10 44				10 59					11 14				11 29					11 44				11 59
Peckham Rye 4	d		10 48				11 03					11 18				11 33					11 48				12 03
Denmark Hill 4	d		10 52				11 07					11 22				11 37					11 52				12 07
Clapham High Street ⊖	d		10 56				11 11					11 26				11 41					11 56				12 11
Wandsworth Road	d		10 58				11 13					11 28				11 43					11 58				12 13
Clapham Junction	a		11 05				11 19					11 35				11 49					12 05				12 19

Station		LO	LO	LO		LO	LO	LO	LO	LO	LO	LO	LO	LO		LO	LO	LO	LO	LO	LO	LO	LO	LO	
Highbury & Islington	d	11 32		11 40			11 47		11 55		12 02		12 10			12 17		12 25		12 32		12 40		12 47	
Canonbury	d	11 34		11 42			11 49		11 57		12 04		12 12			12 19		12 27		12 34		12 42		12 49	
Dalston Junction	d	11 37	11 42	11 45		11 49	11 52	11 57	12 00	12 04	12 07	12 12	12 15	12 19		12 22	12 27	12 30	12 34	12 37	12 42	12 45	12 49	12 52	
Haggerston	d	11 39	11 44	11 47		11 51	11 54	11 59	12 02	12 06	12 09	12 14	12 17	12 21		12 24	12 29	12 32	12 36	12 39	12 44	12 47	12 51	12 54	
Hoxton	d	11 41	11 46	11 49		11 53	11 56	12 01	12 04	12 08	12 11	12 16	12 19	12 23		12 26	12 31	12 34	12 38	12 41	12 46	12 49	12 53	12 56	
Shoreditch High Street	d	11 43	11 48	11 52		11 55	11 58	12 03	12 07	12 10	12 13	12 18	12 22	12 25		12 28	12 33	12 37	12 40	12 43	12 48	12 52	12 55	12 58	
Whitechapel	d	11 46	11 51	11 54		11 58	12 01	12 06	12 09	12 13	12 16	12 21	12 24	12 28		12 31	12 36	12 39	12 43	12 46	12 51	12 54	12 58	13 01	
Shadwell	d	11 48	11 53	11 56		12 00	12 03	12 08	12 11	12 15	12 18	12 23	12 26	12 30		12 33	12 38	12 41	12 45	12 48	12 53	12 56	13 00	13 03	
Wapping	d	11 50	11 55	11 58		12 02	12 05	12 10	12 13	12 17	12 20	12 25	12 28	12 32		12 35	12 40	12 43	12 47	12 50	12 55	12 58	13 02	13 05	
Rotherhithe	d	11 51	11 56	12 00		12 03	12 06	12 11	12 15	12 18	12 21	12 26	12 30	12 33		12 36	12 41	12 45	12 48	12 51	12 56	13 00	13 03	13 06	
Canada Water	d	11 53	11 58	12 02		12 05	12 08	12 13	12 17	12 20	12 23	12 28	12 32	12 35		12 38	12 43	12 47	12 50	12 53	12 58	13 02	13 05	13 08	
Surrey Quays	d	11 55	12 00	12 04		12 07	12 10	12 15	12 19	12 22	12 25	12 30	12 34	12 37		12 40	12 45	12 49	12 52	12 55	13 00	13 04	13 07	13 10	
New Cross	a		12 04					12 19				12 34					12 49				13 04				
New Cross Gate 4	d	12 00		12 08			12 15		12 23		12 30		12 38			12 45		12 53		13 00		13 08		13 15	
Brockley	d	12 02		12 11			12 17		12 26		12 32		12 41			12 47		12 56		13 02		13 11		13 17	
Honor Oak Park	d	12 05		12 13			12 20		12 28		12 35		12 43			12 50		12 58		13 05		13 13		13 20	
Forest Hill 4	d	12 07		12 16			12 22		12 31		12 37		12 46			12 52		13 01		13 07		13 16		13 22	
Sydenham	d	12 11		12 19			12 26		12 34		12 41		12 49			12 56		13 04		13 11		13 19		13 26	
Crystal Palace 4	a			12 24					12 39				12 54					13 09				13 24			
Penge West	d	12 13					12 28				12 43					12 58				13 13				13 28	
Anerley	d	12 15					12 30				12 45					13 00				13 15				13 30	
Norwood Junction 2	d	12 18					12 33				12 48					13 03				13 18				13 33	
West Croydon 4	a	12 24					12 39				12 54					13 09				13 24				13 39	
Queens Rd Peckham	d					12 14				12 29				12 44					12 59				13 14		
Peckham Rye 4	d					12 18				12 33				12 48					13 03				13 18		
Denmark Hill 4	d					12 22				12 37				12 52					13 07				13 22		
Clapham High Street ⊖	d					12 26				12 41				12 56					13 11				13 26		
Wandsworth Road	d					12 28				12 43				12 58					13 13				13 28		
Clapham Junction	a					12 35				12 54				13 05					13 20				13 35		

Table T178-F

Mondays to Fridays
16 December to 15 May

Highbury & Islington - New Cross, Crystal Palace, West Croydon and Clapham Junction

		LO	LO	LO	LO	LO	LO	LO	LO	LO		LO	LO	LO	LO	LO	LO	LO	LO	LO		LO	LO	LO	LO
Highbury & Islington	d		12 55		13 02		13 10		13 17			13 25		13 32		13 40		13 47		13 55			14 02		14 10
Canonbury	d		12 57		13 04		13 12		13 19			13 27		13 34		13 42		13 49		13 57			14 04		14 12
Dalston Junction	d	12 57	13 00	13 04	13 07	13 12	13 15	13 19	13 22	13 27		13 30	13 34	13 37	13 42	13 45	13 49	13 52	13 57	14 00		14 04	14 07	14 12	14 15
Haggerston	d	12 59	13 02	13 06	13 09	13 14	13 17	13 21	13 24	13 29		13 32	13 36	13 39	13 44	13 47	13 51	13 54	13 59	14 02		14 06	14 09	14 14	14 17
Hoxton	d	13 01	13 04	13 08	13 11	13 16	13 19	13 23	13 26	13 31		13 34	13 38	13 41	13 46	13 49	13 53	13 56	14 01	14 04		14 08	14 11	14 16	14 19
Shoreditch High Street	d	13 03	13 07	13 10	13 13	13 18	13 22	13 25	13 28	13 33		13 37	13 40	13 43	13 48	13 52	13 55	13 58	14 03	14 07		14 10	14 13	14 18	14 22
Whitechapel	d	13 06	13 09	13 13	13 16	13 21	13 24	13 28	13 31	13 36		13 39	13 43	13 46	13 51	13 54	13 58	14 01	14 06	14 09		14 13	14 16	14 21	14 24
Shadwell	d	13 08	13 11	13 15	13 18	13 23	13 26	13 30	13 33	13 38		13 41	13 45	13 48	13 53	13 56	14 00	14 03	14 08	14 11		14 15	14 18	14 23	14 26
Wapping	d	13 10	13 13	13 17	13 20	13 25	13 28	13 32	13 35	13 40		13 43	13 47	13 50	13 55	13 58	14 02	14 05	14 10	14 13		14 17	14 20	14 25	14 28
Rotherhithe	d	13 11	13 15	13 18	13 21	13 26	13 30	13 33	13 36	13 41		13 45	13 48	13 51	13 56	14 00	14 03	14 06	14 11	14 15		14 18	14 21	14 26	14 30
Canada Water	d	13 13	13 17	13 20	13 23	13 28	13 32	13 35	13 38	13 43		13 47	13 50	13 53	13 58	14 02	14 05	14 08	14 13	14 17		14 20	14 23	14 28	14 32
Surrey Quays	d	13 15	13 19	13 22	13 25	13 30	13 34	13 37	13 40	13 45		13 49	13 52	13 55	14 00	14 04	14 07	14 10	14 15	14 19		14 22	14 25	14 30	14 34
New Cross	a	13 19				13 34				13 49					14 04				14 19					14 34	
New Cross Gate 4	d		13 23		13 30		13 38		13 45			13 53		14 00		14 08		14 15		14 23			14 30		14 38
Brockley	d		13 26		13 32		13 41		13 47			13 56		14 02		14 11		14 17		14 26			14 32		14 41
Honor Oak Park	d		13 28		13 35		13 43		13 50			13 58		14 05		14 13		14 20		14 28			14 35		14 43
Forest Hill 4	d		13 31		13 37		13 46		13 52			14 01		14 07		14 16		14 22		14 31			14 37		14 46
Sydenham	d		13 34		13 41		13 49		13 56			14 04		14 11		14 19		14 26		14 34			14 41		14 49
Crystal Palace 4	a		13 39				13 54					14 09				14 24				14 39					14 54
Penge West	d				13 43				13 58					14 13				14 28					14 43		
Anerley	d				13 45				14 00					14 15				14 30					14 45		
Norwood Junction 2	d				13 48				14 03					14 18				14 33					14 48		
West Croydon 4	a				13 54				14 09					14 25				14 39					14 54		
Queens Rd Peckham	d			13 29				13 44					13 59				14 14					14 29			
Peckham Rye 4	d			13 33				13 48					14 03				14 18					14 33			
Denmark Hill 4	d			13 37				13 52					14 07				14 22					14 37			
Clapham High Street ⊖	d			13 41				13 56					14 11				14 26					14 41			
Wandsworth Road	d			13 43				13 58					14 13				14 28					14 43			
Clapham Junction	a			13 49				14 05					14 24				14 35					14 49			

		LO	LO	LO	LO	LO		LO	LO	LO	LO	LO	LO	LO	LO	LO		LO	LO	LO	LO	LO	LO	LO	LO
Highbury & Islington	d		14 17		14 25			14 32		14 40		14 47		14 55		15 02			15 10		15 17		15 25		15 32
Canonbury	d		14 19		14 27			14 34		14 42		14 49		14 57		15 04			15 12		15 19		15 27		15 34
Dalston Junction	d	14 19	14 22	14 27	14 30	14 34		14 37	14 42	14 45	14 49	14 52	14 57	15 00	15 04	15 07		15 12	15 15	15 19	15 22	15 27	15 30	15 34	15 37
Haggerston	d	14 21	14 24	14 29	14 32	14 36		14 39	14 44	14 47	14 51	14 54	14 59	15 02	15 06	15 09		15 14	15 17	15 21	15 24	15 29	15 32	15 36	15 39
Hoxton	d	14 23	14 26	14 31	14 34	14 38		14 41	14 46	14 49	14 53	14 56	15 01	15 04	15 08	15 11		15 16	15 19	15 23	15 26	15 31	15 34	15 38	15 41
Shoreditch High Street	d	14 25	14 28	14 33	14 37	14 40		14 43	14 48	14 52	14 55	14 58	15 03	15 07	15 10	15 13		15 18	15 22	15 25	15 28	15 33	15 37	15 40	15 43
Whitechapel	d	14 28	14 31	14 36	14 39	14 43		14 46	14 51	14 54	14 58	15 01	15 06	15 09	15 13	15 16		15 21	15 24	15 28	15 31	15 36	15 39	15 43	15 46
Shadwell	d	14 30	14 33	14 38	14 41	14 45		14 48	14 53	14 56	15 00	15 03	15 08	15 11	15 15	15 18		15 23	15 26	15 30	15 33	15 38	15 41	15 45	15 48
Wapping	d	14 32	14 35	14 40	14 43	14 47		14 50	14 55	14 58	15 02	15 05	15 10	15 13	15 17	15 20		15 25	15 28	15 32	15 35	15 40	15 43	15 47	15 50
Rotherhithe	d	14 33	14 36	14 41	14 45	14 48		14 51	14 56	15 00	15 03	15 06	15 11	15 15	15 18	15 21		15 26	15 30	15 33	15 36	15 41	15 45	15 48	15 51
Canada Water	d	14 35	14 38	14 43	14 47	14 50		14 53	14 58	15 02	15 05	15 08	15 13	15 17	15 20	15 23		15 28	15 32	15 35	15 38	15 43	15 47	15 50	15 53
Surrey Quays	d	14 37	14 40	14 45	14 49	14 52		14 55	15 00	15 04	15 07	15 10	15 15	15 19	15 22	15 25		15 30	15 34	15 37	15 40	15 45	15 49	15 52	15 55
New Cross	a			14 49					15 04				15 19					15 34				15 49			
New Cross Gate 4	d		14 45		14 53			15 00		15 08		15 15		15 23		15 30			15 38		15 45		15 53		16 00
Brockley	d		14 47		14 56			15 02		15 11		15 17		15 26		15 32			15 41		15 47		15 56		16 02
Honor Oak Park	d		14 50		14 58			15 05		15 13		15 20		15 28		15 35			15 43		15 50		15 58		16 05
Forest Hill 4	d		14 52		15 01			15 07		15 16		15 22		15 31		15 37			15 46		15 52		16 01		16 07
Sydenham	d		14 56		15 04			15 11		15 19		15 26		15 34		15 41			15 49		15 56		16 04		16 11
Crystal Palace 4	a				15 09					15 24				15 39					15 54				16 09		
Penge West	d		14 58					15 13				15 28				15 43					15 58				16 13
Anerley	d		15 00					15 15				15 30				15 45					16 00				16 15
Norwood Junction 2	d		15 03					15 18				15 33				15 48					16 03				16 18
West Croydon 4	a		15 09					15 24				15 39				15 54					16 09				16 28
Queens Rd Peckham	d	14 44				14 59					15 14				15 29					15 44				15 59	
Peckham Rye 4	d	14 48				15 03					15 18				15 33					15 48				16 03	
Denmark Hill 4	d	14 52				15 07					15 22				15 37					15 52				16 07	
Clapham High Street ⊖	d	14 56				15 11					15 26				15 41					15 56				16 11	
Wandsworth Road	d	14 58				15 13					15 28				15 43					15 58				16 13	
Clapham Junction	a	15 05				15 19					15 35				15 49					16 05				16 19	

		LO		LO	LO	LO	LO	LO	LO	LO	LO	LO		LO	LO	LO	LO	LO	LO	LO	LO	LO		LO	LO
Highbury & Islington	d			15 40		15 47		15 55		16 02		16 10			16 17		16 25		16 32		16 40			16 47	
Canonbury	d			15 42		15 49		15 57		16 04		16 12			16 19		16 27		16 34		16 42			16 49	
Dalston Junction	d	15 42		15 45	15 49	15 52	15 57	16 00	16 04	16 07	16 12	16 15		16 19	16 22	16 27	16 30	16 34	16 37	16 42	16 45	16 49		16 52	16 57
Haggerston	d	15 44		15 47	15 51	15 54	15 59	16 02	16 06	16 09	16 14	16 17		16 21	16 24	16 29	16 32	16 36	16 39	16 44	16 47	16 51		16 54	16 59
Hoxton	d	15 46		15 49	15 53	15 56	16 01	16 04	16 08	16 11	16 16	16 19		16 23	16 26	16 31	16 34	16 38	16 41	16 46	16 49	16 53		16 56	17 01
Shoreditch High Street	d	15 48		15 52	15 55	15 58	16 03	16 07	16 10	16 13	16 18	16 22		16 25	16 28	16 33	16 37	16 40	16 43	16 48	16 52	16 55		16 58	17 03
Whitechapel	d	15 51		15 54	15 58	16 01	16 06	16 09	16 13	16 16	16 21	16 24		16 28	16 31	16 36	16 39	16 43	16 46	16 51	16 54	16 58		17 01	17 06
Shadwell	d	15 53		15 56	16 00	16 03	16 08	16 11	16 15	16 18	16 23	16 26		16 30	16 33	16 38	16 41	16 45	16 48	16 53	16 56	17 00		17 03	17 08
Wapping	d	15 55		15 58	16 02	16 05	16 10	16 13	16 17	16 20	16 25	16 28		16 32	16 35	16 40	16 43	16 47	16 50	16 55	16 58	17 02		17 05	17 10
Rotherhithe	d	15 56		16 00	16 03	16 06	16 11	16 15	16 18	16 21	16 26	16 30		16 33	16 36	16 41	16 45	16 48	16 51	16 56	17 00	17 03		17 06	17 11
Canada Water	d	15 58		16 02	16 05	16 08	16 13	16 17	16 20	16 23	16 28	16 32		16 35	16 38	16 43	16 47	16 50	16 53	16 58	17 02	17 05		17 08	17 13
Surrey Quays	d	16 00		16 04	16 07	16 10	16 15	16 19	16 22	16 25	16 30	16 34		16 37	16 40	16 45	16 49	16 52	16 55	17 00	17 04	17 07		17 10	17 15
New Cross	a	16 04					16 19				16 34					16 49				17 04					17 19
New Cross Gate 4	d			16 08		16 15		16 23		16 30		16 38			16 45		16 53		17 00		17 08			17 15	
Brockley	d			16 11		16 17		16 26		16 32		16 41			16 47		16 56		17 02		17 11			17 17	
Honor Oak Park	d			16 13		16 20		16 28		16 35		16 43			16 50		16 58		17 05		17 13			17 20	
Forest Hill 4	d			16 16		16 22		16 31		16 37		16 46			16 52		17 01		17 07		17 16			17 22	
Sydenham	d			16 19		16 26		16 34		16 41		16 49			16 56		17 04		17 11		17 19			17 26	
Crystal Palace 4	a			16 24				16 39				16 54					17 09				17 24				
Penge West	d					16 28				16 43					16 58				17 13					17 28	
Anerley	d					16 30				16 45					17 00				17 15					17 30	
Norwood Junction 2	d					16 33				16 48					17 03				17 18					17 33	
West Croydon 4	a					16 43				16 58					17 13				17 28					17 43	
Queens Rd Peckham	d				16 14				16 29					16 44				16 59				17 14			
Peckham Rye 4	d				16 18				16 33					16 48				17 01				17 18			
Denmark Hill 4	d				16 22				16 37					16 52				17 07				17 22			
Clapham High Street ⊖	d				16 26				16 41					16 56				17 11				17 26			
Wandsworth Road	d				16 28				16 43					16 58				17 13				17 28			
Clapham Junction	a				16 35				16 49					17 05				17 19				17 35			

Table T178-F

Mondays to Fridays
16 December to 15 May

Highbury & Islington - New Cross, Crystal Palace, West Croydon and Clapham Junction

		LO	LO	LO	LO	LO	LO	LO		LO	LO	LO	LO	LO	LO	LO	LO	LO		LO	LO	LO	LO	LO	LO
Highbury & Islington	d	16 55		17 02		17 10		17 17			17 25		17 32		17 40		17 47			17 55		18 02		18 10	
Canonbury	d	16 57		17 04		17 12		17 19			17 27		17 34		17 42		17 49			17 57		18 04		18 12	
Dalston Junction	d	17 00	17 04	17 07	17 12	17 15	17 19	17 22		17 27	17 30	17 34	17 37	17 42	17 45	17 49	17 52	17 57		18 00	18 04	18 07	18 12	18 15	18 19
Haggerston	d	17 02	17 06	17 09	17 14	17 17	17 21	17 24		17 29	17 32	17 36	17 39	17 44	17 47	17 51	17 54	17 59		18 02	18 06	18 09	18 14	18 17	18 21
Hoxton	d	17 04	17 08	17 11	17 16	17 19	17 23	17 26		17 31	17 34	17 38	17 41	17 46	17 49	17 53	17 56	18 01		18 04	18 08	18 11	18 16	18 19	18 23
Shoreditch High Street	d	17 07	17 10	17 13	17 18	17 22	17 25	17 28		17 33	17 37	17 40	17 43	17 48	17 52	17 55	17 58	18 03		18 07	18 10	18 13	18 18	18 22	18 25
Whitechapel	d	17 09	17 13	17 16	17 21	17 24	17 28	17 31		17 36	17 39	17 43	17 46	17 51	17 54	17 58	18 01	18 06		18 09	18 13	18 16	18 21	18 24	18 28
Shadwell	d	17 11	17 15	17 18	17 23	17 26	17 30	17 33		17 38	17 41	17 45	17 48	17 53	17 56	18 00	18 03	18 08		18 11	18 15	18 18	18 23	18 26	18 30
Wapping	d	17 13	17 17	17 20	17 25	17 28	17 32	17 35		17 40	17 43	17 47	17 50	17 55	17 58	18 02	18 05	18 10		18 13	18 17	18 20	18 25	18 28	18 32
Rotherhithe	d	17 15	17 18	17 21	17 26	17 30	17 33	17 36		17 41	17 45	17 48	17 51	17 56	18 00	18 03	18 06	18 11		18 15	18 18	18 21	18 26	18 30	18 33
Canada Water	d	17 17	17 20	17 23	17 28	17 32	17 35	17 38		17 43	17 47	17 50	17 53	17 58	18 02	18 05	18 08	18 13		18 17	18 20	18 23	18 28	18 32	18 35
Surrey Quays	d	17 19	17 22	17 25	17 30	17 34	17 37	17 40		17 45	17 49	17 52	17 55	18 00	18 04	18 07	18 10	18 15		18 19	18 22	18 25	18 30	18 34	18 37
New Cross	a				17 34					17 49				18 04				18 19					18 34		
New Cross Gate 4	d	17 23		17 30		17 38		17 45			17 53		18 00		18 08		18 15			18 23		18 30		18 38	
Brockley	d	17 26		17 32		17 41		17 47			17 56		18 02		18 11		18 17			18 26		18 32		18 41	
Honor Oak Park	d	17 28		17 35		17 43		17 50			17 58		18 05		18 13		18 20			18 28		18 35		18 43	
Forest Hill 4	d	17 31		17 37		17 46		17 52			18 01		18 07		18 16		18 22			18 31		18 37		18 46	
Sydenham	d	17 34		17 41		17 49		17 56			18 04		18 11		18 19		18 26			18 34		18 41		18 49	
Crystal Palace 4	a	17 39				17 54					18 09				18 24					18 39				18 54	
Penge West	d			17 43				17 58					18 13				18 28					18 43			
Anerley	d			17 45				18 00					18 15				18 30					18 45			
Norwood Junction 2	d			17 48				18 03					18 18				18 33					18 48			
West Croydon 4	a			17 58				18 13					18 28				18 43					18 58			
Queens Rd Peckham	d		17 29				17 44					17 59				18 14					18 29				18 44
Peckham Rye 4	d		17 31				17 48					18 01				18 18					18 31				18 48
Denmark Hill 4	d		17 37				17 52					18 07				18 22					18 37				18 52
Clapham High Street ⊖	d		17 41				17 56					18 11				18 26					18 41				18 56
Wandsworth Road	d		17 43				17 58					18 13				18 28					18 43				18 58
Clapham Junction	a		17 49				18 05					18 19				18 35					18 49				19 05

		LO	LO	LO		LO	LO	LO	LO	LO	LO	LO	LO	LO		LO	LO	LO	LO	LO	LO	LO	LO	LO	
Highbury & Islington	d	18 17		18 25			18 32		18 40		18 47		18 55			19 02		19 10		19 17		19 25		19 32	
Canonbury	d	18 19		18 27			18 34		18 42		18 49		18 57			19 04		19 12		19 19		19 27		19 34	
Dalston Junction	d	18 22	18 27	18 30		18 34	18 37	18 42	18 45	18 49	18 52	18 57	19 00	19 04		19 07	19 12	19 15	19 19	19 22	19 27	19 30	19 34	19 37	
Haggerston	d	18 24	18 29	18 32		18 36	18 39	18 44	18 47	18 51	18 54	18 59	19 02	19 06		19 09	19 14	19 17	19 21	19 24	19 29	19 32	19 36	19 39	
Hoxton	d	18 26	18 31	18 34		18 38	18 41	18 46	18 49	18 53	18 56	19 01	19 04	19 08		19 11	19 16	19 19	19 23	19 26	19 31	19 34	19 38	19 41	
Shoreditch High Street	d	18 28	18 33	18 37		18 40	18 43	18 48	18 52	18 55	18 58	19 03	19 07	19 10		19 13	19 18	19 22	19 25	19 28	19 33	19 37	19 40	19 43	
Whitechapel	d	18 31	18 36	18 39		18 43	18 46	18 51	18 54	18 58	19 01	19 06	19 09	19 13		19 16	19 21	19 24	19 28	19 31	19 36	19 39	19 43	19 46	
Shadwell	d	18 33	18 38	18 41		18 45	18 48	18 53	18 56	19 00	19 03	19 08	19 11	19 15		19 18	19 23	19 26	19 30	19 33	19 38	19 41	19 45	19 48	
Wapping	d	18 35	18 40	18 43		18 47	18 50	18 55	18 58	19 02	19 05	19 10	19 13	19 17		19 20	19 25	19 28	19 32	19 35	19 40	19 43	19 47	19 50	
Rotherhithe	d	18 36	18 41	18 45		18 48	18 51	18 56	19 00	19 03	19 06	19 11	19 15	19 18		19 21	19 26	19 30	19 33	19 36	19 41	19 45	19 48	19 51	
Canada Water	d	18 38	18 43	18 47		18 50	18 53	18 58	19 02	19 05	19 08	19 13	19 17	19 20		19 23	19 28	19 32	19 35	19 38	19 43	19 47	19 50	19 53	
Surrey Quays	d	18 40	18 45	18 49		18 52	18 55	19 00	19 04	19 07	19 10	19 15	19 19	19 22		19 25	19 30	19 34	19 37	19 40	19 45	19 49	19 52	19 55	
New Cross	a		18 49					19 04				19 19					19 34				19 49				
New Cross Gate 4	d	18 45		18 53			19 00		19 08		19 15		19 23			19 30		19 38		19 45		19 53		20 00	
Brockley	d	18 47		18 56			19 02		19 11		19 17		19 26			19 32		19 41		19 47		19 56		20 02	
Honor Oak Park	d	18 50		18 58			19 05		19 13		19 20		19 28			19 35		19 43		19 50		19 58		20 05	
Forest Hill 4	d	18 52		19 01			19 07		19 16		19 22		19 31			19 37		19 46		19 52		20 01		20 07	
Sydenham	d	18 56		19 04			19 11		19 19		19 26		19 34			19 41		19 49		19 56		20 04		20 11	
Crystal Palace 4	a			19 09					19 24				19 39					19 54				20 09			
Penge West	d	18 58					19 13				19 28					19 43				19 58				20 13	
Anerley	d	19 00					19 15				19 30					19 45				20 00				20 15	
Norwood Junction 2	d	19 03					19 18				19 33					19 48				20 03				20 18	
West Croydon 4	a	19 13					19 28				19 43					19 59				20 13				20 28	
Queens Rd Peckham	d					18 59				19 14				19 29					19 44				19 59		
Peckham Rye 4	d					19 03				19 18				19 33					19 48				20 03		
Denmark Hill 4	d					19 07				19 22				19 37					19 52				20 07		
Clapham High Street ⊖	d					19 11				19 26				19 41					19 56				20 11		
Wandsworth Road	d					19 13				19 28				19 43					19 58				20 13		
Clapham Junction	a					19 19				19 35				19 49					20 05				20 19		

		LO	LO	LO	LO	LO	LO	LO	LO	LO		LO	LO	LO	LO	LO	LO	LO	LO	LO		LO	LO	LO	LO
Highbury & Islington	d		19 40		19 47		19 55		20 02			20 10		20 17		20 25		20 32		20 40			20 47		20 55
Canonbury	d		19 42		19 49		19 57		20 04			20 12		20 19		20 27		20 34		20 42			20 49		20 57
Dalston Junction	d	19 42	19 45	19 49	19 52	19 57	20 00	20 04	20 07	20 12		20 15	20 19	20 22	20 27	20 30	20 34	20 37	20 42	20 45		20 49	20 52	20 57	21 00
Haggerston	d	19 44	19 47	19 51	19 54	19 59	20 02	20 06	20 09	20 14		20 17	20 21	20 24	20 29	20 32	20 36	20 39	20 44	20 47		20 51	20 54	20 59	21 02
Hoxton	d	19 46	19 49	19 53	19 56	20 01	20 04	20 08	20 11	20 16		20 19	20 23	20 26	20 31	20 34	20 38	20 41	20 46	20 49		20 53	20 56	21 01	21 04
Shoreditch High Street	d	19 48	19 52	19 55	19 58	20 03	20 07	20 10	20 13	20 18		20 22	20 25	20 28	20 33	20 37	20 40	20 43	20 48	20 52		20 55	20 58	21 03	21 07
Whitechapel	d	19 51	19 54	19 58	20 01	20 06	20 09	20 13	20 16	20 21		20 24	20 28	20 31	20 36	20 39	20 43	20 46	20 51	20 54		20 58	21 01	21 06	21 09
Shadwell	d	19 53	19 56	20 00	20 03	20 08	20 11	20 15	20 18	20 23		20 26	20 30	20 33	20 38	20 41	20 45	20 48	20 53	20 56		21 00	21 03	21 08	21 11
Wapping	d	19 55	19 58	20 02	20 05	20 10	20 13	20 17	20 20	20 25		20 28	20 32	20 35	20 40	20 43	20 47	20 50	20 55	20 58		21 02	21 05	21 10	21 13
Rotherhithe	d	19 56	20 00	20 03	20 06	20 11	20 15	20 18	20 21	20 26		20 30	20 33	20 36	20 41	20 45	20 48	20 51	20 56	21 00		21 03	21 06	21 11	21 15
Canada Water	d	19 58	20 02	20 05	20 08	20 13	20 17	20 20	20 23	20 28		20 32	20 35	20 38	20 43	20 47	20 50	20 53	20 58	21 02		21 05	21 08	21 13	21 17
Surrey Quays	d	20 00	20 04	20 07	20 10	20 15	20 19	20 22	20 25	20 30		20 34	20 37	20 40	20 45	20 49	20 52	20 55	21 00	21 04		21 07	21 10	21 15	21 19
New Cross	a	20 04				20 19				20 34					20 49				21 04					21 19	
New Cross Gate 4	d		20 08		20 15		20 23		20 30			20 38		20 45		20 53		21 00		21 08			21 15		21 23
Brockley	d		20 11		20 17		20 26		20 32			20 41		20 47		20 56		21 02		21 11			21 17		21 26
Honor Oak Park	d		20 13		20 20		20 28		20 35			20 43		20 50		20 58		21 05		21 13			21 20		21 28
Forest Hill 4	d		20 16		20 22		20 31		20 37			20 46		20 52		21 01		21 07		21 16			21 22		21 31
Sydenham	d		20 19		20 26		20 34		20 41			20 49		20 56		21 04		21 11		21 19			21 26		21 34
Crystal Palace 4	a		20 24				20 39					20 54				21 09				21 24					21 39
Penge West	d				20 28				20 43					20 58				21 13					21 28		
Anerley	d				20 30				20 45					21 00				21 15					21 30		
Norwood Junction 2	d				20 33				20 48					21 03				21 18					21 33		
West Croydon 4	a				20 43				20 58					21 09				21 24					21 39		
Queens Rd Peckham	d			20 14				20 29					20 43				20 59					21 14			
Peckham Rye 4	d			20 18				20 33					20 48				21 03					21 18			
Denmark Hill 4	d			20 22				20 37					20 52				21 07					21 22			
Clapham High Street ⊖	d			20 26				20 41					20 56				21 11					21 26			
Wandsworth Road	d			20 28				20 43					20 58				21 13					21 28			
Clapham Junction	a			20 35				20 49					21 05				21 19					21 35			

Table T178-F

Mondays to Fridays

16 December to 15 May

Highbury & Islington - New Cross, Crystal Palace, West Croydon and Clapham Junction

		LO	LO	LO	LO	LO	LO	LO	LO	LO	LO	LO	LO	LO	LO	LO	LO	LO A	LO	LO	LO	LO	LO
Highbury & Islington	d		21 02		21 10		21 17		21 25		21 32		21 40		21 47		21 55		22 02		22 10		22 17
Canonbury	d		21 04		21 12		21 19		21 27		21 34		21 42		21 49		21 57		22 04		22 12		22 19
Dalston Junction	d	21 04	21 07	21 12	21 15	21 19	21 22	21 27	21 30	21 34	21 37	21 42	21 45	21 49	21 52	21 57	22 00	22 04	22 07	22 12	22 15	22 19	22 22
Haggerston	d	21 06	21 09	21 14	21 17	21 21	21 24	21 29	21 32	21 36	21 39	21 44	21 47	21 51	21 54	21 59	22 02	22 06	22 09	22 14	22 17	22 21	22 24
Hoxton	d	21 08	21 11	21 16	21 19	21 23	21 26	21 31	21 34	21 38	21 41	21 46	21 49	21 53	21 56	22 01	22 04	22 08	22 11	22 16	22 19	22 23	22 26
Shoreditch High Street	d	21 10	21 13	21 18	21 22	21 25	21 28	21 33	21 37	21 40	21 43	21 48	21 52	21 55	21 58	22 03	22 07	22 10	22 13	22 18	22 22	22 25	22 28
Whitechapel	d	21 13	21 16	21 21	21 24	21 28	21 31	21 36	21 39	21 43	21 46	21 51	21 54	21 58	22 01	22 06	22 09	22 13	22 16	22 21	22 24	22 28	22 31
Shadwell	d	21 15	21 18	21 23	21 26	21 30	21 33	21 38	21 41	21 45	21 48	21 53	21 56	22 00	22 03	22 08	22 11	22 15	22 18	22 23	22 26	22 30	22 33
Wapping	d	21 17	21 20	21 25	21 28	21 32	21 35	21 40	21 43	21 47	21 50	21 55	21 58	22 02	22 05	22 10	22 13	22 17	22 20	22 25	22 28	22 32	22 35
Rotherhithe	d	21 18	21 21	21 26	21 30	21 33	21 36	21 41	21 45	21 48	21 51	21 56	22 00	22 03	22 06	22 11	22 15	22 18	22 21	22 26	22 30	22 33	22 36
Canada Water	d	21 20	21 23	21 28	21 32	21 35	21 38	21 43	21 47	21 50	21 53	21 58	22 02	22 05	22 08	22 13	22 17	22 20	22 23	22 28	22 32	22 35	22 38
Surrey Quays	d	21 22	21 25	21 30	21 34	21 37	21 40	21 45	21 49	21 52	21 55	22 00	22 04	22 07	22 10	22 15	22 19	22 22	22 25	22 30	22 34	22 37	22 40
New Cross	a			21 34				21 49				22 04				22 19				22 34			
New Cross Gate	d		21 30		21 38		21 45		21 53		22 00		22 08		22 15		22 23		22 30		22 38		22 45
Brockley	d		21 32		21 41		21 47		21 56		22 02		22 11		22 17		22 26		22 32		22 41		22 47
Honor Oak Park	d		21 35		21 43		21 50		21 58		22 05		22 13		22 20		22 28		22 35		22 43		22 50
Forest Hill	d		21 37		21 46		21 52		22 01		22 07		22 16		22 22		22 31		22 37		22 46		22 52
Sydenham	d		21 41		21 49		21 56		22 04		22 11		22 19		22 26		22 34		22 41		22 49		22 56
Crystal Palace	a				21 54				22 09				22 24				22 39				22 54		
Penge West	d		21 43				21 58				22 13				22 28				22 43				22 58
Anerley	d		21 45				22 00				22 15				22 30				22 45				23 00
Norwood Junction	d		21 48				22 03				22 18				22 33				22 48				23 03
West Croydon	a		21 54				22 09				22 24				22 39				22 54				23 09
Queens Rd Peckham	d	21 29				21 44				21 59				22 14				22 29				22 44	
Peckham Rye	d	21 33				21 48				22 03				22 18				22 33				22 48	
Denmark Hill	d	21 37				21 52				22 07				22 22				22 37				22 52	
Clapham High Street	d	21 41				21 56				22 11				22 26				22 41				22 56	
Wandsworth Road	d	21 43				21 58				22 13				22 28				22a43				22 58	
Clapham Junction	a	21 49				22 05				22 19				22 35								23 05	

		LO	LO	LO	LO	LO	LO	LO	LO	LO	LO	LO	LO	LO	LO	LO	LO	LO	LO	LO	LO	LO
Highbury & Islington	d		22 25		22 32		22 40		22 47		22 55		23 02		23 10		23 17		23 25	23 30		
Canonbury	d		22 27		22 34		22 42		22 49		22 57		23 04		23 12		23 19		23 27	23 32		
Dalston Junction	d	22 27	22 30	22 34	22 37	22 42	22 45	22 49	22 52	22 57	23 00	23 04	23 07	23 12	23 15	23 19	23 22	23 27	23 30	23 35	23 38	23 42
Haggerston	d	22 29	22 32	22 36	22 39	22 44	22 47	22 51	22 54	22 59	23 02	23 06	23 09	23 14	23 17	23 21	23 24	23 29	23 32	23 36	23 39	23 44
Hoxton	d	22 31	22 34	22 38	22 41	22 46	22 49	22 53	22 56	23 01	23 04	23 08	23 11	23 16	23 19	23 23	23 26	23 31	23 34	23 38	23 41	23 46
Shoreditch High Street	d	22 33	22 37	22 40	22 43	22 48	22 52	22 55	22 58	23 03	23 07	23 10	23 13	23 18	23 22	23 25	23 28	23 33	23 37	23 40	23 43	23 48
Whitechapel	d	22 36	22 39	22 43	22 46	22 51	22 54	22 58	23 01	23 06	23 09	23 13	23 16	23 21	23 24	23 28	23 31	23 36	23 39	23 43	23 46	23 51
Shadwell	d	22 38	22 41	22 45	22 48	22 53	22 56	23 00	23 03	23 08	23 11	23 15	23 18	23 23	23 26	23 30	23 33	23 38	23 41	23 45	23 48	23 53
Wapping	d	22 40	22 43	22 47	22 50	22 55	22 58	23 02	23 05	23 10	23 13	23 17	23 20	23 25	23 28	23 32	23 35	23 40	23 43	23 47	23 50	23 55
Rotherhithe	d	22 41	22 45	22 48	22 51	22 56	23 00	23 03	23 06	23 11	23 15	23 18	23 21	23 26	23 30	23 33	23 36	23 41	23 45	23 48	23 51	23 56
Canada Water	d	22 43	22 47	22 50	22 53	22 58	23 02	23 05	23 08	23 13	23 17	23 20	23 23	23 28	23 32	23 35	23 38	23 43	23 47	23 50	23 53	23 58
Surrey Quays	d	22 45	22 49	22 52	22 55	23 00	23 04	23 07	23 10	23 15	23 19	23 22	23 25	23 30	23 34	23 37	23 40	23 45	23 49	23 52	23 55	00 01
New Cross	a	22 49				23 04				23 19				23 34				23 49				00 04
New Cross Gate	d		22 53		23 00		23 08		23 15		23 23		23 30		23 38		23 45		23 53		00 01	
Brockley	d		22 56		23 02		23 11		23 17		23 26		23 32		23 41		23 47		23 56		00 02	
Honor Oak Park	d		22 58		23 05		23 13		23 20		23 28		23 35		23 43		23 50		23 58		00 05	
Forest Hill	d		23 01		23 07		23 16		23 22		23 31		23 37		23 46		23 52		00 01		00 07	
Sydenham	d		23 04		23 11		23 19		23 26		23 34		23 41		23 49		23 56		00 04		00 11	
Crystal Palace	a		23 09				23 24				23 39				23 54				00 09			
Penge West	d				23 13				23 28				23 43				23 58				00 13	
Anerley	d				23 15				23 30				23 45				00 01				00 15	
Norwood Junction	d				23 18				23 33				23 48				00 03				00 18	
West Croydon	a				23 24				23 39				23 58				00 13				00 29	
Queens Rd Peckham	d			22 59				23 14				23 29				23 44				23 59		
Peckham Rye	d			23 03				23 18				23 33				23 48				00 02		
Denmark Hill	d			23 07				23 22				23 37				23 52				00 06		
Clapham High Street	d			23 11				23 26				23 41				23 56				00 10		
Wandsworth Road	d			23 13				23 28				23 43				23 58				00 12		
Clapham Junction	a			23 19				23 39				23 49				00 09				00 20		

		LO	LO	LO
Highbury & Islington	d	23 40		23 50
Canonbury	d	23 42		23 52
Dalston Junction	d	23 45	23 49	23 55
Haggerston	d	23 47	23 51	23 57
Hoxton	d	23 49	23 53	23 59
Shoreditch High Street	d	23 52	23 55	00 01
Whitechapel	d	23 54	23 58	00 04
Shadwell	d	23 56	23 59	00 06
Wapping	d	23 58	00 02	00 08
Rotherhithe	d	23 59	00 03	00 09
Canada Water	d	00 02	00 05	00 11
Surrey Quays	d	00 04	00 07	00 13
New Cross	a			
New Cross Gate	d	00 08		00a20
Brockley	d	00 11		
Honor Oak Park	d	00 13		
Forest Hill	d	00 16		
Sydenham	d	00 19		
Crystal Palace	a	00 24		
Penge West	d			
Anerley	d			
Norwood Junction	d			
West Croydon	a			
Queens Rd Peckham	d		00 14	
Peckham Rye	d		00 18	
Denmark Hill	d		00 22	
Clapham High Street	d		00 26	
Wandsworth Road	d		00 28	
Clapham Junction	a		00 35	

A To Battersea Park

NRT DECEMBER 19 EDITION

Table T178-F

Saturdays

21 December to 16 May

Highbury & Islington - New Cross, Crystal Palace, West Croydon and Clapham Junction

		LO A	LO A	LO B	LO B	LO A	LO A	LO B	LO A	LO	LO		LO	LO	LO	LO	LO	LO	LO	LO	LO	LO
Highbury & Islington	d									00 01	00 10		04 25	04 40	04 55	05 10	05 25			05 40		05 47
Canonbury	d									00 03	00 12		04 27	04 42	04 57	05 12	05 27			05 42		05 49
Dalston Junction	d									00 06	00 15		04 30	04 45	05 00	05 15	05 30	05 37	05 42	05 45	05 49	05 52
Haggerston	d									00 08	00 17		04 32	04 47	05 02	05 17	05 32	05 39	05 44	05 47	05 51	05 54
Hoxton	d									00 10	00 19		04 34	04 49	05 04	05 19	05 34	05 41	05 46	05 49	05 53	05 56
Shoreditch High Street	d								00 01	00 13	00 21		04 36	04 51	05 06	05 21	05 37	05 43	05 48	05 52	05 55	05 58
Whitechapel	d								00 04	00 15	00 24		04 39	04 54	05 09	05 24	05 39	05 46	05 51	05 54	05 58	06 01
Shadwell	d								00 06	00 17	00 26		04 41	04 56	05 11	05 26	05 41	05 48	05 53	05 56	06 00	06 03
Wapping	d							00 02	00 08	00 19	00 28		04 43	04 58	05 13	05 28	05 43	05 50	05 55	05 58	06 02	06 05
Rotherhithe	d							00 03	00 09	00 21	00 29		04 44	04 59	05 14	05 29	05 45	05 51	05 56	06 00	06 03	06 06
Canada Water	d						00 02	00 05	00 11	00 23	00 31		04 46	05 01	05 16	05 31	05 47	05 53	05 58	06 02	06 05	06 08
Surrey Quays	d				00 01		00 04	00 07	00 13	00 25	00 33		04 48	05 03	05 18	05 33	05 49	05 55	06 00	06 04	06 07	06 10
New Cross	a				00 04							and every 15 minutes until							06 04			
New Cross Gate	d			00 01			00 08		00a20		00a40		04a55	05a12	05a25	05a40	05 53	06 00		06 08		06 15
Brockley	d			00 02			00 11										05 56	06 02		06 11		06 17
Honor Oak Park	d			00 05			00 13										05 58	06 05		06 13		06 20
Forest Hill	d		00 01	00 07			00 16										06 01	06 07		06 16		06 22
Sydenham	d		00 04	00 11			00 19										06 04	06 11		06 19		06 26
Crystal Palace	a		00 09				00 24										06 08			06 23		
Penge West	d			00 13														06 13				06 28
Anerley	d	00 01		00 15														06 15				06 30
Norwood Junction	d	00 03		00 18														06 18				06 33
West Croydon	a	00 13		00 29														06 24				06 39
Queens Rd Peckham	d							00 14		00 29											06 14	
Peckham Rye	d					00 02		00 18		00 33											06 18	
Denmark Hill	d					00 06		00 22		00 37											06 22	
Clapham High Street	d					00 10		00 26		00 41											06 26	
Wandsworth Road	d					00 12		00 28		00 43											06 28	
Clapham Junction	a					00 20		00 35		00 51											06 35	

		LO	LO	LO	LO	LO	LO	LO	LO	LO	LO	LO	LO	LO	LO	LO	LO	LO	LO	LO	LO	LO	LO
Highbury & Islington	d	05 55		06 02		06 10		06 17		06 25		06 32		06 40		06 47		06 55		07 02		07 10	
Canonbury	d	05 57		06 04		06 12		06 19		06 27		06 34		06 42		06 49		06 57		07 04		07 12	
Dalston Junction	d	06 00	06 04	06 07	06 12	06 15	06 19	06 22	06 27	06 30	06 34	06 37	06 42	06 45	06 49	06 52	06 57	07 00	07 04	07 07	07 12	07 15	07 19
Haggerston	d	06 02	06 06	06 09	06 14	06 17	06 21	06 24	06 29	06 32	06 36	06 39	06 44	06 47	06 51	06 54	06 59	07 02	07 06	07 09	07 14	07 17	07 21
Hoxton	d	06 04	06 08	06 11	06 16	06 19	06 23	06 26	06 31	06 34	06 38	06 41	06 46	06 49	06 53	06 56	07 01	07 04	07 08	07 11	07 16	07 19	07 23
Shoreditch High Street	d	06 07	06 10	06 13	06 18	06 22	06 25	06 28	06 33	06 37	06 40	06 43	06 48	06 52	06 55	06 58	07 03	07 07	07 10	07 13	07 18	07 22	07 25
Whitechapel	d	06 09	06 13	06 16	06 21	06 24	06 28	06 31	06 36	06 39	06 43	06 46	06 51	06 54	06 58	07 01	07 06	07 09	07 13	07 16	07 21	07 24	07 28
Shadwell	d	06 11	06 15	06 18	06 23	06 26	06 30	06 33	06 38	06 41	06 45	06 48	06 53	06 56	07 00	07 03	07 08	07 11	07 15	07 18	07 23	07 26	07 30
Wapping	d	06 13	06 17	06 20	06 25	06 28	06 32	06 35	06 40	06 43	06 47	06 50	06 55	06 58	07 02	07 05	07 10	07 13	07 17	07 20	07 25	07 28	07 32
Rotherhithe	d	06 15	06 18	06 21	06 26	06 30	06 33	06 36	06 41	06 45	06 48	06 51	06 56	07 00	07 03	07 06	07 11	07 15	07 18	07 21	07 26	07 30	07 33
Canada Water	d	06 17	06 20	06 23	06 28	06 32	06 35	06 38	06 43	06 47	06 50	06 53	06 58	07 02	07 05	07 08	07 13	07 17	07 20	07 23	07 28	07 32	07 35
Surrey Quays	d	06 19	06 22	06 25	06 30	06 34	06 37	06 40	06 45	06 49	06 52	06 55	07 00	07 04	07 07	07 10	07 15	07 19	07 22	07 25	07 30	07 34	07 37
New Cross	a				06 34				06 49				07 04				07 19				07 34		
New Cross Gate	d	06 23		06 30		06 38		06 45		06 53		07 00		07 08		07 15		07 23		07 30		07 38	
Brockley	d	06 26		06 32		06 41		06 47		06 56		07 02		07 11		07 17		07 26		07 32		07 41	
Honor Oak Park	d	06 28		06 35		06 43		06 50		06 58		07 05		07 13		07 20		07 28		07 35		07 43	
Forest Hill	d	06 31		06 37		06 46		06 52		07 01		07 07		07 16		07 22		07 31		07 37		07 46	
Sydenham	d	06 34		06 41		06 49		06 56		07 04		07 11		07 19		07 26		07 34		07 41		07 49	
Crystal Palace	a	06 38				06 53				07 08				07 23				07 38				07 53	
Penge West	d			06 43				06 58				07 13				07 28				07 43			
Anerley	d			06 45				07 00				07 15				07 30				07 45			
Norwood Junction	d			06 48				07 03				07 18				07 33				07 48			
West Croydon	a			06 54				07 09				07 25				07 39				07 54			
Queens Rd Peckham	d		06 29				06 44				06 59				07 14				07 29				07 44
Peckham Rye	d		06 33				06 48				07 03				07 18				07 33				07 48
Denmark Hill	d		06 37				06 52				07 07				07 22				07 37				07 52
Clapham High Street	d		06 41				06 56				07 11				07 26				07 41				07 56
Wandsworth Road	d		06 43				06 58				07 13				07 28				07 43				07 58
Clapham Junction	a		06 49				07 05				07 19				07 35				07 49				08 05

		LO	LO	LO	LO	LO	LO	LO	LO	LO	LO	LO	LO	LO	LO	LO	LO	LO	LO	LO	LO	LO	LO
Highbury & Islington	d	07 17		07 25		07 32		07 40		07 47		07 55		08 02		08 10		08 17		08 25		08 32	
Canonbury	d	07 19		07 27		07 34		07 42		07 49		07 57		08 04		08 12		08 19		08 27		08 34	
Dalston Junction	d	07 22	07 27	07 30	07 34	07 37	07 42	07 45	07 49	07 52	07 57	08 00	08 04	08 07	08 12	08 15	08 19	08 22	08 27	08 30	08 34	08 37	08 42
Haggerston	d	07 24	07 29	07 32	07 36	07 39	07 44	07 47	07 51	07 54	07 59	08 02	08 06	08 09	08 14	08 17	08 21	08 24	08 29	08 32	08 36	08 39	08 44
Hoxton	d	07 26	07 31	07 34	07 38	07 41	07 46	07 49	07 53	07 56	08 01	08 04	08 08	08 11	08 16	08 19	08 23	08 26	08 31	08 34	08 38	08 41	08 46
Shoreditch High Street	d	07 28	07 33	07 37	07 40	07 43	07 48	07 52	07 55	07 58	08 03	08 07	08 10	08 13	08 18	08 22	08 25	08 28	08 33	08 37	08 40	08 43	08 48
Whitechapel	d	07 31	07 36	07 39	07 43	07 46	07 51	07 54	07 58	08 01	08 06	08 09	08 13	08 16	08 21	08 24	08 28	08 31	08 36	08 39	08 43	08 46	08 51
Shadwell	d	07 33	07 38	07 41	07 45	07 48	07 53	07 56	08 00	08 03	08 08	08 11	08 15	08 18	08 23	08 26	08 30	08 33	08 38	08 41	08 45	08 48	08 53
Wapping	d	07 35	07 40	07 43	07 47	07 50	07 55	07 58	08 02	08 05	08 10	08 13	08 17	08 20	08 25	08 28	08 32	08 35	08 40	08 43	08 47	08 50	08 55
Rotherhithe	d	07 36	07 41	07 45	07 48	07 51	07 56	08 00	08 03	08 06	08 11	08 15	08 18	08 21	08 26	08 30	08 33	08 36	08 41	08 45	08 48	08 51	08 56
Canada Water	d	07 38	07 43	07 47	07 50	07 53	07 58	08 02	08 05	08 08	08 13	08 17	08 20	08 23	08 28	08 32	08 35	08 38	08 43	08 47	08 50	08 53	08 58
Surrey Quays	d	07 40	07 45	07 49	07 52	07 55	08 00	08 04	08 07	08 10	08 15	08 19	08 22	08 25	08 30	08 34	08 37	08 40	08 45	08 49	08 52	08 55	09 00
New Cross	a		07 49				08 04				08 19				08 34				08 49				09 04
New Cross Gate	d	07 45		07 53		08 00		08 08		08 15		08 23		08 30		08 38		08 45		08 53		09 00	
Brockley	d	07 47		07 56		08 02		08 11		08 17		08 26		08 32		08 41		08 47		08 56		09 02	
Honor Oak Park	d	07 50		07 58		08 05		08 13		08 20		08 28		08 35		08 43		08 50		08 58		09 05	
Forest Hill	d	07 52		08 01		08 07		08 16		08 22		08 31		08 37		08 46		08 52		09 01		09 07	
Sydenham	d	07 56		08 04		08 11		08 19		08 26		08 34		08 41		08 49		08 56		09 04		09 11	
Crystal Palace	a			08 08				08 23				08 39				08 54				09 09			
Penge West	d	07 58				08 13				08 28				08 43				08 58				09 13	
Anerley	d	08 00				08 15				08 30				08 45				09 00				09 15	
Norwood Junction	d	08 03				08 18				08 33				08 48				09 03				09 18	
West Croydon	a	08 09				08 24				08 39				08 58				09 13				09 28	
Queens Rd Peckham	d				07 59				08 14				08 29				08 44				08 59		
Peckham Rye	d				08 03				08 18				08 33				08 48				09 03		
Denmark Hill	d				08 07				08 22				08 37				08 52				09 07		
Clapham High Street	d				08 11				08 26				08 41				08 56				09 11		
Wandsworth Road	d				08 13				08 28				08 43				08 58				09 13		
Clapham Junction	a				08 19				08 35				08 49				09 05				09 19		

A From Highbury and Islington Ell

B From Dalston Junction Stn Ell

Table T178-F

Saturdays

21 December to 16 May

Highbury & Islington - New Cross, Crystal Palace, West Croydon and Clapham Junction

		LO		LO	LO	LO	LO	LO	LO	LO	LO	LO		LO	LO	LO	LO	LO	LO	LO	LO	LO		LO	LO
Highbury & Islington	d	08 40			08 47		08 55		09 02		09 10			09 17		09 25		09 32		09 40		09 47			09 55
Canonbury	d	08 42			08 49		08 57		09 04		09 12			09 19		09 27		09 34		09 42		09 49			09 57
Dalston Junction	d	08 45		08 49	08 52	08 57	09 00	09 04	09 07	09 12	09 15	09 19		09 22	09 27	09 30	09 34	09 37	09 42	09 45	09 49	09 52		09 57	10 00
Haggerston	d	08 47		08 51	08 54	08 59	09 02	09 06	09 09	09 14	09 17	09 21		09 24	09 29	09 32	09 36	09 39	09 44	09 47	09 51	09 54		09 59	10 02
Hoxton	d	08 49		08 53	08 56	09 01	09 04	09 08	09 11	09 16	09 19	09 23		09 26	09 31	09 34	09 38	09 41	09 46	09 49	09 53	09 56		10 01	10 04
Shoreditch High Street	d	08 52		08 55	08 58	09 03	09 07	09 10	09 13	09 18	09 22	09 25		09 28	09 33	09 37	09 40	09 43	09 48	09 52	09 55	09 58		10 03	10 07
Whitechapel	d	08 54		08 58	09 01	09 06	09 09	09 13	09 16	09 21	09 24	09 28		09 31	09 36	09 39	09 43	09 46	09 51	09 54	09 58	10 01		10 06	10 09
Shadwell	d	08 56		09 00	09 03	09 08	09 11	09 15	09 18	09 23	09 26	09 30		09 33	09 38	09 41	09 45	09 48	09 53	09 56	10 00	10 03		10 08	10 11
Wapping	d	08 58		09 02	09 05	09 10	09 13	09 17	09 20	09 25	09 28	09 32		09 35	09 40	09 43	09 47	09 50	09 55	09 58	10 02	10 05		10 10	10 13
Rotherhithe	d	09 00		09 03	09 06	09 11	09 15	09 18	09 21	09 26	09 30	09 33		09 36	09 41	09 45	09 48	09 51	09 56	10 00	10 03	10 06		10 11	10 15
Canada Water	d	09 02		09 05	09 08	09 13	09 17	09 20	09 23	09 28	09 32	09 35		09 38	09 43	09 47	09 50	09 53	09 58	10 02	10 05	10 08		10 13	10 17
Surrey Quays	d	09 04		09 07	09 10	09 15	09 19	09 22	09 25	09 30	09 34	09 37		09 40	09 45	09 49	09 52	09 55	10 00	10 04	10 07	10 10		10 15	10 19
New Cross	a					09 19				09 34					09 49				10 04					10 19	
New Cross Gate 4	d	09 08			09 15		09 23		09 30		09 38			09 45		09 53		10 00		10 08		10 15			10 23
Brockley	d	09 11			09 17		09 26		09 32		09 41			09 47		09 56		10 02		10 11		10 17			10 26
Honor Oak Park	d	09 13			09 20		09 28		09 35		09 43			09 50		09 58		10 05		10 13		10 20			10 28
Forest Hill 4	d	09 16			09 22		09 31		09 37		09 46			09 52		10 01		10 07		10 16		10 22			10 31
Sydenham	d	09 19			09 26		09 34		09 41		09 49			09 56		10 04		10 11		10 19		10 26			10 34
Crystal Palace 4	a	09 24					09 38				09 53					10 08				10 23					10 38
Penge West	d				09 28				09 43					09 58				10 13				10 28			
Anerley	d				09 30				09 45					10 00				10 15				10 30			
Norwood Junction 2	d				09 33				09 48					10 03				10 18				10 33			
West Croydon 4	a				09 43				09 58					10 13				10 28				10 43			
Queens Rd Peckham	d			09 14				09 29				09 44					09 59				10 14				
Peckham Rye 4	d			09 18				09 33				09 48					10 03				10 18				
Denmark Hill 4	d			09 22				09 37				09 52					10 07				10 22				
Clapham High Street ⊖	d			09 26				09 41				09 56					10 11				10 26				
Wandsworth Road	d			09 28				09 43				09 58					10 13				10 28				
Clapham Junction	a			09 35				09 49				10 05					10 19				10 35				

		LO	LO	LO	LO	LO	LO	LO		LO	LO	LO	LO	LO	LO	LO	LO	LO		LO	LO	LO	LO	LO	LO
Highbury & Islington	d		10 02		10 10		10 17			10 25		10 32		10 40		10 47		10 55			11 02		11 10		11 17
Canonbury	d		10 04		10 12		10 19			10 27		10 34		10 42		10 49		10 57			11 04		11 12		11 19
Dalston Junction	d	10 04	10 07	10 12	10 15	10 19	10 22	10 27		10 30	10 34	10 37	10 42	10 45	10 49	10 52	10 57	11 00		11 04	11 07	11 12	11 15	11 19	11 22
Haggerston	d	10 06	10 09	10 14	10 17	10 21	10 24	10 29		10 32	10 36	10 39	10 44	10 47	10 51	10 54	10 59	11 02		11 06	11 09	11 14	11 17	11 21	11 24
Hoxton	d	10 08	10 11	10 16	10 19	10 23	10 26	10 31		10 34	10 38	10 41	10 46	10 49	10 53	10 56	11 01	11 04		11 08	11 11	11 16	11 19	11 23	11 26
Shoreditch High Street	d	10 10	10 13	10 18	10 22	10 25	10 28	10 33		10 37	10 40	10 43	10 48	10 52	10 55	10 58	11 03	11 07		11 10	11 13	11 18	11 22	11 25	11 28
Whitechapel	d	10 13	10 16	10 21	10 24	10 28	10 31	10 36		10 39	10 43	10 46	10 51	10 54	10 58	11 01	11 06	11 09		11 13	11 16	11 21	11 24	11 28	11 31
Shadwell	d	10 15	10 18	10 23	10 26	10 30	10 33	10 38		10 41	10 45	10 48	10 53	10 56	11 00	11 03	11 08	11 11		11 15	11 18	11 23	11 26	11 30	11 33
Wapping	d	10 17	10 20	10 25	10 28	10 32	10 35	10 40		10 43	10 47	10 50	10 55	10 58	11 02	11 05	11 10	11 13		11 17	11 20	11 25	11 28	11 32	11 35
Rotherhithe	d	10 18	10 21	10 26	10 30	10 33	10 36	10 41		10 45	10 48	10 51	10 56	11 00	11 03	11 06	11 11	11 15		11 18	11 21	11 26	11 30	11 33	11 36
Canada Water	d	10 20	10 23	10 28	10 32	10 35	10 38	10 43		10 47	10 50	10 53	10 58	11 02	11 05	11 08	11 13	11 17		11 20	11 23	11 28	11 32	11 35	11 38
Surrey Quays	d	10 22	10 25	10 30	10 34	10 37	10 40	10 45		10 49	10 52	10 55	11 00	11 04	11 07	11 10	11 15	11 19		11 22	11 25	11 30	11 34	11 37	11 40
New Cross	a			10 34				10 49					11 04				11 19					11 34			
New Cross Gate 4	d		10 30		10 38		10 45			10 53		11 00		11 08		11 15		11 23			11 30		11 38		11 45
Brockley	d		10 32		10 41		10 47			10 56		11 02		11 11		11 17		11 26			11 32		11 41		11 47
Honor Oak Park	d		10 35		10 43		10 50			10 58		11 05		11 13		11 20		11 28			11 35		11 43		11 50
Forest Hill 4	d		10 37		10 46		10 52			11 01		11 07		11 16		11 22		11 31			11 37		11 46		11 52
Sydenham	d		10 41		10 49		10 56			11 04		11 11		11 19		11 26		11 34			11 41		11 49		11 56
Crystal Palace 4	a				10 53					11 08				11 23				11 38					11 53		
Penge West	d		10 43				10 58					11 13				11 28					11 43				11 58
Anerley	d		10 45				11 00					11 15				11 30					11 45				12 00
Norwood Junction 2	d		10 48				11 03					11 18				11 33					11 48				12 03
West Croydon 4	a		10 54				11 09					11 24				11 39					11 54				12 09
Queens Rd Peckham	d	10 29				10 44					10 59				11 14					11 29				11 44	
Peckham Rye 4	d	10 33				10 48					11 03				11 18					11 33				11 48	
Denmark Hill 4	d	10 37				10 52					11 07				11 22					11 37				11 52	
Clapham High Street ⊖	d	10 41				10 56					11 11				11 26					11 41				11 56	
Wandsworth Road	d	10 43				10 58					11 13				11 28					11 43				11 58	
Clapham Junction	a	10 49				11 05					11 19				11 35					11 49				12 05	

		LO	LO	LO		LO	LO	LO	LO	LO	LO	LO	LO	LO		LO	LO	LO	LO	LO	LO	LO	LO	LO	
Highbury & Islington	d		11 25			11 32		11 40		11 47		11 55		12 02			12 10		12 17		12 25		12 32		
Canonbury	d		11 27			11 34		11 42		11 49		11 57		12 04			12 12		12 19		12 27		12 34		
Dalston Junction	d	11 27	11 30	11 34		11 37	11 42	11 45	11 49	11 52	11 57	12 00	12 04	12 07		12 12	12 15	12 19	12 22	12 27	12 30	12 34	12 37	12 42	
Haggerston	d	11 29	11 32	11 36		11 39	11 44	11 47	11 51	11 54	11 59	12 02	12 06	12 09		12 14	12 17	12 21	12 24	12 29	12 32	12 36	12 39	12 44	
Hoxton	d	11 31	11 34	11 38		11 41	11 46	11 49	11 53	11 56	12 01	12 04	12 08	12 11		12 16	12 19	12 23	12 26	12 31	12 34	12 38	12 41	12 46	
Shoreditch High Street	d	11 33	11 37	11 40		11 43	11 48	11 52	11 55	11 58	12 03	12 07	12 10	12 13		12 18	12 22	12 25	12 28	12 33	12 37	12 40	12 43	12 48	
Whitechapel	d	11 36	11 39	11 43		11 46	11 51	11 54	11 58	12 01	12 06	12 09	12 13	12 16		12 21	12 24	12 28	12 31	12 36	12 39	12 43	12 46	12 51	
Shadwell	d	11 38	11 41	11 45		11 48	11 53	11 56	12 00	12 03	12 08	12 11	12 15	12 18		12 23	12 26	12 30	12 33	12 38	12 41	12 45	12 48	12 53	
Wapping	d	11 40	11 43	11 47		11 50	11 55	11 58	12 02	12 05	12 10	12 13	12 17	12 20		12 25	12 28	12 32	12 35	12 40	12 43	12 47	12 50	12 55	
Rotherhithe	d	11 41	11 45	11 48		11 51	11 56	12 00	12 03	12 06	12 11	12 15	12 18	12 21		12 26	12 30	12 33	12 36	12 41	12 45	12 48	12 51	12 56	
Canada Water	d	11 43	11 47	11 50		11 53	11 58	12 02	12 05	12 08	12 13	12 17	12 20	12 23		12 28	12 32	12 35	12 38	12 43	12 47	12 50	12 53	12 58	
Surrey Quays	d	11 45	11 49	11 52		11 55	12 00	12 04	12 07	12 10	12 15	12 19	12 22	12 25		12 30	12 34	12 37	12 40	12 45	12 49	12 52	12 55	13 00	
New Cross	a	11 49					12 04				12 19					12 34				12 49				13 04	
New Cross Gate 4	d		11 53			12 00		12 08		12 15		12 23		12 30			12 38		12 45		12 53		13 00		
Brockley	d		11 56			12 02		12 11		12 17		12 26		12 32			12 41		12 47		12 56		13 02		
Honor Oak Park	d		11 58			12 05		12 13		12 20		12 28		12 35			12 43		12 50		12 58		13 05		
Forest Hill 4	d		12 01			12 07		12 16		12 22		12 31		12 37			12 46		12 52		13 01		13 07		
Sydenham	d		12 04			12 11		12 19		12 26		12 34		12 41			12 49		12 56		13 04		13 11		
Crystal Palace 4	a		12 08					12 23				12 38					12 53				13 08				
Penge West	d					12 13				12 28				12 43					12 58				13 13		
Anerley	d					12 15				12 30				12 45					13 00				13 15		
Norwood Junction 2	d					12 18				12 33				12 48					13 03				13 18		
West Croydon 4	a					12 24				12 39				12 54					13 09				13 24		
Queens Rd Peckham	d			11 59					12 14				12 29					12 44				12 59			
Peckham Rye 4	d			12 03					12 18				12 33					12 48				13 03			
Denmark Hill 4	d			12 07					12 22				12 37					12 52				13 07			
Clapham High Street ⊖	d			12 11					12 26				12 41					12 56				13 11			
Wandsworth Road	d			12 13					12 28				12 43					12 58				13 13			
Clapham Junction	a			12 19					12 35				12 49					13 05				13 19			

Table T178-F

Saturdays

21 December to 16 May

Highbury & Islington - New Cross, Crystal Palace, West Croydon and Clapham Junction

		LO	LO	LO	LO	LO	LO	LO	LO	LO		LO	LO	LO	LO	LO	LO	LO	LO	LO		LO	LO	LO	LO
Highbury & Islington	d	12 40		12 47		12 55		13 02		13 10			13 17		13 25		13 32		13 40			13 47		13 55	
Canonbury	d	12 42		12 49		12 57		13 04		13 12			13 19		13 27		13 34		13 42			13 49		13 57	
Dalston Junction	d	12 45	12 49	12 52	12 57	13 00	13 04	13 07	13 12	13 15		13 19	13 22	13 27	13 30	13 34	13 37	13 42	13 45	13 49		13 52	13 57	14 00	14 04
Haggerston	d	12 47	12 51	12 54	12 59	13 02	13 06	13 09	13 14	13 17		13 21	13 24	13 29	13 32	13 36	13 39	13 44	13 47	13 51		13 54	13 59	14 02	14 06
Hoxton	d	12 49	12 53	12 56	13 01	13 04	13 08	13 11	13 16	13 19		13 23	13 26	13 31	13 34	13 38	13 41	13 46	13 49	13 53		13 56	14 01	14 04	14 08
Shoreditch High Street	d	12 52	12 55	12 58	13 03	13 07	13 10	13 13	13 18	13 22		13 25	13 28	13 33	13 37	13 40	13 43	13 48	13 52	13 55		13 58	14 03	14 07	14 10
Whitechapel	d	12 54	12 58	13 01	13 06	13 09	13 13	13 16	13 21	13 24		13 28	13 31	13 36	13 39	13 43	13 46	13 51	13 54	13 58		14 01	14 06	14 09	14 13
Shadwell	d	12 56	13 00	13 03	13 08	13 11	13 15	13 18	13 23	13 26		13 30	13 33	13 38	13 41	13 45	13 48	13 53	13 56	14 00		14 03	14 08	14 11	14 15
Wapping	d	12 58	13 02	13 05	13 10	13 13	13 17	13 20	13 25	13 28		13 32	13 35	13 40	13 43	13 47	13 50	13 55	13 58	14 02		14 05	14 10	14 13	14 17
Rotherhithe	d	13 00	13 03	13 06	13 11	13 15	13 18	13 21	13 26	13 30		13 33	13 36	13 41	13 45	13 48	13 51	13 56	14 00	14 03		14 06	14 11	14 15	14 18
Canada Water	d	13 02	13 05	13 08	13 13	13 17	13 20	13 23	13 28	13 32		13 35	13 38	13 43	13 47	13 50	13 53	13 58	14 02	14 05		14 08	14 13	14 17	14 20
Surrey Quays	d	13 04	13 07	13 10	13 15	13 19	13 22	13 25	13 30	13 34		13 37	13 40	13 45	13 49	13 52	13 55	14 00	14 04	14 07		14 10	14 15	14 19	14 22
New Cross	a				13 19				13 34					13 49				14 04					14 19		
New Cross Gate 4	d	13 08		13 15		13 23		13 30		13 38			13 45		13 53		14 00		14 08			14 15		14 23	
Brockley	d	13 11		13 17		13 26		13 32		13 41			13 47		13 56		14 02		14 11			14 17		14 26	
Honor Oak Park	d	13 13		13 20		13 28		13 35		13 43			13 50		13 58		14 05		14 13			14 20		14 28	
Forest Hill 4	d	13 16		13 22		13 31		13 37		13 46			13 52		14 01		14 07		14 16			14 22		14 31	
Sydenham	d	13 19		13 26		13 34		13 41		13 49			13 56		14 04		14 11		14 19			14 26		14 34	
Crystal Palace 4	a	13 23				13 38				13 53					14 08				14 23					14 38	
Penge West	d			13 28				13 43					13 58				14 13					14 28			
Anerley	d			13 30				13 45					14 00				14 15					14 30			
Norwood Junction 2	d			13 33				13 48					14 03				14 18					14 33			
West Croydon 4	a			13 39				13 54					14 09				14 24					14 39			
Queens Rd Peckham	d		13 14				13 29					13 44				13 59				14 14					14 29
Peckham Rye 4	d		13 16				13 33					13 48				14 03				14 18					14 33
Denmark Hill 4	d		13 22				13 37					13 52				14 07				14 22					14 37
Clapham High Street ⊖	d		13 26				13 41					13 56				14 11				14 26					14 41
Wandsworth Road	d		13 28				13 43					13 58				14 13				14 28					14 43
Clapham Junction	a		13 35				13 49					14 05				14 19				14 35					14 49

		LO	LO	LO	LO	LO		LO	LO	LO	LO	LO	LO	LO	LO	LO		LO	LO	LO	LO	LO	LO	LO	LO
Highbury & Islington	d	14 02		14 10		14 17			14 25		14 32		14 40		14 47			14 55		15 02		15 10		15 17	
Canonbury	d	14 04		14 12		14 19			14 27		14 34		14 42		14 49			14 57		15 04		15 12		15 19	
Dalston Junction	d	14 07	14 12	14 15	14 19	14 22		14 27	14 30	14 34	14 37	14 42	14 45	14 49	14 52	14 57		15 00	15 04	15 07	15 12	15 15	15 19	15 22	15 27
Haggerston	d	14 09	14 14	14 17	14 21	14 24		14 29	14 32	14 36	14 39	14 44	14 47	14 51	14 54	14 59		15 02	15 06	15 09	15 14	15 17	15 21	15 24	15 29
Hoxton	d	14 11	14 16	14 19	14 23	14 26		14 31	14 34	14 38	14 41	14 46	14 49	14 53	14 56	15 01		15 04	15 08	15 11	15 16	15 19	15 23	15 26	15 31
Shoreditch High Street	d	14 13	14 18	14 22	14 25	14 28		14 33	14 37	14 40	14 43	14 48	14 52	14 55	14 58	15 03		15 07	15 10	15 13	15 18	15 22	15 25	15 28	15 33
Whitechapel	d	14 16	14 21	14 24	14 28	14 31		14 36	14 39	14 43	14 46	14 51	14 54	14 58	15 01	15 06		15 09	15 13	15 16	15 21	15 24	15 28	15 31	15 36
Shadwell	d	14 18	14 23	14 26	14 30	14 33		14 38	14 41	14 45	14 48	14 53	14 56	15 00	15 03	15 08		15 11	15 15	15 18	15 23	15 26	15 30	15 33	15 38
Wapping	d	14 20	14 25	14 28	14 32	14 35		14 40	14 43	14 47	14 50	14 55	14 58	15 02	15 05	15 10		15 13	15 17	15 20	15 25	15 28	15 32	15 35	15 40
Rotherhithe	d	14 21	14 26	14 30	14 33	14 36		14 41	14 45	14 48	14 51	14 56	15 00	15 03	15 06	15 11		15 15	15 18	15 21	15 26	15 30	15 33	15 36	15 41
Canada Water	d	14 23	14 28	14 32	14 35	14 38		14 43	14 47	14 50	14 53	14 58	15 02	15 05	15 08	15 13		15 17	15 20	15 23	15 28	15 32	15 35	15 38	15 43
Surrey Quays	d	14 25	14 30	14 34	14 37	14 40		14 45	14 49	14 52	14 55	15 00	15 04	15 07	15 10	15 15		15 19	15 22	15 25	15 30	15 34	15 37	15 40	15 45
New Cross	a		14 34					14 49				15 04				15 19					15 34				15 49
New Cross Gate 4	d	14 30		14 38		14 45			14 53		15 00		15 08		15 15			15 23		15 30		15 38		15 45	
Brockley	d	14 32		14 41		14 47			14 56		15 02		15 11		15 17			15 26		15 32		15 41		15 47	
Honor Oak Park	d	14 35		14 43		14 50			14 58		15 05		15 13		15 20			15 28		15 35		15 43		15 50	
Forest Hill 4	d	14 37		14 46		14 52			15 01		15 07		15 16		15 22			15 31		15 37		15 46		15 52	
Sydenham	d	14 41		14 49		14 56			15 04		15 11		15 19		15 26			15 34		15 41		15 49		15 56	
Crystal Palace 4	a			14 53					15 08				15 23					15 38				15 53			
Penge West	d	14 43				14 58					15 13				15 28					15 43				15 58	
Anerley	d	14 45				15 00					15 15				15 30					15 45				16 00	
Norwood Junction 2	d	14 48				15 03					15 18				15 33					15 48				16 03	
West Croydon 4	a	14 54				15 09					15 24				15 39					15 58				16 13	
Queens Rd Peckham	d				14 44					14 59				15 14					15 29				15 44		
Peckham Rye 4	d				14 48					15 03				15 18					15 33				15 48		
Denmark Hill 4	d				14 52					15 07				15 22					15 37				15 52		
Clapham High Street ⊖	d				14 56					15 11				15 26					15 41				15 56		
Wandsworth Road	d				14 58					15 13				15 28					15 43				15 58		
Clapham Junction	a				15 05					15 19				15 35					15 49				16 05		

		LO		LO	LO	LO	LO	LO	LO	LO	LO	LO		LO	LO	LO	LO	LO	LO	LO	LO	LO		LO	LO
Highbury & Islington	d	15 25			15 32		15 40		15 47		15 55			16 02		16 10		16 17		16 25		16 32			16 40
Canonbury	d	15 27			15 34		15 42		15 49		15 57			16 04		16 12		16 19		16 27		16 34			16 42
Dalston Junction	d	15 30		15 34	15 37	15 42	15 45	15 49	15 52	15 57	16 00	16 04		16 07	16 12	16 15	16 19	16 22	16 27	16 30	16 34	16 37		16 42	16 45
Haggerston	d	15 32		15 36	15 39	15 44	15 47	15 51	15 54	15 59	16 02	16 06		16 09	16 14	16 17	16 21	16 24	16 29	16 32	16 36	16 39		16 44	16 47
Hoxton	d	15 34		15 38	15 41	15 46	15 49	15 53	15 56	16 01	16 04	16 08		16 11	16 16	16 19	16 23	16 26	16 31	16 34	16 38	16 41		16 46	16 49
Shoreditch High Street	d	15 37		15 40	15 43	15 48	15 52	15 55	15 58	16 03	16 07	16 10		16 13	16 18	16 22	16 25	16 28	16 33	16 37	16 40	16 43		16 48	16 52
Whitechapel	d	15 39		15 43	15 46	15 51	15 54	15 58	16 01	16 06	16 09	16 13		16 16	16 21	16 24	16 28	16 31	16 36	16 39	16 43	16 46		16 51	16 54
Shadwell	d	15 41		15 45	15 48	15 53	15 56	16 00	16 03	16 08	16 11	16 15		16 18	16 23	16 26	16 30	16 33	16 38	16 41	16 45	16 48		16 53	16 56
Wapping	d	15 43		15 47	15 50	15 55	15 58	16 02	16 05	16 10	16 13	16 17		16 20	16 25	16 28	16 32	16 35	16 40	16 43	16 47	16 50		16 55	16 58
Rotherhithe	d	15 45		15 48	15 51	15 56	16 00	16 03	16 06	16 11	16 15	16 18		16 21	16 26	16 30	16 33	16 36	16 41	16 45	16 48	16 51		16 56	17 00
Canada Water	d	15 47		15 50	15 53	15 58	16 02	16 05	16 08	16 13	16 17	16 20		16 23	16 28	16 32	16 35	16 38	16 43	16 47	16 50	16 53		16 58	17 02
Surrey Quays	d	15 49		15 52	15 55	16 00	16 04	16 07	16 10	16 15	16 19	16 22		16 25	16 30	16 34	16 37	16 40	16 45	16 49	16 52	16 55		17 00	17 04
New Cross	a					16 04				16 19					16 34				16 49					17 04	
New Cross Gate 4	d	15 53			16 00		16 08		16 15		16 23			16 30		16 38		16 45		16 53		17 00			17 08
Brockley	d	15 56			16 02		16 11		16 17		16 26			16 32		16 41		16 47		16 56		17 02			17 11
Honor Oak Park	d	15 58			16 05		16 13		16 20		16 28			16 35		16 43		16 50		16 58		17 05			17 13
Forest Hill 4	d	16 01			16 07		16 16		16 22		16 31			16 37		16 46		16 52		17 01		17 07			17 16
Sydenham	d	16 04			16 11		16 19		16 26		16 34			16 41		16 49		16 56		17 04		17 11			17 19
Crystal Palace 4	a	16 08					16 23				16 38					16 53				17 08					17 23
Penge West	d				16 13				16 28					16 43				16 58				17 13			
Anerley	d				16 15				16 30					16 45				17 00				17 15			
Norwood Junction 2	d				16 18				16 33					16 48				17 03				17 18			
West Croydon 4	a				16 28				16 43					16 58				17 13				17 28			
Queens Rd Peckham	d			15 59				16 14				16 29					16 44				16 59				
Peckham Rye 4	d			16 03				16 18				16 33					16 48				17 03				
Denmark Hill 4	d			16 07				16 22				16 37					16 52				17 07				
Clapham High Street ⊖	d			16 11				16 26				16 41					16 56				17 11				
Wandsworth Road	d			16 13				16 28				16 43					16 58				17 13				
Clapham Junction	a			16 19				16 35				16 49					17 05				17 19				

Table T178-F

Saturdays

21 December to 16 May

Highbury & Islington - New Cross, Crystal Palace, West Croydon and Clapham Junction

		LO	LO	LO	LO	LO	LO	LO		LO	LO	LO	LO	LO	LO	LO	LO	LO		LO	LO	LO	LO	LO	LO
Highbury & Islington	d		16 47		16 55		17 02			17 10		17 17		17 25		17 32		17 40			17 47		17 55		18 02
Canonbury	d		16 49		16 57		17 04			17 12		17 19		17 27		17 34		17 42			17 49		17 57		18 04
Dalston Junction	d	16 49	16 52	16 57	17 00	17 04	17 07	17 12		17 15	17 19	17 22	17 27	17 30	17 34	17 37	17 42	17 45		17 49	17 52	17 57	18 00	18 04	18 07
Haggerston	d	16 51	16 54	16 59	17 02	17 06	17 09	17 14		17 17	17 21	17 24	17 29	17 32	17 36	17 39	17 44	17 47		17 51	17 54	17 59	18 02	18 06	18 09
Hoxton	d	16 53	16 56	17 01	17 04	17 08	17 11	17 16		17 19	17 23	17 26	17 31	17 34	17 38	17 41	17 46	17 49		17 53	17 56	18 01	18 04	18 08	18 11
Shoreditch High Street	d	16 55	16 58	17 03	17 07	17 10	17 13	17 18		17 22	17 25	17 28	17 33	17 37	17 40	17 43	17 48	17 52		17 55	17 58	18 03	18 07	18 10	18 13
Whitechapel	d	16 58	17 01	17 06	17 09	17 13	17 16	17 21		17 24	17 28	17 31	17 36	17 39	17 43	17 46	17 51	17 54		17 58	18 01	18 06	18 09	18 13	18 16
Shadwell	d	17 00	17 03	17 08	17 11	17 15	17 18	17 23		17 26	17 30	17 33	17 38	17 41	17 45	17 48	17 53	17 56		18 00	18 03	18 08	18 11	18 15	18 18
Wapping	d	17 02	17 05	17 10	17 13	17 17	17 20	17 25		17 28	17 32	17 35	17 40	17 43	17 47	17 50	17 55	17 58		18 02	18 05	18 10	18 13	18 17	18 20
Rotherhithe	d	17 03	17 06	17 11	17 15	17 18	17 21	17 26		17 30	17 33	17 36	17 41	17 45	17 48	17 51	17 56	18 00		18 03	18 06	18 11	18 15	18 18	18 21
Canada Water	d	17 05	17 08	17 13	17 17	17 20	17 23	17 28		17 32	17 35	17 38	17 43	17 47	17 50	17 53	17 58	18 02		18 05	18 08	18 13	18 17	18 20	18 23
Surrey Quays	d	17 07	17 10	17 15	17 19	17 22	17 25	17 30		17 34	17 37	17 40	17 45	17 49	17 52	17 55	18 00	18 04		18 07	18 10	18 15	18 19	18 22	18 25
New Cross	a			17 19				17 34					17 49				18 04					18 19			
New Cross Gate 4	d		17 15		17 23		17 30			17 38		17 45		17 53		18 00		18 08			18 15		18 23		18 30
Brockley	d		17 17		17 26		17 32			17 41		17 47		17 56		18 02		18 11			18 17		18 26		18 32
Honor Oak Park	d		17 20		17 28		17 35			17 43		17 50		17 58		18 05		18 13			18 20		18 28		18 35
Forest Hill 4	d		17 22		17 31		17 37			17 46		17 52		18 01		18 07		18 16			18 22		18 31		18 37
Sydenham	d		17 26		17 34		17 41			17 49		17 56		18 04		18 11		18 19			18 26		18 34		18 41
Crystal Palace 4	a				17 38					17 53				18 08				18 23					18 38		
Penge West	d		17 28				17 43					17 58				18 13					18 28				18 43
Anerley	d		17 30				17 45					18 00				18 15					18 30				18 45
Norwood Junction 2	d		17 33				17 48					18 03				18 18					18 33				18 48
West Croydon 4	a		17 43				17 58					18 13				18 28					18 43				18 58
Queens Rd Peckham	d	17 14				17 29					17 44				17 59					18 14				18 29	
Peckham Rye 4	d	17 18				17 33					17 48				18 03					18 18				18 33	
Denmark Hill 4	d	17 22				17 37					17 52				18 07					18 22				18 37	
Clapham High Street ⊖	d	17 26				17 41					17 56				18 11					18 26				18 41	
Wandsworth Road	d	17 28				17 43					17 58				18 13					18 28				18 43	
Clapham Junction	a	17 35				17 49					18 05				18 19					18 35				18 49	

		LO	LO	LO		LO	LO	LO	LO	LO	LO	LO	LO	LO		LO	LO	LO	LO	LO	LO	LO	LO	LO	
Highbury & Islington	d		18 10			18 17		18 25		18 32		18 40		18 47			18 55		19 02		19 10		19 17		
Canonbury	d		18 12			18 19		18 27		18 34		18 42		18 49			18 57		19 04		19 12		19 19		
Dalston Junction	d	18 12	18 15	18 19		18 22	18 27	18 30	18 34	18 37	18 42	18 45	18 49	18 52		18 57	19 00	19 04	19 07	19 12	19 15	19 19	19 22	19 27	
Haggerston	d	18 14	18 17	18 21		18 24	18 29	18 32	18 36	18 39	18 44	18 47	18 51	18 54		18 59	19 02	19 06	19 09	19 14	19 17	19 21	19 24	19 29	
Hoxton	d	18 16	18 19	18 23		18 26	18 31	18 34	18 38	18 41	18 46	18 49	18 53	18 56		19 01	19 04	19 08	19 11	19 16	19 19	19 23	19 26	19 31	
Shoreditch High Street	d	18 18	18 22	18 25		18 28	18 33	18 37	18 40	18 43	18 48	18 52	18 55	18 58		19 03	19 07	19 10	19 13	19 18	19 22	19 25	19 28	19 33	
Whitechapel	d	18 21	18 24	18 28		18 31	18 36	18 39	18 43	18 46	18 51	18 54	18 58	19 01		19 06	19 09	19 13	19 16	19 21	19 24	19 28	19 31	19 36	
Shadwell	d	18 23	18 26	18 30		18 33	18 38	18 41	18 45	18 48	18 53	18 56	19 00	19 03		19 08	19 11	19 15	19 18	19 23	19 26	19 30	19 33	19 38	
Wapping	d	18 25	18 28	18 32		18 35	18 40	18 43	18 47	18 50	18 55	18 58	19 02	19 05		19 10	19 13	19 17	19 20	19 25	19 28	19 32	19 35	19 40	
Rotherhithe	d	18 26	18 30	18 33		18 36	18 41	18 45	18 48	18 51	18 56	19 00	19 03	19 06		19 11	19 15	19 18	19 21	19 26	19 30	19 33	19 36	19 41	
Canada Water	d	18 28	18 32	18 35		18 38	18 43	18 47	18 50	18 53	18 58	19 02	19 05	19 08		19 13	19 17	19 20	19 23	19 28	19 32	19 35	19 38	19 43	
Surrey Quays	d	18 30	18 34	18 37		18 40	18 45	18 49	18 52	18 55	19 00	19 04	19 07	19 10		19 15	19 19	19 22	19 25	19 30	19 34	19 37	19 40	19 45	
New Cross	a	18 34					18 49				19 04					19 19				19 34				19 49	
New Cross Gate 4	d		18 38			18 45		18 53		19 00		19 08		19 15			19 23		19 30		19 38		19 45		
Brockley	d		18 41			18 47		18 56		19 02		19 11		19 17			19 26		19 32		19 41		19 47		
Honor Oak Park	d		18 43			18 50		18 58		19 05		19 13		19 20			19 28		19 35		19 43		19 50		
Forest Hill 4	d		18 46			18 52		19 01		19 07		19 16		19 22			19 31		19 37		19 46		19 52		
Sydenham	d		18 49			18 56		19 04		19 11		19 19		19 26			19 34		19 41		19 49		19 56		
Crystal Palace 4	a		18 53					19 08				19 23					19 38				19 53				
Penge West	d					18 58				19 13				19 28					19 43				19 58		
Anerley	d					19 00				19 15				19 30					19 45				20 00		
Norwood Junction 2	d					19 03				19 18				19 33					19 48				20 03		
West Croydon 4	a					19 13				19 28				19 43					19 58				20 13		
Queens Rd Peckham	d			18 44					18 59				19 14					19 29				19 44			
Peckham Rye 4	d			18 48					19 03				19 18					19 33				19 48			
Denmark Hill 4	d			18 52					19 07				19 22					19 37				19 52			
Clapham High Street ⊖	d			18 56					19 11				19 26					19 41				19 56			
Wandsworth Road	d			18 58					19 13				19 28					19 43				19 58			
Clapham Junction	a			19 05					19 20				19 35					19 49				20 05			

		LO	LO	LO	LO	LO	LO	LO	LO	LO		LO	LO	LO	LO	LO	LO	LO	LO	LO		LO	LO	LO	LO
Highbury & Islington	d	19 25		19 32		19 40		19 47		19 55			20 02		20 10		20 17		20 25			20 32		20 40	
Canonbury	d	19 27		19 34		19 42		19 49		19 57			20 04		20 12		20 19		20 27			20 34		20 42	
Dalston Junction	d	19 30	19 34	19 37	19 42	19 45	19 49	19 52	19 57	20 00		20 04	20 07	20 12	20 15	20 19	20 22	20 27	20 30	20 34		20 37	20 42	20 45	20 49
Haggerston	d	19 32	19 36	19 39	19 44	19 47	19 51	19 54	19 59	20 02		20 06	20 09	20 14	20 17	20 21	20 24	20 29	20 32	20 36		20 39	20 44	20 47	20 51
Hoxton	d	19 34	19 38	19 41	19 46	19 49	19 53	19 56	20 01	20 04		20 08	20 11	20 16	20 19	20 23	20 26	20 31	20 34	20 38		20 41	20 46	20 49	20 53
Shoreditch High Street	d	19 37	19 40	19 43	19 48	19 52	19 55	19 58	20 03	20 07		20 10	20 13	20 18	20 22	20 25	20 28	20 33	20 37	20 40		20 43	20 48	20 52	20 55
Whitechapel	d	19 39	19 43	19 46	19 51	19 54	19 58	20 01	20 06	20 09		20 13	20 16	20 21	20 24	20 28	20 31	20 36	20 39	20 43		20 46	20 51	20 54	20 58
Shadwell	d	19 41	19 45	19 48	19 53	19 56	20 00	20 03	20 08	20 11		20 15	20 18	20 23	20 26	20 30	20 33	20 38	20 41	20 45		20 48	20 53	20 56	21 00
Wapping	d	19 43	19 47	19 50	19 55	19 58	20 02	20 05	20 10	20 13		20 17	20 20	20 25	20 28	20 32	20 35	20 40	20 43	20 47		20 50	20 55	20 58	21 02
Rotherhithe	d	19 45	19 48	19 51	19 56	20 00	20 03	20 06	20 11	20 15		20 18	20 21	20 26	20 30	20 33	20 36	20 41	20 45	20 48		20 51	20 56	21 00	21 03
Canada Water	d	19 47	19 50	19 53	19 58	20 02	20 05	20 08	20 13	20 17		20 20	20 23	20 28	20 32	20 35	20 38	20 43	20 47	20 50		20 53	20 58	21 02	21 05
Surrey Quays	d	19 49	19 52	19 55	20 00	20 04	20 07	20 10	20 15	20 19		20 22	20 25	20 30	20 34	20 37	20 40	20 45	20 49	20 52		20 55	21 00	21 04	21 07
New Cross	a				20 04				20 19					20 34				20 49					21 04		
New Cross Gate 4	d	19 53		20 00		20 08		20 15		20 23			20 30		20 38		20 45		20 53			21 00		21 08	
Brockley	d	19 56		20 02		20 11		20 17		20 26			20 32		20 41		20 47		20 56			21 02		21 11	
Honor Oak Park	d	19 58		20 05		20 13		20 20		20 28			20 35		20 43		20 50		20 58			21 05		21 13	
Forest Hill 4	d	20 01		20 07		20 16		20 22		20 31			20 37		20 46		20 52		21 01			21 07		21 16	
Sydenham	d	20 04		20 11		20 19		20 26		20 34			20 41		20 49		20 56		21 04			21 11		21 19	
Crystal Palace 4	a	20 08				20 23				20 38					20 53				21 08					21 23	
Penge West	d			20 13				20 28					20 43				20 58					21 13			
Anerley	d			20 15				20 30					20 45				21 00					21 15			
Norwood Junction 2	d			20 18				20 33					20 48				21 03					21 18			
West Croydon 4	a			20 28				20 43					20 58				21 13					21 24			
Queens Rd Peckham	d		19 59				20 14					20 29				20 44				20 59					21 14
Peckham Rye 4	d		20 03				20 18					20 33				20 48				21 03					21 18
Denmark Hill 4	d		20 07				20 22					20 37				20 52				21 07					21 22
Clapham High Street ⊖	d		20 11				20 26					20 41				20 56				21 11					21 26
Wandsworth Road	d		20 13				20 28					20 43				20 58				21 13					21 28
Clapham Junction	a		20 19				20 35					20 49				21 05				21 19					21 36

Table T178-F

Saturdays

21 December to 16 May

Highbury & Islington - New Cross, Crystal Palace, West Croydon and Clapham Junction

		LO	LO	LO	LO	LO		LO	LO	LO	LO	LO	LO	LO	LO	LO		LO	LO	LO	LO	LO	LO	LO	LO
Highbury & Islington	d	20 47		20 55		21 02			21 10		21 17		21 25		21 32			21 40		21 47		21 55		22 02	
Canonbury	d	20 49		20 57		21 04			21 12		21 19		21 27		21 34			21 42		21 49		21 57		22 04	
Dalston Junction	d	20 52	20 57	21 00	21 04	21 07		21 12	21 15	21 19	21 22	21 27	21 30	21 34	21 37	21 42		21 45	21 49	21 52	21 57	22 00	22 04	22 07	22 12
Haggerston	d	20 54	20 59	21 02	21 06	21 09		21 14	21 17	21 21	21 24	21 29	21 32	21 36	21 39	21 44		21 47	21 51	21 54	21 59	22 02	22 06	22 09	22 14
Hoxton	d	20 56	21 01	21 04	21 08	21 11		21 16	21 19	21 23	21 26	21 31	21 34	21 38	21 41	21 46		21 49	21 53	21 56	22 01	22 04	22 08	22 11	22 16
Shoreditch High Street	d	20 58	21 03	21 07	21 10	21 13		21 18	21 22	21 25	21 28	21 33	21 37	21 40	21 43	21 48		21 52	21 55	21 58	22 03	22 07	22 10	22 13	22 18
Whitechapel	d	21 01	21 06	21 09	21 13	21 16		21 21	21 24	21 28	21 31	21 36	21 39	21 43	21 46	21 51		21 54	21 58	22 01	22 06	22 09	22 13	22 16	22 21
Shadwell	d	21 03	21 08	21 11	21 15	21 18		21 23	21 26	21 30	21 33	21 38	21 41	21 45	21 48	21 53		21 56	22 00	22 03	22 08	22 11	22 15	22 18	22 23
Wapping	d	21 05	21 10	21 13	21 17	21 20		21 25	21 28	21 32	21 35	21 40	21 43	21 47	21 50	21 55		21 58	22 02	22 05	22 10	22 13	22 17	22 20	22 25
Rotherhithe	d	21 06	21 11	21 15	21 18	21 21		21 26	21 30	21 33	21 36	21 41	21 45	21 48	21 51	21 56		22 00	22 03	22 06	22 11	22 15	22 18	22 21	22 26
Canada Water	d	21 08	21 13	21 17	21 20	21 23		21 28	21 32	21 35	21 38	21 43	21 47	21 50	21 53	21 58		22 02	22 05	22 08	22 13	22 17	22 20	22 23	22 28
Surrey Quays	d	21 10	21 15	21 19	21 22	21 25		21 30	21 34	21 37	21 40	21 45	21 49	21 52	21 55	22 00		22 04	22 07	22 10	22 15	22 19	22 22	22 25	22 30
New Cross	a		21 19					21 34				21 49				22 04					22 19				22 34
New Cross Gate 4	d	21 15		21 23		21 30			21 38		21 45		21 53		22 00			22 08		22 15		22 23		22 30	
Brockley	d	21 17		21 26		21 32			21 41		21 47		21 56		22 02			22 11		22 17		22 26		22 32	
Honor Oak Park	d	21 20		21 28		21 35			21 43		21 50		21 58		22 05			22 13		22 20		22 28		22 35	
Forest Hill 4	d	21 22		21 31		21 37			21 46		21 52		22 01		22 07			22 16		22 22		22 31		22 37	
Sydenham	d	21 26		21 34		21 41			21 49		21 56		22 04		22 11			22 19		22 26		22 34		22 41	
Crystal Palace 4	a			21 38					21 53				22 08					22 23				22 38			
Penge West	d	21 28				21 43					21 58				22 13					22 28				22 43	
Anerley	d	21 30				21 45					22 00				22 15					22 30				22 45	
Norwood Junction 2	d	21 33				21 48					22 03				22 18					22 33				22 48	
West Croydon 4	a	21 39				21 54					22 09				22 24					22 39				22 54	
Queens Rd Peckham	d				21 29					21 44				21 59					22 14				22 29		
Peckham Rye 4	d				21 33					21 48				22 03					22 18				22 33		
Denmark Hill 4	d				21 37					21 52				22 07					22 22				22 37		
Clapham High Street ⊖	d				21 41					21 56				22 11					22 26				22 41		
Wandsworth Road	d				21 43					21 58				22 13					22 28				22 43		
Clapham Junction	a				21 49					22 05				22 19					22 35				22 49		

		LO		LO	LO	LO	LO	LO	LO	LO	LO	LO		LO	LO	LO	LO	LO	LO	LO	LO	LO		LO	LO
Highbury & Islington	d	22 10			22 17		22 25		22 32		22 40			22 47		22 55		23 02		23 10		23 17			23 25
Canonbury	d	22 12			22 19		22 27		22 34		22 42			22 49		22 57		23 04		23 12		23 19			23 27
Dalston Junction	d	22 15		22 19	22 22	22 27	22 30	22 34	22 37	22 42	22 45	22 49		22 52	22 57	23 00	23 04	23 07	23 12	23 15	23 19	23 22		23 27	23 30
Haggerston	d	22 17		22 21	22 24	22 29	22 32	22 36	22 39	22 44	22 47	22 51		22 54	22 59	23 02	23 06	23 09	23 14	23 17	23 21	23 24		23 29	23 32
Hoxton	d	22 19		22 23	22 26	22 31	22 34	22 38	22 41	22 46	22 49	22 53		22 56	23 01	23 04	23 08	23 11	23 16	23 19	23 23	23 26		23 31	23 34
Shoreditch High Street	d	22 22		22 25	22 28	22 33	22 37	22 40	22 43	22 48	22 52	22 55		22 58	23 03	23 07	23 10	23 13	23 18	23 22	23 25	23 28		23 33	23 37
Whitechapel	d	22 24		22 28	22 31	22 36	22 39	22 43	22 46	22 51	22 54	22 58		23 01	23 06	23 09	23 13	23 16	23 21	23 24	23 28	23 31		23 36	23 39
Shadwell	d	22 26		22 30	22 33	22 38	22 41	22 45	22 48	22 53	22 56	23 00		23 03	23 08	23 11	23 15	23 18	23 23	23 26	23 30	23 33		23 38	23 41
Wapping	d	22 28		22 32	22 35	22 40	22 43	22 47	22 50	22 55	22 58	23 02		23 05	23 10	23 13	23 17	23 20	23 25	23 28	23 32	23 35		23 40	23 43
Rotherhithe	d	22 30		22 33	22 36	22 41	22 45	22 48	22 51	22 56	23 00	23 03		23 06	23 11	23 15	23 18	23 21	23 26	23 30	23 33	23 36		23 41	23 45
Canada Water	d	22 32		22 35	22 38	22 43	22 47	22 50	22 53	22 58	23 02	23 05		23 08	23 13	23 17	23 20	23 23	23 28	23 32	23 35	23 38		23 43	23 47
Surrey Quays	d	22 34		22 37	22 40	22 45	22 49	22 52	22 55	23 00	23 04	23 07		23 10	23 15	23 19	23 22	23 25	23 30	23 34	23 37	23 40		23 45	23 49
New Cross	a					22 49				23 04					23 19				23 34					23 49	
New Cross Gate 4	d	22 38			22 45		22 53		23 00		23 08			23 15		23 23		23 30		23 38		23 45			23 53
Brockley	d	22 41			22 47		22 56		23 02		23 11			23 17		23 26		23 32		23 41		23 47			23 56
Honor Oak Park	d	22 43			22 50		22 58		23 05		23 13			23 20		23 28		23 35		23 43		23 50			23 58
Forest Hill 4	d	22 46			22 52		23 01		23 07		23 16			23 22		23 31		23 37		23 46		23 52			00 01
Sydenham	d	22 49			22 56		23 04		23 11		23 19			23 26		23 34		23 41		23 49		23 56			00 04
Crystal Palace 4	a	22 53					23 08				23 23					23 38				23 53					00 08
Penge West	d				22 58				23 13					23 28				23 43				23 58			
Anerley	d				23 00				23 15					23 30				23 45				00 01			
Norwood Junction 2	d				23 03				23 18					23 33				23 48				00 03			
West Croydon 4	a				23 13				23 28					23 43				23 58				00 13			
Queens Rd Peckham	d			22 44				22 59				23 15					23 29				23 44				
Peckham Rye 4	d			22 48				23 03				23 18					23 33				23 48				
Denmark Hill 4	d			22 52				23 07				23 22					23 37				23 52				
Clapham High Street ⊖	d			22 56				23 11				23 26					23 41				23 56				
Wandsworth Road	d			22 58				23 13				23 28					23 43				23 58				
Clapham Junction	a			23 05				23 19				23 35					23 49				00 05				

		LO	LO	LO	LO	LO	LO
Highbury & Islington	d		23 32		23 40		23 50
Canonbury	d		23 34		23 42		23 52
Dalston Junction	d	23 34	23 37	23 42	23 45	23 49	23 55
Haggerston	d	23 36	23 39	23 44	23 47	23 51	23 57
Hoxton	d	23 38	23 41	23 46	23 49	23 53	23 59
Shoreditch High Street	d	23 40	23 43	23 48	23 52	23 55	00 01
Whitechapel	d	23 43	23 46	23 51	23 54	23 58	00 04
Shadwell	d	23 45	23 48	23 53	23 56	23 59	00 06
Wapping	d	23 47	23 50	23 55	23 58	00 02	00 08
Rotherhithe	d	23 48	23 51	23 56	23 59	00 03	00 09
Canada Water	d	23 50	23 53	23 58	00 02	00 05	00 11
Surrey Quays	d	23 52	23 55	00 02	00 04	00 07	00 13
New Cross	a			00 04			
New Cross Gate 4	d		00 01		00 08		00a20
Brockley	d		00 03		00 11		
Honor Oak Park	d		00 06		00 13		
Forest Hill 4	d		00 08		00 16		
Sydenham	d		00 11		00 19		
Crystal Palace 4	a				00 23		
Penge West	d		00 13				
Anerley	d		00 15				
Norwood Junction 2	d		00 19				
West Croydon 4	a		00 28				
Queens Rd Peckham	d	23 59				00 14	
Peckham Rye 4	d	00 02				00 18	
Denmark Hill 4	d	00 06				00 22	
Clapham High Street ⊖	d	00 10				00 26	
Wandsworth Road	d	00 12				00 28	
Clapham Junction	a	00 19				00 35	

Table T178-F

Sundays

15 December to 10 May

Highbury & Islington - New Cross, Crystal Palace, West Croydon and Clapham Junction

		LO A	LO A	LO A	LO B	LO B	LO A	LO B	LO A	LO	LO		LO	LO	LO	LO	LO	LO	LO	LO	LO	LO
Highbury & Islington	d									00 01	00 10		05 55	06 08	06 20	06 35	06 51		07 11	07 21	07 26	
Canonbury	d									00 03	00 12		05 57	06 10	06 22	06 37	06 53		07 13	07 23	07 28	
Dalston Junction	d									00 06	00 15		06 00	06 13	06 25	06 40	06 56	07 12	07 16	07 26	07 31	07 42
Haggerston	d									00 08	00 17		06 02	06 14	06 27	06 42	06 57	07 13	07 17	07 27	07 32	07 43
Hoxton	d									00 10	00 19		06 04	06 16	06 29	06 44	06 59	07 15	07 19	07 29	07 34	07 45
Shoreditch High Street	d								00 01	00 13	00 21		06 06	06 19	06 31	06 46	07 02	07 18	07 22	07 32	07 37	07 48
Whitechapel	d								00 04	00 15	00 24		06 09	06 21	06 34	06 49	07 04	07 20	07 24	07 34	07 39	07 50
Shadwell	d								00 06	00 17	00 26		06 11	06 23	06 36	06 51	07 06	07 22	07 26	07 36	07 41	07 52
Wapping	d							00 02	00 08	00 19	00 28		06 13	06 25	06 38	06 53	07 08	07 24	07 28	07 38	07 43	07 54
Rotherhithe	d							00 03	00 09	00 21	00 29		06 14	06 27	06 39	06 54	07 10	07 26	07 30	07 40	07 45	07 56
Canada Water	d						00 02	00 05	00 11	00 23	00 31		06 16	06 29	06 41	06 56	07 12	07 28	07 32	07 42	07 47	07 58
Surrey Quays	d					00 02	00 04	00 07	00 13	00 25	00 33	and	06 18	06 31	06 43	06 58	07 14	07 30	07 34	07 44	07 49	08 00
New Cross	a					00 04						every 15										
New Cross Gate	d			00 01			00 08		00a20		00a40	minutes	06a25	06a38	06a50	07 04	07 18	07 34		07 48		08 04
Brockley	d			00 03			00 11					until				07 07	07 21	07 37		07 51		08 07
Honor Oak Park	d			00 06			00 13									07 09	07 23	07 39		07 53		08 09
Forest Hill	d		00 01	00 08			00 16									07 12	07 26	07 42		07 56		08 12
Sydenham	d		00 04	00 11			00 19									07 15	07 29	07 45		07 59		08 15
Crystal Palace	a		00 08				00 23										07 34			08 04		
Penge West	d			00 13												07 17		07 47				08 17
Anerley	d	00 01		00 15												07 19		07 49				08 19
Norwood Junction	d	00 03		00 19												07 22		07 52				08 22
West Croydon	a	00 13		00 28												07 27		07 58				08 28
Queens Rd Peckham	d							00 14		00 31									07 38		07 53	
Peckham Rye	d				00 02			00 18		00 34									07 42		07 57	
Denmark Hill	d				00 06			00 22		00 38									07 44		07 59	
Clapham High Street	d				00 10			00 26		00 42									07 49		08 04	
Wandsworth Road	d				00 12			00 28		00 44									07 50		08 05	
Clapham Junction	a				00 19			00 35		00 52									08 02		08 17	

		LO	LO	LO	LO	LO	LO	LO	LO	LO	LO	LO	LO	LO	LO	LO	LO	LO	LO	LO	LO	LO	LO
Highbury & Islington	d	07 41	07 51	07 56	08 07	08 11		08 21	08 26		08 37	08 41		08 51	08 56		09 07	09 11		09 21	09 26		09 37
Canonbury	d	07 43	07 53	07 58	08 09	08 13		08 23	08 28		08 39	08 43		08 53	08 58		09 09	09 13		09 23	09 28		09 39
Dalston Junction	d	07 46	07 56	08 01	08 12	08 16	08 23	08 26	08 31	08 38	08 42	08 46	08 53	08 56	09 01	09 08	09 12	09 16	09 23	09 26	09 31	09 38	09 42
Haggerston	d	07 47	07 57	08 02	08 13	08 17	08 24	08 27	08 32	08 39	08 43	08 47	08 54	08 57	09 02	09 09	09 13	09 17	09 24	09 27	09 32	09 39	09 43
Hoxton	d	07 49	07 59	08 04	08 15	08 19	08 26	08 29	08 34	08 41	08 45	08 49	08 56	08 59	09 04	09 11	09 15	09 19	09 26	09 29	09 34	09 41	09 45
Shoreditch High Street	d	07 52	08 02	08 07	08 18	08 22	08 29	08 32	08 37	08 44	08 48	08 52	08 59	09 02	09 07	09 14	09 18	09 22	09 29	09 32	09 37	09 44	09 48
Whitechapel	d	07 54	08 04	08 09	08 20	08 24	08 31	08 34	08 39	08 46	08 50	08 54	09 01	09 04	09 09	09 16	09 20	09 24	09 31	09 34	09 39	09 46	09 50
Shadwell	d	07 56	08 06	08 11	08 22	08 26	08 33	08 36	08 41	08 48	08 52	08 56	09 03	09 06	09 11	09 18	09 22	09 26	09 33	09 36	09 41	09 48	09 52
Wapping	d	07 58	08 08	08 13	08 24	08 28	08 35	08 38	08 43	08 50	08 54	08 58	09 05	09 08	09 13	09 20	09 24	09 28	09 35	09 38	09 43	09 50	09 54
Rotherhithe	d	08 00	08 10	08 15	08 26	08 30	08 37	08 40	08 45	08 52	08 56	09 00	09 07	09 10	09 15	09 22	09 26	09 30	09 37	09 40	09 45	09 52	09 56
Canada Water	d	08 02	08 12	08 17	08 28	08 32	08 39	08 42	08 47	08 54	08 58	09 02	09 09	09 12	09 17	09 24	09 28	09 32	09 39	09 42	09 47	09 54	09 58
Surrey Quays	d	08 04	08 14	08 19	08 30	08 34	08 41	08 44	08 49	08 56	09 00	09 04	09 11	09 14	09 19	09 26	09 30	09 34	09 41	09 44	09 49	09 56	10 00
New Cross	a						08 45			09 00			09 15			09 30			09 45			10 00	
New Cross Gate	d		08 18		08 34			08 48			09 04			09 18			09 34			09 48			10 04
Brockley	d		08 21		08 37			08 51			09 07			09 21			09 37			09 51			10 07
Honor Oak Park	d		08 23		08 39			08 53			09 09			09 23			09 39			09 53			10 09
Forest Hill	d		08 26		08 42			08 56			09 12			09 26			09 42			09 56			10 12
Sydenham	d		08 29		08 45			08 59			09 15			09 29			09 45			09 59			10 15
Crystal Palace	a		08 34					09 04						09 34						10 04			
Penge West	d				08 47						09 17						09 47						10 17
Anerley	d				08 49						09 19						09 49						10 19
Norwood Junction	d				08 52						09 22						09 52						10 22
West Croydon	a				08 59						09 29						09 59						10 29
Queens Rd Peckham	d	08 08		08 23		08 38			08 53			09 08			09 23			09 38			09 53		
Peckham Rye	d	08 12		08 27		08 42			08 57			09 12			09 27			09 42			09 57		
Denmark Hill	d	08 14		08 29		08 44			08 59			09 14			09 29			09 44			09 59		
Clapham High Street	d	08 19		08 34		08 49			09 04			09 19			09 34			09 49			10 04		
Wandsworth Road	d	08 20		08 35		08 50			09 05			09 20			09 35			09 50			10 05		
Clapham Junction	a	08 32		08 46		09 01			09 16			09 31			09 46			10 01			10 16		

		LO	LO	LO	LO	LO	LO	LO	LO	LO	LO	LO	LO	LO	LO	LO	LO	LO	LO	LO	LO	LO	LO
Highbury & Islington	d	09 41		09 51	09 56		10 07	10 11		10 21	10 26		10 37	10 41		10 51	10 56		11 07	11 11		11 21	11 26
Canonbury	d	09 43		09 53	09 58		10 09	10 13		10 23	10 28		10 39	10 43		10 53	10 58		11 09	11 13		11 23	11 28
Dalston Junction	d	09 46	09 53	09 56	10 01	10 08	10 12	10 16	10 23	10 26	10 31	10 38	10 42	10 46	10 53	10 56	11 01	11 08	11 12	11 16	11 23	11 26	11 31
Haggerston	d	09 47	09 54	09 57	10 02	10 09	10 13	10 17	10 24	10 27	10 32	10 39	10 43	10 47	10 54	10 57	11 02	11 09	11 13	11 17	11 24	11 27	11 32
Hoxton	d	09 49	09 56	09 59	10 04	10 11	10 15	10 19	10 26	10 29	10 34	10 41	10 45	10 49	10 56	10 59	11 04	11 11	11 15	11 19	11 26	11 29	11 34
Shoreditch High Street	d	09 52	09 59	10 02	10 07	10 14	10 18	10 22	10 29	10 32	10 37	10 44	10 48	10 52	10 59	11 02	11 07	11 14	11 18	11 22	11 29	11 32	11 37
Whitechapel	d	09 54	10 01	10 04	10 09	10 16	10 20	10 24	10 31	10 34	10 39	10 46	10 50	10 54	11 01	11 04	11 09	11 16	11 20	11 24	11 31	11 34	11 39
Shadwell	d	09 56	10 03	10 06	10 11	10 18	10 22	10 26	10 33	10 36	10 41	10 48	10 52	10 56	11 03	11 06	11 11	11 18	11 22	11 26	11 33	11 36	11 41
Wapping	d	09 58	10 05	10 08	10 13	10 20	10 24	10 28	10 35	10 38	10 43	10 50	10 54	10 58	11 05	11 08	11 13	11 20	11 24	11 28	11 35	11 38	11 43
Rotherhithe	d	10 00	10 07	10 10	10 15	10 22	10 26	10 30	10 37	10 40	10 45	10 52	10 56	11 00	11 07	11 10	11 15	11 22	11 26	11 30	11 37	11 40	11 45
Canada Water	d	10 02	10 09	10 12	10 17	10 24	10 28	10 32	10 39	10 42	10 47	10 54	10 58	11 02	11 09	11 12	11 17	11 24	11 28	11 32	11 39	11 42	11 47
Surrey Quays	d	10 04	10 11	10 14	10 19	10 26	10 30	10 34	10 41	10 44	10 49	10 56	11 00	11 04	11 11	11 14	11 19	11 26	11 30	11 34	11 41	11 44	11 49
New Cross	a		10 15			10 30			10 45			11 00			11 15			11 30			11 45		
New Cross Gate	d			10 18			10 34			10 48			11 04			11 18			11 34			11 48	
Brockley	d			10 21			10 37			10 51			11 07			11 21			11 37			11 51	
Honor Oak Park	d			10 23			10 39			10 53			11 09			11 23			11 39			11 53	
Forest Hill	d			10 26			10 42			10 56			11 12			11 26			11 42			11 56	
Sydenham	d			10 29			10 45			10 59			11 15			11 29			11 45			11 59	
Crystal Palace	a			10 34						11 04						11 34						12 04	
Penge West	d						10 47						11 17						11 47				
Anerley	d						10 49						11 19						11 49				
Norwood Junction	d						10 52						11 22						11 52				
West Croydon	a						10 59						11 29						11 59				
Queens Rd Peckham	d	10 08			10 23			10 38			10 53			11 08			11 23			11 38			11 53
Peckham Rye	d	10 12			10 27			10 42			10 57			11 12			11 27			11 42			11 57
Denmark Hill	d	10 14			10 29			10 44			10 59			11 14			11 29			11 44			11 59
Clapham High Street	d	10 19			10 34			10 49			11 04			11 19			11 34			11 49			12 04
Wandsworth Road	d	10 20			10 35			10 50			11 05			11 20			11 35			11 50			12 05
Clapham Junction	a	10 31			10 46			11 01			11 16			11 31			11 46			12 01			12 16

A not 15 December. From Highbury and Islington Ell
B not 15 December. From Dalston Junction Stn Ell

Table T178-F

Sundays

15 December to 10 May

Highbury & Islington - New Cross, Crystal Palace, West Croydon and Clapham Junction

		LO	LO	LO	LO	LO	LO	LO	LO	LO	LO	LO	LO	LO	LO	LO	LO	LO	LO	LO	LO	LO
Highbury & Islington	d		11 35	11 37			11 50	11 53			12 05	12 08			12 20		12 28		12 35		12 43	
Canonbury	d		11 37	11 39			11 52	11 55			12 07	12 10			12 22		12 30		12 37		12 45	
Dalston Junction	d	11 38	11 40	11 42	11 48	11 53	11 55	11 58	12 03	12 08	12 10	12 13	12 18	12 23	12 25	12 28	12 33	12 38	12 40	12 43	12 48	12 53
Haggerston	d	11 39	11 41	11 43	11 49	11 54	11 56	11 59	12 04	12 09	12 11	12 14	12 19	12 24	12 26	12 29	12 34	12 39	12 41	12 44	12 49	12 54
Hoxton	d	11 41	11 43	11 45	11 51	11 56	11 58	12 01	12 06	12 11	12 13	12 16	12 21	12 26	12 28	12 31	12 36	12 41	12 43	12 46	12 51	12 56
Shoreditch High Street	d	11 44	11 46	11 48	11 54	11 59	12 01	12 04	12 09	12 14	12 16	12 19	12 24	12 29	12 31	12 34	12 39	12 44	12 46	12 49	12 54	12 59
Whitechapel	d	11 46	11 48	11 50	11 56	12 01	12 03	12 06	12 11	12 16	12 18	12 21	12 26	12 31	12 33	12 36	12 41	12 46	12 48	12 51	12 56	13 01
Shadwell	d	11 48	11 50	11 52	11 58	12 03	12 05	12 08	12 13	12 18	12 20	12 23	12 28	12 33	12 35	12 38	12 43	12 48	12 50	12 53	12 58	13 03
Wapping	d	11 50	11 52	11 54	12 00	12 05	12 07	12 10	12 15	12 20	12 22	12 25	12 30	12 35	12 37	12 40	12 45	12 50	12 52	12 55	13 00	13 05
Rotherhithe	d	11 52	11 54	11 56	12 02	12 07	12 09	12 12	12 17	12 22	12 24	12 27	12 32	12 37	12 39	12 42	12 47	12 52	12 54	12 57	13 02	13 07
Canada Water	d	11 54	11 56	11 58	12 04	12 09	12 11	12 14	12 19	12 24	12 26	12 29	12 34	12 39	12 41	12 44	12 49	12 54	12 56	12 59	13 04	13 09
Surrey Quays	d	11 56	11 58	12 00	12 06	12 11	12 13	12 16	12 21	12 26	12 28	12 31	12 36	12 41	12 43	12 46	12 51	12 56	12 58	13 01	13 06	13 11
New Cross	a	12 00				12 15				12 30				12 45				13 00				13 15
New Cross Gate	d			12 04	12 10			12 20	12 25			12 35	12 40			12 50	12 55			13 05	13 10	
Brockley	d			12 07	12 13			12 23	12 28			12 38	12 43			12 53	12 58			13 08	13 13	
Honor Oak Park	d			12 09	12 15			12 25	12 30			12 40	12 45			12 55	13 00			13 10	13 15	
Forest Hill	d			12 12	12 18			12 28	12 33			12 43	12 48			12 58	13 03			13 13	13 18	
Sydenham	d			12 15	12 21			12 31	12 36			12 46	12 51			13 01	13 06			13 16	13 21	
Crystal Palace	a				12 25				12 40				12 55				13 11				13 26	
Penge West	d			12 17				12 33				12 48				13 03				13 18		
Anerley	d			12 19				12 35				12 50				13 05				13 20		
Norwood Junction	d			12 22				12 38				12 53				13 08				13 23		
West Croydon	a			12 29				12 45				13 00				13 14				13 30		
Queens Rd Peckham	d		12 02				12 17				12 32				12 47				13 02			
Peckham Rye	d		12 06				12 20				12 36				12 50				13 06			
Denmark Hill	d		12 08				12 22				12 38				12 53				13 08			
Clapham High Street	d		12 13				12 27				12 43				12 57				13 13			
Wandsworth Road	d		12 14				12 28				12 44				12 59				13 14			
Clapham Junction	a		12 25				12 40				12 55				13 10				13 25			

		LO	LO	LO	LO	LO	LO	LO	LO	LO	LO	LO	LO	LO	LO	LO	LO	LO	LO	LO	LO	LO	LO
Highbury & Islington	d	12 50		12 58		13 05		13 13		13 20		13 28		13 35		13 43		13 50		13 58		14 05	
Canonbury	d	12 52		13 00		13 07		13 15		13 22		13 30		13 37		13 45		13 52		14 00		14 07	
Dalston Junction	d	12 55	12 58	13 03	13 07	13 10	13 13	13 18	13 22	13 25	13 28	13 33	13 37	13 40	13 43	13 48	13 52	13 55	13 58	14 03	14 07	14 10	14 13
Haggerston	d	12 56	12 59	13 04	13 08	13 11	13 14	13 19	13 23	13 26	13 29	13 34	13 38	13 41	13 44	13 49	13 53	13 56	13 59	14 04	14 08	14 11	14 14
Hoxton	d	12 58	13 01	13 06	13 10	13 13	13 16	13 21	13 25	13 28	13 31	13 36	13 40	13 43	13 46	13 51	13 55	13 58	14 01	14 06	14 10	14 13	14 16
Shoreditch High Street	d	13 01	13 04	13 09	13 13	13 16	13 19	13 24	13 28	13 31	13 34	13 39	13 43	13 46	13 49	13 54	13 58	14 01	14 04	14 09	14 13	14 16	14 19
Whitechapel	d	13 03	13 06	13 11	13 15	13 18	13 21	13 26	13 30	13 33	13 36	13 41	13 45	13 48	13 51	13 56	14 00	14 03	14 06	14 11	14 15	14 18	14 21
Shadwell	d	13 05	13 08	13 13	13 17	13 20	13 23	13 28	13 32	13 35	13 38	13 43	13 47	13 50	13 53	13 58	14 02	14 05	14 08	14 13	14 17	14 20	14 23
Wapping	d	13 07	13 10	13 15	13 19	13 22	13 25	13 30	13 34	13 37	13 40	13 45	13 49	13 52	13 55	14 00	14 04	14 07	14 10	14 15	14 19	14 22	14 25
Rotherhithe	d	13 09	13 12	13 17	13 21	13 24	13 27	13 32	13 36	13 39	13 42	13 47	13 51	13 54	13 57	14 02	14 06	14 09	14 12	14 17	14 21	14 24	14 27
Canada Water	d	13 11	13 14	13 19	13 23	13 26	13 29	13 34	13 38	13 41	13 44	13 49	13 53	13 56	13 59	14 04	14 08	14 11	14 14	14 19	14 23	14 26	14 29
Surrey Quays	d	13 13	13 16	13 21	13 25	13 28	13 31	13 36	13 40	13 43	13 46	13 51	13 55	13 58	14 01	14 06	14 10	14 13	14 16	14 21	14 25	14 28	14 31
New Cross	a				13 29				13 44				13 59				14 14				14 29		
New Cross Gate	d		13 20	13 25			13 35	13 40			13 50	13 55			14 05	14 10			14 20	14 25			14 35
Brockley	d		13 23	13 28			13 38	13 43			13 53	13 58			14 08	14 13			14 23	14 28			14 38
Honor Oak Park	d		13 25	13 30			13 40	13 45			13 55	14 00			14 10	14 15			14 25	14 30			14 40
Forest Hill	d		13 28	13 33			13 43	13 48			13 58	14 03			14 13	14 18			14 28	14 33			14 43
Sydenham	d		13 31	13 36			13 46	13 51			14 01	14 06			14 16	14 21			14 31	14 36			14 46
Crystal Palace	a			13 41				13 56				14 11				14 26				14 41			
Penge West	d		13 33				13 48				14 03				14 18				14 33				14 48
Anerley	d		13 35				13 50				14 05				14 20				14 35				14 50
Norwood Junction	d		13 38				13 53				14 08				14 23				14 38				14 53
West Croydon	a		13 44				13 59				14 14				14 29				14 44				14 59
Queens Rd Peckham	d	13 17				13 32				13 47				14 02				14 17				14 32	
Peckham Rye	d	13 21				13 36				13 50				14 06				14 20				14 36	
Denmark Hill	d	13 23				13 38				13 53				14 08				14 23				14 38	
Clapham High Street	d	13 28				13 43				13 57				14 13				14 27				14 43	
Wandsworth Road	d	13 29				13 44				13 59				14 14				14 29				14 44	
Clapham Junction	a	13 40				13 55				14 10				14 25				14 40				14 55	

		LO	LO	LO	LO	LO	LO	LO	LO	LO	LO	LO	LO	LO	LO	LO	LO	LO	LO	LO	LO	LO
Highbury & Islington	d	14 13		14 20		14 28		14 35		14 43		14 50		14 58		15 05		15 13		15 20		15 28
Canonbury	d	14 15		14 22		14 30		14 37		14 45		14 52		15 00		15 07		15 15		15 22		15 30
Dalston Junction	d	14 18	14 22	14 25	14 28	14 33	14 37	14 40	14 43	14 48	14 52	14 55	14 58	15 03	15 07	15 10	15 13	15 18	15 22	15 25	15 28	15 33
Haggerston	d	14 19	14 23	14 26	14 29	14 34	14 38	14 41	14 44	14 49	14 53	14 56	14 59	15 04	15 08	15 11	15 14	15 19	15 23	15 26	15 29	15 34
Hoxton	d	14 21	14 25	14 28	14 31	14 36	14 40	14 43	14 46	14 51	14 55	14 58	15 01	15 06	15 10	15 13	15 16	15 21	15 25	15 28	15 31	15 36
Shoreditch High Street	d	14 24	14 28	14 31	14 34	14 39	14 43	14 46	14 49	14 54	14 58	15 01	15 04	15 09	15 13	15 16	15 19	15 24	15 28	15 31	15 34	15 39
Whitechapel	d	14 26	14 30	14 33	14 36	14 41	14 45	14 48	14 51	14 56	15 00	15 03	15 06	15 11	15 15	15 18	15 21	15 26	15 30	15 33	15 36	15 41
Shadwell	d	14 28	14 32	14 35	14 38	14 43	14 47	14 50	14 53	14 58	15 02	15 05	15 08	15 13	15 17	15 20	15 23	15 28	15 32	15 35	15 38	15 43
Wapping	d	14 30	14 34	14 37	14 40	14 45	14 49	14 52	14 55	15 00	15 04	15 07	15 10	15 15	15 19	15 22	15 25	15 30	15 34	15 37	15 40	15 45
Rotherhithe	d	14 32	14 36	14 39	14 42	14 47	14 51	14 54	14 57	15 02	15 06	15 09	15 12	15 17	15 21	15 24	15 27	15 32	15 36	15 39	15 42	15 47
Canada Water	d	14 34	14 38	14 41	14 44	14 49	14 53	14 56	14 59	15 04	15 08	15 11	15 14	15 19	15 23	15 26	15 29	15 34	15 38	15 41	15 44	15 49
Surrey Quays	d	14 36	14 40	14 43	14 46	14 51	14 55	14 58	15 01	15 06	15 10	15 13	15 16	15 21	15 25	15 28	15 31	15 36	15 40	15 43	15 46	15 51
New Cross	a		14 44				14 59				15 14				15 29				15 44			
New Cross Gate	d	14 40			14 50	14 55			15 05	15 10			15 20	15 25			15 35	15 40			15 50	15 55
Brockley	d	14 43			14 53	14 58			15 08	15 13			15 23	15 28			15 38	15 43			15 53	15 58
Honor Oak Park	d	14 45			14 55	15 00			15 10	15 15			15 25	15 30			15 40	15 45			15 55	16 00
Forest Hill	d	14 48			14 58	15 03			15 13	15 18			15 28	15 33			15 43	15 48			15 58	16 03
Sydenham	d	14 51			15 01	15 06			15 16	15 21			15 31	15 36			15 46	15 51			16 01	16 06
Crystal Palace	a	14 56				15 11				15 26				15 41				15 56				16 11
Penge West	d				15 03				15 18				15 33				15 48				16 03	
Anerley	d				15 05				15 20				15 35				15 50				16 05	
Norwood Junction	d				15 08				15 23				15 38				15 53				16 08	
West Croydon	a				15 14				15 29				15 44				15 59				16 14	
Queens Rd Peckham	d			14 47				15 02				15 17				15 32				15 47		
Peckham Rye	d			14 50				15 06				15 20				15 36				15 50		
Denmark Hill	d			14 53				15 08				15 23				15 38				15 53		
Clapham High Street	d			14 57				15 13				15 27				15 43				15 57		
Wandsworth Road	d			14 59				15 14				15 29				15 44				15 59		
Clapham Junction	a			15 10				15 25				15 40				15 55				16 10		

Table T178-F

Sundays

15 December to 10 May

Highbury & Islington - New Cross, Crystal Palace, West Croydon and Clapham Junction

		LO	LO	LO	LO	LO	LO	LO	LO	LO		LO	LO	LO	LO	LO	LO	LO	LO	LO		LO	LO	LO	LO
Highbury & Islington	d		15 35		15 43		15 50		15 58			16 05		16 13		16 20		16 28		16 35			16 43		16 50
Canonbury	d		15 37		15 45		15 52		16 00			16 07		16 15		16 22		16 30		16 37			16 45		16 52
Dalston Junction	d	15 37	15 40	15 43	15 48	15 52	15 55	15 58	16 03	16 07		16 10	16 13	16 18	16 22	16 25	16 28	16 33	16 37	16 40		16 43	16 48	16 52	16 55
Haggerston	d	15 38	15 41	15 44	15 49	15 53	15 56	15 59	16 04	16 08		16 11	16 14	16 19	16 23	16 26	16 29	16 34	16 38	16 41		16 44	16 49	16 53	16 56
Hoxton	d	15 40	15 43	15 46	15 51	15 55	15 58	16 01	16 06	16 10		16 13	16 16	16 21	16 25	16 28	16 31	16 36	16 40	16 43		16 46	16 51	16 55	16 58
Shoreditch High Street	d	15 43	15 46	15 49	15 54	15 58	16 01	16 04	16 09	16 13		16 16	16 19	16 24	16 28	16 31	16 34	16 39	16 43	16 46		16 49	16 54	16 58	17 01
Whitechapel	d	15 45	15 48	15 51	15 56	16 00	16 03	16 06	16 11	16 15		16 18	16 21	16 26	16 30	16 33	16 36	16 41	16 45	16 48		16 51	16 56	17 00	17 03
Shadwell	d	15 47	15 50	15 53	15 58	16 02	16 05	16 08	16 13	16 17		16 20	16 23	16 28	16 32	16 35	16 38	16 43	16 47	16 50		16 53	16 58	17 02	17 05
Wapping	d	15 49	15 52	15 55	16 00	16 04	16 07	16 10	16 15	16 19		16 22	16 25	16 30	16 34	16 37	16 40	16 45	16 49	16 52		16 55	17 00	17 04	17 07
Rotherhithe	d	15 51	15 54	15 57	16 02	16 06	16 09	16 12	16 17	16 21		16 24	16 27	16 32	16 36	16 39	16 42	16 47	16 51	16 54		16 57	17 02	17 06	17 09
Canada Water	d	15 53	15 56	15 59	16 04	16 08	16 11	16 14	16 19	16 23		16 26	16 29	16 34	16 38	16 41	16 44	16 49	16 53	16 56		16 59	17 04	17 08	17 11
Surrey Quays	d	15 55	15 58	16 01	16 06	16 10	16 13	16 16	16 21	16 25		16 28	16 31	16 36	16 40	16 43	16 46	16 51	16 55	16 58		17 01	17 06	17 10	17 13
New Cross	a	15 59				16 14				16 29					16 44				16 59					17 14	
New Cross Gate 4	d			16 05	16 10			16 20	16 25				16 35	16 40			16 50	16 55				17 05	17 10		
Brockley	d			16 08	16 13			16 23	16 28				16 38	16 43			16 53	16 58				17 08	17 13		
Honor Oak Park	d			16 10	16 15			16 25	16 30				16 40	16 45			16 55	17 00				17 10	17 15		
Forest Hill 4	d			16 13	16 18			16 28	16 33				16 43	16 48			16 58	17 03				17 13	17 18		
Sydenham	d			16 16	16 21			16 31	16 36				16 46	16 51			17 01	17 06				17 16	17 21		
Crystal Palace 4	a				16 26				16 41					16 56				17 11					17 26		
Penge West	d			16 18				16 33					16 48				17 03					17 18			
Anerley	d			16 20				16 35					16 50				17 05					17 20			
Norwood Junction 2	d			16 23				16 38					16 53				17 08					17 23			
West Croydon 4	a			16 29				16 44					16 59				17 15					17 30			
Queens Rd Peckham	d		16 02				16 17					16 32				16 47				17 02					17 17
Peckham Rye 4	d		16 06				16 20					16 36				16 50				17 06					17 20
Denmark Hill 4	d		16 08				16 23					16 38				16 53				17 08					17 23
Clapham High Street ⊖	d		16 13				16 27					16 43				16 57				17 13					17 27
Wandsworth Road	d		16 14				16 29					16 44				16 59				17 14					17 29
Clapham Junction	a		16 25				16 40					16 55				17 10				17 25					17 40

		LO	LO	LO	LO	LO		LO	LO	LO	LO	LO	LO	LO	LO	LO		LO	LO	LO	LO	LO	LO	LO	LO
Highbury & Islington	d		16 58		17 05			17 13		17 20		17 28		17 35		17 43			17 50		17 58		18 05		18 13
Canonbury	d		17 00		17 07			17 15		17 22		17 30		17 37		17 45			17 52		18 00		18 07		18 15
Dalston Junction	d	16 58	17 03	17 07	17 10	17 13		17 18	17 22	17 25	17 28	17 33	17 37	17 40	17 43	17 48		17 52	17 55	17 58	18 03	18 07	18 10	18 13	18 18
Haggerston	d	16 59	17 04	17 08	17 11	17 14		17 19	17 23	17 26	17 29	17 34	17 38	17 41	17 44	17 49		17 53	17 56	17 59	18 04	18 08	18 11	18 14	18 19
Hoxton	d	17 01	17 06	17 10	17 13	17 16		17 21	17 25	17 28	17 31	17 36	17 40	17 43	17 46	17 51		17 55	17 58	18 01	18 06	18 10	18 13	18 16	18 21
Shoreditch High Street	d	17 04	17 09	17 13	17 16	17 19		17 24	17 28	17 31	17 34	17 39	17 43	17 46	17 49	17 54		17 58	18 01	18 04	18 09	18 13	18 16	18 19	18 24
Whitechapel	d	17 06	17 11	17 15	17 18	17 21		17 26	17 30	17 33	17 36	17 41	17 45	17 48	17 51	17 56		18 00	18 03	18 06	18 11	18 15	18 18	18 21	18 26
Shadwell	d	17 08	17 13	17 17	17 20	17 23		17 28	17 32	17 35	17 38	17 43	17 47	17 50	17 53	17 58		18 02	18 05	18 08	18 13	18 17	18 20	18 23	18 28
Wapping	d	17 10	17 15	17 19	17 22	17 25		17 30	17 34	17 37	17 40	17 45	17 49	17 52	17 55	18 00		18 04	18 07	18 10	18 15	18 19	18 22	18 25	18 30
Rotherhithe	d	17 12	17 17	17 21	17 24	17 27		17 32	17 36	17 39	17 42	17 47	17 51	17 54	17 57	18 02		18 06	18 09	18 12	18 17	18 21	18 24	18 27	18 32
Canada Water	d	17 14	17 19	17 23	17 26	17 29		17 34	17 38	17 41	17 44	17 49	17 53	17 56	17 59	18 04		18 08	18 11	18 14	18 19	18 23	18 26	18 29	18 34
Surrey Quays	d	17 16	17 21	17 25	17 28	17 31		17 36	17 40	17 43	17 46	17 51	17 55	17 58	18 01	18 06		18 10	18 13	18 16	18 21	18 25	18 28	18 31	18 36
New Cross	a			17 29					17 44				17 59					18 14				18 29			
New Cross Gate 4	d	17 20	17 25			17 35		17 40			17 50	17 55			18 05	18 10				18 20	18 25			18 35	18 40
Brockley	d	17 23	17 28			17 38		17 43			17 53	17 58			18 08	18 13				18 23	18 28			18 38	18 43
Honor Oak Park	d	17 25	17 30			17 40		17 45			17 55	18 00			18 10	18 15				18 25	18 30			18 40	18 45
Forest Hill 4	d	17 28	17 33			17 43		17 48			17 58	18 03			18 13	18 18				18 28	18 33			18 43	18 48
Sydenham	d	17 31	17 36			17 46		17 51			18 01	18 06			18 16	18 21				18 31	18 36			18 46	18 51
Crystal Palace 4	a		17 41					17 56				18 11				18 26					18 41				18 56
Penge West	d	17 33				17 48					18 03				18 18					18 33				18 48	
Anerley	d	17 35				17 50					18 05				18 20					18 35				18 50	
Norwood Junction 2	d	17 38				17 53					18 08				18 23					18 38				18 53	
West Croydon 4	a	17 45				18 00					18 15				18 30					18 45				19 00	
Queens Rd Peckham	d				17 32					17 47				18 02					18 17				18 32		
Peckham Rye 4	d				17 36					17 50				18 06					18 20				18 36		
Denmark Hill 4	d				17 38					17 53				18 08					18 23				18 38		
Clapham High Street ⊖	d				17 43					17 57				18 13					18 27				18 43		
Wandsworth Road	d				17 44					17 59				18 14					18 29				18 44		
Clapham Junction	a				17 55					18 10				18 25					18 40				18 55		

		LO		LO	LO	LO	LO	LO	LO	LO	LO	LO	LO	LO	LO	LO	LO	LO	LO	LO	LO			
Highbury & Islington	d			18 20		18 28		18 35		18 43		18 50		18 58		19 05		19 13		19 20				
Canonbury	d			18 22		18 30		18 37		18 45		18 52		19 00		19 07		19 15		19 22				
Dalston Junction	d	18 22		18 25	18 28	18 33	18 37	18 40	18 43	18 48	18 52	18 55	18 58	19 03	19 07	19 10	19 13	19 18	19 22	19 25	19 28			
Haggerston	d	18 23		18 26	18 29	18 34	18 38	18 41	18 44	18 49	18 53	18 56	18 59	19 04	19 08	19 11	19 14	19 19	19 23	19 26	19 29			
Hoxton	d	18 25		18 28	18 31	18 36	18 40	18 43	18 46	18 51	18 55	18 58	19 01	19 06	19 10	19 13	19 16	19 21	19 25	19 28	19 31			
Shoreditch High Street	d	18 28		18 31	18 34	18 39	18 43	18 46	18 49	18 54	18 58	19 01	19 04	19 09	19 13	19 16	19 19	19 24	19 28	19 31	19 34			
Whitechapel	d	18 30		18 33	18 36	18 41	18 45	18 48	18 51	18 56	19 00	19 03	19 06	19 11	19 15	19 18	19 21	19 26	19 30	19 33	19 36			
Shadwell	d	18 32		18 35	18 38	18 43	18 47	18 50	18 53	18 58	19 02	19 05	19 08	19 13	19 17	19 20	19 23	19 28	19 32	19 35	19 38			
Wapping	d	18 34		18 37	18 40	18 45	18 49	18 52	18 55	19 00	19 04	19 07	19 10	19 15	19 19	19 22	19 25	19 30	19 34	19 37	19 40			
Rotherhithe	d	18 36		18 39	18 42	18 47	18 51	18 54	18 57	19 02	19 06	19 09	19 12	19 17	19 21	19 24	19 27	19 32	19 36	19 39	19 42			
Canada Water	d	18 38		18 41	18 44	18 49	18 53	18 56	18 59	19 04	19 08	19 11	19 14	19 19	19 23	19 26	19 29	19 34	19 38	19 41	19 44	and at		
Surrey Quays	d	18 40		18 43	18 46	18 51	18 55	18 58	19 01	19 06	19 10	19 13	19 16	19 21	19 25	19 28	19 31	19 36	19 40	19 43	19 46	the same		
New Cross	a	18 44					18 59				19 14				19 29				19 44			minutes		
New Cross Gate 4	d				18 50	18 55			19 05	19 10			19 20	19 25			19 35	19 40			19 50	past		
Brockley	d				18 53	18 58			19 08	19 13			19 23	19 28			19 38	19 43			19 53	each		
Honor Oak Park	d				18 55	19 00			19 10	19 15			19 25	19 30			19 40	19 45			19 55	hour until		
Forest Hill 4	d				18 58	19 03			19 13	19 18			19 28	19 33			19 43	19 48			19 58			
Sydenham	d				19 01	19 06			19 16	19 21			19 31	19 36			19 46	19 51			20 01			
Crystal Palace 4	a					19 11				19 26				19 41				19 56						
Penge West	d				19 03				19 18				19 33				19 48				20 03			
Anerley	d				19 05				19 20				19 35				19 50				20 05			
Norwood Junction 2	d				19 08				19 23				19 38				19 53				20 08			
West Croydon 4	a				19 15				19 29				19 44				19 59				20 14			
Queens Rd Peckham	d			18 47				19 02				19 17				19 32				19 47				
Peckham Rye 4	d			18 50				19 06				19 20				19 36				19 50				
Denmark Hill 4	d			18 53				19 08				19 23				19 38				19 53				
Clapham High Street ⊖	d			18 57				19 13				19 27				19 43				19 57				
Wandsworth Road	d			18 59				19 14				19 29				19 44				19 59				
Clapham Junction	a			19 10				19 25				19 40				19 55				20 10				

Table T178-F

Sundays

15 December to 10 May

Highbury & Islington - New Cross, Crystal Palace, West Croydon and Clapham Junction

		LO	LO	LO	LO	LO	LO	LO	LO	LO	LO	LO	LO	LO	LO	LO	LO		LO	LO	LO	LO	LO	LO	LO
Highbury & Islington	d	21 28		21 35		21 43		21 50		21 58		22 05		22 13		22 20				22 35		22 43		22 50	
Canonbury	d	21 30		21 37		21 45		21 52		22 00		22 07		22 15		22 22				22 37		22 45		22 52	
Dalston Junction	d	21 33	21 37	21 40	21 43	21 48	21 52	21 55	21 58	22 03	22 07	22 10	22 13	22 18	22 22	22 25	22 28		22 37	22 40	22 43	22 48	22 52	22 55	22 58
Haggerston	d	21 34	21 38	21 41	21 44	21 49	21 53	21 56	21 59	22 04	22 08	22 11	22 14	22 19	22 23	22 26	22 29		22 38	22 41	22 44	22 49	22 53	22 56	22 59
Hoxton	d	21 36	21 40	21 43	21 46	21 51	21 55	21 58	22 01	22 06	22 10	22 13	22 16	22 21	22 25	22 28	22 31		22 40	22 43	22 46	22 51	22 55	22 58	23 01
Shoreditch High Street	d	21 39	21 43	21 46	21 49	21 54	21 58	22 01	22 04	22 09	22 13	22 16	22 19	22 24	22 28	22 31	22 34		22 43	22 46	22 49	22 54	22 58	23 01	23 04
Whitechapel	d	21 41	21 45	21 48	21 51	21 56	22 00	22 03	22 06	22 11	22 15	22 18	22 21	22 26	22 30	22 33	22 36		22 45	22 48	22 51	22 56	23 00	23 03	23 06
Shadwell	d	21 43	21 47	21 50	21 53	21 58	22 02	22 05	22 08	22 13	22 17	22 20	22 23	22 28	22 32	22 35	22 38		22 47	22 50	22 53	22 58	23 02	23 05	23 08
Wapping	d	21 45	21 49	21 52	21 55	22 00	22 04	22 07	22 10	22 15	22 19	22 22	22 25	22 30	22 34	22 37	22 40		22 49	22 52	22 55	23 00	23 04	23 07	23 10
Rotherhithe	d	21 47	21 51	21 54	21 57	22 02	22 06	22 09	22 12	22 17	22 21	22 24	22 27	22 32	22 36	22 39	22 42		22 51	22 54	22 57	23 02	23 06	23 09	23 12
Canada Water	d	21 49	21 53	21 56	21 59	22 04	22 08	22 11	22 14	22 19	22 23	22 26	22 29	22 34	22 38	22 41	22 44		22 53	22 56	22 59	23 04	23 08	23 11	23 14
Surrey Quays	d	21 51	21 55	21 58	22 01	22 06	22 10	22 13	22 16	22 21	22 25	22 28	22 31	22 36	22 40	22 43	22 46		22 55	22 58	23 01	23 06	23 10	23 13	23 16
New Cross	a		21 59				22 14				22 29				22 44				22 59				23 14		
New Cross Gate 4	d	21 55			22 05	22 10			22 20	22 25			22 35	22 40			22 50				23 05	23 10			23 20
Brockley	d	21 58			22 08	22 13			22 23	22 28			22 38	22 43			22 53				23 08	23 13			23 23
Honor Oak Park	d	22 00			22 10	22 15			22 25	22 30			22 40	22 45			22 55				23 10	23 15			23 25
Forest Hill 4	d	22 03			22 13	22 18			22 28	22 33			22 43	22 48			22 58				23 13	23 18			23 28
Sydenham	d	22 06			22 16	22 21			22 31	22 36			22 46	22 51			23 01				23 16	23 21			23 31
Crystal Palace 4	a	22 11				22 26				22 41				22 56								23 26			
Penge West	d				22 18				22 33				22 48				23 03				23 18				23 33
Anerley	d				22 20				22 35				22 50				23 05				23 20				23 35
Norwood Junction 2	d				22 23				22 38				22 53				23 08				23 23				23 38
West Croydon 4	a				22 29				22 44				22 59				23 14				23 29				23 45
Queens Rd Peckham	d			22 02				22 17				22 32				22 47				23 02				23 17	
Peckham Rye 4	d			22 06				22 20				22 36				22 50				23 06				23 20	
Denmark Hill 4	d			22 08				22 23				22 38				22 53				23 08				23 23	
Clapham High Street ⊖	d			22 13				22 27				22 43				22 57				23 13				23 27	
Wandsworth Road	d			22 14				22 29				22 44				22 59				23 14				23 29	
Clapham Junction	a			22 25				22 40				22 55				23 10				23 25				23 40	

		LO	LO		LO	LO	LO
Highbury & Islington	d		23 05			23 13	23 23
Canonbury	d		23 07			23 15	23 25
Dalston Junction	d	23 07	23 10		23 13	23 18	23 28
Haggerston	d	23 08	23 11		23 14	23 19	23 29
Hoxton	d	23 10	23 13		23 16	23 21	23 31
Shoreditch High Street	d	23 13	23 16		23 19	23 24	23 34
Whitechapel	d	23 15	23 18		23 21	23 26	23 36
Shadwell	d	23 17	23 20		23 23	23 28	23 38
Wapping	d	23 19	23 22		23 25	23 30	23 40
Rotherhithe	d	23 21	23 24		23 27	23 32	23 42
Canada Water	d	23 23	23 26		23 29	23 34	23 44
Surrey Quays	d	23 25	23 28		23 31	23 36	23 46
New Cross	a	23 29					
New Cross Gate 4	d				23 35	23 42	23 50
Brockley	d				23 38	23 45	23 53
Honor Oak Park	d				23 40	23 47	23 55
Forest Hill 4	d				23 43	23 50	23 58
Sydenham	d				23 46	23 53	00 01
Crystal Palace 4	a					23 57	
Penge West	d				23 48		00 03
Anerley	d				23 50		00 05
Norwood Junction 2	d				23 53		00 08
West Croydon 4	a				23 59		00 16
Queens Rd Peckham	d		23 32				
Peckham Rye 4	d		23 36				
Denmark Hill 4	d		23 38				
Clapham High Street ⊖	d		23 43				
Wandsworth Road	d		23 44				
Clapham Junction	a		23 55				

Clapham Junction and West Croydon, Crystal Palace, New Cross - Highbury & Islington

Miles	Miles	Miles	Miles			LO MX A	LO MX B	LO MX C	LO MX D	LO MX C	LO MX B	LO	LO	LO	LO	LO	LO	LO	LO	LO	LO	LO	LO
0	—	—	—	Clapham Junction	d														06 00				06 15
1½	—	—	—	**Wandsworth Road**	d														06 06				06 21
1¾	—	—	—	**Clapham High Street**	d														06 08				06 23
3¾	—	—	—	Denmark Hill	d														06 13				06 28
4¾	—	—	—	Peckham Rye	d					00 01									06 15				06 30
5¼	—	—	—	Queens Rd Peckham	d					00 03									06 17				06 32
—	—	0	—	West Croydon	d								05 31			05 46				06 01			
—	—	1¾	—	Norwood Junction	d								05 37			05 52				06 07			
—	—	2¾	—	Anerley	d								05 40			05 55				06 10			
—	—	3¼	—	Penge West	d								05 41			05 56				06 11			
—	0	—	—	Crystal Palace	d							05 32			05 47			06 02				06 17	
—	1¼	4	—	Sydenham	d							05 36	05 44		05 51	05 59		06 06		06 14		06 21	
—	2	4¾	—	Forest Hill	d							05 39	05 47		05 54	06 02		06 09		06 17		06 24	
—	3	5¾	—	Honor Oak Park	d							05 41	05 49		05 56	06 04		06 11		06 19		06 26	
—	4	6¾	—	Brockley	d						00 01	05 44	05 52		05 59	06 07		06 14		06 22		06 29	
—	4¾	7½	—	New Cross Gate	d						00 03	05 46	05 54		06 01	06 09		06 16		06 24		06 31	
—	—	—	0	New Cross	d									05 57			06 12				06 27		
6¾	6	8¾	1½	**Surrey Quays**	d					00 06	00 09	05 50	05 57	06 01	06 05	06 12	06 16	06 20	06 23	06 27	06 31	06 35	06 38
7	6¼	9¼	1¾	**Canada Water**	d					00 08	00 11	05 52	05 59	06 03	06 07	06 14	06 18	06 22	06 25	06 29	06 33	06 37	06 40
7¼	6½	9½	2	**Rotherhithe**	d				00 01	00 10	00 12	05 54	06 01	06 05	06 08	06 16	06 20	06 23	06 27	06 31	06 35	06 38	06 42
7½	6¾	9¾	2¼	**Wapping**	d				00 02	00 11	00 14	05 55	06 02	06 06	06 10	06 17	06 21	06 25	06 28	06 32	06 36	06 40	06 43
8¼	7¼	10¼	2¾	**Shadwell**	d			00 01	00 04	00 13	00 16	05 57	06 04	06 08	06 12	06 19	06 23	06 27	06 30	06 34	06 38	06 42	06 45
9	8	11	3½	**Whitechapel**	d			00 03	00 07	00 16	00 18	06 00	06 07	06 11	06 14	06 22	06 26	06 29	06 33	06 37	06 41	06 44	06 48
9¾	8¾	11¾	4¼	**Shoreditch High Street**	d		00 02	00 05	00 09	00 18	00 21	06 02	06 09	06 13	06 17	06 24	06 28	06 32	06 35	06 39	06 43	06 47	06 50
10¼	9½	12¼	5	**Hoxton**	d	00 01	00 04	00 07	00 11	00 20	00 23	06 04	06 11	06 15	06 19	06 26	06 30	06 34	06 37	06 41	06 45	06 49	06 52
10¾	10	12¾	5½	**Haggerston**	d	00 02	00 06	00 09	00 13	00 22	00 25	06 06	06 13	06 17	06 21	06 28	06 32	06 36	06 39	06 43	06 47	06 51	06 54
11¼	10½	13¼	5¾	**Dalston Junction**	a	00 04	00 08	00 14	00 15	00 29	00 27	06 08	06 15	06 19	06 23	06 30	06 34	06 38	06 44	06 45	06 49	06 53	06 59
12¼	11½	—	—	Canonbury	a		00 11		00 18		00 30	06 11	06 18		06 26	06 33		06 41		06 48		06 56	
12¾	12	—	—	Highbury & Islington	a		00 15		00 25		00 32	06 15	06 23		06 30	06 38		06 45		06 53		07 00	

		LO	LO	LO	LO E	LO	LO	LO	LO	LO	LO	LO	LO	LO	LO	LO	LO	LO	LO	LO	LO	LO	LO
Clapham Junction	d								06 45				07 00				07 15				07 30		
Wandsworth Road	d				06 36				06 51				07 06				07 21				07 36		
Clapham High Street	d				06 38				06 53				07 08				07 23				07 38		
Denmark Hill	d				06 43				06 58				07 13				07 28				07 43		
Peckham Rye	d				06 45				07 00				07 15				07 30				07 45		
Queens Rd Peckham	d				06 47				07 02				07 17				07 32				07 47		
West Croydon	d	06 16				06 31				06 46				07 01				07 15				07 31	
Norwood Junction	d	06 22				06 37				06 52				07 07				07 22				07 37	
Anerley	d	06 25				06 40				06 55				07 10				07 25				07 40	
Penge West	d	06 26				06 41				06 56				07 11				07 26				07 41	
Crystal Palace	d			06 32				06 47				07 02				07 17				07 32			
Sydenham	d	06 29		06 36		06 44		06 51		06 59		07 06		07 14		07 21		07 29		07 36		07 44	
Forest Hill	d	06 32		06 39		06 47		06 54		07 02		07 09		07 17		07 24		07 32		07 39		07 47	
Honor Oak Park	d	06 34		06 41		06 49		06 56		07 04		07 11		07 19		07 26		07 34		07 41		07 49	
Brockley	d	06 37		06 44		06 52		06 59		07 07		07 14		07 22		07 29		07 37		07 44		07 52	
New Cross Gate	d	06 39		06 46		06 54		07 01		07 09		07 16		07 24		07 31		07 39		07 46		07 54	
New Cross	d		06 42				06 57				07 12				07 27				07 42				07 57
Surrey Quays	d	06 42	06 46	06 50	06 53	06 57	07 01	07 05	07 08	07 12	07 16	07 20	07 23	07 27	07 31	07 35	07 38	07 42	07 46	07 50	07 53	07 57	08 01
Canada Water	d	06 44	06 48	06 52	06 55	06 59	07 03	07 07	07 10	07 14	07 18	07 22	07 25	07 29	07 33	07 37	07 40	07 44	07 48	07 52	07 55	07 59	08 03
Rotherhithe	d	06 46	06 50	06 53	06 57	07 01	07 05	07 08	07 12	07 16	07 20	07 23	07 27	07 31	07 35	07 38	07 42	07 46	07 50	07 53	07 57	08 01	08 05
Wapping	d	06 47	06 51	06 55	06 58	07 02	07 06	07 10	07 13	07 17	07 21	07 25	07 28	07 32	07 36	07 40	07 43	07 47	07 51	07 55	07 58	08 02	08 06
Shadwell	d	06 49	06 53	06 57	07 00	07 04	07 08	07 12	07 15	07 19	07 23	07 27	07 30	07 34	07 38	07 42	07 45	07 49	07 53	07 57	08 00	08 04	08 08
Whitechapel	d	06 52	06 56	06 59	07 03	07 07	07 11	07 14	07 18	07 22	07 26	07 29	07 33	07 37	07 41	07 44	07 48	07 52	07 56	07 59	08 03	08 07	08 11
Shoreditch High Street	d	06 54	06 58	07 02	07 05	07 09	07 13	07 17	07 20	07 24	07 28	07 32	07 35	07 39	07 43	07 47	07 50	07 54	07 58	08 02	08 05	08 09	08 13
Hoxton	d	06 56	07 00	07 04	07 07	07 11	07 15	07 19	07 22	07 26	07 30	07 34	07 37	07 41	07 45	07 49	07 52	07 56	08 00	08 04	08 07	08 11	08 15
Haggerston	d	06 58	07 02	07 06	07 09	07 13	07 17	07 21	07 24	07 28	07 32	07 36	07 39	07 43	07 47	07 51	07 54	07 58	08 02	08 06	08 09	08 13	08 17
Dalston Junction	a	07 00	07 04	07 08	07 14	07 15	07 19	07 23	07 29	07 30	07 34	07 38	07 44	07 46	07 49	07 53	07 59	08 01	08 04	08 08	08 14	08 16	08 19
Canonbury	a	07 03		07 11		07 18		07 26		07 33		07 41		07 48		07 56		08 03		08 11		08 18	
Highbury & Islington	a	07 08		07 15		07 23		07 30		07 38		07 45		07 55		08 00		08 09		08 17		08 25	

		LO	LO	LO	LO	LO	LO	LO	LO	LO	LO	LO	LO	LO	LO	LO	LO	LO	LO	LO	LO	LO	LO
Clapham Junction	d		07 45				08 00				08 15				08 30				08 45				09 00
Wandsworth Road	d		07 51				08 06				08 21				08 36				08 51				09 06
Clapham High Street	d		07 53				08 08				08 23				08 38				08 53				09 08
Denmark Hill	d		07 58				08 13				08 28				08 43				08 58				09 13
Peckham Rye	d		08 00				08 15				08 30				08 45				09 00				09 15
Queens Rd Peckham	d		08 02				08 17				08 32				08 47				09 02				09 17
West Croydon	d			07 46				08 01				08 15				08 31				08 45			
Norwood Junction	d			07 52				08 07				08 22				08 37				08 52			
Anerley	d			07 55				08 10				08 25				08 40				08 55			
Penge West	d			07 56				08 11				08 26				08 41				08 56			
Crystal Palace	d	07 47				08 03				08 17				08 33				08 47				09 02	
Sydenham	d	07 51		07 59		08 06		08 14		08 21		08 29		08 36		08 44		08 51		08 59		09 06	
Forest Hill	d	07 54		08 02		08 09		08 17		08 24		08 32		08 39		08 47		08 54		09 02		09 09	
Honor Oak Park	d	07 56		08 04		08 11		08 19		08 26		08 34		08 41		08 49		08 56		09 04		09 11	
Brockley	d	07 59		08 07		08 14		08 22		08 29		08 37		08 44		08 52		08 59		09 07		09 14	
New Cross Gate	d	08 01		08 09		08 16		08 24		08 31		08 39		08 46		08 54		09 01		09 09		09 16	
New Cross	d				08 12				08 27				08 42				08 57				09 12		
Surrey Quays	d	08 05	08 08	08 12	08 16	08 20	08 23	08 27	08 31	08 35	08 38	08 42	08 46	08 50	08 53	08 57	09 01	09 05	09 08	09 12	09 16	09 20	09 23
Canada Water	d	08 07	08 10	08 14	08 18	08 22	08 25	08 29	08 33	08 37	08 40	08 44	08 48	08 52	08 55	08 59	09 03	09 07	09 10	09 14	09 18	09 22	09 25
Rotherhithe	d	08 08	08 12	08 16	08 20	08 23	08 27	08 31	08 35	08 38	08 42	08 46	08 50	08 53	08 57	09 01	09 05	09 08	09 12	09 16	09 20	09 23	09 27
Wapping	d	08 10	08 13	08 17	08 21	08 25	08 28	08 32	08 36	08 40	08 43	08 47	08 51	08 55	08 58	09 02	09 06	09 10	09 13	09 17	09 21	09 25	09 28
Shadwell	d	08 12	08 15	08 19	08 23	08 27	08 30	08 34	08 38	08 42	08 45	08 49	08 53	08 57	09 00	09 04	09 08	09 12	09 15	09 19	09 23	09 27	09 30
Whitechapel	d	08 14	08 18	08 22	08 26	08 29	08 33	08 37	08 41	08 44	08 48	08 52	08 56	08 59	09 03	09 07	09 11	09 14	09 18	09 22	09 26	09 29	09 33
Shoreditch High Street	d	08 17	08 20	08 24	08 28	08 32	08 35	08 39	08 43	08 47	08 50	08 54	08 58	09 02	09 05	09 09	09 13	09 17	09 20	09 24	09 28	09 32	09 35
Hoxton	d	08 19	08 22	08 26	08 30	08 34	08 37	08 41	08 45	08 49	08 52	08 56	09 00	09 04	09 07	09 11	09 15	09 19	09 22	09 26	09 30	09 34	09 37
Haggerston	d	08 21	08 24	08 28	08 32	08 36	08 39	08 43	08 47	08 51	08 54	08 58	09 02	09 06	09 09	09 13	09 17	09 21	09 24	09 28	09 32	09 36	09 39
Dalston Junction	a	08 23	08 29	08 31	08 35	08 39	08 45	08 46	08 50	08 53	09 00	09 01	09 04	09 09	09 15	09 16	09 19	09 23	09 29	09 31	09 34	09 38	09 44
Canonbury	a	08 26		08 33		08 41		08 48		08 56		09 03		09 11		09 18		09 26		09 33		09 41	
Highbury & Islington	a	08 32		08 40		08 47		08 55		09 02		09 09		09 17		09 25		09 32		09 39		09 47	

A From New Cross ELL
B From Crystal Palace
C From Clapham Junction Plats 0-2
D From West Croydon
E From Battersea Park

Table T178-R

Mondays to Fridays
16 December to 15 May

Clapham Junction and West Croydon, Crystal Palace, New Cross - Highbury & Islington

		LO	LO	LO	LO	LO	LO	LO	LO	LO	LO	LO	LO	LO	LO	LO	LO	LO	LO	LO	LO	LO
Clapham Junction	d				09 15				09 30				09 45				10 00				10 15	
Wandsworth Road	d				09 21				09 36				09 51				10 06				10 21	
Clapham High Street	d				09 23				09 38				09 53				10 08				10 23	
Denmark Hill	d				09 28				09 43				09 58				10 13				10 28	
Peckham Rye	d				09 30				09 45				10 00				10 15				10 30	
Queens Rd Peckham	d				09 32				09 47				10 02				10 17				10 32	
West Croydon	d	09 01				09 16				09 31				09 46				10 01				10 15
Norwood Junction	d	09 07				09 22				09 37				09 52				10 07				10 21
Anerley	d	09 10				09 25				09 40				09 55				10 10				10 24
Penge West	d	09 11				09 26				09 41				09 56				10 11				10 25
Crystal Palace	d			09 17				09 32				09 47				10 02				10 17		
Sydenham	d	09 14		09 21		09 29		09 36		09 44		09 51		09 59		10 06		10 14		10 21		10 28
Forest Hill	d	09 17		09 24		09 32		09 39		09 47		09 54		10 02		10 09		10 17		10 24		10 32
Honor Oak Park	d	09 19		09 26		09 34		09 41		09 49		09 56		10 04		10 11		10 19		10 26		10 34
Brockley	d	09 22		09 29		09 37		09 44		09 52		09 59		10 07		10 14		10 22		10 29		10 37
New Cross Gate	d	09 24		09 31		09 39		09 46		09 54		10 01		10 09		10 16		10 24		10 31		10 39
New Cross	d		09 27				09 42				09 57				10 12				10 27			
Surrey Quays	d	09 27	09 31	09 35	09 38	09 42	09 46	09 50	09 53	09 57	10 01	10 05	10 08	10 12	10 16	10 20	10 23	10 27	10 31	10 35	10 38	10 42
Canada Water	d	09 29	09 33	09 37	09 40	09 44	09 48	09 52	09 55	09 59	10 03	10 07	10 10	10 14	10 18	10 22	10 25	10 29	10 33	10 37	10 40	10 44
Rotherhithe	d	09 31	09 35	09 38	09 42	09 46	09 50	09 53	09 57	10 01	10 05	10 08	10 12	10 16	10 20	10 23	10 27	10 31	10 35	10 38	10 42	10 46
Wapping	d	09 32	09 36	09 40	09 43	09 47	09 51	09 55	09 58	10 02	10 06	10 10	10 13	10 17	10 21	10 25	10 28	10 32	10 36	10 40	10 43	10 47
Shadwell	d	09 34	09 38	09 42	09 45	09 49	09 53	09 57	10 00	10 04	10 08	10 12	10 15	10 19	10 23	10 27	10 30	10 34	10 38	10 42	10 45	10 49
Whitechapel	d	09 37	09 41	09 44	09 48	09 52	09 56	09 59	10 03	10 07	10 11	10 14	10 18	10 22	10 26	10 29	10 33	10 37	10 41	10 44	10 48	10 52
Shoreditch High Street	d	09 39	09 43	09 47	09 50	09 54	09 58	10 02	10 05	10 09	10 13	10 17	10 20	10 24	10 28	10 32	10 35	10 39	10 43	10 47	10 50	10 54
Hoxton	d	09 41	09 45	09 49	09 52	09 56	10 00	10 04	10 07	10 11	10 15	10 19	10 22	10 26	10 30	10 34	10 37	10 41	10 45	10 49	10 52	10 56
Haggerston	d	09 43	09 47	09 51	09 54	09 58	10 02	10 06	10 09	10 13	10 17	10 21	10 24	10 28	10 32	10 36	10 39	10 43	10 47	10 51	10 54	10 58
Dalston Junction	a	09 45	09 49	09 53	09 59	10 00	10 04	10 08	10 14	10 15	10 19	10 23	10 29	10 30	10 34	10 38	10 44	10 45	10 49	10 53	10 59	11 00
Canonbury	a	09 48		09 56		10 03		10 11		10 18		10 26		10 33		10 41		10 48		10 56		11 03
Highbury & Islington	a	09 55		10 00		10 08		10 15		10 25		10 30		10 40		10 45		10 55		11 00		11 09

		LO	LO	LO	LO	LO	LO	LO	LO	LO	LO	LO	LO	LO	LO	LO	LO	LO	LO	LO	LO	LO	LO
Clapham Junction	d			10 30				10 45				11 00				11 15				11 30			
Wandsworth Road	d			10 36				10 51				11 06				11 21				11 36			
Clapham High Street	d			10 38				10 53				11 08				11 23				11 38			
Denmark Hill	d			10 43				10 58				11 13				11 28				11 43			
Peckham Rye	d			10 45				11 00				11 15				11 30				11 45			
Queens Rd Peckham	d			10 47				11 02				11 17				11 32				11 47			
West Croydon	d				10 31				10 46				11 01				11 16				11 31		
Norwood Junction	d				10 37				10 52				11 07				11 22				11 37		
Anerley	d				10 40				10 55				11 10				11 25				11 40		
Penge West	d				10 41				10 56				11 11				11 26				11 41		
Crystal Palace	d		10 32				10 47				11 02				11 17				11 32				11 47
Sydenham	d		10 36		10 44		10 51		10 59		11 06		11 14		11 21		11 29		11 36		11 44		11 51
Forest Hill	d		10 39		10 47		10 54		11 02		11 09		11 17		11 24		11 32		11 39		11 47		11 54
Honor Oak Park	d		10 41		10 49		10 56		11 04		11 11		11 19		11 26		11 34		11 41		11 49		11 56
Brockley	d		10 44		10 52		10 59		11 07		11 14		11 22		11 29		11 37		11 44		11 52		11 59
New Cross Gate	d		10 46		10 54		11 01		11 09		11 16		11 24		11 31		11 39		11 46		11 54		12 01
New Cross	d	10 42				10 57				11 12				11 27				11 42				11 57	
Surrey Quays	d	10 46	10 50	10 53	10 57	11 01	11 05	11 08	11 12	11 16	11 20	11 23	11 27	11 31	11 35	11 38	11 42	11 46	11 50	11 53	11 57	12 01	12 05
Canada Water	d	10 48	10 52	10 55	10 59	11 03	11 07	11 10	11 14	11 18	11 22	11 25	11 29	11 33	11 37	11 40	11 44	11 48	11 52	11 55	11 59	12 03	12 07
Rotherhithe	d	10 50	10 53	10 57	11 01	11 05	11 08	11 12	11 16	11 20	11 23	11 27	11 31	11 35	11 38	11 42	11 46	11 50	11 53	11 57	12 01	12 05	12 08
Wapping	d	10 51	10 55	10 58	11 02	11 06	11 10	11 13	11 17	11 21	11 25	11 28	11 32	11 36	11 40	11 43	11 47	11 51	11 55	11 58	12 02	12 06	12 10
Shadwell	d	10 53	10 57	11 00	11 04	11 08	11 12	11 15	11 19	11 23	11 27	11 30	11 34	11 38	11 42	11 45	11 49	11 53	11 57	12 00	12 04	12 08	12 12
Whitechapel	d	10 56	10 59	11 03	11 07	11 11	11 14	11 18	11 22	11 26	11 29	11 33	11 37	11 41	11 44	11 48	11 52	11 56	11 59	12 03	12 07	12 11	12 14
Shoreditch High Street	d	10 58	11 02	11 05	11 09	11 13	11 17	11 20	11 24	11 28	11 32	11 35	11 39	11 43	11 47	11 50	11 54	11 58	12 02	12 05	12 09	12 13	12 17
Hoxton	d	11 00	11 04	11 07	11 11	11 15	11 19	11 22	11 26	11 30	11 34	11 37	11 41	11 45	11 49	11 52	11 56	12 00	12 04	12 07	12 11	12 15	12 19
Haggerston	d	11 02	11 06	11 09	11 13	11 17	11 21	11 24	11 28	11 32	11 36	11 39	11 43	11 47	11 51	11 54	11 58	12 02	12 06	12 09	12 13	12 17	12 21
Dalston Junction	a	11 04	11 08	11 14	11 15	11 19	11 23	11 29	11 30	11 34	11 38	11 44	11 45	11 49	11 53	11 59	12 00	12 04	12 08	12 14	12 15	12 19	12 23
Canonbury	a		11 11		11 18		11 26		11 33		11 41		11 48		11 56		12 03		12 11		12 18		12 26
Highbury & Islington	a		11 15		11 23		11 30		11 38		11 45		11 55		12 00		12 08		12 15		12 25		12 30

		LO	LO	LO	LO	LO	LO	LO	LO	LO	LO	LO	LO	LO	LO	LO	LO	LO	LO	LO	LO	LO
Clapham Junction	d	11 45				12 00				12 15				12 30				12 45				13 00
Wandsworth Road	d	11 51				12 06				12 21				12 36				12 51				13 06
Clapham High Street	d	11 53				12 08				12 23				12 38				12 53				13 08
Denmark Hill	d	11 58				12 13				12 28				12 43				12 58				13 13
Peckham Rye	d	12 00				12 15				12 30				12 45				13 00				13 15
Queens Rd Peckham	d	12 02				12 17				12 32				12 47				13 02				13 17
West Croydon	d		11 46				12 01				12 16				12 31				12 46			
Norwood Junction	d		11 52				12 07				12 22				12 37				12 52			
Anerley	d		11 55				12 10				12 25				12 40				12 55			
Penge West	d		11 56				12 11				12 26				12 41				12 56			
Crystal Palace	d				12 02				12 17				12 32				12 47				13 02	
Sydenham	d		11 59		12 06		12 14		12 21		12 29		12 36		12 44		12 51		12 59		13 06	
Forest Hill	d		12 02		12 09		12 17		12 24		12 32		12 39		12 47		12 54		13 02		13 09	
Honor Oak Park	d		12 04		12 11		12 19		12 26		12 34		12 41		12 49		12 56		13 04		13 11	
Brockley	d		12 07		12 14		12 22		12 29		12 37		12 44		12 52		12 59		13 07		13 14	
New Cross Gate	d		12 09		12 16		12 24		12 31		12 39		12 46		12 54		13 01		13 09		13 16	
New Cross	d			12 12				12 27				12 42				12 57				13 12		
Surrey Quays	d	12 08	12 12	12 16	12 20	12 23	12 27	12 31	12 35	12 38	12 42	12 46	12 50	12 53	12 57	13 01	13 05	13 08	13 12	13 16	13 20	13 23
Canada Water	d	12 10	12 14	12 18	12 22	12 25	12 29	12 33	12 37	12 40	12 44	12 48	12 52	12 55	12 59	13 03	13 07	13 10	13 14	13 18	13 22	13 25
Rotherhithe	d	12 12	12 16	12 20	12 23	12 27	12 31	12 35	12 38	12 42	12 46	12 50	12 53	12 57	13 01	13 05	13 08	13 12	13 16	13 20	13 23	13 27
Wapping	d	12 13	12 17	12 21	12 25	12 28	12 32	12 36	12 40	12 43	12 47	12 51	12 55	12 58	13 02	13 06	13 10	13 13	13 17	13 21	13 25	13 28
Shadwell	d	12 15	12 19	12 23	12 27	12 30	12 34	12 38	12 42	12 45	12 49	12 53	12 57	13 00	13 04	13 08	13 12	13 15	13 19	13 23	13 27	13 30
Whitechapel	d	12 18	12 22	12 26	12 29	12 33	12 37	12 41	12 44	12 48	12 52	12 56	12 59	13 03	13 07	13 11	13 14	13 18	13 22	13 26	13 29	13 33
Shoreditch High Street	d	12 20	12 24	12 28	12 32	12 35	12 39	12 43	12 47	12 50	12 54	12 58	13 02	13 05	13 09	13 13	13 17	13 20	13 24	13 28	13 32	13 35
Hoxton	d	12 22	12 26	12 30	12 34	12 37	12 41	12 45	12 49	12 52	12 56	13 00	13 04	13 07	13 11	13 15	13 19	13 22	13 26	13 30	13 34	13 37
Haggerston	d	12 24	12 28	12 32	12 36	12 39	12 43	12 47	12 51	12 54	12 58	13 02	13 06	13 09	13 13	13 17	13 21	13 24	13 28	13 32	13 36	13 39
Dalston Junction	a	12 29	12 30	12 34	12 38	12 44	12 45	12 49	12 53	12 59	13 00	13 04	13 08	13 14	13 15	13 19	13 23	13 29	13 30	13 34	13 38	13 44
Canonbury	a		12 33		12 41		12 48		12 56		13 03		13 11		13 18		13 26		13 33		13 41	
Highbury & Islington	a		12 38		12 45		12 53		13 00		13 08		13 15		13 23		13 30		13 38		13 45	

Table T178-R

Mondays to Fridays

16 December to 15 May

Clapham Junction and West Croydon, Crystal Palace, New Cross - Highbury & Islington

		LO	LO	LO	LO	LO	LO	LO	LO	LO	LO	LO	LO	LO	LO	LO	LO	LO	LO	LO	LO	LO	LO
Clapham Junction	d				13 15				13 30				13 45				14 00				14 15		
Wandsworth Road	d				13 21				13 36				13 51				14 06				14 21		
Clapham High Street ⊖	d				13 23				13 38				13 53				14 08				14 23		
Denmark Hill 4	d				13 28				13 43				13 58				14 13				14 28		
Peckham Rye 4	d				13 30				13 45				14 00				14 15				14 30		
Queens Rd Peckham	d				13 32				13 47				14 02				14 17				14 32		
West Croydon 4	d	13 01				13 16				13 31				13 46				14 01				14 16	
Norwood Junction 2	d	13 07				13 22				13 37				13 52				14 07				14 22	
Anerley	d	13 10				13 25				13 40				13 55				14 10				14 25	
Penge West	d	13 11				13 26				13 41				13 56				14 11				14 26	
Crystal Palace 4	d			13 17				13 32				13 47				14 02				14 17			
Sydenham	d	13 14		13 21		13 29		13 36		13 44		13 51		13 59		14 06		14 14		14 21		14 29	
Forest Hill 4	d	13 17		13 24		13 32		13 39		13 47		13 54		14 02		14 09		14 17		14 24		14 32	
Honor Oak Park	d	13 19		13 26		13 34		13 41		13 49		13 56		14 04		14 11		14 19		14 26		14 34	
Brockley	d	13 22		13 29		13 37		13 44		13 52		13 59		14 07		14 14		14 22		14 29		14 37	
New Cross Gate	d	13 24		13 31		13 39		13 46		13 54		14 01		14 09		14 16		14 24		14 31		14 39	
New Cross 4	d		13 27				13 42				13 57				14 12				14 27				14 42
Surrey Quays	d	13 27	13 31	13 35	13 38	13 42	13 46	13 50	13 53	13 57	14 01	14 05	14 08	14 12	14 16	14 20	14 23	14 27	14 31	14 35	14 38	14 42	14 46
Canada Water	d	13 29	13 33	13 37	13 40	13 44	13 48	13 52	13 55	13 59	14 03	14 07	14 10	14 14	14 18	14 22	14 25	14 29	14 33	14 37	14 40	14 44	14 48
Rotherhithe	d	13 31	13 35	13 38	13 42	13 46	13 50	13 53	13 57	14 01	14 05	14 08	14 12	14 16	14 20	14 23	14 27	14 31	14 35	14 38	14 42	14 46	14 50
Wapping	d	13 32	13 36	13 40	13 43	13 47	13 51	13 55	13 58	14 02	14 06	14 10	14 13	14 17	14 21	14 25	14 28	14 32	14 36	14 40	14 43	14 47	14 51
Shadwell	d	13 34	13 38	13 42	13 45	13 49	13 53	13 57	14 00	14 04	14 08	14 12	14 15	14 19	14 23	14 27	14 30	14 34	14 38	14 42	14 45	14 49	14 53
Whitechapel	d	13 37	13 41	13 44	13 48	13 52	13 56	13 59	14 03	14 07	14 11	14 14	14 18	14 22	14 26	14 29	14 33	14 37	14 41	14 44	14 48	14 52	14 56
Shoreditch High Street	d	13 39	13 43	13 47	13 50	13 54	13 58	14 02	14 05	14 09	14 13	14 17	14 20	14 24	14 28	14 32	14 35	14 39	14 43	14 47	14 50	14 54	14 58
Hoxton	d	13 41	13 45	13 49	13 52	13 56	14 00	14 04	14 07	14 11	14 15	14 19	14 22	14 26	14 30	14 34	14 37	14 41	14 45	14 49	14 52	14 56	15 00
Haggerston	d	13 43	13 47	13 51	13 54	13 58	14 02	14 06	14 09	14 13	14 17	14 21	14 24	14 28	14 32	14 36	14 39	14 43	14 47	14 51	14 54	14 58	15 02
Dalston Junction	a	13 45	13 49	13 53	13 59	14 00	14 04	14 08	14 14	14 15	14 19	14 23	14 29	14 30	14 34	14 38	14 44	14 45	14 49	14 53	14 59	15 00	15 04
Canonbury	a	13 48		13 56		14 03		14 11		14 18		14 26		14 33		14 41		14 48		14 56		15 03	
Highbury & Islington	a	13 53		14 00		14 08		14 15		14 23		14 30		14 38		14 45		14 53		15 00		15 08	

		LO	LO	LO	LO	LO	LO	LO	LO	LO	LO	LO	LO	LO	LO	LO	LO	LO	LO	LO	LO	LO	LO
Clapham Junction	d		14 30				14 45				15 00				15 15				15 30				15 45
Wandsworth Road	d		14 36				14 51				15 06				15 21				15 36				15 51
Clapham High Street ⊖	d		14 38				14 53				15 08				15 23				15 38				15 53
Denmark Hill 4	d		14 43				14 58				15 13				15 28				15 43				15 58
Peckham Rye 4	d		14 45				15 00				15 15				15 30				15 45				16 00
Queens Rd Peckham	d		14 47				15 02				15 17				15 32				15 47				16 02
West Croydon 4	d			14 31				14 46				15 01				15 16				15 31			
Norwood Junction 2	d			14 37				14 52				15 07				15 22				15 37			
Anerley	d			14 40				14 55				15 10				15 25				15 40			
Penge West	d			14 41				14 56				15 11				15 26				15 41			
Crystal Palace 4	d	14 32				14 47				15 02				15 17				15 32				15 47	
Sydenham	d	14 36		14 44		14 51		14 59		15 06		15 14		15 21		15 29		15 36		15 44		15 51	
Forest Hill 4	d	14 39		14 47		14 54		15 02		15 09		15 17		15 24		15 32		15 39		15 47		15 54	
Honor Oak Park	d	14 41		14 49		14 56		15 04		15 11		15 19		15 26		15 34		15 41		15 49		15 56	
Brockley	d	14 44		14 52		14 59		15 07		15 14		15 22		15 29		15 37		15 44		15 52		15 59	
New Cross Gate	d	14 46		14 54		15 01		15 09		15 16		15 24		15 31		15 39		15 46		15 54		16 01	
New Cross 4	d				14 57				15 12				15 27				15 42				15 57		
Surrey Quays	d	14 50	14 53	14 57	15 01	15 05	15 08	15 12	15 16	15 20	15 23	15 27	15 31	15 35	15 38	15 42	15 46	15 50	15 53	15 57	16 01	16 05	16 08
Canada Water	d	14 52	14 55	14 59	15 03	15 07	15 10	15 14	15 18	15 22	15 25	15 29	15 33	15 37	15 40	15 44	15 48	15 52	15 55	15 59	16 03	16 07	16 10
Rotherhithe	d	14 53	14 57	15 01	15 05	15 08	15 12	15 16	15 20	15 23	15 27	15 31	15 35	15 38	15 42	15 46	15 50	15 53	15 57	16 01	16 05	16 08	16 12
Wapping	d	14 55	14 58	15 02	15 06	15 10	15 13	15 17	15 21	15 25	15 28	15 32	15 36	15 40	15 43	15 47	15 51	15 55	15 58	16 02	16 06	16 10	16 13
Shadwell	d	14 57	15 00	15 04	15 08	15 12	15 15	15 19	15 23	15 27	15 30	15 34	15 38	15 42	15 45	15 49	15 53	15 57	16 00	16 04	16 08	16 12	16 15
Whitechapel	d	14 59	15 03	15 07	15 11	15 14	15 18	15 22	15 26	15 29	15 33	15 37	15 41	15 44	15 48	15 52	15 56	15 59	16 03	16 07	16 11	16 14	16 18
Shoreditch High Street	d	15 02	15 05	15 09	15 13	15 17	15 20	15 24	15 28	15 32	15 35	15 39	15 43	15 47	15 50	15 54	15 58	16 02	16 05	16 09	16 13	16 17	16 20
Hoxton	d	15 04	15 07	15 11	15 15	15 19	15 22	15 26	15 30	15 34	15 37	15 41	15 45	15 49	15 52	15 56	16 00	16 04	16 07	16 11	16 15	16 19	16 22
Haggerston	d	15 06	15 09	15 13	15 17	15 21	15 24	15 28	15 32	15 36	15 39	15 43	15 47	15 51	15 54	15 58	16 02	16 06	16 09	16 13	16 17	16 21	16 24
Dalston Junction	a	15 08	15 14	15 15	15 19	15 23	15 29	15 30	15 34	15 38	15 44	15 45	15 49	15 53	15 59	16 00	16 04	16 08	16 14	16 15	16 19	16 23	16 29
Canonbury	a	15 11		15 18		15 26		15 33		15 41		15 48		15 56		16 03		16 11		16 18		16 26	
Highbury & Islington	a	15 15		15 23		15 30		15 38		15 45		15 53		16 00		16 08		16 15		16 23		16 30	

		LO	LO	LO	LO	LO	LO	LO	LO	LO	LO	LO	LO	LO	LO	LO	LO	LO	LO	LO	LO	LO
Clapham Junction	d				16 00				16 15				16 30				16 45				17 00	
Wandsworth Road	d				16 06				16 21				16 36				16 51				17 06	
Clapham High Street ⊖	d				16 08				16 23				16 38				16 53				17 08	
Denmark Hill 4	d				16 13				16 28				16 43				16 58				17 13	
Peckham Rye 4	d				16 15				16 30				16 45				17 00				17 15	
Queens Rd Peckham	d				16 17				16 32				16 47				17 02				17 17	
West Croydon 4	d	15 46				16 01				16 16				16 31				16 46				17 01
Norwood Junction 2	d	15 52				16 07				16 22				16 37				16 52				17 07
Anerley	d	15 55				16 10				16 25				16 40				16 55				17 10
Penge West	d	15 56				16 11				16 26				16 41				16 56				17 11
Crystal Palace 4	d			16 02				16 17				16 32				16 47				17 02		
Sydenham	d	15 59		16 06		16 14		16 21		16 29		16 36		16 44		16 51		16 59		17 06		17 14
Forest Hill 4	d	16 02		16 09		16 17		16 24		16 32		16 39		16 47		16 54		17 02		17 09		17 17
Honor Oak Park	d	16 04		16 11		16 19		16 26		16 34		16 41		16 49		16 56		17 04		17 11		17 19
Brockley	d	16 07		16 14		16 22		16 29		16 37		16 44		16 52		16 59		17 07		17 14		17 22
New Cross Gate	d	16 09		16 16		16 24		16 31		16 39		16 46		16 54		17 01		17 09		17 16		17 24
New Cross 4	d		16 12				16 27				16 42				16 57				17 12			
Surrey Quays	d	16 12	16 16	16 20	16 23	16 27	16 31	16 35	16 38	16 42	16 46	16 50	16 53	16 57	17 01	17 05	17 08	17 12	17 16	17 20	17 23	17 27
Canada Water	d	16 14	16 18	16 22	16 25	16 29	16 33	16 37	16 40	16 44	16 48	16 52	16 55	16 59	17 03	17 07	17 10	17 14	17 18	17 22	17 25	17 29
Rotherhithe	d	16 16	16 20	16 23	16 27	16 31	16 35	16 38	16 42	16 46	16 50	16 53	16 57	17 01	17 05	17 08	17 12	17 16	17 20	17 23	17 27	17 31
Wapping	d	16 17	16 21	16 25	16 28	16 32	16 36	16 40	16 43	16 47	16 51	16 55	16 58	17 02	17 06	17 10	17 13	17 17	17 21	17 25	17 28	17 32
Shadwell	d	16 19	16 23	16 27	16 30	16 34	16 38	16 42	16 45	16 49	16 53	16 57	17 00	17 04	17 08	17 12	17 15	17 19	17 23	17 27	17 30	17 34
Whitechapel	d	16 22	16 26	16 29	16 33	16 37	16 41	16 44	16 48	16 52	16 56	16 59	17 03	17 07	17 11	17 14	17 18	17 22	17 26	17 29	17 33	17 37
Shoreditch High Street	d	16 24	16 28	16 32	16 35	16 39	16 43	16 47	16 50	16 54	16 58	17 02	17 05	17 09	17 13	17 17	17 20	17 24	17 28	17 32	17 35	17 39
Hoxton	d	16 26	16 30	16 34	16 37	16 41	16 45	16 49	16 52	16 56	17 00	17 04	17 07	17 11	17 15	17 19	17 22	17 26	17 30	17 34	17 37	17 41
Haggerston	d	16 28	16 32	16 36	16 39	16 43	16 47	16 51	16 54	16 58	17 02	17 06	17 09	17 13	17 17	17 21	17 24	17 28	17 32	17 36	17 39	17 43
Dalston Junction	a	16 30	16 34	16 38	16 44	16 46	16 49	16 53	16 59	17 00	17 04	17 08	17 14	17 16	17 19	17 23	17 29	17 30	17 34	17 38	17 44	17 46
Canonbury	a	16 33		16 41		16 48		16 56		17 03		17 11		17 18		17 26		17 33		17 41		17 48
Highbury & Islington	a	16 40		16 45		16 55		17 00		17 10		17 15		17 25		17 30		17 40		17 45		17 55

Table T178-R

Mondays to Fridays

16 December to 15 May

Clapham Junction and West Croydon, Crystal Palace, New Cross - Highbury & Islington

		LO	LO	LO	LO	LO	LO	LO	LO	LO	LO	LO	LO	LO	LO	LO	LO	LO	LO	LO	LO	LO	LO
Clapham Junction	d			17 15				17 30				17 45				18 00				18 15			
Wandsworth Road	d			17 21				17 36				17 51				18 06				18 21			
Clapham High Street ⊖	d			17 23				17 38				17 53				18 08				18 23			
Denmark Hill 4	d			17 28				17 43				17 58				18 13				18 28			
Peckham Rye 4	d			17 30				17 45				18 00				18 15				18 30			
Queens Rd Peckham	d			17 32				17 47				18 02				18 17				18 32			
West Croydon 4	d				17 16				17 31				17 46				18 01				18 16		
Norwood Junction 2	d				17 22				17 37				17 52				18 07				18 22		
Anerley	d				17 25				17 40				17 55				18 10				18 25		
Penge West	d				17 26				17 41				17 56				18 11				18 26		
Crystal Palace 4	d		17 17				17 32				17 47				18 02				18 17				18 32
Sydenham	d		17 21		17 29		17 36		17 44		17 51		17 59		18 06		18 14		18 21		18 29		18 36
Forest Hill 4	d		17 24		17 32		17 39		17 47		17 54		18 02		18 09		18 17		18 24		18 32		18 39
Honor Oak Park	d		17 26		17 34		17 41		17 49		17 56		18 04		18 11		18 19		18 26		18 34		18 41
Brockley	d		17 29		17 37		17 44		17 52		17 59		18 07		18 14		18 22		18 29		18 37		18 44
New Cross Gate	d		17 31		17 39		17 46		17 54		18 01		18 09		18 16		18 24		18 31		18 39		18 46
New Cross 4	d	17 27				17 42				17 57				18 12				18 27				18 42	
Surrey Quays	d	17 31	17 35	17 38	17 42	17 46	17 50	17 53	17 57	18 01	18 05	18 08	18 12	18 16	18 20	18 23	18 27	18 31	18 35	18 38	18 42	18 46	18 50
Canada Water	d	17 33	17 37	17 40	17 44	17 48	17 52	17 55	17 59	18 03	18 07	18 10	18 14	18 18	18 22	18 25	18 29	18 33	18 37	18 40	18 44	18 48	18 52
Rotherhithe	d	17 35	17 38	17 42	17 46	17 50	17 53	17 57	18 01	18 05	18 08	18 12	18 16	18 20	18 23	18 27	18 31	18 35	18 38	18 42	18 46	18 50	18 53
Wapping	d	17 36	17 40	17 43	17 47	17 51	17 55	17 58	18 02	18 06	18 10	18 13	18 17	18 21	18 25	18 28	18 32	18 36	18 40	18 43	18 47	18 51	18 55
Shadwell	d	17 38	17 42	17 45	17 49	17 53	17 57	18 00	18 04	18 08	18 12	18 15	18 19	18 23	18 27	18 30	18 34	18 38	18 42	18 45	18 49	18 53	18 57
Whitechapel	d	17 41	17 44	17 48	17 52	17 56	17 59	18 03	18 07	18 11	18 14	18 18	18 22	18 26	18 29	18 33	18 37	18 41	18 44	18 48	18 52	18 56	18 59
Shoreditch High Street	d	17 43	17 47	17 50	17 54	17 58	18 02	18 05	18 09	18 13	18 17	18 20	18 24	18 28	18 32	18 35	18 39	18 43	18 47	18 50	18 54	18 58	19 02
Hoxton	d	17 45	17 49	17 52	17 56	18 00	18 04	18 07	18 11	18 15	18 19	18 22	18 26	18 30	18 34	18 37	18 41	18 45	18 49	18 52	18 56	19 00	19 04
Haggerston	d	17 47	17 51	17 54	17 58	18 02	18 06	18 09	18 13	18 17	18 21	18 24	18 28	18 32	18 36	18 39	18 43	18 47	18 51	18 54	18 58	19 02	19 06
Dalston Junction	a	17 49	17 53	17 59	18 00	18 04	18 08	18 14	18 15	18 19	18 23	18 29	18 30	18 34	18 38	18 44	18 45	18 49	18 53	18 59	19 00	19 04	19 08
Canonbury	a		17 56		18 03		18 11		18 18		18 26		18 33		18 41		18 48		18 56		19 03		19 11
Highbury & Islington	a		18 00		18 08		18 15		18 25		18 30		18 40		18 45		18 55		19 00		19 10		19 15

		LO	LO	LO	LO	LO	LO	LO	LO	LO	LO	LO	LO	LO	LO	LO	LO	LO	LO	LO	LO	LO
Clapham Junction	d	18 30				18 45				19 00				19 15				19 30				19 45
Wandsworth Road	d	18 36				18 51				19 06				19 21				19 36				19 51
Clapham High Street ⊖	d	18 38				18 53				19 08				19 23				19 38				19 53
Denmark Hill 4	d	18 43				18 58				19 13				19 28				19 43				19 58
Peckham Rye 4	d	18 45				19 00				19 15				19 30				19 45				20 00
Queens Rd Peckham	d	18 47				19 02				19 17				19 32				19 47				20 02
West Croydon 4	d		18 31				18 46				19 01				19 16				19 31			
Norwood Junction 2	d		18 37				18 52				19 07				19 22				19 37			
Anerley	d		18 40				18 55				19 10				19 25				19 40			
Penge West	d		18 41				18 56				19 11				19 26				19 41			
Crystal Palace 4	d				18 47				19 02				19 17				19 32				19 47	
Sydenham	d		18 44		18 51		18 59		19 06		19 14		19 21		19 29		19 36		19 44		19 51	
Forest Hill 4	d		18 47		18 54		19 02		19 09		19 17		19 24		19 32		19 39		19 47		19 54	
Honor Oak Park	d		18 49		18 56		19 04		19 11		19 19		19 26		19 34		19 41		19 49		19 56	
Brockley	d		18 52		18 59		19 07		19 14		19 22		19 29		19 37		19 44		19 52		19 59	
New Cross Gate	d		18 54		19 01		19 09		19 16		19 24		19 31		19 39		19 46		19 54		20 01	
New Cross 4	d			18 57				19 12				19 27				19 42				19 57		
Surrey Quays	d	18 53	18 57	19 01	19 05	19 08	19 12	19 16	19 20	19 23	19 27	19 31	19 35	19 38	19 42	19 46	19 50	19 53	19 57	20 01	20 05	20 08
Canada Water	d	18 55	18 59	19 03	19 07	19 10	19 14	19 18	19 22	19 25	19 29	19 33	19 37	19 40	19 44	19 48	19 52	19 55	19 59	20 03	20 07	20 10
Rotherhithe	d	18 57	19 01	19 05	19 08	19 12	19 16	19 20	19 23	19 27	19 31	19 35	19 38	19 42	19 46	19 50	19 53	19 57	20 01	20 05	20 08	20 12
Wapping	d	18 58	19 02	19 06	19 10	19 13	19 17	19 21	19 25	19 28	19 32	19 36	19 40	19 43	19 47	19 51	19 55	19 58	20 02	20 06	20 10	20 13
Shadwell	d	19 00	19 04	19 08	19 12	19 15	19 19	19 23	19 27	19 30	19 34	19 38	19 42	19 45	19 49	19 53	19 57	20 00	20 04	20 08	20 12	20 15
Whitechapel	d	19 03	19 07	19 11	19 14	19 18	19 22	19 26	19 29	19 33	19 37	19 41	19 44	19 48	19 52	19 56	19 59	20 03	20 07	20 11	20 14	20 18
Shoreditch High Street	d	19 05	19 09	19 13	19 17	19 20	19 24	19 28	19 32	19 35	19 39	19 43	19 47	19 50	19 54	19 58	20 02	20 05	20 09	20 13	20 17	20 20
Hoxton	d	19 07	19 11	19 15	19 19	19 22	19 26	19 30	19 34	19 37	19 41	19 45	19 49	19 52	19 56	20 00	20 04	20 07	20 11	20 15	20 19	20 22
Haggerston	d	19 09	19 13	19 17	19 21	19 24	19 28	19 32	19 36	19 39	19 43	19 47	19 51	19 54	19 58	20 02	20 06	20 09	20 13	20 17	20 21	20 24
Dalston Junction	a	19 14	19 15	19 19	19 23	19 29	19 30	19 34	19 38	19 44	19 45	19 49	19 53	19 59	20 00	20 04	20 08	20 14	20 15	20 19	20 23	20 29
Canonbury	a		19 18		19 26		19 33		19 41		19 48		19 56		20 03		20 11		20 18		20 26	
Highbury & Islington	a		19 25		19 30		19 40		19 45		19 55		20 00		20 10		20 15		20 25		20 30	

		LO	LO	LO	LO	LO	LO	LO	LO	LO	LO	LO	LO	LO	LO	LO	LO	LO	LO	LO	LO	LO	LO
Clapham Junction	d				20 00				20 15				20 30				20 45				21 00		
Wandsworth Road	d				20 06				20 21				20 36				20 51				21 06		
Clapham High Street ⊖	d				20 08				20 23				20 38				20 53				21 08		
Denmark Hill 4	d				20 13				20 28				20 43				20 58				21 13		
Peckham Rye 4	d				20 15				20 30				20 45				21 00				21 15		
Queens Rd Peckham	d				20 17				20 32				20 47				21 02				21 17		
West Croydon 4	d	19 46				20 01				20 16				20 31				20 46				21 01	
Norwood Junction 2	d	19 52				20 07				20 22				20 37				20 52				21 07	
Anerley	d	19 55				20 10				20 25				20 40				20 55				21 10	
Penge West	d	19 56				20 11				20 26				20 41				20 57				21 11	
Crystal Palace 4	d			20 02				20 17				20 32				20 47				21 02			
Sydenham	d	19 59		20 06		20 14		20 21		20 29		20 36		20 44		20 51		20 59		21 06		21 14	
Forest Hill 4	d	20 02		20 09		20 17		20 24		20 32		20 39		20 47		20 54		21 02		21 09		21 17	
Honor Oak Park	d	20 04		20 11		20 19		20 26		20 34		20 41		20 49		20 56		21 04		21 11		21 19	
Brockley	d	20 07		20 14		20 22		20 29		20 37		20 44		20 52		20 59		21 07		21 14		21 22	
New Cross Gate	d	20 09		20 16		20 24		20 31		20 39		20 46		20 54		21 01		21 09		21 16		21 24	
New Cross 4	d		20 11				20 27				20 42				20 57				21 12				21 27
Surrey Quays	d	20 12	20 16	20 20	20 23	20 27	20 31	20 35	20 38	20 42	20 46	20 50	20 53	20 57	21 01	21 05	21 08	21 12	21 16	21 20	21 23	21 27	21 31
Canada Water	d	20 14	20 18	20 22	20 25	20 29	20 33	20 37	20 40	20 44	20 48	20 52	20 55	20 59	21 03	21 07	21 10	21 14	21 18	21 22	21 25	21 29	21 33
Rotherhithe	d	20 16	20 20	20 23	20 27	20 31	20 35	20 38	20 42	20 46	20 50	20 53	20 57	21 01	21 05	21 08	21 12	21 16	21 20	21 23	21 27	21 31	21 35
Wapping	d	20 17	20 21	20 25	20 28	20 32	20 36	20 40	20 43	20 47	20 51	20 55	20 58	21 02	21 06	21 10	21 13	21 17	21 21	21 25	21 28	21 32	21 36
Shadwell	d	20 19	20 23	20 27	20 30	20 34	20 38	20 42	20 45	20 49	20 53	20 57	21 00	21 04	21 08	21 12	21 15	21 19	21 23	21 27	21 30	21 34	21 38
Whitechapel	d	20 22	20 26	20 29	20 33	20 37	20 41	20 44	20 48	20 52	20 56	20 59	21 03	21 07	21 11	21 14	21 18	21 22	21 26	21 29	21 33	21 37	21 41
Shoreditch High Street	d	20 24	20 28	20 32	20 35	20 39	20 43	20 47	20 50	20 54	20 58	21 02	21 05	21 09	21 13	21 17	21 20	21 24	21 28	21 32	21 35	21 39	21 43
Hoxton	d	20 26	20 30	20 34	20 37	20 41	20 45	20 49	20 52	20 56	21 00	21 04	21 07	21 11	21 15	21 19	21 22	21 26	21 30	21 34	21 37	21 41	21 45
Haggerston	d	20 28	20 32	20 36	20 39	20 43	20 47	20 51	20 54	20 58	21 02	21 06	21 09	21 13	21 17	21 21	21 24	21 28	21 32	21 36	21 39	21 43	21 47
Dalston Junction	a	20 30	20 34	20 38	20 44	20 45	20 49	20 53	20 59	21 00	21 04	21 08	21 14	21 15	21 19	21 23	21 29	21 30	21 34	21 38	21 44	21 45	21 49
Canonbury	a	20 33		20 41		20 48		20 56		21 03		21 11		21 18		21 26		21 33		21 41		21 48	
Highbury & Islington	a	20 40		20 45		20 53		21 00		21 08		21 15		21 23		21 30		21 38		21 45		21 53	

Mondays to Fridays

16 December to 15 May

Clapham Junction and West Croydon, Crystal Palace, New Cross - Highbury & Islington

		LO	LO	LO	LO	LO		LO	LO	LO	LO	LO	LO	LO	LO	LO		LO	LO	LO	LO	LO	LO	LO	LO
Clapham Junction	d		21 15					21 30				21 45				22 00					22 15				22 30
Wandsworth Road	d		21 21					21 36				21 51				22 06					22 21				22 36
Clapham High Street ⊖	d		21 23					21 38				21 53				22 08					22 23				22 38
Denmark Hill 4	d		21 28					21 43				21 58				22 13					22 28				22 43
Peckham Rye 4	d		21 30					21 45				22 00				22 15					22 30				22 45
Queens Rd Peckham	d		21 32					21 47				22 02				22 17					22 32				22 47
West Croydon 4	d			21 16					21 31				21 46					22 01				22 16			
Norwood Junction 2	d			21 22					21 37				21 52					22 07				22 22			
Anerley	d			21 25					21 40				21 55					22 10				22 25			
Penge West	d			21 26					21 41				21 56					22 11				22 26			
Crystal Palace 4	d	21 17				21 32					21 47				22 02					22 17				22 32	
Sydenham	d	21 21		21 29		21 36			21 44		21 51		21 59		22 06			22 14		22 21		22 29		22 36	
Forest Hill 4	d	21 24		21 32		21 39			21 47		21 54		22 02		22 09			22 17		22 24		22 32		22 39	
Honor Oak Park	d	21 26		21 34		21 41			21 49		21 56		22 04		22 11			22 19		22 26		22 34		22 41	
Brockley	d	21 29		21 37		21 44			21 52		21 59		22 07		22 14			22 22		22 29		22 37		22 44	
New Cross Gate	d	21 31		21 39		21 46			21 54		22 01		22 09		22 16			22 24		22 31		22 39		22 46	
New Cross 4	d				21 42					21 57				22 12					22 27				22 42		
Surrey Quays	d	21 35	21 38	21 42	21 46	21 50		21 53	21 57	22 01	22 05	22 08	22 12	22 16	22 20	22 23		22 27	22 31	22 35	22 38	22 42	22 46	22 50	22 53
Canada Water	d	21 37	21 40	21 44	21 48	21 52		21 55	21 59	22 03	22 07	22 10	22 14	22 18	22 22	22 25		22 29	22 33	22 37	22 40	22 44	22 48	22 52	22 55
Rotherhithe	d	21 38	21 42	21 46	21 50	21 53		21 57	22 01	22 05	22 08	22 12	22 16	22 20	22 23	22 27		22 31	22 35	22 38	22 42	22 46	22 50	22 53	22 57
Wapping	d	21 40	21 43	21 47	21 51	21 55		21 58	22 02	22 06	22 10	22 13	22 17	22 21	22 25	22 28		22 32	22 36	22 40	22 43	22 47	22 51	22 55	22 58
Shadwell	d	21 42	21 45	21 49	21 53	21 57		22 00	22 04	22 08	22 12	22 15	22 19	22 23	22 27	22 30		22 34	22 38	22 42	22 45	22 49	22 53	22 57	23 00
Whitechapel	d	21 44	21 48	21 52	21 56	21 59		22 03	22 07	22 11	22 14	22 18	22 22	22 26	22 29	22 33		22 37	22 41	22 44	22 48	22 52	22 56	22 59	23 03
Shoreditch High Street	d	21 47	21 50	21 54	21 58	22 02		22 05	22 09	22 13	22 17	22 20	22 24	22 28	22 32	22 35		22 39	22 43	22 47	22 50	22 54	22 58	23 02	23 05
Hoxton	d	21 49	21 52	21 56	22 00	22 04		22 07	22 11	22 15	22 19	22 22	22 26	22 30	22 34	22 37		22 41	22 45	22 49	22 52	22 56	23 00	23 04	23 07
Haggerston	d	21 51	21 54	21 58	22 02	22 06		22 09	22 13	22 17	22 21	22 24	22 28	22 32	22 36	22 39		22 43	22 47	22 51	22 54	22 58	23 02	23 06	23 09
Dalston Junction	a	21 53	21 59	22 00	22 04	22 08		22 14	22 15	22 19	22 23	22 29	22 30	22 34	22 38	22 44		22 45	22 49	22 53	22 59	23 00	23 04	23 08	23 14
Canonbury	a	21 56		22 03		22 11			22 18		22 26		22 33		22 41			22 48		22 56		23 03		23 11	
Highbury & Islington	a	22 00		22 08		22 15			22 23		22 30		22 38		22 45			22 55		23 00		23 10		23 15	

		LO		LO	LO	LO	LO	LO	LO	LO A	LO	LO		LO	LO	LO	LO	LO	LO	LO	LO	LO
Clapham Junction	d					22 45									23 15				23 30		23 44	
Wandsworth Road	d					22 51				23 06					23 21				23 36		23 51	
Clapham High Street ⊖	d					22 53				23 08					23 23				23 38		23 52	
Denmark Hill 4	d					22 58				23 13					23 28				23 43		23 57	
Peckham Rye 4	d					23 00				23 15					23 30				23 45		00 01	
Queens Rd Peckham	d					23 02				23 17					23 32				23 47		00 03	
West Croydon 4	d	22 31					22 46				23 01					23 16				23 31		
Norwood Junction 2	d	22 37					22 52				23 07					23 22				23 37		
Anerley	d	22 40					22 55				23 10					23 25				23 40		
Penge West	d	22 41					22 56				23 11					23 26				23 41		
Crystal Palace 4	d				22 47				23 02					23 17				23 32				23 50
Sydenham	d	22 44			22 51		22 59		23 06		23 14			23 21		23 29		23 36		23 44		23 54
Forest Hill 4	d	22 47			22 54		23 02		23 09		23 17			23 24		23 32		23 39		23 47		23 56
Honor Oak Park	d	22 49			22 56		23 04		23 11		23 19			23 26		23 34		23 41		23 49		23 59
Brockley	d	22 52			22 59		23 07		23 14		23 22			23 29		23 37		23 44		23 52		00 01
New Cross Gate	d	22 54			23 01		23 09		23 16		23 24			23 31		23 39		23 46		23 54		00 03
New Cross 4	d			22 57				23 12				23 27					23 42					
Surrey Quays	d	22 57		23 01	23 05	23 08	23 12	23 16	23 20	23 23	23 27	23 31		23 35	23 38	23 42	23 46	23 50	23 53	23 57	00 06	00 09
Canada Water	d	22 59		23 03	23 07	23 10	23 14	23 18	23 22	23 25	23 29	23 33		23 37	23 40	23 44	23 48	23 52	23 55	23 59	00 08	00 11
Rotherhithe	d	23 01		23 05	23 08	23 12	23 16	23 20	23 23	23 27	23 31	23 35		23 38	23 42	23 46	23 50	23 53	23 57	00 01	00 10	00 12
Wapping	d	23 02		23 06	23 10	23 13	23 17	23 21	23 25	23 28	23 32	23 36		23 40	23 43	23 47	23 51	23 55	23 58	00 02	00 11	00 14
Shadwell	d	23 04		23 08	23 12	23 15	23 19	23 23	23 27	23 30	23 34	23 38		23 42	23 45	23 49	23 53	23 57	00 01	00 04	00 13	00 16
Whitechapel	d	23 07		23 11	23 14	23 18	23 22	23 26	23 29	23 33	23 37	23 41		23 44	23 48	23 52	23 56	23 59	00 03	00 07	00 16	00 18
Shoreditch High Street	d	23 09		23 13	23 17	23 20	23 24	23 28	23 32	23 35	23 39	23 43		23 47	23 50	23 54	23 58	00 02	00 05	00 09	00 18	00 21
Hoxton	d	23 11		23 15	23 19	23 22	23 26	23 30	23 34	23 37	23 41	23 45		23 49	23 52	23 56	00 01	00 04	00 07	00 11	00 20	00 23
Haggerston	d	23 13		23 17	23 21	23 24	23 28	23 32	23 36	23 39	23 43	23 47		23 51	23 54	23 58	00 02	00 06	00 09	00 13	00 22	00 25
Dalston Junction	a	23 15		23 19	23 23	23 29	23 32	23 34	23 38	23 44	23 45	23 49		23 53	23 59	00 01	00 04	00 08	00 14	00 15	00 29	00 27
Canonbury	a	23 18			23 26			23 37	23 41		23 50			23 56		00 03		00 11		00 18		00 30
Highbury & Islington	a	23 25			23 30			23 39	23 45		23 55			23 59		00 10		00 15		00 25		00 32

Saturdays

21 December to 16 May

		LO B	LO C	LO D	LO E	LO D	LO C	LO	LO		LO		LO	LO	LO	LO	LO	LO	LO	LO	LO		LO	LO
Clapham Junction	d																			06 00				
Wandsworth Road	d																			06 06				
Clapham High Street ⊖	d																			06 08				
Denmark Hill 4	d																			06 13				
Peckham Rye 4	d					00 01														06 15				
Queens Rd Peckham	d					00 03														06 17				
West Croydon 4	d													05 31			05 46				06 01			
Norwood Junction 2	d													05 37			05 52				06 07			
Anerley	d													05 40			05 55				06 10			
Penge West	d													05 41			05 56				06 11			
Crystal Palace 4	d							00 04					05 32			05 47			06 02					06 17
Sydenham	d							00 08		and every 15 minutes until			05 36	05 44		05 51	05 59		06 06		06 14			06 21
Forest Hill 4	d							00 11					05 39	05 47		05 54	06 02		06 09		06 17			06 24
Honor Oak Park	d							00 13					05 41	05 49		05 56	06 04		06 11		06 19			06 26
Brockley	d						00 01	00 16					05 44	05 52		05 59	06 07		06 14		06 22			06 29
New Cross Gate	d						00 03	00 18	00 33		05 33		05 46	05 54		06 01	06 09		06 16		06 24			06 31
New Cross 4	d														05 57			06 12					06 27	
Surrey Quays	d					00 06	00 09	00 22	00 37		05 37		05 50	05 57	06 01	06 05	06 12	06 16	06 20	06 23	06 27		06 31	06 35
Canada Water	d					00 08	00 11	00 24	00 39		05 39		05 52	05 59	06 03	06 07	06 14	06 18	06 22	06 25	06 29		06 33	06 37
Rotherhithe	d				00 01	00 10	00 12	00 25	00 40		05 40		05 53	06 01	06 05	06 08	06 16	06 20	06 23	06 27	06 31		06 35	06 38
Wapping	d				00 02	00 11	00 14	00 27	00 42		05 42		05 55	06 02	06 06	06 10	06 17	06 21	06 25	06 28	06 32		06 36	06 40
Shadwell	d			00 01	00 04	00 13	00 16	00 29	00 44		05 44		05 57	06 04	06 08	06 12	06 19	06 23	06 27	06 30	06 34		06 38	06 42
Whitechapel	d			00 03	00 07	00 16	00 18	00 31	00 46		05 46		05 59	06 07	06 11	06 14	06 22	06 26	06 29	06 33	06 37		06 41	06 44
Shoreditch High Street	d		00 02	00 05	00 09	00 18	00 21	00 34	00 49		05 49		06 02	06 09	06 13	06 17	06 24	06 28	06 32	06 35	06 39		06 43	06 47
Hoxton	d	00 01	00 04	00 07	00 11	00 20	00 23	00 36	00 51		05 51		06 04	06 11	06 15	06 19	06 26	06 30	06 34	06 37	06 41		06 45	06 49
Haggerston	d	00 02	00 06	00 09	00 13	00 22	00 25	00 38	00 53		05 53		06 06	06 13	06 17	06 21	06 28	06 32	06 36	06 39	06 43		06 47	06 51
Dalston Junction	a	00 04	00 08	00 14	00 15	00 29	00 27	00 40	00 55		05 55		06 08	06 15	06 19	06 23	06 30	06 34	06 38	06 44	06 45		06 49	06 53
Canonbury	a		00 11		00 18		00 30	00 43	00 58		05 58		06 11	06 18		06 26	06 33		06 41		06 48			06 56
Highbury & Islington	a		00 15		00 25		00 32	00 47	01 03		06 03		06 15	06 23		06 30	06 38		06 45		06 53			07 00

A From Battersea Park
B From New Cross ELL
C From Crystal Palace
D From Clapham Junction Plats 0-2
E From West Croydon

Saturdays

21 December to 16 May

Clapham Junction and West Croydon, Crystal Palace, New Cross - Highbury & Islington

		LO	LO	LO	LO	LO	LO	LO		LO	LO	LO	LO	LO	LO	LO	LO	LO		LO	LO	LO	LO	LO	LO
Clapham Junction	d	06 15				06 30					06 45				07 00					07 15				07 30	
Wandsworth Road	d	06 21				06 36					06 51				07 06					07 21				07 36	
Clapham High Street ⊖	d	06 23				06 38					06 53				07 08					07 23				07 38	
Denmark Hill 4	d	06 28				06 43					06 58				07 13					07 28				07 43	
Peckham Rye 4	d	06 30				06 45					07 00				07 15					07 30				07 45	
Queens Rd Peckham	d	06 32				06 47					07 02				07 17					07 32				07 47	
West Croydon 4	d		06 16				06 31					06 46				07 01					07 16				07 31
Norwood Junction 2	d		06 22				06 37					06 52				07 07					07 22				07 37
Anerley	d		06 25				06 40					06 55				07 10					07 25				07 40
Penge West	d		06 26				06 41					06 56				07 11					07 26				07 41
Crystal Palace 4	d				06 32					06 47				07 02				07 17					07 32		
Sydenham	d		06 29		06 36		06 44			06 51		06 59		07 06		07 14		07 21			07 29		07 36		07 44
Forest Hill 4	d		06 32		06 39		06 47			06 54		07 02		07 09		07 17		07 24			07 32		07 39		07 47
Honor Oak Park	d		06 34		06 41		06 49			06 56		07 04		07 11		07 19		07 26			07 34		07 41		07 49
Brockley	d		06 37		06 44		06 52			06 59		07 07		07 14		07 22		07 29			07 37		07 44		07 52
New Cross Gate	d		06 39		06 46		06 54			07 01		07 09		07 16		07 24		07 31			07 39		07 46		07 54
New Cross 4	d			06 42				06 57					07 12				07 27					07 42			
Surrey Quays	d	06 38	06 42	06 46	06 50	06 53	06 57	07 01		07 05	07 08	07 12	07 16	07 20	07 23	07 27	07 31	07 35		07 38	07 42	07 46	07 50	07 53	07 57
Canada Water	d	06 40	06 44	06 48	06 52	06 55	06 59	07 03		07 07	07 10	07 14	07 18	07 22	07 25	07 29	07 33	07 37		07 40	07 44	07 48	07 52	07 55	07 59
Rotherhithe	d	06 42	06 46	06 50	06 53	06 57	07 01	07 05		07 08	07 12	07 16	07 20	07 23	07 27	07 31	07 35	07 38		07 42	07 46	07 50	07 53	07 57	08 01
Wapping	d	06 43	06 47	06 51	06 55	06 58	07 02	07 06		07 10	07 13	07 17	07 21	07 25	07 28	07 32	07 36	07 40		07 43	07 47	07 51	07 55	07 58	08 02
Shadwell	d	06 45	06 49	06 53	06 57	07 00	07 04	07 08		07 12	07 15	07 19	07 23	07 27	07 30	07 34	07 38	07 42		07 45	07 49	07 53	07 57	08 00	08 04
Whitechapel	d	06 48	06 52	06 56	06 59	07 03	07 07	07 11		07 14	07 18	07 22	07 26	07 29	07 33	07 37	07 41	07 44		07 48	07 52	07 56	07 59	08 03	08 07
Shoreditch High Street	d	06 50	06 54	06 58	07 02	07 05	07 09	07 13		07 17	07 20	07 24	07 28	07 32	07 35	07 39	07 43	07 47		07 50	07 54	07 58	08 02	08 05	08 09
Hoxton	d	06 52	06 56	07 00	07 04	07 07	07 11	07 15		07 19	07 22	07 26	07 30	07 34	07 37	07 41	07 45	07 49		07 52	07 56	08 00	08 04	08 07	08 11
Haggerston	d	06 54	06 58	07 02	07 06	07 09	07 13	07 17		07 21	07 24	07 28	07 32	07 36	07 39	07 43	07 47	07 51		07 54	07 58	08 02	08 06	08 09	08 13
Dalston Junction	a	06 59	07 00	07 04	07 08	07 14	07 15	07 19		07 23	07 29	07 30	07 34	07 38	07 44	07 45	07 49	07 53		07 59	08 00	08 04	08 08	08 14	08 15
Canonbury	a		07 03		07 11		07 18			07 26		07 33		07 41		07 48		07 56			08 03		08 11		08 18
Highbury & Islington	a		07 10		07 15		07 25			07 30		07 40		07 45		07 55		08 00			08 10		08 15		08 25

		LO	LO	LO		LO	LO	LO	LO	LO	LO	LO	LO	LO		LO	LO	LO	LO	LO	LO	LO	LO	LO	
Clapham Junction	d			07 45					08 00				08 15					08 30				08 45			
Wandsworth Road	d			07 51					08 06				08 21					08 36				08 51			
Clapham High Street ⊖	d			07 53					08 08				08 23					08 38				08 53			
Denmark Hill 4	d			07 58					08 13				08 28					08 43				08 58			
Peckham Rye 4	d			08 00					08 15				08 30					08 45				09 00			
Queens Rd Peckham	d			08 02					08 17				08 32					08 47				09 02			
West Croydon 4	d					07 46				08 01				08 16					08 31				08 46		
Norwood Junction 2	d					07 52				08 07				08 22					08 37				08 52		
Anerley	d					07 55				08 10				08 25					08 40				08 55		
Penge West	d					07 57				08 11				08 26					08 41				08 57		
Crystal Palace 4	d		07 47					08 02				08 17					08 32				08 47				
Sydenham	d		07 51			07 59		08 06		08 14		08 21		08 29			08 36		08 44		08 51		08 59		
Forest Hill 4	d		07 54			08 02		08 09		08 17		08 24		08 32			08 39		08 47		08 54		09 02		
Honor Oak Park	d		07 56			08 04		08 11		08 19		08 26		08 34			08 41		08 49		08 56		09 04		
Brockley	d		07 59			08 07		08 14		08 22		08 29		08 37			08 44		08 52		08 59		09 07		
New Cross Gate	d		08 01			08 09		08 16		08 24		08 31		08 39			08 46		08 54		09 01		09 09		
New Cross 4	d	07 57					08 12				08 27					08 42				08 57				09 12	
Surrey Quays	d	08 01	08 05	08 08		08 12	08 16	08 20	08 23	08 27	08 31	08 35	08 38	08 42		08 46	08 50	08 53	08 57	09 01	09 05	09 08	09 12	09 16	
Canada Water	d	08 03	08 07	08 10		08 14	08 18	08 22	08 25	08 29	08 33	08 37	08 40	08 44		08 48	08 52	08 55	08 59	09 03	09 07	09 10	09 14	09 18	
Rotherhithe	d	08 05	08 08	08 12		08 16	08 20	08 23	08 27	08 31	08 35	08 38	08 42	08 46		08 50	08 53	08 57	09 01	09 05	09 08	09 12	09 16	09 20	
Wapping	d	08 06	08 10	08 13		08 17	08 21	08 25	08 28	08 32	08 36	08 40	08 43	08 47		08 51	08 55	08 58	09 02	09 06	09 10	09 13	09 17	09 21	
Shadwell	d	08 08	08 12	08 15		08 19	08 23	08 27	08 30	08 34	08 38	08 42	08 45	08 49		08 53	08 57	09 00	09 04	09 08	09 12	09 15	09 19	09 23	
Whitechapel	d	08 11	08 14	08 18		08 22	08 26	08 29	08 33	08 37	08 41	08 44	08 48	08 52		08 56	08 59	09 03	09 07	09 11	09 14	09 18	09 22	09 26	
Shoreditch High Street	d	08 13	08 17	08 20		08 24	08 28	08 32	08 35	08 39	08 43	08 47	08 50	08 54		08 58	09 02	09 05	09 09	09 13	09 17	09 20	09 24	09 28	
Hoxton	d	08 15	08 19	08 22		08 26	08 30	08 34	08 37	08 41	08 45	08 49	08 52	08 56		09 00	09 04	09 07	09 11	09 15	09 19	09 22	09 26	09 30	
Haggerston	d	08 17	08 21	08 24		08 28	08 32	08 36	08 39	08 43	08 47	08 51	08 54	08 58		09 02	09 06	09 09	09 13	09 17	09 21	09 24	09 28	09 32	
Dalston Junction	a	08 19	08 23	08 29		08 30	08 34	08 38	08 44	08 45	08 50	08 53	09 00	09 00		09 05	09 08	09 15	09 15	09 19	09 23	09 30	09 30	09 34	
Canonbury	a		08 26			08 33		08 41		08 48		08 56		09 03			09 11		09 18		09 26		09 33		
Highbury & Islington	a		08 30			08 40		08 47		08 55		09 02		09 10			09 17		09 25		09 30		09 40		

		LO	LO	LO	LO	LO	LO	LO	LO	LO		LO	LO	LO	LO	LO	LO	LO	LO	LO		LO	LO	LO	LO
Clapham Junction	d		09 00				09 15					09 30				09 45				10 00					10 15
Wandsworth Road	d		09 06				09 21					09 36				09 51				10 06					10 21
Clapham High Street ⊖	d		09 08				09 23					09 38				09 53				10 08					10 23
Denmark Hill 4	d		09 13				09 28					09 43				09 58				10 13					10 28
Peckham Rye 4	d		09 15				09 30					09 45				10 00				10 15					10 30
Queens Rd Peckham	d		09 17				09 32					09 47				10 02				10 17					10 32
West Croydon 4	d			09 01				09 16					09 31				09 46					10 01			
Norwood Junction 2	d			09 07				09 22					09 37				09 52					10 07			
Anerley	d			09 10				09 25					09 40				09 55					10 10			
Penge West	d			09 11				09 26					09 41				09 57					10 11			
Crystal Palace 4	d	09 02				09 17				09 32					09 47				10 02					10 17	
Sydenham	d	09 06		09 14		09 21		09 29		09 36			09 44		09 51		09 59		10 06			10 14		10 21	
Forest Hill 4	d	09 09		09 17		09 24		09 32		09 39			09 47		09 54		10 02		10 09			10 17		10 24	
Honor Oak Park	d	09 11		09 19		09 26		09 34		09 41			09 49		09 56		10 04		10 11			10 19		10 26	
Brockley	d	09 14		09 22		09 29		09 37		09 44			09 52		09 59		10 07		10 14			10 22		10 29	
New Cross Gate	d	09 16		09 24		09 31		09 39		09 46			09 54		10 01		10 09		10 16			10 24		10 31	
New Cross 4	d				09 27				09 42					09 57				10 12					10 27		
Surrey Quays	d	09 20	09 23	09 27	09 31	09 35	09 38	09 42	09 46	09 50		09 53	09 57	10 01	10 05	10 08	10 12	10 16	10 20	10 23		10 27	10 31	10 35	10 38
Canada Water	d	09 22	09 25	09 29	09 33	09 37	09 40	09 44	09 48	09 52		09 55	09 59	10 03	10 07	10 10	10 14	10 18	10 22	10 25		10 29	10 33	10 37	10 40
Rotherhithe	d	09 23	09 27	09 31	09 35	09 38	09 42	09 46	09 50	09 53		09 57	10 01	10 05	10 08	10 12	10 16	10 20	10 23	10 27		10 31	10 35	10 38	10 42
Wapping	d	09 25	09 28	09 32	09 36	09 40	09 43	09 47	09 51	09 55		09 58	10 02	10 06	10 10	10 13	10 17	10 21	10 25	10 28		10 32	10 36	10 40	10 43
Shadwell	d	09 27	09 30	09 34	09 38	09 42	09 45	09 49	09 53	09 57		10 00	10 04	10 08	10 12	10 15	10 19	10 23	10 27	10 30		10 34	10 38	10 42	10 45
Whitechapel	d	09 29	09 33	09 37	09 41	09 44	09 48	09 52	09 56	09 59		10 03	10 07	10 11	10 14	10 18	10 22	10 26	10 29	10 33		10 37	10 41	10 44	10 48
Shoreditch High Street	d	09 32	09 35	09 39	09 43	09 47	09 50	09 54	09 58	10 02		10 05	10 09	10 13	10 17	10 20	10 24	10 28	10 32	10 35		10 39	10 43	10 47	10 50
Hoxton	d	09 34	09 37	09 41	09 45	09 49	09 52	09 56	10 00	10 04		10 07	10 11	10 15	10 19	10 22	10 26	10 30	10 34	10 37		10 41	10 45	10 49	10 52
Haggerston	d	09 36	09 39	09 43	09 47	09 51	09 54	09 58	10 02	10 06		10 09	10 13	10 17	10 21	10 24	10 28	10 32	10 36	10 39		10 43	10 47	10 51	10 54
Dalston Junction	a	09 38	09 44	09 45	09 49	09 53	09 59	10 00	10 04	10 08		10 14	10 15	10 19	10 23	10 29	10 30	10 34	10 38	10 44		10 45	10 49	10 53	10 59
Canonbury	a	09 41		09 48		09 56		10 03		10 11			10 18		10 26		10 33		10 41			10 48		10 56	
Highbury & Islington	a	09 45		09 55		10 00		10 10		10 15			10 25		10 30		10 40		10 45			10 55		11 00	

Table T178-R

Saturdays

21 December to 16 May

Clapham Junction and West Croydon, Crystal Palace, New Cross - Highbury & Islington

		LO	LO	LO	LO	LO	LO	LO	LO	LO	LO	LO	LO	LO	LO	LO	LO	LO	LO	LO	LO	LO	LO
Clapham Junction	d				10 30				10 45				11 00				11 15				11 30		
Wandsworth Road	d				10 36				10 51				11 06				11 21				11 36		
Clapham High Street ⊖	d				10 38				10 53				11 08				11 23				11 38		
Denmark Hill 4	d				10 43				10 58				11 13				11 28				11 43		
Peckham Rye 4	d				10 45				11 00				11 15				11 30				11 45		
Queens Rd Peckham	d				10 47				11 02				11 17				11 32				11 47		
West Croydon 4	d	10 16				10 31				10 46				11 01				11 16				11 31	
Norwood Junction 2	d	10 22				10 37				10 52				11 07				11 22				11 37	
Anerley	d	10 25				10 40				10 55				11 10				11 25				11 40	
Penge West	d	10 26				10 41				10 57				11 11				11 26				11 41	
Crystal Palace 4	d			10 32				10 47				11 02				11 17				11 32			
Sydenham	d	10 29		10 36		10 44		10 51		10 59		11 06		11 14		11 21		11 29		11 36		11 44	
Forest Hill 4	d	10 32		10 39		10 47		10 54		11 02		11 09		11 17		11 24		11 32		11 39		11 47	
Honor Oak Park	d	10 34		10 41		10 49		10 56		11 04		11 11		11 19		11 26		11 34		11 41		11 49	
Brockley	d	10 37		10 44		10 52		10 59		11 07		11 14		11 22		11 29		11 37		11 44		11 52	
New Cross Gate	d	10 39		10 46		10 54		11 01		11 09		11 16		11 24		11 31		11 39		11 46		11 54	
New Cross 4	d		10 42				10 57				11 12				11 27				11 42				11 57
Surrey Quays	d	10 42	10 46	10 50	10 53	10 57	11 01	11 05	11 08	11 12	11 16	11 20	11 23	11 27	11 31	11 35	11 38	11 42	11 46	11 50	11 53	11 57	12 01
Canada Water	d	10 44	10 48	10 52	10 55	10 59	11 03	11 07	11 10	11 14	11 18	11 22	11 25	11 29	11 33	11 37	11 40	11 44	11 48	11 52	11 55	11 59	12 03
Rotherhithe	d	10 46	10 50	10 53	10 57	11 01	11 05	11 08	11 12	11 16	11 20	11 23	11 27	11 31	11 35	11 38	11 42	11 46	11 50	11 53	11 57	12 01	12 05
Wapping	d	10 47	10 51	10 55	10 58	11 02	11 06	11 10	11 13	11 17	11 21	11 25	11 28	11 32	11 36	11 40	11 43	11 47	11 51	11 55	11 58	12 02	12 06
Shadwell	d	10 49	10 53	10 57	11 00	11 04	11 08	11 12	11 15	11 19	11 23	11 27	11 30	11 34	11 38	11 42	11 45	11 49	11 53	11 57	12 00	12 04	12 08
Whitechapel	d	10 52	10 56	10 59	11 03	11 07	11 11	11 14	11 18	11 22	11 26	11 29	11 33	11 37	11 41	11 44	11 48	11 52	11 56	11 59	12 03	12 07	12 11
Shoreditch High Street	d	10 54	10 58	11 02	11 05	11 09	11 13	11 17	11 20	11 24	11 28	11 32	11 35	11 39	11 43	11 47	11 50	11 54	11 58	12 02	12 05	12 09	12 13
Hoxton	d	10 56	11 00	11 04	11 07	11 11	11 15	11 19	11 22	11 26	11 30	11 34	11 37	11 41	11 45	11 49	11 52	11 56	12 00	12 04	12 07	12 11	12 15
Haggerston	d	10 58	11 02	11 06	11 09	11 13	11 17	11 21	11 24	11 28	11 32	11 36	11 39	11 43	11 47	11 51	11 54	11 58	12 02	12 06	12 09	12 13	12 17
Dalston Junction	a	11 00	11 04	11 08	11 14	11 15	11 19	11 23	11 29	11 30	11 34	11 38	11 44	11 45	11 49	11 53	11 59	12 00	12 04	12 08	12 14	12 15	12 19
Canonbury	a	11 03		11 11		11 18		11 26		11 33		11 41		11 48		11 56		12 03		12 11		12 18	
Highbury & Islington	a	11 08		11 15		11 23		11 30		11 38		11 45		11 53		12 00		12 08		12 15		12 23	

		LO	LO	LO	LO	LO	LO	LO	LO	LO	LO	LO	LO	LO	LO	LO	LO	LO	LO	LO	LO	LO
Clapham Junction	d		11 45				12 00				12 15				12 30				12 45			
Wandsworth Road	d		11 51				12 06				12 21				12 36				12 51			
Clapham High Street ⊖	d		11 53				12 08				12 23				12 38				12 53			
Denmark Hill 4	d		11 58				12 13				12 28				12 43				12 58			
Peckham Rye 4	d		12 00				12 15				12 30				12 45				13 00			
Queens Rd Peckham	d		12 02				12 17				12 32				12 47				13 02			
West Croydon 4	d			11 46				12 01				12 16				12 31				12 46		
Norwood Junction 2	d			11 52				12 07				12 22				12 37				12 52		
Anerley	d			11 55				12 10				12 25				12 40				12 55		
Penge West	d			11 57				12 11				12 26				12 41				12 57		
Crystal Palace 4	d	11 47				12 02				12 17				12 32				12 47				13 02
Sydenham	d	11 51		11 59		12 06		12 14		12 21		12 29		12 36		12 44		12 51		12 59		13 06
Forest Hill 4	d	11 54		12 02		12 09		12 17		12 24		12 32		12 39		12 47		12 54		13 02		13 09
Honor Oak Park	d	11 56		12 04		12 11		12 19		12 26		12 34		12 41		12 49		12 56		13 04		13 11
Brockley	d	11 59		12 07		12 14		12 22		12 29		12 37		12 44		12 52		12 59		13 07		13 14
New Cross Gate	d	12 01		12 09		12 16		12 24		12 31		12 39		12 46		12 54		13 01		13 09		13 16
New Cross 4	d				12 12				12 27				12 42				12 57				13 12	
Surrey Quays	d	12 05	12 08	12 12	12 16	12 20	12 23	12 27	12 31	12 35	12 38	12 42	12 46	12 50	12 53	12 57	13 01	13 05	13 08	13 12	13 16	13 20
Canada Water	d	12 07	12 10	12 14	12 18	12 22	12 25	12 29	12 33	12 37	12 40	12 44	12 48	12 52	12 55	12 59	13 03	13 07	13 10	13 14	13 18	13 22
Rotherhithe	d	12 08	12 12	12 16	12 20	12 23	12 27	12 31	12 35	12 38	12 42	12 46	12 50	12 53	12 57	13 01	13 05	13 08	13 12	13 16	13 20	13 23
Wapping	d	12 10	12 13	12 17	12 21	12 25	12 28	12 32	12 36	12 40	12 43	12 47	12 51	12 55	12 58	13 02	13 06	13 10	13 13	13 17	13 21	13 25
Shadwell	d	12 12	12 15	12 19	12 23	12 27	12 30	12 34	12 38	12 42	12 45	12 49	12 53	12 57	13 00	13 04	13 08	13 12	13 15	13 19	13 23	13 27
Whitechapel	d	12 14	12 18	12 22	12 26	12 29	12 33	12 37	12 41	12 44	12 48	12 52	12 56	12 59	13 03	13 07	13 11	13 14	13 18	13 22	13 26	13 29
Shoreditch High Street	d	12 17	12 20	12 24	12 28	12 32	12 35	12 39	12 43	12 47	12 50	12 54	12 58	13 02	13 05	13 09	13 13	13 17	13 20	13 24	13 28	13 32
Hoxton	d	12 19	12 22	12 26	12 30	12 34	12 37	12 41	12 45	12 49	12 52	12 56	13 00	13 04	13 07	13 11	13 15	13 19	13 22	13 26	13 30	13 34
Haggerston	d	12 21	12 24	12 28	12 32	12 36	12 39	12 43	12 47	12 51	12 54	12 58	13 02	13 06	13 09	13 13	13 17	13 21	13 24	13 28	13 32	13 36
Dalston Junction	a	12 23	12 29	12 30	12 34	12 38	12 44	12 45	12 49	12 53	12 59	13 00	13 04	13 08	13 14	13 15	13 19	13 23	13 29	13 30	13 34	13 38
Canonbury	a	12 26		12 33		12 41		12 48		12 56		13 03		13 11		13 18		13 26		13 33		13 41
Highbury & Islington	a	12 30		12 38		12 45		12 53		13 00		13 08		13 15		13 23		13 30		13 38		13 45

		LO	LO	LO	LO	LO	LO	LO	LO	LO	LO	LO	LO	LO	LO	LO	LO	LO	LO	LO	LO	LO	LO
Clapham Junction	d	13 00				13 15				13 30				13 45				14 00				14 15	
Wandsworth Road	d	13 06				13 21				13 36				13 51				14 06				14 21	
Clapham High Street ⊖	d	13 08				13 23				13 38				13 53				14 08				14 23	
Denmark Hill 4	d	13 13				13 28				13 43				13 58				14 13				14 28	
Peckham Rye 4	d	13 15				13 30				13 45				14 00				14 15				14 30	
Queens Rd Peckham	d	13 17				13 32				13 47				14 02				14 17				14 32	
West Croydon 4	d		13 01				13 16				13 31				13 46				14 01				14 16
Norwood Junction 2	d		13 07				13 22				13 37				13 52				14 07				14 22
Anerley	d		13 10				13 25				13 40				13 55				14 10				14 25
Penge West	d		13 11				13 26				13 41				13 57				14 11				14 26
Crystal Palace 4	d				13 17				13 32				13 47				14 02				14 17		
Sydenham	d		13 14		13 21		13 29		13 36		13 44		13 51		13 59		14 06		14 14		14 21		14 29
Forest Hill 4	d		13 17		13 24		13 32		13 39		13 47		13 54		14 02		14 09		14 17		14 24		14 32
Honor Oak Park	d		13 19		13 26		13 34		13 41		13 49		13 56		14 04		14 11		14 19		14 26		14 34
Brockley	d		13 22		13 29		13 37		13 44		13 52		13 59		14 07		14 14		14 22		14 29		14 37
New Cross Gate	d		13 24		13 31		13 39		13 46		13 54		14 01		14 09		14 16		14 24		14 31		14 39
New Cross 4	d			13 27				13 42				13 57				14 12				14 27			
Surrey Quays	d	13 23	13 27	13 31	13 35	13 38	13 42	13 46	13 50	13 53	13 57	14 01	14 05	14 08	14 12	14 16	14 20	14 23	14 27	14 31	14 35	14 38	14 42
Canada Water	d	13 25	13 29	13 33	13 37	13 40	13 44	13 48	13 52	13 55	13 59	14 03	14 07	14 10	14 14	14 18	14 22	14 25	14 29	14 33	14 37	14 40	14 44
Rotherhithe	d	13 27	13 31	13 35	13 38	13 42	13 46	13 50	13 53	13 57	14 01	14 05	14 08	14 12	14 16	14 20	14 23	14 27	14 31	14 35	14 38	14 42	14 46
Wapping	d	13 28	13 32	13 36	13 40	13 43	13 47	13 51	13 55	13 58	14 02	14 06	14 10	14 13	14 17	14 21	14 25	14 28	14 32	14 36	14 40	14 43	14 47
Shadwell	d	13 30	13 34	13 38	13 42	13 45	13 49	13 53	13 57	14 00	14 04	14 08	14 12	14 15	14 19	14 23	14 27	14 30	14 34	14 38	14 42	14 45	14 49
Whitechapel	d	13 33	13 37	13 41	13 44	13 48	13 52	13 56	13 59	14 03	14 07	14 11	14 14	14 18	14 22	14 26	14 29	14 33	14 37	14 41	14 44	14 48	14 52
Shoreditch High Street	d	13 35	13 39	13 43	13 47	13 50	13 54	13 58	14 02	14 05	14 09	14 13	14 17	14 20	14 24	14 28	14 32	14 35	14 39	14 43	14 47	14 50	14 54
Hoxton	d	13 37	13 41	13 45	13 49	13 52	13 56	14 00	14 04	14 07	14 11	14 15	14 19	14 22	14 26	14 30	14 34	14 37	14 41	14 45	14 49	14 52	14 56
Haggerston	d	13 39	13 43	13 47	13 51	13 54	13 58	14 02	14 06	14 09	14 13	14 17	14 21	14 24	14 28	14 32	14 36	14 39	14 43	14 47	14 51	14 54	14 58
Dalston Junction	a	13 44	13 45	13 49	13 53	13 59	14 00	14 04	14 08	14 14	14 15	14 19	14 23	14 29	14 30	14 34	14 38	14 44	14 45	14 49	14 53	14 59	15 00
Canonbury	a		13 48		13 56		14 03		14 11		14 18		14 26		14 33		14 41		14 48		14 56		15 03
Highbury & Islington	a		13 53		14 00		14 08		14 15		14 23		14 30		14 38		14 45		14 53		15 00		15 08

Table T178-R

Saturdays

21 December to 16 May

Clapham Junction and West Croydon, Crystal Palace, New Cross - Highbury & Islington

		LO	LO	LO	LO	LO	LO	LO	LO	LO	LO	LO	LO	LO	LO	LO	LO	LO	LO	LO	LO	LO
Clapham Junction	d			14 30				14 45				15 00				15 15				15 30		
Wandsworth Road	d			14 36				14 51				15 06				15 21				15 36		
Clapham High Street ⊖	d			14 38				14 53				15 08				15 23				15 38		
Denmark Hill 4	d			14 43				14 58				15 13				15 28				15 43		
Peckham Rye 4	d			14 45				15 00				15 15				15 30				15 45		
Queens Rd Peckham	d			14 47				15 02				15 17				15 32				15 47		
West Croydon 4	d				14 31				14 46				15 01				15 16				15 31	
Norwood Junction 2	d				14 37				14 52				15 07				15 22				15 37	
Anerley	d				14 40				14 55				15 10				15 25				15 40	
Penge West	d				14 41				14 57				15 11				15 26				15 41	
Crystal Palace 4	d		14 32				14 47				15 02				15 17				15 32			
Sydenham	d		14 36		14 44		14 51		14 59		15 06		15 14		15 21		15 29		15 36		15 44	
Forest Hill 4	d		14 39		14 47		14 54		15 02		15 09		15 17		15 24		15 32		15 39		15 47	
Honor Oak Park	d		14 41		14 49		14 56		15 04		15 11		15 19		15 26		15 34		15 41		15 49	
Brockley	d		14 44		14 52		14 59		15 07		15 14		15 22		15 29		15 37		15 44		15 52	
New Cross Gate	d		14 46		14 54		15 01		15 09		15 16		15 24		15 31		15 39		15 46		15 54	
New Cross 4	d	14 42				14 57				15 12				15 27				15 42				15 57
Surrey Quays	d	14 46	14 50	14 53	14 57	15 01	15 05	15 08	15 12	15 16	15 20	15 23	15 27	15 31	15 35	15 38	15 42	15 46	15 50	15 53	15 57	16 01
Canada Water	d	14 48	14 52	14 55	14 59	15 03	15 07	15 10	15 14	15 18	15 22	15 25	15 29	15 33	15 37	15 40	15 44	15 48	15 52	15 55	15 59	16 03
Rotherhithe	d	14 50	14 53	14 57	15 01	15 05	15 08	15 12	15 16	15 20	15 23	15 27	15 31	15 35	15 38	15 42	15 46	15 50	15 53	15 57	16 01	16 05
Wapping	d	14 51	14 55	14 58	15 02	15 06	15 10	15 13	15 17	15 21	15 25	15 28	15 32	15 36	15 40	15 43	15 47	15 51	15 55	15 58	16 02	16 06
Shadwell	d	14 53	14 57	15 00	15 04	15 08	15 12	15 15	15 19	15 23	15 27	15 30	15 34	15 38	15 42	15 45	15 49	15 53	15 57	16 00	16 04	16 08
Whitechapel	d	14 56	14 59	15 03	15 07	15 11	15 14	15 18	15 22	15 26	15 29	15 33	15 37	15 41	15 44	15 48	15 52	15 56	15 59	16 03	16 07	16 11
Shoreditch High Street	d	14 58	15 02	15 05	15 09	15 13	15 17	15 20	15 24	15 28	15 32	15 35	15 39	15 43	15 47	15 50	15 54	15 58	16 02	16 05	16 09	16 13
Hoxton	d	15 00	15 04	15 07	15 11	15 15	15 19	15 22	15 26	15 30	15 34	15 37	15 41	15 45	15 49	15 52	15 56	16 00	16 04	16 07	16 11	16 15
Haggerston	d	15 02	15 06	15 09	15 13	15 17	15 21	15 24	15 28	15 32	15 36	15 39	15 43	15 47	15 51	15 54	15 58	16 02	16 06	16 09	16 13	16 17
Dalston Junction	a	15 04	15 08	15 14	15 15	15 19	15 23	15 29	15 30	15 34	15 38	15 44	15 45	15 49	15 53	15 59	16 00	16 04	16 08	16 14	16 15	16 19
Canonbury	a		15 11		15 18		15 26		15 33		15 41		15 48		15 56		16 03		16 11		16 18	
Highbury & Islington	a		15 15		15 23		15 30		15 38		15 45		15 53		16 00		16 10		16 15		16 25	

		LO	LO	LO	LO	LO	LO	LO	LO	LO	LO	LO	LO	LO	LO	LO	LO	LO	LO	LO	LO	LO	LO
Clapham Junction	d		15 45				16 00				16 15				16 30				16 45				17 00
Wandsworth Road	d		15 51				16 06				16 21				16 36				16 51				17 06
Clapham High Street ⊖	d		15 53				16 08				16 23				16 38				16 53				17 08
Denmark Hill 4	d		15 58				16 13				16 28				16 43				16 58				17 13
Peckham Rye 4	d		16 00				16 15				16 30				16 45				17 00				17 15
Queens Rd Peckham	d		16 02				16 17				16 32				16 47				17 02				17 17
West Croydon 4	d			15 46				16 01				16 16				16 31				16 46			
Norwood Junction 2	d			15 52				16 07				16 22				16 37				16 52			
Anerley	d			15 55				16 10				16 25				16 40				16 55			
Penge West	d			15 57				16 11				16 26				16 41				16 57			
Crystal Palace 4	d	15 47				16 02				16 17				16 32				16 47				17 02	
Sydenham	d	15 51		15 59		16 06		16 14		16 21		16 29		16 36		16 44		16 51		16 59		17 06	
Forest Hill 4	d	15 54		16 02		16 09		16 17		16 24		16 32		16 39		16 47		16 54		17 02		17 09	
Honor Oak Park	d	15 56		16 04		16 11		16 19		16 26		16 34		16 41		16 49		16 56		17 04		17 11	
Brockley	d	15 59		16 07		16 14		16 22		16 29		16 37		16 44		16 52		16 59		17 07		17 14	
New Cross Gate	d	16 01		16 09		16 16		16 24		16 31		16 39		16 46		16 54		17 01		17 09		17 16	
New Cross 4	d				16 12				16 27				16 42				16 57				17 12		
Surrey Quays	d	16 05	16 08	16 12	16 16	16 20	16 23	16 27	16 31	16 35	16 38	16 42	16 46	16 50	16 53	16 57	17 01	17 05	17 08	17 12	17 16	17 20	17 23
Canada Water	d	16 07	16 10	16 14	16 18	16 22	16 25	16 29	16 33	16 37	16 40	16 44	16 48	16 52	16 55	16 59	17 03	17 07	17 10	17 14	17 18	17 22	17 25
Rotherhithe	d	16 08	16 12	16 16	16 20	16 23	16 27	16 31	16 35	16 38	16 42	16 46	16 50	16 53	16 57	17 01	17 05	17 08	17 12	17 16	17 20	17 23	17 27
Wapping	d	16 10	16 13	16 17	16 21	16 25	16 28	16 32	16 36	16 40	16 43	16 47	16 51	16 55	16 58	17 02	17 06	17 10	17 13	17 17	17 21	17 25	17 28
Shadwell	d	16 12	16 15	16 19	16 23	16 27	16 30	16 34	16 38	16 42	16 45	16 49	16 53	16 57	17 00	17 04	17 08	17 12	17 15	17 19	17 23	17 27	17 30
Whitechapel	d	16 14	16 18	16 22	16 26	16 29	16 33	16 37	16 41	16 44	16 48	16 52	16 56	16 59	17 03	17 07	17 11	17 14	17 18	17 22	17 26	17 29	17 33
Shoreditch High Street	d	16 17	16 20	16 24	16 28	16 32	16 35	16 39	16 43	16 47	16 50	16 54	16 58	17 02	17 05	17 09	17 13	17 17	17 20	17 24	17 28	17 32	17 35
Hoxton	d	16 19	16 22	16 26	16 30	16 34	16 37	16 41	16 45	16 49	16 52	16 56	17 00	17 04	17 07	17 11	17 15	17 19	17 22	17 26	17 30	17 34	17 37
Haggerston	d	16 21	16 24	16 28	16 32	16 36	16 39	16 43	16 47	16 51	16 54	16 58	17 02	17 06	17 09	17 13	17 17	17 21	17 24	17 28	17 32	17 36	17 39
Dalston Junction	a	16 23	16 29	16 30	16 34	16 38	16 44	16 45	16 49	16 53	16 59	17 00	17 04	17 08	17 14	17 15	17 19	17 23	17 29	17 30	17 34	17 38	17 44
Canonbury	a	16 26		16 33		16 41		16 48		16 56		17 03		17 11		17 18		17 26		17 33		17 41	
Highbury & Islington	a	16 30		16 40		16 45		16 55		17 00		17 10		17 15		17 25		17 30		17 40		17 45	

		LO	LO	LO	LO	LO	LO	LO	LO	LO	LO	LO	LO	LO	LO	LO	LO	LO	LO	LO	LO	LO	LO
Clapham Junction	d				17 15				17 30				17 45				18 00				18 15		
Wandsworth Road	d				17 21				17 36				17 51				18 06				18 21		
Clapham High Street ⊖	d				17 23				17 38				17 53				18 08				18 23		
Denmark Hill 4	d				17 28				17 43				17 58				18 13				18 28		
Peckham Rye 4	d				17 30				17 45				18 00				18 15				18 30		
Queens Rd Peckham	d				17 32				17 47				18 02				18 17				18 32		
West Croydon 4	d	17 01				17 16				17 31				17 46				18 01				18 16	
Norwood Junction 2	d	17 07				17 22				17 37				17 52				18 07				18 22	
Anerley	d	17 10				17 25				17 40				17 55				18 10				18 25	
Penge West	d	17 11				17 26				17 41				17 57				18 11				18 26	
Crystal Palace 4	d			17 17				17 32				17 47				18 02				18 17			
Sydenham	d	17 14		17 21		17 29		17 36		17 44		17 51		17 59		18 06		18 14		18 21		18 29	
Forest Hill 4	d	17 17		17 24		17 32		17 39		17 47		17 54		18 02		18 09		18 17		18 24		18 32	
Honor Oak Park	d	17 19		17 26		17 34		17 41		17 49		17 56		18 04		18 11		18 19		18 26		18 34	
Brockley	d	17 22		17 29		17 37		17 44		17 52		17 59		18 07		18 14		18 22		18 29		18 37	
New Cross Gate	d	17 24		17 31		17 39		17 46		17 54		18 01		18 09		18 16		18 24		18 31		18 39	
New Cross 4	d		17 27				17 42				17 57				18 12				18 27				18 42
Surrey Quays	d	17 27	17 31	17 35	17 38	17 42	17 46	17 50	17 53	17 57	18 01	18 05	18 08	18 12	18 16	18 20	18 23	18 27	18 31	18 35	18 38	18 42	18 46
Canada Water	d	17 29	17 33	17 37	17 40	17 44	17 48	17 52	17 55	17 59	18 03	18 07	18 10	18 14	18 18	18 22	18 25	18 29	18 33	18 37	18 40	18 44	18 48
Rotherhithe	d	17 31	17 35	17 38	17 42	17 46	17 50	17 53	17 57	18 01	18 05	18 08	18 12	18 16	18 20	18 23	18 27	18 31	18 35	18 38	18 42	18 46	18 50
Wapping	d	17 32	17 36	17 40	17 43	17 47	17 51	17 55	17 58	18 02	18 06	18 10	18 13	18 17	18 21	18 25	18 28	18 32	18 36	18 40	18 43	18 47	18 51
Shadwell	d	17 34	17 38	17 42	17 45	17 49	17 53	17 57	18 00	18 04	18 08	18 12	18 15	18 19	18 23	18 27	18 30	18 34	18 38	18 42	18 45	18 49	18 53
Whitechapel	d	17 37	17 41	17 44	17 48	17 52	17 56	17 59	18 03	18 07	18 11	18 14	18 18	18 22	18 26	18 29	18 33	18 37	18 41	18 44	18 48	18 52	18 56
Shoreditch High Street	d	17 39	17 43	17 47	17 50	17 54	17 58	18 02	18 05	18 09	18 13	18 17	18 20	18 24	18 28	18 32	18 35	18 39	18 43	18 47	18 50	18 54	18 58
Hoxton	d	17 41	17 45	17 49	17 52	17 56	18 00	18 04	18 07	18 11	18 15	18 19	18 22	18 26	18 30	18 34	18 37	18 41	18 45	18 49	18 52	18 56	19 00
Haggerston	d	17 43	17 47	17 51	17 54	17 58	18 02	18 06	18 09	18 13	18 17	18 21	18 24	18 28	18 32	18 36	18 39	18 43	18 47	18 51	18 54	18 58	19 02
Dalston Junction	a	17 45	17 49	17 53	17 59	18 00	18 04	18 08	18 14	18 15	18 19	18 23	18 29	18 30	18 34	18 38	18 44	18 45	18 49	18 53	18 59	19 00	19 04
Canonbury	a	17 48		17 56		18 03		18 11		18 18		18 26		18 33		18 41		18 48		18 56		19 03	
Highbury & Islington	a	17 55		18 00		18 10		18 15		18 25		18 30		18 40		18 45		18 55		19 00		19 10	

Table T178-R

Saturdays

21 December to 16 May

Clapham Junction and West Croydon, Crystal Palace, New Cross - Highbury & Islington

		LO		LO	LO	LO	LO	LO	LO	LO	LO	LO		LO	LO	LO	LO	LO	LO	LO	LO	LO		LO	LO
Clapham Junction	d			18 30				18 45				19 00					19 15				19 30				
Wandsworth Road	d			18 36				18 51				19 06					19 21				19 36				
Clapham High Street ⊖	d			18 38				18 53				19 08					19 23				19 38				
Denmark Hill	d			18 43				18 58				19 13					19 28				19 43				
Peckham Rye	d			18 45				19 00				19 15					19 30				19 45				
Queens Rd Peckham	d			18 47				19 02				19 17					19 32				19 47				
West Croydon	d				18 31				18 46					19 01				19 16				19 31			
Norwood Junction	d				18 37				18 52					19 07				19 22				19 37			
Anerley	d				18 40				18 55					19 10				19 25				19 40			
Penge West	d				18 41				18 57					19 11				19 26				19 41			
Crystal Palace	d	18 32					18 47				19 02					19 17				19 32					19 47
Sydenham	d	18 36			18 44		18 51		18 59		19 06			19 14		19 21		19 29		19 36		19 44			19 51
Forest Hill	d	18 39			18 47		18 54		19 02		19 09			19 17		19 24		19 32		19 39		19 47			19 54
Honor Oak Park	d	18 41			18 49		18 56		19 04		19 11			19 19		19 26		19 34		19 41		19 49			19 56
Brockley	d	18 44			18 52		18 59		19 07		19 14			19 22		19 29		19 37		19 44		19 52			19 59
New Cross Gate	d	18 46			18 54		19 01		19 09		19 16			19 24		19 31		19 39		19 46		19 54			20 01
New Cross	d					18 57				19 12					19 27				19 42					19 57	
Surrey Quays	d	18 50		18 53	18 57	19 01	19 05	19 08	19 12	19 16	19 20	19 23		19 27	19 31	19 35	19 38	19 42	19 46	19 50	19 53	19 57		20 01	20 05
Canada Water	d	18 52		18 55	18 59	19 03	19 07	19 10	19 14	19 18	19 22	19 25		19 29	19 33	19 37	19 40	19 44	19 48	19 52	19 55	19 59		20 03	20 07
Rotherhithe	d	18 53		18 57	19 01	19 05	19 08	19 12	19 16	19 20	19 23	19 27		19 31	19 35	19 38	19 42	19 46	19 50	19 53	19 57	20 01		20 05	20 08
Wapping	d	18 55		18 58	19 02	19 06	19 10	19 13	19 17	19 21	19 25	19 28		19 32	19 36	19 40	19 43	19 47	19 51	19 55	19 58	20 02		20 06	20 10
Shadwell	d	18 57		19 00	19 04	19 08	19 12	19 15	19 19	19 23	19 27	19 30		19 34	19 38	19 42	19 45	19 49	19 53	19 57	20 00	20 04		20 08	20 12
Whitechapel	d	18 59		19 03	19 07	19 11	19 14	19 18	19 22	19 26	19 29	19 33		19 37	19 41	19 44	19 48	19 52	19 56	19 59	20 03	20 07		20 11	20 14
Shoreditch High Street	d	19 02		19 05	19 09	19 13	19 17	19 20	19 24	19 28	19 32	19 35		19 39	19 43	19 47	19 50	19 54	19 58	20 02	20 05	20 09		20 13	20 17
Hoxton	d	19 04		19 07	19 11	19 15	19 19	19 22	19 26	19 30	19 34	19 37		19 41	19 45	19 49	19 52	19 56	20 00	20 04	20 07	20 11		20 15	20 19
Haggerston	d	19 06		19 09	19 13	19 17	19 21	19 24	19 28	19 32	19 36	19 39		19 43	19 47	19 51	19 54	19 58	20 02	20 06	20 09	20 13		20 17	20 21
Dalston Junction	a	19 08		19 14	19 15	19 19	19 23	19 29	19 30	19 34	19 38	19 44		19 45	19 49	19 53	19 59	20 00	20 04	20 08	20 14	20 15		20 19	20 23
Canonbury	a	19 11			19 18		19 26		19 33		19 41			19 48		19 56		20 03		20 11		20 18			20 26
Highbury & Islington	a	19 15			19 25		19 30		19 40		19 45			19 53		20 00		20 08		20 15		20 23			20 30

		LO	LO	LO	LO	LO	LO	LO		LO	LO	LO	LO	LO	LO	LO	LO	LO		LO	LO	LO	LO	LO	LO
Clapham Junction	d	19 45				20 00					20 15				20 30					20 45				21 00	
Wandsworth Road	d	19 51				20 06					20 21				20 36					20 51				21 06	
Clapham High Street ⊖	d	19 53				20 08					20 23				20 38					20 53				21 08	
Denmark Hill	d	19 58				20 13					20 28				20 43					20 58				21 13	
Peckham Rye	d	20 00				20 15					20 30				20 45					21 00				21 15	
Queens Rd Peckham	d	20 02				20 17					20 32				20 47					21 02				21 17	
West Croydon	d		19 46				20 01					20 16				20 31					20 46				21 01
Norwood Junction	d		19 52				20 07					20 22				20 37					20 52				21 07
Anerley	d		19 55				20 10					20 25				20 40					20 55				21 10
Penge West	d		19 57				20 11					20 26				20 41					20 57				21 11
Crystal Palace	d				20 02					20 17				20 32				20 47					21 02		
Sydenham	d		19 59		20 06		20 14			20 21		20 29		20 36		20 44		20 51			20 59		21 06		21 14
Forest Hill	d		20 02		20 09		20 17			20 24		20 32		20 39		20 47		20 54			21 02		21 09		21 17
Honor Oak Park	d		20 04		20 11		20 19			20 26		20 34		20 41		20 49		20 56			21 04		21 11		21 19
Brockley	d		20 07		20 14		20 22			20 29		20 37		20 44		20 52		20 59			21 07		21 14		21 22
New Cross Gate	d		20 09		20 16		20 24			20 31		20 39		20 46		20 54		21 01			21 09		21 16		21 24
New Cross	d			20 12				20 27					20 42				20 57					21 12			
Surrey Quays	d	20 08	20 12	20 16	20 20	20 23	20 27	20 31		20 35	20 38	20 42	20 46	20 50	20 53	20 57	21 01	21 05		21 08	21 12	21 16	21 20	21 23	21 27
Canada Water	d	20 10	20 14	20 18	20 22	20 25	20 29	20 33		20 37	20 40	20 44	20 48	20 52	20 55	20 59	21 03	21 07		21 10	21 14	21 18	21 22	21 25	21 29
Rotherhithe	d	20 12	20 16	20 20	20 23	20 27	20 31	20 35		20 38	20 42	20 46	20 50	20 53	20 57	21 01	21 05	21 08		21 12	21 16	21 20	21 23	21 27	21 31
Wapping	d	20 13	20 17	20 21	20 25	20 28	20 32	20 36		20 40	20 43	20 47	20 51	20 55	20 58	21 02	21 06	21 10		21 13	21 17	21 21	21 25	21 28	21 32
Shadwell	d	20 15	20 19	20 23	20 27	20 30	20 34	20 38		20 42	20 45	20 49	20 53	20 57	21 00	21 04	21 08	21 12		21 15	21 19	21 23	21 27	21 30	21 34
Whitechapel	d	20 18	20 22	20 26	20 29	20 33	20 37	20 41		20 44	20 48	20 52	20 56	20 59	21 03	21 07	21 11	21 14		21 18	21 22	21 26	21 29	21 33	21 37
Shoreditch High Street	d	20 20	20 24	20 28	20 32	20 35	20 39	20 43		20 47	20 50	20 54	20 58	21 02	21 05	21 09	21 13	21 17		21 20	21 24	21 28	21 32	21 35	21 39
Hoxton	d	20 22	20 26	20 30	20 34	20 37	20 41	20 45		20 49	20 52	20 56	21 00	21 04	21 07	21 11	21 15	21 19		21 22	21 26	21 30	21 34	21 37	21 41
Haggerston	d	20 24	20 28	20 32	20 36	20 39	20 43	20 47		20 51	20 54	20 58	21 02	21 06	21 09	21 13	21 17	21 21		21 24	21 28	21 32	21 36	21 39	21 43
Dalston Junction	a	20 29	20 30	20 34	20 38	20 44	20 45	20 49		20 53	20 59	21 00	21 04	21 08	21 14	21 15	21 19	21 23		21 29	21 30	21 34	21 38	21 44	21 45
Canonbury	a		20 33		20 41		20 48			20 56		21 03		21 11		21 18		21 26			21 33		21 41		21 48
Highbury & Islington	a		20 38		20 45		20 53			21 00		21 08		21 15		21 23		21 30			21 38		21 45		21 53

		LO	LO	LO		LO	LO	LO	LO	LO	LO	LO	LO	LO		LO	LO	LO	LO	LO	LO	LO	LO	LO	
Clapham Junction	d			21 15					21 30				21 45					22 00				22 15			
Wandsworth Road	d			21 21					21 36				21 51					22 06				22 21			
Clapham High Street ⊖	d			21 23					21 38				21 53					22 08				22 23			
Denmark Hill	d			21 28					21 43				21 58					22 13				22 28			
Peckham Rye	d			21 30					21 45				22 00					22 15				22 32			
Queens Rd Peckham	d			21 32					21 47				22 02					22 17				22 34			
West Croydon	d					21 16				21 31				21 46					22 01				22 16		
Norwood Junction	d					21 22				21 37				21 52					22 07				22 22		
Anerley	d					21 25				21 40				21 55					22 10				22 25		
Penge West	d					21 26				21 41				21 57					22 11				22 26		
Crystal Palace	d		21 17					21 32				21 47					22 02				22 17				
Sydenham	d		21 21			21 29		21 36		21 44		21 51		21 59			22 06		22 14		22 21		22 29		
Forest Hill	d		21 24			21 32		21 39		21 47		21 54		22 02			22 09		22 17		22 24		22 32		
Honor Oak Park	d		21 26			21 34		21 41		21 49		21 56		22 04			22 11		22 19		22 26		22 34		
Brockley	d		21 29			21 37		21 44		21 52		21 59		22 07			22 14		22 22		22 29		22 37		
New Cross Gate	d		21 31			21 39		21 46		21 54		22 01		22 09			22 16		22 24		22 31		22 39		
New Cross	d	21 27					21 42				21 57					22 12				22 27				22 42	
Surrey Quays	d	21 31	21 35	21 38		21 42	21 46	21 50	21 53	21 57	22 01	22 05	22 08	22 12		22 16	22 20	22 23	22 27	22 31	22 35	22 38	22 42	22 46	
Canada Water	d	21 33	21 37	21 40		21 44	21 48	21 52	21 55	21 59	22 03	22 07	22 10	22 14		22 18	22 22	22 25	22 29	22 33	22 37	22 40	22 44	22 48	
Rotherhithe	d	21 35	21 38	21 42		21 46	21 50	21 53	21 57	22 01	22 05	22 08	22 12	22 16		22 20	22 23	22 27	22 31	22 35	22 38	22 42	22 46	22 50	
Wapping	d	21 36	21 40	21 43		21 47	21 51	21 55	21 58	22 02	22 06	22 10	22 13	22 17		22 21	22 25	22 28	22 32	22 36	22 40	22 43	22 47	22 51	
Shadwell	d	21 38	21 42	21 45		21 49	21 53	21 57	22 00	22 04	22 08	22 12	22 15	22 19		22 23	22 27	22 30	22 34	22 38	22 42	22 45	22 49	22 53	
Whitechapel	d	21 41	21 44	21 48		21 52	21 56	21 59	22 03	22 07	22 11	22 14	22 18	22 22		22 26	22 29	22 33	22 37	22 41	22 44	22 48	22 52	22 56	
Shoreditch High Street	d	21 43	21 47	21 50		21 54	21 58	22 02	22 05	22 09	22 13	22 17	22 20	22 24		22 28	22 32	22 35	22 39	22 43	22 47	22 50	22 54	22 58	
Hoxton	d	21 45	21 49	21 52		21 56	22 00	22 04	22 07	22 11	22 15	22 19	22 22	22 26		22 30	22 34	22 37	22 41	22 45	22 49	22 52	22 56	23 00	
Haggerston	d	21 47	21 51	21 54		21 58	22 02	22 06	22 09	22 13	22 17	22 21	22 24	22 28		22 32	22 36	22 39	22 43	22 47	22 51	22 54	22 58	23 02	
Dalston Junction	a	21 49	21 53	21 59		22 00	22 04	22 08	22 14	22 15	22 19	22 23	22 29	22 30		22 34	22 38	22 44	22 45	22 49	22 53	22 59	23 00	23 04	
Canonbury	a		21 56			22 03		22 11		22 18		22 26		22 33			22 41		22 48		22 56		23 03		
Highbury & Islington	a		22 00			22 08		22 15		22 23		22 30		22 38			22 45		22 53		23 00		23 10		

Table T178-R

Saturdays

21 December to 16 May

Clapham Junction and West Croydon, Crystal Palace, New Cross - Highbury & Islington

		LO	LO	LO	LO	LO	LO	LO	LO	LO		LO	LO	LO	LO	LO	LO	LO	LO	LO		LO	LO	LO	
Clapham Junction	d		22 30				22 45					23 00				23 15				23 30			23 44		
Wandsworth Road	d		22 36				22 51					23 06				23 21				23 36			23 50		
Clapham High Street ⊖	d		22 38				22 53					23 08				23 23				23 38			23 52		
Denmark Hill	d		22 43				22 58					23 13				23 28				23 43			23 57		
Peckham Rye	d		22 45				23 00					23 15				23 30				23 45			23 59		
Queens Rd Peckham	d		22 47				23 02					23 17				23 32				23 47			00 01		
West Croydon	d			22 31				22 46					23 01				23 16					23 31			
Norwood Junction	d			22 37				22 52					23 07				23 22					23 37			
Anerley	d			22 40				22 55					23 10				23 25					23 40			
Penge West	d			22 41				22 56					23 11				23 26					23 41			
Crystal Palace	d	22 32				22 47				23 02					23 17				23 32					23 50	
Sydenham	d	22 36		22 44		22 51		22 59		23 06			23 14		23 21		23 29		23 36			23 44		23 54	
Forest Hill	d	22 39		22 47		22 54		23 02		23 09			23 17		23 24		23 32		23 39			23 47		23 56	
Honor Oak Park	d	22 41		22 49		22 56		23 04		23 11			23 19		23 26		23 34		23 41			23 49		23 59	
Brockley	d	22 44		22 52		22 59		23 07		23 14			23 22		23 29		23 37		23 44			23 52		00 01	
New Cross Gate	d	22 46		22 54		23 01		23 09		23 16			23 24		23 31		23 39		23 46			23 54		00 03	
New Cross	d				22 57				23 12					23 27				23 42							
Surrey Quays	d	22 50	22 53	22 57	23 01	23 05	23 08	23 12	23 16	23 20		23 23	23 27	23 31	23 35	23 38	23 42	23 46	23 50	23 53		23 57	00 05	00 09	
Canada Water	d	22 52	22 55	22 59	23 03	23 07	23 10	23 14	23 18	23 22		23 25	23 29	23 33	23 37	23 40	23 44	23 48	23 52	23 55		23 59	00 07	00 11	
Rotherhithe	d	22 53	22 57	23 01	23 05	23 08	23 12	23 16	23 20	23 23		23 27	23 31	23 35	23 38	23 42	23 46	23 50	23 53	23 57		00 01	00 09	00 12	
Wapping	d	22 55	22 58	23 02	23 06	23 10	23 13	23 17	23 21	23 25		23 28	23 32	23 36	23 40	23 43	23 47	23 51	23 55	23 58		00 02	00 10	00 14	
Shadwell	d	22 57	23 00	23 04	23 08	23 12	23 15	23 19	23 23	23 27		23 30	23 34	23 38	23 42	23 45	23 49	23 53	23 57	00 01		00 04	00 12	00 16	
Whitechapel	d	22 59	23 03	23 07	23 11	23 14	23 18	23 22	23 26	23 29		23 33	23 37	23 41	23 44	23 48	23 52	23 56	23 59	00 03		00 07	00 15	00 18	
Shoreditch High Street	d	23 02	23 05	23 09	23 13	23 17	23 20	23 24	23 28	23 32		23 35	23 39	23 43	23 47	23 50	23 54	23 58	00 02	00 05		00 09	00 17	00 21	
Hoxton	d	23 04	23 07	23 11	23 15	23 19	23 22	23 26	23 30	23 34		23 37	23 41	23 45	23 49	23 52	23 56	00 01	00 04	00 07		00 11	00 19	00 23	
Haggerston	d	23 06	23 09	23 13	23 17	23 21	23 24	23 28	23 32	23 36		23 39	23 43	23 47	23 51	23 54	23 58	00 02	00 06	00 09		00 13	00 21	00 25	
Dalston Junction	a	23 08	23 14	23 15	23 19	23 23	23 29	23 34	23 34	23 38		23 44	23 45	23 49	23 53	23 59	00 01	00 04	00 08	00 14		00 15	00 28	00 27	
Canonbury	a	23 11		23 18		23 26			23 37	23 41			23 50		23 56		00 03		00 11			00 18		00 30	
Highbury & Islington	a	23 15		23 25		23 30			23 40	23 45			23 58		23 59		00 10		00 15			00 25		00 32	

Sundays

15 December to 10 May

		LO	LO	LO	LO	LO	LO	LO	LO		LO		LO	LO	LO	LO	LO	LO	LO	LO	LO		LO	LO
		A	B	C	D	C	B												E					
Clapham Junction	d																				07 35			07 55
Wandsworth Road	d																		07 29		07 41			08 01
Clapham High Street ⊖	d																		07 30		07 43			08 03
Denmark Hill	d																		07 37		07 48			08 11
Peckham Rye	d																		07 39		07 50			08 14
Queens Rd Peckham	d					00 01													07 41		07 52			08 16
West Croydon	d															06 43		07 12					07 47	
Norwood Junction	d															06 48		07 18					07 52	
Anerley	d															06 51		07 21					07 55	
Penge West	d															06 53		07 23					07 57	
Crystal Palace	d							00 04							06 36		07 07			07 37				
Sydenham	d							00 08		and every 15 minutes until					06 40	06 55	07 11	07 25		07 41			07 59	
Forest Hill	d							00 11							06 42	06 58	07 13	07 28		07 43			08 02	
Honor Oak Park	d							00 13							06 45	07 00	07 16	07 30		07 46			08 04	
Brockley	d						00 01	00 16							06 47	07 03	07 18	07 33		07 48			08 07	
New Cross Gate	d						00 03	00 18	00 33		06 03		06 15	06 32	06 49	07 05	07 20	07 35		07 50			08 09	
New Cross	d																							
Surrey Quays	d					00 05	00 09	00 22	00 37		06 07		06 19	06 36	06 53	07 08	07 24	07 38	07 48	07 54	08 00		08 12	08 19
Canada Water	d					00 07	00 11	00 24	00 39		06 09		06 21	06 38	06 55	07 10	07 26	07 40	07 50	07 56	08 02		08 14	08 21
Rotherhithe	d				00 01	00 09	00 12	00 25	00 40		06 10		06 22	06 39	06 56	07 12	07 27	07 42	07 51	07 57	08 04		08 16	08 23
Wapping	d				00 02	00 10	00 14	00 27	00 42		06 12		06 24	06 41	06 58	07 13	07 29	07 43	07 53	07 59	08 05		08 17	08 24
Shadwell	d			00 01	00 04	00 12	00 16	00 29	00 44		06 14		06 26	06 43	07 00	07 15	07 31	07 45	07 55	08 01	08 07		08 19	08 26
Whitechapel	d			00 03	00 07	00 15	00 18	00 31	00 46		06 16		06 28	06 45	07 02	07 18	07 33	07 48	07 57	08 03	08 10		08 22	08 29
Shoreditch High Street	d		00 02	00 05	00 09	00 17	00 21	00 34	00 49		06 19		06 31	06 48	07 04	07 20	07 35	07 50	07 59	08 05	08 12		08 24	08 31
Hoxton	d	00 01	00 04	00 07	00 11	00 19	00 23	00 36	00 51		06 21		06 33	06 50	07 06	07 22	07 37	07 52	08 01	08 07	08 14		08 26	08 33
Haggerston	d	00 02	00 06	00 09	00 13	00 21	00 25	00 38	00 53		06 23		06 35	06 52	07 08	07 24	07 39	07 54	08 03	08 09	08 16		08 28	08 35
Dalston Junction	a	00 04	00 08	00 14	00 15	00 28	00 27	00 40	00 55		06 25		06 37	06 54	07 10	07 26	07 41	07 56	08 05	08 11	08 19		08 30	08 37
Canonbury	a		00 11		00 18		00 30	00 43	00 58		06 28		06 40	06 57	07 13	07 29	07 44	07 59	08 08	08 14			08 33	08 40
Highbury & Islington	a		00 15		00 25		00 32	00 46	01 03		06 33		06 45	07 02	07 19	07 34	07 50	08 03	08 14	08 20			08 38	08 44

		LO	LO	LO	LO	LO	LO	LO		LO	LO	LO	LO	LO	LO	LO	LO	LO		LO	LO	LO	LO	LO	LO
Clapham Junction	d		08 05		08 20			08 35				08 50			09 05			09 20				09 35			09 50
Wandsworth Road	d		08 11		08 26			08 41				08 56			09 11			09 26				09 41			09 56
Clapham High Street ⊖	d		08 13		08 28			08 43				08 58			09 13			09 28				09 43			09 58
Denmark Hill	d		08 18		08 33			08 48				09 03			09 18			09 33				09 48			10 03
Peckham Rye	d		08 20		08 35			08 50				09 05			09 20			09 35				09 50			10 05
Queens Rd Peckham	d		08 22		08 37			08 52				09 07			09 22			09 37				09 52			10 07
West Croydon	d			08 12						08 42						09 13							09 42		
Norwood Junction	d			08 18						08 48						09 18							09 48		
Anerley	d			08 21						08 51						09 21							09 51		
Penge West	d			08 23						08 53						09 23							09 53		
Crystal Palace	d	08 07				08 37							09 07							09 37					
Sydenham	d	08 11		08 25		08 41				08 55			09 11			09 25				09 41			09 55		
Forest Hill	d	08 13		08 28		08 43				08 58			09 13			09 28				09 43			09 58		
Honor Oak Park	d	08 16		08 30		08 46				09 00			09 16			09 30				09 46			10 00		
Brockley	d	08 18		08 33		08 48				09 03			09 18			09 33				09 48			10 03		
New Cross Gate	d	08 20		08 35		08 50				09 05			09 20			09 35				09 50			10 05		
New Cross	d						08 55				09 10			09 25			09 40				09 55			10 10	
Surrey Quays	d	08 24	08 33	08 38	08 48	08 54	08 59	09 03		09 08	09 14	09 18	09 24	09 29	09 33	09 38	09 44	09 48		09 54	09 59	10 03	10 08	10 14	10 18
Canada Water	d	08 26	08 35	08 40	08 50	08 56	09 01	09 05		09 10	09 16	09 20	09 26	09 31	09 35	09 40	09 46	09 50		09 56	10 01	10 05	10 10	10 16	10 20
Rotherhithe	d	08 27	08 36	08 42	08 51	08 57	09 03	09 06		09 12	09 18	09 21	09 27	09 33	09 36	09 42	09 48	09 51		09 57	10 03	10 06	10 12	10 18	10 21
Wapping	d	08 29	08 38	08 43	08 53	08 59	09 04	09 08		09 13	09 19	09 23	09 29	09 34	09 38	09 43	09 49	09 53		09 59	10 04	10 08	10 13	10 19	10 23
Shadwell	d	08 31	08 40	08 45	08 55	09 01	09 06	09 10		09 15	09 21	09 25	09 31	09 36	09 40	09 45	09 51	09 55		10 01	10 06	10 10	10 15	10 21	10 25
Whitechapel	d	08 33	08 42	08 48	08 57	09 03	09 09	09 12		09 18	09 24	09 27	09 33	09 39	09 42	09 48	09 54	09 57		10 03	10 09	10 12	10 18	10 24	10 27
Shoreditch High Street	d	08 35	08 44	08 50	08 59	09 05	09 11	09 14		09 20	09 26	09 29	09 35	09 41	09 44	09 50	09 56	09 59		10 05	10 11	10 14	10 20	10 26	10 29
Hoxton	d	08 37	08 46	08 52	09 01	09 07	09 13	09 16		09 22	09 28	09 31	09 37	09 43	09 46	09 52	09 58	10 01		10 07	10 13	10 16	10 22	10 28	10 31
Haggerston	d	08 39	08 48	08 54	09 03	09 09	09 15	09 18		09 24	09 30	09 33	09 39	09 45	09 48	09 54	10 00	10 03		10 09	10 15	10 18	10 24	10 30	10 33
Dalston Junction	a	08 41	08 50	08 56	09 05	09 11	09 17	09 20		09 26	09 32	09 35	09 41	09 47	09 50	09 56	10 02	10 05		10 11	10 17	10 20	10 26	10 32	10 35
Canonbury	a	08 44	08 53	08 59	09 08	09 14		09 23		09 29		09 38	09 44		09 53	09 59		10 08		10 14		10 23	10 29		10 38
Highbury & Islington	a	08 50	08 56	09 03	09 11	09 20		09 26		09 33		09 41	09 50		09 56	10 04		10 11		10 20		10 26	10 33		10 41

A not 15 December. From New Cross Ell
B not 15 December. From Crystal Palace
C not 15 December. From Clapham Junction Plats
D not 15 December. From West Croydon

Table T178-R

Sundays

15 December to 10 May

Clapham Junction and West Croydon, Crystal Palace, New Cross - Highbury & Islington

		LO	LO	LO		LO	LO	LO	LO	LO	LO	LO	LO	LO		LO	LO	LO	LO	LO	LO	LO	LO	LO	
Clapham Junction	d			10 05				10 20			10 35			10 50					11 05				11 20		
Wandsworth Road	d			10 11				10 26			10 41			10 56					11 11				11 26		
Clapham High Street ⊖	d			10 13				10 28			10 43			10 58					11 13				11 28		
Denmark Hill 4	d			10 18				10 33			10 48			11 03					11 18				11 33		
Peckham Rye 4	d			10 20				10 35			10 50			11 05					11 20				11 35		
Queens Rd Peckham	d			10 22				10 37			10 52			11 07					11 22				11 37		
West Croydon 4 (tram)	d					10 12						10 42									11 12				
Norwood Junction 2	d					10 18						10 48									11 18				
Anerley	d					10 21						10 51									11 21				
Penge West	d					10 23						10 53									11 23				
Crystal Palace 4	d	10 07							10 37								11 07								
Sydenham	d	10 11				10 25			10 41			10 55					11 11				11 25				
Forest Hill 4	d	10 13				10 28			10 43			10 58					11 13				11 28				
Honor Oak Park	d	10 16				10 30			10 46			11 00					11 16				11 30				
Brockley	d	10 18				10 33			10 48			11 03					11 18				11 33				
New Cross Gate	d	10 20				10 35			10 50			11 05					11 20				11 35				
New Cross 4	d		10 25				10 40			10 55			11 10					11 25				11 40			
Surrey Quays	d	10 24	10 29	10 33		10 38	10 44	10 48	10 54	10 59	11 03	11 08	11 14	11 18		11 21	11 24	11 29	11 32	11 35	11 38	11 44	11 48	11 51	
Canada Water	d	10 26	10 31	10 35		10 40	10 46	10 50	10 56	11 01	11 05	11 10	11 16	11 20		11 23	11 26	11 31	11 34	11 37	11 40	11 46	11 50	11 53	
Rotherhithe	d	10 27	10 33	10 36		10 42	10 48	10 51	10 57	11 03	11 06	11 12	11 18	11 21		11 24	11 27	11 33	11 36	11 38	11 42	11 48	11 51	11 54	
Wapping	d	10 29	10 34	10 38		10 43	10 49	10 53	10 59	11 04	11 08	11 13	11 19	11 23		11 26	11 29	11 34	11 37	11 40	11 43	11 49	11 53	11 56	
Shadwell	d	10 31	10 36	10 40		10 45	10 51	10 55	11 01	11 06	11 10	11 15	11 21	11 25		11 28	11 31	11 36	11 39	11 42	11 45	11 51	11 55	11 58	
Whitechapel	d	10 33	10 39	10 42		10 48	10 54	10 57	11 03	11 09	11 12	11 18	11 24	11 27		11 30	11 33	11 39	11 42	11 44	11 48	11 54	11 57	12 00	
Shoreditch High Street	d	10 35	10 41	10 44		10 50	10 56	10 59	11 05	11 11	11 14	11 20	11 26	11 29		11 32	11 35	11 41	11 44	11 46	11 50	11 56	11 59	12 02	
Hoxton	d	10 37	10 43	10 46		10 52	10 58	11 01	11 07	11 13	11 16	11 22	11 28	11 31		11 34	11 37	11 43	11 46	11 48	11 52	11 58	12 01	12 04	
Haggerston	d	10 39	10 45	10 48		10 54	11 00	11 03	11 09	11 15	11 18	11 24	11 30	11 33		11 36	11 39	11 45	11 48	11 50	11 54	12 00	12 03	12 06	
Dalston Junction	a	10 41	10 47	10 50		10 56	11 02	11 05	11 11	11 17	11 20	11 26	11 32	11 35		11 41	11 41	11 47	11 50	11 52	11 57	12 02	12 05	12 11	
Canonbury	a	10 44		10 53		10 59		11 08	11 14		11 23	11 29		11 38			11 44		11 53	11 55			12 08		
Highbury & Islington	a	10 50		10 56		11 03		11 11	11 20		11 26	11 33		11 41			11 50		11 55	12 01			12 11		

		LO	LO	LO	LO	LO	LO	LO	LO	LO		LO	LO	LO	LO	LO	LO	LO	LO	LO		LO	LO	LO	LO
Clapham Junction	d			11 35				11 50					12 05			12 17				12 32					12 47
Wandsworth Road	d			11 41				11 56					12 11			12 23				12 38					12 53
Clapham High Street ⊖	d			11 43				11 58					12 13			12 25				12 40					12 55
Denmark Hill 4	d			11 48				12 03					12 18			12 30				12 45					13 00
Peckham Rye 4	d			11 50				12 05					12 20			12 32				12 47					13 02
Queens Rd Peckham	d			11 52				12 07					12 22			12 34				12 49					13 04
West Croydon 4 (tram)	d					11 42									12 12									12 42	
Norwood Junction 2	d					11 47									12 17									12 47	
Anerley	d					11 50									12 20									12 50	
Penge West	d					11 52									12 22									12 52	
Crystal Palace 4	d	11 37								12 07				12 16				12 31					12 46		
Sydenham	d	11 41				11 54				12 11				12 20	12 24			12 35					12 50	12 54	
Forest Hill 4	d	11 43				11 57				12 13				12 22	12 27			12 37					12 52	12 57	
Honor Oak Park	d	11 46				11 59				12 16				12 25	12 29			12 40					12 55	12 59	
Brockley	d	11 48				12 02				12 18				12 27	12 32			12 42					12 57	13 02	
New Cross Gate	d	11 50				12 04				12 20				12 29	12 34			12 44					12 59	13 04	
New Cross 4	d		11 55				12 10					12 25					12 40					12 55			
Surrey Quays	d	11 54	11 59	12 02	12 05	12 07	12 14	12 17	12 21	12 24		12 29	12 32	12 35	12 37	12 41	12 44	12 48	12 53	12 56		12 59	13 03	13 07	13 11
Canada Water	d	11 56	12 01	12 04	12 07	12 09	12 16	12 19	12 23	12 26		12 31	12 34	12 37	12 39	12 43	12 46	12 50	12 55	12 58		13 01	13 05	13 09	13 13
Rotherhithe	d	11 57	12 03	12 06	12 08	12 11	12 18	12 21	12 24	12 27		12 33	12 36	12 39	12 41	12 45	12 48	12 51	12 56	12 59		13 03	13 06	13 11	13 14
Wapping	d	11 59	12 04	12 07	12 10	12 12	12 19	12 22	12 26	12 29		12 34	12 37	12 40	12 42	12 46	12 49	12 53	12 58	13 01		13 04	13 08	13 12	13 16
Shadwell	d	12 01	12 06	12 09	12 12	12 14	12 21	12 24	12 28	12 31		12 36	12 39	12 42	12 44	12 48	12 51	12 55	13 00	13 03		13 06	13 10	13 14	13 18
Whitechapel	d	12 03	12 09	12 12	12 14	12 17	12 24	12 27	12 30	12 33		12 39	12 42	12 45	12 47	12 51	12 54	12 57	13 02	13 05		13 09	13 12	13 17	13 20
Shoreditch High Street	d	12 05	12 11	12 14	12 16	12 19	12 26	12 29	12 32	12 35		12 41	12 44	12 47	12 49	12 53	12 56	12 59	13 04	13 07		13 11	13 14	13 19	13 22
Hoxton	d	12 07	12 13	12 16	12 18	12 21	12 28	12 31	12 34	12 37		12 43	12 46	12 49	12 51	12 55	12 58	13 01	13 06	13 09		13 13	13 16	13 21	13 24
Haggerston	d	12 09	12 15	12 18	12 20	12 23	12 30	12 33	12 36	12 39		12 45	12 48	12 51	12 53	12 57	13 00	13 03	13 08	13 11		13 15	13 18	13 23	13 26
Dalston Junction	a	12 11	12 17	12 20	12 25	12 26	12 32	12 35	12 41	12 41		12 47	12 50	12 55	12 57	12 59	13 02	13 05	13 13	13 13		13 17	13 20	13 27	13 28
Canonbury	a	12 14		12 23		12 29		12 38		12 44			12 53			13 02		13 08		13 16			13 23		13 31
Highbury & Islington	a	12 20		12 25		12 33		12 40		12 50			12 55			13 06		13 16		13 22			13 29		13 37

		LO	LO	LO	LO	LO		LO	LO	LO	LO	LO	LO	LO	LO	LO		LO	LO	LO	LO	LO	LO	LO	LO
Clapham Junction	d				13 02					13 17				13 32					13 47				14 02		
Wandsworth Road	d				13 08					13 23				13 38					13 53				14 08		
Clapham High Street ⊖	d				13 10					13 25				13 40					13 55				14 10		
Denmark Hill 4	d				13 15					13 30				13 45					14 00				14 15		
Peckham Rye 4	d				13 17					13 32				13 47					14 02				14 17		
Queens Rd Peckham	d				13 19					13 34				13 49					14 04				14 19		
West Croydon 4 (tram)	d			12 57					13 12				13 27					13 42				13 57			
Norwood Junction 2	d			13 02					13 17				13 32					13 47				14 02			
Anerley	d			13 05					13 20				13 35					13 50				14 05			
Penge West	d			13 07					13 22				13 37					13 52				14 07			
Crystal Palace 4	d		13 01					13 16				13 31				13 46					14 01				14 16
Sydenham	d		13 05	13 09				13 20	13 24			13 35	13 39			13 50		13 54			14 05	14 09			14 20
Forest Hill 4	d		13 07	13 12				13 22	13 27			13 37	13 42			13 52		13 57			14 07	14 12			14 22
Honor Oak Park	d		13 10	13 14				13 25	13 29			13 40	13 44			13 55		13 59			14 10	14 14			14 25
Brockley	d		13 12	13 17				13 27	13 32			13 42	13 47			13 57		14 02			14 12	14 17			14 27
New Cross Gate	d		13 14	13 19				13 29	13 34			13 44	13 49			13 59		14 04			14 14	14 19			14 29
New Cross 4	d	13 10				13 25					13 40				13 55					14 10				14 25	
Surrey Quays	d	13 14	13 18	13 22	13 26	13 29		13 33	13 37	13 41	13 44	13 48	13 52	13 56	13 59	14 03		14 07	14 11	14 14	14 18	14 22	14 26	14 29	14 33
Canada Water	d	13 16	13 20	13 24	13 28	13 31		13 35	13 39	13 43	13 46	13 50	13 54	13 58	14 01	14 05		14 09	14 13	14 16	14 20	14 24	14 28	14 31	14 35
Rotherhithe	d	13 18	13 21	13 26	13 29	13 33		13 36	13 41	13 44	13 48	13 51	13 56	13 59	14 03	14 06		14 11	14 14	14 18	14 21	14 26	14 29	14 33	14 36
Wapping	d	13 19	13 23	13 27	13 31	13 34		13 38	13 42	13 46	13 49	13 53	13 57	14 01	14 04	14 08		14 12	14 16	14 19	14 23	14 27	14 31	14 34	14 38
Shadwell	d	13 21	13 25	13 29	13 33	13 36		13 40	13 44	13 48	13 51	13 55	13 59	14 03	14 06	14 10		14 14	14 18	14 21	14 25	14 29	14 33	14 36	14 40
Whitechapel	d	13 24	13 27	13 32	13 35	13 39		13 42	13 47	13 50	13 54	13 57	14 02	14 05	14 09	14 12		14 17	14 20	14 24	14 27	14 32	14 35	14 39	14 42
Shoreditch High Street	d	13 26	13 29	13 34	13 37	13 41		13 44	13 49	13 52	13 56	13 59	14 04	14 07	14 11	14 14		14 19	14 22	14 26	14 29	14 34	14 37	14 41	14 44
Hoxton	d	13 28	13 31	13 36	13 39	13 43		13 46	13 51	13 54	13 58	14 01	14 06	14 09	14 13	14 16		14 21	14 24	14 28	14 31	14 36	14 39	14 43	14 46
Haggerston	d	13 30	13 33	13 38	13 41	13 45		13 48	13 53	13 56	14 00	14 03	14 08	14 11	14 15	14 18		14 23	14 26	14 30	14 33	14 38	14 41	14 45	14 48
Dalston Junction	a	13 32	13 35	13 42	13 43	13 47		13 50	13 57	13 58	14 02	14 05	14 12	14 13	14 17	14 20		14 27	14 28	14 32	14 35	14 42	14 43	14 47	14 50
Canonbury	a		13 38		13 46			13 53		14 01		14 08		14 16		14 23			14 31		14 38		14 46		14 53
Highbury & Islington	a		13 44		13 52			13 59		14 07		14 14		14 22		14 29			14 37		14 44		14 52		14 59

Table T178-R

Sundays

15 December to 10 May

Clapham Junction and West Croydon, Crystal Palace, New Cross - Highbury & Islington

		LO		LO	LO	LO	LO	LO	LO	LO	LO	LO		LO	LO	LO	LO	LO	LO	LO	LO	LO		LO	LO
Clapham Junction	d			14 17				14 32				14 47					15 02				15 17				
Wandsworth Road	d			14 23				14 38				14 53					15 08				15 23				
Clapham High Street ⊖	d			14 25				14 40				14 55					15 10				15 25				
Denmark Hill 4	d			14 30				14 45				15 00					15 15				15 30				
Peckham Rye 4	d			14 32				14 47				15 02					15 17				15 32				
Queens Rd Peckham	d			14 34				14 49				15 04					15 19				15 34				
West Croydon 4 (tram)	d	14 12					14 27				14 42					14 57				15 12					15 27
Norwood Junction 2	d	14 17					14 32				14 47					15 02				15 17					15 32
Anerley	d	14 20					14 35				14 50					15 05				15 20					15 35
Penge West	d	14 22					14 37				14 52					15 07				15 22					15 37
Crystal Palace 4	d					14 31				14 46					15 01				15 16					15 31	
Sydenham	d	14 24				14 35	14 39			14 50	14 54				15 05	15 09			15 20	15 24				15 35	15 39
Forest Hill 4	d	14 27				14 37	14 42			14 52	14 57				15 07	15 12			15 22	15 27				15 37	15 42
Honor Oak Park	d	14 29				14 40	14 44			14 55	14 59				15 10	15 14			15 25	15 29				15 40	15 44
Brockley	d	14 32				14 42	14 47			14 57	15 02				15 12	15 17			15 27	15 32				15 42	15 47
New Cross Gate	d	14 34				14 44	14 49			14 59	15 04				15 14	15 19			15 29	15 34				15 44	15 49
New Cross 4	d				14 40				14 55					15 10				15 25				15 40			
Surrey Quays	d	14 37		14 41	14 44	14 48	14 52	14 56	14 59	15 03	15 07	15 11		15 14	15 18	15 22	15 26	15 29	15 33	15 37	15 41	15 44		15 48	15 52
Canada Water	d	14 39		14 43	14 46	14 50	14 54	14 58	15 01	15 05	15 09	15 13		15 16	15 20	15 24	15 28	15 31	15 35	15 39	15 43	15 46		15 50	15 54
Rotherhithe	d	14 41		14 44	14 48	14 51	14 56	14 59	15 03	15 06	15 11	15 14		15 18	15 21	15 26	15 29	15 33	15 36	15 41	15 44	15 48		15 51	15 56
Wapping	d	14 42		14 46	14 49	14 53	14 57	15 01	15 04	15 08	15 12	15 16		15 19	15 23	15 27	15 31	15 34	15 38	15 42	15 46	15 49		15 53	15 57
Shadwell	d	14 44		14 48	14 51	14 55	14 59	15 03	15 06	15 10	15 14	15 18		15 21	15 25	15 29	15 33	15 36	15 40	15 44	15 48	15 51		15 55	15 59
Whitechapel	d	14 47		14 50	14 54	14 57	15 02	15 05	15 09	15 12	15 17	15 20		15 24	15 27	15 32	15 35	15 39	15 42	15 47	15 50	15 54		15 57	16 02
Shoreditch High Street	d	14 49		14 52	14 56	14 59	15 04	15 07	15 11	15 14	15 19	15 22		15 26	15 29	15 34	15 37	15 41	15 44	15 49	15 52	15 56		15 59	16 04
Hoxton	d	14 51		14 54	14 58	15 01	15 06	15 09	15 13	15 16	15 21	15 24		15 28	15 31	15 36	15 39	15 43	15 46	15 51	15 54	15 58		16 01	16 06
Haggerston	d	14 53		14 56	15 00	15 03	15 08	15 11	15 15	15 18	15 23	15 26		15 30	15 33	15 38	15 41	15 45	15 48	15 53	15 56	16 00		16 03	16 08
Dalston Junction	a	14 57		14 58	15 02	15 05	15 12	15 13	15 17	15 20	15 27	15 28		15 32	15 35	15 42	15 43	15 47	15 50	15 57	15 58	16 02		16 05	16 12
Canonbury	a			15 01		15 08		15 16		15 23		15 31			15 38		15 46		15 53		16 01			16 08	
Highbury & Islington	a			15 07		15 14		15 22		15 29		15 37			15 44		15 52		15 59		16 07			16 14	

		LO	LO	LO	LO	LO	LO	LO		LO	LO	LO	LO	LO	LO	LO	LO	LO		LO	LO	LO	LO	LO	LO
Clapham Junction	d	15 32				15 47					16 02				16 17					16 32				16 47	
Wandsworth Road	d	15 38				15 53					16 08				16 23					16 38				16 53	
Clapham High Street ⊖	d	15 40				15 55					16 10				16 25					16 40				16 55	
Denmark Hill 4	d	15 45				16 00					16 15				16 30					16 45				17 00	
Peckham Rye 4	d	15 47				16 02					16 17				16 32					16 47				17 02	
Queens Rd Peckham	d	15 49				16 04					16 19				16 34					16 49				17 04	
West Croydon 4 (tram)	d				15 42					15 57				16 12				16 27					16 42		
Norwood Junction 2	d				15 47					16 02				16 17				16 32					16 47		
Anerley	d				15 50					16 05				16 20				16 35					16 50		
Penge West	d				15 52					16 07				16 22				16 37					16 52		
Crystal Palace 4	d			15 46				16 01					16 16				16 31					16 46			
Sydenham	d			15 50	15 54			16 05		16 09			16 20	16 24			16 35	16 39				16 50	16 54		
Forest Hill 4	d			15 52	15 57			16 07		16 12			16 22	16 27			16 37	16 42				16 52	16 57		
Honor Oak Park	d			15 55	15 59			16 10		16 14			16 25	16 29			16 40	16 44				16 55	16 59		
Brockley	d			15 57	16 02			16 12		16 17			16 27	16 32			16 42	16 47				16 57	17 02		
New Cross Gate	d			15 59	16 04			16 14		16 19			16 29	16 34			16 44	16 49				16 59	17 04		
New Cross 4	d		15 55				16 10					16 25				16 40					16 55				17 10
Surrey Quays	d	15 56	15 59	16 03	16 07	16 11	16 14	16 18		16 22	16 26	16 29	16 33	16 37	16 41	16 44	16 48	16 52		16 56	16 59	17 03	17 07	17 11	17 14
Canada Water	d	15 58	16 01	16 05	16 09	16 13	16 16	16 20		16 24	16 28	16 31	16 35	16 39	16 43	16 46	16 50	16 54		16 58	17 01	17 05	17 09	17 13	17 16
Rotherhithe	d	15 59	16 03	16 06	16 11	16 14	16 18	16 21		16 26	16 29	16 33	16 36	16 41	16 44	16 48	16 51	16 56		16 59	17 03	17 06	17 11	17 14	17 18
Wapping	d	16 01	16 04	16 08	16 12	16 16	16 19	16 23		16 27	16 31	16 34	16 38	16 42	16 46	16 49	16 53	16 57		17 01	17 04	17 08	17 12	17 16	17 19
Shadwell	d	16 03	16 06	16 10	16 14	16 18	16 21	16 25		16 29	16 33	16 36	16 40	16 44	16 48	16 51	16 55	16 59		17 03	17 06	17 10	17 14	17 18	17 21
Whitechapel	d	16 05	16 09	16 12	16 17	16 20	16 24	16 27		16 32	16 35	16 39	16 42	16 47	16 50	16 54	16 57	17 02		17 05	17 09	17 12	17 17	17 20	17 24
Shoreditch High Street	d	16 07	16 11	16 14	16 19	16 22	16 26	16 29		16 34	16 37	16 41	16 44	16 49	16 52	16 56	16 59	17 04		17 07	17 11	17 14	17 19	17 22	17 26
Hoxton	d	16 09	16 13	16 16	16 21	16 24	16 28	16 31		16 36	16 39	16 43	16 46	16 51	16 54	16 58	17 01	17 06		17 09	17 13	17 16	17 21	17 24	17 28
Haggerston	d	16 11	16 15	16 18	16 23	16 26	16 30	16 33		16 38	16 41	16 45	16 48	16 53	16 56	17 00	17 03	17 08		17 11	17 15	17 18	17 23	17 26	17 30
Dalston Junction	a	16 13	16 17	16 20	16 27	16 28	16 32	16 35		16 42	16 43	16 47	16 50	16 57	16 58	17 02	17 05	17 12		17 13	17 17	17 20	17 27	17 28	17 32
Canonbury	a	16 16		16 23		16 31		16 38			16 46		16 53		17 01		17 08			17 16		17 23		17 31	
Highbury & Islington	a	16 22		16 29		16 37		16 44			16 52		16 59		17 07		17 14			17 22		17 29		17 37	

		LO	LO	LO		LO	LO	LO	LO	LO	LO	LO	LO	LO		LO	LO	LO	LO	LO	LO	LO	LO	LO	
Clapham Junction	d			17 02					17 17				17 32					17 47				18 02			
Wandsworth Road	d			17 08					17 23				17 38					17 53				18 08			
Clapham High Street ⊖	d			17 10					17 25				17 40					17 55				18 10			
Denmark Hill 4	d			17 15					17 30				17 45					18 00				18 15			
Peckham Rye 4	d			17 17					17 32				17 47					18 02				18 17			
Queens Rd Peckham	d			17 19					17 34				17 49					18 04				18 19			
West Croydon 4 (tram)	d		16 57					17 12				17 27					17 42				17 57				
Norwood Junction 2	d		17 02					17 17				17 32					17 47				18 02				
Anerley	d		17 05					17 20				17 35					17 50				18 05				
Penge West	d		17 07					17 22				17 37					17 52				18 07				
Crystal Palace 4	d	17 01					17 16				17 31					17 46				18 01				18 16	
Sydenham	d	17 05	17 09				17 20	17 24			17 35	17 39				17 50	17 54			18 05	18 09			18 20	
Forest Hill 4	d	17 07	17 12				17 22	17 27			17 37	17 42				17 52	17 57			18 07	18 12			18 22	
Honor Oak Park	d	17 10	17 14				17 25	17 29			17 40	17 44				17 55	17 59			18 10	18 14			18 25	
Brockley	d	17 12	17 17				17 27	17 32			17 42	17 47				17 57	18 02			18 12	18 17			18 27	
New Cross Gate	d	17 14	17 19				17 29	17 34			17 44	17 49				17 59	18 04			18 14	18 19			18 29	
New Cross 4	d					17 25				17 40				17 55					18 10				18 25		
Surrey Quays	d	17 18	17 22	17 26		17 29	17 33	17 37	17 41	17 44	17 48	17 52	17 56	17 59		18 03	18 07	18 11	18 14	18 18	18 22	18 26	18 29	18 33	
Canada Water	d	17 20	17 24	17 28		17 31	17 35	17 39	17 43	17 46	17 50	17 54	17 58	18 01		18 05	18 09	18 13	18 16	18 20	18 24	18 28	18 31	18 35	
Rotherhithe	d	17 21	17 26	17 29		17 33	17 36	17 41	17 44	17 48	17 51	17 56	17 59	18 03		18 06	18 11	18 14	18 18	18 21	18 26	18 29	18 33	18 36	
Wapping	d	17 23	17 27	17 31		17 34	17 38	17 42	17 46	17 49	17 53	17 57	18 01	18 04		18 08	18 12	18 16	18 19	18 23	18 27	18 31	18 34	18 38	
Shadwell	d	17 25	17 29	17 33		17 36	17 40	17 44	17 48	17 51	17 55	17 59	18 03	18 06		18 10	18 14	18 18	18 21	18 25	18 29	18 33	18 36	18 40	
Whitechapel	d	17 27	17 32	17 35		17 39	17 42	17 47	17 50	17 54	17 57	18 02	18 05	18 09		18 12	18 17	18 20	18 24	18 27	18 32	18 35	18 39	18 42	
Shoreditch High Street	d	17 29	17 34	17 37		17 41	17 44	17 49	17 52	17 56	17 59	18 04	18 07	18 11		18 14	18 19	18 22	18 26	18 29	18 34	18 37	18 41	18 44	
Hoxton	d	17 31	17 36	17 39		17 43	17 46	17 51	17 54	17 58	18 01	18 06	18 09	18 13		18 16	18 21	18 24	18 28	18 31	18 36	18 39	18 43	18 46	
Haggerston	d	17 33	17 38	17 41		17 45	17 48	17 53	17 56	18 00	18 03	18 08	18 11	18 15		18 18	18 23	18 26	18 30	18 33	18 38	18 41	18 45	18 48	
Dalston Junction	a	17 35	17 42	17 43		17 47	17 50	17 57	17 58	18 02	18 05	18 12	18 13	18 17		18 20	18 27	18 28	18 32	18 35	18 42	18 43	18 48	18 50	
Canonbury	a	17 38		17 46			17 53		18 01		18 08		18 16			18 23		18 31		18 38		18 46		18 53	
Highbury & Islington	a	17 44		17 52			17 59		18 07		18 14		18 22			18 29		18 37		18 44		18 52		18 59	

Table T178-R

Sundays
15 December to 10 May

Clapham Junction and West Croydon, Crystal Palace, New Cross - Highbury & Islington

		LO	LO	LO	LO	LO	LO	LO	LO	LO		LO	LO	LO	LO	LO	LO	LO	LO	LO		LO	LO	LO	LO
Clapham Junction	d		18 17				18 32					18 47				19 02				19 17					19 32
Wandsworth Road	d		18 23				18 38					18 53				19 08				19 23					19 38
Clapham High Street ⊖	d		18 25				18 40					18 55				19 10				19 25					19 40
Denmark Hill 4	d		18 30				18 45					19 00				19 15				19 30					19 45
Peckham Rye 4	d		18 32				18 47					19 02				19 17				19 32					19 47
Queens Rd Peckham	d		18 34				18 49					19 04				19 19				19 34					19 49
West Croydon 4	d	18 12				18 27				18 42					18 57				19 12					19 27	
Norwood Junction 2	d	18 17				18 32				18 47					19 02				19 17					19 32	
Anerley	d	18 20				18 35				18 50					19 05				19 20					19 35	
Penge West	d	18 22				18 37				18 52					19 07				19 22					19 37	
Crystal Palace 4	d				18 31				18 46					19 01				19 16					19 31		
Sydenham	d	18 24			18 35	18 39			18 50	18 54				19 05	19 09			19 20	19 24				19 35	19 39	
Forest Hill 4	d	18 27			18 37	18 42			18 52	18 57				19 07	19 12			19 22	19 27				19 37	19 42	
Honor Oak Park	d	18 29			18 40	18 44			18 55	18 59				19 10	19 14			19 25	19 29				19 40	19 44	
Brockley	d	18 32			18 42	18 47			18 57	19 02				19 12	19 17			19 27	19 32				19 42	19 47	
New Cross Gate	d	18 34			18 44	18 49			18 59	19 04				19 14	19 19			19 29	19 34				19 44	19 49	
New Cross 4	d			18 40				18 55					19 10				19 25					19 40			
Surrey Quays	d	18 37	18 41	18 44	18 48	18 52	18 56	18 59	19 03	19 07		19 11	19 14	19 18	19 22	19 26	19 29	19 33	19 37	19 41		19 44	19 48	19 52	19 55
Canada Water	d	18 39	18 43	18 46	18 50	18 54	18 58	19 01	19 05	19 09		19 13	19 16	19 20	19 24	19 28	19 31	19 35	19 39	19 43		19 46	19 50	19 54	19 57
Rotherhithe	d	18 41	18 44	18 48	18 51	18 56	18 59	19 03	19 06	19 11		19 14	19 18	19 21	19 26	19 29	19 33	19 36	19 41	19 44		19 48	19 51	19 56	19 58
Wapping	d	18 42	18 46	18 49	18 53	18 57	19 01	19 04	19 08	19 12		19 16	19 19	19 23	19 27	19 31	19 34	19 38	19 42	19 46		19 49	19 53	19 57	20 00
Shadwell	d	18 44	18 48	18 51	18 55	18 59	19 03	19 06	19 10	19 14		19 18	19 21	19 25	19 29	19 33	19 36	19 40	19 44	19 48		19 51	19 55	19 59	20 02
Whitechapel	d	18 47	18 50	18 54	18 57	19 02	19 05	19 09	19 12	19 17		19 20	19 24	19 27	19 32	19 35	19 39	19 42	19 47	19 50		19 54	19 57	20 02	20 04
Shoreditch High Street	d	18 49	18 52	18 56	18 59	19 04	19 07	19 11	19 14	19 19		19 22	19 26	19 29	19 34	19 37	19 41	19 44	19 49	19 52		19 56	19 59	20 04	20 06
Hoxton	d	18 51	18 54	18 58	19 01	19 06	19 09	19 13	19 16	19 21		19 24	19 28	19 31	19 36	19 39	19 43	19 46	19 51	19 54		19 58	20 01	20 06	20 08
Haggerston	d	18 53	18 56	19 00	19 03	19 08	19 11	19 15	19 18	19 23		19 26	19 30	19 33	19 38	19 41	19 45	19 48	19 53	19 56		20 00	20 03	20 08	20 10
Dalston Junction	a	18 57	18 58	19 02	19 05	19 12	19 13	19 17	19 20	19 27		19 28	19 32	19 35	19 42	19 43	19 47	19 50	19 57	19 58		20 02	20 05	20 12	20 12
Canonbury	a		19 01		19 08		19 16		19 23			19 31		19 38		19 46		19 53		20 01			20 08		20 15
Highbury & Islington	a		19 07		19 14		19 22		19 29			19 37		19 44		19 52		19 59		20 07			20 14		20 22

		LO	LO	LO	LO	LO		LO	LO	LO	LO	LO	LO	LO	LO	LO		LO	LO	LO	LO	LO	LO	LO	LO
Clapham Junction	d				19 47					20 02				20 17					20 32				20 47		
Wandsworth Road	d				19 53					20 08				20 23					20 38				20 53		
Clapham High Street ⊖	d				19 55					20 10				20 25					20 40				20 55		
Denmark Hill 4	d				20 00					20 15				20 30					20 45				21 00		
Peckham Rye 4	d				20 02					20 17				20 32					20 47				21 02		
Queens Rd Peckham	d				20 04					20 19				20 34					20 49				21 04		
West Croydon 4	d			19 42					19 57				20 12					20 27				20 42			
Norwood Junction 2	d			19 47					20 02				20 17					20 32				20 47			
Anerley	d			19 50					20 05				20 20					20 35				20 50			
Penge West	d			19 52					20 07				20 22					20 37				20 52			
Crystal Palace 4	d		19 46					20 01				20 16				20 31					20 46				21 01
Sydenham	d		19 50	19 54				20 05	20 09			20 20	20 24			20 35		20 39			20 50	20 54			21 05
Forest Hill 4	d		19 52	19 57				20 07	20 12			20 22	20 27			20 37		20 42			20 52	20 57			21 07
Honor Oak Park	d		19 55	19 59				20 10	20 14			20 25	20 29			20 40		20 44			20 55	20 59			21 10
Brockley	d		19 57	20 02				20 12	20 17			20 27	20 32			20 42		20 47			20 57	21 02			21 12
New Cross Gate	d		19 59	20 04				20 14	20 19			20 29	20 34			20 44		20 49			20 59	21 04			21 14
New Cross 4	d	19 55				20 10					20 25				20 40					20 55				21 10	
Surrey Quays	d	19 59	20 03	20 07	20 11	20 14		20 18	20 22	20 26	20 29	20 33	20 37	20 41	20 44	20 48		20 52	20 56	20 59	21 03	21 07	21 11	21 14	21 18
Canada Water	d	20 01	20 05	20 09	20 13	20 16		20 20	20 24	20 28	20 31	20 35	20 39	20 43	20 46	20 50		20 54	20 58	21 01	21 05	21 09	21 13	21 16	21 20
Rotherhithe	d	20 03	20 06	20 11	20 14	20 18		20 21	20 26	20 29	20 33	20 36	20 41	20 44	20 48	20 51		20 56	20 59	21 03	21 06	21 11	21 14	21 18	21 21
Wapping	d	20 04	20 08	20 12	20 16	20 19		20 23	20 27	20 31	20 34	20 38	20 42	20 46	20 49	20 53		20 57	21 01	21 04	21 08	21 12	21 16	21 19	21 23
Shadwell	d	20 06	20 10	20 14	20 18	20 21		20 25	20 29	20 33	20 36	20 40	20 44	20 48	20 51	20 55		20 59	21 03	21 06	21 10	21 14	21 18	21 21	21 25
Whitechapel	d	20 09	20 12	20 17	20 20	20 24		20 27	20 32	20 35	20 39	20 42	20 47	20 50	20 54	20 57		21 02	21 05	21 09	21 12	21 17	21 20	21 24	21 27
Shoreditch High Street	d	20 11	20 14	20 19	20 22	20 26		20 29	20 34	20 37	20 41	20 44	20 49	20 52	20 56	20 59		21 04	21 07	21 11	21 14	21 19	21 22	21 26	21 29
Hoxton	d	20 13	20 16	20 21	20 24	20 28		20 31	20 36	20 39	20 43	20 46	20 51	20 54	20 58	21 01		21 06	21 09	21 13	21 16	21 21	21 24	21 28	21 31
Haggerston	d	20 15	20 18	20 23	20 26	20 30		20 33	20 38	20 41	20 45	20 48	20 53	20 56	21 00	21 03		21 08	21 11	21 15	21 18	21 23	21 26	21 30	21 33
Dalston Junction	a	20 17	20 20	20 27	20 28	20 32		20 35	20 42	20 43	20 47	20 50	20 57	20 58	21 02	21 05		21 12	21 13	21 17	21 20	21 27	21 28	21 32	21 35
Canonbury	a		20 23		20 31			20 38		20 46		20 53		21 01		21 08			21 16		21 23		21 31		21 38
Highbury & Islington	a		20 29		20 37			20 44		20 52		20 59		21 07		21 14			21 22		21 29		21 37		21 44

		LO		LO	LO	LO	LO	LO	LO	LO	LO	LO		LO	LO	LO	LO	LO	LO	LO	LO	LO		LO	LO
Clapham Junction	d			21 02				21 17				21 32					21 47				22 02				
Wandsworth Road	d			21 08				21 23				21 38					21 53				22 08				
Clapham High Street ⊖	d			21 10				21 25				21 40					21 55				22 10				
Denmark Hill 4	d			21 15				21 30				21 45					22 00				22 15				
Peckham Rye 4	d			21 17				21 32				21 47					22 02				22 17				
Queens Rd Peckham	d			21 19				21 34				21 49					22 04				22 19				
West Croydon 4	d	20 57					21 12				21 27					21 42				21 57					22 12
Norwood Junction 2	d	21 02					21 17				21 32					21 47				22 02					22 17
Anerley	d	21 05					21 20				21 35					21 50				22 05					22 20
Penge West	d	21 07					21 22				21 37					21 52				22 07					22 22
Crystal Palace 4	d					21 16				21 31					21 46				22 01					22 16	
Sydenham	d	21 09				21 20	21 24			21 35	21 39				21 50	21 54			22 05	22 09				22 20	22 24
Forest Hill 4	d	21 12				21 22	21 27			21 37	21 42				21 52	21 57			22 07	22 12				22 22	22 27
Honor Oak Park	d	21 14				21 25	21 29			21 40	21 44				21 55	21 59			22 10	22 14				22 25	22 29
Brockley	d	21 17				21 27	21 32			21 42	21 47				21 57	22 02			22 12	22 17				22 27	22 32
New Cross Gate	d	21 19				21 29	21 34			21 44	21 49				21 59	22 04			22 14	22 19				22 29	22 34
New Cross 4	d				21 25				21 40					21 55				22 10				22 25			
Surrey Quays	d	21 22		21 26	21 29	21 33	21 37	21 41	21 44	21 48	21 52	21 56		21 59	22 03	22 07	22 11	22 14	22 18	22 22	22 26	22 29		22 33	22 37
Canada Water	d	21 24		21 28	21 31	21 35	21 39	21 43	21 46	21 50	21 54	21 58		22 01	22 05	22 09	22 13	22 16	22 20	22 24	22 28	22 31		22 35	22 39
Rotherhithe	d	21 26		21 29	21 33	21 36	21 41	21 44	21 48	21 51	21 56	21 59		22 03	22 06	22 11	22 14	22 18	22 21	22 26	22 29	22 33		22 36	22 41
Wapping	d	21 27		21 31	21 34	21 38	21 42	21 46	21 49	21 53	21 57	22 01		22 04	22 08	22 12	22 16	22 19	22 23	22 27	22 31	22 34		22 38	22 42
Shadwell	d	21 29		21 33	21 36	21 40	21 44	21 48	21 51	21 55	21 59	22 03		22 06	22 10	22 14	22 18	22 21	22 25	22 29	22 33	22 36		22 40	22 44
Whitechapel	d	21 32		21 35	21 39	21 42	21 47	21 50	21 54	21 57	22 02	22 05		22 09	22 12	22 17	22 20	22 24	22 27	22 32	22 35	22 39		22 42	22 47
Shoreditch High Street	d	21 34		21 37	21 41	21 44	21 49	21 52	21 56	21 59	22 04	22 07		22 11	22 14	22 19	22 22	22 26	22 29	22 34	22 37	22 41		22 44	22 49
Hoxton	d	21 36		21 39	21 43	21 46	21 51	21 54	21 58	22 01	22 06	22 09		22 13	22 16	22 21	22 24	22 28	22 31	22 36	22 39	22 43		22 46	22 51
Haggerston	d	21 38		21 41	21 45	21 48	21 53	21 56	22 00	22 03	22 08	22 11		22 15	22 18	22 23	22 26	22 30	22 33	22 38	22 41	22 45		22 48	22 53
Dalston Junction	a	21 42		21 43	21 47	21 50	21 57	21 58	22 02	22 05	22 12	22 13		22 17	22 20	22 27	22 28	22 32	22 35	22 42	22 43	22 47		22 50	22 57
Canonbury	a			21 46		21 53		22 01		22 08		22 16			22 23		22 31		22 38		22 46			22 53	
Highbury & Islington	a			21 52		21 59		22 07		22 14		22 22			22 29		22 37		22 44		22 52			22 59	

Table T178-R

Sundays
15 December to 10 May

Clapham Junction and West Croydon, Crystal Palace, New Cross - Highbury & Islington

		LO	LO	LO	LO	LO	LO	LO		LO	LO	LO	LO	LO	LO
Clapham Junction	d	22 17			22 32					22 47			23 02		23 17
Wandsworth Road	d	22 23			22 38					22 53			23 08		23 23
Clapham High Street ⊖	d	22 25			22 40					22 55			23 10		23 25
Denmark Hill 4	d	22 30			22 45					23 00			23 15		23 30
Peckham Rye 4	d	22 32			22 47					23 02			23 17		23 32
Queens Rd Peckham	d	22 34			22 49					23 04			23 19		23 34
West Croydon 4	d			22 27				22 42				22 57			
Norwood Junction 2	d			22 32				22 47				23 02			
Anerley	d			22 35				22 50				23 05			
Penge West	d			22 37				22 52				23 07			
Crystal Palace 4	d						22 46							23 16	
Sydenham	d			22 39			22 50	22 54				23 09		23 20	
Forest Hill 4	d			22 42			22 52	22 57				23 12		23 22	
Honor Oak Park	d			22 44			22 55	22 59				23 14		23 25	
Brockley	d			22 47			22 57	23 02				23 17		23 27	
New Cross Gate	d			22 49			22 59	23 04				23 19		23 29	
New Cross 4	d		22 40			22 55					23 10				
Surrey Quays	d	22 41	22 44	22 52	22 56	22 59	23 03	23 07		23 11	23 14	23 22	23 26	23 33	23 41
Canada Water	d	22 43	22 46	22 54	22 58	23 01	23 05	23 09		23 13	23 16	23 24	23 28	23 35	23 43
Rotherhithe	d	22 44	22 48	22 56	22 59	23 03	23 06	23 11		23 14	23 18	23 26	23 29	23 36	23 44
Wapping	d	22 46	22 49	22 57	23 01	23 04	23 08	23 12		23 16	23 19	23 27	23 31	23 38	23 46
Shadwell	d	22 48	22 51	22 59	23 03	23 06	23 10	23 14		23 18	23 21	23 29	23 33	23 40	23 48
Whitechapel	d	22 50	22 54	23 02	23 05	23 09	23 12	23 17		23 20	23 24	23 32	23 35	23 42	23 50
Shoreditch High Street	d	22 52	22 56	23 04	23 07	23 11	23 14	23 19		23 22	23 26	23 34	23 37	23 44	23 52
Hoxton	d	22 54	22 58	23 06	23 09	23 13	23 16	23 21		23 24	23 28	23 36	23 39	23 46	23 54
Haggerston	d	22 56	23 00	23 08	23 11	23 15	23 18	23 23		23 26	23 30	23 38	23 41	23 48	23 56
Dalston Junction	a	22 58	23 02	23 12	23 13	23 17	23 20	23 27		23 28	23 34	23 42	23 43	23 50	23 58
Canonbury	a	23 06			23 16		23 23			23 31			23 46	23 53	00 01
Highbury & Islington	a	23 12			23 22		23 29			23 37			23 52	23 59	00 07

Table T179-F

Mondays to Fridays

16 December to 15 May

Thameslink - Wimbledon and Sutton

Miles	Miles	Station		TL MX A	TL MX B	TL B	TL	SN	TL B	TL C	SN	TL B	TL B	SN	TL	TL	SN	TL	TL	SN	TL	TL	TL
0	0	St Albans City	d			04 35			05 05			05 35	05 51		06 07	06 22		06 34	06 52		07 07	07 22	07 36
16	16	West Hampstead Thameslink	d			04 59	05 16		05 31			05 59	06 17		06 32	06 47		07 02	07 17		07 32	07 47	08 02
20	20	St Pancras International 15	d			05 12	05 27		05 42	05 57		06 12	06 27		06 42	06 57		07 12	07 27		07 42	07 57	08 12
21¼	21¼	Farringdon 3	d			05 17	05 32		05 47	06 02		06 17	06 32		06 47	07 02		07 17	07 32		07 47	08 02	08 17
21½	21½	City Thameslink 3	d			05 19	05 34		05 49	06 04		06 19	06 34		06 49	07 04		07 19	07 34		07 49	08 04	08 19
22	22	London Blackfriars 3	d			05 21	05 36		05 51	06 06		06 21	06 36		06 51	07 06		07 21	07 36		07 51	08 06	08 21
23¾	23¾	Elephant & Castle	d			05 25	05 40		05 55	06 10		06 25	06 40		06 55	07 10		07 25	07 40		07 55	08 10	08 25
25	25	Loughborough Jn	d		00 02	05 30	05 45		06 00	06 15		06 30	06 45		07 00	07 15		07 30	07 45		08 00	08 15	08 30
26	26	Herne Hill 4	d		00 06	05 35	05 50		06 05	06 20		06 35	06 50		07 05	07 20		07 35	07 50		08 05	08 20	08 35
—	—	London Bridge 4	d					05 39			06 08			06 38			07 07			07 37			
27	27	Tulse Hill 3	a		00 10	05 39	05 54	05 59	06 09	06 24	06 29	06 39	06 54	06 59	07 09	07 24	07 29	07 39	07 54	07 59	08 09	08 24	08 39
—	—		d		00 11	05 40	05 56	05 59	06 10	06 26	06 29	06 40	06 56	06 59	07 10	07 26	07 29	07 40	07 56	07 59	08 10	08 27	08 40
28¾	28¾	Streatham 4	d		00 14	05 44	06 00	06 04	06 14	06 30	06 34	06 44	07 00	07 04	07 14	07 30	07 34	07 44	08 00	08 04	08 14	08 30	08 44
30¼	—	**Tooting**	d		00 19	05 49		06 09	06 19		06 39	06 49		07 09	07 19		07 39	07 49		08 09	08 19		08 49
31½	—	**Haydons Road**	d		00 22	05 52		06 12	06 22		06 42	06 52		07 12	07 22		07 42	07 52		08 12	08 22		08 52
32¼	—	Wimbledon 6	a		00 24	05 54		06 14	06 24		06 44	06 54		07 14	07 24		07 44	07 54		08 14	08 24		08 54
—	—		d		00 25	05 55		06 15	06 25		06 45	06 55		07 15	07 25		07 45	07 55		08 15	08 25		08 55
33¼	—	**Wimbledon Chase**	d		00 28	05 58		06 18	06 28		06 48	06 58		07 18	07 28		07 48	07 58		08 18	08 28		08 58
34	—	**South Merton**	d	00 01	00 30	06 00		06 20	06 30		06 50	07 00		07 20	07 30		07 50	08 00		08 20	08 30		09 00
34½	—	**Morden South**	d	00 04	00 33	06 03		06 23	06 33		06 53	07 03		07 23	07 33		07 53	08 03		08 23	08 33		09 03
35	—	**St Helier**	d	00 06	00 35	06 05		06 25	06 35		06 55	07 05		07 25	07 35		07 55	08 05		08 25	08 35		09 05
36	—	**Sutton Common**	d	00 08	00 37	06 07		06 27	06 37		06 57	07 07		07 27	07 37		07 57	08 07		08 27	08 37		09 07
36½	—	**West Sutton**	d	00 11	00 40	06 10		06 30	06 40		07 00	07 10		07 30	07 40		08 00	08 10		08 30	08 40		09 10
—	30¼	Mitcham Eastfields	d				06 04			06 34			07 04			07 34			08 04			08 34	
—	31½	Mitcham Junction	d				06 07			06 37			07 07			07 37			08 07			08 37	
—	32½	Hackbridge	d				06 10			06 40			07 10			07 40			08 10			08 40	
—	33½	Carshalton	d				06 13			06 43			07 13			07 43			08 13			08 43	
37¾	34¾	Sutton 4	a	00 14	00 44	06 14	06 17	06 34	06 44	06 47	07 04	07 14	07 17	07 34	07 44	07 47	08 04	08 14	08 17	08 34	08 44	08 47	09 14

Station		TL	TL	TL	TL	TL	TL	TL	TL	TL	TL	TL	TL	TL	TL	TL	TL	TL	TL	TL	TL	TL	TL
St Albans City	d	07 52	08 07	08 22	08 37	08 52	09 07	09 22	09 37	09 51	10 07	10 22	10 38	10 52	11 07	11 22	11 37	11 53	12 07	12 22	12 37	12 52	13 07
West Hampstead Thameslink	d	08 17	08 32	08 47	09 02	09 17	09 32	09 47	10 01	10 16	10 31	10 46	11 01	11 16	11 32	11 46	12 01	12 16	12 31	12 46	13 01	13 16	13 31
St Pancras International 15	d	08 27	08 42	08 57	09 12	09 27	09 42	09 57	10 12	10 27	10 42	10 57	11 12	11 27	11 42	11 57	12 12	12 27	12 42	12 57	13 12	13 27	13 42
Farringdon 3	d	08 32	08 47	09 02	09 17	09 32	09 47	10 02	10 17	10 32	10 47	11 02	11 17	11 32	11 47	12 02	12 17	12 32	12 47	13 02	13 17	13 32	13 47
City Thameslink 3	d	08 34	08 49	09 04	09 19	09 34	09 49	10 04	10 19	10 34	10 49	11 04	11 19	11 34	11 49	12 04	12 19	12 34	12 49	13 04	13 19	13 34	13 49
London Blackfriars 3	d	08 36	08 51	09 06	09 21	09 36	09 51	10 06	10 21	10 36	10 51	11 06	11 21	11 36	11 51	12 06	12 21	12 36	12 51	13 06	13 21	13 36	13 51
Elephant & Castle	d	08 40	08 55	09 10	09 25	09 40	09 55	10 10	10 25	10 40	10 55	11 10	11 25	11 40	11 55	12 10	12 25	12 40	12 55	13 10	13 25	13 40	13 55
Loughborough Jn	d	08 45	09 00	09 15	09 30	09 45	10 00	10 15	10 30	10 45	11 00	11 15	11 30	11 45	12 00	12 15	12 30	12 45	13 00	13 15	13 30	13 45	14 00
Herne Hill 4	d	08 50	09 05	09 20	09 35	09 50	10 05	10 20	10 35	10 50	11 05	11 20	11 35	11 50	12 05	12 20	12 35	12 50	13 05	13 20	13 35	13 50	14 05
London Bridge 4	d																						
Tulse Hill 3	a	08 54	09 09	09 24	09 39	09 54	10 09	10 24	10 39	10 54	11 09	11 24	11 39	11 54	12 09	12 24	12 39	12 54	13 09	13 24	13 39	13 54	14 09
	d	08 57	09 10	09 27	09 40	09 56	10 10	10 26	10 40	10 56	11 10	11 26	11 40	11 56	12 10	12 26	12 40	12 56	13 10	13 26	13 40	13 56	14 10
Streatham 4	d	09 00	09 14	09 30	09 44	10 00	10 14	10 30	10 44	11 00	11 14	11 30	11 44	12 00	12 14	12 30	12 44	13 00	13 14	13 30	13 44	14 00	14 14
Tooting	d		09 19		09 49		10 19		10 49		11 19		11 49		12 19		12 49		13 19		13 49		14 19
Haydons Road	d		09 22		09 52		10 22		10 52		11 22		11 52		12 22		12 52		13 22		13 52		14 22
Wimbledon 6	a		09 24		09 54		10 24		10 54		11 24		11 54		12 24		12 54		13 24		13 54		14 24
	d		09 25		09 55		10 25		10 55		11 25		11 55		12 25		12 55		13 25		13 55		14 25
Wimbledon Chase	d		09 28		09 58		10 28		10 58		11 28		11 58		12 28		12 58		13 28		13 58		14 28
South Merton	d		09 30		10 00		10 30		11 00		11 30		12 00		12 30		13 00		13 30		14 00		14 30
Morden South	d		09 33		10 03		10 33		11 03		11 33		12 03		12 33		13 03		13 33		14 03		14 33
St Helier	d		09 35		10 05		10 35		11 05		11 35		12 05		12 35		13 05		13 35		14 05		14 35
Sutton Common	d		09 37		10 07		10 37		11 07		11 37		12 07		12 37		13 07		13 37		14 07		14 37
West Sutton	d		09 40		10 10		10 40		11 10		11 40		12 10		12 40		13 10		13 40		14 10		14 40
Mitcham Eastfields	d	09 04		09 34		10 04		10 34		11 04		11 34		12 04		12 34		13 04		13 34		14 04	
Mitcham Junction	d	09 07		09 37		10 07		10 37		11 07		11 37		12 07		12 37		13 07		13 37		14 07	
Hackbridge	d	09 10		09 40		10 10		10 40		11 10		11 40		12 10		12 40		13 10		13 40		14 10	
Carshalton	d	09 13		09 43		10 13		10 43		11 13		11 43		12 13		12 43		13 13		13 43		14 13	
Sutton 4	a	09 17	09 44	09 47	10 14	10 17	10 44	10 47	11 14	11 17	11 44	11 47	12 14	12 17	12 44	12 47	13 14	13 17	13 44	13 47	14 14	14 17	14 44

Station		TL	TL	TL	TL	TL	TL	TL	TL	TL	TL	TL	TL	SN	TL	TL	SN	TL	TL	SN	TL	TL
St Albans City	d	13 22	13 37	13 52	14 07	14 22	14 37	14 52	15 07	15 22	15 37	15 52	16 07		16 22	16 38		16 52	17 07		17 22	17 37
West Hampstead Thameslink	d	13 46	14 01	14 16	14 31	14 46	15 01	15 16	15 31	15 46	16 01	16 17	16 32		16 47	17 02		17 17	17 32		17 47	18 01
St Pancras International 15	d	13 57	14 12	14 27	14 42	14 57	15 12	15 27	15 42	15 57	16 12	16 27	16 42		16 57	17 12		17 27	17 42		17 57	18 12
Farringdon 3	d	14 02	14 17	14 32	14 47	15 02	15 17	15 32	15 47	16 02	16 17	16 32	16 47		17 02	17 17		17 32	17 47		18 02	18 17
City Thameslink 3	d	14 04	14 19	14 34	14 49	15 04	15 19	15 34	15 49	16 04	16 19	16 34	16 49		17 04	17 19		17 34	17 49		18 04	18 19
London Blackfriars 3	d	14 06	14 21	14 36	14 51	15 06	15 21	15 36	15 51	16 06	16 21	16 36	16 51		17 06	17 21		17 36	17 51		18 06	18 21
Elephant & Castle	d	14 10	14 25	14 40	14 55	15 10	15 25	15 40	15 55	16 10	16 25	16 40	16 55		17 10	17 25		17 40	17 55		18 10	18 25
Loughborough Jn	d	14 15	14 30	14 45	15 00	15 15	15 30	15 45	16 00	16 15	16 30	16 45	17 00		17 15	17 30		17 45	18 00		18 15	18 30
Herne Hill 4	d	14 20	14 35	14 50	15 05	15 20	15 35	15 50	16 05	16 20	16 35	16 50	17 05		17 20	17 35		17 50	18 05		18 20	18 35
London Bridge 4	d													16 52			17 22			17 52		
Tulse Hill 3	a	14 24	14 39	14 54	15 09	15 24	15 39	15 54	16 09	16 24	16 39	16 54	17 09	17 14	17 24	17 39	17 44	17 54	18 09	18 14	18 24	18 39
	d	14 26	14 39	14 56	15 10	15 26	15 40	15 56	16 10	16 26	16 40	16 56	17 10	17 16	17 26	17 40	17 46	17 56	18 10	18 16	18 26	18 40
Streatham 4	d	14 30	14 42	15 00	15 14	15 30	15 44	16 00	16 14	16 30	16 44	17 00	17 14	17 20	17 30	17 44	17 50	18 00	18 14	18 20	18 30	18 44
Tooting	d		14 47		15 19		15 49		16 19		16 49		17 19			17 49			18 19			18 49
Haydons Road	d		14 50		15 22		15 52		16 22		16 52		17 22			17 52			18 22			18 52
Wimbledon 6	a		14 52		15 24		15 54		16 24		16 54		17 24			17 54			18 24			18 54
	d		14 55		15 25		15 55		16 25		16 55		17 25			17 55			18 25			18 55
Wimbledon Chase	d		14 58		15 28		15 58		16 28		16 58		17 28			17 58			18 28			18 58
South Merton	d		15 00		15 30		16 00		16 30		17 00		17 30			18 00			18 30			19 00
Morden South	d		15 03		15 33		16 03		16 33		17 03		17 33			18 03			18 33			19 03
St Helier	d		15 05		15 35		16 05		16 35		17 05		17 35			18 05			18 35			19 05
Sutton Common	d		15 07		15 37		16 07		16 37		17 07		17 37			18 07			18 37			19 07
West Sutton	d		15 10		15 40		16 10		16 40		17 10		17 40			18 10			18 40			19 10
Mitcham Eastfields	d	14 34		15 04		15 34		16 04		16 34		17 04		17 24	17 34		17 54	18 04		18 24	18 34	
Mitcham Junction	d	14 37		15 07		15 37		16 07		16 37		17 07		17 27	17 37		17 57	18 07		18 27	18 37	
Hackbridge	d	14 40		15 10		15 40		16 10		16 40		17 10		17 30	17 40		18 00	18 10		18 30	18 40	
Carshalton	d	14 43		15 13		15 43		16 13		16 43		17 13		17 33	17 43		18 03	18 13		18 33	18 43	
Sutton 4	a	14 47	15 14	15 17	15 44	15 47	16 14	16 17	16 44	16 47	17 14	17 17	17 44	17 37	17 47	18 14	18 07	18 17	18 44	18 37	18 47	19 14

A From St Albans City B From Luton C From Kentish Town

For more London Bridge connections, refer to Table T173

Most Thameslink services from Blackfriars via Wimbledon and Hackbridge continue back towards Blackfriars.

Table T179-F

Mondays to Fridays

16 December to 15 May

Thameslink - Wimbledon and Sutton

Station		SN	TL	TL	TL	TL	TL	TL	TL	TL	TL	TL	TL	TL	TL	TL	TL	TL	TL	TL	TL	TL	TL A
St Albans City	d		17 52	18 07	18 22	18 37	18 52	19 07	19 22	19 37	19 52	20 08	20 22	20 37	20 52	21 07	21 22	21 37	21 52	22 08	22 22	22 37	23 09
West Hampstead Thameslink	d		18 17	18 31	18 47	19 00	19 16	19 31	19 46	20 01	20 16	20 31	20 46	21 01	21 16	21 31	21 46	22 01	22 16	22 31	22 46	23 01	23 33
St Pancras International 15	d		18 27	18 42	18 57	19 12	19 27	19 42	19 57	20 12	20 27	20 42	20 57	21 12	21 27	21 42	21 57	22 12	22 27	22 42	22 57	23 12	23 44
Farringdon 3	d		18 32	18 47	19 02	19 17	19 32	19 47	20 02	20 17	20 32	20 47	21 02	21 17	21 32	21 47	22 02	22 17	22 32	22 47	23 02	23 17	23 49
City Thameslink 3	d		18 34	18 49	19 04	19 19	19 34	19 49	20 04	20 19	20 34	20 49	21 04	21 19	21 34	21 49	22 04	22 19	22 34	22 49			
London Blackfriars 3	d		18 36	18 51	19 06	19 21	19 36	19 51	20 06	20 21	20 36	20 51	21 06	21 21	21 36	21 51	22 06	22 21	22 36	22 51	23 06	23 21	23 53
Elephant & Castle	d		18 40	18 55	19 10	19 25	19 40	19 55	20 10	20 25	20 40	20 55	21 10	21 25	21 40	21 55	22 10	22 25	22 40	22 55	23 10	23 25	23 57
Loughborough Jn	d		18 45	19 00	19 15	19 30	19 45	20 00	20 15	20 30	20 45	21 00	21 15	21 30	21 45	22 00	22 15	22 30	22 45	23 00	23 15	23 30	00 02
Herne Hill 4	d		18 50	19 05	19 20	19 35	19 50	20 05	20 20	20 35	20 50	21 05	21 20	21 35	21 50	22 05	22 20	22 35	22 50	23 05	23 20	23 35	00 06
London Bridge 4	d	18 22																					
Tulse Hill 3	a	18 44	18 54	19 09	19 24	19 39	19 54	20 09	20 24	20 39	20 54	21 09	21 24	21 41	21 54	22 09	22 24	22 39	22 54	23 09	23 24	23 39	00 10
	d	18 46	18 56	19 10	19 26	19 40	19 56	20 10	20 26	20 40	20 56	21 10	21 26	21 41	21 56	22 10	22 26	22 40	22 56	23 10	23 26	23 40	00 11
Streatham 4	d	18 50	19 00	19 14	19 30	19 44	20 00	20 14	20 30	20 44	21 00	21 14	21 30	21 44	22 00	22 14	22 30	22 44	23 00	23 14	23 30	23 44	00 14
Tooting	d			19 19		19 49		20 19		20 49		21 19		21 49		22 19		22 49		23 19		23 49	00 19
Haydons Road	d			19 22		19 52		20 22		20 52		21 22		21 52		22 22		22 52		23 22		23 52	00 22
Wimbledon 6	a			19 24		19 54		20 24		20 54		21 24		21 54		22 24		22 54		23 24		23 54	00 24
	d			19 25		19 55		20 25		20 55		21 25		21 55		22 25		22 55		23 25		23 55	00 25
Wimbledon Chase	d			19 28		19 58		20 28		20 58		21 28		21 58		22 28		22 58		23 28		23 58	00 28
South Merton	d			19 30		20 00		20 30		21 00		21 30		22 00		22 30		23 00		23 30		00 01	00 30
Morden South	d			19 33		20 03		20 33		21 03		21 33		22 03		22 33		23 03		23 33		00 04	00 33
St Helier	d			19 35		20 05		20 35		21 05		21 35		22 05		22 35		23 05		23 35		00 06	00 35
Sutton Common	d			19 37		20 07		20 37		21 07		21 37		22 07		22 37		23 07		23 37		00 08	00 37
West Sutton	d			19 40		20 10		20 40		21 10		21 40		22 10		22 40		23 10		23 40		00 11	00 40
Mitcham Eastfields	d	18 54	19 04		19 34		20 04		20 34		21 04		21 34		22 04		22 34		23 04		23 34		
Mitcham Junction	d	18 57	19 07		19 37		20 07		20 37		21 07		21 37		22 07		22 37		23 07		23 37		
Hackbridge	d	19 00	19 10		19 40		20 10		20 40		21 10		21 40		22 10		22 40		23 10		23 40		
Carshalton	d	19 03	19 13		19 43		20 13		20 43		21 13		21 43		22 13		22 43		23 13		23 43		
Sutton 4	a	19 07	19 17	19 44	19 47	20 14	20 17	20 44	20 47	21 14	21 17	21 44	21 47	22 14	22 17	22 44	22 47	23 14	23 17	23 44	23 47	00 14	00 44

Saturdays

21 December to 16 May

Station		TL B	TL A	TL A	TL	TL A	TL	TL A	TL A	TL	TL	TL C	ZZ	TL	TL	TL	TL	TL	TL	TL	TL	TL
St Albans City	d			04 35		05 05		05 35	05 51	06 07	06 23	06 37	06 37	06 52	07 07	07 22	07 37	07 52	08 07	08 22	08 37	08 52
West Hampstead Thameslink	d			04 59	05 16	05 29	05 46	05 59	06 17	06 31	06 46	07 01	07 01	07 16	07 31	07 46	08 01	08 16	08 31	08 46	09 01	09 16
St Pancras International 15	d			05 12	05 27	05 42	05 57	06 12	06 27	06 42	06 57	07 12	07 12	07 27	07 42	07 57	08 12	08 27	08 42	08 57	09 12	09 27
Farringdon 3	d			05 17	05 32	05 47	06 02	06 17	06 32	06 47	07 02	07 17	07 17	07 32	07 47	08 02	08 17	08 32	08 47	09 02	09 17	09 32
City Thameslink 3	d																			09 04	09 19	09 34
London Blackfriars 3	d			05 21	05 36	05 51	06 06	06 21	06 36	06 51	07 06	07 21	07 21	07 36	07 51	08 06	08 21	08 36	08 51	09 06	09 21	09 36
Elephant & Castle	d			05 25	05 40	05 55	06 10	06 25	06 40	06 55	07 10	07 25	07 25	07 40	07 55	08 10	08 25	08 40	08 55	09 10	09 25	09 40
Loughborough Jn	d		00 02	05 30	05 45	06 00	06 15	06 30	06 45	07 00	07 15	07 30	07 30	07 45	08 00	08 15	08 30	08 45	09 00	09 15	09 30	09 45
Herne Hill 4	d		00 06	05 35	05 50	06 05	06 20	06 35	06 50	07 05	07 20	07 35	07 35	07 50	08 05	08 20	08 35	08 50	09 05	09 20	09 35	09 50
London Bridge 4	d																					
Tulse Hill 3	a		00 10	05 39	05 54	06 09	06 24	06 39	06 54	07 09	07 24	07 39	07 39	07 54	08 09	08 24	08 39	08 54	09 09	09 24	09 39	09 54
	d		00 11	05 40	05 56	06 10	06 26	06 40	06 56	07 10	07 26	07 40	07 40	07 56	08 10	08 26	08 40	08 56	09 10	09 26	09 40	09 56
Streatham 4	d		00 14	05 44	06 00	06 14	06 30	06 44	07 00	07 14	07 30	07 44	07 44	08 00	08 14	08 30	08 44	09 00	09 14	09 30	09 44	10 00
Tooting	d		00 19	05 49		06 19		06 49		07 19		07 49	07 49		08 19		08 49		09 19		09 49	
Haydons Road	d		00 22	05 52		06 22		06 52		07 22		07 52	07 52		08 22		08 52		09 22		09 52	
Wimbledon 6	a		00 24	05 54		06 24		06 54		07 24		07 54	07 54		08 24		08 54		09 24		09 54	
	d		00 25	05 55		06 25		06 55		07 25		07 55	07 55		08 25		08 55		09 25		09 55	
Wimbledon Chase	d		00 28	05 58		06 28		06 58		07 28		07 58	07 58		08 28		08 58		09 28		09 58	
South Merton	d	00 01	00 30	06 00		06 30		07 00		07 30		08 00	08 00		08 30		09 00		09 30		10 00	
Morden South	d	00 04	00 33	06 03		06 33		07 03		07 33		08 03	08 03		08 33		09 03		09 33		10 03	
St Helier	d	00 06	00 35	06 05		06 35		07 05		07 35		08 05	08 05		08 35		09 05		09 35		10 05	
Sutton Common	d	00 08	00 37	06 07		06 37		07 07		07 37		08 07	08 07		08 37		09 07		09 37		10 07	
West Sutton	d	00 11	00 40	06 10		06 40		07 10		07 40		08 10	08 10		08 40		09 10		09 40		10 10	
Mitcham Eastfields	d				06 04		06 34		07 04		07 34			08 04		08 34		09 04		09 34		10 04
Mitcham Junction	d				06 07		06 37		07 07		07 37			08 07		08 37		09 07		09 37		10 07
Hackbridge	d				06 10		06 40		07 10		07 40			08 10		08 40		09 10		09 40		10 10
Carshalton	d				06 13		06 43		07 13		07 43			08 13		08 43		09 13		09 43		10 13
Sutton 4	a	00 14	00 44	06 14	06 17	06 44	06 47	07 14	07 17	07 44	07 47	08 14	08 14	08 17	08 44	08 47	09 14	09 17	09 44	09 47	10 14	10 17

A From Luton B From St Albans City C From Bedford

For more London Bridge connections, refer to Table T173

Most Thameslink services from Blackfriars via Wimbledon and Hackbridge continue back towards Blackfriars.

Table T179-F

Saturdays
21 December to 16 May

Thameslink - Wimbledon and Sutton

		TL		TL	TL	TL	TL	TL	TL	TL	TL	TL	TL	TL	TL	TL	TL	TL A
St Albans City	d	09 07	and at the same minutes past each hour until	19 22	19 37	19 52	20 07	20 22	20 37	20 52	21 07	21 22	21 37	21 52	22 07	22 22	22 37	23 09
West Hampstead Thameslink	d	09 31		19 46	20 01	20 16	20 31	20 46	21 01	21 16	21 31	21 46	22 01	22 16	22 31	22 46	23 01	23 33
St Pancras International 15 ⊖	d	09 42		19 57	20 12	20 27	20 42	20 57	21 12	21 27	21 42	21 57	22 12	22 27	22 42	22 57	23 12	23 44
Farringdon 3 ⊖	d	09 47		20 02	20 17	20 32	20 47	21 02	21 17	21 32	21 47	22 02	22 17	22 32	22 47	23 02	23 17	23 49
City Thameslink 3	d	09 49		20 04	20 19	20 34	20 49											
London Blackfriars 3 ⊖	d	09 51		20 06	20 21	20 36	20 51	21 06	21 21	21 36	21 51	22 06	22 21	22 36	22 51	23 06	23 21	23 53
Elephant & Castle ⊖	d	09 55		20 10	20 25	20 40	20 55	21 10	21 25	21 40	21 55	22 10	22 25	22 40	22 55	23 10	23 25	23 57
Loughborough Jn	d	10 00		20 15	20 30	20 45	21 00	21 15	21 30	21 45	22 00	22 15	22 30	22 45	23 00	23 15	23 30	00 02
Herne Hill 4	d	10 05		20 20	20 35	20 50	21 05	21 20	21 35	21 50	22 05	22 20	22 35	22 50	23 05	23 20	23 35	00 06
London Bridge 4 ⊖	d																	
Tulse Hill 3	a	10 09		20 24	20 39	20 54	21 09	21 24	21 39	21 54	22 09	22 24	22 39	22 54	23 09	23 24	23 39	00 10
	d	10 10		20 26	20 40	20 56	21 10	21 26	21 40	21 56	22 10	22 26	22 40	22 56	23 10	23 26	23 40	00 11
Streatham 4	d	10 14		20 30	20 44	21 00	21 14	21 30	21 44	22 00	22 14	22 30	22 44	23 00	23 14	23 30	23 44	00 14
Tooting	d	10 19			20 49		21 19		21 49		22 19		22 49		23 19		23 49	00 19
Haydons Road	d	10 22			20 52		21 22		21 52		22 22		22 52		23 22		23 52	00 22
Wimbledon 6 ⊖ ⇌	a	10 24			20 54		21 24		21 54		22 24		22 54		23 24		23 54	00 24
	d	10 25			20 55		21 25		21 55		22 25		22 55		23 25		23 55	00 25
Wimbledon Chase	d	10 28			20 58		21 28		21 58		22 28		22 58		23 28		23 58	00 28
South Merton	d	10 30			21 00		21 30		22 00		22 30		23 00		23 30		00 01	00 30
Morden South	d	10 33			21 03		21 33		22 03		22 33		23 03		23 33		00 04	00 33
St Helier	d	10 35			21 05		21 35		22 05		22 35		23 05		23 35		00 06	00 35
Sutton Common	d	10 37			21 07		21 37		22 07		22 37		23 07		23 37		00 08	00 37
West Sutton	d	10 40			21 10		21 40		22 10		22 40		23 10		23 40		00 11	00 40
Mitcham Eastfields	d			20 34		21 04		21 34		22 04		22 34		23 04		23 34		
Mitcham Junction ⇌	d			20 37		21 07		21 37		22 07		22 37		23 07		23 37		
Hackbridge	d			20 40		21 10		21 40		22 10		22 40		23 10		23 40		
Carshalton	d			20 43		21 13		21 43		22 13		22 43		23 13		23 43		
Sutton 4	a	10 44		20 47	21 14	21 17	21 44	21 47	22 14	22 17	22 44	22 47	23 14	23 17	23 44	23 47	00 14	00 44

Sundays
15 December to 10 May

		TL B	TL C	TL	TL	TL	TL A	TL	TL A	TL	TL A	TL	TL A	TL	TL A	TL	TL A	TL	TL A	TL A	TL A	TL
St Albans City	d						09 03		09 33		10 03		10 33		11 03		11 33		12 03	12 16	12 37	12 46
West Hampstead Thameslink	d						09 26		09 56		10 26		10 56		11 26		11 56		12 26	12 39	12 56	13 09
St Pancras International 15 ⊖	d						09 38		10 08		10 38		11 08		11 38		12 08	12 21	12 38	12 51	13 08	13 21
Farringdon 3 ⊖	d						09 42		10 12		10 42		11 12		11 42		12 12	12 25	12 42	12 55	13 12	13 25
City Thameslink 3	d																					
London Blackfriars 3 ⊖	d					09 30	09 47	10 00	10 17	10 30	10 47	11 00	11 17	11 30	11 47	12 00	12 17	12 30	12 47	13 00	13 17	13 30
Elephant & Castle ⊖	d					09 34	09 51	10 04	10 21	10 34	10 51	11 04	11 21	11 34	11 51	12 04	12 21	12 34	12 51	13 04	13 21	13 34
Loughborough Jn	d		00 02			09 39	09 56	10 09	10 26	10 39	10 56	11 09	11 26	11 39	11 56	12 09	12 26	12 39	12 56	13 09	13 26	13 39
Herne Hill 4	d		00 06			09 44	10 00	10 14	10 30	10 44	11 00	11 14	11 30	11 44	12 00	12 14	12 30	12 44	13 00	13 14	13 30	13 44
London Bridge 4 ⊖	d			08 30	09 00																	
Tulse Hill 3	a		00 10	08 43	09 13	09 48	10 04	10 18	10 34	10 48	11 04	11 18	11 34	11 48	12 04	12 18	12 34	12 48	13 04	13 18	13 34	13 48
	d		00 11	08 46	09 16	09 48	10 04	10 18	10 34	10 48	11 04	11 18	11 34	11 48	12 04	12 18	12 34	12 48	13 04	13 18	13 34	13 48
Streatham 4	d		00 14	08 50	09 20	09 52	10 08	10 22	10 38	10 52	11 08	11 22	11 38	11 52	12 08	12 22	12 38	12 52	13 08	13 22	13 38	13 52
Tooting	d		00 19				10 13		10 43		11 13		11 43		12 13		12 43		13 13		13 43	
Haydons Road	d		00 22				10 16		10 46		11 16		11 46		12 16		12 46		13 16		13 46	
Wimbledon 6 ⊖ ⇌	a		00 24				10 18		10 48		11 18		11 48		12 18		12 48		13 18		13 48	
	d		00 25				10 19		10 49		11 19		11 49		12 19		12 49		13 19		13 49	
Wimbledon Chase	d		00 28				10 22		10 52		11 22		11 52		12 22		12 52		13 22		13 52	
South Merton	d	00 01	00 30				10 24		10 54		11 24		11 54		12 24		12 54		13 24		13 54	
Morden South	d	00 04	00 33				10 27		10 57		11 27		11 57		12 27		12 57		13 27		13 57	
St Helier	d	00 06	00 35				10 29		10 59		11 29		11 59		12 29		12 59		13 29		13 59	
Sutton Common	d	00 08	00 37				10 31		11 01		11 31		12 01		12 31		13 01		13 31		14 01	
West Sutton	d	00 11	00 40				10 34		11 04		11 34		12 04		12 34		13 04		13 34		14 04	
Mitcham Eastfields	d			08 53	09 23	09 55		10 25		10 55		11 25		11 55		12 25		12 55		13 25		13 55
Mitcham Junction ⇌	d			08 56	09 26	09 58		10 28		10 58		11 28		11 58		12 28		12 58		13 28		13 58
Hackbridge	d			08 59	09 29	10 01		10 31		11 01		11 31		12 01		12 31		13 01		13 31		14 01
Carshalton	d			09 02	09 32	10 04		10 34		11 04		11 34		12 04		12 34		13 04		13 34		14 04
Sutton 4	a	00 14	00 44	09 05	09 35	10 07	10 38	10 37	11 08	11 07	11 38	11 37	12 08	12 07	12 38	12 37	13 08	13 07	13 38	13 37	14 08	14 07

A From Luton   B not 15 December. From St Albans City   C not 15 December. From Luton

For more London Bridge connections, refer to Table T173

Most Thameslink services from Blackfriars via Wimbledon and Hackbridge continue back towards Blackfriars.

Table T179-F

Sundays
15 December to 10 May

Thameslink - Wimbledon and Sutton

		TL A	TL	TL A	TL		TL A	TL	TL A	TL	TL A	TL	TL A	TL	TL A	TL	TL A	TL	TL A	TL	TL A	TL
St Albans City	d	13 07	13 16	13 37	13 47	and at the same minutes past each hour until	17 07	17 16	17 37	17 47	18 07	18 16	18 37	18 46	19 07	19 16	19 37	19 47	20 07	20 17	20 37	20 46
West Hampstead Thameslink	d	13 26	13 39	13 56	14 09		17 26	17 39	17 56	18 09	18 26	18 39	18 57	19 09	19 26	19 39	19 56	20 09	20 26	20 39	20 57	21 09
St Pancras International 15 ⊖	d	13 38	13 51	14 08	14 21		17 38	17 51	18 08	18 21	18 38	18 51	19 08	19 21	19 38	19 51	20 08	20 21	20 38	20 51	21 08	21 21
Farringdon 3 ⊖	d	13 42	13 55	14 12	14 25		17 42	17 55	18 12	18 25	18 42	18 55	19 12	19 25	19 42	19 55	20 12	20 25	20 42	20 55	21 12	21 25
City Thameslink 3	d																					
London Blackfriars 3 ⊖	d	13 47	14 00	14 17	14 30		17 47	18 00	18 17	18 30	18 47	19 00	19 17	19 30	19 47	20 00	20 17	20 30	20 47	21 00	21 17	21 30
Elephant & Castle ⊖	d	13 51	14 04	14 21	14 34		17 51	18 04	18 21	18 34	18 51	19 04	19 21	19 34	19 51	20 04	20 21	20 34	20 51	21 04	21 21	21 34
Loughborough Jn	d	13 56	14 09	14 26	14 39		17 56	18 09	18 26	18 39	18 56	19 09	19 26	19 39	19 56	20 09	20 26	20 39	20 56	21 09	21 26	21 39
Herne Hill 4	d	14 00	14 14	14 30	14 44		18 00	18 14	18 30	18 44	19 00	19 14	19 30	19 44	20 00	20 14	20 30	20 44	21 00	21 14	21 30	21 44
London Bridge 4 ⊖	d																					
Tulse Hill 3	a	14 04	14 18	14 34	14 48		18 04	18 18	18 34	18 48	19 04	19 18	19 34	19 48	20 04	20 18	20 34	20 48	21 04	21 18	21 34	21 48
	d	14 04	14 18	14 34	14 48		18 04	18 18	18 34	18 48	19 04	19 18	19 34	19 48	20 04	20 18	20 34	20 48	21 04	21 18	21 34	21 48
Streatham 4	d	14 08	14 22	14 38	14 52		18 08	18 22	18 38	18 52	19 08	19 22	19 38	19 52	20 08	20 22	20 38	20 52	21 08	21 22	21 38	21 52
Tooting	d	14 13		14 43			18 13		18 43		19 13		19 43		20 13		20 43		21 13		21 43	
Haydons Road	d	14 16		14 46			18 16		18 46		19 16		19 46		20 16		20 46		21 16		21 46	
Wimbledon 6 ⊖ ⇌	a	14 18		14 48			18 18		18 48		19 18		19 48		20 18		20 48		21 18		21 48	
	d	14 19		14 49			18 19		18 49		19 19		19 49		20 19		20 49		21 19		21 49	
Wimbledon Chase	d	14 22		14 52			18 22		18 52		19 22		19 52		20 22		20 52		21 22		21 52	
South Merton	d	14 24		14 54			18 24		18 54		19 24		19 54		20 24		20 54		21 24		21 54	
Morden South	d	14 27		14 57			18 27		18 57		19 27		19 57		20 27		20 57		21 27		21 57	
St Helier	d	14 29		14 59			18 29		18 59		19 29		19 59		20 29		20 59		21 29		21 59	
Sutton Common	d	14 31		15 01			18 31		19 01		19 31		20 01		20 31		21 01		21 31		22 01	
West Sutton	d	14 34		15 04			18 34		19 04		19 34		20 04		20 34		21 04		21 34		22 04	
Mitcham Eastfields	d		14 25		14 55			18 25		18 55		19 25		19 55		20 25		20 55		21 25		21 55
Mitcham Junction ⇌	d		14 28		14 58			18 28		18 58		19 28		19 58		20 28		20 58		21 28		21 58
Hackbridge	d		14 31		15 01			18 31		19 01		19 31		20 01		20 31		21 01		21 31		22 01
Carshalton	d		14 34		15 04			18 34		19 04		19 34		20 04		20 34		21 04		21 34		22 04
Sutton 4	a	14 38	14 37	15 08	15 07		18 38	18 37	19 08	19 07	19 38	19 37	20 08	20 07	20 38	20 37	21 08	21 07	21 38	21 37	22 08	22 07

		TL A
St Albans City	d	21 07
West Hampstead Thameslink	d	21 26
St Pancras International 15 ⊖	d	21 38
Farringdon 3 ⊖	d	21 42
City Thameslink 3	d	
London Blackfriars 3 ⊖	d	21 47
Elephant & Castle ⊖	d	21 51
Loughborough Jn	d	21 56
Herne Hill 4	d	22 00
London Bridge 4 ⊖	d	
Tulse Hill 3	a	22 04
	d	22 04
Streatham 4	d	22 08
Tooting	d	22 13
Haydons Road	d	22 16
Wimbledon 6 ⊖ ⇌	a	22 18
	d	22 19
Wimbledon Chase	d	22 22
South Merton	d	22 24
Morden South	d	22 27
St Helier	d	22 29
Sutton Common	d	22 31
West Sutton	d	22 34
Mitcham Eastfields	d	
Mitcham Junction ⇌	d	
Hackbridge	d	
Carshalton	d	
Sutton 4	a	22 38

A From Luton

For more London Bridge connections, refer to Table T173

Most Thameslink services from Blackfriars via Wimbledon and Hackbridge continue back towards Blackfriars.

Table T179-R

Wimbledon and Sutton - Thameslink

Mondays to Fridays

16 December to 15 May

Miles	Miles			TL MX A	TL MX A	TL MX A	TL	TL	TL	TL	SN	TL	TL	SN	TL	TL	SN	TL	TL	SN	TL	TL	SN
0	0	Sutton 4	d				05 46	05 49	06 16	06 19	06 36	06 46	06 49	07 06	07 16	07 19	07 36	07 46	07 49	08 06	08 16	08 19	08 36
—	1¼	Carshalton	d				05 49		06 19		06 39	06 49		07 09	07 19		07 39	07 49		08 09	08 19		08 39
—	2¼	Hackbridge	d				05 52		06 22		06 42	06 52		07 12	07 22		07 42	07 52		08 12	08 22		08 42
—	3¼	Mitcham Junction	d				05 55		06 25		06 45	06 55		07 15	07 25		07 45	07 55		08 15	08 25		08 45
—	4½	Mitcham Eastfields	d				05 58		06 28		06 48	06 58		07 18	07 28		07 49	07 58		08 19	08 28		08 49
1	—	**West Sutton**	d					05 52		06 22			06 52			07 22			07 52			08 22	
2	—	**Sutton Common**	d					05 54		06 24			06 54			07 24			07 54			08 24	
2¾	—	**St Helier**	d					05 57		06 27			06 57			07 27			07 57			08 27	
3¼	—	**Morden South**	d					05 59		06 29			06 59			07 29			07 59			08 29	
4	—	**South Merton**	d					06 01		06 31			07 01			07 31			08 01			08 31	
4½	—	**Wimbledon Chase**	d					06 03		06 33			07 03			07 33			08 03			08 33	
5½	—	Wimbledon 6	a					06 06		06 36			07 06			07 36			08 06			08 36	
—	—		d					06 07		06 37			07 07			07 37			08 07			08 37	
6¼	—	**Haydons Road**	d					06 10		06 40			07 10			07 40			08 10			08 40	
7½	—	**Tooting**	d					06 13		06 43			07 13			07 43			08 13			08 43	
9	6	Streatham 4	d				06 03	06 18	06 33	06 48	06 53	07 03	07 18	07 23	07 33	07 48	07 53	08 03	08 18	08 23	08 33	08 48	08 53
10½	7½	Tulse Hill 3	a				06 07	06 22	06 37	06 52	06 56	07 07	07 22	07 26	07 37	07 52	07 56	08 07	08 22	08 26	08 37	08 52	08 56
—	—		d				06 08	06 23	06 38	06 53	06 57	07 08	07 23	07 27	07 38	07 53	07 57	08 08	08 23	08 27	08 38	08 53	08 57
—	—	London Bridge 4	a								07 15			07 45			08 15			08 47			09 17
11¾	8¾	Herne Hill 4	d				06 12	06 27	06 42	06 57		07 12	07 27		07 42	07 57		08 12	08 27		08 42	08 57	
12¾	9¾	Loughborough Jn	d				06 15	06 30	06 45	07 00		07 15	07 30		07 45	08 00		08 15	08 30		08 45	09 00	
14½	11½	Elephant & Castle	d			00 04	06 19	06 34	06 49	07 04		07 19	07 34		07 49	08 04		08 19	08 34		08 49	09 04	
15¾	12¾	London Blackfriars 3	d		00 02	00 09	06 24	06 39	06 54	07 09		07 24	07 39		07 54	08 09		08 24	08 39		08 54	09 09	
16	13¼	City Thameslink 3	d				06 26	06 41	06 56	07 11		07 26	07 41		07 56	08 11		08 26	08 41		08 56	09 11	
16½	13½	Farringdon 3	d		00 06	00 13	06 29	06 44	06 59	07 14		07 29	07 44		07 59	08 14		08 29	08 44		08 59	09 14	
17¾	14¾	St Pancras International 15	d		00 11	00 18	06 33	06 48	07 03	07 18		07 33	07 48		08 03	08 18		08 33	08 48		09 03	09 18	
21¾	18¾	West Hampstead Thameslink	d	00 06	00 20	00 26	06 44	06 58	07 14	07 28		07 43	07 58		08 13	08 29		08 43	08 58		09 14	09 28	
37¾	34¾	St Albans City	a	00 31	00 35	00 51	07 07	07 21	07 37	07 51		08 06	08 21		08 36	08 51		09 06	09 21		09 36	09 51	

		TL	TL	TL	TL	TL	TL	TL	TL	TL	TL	TL	TL	TL	TL	TL	TL	TL	TL	TL	TL	TL	TL
Sutton 4	d	08 46	08 49	09 16	09 19	09 46	09 49	10 16	10 19	10 46	10 49	11 16	11 19	11 46	11 49	12 16	12 19	12 46	12 49	13 16	13 19	13 46	13 49
Carshalton	d	08 49		09 19		09 49		10 19		10 49		11 19		11 49		12 19		12 49		13 19		13 49	
Hackbridge	d	08 52		09 22		09 52		10 22		10 52		11 22		11 52		12 22		12 52		13 22		13 52	
Mitcham Junction	d	08 55		09 25		09 55		10 25		10 55		11 25		11 55		12 25		12 55		13 25		13 55	
Mitcham Eastfields	d	08 58		09 28		09 58		10 28		10 58		11 28		11 58		12 28		12 58		13 28		13 58	
West Sutton	d		08 52		09 22		09 52		10 22		10 52		11 22		11 52		12 22		12 52		13 22		13 52
Sutton Common	d		08 54		09 24		09 54		10 24		10 54		11 24		11 54		12 24		12 54		13 24		13 54
St Helier	d		08 57		09 27		09 57		10 27		10 57		11 27		11 57		12 27		12 57		13 27		13 57
Morden South	d		08 59		09 29		09 59		10 29		10 59		11 29		11 59		12 29		12 59		13 29		13 59
South Merton	d		09 01		09 31		10 01		10 31		11 01		11 31		12 01		12 31		13 01		13 31		14 01
Wimbledon Chase	d		09 03		09 33		10 03		10 33		11 03		11 33		12 03		12 33		13 03		13 33		14 03
Wimbledon 6	a		09 06		09 36		10 06		10 36		11 06		11 36		12 06		12 36		13 06		13 36		14 06
	d		09 07		09 37		10 07		10 37		11 07		11 37		12 07		12 37		13 07		13 37		14 07
Haydons Road	d		09 10		09 40		10 10		10 40		11 10		11 40		12 10		12 40		13 10		13 40		14 10
Tooting	d		09 13		09 43		10 13		10 43		11 13		11 43		12 13		12 43		13 13		13 43		14 13
Streatham 4	d	09 03	09 18	09 33	09 48	10 03	10 18	10 33	10 48	11 03	11 18	11 33	11 48	12 03	12 18	12 33	12 48	13 03	13 18	13 33	13 48	14 03	14 18
Tulse Hill 3	a	09 07	09 22	09 37	09 52	10 07	10 22	10 37	10 52	11 07	11 22	11 37	11 52	12 07	12 22	12 37	12 52	13 07	13 22	13 37	13 52	14 07	14 22
	d	09 08	09 23	09 38	09 53	10 08	10 23	10 38	10 53	11 08	11 23	11 38	11 53	12 08	12 23	12 38	12 53	13 08	13 23	13 38	13 53	14 08	14 23
London Bridge 4	a																						
Herne Hill 4	d	09 12	09 27	09 42	09 57	10 12	10 27	10 42	10 57	11 12	11 27	11 42	11 57	12 12	12 27	12 42	12 57	13 12	13 27	13 42	13 57	14 12	14 27
Loughborough Jn	d	09 15	09 30	09 45	10 00	10 15	10 30	10 45	11 00	11 15	11 30	11 45	12 00	12 15	12 30	12 45	13 00	13 15	13 30	13 45	14 00	14 15	14 30
Elephant & Castle	d	09 19	09 34	09 49	10 04	10 19	10 34	10 49	11 04	11 19	11 34	11 49	12 04	12 19	12 34	12 49	13 04	13 19	13 34	13 49	14 04	14 19	14 34
London Blackfriars 3	d	09 24	09 39	09 54	10 09	10 24	10 39	10 54	11 09	11 24	11 39	11 54	12 09	12 24	12 39	12 54	13 09	13 24	13 39	13 54	14 09	14 24	14 39
City Thameslink 3	d	09 26	09 41	09 56	10 11	10 26	10 41	10 56	11 11	11 26	11 41	11 56	12 11	12 26	12 41	12 56	13 11	13 26	13 41	13 56	14 11	14 26	14 41
Farringdon 3	d	09 29	09 44	09 59	10 14	10 29	10 44	10 59	11 14	11 29	11 44	11 59	12 14	12 29	12 44	12 59	13 14	13 29	13 44	13 59	14 14	14 29	14 44
St Pancras International 15	d	09 33	09 48	10 03	10 18	10 33	10 48	11 03	11 18	11 33	11 48	12 03	12 18	12 33	12 48	13 03	13 18	13 33	13 48	14 03	14 18	14 33	14 48
West Hampstead Thameslink	d	09 44	09 59	10 14	10 29	10 44	10 59	11 14	11 29	11 44	11 59	12 14	12 29	12 44	12 59	13 14	13 29	13 44	13 59	14 15	14 29	14 44	14 59
St Albans City	a	10 06	10 23	10 37	10 52	11 07	11 22	11 38	11 52	12 07	12 22	12 37	12 52	13 07	13 22	13 37	13 52	14 07	14 22	14 37	14 52	15 07	15 22

		TL	TL	TL	TL	TL	TL	TL	TL	TL	TL	TL	TL	TL	TL	TL	SN	TL	TL	SN	TL	TL
Sutton 4	d	14 16	14 18	14 46	14 49	15 16	15 19	15 46	15 49	16 16	16 19	16 46	16 49	17 16	17 19	17 46	17 38	17 49	18 16	18 08	18 19	18 46
Carshalton	d	14 19		14 49		15 19		15 49		16 19		16 49		17 19		17 49			18 19			18 49
Hackbridge	d	14 22		14 52		15 22		15 52		16 22		16 52		17 22		17 52			18 22			18 52
Mitcham Junction	d	14 25		14 55		15 25		15 55		16 25		16 55		17 25		17 55			18 25			18 55
Mitcham Eastfields	d	14 28		14 58		15 28		15 58		16 28		16 58		17 28		17 58			18 28			18 58
West Sutton	d		14 21		14 52		15 22		15 52		16 22		16 52		17 22		17 42	17 52		18 12	18 22	
Sutton Common	d		14 23		14 54		15 24		15 54		16 24		16 54		17 24		17 44	17 54		18 14	18 24	
St Helier	d		14 26		14 57		15 27		15 57		16 27		16 57		17 27		17 47	17 57		18 17	18 27	
Morden South	d		14 28		14 59		15 29		15 59		16 29		16 59		17 29		17 49	17 59		18 19	18 29	
South Merton	d		14 30		15 01		15 31		16 01		16 31		17 01		17 31		17 51	18 01		18 21	18 31	
Wimbledon Chase	d		14 32		15 03		15 33		16 03		16 33		17 03		17 33		17 53	18 03		18 23	18 33	
Wimbledon 6	a		14 35		15 06		15 36		16 06		16 36		17 06		17 36		17 58	18 06		18 28	18 36	
	d		14 36		15 07		15 37		16 07		16 37		17 07		17 37		17 59	18 07		18 29	18 37	
Haydons Road	d		14 38		15 10		15 40		16 10		16 40		17 10		17 40		18 01	18 10		18 31	18 40	
Tooting	d		14 41		15 13		15 43		16 13		16 43		17 13		17 43		18 05	18 13		18 35	18 43	
Streatham 4	d	14 33	14 46	15 03	15 18	15 33	15 48	16 03	16 18	16 33	16 48	17 03	17 18	17 33	17 48	18 03	18 10	18 18	18 33	18 40	18 48	19 03
Tulse Hill 3	a	14 37	14 50	15 07	15 22	15 37	15 52	16 07	16 22	16 37	16 52	17 07	17 22	17 37	17 52	18 07	18 14	18 22	18 37	18 43	18 52	19 07
	d	14 38	14 53	15 08	15 23	15 38	15 53	16 08	16 23	16 38	16 53	17 08	17 23	17 38	17 53	18 08	18 14	18 23	18 38	18 44	18 53	19 08
London Bridge 4	a																18 33			19 03		
Herne Hill 4	d	14 42	14 57	15 12	15 27	15 42	15 57	16 12	16 27	16 42	16 57	17 12	17 27	17 42	17 57	18 12		18 27	18 42		18 57	19 12
Loughborough Jn	d	14 45	15 00	15 15	15 30	15 45	16 00	16 15	16 30	16 45	17 00	17 15	17 30	17 45	18 00	18 15		18 30	18 45		19 00	19 15
Elephant & Castle	d	14 49	15 04	15 19	15 34	15 49	16 04	16 19	16 34	16 49	17 04	17 19	17 34	17 49	18 04	18 19		18 34	18 49		19 04	19 19
London Blackfriars 3	d	14 54	15 09	15 24	15 39	15 54	16 09	16 24	16 39	16 54	17 09	17 24	17 39	17 54	18 09	18 24		18 39	18 54		19 09	19 24
City Thameslink 3	d	14 56	15 11	15 26	15 41	15 56	16 11	16 26	16 41	16 56	17 11	17 26	17 41	17 56	18 11	18 26		18 41	18 56		19 11	19 26
Farringdon 3	d	14 59	15 14	15 29	15 44	15 59	16 14	16 29	16 44	16 59	17 14	17 29	17 44	17 59	18 14	18 29		18 44	18 59		19 14	19 29
St Pancras International 15	d	15 03	15 18	15 33	15 48	16 03	16 18	16 33	16 48	17 03	17 18	17 33	17 48	18 03	18 18	18 33		18 48	19 03		19 18	19 33
West Hampstead Thameslink	d	15 14	15 29	15 44	15 59	16 14	16 29	16 44	16 59	17 14	17 29	17 44	17 59	18 14	18 29	18 44		18 59	19 14		19 29	19 44
St Albans City	a	15 37	15 52	16 07	16 23	16 37	16 51	17 06	17 21	17 36	17 51	18 06	18 23	18 36	18 51	19 06		19 21	19 36		19 53	20 07

A From Sutton (Surrey) to Bedford

NRT DECEMBER 19 EDITION

Table T179-R

Wimbledon and Sutton - Thameslink

Mondays to Fridays

16 December to 15 May

		SN	TL	TL	SN	TL	TL	TL	TL	TL	TL	TL	TL	TL A	TL A	TL A	TL A	TL A	TL A	TL A	TL A	TL A
Sutton 4	d	18 38	18 49	19 16	19 08	19 19	19 46	19 49	20 16	20 21	20 46	20 49	21 16	21 19	21 46	21 49	22 18	22 19	22 48	22 49	23 18	23 19
Carshalton	d			19 19			19 49		20 19		20 49		21 19		21 49		22 21		22 51		23 21	
Hackbridge	d			19 22			19 52		20 22		20 52		21 22		21 52		22 24		22 54		23 24	
Mitcham Junction	d			19 25			19 55		20 25		20 55		21 25		21 55		22 27		22 57		23 27	
Mitcham Eastfields	d			19 28			19 58		20 28		20 58		21 28		21 58		22 30		23 00		23 30	
West Sutton	d	18 42	18 52		19 12	19 22		19 52		20 24		20 52		21 22		21 52		22 22		22 52		23 22
Sutton Common	d	18 44	18 54		19 14	19 24		19 54		20 26		20 54		21 24		21 54		22 24		22 54		23 24
St Helier	d	18 47	18 57		19 17	19 27		19 57		20 29		20 57		21 27		21 57		22 27		22 57		23 27
Morden South	d	18 49	18 59		19 19	19 29		19 59		20 31		20 59		21 29		21 59		22 29		22 59		23 29
South Merton	d	18 51	19 01		19 21	19 31		20 01		20 33		21 01		21 31		22 01		22 31		23 01		23 31
Wimbledon Chase	d	18 53	19 03		19 23	19 33		20 03		20 35		21 03		21 33		22 03		22 33		23 03		23 33
Wimbledon 6	a	18 58	19 06		19 28	19 36		20 06		20 41		21 06		21 36		22 06		22 36		23 06		23 36
	d	18 59	19 07		19 29	19 37		20 07		20 43		21 07		21 37		22 07		22 41		23 11		23 37
Haydons Road	d	19 01	19 10		19 31	19 40		20 10		20 46		21 10		21 40		22 10		22 44		23 14		23 40
Tooting	d	19 05	19 13		19 35	19 43		20 13		20 49		21 13		21 43		22 13		22 47		23 17		23 43
Streatham 4	d	19 10	19 18	19 33	19 40	19 48	20 03	20 18	20 33	20 54	21 03	21 18	21 33	21 48	22 03	22 18	22 35	22 52	23 05	23 22	23 35	23 48
Tulse Hill 3	a	19 13	19 22	19 37	19 43	19 52	20 07	20 22	20 37	20 58	21 07	21 22	21 37	21 52	22 07	22 22	22 39	22 56	23 09	23 26	23 39	23 52
	d	19 14	19 23	19 38	19 44	19 53	20 08	20 23	20 38	20 59	21 08	21 23	21 38	21 53	22 08	22 23	22 40	22 57	23 10	23 27	23 40	23 53
London Bridge 4	a	19 33			20 03																	
Herne Hill 4	d		19 27	19 42		19 57	20 12	20 27	20 42	21 04	21 12	21 27	21 42	21 57	22 12	22 27	22 44	23 04	23 14	23 34	23 44	23 57
Loughborough Jn	d		19 30	19 45		20 00	20 15	20 30	20 45	21 07	21 15	21 30	21 45	22 00	22 15	22 30	22 47	23 07	23 17	23 37	23 47	
Elephant & Castle	d		19 34	19 49		20 04	20 19	20 34	20 49	21 11	21 19	21 34	21 49	22 04	22 19	22 34	22 51	23 11	23 21	23 41	23 54	00 04
London Blackfriars 3	d		19 39	19 54		20 09	20 24	20 39	20 54	21 17	21 24	21 39	21 54	22 09	22 24	22 39	22 59	23 17	23 29	23 49	00 02	00 09
City Thameslink 3	d		19 41	19 56		20 11	20 26	20 41	20 56	21 19	21 26	21 41	21 56	22 11	22 26	22 41						
Farringdon 3	d		19 44	19 59		20 14	20 29	20 44	20 59	21 21	21 29	21 44	21 59	22 14	22 29	22 44	23 04	23 21	23 33	23 53	00 06	00 13
St Pancras International 15	d		19 48	20 03		20 18	20 33	20 48	21 03	21 26	21 33	21 48	22 03	22 18	22 33	22 48	23 08	23 26	23 38	23 58	00 11	00 18
West Hampstead Thameslink	d		19 59	20 14		20 29	20 44	20 59	21 14	21 34	21 44	21 59	22 14	22 29	22 44	23 02	23 18	23 35	23 46	00 06	00 20	00 26
St Albans City	a		20 22	20 37		20 52	21 08	21 22	21 37	21 54	22 07	22 23	22 37	22 51	23 08	23 26	23 41	23 58	00 11	00 31	00 35	00 51

Saturdays

21 December to 16 May

		TL B	TL B	TL B	TL	TL	TL	TL	TL	TL	TL	TL	TL	TL	TL	TL	TL	TL	TL	
Sutton 4	d				05 46	05 49	06 16	06 19	06 46	06 49	07 16	07 19	07 46	07 49	08 16	08 19	08 46	08 49	09 16	and at the same minutes past each hour until
Carshalton	d				05 49		06 19		06 49		07 19		07 49		08 19		08 49		09 19	
Hackbridge	d				05 52		06 22		06 52		07 22		07 52		08 22		08 52		09 22	
Mitcham Junction	d				05 55		06 25		06 55		07 25		07 55		08 25		08 55		09 25	
Mitcham Eastfields	d				05 58		06 28		06 58		07 28		07 58		08 28		08 58		09 28	
West Sutton	d					05 52		06 22		06 52		07 22		07 52		08 22		08 52		
Sutton Common	d					05 54		06 24		06 54		07 24		07 54		08 24		08 54		
St Helier	d					05 57		06 27		06 57		07 27		07 57		08 27		08 57		
Morden South	d					05 59		06 29		06 59		07 29		07 59		08 29		08 59		
South Merton	d					06 01		06 31		07 01		07 31		08 01		08 31		09 01		
Wimbledon Chase	d					06 03		06 33		07 03		07 33		08 03		08 33		09 03		
Wimbledon 6	a					06 06		06 36		07 06		07 36		08 06		08 36		09 06		
	d					06 07		06 37		07 07		07 37		08 07		08 37		09 07		
Haydons Road	d					06 10		06 40		07 10		07 40		08 10		08 40		09 10		
Tooting	d					06 13		06 43		07 13		07 43		08 13		08 43		09 13		
Streatham 4	d				06 03	06 18	06 33	06 48	07 03	07 18	07 33	07 48	08 03	08 18	08 33	08 48	09 03	09 18	09 33	
Tulse Hill 3	a				06 07	06 22	06 37	06 52	07 07	07 22	07 37	07 52	08 07	08 22	08 37	08 52	09 07	09 22	09 37	
	d				06 08	06 23	06 38	06 53	07 08	07 23	07 38	07 53	08 08	08 23	08 38	08 53	09 08	09 23	09 38	
London Bridge 4	a																			
Herne Hill 4	d				06 12	06 27	06 42	06 57	07 12	07 27	07 42	07 57	08 12	08 27	08 42	08 57	09 12	09 27	09 42	
Loughborough Jn	d				06 15	06 30	06 45	07 00	07 15	07 30	07 45	08 00	08 15	08 30	08 45	09 00	09 15	09 30	09 45	
Elephant & Castle	d			00 04	06 19	06 34	06 49	07 04	07 19	07 34	07 49	08 04	08 19	08 34	08 49	09 04	09 19	09 34	09 49	
London Blackfriars 3	d		00 02	00 09	06 24	06 39	06 54	07 09	07 24	07 39	07 54	08 09	08 24	08 39	08 54	09 09	09 24	09 39	09 54	
City Thameslink 3	d															09 11	09 26	09 41	09 56	
Farringdon 3	d		00 06	00 13	06 29	06 44	06 59	07 14	07 29	07 44	07 59	08 14	08 29	08 44	08 59	09 14	09 29	09 44	09 59	
St Pancras International 15	d		00 11	00 18	06 33	06 48	07 03	07 18	07 33	07 48	08 03	08 18	08 33	08 48	09 03	09 18	09 33	09 48	10 03	
West Hampstead Thameslink	d	00 06	00 20	00 26	06 44	06 59	07 14	07 29	07 44	07 59	08 14	08 29	08 44	08 59	09 14	09 29	09 44	09 59	10 14	
St Albans City	a	00 31	00 35	00 51	07 07	07 22	07 37	07 52	08 07	08 22	08 37	08 52	09 07	09 22	09 37	09 52	10 07	10 22	10 37	

A To Bedford

B From Sutton (Surrey) to Bedford

For more London Bridge connections, refer to Table T173

Most Thameslink services from Blackfriars via Wimbledon and Hackbridge continue back towards Blackfriars.

Table T179-R

Wimbledon and Sutton - Thameslink

Saturdays
21 December to 16 May

		TL	TL	TL	TL	TL	TL	TL	TL	TL A	TL A	TL A	TL A	TL A	TL A	TL A	TL A	TL A
Sutton 4	d	19 19	19 46	19 49	20 16	20 19	20 46	20 49	21 16	21 19	21 46	21 49	22 18	22 19	22 48	22 49	23 18	23 19
Carshalton	d		19 49		20 19		20 49		21 19		21 49		22 21		22 51		23 21	
Hackbridge	d		19 52		20 22		20 52		21 22		21 52		22 24		22 54		23 24	
Mitcham Junction	d		19 55		20 25		20 55		21 25		21 55		22 27		22 57		23 27	
Mitcham Eastfields	d		19 58		20 28		20 58		21 28		21 58		22 30		23 00		23 30	
West Sutton	d	19 22		19 52		20 22		20 52		21 22		21 52		22 22		22 52		23 22
Sutton Common	d	19 24		19 54		20 24		20 54		21 24		21 54		22 24		22 54		23 24
St Helier	d	19 27		19 57		20 27		20 57		21 27		21 57		22 27		22 57		23 27
Morden South	d	19 29		19 59		20 29		20 59		21 29		21 59		22 29		22 59		23 29
South Merton	d	19 31		20 01		20 31		21 01		21 31		22 01		22 31		23 01		23 31
Wimbledon Chase	d	19 33		20 03		20 33		21 03		21 33		22 03		22 33		23 03		23 33
Wimbledon 6	a	19 36		20 06		20 36		21 06		21 36		22 06		22 36		23 06		23 36
	d	19 37		20 07		20 37		21 07		21 37		22 07		22 41		23 11		23 37
Haydons Road	d	19 40		20 10		20 40		21 10		21 40		22 10		22 44		23 14		23 40
Tooting	d	19 43		20 13		20 43		21 13		21 43		22 13		22 47		23 17		23 43
Streatham 4	d	19 48	20 03	20 18	20 33	20 48	21 03	21 18	21 33	21 48	22 03	22 18	22 35	22 52	23 05	23 22	23 35	23 48
Tulse Hill 3	a	19 52	20 07	20 22	20 37	20 52	21 07	21 22	21 37	21 52	22 07	22 22	22 39	22 56	23 09	23 26	23 39	23 52
	d	19 53	20 08	20 23	20 38	20 53	21 08	21 23	21 38	21 53	22 08	22 23	22 40	22 57	23 10	23 27	23 40	23 53
London Bridge 4	a																	
Herne Hill 4	d	19 57	20 12	20 27	20 42	20 57	21 12	21 27	21 42	21 57	22 12	22 27	22 44	23 04	23 14	23 34	23 44	23 57
Loughborough Jn.	d	20 00	20 15	20 30	20 45	21 00	21 15	21 30	21 45	22 00	22 15	22 30	22 47	23 07	23 17	23 37	23 47	
Elephant & Castle	d	20 04	20 19	20 34	20 49	21 04	21 19	21 34	21 49	22 04	22 19	22 34	22 51	23 11	23 21	23 41	23 54	00 04
London Blackfriars 3	d	20 09	20 24	20 39	20 54	21 09	21 24	21 39	21 54	22 09	22 24	22 39	22 59	23 17	23 27	23 49	00 02	00 09
City Thameslink 3	d	20 11	20 26	20 41	20 56													
Farringdon 3	d	20 14	20 29	20 44	20 59	21 14	21 29	21 44	21 59	22 14	22 29	22 44	23 04	23 21	23 31	23 53	00 06	00 13
St Pancras International 15	d	20 18	20 33	20 48	21 03	21 18	21 33	21 48	22 03	22 18	22 33	22 48	23 08	23 26	23 36	23 58	00 11	00 18
West Hampstead Thameslink	d	20 29	20 44	20 59	21 14	21 29	21 44	21 59	22 14	22 29	22 44	23 02	23 17	23 34	23 44	00 06	00 19	00 26
St Albans City	a	20 52	21 07	21 22	21 37	21 52	22 07	22 22	22 37	22 51	23 08	23 26	23 41	23 58	00 09	00 31	00 35	00 51

Sundays
15 December to 10 May

		TL B	TL B	TL B	TL C	TL C	TL C	TL	TL C	TL	TL	TL C	TL	TL C	TL	TL C	TL	TL C	TL	TL C	TL	TL C	TL
Sutton 4	d				09 09	09 39	10 09	10 40	10 39	11 10	11 09	11 40	11 39	12 10	12 09	12 40	12 39	13 10	13 09	13 40	13 39	14 10	14 09
Carshalton	d							10 43		11 13		11 43		12 13		12 43		13 13		13 43		14 13	
Hackbridge	d							10 45		11 15		11 45		12 15		12 45		13 15		13 45		14 15	
Mitcham Junction	d							10 48		11 18		11 48		12 18		12 48		13 18		13 48		14 18	
Mitcham Eastfields	d							10 51		11 21		11 51		12 21		12 51		13 21		13 51		14 21	
West Sutton	d				09 12	09 42	10 12		10 42		11 12		11 42		12 12		12 42		13 12		13 42		14 12
Sutton Common	d				09 14	09 44	10 14		10 44		11 14		11 44		12 14		12 44		13 14		13 44		14 14
St Helier	d				09 17	09 47	10 17		10 47		11 17		11 47		12 17		12 47		13 17		13 47		14 17
Morden South	d				09 19	09 49	10 19		10 49		11 19		11 49		12 19		12 49		13 19		13 49		14 19
South Merton	d				09 21	09 51	10 21		10 51		11 21		11 51		12 21		12 51		13 21		13 51		14 21
Wimbledon Chase	d				09 23	09 53	10 23		10 53		11 23		11 53		12 23		12 53		13 23		13 53		14 23
Wimbledon 6	a				09 26	09 56	10 26		10 56		11 26		11 56		12 26		12 56		13 26		13 56		14 26
	d				09 27	09 57	10 27		10 57		11 27		11 57		12 27		12 57		13 27		13 57		14 27
Haydons Road	d				09 29	09 59	10 29		10 59		11 29		11 59		12 29		12 59		13 29		13 59		14 29
Tooting	d				09 32	10 02	10 32		11 02		11 32		12 02		12 32		13 02		13 32		14 02		14 32
Streatham 4	d				09 37	10 07	10 37	10 55	11 07	11 25	11 37	11 55	12 07	12 25	12 37	12 55	13 07	13 25	13 37	13 55	14 07	14 25	14 37
Tulse Hill 3	a				09 41	10 11	10 41	10 59	11 11	11 29	11 41	11 59	12 11	12 29	12 41	12 59	13 11	13 29	13 41	13 59	14 11	14 29	14 41
	d				09 41	10 11	10 41	10 59	11 11	11 29	11 41	11 59	12 11	12 29	12 41	12 59	13 11	13 29	13 41	13 59	14 11	14 29	14 41
London Bridge 4	a																						
Herne Hill 4	d				09 45	10 15	10 45	11 03	11 15	11 33	11 45	12 03	12 15	12 33	12 45	13 03	13 15	13 33	13 45	14 03	14 15	14 33	14 45
Loughborough Jn.	d				09 48	10 18	10 48	11 06	11 18	11 36	11 48	12 06	12 18	12 36	12 48	13 06	13 18	13 36	13 48	14 06	14 18	14 36	14 48
Elephant & Castle	d			00 04	09 53	10 23	10 53	11 11	11 23	11 41	11 53	12 11	12 23	12 41	12 53	13 11	13 23	13 41	13 53	14 11	14 23	14 41	14 53
London Blackfriars 3	d		00 02	00 09	09 58	10 28	10 58	11a15	11 28	11a45	11 58	12 16	12 28	12 46	12 58	13 16	13 28	13 46	13 58	14 16	14 28	14 46	14 58
City Thameslink 3	d																						
Farringdon 3	d		00 06	00 13	10 02	10 32	11 02		11 32		12 02	12 20	12 32	12 50	13 02	13 20	13 32	13 50	14 02	14 20	14 32	14 50	15 02
St Pancras International 15	d		00 11	00 18	10 07	10 37	11 07		11 37		12 07	12 25	12 37	12 55	13 07	13 25	13 37	13 55	14 07	14 25	14 37	14 55	15 07
West Hampstead Thameslink	d	00 06	00 19	00 26	10 15	10 45	11 15		11 45		12 16	12 34	12 46	13 04	13 16	13 34	13 46	14 04	14 16	14 34	14 46	15 04	15 16
St Albans City	a	00 31	00 35	00 51	10 38	11 08	11 38		12 10		12 42	12 54	13 12	13 24	13 42	13 54	14 14	14 24	14 44	14 54	15 14	15 24	15 42

A To Bedford

B not 15 December. From Sutton (Surrey) to Bedford

C To Luton

For more London Bridge connections, refer to Table T173

Most Thameslink services from Blackfriars via Wimbledon and Hackbridge continue back towards Blackfriars.

Table T179-R

Wimbledon and Sutton - Thameslink

Sundays
15 December to 10 May

		TL A	TL	TL A	TL	TL A	TL	TL A	TL	TL A	TL	TL A	TL	TL A	TL	TL A	TL	TL A	TL	TL A	TL	TL A
Sutton 4	d	14 40	14 39	15 10	15 09	15 40	15 39	16 10	16 09	16 40	16 39	17 10	17 09	17 40	17 39	18 10	18 09	18 40	18 39	19 10	19 09	19 40
Carshalton	d	14 43		15 13		15 43		16 13		16 43		17 13		17 43		18 13		18 43		19 13		19 43
Hackbridge	d	14 45		15 15		15 45		16 15		16 45		17 15		17 45		18 15		18 45		19 15		19 45
Mitcham Junction	d	14 48		15 18		15 48		16 18		16 48		17 18		17 48		18 18		18 48		19 18		19 48
Mitcham Eastfields	d	14 51		15 21		15 51		16 21		16 51		17 21		17 51		18 21		18 51		19 21		19 51
West Sutton	d		14 42		15 12		15 42		16 12		16 42		17 12		17 42		18 12		18 42		19 12	
Sutton Common	d		14 44		15 14		15 44		16 14		16 44		17 14		17 44		18 14		18 44		19 14	
St Helier	d		14 47		15 17		15 47		16 17		16 47		17 17		17 47		18 17		18 47		19 17	
Morden South	d		14 49		15 19		15 49		16 19		16 49		17 19		17 49		18 19		18 49		19 19	
South Merton	d		14 51		15 21		15 51		16 21		16 51		17 21		17 51		18 21		18 51		19 21	
Wimbledon Chase	d		14 53		15 23		15 53		16 23		16 53		17 23		17 53		18 23		18 53		19 23	
Wimbledon 6	a		14 56		15 26		15 56		16 26		16 56		17 26		17 56		18 26		18 56		19 26	
	d		14 57		15 27		15 57		16 27		16 57		17 27		17 57		18 27		18 57		19 27	
Haydons Road	d		14 59		15 29		15 59		16 29		16 59		17 29		17 59		18 29		18 59		19 29	
Tooting	d		15 02		15 32		16 02		16 32		17 02		17 32		18 02		18 32		19 02		19 32	
Streatham 4	d	14 55	15 07	15 25	15 37	15 55	16 07	16 25	16 37	16 55	17 07	17 25	17 37	17 55	18 07	18 25	18 37	18 55	19 07	19 25	19 37	19 55
Tulse Hill 3	a	14 59	15 11	15 29	15 41	15 59	16 11	16 29	16 41	16 59	17 11	17 29	17 41	17 59	18 11	18 29	18 41	18 59	19 11	19 29	19 41	19 59
	d	14 59	15 11	15 29	15 41	15 59	16 11	16 29	16 41	16 59	17 11	17 29	17 41	17 59	18 11	18 29	18 41	18 59	19 11	19 29	19 41	19 59
London Bridge 4	a																					
Herne Hill 4	d	15 03	15 15	15 33	15 45	16 03	16 15	16 33	16 45	17 03	17 15	17 33	17 45	18 03	18 15	18 33	18 45	19 03	19 15	19 33	19 45	20 03
Loughborough Jn.	d	15 06	15 18	15 36	15 48	16 06	16 18	16 36	16 48	17 06	17 18	17 36	17 48	18 06	18 18	18 36	18 48	19 06	19 18	19 36	19 48	20 06
Elephant & Castle	d	15 11	15 23	15 41	15 53	16 11	16 23	16 41	16 53	17 11	17 23	17 41	17 53	18 11	18 23	18 41	18 53	19 11	19 23	19 41	19 53	20 11
London Blackfriars 3	d	15 16	15 28	15 46	15 58	16 16	16 28	16 46	16 58	17 16	17 28	17 46	17 58	18 16	18 28	18 46	18 58	19 16	19 28	19 46	19 58	20 16
City Thameslink 3	d																					
Farringdon 3	d	15 20	15 32	15 50	16 02	16 20	16 32	16 50	17 02	17 20	17 32	17 50	18 02	18 20	18 32	18 50	19 02	19 20	19 32	19 50	20 02	20 20
St Pancras International 15	d	15 25	15 37	15 55	16 07	16 25	16 37	16 55	17 07	17 25	17 37	17 55	18 07	18 25	18 37	18 55	19 07	19 25	19 37	19 55	20 07	20 25
West Hampstead Thameslink	d	15 34	15 46	16 04	16 16	16 34	16 46	17 04	17 16	17 34	17 46	18 04	18 16	18 34	18 46	19 04	19 16	19 34	19 46	20 04	20 16	20 34
St Albans City	a	15 54	16 14	16 24	16 42	16 54	17 12	17 24	17 44	17 54	18 12	18 24	18 42	18 54	19 12	19 24	19 44	19 54	20 12	20 24	20 42	20 54

		TL	TL A	TL	TL A	TL	TL A	TL B	TL	TL A	TL	TL B	TL B
Sutton 4	d	19 39	20 10	20 09	20 40	20 39	21 10	21 09	21 40	21 39	22 10	22 09	22 40
Carshalton	d		20 13		20 43		21 13		21 43		22 13		22 43
Hackbridge	d		20 15		20 45		21 15		21 45		22 15		22 45
Mitcham Junction	d		20 18		20 48		21 18		21 48		22 18		22 48
Mitcham Eastfields	d		20 21		20 51		21 21		21 51		22 21		22 51
West Sutton	d	19 42		20 12		20 42		21 12		21 42		22 12	
Sutton Common	d	19 44		20 14		20 44		21 14		21 44		22 14	
St Helier	d	19 47		20 17		20 47		21 17		21 47		22 17	
Morden South	d	19 49		20 19		20 49		21 19		21 49		22 19	
South Merton	d	19 51		20 21		20 51		21 21		21 51		22 21	
Wimbledon Chase	d	19 53		20 23		20 53		21 23		21 53		22 23	
Wimbledon 6	a	19 56		20 26		20 56		21 26		21 56		22 26	
	d	19 57		20 27		20 57		21 27		21 57		22 27	
Haydons Road	d	19 59		20 29		20 59		21 29		21 59		22 29	
Tooting	d	20 02		20 32		21 02		21 32		22 02		22 32	
Streatham 4	d	20 07	20 25	20 37	20 55	21 07	21 25	21 37	21 55	22 07	22 25	22 37	22 55
Tulse Hill 3	a	20 11	20 29	20 41	20 59	21 11	21 29	21 41	21 59	22 11	22 29	22 41	22 59
	d	20 11	20 29	20 41	20 59	21 11	21 29	21 41	21 59	22 11	22 29	22 41	22 59
London Bridge 4	a												
Herne Hill 4	d	20 15	20 33	20 45	21 03	21 15	21 33	21 45	22 03	22 15	22 33	22 45	23 03
Loughborough Jn.	d	20 18	20 36	20 48	21 06	21 18	21 36	21 48	22 06	22 18	22 36	22 48	23 06
Elephant & Castle	d	20 23	20 41	20 53	21 11	21 23	21 41	21 53	22 11	22 23	22 41	22 53	23 11
London Blackfriars 3	d	20 28	20 46	20 58	21 16	21 28	21 46	21 58	22 16	22 28	22a45	22 58	23 16
City Thameslink 3	d												
Farringdon 3	d	20 32	20 50	21 02	21 20	21 32	21 50	22 02	22 20	22 32		23 02	23 20
St Pancras International 15	d	20 37	20 55	21 07	21 25	21 37	21 55	22 07	22 25	22 37		23 07	23 25
West Hampstead Thameslink	d	20 46	21 04	21 16	21 34	21 46	22 04	22 15	22a33	22 45		23 15	23 33
St Albans City	a	21 12	21 24	21 42	21 54	22 12	22 24	22 40		23 10		23 40	23 58

A To Luton

B To Bedford

For more London Bridge connections, refer to Table T173

Most Thameslink services from Blackfriars via Wimbledon and Hackbridge continue back towards Blackfriars.

Table T180-F

Mondays to Fridays

16 December to 15 May

London - Hackbridge, Sutton, Epsom, Leatherhead, Dorking and Horsham

Miles	Miles	Miles	Miles		SN MO	SN MO	SN MX	SW MX	SW MX	SW	SN	TL	SN	SN	TL	SW	SN	SW	SN	TL	SW	SN
0	—	—	0	London Victoria 15 ⊖ d							05 41			06 11			06 25		06 41			06 55
—	0	—	—	London Waterloo 15 ⊖ d					00 15	05 39						06 24		06 39			06 54	
2¾	4¼	—	2¾	Clapham Junction 10 d					00 26	05 48	05 48			06 18		06 33	06 32	06 48	06 48		07 03	07 02
4½	—	—	4½	Balham 4 ⊖ d							05 53			06 23					06 53			
—	—	0	—	St Pancras International d								05 27			05 57					06 27		
—	—	1¼	—	Farringdon d								05 32			06 02					06 32		
—	—	1¾	—	City Thameslink d								05 34			06 04					06 34		
—	—	2¼	—	London Blackfriars d								05 36			06 06					06 36		
—	—	3¼	—	Elephant & Castle d								05 40			06 10					06 40		
—	—	5¼	—	Loughborough Jn d								05 45			06 15					06 45		
—	—	6½	—	Herne Hill d								05 50			06 20					06 50		
—	—	—	—	London Bridge d									05 55									
—	—	7½	—	Tulse Hill a								05 54			06 24					06 54		
—	—	—	—	Tulse Hill 3 d								05 56			06 26					06 56		
—	—	9¼	—	Streatham d								06 00			06 30					07 00		
7¼	—	10¼	—	**Mitcham Eastfields** d							06 00	06 04		06 30	06 34				07 00	07 04		
8¼	—	11¼	—	**Mitcham Junction** d							06 03	06 07		06 33	06 37				07 03	07 07		
9½	—	12½	—	**Hackbridge** d							06 06	06 10		06 36	06 40				07 06	07 10		
10¼	—	13¼	—	**Carshalton** d							06 09	06 13		06 39	06 43		06 49		07 09	07 13		07 19
11½	—	14½	12¾	Sutton a							06 13	06 17		06 43	06 47		06 53		07 13	07 17		07 23
—	—	—	—	Norwood Junction d									06 09									
—	—	—	—	West Croydon d									06 15									
—	—	—	—	Sutton a									06 28									
—	—	—	—	Sutton d							06 13		06 28	06 43			06 54		07 13			07 24
12¾	—	—	—	**Cheam** d			00 02				06 16		06 31	06 46			06 57		07 16			07 27
14¼	—	—	—	**Ewell East** d	00 01		00 05				06 19		06 34	06 49					07 19			
15½	14¼	—	—	**Epsom** 3 a	00 05		00 09		00 51	06 13	06 23		06 38	06 53		06 58	07 03	07 13	07 23		07 28	07 33
—	—	—	—	**Epsom** d			00 09	00 19		06 13			06 39			06 58	07 04	07 13			07 28	07 34
17¼	16½	—	—	**Ashtead** d			00 14	00 23		06 17						07 02	07 09	07 17			07 32	07 39
19¼	18½	—	—	**Leatherhead** d		00 02	00 18	00a26		06a21			06a45			07 06	07 12	07a21			07 36	07 43
—	—	—	—	**Box Hill & Westhumble** d		00 07	00 23									07 11	07 17				07 41	
23½	—	—	—	**Dorking** 4 a		00 09	00 26									07 13	07 20				07 43	07 50
—	—	—	—	**Dorking** d			00 26										07 21					
28½	—	—	—	**Holmwood** d			00s33										07 28					
30¾	—	—	—	**Ockley** d			00s37										07 32					
35	—	—	—	**Warnham** d			00s43										07 38					
37¼	—	—	—	Horsham 4 a			00 48										07 46					

	SN	SW	SN	TL	SW	SN	SW	SN	TL	SW	SN	SN	SW	SN	TL	SW	SN	SN	SW	SN	TL	SW
London Victoria 15 ⊖ d			07 11			07 25		07 41			07 55			08 11			08 25			08 41		
London Waterloo 15 ⊖ d		07 09			07 24		07 39			07 54			08 09			08 24			08 39			08 54
Clapham Junction 10 d		07 18	07 18		07 33	07 32	07 48	07 48		08 03	08 02		08 18	08 18		08 33	08 32		08 48	08 48		09 03
Balham 4 ⊖ d			07 23					07 53						08 23						08 53		
St Pancras International d				06 57					07 27						07 57						08 27	
Farringdon d				07 02					07 32						08 02						08 32	
City Thameslink d				07 04					07 34						08 04						08 34	
London Blackfriars d				07 06					07 36						08 06						08 36	
Elephant & Castle d				07 10					07 40						08 10						08 40	
Loughborough Jn d				07 15					07 45						08 15						08 45	
Herne Hill d				07 20					07 50						08 20						08 50	
London Bridge d	06 55											07 55						08 25				
Tulse Hill a				07 24					07 54						08 24						08 54	
Tulse Hill 3 d				07 26					07 56						08 27						08 57	
Streatham d				07 30					08 00						08 30						09 00	
Mitcham Eastfields d			07 30	07 34				08 00	08 04					08 30	08 34					09 00	09 04	
Mitcham Junction d			07 33	07 37				08 03	08 07					08 33	08 37					09 03	09 07	
Hackbridge d			07 36	07 40				08 06	08 10					08 36	08 40					09 06	09 10	
Carshalton d			07 39	07 43		07 50		08 09	08 13		08 19			08 39	08 43		08 49			09 09	09 13	
Sutton a			07 43	07 47		07 53		08 13	08 17		08 23			08 43	08 47		08 53			09 13	09 17	
Norwood Junction d	07 09											08 09						08 39				
West Croydon d	07 16											08 16						08 45				
Sutton a	07 28											08 28						08 58				
Sutton d	07 28		07 43			07 54		08 13			08 24	08 28		08 43			08 54	08 58		09 13		
Cheam d	07 31		07 46			07 57		08 16			08 27	08 31		08 46			08 57	09 01		09 16		
Ewell East d	07 34		07 49					08 19				08 34		08 49				09 04		09 19		
Epsom 3 a	07 38	07 47	07 53		07 59	08 04	08 14	08 23		08 28	08 34	08 38	08 43	08 53		08 58	09 04	09 08	09 17	09 23		09 28
Epsom d		07 47			07 59	08 05	08 17			08 28	08 35		08 47			08 58	09 05		09 17			09 28
Ashtead d		07 51			08 02	08 10	08 21			08 32	08 40		08 51			09 02	09 10		09 21			09 32
Leatherhead d		07a55			08 06	08 14	08a25			08 36	08 44		08a55			09 06	09 14		09a25			09 36
Box Hill & Westhumble d					08 11	08 19				08 41						09 11	09 19					09 41
Dorking 4 a					08 14	08 21				08 43	08 51					09 13	09 21					09 43
Dorking d						08 22											09 22					
Holmwood d						08 29											09 29					
Ockley d						08 33											09 33					
Warnham d						08 39											09 39					
Horsham 4 a						08 43											09 43					

For faster trains from London and Clapham Junction to Horsham refer to Table T186

NRT DECEMBER 19 EDITION

Table T180-F

Mondays to Fridays

16 December to 15 May

London - Hackbridge, Sutton, Epsom, Leatherhead, Dorking and Horsham

	SN	SN	SW	SN	TL	SW	SN	SN	SW	SN	TL	SW	SN	SN	SW	SN	TL	SW	SN	SN	SW	SN
London Victoria 15 ⊖ d	08 55			09 11			09 25			09 41			09 55			10 11			10 25			10 41
London Waterloo 15 ⊖ d			09 09			09 24			09 39			09 54			10 09			10 24			10 39	
Clapham Junction 10 d	09 02		09 18	09 19		09 33	09 32		09 48	09 48		10 03	10 02		10 18	10 18		10 33	10 32		10 48	10 48
Balham 4 ⊖ d				09 24						09 53						10 23						10 53
St Pancras International d					08 57						09 27						09 57					
Farringdon d					09 02						09 32						10 02					
City Thameslink d					09 04						09 34						10 04					
London Blackfriars d					09 06						09 36						10 06					
Elephant & Castle d					09 10						09 40						10 10					
Loughborough Jn d					09 15						09 45						10 15					
Herne Hill d					09 20						09 50						10 20					
London Bridge d		08 55						09 25						09 55						10 25		
Tulse Hill a					09 24						09 54						10 24					
Tulse Hill 3 d					09 27						09 56						10 26					
Streatham d					09 30						10 00						10 30					
Mitcham Eastfields d				09 30	09 34					10 00	10 04					10 30	10 34					11 00
Mitcham Junction d				09 33	09 37					10 03	10 07					10 33	10 37					11 03
Hackbridge d				09 36	09 40					10 06	10 10					10 36	10 40					11 06
Carshalton d	09 19			09 39	09 43		09 49			10 09	10 13		10 19			10 39	10 43		10 49			11 09
Sutton a	09 23			09 43	09 47		09 53			10 13	10 17		10 23			10 43	10 47		10 53			11 13
Norwood Junction d		09 09						09 39						10 09						10 39		
West Croydon d		09 15						09 45						10 15						10 45		
Sutton a		09 28						09 58						10 28						10 58		
Sutton d	09 24	09 28		09 43			09 54	09 58		10 13			10 24	10 28		10 43			10 54	10 58		11 13
Cheam d	09 27	09 31		09 46			09 57	10 01		10 16			10 27	10 31		10 46			10 57	11 01		11 16
Ewell East d		09 34		09 49				10 04		10 19				10 34		10 49				11 04		11 19
Epsom 3 a	09 34	09 38	09 43	09 53		09 58	10 04	10 08	10 13	10 23		10 28	10 34	10 38	10 43	10 53		10 58	11 04	11 08	11 13	11 23
Epsom d	09 35		09 43			09 58	10 05		10 13			10 28	10 35		10 43			10 58	11 05		11 13	
Ashtead d	09 40		09 47			10 02	10 10		10 17			10 32	10 40		10 47			11 02	11 10		11 17	
Leatherhead d	09 44		09a51			10 06	10 14		10a21			10 36	10 44		10a51			11 06	11 13		11a21	
Box Hill & Westhumble d						10 11	10 19					10 41						11 11	11 18			
Dorking 4 a	09 51					10 13	10 21					10 43	10 51					11 13	11 21			
Dorking d							10 22												11 22			
Holmwood d							10 29												11 29			
Ockley d							10 33												11 33			
Warnham d							10 39												11 39			
Horsham 4 a							10 43												11 43			

	TL	SW	SN	SN	SW	SN	TL	SW	SN	SN	SW	SN	TL	SW	SN	SN	SW	SN	TL	SW	SN
London Victoria 15 ⊖ d			10 55			11 11			11 25			11 41			11 55			12 11			12 25
London Waterloo 15 ⊖ d		10 54			11 09			11 24			11 39			11 54			12 09			12 24	
Clapham Junction 10 d		11 03	11 02		11 18	11 18		11 33	11 32		11 48	11 48		12 03	12 02		12 18	12 18		12 33	12 32
Balham 4 ⊖ d						11 23						11 53						12 23			
St Pancras International d	10 27						10 57						11 27						11 57		
Farringdon d	10 32						11 02						11 32						12 02		
City Thameslink d	10 34						11 04						11 34						12 04		
London Blackfriars d	10 36						11 06						11 36						12 06		
Elephant & Castle d	10 40						11 10						11 40						12 10		
Loughborough Jn d	10 45						11 15						11 45						12 15		
Herne Hill d	10 50						11 20						11 50						12 20		
London Bridge d				10 55						11 25						11 55					
Tulse Hill a	10 54						11 24						11 54						12 24		
Tulse Hill 3 d	10 56						11 26						11 56						12 26		
Streatham d	11 00						11 30						12 00						12 30		
Mitcham Eastfields d	11 04					11 30	11 34					12 00	12 04					12 30	12 34		
Mitcham Junction d	11 07					11 33	11 37					12 03	12 07					12 33	12 37		
Hackbridge d	11 10					11 36	11 40					12 06	12 10					12 36	12 40		
Carshalton d	11 13		11 19			11 39	11 43		11 49			12 09	12 13		12 19			12 39	12 43		12 49
Sutton a	11 17		11 23			11 43	11 47		11 53			12 13	12 17		12 23			12 43	12 47		12 53
Norwood Junction d				11 09						11 39						12 09					
West Croydon d				11 15						11 45						12 15					
Sutton a				11 28						11 58						12 28					
Sutton d			11 24	11 28		11 43			11 54	11 58		12 13			12 24	12 28		12 43			12 54
Cheam d			11 27	11 31		11 46			11 57	12 01		12 16			12 27	12 31		12 46			12 57
Ewell East d				11 34		11 49				12 04		12 19				12 34		12 49			
Epsom 3 a		11 28	11 34	11 38	11 43	11 53		11 58	12 04	12 08	12 12	12 23		12 28	12 34	12 38	12 43	12 53		12 58	13 04
Epsom d		11 28	11 35		11 43			11 58	12 05		12 13			12 28	12 35		12 43			12 58	13 05
Ashtead d		11 32	11 40		11 47			12 02	12 10		12 17			12 32	12 40		12 47			13 02	13 10
Leatherhead d		11 36	11 43		11a51			12 06	12 14		12a21			12 36	12 44		12a51			13 06	13 14
Box Hill & Westhumble d		11 41						12 11	12 19					12 41						13 11	13 19
Dorking 4 a		11 43	11 51					12 13	12 21					12 43	12 51					13 13	13 21
Dorking d									12 22												13 22
Holmwood d									12 29												13 29
Ockley d									12 33												13 33
Warnham d									12 39												13 39
Horsham 4 a									12 43												13 43

For faster trains from London and Clapham Junction to Horsham refer to Table T186

Table T180-F

Mondays to Fridays

16 December to 15 May

London - Hackbridge, Sutton, Epsom, Leatherhead, Dorking and Horsham

		SN	SW	SN	TL	SW	SN	SN		SW	SN	TL	SW	SN	SN	SW	SN	TL		SW	SN	SN	SW	SN	TL
London Victoria 15 ⊖	d			12 41			12 55				13 11			13 25			13 41				13 55			14 11	
London Waterloo 15 ⊖	d		12 39			12 54				13 09			13 24			13 39				13 54			14 09		
Clapham Junction 10	d		12 48	12 48		13 03	13 02			13 18	13 18		13 33	13 32		13 48	13 48			14 03	14 02		14 18	14 18	
Balham 4 ⊖	d			12 54							13 23						13 53							14 23	
St Pancras International	d				12 27							12 57						13 27							13 57
Farringdon	d				12 32							13 02						13 32							14 02
City Thameslink	d				12 34							13 04						13 34							14 04
London Blackfriars	d				12 36							13 06						13 36							14 06
Elephant & Castle	d				12 40							13 10						13 40							14 10
Loughborough Jn	d				12 45							13 15						13 45							14 15
Herne Hill	d				12 50							13 20						13 50							14 20
London Bridge	d	12 25						12 55							13 25							13 55			
Tulse Hill	a				12 54							13 24						13 54							14 24
Tulse Hill 3	d				12 56							13 26						13 56							14 26
Streatham	d				13 00							13 30						14 00							14 30
Mitcham Eastfields	d			13 01	13 04						13 30	13 34					14 00	14 04						14 30	14 34
Mitcham Junction	d			13 04	13 07						13 33	13 37					14 03	14 07						14 33	14 37
Hackbridge	d			13 07	13 10						13 36	13 40					14 06	14 10						14 36	14 40
Carshalton	d			13 09	13 13		13 19				13 39	13 43		13 49			14 09	14 13			14 19			14 39	14 43
Sutton	a			13 13	13 17		13 23				13 43	13 47		13 53			14 13	14 17			14 23			14 43	14 47
Norwood Junction	d	12 39						13 09							13 39							14 09			
West Croydon	d	12 45						13 15							13 45							14 15			
Sutton	a	12 58						13 28							13 58							14 28			
Sutton	d	12 58		13 13			13 24	13 28			13 43			13 54	13 58		14 13				14 24	14 28		14 43	
Cheam	d	13 01		13 16			13 27	13 31			13 46			13 57	14 01		14 16				14 27	14 31		14 46	
Ewell East	d	13 04		13 19				13 34			13 49				14 04		14 19					14 34		14 49	
Epsom 3	a	13 08	13 13	13 23		13 28	13 34	13 38		13 43	13 53		13 59	14 04	14 08	14 13	14 23			14 28	14 34	14 38	14 43	14 53	
Epsom	d		13 13			13 28	13 35			13 43			14 00	14 05		14 13				14 28	14 35		14 43		
Ashtead	d		13 17			13 32	13 40			13 47			14 04	14 10		14 17				14 32	14 40		14 47		
Leatherhead	d		13a21			13 36	13 44			13a51			14 07	14 14		14a21				14 36	14 44		14a51		
Box Hill & Westhumble	d					13 41							14 12	14 19						14 41					
Dorking 4	a					13 43	13 51						14 15	14 21						14 43	14 51				
Dorking	d													14 22											
Holmwood	d													14 29											
Ockley	d													14 33											
Warnham	d													14 39											
Horsham 4	a													14 43											

		SW	SN	SN		SW	SN	TL	SW	SN	SN	SW	SN	TL		SW	SN	SN	SW	SN	TL	SW	SN	SN	
London Victoria 15 ⊖	d		14 25				14 41			14 55			15 11				15 25			15 41			15 55		
London Waterloo 15 ⊖	d	14 24				14 39			14 54			15 09				15 24			15 39			15 54			
Clapham Junction 10	d	14 33	14 32			14 48	14 48		15 03	15 02		15 18	15 18			15 33	15 32		15 48	15 48		16 03	16 02		
Balham 4 ⊖	d						14 53						15 23							15 53					
St Pancras International	d							14 27						14 57							15 27				
Farringdon	d							14 32						15 02							15 32				
City Thameslink	d							14 34						15 04							15 34				
London Blackfriars	d							14 36						15 06							15 36				
Elephant & Castle	d							14 40						15 10							15 40				
Loughborough Jn	d							14 45						15 15							15 45				
Herne Hill	d							14 50						15 20							15 50				
London Bridge	d			14 25							14 55							15 25						15 55	
Tulse Hill	a							14 54						15 24							15 54				
Tulse Hill 3	d							14 56						15 26							15 56				
Streatham	d							15 00						15 30							16 00				
Mitcham Eastfields	d						15 00	15 04					15 30	15 34						16 00	16 04				
Mitcham Junction	d						15 03	15 07					15 33	15 37						16 03	16 07				
Hackbridge	d						15 06	15 10					15 36	15 40						16 06	16 10				
Carshalton	d		14 49				15 09	15 13		15 19			15 39	15 43			15 49			16 09	16 13		16 19		
Sutton	a		14 53				15 13	15 17		15 23			15 43	15 47			15 53			16 13	16 17		16 23		
Norwood Junction	d			14 39							15 09							15 39						16 09	
West Croydon	d			14 45							15 15							15 45						16 15	
Sutton	a			14 58							15 28							15 58						16 28	
Sutton	d		14 54	14 58			15 13			15 24	15 28		15 43				15 54	15 58		16 13			16 24	16 28	
Cheam	d		14 57	15 01			15 16			15 27	15 31		15 46				15 57	16 01		16 16			16 27	16 31	
Ewell East	d			15 04			15 19				15 34		15 49					16 04		16 19				16 34	
Epsom 3	a	14 58	15 04	15 08		15 13	15 23		15 28	15 34	15 38	15 43	15 53			15 58	16 04	16 08	16 13	16 23		16 28	16 34	16 38	
Epsom	d	14 58	15 05			15 13			15 28	15 35		15 43				15 58	16 05		16 13			16 28	16 35		
Ashtead	d	15 02	15 10			15 17			15 32	15 40		15 47				16 02	16 10		16 17			16 32	16 40		
Leatherhead	d	15 06	15 14			15a21			15 36	15 44		15a51				16 06	16 14		16a21			16 36	16 44		
Box Hill & Westhumble	d	15 11	15 19						15 41							16 11	16 19					16 41			
Dorking 4	a	15 13	15 21						15 43	15 51						16 13	16 22					16 43	16 51		
Dorking	d		15 22														16 22								
Holmwood	d		15 29														16 29								
Ockley	d		15 33														16 33								
Warnham	d		15 39														16 39								
Horsham 4	a		15 43														16 43								

For faster trains from London and Clapham Junction to Horsham refer to Table T186

Table T180-F

Mondays to Fridays

16 December to 15 May

London - Hackbridge, Sutton, Epsom, Leatherhead, Dorking and Horsham

		SW	SN	TL	SW	SN	SN	SW	SN	TL		SW	SN	SN	SN	SW	SN	TL	SW	SN		SN	SW	SN	SW
London Victoria 15 ⊖	d		16 12			16 25			16 41				16 55				17 11			17 25					
London Waterloo 15 ⊖	d	16 09			16 24			16 39				16 54				17 09			17 24				17 31		17 39
Clapham Junction 10	d	16 18	16 19		16 33	16 32		16 48	16 48			17 03	17 02			17 18	17 18		17 33	17 32			17 40		17 49
Balham 4 ⊖	d		16 24						16 53								17 23								
St Pancras International	d			15 57						16 27								16 57							
Farringdon	d			16 02						16 32								17 02							
City Thameslink	d			16 04						16 34								17 04							
London Blackfriars	d			16 06						16 36								17 06							
Elephant & Castle	d			16 10						16 40								17 10							
Loughborough Jn	d			16 15						16 45								17 15							
Herne Hill	d			16 20						16 50								17 20							
London Bridge	d						16 25							16 52	16 55							17 22		17 25	
Tulse Hill	a			16 24						16 54				17 14				17 24				17 44			
Tulse Hill 3	d			16 26						16 56				17 16				17 26				17 46			
Streatham	d			16 30						17 00				17 20				17 30				17 50			
Mitcham Eastfields	d		16 30	16 34					17 00	17 04				17 24			17 30	17 34		17 43		17 54			
Mitcham Junction	d		16 33	16 37					17 03	17 07				17 27			17 33	17 37		17 46		17 57			
Hackbridge	d		16 36	16 40					17 06	17 10				17 30			17 36	17 40		17 49		18 00			
Carshalton	d		16 39	16 43		16 49			17 09	17 13			17 19	17 33			17 39	17 43		17 52		18 03			
Sutton	a		16 43	16 47		16 53			17 13	17 17			17 23	17 37			17 43	17 47		17 56		18 07			
Norwood Junction	d						16 39								17 09									17 39	
West Croydon	d						16 46								17 16									17 46	
Sutton	a						16 58								17 28									17 59	
Sutton	d		16 43			16 54	16 58		17 13				17 24		17 28		17 43			17 56				18 00	
Cheam	d		16 46			16 57	17 01		17 16				17 27		17 31		17 46			17 59				18 03	
Ewell East	d		16 49				17 04		17 19						17 34		17 49							18 06	
Epsom 3	a	16 43	16 53		16 58	17 04	17 08	17 13	17 23			17 28	17 34		17 38	17 43	17 53		17 57	18 05			18 08	18 10	18 19
Epsom	d	16 43			16 58	17 05		17 17				17 28	17 35		17 39	17 47			17 57	18 05				18 10	18 19
Ashtead	d	16 47			17 02	17 10		17 21				17 32	17 40		17 44	17 51			18 01	18 10				18 15	18 23
Leatherhead	d	16a51			17 06	17 14		17a24				17 36	17 44		17 48	17a55			18 05	18 14				18a18	18a27
Box Hill & Westhumble	d				17 11	17 19						17 41	17 49						18 10	18 19					
Dorking 4	a				17 13	17 22						17 43	17 52		17 55				18 15	18 21					
Dorking	d					17 22							17 52							18 22					
Holmwood	d					17 29							17 59							18 29					
Ockley	d					17 34							18 04							18 34					
Warnham	d					17 41							18 11							18 41					
Horsham 4	a					17 47							18 17							18 47					

		SN	TL	SW	SN	SN		SW	SN	SW	SN	TL	SW	SN	SN	SW		SN	SW	SN	TL	SW	SN	SW	SN
London Victoria 15 ⊖	d	17 41			17 55						18 11			18 26						18 41			18 55		
London Waterloo 15 ⊖	d			17 54				18 01		18 09			18 24			18 31			18 40			18 54		19 01	
Clapham Junction 10	d	17 48		18 03	18 02			18 10		18 19	18 18		18 33	18 33		18 40			18 49	18 48		19 03	19 02	19 10	
Balham 4 ⊖	d	17 53									18 23									18 53					
St Pancras International	d		17 27									17 57									18 27				
Farringdon	d		17 32									18 02									18 32				
City Thameslink	d		17 34									18 04									18 34				
London Blackfriars	d		17 36									18 06									18 36				
Elephant & Castle	d		17 40									18 10									18 40				
Loughborough Jn	d		17 45									18 15									18 45				
Herne Hill	d		17 50									18 20									18 50				
London Bridge	d					17 52			17 55						18 22			18 25							18 55
Tulse Hill	a		17 54			18 14						18 24			18 44						18 54				
Tulse Hill 3	d		17 56			18 16						18 26			18 46						18 56				
Streatham	d		18 00			18 20						18 30			18 50						19 00				
Mitcham Eastfields	d	18 00	18 04		18 13	18 24					18 30	18 34		18 43	18 54					19 00	19 04		19 13		
Mitcham Junction	d	18 03	18 07		18 16	18 27					18 33	18 37		18 46	18 57					19 03	19 07		19 16		
Hackbridge	d	18 06	18 10		18 19	18 30					18 36	18 40		18 49	19 00					19 06	19 10		19 19		
Carshalton	d	18 09	18 13		18 22	18 33					18 39	18 43		18 52	19 03					19 09	19 13		19 22		
Sutton	a	18 13	18 17		18 25	18 37					18 43	18 47		18 55	19 07					19 13	19 17		19 25		
Norwood Junction	d								18 09									18 39							19 09
West Croydon	d								18 16									18 46							19 15
Sutton	a								18 29									18 59							19 29
Sutton	d	18 13			18 26				18 30		18 43			18 56				19 00		19 13			19 26		19 30
Cheam	d	18 16			18 29				18 33		18 46			18 59				19 03		19 16			19 29		19 33
Ewell East	d	18 19							18 36		18 49							19 06		19 19					19 36
Epsom 3	a	18 23		18 27	18 35			18 38	18 40	18 50	18 53		18 57	19 05		19 08		19 10	19 19	19 23		19 30	19 35	19 38	19 40
Epsom	d			18 27	18 35				18 40	18 53			18 57	19 05				19 10	19 20			19 31	19 35		19 40
Ashtead	d			18 31	18 40				18 45	18 57			19 01	19 10				19 15	19 24			19 35	19 41		19 45
Leatherhead	d			18 35	18 44				18 49	19a00			19 05	19 14				19 19	19a27			19 38	19 44		19a48
Box Hill & Westhumble	d			18 40	18 49								19 10	19 19								19 43			
Dorking 4	a			18 45	18 51				18 55				19 13	19 21				19 25				19 46	19 52		
Dorking	d				18 52									19 22											
Holmwood	d				18 59									19 29											
Ockley	d				19 03									19 33											
Warnham	d				19 09									19 39											
Horsham 4	a				19 15									19 45											

For faster trains from London and Clapham Junction to Horsham refer to Table T186

Table T180-F

Mondays to Fridays
16 December to 15 May

London - Hackbridge, Sutton, Epsom, Leatherhead, Dorking and Horsham

		SW		SN	TL	SW	SN	SN	SW	SN	TL	SW		SN	SN	SW	SN	TL	SW	SN	SN	SW		SN	TL
London Victoria 15 ⊖	d			19 11			19 25			19 41				19 55			20 11			20 25				20 41	
London Waterloo 15 ⊖	d	19 09				19 24			19 38			19 54				20 09			20 24			20 39			
Clapham Junction 10	d	19 19		19 18		19 33	19 32		19 48	19 48		20 03		20 02		20 18	20 18		20 33	20 32		20 48		20 48	
Balham 4 ⊖	d			19 23						19 53							20 23							20 53	
St Pancras International	d				18 57						19 27							19 57							20 27
Farringdon	d				19 02						19 32							20 02							20 32
City Thameslink	d				19 04						19 34							20 04							20 34
London Blackfriars	d				19 06						19 36							20 06							20 36
Elephant & Castle	d				19 10						19 40							20 10							20 40
Loughborough Jn	d				19 15						19 45							20 15							20 45
Herne Hill	d				19 20						19 50							20 20							20 50
London Bridge	d							19 25							19 55						20 25				
Tulse Hill	a				19 24						19 54							20 24							20 54
Tulse Hill 3	d				19 26						19 56							20 26							20 56
Streatham	d				19 30						20 00							20 30							21 00
Mitcham Eastfields	d			19 30	19 34					20 00	20 04						20 30	20 34						21 00	21 04
Mitcham Junction	d			19 33	19 37					20 03	20 07						20 33	20 37						21 03	21 07
Hackbridge	d			19 36	19 40					20 06	20 10						20 36	20 40						21 06	21 10
Carshalton	d			19 39	19 43		19 49			20 09	20 13			20 19			20 39	20 43		20 49				21 09	21 13
Sutton	a			19 43	19 47		19 53			20 13	20 17			20 24			20 43	20 47		20 53				21 13	21 17
Norwood Junction	d							19 39							20 09						20 39				
West Croydon	d							19 45							20 15						20 45				
Sutton	a							19 58							20 28						20 58				
Sutton	d			19 43			19 54	19 58		20 13				20 24	20 28		20 43			20 54	20 58			21 13	
Cheam	d			19 46			19 57	20 01		20 16				20 27	20 31		20 46			20 57	21 01			21 16	
Ewell East	d			19 49				20 04		20 19					20 34		20 49				21 04			21 19	
Epsom 3	a	19 48		19 53		19 58	20 04	20 08	20 13	20 23		20 28		20 34	20 38	20 43	20 53		20 58	21 05	21 08	21 13		21 23	
Epsom	d	19 50				19 58	20 05		20 13			20 28		20 35		20 43			20 58	21 05		21 13			
Ashtead	d	19 54				20 02	20 10		20 17			20 32		20 40		20 47			21 02	21 10		21 17			
Leatherhead	d	19a57				20 06	20 14		20a21			20 36		20 43		20a51			21 06	21 14		21a21			
Box Hill & Westhumble	d					20 11	20 19					20 41							21 11	21 19					
Dorking 4	a					20 13	20 22					20 43		20 51					21 13	21 22					
Dorking	d						20 22													21 22					
Holmwood	d						20 29													21 29					
Ockley	d						20 33													21 33					
Warnham	d						20 39													21 39					
Horsham 4	a						20 45													21 43					

		SW	SN	SN	SW	SN	TL	SW		SN	SN	SW	SN	TL	SW	SN	SN	SW		SN	TL	SN	SN	SW	SN
London Victoria 15 ⊖	d		20 55			21 11				21 25			21 41			21 55				22 11		22 25			22 41
London Waterloo 15 ⊖	d	20 54			21 09			21 24				21 39			21 54			22 09						22 39	
Clapham Junction 10	d	21 03	21 02		21 18	21 18		21 33		21 32		21 48	21 48		22 03	22 03		22 18		22 18		22 32		22 48	22 48
Balham 4 ⊖	d					21 23							21 54							22 23					22 53
St Pancras International	d						20 57							21 27							21 57				
Farringdon	d						21 02							21 32							22 02				
City Thameslink	d						21 04							21 34							22 04				
London Blackfriars	d						21 06							21 36							22 06				
Elephant & Castle	d						21 10							21 40							22 10				
Loughborough Jn	d						21 15							21 45							22 15				
Herne Hill	d						21 20							21 50							22 20				
London Bridge	d			20 55							21 25						21 55						22 25		
Tulse Hill	a						21 24							21 54							22 24				
Tulse Hill 3	d						21 26							21 56							22 26				
Streatham	d						21 30							22 00							22 30				
Mitcham Eastfields	d					21 30	21 34						22 01	22 04						22 30	22 34				23 00
Mitcham Junction	d					21 33	21 37						22 04	22 07						22 33	22 37				23 03
Hackbridge	d					21 36	21 40						22 07	22 10						22 36	22 40				23 06
Carshalton	d		21 19			21 39	21 43			21 49			22 09	22 13		22 20				22 39	22 43	22 49			23 09
Sutton	a		21 23			21 43	21 47			21 53			22 13	22 17		22 24				22 43	22 47	22 53			23 13
Norwood Junction	d			21 09							21 39						22 09						22 39		
West Croydon	d			21 15							21 45						22 15						22 45		
Sutton	a			21 28							21 58						22 28						22 58		
Sutton	d		21 24	21 28		21 43				21 54	21 58		22 13			22 25	22 28			22 43		22 54	22 58		23 13
Cheam	d		21 27	21 31		21 46				21 57	22 01		22 16			22 28	22 31			22 46		22 57	23 01		23 16
Ewell East	d			21 34		21 49					22 04		22 19				22 34			22 49			23 04		23 19
Epsom 3	a	21 28	21 34	21 38	21 43	21 53		21 58		22 04	22 08	22 13	22 23		22 28	22 34	22 38	22 43		22 53		23 04	23 08	23 13	23 23
Epsom	d	21 28	21 35		21 43			21 58		22 05		22 13				22 35		22 43				23 05		23 13	
Ashtead	d	21 32	21 40		21 47			22 02		22 10		22 17				22 40		22 47				23 10		23 17	
Leatherhead	d	21 36	21 44		21a51			22 06		22 14		22a21				22 44		22 51				23 14		23a21	
Box Hill & Westhumble	d	21 41						22 11		22 19								22 56				23 19			
Dorking 4	a	21 43	21 51					22 13		22 22						22 51		22 58				23 22			
Dorking	d									22 22												23 22			
Holmwood	d									22 29												23 29			
Ockley	d									22 33												23 33			
Warnham	d									22 39												23 39			
Horsham 4	a									22 43												23 43			

For faster trains from London and Clapham Junction to Horsham refer to Table T186

Table T180-F

Mondays to Fridays
16 December to 15 May

London - Hackbridge, Sutton, Epsom, Leatherhead, Dorking and Horsham

		TL	SN	SN		SW	SN	TL	SN	SW
London Victoria 15 ⊖	d		22 56				23 11		23 25	
London Waterloo 15 ⊖	d					23 09				23 42
Clapham Junction 10	d		23 03			23 18	23 18		23 32	23 51
Balham 4 ⊖	d						23 23		23 37	
St Pancras International	d	22 27						22 57		
Farringdon	d	22 32						23 02		
City Thameslink	d	22 34								
London Blackfriars	d	22 36						23 06		
Elephant & Castle	d	22 40						23 10		
Loughborough Jn	d	22 45						23 15		
Herne Hill	d	22 50						23 20		
London Bridge	d			22 55						
Tulse Hill	a	22 54						23 24		
Tulse Hill 3	d	22 56						23 26		
Streatham	d	23 00						23 30		
Mitcham Eastfields	d	23 04					23 30	23 34	23 45	
Mitcham Junction	d	23 07					23 33	23 37	23 48	
Hackbridge	d	23 10					23 36	23 40	23 51	
Carshalton	d	23 13	23 19				23 39	23 43	23 54	
Sutton	a	23 17	23 23				23 43	23 47	23 58	
Norwood Junction	d			23 09						
West Croydon	d			23 15						
Sutton	a			23 28						
Sutton	d		23 24	23 28			23 43		23 59	
Cheam	d		23 27	23 31			23 46		00 02	
Ewell East	d			23 34			23 49		00 05	
Epsom 3	a		23 34	23 38		23 43	23 53		00 09	00 16
Epsom	d		23 35			23 43			00 09	00 19
Ashtead	d		23 40			23 47			00 14	00 23
Leatherhead	d		23 43			23 51			00 18	00a26
Box Hill & Westhumble	d					23 56			00 23	
Dorking 4	a		23 51			23 58			00 26	
Dorking	d								00 26	
Holmwood	d								00s33	
Ockley	d								00s37	
Warnham	d								00s43	
Horsham 4	a								00 48	

Saturdays
21 December to 16 May

		SN	SW	SW	SN	TL	SN	TL	SN	SW		SN	TL	SN	SN	SW	SN	TL	SW	SN		SN	SW	SN	TL
London Victoria 15 ⊖	d				00 20		06 11		06 25			06 41		06 55			07 11			07 25				07 41	
London Waterloo 15 ⊖	d			00 15						06 39						07 09			07 24				07 39		
Clapham Junction 10	d			00 26	00 27		06 18		06 32	06 48		06 48		07 02		07 18	07 18		07 33	07 32			07 48	07 48	
Balham 4 ⊖	d				00 33		06 23					06 53					07 23							07 53	
St Pancras International	d					05 27		05 57					06 27					06 57							07 27
Farringdon	d					05 32		06 02					06 32					07 02							07 32
City Thameslink	d																								
London Blackfriars	d					05 36		06 06					06 36					07 06							07 36
Elephant & Castle	d					05 40		06 10					06 40					07 10							07 40
Loughborough Jn	d					05 45		06 15					06 45					07 15							07 45
Herne Hill	d					05 50		06 20					06 50					07 20							07 50
London Bridge	d														06 55							07 25			
Tulse Hill	a					05 54		06 24					06 54					07 24							07 54
Tulse Hill 3	d					05 56		06 26					06 56					07 26							07 56
Streatham	d					06 00		06 30					07 00					07 30							08 00
Mitcham Eastfields	d				00 40	06 04	06 30	06 34				07 00	07 04				07 30	07 34						08 00	08 04
Mitcham Junction	d				00 43	06 07	06 33	06 37				07 03	07 07				07 33	07 37						08 03	08 07
Hackbridge	d				00 46	06 10	06 36	06 40				07 06	07 10				07 36	07 40						08 06	08 10
Carshalton	d				00 49	06 13	06 39	06 43	06 49			07 09	07 13	07 19			07 39	07 43		07 49				08 09	08 13
Sutton	a				00 53	06 17	06 43	06 47	06 53			07 13	07 17	07 23			07 43	07 47		07 53				08 13	08 17
Norwood Junction	d														07 09							07 39			
West Croydon	d														07 15							07 45			
Sutton	a														07 28							07 58			
Sutton	d				00 53		06 43		06 54			07 13		07 24	07 28		07 43			07 54		07 58		08 13	
Cheam	d	00 02			00 56		06 46		06 57			07 16		07 27	07 31		07 46			07 57		08 01		08 16	
Ewell East	d	00 05			00 59		06 49					07 19			07 34		07 49					08 04		08 19	
Epsom 3	a	00 09		00 51	01 03		06 53		07 04	07 13		07 23		07 34	07 38	07 43	07 53		07 58	08 04		08 08	08 13	08 23	
Epsom	d	00 09	00 19						07 05	07 13				07 35		07 43			07 58	08 05			08 13		
Ashtead	d	00 14	00 23						07 10	07 17				07 40		07 47			08 02	08 10			08 17		
Leatherhead	d	00 18	00a26						07 13	07a21				07 44		07a51			08 06	08 14			08a21		
Box Hill & Westhumble	d	00 23							07 18										08 11	08 19					
Dorking 4	a	00 26							07 21					07 51					08 13	08 21					
Dorking	d	00 26																		08 22					
Holmwood	d	00s33																		08 29					
Ockley	d	00s37																		08 33					
Warnham	d	00s43																		08 39					
Horsham 4	a	00 48																		08 43					

For faster trains from London and Clapham Junction to Horsham refer to Table T186

Table T180-F

Saturdays
21 December to 16 May

London - Hackbridge, Sutton, Epsom, Leatherhead, Dorking and Horsham

		SW	SN	SN	SW	SN		TL	SW	SN	SN	SW	SN	TL	SW	SN		SN	SW	SN	TL	SW	SN	SN	SW
London Victoria 15 ⊖	d		07 55			08 11				08 25			08 41			08 55				09 11			09 25		
London Waterloo 15 ⊖	d	07 54			08 09				08 24			08 39			08 54				09 09			09 24			09 39
Clapham Junction 10	d	08 03	08 02		08 18	08 18			08 33	08 32		08 48	08 48		09 03	09 02			09 18	09 18		09 33	09 32		09 48
Balham 4 ⊖	d					08 23							08 53							09 23					
St Pancras International	d							07 57						08 27							08 57				
Farringdon	d							08 02						08 32							09 02				
City Thameslink	d																				09 04				
London Blackfriars	d							08 06						08 36							09 06				
Elephant & Castle	d							08 10						08 40							09 10				
Loughborough Jn	d							08 15						08 45							09 15				
Herne Hill	d							08 20						08 50							09 20				
London Bridge	d			07 55							08 25							08 55						09 25	
Tulse Hill	a							08 24						08 54							09 24				
Tulse Hill 3	d							08 26						08 56							09 26				
Streatham	d							08 30						09 00							09 30				
Mitcham Eastfields	d					08 30		08 34					09 00	09 04						09 30	09 34				
Mitcham Junction	d					08 33		08 37					09 03	09 07						09 33	09 37				
Hackbridge	d					08 36		08 40					09 06	09 10						09 36	09 40				
Carshalton	d		08 19			08 39		08 43		08 49			09 09	09 13		09 19				09 39	09 43		09 49		
Sutton	a		08 23			08 43		08 47		08 53			09 13	09 17		09 23				09 43	09 47		09 53		
Norwood Junction	d			08 09							08 39							09 09						09 39	
West Croydon	d			08 15							08 45							09 15						09 45	
Sutton	a			08 28							08 58							09 28						09 58	
Sutton	d		08 24	08 28		08 43				08 54	08 58		09 13			09 24		09 28		09 43			09 54	09 58	
Cheam	d		08 27	08 31		08 46				08 57	09 01		09 16			09 27		09 31		09 46			09 57	10 01	
Ewell East	d			08 34		08 49					09 04		09 19					09 34		09 49				10 04	
Epsom 3	a	08 28	08 34	08 38	08 43	08 53			08 58	09 04	09 08	09 13	09 23		09 28	09 34		09 38	09 43	09 53		09 58	10 04	10 08	10 13
Epsom	d	08 28	08 35		08 43				08 58	09 05		09 13			09 28	09 35			09 43			09 58	10 05		10 13
Ashtead	d	08 32	08 40		08 47				09 02	09 10		09 17			09 32	09 40			09 47			10 02	10 10		10 17
Leatherhead	d	08 36	08 44		08a51				09 06	09 14		09a21			09 36	09 44			09a51			10 06	10 14		10a21
Box Hill & Westhumble	d	08 41							09 11	09 19					09 41							10 11	10 19		
Dorking 4	a	08 43	08 51						09 13	09 21					09 43	09 51						10 13	10 21		
Dorking	d									09 22													10 22		
Holmwood	d									09 29													10 29		
Ockley	d									09 33													10 33		
Warnham	d									09 39													10 39		
Horsham 4	a									09 43													10 43		

		SN		TL	SW	SN	SN	SW	SN	TL	SW	SN		SN	SW	SN	TL	SW	SN	SN	SW	SN		TL	SW
London Victoria 15 ⊖	d	09 41				09 55			10 11			10 25				10 41			10 55			11 11			
London Waterloo 15 ⊖	d				09 54			10 09			10 24				10 39			10 54			11 09				11 24
Clapham Junction 10	d	09 48			10 03	10 02		10 18	10 18		10 33	10 32			10 48	10 48		11 03	11 02		11 18	11 18			11 33
Balham 4 ⊖	d	09 53							10 23							10 53						11 23			
St Pancras International	d			09 27						09 57							10 27							10 57	
Farringdon	d			09 32						10 02							10 32							11 02	
City Thameslink	d			09 34						10 04							10 34							11 04	
London Blackfriars	d			09 36						10 06							10 36							11 06	
Elephant & Castle	d			09 40						10 10							10 40							11 10	
Loughborough Jn	d			09 45						10 15							10 45							11 15	
Herne Hill	d			09 50						10 20							10 50							11 20	
London Bridge	d						09 55							10 25						10 55					
Tulse Hill	a			09 54						10 24							10 54							11 24	
Tulse Hill 3	d			09 56						10 26							10 56							11 26	
Streatham	d			10 00						10 30							11 00							11 30	
Mitcham Eastfields	d	10 00		10 04					10 30	10 34						11 00	11 04					11 30		11 34	
Mitcham Junction	d	10 03		10 07					10 33	10 37						11 03	11 07					11 33		11 37	
Hackbridge	d	10 06		10 10					10 36	10 40						11 06	11 10					11 36		11 40	
Carshalton	d	10 09		10 13		10 19			10 39	10 43		10 49				11 09	11 13		11 19			11 39		11 43	
Sutton	a	10 13		10 17		10 23			10 43	10 47		10 53				11 13	11 17		11 23			11 43		11 47	
Norwood Junction	d						10 09							10 39						11 09					
West Croydon	d						10 15							10 45						11 15					
Sutton	a						10 28							10 58						11 28					
Sutton	d	10 13				10 24	10 28		10 43			10 54		10 58		11 13			11 24	11 28		11 43			
Cheam	d	10 16				10 27	10 31		10 46			10 57		11 01		11 16			11 27	11 31		11 46			
Ewell East	d	10 19					10 34		10 49					11 04		11 19				11 34		11 49			
Epsom 3	a	10 23			10 28	10 34	10 38	10 43	10 53		10 58	11 04		11 08	11 13	11 23		11 28	11 34	11 38	11 43	11 53			11 58
Epsom	d				10 28	10 35		10 43			10 58	11 05			11 13			11 28	11 35		11 43				11 58
Ashtead	d				10 32	10 40		10 47			11 02	11 10			11 17			11 32	11 40		11 47				12 02
Leatherhead	d				10 36	10 44		10a51			11 06	11 14			11a21			11 36	11 44		11a51				12 06
Box Hill & Westhumble	d				10 41						11 11	11 19						11 41							12 11
Dorking 4	a				10 43	10 51					11 13	11 21						11 43	11 51						12 13
Dorking	d											11 22													
Holmwood	d											11 29													
Ockley	d											11 33													
Warnham	d											11 39													
Horsham 4	a											11 43													

For faster trains from London and Clapham Junction to Horsham refer to Table T186

Table T180-F

Saturdays
21 December to 16 May

London - Hackbridge, Sutton, Epsom, Leatherhead, Dorking and Horsham

		SN	SN	SW	SN	TL	SW	SN		SN	SW	SN	TL	SW	SN	SN	SW	SN		TL	SW	SN	SN	SW	SN
London Victoria 15 ⊖	d	11 25			11 41			11 55				12 11			12 25			12 41				12 55			13 11
London Waterloo 15 ⊖	d			11 39			11 54				12 09			12 24			12 39				12 54			13 09	
Clapham Junction 10	d	11 32		11 48	11 48		12 03	12 02			12 18	12 18		12 33	12 32		12 48	12 48			13 03	13 02		13 18	13 18
Balham 4 ⊖	d				11 53							12 23						12 53							13 23
St Pancras International	d					11 27							11 57							12 27					
Farringdon	d					11 32							12 02							12 32					
City Thameslink	d					11 34							12 04							12 34					
London Blackfriars	d					11 36							12 06							12 36					
Elephant & Castle	d					11 40							12 10							12 40					
Loughborough Jn	d					11 45							12 15							12 45					
Herne Hill	d					11 50							12 20							12 50					
London Bridge	d		11 25							11 55						12 25							12 55		
Tulse Hill	a					11 54							12 24							12 54					
Tulse Hill 3	d					11 56							12 26							12 56					
Streatham	d					12 00							12 30							13 00					
Mitcham Eastfields	d				12 00	12 04						12 30	12 34					13 00		13 04					13 30
Mitcham Junction	d				12 03	12 07						12 33	12 37					13 03		13 07					13 33
Hackbridge	d				12 06	12 10						12 36	12 40					13 06		13 10					13 36
Carshalton	d	11 49			12 09	12 13		12 19				12 39	12 43		12 49			13 09		13 13		13 19			13 39
Sutton	a	11 53			12 13	12 17		12 23				12 43	12 47		12 53			13 13		13 17		13 23			13 43
Norwood Junction	d		11 39							12 09						12 39							13 09		
West Croydon	d		11 45							12 15						12 45							13 15		
Sutton	a		11 58							12 28						12 58							13 28		
Sutton	d	11 54	11 58		12 13			12 24		12 28		12 43			12 54	12 58		13 13				13 24	13 28		13 43
Cheam	d	11 57	12 01		12 16			12 27		12 31		12 46			12 57	13 01		13 16				13 27	13 31		13 46
Ewell East	d		12 04		12 19					12 34		12 49				13 04		13 19					13 34		13 49
Epsom 3	a	12 04	12 08	12 13	12 23		12 28	12 34		12 38	12 43	12 53		12 58	13 04	13 08	13 13	13 23			13 28	13 34	13 38	13 43	13 53
Epsom	d	12 05		12 13			12 28	12 35			12 43			12 58	13 05		13 13				13 28	13 35		13 43	
Ashtead	d	12 10		12 17			12 32	12 40			12 47			13 02	13 10		13 17				13 32	13 40		13 47	
Leatherhead	d	12 14		12a21			12 36	12 44			12a51			13 06	13 14		13a21				13 36	13 44		13a51	
Box Hill & Westhumble	d	12 19					12 41							13 11	13 19						13 41				
Dorking 4	a	12 21					12 43	12 51						13 13	13 21						13 43	13 51			
Dorking	d	12 22													13 22										
Holmwood	d	12 29													13 29										
Ockley	d	12 33													13 33										
Warnham	d	12 39													13 39										
Horsham 4	a	12 43													13 43										

		TL	SW	SN		SN	SW	SN	TL	SW	SN	SN	SW	SN		TL	SW	SN	SN	SW	SN	TL	SW	SN
London Victoria 15 ⊖	d			13 25				13 41			13 55			14 11				14 25			14 41			14 55
London Waterloo 15 ⊖	d		13 24				13 39			13 54			14 09				14 24			14 39			14 54	
Clapham Junction 10	d		13 33	13 32			13 48	13 48		14 03	14 02		14 18	14 18			14 33	14 32		14 48	14 48		15 03	15 02
Balham 4 ⊖	d							13 53						14 23							14 53			
St Pancras International	d	12 57							13 27							13 57						14 27		
Farringdon	d	13 02							13 32							14 02						14 32		
City Thameslink	d	13 04							13 34							14 04						14 34		
London Blackfriars	d	13 06							13 36							14 06						14 36		
Elephant & Castle	d	13 10							13 40							14 10						14 40		
Loughborough Jn	d	13 15							13 45							14 15						14 45		
Herne Hill	d	13 20							13 50							14 20						14 50		
London Bridge	d					13 25						13 55							14 25					
Tulse Hill	a	13 24							13 54							14 24						14 54		
Tulse Hill 3	d	13 26							13 56							14 26						14 56		
Streatham	d	13 30							14 00							14 30						15 00		
Mitcham Eastfields	d	13 34						14 00	14 04					14 30		14 34					15 00	15 04		
Mitcham Junction	d	13 37						14 03	14 07					14 33		14 37					15 03	15 07		
Hackbridge	d	13 40						14 06	14 10					14 36		14 40					15 06	15 10		
Carshalton	d	13 43		13 49				14 09	14 13		14 19			14 39		14 43		14 49			15 09	15 13		15 19
Sutton	a	13 47		13 53				14 13	14 17		14 23			14 43		14 47		14 53			15 13	15 17		15 23
Norwood Junction	d					13 39						14 09							14 39					
West Croydon	d					13 45						14 15							14 45					
Sutton	a					13 58						14 28							14 58					
Sutton	d			13 54		13 58		14 13			14 24	14 28		14 43				14 54	14 58		15 13			15 24
Cheam	d			13 57		14 01		14 16			14 27	14 31		14 46				14 57	15 01		15 16			15 27
Ewell East	d					14 04		14 19				14 34		14 49					15 04		15 19			
Epsom 3	a		13 58	14 04		14 08	14 13	14 23		14 27	14 34	14 38	14 43	14 53			14 58	15 04	15 08	15 13	15 23		15 28	15 34
Epsom	d		13 58	14 05			14 13			14 28	14 35		14 43				14 58	15 05		15 13			15 28	15 35
Ashtead	d		14 02	14 10			14 17			14 32	14 40		14 47				15 02	15 10		15 17			15 32	15 40
Leatherhead	d		14 06	14 14			14a21			14 36	14 44		14a51				15 06	15 14		15a21			15 36	15 44
Box Hill & Westhumble	d		14 11	14 19						14 41							15 11	15 19					15 41	
Dorking 4	a		14 13	14 21						14 45	14 51						15 13	15 21					15 43	15 51
Dorking	d			14 22														15 22						
Holmwood	d			14 29														15 29						
Ockley	d			14 33														15 33						
Warnham	d			14 39														15 39						
Horsham 4	a			14 43														15 43						

For faster trains from London and Clapham Junction to Horsham refer to Table T186

Table T180-F

Saturdays

21 December to 16 May

London - Hackbridge, Sutton, Epsom, Leatherhead, Dorking and Horsham

		SN	SW	SN	TL	SW	SN	SN	SW	SN		TL	SW	SN	SN	SW	SN	TL	SW	SN		SN	SW	SN	TL
London Victoria 15	⊖ d			15 11			15 25			15 41				15 55			16 11			16 25				16 41	
London Waterloo 15	⊖ d		15 09			15 24			15 39				15 54			16 09			16 24				16 39		
Clapham Junction 10	d		15 18	15 18		15 33	15 32		15 48	15 48			16 03	16 02		16 18	16 18		16 33	16 32			16 48	16 48	
Balham 4	⊖ d			15 23						15 53							16 23							16 53	
St Pancras International	d				14 57							15 27						15 57							16 27
Farringdon	d				15 02							15 32						16 02							16 32
City Thameslink	d				15 04							15 34						16 04							16 34
London Blackfriars	d				15 06							15 36						16 06							16 36
Elephant & Castle	d				15 10							15 40						16 10							16 40
Loughborough Jn	d				15 15							15 45						16 15							16 45
Herne Hill	d				15 20							15 50						16 20							16 50
London Bridge	d	14 55						15 25							15 55							16 25			
Tulse Hill	a				15 24							15 54						16 24							16 54
Tulse Hill 3	d				15 26							15 56						16 26							16 56
Streatham	d				15 30							16 00						16 30							17 00
Mitcham Eastfields	d			15 30	15 34					16 00		16 04					16 30	16 34						17 00	17 04
Mitcham Junction	d			15 33	15 37					16 03		16 07					16 33	16 37						17 03	17 07
Hackbridge	d			15 36	15 40					16 06		16 10					16 36	16 40						17 06	17 10
Carshalton	d			15 39	15 43		15 49			16 09		16 13		16 19			16 39	16 43		16 49				17 09	17 13
Sutton	a			15 43	15 47		15 53			16 13		16 17		16 23			16 43	16 47		16 53				17 13	17 17
Norwood Junction	d	15 09						15 39							16 09							16 39			
West Croydon	d	15 15						15 45							16 15							16 45			
Sutton	a	15 28						15 58							16 28							16 58			
Sutton	d	15 28		15 43			15 54	15 58		16 13				16 24	16 28		16 43			16 54		16 58		17 13	
Cheam	d	15 31		15 46			15 57	16 01		16 16				16 27	16 31		16 46			16 57		17 01		17 16	
Ewell East	d	15 34		15 49				16 04		16 19					16 34		16 49					17 04		17 19	
Epsom 3	a	15 38	15 43	15 53		15 58	16 04	16 08	16 13	16 23			16 28	16 34	16 38	16 43	16 53		16 58	17 04		17 08	17 13	17 23	
Epsom	d		15 43			15 58	16 05		16 13				16 28	16 35		16 43			16 58	17 05			17 13		
Ashtead	d		15 47			16 02	16 10		16 17				16 32	16 40		16 47			17 02	17 10			17 17		
Leatherhead	d		15a51			16 06	16 14		16a21				16 36	16 44		16a51			17 06	17 14			17a21		
Box Hill & Westhumble	d					16 11	16 19						16 41						17 11	17 19					
Dorking 4	a					16 13	16 22						16 43	16 51					17 13	17 22					
Dorking	d						16 22													17 22					
Holmwood	d						16 29													17 29					
Ockley	d						16 33													17 33					
Warnham	d						16 39													17 39					
Horsham 4	a						16 43													17 43					

		SW	SN	SN	SW	SN		TL	SW	SN	SN	SW	SN	TL	SW	SN		SN	SW	SN	TL	SW	SN	SN	SW
London Victoria 15	⊖ d		16 55			17 11				17 25			17 41			17 55				18 11			18 25		
London Waterloo 15	⊖ d	16 54			17 09				17 24			17 39			17 54				18 09			18 24			18 39
Clapham Junction 10	d	17 03	17 02		17 18	17 18			17 33	17 32		17 48	17 48		18 03	18 02			18 18	18 18		18 33	18 32		18 48
Balham 4	⊖ d					17 23							17 53							18 23					
St Pancras International	d							16 57						17 27							17 57				
Farringdon	d							17 02						17 32							18 02				
City Thameslink	d							17 04						17 34							18 04				
London Blackfriars	d							17 06						17 36							18 06				
Elephant & Castle	d							17 10						17 40							18 10				
Loughborough Jn	d							17 15						17 45							18 15				
Herne Hill	d							17 20						17 50							18 20				
London Bridge	d			16 55							17 25							17 55						18 25	
Tulse Hill	a							17 24						17 54							18 24				
Tulse Hill 3	d							17 26						17 56							18 26				
Streatham	d							17 30						18 00							18 30				
Mitcham Eastfields	d					17 30		17 34					18 00	18 04						18 30	18 34				
Mitcham Junction	d					17 33		17 37					18 03	18 07						18 33	18 37				
Hackbridge	d					17 36		17 40					18 06	18 10						18 36	18 40				
Carshalton	d		17 19			17 39		17 43		17 49			18 09	18 13		18 19				18 39	18 43		18 49		
Sutton	a		17 23			17 43		17 47		17 53			18 13	18 17		18 23				18 43	18 47		18 53		
Norwood Junction	d			17 09							17 39							18 09						18 39	
West Croydon	d			17 15							17 45							18 15						18 45	
Sutton	a			17 28							17 58							18 28						18 58	
Sutton	d		17 24	17 28		17 43				17 54	17 58		18 13			18 24		18 28		18 43			18 54	18 58	
Cheam	d		17 27	17 31		17 46				17 57	18 01		18 16			18 27		18 31		18 46			18 57	19 01	
Ewell East	d			17 34		17 49					18 04		18 19					18 34		18 49				19 04	
Epsom 3	a	17 28	17 34	17 38	17 43	17 53			17 58	18 04	18 08	18 13	18 23		18 29	18 34		18 38	18 43	18 53		18 58	19 04	19 08	19 13
Epsom	d	17 28	17 35		17 43				17 58	18 05		18 13			18 30	18 35			18 43			18 58	19 05		19 13
Ashtead	d	17 32	17 40		17 47				18 02	18 10		18 17			18 34	18 40			18 47			19 02	19 10		19 17
Leatherhead	d	17 36	17 44		17a51				18 06	18 14		18a21			18 37	18 44			18a51			19 06	19 14		19a21
Box Hill & Westhumble	d	17 41							18 11	18 19					18 42							19 11	19 19		
Dorking 4	a	17 43	17 51						18 13	18 22					18 45	18 51						19 13	19 21		
Dorking	d									18 22															
Holmwood	d									18 29															
Ockley	d									18 33															
Warnham	d									18 39															
Horsham 4	a									18 43															

For faster trains from London and Clapham Junction to Horsham refer to Table T186

Table T180-F

Saturdays

21 December to 16 May

London - Hackbridge, Sutton, Epsom, Leatherhead, Dorking and Horsham

		SN		TL	SW	SN	SN	SW	SN	TL	SW	SN		SN	SW	SN	TL	SW	SN	SN	SW	SN		TL	SW
London Victoria 15	⊖ d	18 41				18 55			19 11			19 25				19 41			19 55			20 11			
London Waterloo 15	⊖ d				18 54			19 09			19 24				19 39			19 54			20 09				20 24
Clapham Junction 10	d	18 48			19 03	19 02		19 18	19 18		19 33	19 32			19 48	19 48		20 03	20 02		20 18	20 18			20 33
Balham 4	⊖ d	18 53							19 23							19 53						20 23			
St Pancras International	d			18 27						18 57							19 27							19 57	
Farringdon	d			18 32						19 02							19 32							20 02	
City Thameslink	d			18 34						19 04							19 34							20 04	
London Blackfriars	d			18 36						19 06							19 36							20 06	
Elephant & Castle	d			18 40						19 10							19 40							20 10	
Loughborough Jn	d			18 45						19 15							19 45							20 15	
Herne Hill	d			18 50						19 20							19 50							20 20	
London Bridge	d						18 55							19 25						19 55					
Tulse Hill	a			18 54						19 24							19 54							20 24	
Tulse Hill 3	d			18 56						19 26							19 56							20 26	
Streatham	d			19 00						19 30							20 00							20 30	
Mitcham Eastfields	d	19 00		19 04					19 30	19 34						20 00	20 04					20 30		20 34	
Mitcham Junction	d	19 03		19 07					19 33	19 37						20 03	20 07					20 33		20 37	
Hackbridge	d	19 06		19 10					19 36	19 40						20 06	20 10					20 36		20 40	
Carshalton	d	19 09		19 13		19 19			19 39	19 43		19 49				20 09	20 13		20 19			20 39		20 43	
Sutton	a	19 13		19 17		19 23			19 43	19 47		19 53				20 13	20 17		20 23			20 43		20 47	
Norwood Junction	d						19 09							19 39						20 09					
West Croydon	d						19 15							19 45						20 15					
Sutton	a						19 28							19 58						20 28					
Sutton	d	19 13				19 24	19 28		19 43			19 54		19 58		20 13			20 24	20 28		20 43			
Cheam	d	19 16				19 27	19 31		19 46			19 57		20 01		20 16			20 27	20 31		20 46			
Ewell East	d	19 19					19 34		19 49					20 04		20 19				20 34		20 49			
Epsom 3	a	19 23			19 28	19 34	19 38	19 43	19 53		19 58	20 04		20 08	20 13	20 23		20 28	20 34	20 38	20 43	20 53			20 58
Epsom	d				19 28	19 35		19 43			19 58	20 05			20 13			20 28	20 35		20 43				20 58
Ashtead	d				19 32	19 40		19 47			20 02	20 10			20 17			20 32	20 40		20 47				21 02
Leatherhead	d				19 36	19 44		19a51			20 06	20 14			20a21			20 36	20 44		20a51				21 06
Box Hill & Westhumble	d				19 41						20 11	20 19						20 41							21 11
Dorking 4	a				19 43	19 51					20 13	20 21						20 43	20 51						21 13
Dorking	d																								
Holmwood	d																								
Ockley	d																								
Warnham	d																								
Horsham 4	a																								

		SN	SN	SW	SN	TL	SW	SN		SN	SW	SN	TL	SW	SN	SN	SW	SN		TL	SW	SN	SN	SW	SN
London Victoria 15	⊖ d	20 25			20 41			20 55				21 11			21 25			21 41				21 55			22 11
London Waterloo 15	⊖ d			20 39			20 54				21 09			21 24			21 39				21 54			22 09	
Clapham Junction 10	d	20 32		20 48	20 48		21 03	21 02			21 18	21 18		21 33	21 32		21 48	21 48			22 03	22 02		22 18	22 18
Balham 4	⊖ d				20 53							21 23						21 53							22 23
St Pancras International	d					20 27							20 57							21 27					
Farringdon	d					20 32							21 02							21 32					
City Thameslink	d					20 34																			
London Blackfriars	d					20 36							21 06							21 36					
Elephant & Castle	d					20 40							21 10							21 40					
Loughborough Jn	d					20 45							21 15							21 45					
Herne Hill	d					20 50							21 20							21 50					
London Bridge	d		20 25							20 55						21 25							21 55		
Tulse Hill	a					20 54							21 24							21 54					
Tulse Hill 3	d					20 56							21 26							21 56					
Streatham	d					21 00							21 30							22 00					
Mitcham Eastfields	d				21 00	21 04						21 30	21 34					22 00		22 04					22 30
Mitcham Junction	d				21 03	21 07						21 33	21 37					22 03		22 07					22 33
Hackbridge	d				21 06	21 10						21 36	21 40					22 06		22 10					22 36
Carshalton	d	20 49			21 09	21 13		21 19				21 39	21 43		21 49			22 09		22 13		22 19			22 39
Sutton	a	20 53			21 13	21 17		21 23				21 43	21 47		21 53			22 13		22 17		22 23			22 43
Norwood Junction	d		20 39							21 09						21 39							22 09		
West Croydon	d		20 45							21 15						21 45							22 15		
Sutton	a		20 58							21 28						21 58							22 28		
Sutton	d	20 54	20 58		21 13			21 24		21 28		21 43			21 54	21 58		22 13				22 24	22 28		22 43
Cheam	d	20 57	21 01		21 16			21 27		21 31		21 46			21 57	22 01		22 16				22 27	22 31		22 46
Ewell East	d		21 04		21 19					21 34		21 49				22 04		22 19					22 34		22 49
Epsom 3	a	21 04	21 08	21 13	21 23		21 28	21 34		21 38	21 43	21 53		21 58	22 04	22 08	22 13	22 23			22 28	22 34	22 38	22 43	22 53
Epsom	d	21 05		21 13			21 28	21 35			21 43			21 58	22 05		22 13					22 35		22 43	
Ashtead	d	21 10		21 17			21 32	21 40			21 47			22 02	22 10		22 17					22 40		22 47	
Leatherhead	d	21 14		21a21			21 36	21 44			21a51			22 06	22 14		22a21					22 44		22 51	
Box Hill & Westhumble	d	21 19					21 41							22 11	22 19									22 56	
Dorking 4	a	21 21					21 43	21 51						22 13	22 21							22 51		22 58	
Dorking	d																								
Holmwood	d																								
Ockley	d																								
Warnham	d																								
Horsham 4	a																								

For faster trains from London and Clapham Junction to Horsham refer to Table T186

Table T180-F

London - Hackbridge, Sutton, Epsom, Leatherhead, Dorking and Horsham

Saturdays
21 December to 16 May

		TL	SN	SN	SW	SN	TL	SN	SN	SW	SN	TL	SN	SW	SN
London Victoria ⊖	d		22 25			22 41		22 55			23 11		23 25		23 45
London Waterloo ⊖	d				22 39					23 09				23 42	
Clapham Junction	d		22 33		22 48	22 49		23 02		23 18	23 18		23 32	23 51	23 53
Balham ⊖	d					22 53					23 23				23 57
St Pancras International	d	21 57					22 27					22 57			
Farringdon	d	22 02					22 32					23 02			
City Thameslink	d														
London Blackfriars	d	22 06					22 36					23 06			
Elephant & Castle	d	22 10					22 40					23 10			
Loughborough Jn	d	22 15					22 45					23 15			
Herne Hill	d	22 20					22 50					23 20			
London Bridge	d			22 25					22 55						
Tulse Hill	a	22 24					22 54					23 24			
Tulse Hill	d	22 26					22 56					23 26			
Streatham	d	22 30					23 00					23 30			
Mitcham Eastfields	d	22 34				23 00	23 04				23 30	23 34			00 04
Mitcham Junction	d	22 37				23 03	23 07				23 33	23 37			00 07
Hackbridge	d	22 40				23 06	23 10				23 36	23 40			00 10
Carshalton	d	22 43	22 49			23 09	23 13	23 19			23 39	23 43	23 52		00 13
Sutton	a	22 47	22 53			23 13	23 17	23 23			23 43	23 47	23 58		00 17
Norwood Junction	d			22 39					23 09						
West Croydon	d			22 45					23 15						
Sutton	a			22 58					23 28						
Sutton	d		22 54	22 58		23 13		23 24	23 28		23 43		23 59		00 17
Cheam	d		22 57	23 01		23 16		23 27	23 31		23 46		00 02		00 20
Ewell East	d			23 04		23 19			23 34		23 49				00 23
Epsom	a		23 04	23 08	23 13	23 23		23 34	23 38	23 43	23 53		00 07	00 16	00 27
Epsom	d		23 05		23 13			23 35		23 43			00 08	00 19	
Ashtead	d		23 10		23 17			23 40		23 47			00 13	00 23	
Leatherhead	d		23 14		23a21			23 43		23 51			00 16	00a26	
Box Hill & Westhumble	d		23 19							23 56			00 21		
Dorking	a		23 21					23 51		23 58			00 24		
Dorking	d														
Holmwood	d														
Ockley	d														
Warnham	d														
Horsham	a														

Sundays
15 December to 10 May

		SN A	SW A	SN A	SW	SN	SN	SW	SN	SW	SN	TL	SW	SN	SN	TL	SW	SN	SN	TL	SW	SN	SN
London Victoria ⊖	d					06 40	07 10		07 40		08 10			08 42	08 52			09 12	09 22			09 42	09 52
London Waterloo ⊖	d				00 15					08 02			08 33				09 02				09 32		
Clapham Junction	d				00 26	06 47	07 17		07 47	08 11	08 17		08 41	08 50	08 58		09 11	09 20	09 28		09 41	09 50	09 58
Balham ⊖	d					06 53	07 23		07 53		08 23				09 03				09 33				10 03
St Pancras International	d																						
Farringdon	d																						
City Thameslink	d																						
London Blackfriars	d																			09 30			
Elephant & Castle	d																			09 34			
Loughborough Jn	d																			09 39			
Herne Hill	d																			09 44			
London Bridge	d											08 30				09 00							
Tulse Hill	a											08 43				09 13				09 48			
Tulse Hill	d											08 46				09 16				09 48			
Streatham	d											08 50				09 20				09 52			
Mitcham Eastfields	d			00 04		07 00	07 30		08 00		08 30	08 53			09 10	09 23			09 40	09 55			10 10
Mitcham Junction	d			00 07		07 03	07 33		08 03		08 33	08 56			09 13	09 26			09 43	09 58			10 13
Hackbridge	d			00 10		07 06	07 36		08 06		08 36	08 59			09 16	09 29			09 46	10 01			10 16
Carshalton	d			00 13		07 09	07 39		08 09		08 39	09 02		09 09	09 19	09 32		09 39	09 49	10 04		10 09	10 19
Sutton	a			00 17		07 12	07 42		08 12		08 42	09 05		09 12	09 23	09 35		09 42	09 53	10 07		10 12	10 23
Norwood Junction	d																						
West Croydon	d																						
Sutton	a																						
Sutton	d			00 17		07 13	07 43		08 13		08 43			09 13	09 24			09 43	09 54			10 13	10 24
Cheam	d	00 02		00 20		07 16	07 46		08 16		08 46			09 16	09 27			09 46	09 57			10 16	10 27
Ewell East	d			00 23		07 19	07 49		08 19		08 49			09 19	09 30			09 49	10 00			10 19	10 30
Epsom	a	00 07		00 27	00 51	07 23	07 53		08 23	08 36	08 53		09 07	09 23	09 34		09 37	09 53	10 04		10 07	10 23	10 34
Epsom	d	00 08	00 19			07 23	07 53	08 08	08 23	08 38	08 53		09 08	09 23			09 38	09 53			10 08	10 23	
Ashtead	d	00 13	00 23			07 28	07 58	08 12	08 28	08 42	08 58		09 12	09 28			09 42	09 58			10 12	10 28	
Leatherhead	d	00 16	00a26			07 32	08 02	08a16	08 32	08 46	09 02		09a16	09 32			09 46	10 02			10a16	10 32	
Box Hill & Westhumble	d	00 21				07 37	08 07		08 37	08 51	09 07			09 37			09 51	10 07				10 37	
Dorking	a	00 24				07 39	08 09		08 39	08 53	09 09			09 39			09 53	10 09				10 39	
Dorking	d																						
Holmwood	d																						
Ockley	d																						
Warnham	d																						
Horsham	a																						

A not 15 December

For faster trains from London and Clapham Junction to Horsham refer to Table T186

Table T180-F

London - Hackbridge, Sutton, Epsom, Leatherhead, Dorking and Horsham

Sundays
15 December to 10 May

		TL	SW	SN	SN	TL	SW	SN	SN	TL	SW	SN	SN	TL	SW	SN	SN	TL	SW	SN	SN	TL	SW
London Victoria ⊖	d			10 12	10 22			10 42	10 52			11 12	11 22			11 42	11 52			12 12	12 22		
London Waterloo ⊖	d		10 02				10 32				11 02				11 32				12 02				12 32
Clapham Junction	d		10 11	10 20	10 28		10 41	10 50	10 58		11 12	11 20	11 28		11 42	11 50	11 58		12 11	12 20	12 28		12 42
Balham ⊖	d				10 33				11 03				11 33				12 03				12 33		
St Pancras International	d																					12 21	
Farringdon	d																					12 25	
City Thameslink	d																						
London Blackfriars	d	10 00				10 30				11 00				11 30				12 00				12 30	
Elephant & Castle	d	10 04				10 34				11 04				11 34				12 04				12 34	
Loughborough Jn	d	10 09				10 39				11 09				11 39				12 09				12 39	
Herne Hill	d	10 14				10 44				11 14				11 44				12 14				12 44	
London Bridge	d																						
Tulse Hill	a	10 18				10 48				11 18				11 48				12 18				12 48	
Tulse Hill	d	10 18				10 48				11 18				11 48				12 18				12 48	
Streatham	d	10 22				10 52				11 22				11 52				12 22				12 52	
Mitcham Eastfields	d	10 25			10 40	10 55			11 10	11 25			11 40	11 55			12 10	12 25			12 40	12 55	
Mitcham Junction	d	10 28			10 43	10 58			11 13	11 28			11 43	11 58			12 13	12 28			12 43	12 58	
Hackbridge	d	10 31			10 46	11 01			11 16	11 31			11 46	12 01			12 16	12 31			12 46	13 01	
Carshalton	d	10 34		10 39	10 49	11 04		11 09	11 19	11 34		11 39	11 49	12 04		12 09	12 19	12 34		12 39	12 49	13 04	
Sutton	a	10 37		10 42	10 53	11 07		11 12	11 23	11 37		11 42	11 53	12 07		12 12	12 23	12 37		12 42	12 53	13 07	
Norwood Junction	d																						
West Croydon	d																						
Sutton	a																						
Sutton	d			10 43	10 54			11 13	11 24			11 43	11 54			12 13	12 24			12 43	12 54		
Cheam	d			10 46	10 57			11 16	11 27			11 46	11 57			12 16	12 27			12 46	12 57		
Ewell East	d			10 49	11 00			11 19	11 30			11 49	12 00			12 19	12 30			12 49	13 00		
Epsom	a		10 37	10 53	11 04		11 07	11 23	11 34		11 37	11 53	12 04		12 07	12 23	12 34		12 37	12 53	13 04		13 07
Epsom	d		10 38	10 53			11 08	11 23			11 38	11 53			12 08	12 23			12 38	12 53			13 08
Ashtead	d		10 42	10 58			11 12	11 28			11 42	11 58			12 12	12 28			12 42	12 58			13 12
Leatherhead	d		10 46	11 02			11a16	11 32			11 46	12 02			12a16	12 32			12 46	13 02			13a16
Box Hill & Westhumble	d		10 51	11 07				11 37			11 51	12 07				12 37			12 51	13 07			
Dorking	a		10 53	11 09				11 39			11 53	12 09				12 39			12 53	13 09			
Dorking	d																						
Holmwood	d																						
Ockley	d																						
Warnham	d																						
Horsham	a																						

		SN	SN	TL	SW	SN	SN	TL	SW		SN	SN	TL	SW	SN	SN	TL	SW	SN	SN	TL	SW	SN
London Victoria ⊖	d	12 42	12 52			13 12	13 22				19 42	19 52			20 12	20 22			20 42	20 52			21 12
London Waterloo ⊖	d				13 02				13 32					20 02				20 32				21 02	
Clapham Junction	d	12 50	12 58		13 11	13 20	13 28		13 41		19 50	19 58		20 11	20 20	20 28		20 41	20 50	20 58		21 11	21 20
Balham ⊖	d		13 03				13 33					20 03				20 33				21 03			
St Pancras International	d			12 51				13 21					19 51				20 21				20 51		
Farringdon	d			12 55				13 25					19 55				20 25				20 55		
City Thameslink	d																						
London Blackfriars	d			13 00				13 30					20 00				20 30				21 00		
Elephant & Castle	d			13 04				13 34					20 04				20 34				21 04		
Loughborough Jn	d			13 09				13 39					20 09				20 39				21 09		
Herne Hill	d			13 14				13 44					20 14				20 44				21 14		
London Bridge	d																						
Tulse Hill	a			13 18				13 48					20 18				20 48				21 18		
Tulse Hill	d			13 18				13 48					20 18				20 48				21 18		
Streatham	d			13 22				13 52					20 22				20 52				21 22		
Mitcham Eastfields	d		13 10	13 25			13 40	13 55		and at the same minutes past each hour until		20 10	20 25			20 40	20 55			21 10	21 25		
Mitcham Junction	d		13 13	13 28			13 43	13 58				20 13	20 28			20 43	20 58			21 13	21 28		
Hackbridge	d		13 16	13 31			13 46	14 01				20 16	20 31			20 46	21 01			21 16	21 31		
Carshalton	d	13 09	13 19	13 34		13 39	13 49	14 04			20 09	20 19	20 34		20 39	20 49	21 04		21 09	21 19	21 34		21 39
Sutton	a	13 12	13 23	13 37		13 42	13 53	14 07			20 12	20 23	20 37		20 42	20 53	21 07		21 12	21 23	21 37		21 42
Norwood Junction	d																						
West Croydon	d																						
Sutton	a																						
Sutton	d	13 13	13 24			13 43	13 54				20 13	20 24			20 43	20 54			21 13	21 24			21 43
Cheam	d	13 16	13 27			13 46	13 57				20 16	20 27			20 46	20 57			21 16	21 27			21 46
Ewell East	d	13 19	13 30			13 49	14 00				20 19	20 30			20 49	21 00			21 19	21 30			21 49
Epsom	a	13 23	13 34		13 37	13 53	14 04		14 07		20 23	20 34		20 37	20 53	21 04		21 07	21 23	21 34		21 37	21 53
Epsom	d	13 23			13 38	13 53			14 08		20 23			20 38	20 53			21 08	21 23			21 38	21 53
Ashtead	d	13 28			13 42	13 58			14 12		20 28			20 42	20 58			21 12	21 28			21 42	21 58
Leatherhead	d	13 32			13 46	14 02			14a16		20 32			20 46	21 02			21a16	21 32			21 46	22 02
Box Hill & Westhumble	d	13 37			13 51	14 07					20 37			20 51	21 07				21 37			21 51	22 07
Dorking	a	13 39			13 53	14 09					20 39			20 53	21 09				21 39			21 53	22 09
Dorking	d																						
Holmwood	d																						
Ockley	d																						
Warnham	d																						
Horsham	a																						

For faster trains from London and Clapham Junction to Horsham refer to Table T186

Table T180-F

Sundays
15 December to 10 May

London - Hackbridge, Sutton, Epsom, Leatherhead, Dorking and Horsham

		SN	TL	SW	SN	SN	SW	SN	SN	SW	SN	SN	SW	SN	SN	SW
London Victoria 15	⊖ d	21 22			21 42	21 52		22 12	22 22		22 42	22 52		23 12	23 22	
London Waterloo 15	⊖ d			21 32			22 02			22 32			23 02			23 32
Clapham Junction 10	d	21 28		21 41	21 50	21 58	22 11	22 20	22 28	22 41	22 50	22 58	23 11	23 20	23 29	23 41
Balham 4	⊖ d	21 33				22 03			22 33			23 03			23 35	
St Pancras International	d		21 21													
Farringdon	d		21 25													
City Thameslink	d															
London Blackfriars	d		21 30													
Elephant & Castle	d		21 34													
Loughborough Jn	d		21 39													
Herne Hill	d		21 44													
London Bridge	d															
Tulse Hill	a		21 48													
Tulse Hill 3	d		21 48													
Streatham	d		21 52													
Mitcham Eastfields	d	21 40	21 55			22 10			22 40			23 10			23 41	
Mitcham Junction	d	21 43	21 58			22 13			22 43			23 13			23 44	
Hackbridge	d	21 46	22 01			22 16			22 46			23 16			23 47	
Carshalton	d	21 49	22 04		22 09	22 19		22 39	22 49		23 09	23 19		23 39	23 50	
Sutton	a	21 53	22 07		22 12	22 23		22 42	22 53		23 12	23 23		23 42	23 54	
Norwood Junction	d															
West Croydon	d															
Sutton	a															
Sutton	d	21 54			22 13	22 24		22 43	22 54		23 13	23 24		23 43	23 54	
Cheam	d	21 57			22 16	22 27		22 46	22 57		23 16	23 27		23 46	23 57	
Ewell East	d	22 00			22 19	22 30		22 49	23 00		23 19	23 30		23 49	00 01	
Epsom 3	a	22 04		22 07	22 23	22 34	22 37	22 53	23 04	23 07	23 23	23 34	23 37	23 53	00 05	00 07
Epsom	d			22 08	22 23		22 38	22 53		23 08	23 23			23 53		
Ashtead	d			22 12	22 28		22 42	22 58		23 12	23 28			23 58		
Leatherhead	d			22a16	22 32		22 46	23 02		23a16	23 32			00 02		
Box Hill & Westhumble	d				22 37		22 51	23 07			23 37			00 07		
Dorking 4	a				22 39		22 53	23 09			23 39			00 09		
Dorking	d															
Holmwood	d															
Ockley	d															
Warnham	d															
Horsham 4	a															

For faster trains from London and Clapham Junction to Horsham refer to Table T186

NRT DECEMBER 19 EDITION

Table T180-R

Mondays to Fridays
16 December to 15 May

Horsham and Dorking, Leatherhead, Epsom, Sutton, Hackbridge - London

		SN	SW	SN	TL	SN	SN	SW	SN	TL	SW	SN	SN	SN	SW	TL	SN	SW	SN	SN	SN	SW	TL
Horsham 4	d											05 44							06 14				
Warnham	d											05 48							06 18				
Ockley	d											05 54							06 24				
Holmwood	d											05 58							06 28				
Dorking 4	a											06 06							06 36				
Dorking	d					05 37		05 46				06 07					06 27	06 31	06 37				
Box Hill & Westhumble	d					05 40		05 49				06 10						06 33	06 40				
Leatherhead	d		05 23			05 44		05 55				06 14			06 23		06 34	06 38	06 44			06 54	
Ashtead	d		05 27			05 48		05 58				06 18			06 27		06 38	06 42	06 48			06 57	
Epsom 3	a		05 31			05 53		06 03				06 23			06 31		06 43	06 46	06 53			07 02	
Epsom	d	05 31	05 33	05 45		05 53	06 01	06 04	06 15		06 18	06 23		06 31	06 33		06 45	06 47	06 53		07 00	07 03	
Ewell East	d	05 35		05 49			06 05		06 19					06 35			06 49				07 05		
Cheam	d	05 38		05 52		05 59	06 08		06 22			06 29		06 38			06 52		06 59		07 08		
Sutton	a	05 41		05 55		06 01	06 11		06 25			06 31		06 41			06 55		07 01		07 11		
Sutton	d	05 42		05 56					06 26								06 56						
West Croydon	a	05 55		06 09					06 39								07 09						
Norwood Junction	a	06 02		06 15					06 45								07 15						
Sutton	d				05 46	06 02	06 12			06 16		06 32	06 36	06 42		06 46			07 02	07 06	07 12		07 16
Carshalton	d				05 49	06 05	06 15			06 19		06 35	06 39	06 45		06 49			07 05	07 09	07 15		07 19
Hackbridge	d				05 52		06 18			06 22			06 42	06 48		06 52				07 12	07 18		07 22
Mitcham Junction	d				05 55		06 21			06 25			06 45	06 51		06 55				07 15	07 21		07 25
Mitcham Eastfields	a				05 58		06 24			06 28			06 48	06 54		06 58				07 18	07 24		07 28
Streatham	d				06 03					06 33			06 53			07 03				07 23			07 33
Tulse Hill 3	a				06 07					06 37			06 56			07 07				07 26			07 37
Tulse Hill	d				06 08					06 38			06 57			07 08				07 27			07 38
London Bridge	a	06 31		06 28					06 58				07 15				07 28			07 45			
Herne Hill	a				06 11					06 41						07 11							07 41
Loughborough Jn	a				06 15					06 45						07 15							07 45
Elephant & Castle	a				06 19					06 49						07 19							07 49
London Blackfriars	a				06 24					06 54						07 24							07 54
City Thameslink	a				06 26					06 56						07 26							07 56
Farringdon	a				06 28					06 58						07 28							07 58
St Pancras International	a				06 33					07 03						07 33							08 03
Balham 4	⊖ a						06 33							07 03							07 32		
Clapham Junction 10	a		06 01			06 23	06 37	06 30			06 46	06 53		07 07	07 00			07 15	07 23		07 37	07 29	
London Waterloo 15	⊖ a		06 11					06 40			06 56				07 12			07 27				07 41	
London Victoria 15	⊖ a					06 33	06 45					07 02		07 15					07 32		07 46		

		SN	SW	SW	SN	SN	SN	SW	TL	SN	SW	SW	SN	SN	SN	SW	TL	SN	SW	SW	SN	SN
Horsham 4	d				06 45								07 13									
Warnham	d				06 49								07 18									
Ockley	d				06 55								07 24									
Holmwood	d				06 59								07 28									
Dorking 4	a				07 06								07 36									
Dorking	d		07 01		07 07						07 31		07 37					07 56	08 01		08 07	
Box Hill & Westhumble	d		07 04		07 10						07 34		07 40						08 04			
Leatherhead	d	07 05	07 09		07 14			07 24		07 35	07 39		07 44			07 55		08 02	08 09		08 13	
Ashtead	d	07 09	07 12		07 18			07 27		07 39	07 42		07 48			07 58		08 06	08 12		08 17	
Epsom 3	a	07 13	07 17		07 23			07 32		07 43	07 47		07 53			08 03		08 11	08 17		08 23	
Epsom	d	07 15	07 17	07 21	07 23		07 30	07 34		07 45	07 47	07 51	07 53		08 01	08 03		08 15	08 17	08 21	08 23	
Ewell East	d	07 19					07 35			07 49					08 05			08 20				
Cheam	d	07 22			07 29		07 38			07 52			07 59		08 08			08 23			08 29	
Sutton	a	07 25			07 31		07 41			07 55			08 01		08 11			08 25			08 31	
Sutton	d	07 26								07 56								08 26				
West Croydon	a	07 39								08 09								08 39				
Norwood Junction	a	07 45								08 15								08 45				
Sutton	d				07 32	07 36	07 42		07 46				08 02	08 06	08 12		08 16				08 32	08 36
Carshalton	d				07 35	07 39	07 45		07 49				08 05	08 09	08 15		08 19				08 35	08 39
Hackbridge	d				07 38	07 42	07 48		07 52				08 08	08 12	08 18		08 22				08 38	08 42
Mitcham Junction	d				07 42	07 45	07 51		07 55				08 12	08 15	08 21		08 25				08 42	08 45
Mitcham Eastfields	a				07 45	07 48	07 54		07 58				08 15	08 18	08 24		08 28				08 45	08 48
Streatham	d					07 53			08 03					08 23			08 33					08 53
Tulse Hill 3	a					07 56			08 07					08 26			08 37					08 56
Tulse Hill	d					07 57			08 08					08 27			08 38					08 57
London Bridge	a	07 58				08 15				08 28				08 47				08 58				09 17
Herne Hill	a								08 11								08 41					
Loughborough Jn	a								08 15								08 45					
Elephant & Castle	a								08 19								08 49					
London Blackfriars	a								08 24								08 54					
City Thameslink	a								08 26								08 56					
Farringdon	a								08 28								08 58					
St Pancras International	a								08 33								09 03					
Balham 4	⊖ a						08 02								08 32							
Clapham Junction 10	a		07 42	07 48	07 54		08 07	08 01			08 12	08 18	08 24		08 37	08 31			08 42	08 48	08 54	
London Waterloo 15	⊖ a		07 55	08 02				08 13			08 24	08 32				08 43			08 54	09 02		
London Victoria 15	⊖ a				08 04		08 16						08 33		08 45						09 03	

Table T180-R

Mondays to Fridays
16 December to 15 May

Horsham and Dorking, Leatherhead, Epsom, Sutton, Hackbridge - London

		SN	SW	SN	SW	TL	SN	SN		SW	SN	SW	TL	SN	SN	SW	SN	SW		TL	SN	SN	SW	SN	SW
Horsham 4	d						08 14														09 14				
Warnham	d						08 18														09 18				
Ockley	d						08 24														09 24				
Holmwood	d						08 28														09 28				
Dorking 4	a						08 36														09 36				
Dorking	d				08 31		08 37					09 01		09 07				09 32			09 37				10 02
Box Hill & Westhumble	d				08 34		08 40					09 04						09 35			09 40				10 05
Leatherhead	d		08 24		08 39		08 44			08 54		09 09		09 13		09 23		09 40			09 44		09 53		10 10
Ashtead	d		08 27		08 42		08 48			08 57		09 12		09 17		09 27		09 43			09 48		09 57		10 13
Epsom 3	a		08 32		08 47		08 53			09 02		09 17		09 23		09 31		09 48			09 53		10 01		10 18
Epsom	d	08 31	08 34	08 45	08 47		08 53	09 01		09 04	09 15	09 17		09 23	09 31	09 34	09 45	09 49			09 53	10 01	10 04	10 15	10 19
Ewell East	d	08 35		08 49				09 05			09 19				09 35		09 49					10 05		10 19	
Cheam	d	08 38		08 52			08 59	09 08			09 22			09 29	09 38		09 52				09 59	10 08		10 22	
Sutton	a	08 41		08 55			09 01	09 11			09 25			09 31	09 41		09 55				10 01	10 11		10 25	
Sutton	d			08 56							09 26						09 56							10 26	
West Croydon	a			09 09							09 39						10 09							10 39	
Norwood Junction	a			09 15							09 45						10 15							10 45	
Sutton	d	08 42				08 46	09 02	09 12					09 16	09 32	09 42					09 46	10 02	10 12			
Carshalton	d	08 45				08 49	09 05	09 15					09 19	09 35	09 45					09 49	10 05	10 15			
Hackbridge	d	08 48				08 52		09 18					09 22		09 48					09 52		10 18			
Mitcham Junction	d	08 51				08 55		09 21					09 25		09 51					09 55		10 21			
Mitcham Eastfields	a	08 54				08 58		09 24					09 28		09 54					09 58		10 24			
Streatham	d					09 03							09 33							10 03					
Tulse Hill 3	a					09 07							09 37							10 07					
Tulse Hill	d					09 08							09 38							10 08					
London Bridge	a			09 28							09 58						10 28							10 58	
Herne Hill	a					09 11							09 41							10 11					
Loughborough Jn	a					09 15							09 45							10 15					
Elephant & Castle	a					09 19							09 49							10 19					
London Blackfriars	a					09 24							09 54							10 24					
City Thameslink	a					09 26							09 56							10 26					
Farringdon	a					09 28							09 58							10 28					
St Pancras International	a					09 33							10 03							10 33					
Balham 4 ⊖	a	09 03						09 33							10 03							10 33			
Clapham Junction 10	a	09 07	09 01		09 15		09 23	09 37		09 30		09 45		09 53	10 07	10 00		10 15			10 23	10 37	10 30		10 45
London Waterloo 15 ⊖	a		09 13		09 27					09 42		09 57				10 10		10 25					10 40		10 55
London Victoria 15 ⊖	a	09 19					09 32	09 45						10 03	10 15						10 31	10 45			

		TL	SN	SN		SW	SN	SW	TL	SN	SN	SW	SN	SW		TL	SN	SN	SW	SN	SW	TL	SN	SN	
Horsham 4	d									10 14													11 14		
Warnham	d									10 18													11 18		
Ockley	d									10 24													11 24		
Holmwood	d									10 28													11 28		
Dorking 4	a									10 36													11 36		
Dorking	d		10 07					10 32		10 37				11 02			11 07				11 32		11 37		
Box Hill & Westhumble	d							10 35		10 40				11 05							11 35		11 40		
Leatherhead	d		10 13			10 23		10 40		10 44		10 53		11 10			11 13		11 23		11 40		11 44		
Ashtead	d		10 17			10 27		10 43		10 48		10 57		11 13			11 17		11 27		11 43		11 48		
Epsom 3	a		10 23			10 31		10 48		10 53		11 01		11 18			11 23		11 31		11 48		11 53		
Epsom	d		10 23	10 31		10 34	10 45	10 49		10 53	11 01	11 04	11 15	11 19			11 23	11 31	11 34	11 45	11 49		11 53	12 01	
Ewell East	d			10 35			10 49				11 05		11 19					11 35		11 49				12 05	
Cheam	d		10 29	10 38			10 52			10 59	11 08		11 22				11 29	11 38		11 52			11 59	12 08	
Sutton	a		10 31	10 41			10 55			11 01	11 11		11 25				11 31	11 41		11 55			12 01	12 11	
Sutton	d						10 56						11 26							11 56					
West Croydon	a						11 09						11 39							12 09					
Norwood Junction	a						11 15						11 45							12 15					
Sutton	d	10 16	10 32	10 42					10 46	11 02	11 12					11 16	11 32	11 42				11 46	12 02	12 12	
Carshalton	d	10 19	10 35	10 45					10 49	11 05	11 15					11 19	11 35	11 45				11 49	12 05	12 15	
Hackbridge	d	10 22		10 48					10 52		11 18					11 22		11 48				11 52		12 18	
Mitcham Junction	d	10 25		10 51					10 55		11 21					11 25		11 51				11 55		12 21	
Mitcham Eastfields	d	10 28		10 54					10 58		11 24					11 28		11 54				11 58		12 24	
Streatham	d	10 33							11 03							11 33						12 03			
Tulse Hill 3	a	10 37							11 07							11 37						12 07			
Tulse Hill	d	10 38							11 08							11 38						12 08			
London Bridge	a						11 28						11 58							12 28					
Herne Hill	a	10 41							11 11							11 41						12 11			
Loughborough Jn	a	10 45							11 15							11 45						12 15			
Elephant & Castle	a	10 49							11 19							11 49						12 19			
London Blackfriars	a	10 54							11 24							11 54						12 24			
City Thameslink	a	10 56							11 26							11 56						12 26			
Farringdon	a	10 58							11 28							11 58						12 28			
St Pancras International	a	11 03							11 33							12 03						12 33			
Balham 4 ⊖	a			11 03							11 33							12 03						12 33	
Clapham Junction 10	a		10 53	11 07		11 00		11 15		11 23	11 37	11 30		11 45			11 53	12 07	12 00		12 15		12 23	12 37	
London Waterloo 15 ⊖	a					11 10		11 25				11 40		11 55					12 10		12 25				
London Victoria 15 ⊖	a		11 01	11 15						11 32	11 45						12 02	12 15					12 33	12 45	

Table T180-R

Mondays to Fridays
16 December to 15 May

Horsham and Dorking, Leatherhead, Epsom, Sutton, Hackbridge - London

		SW	SN	SW	TL	SN	SN	SW	SN	SW		TL	SN	SN	SW	SN	SW	TL	SN	SN		SW	SN	SW	TL
Horsham 4	d												12 14												
Warnham	d												12 18												
Ockley	d												12 24												
Holmwood	d												12 28												
Dorking 4	a												12 36												
Dorking	d			12 02		12 07				12 32			12 37				13 02		13 07					13 32	
Box Hill & Westhumble	d			12 05						12 35			12 40				13 05							13 35	
Leatherhead	d	11 53		12 10		12 13		12 23		12 40			12 44		12 53		13 10		13 13			13 23		13 40	
Ashtead	d	11 57		12 13		12 17		12 27		12 43			12 48		12 57		13 13		13 17			13 27		13 43	
Epsom 3	a	12 01		12 18		12 23		12 31		12 48			12 53		13 01		13 18		13 23			13 31		13 48	
Epsom	d	12 04	12 15	12 19		12 23	12 31	12 34	12 45	12 49			12 53	13 01	13 04	13 15	13 19		13 23	13 31		13 34	13 45	13 49	
Ewell East	d		12 19				12 35		12 49					13 05		13 19				13 35			13 49		
Cheam	d		12 22			12 29	12 38		12 52				12 59	13 08		13 22			13 29	13 38			13 52		
Sutton	a		12 25			12 31	12 41		12 55				13 01	13 11		13 25			13 31	13 41			13 55		
Sutton	d		12 26						12 56							13 26							13 56		
West Croydon	a		12 39						13 09							13 39							14 09		
Norwood Junction	a		12 45						13 15							13 45							14 15		
Sutton	d				12 16	12 32	12 42					12 46	13 02	13 12				13 16	13 32	13 42					13 46
Carshalton	d				12 19	12 35	12 45					12 49	13 05	13 15				13 19	13 35	13 45					13 49
Hackbridge	d				12 22		12 48					12 52		13 18				13 22		13 48					13 52
Mitcham Junction	d				12 25		12 51					12 55		13 21				13 25		13 51					13 55
Mitcham Eastfields	a				12 28		12 54					12 58		13 24				13 28		13 54					13 58
Streatham	d				12 33							13 03						13 33							14 03
Tulse Hill 3	a				12 37							13 07						13 37							14 07
Tulse Hill	d				12 38							13 08						13 38							14 08
London Bridge	a		12 58						13 28							13 58							14 28		
Herne Hill	a				12 41							13 11						13 41							14 11
Loughborough Jn	a				12 45							13 15						13 45							14 15
Elephant & Castle	a				12 49							13 19						13 49							14 19
London Blackfriars	a				12 54							13 24						13 54							14 24
City Thameslink	a				12 56							13 26						13 56							14 26
Farringdon	a				12 58							13 28						13 58							14 28
St Pancras International	a				13 03							13 33						14 03							14 33
Balham 4 ⊖	a						13 03							13 33						14 03					
Clapham Junction 10	a	12 30		12 45		12 53	13 07	13 00		13 15			13 23	13 37	13 30		13 45		13 53	14 07		14 00		14 15	
London Waterloo 15 ⊖	a	12 40		12 55				13 10		13 25					13 40		13 55					14 10		14 25	
London Victoria 15 ⊖	a					13 02	13 15						13 32	13 45					14 02	14 15					

		SN	SN	SW	SN	SW		TL	SN	SN	SW	SN	SW	TL	SN	SN		SW	SN	SW	TL	SN	SN	SW	SN
Horsham 4	d	13 14													14 14										
Warnham	d	13 18													14 18										
Ockley	d	13 24													14 24										
Holmwood	d	13 28													14 28										
Dorking 4	a	13 36													14 36										
Dorking	d	13 37				14 02			14 07				14 32		14 37					15 02		15 07			
Box Hill & Westhumble	d	13 40				14 05							14 35		14 40					15 05					
Leatherhead	d	13 44		13 53		14 10			14 13		14 23		14 40		14 44			14 53		15 10		15 13		15 23	
Ashtead	d	13 48		13 57		14 13			14 17		14 27		14 43		14 48			14 57		15 13		15 17		15 27	
Epsom 3	a	13 53		14 01		14 18			14 22		14 31		14 48		14 53			15 01		15 18		15 23		15 31	
Epsom	d	13 53	14 01	14 04	14 15	14 19			14 22	14 31	14 34	14 45	14 49		14 53	15 01		15 04	15 15	15 19		15 23	15 31	15 34	15 45
Ewell East	d		14 05		14 19					14 35		14 49				15 05			15 19				15 35		15 49
Cheam	d	13 59	14 08		14 22				14 28	14 38		14 52			14 59	15 08			15 22			15 29	15 38		15 52
Sutton	a	14 01	14 11		14 25				14 30	14 41		14 55			15 01	15 11			15 25			15 31	15 41		15 55
Sutton	d				14 26							14 56							15 26						15 56
West Croydon	a				14 39							15 09							15 39						16 09
Norwood Junction	a				14 45							15 15							15 45						16 15
Sutton	d	14 02	14 12					14 16	14 31	14 42				14 46	15 02	15 12					15 16	15 32	15 42		
Carshalton	d	14 05	14 15					14 19	14 34	14 45				14 49	15 05	15 15					15 19	15 35	15 45		
Hackbridge	d		14 18					14 22		14 48				14 52		15 18					15 22		15 48		
Mitcham Junction	d		14 21					14 25		14 51				14 55		15 21					15 25		15 51		
Mitcham Eastfields	a		14 24					14 28		14 54				14 58		15 24					15 28		15 54		
Streatham	d							14 33						15 03							15 33				
Tulse Hill 3	a							14 37						15 07							15 37				
Tulse Hill	d							14 38						15 08							15 38				
London Bridge	a				14 58							15 28							15 58						16 28
Herne Hill	a							14 41						15 11							15 41				
Loughborough Jn	a							14 45						15 15							15 45				
Elephant & Castle	a							14 49						15 19							15 49				
London Blackfriars	a							14 54						15 24							15 54				
City Thameslink	a							14 56						15 26							15 56				
Farringdon	a							14 58						15 28							15 58				
St Pancras International	a							15 03						15 33							16 03				
Balham 4 ⊖	a		14 33							15 03						15 33							16 03		
Clapham Junction 10	a	14 23	14 37	14 30		14 45			14 53	15 07	15 00		15 15		15 23	15 37		15 30		15 45		15 53	16 07	16 00	
London Waterloo 15 ⊖	a			14 40		14 55					15 10		15 25					15 40		15 55				16 10	
London Victoria 15 ⊖	a	14 32	14 45						15 02	15 15					15 32	15 45						16 02	16 15		

Table T180-R

Mondays to Fridays
16 December to 15 May

Horsham and Dorking, Leatherhead, Epsom, Sutton, Hackbridge - London

		SW		TL	SN	SN	SW	SN	SW	TL	SN	SN		SW	SN	SW	TL	SN	SN	SW	SN	SW		TL	SN
Horsham 4	d				15 14													16 14							
Warnham	d				15 18													16 18							
Ockley	d				15 24													16 24							
Holmwood	d				15 28													16 28							
Dorking 4	a				15 36													16 36							
Dorking	d	15 32			15 37				16 02		16 07					16 32		16 37				17 02			17 07
Box Hill & Westhumble	d	15 35			15 40				16 05							16 35		16 40				17 05			
Leatherhead	d	15 40			15 44		15 53		16 10		16 13			16 23		16 40		16 44		16 53		17 10			17 13
Ashtead	d	15 43			15 48		15 57		16 13		16 17			16 27		16 43		16 48		16 57		17 13			17 17
Epsom 3	a	15 48			15 53		16 01		16 18		16 23			16 31		16 48		16 53		17 01		17 18			17 23
Epsom	d	15 49			15 53	16 01	16 04	16 15	16 19		16 23	16 31		16 34	16 45	16 49		16 53	17 01	17 04	17 15	17 19			17 23
Ewell East	d					16 05		16 19				16 35			16 49				17 05		17 19				
Cheam	d				15 59	16 08		16 22			16 29	16 38			16 52			16 59	17 08		17 22				17 29
Sutton	a				16 01	16 11		16 25			16 31	16 41			16 55			17 01	17 11		17 25				17 31
Sutton	d							16 26							16 56						17 26				
West Croydon	a							16 39							17 09						17 39				
Norwood Junction	a							16 45							17 15						17 45				
Sutton	d			15 46	16 02	16 12				16 16	16 32	16 42					16 46	17 02	17 12					17 16	17 32
Carshalton	d			15 49	16 05	16 15				16 19	16 35	16 45					16 49	17 05	17 15					17 19	17 35
Hackbridge	d			15 52		16 18				16 22		16 48					16 52		17 18					17 22	
Mitcham Junction	d			15 55		16 21				16 25		16 51					16 55		17 21					17 25	
Mitcham Eastfields	a			15 58		16 24				16 28		16 54					16 58		17 24					17 28	
Streatham	d			16 03						16 33							17 03							17 33	
Tulse Hill 3	a			16 07						16 37							17 07							17 37	
Tulse Hill	d			16 08						16 38							17 08							17 38	
London Bridge	a							16 58							17 28						17 58				
Herne Hill	a			16 11						16 41							17 11							17 41	
Loughborough Jn	a			16 15						16 45							17 15							17 45	
Elephant & Castle	a			16 19						16 49							17 19							17 49	
London Blackfriars	a			16 24						16 54							17 24							17 54	
City Thameslink	a			16 26						16 56							17 26							17 56	
Farringdon	a			16 28						16 58							17 28							17 58	
St Pancras International	a			16 33						17 03							17 33							18 03	
Balham 4 ⊖	a					16 33						17 03							17 33						
Clapham Junction 10	a	16 15			16 23	16 37	16 30		16 45		16 53	17 07		17 00		17 15		17 23	17 37	17 30		17 45			17 53
London Waterloo 15 ⊖	a	16 25					16 40		16 55					17 10		17 25				17 40		17 55			
London Victoria 15 ⊖	a				16 33	16 45					17 03	17 15						17 33	17 45						18 02

		SN	SW	SW	TL	SN	SN	SW		SN	SW	TL	SN	SN	SW	SW	TL	SN		SN	SW	SN	SW	TL	SN
Horsham 4	d					17 14							17 42					18 12							18 42
Warnham	d					17 18							17 46					18 16							18 46
Ockley	d					17 24							17 52					18 22							18 52
Holmwood	d					17 28							17 56					18 26							18 56
Dorking 4	a					17 36							18 03					18 33							19 03
Dorking	d			17 32		17 37					17 53		18 07			18 32		18 37					19 03		19 07
Box Hill & Westhumble	d			17 35		17 40					17 56		18 10			18 35		18 40					19 05		19 10
Leatherhead	d		17 23	17 40		17 44		17 53			18 01		18 14		18 23	18 40		18 44			18 55		19 10		19 14
Ashtead	d		17 27	17 43		17 48		17 57			18 04		18 18		18 27	18 43		18 48			18 58		19 14		19 18
Epsom 3	a		17 31	17 48		17 53		18 01			18 09		18 23		18 31	18 48		18 53			19 03		19 18		19 23
Epsom	d	17 31	17 34	17 48		17 53	18 01	18 04		18 15	18 19		18 23	18 31	18 34	18 49		18 53		19 01	19 04	19 15	19 19		19 23
Ewell East	d	17 35					18 05			18 19				18 35						19 05		19 19			
Cheam	d	17 38				17 59	18 08			18 22			18 29	18 38				18 59		19 08		19 22			19 29
Sutton	a	17 41				18 01	18 11			18 25			18 31	18 41				19 01		19 11		19 25			19 31
Sutton	d									18 26												19 26			
West Croydon	a									18 39												19 39			
Norwood Junction	a									18 45												19 45			
Sutton	d	17 42			17 46	18 02	18 12					18 16	18 32	18 42			18 46	19 02		19 12				19 16	19 32
Carshalton	d	17 45			17 49	18 05	18 15					18 19	18 35	18 45			18 49	19 05		19 15				19 19	19 35
Hackbridge	d	17 48			17 52		18 18					18 22		18 48			18 52			19 18				19 22	
Mitcham Junction	d	17 51			17 55		18 21					18 25		18 51			18 55			19 21				19 25	
Mitcham Eastfields	a	17 54			17 58		18 24					18 28		18 54			18 58			19 24				19 28	
Streatham	d				18 03							18 33					19 03							19 33	
Tulse Hill 3	a				18 07							18 37					19 07							19 37	
Tulse Hill	d				18 08							18 38					19 08							19 38	
London Bridge	a									18 58												19 58			
Herne Hill	a				18 11							18 41					19 11							19 41	
Loughborough Jn	a				18 15							18 45					19 15							19 45	
Elephant & Castle	a				18 19							18 49					19 19							19 49	
London Blackfriars	a				18 24							18 54					19 24							19 54	
City Thameslink	a				18 26							18 56					19 26							19 56	
Farringdon	a				18 28							18 58					19 28							19 58	
St Pancras International	a				18 33							19 03					19 33							20 03	
Balham 4 ⊖	a	18 03					18 33							19 03						19 33					
Clapham Junction 10	a	18 07	18 00	18 14		18 23	18 37	18 30			18 45		18 53	19 07	19 00	19 15		19 23		19 37	19 30		19 45		19 53
London Waterloo 15 ⊖	a		18 10	18 24				18 41			18 55				19 11	19 26					19 41		19 55		
London Victoria 15 ⊖	a	18 19				18 34	18 45						19 02	19 15				19 33		19 45					20 02

NRT DECEMBER 19 EDITION

Table T180-R

Mondays to Fridays
16 December to 15 May

Horsham and Dorking, Leatherhead, Epsom, Sutton, Hackbridge - London

		SN	SW	TL		SN	SW	SN	SN	SW	SN	SW	TL	SN		SN	SW	SN	SW	TL	SN	SN	SW	SN	
Horsham 4	d							19 12													20 14				
Warnham	d							19 16													20 18				
Ockley	d							19 22													20 24				
Holmwood	d							19 26													20 28				
Dorking 4	a							19 33													20 36				
Dorking	d						19 32	19 37				20 02		20 07					20 32		20 37				
Box Hill & Westhumble	d						19 35	19 40				20 05							20 35		20 40				
Leatherhead	d		19 23			19 29	19 40	19 44		19 53		20 10		20 13			20 23		20 40		20 44		20 55		
Ashtead	d		19 27			19 34	19 43	19 48		19 57		20 13		20 17			20 27		20 43		20 48		20 59		
Epsom 3	a		19 31			19 41	19 48	19 53		20 01		20 18		20 23			20 31		20 48		20 53		21 03		
Epsom	d	19 31	19 34			19 42	19 49	19 53	20 01	20 04	20 15	20 19		20 23		20 31	20 34	20 45	20 49		20 53	21 01	21 04	21 15	
Ewell East	d	19 35				19 49			20 05		20 19					20 35		20 49				21 06		21 19	
Cheam	d	19 38				19 52		19 59	20 08		20 22			20 29		20 38		20 52			20 59	21 09		21 22	
Sutton	a	19 41				19 55		20 01	20 11		20 25			20 31		20 41		20 55			21 01	21 11		21 25	
Sutton	d					19 56					20 26							20 56						21 26	
West Croydon	a					20 09					20 39							21 09						21 39	
Norwood Junction	a					20 15					20 45							21 15						21 45	
Sutton	d	19 42		19 46				20 02	20 12				20 16	20 32		20 42				20 46	21 02	21 12			
Carshalton	d	19 45		19 49				20 05	20 15				20 19	20 35		20 45				20 49	21 05	21 15			
Hackbridge	d	19 48		19 52					20 18				20 22			20 48				20 52		21 18			
Mitcham Junction	d	19 51		19 55					20 21				20 25			20 51				20 55		21 21			
Mitcham Eastfields	a	19 54		19 58					20 24				20 28			20 54				20 58		21 24			
Streatham	d			20 03									20 33							21 03					
Tulse Hill 3	a			20 07									20 37							21 07					
Tulse Hill	d			20 08									20 38							21 08					
London Bridge	a					20 28					20 58							21 28						21 58	
Herne Hill	a			20 11									20 41							21 11					
Loughborough Jn	a			20 15									20 45							21 15					
Elephant & Castle	a			20 19									20 49							21 19					
London Blackfriars	a			20 24									20 54							21 24					
City Thameslink	a			20 26									20 56							21 26					
Farringdon	a			20 28									20 58							21 28					
St Pancras International	a			20 33									21 03							21 33					
Balham 4 ⊖	a	20 03							20 33							21 03						21 33			
Clapham Junction 10	a	20 07	20 00				20 15	20 23	20 37	20 30		20 45		20 55		21 07	21 00		21 15		21 23	21 37	21 31		
London Waterloo 15 ⊖	a		20 10				20 25			20 40		20 55					21 10		21 25				21 41		
London Victoria 15 ⊖	a	20 17						20 32	20 45					21 03		21 15					21 33	21 46			

		SW	TL	SN	SN	SW	SN	SW	TL	SN		SN	SW	SN	SW	TL	SN	SN	SW	SN		SW	TL	SN	TL
Horsham 4	d									21 14															
Warnham	d									21 18															
Ockley	d									21 24															
Holmwood	d									21 28															
Dorking 4	a									21 36															
Dorking	d	21 02		21 07				21 32		21 37					22 02		22 07					22 32			
Box Hill & Westhumble	d	21 05						21 35		21 40					22 05							22 35			
Leatherhead	d	21 10		21 13		21 23		21 40		21 44			21 53		22 10		22 13		22 23			22 40			
Ashtead	d	21 12		21 17		21 27		21 43		21 48			21 57		22 12		22 17		22 27			22 43			
Epsom 3	a	21 18		21 23		21 31		21 48		21 53			22 01		22 18		22 23		22 31			22 48			
Epsom	d	21 19		21 23	21 31	21 34	21 45	21 49		21 53		22 01	22 04	22 15	22 19		22 23	22 31	22 34	22 45		22 49		23 01	
Ewell East	d				21 35		21 49					22 05		22 19				22 35		22 49				23 05	
Cheam	d			21 29	21 38		21 52			21 59		22 08		22 22			22 29	22 38		22 52				23 08	
Sutton	a			21 31	21 41		21 55			22 01		22 11		22 25			22 31	22 41		22 55				23 11	
Sutton	d						21 56							22 26						22 56					
West Croydon	a						22 09							22 39						23 09					
Norwood Junction	a						22 15							22 45						23 15					
Sutton	d		21 16	21 32	21 42				21 46	22 02		22 12				22 18	22 32	22 42					22 48	23 12	23 18
Carshalton	d		21 19	21 35	21 45				21 49	22 05		22 15				22 21	22 35	22 45					22 51	23 15	23 21
Hackbridge	d		21 22		21 48				21 52			22 18				22 24		22 48					22 54	23 18	23 24
Mitcham Junction	d		21 25		21 51				21 55			22 21				22 27		22 51					22 57	23 21	23 27
Mitcham Eastfields	a		21 28		21 54				21 58			22 24				22 30		22 54					23 00	23 24	23 30
Streatham	d		21 33						22 03							22 35							23 05		23 35
Tulse Hill 3	a		21 37						22 07							22 39							23 09		23 39
Tulse Hill	d		21 38						22 08							22 40							23 10		23 40
London Bridge	a						22 28							22 58						23 28					
Herne Hill	a		21 41						22 11							22 43							23 13		23 43
Loughborough Jn	a		21 45						22 15							22 47							23 17		23 47
Elephant & Castle	a		21 49						22 19							22 51							23 21		23 51
London Blackfriars	a		21 54						22 24							22 56							23 26		00 01
City Thameslink	a		21 56						22 26																
Farringdon	a		21 58						22 28							23 03							23 33		00 06
St Pancras International	a		22 03						22 33							23 08							23 37		00 10
Balham 4 ⊖	a				22 03							22 33						23 03						23 33	
Clapham Junction 10	a	21 45		21 53	22 07	22 00		22 15		22 23		22 37	22 30		22 45		22 53	23 07	23 00			23 15		23 37	
London Waterloo 15 ⊖	a	21 55				22 10		22 25					22 40		22 56				23 12			23 28			
London Victoria 15 ⊖	a			22 03	22 16					22 33		22 45					23 03	23 15						23 47	

Table T180-R

Horsham and Dorking, Leatherhead, Epsom, Sutton, Hackbridge - London

Mondays to Fridays
16 December to 15 May

Station		SN	SW FO	SW FX
Horsham 4	d			
Warnham	d			
Ockley	d			
Holmwood	d			
Dorking 4	a			
Dorking	d	22 59		
Box Hill & Westhumble	d	23 02		
Leatherhead	d	23 06	23 11	23 11
Ashtead	d	23 10	23 14	23 14
Epsom 3	a	23 15	23 19	23 19
Epsom	d	23 16	23 19	23 19
Ewell East	d	23 20		
Cheam	d	23 23		
Sutton	a	23 26		
Sutton	d	23 26		
West Croydon	a	23 39		
Norwood Junction	a			
Sutton	d			
Carshalton	d			
Hackbridge	d			
Mitcham Junction	d			
Mitcham Eastfields	a			
Streatham	d			
Tulse Hill 3	a			
Tulse Hill	d			
London Bridge	a			
Herne Hill	a			
Loughborough Jn	a			
Elephant & Castle	a			
London Blackfriars	a			
City Thameslink	a			
Farringdon	a			
St Pancras International	a			
Balham 4 ⊖	a			
Clapham Junction 10	a		23 45	23 45
London Waterloo 15 ⊖	a		23 58	23 59
London Victoria 15 ⊖	a			

Saturdays
21 December to 16 May

Station		SW	TL	SW	TL	SN	SW	TL	SN	SN	SN	SW	SN	TL	SN	SN	SW	SN	TL	SN	SN	SW	SN
Horsham 4	d																						
Warnham	d																						
Ockley	d																						
Holmwood	d																						
Dorking 4	a																						
Dorking	d									06 37					07 07					07 37			
Box Hill & Westhumble	d									06 40										07 40			
Leatherhead	d									06 44		06 55			07 13		07 23			07 44		07 53	
Ashtead	d									06 48		06 59			07 17		07 27			07 48		07 57	
Epsom 3	a									06 53		07 04			07 23		07 31			07 53		08 01	
Epsom	d	05 34		06 04		06 31	06 34		06 45	06 53	07 01	07 04	07 15		07 23	07 31	07 34	07 45		07 53	08 01	08 04	08 15
Ewell East	d					06 35			06 49		07 05		07 19			07 35		07 49			08 05		08 19
Cheam	d					06 38			06 52	06 59	07 08		07 22		07 29	07 38		07 52		07 59	08 08		08 22
Sutton	a					06 41			06 55	07 01	07 11		07 25		07 31	07 41		07 55		08 01	08 11		08 25
Sutton	d								06 56				07 26					07 56					08 26
West Croydon	a								07 09				07 39					08 09					08 39
Norwood Junction	a								07 15				07 45					08 15					08 45
Sutton	d		05 46		06 16	06 42		06 46		07 02	07 12			07 16	07 32	07 42			07 46	08 02	08 12		
Carshalton	d		05 49		06 19	06 45		06 49		07 05	07 15			07 19	07 35	07 45			07 49	08 05	08 15		
Hackbridge	d		05 52		06 22	06 48		06 52			07 18			07 22		07 48			07 52		08 18		
Mitcham Junction	d		05 55		06 25	06 51		06 55			07 21			07 25		07 51			07 55		08 21		
Mitcham Eastfields	a		05 58		06 28	06 54		06 58			07 24			07 28		07 54			07 58		08 24		
Streatham	d		06 03		06 33			07 03						07 33					08 03				
Tulse Hill 3	a		06 07		06 37			07 07						07 37					08 07				
Tulse Hill	d		06 08		06 38			07 08						07 38					08 08				
London Bridge	a								07 28				07 58					08 28					08 58
Herne Hill	a		06 11		06 41			07 11						07 41					08 11				
Loughborough Jn	a		06 15		06 45			07 15						07 45					08 15				
Elephant & Castle	a		06 19		06 49			07 19						07 49					08 19				
London Blackfriars	a		06 24		06 54			07 24						07 54					08 24				
City Thameslink	a																						
Farringdon	a		06 28		06 58			07 28						07 58					08 28				
St Pancras International	a		06 33		07 03			07 33						08 03					08 33				
Balham 4 ⊖	a					07 03					07 33					08 03					08 33		
Clapham Junction 10	a	06 01		06 30		07 07	07 00			07 23	07 37	07 30			07 53	08 07	08 00			08 23	08 37	08 30	
London Waterloo 15 ⊖	a	06 11		06 40			07 10					07 40					08 10					08 40	
London Victoria 15 ⊖	a					07 15				07 32	07 45				08 02	08 15				08 32	08 45		

Table T180-R

Horsham and Dorking, Leatherhead, Epsom, Sutton, Hackbridge - London

Saturdays
21 December to 16 May

Station		SW	TL	SN	SN	SW	SN	SW	TL	SN	SN	SW	SN	SW	TL	SN	SN	SW	SN	SW	TL	SN	SN
Horsham 4	d									08 14												09 14	
Warnham	d									08 18												09 18	
Ockley	d									08 24												09 24	
Holmwood	d									08 28												09 28	
Dorking 4	a									08 36												09 36	
Dorking	d	08 02		08 07				08 32		08 37				09 02		09 07				09 32		09 37	
Box Hill & Westhumble	d	08 05						08 35		08 40				09 05						09 35		09 40	
Leatherhead	d	08 10		08 13		08 23		08 40		08 44		08 53		09 10		09 13		09 23		09 40		09 44	
Ashtead	d	08 13		08 17		08 27		08 43		08 48		08 57		09 13		09 17		09 27		09 43		09 48	
Epsom 3	a	08 18		08 23		08 31		08 48		08 53		09 01		09 18		09 23		09 31		09 48		09 53	
Epsom	d	08 19		08 23	08 31	08 34	08 45	08 49		08 53	09 01	09 04	09 15	09 19		09 23	09 31	09 34	09 45	09 49		09 53	10 01
Ewell East	d				08 35		08 49				09 05		09 19				09 35		09 49				10 05
Cheam	d			08 29	08 38		08 52			08 59	09 08		09 22			09 29	09 38		09 52			09 59	10 08
Sutton	a			08 31	08 41		08 55			09 01	09 11		09 25			09 31	09 41		09 55			10 01	10 11
Sutton	d						08 55						09 26						09 56				
West Croydon	a						09 09						09 39						10 09				
Norwood Junction	a						09 15						09 45						10 15				
Sutton	d		08 16	08 32	08 42				08 46	09 02	09 12				09 16	09 32	09 42				09 46	10 02	10 12
Carshalton	d		08 19	08 35	08 45				08 49	09 05	09 15				09 19	09 35	09 45				09 49	10 05	10 15
Hackbridge	d		08 22		08 48				08 52		09 18				09 22		09 48				09 52		10 18
Mitcham Junction	d		08 25		08 51				08 55		09 21				09 25		09 51				09 55		10 21
Mitcham Eastfields	a		08 28		08 54				08 58		09 24				09 28		09 54				09 58		10 24
Streatham	d		08 33						09 03						09 33						10 03		
Tulse Hill 3	a		08 37						09 07						09 37						10 07		
Tulse Hill	d		08 38						09 08						09 38						10 08		
London Bridge	a						09 28						09 58						10 28				
Herne Hill	a		08 41						09 11						09 41						10 11		
Loughborough Jn	a		08 45						09 15						09 45						10 15		
Elephant & Castle	a		08 49						09 19						09 49						10 19		
London Blackfriars	a		08 54						09 24						09 54						10 24		
City Thameslink	a								09 26						09 56						10 26		
Farringdon	a		08 58						09 28						09 58						10 28		
St Pancras International	a		09 03						09 33						10 03						10 33		
Balham 4 ⊖	a				09 03						09 33						10 03						10 33
Clapham Junction 10	a	08 45		08 53	09 07	09 00		09 15		09 23	09 37	09 30		09 45		09 53	10 07	10 00		10 15		10 23	10 37
London Waterloo 15 ⊖	a	08 55				09 10		09 25				09 40		09 55				10 10		10 25			
London Victoria 15 ⊖	a			09 02	09 15					09 32	09 45					10 02	10 15					10 32	10 45

Station		SW	SN	SW	TL	SN	SN	SW	SN	SW	TL	SN	SN	SW	SN	SW	TL	SN	SN	SW	SN	SW
Horsham 4	d											10 14										
Warnham	d											10 18										
Ockley	d											10 24										
Holmwood	d											10 28										
Dorking 4	a											10 36										
Dorking	d			10 02		10 07				10 32		10 37				11 02		11 07				11 32
Box Hill & Westhumble	d			10 05						10 35		10 40				11 05						11 35
Leatherhead	d	09 53		10 10		10 13		10 23		10 40		10 44		10 53		11 10		11 13		11 23		11 40
Ashtead	d	09 57		10 13		10 17		10 27		10 43		10 48		10 57		11 13		11 17		11 27		11 43
Epsom 3	a	10 01		10 18		10 23		10 31		10 48		10 53		11 01		11 18		11 23		11 31		11 48
Epsom	d	10 04	10 15	10 19		10 23	10 31	10 34	10 45	10 49		10 53	11 01	11 04	11 15	11 19		11 23	11 31	11 34	11 45	11 49
Ewell East	d		10 19				10 35		10 49				11 05		11 19				11 35		11 49	
Cheam	d		10 22			10 29	10 38		10 52			10 59	11 08		11 22			11 29	11 38		11 52	
Sutton	a		10 25			10 31	10 41		10 55			11 01	11 11		11 25			11 31	11 41		11 55	
Sutton	d		10 26						10 56						11 26						11 56	
West Croydon	a		10 39						11 09						11 39						12 09	
Norwood Junction	a		10 45						11 15						11 45						12 15	
Sutton	d				10 16	10 32	10 42				10 46	11 02	11 12				11 16	11 32	11 42			
Carshalton	d				10 19	10 35	10 45				10 49	11 05	11 15				11 19	11 35	11 45			
Hackbridge	d				10 22		10 48				10 52		11 18				11 22		11 48			
Mitcham Junction	d				10 25		10 51				10 55		11 21				11 25		11 51			
Mitcham Eastfields	a				10 28		10 54				10 58		11 24				11 28		11 54			
Streatham	d				10 33						11 03						11 33					
Tulse Hill 3	a				10 37						11 07						11 37					
Tulse Hill	d				10 38						11 08						11 38					
London Bridge	a		10 58						11 28						11 58						12 28	
Herne Hill	a				10 41						11 11						11 41					
Loughborough Jn	a				10 45						11 15						11 45					
Elephant & Castle	a				10 49						11 19						11 49					
London Blackfriars	a				10 54						11 24						11 54					
City Thameslink	a				10 56						11 26						11 56					
Farringdon	a				10 58						11 28						11 58					
St Pancras International	a				11 03						11 33						12 03					
Balham 4 ⊖	a						11 03						11 33						12 03			
Clapham Junction 10	a	10 30		10 45		10 53	11 07	11 00		11 15		11 23	11 37	11 30		11 45		11 53	12 07	12 00		12 15
London Waterloo 15 ⊖	a	10 40		10 55				11 10		11 25				11 40		11 55				12 10		12 25
London Victoria 15 ⊖	a					11 02	11 15					11 32	11 45					12 02	12 15			

Table T180-R

Saturdays

21 December to 16 May

Horsham and Dorking, Leatherhead, Epsom, Sutton, Hackbridge - London

		TL	SN	SN	SW	SN	SW	TL		SN	SN	SW	SN	SW	TL	SN	SN	SW		SN	SW	TL	SN	SN	SW
Horsham 4	d		11 14													12 14									
Warnham	d		11 18													12 18									
Ockley	d		11 24													12 24									
Holmwood	d		11 28													12 28									
Dorking 4	a		11 36													12 36									
Dorking	d		11 37				12 02			12 07				12 32		12 37					13 02		13 07		
Box Hill & Westhumble	d		11 40				12 05							12 35		12 40					13 05				
Leatherhead	d		11 44		11 53		12 10			12 13		12 23		12 40		12 44		12 53			13 10		13 13		13 23
Ashtead	d		11 48		11 57		12 13			12 17		12 27		12 43		12 48		12 57			13 13		13 17		13 27
Epsom 3	a		11 53		12 01		12 18			12 23		12 31		12 48		12 53		13 01			13 18		13 23		13 31
Epsom	d		11 53	12 01	12 04	12 15	12 19			12 23	12 31	12 34	12 45	12 49		12 53	13 01	13 04		13 15	13 19		13 23	13 31	13 34
Ewell East	d			12 05		12 19					12 35		12 49				13 05			13 19				13 35	
Cheam	d		11 59	12 08		12 22				12 29	12 38		12 52			12 59	13 08			13 22			13 29	13 38	
Sutton	a		12 01	12 11		12 25				12 31	12 41		12 55			13 01	13 11			13 25			13 31	13 41	
Sutton	d					12 26							12 56							13 26					
West Croydon	a					12 39							13 09							13 39					
Norwood Junction	a					12 45							13 15							13 45					
Sutton	d	11 46	12 02	12 12				12 16		12 32	12 42				12 46	13 02	13 12					13 16	13 32	13 42	
Carshalton	d	11 49	12 05	12 15				12 19		12 35	12 45				12 49	13 05	13 15					13 19	13 35	13 45	
Hackbridge	d	11 52		12 18				12 22			12 48				12 52		13 18					13 22		13 48	
Mitcham Junction	d	11 55		12 21				12 25			12 51				12 55		13 21					13 25		13 51	
Mitcham Eastfields	a	11 58		12 24				12 28			12 54				12 58		13 24					13 28		13 54	
Streatham	d	12 03						12 33							13 03							13 33			
Tulse Hill 3	a	12 07						12 37							13 07							13 37			
Tulse Hill	d	12 08						12 38							13 08							13 38			
London Bridge	a					12 58							13 28							13 58					
Herne Hill	a	12 11						12 41							13 11							13 41			
Loughborough Jn	a	12 15						12 45							13 15							13 45			
Elephant & Castle	a	12 19						12 49							13 19							13 49			
London Blackfriars	a	12 24						12 54							13 24							13 54			
City Thameslink	a	12 26						12 56							13 26							13 56			
Farringdon	a	12 28						12 58							13 28							13 58			
St Pancras International	a	12 33						13 03							13 33							14 03			
Balham 4 ⊖	a			12 33							13 03						13 33							14 03	
Clapham Junction 10	a		12 23	12 37	12 30		12 45			12 53	13 07	13 00		13 15		13 23	13 37	13 30			13 45		13 53	14 07	14 00
London Waterloo 15 ⊖	a				12 40		12 55					13 10		13 25				13 40			13 55				14 10
London Victoria 15 ⊖	a		12 32	12 45						13 02	13 15					13 32	13 45						14 02	14 15	

		SN	SW	TL		SN	SN	SW	SN	SW	TL	SN	SN	SW		SN	SW	TL	SN	SN	SW	SN	SW	TL	
Horsham 4	d					13 14													14 14						
Warnham	d					13 18													14 18						
Ockley	d					13 24													14 24						
Holmwood	d					13 28													14 28						
Dorking 4	a					13 36													14 36						
Dorking	d		13 32			13 37				14 02		14 07					14 32		14 37				15 02		
Box Hill & Westhumble	d		13 35			13 40				14 05							14 35		14 40				15 05		
Leatherhead	d		13 40			13 44		13 53		14 10		14 13		14 23			14 40		14 44		14 53		15 10		
Ashtead	d		13 43			13 48		13 57		14 13		14 17		14 27			14 43		14 48		14 57		15 13		
Epsom 3	a		13 48			13 53		14 01		14 18		14 22		14 31			14 48		14 53		15 01		15 18		
Epsom	d	13 45	13 49			13 53	14 01	14 04	14 15	14 19		14 22	14 31	14 34		14 45	14 49		14 53	15 01	15 04	15 15	15 19		
Ewell East	d	13 49					14 05		14 19				14 35			14 49				15 05		15 19			
Cheam	d	13 52				13 59	14 08		14 22			14 29	14 38			14 52			14 59	15 08		15 22			
Sutton	a	13 55				14 01	14 11		14 25			14 31	14 41			14 55			15 01	15 11		15 25			
Sutton	d	13 56							14 26							14 56						15 26			
West Croydon	a	14 09							14 39							15 09						15 39			
Norwood Junction	a	14 15							14 45							15 15						15 45			
Sutton	d			13 46		14 02	14 12				14 16	14 32	14 42					14 46	15 02	15 12				15 16	
Carshalton	d			13 49		14 05	14 15				14 19	14 35	14 45					14 49	15 05	15 15				15 19	
Hackbridge	d			13 52			14 18				14 22		14 48					14 52		15 18				15 22	
Mitcham Junction	d			13 55			14 21				14 25		14 51					14 55		15 21				15 25	
Mitcham Eastfields	a			13 58			14 24				14 28		14 54					14 58		15 24				15 28	
Streatham	d			14 03							14 33							15 03						15 33	
Tulse Hill 3	a			14 07							14 37							15 07						15 37	
Tulse Hill	d			14 08							14 38							15 08						15 38	
London Bridge	a	14 28							14 58							15 28						15 58			
Herne Hill	a			14 11							14 41							15 11						15 41	
Loughborough Jn	a			14 15							14 45							15 15						15 45	
Elephant & Castle	a			14 19							14 49							15 19						15 49	
London Blackfriars	a			14 24							14 54							15 24						15 54	
City Thameslink	a			14 26							14 56							15 26						15 56	
Farringdon	a			14 28							14 58							15 28						15 58	
St Pancras International	a			14 33							15 03							15 33						16 03	
Balham 4 ⊖	a						14 33						15 03							15 33					
Clapham Junction 10	a		14 15			14 23	14 37	14 30		14 45		14 53	15 07	15 00			15 15		15 23	15 37	15 30		15 45		
London Waterloo 15 ⊖	a		14 25					14 40		14 55				15 10			15 25				15 40		15 55		
London Victoria 15 ⊖	a					14 32	14 45					15 02	15 15						15 32	15 45					

Table T180-R

Saturdays

21 December to 16 May

Horsham and Dorking, Leatherhead, Epsom, Sutton, Hackbridge - London

		SN	SN	SW	SN	SW	TL	SN	SN	SW		SN	SW	TL	SN	SN	SW	SN	SW	TL		SN	SN	SW	SN
Horsham 4	d							15 14														16 14			
Warnham	d							15 18														16 18			
Ockley	d							15 24														16 24			
Holmwood	d							15 28														16 28			
Dorking 4	a							15 36														16 36			
Dorking	d	15 07				15 32		15 37					16 02		16 07				16 32			16 37			
Box Hill & Westhumble	d					15 35		15 40					16 05						16 35			16 40			
Leatherhead	d	15 13		15 23		15 40		15 44		15 53			16 10		16 13		16 23		16 40			16 44		16 53	
Ashtead	d	15 17		15 27		15 43		15 48		15 57			16 13		16 17		16 27		16 43			16 48		16 57	
Epsom 3	a	15 23		15 31		15 48		15 53		16 01			16 18		16 22		16 31		16 48			16 53		17 01	
Epsom	d	15 23	15 31	15 34	15 45	15 49		15 53	16 01	16 04		16 15	16 19		16 22	16 31	16 34	16 45	16 49			16 53	17 01	17 04	17 15
Ewell East	d		15 35		15 49				16 05			16 19				16 35		16 49					17 05		17 19
Cheam	d	15 29	15 38		15 52			15 59	16 08			16 22			16 29	16 38		16 52				16 59	17 08		17 22
Sutton	a	15 31	15 41		15 55			16 01	16 11			16 25			16 31	16 41		16 55				17 01	17 11		17 25
Sutton	d				15 56							16 26						16 56							17 26
West Croydon	a				16 09							16 39						17 09							17 39
Norwood Junction	a				16 15							16 45						17 15							17 45
Sutton	d	15 32	15 42				15 46	16 02	16 12					16 16	16 32	16 42				16 46		17 02	17 12		
Carshalton	d	15 35	15 45				15 49	16 05	16 15					16 19	16 35	16 45				16 49		17 05	17 15		
Hackbridge	d		15 48				15 52		16 18					16 22		16 48				16 52			17 18		
Mitcham Junction	d		15 51				15 55		16 21					16 25		16 51				16 55			17 21		
Mitcham Eastfields	a		15 54				15 58		16 24					16 28		16 54				16 58			17 24		
Streatham	d						16 03							16 33						17 03					
Tulse Hill 3	a						16 07							16 37						17 07					
Tulse Hill	d						16 08							16 38						17 08					
London Bridge	a				16 28							16 58						17 28							17 58
Herne Hill	a						16 11							16 41						17 11					
Loughborough Jn	a						16 15							16 45						17 15					
Elephant & Castle	a						16 19							16 49						17 19					
London Blackfriars	a						16 24							16 54						17 24					
City Thameslink	a						16 26							16 56						17 26					
Farringdon	a						16 28							16 58						17 28					
St Pancras International	a						16 33							17 03						17 33					
Balham 4 ⊖	a		16 03						16 33							17 03							17 33		
Clapham Junction 10	a	15 53	16 07	16 00		16 15		16 23	16 37	16 30			16 45		16 53	17 07	17 00		17 15			17 23	17 37	17 30	
London Waterloo 15 ⊖	a			16 10		16 25				16 40			16 55				17 10		17 25					17 40	
London Victoria 15 ⊖	a	16 02	16 15					16 32	16 45						17 02	17 15						17 32	17 45		

		SW	TL	SN	SN	SW		SN	SW	TL	SN	SN	SW	SN	SW	TL		SN	SN	SW	SN	SW	TL	SN	SN
Horsham 4	d										17 14													18 14	
Warnham	d										17 18													18 18	
Ockley	d										17 24													18 24	
Holmwood	d										17 28													18 28	
Dorking 4	a										17 36													18 36	
Dorking	d	17 02		17 07					17 32		17 37				18 02			18 07				18 32		18 37	
Box Hill & Westhumble	d	17 05							17 35		17 40				18 05							18 35		18 40	
Leatherhead	d	17 10		17 13		17 23			17 40		17 44		17 53		18 10			18 13		18 23		18 40		18 44	
Ashtead	d	17 13		17 17		17 27			17 43		17 48		17 57		18 13			18 17		18 27		18 43		18 48	
Epsom 3	a	17 18		17 23		17 31			17 48		17 53		18 01		18 18			18 23		18 31		18 48		18 53	
Epsom	d	17 19		17 23	17 31	17 34		17 45	17 49		17 53	18 01	18 04	18 15	18 19			18 23	18 31	18 34	18 45	18 49		18 53	19 01
Ewell East	d				17 35			17 49				18 05		18 19					18 35		18 49				19 05
Cheam	d			17 29	17 38			17 52			17 59	18 08		18 22				18 29	18 38		18 52			18 59	19 08
Sutton	a			17 31	17 41			17 55			18 01	18 11		18 25				18 31	18 41		18 55			19 02	19 11
Sutton	d							17 56						18 26							18 55				
West Croydon	a							18 09						18 39							19 09				
Norwood Junction	a							18 15						18 45							19 15				
Sutton	d		17 16	17 32	17 42					17 46	18 02	18 12				18 16		18 32	18 42				18 46	19 02	19 12
Carshalton	d		17 19	17 35	17 45					17 49	18 05	18 15				18 19		18 35	18 45				18 49	19 05	19 15
Hackbridge	d		17 22		17 48					17 52		18 18				18 22			18 48				18 52		19 18
Mitcham Junction	d		17 25		17 51					17 55		18 21				18 25			18 51				18 55		19 21
Mitcham Eastfields	a		17 28		17 54					17 58		18 24				18 28			18 54				18 58		19 24
Streatham	d		17 33							18 03						18 33							19 03		
Tulse Hill 3	a		17 37							18 07						18 37							19 07		
Tulse Hill	d		17 38							18 08						18 38							19 08		
London Bridge	a							18 28						18 58							19 28				
Herne Hill	a		17 41							18 11						18 41							19 11		
Loughborough Jn	a		17 45							18 15						18 45							19 15		
Elephant & Castle	a		17 49							18 19						18 49							19 19		
London Blackfriars	a		17 54							18 24						18 54							19 24		
City Thameslink	a		17 56							18 26						18 56							19 26		
Farringdon	a		17 58							18 28						18 58							19 28		
St Pancras International	a		18 03							18 33						19 03							19 33		
Balham 4 ⊖	a				18 03							18 33							19 03						19 33
Clapham Junction 10	a	17 45		17 53	18 07	18 00			18 15		18 23	18 37	18 30		18 45			18 53	19 07	19 00		19 15		19 23	19 37
London Waterloo 15 ⊖	a	17 55				18 10			18 25				18 40		18 55					19 10		19 25			
London Victoria 15 ⊖	a			18 02	18 15						18 32	18 45						19 02	19 15					19 32	19 45

Table T180-R

Saturdays
21 December to 16 May

Horsham and Dorking, Leatherhead, Epsom, Sutton, Hackbridge - London

Station		SW		SN	SW	TL	SN	SN	SW	SN	SW	TL		SN	SN	SW	SN	SW	TL	SN	SN	SW		SN	SW
Horsham 4	d																								
Warnham	d																								
Ockley	d																								
Holmwood	d																								
Dorking 4	a																								
Dorking	d				19 02		19 07				19 32			19 37				20 02		20 07					20 32
Box Hill & Westhumble	d				19 05						19 35			19 40				20 05							20 35
Leatherhead	d	18 53			19 10		19 13		19 23		19 40			19 44		19 53		20 10		20 13		20 23			20 40
Ashtead	d	18 57			19 13		19 17		19 27		19 43			19 48		19 57		20 13		20 17		20 27			20 43
Epsom 3	a	19 01			19 18		19 23		19 31		19 48			19 53		20 01		20 18		20 23		20 31			20 48
Epsom	d	19 04		19 15	19 19		19 23	19 31	19 34	19 45	19 49			19 53	20 01	20 04	20 15	20 19		20 23	20 31	20 34		20 45	20 49
Ewell East	d			19 19				19 35		19 49					20 05		20 19				20 35			20 49	
Cheam	d			19 22			19 29	19 38		19 52				19 59	20 08		20 22			20 29	20 38			20 52	
Sutton	a			19 25			19 31	19 41		19 55				20 01	20 11		20 25			20 31	20 41			20 55	
Sutton	d			19 26						19 56							20 26							20 56	
West Croydon	a			19 39						20 09							20 39							21 09	
Norwood Junction	a			19 45						20 15							20 45							21 15	
Sutton	d					19 16	19 32	19 42				19 46		20 02	20 12				20 16	20 32	20 42				
Carshalton	d					19 19	19 35	19 45				19 49		20 05	20 15				20 19	20 35	20 45				
Hackbridge	d					19 22		19 48				19 52			20 18				20 22		20 48				
Mitcham Junction	d					19 25		19 51				19 55			20 21				20 25		20 51				
Mitcham Eastfields	a					19 28		19 54				19 58			20 24				20 28		20 54				
Streatham	d					19 33						20 03							20 33						
Tulse Hill 3	a					19 37						20 07							20 37						
Tulse Hill	d					19 38						20 08							20 38						
London Bridge	a			19 58						20 28							20 58							21 28	
Herne Hill	a					19 41						20 11							20 41						
Loughborough Jn	a					19 45						20 15							20 45						
Elephant & Castle	a					19 49						20 19							20 49						
London Blackfriars	a					19 54						20 24							20 54						
City Thameslink	a					19 56						20 26							20 56						
Farringdon	a					19 58						20 28							20 58						
St Pancras International	a					20 03						20 33							21 03						
Balham 4 ⊖	a							20 03							20 33						21 03				
Clapham Junction 10	a	19 30			19 45		19 53	20 07	20 00		20 15			20 23	20 37	20 30		20 45		20 53	21 07	21 00			21 15
London Waterloo 15 ⊖	a	19 40			19 55				20 10		20 25					20 40		20 55				21 10			21 25
London Victoria 15 ⊖	a						20 02	20 15						20 32	20 45					21 02	21 15				

Station		TL	SN	SN	SW	SN	SW	TL		SN	SN	SW	SN	SW	TL	SN	SN	SW		SN	SW	TL	SN	SN	SW
Horsham 4	d																								
Warnham	d																								
Ockley	d																								
Holmwood	d																								
Dorking 4	a																								
Dorking	d		20 37				21 02			21 07				21 32		21 37					22 02		22 07		
Box Hill & Westhumble	d		20 40				21 05							21 35		21 40					22 05				
Leatherhead	d		20 44		20 53		21 10			21 13		21 23		21 40		21 44		21 53			22 10		22 13		22 23
Ashtead	d		20 48		20 57		21 12			21 17		21 27		21 43		21 48		21 57			22 12		22 17		22 27
Epsom 3	a		20 53		21 01		21 18			21 23		21 31		21 48		21 53		22 01			22 18		22 23		22 31
Epsom	d		20 53	21 01	21 04	21 15	21 19			21 23	21 31	21 34	21 45	21 49		21 53	22 01	22 04		22 15	22 19		22 23	22 31	22 34
Ewell East	d			21 05		21 19					21 35		21 49				22 05			22 19				22 35	
Cheam	d		20 59	21 08		21 22				21 29	21 38		21 52			21 59	22 08			22 22			22 29	22 38	
Sutton	a		21 01	21 11		21 25				21 31	21 41		21 55			22 01	22 11			22 25			22 31	22 41	
Sutton	d					21 26							21 56							22 26					
West Croydon	a					21 39							22 09							22 39					
Norwood Junction	a					21 45							22 15							22 45					
Sutton	d	20 46	21 02	21 12				21 16		21 32	21 42				21 46	22 02	22 12					22 18	22 32	22 42	
Carshalton	d	20 49	21 05	21 15				21 19		21 35	21 45				21 49	22 05	22 15					22 21	22 35	22 45	
Hackbridge	d	20 52		21 18				21 22			21 48				21 52		22 18					22 24		22 48	
Mitcham Junction	d	20 55		21 21				21 25			21 51				21 55		22 21					22 27		22 51	
Mitcham Eastfields	a	20 58		21 24				21 28			21 54				21 58		22 24					22 30		22 54	
Streatham	d	21 03						21 33							22 03							22 35			
Tulse Hill 3	a	21 07						21 37							22 07							22 39			
Tulse Hill	d	21 08						21 38							22 08							22 40			
London Bridge	a					21 58							22 28							22 58					
Herne Hill	a	21 11						21 41							22 11							22 43			
Loughborough Jn	a	21 15						21 45							22 15							22 47			
Elephant & Castle	a	21 19						21 49							22 19							22 51			
London Blackfriars	a	21 24						21 54							22 24							22 59			
City Thameslink	a																								
Farringdon	a	21 28						21 58							22 28							23 03			
St Pancras International	a	21 33						22 03							22 33							23 08			
Balham 4 ⊖	a			21 33							22 03						22 33							23 03	
Clapham Junction 10	a		21 23	21 37	21 30		21 45			21 53	22 07	22 00		22 15		22 23	22 37	22 30			22 45		22 53	23 07	23 00
London Waterloo 15 ⊖	a				21 40		21 55					22 10		22 25				22 41			22 55				23 11
London Victoria 15 ⊖	a		21 32	21 45						22 01	22 15					22 32	22 45						23 02	23 15	

Table T180-R

Saturdays
21 December to 16 May

Horsham and Dorking, Leatherhead, Epsom, Sutton, Hackbridge - London

Station		SN	SW	TL		SN	SN	SW	TL	SN	SN
Horsham 4	d										
Warnham	d										
Ockley	d										
Holmwood	d										
Dorking 4	a										
Dorking	d		22 32			22 37				23 07	23 37
Box Hill & Westhumble	d		22 35			22 40				23 10	23 40
Leatherhead	d		22 40			22 44		23 11		23 14	23 44
Ashtead	d		22 43			22 48		23 14		23 18	23 48
Epsom 3	a		22 48			22 53		23 19		23 23	23 53
Epsom	d	22 45	22 49			22 53	23 01	23 19		23 23	23 53
Ewell East	d	22 49					23 05				
Cheam	d	22 52				22 59	23 08			23 29	23 59
Sutton	a	22 55				23 01	23 11			23 31	00 02
Sutton	d	22 56								23 32	00 03
West Croydon	a	23 09								23 45	00 15
Norwood Junction	a	23 15									
Sutton	d			22 48		23 02	23 12		23 18		
Carshalton	d			22 51		23 05	23 15		23 21		
Hackbridge	d			22 54			23 18		23 24		
Mitcham Junction	d			22 57			23 21		23 27		
Mitcham Eastfields	a			23 00			23 24		23 30		
Streatham	d			23 05					23 35		
Tulse Hill 3	a			23 09					23 39		
Tulse Hill	d			23 10					23 40		
London Bridge	a	23 28									
Herne Hill	a			23 13					23 43		
Loughborough Jn	a			23 17					23 47		
Elephant & Castle	a			23 21					23 51		
London Blackfriars	a			23 26					00 01		
City Thameslink	a										
Farringdon	a			23 31					00 06		
St Pancras International	a			23 35					00 10		
Balham 4 ⊖	a						23 33				
Clapham Junction 10	a		23 15			23 23	23 37	23 45			
London Waterloo 15 ⊖	a		23 28					23 59			
London Victoria 15 ⊖	a					23 32	23 48				

Sundays
15 December to 10 May

Station		SN A	SN	SN	SW	SN	SW	SN	SN	SW		SN	SN	SW	SN	SN	SW	SN	SN	SW		SN	SN	SW	TL
Horsham 4	d																								
Warnham	d																								
Ockley	d																								
Holmwood	d																								
Dorking 4	a																								
Dorking	d					07 16		07 46				08 16			08 46		09 07	09 16				09 46		10 07	
Box Hill & Westhumble	d					07 19		07 49				08 19			08 49		09 10	09 19				09 49		10 10	
Leatherhead	d					07 24		07 54				08 24		08 45	08 54		09 15	09 24		09 45		09 54		10 15	
Ashtead	d					07 28		07 58				08 28		08 48	08 58		09 18	09 28		09 48		09 58		10 18	
Epsom 3	a					07 32		08 02				08 32		08 53	09 02		09 23	09 32		09 53		10 02		10 23	
Epsom	d		06 43	07 03	07 23	07 33	07 53	08 03	08 14	08 23		08 33	08 44	08 53	09 03	09 14	09 23	09 33	09 44	09 53		10 03	10 14	10 23	
Ewell East	d		06 47	07 07		07 37		08 07	08 18			08 37	08 48		09 07	09 18		09 37	09 48			10 07	10 18		
Cheam	d		06 50	07 10		07 40		08 10	08 21			08 40	08 51		09 10	09 21		09 40	09 51			10 10	10 21		
Sutton	a		06 53	07 13		07 43		08 13	08 24			08 43	08 54		09 13	09 24		09 43	09 54			10 13	10 24		
Sutton	d	00 03	06 53																						
West Croydon	a	00 15	07 06																						
Norwood Junction	a																								
Sutton	d			07 14		07 44		08 14	08 26			08 46	08 56		09 16	09 26		09 46	09 56			10 16	10 26		10 40
Carshalton	d			07 17		07 47		08 17	08 29			08 49	08 59		09 19	09 29		09 49	09 59			10 19	10 29		10 43
Hackbridge	d			07 20		07 50		08 20	08 32				09 02			09 32			10 02				10 32		10 45
Mitcham Junction	d			07 24		07 54		08 24	08 35				09 05			09 35			10 05				10 35		10 48
Mitcham Eastfields	a			07 27		07 57		08 27	08 38				09 08			09 38			10 08				10 38		10 51
Streatham	d																								10 55
Tulse Hill 3	a																								10 59
Tulse Hill	d																								10 59
London Bridge	a																								
Herne Hill	a																								11 03
Loughborough Jn	a																								11 06
Elephant & Castle	a																								11 10
London Blackfriars	a																								11 15
City Thameslink	a																								
Farringdon	a																								
St Pancras International	a																								
Balham 4 ⊖	a		07 24	07 35		08 05		08 34	08 48				09 16			09 46			10 16				10 46		
Clapham Junction 10	a		07 30	07 40	07 50	08 10	08 21	08 41	08 53	08 50		09 06	09 21	09 20	09 36	09 51	09 51	10 06	10 21	10 20		10 36	10 51	10 49	
London Waterloo 15 ⊖	a				08 02		08 36			09 02				09 32			10 03			10 34				10 59	
London Victoria 15 ⊖	a		07 39	07 48		08 19		08 49	09 00			09 15	09 29		09 45	09 59		10 15	10 29			10 45	10 59		

A not 15 December

Table T180-R

Sundays
15 December to 10 May

Horsham and Dorking, Leatherhead, Epsom, Sutton, Hackbridge - London

		SN	SN	SW	TL	SN	SN	SW	TL	SN	SN	SW	TL		SN	SN	SW	TL	SN	SN	SW	TL		SN
Horsham 4	d																							
Warnham	d																							
Ockley	d																							
Holmwood	d																							
Dorking 4	a																							
Dorking	d	10 16				10 46		11 07		11 16					16 46		17 07		17 16					17 46
Box Hill & Westhumble	d	10 19				10 49		11 10		11 19					16 49		17 10		17 19					17 49
Leatherhead	d	10 24		10 45		10 54		11 15		11 24		11 45			16 54		17 15		17 24		17 45			17 54
Ashtead	d	10 28		10 48		10 58		11 18		11 28		11 48			16 58		17 18		17 28		17 48			17 58
Epsom 3	a	10 32		10 53		11 02		11 23		11 32		11 53			17 02		17 23		17 32		17 53			18 02
Epsom	d	10 33	10 44	10 53		11 03	11 14	11 23		11 33	11 44	11 53			17 03	17 14	17 23		17 33	17 44	17 53			18 03
Ewell East	d	10 37	10 48			11 07	11 18			11 37	11 48				17 07	17 18			17 37	17 48				18 07
Cheam	d	10 40	10 51			11 10	11 21			11 40	11 51				17 10	17 21			17 40	17 51				18 10
Sutton	a	10 43	10 54			11 13	11 24			11 43	11 54				17 13	17 24			17 43	17 54				18 13
Sutton	d																							
West Croydon	a																							
Norwood Junction	a																							
Sutton	d	10 46	10 56		11 10	11 16	11 26		11 40	11 46	11 56		12 10	and at the same minutes past each hour until	17 16	17 26		17 40	17 46	17 56		18 10		18 16
Carshalton	d	10 49	10 59		11 13	11 19	11 29		11 43	11 49	11 59		12 13		17 19	17 29		17 43	17 49	17 59		18 13		18 19
Hackbridge	d		11 02		11 15		11 32		11 45		12 02		12 15			17 32		17 45		18 02		18 15		
Mitcham Junction	d		11 05		11 18		11 35		11 48		12 05		12 18			17 35		17 48		18 05		18 18		
Mitcham Eastfields	a		11 08		11 21		11 38		11 51		12 08		12 21			17 38		17 51		18 08		18 21		
Streatham	d				11 25				11 55				12 25					17 55				18 25		
Tulse Hill 3	a				11 29				11 59				12 29					17 59				18 29		
Tulse Hill	d				11 29				11 59				12 29					17 59				18 29		
London Bridge	a																							
Herne Hill	a				11 33				12 03				12 33					18 03				18 33		
Loughborough Jn	a				11 36				12 06				12 36					18 06				18 36		
Elephant & Castle	a				11 40				12 10				12 40					18 10				18 40		
London Blackfriars	a				11 45				12 15				12 45					18 15				18 45		
City Thameslink	a																							
Farringdon	a								12 20				12 50					18 20				18 50		
St Pancras International	a								12 24				12 54					18 24				18 54		
Balham 4 ⊖	a		11 16				11 46				12 16					17 46				18 16				
Clapham Junction 10	a	11 06	11 21	11 19		11 36	11 51	11 49		12 06	12 21	12 19			17 36	17 51	17 49		18 06	18 21	18 19			18 36
London Waterloo 15 ⊖	a			11 29				11 59				12 29					17 59				18 29			
London Victoria 15 ⊖	a	11 15	11 29			11 45	11 59			12 15	12 29				17 45	17 59			18 15	18 29				18 45

		SN	SW	TL	SN	SN	SW	TL	SN		SN	SW	TL	SN	SN	SW	TL	SN	SN		SW	TL	SN	SN	SW
Horsham 4	d																								
Warnham	d																								
Ockley	d																								
Holmwood	d																								
Dorking 4	a																								
Dorking	d		18 07		18 16				18 46			19 07		19 16				19 46			20 07		20 16		
Box Hill & Westhumble	d		18 10		18 19				18 49			19 10		19 19				19 49			20 10		20 19		
Leatherhead	d		18 15		18 24		18 45		18 54			19 15		19 24		19 45		19 54			20 15		20 24		20 45
Ashtead	d		18 18		18 28		18 48		18 58			19 18		19 28		19 48		19 58			20 18		20 28		20 48
Epsom 3	a		18 23		18 32		18 53		19 02			19 23		19 32		19 53		20 02			20 23		20 32		20 53
Epsom	d	18 17	18 23		18 33	18 44	18 53		19 03		19 14	19 23		19 33	19 44	19 53		20 03	20 14		20 23		20 33	20 44	20 53
Ewell East	d	18 21			18 37	18 48			19 07		19 18			19 37	19 48			20 07	20 18				20 37	20 48	
Cheam	d	18 24			18 40	18 51			19 10		19 21			19 40	19 51			20 10	20 21				20 40	20 51	
Sutton	a	18 28			18 43	18 54			19 13		19 24			19 43	19 54			20 13	20 24				20 43	20 54	
Sutton	d																								
West Croydon	a																								
Norwood Junction	a																								
Sutton	d	18 28		18 40	18 46	18 56		19 10	19 16		19 26		19 40	19 46	19 56		20 10	20 16	20 26			20 40	20 46	20 56	
Carshalton	d	18 31		18 43	18 49	18 59		19 13	19 19		19 29		19 43	19 49	19 59		20 13	20 19	20 29			20 43	20 49	20 59	
Hackbridge	d	18 34		18 45		19 02		19 15			19 32		19 45		20 02		20 15		20 32			20 45		21 02	
Mitcham Junction	d	18 37		18 48		19 05		19 18			19 35		19 48		20 05		20 18		20 35			20 48		21 05	
Mitcham Eastfields	a	18 40		18 51		19 08		19 21			19 38		19 51		20 08		20 21		20 38			20 51		21 08	
Streatham	d			18 55				19 25					19 55				20 25					20 55			
Tulse Hill 3	a			18 59				19 29					19 59				20 29					20 59			
Tulse Hill	d			18 59				19 29					19 59				20 29					20 59			
London Bridge	a																								
Herne Hill	a			19 03				19 33					20 03				20 33					21 03			
Loughborough Jn	a			19 06				19 36					20 06				20 36					21 06			
Elephant & Castle	a			19 10				19 40					20 10				20 40					21 10			
London Blackfriars	a			19 15				19 45					20 15				20 45					21 15			
City Thameslink	a																								
Farringdon	a			19 20				19 50					20 20				20 50					21 20			
St Pancras International	a			19 24				19 54					20 24				20 54					21 24			
Balham 4 ⊖	a	18 47				19 16					19 46				20 16				20 46					21 16	
Clapham Junction 10	a	18 51	18 49		19 07	19 21	19 19		19 36		19 51	19 49		20 07	20 21	20 19		20 36	20 51		20 49		21 06	21 21	21 19
London Waterloo 15 ⊖	a		18 59				19 29					20 00				20 29					21 01				21 29
London Victoria 15 ⊖	a	18 59			19 15	19 29			19 45		19 59			20 15	20 29			20 45	20 59				21 15	21 29	

NRT DECEMBER 19 EDITION

Table T180-R

Sundays
15 December to 10 May

Horsham and Dorking, Leatherhead, Epsom, Sutton, Hackbridge - London

		TL	SN	SN	SW		TL	SN	SN	SW	TL	SN	SN	SW	TL		SN	SN	SW	SN	SW	SN
Horsham 4	d																					
Warnham	d																					
Ockley	d																					
Holmwood	d																					
Dorking 4	a																					
Dorking	d		20 46		21 07			21 16				21 46		22 07			22 16			22 46	23 07	23 16
Box Hill & Westhumble	d		20 49		21 10			21 19				21 49		22 10			22 19			22 49	23 10	23 19
Leatherhead	d		20 54		21 15			21 24		21 45		21 54		22 15			22 24		22 45	22 54	23 15	23 24
Ashtead	d		20 58		21 18			21 28		21 48		21 58		22 18			22 28		22 48	22 58	23 18	23 28
Epsom 3	a		21 02		21 23			21 32		21 53		22 02		22 23			22 32		22 53	23 02	23 23	23 32
Epsom	d		21 03	21 14	21 23			21 33	21 44	21 53		22 03	22 14	22 23			22 33	22 44	22 53	23 03	23 23	23 33
Ewell East	d		21 07	21 18				21 37	21 48			22 07	22 18				22 37	22 48		23 07		23 37
Cheam	d		21 10	21 21				21 40	21 51			22 10	22 21				22 40	22 51		23 10		23 40
Sutton	a		21 13	21 24				21 43	21 54			22 13	22 24				22 43	22 54		23 13		23 43
Sutton	d																					
West Croydon	a																					
Norwood Junction	a																					
Sutton	d	21 10	21 16	21 26			21 40	21 46	21 56		22 10	22 16	22 26		22 40		22 46	22 56		23 16		23 46
Carshalton	d	21 13	21 19	21 29			21 43	21 49	21 59		22 13	22 19	22 29		22 43		22 49	22 59		23 19		23 49
Hackbridge	d	21 15		21 32			21 45		22 02		22 15		22 32		22 45			23 02				23 52
Mitcham Junction	d	21 18		21 35			21 48		22 05		22 18		22 35		22 48			23 05				23 55
Mitcham Eastfields	a	21 21		21 38			21 51		22 08		22 21		22 38		22 51			23 08				23 58
Streatham	d	21 25					21 55				22 25				22 55							
Tulse Hill 3	a	21 29					21 59				22 29				22 59							
Tulse Hill	d	21 29					21 59				22 29				22 59							
London Bridge	a																					
Herne Hill	a	21 33					22 03				22 33				23 03							
Loughborough Jn	a	21 36					22 06				22 36				23 06							
Elephant & Castle	a	21 40					22 10				22 40				23 10							
London Blackfriars	a	21 45					22 15				22 45				23 15							
City Thameslink	a																					
Farringdon	a	21 50					22 20								23 20							
St Pancras International	a	21 54					22 24								23 24							
Balham 4 ⊖	a			21 46					22 16				22 46					23 16				00 06
Clapham Junction 10	a		21 36	21 51	21 49			22 06	22 21	22 19		22 36	22 51	22 49			23 06	23 21	23 19	23 36	23 49	00 12
London Waterloo 15 ⊖	a				22 00					22 29				23 00					23 29		00 01	
London Victoria 15 ⊖	a		21 45	21 59				22 15	22 29			22 45	22 59				23 15	23 30		23 45		00 21

AVAILABLE FROM MP Middleton Press

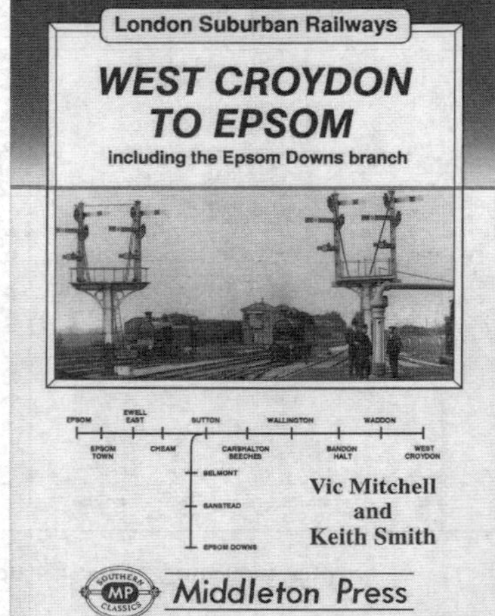

London and Croydon - Purley, Caterham and Tattenham Corner

Miles	Miles	Miles	Station		SN MO	TL MO 1	SN MX	SN MX	SN MO	SN MX	SN MX 1	SN MX	SN MO	SN 1	SN MX	TL MO 1	TL MX 1	TL 1	TL 1	TL 1	SN 1	TL 1	SN 1
0	—	0	London Victoria (15) ⊖	d										00 08							04 35		05 20
2¾	—	2¾	Clapham Junction (10)	d										00 15							04 42		05 29
—	—	10	East Croydon	a										00 30							04 57		05 41
—	—	—	St Pancras International	d												00 51	00 52	01 32	02 32	03 32		04 32	
—	—	—	Farringdon	d																			
—	—	—	City Thameslink	d																			
—	—	—	London Blackfriars	d												01 01	01 02	01 40	02 40	03 40		04 40	
—	0	—	London Bridge (4) ⊖	d											00 17								
—	8½	—	New Cross Gate (4) ⊖	d																			
—	8¾	—	Norwood Junction (2)	d									00 16		00 30								
10	10	—	East Croydon	a									00 19		00 34	01 27	01 28	02 06	03 06	04 06		05 06	
10	10	—	East Croydon	d		00 01		00 02	00 03		00 14		00 20	00 31	00 34	01 28	01 28	02 07	03 07	04 07	04 58	05 07	05 41
11½	11	—	**South Croydon (4)**	d				00 04	00 05		00 17		00 22		00 37								
12½	12	—	**Purley Oaks**	d				00 07	00 08				00 25		00 40								
—	—	12½	**Sanderstead**	d						←	00 20												05 46
13½	13	—	**Purley (4)**	a		00 06		00 10	00 11	00 10			00 28	00 36	00 43	01 33	01 34	02 12	03 12	04 12	05 04	05 12	
—	—	—	**Purley**	d				00 15	00 12	00 15		00 18	00 29		00 44								
—	14¼	—	**Kenley**	d				→	00 15	00 18			00 32		00 47								
—	15½	—	**Whyteleafe**	d					00 18	00 21			00 35		00 50								
—	—	15½	**Upper Warlingham**	a							00 27												05 53
—	16	—	**Whyteleafe South**	d					00 20	00 23			00 37		00 52								
—	17¾	—	**Caterham**	a					00 25	00 28			00 42		00 57								
14¼	—	—	**Reedham**	d								00 20											
15	—	—	**Coulsdon Town**	d								00 23											
15¾	—	—	**Woodmansterne**	d								00 26											
16¾	—	—	**Chipstead**	d								00 29											
19¼	—	—	**Kingswood**	d			00 05					00 35											
20½	—	—	**Tadworth**	d	00 01		00 08					00 38											
21¾	—	—	**Tattenham Corner**	a	00 05		00 12					00 42											

Station		SN 1	TL 1	SN 1	SN		SN 1	TL 1	SN	TL 1	SN 1	SN		SN 1	TL 1	SN		TL 1	SN 1	SN		SN 1
London Victoria (15) ⊖	d	05 32		05 39			05 50		06 02		06 09			06 20		06 32			06 39			06 50
Clapham Junction (10)	d	05 42		05 46			05 57		06 09		06 16			06 27		06 39			06 46			06 57
East Croydon	a	05 51		05 55			06 09		06 19		06 26			06 39		06 49			06 56			07 09
St Pancras International	d							05 45		05 55					06 15			06 25				
Farringdon	d							05 49		05 59					06 19			06 29				
City Thameslink	d							05 51		06 01					06 21			06 31				
London Blackfriars	d							05 54		06 04					06 24			06 34				
London Bridge (4) ⊖	d		05 37		05 34			06 00		06 11		06 17			06 30			06 41		06 47		
New Cross Gate (4) ⊖	d				05 40																	
Norwood Junction (2)	d		05 51		05 58			06 12							06 42							
East Croydon	a		05 54		06 02			06 16		06 24		06 31			06 46			06 54		07 01		
East Croydon	d	05 52	05 55	05 55	06 02		06 10	06 16	06 20	06 25	06 27	06 32		06 40	06 46	06 50		06 55	06 57	07 02		07 10
South Croydon (4)	d		05 58		06 05				06 23	06 28		06 35				06 53		06 58		07 05		
Purley Oaks	d				06 08				06 26			06 38				06 56				07 08		
Sanderstead	d		06a01				06 15			06a31				06 45				07a01				07 15
Purley (4)	a	05 56		06 01	06 11			06 22	06 29		06 32	06 41			06 53	06 59			07 02	07 11		
Purley	d				06 15	06 18			06 33			06 45	06 48			07 05	07 08			07 15	07 18	
Kenley	d				06 18							06 48				07 08				07 18		
Whyteleafe	d				06 21							06 51				07 11				07 21		
Upper Warlingham	a						06 22							06 52								07 22
Whyteleafe South	d				06 23							06 53				07 13				07 23		
Caterham	a				06 28							06 58				07 18				07 28		
Reedham	d					06 20			06 35				06 50				07 10				07 20	
Coulsdon Town	d					06 23			06 38				06 53				07 13				07 23	
Woodmansterne	d					06 26			06 41				06 56				07 16				07 26	
Chipstead	d					06 29			06 44				06 59				07 19				07 29	
Kingswood	d					06 35			06 50				07 05				07 25				07 35	
Tadworth	d					06 38			06 53				07 08				07 28				07 38	
Tattenham Corner	a					06 42			06 57				07 12				07 32				07 42	

Station		SN		TL 1	SN 1	SN		SN 1	SN	TL 1	SN 1	SN		SN 1	SN	TL 1	SN 1	SN		TL 1	SN 1	SN	SN 1
London Victoria (15) ⊖	d	07 02			07 09			07 20	07 32		07 39			07 50	08 01		08 09				08 20		08 39
Clapham Junction (10)	d	07 09			07 16			07 27	07 39		07 46			07 57	08 08		08 16				08 27		08 46
East Croydon	a	07 19			07 27			07 39	07 49		07 57			08 09	08 19		08 27				08 39		08 57
St Pancras International	d			06 55						07 25						07 55				08 05			
Farringdon	d			06 59						07 29						07 59				08 09			
City Thameslink	d			07 01						07 31						08 01				08 11			
London Blackfriars	d			07 04						07 34						08 04				08 14			
London Bridge (4) ⊖	d			07 11		07 17				07 41		07 47				08 11		08 17		08 21		08 10	
New Cross Gate (4) ⊖	d																					08 18	
Norwood Junction (2)	d																			08 32		08 39	
East Croydon	a			07 24		07 32				07 54		08 03				08 24		08 33		08 36		08 42	
East Croydon	d	07 20		07 25	07 27	07 33		07 40	07 50	07 55	07 57	08 04		08 10	08 20	08 25	08 28	08 34		08 37	08 40	08 43	08 57
South Croydon (4)	d	07 23		07 28		07 35			07 53	07 58		08 06			08 23	08 28		08 36					
Purley Oaks	d	07 26				07 38			07 56			08 09			08 26			08 39					
Sanderstead	d			07a31				07 45		08 02				08 15		08a31					08 45		
Purley (4)	a	07 29			07 32	07 41			07 59		08 02	08 12			08 29		08 32	08 42		08 44		08 50	09 02
Purley	d	07 35	07 38			07 45	07 48		08 05			08 15	08 18		08 32			08 45	08 48			08 53	
Kenley	d	07 38				07 48			08 08			08 18			08 35			08 48				08 56	
Whyteleafe	d	07 41				07 51			08 11			08 22			08 38			08 52				08 59	
Upper Warlingham	a							07 52		08 09				08 22							08 52		
Whyteleafe South	d	07 43				07 53			08 13			08 24			08 40			08 54				09 01	
Caterham	a	07 48				07 58			08 18			08 28			08 45			08 58				09 06	
Reedham	d		07 40				07 50						08 20						08 50				
Coulsdon Town	d		07 43				07 53						08 23						08 53				
Woodmansterne	d		07 46				07 56						08 26						08 56				
Chipstead	d		07 49				07 59						08 29						08 59				
Kingswood	d		07 55				08 05						08 35						09 05				
Tadworth	d		07 58				08 08						08 38						09 08				
Tattenham Corner	a		08 02				08 12						08 42						09 12				

London and Croydon - Purley, Caterham and Tattenham Corner

Station		SN		TL 1	SN 1	SN	SN 1	SN		TL 1	SN 1	SN	SN 1	SN		TL 1	SN 1	SN	SN	SN 1	SN	
London Victoria (15) ⊖	d				08 50		09 09				09 20		09 39				09 50			10 09		
Clapham Junction (10)	d				08 57		09 16				09 27		09 46				09 57			10 16		
East Croydon	a				09 09		09 26				09 39		09 56				10 09			10 26		
St Pancras International	d			08 35						09 05						09 35						
Farringdon	d			08 39						09 09						09 39						
City Thameslink	d			08 41						09 11						09 41						
London Blackfriars	d			08 44						09 14						09 44						
London Bridge (4) ⊖	d	08 47		08 51		08 40		09 17		09 21		09 10		09 47		09 51		09 40	09 44		10 17	
New Cross Gate (4) ⊖	d					08 48						09 18						09 48				
Norwood Junction (2)	d			09 02		09 09				09 32		09 39				10 02		10 09				
East Croydon	a	09 03		09 06		09 12		09 32		09 36		09 42		10 02		10 06		10 13	10 24		10 31	
East Croydon	d	09 04		09 07	09 10	09 14	09 27	09 33		09 37	09 40	09 44	09 57	10 03		10 07	10 10	10 14	10 24	10 27	10 32	
South Croydon (4)	d	09 06				09 17		09 35				09 47		10 06				10 17			10 35	
Purley Oaks	d	09 09				09 21		09 38				09 50		10 08				10 20			10 38	
Sanderstead	d				09 15						09 45						10 15					
Purley (4)	a	09 12		09 14		09 24	09 33	09 41		09 43		09 54	10 03	10 11		10 13		10 24	10 31	10 33	10 41	
Purley	d	09 15	09 18			09 27		09 44	09 48			09 57		10 15	10 18			10 25	10 33		10 45	10 48
Kenley	d	09 18				09 30		09 47				10 00		10 18					10 36		10 48	
Whyteleafe	d	09 22				09 33		09 51				10 03		10 21					10 40		10 51	
Upper Warlingham	a				09 22						09 52						10 22					
Whyteleafe South	d	09 24				09 35		09 53				10 05		10 23					10 42		10 53	
Caterham	a	09 28				09 40		09 57				10 10		10 28					10 47		10 58	
Reedham	d		09 20						09 50						10 20			10 27				10 50
Coulsdon Town	d		09 23						09 53						10 23			10a30				10 53
Woodmansterne	d		09 26						09 56						10 26							10 56
Chipstead	d		09 29						09 59						10 29							10 59
Kingswood	d		09 35						10 05						10 35							11 05
Tadworth	d		09 38						10 08						10 38							11 08
Tattenham Corner	a		09 42						10 12						10 42							11 12

Station		TL 1	SN 1	SN	SN	SN 1	SN		TL 1	SN 1	SN	SN	SN 1	SN		TL 1	SN 1	SN	SN	SN 1	SN		TL 1
London Victoria (15) ⊖	d		10 20			10 39				10 50			11 09				11 20			11 39			
Clapham Junction (10)	d		10 27			10 46				10 57			11 16				11 27			11 46			
East Croydon	a		10 39			10 56				11 09			11 26				11 39			11 56			
St Pancras International	d	10 05							10 35							11 05							11 35
Farringdon	d	10 09							10 39							11 09							11 39
City Thameslink	d	10 11							10 41							11 11							11 41
London Blackfriars	d	10 14							10 44							11 14							11 44
London Bridge (4) ⊖	d	10 21		10 10	10 14		10 47		10 51		10 40	10 44		11 17		11 21		11 10	11 14		11 47		11 51
New Cross Gate (4) ⊖	d			10 18							10 48							11 18					
Norwood Junction (2)	d	10 32		10 39					11 02		11 09					11 32		11 39					12 02
East Croydon	a	10 36		10 43	10 54		11 01		11 06		11 13	11 24		11 31		11 36		11 43	11 54		12 01		12 06
East Croydon	d	10 37	10 40	10 44	10 54	10 57	11 02		11 07	11 10	11 14	11 24	11 27	11 32		11 37	11 40	11 44	11 54	11 57	12 02		12 07
South Croydon (4)	d			10 47			11 05				11 17			11 35				11 47			12 05		
Purley Oaks	d			10 50			11 08				11 20			11 38				11 50			12 08		
Sanderstead	d		10 45							11 15							11 45						
Purley (4)	a	10 43		10 54	11 01	11 03	11 11		11 13		11 24	11 31	11 33	11 41		11 43		11 54	12 01	12 03	12 11		12 13
Purley	d			10 55	11 03		11 15	11 18			11 25	11 33		11 45	11 48			11 55	12 03		12 15	12 18	
Kenley	d				11 06		11 18					11 36		11 48					12 06		12 18		
Whyteleafe	d				11 10		11 21					11 40		11 51					12 10		12 21		
Upper Warlingham	a		10 52							11 22							11 52						
Whyteleafe South	d				11 12		11 23					11 42		11 53					12 12		12 23		
Caterham	a				11 17		11 28					11 47		11 58					12 17		12 28		
Reedham	d			10 57				11 20			11 27				11 50			11 57				12 20	
Coulsdon Town	d			11a01				11 23			11a30				11 53			12a00				12 23	
Woodmansterne	d							11 26							11 56							12 26	
Chipstead	d							11 29							11 59							12 29	
Kingswood	d							11 35							12 05							12 35	
Tadworth	d							11 38							12 08							12 38	
Tattenham Corner	a							11 42							12 12							12 42	

Station		SN 1	SN	SN	SN 1	SN		TL 1	SN 1	SN	SN	SN 1	SN		TL 1	SN 1	SN	SN	SN 1	SN		TL 1	SN 1
London Victoria (15) ⊖	d	11 50			12 09				12 20			12 39				12 50			13 09				13 20
Clapham Junction (10)	d	11 57			12 16				12 27			12 46				12 57			13 16				13 27
East Croydon	a	12 09			12 26				12 39			12 56				13 09			13 26				13 39
St Pancras International	d							12 05							12 35							13 05	
Farringdon	d							12 09							12 39							13 09	
City Thameslink	d							12 11							12 41							13 11	
London Blackfriars	d							12 14							12 44							13 14	
London Bridge (4) ⊖	d		11 40	11 44		12 17		12 21		12 10	12 14		12 47		12 51		12 40	12 44		13 17		13 21	
New Cross Gate (4) ⊖	d		11 48							12 18							12 48						
Norwood Junction (2)	d		12 09					12 32		12 39					13 02		13 09					13 32	
East Croydon	a		12 13	12 24		12 31		12 36		12 43	12 54		13 01		13 06		13 13	13 24		13 31		13 36	
East Croydon	d	12 10	12 14	12 24	12 27	12 32		12 37	12 40	12 44	12 54	12 57	13 02		13 07	13 10	13 14	13 24	13 27	13 32		13 37	13 40
South Croydon (4)	d		12 17			12 35				12 47			13 05				13 17			13 35			
Purley Oaks	d		12 20			12 38				12 50			13 08				13 21			13 38			
Sanderstead	d	12 15							12 45							13 15							13 45
Purley (4)	a		12 24	12 31	12 33	12 41		12 43		12 54	13 01	13 03	13 11		13 13		13 24	13 31	13 33	13 41		13 43	
Purley	d		12 25	12 33		12 45	12 48			12 55	13 03		13 15	13 18			13 25	13 33		13 45	13 48		
Kenley	d			12 36		12 48					13 06		13 18					13 36		13 48			
Whyteleafe	d			12 40		12 51					13 10		13 21					13 40		13 51			
Upper Warlingham	a	12 22							12 52							13 22							13 52
Whyteleafe South	d			12 42		12 53					13 12		13 23					13 42		13 53			
Caterham	a			12 47		12 58					13 17		13 28					13 47		13 58			
Reedham	d		12 27				12 50			12 57				13 20			13 27				13 50		
Coulsdon Town	d		12a30				12 53			13a00				13 23			13a30				13 53		
Woodmansterne	d						12 56							13 26							13 56		
Chipstead	d						12 59							13 29							13 59		
Kingswood	d						13 05							13 35							14 05		
Tadworth	d						13 08							13 38							14 08		
Tattenham Corner	a						13 12							13 42							14 12		

Table T181-F

Mondays to Fridays

16 December to 15 May

London and Croydon - Purley, Caterham and Tattenham Corner

Station		SN	SN	SN 1	SN		TL 1	SN 1	SN	SN	SN 1	SN		TL 1	SN 1	SN	SN	SN 1	SN		TL 1	SN 1
London Victoria 15 ⊖	d			13 39				13 50			14 09				14 20			14 39				14 50
Clapham Junction 10	d			13 46				13 57			14 16				14 27			14 46				14 57
East Croydon	a			13 56				14 09			14 26				14 39			14 56				15 09
St Pancras International	d						13 35							14 05							14 35	
Farringdon	d						13 39							14 09							14 39	
City Thameslink	d						13 41							14 11							14 41	
London Blackfriars	d						13 44							14 14							14 44	
London Bridge 4 ⊖	d	13 10	13 14		13 47		13 51		13 40	13 44		14 17		14 21		14 10	14 14		14 47		14 51	
New Cross Gate 4 ⊖	d	13 18							13 48							14 18						
Norwood Junction 2	d	13 39					14 02		14 09					14 32		14 39					15 02	
East Croydon	a	13 43	13 54		14 01		14 06		14 13	14 24		14 31		14 36		14 43	14 54		15 01		15 06	
East Croydon	d	13 44	13 54	13 57	14 02		14 07	14 10	14 14	14 24	14 27	14 32		14 37	14 40	14 44	14 54	14 57	15 02		15 07	15 10
South Croydon 4	d	13 47			14 05				14 17			14 35				14 47			15 05			
Purley Oaks	d	13 50			14 08				14 20			14 38				14 50			15 08			
Sanderstead	d							14 15							14 45							15 15
Purley 4	a	13 54	14 01	14 03	14 11		14 13		14 24	14 31	14 33	14 41		14 43		14 54	15 01	15 03	15 11		15 13	
Purley	d	13 56	14 03		14 15	14 18			14 25	14 33		14 45	14 48			14 55	15 03		15 15	15 18		
Kenley	d		14 06		14 18					14 36		14 48					15 06		15 18			
Whyteleafe	d		14 10		14 21					14 40		14 51					15 10		15 21			
Upper Warlingham	a							14 22							14 52							15 22
Whyteleafe South	d		14 12		14 23					14 42		14 53					15 12		15 23			
Caterham	a		14 17		14 28					14 47		14 58					15 17		15 28			
Reedham	d	13 58				14 20			14 27				14 50			14 57				15 20		
Coulsdon Town	d	14a01				14 23			14a30				14 53			15a00				15 23		
Woodmansterne	d					14 26							14 56							15 26		
Chipstead	d					14 29							14 59							15 29		
Kingswood	d					14 35							15 05							15 35		
Tadworth	d					14 38							15 08							15 38		
Tattenham Corner	a					14 42							15 12							15 42		

Station		SN	SN	SN 1	SN		TL 1	SN 1	SN	SN	SN 1	SN		TL 1	SN 1	SN	SN	SN 1	SN		TL 1	SN 1	SN
London Victoria 15 ⊖	d			15 09				15 20			15 39				15 50			16 09				16 20	16 31
Clapham Junction 10	d			15 16				15 27			15 46				15 57			16 16				16 27	16 38
East Croydon	a			15 26				15 39			15 56				16 09			16 26				16 39	16 49
St Pancras International	d						15 05							15 35							16 05		
Farringdon	d						15 09							15 39							16 09		
City Thameslink	d						15 11							15 41							16 11		
London Blackfriars	d						15 14							15 44							16 14		
London Bridge 4 ⊖	d	14 40	14 44		15 17		15 21		15 10	15 14		15 47		15 51		15 40	15 44		16 17		16 21		
New Cross Gate 4 ⊖	d	14 48							15 18							15 48							
Norwood Junction 2	d	15 09					15 32		15 39					16 02		16 09					16 32		
East Croydon	a	15 13	15 24		15 31		15 36		15 43	15 54		16 02		16 06		16 13	16 24		16 32		16 36		
East Croydon	d	15 14	15 24	15 27	15 32		15 37	15 40	15 44	15 54	15 57	16 03		16 07	16 10	16 14	16 24	16 27	16 33		16 37	16 40	16 50
South Croydon 4	d	15 17			15 35			15 42	15 47			16 06			16 12	16 17			16 36			16 42	16 53
Purley Oaks	d	15 20			15 38				15 50			16 08				16 20			16 38				16 56
Sanderstead	d							15 45							16 15							16 45	
Purley 4	a	15 24	15 31	15 35	15 41		15 43		15 54	16 01	16 03	16 11		16 13		16 24	16 31	16 33	16 41		16 43		16 59
Purley	d	15 25	15 33		15 45	15 48			15 55	16 03		16 15	16 18			16 25	16 33		16 45	16 48			17 01
Kenley	d		15 36		15 48					16 06		16 18					16 36		16 48				17 04
Whyteleafe	d		15 40		15 51					16 10		16 21					16 40		16 51				17 07
Upper Warlingham	a							15 52							16 22							16 52	
Whyteleafe South	d		15 42		15 53					16 12		16 23					16 42		16 53				17 09
Caterham	a		15 47		15 58					16 17		16 28					16 47		16 58				17 14
Reedham	d	15 27				15 50			15 57				16 20			16 27				16 50			
Coulsdon Town	d	15a30				15 53			16a00				16 23			16a30				16 53			
Woodmansterne	d					15 56							16 26							16 56			
Chipstead	d					15 59							16 29							16 59			
Kingswood	d					16 05							16 35							17 05			
Tadworth	d					16 08							16 38							17 08			
Tattenham Corner	a					16 12							16 42							17 12			

Station		TL 1	SN 1	SN		TL 1	SN 1	SN		TL 1	SN		TL 1	SN 1	SN		TL 1	SN		TL 1	SN 1	SN	
London Victoria 15 ⊖	d		16 39				16 50	17 02						17 20	17 32						17 50	18 02	
Clapham Junction 10	d		16 46				16 57	17 09						17 28	17 39						17 58	18 09	
East Croydon	a		16 56				17 09	17 19						17 39	17 49						18 09	18 19	
St Pancras International	d	16 25				16 35				16 55			17 05				17 25			17 35			
Farringdon	d	16 29				16 39				16 59			17 09				17 29			17 39			
City Thameslink	d	16 31				16 41				17 01			17 11				17 31			17 41			
London Blackfriars	d	16 34				16 44				17 04			17 14				17 34			17 44			
London Bridge 4 ⊖	d	16 41		16 47		16 51				17 11	17 17		17 21				17 41	17 47		17 51			
New Cross Gate 4 ⊖	d																						
Norwood Junction 2	d					17 02							17 32							18 02			
East Croydon	a	16 54		17 02		17 06				17 24	17 32		17 36				17 54	18 02		18 06			
East Croydon	d	16 55	16 57	17 03		17 07	17 10	17 20		17 25	17 33		17 37	17 40	17 50		17 56	18 03		18 07	18 10	18 20	
South Croydon 4	d	16 58		17 06				17 23		17 28	17 36				17 53		17 59	18 06				18 23	
Purley Oaks	d			17 08				17 26			17 38				17 56			18 08				18 26	
Sanderstead	d	17 02					17 15			17 32				17 45			18 02				18 15		
Purley 4	a		17 03	17 11		17 13		17 29			17 41		17 43		17 59			18 11		18 13		18 29	
Purley	d			17 15	17 18			17 35	17 38		17 45	17 48			18 05	18 08		18 15	18 18			18 35	18 38
Kenley	d			17 18				17 38			17 48				18 08			18 18				18 38	
Whyteleafe	d			17 21				17 41			17 51				18 11			18 21				18 41	
Upper Warlingham	a	17 09					17 22			17 39				17 52			18 09				18 22		
Whyteleafe South	d			17 23				17 43			17 53				18 13			18 23				18 43	
Caterham	a			17 28				17 48			17 58				18 18			18 28				18 48	
Reedham	d				17 20				17 40			17 50				18 10			18 20				18 40
Coulsdon Town	d				17 23				17 43			17 53				18 13			18 23				18 43
Woodmansterne	d				17 26				17 46			17 56				18 16			18 26				18 46
Chipstead	d				17 29				17 49			17 59				18 19			18 29				18 49
Kingswood	d				17 35				17 55			18 05				18 25			18 35				18 55
Tadworth	d				17 38				17 58			18 08				18 28			18 38				18 58
Tattenham Corner	a				17 42				18 02			18 12				18 32			18 42				19 02

Table T181-F

Mondays to Fridays

16 December to 15 May

London and Croydon - Purley, Caterham and Tattenham Corner

Station		TL 1	SN		TL 1	SN 1	SN		TL 1	SN		TL 1	SN 1	SN	TL 1	SN 1	SN		TL 1	SN 1	SN	SN
London Victoria 15 ⊖	d					18 20	18 32						18 50			19 09				19 20		
Clapham Junction 10	d					18 27	18 39						18 57			19 16				19 27		
East Croydon	a					18 39	18 49						19 09			19 27				19 39		
St Pancras International	d	17 55			18 05				18 25			18 35			18 55				19 05			
Farringdon	d	17 59			18 09				18 29			18 39			18 59				19 09			
City Thameslink	d	18 01			18 11				18 31			18 41			19 01				19 11			
London Blackfriars	d	18 04			18 14				18 34			18 44			19 04				19 14			
London Bridge 4 ⊖	d	18 11	18 17		18 21				18 41	18 47		18 51		18 41	19 11		19 17		19 21		19 10	19 14
New Cross Gate 4 ⊖	d													18 48							19 18	
Norwood Junction 2	d				18 32							19 02		19 09					19 32		19 39	
East Croydon	a	18 24	18 33		18 36				18 54	19 03		19 06		19 13	19 24		19 32		19 36		19 43	19 54
East Croydon	d	18 25	18 33		18 37	18 40	18 50		18 55	19 03		19 07	19 10	19 13	19 25	19 27	19 33		19 37	19 40	19 44	19 54
South Croydon 4	d	18 28	18 36				18 53		18 58	19 06				19 16	19 28		19 35				19 47	
Purley Oaks	d		18 38				18 56			19 08				19 19			19 38				19 50	
Sanderstead	d	18 32				18 45			19 02				19 15		19 32					19 45		
Purley 4	a		18 41		18 43		18 59			19 11		19 13		19 22		19 32	19 41		19 43		19 54	20 01
Purley	d		18 45	18 48			19 05	19 08		19 15	19 18			19 25			19 45	19 48			19 55	20 03
Kenley	d		18 48				19 08			19 18							19 48					20 06
Whyteleafe	d		18 51				19 11			19 21							19 51					20 10
Upper Warlingham	a	18 39				18 52			19 09				19 22		19 39					19 52		
Whyteleafe South	d		18 53				19 13			19 23							19 53					20 12
Caterham	a		18 58				19 18			19 28							19 58					20 17
Reedham	d			18 50				19 10			19 20			19 27				19 50			19 57	
Coulsdon Town	d			18 53				19 13			19 23			19a30				19 53			20a02	
Woodmansterne	d			18 56				19 16			19 26							19 56				
Chipstead	d			18 59				19 19			19 29							19 59				
Kingswood	d			19 05				19 25			19 35							20 05				
Tadworth	d			19 08				19 28			19 38							20 08				
Tattenham Corner	a			19 12				19 32			19 42							20 12				

Station		SN 1	SN		TL 1	SN 1	SN	SN	SN 1	SN		TL 1	SN 1	SN	SN	SN 1	SN		TL 1	SN 1	SN	SN	SN 1
London Victoria 15 ⊖	d	19 39				19 50			20 09				20 20			20 39				20 50			21 09
Clapham Junction 10	d	19 46				19 57			20 16				20 27			20 46				20 57			21 16
East Croydon	a	19 57				20 09			20 26				20 39			20 57				21 09			21 27
St Pancras International	d				19 35							20 05							20 35				
Farringdon	d				19 39							20 09							20 39				
City Thameslink	d				19 41							20 11							20 41				
London Blackfriars	d				19 44							20 14							20 44				
London Bridge 4 ⊖	d		19 47		19 51		19 40	19 44		20 17		20 21		20 12	20 14		20 47		20 51		20 40	20 44	
New Cross Gate 4 ⊖	d						19 48							20 18							20 48		
Norwood Junction 2	d				20 02		20 09					20 32		20 39					21 02		21 09		
East Croydon	a		20 02		20 06		20 13	20 24		20 31		20 36		20 43	20 53		21 02		21 06		21 13	21 24	
East Croydon	d	19 58	20 03		20 07	20 10	20 14	20 24	20 27	20 32		20 37	20 40	20 44	20 54	20 58	21 03		21 07	21 10	21 14	21 24	21 28
South Croydon 4	d		20 06				20 17			20 35				20 47			21 06				21 17		
Purley Oaks	d		20 08				20 20			20 38				20 50			21 08				21 20		
Sanderstead	d					20 15							20 45							21 15			
Purley 4	a	20 03	20 12		20 15		20 25	20 31	20 33	20 41		20 43		20 54	21 01	21 04	21 11		21 13		21 25	21 32	21 33
Purley	d		20 15	20 19			20 25	20 33		20 45	20 48			20 55	21 03		21 15	21 18			21 27	21 34	
Kenley	d		20 18					20 36		20 48					21 06		21 18					21 37	
Whyteleafe	d		20 22					20 40		20 51					21 10		21 21					21 41	
Upper Warlingham	a					20 22							20 52							21 22			
Whyteleafe South	d		20 24					20 42		20 53					21 12		21 23					21 43	
Caterham	a		20 28					20 47		20 58					21 17		21 28					21 47	
Reedham	d			20 21			20 28				20 50			20 57				21 20			21 29		
Coulsdon Town	d			20 24			20a31				20 53			21a00				21 23			21a32		
Woodmansterne	d			20 27							20 56							21 26					
Chipstead	d			20 30							20 59							21 29					
Kingswood	d			20 36							21 05							21 35					
Tadworth	d			20 39							21 08							21 38					
Tattenham Corner	a			20 43							21 12							21 42					

Station		SN		TL 1	SN 1	SN	SN	SN 1	SN		TL 1	SN 1	SN	SN	SN 1	SN		TL 1	SN 1	SN	SN	SN 1
London Victoria 15 ⊖	d				21 20			21 39				21 50			22 09				22 20			22 39
Clapham Junction 10	d				21 27			21 46				21 57			22 16				22 27			22 46
East Croydon	a				21 39			21 57				22 09			22 26				22 39			22 56
St Pancras International	d			21 05							21 35							22 05				
Farringdon	d			21 09							21 39							22 09				
City Thameslink	d			21 11							21 41							22 11				
London Blackfriars	d			21 14							21 44							22 14				
London Bridge 4 ⊖	d	21 17		21 21		21 10	21 14		21 47		21 51		21 40	21 44		22 17		22 21		22 10	22 14	
New Cross Gate 4 ⊖	d					21 18							21 48							22 18		
Norwood Junction 2	d			21 32		21 39					22 02		22 09					22 32		22 39		
East Croydon	a	21 31		21 36		21 43	21 54		22 01		22 06		22 13	22 24		22 31		22 36		22 43	22 54	
East Croydon	d	21 32		21 37	21 40	21 44	21 54	21 57	22 02		22 07	22 10	22 14	22 24	22 27	22 32		22 37	22 40	22 43	22 54	22 57
South Croydon 4	d	21 35				21 47			22 05				22 17			22 35				22 46		
Purley Oaks	d	21 38				21 50			22 08				22 21			22 38				22 50		
Sanderstead	d				21 45							22 15							22 45			
Purley 4	a	21 41		21 43		21 54	22 01	22 04	22 11		22 13		22 24	22 31	22 33	22 41		22 43		22 53	23 01	23 03
Purley	d	21 45	21 48			21 55	22 03		22 15	22 18			22 25	22 33		22 45	22 48			22 55	23 04	
Kenley	d	21 48					22 06		22 18					22 36		22 48					23 07	
Whyteleafe	d	21 51					22 10		22 21					22 40		22 51					23 10	
Upper Warlingham	a				21 52							22 22							22 52			
Whyteleafe South	d	21 53					22 12		22 23					22 42		22 53					23 12	
Caterham	a	21 58					22 17		22 28					22 47		22 58					23 17	
Reedham	d		21 50			21 57				22 20			22 27				22 50			22 57		
Coulsdon Town	d		21 53			22a00				22 23			22a30				22 53			23a00		
Woodmansterne	d		21 56							22 26							22 56					
Chipstead	d		21 59							22 29							22 59					
Kingswood	d		22 05							22 35							23 05					
Tadworth	d		22 08							22 38							23 08					
Tattenham Corner	a		22 12							22 42							23 12					

Table T181-F

London and Croydon - Purley, Caterham and Tattenham Corner

Mondays to Fridays

16 December to 15 May

		SN		TL	SN	SN	SN	SN		TL	SN	SN	SN	SN	SN
				1	1		1			1	1	1		FO	1
London Victoria 15 ⊖	d				22 52		23 09				23 22	23 36			23 53
Clapham Junction 10	d				23 00		23 16				23 29	23 43			23 59
East Croydon	a				23 10		23 26				23 39	23 58			00 14
St Pancras International	d			22 35						23 05					
Farringdon	d			22 39						23 10					
City Thameslink	d			22 41											
London Blackfriars	d			22 44						23 14					
London Bridge 4 ⊖	d	22 47		22 51		22 40		23 17		23 21			23 47	23 47	
New Cross Gate 4 ⊖	d					22 48									
Norwood Junction 2	d			23 02		23 09				23 32					
East Croydon	a	23 01		23 06		23 13		23 31		23 36			00 01	00 01	
East Croydon	d	23 02		23 07	23 11	23 14	23 27	23 32		23 37	23 40	23 59	00 02	00 02	00 14
South Croydon 4	d	23 05				23 17		23 34					00 04	00 04	00 17
Purley Oaks	d	23 08				23 20		23 37					00 07	00 07	
Sanderstead	d				23 15						23 45				00 20
Purley 4	a	23 11		23 13		23 24	23 32	23 40		23 42		00 04	00 10	00 10	
Purley	d	23 15	23 18			23 25		23 45	23 48				00 15	00 18	
Kenley	d	23 18						23 48					00 18		
Whyteleafe	d	23 21						23 51					00 21		
Upper Warlingham	a				23 22						23 52				00 27
Whyteleafe South	d	23 23						23 53					00 23		
Caterham	a	23 28						23 58					00 28		
Reedham	d		23 20			23 27			23 50					00 20	
Coulsdon Town	d		23 23			23a31			23 53					00 23	
Woodmansterne	d		23 26						23 56					00 26	
Chipstead	d		23 29						23 59					00 29	
Kingswood	d		23 35						00 05					00 35	
Tadworth	d		23 38						00 08					00 38	
Tattenham Corner	a		23 42						00 12					00 42	

Saturdays

21 December to 16 May

		SN	SN		SN	SN	SN		TL	SN	TL	SN	TL	SN	TL	SN	TL	SN	SN	TL	SN	SN	
					1	1 A			1	1	1	1	1	1	1	1	1	1	1	1	1		
London Victoria 15 ⊖	d					00 08				01 10		02 10		03 10		04 10		05 08	05 39		06 09		
Clapham Junction 10	d					00 15				01 17		02 17		03 17		04 17		05 16	05 46		06 16		
East Croydon	a					00 30				01 32		02 32		03 32		04 31		05 31	05 56		06 26		
St Pancras International	d								00 52		01 32		02 32		03 32		04 32			05 45			
Farringdon	d																			05 49			
City Thameslink	d																						
London Blackfriars	d								01 02		01 40		02 40		03 40		04 40			05 54			
London Bridge 4 ⊖	d						00 17													06 00		06 17	
New Cross Gate 4 ⊖	d																						
Norwood Junction 2	d						00 31																
East Croydon	a						00 34		01 28		02 06		03 06		04 06		05 06			06 14		06 32	
East Croydon	d		00 02		00 14	00 31	00 35		01 28	01 33	02 07	02 32	03 07	03 32	04 07	04 31	05 07	05 31	05 57	06 16	06 27	06 33	
South Croydon 4	d		00 04		00 17		00 38															06 35	
Purley Oaks	d		00 07				00 41															06 38	
Sanderstead	d				00 20																		
Purley 4	a		00 10			00 36	00 44		01 34	01 38	02 12	02 38	03 12	03 38	04 12	04 37	05 12	05 37	06 03	06 22	06 33	06 41	
Purley	d		00 15	00 18			00 48	00 50														06 45	06 48
Kenley	d		00 18				00 51															06 48	
Whyteleafe	d		00 21				00 54															06 51	
Upper Warlingham	a				00 27																		
Whyteleafe South	d		00 23				00 56															06 53	
Caterham	a		00 28				01 01															06 58	
Reedham	d			00 20				00 52															06 50
Coulsdon Town	d			00 23				00 55															06 53
Woodmansterne	d			00 26				00 58															06 56
Chipstead	d			00 29				01 01															06 59
Kingswood	d	00 05		00 35				01 07															07 05
Tadworth	d	00 08		00 38				01 10															07 08
Tattenham Corner	a	00 12		00 42				01 14															07 12

A not 16 May

Table T181-F

London and Croydon - Purley, Caterham and Tattenham Corner

Saturdays

21 December to 16 May

		SN	SN	SN	SN	SN		SN	SN	SN	SN	SN		TL	SN	SN	SN	SN	SN		TL	SN
		1			1			1			1			1	1			1			1	1
London Victoria 15 ⊖	d	06 20			06 39			06 50			07 09				07 20			07 39				07 50
Clapham Junction 10	d	06 27			06 46			06 57			07 16				07 27			07 46				07 57
East Croydon	a	06 39			06 56			07 09			07 26				07 39			07 56				08 09
St Pancras International	d													07 05							07 35	
Farringdon	d													07 09							07 39	
City Thameslink	d																					
London Blackfriars	d													07 14							07 44	
London Bridge 4 ⊖	d		06 11	06 14		06 47			06 40	06 44		07 17		07 21		07 10	07 14		07 47		07 51	
New Cross Gate 4 ⊖	d		06 18						06 48							07 18						
Norwood Junction 2	d		06 39						07 09					07 32		07 39					08 02	
East Croydon	a		06 43	06 54		07 01			07 13	07 24		07 31		07 36		07 43	07 54		08 01		08 06	
East Croydon	d	06 40	06 44	06 54	06 57	07 02		07 10	07 14	07 24	07 27	07 32		07 37	07 40	07 44	07 54	07 57	08 02		08 07	08 10
South Croydon 4	d		06 47			07 05			07 17			07 35				07 47			08 05			
Purley Oaks	d		06 50			07 08			07 20			07 38				07 50			08 08			
Sanderstead	d	06 45						07 15							07 45							08 15
Purley 4	a		06 54	07 01	07 03	07 11			07 24	07 31	07 33	07 41		07 43		07 54	08 01	08 03	08 11		08 13	
Purley	d		06 56	07 03		07 15	07 18		07 25	07 33		07 45	07 48			07 55	08 03		08 15	08 18		
Kenley	d			07 06		07 18				07 36		07 48					08 06		08 18			
Whyteleafe	d			07 10		07 21				07 40		07 51					08 10		08 21			
Upper Warlingham	a	06 52						07 22							07 52							08 22
Whyteleafe South	d			07 12		07 23				07 42		07 53					08 12		08 23			
Caterham	a			07 17		07 28				07 47		07 58					08 17		08 28			
Reedham	d		06 58				07 20		07 27				07 50			07 57				08 20		
Coulsdon Town	d		07a02				07 23		07a31				07 53			08a01				08 23		
Woodmansterne	d						07 26						07 56							08 26		
Chipstead	d						07 29						07 59							08 29		
Kingswood	d						07 35						08 05							08 35		
Tadworth	d						07 38						08 08							08 38		
Tattenham Corner	a						07 42						08 12							08 42		

		SN	SN	SN	SN		TL	SN	SN	SN	SN	SN		TL	SN	SN	SN	SN	SN		TL	SN	SN
				1			1	1			1			1	1			1			1	1	
London Victoria 15 ⊖	d			08 09				08 20			08 39				08 50			09 09				09 20	
Clapham Junction 10	d			08 16				08 27			08 46				08 57			09 16				09 27	
East Croydon	a			08 26				08 39			08 56				09 09			09 26				09 39	
St Pancras International	d						08 05							08 35							09 05		
Farringdon	d						08 09							08 39							09 09		
City Thameslink	d																				09 11		
London Blackfriars	d						08 14							08 44							09 14		
London Bridge 4 ⊖	d	07 40	07 44		08 17		08 21		08 10	08 14		08 47		08 51		08 40	08 44		09 17		09 21		09 10
New Cross Gate 4 ⊖	d	07 48							08 18							08 48							09 18
Norwood Junction 2	d	08 09					08 32		08 39					09 02		09 09					09 32		09 39
East Croydon	a	08 13	08 24		08 31		08 36		08 43	08 54		09 01		09 06		09 13	09 24		09 31		09 36		09 43
East Croydon	d	08 14	08 24	08 27	08 32		08 37	08 40	08 44	08 54	08 57	09 02		09 07	09 10	09 14	09 24	09 27	09 32		09 37	09 40	09 44
South Croydon 4	d	08 17			08 35				08 47			09 05				09 17			09 35				09 47
Purley Oaks	d	08 20			08 38				08 50			09 08				09 20			09 38				09 50
Sanderstead	d							08 45							09 15							09 45	
Purley 4	a	08 24	08 31	08 33	08 41		08 43		08 54	09 01	09 03	09 11		09 13		09 24	09 31	09 33	09 41		09 43		09 54
Purley	d	08 25	08 33		08 45	08 48			08 55	09 03		09 15	09 18			09 25	09 33		09 45	09 48			09 55
Kenley	d		08 36		08 48					09 06		09 18					09 36		09 48				
Whyteleafe	d		08 40		08 51					09 10		09 21					09 40		09 51				
Upper Warlingham	a							08 52							09 22							09 52	
Whyteleafe South	d		08 42		08 53					09 12		09 23					09 42		09 53				
Caterham	a		08 47		08 58					09 17		09 28					09 47		09 58				
Reedham	d	08 27				08 50			08 57				09 20			09 27				09 50			09 57
Coulsdon Town	d	08a31				08 53			09a00				09 23			09a31				09 53			10a01
Woodmansterne	d					08 56							09 26							09 56			
Chipstead	d					08 59							09 29							09 59			
Kingswood	d					09 05							09 35							10 05			
Tadworth	d					09 08							09 38							10 08			
Tattenham Corner	a					09 12							09 42							10 12			

		SN	SN	SN		TL	SN	SN	SN	SN	SN		TL	SN	SN	SN	SN	SN		TL	SN	SN	SN
			1			1	1			1			1	1			1			1	1		
London Victoria 15 ⊖	d		09 39				09 50			10 09				10 20			10 39				10 50		
Clapham Junction 10	d		09 46				09 57			10 16				10 27			10 46				10 57		
East Croydon	a		09 56				10 09			10 26				10 39			10 56				11 09		
St Pancras International	d					09 35							10 05							10 35			
Farringdon	d					09 39							10 09							10 39			
City Thameslink	d					09 41							10 11							10 41			
London Blackfriars	d					09 44							10 14							10 44			
London Bridge 4 ⊖	d	09 14		09 47		09 51		09 40	09 44		10 17		10 21		10 10	10 14		10 47		10 51		10 40	10 44
New Cross Gate 4 ⊖	d							09 48							10 18							10 48	
Norwood Junction 2	d					10 02		10 09					10 32		10 39					11 02		11 09	
East Croydon	a	09 54		10 01		10 06		10 13	10 24		10 31		10 36		10 43	10 54		11 01		11 06		11 13	11 24
East Croydon	d	09 54	09 57	10 02		10 07	10 10	10 14	10 24	10 27	10 32		10 37	10 40	10 44	10 54	10 57	11 02		11 07	11 10	11 14	11 24
South Croydon 4	d			10 05				10 17			10 35				10 47			11 05				11 17	
Purley Oaks	d			10 08				10 20			10 38				10 50			11 08				11 20	
Sanderstead	d						10 15							10 45							11 15		
Purley 4	a	10 01	10 03	10 11		10 13		10 24	10 31	10 33	10 41		10 43		10 54	11 01	11 03	11 11		11 13		11 24	11 31
Purley	d	10 03		10 15	10 18			10 25	10 33		10 45	10 48			10 55	11 03		11 15	11 18			11 25	11 33
Kenley	d	10 06		10 18					10 36		10 48					11 06		11 18					11 36
Whyteleafe	d	10 10		10 21					10 40		10 51					11 10		11 21					11 40
Upper Warlingham	a						10 22							10 52							11 22		
Whyteleafe South	d	10 12		10 23					10 42		10 53					11 12		11 23					11 42
Caterham	a	10 17		10 28					10 47		10 58					11 17		11 28					11 47
Reedham	d				10 20			10 27				10 50			10 57				11 20			11 27	
Coulsdon Town	d				10 23			10a31				10 53			11a01				11 23			11a31	
Woodmansterne	d				10 26							10 56							11 26				
Chipstead	d				10 29							10 59							11 29				
Kingswood	d				10 35							11 05							11 35				
Tadworth	d				10 38							11 08							11 38				
Tattenham Corner	a				10 42							11 12							11 42				

Table T181-F

London and Croydon - Purley, Caterham and Tattenham Corner

Saturdays

21 December to 16 May

		SN 1	SN		TL 1	SN 1	SN	SN	SN 1	SN		TL 1	SN 1	SN	SN	SN 1	SN		TL 1	SN 1	SN	SN
London Victoria 15 ⊖	d	11 09				11 20			11 39				11 50			12 09				12 20		
Clapham Junction 10	d	11 16				11 27			11 46				11 57			12 16				12 27		
East Croydon	a	11 26				11 39			11 56				12 09			12 26				12 39		
St Pancras International	d				11 05							11 35							12 05			
Farringdon	d				11 09							11 39							12 09			
City Thameslink	d				11 11							11 41							12 11			
London Blackfriars	d				11 14							11 44							12 14			
London Bridge 4 ⊖	d		11 17		11 21		11 10	11 14		11 47		11 51		11 40	11 44		12 17		12 21		12 10	12 14
New Cross Gate 4 ⊖	d						11 18							11 48							12 18	
Norwood Junction 2	d				11 32		11 39					12 02		12 09					12 32		12 39	
East Croydon	a		11 31		11 36		11 43	11 54		12 01		12 06		12 13	12 24		12 31		12 36		12 43	12 54
East Croydon	d	11 27	11 32		11 37	11 40	11 44	11 54	11 57	12 02		12 07	12 10	12 14	12 24	12 27	12 32		12 37	12 40	12 44	12 54
South Croydon 4	d		11 35				11 47			12 05				12 17			12 35				12 47	
Purley Oaks	d		11 38				11 50			12 08				12 20			12 38				12 50	
Sanderstead	d					11 45							12 15							12 45		
Purley 4	a	11 33	11 41		11 43		11 54	12 01	12 03	12 11		12 13		12 24	12 31	12 33	12 41		12 43		12 54	13 01
Purley	d		11 45	11 48			11 55	12 03		12 15	12 18			12 25	12 33		12 45	12 48			12 55	13 03
Kenley	d		11 48					12 06		12 18					12 36		12 48					13 06
Whyteleafe	d		11 51					12 10		12 21					12 40		12 51					13 10
Upper Warlingham	a					11 52							12 22							12 52		
Whyteleafe South	d		11 53					12 12		12 23					12 42		12 53					13 12
Caterham	a		11 58					12 17		12 28					12 47		12 58					13 17
Reedham	d			11 50			11 57				12 20			12 27				12 50			12 57	
Coulsdon Town	d			11 53			12a01				12 23			12a31				12 53			13a01	
Woodmansterne	d			11 56							12 26							12 56				
Chipstead	d			11 59							12 29							12 59				
Kingswood	d			12 05							12 35							13 05				
Tadworth	d			12 08							12 38							13 08				
Tattenham Corner	a			12 12							12 42							13 12				

		SN 1	SN		TL 1	SN 1	SN	SN	SN 1	SN		TL 1	SN 1	SN	SN	SN 1	SN		TL 1	SN 1	SN	SN	SN 1
London Victoria 15 ⊖	d	12 39				12 50			13 09				13 20			13 39				13 50			14 09
Clapham Junction 10	d	12 46				12 57			13 16				13 27			13 46				13 57			14 16
East Croydon	a	12 56				13 09			13 26				13 39			13 56				14 09			14 26
St Pancras International	d				12 35							13 05							13 35				
Farringdon	d				12 39							13 09							13 39				
City Thameslink	d				12 41							13 11							13 41				
London Blackfriars	d				12 44							13 14							13 44				
London Bridge 4 ⊖	d		12 47		12 51		12 40	12 44		13 17		13 21		13 10	13 14		13 47		13 51		13 40	13 44	
New Cross Gate 4 ⊖	d						12 48							13 18							13 48		
Norwood Junction 2	d				13 02		13 09					13 32		13 39					14 02		14 09		
East Croydon	a		13 01		13 06		13 13	13 24		13 31		13 36		13 43	13 54		14 01		14 06		14 13	14 24	
East Croydon	d	12 57	13 02		13 07	13 10	13 14	13 24	13 27	13 32		13 37	13 40	13 44	13 54	13 57	14 02		14 07	14 10	14 14	14 24	14 27
South Croydon 4	d		13 05				13 17			13 35				13 47			14 05				14 17		
Purley Oaks	d		13 08				13 20			13 38				13 50			14 08				14 20		
Sanderstead	d					13 15							13 45							14 15			
Purley 4	a	13 03	13 11		13 13		13 24	13 31	13 33	13 41		13 43		13 54	14 01	14 04	14 11		14 13		14 24	14 31	14 33
Purley	d		13 15	13 18			13 25	13 33		13 45	13 48			13 55	14 04		14 15	14 18			14 25	14 33	
Kenley	d		13 18					13 36		13 48					14 07		14 18					14 36	
Whyteleafe	d		13 21					13 40		13 51					14 10		14 21					14 40	
Upper Warlingham	a					13 22							13 52							14 22			
Whyteleafe South	d		13 23					13 42		13 53					14 12		14 23					14 42	
Caterham	a		13 28					13 47		13 58					14 17		14 28					14 47	
Reedham	d			13 20			13 27				13 50			13 57				14 20			14 27		
Coulsdon Town	d			13 23			13a31				13 53			14a01				14 23			14a31		
Woodmansterne	d			13 26							13 56							14 26					
Chipstead	d			13 29							13 59							14 29					
Kingswood	d			13 35							14 05							14 35					
Tadworth	d			13 38							14 08							14 38					
Tattenham Corner	a			13 42							14 12							14 42					

		SN		TL 1	SN 1	SN	SN	SN 1	SN		TL 1	SN 1	SN	SN	SN 1	SN		TL 1	SN 1	SN	SN	SN 1
London Victoria 15 ⊖	d				14 20			14 39				14 50			15 09				15 20			15 39
Clapham Junction 10	d				14 27			14 46				14 57			15 16				15 27			15 46
East Croydon	a				14 39			14 56				15 09			15 26				15 39			15 56
St Pancras International	d			14 05							14 35							15 05				
Farringdon	d			14 09							14 39							15 09				
City Thameslink	d			14 11							14 41							15 11				
London Blackfriars	d			14 14							14 44							15 14				
London Bridge 4 ⊖	d	14 17		14 21		14 10	14 14		14 47		14 51		14 40	14 44		15 17		15 21		15 10	15 14	
New Cross Gate 4 ⊖	d					14 18							14 48							15 18		
Norwood Junction 2	d			14 32		14 38					15 02		15 09					15 32		15 39		
East Croydon	a	14 31		14 36		14 43	14 54		15 01		15 06		15 13	15 24		15 31		15 36		15 43	15 54	
East Croydon	d	14 32		14 37	14 40	14 44	14 54	14 57	15 02		15 07	15 10	15 14	15 24	15 27	15 32		15 37	15 40	15 44	15 54	15 57
South Croydon 4	d	14 35				14 47			15 05				15 17			15 35				15 47		
Purley Oaks	d	14 38				14 50			15 08				15 20			15 38				15 50		
Sanderstead	d				14 45							15 15							15 45			
Purley 4	a	14 41		14 43		14 54	15 01	15 03	15 11		15 13		15 24	15 31	15 33	15 41		15 43		15 54	16 01	16 03
Purley	d	14 45	14 48			14 55	15 03		15 15	15 18			15 25	15 33		15 45	15 48			15 55	16 03	
Kenley	d	14 48					15 06		15 18					15 36		15 48					16 06	
Whyteleafe	d	14 51					15 10		15 21					15 40		15 51					16 10	
Upper Warlingham	a				14 52							15 22							15 52			
Whyteleafe South	d	14 53					15 12		15 23					15 42		15 53					16 12	
Caterham	a	14 58					15 17		15 28					15 47		15 58					16 17	
Reedham	d		14 50			14 57				15 20			15 27				15 50			15 57		
Coulsdon Town	d		14 53			15a01				15 23			15a31				15 53			16a01		
Woodmansterne	d		14 56							15 26							15 56					
Chipstead	d		14 59							15 29							15 59					
Kingswood	d		15 05							15 35							16 05					
Tadworth	d		15 08							15 38							16 08					
Tattenham Corner	a		15 12							15 42							16 12					

Table T181-F

London and Croydon - Purley, Caterham and Tattenham Corner

Saturdays

21 December to 16 May

		SN		TL 1	SN 1	SN	SN	SN 1	SN		TL 1	SN 1	SN	SN	SN 1	SN		TL 1	SN 1	SN	SN	SN 1
London Victoria 15 ⊖	d				15 50			16 09				16 20			16 39				16 50			17 09
Clapham Junction 10	d				15 57			16 16				16 27			16 46				16 57			17 16
East Croydon	a				16 09			16 26				16 39			16 56				17 09			17 26
St Pancras International	d			15 35							16 05							16 35				
Farringdon	d			15 39							16 09							16 39				
City Thameslink	d			15 41							16 11							16 41				
London Blackfriars	d			15 44							16 14							16 44				
London Bridge 4 ⊖	d	15 47		15 51		15 40	15 44		16 17		16 21		16 10	16 14		16 47		16 51		16 40	16 44	
New Cross Gate 4 ⊖	d					15 48							16 18							16 48		
Norwood Junction 2	d			16 02		16 09					16 32		16 39					17 02		17 09		
East Croydon	a	16 01		16 06		16 13	16 24		16 31		16 36		16 43	16 54		17 01		17 06		17 13	17 24	
East Croydon	d	16 02		16 07	16 10	16 14	16 24	16 27	16 32		16 37	16 40	16 44	16 54	16 57	17 02		17 07	17 10	17 14	17 24	17 27
South Croydon 4	d	16 05				16 17			16 35				16 47			17 05				17 17		
Purley Oaks	d	16 08				16 20			16 38				16 50			17 08				17 20		
Sanderstead	d				16 15							16 45							17 15			
Purley 4	a	16 11		16 13		16 24	16 31	16 33	16 41		16 43		16 54	17 01	17 03	17 11		17 13		17 24	17 31	17 33
Purley	d	16 15	16 18			16 25	16 33		16 45	16 48			16 55	17 03		17 15	17 18			17 25	17 33	
Kenley	d	16 18					16 36		16 48					17 06		17 18					17 36	
Whyteleafe	d	16 21					16 40		16 51					17 10		17 21					17 40	
Upper Warlingham	a				16 22							16 52							17 22			
Whyteleafe South	d	16 23					16 42		16 53					17 12		17 23					17 42	
Caterham	a	16 28					16 47		16 58					17 17		17 28					17 47	
Reedham	d		16 20			16 27				16 50			16 57				17 20			17 27		
Coulsdon Town	d		16 23			16a31				16 53			17a01				17 23			17a31		
Woodmansterne	d		16 26							16 56							17 26					
Chipstead	d		16 29							16 59							17 29					
Kingswood	d		16 35							17 05							17 35					
Tadworth	d		16 38							17 08							17 38					
Tattenham Corner	a		16 42							17 12							17 42					

		SN		TL 1	SN 1	SN	SN	SN 1	SN		TL 1	SN 1	SN	SN	SN 1	SN		TL 1	SN 1	SN	SN	SN 1
London Victoria 15 ⊖	d				17 20			17 39				17 50			18 09				18 20			18 39
Clapham Junction 10	d				17 27			17 46				17 57			18 16				18 27			18 46
East Croydon	a				17 39			17 56				18 09			18 26				18 39			18 56
St Pancras International	d			17 05							17 35							18 05				
Farringdon	d			17 09							17 39							18 09				
City Thameslink	d			17 11							17 41							18 11				
London Blackfriars	d			17 14							17 44							18 14				
London Bridge 4 ⊖	d	17 17		17 21		17 10	17 14		17 47		17 51		17 40	17 44		18 17		18 21		18 10	18 14	
New Cross Gate 4 ⊖	d					17 18							17 48							18 18		
Norwood Junction 2	d			17 32		17 39					18 02		18 09					18 32		18 39		
East Croydon	a	17 31		17 36		17 43	17 54		18 01		18 06		18 13	18 24		18 31		18 36		18 43	18 54	
East Croydon	d	17 32		17 37	17 40	17 44	17 54	17 57	18 02		18 07	18 10	18 14	18 24	18 27	18 32		18 37	18 40	18 44	18 54	18 57
South Croydon 4	d	17 35				17 47			18 05				18 17			18 35				18 47		
Purley Oaks	d	17 38				17 50			18 08				18 20			18 38				18 50		
Sanderstead	d				17 45							18 15							18 45			
Purley 4	a	17 41		17 43		17 54	18 01	18 03	18 11		18 13		18 24	18 31	18 33	18 41		18 43		18 54	19 01	19 03
Purley	d	17 45	17 48			17 55	18 03		18 15	18 18			18 25	18 33		18 45	18 48			18 55	19 03	
Kenley	d	17 48					18 06		18 18					18 36		18 48					19 06	
Whyteleafe	d	17 51					18 10		18 21					18 40		18 51					19 10	
Upper Warlingham	a				17 52							18 22							18 52			
Whyteleafe South	d	17 53					18 12		18 23					18 42		18 53					19 12	
Caterham	a	17 58					18 17		18 28					18 47		18 58					19 17	
Reedham	d		17 50			17 57				18 20			18 27				18 50			18 57		
Coulsdon Town	d		17 53			18a01				18 23			18a31				18 53			19a01		
Woodmansterne	d		17 56							18 26							18 56					
Chipstead	d		17 59							18 29							18 59					
Kingswood	d		18 05							18 35							19 05					
Tadworth	d		18 08							18 38							19 08					
Tattenham Corner	a		18 12							18 42							19 12					

		SN		TL 1	SN 1	SN	SN	SN 1	SN		TL 1	SN 1	SN	SN	SN 1	SN		TL 1	SN 1	SN	SN	SN 1
London Victoria 15 ⊖	d				18 50			19 09				19 20			19 39				19 50			20 09
Clapham Junction 10	d				18 57			19 16				19 27			19 46				19 57			20 16
East Croydon	a				19 09			19 26				19 39			19 56				20 09			20 26
St Pancras International	d			18 35							19 05							19 35				
Farringdon	d			18 39							19 09							19 39				
City Thameslink	d			18 41							19 11							19 41				
London Blackfriars	d			18 44							19 14							19 44				
London Bridge 4 ⊖	d	18 47		18 51		18 40	18 44		19 17		19 21		19 10	19 14		19 47		19 51		19 40	19 44	
New Cross Gate 4 ⊖	d					18 48							19 18							19 48		
Norwood Junction 2	d			19 02		19 09					19 32		19 39					20 02		20 09		
East Croydon	a	19 01		19 06		19 13	19 24		19 31		19 36		19 43	19 54		20 01		20 06		20 13	20 24	
East Croydon	d	19 02		19 07	19 10	19 14	19 24	19 27	19 32		19 37	19 40	19 44	19 54	19 57	20 02		20 07	20 10	20 14	20 24	20 27
South Croydon 4	d	19 05				19 17			19 35				19 47			20 05				20 17		
Purley Oaks	d	19 08				19 20			19 38				19 50			20 08				20 20		
Sanderstead	d				19 15							19 45							20 15			
Purley 4	a	19 11		19 13		19 24	19 31	19 33	19 41		19 43		19 54	20 01	20 03	20 12		20 14		20 24	20 31	20 33
Purley	d	19 15	19 18			19 25	19 33		19 45	19 48			19 55	20 03		20 16	20 19			20 25	20 33	
Kenley	d	19 18					19 36		19 48					20 06		20 19					20 36	
Whyteleafe	d	19 21					19 40		19 51					20 10		20 22					20 40	
Upper Warlingham	a				19 22							19 52							20 22			
Whyteleafe South	d	19 23					19 42		19 53					20 12		20 24					20 42	
Caterham	a	19 28					19 47		19 58					20 17		20 29					20 47	
Reedham	d		19 20			19 27				19 50			19 57				20 21			20 27		
Coulsdon Town	d		19 23			19a31				19 53			20a01				20 24			20a32		
Woodmansterne	d		19 26							19 56							20 27					
Chipstead	d		19 29							19 59							20 30					
Kingswood	d		19 35							20 05							20 36					
Tadworth	d		19 38							20 08							20 39					
Tattenham Corner	a		19 42							20 12							20 43					

Table T181-F

Saturdays

21 December to 16 May

London and Croydon - Purley, Caterham and Tattenham Corner

		SN		TL [1]	SN [1]	SN	SN	SN [1]	SN		TL [1]	SN [1]	SN	SN	SN [1]	SN		TL [1]	SN [1]	SN	SN	SN [1]
London Victoria [15] ⊖	d				20 20			20 39				20 50			21 09				21 20			21 39
Clapham Junction [10]	d				20 27			20 46				20 57			21 16				21 27			21 46
East Croydon	a				20 39			20 57				21 09			21 26				21 39			21 56
St Pancras International	d			20 05							20 35							21 05				
Farringdon	d			20 09							20 39							21 09				
City Thameslink	d			20 11							20 41											
London Blackfriars	d			20 14							20 44							21 14				
London Bridge [4] ⊖	d	20 17		20 21		20 10	20 14		20 47		20 51		20 40	20 44		21 17		21 21		21 10	21 14	
New Cross Gate [4] ⊖	d					20 18							20 48							21 18		
Norwood Junction [2]	d			20 32		20 39					21 02		21 09					21 32		21 39		
East Croydon	a	20 31		20 36		20 43	20 54		21 01		21 06		21 13	21 24		21 31		21 36		21 43	21 54	
East Croydon	d	20 32		20 37	20 40	20 44	20 54	20 57	21 02		21 07	21 10	21 14	21 24	21 27	21 32		21 37	21 40	21 44	21 54	21 57
South Croydon [4]	d	20 35				20 47			21 05				21 17			21 35				21 47		
Purley Oaks	d	20 38				20 50			21 08				21 20			21 38				21 50		
Sanderstead	d				20 45							21 15							21 45			
Purley [4]	a	20 41		20 43		20 54	21 01	21 03	21 11		21 13		21 24	21 31	21 34	21 41		21 43		21 54	22 01	22 04
Purley	d	20 45	20 48			20 55	21 03		21 15	21 18			21 25	21 33		21 45	21 48			21 55	22 03	
Kenley	d	20 48					21 06		21 18					21 36		21 48					22 06	
Whyteleafe	d	20 51					21 10		21 21					21 40		21 51					22 10	
Upper Warlingham	a				20 52							21 22							21 52			
Whyteleafe South	d	20 53					21 12		21 23					21 42		21 53					22 12	
Caterham	a	20 58					21 17		21 28					21 47		21 58					22 17	
Reedham	d		20 50			20 57				21 20			21 27				21 50			21 57		
Coulsdon Town	d		20 53			21a02				21 23			21a31				21 53			22a01		
Woodmansterne	d		20 56							21 26							21 56					
Chipstead	d		20 59							21 29							21 59					
Kingswood	d		21 05							21 35							22 05					
Tadworth	d		21 08							21 38							22 08					
Tattenham Corner	a		21 12							21 42							22 12					

		SN		TL [1]	SN [1]	SN	SN	SN [1]	SN		TL [1]	SN [1]	SN	SN	SN [1]	SN		TL [1]	SN [1]	SN	SN [1]	SN	
London Victoria [15] ⊖	d				21 50			22 09				22 20			22 39				22 50		23 09		
Clapham Junction [10]	d				21 57			22 16				22 27			22 46				22 57		23 16		
East Croydon	a				22 09			22 26				22 39			22 56				23 09		23 26		
St Pancras International	d			21 35							22 05							22 35					
Farringdon	d			21 39							22 09							22 39					
City Thameslink	d																						
London Blackfriars	d			21 44							22 14							22 44					
London Bridge [4] ⊖	d	21 47		21 51		21 40	21 44		22 17		22 21		22 10	22 14		22 47		22 51		22 40		23 17	
New Cross Gate [4] ⊖	d					21 48							22 18							22 48			
Norwood Junction [2]	d			22 02		22 09					22 32		22 39					23 02		23 09			
East Croydon	a	22 01		22 06		22 13	22 24		22 31		22 36		22 43	22 54		23 01		23 06		23 13		23 31	
East Croydon	d	22 02		22 07	22 10	22 14	22 24	22 27	22 32		22 37	22 40	22 44	22 54	22 57	23 02		23 07	23 10	23 14	23 27	23 32	
South Croydon [4]	d	22 05				22 17			22 35				22 47			23 05				23 17		23 34	
Purley Oaks	d	22 08				22 20			22 38				22 50			23 08				23 20		23 37	
Sanderstead	d				22 15							22 45							23 15				
Purley [4]	a	22 11		22 13		22 24	22 31	22 33	22 41		22 43		22 54	23 01	23 03	23 11		23 13		23 24	23 33	23 40	
Purley	d	22 15	22 18			22 25	22 33		22 45	22 48			22 55	23 03		23 15	23 18			23 25		23 45	23 48
Kenley	d	22 18					22 36		22 48					23 06		23 18						23 48	
Whyteleafe	d	22 21					22 40		22 51					23 10		23 21						23 51	
Upper Warlingham	a				22 22							22 52							23 22				
Whyteleafe South	d	22 23					22 42		22 53					23 12		23 23						23 53	
Caterham	a	22 28					22 47		22 58					23 17		23 28						23 58	
Reedham	d		22 20			22 27				22 50			22 57				23 20			23 27			23 50
Coulsdon Town	d		22 23			22a31				22 53			23a01				23 23			23a30			23 53
Woodmansterne	d		22 26							22 56							23 26						23 56
Chipstead	d		22 29							22 59							23 29						23 59
Kingswood	d		22 35							23 05							23 35						00 05
Tadworth	d		22 38							23 08							23 38						00 08
Tattenham Corner	a		22 42							23 12							23 42						00 12

		TL [1]	SN [1]	SN [1]	SN	SN [1]
London Victoria [15] ⊖	d		23 20	23 36		23 53
Clapham Junction [10]	d		23 27	23 43		23 59
East Croydon	a		23 39	23 58		00 14
St Pancras International	d	23 05				
Farringdon	d	23 10				
City Thameslink	d					
London Blackfriars	d	23 14				
London Bridge [4] ⊖	d	23 21			23 47	
New Cross Gate [4] ⊖	d					
Norwood Junction [2]	d	23 32				
East Croydon	a	23 36			00 01	
East Croydon	d	23 37	23 40	23 59	00 02	00 14
South Croydon [4]	d				00 05	00 17
Purley Oaks	d				00 08	
Sanderstead	d		23 45			00 20
Purley [4]	a	23 42		00 04	00 11	
Purley	d				00 15	
Kenley	d				00 18	
Whyteleafe	d				00 21	
Upper Warlingham	a		23 52			00 27
Whyteleafe South	d				00 23	
Caterham	a				00 28	
Reedham	d					
Coulsdon Town	d					
Woodmansterne	d					
Chipstead	d					
Kingswood	d					
Tadworth	d					
Tattenham Corner	a					

Table T181-F

Sundays

15 December to 10 May

London and Croydon - Purley, Caterham and Tattenham Corner

		SN A	SN A	SN [1] A	SN	SN [1]	SN		TL [1] A	SN [1]	SN [1]	SN [1]	SN [1]	SN [1]	SN [1]	SN	SN [1]	TL [1]	SN		SN [1]	SN [1]
London Victoria [15] ⊖	d					00 08				01 08	02 08	03 08	04 10	05 02	06 32		07 02				07 43	08 02
Clapham Junction [10]	d					00 15				01 17	02 17	03 17	04 17	05 10	06 40		07 10				07 51	08 10
East Croydon	a					00 31				01 32	02 32	03 31	04 31	05 23	06 53		07 26				08 08	08 26
St Pancras International	d								00 51													
Farringdon	d																					
City Thameslink	d																					
London Blackfriars	d								01 01													
London Bridge [4] ⊖	d						00 17											07 19	07 31			
New Cross Gate [4] ⊖	d																		07 38			
Norwood Junction [2]	d						00 30											07 31	07 56			
East Croydon	a						00 34		01 27									07 35	08 02			
East Croydon	d	00 02		00 14		00 32	00 35		01 28	01 33	02 32	03 32	04 31	05 24	06 54	07 01	07 27	07 35	08 03		08 09	08 27
South Croydon [4]	d	00 05		00 17			00 37									07 03			08 05			
Purley Oaks	d	00 08					00 40									07 06			08 08			
Sanderstead	d			00 20																	08 14	
Purley [4]	a	00 11				00 37	00 43		01 33	01 38	02 38	03 37	04 37	05 29	06 58	07 09	07 32	07 40	08 11			08 32
Purley	d	00 15			00 18		00 47	00 50								07 12			08 14	08 17		
Kenley	d	00 18					00 50									07 15			08 17			
Whyteleafe	d	00 21					00 53									07 18			08 21			
Upper Warlingham	a			00 27																	08 21	
Whyteleafe South	d	00 23					00 55									07 20			08 23			
Caterham	a	00 28					01 00									07 25			08 27			
Reedham	d				00 20			00 52												08 19		
Coulsdon Town	d				00 23			00 55												08 22		
Woodmansterne	d				00 26			00 58												08 25		
Chipstead	d				00 29			01 01												08 28		
Kingswood	d		00 05		00 35			01 07												08 34		
Tadworth	d		00 08		00 38			01 10												08 37		
Tattenham Corner	a		00 12		00 42			01 14												08 41		

		SN		TL [1]	SN		SN [1]	SN	SN		SN [1]	TL [1]	SN		SN [1]	TL [1]	SN	SN		SN [1]	TL [1]	SN	
London Victoria [15] ⊖	d						08 51	09 05			09 21				09 51		10 05			10 21			
Clapham Junction [10]	d						08 58	09 12			09 28				09 58		10 12			10 28			
East Croydon	a						09 08	09 23			09 38				10 08		10 23			10 38			
St Pancras International	d															09 41					10 11		
Farringdon	d															09 45					10 15		
City Thameslink	d																						
London Blackfriars	d															09 50					10 20		
London Bridge [4] ⊖	d	08 01		08 19	08 24				08 54			09 27	09 24			09 56		09 54			10 26	10 24	
New Cross Gate [4] ⊖	d	08 08			08 30				09 00				09 30					10 00				10 30	
Norwood Junction [2]	d	08 26		08 31	08 52				09 22				09 52					10 22				10 52	
East Croydon	a	08 32		08 35	08 55				09 25			09 41	09 55			10 10		10 25			10 40	10 55	
East Croydon	d	08 33		08 37	08 56		09 09	09 23	09 26		09 39	09 41	09 56		10 09	10 11	10 23	10 26		10 39	10 41	10 56	
South Croydon [4]	d	08 35			08 59				09 29				09 59					10 29				10 59	
Purley Oaks	d	08 38			09 01				09 31				10 01					10 31				11 01	
Sanderstead	d						09 14				09 44				10 14					10 44			
Purley [4]	a	08 41		08 42	09 04			09 28	09 34			09 46	10 04			10 16	10 28	10 34			10 46	11 04	
Purley	d	08 44	08 47		09 08	09 11			09 38	09 41			10 08	10 11				10 38	10 41			11 08	11 11
Kenley	d	08 47			09 11				09 41				10 11					10 41				11 11	
Whyteleafe	d	08 51			09 14				09 44				10 14					10 44				11 14	
Upper Warlingham	a						09 21				09 51				10 21					10 51			
Whyteleafe South	d	08 53			09 16				09 46				10 16					10 46				11 16	
Caterham	a	08 57			09 22				09 52				10 22					10 52				11 22	
Reedham	d		08 49			09 13				09 43				10 13					10 43				11 13
Coulsdon Town	d		08 52			09 16				09 46				10 16					10 46				11 16
Woodmansterne	d		08 55			09 19				09 49				10 19					10 49				11 19
Chipstead	d		08 58			09 22				09 52				10 22					10 52				11 22
Kingswood	d		09 04			09 28				09 58				10 28					10 58				11 28
Tadworth	d		09 07			09 31				10 01				10 31					11 01				11 31
Tattenham Corner	a		09 11			09 35				10 05				10 35					11 05				11 35

		SN [1]	TL [1]	SN	SN		SN [1]	TL [1]	SN		SN [1]	TL [1]	SN	SN		SN [1]	TL [1]	SN		TL [1]	SN [1]	SN
London Victoria [15] ⊖	d	10 51		11 05			11 21				11 51		12 05			12 21					12 51	13 05
Clapham Junction [10]	d	10 58		11 12			11 28				11 58		12 12			12 28					12 58	13 12
East Croydon	a	11 08		11 23			11 38				12 08		12 23			12 38					13 11	13 23
St Pancras International	d		10 41					11 11				11 41					12 11			12 41		
Farringdon	d		10 45					11 15				11 45					12 15			12 45		
City Thameslink	d																					
London Blackfriars	d		10 50					11 20				11 50					12 20			12 50		
London Bridge [4] ⊖	d		10 56		10 54			11 26	11 24			11 56		11 54			12 26	12 24		12 56		
New Cross Gate [4] ⊖	d				11 00				11 30					12 00				12 30				
Norwood Junction [2]	d				11 22				11 52					12 22				12 52				
East Croydon	a		11 10		11 25			11 40	11 55			12 10		12 25			12 40	12 55		13 10		
East Croydon	d	11 09	11 11	11 23	11 26		11 39	11 41	11 56		12 09	12 11	12 23	12 26		12 39	12 41	12 56		13 11	13 12	13 23
South Croydon [4]	d				11 29				11 59					12 29				12 59				
Purley Oaks	d				11 31				12 01					12 31				13 01				
Sanderstead	d	11 14					11 44				12 14					12 44					13 17	
Purley [4]	a		11 16	11 28	11 34			11 46	12 04			12 16	12 28	12 34			12 46	13 04		13 16		13 28
Purley	d				11 38	11 41			12 08	12 11				12 38	12 41			13 08	13 11			
Kenley	d				11 41				12 11					12 41				13 11				
Whyteleafe	d				11 44				12 14					12 44				13 14				
Upper Warlingham	a	11 21					11 51				12 21					12 51					13 24	
Whyteleafe South	d				11 46				12 16					12 46				13 16				
Caterham	a				11 52				12 22					12 52				13 22				
Reedham	d					11 43				12 13					12 43				13 13			
Coulsdon Town	d					11 46				12 16					12 46				13 16			
Woodmansterne	d					11 49				12 19					12 49				13 19			
Chipstead	d					11 52				12 22					12 52				13 22			
Kingswood	d					11 58				12 28					12 58				13 28			
Tadworth	d					12 01				12 31					13 01				13 31			
Tattenham Corner	a					12 05				12 35					13 05				13 35			

A not 15 December

Table T181-F

Sundays
15 December to 10 May

London and Croydon - Purley, Caterham and Tattenham Corner

		SN		SN 1	TL 1	SN		SN 1	TL 1	SN		SN		SN 1	TL 1	SN		SN 1	TL 1	SN		SN		SN 1	TL 1
London Victoria 15 ⊖	d			13 21				13 51		14 05				14 21				14 51		15 05				15 21	
Clapham Junction 10	d			13 28				13 58		14 12				14 28				14 58		15 12				15 28	
East Croydon	a			13 38				14 08		14 23				14 38				15 08		15 23				15 38	
St Pancras International	d				13 11				13 41						14 11				14 41						15 11
Farringdon	d				13 15				13 45						14 15				14 45						15 15
City Thameslink	d																								
London Blackfriars	d				13 20				13 50						14 20				14 50						15 20
London Bridge 4 ⊖	d	12 54			13 26	13 24			13 56			13 54			14 26	14 24			14 56			14 54			15 26
New Cross Gate 4 ⊖	d	13 00				13 30						14 00				14 30						15 00			
Norwood Junction 2	d	13 22				13 52						14 22				14 52						15 22			
East Croydon	a	13 25			13 40	13 55			14 10			14 25			14 40	14 55			15 10			15 25			15 40
East Croydon	d	13 26		13 39	13 41	13 56		14 09	14 11	14 23		14 26		14 39	14 41	14 56		15 09	15 11	15 23		15 26		15 39	15 41
South Croydon 4	d	13 29				13 59						14 29				14 59						15 29			
Purley Oaks	d	13 31				14 01						14 31				15 01						15 31			
Sanderstead	d			13 44				14 14						14 44				15 14						15 44	
Purley 4	a	13 34			13 46	14 04			14 16	14 28		14 34			14 46	15 04			15 16	15 28		15 34			15 46
Purley	d	13 38	13 41			14 08	14 11					14 38	14 41			15 08	15 11					15 38	15 41		
Kenley	d	13 41				14 11						14 41				15 11						15 41			
Whyteleafe	d	13 44				14 14						14 44				15 14						15 44			
Upper Warlingham	a			13 51				14 21						14 51				15 21						15 51	
Whyteleafe South	d	13 46				14 16						14 46				15 16						15 46			
Caterham	a	13 52				14 22						14 52				15 22						15 52			
Reedham	d		13 43				14 13						14 43				15 13						15 43		
Coulsdon Town	d		13 46				14 16						14 46				15 16						15 46		
Woodmansterne	d		13 49				14 19						14 49				15 19						15 49		
Chipstead	d		13 52				14 22						14 52				15 22						15 52		
Kingswood	d		13 58				14 28						14 58				15 28						15 58		
Tadworth	d		14 01				14 31						15 01				15 31						16 01		
Tattenham Corner	a		14 05				14 35						15 05				15 35						16 05		

		SN		TL 1	SN 1	SN		SN		SN 1	TL 1	SN		TL 1	SN 1	SN		SN		SN 1	TL 1	SN			
London Victoria 15 ⊖	d				15 51	16 05				16 21					16 51	17 05				17 21					
Clapham Junction 10	d				15 58	16 12				16 28					16 58	17 12				17 28					
East Croydon	a				16 11	16 23				16 38					17 11	17 23				17 38					
St Pancras International	d			15 41							16 11			16 41							17 11				
Farringdon	d			15 45							16 15			16 45							17 15				
City Thameslink	d																								
London Blackfriars	d			15 50							16 20			16 50							17 20				
London Bridge 4 ⊖	d	15 24		15 56				15 54			16 26	16 24		16 56				16 54			17 26	17 24			
New Cross Gate 4 ⊖	d	15 30						16 00				16 30						17 00				17 30			
Norwood Junction 2	d	15 52						16 22				16 52						17 22				17 51			
East Croydon	a	15 55		16 10				16 25			16 40	16 55		17 10				17 25			17 40	17 55			
East Croydon	d	15 56		16 11	16 12	16 23		16 26		16 39	16 41	16 56		17 11	17 12	17 23		17 26		17 39	17 41	17 56			
South Croydon 4	d	15 59						16 29				16 59						17 29				17 59			
Purley Oaks	d	16 01						16 31				17 01						17 31				18 01			
Sanderstead	d				16 17					16 44					17 17					17 44					
Purley 4	a	16 04		16 16		16 28		16 34			16 46	17 04		17 16		17 28		17 34			17 46	18 04			
Purley	d	16 08	16 11					16 38	16 41			17 08	17 11					17 38	17 41			18 08	18 11		
Kenley	d	16 11						16 41				17 11						17 41				18 11			
Whyteleafe	d	16 14						16 44				17 14						17 44				18 14			
Upper Warlingham	a				16 24					16 51					17 24					17 51					
Whyteleafe South	d	16 16						16 46				17 16						17 46				18 16			
Caterham	a	16 22						16 52				17 22						17 52				18 22			
Reedham	d		16 13						16 43				17 13						17 43				18 13		
Coulsdon Town	d		16 16						16 46				17 16						17 46				18 16		
Woodmansterne	d		16 19						16 49				17 19						17 49				18 19		
Chipstead	d		16 22						16 52				17 22						17 52				18 22		
Kingswood	d		16 28						16 58				17 28						17 58				18 28		
Tadworth	d		16 31						17 01				17 31						18 01				18 31		
Tattenham Corner	a		16 35						17 05				17 35						18 05				18 35		

		SN 1	TL 1	SN	SN		SN 1	TL 1	SN			SN 1	TL 1	SN	SN		SN 1	TL 1	SN			SN 1	TL 1	SN
London Victoria 15 ⊖	d	17 51		18 05			18 21					20 51		21 05			21 21					21 51		22 05
Clapham Junction 10	d	17 58		18 12			18 28					20 58		21 12			21 28					21 58		22 13
East Croydon	a	18 08		18 23			18 38					21 08		21 23			21 38					22 08		22 23
St Pancras International	d		17 41					18 11					20 41					21 11					21 41	
Farringdon	d		17 45					18 15					20 45					21 15					21 45	
City Thameslink	d																							
London Blackfriars	d		17 50					18 20					20 50					21 20					21 50	
London Bridge 4 ⊖	d		17 56		17 54			18 26	18 24				20 56		20 54			21 26	21 24				21 56	
New Cross Gate 4 ⊖	d				18 00				18 30						21 00				21 30					
Norwood Junction 2	d				18 22				18 52						21 22				21 52					
East Croydon	a		18 10		18 25			18 40	18 55		and at		21 10		21 25			21 40	21 55				22 10	
East Croydon	d	18 09	18 11	18 23	18 26		18 39	18 41	18 56		the same	21 09	21 11	21 23	21 26		21 39	21 41	21 56			22 09	22 11	22 24
South Croydon 4	d				18 29				18 59		minutes				21 29				21 59					
Purley Oaks	d				18 31				19 01		past				21 31				22 01					
Sanderstead	d	18 14					18 44				each	21 14					21 44					22 14		
Purley 4	a		18 16	18 28	18 34			18 46	19 04		hour until		21 16	21 28	21 34			21 46	22 04				22 16	22 28
Purley	d				18 38	18 41			19 08	19 11					21 38	21 41			22 08	22 11				
Kenley	d				18 41				19 11						21 41				22 11					
Whyteleafe	d				18 44				19 14						21 44				22 14					
Upper Warlingham	a	18 21					18 51					21 21					21 51					22 21		
Whyteleafe South	d				18 46				19 16						21 46				22 16					
Caterham	a				18 52				19 22						21 52				22 22					
Reedham	d					18 43				19 13						21 43				22 13				
Coulsdon Town	d					18 46				19 16						21 46				22 16				
Woodmansterne	d					18 49				19 19						21 49				22 19				
Chipstead	d					18 52				19 22						21 52				22 22				
Kingswood	d					18 58				19 28						21 58				22 28				
Tadworth	d					19 01				19 31						22 01				22 31				
Tattenham Corner	a					19 05				19 35						22 05				22 35				

Table T181-F

Sundays
15 December to 10 May

London and Croydon - Purley, Caterham and Tattenham Corner

		SN		SN 1	TL 1	SN			TL 1	SN 1	SN 1	SN		SN 1	TL 1	SN	SN
London Victoria 15 ⊖	d			22 21						22 51	23 05			23 32			
Clapham Junction 10	d			22 28						22 58	23 12			23 40			
East Croydon	a			22 38						23 08	23 22			23 56			
St Pancras International	d				22 11				22 35								
Farringdon	d				22 15				22 39								
City Thameslink	d																
London Blackfriars	d				22 20				22 44								
London Bridge 4 ⊖	d	21 54			22 26	22 24			22 51			22 54			23 45	23 31	23 50
New Cross Gate 4 ⊖	d	22 00				22 30						23 00				23 39	23 57
Norwood Junction 2	d	22 22				22 52			23 03			23 22				23 58	00 16
East Croydon	a	22 25			22 40	22 55			23 07			23 25			23 59	00 02	00 19
East Croydon	d	22 26		22 39	22 41	22 56			23 08	23 09	23 23	23 26		23 57	00 01	00 03	00 20
South Croydon 4	d	22 29				22 59						23 29				00 05	00 22
Purley Oaks	d	22 31				23 01						23 31				00 08	00 25
Sanderstead	d			22 44						23 14							
Purley 4	a	22 34			22 46	23 04			23 13		23 27	23 34		00 02	00 06	00 11	00 28
Purley	d	22 38	22 41			23 08	23 11					23 38	23 41			00 12	00 29
Kenley	d	22 41				23 11						23 41				00 15	00 32
Whyteleafe	d	22 44				23 14						23 44				00 18	00 35
Upper Warlingham	a			22 51						23 21							
Whyteleafe South	d	22 46				23 16						23 46				00 20	00 37
Caterham	a	22 52				23 22						23 52				00 25	00 42
Reedham	d		22 43				23 13						23 43				
Coulsdon Town	d		22 46				23 16						23 46				
Woodmansterne	d		22 49				23 19						23 49				
Chipstead	d		22 52				23 22						23 52				
Kingswood	d		22 58				23 28						23 58				
Tadworth	d		23 01				23 31						00 01				
Tattenham Corner	a		23 05				23 35						00 05				

AVAILABLE FROM MP Middleton Press

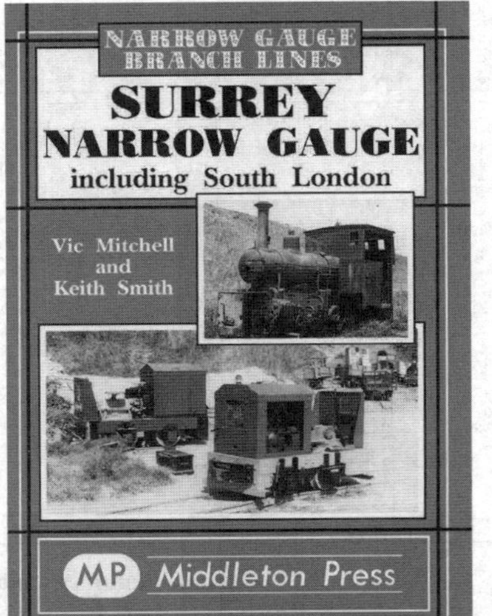

Tattenham Corner and Caterham, Purley - London and Croydon

Miles	Miles	Miles	Station		SN MO ■	TL MX ■	TL ■	TL ■	TL ■	TL ■	TL ■	SN	SN ■	TL ■	SN ■	SN	SN	TL ■	SN	SN	TL ■	SN ■	SN ■
0	—	—	Tattenham Corner	d													05 39			05 49			
1¼	—	—	Tadworth	d													05 43			05 53			
2½	—	—	Kingswood	d													05 46			05 56			
5	—	—	Chipstead	d													05 52			06 02			
6	—	—	Woodmansterne	d													05 55			06 05			
6¾	—	—	Coulsdon Town	d													05 59			06 09			
7½	—	—	Reedham	d													06 02			06 12			
—	0	—	Caterham	d												05 50			06 00				
—	1¾	—	Whyteleafe South	d												05 53			06 03				
—	—	0	Upper Warlingham	d											06 02			06 11					06 32
—	2¼	—	Whyteleafe	d												05 55			06 05				
—	3½	—	Kenley	d												05 58			06 08				
—	—	—	Purley	a												06 02	06 05		06 12	06 15			
8¼	4¾	—	Purley [4]	d		00 03	01 03	02 04	03 03	04 03	05 01	05 11	05 52	05 58		06 09			06 19		06 24	06 28	
—	—	3¾	Sanderstead	d											06 09			06 18					06 39
9¼	5¾	—	Purley Oaks	d								05 14	05 54			06 12			06 22				
10¼	6¾	—	South Croydon [4]	d								05 17	05 57			06 15		06 21	06 25		06 28		
11¼	7¾	5¾	East Croydon ⇌	a		00 09	01 09	02 10	03 09	04 09	05 08	05 19	06 00	06 03	06 15	06 18		06 24	06 28		06 31	06 34	06 44
—	—	—	East Croydon	d		00 09	01 10	02 10	03 10	04 10	05 10	05 20		06 03		06 18		06 25			06 31		
—	9	—	Norwood Junction [2]	a								05 24		06 07							06 36		
—	15	—	New Cross Gate [4] ⊖	a							05 24	05 42		06 20				06 40			06 50		
—	17¾	—	London Bridge [4] ⊖	a								05 50				06 34							
—	—	—	London Blackfriars	a		00 36	01 36	02 36	03 36	04 36	05 31			06 26				06 46			06 56		
—	—	—	City Thameslink	a							05 33			06 28				06 48			06 58		
—	—	—	Farringdon	a		00 41					05 35			06 31				06 51			07 01		
—	—	—	St Pancras International	a		00 45	01 43	02 43	03 43	04 43	05 40			06 35				06 55			07 05		
—	—	—	East Croydon	d	00 06								06 00		06 15				06 28			06 34	06 45
19	—	13½	Clapham Junction [10]	a	00 18								06 11		06 25				06 39			06 44	06 55
21¾	—	15½	London Victoria [15] ⊖	a	00 27								06 18		06 32				06 49			06 52	07 03

Station		SN	SN	TL ■	SN	SN	TL ■	SN ■	SN ■	SN	SN	TL ■	SN	SN	TL ■	SN ■	SN ■	SN	SN	TL ■	SN	SN	TL ■
Tattenham Corner	d		06 09			06 19					06 39			06 49					07 09			07 19	
Tadworth	d		06 13			06 23					06 43			06 53					07 13			07 23	
Kingswood	d		06 16			06 26					06 46			06 56					07 16			07 26	
Chipstead	d		06 22			06 32					06 52			07 02					07 22			07 32	
Woodmansterne	d		06 25			06 35					06 55			07 05					07 25			07 35	
Coulsdon Town	d		06 29			06 39					06 59			07 09					07 29			07 39	
Reedham	d		06 32			06 42					07 02			07 12					07 32			07 42	
Caterham	d	06 20			06 30					06 50			07 00					07 20			07 30		
Whyteleafe South	d	06 23			06 33					06 53			07 03					07 23			07 33		
Upper Warlingham	d			06 39					07 02			07 11					07 32			07 41			
Whyteleafe	d	06 25			06 35					06 55			07 05					07 25			07 35		
Kenley	d	06 28			06 38					06 58			07 08					07 28			07 38		
Purley	a	06 32	06 35		06 42	06 45				07 02	07 05		07 12	07 15				07 32	07 35		07 42	07 45	
Purley [4]	d	06 39			06 49		06 54	06 58		07 09			07 19		07 24	07 28		07 39			07 49		07 54
Sanderstead	d			06 45					07 09			07 18					07 39			07 48			
Purley Oaks	d	06 42			06 52					07 12			07 22					07 42			07 52		
South Croydon [4]	d	06 45		06 48	06 55		06 58			07 15		07 21	07 25		07 28			07 45		07 51	07 55		07 58
East Croydon ⇌	a	06 48		06 51	06 58		07 01	07 04	07 15	07 18		07 24	07 28		07 31	07 34	07 45	07 48		07 54	07 58		08 01
East Croydon	d	06 48		06 51			07 01			07 18		07 25			07 31			07 48		07 55			08 01
Norwood Junction [2]	a						07 06								07 36								08 06
New Cross Gate [4] ⊖	a			07 05			07 20					07 40			07 50					08 10			08 20
London Bridge [4] ⊖	a	07 04								07 34								08 04					
London Blackfriars	a			07 11			07 26					07 46			07 56					08 16			08 26
City Thameslink	a			07 13			07 28					07 48			07 58					08 18			08 28
Farringdon	a			07 16			07 31					07 51			08 01					08 21			08 31
St Pancras International	a			07 20			07 35					07 55			08 05					08 25			08 35
East Croydon	d				06 58			07 04	07 15				07 28			07 34	07 45				07 58		
Clapham Junction [10]	a				07 10			07 14	07 25				07 40			07 44	07 57				08 10		
London Victoria [15] ⊖	a				07 19			07 22	07 32				07 49			07 52	08 06				08 19		

Station		SN ■	SN ■	SN	SN	TL ■	SN	SN	TL ■	SN ■	SN ■	SN	SN	TL ■	SN	SN	TL ■	SN ■	SN ■	SN	SN	SN	TL ■
Tattenham Corner	d				07 39			07 49					08 09			08 19					08 39		
Tadworth	d				07 43			07 53					08 13			08 23					08 43		
Kingswood	d				07 46			07 56					08 16			08 26					08 46		
Chipstead	d				07 52			08 02					08 22			08 32					08 52		
Woodmansterne	d				07 55			08 05					08 25			08 35					08 55		
Coulsdon Town	d				07 59			08 09					08 29			08 39					08 59		
Reedham	d				08 02			08 12					08 32			08 42					09 02		
Caterham	d			07 50			08 00					08 20			08 30					08 50		09 00	
Whyteleafe South	d			07 53			08 03					08 23			08 33					08 53		09 03	
Upper Warlingham	d		08 02			08 11					08 32			08 41					09 02				09 11
Whyteleafe	d			07 55			08 05					08 25			08 35					08 55		09 05	
Kenley	d			07 58			08 08					08 28			08 38					08 58		09 08	
Purley	a			08 02	08 05		08 12	08 15				08 32	08 35		08 42	08 45				09 02	09 05	09 12	
Purley [4]	d	07 58		08 09			08 19		08 24	08 28		08 39			08 49		08 54	08 58		09 09		09 15	
Sanderstead	d		08 09			08 18					08 39			08 48					09 09				09 18
Purley Oaks	d			08 12			08 22					08 42			08 52					09 12			
South Croydon [4]	d			08 15		08 21	08 25		08 28			08 45		08 51	08 55		08 58			09 15			09 21
East Croydon ⇌	a	08 04	08 15	08 18		08 24	08 28		08 31	08 34	08 45	08 48		08 54	08 58		09 01	09 04	09 15	09 18		09 21	09 24
East Croydon	d			08 18		08 25			08 31			08 48		08 55			09 01			09 18		09 21	09 25
Norwood Junction [2]	a								08 36								09 06						
New Cross Gate [4] ⊖	a					08 40			08 50					09 10			09 20						09 40
London Bridge [4] ⊖	a			08 34								09 04								09 34		10 06	
London Blackfriars	a					08 46			08 56					09 16			09 26						09 46
City Thameslink	a					08 48			08 58					09 18			09 28						09 48
Farringdon	a					08 51			09 01					09 21			09 31						09 51
St Pancras International	a					08 55			09 05					09 25			09 35						09 55
East Croydon	d	08 04	08 15				08 28			08 34	08 45				08 58			09 04	09 15				
Clapham Junction [10]	a	08 14	08 27				08 40			08 44	08 57				09 10			09 14	09 25				
London Victoria [15] ⊖	a	08 22	08 35				08 49			08 52	09 05				09 19			09 24	09 32				

Table T181-R

Mondays to Fridays

16 December to 15 May

Tattenham Corner and Caterham, Purley - London and Croydon

Station		TL ■	SN ■	SN ■	SN	SN	SN	TL ■	SN ■	TL ■	SN ■	SN	SN	SN	SN ■	TL ■	SN ■	SN	SN	SN	SN	SN ■
Tattenham Corner	d					09 09							09 39						10 09			
Tadworth	d					09 13							09 43						10 13			
Kingswood	d					09 16							09 46						10 16			
Chipstead	d					09 22							09 52						10 22			
Woodmansterne	d					09 25							09 55						10 25			
Coulsdon Town	d					09 29							09 59						10 29		10 42	
Reedham	d					09 32							10 02						10 32		10 45	
Caterham	d				09 20		09 30					09 50		10 00				10 20		10 30		
Whyteleafe South	d				09 23		09 33					09 53		10 03				10 23		10 33		
Upper Warlingham	d			09 32							10 02						10 32					
Whyteleafe	d				09 25		09 35					09 55		10 05				10 25		10 35		
Kenley	d				09 28		09 38					09 58		10 08				10 28		10 38		
Purley	a				09 32	09 35	09 42					10 02	10 05	10 12				10 32	10 35	10 42	10 47	
Purley [4]	d	09 24	09 28		09 39		09 45		09 55	09 58		10 09		10 15	10 25	10 28		10 39		10 45	10 48	10 55
Sanderstead	d			09 39				09 48			10 09						10 39					
Purley Oaks	d				09 42							10 12						10 42			10 51	
South Croydon [4]	d	09 28			09 45			09 51				10 15						10 45			10 54	
East Croydon ⇌	a	09 31	09 34	09 45	09 48		09 51	09 54	10 00	10 03	10 15	10 18		10 21	10 30	10 33	10 45	10 48		10 51	10 57	11 00
East Croydon	d	09 31			09 48		09 51	09 54		10 03		10 18		10 22		10 33		10 48		10 52	10 57	
Norwood Junction [2]	a	09 36								10 07						10 37					11 02	
New Cross Gate [4] ⊖	a	09 50								10 20						10 50					11 20	
London Bridge [4] ⊖	a				10 04		10 36	10 11				10 34		11 06				11 04		11 36	11 31	
London Blackfriars	a	09 56								10 26						10 56						
City Thameslink	a	09 58								10 28						10 58						
Farringdon	a	10 01								10 31						11 01						
St Pancras International	a	10 05								10 35						11 05						
East Croydon	d		09 34	09 45					10 00		10 15				10 30		10 45					11 00
Clapham Junction [10]	a		09 44	09 55					10 10		10 25				10 40		10 55					11 10
London Victoria [15] ⊖	a		09 52	10 02					10 18		10 35				10 48		11 02					11 18

Station		TL ■	SN ■	SN	SN	SN	SN	SN ■	TL ■	SN ■	SN	SN	SN	SN	SN ■	TL ■	SN ■	SN	SN	SN	SN	SN ■	TL ■
Tattenham Corner	d				10 39							11 09							11 39				
Tadworth	d				10 43							11 13							11 43				
Kingswood	d				10 46							11 16							11 46				
Chipstead	d				10 52							11 22							11 52				
Woodmansterne	d				10 55							11 25							11 55				
Coulsdon Town	d				10 59		11 12					11 29		11 42					11 59		12 12		
Reedham	d				11 02		11 15					11 32		11 45					12 02		12 15		
Caterham	d			10 50		11 00					11 20		11 30					11 50		12 00			
Whyteleafe South	d			10 53		11 03					11 23		11 33					11 53		12 03			
Upper Warlingham	d		11 02							11 32							12 02						
Whyteleafe	d			10 55		11 05					11 25		11 35					11 55		12 05			
Kenley	d			10 58		11 08					11 28		11 38					11 58		12 08			
Purley	a			11 02	11 05	11 12	11 17				11 32	11 35	11 42	11 47				12 02	12 05	12 12	12 17		
Purley [4]	d	10 58		11 09		11 15	11 18	11 25	11 28		11 39		11 45	11 48	11 55	11 58		12 09		12 15	12 18	12 25	12 28
Sanderstead	d		11 09							11 39							12 09						
Purley Oaks	d			11 12			11 21				11 42			11 51				12 12			12 21		
South Croydon [4]	d			11 15			11 24				11 45			11 54				12 15			12 24		
East Croydon ⇌	a	11 03	11 15	11 18		11 21	11 27	11 30	11 33	11 45	11 48		11 51	11 57	12 00	12 03	12 15	12 18		12 21	12 27	12 30	12 33
East Croydon	d	11 03		11 18		11 22	11 27		11 33		11 48		11 52	11 57		12 03		12 18		12 22	12 27		12 33
Norwood Junction [2]	a	11 07					11 32		11 37					12 02		12 07					12 32		12 37
New Cross Gate [4] ⊖	a	11 20					11 50		11 50					12 20		12 20					12 50		12 50
London Bridge [4] ⊖	a			11 34		12 06	12 01				12 04		12 36	12 31				12 34		13 06	13 01		
London Blackfriars	a	11 26							11 56							12 26							12 56
City Thameslink	a	11 28							11 58							12 28							12 58
Farringdon	a	11 31							12 01							12 31							13 01
St Pancras International	a	11 35							12 05							12 35							13 05
East Croydon	d		11 15					11 30		11 45					12 00		12 15					12 30	
Clapham Junction [10]	a		11 25					11 40		11 55					12 10		12 25					12 40	
London Victoria [15] ⊖	a		11 32					11 48		12 02					12 18		12 32					12 48	

Station		SN ■	SN	SN	SN	SN	SN ■	TL ■	SN ■	SN	SN	SN	SN	SN ■	TL ■	SN ■	SN	SN	SN	SN	SN ■	TL ■
Tattenham Corner	d			12 09							12 39							13 09				
Tadworth	d			12 13							12 43							13 13				
Kingswood	d			12 16							12 46							13 16				
Chipstead	d			12 22							12 52							13 22				
Woodmansterne	d			12 25							12 55							13 25				
Coulsdon Town	d			12 29		12 42					12 59		13 12					13 29		13 42		
Reedham	d			12 32		12 45					13 02		13 15					13 32		13 45		
Caterham	d		12 20		12 30					12 50		13 00					13 20		13 30			
Whyteleafe South	d		12 23		12 33					12 53		13 03					13 23		13 33			
Upper Warlingham	d	12 32							13 02							13 32						
Whyteleafe	d		12 25		12 35					12 55		13 05					13 25		13 35			
Kenley	d		12 28		12 38					12 58		13 08					13 28		13 38			
Purley	a		12 32	12 35	12 42	12 47				13 02	13 05	13 12	13 17				13 32	13 35	13 42	13 47		
Purley [4]	d		12 39		12 45	12 48	12 55	12 58		13 09		13 15	13 18	13 25	13 28		13 39		13 45	13 48	13 55	13 58
Sanderstead	d	12 39							13 09							13 39						
Purley Oaks	d		12 42			12 51				13 12			13 21				13 42			13 51		
South Croydon [4]	d		12 45			12 54				13 15			13 24				13 45			13 54		
East Croydon ⇌	a	12 45	12 48		12 51	12 57	13 00	13 03	13 15	13 18		13 21	13 27	13 30	13 33	13 45	13 48		13 51	13 57	14 00	14 03
East Croydon	d		12 48		12 52	12 57		13 03		13 18		13 22	13 27		13 33		13 48		13 52	13 57		14 03
Norwood Junction [2]	a					13 02		13 07					13 32		13 37					14 02		14 07
New Cross Gate [4] ⊖	a					13 20		13 20					13 50		13 50					14 20		14 20
London Bridge [4] ⊖	a		13 04		13 36	13 31				13 34		14 06	14 01				14 04		14 36	14 31		
London Blackfriars	a							13 26							13 56							14 26
City Thameslink	a							13 28							13 58							14 28
Farringdon	a							13 31							14 01							14 31
St Pancras International	a							13 35							14 05							14 35
East Croydon	d	12 45					13 00		13 15					13 30		13 45					14 00	
Clapham Junction [10]	a	12 55					13 10		13 25					13 40		13 55					14 10	
London Victoria [15] ⊖	a	13 02					13 18		13 32					13 48		14 02					14 18	

Table T181-R

Mondays to Fridays
16 December to 15 May

Tattenham Corner and Caterham, Purley - London and Croydon

		SN 1	SN	SN	SN	SN	SN 1	TL 1	SN 1	SN	SN	SN	SN	SN 1	TL 1	SN 1	SN	SN	SN	SN	SN 1	TL 1	SN 1
Tattenham Corner	d			13 39							14 09							14 39					
Tadworth	d			13 43							14 13							14 43					
Kingswood	d			13 46							14 16							14 46					
Chipstead	d			13 52							14 22							14 52					
Woodmansterne	d			13 55							14 25							14 55					
Coulsdon Town	d			13 59		14 12					14 29		14 42					14 59		15 12			
Reedham	d			14 02		14 15					14 32		14 45					15 02		15 15			
Caterham	d		13 50		14 00					14 20		14 30					14 50		15 00				
Whyteleafe South	d		13 53		14 03					14 23		14 33					14 53		15 03				
Upper Warlingham	d	14 02							14 32							15 02							
Whyteleafe	d		13 55		14 05					14 25		14 35					14 55		15 05				
Kenley	d		13 58		14 08					14 28		14 38					14 58		15 08				
Purley	a		14 02	14 05	14 12	14 17				14 32	14 35	14 42	14 47				15 02	15 05	15 12	15 17			
Purley 4	d		14 09		14 15	14 18	14 25	14 28		14 39		14 45	14 48	14 55	14 58		15 09		15 15	15 18	15 25	15 28	
Sanderstead	d	14 09							14 39							15 09							
Purley Oaks	d		14 12			14 21				14 42			14 51				15 12			15 21			
South Croydon 4	d		14 15			14 24				14 45			14 54				15 15			15 24			15 36
East Croydon	a	14 15	14 18		14 21	14 27	14 30	14 33	14 45	14 48		14 51	14 57	15 00	15 03	15 15	15 18		15 21	15 27	15 30	15 33	15 39
East Croydon	d		14 18		14 22	14 27		14 33		14 48		14 52	14 57		15 03		15 18		15 22	15 27		15 33	
Norwood Junction 2	a					14 32		14 37					15 02		15 07					15 32		15 37	
New Cross Gate 4 ⊖	a					14 50		14 50					15 20		15 20					15 50		15 50	
London Bridge 4 ⊖	a		14 34		15 06	15 01				15 04		15 36	15 31				15 34		16 06	16 01			
London Blackfriars	a							14 56							15 26							15 56	
City Thameslink	a							14 58							15 28							15 58	
Farringdon	a							15 01							15 31							16 01	
St Pancras International	a							15 05							15 35							16 05	
East Croydon	d	14 15					14 30		14 45					15 00		15 15					15 30		15 43
Clapham Junction 10	a	14 25					14 40		14 55					15 10		15 25					15 40		→
London Victoria 15 ⊖	a	14 32					14 48		15 02					15 18		15 32					15 49		

		SN 1	SN 1	SN	SN	SN	TL 1	SN	SN 1	TL 1	SN	SN 1	SN	SN	SN	TL 1	SN	SN 1	TL 1	SN	SN 1	SN	SN
Tattenham Corner	d				15 09									15 39									16 09
Tadworth	d				15 13									15 43									16 13
Kingswood	d				15 16									15 46									16 16
Chipstead	d				15 22									15 52									16 22
Woodmansterne	d				15 25									15 55									16 25
Coulsdon Town	d				15 29			15 42						15 59			16 12						16 29
Reedham	d				15 32			15 45						16 02			16 15						16 32
Caterham	d			15 20		15 30							15 50		16 00							16 20	
Whyteleafe South	d			15 23		15 33							15 53		16 03							16 23	
Upper Warlingham	d	15 32										16 02									16 32		
Whyteleafe	d			15 25		15 35							15 55		16 05							16 25	
Kenley	d			15 28		15 38							15 58		16 08							16 28	
Purley	a			15 32	15 35	15 42		15 47					16 02	16 05	16 12		16 17					16 32	16 35
Purley 4	d			15 39		15 45	15 48	15 50	15 55	15 58			16 09		16 15	16 18	16 20	16 25	16 28			16 39	
Sanderstead	d	15 39										16 09									16 39		
Purley Oaks	d			15 42									16 12									16 42	
South Croydon 4	d			15 45				15 54					16 15				16 24					16 45	
East Croydon	a	15 45		15 48		15 51	15 54	15 57	16 00	16 03		16 15	16 18		16 21	16 24	16 27	16 30	16 33		16 45	16 48	
East Croydon	d			15 48		15 51	15 54	15 57		16 03			16 18		16 21	16 24	16 27		16 33			16 48	
Norwood Junction 2	a							16 03		16 07	←						16 33		16 37	←			
New Cross Gate 4 ⊖	a						16 10	16 21		16 20	16 21					16 40	16 51		16 50	16 51			
London Bridge 4 ⊖	a			16 04		16 36		→			16 31		16 34		17 06		→			17 01		17 04	
London Blackfriars	a						16 16			16 26						16 46			16 56				
City Thameslink	a						16 18			16 28						16 48			16 58				
Farringdon	a						16 21			16 31						16 51			17 01				
St Pancras International	a		←				16 25			16 35						16 55			17 05				
East Croydon	d	15 46	15 43						16 00			16 15						16 30			16 45		
Clapham Junction 10	a	15 56	16 04						16 11			16 25						16 41			16 55		
London Victoria 15 ⊖	a	16 03	16 13						16 19			16 32						16 48			17 02		

		SN	TL 1	SN	SN 1	TL 1	SN	SN 1	SN	SN	SN	TL 1	SN 1	TL 1	SN 1	SN	SN	SN	TL 1	SN 1	TL 1	SN 1
Tattenham Corner	d									16 39							17 09					
Tadworth	d									16 43							17 13					
Kingswood	d									16 46							17 16					
Chipstead	d									16 52							17 22					
Woodmansterne	d									16 55							17 25					
Coulsdon Town	d			16 42						16 59							17 29					
Reedham	d			16 45						17 02							17 32					
Caterham	d	16 30							16 50		17 00					17 20		17 30				
Whyteleafe South	d	16 33							16 53		17 03					17 23		17 33				
Upper Warlingham	d							17 02							17 32							18 02
Whyteleafe	d	16 35							16 55		17 05					17 25		17 35				
Kenley	d	16 38							16 58		17 08					17 28		17 38				
Purley	a	16 42		16 47					17 02	17 05	17 12					17 32	17 35	17 42				
Purley 4	d	16 45	16 48	16 50	16 55	16 58			17 09		17 15	17 18	17 25	17 28		17 39		17 45	17 48	17 55	17 58	
Sanderstead	d							17 09							17 39							18 09
Purley Oaks	d								17 12							17 42						
South Croydon 4	d			16 54					17 15							17 45						
East Croydon	a	16 51	16 54	16 57	17 00	17 03		17 15	17 18		17 21	17 24	17 30	17 33	17 45	17 48		17 51	17 54	18 00	18 03	18 15
East Croydon	d	16 51	16 54	16 57		17 03			17 18		17 21	17 25		17 33		17 48		17 51	17 55		18 03	
Norwood Junction 2	a			17 03		17 07	←							17 37							18 07	
New Cross Gate 4 ⊖	a		17 10	17 21		17 20	17 21					17 40		17 50					18 10		18 20	
London Bridge 4 ⊖	a	17 36		→			17 31		17 34		18 06					18 04		18 36				
London Blackfriars	a		17 16			17 26						17 46		17 56					18 16		18 26	
City Thameslink	a		17 18			17 28						17 48		17 58					18 18		18 28	
Farringdon	a		17 21			17 31						17 51		18 01					18 21		18 31	
St Pancras International	a		17 25			17 35						17 55		18 05					18 25		18 35	
East Croydon	d				17 00			17 15					17 30		17 45					18 00		18 15
Clapham Junction 10	a				17 13			17 25					17 40		17 55					18 10		18 25
London Victoria 15 ⊖	a				17 21			17 34					17 50		18 02					18 18		18 32

Table T181-R

Mondays to Fridays
16 December to 15 May

Tattenham Corner and Caterham, Purley - London and Croydon

		SN	SN	SN	TL 1	SN 1	TL 1	SN 1	SN	SN	SN	TL 1	SN 1	TL 1	SN 1	SN	SN	SN	TL 1	SN 1	TL 1	SN 1
Tattenham Corner	d		17 39							18 09							18 39					
Tadworth	d		17 43							18 13							18 43					
Kingswood	d		17 46							18 16							18 46					
Chipstead	d		17 52							18 22							18 52					
Woodmansterne	d		17 55							18 25							18 55					
Coulsdon Town	d		17 59							18 29							18 59					
Reedham	d		18 02							18 32							19 02					
Caterham	d	17 50		18 00					18 20		18 30					18 50		19 00				
Whyteleafe South	d	17 53		18 03					18 23		18 33					18 53		19 03				
Upper Warlingham	d							18 32							19 02							19 32
Whyteleafe	d	17 55		18 05					18 25		18 35					18 55		19 05				
Kenley	d	17 58		18 08					18 28		18 38					18 58		19 08				
Purley	a	18 02	18 05	18 12					18 32	18 35	18 42					19 02	19 05	19 12				
Purley 4	d	18 09				18 25	18 28		18 39				18 55	18 58		19 09				19 25	19 28	
Sanderstead	d				18 18			18 39				18 48			19 09				19 18			19 39
Purley Oaks	d	18 12							18 42							19 12						
South Croydon 4	d	18 15							18 45							19 15						
East Croydon	a	18 18			18 24	18 30	18 33	18 45	18 48			18 54	19 00	19 03	19 15	19 18			19 24	19 30	19 33	19 45
East Croydon	d	18 18			18 25		18 33		18 48			18 55		19 03		19 18			19 25		19 33	
Norwood Junction 2	a						18 37							19 07							19 37	
New Cross Gate 4 ⊖	a				18 40		18 50					19 10		19 20					19 40		19 50	
London Bridge 4 ⊖	a	18 34							19 04							19 34						
London Blackfriars	a				18 46		18 56					19 16		19 26					19 46		19 56	
City Thameslink	a				18 48		18 58					19 18		19 28					19 48		19 58	
Farringdon	a				18 51		19 01					19 21		19 31					19 51		20 01	
St Pancras International	a				18 55		19 05					19 25		19 35					19 55		20 05	
East Croydon	d					18 30		18 45					19 00		19 15					19 30		19 45
Clapham Junction 10	a					18 40		18 55					19 10		19 25					19 41		19 55
London Victoria 15 ⊖	a					18 48		19 03					19 18		19 32					19 49		20 02

		SN	SN	TL 1	SN	SN 1	TL 1	SN 1	SN	SN	TL 1	SN	SN 1	TL 1	SN 1	SN	SN	TL 1	SN	SN	SN 1	TL 1	SN 1
Tattenham Corner	d		19 09							19 39							20 09						
Tadworth	d		19 13							19 43							20 13						
Kingswood	d		19 16							19 46							20 16						
Chipstead	d		19 22							19 52							20 22						
Woodmansterne	d		19 25							19 55							20 25						
Coulsdon Town	d		19 29		19 42					19 59		20 12					20 29			20 42			
Reedham	d		19 32		19 45					20 02		20 15					20 32			20 45			
Caterham	d	19 20							19 50							20 20			20 30				
Whyteleafe South	d	19 23							19 53							20 23			20 33				
Upper Warlingham	d							20 02							20 32								21 02
Whyteleafe	d	19 25							19 55							20 25			20 35				
Kenley	d	19 28							19 58							20 28			20 38				
Purley	a	19 32	19 35		19 47				20 02	20 05		20 18				20 32	20 35		20 42	20 47			
Purley 4	d	19 39			19 48	19 55	19 58		20 09			20 19	20 25	20 28		20 39			20 45	20 48	20 55	20 58	
Sanderstead	d			19 45				20 09			20 18				20 39			20 45					21 09
Purley Oaks	d	19 42			19 51				20 12			20 22				20 42				20 51			
South Croydon 4	d	19 45			19 54				20 15			20 25				20 45				20 54			
East Croydon	a	19 48		19 52	19 57	20 00	20 03	20 15	20 18		20 24	20 27	20 30	20 33	20 45	20 48		20 52	20 54	20 57	21 00	21 03	21 15
East Croydon	d	19 48		19 52	19 57		20 03		20 18		20 24	20 28		20 33		20 48		20 52	20 54	20 57		21 03	
Norwood Junction 2	a				20 02		20 07					20 32		20 37						21 02		21 07	
New Cross Gate 4 ⊖	a				20 20		20 20					20 50		20 50						21 20		21 20	
London Bridge 4 ⊖	a	20 05		20 12	20 31				20 34		20 41	21 01				21 04		21 11	21 36	21 31			
London Blackfriars	a						20 26							20 56								21 26	
City Thameslink	a						20 28							20 58								21 28	
Farringdon	a						20 31							21 01								21 31	
St Pancras International	a						20 35							21 05								21 35	
East Croydon	d					20 00		20 15					20 30		20 45						21 00		21 15
Clapham Junction 10	a					20 10		20 25					20 41		20 58						21 12		21 25
London Victoria 15 ⊖	a					20 19		20 32					20 49		21 05						21 19		21 32

		SN	SN	SN	SN	SN 1	TL 1	SN 1	SN	SN	SN	SN	SN 1	TL 1	SN 1	SN	SN	SN	SN	SN 1	SN 1	SN	SN
Tattenham Corner	d		20 39							21 09							21 39						22 09
Tadworth	d		20 43							21 13							21 43						22 13
Kingswood	d		20 46							21 16							21 46						22 16
Chipstead	d		20 52							21 22							21 52						22 22
Woodmansterne	d		20 55							21 25							21 55						22 25
Coulsdon Town	d		20 59		21 12					21 29		21 42					21 59		22 12				22 29
Reedham	d		21 02		21 15					21 32		21 45					22 02		22 15				22 32
Caterham	d	20 50		21 00					21 20		21 30					21 50		22 00				22 20	
Whyteleafe South	d	20 53		21 03					21 23		21 33					21 53		22 03				22 23	
Upper Warlingham	d							21 32							22 02						22 32		
Whyteleafe	d	20 55		21 05					21 25		21 35					21 55		22 05				22 25	
Kenley	d	20 58		21 08					21 28		21 38					21 58		22 08				22 28	
Purley	a	21 02	21 05	21 12	21 17				21 32	21 35	21 42	21 47				22 02	22 05	22 12	22 17			22 32	22 35
Purley 4	d	21 09		21 15	21 18	21 25	21 28		21 39		21 45	21 48	21 55	21 58		22 09		22 15	22 18	22 25		22 39	
Sanderstead	d							21 39							22 09						22 39		
Purley Oaks	d	21 12			21 21				21 42			21 51				22 12			22 21			22 42	
South Croydon 4	d	21 15			21 24				21 45			21 54				22 15			22 24			22 45	
East Croydon	a	21 18		21 24	21 27	21 30	21 33	21 45	21 48		21 51	21 57	22 00	22 03	22 15	22 18		22 21	22 27	22 30	22 45	22 48	
East Croydon	d	21 18		21 24	21 27		21 33		21 48		21 52	21 57		22 03		22 18		22 22	22 27			22 48	
Norwood Junction 2	a				21 32		21 37					22 02		22 07					22 32				
New Cross Gate 4 ⊖	a				21 50		21 50					22 20		22 20					22 50				
London Bridge 4 ⊖	a	21 34		22 06	22 01				22 04		22 36	22 31				22 34		23 06	23 01			23 04	
London Blackfriars	a						21 56							22 26									
City Thameslink	a						21 58							22 28									
Farringdon	a						22 01							22 31									
St Pancras International	a						22 05							22 35									
East Croydon	d					21 30		21 45					22 00		22 15					22 30	22 45		
Clapham Junction 10	a					21 40		21 55					22 10		22 25					22 40	22 55		
London Victoria 15 ⊖	a					21 49		22 02					22 18		22 35					22 49	23 02		

Table T181-R

Tattenham Corner and Caterham, Purley - London and Croydon

Mondays to Fridays
16 December to 15 May

		SN	SN	SN 1	SN 1	SN	SN	SN 1	SN 1
Tattenham Corner	d						22 39		
Tadworth	d						22 43		
Kingswood	d						22 46		
Chipstead	d						22 52		
Woodmansterne	d						22 55		
Coulsdon Town	d		22 42				22 59		
Reedham	d		22 45				23 02		
Caterham	d	22 30				22 50			
Whyteleafe South	d	22 33				22 53			
Upper Warlingham	d				23 02				23 32
Whyteleafe	d	22 35				22 55			
Kenley	d	22 38				22 58			
Purley	a	22 42	22 47			23 02	23 05		
Purley 4	d	22 45	22 48	22 55		23 09		23 25	
Sanderstead	d				23 09				23 39
Purley Oaks	d		22 51			23 12			
South Croydon 4	d		22 54			23 15			
East Croydon	a	22 51	22 57	23 00	23 15	23 18		23 30	23 45
East Croydon	d	22 52	22 57			23 18			
Norwood Junction 2	a		23 02						
New Cross Gate 4	a		23 20						
London Bridge 4	a	23 36	23 31			23 34			
London Blackfriars	a								
City Thameslink	a								
Farringdon	a								
St Pancras International	a								
East Croydon	d			23 00	23 15			23 30	23 45
Clapham Junction 10	a			23 11	23 25			23 44	23 59
London Victoria 15	a			23 19	23 32			23 52	00 08

Saturdays
21 December to 16 May

		TL 1	TL 1	TL 1	SN 1	TL 1	SN 1	TL 1	SN 1	TL 1	SN 1	SN 1	TL 1	TL 1	SN	SN	SN 1	TL 1	SN 1	SN	SN	SN	SN
Tattenham Corner	d															06 09					06 39		
Tadworth	d															06 13					06 43		
Kingswood	d															06 16					06 46		
Chipstead	d															06 22					06 52		
Woodmansterne	d															06 25					06 55		
Coulsdon Town	d															06 29					06 59		07 12
Reedham	d															06 32					07 02		07 15
Caterham	d														06 20					06 50		07 00	
Whyteleafe South	d														06 23					06 53		07 03	
Upper Warlingham	d																		07 02				
Whyteleafe	d														06 25					06 55		07 05	
Kenley	d														06 28					06 58		07 08	
Purley	a														06 32	06 35				07 02	07 05	07 12	07 17
Purley 4	d	00 03	01 03	02 03	02 29	03 03	03 29	04 03	04 29	05 03	05 24	05 55	05 58	06 28	06 39		06 55	06 58		07 09		07 15	07 18
Sanderstead	d																		07 09				
Purley Oaks	d														06 42					07 12			07 21
South Croydon 4	d														06 45					07 15			07 24
East Croydon	a	00 09	01 09	02 09	02 36	03 09	03 36	04 09	04 36	05 09	05 30	06 00	06 03	06 33	06 48		07 00	07 03	07 15	07 18		07 21	07 27
East Croydon	d	00 09	01 10	02 10		03 10		04 10		05 10			06 03	06 33	06 48			07 03		07 18		07 23	07 27
Norwood Junction 2	a												06 07	06 37				07 07					07 32
New Cross Gate 4	a									05 25			06 20	06 50				07 20					07 50
London Bridge 4	a														07 05					07 35		08 07	08 01
London Blackfriars	a	00 36	01 36	02 36		03 36		04 36		05 31			06 26	06 56				07 26					
City Thameslink	a																						
Farringdon	a	00 41								05 36			06 31	07 01				07 31					
St Pancras International	a	00 45	01 43	02 43		03 43		04 43		05 40			06 35	07 05				07 35					
East Croydon	d				02 36		03 36		04 36		05 30	06 00					07 00		07 15				
Clapham Junction 10	a				02 50		03 50		04 50		05 50	06 10					07 10		07 25				
London Victoria 15	a				02 58		03 58		04 58		05 59	06 18					07 18		07 32				

Table T181-R

Saturdays
21 December to 16 May

Tattenham Corner and Caterham, Purley - London and Croydon

		SN 1	TL 1	SN 1	SN	SN	SN	SN	SN 1	TL 1	SN 1	SN	SN	SN	SN	SN 1	TL 1	SN 1	SN	SN	SN	SN
Tattenham Corner	d					07 09							07 39							08 09		
Tadworth	d					07 13							07 43							08 13		
Kingswood	d					07 16							07 46							08 16		
Chipstead	d					07 22							07 52							08 22		
Woodmansterne	d					07 25							07 55							08 25		
Coulsdon Town	d					07 29		07 42					07 59		08 12					08 29		08 42
Reedham	d					07 32		07 45					08 02		08 15					08 32		08 45
Caterham	d				07 20		07 30					07 50		08 00					08 20		08 30	
Whyteleafe South	d				07 23		07 33					07 53		08 03					08 23		08 33	
Upper Warlingham	d			07 32							08 02							08 32				
Whyteleafe	d				07 25		07 35					07 55		08 05					08 25		08 35	
Kenley	d				07 28		07 38					07 58		08 08					08 28		08 38	
Purley	a				07 32	07 35	07 42	07 47				08 02	08 05	08 12	08 17				08 32	08 35	08 42	08 47
Purley 4	d	07 25	07 28		07 39		07 45	07 48	07 55	07 58		08 09		08 15	08 18	08 25	08 28		08 39		08 45	08 48
Sanderstead	d			07 39							08 09							08 39				
Purley Oaks	d				07 42			07 51				08 12			08 21				08 42			08 51
South Croydon 4	d				07 45			07 54				08 15			08 24				08 45			08 54
East Croydon	a	07 30	07 33	07 45	07 48		07 51	07 57	08 00	08 03	08 15	08 18		08 21	08 27	08 30	08 33	08 45	08 48		08 51	08 57
East Croydon	d		07 33		07 48		07 53	07 57		08 03		08 18		08 23	08 27		08 33		08 48		08 53	08 57
Norwood Junction 2	a		07 37					08 02		08 07					08 32		08 37					09 02
New Cross Gate 4	a		07 50					08 20		08 20					08 50		08 50					09 20
London Bridge 4	a				08 05		08 37	08 31				08 35		09 07	09 01				09 05		09 37	09 31
London Blackfriars	a		07 56							08 26							08 56					
City Thameslink	a																					
Farringdon	a		08 01							08 31							09 01					
St Pancras International	a		08 05							08 35							09 05					
East Croydon	d	07 30		07 45					08 00		08 15					08 30		08 45				
Clapham Junction 10	a	07 40		07 55					08 10		08 25					08 40		08 55				
London Victoria 15	a	07 48		08 02					08 18		08 32					08 48		09 02				

		SN 1	TL 1	SN 1	SN	SN	SN	SN	SN 1	TL 1	SN 1	SN	SN	SN	SN	SN 1	TL 1	SN 1	SN	SN	SN	SN	SN 1
Tattenham Corner	d					08 39							09 09							09 39			
Tadworth	d					08 43							09 13							09 43			
Kingswood	d					08 46							09 16							09 46			
Chipstead	d					08 52							09 22							09 52			
Woodmansterne	d					08 55							09 25							09 55			
Coulsdon Town	d					08 59		09 12					09 29		09 42					09 59		10 12	
Reedham	d					09 02		09 15					09 32		09 45					10 02		10 15	
Caterham	d				08 50		09 00					09 20		09 30					09 50		10 00		
Whyteleafe South	d				08 53		09 03					09 23		09 33					09 53		10 03		
Upper Warlingham	d			09 02							09 32							10 02					
Whyteleafe	d				08 55		09 05					09 25		09 35					09 55		10 05		
Kenley	d				08 58		09 08					09 28		09 38					09 58		10 08		
Purley	a				09 02	09 05	09 12	09 17				09 32	09 35	09 42	09 47				10 02	10 05	10 12	10 17	
Purley 4	d	08 55	08 58		09 09		09 15	09 18	09 25	09 28		09 39		09 45	09 48	09 55	09 58		10 09		10 15	10 18	10 25
Sanderstead	d			09 09							09 39							10 09					
Purley Oaks	d				09 12			09 21				09 42			09 51				10 12			10 21	
South Croydon 4	d				09 15			09 24				09 45			09 54				10 15			10 24	
East Croydon	a	09 00	09 03	09 15	09 18		09 21	09 27	09 30	09 33	09 45	09 48		09 51	09 57	10 00	10 03	10 15	10 18		10 21	10 27	10 30
East Croydon	d		09 03		09 18		09 23	09 27		09 33		09 48		09 53	09 57		10 03		10 18		10 23	10 27	
Norwood Junction 2	a		09 07					09 32		09 37					10 02		10 07					10 32	
New Cross Gate 4	a		09 20					09 50		09 50					10 20		10 20					10 50	
London Bridge 4	a				09 35		10 07	10 01				10 05		10 37	10 31				10 35		11 07	11 01	
London Blackfriars	a		09 26							09 56							10 26						
City Thameslink	a		09 28							09 58							10 28						
Farringdon	a		09 31							10 01							10 31						
St Pancras International	a		09 35							10 05							10 35						
East Croydon	d	09 00		09 15					09 30		09 45					10 00		10 15					10 30
Clapham Junction 10	a	09 10		09 25					09 40		09 55					10 10		10 25					10 40
London Victoria 15	a	09 18		09 32					09 48		10 02					10 18		10 32					10 48

		TL 1	SN 1	SN	SN	SN	SN	SN 1	TL 1	SN 1	SN	SN	SN	SN	SN 1	TL 1	SN 1	SN	SN	SN	SN	SN 1	TL 1
Tattenham Corner	d				10 09							10 39							11 09				
Tadworth	d				10 13							10 43							11 13				
Kingswood	d				10 16							10 46							11 16				
Chipstead	d				10 22							10 52							11 22				
Woodmansterne	d				10 25							10 55							11 25				
Coulsdon Town	d				10 29		10 42					10 59		11 12					11 29		11 42		
Reedham	d				10 32		10 45					11 02		11 15					11 32		11 45		
Caterham	d			10 20		10 30					10 50		11 00					11 20		11 30			
Whyteleafe South	d			10 23		10 33					10 53		11 03					11 23		11 33			
Upper Warlingham	d		10 32							11 02							11 32						
Whyteleafe	d			10 25		10 35					10 55		11 05					11 25		11 35			
Kenley	d			10 28		10 38					10 58		11 08					11 28		11 38			
Purley	a			10 32	10 35	10 42	10 47				11 02	11 05	11 12	11 17				11 32	11 35	11 42	11 47		
Purley 4	d	10 28		10 39		10 45	10 48	10 55	10 58		11 09		11 15	11 18	11 25	11 28		11 39		11 45	11 48	11 55	11 58
Sanderstead	d		10 39							11 09							11 39						
Purley Oaks	d			10 42			10 51				11 12			11 21				11 42			11 51		
South Croydon 4	d			10 45			10 54				11 15			11 24				11 45			11 54		
East Croydon	a	10 33	10 45	10 48		10 51	10 57	11 00	11 03	11 15	11 18		11 21	11 27	11 30	11 33	11 45	11 48		11 51	11 57	12 00	12 03
East Croydon	d	10 33		10 48		10 53	10 57		11 03		11 18		11 23	11 27		11 33		11 48		11 53	11 57		12 03
Norwood Junction 2	a	10 37					11 02		11 07					11 32		11 37					12 02		12 07
New Cross Gate 4	a	10 50					11 20		11 20					11 50		11 50					12 20		12 20
London Bridge 4	a			11 05		11 37	11 31				11 35		12 07	12 01				12 05		12 37	12 31		
London Blackfriars	a	10 56							11 26							11 56							12 26
City Thameslink	a	10 58							11 28							11 58							12 28
Farringdon	a	11 01							11 31							12 01							12 31
St Pancras International	a	11 05							11 35							12 05							12 35
East Croydon	d		10 45					11 00		11 15					11 30		11 45					12 00	
Clapham Junction 10	a		10 55					11 10		11 25					11 40		11 55					12 10	
London Victoria 15	a		11 02					11 18		11 32					11 48		12 02					12 18	

Table T181-R

Tattenham Corner and Caterham, Purley - London and Croydon

			SN 1	SN	SN	SN	SN	SN 1	TL 1	SN 1	SN	SN		SN	SN	SN 1	TL 1	SN 1	SN	SN	SN	SN		SN 1	TL 1
Tattenham Corner	d				11 39							12 09								12 39					
Tadworth	d				11 43							12 13								12 43					
Kingswood	d				11 46							12 16								12 46					
Chipstead	d				11 52							12 22								12 52					
Woodmansterne	d				11 55							12 25								12 55					
Coulsdon Town	d				11 59		12 12					12 29			12 42					12 59		13 12			
Reedham	d				12 02		12 15					12 32			12 45					13 02		13 15			
Caterham	d			11 50		12 00					12 20			12 30					12 50		13 00				
Whyteleafe South	d			11 53		12 03					12 23			12 33					12 53		13 03				
Upper Warlingham	d		12 02							12 32								13 02							
Whyteleafe	d			11 55		12 05					12 25			12 35					12 55		13 05				
Kenley	d			11 58		12 08					12 28			12 38					12 58		13 08				
Purley	a			12 02	12 05	12 12	12 17				12 32	12 35		12 42	12 47				13 02	13 05	13 12	13 17			
Purley 4	d				12 09	12 15	12 18	12 25	12 28			12 39		12 45	12 48	12 55	12 58			13 09	13 15	13 18		13 25	13 28
Sanderstead	d		12 09							12 39								13 09							
Purley Oaks	d				12 12		12 21					12 42			12 51					13 12		13 21			
South Croydon 4	d				12 15		12 24					12 45			12 54					13 15		13 24			
East Croydon	a		12 15		12 18	12 21	12 27	12 30	12 33	12 45		12 48		12 51	12 57	13 00	13 03	13 15		13 18	13 21	13 27		13 30	13 33
East Croydon	d				12 18	12 23	12 27		12 33			12 48		12 53	12 57		13 03			13 18	13 23	13 27			13 33
Norwood Junction 2	a						12 32		12 37						13 02		13 07					13 32			13 37
New Cross Gate 4 ⊖	a						12 50		12 50						13 20		13 20					13 50			13 50
London Bridge 4 ⊖	a				12 35	13 07	13 01					13 05		13 37	13 31					13 35	14 07	14 01			
London Blackfriars	a								12 56								13 26								13 56
City Thameslink	a								12 58								13 28								13 58
Farringdon	a								13 01								13 31								14 01
St Pancras International	a								13 05								13 35								14 05
East Croydon	d		12 15					12 30		12 45						13 00		13 15						13 30	
Clapham Junction 10	a		12 25					12 40		12 55						13 10		13 25						13 40	
London Victoria 15 ⊖	a		12 32					12 48		13 02						13 18		13 32						13 48	

		SN 1	SN	SN	SN	SN	SN 1	TL 1		SN 1	SN	SN	SN	SN	SN 1	TL 1	SN 1	SN	SN		SN	SN	SN 1	TL 1	SN 1
Tattenham Corner	d			13 09								13 39							14 09						
Tadworth	d			13 13								13 43							14 13						
Kingswood	d			13 16								13 46							14 16						
Chipstead	d			13 22								13 52							14 22						
Woodmansterne	d			13 25								13 55							14 25						
Coulsdon Town	d			13 29		13 42						13 59		14 12					14 29			14 42			
Reedham	d			13 32		13 45						14 02		14 15					14 32			14 45			
Caterham	d		13 20		13 30						13 50		14 00					14 20			14 30				
Whyteleafe South	d		13 23		13 33						13 53		14 03					14 23			14 33				
Upper Warlingham	d	13 32								14 02							14 32								15 02
Whyteleafe	d		13 25		13 35						13 55		14 05					14 25			14 35				
Kenley	d		13 28		13 38						13 58		14 08					14 28			14 38				
Purley	a		13 32	13 35	13 42	13 47					14 02	14 05	14 12	14 17				14 32	14 35		14 42	14 47			
Purley 4	d			13 39	13 45	13 48	13 55	13 58				14 09	14 15	14 18	14 25	14 28			14 39		14 45	14 48	14 55	14 58	
Sanderstead	d	13 39								14 09							14 39								15 09
Purley Oaks	d			13 42		13 51						14 12		14 21					14 42			14 51			
South Croydon 4	d			13 45		13 54						14 15		14 24					14 45			14 54			
East Croydon	a	13 45		13 48	13 51	13 57	14 00	14 03		14 15		14 18	14 21	14 27	14 30	14 33	14 45		14 48		14 51	14 57	15 00	15 03	15 15
East Croydon	d			13 48	13 53	13 57		14 03				14 18	14 23	14 27		14 33			14 48		14 53	14 57		15 03	
Norwood Junction 2	a					14 02		14 07						14 32		14 37						15 02		15 07	
New Cross Gate 4 ⊖	a					14 20		14 20						14 50		14 50						15 20		15 20	
London Bridge 4 ⊖	a			14 05	14 37	14 31						14 35	15 07	15 01					15 05		15 37	15 31			
London Blackfriars	a							14 26								14 56								15 26	
City Thameslink	a							14 28								14 58								15 28	
Farringdon	a							14 31								15 01								15 31	
St Pancras International	a							14 35								15 05								15 35	
East Croydon	d	13 45					14 00			14 15					14 30		14 45						15 00		15 15
Clapham Junction 10	a	13 55					14 10			14 25					14 40		14 55						15 10		15 25
London Victoria 15 ⊖	a	14 02					14 18			14 32					14 48		15 02						15 18		15 32

		SN	SN	SN	SN		SN 1	TL 1	SN 1	SN	SN	SN	SN	SN 1	TL 1		SN 1	SN	SN	SN	SN	SN 1	TL 1	SN 1	
Tattenham Corner	d		14 39								15 09								15 39						
Tadworth	d		14 43								15 13								15 43						
Kingswood	d		14 46								15 16								15 46						
Chipstead	d		14 52								15 22								15 52						
Woodmansterne	d		14 55								15 25								15 55						
Coulsdon Town	d		14 59		15 12						15 29		15 42						15 59		16 12				
Reedham	d		15 02		15 15						15 32		15 45						16 02		16 15				
Caterham	d	14 50		15 00						15 20		15 30						15 50		16 00					
Whyteleafe South	d	14 53		15 03						15 23		15 33						15 53		16 03					
Upper Warlingham	d								15 32								16 02							16 32	
Whyteleafe	d	14 55		15 05						15 25		15 35						15 55		16 05					
Kenley	d	14 58		15 08						15 28		15 38						15 58		16 08					
Purley	a	15 02	15 05	15 12	15 17					15 32	15 35	15 42	15 47					16 02	16 05	16 12	16 17				
Purley 4	d		15 09	15 15	15 18		15 25	15 28			15 39	15 45	15 48	15 55	15 58				16 09	16 15	16 18	16 25	16 28		
Sanderstead	d								15 39								16 09							16 39	
Purley Oaks	d		15 12		15 21						15 42		15 51						16 12		16 21				
South Croydon 4	d		15 15		15 24						15 45		15 54						16 15		16 24				
East Croydon	a		15 18	15 21	15 27		15 30	15 33	15 45		15 48	15 51	15 57	16 00	16 03		16 15		16 18	16 21	16 27	16 30	16 33	16 45	
East Croydon	d		15 18	15 23	15 27			15 33			15 48	15 53	15 57		16 03				16 18	16 23	16 27		16 33		
Norwood Junction 2	a				15 32			15 37					16 02		16 07						16 32		16 37		
New Cross Gate 4 ⊖	a				15 50			15 50					16 20		16 20						16 50		16 50		
London Bridge 4 ⊖	a		15 35	16 07	16 01						16 05	16 37	16 31						16 35	17 07	17 01				
London Blackfriars	a							15 56							16 26								16 56		
City Thameslink	a							15 58							16 28								16 58		
Farringdon	a							16 01							16 31								17 01		
St Pancras International	a							16 05							16 35								17 05		
East Croydon	d						15 30		15 45					16 00			16 15					16 30		16 45	
Clapham Junction 10	a						15 40		15 55					16 10			16 25					16 40		16 55	
London Victoria 15 ⊖	a						15 48		16 02					16 18			16 32					16 48		17 02	

Table T181-R

Tattenham Corner and Caterham, Purley - London and Croydon

		SN	SN		SN	SN	SN 1	TL 1	SN 1	SN	SN	SN	SN		SN 1	TL 1	SN 1	SN	SN	SN	SN	SN 1	TL 1		SN 1
Tattenham Corner	d		16 09								16 39								17 09						
Tadworth	d		16 13								16 43								17 13						
Kingswood	d		16 16								16 46								17 16						
Chipstead	d		16 22								16 52								17 22						
Woodmansterne	d		16 25								16 55								17 25						
Coulsdon Town	d		16 29			16 42					16 59		17 12						17 29		17 42				
Reedham	d		16 32			16 45					17 02		17 15						17 32		17 45				
Caterham	d	16 20			16 30					16 50		17 00						17 20		17 30					
Whyteleafe South	d	16 23			16 33					16 53		17 03						17 23		17 33					
Upper Warlingham	d								17 02								17 32								18 02
Whyteleafe	d	16 25			16 35					16 55		17 05						17 25		17 35					
Kenley	d	16 28			16 38					16 58		17 08						17 28		17 38					
Purley	a	16 32	16 35		16 42	16 47				17 02	17 05	17 12	17 17					17 32	17 35	17 42	17 47				
Purley 4	d		16 39		16 45	16 48	16 55	16 58			17 09	17 15	17 18		17 25	17 28			17 39	17 45	17 48	17 55	17 58		
Sanderstead	d								17 09								17 39								18 09
Purley Oaks	d		16 42			16 51					17 12		17 21						17 42		17 51				
South Croydon 4	d		16 45			16 54					17 15		17 24						17 45		17 54				
East Croydon	a		16 48		16 51	16 57	17 00	17 03	17 15		17 18	17 21	17 27		17 30	17 33	17 45		17 48	17 51	17 57	18 00	18 03		18 15
East Croydon	d		16 48		16 53	16 57		17 03			17 18	17 23	17 27			17 33			17 48	17 53	17 57		18 03		
Norwood Junction 2	a					17 02		17 07					17 32			17 37					18 02		18 07		
New Cross Gate 4 ⊖	a					17 20		17 20					17 50			17 50					18 20		18 20		
London Bridge 4 ⊖	a		17 05		17 37	17 31					17 35	18 07	18 01						18 05	18 37	18 31				
London Blackfriars	a							17 26								17 56							18 26		
City Thameslink	a							17 28								17 58							18 28		
Farringdon	a							17 31								18 01							18 31		
St Pancras International	a							17 35								18 05							18 35		
East Croydon	d						17 00		17 15						17 30		17 45					18 00			18 15
Clapham Junction 10	a						17 11		17 25						17 40		17 55					18 10			18 25
London Victoria 15 ⊖	a						17 19		17 32						17 48		18 02					18 18			18 32

		SN	SN	SN	SN	SN 1	TL 1	SN 1	SN	SN		SN	SN	SN 1	TL 1	SN 1	SN	SN	SN	SN		SN 1	TL 1	SN 1	
Tattenham Corner	d		17 39							18 09								18 39							
Tadworth	d		17 43							18 13								18 43							
Kingswood	d		17 46							18 16								18 46							
Chipstead	d		17 52							18 22								18 52							
Woodmansterne	d		17 55							18 25								18 55							
Coulsdon Town	d		17 59		18 12					18 29			18 42					18 59		19 12					
Reedham	d		18 02		18 15					18 32			18 45					19 02		19 15					
Caterham	d	17 50		18 00					18 20			18 30					18 50		19 00						
Whyteleafe South	d	17 53		18 03					18 23			18 33					18 53		19 03						
Upper Warlingham	d							18 32								19 02								19 32	
Whyteleafe	d	17 55		18 05					18 25			18 35					18 55		19 05						
Kenley	d	17 58		18 08					18 28			18 38					18 58		19 08						
Purley	a	18 02	18 05	18 12	18 17				18 32	18 35		18 42	18 47				19 02	19 05	19 12	19 17					
Purley 4	d		18 09	18 15	18 18	18 25	18 28			18 39		18 45	18 48	18 55	18 58			19 09	19 15	19 18		19 25	19 28		
Sanderstead	d							18 39								19 09								19 39	
Purley Oaks	d		18 12		18 21					18 42			18 51					19 12		19 21					
South Croydon 4	d		18 15		18 24					18 45			18 54					19 15		19 24					
East Croydon	a		18 18	18 21	18 27	18 30	18 33	18 45		18 48		18 51	18 57	19 00	19 03	19 15		19 18	19 21	19 27		19 30	19 33	19 45	
East Croydon	d		18 18	18 23	18 27		18 33			18 48		18 53	18 57		19 03			19 18	19 23	19 27			19 33		
Norwood Junction 2	a				18 32		18 37						19 02		19 07					19 32			19 37		
New Cross Gate 4 ⊖	a				18 50		18 50						19 20		19 20					19 50			19 50		
London Bridge 4 ⊖	a		18 35	19 07	19 01					19 05		19 37	19 31					19 35	20 07	20 01					
London Blackfriars	a						18 56								19 26								19 56		
City Thameslink	a						18 58								19 28								19 58		
Farringdon	a						19 01								19 31								20 01		
St Pancras International	a						19 05								19 35								20 05		
East Croydon	d					18 30		18 45						19 00		19 15						19 30		19 45	
Clapham Junction 10	a					18 40		18 55						19 10		19 25						19 40		19 55	
London Victoria 15 ⊖	a					18 48		19 02						19 18		19 32						19 48		20 02	

		SN	SN	SN	SN	SN 1	TL 1		SN 1	SN	SN	SN	SN	SN 1	TL 1	SN 1	SN	SN		SN	SN	SN 1	TL 1	SN 1	
Tattenham Corner	d		19 09								19 39							20 09							
Tadworth	d		19 13								19 43							20 13							
Kingswood	d		19 16								19 46							20 16							
Chipstead	d		19 22								19 52							20 22							
Woodmansterne	d		19 25								19 55							20 25							
Coulsdon Town	d		19 29		19 42						19 59		20 12					20 29			20 42				
Reedham	d		19 32		19 45						20 02		20 15					20 32			20 45				
Caterham	d	19 20		19 30						19 50		20 00					20 20			20 30					
Whyteleafe South	d	19 23		19 33						19 53		20 03					20 23			20 33					
Upper Warlingham	d								20 02							20 32								21 02	
Whyteleafe	d	19 25		19 35						19 55		20 05					20 25			20 35					
Kenley	d	19 28		19 38						19 58		20 08					20 28			20 38					
Purley	a	19 32	19 35	19 42	19 47					20 02	20 05	20 12	20 17				20 32	20 35		20 42	20 47				
Purley 4	d		19 39	19 45	19 48	19 55	19 58				20 09	20 15	20 18	20 25	20 28			20 39		20 45	20 48	20 55	20 58		
Sanderstead	d								20 09							20 39								21 09	
Purley Oaks	d		19 42		19 51						20 12		20 21					20 42			20 51				
South Croydon 4	d		19 45		19 54						20 15		20 24					20 45			20 54				
East Croydon	a		19 48	19 52	19 57	20 00	20 03		20 15		20 18	20 21	20 27	20 30	20 33	20 45		20 48		20 51	20 57	21 00	21 03	21 15	
East Croydon	d		19 48	19 54	19 57		20 03				20 18	20 23	20 27		20 33			20 48		20 53	20 57		21 03		
Norwood Junction 2	a				20 02		20 07						20 32		20 37						21 02		21 07		
New Cross Gate 4 ⊖	a				20 20		20 20						20 50		20 50						21 20		21 20		
London Bridge 4 ⊖	a		20 05	20 37	20 31						20 35	21 07	21 01					21 05		21 37	21 31				
London Blackfriars	a						20 26								20 56								21 26		
City Thameslink	a						20 28								20 58										
Farringdon	a						20 31								21 01								21 31		
St Pancras International	a						20 35								21 05								21 35		
East Croydon	d					20 00			20 15					20 30		20 45						21 00		21 15	
Clapham Junction 10	a					20 10			20 25					20 40		20 55						21 10		21 25	
London Victoria 15 ⊖	a					20 18			20 32					20 48		21 02						21 18		21 32	

Table T181-R

Saturdays
21 December to 16 May

Tattenham Corner and Caterham, Purley - London and Croydon

		SN	SN	SN	SN	SN [1]	TL [1]	SN [1]	SN	SN	SN	SN	SN [1]	TL [1]	SN [1]	SN	SN	SN	SN	SN [1]	SN [1]	SN	SN
Tattenham Corner	d		20 39							21 09							21 39						22 09
Tadworth	d		20 43							21 13							21 43						22 13
Kingswood	d		20 46							21 16							21 46						22 16
Chipstead	d		20 52							21 22							21 52						22 22
Woodmansterne	d		20 55							21 25							21 55						22 25
Coulsdon Town	d		20 59		21 12					21 29		21 42					21 59		22 12				22 29
Reedham	d		21 02		21 15					21 32		21 45					22 02		22 15				22 32
Caterham	d	20 50		21 00					21 20		21 30					21 50		22 00				22 20	
Whyteleafe South	d	20 53		21 03					21 23		21 33					21 53		22 03				22 23	
Upper Warlingham	d							21 32							22 02						22 32		
Whyteleafe	d	20 55		21 05					21 25		21 35					21 55		22 05				22 25	
Kenley	d	20 58		21 08					21 28		21 38					21 58		22 08				22 28	
Purley	a	21 02	21 05	21 12	21 17				21 32	21 35	21 42	21 47				22 02	22 05	22 12	22 17			22 32	22 35
Purley 4	d	21 09		21 15	21 18	21 25	21 28		21 39		21 45	21 48	21 55	21 58		22 09		22 15	22 18	22 25		22 39	
Sanderstead	d							21 39							22 09						22 39		
Purley Oaks	d	21 12			21 21				21 42			21 51				22 12			22 21			22 42	
South Croydon 4	d	21 15			21 24				21 45			21 54				22 15			22 24			22 45	
East Croydon	a	21 18		21 21	21 27	21 30	21 33	21 45	21 48		21 51	21 57	22 00	22 03	22 15	22 18		22 21	22 27	22 30	22 45	22 48	
East Croydon	d	21 18		21 23	21 27		21 33		21 48		21 53	21 57		22 03		22 18		22 23	22 27			22 48	
Norwood Junction 2	a				21 32		21 37					22 02		22 07					22 32				
New Cross Gate 4 ⊖	a				21 50		21 50					22 20		22 20					22 50				
London Bridge 4 ⊖	a	21 35		22 07	22 01				22 05		22 37	22 31				22 35		23 07	23 01			23 05	
London Blackfriars	a						21 56							22 26									
City Thameslink	a																						
Farringdon	a						22 01							22 31									
St Pancras International	a						22 05							22 35									
East Croydon	d					21 30		21 45					22 00		22 15					22 30	22 45		
Clapham Junction 10	a					21 40		21 55					22 10		22 25					22 40	22 55		
London Victoria 15 ⊖	a					21 48		22 02					22 18		22 32					22 48	23 02		

		SN	SN	SN [1]	SN [1]	SN	SN	SN	SN [1]	SN [1]	SN	SN
Tattenham Corner	d						22 39					23 09
Tadworth	d						22 43					23 13
Kingswood	d						22 46					23 16
Chipstead	d						22 52					23 22
Woodmansterne	d						22 55					23 25
Coulsdon Town	d		22 42				22 59					23 29
Reedham	d		22 45				23 02					23 32
Caterham	d	22 30				22 50		23 00			23 20	
Whyteleafe South	d	22 33				22 53		23 03			23 23	
Upper Warlingham	d				23 02					23 32		
Whyteleafe	d	22 35				22 55		23 05			23 25	
Kenley	d	22 38				22 58		23 08			23 28	
Purley	a	22 42	22 47			23 02	23 05	23 12			23 32	23 35
Purley 4	d	22 45	22 48	22 55		23 09		23 15	23 25		23 39	
Sanderstead	d				23 09					23 39		
Purley Oaks	d		22 51			23 12					23 42	
South Croydon 4	d		22 54			23 15					23 45	
East Croydon	a	22 51	22 57	23 00	23 15	23 18		23 21	23 30	23 45	23 48	
East Croydon	d	22 53	22 57			23 18		23 23			23 48	
Norwood Junction 2	a		23 02								23 52	
New Cross Gate 4 ⊖	a		23 20									
London Bridge 4 ⊖	a	23 37	23 31			23 35		00 06			00 06	
London Blackfriars	a											
City Thameslink	a											
Farringdon	a											
St Pancras International	a											
East Croydon	d			23 00	23 15				23 30	23 45		
Clapham Junction 10	a			23 10	23 25				23 41	00 04		
London Victoria 15 ⊖	a			23 18	23 32				23 50	00 12		

Table T181-R

Sundays
15 December to 10 May

Tattenham Corner and Caterham, Purley - London and Croydon

		TL [1] A	TL [1]	SN [1]	SN [1]	SN [1]	SN [1]	TL [1]	SN [1]	SN	TL [1]	SN	SN [1]	SN	SN	TL [1]	SN [1]	SN	SN	TL [1]	SN [1]	SN	SN
Tattenham Corner	d														07 50				08 20				08 50
Tadworth	d														07 54				08 24				08 54
Kingswood	d														07 57				08 27				08 57
Chipstead	d														08 03				08 33				09 03
Woodmansterne	d														08 06				08 36				09 06
Coulsdon Town	d														08 10				08 40				09 10
Reedham	d														08 13				08 43				09 13
Caterham	d									07 05		07 35		08 02				08 32				09 02	
Whyteleafe South	d									07 08		07 38		08 05				08 35				09 05	
Upper Warlingham	d																08 38				09 08		
Whyteleafe	d									07 10		07 40		08 07				08 37				09 07	
Kenley	d									07 13		07 43		08 10				08 40				09 10	
Purley	a									07 17		07 47		08 13	08 16			08 43	08 46			09 13	09 16
Purley 4	d	00 03	01 03	02 29	03 30	04 29	05 23	06 27	07 16	07 20	07 25	07 50	08 16	08 20		08 25		08 50		09 12		09 20	
Sanderstead	d																08 45				09 15		
Purley Oaks	d									07 22		07 52		08 22				08 52				09 23	
South Croydon 4	d									07 25		07 55		08 25				08 55				09 26	
East Croydon	a	00 09	01 09	02 35	03 36	04 35	05 29	06 33	07 22	07 28	07 31	07 58	08 22	08 28		08 31	08 51	08 58		09 17	09 21	09 29	
East Croydon	d	00 10	01 10					06 34		07 29	07 32	07 59		08 29		08 32		08 59		09 18		09 31	
Norwood Junction 2	a							06 38		07 33	07 36	08 05		08 33		08 36		09 03				09 35	
New Cross Gate 4 ⊖	a									07 55		08 25		08 55				09 25		09 32		09 55	
London Bridge 4 ⊖	a							06 52		08 05	07 50	08 36		09 02		08 50		09 32				10 02	
London Blackfriars	a	00 36	01 36																	09 38			
City Thameslink	a																						
Farringdon	a	00 41																		09 43			
St Pancras International	a	00 45	01 43																	09 47			
East Croydon	d			02 36	03 37	04 36	05 30		07 23				08 23				08 51				09 21		
Clapham Junction 10	a			02 49	03 50	04 49	05 51		07 37				08 38				09 02				09 32		
London Victoria 15 ⊖	a			02 58	03 58	04 58	05 59		07 46				08 46				09 09				09 39		

		SN	TL [1]	SN [1]	SN	SN	TL [1]	SN [1]	SN	SN	SN	TL [1]	SN [1]	SN	SN	TL [1]	SN [1]	SN	SN	SN	TL [1]	SN [1]
Tattenham Corner	d					09 20				09 50					10 20				10 50			
Tadworth	d					09 24				09 54					10 24				10 54			
Kingswood	d					09 27				09 57					10 27				10 57			
Chipstead	d					09 33				10 03					10 33				11 03			
Woodmansterne	d					09 36				10 06					10 36				11 06			
Coulsdon Town	d					09 40				10 10					10 40				11 10			
Reedham	d					09 43				10 13					10 43				11 13			
Caterham	d				09 32				10 02					10 32				11 02				
Whyteleafe South	d				09 35				10 05					10 35				11 05				
Upper Warlingham	d			09 38				10 08					10 38				11 08					11 38
Whyteleafe	d				09 37				10 07					10 37				11 07				
Kenley	d				09 40				10 10					10 40				11 10				
Purley	a				09 43	09 46			10 13	10 16				10 43	10 46			11 13	11 16			
Purley 4	d	09 25	09 42		09 50		10 12		10 20		10 25	10 42		10 50		11 12		11 20		11 25	11 42	
Sanderstead	d			09 45				10 15					10 45				11 15					11 45
Purley Oaks	d				09 53				10 23					10 53				11 23				
South Croydon 4	d				09 56				10 26					10 56				11 26				
East Croydon	a	09 29	09 47	09 51	09 59		10 17	10 21	10 29		10 29	10 47	10 51	10 59		11 17	11 21	11 29		11 29	11 47	11 51
East Croydon	d		09 48		10 01		10 18		10 31			10 48		11 01		11 18		11 31			11 48	
Norwood Junction 2	a				10 05				10 35					11 05				11 35				
New Cross Gate 4 ⊖	a		10 02		10 25		10 32		10 55			11 02		11 25		11 32		11 55			12 02	
London Bridge 4 ⊖	a				10 32				11 02					11 32				12 02				
London Blackfriars	a		10 08				10 38					11 08				11 38					12 08	
City Thameslink	a																					
Farringdon	a		10 13				10 43					11 13				11 43					12 13	
St Pancras International	a		10 17				10 47					11 17				11 47					12 17	
East Croydon	d	09 30		09 51				10 21			10 30		10 51				11 21			11 30		11 51
Clapham Junction 10	a	09 39		10 02				10 32			10 39		11 02				11 32			11 39		12 02
London Victoria 15 ⊖	a	09 47		10 09				10 39			10 47		11 09				11 39			11 47		12 09

		SN	SN	TL [1]	SN [1]	SN	SN	SN	TL [1]	SN [1]	SN	SN	TL [1]		SN [1]	SN	SN	SN	TL [1]	SN [1]	SN	SN	TL [1]
Tattenham Corner	d		11 20				11 50					12 20					19 50					20 20	
Tadworth	d		11 24				11 54					12 24					19 54					20 24	
Kingswood	d		11 27				11 57					12 27					19 57					20 27	
Chipstead	d		11 33				12 03					12 33					20 03					20 33	
Woodmansterne	d		11 36				12 06					12 36					20 06					20 36	
Coulsdon Town	d		11 40				12 10					12 40					20 10					20 40	
Reedham	d		11 43				12 13					12 43					20 13					20 43	
Caterham	d	11 32				12 02					12 32					20 02					20 32		
Whyteleafe South	d	11 35				12 05					12 35					20 05					20 35		
Upper Warlingham	d				12 08					12 38					20 08					20 38			
Whyteleafe	d	11 37				12 07					12 37			and at the same minutes past each hour until		20 07					20 37		
Kenley	d	11 40				12 10					12 40					20 10					20 40		
Purley	a	11 43	11 46			12 13	12 16				12 43	12 46				20 13	20 16				20 43	20 46	
Purley 4	d	11 50		12 12		12 20		12 25	12 42		12 50		13 12			20 20		20 25	20 42		20 50		21 12
Sanderstead	d				12 15					12 45					20 15					20 45			
Purley Oaks	d	11 53				12 23					12 53					20 23					20 53		
South Croydon 4	d	11 56				12 26					12 56					20 26					20 56		
East Croydon	a	11 59		12 17	12 21	12 29		12 29	12 47	12 51	12 59		13 17		20 21	20 29		20 29	20 47	20 51	20 59		21 17
East Croydon	d	12 01		12 18		12 31			12 48		13 01		13 18			20 31			20 48		21 01		21 18
Norwood Junction 2	a	12 05				12 35					13 05					20 35					21 05		
New Cross Gate 4 ⊖	a	12 25		12 32		12 53			13 02		13 23		13 32			20 53			21 02		21 23		21 32
London Bridge 4 ⊖	a	12 32				13 02					13 32					21 02					21 32		
London Blackfriars	a			12 38					13 08				13 38						21 08				21 38
City Thameslink	a																						
Farringdon	a			12 45					13 13				13 43						21 13				21 43
St Pancras International	a			12 49					13 17				13 47						21 17				21 47
East Croydon	d				12 21			12 30		12 51					20 21			20 30		20 51			
Clapham Junction 10	a				12 32			12 39		13 02					20 32			20 39		21 02			
London Victoria 15 ⊖	a				12 39			12 47		13 09					20 39			20 47		21 09			

A not 15 December

Table T181-R

Sundays

15 December to 10 May

Tattenham Corner and Caterham, Purley - London and Croydon

		SN 1	SN	SN	SN	TL 1	SN 1	SN	SN	SN 1	SN	SN	SN	TL 1	SN 1	SN	SN	TL 1	SN 1	SN	SN	SN 1	SN 1
Tattenham Corner	d			20 50					21 20			21 50					22 20				22 50		
Tadworth	d			20 54					21 24			21 54					22 24				22 54		
Kingswood	d			20 57					21 27			21 57					22 27				22 57		
Chipstead	d			21 03					21 33			22 03					22 33				23 03		
Woodmansterne	d			21 06					21 36			22 06					22 36				23 06		
Coulsdon Town	d			21 10					21 40			22 10					22 40				23 10		
Reedham	d			21 13					21 43			22 13					22 43				23 13		
Caterham	d		21 02					21 32			22 02					22 32				23 02			
Whyteleafe South	d		21 05					21 35			22 05					22 35				23 05			
Upper Warlingham	d	21 08					21 38			22 08					22 38				23 08			23 40	
Whyteleafe	d		21 07					21 37			22 07					22 37				23 07			
Kenley	d		21 10					21 40			22 10					22 40				23 10			
Purley	a		21 13	21 16				21 43	21 46		22 13	22 16				22 43	22 46			23 13	23 16		
Purley 4	d		21 20		21 25	21 42		21 50			22 20		22 25	22 38		22 50		23 07		23 20			23 59
Sanderstead	d	21 15					21 45			22 15					22 45				23 15			23 47	
Purley Oaks	d		21 23					21 53			22 23					22 53				23 23			
South Croydon 4	d		21 26					21 56			22 26					22 56				23 26			
East Croydon ⇌	a	21 21	21 29		21 29	21 47	21 51	21 59		22 21	22 29		22 29	22 45	22 51	22 59		23 12	23 21	23 29		23 54	00 05
East Croydon	d		21 31			21 48		22 01			22 31			22 47		23 01		23 12		23 31			
Norwood Junction 2	a		21 35					22 05			22 35			22 51		23 05		23 16		23 35			
New Cross Gate 4 ⊖	a		21 53			22 02		22 23			22 53					23 23				23 53			
London Bridge 4 ⊖	a		22 02					22 32			23 02			23 05		23 32		23 30		00 03			
London Blackfriars	a					22 08																	
City Thameslink	a																						
Farringdon	a					22 13																	
St Pancras International	a					22 17																	
East Croydon	d	21 21			21 30		21 51			22 21			22 30		22 51				23 21			23 55	00 06
Clapham Junction 10	a	21 32			21 39		22 02			22 32			22 39		23 02				23 32			00 15	00 18
London Victoria 15 ⊖	a	21 39			21 47		22 09			22 39			22 47		23 09				23 39			00 23	00 27

Table T182-F

Mondays to Fridays

16 December to 15 May

London - Oxted, East Grinstead and Uckfield

Miles	Miles			SN MX 1	SN MX 1	SN MX 1	SN 1	SN 1	TL 1	SN 1	SN 1	TL 1	SN 1	SN 1	TL 1	SN 1	SN 1	TL 1	SN 1	TL 1	SN 1	SN 1	TL 1
0	—	London Victoria 15 ⊖175,177	d					05 20		05 50			06 20			06 50			07 20		07 50		
—	—	Clapham Junction	a					05 28		05 56			06 26			06 56			07 26		07 56		
—	—	Clapham Junction 10 175,177	d					05 29		05 57			06 27			06 57			07 27		07 57		
—	—	East Croydon	a					05 41		06 09			06 39			07 09			07 39		08 09		
—	—	St Pancras International	d									05 55			06 25			06 55		07 25			07 55
—	—	Farringdon	d									05 59			06 29			06 59		07 29			07 59
—	—	City Thameslink	a									06 01			06 31			07 01		07 31			08 01
—	—		d									06 01			06 31			07 01		07 31			08 01
—	—	London Blackfriars	a									06 03			06 33			07 03		07 33			08 03
—	—		d									06 04			06 34			07 04		07 34			08 04
—	0	London Bridge 4 ⊖175,177	a									06 10			06 40			07 10		07 40			08 10
—	—		d						05 37		06 07	06 11		06 37	06 41		07 07	07 11		07 41		08 07	08 11
10½	10¼	East Croydon 175,177 ⇌	a						05 54		06 21	06 24		06 51	06 54		07 21	07 24		07 54		08 21	08 24
—	—	East Croydon	d			00 14	05 20	05 41	05 55	06 10	06 22	06 25	06 40	06 52	06 55	07 10	07 22	07 25	07 40	07 55	08 10	08 22	08 25
11½	—	South Croydon 4 175	d			00 17			05 58			06 28			06 58			07 28		07 58			08 28
12½	—	**Sanderstead**	d			00 20		05 46	06 02	06 15		06 32	06 45		07 02	07 15		07 32	07 45	08 02	08 15		08 32
13¾	—	**Riddlesdown**	d			00 23		05 49		06 18			06 48			07 18			07 48	08 05	08 18		
15½	—	**Upper Warlingham**	d			00 27		05 53		06 22			06 52			07 22			07 52	08 09	08 22		
17¼	—	**Woldingham**	d			00 31		05 57		06 26			06 56			07 26			07 56	08 13	08 26		
20½	20½	**Oxted** 3	a			00 37	05 33	06 02	06 13	06 31	06 35	06 43	07 01	07 05	07 13	07 31	07 35	07 43	08 01	08 18	08 31	08 35	08 43
—	—	**Oxted**	d	00 02			05 33	06 03	06 15	06 32	06 36	06 45	07 02	07 06	07 15	07 32	07 36	07 45	08 02	08 18	08 32	08 36	08 45
21½	21½	**Hurst Green**	d	00 05			05 36	06 06	06 18	06 35	06 39	06 48	07 05	07 09	07 18	07 35	07 39	07 48	08 05	08 21	08 35	08 39	08 48
26¼	—	**Lingfield**	d	00 11				06 12	06 24	06 41		06 54	07 11		07 24	07 41		07 54	08 11	08 27	08 41		08 54
28	—	**Dormans**	d	00 14				06 15	06 27	06 44		06 57	07 14		07 27	07 44		07 57	08 14	08 30	08 44		08 57
30¼	—	**East Grinstead**	a	00 20				06 20	06 33	06 50		07 03	07 20		07 33	07 50		08 03	08 20	08 35	08 50		09 03
—	25½	**Edenbridge Town**	d				05 42				06 45			07 15			07 45					08 45	
—	27½	**Hever**	d				05 46				06 49			07 19			07 49					08 49	
—	29¼	**Cowden**	d				05 50				06 53			07 23			07 53					08 53	
—	32¼	**Ashurst**	d				05 57				06 58			07 28			07 58					08 58	
—	35¾	**Eridge**	d				06 02				07 03			07 33			08 03					09 03	
—	39¼	**Crowborough**	d		00 04		06 09				07 10			07 40			08 10					09 10	
—	43¾	**Buxted**	d		00 10		06 15				07 16			07 46			08 16					09 16	
—	46¼	**Uckfield**	a		00 16		06 21				07 22			07 52			08 22					09 22	

		SN 1	SN 1	SN 1	SN 1	SN 1	SN 1	SN 1	SN 1	SN 1		SN 1	SN 1	SN 1	SN 1	SN 1	SN 1	SN 1	SN 1	SN 1	TL 1	SN 1	SN 1
London Victoria 15 ⊖175,177	d	08 20		08 50		09 20	09 50		10 20	10 50			14 20	14 50		15 20	15 50		16 20			16 50	
Clapham Junction	a	08 26		08 56		09 26	09 57		10 26	10 56			14 26	14 56		15 26	15 56		16 26			16 56	
Clapham Junction 10 175,177	d	08 27		08 57		09 27	09 57		10 27	10 57			14 27	14 57		15 27	15 57		16 27			16 57	
East Croydon	a	08 39		09 09		09 39	10 09		10 39	11 09			14 39	15 09		15 39	16 09		16 39			17 09	
St Pancras International	d																				16 25		
Farringdon	d																				16 29		
City Thameslink	a																				16 31		
	d																				16 31		
London Blackfriars	a																				16 33		
	d																				16 34		
London Bridge 4 ⊖175,177	a																				16 40		
	d		08 37		09 07			10 07				14 07			15 07			16 07		16 37	16 41		17 07
East Croydon 175,177 ⇌	a		08 51		09 21			10 21			and at the same minutes past each hour until	14 21			15 21			16 21		16 51	16 54		17 21
East Croydon	d	08 40	08 52	09 10	09 22	09 40	10 10	10 22	10 40	11 10		14 22	14 40	15 10	15 22	15 40	16 10	16 22	16 40	16 52	16 55	17 10	17 22
South Croydon 4 175	d															15 42	16 12		16 42		16 58		
Sanderstead	d	08 45		09 15		09 45	10 15		10 45	11 15			14 45	15 15		15 45	16 15		16 45		17 02	17 15	
Riddlesdown	d	08 48		09 18		09 48	10 18		10 48	11 18			14 48	15 18		15 48	16 18		16 48		17 05	17 18	
Upper Warlingham	d	08 52		09 22		09 52	10 22		10 52	11 22			14 52	15 22		15 52	16 22		16 52		17 09	17 22	
Woldingham	d	08 56		09 26		09 56	10 26		10 56	11 26			14 56	15 26		15 56	16 26		16 56		17 13	17 26	
Oxted 3	a	09 01	09 05	09 31	09 35	10 01	10 31	10 35	11 01	11 31		14 35	15 01	15 31	15 35	16 01	16 31	16 35	17 01	17 05	17 18	17 31	17 35
Oxted	d	09 02	09 06	09 32	09 36	10 02	10 32	10 36	11 02	11 32		14 36	15 02	15 32	15 36	16 02	16 32	16 36	17 02	17 06	17 19	17 32	17 36
Hurst Green	d	09 05	09 09	09 35	09 39	10 05	10 35	10 39	11 05	11 35		14 39	15 05	15 35	15 39	16 05	16 35	16 39	17 05	17 09	17 22	17 35	17 39
Lingfield	d	09 11		09 41		10 11	10 41		11 11	11 41			15 11	15 41		16 11	16 41		17 11		17 28	17 41	
Dormans	d	09 14		09 44		10 14	10 44		11 14	11 44			15 14	15 44		16 14	16 44		17 14		17 31	17 44	
East Grinstead	a	09 22		09 50		10 20	10 50		11 20	11 50			15 20	15 50		16 20	16 50		17 20		17 37	17 50	
Edenbridge Town	d		09 15		09 45			10 45				14 45			15 45			16 45		17 15			17 45
Hever	d		09 19		09 49			10 49				14 49			15 49			16 49		17 19			17 49
Cowden	d		09 23		09 53			10 53				14 53			15 53			16 53		17 23			17 53
Ashurst	d		09 28		09 58			10 58				14 58			15 58			16 58		17 28			17 58
Eridge	d		09 33		10 03			11 03				15 03			16 03			17 03		17 33			18 03
Crowborough	d		09 40		10 10			11 10				15 10			16 10			17 10		17 40			18 10
Buxted	d		09 46		10 16			11 16				15 16			16 16			17 16		17 46			18 16
Uckfield	a		09 52		10 22			11 22				15 22			16 22			17 22		17 52			18 22

Table T182-F

London - Oxted, East Grinstead and Uckfield

Mondays to Fridays

16 December to 15 May

		TL 1	SN 1	SN 1	TL 1	SN 1	SN 1	TL 1	SN 1	TL 1	SN 1	SN 1	TL 1	SN 1	SN 1	SN 1	SN 1	SN 1	SN 1	SN 1	SN 1	SN 1
London Victoria 15 ⊖175,177	d		17 20			17 50			18 20		18 50			19 20	19 50		20 20	20 50		21 20	21 50	
Clapham Junction	a		17 28			17 57			18 26		18 56			19 26	19 56		20 26	20 56		21 26	21 56	
Clapham Junction 10 175,177	d		17 28			17 58			18 27		18 57			19 27	19 57		20 27	20 57		21 27	21 57	
East Croydon	a		17 39			18 09			18 39		19 09			19 39	20 09		20 39	21 09		21 39	22 09	
St Pancras International	d	16 55			17 25			17 55		18 25			18 55									
Farringdon	d	16 59			17 29			17 59		18 29			18 59									
City Thameslink	a	17 01			17 31			18 01		18 31			19 01									
	d	17 01			17 31			18 01		18 31			19 01									
London Blackfriars	a	17 03			17 33			18 03		18 33			19 03									
	d	17 04			17 34			18 04		18 34			19 04									
London Bridge 4 ⊖175,177	a	17 10			17 40			18 10		18 40			19 10									
	d	17 11		17 37	17 41		18 07	18 11		18 41		19 07	19 11			20 07			21 07			22 07
East Croydon 175,177 ⇌	a	17 24		17 51	17 54		18 21	18 24		18 54		19 21	19 24			20 21			21 21			22 21
East Croydon	d	17 25	17 40	17 52	17 56	18 10	18 22	18 25	18 40	18 55	19 10	19 22	19 25	19 40	20 10	20 22	20 40	21 10	21 22	21 40	22 10	22 22
South Croydon 4 175	d	17 28			17 59			18 28		18 58			19 28									
Sanderstead	d	17 32	17 45		18 02	18 15		18 32	18 45	19 02	19 15		19 32	19 45	20 15		20 45	21 15		21 45	22 15	
Riddlesdown	d	17 35	17 48		18 05	18 18		18 35	18 48	19 05	19 18		19 35	19 48	20 18		20 48	21 18		21 48	22 18	
Upper Warlingham	d	17 39	17 52		18 09	18 22		18 39	18 52	19 09	19 22		19 39	19 52	20 22		20 52	21 22		21 52	22 22	
Woldingham	d	17 43	17 56		18 13	18 26		18 43	18 56	19 13	19 26		19 43	19 56	20 26		20 56	21 26		21 56	22 26	
Oxted 3	a	17 48	18 01	18 05	18 18	18 31	18 35	18 48	19 01	19 18	19 31	19 35	19 48	20 01	20 31	20 35	21 01	21 31	21 35	22 01	22 31	22 35
Oxted	d	17 49	18 02	18 06	18 19	18 32	18 36	18 49	19 02	19 19	19 32	19 36	19 49	20 02	20 32	20 36	21 02	21 32	21 36	22 02	22 32	22 36
Hurst Green	d	17 52	18 05	18 09	18 22	18 35	18 39	18 52	19 05	19 22	19 35	19 39	19 52	20 05	20 35	20 39	21 05	21 35	21 39	22 05	22 35	22 39
Lingfield	d	17 58	18 11		18 28	18 41		18 58	19 11	19 28	19 41		19 58	20 11	20 41		21 11	21 41		22 11	22 41	
Dormans	d	18 01	18 14		18 31	18 44		19 01	19 14	19 31	19 44		20 01	20 14	20 44		21 14	21 44		22 14	22 44	
East Grinstead	a	18 07	18 20		18 37	18 50		19 07	19 20	19 37	19 50		20 07	20 20	20 50		21 20	21 50		22 20	22 50	
Edenbridge Town	d			18 15			18 45					19 45				20 45			21 45			22 45
Hever	d			18 19			18 49					19 49				20 49			21 49			22 49
Cowden	d			18 23			18 53					19 53				20 53			21 53			22 53
Ashurst	d			18 28			18 58					19 58				20 58			21 58			22 58
Eridge	d			18 33			19 03					20 03				21 03			22 03			23 03
Crowborough	d			18 40			19 10					20 10				21 10			22 10			23 10
Buxted	d			18 46			19 16					20 16				21 16			22 16			23 16
Uckfield	a			18 52			19 22					20 22				21 22			22 22			23 22

		SN 1	SN 1	SN 1	SN 1	SN 1
London Victoria 15 ⊖175,177	d	22 20	22 52		23 22	23 53
Clapham Junction	a	22 26	22 59		23 28	23 59
Clapham Junction 10 175,177	d	22 27	23 00		23 29	23 59
East Croydon	a	22 39	23 10		23 39	00 14
St Pancras International	d					
Farringdon	d					
City Thameslink	a					
	d					
London Blackfriars	a					
	d					
London Bridge 4 ⊖175,177	a					
	d			23 07		
East Croydon 175,177 ⇌	a			23 21		
East Croydon	d	22 40	23 11	23 22	23 40	00 14
South Croydon 4 175	d					00 17
Sanderstead	d	22 45	23 15		23 45	00 20
Riddlesdown	d	22 48	23 18		23 48	00 23
Upper Warlingham	d	22 52	23 22		23 52	00 27
Woldingham	d	22 56	23 26		23 56	00 31
Oxted 3	a	23 01	23 31	23 35	00 01	00 37
Oxted	d	23 02	23 32	23 36	00 02	
Hurst Green	d	23 05	23 35	23 39	00 05	
Lingfield	d	23 11	23 41		00 11	
Dormans	d	23 14	23 44		00 14	
East Grinstead	a	23 20	23 50		00 20	
Edenbridge Town	d			23 45		
Hever	d					
Cowden	d					
Ashurst	d					
Eridge	d			23 57		
Crowborough	d			00 04		
Buxted	d			00 10		
Uckfield	a			00 16		

Table T182-F

London - Oxted, East Grinstead and Uckfield

Saturdays

21 December to 16 May

		SN 1	SN 1	SN 1	SN 1	SN 1	SN 1	SN 1		SN 1	SN 1	SN 1	SN 1	SN 1	SN 1	SN 1	SN 1	SN 1
London Victoria 15 ⊖175,177	d				05 20		06 20	06 50			21 20	21 50		22 20	22 50		23 20	23 53
Clapham Junction	a				05 27		06 26	06 56			21 26	21 56		22 26	22 56		23 26	23 59
Clapham Junction 10 175,177	d				05 28		06 27	06 57			21 27	21 57		22 27	22 57		23 27	23 59
East Croydon	a				05 44		06 39	07 09			21 39	22 09		22 39	23 09		23 39	00 14
St Pancras International	d																	
Farringdon	d																	
City Thameslink	a																	
	d																	
London Blackfriars	a																	
	d																	
London Bridge 4 ⊖175,177	a																	
	d					06 07				21 07			22 07			23 07		
East Croydon 175,177 ⇌	a					06 21				21 21			22 21			23 21		
East Croydon	d			00 14	05 45	06 22	06 40	07 10	and at the same minutes past each hour until	21 22	21 40	22 10	22 22	22 40	23 10	23 22	23 40	00 14
South Croydon 4 175	d			00 17														00 17
Sanderstead	d			00 20			06 45	07 15			21 45	22 15		22 45	23 15		23 45	00 20
Riddlesdown	d			00 23			06 48	07 18			21 48	22 18		22 48	23 18		23 48	00 23
Upper Warlingham	d			00 27			06 52	07 22			21 52	22 22		22 52	23 22		23 52	00 27
Woldingham	d			00 31			06 56	07 26			21 56	22 26		22 56	23 26		23 56	00 31
Oxted 3	a			00 37	05 58	06 35	07 01	07 31		21 35	22 01	22 31	22 35	23 01	23 31	23 35	00 01	00 37
Oxted	d	00 02			05 59	06 36	07 02	07 32		21 36	22 02	22 32	22 36	23 02	23 32	23 36	00 02	
Hurst Green	d	00 05			06 02	06 39	07 05	07 35		21 39	22 05	22 35	22 39	23 05	23 35	23 39	00 05	
Lingfield	d	00 11			06 08		07 11	07 41			22 11	22 41		23 11	23 41		00 11	
Dormans	d	00 14			06 11		07 14	07 44			22 14	22 44		23 14	23 44		00 14	
East Grinstead	a	00 20			06 17		07 20	07 50			22 20	22 50		23 20	23 50		00 20	
Edenbridge Town	d					06 45				21 45			22 45			23 45		
Hever	d					06 49				21 49			22 49					
Cowden	d					06 53				21 53			22 53					
Ashurst	d					06 58				21 58			22 58					
Eridge	d					07 03				22 03			23 03			23 57		
Crowborough	d		00 04			07 10				22 10			23 10			00 04		
Buxted	d		00 10			07 16				22 16			23 18			00 10		
Uckfield	a		00 16			07 22				22 22			23 24			00 16		

Sundays

15 December to 10 May

		SN 1 A	SN 1 A	SN 1 A	SN 1	SN 1	SN 1	SN 1	SN 1	SN 1	SN 1	SN 1	SN 1	SN 1	SN 1	SN 1	SN 1	SN 1	SN 1	SN 1	SN 1	SN 1	SN
London Victoria 15 ⊖175,177	d				07 43		08 51		09 21	09 51		10 21	10 51		11 21	11 51		12 21	12 51		13 21	13 51	
Clapham Junction	a				07 50		08 57		09 27	09 57		10 27	10 57		11 27	11 57		12 27	12 57		13 27	13 57	
Clapham Junction 10 175,177	d				07 51		08 58		09 28	09 58		10 28	10 58		11 28	11 58		12 28	12 58		13 28	13 58	
East Croydon	a				08 08		09 08		09 38	10 08		10 38	11 08		11 38	12 08		12 38	13 11		13 38	14 08	
St Pancras International	d																						
Farringdon	d																						
City Thameslink	a																						
	d																						
London Blackfriars	a																						
	d																						
London Bridge 4 ⊖175,177	a																						
	d																						
East Croydon 175,177 ⇌	a																						
East Croydon	d			00 14	08 09	08 17	09 09	09 23	09 39	10 09		10 39	11 09		11 39	12 09		12 39	13 12		13 39	14 09	
South Croydon 4 175	d			00 17																			
Sanderstead	d			00 20	08 14		09 14		09 44	10 14		10 44	11 14		11 44	12 14		12 44	13 17		13 44	14 14	
Riddlesdown	d			00 23	08 17		09 17		09 47	10 17		10 47	11 17		11 47	12 17		12 47	13 20		13 47	14 17	
Upper Warlingham	d			00 27	08 21		09 21		09 51	10 21		10 51	11 21		11 51	12 21		12 51	13 24		13 51	14 21	
Woldingham	d			00 31	08 25		09 25		09 55	10 25		10 55	11 25		11 55	12 25		12 55	13 28		13 55	14 25	
Oxted 3	a			00 37	08 30	08 36	09 30	09 36	10 00	10 33		11 00	11 33		12 00	12 33		13 00	13 33		14 00	14 33	
Oxted	d	00 02			08 30	08 37	09 31	09 37	10 01	10 34	10 38	11 01	11 34	11 38	12 01	12 34	12 38	13 01	13 34	13 38	14 01	14 34	14 38
Hurst Green	d	00 05			08 33	08 40	09 34	09 40	10 04	10 37	10 41	11 04	11 37	11 41	12 04	12 37	12 41	13 04	13 37	13 41	14 04	14 37	14 41
Lingfield	d	00 11			08 39		09 40		10 10	10 43		11 10	11 43		12 10	12 43		13 10	13 43		14 10	14 43	
Dormans	d	00 14			08 43		09 43		10 13	10 46		11 13	11 46		12 13	12 46		13 13	13 46		14 13	14 46	
East Grinstead	a	00 20			08 48		09 48		10 18	10 51		11 18	11 51		12 18	12 51		13 18	13 51		14 18	14 51	
Edenbridge Town	d					08 46		09 46			10 47			11 47			12 47			13 47			14 47
Hever	d					08 50		09 50			10 51			11 51			12 51			13 51			14 51
Cowden	d					08 54		09 54			10 55			11 55			12 55			13 55			14 55
Ashurst	d					08 58		09 58			10 59			11 59			12 59			13 59			14 59
Eridge	d					09 04		10 04			11 05			12 05			13 05			14 05			15 05
Crowborough	d		00 04			09 11		10 11			11 12			12 12			13 12			14 12			15 12
Buxted	d		00 10			09 17		10 17			11 18			12 18			13 18			14 18			15 18
Uckfield	a		00 16			09 23		10 23			11 24			12 24			13 24			14 24			15 24

A not 15 December

NRT DECEMBER 19 EDITION

Table T182-F

Sundays

15 December to 10 May

London - Oxted, East Grinstead and Uckfield

		SN	SN	SN	SN	SN	SN	SN	SN	SN	SN	SN		SN	SN	SN	SN	SN	SN
London Victoria 15 ⊖175,177	d	14 21	14 51		15 21	15 51		16 21	16 51		17 21	17 51			21 21	21 51		22 21	22 51
Clapham Junction	a	14 27	14 57		15 27	15 57		16 27	16 57		17 27	17 57			21 27	21 57		22 27	22 57
Clapham Junction 10 175,177	d	14 28	14 58		15 28	15 58		16 28	16 58		17 28	17 58			21 28	21 58		22 28	22 58
East Croydon	a	14 38	15 08		15 38	16 11		16 38	17 11		17 38	18 08			21 38	22 08		22 38	23 08
St Pancras International	d																		
Farringdon	d																		
City Thameslink	a																		
	d																		
London Blackfriars	a																		
	d																		
London Bridge 4 ⊖175,177	a																		
	d																		
East Croydon 175,177	a																		
East Croydon	d	14 39	15 09		15 39	16 12		16 39	17 12		17 39	18 09	and at the same minutes past each hour until		21 39	22 09		22 39	23 09
South Croydon 4 175	d																		
Sanderstead	d	14 44	15 14		15 44	16 17		16 44	17 17		17 44	18 14			21 44	22 14		22 44	23 14
Riddlesdown	d	14 47	15 17		15 47	16 20		16 47	17 20		17 47	18 17			21 47	22 17		22 47	23 17
Upper Warlingham	d	14 51	15 21		15 51	16 24		16 51	17 24		17 51	18 21			21 51	22 21		22 51	23 21
Woldingham	d	14 55	15 25		15 55	16 28		16 55	17 28		17 55	18 25			21 55	22 25		22 55	23 25
Oxted 3	a	15 00	15 33		16 00	16 33		17 00	17 33		18 00	18 33			22 00	22 33		23 00	23 30
Oxted	d	15 01	15 34	15 38	16 01	16 34	16 38	17 01	17 34	17 38	18 01	18 34		21 38	22 01	22 34	22 38	23 01	23 31
Hurst Green	d	15 04	15 37	15 41	16 04	16 37	16 41	17 04	17 37	17 41	18 04	18 37		21 41	22 04	22 37	22 41	23 04	23 34
Lingfield	d	15 10	15 43		16 10	16 43		17 10	17 43		18 10	18 43			22 10	22 43		23 10	23 40
Dormans	d	15 13	15 46		16 13	16 46		17 13	17 46		18 13	18 46			22 13	22 46		23 13	23 43
East Grinstead	a	15 18	15 51		16 18	16 51		17 18	17 51		18 18	18 51			22 18	22 51		23 18	23 48
Edenbridge Town	d			15 47			16 47			17 47				21 47			22 47		
Hever	d			15 51			16 51			17 51				21 51			22 51		
Cowden	d			15 55			16 55			17 55				21 55			22 55		
Ashurst	d			15 59			16 59			17 59				21 59			22 59		
Eridge	d			16 05			17 05			18 05				22 05			23 05		
Crowborough	d			16 12			17 12			18 12				22 12			23 12		
Buxted	d			16 18			17 18			18 18				22 18			23 18		
Uckfield	a			16 24			17 24			18 24				22 24			23 24		

Table T182-R

Mondays to Fridays

16 December to 15 May

Uckfield, East Grinstead and Oxted - London

		SN MX	SN MO	SN	SN	TL	SN	SN	TL	SN	TL	SN	SN	TL	SN	SN	TL	SN	SN	TL	SN	SN	TL
Uckfield	d			05 10			05 31					06 33			07 03			07 33			08 03		
Buxted	d			05 14			05 35					06 37			07 07			07 37			08 07		
Crowborough	d			05 21			05 42					06 44			07 14			07 44			08 14		
Eridge	d			05 27			05 48					06 50			07 20			07 50			08 20		
Ashurst	d						05 54					06 56			07 26			07 56			08 26		
Cowden	d			05 35			05 58					07 00			07 30			08 00			08 30		
Hever	d						06 03					07 05			07 35			08 05			08 35		
Edenbridge Town	a			05 40			06 06					07 08			07 38			08 08			08 38		
East Grinstead	d				05 36	05 45		06 04	06 13	06 36	06 45		07 06	07 15		07 36	07 45		08 06	08 15		08 36	08 45
Dormans	d				05 40	05 49		06 08	06 17	06 40	06 49		07 10	07 19		07 40	07 49		08 10	08 19		08 40	08 49
Lingfield	d				05 43	05 52		06 11	06 20	06 43	06 52		07 13	07 22		07 43	07 52		08 13	08 22		08 43	08 52
Hurst Green	d				05 50	05 59	06 14	06 18	06 27	06 50	06 59	07 16	07 20	07 29	07 46	07 50	07 59	08 16	08 20	08 29	08 46	08 50	08 59
Oxted	a			05 48	05 53	06 02	06 17	06 22	06 29	06 53	07 02	07 19	07 23	07 32	07 49	07 53	08 02	08 19	08 23	08 32	08 49	08 53	09 02
Oxted 3	d			05 49	05 53	06 02	06 19	06 23	06 30	06 53	07 02	07 20	07 23	07 32	07 50	07 53	08 02	08 20	08 23	08 32	08 50	08 53	09 02
Woldingham	d				05 59	06 08		06 28	06 35	06 59	07 08		07 29	07 38		07 59	08 08		08 29	08 38		08 59	09 08
Upper Warlingham	d				06 02	06 11		06 32	06 39	07 02	07 11		07 32	07 41		08 02	08 11		08 32	08 41		09 02	09 11
Riddlesdown	d				06 06	06 15		06 35	06 42	07 06	07 15		07 36	07 45		08 06	08 15		08 36	08 45		09 06	09 15
Sanderstead	d				06 09	06 18		06 39	06 45	07 09	07 18		07 39	07 48		08 09	08 18		08 39	08 48		09 09	09 18
South Croydon 4 175	d					06 21			06 48		07 21			07 51			08 21			08 51			09 21
East Croydon	a			06 06	06 15	06 24	06 37	06 44	06 51	07 15	07 24	07 37	07 45	07 54	08 07	08 15	08 24	08 37	08 45	08 54	09 07	09 15	09 24
East Croydon 175,177	d			06 08		06 25	06 38		06 51		07 25	07 38		07 55	08 08		08 25	08 38		08 55	09 08		09 25
London Bridge	a			06 23		06 40	06 53		07 05		07 40	07 53		08 10	08 23		08 40	08 53		09 10	09 23		09 40
	d					06 41			07 06		07 41			08 11			08 41			09 11			09 41
London Blackfriars	a					06 46			07 11		07 46			08 16			08 46			09 16			09 46
	d					06 47			07 12		07 47			08 17			08 47			09 17			09 47
City Thameslink	d					06 49			07 14		07 49			08 19			08 49			09 19			09 49
Farringdon	d					06 51			07 16		07 51			08 21			08 51			09 21			09 51
St Pancras International	a					06 55			07 20		07 55			08 25			08 55			09 25			09 55
East Croydon	d				06 15			06 45		07 15			07 45			08 15			08 45			09 15	
Clapham Junction 10 175,177	d	00 01	00 16		06 26			06 56		07 26			07 58			08 28			08 58			09 26	
London Victoria 15 ⊖175,177	a	00 08	00 23		06 32			07 03		07 32			08 06			08 35			09 05			09 32	

		SN	SN	TL	SN	SN	SN	SN	SN	SN	SN	SN	SN	SN	SN	SN	SN	SN	SN	SN	SN	SN	SN
Uckfield	d	08 33				09 33		10 03		10 33			11 33			12 33			13 33				14 33
Buxted	d	08 37				09 37		10 07		10 37			11 37			12 37			13 37				14 37
Crowborough	d	08 44				09 44		10 14		10 44			11 44			12 44			13 44				14 44
Eridge	d	08 50				09 50		10 20		10 50			11 50			12 50			13 50				14 50
Ashurst	d	08 56				09 56		10 26		10 56			11 56			12 56			13 56				14 56
Cowden	d	09 00				10 00		10 30		11 00			12 00			13 00			14 00				15 00
Hever	d	09 05				10 05		10 35		11 05			12 05			13 05			14 05				15 05
Edenbridge Town	a	09 08				10 08		10 38		11 08			12 08			13 08			14 08				15 08
East Grinstead	d		09 06	09 19	09 36		10 06		10 36		11 06	11 36		12 06	12 36		13 06	13 36		14 06	14 36		
Dormans	d		09 10	09 23	09 40		10 10		10 40		11 10	11 40		12 10	12 40		13 10	13 40		14 10	14 40		
Lingfield	d		09 13	09 26	09 43		10 13		10 43		11 13	11 43		12 13	12 43		13 13	13 43		14 13	14 43		
Hurst Green	d	09 16	09 20	09 33	09 50	10 16	10 20	10 46	10 50	11 16	11 20	11 50	12 16	12 20	12 50	13 16	13 20	13 50	14 16	14 20	14 50		15 16
Oxted	a	09 19	09 23	09 36	09 53	10 19	10 23	10 49	10 53	11 19	11 23	11 53	12 19	12 23	12 53	13 19	13 23	13 53	14 19	14 23	14 53		15 19
Oxted 3	d	09 20	09 23	09 38	09 53	10 20	10 23	10 50	10 53	11 20	11 23	11 53	12 20	12 23	12 53	13 20	13 23	13 53	14 20	14 23	14 53		15 20
Woldingham	d		09 29		09 59		10 29		10 59		11 29	11 59		12 29	12 59		13 29	13 59		14 29	14 59		
Upper Warlingham	d		09 32		10 02		10 32		11 02		11 32	12 02		12 32	13 02		13 32	14 02		14 32	15 02		
Riddlesdown	d		09 36		10 06		10 36		11 06		11 36	12 06		12 36	13 06		13 36	14 06		14 36	15 06		
Sanderstead	d		09 39	09 48	10 09		10 39		11 09		11 39	12 09		12 39	13 09		13 39	14 09		14 39	15 09		
South Croydon 4 175	d			09 51																			
East Croydon	a	09 37	09 45	09 54	10 15	10 36	10 45	11 08	11 15	11 36	11 45	12 15	12 36	12 45	13 15	13 36	13 45	14 15	14 36	14 45	15 15		15 36
East Croydon 175,177	d	09 38		09 54		10 38				11 38			12 38			13 39			14 38				15 38
London Bridge	a	09 53		10 11		10 53				11 53			12 53			13 55			14 53				15 53
	d																						
London Blackfriars	a																						
	d																						
City Thameslink	d																						
Farringdon	d																						
St Pancras International	a																						
East Croydon	d		09 45		10 15		10 45		11 15		11 45	12 15		12 45	13 15		13 45	14 15		14 45	15 15		
Clapham Junction 10 175,177	d		09 56		10 26		10 56		11 26		11 56	12 26		12 56	13 26		13 56	14 26		14 56	15 26		
London Victoria 15 ⊖175,177	a		10 02		10 35		11 02		11 32		12 02	12 32		13 02	13 32		14 02	14 32		15 02	15 32		

		SN	SN	SN	SN	SN	SN	SN	SN	TL	SN	SN	TL	SN	SN	TL	SN	SN	TL	SN	SN	TL	SN
Uckfield	d			15 33			16 33				17 33			18 03			18 33			19 03			19 33
Buxted	d			15 37			16 37				17 37			18 07			18 37			19 07			19 37
Crowborough	d			15 44			16 44				17 44			18 14			18 44			19 14			19 44
Eridge	d			15 50			16 50				17 50			18 20			18 50			19 20			19 50
Ashurst	d			15 56			16 56				17 56			18 26			18 56			19 26			19 56
Cowden	d			16 00			17 00				18 00			18 30			19 00			19 30			20 00
Hever	d			16 05			17 05				18 05			18 35			19 05			19 35			20 05
Edenbridge Town	a			16 08			17 08				18 08			18 38			19 08			19 38			20 08
East Grinstead	d	15 06	15 36		16 06	16 36		17 06	17 36	17 51		18 06	18 21		18 36	18 51		19 06	19 17		19 36	19 51	
Dormans	d	15 10	15 40		16 10	16 40		17 10	17 40	17 55		18 10	18 25		18 40	18 55		19 10	19 21		19 40	19 55	
Lingfield	d	15 13	15 43		16 13	16 43		17 13	17 43	17 58		18 13	18 28		18 43	18 58		19 13	19 24		19 43	19 58	
Hurst Green	d	15 20	15 50	16 16	16 20	16 50	17 16	17 20	17 50	18 05	18 16	18 20	18 35	18 46	18 50	19 05	19 16	19 20	19 31	19 46	19 50	20 05	20 16
Oxted	a	15 23	15 53	16 19	16 23	16 53	17 19	17 23	17 53	18 08	18 19	18 23	18 38	18 49	18 53	19 08	19 19	19 23	19 34	19 49	19 53	20 08	20 19
Oxted 3	d	15 23	15 53	16 20	16 23	16 53	17 20	17 23	17 53	18 08	18 20	18 23	18 38	18 50	18 53	19 08	19 20	19 23	19 34	19 50	19 53	20 08	20 20
Woldingham	d	15 29	15 59		16 29	16 59		17 29	17 59			18 29			18 59			19 29			19 59		
Upper Warlingham	d	15 32	16 02		16 32	17 02		17 32	18 02			18 32			19 02			19 32			20 02		
Riddlesdown	d	15 36	16 06		16 36	17 06		17 36	18 06			18 36			19 06			19 36			20 06		
Sanderstead	d	15 39	16 09		16 39	17 09		17 39	18 09	18 18		18 39	18 48		19 09	19 18		19 39	19 45		20 09	20 18	
South Croydon 4 175	d																						
East Croydon	a	15 45	16 15	16 36	16 45	17 15	17 36	17 45	18 15	18 24	18 36	18 45	18 54	19 06	19 15	19 24	19 36	19 45	19 52	20 06	20 15	20 24	20 36
East Croydon 175,177	d			16 38			17 38			18 25	18 38		18 55	19 08		19 25	19 38		19 52	20 08		20 24	20 38
London Bridge	a			16 54			17 54			18 40	18 53		19 10	19 23		19 40	19 53		20 12	20 23		20 41	20 54
	d									18 41			19 11			19 41							
London Blackfriars	a									18 46			19 16			19 46							
	d									18 47			19 17			19 47							
City Thameslink	d									18 49			19 19			19 49							
Farringdon	d									18 51			19 21			19 51							
St Pancras International	a									18 55			19 25			19 55							
East Croydon	d	15 46	16 15		16 45	17 15		17 45	18 15			18 45			19 15			19 45			20 15		
Clapham Junction 10 175,177	d	15 57	16 26		16 56	17 26		17 56	18 26			18 56			19 26			19 56			20 26		
London Victoria 15 ⊖175,177	a	16 03	16 32		17 02	17 34		18 02	18 32			19 03			19 32			20 02			20 32		

Table T182-R

Mondays to Fridays
16 December to 15 May

Uckfield, East Grinstead and Oxted - London

		SN 1	TL 1	SN 1	SN 1	SN 1	SN 1	SN 1	SN 1	SN 1	SN 1	SN 1
Uckfield	d				20 33			21 33			22 33	
Buxted	d				20 37			21 37			22 37	
Crowborough	d				20 44			21 44			22 44	
Eridge	d				20 50			21 50			22 50	
Ashurst	d				20 56			21 56			22 56	
Cowden	d				21 00			22 00			23 00	
Hever	d				21 05			22 05			23 05	
Edenbridge Town	a				21 08			22 08			23 08	
East Grinstead	d	20 06	20 17	20 36		21 06	21 36		22 06	22 36		23 06
Dormans	d	20 10	20 21	20 40		21 10	21 40		22 10	22 40		23 10
Lingfield	d	20 13	20 24	20 43		21 13	21 43		22 13	22 43		23 13
Hurst Green	d	20 20	20 31	20 50	21 16	21 20	21 50	22 16	22 20	22 50	23 16	23 20
Oxted	a	20 23	20 34	20 53	21 19	21 23	21 53	22 19	22 23	22 53	23 19	23 23
Oxted 3	d	20 23	20 34	20 53	21 20	21 23	21 53	22 20	22 23	22 53	23 20	23 23
Woldingham	d	20 29		20 59		21 29	21 59		22 29	22 59		23 29
Upper Warlingham	d	20 32		21 02		21 32	22 02		22 32	23 02		23 32
Riddlesdown	d	20 36		21 06		21 36	22 06		22 36	23 06		23 36
Sanderstead	d	20 39	20 45	21 09		21 39	22 09		22 39	23 09		23 39
South Croydon 4 175	d											
East Croydon	a	20 45	20 52	21 15	21 36	21 45	22 15	22 36	22 45	23 15	23 36	23 45
East Croydon 175,177 ⛴	d		20 52		21 39			22 38			23 38	
London Bridge	a		21 11		21 55			22 53			23 53	
	d											
London Blackfriars	a											
	d											
City Thameslink	d											
Farringdon	d											
St Pancras International	a											
East Croydon	d	20 45		21 15		21 45	22 15		22 45	23 15		23 45
Clapham Junction 10 175,177	d	20 59		21 26		21 56	22 26		22 56	23 26		00 01
London Victoria 15 ⊖175,177	a	21 05		21 32		22 02	22 35		23 02	23 32		00 08

Saturdays
21 December to 16 May

		SN 1	SN 1	SN 1	SN 1		SN 1	SN 1	SN 1	SN 1	SN 1	SN 1	SN 1	SN 1	SN 1
Uckfield	d			06 33				20 33			21 33			22 33	
Buxted	d			06 37				20 37			21 37			22 37	
Crowborough	d			06 44				20 44			21 44			22 44	
Eridge	d			06 50				20 50			21 50			22 50	
Ashurst	d			06 56				20 56			21 56			22 56	
Cowden	d			07 00				21 00			22 00			23 00	
Hever	d			07 05				21 05			22 05			23 05	
Edenbridge Town	a			07 08				21 08			22 08			23 08	
East Grinstead	d		06 36		07 06		20 36		21 06	21 36		22 06	22 36		23 06
Dormans	d		06 40		07 10		20 40		21 10	21 40		22 10	22 40		23 10
Lingfield	d		06 43		07 13	and at	20 43		21 13	21 43		22 13	22 43		23 13
Hurst Green	d		06 50	07 16	07 20	the same	20 50	21 16	21 20	21 50	22 16	22 20	22 50	23 16	23 20
Oxted	a		06 53	07 19	07 23	minutes	20 53	21 19	21 23	21 53	22 19	22 23	22 53	23 19	23 23
Oxted 3	d		06 53	07 20	07 23	past	20 53	21 20	21 23	21 53	22 20	22 23	22 53	23 20	23 23
Woldingham	d		06 59		07 29	each	20 59		21 29	21 59		22 29	22 59		23 29
Upper Warlingham	d		07 02		07 32	hour until	21 02		21 32	22 02		22 32	23 02		23 32
Riddlesdown	d		07 06		07 36		21 06		21 36	22 06		22 36	23 06		23 36
Sanderstead	d		07 09		07 39		21 09		21 39	22 09		22 39	23 09		23 39
South Croydon 4 175	d														
East Croydon	a		07 15	07 36	07 45		21 15	21 36	21 45	22 15	22 36	22 45	23 15	23 36	23 45
East Croydon 175,177 ⛴	d			07 37				21 37			22 37			23 38	
London Bridge	a			07 53				21 53			22 54			23 53	
	d														
London Blackfriars	a														
	d														
City Thameslink	d														
Farringdon	d														
St Pancras International	a														
East Croydon	d		07 15		07 45		21 15		21 45	22 15		22 45	23 15		23 45
Clapham Junction 10 175,177	d	00 01	07 26		07 56		21 26		21 56	22 26		22 56	23 26		00 05
London Victoria 15 ⊖175,177	a	00 08	07 32		08 02		21 32		22 02	22 32		23 02	23 32		00 12

Table T182-R

Sundays
15 December to 10 May

Uckfield, East Grinstead and Oxted - London

		SN 1 A	SN 1		SN 1	SN 1	SN 1	SN 1		SN 1	SN 1	SN 1	SN 1	SN 1
Uckfield	d					09 34				21 34			22 34	
Buxted	d					09 38				21 38			22 38	
Crowborough	d					09 45				21 45			22 45	
Eridge	d					09 51				21 51			22 51	
Ashurst	d					09 58				21 58			22 58	
Cowden	d					10 02				22 02			23 02	
Hever	d					10 07				22 07			23 07	
Edenbridge Town	a					10 10				22 10			23 10	
East Grinstead	d		08 12		09 42		10 12	10 42			22 12	22 42		23 14
Dormans	d		08 16		09 46		10 16	10 46			22 16	22 46		23 18
Lingfield	d		08 19		09 49		10 19	10 49	and at		22 19	22 49		23 21
Hurst Green	d		08 26	and	09 56	10 17	10 26	10 56	the same	22 17	22 26	22 56	23 17	23 28
Oxted	a		08 29	every 30	09 59	10 20	10 29	10 59	minutes	22 20	22 29	22 59	23 20	23 31
Oxted 3	d		08 29	minutes	09 59		10 29	10 59	past		22 29	22 59	23 21	23 31
Woldingham	d		08 35	until	10 05		10 35	11 05	each		22 35	23 05		23 37
Upper Warlingham	d		08 38		10 08		10 38	11 08	hour until		22 38	23 08		23 40
Riddlesdown	d		08 42		10 12		10 42	11 12			22 42	23 12		23 44
Sanderstead	d		08 45		10 15		10 45	11 15			22 45	23 15		23 47
South Croydon 4 175	d													
East Croydon	a		08 51		10 21		10 51	11 21			22 51	23 21	23 34	23 54
East Croydon 175,177 ⛴	d													
London Bridge	a													
	d													
London Blackfriars	a													
	d													
City Thameslink	d													
Farringdon	d													
St Pancras International	a													
East Croydon	d		08 51		10 21		10 51	11 21			22 51	23 21		23 55
Clapham Junction 10 175,177	d	00 05	09 02		10 32		11 02	11 32			23 02	23 32		00 16
London Victoria 15 ⊖175,177	a	00 12	09 09		10 39		11 09	11 39			23 09	23 39		00 23

A not 15 December

AVAILABLE FROM MP Middleton Press

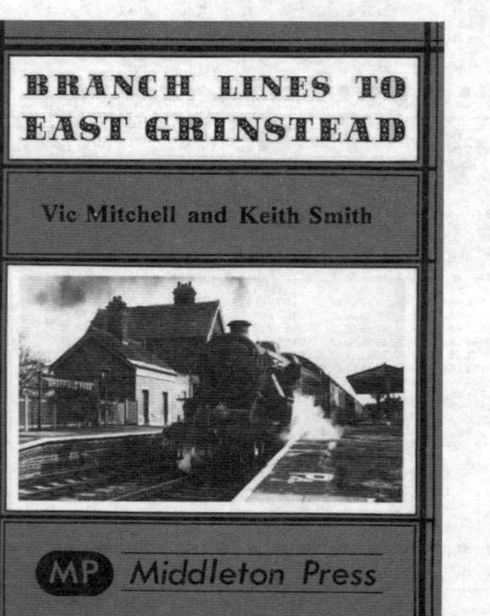

Table T183-F

Mondays to Fridays

16 December to 15 May

London - Redhill / Reigate / Tonbridge / Gatwick Airport - Horsham

Miles	Miles	Miles			SN MX	GW MO	SN MX	SN MO	GW MX	TL	TL MO	TL MX	TL		TL	TL	GW	SN	SN	TL	GW	SN	GW		SN
						1	1	1	1	1	1	1	1		1	1	1	1		1	1	1	1		
0	—	—	London Victoria	d			00 08	00 08										04 35							
2¼	—	—	Clapham Junction	d			00 15	00 15										04 42							
10½	—	—	East Croydon	a			00 30	00 30										04 57							
—	—	0	St Pancras International	d						00 21	00 51	00 52	01 32		02 32	03 32				04 32					
—	—	1¼	Farringdon	d						00 26															
—	—	1¾	City Thameslink	d																					
—	—	2	London Blackfriars	d						00 31	01 01	01 02	01 40		02 40	03 40				04 40					
—	0	—	London Bridge	d																					
—	8½	—	Norwood Junction	d																					
—	—	—	East Croydon	a						00 57	01 27	01 28	02 06		03 06	04 06				05 06					
—	10¼	—	East Croydon	d			00 31	00 31		00 58	01 28	01 28	02 07		03 07	04 07		04 58		05 07					
13¼	13¼	—	Purley	d			00 37	00 37			01 34	01 34	02 13		03 13	04 13		05 04		05 13					
15¼	15¼	—	**Coulsdon South**	d			00 41	00 41										05 08							
19	19	—	**Merstham**	d			00 46	00 46										05 13							
20½	20½	—	**Redhill**	a			00 50	00 52		01 11		01 45						05 17							
—	—	—	**Redhill**	d	00 16														05 23				05 35		05 53
—	—	—	**Reigate**	a																			05 39		
—	22¾	—	**Nutfield**	a	00 20														05 27						05 57
—	26¼	—	**Godstone**	a	00 26														05 33						06 03
—	31	—	**Edenbridge**	a	00 32														05 38						06 09
—	36	—	**Penshurst**	a	00 38														05 45						06 15
—	37¾	—	**Leigh (Kent)**	a	00 42														05 48						06 19
—	40¼	—	Tonbridge	a	00 46														05 53						06 23
—	—	—	Tonbridge	d																					
—	—	—	Redhill	a																					
—	—	—	Reigate	d		00 27			00 51												05 37				
—	—	—	Redhill	a		00 31			00 55												05 41				
—	—	—	**Redhill**	d		00 34	00 53	00 53	00 58	01 11		01 46					04 53	05 18			05 47				
21	—	—	**Earlswood (Surrey)**	d																					
22¼	—	—	**Salfords**	d																					
25¼	—	—	**Horley**	d			01 00	00 59			01 52	01 52	02 26		03 26	04 26		05 24		05 26					
26¼	—	—	Gatwick Airport	a		00 42	01 03	01 03	01 06	01 20	01 56	01 56	02 30		03 30	04 30	05 01	05 28		05 31	05 54				
—	—	—	Gatwick Airport	d						01 21	01 58	01 58	02 31		03 31	04 35				05 32		05 56			
29	—	—	Three Bridges	a						01 26	02 03	02 03	02 36		03 36	04 40				05 37		06 00			
—	—	—	Three Bridges	d																		06 01			
30¾	—	—	**Crawley**	d																		06 05			
32	—	—	**Ifield**	d																		06 08			
34½	—	—	**Faygate**	d																					
36¼	—	—	**Littlehaven**	d																		06 14			
38	—	—	Horsham	a																		06 17			

		SN	GW	SN	SN	SN	TL	GW	GW		SN	SN	TL	GW	SN	SN	TL	SN	GW		TL	SN	GW	SN	
		1	1		1	1	1		1		1		1	1	1	1	1				1	1	1		
London Victoria	d	05 32			05 39	05 54					06 09				06 36	06 39						07 06			
Clapham Junction	d	05 42			05 46	06 01					06 16				06 43	06 46						07 13			
East Croydon	a	05 51			05 55	06 10					06 26				06 52	06 56						07 22			
St Pancras International	d						05 45						06 15				06 35				06 45				
Farringdon	d						05 49						06 19				06 39				06 49				
City Thameslink	d						05 51						06 21				06 41				06 51				
London Blackfriars	d						05 54						06 24				06 44				06 54				
London Bridge	d						06 00						06 30				06 51				07 00				
Norwood Junction	d						06 12						06 42				07 02				07 12				
East Croydon	a						06 16						06 46				07 06				07 16				
East Croydon	d	05 52			05 55	06 10	06 16				06 27		06 46		06 52	06 57	07 07				07 16	07 22			
Purley	d	05 56			06 02		06 23				06 33		06 53			07 03									
Coulsdon South	d				06 06		06 27				06 37		06 57			07 07					07 24				
Merstham	d				06 11		06 32				06 43		07 02			07 13					07 29				
Redhill	a	06 05			06 15		06 36				06 47		07 06			07 17	07 20				07 33				
Redhill	d		06 17	06 22	06 24			06 44			06 48	06 52		07 14		07 18		07 23	07 32					07 52	
Reigate	a		06 21		06 28			06 48			06 52			07 18		07 22			07 39						
Nutfield	a			06 26								06 56						07 27						07 56	
Godstone	a			06 32								07 02						07 33						08 02	
Edenbridge	a			06 38								07 08						07 38						08 08	
Penshurst	a			06 44								07 14						07 45						08 14	
Leigh (Kent)	a			06 48								07 18						07 48						08 18	
Tonbridge	a			06 53								07 23						07 53						08 23	
Tonbridge	d																								
Redhill	a																								
Reigate	d								06 32														07 41		
Redhill	a								06 36														07 46		
Redhill	d	06 05					06 37		06 46				07 07				07 21				07 34		07 49		
Earlswood (Surrey)	d	06 08					06 39						07 09								07 36				
Salfords	d	06 11					06 43						07 13								07 40				
Horley	d	06 15					06 46						07 16								07 43				
Gatwick Airport	a	06 17				06 25	06 50		06 54				07 19		07 07		07 28				07 46	07 37	07 57		
Gatwick Airport	d	06 18				06 26	06 51						07 21		07 08						07 47	07 38			
Three Bridges	a	06 23				06 31	06 56						07 26		07 13						07 52	07 42			
Three Bridges	d					06 32	06 57						07 27		07 13						07 53	07 45			
Crawley	d					06 36	07 01						07 31		07 17						07 57	07 49			
Ifield	d					06 38	07 03						07 33								07 59				
Faygate	d					06 42							07 37								08 03				
Littlehaven	d					06 46	07 09						07 41		07 25						08 07				
Horsham	a					06 50	07 13						07 45		07 28						08 11	07 57			

Table T183-F

Mondays to Fridays

16 December to 15 May

London - Redhill / Reigate / Tonbridge / Gatwick Airport - Horsham

		SN		TL	GW	SN		SN	SN		TL	SN	GW	GW	SN			TL	SN	TL	SN	TL	GW	SN	TL
		1		1	1	1			1		1	1	1		1			1		1	1	1	1	1	1
London Victoria	d	07 09				07 36			07 39			08 06			08 09						08 36			08 39	
Clapham Junction	d	07 16				07 43			07 46			08 13			08 16						08 43			08 46	
East Croydon	a	07 27				07 52			07 57			08 22			08 27						08 52			08 57	
St Pancras International	d			07 15							07 45							08 05		08 15		08 25			08 35
Farringdon	d			07 19							07 49							08 09		08 19		08 29			08 39
City Thameslink	d			07 21							07 51							08 11		08 21		08 31			08 41
London Blackfriars	d			07 24							07 54							08 14		08 24		08 34			08 44
London Bridge	d			07 30							08 00							08 21		08 30		08 41			08 51
Norwood Junction	d			07 42							08 12							08 32		08 42					09 02
East Croydon	a			07 46							08 16							08 36		08 46		08 54			09 06
East Croydon	d	07 27		07 46		07 52			07 57		08 16	08 22			08 28			08 37		08 46	08 53	08 55		08 57	09 07
Purley	d	07 33							08 03						08 33			08 44						09 03	09 14
Coulsdon South	d	07 37		07 56					08 07		08 25				08 37					08 56				09 07	
Merstham	d	07 43		08 02					08 13		08 31				08 43					09 01				09 13	
Redhill	a	07 47		08 06					08 17		08 35				08 49			08 53		09 05		09 09		09 17	09 22
Redhill	d		07 54		08 16			08 22		08 24				08 51		08 55			08 56				09 15	09 20	
Reigate	a		07 58		08 20					08 28				08 55		09 00							09 19	09 26	
Nutfield	a							08 26											09 00						
Godstone	a							08 32											09 06						
Edenbridge	a							08 38											09 12						
Penshurst	a							08 44											09 18						
Leigh (Kent)	a							08 48											09 22						
Tonbridge	a							08 53											09 27						
Tonbridge	d																								
Redhill	a																								
Reigate	d												08 32												
Redhill	a												08 38												
Redhill	d	07 57		08 07					08 27		08 36		08 42		08 59			08 53		09 06		09 10			09 23
Earlswood (Surrey)	d	08 00							08 30									08 56							09 25
Salfords	d	08 04							08 34									08 59							09 29
Horley	d	08 08		08 13					08 38		08 42				09 06			09 03		09 12					09 33
Gatwick Airport	a	08 12		08 16		08 07			08 41		08 45	08 37	08 51		09 09			09 05		09 15	09 08	09 19			09 35
Gatwick Airport	d			08 17		08 08					08 46	08 38						09 06		09 16	09 09				09 36
Three Bridges	a			08 22		08 13					08 51	08 43						09 11		09 21	09 14				09 41
Three Bridges	d			08 23		08 14					08 52	08 44								09 22	09 15				
Crawley	d			08 27		08 18					08 56	08 48								09 26	09 19				
Ifield	d			08 30							08 59									09 29					
Faygate	d			08 34							09 03														
Littlehaven	d			08 38							09 07									09 35					
Horsham	a			08 42		08 27					09 11	08 57								09 39	09 27				

		SN		TL	GW	SN	TL	GW	SN	TL	SN	TL		GW	SN	SN	TL	GW	TL	SN	GW	SN		TL	SN
				1		1	1	1	1	1		1		1	1	1	1		1	1	1	1		1	
London Victoria	d					09 06			09 09						09 36	09 39				10 06		10 09			
Clapham Junction	d					09 13			09 16						09 43	09 46				10 13		10 16			
East Croydon	a					09 22			09 26						09 52	09 56				10 22		10 26			
St Pancras International	d			08 45			08 55			09 05		09 15					09 35		09 45					10 05	
Farringdon	d			08 49			08 59			09 09		09 19					09 39		09 49					10 09	
City Thameslink	d			08 51			09 01			09 11		09 21					09 41		09 51					10 11	
London Blackfriars	d			08 54			09 04			09 14		09 24					09 44		09 54					10 14	
London Bridge	d			09 00			09 11			09 21		09 30					09 51		10 00					10 21	
Norwood Junction	d									09 32							10 02							10 32	
East Croydon	a			09 14			09 24			09 36		09 44					10 06		10 14					10 36	
East Croydon	d			09 16		09 23	09 25		09 27	09 37		09 46			09 53	09 57	10 07		10 16	10 23		10 27		10 37	
Purley	d								09 34	09 44						10 04	10 14					10 34		10 44	
Coulsdon South	d			09 23					09 38			09 53				10 08			10 23			10 38			
Merstham	d			09 28					09 44			09 58				10 14			10 28			10 44			
Redhill	a			09 32			09 38		09 48	09 53		10 02				10 18	10 22		10 32			10 48		10 52	
Redhill	d	09 25			09 32				09 50		10 00			10 14		10 19		10 30				10 49			11 00
Reigate	a				09 36				09 55					10 18		10 23		10 34				10 54			
Nutfield	a	09 29									10 04														11 04
Godstone	a	09 35									10 10														11 10
Edenbridge	a	09 41									10 16														11 16
Penshurst	a	09 47									10 22														11 22
Leigh (Kent)	a	09 51									10 26														11 26
Tonbridge	a	09 57									10 31														11 31
Tonbridge	d																								
Redhill	a																								
Reigate	d							09 41													10 38				
Redhill	a							09 45													10 42				
Redhill	d			09 33			09 39	09 48		09 55		10 03					10 25		10 33		10 47			10 55	
Earlswood (Surrey)	d									09 57							10 27							10 57	
Salfords	d									10 01							10 31							11 01	
Horley	d			09 39						10 05		10 09					10 35		10 39					11 05	
Gatwick Airport	a			09 43		09 38	09 47	09 56		10 08		10 13			10 08		10 38		10 43	10 38	10 55			11 08	
Gatwick Airport	d			09 44		09 39						10 14			10 09				10 44	10 39					
Three Bridges	a			09 49		09 44						10 19			10 14				10 49	10 44					
Three Bridges	d			09 50		09 44						10 20			10 14				10 50	10 44					
Crawley	d			09 54		09 48						10 24			10 18				10 54	10 48					
Ifield	d			09 56								10 26							10 56						
Faygate	d																								
Littlehaven	d			10 02								10 32							11 02						
Horsham	a			10 08		09 57						10 38			10 27				11 08	10 57					

Table T183-F

Mondays to Fridays
16 December to 15 May

London - Redhill / Reigate / Tonbridge / Gatwick Airport - Horsham

		TL [1]	GW	SN [1]	SN [1]	TL [1]	GW	TL [1]		SN [1]	GW [1]	SN [1]	TL [1]	SN	TL [1]	GW [1]	SN [1]	SN [1]		TL [1]	GW	TL [1]	SN [1]	GW [1]	SN [1]
London Victoria	d			10 36	10 39					11 06		11 09					11 36	11 39					12 06		12 09
Clapham Junction	d			10 43	10 46					11 13		11 16					11 43	11 46					12 13		12 16
East Croydon	a			10 52	10 56					11 22		11 26					11 52	11 56					12 22		12 26
St Pancras International	d	10 15				10 35		10 45					11 05		11 15					11 35		11 45			
Farringdon	d	10 19				10 39		10 49					11 09		11 19					11 39		11 49			
City Thameslink	d	10 21				10 41		10 51					11 11		11 21					11 41		11 51			
London Blackfriars	d	10 24				10 44		10 54					11 14		11 24					11 44		11 54			
London Bridge	d	10 30				10 51		11 00					11 21		11 30					11 51		12 00			
Norwood Junction	d					11 02							11 32							12 02					
East Croydon	a	10 44				11 06		11 14					11 36		11 44					12 06		12 14			
East Croydon	d	10 46		10 53	10 57	11 07		11 16		11 23		11 27	11 37		11 46		11 53	11 57		12 07		12 16	12 23		12 27
Purley	d				11 04	11 14						11 34	11 44					12 04		12 14					12 34
Coulsdon South	d	10 53			11 08			11 23				11 38			11 53			12 08				12 23			12 38
Merstham	d	10 58			11 14			11 28				11 44			11 58			12 14				12 28			12 44
Redhill	a	11 02			11 18	11 22		11 32				11 48	11 52		12 02			12 18		12 22		12 32			12 48
Redhill	d		11 15		11 19		11 30					11 49		12 00		12 14		12 20			12 30				12 49
Reigate	a		11 19		11 23		11 38					11 53				12 18		12 24			12 34				12 53
Nutfield	a													12 04											
Godstone	a													12 10											
Edenbridge	a													12 16											
Penshurst	a													12 22											
Leigh (Kent)	a													12 26											
Tonbridge	a													12 31											
Tonbridge	d																								
Redhill	a																								
Reigate	d										11 35													12 37	
Redhill	a										11 40													12 41	
Redhill	d	11 03				11 25		11 33			11 43		11 55		12 03					12 25		12 33		12 46	
Earlswood (Surrey)	d					11 27							11 57							12 27					
Salfords	d					11 31							12 01							12 31					
Horley	d	11 09				11 35		11 39					12 05		12 09					12 35		12 39			
Gatwick Airport	a	11 12		11 08		11 38		11 43		11 38	11 50		12 08		12 13		12 08			12 38		12 43	12 38	12 54	
Gatwick Airport	d	11 14		11 09				11 44		11 39					12 14		12 09					12 44	12 39		
Three Bridges	a	11 19		11 14				11 49		11 44					12 19		12 14					12 49	12 44		
Three Bridges	d	11 20		11 14				11 50		11 44					12 20		12 14					12 50	12 44		
Crawley	d	11 24		11 18				11 54		11 48					12 24		12 18					12 54	12 48		
Ifield	d	11 26						11 56							12 26							12 56			
Faygate	d							12 00																	
Littlehaven	d	11 32						12 04							12 32							13 02			
Horsham	a	11 38		11 27				12 08		11 57					12 38		12 27					13 08	12 57		

		TL [1]	SN	TL [1]		GW [1]	SN [1]	SN [1]	TL [1]	GW	TL [1]	SN [1]	GW [1]	SN [1]		TL [1]	SN	TL [1]	GW [1]	SN [1]	SN [1]	TL [1]	GW	TL [1]	
London Victoria	d						12 36	12 39				13 06		13 09						13 36	13 39				
Clapham Junction	d						12 43	12 46				13 13		13 16						13 43	13 46				
East Croydon	a						12 52	12 56				13 22		13 26						13 52	13 56				
St Pancras International	d	12 05		12 15					12 35		12 45					13 05		13 15				13 35		13 45	
Farringdon	d	12 09		12 19					12 39		12 49					13 09		13 19				13 39		13 49	
City Thameslink	d	12 11		12 21					12 41		12 51					13 11		13 21				13 41		13 51	
London Blackfriars	d	12 14		12 24					12 44		12 54					13 14		13 24				13 44		13 54	
London Bridge	d	12 21		12 30					12 51		13 00					13 21		13 30				13 51		14 00	
Norwood Junction	d	12 32							13 02							13 32						14 02			
East Croydon	a	12 36		12 44					13 06		13 14					13 36		13 44				14 06		14 14	
East Croydon	d	12 37		12 46			12 53	12 57	13 07		13 16	13 23		13 27		13 37		13 46		13 53	13 57	14 07		14 16	
Purley	d	12 44						13 04	13 14					13 34		13 44					14 04	14 14			
Coulsdon South	d			12 53				13 08			13 23			13 38				13 53			14 08			14 23	
Merstham	d			12 58				13 14			13 28			13 44				13 58			14 14			14 28	
Redhill	a	12 52		13 02				13 18	13 22		13 32			13 48		13 52		14 02			14 18	14 22		14 32	
Redhill	d		13 00			13 14		13 19		13 30				13 49			14 00		14 14		14 19		14 30		
Reigate	a					13 18		13 23		13 34				13 53					14 18		14 23		14 34		
Nutfield	a		13 04														14 04								
Godstone	a		13 10														14 10								
Edenbridge	a		13 16														14 16								
Penshurst	a		13 22														14 22								
Leigh (Kent)	a		13 26														14 26								
Tonbridge	a		13 31														14 31								
Tonbridge	d																								
Redhill	a																								
Reigate	d												13 37												
Redhill	a												13 41												
Redhill	d	12 55		13 03					13 25		13 33		13 46			13 55		14 03				14 25		14 33	
Earlswood (Surrey)	d	12 57							13 27							13 57						14 27			
Salfords	d	13 01							13 31							14 01						14 31			
Horley	d	13 05		13 09					13 35		13 39					14 05		14 09				14 35		14 39	
Gatwick Airport	a	13 08		13 13			13 08		13 38		13 43	13 38	13 54			14 08		14 13		14 08		14 38		14 43	
Gatwick Airport	d			13 14			13 09				13 44	13 39						14 14		14 09				14 44	
Three Bridges	a			13 19			13 14				13 49	13 44						14 19		14 14				14 49	
Three Bridges	d			13 20			13 14				13 50	13 44						14 20		14 14				14 50	
Crawley	d			13 24			13 18				13 54	13 48						14 24		14 18				14 54	
Ifield	d			13 26							13 56							14 26						14 56	
Faygate	d																								
Littlehaven	d			13 32							14 02							14 32						15 02	
Horsham	a			13 38			13 27				14 08	13 57						14 38		14 27				15 08	

Table T183-F

Mondays to Fridays
16 December to 15 May

London - Redhill / Reigate / Tonbridge / Gatwick Airport - Horsham

		SN [1]	GW [1]	SN [1]	TL [1]	SN	TL [1]	GW [1]	SN [1]	SN [1]		TL [1]	GW	SN	TL [1]	SN [1]	GW [1]	SN [1]	TL [1]	SN		TL [1]	GW [1]	SN [1]	SN [1]
London Victoria	d	14 06		14 09					14 36	14 39						15 06		15 09						15 36	15 39
Clapham Junction	d	14 13		14 16					14 43	14 46						15 13		15 16						15 43	15 46
East Croydon	a	14 22		14 26					14 53	14 56						15 22		15 26						15 52	15 56
St Pancras International	d				14 05		14 15					14 35			14 45				15 05			15 15			
Farringdon	d				14 09		14 19					14 39			14 49				15 09			15 19			
City Thameslink	d				14 11		14 21					14 41			14 51				15 11			15 21			
London Blackfriars	d				14 14		14 24					14 44			14 54				15 14			15 24			
London Bridge	d				14 21		14 30					14 51			15 00				15 21			15 30			
Norwood Junction	d				14 32							15 02							15 32						
East Croydon	a				14 36		14 44					15 06			15 14				15 36			15 44			
East Croydon	d	14 23		14 27	14 37		14 46		14 53	14 57		15 07			15 16	15 23		15 27	15 37			15 46		15 53	15 57
Purley	d			14 34	14 44					15 04		15 14						15 36	15 44						16 04
Coulsdon South	d			14 38			14 53			15 08					15 23			15 40				15 53			16 08
Merstham	d			14 44			14 58			15 14					15 28			15 45				15 58			16 14
Redhill	a			14 48	14 52		15 02			15 18		15 22			15 32			15 49	15 52			16 02			16 18
Redhill	d			14 49		15 00		15 14		15 19			15 28	15 30				15 50		16 00			16 14		16 22
Reigate	a			14 53				15 18		15 23			15 33					15 54					16 18		16 26
Nutfield	a					15 04								15 34						16 04					
Godstone	a					15 10								15 40						16 10					
Edenbridge	a					15 16								15 46						16 16					
Penshurst	a					15 22								15 52						16 22					
Leigh (Kent)	a					15 26								15 56						16 26					
Tonbridge	a					15 31								16 01						16 31					
Tonbridge	d																								
Redhill	a																								
Reigate	d		14 36														15 36								
Redhill	a		14 40														15 41								
Redhill	d		14 46		14 55		15 03					15 25			15 33		15 46		15 55			16 03			
Earlswood (Surrey)	d				14 57							15 27							15 57						
Salfords	d				15 01							15 31							16 01						
Horley	d				15 05		15 09					15 35			15 39				16 05			16 09			
Gatwick Airport	a	14 38	14 54		15 08		15 13		15 08			15 38			15 43	15 38	15 54		16 08			16 13		16 08	
Gatwick Airport	d	14 39					15 14		15 09						15 44	15 39						16 14		16 09	
Three Bridges	a	14 44					15 19		15 14						15 49	15 44						16 19		16 14	
Three Bridges	d	14 44					15 20		15 14						15 50	15 44						16 20		16 14	
Crawley	d	14 48					15 24		15 18						15 54	15 48						16 24		16 18	
Ifield	d						15 26								15 56							16 26			
Faygate	d																								
Littlehaven	d						15 32								16 02							16 32			
Horsham	a	14 57					15 38		15 27						16 08	15 57						16 38		16 27	

		TL [1]	SN	GW	TL [1]	SN [1]		GW [1]	SN [1]		TL [1]	SN	TL [1]	GW [1]	SN [1]	SN [1]			SN [1]	TL [1]	SN	TL [1]	GW	SN [1]	SN [1]
London Victoria	d					16 06			16 09						16 36	16 39			16 45						17 06
Clapham Junction	d					16 13			16 16						16 43	16 46			16 52						17 13
East Croydon	a					16 23			16 26						16 52	16 56			17 01						17 22
St Pancras International	d	15 35			15 45						16 05		16 15							16 35		16 45			
Farringdon	d	15 39			15 49						16 09		16 19							16 39		16 49			
City Thameslink	d	15 41			15 51						16 11		16 21							16 41		16 51			
London Blackfriars	d	15 44			15 54						16 14		16 24							16 44		16 54			
London Bridge	d	15 51			16 00						16 21		16 30							16 51		17 00		17 02	
Norwood Junction	d	16 02									16 32									17 02					
East Croydon	a	16 06			16 14						16 36		16 44							17 06		17 14		17 16	
East Croydon	d	16 07			16 16	16 23			16 27		16 37		16 46		16 53	16 57			17 02	17 07		17 16		17 16	17 23
Purley	d	16 14							16 34		16 44					17 04				17 14					
Coulsdon South	d				16 23				16 38		16 48		16 56			17 08				17 18		17 25			
Merstham	d				16 28				16 44		16 53		17 02			17 14				17 23		17 30			
Redhill	a	16 23			16 32				16 48		16 57		17 06			17 18				17 27		17 34			
Redhill	d		16 30	16 30					16 52			17 00		17 14		17 22					17 30		17 43		
Reigate	a			16 34					16 56					17 19		17 26							17 47		
Nutfield	a		16 34									17 04									17 34				
Godstone	a		16 40									17 10									17 40				
Edenbridge	a		16 46									17 16									17 46				
Penshurst	a		16 52									17 22									17 52				
Leigh (Kent)	a		16 56									17 26									17 56				
Tonbridge	a		17 01									17 31									18 01				
Tonbridge	d																								
Redhill	a																								
Reigate	d							16 38																	
Redhill	a							16 42																	
Redhill	d	16 25			16 33			16 46		16 54	16 58		17 06				17 24			17 28		17 36			
Earlswood (Surrey)	d	16 27								16 57	17 00						17 27			17 30					
Salfords	d	16 31								17 00	17 04						17 30			17 34					
Horley	d	16 35			16 39					17 04	17 08						17 34		17 16	17 38					
Gatwick Airport	a	16 38			16 43	16 38		16 53		17 07	17 11		17 15		17 08		17 39		17 19	17 41		17 45			17 38
Gatwick Airport	d				16 44	16 39							17 16		17 09							17 46			17 39
Three Bridges	a				16 49	16 44							17 21		17 14							17 51		17 35	17 44
Three Bridges	d				16 50	16 44							17 25		17 14							17 52		17 35	17 44
Crawley	d				16 54	16 48							17 29		17 18							17 56		17 39	17 48
Ifield	d				16 56								17 31									17 59			17 51
Faygate	d												17 35									18 03			
Littlehaven	d				17 02								17 40									18 07		17 47	17 58
Horsham	a				17 10	16 57							17 45		17 27							18 12		17 51	18 01

Table T183-F

Mondays to Fridays

16 December to 15 May

London - Redhill / Reigate / Tonbridge / Gatwick Airport - Horsham

		GW	SN			SN	TL	SN	TL	GW	SN	SN		SN		TL	SN	TL	GW	SN	SN	GW	SN		
		1	1			1	1		1	1	1	1		1		1		1		1	1	1	1		
London Victoria	d		17 09			17 15					17 36	17 39		17 45							18 06		18 09		
Clapham Junction	d		17 16			17 22					17 43	17 46		17 52							18 13		18 16		
East Croydon	a		17 26			17 31					17 52	17 56		18 01							18 22		18 27		
St Pancras International	d						17 05		17 15							17 35		17 45							
Farringdon	d						17 09		17 19							17 39		17 49							
City Thameslink	d						17 11		17 21							17 41		17 51							
London Blackfriars	d						17 14		17 24							17 44		17 54							
London Bridge	d						17 21		17 30							17 51		18 00		18 03					
Norwood Junction	d						17 32									18 02									
East Croydon	a						17 36		17 45							18 06		18 14		18 16					
East Croydon	d		17 27			17 32	17 37		17 46		17 53	17 57		18 02		18 07		18 16		18 17	18 23		18 27		
Purley	d						17 44									18 14									
Coulsdon South	d		17 35				17 48		17 55			18 05				18 18		18 25					18 35		
Merstham	d		17 41				17 53		18 00			18 11				18 23		18 30					18 41		
Redhill	a		17 45				17 57		18 04			18 15				18 27		18 34					18 45		
Redhill	d		17 51					18 00		18 14		18 21					18 30		18 43				18 51		
Reigate	a		17 55							18 18		18 25							18 47				18 55		
Nutfield	a							18 04									18 34								
Godstone	a							18 10									18 40								
Edenbridge	a							18 16									18 46								
Penshurst	a							18 22																	
Leigh (Kent)	a							18 26																	
Tonbridge	a							18 31									18 55								
Tonbridge	d																								
Redhill	a																								
Reigate	d	17 36																				18 35			
Redhill	a	17 40																				18 39			
Redhill	d	17 44		17 54			17 58		18 06				18 24			18 28		18 36				18 43		18 54	
Earlswood (Surrey)	d			17 56			18 00						18 26			18 30								18 56	
Salfords	d			18 00			18 04						18 30			18 34								19 00	
Horley	d			18 04		17 46	18 08						18 34	18 16		18 38								19 04	
Gatwick Airport	a	17 51		18 07		17 49	18 11		18 15		18 08		18 37	18 19		18 41		18 45			18 38	18 50		19 07	
Gatwick Airport	d			18 08					18 16		18 09		18 38					18 46			18 39			19 08	
Three Bridges	a			18 16					18 21		18 14		18 43					18 51		18 35	18 44			19 16	
Three Bridges	d								18 22		18 14							18 52		18 35	18 44				
Crawley	d								18 26		18 18							18 56		18 39	18 48				
Ifield	d								18 29									18 59			18 51				
Faygate	d								18 33									19 03							
Littlehaven	d								18 37									19 07		18 47	18 58				
Horsham	a								18 42		18 27							19 12		18 51	19 01				

		SN	TL	SN	TL	GW	SN	SN		SN		TL	SN	TL	SN	GW	SN		TL	SN		TL	GW	SN	SN
		1	1		1	1	1	1		1		1		1	1	1	1		1			1	1	1	1
London Victoria	d	18 15					18 36	18 39		18 45					19 06		19 09							19 36	19 39
Clapham Junction	d	18 22					18 43	18 46		18 52					19 13		19 16							19 43	19 46
East Croydon	a	18 31					18 52	18 57		19 01					19 22		19 27							19 52	19 57
St Pancras International	d		18 05		18 15							18 35		18 45					19 05			19 15			
Farringdon	d		18 09		18 19							18 39		18 49					19 09			19 19			
City Thameslink	d		18 11		18 21							18 41		18 51					19 11			19 21			
London Blackfriars	d		18 14		18 24							18 44		18 54					19 14			19 24			
London Bridge	d		18 21		18 30							18 51		19 00					19 21			19 30			
Norwood Junction	d		18 32									19 02							19 32						
East Croydon	a		18 36		18 44							19 06		19 14					19 36			19 44			
East Croydon	d	18 32	18 37		18 46		18 53	18 57		19 02		19 07		19 16	19 23		19 27		19 37			19 46		19 53	19 58
Purley	d		18 44									19 14					19 33		19 44						20 04
Coulsdon South	d		18 48		18 55			19 06				19 18		19 23			19 37		19 48			19 53			20 08
Merstham	d		18 53		19 00			19 12				19 23		19 28			19 43		19 53			19 58			20 14
Redhill	a		18 57		19 04			19 16				19 27		19 32			19 47		19 57			20 02			20 18
Redhill	d			19 00		19 14		19 21					19 30				19 51			20 00			20 12		20 19
Reigate	a					19 18		19 25									19 55						20 16		20 23
Nutfield	a			19 04									19 34							20 04					
Godstone	a			19 10									19 40							20 10					
Edenbridge	a			19 16									19 46							20 16					
Penshurst	a			19 22									19 52							20 22					
Leigh (Kent)	a			19 26									19 56							20 26					
Tonbridge	a			19 31									20 04							20 31					
Tonbridge	d																								
Redhill	a																								
Reigate	d															19 36									
Redhill	a															19 40									
Redhill	d		18 58		19 06				19 24			19 28		19 36		19 42		19 54	19 58			20 05			
Earlswood (Surrey)	d		19 00						19 26			19 30						19 56	20 00						
Salfords	d		19 04						19 30			19 34						20 00	20 04						
Horley	d	18 46	19 08						19 34	19 17		19 38						20 04	20 08			20 12			
Gatwick Airport	a	18 49	19 11		19 15		19 08		19 37	19 19		19 41		19 45	19 38	19 51		20 07	20 11			20 14		20 08	
Gatwick Airport	d				19 16		19 09		19 38					19 46	19 39			20 08				20 16		20 09	
Three Bridges	a				19 21		19 14		19 46					19 51	19 44			20 16				20 21		20 14	
Three Bridges	d				19 22		19 14							19 52	19 44							20 22		20 14	
Crawley	d				19 26		19 18							19 56	19 48							20 26		20 18	
Ifield	d				19 29									19 59								20 29			
Faygate	d				19 33									20 03											
Littlehaven	d				19 37									20 07								20 35			
Horsham	a				19 42		19 27							20 12	19 57							20 39		20 27	

Table T183-F

Mondays to Fridays

16 December to 15 May

London - Redhill / Reigate / Tonbridge / Gatwick Airport - Horsham

		TL	GW	TL	SN	GW		SN	TL	SN	TL	TL	GW	SN	SN	TL		TL	GW	SN	GW	SN	TL	SN	TL
		1		1	1	1		1	1		1	1	1	1	1	1		1		1	1	1	1		1
London Victoria	d				20 06			20 09						20 36	20 39					21 06		21 09			
Clapham Junction	d				20 13			20 16						20 43	20 46					21 13		21 16			
East Croydon	a				20 22			20 26						20 52	20 57					21 24		21 27			
St Pancras International	d	19 35		19 45					20 05			20 15				20 35		20 45					21 05		21 15
Farringdon	d	19 39		19 49					20 09			20 19				20 39		20 49					21 09		21 19
City Thameslink	d	19 41		19 51					20 11			20 21				20 41		20 51					21 11		21 21
London Blackfriars	d	19 44		19 54					20 14			20 24				20 44		20 54					21 14		21 24
London Bridge	d	19 51		20 00					20 21		20 22	20 30				20 51		21 00					21 21		21 30
Norwood Junction	d	20 02							20 32							21 02							21 32		
East Croydon	a	20 06		20 14					20 36		20 38	20 44				21 06		21 14					21 36		21 44
East Croydon	d	20 07		20 16	20 23			20 27	20 37		20 38	20 46		20 53	20 58	21 07		21 16		21 25		21 28	21 37		21 46
Purley	d	20 16						20 34	20 44						21 04	21 14						21 34	21 44		
Coulsdon South	d			20 23				20 38				20 53			21 08			21 23				21 38			21 53
Merstham	d			20 28				20 44				20 58			21 14			21 28				21 44			21 58
Redhill	a	20 24		20 32				20 48	20 52			21 02			21 18	21 22		21 32				21 48	21 52		22 02
Redhill	d		20 32					20 49		21 00			21 14		21 19				21 35			21 49		22 00	
Reigate	a		20 36					20 53					21 18		21 23				21 39			21 53			
Nutfield	a									21 04														22 04	
Godstone	a									21 10														22 10	
Edenbridge	a									21 16														22 16	
Penshurst	a									21 22														22 22	
Leigh (Kent)	a									21 26														22 26	
Tonbridge	a									21 31														22 31	
Tonbridge	d																								
Redhill	a																								
Reigate	d					20 37															21 38				
Redhill	a					20 42															21 42				
Redhill	d	20 25		20 33		20 46			20 55			21 03				21 25		21 33			21 46		21 55		22 03
Earlswood (Surrey)	d	20 27							20 57							21 27							21 57		
Salfords	d	20 31							21 01							21 31							22 01		
Horley	d	20 35		20 39					21 05			21 09				21 35		21 39					22 05		22 09
Gatwick Airport	a	20 38		20 43	20 38	20 55			21 08		20 53	21 13		21 08		21 38		21 43		21 39	21 54		22 08		22 13
Gatwick Airport	d			20 44	20 39						20 54	21 14		21 09				21 44		21 40					22 14
Three Bridges	a			20 49	20 44						20 59	21 19		21 14				21 49		21 45					22 19
Three Bridges	d			20 50	20 44						21 00	21 20		21 14				21 50		21 45					22 20
Crawley	d			20 54	20 48						21 04	21 24		21 18				21 54		21 49					22 24
Ifield	d			20 56								21 26						21 56							22 26
Faygate	d																								
Littlehaven	d			21 02								21 32						22 02							22 32
Horsham	a			21 08	20 57						21 13	21 38		21 27				22 08		21 58					22 38

		GW		SN	SN	TL	TL	SN	GW	SN	TL	SN		TL	SN	SN	TL	GW	TL	SN	SN	TL		TL	GW
		1		1	1	1	1	1	1	1	1			1	1	1	1	1	1	1	1	1		1	1
London Victoria	d			21 36	21 39			22 06		22 09					22 36	22 39				23 06	23 09				
Clapham Junction	d			21 43	21 46			22 13		22 16					22 43	22 46				23 13	23 16				
East Croydon	a			21 52	21 57			22 22		22 26					22 52	22 56				23 22	23 26				
St Pancras International	d					21 35	21 45				22 05			22 15			22 35		22 45			23 05		23 15	
Farringdon	d					21 39	21 49				22 09			22 19			22 39		22 49			23 10		23 19	
City Thameslink	d					21 41	21 51				22 11			22 21			22 41		22 51						
London Blackfriars	d					21 44	21 54				22 14			22 24			22 44		22 54			23 14		23 24	
London Bridge	d					21 51	22 00				22 21			22 30			22 51		23 00			23 21		23 30	
Norwood Junction	d					22 02					22 32						23 02					23 32			
East Croydon	a					22 06	22 14				22 36			22 44			23 06		23 15			23 36		23 44	
East Croydon	d			21 53	21 57	22 07	22 16	22 23		22 27	22 37			22 46	22 53	22 57	23 07		23 16	23 23	23 27	23 37		23 46	
Purley	d				22 04	22 14				22 34	22 44					23 04	23 14				23 33	23 43			
Coulsdon South	d				22 08		22 23			22 38				22 53		23 08			23 23		23 37				
Merstham	d				22 14		22 28			22 44				22 58		23 14			23 28		23 43				
Redhill	a				22 18	22 22	22 32			22 48	22 52			23 02		23 18	23 22		23 32		23 47	23 51		23 59	
Redhill	d	22 13			22 19					22 49		23 00				23 19		23 32			23 48				
Reigate	a	22 17			22 23					22 53						23 23		23 36			23 52				
Nutfield	a											23 04													
Godstone	a											23 10													
Edenbridge	a											23 16													
Penshurst	a											23 22													
Leigh (Kent)	a											23 26													
Tonbridge	a											23 31													
Tonbridge	d																								
Redhill	a																								
Reigate	d								22 36																23 56
Redhill	a								22 40																00 01
Redhill	d					22 25	22 33		22 43		22 55			23 03			23 25		23 33			23 52		23 59	00 05
Earlswood (Surrey)	d					22 27					22 57						23 27							00 02	
Salfords	d					22 31					23 01						23 31							00 05	
Horley	d					22 35	22 39				23 05			23 09			23 35		23 39					00 09	
Gatwick Airport	a			22 08		22 38	22 43	22 38	22 52		23 08			23 12	23 08		23 37		23 41	23 38		00 01		00 12	00 14
Gatwick Airport	d			22 09			22 44	22 39						23 14	23 09		23 38		23 42	23 39				00 14	
Three Bridges	a			22 14			22 49	22 44						23 19	23 14		23 43		23 47	23 44				00 19	
Three Bridges	d			22 14			22 50	22 44						23 20	23 14				23 49	23 44				00 20	
Crawley	d			22 18			22 54	22 48						23 24	23 18				23 53	23 48				00 24	
Ifield	d						22 56							23 26					23 56					00 26	
Faygate	d																								
Littlehaven	d						23 02							23 32					00 02					00 32	
Horsham	a			22 27			23 08	22 57						23 38	23 27				00 06	23 57				00 36	

Table T183-F

Mondays to Fridays

16 December to 15 May

London - Redhill / Reigate / Tonbridge / Gatwick Airport - Horsham

		TL 1	SN 1
London Victoria	d		23 36
Clapham Junction	d		23 43
East Croydon	a		23 58
St Pancras International	d	23 22	
Farringdon	d	23 27	
City Thameslink	d		
London Blackfriars	d	23 31	
London Bridge	d	23 37	
Norwood Junction	d		
East Croydon	a	23 50	
East Croydon	d	23 51	23 59
Purley	d		00 05
Coulsdon South	d	23 59	00 09
Merstham	d	00 04	00 14
Redhill	a	00 09	00 18
Redhill	d		
Reigate	a		
Nutfield	a		
Godstone	a		
Edenbridge	a		
Penshurst	a		
Leigh (Kent)	a		
Tonbridge	a		
Tonbridge	d		
Redhill	a		
Reigate	d		
Redhill	a		
Redhill	d	00 10	00 19
Earlswood (Surrey)	d		
Salfords	d		
Horley	d		00 25
Gatwick Airport	a	00 18	00 29
Gatwick Airport	d	00 19	00 31
Three Bridges	a	00 24	00 36
Three Bridges	d		00 36
Crawley	d		00 40
Ifield	d		
Faygate	d		
Littlehaven	d		
Horsham	a		00 49

Saturdays

21 December to 16 May

		SN A	SN 1 A	GW 1	TL 1	TL 1	SN 1	TL 1	SN 1	TL 1	SN 1	TL 1	SN 1	GW 1	GW 1	TL 1	GW 1	SN 1	SN 1	GW 1	SN 1	SN	GW 1
London Victoria	d		00 08				01 10		02 10		03 10		04 10						05 08		05 39		
Clapham Junction	d		00 15				01 17		02 17		03 17		04 17						05 16		05 46		
East Croydon	a		00 30				01 32		02 32		03 32		04 31						05 31		05 56		
St Pancras International	d				00 21	00 52		01 32		02 32		03 32				04 32							
Farringdon	d				00 26																		
City Thameslink	d																						
London Blackfriars	d				00 31	01 02		01 40		02 40		03 40				04 40							
London Bridge	d																						
Norwood Junction	d																						
East Croydon	a				00 57	01 28		02 06		03 06		04 06				05 06							
East Croydon	d		00 31		00 58	01 28	01 33	02 07	02 32	03 07	03 32	04 07	04 31			05 07			05 31		05 57		
Purley	d		00 37			01 34	01 39	02 13	02 38	03 13	03 38	04 13	04 37			05 13			05 37		06 04		
Coulsdon South	d		00 41				01s43												05 41		06 08		
Merstham	d		00 46				01s48												05 46		06 14		
Redhill	a		00 50		01 11	01 45	01s54						04 48						05 50		06 18		
Redhill	d	00 16												05 42						06 12	06 19	06 25	06 30
Reigate	a													05 46						06 16	06 23		06 34
Nutfield	a	00 20																				06 29	
Godstone	a	00 26																				06 35	
Edenbridge	a	00 32																				06 41	
Penshurst	a	00 38																				06 47	
Leigh (Kent)	a	00 42																				06 51	
Tonbridge	a	00 46																				06 55	
Tonbridge	d																						
Redhill	a																						
Reigate	d			00 51													05 35						
Redhill	a			00 55													05 39						
Redhill	d		00 53	00 58	01 11	01 46							04 49		05 08		05 44		05 51				
Earlswood (Surrey)	d																						
Salfords	d																						
Horley	d		01 00			01 52	02 02	02 26	02 51	03 26	03 51	04 26	04 55			05 28			05 57				
Gatwick Airport	a		01 03	01 06	01 20	01 56	02 06	02 30	02 55	03 30	03 55	04 30	04 59		05 16	05 31	05 51		06 00				
Gatwick Airport	d				01 21	01 58	02 13	02 31	02 56	03 31	03 56	04 35	05 00			05 32		05 56	06 01				
Three Bridges	a				01 26	02 03	02 18	02 36	03 01	03 36	04 01	04 40	05 05			05 36		06 02	06 06				
Three Bridges	d																	06 02					
Crawley	d																	06 06					
Ifield	d																	06 09					
Faygate	d																						
Littlehaven	d																	06 15					
Horsham	a																	06 18					

A not 16 May

Table T183-F

Saturdays

21 December to 16 May

London - Redhill / Reigate / Tonbridge / Gatwick Airport - Horsham

		TL 1	SN 1	GW 1	SN 1	SN	TL 1	GW 1	SN 1	SN 1	GW 1	TL 1	SN 1	GW 1	SN 1	TL 1	SN	TL 1	GW 1	SN 1	SN 1	TL 1	GW 1
London Victoria	d		06 06		06 09				06 36	06 39			07 06		07 09					07 36	07 39		
Clapham Junction	d		06 13		06 16				06 43	06 46			07 13		07 16					07 43	07 46		
East Croydon	a		06 22		06 26				06 52	06 56			07 22		07 26					07 52	07 56		
St Pancras International	d	05 45					06 15					06 45				07 05		07 15				07 35	
Farringdon	d	05 49					06 19					06 49				07 09		07 19				07 39	
City Thameslink	d																						
London Blackfriars	d	05 54					06 24					06 54				07 14		07 24				07 44	
London Bridge	d	06 00					06 30					07 00				07 21		07 30				07 51	
Norwood Junction	d															07 32						08 02	
East Croydon	a	06 14					06 44					07 14				07 36		07 44				08 06	
East Croydon	d	06 16	06 23		06 27		06 46		06 53	06 57		07 16	07 23		07 27	07 37		07 46		07 53	07 57	08 07	
Purley	d	06 23			06 34					07 04					07 34	07 44					08 04	08 14	
Coulsdon South	d	06 27			06 38		06 53			07 08		07 23			07 38			07 53			08 08		
Merstham	d	06 32			06 44		06 58			07 14		07 28			07 44			07 58			08 14		
Redhill	a	06 36			06 48		07 02			07 18		07 32			07 48	07 52		08 02			08 18	08 22	
Redhill	d				06 49	07 00		07 14		07 19	07 30				07 49		08 00		08 14		08 19		08 30
Reigate	a				06 53			07 18		07 23	07 34				07 53				08 18		08 23		08 34
Nutfield	a					07 04											08 04						
Godstone	a					07 10											08 10						
Edenbridge	a					07 16											08 16						
Penshurst	a					07 22											08 22						
Leigh (Kent)	a					07 26											08 26						
Tonbridge	a					07 34											08 31						
Tonbridge	d																						
Redhill	a																						
Reigate	d			06 36										07 35									
Redhill	a			06 40										07 39									
Redhill	d	06 37		06 44			07 03					07 33		07 42		07 55		08 03				08 25	
Earlswood (Surrey)	d	06 39														07 57						08 27	
Salfords	d	06 43														08 01						08 31	
Horley	d	06 46					07 09					07 39				08 05		08 09				08 35	
Gatwick Airport	a	06 50	06 38	06 54			07 12		07 08			07 42	07 38	07 50		08 08		08 12		08 08		08 38	
Gatwick Airport	d	06 51	06 39				07 14		07 09			07 44	07 39					08 14		08 09			
Three Bridges	a	06 56	06 44				07 19		07 14			07 49	07 44					08 19		08 14			
Three Bridges	d	06 58	06 44				07 20		07 14			07 50	07 44					08 20		08 14			
Crawley	d	07 02	06 48				07 24		07 18			07 54	07 48					08 24		08 18			
Ifield	d	07 05					07 26					07 56						08 26					
Faygate	d																						
Littlehaven	d	07 11					07 32					08 02						08 32					
Horsham	a	07 14	06 57				07 38		07 27			08 08	07 57					08 38		08 27			

		TL 1	SN 1	GW 1	SN 1	TL 1	SN	TL 1	GW 1	SN 1	SN 1	TL 1	GW 1	TL 1	SN 1	GW 1	SN 1	TL 1	SN	TL 1	GW 1	SN 1
London Victoria	d		08 06		08 09					08 36	08 39				09 06		09 09					09 36
Clapham Junction	d		08 13		08 16					08 43	08 46				09 13		09 16					09 43
East Croydon	a		08 22		08 26					08 52	08 56				09 22		09 26					09 52
St Pancras International	d	07 45				08 05		08 15				08 35		08 45				09 05		09 15		
Farringdon	d	07 49				08 09		08 19				08 39		08 49				09 09		09 19		
City Thameslink	d																	09 11		09 21		
London Blackfriars	d	07 54				08 14		08 24				08 44		08 54				09 14		09 24		
London Bridge	d	08 00				08 21		08 30				08 51		09 00				09 21		09 30		
Norwood Junction	d					08 32						09 02						09 32				
East Croydon	a	08 14				08 36		08 44				09 06		09 14				09 36		09 44		
East Croydon	d	08 16	08 23		08 27	08 37		08 46		08 53	08 57	09 07		09 16	09 23		09 27	09 37		09 46		09 53
Purley	d				08 34	08 44					09 04	09 14					09 34	09 44				
Coulsdon South	d	08 23			08 38			08 53			09 08			09 23			09 38			09 53		
Merstham	d	08 28			08 44			08 58			09 14			09 28			09 44			09 58		
Redhill	a	08 32			08 48	08 52		09 02			09 18	09 22		09 32			09 48	09 52		10 02		
Redhill	d				08 49		09 00		09 14		09 19		09 30				09 49		10 00		10 14	
Reigate	a				08 53				09 18		09 23		09 34				09 53				10 18	
Nutfield	a						09 04												10 04			
Godstone	a						09 10												10 10			
Edenbridge	a						09 16												10 16			
Penshurst	a						09 22												10 22			
Leigh (Kent)	a						09 26												10 26			
Tonbridge	a						09 31												10 31			
Tonbridge	d																					
Redhill	a																					
Reigate	d			08 36												09 36						
Redhill	a			08 40												09 40						
Redhill	d	08 33		08 44		08 55		09 03				09 25		09 33		09 44		09 55		10 03		
Earlswood (Surrey)	d					08 57						09 27						09 57				
Salfords	d					09 01						09 31						10 01				
Horley	d	08 39				09 05		09 09				09 35		09 39				10 05		10 09		
Gatwick Airport	a	08 42	08 38	08 51		09 08		09 12		09 08		09 38		09 42	09 38	09 51		10 08		10 12		10 08
Gatwick Airport	d	08 44	08 39					09 14		09 09				09 44	09 39					10 14		10 09
Three Bridges	a	08 49	08 44					09 19		09 14				09 49	09 44					10 19		10 14
Three Bridges	d	08 50	08 44					09 20		09 14				09 50	09 44					10 20		10 14
Crawley	d	08 54	08 48					09 24		09 18				09 54	09 48					10 24		10 18
Ifield	d	08 56						09 26						09 56						10 26		
Faygate	d																					
Littlehaven	d	09 02						09 32						10 02						10 32		
Horsham	a	09 08	08 57					09 38		09 27				10 08	09 57					10 38		10 27

Table T183-F

Saturdays

21 December to 16 May

London - Redhill / Reigate / Tonbridge / Gatwick Airport - Horsham

		SN 1	TL 1	GW 1	TL 1	SN 1	GW 1	SN 1		TL 1	SN	TL 1	GW 1	SN 1	SN 1	TL 1	GW 1	TL 1		SN 1	GW 1	SN 1	TL 1	SN	TL 1
London Victoria	d	09 39				10 06		10 09						10 36	10 39					11 06		11 09			
Clapham Junction	d	09 46				10 13		10 16						10 43	10 46					11 13		11 16			
East Croydon	a	09 56				10 22		10 26						10 52	10 56					11 22		11 26			
St Pancras International	d		09 35		09 45					10 05		10 15				10 35		10 45					11 05		11 15
Farringdon	d		09 39		09 49					10 09		10 19				10 39		10 49					11 09		11 19
City Thameslink	d		09 41		09 51					10 11		10 21				10 41		10 51					11 11		11 21
London Blackfriars	d		09 44		09 54					10 14		10 24				10 44		10 54					11 14		11 24
London Bridge	d		09 51		10 00					10 21		10 30				10 51		11 00					11 21		11 30
Norwood Junction	d		10 02							10 32						11 02							11 32		
East Croydon	a		10 06		10 14					10 36		10 44				11 06		11 14					11 36		11 44
East Croydon	d	09 57	10 07		10 16	10 23		10 27		10 37		10 46		10 53	10 57	11 07		11 16		11 23		11 27	11 37		11 46
Purley	d	10 04	10 14					10 34		10 44					11 04	11 14						11 34	11 44		
Coulsdon South	d	10 08			10 23			10 38				10 53			11 08			11 23				11 38			11 53
Merstham	d	10 14			10 28			10 44				10 58			11 14			11 28				11 44			11 58
Redhill	a	10 18	10 22		10 32			10 48		10 52		11 02			11 18	11 22		11 32				11 48	11 52		12 02
Redhill	d	10 19		10 30				10 49			11 00		11 14		11 19		11 30					11 49		12 00	
Reigate	a	10 23		10 34				10 53					11 18		11 23		11 34					11 53			
Nutfield	a										11 04													12 04	
Godstone	a										11 10													12 10	
Edenbridge	a										11 16													12 16	
Penshurst	a										11 22													12 24	
Leigh (Kent)	a										11 26													12 30	
Tonbridge	a										11 31													12 37	
Tonbridge	d																								
Redhill	a																								
Reigate	d						10 36														11 36				
Redhill	a						10 40														11 40				
Redhill	d		10 25		10 33		10 44			10 55		11 03				11 25		11 33			11 44		11 55		12 03
Earlswood (Surrey)	d		10 27							10 57						11 27							11 57		
Salfords	d		10 31							11 01						11 31							12 01		
Horley	d		10 35		10 39					11 05		11 09				11 35		11 39					12 05		12 09
Gatwick Airport	a		10 38		10 42	10 38	10 51			11 08		11 12		11 08		11 38		11 42		11 38	11 51		12 08		12 12
Gatwick Airport	d				10 44	10 39						11 14		11 09				11 44		11 39					12 14
Three Bridges	a				10 49	10 44						11 19		11 14				11 49		11 44					12 19
Three Bridges	d				10 50	10 44						11 20		11 14				11 50		11 44					12 20
Crawley	d				10 54	10 48						11 24		11 18				11 54		11 48					12 24
Ifield	d				10 56							11 26						11 56							12 26
Faygate	d																								
Littlehaven	d				11 02							11 32						12 02							12 32
Horsham	a				11 08	10 57						11 38		11 27				12 08		11 57					12 38

		GW 1	SN 1	SN 1		TL 1	GW 1	TL 1	SN 1	GW 1	SN 1	TL 1	SN	TL 1		GW 1	SN 1	SN 1	TL 1	GW 1	TL 1	SN 1	GW 1	SN 1	
London Victoria	d		11 36	11 39					12 06		12 09						12 36	12 39				13 06		13 09	
Clapham Junction	d		11 43	11 46					12 13		12 16						12 43	12 46				13 13		13 16	
East Croydon	a		11 52	11 56					12 22		12 26						12 52	12 56				13 22		13 26	
St Pancras International	d					11 35		11 45				12 05		12 15					12 35		12 45				
Farringdon	d					11 39		11 49				12 09		12 19					12 39		12 49				
City Thameslink	d					11 41		11 51				12 11		12 21					12 41		12 51				
London Blackfriars	d					11 44		11 54				12 14		12 24					12 44		12 54				
London Bridge	d					11 51		12 00				12 21		12 30					12 51		13 00				
Norwood Junction	d					12 02						12 32							13 02						
East Croydon	a					12 06		12 14				12 36		12 44					13 06		13 14				
East Croydon	d		11 53	11 57		12 07		12 16	12 23		12 27	12 37		12 46			12 53	12 57	13 07		13 16	13 23		13 27	
Purley	d			12 04		12 14					12 34	12 44						13 04	13 14					13 34	
Coulsdon South	d			12 08				12 23			12 38			12 53				13 08			13 23			13 38	
Merstham	d			12 14				12 28			12 44			12 58				13 14			13 28			13 44	
Redhill	a			12 18		12 22		12 32			12 48	12 52		13 02				13 18	13 22		13 32			13 48	
Redhill	d	12 14		12 19			12 30				12 49		13 00			13 14		13 19		13 30				13 49	
Reigate	a	12 18		12 23			12 34				12 53					13 18		13 23		13 34				13 53	
Nutfield	a												13 04												
Godstone	a												13 10												
Edenbridge	a												13 16												
Penshurst	a												13 22												
Leigh (Kent)	a												13 26												
Tonbridge	a												13 31												
Tonbridge	d																								
Redhill	a																								
Reigate	d									12 36													13 36		
Redhill	a									12 40													13 40		
Redhill	d					12 25		12 33		12 44		12 55		13 03					13 25		13 33		13 44		
Earlswood (Surrey)	d					12 27						12 57							13 27						
Salfords	d					12 31						13 01							13 31						
Horley	d					12 35		12 39				13 05		13 09					13 35		13 39				
Gatwick Airport	a		12 08			12 38		12 42	12 38	12 51		13 08		13 12			13 08		13 38		13 42	13 38	13 51		
Gatwick Airport	d		12 09					12 44	12 39					13 14			13 09				13 44	13 39			
Three Bridges	a		12 14					12 49	12 44					13 19			13 14				13 49	13 44			
Three Bridges	d		12 14					12 50	12 44					13 20			13 14				13 50	13 44			
Crawley	d		12 18					12 54	12 48					13 24			13 18				13 54	13 48			
Ifield	d							12 56						13 26							13 56				
Faygate	d																								
Littlehaven	d							13 02						13 32							14 02				
Horsham	a		12 27					13 08	12 57					13 38			13 27				14 08	13 57			

Table T183-F

Saturdays

21 December to 16 May

London - Redhill / Reigate / Tonbridge / Gatwick Airport - Horsham

		TL 1	SN	TL 1	GW 1	SN 1	SN 1	TL 1	GW 1	TL 1		SN 1	GW 1	SN 1	TL 1	SN	TL 1	GW 1	SN 1	SN 1		TL 1	GW 1	TL 1	SN 1
London Victoria	d					13 36	13 39					14 06		14 09					14 36	14 39					15 06
Clapham Junction	d					13 43	13 46					14 13		14 16					14 43	14 46					15 13
East Croydon	a					13 52	13 56					14 22		14 26					14 52	14 56					15 22
St Pancras International	d	13 05		13 15				13 35		13 45					14 05		14 15					14 35		14 45	
Farringdon	d	13 09		13 19				13 39		13 49					14 09		14 19					14 39		14 49	
City Thameslink	d	13 11		13 21				13 41		13 51					14 11		14 21					14 41		14 51	
London Blackfriars	d	13 14		13 24				13 44		13 54					14 14		14 24					14 44		14 54	
London Bridge	d	13 21		13 30				13 51		14 00					14 21		14 30					14 51		15 00	
Norwood Junction	d	13 32						14 02							14 32							15 02			
East Croydon	a	13 36		13 44				14 06		14 14					14 36		14 44					15 06		15 14	
East Croydon	d	13 37		13 46		13 53	13 57	14 07		14 16		14 23		14 27	14 37		14 46		14 53	14 57		15 07		15 16	15 23
Purley	d	13 44					14 04	14 14						14 34	14 44					15 04		15 14			
Coulsdon South	d			13 53			14 08			14 23				14 38			14 53			15 08				15 23	
Merstham	d			13 58			14 14			14 28				14 44			14 58			15 14				15 28	
Redhill	a	13 52		14 02			14 18	14 22		14 32				14 48	14 52		15 02			15 18		15 22		15 32	
Redhill	d		14 00		14 14		14 19		14 30					14 49		15 00		15 14		15 19			15 30		
Reigate	a				14 18		14 23		14 34					14 53				15 18		15 23			15 34		
Nutfield	a		14 04													15 04									
Godstone	a		14 10													15 10									
Edenbridge	a		14 16													15 16									
Penshurst	a		14 22													15 22									
Leigh (Kent)	a		14 26													15 26									
Tonbridge	a		14 31													15 31									
Tonbridge	d																								
Redhill	a																								
Reigate	d												14 36												
Redhill	a												14 40												
Redhill	d	13 55		14 03				14 25		14 33			14 44		14 55		15 03					15 25		15 33	
Earlswood (Surrey)	d	13 57						14 27							14 57							15 27			
Salfords	d	14 01						14 31							15 01							15 31			
Horley	d	14 05		14 09				14 35		14 39					15 05		15 09					15 35		15 39	
Gatwick Airport	a	14 08		14 12		14 08		14 38		14 42		14 38	14 51		15 08		15 12		15 08			15 38		15 42	15 38
Gatwick Airport	d			14 14		14 09				14 44		14 39					15 14		15 09					15 44	15 39
Three Bridges	a			14 19		14 14				14 49		14 44					15 19		15 14					15 49	15 44
Three Bridges	d			14 20		14 14				14 50		14 44					15 20		15 14					15 50	15 44
Crawley	d			14 24		14 18				14 54		14 48					15 24		15 18					15 54	15 48
Ifield	d			14 26						14 56							15 26							15 56	
Faygate	d																								
Littlehaven	d			14 32						15 02							15 32							16 02	
Horsham	a			14 38		14 27				15 08		14 57					15 38		15 27					16 08	15 57

		GW 1	SN 1	TL 1	SN	TL 1		GW 1	SN 1	SN 1	TL 1	GW 1	TL 1	SN 1	GW 1	SN 1		TL 1	SN	TL 1	GW 1	SN 1	SN 1	TL 1	GW 1
London Victoria	d		15 09						15 36	15 39				16 06		16 09						16 36	16 39		
Clapham Junction	d		15 16						15 43	15 46				16 13		16 16						16 43	16 46		
East Croydon	a		15 26						15 52	15 56				16 22		16 26						16 52	16 56		
St Pancras International	d			15 05		15 15					15 35		15 45					16 05		16 15				16 35	
Farringdon	d			15 09		15 19					15 39		15 49					16 09		16 19				16 39	
City Thameslink	d			15 11		15 21					15 41		15 51					16 11		16 21				16 41	
London Blackfriars	d			15 14		15 24					15 44		15 54					16 14		16 24				16 44	
London Bridge	d			15 21		15 30					15 51		16 00					16 21		16 30				16 51	
Norwood Junction	d			15 32							16 02							16 32						17 02	
East Croydon	a			15 36		15 44					16 06		16 14					16 36		16 44				17 06	
East Croydon	d		15 27	15 37		15 46			15 53	15 57	16 07		16 16	16 23		16 27		16 37		16 46		16 53	16 57	17 07	
Purley	d		15 34	15 44						16 04	16 14					16 34		16 44					17 04	17 14	
Coulsdon South	d		15 38			15 53				16 08			16 23			16 38				16 53			17 08		
Merstham	d		15 44			15 58				16 14			16 28			16 44				16 58			17 14		
Redhill	a		15 48	15 52		16 02				16 18	16 22		16 32			16 48		16 52		17 02			17 18	17 22	
Redhill	d		15 49		16 00			16 14		16 19		16 30				16 49			17 00		17 14		17 19		17 30
Reigate	a		15 53					16 18		16 23		16 34				16 53					17 18		17 23		17 34
Nutfield	a				16 04														17 04						
Godstone	a				16 10														17 10						
Edenbridge	a				16 16														17 16						
Penshurst	a				16 22														17 22						
Leigh (Kent)	a				16 26														17 26						
Tonbridge	a				16 31														17 31						
Tonbridge	d																								
Redhill	a																								
Reigate	d	15 36													16 36										
Redhill	a	15 40													16 40										
Redhill	d	15 46		15 55		16 03					16 25		16 33		16 44			16 55		17 03				17 25	
Earlswood (Surrey)	d			15 57							16 27							16 57						17 27	
Salfords	d			16 01							16 31							17 01						17 31	
Horley	d			16 05		16 09					16 35		16 39					17 05		17 09				17 35	
Gatwick Airport	a	15 55		16 08		16 12			16 08		16 38		16 42	16 38	16 51			17 08		17 12		17 08		17 38	
Gatwick Airport	d					16 14			16 09				16 44	16 39						17 14		17 09			
Three Bridges	a					16 19			16 14				16 49	16 44						17 19		17 14			
Three Bridges	d					16 20			16 14				16 50	16 44						17 20		17 14			
Crawley	d					16 24			16 18				16 54	16 48						17 24		17 18			
Ifield	d					16 26							16 56							17 26					
Faygate	d																								
Littlehaven	d					16 32							17 02							17 32					
Horsham	a					16 38			16 27				17 08	16 57						17 38		17 27			

Table T183-F

London - Redhill / Reigate / Tonbridge / Gatwick Airport - Horsham

Saturdays

21 December to 16 May

		TL 1		SN 1	GW 1	SN 1	TL 1	SN	TL 1	GW 1	SN 1	SN 1		TL 1	GW 1	TL 1	SN 1	GW 1	SN 1	TL 1	SN	TL 1		GW 1	SN 1
London Victoria	d			17 06		17 09					17 36	17 39					18 06		18 09						18 36
Clapham Junction	d			17 13		17 16					17 43	17 46					18 13		18 16						18 43
East Croydon	a			17 22		17 26					17 52	17 56					18 22		18 26						18 52
St Pancras International	d	16 45					17 05		17 15					17 35		17 45				18 05		18 15			
Farringdon	d	16 49					17 09		17 19					17 39		17 49				18 09		18 19			
City Thameslink	d	16 51					17 11		17 21					17 41		17 51				18 11		18 21			
London Blackfriars	d	16 54					17 14		17 24					17 44		17 54				18 14		18 24			
London Bridge	d	17 00					17 21		17 30					17 51		18 00				18 21		18 30			
Norwood Junction	d						17 32							18 02						18 32					
East Croydon	a	17 14					17 36		17 44					18 06		18 14				18 36		18 44			
East Croydon	d	17 16		17 23		17 27	17 37		17 46		17 53	17 57		18 07		18 16	18 23		18 27	18 37		18 46			18 53
Purley	d					17 34	17 44					18 04		18 14					18 34	18 44					
Coulsdon South	d	17 23				17 38			17 53			18 08				18 23			18 38			18 53			
Merstham	d	17 28				17 44			17 58			18 14				18 28			18 44			18 58			
Redhill	a	17 32				17 48	17 52		18 02			18 18		18 22		18 32			18 48	18 52		19 02			
Redhill	d					17 49		18 00		18 14		18 19			18 30				18 49		19 00			19 14	
Reigate	a					17 53				18 18		18 23			18 34				18 53					19 18	
Nutfield	a							18 04													19 04				
Godstone	a							18 10													19 10				
Edenbridge	a							18 16													19 16				
Penshurst	a							18 22													19 22				
Leigh (Kent)	a							18 26													19 26				
Tonbridge	a							18 31													19 31				
Tonbridge	d																								
Redhill	a																								
Reigate	d				17 36													18 36							
Redhill	a				17 40													18 40							
Redhill	d	17 33			17 44		17 55		18 03					18 25		18 33		18 44		18 55		19 03			
Earlswood (Surrey)	d						17 57							18 27						18 57					
Salfords	d						18 01							18 31						19 01					
Horley	d	17 39					18 05		18 09					18 35		18 39				19 05		19 09			
Gatwick Airport	a	17 42		17 38	17 51		18 08		18 12		18 08			18 38		18 42	18 38	18 51		19 08		19 12			19 08
Gatwick Airport	d	17 44		17 39					18 14		18 09					18 44	18 39					19 14			19 09
Three Bridges	a	17 49		17 44					18 19		18 14					18 49	18 44					19 19			19 14
Three Bridges	d	17 50		17 44					18 20		18 14					18 50	18 44					19 20			19 14
Crawley	d	17 54		17 48					18 24		18 18					18 54	18 48					19 24			19 18
Ifield	d	17 56							18 26							18 56						19 26			
Faygate	d																								
Littlehaven	d	18 02							18 32							19 02						19 32			
Horsham	a	18 08		17 57					18 38		18 27					19 08	18 57					19 38			19 27

		SN 1	TL 1	GW 1	TL 1	SN 1	GW 1	SN 1		TL 1	SN	TL 1	GW 1	SN 1	SN 1	TL 1	GW 1	TL 1		SN 1	GW 1	SN 1	TL 1	SN	TL 1
London Victoria	d	18 39				19 06		19 09						19 36	19 39					20 06		20 09			
Clapham Junction	d	18 46				19 13		19 16						19 43	19 46					20 13		20 16			
East Croydon	a	18 56				19 22		19 26						19 52	19 56					20 22		20 26			
St Pancras International	d		18 35		18 45					19 05		19 15				19 35		19 45				20 05		20 15
Farringdon	d		18 39		18 49					19 09		19 19				19 39		19 49				20 09		20 19
City Thameslink	d		18 41		18 51					19 11		19 21				19 41		19 51				20 11		20 21
London Blackfriars	d		18 44		18 54					19 14		19 24				19 44		19 54				20 14		20 24
London Bridge	d		18 51		19 00					19 21		19 30				19 51		20 00				20 21		20 30
Norwood Junction	d		19 02							19 32						20 02						20 32		
East Croydon	a		19 06		19 14					19 36		19 44				20 06		20 14				20 36		20 44
East Croydon	d	18 57	19 07		19 16	19 23		19 27		19 37		19 46		19 53	19 57	20 07		20 16		20 23		20 27	20 37		20 46
Purley	d	19 04	19 14					19 34		19 44					20 04	20 15						20 34	20 44		
Coulsdon South	d	19 08			19 23			19 38				19 53			20 08			20 23				20 38			20 53
Merstham	d	19 14			19 28			19 44				19 58			20 14			20 28				20 44			20 58
Redhill	a	19 18	19 22		19 32			19 48		19 52		20 02			20 18	20 23		20 32				20 48	20 52		21 02
Redhill	d	19 19		19 30				19 49			20 00		20 14		20 19		20 30					20 49		21 00	
Reigate	a	19 23		19 34				19 53					20 18		20 23		20 34					20 53			
Nutfield	a										20 04													21 04	
Godstone	a										20 10													21 10	
Edenbridge	a										20 16													21 16	
Penshurst	a										20 22													21 22	
Leigh (Kent)	a										20 26													21 26	
Tonbridge	a										20 31													21 31	
Tonbridge	d																								
Redhill	a																								
Reigate	d						19 36														20 36				
Redhill	a						19 40														20 40				
Redhill	d		19 25		19 33		19 44			19 55		20 03				20 25		20 33			20 44		20 55		21 03
Earlswood (Surrey)	d		19 27							19 57						20 27							20 57		
Salfords	d		19 31							20 01						20 31							21 01		
Horley	d		19 35		19 39					20 05		20 09				20 35		20 39					21 05		21 09
Gatwick Airport	a		19 38		19 42	19 38	19 51			20 08		20 12		20 08		20 38		20 42		20 38	20 51		21 08		21 12
Gatwick Airport	d				19 44	19 39						20 14		20 09				20 44		20 39					21 14
Three Bridges	a				19 49	19 44						20 19		20 14				20 49		20 44					21 19
Three Bridges	d				19 50	19 44						20 20		20 14				20 50		20 44					21 20
Crawley	d				19 54	19 48						20 24		20 18				20 54		20 48					21 24
Ifield	d				19 56							20 26						20 56							21 26
Faygate	d																								
Littlehaven	d				20 02							20 32						21 02							21 32
Horsham	a				20 08	19 57						20 38		20 27				21 08		20 57					21 38

Table T183-F

London - Redhill / Reigate / Tonbridge / Gatwick Airport - Horsham

Saturdays

21 December to 16 May

		GW 1	SN 1	SN 1		TL 1	TL 1	GW 1	SN 1	GW 1	SN 1	TL 1	SN	TL 1		SN 1	SN 1	TL 1	GW 1	TL 1	SN 1	GW 1	SN 1	TL 1	
London Victoria	d		20 36	20 39					21 06		21 09					21 36	21 39				22 06		22 09		
Clapham Junction	d		20 43	20 46					21 13		21 16					21 43	21 46				22 13		22 16		
East Croydon	a		20 52	20 57					21 22		21 26					21 52	21 56				22 22		22 26		
St Pancras International	d					20 35	20 45					21 05		21 15				21 35		21 45				22 05	
Farringdon	d					20 39	20 49					21 09		21 19				21 39		21 49				22 09	
City Thameslink	d					20 41	20 51																		
London Blackfriars	d					20 44	20 54					21 14		21 24				21 44		21 54				22 14	
London Bridge	d					20 51	21 00					21 21		21 30				21 51		22 00				22 21	
Norwood Junction	d					21 02						21 32						22 02						22 32	
East Croydon	a					21 06	21 14					21 36		21 44				22 06		22 14				22 36	
East Croydon	d		20 53	20 57		21 07	21 16		21 23		21 27	21 37		21 46		21 53	21 57	22 07		22 16	22 23		22 27	22 37	
Purley	d			21 04		21 14					21 35	21 44					22 05	22 14					22 34	22 44	
Coulsdon South	d			21 08			21 23				21 38			21 53			22 08			22 23			22 38		
Merstham	d			21 14			21 28				21 44			21 58			22 14			22 28			22 44		
Redhill	a			21 18		21 22	21 32				21 48	21 52		22 02			22 18	22 22		22 32			22 48	22 53	
Redhill	d	21 14		21 19				21 35			21 49		22 00				22 19		22 30				22 48		
Reigate	a	21 18		21 23				21 39			21 54						22 23		22 34				22 53		
Nutfield	a												22 04												
Godstone	a												22 10												
Edenbridge	a												22 16												
Penshurst	a												22 22												
Leigh (Kent)	a												22 26												
Tonbridge	a												22 31												
Tonbridge	d																								
Redhill	a																								
Reigate	d									21 43												22 40			
Redhill	a									21 47												22 44			
Redhill	d					21 25	21 33			21 52		21 55		22 03				22 25		22 33		22 50		22 55	
Earlswood (Surrey)	d					21 27						21 57						22 27						22 57	
Salfords	d					21 31						22 01						22 31						23 01	
Horley	d					21 35	21 39					22 05		22 09				22 35		22 39				23 05	
Gatwick Airport	a		21 08			21 38	21 42		21 38	22 00		22 08		22 12		22 07		22 38		22 42	22 38	22 58		23 08	
Gatwick Airport	d		21 09				21 44		21 39					22 14		22 09				22 44	22 39				
Three Bridges	a		21 14				21 49		21 44					22 19		22 14				22 49	22 44				
Three Bridges	d		21 14				21 50		21 45					22 20		22 14				22 50	22 44				
Crawley	d		21 18				21 54		21 49					22 24		22 18				22 54	22 48				
Ifield	d						21 56							22 26						22 56					
Faygate	d																								
Littlehaven	d						22 02							22 32						23 02					
Horsham	a		21 27				22 08		21 57					22 38		22 27				23 08	22 57				

		SN	TL 1	SN 1	SN 1	TL 1	GW 1	TL 1	SN 1	SN 1		TL 1	TL 1	TL 1	GW 1	SN 1
London Victoria	d			22 36	22 39				23 06	23 09						23 36
Clapham Junction	d			22 43	22 46				23 13	23 16						23 43
East Croydon	a			22 52	22 56				23 22	23 26						23 58
St Pancras International	d		22 15			22 35		22 45				23 05	23 15	23 22		
Farringdon	d		22 19			22 39		22 49				23 10	23 19	23 27		
City Thameslink	d															
London Blackfriars	d		22 24			22 44		22 54				23 14	23 24	23 31		
London Bridge	d		22 30			22 51		23 00				23 21	23 30	23 37		
Norwood Junction	d					23 02						23 32				
East Croydon	a		22 44			23 06		23 14				23 36	23 44	23 50		
East Croydon	d		22 46	22 53	22 57	23 07		23 16	23 23	23 27		23 37	23 46	23 51		23 59
Purley	d				23 04	23 14				23 34		23 43				00 05
Coulsdon South	d		22 53		23 08			23 23		23 38				23 59		00 09
Merstham	d		22 58		23 14			23 28		23 44				00 04		00 14
Redhill	a		23 02		23 18	23 22		23 32		23 48		23 52	23 59	00 08		00 18
Redhill	d	23 00			23 19		23 32			23 49						
Reigate	a				23 23		23 37			23 53						
Nutfield	a	23 04														
Godstone	a	23 10														
Edenbridge	a	23 16														
Penshurst	a	23 22														
Leigh (Kent)	a	23 26														
Tonbridge	a	23 31														
Tonbridge	d															
Redhill	a															
Reigate	d														23 57	
Redhill	a														00 02	
Redhill	d		23 03			23 25		23 33				23 52	23 59	00 09	00 12	00 19
Earlswood (Surrey)	d					23 27							00 02			
Salfords	d					23 31							00 05			
Horley	d		23 09			23 35		23 39					00 09			00 25
Gatwick Airport	a		23 12	23 08		23 37		23 42	23 38			00 01	00 12	00 17	00 20	00 29
Gatwick Airport	d		23 14	23 09		23 38		23 44	23 39				00 14	00 18		00 31
Three Bridges	a		23 19	23 14		23 43		23 49	23 44				00 19	00 23		00 36
Three Bridges	d		23 20	23 14				23 50	23 44				00 20			00 36
Crawley	d		23 24	23 18				23 54	23 48				00 24			00 40
Ifield	d		23 26					23 56					00 26			
Faygate	d															
Littlehaven	d		23 32					00 02					00 32			
Horsham	a		23 38	23 27				00 06	23 57				00 36			00 49

Table T183-F

Sundays

15 December to 10 May

London - Redhill / Reigate / Tonbridge / Gatwick Airport - Horsham

		SN	SN ■	GW ■ A	TL ■ A	SN ■	SN ■	SN ■	SN ■	SN ■		SN ■	GW ■	SN ■	GW ■	GW ■	SN ■	SN	TL ■	SN ■		GW ■	GW ■	SN ■	GW
London Victoria	d		00 08			01 08	02 08	03 08	04 10	05 02		05 45		06 32			07 02			07 32				08 02	
Clapham Junction	d		00 15			01 17	02 17	03 17	04 17	05 10		05 53		06 40			07 10			07 40				08 10	
East Croydon	a		00 31			01 32	02 32	03 31	04 31	05 23		06 08		06 53			07 26			07 56				08 26	
St Pancras International	d				00 51																				
Farringdon	d																								
City Thameslink	d																								
London Blackfriars	d				01 01																				
London Bridge	d																		07 19						
Norwood Junction	d																		07 31						
East Croydon	a				01 27														07 35						
East Croydon	d		00 32		01 28	01 33	02 32	03 32	04 31	05 24		06 09		06 54			07 27		07 35	07 57				08 27	
Purley	d		00 37		01 34	01 39	02 38	03 37	04 37	05 30				06 59			07 33		07 40					08 33	
Coulsdon South	d		00 40											07 03					07 44						
Merstham	d		00 46											07 08					07 49						
Redhill	a		00 50									06 21		07 12			07 42		07 53	08 10				08 42	
Redhill	d	00 16											06 23		07 23			07 50				08 26			08 43
Reigate	a												06 26		07 26							08 30			08 47
Nutfield	a																	07 54							
Godstone	a																	08 00							
Edenbridge	a	00 27																08 05							
Penshurst	a																	08 12							
Leigh (Kent)	a																	08 16							
Tonbridge	a	00 36																08 20							
Tonbridge	d																								
Redhill	a																								
Reigate	d			00 49												07 09							08 03		
Redhill	a			00 53												07 13							08 07		
Redhill	d		00 50	00 56								06 22		07 13		07 15	07 42		07 53	08 10			08 13	08 42	
Earlswood (Surrey)	d																		07 56						
Salfords	d																		07 59						
Horley	d		00 57		01 52	02 02	02 51	03 50	04 53	05 46		06 28		07 19			07 49		08 03					08 49	
Gatwick Airport	a		01 01	01 04	01 56	02 06	02 55	03 54	04 57	05 50		06 32		07 23		07 26	07 52		08 06	08 19			08 24	08 52	
Gatwick Airport	d				01 58	02 08	02 56	03 55	04 58	05 51		06 33		07 24			07 53		08 09	08 20				08 54	
Three Bridges	a				02 03	02 13	03 01	04 00	05 03	05 56		06 37		07 28			07 58		08 14	08 24				08 58	
Three Bridges	d																		08 15	08 25					
Crawley	d																		08 19	08 29					
Ifield	d																		08 21						
Faygate	d																								
Littlehaven	d																		08 27						
Horsham	a																		08 31	08 37					

		SN	TL ■	SN ■	SN	GW ■		GW ■	GW	SN	TL ■	TL ■	SN ■	SN	TL ■	GW ■		TL ■	GW ■	GW	SN	TL ■	TL ■	SN ■	SN
London Victoria	d			08 32						09 05			09 33								10 05			10 33	
Clapham Junction	d			08 40						09 12			09 40								10 12			10 40	
East Croydon	a			08 51						09 23			09 49								10 23			10 49	
St Pancras International	d														09 35			09 41					10 11		
Farringdon	d														09 39			09 45					10 15		
City Thameslink	d																								
London Blackfriars	d														09 44			09 50					10 20		
London Bridge	d		08 19								09 19	09 27			09 51			09 56				10 21	10 26		
Norwood Junction	d		08 31								09 33				10 03							10 33			
East Croydon	a		08 35								09 37	09 41			10 07			10 10				10 37	10 40		
East Croydon	d		08 37	08 51						09 23	09 37	09 41	09 49		10 07			10 11			10 23	10 37	10 41	10 49	
Purley	d		08 42							09 28		09 47						10 17			10 28		10 47		
Coulsdon South	d		08 46	08 58						09 32	09 44		09 56								10 32	10 44		10 56	
Merstham	d		08 51							09 37	09 49										10 37	10 49			
Redhill	a		08 55	09 05						09 41	09 53	09 56	10 03		10 19			10 25			10 41	10 53	10 56	11 03	
Redhill	d	08 48			09 11			09 30	09 43	09 49				10 07					10 29	10 43	10 50				11 07
Reigate	a							09 33	09 47	09 54									10 32	10 47	10 54				
Nutfield	a	08 52			09 15									10 11											11 11
Godstone	a	08 58			09 21									10 17											11 17
Edenbridge	a	09 03			09 26									10 22											11 22
Penshurst	a	09 10			09 33									10 29											11 29
Leigh (Kent)	a	09 14			09 37									10 33											11 33
Tonbridge	a	09 18			09 41									10 37											11 37
Tonbridge	d																								
Redhill	a																								
Reigate	d					09 17										10 17									
Redhill	a					09 24										10 24									
Redhill	d		08 55	09 06		09 27					09 53	09 57	10 04		10 19	10 27		10 30				10 53	10 57	11 04	
Earlswood (Surrey)	d		08 58									09 59						10 32					10 59		
Salfords	d		09 01									10 03						10 36					11 03		
Horley	d		09 05								09 59	10 06						10 39				10 59	11 06		
Gatwick Airport	a		09 07	09 13		09 35					10 02	10 09	10 12		10 27	10 35		10 42				11 02	11 09	11 12	
Gatwick Airport	d		09 09	09 14							10 03		10 13					10 43				11 03		11 13	
Three Bridges	a		09 14	09 19							10 08		10 18					10 47				11 08		11 18	
Three Bridges	d		09 15	09 19							10 09		10 19									11 09		11 18	
Crawley	d		09 19	09 23							10 13		10 23									11 13		11 22	
Ifield	d		09 21								10 15											11 15			
Faygate	d																								
Littlehaven	d		09 27								10 21											11 21			
Horsham	a		09 31	09 34							10 25		10 32									11 25		11 31	

A not 15 December

Table T183-F

Sundays

15 December to 10 May

London - Redhill / Reigate / Tonbridge / Gatwick Airport - Horsham

		TL ■		GW ■	TL ■	GW ■	GW	SN	TL ■	TL ■	SN ■	SN		TL ■	GW ■	TL ■	GW ■	GW	SN	TL ■	TL ■	SN ■		SN	TL ■
London Victoria	d							11 05			11 33								12 05			12 33			
Clapham Junction	d							11 12			11 40								12 12			12 40			
East Croydon	a							11 23			11 49								12 23			12 49			
St Pancras International	d	10 35			10 41					11 11				11 35		11 41					12 11				12 35
Farringdon	d	10 39			10 45					11 15				11 39		11 45					12 15				12 39
City Thameslink	d																								
London Blackfriars	d	10 44			10 50					11 20				11 44		11 50					12 20				12 44
London Bridge	d	10 51			10 56				11 21	11 26				11 51		11 56				12 21	12 26				12 51
Norwood Junction	d	11 03							11 33					12 03						12 33					13 03
East Croydon	a	11 07			11 10				11 37	11 40				12 07		12 10				12 37	12 40				13 07
East Croydon	d	11 07			11 11			11 23	11 37	11 41	11 49			12 07		12 11			12 23	12 37	12 41	12 49			13 07
Purley	d				11 17			11 28		11 47						12 17			12 28		12 47				
Coulsdon South	d							11 32	11 44		11 56								12 32	12 44		12 56			
Merstham	d							11 37	11 49										12 37	12 49					
Redhill	a	11 19			11 25			11 41	11 53	11 56	12 03			12 19		12 25			12 41	12 53	12 56	13 03			13 19
Redhill	d					11 29	11 43	11 50				12 07					12 29	12 43	12 50					13 07	
Reigate	a					11 32	11 47	11 54									12 32	12 47	12 54						
Nutfield	a											12 11												13 11	
Godstone	a											12 17												13 17	
Edenbridge	a											12 22												13 22	
Penshurst	a											12 29												13 29	
Leigh (Kent)	a											12 33												13 33	
Tonbridge	a											12 37												13 37	
Tonbridge	d																								
Redhill	a																								
Reigate	d			11 17											12 17										
Redhill	a			11 24											12 24										
Redhill	d	11 19		11 27	11 30				11 53	11 57	12 04			12 19	12 27	12 30				12 53	12 57	13 04			13 19
Earlswood (Surrey)	d				11 32					11 59						12 32					12 59				
Salfords	d				11 36					12 03						12 36					13 03				
Horley	d				11 39				11 59	12 06						12 39				12 59	13 06				
Gatwick Airport	a	11 27		11 35	11 42				12 02	12 09	12 12			12 27	12 35	12 42				13 02	13 09	13 12			13 27
Gatwick Airport	d				11 43				12 03		12 13					12 43				13 03		13 13			
Three Bridges	a				11 48				12 08		12 18					12 48				13 08		13 18			
Three Bridges	d								12 09		12 18									13 09		13 18			
Crawley	d								12 13		12 22									13 13		13 22			
Ifield	d								12 15											13 15					
Faygate	d																								
Littlehaven	d								12 21											13 21					
Horsham	a								12 25		12 31									13 25		13 31			

		GW ■	TL ■	GW ■	GW	SN	TL ■	TL ■		SN ■	SN	TL ■	GW ■	TL ■	GW ■	GW	SN	TL ■		TL ■	SN ■	SN	TL ■	GW ■	TL ■
London Victoria	d					13 05				13 33							14 05				14 33				
Clapham Junction	d					13 12				13 40							14 12				14 40				
East Croydon	a					13 23				13 49							14 23				14 49				
St Pancras International	d		12 41					13 11				13 35		13 41						14 11			14 35		14 41
Farringdon	d		12 45					13 15				13 39		13 45						14 15			14 39		14 45
City Thameslink	d																								
London Blackfriars	d		12 50					13 20				13 44		13 50						14 20			14 44		14 50
London Bridge	d		12 56				13 21	13 26				13 51		13 56				14 21		14 26			14 51		14 56
Norwood Junction	d						13 33					14 03						14 33					15 03		
East Croydon	a		13 10				13 37	13 40				14 07		14 10				14 37		14 40			15 07		15 10
East Croydon	d		13 11			13 23	13 37	13 41		13 49		14 07		14 11			14 23	14 37		14 41	14 49		15 07		15 11
Purley	d		13 17			13 28		13 47						14 17			14 28			14 47					15 17
Coulsdon South	d					13 32	13 44			13 56							14 32	14 44			14 56				
Merstham	d					13 37	13 49										14 37	14 49							
Redhill	a		13 25			13 41	13 53	13 56		14 03		14 19		14 25			14 41	14 53		14 56	15 03		15 19		15 25
Redhill	d			13 29	13 43	13 50					14 07				14 29	14 43	14 50					15 07			
Reigate	a			13 32	13 47	13 54									14 32	14 47	14 54								
Nutfield	a										14 11											15 11			
Godstone	a										14 17											15 17			
Edenbridge	a										14 22											15 22			
Penshurst	a										14 29											15 29			
Leigh (Kent)	a										14 33											15 33			
Tonbridge	a										14 37											15 37			
Tonbridge	d																								
Redhill	a																								
Reigate	d	13 17											14 17											15 17	
Redhill	a	13 24											14 24											15 24	
Redhill	d	13 27	13 30				13 53	13 57		14 04		14 19	14 27	14 30				14 53		14 57	15 04		15 19	15 27	15 30
Earlswood (Surrey)	d		13 32					13 59						14 32						14 59					15 32
Salfords	d		13 36					14 03						14 36						15 03					15 36
Horley	d		13 39				13 59	14 06						14 39				14 59		15 06					15 39
Gatwick Airport	a	13 35	13 42				14 02	14 09		14 12		14 27	14 35	14 42				15 02		15 09	15 12		15 27	15 35	15 42
Gatwick Airport	d		13 43				14 03			14 13				14 43				15 03			15 13				15 43
Three Bridges	a		13 47				14 08			14 18				14 47				15 08			15 18				15 48
Three Bridges	d						14 09			14 18								15 09			15 18				
Crawley	d						14 13			14 22								15 13			15 22				
Ifield	d						14 15											15 15							
Faygate	d																								
Littlehaven	d						14 21											15 21							
Horsham	a						14 25			14 31								15 25			15 31				

Table T183-F

Sundays
15 December to 10 May

London - Redhill / Reigate / Tonbridge / Gatwick Airport - Horsham

		GW 1	GW	SN	TL 1	TL 1	SN 1	SN	TL 1	GW 1	TL 1	GW 1	GW	SN	TL 1	TL 1	SN 1	SN	TL 1	GW 1	TL 1	GW 1
London Victoria	d			15 05			15 33							16 05			16 33					
Clapham Junction	d			15 12			15 40							16 12			16 40					
East Croydon	a			15 23			15 49							16 23			16 49					
St Pancras International	d					15 11			15 35		15 41					16 11			16 35		16 41	
Farringdon	d					15 15			15 39		15 45					16 15			16 39		16 45	
City Thameslink	d																					
London Blackfriars	d					15 20			15 44		15 50					16 20			16 44		16 50	
London Bridge	d				15 21	15 26			15 51		15 56				16 21	16 26			16 51		16 56	
Norwood Junction	d				15 33				16 03						16 33				17 03			
East Croydon	a				15 37	15 40			16 07		16 10				16 37	16 40			17 07		17 10	
East Croydon	d			15 23	15 37	15 41	15 49		16 07		16 11			16 23	16 37	16 41	16 49		17 07		17 11	
Purley	d			15 28		15 47					16 17			16 28		16 47					17 17	
Coulsdon South	d			15 32	15 44		15 56							16 32	16 44		16 56					
Merstham	d			15 37	15 49									16 37	16 49							
Redhill	a			15 41	15 53	15 56	16 03		16 19		16 25			16 41	16 53	16 56	17 03		17 19		17 25	
Redhill	d	15 29	15 43	15 50				16 07				16 29	16 43	16 50				17 07				17 29
Reigate	a	15 32	15 47	15 54								16 32	16 47	16 54								17 32
Nutfield	a							16 11										17 11				
Godstone	a							16 17										17 17				
Edenbridge	a							16 22										17 22				
Penshurst	a							16 29										17 29				
Leigh (Kent)	a							16 33										17 33				
Tonbridge	a							16 37										17 37				
Tonbridge	d																					
Redhill	a																					
Reigate	d									16 16										17 17		
Redhill	a									16 24										17 24		
Redhill	d				15 53	15 57	16 04		16 19	16 27	16 30				16 53	16 57	17 04		17 19	17 27	17 30	
Earlswood (Surrey)	d					15 59					16 32					16 59					17 32	
Salfords	d					16 03					16 36					17 03					17 36	
Horley	d				15 59	16 06					16 39				16 59	17 06					17 39	
Gatwick Airport	a				16 02	16 09	16 12		16 27	16 35	16 42				17 02	17 09	17 12		17 27	17 35	17 42	
Gatwick Airport	d				16 03		16 13				16 43				17 03		17 13				17 43	
Three Bridges	a				16 08		16 18				16 48				17 08		17 18				17 48	
Three Bridges	d				16 09		16 18								17 09		17 18					
Crawley	d				16 13		16 22								17 13		17 22					
Ifield	d				16 15										17 15							
Faygate	d																					
Littlehaven	d				16 21										17 21							
Horsham	a				16 25		16 31								17 25		17 31					

		GW	SN	TL 1	TL 1	SN 1	SN	TL 1	GW 1	TL 1	GW 1	GW	SN	TL 1	TL 1	SN 1	SN	TL 1	GW 1	TL 1	GW 1	GW	SN
London Victoria	d		17 05			17 33							18 05			18 33							19 05
Clapham Junction	d		17 12			17 40							18 12			18 40							19 12
East Croydon	a		17 23			17 49							18 23			18 49							19 23
St Pancras International	d				17 11			17 35		17 41					18 11			18 35		18 41			
Farringdon	d				17 15			17 39		17 45					18 15			18 39		18 45			
City Thameslink	d																						
London Blackfriars	d				17 20			17 44		17 50					18 20			18 44		18 50			
London Bridge	d			17 21	17 26			17 51		17 56				18 21	18 26			18 51		18 56			
Norwood Junction	d			17 33				18 03						18 33				19 03					
East Croydon	a			17 37	17 40			18 07		18 10				18 37	18 40			19 07		19 10			
East Croydon	d		17 23	17 37	17 41	17 49		18 07		18 11			18 23	18 37	18 41	18 49		19 07		19 11			19 23
Purley	d		17 28		17 47					18 17			18 28		18 47					19 17			19 28
Coulsdon South	d		17 32	17 44		17 56							18 32	18 44		18 56							19 32
Merstham	d		17 37	17 49									18 37	18 49									19 37
Redhill	a		17 41	17 53	17 56	18 03		18 19		18 25			18 41	18 53	18 56	19 03		19 19		19 25			19 41
Redhill	d	17 43	17 50				18 07				18 29	18 43	18 50				19 07				19 29	19 43	19 50
Reigate	a	17 47	17 54								18 32	18 47	18 54								19 32	19 47	19 54
Nutfield	a						18 11										19 11						
Godstone	a						18 17										19 17						
Edenbridge	a						18 22										19 22						
Penshurst	a						18 29										19 29						
Leigh (Kent)	a						18 33										19 33						
Tonbridge	a						18 37										19 37						
Tonbridge	d																						
Redhill	a																						
Reigate	d								18 17										19 17				
Redhill	a								18 24										19 24				
Redhill	d			17 53	17 57	18 04		18 19	18 27	18 30				18 53	18 57	19 04		19 19	19 27	19 30			
Earlswood (Surrey)	d				17 59					18 32					18 59					19 32			
Salfords	d				18 03					18 36					19 03					19 36			
Horley	d			17 59	18 06					18 39				18 59	19 06					19 39			
Gatwick Airport	a			18 02	18 09	18 12		18 27	18 35	18 42				19 02	19 09	19 12		19 27	19 35	19 42			
Gatwick Airport	d			18 03		18 13				18 43				19 03		19 13				19 43			
Three Bridges	a			18 08		18 18				18 47				19 08		19 18				19 47			
Three Bridges	d			18 09		18 18								19 09		19 18							
Crawley	d			18 13		18 22								19 13		19 22							
Ifield	d			18 15										19 15									
Faygate	d																						
Littlehaven	d			18 21										19 21									
Horsham	a			18 25		18 31								19 25		19 31							

Table T183-F

Sundays
15 December to 10 May

London - Redhill / Reigate / Tonbridge / Gatwick Airport - Horsham

		TL 1	TL 1	SN 1	SN	TL 1	GW 1	TL 1	GW 1	SN	TL 1	TL 1	SN 1	SN	GW 1	TL 1	TL 1	GW 1	SN	TL 1	TL 1	SN 1	SN
London Victoria	d			19 33						20 05			20 33						21 05			21 33	
Clapham Junction	d			19 40						20 12			20 40						21 12			21 40	
East Croydon	a			19 49						20 23			20 49						21 23			21 49	
St Pancras International	d		19 11			19 35		19 41				20 11				20 35	20 41				21 11		
Farringdon	d		19 15			19 39		19 45				20 15				20 39	20 45				21 15		
City Thameslink	d																						
London Blackfriars	d		19 20			19 44		19 50				20 20				20 44	20 50				21 20		
London Bridge	d	19 21	19 26			19 51		19 56			20 21	20 26				20 51	20 56			21 21	21 26		
Norwood Junction	d	19 33				20 03					20 33					21 03				21 33			
East Croydon	a	19 37	19 40			20 07		20 10			20 37	20 40				21 07	21 10			21 37	21 40		
East Croydon	d	19 37	19 41	19 49		20 07		20 11		20 23	20 37	20 41	20 49			21 07	21 11		21 23	21 37	21 41	21 49	
Purley	d		19 47					20 17		20 28		20 47					21 17		21 28		21 47		
Coulsdon South	d	19 44		19 56						20 32	20 44		20 56						21 32	21 44		21 56	
Merstham	d	19 49								20 37	20 49								21 37	21 49			
Redhill	a	19 53	19 56	20 03		20 19		20 25		20 41	20 53	20 56	21 03			21 19	21 25		21 41	21 53	21 56	22 03	
Redhill	d				20 07				20 29	20 43				21 07	21 16				21 43				22 07
Reigate	a								20 32	20 47					21 18				21 47				
Nutfield	a				20 11									21 11									22 11
Godstone	a				20 17									21 17									22 17
Edenbridge	a				20 22									21 22									22 22
Penshurst	a				20 29									21 29									22 29
Leigh (Kent)	a				20 33									21 33									22 33
Tonbridge	a				20 37									21 37									22 37
Tonbridge	d																						
Redhill	a																						
Reigate	d						20 17											21 37					
Redhill	a						20 24											21 43					
Redhill	d	19 53	19 57	20 04		20 19	20 27	20 30			20 53	20 57	21 04			21 19	21 27	21 48		21 53	21 57	22 04	
Earlswood (Surrey)	d		19 59					20 32				20 59					21 29				21 59		
Salfords	d		20 03					20 36				21 03					21 33				22 03		
Horley	d	19 59	20 06					20 39			20 59	21 06					21 36			21 59	22 06		
Gatwick Airport	a	20 02	20 09	20 12		20 27	20 35	20 42			21 02	21 09	21 12			21 27	21 39	21 58		22 02	22 09	22 12	
Gatwick Airport	d	20 03		20 13				20 43			21 03		21 13							22 03	22 10	22 14	
Three Bridges	a	20 08		20 18				20 47			21 08		21 18							22 08	22 15	22 19	
Three Bridges	d	20 09		20 18							21 09		21 18							22 09		22 20	
Crawley	d	20 13		20 22							21 13		21 22							22 13		22 24	
Ifield	d	20 15									21 15									22 15			
Faygate	d																						
Littlehaven	d	20 21									21 21									22 21			
Horsham	a	20 25		20 31							21 25		21 31							22 25		22 32	

		TL 1	TL 1	GW 1	GW 1	SN	TL 1	TL 1	SN 1	SN	GW 1	TL 1	SN 1	GW 1	SN 1	TL 1
London Victoria	d					22 05			22 33				23 05		23 32	
Clapham Junction	d					22 13			22 40				23 12		23 40	
East Croydon	a					22 23			22 49				23 22		23 56	
St Pancras International	d	21 35	21 41					22 11				22 35				
Farringdon	d	21 39	21 45					22 15				22 39				
City Thameslink	d															
London Blackfriars	d	21 44	21 50					22 20				22 44				
London Bridge	d	21 51	21 56				22 21	22 26				22 51				23 45
Norwood Junction	d	22 03					22 33					23 03				
East Croydon	a	22 07	22 10				22 37	22 40				23 07				23 59
East Croydon	d	22 07	22 11			22 24	22 37	22 41	22 49			23 08	23 23		23 57	00 01
Purley	d		22 17			22 29		22 47				23 13	23 28		00 03	00 06
Coulsdon South	d					22 32	22 44		22 56				23 32			
Merstham	d					22 38	22 49						23 37			
Redhill	a	22 19	22 25			22 42	22 53	22 56	23 03			23 22	23 41		00 12	00 15
Redhill	d			22 34						23 07	23 17					
Reigate	a			22 37							23 20					
Nutfield	a									23 11						
Godstone	a									23 17						
Edenbridge	a									23 22						
Penshurst	a									23 29						
Leigh (Kent)	a									23 33						
Tonbridge	a									23 37						
Tonbridge	d															
Redhill	a															
Reigate	d				22 29									23 33		
Redhill	a				22 35									23 39		
Redhill	d	22 19	22 27		22 38	22 44	22 53	22 57	23 04			23 23	23 42	23 46	00 13	00 16
Earlswood (Surrey)	d		22 29					22 59				23 25				00 18
Salfords	d		22 33					23 03				23 29				00 22
Horley	d		22 36				22 59	23 06				23 32				00 25
Gatwick Airport	a	22 26	22 39		22 47	22 51	23 02	23 09	23 12			23 35	23 50	23 57	00 21	00 29
Gatwick Airport	d	22 27	22 41			22 52	23 03		23 13			23 36	23 51		00 23	00 30
Three Bridges	a	22 32	22 45			22 56	23 08		23 18			23 40	23 56		00 27	00 35
Three Bridges	d					22 57	23 09		23 18				23 56			
Crawley	d					23 01	23 13		23 22				00 02			
Ifield	d						23 15						00 04			
Faygate	d															
Littlehaven	d						23 21						00 10			
Horsham	a					23 09	23 25		23 31				00 14			

Table T183-R

Mondays to Fridays
16 December to 15 May

Horsham / Gatwick Airport / Tonbridge / Reigate / Redhill - London

		GW MX	GW MO 1	TL 1	GW MX 1	TL 1	TL 1	TL 1	TL 1	SN		GW 1	TL 1	SN 1	GW 1	TL 1	SN 1	TL 1	SN	TL 1		GW 1	SN 1	SN 1	SN 1
Horsham	d																05 15	05 25					05 41		
Littlehaven	d																05 18	05 29					05 45		
Faygate	d																								
Ifield	d																05 24	05 35					05 51		
Crawley	d																05 28	05 38					05 55		
Three Bridges	a																05 32	05 42					06 00		
Three Bridges	d			00 37		01 41	02 41	03 41	04 35				05 14			05 27	05 33	05 43		05 51			06 02		
Gatwick Airport	a			00 41		01 45	02 45	03 45	04 40				05 18			05 31	05 37	05 47		05 55			06 06		
Gatwick Airport	d	00 24		00 42		01 46	02 46	03 46	04 41			05 08	05 19	05 28		05 32	05 38	05 49		05 56		06 01	06 08	05 52	
Horley	d			00 45		01 49	02 49	03 49	04 43					05 31		05 35		05 51		05 59				05 55	
Salfords	d															05 39				06 03					
Earlswood (Surrey)	d															05 42				06 06				06 00	
Redhill	a	00 35		00 52					04 51			05 17	05 27	05 38		05 46		05 59		06 10		06 14		06 05	
Redhill	d											05 35										06 17			
Reigate	a											05 39										06 21			
Redhill	d																								
Tonbridge	a																								
Tonbridge	d									04 40									05 28						
Leigh (Kent)	a									04 44									05 32						
Penshurst	a									04 48									05 36						
Edenbridge	a									04 55									05 43						
Godstone	a									05 01									05 49						
Nutfield	a									05 07									05 55						
Reigate	d		00 27		00 51										05 37										06 06
Redhill	a		00 31		00 55					05 13					05 41				06 01						06 11
Redhill	d			00 53					04 52				05 28	05 39		05 49		05 59		06 11					06 15
Merstham	d													05 43				06 03		06 15					06 19
Coulsdon South	d													05 48				06 09		06 20					06 24
Purley	d			01 03		02 04	03 03	04 03	05 01					05 52		05 58				06 24					06 28
East Croydon	a			01 09		02 10	03 09	04 09	05 08				05 39	06 00		06 03	05 53	06 15		06 31			06 23		06 34
East Croydon	d			01 10		02 10	03 10	04 10	05 10				05 40			06 03		06 16		06 31					
Norwood Junction	a															06 07				06 36					
London Bridge	a								05 24				05 54			06 20		06 30		06 50					
London Blackfriars	a			01 36		02 36	03 36	04 36	05 31				06 01			06 26		06 36		06 56					
City Thameslink	a								05 33				06 03			06 28		06 38		06 58					
Farringdon	a								05 35				06 05			06 31		06 41		07 01					
St Pancras International	a			01 43		02 43	03 43	04 43	05 40				06 10			06 35		06 45		07 05					
East Croydon	d													06 00			05 53						06 24		06 34
Clapham Junction	a													06 11			06 02						06 33		06 44
London Victoria	a													06 18			06 12						06 42		06 52

		TL 1	SN	GW 1	TL 1	SN 1		SN 1	SN 1	TL 1	SN	TL 1	GW 1	SN 1	SN 1	SN 1	SN 1		GW 1	TL 1	SN	SN 1	TL 1	SN 1	
Horsham	d				06 04	06 19				06 24		06 34		06 40	06 50								07 04	07 16	
Littlehaven	d				06 08							06 38		06 44	06 54								07 08	07 20	
Faygate	d				06 11							06 41											07 11		
Ifield	d				06 15							06 45		06 50									07 15		
Crawley	d				06 19	06 28				06 33		06 49		06 54	07 02								07 19	07 28	
Three Bridges	a				06 22	06 32				06 36		06 52		06 58	07 07								07 22	07 32	
Three Bridges	d	06 07			06 24	06 33				06 37		06 54		07 03	07 07								07 24	07 33	
Gatwick Airport	a	06 12			06 28	06 37				06 42		06 58		07 08									07 28	07 37	
Gatwick Airport	d	06 13			06 29	06 38		06 19		06 43		06 59	07 03	07 09		06 49				07 13		07 20	07 29	07 39	
Horley	d	06 16						06 22		06 46						06 52				07 16		07 23			
Salfords	d	06 20						06 26		06 50						06 56				07 20					
Earlswood (Surrey)	d	06 24						06 30		06 54						07 00				07 24					
Redhill	a	06 28			06 37			06 34		06 58		07 07	07 11			07 04				07 28			07 38		
Redhill	d												07 14												
Reigate	a												07 18												
Redhill	d																								
Tonbridge	a																								
Tonbridge	d		05 58								06 28										06 58				
Leigh (Kent)	a		06 02								06 32										07 02				
Penshurst	a		06 06								06 36										07 06				
Edenbridge	a		06 13								06 43										07 13				
Godstone	a		06 19								06 49										07 19				
Nutfield	a		06 25								06 55										07 25				
Reigate	d			06 32					06 36								07 06		07 18						
Redhill	a		06 31	06 36					06 41		07 01						07 11		07 22		07 31				
Redhill	d	06 29			06 39				06 45	06 59		07 09					07 15			07 29			07 39		
Merstham	d	06 33			06 43				06 49	07 03		07 13					07 19			07 33			07 43		
Coulsdon South	d	06 39			06 48				06 54	07 09		07 18					07 24			07 39			07 48		
Purley	d				06 54				06 58			07 24					07 28						07 54		
East Croydon	a	06 45			07 01	06 53			07 04	07 15		07 31		07 23	07 26		07 34			07 46		07 37	08 01	07 54	
East Croydon	d	06 46			07 01					07 16		07 31			07 27					07 46			08 01		
Norwood Junction	a				07 06							07 36											08 06		
London Bridge	a	07 00			07 20					07 30		07 50			07 43					08 00			08 20		
London Blackfriars	a	07 06			07 26					07 36		07 56								08 06			08 26		
City Thameslink	a	07 08			07 28					07 38		07 58								08 08			08 28		
Farringdon	a	07 11			07 31					07 41		08 01								08 11			08 31		
St Pancras International	a	07 15			07 35					07 45		08 05								08 15			08 35		
East Croydon	d					06 53			07 04					07 24			07 34					07 38		07 55	
Clapham Junction	a					07 02			07 14					07 33			07 44					07 47		08 04	
London Victoria	a					07 12			07 22					07 40			07 52					07 54		08 12	

Table T183-R

Mondays to Fridays
16 December to 15 May

Horsham / Gatwick Airport / Tonbridge / Reigate / Redhill - London

		SN 1	SN 1	GW 1		TL 1	SN	SN 1	TL 1	GW 1	SN 1	SN 1	SN 1	SN 1		TL 1	SN	GW 1	SN 1	TL 1	SN 1	SN 1	SN 1	TL 1	
Horsham	d								07 34		07 40	07 50								08 04	08 19				
Littlehaven	d								07 38		07 44	07 54								08 08					
Faygate	d								07 41											08 11					
Ifield	d								07 45		07 50									08 15					
Crawley	d								07 49		07 54	08 02								08 19	08 28				
Three Bridges	a								07 52		07 58	08 07								08 22	08 32				
Three Bridges	d								07 54		08 01	08 07								08 24	08 33				
Gatwick Airport	a								07 58		08 05									08 28	08 37				
Gatwick Airport	d	07 20				07 43		07 50	07 59	08 02	08 08		07 50			08 13			08 20	08 29	08 39	08 19		08 43	
Horley	d	07 23				07 46		07 53					07 53			08 16			08 23			08 22		08 46	
Salfords	d	07 27				07 50							07 57			08 20						08 26		08 50	
Earlswood (Surrey)	d	07 31				07 54							08 00			08 24						08 30		08 54	
Redhill	a	07 35				07 58			08 07	08 11			08 04			08 28				08 37		08 34		08 58	
Redhill	d									08 16															
Reigate	a									08 20															
Redhill	d																								
Tonbridge	a																								
Tonbridge	d						07 28										07 58								
Leigh (Kent)	a						07 32										08 02								
Penshurst	a						07 36										08 06								
Edenbridge	a						07 43										08 13								
Godstone	a						07 49										08 19								
Nutfield	a						07 55										08 25								
Reigate	d		07 36	07 41										08 04				08 32					08 36		
Redhill	a		07 41	07 46			08 01							08 10			08 31	08 38					08 41		
Redhill	d		07 45			07 59			08 09					08 15		08 29				08 39			08 45	08 59	
Merstham	d		07 49			08 03			08 13					08 19		08 33				08 43			08 49	09 03	
Coulsdon South	d		07 54			08 09			08 18					08 24		08 39				08 48			08 54	09 09	
Purley	d		07 58						08 24					08 28						08 54			08 58		
East Croydon	a		08 04			08 15		08 07	08 31		08 23	08 26		08 34		08 45			08 37	09 01	08 54		09 04	09 15	
East Croydon	d					08 16			08 31			08 27				08 46				09 01				09 16	
Norwood Junction	a								08 36											09 06					
London Bridge	a					08 30			08 50			08 43				09 00				09 20				09 30	
London Blackfriars	a					08 36			08 56							09 06				09 26				09 36	
City Thameslink	a					08 38			08 58							09 08				09 28				09 38	
Farringdon	a					08 41			09 01							09 11				09 31				09 41	
St Pancras International	a					08 45			09 05							09 15				09 35				09 45	
East Croydon	d		08 04					08 08			08 24			08 34					08 38		08 54		09 04		
Clapham Junction	a		08 14					08 17			08 33			08 44					08 47		09 03		09 14		
London Victoria	a		08 22					08 24			08 40			08 52					08 54		09 10		09 24		

		SN	SN 1	TL 1	GW 1	SN 1	SN 1	SN 1	GW 1	TL 1		SN	SN 1	SN 1	GW 1	TL 1	SN 1	TL 1	GW 1	SN 1		SN	TL 1	SN 1	GW
Horsham	d			08 34		08 50				08 55							09 20	09 25						09 50	
Littlehaven	d			08 38						08 59								09 29							
Faygate	d			08 41																					
Ifield	d			08 45						09 05								09 35							
Crawley	d			08 49		08 59				09 08							09 29	09 38						09 59	
Three Bridges	a			08 52		09 03				09 12							09 33	09 42						10 03	
Three Bridges	d			08 54		09 04				09 13							09 34	09 43						10 04	
Gatwick Airport	a			08 58		09 08				09 17							09 38	09 47						10 08	
Gatwick Airport	d		08 51	08 59	09 02	09 09	08 49			09 19			09 23			09 33	09 39	09 49	10 00				10 03	10 09	
Horley	d		08 54				08 52			09 21			09 26			09 35		09 51					10 05		
Salfords	d						08 56									09 39							10 09		
Earlswood (Surrey)	d						09 00						09 31			09 43							10 13		
Redhill	a			09 07	09 11		09 04			09 29			09 35			09 48		09 59	10 09				10 17		
Redhill	d				09 15														10 14						
Reigate	a				09 19														10 18						
Redhill	d																								
Tonbridge	a																								
Tonbridge	d	08 28										08 58										09 32			
Leigh (Kent)	a	08 32										09 02										09 36			
Penshurst	a	08 36										09 06										09 40			
Edenbridge	a	08 43										09 13										09 47			
Godstone	a	08 49										09 19										09 53			
Nutfield	a	08 55										09 25										09 59			
Reigate	d							09 06	09 24					09 32	09 41					10 00					10 19
Redhill	a	09 02						09 11	09 28			09 31		09 37	09 45					10 05		10 06			10 23
Redhill	d			09 09				09 15		09 29				09 41		09 49		09 59		10 11			10 19		
Merstham	d			09 13				09 19		09 33				09 45				10 03		10 15					
Coulsdon South	d			09 18				09 24		09 39				09 50				10 09		10 20					
Purley	d			09 24				09 28						09 55		09 58				10 25			10 28		
East Croydon	a		09 09	09 31		09 24		09 34		09 45				10 00		10 03	09 54	10 15		10 30			10 33	10 24	
East Croydon	d			09 31						09 45						10 03		10 15					10 33		
Norwood Junction	a			09 36												10 07							10 37		
London Bridge	a			09 50						10 00						10 20		10 30					10 50		
London Blackfriars	a			09 56						10 06						10 26		10 36					10 56		
City Thameslink	a			09 58						10 08						10 28		10 38					10 58		
Farringdon	a			10 01						10 11						10 31		10 41					11 01		
St Pancras International	a			10 05						10 15						10 35		10 45					11 05		
East Croydon	d		09 09			09 24		09 34						10 00			09 54			10 30				10 24	
Clapham Junction	a		09 18			09 33		09 44						10 10			10 03			10 40				10 33	
London Victoria	a		09 26			09 40		09 52						10 18			10 11			10 48				10 41	

Table T183-R

Mondays to Fridays

16 December to 15 May

Horsham / Gatwick Airport / Tonbridge / Reigate / Redhill - London

		TL 1	SN 1	SN	GW 1	TL 1	SN 1	TL 1	SN 1	GW	GW 1	TL 1	SN 1	TL 1	SN 1	SN	GW 1	TL 1	SN 1	TL 1	GW 1	SN 1	TL 1
Horsham	d	09 55					10 20	10 25					10 50	10 55					11 20	11 25			
Littlehaven	d	09 59						10 29						10 59						11 29			
Faygate	d																						
Ifield	d	10 05						10 35						11 05						11 35			
Crawley	d	10 08					10 29	10 38					10 59	11 08					11 29	11 38			
Three Bridges	a	10 12					10 33	10 42					11 03	11 12					11 33	11 42			
Three Bridges	d	10 13					10 34	10 43					11 04	11 13					11 34	11 43			
Gatwick Airport	a	10 17					10 38	10 47					11 08	11 17					11 38	11 47			
Gatwick Airport	d	10 19				10 33	10 39	10 49			10 59	11 03	11 09	11 19				11 33	11 39	11 49	12 00		12 03
Horley	d	10 21				10 35		10 51				11 05		11 21				11 35		11 51			12 05
Salfords	d					10 39						11 09						11 39					12 09
Earlswood (Surrey)	d					10 43						11 13						11 43					12 13
Redhill	a	10 29				10 47		10 59			11 07	11 17		11 29				11 47		11 59	12 09		12 17
Redhill	d										11 15										12 14		
Reigate	a										11 19										12 18		
Redhill	d																						
Tonbridge	a																						
Tonbridge	d			10 01												11 01							
Leigh (Kent)	a			10 05												11 05							
Penshurst	a			10 09												11 09							
Edenbridge	a			10 16												11 16							
Godstone	a			10 22												11 22							
Nutfield	a			10 28												11 28							
Reigate	d		10 30		10 38				11 00	11 08					11 30		11 35					12 00	
Redhill	a		10 34	10 36	10 42				11 04	11 14					11 34	11 36	11 40					12 04	
Redhill	d	10 29	10 41			10 49		10 59	11 11			11 19		11 29	11 41			11 49		11 59		12 11	12 19
Merstham	d	10 33	10 45					11 03	11 15					11 33	11 45					12 03		12 15	
Coulsdon South	d	10 39	10 50					11 09	11 20					11 39	11 50					12 09		12 20	
Purley	d		10 55			10 58			11 25			11 28			11 55			11 58				12 25	12 28
East Croydon	a	10 45	11 00			11 03	10 54	11 15	11 30			11 33	11 24	11 45	12 00			12 03	11 54	12 15		12 30	12 33
East Croydon	d	10 45				11 03		11 15				11 33		11 45				12 03		12 15			12 33
Norwood Junction	a					11 07						11 37						12 07					12 37
London Bridge	a	11 00				11 20		11 30				11 50		12 00				12 20		12 30			12 50
London Blackfriars	a	11 06				11 26		11 36				11 56		12 06				12 26		12 36			12 56
City Thameslink	a	11 08				11 28		11 38				11 58		12 08				12 28		12 38			12 58
Farringdon	a	11 11				11 31		11 41				12 01		12 11				12 31		12 41			13 01
St Pancras International	a	11 15				11 35		11 45				12 05		12 15				12 35		12 45			13 05
East Croydon	d		11 00				10 54		11 30				11 24		12 00				11 54			12 30	
Clapham Junction	a		11 10				11 03		11 40				11 33		12 10				12 03			12 40	
London Victoria	a		11 18				11 11		11 48				11 41		12 18				12 11			12 48	

		SN 1	GW	TL 1	SN 1	SN	GW 1	TL 1	SN 1	TL 1	GW 1	SN 1	TL 1	SN 1	GW	TL 1	SN 1	SN	GW 1	TL 1	SN 1	TL 1
Horsham	d	11 50		11 55					12 20	12 23				12 50		12 55					13 20	13 25
Littlehaven	d			11 59						12 27						12 59						13 29
Faygate	d									12 30												
Ifield	d			12 05						12 34						13 05						13 35
Crawley	d	11 59		12 08					12 29	12 38				12 59		13 08					13 29	13 38
Three Bridges	a	12 03		12 12					12 33	12 41				13 03		13 12					13 33	13 42
Three Bridges	d	12 04		12 13					12 34	12 43				13 04		13 13					13 34	13 43
Gatwick Airport	a	12 08		12 17					12 38	12 47				13 08		13 17					13 38	13 47
Gatwick Airport	d	12 09		12 19				12 32	12 39	12 49	13 00		13 03	13 09		13 19				13 32	13 39	13 49
Horley	d			12 21				12 34		12 51			13 05			13 21				13 34		13 51
Salfords	d							12 38					13 09							13 38		
Earlswood (Surrey)	d							12 42					13 13							13 42		
Redhill	a			12 29				12 46		12 59	13 09		13 17			13 29				13 46		13 59
Redhill	d										13 14											
Reigate	a										13 18											
Redhill	d																					
Tonbridge	a																					
Tonbridge	d					12 01												13 01				
Leigh (Kent)	a					12 05												13 05				
Penshurst	a					12 09												13 09				
Edenbridge	a					12 16												13 16				
Godstone	a					12 22												13 22				
Nutfield	a					12 28												13 28				
Reigate	d		12 16		12 30		12 37					13 00			13 19		13 30		13 37			
Redhill	a		12 22		12 34	12 36	12 41					13 04			13 23		13 34	13 36	13 41			
Redhill	d			12 29	12 41			12 49		12 59		13 11	13 19			13 29	13 41			13 49		13 59
Merstham	d			12 33	12 45					13 03		13 15				13 33	13 45					14 03
Coulsdon South	d			12 39	12 50					13 09		13 20				13 39	13 50					14 09
Purley	d				12 55			12 58				13 25	13 28				13 55			13 58		
East Croydon	a	12 24		12 45	13 00			13 03	12 54	13 15		13 30	13 33	13 24		13 45	14 00			14 03	13 54	14 15
East Croydon	d			12 45				13 03		13 15			13 33			13 45				14 03		14 15
Norwood Junction	a							13 07					13 37							14 07		
London Bridge	a			13 00				13 20		13 30			13 50			14 00				14 20		14 30
London Blackfriars	a			13 06				13 26		13 36			13 56			14 06				14 26		14 36
City Thameslink	a			13 08				13 28		13 38			13 58			14 08				14 28		14 38
Farringdon	a			13 11				13 31		13 41			14 01			14 11				14 31		14 41
St Pancras International	a			13 15				13 35		13 45			14 05			14 15				14 35		14 45
East Croydon	d	12 24			13 00				12 54			13 30		13 24			14 00				13 54	
Clapham Junction	a	12 33			13 10				13 03			13 40		13 33			14 10				14 03	
London Victoria	a	12 41			13 18				13 11			13 48		13 41			14 18				14 11	

Table T183-R

Mondays to Fridays

16 December to 15 May

Horsham / Gatwick Airport / Tonbridge / Reigate / Redhill - London

		GW 1	SN 1	GW	TL 1	SN 1	TL 1	SN 1	SN	GW 1	TL 1	SN 1	TL 1	GW 1	SN 1	TL 1	SN 1	GW	TL 1	TL 1	SN 1	SN	GW 1
Horsham	d					13 50	13 55					14 20	14 25				14 50		14 55				
Littlehaven	d						13 59						14 29						14 59				
Faygate	d																						
Ifield	d						14 05						14 35						15 05				
Crawley	d					13 59	14 08					14 29	14 38				14 59		15 08				
Three Bridges	a					14 03	14 12					14 33	14 42				15 03		15 12				
Three Bridges	d					14 04	14 13					14 34	14 43				15 04		15 13				
Gatwick Airport	a					14 08	14 17					14 38	14 47				15 08		15 17				
Gatwick Airport	d	14 00			14 03	14 09	14 19				14 32	14 39	14 49	15 00		15 03	15 09		15 19	15 27			
Horley	d				14 05		14 21				14 34		14 51			15 05			15 21				
Salfords	d				14 09						14 38					15 09							
Earlswood (Surrey)	d				14 13						14 42					15 13							
Redhill	a	14 08			14 17		14 29				14 46		14 59	15 09		15 17			15 29	15 35			
Redhill	d	14 14												15 14									
Reigate	a	14 18												15 18									
Redhill	d																						
Tonbridge	a																						
Tonbridge	d								14 01													15 01	
Leigh (Kent)	a								14 05													15 05	
Penshurst	a								14 09													15 09	
Edenbridge	a								14 16													15 16	
Godstone	a								14 22													15 22	
Nutfield	a								14 28													15 28	
Reigate	d		14 00	14 14				14 30		14 36					15 00			15 17			15 30		15 36
Redhill	a		14 04	14 18				14 34	14 36	14 40					15 04			15 23			15 34	15 36	15 41
Redhill	d		14 11		14 19		14 29	14 41			14 49		14 59		15 11	15 19			15 29	15 36	15 41		
Merstham	d		14 15				14 33	14 45					15 03		15 15				15 33		15 45		
Coulsdon South	d		14 20				14 39	14 50					15 09		15 20				15 39		15 50		
Purley	d		14 25		14 28			14 55			14 58				15 25	15 28				15 48	15 55		
East Croydon	a		14 30		14 33	14 24	14 45	15 00			15 03	14 54	15 15		15 30	15 33	15 24		15 45	15 54	16 00		
East Croydon	d				14 33		14 45				15 03		15 15			15 33			15 45	15 54			
Norwood Junction	a				14 37						15 07					15 37							
London Bridge	a				14 50		15 00				15 20		15 30			15 50			16 00	16 10			
London Blackfriars	a				14 56		15 06				15 26		15 36			15 56			16 06	16 16			
City Thameslink	a				14 58		15 08				15 28		15 38			15 58			16 08	16 18			
Farringdon	a				15 01		15 11				15 31		15 41			16 01			16 11	16 21			
St Pancras International	a				15 05		15 15				15 35		15 45			16 05			16 15	16 25			
East Croydon	d		14 30			14 24		15 00				14 54			15 30		15 24				16 00		
Clapham Junction	a		14 40			14 33		15 10				15 03			15 40		15 33				16 11		
London Victoria	a		14 48			14 41		15 18				15 11			15 49		15 41				16 19		

		TL 1	SN 1	TL 1	TL 1	GW 1	SN 1	TL 1	SN	SN 1	GW	TL 1	TL 1	SN 1	GW 1	TL 1	SN	SN 1	TL 1	TL 1	GW 1	SN 1
Horsham	d		15 20	15 25						15 50		15 55						16 22	16 25			
Littlehaven	d			15 29								15 59							16 28			
Faygate	d																		16 32			
Ifield	d			15 35								16 05							16 36			
Crawley	d		15 29	15 38						15 59		16 08						16 31	16 39			
Three Bridges	a		15 33	15 42						16 03		16 12						16 35	16 43			
Three Bridges	d		15 34	15 43						16 04		16 13						16 36	16 44			
Gatwick Airport	a		15 38	15 47						16 08		16 17						16 40	16 48			
Gatwick Airport	d	15 32	15 39	15 49	15 57	16 00		16 03		16 09		16 19	16 27			16 33		16 41	16 49	16 57	17 00	
Horley	d	15 34		15 51				16 05				16 21				16 35			16 52			
Salfords	d	15 38						16 09								16 39						
Earlswood (Surrey)	d	15 42						16 13								16 43						
Redhill	a	15 46		15 59	16 05	16 09		16 17				16 29	16 35			16 47			16 59	17 05	17 08	
Redhill	d					16 14															17 14	
Reigate	a					16 18															17 19	
Redhill	d																					
Tonbridge	a																					
Tonbridge	d								15 47								16 17					
Leigh (Kent)	a								15 51								16 21					
Penshurst	a								15 55								16 25					
Edenbridge	a								16 02								16 32					
Godstone	a								16 08								16 38					
Nutfield	a								16 14								16 44					
Reigate	d						16 00				16 21			16 30	16 38							17 00
Redhill	a						16 04		16 20		16 26			16 34	16 42		16 50					17 04
Redhill	d	15 49		15 59	16 06		16 11	16 19				16 29	16 36	16 41		16 49			17 00	17 06		17 11
Merstham	d			16 03			16 15					16 33		16 45					17 04			17 15
Coulsdon South	d			16 09			16 20					16 39		16 50					17 09			17 20
Purley	d	15 58			16 18		16 25	16 28					16 48	16 55		16 58				17 18		17 25
East Croydon	a	16 03	15 54	16 15	16 24		16 30	16 33		16 24		16 45	16 54	17 00		17 03		16 56	17 15	17 24		17 30
East Croydon	d	16 03		16 15	16 24			16 33				16 45	16 54			17 03			17 15	17 25		
Norwood Junction	a	16 07						16 37								17 07						
London Bridge	a	16 20		16 30	16 40			16 50				17 00	17 10			17 20			17 30	17 40		
London Blackfriars	a	16 26		16 36	16 46			16 56				17 06	17 16			17 26			17 36	17 46		
City Thameslink	a	16 28		16 38	16 48			16 58				17 08	17 18			17 28			17 38	17 48		
Farringdon	a	16 31		16 41	16 51			17 01				17 11	17 21			17 31			17 41	17 51		
St Pancras International	a	16 35		16 45	16 55			17 05				17 15	17 25			17 35			17 45	17 55		
East Croydon	d		15 54				16 30			16 24				17 00				16 56				17 30
Clapham Junction	a		16 03				16 41			16 33				17 13				17 05				17 40
London Victoria	a		16 11				16 48			16 41				17 21				17 13				17 50

Table T183-R

Mondays to Fridays

16 December to 15 May

Horsham / Gatwick Airport / Tonbridge / Reigate / Redhill - London

		TL 1	SN	SN 1	TL 1	GW	TL 1	SN 1	GW 1	TL 1		SN	SN 1	TL 1	GW 1	SN 1	TL 1	SN	SN 1	TL 1		GW	SN 1	GW 1	TL 1
Horsham	d			16 50	16 55								17 20	17 25					17 50	17 55					
Littlehaven	d				16 58									17 28						17 58					
Faygate	d				17 02									17 32						18 02					
Ifield	d				17 06									17 36						18 06					
Crawley	d			16 59	17 09								17 29	17 39					17 59	18 09					
Three Bridges	a			17 03	17 13								17 33	17 43					18 03	18 13					
Three Bridges	d			17 04	17 14								17 34	17 44					18 04	18 14					
Gatwick Airport	a			17 08	17 18								17 38	17 48					18 08	18 18					
Gatwick Airport	d	17 03		17 09	17 19		17 27			17 33			17 39	17 49	18 00		18 03		18 09	18 19					18 33
Horley	d	17 05			17 22					17 35				17 52			18 05			18 22					18 35
Salfords	d	17 09								17 39							18 09								18 39
Earlswood (Surrey)	d	17 13								17 43							18 13								18 43
Redhill	a	17 17			17 29		17 35			17 48				17 59	18 09		18 17			18 29					18 47
Redhill	d														18 14										
Reigate	a														18 18										
Redhill	d																								
Tonbridge	a																								
Tonbridge	d		16 47									17 17						17 47							
Leigh (Kent)	a		16 51									17 21						17 51							
Penshurst	a		16 55									17 25						17 55							
Edenbridge	a		17 02									17 32						18 02							
Godstone	a		17 08									17 38						18 08							
Nutfield	a		17 14									17 44						18 14							
Reigate	d					17 27		17 31	17 36							18 00						18 26	18 30	18 35	
Redhill	a		17 20			17 33		17 36	17 40			17 50				18 04		18 20				18 30	18 35	18 39	
Redhill	d	17 19			17 30		17 36	17 41		17 49				18 00		18 11	18 19			18 30			18 41		18 49
Merstham	d				17 34			17 45						18 04		18 15				18 34			18 45		
Coulsdon South	d				17 39			17 50						18 09		18 20				18 39			18 50		
Purley	d	17 28					17 48	17 55		17 58						18 25	18 28						18 55		18 58
East Croydon	a	17 33		17 24	17 45		17 54	18 00		18 03			17 54	18 15		18 30	18 33		18 24	18 45			19 00		19 03
East Croydon	d	17 33			17 45		17 55			18 03				18 15			18 33			18 45					19 03
Norwood Junction	a	17 37								18 07							18 37								19 07
London Bridge	a	17 50			18 00		18 10			18 20				18 30			18 50			19 00					19 20
London Blackfriars	a	17 56			18 06		18 16			18 26				18 36			18 56			19 06					19 26
City Thameslink	a	17 58			18 08		18 18			18 28				18 38			18 58			19 08					19 28
Farringdon	a	18 01			18 11		18 21			18 31				18 41			19 01			19 11					19 31
St Pancras International	a	18 05			18 15		18 25			18 35				18 45			19 05			19 15					19 35
East Croydon	d			17 24				18 00					17 54			18 30			18 24				19 00		
Clapham Junction	a			17 33				18 10					18 03			18 40			18 34				19 10		
London Victoria	a			17 41				18 18					18 12			18 48			18 42				19 18		

		SN	SN 1	TL 1	GW 1	SN 1		TL 1	SN	SN 1	TL 1	GW	SN 1	GW 1	TL 1	SN 1		SN	TL 1	SN 1	GW 1	TL 1	SN 1	TL 1	SN
Horsham	d		18 20	18 25						18 52	18 55					19 20			19 25				19 52	19 55	
Littlehaven	d			18 28							18 59								19 29					19 59	
Faygate	d			18 32																					
Ifield	d			18 36							19 05								19 35					20 05	
Crawley	d		18 29	18 39						19 01	19 08					19 29			19 38				20 01	20 08	
Three Bridges	a		18 33	18 43						19 05	19 12					19 33			19 42				20 05	20 12	
Three Bridges	d		18 34	18 44						19 06	19 13					19 34			19 43				20 06	20 13	
Gatwick Airport	a		18 38	18 48						19 10	19 17					19 38			19 47				20 10	20 18	
Gatwick Airport	d		18 39	18 49	19 00			19 03		19 11	19 19				19 33	19 39			19 49		19 58	20 03	20 11	20 19	
Horley	d			18 52				19 05			19 21				19 35				19 51			20 05		20 21	
Salfords	d							19 09							19 39							20 09			
Earlswood (Surrey)	d							19 13							19 43							20 13			
Redhill	a			18 59	19 08			19 17			19 29				19 47				19 59		20 06	20 17		20 29	
Redhill	d				19 14																20 12				
Reigate	a				19 18																20 16				
Redhill	d																								
Tonbridge	a																								
Tonbridge	d	18 17							18 47									19 22							20 01
Leigh (Kent)	a	18 21							18 51																20 05
Penshurst	a	18 25							18 55																20 09
Edenbridge	a	18 32							19 02									19 32							20 16
Godstone	a	18 38							19 08									19 39							20 22
Nutfield	a	18 44							19 14									19 44							20 28
Reigate	d					19 00						19 27	19 31	19 36						20 00					
Redhill	a	18 50				19 04			19 20			19 33	19 36	19 40				19 50		20 04					20 36
Redhill	d			19 00		19 11		19 19			19 29		19 41		19 49				19 59	20 11		20 19		20 29	
Merstham	d			19 04		19 15					19 33		19 45						20 03	20 15				20 33	
Coulsdon South	d			19 09		19 20					19 39		19 50						20 09	20 20				20 39	
Purley	d					19 25		19 28					19 55		19 58					20 25		20 28			
East Croydon	a		18 54	19 15		19 30		19 33		19 26	19 45		20 00		20 03	19 54			20 15	20 30		20 33	20 26	20 45	
East Croydon	d			19 15				19 33			19 45				20 03				20 15			20 33		20 45	
Norwood Junction	a							19 37							20 07							20 37			
London Bridge	a			19 30				19 50			20 00				20 20				20 30			20 50		21 00	
London Blackfriars	a			19 36				19 56			20 06				20 26				20 36			20 56		21 06	
City Thameslink	a			19 38				19 58			20 08				20 28				20 38			20 58		21 08	
Farringdon	a			19 41				20 01			20 11				20 31				20 41			21 01		21 11	
St Pancras International	a			19 45				20 05			20 15				20 35				20 45			21 05		21 15	
East Croydon	d		18 54			19 30				19 26			20 00			19 54				20 30			20 26		
Clapham Junction	a		19 03			19 41				19 35			20 10			20 04				20 41			20 35		
London Victoria	a		19 11			19 49				19 43			20 19			20 11				20 49			20 43		

NRT DECEMBER 19 EDITION

Table T183-R

Mondays to Fridays

16 December to 15 May

Horsham / Gatwick Airport / Tonbridge / Reigate / Redhill - London

		SN 1		GW 1	TL 1	SN 1	TL 1	GW 1	SN 1	TL 1	SN 1	TL 1		GW	SN 1	SN	GW 1	TL 1	SN 1	TL 1	GW 1	SN 1		SN 1	TL 1
Horsham	d					20 20	20 25				20 50	20 55							21 20	21 26		21 50			21 55
Littlehaven	d						20 29					20 59								21 29					21 59
Faygate	d																								
Ifield	d						20 35					21 05								21 35					22 05
Crawley	d					20 29	20 38				20 59	21 08							21 29	21 39		21 59			22 08
Three Bridges	a					20 33	20 42				21 03	21 12							21 33	21 42		22 03			22 12
Three Bridges	d					20 34	20 43				21 04	21 13							21 34	21 43		22 04			22 13
Gatwick Airport	a					20 38	20 47				21 08	21 17							21 38	21 48		22 08			22 17
Gatwick Airport	d				20 32	20 39	20 49	21 00		21 03	21 09	21 19						21 32	21 39	21 49	22 00	22 09			22 19
Horley	d				20 34		20 51			21 05		21 21						21 34		21 51					22 21
Salfords	d				20 38					21 09								21 38							22 25
Earlswood (Surrey)	d				20 42					21 13								21 42							22 29
Redhill	a				20 46		20 59	21 08		21 17		21 29						21 46		21 59	22 09				22 33
Redhill	d							21 14													22 13				
Reigate	a							21 18													22 17				
Redhill	d																								
Tonbridge	a																								
Tonbridge	d															21 01									
Leigh (Kent)	a															21 05									
Penshurst	a															21 09									
Edenbridge	a															21 16									
Godstone	a															21 22									
Nutfield	a															21 28									
Reigate	d	20 30		20 37					21 00					21 26	21 30		21 38							22 00	
Redhill	a	20 36		20 42					21 04					21 31	21 34	21 36	21 42							22 04	
Redhill	d	20 41			20 49		20 59		21 11	21 19		21 29			21 41			21 49		21 59				22 11	22 34
Merstham	d	20 45					21 03		21 15			21 33			21 45					22 03				22 15	
Coulsdon South	d	20 50					21 09		21 20			21 39			21 50					22 09				22 20	
Purley	d	20 55			20 58				21 25	21 28					21 55			21 58						22 25	
East Croydon	a	21 00			21 03	20 54	21 15		21 30	21 33	21 24	21 45			22 00			22 03	21 54	22 15		22 24		22 30	22 45
East Croydon	d				21 03		21 15			21 33		21 45						22 03		22 15					22 45
Norwood Junction	a				21 07					21 37								22 07							
London Bridge	a				21 20		21 30			21 50		22 00						22 20		22 30					23 00
London Blackfriars	a				21 26		21 36			21 56		22 06						22 26		22 36					23 06
City Thameslink	a				21 28		21 38			21 58		22 08						22 28		22 38					
Farringdon	a				21 31		21 41			22 01		22 11						22 31		22 41					23 11
St Pancras International	a				21 35		21 45			22 05		22 15						22 35		22 45					23 15
East Croydon	d	21 00				20 54			21 30		21 24				22 00				21 54			22 24		22 30	
Clapham Junction	a	21 12				21 06			21 40		21 33				22 10				22 03			22 33		22 40	
London Victoria	a	21 19				21 13			21 49		21 41				22 18				22 11			22 42		22 49	

		SN 1	SN 1	SN	GW 1	TL 1	SN 1	GW 1		SN	TL 1	SN 1	GW 1	SN
Horsham	d	22 20				22 25					23 11	23 27		
Littlehaven	d					22 29					23 15	23 30		
Faygate	d													
Ifield	d					22 35					23 21	23 36		
Crawley	d	22 29				22 38					23 24	23 40		
Three Bridges	a	22 33				22 42					23 28	23 43		
Three Bridges	d	22 34				22 43					23 29	23 44		
Gatwick Airport	a	22 38				22 47					23 33	23 49		
Gatwick Airport	d	22 39				22 49		23 18			23 35			
Horley	d					22 51					23 37			
Salfords	d					22 55					23 41			
Earlswood (Surrey)	d					22 59					23 45			
Redhill	a					23 03		23 26			23 49			
Redhill	d							23 32						
Reigate	a							23 36						
Redhill	d													
Tonbridge	a													
Tonbridge	d			22 01						23 01				23 36
Leigh (Kent)	a			22 05						23 05				23 40
Penshurst	a			22 09						23 09				23 44
Edenbridge	a			22 16						23 16				23 51
Godstone	a			22 22						23 22				23 57
Nutfield	a			22 28						23 28				00 03
Reigate	d		22 30		22 36		23 00						23 56	
Redhill	a		22 34	22 36	22 40		23 04			23 36			00 01	00 09
Redhill	d		22 41			23 04	23 11				23 49			
Merstham	d		22 45				23 15				23 53			
Coulsdon South	d		22 50				23 20				23 59			
Purley	d		22 55				23 25				00 03			
East Croydon	a	22 54	23 00			23 15	23 30				00 09			
East Croydon	d					23 15					00 09			
Norwood Junction	a													
London Bridge	a					23 30								
London Blackfriars	a					23 36					00 36			
City Thameslink	a													
Farringdon	a					23 41					00 41			
St Pancras International	a					23 45					00 45			
East Croydon	d	22 54	23 00				23 30							
Clapham Junction	a	23 03	23 11				23 44							
London Victoria	a	23 12	23 19				23 52							

Table T183-R

Saturdays

21 December to 16 May

Horsham / Gatwick Airport / Tonbridge / Reigate / Redhill - London

		GW	TL 1	GW 1	TL 1	SN 1	TL 1	SN 1	TL 1	SN 1	TL 1	SN 1	GW 1	GW 1	SN 1	TL 1	TL 1	SN	GW 1	TL 1	SN 1	TL 1	SN 1
Horsham	d																05 25				05 41	05 55	
Littlehaven	d																05 29				05 45	05 59	
Faygate	d																						
Ifield	d																05 35				05 51	06 05	
Crawley	d																05 38				05 55	06 08	
Three Bridges	a																05 42				06 00	06 12	
Three Bridges	d		00 37		01 41	02 08	02 41	03 08	03 41	04 08	04 35	04 58			05 22	05 27	05 43				06 03	06 13	
Gatwick Airport	a		00 41		01 45	02 12	02 45	03 12	03 45	04 12	04 40	05 02			05 26	05 31	05 48				06 08	06 17	
Gatwick Airport	d	00 24	00 42		01 46	02 13	02 46	03 13	03 46	04 13	04 41	05 03		05 24	05 28	05 33	05 49		05 55	06 03	06 09	06 19	
Horley	d		00 45		01 49	02 16	02 49	03 16	03 49	04 16	04 43	05 06			05 31	05 35	05 51			06 05		06 21	
Salfords	d															05 39				06 09			
Earlswood (Surrey)	d															05 43				06 13			
Redhill	a	00 35	00 52								04 51	05 14		05 33	05 39	05 48	05 59		06 04	06 17		06 29	
Redhill	d													05 42					06 12				
Reigate	a													05 46					06 16				
Redhill	d																						
Tonbridge	a																						
Tonbridge	d																	05 33					
Leigh (Kent)	a																	05 37					
Penshurst	a																	05 41					
Edenbridge	a																	05 48					
Godstone	a																	05 54					
Nutfield	a																	06 00					
Reigate	d			00 51									05 35										06 30
Redhill	a			00 55									05 39					06 06					06 34
Redhill	d		00 53								04 54	05 14			05 41	05 49	05 59			06 19		06 29	06 41
Merstham	d														05 45		06 03					06 33	06 45
Coulsdon South	d														05 50		06 09					06 39	06 50
Purley	d		01 03		02 03	02 29	03 03	03 29	04 03	04 29	05 03	05 24			05 55	05 58				06 28			06 55
East Croydon	a		01 09		02 09	02 36	03 09	03 36	04 09	04 36	05 09	05 30			06 00	06 03	06 15			06 33	06 24	06 45	07 00
East Croydon	d		01 10		02 10		03 10		04 10		05 10					06 03	06 15			06 33		06 45	
Norwood Junction	a															06 07				06 37			
London Bridge	a										05 25					06 20	06 30			06 50		07 00	
London Blackfriars	a		01 36		02 36		03 36		04 36		05 31					06 26	06 36			06 56		07 06	
City Thameslink	a																						
Farringdon	a										05 36					06 31	06 41			07 01		07 11	
St Pancras International	a		01 43		02 43		03 43		04 43		05 40					06 35	06 45			07 05		07 15	
East Croydon	d					02 36		03 36		04 36		05 30			06 00						06 24		07 00
Clapham Junction	a					02 50		03 50		04 50		05 50			06 10						06 33		07 10
London Victoria	a					02 58		03 58		04 58		05 59			06 18						06 41		07 18

		SN 1	GW 1	TL 1	SN 1	TL 1	GW 1	SN 1	TL 1	SN 1	GW 1	TL 1	SN 1	SN	GW 1	TL 1	SN 1	TL 1	GW 1	SN 1	TL 1	SN 1	GW 1
Horsham	d				06 20	06 25				06 50		06 55					07 20	07 25				07 50	
Littlehaven	d					06 29						06 59						07 29					
Faygate	d																						
Ifield	d					06 35						07 05						07 35					
Crawley	d				06 29	06 38				06 59		07 08					07 29	07 38				07 59	
Three Bridges	a				06 33	06 42				07 03		07 12					07 33	07 42				08 03	
Three Bridges	d				06 34	06 43				07 04		07 13					07 34	07 43				08 04	
Gatwick Airport	a				06 38	06 47				07 08		07 17					07 38	07 47				08 08	
Gatwick Airport	d			06 33	06 39	06 49	07 00		07 03	07 09		07 19				07 33	07 39	07 49	08 00		08 03	08 09	
Horley	d			06 35		06 51			07 05			07 21				07 35		07 51			08 05		
Salfords	d			06 39					07 09							07 39					08 09		
Earlswood (Surrey)	d			06 43					07 13							07 43					08 13		
Redhill	a			06 48		06 59	07 09		07 17			07 29				07 47		07 59	08 09		08 17		
Redhill	d						07 14												08 14				
Reigate	a						07 18												08 18				
Redhill	d																						
Tonbridge	a																						
Tonbridge	d	06 03												07 01									
Leigh (Kent)	a	06 07												07 05									
Penshurst	a	06 11												07 09									
Edenbridge	a	06 18												07 16									
Godstone	a	06 24												07 22									
Nutfield	a	06 30												07 28									
Reigate	d		06 36					07 00			07 17		07 30		07 35					08 00			08 18
Redhill	a	06 36	06 40					07 04			07 23		07 34	07 36	07 39					08 04			08 24
Redhill	d			06 49		06 59		07 11	07 19			07 29	07 41			07 49		07 59		08 11	08 19		
Merstham	d					07 03		07 15				07 33	07 45					08 03		08 15			
Coulsdon South	d					07 09		07 20				07 39	07 50					08 09		08 20			
Purley	d			06 58				07 25	07 28				07 55			07 58				08 25	08 28		
East Croydon	a			07 03	06 54	07 15		07 30	07 33	07 24		07 45	08 00			08 03	07 54	08 15		08 30	08 33	08 24	
East Croydon	d			07 03		07 15			07 33			07 45				08 03		08 15			08 33		
Norwood Junction	a			07 07					07 37							08 07					08 37		
London Bridge	a			07 20		07 30			07 50			08 00				08 20		08 30			08 50		
London Blackfriars	a			07 26		07 36			07 56			08 06				08 26		08 36			08 56		
City Thameslink	a																						
Farringdon	a			07 31		07 41			08 01			08 11				08 31		08 41			09 01		
St Pancras International	a			07 35		07 45			08 05			08 15				08 35		08 45			09 05		
East Croydon	d				06 54			07 30		07 24			08 00				07 54			08 30		08 24	
Clapham Junction	a				07 03			07 40		07 33			08 10				08 03			08 40		08 33	
London Victoria	a				07 11			07 48		07 41			08 18				08 11			08 48		08 41	

Table T183-R

Saturdays

21 December to 16 May

Horsham / Gatwick Airport / Tonbridge / Reigate / Redhill - London

		TL 1	SN 1	SN	GW 1	TL 1	SN 1	TL 1	GW 1	SN 1	TL 1	SN 1	GW 1	TL 1	SN 1	SN	GW 1	TL 1	SN 1	TL 1	GW 1	SN 1
Horsham	d	07 55					08 20	08 25				08 50		08 55					09 20	09 25		
Littlehaven	d	07 59						08 29						08 59						09 29		
Faygate	d																					
Ifield	d	08 05						08 35						09 05						09 35		
Crawley	d	08 08					08 29	08 38				08 59		09 08					09 29	09 38		
Three Bridges	a	08 12					08 33	08 42				09 03		09 12					09 33	09 42		
Three Bridges	d	08 13					08 34	08 43				09 04		09 13					09 34	09 43		
Gatwick Airport	a	08 17					08 38	08 47				09 08		09 17					09 38	09 47		
Gatwick Airport	d	08 19				08 33	08 39	08 49	09 00		09 03	09 09		09 19				09 33	09 39	09 49	10 00	
Horley	d	08 21				08 36		08 51			09 05			09 21				09 36		09 51		
Salfords	d					08 40					09 09							09 40				
Earlswood (Surrey)	d					08 44					09 13							09 44				
Redhill	a	08 29				08 48		08 59	09 09		09 17			09 29				09 48		09 59	10 09	
Redhill	d								09 14												10 14	
Reigate	a								09 18												10 18	
Redhill	d																					
Tonbridge	a																					
Tonbridge	d			08 01												09 01						
Leigh (Kent)	a			08 05												09 05						
Penshurst	a			08 09												09 09						
Edenbridge	a			08 16												09 16						
Godstone	a			08 22												09 22						
Nutfield	a			08 28												09 28						
Reigate	d		08 30		08 36					09 00			09 17		09 30		09 36					10 00
Redhill	a		08 34	08 36	08 40					09 04			09 23		09 34	09 36	09 40					10 04
Redhill	d	08 29	08 41			08 49		08 59		09 11	09 19			09 29	09 41			09 49		09 59		10 11
Merstham	d	08 33	08 45					09 03		09 15				09 33	09 45					10 03		10 15
Coulsdon South	d	08 39	08 50					09 09		09 20				09 39	09 50					10 09		10 20
Purley	d		08 55			08 58				09 25	09 28				09 55			09 58				10 25
East Croydon	a	08 45	09 00			09 03	08 54	09 15		09 30	09 33	09 24		09 45	10 00			10 03	09 54	10 15		10 30
East Croydon	d	08 45				09 03		09 15			09 33			09 45				10 03		10 15		
Norwood Junction	a					09 07					09 37							10 07				
London Bridge	a	09 00				09 20		09 30			09 50			10 00				10 20		10 30		
London Blackfriars	a	09 06				09 26		09 36			09 56			10 06				10 26		10 36		
City Thameslink	a	09 08				09 28		09 38			09 58			10 08				10 28		10 38		
Farringdon	a	09 11				09 31		09 41			10 01			10 11				10 31		10 41		
St Pancras International	a	09 15				09 35		09 45			10 05			10 15				10 35		10 45		
East Croydon	d		09 00				08 54			09 30		09 24			10 00				09 54			10 30
Clapham Junction	a		09 10				09 03			09 40		09 33			10 10				10 03			10 40
London Victoria	a		09 18				09 11			09 48		09 41			10 18				10 11			10 48

		TL 1	SN 1	GW 1	TL 1	SN 1	SN	GW 1	TL 1	SN 1	TL 1	GW 1	SN 1	TL 1	SN 1	GW 1	TL 1	SN 1	SN	GW 1	TL 1	SN 1	TL 1
Horsham	d		09 50		09 55					10 20	10 25				10 50		10 55					11 20	11 25
Littlehaven	d				09 59						10 29						10 59						11 29
Faygate	d																						
Ifield	d				10 05						10 35						11 05						11 35
Crawley	d		09 59		10 08					10 29	10 38				10 59		11 08					11 29	11 38
Three Bridges	a		10 03		10 12					10 33	10 42				11 03		11 12					11 33	11 42
Three Bridges	d		10 04		10 13					10 34	10 43				11 04		11 13					11 34	11 43
Gatwick Airport	a		10 08		10 17					10 38	10 47				11 08		11 17					11 38	11 47
Gatwick Airport	d	10 03	10 09		10 19				10 33	10 39	10 49	11 00		11 03	11 09		11 19				11 33	11 39	11 49
Horley	d	10 05			10 21				10 36		10 51			11 05			11 21				11 36		11 51
Salfords	d	10 09							10 40					11 09							11 40		
Earlswood (Surrey)	d	10 13							10 44					11 13							11 44		
Redhill	a	10 17			10 29				10 48		10 59	11 09		11 17			11 29				11 48		11 59
Redhill	d											11 14											
Reigate	a											11 18											
Redhill	d																						
Tonbridge	a																						
Tonbridge	d						10 01												11 01				
Leigh (Kent)	a						10 05												11 05				
Penshurst	a						10 09												11 09				
Edenbridge	a						10 16												11 16				
Godstone	a						10 22												11 22				
Nutfield	a						10 28												11 28				
Reigate	d			10 18		10 30		10 36					11 00			11 17		11 30		11 36			
Redhill	a			10 24		10 34	10 36	10 40					11 04			11 23		11 34	11 36	11 40			
Redhill	d	10 19			10 29	10 41			10 49		10 59		11 11	11 19			11 29	11 41			11 49		11 59
Merstham	d				10 33	10 45					11 03		11 15				11 33	11 45					12 03
Coulsdon South	d				10 39	10 50					11 09		11 20				11 39	11 50					12 09
Purley	d	10 28				10 55			10 58				11 25	11 28				11 55			11 58		
East Croydon	a	10 33	10 24		10 45	11 00			11 03	10 54	11 15		11 30	11 33	11 24		11 45	12 00			12 03	11 54	12 15
East Croydon	d	10 33			10 45				11 03		11 15			11 33			11 45				12 03		12 15
Norwood Junction	a	10 37							11 07					11 37							12 07		
London Bridge	a	10 50			11 00				11 20		11 30			11 50			12 00				12 20		12 30
London Blackfriars	a	10 56			11 06				11 26		11 36			11 56			12 06				12 26		12 36
City Thameslink	a	10 58			11 08				11 28		11 38			11 58			12 08				12 28		12 38
Farringdon	a	11 01			11 11				11 31		11 41			12 01			12 11				12 31		12 41
St Pancras International	a	11 05			11 15				11 35		11 45			12 05			12 15				12 35		12 45
East Croydon	d		10 24			11 00				10 54			11 30		11 24			12 00				11 54	
Clapham Junction	a		10 33			11 10				11 03			11 40		11 33			12 10				12 03	
London Victoria	a		10 41			11 18				11 11			11 48		11 41			12 18				12 11	

Table T183-R

Saturdays

21 December to 16 May

Horsham / Gatwick Airport / Tonbridge / Reigate / Redhill - London

Station		GW	SN	TL	SN	GW	TL	SN	SN	GW	TL	SN	TL	GW	SN	TL	SN	GW	TL	SN	SN	GW
Horsham	d				11 50		11 55					12 20	12 25				12 50		12 55			
Littlehaven	d						11 59						12 29						12 59			
Faygate	d																					
Ifield	d						12 05						12 35						13 05			
Crawley	d				11 59		12 08					12 29	12 38				12 59		13 08			
Three Bridges	a				12 03		12 12					12 33	12 42				13 03		13 12			
Three Bridges	d				12 04		12 13					12 34	12 43				13 04		13 13			
Gatwick Airport	a				12 08		12 17					12 38	12 47				13 08		13 17			
Gatwick Airport	d	12 00		12 03	12 09		12 19				12 33	12 39	12 49	13 00		13 03	13 09		13 19			
Horley	d			12 05			12 21				12 36		12 51			13 05			13 21			
Salfords	d			12 09							12 40					13 09						
Earlswood (Surrey)	d			12 13							12 44					13 13						
Redhill	a	12 09		12 17			12 29				12 48		12 59	13 09		13 17			13 29			
Redhill	d	12 14												13 14								
Reigate	a	12 18												13 18								
Redhill	d																					
Tonbridge	a																					
Tonbridge	d								12 01												13 01	
Leigh (Kent)	a								12 05												13 05	
Penshurst	a								12 09												13 09	
Edenbridge	a								12 16												13 16	
Godstone	a								12 22												13 22	
Nutfield	a								12 28												13 28	
Reigate	d		12 00			12 18		12 30		12 36					13 00			13 17		13 30		13 36
Redhill	a		12 04			12 24		12 34	12 36	12 40					13 04			13 23		13 34	13 36	13 40
Redhill	d		12 11	12 19			12 29	12 41			12 49		12 59		13 11	13 19			13 29	13 41		
Merstham	d		12 15				12 33	12 45					13 03		13 15				13 33	13 45		
Coulsdon South	d		12 20				12 39	12 50					13 09		13 20				13 39	13 50		
Purley	d		12 25	12 28				12 55			12 58				13 25	13 28				13 55		
East Croydon	a		12 30	12 33	12 24		12 45	13 00			13 03	12 54	13 15		13 30	13 33	13 24		13 45	14 00		
East Croydon	d			12 33			12 45				13 03		13 15			13 33			13 45			
Norwood Junction	a			12 37							13 07					13 37						
London Bridge	a			12 50			13 00				13 20		13 30			13 50			14 00			
London Blackfriars	a			12 56			13 06				13 26		13 36			13 56			14 06			
City Thameslink	a			12 58			13 08				13 28		13 38			13 58			14 08			
Farringdon	a			13 01			13 11				13 31		13 41			14 01			14 11			
St Pancras International	a			13 05			13 15				13 35		13 45			14 05			14 15			
East Croydon	d		12 30		12 24			13 00				12 54			13 30		13 24			14 00		
Clapham Junction	a		12 40		12 33			13 10				13 03			13 40		13 33			14 10		
London Victoria	a		12 48		12 41			13 18				13 11			13 48		13 41			14 18		

Station		TL	SN	TL	GW	SN	TL	SN	GW	TL	SN	SN	GW	TL	SN	TL	GW	SN	TL	SN	GW	TL	SN
Horsham	d		13 20	13 25				13 50		13 55					14 20	14 25				14 50		14 55	
Littlehaven	d			13 29						13 59						14 29						14 59	
Faygate	d																						
Ifield	d			13 35						14 05						14 35						15 05	
Crawley	d		13 29	13 38				13 59		14 08					14 29	14 38				14 59		15 08	
Three Bridges	a		13 33	13 42				14 03		14 12					14 33	14 42				15 03		15 12	
Three Bridges	d		13 34	13 43				14 04		14 13					14 34	14 43				15 04		15 13	
Gatwick Airport	a		13 38	13 47				14 08		14 17					14 38	14 47				15 08		15 17	
Gatwick Airport	d	13 33	13 39	13 49	14 00		14 03	14 09		14 19				14 33	14 39	14 49	15 00		15 03	15 09		15 19	
Horley	d	13 36		13 51			14 05			14 21				14 36		14 51			15 05			15 21	
Salfords	d	13 40					14 09							14 40					15 09				
Earlswood (Surrey)	d	13 44					14 13							14 44					15 13				
Redhill	a	13 48		13 59	14 09		14 17			14 29				14 48		14 59	15 09		15 17			15 29	
Redhill	d				14 14												15 14						
Reigate	a				14 18												15 18						
Redhill	d																						
Tonbridge	a																						
Tonbridge	d											14 01											
Leigh (Kent)	a											14 05											
Penshurst	a											14 09											
Edenbridge	a											14 16											
Godstone	a											14 22											
Nutfield	a											14 28											
Reigate	d					14 00			14 18		14 30		14 36					15 00			15 18		15 30
Redhill	a					14 04			14 24		14 34	14 36	14 40					15 04			15 24		15 34
Redhill	d	13 49		13 59		14 11	14 19			14 29	14 41			14 49		14 59		15 11	15 19			15 29	15 41
Merstham	d			14 03		14 15				14 33	14 45					15 03		15 15				15 33	15 45
Coulsdon South	d			14 09		14 20				14 39	14 50					15 09		15 20				15 39	15 50
Purley	d	13 58				14 25	14 28				14 55			14 58				15 25	15 28				15 55
East Croydon	a	14 03	13 54	14 15		14 30	14 33	14 24		14 45	15 00			15 03	14 54	15 15		15 30	15 33	15 24		15 45	16 00
East Croydon	d	14 03		14 15			14 33			14 45				15 03		15 15			15 33			15 45	
Norwood Junction	a	14 07					14 37							15 07					15 37				
London Bridge	a	14 20		14 30			14 50			15 00				15 20		15 30			15 50			16 00	
London Blackfriars	a	14 26		14 36			14 56			15 06				15 26		15 36			15 56			16 06	
City Thameslink	a	14 28		14 38			14 58			15 08				15 28		15 38			15 58			16 08	
Farringdon	a	14 31		14 41			15 01			15 11				15 31		15 41			16 01			16 11	
St Pancras International	a	14 35		14 45			15 05			15 15				15 35		15 45			16 05			16 15	
East Croydon	d		13 54			14 30		14 24			15 00				14 54			15 30		15 24			16 00
Clapham Junction	a		14 03			14 40		14 33			15 10				15 03			15 40		15 33			16 10
London Victoria	a		14 11			14 48		14 41			15 18				15 11			15 48		15 41			16 18

NRT DECEMBER 19 EDITION

Table T183-R

Saturdays

21 December to 16 May

Horsham / Gatwick Airport / Tonbridge / Reigate / Redhill - London

Station		SN	GW	TL	SN	TL	GW	SN	TL	SN	GW	TL	SN	SN	GW	TL	SN	TL	GW	SN	TL	SN	GW
Horsham	d				15 20	15 25				15 50		15 55					16 22	16 25				16 50	
Littlehaven	d					15 29						15 59						16 29					
Faygate	d																						
Ifield	d					15 35						16 05						16 35					
Crawley	d				15 29	15 38				15 59		16 08					16 31	16 38				16 59	
Three Bridges	a				15 33	15 42				16 03		16 12					16 35	16 42				17 03	
Three Bridges	d				15 34	15 43				16 04		16 13					16 36	16 43				17 04	
Gatwick Airport	a				15 38	15 47				16 08		16 17					16 40	16 47				17 08	
Gatwick Airport	d			15 32	15 39	15 49	16 00		16 03	16 09		16 19				16 33	16 41	16 49	17 00		17 03	17 09	
Horley	d			15 34		15 51			16 05			16 21				16 36		16 51			17 05		
Salfords	d			15 38					16 09							16 40					17 09		
Earlswood (Surrey)	d			15 42					16 13							16 44					17 13		
Redhill	a			15 46		15 59	16 10		16 17			16 29				16 48		16 59	17 10		17 17		
Redhill	d						16 14												17 14				
Reigate	a						16 18												17 18				
Redhill	d																						
Tonbridge	a																						
Tonbridge	d	15 01												16 01									
Leigh (Kent)	a	15 05												16 05									
Penshurst	a	15 09												16 09									
Edenbridge	a	15 16												16 16									
Godstone	a	15 22												16 22									
Nutfield	a	15 28												16 28									
Reigate	d		15 36					16 00			16 18		16 30		16 36					17 00			17 17
Redhill	a	15 36	15 40					16 04			16 24		16 34	16 36	16 40					17 04			17 23
Redhill	d			15 49		15 59		16 11	16 19			16 29	16 41			16 49		16 59		17 11	17 19		
Merstham	d					16 03		16 15				16 33	16 45					17 03		17 15			
Coulsdon South	d					16 09		16 20				16 39	16 50					17 09		17 20			
Purley	d			15 58				16 25	16 28				16 55			16 58				17 25	17 28		
East Croydon	a			16 03	15 54	16 15		16 30	16 33	16 24		16 45	17 00			17 03	16 56	17 15		17 30	17 33	17 24	
East Croydon	d			16 03		16 15			16 33			16 45				17 03		17 15			17 33		
Norwood Junction	a			16 07					16 37							17 07					17 37		
London Bridge	a			16 20		16 30			16 50			17 00				17 20		17 30			17 50		
London Blackfriars	a			16 26		16 36			16 56			17 06				17 26		17 36			17 56		
City Thameslink	a			16 28		16 38			16 58			17 08				17 28		17 38			17 58		
Farringdon	a			16 31		16 41			17 01			17 11				17 31		17 41			18 01		
St Pancras International	a			16 35		16 45			17 05			17 15				17 35		17 45			18 05		
East Croydon	d				15 54			16 30		16 24			17 00				16 56			17 30		17 24	
Clapham Junction	a				16 03			16 40		16 33			17 11				17 05			17 40		17 33	
London Victoria	a				16 11			16 48		16 41			17 19				17 13			17 48		17 41	

Station		TL	SN	SN	GW	TL	SN	TL	GW	SN	TL	SN	GW	TL	SN	SN	GW	TL	SN	TL	GW	SN
Horsham	d	16 55					17 20	17 25				17 50		17 55					18 20	18 25		
Littlehaven	d	16 59						17 29						17 59						18 29		
Faygate	d																					
Ifield	d	17 05						17 35						18 05						18 35		
Crawley	d	17 08					17 29	17 38				17 59		18 08					18 29	18 38		
Three Bridges	a	17 12					17 33	17 42				18 03		18 12					18 33	18 42		
Three Bridges	d	17 13					17 34	17 43				18 04		18 13					18 34	18 43		
Gatwick Airport	a	17 17					17 38	17 47				18 08		18 17					18 38	18 47		
Gatwick Airport	d	17 19				17 33	17 39	17 49	18 00		18 03	18 09		18 19				18 33	18 39	18 49	19 00	
Horley	d	17 21				17 36		17 51			18 05			18 21				18 36		18 51		
Salfords	d					17 40					18 09							18 40				
Earlswood (Surrey)	d					17 44					18 13							18 44				
Redhill	a	17 29				17 48		17 59	18 09		18 17			18 29				18 48		18 59	19 10	
Redhill	d								18 14												19 14	
Reigate	a								18 18												19 18	
Redhill	d																					
Tonbridge	a																					
Tonbridge	d			17 01												18 01						
Leigh (Kent)	a			17 05												18 05						
Penshurst	a			17 09												18 09						
Edenbridge	a			17 16												18 16						
Godstone	a			17 22												18 22						
Nutfield	a			17 28												18 28						
Reigate	d		17 30		17 36					18 00			18 18		18 30		18 36					19 00
Redhill	a		17 34	17 36	17 40					18 04			18 24		18 34	18 36	18 40					19 04
Redhill	d	17 29	17 41			17 49		17 59		18 11	18 19			18 29	18 41			18 49		18 59		19 11
Merstham	d	17 33	17 45					18 03		18 15				18 33	18 45					19 03		19 15
Coulsdon South	d	17 39	17 50					18 09		18 20				18 39	18 50					19 09		19 20
Purley	d		17 55			17 58				18 25	18 28				18 55			18 58				19 25
East Croydon	a	17 45	18 00			18 03	17 54	18 15		18 30	18 33	18 24		18 45	19 00			19 03	18 54	19 15		19 30
East Croydon	d	17 45				18 03		18 15			18 33			18 45				19 03		19 15		
Norwood Junction	a					18 07					18 37							19 07				
London Bridge	a	18 00				18 20		18 30			18 50			19 00				19 20		19 30		
London Blackfriars	a	18 06				18 26		18 36			18 56			19 06				19 26		19 36		
City Thameslink	a	18 08				18 28		18 38			18 58			19 08				19 28		19 38		
Farringdon	a	18 11				18 31		18 41			19 01			19 11				19 31		19 41		
St Pancras International	a	18 15				18 35		18 45			19 05			19 15				19 35		19 45		
East Croydon	d		18 00				17 54			18 30		18 24			19 00				18 54			19 30
Clapham Junction	a		18 10				18 03			18 40		18 33			19 10				19 03			19 40
London Victoria	a		18 18				18 11			18 48		18 41			19 18				19 11			19 48

Table T183-R

Saturdays
21 December to 16 May

Horsham / Gatwick Airport / Tonbridge / Reigate / Redhill - London

		TL	SN	GW	TL	SN	SN	GW	TL	SN	TL	GW	SN	TL	SN	GW	TL	SN	SN	GW	TL	SN	TL
Horsham	d		18 50		18 55					19 20	19 25				19 50		19 55					20 20	20 25
Littlehaven	d				18 59						19 29						19 59						20 29
Faygate	d																						
Ifield	d				19 05						19 35						20 05						20 35
Crawley	d		18 59		19 08					19 29	19 38				19 59		20 08					20 29	20 38
Three Bridges	a		19 03		19 12					19 33	19 42				20 03		20 12					20 33	20 42
Three Bridges	d		19 04		19 13					19 34	19 43				20 04		20 13					20 34	20 43
Gatwick Airport	a		19 08		19 17					19 38	19 47				20 08		20 17					20 38	20 47
Gatwick Airport	d	19 03	19 09		19 19				19 33	19 39	19 49	20 00		20 03	20 09		20 19				20 33	20 39	20 49
Horley	d	19 05			19 21				19 36		19 51			20 05			20 21				20 36		20 51
Salfords	d	19 09							19 40					20 09							20 40		
Earlswood (Surrey)	d	19 13							19 44					20 13							20 44		
Redhill	a	19 17			19 29				19 48		19 59	20 10		20 17			20 29				20 48		20 59
Redhill	d											20 14											
Reigate	a											20 18											
Redhill	d																						
Tonbridge	a																						
Tonbridge	d						19 01												20 01				
Leigh (Kent)	a						19 05												20 05				
Penshurst	a						19 09												20 09				
Edenbridge	a						19 16												20 16				
Godstone	a						19 22												20 22				
Nutfield	a						19 28												20 28				
Reigate	d			19 17		19 30		19 36					20 00			20 18		20 30		20 36			
Redhill	a			19 23		19 34	19 36	19 40					20 04			20 24		20 34	20 36	20 40			
Redhill	d	19 19			19 29	19 41			19 49		19 59		20 11	20 19			20 29	20 41			20 49		20 59
Merstham	d				19 33	19 45					20 03		20 15				20 33	20 45					21 03
Coulsdon South	d				19 39	19 50					20 09		20 20				20 39	20 50					21 09
Purley	d	19 28				19 55			19 58				20 25	20 28				20 55			20 58		
East Croydon	a	19 33	19 24		19 45	20 00			20 03	19 54	20 15		20 30	20 33	20 24		20 45	21 00			21 03	20 54	21 15
East Croydon	d	19 33			19 45				20 03		20 15			20 33			20 45				21 03		21 15
Norwood Junction	a	19 37							20 07					20 37							21 07		
London Bridge	a	19 50			20 00				20 20		20 30			20 50			21 00				21 20		21 30
London Blackfriars	a	19 56			20 06				20 26		20 36			20 56			21 06				21 26		21 36
City Thameslink	a	19 58			20 08				20 28		20 38			20 58									
Farringdon	a	20 01			20 11				20 31		20 41			21 01			21 11				21 31		21 41
St Pancras International	a	20 05			20 15				20 35		20 45			21 05			21 15				21 35		21 45
East Croydon	d		19 24			20 00				19 54			20 30		20 24			21 00				20 54	
Clapham Junction	a		19 33			20 10				20 03			20 40		20 33			21 10				21 03	
London Victoria	a		19 41			20 18				20 11			20 48		20 41			21 18				21 11	

		GW	SN	TL	SN	GW	TL	SN	SN	GW	TL	SN	TL	SN	GW	SN	TL	SN	SN	SN	GW	TL
Horsham	d				20 50		20 55					21 20	21 25	21 50			21 55	22 20				22 25
Littlehaven	d						20 59						21 29				21 59					22 29
Faygate	d																					
Ifield	d						21 05						21 35				22 05					22 35
Crawley	d				20 59		21 08					21 29	21 38	21 59			22 08	22 29				22 38
Three Bridges	a				21 03		21 12					21 33	21 42	22 03			22 12	22 33				22 42
Three Bridges	d				21 04		21 13					21 34	21 43	22 04			22 13	22 34				22 43
Gatwick Airport	a				21 08		21 17					21 38	21 47	22 08			22 17	22 38				22 47
Gatwick Airport	d	21 00		21 03	21 09		21 19				21 33	21 39	21 49	22 09	22 16		22 19	22 39				22 49
Horley	d			21 05			21 21				21 35		21 51				22 22					22 51
Salfords	d			21 09							21 39						22 26					22 55
Earlswood (Surrey)	d			21 13							21 43						22 29					22 59
Redhill	a	21 10		21 17			21 29				21 47		21 59		22 25		22 33					23 03
Redhill	d	21 14													22 30							
Reigate	a	21 18													22 34							
Redhill	d																					
Tonbridge	a																					
Tonbridge	d								21 01											22 01		
Leigh (Kent)	a								21 05											22 05		
Penshurst	a								21 09											22 09		
Edenbridge	a								21 16											22 16		
Godstone	a								21 22											22 22		
Nutfield	a								21 28											22 28		
Reigate	d		21 00			21 17		21 30		21 43						22 00			22 31		22 40	
Redhill	a		21 04			21 23		21 34	21 36	21 47						22 04			22 36	22 38	22 44	
Redhill	d		21 11	21 19			21 29	21 41			21 49		21 59			22 11	22 34		22 41			23 04
Merstham	d		21 15				21 33	21 45					22 03			22 15			22 45			
Coulsdon South	d		21 20				21 39	21 50					22 09			22 20			22 50			
Purley	d		21 25	21 28				21 55			21 58					22 25			22 55			
East Croydon	a		21 30	21 33	21 24		21 45	22 00			22 03	21 54	22 15	22 24		22 30	22 45	22 54	23 00			23 15
East Croydon	d			21 33			21 45				22 03		22 16				22 46					23 15
Norwood Junction	a			21 37							22 07											
London Bridge	a			21 50			22 00				22 20		22 30				23 00					23 30
London Blackfriars	a			21 56			22 06				22 26		22 36				23 06					23 36
City Thameslink	a																					
Farringdon	a			22 01			22 11				22 31		22 41				23 11					23 41
St Pancras International	a			22 05			22 15				22 35		22 45				23 15					23 45
East Croydon	d		21 30		21 24			22 00				21 54		22 24		22 30		22 54	23 00			
Clapham Junction	a		21 40		21 33			22 10				22 03		22 33		22 40		23 04	23 10			
London Victoria	a		21 48		21 41			22 18				22 11		22 41		22 48		23 11	23 18			

Table T183-R

Saturdays
21 December to 16 May

Horsham / Gatwick Airport / Tonbridge / Reigate / Redhill - London

		SN	GW	SN	TL	SN	GW
Horsham	d				23 11	23 27	
Littlehaven	d				23 15	23 30	
Faygate	d						
Ifield	d				23 21	23 36	
Crawley	d				23 24	23 40	
Three Bridges	a				23 28	23 43	
Three Bridges	d				23 29	23 44	
Gatwick Airport	a				23 33	23 49	
Gatwick Airport	d		23 18		23 34		
Horley	d				23 37		
Salfords	d				23 41		
Earlswood (Surrey)	d				23 44		
Redhill	a		23 28		23 48		
Redhill	d		23 32				
Reigate	a		23 37				
Redhill	d						
Tonbridge	a						
Tonbridge	d			23 03			
Leigh (Kent)	a			23 07			
Penshurst	a			23 11			
Edenbridge	a			23 18			
Godstone	a			23 24			
Nutfield	a			23 30			
Reigate	d	23 00					23 57
Redhill	a	23 04		23 36			00 02
Redhill	d	23 11			23 49		
Merstham	d	23 15			23 53		
Coulsdon South	d	23 20			23 59		
Purley	d	23 25			00 03		
East Croydon	a	23 30			00 09		
East Croydon	d				00 10		
Norwood Junction	a						
London Bridge	a						
London Blackfriars	a				00 36		
City Thameslink	a						
Farringdon	a				00 41		
St Pancras International	a				00 45		
East Croydon	d	23 30					
Clapham Junction	a	23 41					
London Victoria	a	23 50					

Sundays
15 December to 10 May

		SN	TL	GW A	SN	SN	SN	SN	TL	GW	SN	SN	GW	TL	GW	SN	SN	SN	GW	SN	TL	GW	SN
Horsham	d										06 01	06 31		06 39			07 05				07 35		
Littlehaven	d										06 04	06 34		06 42							07 38		
Faygate	d																						
Ifield	d										06 10	06 40		06 48							07 44		
Crawley	d										06 14	06 44		06 52			07 14				07 48		
Three Bridges	a										06 19	06 47		06 55			07 19				07 51		
Three Bridges	d		00 37		02 08	03 08	04 08	04 58	05 54		06 23	06 49		06 56			07 23				07 52		
Gatwick Airport	a		00 41		02 12	03 12	04 12	05 02	05 58		06 27	06 53		07 01			07 27				07 57		
Gatwick Airport	d		00 42		02 13	03 13	04 13	05 03	06 00	06 11	06 28	06 54		07 02	07 11		07 28	07 54			07 58	08 11	08 25
Horley	d		00 45		02 16	03 16	04 16	05 06	06 02					07 04							08 00		
Salfords	d								06 06					07 08							08 04		
Earlswood (Surrey)	d								06 10					07 12							08 08		
Redhill	a		00 52						06 14	06 18	06 36	07 03		07 16	07 18		07 36	08 03			08 12	08 20	08 34
Redhill	d									06 23					07 23							08 26	
Reigate	a									06 26					07 26							08 30	
Redhill	d	00 16																					
Tonbridge	a																						
Tonbridge	d															07 00				07 35			
Leigh (Kent)	a															07 04				07 39			
Penshurst	a															07 08				07 43			
Edenbridge	a	00 27														07 14				07 49			
Godstone	a															07 21				07 56			
Nutfield	a															07 27				08 02			
Reigate	d			00 49									07 09						08 03				
Redhill	a			00 53									07 13			07 32			08 07	08 08			
Redhill	d		00 53						06 14		06 37	07 03		07 16			07 37	08 03			08 12		08 34
Merstham	d								06 18			07 07						08 07			08 16		
Coulsdon South	d								06 23			07 12						08 12			08 21		
Purley	d		01 03		02 29	03 30	04 29	05 23	06 27			07 16		07 25				08 16			08 25		
East Croydon	a		01 09		02 35	03 36	04 35	05 29	06 33		06 50	07 22		07 31			07 50	08 22			08 31		08 45
East Croydon	d		01 10						06 34					07 32							08 32		
Norwood Junction	a								06 38					07 36							08 36		
London Bridge	a								06 52					07 50							08 50		
London Blackfriars	a		01 36																				
City Thameslink	a																						
Farringdon	a																						
St Pancras International	a		01 43																				
East Croydon	d				02 36	03 37	04 36	05 30			06 51	07 23					07 51	08 23					08 46
Clapham Junction	a				02 49	03 50	04 49	05 51			07 05	07 37					08 07	08 38					08 55
London Victoria	a				02 58	03 58	04 58	05 59			07 15	07 46					08 17	08 46					09 02

A not 15 December

Table T183-R

Sundays
15 December to 10 May

Horsham / Gatwick Airport / Tonbridge / Reigate / Redhill - London

		SN 1	TL 1	SN	TL 1	GW	SN	TL 1	GW 1	GW 1	TL 1	SN 1	TL 1	SN	TL 1	GW	SN	TL 1	GW 1	GW 1	TL 1	SN 1	TL 1
Horsham	d	08 17						08 48				09 21						09 48				10 21	
Littlehaven	d							08 51										09 51					
Faygate	d																						
Ifield	d							08 57										09 57					
Crawley	d	08 26						09 01				09 30						10 01				10 30	
Three Bridges	a	08 30						09 04				09 35						10 04				10 35	
Three Bridges	d	08 31			08 43			09 05			09 13	09 35			09 43			10 05				10 35	
Gatwick Airport	a	08 35			08 47			09 10			09 17	09 40			09 47			10 10				10 40	
Gatwick Airport	d	08 36	08 46		08 49			09 11		09 15	09 19	09 41	09 46		09 49			10 11		10 15	10 19	10 41	10 46
Horley	d				08 51			09 13			09 21				09 51			10 13			10 21		
Salfords	d				08 55						09 25				09 55						10 25		
Earlswood (Surrey)	d				08 59						09 29				09 59						10 29		
Redhill	a	08 44	08 54		09 03			09 21		09 24	09 33	09 49	09 54		10 03			10 21		10 25	10 33	10 49	10 54
Redhill	d									09 30										10 29			
Reigate	a									09 33										10 32			
Redhill	d																						
Tonbridge	a																						
Tonbridge	d			08 29										09 29									
Leigh (Kent)	a			08 33										09 33									
Penshurst	a			08 37										09 37									
Edenbridge	a			08 43										09 43									
Godstone	a			08 50										09 50									
Nutfield	a			08 56										09 56									
Reigate	d					09 01	09 06		09 17							10 02	10 06		10 17				
Redhill	a			09 00		09 05	09 10		09 24					10 00		10 06	10 10		10 24				
Redhill	d	08 45	08 54		09 03		09 11	09 21			09 33	09 50	09 54		10 03		10 11	10 21			10 33	10 50	10 54
Merstham	d						09 15	09 25									10 15	10 25					
Coulsdon South	d	08 52					09 20	09 30				09 57					10 20	10 30				10 57	
Purley	d				09 12		09 25				09 42				10 12		10 25				10 42		
East Croydon	a	08 58	09 06		09 17		09 29	09 37			09 47	10 03	10 07		10 17		10 29	10 37			10 47	11 03	11 07
East Croydon	d		09 07		09 18			09 37			09 48		10 07		10 18			10 37			10 48		11 07
Norwood Junction	a		09 11					09 41					10 11					10 41					11 11
London Bridge	a		09 24		09 32			09 57			10 02		10 24		10 32			10 58			11 02		11 24
London Blackfriars	a		09 30		09 38						10 08		10 30		10 38						11 08		11 30
City Thameslink	a																						
Farringdon	a		09 35		09 43						10 13		10 35		10 43						11 13		11 35
St Pancras International	a		09 39		09 47						10 17		10 39		10 47						11 17		11 39
East Croydon	d	08 59					09 30					10 04					10 30					11 04	
Clapham Junction	a	09 08					09 39					10 14					10 39					11 14	
London Victoria	a	09 15					09 47					10 21					10 47					11 21	

		SN	TL 1	GW	SN	TL 1	GW 1	GW 1	TL 1	SN 1	TL 1	SN	TL 1	GW	SN	TL 1	GW 1	GW 1	TL 1	SN 1	TL 1	SN
Horsham	d					10 48				11 21						11 48				12 21		
Littlehaven	d					10 51										11 51						
Faygate	d																					
Ifield	d					10 57										11 57						
Crawley	d					11 01				11 30						12 01				12 30		
Three Bridges	a					11 04				11 35						12 04				12 35		
Three Bridges	d		10 43			11 05				11 35			11 43			12 05				12 35		
Gatwick Airport	a		10 47			11 10				11 40			11 47			12 10				12 40		
Gatwick Airport	d		10 49			11 11		11 15	11 19	11 41	11 46		11 49			12 11		12 15	12 19	12 41	12 46	
Horley	d		10 51			11 13			11 21				11 51			12 13			12 21			
Salfords	d		10 55						11 25				11 55						12 25			
Earlswood (Surrey)	d		10 59						11 29				11 59						12 29			
Redhill	a		11 03			11 21		11 23	11 33	11 49	11 54		12 03			12 21		12 26	12 33	12 49	12 54	
Redhill	d							11 29										12 29				
Reigate	a							11 32										12 32				
Redhill	d																					
Tonbridge	a																					
Tonbridge	d	10 29										11 29										12 29
Leigh (Kent)	a	10 33										11 33										12 33
Penshurst	a	10 37										11 37										12 37
Edenbridge	a	10 43										11 43										12 43
Godstone	a	10 50										11 50										12 50
Nutfield	a	10 56										11 56										12 56
Reigate	d			11 02	11 06		11 17							12 02	12 06		12 17					
Redhill	a	11 00		11 06	11 10		11 24					12 00		12 06	12 10		12 24					13 00
Redhill	d		11 03		11 11	11 21			11 33	11 50	11 54		12 03		12 11	12 21			12 33	12 50	12 54	
Merstham	d				11 15	11 25									12 15	12 25						
Coulsdon South	d				11 20	11 30				11 57					12 20	12 30				12 57		
Purley	d		11 12		11 25				11 42				12 12		12 25				12 42			
East Croydon	a		11 17		11 29	11 37			11 47	12 03	12 07		12 17		12 29	12 37			12 47	13 06	13 06	
East Croydon	d		11 18			11 37			11 48		12 07		12 18			12 37			12 48		13 07	
Norwood Junction	a					11 41					12 11					12 41					13 11	
London Bridge	a		11 32			11 57			12 02		12 24		12 32			12 57			13 02		13 24	
London Blackfriars	a		11 38						12 08		12 30		12 38						13 08		13 30	
City Thameslink	a																					
Farringdon	a		11 43						12 13		12 35		12 45						13 13		13 35	
St Pancras International	a		11 47						12 17		12 39		12 49						13 17		13 39	
East Croydon	d				11 30					12 04					12 30					13 06		
Clapham Junction	a				11 39					12 14					12 39					13 16		
London Victoria	a				11 47					12 21					12 47					13 23		

Table T183-R

Sundays
15 December to 10 May

Horsham / Gatwick Airport / Tonbridge / Reigate / Redhill - London

		TL 1	GW	SN	TL 1	GW 1	GW 1	TL 1	SN 1	TL 1	SN	TL 1	GW	SN	TL 1	GW 1	GW 1	TL 1	SN 1	TL 1	SN	TL 1	GW
Horsham	d				12 48				13 21						13 48				14 21				
Littlehaven	d				12 51										13 51								
Faygate	d																						
Ifield	d				12 57										13 57								
Crawley	d				13 01				13 30						14 01				14 30				
Three Bridges	a				13 04				13 35						14 04				14 35				
Three Bridges	d	12 43			13 05				13 35			13 43			14 05				14 35			14 43	
Gatwick Airport	a	12 47			13 10				13 40			13 47			14 10				14 40			14 47	
Gatwick Airport	d	12 49			13 11		13 15	13 19	13 41	13 46		13 49			14 11		14 15	14 19	14 41	14 46		14 49	
Horley	d	12 51			13 13			13 21				13 51			14 13			14 21				14 51	
Salfords	d	12 55						13 25				13 55						14 25				14 55	
Earlswood (Surrey)	d	12 59						13 29				13 59						14 29				14 59	
Redhill	a	13 03			13 21		13 26	13 33	13 49	13 54		14 03			14 21		14 26	14 33	14 49	14 54		15 03	
Redhill	d						13 29										14 29						
Reigate	a						13 32										14 32						
Redhill	d																						
Tonbridge	a																						
Tonbridge	d										13 29										14 29		
Leigh (Kent)	a										13 33										14 33		
Penshurst	a										13 37										14 37		
Edenbridge	a										13 43										14 43		
Godstone	a										13 50										14 50		
Nutfield	a										13 56										14 56		
Reigate	d		13 02	13 06		13 17							14 01	14 06		14 17							15 02
Redhill	a		13 06	13 10		13 24					14 00		14 05	14 10		14 24					15 00		15 06
Redhill	d	13 03		13 11	13 21			13 33	13 50	13 54		14 03		14 11	14 21			14 33	14 50	14 54		15 03	
Merstham	d			13 15	13 25									14 15	14 25								
Coulsdon South	d			13 20	13 30				13 57					14 20	14 30				14 57				
Purley	d	13 12		13 25				13 42				14 12		14 25				14 42				15 12	
East Croydon	a	13 17		13 29	13 37			13 47	14 03	14 07		14 17		14 29	14 37			14 47	15 03	15 07		15 17	
East Croydon	d	13 18			13 37			13 48		14 07		14 18			14 37			14 48		15 07		15 18	
Norwood Junction	a				13 41					14 11					14 41					15 11			
London Bridge	a	13 32			13 57			14 02		14 24		14 32			14 57			15 02		15 24		15 32	
London Blackfriars	a	13 38						14 08		14 30		14 38						15 08		15 30		15 38	
City Thameslink	a																						
Farringdon	a	13 43						14 13		14 35		14 43						15 13		15 35		15 43	
St Pancras International	a	13 47						14 17		14 39		14 47						15 17		15 39		15 47	
East Croydon	d			13 30					14 04					14 30					15 04				
Clapham Junction	a			13 39					14 14					14 39					15 14				
London Victoria	a			13 47					14 21					14 47					15 21				

		SN	TL 1	GW 1	GW 1	TL 1	SN 1	TL 1	SN	TL 1	GW	SN	TL 1	GW 1	GW 1	TL 1	SN 1	TL 1	SN	TL 1	GW	SN
Horsham	d		14 48				15 21						15 48				16 21					
Littlehaven	d		14 51										15 51									
Faygate	d																					
Ifield	d		14 57										15 57									
Crawley	d		15 01				15 30						16 01				16 30					
Three Bridges	a		15 04				15 35						16 04				16 35					
Three Bridges	d		15 05				15 35			15 43			16 05				16 35			16 43		
Gatwick Airport	a		15 10				15 40			15 47			16 10				16 40			16 47		
Gatwick Airport	d		15 11		15 15	15 19	15 41	15 46		15 49			16 11		16 15	16 19	16 41	16 46		16 49		
Horley	d		15 13			15 21				15 51			16 13			16 21				16 51		
Salfords	d					15 25				15 55						16 25				16 55		
Earlswood (Surrey)	d					15 29				15 59						16 29				16 59		
Redhill	a		15 21		15 26	15 33	15 49	15 54		16 03			16 21		16 26	16 33	16 49	16 54		17 03		
Redhill	d				15 29										16 29							
Reigate	a				15 32										16 32							
Redhill	d																					
Tonbridge	a																					
Tonbridge	d								15 29										16 29			
Leigh (Kent)	a								15 33										16 33			
Penshurst	a								15 37										16 37			
Edenbridge	a								15 43										16 43			
Godstone	a								15 50										16 50			
Nutfield	a								15 56										16 56			
Reigate	d	15 06		15 17							16 02	16 06		16 16							17 02	17 06
Redhill	a	15 10		15 24					16 00		16 06	16 10		16 24					17 00		17 06	17 10
Redhill	d	15 11	15 21			15 33	15 50	15 54		16 03		16 11	16 21			16 33	16 50	16 54		17 03		17 11
Merstham	d	15 15	15 25									16 15	16 25									17 15
Coulsdon South	d	15 20	15 30				15 57					16 20	16 30				16 57					17 20
Purley	d	15 25				15 42				16 12		16 25				16 42				17 12		17 25
East Croydon	a	15 29	15 37			15 47	16 06	16 06		16 17		16 29	16 37			16 47	17 06	17 06		17 17		17 29
East Croydon	d		15 37			15 48		16 07		16 18			16 37			16 48		17 07		17 18		
Norwood Junction	a		15 41					16 11					16 41					17 11				
London Bridge	a		15 57			16 02		16 24		16 32			16 57			17 02		17 24		17 32		
London Blackfriars	a					16 08		16 30		16 38						17 08		17 30		17 38		
City Thameslink	a																					
Farringdon	a					16 13		16 35		16 43						17 13		17 35		17 43		
St Pancras International	a					16 17		16 39		16 47						17 17		17 39		17 47		
East Croydon	d	15 30					16 06					16 30					17 06					17 30
Clapham Junction	a	15 39					16 16					16 39					17 16					17 39
London Victoria	a	15 47					16 23					16 47					17 23					17 47

Table T183-R

Sundays

15 December to 10 May

Horsham / Gatwick Airport / Tonbridge / Reigate / Redhill - London

		TL	GW	GW	TL	SN	TL	SN	TL	GW		SN	TL	GW	GW	TL	SN	TL	SN	TL		GW	SN	TL	GW
		1	1	1	1	1	1		1				1	1	1	1	1	1		1				1	1
Horsham	d	16 48				17 21							17 48				18 21							18 48	
Littlehaven	d	16 51											17 51											18 51	
Faygate	d																								
Ifield	d	16 57											17 57											18 57	
Crawley	d	17 01				17 30							18 01				18 30							19 01	
Three Bridges	a	17 04				17 35							18 04				18 35							19 04	
Three Bridges	d	17 05				17 35			17 43				18 05				18 35			18 43				19 05	
Gatwick Airport	a	17 10				17 40			17 47				18 10				18 40			18 47				19 10	
Gatwick Airport	d	17 11		17 15	17 19	17 41	17 46		17 49				18 11		18 15	18 19	18 41	18 46		18 49				19 11	
Horley	d	17 13			17 21				17 51				18 13			18 21				18 51				19 13	
Salfords	d				17 25				17 55							18 25				18 55					
Earlswood (Surrey)	d				17 29				17 59							18 29				18 59					
Redhill	a	17 21		17 26	17 33	17 49	17 54		18 03				18 21		18 26	18 33	18 49	18 54		19 03				19 21	
Redhill	d			17 29											18 29										
Reigate	a			17 32											18 32										
Redhill	d																								
Tonbridge	a																								
Tonbridge	d							17 29											18 29						
Leigh (Kent)	a							17 33											18 33						
Penshurst	a							17 37											18 37						
Edenbridge	a							17 43											18 43						
Godstone	a							17 50											18 50						
Nutfield	a							17 56											18 56						
Reigate	d		17 17							18 02		18 06		18 17								19 02	19 06		19 17
Redhill	a		17 24					18 00		18 06		18 10		18 24					19 00			19 06	19 10		19 24
Redhill	d	17 21			17 33	17 50	17 54		18 03			18 11	18 21			18 33	18 50	18 54		19 03			19 11	19 21	
Merstham	d	17 25										18 15	18 25										19 15	19 25	
Coulsdon South	d	17 30				17 57						18 20	18 30				18 57						19 20	19 30	
Purley	d				17 42				18 12			18 25				18 42				19 12			19 25		
East Croydon	a	17 37			17 47	18 03	18 07		18 17			18 29	18 37			18 47	19 03	19 07		19 17			19 29	19 37	
East Croydon	d	17 37			17 48		18 07		18 18				18 37			18 48		19 07		19 18				19 37	
Norwood Junction	a	17 41					18 11						18 41					19 11						19 41	
London Bridge	a	17 57			18 02		18 24		18 32				18 57			19 02		19 24		19 32				19 57	
London Blackfriars	a				18 08		18 30		18 38							19 08		19 30		19 38					
City Thameslink	a																								
Farringdon	a				18 13		18 35		18 43							19 13		19 35		19 43					
St Pancras International	a				18 17		18 39		18 47							19 17		19 39		19 47					
East Croydon	d					18 04						18 30					19 04						19 30		
Clapham Junction	a					18 14						18 39					19 14						19 39		
London Victoria	a					18 21						18 47					19 21						19 47		

		GW	TL	SN	TL	SN		TL	GW	SN	TL	GW	GW	TL	SN	TL		SN	TL	SN	GW	TL	TL	GW	SN
		1	1	1	1			1			1	1	1	1	1	1			1		1	1	1	1	1
Horsham	d			19 21							19 48				20 21							20 48			21 21
Littlehaven	d										19 51											20 51			
Faygate	d																								
Ifield	d										19 57											20 57			
Crawley	d			19 30							20 01				20 30							21 01			21 30
Three Bridges	a			19 35							20 04				20 35							21 04			21 35
Three Bridges	d			19 35				19 43			20 05				20 35				20 43			21 05			21 35
Gatwick Airport	a			19 40				19 47			20 10				20 40				20 47			21 10			21 40
Gatwick Airport	d	19 15	19 19	19 41	19 46			19 49			20 11		20 15	20 19	20 41	20 46			20 49		21 03	21 11	21 19		21 41
Horley	d		19 21					19 51			20 13			20 21					20 51			21 13	21 21		
Salfords	d		19 25					19 55						20 25					20 55				21 25		
Earlswood (Surrey)	d		19 29					19 59						20 29					20 59				21 29		
Redhill	a	19 26	19 33	19 49	19 54			20 03			20 21		20 26	20 33	20 49	20 54			21 03		21 12	21 21	21 33		21 49
Redhill	d	19 29											20 29								21 16				
Reigate	a	19 32											20 32								21 18				
Redhill	d																								
Tonbridge	a																								
Tonbridge	d					19 29												20 29							
Leigh (Kent)	a					19 33												20 33							
Penshurst	a					19 37												20 37							
Edenbridge	a					19 43												20 43							
Godstone	a					19 50												20 50							
Nutfield	a					19 56												20 56							
Reigate	d								20 02	20 06		20 17								21 06				21 37	
Redhill	a					20 00			20 06	20 10		20 24						21 00		21 10				21 43	
Redhill	d		19 33	19 50	19 54			20 03		20 11	20 21			20 33	20 50	20 54			21 03	21 11		21 21	21 33		21 50
Merstham	d									20 15	20 25									21 15		21 25			
Coulsdon South	d			19 57						20 20	20 30				20 57					21 20		21 30			21 57
Purley	d		19 42					20 12		20 25				20 42					21 12	21 25			21 42		
East Croydon	a		19 47	20 03	20 07			20 17		20 29	20 37			20 47	21 03	21 07			21 17	21 29		21 37	21 47		22 03
East Croydon	d		19 48		20 07			20 18			20 37			20 48		21 07			21 18			21 37	21 48		
Norwood Junction	a				20 11						20 41					21 11						21 41			
London Bridge	a		20 02		20 24			20 32			20 57			21 02		21 24			21 32			21 57	22 02		
London Blackfriars	a		20 08		20 30			20 38						21 08		21 30			21 38				22 08		
City Thameslink	a																								
Farringdon	a		20 13		20 35			20 43						21 13		21 35			21 43				22 13		
St Pancras International	a		20 17		20 39			20 47						21 17		21 39			21 47				22 17		
East Croydon	d			20 04						20 30					21 04					21 30					22 04
Clapham Junction	a			20 14						20 39					21 14					21 39					22 14
London Victoria	a			20 21						20 47					21 21					21 47					22 21

Table T183-R

Sundays

15 December to 10 May

Horsham / Gatwick Airport / Tonbridge / Reigate / Redhill - London

		TL		SN	SN	TL	GW	GW	TL	SN	SN	TL		GW	SN	GW	SN
		1				1	1	1	1	1		1		1	1	1	1
Horsham	d					21 48				22 21		22 41					23 14
Littlehaven	d					21 51						22 44					23 17
Faygate	d																
Ifield	d					21 57						22 50					23 23
Crawley	d					22 01				22 30		22 54					23 27
Three Bridges	a					22 04				22 35		22 58					23 30
Three Bridges	d					22 05			22 31	22 35					23 25		23 31
Gatwick Airport	a					22 10			22 35	22 40					23 29		23 35
Gatwick Airport	d	21 46				22 11		22 18	22 39	22 41				23 04	23 30		23 36
Horley	d					22 13			22 42								23 38
Salfords	d					22 17			22 46								
Earlswood (Surrey)	d					22 21			22 49								
Redhill	a	21 54				22 25		22 28	22 53	22 49				23 14	23 38		23 46
Redhill	d							22 34						23 17			
Reigate	a							22 37						23 20			
Redhill	d																
Tonbridge	a																
Tonbridge	d			21 29							22 29						
Leigh (Kent)	a			21 33							22 33						
Penshurst	a			21 37							22 37						
Edenbridge	a			21 43							22 43						
Godstone	a			21 50							22 50						
Nutfield	a			21 56							22 56						
Reigate	d				22 06		22 29									23 33	
Redhill	a			22 00	22 10		22 35				23 00					23 39	
Redhill	d	21 54			22 11	22 25			22 54	22 50					23 38		23 47
Merstham	d				22 15	22 29			22 58								23 51
Coulsdon South	d				22 20	22 34			23 03	22 57							23 56
Purley	d				22 25	22 38			23 07								23 59
East Croydon	a	22 07			22 29	22 45			23 12	23 03					23 51		00 05
East Croydon	d	22 07				22 47			23 12								
Norwood Junction	a	22 11				22 51			23 16								
London Bridge	a	22 24				23 05			23 30								
London Blackfriars	a	22 30															
City Thameslink	a																
Farringdon	a	22 35															
St Pancras International	a	22 39															
East Croydon	d				22 30					23 04					23 52		00 06
Clapham Junction	a				22 39					23 14					00 08		00 18
London Victoria	a				22 47					23 21					00 17		00 27

Table T184-F

Mondays to Fridays

16 December to 15 May

London - Gatwick Airport - Haywards Heath - Brighton/Hove/Lewes

Miles	Miles			SN MX		TL MO	TL MX	TL	TL	TL	GX	TL	SN	GX	TL	GX	TL	GX	TL	GX	TL	SN	GX
0	—	London Victoria	d	00 02							05 14		05 32	06 00		06 13		06 30		06 43		06 46	07 00
2¾	—	Clapham Junction	d	00 09									05 42									06 53	
10½	—	East Croydon	a	00 23									05 51									07 02	
—	0	St Pancras International	d			00 51	00 52	04 02	04 32	04 52		05 20			05 50		06 00		06 20		06 30		
—	1¼	Farringdon	d							04 56		05 24			05 54		06 04		06 24		06 34		
—	1¾	City Thameslink	d							04 58		05 26			05 56		06 06		06 26		06 36		
—	2	London Blackfriars	d			01 01	01 02	04 10	04 40	05 01		05 29			05 59		06 09		06 29		06 39		
—	—	London Bridge	d									05 35			06 05		06 15		06 35		06 45		
—	—	East Croydon	a			01 27	01 28	04 36	05 06	05 27		05 48			06 18		06 28		06 48		06 59		
—	12¾	East Croydon	d	00 24		01 28	01 28	04 37	05 07	05 28		05 49	05 52		06 19		06 29		06 49		07 00	07 03	
26¾	29	Gatwick Airport	a	00 43		01 56	01 56	04 57	05 31	05 47	05 50	06 04	06 17	06 28	06 34	06 41	06 44	06 58	07 04	07 11	07 14	07 17	07 28
—	—	Gatwick Airport	d	00 44		01 58	01 58	04 58	05 32	05 48	05 51	06 05	06 18	06 31	06 35	06 42	06 45	07 00	07 05	07 12	07 15	07 20	07 31
29¼	31½	Three Bridges	a	00 48		02 03	02 03	05 03	05 37	05 53		06 09	06 23		06 39		06 49		07 09		07 19	07 24	
—	—	Three Bridges	d	00 49		02 04	02 04	05 04	05 38	05 54		06 10	06 23		06 40		06 50		07 10		07 20	07 24	
—	36	**Balcombe**	d							06 00		06 16			06 46				07 16				
37¾	40	**Haywards Heath**	a	00 58		02 13	02 13	05 13	05 47	06 05		06 21	06 32		06 51		06 59		07 21		07 29	07 33	
—	—	**Haywards Heath**	d	01 02	01 08	02 14	02 14	05 14	05 48	06 06		06 22	06 33		06 54		06 59		07 24		07 30	07 34	
40¾	43	**Wivelsfield**	d						05 52	06 10		06 26	06 37		06 58				07 28				
41½	43¾	**Burgess Hill**	d						05 54	06 12		06 28			07 00		07 05		07 30		07 35		07 44
43¾	46	**Hassocks**	d						05 58	06 16		06 32			07 04		07 08				07 38		07 47
49½	51½	**Preston Park**	d						06 04	06 22		06 38			07 10		07 15				07 45		07 54
—	53	**Brighton**	a	01s16		02 28	02 28	05 32	06 10	06 26	06 13	06 42		06 53	07 14	07 05	07 22	07 26	07 42	07 35	07 49		07 58
50¾	—	Hove	a	01s25																			
—	—	Lewes	a		01 23								06 53									07 54	

		TL	GX	TL	SN	GX	TL	GX	TL	SN		SN	TL	GX	TL	SN	TL	SN	TL	GX	TL	SN	
London Victoria	d		07 13		07 16	07 30		07 43		07 46		07 55		08 13		08 16		08 25		08 43		08 46	
Clapham Junction	d				07 23					07 53		08 02				08 23		08 32				08 53	
East Croydon	a				07 32					08 03		08 11				08 33		08 41				09 02	
St Pancras International	d	06 50		07 00			07 20		07 30				07 50		08 00		08 10		08 20		08 30		
Farringdon	d	06 54		07 04			07 24		07 34				07 54		08 04		08 14		08 24		08 34		
City Thameslink	d	06 56		07 06			07 26		07 36				07 56		08 06		08 16		08 26		08 36		
London Blackfriars	d	06 59		07 09			07 29		07 39				07 59		08 09		08 19		08 29		08 39		
London Bridge	d	07 05		07 15			07 35		07 45				08 05		08 15		08 25		08 35		08 45		
East Croydon	a	07 18		07 29			07 48		08 00				08 18		08 29		08 38		08 48		08 58		
East Croydon	d	07 19		07 30	07 33		07 49		08 00	08 03		08 11	08 19		08 29	08 33	08 38	08 41	08 49		08 59	09 03	
Gatwick Airport	a	07 34	07 41	07 44	07 47	07 58	08 04	08 11	08 15	08 18		08 26	08 34	08 41	08 44	08 48		08 56	09 04	09 11	09 14	09 17	
Gatwick Airport	d	07 35	07 42	07 45	07 50	08 00	08 05	08 12	08 16	08 20		08 27	08 35	08 42	08 45	08 49		08 58	09 05	09 12	09 15	09 20	
Three Bridges	a	07 39		07 49			08 09		08 20				08 39		08 49		08 57		09 09		09 19		
Three Bridges	d	07 40		07 50			08 10		08 20				08 40		08 50		08 57		09 10		09 20		
Balcombe	d	07 46					08 16						08 46						09 16				
Haywards Heath	a	07 51		07 59	08 01		08 21		08 29	08 31		08 38	08 51		08 59	09 02	09 06	09 09	09 21		09 29	09 31	
Haywards Heath	d	07 54		08 00	08 03		08 24		08 30	08 35	08 38	08 41	08 54		08 59	09 03	09 07	09 11	09 24		09 29	09 35	09 38
Wivelsfield	d	07 58			08 08		08 28						08 58			09 08			09 28				
Burgess Hill	d	08 00		08 05			08 30		08 35			08 46	09 00		09 05			09 16	09 30		09 35		
Hassocks	d			08 08					08 39			08 50			09 08			09 20			09 38		
Preston Park	d			08 15					08 46						09 15		09 18				09 45		
Brighton	a	08 12	08 05	08 19		08 23	08 42	08 36	08 50			09 01	09 12	09 05	09 20			09 32	09 42	09 37	09 49		
Hove	a										08 52						09 23						09 52
Lewes	a				08 22					08 53						09 22						09 53	

		SN	TL	GX	TL	SN		SN	TL	GX	TL	SN		SN	TL	GX	TL	SN		SN	TL	GX
London Victoria	d	08 55		09 14		09 16		09 25		09 44		09 46		09 55		10 14		10 16		10 25		10 44
Clapham Junction	d	09 02				09 23		09 32				09 53		10 02				10 23		10 32		
East Croydon	a	09 11				09 32		09 41				10 02		10 11				10 32		10 41		
St Pancras International	d		08 50		09 00				09 20		09 30				09 50		10 00				10 20	
Farringdon	d		08 54		09 04				09 24		09 34				09 54		10 04				10 24	
City Thameslink	d		08 56		09 06				09 26		09 36				09 56		10 06				10 26	
London Blackfriars	d		08 59		09 09				09 29		09 39				09 59		10 09				10 29	
London Bridge	d		09 05		09 15				09 35		09 45				10 05		10 15				10 35	
East Croydon	a		09 18		09 28				09 48		09 58				10 18		10 28				10 48	
East Croydon	d	09 11	09 19		09 29	09 33		09 41	09 49		09 59	10 03		10 11	10 19		10 29	10 33		10 41	10 49	
Gatwick Airport	a	09 26	09 34	09 41	09 44	09 47		09 57	10 04	10 11	10 14	10 17		10 27	10 34	10 41	10 44	10 47		10 56	11 04	11 11
Gatwick Airport	d	09 28	09 35	09 42	09 45	09 50		10 01	10 05	10 12	10 15	10 20		10 31	10 35	10 42	10 45	10 50		10 58	11 05	11 12
Three Bridges	a		09 39		09 49				10 09		10 19				10 39		10 49				11 09	
Three Bridges	d		09 40		09 50				10 10		10 20				10 40		10 50				11 10	
Balcombe	d		09 46						10 16						10 46						11 16	
Haywards Heath	a	09 41	09 51		09 59	10 01		10 14	10 21		10 29	10 31		10 42	10 51		10 59	11 01		11 09	11 21	
Haywards Heath	d	09 41	09 54		10 00	10 05	10 07	10 14	10 24		10 29	10 35	10 38	10 43	10 54		10 59	11 05	11 07	11 11	11 24	
Wivelsfield	d		09 58				10 11		10 28						10 58				11 11		11 28	
Burgess Hill	d	09 46	10 00		10 05			10 20	10 30		10 35			10 48	11 00		11 05			11 16	11 30	
Hassocks	d	09 50			10 09			10 23			10 38			10 51			11 08			11 20		
Preston Park	d				10 15	10 18					10 45						11 15	11 18				
Brighton	a	10 02	10 12	10 07	10 19			10 33	10 42	10 37	10 49			11 02	11 12	11 07	11 19			11 32	11 42	11 37
Hove	a					10 22							10 52					11 22				
Lewes	a						10 25					10 53							11 25			

Table T184-F

Mondays to Fridays

16 December to 15 May

London - Gatwick Airport - Haywards Heath - Brighton/Hove/Lewes

		TL	SN		SN	TL	GX	TL	SN		SN	TL	GX	TL	SN		SN	TL	GX	TL	SN		SN
London Victoria	d		10 46		10 55		11 14		11 16		11 25		11 44		11 46		11 55		12 14		12 16		12 25
Clapham Junction	d		10 53		11 02				11 23		11 32				11 53		12 02				12 23		12 32
East Croydon	a		11 02		11 11				11 32		11 41				12 02		12 11				12 32		12 41
St Pancras International	d	10 30				10 50		11 00				11 20		11 30				11 50		12 00			
Farringdon	d	10 34				10 54		11 04				11 24		11 34				11 54		12 04			
City Thameslink	d	10 36				10 56		11 06				11 26		11 36				11 56		12 06			
London Blackfriars	d	10 39				10 59		11 09				11 29		11 39				11 59		12 09			
London Bridge	d	10 45				11 05		11 15				11 35		11 45				12 05		12 15			
East Croydon	a	10 58				11 18		11 28				11 48		11 58				12 18		12 28			
East Croydon	d	10 59	11 03		11 11	11 19		11 29	11 33		11 41	11 49		11 59	12 03		12 11	12 19		12 29	12 33		12 41
Gatwick Airport	a	11 14	11 17		11 26	11 34	11 41	11 44	11 47		11 56	12 04	12 11	12 14	12 17		12 26	12 34	12 41	12 44	12 47		12 56
Gatwick Airport	d	11 15	11 20		11 28	11 35	11 42	11 45	11 50		11 58	12 05	12 12	12 15	12 20		12 28	12 35	12 42	12 45	12 50		12 58
Three Bridges	a	11 19				11 39		11 49				12 09		12 19				12 39		12 49			
Three Bridges	d	11 20				11 40		11 50				12 10		12 20				12 40		12 50			
Balcombe	d					11 46						12 16						12 46					
Haywards Heath	a	11 29	11 31		11 39	11 51		11 59	12 01		12 09	12 21		12 29	12 31		12 39	12 51		12 59	13 01		13 09
Haywards Heath	d	11 29	11 35	11 38	11 41	11 54		11 59	12 05	12 07	12 11	12 24		12 29	12 35	12 38	12 41	12 54		12 59	13 05	13 07	13 11
Wivelsfield	d					11 58				12 11		12 28						12 58				13 11	
Burgess Hill	d	11 35			11 46	12 00		12 05			12 16	12 30		12 35			12 46	13 00		13 05			13 16
Hassocks	d	11 38			11 50			12 08			12 20			12 38			12 50			13 08			13 20
Preston Park	d	11 45						12 15	12 18					12 45						13 15	13 18		
Brighton	a	11 49			12 02	12 12	12 07	12 19			12 32	12 42	12 37	12 49			13 02	13 12	13 07	13 19			13 32
Hove	a			11 52					12 22							12 52					13 22		
Lewes	a		11 53							12 25					12 53							13 25	

		TL	GX	TL	SN		SN	TL	GX	TL	SN		SN	TL	GX	TL	SN		SN	TL	GX	TL
London Victoria	d		12 44		12 46		12 55		13 14		13 16		13 25		13 44		13 46		13 55		14 14	
Clapham Junction	d				12 53		13 02				13 23		13 32				13 53		14 02			
East Croydon	a				13 02		13 11				13 32		13 41				14 02		14 11			
St Pancras International	d	12 20		12 30				12 50		13 00				13 20		13 30				13 50		14 00
Farringdon	d	12 24		12 34				12 54		13 04				13 24		13 34				13 54		14 04
City Thameslink	d	12 26		12 36				12 56		13 06				13 26		13 36				13 56		14 06
London Blackfriars	d	12 29		12 39				12 59		13 09				13 29		13 39				13 59		14 09
London Bridge	d	12 35		12 45				13 05		13 15				13 35		13 45				14 05		14 15
East Croydon	a	12 48		12 58				13 18		13 28				13 48		13 58				14 18		14 28
East Croydon	d	12 49		12 59	13 03		13 11	13 19		13 29	13 33		13 41	13 49		13 59	14 03		14 11	14 19		14 29
Gatwick Airport	a	13 04	13 11	13 14	13 17		13 26	13 34	13 41	13 44	13 47		13 56	14 04	14 11	14 14	14 17		14 26	14 34	14 41	14 44
Gatwick Airport	d	13 05	13 12	13 15	13 20		13 28	13 35	13 42	13 45	13 50		13 58	14 05	14 12	14 15	14 20		14 28	14 35	14 42	14 45
Three Bridges	a	13 09		13 19				13 39		13 49				14 09		14 19				14 39		14 49
Three Bridges	d	13 10		13 20				13 40		13 50				14 10		14 20				14 40		14 50
Balcombe	d	13 16						13 46						14 16						14 46		
Haywards Heath	a	13 21		13 29	13 31		13 39	13 51		13 59	14 01		14 09	14 21		14 29	14 31		14 39	14 51		14 59
Haywards Heath	d	13 24		13 29	13 35	13 38	13 41	13 54		13 59	14 05	14 07	14 11	14 24		14 29	14 35	14 38	14 41	14 54		14 59
Wivelsfield	d	13 28						13 58				14 11		14 28						14 58		
Burgess Hill	d	13 30		13 35			13 46	14 00		14 05			14 16	14 30		14 35			14 46	15 00		15 05
Hassocks	d			13 38			13 50			14 08			14 20			14 38			14 50			15 08
Preston Park	d			13 45						14 15	14 18					14 45						15 15
Brighton	a	13 42	13 37	13 49			14 02	14 12	14 07	14 19			14 31	14 42	14 37	14 49			15 02	15 12	15 07	15 19
Hove	a					13 52					14 22							14 52				
Lewes	a				13 53							14 25					14 53					

		SN		SN	TL	GX	TL	SN		SN	TL	GX	TL	SN		SN	TL	GX	TL	SN		SN
London Victoria	d	14 16		14 25		14 44		14 46		14 55		15 14		15 16		15 25		15 44		15 46		15 55
Clapham Junction	d	14 23		14 32				14 53		15 02				15 23		15 32				15 53		16 02
East Croydon	a	14 32		14 41				15 02		15 11				15 32		15 41				16 02		16 11
St Pancras International	d				14 20		14 30				14 50		15 00				15 20		15 30			
Farringdon	d				14 24		14 34				14 54		15 04				15 24		15 34			
City Thameslink	d				14 26		14 36				14 56		15 06				15 26		15 36			
London Blackfriars	d				14 29		14 39				14 59		15 09				15 29		15 39			
London Bridge	d				14 35		14 45				15 05		15 15				15 35		15 45			
East Croydon	a				14 48		14 58				15 18		15 28				15 48		15 58			
East Croydon	d	14 33		14 41	14 49		14 59	15 03		15 11	15 19		15 29	15 33		15 41	15 49		15 59	16 03		16 11
Gatwick Airport	a	14 47		14 56	15 04	15 11	15 14	15 17		15 26	15 34	15 41	15 44	15 47		15 56	16 04	16 11	16 14	16 17		16 26
Gatwick Airport	d	14 50		14 58	15 05	15 12	15 15	15 20		15 28	15 35	15 42	15 45	15 50		15 58	16 05	16 12	16 15	16 20		16 28
Three Bridges	a				15 09		15 19				15 39		15 49				16 09		16 19			
Three Bridges	d				15 10		15 20				15 40		15 50				16 10		16 20			
Balcombe	d				15 16						15 46						16 16					
Haywards Heath	a	15 01		15 09	15 21		15 29	15 31		15 39	15 51		15 59	16 02		16 10	16 21		16 29	16 31		16 39
Haywards Heath	d	15 05	15 07	15 11	15 24		15 29	15 35	15 38	15 41	15 54		15 59	16 06	16 08	16 11	16 24		16 29	16 35	16 38	16 41
Wivelsfield	d		15 11		15 28						15 58				16 12		16 28					
Burgess Hill	d			15 16	15 30		15 35			15 46	16 00		16 05			16 17	16 30		16 35			16 46
Hassocks	d			15 20			15 38			15 50			16 08			16 21			16 38			16 50
Preston Park	d	15 18					15 45						16 15	16 18					16 45			
Brighton	a			15 32	15 42	15 37	15 49			16 02	16 12	16 07	16 19			16 32	16 42	16 37	16 49			17 02
Hove	a	15 22							15 52					16 22							16 52	
Lewes	a		15 25					15 53							16 26					16 53		

Table T184-F

Mondays to Fridays

16 December to 15 May

London - Gatwick Airport - Haywards Heath - Brighton/Hove/Lewes

Station		TL	GX	TL	SN	SN	SN	TL	GX	TL	SN	TL	SN	GX	TL	GX	TL	TL	SN	SN	GX	SN	TL
London Victoria	d		16 14		16 16		16 25		16 43		16 45		16 54	16 59		17 13			17 15	17 24	17 29		
Clapham Junction	d				16 23		16 32				16 52		17 02						17 22	17 32			
East Croydon	a				16 32		16 41				17 01		17 11						17 31	17 41			
St Pancras International	d	15 50		16 00				16 20		16 30		16 40			16 50			17 00					17 20
Farringdon	d	15 54		16 04				16 24		16 34		16 44			16 54			17 04					17 24
City Thameslink	d	15 56		16 06				16 26		16 36		16 46			16 56			17 06					17 26
London Blackfriars	d	15 59		16 09				16 29		16 39		16 49			16 59			17 09					17 29
London Bridge	d	16 05		16 15				16 35		16 45		16 55			17 05			17 15				17 32	17 35
East Croydon	a	16 19		16 29				16 49		16 59		17 08			17 19			17 29				17 46	17 49
East Croydon	d	16 20		16 29	16 33		16 41	16 50		16 59	17 02	17 08	17 11		17 20			17 29	17 32	17 41		17 47	17 50
Gatwick Airport	a	16 35	16 41	16 44	16 47		16 56	17 04	17 11	17 14	17 19		17 26	17 29	17 35	17 41		17 44	17 49	17 56	17 59	18 02	18 05
Gatwick Airport	d	16 36	16 42	16 45	16 50		16 58	17 06	17 12	17 15	17 20		17 27	17 33	17 36	17 42	←	17 45	17 50	17 57	18 00	18 03	18 06
Three Bridges	a	16 40		16 49				17 10		17 19		17 27			17 40		17 40	17 49					18 10
Three Bridges	d	16 41		16 50				17 11		17 20		17 28			17 41		17 41	17 50					18 11
Balcombe	d	16 47						17 17							→		17 47						→
Haywards Heath	a	16 52		16 59	17 01		17 09	17 22		17 29	17 32	17 37	17 39	17 44			17 52	17 59	18 02	18 09	18 12	18 15	
Haywards Heath	d	16 54		16 59	17 05	17 07	17 12	17 24		17 30	17 33	17 37	17 40	17 45			17 54	18 00	18 03	18 09	18 14	18 16	
Wivelsfield	d	16 59				17 11		17 29			17 37						17 59		18 07			18 21	
Burgess Hill	d	17 01		17 05			17 17	17 31		17 35			17 46			17 57	18 01	18 05		18 15			
Hassocks	d			17 09			17 21	17 35		17 39				17 52		18 01		18 09		18 19	18 22		
Preston Park	d			17 16	17 20			17 42		17 46		17 50	17 55			18 08		18 16		18 26			
Brighton	a	17 13	17 07	17 21			17 32	17 46	17 37	17 51				18 02		18 12	18 15	18 21			18 32		
Hove	a				17 24							17 54	18 00							18 30			
Lewes	a					17 25					17 52								18 22			18 38	

Station		GX	TL	TL	SN	TL	SN	GX	TL	GX	TL	TL	SN	SN	GX	SN	TL	GX	TL	TL	SN	SN	GX
London Victoria	d	17 43			17 45		17 54	17 59		18 13			18 15	18 24	18 29			18 43			18 45	18 54	18 59
Clapham Junction	d				17 52		18 02						18 22	18 32							18 52	19 02	
East Croydon	a				18 01		18 11						18 31	18 41							19 01	19 11	
St Pancras International	d			17 30		17 40			17 50			18 00					18 20			18 30			
Farringdon	d			17 34		17 44			17 54			18 04					18 24			18 34			
City Thameslink	d			17 36		17 46			17 56			18 06					18 26			18 36			
London Blackfriars	d			17 39		17 49			17 59			18 09					18 29			18 39			
London Bridge	d			17 45		17 55			18 05			18 15				18 32	18 35			18 45			
East Croydon	a			17 59		18 08			18 19			18 29				18 46	18 49			18 59			
East Croydon	d			17 59	18 02	18 08	18 11		18 20			18 29	18 32	18 41		18 47	18 50			18 59	19 02	19 11	
Gatwick Airport	a	18 11		18 14	18 19		18 26	18 29	18 35	18 41		18 44	18 49	18 56	18 59	19 02	19 05	19 11		19 14	19 19	19 26	19 29
Gatwick Airport	d	18 12	←	18 15	18 20		18 27	18 33	18 36	18 42	←	18 45	18 50	18 57	19 00	19 03	19 06	19 12	←	19 15	19 20	19 27	19 30
Three Bridges	a		18 10	18 19		18 27			18 40		18 40	18 49					19 10		19 10	19 19			
Three Bridges	d		18 11	18 20		18 28			18 41		18 41	18 50					19 11		19 11	19 20			
Balcombe	d		18 17						→		18 47						→		19 17				
Haywards Heath	a		18 22	18 29	18 32	18 37	18 39	18 44			18 52	18 59	19 02	19 08	19 11	19 15			19 22	19 29	19 32	19 38	19 41
Haywards Heath	d		18 24	18 30	18 33	18 37	18 40	18 45			18 54	19 00	19 03	19 10	19 13	19 16			19 24	19 30	19 33	19 40	19 43
Wivelsfield	d		18 29		18 37						18 59		19 07			19 21			19 29		19 37		
Burgess Hill	d	18 27	18 31	18 35			18 46			18 57	19 01	19 05		19 16				19 27	19 31	19 35		19 46	
Hassocks	d	18 31	18 35	18 39				18 52		19 01		19 09			19 22			19 31	19 35	19 39			19 52
Preston Park	d	18 38	18 42	18 46		18 50	18 55			19 08		19 16		19 25				19 38	19 42	19 46		19 55	
Brighton	a	18 42	18 46	18 51				19 02		19 12	19 15	19 21			19 32			19 42	19 46	19 51			20 02
Hove	a					18 54	19 00							19 30								19 59	
Lewes	a				18 52								19 22			19 38					19 52		

Station		TL	GX	TL	SN	SN	SN	TL	GX	TL	SN	SN	SN	TL	GX	TL	SN	SN	SN	TL	GX
London Victoria	d		19 14		19 16		19 25		19 44		19 46		19 55		20 14		20 16		20 25		20 44
Clapham Junction	d				19 23		19 32				19 53		20 02				20 23		20 32		
East Croydon	a				19 32		19 41				20 02		20 11				20 32		20 41		
St Pancras International	d	18 50		19 00				19 20		19 30				19 50		20 00				20 20	
Farringdon	d	18 54		19 04				19 24		19 34				19 54		20 04				20 24	
City Thameslink	d	18 56		19 06				19 26		19 36				19 56		20 06				20 26	
London Blackfriars	d	18 59		19 09				19 29		19 39				19 59		20 09				20 29	
London Bridge	d	19 05		19 15				19 35		19 45				20 05		20 15				20 35	
East Croydon	a	19 19		19 29				19 48		19 58				20 18		20 28				20 48	
East Croydon	d	19 20		19 29	19 33		19 41	19 49		19 59	20 03		20 11	20 19		20 29	20 33		20 41	20 49	
Gatwick Airport	a	19 35	19 41	19 44	19 47		19 56	20 04	20 11	20 14	20 17		20 26	20 34	20 41	20 44	20 47		20 56	21 04	21 11
Gatwick Airport	d	19 36	19 42	19 45	19 50		19 58	20 05	20 12	20 15	20 20		20 28	20 35	20 42	20 45	20 50		20 58	21 05	21 12
Three Bridges	a	19 40		19 49				20 09		20 19				20 39		20 49				21 09	
Three Bridges	d	19 41		19 50				20 10		20 20				20 40		20 50				21 10	
Balcombe	d	19 47						20 16						20 46						21 16	
Haywards Heath	a	19 52		19 59	20 01		20 09	20 21		20 29	20 31		20 39	20 51		20 59	21 01		21 09	21 21	
Haywards Heath	d	19 54		20 00	20 05	20 07	20 11	20 24		20 29	20 35	20 38	20 41	20 54		20 59	21 05	21 07	21 11	21 24	
Wivelsfield	d	19 59				20 11		20 28						20 58				21 11		21 28	
Burgess Hill	d	20 01		20 05			20 17	20 30		20 35			20 47	21 00		21 05			21 17	21 30	
Hassocks	d			20 09			20 21			20 38			20 51			21 08			21 21	21 34	
Preston Park	d			20 15	20 18					20 45						21 15	21 18			21 40	
Brighton	a	20 13	20 07	20 19			20 32	20 42	20 37	20 49			21 02	21 12	21 07	21 19			21 32	21 45	21 37
Hove	a				20 22							20 52					21 22				
Lewes	a					20 25					20 53							21 25			

Table T184-F

Mondays to Fridays

16 December to 15 May

London - Gatwick Airport - Haywards Heath - Brighton/Hove/Lewes

Station		SN	SN	SN	TL	GX	TL	SN	SN	SN	TL	GX	SN	SN	SN	TL	GX	TL	SN	SN	SN	TL	GX
London Victoria	d	20 46		20 55		21 14		21 16		21 25		21 44	21 46		21 55		22 14		22 16		22 25		22 44
Clapham Junction	d	20 53		21 02				21 23		21 32			21 53		22 02				22 23		22 32		
East Croydon	a	21 02		21 11				21 32		21 41			22 02		22 11				22 32		22 41		
St Pancras International	d				20 50		21 00				21 20					21 50		22 00				22 20	
Farringdon	d				20 54		21 04				21 24					21 54		22 04				22 24	
City Thameslink	d				20 56		21 06				21 26					21 56		22 06				22 26	
London Blackfriars	d				20 59		21 09				21 29					21 59		22 09				22 29	
London Bridge	d				21 05		21 15				21 35					22 05		22 15				22 35	
East Croydon	a				21 21		21 28				21 48					22 18		22 28				22 48	
East Croydon	d	21 03		21 11	21 22		21 30	21 33		21 41	21 49		22 03		22 11	22 19		22 29	22 33		22 41	22 49	
Gatwick Airport	a	21 17		21 26	21 36	21 42	21 44	21 47		21 56	22 04	22 11	22 17		22 26	22 34	22 41	22 44	22 47		22 56	23 04	23 11
Gatwick Airport	d	21 20		21 28	21 37	21 43	21 45	21 50		21 58	22 05	22 12	22 20		22 28	22 35	22 42	22 45	22 50		22 58	23 05	23 12
Three Bridges	a				21 41		21 49				22 09					22 39		22 49				23 09	
Three Bridges	d				21 42		21 50				22 10					22 40		22 50				23 10	
Balcombe	d				21 48						22 16					22 46						23 16	
Haywards Heath	a	21 31		21 39	21 53		21 59	22 01		22 09	22 21		22 31		22 39	22 51		22 59	23 01		23 09	23 21	
Haywards Heath	d	21 35	21 38	21 41	21 56		22 01	22 05	22 07	22 11	22 24		22 35	22 38	22 41	22 54		23 00	23 05	23 07	23 11	23 24	
Wivelsfield	d				22 00				22 11		22 28					22 58				23 11		23 28	
Burgess Hill	d			21 47	22 02		22 06			22 17	22 30				22 47	23 00		23 05			23 17	23 30	
Hassocks	d			21 51			22 09			22 21	22 34				22 51			23 08			23 21	23 34	
Preston Park	d						22 16	22 18			22 40							23 15	23 18			23 40	
Brighton	a			22 02	22 13	22 07	22 20			22 32	22 45	22 37			23 03	23 12	23 07	23 19			23 32	23 45	23 37
Hove	a		21 52					22 22						22 52					23 22				
Lewes	a	21 53							22 25				22 53							23 25			

Station		SN	SN	SN	TL	TL	SN	SN	TL	TL
London Victoria	d	22 46		22 56			23 16	23 25		
Clapham Junction	d	22 53		23 03			23 23	23 32		
East Croydon	a	23 02		23 12			23 32	23 41		
St Pancras International	d				22 50	23 00			23 22	23 51
Farringdon	d				22 54	23 04			23 27	23 56
City Thameslink	d				22 56					
London Blackfriars	d				22 59	23 09			23 31	00 02
London Bridge	d				23 05	23 15			23 37	
East Croydon	a				23 18	23 28			23 50	00 27
East Croydon	d	23 03		23 12	23 19	23 29	23 33	23 43	23 51	00 28
Gatwick Airport	a	23 17		23 27	23 34	23 47	23 52	00 03	00 18	00 47
Gatwick Airport	d	23 20		23 28	23 35	23 48	23 56	00 04	00 19	00 48
Three Bridges	a				23 39	23 53			00 24	00 53
Three Bridges	d				23 40	23 54			00 25	00 54
Balcombe	d				23 46				00 31	
Haywards Heath	a	23 31		23 39	23 51	00 03	00 08	00 17	00 36	01 04
Haywards Heath	d	23 35	23 38	23 41	23 54	00 04	00 09	00 17	00 37	01 04
Wivelsfield	d	23 39			23 58		00 13		00 41	01 08
Burgess Hill	d			23 46	00 01	00 09		00 22	00 43	01 10
Hassocks	d			23 50		00 12		00 26	00 47	01 13
Preston Park	d					00 19	00 22		00 53	01 20
Brighton	a			00 02	00 12	00 23		00 35	00 57	01 24
Hove	a		23 52				00 26			
Lewes	a	23 55								

Saturdays

21 December to 16 May

Station		SN A	SN A	TL	SN	SN	TL	TL	TL	SN	TL	GX	TL	SN	TL	GX	TL	TL	GX	SN	SN	SN	TL
London Victoria	d	00 02			01 10	04 10				05 08		05 44				06 14			06 44			06 55	
Clapham Junction	d	00 09			01 17	04 17				05 16												07 02	
East Croydon	a	00 23			01 32	04 31				05 31												07 11	
St Pancras International	d			00 52			04 02	04 32	04 51		05 20				05 50		06 00	06 20					06 50
Farringdon	d								04 56		05 24				05 54		06 04	06 24					06 54
City Thameslink	d																						
London Blackfriars	d			01 02			04 10	04 40	05 01		05 29				05 59		06 09	06 29					06 59
London Bridge	d										05 35				06 05		06 15	06 35					07 05
East Croydon	a			01 28			04 36	05 06	05 27		05 48				06 18		06 28	06 48					07 18
East Croydon	d	00 24		01 28	01 33	04 31	04 37	05 07	05 28	05 31	05 49				06 19		06 29	06 49				07 11	07 19
Gatwick Airport	a	00 43		01 56	02 06	04 59	05 02	05 31	05 47	06 00	06 04	06 11			06 34	06 41	06 44	07 04	07 11			07 26	07 34
Gatwick Airport	d	00 44		01 58	02 13	05 00	05 04	05 32	05 48	06 01	06 05	06 12		06 13	06 35	06 42	06 45	07 05	07 12			07 28	07 35
Three Bridges	a	00 48		02 03	02 18	05 05	05 09	05 36	05 53	06 06	06 09			06 19	06 39		06 49	07 09					07 39
Three Bridges	d	00 49		02 04	02 19	05 06	05 09	05 37	05 54	06 07	06 10			06 20	06 40		06 50	07 10					07 40
Balcombe	d								06 00		06 16		←		06 46			07 16					07 46
Haywards Heath	a	00 58		02 13	02 28	05 15	05 20	05 46	06 05	06 16	06 21	06 23	06 21	06 29	06 51	06 53	06 59	07 21				07 39	07 51
Haywards Heath	d	01 02	01 08	02 14	02 29	05 17	05 20	05 47	06 06	06 17	06 25	06 23	06 25	06 31	06 52	06 55	06 59	07 24		07 35	07 38	07 41	07 54
Wivelsfield	d							05 51	06 10		→		06 29				07 03	07 28					07 58
Burgess Hill	d							05 53	06 12	06 22			06 32				07 06	07 30				07 46	08 00
Hassocks	d							05 57	06 16	06 26			06 35				07 09	07 34				07 50	
Preston Park	d							06 03	06 22				06 42				07 16	07 40					
Brighton	a	01s16		02 28	02 43	05 32	05 38	06 07	06 26	06 37		06 40	06 46		07 06	07 09	07 22	07 44	07 37			08 02	08 12
Hove	a	01s25																			07 52		
Lewes	a		01 23											06 49						07 53			

A not 16 May

Table T184-F

Saturdays

21 December to 16 May

London - Gatwick Airport - Haywards Heath - Brighton/Hove/Lewes

		GX 1	TL 1	SN 1	TL 1	GX 1	SN 1		SN 1	TL 1	GX 1	TL 1	SN 1		SN 1	TL 1	GX 1	SN 1		SN 1	TL 1
London Victoria	d	07 14		07 25		07 44	07 46		07 55		08 14		08 16		08 25		08 44	08 46		08 55	
Clapham Junction	d			07 32			07 53		08 02				08 23		08 32			08 53		09 02	
East Croydon	a			07 41			08 02		08 11				08 32		08 41			09 02		09 11	
St Pancras International	d		07 00		07 20					07 50		08 00				08 20					08 50
Farringdon	d		07 04		07 24					07 54		08 04				08 24					08 54
City Thameslink	d																				
London Blackfriars	d		07 09		07 29					07 59		08 09				08 29					08 59
London Bridge	d		07 15		07 35					08 05		08 15				08 35					09 05
East Croydon	a		07 28		07 48					08 18		08 28				08 48					09 18
East Croydon	d		07 29	07 41	07 49		08 03		08 11	08 19		08 29	08 33		08 41	08 49		09 03		09 11	09 19
Gatwick Airport	a	07 41	07 44	07 56	08 04	08 11	08 18		08 26	08 34	08 41	08 44	08 47		08 56	09 04	09 11	09 18		09 26	09 34
Gatwick Airport	d	07 42	07 45	07 58	08 05	08 12	08 20		08 28	08 35	08 42	08 45	08 50		08 58	09 05	09 12	09 20		09 28	09 35
Three Bridges	a		07 49		08 09					08 39		08 49				09 09					09 39
Three Bridges	d		07 50		08 10					08 40		08 50				09 10					09 40
Balcombe	d				08 16					08 46						09 16					09 46
Haywards Heath	a		07 59	08 09	08 21		08 31		08 39	08 51		08 59	09 01		09 09	09 21		09 31		09 39	09 51
Haywards Heath	d		07 59	08 11	08 24		08 35	08 38	08 41	08 54		08 59	09 05	09 07	09 11	09 24		09 35	09 38	09 41	09 54
Wivelsfield	d				08 28					08 58				09 11		09 28					09 58
Burgess Hill	d		08 05	08 16	08 30				08 46	09 00		09 05			09 16	09 30				09 46	10 00
Hassocks	d		08 08	08 20	08 34				08 50			09 08			09 20	09 34				09 50	
Preston Park	d		08 15		08 40							09 15	09 18			09 40					
Brighton	a	08 07	08 19	08 32	08 46	08 37			09 02	09 12	09 07	09 19			09 32	09 44	09 37			10 02	10 12
Hove	a							08 52					09 22						09 52		
Lewes	a						08 53							09 25				09 53			

		GX 1	TL 1	SN 1		SN 1	TL 1	GX 1	SN 1		SN 1	TL 1		GX 1	TL 1	SN 1		SN 1	TL 1	GX 1	SN 1		SN 1	TL 1
London Victoria	d	09 14		09 16		09 25		09 44	09 46		09 55			14 14		14 16		14 25		14 44	14 46		14 55	
Clapham Junction	d			09 23		09 32			09 53		10 02					14 23		14 32			14 53		15 02	
East Croydon	a			09 32		09 41			10 02		10 11					14 32		14 41			15 02		15 11	
St Pancras International	d		09 00				09 20					09 50			14 00				14 20					14 50
Farringdon	d		09 04				09 24					09 54			14 04				14 24					14 54
City Thameslink	d		09 06				09 26					09 56			14 06				14 26					14 56
London Blackfriars	d		09 09				09 29					09 59			14 09				14 29					14 59
London Bridge	d		09 15				09 35					10 05			14 15				14 35					15 05
East Croydon	a		09 28				09 48					10 18	and at		14 28				14 48					15 18
East Croydon	d		09 29	09 33		09 41	09 49		10 03		10 11	10 19	the same		14 29	14 33		14 41	14 49		15 03		15 11	15 19
Gatwick Airport	a	09 41	09 44	09 47		09 56	10 04	10 11	10 18		10 26	10 34	minutes	14 41	14 44	14 47		14 56	15 04	15 11	15 18		15 26	15 34
Gatwick Airport	d	09 42	09 45	09 50		09 58	10 05	10 12	10 20		10 28	10 35	past	14 42	14 45	14 50		14 58	15 05	15 12	15 20		15 28	15 35
Three Bridges	a		09 49				10 09					10 39	each		14 49				15 09					15 39
Three Bridges	d		09 50				10 10					10 40	hour until		14 50				15 10					15 40
Balcombe	d						10 16					10 46							15 16					15 46
Haywards Heath	a		09 59	10 01		10 09	10 21		10 31		10 39	10 51			14 59	15 01		15 09	15 21		15 31		15 39	15 51
Haywards Heath	d		09 59	10 05	10 07	10 11	10 24		10 35	10 38	10 41	10 54			14 59	15 05	15 07	15 11	15 24		15 35	15 38	15 41	15 54
Wivelsfield	d				10 11		10 28					10 58					15 11		15 28					15 58
Burgess Hill	d		10 05			10 16	10 30				10 46	11 00			15 05			15 16	15 30				15 46	16 00
Hassocks	d		10 08			10 20	10 34				10 50				15 08			15 20	15 34				15 50	
Preston Park	d		10 15	10 18			10 40								15 15	15 18			15 40					
Brighton	a	10 07	10 19			10 32	10 44	10 37			11 02	11 12		15 07	15 19			15 32	15 44	15 37			16 02	16 12
Hove	a			10 22						10 52						15 22						15 52		
Lewes	a				10 25				10 53								15 25				15 53			

		GX 1	TL 1	SN 1		SN 1	TL 1	GX 1	SN 1		SN 1	TL 1	GX 1	TL 1		SN 1		SN 1	TL 1	GX 1
London Victoria	d	15 14		15 16		15 25		15 44	15 46		15 55		16 14			19 16		19 25		19 44
Clapham Junction	d			15 23		15 32			15 53		16 02					19 23		19 32		
East Croydon	a			15 32		15 41			16 02		16 11					19 32		19 41		
St Pancras International	d		15 00				15 20					15 50		16 00					19 20	
Farringdon	d		15 04				15 24					15 54		16 04					19 24	
City Thameslink	d		15 06				15 26					15 56		16 06					19 26	
London Blackfriars	d		15 09				15 29					15 59		16 09					19 29	
London Bridge	d		15 15				15 35					16 05		16 15	and at				19 35	
East Croydon	a		15 28				15 48					16 18		16 28	the same				19 48	
East Croydon	d		15 29	15 33		15 41	15 49		16 03		16 11	16 19		16 29	minutes	19 33		19 41	19 49	
Gatwick Airport	a	15 41	15 44	15 47		15 56	16 04	16 11	16 18		16 26	16 34	16 41	16 44	past	19 47		19 56	20 04	20 11
Gatwick Airport	d	15 42	15 45	15 50		15 58	16 05	16 12	16 20		16 28	16 35	16 42	16 45	each	19 50		19 58	20 05	20 12
Three Bridges	a		15 49				16 09					16 39		16 49	hour until				20 09	
Three Bridges	d		15 50				16 10					16 40		16 50					20 10	
Balcombe	d						16 16					16 46							20 16	
Haywards Heath	a		15 59	16 01		16 09	16 21		16 31		16 39	16 51		16 59		20 01		20 09	20 21	
Haywards Heath	d		16 00	16 05	16 07	16 11	16 24		16 35	16 38	16 41	16 54		16 59		20 05	20 07	20 11	20 24	
Wivelsfield	d				16 11		16 28					16 58					20 11		20 28	
Burgess Hill	d		16 05			16 16	16 30				16 46	17 00		17 05				20 16	20 30	
Hassocks	d		16 08			16 20	16 34				16 50			17 08				20 20	20 34	
Preston Park	d		16 15	16 18			16 40							17 15		20 18			20 40	
Brighton	a	16 07	16 19			16 32	16 44	16 37			17 02	17 12	17 07	17 19				20 32	20 44	20 37
Hove	a			16 22						16 52						20 22				
Lewes	a				16 25				16 53								20 25			

NRT DECEMBER 19 EDITION

Table T184-F

Saturdays

21 December to 16 May

London - Gatwick Airport - Haywards Heath - Brighton/Hove/Lewes

		SN 1		SN 1	TL 1	GX 1	TL 1	SN 1		SN 1	TL 1	GX 1	SN 1		SN 1	TL 1	GX 1	TL 1	SN 1		SN 1	TL 1	GX 1
London Victoria	d	19 46		19 55		20 14		20 16		20 25		20 44	20 46		20 55		21 14		21 16		21 25		21 44
Clapham Junction	d	19 53		20 02				20 23		20 32			20 53		21 02				21 23		21 32		
East Croydon	a	20 02		20 11				20 32		20 41			21 02		21 11				21 32		21 41		
St Pancras International	d				19 50		20 00				20 20					20 50		21 00				21 20	
Farringdon	d				19 54		20 04				20 24					20 54		21 04				21 24	
City Thameslink	d				19 56		20 06				20 26					20 56							
London Blackfriars	d				19 59		20 09				20 29					20 59		21 09				21 29	
London Bridge	d				20 05		20 15				20 35					21 05		21 15				21 35	
East Croydon	a				20 18		20 28				20 48					21 18		21 28				21 48	
East Croydon	d	20 03		20 11	20 19		20 29	20 33		20 41	20 49		21 03		21 11	21 19		21 29	21 33		21 41	21 49	
Gatwick Airport	a	20 18		20 26	20 34	20 41	20 44	20 47		20 56	21 04	21 11	21 18		21 26	21 34	21 41	21 44	21 47		21 56	22 04	22 11
Gatwick Airport	d	20 20		20 28	20 35	20 42	20 45	20 50		20 58	21 05	21 12	21 20		21 28	21 35	21 42	21 45	21 50		21 58	22 05	22 12
Three Bridges	a				20 39		20 49				21 09					21 39		21 49				22 09	
Three Bridges	d				20 40		20 50				21 10					21 40		21 50				22 10	
Balcombe	d				20 46						21 16					21 46						22 16	
Haywards Heath	a	20 31		20 39	20 51		20 59	21 01		21 09	21 21		21 31		21 39	21 51		21 59	22 01		22 09	22 21	
Haywards Heath	d	20 35	20 38	20 41	20 54		20 59	21 05	21 07	21 11	21 24		21 35	21 38	21 41	21 54		21 59	22 05	22 07	22 11	22 24	
Wivelsfield	d				20 58				21 11		21 28					21 58				22 11		22 28	
Burgess Hill	d			20 46	21 00		21 05			21 16	21 30				21 46	22 00		22 05			22 16	22 30	
Hassocks	d			20 50			21 08			21 20	21 34				21 50			22 08			22 20	22 34	
Preston Park	d						21 15	21 18			21 40							22 15	22 18			22 40	
Brighton	a			21 02	21 12	21 07	21 19			21 32	21 44	21 37			22 02	22 12	22 07	22 19			22 32	22 44	22 37
Hove	a		20 52					21 22						21 52					22 22				
Lewes	a	20 53							21 25				21 53							22 25			

		SN 1		SN 1	TL 1	GX 1	TL 1	SN 1		SN 1	TL 1	GX 1	SN 1		SN 1	TL 1	TL 1	SN 1	SN 1 A	SN 1	TL 1	TL 1
London Victoria	d	21 46		21 55		22 14		22 16		22 25		22 44	22 46		22 55			23 16	23 16	23 25		
Clapham Junction	d	21 53		22 02				22 23		22 32			22 53		23 02			23 23	23 23	23 32		
East Croydon	a	22 02		22 11				22 32		22 41			23 02		23 11			23 32	23 32	23 41		
St Pancras International	d				21 50		22 00				22 20					22 50	23 00				23 22	23 51
Farringdon	d				21 54		22 04				22 24					22 54	23 04				23 27	23 56
City Thameslink	d																					
London Blackfriars	d				21 59		22 09				22 29					22 59	23 09				23 31	00 01
London Bridge	d				22 05		22 15				22 35					23 05	23 15				23 37	
East Croydon	a				22 18		22 28				22 48					23 18	23 28				23 50	00 27
East Croydon	d	22 03		22 11	22 19		22 29	22 33		22 41	22 49		23 03		23 11	23 19	23 29	23 33	23 33	23 43	23 51	00 28
Gatwick Airport	a	22 18		22 26	22 34	22 41	22 44	22 47		22 56	23 04	23 11	23 18		23 26	23 34	23 47	23 52	23 52	00 04	00 17	00 47
Gatwick Airport	d	22 20		22 28	22 35	22 42	22 45	22 50		22 58	23 05	23 12	23 20		23 28	23 35	23 48	23 54	23 54	00 05	00 18	00 48
Three Bridges	a				22 39		22 49				23 09					23 39	23 53				00 23	00 53
Three Bridges	d				22 40		22 50				23 10					23 40	23 54				00 24	00 54
Balcombe	d				22 46						23 16					23 46					00 30	
Haywards Heath	a	22 31		22 39	22 51		22 59	23 01		23 09	23 21		23 31		23 39	23 51	00 03	00 05	00 05	00 17	00 35	01 04
Haywards Heath	d	22 35	22 38	22 41	22 54		22 59	23 05	23 07	23 11	23 24		23 35	23 38	23 41	23 54	00 04	00 09	00 11	00 17	00 36	01 04
Wivelsfield	d				22 58				23 11		23 28					23 58			00 15		00 40	01 08
Burgess Hill	d			22 46	23 00		23 05			23 16	23 30				23 46	00 01	00 09			00 22	00 42	01 10
Hassocks	d			22 50			23 08			23 20	23 35				23 50		00 12			00 26	00 46	01 14
Preston Park	d						23 15	23 18			23 41						00 19	00 21			00 52	01 20
Brighton	a			23 02	23 12	23 07	23 19			23 32	23 45	23 37			00 02	00 12	00 23			00 35	00 56	01 24
Hove	a		22 52					23 22						23 52				00 25				
Lewes	a	22 53							23 25				23 55						00 27			

Sundays

15 December to 10 May

		SN	SN 1		TL 1 B	SN 1	SN 1	SN 1	SN 1	SN 1	TL 1	SN 1	TL 1	TL 1	SN 1	SN 1	SN 1	TL 1	SN 1	SN 1	TL 1	SN 1	SN 1
London Victoria	d		00 02			01 08	04 10	05 02	05 45	06 32		07 02			08 02	08 14			08 46	08 55		09 16	09 25
Clapham Junction	d		00 09			01 17	04 17	05 10	05 53	06 40		07 10			08 10	08 21			08 53	09 02		09 23	09 32
East Croydon	a		00 23			01 32	04 31	05 23	06 08	06 53		07 26			08 26	08 39			09 02	09 11		09 32	09 41
St Pancras International	d				00 51																		
Farringdon	d																						
City Thameslink	d																						
London Blackfriars	d				01 01																		
London Bridge	d										07 11		07 41	08 11				08 41			09 11		
East Croydon	a				01 27						07 24		07 54	08 24				08 54			09 24		
East Croydon	d		00 24		01 28	01 33	04 31	05 24	06 09	06 54	07 25	07 27	07 55	08 25	08 27	08 40		08 55	09 03	09 12	09 25	09 33	09 42
Gatwick Airport	a		00 43		01 56	02 06	04 57	05 50	06 32	07 23	07 43	07 52	08 14	08 43	08 52	08 58		09 09	09 18	09 26	09 39	09 47	09 56
Gatwick Airport	d		00 44		01 58	02 08	04 58	05 51	06 33	07 24	07 45	07 53	08 15	08 44	08 54	08 59	←	09 10	09 20	09 28	09 40	09 50	09 58
Three Bridges	a		00 48		02 03	02 13	05 03	05 56	06 37	07 28	07 50	07 58	08 19	08 48	08 58		08 58	09 14		09 32	09 44		
Three Bridges	d		00 49		02 04	02 14	05 04	05 57	06 38	07 29	07 51	07 58	08 20	08 49	09 03		09 03	09 15		09 32	09 45		
Balcombe	d									07 35			08 26		→			09 21					
Haywards Heath	a		00 58		02 13	02 23	05 13	06 06	06 47	07 40	08 00	08 07	08 31	09 00		09 09	09 12	09 26	09 30	09 41	09 54	10 00	10 09
Haywards Heath	d	00 11	01 02	01 08	02 14	02 24	05 13	06 07	06 48	07 40	08 01	08 08	08 32	09 01		09 10	09 13	09 27	09 31	09 42	09 55	10 02	10 12
Wivelsfield	d	00 15							06 52	07 44	08 05	08 12	08 36	09 05			09 17	09 31	09 35		09 59		
Burgess Hill	d								06 54	07 47	08 07	08 14	08 38	09 07			09 19	09 33		09 47	10 01		10 17
Hassocks	d								06 58	07 50	08 10	08 18	08 41	09 10			09 22	09 36		09 51	10 04		10 21
Preston Park	d								07 05	07 57	08 17	08 24	08 48	09 17		09 22	09 29	09 43			10 11	10 14	
Brighton	a		01s16		02 28	02 38	05 28	06 21	07 12	08 01	08 21	08 31	08 52	09 21			09 33	09 47		10 01	10 15		10 31
Hove	a		01s25													09 25						10 17	
Lewes	a	00 27		01s23															09 49				

A not 16 May. 1 to Haywards Heath

B not 15 December

Table T184-F

Sundays
15 December to 10 May

London - Gatwick Airport - Haywards Heath - Brighton/Hove/Lewes

		TL 1	SN 1	SN 1	TL 1	SN 1		SN 1	TL 1	SN 1	SN 1	TL 1	SN 1	SN 1	TL 1	SN 1		SN 1	TL 1	SN 1	SN 1	TL 1	SN 1	SN 1	TL 1
London Victoria	d		09 46	09 55		10 16		10 25		10 46	10 55		11 16	11 25		11 46		11 55		12 16	12 25		12 46	12 55	
Clapham Junction	d		09 53	10 02		10 23		10 32		10 53	11 02		11 23	11 32		11 53		12 02		12 23	12 32		12 53	13 02	
East Croydon	a		10 02	10 11		10 32		10 41		11 02	11 11		11 32	11 41		12 02		12 11		12 32	12 41		13 02	13 12	
St Pancras International	d	09 26			09 56				10 26			10 56			11 26				11 56			12 26			12 56
Farringdon	d	09 30			10 00				10 30			11 00			11 30				12 00			12 30			13 00
City Thameslink	d																								
London Blackfriars	d	09 35			10 05				10 35			11 05			11 35				12 05			12 35			13 05
London Bridge	d	09 41			10 11				10 41			11 11			11 41				12 11			12 41			13 11
East Croydon	a	09 54			10 24				10 54			11 24			11 54				12 24			12 54			13 24
East Croydon	d	09 55	10 03	10 12	10 25	10 33		10 42	10 55	11 03	11 12	11 25	11 33	11 42	11 55	12 03		12 12	12 25	12 33	12 42	12 55	13 03	13 13	13 25
Gatwick Airport	a	10 09	10 18	10 26	10 39	10 47		10 56	11 09	11 18	11 26	11 39	11 47	11 56	12 09	12 18		12 26	12 39	12 47	12 56	13 09	13 18	13 27	13 39
Gatwick Airport	d	10 10	10 20	10 28	10 40	10 50		10 58	11 10	11 20	11 28	11 40	11 50	11 58	12 10	12 20		12 28	12 40	12 50	12 58	13 10	13 20	13 28	13 40
Three Bridges	a	10 14		10 32	10 44				11 14		11 32	11 44			12 14			12 32	12 44			13 14		13 32	13 44
Three Bridges	d	10 15		10 32	10 45				11 15		11 32	11 45			12 15			12 32	12 45			13 15		13 33	13 45
Balcombe	d	10 21							11 21						12 21							13 21			
Haywards Heath	a	10 26	10 30	10 41	10 54	11 00		11 09	11 26	11 30	11 41	11 54	12 00	12 09	12 26	12 30		12 41	12 54	13 00	13 09	13 26	13 30	13 42	13 54
Haywards Heath	d	10 27	10 31	10 42	10 55	11 02		11 12	11 27	11 31	11 42	11 55	12 02	12 12	12 27	12 31		12 42	12 55	13 02	13 12	13 27	13 31	13 42	13 55
Wivelsfield	d	10 31	10 35		10 59				11 31	11 35		11 59			12 31	12 35			12 59			13 31	13 35		13 59
Burgess Hill	d	10 33		10 47	11 01			11 17	11 33		11 47	12 01		12 17	12 33			12 47	13 01		13 17	13 33		13 48	14 01
Hassocks	d	10 36		10 51	11 04			11 21	11 36		11 51	12 04		12 21	12 36			12 51	13 04		13 21	13 36		13 52	14 04
Preston Park	d	10 43			11 11	11 14			11 43			12 11	12 14		12 43				13 11	13 14		13 43			14 11
Brighton	a	10 47		11 01	11 15			11 31	11 47		12 01	12 15		12 31	12 47			13 01	13 15		13 31	13 47		14 01	14 15
Hove	a					11 20							12 17							13 17					
Lewes	a		10 49							11 49						12 49							13 49		

		SN 1		SN 1	TL 1	SN 1	SN 1	TL 1	SN 1	SN 1	TL 1	SN 1		SN 1	TL 1	SN 1	SN 1	TL 1	SN 1	SN 1	TL 1	SN 1		SN 1	TL 1
London Victoria	d	13 16		13 25		13 46	13 55		14 16	14 25		14 46		14 55		15 16	15 25		15 46	15 55		16 16		16 25	
Clapham Junction	d	13 23		13 32		13 53	14 02		14 23	14 32		14 53		15 02		15 23	15 32		15 53	16 02		16 23		16 32	
East Croydon	a	13 32		13 41		14 02	14 11		14 32	14 41		15 02		15 11		15 32	15 41		16 02	16 12		16 32		16 41	
St Pancras International	d				13 26			13 56			14 26				14 56			15 26			15 56				16 26
Farringdon	d				13 30			14 00			14 30				15 00			15 30			16 00				16 30
City Thameslink	d																								
London Blackfriars	d				13 35			14 05			14 35				15 05			15 35			16 05				16 35
London Bridge	d				13 41			14 11			14 41				15 11			15 41			16 11				16 41
East Croydon	a				13 54			14 24			14 54				15 24			15 54			16 24				16 54
East Croydon	d	13 33		13 42	13 55	14 03	14 12	14 25	14 33	14 42	14 55	15 03		15 12	15 25	15 33	15 42	15 55	16 03	16 13	16 25	16 33		16 42	16 55
Gatwick Airport	a	13 47		13 56	14 09	14 18	14 26	14 39	14 47	14 56	15 09	15 18		15 26	15 39	15 47	15 56	16 09	16 18	16 27	16 39	16 47		16 56	17 09
Gatwick Airport	d	13 50		13 58	14 10	14 20	14 28	14 40	14 50	14 58	15 10	15 20		15 28	15 40	15 50	15 58	16 10	16 20	16 28	16 40	16 50		16 58	17 10
Three Bridges	a				14 14		14 32	14 44			15 14			15 32	15 44			16 14		16 32	16 44				17 14
Three Bridges	d				14 15		14 32	14 45			15 15			15 32	15 45			16 15		16 33	16 45				17 15
Balcombe	d				14 21						15 21							16 21							17 21
Haywards Heath	a	14 00		14 09	14 26	14 30	14 41	14 54	15 00	15 09	15 26	15 30		15 41	15 54	16 00	16 09	16 26	16 30	16 42	16 54	17 00		17 09	17 26
Haywards Heath	d	14 02		14 12	14 27	14 31	14 42	14 55	15 02	15 12	15 27	15 31		15 42	15 55	16 02	16 12	16 27	16 31	16 42	16 55	17 02		17 12	17 27
Wivelsfield	d				14 31	14 35		14 59			15 31	15 35			15 59			16 31	16 35		16 59				17 31
Burgess Hill	d			14 17	14 33		14 47	15 01		15 17	15 33			15 47	16 01		16 17	16 33		16 48	17 01			17 17	17 33
Hassocks	d			14 21	14 36		14 51	15 04		15 21	15 36			15 51	16 04		16 21	16 36		16 52	17 04			17 21	17 36
Preston Park	d	14 14			14 43			15 11	15 14		15 43				16 11	16 14		16 43			17 11	17 14			17 43
Brighton	a			14 31	14 47		15 01	15 15		15 31	15 47			16 01	16 15		16 31	16 47		17 01	17 15			17 31	17 47
Hove	a	14 17							15 17							16 17						17 17			
Lewes	a					14 49						15 49							16 49						

		SN 1	SN 1	TL 1	SN 1	SN 1	TL 1	SN 1	SN 1		TL 1	SN 1	SN 1	TL 1	SN 1	SN 1		TL 1	SN 1		SN 1	TL 1	SN 1	SN 1
London Victoria	d	16 46	16 55		17 16	17 25		17 46	17 55	and at the same minutes past each hour until		20 16	20 25		20 46	20 55			21 16		21 25		21 46	21 55
Clapham Junction	d	16 53	17 02		17 23	17 32		17 53	18 02			20 23	20 32		20 53	21 02			21 23		21 32		21 53	22 02
East Croydon	a	17 02	17 12		17 32	17 41		18 02	18 11			20 32	20 41		21 02	21 11			21 32		21 41		22 02	22 11
St Pancras International	d			16 56			17 26				19 56			20 26				20 56				21 26		
Farringdon	d			17 00			17 30				20 00			20 30				21 00				21 30		
City Thameslink	d																							
London Blackfriars	d			17 05			17 35				20 05			20 35				21 05				21 35		
London Bridge	d			17 11			17 41				20 11			20 41				21 11				21 41		
East Croydon	a			17 24			17 54				20 24			20 54				21 24				21 54		
East Croydon	d	17 03	17 13	17 25	17 33	17 42	17 55	18 03	18 12		20 25	20 33	20 42	20 55	21 03	21 12		21 25	21 33		21 42	21 55	22 03	22 12
Gatwick Airport	a	17 18	17 27	17 39	17 47	17 56	18 09	18 18	18 26		20 39	20 47	20 56	21 09	21 18	21 26		21 39	21 47		21 56	22 09	22 18	22 26
Gatwick Airport	d	17 20	17 28	17 40	17 50	17 58	18 10	18 20	18 28		20 40	20 50	20 58	21 10	21 20	21 28		21 40	21 50		21 58	22 10	22 20	22 28
Three Bridges	a		17 32	17 44			18 14		18 32		20 44			21 14		21 32		21 44				22 14		22 32
Three Bridges	d		17 33	17 45			18 15		18 32		20 45			21 15		21 32		21 45				22 15		22 32
Balcombe	d						18 21							21 21								22 21		
Haywards Heath	a	17 30	17 42	17 54	18 00	18 09	18 26	18 30	18 41		20 54	21 00	21 09	21 26	21 30	21 41		21 54	22 00		22 09	22 26	22 30	22 41
Haywards Heath	d	17 31	17 42	17 55	18 02	18 12	18 27	18 31	18 42		20 55	21 02	21 12	21 27	21 31	21 42		21 55	22 04	22 07	22 12	22 27	22 31	22 42
Wivelsfield	d	17 35		17 59			18 31	18 35			20 59			21 31	21 35			21 59				22 31	22 35	
Burgess Hill	d		17 48	18 01		18 17	18 33		18 47		21 01		21 17	21 33		21 47		22 01			22 17	22 33		22 47
Hassocks	d		17 52	18 04		18 21	18 36		18 51		21 04		21 21	21 36		21 51		22 04			22 21	22 36		22 51
Preston Park	d			18 11	18 14		18 43				21 11	21 14		21 43				22 11		22 18		22 43		
Brighton	a		18 01	18 15		18 31	18 47		19 01		21 15		21 31	21 47		22 01		22 15			22 31	22 47		23 01
Hove	a				18 17							21 17							22 18	22 22				
Lewes	a	17 49						18 49							21 49								22 49	

Table T184-F

Sundays
15 December to 10 May

London - Gatwick Airport - Haywards Heath - Brighton/Hove/Lewes

		TL 1	SN 1		SN 1	TL 1	SN 1	TL 1	SN 1	TL 1	SN 1	TL 1
London Victoria	d		22 16		22 25		22 46		23 16		23 32	
Clapham Junction	d		22 23		22 32		22 53		23 23		23 40	
East Croydon	a		22 32		22 41		23 02		23 32		23 56	
St Pancras International	d	21 56				22 26		22 56		23 26		23 51
Farringdon	d	22 00				22 30		23 00		23 30		23 56
City Thameslink	d											
London Blackfriars	d	22 05				22 35		23 05		23 35		00 01
London Bridge	d	22 11				22 41		23 11		23 41		
East Croydon	a	22 24				22 54		23 24		23 54		00 27
East Croydon	d	22 25	22 33		22 42	22 55	23 03	23 25	23 33	23 55	23 57	00 28
Gatwick Airport	a	22 39	22 47		22 56	23 09	23 18	23 42	23 54	00 17	00 21	00 47
Gatwick Airport	d	22 40	22 50		22 58	23 10	23 20	23 44	23 55	00 18	00 23	00 48
Three Bridges	a	22 44				23 14		23 48		00 22	00 27	00 53
Three Bridges	d	22 45				23 15		23 49		00 23	00 28	00 54
Balcombe	d					23 21				00 29	00 34	
Haywards Heath	a	22 54	23 00		23 09	23 26	23 30	23 58	00 07	00 34	00 39	01 03
Haywards Heath	d	22 55	23 02		23 12	23 27	23 31	23 59	00 08	00 35	00 39	01 04
Wivelsfield	d	22 59				23 31	23 35	00 03			00 43	01 08
Burgess Hill	d	23 01			23 17	23 33		00 05		00 40	00 45	01 10
Hassocks	d	23 04			23 21	23 36		00 08		00 43	00 49	01 13
Preston Park	d	23 11	23 14			23 43		00 15	00 19	00 50	00 55	01 20
Brighton	a	23 15			23 31	23 47		00 19		00 54	00 59	01 24
Hove	a		23 17						00 23			
Lewes	a						23 49					

AVAILABLE FROM MP Middleton Press

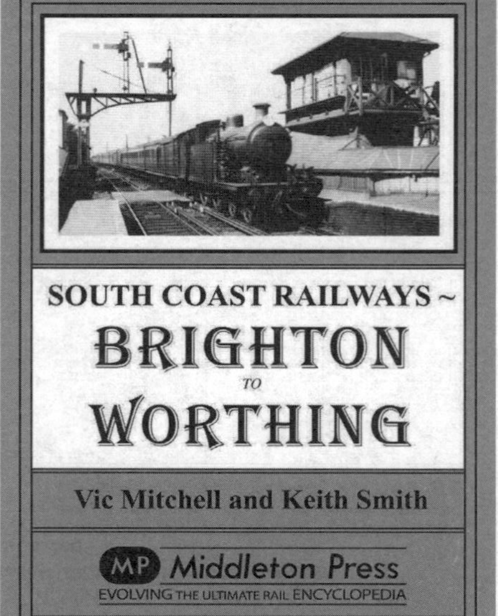

Table T184-R

Mondays to Fridays

16 December to 15 May

Brighton/Hove/Lewes - Haywards Heath - Gatwick Airport - London

		TL	TL	TL	SN	SN	TL ◇	TL	TL	SN	SN	SN	TL	GX	TL	TL	SN	SN	GX	TL	TL	GX	TL
Lewes	d				05 11					05 46		06 00					06 16						
Hove	d										05 53							06 23		06 32			
Brighton	d	00 04	04 12	05 06		05 19	05 28	05 38	05 52				06 05	06 12		06 22			06 29		06 37	06 42	
Preston Park	d	00 08		05 10				05 42			05 58		06 09	06 16				06 29		06 38	06 41	06 46	
Hassocks	d	00 14		05 16				05 48					06 16	06 23					06 38		06 48	06 53	
Burgess Hill	d	00 18		05 20		05 29	05 38	05 52	06 03		06 07		06 20	06 27	←	06 33		06 38			06 52	06 57	
Wivelsfield	d	00 20		05 22			05 40		06 06	06 02		06 20	06 23		06 23	06 36	06 33						←
Haywards Heath	a	00 24	04 25	05 27	05 31	05 35	05 45	05 57	06 10	06 07	06 13	06 24	→		06 28	06 40	06 37	06 44	06 46	06 50	06 58		06 58
Haywards Heath	d	00 25	04 26	05 28	05 39		05 46	06 01	06 11	06 17		06 25			06 31	06 41	06 49		06 47	06 51	07 01		07 01
Balcombe	d	00 30		05 34			05 52					06 30								06 57	→		
Three Bridges	a	00 36	04 34	05 39	05 47		05 57	06 09	06 19	06 25					06 40	06 49	06 57			07 03			07 10
Three Bridges	d	00 37	04 35	05 40	05 48		05 59	06 10	06 20	06 26					06 41	06 50	06 58			07 04			07 11
Gatwick Airport	a	00 41	04 40	05 44	05 53		06 03	06 14	06 24	06 31		06 39		06 42	06 45	06 54	07 02		06 58			07 12	07 15
Gatwick Airport	d	00 42	04 41	05 46	05 54		06 06	06 16	06 25	06 33		06 41		06 44	06 46	06 55	07 03		06 59			07 14	07 16
East Croydon	a	01 09	05 08	06 00	06 08		06 21	06 30	06 40	06 48		06 56			07 01	07 10	07 18			07 20			07 31
East Croydon	d	01 10	05 10	06 01			06 21	06 31	06 41			06 57			07 01	07 10				07 21			07 31
London Bridge	d		05 25	06 16			06 35	06 46	06 54			07a13			07 16	07 24				07 35			07 46
London Blackfriars	d	01 36	05 31	06 22			06 42	06 52	07 02						07 22	07 32				07 42			07 52
City Thameslink	d		05 33	06 24			06 44	06 54	07 04						07 24	07 34				07 44			07 54
Farringdon	d		05 36	06 26			06 46	06 56	07 06						07 26	07 36				07 46			07 56
St Pancras International	a	01 43	05 40	06 30			06 50	07 00	07 10						07 30	07 40				07 50			08 00
East Croydon	d				06 09					06 49							07 19						
Clapham Junction	a				06 20					06 58							07 28						
London Victoria	a				06 27					07 05				07 14			07 35		07 28			07 43	

		SN	TL	GX	SN	SN	TL	GX	TL	SN	TL	GX	SN	TL	TL	GX	TL	SN	GX	SN	TL	TL
Lewes	d	06 46				07 02				07 16								07 46				
Hove	d				06 57								07 27	07 33						07 52		
Brighton	d		06 48	06 57			07 07	07 12			07 18	07 27			07 37	07 42			07 54		08 00	08 07
Preston Park	d		06 52		07 03		07 11	07 16			07 22		07 33	07 38	07 41	07 46				07 59		08 11
Hassocks	d		06 59	07 06	07 10		07 18	07 23			07 29	07 36			07 48	07 53			08 03			08 18
Burgess Hill	d		07 03		07 14		07 22	07 27			07 33		07 42		07 52	07 57				08 08	08 11	08 22
Wivelsfield	d	07 02	07 06			07 21			←	07 32	07 36						←	08 02			08 14	
Haywards Heath	a	07 06	07 10	07 13	07 19	07 26	07 28		07 28	07 36	07 40	07 43	07 47	07 50	07 58		07 58	08 06	08 10	08 14	08 18	08 28
Haywards Heath	d	07 07	07 11	07 14	07 19	07 26	07 31		07 31	07 37	07 41	07 44	07 47	07 51	08 01		08 01	08 07	08 11	08 16	08 19	08 31
Balcombe	d				07 25		→							07 57	→						08 25	→
Three Bridges	a		07 19		07 31				07 40		07 49		07 56	08 02			08 10			08 24	08 30	
Three Bridges	d		07 20		07 31				07 41		07 50		07 57	08 03			08 11			08 25	08 31	
Gatwick Airport	a	07 19	07 24	07 28	07 36	07 40		07 40	07 45	07 49	07 54	07 58	08 02			08 11	08 15	08 19	08 23	08 31	08 35	
Gatwick Airport	d	07 20	07 25	07 29	07 37	07 41		07 44	07 46	07 50	07 55	07 59	08 03			08 14	08 16	08 20	08 28	08 33	08 36	
East Croydon	a	07 37	07 40		07 52	07 57			08 01	08 07	08 09		08 18	08 20			08 31	08 37		08 48	08 51	
East Croydon	d		07 40			07 57			08 01		08 10			08 21			08 31				08 51	
London Bridge	d		07 54			08a13			08 16		08 24			08 35			08 46				09 05	
London Blackfriars	d		08 02						08 22		08 32			08 42			08 52				09 12	
City Thameslink	d		08 04						08 24		08 34			08 44			08 54				09 14	
Farringdon	d		08 06						08 26		08 36			08 46			08 56				09 16	
St Pancras International	a		08 10						08 30		08 40			08 50			09 00				09 20	
East Croydon	d	07 38			07 52					08 08			08 20					08 38		08 50		
Clapham Junction	a	07 47			08 01					08 17			08 30					08 47		09 00		
London Victoria	a	07 54		07 58	08 09			08 14		08 24		08 29	08 37			08 43		08 54	08 58	09 08		

		GX	TL	SN	GX	SN	TL	TL	GX	TL	GX	SN	SN	TL	TL	GX	TL	SN	SN	TL	SN	TL	TL
Lewes	d			08 14								08 46							09 21				
Hove	d					08 24							08 52					09 21					
Brighton	d	08 12			08 24		08 30	08 37	08 42		08 57			09 02	09 08	09 18	←			09 28	09 33		09 38
Preston Park	d	08 16				08 29		08 41	08 46				08 57		09 12		09 12						09 42
Hassocks	d	08 23			08 33			08 48	08 53		09 07				→		09 18				09 41		→
Burgess Hill	d	08 27				08 38	08 41	08 52	08 57					09 12			09 22			09 38	09 45		
Wivelsfield	d		←	08 33			08 44			←		09 03		09 14						09 40			
Haywards Heath	a		08 28	08 38	08 40	08 44	08 48	08 58		08 58		09 07	09 11	09 18			09 27	09 36	09 40	09 44	09 50		
Haywards Heath	d		08 31	08 38	08 41	08 45	08 49	09 01		09 01		09 15		09 19			09 31	09 44		09 46	09 51	←	
Balcombe	d						08 55	→						09 24						09 52		09 52	
Three Bridges	a		08 40			08 53	09 00			09 10				09 30			09 39			→		09 57	
Three Bridges	d		08 41			08 55	09 01			09 10				09 31			09 40					09 59	
Gatwick Airport	a	08 41	08 45	08 50	08 54	09 01	09 05		09 11	09 15	09 23	09 27		09 35		09 41	09 45	09 56			10 02	10 03	
Gatwick Airport	d	08 44	08 46	08 51	08 58	09 03	09 06		09 12	09 16	09 24	09 28		09 36		09 42	09 46	09 57			10 03	10 06	
East Croydon	a		09 01	09 09		09 18	09 21			09 31		09 42		09 51			10 01	10 11			10 18	10 21	
East Croydon	d		09 01				09 21			09 31				09 51			10 01					10 21	
London Bridge	d		09 16				09 35			09 46				10 05			10 16					10 35	
London Blackfriars	d		09 22				09 42			09 52				10 12			10 22					10 42	
City Thameslink	d		09 24				09 44			09 54				10 14			10 24					10 44	
Farringdon	d		09 26				09 46			09 56				10 16			10 26					10 46	
St Pancras International	a		09 30				09 50			10 00				10 20			10 30					10 50	
East Croydon	d			09 09		09 19						09 43						10 12			10 19		
Clapham Junction	a			09 18		09 28						09 52						10 21			10 28		
London Victoria	a	09 13		09 26	09 29	09 35			09 43		09 54	09 59				10 13		10 29			10 39		

NRT DECEMBER 19 EDITION

Table T184-R

Mondays to Fridays

16 December to 15 May

Brighton/Hove/Lewes - Haywards Heath - Gatwick Airport - London

		GX	TL	SN	SN	TL	SN	TL	TL	GX	TL	SN	SN	TL	SN	TL	TL	GX	TL	SN	TL	TL	SN
Lewes	d			09 45									10 21							10 45			
Hove	d				09 51							10 21									10 51		
Brighton	d	09 48	←			09 58	10 03		10 08	10 18	←			10 28	10 33		10 38	10 48	←			10 58	11 03
Preston Park	d		09 42		09 57				10 12		10 12						10 42		10 42		10 57		
Hassocks	d		09 48				10 11		→		10 18				10 41		→		10 48				11 11
Burgess Hill	d		09 52			10 08	10 15				10 22			10 38	10 45				10 52			11 08	11 15
Wivelsfield	d			10 01		10 10								10 40						11 01		11 10	
Haywards Heath	a		09 57	10 06	10 10	10 16	10 20				10 27	10 36	10 40	10 45	10 50				10 57	11 06	11 09	11 15	11 20
Haywards Heath	d		10 01	10 14		10 16	10 21	←			10 31	10 44		10 46	10 51	←			11 01	11 14		11 17	11 21
Balcombe	d					10 22		10 22						10 52		10 52						11 22	
Three Bridges	a		10 10			→		10 27			10 39			→		10 57			11 09			→	
Three Bridges	d		10 10					10 29			10 40					10 59			11 10				
Gatwick Airport	a	10 12	10 16	10 26			10 32	10 33		10 41	10 45	10 56			11 02	11 03		11 11	11 15	11 26			11 32
Gatwick Airport	d	10 13	10 17	10 27			10 33	10 36		10 42	10 46	10 57			11 03	11 06		11 12	11 16	11 27			11 33
East Croydon	a		10 31	10 41			10 48	10 51			11 01	11 11			11 18	11 21			11 31	11 41			11 48
East Croydon	d		10 32					10 51			11 01					11 21			11 31				
London Bridge	d		10 46					11 05			11 16					11 35			11 46				
London Blackfriars	d		10 52					11 12			11 22					11 42			11 52				
City Thameslink	d		10 54					11 14			11 24					11 44			11 54				
Farringdon	d		10 56					11 16			11 26					11 46			11 56				
St Pancras International	a		11 00					11 20			11 30					11 50			12 00				
East Croydon	d			10 42			10 49					11 12			11 19					11 42			11 49
Clapham Junction	a			10 51			10 58					11 21			11 28					11 51			11 58
London Victoria	a	10 43		10 59			11 05			11 13		11 29			11 35			11 43		11 59			12 05

		TL	TL	GX	TL	SN	SN	TL	SN	TL	TL	GX	TL	SN	SN	TL	SN	TL	TL	GX	TL
Lewes	d						11 21							11 45							
Hove	d					11 21									11 51						
Brighton	d		11 08	11 18	←			11 28	11 33		11 38	11 48	←			11 58	12 03		12 08	12 18	←
Preston Park	d		11 12		11 12						11 42		11 42		11 57				12 12		12 12
Hassocks	d		→		11 18				11 41		→		11 48				12 11		→		12 18
Burgess Hill	d				11 22			11 38	11 45				11 52			12 08	12 15				12 22
Wivelsfield	d							11 40						12 01		12 10					
Haywards Heath	a				11 27	11 36	11 40	11 45	11 50				11 57	12 06	12 10	12 15	12 20				12 27
Haywards Heath	d	←			11 31	11 44		11 46	11 51	←			12 01	12 14		12 16	12 21	←			12 31
Balcombe	d	11 22						11 52		11 52						12 22		12 22			
Three Bridges	a	11 28			11 39			→		11 57			12 09			→		12 27			12 39
Three Bridges	d	11 29			11 40					11 59			12 10					12 29			12 40
Gatwick Airport	a	11 33		11 41	11 45	11 56			12 02	12 03		12 11	12 15	12 26			12 32	12 33		12 41	12 45
Gatwick Airport	d	11 36		11 42	11 46	11 57			12 03	12 06		12 12	12 16	12 27			12 33	12 36		12 42	12 46
East Croydon	a	11 51			12 01	12 11			12 18	12 21			12 31	12 41			12 48	12 51			13 01
East Croydon	d	11 51			12 01					12 21			12 31					12 51			13 01
London Bridge	d	12 05			12 16					12 35			12 46					13 05			13 16
London Blackfriars	d	12 12			12 22					12 42			12 52					13 12			13 22
City Thameslink	d	12 14			12 24					12 44			12 54					13 14			13 24
Farringdon	d	12 16			12 26					12 46			12 56					13 16			13 26
St Pancras International	a	12 20			12 30					12 50			13 00					13 20			13 30
East Croydon	d					12 12			12 19					12 42			12 49				
Clapham Junction	a					12 22			12 28					12 51			12 58				
London Victoria	a			12 13		12 29			12 35			12 43		12 59			13 05			13 13	

		SN	SN	TL	SN	TL	TL	GX	TL	SN	SN	TL	SN	TL	TL	GX	TL	SN	SN	TL	SN	TL	TL
Lewes	d		12 21							12 45									13 21				
Hove	d	12 21									12 51							13 21					
Brighton	d			12 28	12 33		12 38	12 48	←			12 58	13 03		13 08	13 18	←			13 28	13 33		13 38
Preston Park	d						12 42		12 42		12 57				13 12		13 12						13 42
Hassocks	d				12 41		→		12 48				13 11		→		13 18				13 41		→
Burgess Hill	d			12 38	12 45				12 52			13 08	13 15				13 22			13 38	13 45		
Wivelsfield	d			12 40						13 01		13 10								13 40			
Haywards Heath	a	12 36	12 40	12 45	12 50				12 58	13 06	13 10	13 15	13 20				13 27	13 36	13 40	13 45	13 50		
Haywards Heath	d	12 44		12 46	12 50	←			13 01	13 14		13 16	13 21	←			13 31	13 44		13 46	13 51	←	
Balcombe	d			12 52		12 52						13 22		13 22						13 52		13 52	
Three Bridges	a			→		12 57			13 09			→		13 27			13 39			→		13 57	
Three Bridges	d					12 59			13 10					13 29			13 40					13 59	
Gatwick Airport	a	12 56			13 02	13 03		13 11	13 15	13 26			13 32	13 33		13 41	13 45	13 56			14 02	14 03	
Gatwick Airport	d	12 57			13 03	13 06		13 12	13 16	13 27			13 33	13 36		13 42	13 46	13 57			14 03	14 06	
East Croydon	a	13 11			13 18	13 21			13 31	13 41			13 48	13 51			14 01	14 11			14 18	14 21	
East Croydon	d					13 21			13 31					13 51			14 01					14 21	
London Bridge	d					13 35			13 46					14 05			14 16					14 35	
London Blackfriars	d					13 42			13 52					14 12			14 22					14 42	
City Thameslink	d					13 44			13 54					14 14			14 24					14 44	
Farringdon	d					13 46			13 56					14 16			14 26					14 46	
St Pancras International	a					13 50			14 00					14 20			14 30					14 50	
East Croydon	d	13 12			13 19					13 42			13 49					14 12			14 19		
Clapham Junction	a	13 21			13 28					13 51			13 58					14 21			14 28		
London Victoria	a	13 29			13 35			13 43		13 59			14 05			14 13		14 29			14 35		

Table T184-R

Mondays to Fridays

16 December to 15 May

Brighton/Hove/Lewes - Haywards Heath - Gatwick Airport - London

		GX 1	TL 1	SN 1	SN 1	TL 1		SN 1	TL 1	TL 1	GX 1	TL 1	SN 1	SN 1	TL 1	SN 1		TL 1	TL 1	GX 1	TL 1	SN 1	SN 1	TL 1	SN 1
Lewes	d			13 45										14 21								14 45			
Hove	d				13 51								14 21										14 51		
Brighton	d	13 48	←			13 58		14 03		14 08	14 18	←			14 28	14 33			14 38	14 48	←			14 56	15 03
Preston Park	d		13 42		13 57					14 12		14 12							14 42		14 42		14 57	15 00	
Hassocks	d		13 48					14 11		→		14 18				14 41			→		14 48			15 06	15 11
Burgess Hill	d		13 52			14 08		14 15				14 22			14 38	14 45					14 52			15 10	15 15
Wivelsfield	d			14 01		14 10									14 40							15 01		15 12	
Haywards Heath	a		13 57	14 06	14 10	14 15		14 20				14 27	14 36	14 40	14 45	14 50					14 57	15 06	15 10	15 16	15 20
Haywards Heath	d		14 01	14 14		14 16		14 21	←			14 31	14 44		14 46	14 51		←			15 01	15 14		15 17	15 21
Balcombe	d					14 22			14 22						14 52			14 52						15 22	
Three Bridges	a		14 09			→			14 27			14 39			→			14 57			15 09			→	
Three Bridges	d		14 10						14 29			14 40						14 59			15 10				
Gatwick Airport	a	14 11	14 15	14 26				14 32	14 33		14 41	14 45	14 56			15 02		15 03		15 11	15 15	15 26			15 32
Gatwick Airport	d	14 12	14 16	14 27				14 33	14 36		14 42	14 46	14 57			15 03		15 06		15 12	15 16	15 27			15 33
East Croydon	a		14 31	14 41				14 48	14 51			15 01	15 11			15 18		15 21			15 31	15 41			15 48
East Croydon	d		14 31						14 51			15 01						15 21			15 31				
London Bridge	d		14 46						15 05			15 16						15 35			15 46				
London Blackfriars	d		14 52						15 12			15 22						15 42			15 52				
City Thameslink	d		14 54						15 14			15 24						15 44			15 54				
Farringdon	d		14 56						15 16			15 26						15 46			15 56				
St Pancras International	a		15 00						15 20			15 30						15 50			16 00				
East Croydon	d			14 42				14 49					15 12			15 19						15 42			15 49
Clapham Junction	a			14 51				14 58					15 21			15 28						15 51			15 59
London Victoria	a	14 43		14 59				15 05			15 13		15 29			15 35				15 43		16 00			16 09

		TL 1		TL 1	GX 1	TL 1	SN 1	SN 1	TL 1	SN 1	TL 1	TL 1		GX 1	TL 1	SN 1	SN 1	TL 1	SN 1	TL 1	TL 1	GX 1		TL 1	
Lewes	d							15 21								15 45									
Hove	d						15 21										15 52								
Brighton	d			15 08	15 18	←			15 26	15 33		15 38		15 48	←			15 58	16 03		16 08	16 18		←	
Preston Park	d			15 12		15 12			15 30			15 42			15 42		15 58				16 12			16 12	
Hassocks	d			→		15 18			15 36	15 41		→			15 48				16 11		→			16 18	
Burgess Hill	d					15 22			15 40	15 45					15 52			16 08	16 15					16 22	
Wivelsfield	d								15 42							16 01		16 10							
Haywards Heath	a					15 27	15 36	15 40	15 46	15 50					15 57	16 06	16 10	16 15	16 20					16 27	
Haywards Heath	d	←				15 31	15 44		15 47	15 51	←				16 01	16 14		16 16	16 21	←				16 31	
Balcombe	d	15 22							15 52		15 52							16 22		16 22					
Three Bridges	a	15 28				15 39			→		15 58				16 09			→		16 28				16 39	
Three Bridges	d	15 29				15 40					15 59				16 10					16 29				16 40	
Gatwick Airport	a	15 33			15 41	15 45	15 56			16 02	16 03			16 11	16 15	16 26			16 32	16 33		16 43		16 45	
Gatwick Airport	d	15 36			15 42	15 46	15 57			16 03	16 06			16 12	16 16	16 27			16 33	16 36		16 44		16 46	
East Croydon	a	15 51				16 01	16 11			16 18	16 21				16 31	16 42			16 48	16 51				17 01	
East Croydon	d	15 51				16 01					16 21				16 31					16 51				17 01	
London Bridge	d	16 05				16 16					16 35				16 46					17 05				17 16	
London Blackfriars	d	16 12				16 22					16 42				16 52					17 12				17 22	
City Thameslink	d	16 14				16 24					16 44				16 54					17 14				17 24	
Farringdon	d	16 16				16 26					16 46				16 56					17 16				17 26	
St Pancras International	a	16 20				16 30					16 50				17 00					17 20				17 30	
East Croydon	d						16 12			16 19						16 42			16 49						
Clapham Junction	a						16 21			16 28						16 51			16 58						
London Victoria	a				16 15		16 29			16 35				16 43		16 59			17 10			17 18			

		SN 1	SN 1	TL 1	SN 1	TL 1	TL 1	GX 1	TL 1		SN 1	SN 1	TL 1	SN 1	TL 1	TL 1	GX 1	TL 1	SN 1	SN 1		TL 1	SN 1	TL 1	TL 1
Lewes	d		16 21								16 45									17 21					
Hove	d	16 21										16 51							17 21						
Brighton	d			16 28	16 33		16 38	16 48	←				16 58	17 03		17 08	17 16	←				17 28	17 33		17 38
Preston Park	d						16 42		16 42			16 57				17 12		17 12							17 42
Hassocks	d				16 41		→		16 48					17 11		→		17 18					17 41		→
Burgess Hill	d			16 40	16 45				16 52				17 08	17 15				17 22				17 38	17 45		
Wivelsfield	d			16 42							17 02		17 10									17 40			
Haywards Heath	a	16 36	16 40	16 46	16 50				16 57		17 07	17 11	17 15	17 20				17 27	17 36	17 40		17 45	17 50		
Haywards Heath	d	16 44		16 46	16 51	←			17 01		17 15		17 17	17 21	←			17 31	17 44			17 46	17 51	←	
Balcombe	d			16 52		16 52							17 22		17 22							17 52		17 52	
Three Bridges	a			→		16 58			17 09				→		17 28			17 39				→		17 57	
Three Bridges	d					16 59			17 10						17 29			17 40						17 59	
Gatwick Airport	a	16 56			17 02	17 03		17 11	17 15		17 26			17 32	17 34		17 41	17 45	17 56				18 02	18 03	
Gatwick Airport	d	16 57			17 03	17 06		17 12	17 16		17 27			17 33	17 36		17 42	17 46	17 57				18 03	18 06	
East Croydon	a	17 12			17 18	17 21			17 31		17 42			17 48	17 51			18 01	18 12				18 18	18 21	
East Croydon	d					17 21			17 31						17 51			18 01						18 21	
London Bridge	d					17 35			17 46						18 05			18 16						18 35	
London Blackfriars	d					17 42			17 52						18 12			18 22						18 42	
City Thameslink	d					17 44			17 54						18 14			18 24						18 44	
Farringdon	d					17 46			17 56						18 16			18 26						18 46	
St Pancras International	a					17 50			18 00						18 20			18 30						18 50	
East Croydon	d	17 12			17 18						17 42			17 48					18 12				18 18		
Clapham Junction	a	17 21			17 28						17 51			17 58					18 21				18 28		
London Victoria	a	17 30			17 35			17 43			17 59			18 05			18 13		18 29				18 35		

Table T184-R

Mondays to Fridays

16 December to 15 May

Brighton/Hove/Lewes - Haywards Heath - Gatwick Airport - London

		GX 1	TL 1	SN 1	SN 1	TL 1		SN 1	TL 1	TL 1	GX 1	TL 1	SN 1	SN 1	TL 1	SN 1		TL 1	TL 1	GX 1	TL 1	SN 1	SN 1	TL 1	SN 1
Lewes	d			17 45										18 21								18 45			
Hove	d				17 51								18 21										18 53		
Brighton	d	17 46	←			17 58		18 03		18 08	18 16	←			18 28	18 33			18 38	18 46	←			18 58	19 03
Preston Park	d		17 42		17 57					18 12		18 12							18 42		18 42		18 58		
Hassocks	d		17 48					18 11		→		18 18				18 41			→		18 48				19 11
Burgess Hill	d		17 52			18 08		18 15				18 22			18 38	18 45					18 52			19 08	19 15
Wivelsfield	d			18 02		18 10									18 40							19 02		19 10	
Haywards Heath	a		17 57	18 07	18 11	18 15		18 20				18 27	18 36	18 40	18 45	18 50					18 57	19 07	19 11	19 15	19 20
Haywards Heath	d		18 01	18 15		18 17		18 21	←			18 31	18 44		18 46	18 51		←			19 01	19 15		19 17	19 21
Balcombe	d					18 22			18 22						18 52			18 52						19 22	
Three Bridges	a		18 09			→			18 28			18 39			→			18 57			19 09			→	
Three Bridges	d		18 10						18 29			18 40						18 59			19 10				
Gatwick Airport	a	18 11	18 15	18 26				18 32	18 34		18 41	18 45	18 56			19 02		19 03		19 13	19 15	19 26			19 32
Gatwick Airport	d	18 12	18 16	18 27				18 33	18 36		18 42	18 46	18 57			19 03		19 06		19 14	19 16	19 27			19 33
East Croydon	a		18 31	18 42				18 48	18 51			19 01	19 11			19 18		19 21			19 31	19 42			19 48
East Croydon	d		18 31						18 51			19 01						19 21			19 31				
London Bridge	d		18 46						19 05			19 16						19 35			19 46				
London Blackfriars	d		18 52						19 12			19 22						19 42			19 52				
City Thameslink	d		18 54						19 14			19 24						19 44			19 54				
Farringdon	d		18 56						19 16			19 26						19 46			19 56				
St Pancras International	a		19 00						19 20			19 30						19 50			20 00				
East Croydon	d			18 42				18 48					19 12			19 18						19 42			19 49
Clapham Junction	a			18 51				18 58					19 21			19 28						19 51			19 58
London Victoria	a	18 44		18 59				19 05			19 14		19 29			19 35				19 45		19 59			20 05

		TL 1		TL 1	GX 1	TL 1	SN 1	SN 1	TL 1	SN 1	TL 1	GX 1		SN 1	SN 1	TL 1	SN 1	TL 1	TL 1	GX 1	TL 1	SN 1	SN 1		TL 1
Lewes	d							19 21						19 46									20 21		
Hove	d						19 21								19 52							20 21			
Brighton	d			19 08	19 16	←			19 26	19 33		19 48				19 58	20 03		20 08	20 18	←				20 26
Preston Park	d			19 12		19 12			19 30						19 58				20 12		20 12				20 30
Hassocks	d			→		19 18			19 36	19 41							20 11		→		20 18				20 36
Burgess Hill	d					19 22			19 40	19 45						20 08	20 15				20 22				20 40
Wivelsfield	d								19 42					20 02		20 10									20 42
Haywards Heath	a					19 27	19 36	19 40	19 46	19 50				20 07	20 11	20 15	20 20				20 27	20 37	20 40		20 46
Haywards Heath	d	←				19 31	19 44		19 47	19 51	←			20 15		20 16	20 21	←			20 31	20 44			20 47
Balcombe	d	19 22							19 52		19 52					20 22		20 22							20 52
Three Bridges	a	19 28				19 39			→		19 58					→		20 27			20 39				→
Three Bridges	d	19 29				19 40					19 59							20 29			20 40				
Gatwick Airport	a	19 33			19 41	19 45	19 56			20 02	20 03	20 13		20 27			20 32	20 33		20 41	20 45	20 56			
Gatwick Airport	d	19 36			19 42	19 46	19 57			20 03	20 06	20 14		20 28			20 33	20 36		20 42	20 46	20 57			
East Croydon	a	19 51				20 01	20 11			20 18	20 21			20 42			20 48	20 51			21 01	21 11			
East Croydon	d	19 51				20 01					20 21							20 51			21 01				
London Bridge	d	20 05				20 16					20 35							21 05			21 16				
London Blackfriars	d	20 12				20 22					20 42							21 12			21 22				
City Thameslink	d	20 14				20 24					20 44							21 14			21 24				
Farringdon	d	20 16				20 26					20 46							21 16			21 26				
St Pancras International	a	20 20				20 30					20 50							21 20			21 30				
East Croydon	d						20 12			20 19				20 43			20 49					21 12			
Clapham Junction	a						20 21			20 28				20 52			21 01					21 21			
London Victoria	a				20 13		20 30			20 35		20 45		20 59			21 08			21 15		21 29			

		SN 1	TL 1	GX	SN 1	SN 1	TL 1	SN 1	TL 1		TL 1	GX	TL 1	SN 1	SN 1	TL 1	SN 1	TL 1	GX		SN 1	SN 1	TL 1	SN 1	TL 1
Lewes	d				20 48										21 21						21 45				
Hove	d					20 51								21 21								21 51			
Brighton	d	20 33		20 48			20 58	21 03			21 08	21 18	←			21 26	21 33		21 48				21 58	22 03	
Preston Park	d					20 57					21 12		21 12			21 30						21 57			
Hassocks	d	20 41						21 11			→		21 18			21 36	21 41							22 11	
Burgess Hill	d	20 45					21 08	21 15					21 22			21 40	21 45						22 08	22 15	
Wivelsfield	d				21 02		21 10									21 42					22 03		22 10		
Haywards Heath	a	20 50			21 06	21 10	21 15	21 20					21 27	21 36	21 40	21 46	21 50				22 08	22 11	22 15	22 20	
Haywards Heath	d	20 51	←		21 14		21 16	21 21	←				21 31	21 44		21 47	21 51	←			22 15		22 17	22 21	←
Balcombe	d		20 52				21 22		21 22							21 52		21 52					22 22		22 22
Three Bridges	a		20 58				→		21 27				21 39			→		21 58					→		22 28
Three Bridges	d		20 59						21 29				21 40					21 59							22 29
Gatwick Airport	a	21 02	21 03	21 11	21 26			21 32	21 33			21 41	21 45	21 56			22 02	22 03	22 11		22 26			22 32	22 33
Gatwick Airport	d	21 03	21 06	21 12	21 27			21 33	21 36			21 42	21 46	21 57			22 03	22 06	22 12		22 27			22 33	22 36
East Croydon	a	21 18	21 21		21 41			21 48	21 51				22 01	22 12			22 18	22 21			22 42			22 48	22 51
East Croydon	d		21 21						21 51				22 01					22 21							22 51
London Bridge	d		21 35						22 05				22 16					22 35							23 05
London Blackfriars	d		21 42						22 12				22 22					22 42							23 12
City Thameslink	d		21 44						22 14				22 24					22 44							
Farringdon	d		21 46						22 16				22 26					22 46							23 16
St Pancras International	a		21 50						22 20				22 30					22 50							23 20
East Croydon	d	21 19			21 42			21 49						22 12			22 19				22 43			22 49	
Clapham Junction	a	21 28			21 51			21 58						22 21			22 28				22 52			22 58	
London Victoria	a	21 35		21 43	21 59			22 05				22 13		22 29			22 37		22 43		23 00			23 05	

Table T184-R

Brighton/Hove/Lewes - Haywards Heath - Gatwick Airport - London

Mondays to Fridays

16 December to 15 May

		TL 1	GX	TL 1	SN 1	SN 1	TL 1	SN 1	TL 1	GX 1	SN 1	SN 1	TL 1	SN FO 1	SN FX 1	TL 1	TL 1
Lewes	d					22 21					22 45						
Hove	d				22 21							22 51					
Brighton	d	22 08	22 18	←			22 26	22 33		22 48			22 56	23 13	23 13	23 24	23 42
Preston Park	d	22 12		22 12			22 30					22 57	23 00			23 28	23 46
Hassocks	d	→		22 18			22 36	22 41					23 06	23 21	23 21	23 34	23 52
Burgess Hill	d			22 22			22 40	22 45					23 10	23 25	23 25	23 38	23 56
Wivelsfield	d						22 42				23 01		23 12			23 40	23 58
Haywards Heath	a			22 27	22 36	22 40	22 46	22 50			23 06	23 10	23 16	23 30	23 30	23 45	00 02
Haywards Heath	d			22 31		22 44	22 47	22 51	←			23 14	23 17	23 30	23 30	23 46	00 03
Balcombe	d						22 52		22 52				23 22			23 52	00 08
Three Bridges	a			22 39			→		22 58				23 28	23 39	23 39	23 57	00 14
Three Bridges	d			22 40					22 59				23 29	23 40	23 40	23 58	00 15
Gatwick Airport	a		22 41	22 45		22 56		23 02	23 03	23 10		23 26	23 33	23 44	23 44	00 03	00 19
Gatwick Airport	d		22 42	22 46		22 57		23 03	23 06	23 11		23 27	23 34	23 55	23 55	00 04	00 21
East Croydon	a			23 01		23 11		23 18	23 21			23 42	23 52	00 16	00 17	00 22	00 39
East Croydon	d			23 01					23 21				23 53			00 23	00 40
London Bridge	d			23 16					23 35								
London Blackfriars	d			23 22					23 42				00 22			00 50	01 06
City Thameslink	d																
Farringdon	d			23 26					23 46				00 26				
St Pancras International	a			23 30					23 50				00 30			00 59	01 13
East Croydon	d					23 12		23 19				23 42		00 16	00 17		
Clapham Junction	a					23 21		23 28				23 57		00 33	00 33		
London Victoria	a		23 13			23 30		23 35		23 43		00 05		00 41	00 41		

Saturdays

21 December to 16 May

		TL 1	TL 1	SN 1	TL 1	SN 1	TL 1	SN 1	TL 1	SN 1	SN 1	TL 1	SN 1	TL 1	TL 1	GX 1	TL 1	SN 1	SN 1	TL 1	SN 1	TL 1	GX 1
Lewes	d					05 24													06 21				
Hove	d										05 55							06 21					
Brighton	d	00 04	04 12	04 33	05 06		05 26	05 33		05 44		05 58	06 03		06 08	06 18	←			06 26	06 33		06 48
Preston Park	d	00 08			05 10		05 30			05 48					06 12		06 12			06 30			
Hassocks	d	00 14			05 16		05 36	05 41		05 54			06 11		→		06 18			06 36	06 41		
Burgess Hill	d	00 18			05 20		05 40	05 45		05 58		06 08	06 15				06 22			06 40	06 45		
Wivelsfield	d	00 20			05 22		05 42			06 01		06 10								06 42			
Haywards Heath	a	00 24	04 25	04 46	05 27	05 40	05 46	05 50		06 06	06 10	06 15	06 20				06 27	06 36	06 40	06 46	06 50		
Haywards Heath	d	00 25	04 26	04 47	05 28	05 43	05 47	05 51	←		06 14	06 16	06 21	←			06 31		06 44	06 47	06 51	←	
Balcombe	d	00 30			05 34		05 52		05 52			06 22		06 22						06 52		06 52	
Three Bridges	a	00 36	04 34	04 56	05 39	05 52	→		05 58			→		06 27			06 39			→		06 58	
Three Bridges	d	00 37	04 35	04 58	05 40	05 55			05 59					06 29			06 40					06 59	
Gatwick Airport	a	00 41	04 40	05 02	05 44	06 00		06 02	06 05		06 26		06 32	06 33		06 41	06 45		06 56		07 02	07 03	07 11
Gatwick Airport	d	00 42	04 41	05 03	05 46			06 03	06 06		06 27		06 33	06 36		06 42	06 46		06 57		07 03	07 06	07 12
East Croydon	a	01 09	05 09	05 30	06 00			06 18	06 21		06 41		06 48	06 51			07 01		07 11		07 18	07 21	
East Croydon	d	01 10	05 10		06 01				06 21					06 51			07 01					07 21	
London Bridge	d		05 26		06 16				06 35					07 05			07 16					07 35	
London Blackfriars	d	01 36	05 32		06 22				06 42					07 12			07 22					07 42	
City Thameslink	d																						
Farringdon	d		05 36		06 26				06 46					07 16			07 26					07 46	
St Pancras International	a	01 43	05 40		06 30				06 50					07 20			07 30					07 50	
East Croydon	d			05 30				06 19			06 42		06 49						07 12		07 19		
Clapham Junction	a			05 50				06 28			06 51		06 58						07 21		07 28		
London Victoria	a			05 59				06 35			06 59		07 05			07 13			07 29		07 35		07 43

		SN 1	SN 1	TL 1	SN 1	TL 1	TL 1	GX 1	TL 1	SN 1	SN 1	TL 1	SN 1	TL 1	GX 1	SN 1	SN 1	TL 1	SN 1	TL 1	TL 1	GX 1	TL 1
Lewes	d	06 45									07 21					07 45							
Hove	d		06 51							07 21							07 51						
Brighton	d			06 58	07 03		07 08	07 18	←			07 26	07 33		07 48			07 58	08 03		08 08	08 18	←
Preston Park	d		06 57				07 12		07 12			07 30					07 57				08 12		08 12
Hassocks	d				07 11		→		07 18			07 36	07 41						08 11		→		08 18
Burgess Hill	d			07 08	07 15				07 22			07 40	07 45					08 08	08 15				08 22
Wivelsfield	d	07 01		07 10								07 42				08 01		08 10					
Haywards Heath	a	07 06	07 10	07 15	07 20				07 27	07 36	07 40	07 46	07 50			08 06	08 10	08 15	08 20				08 27
Haywards Heath	d		07 14	07 16	07 21	←			07 31		07 44	07 47	07 51	←			08 14	08 16	08 21	←			08 31
Balcombe	d			07 22		07 22						07 52		07 52				08 22		08 22			
Three Bridges	a			→		07 27			07 39			→		07 58				→		08 27			08 39
Three Bridges	d					07 29			07 40					07 59						08 29			08 40
Gatwick Airport	a		07 26		07 32	07 33		07 41	07 45		07 56		08 02	08 03	08 11		08 26		08 32	08 33		08 41	08 45
Gatwick Airport	d		07 27		07 33	07 36		07 42	07 46		07 57		08 03	08 06	08 12		08 27		08 33	08 36		08 42	08 46
East Croydon	a		07 41		07 48	07 51			08 01		08 11		08 18	08 21			08 41		08 48	08 51			09 01
East Croydon	d					07 51			08 01					08 21						08 51			09 01
London Bridge	d					08 05			08 16					08 35						09 05			09 16
London Blackfriars	d					08 12			08 22					08 42						09 12			09 22
City Thameslink	d																			09 14			09 24
Farringdon	d					08 16			08 26					08 46						09 16			09 26
St Pancras International	a					08 20			08 30					08 50						09 20			09 30
East Croydon	d		07 42		07 49						08 12		08 19				08 42		08 49				
Clapham Junction	a		07 51		07 58						08 21		08 28				08 51		08 58				
London Victoria	a		07 59		08 05			08 13			08 29		08 35		08 43		08 59		09 05			09 13	

Table T184-R

Saturdays

21 December to 16 May

Brighton/Hove/Lewes - Haywards Heath - Gatwick Airport - London

		SN 1	SN 1	TL 1	SN 1	TL 1	GX 1	SN 1	SN 1	TL 1	SN 1	TL 1	TL 1	GX 1	TL 1	SN 1	SN 1	TL 1	SN 1	TL 1	GX 1	SN 1	SN 1
Lewes	d		08 21					08 45									09 21					09 45	
Hove	d	08 21							08 51							09 21							09 51
Brighton	d			08 26	08 33		08 48			08 58	09 03		09 08	09 18	←			09 26	09 33		09 48		
Preston Park	d			08 30					08 57				09 12		09 12			09 30					09 57
Hassocks	d			08 36	08 41						09 11		→		09 18			09 36	09 41				
Burgess Hill	d			08 40	08 45					09 08	09 15				09 22			09 40	09 45				
Wivelsfield	d			08 42				09 01		09 10								09 42				10 01	
Haywards Heath	a	08 36	08 40	08 46	08 50			09 06	09 10	09 15	09 20				09 27	09 36	09 40	09 46	09 50			10 06	10 10
Haywards Heath	d		08 44	08 47	08 51	←			09 14	09 16	09 21	←			09 31		09 44	09 47	09 51	←			10 14
Balcombe	d			08 52		08 52				09 22		09 22						09 52		09 52			
Three Bridges	a			→		08 58				→		09 27			09 39			→		09 58			
Three Bridges	d					08 59						09 29			09 40					09 59			
Gatwick Airport	a		08 56		09 02	09 03	09 11		09 26		09 32	09 33		09 41	09 45		09 56		10 02	10 03	10 11		10 26
Gatwick Airport	d		08 57		09 03	09 06	09 12		09 27		09 33	09 36		09 42	09 46		09 57		10 03	10 06	10 12		10 27
East Croydon	a		09 11		09 18	09 21			09 41		09 48	09 51			10 01		10 11		10 18	10 21			10 41
East Croydon	d					09 21						09 51			10 01					10 21			
London Bridge	d					09 35						10 05			10 16					10 35			
London Blackfriars	d					09 42						10 12			10 22					10 42			
City Thameslink	d					09 44						10 14			10 24					10 44			
Farringdon	d					09 46						10 16			10 26					10 46			
St Pancras International	a					09 50						10 20			10 30					10 50			
East Croydon	d		09 12		09 19				09 42		09 49						10 12		10 19				10 42
Clapham Junction	a		09 21		09 28				09 51		09 58						10 21		10 28				10 51
London Victoria	a		09 29		09 35		09 43		09 59		10 05			10 13			10 29		10 35		10 43		10 59

		TL 1	SN 1	TL 1	TL 1	GX 1	TL 1	SN 1	SN 1	TL 1	SN 1	TL 1	GX 1	SN 1	SN 1	TL 1	SN 1	TL 1	TL 1	GX 1	TL 1
Lewes	d								10 21					10 45							
Hove	d							10 21							10 51						
Brighton	d	09 58	10 03		10 08	10 18	←			10 26	10 33		10 48			10 58	11 03		11 08	11 18	←
Preston Park	d				10 12		10 12			10 30					10 57				11 12		11 12
Hassocks	d		10 11		→		10 18			10 36	10 41						11 11		→		11 18
Burgess Hill	d	10 08	10 15				10 22			10 40	10 45					11 08	11 15				11 22
Wivelsfield	d	10 10								10 42				11 01		11 10					
Haywards Heath	a	10 15	10 20				10 27	10 36	10 40	10 46	10 50			11 06	11 10	11 15	11 20				11 27
Haywards Heath	d	10 16	10 21	←			10 31		10 44	10 47	10 51	←			11 14	11 16	11 21	←			11 31
Balcombe	d	10 22		10 22						10 52		10 52				11 22		11 22			
Three Bridges	a	→		10 27			10 39			→		10 58				→		11 27			11 39
Three Bridges	d			10 29			10 40					10 59						11 29			11 40
Gatwick Airport	a		10 32	10 33		10 41	10 45		10 56		11 02	11 03	11 11		11 26		11 32	11 33		11 41	11 45
Gatwick Airport	d		10 33	10 36		10 42	10 46		10 57		11 03	11 06	11 12		11 27		11 33	11 36		11 42	11 46
East Croydon	a		10 48	10 51			11 01		11 11		11 18	11 21			11 41		11 48	11 51			12 01
East Croydon	d			10 51			11 01					11 21						11 51			12 01
London Bridge	d			11 05			11 16					11 35						12 05			12 16
London Blackfriars	d			11 12			11 22					11 42						12 12			12 22
City Thameslink	d			11 14			11 24					11 44						12 14			12 24
Farringdon	d			11 16			11 26					11 46						12 16			12 26
St Pancras International	a			11 20			11 30					11 50						12 20			12 30
East Croydon	d		10 49						11 12		11 19				11 42		11 49				
Clapham Junction	a		10 58						11 21		11 28				11 51		11 58				
London Victoria	a		11 05			11 13			11 29		11 35		11 43		11 59		12 05			12 13	

		SN 1	SN 1	TL 1	SN 1	TL 1	GX 1	SN 1	SN 1	TL 1	SN 1	TL 1	TL 1	GX 1	TL 1	SN 1	SN 1	TL 1	SN 1	TL 1	GX 1	SN 1	SN 1
Lewes	d		11 21					11 45									12 21					12 45	
Hove	d	11 21							11 51							12 21							12 51
Brighton	d			11 26	11 33		11 48			11 58	12 03		12 08	12 18	←			12 26	12 33		12 48		
Preston Park	d			11 30					11 57				12 12		12 12			12 30					12 57
Hassocks	d			11 36	11 41						12 11		→		12 18			12 36	12 41				
Burgess Hill	d			11 40	11 45					12 08	12 15				12 22			12 40	12 45				
Wivelsfield	d			11 42				12 01		12 10								12 42				13 01	
Haywards Heath	a	11 36	11 40	11 46	11 50			12 06	12 10	12 15	12 20				12 27	12 36	12 40	12 46	12 50			13 06	13 10
Haywards Heath	d		11 44	11 47	11 51	←			12 14	12 16	12 21	←			12 31		12 44	12 47	12 51	←			13 14
Balcombe	d			11 52		11 52				12 22		12 22						12 52		12 52			
Three Bridges	a			→		11 58				→		12 27			12 39			→		12 58			
Three Bridges	d					11 59						12 29			12 40					12 59			
Gatwick Airport	a		11 56		12 02	12 03	12 11		12 26		12 32	12 33		12 41	12 45		12 56		13 02	13 03	13 11		13 26
Gatwick Airport	d		11 57		12 03	12 06	12 12		12 27		12 33	12 36		12 42	12 46		12 57		13 03	13 06	13 12		13 27
East Croydon	a		12 11		12 18	12 21			12 41		12 48	12 51			13 01		13 11		13 18	13 21			13 41
East Croydon	d					12 21						12 51			13 01					13 21			
London Bridge	d					12 35						13 05			13 16					13 35			
London Blackfriars	d					12 42						13 12			13 22					13 42			
City Thameslink	d					12 44						13 14			13 24					13 44			
Farringdon	d					12 46						13 16			13 26					13 46			
St Pancras International	a					12 50						13 20			13 30					13 50			
East Croydon	d		12 12		12 19				12 42		12 49						13 12		13 19				13 42
Clapham Junction	a		12 21		12 28				12 51		12 58						13 21		13 28				13 51
London Victoria	a		12 29		12 35		12 43		12 59		13 05			13 13			13 29		13 35		13 43		13 59

Brighton/Hove/Lewes - Haywards Heath - Gatwick Airport - London

		TL	SN	TL	TL	GX	TL	SN	SN	TL	SN	TL	GX	SN	SN	TL	SN	TL	TL	GX	TL	SN	SN
Lewes	d								13 21					13 45									14 21
Hove	d							13 21							13 51							14 21	
Brighton	d	12 58	13 03		13 08	13 18	←			13 26	13 33		13 48			13 58	14 03		14 08	14 18	←		
Preston Park	d				13 12		13 12			13 30					13 57				14 12		14 12		
Hassocks	d		13 11		→		13 18			13 36	13 41						14 11		→		14 18		
Burgess Hill	d	13 08	13 15				13 22			13 40	13 45					14 08	14 15				14 22		
Wivelsfield	d	13 10								13 42				14 01		14 10							
Haywards Heath	a	13 15	13 20				13 27	13 36	13 40	13 46	13 50			14 06	14 10	14 15	14 20				14 27	14 36	14 40
Haywards Heath	d	13 16	13 21	←			13 31	13 44		13 47	13 51	←		14 14		14 16	14 21	←			14 31	14 44	
Balcombe	d	13 22		13 22						13 52		13 52				14 22		14 22					
Three Bridges	a	→		13 27			13 39			→		13 58				→		14 27			14 39		
Three Bridges	d			13 29			13 40					13 59						14 29			14 40		
Gatwick Airport	a		13 32	13 33		13 41	13 45	13 56			14 02	14 03	14 11	14 26			14 32	14 33		14 41	14 45	14 56	
Gatwick Airport	d		13 33	13 36		13 42	13 46	13 57			14 03	14 06	14 12	14 27			14 33	14 36		14 42	14 46	14 57	
East Croydon	a		13 48	13 51			14 01	14 11			14 18	14 21		14 41			14 48	14 51			15 01	15 11	
East Croydon	d			13 51			14 01					14 21						14 51			15 01		
London Bridge	d			14 05			14 16					14 35						15 05			15 16		
London Blackfriars	d			14 12			14 22					14 42						15 12			15 22		
City Thameslink	d			14 14			14 24					14 44						15 14			15 24		
Farringdon	d			14 16			14 26					14 46						15 16			15 26		
St Pancras International	a			14 20			14 30					14 50						15 20			15 30		
East Croydon	d		13 49					14 12			14 19			14 42			14 49					15 12	
Clapham Junction	a		13 58					14 21			14 28			14 51			14 58					15 21	
London Victoria	a		14 05			14 13		14 30			14 36		14 43	14 59			15 05			15 13		15 29	

		TL	SN	TL	GX	SN	SN	TL	SN	TL	TL	GX	TL	SN	SN	TL	SN	TL	GX	SN	SN	TL
Lewes	d					14 45									15 21					15 45		
Hove	d						14 51							15 21							15 51	
Brighton	d	14 26	14 33		14 48			14 58	15 03		15 08	15 18	←			15 26	15 33		15 48			15 58
Preston Park	d	14 30					14 57				15 12		15 12			15 30					15 57	
Hassocks	d	14 36	14 41						15 11		→		15 18			15 36	15 41					
Burgess Hill	d	14 40	14 45					15 08	15 15				15 22			15 40	15 45					16 08
Wivelsfield	d	14 42				15 01		15 10								15 42				16 01		16 10
Haywards Heath	a	14 46	14 50			15 06	15 10	15 15	15 20				15 27	15 36	15 40	15 46	15 50			16 06	16 10	16 15
Haywards Heath	d	14 47	14 51	←		15 14		15 16	15 21	←			15 31	15 44		15 47	15 51	←		16 14		16 16
Balcombe	d	14 52		14 52				15 22		15 22						15 52		15 52				16 22
Three Bridges	a	→		14 58				→		15 28			15 39			→		15 58				→
Three Bridges	d			14 59						15 29			15 40					15 59				
Gatwick Airport	a		15 02	15 03	15 11	15 26			15 32	15 33		15 41	15 45	15 56			16 02	16 03	16 11	16 26		
Gatwick Airport	d		15 03	15 06	15 12	15 27			15 33	15 36		15 42	15 46	15 57			16 03	16 06	16 12	16 27		
East Croydon	a		15 18	15 21		15 41			15 48	15 51			16 01	16 11			16 18	16 21		16 41		
East Croydon	d			15 21						15 51			16 01					16 21				
London Bridge	d			15 35						16 05			16 16					16 35				
London Blackfriars	d			15 42						16 12			16 22					16 42				
City Thameslink	d			15 44						16 14			16 24					16 44				
Farringdon	d			15 46						16 16			16 26					16 46				
St Pancras International	a			15 50						16 20			16 30					16 50				
East Croydon	d		15 19			15 42			15 49					16 12			16 19			16 42		
Clapham Junction	a		15 28			15 51			15 58					16 21			16 28			16 51		
London Victoria	a		15 35		15 43	15 59			16 05			16 13		16 29			16 35		16 43	16 59		

		SN	TL	TL	GX	TL	SN	SN	TL	SN	TL	GX	SN	SN	TL	SN	TL	TL	GX	TL	SN	SN	TL
Lewes	d							16 21					16 45									17 21	
Hove	d						16 21							16 51							17 21		
Brighton	d	16 03		16 08	16 18	←			16 26	16 33		16 48			16 58	17 03		17 08	17 18	←			17 26
Preston Park	d			16 12		16 12			16 30					16 57				17 12		17 12			17 30
Hassocks	d	16 11		→		16 18			16 36	16 41						17 11		→		17 18			17 36
Burgess Hill	d	16 15				16 22			16 40	16 45					17 08	17 15				17 22			17 40
Wivelsfield	d								16 42				17 01		17 10								17 42
Haywards Heath	a	16 20				16 27	16 36	16 40	16 46	16 50			17 06	17 10	17 15	17 20				17 27	17 36	17 40	17 46
Haywards Heath	d	16 21	←			16 31	16 44		16 47	16 51	←		17 14		17 16	17 21	←			17 31	17 44		17 47
Balcombe	d		16 22						16 52		16 52				17 22		17 22						17 52
Three Bridges	a		16 27			16 39			→		16 58				→		17 27			17 39			→
Three Bridges	d		16 29			16 40					16 59						17 29			17 40			
Gatwick Airport	a	16 32	16 33		16 43	16 45	16 56			17 02	17 03	17 11	17 26			17 32	17 33		17 41	17 45	17 56		
Gatwick Airport	d	16 33	16 36		16 44	16 46	16 57			17 03	17 06	17 12	17 27			17 33	17 36		17 42	17 46	17 57		
East Croydon	a	16 48	16 51			17 01	17 11			17 18	17 21		17 41			17 48	17 51			18 01	18 11		
East Croydon	d		16 51			17 01					17 21						17 51			18 01			
London Bridge	d		17 05			17 16					17 35						18 05			18 16			
London Blackfriars	d		17 12			17 22					17 42						18 12			18 22			
City Thameslink	d		17 14			17 24					17 44						18 14			18 24			
Farringdon	d		17 16			17 26					17 46						18 16			18 26			
St Pancras International	a		17 20			17 30					17 50						18 20			18 30			
East Croydon	d	16 49					17 12			17 19			17 42			17 49					18 12		
Clapham Junction	a	16 58					17 21			17 28			17 51			17 58					18 21		
London Victoria	a	17 05			17 15		17 29			17 35		17 43	17 59			18 05			18 13		18 29		

		SN	TL	GX	SN	SN	TL	SN	TL	TL	GX	TL	SN	SN	TL	SN	TL	GX	SN	SN	TL	SN	TL
Lewes	d				17 45									18 21					18 45				
Hove	d					17 51							18 21							18 51			
Brighton	d	17 33		17 48			17 58	18 03		18 08	18 18	←			18 26	18 33		18 48			18 58	19 03	
Preston Park	d					17 57				18 12		18 12			18 30					18 57			
Hassocks	d	17 41						18 11		→		18 18			18 36	18 41						19 11	
Burgess Hill	d	17 45					18 08	18 15				18 22			18 40	18 45					19 08	19 15	
Wivelsfield	d				18 01		18 10								18 42				19 01		19 10		
Haywards Heath	a	17 50			18 06	18 10	18 15	18 20				18 27	18 36	18 40	18 46	18 50			19 06	19 10	19 15	19 20	
Haywards Heath	d	17 51	←		18 14		18 16	18 21	←			18 31	18 44		18 47	18 51	←		19 14		19 16	19 21	←
Balcombe	d		17 52				18 22		18 22						18 52		18 52				19 22		19 22
Three Bridges	a		17 58				→		18 27			18 39			→		18 58				→		19 27
Three Bridges	d		17 59						18 29			18 40					18 59						19 29
Gatwick Airport	a	18 02	18 03	18 11	18 26			18 32	18 33		18 41	18 45	18 56			19 02	19 03	19 11	19 26			19 32	19 33
Gatwick Airport	d	18 03	18 06	18 12	18 27			18 33	18 36		18 42	18 46	18 57			19 03	19 06	19 12	19 27			19 33	19 36
East Croydon	a	18 18	18 21		18 41			18 48	18 51			19 01	19 11			19 18	19 21		19 41			19 48	19 51
East Croydon	d		18 21						18 51			19 01					19 21						19 51
London Bridge	d		18 35						19 05			19 16					19 35						20 05
London Blackfriars	d		18 42						19 12			19 22					19 42						20 12
City Thameslink	d		18 44						19 14			19 24					19 44						20 14
Farringdon	d		18 46						19 16			19 26					19 46						20 16
St Pancras International	a		18 50						19 20			19 30					19 50						20 20
East Croydon	d	18 19			18 42			18 49					19 12			19 19			19 42			19 49	
Clapham Junction	a	18 28			18 51			18 58					19 21			19 28			19 51			19 58	
London Victoria	a	18 35		18 43	18 59			19 05			19 13		19 29			19 35		19 43	19 59			20 05	

		TL	GX	TL	SN	SN	TL	SN	TL	GX	SN	SN	TL	SN	TL	TL	GX	TL	SN	SN	TL	SN
Lewes	d					19 21					19 45									20 21		
Hove	d				19 21							19 51							20 21			
Brighton	d	19 08	19 18	←			19 26	19 33		19 48			19 58	20 03		20 08	20 18	←			20 26	20 33
Preston Park	d	19 12		19 12			19 30					19 57				20 12		20 12			20 30	
Hassocks	d	→		19 18			19 36	19 41						20 11		→		20 18			20 36	20 41
Burgess Hill	d			19 22			19 40	19 45					20 08	20 15				20 22			20 40	20 45
Wivelsfield	d						19 42				20 01		20 10								20 42	
Haywards Heath	a			19 27	19 36	19 40	19 46	19 50			20 06	20 10	20 15	20 20				20 27	20 36	20 40	20 46	20 50
Haywards Heath	d			19 31	19 44		19 47	19 51	←		20 14		20 16	20 21	←			20 31	20 44		20 47	20 51
Balcombe	d						19 52		19 52				20 22		20 22						20 52	
Three Bridges	a			19 39			→		19 58				→		20 27			20 39			→	
Three Bridges	d			19 40					19 59						20 29			20 40				
Gatwick Airport	a		19 41	19 45	19 56			20 02	20 03	20 11	20 26			20 32	20 33		20 41	20 45	20 56			21 02
Gatwick Airport	d		19 42	19 46	19 57			20 03	20 06	20 12	20 27			20 33	20 36		20 42	20 46	20 57			21 03
East Croydon	a			20 01	20 11			20 18	20 21		20 41			20 48	20 51			21 01	21 11			21 18
East Croydon	d			20 01					20 21						20 51			21 01				
London Bridge	d			20 16					20 35						21 05			21 16				
London Blackfriars	d			20 22					20 42						21 12			21 22				
City Thameslink	d			20 24					20 44													
Farringdon	d			20 26					20 46						21 16			21 26				
St Pancras International	a			20 30					20 50						21 20			21 30				
East Croydon	d				20 12			20 19			20 42			20 49					21 12			21 19
Clapham Junction	a				20 21			20 28			20 51			20 58					21 21			21 28
London Victoria	a		20 13		20 29			20 35		20 43	20 59			21 05			21 13		21 29			21 35

		TL	GX	SN	SN	TL	SN	TL	TL	GX	TL	SN	SN	TL	SN	TL	GX	SN	SN	TL	SN	TL	TL
Lewes	d			20 45									21 21					21 45					
Hove	d				20 51							21 21							21 51				
Brighton	d		20 48			20 58	21 03		21 08	21 18	←			21 26	21 33		21 48			21 58	22 03		22 08
Preston Park	d				20 57				21 12		21 12			21 30					21 57				22 12
Hassocks	d						21 11		→		21 18			21 36	21 41						22 11		→
Burgess Hill	d					21 08	21 15				21 22			21 40	21 45					22 08	22 15		
Wivelsfield	d			21 01		21 10								21 42				22 01		22 10			
Haywards Heath	a			21 06	21 10	21 15	21 20				21 27	21 36	21 40	21 46	21 50			22 06	22 10	22 15	22 20		
Haywards Heath	d	←		21 14		21 16	21 21	←			21 31	21 44		21 47	21 51	←		22 14		22 16	22 21	←	
Balcombe	d	20 52				21 22		21 22						21 52		21 52				22 22		22 22	
Three Bridges	a	20 58				→		21 27			21 39			→		21 58				→		22 27	
Three Bridges	d	20 59						21 29			21 40					21 59						22 29	
Gatwick Airport	a	21 03	21 11	21 26			21 32	21 33		21 41	21 45	21 56			22 02	22 03	22 11	22 27			22 32	22 33	
Gatwick Airport	d	21 06	21 12	21 27			21 33	21 36		21 42	21 46	21 57			22 03	22 06	22 12	22 28			22 33	22 36	
East Croydon	a	21 21		21 41			21 48	21 51			22 01	22 12			22 18	22 21		22 42			22 48	22 51	
East Croydon	d	21 21						21 51			22 01					22 21						22 51	
London Bridge	d	21 35						22 05			22 16					22 35						23 05	
London Blackfriars	d	21 42						22 12			22 22					22 42						23 12	
City Thameslink	d																						
Farringdon	d	21 46						22 16			22 26					22 46						23 16	
St Pancras International	a	21 50						22 20			22 30					22 50						23 20	
East Croydon	d			21 42			21 49					22 12			22 19			22 43			22 49		
Clapham Junction	a			21 51			21 58					22 21			22 28			22 52			22 58		
London Victoria	a		21 43	21 59			22 05			22 13		22 28			22 35		22 43	23 00			23 05		

Table T184-R

Saturdays
21 December to 16 May

Brighton/Hove/Lewes - Haywards Heath - Gatwick Airport - London

		GX	TL	SN	SN	TL		SN	TL	GX	TL	SN	TL	TL
Lewes	d				22 21									
Hove	d			22 21										
Brighton	d	22 18	←			22 26		22 33		22 48	22 56	23 13	23 24	23 42
Preston Park	d		22 12			22 30					23 00		23 28	23 46
Hassocks	d		22 18			22 36		22 41			23 06	23 21	23 34	23 52
Burgess Hill	d		22 22			22 40		22 45			23 10	23 25	23 38	23 56
Wivelsfield	d					22 42					23 12		23 40	23 58
Haywards Heath	a		22 27	22 36	22 40	22 46		22 50			23 16	23 30	23 45	00 02
Haywards Heath	d		22 31	22 44		22 47		22 51	←		23 17	23 30	23 46	00 03
Balcombe	d					22 52			22 52		23 22		23 52	00 08
Three Bridges	a		22 39			→			22 58		23 28	23 39	23 57	00 14
Three Bridges	d		22 40						22 59		23 29	23 40	23 58	00 15
Gatwick Airport	a	22 41	22 45	22 56				23 02	23 03	23 11	23 33	23 44	00 03	00 19
Gatwick Airport	d	22 42	22 46	22 57				23 03	23 06	23 12	23 34	23 55	00 04	00 21
East Croydon	a		23 01	23 11				23 18	23 21		23 52	00 15	00 22	00 39
East Croydon	d		23 01						23 21		23 53		00 23	00 40
London Bridge	d		23 16						23 35					
London Blackfriars	d		23 22						23 42		00 22		00 50	01 06
City Thameslink	d													
Farringdon	d		23 26						23 46		00 26			
St Pancras International	a		23 30						23 50		00 30		00 59	01 15
East Croydon	d			23 12				23 19				00 16		
Clapham Junction	a			23 21				23 28				00 33		
London Victoria	a	23 13		23 29				23 35		23 43		00 41		

Sundays
15 December to 10 May

		TL	SN	TL	SN	TL	TL	SN	TL	SN	SN		TL	SN	SN	TL	SN	SN	TL	SN	SN		TL	SN	SN
Lewes	d										07 19						08 18							09 21	
Hove	d														07 52					08 52					
Brighton	d	00 04	04 33	05 42	05 47	06 08	06 42	06 47	07 08	07 17			07 42	07 47		08 08		08 27	08 42		08 57		09 08		09 27
Preston Park	d	00 08		05 46	05 51	06 12	06 46	06 51	07 12				07 46		07 57	08 12			08 46	08 57			09 12		
Hassocks	d	00 14		05 52	05 57	06 18	06 52	06 57	07 18	07 25			07 52	07 56		08 18		08 36	08 52		09 06		09 18		09 36
Burgess Hill	d	00 18		05 56	06 01	06 22	06 56	07 01	07 22	07 29			07 56	08 00		08 22		08 40	08 56		09 10		09 22		09 40
Wivelsfield	d	00 20		05 58	06 03	06 24	06 58	07 03	07 24				07 58			08 24	08 35		08 58				09 24	09 36	
Haywards Heath	a	00 24	04 46	06 03	06 07	06 29	07 03	07 07	07 29	07 34	07 38		08 03	08 06	08 09	08 29	08 39	08 45	09 03	09 08	09 15		09 29	09 41	09 45
Haywards Heath	d	00 25	04 47	06 04	06 08	06 30	07 04	07 08	07 30	07 42			08 04	08 13		08 30	08 41	08 46	09 04	09 11	09 16		09 30	09 41	09 46
Balcombe	d	00 30				06 36			07 36							08 35							09 36		
Three Bridges	a	00 36	04 56	06 12	06 16	06 42	07 12	07 16	07 42				08 12			08 41			09 12		09 24		09 42		
Three Bridges	d	00 37	04 58	06 13	06 23	06 43	07 13	07 23	07 43				08 13			08 42			09 13		09 25		09 43		
Gatwick Airport	a	00 41	05 02	06 18	06 27	06 48	07 18	07 27	07 48	07 53			08 17	08 24		08 46	08 52	08 58	09 17	09 24	09 29		09 47	09 53	09 58
Gatwick Airport	d	00 42	05 03	06 21	06 28	06 51	07 21	07 28	07 51	07 54			08 21	08 25		08 47	08 56	09 00	09 19	09 25	09 30		09 49	09 56	10 00
East Croydon	a	01 09	05 29	06 40	06 50	07 09	07 39	07 50	08 09	08 22			08 39	08 45		09 02	09 10	09 14	09 33	09 40	09 44		10 03	10 10	10 14
East Croydon	d	01 10		06 41		07 10	07 40		08 10				08 40			09 02			09 34				10 04		
London Bridge	d			06a56		07a25	07a55		08a25				08a55			09a17			09 49				10 19		
London Blackfriars	d	01 36																	09 55				10 25		
City Thameslink	d																								
Farringdon	d																		09 59				10 29		
St Pancras International	a	01 43																	10 03				10 33		
East Croydon	d		05 30		06 51			07 51		08 23				08 46			09 11	09 15		09 41	09 45			10 11	10 15
Clapham Junction	a		05 51		07 05			08 07		08 38				08 55			09 20	09 24		09 50	09 54			10 20	10 24
London Victoria	a		05 59		07 15			08 17		08 46				09 02			09 28	09 32		09 58	10 02			10 28	10 32

		TL	SN	SN	TL	SN	SN		TL	SN	SN	TL	SN	SN	TL	SN	SN		TL	SN	SN	TL	SN	SN	TL
Lewes	d					10 21							11 21							12 21					
Hove	d		09 52							10 52						11 52							12 52		
Brighton	d	09 42		09 57	10 08		10 27		10 42		10 57	11 08		11 27	11 42		11 57		12 08		12 27	12 42		12 57	13 08
Preston Park	d	09 46	09 57		10 12				10 46	10 57		11 12			11 46	11 57			12 12			12 46	12 57		13 12
Hassocks	d	09 52		10 06	10 18		10 36		10 52		11 06	11 18		11 36	11 52		12 06		12 18		12 36	12 52		13 06	13 18
Burgess Hill	d	09 56		10 10	10 22		10 40		10 56		11 10	11 22		11 40	11 56		12 10		12 22		12 40	12 56		13 10	13 22
Wivelsfield	d	09 58			10 24	10 36			10 58			11 24	11 36		11 58				12 24	12 36		12 58			13 24
Haywards Heath	a	10 03	10 08	10 15	10 29	10 41	10 45		11 03	11 08	11 15	11 29	11 41	11 45	12 03	12 08	12 15		12 29	12 41	12 45	13 03	13 08	13 15	13 29
Haywards Heath	d	10 04	10 11	10 16	10 30	10 41	10 46		11 04	11 11	11 16	11 30	11 41	11 46	12 04	12 11	12 16		12 30	12 41	12 46	13 04	13 11	13 16	13 30
Balcombe	d				10 36							11 36							12 36						13 36
Three Bridges	a	10 12		10 24	10 42				11 12		11 24	11 42			12 12		12 24		12 42			13 12		13 24	13 42
Three Bridges	d	10 13		10 25	10 43				11 13		11 25	11 43			12 13		12 25		12 43			13 13		13 25	13 43
Gatwick Airport	a	10 17	10 24	10 29	10 47	10 53	10 58		11 17	11 23	11 29	11 47	11 54	11 58	12 17	12 24	12 29		12 47	12 54	12 58	13 17	13 24	13 29	13 47
Gatwick Airport	d	10 19	10 25	10 30	10 49	10 56	11 00		11 19	11 25	11 30	11 49	11 56	12 00	12 19	12 25	12 30		12 49	12 56	13 00	13 19	13 25	13 30	13 49
East Croydon	a	10 33	10 40	10 44	11 03	11 10	11 14		11 33	11 39	11 44	12 03	12 10	12 14	12 33	12 40	12 44		13 03	13 10	13 14	13 33	13 40	13 44	14 03
East Croydon	d	10 34			11 04				11 34			12 04			12 34				13 04			13 34			14 04
London Bridge	d	10 49			11 19				11 49			12 19			12 49				13 19			13 49			14 19
London Blackfriars	d	10 55			11 25				11 55			12 25			12 55				13 25			13 55			14 25
City Thameslink	d																								
Farringdon	d	10 59			11 29				11 59			12 29			12 59				13 29			13 59			14 29
St Pancras International	a	11 03			11 33				12 03			12 33			13 03				13 33			14 03			14 33
East Croydon	d		10 41	10 45		11 11	11 15			11 40	11 45		12 11	12 15		12 41	12 45			13 11	13 15		13 41	13 45	
Clapham Junction	a		10 50	10 54		11 20	11 24			11 50	11 54		12 20	12 24		12 50	12 54			13 22	13 25		13 50	13 54	
London Victoria	a		10 58	11 02		11 28	11 32			11 58	12 02		12 28	12 32		12 58	13 02			13 30	13 32		13 58	14 02	

NRT DECEMBER 19 EDITION

Table T184-R

Sundays
15 December to 10 May

Brighton/Hove/Lewes - Haywards Heath - Gatwick Airport - London

		SN	SN		TL	SN	SN	TL	SN	SN	TL	SN	SN		TL	SN	SN	TL	SN	SN	TL	SN	SN		TL
Lewes	d	13 21							14 21							15 21						16 21			
Hove	d					13 52						14 52							15 52						
Brighton	d		13 27		13 42		13 57	14 08		14 27	14 42		14 57		15 08		15 27	15 42		15 57	16 08		16 27		16 42
Preston Park	d				13 46	13 57		14 12			14 46	14 57			15 12			15 46	15 57		16 12				16 46
Hassocks	d		13 36		13 52		14 06	14 18		14 36	14 52		15 06		15 18		15 36	15 52		16 06	16 18		16 36		16 52
Burgess Hill	d		13 40		13 56		14 10	14 22		14 40	14 56		15 10		15 22		15 40	15 56		16 10	16 22		16 40		16 56
Wivelsfield	d	13 36			13 58			14 24	14 36		14 58				15 24	15 36		15 58			16 24	16 36			16 58
Haywards Heath	a	13 41	13 45		14 03	14 08	14 15	14 29	14 41	14 45	15 03	15 08	15 15		15 29	15 41	15 45	16 03	16 08	16 15	16 29	16 41	16 45		17 03
Haywards Heath	d	13 41	13 46		14 04	14 11	14 16	14 30	14 41	14 46	15 04	15 11	15 16		15 30	15 41	15 46	16 04	16 11	16 16	16 30	16 41	16 46		17 04
Balcombe	d							14 36							15 36						16 36				
Three Bridges	a				14 12		14 24	14 42			15 12		15 24		15 42			16 12		16 24	16 42				17 12
Three Bridges	d				14 13		14 25	14 43			15 13		15 25		15 43			16 13		16 25	16 43				17 13
Gatwick Airport	a	13 53	13 58		14 17	14 24	14 29	14 47	14 53	14 58	15 17	15 24	15 29		15 47	15 54	15 58	16 17	16 24	16 29	16 47	16 54	16 58		17 17
Gatwick Airport	d	13 56	14 00		14 19	14 25	14 30	14 49	14 56	15 00	15 19	15 25	15 30		15 49	15 56	16 00	16 19	16 25	16 30	16 49	16 56	17 00		17 19
East Croydon	a	14 10	14 14		14 33	14 40	14 44	15 03	15 10	15 14	15 33	15 40	15 44		16 03	16 10	16 14	16 33	16 40	16 44	17 03	17 10	17 14		17 33
East Croydon	d				14 34			15 04			15 34				16 04			16 34			17 04				17 34
London Bridge	d				14 49			15 19			15 49				16 19			16 49			17 19				17 49
London Blackfriars	d				14 55			15 25			15 55				16 25			16 55			17 25				17 55
City Thameslink	d																								
Farringdon	d				14 59			15 29			15 59				16 29			16 59			17 29				17 59
St Pancras International	a				15 03			15 33			16 03				16 33			17 03			17 33				18 03
East Croydon	d	14 11	14 15			14 41	14 45		15 11	15 15		15 41	15 45			16 11	16 15		16 41	16 45		17 11	17 15		
Clapham Junction	a	14 20	14 24			14 50	14 54		15 20	15 24		15 50	15 54			16 22	16 25		16 50	16 54		17 22	17 25		
London Victoria	a	14 28	14 32			14 58	15 02		15 28	15 32		15 58	16 02			16 30	16 32		16 58	17 02		17 30	17 32		

		SN	SN	TL	SN	SN	TL	SN	SN		TL	SN	SN	TL	SN	SN	TL	SN	SN		TL	SN	SN	TL	SN
Lewes	d				17 21							18 21						19 21							20 21
Hove	d	16 52						17 52							18 52							19 52			
Brighton	d		16 57	17 08		17 27	17 42		17 57		18 08		18 27	18 42		18 57	19 08		19 27		19 42		19 57	20 08	
Preston Park	d	16 57		17 12			17 46	17 57			18 12			18 46	18 57		19 12				19 46	19 57		20 12	
Hassocks	d		17 06	17 18		17 36	17 52		18 06		18 18		18 36	18 52		19 06	19 18		19 36		19 52		20 06	20 18	
Burgess Hill	d		17 10	17 22		17 40	17 56		18 10		18 22		18 40	18 56		19 10	19 22		19 40		19 56		20 10	20 22	
Wivelsfield	d			17 24	17 36		17 58				18 24	18 36		18 58			19 24	19 36			19 58			20 24	20 36
Haywards Heath	a	17 08	17 15	17 29	17 41	17 45	18 03	18 08	18 15		18 29	18 41	18 45	19 03	19 08	19 15	19 29	19 41	19 45		20 03	20 08	20 15	20 29	20 41
Haywards Heath	d	17 11	17 16	17 30	17 41	17 46	18 04	18 11	18 16		18 30	18 41	18 46	19 04	19 11	19 16	19 30	19 41	19 46		20 04	20 11	20 16	20 30	20 41
Balcombe	d			17 36							18 36						19 36							20 36	
Three Bridges	a		17 24	17 42			18 12		18 24		18 42			19 12		19 24	19 42				20 12		20 24	20 42	
Three Bridges	d		17 25	17 43			18 13		18 25		18 43			19 13		19 25	19 43				20 13		20 25	20 43	
Gatwick Airport	a	17 24	17 29	17 47	17 54	17 58	18 17	18 24	18 29		18 47	18 53	18 58	19 17	19 24	19 29	19 47	19 53	19 58		20 17	20 24	20 29	20 47	20 53
Gatwick Airport	d	17 25	17 30	17 49	17 56	18 00	18 19	18 25	18 30		18 49	18 56	19 00	19 19	19 25	19 30	19 49	19 56	20 00		20 19	20 25	20 30	20 49	20 56
East Croydon	a	17 40	17 44	18 03	18 10	18 14	18 33	18 40	18 44		19 03	19 10	19 14	19 33	19 40	19 44	20 03	20 10	20 14		20 33	20 40	20 44	21 03	21 10
East Croydon	d			18 04			18 34				19 04			19 34			20 04				20 34			21 04	
London Bridge	d			18 19			18 49				19 19			19 49			20 19				20 49			21 19	
London Blackfriars	d			18 25			18 55				19 25			19 55			20 25				20 55			21 25	
City Thameslink	d																								
Farringdon	d			18 29			18 59				19 29			19 59			20 29				20 59			21 29	
St Pancras International	a			18 33			19 03				19 33			20 03			20 33				21 03			21 33	
East Croydon	d	17 41	17 45		18 11	18 15		18 41	18 45			19 11	19 15		19 41	19 45		20 11	20 15			20 41	20 45		21 11
Clapham Junction	a	17 50	17 54		18 20	18 24		18 50	18 54			19 20	19 24		19 50	19 54		20 20	20 24			20 50	20 54		21 20
London Victoria	a	17 58	18 02		18 28	18 32		18 58	19 02			19 28	19 32		19 58	20 02		20 28	20 32			20 58	21 02		21 28

		SN	TL	SN	SN		TL	SN	SN	TL	SN	TL	SN	TL	SN		TL	TL
Lewes	d							21 21										
Hove	d			20 52														
Brighton	d	20 27	20 42		20 57		21 08		21 27	21 42	21 54	22 08	22 27	22 42	22 54		23 08	23 42
Preston Park	d		20 46	20 57			21 12			21 46	21 58	22 12		22 46	22 58		23 12	23 46
Hassocks	d	20 36	20 52		21 06		21 18		21 36	21 52	22 05	22 18	22 36	22 52	23 05		23 18	23 52
Burgess Hill	d	20 40	20 56		21 10		21 22		21 40	21 56	22 09	22 22	22 40	22 56	23 09		23 22	23 56
Wivelsfield	d		20 58				21 24	21 36		21 58	22 11	22 24		22 58	23 11		23 24	23 58
Haywards Heath	a	20 45	21 03	21 08	21 15		21 29	21 41	21 45	22 03	22 15	22 29	22 45	23 03	23 15		23 29	00 03
Haywards Heath	d	20 46	21 04	21 11	21 16		21 30	21 41	21 46	22 04	22 16	22 30	22 46	23 04	23 16		23 30	00 04
Balcombe	d						21 36					22 36					23 36	
Three Bridges	a		21 12		21 24		21 42			22 12	22 24	22 42	22 54	23 13	23 24		23 42	00 13
Three Bridges	d		21 13		21 25		21 43			22 13	22 25	22 43	22 55	23 15	23 25		23 45	00 15
Gatwick Airport	a	20 58	21 17	21 24	21 29		21 48	21 53	21 58	22 17	22 29	22 47	22 59	23 19	23 29		23 49	00 19
Gatwick Airport	d	21 00	21 19	21 25	21 30		21 49	21 56	22 00	22 19	22 30	22 49	23 00	23 21	23 30		23 50	00 21
East Croydon	a	21 14	21 33	21 40	21 44		22 03	22 10	22 14	22 33	22 44	23 03	23 14	23 39	23 51		00 09	00 39
East Croydon	d		21 34				22 04			22 34		23 04		23 40			00 10	00 40
London Bridge	d		21 49				22 19			22 49		23 19						
London Blackfriars	d		21 55				22 25			22 55		23 27		00 06			00 36	01 06
City Thameslink	d																	
Farringdon	d		21 59				22 29			22 59		23 31		00 11				
St Pancras International	a		22 03				22 33			23 03		23 35		00 15			00 45	01 15
East Croydon	d	21 15		21 41	21 45			22 11	22 15		22 45		23 15		23 52			
Clapham Junction	a	21 24		21 50	21 54			22 20	22 24		22 54		23 24		00 08			
London Victoria	a	21 32		21 58	22 02			22 28	22 32		23 02		23 31		00 17			

Table T185-F

Mondays to Fridays

16 December to 15 May

London - Gatwick Airport - Three Bridges - Horsham : Summary of Fast Trains

		SN MX	SN	TL	TL MO	TL MX	TL	TL	TL	TL		TL	SN	SN	TL	GX	TL	GX	GX	TL		SN	GX	SN	GX
London Victoria	d	00 02	00 08										04 30	04 35		05 00		05 14	05 30			05 32	05 44	05 54	06 00
Clapham Junction	d	00 09	00 15										04 38	04 42								05 42		06 01	
East Croydon	a	00 23	00 30											04 57								05 51		06 10	
St Pancras International	d			00 21	00 51	00 52	01 32	02 32	03 02	03 32		04 02			04 32		04 52			05 20					
Farringdon	d			00 26													04 56			05 24					
City Thameslink	d																04 58			05 26					
London Blackfriars	d			00 31	01 01	01 02	01 40	02 40	03 10	03 40		04 10			04 40		05 01			05 29					
London Bridge	d																			05 35					
East Croydon	a			00 57	01 27	01 28	02 06	03 06	03 36	04 06		04 36			05 06		05 27			05 48					
East Croydon	d	00 24	00 31	00 58	01 28	01 28	02 07	03 07	03 37	04 07		04 37		04 58	05 07		05 28			05 49		05 52		06 10	
Gatwick Airport	a	00 43	01 03	01 20	01 56	01 56	02 30	03 30	03 56	04 30		04 57	05 12	05 28	05 31	05 39	05 47	05 50	05 59	06 04		06 17	06 12	06 25	06 28
Three Bridges	a	00 48		01 26	02 03	02 03	02 36	03 36	04 02	04 40		05 03			05 37		05 53			06 09		06 23		06 31	
Crawley	a																							06 35	
Horsham	a																							06 50	

		TL	TL	GX	TL	TL		SN	GX	TL	TL	SN	GX	TL	SN	TL		TL	GX	TL	TL	SN	SN	GX	TL
London Victoria	d			06 13				06 25	06 30			06 36	06 43		06 46				07 00			07 06	07 09	07 13	
Clapham Junction	d							06 32				06 43			06 53							07 13	07 16		
East Croydon	a											06 52			07 02							07 22	07 27		
St Pancras International	d	05 45	05 50		06 00					06 15	06 20			06 30				06 35		06 45	06 50				07 00
Farringdon	d	05 49	05 54		06 04					06 19	06 24			06 34				06 39		06 49	06 54				07 04
City Thameslink	d	05 51	05 56		06 06					06 21	06 26			06 36				06 41		06 51	06 56				07 06
London Blackfriars	d	05 54	05 59		06 09					06 24	06 29			06 39				06 44		06 54	06 59				07 09
London Bridge	d	06 00	06 05		06 15					06 30	06 35			06 45				06 51		07 00	07 05				07 15
East Croydon	a	06 16	06 18		06 28					06 46	06 48			06 59				07 06		07 16	07 18				07 29
East Croydon	d	06 16	06 19		06 29	←				06 46	06 49	06 52		07 00	07 03	←		07 07		07 16	07 19	07 22	07 27		07 30
Gatwick Airport	a	06 50	06 34	06 41	06 44	06 50			06 58	07 19	07 04	07 07	07 11	07 14	07 17	07 19		07 28	07 28	07 46	07 34	07 37	08 12	07 41	07 44
Three Bridges	a	→	06 39		06 49	06 56				→	07 09	07 13		07 19	07 24	07 26				→	07 39	07 42			07 49
Crawley	a					07 00						07 17				07 30						07 48			
Horsham	a					07 13		07 46				07 28				07 45						07 57			

		TL		SN	TL	SN	GX	TL	TL	SN	SN	GX		TL	TL	SN	TL	SN	GX	TL	TL	SN		SN	GX
London Victoria	d			07 16		07 25	07 30			07 36	07 39	07 43				07 46		07 55	07 59			08 06		08 09	08 13
Clapham Junction	d			07 23		07 32				07 43	07 46					07 53		08 02				08 13		08 16	
East Croydon	a			07 32						07 52	07 57					08 03		08 11				08 22		08 27	
St Pancras International	d				07 10			07 15	07 20					07 30			07 40			07 45	07 50				
Farringdon	d				07 14			07 19	07 24					07 34			07 44			07 49	07 54				
City Thameslink	d				07 16			07 21	07 26					07 36			07 46			07 51	07 56				
London Blackfriars	d				07 19			07 24	07 29					07 39			07 49			07 54	07 59				
London Bridge	d				07 25			07 30	07 35					07 45			07 55			08 00	08 05				
East Croydon	a				07 38			07 46	07 48					08 00			08 08			08 16	08 18				
East Croydon	d	←		07 33	07 38			07 46	07 49	07 52	07 57			08 00	←	08 03	08 08	08 11		08 16	08 19	08 22		08 28	
Gatwick Airport	a	07 46		07 47	07 53		07 58	08 16	08 04	08 07	08 41	08 11		08 15	08 16	08 18	08 23	08 26	08 30	08 45	08 34	08 37		09 09	08 41
Three Bridges	a	07 52						→	08 09	08 13				08 20	08 22					→	08 39	08 43			
Crawley	a	07 56								08 18					08 27							08 48			
Horsham	a	08 11				08 43				08 27					08 42							08 57			

		TL	TL	SN	SN	TL	SN	GX		TL	TL	TL	SN	GX	TL	TL	TL	SN		TL	TL	SN	GX	TL	TL
London Victoria	d			08 16	08 25		08 25	08 30					08 36	08 43				08 46				08 55	09 00		
Clapham Junction	d			08 23	08 32		08 32						08 43					08 53				09 02			
East Croydon	a			08 33			08 41						08 52					09 02				09 11			
St Pancras International	d	08 00				08 05				08 15	08 20				08 25	08 30				08 35	08 40			08 45	08 50
Farringdon	d	08 04				08 09				08 19	08 24				08 29	08 34				08 39	08 44			08 49	08 54
City Thameslink	d	08 06				08 11				08 21	08 26				08 31	08 36				08 41	08 46			08 51	08 56
London Blackfriars	d	08 09				08 14				08 24	08 29				08 34	08 39				08 44	08 49			08 54	08 59
London Bridge	d	08 15				08 21				08 30	08 35				08 41	08 45				08 51	08 55			09 00	09 05
East Croydon	a	08 29				08 36				08 46	08 48				08 54	08 58				09 06	09 08			09 14	09 18
East Croydon	d	08 29	←	08 33		08 37	08 41			08 46	08 49	←	08 53		08 55	08 59	←	09 03		09 07	09 08	09 11		09 16	09 19
Gatwick Airport	a	08 44	08 45	08 48		09 05	08 56	09 00		09 15	09 04	09 05	09 08	09 11	09 19	09 14	09 15	09 17		09 35	09 23	09 26	09 30	09 43	09 34
Three Bridges	a	08 49	08 51			→				→	09 09	09 11	09 14			09 19	09 21			→	09 28			→	09 39
Crawley	a		08 56										09 18				09 26								
Horsham	a		09 11		09 43								09 27				09 39								

		TL	SN	GX		TL	TL	TL	SN	TL	TL	SN	SN	GX		TL	TL	SN	GX	TL	TL	SN	TL	TL	
London Victoria	d		09 06	09 14					09 16			09 25	09 25	09 30				09 36	09 44			09 46			
Clapham Junction	d		09 13						09 23			09 32	09 32					09 43				09 53			
East Croydon	a		09 22						09 32			09 41						09 52				10 02			
St Pancras International	d						08 55	09 00		09 05	09 10					09 15	09 20				09 30		09 35	09 40	
Farringdon	d						08 59	09 04		09 09	09 14					09 19	09 24				09 34		09 39	09 44	
City Thameslink	d						09 01	09 06		09 11	09 16					09 21	09 26				09 36		09 41	09 46	
London Blackfriars	d						09 04	09 09		09 14	09 19					09 24	09 29				09 39		09 44	09 49	
London Bridge	d						09 11	09 15		09 21	09 25					09 30	09 35				09 45		09 51	09 55	
East Croydon	a						09 24	09 28		09 36	09 38					09 44	09 48				09 58		10 06	10 08	
East Croydon	d	←	09 23			←	09 25	09 29	09 33	09 37	09 38	09 41				09 46	09 49	09 53		←	09 59	10 03	10 07	10 08	
Gatwick Airport	a	09 35	09 38	09 41		09 43	09 47	09 44	09 47	10 08	09 53	09 57		10 00		10 13	10 04	10 08	10 11	10 13	10 14	10 17	10 38	10 23	
Three Bridges	a	09 41	09 44			09 49		09 49			10 02					→	10 09	10 14		10 19	10 19			10 32	
Crawley	a		09 48			09 53												10 18		10 23					
Horsham	a		09 57			10 08							10 43					10 27		10 38					

		SN	GX	TL	TL	SN		GX	TL	TL	SN	TL	TL	SN	SN	GX		TL	TL	SN	GX	TL	TL	SN	TL
London Victoria	d	09 55	10 00			10 06		10 14			10 16			10 25	10 25	10 30				10 36	10 44			10 46	
Clapham Junction	d	10 02				10 13					10 23			10 32	10 32					10 43				10 53	
East Croydon	a	10 11				10 22					10 32			10 41						10 52				11 02	
St Pancras International	d			09 45	09 50					10 00		10 05						10 15	10 20				10 30		10 35
Farringdon	d			09 49	09 54					10 04		10 09						10 19	10 24				10 34		10 39
City Thameslink	d			09 51	09 56					10 06		10 11						10 21	10 26				10 36		10 41
London Blackfriars	d			09 54	09 59					10 09		10 14						10 24	10 29				10 39		10 44
London Bridge	d			10 00	10 05					10 15		10 21	10 22					10 30	10 35				10 45		10 51
East Croydon	a			10 14	10 18					10 28		10 36	10 38					10 44	10 48				10 58		11 06
East Croydon	d	10 11		10 16	10 19	10 23			←	10 29	10 33	10 37	10 38	10 41				10 46	10 49	10 53		←	10 59	11 03	11 07
Gatwick Airport	a	10 27	10 30	10 43	10 34	10 38		10 41	10 43	10 44	10 47	11 08	10 53	10 56		11 00		11 12	11 04	11 08	11 11	11 12	11 14	11 17	11 38
Three Bridges	a			→	10 39	10 44			10 49	10 49								→	11 09	11 14		11 19	11 19		
Crawley	a					10 48			10 53											11 18		11 23			
Horsham	a					10 57			11 08						11 43					11 27		11 38			

		SN		GX	TL	TL	SN	GX	TL	TL	SN	TL		SN	SN	GX	TL	TL	SN	GX	TL	TL		SN	TL
London Victoria	d	10 55		11 00			11 06	11 14			11 16			11 25	11 25	11 30			11 36	11 44				11 46	
Clapham Junction	d	11 02					11 13				11 23			11 32	11 32				11 43					11 53	
East Croydon	a	11 11					11 22				11 32			11 41					11 52					12 02	
St Pancras International	d				10 45	10 50				11 00		11 05					11 15	11 20				11 30			11 35
Farringdon	d				10 49	10 54				11 04		11 09					11 19	11 24				11 34			11 39
City Thameslink	d				10 51	10 56				11 06		11 11					11 21	11 26				11 36			11 41
London Blackfriars	d				10 54	10 59				11 09		11 14					11 24	11 29				11 39			11 44
London Bridge	d				11 00	11 05				11 15		11 21					11 30	11 35				11 45			11 51
East Croydon	a				11 14	11 18				11 28		11 36					11 44	11 48				11 58			12 06
East Croydon	d	11 11			11 16	11 19	11 23		←	11 29	11 33	11 37		11 41			11 46	11 49	11 53		←	11 59		12 03	12 07
Gatwick Airport	a	11 26		11 30	11 43	11 34	11 38	11 41	11 43	11 44	11 47	12 08		11 56		12 00	12 13	12 04	12 08	12 11	12 13	12 14		12 17	12 38
Three Bridges	a				→	11 39	11 44		11 49	11 49							→	12 09	12 14		12 19	12 19			
Crawley	a						11 48		11 53										12 18		12 23				
Horsham	a						11 57		12 08						12 43				12 27		12 38				

		SN	GX	TL	TL	SN	GX	TL		TL	SN	TL	SN	SN	GX	TL	TL	SN		GX	TL	TL	SN	TL	SN
London Victoria	d	11 55	12 00			12 06	12 14				12 16		12 25	12 25	12 30			12 36		12 44			12 46		12 55
Clapham Junction	d	12 02				12 13					12 23		12 32	12 32				12 43					12 53		13 02
East Croydon	a	12 11				12 22					12 32		12 41					12 52					13 02		13 11
St Pancras International	d			11 45	11 50					12 00		12 05				12 15	12 20					12 30		12 35	
Farringdon	d			11 49	11 54					12 04		12 09				12 19	12 24					12 34		12 39	
City Thameslink	d			11 51	11 56					12 06		12 11				12 21	12 26					12 36		12 41	
London Blackfriars	d			11 54	11 59					12 09		12 14				12 24	12 29					12 39		12 44	
London Bridge	d			12 00	12 05					12 15		12 21				12 30	12 35					12 45		12 51	
East Croydon	a			12 14	12 18					12 28		12 36				12 44	12 48					12 58		13 06	
East Croydon	d	12 11		12 16	12 19	12 23		←		12 29	12 33	12 37	12 41			12 46	12 49	12 53			←	12 59	13 03	13 07	13 11
Gatwick Airport	a	12 26	12 30	12 43	12 34	12 38	12 41	12 43		12 44	12 47	13 08	12 56		13 00	13 13	13 04	13 08		13 11	13 13	13 14	13 17	13 38	13 26
Three Bridges	a			→	12 39	12 44		12 49		12 49						→	13 09	13 14			13 19	13 19			
Crawley	a					12 48		12 53										13 18			13 23				
Horsham	a					12 57		13 08						13 43				13 27			13 38				

		GX	TL	TL		SN	GX	TL	TL	SN	TL	SN	SN	GX		TL	TL	SN	GX	TL	TL	SN	TL	SN	
London Victoria	d	13 00				13 06	13 14			13 16		13 25	13 25	13 30				13 36	13 44			13 46		13 55	
Clapham Junction	d					13 13				13 23		13 32	13 32					13 43				13 53		14 02	
East Croydon	a					13 22				13 32		13 41						13 52				14 02		14 11	
St Pancras International	d		12 45	12 50					13 00		13 05					13 15	13 20				13 30		13 35		
Farringdon	d		12 49	12 54					13 04		13 09					13 19	13 24				13 34		13 39		
City Thameslink	d		12 51	12 56					13 06		13 11					13 21	13 26				13 36		13 41		
London Blackfriars	d		12 54	12 59					13 09		13 14					13 24	13 29				13 39		13 44		
London Bridge	d		13 00	13 05					13 15		13 21					13 30	13 35				13 45		13 51		
East Croydon	a		13 14	13 18					13 28		13 36					13 44	13 48				13 58		14 06		
East Croydon	d		13 16	13 19		13 23		←	13 29	13 33	13 37	13 41				13 46	13 49	13 53		←	13 59	14 03	14 07	14 11	
Gatwick Airport	a	13 30	13 43	13 34		13 38	13 41	13 43	13 44	13 47	14 08	13 56		14 00		14 13	14 04	14 08	14 11	14 13	14 14	14 17	14 38	14 26	
Three Bridges	a		→	13 39		13 44		13 49	13 49							→	14 09	14 14		14 19	14 19				
Crawley	a					13 48		13 53										14 18		14 23					
Horsham	a					13 57		14 08					14 43					14 27		14 38					

		GX	TL	TL	SN	GX	TL	TL	SN	TL		SN	SN	GX	TL	TL	SN	GX	TL	TL		SN	TL	SN	GX
London Victoria	d	14 00			14 06	14 14			14 16			14 25	14 25	14 30			14 36	14 44				14 46		14 55	15 00
Clapham Junction	d				14 13				14 23			14 32	14 32				14 43					14 53		15 02	
East Croydon	a				14 22				14 32			14 41					14 53					15 02		15 11	
St Pancras International	d		13 45	13 50				14 00		14 05					14 15	14 20				14 30			14 35		
Farringdon	d		13 49	13 54				14 04		14 09					14 19	14 24				14 34			14 39		
City Thameslink	d		13 51	13 56				14 06		14 11					14 21	14 26				14 36			14 41		
London Blackfriars	d		13 54	13 59				14 09		14 14					14 24	14 29				14 39			14 44		
London Bridge	d		14 00	14 05				14 15		14 21					14 30	14 35				14 45			14 51		
East Croydon	a		14 14	14 18				14 28		14 36					14 44	14 48				14 58			15 06		
East Croydon	d		14 16	14 19	14 23		←	14 29	14 33	14 37		14 41			14 46	14 49	14 53		←	14 59		15 03	15 07	15 11	
Gatwick Airport	a	14 30	14 43	14 34	14 38	14 41	14 43	14 44	14 47	15 08		14 56		15 00	15 13	15 04	15 08	15 11	15 13	15 14		15 17	15 38	15 26	15 30
Three Bridges	a		→	14 39	14 44		14 49	14 49							→	15 09	15 14		15 19	15 19					
Crawley	a				14 48		14 53										15 18		15 23						
Horsham	a				14 57		15 08						15 43				15 27		15 38						

Table T185-F

Mondays to Fridays

16 December to 15 May

London - Gatwick Airport - Three Bridges - Horsham : Summary of Fast Trains

		TL 1		TL 1	SN 1	GX 1	TL 1	TL 1	SN 1	TL 1	SN 1	SN		GX 1	TL 1	TL 1	SN 1	GX 1	TL 1	TL 1	SN 1	TL 1		SN 1	GX 1
London Victoria	d				15 06	15 14			15 16		15 25	15 25		15 30			15 36	15 44			15 46			15 55	16 00
Clapham Junction	d				15 13				15 23		15 32	15 32					15 43				15 53			16 02	
East Croydon	a				15 22				15 32		15 41						15 52				16 02			16 11	
St Pancras International	d	14 45		14 50				15 00		15 05					15 15	15 20				15 30		15 35			
Farringdon	d	14 49		14 54				15 04		15 09					15 19	15 24				15 34		15 39			
City Thameslink	d	14 51		14 56				15 06		15 11					15 21	15 26				15 36		15 41			
London Blackfriars	d	14 54		14 59				15 09		15 14					15 24	15 29				15 39		15 44			
London Bridge	d	15 00		15 05				15 15		15 21					15 30	15 35				15 45		15 51			
East Croydon	a	15 14		15 18				15 28		15 36					15 44	15 48				15 58		16 06			
East Croydon	d	15 16		15 19	15 23		←	15 29	15 33	15 37	15 41				15 46	15 49	15 53		←	15 59	16 03	16 07		16 11	
Gatwick Airport	a	15 43		15 34	15 38	15 41	15 43	15 44	15 47	16 08	15 56			16 00	16 13	16 04	16 08	16 11	16 13	16 14	16 17	16 38		16 26	16 30
Three Bridges	a	→		15 39	15 44		15 49	15 49							→	16 09	16 14		16 19	16 19					
Crawley	a				15 48		15 53										16 18		16 23						
Horsham	a				15 57		16 08					16 43					16 27		16 38						

		TL 1	TL 1	SN 1	SN 1	GX 1	TL 1	TL 1		SN 1	TL 1	SN 1	SN	GX 1	TL 1	TL 1	SN 1	SN 1		GX 1	TL 1	TL 1	SN 1	TL 1	SN 1
London Victoria	d			16 06	16 09	16 14				16 16		16 25	16 25	16 29			16 36	16 39		16 43			16 45		16 54
Clapham Junction	d			16 13	16 16					16 23		16 32	16 32				16 43	16 46					16 52		17 02
East Croydon	a			16 23	16 26					16 32		16 41					16 52	16 56					17 01		17 11
St Pancras International	d	15 45	15 50					16 00			16 05				16 15	16 20					16 30			16 35	
Farringdon	d	15 49	15 54					16 04			16 09				16 19	16 24					16 34			16 39	
City Thameslink	d	15 51	15 56					16 06			16 11				16 21	16 26					16 36			16 41	
London Blackfriars	d	15 54	15 59					16 09			16 14				16 24	16 29					16 39			16 44	
London Bridge	d	16 00	16 05					16 15			16 21				16 30	16 35					16 45			16 51	
East Croydon	a	16 14	16 19					16 29			16 36				16 44	16 49					16 59			17 06	
East Croydon	d	16 16	16 20	16 23	16 27		←	16 29		16 33	16 37	16 41			16 46	16 50	16 53	16 57			16 59	←	17 02	17 07	17 11
Gatwick Airport	a	16 43	16 35	16 38	17 07	16 41	16 43	16 44		16 47	17 11	16 56		16 59	17 15	17 04	17 08	17 39		17 11	17 14	17 15	17 19	17 41	17 26
Three Bridges	a	→	16 40	16 44			16 49	16 49							→	17 10	17 14				17 19	17 21			
Crawley	a			16 48			16 53										17 18					17 28			
Horsham	a			16 57			17 10						17 47				17 27					17 45			

		TL 1	SN 1	SN		GX 1	TL 1	SN 1	SN 1	GX 1	TL 1	TL 1	SN 1	TL 1		SN 1	SN	GX 1	TL 1	SN 1	TL 1	SN 1	SN 1	SN 1	
London Victoria	d			16 55		16 59		17 06	17 09	17 13			17 15			17 24	17 25	17 29					17 36	17 39	
Clapham Junction	d			17 02				17 13	17 16				17 22			17 32	17 32						17 43	17 46	
East Croydon	a							17 22	17 26				17 31			17 41							17 52	17 56	
St Pancras International	d	16 45					16 50				17 00			17 05					17 15		17 20				
Farringdon	d	16 49					16 54				17 04			17 09					17 19		17 24				
City Thameslink	d	16 51					16 56				17 06			17 11					17 21		17 26				
London Blackfriars	d	16 54					16 59				17 09			17 14					17 24		17 29				
London Bridge	d	17 00	17 02				17 05				17 15			17 21					17 30	17 32	17 35				
East Croydon	a	17 14	17 16				17 19				17 29			17 36					17 45	17 46	17 49				
East Croydon	d	17 16	17 16				17 20	17 23	17 27		17 29	←	17 32	17 37		17 41			17 46	17 47	17 50	←	17 53	17 57	
Gatwick Airport	a	17 45				17 29	17 35	17 38	18 07	17 41	17 44	17 45	17 49	18 11		17 56		17 59	18 15	18 02	18 05	18 07	18 08	18 37	
Three Bridges	a	→	17 35				17 40	17 44	→		17 49	17 51							→		18 10	18 16	18 14	→	
Crawley	a		17 39					17 48				17 56											18 18		
Horsham	a		17 51	18 17				18 01				18 12					18 47						18 27		

		GX 1	TL 1	TL 1	SN 1	TL 1	SN 1	TL 1	SN 1	SN		GX 1	TL 1	SN 1	SN 1	SN 1	GX 1	TL 1	TL 1	SN 1		TL 1	SN 1	SN	GX 1
London Victoria	d	17 43			17 45		17 54			17 55		17 59			18 06	18 09	18 13			18 15			18 24	18 26	18 29
Clapham Junction	d				17 52		18 02			18 02					18 13	18 16				18 22			18 32	18 33	
East Croydon	a				18 01		18 11								18 22	18 27				18 31			18 41		
St Pancras International	d		17 30			17 35		17 45					17 50					18 00				18 05			
Farringdon	d		17 34			17 39		17 49					17 54					18 04				18 09			
City Thameslink	d		17 36			17 41		17 51					17 56					18 06				18 11			
London Blackfriars	d		17 39			17 44		17 54					17 59					18 09				18 14			
London Bridge	d		17 45			17 51		18 00	18 03				18 05					18 15				18 21			
East Croydon	a		17 59			18 06		18 14	18 16				18 19					18 29				18 36			
East Croydon	d		17 59	←	18 02	18 07	18 11	18 16	18 17				18 20	←	18 23	18 27		18 29	←	18 32		18 37	18 41		
Gatwick Airport	a	18 11	18 14	18 15	18 19	18 41	18 26	18 45				18 29	18 35	18 37	18 38	19 07	18 41	18 44	18 45	18 49		19 11	18 56		18 59
Three Bridges	a		18 19	18 21				→	18 35				18 40	18 43	18 44	→		18 49	18 51						
Crawley	a			18 26					18 39						18 48				18 56						
Horsham	a			18 42					18 51	19 15					19 01				19 12					19 45	

		TL 1	SN 1	TL 1	SN 1	SN 1		SN 1	GX 1	TL 1	TL 1	SN 1	TL 1	SN 1	GX 1	TL 1		TL 1	SN 1	SN 1	SN 1	GX 1	TL 1	TL 1	SN 1
London Victoria	d					18 36		18 39	18 43			18 45		18 54	18 59					19 06	19 09	19 14			19 16
Clapham Junction	d					18 43		18 46				18 52		19 02						19 13	19 16				19 23
East Croydon	a					18 52		18 57				19 01		19 11						19 22	19 27				19 32
St Pancras International	d	18 15		18 20						18 30			18 35			18 45		18 50					19 00		
Farringdon	d	18 19		18 24						18 34			18 39			18 49		18 54					19 04		
City Thameslink	d	18 21		18 26						18 36			18 41			18 51		18 56					19 06		
London Blackfriars	d	18 24		18 29						18 39			18 44			18 54		18 59					19 09		
London Bridge	d	18 30	18 32	18 35						18 45			18 51			19 00		19 05					19 15		
East Croydon	a	18 44	18 46	18 49						18 59			19 06			19 14		19 19					19 29		
East Croydon	d	18 46	18 47	18 50	←	18 53		18 57		18 59	←	19 02	19 07	19 11		19 16		19 20	←	19 23	19 27		19 29	←	19 33
Gatwick Airport	a	19 15	19 02	19 05	19 07	19 08		19 37	19 11	19 14	19 15	19 19	19 41	19 26	19 29	19 45		19 35	19 37	19 38	20 07	19 41	19 44	19 45	19 47
Three Bridges	a	→		19 10	19 16	19 14		→		19 19	19 21					→		19 40	19 46	19 44	→		19 49	19 51	
Crawley	a					19 18					19 26									19 48				19 56	
Horsham	a					19 27					19 42									19 57				20 12	

NRT DECEMBER 19 EDITION

Table T185-F

Mondays to Fridays

16 December to 15 May

London - Gatwick Airport - Three Bridges - Horsham : Summary of Fast Trains

		TL 1	SN 1	SN	GX 1	TL 1	TL 1	SN 1		SN 1	GX 1	TL 1	TL 1	SN 1	TL 1	SN 1	GX 1	TL 1		TL 1	SN 1	GX 1	TL 1	TL 1	SN 1
London Victoria	d		19 25	19 25	19 30					19 36	19 44			19 46		19 55	20 00				20 06	20 14			20 16
Clapham Junction	d		19 32	19 32						19 43				19 53		20 02					20 13				20 23
East Croydon	a		19 41							19 52				20 02		20 11					20 22				20 32
St Pancras International	d	19 05				19 15	19 20					19 30			19 35			19 45		19 50				20 00	
Farringdon	d	19 09				19 19	19 24					19 34			19 39			19 49		19 54				20 04	
City Thameslink	d	19 11				19 21	19 26					19 36			19 41			19 51		19 56				20 06	
London Blackfriars	d	19 14				19 24	19 29					19 39			19 44			19 54		19 59				20 09	
London Bridge	d	19 21				19 30	19 35					19 45			19 51			20 00		20 05				20 15	
East Croydon	a	19 36				19 44	19 48					19 58			20 06			20 14		20 18				20 28	
East Croydon	d	19 37	19 41			19 46	19 49	←		19 53		19 59	←	20 03	20 07	20 11		20 16		20 19	20 23		←	20 29	20 33
Gatwick Airport	a	20 11	19 56		20 00	20 14	20 04	20 07		20 08	20 11	20 14	20 14	20 17	20 38	20 26	20 30	20 43		20 34	20 38	20 41	20 43	20 44	20 47
Three Bridges	a					→	20 09	20 16		20 14		20 19	20 21					→		20 39	20 44		20 49	20 49	
Crawley	a									20 18			20 26								20 48		20 53		
Horsham	a			20 45						20 27			20 39								20 57		21 08		

		TL 1	TL 1	SN 1		SN	GX 1	TL 1	TL 1	SN 1	GX 1	TL 1	SN 1	TL 1		TL 1	SN 1	GX 1	TL 1	TL 1	SN 1	GX 1	TL 1	TL 1	
London Victoria	d			20 25		20 25	20 30			20 36	20 44		20 46				20 55	21 00			21 06	21 14			
Clapham Junction	d			20 32		20 32				20 43			20 53				21 02				21 13				
East Croydon	a			20 41						20 52			21 02				21 11				21 24				
St Pancras International	d	20 05						20 15	20 20					20 35					20 45	20 50				21 00	
Farringdon	d	20 09						20 19	20 24					20 39					20 49	20 54				21 04	
City Thameslink	d	20 11						20 21	20 26					20 41					20 51	20 56				21 06	
London Blackfriars	d	20 14						20 24	20 29					20 44					20 54	20 59				21 09	
London Bridge	d	20 21	20 22					20 30	20 35					20 51		20 52			21 00	21 05				21 15	
East Croydon	a	20 36	20 38					20 44	20 48					21 06		21 08			21 14	21 21				21 28	
East Croydon	d	20 37	20 38	20 41				20 46	20 49	20 53		←	21 03	21 07		21 08	21 11		21 16	21 22	21 25		←	21 30	
Gatwick Airport	a	21 08	20 53	20 56			21 00	21 13	21 04	21 08	21 11	21 13	21 17	21 38		21 23	21 26	21 30	21 43	21 36	21 39	21 42	21 43	21 44	
Three Bridges	a		20 59					→	21 09	21 14		21 19				21 29			→	21 41	21 45		21 49	21 49	
Crawley	a		21 04							21 18		21 23									21 49		21 53		
Horsham	a		21 13			21 43				21 27		21 38									21 58		22 08		

		SN 1	TL 1	TL 1	SN 1	SN	GX 1	TL 1	TL 1	SN 1		GX 1	TL 1	SN 1	TL 1	SN 1	GX 1	TL 1	TL 1	SN 1		GX 1	TL 1	TL 1	SN 1
London Victoria	d	21 16			21 25	21 25	21 30			21 36		21 44		21 46		21 55	22 00			22 06		22 14			22 16
Clapham Junction	d	21 23			21 32	21 32				21 43				21 53		22 02				22 13					22 23
East Croydon	a	21 32			21 41					21 52				22 02		22 11				22 22					22 32
St Pancras International	d		21 05					21 15	21 20						21 35			21 45	21 50					22 00	
Farringdon	d		21 09					21 19	21 24						21 39			21 49	21 54					22 04	
City Thameslink	d		21 11					21 21	21 26						21 41			21 51	21 56					22 06	
London Blackfriars	d		21 14					21 24	21 29						21 44			21 54	21 59					22 09	
London Bridge	d		21 21	21 22				21 30	21 35						21 51			22 00	22 05					22 15	
East Croydon	a		21 36	21 38				21 44	21 48						22 06			22 14	22 18					22 28	
East Croydon	d	21 33	21 37	21 38	21 41			21 46	21 49	21 53			←	22 03	22 07	22 11		22 16	22 19	22 23			←	22 29	22 33
Gatwick Airport	a	21 47	22 08	21 53	21 56		22 00	22 13	22 04	22 08		22 11	22 13	22 17	22 38	22 26	22 30	22 43	22 34	22 38		22 41	22 43	22 44	22 47
Three Bridges	a							→	22 09	22 14			22 19					→	22 39	22 44			22 49	22 49	
Crawley	a									22 18			22 23							22 48			22 53		
Horsham	a					22 43				22 27			22 38							22 57			23 08		

		TL 1	SN 1	SN	TL 1	TL 1		SN 1	GX 1	TL 1	SN 1	TL 1	SN 1	TL 1	TL 1	TL 1		SN 1	TL 1	TL 1	SN 1	TL 1	SN 1	TL 1	TL 1
London Victoria	d		22 25	22 25				22 36	22 44		22 46		22 56					23 06			23 16		23 25		
Clapham Junction	d		22 32	22 32				22 43			22 53		23 03					23 13			23 23		23 32		
East Croydon	a		22 41					22 52			23 02		23 12					23 22			23 32		23 41		
St Pancras International	d	22 05			22 15	22 20						22 35		22 45	22 50					23 00		23 05		23 15	23 22
Farringdon	d	22 09			22 19	22 24						22 39		22 49	22 54					23 04		23 10		23 19	23 27
City Thameslink	d	22 11			22 21	22 26						22 41		22 51	22 56										
London Blackfriars	d	22 14			22 24	22 29						22 44		22 54	22 59					23 09		23 14		23 24	23 31
London Bridge	d	22 21			22 30	22 35						22 51		23 00	23 05					23 15		23 21		23 30	23 37
East Croydon	a	22 36			22 44	22 48						23 06		23 15	23 18					23 28		23 36		23 44	23 50
East Croydon	d	22 37	22 41		22 46	22 49		22 53		←	23 03	23 07	23 12	23 16	23 19	←		23 23	←	23 29	23 33	23 37	23 43	23 46	23 51
Gatwick Airport	a	23 08	22 56		23 12	23 04		23 08	23 11	23 12	23 17	23 37	23 27	23 41	23 34	23 37		23 38	23 41	23 47	23 52	00 01	00 03	00 12	00 18
Three Bridges	a				→	23 09		23 14		23 19		→		→	23 39	23 43		23 44	23 47	23 53				00 19	00 24
Crawley	a							23 18		23 23								23 48	23 53					00 23	
Horsham	a			23 43				23 27		23 38								23 57	00 06					00 36	

		SN		SN 1	TL 1
London Victoria	d	23 25		23 36	
Clapham Junction	d	23 32		23 43	
East Croydon	a			23 58	
St Pancras International	d				23 51
Farringdon	d				23 56
City Thameslink	d				
London Blackfriars	d				00 02
London Bridge	d				
East Croydon	a				00 27
East Croydon	d			23 59	00 28
Gatwick Airport	a			00 29	00 47
Three Bridges	a			00 36	00 53
Crawley	a			00 40	
Horsham	a	00 48		00 49	

Table T185-F

Saturdays

21 December to 16 May

London - Gatwick Airport - Three Bridges - Horsham : Summary of Fast Trains

Station		SN A	SN A	TL	TL	SN		TL	SN	TL	SN	TL	TL	SN	TL	SN		TL	GX	TL	SN	GX	GX	TL	GX
London Victoria	d	00 02	00 08			01 10			02 10		03 10			04 10		04 30			05 00		05 08	05 15	05 30		05 44
Clapham Junction	d	00 09	00 15			01 17			02 17		03 17			04 17		04 38					05 16				
East Croydon	a	00 23	00 30			01 32			02 32		03 32			04 31							05 31				
St Pancras International	d			00 21	00 52			01 32		02 32		03 02	03 32		04 02			04 32		04 51				05 20	
Farringdon	d			00 26																04 56				05 24	
City Thameslink	d																								
London Blackfriars	d			00 31	01 02			01 40		02 40		03 10	03 40		04 10			04 40		05 01				05 29	
London Bridge	d																							05 35	
East Croydon	a			00 57	01 28			02 06		03 06		03 36	04 06		04 36			05 06		05 27				05 48	
East Croydon	d	00 24	00 31	00 58	01 28	01 33		02 07	02 32	03 07	03 32	03 37	04 07	04 31	04 37			05 07		05 28	05 31			05 49	
Gatwick Airport	a	00 43	01 03	01 20	01 56	02 06		02 30	02 55	03 30	03 55	03 58	04 30	04 59	05 02	05 12		05 31	05 37	05 47	06 00	05 49	06 01	06 04	06 11
Three Bridges	a	00 48		01 26	02 03	02 18		02 36	03 01	03 36	04 01	04 05	04 40	05 05	05 09			05 36		05 53	06 06			06 09	
Crawley	a																								
Horsham	a																								

Station		GX		TL	TL	SN	GX	TL	TL	GX	TL	TL		SN	GX	TL	SN	GX	TL	TL	SN	GX		TL	TL
London Victoria	d	06 00				06 06	06 14			06 30				06 36	06 44		06 55	07 00			07 06	07 14			
Clapham Junction	d					06 13								06 43			07 02				07 13				
East Croydon	a					06 22								06 52			07 11				07 22				
St Pancras International	d			05 45	05 50			06 00			06 15	06 20							06 45	06 50					07 00
Farringdon	d			05 49	05 54			06 04			06 19	06 24							06 49	06 54					07 04
City Thameslink	d																								
London Blackfriars	d			05 54	05 59			06 09			06 24	06 29							06 54	06 59					07 09
London Bridge	d			06 00	06 05			06 15			06 30	06 35							07 00	07 05					07 15
East Croydon	a			06 14	06 18			06 28			06 44	06 48							07 14	07 18					07 28
East Croydon	d			06 16	06 19	06 23		06 29	←		06 46	06 49		06 53		←	07 11		07 16	07 19	07 23			←	07 29
Gatwick Airport	a	06 30		06 50	06 34	06 38	06 41	06 44	06 50	07 00	07 12	07 04		07 08	07 11	07 12	07 26	07 30	07 42	07 34	07 38	07 41		07 42	07 44
Three Bridges	a			→	06 39	06 44		06 49	06 56		→	07 09		07 14		07 19			→	07 39	07 44			07 49	07 49
Crawley	a					06 48			07 02					07 18		07 23					07 48			07 53	
Horsham	a					06 57			07 14					07 27		07 38					07 57			08 08	

Station		TL	SN	SN	GX	TL	TL	SN		GX	TL	SN	TL	SN	GX	TL	TL	SN		GX	TL	TL	SN	TL	SN
London Victoria	d		07 25	07 25	07 30			07 36		07 44		07 46		07 55	08 00			08 06		08 14			08 16		08 25
Clapham Junction	d		07 32	07 32				07 43				07 53		08 02				08 13					08 23		08 32
East Croydon	a		07 41					07 52				08 02		08 11				08 22					08 32		08 41
St Pancras International	d	07 05				07 15	07 20						07 35			07 45	07 50					08 00		08 05	
Farringdon	d	07 09				07 19	07 24						07 39			07 49	07 54					08 04		08 09	
City Thameslink	d																								
London Blackfriars	d	07 14				07 24	07 29						07 44			07 54	07 59					08 09		08 14	
London Bridge	d	07 21				07 30	07 35						07 51			08 00	08 05					08 15		08 21	
East Croydon	a	07 36				07 44	07 48						08 06			08 14	08 18					08 28		08 36	
East Croydon	d	07 37	07 41			07 46	07 49	07 53			←	08 03	08 07	08 11		08 16	08 19	08 23			←	08 29	08 33	08 37	08 41
Gatwick Airport	a	08 08	07 56		08 00	08 12	08 04	08 08		08 11	08 12	08 18	08 38	08 26	08 30	08 42	08 34	08 38		08 41	08 42	08 44	08 47	09 08	08 56
Three Bridges	a					→	08 09	08 14			08 19					→	08 39	08 44			08 49	08 49			
Crawley	a							08 18			08 23							08 48			08 53				
Horsham	a			08 43				08 27			08 38							08 57			09 08				

Station		SN	GX	TL		TL	SN	GX	TL	SN	TL	SN	GX	TL		TL	SN	GX	TL	TL	SN	TL	SN	SN	
London Victoria	d	08 25	08 30				08 36	08 44		08 46		08 55	09 00				09 06	09 14			09 16		09 25	09 25	
Clapham Junction	d	08 32					08 43			08 53		09 02					09 13				09 23		09 32	09 32	
East Croydon	a						08 52			09 02		09 11					09 22				09 32		09 41		
St Pancras International	d			08 15		08 20					08 35			08 45		08 50				09 00		09 05			
Farringdon	d			08 19		08 24					08 39			08 49		08 54				09 04		09 09			
City Thameslink	d																			09 06		09 11			
London Blackfriars	d			08 24		08 29					08 44			08 54		08 59				09 09		09 14			
London Bridge	d			08 30		08 35					08 51			09 00		09 05				09 15		09 21			
East Croydon	a			08 44		08 48					09 06			09 14		09 18				09 28		09 36			
East Croydon	d			08 46		08 49	08 53		←	09 03	09 07	09 11		09 16		09 19	09 23		←	09 29	09 33	09 37	09 41		
Gatwick Airport	a		09 00	09 12		09 04	09 08	09 11	09 12	09 18	09 38	09 26	09 30	09 42		09 34	09 38	09 41	09 42	09 44	09 47	10 08	09 56		
Three Bridges	a			→		09 09	09 14		09 19					→		09 39	09 44		09 49	09 49					
Crawley	a						09 18		09 23								09 48		09 53						
Horsham	a	09 43					09 27		09 38								09 57		10 08					10 43	

Station		GX	TL	TL	SN	GX	TL	SN	TL	SN		GX	TL	TL	SN	GX	TL	TL	SN	TL		SN	SN	GX	TL
London Victoria	d	09 30			09 36	09 44		09 46		09 55		10 00			10 06	10 14			10 16			10 25	10 25	10 30	
Clapham Junction	d				09 43			09 53		10 02					10 13				10 23			10 32	10 32		
East Croydon	a				09 52			10 02		10 11					10 22				10 32			10 41			
St Pancras International	d		09 15	09 20					09 35				09 45	09 50				10 00		10 05					10 15
Farringdon	d		09 19	09 24					09 39				09 49	09 54				10 04		10 09					10 19
City Thameslink	d		09 21	09 26					09 41				09 51	09 56				10 06		10 11					10 21
London Blackfriars	d		09 24	09 29					09 44				09 54	09 59				10 09		10 14					10 24
London Bridge	d		09 30	09 35					09 51				10 00	10 05				10 15		10 21					10 30
East Croydon	a		09 44	09 48					10 06				10 14	10 18				10 28		10 36					10 44
East Croydon	d		09 46	09 49	09 53		←	10 03	10 07	10 11			10 16	10 19	10 23		←	10 29	10 33	10 37		10 41			10 46
Gatwick Airport	a	10 00	10 12	10 04	10 08	10 11	10 12	10 18	10 38	10 26		10 30	10 42	10 34	10 38	10 41	10 42	10 44	10 47	11 08		10 56		11 00	11 12
Three Bridges	a		→	10 09	10 14		10 19						→	10 39	10 44		10 49	10 49							→
Crawley	a				10 18		10 23								10 48		10 53								
Horsham	a				10 27		10 38								10 57		11 08						11 43		

A not 16 May

Table T185-F

Saturdays

21 December to 16 May

London - Gatwick Airport - Three Bridges - Horsham : Summary of Fast Trains

Station		TL		SN	GX	TL	SN	TL	SN	GX	TL	TL		SN	GX	TL	TL	SN	TL	SN	SN	GX		TL	TL
London Victoria	d			10 36	10 44		10 46		10 55	11 00				11 06	11 14			11 16		11 25	11 25	11 30			
Clapham Junction	d			10 43			10 53		11 02					11 13				11 23		11 32	11 32				
East Croydon	a			10 52			11 02		11 11					11 22				11 32		11 41					
St Pancras International	d	10 20						10 35			10 45	10 50					11 00		11 05					11 15	11 20
Farringdon	d	10 24						10 39			10 49	10 54					11 04		11 09					11 19	11 24
City Thameslink	d	10 26						10 41			10 51	10 56					11 06		11 11					11 21	11 26
London Blackfriars	d	10 29						10 44			10 54	10 59					11 09		11 14					11 24	11 29
London Bridge	d	10 35						10 51			11 00	11 05					11 15		11 21					11 30	11 35
East Croydon	a	10 48						11 06			11 14	11 18					11 28		11 36					11 44	11 48
East Croydon	d	10 49		10 53		←	11 03	11 07	11 11		11 16	11 19		11 23		←	11 29	11 33	11 37	11 41				11 46	11 49
Gatwick Airport	a	11 04		11 08	11 11	11 12	11 18	11 38	11 26	11 30	11 42	11 34		11 38	11 41	11 42	11 44	11 47	12 08	11 56		12 00		12 12	12 04
Three Bridges	a	11 09		11 14		11 19					→	11 39		11 44		11 49	11 49							→	12 09
Crawley	a			11 18		11 23								11 48		11 53									
Horsham	a			11 27		11 38								11 57		12 08					12 43				

Station		SN	GX	TL	SN	TL	SN	GX		TL	TL	SN	GX	TL	TL	SN	TL	SN		SN	GX	TL	TL	SN	GX
London Victoria	d	11 36	11 44		11 46		11 55	12 00				12 06	12 14			12 16		12 25		12 25	12 30			12 36	12 44
Clapham Junction	d	11 43			11 53		12 02					12 13				12 23		12 32		12 32				12 43	
East Croydon	a	11 52			12 02		12 11					12 22				12 32		12 41						12 52	
St Pancras International	d					11 35				11 45	11 50				12 00		12 05					12 15	12 20		
Farringdon	d					11 39				11 49	11 54				12 04		12 09					12 19	12 24		
City Thameslink	d					11 41				11 51	11 56				12 06		12 11					12 21	12 26		
London Blackfriars	d					11 44				11 54	11 59				12 09		12 14					12 24	12 29		
London Bridge	d					11 51				12 00	12 05				12 15		12 21					12 30	12 35		
East Croydon	a					12 06				12 14	12 18				12 28		12 36					12 44	12 48		
East Croydon	d	11 53		←	12 03	12 07	12 11			12 16	12 19	12 23		←	12 29	12 33	12 37	12 41				12 46	12 49	12 53	
Gatwick Airport	a	12 08	12 11	12 12	12 18	12 38	12 26	12 30		12 42	12 34	12 38	12 41	12 42	12 44	12 47	13 08	12 56			13 00	13 12	13 04	13 08	13 11
Three Bridges	a	12 14		12 19						→	12 39	12 44		12 49	12 49							→	13 09	13 14	
Crawley	a	12 18		12 23								12 48		12 53										13 18	
Horsham	a	12 27		12 38								12 57		13 08						13 43				13 27	

Station		TL	SN	TL		SN	GX	TL	TL	SN	GX	TL	TL	SN		TL	SN	SN	GX	TL	TL	SN	GX	TL	
London Victoria	d		12 46			12 55	13 00			13 06	13 14			13 16			13 25	13 25	13 30			13 36	13 44		
Clapham Junction	d		12 53			13 02				13 13				13 23			13 32	13 32				13 43			
East Croydon	a		13 02			13 11				13 22				13 32			13 41					13 52			
St Pancras International	d			12 35				12 45	12 50				13 00			13 05				13 15	13 20				
Farringdon	d			12 39				12 49	12 54				13 04			13 09				13 19	13 24				
City Thameslink	d			12 41				12 51	12 56				13 06			13 11				13 21	13 26				
London Blackfriars	d			12 44				12 54	12 59				13 09			13 14				13 24	13 29				
London Bridge	d			12 51				13 00	13 05				13 15			13 21				13 30	13 35				
East Croydon	a			13 06				13 14	13 18				13 28			13 36				13 44	13 48				
East Croydon	d	←	13 03	13 07		13 11		13 16	13 19	13 23		←	13 29	13 33		13 37	13 41			13 46	13 49	13 53		←	
Gatwick Airport	a	13 12	13 18	13 38		13 26	13 30	13 42	13 34	13 38	13 41	13 42	13 44	13 47		14 08	13 56		14 00	14 12	14 04	14 08	14 11	14 12	
Three Bridges	a	13 19						→	13 39	13 44		13 49	13 49							→	14 09	14 14		14 19	
Crawley	a	13 23								13 48		13 53										14 18		14 23	
Horsham	a	13 38								13 57		14 08						14 43				14 27		14 38	

Station		SN	TL	SN	GX	TL	TL	SN	GX	TL		TL	SN	TL	SN	SN	GX	TL	TL	SN		GX	TL	SN	TL
London Victoria	d	13 46		13 55	14 00			14 06	14 14				14 16		14 25	14 25	14 30			14 36		14 44		14 46	
Clapham Junction	d	13 53		14 02				14 13					14 23		14 32	14 32				14 43				14 53	
East Croydon	a	14 02		14 11				14 22					14 32		14 41					14 52				15 02	
St Pancras International	d		13 35			13 45	13 50					14 00		14 05				14 15	14 20						14 35
Farringdon	d		13 39			13 49	13 54					14 04		14 09				14 19	14 24						14 39
City Thameslink	d		13 41			13 51	13 56					14 06		14 11				14 21	14 26						14 41
London Blackfriars	d		13 44			13 54	13 59					14 09		14 14				14 24	14 29						14 44
London Bridge	d		13 51			14 00	14 05					14 15		14 21				14 30	14 35						14 51
East Croydon	a		14 06			14 14	14 18					14 28		14 36				14 44	14 48						15 06
East Croydon	d	14 03	14 07	14 11		14 16	14 19	14 23		←		14 29	14 33	14 37	14 41			14 46	14 49	14 53			←	15 03	15 07
Gatwick Airport	a	14 18	14 38	14 26	14 30	14 42	14 34	14 38	14 41	14 42		14 44	14 47	15 08	14 56		15 00	15 12	15 04	15 08		15 11	15 12	15 18	15 38
Three Bridges	a					→	14 39	14 44		14 49		14 49						→	15 09	15 14			15 19		
Crawley	a							14 48		14 53										15 18			15 23		
Horsham	a							14 57		15 08						15 43				15 27			15 38		

Station		SN	GX	TL	TL	SN		GX	TL	TL	SN	TL	SN	SN	GX	TL		TL	SN	GX	TL	SN	TL	SN	GX
London Victoria	d	14 55	15 00			15 06		15 14			15 16		15 25	15 25	15 30				15 36	15 44		15 46		15 55	16 00
Clapham Junction	d	15 02				15 13					15 23		15 32	15 32					15 43			15 53		16 02	
East Croydon	a	15 11				15 22					15 32		15 41						15 52			16 02		16 11	
St Pancras International	d			14 45	14 50					15 00		15 05				15 15		15 20					15 35		
Farringdon	d			14 49	14 54					15 04		15 09				15 19		15 24					15 39		
City Thameslink	d			14 51	14 56					15 06		15 11				15 21		15 26					15 41		
London Blackfriars	d			14 54	14 59					15 09		15 14				15 24		15 29					15 44		
London Bridge	d			15 00	15 05					15 15		15 21				15 30		15 35					15 51		
East Croydon	a			15 14	15 18					15 28		15 36				15 44		15 48					16 06		
East Croydon	d	15 11		15 16	15 19	15 23			←	15 29	15 33	15 37	15 41			15 46		15 49	15 53		←	16 03	16 07	16 11	
Gatwick Airport	a	15 26	15 30	15 42	15 34	15 38		15 41	15 42	15 44	15 47	16 08	15 56		16 00	16 12		16 04	16 08	16 11	16 12	16 18	16 38	16 26	16 30
Three Bridges	a			→	15 39	15 44			15 49	15 49						→		16 09	16 14		16 19				
Crawley	a					15 48			15 53										16 18		16 23				
Horsham	a					15 57			16 08					16 43					16 27		16 38				

Table T185-F

Saturdays

21 December to 16 May

London - Gatwick Airport - Three Bridges - Horsham : Summary of Fast Trains

		TL	TL	SN	GX	TL	TL	SN	TL	SN	SN	GX	TL	TL	SN	GX	TL	SN	TL	SN	GX	TL	TL
London Victoria	d			16 06	16 14			16 16		16 25	16 25	16 30			16 36	16 44		16 46		16 55	17 00		
Clapham Junction	d			16 13				16 23		16 32	16 32				16 43			16 53		17 02			
East Croydon	a			16 22				16 32		16 41					16 52			17 02		17 11			
St Pancras International	d	15 45	15 50				16 00		16 05				16 15	16 20					16 35			16 45	16 50
Farringdon	d	15 49	15 54				16 04		16 09				16 19	16 24					16 39			16 49	16 54
City Thameslink	d	15 51	15 56				16 06		16 11				16 21	16 26					16 41			16 51	16 56
London Blackfriars	d	15 54	15 59				16 09		16 14				16 24	16 29					16 44			16 54	16 59
London Bridge	d	16 00	16 05				16 15		16 21				16 30	16 35					16 51			17 00	17 05
East Croydon	a	16 14	16 18				16 28		16 36				16 44	16 48					17 06			17 14	17 18
East Croydon	d	16 16	16 19	16 23		←	16 29	16 33	16 37	16 41			16 46	16 49	16 53		←	17 03	17 07	17 11		17 16	17 19
Gatwick Airport	a	16 42	16 34	16 38	16 41	16 42	16 44	16 47	17 08	16 56		17 00	17 12	17 04	17 08	17 11	17 12	17 18	17 38	17 26	17 30	17 42	17 34
Three Bridges	a	→	16 39	16 44		16 49	16 49						→	17 09	17 14		17 19					→	17 39
Crawley	a			16 48		16 53									17 18		17 23						
Horsham	a			16 57		17 08					17 43				17 27		17 38						

		SN	GX	TL	TL	SN	TL	SN	SN	GX	TL	TL	SN	GX	TL	SN	TL	SN	GX	TL	TL	SN
London Victoria	d	17 06	17 14			17 16		17 25	17 25	17 30			17 36	17 44		17 46		17 55	18 00			18 06
Clapham Junction	d	17 13				17 23		17 32	17 32				17 43			17 53		18 02				18 13
East Croydon	a	17 22				17 32		17 41					17 52			18 02		18 11				18 22
St Pancras International	d				17 00		17 05				17 15	17 20					17 35			17 45	17 50	
Farringdon	d				17 04		17 09				17 19	17 24					17 39			17 49	17 54	
City Thameslink	d				17 06		17 11				17 21	17 26					17 41			17 51	17 56	
London Blackfriars	d				17 09		17 14				17 24	17 29					17 44			17 54	17 59	
London Bridge	d				17 15		17 21				17 30	17 35					17 51			18 00	18 05	
East Croydon	a				17 28		17 36				17 44	17 48					18 06			18 14	18 18	
East Croydon	d	17 23		←	17 29	17 33	17 37	17 41			17 46	17 49	17 53		←	18 03	18 07	18 11		18 16	18 19	18 23
Gatwick Airport	a	17 38	17 41	17 42	17 44	17 47	18 08	17 56		18 00	18 12	18 04	18 08	18 11	18 12	18 18	18 38	18 26	18 30	18 42	18 34	18 38
Three Bridges	a	17 44		17 49	17 49						→	18 09	18 14		18 19					→	18 39	18 44
Crawley	a	17 48		17 53									18 18		18 23							18 48
Horsham	a	17 57		18 08					18 43				18 27		18 38							18 57

		GX	TL	TL	SN	TL	SN	GX	TL	TL	SN	GX	TL	SN	TL	SN	GX	TL	TL	SN	GX	TL	TL
London Victoria	d	18 14			18 16		18 25	18 30			18 36	18 44		18 46		18 55	19 00			19 06	19 14		
Clapham Junction	d				18 23		18 32				18 43			18 53		19 02				19 13			
East Croydon	a				18 32		18 41				18 52			19 02		19 11				19 22			
St Pancras International	d			18 00		18 05			18 15	18 20					18 35			18 45	18 50				19 00
Farringdon	d			18 04		18 09			18 19	18 24					18 39			18 49	18 54				19 04
City Thameslink	d			18 06		18 11			18 21	18 26					18 41			18 51	18 56				19 06
London Blackfriars	d			18 09		18 14			18 24	18 29					18 44			18 54	18 59				19 09
London Bridge	d			18 15		18 21			18 30	18 35					18 51			19 00	19 05				19 15
East Croydon	a			18 28		18 36			18 44	18 48					19 06			19 14	19 18				19 28
East Croydon	d		←	18 29	18 33	18 37	18 41		18 46	18 49	18 53		←	19 03	19 07	19 11		19 16	19 19	19 23		←	19 29
Gatwick Airport	a	18 41	18 42	18 44	18 47	19 08	18 56	19 00	19 12	19 04	19 08	19 11	19 12	19 18	19 38	19 26	19 30	19 42	19 34	19 38	19 41	19 42	19 44
Three Bridges	a		18 49	18 49					→	19 09	19 14		19 19					→	19 39	19 44		19 49	19 49
Crawley	a		18 53								19 18		19 23							19 48		19 53	
Horsham	a		19 08								19 27		19 38							19 57		20 08	

		SN	TL	SN	GX	TL	TL	SN	GX	TL	SN	TL	SN	GX	TL	TL	SN	GX	TL	TL	SN	TL	SN
London Victoria	d	19 16		19 25	19 30			19 36	19 44		19 46		19 55	20 00			20 06	20 14			20 16		20 25
Clapham Junction	d	19 23		19 32				19 43			19 53		20 02				20 13				20 23		20 32
East Croydon	a	19 32		19 41				19 52			20 02		20 11				20 22				20 32		20 41
St Pancras International	d		19 05			19 15	19 20					19 35			19 45	19 50				20 00		20 05	
Farringdon	d		19 09			19 19	19 24					19 39			19 49	19 54				20 04		20 09	
City Thameslink	d		19 11			19 21	19 26					19 41			19 51	19 56				20 06		20 11	
London Blackfriars	d		19 14			19 24	19 29					19 44			19 54	19 59				20 09		20 14	
London Bridge	d		19 21			19 30	19 35					19 51			20 00	20 05				20 15		20 21	
East Croydon	a		19 36			19 44	19 48					20 06			20 14	20 18				20 28		20 36	
East Croydon	d	19 33	19 37	19 41		19 46	19 49	19 53		←	20 03	20 07	20 11		20 16	20 19	20 23		←	20 29	20 33	20 37	20 41
Gatwick Airport	a	19 47	20 08	19 56	20 00	20 12	20 04	20 08	20 11	20 12	20 18	20 38	20 26	20 30	20 42	20 34	20 38	20 41	20 42	20 44	20 47	21 08	20 56
Three Bridges	a					→	20 09	20 14		20 19					→	20 39	20 44		20 49	20 49			
Crawley	a							20 18		20 23							20 48		20 53				
Horsham	a							20 27		20 38							20 57		21 08				

		GX	TL	TL	SN	GX	TL	SN	TL	SN	GX	TL	TL	SN	GX	TL	TL	SN	TL	SN	GX	TL
London Victoria	d	20 30			20 36	20 44		20 46		20 55	21 00			21 06	21 14			21 16		21 25	21 30	
Clapham Junction	d				20 43			20 53		21 02				21 13				21 23		21 32		
East Croydon	a				20 52			21 02		21 11				21 22				21 32		21 41		
St Pancras International	d		20 15	20 20					20 35			20 45	20 50				21 00		21 05			21 15
Farringdon	d		20 19	20 24					20 39			20 49	20 54				21 04		21 09			21 19
City Thameslink	d		20 21	20 26					20 41			20 51	20 56									
London Blackfriars	d		20 24	20 29					20 44			20 54	20 59				21 09		21 14			21 24
London Bridge	d		20 30	20 35					20 51			21 00	21 05				21 15		21 21			21 30
East Croydon	a		20 44	20 48					21 06			21 14	21 18				21 28		21 36			21 44
East Croydon	d		20 46	20 49	20 53		←	21 03	21 07	21 11		21 16	21 19	21 23		←	21 29	21 33	21 37	21 41		21 46
Gatwick Airport	a	21 00	21 12	21 04	21 08	21 11	21 12	21 18	21 38	21 26	21 30	21 42	21 34	21 38	21 41	21 42	21 44	21 47	22 08	21 56	22 00	22 12
Three Bridges	a		→	21 09	21 14		21 19					→	21 39	21 44		21 49	21 49					→
Crawley	a				21 18		21 23							21 48		21 53						
Horsham	a				21 27		21 38							21 57		22 08						

Table T185-F

Saturdays

21 December to 16 May

London - Gatwick Airport - Three Bridges - Horsham : Summary of Fast Trains

		TL	SN	GX	TL	SN	TL	SN	GX	TL	TL	SN	GX	TL	TL	SN	TL	SN	TL	TL	SN	GX
London Victoria	d		21 36	21 44		21 46		21 55	22 00			22 06	22 14			22 16		22 25			22 36	22 44
Clapham Junction	d		21 43			21 53		22 02				22 13				22 23		22 32			22 43	
East Croydon	a		21 52			22 02		22 11				22 22				22 32		22 41			22 52	
St Pancras International	d	21 20					21 35			21 45	21 50				22 00		22 05		22 15	22 20		
Farringdon	d	21 24					21 39			21 49	21 54				22 04		22 09		22 19	22 24		
City Thameslink	d																					
London Blackfriars	d	21 29					21 44			21 54	21 59				22 09		22 14		22 24	22 29		
London Bridge	d	21 35					21 51			22 00	22 05				22 15		22 21		22 30	22 35		
East Croydon	a	21 48					22 06			22 14	22 18				22 28		22 36		22 44	22 48		
East Croydon	d	21 49	21 53		←	22 03	22 07	22 11		22 16	22 19	22 23		←	22 29	22 33	22 37	22 41	22 46	22 49	22 53	
Gatwick Airport	a	22 04	22 07	22 11	22 12	22 18	22 38	22 26	22 30	22 42	22 34	22 38	22 41	22 42	22 44	22 47	23 08	22 56	23 12	23 04	23 08	23 11
Three Bridges	a	22 09	22 14		22 19					→	22 39	22 44		22 49	22 49				→	23 09	23 14	
Crawley	a		22 18		22 23							22 48		22 53							23 18	
Horsham	a		22 27		22 38							22 57		23 08							23 27	

		TL	SN	TL	SN	TL	TL	TL	SN	TL	TL	SN	TL	SN	TL	TL	SN	TL
London Victoria	d		22 46		22 55				23 06			23 16		23 25			23 36	
Clapham Junction	d		22 53		23 02				23 13			23 23		23 32			23 43	
East Croydon	a		23 02		23 11				23 22			23 32		23 41			23 58	
St Pancras International	d			22 35		22 45	22 50				23 00		23 05		23 15	23 22		23 51
Farringdon	d			22 39		22 49	22 54				23 04		23 10		23 19	23 27		23 56
City Thameslink	d																	
London Blackfriars	d			22 44		22 54	22 59				23 09		23 14		23 24	23 31		00 01
London Bridge	d			22 51		23 00	23 05				23 15		23 21		23 30	23 37		
East Croydon	a			23 06		23 14	23 18				23 28		23 36		23 44	23 50		00 27
East Croydon	d	←	23 03	23 07	23 11	23 16	23 19	←	23 23	←	23 29	23 33	23 37	23 43	23 46	23 51	23 59	00 28
Gatwick Airport	a	23 12	23 18	23 37	23 26	23 42	23 34	23 37	23 38	23 42	23 47	23 52	00 01	00 04	00 12	00 17	00 29	00 47
Three Bridges	a	23 19		→		→	23 39	23 43	23 44	23 49	23 53				00 19	00 23	00 36	00 53
Crawley	a	23 23							23 48	23 53					00 23		00 40	
Horsham	a	23 38							23 57	00 06					00 36		00 49	

Sundays

15 December to 10 May

		SN	SN	TL	TL	TL	SN	SN	SN	SN	GX	SN	GX	SN	GX	GX	SN	GX	TL	SN	TL	GX	TL
				A	B	C																	
London Victoria	d	00 02	00 08				01 08	02 08	03 08	04 10	05 00	05 02	05 30	05 45	06 00	06 30	06 32	07 00		07 02		07 30	
Clapham Junction	d	00 09	00 15				01 17	02 17	03 17	04 17		05 10		05 53			06 40			07 10			
East Croydon	a	00 23	00 31				01 32	02 32	03 31	04 31		05 23		06 08			06 53			07 26			
St Pancras International	d			00 21	00 21	00 51																	
Farringdon	d			00 26	00 26																		
City Thameslink	d																						
London Blackfriars	d			00 31	00 31	01 01																	
London Bridge	d																		07 11		07 19		07 41
East Croydon	a			00 57	00 57	01 27													07 24		07 35		07 54
East Croydon	d	00 24	00 32	00 58	00 58	01 28	01 33	02 32	03 32	04 31		05 24		06 09			06 54		07 25	07 27	07 35		07 55
Gatwick Airport	a	00 43	01 01	01 20	01 28	01 56	02 06	02 55	03 54	04 57	05 36	05 50	06 06	06 32	06 37	07 06	07 23	07 37	07 43	07 52	08 06	08 09	08 14
Three Bridges	a	00 48		01 26	01 33	02 03	02 13	03 01	04 00	05 03		05 56		06 37			07 28		07 50	07 58	08 14		08 19
Crawley	a																				08 18		
Horsham	a																				08 31		

		SN	GX	TL	SN	TL	SN	GX	SN	TL	SN	SN	SN	GX	TL	GX	SN	TL	TL	SN	GX	SN	TL
London Victoria	d	07 32	08 00		08 02		08 14	08 30	08 32			08 46	08 55	09 00		09 14	09 16			09 25	09 30	09 33	
Clapham Junction	d	07 40			08 10		08 21		08 40			08 53	09 02				09 23			09 32		09 40	
East Croydon	a	07 56			08 26		08 39		08 51			09 02	09 11				09 32			09 41		09 49	
St Pancras International	d																						09 26
Farringdon	d																						09 30
City Thameslink	d																						
London Blackfriars	d																						09 35
London Bridge	d			08 11		08 19				08 41					09 11			09 19	09 27				09 41
East Croydon	a			08 24		08 35				08 54					09 24			09 37	09 41				09 54
East Croydon	d	07 57		08 25	08 27	08 37	08 40		08 51	08 55	←	09 03	09 12		09 25		09 33	09 37	09 41	09 42		09 49	09 55
Gatwick Airport	a	08 19	08 39	08 43	08 52	09 07	08 58	09 00	09 13	09 09	09 13	09 18	09 26	09 29	09 39	09 43	09 47	10 02	10 09	09 56	09 59	10 12	10 09
Three Bridges	a	08 24		08 48	08 58	09 14			→	09 14	09 19		09 32		09 44			10 08				→	10 14
Crawley	a	08 28				09 18					09 23							10 12					
Horsham	a	08 37				09 31					09 34							10 25					

		SN	GX	SN	TL	TL	SN	GX	TL	TL	GX	SN	TL	TL	SN	GX	SN	TL	SN	GX	SN	TL
London Victoria	d		09 44	09 46			09 55	10 00			10 14	10 16			10 25	10 30	10 33			10 44	10 46	
Clapham Junction	d			09 53			10 02					10 23			10 32		10 40				10 53	
East Croydon	a			10 02			10 11					10 32			10 41		10 49				11 02	
St Pancras International	d				09 35	09 41			09 56					10 11				10 26				10 35
Farringdon	d				09 39	09 45			10 00					10 15				10 30				10 39
City Thameslink	d																					
London Blackfriars	d				09 44	09 50			10 05					10 20				10 35				10 44
London Bridge	d				09 51	09 56			10 11				10 21	10 26				10 41				10 51
East Croydon	a				10 07	10 10			10 24				10 37	10 40				10 54				11 07
East Croydon	d	←		10 03	10 07	10 11	10 12		10 25	←		10 33	10 37	10 41	10 42		10 49	10 55	←		11 03	11 07
Gatwick Airport	a	10 12	10 13	10 18	10 27	10 42	10 26	10 29	10 39	10 42	10 43	10 47	11 02	11 09	10 56	10 59	11 12	11 09	11 12	11 13	11 18	11 27
Three Bridges	a	10 18				→	10 32		10 44	10 47			11 08				→	11 14	11 18			
Crawley	a	10 22											11 12						11 22			
Horsham	a	10 32											11 25						11 31			

A not 15 December, 5 January

B 5 January

C not 15 December

Table T185-F

Sundays

15 December to 10 May

London - Gatwick Airport - Three Bridges - Horsham : Summary of Fast Trains

		TL	SN	GX	TL	TL	GX	SN	TL	TL	SN	GX	SN	TL	SN	GX	SN	TL	TL	SN	GX	TL
London Victoria	d		10 55	11 00			11 14	11 16			11 25	11 30	11 33			11 44	11 46			11 55	12 00	
Clapham Junction	d		11 02					11 23			11 32		11 40				11 53			12 02		
East Croydon	a		11 11					11 32			11 41		11 49				12 02			12 11		
St Pancras International	d	10 41			10 56					11 11				11 26				11 35	11 41			11 56
Farringdon	d	10 45			11 00					11 15				11 30				11 39	11 45			12 00
City Thameslink	d																					
London Blackfriars	d	10 50			11 05					11 20				11 35				11 44	11 50			12 05
London Bridge	d	10 56			11 11				11 21	11 26				11 41				11 51	11 56			12 11
East Croydon	a	11 10			11 24				11 37	11 40				11 54				12 07	12 10			12 24
East Croydon	d	11 11	11 12		11 25	←		11 33	11 37	11 41	11 42		11 49	11 55	←		12 03	12 07	12 11	12 12		12 25
Gatwick Airport	a	11 42	11 26	11 29	11 39	11 42	11 43	11 47	12 02	12 09	11 56	11 59	12 12	12 09	12 12	12 13	12 18	12 27	12 42	12 26	12 29	12 39
Three Bridges	a	→	11 32		11 44	11 48			12 08				→	12 14	12 18				→	12 32		12 44
Crawley	a								12 12						12 22							
Horsham	a								12 25						12 31							

		TL	GX	SN	TL	TL	SN	GX	SN	TL	SN	GX	SN	TL	TL	SN	GX	TL	TL	GX	SN	TL	TL
London Victoria	d		12 14	12 16			12 25	12 30	12 33			12 44	12 46			12 55	13 00			13 14	13 16		
Clapham Junction	d			12 23			12 32		12 40				12 53			13 02					13 23		
East Croydon	a			12 32			12 41		12 49				13 02			13 12					13 32		
St Pancras International	d					12 11				12 26				12 35	12 41			12 56					13 11
Farringdon	d					12 15				12 30				12 39	12 45			13 00					13 15
City Thameslink	d																						
London Blackfriars	d					12 20				12 35				12 44	12 50			13 05					13 20
London Bridge	d				12 21	12 26				12 41				12 51	12 56			13 11				13 21	13 26
East Croydon	a				12 37	12 40				12 54				13 07	13 10			13 24				13 37	13 40
East Croydon	d	←		12 33	12 37	12 41	12 42		12 49	12 55	←		13 03	13 07	13 11	13 13		13 25	←		13 33	13 37	13 41
Gatwick Airport	a	12 42	12 43	12 47	13 02	13 09	12 56	12 59	13 12	13 09	13 12	13 14	13 18	13 27	13 42	13 27	13 30	13 39	13 42	13 43	13 47	14 02	14 09
Three Bridges	a	12 48			13 08				→	13 14	13 18				→	13 32		13 44	13 47			14 08	
Crawley	a				13 12						13 22											14 12	
Horsham	a				13 25						13 31											14 25	

		SN	GX	SN	TL	SN	GX	SN	TL	TL	SN	GX	TL	TL	GX	SN	TL	TL	SN	GX	SN	TL	SN
London Victoria	d	13 25	13 30	13 33			13 44	13 46			13 55	14 00			14 14	14 16			14 25	14 30	14 33		
Clapham Junction	d	13 32		13 40				13 53			14 02					14 23			14 32		14 40		
East Croydon	a	13 41		13 49				14 02			14 11					14 32			14 41		14 49		
St Pancras International	d				13 26				13 35	13 41			13 56					14 11				14 26	
Farringdon	d				13 30				13 39	13 45			14 00					14 15				14 30	
City Thameslink	d																						
London Blackfriars	d				13 35				13 44	13 50			14 05					14 20				14 35	
London Bridge	d				13 41				13 51	13 56			14 11				14 21	14 26				14 41	
East Croydon	a				13 54				14 07	14 10			14 24				14 37	14 40				14 54	
East Croydon	d	13 42		13 49	13 55	←		14 03	14 07	14 11	14 12		14 25	←		14 33	14 37	14 41	14 42		14 49	14 55	←
Gatwick Airport	a	13 56	13 59	14 12	14 09	14 12	14 13	14 18	14 27	14 42	14 26	14 29	14 39	14 42	14 43	14 47	15 02	15 09	14 56	14 59	15 12	15 09	15 12
Three Bridges	a			→	14 14	14 18				→	14 32		14 44	14 47			15 08				→	15 14	15 18
Crawley	a					14 22											15 12						15 22
Horsham	a					14 31											15 25						15 31

		GX	SN	TL	TL	SN	GX	TL	TL	GX	SN	TL	TL	SN	GX	SN	TL	SN	GX	SN	TL	TL
London Victoria	d	14 44	14 46			14 55	15 00			15 14	15 16			15 25	15 30	15 33			15 44	15 46		
Clapham Junction	d		14 53			15 02					15 23			15 32		15 40				15 53		
East Croydon	a		15 02			15 11					15 32			15 41		15 49				16 02		
St Pancras International	d			14 35	14 41			14 56					15 11				15 26				15 35	15 41
Farringdon	d			14 39	14 45			15 00					15 15				15 30				15 39	15 45
City Thameslink	d																					
London Blackfriars	d			14 44	14 50			15 05					15 20				15 35				15 44	15 50
London Bridge	d			14 51	14 56			15 11				15 21	15 26				15 41				15 51	15 56
East Croydon	a			15 07	15 10			15 24				15 37	15 40				15 54				16 07	16 10
East Croydon	d		15 03	15 07	15 11	15 12		15 25	←		15 33	15 37	15 41	15 42		15 49	15 55	←		16 03	16 07	16 11
Gatwick Airport	a	15 13	15 18	15 27	15 42	15 26	15 29	15 39	15 42	15 43	15 47	16 02	16 09	15 56	15 59	16 12	16 09	16 12	16 14	16 18	16 27	16 42
Three Bridges	a				→	15 32		15 44	15 48			16 08				→	16 14	16 18				→
Crawley	a											16 12						16 22				
Horsham	a											16 25						16 31				

		SN	GX	TL	TL	GX	SN	TL	TL	SN	GX	SN	TL	SN	GX	SN	TL	TL	SN	GX	TL	TL	GX
London Victoria	d	15 55	16 00			16 14	16 16			16 25	16 30	16 33			16 44	16 46			16 55	17 00			17 14
Clapham Junction	d	16 02					16 23			16 32		16 40				16 53			17 02				
East Croydon	a	16 12					16 32			16 41		16 49				17 02			17 12				
St Pancras International	d			15 56					16 11				16 26				16 35	16 41			16 56		
Farringdon	d			16 00					16 15				16 30				16 39	16 45			17 00		
City Thameslink	d																						
London Blackfriars	d			16 05					16 20				16 35				16 44	16 50			17 05		
London Bridge	d			16 11				16 21	16 26				16 41				16 51	16 56			17 11		
East Croydon	a			16 24				16 37	16 40				16 54				17 07	17 10			17 24		
East Croydon	d	16 13		16 25	←		16 33	16 37	16 41	16 42		16 49	16 55	←		17 03	17 07	17 11	17 13		17 25	←	
Gatwick Airport	a	16 27	16 30	16 39	16 42	16 43	16 47	17 02	17 09	16 56	16 59	17 12	17 09	17 12	17 14	17 18	17 27	17 42	17 27	17 30	17 39	17 42	17 43
Three Bridges	a	16 32		16 44	16 48			17 08				→	17 14	17 18				→	17 32		17 44	17 48	
Crawley	a							17 12						17 22									
Horsham	a							17 25						17 31									

Table T185-F

Sundays

15 December to 10 May

London - Gatwick Airport - Three Bridges - Horsham : Summary of Fast Trains

		SN	TL	TL	SN	GX	SN	TL	SN	GX	SN	TL	TL	SN	GX	TL	TL	GX	SN	TL	TL	SN	GX
London Victoria	d	17 16			17 25	17 30	17 33			17 44	17 46			17 55	18 00			18 14	18 16			18 25	18 30
Clapham Junction	d	17 23			17 32		17 40				17 53			18 02					18 23			18 32	
East Croydon	a	17 32			17 41		17 49				18 02			18 11					18 32			18 41	
St Pancras International	d			17 11				17 26				17 35	17 41			17 56					18 11		
Farringdon	d			17 15				17 30				17 39	17 45			18 00					18 15		
City Thameslink	d																						
London Blackfriars	d			17 20				17 35				17 44	17 50			18 05					18 20		
London Bridge	d		17 21	17 26				17 41				17 51	17 56			18 11				18 21	18 26		
East Croydon	a		17 37	17 40				17 54				18 07	18 10			18 24				18 37	18 40		
East Croydon	d	17 33	17 37	17 41	17 42		17 49	17 55	←		18 03	18 07	18 11	18 12		18 25	←		18 33	18 37	18 41	18 42	
Gatwick Airport	a	17 47	18 02	18 09	17 56	17 59	18 12	18 09	18 12	18 13	18 18	18 27	18 42	18 26	18 29	18 39	18 42	18 43	18 47	19 02	19 09	18 56	18 59
Three Bridges	a		18 08				→	18 14	18 18				→	18 32		18 44	18 47			19 08			
Crawley	a		18 12						18 22											19 12			
Horsham	a		18 25						18 31											19 25			

		SN	TL	SN	GX	SN	TL	TL	SN	GX	TL	TL	GX	SN	TL	TL	SN	GX	SN	TL	SN	GX	SN
London Victoria	d	18 33			18 44	18 46			18 55	19 00			19 14	19 16			19 25	19 30	19 33			19 44	19 46
Clapham Junction	d	18 40				18 53			19 02					19 23			19 32		19 40				19 53
East Croydon	a	18 49				19 02			19 11					19 32			19 41		19 49				20 02
St Pancras International	d		18 26				18 35	18 41			18 56					19 11				19 26			
Farringdon	d		18 30				18 39	18 45			19 00					19 15				19 30			
City Thameslink	d																						
London Blackfriars	d		18 35				18 44	18 50			19 05					19 20				19 35			
London Bridge	d		18 41				18 51	18 56			19 11				19 21	19 26				19 41			
East Croydon	a		18 54				19 07	19 10			19 24				19 37	19 40				19 54			
East Croydon	d	18 49	18 55	←		19 03	19 07	19 11	19 12		19 25	←		19 33	19 37	19 41	19 42		19 49	19 55	←		20 03
Gatwick Airport	a	19 12	19 09	19 12	19 13	19 18	19 27	19 42	19 26	19 29	19 39	19 42	19 43	19 47	20 02	20 09	19 56	19 59	20 12	20 09	20 12	20 13	20 18
Three Bridges	a	→	19 14	19 18				→	19 32		19 44	19 47			20 08				→	20 14	20 18		
Crawley	a			19 22											20 12						20 22		
Horsham	a			19 31											20 25						20 31		

		TL	TL	SN	GX	TL	TL	GX	SN	TL	TL	SN	GX	SN	TL	SN	GX	SN	TL	TL	SN	GX
London Victoria	d			19 55	20 00			20 14	20 16			20 25	20 30	20 33			20 44	20 46			20 55	21 00
Clapham Junction	d			20 02					20 23			20 32		20 40				20 53			21 02	
East Croydon	a			20 11					20 32			20 41		20 49				21 02			21 11	
St Pancras International	d	19 35	19 41			19 56					20 11				20 26				20 35	20 41		
Farringdon	d	19 39	19 45			20 00					20 15				20 30				20 39	20 45		
City Thameslink	d																					
London Blackfriars	d	19 44	19 50			20 05					20 20				20 35				20 44	20 50		
London Bridge	d	19 51	19 56			20 11				20 21	20 26				20 41				20 51	20 56		
East Croydon	a	20 07	20 10			20 24				20 37	20 40				20 54				21 07	21 10		
East Croydon	d	20 07	20 11	20 12		20 25	←		20 33	20 37	20 41	20 42		20 49	20 55	←		21 03	21 07	21 11	21 12	
Gatwick Airport	a	20 27	20 42	20 26	20 29	20 39	20 42	20 43	20 47	21 02	21 09	20 56	20 59	21 12	21 09	21 12	21 13	21 18	21 27	21 39	21 26	21 29
Three Bridges	a		→	20 32		20 44	20 47			21 08				→	21 14	21 18					21 32	
Crawley	a									21 12						21 22						
Horsham	a									21 25						21 31						

		TL	SN	TL	TL	SN	GX	SN	TL	SN	SN	TL	TL	SN	GX	SN	TL	TL	SN	SN	TL	TL	SN
London Victoria	d		21 16			21 25	21 30	21 33			21 46			21 55	22 00	22 05			22 16				22 25
Clapham Junction	d		21 23			21 32		21 40			21 53			22 02		22 13			22 23				22 32
East Croydon	a		21 32			21 41		21 49			22 02			22 11		22 23			22 32				22 41
St Pancras International	d	20 56			21 11				21 26			21 35	21 41				21 56					22 11	
Farringdon	d	21 00			21 15				21 30			21 39	21 45				22 00					22 15	
City Thameslink	d																						
London Blackfriars	d	21 05			21 20				21 35			21 44	21 50				22 05					22 20	
London Bridge	d	21 11		21 21	21 26				21 41			21 51	21 56				22 11				22 21	22 26	
East Croydon	a	21 24		21 37	21 40				21 54			22 07	22 10				22 24				22 37	22 40	
East Croydon	d	21 25	21 33	21 37	21 41	21 42		21 49	21 55	←	22 03	22 07	22 11	22 12		22 24	22 25	←	22 33	←	22 37	22 41	22 42
Gatwick Airport	a	21 39	21 47	22 02	22 09	21 56	21 59	22 12	22 09	22 12	22 18	22 26	22 39	22 26	22 29	22 51	22 39	22 39	22 47	22 51	23 02	23 09	22 56
Three Bridges	a	21 44		22 08	22 15			→	22 14	22 19		22 32	→	22 32		→	22 44	22 45		22 56	23 08		
Crawley	a			22 12						22 23										23 00	23 12		
Horsham	a			22 25						22 32										23 09	23 25		

		GX	SN	TL	SN	SN	TL	SN	TL	SN	SN	TL	SN	TL	TL
London Victoria	d	22 30	22 33			22 46		23 05			23 16		23 32		
Clapham Junction	d		22 40			22 53		23 12			23 23		23 40		
East Croydon	a		22 49			23 02		23 22			23 32		23 56		
St Pancras International	d			22 26			22 35		22 56			23 26			23 51
Farringdon	d			22 30			22 39		23 00			23 30			23 56
City Thameslink	d														
London Blackfriars	d			22 35			22 44		23 05			23 35			00 01
London Bridge	d			22 41			22 51		23 11			23 41		23 45	
East Croydon	a			22 54			23 07		23 24			23 54		23 59	00 27
East Croydon	d		22 49	22 55	←	23 03	23 08	23 23	23 25	←	23 33	23 55	23 57	00 01	00 28
Gatwick Airport	a	22 59	23 12	23 09	23 12	23 18	23 35	23 50	23 42	23 50	23 54	00 17	00 21	00 29	00 47
Three Bridges	a		→	23 14	23 18		23 40	→	23 48	23 56		00 22	00 27	00 35	00 53
Crawley	a				23 22					00 01					
Horsham	a				23 31					00 14					

Table T185-R

Mondays to Fridays

16 December to 15 May

Horsham - Three Bridges - Gatwick Airport - London : Summary of Fast Trains

		TL MX	TL MO	TL	TL	TL		TL	TL	TL	TL	TL	TL	SN	TL	SN		GX	SN	TL	TL	SN	SN	TL	GX
Horsham	d															05 15					05 25				
Crawley	d															05 28					05 38				
Three Bridges	d	00 15	00 15	00 37	01 41	02 15		02 41	03 15	03 41	04 15	04 35	05 14		05 27	05 33				05 40	05 43		05 48	05 51	
Gatwick Airport	d	00 21	00 21	00 42	01 46	02 21		02 46	03 21	03 46	04 21	04 41	05 19	05 28	05 32	05 38		05 41		05 46	05 49	05 52	05 54	05 56	05 59
East Croydon	a	00 39	00 39	01 09	02 10	02 39		03 09	03 39	04 09	04 39	05 08	05 39	06 00	06 03	05 53				06 00	06 15	06 34	06 08	06 31	
East Croydon	d	00 40	00 40	01 10	02 10	02 40		03 10	03 40	04 10	04 40	05 10	05 40		06 03					06 01	06 16			06 31	
London Bridge	d											05 25	05 55		06 21					06 16	06 31			06 51	
London Blackfriars	d	01 06	01 06	01 36	02 36	03 06		03 36	04 06	04 36	05 06	05 31	06 01		06 27					06 22	06 37			06 57	
City Thameslink	d										05 08	05 33	06 03		06 29					06 24	06 39			06 59	
Farringdon	d										05 11	05 36	06 06		06 31					06 26	06 41			07 01	
St Pancras International	a	01 13	01 15	01 43	02 43	03 13		03 43	04 13	04 43	05 15	05 40	06 10		06 35				←	06 30	06 45			07 05	
East Croydon	d													06 00		05 53			06 00			06 34	06 09		
Clapham Junction	a													→		06 02			06 11			→	06 20		
London Victoria	a															06 12		06 14	06 18				06 27		06 35

		TL ◇		SN	TL	GX	SN	TL	SN	TL	GX	SN		TL	SN	SN	SN	SN	TL	GX	SN	TL		SN	TL
Horsham	d			05 41								05 44		06 04		06 14	06 19		06 24						
Crawley	d			05 55										06 19			06 28		06 33						
Three Bridges	d	05 59		06 02	06 07			06 10		06 20				06 24	06 26		06 33		06 37			06 41			06 50
Gatwick Airport	d	06 06		06 08	06 13	06 13		06 16	06 19	06 25	06 28			06 29	06 33		06 38	06 41	06 43	06 44		06 46		06 49	06 55
East Croydon	a	06 21		06 23	06 45			06 30	07 04	06 40				07 01	06 48		06 53	06 56	07 15			07 01		07 34	07 10
East Croydon	d	06 21			06 46			06 31		06 41				07 01				06 57	07 16			07 01			07 10
London Bridge	d	06 35			07 01			06 46		06 54				07 21				07a13	07 31			07 16			07 24
London Blackfriars	d	06 42			07 07			06 52		07 02				07 27					07 37			07 22			07 32
City Thameslink	d	06 44			07 09			06 54		07 04				07 29					07 39			07 24			07 34
Farringdon	d	06 46			07 11			06 56		07 06				07 31					07 41			07 26			07 36
St Pancras International	a	06 50			07 15		←	07 00		07 10				07 35					07 45		←	07 30			07 40
East Croydon	d			06 24			06 34		07 04						06 49		06 53				07 04			07 34	
Clapham Junction	a			06 33			06 44		→			06 53			06 58	07 23	07 02				07 14			→	
London Victoria	a			06 42		06 43	06 52				06 58	07 02			07 05	07 32	07 12			07 14	07 22				

		TL	GX	SN	SN	TL	GX	SN		TL	SN	SN	TL	GX	SN	SN	TL	SN		SN	SN	SN	TL	GX	SN
Horsham	d	06 34			06 40										06 45	06 50	07 04			07 13	07 16				
Crawley	d	06 49			06 54											07 02	07 19				07 28				
Three Bridges	d	06 54		06 58	07 03					07 11			07 20			07 07	07 24	07 31			07 33				
Gatwick Airport	d	06 59	06 59	07 03	07 09	07 13	07 14			07 16	07 20	07 20	07 25	07 29			07 29	07 37			07 39	07 41	07 43	07 44	
East Croydon	a	07 31		07 18	07 23	07 46				07 31	07 37	08 04	07 40			07 26	08 01	07 52			07 54	07 57	08 15		
East Croydon	d	07 31				07 46				07 31			07 40			07 27	08 01					07 57	08 16		
London Bridge	d	07 51				08 01				07 46			07 54			07a43	08 21					08a13	08 31		
London Blackfriars	d	07 57				08 07				07 52			08 02				08 27						08 37		
City Thameslink	d	07 59				08 09				07 54			08 04				08 29						08 39		
Farringdon	d	08 01				08 11				07 56			08 06				08 31						08 41		
St Pancras International	a	08 05				08 15		←		08 00			08 10				08 35						08 45		←
East Croydon	d			07 19	07 24			07 34			07 38	08 04						07 52			07 55				08 04
Clapham Junction	a			07 28	07 33			07 44			07 47	→			07 54			08 01		08 24	08 04				08 14
London Victoria	a		07 28	07 35	07 40		07 43	07 52			07 54			07 58	08 04			08 09		08 33	08 12			08 14	08 22

		TL	SN	SN		TL	TL	GX	SN	SN	SN	TL	GX	SN		TL	SN	SN	GX	TL	SN	SN	TL	SN	
Horsham	d						07 34			07 40	07 50									08 04		08 14		08 19	
Crawley	d						07 49			07 54	08 02									08 19				08 28	
Three Bridges	d	07 41				07 50	07 54		07 57	08 01	08 07					08 11				08 24	08 25		08 31	08 33	
Gatwick Airport	d	07 46	07 50	07 50		07 55	07 59	07 59	08 03	08 08		08 13	08 14			08 16	08 19	08 20	08 28	08 29	08 33		08 36	08 39	
East Croydon	a	08 01	08 07	08 34		08 09	08 31		08 18	08 23	08 26	08 45				08 31	09 04	08 37		09 01	08 48		08 51	08 54	
East Croydon	d	08 01				08 10	08 31				08 27	08 46				08 31				09 01			08 51		
London Bridge	d	08 16				08 24	08 51				08a43	09 01				08 46				09 21			09 05		
London Blackfriars	d	08 22				08 32	08 57					09 07				08 52				09 27			09 12		
City Thameslink	d	08 24				08 34	08 59					09 09				08 54				09 29			09 14		
Farringdon	d	08 26				08 36	09 01					09 11				08 56				09 31			09 16		
St Pancras International	a	08 30				08 40	09 05					09 15		←		09 00				09 35			09 20		
East Croydon	d		08 08	08 34					08 20	08 24				08 34			09 04	08 38			08 50			08 54	
Clapham Junction	a		08 17	→					08 30	08 33				08 44			→	08 47			09 00	09 23		09 03	
London Victoria	a		08 24					08 29	08 37	08 40			08 43	08 52				08 54	08 58		09 08	09 32		09 10	

		TL	GX	SN	TL	SN	SN	GX	TL	SN		TL	SN	GX	SN	TL	TL	SN	GX	SN		SN	TL	TL	SN
Horsham	d								08 34				08 50				08 55					09 14			09 20
Crawley	d								08 49				08 59				09 08								09 29
Three Bridges	d				08 41				08 54	08 55		09 01	09 04			09 10	09 13							09 31	09 34
Gatwick Airport	d	08 43	08 44		08 46	08 49	08 51	08 58	08 59	09 03		09 06	09 09	09 12	←	09 16	09 19	09 23	09 24	09 28			09 33	09 36	09 39
East Croydon	a	09 15			09 01	09 34	09 09		09 31	09 18		09 21	09 24		09 34	09 31	09 45	10 00		09 42			10 03	09 51	09 54
East Croydon	d	09 16			09 01	→			09 31			09 21				09 31	09 45						10 03	09 51	
London Bridge	d	09 31			09 16				09 51			09 35				09 46	10 01						10 21	10 05	
London Blackfriars	d	09 37			09 22				09 57			09 42				09 52	10 07						10 27	10 12	
City Thameslink	d	09 39			09 24				09 59			09 44				09 54	10 09						10 29	10 14	
Farringdon	d	09 41			09 26				10 01			09 46				09 56	10 11						10 31	10 16	
St Pancras International	a	09 45		←	09 30				10 05			09 50				10 00	10 15						10 35	10 20	
East Croydon	d			09 04			09 09			09 19			09 24		09 34			10 00		09 43					09 54
Clapham Junction	a			09 14			09 18			09 28			09 33		09 44			→		09 52		10 23			10 03
London Victoria	a		09 13	09 24			09 26	09 29		09 35			09 40	09 43	09 52				09 54	09 59		10 31			10 11

		GX		SN	TL	TL	GX	SN	SN	TL	TL	SN		GX	TL	TL	GX	SN	SN	SN	TL	TL		SN	GX
Horsham	d					09 25						09 50				09 55				10 14				10 20	
Crawley	d					09 38						09 59				10 08								10 29	
Three Bridges	d				09 40	09 43					09 59	10 04			10 10	10 13						10 29		10 34	
Gatwick Airport	d	09 42			09 46	09 49	09 53	09 57	10 03	10 03	10 06	10 09		10 13	10 17	10 19	10 23	10 27	10 33		10 33	10 36		10 39	10 42
East Croydon	a				10 01	10 15		10 11	10 18	10 33	10 21	10 24			10 31	10 45		10 41	10 48		11 03	10 51		10 54	
East Croydon	d				10 01	10 15				10 33	10 21				10 32	10 45					11 03	10 51			
London Bridge	d				10 16	10 31				10 51	10 35				10 46	11 01					11 21	11 05			
London Blackfriars	d				10 22	10 37				10 57	10 42				10 52	11 07					11 27	11 12			
City Thameslink	d				10 24	10 39				10 59	10 44				10 54	11 09					11 29	11 14			
Farringdon	d				10 26	10 41				11 01	10 46				10 56	11 11					11 31	11 16			
St Pancras International	a			←	10 30	10 45				11 05	10 50				11 00	11 15					11 35	11 20			
East Croydon	d			10 00				10 12	10 19			10 24						10 42	10 49					10 54	
Clapham Junction	a			10 10				10 21	10 28			10 33						10 51	10 58	11 23				11 03	
London Victoria	a	10 13		10 18			10 23	10 29	10 39			10 41		10 43			10 53	10 59	11 05	11 32				11 11	11 13

		TL	TL	GX	SN	SN	TL	TL		SN	GX	TL	TL	GX	SN	SN	SN	TL		TL	SN	GX	TL	TL	GX
Horsham	d		10 25							10 50			10 55				11 14				11 20			11 25	
Crawley	d		10 38							10 59			11 08								11 29			11 38	
Three Bridges	d	10 40	10 43					10 59		11 04		11 10	11 13							11 29	11 34		11 40	11 43	
Gatwick Airport	d	10 46	10 49	10 54	10 57	11 03	11 03	11 06		11 09	11 12	11 16	11 19	11 23	11 27	11 33		11 33		11 36	11 39	11 42	11 46	11 49	11 53
East Croydon	a	11 01	11 15		11 11	11 18	11 33	11 21		11 24		11 31	11 45		11 41	11 48		12 03		11 51	11 54		12 01	12 15	
East Croydon	d	11 01	11 15				11 33	11 21				11 31	11 45					12 03		11 51			12 01	12 15	
London Bridge	d	11 16	11 31				11 51	11 35				11 46	12 01					12 21		12 05			12 16	12 31	
London Blackfriars	d	11 22	11 37				11 57	11 42				11 52	12 07					12 27		12 12			12 22	12 37	
City Thameslink	d	11 24	11 39				11 59	11 44				11 54	12 09					12 29		12 14			12 24	12 39	
Farringdon	d	11 26	11 41				12 01	11 46				11 56	12 11					12 31		12 16			12 26	12 41	
St Pancras International	a	11 30	11 45				12 05	11 50				12 00	12 15					12 35		12 20			12 30	12 45	
East Croydon	d				11 12	11 19				11 24					11 42	11 49					11 54				
Clapham Junction	a				11 21	11 28				11 33					11 51	11 58	12 23				12 03				
London Victoria	a			11 23	11 29	11 35				11 41	11 43			11 53	11 59	12 05	12 33				12 11	12 13			12 23

		SN	SN	TL		TL	SN	GX	TL	TL	GX	SN	TL	SN		SN	TL	SN	GX	TL	TL	GX	SN	SN	
Horsham	d						11 50			11 55						12 14		12 20			12 23				
Crawley	d						11 59			12 08								12 29			12 38				
Three Bridges	d					11 59	12 04		12 10	12 13							12 29	12 34		12 40	12 43				
Gatwick Airport	d	11 57	12 03	12 03		12 06	12 09	12 12	12 16	12 19	12 23	12 27	12 32	12 33			12 36	12 39	12 42	12 46	12 49	12 53	12 57	13 03	
East Croydon	a	12 11	12 18	12 33		12 21	12 24		12 31	12 45		12 41	13 03	12 48			12 51	12 54		13 01	13 15		13 11	13 18	
East Croydon	d			12 33		12 21			12 31	12 45			13 03				12 51			13 01	13 15				
London Bridge	d			12 51		12 35			12 46	13 01			13 21				13 05			13 16	13 31				
London Blackfriars	d			12 57		12 42			12 52	13 07			13 27				13 12			13 22	13 37				
City Thameslink	d			12 59		12 44			12 54	13 09			13 29				13 14			13 24	13 39				
Farringdon	d			13 01		12 46			12 56	13 11			13 31				13 16			13 26	13 41				
St Pancras International	a			13 05		12 50			13 00	13 15			13 35				13 20			13 30	13 45				
East Croydon	d	12 12	12 19				12 24					12 42		12 49				12 54					13 12	13 19	
Clapham Junction	a	12 22	12 28				12 33					12 51		12 58		13 23		13 03					13 21	13 28	
London Victoria	a	12 29	12 35				12 41	12 43			12 53	12 59		13 05		13 32		13 11	13 13			13 23	13 29	13 35	

		TL	TL	SN	GX	TL	TL	GX	SN	TL		SN	SN	TL	SN	GX	TL	TL	GX	SN		SN	TL	TL	SN
Horsham	d			12 50			12 55						13 14		13 20			13 25							13 50
Crawley	d			12 59			13 08								13 29			13 38							13 59
Three Bridges	d		12 59	13 04		13 10	13 13							13 29	13 34		13 40	13 43						13 59	14 04
Gatwick Airport	d	13 03	13 06	13 09	13 12	13 16	13 19	13 23	13 27	13 32		13 33		13 36	13 39	13 42	13 46	13 49	13 53	13 57		14 03	14 03	14 06	14 09
East Croydon	a	13 33	13 21	13 24		13 31	13 45		13 41	14 03		13 48		13 51	13 54		14 01	14 15		14 11		14 18	14 33	14 21	14 24
East Croydon	d	13 33	13 21			13 31	13 45			14 03				13 51			14 01	14 15					14 33	14 21	
London Bridge	d	13 51	13 35			13 46	14 01			14 21				14 05			14 16	14 31					14 51	14 35	
London Blackfriars	d	13 57	13 42			13 52	14 07			14 27				14 12			14 22	14 37					14 57	14 42	
City Thameslink	d	13 59	13 44			13 54	14 09			14 29				14 14			14 24	14 39					14 59	14 44	
Farringdon	d	14 01	13 46			13 56	14 11			14 31				14 16			14 26	14 41					15 01	14 46	
St Pancras International	a	14 05	13 50			14 00	14 15			14 35				14 20			14 30	14 45					15 05	14 50	
East Croydon	d			13 24					13 42			13 49			13 54					14 12		14 19			14 24
Clapham Junction	a			13 33					13 51			13 58	14 23		14 03					14 21		14 28			14 33
London Victoria	a			13 41	13 43			13 53	13 59			14 05	14 32		14 11	14 13			14 23	14 29		14 35			14 41

		GX	TL	TL	GX	SN		TL	SN	SN	TL	SN	GX	TL	TL	GX		SN	SN	TL	TL	SN	GX	TL	TL
Horsham	d			13 55						14 14		14 20			14 25							14 50			14 55
Crawley	d			14 08								14 29			14 38							14 59			15 08
Three Bridges	d		14 10	14 13							14 29	14 34		14 40	14 43						14 59	15 04		15 10	15 13
Gatwick Airport	d	14 12	14 16	14 19	14 23	14 27		14 32	14 33		14 36	14 39	14 42	14 46	14 49	14 53		14 57	15 03	15 03	15 06	15 09	15 12	15 16	15 19
East Croydon	a		14 31	14 45		14 41		15 03	14 48		14 51	14 54		15 01	15 15			15 11	15 18	15 33	15 21	15 24		15 31	15 45
East Croydon	d		14 31	14 45				15 03			14 51			15 01	15 15					15 33	15 21			15 31	15 45
London Bridge	d		14 46	15 01				15 21			15 05			15 16	15 31					15 51	15 35			15 46	16 01
London Blackfriars	d		14 52	15 07				15 27			15 12			15 22	15 37					15 57	15 42			15 52	16 07
City Thameslink	d		14 54	15 09				15 29			15 14			15 24	15 39					15 59	15 44			15 54	16 09
Farringdon	d		14 56	15 11				15 31			15 16			15 26	15 41					16 01	15 46			15 56	16 11
St Pancras International	a		15 00	15 15				15 35			15 20			15 30	15 45					16 05	15 50			16 00	16 15
East Croydon	d					14 42			14 49			14 54						15 12	15 19			15 24			
Clapham Junction	a					14 51			14 58	15 23		15 03						15 21	15 28			15 33			
London Victoria	a	14 43			14 53	14 59			15 05	15 32		15 11	15 13			15 23		15 29	15 35			15 41	15 43		

Table T185-R

Mondays to Fridays

16 December to 15 May

Horsham - Three Bridges - Gatwick Airport - London : Summary of Fast Trains

Station		GX	SN	TL	TL	SN	SN	TL	SN	GX	TL	TL	GX	SN	TL	SN	TL	TL	SN	GX	TL	TL	GX
Horsham	d						15 14		15 20			15 25							15 50			15 55	
Crawley	d								15 29			15 38							15 59			16 08	
Three Bridges	d							15 29	15 34		15 40	15 43						15 59	16 04		16 10	16 13	
Gatwick Airport	d	15 23	15 27	15 27	15 32	15 33		15 36	15 39	15 42	15 46	15 49	15 53	15 57	15 57	16 03	16 03	16 06	16 09	16 12	16 16	16 19	16 22
East Croydon	a		15 41	15 54	16 03	15 48		15 51	15 54		16 01	16 15		16 11	16 24	16 18	16 33	16 21	16 24		16 31	16 45	
East Croydon	d			15 54	16 03			15 51			16 01	16 15			16 24		16 33	16 21			16 31	16 45	
London Bridge	d			16 11	16 21			16 05			16 16	16 31			16 41		16 51	16 35			16 46	17 01	
London Blackfriars	d			16 17	16 27			16 12			16 22	16 37			16 47		16 57	16 42			16 52	17 07	
City Thameslink	d			16 19	16 29			16 14			16 24	16 39			16 49		16 59	16 44			16 54	17 09	
Farringdon	d			16 21	16 31			16 16			16 26	16 41			16 51		17 01	16 46			16 56	17 11	
St Pancras International	a			16 25	16 35			16 20			16 30	16 45			16 55		17 05	16 50			17 00	17 15	
East Croydon	d		15 42			15 49			15 54					16 12		16 19			16 24				
Clapham Junction	a		15 51			15 59	16 23		16 03					16 21		16 28			16 33				
London Victoria	a	15 53	16 00			16 09	16 33		16 11	16 15			16 23	16 29		16 35			16 41	16 43			16 53

Station		TL	SN	TL	SN	SN	TL	TL	SN	GX	TL	TL	GX	TL	SN	TL	SN	TL	TL	SN	GX	TL
Horsham	d					16 14			16 22			16 25								16 50		
Crawley	d								16 31			16 39								16 59		
Three Bridges	d	16 19						16 29	16 36		16 40	16 44		16 49					16 59	17 04		17 10
Gatwick Airport	d	16 24	16 27	16 27	16 33		16 33	16 36	16 41	16 44	16 46	16 49	16 52	16 54	16 57	16 57	17 03	17 03	17 06	17 09	17 12	17 16
East Croydon	a	16 39	16 42	16 54	16 48		17 03	16 51	16 56		17 01	17 15		17 09	17 12	17 24	17 18	17 33	17 21	17 24		17 31
East Croydon	d	16 40		16 54			17 03	16 51			17 01	17 15		17 10		17 25		17 33	17 21			17 31
London Bridge	d	16 55		17 11			17 21	17 05			17 16	17 31		17 24		17 41		17 51	17 35			17 46
London Blackfriars	d	17 02		17 17			17 27	17 12			17 22	17 37		17 32		17 47		17 57	17 42			17 52
City Thameslink	d	17 04		17 19			17 29	17 14			17 24	17 39		17 34		17 49		17 59	17 44			17 54
Farringdon	d	17 06		17 21			17 31	17 16			17 26	17 41		17 36		17 51		18 01	17 46			17 56
St Pancras International	a	17 10		17 25			17 35	17 20			17 30	17 45		17 40		17 55		18 05	17 50			18 00
East Croydon	d		16 42		16 49				16 56						17 12		17 18			17 24		
Clapham Junction	a		16 51		16 58	17 23			17 05						17 21		17 28			17 33		
London Victoria	a		16 59		17 10	17 33			17 13	17 18			17 24		17 30		17 35			17 41	17 43	

Station		TL	GX	TL	SN	TL	SN	SN	TL	TL	SN	GX	TL	TL	GX	SN	SN	SN	TL	TL	SN	GX	TL
Horsham	d	16 55						17 14			17 20			17 25				17 42			17 50		
Crawley	d	17 09									17 29			17 39							17 59		
Three Bridges	d	17 14		17 19						17 29	17 34		17 40	17 44						17 59	18 04		18 10
Gatwick Airport	d	17 19	17 22	17 24	17 27	17 27	17 33		17 33	17 36	17 39	17 42	17 46	17 49	17 52	17 57	18 03		18 03	18 06	18 09	18 12	18 16
East Croydon	a	17 45		17 39	17 42	17 54	17 48		18 03	17 51	17 54		18 01	18 15		18 12	18 18		18 33	18 21	18 24		18 31
East Croydon	d	17 45		17 40		17 55			18 03	17 51			18 01	18 15					18 33	18 21			18 31
London Bridge	d	18 01		17 54		18 11			18 21	18 05			18 16	18 31					18 51	18 35			18 46
London Blackfriars	d	18 07		18 02		18 17			18 27	18 12			18 22	18 37					18 57	18 42			18 52
City Thameslink	d	18 09		18 04		18 19			18 29	18 14			18 24	18 39					18 59	18 44			18 54
Farringdon	d	18 11		18 06		18 21			18 31	18 16			18 26	18 41					19 01	18 46			18 56
St Pancras International	a	18 15		18 10		18 25			18 35	18 20			18 30	18 45					19 05	18 50			19 00
East Croydon	d				17 42		17 48				17 54					18 12	18 18				18 24		
Clapham Junction	a				17 51		17 58	18 23			18 03					18 21	18 28	18 53			18 34		
London Victoria	a		17 53		17 59		18 05	18 34			18 12	18 13			18 23	18 29	18 35	19 02			18 42	18 44	

Station		TL	GX	SN	SN	SN	TL	TL	SN	GX	TL	TL	GX	SN	SN	SN	TL	TL	SN	GX	TL	TL	GX
Horsham	d	17 55				18 12			18 20			18 25				18 42			18 52			18 55	
Crawley	d	18 09							18 29			18 39							19 01			19 08	
Three Bridges	d	18 14						18 29	18 34		18 40	18 44						18 59	19 06		19 10	19 13	
Gatwick Airport	d	18 19	18 22	18 27	18 33		18 33	18 36	18 39	18 42	18 46	18 49	18 53	18 57	19 03		19 03	19 06	19 11	19 14	19 16	19 19	19 23
East Croydon	a	18 45		18 42	18 48		19 03	18 51	18 54		19 01	19 15		19 11	19 18		19 33	19 21	19 26		19 31	19 45	
East Croydon	d	18 45					19 03	18 51			19 01	19 15					19 33	19 21			19 31	19 45	
London Bridge	d	19 01					19 21	19 05			19 16	19 31					19 51	19 35			19 46	20 01	
London Blackfriars	d	19 07					19 27	19 12			19 22	19 37					19 57	19 42			19 52	20 07	
City Thameslink	d	19 09					19 29	19 14			19 24	19 39					19 59	19 44			19 54	20 09	
Farringdon	d	19 11					19 31	19 16			19 26	19 41					20 01	19 46			19 56	20 11	
St Pancras International	a	19 15					19 35	19 20			19 30	19 45					20 05	19 50			20 00	20 15	
East Croydon	d			18 42	18 48				18 54					19 12	19 18				19 26				
Clapham Junction	a			18 51	18 58	19 23			19 03					19 21	19 28	19 53			19 35				
London Victoria	a		18 53	18 59	19 05	19 33			19 11	19 14			19 23	19 29	19 35	20 02			19 43	19 45			19 53

Station		SN	SN	SN	TL	TL	SN	GX	TL	TL	GX	SN	SN	TL	TL	SN	GX	TL	GX	SN	TL	SN
Horsham	d			19 12			19 20			19 25						19 52		19 55				
Crawley	d						19 29			19 38						20 01		20 08				
Three Bridges	d					19 29	19 34		19 40	19 43					19 59	20 06		20 13				
Gatwick Airport	d	19 27	19 33		19 33	19 36	19 39	19 42	19 46	19 49	19 53	19 57	20 03	20 03	20 06	20 11	20 14	20 19	20 23	20 28	20 32	20 33
East Croydon	a	19 42	19 48		20 03	19 51	19 54		20 01	20 15		20 11	20 18	20 33	20 21	20 26		20 45		20 42	21 03	20 48
East Croydon	d				20 03	19 51			20 01	20 15				20 33	20 21			20 45			21 03	
London Bridge	d				20 21	20 05			20 16	20 31				20 51	20 35			21 01			21 21	
London Blackfriars	d				20 27	20 12			20 22	20 37				20 57	20 42			21 07			21 27	
City Thameslink	d				20 29	20 14			20 24	20 39				20 59	20 44			21 09			21 29	
Farringdon	d				20 31	20 16			20 26	20 41				21 01	20 46			21 11			21 31	
St Pancras International	a				20 35	20 20			20 30	20 45				21 05	20 50			21 15			21 35	
East Croydon	d	19 42	19 49				19 54					20 12	20 19			20 26				20 43		20 49
Clapham Junction	a	19 51	19 58	20 23			20 04					20 21	20 28			20 35				20 52		21 01
London Victoria	a	19 59	20 05	20 32			20 11	20 13			20 23	20 30	20 35			20 43	20 45		20 53	20 59		21 08

Table T185-R

Mondays to Fridays

16 December to 15 May

Horsham - Three Bridges - Gatwick Airport - London : Summary of Fast Trains

Station		SN	TL	SN	GX	TL	TL	GX	SN	SN	TL	TL	SN	GX	TL	GX	SN	TL	SN	SN	TL	SN
Horsham	d	20 14		20 20			20 25						20 50		20 55					21 14		21 20
Crawley	d			20 29			20 38						20 59		21 08							21 29
Three Bridges	d		20 29	20 34		20 40	20 43					20 59	21 04		21 13						21 29	21 34
Gatwick Airport	d		20 36	20 39	20 42	20 46	20 49	20 54	20 57	21 03	21 03	21 06	21 09	21 12	21 19	21 24	21 27	21 32	21 33		21 36	21 39
East Croydon	a		20 51	20 54		21 01	21 15		21 11	21 18	21 33	21 21	21 24		21 45		21 41	22 03	21 48		21 51	21 54
East Croydon	d		20 51			21 01	21 15				21 33	21 21			21 45			22 03			21 51	
London Bridge	d		21 05			21 16	21 31				21 51	21 35			22 01			22 21			22 05	
London Blackfriars	d		21 12			21 22	21 37				21 57	21 42			22 07			22 27			22 12	
City Thameslink	d		21 14			21 24	21 39				21 59	21 44			22 09			22 29			22 14	
Farringdon	d		21 16			21 26	21 41				22 01	21 46			22 11			22 31			22 16	
St Pancras International	a		21 20			21 30	21 45				22 05	21 50			22 15			22 35			22 20	
East Croydon	d			20 54					21 12	21 19			21 24				21 42		21 49			21 54
Clapham Junction	a	21 23		21 06					21 21	21 28			21 33				21 51		21 58	22 23		22 03
London Victoria	a	21 33		21 13	21 15			21 24	21 29	21 35			21 41	21 43		21 53	21 59		22 05	22 33		22 11

Station		GX	TL	TL	GX	SN	SN	TL	SN	GX	TL	GX	SN	SN	TL	SN	GX	TL	TL	GX	SN	SN	TL
Horsham	d			21 26					21 50		21 55					22 20			22 25				
Crawley	d			21 39					21 59		22 08					22 29			22 38				
Three Bridges	d		21 40	21 43				21 59	22 04		22 13				22 29	22 34		22 40	22 43				22 59
Gatwick Airport	d	21 42	21 46	21 49	21 54	21 57	22 03	22 06	22 09	22 12	22 19	22 23	22 27	22 33	22 36	22 39	22 42	22 46	22 49	22 53	22 57	23 03	23 06
East Croydon	a		22 01	22 15		22 12	22 18	22 21	22 24		22 45		22 42	22 48	22 51	22 54		23 01	23 15		23 11	23 18	23 21
East Croydon	d		22 01	22 15				22 21			22 45				22 51			23 01	23 15				23 21
London Bridge	d		22 16	22 31				22 35			23 01				23 05			23 16	23 31				23 35
London Blackfriars	d		22 22	22 37				22 42			23 07				23 12			23 22	23 37				23 42
City Thameslink	d		22 24	22 39				22 44															
Farringdon	d		22 26	22 41				22 46			23 11				23 16			23 26	23 41				23 46
St Pancras International	a		22 30	22 45				22 50			23 15				23 20			23 30	23 45				23 50
East Croydon	d					22 12	22 19		22 24				22 43	22 49		22 54					23 12	23 19	
Clapham Junction	a					22 21	22 28		22 33				22 52	22 58		23 03					23 21	23 28	
London Victoria	a	22 13			22 23	22 29	22 37		22 42	22 43		22 51	23 00	23 05		23 12	23 13			23 23	23 30	23 35	

Station		GX	SN	TL	TL	SN FO	SN FX	SN	TL
Horsham	d				23 11			23 27	
Crawley	d				23 24			23 40	
Three Bridges	d			23 29	23 29	23 40	23 40	23 44	23 58
Gatwick Airport	d	23 11	23 27	23 34	23 35	23 55	23 55	23a49	00 04
East Croydon	a		23 42	23 52	00 09	00 16	00 17		00 22
East Croydon	d			23 53	00 09				00 23
London Bridge	d								
London Blackfriars	d			00 22	00 37				00 50
City Thameslink	d								
Farringdon	d			00 26	00 41				
St Pancras International	a			00 30	00 45				00 59
East Croydon	d		23 42			00 16	00 17		
Clapham Junction	a		23 57			00 33	00 33		
London Victoria	a	23 43	00 05			00 41	00 41		

Saturdays

21 December to 16 May

Station		TL	TL	TL	SN	TL	TL	SN	TL	TL	SN	TL	TL	SN	TL	SN	TL	GX	TL	TL	GX	SN	TL
Horsham	d																			05 25			
Crawley	d																			05 38			
Three Bridges	d	00 15	00 37	01 41	02 08	02 15	02 41	03 08	03 15	03 41	04 08	04 15	04 35	04 58	05 15	05 22	05 27		05 40	05 43			
Gatwick Airport	d	00 21	00 42	01 46	02 13	02 21	02 46	03 13	03 21	03 46	04 13	04 21	04 41	05 03	05 20	05 28	05 33	05 40	05 46	05 49	05 57	06 03	06 03
East Croydon	a	00 39	01 09	02 09	02 36	02 39	03 09	03 36	03 39	04 09	04 36	04 39	05 09	05 30	05 38	06 00	06 03		06 00	06 15		06 18	06 33
East Croydon	d	00 40	01 10	02 10		02 40	03 10		03 40	04 10		04 40	05 10		05 39		06 03		06 01	06 15			06 33
London Bridge	d												05 26		05 55		06 21		06 16	06 31			06 51
London Blackfriars	d	01 06	01 36	02 36		03 06	03 36		04 06	04 36		05 06	05 32		06 02		06 27		06 22	06 37			06 57
City Thameslink	d																						
Farringdon	d											05 11	05 36		06 06		06 31		06 26	06 41			07 01
St Pancras International	a	01 13	01 43	02 43		03 13	03 43		04 13	04 43		05 15	05 40		06 10		06 35		06 30	06 45			07 05
East Croydon	d				02 36			03 36			04 36			05 30		06 00						06 19	
Clapham Junction	a				02 50			03 50			04 50			05 50		06 10						06 28	
London Victoria	a				02 58			03 58			04 58			05 59		06 18		06 12			06 25	06 35	

Station		TL	SN	GX	TL	GX	SN	SN	TL	TL	SN	GX	TL	TL	GX	SN	SN	TL	TL	SN	GX	TL	GX
Horsham	d		05 41		05 55						06 20			06 25						06 50		06 55	
Crawley	d		05 55		06 08						06 29			06 38						06 59		07 08	
Three Bridges	d	05 59	06 03		06 13					06 29	06 34		06 40	06 43					06 59	07 04		07 13	
Gatwick Airport	d	06 06	06 09	06 12	06 19	06 23	06 27	06 33	06 33	06 36	06 39	06 42	06 46	06 49	06 53	06 57	07 03	07 03	07 06	07 09	07 12	07 19	07 23
East Croydon	a	06 21	06 24		06 45		06 41	06 48	07 03	06 51	06 54		07 01	07 15		07 11	07 18	07 33	07 21	07 24		07 45	
East Croydon	d	06 21			06 45				07 03	06 51			07 01	07 15				07 33	07 21			07 45	
London Bridge	d	06 35			07 01				07 21	07 05			07 16	07 31				07 51	07 35			08 01	
London Blackfriars	d	06 42			07 07				07 27	07 12			07 22	07 37				07 57	07 42			08 07	
City Thameslink	d																						
Farringdon	d	06 46			07 11				07 31	07 16			07 26	07 41				08 01	07 46			08 11	
St Pancras International	a	06 50			07 15				07 35	07 20			07 30	07 45				08 05	07 50			08 15	
East Croydon	d		06 24				06 42	06 49			06 54					07 12	07 19			07 24			
Clapham Junction	a		06 33				06 51	06 58			07 03					07 21	07 28			07 33			
London Victoria	a		06 41	06 43		06 53	06 59	07 05			07 11	07 13			07 23	07 29	07 35			07 41	07 43		07 53

Table T185-R

Saturdays

21 December to 16 May

Horsham - Three Bridges - Gatwick Airport - London : Summary of Fast Trains

		SN	SN	TL	TL	SN	GX	TL		TL	GX	SN	SN	TL	TL	SN	GX	TL		GX	SN	SN	SN	TL	TL
Horsham	d					07 20				07 25						07 50		07 55					08 14		
Crawley	d					07 29				07 38						07 59		08 08							
Three Bridges	d				07 29	07 34		07 40		07 43					07 59	08 04		08 13							08 29
Gatwick Airport	d	07 27	07 33	07 33	07 36	07 39	07 42	07 46		07 49	07 53	07 57	08 03	08 03	08 06	08 09	08 12	08 19		08 23	08 27	08 33		08 33	08 36
East Croydon	a	07 41	07 48	08 03	07 51	07 54		08 01		08 15		08 11	08 18	08 33	08 21	08 24		08 45			08 41	08 48		09 03	08 51
East Croydon	d			08 03	07 51			08 01		08 15				08 33	08 21			08 45						09 03	08 51
London Bridge	d			08 21	08 05			08 16		08 31				08 51	08 35			09 01						09 21	09 05
London Blackfriars	d			08 27	08 12			08 22		08 37				08 57	08 42			09 07						09 27	09 12
City Thameslink	d																	09 09						09 29	09 14
Farringdon	d			08 31	08 16			08 26		08 41				09 01	08 46			09 11						09 31	09 16
St Pancras International	a			08 35	08 20			08 30		08 45				09 05	08 50			09 15						09 35	09 20
East Croydon	d	07 42	07 49			07 54						08 12	08 19			08 24					08 42	08 49			
Clapham Junction	a	07 51	07 58			08 03						08 21	08 28			08 33					08 51	08 58	09 23		
London Victoria	a	07 59	08 05			08 11	08 13				08 23	08 29	08 35			08 41	08 43			08 53	08 59	09 05	09 32		

		SN	GX	TL		TL	GX	SN	SN	TL	TL	SN	GX	TL		GX	SN	SN	SN	TL	TL	SN	GX	TL	
Horsham	d	08 20				08 25						08 50		08 55					09 14			09 20			
Crawley	d	08 29				08 38						08 59		09 08								09 29			
Three Bridges	d	08 34		08 40		08 43					08 59	09 04		09 13							09 29	09 34		09 40	
Gatwick Airport	d	08 39	08 42	08 46		08 49	08 53	08 57	09 03	09 03	09 06	09 09	09 12	09 19		09 23	09 27	09 33		09 33	09 36	09 39	09 42	09 46	
East Croydon	a	08 54		09 01		09 15		09 11	09 18	09 33	09 21	09 24		09 45			09 41	09 48		10 03	09 51	09 54		10 01	
East Croydon	d			09 01		09 15				09 33	09 21			09 45						10 03	09 51			10 01	
London Bridge	d			09 16		09 31				09 51	09 35			10 01						10 21	10 05			10 16	
London Blackfriars	d			09 22		09 37				09 57	09 42			10 07						10 27	10 12			10 22	
City Thameslink	d			09 24		09 39				09 59	09 44			10 09						10 29	10 14			10 24	
Farringdon	d			09 26		09 41				10 01	09 46			10 11						10 31	10 16			10 26	
St Pancras International	a			09 30		09 45				10 05	09 50			10 15						10 35	10 20			10 30	
East Croydon	d	08 54						09 12	09 19			09 24					09 42	09 49				09 54			
Clapham Junction	a	09 03						09 21	09 28			09 33					09 51	09 58	10 23			10 03			
London Victoria	a	09 11	09 13				09 23	09 29	09 35			09 41	09 43			09 53	09 59	10 05	10 32			10 11	10 13		

		TL	GX	SN	SN	TL	TL	SN	GX	TL		GX	SN	SN	SN	TL	TL	SN	GX	TL		TL	GX	SN	SN
Horsham	d	09 25						09 50		09 55					10 14			10 20				10 25			
Crawley	d	09 38						09 59		10 08								10 29				10 38			
Three Bridges	d	09 43					09 59	10 04		10 13							10 29	10 34		10 40		10 43			
Gatwick Airport	d	09 49	09 53	09 57	10 03	10 03	10 06	10 09	10 12	10 19		10 23	10 27	10 33		10 33	10 36	10 39	10 42	10 46		10 49	10 53	10 57	11 03
East Croydon	a	10 15		10 11	10 18	10 33	10 21	10 24		10 45			10 41	10 48		11 03	10 51	10 54		11 01		11 15		11 11	11 18
East Croydon	d	10 15				10 33	10 21			10 45						11 03	10 51			11 01		11 15			
London Bridge	d	10 31				10 51	10 35			11 01						11 21	11 05			11 16		11 31			
London Blackfriars	d	10 37				10 57	10 42			11 07						11 27	11 12			11 22		11 37			
City Thameslink	d	10 39				10 59	10 44			11 09						11 29	11 14			11 24		11 39			
Farringdon	d	10 41				11 01	10 46			11 11						11 31	11 16			11 26		11 41			
St Pancras International	a	10 45				11 05	10 50			11 15						11 35	11 20			11 30		11 45			
East Croydon	d			10 12	10 19			10 24					10 42	10 49				10 54						11 12	11 19
Clapham Junction	a			10 21	10 28			10 33					10 51	10 58	11 23			11 03						11 21	11 28
London Victoria	a		10 23	10 29	10 35			10 41	10 43			10 53	10 59	11 05	11 32			11 11	11 13				11 23	11 29	11 35

		TL	TL	SN	GX	TL		GX	SN	SN	SN	TL	TL	SN	GX	TL		TL	GX	SN	SN	TL	TL	SN	GX
Horsham	d			10 50		10 55					11 14			11 20				11 25						11 50	
Crawley	d			10 59		11 08								11 29				11 38						11 59	
Three Bridges	d		10 59	11 04		11 13							11 29	11 34		11 40		11 43					11 59	12 04	
Gatwick Airport	d	11 03	11 06	11 09	11 12	11 19		11 23	11 27	11 33		11 33	11 36	11 39	11 42	11 46		11 49	11 53	11 57	12 03	12 03	12 06	12 09	12 12
East Croydon	a	11 33	11 21	11 24		11 45			11 41	11 48		12 03	11 51	11 54		12 01		12 15		12 11	12 18	12 33	12 21	12 24	
East Croydon	d	11 33	11 21			11 45						12 03	11 51			12 01		12 15				12 33	12 21		
London Bridge	d	11 51	11 35			12 01						12 21	12 05			12 16		12 31				12 51	12 35		
London Blackfriars	d	11 57	11 42			12 07						12 27	12 12			12 22		12 37				12 57	12 42		
City Thameslink	d	11 59	11 44			12 09						12 29	12 14			12 24		12 39				12 59	12 44		
Farringdon	d	12 01	11 46			12 11						12 31	12 16			12 26		12 41				13 01	12 46		
St Pancras International	a	12 05	11 50			12 15						12 35	12 20			12 30		12 45				13 05	12 50		
East Croydon	d			11 24					11 42	11 49				11 54						12 12	12 19			12 24	
Clapham Junction	a			11 33					11 51	11 58	12 23			12 03						12 21	12 28			12 33	
London Victoria	a			11 41	11 43			11 53	11 59	12 05	12 32			12 11	12 13				12 23	12 29	12 35			12 41	12 43

		TL		GX	SN	SN	SN	TL	TL	SN	GX	TL		TL	GX	SN	SN	TL	TL	SN	GX	TL		GX	SN
Horsham	d	11 55					12 14			12 20				12 25						12 50		12 55			
Crawley	d	12 08								12 29				12 38						12 59		13 08			
Three Bridges	d	12 13							12 29	12 34		12 40		12 43					12 59	13 04		13 13			
Gatwick Airport	d	12 19		12 23	12 27	12 33		12 33	12 36	12 39	12 42	12 46		12 49	12 53	12 57	13 03	13 03	13 06	13 09	13 12	13 19		13 23	13 27
East Croydon	a	12 45			12 41	12 48		13 03	12 51	12 54		13 01		13 15		13 11	13 18	13 33	13 21	13 24		13 45			13 41
East Croydon	d	12 45						13 03	12 51			13 01		13 15				13 33	13 21			13 45			
London Bridge	d	13 01						13 21	13 05			13 16		13 31				13 51	13 35			14 01			
London Blackfriars	d	13 07						13 27	13 12			13 22		13 37				13 57	13 42			14 07			
City Thameslink	d	13 09						13 29	13 14			13 24		13 39				13 59	13 44			14 09			
Farringdon	d	13 11						13 31	13 16			13 26		13 41				14 01	13 46			14 11			
St Pancras International	a	13 15						13 35	13 20			13 30		13 45				14 05	13 50			14 15			
East Croydon	d				12 42	12 49				12 54						13 12	13 19			13 24					13 42
Clapham Junction	a				12 51	12 58	13 23			13 03						13 21	13 28			13 33					13 51
London Victoria	a			12 53	12 59	13 05	13 32			13 11	13 13				13 23	13 29	13 35			13 41	13 43			13 53	13 59

Table T185-R

Saturdays

21 December to 16 May

Horsham - Three Bridges - Gatwick Airport - London : Summary of Fast Trains

		SN	SN	TL		TL	SN	GX	TL	TL	GX	SN	SN	TL		TL	SN	GX	TL	GX	SN	SN	SN	TL	
Horsham	d		13 14				13 20			13 25							13 50		13 55				14 14		
Crawley	d						13 29			13 38							13 59		14 08						
Three Bridges	d					13 29	13 34		13 40	13 43						13 59	14 04		14 13						
Gatwick Airport	d	13 33		13 33		13 36	13 39	13 42	13 46	13 49	13 53	13 57	14 03	14 03		14 06	14 09	14 12	14 19	14 23	14 27	14 33		14 33	
East Croydon	a	13 48		14 03		13 51	13 54		14 01	14 15		14 11	14 18	14 33		14 21	14 24		14 45		14 41	14 48		15 03	
East Croydon	d			14 03		13 51			14 01	14 15				14 33		14 21			14 45					15 03	
London Bridge	d			14 21		14 05			14 16	14 31				14 51		14 35			15 01					15 21	
London Blackfriars	d			14 27		14 12			14 22	14 37				14 57		14 42			15 07					15 27	
City Thameslink	d			14 29		14 14			14 24	14 39				14 59		14 44			15 09					15 29	
Farringdon	d			14 31		14 16			14 26	14 41				15 01		14 46			15 11					15 31	
St Pancras International	a			14 35		14 20			14 30	14 45				15 05		14 50			15 15					15 35	
East Croydon	d	13 49					13 54					14 12	14 19				14 24				14 42	14 49			
Clapham Junction	a	13 58	14 23				14 03					14 21	14 28				14 33				14 51	14 58	15 23		
London Victoria	a	14 05	14 32				14 11	14 13			14 23	14 30	14 36				14 41	14 43		14 53	14 59	15 05	15 32		

		TL	SN	GX	TL	TL	GX	SN	SN	TL		TL	SN	GX	TL	GX	SN	TL	SN	SN		TL	SN	GX	TL
Horsham	d		14 20			14 25							14 50		14 55					15 14			15 20		
Crawley	d		14 29			14 38							14 59		15 08								15 29		
Three Bridges	d	14 29	14 34		14 40	14 43						14 59	15 04		15 13							15 29	15 34		15 40
Gatwick Airport	d	14 36	14 39	14 42	14 46	14 49	14 53	14 57	15 03	15 03		15 06	15 09	15 12	15 19	15 23	15 27	15 32	15 33			15 36	15 39	15 42	15 46
East Croydon	a	14 51	14 54		15 01	15 15		15 11	15 18	15 33		15 21	15 24		15 45		15 41	16 03	15 48			15 51	15 54		16 01
East Croydon	d	14 51			15 01	15 15				15 33		15 21			15 45			16 03				15 51			16 01
London Bridge	d	15 05			15 16	15 31				15 51		15 35			16 01			16 21				16 05			16 16
London Blackfriars	d	15 12			15 22	15 37				15 57		15 42			16 07			16 27				16 12			16 22
City Thameslink	d	15 14			15 24	15 39				15 59		15 44			16 09			16 29				16 14			16 24
Farringdon	d	15 16			15 26	15 41				16 01		15 46			16 11			16 31				16 16			16 26
St Pancras International	a	15 20			15 30	15 45				16 05		15 50			16 15			16 35				16 20			16 30
East Croydon	d		14 54					15 12	15 19				15 24				15 42		15 49				15 54		
Clapham Junction	a		15 03					15 21	15 28				15 33				15 51		15 58	16 23			16 03		
London Victoria	a		15 11	15 13			15 23	15 29	15 35				15 41	15 43		15 53	15 59		16 05	16 32			16 11	16 13	

		TL	GX	SN	SN	TL		TL	SN	GX	TL	GX	SN	SN	SN	TL		TL	SN	GX	TL	TL	GX	SN	SN
Horsham	d	15 25							15 50		15 55				16 14				16 22			16 25			
Crawley	d	15 38							15 59		16 08								16 31			16 38			
Three Bridges	d	15 43						15 59	16 04		16 13							16 29	16 36		16 40	16 43			
Gatwick Airport	d	15 49	15 53	15 57	16 03	16 03		16 06	16 09	16 12	16 19	16 23	16 27	16 33		16 33		16 36	16 41	16 44	16 46	16 49	16 53	16 57	17 03
East Croydon	a	16 15		16 11	16 18	16 33		16 21	16 24		16 45		16 41	16 48		17 03		16 51	16 56		17 01	17 15		17 11	17 18
East Croydon	d	16 15				16 33		16 21			16 45					17 03		16 51			17 01	17 15			
London Bridge	d	16 31				16 51		16 35			17 01					17 21		17 05			17 16	17 31			
London Blackfriars	d	16 37				16 57		16 42			17 07					17 27		17 12			17 22	17 37			
City Thameslink	d	16 39				16 59		16 44			17 09					17 29		17 14			17 24	17 39			
Farringdon	d	16 41				17 01		16 46			17 11					17 31		17 16			17 26	17 41			
St Pancras International	a	16 45				17 05		16 50			17 15					17 35		17 20			17 30	17 45			
East Croydon	d			16 12	16 19				16 24				16 42	16 49					16 56					17 12	17 19
Clapham Junction	a			16 21	16 28				16 33				16 51	16 58	17 23				17 05					17 21	17 28
London Victoria	a		16 23	16 29	16 35				16 41	16 43		16 53	16 59	17 05	17 32				17 13	17 15			17 23	17 29	17 35

		TL		TL	SN	GX	TL	GX	SN	SN	SN	TL		TL	SN	GX	TL	TL	GX	SN	SN	TL		TL	SN
Horsham	d				16 50		16 55				17 14				17 20			17 25							17 50
Crawley	d				16 59		17 08								17 29			17 38							17 59
Three Bridges	d			16 59	17 04		17 13							17 29	17 34		17 40	17 43						17 59	18 04
Gatwick Airport	d	17 03		17 06	17 09	17 12	17 19	17 23	17 27	17 33		17 33		17 36	17 39	17 42	17 46	17 49	17 53	17 57	18 03	18 03		18 06	18 09
East Croydon	a	17 33		17 21	17 24		17 45		17 41	17 48		18 03		17 51	17 54		18 01	18 15		18 11	18 18	18 33		18 21	18 24
East Croydon	d	17 33		17 21			17 45					18 03		17 51			18 01	18 15				18 33		18 21	
London Bridge	d	17 51		17 35			18 01					18 21		18 05			18 16	18 31				18 51		18 35	
London Blackfriars	d	17 57		17 42			18 07					18 27		18 12			18 22	18 37				18 57		18 42	
City Thameslink	d	17 59		17 44			18 09					18 29		18 14			18 24	18 39				18 59		18 44	
Farringdon	d	18 01		17 46			18 11					18 31		18 16			18 26	18 41				19 01		18 46	
St Pancras International	a	18 05		17 50			18 15					18 35		18 20			18 30	18 45				19 05		18 50	
East Croydon	d				17 24				17 42	17 49					17 54					18 12	18 19				18 24
Clapham Junction	a				17 33				17 51	17 58	18 23				18 03					18 21	18 28				18 33
London Victoria	a				17 41	17 43		17 53	17 59	18 05	18 32				18 11	18 13			18 23	18 29	18 35				18 41

		GX	TL	GX	SN	SN	SN	TL		TL	SN	GX	TL	TL	GX	SN	SN	TL		TL	SN	GX	TL	GX	SN
Horsham	d		17 55				18 14				18 20			18 25							18 50		18 55		
Crawley	d		18 08								18 29			18 38							18 59		19 08		
Three Bridges	d		18 13							18 29	18 34		18 40	18 43						18 59	19 04		19 13		
Gatwick Airport	d	18 12	18 19	18 23	18 27	18 33		18 33		18 36	18 39	18 42	18 46	18 49	18 53	18 57	19 03	19 03		19 06	19 09	19 12	19 19	19 23	19 27
East Croydon	a		18 45		18 41	18 48		19 03		18 51	18 54		19 01	19 15		19 11	19 18	19 33		19 21	19 24		19 45		19 41
East Croydon	d		18 45					19 03		18 51			19 01	19 15				19 33		19 21			19 45		
London Bridge	d		19 01					19 21		19 05			19 16	19 31				19 51		19 35			20 01		
London Blackfriars	d		19 07					19 27		19 12			19 22	19 37				19 57		19 42			20 07		
City Thameslink	d		19 09					19 29		19 14			19 24	19 39				19 59		19 44			20 09		
Farringdon	d		19 11					19 31		19 16			19 26	19 41				20 01		19 46			20 11		
St Pancras International	a		19 15					19 35		19 20			19 30	19 45				20 05		19 50			20 15		
East Croydon	d				18 42	18 49					18 54					19 12	19 19				19 24				19 42
Clapham Junction	a				18 51	18 58	19 23				19 03					19 21	19 28				19 33				19 51
London Victoria	a	18 43		18 53	18 59	19 05	19 32				19 11	19 13			19 23	19 29	19 35				19 41	19 43		19 53	19 59

Table T185-R

Saturdays
21 December to 16 May

Horsham - Three Bridges - Gatwick Airport - London : Summary of Fast Trains

		SN	TL	TL	SN	GX	TL	TL	GX	SN	SN	TL	TL	SN	GX	TL	GX	SN	SN	TL	TL	SN	GX
Horsham	d				19 20			19 25						19 50		19 55						20 20	
Crawley	d				19 29			19 38						19 59		20 08						20 29	
Three Bridges	d			19 29	19 34		19 40	19 43					19 59	20 04		20 13					20 29	20 34	
Gatwick Airport	d	19 33	19 33	19 36	19 39	19 42	19 46	19 49	19 53	19 57	20 03	20 03	20 06	20 09	20 12	20 19	20 23	20 27	20 33	20 33	20 36	20 39	20 42
East Croydon	a	19 48	20 03	19 51	19 54		20 01	20 15		20 11	20 18	20 33	20 21	20 24		20 45		20 41	20 48	21 03	20 51	20 54	
East Croydon	d		20 03	19 51			20 01	20 15				20 33	20 21			20 45				21 03	20 51		
London Bridge	d		20 21	20 05			20 16	20 31				20 51	20 35			21 01				21 21	21 05		
London Blackfriars	d		20 27	20 12			20 22	20 37				20 57	20 42			21 07				21 27	21 12		
City Thameslink	d		20 29	20 14			20 24	20 39				20 59	20 44										
Farringdon	d		20 31	20 16			20 26	20 41				21 01	20 46			21 11				21 31	21 16		
St Pancras International	a		20 35	20 20			20 30	20 45				21 05	20 50			21 15				21 35	21 20		
East Croydon	d	19 49			19 54					20 12	20 19			20 24				20 42	20 49			20 54	
Clapham Junction	a	19 58			20 03					20 21	20 28			20 33				20 51	20 58			21 03	
London Victoria	a	20 05			20 11	20 13			20 23	20 29	20 35			20 41	20 43		20 53	20 59	21 05			21 11	21 13

		TL	TL	GX	SN	SN	TL	TL	SN	GX	TL	GX	SN	SN	TL	TL	SN	GX	TL	TL	GX	SN	SN
Horsham	d		20 25						20 50		20 55						21 20			21 25			
Crawley	d		20 38						20 59		21 08						21 29			21 38			
Three Bridges	d	20 40	20 43					20 59	21 04		21 13					21 29	21 34		21 40	21 43			
Gatwick Airport	d	20 46	20 49	20 53	20 57	21 03	21 03	21 06	21 09	21 12	21 19	21 23	21 27	21 33	21 33	21 36	21 39	21 42	21 46	21 49	21 53	21 57	22 03
East Croydon	a	21 01	21 15		21 11	21 18	21 33	21 21	21 24		21 45		21 41	21 48	22 03	21 51	21 54		22 01	22 15		22 12	22 18
East Croydon	d	21 01	21 15				21 33	21 21			21 45				22 03	21 51			22 01	22 16			
London Bridge	d	21 16	21 31				21 51	21 35			22 01				22 21	22 05			22 16	22 31			
London Blackfriars	d	21 22	21 37				21 57	21 42			22 07				22 27	22 12			22 22	22 37			
City Thameslink	d																						
Farringdon	d	21 26	21 41				22 01	21 46			22 11				22 31	22 16			22 26	22 41			
St Pancras International	a	21 30	21 45				22 05	21 50			22 15				22 35	22 20			22 30	22 45			
East Croydon	d				21 12	21 19			21 24				21 42	21 49			21 54					22 12	22 19
Clapham Junction	a				21 21	21 28			21 33				21 51	21 58			22 03					22 21	22 28
London Victoria	a			21 23	21 29	21 35			21 41	21 43		21 53	21 59	22 05			22 11	22 13			22 23	22 28	22 35

		TL	SN	GX	TL	GX	SN	SN	TL	SN	GX	TL	TL	GX	SN	SN	TL	GX	TL	TL	SN	SN
Horsham	d		21 50		21 55					22 20			22 25							23 11		23 27
Crawley	d		21 59		22 08					22 29			22 38							23 24		23 40
Three Bridges	d	21 59	22 04		22 13				22 29	22 34		22 40	22 43				22 59		23 29	23 29	23 40	23 44
Gatwick Airport	d	22 06	22 09	22 12	22 19	22 23	22 28	22 33	22 36	22 39	22 42	22 46	22 49	22 53	22 57	23 03	23 06	23 12	23 34	23 34	23 55	23a49
East Croydon	a	22 21	22 24		22 45		22 42	22 48	22 51	22 54		23 01	23 15		23 11	23 18	23 21		23 52	00 09	00 15	
East Croydon	d	22 21			22 46				22 51			23 01	23 15				23 21		23 53	00 10		
London Bridge	d	22 35			23 01				23 05			23 16	23 31				23 35					
London Blackfriars	d	22 42			23 07				23 12			23 22	23 37				23 42		00 22	00 37		
City Thameslink	d																					
Farringdon	d	22 46			23 11				23 16			23 26	23 41				23 46		00 26	00 41		
St Pancras International	a	22 50			23 15				23 20			23 30	23 45				23 50		00 30	00 45		
East Croydon	d		22 24				22 43	22 49		22 54					23 12	23 19					00 16	
Clapham Junction	a		22 33				22 52	22 58		23 04					23 21	23 28					00 33	
London Victoria	a		22 41	22 43		22 53	23 00	23 05		23 11	23 13			23 23	23 29	23 35		23 43			00 41	

		TL
Horsham	d	
Crawley	d	
Three Bridges	d	23 58
Gatwick Airport	d	00 04
East Croydon	a	00 22
East Croydon	d	00 23
London Bridge	d	
London Blackfriars	d	00 50
City Thameslink	d	
Farringdon	d	
St Pancras International	a	00 59
East Croydon	d	
Clapham Junction	a	
London Victoria	a	

Sundays
15 December to 10 May

		TL A	TL	SN	SN	SN	SN	GX	TL	GX	TL	SN	GX	TL	SN	TL	GX	TL	SN	GX	TL	SN	TL
Horsham	d											06 01			06 31	06 39			07 05				07 35
Crawley	d											06 14			06 44	06 52			07 14				07 48
Three Bridges	d	00 15	00 37	02 08	03 08	04 08	04 58		05 54		06 13	06 23		06 43	06 49	06 56		07 13	07 23		07 43		07 52
Gatwick Airport	d	00 21	00 42	02 13	03 13	04 13	05 03	05 48	06 00	06 18	06 21	06 28	06 48	06 51	06 54	07 02	07 18	07 21	07 28	07 48	07 51	07 54	07 58
East Croydon	a	00 39	01 09	02 35	03 36	04 35	05 29		06 33		06 40	06 50		07 09	07 22	07 31		07 39	07 50		08 09	08 22	08 31
East Croydon	d	00 40	01 10						06 34		06 41			07 10		07 32		07 40			08 10		08 32
London Bridge	d								06a52		06a56			07a25		07a50		07a55			08a25		08a50
London Blackfriars	d	01 06	01 36																				
City Thameslink	d																						
Farringdon	d																						
St Pancras International	a	01 15	01 43																				
East Croydon	d			02 36	03 37	04 36	05 30					06 51			07 23				07 51			08 23	
Clapham Junction	a			02 49	03 50	04 49	05 51					07 05			07 37				08 07			08 38	
London Victoria	a			02 58	03 58	04 58	05 59	06 24		06 58		07 15	07 28		07 46		07 58		08 17	08 28		08 46	

A not 15 December

Table T185-R

Sundays
15 December to 10 May

Horsham - Three Bridges - Gatwick Airport - London : Summary of Fast Trains

		GX	TL	SN	SN	TL	TL	TL	GX	SN	SN	TL	TL	TL	GX	SN	SN	SN	TL	TL	TL	GX
Horsham	d				08 17							08 48						09 21				
Crawley	d				08 26							09 01						09 30				
Three Bridges	d		08 13		08 31		08 42	08 43				09 05	09 13	09 13			09 25	09 35		09 43	09 43	
Gatwick Airport	d	08 15	08 21	08 25	08 36	08 46	08 47	08 49	08 53	08 56	09 00	09 11	09 19	09 19	09 22	09 25	09 30	09 41	09 46	09 49	09 49	09 52
East Croydon	a		08 39	08 45	08 58	09 06	09 02	09 17		09 10	09 14	09 37	09 33	09 47		09 40	09 44	10 03	10 07	10 03	10 17	
East Croydon	d		08 40			09 07	09 02	09 18				09 37	09 34	09 48					10 07	10 04	10 18	
London Bridge	d		08a55			09 25	09a17	09 33				09a57	09 49	10 03					10 25	10 19	10 33	
London Blackfriars	d					09 31		09 39					09 55	10 09					10 31	10 25	10 39	
City Thameslink	d																					
Farringdon	d					09 35		09 43					09 59	10 13					10 35	10 29	10 43	
St Pancras International	a					09 39		09 47					10 03	10 17					10 39	10 33	10 47	
East Croydon	d			08 46	08 59					09 11	09 15					09 41	09 45	10 04				
Clapham Junction	a			08 55	09 08					09 20	09 24					09 50	09 54	10 14				
London Victoria	a	08 54		09 02	09 15				09 20	09 28	09 32				09 50	09 58	10 02	10 21				10 24

		SN	SN	GX	TL	TL	TL	GX	SN	SN	GX	SN	TL	TL	TL	GX	SN	SN	GX	TL	TL	TL	GX
Horsham	d				09 48							10 21								10 48			
Crawley	d				10 01							10 30								11 01			
Three Bridges	d				10 05	10 13				10 25		10 35		10 43	10 43					11 05	11 13		
Gatwick Airport	d	09 56	10 00	10 06	10 11	10 19	10 19	10 22	10 25	10 30	10 36	10 41	10 46	10 49	10 49	10 52	10 56	11 00	11 06	11 11	11 19	11 19	11 22
East Croydon	a	10 10	10 14		10 37	10 33	10 47		10 40	10 44		11 03	11 07	11 03	11 17		11 10	11 14		11 37	11 33	11 47	
East Croydon	d				10 37	10 34	10 48						11 07	11 04	11 18					11 37	11 34	11 48	
London Bridge	d				10a58	10 49	11 03						11 25	11 19	11 33					11a57	11 49	12 03	
London Blackfriars	d					10 55	11 09						11 31	11 25	11 39						11 55	12 09	
City Thameslink	d																						
Farringdon	d					10 59	11 13						11 35	11 29	11 43						11 59	12 13	
St Pancras International	a					11 03	11 17						11 39	11 33	11 47						12 03	12 17	
East Croydon	d	10 11	10 15						10 41	10 45		11 04					11 11	11 15					
Clapham Junction	a	10 20	10 24						10 50	10 54		11 14					11 20	11 24					
London Victoria	a	10 28	10 32	10 36				10 50	10 58	11 02	11 05	11 21				11 24	11 28	11 32	11 36				11 50

		SN	SN	GX	SN	TL	TL	TL	GX	SN	SN	GX	TL	TL	TL	GX	SN	SN	GX	SN	TL	TL
Horsham	d				11 21								11 48							12 21		
Crawley	d				11 30								12 01							12 30		
Three Bridges	d		11 25		11 35		11 43	11 43					12 05	12 13				12 25		12 35		12 43
Gatwick Airport	d	11 25	11 30	11 36	11 41	11 46	11 49	11 49	11 52	11 56	12 00	12 06	12 11	12 19	12 19	12 22	12 25	12 30	12 36	12 41	12 46	12 49
East Croydon	a	11 39	11 44		12 03	12 07	12 03	12 17		12 10	12 14		12 37	12 33	12 47		12 40	12 44		13 06	13 06	13 03
East Croydon	d					12 07	12 04	12 18					12 37	12 34	12 48						13 07	13 04
London Bridge	d					12 25	12 19	12 33					12a57	12 49	13 03						13 25	13 19
London Blackfriars	d					12 31	12 25	12 41						12 55	13 09						13 31	13 25
City Thameslink	d																					
Farringdon	d					12 35	12 29	12 45						12 59	13 13						13 35	13 29
St Pancras International	a					12 39	12 33	12 49						13 03	13 17						13 39	13 33
East Croydon	d	11 40	11 45		12 04					12 11	12 15						12 41	12 45		13 06		
Clapham Junction	a	11 50	11 54		12 14					12 20	12 24						12 50	12 54		13 16		
London Victoria	a	11 58	12 02	12 05	12 21				12 24	12 28	12 32	12 36				12 50	12 58	13 02	13 05	13 23		

		TL	GX	SN	SN	GX	TL	TL	TL	GX	SN	SN	GX	SN	TL	TL	TL	GX	SN	SN	GX	TL	TL
Horsham	d						12 48							13 21								13 48	
Crawley	d						13 01							13 30								14 01	
Three Bridges	d	12 43					13 05	13 13				13 25		13 35		13 43	13 43					14 05	14 13
Gatwick Airport	d	12 49	12 52	12 56	13 00	13 06	13 11	13 19	13 19	13 22	13 25	13 30	13 36	13 41	13 46	13 49	13 49	13 52	13 56	14 00	14 06	14 11	14 19
East Croydon	a	13 17		13 10	13 14		13 37	13 33	13 47		13 40	13 44		14 03	14 07	14 03	14 17		14 10	14 14		14 37	14 33
East Croydon	d	13 18					13 37	13 34	13 48						14 07	14 04	14 18					14 37	14 34
London Bridge	d	13 33					13a57	13 49	14 03						14 25	14 19	14 33					14a57	14 49
London Blackfriars	d	13 39						13 55	14 09						14 31	14 25	14 39						14 55
City Thameslink	d																						
Farringdon	d	13 43						13 59	14 13						14 35	14 29	14 43						14 59
St Pancras International	a	13 47						14 03	14 17						14 39	14 33	14 47						15 03
East Croydon	d			13 11	13 15						13 41	13 45		14 04					14 11	14 15			
Clapham Junction	a			13 22	13 25						13 50	13 54		14 14					14 20	14 24			
London Victoria	a		13 28	13 30	13 32	13 36				13 50	13 58	14 02	14 05	14 21				14 24	14 28	14 32	14 36		

		TL	GX	SN	SN	GX	SN	TL	TL	TL	GX	SN	SN	GX	TL	TL	TL	GX	SN	SN	GX	SN	TL
Horsham	d						14 21								14 48							15 21	
Crawley	d						14 30								15 01							15 30	
Three Bridges	d				14 25		14 35		14 43	14 43					15 05	15 13				15 25		15 35	
Gatwick Airport	d	14 19	14 22	14 25	14 30	14 36	14 41	14 46	14 49	14 49	14 52	14 56	15 00	15 06	15 11	15 19	15 19	15 22	15 25	15 30	15 36	15 41	15 46
East Croydon	a	14 47		14 40	14 44		15 03	15 07	15 03	15 17		15 10	15 14		15 37	15 33	15 47		15 40	15 44		16 06	16 06
East Croydon	d	14 48						15 07	15 04	15 18					15 37	15 34	15 48						16 07
London Bridge	d	15 03						15 25	15 19	15 33					15a57	15 49	16 03						16 25
London Blackfriars	d	15 09						15 31	15 25	15 39						15 55	16 09						16 31
City Thameslink	d																						
Farringdon	d	15 13						15 35	15 29	15 43						15 59	16 13						16 35
St Pancras International	a	15 17						15 39	15 33	15 47						16 03	16 17						16 39
East Croydon	d			14 41	14 45		15 04					15 11	15 15						15 41	15 45		16 06	
Clapham Junction	a			14 50	14 54		15 14					15 20	15 24						15 50	15 54		16 16	
London Victoria	a		14 50	14 58	15 02	15 05	15 21				15 24	15 28	15 32	15 36				15 50	15 58	16 02	16 05	16 23	

Table T185-R

Sundays

15 December to 10 May

Horsham - Three Bridges - Gatwick Airport - London : Summary of Fast Trains

		TL 1	TL 1	GX 1	SN 1	SN 1	GX 1	TL 1		TL 1	TL 1	GX 1	SN 1	SN 1	GX 1	SN 1	TL 1	TL 1		TL 1	GX 1	SN 1	SN 1	GX 1	TL 1
Horsham	d							15 48								16 21									16 48
Crawley	d							16 01								16 30									17 01
Three Bridges	d	15 43	15 43					16 05		16 13				16 25		16 35		16 43		16 43					17 05
Gatwick Airport	d	15 49	15 49	15 52	15 56	16 00	16 06	16 11		16 19	16 19	16 22	16 25	16 30	16 36	16 41	16 46	16 49		16 49	16 52	16 56	17 00	17 06	17 11
East Croydon	a	16 03	16 17		16 10	16 14		16 37		16 33	16 47		16 40	16 44		17 06	17 06	17 03		17 17		17 10	17 14		17 37
East Croydon	d	16 04	16 18					16 37		16 34	16 48						17 07	17 04		17 18					17 37
London Bridge	d	16 19	16 33					16a57		16 49	17 03						17 25	17 19		17 33					17a57
London Blackfriars	d	16 25	16 39							16 55	17 09						17 31	17 25		17 39					
City Thameslink	d																								
Farringdon	d	16 29	16 43							16 59	17 13						17 35	17 29		17 43					
St Pancras International	a	16 33	16 47							17 03	17 17						17 39	17 33		17 47					
East Croydon	d				16 11	16 15							16 41	16 45		17 06						17 11	17 15		
Clapham Junction	a				16 22	16 25							16 50	16 54		17 16						17 22	17 25		
London Victoria	a			16 28	16 30	16 32	16 36					16 50	16 58	17 02	17 05	17 23					17 28	17 30	17 32	17 36	

		TL 1	TL 1	GX 1		SN 1	SN 1	GX 1	SN 1	TL 1	TL 1	TL 1	GX 1	SN 1		SN 1	GX 1	TL 1	TL 1	TL 1	GX 1	SN 1	SN 1	GX 1	
Horsham	d								17 21									17 48							
Crawley	d								17 30									18 01							
Three Bridges	d	17 13					17 25		17 35		17 43	17 43						18 05	18 13				18 25		
Gatwick Airport	d	17 19	17 19	17 22		17 25	17 30	17 36	17 41	17 46	17 49	17 49	17 52	17 56		18 00	18 06	18 11	18 19	18 19	18 22	18 25	18 30	18 36	
East Croydon	a	17 33	17 47			17 40	17 44		18 03	18 07	18 03	18 17		18 10		18 14		18 37	18 33	18 47		18 40	18 44		
East Croydon	d	17 34	17 48							18 07	18 04	18 18						18 37	18 34	18 48					
London Bridge	d	17 49	18 03							18 25	18 19	18 33						18a57	18 49	19 03					
London Blackfriars	d	17 55	18 09							18 31	18 25	18 39							18 55	19 09					
City Thameslink	d																								
Farringdon	d	17 59	18 13							18 35	18 29	18 43							18 59	19 13					
St Pancras International	a	18 03	18 17							18 39	18 33	18 47							19 03	19 17					
East Croydon	d					17 41	17 45		18 04					18 11		18 15						18 41	18 45		
Clapham Junction	a					17 50	17 54		18 14					18 20		18 24						18 50	18 54		
London Victoria	a			17 50		17 58	18 02	18 05	18 21				18 24	18 28		18 32	18 36				18 50	18 58	19 02	19 05	

		SN 1	TL 1	TL 1	TL 1	GX 1	SN 1	SN 1	GX 1	TL 1		TL 1	TL 1	GX 1	SN 1	SN 1	GX 1	SN 1	TL 1	TL 1		TL 1	GX 1	SN 1	SN 1
Horsham	d	18 21								18 48								19 21							
Crawley	d	18 30								19 01								19 30							
Three Bridges	d	18 35		18 43	18 43					19 05		19 13				19 25		19 35		19 43		19 43			
Gatwick Airport	d	18 41	18 46	18 49	18 49	18 52	18 56	19 00	19 06	19 11		19 19	19 19	19 22	19 25	19 30	19 36	19 41	19 46	19 49		19 49	19 52	19 56	20 00
East Croydon	a	19 03	19 07	19 03	19 17		19 10	19 14		19 37		19 33	19 47		19 40	19 44		20 03	20 07	20 03		20 17		20 10	20 14
East Croydon	d		19 07	19 04	19 18					19 37		19 34	19 48						20 07	20 04		20 18			
London Bridge	d		19 25	19 19	19 33					19a57		19 49	20 03						20 25	20 19		20 33			
London Blackfriars	d		19 31	19 25	19 39							19 55	20 09						20 31	20 25		20 39			
City Thameslink	d																								
Farringdon	d		19 35	19 29	19 43							19 59	20 13						20 35	20 29		20 43			
St Pancras International	a		19 39	19 33	19 47							20 03	20 17						20 39	20 33		20 47			
East Croydon	d	19 04					19 11	19 15							19 41	19 45		20 04						20 11	20 15
Clapham Junction	a	19 14					19 20	19 24							19 50	19 54		20 14						20 20	20 24
London Victoria	a	19 21				19 24	19 28	19 32	19 36					19 50	19 58	20 02	20 05	20 21					20 24	20 28	20 32

		GX 1	TL 1	TL 1	TL 1	GX 1		SN 1	SN 1	GX 1	SN 1	TL 1	TL 1	TL 1	GX 1	SN 1		SN 1	GX 1	TL 1	TL 1	TL 1	GX 1	SN 1	SN 1
Horsham	d		19 48								20 21									20 48					
Crawley	d		20 01								20 30									21 01					
Three Bridges	d		20 05	20 13					20 25		20 35		20 43	20 43						21 05	21 13				21 25
Gatwick Airport	d	20 06	20 11	20 19	20 19	20 22		20 25	20 30	20 36	20 41	20 46	20 49	20 49	20 52	20 56		21 00	21 06	21 11	21 19	21 19	21 22	21 25	21 30
East Croydon	a		20 37	20 33	20 47			20 40	20 44		21 03	21 07	21 03	21 17		21 10		21 14		21 37	21 33	21 47		21 40	21 44
East Croydon	d		20 37	20 34	20 48							21 07	21 04	21 18						21 37	21 34	21 48			
London Bridge	d		20a57	20 49	21 03							21 25	21 19	21 33						21a57	21 49	22 03			
London Blackfriars	d			20 55	21 09							21 31	21 25	21 39							21 55	22 09			
City Thameslink	d																								
Farringdon	d			20 59	21 13							21 35	21 29	21 43							21 59	22 13			
St Pancras International	a			21 03	21 17							21 39	21 33	21 47							22 03	22 17			
East Croydon	d							20 41	20 45		21 04					21 11		21 15						21 41	21 45
Clapham Junction	a							20 50	20 54		21 14					21 20		21 24						21 50	21 54
London Victoria	a	20 36				20 50		20 58	21 02	21 05	21 21				21 24	21 28		21 32	21 36				21 50	21 58	22 02

		GX 1		SN 1	TL 1	TL 1	GX 1	SN 1	SN 1	TL 1	TL 1	GX 1		SN 1	TL 1	SN 1	TL 1	GX 1	SN 1	TL 1	GX 1	TL 1		SN 1	SN 1
Horsham	d			21 21						21 48						22 21				22 41					23 14
Crawley	d			21 30						22 01						22 30				22 54					23 27
Three Bridges	d			21 35		21 43				22 05	22 13			22 25	22 31	22 35	22 43		22 55	22a58		23 15		23 25	23 31
Gatwick Airport	d	21 36		21 41	21 46	21 49	21 52	21 56	22 00	22 11	22 19	22 22		22 30	22 39	22 41	22 49	22 52	23 00		23 18	23 21		23 30	23 36
East Croydon	a			22 03	22 07	22 03		22 10	22 14	22 45	22 33			22 44	23 12	23 03	23 03		23 14			23 39		23 51	00 05
East Croydon	d				22 07	22 04				22 47	22 34				23 12		23 04					23 40			
London Bridge	d				22 25	22 19				23a05	22 49				23a30		23 19								
London Blackfriars	d				22 31	22 25					22 55						23 27					00 06			
City Thameslink	d																								
Farringdon	d				22 35	22 29					22 59						23 31					00 11			
St Pancras International	a				22 39	22 33					23 03						23 35					00 15			
East Croydon	d			22 04				22 11	22 15					22 45		23 04			23 15					23 52	00 06
Clapham Junction	a			22 14				22 20	22 24					22 54		23 14			23 24					00 08	00 18
London Victoria	a	22 05		22 21			22 24	22 28	22 32			22 50		23 02		23 21		23 25	23 31		23 49			00 17	00 27

NRT DECEMBER 19 EDITION

Table T185-R

Sundays

15 December to 10 May

Horsham - Three Bridges - Gatwick Airport - London : Summary of Fast Trains

		TL 1
Horsham	d	
Crawley	d	
Three Bridges	d	23 45
Gatwick Airport	d	23 50
East Croydon	a	00 09
East Croydon	d	00 10
London Bridge	d	
London Blackfriars	d	00 36
City Thameslink	d	
Farringdon	d	
St Pancras International	a	00 45
East Croydon	d	
Clapham Junction	a	
London Victoria	a	

AVAILABLE FROM MP Middleton Press

Table T186-F

Mondays to Fridays

16 December to 15 May

London, Gatwick Airport, Arun Valley and Brighton - Bognor Regis, Chichester, Portsmouth and Southampton

Miles	Miles	Miles			SN MX	SN ■	SN	SN ■	SN	SN	SN	SN	SN ■	SN	SN	SN ■	SN	SN	SN	SN ■	SN	SN ■	SN
0	—	—	London Victoria	d																			
2¾	—	—	Clapham Junction	d																			
10½	—	—	East Croydon	a																			
—	0	—	London Bridge	d																			
—	10¼	—	East Croydon	a																			
—	—	—	East Croydon	d																			
26¾	26¾	—	Gatwick Airport	d																05 56			
29¼	29¼	—	Three Bridges	a																06 00			
—	—	—		d																06 01			
30¾	—	—	Crawley	d																06 05			
38	—	—	Horsham	a																06 17			
—	—	—		d																06 18			
39¾	—	—	**Christs Hospital**	d																06 22			
41¾	—	—	**Billingshurst**	d																06 28			
43	—	—	**Pulborough**	d																06 34			
44¼	—	—	**Amberley**	d																06 40			
48	—	—	**Arundel**	d																06 45			
—	50½	0	Brighton	d								05 00				05 27	06 02					06 32	
—	—	1	Hove	d								05 05				05 32	06 06					06 36	
—	—	2½	Portslade	d								05 08				05 37	06 09					06 39	
—	—	3¾	Southwick	d								05 11				05 41	06 12					06 42	
—	—	5½	Shoreham-by-Sea	d								05 14				05 44	06 16					06 46	
—	—	7¾	Lancing	d								05 18				05 48	06 20					06 50	
—	—	10¼	Worthing	d								05 22				05 54	06 24					06 55	
—	—	10¾	West Worthing	d								05 24				05 56	06 27					06 57	
—	—	11¾	Durrington-on-Sea	d								05 27				05 59	06 29					06 59	
—	—	12½	Goring-by-Sea	d								05 29				06 01	06 32					07 02	
—	—	15¼	Angmering	d								05 33				06 05	06 36					07 06	
51¼	—	—	Littlehampton	d				05 04			05 29			05 56	06 00			06 43					07 08
53½	—	19½	**Ford**	d				05 09			05 34			06 01	06 05	06 13		06 48		06 52		07 13	07 17
56¼	—	21¾	**Barnham**	a				05 13			05 39	05 44		06 05	06 09	06 17	06 47	06 52		06 57		07 18	07 22
—	—	—	**Barnham**	d	00 36				05 28		05 46				06 11				06 55				
—	—	—	**Bognor Regis**	a	00 43				05 35		05 53				06 18				07 01		←		
—	—	—	**Barnham**	d		04 59	05 03	05 15		05 21		05 45	06 03	06 06		06 19	06 48	07 02		06 58	07 02	07 19	07 22
62¾	—	28¾	**Chichester**	a		05 06	05 10	05 22		05 28		05 52	06 10	06 13		06 26	06 56	→		07 05	07 09	07 26	07 30
—	—	—		d		05 07	05 11	05 23		05 29		05 53	06 11	06 14		06 27	06 56			07 06	07 10	07 27	07 30
64	—	29¾	**Fishbourne (Sussex)**	d										06 17							07 13		07 33
65¼	—	31¼	**Bosham**	d										06 20							07 16		07 36
66¾	—	32¾	**Nutbourne**	d										06 23							07 19		07 40
67¾	—	33¾	**Southbourne**	d								06 00		06 26		06 34	07 03			07 13	07 22		07 42
69½	—	35¼	**Emsworth**	d								06 03		06 29		06 37	07 06			07 16	07 25	07 35	07 45
70¾	—	36½	**Warblington**	d										06 32							07 28		
71¼	—	37¼	Havant	a		05 17	05 21	05 33		05 39		06 06	06 21	06 34		06 40	07 10			07 19	07 30	07 38	07 49
72	—	—	Bedhampton	a										06 37							07 35		07 52
—	—	41¼	Hilsea	a										06 43							07 40		07 57
—	—	43½	Fratton	a			05 30			05 48		06 15		06 47			07 21				07 44		08 01
—	—	44½	Portsmouth & Southsea	a			05 33			05 52		06 20		06 51			07 25				07 48		08 05
—	—	45¼	Portsmouth Harbour	a			05 37			05 56		06 24		06 57									
75¼	—	—	Cosham	a		05 24		05 41					06 29			06 49				07 27		07 45	
78½	—	—	Portchester	a		05 28		05 46								06 54				07 31			
81¼	—	—	Fareham	a		05 33		05 51					06 38			06 59				07 36		07 56	
84¾	—	—	Swanwick	a		05 40		05 58					06 44			07 06				07 43		08 03	
95¾	—	—	Southampton Central	a		06 00		06 18					07 02			07 25				08 03		08 20	

Table T186-F

Mondays to Fridays

16 December to 15 May

London, Gatwick Airport, Arun Valley and Brighton - Bognor Regis, Chichester, Portsmouth and Southampton

		SN	SN ■	SN	SN	SN	SN ■	SN ■	SN	SN	SN	SN ■	SN	SN	SN	SN ■		SN ■	SN	GW ◇	SN ■		SN
London Victoria	d		05 54				06 36					07 06					07 36					08 06	
Clapham Junction	d		06 01				06 43					07 13					07 43					08 13	
East Croydon	a		06 10				06 52					07 22					07 52					08 22	
London Bridge	d																						
East Croydon	a																						
East Croydon	d		06 10				06 52					07 22					07 52					08 22	
Gatwick Airport	d		06 26				07 08					07 38					08 08					08 38	
Three Bridges	a		06 31				07 13					07 42					08 13					08 43	
	d		06 32				07 13					07 45					08 14					08 44	
Crawley	d		06 36				07 17					07 49					08 18					08 48	
Horsham	a		06 50				07 28					07 57					08 27					08 57	
	d		06 52				07 29					08 00				08 31	08 34				09 01	09 04	
Christs Hospital	d		06 56				07 33					08 04					08 38					09 08	
Billingshurst	d		07 03				07 39					08 10					08 44					09 14	
Pulborough	d		07 09				07 46					08 17					08 51					09 21	
Amberley	d		07 15				07 52					08 23					08 57					09 27	
Arundel	d		07 20				07 57					08 28					09 01					09 32	
Brighton	d				06 59			07 32		07 41			08 00					08 32		09 00			09 05
Hove	d				07 03			07 36		07 45			08 04					08 36		09 04			09 09
Portslade	d				07 06			07 39		07 48			08 07					08 39					09 12
Southwick	d				07 09			07 42		07 51			08 10					08 42					09 16
Shoreham-by-Sea	d				07 13			07 46		07 55			08 14					08 46		09 13			09 20
Lancing	d				07 17			07 50		07 59			08 18					08 50					09 24
Worthing	d				07 22			07 55		08 04			08 25					08 55		09 22			09 29
West Worthing	d							07 57		08 06			08 27					08 57					
Durrington-on-Sea	d							07 59		08 08			08 29					08 59					
Goring-by-Sea	d							08 02		08 11			08 32					09 02					
Angmering	d				07 28			08 06		08 15			08 36					09 06					09 35
Littlehampton	d			07 26		07 53			08 10		08 24				08 55				09 10				
Ford	d		07 26	07 31		07 58	08 03	08 13	08 17	08 23	08 29	08 34			09 00		09 07	09 13	09 17			09 39	
Barnham	a		07 32	07 36	07 39	08 02	08 08	08 18	08 22	08 28	08 33	08 39	08 47		09 04	08 58	09 12	09 18	09 22	09 38	09 28	09 43	09 47
Barnham	d	07 32		07 44			08 10		08 23			08 40		08 52			09 13		09 23			09 44	
Bognor Regis	a	07 38		07 51			08 18		08 30			08 46		08 59			09 19		09 30			09 50	
Barnham	d		07 35		07 40	08 04		08 19		08 28	08 36		08 48		09 05	08 59		09 19		09 38	09 29		09 48
Chichester	a		07 43		07 48	08 11		08 26		08 36	08 44		08 55		09 12	09 06		09 26		09 46	09 37		09 55
	d		07 44		07 48	08 12		08 27		08 36			08 56		09 13	09 07		09 27		09 46	09 37		09 56
Fishbourne (Sussex)	d					08 15									09 16								
Bosham	d					08 18									09 19								
Nutbourne	d					08 21									09 22								
Southbourne	d		07 51		07 55	08 24							09 03		09 25	09 14							10 03
Emsworth	d		07 54		07 58	08 27		08 35					09 06		09 28	09 17		09 35					10 06
Warblington	d		07 57			08 30									09 31								
Havant	a		07 59		08 03	08 32		08 38		08 46			09 09		09 33	09 22		09 39		09 57	09 47		10 09
Bedhampton	a					08 36									09 36								
Hilsea	a					08 41									09 42								
Fratton	a				08 12	08 45				08 56			09 18		09 47						09 56		10 18
Portsmouth & Southsea	a				08 16	08 49				08 59			09 23		09 50						10 00		10 23
Portsmouth Harbour	a				08 22					09 04											10 04		
Cosham	a		08 07					08 46								09 29		09 47		10 04			
Portchester	a		08 12													09 34							
Fareham	a		08 17					08 54								09 39		09 55		10 12			
Swanwick	a		08 24					09 00								09 46		10 01					
Southampton Central	a		08 52					09 20								10 05		10 19		10 40			

Table T186-F

Mondays to Fridays

16 December to 15 May

London, Gatwick Airport, Arun Valley and Brighton - Bognor Regis, Chichester, Portsmouth and Southampton

Station		SN	SN	SN 1		SN 1	SN	SN 1		SN	SN	SN	SN 1		SN 1	SN	SN 1		SN	SN	SN	SN 1	
London Victoria	d			08 36				09 06					09 36				10 06					10 36	
Clapham Junction	d			08 43				09 13					09 43				10 13					10 43	
East Croydon	a			08 52				09 22					09 52				10 22					10 52	
London Bridge	d																						
East Croydon	a																						
East Croydon	d			08 53				09 23					09 53				10 23					10 53	
Gatwick Airport	d			09 09				09 39					10 09				10 39					11 09	
Three Bridges	a			09 14				09 44					10 14				10 44					11 14	
	d			09 15				09 44					10 14				10 44					11 14	
Crawley	d			09 19				09 48					10 18				10 48					11 18	
Horsham	a			09 27				09 57					10 27				10 57					11 27	
	d			09 31	09 34			10 01	10 04				10 31	10 34			11 01	11 04				11 31	11 34
Christs Hospital	d				09 38									10 38									11 38
Billingshurst	d				09 44				10 12					10 44				11 12					11 44
Pulborough	d				09 51				10 19					10 51				11 19					11 51
Amberley	d				09 57									10 57									11 57
Arundel	d				10 01				10 28					11 01				11 28					12 01
Brighton	d					09 32				10 02					10 32				11 02				
Hove	d					09 36				10 06					10 36				11 06				
Portslade	d					09 39				10 09					10 39				11 09				
Southwick	d					09 42				10 12					10 42				11 12				
Shoreham-by-Sea	d					09 46				10 16					10 46				11 16				
Lancing	d					09 50				10 20					10 50				11 20				
Worthing	d					09 55				10 25					10 55				11 25				
West Worthing	d					09 57									10 57								
Durrington-on-Sea	d					09 59									10 59								
Goring-by-Sea	d					10 02									11 02								
Angmering	d					10 06				10 32					11 06				11 32				
Littlehampton	d		09 55				10 10					10 55				11 10					11 55		
Ford	d		10 00		10 07	10 13	10 17		10 34			11 00		11 07	11 13	11 17		11 34			12 00		12 07
Barnham	a		10 04	09 58	10 12	10 18	10 22	10 28	10 39	10 43		11 04	10 58	11 12	11 18	11 22	11 28	11 39	11 43		12 04	11 58	12 12
Barnham	d	09 52			10 13		10 23		10 40		10 52			11 13		11 23		11 40		11 52			12 13
Bognor Regis	a	09 59			10 20		10 30		10 46		10 59			11 20		11 30		11 46		11 59			12 20
Barnham	d		10 05	09 59		10 19		10 29		10 44		11 05	10 59		11 19		11 29		11 44		12 05	11 59	
Chichester	a		10 12	10 06		10 26		10 37		10 51		11 12	11 06		11 26		11 37		11 51		12 12	12 06	
	d		10 13	10 07		10 27		10 37		10 52		11 13	11 07		11 27		11 37		11 52		12 13	12 07	
Fishbourne (Sussex)	d		10 16									11 16									12 16		
Bosham	d		10 19									11 19									12 19		
Nutbourne	d		10 22									11 22									12 22		
Southbourne	d		10 25	10 14						10 59		11 25	11 14						11 59		12 25	12 14	
Emsworth	d		10 28	10 17		10 35				11 02		11 28	11 17		11 35				12 02		12 28	12 17	
Warblington	d		10 31									11 31									12 31		
Havant	a		10 33	10 20		10 38		10 48		11 05		11 33	11 20		11 38		11 48		12 05		12 33	12 20	
Bedhampton	a		10 36									11 36									12 36		
Hilsea	a		10 42									11 42									12 42		
Fratton	a		10 46					10 57		11 14		11 46					11 57		12 14		12 46		
Portsmouth & Southsea	a		10 50					11 01		11 18		11 50					12 01		12 18		12 50		
Portsmouth Harbour	a							11 05		11 22							12 05		12 22				
Cosham	a			10 28		10 46							11 28		11 46							12 28	
Portchester	a			10 33									11 33									12 33	
Fareham	a			10 38		10 54							11 38		11 54							12 38	
Swanwick	a			10 45		11 01							11 45		12 01							12 45	
Southampton Central	a			11 03		11 19							12 02		12 19							13 03	

Table T186-F

Mondays to Fridays

16 December to 15 May

London, Gatwick Airport, Arun Valley and Brighton - Bognor Regis, Chichester, Portsmouth and Southampton

Station		SN 1	SN	SN 1		SN	SN	SN	SN 1		SN 1	SN	SN 1		SN	SN	SN	SN 1		SN 1	SN
London Victoria	d			11 06					11 36				12 06					12 36			
Clapham Junction	d			11 13					11 43				12 13					12 43			
East Croydon	a			11 22					11 52				12 22					12 52			
London Bridge	d																				
East Croydon	a																				
East Croydon	d			11 23					11 53				12 23					12 53			
Gatwick Airport	d			11 39					12 09				12 39					13 09			
Three Bridges	a			11 44					12 14				12 44					13 14			
	d			11 44					12 14				12 44					13 14			
Crawley	d			11 48					12 18				12 48					13 18			
Horsham	a			11 57					12 27				12 57					13 27			
	d			12 01	12 04				12 31	12 34			13 01	13 04				13 31	13 34		
Christs Hospital	d									12 38									13 38		
Billingshurst	d				12 12					12 44				13 12					13 44		
Pulborough	d				12 19					12 51				13 19					13 51		
Amberley	d									12 57									13 57		
Arundel	d				12 28					13 01				13 28					14 01		
Brighton	d	11 32				12 02					12 32				13 02					13 32	
Hove	d	11 36				12 06					12 36				13 06					13 36	
Portslade	d	11 39				12 09					12 39				13 09					13 39	
Southwick	d	11 42				12 12					12 42				13 12					13 42	
Shoreham-by-Sea	d	11 46				12 16					12 46				13 16					13 46	
Lancing	d	11 50				12 20					12 50				13 20					13 50	
Worthing	d	11 55				12 25					12 55				13 25					13 55	
West Worthing	d	11 57									12 57									13 57	
Durrington-on-Sea	d	11 59									12 59									13 59	
Goring-by-Sea	d	12 02									13 02									14 02	
Angmering	d	12 06				12 32					13 06				13 32					14 06	
Littlehampton	d		12 10					12 55				13 10					13 55				14 10
Ford	d	12 13	12 17		12 34			13 00		13 07	13 13	13 17		13 34			14 00		14 07	14 13	14 17
Barnham	a	12 18	12 22	12 28	12 39	12 43		13 05	12 59	13 12	13 18	13 22	13 28	13 39	13 43		14 04	13 58	14 12	14 18	14 22
Barnham	d		12 23		12 40		12 52			13 13		13 23		13 40		13 52			14 13		14 23
Bognor Regis	a		12 30		12 46		12 59			13 20		13 30		13 46		13 59			14 20		14 30
Barnham	d	12 19		12 29		12 44		13 05	12 59		13 19		13 29		13 44		14 05	13 59		14 19	
Chichester	a	12 26		12 37		12 51		13 13	13 07		13 26		13 37		13 51		14 12	14 06		14 26	
	d	12 27		12 37		12 52		13 13	13 07		13 27		13 37		13 52		14 13	14 07		14 27	
Fishbourne (Sussex)	d							13 16									14 16				
Bosham	d							13 19									14 19				
Nutbourne	d							13 23									14 22				
Southbourne	d					12 59		13 25	13 14						13 59		14 25	14 14			
Emsworth	d	12 35				13 02		13 28	13 17		13 35				14 02		14 28	14 17		14 35	
Warblington	d							13 31									14 31				
Havant	a	12 38		12 48		13 05		13 34	13 21		13 38		13 48		14 05		14 33	14 21		14 38	
Bedhampton	a							13 37									14 36				
Hilsea	a							13 42									14 42				
Fratton	a			12 57		13 14		13 46					13 57		14 14		14 46				
Portsmouth & Southsea	a			13 01		13 18		13 50					14 01		14 18		14 50				
Portsmouth Harbour	a			13 05		13 22							14 05		14 22						
Cosham	a	12 46							13 28		13 46							14 28		14 46	
Portchester	a								13 33									14 33			
Fareham	a	12 56							13 38		13 54							14 38		14 54	
Swanwick	a	13 03							13 46		14 01							14 45		15 01	
Southampton Central	a	13 20							14 03		14 19							15 03		15 19	

Table T186-F

Mondays to Fridays

16 December to 15 May

London, Gatwick Airport, Arun Valley and Brighton - Bognor Regis, Chichester, Portsmouth and Southampton

		SN ■		SN	SN	SN	SN ■			SN ■	SN	SN ■		SN	SN	SN	SN ■			SN ■	SN	SN ■		SN	SN
London Victoria	d	13 06					13 36					14 06					14 36					15 06			
Clapham Junction	d	13 13					13 43					14 13					14 43					15 13			
East Croydon	a	13 22					13 52					14 22					14 53					15 22			
London Bridge	d																								
East Croydon	a																								
East Croydon	d	13 23					13 53					14 23					14 53					15 23			
Gatwick Airport	d	13 39					14 09					14 39					15 09					15 39			
Three Bridges	a	13 44					14 14					14 44					15 14					15 44			
	d	13 44					14 14					14 44					15 14					15 44			
Crawley	d	13 48					14 18					14 48					15 18					15 48			
Horsham	a	13 57					14 27					14 57					15 27					15 57			
	d	14 01	14 04				14 31	14 34				15 01	15 04				15 31	15 34				16 01	16 04		
Christs Hospital	d							14 38					15 08					15 38					16 08		
Billingshurst	d		14 12					14 44					15 15					15 44					16 14		
Pulborough	d		14 19					14 51					15 22					15 51					16 21		
Amberley	d							14 57										15 57							
Arundel	d		14 28					15 01					15 31					16 01					16 30		
Brighton	d			14 02						14 32				15 02						15 32				16 02	
Hove	d			14 06						14 36				15 06						15 36				16 06	
Portslade	d			14 09						14 39				15 09						15 39				16 09	
Southwick	d			14 12						14 42				15 12						15 42				16 12	
Shoreham-by-Sea	d			14 16						14 46				15 16						15 46				16 16	
Lancing	d			14 20						14 50				15 20						15 50				16 20	
Worthing	d			14 25						14 55				15 26						15 55				16 27	
West Worthing	d									14 57										15 57					
Durrington-on-Sea	d									14 59										15 59					
Goring-by-Sea	d									15 02										16 02					
Angmering	d			14 32						15 06				15 34						16 06				16 35	
Littlehampton	d					14 55					15 09					15 55					16 10				
Ford	d		14 34			15 00		15 08		15 13	15 17		15 38	15 42		16 00		16 07		16 13	16 17		16 36	16 41	
Barnham	a	14 28	14 39	14 43		15 04	14 58	15 13		15 18	15 22	15 28	15 43	15 47		16 04	15 58	16 12		16 18	16 22	16 28	16 40	16 46	
Barnham	d		14 40		14 54			15 14			15 23		15 43		15 52			16 13			16 23		16 41		16 52
Bognor Regis	a		14 46		15 00			15 21			15 30		15 50		15 59			16 20			16 30		16 48		16 59
Barnham	d	14 29		14 44		15 05	14 59			15 19		15 29		15 48		16 05	15 59			16 19		16 29		16 47	
Chichester	a	14 37		14 51		15 12	15 06			15 26		15 37		15 55		16 12	16 06			16 26		16 37		16 54	
	d	14 37		14 52		15 13	15 07			15 27		15 37		15 56		16 13	16 07			16 27		16 37		16 55	
Fishbourne (Sussex)	d					15 16										16 16									
Bosham	d					15 19										16 19									
Nutbourne	d					15 22										16 22									
Southbourne	d			14 59		15 25	15 14							16 03		16 25	16 14							17 02	
Emsworth	d			15 02		15 28	15 17			15 35				16 06		16 28	16 17			16 35				17 05	
Warblington	d					15 31										16 31									
Havant	a	14 48		15 05		15 33	15 20			15 38		15 48		16 09		16 33	16 20			16 38		16 48		17 08	
Bedhampton	a					15 36										16 36									
Hilsea	a					15 42										16 42									
Fratton	a	14 57		15 14		15 46						15 57		16 18		16 46						16 57		17 18	
Portsmouth & Southsea	a	15 01		15 18		15 50						16 01		16 23		16 50						17 01		17 23	
Portsmouth Harbour	a	15 05		15 22								16 05										17 05			
Cosham	a						15 28			15 46							16 28			16 46					
Portchester	a						15 33										16 33								
Fareham	a						15 38			15 54							16 38			16 54					
Swanwick	a						15 45			16 01							16 45			17 01					
Southampton Central	a						16 03			16 20							17 02			17 19					

Table T186-F

Mondays to Fridays

16 December to 15 May

London, Gatwick Airport, Arun Valley and Brighton - Bognor Regis, Chichester, Portsmouth and Southampton

		SN	SN ■			SN ■	SN	GW ◇	SN ■		SN	SN	SN	SN ■			SN ■	SN	SN ■		SN ■	SN	SN	SN	
London Victoria	d		15 36						16 06					16 36						17 06					
Clapham Junction	d		15 43						16 13					16 43						17 13					
East Croydon	a		15 52						16 23					16 52						17 22					
London Bridge	d																		17 02						
East Croydon	a																		17 16						
East Croydon	d		15 53						16 23					16 53					17 16		17 23				
Gatwick Airport	d		16 09						16 39					17 09							17 39				
Three Bridges	a		16 14						16 44					17 14					17 35		17 44				
	d		16 14						16 44					17 14					17 35		17 44				
Crawley	d		16 18						16 48					17 18					17 39		17 48				
Horsham	a		16 27						16 57					17 27					17 51		18 01				
	d		16 31	16 34					17 01	17 04				17 31	17 34				17 54	17 58	18 02				
Christs Hospital	d			16 38						17 08					17 38					18 02	18 06				
Billingshurst	d			16 44						17 14					17 44					18 08	18 13				
Pulborough	d			16 51						17 21					17 51					18 15	18 20				
Amberley	d			16 57						17 27					17 57						18 26				
Arundel	d			17 01						17 32					18 01					18 25	18 31				
Brighton	d					16 32		17 02			17 05						17 32					18 02			
Hove	d					16 36		17 06			17 10						17 37					18 07			
Portslade	d					16 39					17 13						17 40					18 10			
Southwick	d					16 42					17 16						17 43					18 13			
Shoreham-by-Sea	d					16 46		17 12			17 20						17 47					18 16			
Lancing	d					16 50					17 24						17 51					18 20			
Worthing	d					16 55		17 23			17 28						17 56					18 25			
West Worthing	d					16 57					17 30						17 58					18 27			
Durrington-on-Sea	d					16 59					17 33						18 00					18 29			
Goring-by-Sea	d					17 02					17 35						18 03					18 32			
Angmering	d					17 06					17 39						18 07					18 36			
Littlehampton	d	16 55					17 10						17 55					18 18						18 55	
Ford	d	17 00		17 07		17 13	17 17			17 38	17 47		18 00		18 07		18 14	18 23			18 37	18 43		19 00	
Barnham	a	17 04	16 58	17 12		17 18	17 22	17 38	17 28	17 43	17 52		18 04	17 58	18 12		18 19	18 27	18 23	18 34	18 42	18 48		19 04	
Barnham	d			17 13			17 23			17 44		17 53			18 14			18 28		18 35	18 43		18 52		
Bognor Regis	a			17 20			17 30			17 50		18 00			18 20			18 34		18 43	18 49		18 59		
Barnham	d	17 05	16 59			17 19		17 39	17 29		17 52		18 05	17 59			18 19		18 23			18 49		19 05	
Chichester	a	17 12	17 06			17 26		17 46	17 36		18 00		18 12	18 06			18 27		18 31			18 56		19 12	
	d	17 13	17 07			17 27		17 47	17 37		18 00		18 13	18 07			18 27		18 31			18 57		19 13	
Fishbourne (Sussex)	d	17 16							17 40				18 16						18 34					19 16	
Bosham	d	17 19							17 43				18 19						18 37					19 19	
Nutbourne	d	17 22											18 22											19 22	
Southbourne	d	17 25	17 14						17 47		18 07		18 25	18 14					18 42			19 04		19 25	
Emsworth	d	17 28	17 17			17 35			17 50		18 10		18 28	18 17			18 36		18 45			19 07		19 28	
Warblington	d	17 31											18 31											19 31	
Havant	a	17 33	17 20			17 38		17 57	17 54		18 14		18 34	18 22			18 39		18 48			19 10		19 33	
Bedhampton	a	17 36											18 37											19 36	
Hilsea	a	17 42											18 44											19 42	
Fratton	a	17 46							18 03		18 23		18 48						18 58			19 19		19 46	
Portsmouth & Southsea	a	17 50							18 08		18 28		18 53						19 01			19 23		19 50	
Portsmouth Harbour	a																		19 05						
Cosham	a		17 28			17 46		18 04						18 29			18 46								
Portchester	a		17 33											18 34											
Fareham	a		17 38			17 54		18 12						18 39			18 54								
Swanwick	a		17 45			18 01								18 46			19 01								
Southampton Central	a		18 05			18 19		18 41						19 03			19 20								

Table T186-F

Mondays to Fridays
16 December to 15 May

London, Gatwick Airport, Arun Valley and Brighton - Bogner Regis, Chichester, Portsmouth and Southampton

		SN ■		SN ■	SN	SN ■		SN ■	SN	SN	SN	SN ■		SN ■	SN	SN ■		SN	SN	SN ■		SN ■
London Victoria	d	17 36						18 06				18 36				19 06				19 36		
Clapham Junction	d	17 43						18 13				18 43				19 13				19 43		
East Croydon	a	17 52						18 22				18 52				19 22				19 52		
London Bridge	d					18 03																
East Croydon	a					18 16																
East Croydon	d	17 53				18 17		18 23				18 53				19 23				19 53		
Gatwick Airport	d	18 09						18 39				19 09				19 39				20 09		
Three Bridges	a	18 14				18 35		18 44				19 14				19 44				20 14		
	d	18 14				18 35		18 44				19 14				19 44				20 14		
Crawley	d	18 18				18 39		18 48				19 18				19 48				20 18		
Horsham	a	18 27				18 51		19 01				19 27				19 57				20 27		
	d	18 31	18 34			18 54	18 58	19 02				19 31	19 34			20 01	20 04			20 31	20 34	
Christs Hospital	d		18 38				19 02	19 06					19 38				20 08				20 38	
Billingshurst	d		18 44				19 08	19 13					19 44				20 14				20 44	
Pulborough	d		18 51				19 15	19 20					19 51				20 21				20 51	
Amberley	d		18 57				19 21						19 57				20 27				20 57	
Arundel	d		19 02				19 26	19 31					20 01				20 31				21 01	
Brighton	d			18 32					19 02					19 32				20 02				20 32
Hove	d			18 37					19 07					19 37				20 07				20 36
Portslade	d			18 40					19 10					19 40				20 10				20 39
Southwick	d			18 43					19 13					19 43				20 13				20 42
Shoreham-by-Sea	d			18 47					19 16					19 47				20 16				20 46
Lancing	d			18 51					19 20					19 51				20 20				20 50
Worthing	d			18 56					19 25					19 56				20 25				20 55
West Worthing	d			18 58										19 58				20 27				20 57
Durrington-on-Sea	d			19 00					19 29					20 00				20 29				20 59
Goring-by-Sea	d			19 03					19 31					20 03				20 32				21 02
Angmering	d			19 07					19 35					20 07				20 36				21 06
Littlehampton	d				19 18						19 55				20 14				20 44			
Ford	d		19 08	19 14	19 23			19 38	19 43		20 00		20 07	20 14	20 19		20 37	20 43	20 49		21 07	21 13
Barnham	a	18 58	19 13	19 19	19 27	19 23	19 36	19 42	19 47		20 04	19 58	20 12	20 19	20 24	20 28	20 42	20 48	20 54	20 58	21 12	21 18
Barnham	d		19 14		19 28		19 36	19 43		19 52			20 13		20 24		20 43		20 54		21 13	
Bognor Regis	a		19 20		19 34		19 43	19 49		19 59			20 20		20 31		20 50		21 01		21 20	
Barnham	d	18 59		19 20		19 23			19 48		20 05	19 59		20 20		20 29		20 49		21 03		21 19
Chichester	a	19 06		19 27		19 31			19 56		20 12	20 06		20 27		20 37		20 56		21 10		21 26
	d	19 07		19 28		19 31			19 56		20 13	20 07		20 28		20 37		20 57		21 11		21 27
Fishbourne (Sussex)	d					19 34					20 16									21 14		
Bosham	d					19 37					20 19									21 17		
Nutbourne	d										20 22									21 20		
Southbourne	d	19 14				19 42			20 03		20 25	20 14						21 04		21 23		
Emsworth	d	19 17		19 36		19 45			20 06		20 28	20 17		20 36				21 07		21 26		21 35
Warblington	d										20 31									21 29		
Havant	a	19 20		19 39		19 48			20 10		20 35	20 20		20 39		20 47		21 10		21 33		21 38
Bedhampton	a										20 38											
Hilsea	a										20 44											
Fratton	a					19 58			20 19		20 48					20 56		21 19				
Portsmouth & Southsea	a					20 01			20 23		20 53					21 00		21 23				
Portsmouth Harbour	a					20 05										21 04						
Cosham	a	19 29		19 46								20 28		20 46						21 40		21 45
Portchester	a	19 33										20 33								21 45		
Fareham	a	19 38		19 54								20 38		20 54						21 50		21 55
Swanwick	a	19 45		20 01								20 45		21 01						21 57		22 02
Southampton Central	a	20 03		20 19								21 03		21 20						22 15		22 23

NRT DECEMBER 19 EDITION

Table T186-F

Mondays to Fridays
16 December to 15 May

London, Gatwick Airport, Arun Valley and Brighton - Bogner Regis, Chichester, Portsmouth and Southampton

		SN	SN ■		SN	SN	SN ■		SN	SN	SN	SN ■		SN	SN	SN ■	SN	SN	SN ■		SN ■	SN ■
London Victoria	d		20 06				20 36					21 06				21 36			22 06		22 16	22 36
Clapham Junction	d		20 13				20 43					21 13				21 43			22 13		22 23	22 43
East Croydon	a		20 22				20 52					21 24				21 52			22 22		22 32	22 52
London Bridge	d																					
East Croydon	a																					
East Croydon	d		20 23				20 53					21 25				21 53			22 23		22 33	22 53
Gatwick Airport	d		20 39				21 09					21 40				22 09			22 39		22 50	23 09
Three Bridges	a		20 44				21 14					21 45				22 14			22 44			23 14
	d		20 44				21 14					21 45				22 14			22 44			23 14
Crawley	d		20 48				21 18					21 49				22 18			22 48			23 18
Horsham	a		20 57				21 27					21 58				22 27			22 57			23 27
	d		21 01	21 04			21 31	21 34				22 01	22 05			22 28			22 58			23 30
Christs Hospital	d			21 08				21 38					22 09			22 32			23 02			23 34
Billingshurst	d			21 14				21 44					22 15			22 38			23 08			23 40
Pulborough	d			21 21				21 51					22 21			22 45			23 15			23 46
Amberley	d			21 27				21 57					22 27			22 51			23 21			23 52
Arundel	d			21 31				22 01					22 32			22 55			23 25			23 57
Brighton	d				21 02				21 32					22 02			22 32					
Hove	d				21 07				21 37					22 07			22 37				23 22	
Portslade	d				21 10				21 40					22 10			22 41				23 25	
Southwick	d				21 13				21 43					22 13			22 45				23 28	
Shoreham-by-Sea	d				21 16				21 46					22 16			22 49				23 32	
Lancing	d				21 20				21 50					22 20			22 53				23 36	
Worthing	d				21 25				21 55					22 25			22 59				23 41	
West Worthing	d				21 27				21 57					22 27			23 01				23 43	
Durrington-on-Sea	d				21 29				21 59					22 29			23 03				23 45	
Goring-by-Sea	d				21 32				22 02					22 32			23 06				23 48	
Angmering	d				21 36				22 06					22 36			23 10				23 52	
Littlehampton	d	21 10				21 40					22 10							23 16				
Ford	d	21 17		21 37	21 43	21 47		22 07	22 13		22 17		22 38	22 43		23 02	23 17	23 21	23 32		23 59	00 03
Barnham	a	21 22	21 28	21 42	21 48	21 52	21 58	22 12	22 18		22 23	22 29	22 42	22 48		23 06	23 22	23 26	23 36		00 04	00 08
Barnham	d	21 23		21 43		21 53		22 13		22 19	22 25		22 44		22 52			23 28		23 43	00 12	
Bognor Regis	a	21 33		21 50		22 00		22 20		22 26	22 32		22 50		22 59			23 35		23 49	00 19	
Barnham	d		21 29		21 49		21 59		22 19			22 30		22 49		23 07	23 22		23 40			00 09
Chichester	a		21 37		21 56		22 06		22 27			22 37		22 56		23 15	23 30		23 48			00 17
	d		21 37		21 57		22 07					22 38		22 57		23 15	23 30					
Fishbourne (Sussex)	d						22 10									23 18						
Bosham	d						22 13									23 21						
Nutbourne	d						22 16									23 25						
Southbourne	d				22 04		22 19					22 45		23 04		23 27						
Emsworth	d				22 07		22 22					22 48		23 07		23 30						
Warblington	d						22 25									23 33						
Havant	a		21 50		22 10		22 27					22 52		23 10		23 36	23 41					
Bedhampton	a																					
Hilsea	a																					
Fratton	a		21 59		22 19							23 02		23 19		23 48						
Portsmouth & Southsea	a		22 03		22 23							23 07		23 23		23 52						
Portsmouth Harbour	a		22 07		22 27							23 12		23 28								
Cosham	a						22 34															
Portchester	a						22 39															
Fareham	a						22 44															
Swanwick	a						22 50															
Southampton Central	a						23 08															

Table T186-F

Saturdays
21 December to 16 May

London, Gatwick Airport, Arun Valley and Brighton - Bognor Regis, Chichester, Portsmouth and Southampton

		SN A	SN 1	SN	SN 1	SN 1	SN	SN 1	SN	SN 1		SN	SN 1	SN	SN	SN 1	SN	SN 1	SN	SN 1			SN	SN	SN
London Victoria	d																			06 06					
Clapham Junction	d																			06 13					
East Croydon	a																			06 22					
London Bridge	d																								
East Croydon	a																								
East Croydon	d																			06 23					
Gatwick Airport	d															05 56				06 39					
Three Bridges	a															06 02				06 44					
	d															06 02				06 44					
Crawley	d															06 06				06 48					
Horsham	a															06 18				06 57					
	d															06 19				07 01	07 04				
Christs Hospital	d															06 23									
Billingshurst	d															06 29					07 12				
Pulborough	d															06 35					07 19				
Amberley	d															06 41									
Arundel	d															06 46					07 28				
Brighton	d							05 14		05 32				06 02				06 32					07 02		
Hove	d							05 20		05 36				06 06				06 36					07 06		
Portslade	d							05 23		05 39				06 09				06 39					07 09		
Southwick	d							05 26		05 42				06 12				06 42					07 12		
Shoreham-by-Sea	d							05 29		05 46				06 16				06 46					07 16		
Lancing	d							05 33		05 50				06 20				06 50					07 20		
Worthing	d							05 37		05 55				06 25				06 55					07 25		
West Worthing	d							05 39		05 57								06 57							
Durrington-on-Sea	d							05 42		05 59								06 59							
Goring-by-Sea	d							05 44		06 02								07 02							
Angmering	d							05 48		06 06				06 32				07 06					07 32		
Littlehampton	d								05 55				06 19				06 55		07 10						07 55
Ford	d							05 56	06 00	06 13						06 52	07 00	07 13	07 17		07 34				08 00
Barnham	a							06 00	06 04	06 18			06 27	06 43		06 56	07 04	07 18	07 22	07 28	07 39		07 43		08 04
Barnham	d	00 36										06 22			06 52				07 23		07 40			07 52	
Bognor Regis	a	00 43										06 29			06 59				07 30		07 46			07 59	
Barnham	d		05 00	05 05	05 19	05 30	05 44	06 01	06 05	06 19			06 29	06 44		06 57	07 05	07 19		07 29			07 44		08 05
Chichester	a		05 07	05 12	05 26	05 37	05 51	06 08	06 12	06 26			06 36	06 51		07 04	07 12	07 26		07 37			07 51		08 12
	d		05 08	05 13	05 27	05 39	05 52	06 09	06 13	06 27			06 38	06 52		07 05	07 13	07 27		07 38			07 52		08 13
Fishbourne (Sussex)	d			05 16					06 16								07 16								08 16
Bosham	d			05 19					06 19								07 19								08 19
Nutbourne	d			05 22					06 22								07 22								08 22
Southbourne	d			05 25			05 59		06 25					06 59		07 12	07 25						07 59		08 25
Emsworth	d		05 16	05 28	05 35		06 02	06 17	06 28	06 35				07 02		07 15	07 28	07 35					08 02		08 28
Warblington	d			05 31					06 31								07 31								08 31
Havant	a		05 19	05 33	05 38	05 49	06 05	06 20	06 33	06 38			06 48	07 05		07 18	07 33	07 38		07 48			08 05		08 33
Bedhampton	a			05 36					06 36								07 36								08 36
Hilsea	a			05 42					06 42								07 42								08 42
Fratton	a			05 46		05 58	06 17		06 46				06 57	07 14			07 46			07 57			08 16		08 46
Portsmouth & Southsea	a			05 50		06 01	06 21		06 50				07 01	07 18			07 50			08 01			08 20		08 50
Portsmouth Harbour	a					06 05	06 25						07 05	07 22						08 05			08 24		
Cosham	a		05 27		05 46			06 28		06 46						07 27		07 46							
Portchester	a															07 31									
Fareham	a		05 35		05 54			06 36		06 54						07 36		07 54							
Swanwick	a		05 42		06 01			06 43		07 01						07 43		08 01							
Southampton Central	a		06 01		06 19			07 00		07 18						08 03		08 19							

A not 16 May

Table T186-F

Saturdays
21 December to 16 May

London, Gatwick Airport, Arun Valley and Brighton - Bognor Regis, Chichester, Portsmouth and Southampton

		SN 1		SN 1	SN	SN 1			SN	SN	SN	SN 1		SN 1	SN	SN 1			GW ◇	SN	SN	SN			
London Victoria	d	06 36				07 06						07 36				08 06									
Clapham Junction	d	06 43				07 13						07 43				08 13									
East Croydon	a	06 52				07 22						07 52				08 22									
London Bridge	d																								
East Croydon	a																								
East Croydon	d	06 53				07 23						07 53				08 23									
Gatwick Airport	d	07 09				07 39						08 09				08 39									
Three Bridges	a	07 14				07 44						08 14				08 44									
	d	07 14				07 44						08 14				08 44									
Crawley	d	07 18				07 48						08 18				08 48									
Horsham	a	07 27				07 57						08 27				08 57									
	d	07 31	07 34			08 01	08 04					08 31	08 34			09 01	09 04								
Christs Hospital	d		07 38										08 38												
Billingshurst	d		07 44				08 12						08 44				09 12								
Pulborough	d		07 51				08 19						08 51				09 19								
Amberley	d		07 57										08 57												
Arundel	d		08 02				08 28						09 01				09 28								
Brighton	d			07 32					08 02					08 33					09 00	09 04					
Hove	d			07 36					08 06					08 37					09 04	09 08					
Portslade	d			07 39					08 09					08 40						09 11					
Southwick	d			07 42					08 12					08 43						09 14					
Shoreham-by-Sea	d			07 46					08 16					08 47					09 13	09 18					
Lancing	d			07 50					08 20					08 51						09 22					
Worthing	d			07 55					08 25					08 56					09 23	09 27					
West Worthing	d			07 57										08 58											
Durrington-on-Sea	d			07 59										09 00											
Goring-by-Sea	d			08 02										09 03											
Angmering	d			08 06					08 32					09 07						09 35					
Littlehampton	d				08 10						08 55				09 10							09 55			
Ford	d		08 08	08 13	08 17		08 34				09 00		09 07	09 13	09 17		09 34					10 00			
Barnham	a	07 58	08 13	08 18	08 22	08 28	08 39		08 43		09 04	08 58	09 12	09 18	09 22	09 28	09 39		09 42	09 46		10 04			
Barnham	d		08 14		08 23		08 40			08 52			09 13		09 23		09 40				09 52				
Bognor Regis	a		08 20		08 30		08 46			08 59			09 20		09 30		09 46				09 59				
Barnham	d	07 59		08 19		08 29			08 44		09 05	08 59		09 19		09 29			09 43	09 47		10 05			
Chichester	a	08 06		08 26		08 37			08 51		09 12	09 06		09 26		09 37			09 50	09 55		10 12			
	d	08 07		08 27		08 38			08 52		09 13	09 07		09 27		09 38			09 51	09 55		10 13			
Fishbourne (Sussex)	d										09 16											10 16			
Bosham	d										09 19											10 19			
Nutbourne	d										09 22											10 22			
Southbourne	d	08 14							08 59		09 25	09 14								10 02		10 25			
Emsworth	d	08 17		08 35					09 02		09 28	09 17		09 35						10 05		10 28			
Warblington	d										09 31											10 31			
Havant	a	08 20		08 38		08 48			09 05		09 33	09 20		09 38		09 48			10 01	10 09		10 33			
Bedhampton	a										09 36											10 36			
Hilsea	a										09 42											10 42			
Fratton	a					08 57			09 14		09 46					09 57				10 18		10 46			
Portsmouth & Southsea	a					09 01			09 18		09 50					10 01				10 21		10 50			
Portsmouth Harbour	a					09 05			09 22							10 05				10 25					
Cosham	a	08 28		08 46								09 28		09 46					10 11						
Portchester	a	08 33										09 33													
Fareham	a	08 38		08 54								09 38		09 54					10 19						
Swanwick	a	08 45		09 01								09 45		10 01											
Southampton Central	a	09 03		09 19								10 03		10 19					10 41						

Table T186-F

Saturdays

21 December to 16 May

London, Gatwick Airport, Arun Valley and Brighton - Bognor Regis, Chichester, Portsmouth and Southampton

		SN 1		SN 1	SN	SN 1		SN		SN	SN	SN 1		SN 1	SN	SN 1		SN	SN	SN	SN 1		SN 1
London Victoria	d	08 36				09 06						14 36				15 06					15 36		
Clapham Junction	d	08 43				09 13						14 43				15 13					15 43		
East Croydon	a	08 52				09 22						14 52				15 22					15 52		
London Bridge	d																						
East Croydon	a																						
East Croydon	d	08 53				09 23						14 53				15 23					15 53		
Gatwick Airport	d	09 09				09 39						15 09				15 39					16 09		
Three Bridges	a	09 14				09 44						15 14				15 44					16 14		
	d	09 14				09 44						15 14				15 44					16 14		
Crawley	d	09 18				09 48						15 18				15 48					16 18		
Horsham	a	09 27				09 57						15 27				15 57					16 27		
	d	09 31	09 34			10 01	10 04					15 31	15 34			16 01	16 04				16 31	16 34	
Christs Hospital	d		09 38										15 38									16 38	
Billingshurst	d		09 44				10 12						15 44				16 12					16 44	
Pulborough	d		09 51				10 19						15 51				16 19					16 51	
Amberley	d		09 57										15 57									16 57	
Arundel	d		10 01				10 28						16 01				16 28					17 01	
Brighton	d			09 32				10 02						15 32				16 02					16 32
Hove	d			09 36				10 06						15 36				16 06					16 36
Portslade	d			09 39				10 09						15 39				16 09					16 39
Southwick	d			09 42				10 12						15 42				16 12					16 42
Shoreham-by-Sea	d			09 46				10 16	and at the same minutes past each hour until					15 46				16 16					16 46
Lancing	d			09 50				10 20						15 50				16 20					16 50
Worthing	d			09 55				10 25						15 55				16 25					16 55
West Worthing	d			09 57										15 57									16 57
Durrington-on-Sea	d			09 59										15 59									16 59
Goring-by-Sea	d			10 02										16 02									17 02
Angmering	d			10 06				10 32						16 06				16 32					17 06
Littlehampton	d				10 10						15 55				16 10					16 55			
Ford	d		10 07	10 13	10 17		10 34				16 00		16 07	16 13	16 17		16 34			17 00		17 07	17 13
Barnham	a	09 58	10 12	10 18	10 22	10 28	10 39	10 43			16 04	15 58	16 12	16 18	16 22	16 28	16 39	16 43		17 04	16 58	17 12	17 18
Barnham	d		10 13		10 23		10 40			15 52			16 13		16 23		16 40		16 52			17 13	
Bognor Regis	a		10 20		10 30		10 46			15 59			16 20		16 30		16 46		16 59			17 20	
Barnham	d	09 59		10 19		10 29		10 44			16 05	15 59		16 19		16 29		16 44		17 05	16 59		17 19
Chichester	a	10 06		10 26		10 37		10 51			16 12	16 06		16 26		16 37		16 51		17 12	17 06		17 26
	d	10 07		10 27		10 38		10 52			16 13	16 07		16 27		16 38		16 52		17 13	17 07		17 27
Fishbourne (Sussex)	d										16 16									17 16			
Bosham	d										16 19									17 19			
Nutbourne	d										16 22									17 22			
Southbourne	d	10 14						10 59			16 25	16 14						16 59		17 25	17 14		
Emsworth	d	10 17		10 35				11 02			16 28	16 17		16 35				17 02		17 28	17 17		17 35
Warblington	d										16 31									17 31			
Havant	a	10 20		10 38		10 48		11 05			16 33	16 20		16 38		16 48		17 05		17 33	17 20		17 38
Bedhampton	a										16 36									17 36			
Hilsea	a										16 42									17 42			
Fratton	a					10 57		11 14			16 46					16 57		17 14		17 46			
Portsmouth & Southsea	a					11 01		11 18			16 50					17 01		17 18		17 50			
Portsmouth Harbour	a					11 05		11 22								17 05		17 22					
Cosham	a	10 28		10 46								16 28		16 46							17 28		17 46
Portchester	a	10 33										16 33									17 33		
Fareham	a	10 38		10 54								16 38		16 54							17 38		17 54
Swanwick	a	10 45		11 01								16 45		17 01							17 45		18 01
Southampton Central	a	11 03		11 19								17 03		17 19							18 03		18 20

Table T186-F

Saturdays

21 December to 16 May

London, Gatwick Airport, Arun Valley and Brighton - Bognor Regis, Chichester, Portsmouth and Southampton

		SN	SN 1		GW ◇	SN	SN	SN	SN 1		SN 1	SN	SN 1		SN	SN	SN	SN 1		SN 1	SN	SN 1	
London Victoria	d		16 06						16 36				17 06					17 36				18 06	
Clapham Junction	d		16 13						16 43				17 13					17 43				18 13	
East Croydon	a		16 22						16 52				17 22					17 52				18 22	
London Bridge	d																						
East Croydon	a																						
East Croydon	d		16 23						16 53				17 23					17 53				18 23	
Gatwick Airport	d		16 39						17 09				17 39					18 09				18 39	
Three Bridges	a		16 44						17 14				17 44					18 14				18 44	
	d		16 44						17 14				17 44					18 14				18 44	
Crawley	d		16 48						17 18				17 48					18 18				18 48	
Horsham	a		16 57						17 27				17 57					18 27				18 57	
	d		17 01	17 04					17 31	17 34			18 01	18 04				18 31	18 34			19 01	19 04
Christs Hospital	d									17 38									18 38				
Billingshurst	d			17 12						17 44				18 12					18 44				19 12
Pulborough	d			17 19						17 51				18 19					18 51				19 19
Amberley	d									17 57									18 57				
Arundel	d			17 28						18 01				18 28					19 01				19 28
Brighton	d				17 00	17 04					17 32				18 02					18 32			
Hove	d				17 04	17 08					17 36				18 06					18 36			
Portslade	d					17 11					17 39				18 09					18 39			
Southwick	d					17 14					17 42				18 12					18 42			
Shoreham-by-Sea	d				17 13	17 18					17 46				18 16					18 46			
Lancing	d					17 22					17 50				18 20					18 50			
Worthing	d				17 23	17 27					17 55				18 25					18 55			
West Worthing	d										17 57									18 57			
Durrington-on-Sea	d										17 59									18 59			
Goring-by-Sea	d										18 02									19 02			
Angmering	d					17 34					18 06				18 32					19 06			
Littlehampton	d	17 10						17 55				18 10					18 55				19 10		
Ford	d	17 17		17 34				18 00		18 07	18 13	18 17		18 34			19 00		19 07	19 13	19 17		19 34
Barnham	a	17 22	17 28	17 39	17 42	17 46		18 04	17 58	18 12	18 18	18 22	18 28	18 39	18 43		19 04	18 58	19 12	19 18	19 22	19 28	19 39
Barnham	d	17 23		17 40			17 52			18 13		18 23		18 40		18 52			19 13		19 23		19 40
Bognor Regis	a	17 30		17 46			17 59			18 20		18 30		18 46		18 59			19 20		19 30		19 46
Barnham	d		17 29		17 42	17 47		18 05	17 59		18 19		18 29		18 44		19 05	18 59		19 19		19 29	
Chichester	a		17 37		17 50	17 55		18 12	18 06		18 26		18 37		18 51		19 12	19 06		19 26		19 37	
	d		17 38		17 50	17 55		18 13	18 07		18 27		18 38		18 52		19 13	19 07		19 27		19 38	
Fishbourne (Sussex)	d							18 16									19 16						
Bosham	d							18 19									19 19						
Nutbourne	d							18 22									19 22						
Southbourne	d					18 02		18 25	18 14						18 59		19 25	19 14					
Emsworth	d					18 05		18 28	18 17		18 35				19 02		19 28	19 17		19 35			
Warblington	d							18 31									19 31						
Havant	a		17 48		18 05	18 09		18 33	18 20		18 38		18 48		19 05		19 33	19 20		19 38		19 48	
Bedhampton	a							18 36									19 36						
Hilsea	a							18 42									19 42						
Fratton	a		17 57			18 18		18 46					18 57		19 14		19 46					19 57	
Portsmouth & Southsea	a		18 01			18 21		18 50					19 01		19 18		19 50					20 01	
Portsmouth Harbour	a		18 05			18 25							19 05		19 22							20 05	
Cosham	a				18 12				18 28		18 46							19 28		19 46			
Portchester	a								18 33									19 33					
Fareham	a				18 20				18 38		18 54							19 38		19 54			
Swanwick	a								18 45		19 01							19 45		20 01			
Southampton Central	a				18 43				19 03		19 19							20 03		20 19			

Table T186-F

Saturdays
21 December to 16 May

London, Gatwick Airport, Arun Valley and Brighton - Bognor Regis, Chichester, Portsmouth and Southampton

		SN	SN	SN	SN 1		SN 1	SN	SN 1		SN	SN	SN 1		SN 1	SN	SN 1		SN	SN	SN 1	
London Victoria	d				18 36				19 06				19 36				20 06				20 36	
Clapham Junction	d				18 43				19 13				19 43				20 13				20 43	
East Croydon	a				18 52				19 22				19 52				20 22				20 52	
London Bridge	d																					
East Croydon	a																					
East Croydon	d				18 53				19 23				19 53				20 23				20 53	
Gatwick Airport	d				19 09				19 39				20 09				20 39				21 09	
Three Bridges	a				19 14				19 44				20 14				20 44				21 14	
	d				19 14				19 44				20 14				20 44				21 14	
Crawley	d				19 18				19 48				20 18				20 48				21 18	
Horsham	a				19 27				19 57				20 27				20 57				21 27	
	d				19 31	19 34			20 01	20 04			20 31	20 34			21 01	21 04			21 31	21 34
Christs Hospital	d					19 38								20 38								21 38
Billingshurst	d					19 44				20 12				20 44				21 12				21 44
Pulborough	d					19 51				20 19				20 51				21 19				21 51
Amberley	d					19 57								20 57								21 57
Arundel	d					20 01				20 28				21 01				21 28				22 01
Brighton	d	19 02					19 32				20 02				20 32				21 02			
Hove	d	19 06					19 36				20 06				20 36				21 06			
Portslade	d	19 09					19 39				20 09				20 39				21 09			
Southwick	d	19 12					19 42				20 12				20 42				21 12			
Shoreham-by-Sea	d	19 16					19 46				20 16				20 46				21 16			
Lancing	d	19 20					19 50				20 20				20 50				21 20			
Worthing	d	19 25					19 55				20 25				20 55				21 25			
West Worthing	d						19 57								20 57							
Durrington-on-Sea	d						19 59								20 59							
Goring-by-Sea	d						20 02								21 02							
Angmering	d	19 32					20 06				20 32				21 06				21 32			
Littlehampton	d			19 55				20 10								21 10				21 40		
Ford	d			20 00		20 07	20 13	20 17		20 34				21 07	21 13	21 17		21 34		21 45		22 07
Barnham	a	19 43		20 04	19 58	20 12	20 18	20 22	20 28	20 39	20 43		20 58	21 12	21 18	21 22	21 28	21 39	21 43	21 50	21 58	22 12
Barnham	d		19 52			20 13		20 23		20 40		20 52		21 13		21 23		21 40		21 53		22 13
Bognor Regis	a		19 59			20 20		20 30		20 46		20 59		21 20		21 30		21 46		22 00		22 19
Barnham	d	19 44		20 05	19 59		20 19		20 29		20 44		21 03		21 19		21 29		21 44		21 59	
Chichester	a	19 51		20 12	20 06		20 26		20 37		20 51		21 10		21 26		21 37		21 51		22 06	
	d	19 52		20 13	20 07		20 27		20 38		20 52		21 11		21 27		21 38		21 52		22 07	
Fishbourne (Sussex)	d			20 16									21 14								22 10	
Bosham	d			20 19									21 17								22 13	
Nutbourne	d			20 22									21 20								22 16	
Southbourne	d	19 59		20 25	20 14						20 59		21 23						21 59		22 19	
Emsworth	d	20 02		20 28	20 17		20 35				21 02		21 26		21 35				22 02		22 22	
Warblington	d			20 31									21 29								22 25	
Havant	a	20 05		20 33	20 20		20 38		20 48		21 05		21 31		21 38		21 48		22 05		22 27	
Bedhampton	a			20 36									21 34									
Hilsea	a			20 43																		
Fratton	a	20 14		20 47					20 57		21 14						21 57		22 14			
Portsmouth & Southsea	a	20 18		20 52					21 01		21 18						22 01		22 18			
Portsmouth Harbour	a	20 22							21 05		21 22						22 05		22 22			
Cosham	a				20 28		20 46						21 40		21 46						22 34	
Portchester	a				20 33								21 44								22 39	
Fareham	a				20 38		20 54						21 49		21 55						22 44	
Swanwick	a				20 45		21 01						21 56		22 03						22 51	
Southampton Central	a				21 03		21 19						22 14		22 20						23 08	

Table T186-F

Saturdays
21 December to 16 May

London, Gatwick Airport, Arun Valley and Brighton - Bognor Regis, Chichester, Portsmouth and Southampton

		SN	SN	SN 1	SN	SN 1	SN	SN	SN 1	SN 1	SN 1	SN 1	SN 1
London Victoria	d			21 06		21 36			22 06		22 16	22 36	23 16
Clapham Junction	d			21 13		21 43			22 13		22 23	22 43	23 23
East Croydon	a			21 22		21 52			22 22		22 32	22 52	23 32
London Bridge	d												
East Croydon	a												
East Croydon	d			21 23		21 53			22 23		22 33	22 53	23 33
Gatwick Airport	d			21 39		22 09			22 39		22 50	23 09	23 54
Three Bridges	a			21 44		22 14			22 44			23 14	
	d			21 45		22 14			22 44			23 14	
Crawley	d			21 49		22 18			22 48			23 18	
Horsham	a			21 57		22 27			22 57			23 27	
	d			21 58		22 28			22 58			23 30	
Christs Hospital	d			22 02		22 32			23 02			23 34	
Billingshurst	d			22 08		22 38			23 08			23 40	
Pulborough	d			22 15		22 45			23 15			23 47	
Amberley	d			22 21		22 51			23 21			23 53	
Arundel	d			22 26		22 55			23 25			23 57	
Brighton	d	21 32			22 02		22 32						
Hove	d	21 36			22 06		22 37				23 22		00 25
Portslade	d	21 39			22 09		22 41				23 25		00 28
Southwick	d	21 42			22 12		22 45				23 28		00 31
Shoreham-by-Sea	d	21 46			22 16		22 49				23 32		00 35
Lancing	d	21 50			22 20		22 53				23 36		00 39
Worthing	d	21 55			22 25		22 59				23 41		00 43
West Worthing	d						23 01				23 43		00 45
Durrington-on-Sea	d						23 03				23 45		00 48
Goring-by-Sea	d						23 06				23 48		00 50
Angmering	d	22 02			22 32		23 10				23 52		00 54
Littlehampton	d		22 12					23 17					
Ford	d		22 17			23 02	23 17	23 23	23 32		23 59	00 03	01 02
Barnham	a	22 16	22 22	22 36	22 43	23 06	23 22	23 27	23 36		00 04	00 08	01 06
Barnham	d		22 25	22 37				23 28		23 43	00 12		
Bognor Regis	a		22 32	22 43				23 35		23 49	00 19		
Barnham	d	22 17			22 44	23 07	23 24		23 40			00 09	01 08
Chichester	a	22 24			22 51	23 15	23 31		23 48			00 17	01 15
	d	22 25			22 52	23 15							
Fishbourne (Sussex)	d					23 18							
Bosham	d					23 21							
Nutbourne	d					23 25							
Southbourne	d	22 32			22 59	23 27							
Emsworth	d	22 35			23 02	23 30							
Warblington	d					23 33							
Havant	a	22 38			23 05	23 36							
Bedhampton	a												
Hilsea	a												
Fratton	a	22 48			23 14	23 47							
Portsmouth & Southsea	a	22 52			23 18	23 51							
Portsmouth Harbour	a	22 56			23 22								
Cosham	a												
Portchester	a												
Fareham	a												
Swanwick	a												
Southampton Central	a												

Table T186-F

Sundays

15 December to 10 May

London, Gatwick Airport, Arun Valley and Brighton - Bognor Regis, Chichester, Portsmouth and Southampton

		SN	SN	SN	SN	SN	SN	SN	SN ■	SN		SN ■	SN	SN	SN ■	SN ■	SN	SN	SN	SN ■		SN ■	SN	SN	SN
London Victoria	d											07 32				08 32						09 33			
Clapham Junction	d											07 40				08 40						09 40			
East Croydon	a											07 56				08 51						09 49			
London Bridge	d																								
East Croydon	a																								
East Croydon	d											07 57				08 51						09 49			
Gatwick Airport	d											08 20				09 14						10 13			
Three Bridges	a											08 24				09 19						10 18			
	d											08 25				09 19						10 19			
Crawley	d											08 29				09 23						10 23			
Horsham	a											08 37				09 34						10 32			
	d											08 38				09 35						10 35			
Christs Hospital	d											08 42				09 39						10 39			
Billingshurst	d											08 48				09 45						10 45			
Pulborough	d											08 55				09 52						10 52			
Amberley	d											09 01				09 58						10 58			
Arundel	d											09 06				10 02						11 02			
Brighton	d					07 15	07 30		08 00	08 20			08 30		09 00			09 30		10 00				10 30	
Hove	d					07 19	07 34		08 04	08 24			08 34		09 04			09 34		10 04				10 34	
Portslade	d						07 39		08 09				08 39		09 09			09 39		10 09				10 39	
Southwick	d						07 43		08 13				08 43		09 13			09 43		10 13				10 43	
Shoreham-by-Sea	d					07 26	07 47		08 17	08 31			08 47		09 17			09 47		10 17				10 47	
Lancing	d						07 51		08 21				08 51		09 21			09 51		10 21				10 51	
Worthing	d					07 33	07 57		08 27	08 38			08 57		09 27			09 57		10 27				10 57	
West Worthing	d						07 59		08 29				08 59		09 29			09 59		10 29				10 59	
Durrington-on-Sea	d						08 01		08 31				09 01		09 31			10 01		10 31				11 01	
Goring-by-Sea	d						08 04		08 34				09 04		09 34			10 04		10 34				11 04	
Angmering	d					07 40	08 08		08 38	08 45			09 08		09 38			10 08		10 38				11 08	
Littlehampton	d		06 42	07 31	07 39			08 31						09 31					10 31						11 31
Ford	d		06 47	07 36	07 44	07 49	08 16	08 36	08 46	08 52		09 12	09 16	09 36	09 46	10 08		10 16	10 36	10 46		11 08		11 16	11 36
Barnham	a		06 51	07 41	07 48	07 53	08 20	08 41	08 50	08 57		09 16	09 21	09 41	09 50	10 13		10 20	10 41	10 50		11 13		11 20	11 41
Barnham	d	06 45		07 43				08 43				09 17		09 43			10 18		10 43				11 18		11 43
Bognor Regis	a	06 51		07 49				08 49				09 24		09 49			10 24		10 49				11 24		11 49
Barnham	d		06 52		07 49	07 54	08 21		08 51	08 57			09 22		09 51	10 13		10 21		10 51		11 13		11 21	
Chichester	a		06 59		07 56	08 02	08 28		08 58	09 05			09 29		09 58	10 21		10 28		10 58		11 21		11 28	
	d		07 00		07 57	08 02	08 29		08 59	09 05			09 30		09 59	10 22		10 29		10 59		11 22		11 29	
Fishbourne (Sussex)	d						08 32						09 33					10 32						11 32	
Bosham	d						08 35						09 36					10 35						11 35	
Nutbourne	d						08 38						09 39					10 38						11 38	
Southbourne	d		07 07			08 09	08 41			09 12			09 42			10 29		10 41				11 29		11 41	
Emsworth	d		07 10		08 05	08 12	08 44		09 07	09 15			09 45		10 07	10 33		10 44		11 07		11 33		11 44	
Warblington	d						08 47						09 48					10 47						11 47	
Havant	a		07 14		08 09	08 16	08 49		09 10	09 19			09 50		10 10	10 36		10 49		11 10		11 36		11 49	
Bedhampton	a						08 52						09 53					10 52						11 52	
Hilsea	a																								
Fratton	a		07 23			08 25	09 00			09 28			10 01			10 47		11 00				11 47		12 00	
Portsmouth & Southsea	a		07 27			08 28	09 03			09 31			10 04			10 52		11 03				11 50		12 03	
Portsmouth Harbour	a		07 31			08 32	09 07			09 35			10 08			10 56		11 07				11 55		12 07	
Cosham	a				08 17				09 17						10 17					11 17					
Portchester	a																								
Fareham	a				08 25				09 25						10 25					11 25					
Swanwick	a				08 32				09 32						10 32					11 32					
Southampton Central	a				08 50				09 50						10 50					11 50					

Table T186-F

Sundays

15 December to 10 May

London, Gatwick Airport, Arun Valley and Brighton - Bognor Regis, Chichester, Portsmouth and Southampton

		SN ■	GW ◇	SN ■		SN		SN	SN ■	SN ■		SN	SN	SN ■	SN ■			SN	SN	SN ■	SN ■		SN	SN	SN ■
London Victoria	d			10 33						11 33					12 33						13 33				
Clapham Junction	d			10 40						11 40					12 40						13 40				
East Croydon	a			10 49						11 49					12 49						13 49				
London Bridge	d																								
East Croydon	a																								
East Croydon	d			10 49						11 49					12 49						13 49				
Gatwick Airport	d			11 13						12 13					13 13						14 13				
Three Bridges	a			11 18						12 18					13 18						14 18				
	d			11 18						12 18					13 18						14 18				
Crawley	d			11 22						12 22					13 22						14 22				
Horsham	a			11 31						12 31					13 31						14 31				
	d			11 31						12 31					13 31						14 31				
Christs Hospital	d			11 35						12 35					13 35						14 35				
Billingshurst	d			11 42						12 42					13 42						14 42				
Pulborough	d			11 48						12 48					13 48						14 48				
Amberley	d			11 54						12 54					13 54						14 54				
Arundel	d			11 59						12 59					13 59						14 59				
Brighton	d	11 00	11 10			11 30			12 00			12 30		13 00				13 30		14 00			14 30		15 00
Hove	d	11 04	11 14			11 34			12 04			12 34		13 04				13 34		14 04			14 34		15 04
Portslade	d	11 09				11 39			12 09			12 39		13 09				13 39		14 09			14 39		15 09
Southwick	d	11 13				11 43			12 13			12 43		13 13				13 43		14 13			14 43		15 13
Shoreham-by-Sea	d	11 17	11 21			11 47			12 17			12 47		13 17				13 47		14 17			14 47		15 17
Lancing	d	11 21				11 51			12 21			12 51		13 21				13 51		14 21			14 51		15 21
Worthing	d	11 27	11 31			11 57			12 27			12 57		13 27				13 57		14 27			14 57		15 27
West Worthing	d	11 29				11 59			12 29			12 59		13 29				13 59		14 29			14 59		15 29
Durrington-on-Sea	d	11 31				12 01			12 31			13 01		13 31				14 01		14 31			15 01		15 31
Goring-by-Sea	d	11 34				12 04			12 34			13 04		13 34				14 04		14 34			15 04		15 34
Angmering	d	11 38				12 08			12 38			13 08		13 38				14 08		14 38			15 08		15 38
Littlehampton	d							12 31					13 31						14 31					15 31	
Ford	d	11 46		12 05		12 16		12 36	12 46	13 05		13 16	13 36	13 46	14 05			14 16	14 36	14 46	15 05		15 16	15 36	15 46
Barnham	a	11 50	11 55	12 09		12 20		12 41	12 50	13 09		13 20	13 41	13 50	14 09			14 20	14 41	14 50	15 09		15 20	15 41	15 50
Barnham	d			12 16				12 43		13 16			13 43		14 16				14 43		15 16			15 43	
Bognor Regis	a			12 23				12 49		13 23			13 49		14 23				14 49		15 23			15 49	
Barnham	d	11 51	11 56		12 13	12 21			12 51		13 13	13 21		13 51		14 13		14 21		14 51		15 13	15 21		15 51
Chichester	a	11 58	12 03		12 20	12 28			12 58		13 20	13 28		13 58		14 20		14 28		14 58		15 20	15 28		15 58
	d	11 59	12 04		12 21	12 29			12 59		13 21	13 29		13 59		14 21		14 29		14 59		15 21	15 29		15 59
Fishbourne (Sussex)	d					12 32						13 32						14 32					15 32		
Bosham	d					12 35						13 35						14 35					15 35		
Nutbourne	d					12 38						13 38						14 38					15 38		
Southbourne	d				12 28	12 41					13 28	13 41				14 28		14 41				15 28	15 41		
Emsworth	d	12 07			12 32	12 44			13 07		13 32	13 44		14 07		14 32		14 44		15 07		15 32	15 44		16 07
Warblington	d					12 47						13 47						14 47					15 47		
Havant	a	12 10	12 15		12 36	12 49			13 10		13 36	13 49		14 10		14 36		14 49		15 10		15 36	15 49		16 10
Bedhampton	a					12 52						13 52						14 52					15 52		
Hilsea	a																								
Fratton	a				12 47	13 00					13 45	14 00				14 47		15 00				15 45	16 00		
Portsmouth & Southsea	a				12 52	13 03					13 49	14 03				14 51		15 03				15 49	16 03		
Portsmouth Harbour	a				12 56	13 07					13 53	14 07				14 56		15 07				15 53	16 07		
Cosham	a	12 17	12 25						13 17					14 17						15 17					16 17
Portchester	a																								
Fareham	a	12 25	12 33						13 25					14 25						15 25					16 25
Swanwick	a	12 32							13 32					14 32						15 32					16 32
Southampton Central	a	12 50	12 55						13 50					14 50						15 50					16 50

Table T186-F

Sundays
15 December to 10 May

London, Gatwick Airport, Arun Valley and Brighton - Bognor Regis, Chichester, Portsmouth and Southampton

		SN 1		SN	GW ◇	SN	SN	SN 1	SN 1		SN	SN	SN 1	SN 1		SN	GW ◇	SN	SN	SN 1	SN 1	
London Victoria	d	14 33							15 33					16 33							17 33	
Clapham Junction	d	14 40							15 40					16 40							17 40	
East Croydon	a	14 49							15 49					16 49							17 49	
London Bridge	d																					
East Croydon	a																					
East Croydon	d	14 49							15 49					16 49							17 49	
Gatwick Airport	d	15 13							16 13					17 13							18 13	
Three Bridges	a	15 18							16 18					17 18							18 18	
	d	15 18							16 18					17 18							18 18	
Crawley	d	15 22							16 22					17 22							18 22	
Horsham	a	15 31							16 31					17 31							18 31	
	d	15 31							16 31					17 31							18 31	
Christs Hospital	d	15 35							16 35					17 35							18 35	
Billingshurst	d	15 42							16 42					17 42							18 42	
Pulborough	d	15 48							16 48					17 48							18 48	
Amberley	d	15 54							16 54					17 54							18 54	
Arundel	d	15 59							16 59					17 59							18 59	
Brighton	d			15 30	15 47			16 00			16 30		17 00			17 30	17 46			18 00		
Hove	d			15 34	15 51			16 04			16 34		17 04			17 34	17 50			18 04		
Portslade	d			15 39				16 09			16 39		17 09			17 39				18 09		
Southwick	d			15 43				16 13			16 43		17 13			17 43				18 13		
Shoreham-by-Sea	d			15 47	15 57			16 17			16 47		17 17			17 47	17 56			18 17		
Lancing	d			15 51				16 21			16 51		17 21			17 51				18 21		
Worthing	d			15 57	16 09			16 27			16 57		17 27			17 57	18 08			18 27		
West Worthing	d			15 59				16 29			16 59		17 29			17 59				18 29		
Durrington-on-Sea	d			16 01				16 31			17 01		17 31			18 01				18 31		
Goring-by-Sea	d			16 04				16 34			17 04		17 34			18 04				18 34		
Angmering	d			16 08				16 38			17 08		17 38			18 08				18 38		
Littlehampton	d						16 31					17 31							18 31			
Ford	d	16 05		16 16			16 36	16 46	17 05		17 16	17 36	17 46	18 05		18 16			18 36	18 46	19 05	
Barnham	a	16 09		16 20	16 26		16 41	16 50	17 09		17 20	17 41	17 50	18 09		18 20	18 26		18 41	18 50	19 09	
Barnham	d	16 16					16 43		17 16			17 43		18 16					18 43		19 16	
Bognor Regis	a	16 23				←	16 49		17 23			17 49		18 23				←	18 49		19 23	
Barnham	d		16 13	16 31	16 27	16 31		16 51		17 13	17 21		17 51		18 13	18 31	18 27	18 31		18 51		19 13
Chichester	a		16 20	→	16 34	16 38		16 58		17 20	17 28		17 58		18 20	→	18 34	18 38		18 58		19 20
	d		16 21		16 35	16 39		16 59		17 21	17 29		17 59		18 21		18 35	18 39		18 59		19 21
Fishbourne (Sussex)	d					16 42					17 32							18 42				
Bosham	d					16 45					17 35							18 45				
Nutbourne	d					16 48					17 38							18 48				
Southbourne	d		16 28			16 51				17 28	17 41				18 28			18 51				19 28
Emsworth	d		16 32			16 54		17 07		17 32	17 44		18 07		18 32			18 54		19 07		19 32
Warblington	d					16 57					17 47							18 57				
Havant	a		16 36		16 44	16 59		17 10		17 36	17 49		18 10		18 36		18 50	18 59		19 10		19 36
Bedhampton	a					17 02					17 52							19 02				
Hilsea	a																					
Fratton	a		16 47			17 11				17 47	18 00				18 48			19 14				19 47
Portsmouth & Southsea	a		16 51							17 50	18 03				18 51							19 51
Portsmouth Harbour	a		16 55							17 54	18 07				18 55							19 55
Cosham	a				16 51			17 17					18 17				18 56			19 17		
Portchester	a																					
Fareham	a				16 59			17 25					18 25				19 04			19 25		
Swanwick	a							17 32					18 32							19 32		
Southampton Central	a				17 20			17 50					18 50				19 26			19 50		

Table T186-F

Sundays
15 December to 10 May

London, Gatwick Airport, Arun Valley and Brighton - Bognor Regis, Chichester, Portsmouth and Southampton

		SN	SN	SN 1	SN 1		SN	SN	SN 1	SN 1		SN	SN	SN 1	SN 1		SN	GW	SN	SN	SN 1	SN 1	SN	SN 1
London Victoria	d				18 33					19 33					20 33						21 16	21 33		22 33
Clapham Junction	d				18 40					19 40					20 40						21 23	21 40		22 40
East Croydon	a				18 49					19 49					20 49						21 32	21 49		22 49
London Bridge	d																							
East Croydon	a																							
East Croydon	d				18 49					19 49					20 49						21 33	21 49		22 49
Gatwick Airport	d				19 13					20 13					21 13						21 50	22 14		23 13
Three Bridges	a				19 18					20 18					21 18							22 19		23 18
	d				19 18					20 18					21 18							22 20		23 18
Crawley	d				19 22					20 22					21 22							22 24		23 22
Horsham	a				19 31					20 31					21 31							22 32		23 31
	d				19 31					20 31					21 31							22 33		23 31
Christs Hospital	d				19 35					20 35					21 35							22 37		23 35
Billingshurst	d				19 42					20 42					21 42							22 43		23 42
Pulborough	d				19 48					20 48					21 48							22 50		23 48
Amberley	d				19 54					20 54					21 54							22 56		23 54
Arundel	d				19 59					20 59					21 59							23 00		23 59
Brighton	d	18 30		19 00			19 30		20 00			20 30		21 00			21 30	21 46					22 47	
Hove	d	18 34		19 04			19 34		20 04			20 34		21 04			21 34	21 50			22 19		22 52	
Portslade	d	18 39		19 09			19 39		20 09			20 39		21 09			21 39						22 56	
Southwick	d	18 43		19 13			19 43		20 13			20 43		21 13			21 43						23 00	
Shoreham-by-Sea	d	18 47		19 17			19 47		20 17			20 47		21 17			21 47	21 56			22 25		23 04	
Lancing	d	18 51		19 21			19 51		20 21			20 51		21 21			21 51						23 08	
Worthing	d	18 57		19 27			19 57		20 27			20 57		21 27			21 57	22 03			22 35		23 14	
West Worthing	d	18 59		19 29			19 59		20 29			20 59		21 29			21 59						23 16	
Durrington-on-Sea	d	19 01		19 31			20 01		20 31			21 01		21 31			22 01						23 19	
Goring-by-Sea	d	19 04		19 34			20 04		20 34			21 04		21 34			22 04						23 21	
Angmering	d	19 08		19 38			20 08		20 38			21 08		21 38			22 08						23 26	
Littlehampton	d		19 31					20 31					21 31							22 31			23 42	
Ford	d	19 16	19 36	19 46	20 05		20 16	20 36	20 46	21 05		21 16	21 36	21 46	22 05		22 16			22 36	22 47	23 10	23 47	00 05
Barnham	a	19 20	19 41	19 50	20 09		20 20	20 41	20 50	21 09		21 20	21 41	21 50	22 09		22 20	22 24		22 41	22 51	23 14	23 51	00 09
Barnham	d		19 43		20 16			20 43		21 16			21 43		22 16					22 43		23 20		00 11
Bognor Regis	a		19 49		20 23			20 49		21 23			21 49		22 23				←	22 49		23 26		00 17
Barnham	d	19 21		19 51		20 13	20 21		20 51		21 13	21 21		21 51		22 13	22 29	22 24	22 29		22 52		23 52	
Chichester	a	19 28		19 58		20 20	20 28		20 58		21 20	21 28		21 58		22 20	→	22 32	22 36		22 59		23 59	
	d	19 29		19 59		20 21	20 29		20 59		21 21	21 29		21 59		22 21		22 32	22 37		23 00			
Fishbourne (Sussex)	d	19 32					20 32					21 32							22 40					
Bosham	d	19 35					20 35					21 35							22 43		23 04			
Nutbourne	d	19 38					20 38					21 38							22 46		23 08			
Southbourne	d	19 41				20 28	20 41				21 28	21 41				22 28			22 49		23 10			
Emsworth	d	19 44		20 07		20 32	20 44		21 07		21 32	21 44		22 07		22 32			22 52		23 13			
Warblington	d	19 47					20 47					21 47							22 55					
Havant	a	19 49		20 10		20 36	20 49		21 11		21 36	21 49		22 10		22 36		22 45	22 57		23 17			
Bedhampton	a	19 52					20 52					21 52							23 01					
Hilsea	a																							
Fratton	a	20 00				20 47	21 00				21 45	22 00				22 47		22 59	23 11		23 26			
Portsmouth & Southsea	a	20 03				20 51	21 03				21 49	22 03				22 52		23 02	23 15		23 29			
Portsmouth Harbour	a	20 07				20 55	21 07				21 54	22 07				22 56		23 07	23 20		23 33			
Cosham	a			20 17					21 18					22 17										
Portchester	a																							
Fareham	a			20 25					21 26					22 25										
Swanwick	a			20 32					21 33					22 32										
Southampton Central	a			20 50					21 51					22 50										

Table T186-R

Mondays to Fridays

16 December to 15 May

Bognor Regis, Chichester, Portsmouth and Southampton - London, Gatwick Airport, Arun Valley and Brighton

Miles	Miles	Miles			SN	SN	SN	SN	SN ■	SN	SN	SN ■	SN ■		SN	SN	SN ■	SN ■	SN	SN	SN ■	SN ■	SN		SN
0	—	—	Southampton Central	d																	05 46				
11	—	—	Swanwick	d																	06 04				
14½	—	—	Fareham	d																	06 11				
17¼	—	—	Portchester	d																	06 16				
20½	—	—	Cosham	d																	06 21				
—	—	0	Portsmouth Harbour	d									05 28					05 57					06 12		06 32
—	—	0¾	Portsmouth & Southsea	d									05 32					06 01					06 16		06 36
—	—	1¾	Fratton	d									05 36					06 05					06 20		06 40
—	—	4	Hilsea	d									05 40										06 24		
23¾	—	—	Bedhampton	d									05 45										06 29		
24½	—	8	Havant	d					05 20				05 48					06 14			06 28		06 32		06 51
25¼	—	8¾	**Warblington**	d									05 50										06 34		
26½	—	10	**Emsworth**	d									05 53					06 18			06 31		06 37		06 54
28¼	—	11½	**Southbourne**	d									05 56					06 22			06 34		06 40		06 57
29¼	—	14½	**Nutbourne**	d									05 59										06 42		
30¾	—	16	**Bosham**	d									06 02					06 26			06 39		06 45		
32	—	15½	**Fishbourne (Sussex)**	d									06 05					06 29					06 48		
33½	—	17	**Chichester**	a					05 30				06 08					06 32			06 43		06 51		07 04
—	—	—		d	04 54		05 25		05 31		05 50		06 08			06 16		06 33			06 44		06 54		07 05
39½	—	23½	**Barnham**	a	05 01		05 32		05 39		05 57		06 16			06 24		06 41			06 52		07 01		07 12
—	—	—	**Bognor Regis**	d		04 55		05 29		05 38		05 55			06 10		06 21		06 36	06 44		06 51			
—	—	—	**Barnham**	a		05 02		05 35		05 44		06 01			06 17		06 28		06 43	06 51		06 57			
—	—	—	**Barnham**	d	05 03	05 07	05 33	05 37	05 41	05 45	05 58	06 02	06 17		06 20	06 24	06 29	06 43	06 47		06 55	06 59	07 03		07 13
42½	—	25¾	**Ford**	d	05 07	05 11	05 37	05 41		05 49	06 03	06 07			06 26	06 29	06 33		06 51		06 59	07 03	07 07		07 17
44½	—	—	Littlehampton	a		05 16		05 46		05 54					06 31				06 57				07 15		
—	—	30	Angmering	a	05 14		05 44				06 10					06 36					07 06				07 25
—	—	32¾	Goring-by-Sea	a	05 18		05 48				06 14					06 40					07 11				07 29
—	—	34	Durrington-on-Sea	a	05 21		05 51				06 16					06 43					07 13				07 32
—	—	34½	West Worthing	a	05 23		05 53				06 19					06 46					07 16				07 35
—	—	35	Worthing	a	05 26		05 56				06 21					06 49					07 18				07 38
—	—	37½	Lancing	a	05 32		06 02				06 27					06 53					07 23				07 43
—	—	39¾	Shoreham-by-Sea	a	05 36		06 06				06 32					06 57					07 27				07 47
—	—	41½	Southwick	a	05 39		06 09				06 35					07 01					07 30				07 51
—	—	42¾	Portslade	a	05 43		06 13				06 39					07 05					07 34				07 54
—	—	44¼	Hove	a	05 48		06 18				06 44					07 08					07 37				07 58
—	0	45¼	Brighton	a	05 54		06 24				06 49					07 14					07 44				08 03
48	—	—	**Arundel**	d					05 50			06 13					06 39					07 09			
51¾	—	—	**Amberley**	d					05 54			06 18					06 44					07 14			
53	—	—	**Pulborough**	d					06 01			06 24					06 50					07 21			
53¼	—	—	**Billingshurst**	d					06 08			06 31					06 57					07 28			
55¾	—	—	**Christs Hospital**	d					06 14			06 38					07 04					07 34			
57	—	—	Horsham	a					06 18			06 43	06 46				07 08	07 12				07 38			
—	—	—																							
—	—	—		d					06 19			06 50					07 16					07 40			
64¼	—	—	Crawley	a					06 27			07 02					07 27					07 53			
65¾	21¼	—	Three Bridges	a					06 32			07 07					07 32					07 58			
—	—	—		d					06 33			07 07					07 33					08 01			
68¼	23¾	—	Gatwick Airport	a					06 37								07 37					08 05			
—	—	—	East Croydon	a					06 53			07 26					07 54					08 23			
—	40¼	—	East Croydon	d								07 27													
—	50½	—	London Bridge	a								07 43													
84½	—	—	East Croydon	d					06 53								07 55					08 24			
93	—	—	Clapham Junction	a					07 02								08 04					08 33			
95¾	—	—	London Victoria	a					07 12								08 12					08 40			

NRT DECEMBER 19 EDITION

Table T186-R

Mondays to Fridays

16 December to 15 May

Bognor Regis, Chichester, Portsmouth and Southampton - London, Gatwick Airport, Arun Valley and Brighton

		SN ■	SN ■	SN	SN ■	SN ■	GW	SN	SN		SN	SN ■	SN ■	SN	SN ■	SN	SN	SN ■	SN ■		SN	SN	SN ■	SN ■	SN ■
Southampton Central	d		06 08			06 36							07 12		07 33									08 09	08 28
Swanwick	d		06 27			06 57							07 31		07 51									08 28	08 48
Fareham	d		06 36			07 04							07 38		07 57									08 35	08 56
Portchester	d		06 41			07 09							07 43											08 40	
Cosham	d		06 46			07 13							07 47		08 06									08 44	09 04
Portsmouth Harbour	d						07 09		07 18												08 29				
Portsmouth & Southsea	d						07 13		07 22		07 33					08 01			08 14		08 33				
Fratton	d						07 17		07 26		07 37					08 05			08 18		08 37				
Hilsea	d								07 30							08 09									
Bedhampton	d								07 35										08 25						
Havant	d		06 54			07 20	07 27		07 38		07 46		07 56		08 12	08 15			08 29		08 46			08 52	09 11
Warblington	d								07 40							08 17									
Emsworth	d		06 58			07 23	07 32		07 43		07 50		07 59			08 20					08 49			08 56	09 14
Southbourne	d		07 01			07 26	07 36		07 46		07 53		08 02			08 23					08 52			08 59	
Nutbourne	d								07 49							08 26									
Bosham	d					07 31			07 52							08 29									
Fishbourne (Sussex)	d					07 34			07 55							08 32									
Chichester	a		07 08			07 37	07 42		07 58		08 01		08 09		08 23	08 35			08 39		09 00			09 06	09 22
	d		07 09			07 37	07 43		07 58		08 02		08 10		08 23	08 35			08 39		09 00			09 09	09 23
Barnham	a		07 16			07 45	07 51		08 06		08 09		08 17		08 31	08 43			08 47		09 08			09 16	09 30
Bognor Regis	d	07 00		07 06	07 27			07 41				07 54		08 14			08 36	08 28				09 05	08 56		
Barnham	a	07 06		07 13	07 33			07 47				08 00		08 21			08 43	08 34				09 11	09 02		
Barnham	d	07 07	07 17	07 23	07 34	07 46	07 52	07 54	08 06		08 10	08 01	08 18	08 22	08 31	08 43		08 35	08 47		09 09	09 12	09 03	09 17	09 31
Ford	d			07 28				07 59	08 11		08 14	08 06		08 27	08 36	08 48		08 40				09 17	09 07		09 36
Littlehampton	a			07 33				08 04			08 19			08 32		08 53						09 23			
Angmering	a						08 01		08 18						08 43						09 19				09 43
Goring-by-Sea	a														08 48										09 47
Durrington-on-Sea	a														08 51										09 50
West Worthing	a														08 53										09 52
Worthing	a						08 09		08 25						08 56						09 26				09 55
Lancing	a								08 31						09 00						09 30				10 00
Shoreham-by-Sea	a						08 16		08 35						09 05						09 35				10 04
Southwick	a								08 39						09 08						09 38				10 08
Portslade	a						08 22		08 43						09 12						09 42				10 11
Hove	a						08 26		08 48						09 16						09 45				10 15
Brighton	a						08 30		08 54						09 21						09 51				10 21
Arundel	d	07 16			07 43							08 12						08 45					09 13		
Amberley	d				07 47							08 17						08 50					09 17		
Pulborough	d	07 26			07 54							08 23						08 56					09 24		
Billingshurst	d	07 33			08 01							08 30						09 03					09 31		
Christs Hospital	d	07 39			08 07							08 37											09 37		
Horsham	a	07 43	07 46		08 11	08 15						08 41	08 46					09 11	09 16				09 41	09 46	
	d	07 50			08 19							08 50						09 20					09 50		
Crawley	a	08 02			08 27							08 58						09 28					09 58		
Three Bridges	a	08 07			08 32							09 03						09 33					10 03		
	d	08 07			08 33							09 04						09 34					10 04		
Gatwick Airport	a				08 37							09 08						09 38					10 08		
East Croydon	a	08 26			08 54							09 24						09 54					10 24		
East Croydon	d	08 27																							
London Bridge	a	08 43																							
East Croydon	d				08 54							09 24						09 54					10 24		
Clapham Junction	a				09 03							09 33						10 03					10 33		
London Victoria	a				09 10							09 40						10 11					10 41		

Table T186-R

Mondays to Fridays

16 December to 15 May

Bognor Regis, Chichester, Portsmouth and Southampton - London, Gatwick Airport, Arun Valley and Brighton

		SN	SN	SN ■	SN ■	SN	SN	SN ■	SN ■	SN ■	SN	SN	SN ■	SN ■	SN	SN	SN ■	SN ■	SN ■	SN	SN	SN ■	SN ■
Southampton Central	d								09 13	09 26								10 13	10 28				
Swanwick	d								09 32									10 32	10 46				
Fareham	d								09 39									10 39	10 53				
Portchester	d								09 44									10 44					
Cosham	d								09 48	10 04								10 48	11 02				
Portsmouth Harbour	d				09 11									10 11									11 11
Portsmouth & Southsea	d	08 57			09 15	09 33					09 57			10 15	10 33					10 57			11 15
Fratton	d	09 01			09 19	09 37					10 01			10 19	10 37					11 01			11 19
Hilsea	d	09 05									10 05									11 05			
Bedhampton	d	09 12									10 11									11 10			
Havant	d	09 15			09 29	09 46			09 55	10 10	10 14			10 28	10 46			10 55	11 10	11 13			11 28
Warblington	d	09 17									10 16									11 15			
Emsworth	d	09 20				09 49			09 58	10 14	10 19				10 49			10 58	11 13	11 18			
Southbourne	d	09 23				09 52			10 01		10 22				10 52			11 01		11 21			
Nutbourne	d	09 25									10 25									11 24			
Bosham	d	09 28									10 28									11 27			
Fishbourne (Sussex)	d	09 31									10 31									11 30			
Chichester	a	09 34			09 39	09 59			10 08	10 22	10 34			10 38	10 59			11 08	11 21	11 33			11 38
	d	09 35			09 39	10 00			10 09	10 23	10 34			10 39	11 00			11 09	11 22	11 34			11 39
Barnham	a	09 42			09 47	10 07			10 16	10 30	10 42			10 46	11 07			11 16	11 30	11 41			11 46
Bognor Regis	d		09 36	09 29			10 05	09 56				10 36	10 29			11 05	10 56				11 36	11 29	
Barnham	a		09 43	09 35			10 11	10 02				10 43	10 35			11 11	11 02				11 43	11 35	
Barnham	d	09 43		09 36	09 48	10 09	10 12	10 03	10 17	10 31	10 42		10 36	10 47	11 09	11 12	11 03	11 17	11 31	11 42		11 36	11 47
Ford	d	09 47		09 41			10 17	10 07		10 36	10 47		10 41			11 17	11 07		11 36	11 47		11 41	
Littlehampton	a	09 53					10 23				10 53					11 23				11 53			
Angmering	a					10 19				10 43					11 19				11 43				
Goring-by-Sea	a									10 47									11 47				
Durrington-on-Sea	a									10 50									11 50				
West Worthing	a									10 52									11 52				
Worthing	a					10 26				10 55					11 26				11 55				
Lancing	a					10 30				11 00					11 30				12 00				
Shoreham-by-Sea	a					10 35				11 04					11 35				12 04				
Southwick	a					10 38				11 08					11 38				12 08				
Portslade	a					10 42				11 11					11 42				12 11				
Hove	a					10 45				11 15					11 45				12 15				
Brighton	a					10 51				11 21					11 51				12 21				
Arundel	d			09 46				10 13					10 46				11 13					11 46	
Amberley	d							10 17									11 17						
Pulborough	d			09 55				10 24					10 55				11 24					11 55	
Billingshurst	d			10 02				10 31					11 02				11 31					12 02	
Christs Hospital	d							10 37									11 37						
Horsham	a			10 11	10 16			10 41	10 46				11 11	11 16			11 41	11 46				12 11	12 16
	d				10 20				10 50					11 20				11 50					12 20
Crawley	a				10 28				10 58					11 28				11 58					12 28
Three Bridges	a				10 33				11 03					11 33				12 03					12 33
	d				10 34				11 04					11 34				12 04					12 34
Gatwick Airport	a				10 38				11 08					11 38				12 08					12 38
East Croydon	a				10 54				11 24					11 54				12 24					12 54
East Croydon	d																						
London Bridge	a																						
East Croydon	d				10 54				11 24					11 54				12 24					12 54
Clapham Junction	a				11 03				11 33					12 03				12 33					13 03
London Victoria	a				11 11				11 41					12 11				12 41					13 11

Table T186-R

Mondays to Fridays

16 December to 15 May

Bognor Regis, Chichester, Portsmouth and Southampton - London, Gatwick Airport, Arun Valley and Brighton

		SN	SN	SN ■	SN ■	SN ■	SN	SN	SN ■	SN ■	SN	SN	SN ■	SN ■	SN ■	SN	SN	SN ■	SN ■	SN	SN
Southampton Central	d				11 13	11 26								12 13	12 28						
Swanwick	d				11 32									12 32	12 46						
Fareham	d				11 39									12 39	12 53						
Portchester	d				11 44									12 44							
Cosham	d				11 48	12 02								12 48	13 02						
Portsmouth Harbour	d	11 29								12 11	12 29								13 11	13 29	
Portsmouth & Southsea	d	11 33					11 57			12 15	12 33					12 57			13 15	13 33	
Fratton	d	11 37					12 01			12 19	12 37					13 01			13 19	13 37	
Hilsea	d						12 05									13 05					
Bedhampton	d						12 10									13 11					
Havant	d	11 46			11 55	12 10	12 13			12 28	12 46			12 55	13 10	13 14			13 28	13 46	
Warblington	d						12 15									13 16					
Emsworth	d	11 49			11 58	12 13	12 18				12 49			12 58	13 13	13 19				13 49	
Southbourne	d	11 52			12 01		12 21				12 52			13 01		13 22				13 52	
Nutbourne	d						12 24									13 24					
Bosham	d						12 27									13 27					
Fishbourne (Sussex)	d						12 30									13 30					
Chichester	a	11 59			12 08	12 21	12 33			12 38	12 59			13 08	13 21	13 33			13 38	13 59	
	d	12 00			12 09	12 22	12 34			12 39	13 00			13 09	13 22	13 34			13 39	14 00	
Barnham	a	12 07			12 16	12 30	12 41			12 46	13 07			13 16	13 30	13 42			13 46	14 07	
Bognor Regis	d		12 05	11 56				12 36	12 29			13 05	12 56				13 36	13 29			14 05
Barnham	a		12 11	12 02				12 43	12 35			13 11	13 03				13 43	13 35			14 11
Barnham	d	12 09	12 12	12 03	12 17	12 31	12 42		12 36	12 47	13 09	13 12	13 03	13 17	13 31	13 43		13 36	13 47	14 09	14 12
Ford	d		12 17	12 07		12 36	12 47		12 41			13 17	13 08		13 36	13 47		13 41			14 17
Littlehampton	a		12 23				12 53					13 23				13 53					14 23
Angmering	a	12 19				12 43					13 19				13 43					14 19	
Goring-by-Sea	a					12 47									13 47						
Durrington-on-Sea	a					12 50									13 50						
West Worthing	a					12 52									13 52						
Worthing	a	12 26				12 55					13 26				13 55					14 26	
Lancing	a	12 30				13 00					13 30				14 00					14 30	
Shoreham-by-Sea	a	12 35				13 04					13 35				14 04					14 35	
Southwick	a	12 38				13 08					13 38				14 08					14 38	
Portslade	a	12 42				13 11					13 42				14 11					14 42	
Hove	a	12 45				13 15					13 45				14 15					14 45	
Brighton	a	12 51				13 21					13 51				14 21					14 51	
Arundel	d			12 13					12 46				13 13					13 46			
Amberley	d			12 17									13 18								
Pulborough	d			12 24					12 55				13 24					13 55			
Billingshurst	d			12 31					13 02				13 31					14 02			
Christs Hospital	d			12 37									13 37								
Horsham	a			12 41	12 46				13 11	13 16			13 41	13 46				14 11	14 16		
	d				12 50					13 20				13 50					14 20		
Crawley	a				12 58					13 28				13 58					14 28		
Three Bridges	a				13 03					13 33				14 03					14 33		
	d				13 04					13 34				14 04					14 34		
Gatwick Airport	a				13 08					13 38				14 08					14 38		
East Croydon	a				13 24					13 54				14 24					14 54		
East Croydon	d																				
London Bridge	a																				
East Croydon	d				13 24					13 54				14 24					14 54		
Clapham Junction	a				13 33					14 03				14 33					15 03		
London Victoria	a				13 41					14 11				14 41					15 11		

Table T186-R

Mondays to Fridays

16 December to 15 May

Bognor Regis, Chichester, Portsmouth and Southampton - London, Gatwick Airport, Arun Valley and Brighton

		SN ■	SN ■	SN ■	SN	SN	SN ■	SN ■		SN	SN	SN ■	SN ■	SN ■	GW ◇	SN ■	SN	SN		SN ■	SN ■	SN	SN	SN ■	SN ■
Southampton Central	d		13 13	13 28									14 13	14 28	14 34										15 13
Swanwick	d		13 32	13 46									14 33	14 46											15 32
Fareham	d		13 39	13 53									14 40	14 53	14 57										15 39
Portchester	d		13 44										14 45												15 44
Cosham	d		13 48	14 02									14 49	15 01	15 05										15 49
Portsmouth Harbour	d							14 11		14 29											15 11	15 29			
Portsmouth & Southsea	d				13 57			14 15		14 33							14 57				15 15	15 33			
Fratton	d				14 01			14 19		14 37							15 01				15 19	15 37			
Hilsea	d				14 05												15 05								
Bedhampton	d				14 10												15 13								
Havant	d		13 55	14 10	14 13			14 28		14 46			14 56	15 08	15 12		15 16				15 28	15 46			15 55
Warblington	d				14 15												15 18								
Emsworth	d		13 58	14 13	14 18					14 49			14 59				15 21					15 49			15 59
Southbourne	d		14 01		14 21					14 52			15 02				15 24					15 52			16 02
Nutbourne	d				14 24												15 27								
Bosham	d				14 27												15 30								
Fishbourne (Sussex)	d				14 30												15 33								
Chichester	a		14 08	14 21	14 33			14 38		14 59			15 09	15 18	15 25		15 36				15 40	15 59			16 09
	d		14 09	14 22	14 34			14 39		15 00			15 10	15 18	15 26		15 36				15 40	16 00			16 09
Barnham	a		14 16	14 30	14 41			14 46		15 07			15 17	15 26	15 36		15 44				15 48	16 07			16 17
Bognor Regis	d	13 56				14 36	14 29				15 05	14 56						15 36		15 26			16 05	15 56	
Barnham	a	14 02				14 43	14 35				15 11	15 02						15 44		15 32			16 11	16 02	
Barnham	d	14 03	14 17	14 31	14 42		14 36	14 47		15 09	15 12	15 03	15 18	15 26	15 37		15 44			15 33	15 49	16 09	16 12	16 03	16 17
Ford	d	14 07		14 36	14 47		14 41				15 17	15 07		15 31			15 49			15 37			16 17	16 07	
Littlehampton	a				14 53						15 23						15 54						16 22		
Angmering	a			14 43						15 19				15 38								16 19			
Goring-by-Sea	a			14 47										15 42											
Durrington-on-Sea	a			14 50										15 45											
West Worthing	a			14 52										15 48											
Worthing	a			14 55						15 26				15 51	15 54	←						16 26			
Lancing	a			15 00						15 30				16 03		16 03						16 30			
Shoreham-by-Sea	a			15 04						15 35				→	16 00	16 07						16 35			
Southwick	a			15 08						15 38						16 10						16 38			
Portslade	a			15 11						15 42						16 14						16 42			
Hove	a			15 15						15 45					16 09	16 17						16 45			
Brighton	a			15 21						15 51					16 13	16 24						16 51			
Arundel	d	14 13					14 46					15 13								15 43				16 13	
Amberley	d	14 17										15 17												16 17	
Pulborough	d	14 24					14 55					15 24								15 53				16 24	
Billingshurst	d	14 31					15 02					15 31								16 00				16 31	
Christs Hospital	d	14 37										15 37								16 06				16 37	
Horsham	a	14 41	14 46				15 11	15 16				15 41	15 46							16 11	16 18			16 41	16 46
	d		14 50					15 20					15 50								16 22				16 50
Crawley	a		14 58					15 28					15 58								16 30				16 58
Three Bridges	a		15 03					15 33					16 03								16 35				17 03
	d		15 04					15 34					16 04								16 36				17 04
Gatwick Airport	a		15 08					15 38					16 08								16 40				17 08
East Croydon	a		15 24					15 54					16 24								16 56				17 24
East Croydon	d																								
London Bridge	a																								
East Croydon	d		15 24					15 54					16 24								16 56				17 24
Clapham Junction	a		15 33					16 03					16 33								17 05				17 33
London Victoria	a		15 41					16 11					16 41								17 13				17 41

NRT DECEMBER 19 EDITION

Table T186-R

Mondays to Fridays

16 December to 15 May

Bognor Regis, Chichester, Portsmouth and Southampton - London, Gatwick Airport, Arun Valley and Brighton

		SN ■	SN	SN		SN ■	SN ■	SN	SN	SN ■	SN ■	SN ■	SN	SN		SN ■	SN ■	SN	SN	SN ■	SN ■	SN ■	SN	SN
Southampton Central	d	15 28									16 12	16 28									17 14	17 28		
Swanwick	d	15 46									16 32	16 46									17 32	17 46		
Fareham	d	15 53									16 39	16 53									17 39	17 53		
Portchester	d										16 44										17 44			
Cosham	d	16 02									16 48	17 02									17 48	18 02		
Portsmouth Harbour	d						16 11										17 11							
Portsmouth & Southsea	d		15 57				16 15	16 33					16 57				17 15	17 33					17 57	
Fratton	d		16 01				16 19	16 37					17 01				17 19	17 37					18 02	
Hilsea	d		16 05										17 05										18 06	
Bedhampton	d		16 10										17 10										18 11	
Havant	d	16 10	16 13				16 28	16 46			16 55	17 10	17 13				17 28	17 46			17 55	18 10	18 14	
Warblington	d		16 15										17 15										18 16	
Emsworth	d	16 13	16 18					16 49			16 58	17 13	17 18					17 49			17 58	18 13	18 19	
Southbourne	d		16 21					16 52			17 01		17 21					17 52			18 01		18 22	
Nutbourne	d		16 24										17 24										18 24	
Bosham	d		16 27										17 27										18 27	
Fishbourne (Sussex)	d		16 30										17 30										18 30	
Chichester	a	16 21	16 33				16 38	16 59			17 08	17 21	17 33				17 38	17 59			18 08	18 21	18 33	
	d	16 22	16 34				16 39	17 00			17 09	17 22	17 34				17 39	18 00			18 09	18 22	18 34	
Barnham	a	16 30	16 41				16 46	17 07			17 16	17 30	17 41				17 46	18 07			18 16	18 30	18 41	
Bognor Regis	d			16 36		16 29			17 05	16 56				17 36		17 29			18 05	17 56				18 39
Barnham	a			16 44		16 35			17 11	17 02				17 43		17 35			18 11	18 02				18 46
Barnham	d	16 31	16 42			16 36	16 47	17 09	17 12	17 03	17 17	17 31	17 42			17 36	17 47	18 09	18 14	18 03	18 19	18 31	18 42	
Ford	d	16 36	16 47			16 41			17 17	17 07		17 36	17 47			17 41			18 20	18 07		18 36	18 47	
Littlehampton	a		16 53						17 23				17 53						18 25				18 53	
Angmering	a	16 43						17 19				17 43						18 19				18 43		
Goring-by-Sea	a	16 47										17 47										18 47		
Durrington-on-Sea	a	16 50										17 50										18 50		
West Worthing	a	16 52										17 52										18 52		
Worthing	a	16 55						17 26				17 55						18 26				18 55		
Lancing	a	17 00						17 30				18 00						18 30				19 00		
Shoreham-by-Sea	a	17 04						17 35				18 04						18 35				19 04		
Southwick	a	17 08						17 38				18 08						18 38				19 08		
Portslade	a	17 11						17 42				18 11						18 42				19 11		
Hove	a	17 15						17 45				18 15						18 45				19 15		
Brighton	a	17 21						17 51				18 21						18 51				19 21		
Arundel	d					16 46				17 13						17 46				18 13				
Amberley	d									17 17										18 17				
Pulborough	d					16 55				17 24						17 55				18 24				
Billingshurst	d					17 02				17 31						18 02				18 31				
Christs Hospital	d									17 37										18 37				
Horsham	a					17 11	17 16			17 41	17 46					18 11	18 16			18 41	18 48			
	d						17 20				17 50						18 20				18 52			
Crawley	a						17 28				17 58						18 28				19 00			
Three Bridges	a						17 33				18 03						18 33				19 05			
	d						17 34				18 04						18 34				19 06			
Gatwick Airport	a						17 38				18 08						18 38				19 10			
East Croydon	a						17 54				18 24						18 54				19 26			
East Croydon	d																							
London Bridge	a																							
East Croydon	d						17 54				18 24						18 54				19 26			
Clapham Junction	a						18 03				18 34						19 03				19 35			
London Victoria	a						18 12				18 42						19 11				19 43			

Table T186-R

Mondays to Fridays
16 December to 15 May

Bognor Regis, Chichester, Portsmouth and Southampton - London, Gatwick Airport, Arun Valley and Brighton

		SN 1	SN 1	SN	SN	SN 1	SN 1	SN 1	SN	SN		SN 1	SN 1	SN	SN	SN 1	SN 1	SN 1	SN	SN 1	SN 1		SN	SN
Southampton Central	d						18 13	18 28									19 12	19 28						
Swanwick	d						18 32	18 46									19 32	19 46						
Fareham	d						18 39	18 53									19 39	19 53						
Portchester	d						18 44										19 44							
Cosham	d						18 48	19 02									19 48	20 02						
Portsmouth Harbour	d												19 11								20 11			
Portsmouth & Southsea	d		18 15	18 33					18 57				19 15	19 33					19 57		20 15		20 33	
Fratton	d		18 19	18 37					19 01				19 19	19 37					20 01		20 19		20 37	
Hilsea	d								19 05										20 05					
Bedhampton	d								19 10										20 10					
Havant	d		18 28	18 47			18 55	19 10	19 13				19 28	19 46			19 55	20 10	20 13		20 28		20 46	
Warblington	d								19 15										20 15					
Emsworth	d			18 50			18 58	19 13	19 18					19 49			19 58	20 13	20 18				20 49	
Southbourne	d			18 53			19 01		19 21					19 52			20 01		20 21				20 52	
Nutbourne	d								19 24										20 24					
Bosham	d								19 27										20 27					
Fishbourne (Sussex)	d								19 30										20 30					
Chichester	a		18 38	19 00			19 08	19 21	19 33				19 38	19 59			20 08	20 21	20 33		20 38		20 59	
	d		18 39	19 01			19 09	19 22	19 34				19 39	20 00			20 09	20 22	20 34		20 39		21 00	
Barnham	a		18 46	19 08			19 16	19 30	19 41				19 46	20 07			20 16	20 30	20 41		20 46		21 07	
Bognor Regis	d	18 29			19 05	18 56				19 38		19 29			20 05	19 56				20 29				21 05
Barnham	a	18 35			19 11	19 02				19 44		19 35			20 11	20 02				20 35				21 11
Barnham	d	18 36	18 47	19 09	19 16	19 03	19 19	19 31	19 42			19 36	19 47	20 09	20 12	20 03	20 17	20 31	20 42	20 36	20 47		21 09	21 12
Ford	d	18 41			19 21	19 07		19 36	19 47			19 41			20 17	20 07		20 36	20 47	20 41				21 17
Littlehampton	a				19 26				19 53						20 23				20 53					21 23
Angmering	a			19 19				19 43						20 19				20 43					21 19	
Goring-by-Sea	a							19 47										20 47						
Durrington-on-Sea	a							19 50										20 50						
West Worthing	a							19 52										20 52						
Worthing	a			19 26				19 55						20 26				20 55					21 26	
Lancing	a			19 30				20 00						20 30				21 00					21 30	
Shoreham-by-Sea	a			19 35				20 04						20 35				21 04					21 35	
Southwick	a			19 38				20 08						20 38				21 08					21 38	
Portslade	a			19 42				20 11						20 42				21 11					21 42	
Hove	a			19 45				20 15						20 45				21 15					21 45	
Brighton	a			19 51				20 21						20 51				21 21					21 51	
Arundel	d	18 46				19 13						19 46				20 13				20 46				
Amberley	d					19 17										20 17								
Pulborough	d	18 55				19 24						19 55				20 24				20 55				
Billingshurst	d	19 02				19 31						20 02				20 31				21 02				
Christs Hospital	d					19 37										20 37								
Horsham	a	19 11	19 16			19 41	19 48					20 11	20 16			20 41	20 46			21 11	21 16			
	d	19 20				19 52						20 20				20 50				21 20				
Crawley	a	19 28				20 00						20 28				20 58				21 28				
Three Bridges	a	19 33				20 05						20 33				21 03				21 33				
	d	19 34				20 06						20 34				21 04				21 34				
Gatwick Airport	a	19 38				20 10						20 38				21 08				21 38				
East Croydon	a	19 54				20 26						20 54				21 24				21 54				
East Croydon	d																							
London Bridge	a																							
East Croydon	d	19 54				20 26						20 54				21 24				21 54				
Clapham Junction	a	20 04				20 35						21 06				21 33				22 03				
London Victoria	a	20 11				20 43						21 13				21 41				22 11				

Table T186-R

Mondays to Fridays
16 December to 15 May

Bognor Regis, Chichester, Portsmouth and Southampton - London, Gatwick Airport, Arun Valley and Brighton

		SN 1	SN 1	SN 1	SN	SN 1	SN 1	SN		SN	SN 1	SN	SN 1	SN	SN	SN	SN	SN 1		SN	SN
Southampton Central	d		20 13	20 28							21 13		21 32			22 21		22 33			23 12
Swanwick	d		20 32	20 46							21 33		21 52			22 40		22 51			
Fareham	d		20 39	20 54							21 40		22 00			22 47		22 57			23 38
Portchester	d		20 44								21 45		22 05			22 52					
Cosham	d		20 48	21 02							21 49		22 09			22 56		23 06			23 47
Portsmouth Harbour	d						21 11							22 15	22 40					23 16	
Portsmouth & Southsea	d				20 57		21 15	21 33						22 19	22 44					23 20	
Fratton	d				21 01		21 19	21 37						22 23	22 48					23 24	
Hilsea	d				21 05									22 27	22 52					23 28	
Bedhampton	d				21 11									22 32	22 57					23 33	
Havant	d		20 55	21 10	21 14		21 30	21 47			21 56		22 16	22 35	23 00	23 04		23 12		23 36	23 54
Warblington	d				21 16								22 18							23 38	
Emsworth	d		20 58	21 13	21 19			21 50					22 21	22 38		23 07				23 41	
Southbourne	d		21 01		21 22			21 53					22 24	22 41		23 10				23 44	
Nutbourne	d				21 25								22 26							23 46	
Bosham	d				21 28								22 29							23 49	
Fishbourne (Sussex)	d				21 31								22 32							23 52	
Chichester	a		21 08	21 21	21 34		21 40	22 00			22 06		22 35	22 48	23 10	23 17		23 22		23 56	00 05
	d		21 09	21 22	21 34		21 40	22 01			22 07		22 41	22 49	23 10	23 18		23 23		23 57	00 06
Barnham	a		21 16	21 30	21 42		21 48	22 08			22 14		22 48	22 56	23 18	23 25		23 31		00 04	00 13
Bognor Regis	d	20 55				21 29				22 05		22 36					23 20				
Barnham	a	21 02				21 35				22 12		22 43					23 27				
Barnham	d	21 03	21 17	21 31	21 42	21 36	21 48	22 09			22 16		22 49	22 58	23 19	23 26		23 32		00 06	
Ford	d	21 07		21 36	21 47	21 41					22 20		22 54	23 02	23 23	23 31				00 10	
Littlehampton	a				21 53						22 25				23 28	23 37		23 41		00 16	
Angmering	a			21 43				22 19			22 43			23 09	23 52						
Goring-by-Sea	a			21 47							22 47			23 13	23 56						
Durrington-on-Sea	a			21 50							22 49			23 16	23 58						
West Worthing	a			21 52							22 52			23 18	00 01						
Worthing	a			21 55				22 26			22 54			23 21	00 04						
Lancing	a			22 00				22 30			23 00			23 27	00 10						
Shoreham-by-Sea	a			22 04				22 35			23 04			23 31	00 14						
Southwick	a			22 08				22 38			23 07			23 35	00 17						
Portslade	a			22 11				22 42			23 11			23 39	00 21						
Hove	a			22 15				22 46			23 16			23 44	00 25						
Brighton	a			22 21				22 51			23 20			23 49	00 30						
Arundel	d	21 13				21 46							22 58								
Amberley	d	21 17											23 03								
Pulborough	d	21 24				21 55							23 09								
Billingshurst	d	21 31				22 02							23 16								
Christs Hospital	d	21 37											23 22								
Horsham	a	21 41	21 46			22 11	22 16						23 26								
	d	21 50				22 20							23 27								
Crawley	a	21 58				22 28							23 39								
Three Bridges	a	22 03				22 33							23 43								
	d	22 04				22 34							23 44								
Gatwick Airport	a	22 08				22 38							23 49								
East Croydon	a	22 24				22 54															
East Croydon	d																				
London Bridge	a																				
East Croydon	d	22 24				22 54															
Clapham Junction	a	22 33				23 03															
London Victoria	a	22 42				23 12															

Table T186-R

Saturdays
21 December to 16 May

Bognor Regis, Chichester, Portsmouth and Southampton - London, Gatwick Airport, Arun Valley and Brighton

		SN ■	SN	SN ■	SN	SN ■	SN	SN ■	SN	SN	SN ■	SN ■	SN	SN	SN ■	SN ■	GW	SN ■	SN	SN	SN ■	SN ■	SN
Southampton Central	d															06 13		06 25					
Swanwick	d															06 32		06 43					
Fareham	d															06 39		06 52					
Portchester	d															06 44							
Cosham	d															06 48		07 00					
Portsmouth Harbour	d											06 11	06 29				06 50					07 11	07 29
Portsmouth & Southsea	d			04 55					05 57			06 15	06 33				06 54		06 57			07 15	07 33
Fratton	d			04 59					06 01			06 19	06 37				06 58		07 02			07 19	07 37
Hilsea	d								06 05										07 06				
Bedhampton	d								06 10										07 11				
Havant	d			05 07		05 50			06 13			06 28	06 46			06 55	07 08	07 11	07 14			07 28	07 46
Warblington	d								06 15										07 16				
Emsworth	d					05 53			06 18				06 49			06 58		07 14	07 19				07 49
Southbourne	d					05 56			06 21				06 52			07 01			07 22				07 52
Nutbourne	d								06 24										07 25				
Bosham	d								06 27										07 28				
Fishbourne (Sussex)	d								06 30										07 31				
Chichester	a			05 18		06 03			06 33			06 38	06 59			07 08	07 18	07 23	07 34			07 38	07 59
	d			05 18		06 04		06 23	06 34			06 39	07 00			07 09	07 19	07 24	07 34			07 39	08 00
Barnham	a			05 26		06 11		06 30	06 41			06 46	07 07			07 16	07 27	07 32	07 42			07 46	08 07
Bognor Regis	d		05 05		05 37		06 00			06 36	06 29			07 05	06 56					07 36	07 29		
Barnham	a		05 11		05 43		06 06			06 43	06 35			07 11	07 02					07 43	07 35		
Barnham	d	04 48	05 12	05 26	05 45	06 12	06 16	06 31	06 42		06 36	06 47	07 08	07 12	07 03	07 17	07 27	07 32	07 42		07 36	07 47	08 09
Ford	d	04 53	05 17		05 50	06 16	06 20	06 36	06 47		06 41			07 17	07 07			07 37	07 47		07 41		
Littlehampton	a	04 58	05 23				06 26		06 53					07 23					07 53				
Angmering	a	05 13			05 57			06 43					07 18					07 44					08 19
Goring-by-Sea	a	05 18			06 01			06 47										07 48					
Durrington-on-Sea	a	05 20			06 03			06 50										07 51					
West Worthing	a	05 23			06 06			06 52										07 53					
Worthing	a	05 25		05 41	06 08			06 55					07 26				07 49	07 56					08 26
Lancing	a	05 32			06 14			07 00					07 30					08 01					08 30
Shoreham-by-Sea	a	05 36		05 48	06 19			07 04					07 35				07 59	08 05					08 35
Southwick	a	05 40			06 22			07 08					07 38					08 09					08 38
Portslade	a	05 44			06 26			07 11					07 42					08 12					08 42
Hove	a	05 48		05 54	06 31			07 15					07 45				08 12	08 16					08 45
Brighton	a	05 54			06 36			07 21					07 51				08 18	08 24					08 51
Arundel	d					06 22					06 46				07 13						07 46		
Amberley	d					06 26									07 17								
Pulborough	d					06 32					06 55				07 24						07 55		
Billingshurst	d					06 39					07 02				07 31						08 02		
Christs Hospital	d					06 45									07 37								
Horsham	a					06 49					07 11	07 16			07 41	07 46					08 11	08 16	
	d					06 50					07 20				07 50						08 20		
Crawley	a					06 58					07 28				07 58						08 28		
Three Bridges	a					07 03					07 33				08 03						08 33		
	d					07 04					07 34				08 04						08 34		
Gatwick Airport	a			06 26		07 08					07 38				08 08						08 38		
East Croydon	a			06 41		07 24					07 54				08 24						08 54		
East Croydon	d																						
London Bridge	a																						
East Croydon	d			06 42		07 24					07 54				08 24						08 54		
Clapham Junction	a			06 51		07 33					08 03				08 33						09 03		
London Victoria	a			06 59		07 41					08 11				08 41						09 11		

NRT DECEMBER 19 EDITION

Table T186-R

Saturdays
21 December to 16 May

Bognor Regis, Chichester, Portsmouth and Southampton - London, Gatwick Airport, Arun Valley and Brighton

		SN	SN ■	SN ■	SN ■	SN	SN	SN ■	SN ■	SN	SN	SN ■	SN ■	SN ■	SN	SN	SN ■	SN ■	SN	SN
Southampton Central	d			07 13	07 28								08 13	08 28						
Swanwick	d			07 30	07 46								08 30	08 46						
Fareham	d			07 37	07 53								08 37	08 54						
Portchester	d			07 42									08 42							
Cosham	d			07 46	08 02								08 46	09 03						
Portsmouth Harbour	d								08 11	08 29								09 11	09 29	
Portsmouth & Southsea	d					07 57			08 15	08 33					08 57			09 15	09 33	
Fratton	d					08 01			08 19	08 37					09 01			09 19	09 37	
Hilsea	d					08 05									09 05					
Bedhampton	d					08 10									09 10					
Havant	d			07 53	08 10	08 13			08 28	08 46			08 53	09 10	09 13			09 28	09 46	
Warblington	d					08 15									09 15					
Emsworth	d			07 56	08 13	08 18				08 49			08 56	09 13	09 18				09 49	
Southbourne	d			07 59		08 21				08 52			08 59		09 21				09 52	
Nutbourne	d					08 24									09 24					
Bosham	d					08 27									09 27					
Fishbourne (Sussex)	d					08 30									09 30					
Chichester	a			08 06	08 21	08 33			08 38	08 59			09 06	09 21	09 33			09 38	09 59	
	d			08 07	08 22	08 34			08 39	09 00			09 07	09 22	09 34			09 39	10 00	
Barnham	a			08 16	08 30	08 41			08 46	09 07			09 16	09 30	09 41			09 46	10 07	
Bognor Regis	d	08 05	07 56				08 36	08 29			09 05	08 56				09 36	09 29			10 05
Barnham	a	08 11	08 02				08 43	08 35			09 11	09 02				09 43	09 35			10 11
Barnham	d	08 12	08 03	08 17	08 31	08 42		08 36	08 47	09 09	09 12	09 03	09 17	09 31	09 42		09 36	09 47	10 09	10 12
Ford	d	08 17	08 07		08 36	08 47		08 41			09 17	09 07		09 36	09 47		09 41			10 17
Littlehampton	a	08 23				08 53					09 23				09 53					10 23
Angmering	a				08 43					09 19				09 43					10 19	
Goring-by-Sea	a				08 47									09 47						
Durrington-on-Sea	a				08 50									09 50						
West Worthing	a				08 52									09 52						
Worthing	a				08 55					09 26				09 55					10 26	
Lancing	a				09 00					09 30				10 00					10 30	
Shoreham-by-Sea	a				09 04					09 35				10 04					10 35	
Southwick	a				09 08					09 38				10 08					10 38	
Portslade	a				09 11					09 42				10 11					10 42	
Hove	a				09 15					09 45				10 15					10 45	
Brighton	a				09 21					09 51				10 21					10 51	
Arundel	d		08 13					08 46				09 13					09 46			
Amberley	d		08 17									09 17								
Pulborough	d		08 24					08 55				09 24					09 55			
Billingshurst	d		08 31					09 02				09 31					10 02			
Christs Hospital	d		08 37									09 37								
Horsham	a		08 41	08 46				09 11	09 16			09 41	09 46				10 11	10 16		
	d		08 50					09 20				09 50					10 20			
Crawley	a		08 58					09 28				09 58					10 28			
Three Bridges	a		09 03					09 33				10 03					10 33			
	d		09 04					09 34				10 04					10 34			
Gatwick Airport	a		09 08					09 38				10 08					10 38			
East Croydon	a		09 24					09 54				10 24					10 54			
East Croydon	d																			
London Bridge	a																			
East Croydon	d		09 24					09 54				10 24					10 54			
Clapham Junction	a		09 33					10 03				10 33					11 03			
London Victoria	a		09 41					10 11				10 41					11 11			

Table T186-R

Saturdays

21 December to 16 May

Bognor Regis, Chichester, Portsmouth and Southampton - London, Gatwick Airport, Arun Valley and Brighton

		SN 1	SN 1	SN 1		SN	SN	SN 1	SN 1	SN	SN	SN 1	SN 1	SN 1	SN	SN	SN 1	SN 1	SN	SN	SN 1	SN 1	SN 1
Southampton Central	d		09 13	09 28									13 13	13 28								14 13	14 26
Swanwick	d		09 32	09 46									13 32	13 46								14 32	
Fareham	d		09 39	09 53									13 39	13 53								14 39	15 00
Portchester	d		09 44										13 44									14 44	→
Cosham	d		09 48	10 02									13 48	14 02								14 48	
Portsmouth Harbour	d								13 11	13 29								14 11	14 29				
Portsmouth & Southsea	d					12 57			13 15	13 33					13 57			14 15	14 33				
Fratton	d					13 01			13 19	13 37					14 01			14 19	14 37				
Hilsea	d					13 05									14 05								
Bedhampton	d					13 10									14 10								
Havant	d		09 55	10 10		13 13			13 28	13 46			13 55	14 10	14 13			14 28	14 46			14 55	
Warblington	d					13 15									14 15								
Emsworth	d		09 58	10 13		13 18				13 49			13 58	14 13	14 18				14 49			14 58	
Southbourne	d		10 01			13 21				13 52			14 01		14 21				14 52			15 01	
Nutbourne	d					13 24									14 24								
Bosham	d					13 27									14 27								
Fishbourne (Sussex)	d					13 30									14 30								
Chichester	a		10 08	10 21		13 33			13 38	13 59			14 08	14 21	14 33			14 38	14 59			15 08	
	d		10 09	10 22		13 34			13 39	14 00			14 09	14 22	14 34			14 39	15 00			15 09	
Barnham	a		10 16	10 30		13 41			13 46	14 07			14 16	14 30	14 41			14 46	15 07			15 16	
Bognor Regis	d	09 56					13 36	13 29			14 05	13 56				14 36	14 29			15 05	14 56		
Barnham	a	10 02					13 43	13 35			14 11	14 02				14 43	14 35			15 11	15 02		
Barnham	d	10 03	10 17	10 31	and at the same minutes past each hour until	13 42		13 36	13 47	14 09	14 12	14 03	14 17	14 31	14 42		14 36	14 47	15 09	15 12	15 03	15 17	
Ford	d	10 07		10 36		13 47		13 41			14 17	14 07		14 36	14 47		14 41			15 17	15 07		
Littlehampton	a					13 53					14 23				14 53					15 23			
Angmering	a			10 43						14 19				14 43					15 19				
Goring-by-Sea	a			10 47										14 47									
Durrington-on-Sea	a			10 50										14 50									
West Worthing	a			10 52										14 52									
Worthing	a			10 55						14 26				14 55					15 26				
Lancing	a			11 00						14 30				15 00					15 30				
Shoreham-by-Sea	a			11 04						14 35				15 04					15 35				
Southwick	a			11 08						14 38				15 08					15 38				
Portslade	a			11 11						14 42				15 11					15 42				
Hove	a			11 15						14 45				15 15					15 45				
Brighton	a			11 21						14 51				15 21					15 51				
Arundel	d	10 13						13 46				14 13					14 46				15 13		
Amberley	d	10 17										14 17									15 17		
Pulborough	d	10 24						13 55				14 24					14 55				15 24		
Billingshurst	d	10 31						14 02				14 31					15 02				15 31		
Christs Hospital	d	10 37										14 37									15 37		
Horsham	a	10 41	10 46					14 11	14 16			14 41	14 46				15 11	15 16			15 41	15 46	
	d	10 50						14 20				14 50					15 20				15 50		
Crawley	a	10 58						14 28				14 58					15 28				15 58		
Three Bridges	a	11 03						14 33				15 03					15 33				16 03		
	d	11 04						14 34				15 04					15 34				16 04		
Gatwick Airport	a	11 08						14 38				15 08					15 38				16 08		
East Croydon	a	11 24						14 54				15 24					15 54				16 24		
East Croydon	d																						
London Bridge	a																						
East Croydon	d	11 24						14 54				15 24					15 54				16 24		
Clapham Junction	a	11 33						15 03				15 33					16 03				16 33		
London Victoria	a	11 41						15 11				15 41					16 11				16 41		

Table T186-R

Saturdays

21 December to 16 May

Bognor Regis, Chichester, Portsmouth and Southampton - London, Gatwick Airport, Arun Valley and Brighton

		GW ◇	SN 1	SN	SN	SN 1	SN 1	SN	SN	SN 1	SN 1	SN 1	SN	SN	SN 1	SN 1		SN	SN
Southampton Central	d	14 34									15 13	15 28							
Swanwick	d		←								15 32	15 46							
Fareham	d	14 56	15 00								15 39	15 53							
Portchester	d										15 44								
Cosham	d	15 04									15 48	16 02							
Portsmouth Harbour	d						15 11	15 29								16 11		19 29	
Portsmouth & Southsea	d				14 57		15 15	15 33					15 57			16 15		19 33	
Fratton	d				15 01		15 19	15 37					16 01			16 19		19 37	
Hilsea	d				15 05								16 05						
Bedhampton	d				15 14								16 10						
Havant	d	15 10	15 13		15 17		15 28	15 46			15 55	16 10	16 13			16 28		19 46	
Warblington	d				15 19								16 15						
Emsworth	d				15 22			15 49			15 58	16 13	16 18					19 49	
Southbourne	d				15 25			15 52			16 01		16 21					19 52	
Nutbourne	d				15 28								16 24						
Bosham	d				15 31								16 27						
Fishbourne (Sussex)	d				15 34								16 30						
Chichester	a	15 21	15 24		15 37		15 40	15 59			16 08	16 21	16 33			16 38		19 59	
	d	15 21	15 25		15 37		15 41	16 00			16 09	16 22	16 34			16 39		20 00	
Barnham	a	15 29	15 33		15 45		15 49	16 07			16 16	16 30	16 41			16 46		20 07	
Bognor Regis	d			15 36		15 29			16 05	15 56				16 36	16 29				20 05
Barnham	a			15 43		15 37			16 11	16 02				16 43	16 35				20 11
Barnham	d	15 29	15 33		15 45	15 37	15 50	16 09	16 12	16 03	16 17	16 31	16 42		16 36	16 47	and at the same minutes past each hour until	20 09	20 12
Ford	d		15 38		15 50	15 42			16 17	16 07		16 36	16 47		16 41				20 17
Littlehampton	a				15 55				16 23				16 53						20 23
Angmering	a		15 45					16 19				16 43						20 19	
Goring-by-Sea	a		15 49									16 47							
Durrington-on-Sea	a		15 52									16 50							
West Worthing	a		15 54									16 52							
Worthing	a	15 49	15 57					16 26				16 55						20 26	
Lancing	a		16 01					16 30				17 00						20 30	
Shoreham-by-Sea	a	15 59	16 05					16 35				17 04						20 35	
Southwick	a		16 09					16 38				17 08						20 38	
Portslade	a		16 12					16 42				17 11						20 42	
Hove	a	16 12	16 15					16 45				17 15						20 45	
Brighton	a	16 18	16 24					16 51				17 21						20 51	
Arundel	d					15 47				16 13					16 46				
Amberley	d									16 17									
Pulborough	d					15 56				16 24					16 55				
Billingshurst	d					16 03				16 31					17 02				
Christs Hospital	d									16 37									
Horsham	a					16 12	16 18			16 41	16 46				17 11	17 16			
	d					16 22				16 50					17 20				
Crawley	a					16 30				16 58					17 28				
Three Bridges	a					16 35				17 03					17 33				
	d					16 36				17 04					17 34				
Gatwick Airport	a					16 40				17 08					17 38				
East Croydon	a					16 56				17 24					17 54				
East Croydon	d																		
London Bridge	a																		
East Croydon	d					16 56				17 24					17 54				
Clapham Junction	a					17 05				17 33					18 03				
London Victoria	a					17 13				17 41					18 11				

Table T186-R

Saturdays
21 December to 16 May

Bognor Regis, Chichester, Portsmouth and Southampton - London, Gatwick Airport, Arun Valley and Brighton

		SN 1	SN 1	SN 1	SN	SN	SN 1	SN 1	SN	SN	SN 1	SN 1	SN 1	SN	SN	SN 1	SN 1	SN	SN 1	SN	SN	SN 1	SN
Southampton Central	d		19 13	19 28								20 13	20 28						21 13			21 32	
Swanwick	d		19 32	19 46								20 32	20 46						21 33			21 51	
Fareham	d		19 39	19 53								20 39	20 53						21 40			21 58	
Portchester	d		19 44									20 44							21 45			22 03	
Cosham	d		19 48	20 02								20 48	21 02						21 49			22 07	
Portsmouth Harbour	d							20 11	20 29								21 11			21 40			22 15
Portsmouth & Southsea	d				19 57			20 15	20 33					20 57			21 15			21 44			22 19
Fratton	d				20 01			20 19	20 37					21 01			21 19			21 48			22 23
Hilsea	d				20 05									21 05						21 52			22 27
Bedhampton	d				20 10									21 10						21 57			22 32
Havant	d		19 55	20 10	20 13			20 28	20 46			20 55	21 10	21 13			21 28		21 56	22 00		22 14	22 35
Warblington	d				20 15									21 15								22 16	
Emsworth	d		19 58	20 13	20 18				20 49			20 58	21 13	21 18								22 19	22 39
Southbourne	d		20 01		20 21				20 52			21 01		21 21								22 22	22 42
Nutbourne	d				20 24									21 24								22 24	
Bosham	d				20 27									21 27								22 27	
Fishbourne (Sussex)	d				20 30									21 30								22 30	
Chichester	a		20 08	20 21	20 33			20 38	20 59			21 08	21 21	21 33			21 38		22 06	22 10		22 33	22 49
	d		20 09	20 22	20 34			20 39	21 00			21 09	21 22	21 34			21 39		22 07	22 12		22 40	22 49
Barnham	a		20 16	20 30	20 41			20 46	21 07			21 16	21 30	21 41			21 46		22 14	22 19		22 47	22 57
Bognor Regis	d	19 56				20 36	20 29			21 05	20 56				21 36	21 29		22 05			22 35		
Barnham	a	20 02				20 43	20 35			21 11	21 02				21 43	21 35		22 11			22 41		
Barnham	d	20 03	20 17	20 31	20 42		20 36	20 47	21 09	21 12	21 03	21 17	21 31	21 42		21 36	21 47		22 16	22 20	22 42	22 48	22 58
Ford	d	20 07		20 36	20 47		20 41			21 17	21 07		21 36	21 47		21 41			22 20	22 24	22 46	22 53	23 02
Littlehampton	a				20 53					21 23				21 53					22 25	22 29	22 51		
Angmering	a			20 43					21 19				21 43						22 42				23 09
Goring-by-Sea	a			20 47									21 47						22 46				23 13
Durrington-on-Sea	a			20 50									21 50						22 49				23 16
West Worthing	a			20 52									21 52						22 51				23 18
Worthing	a			20 55					21 26				21 55						22 54				23 21
Lancing	a			21 00					21 30				22 00						23 00				23 27
Shoreham-by-Sea	a			21 04					21 35				22 04						23 04				23 31
Southwick	a			21 08					21 38				22 08						23 07				23 35
Portslade	a			21 11					21 42				22 11						23 11				23 39
Hove	a			21 15					21 45				22 15						23 15				23 44
Brighton	a			21 21					21 51				22 21						23 20				23 49
Arundel	d	20 13					20 46				21 13					21 46						22 58	
Amberley	d	20 17									21 17											23 03	
Pulborough	d	20 24					20 55				21 24					21 55						23 09	
Billingshurst	d	20 31					21 02				21 31					22 02						23 16	
Christs Hospital	d	20 37									21 37											23 22	
Horsham	a	20 41	20 46				21 11	21 16			21 41	21 46				22 11	22 16					23 26	
	d	20 50					21 20				21 50					22 20						23 27	
Crawley	a	20 58					21 28				21 58					22 28						23 39	
Three Bridges	a	21 03					21 33				22 03					22 33						23 43	
	d	21 04					21 34				22 04					22 34						23 44	
Gatwick Airport	a	21 08					21 38				22 08					22 38						23 49	
East Croydon	a	21 24					21 54				22 24					22 54							
East Croydon	d																						
London Bridge	a																						
East Croydon	d	21 24					21 54				22 24					22 54							
Clapham Junction	a	21 33					22 03				22 33					23 04							
London Victoria	a	21 41					22 11				22 41					23 11							

Table T186-R

Saturdays
21 December to 16 May

Bognor Regis, Chichester, Portsmouth and Southampton - London, Gatwick Airport, Arun Valley and Brighton

		SN	SN	SN	SN 1	SN	SN
Southampton Central	d			22 21	22 26		23 16
Swanwick	d			22 38	22 46		
Fareham	d			22 45	22 54		23 38
Portchester	d			22 50			
Cosham	d			22 55	23 03		23 47
Portsmouth Harbour	d	22 40				23 15	
Portsmouth & Southsea	d	22 44				23 19	
Fratton	d	22 48				23 23	
Hilsea	d	22 52				23 27	
Bedhampton	d	22 57				23 32	
Havant	d	23 00		23 04	23 10	23 35	23 54
Warblington	d					23 37	
Emsworth	d			23 08	23 13	23 40	
Southbourne	d			23 11		23 43	
Nutbourne	d					23 45	
Bosham	d					23 48	
Fishbourne (Sussex)	d					23 51	
Chichester	a	23 10		23 18	23 21	23 55	00 05
	d	23 10		23 18	23 22	23 56	00 06
Barnham	a	23 18		23 26	23 30	00 03	00 13
Bognor Regis	d		23 15				
Barnham	a		23 21				
Barnham	d	23 19		23 27	23 31	00 05	00 14
Ford	d	23 23		23 31	23 36	00 10	00 18
Littlehampton	a	23 28		23 37	23 41	00 16	00 24
Angmering	a	23 51					
Goring-by-Sea	a	23 55					
Durrington-on-Sea	a	23 57					
West Worthing	a	23 59					
Worthing	a	00 02					
Lancing	a	00 09					
Shoreham-by-Sea	a	00 13					
Southwick	a	00 16					
Portslade	a	00 20					
Hove	a	00 25					
Brighton	a	00 30					
Arundel	d						
Amberley	d						
Pulborough	d						
Billingshurst	d						
Christs Hospital	d						
Horsham	a						
	d						
Crawley	a						
Three Bridges	a						
	d						
Gatwick Airport	a						
East Croydon	a						
East Croydon	d						
London Bridge	a						
East Croydon	d						
Clapham Junction	a						
London Victoria	a						

Table T186-R

Sundays
15 December to 10 May

Bognor Regis, Chichester, Portsmouth and Southampton - London, Gatwick Airport, Arun Valley and Brighton

		SN	SN	SN ■	SN ■	SN	SN	SN ■	SN ■	SN ■	SN	SN	SN ■	GW	SN ■	SN ■	SN ■	SN	SN	SN	SN ■	SN ■	SN ■
Southampton Central	d							07 30					08 21	08 31							09 30		
Swanwick	d							07 47					08 40								09 47		
Fareham	d							07 54					08 47	08 54							09 54		
Portchester	d																						
Cosham	d							08 03					08 56	09 02							10 03		
Portsmouth Harbour	d					07 14			08 01		08 14					09 01		09 14				10 01	
Portsmouth & Southsea	d					07 18			08 05		08 18					09 05		09 18				10 05	
Fratton	d					07 22			08 09		08 22					09 09		09 22				10 09	
Hilsea	d																						
Bedhampton	d					07 30					08 30							09 30					
Havant	d			07 11		07 33		08 10	08 18		08 33		09 02	09 13		09 18		09 33			10 10	10 18	
Warblington	d					07 35					08 35							09 35					
Emsworth	d			07 15		07 38		08 14	08 21		08 38		09 06			09 21		09 38			10 14	10 21	
Southbourne	d			07 18		07 41			08 24		08 41					09 24		09 41				10 24	
Nutbourne	d					07 44					08 44							09 44					
Bosham	d					07 47					08 47							09 47					
Fishbourne (Sussex)	d					07 50					08 50							09 50					
Chichester	a			07 25		07 53		08 22	08 31		08 53		09 14	09 24		09 31		09 53			10 22	10 31	
	d			07 26		07 53		08 22	08 32		08 53		09 14	09 24		09 32		09 53			10 22	10 32	
Barnham	a			07 35		08 01		08 30	08 40		09 01		09 22	09 31		09 40		10 01			10 30	10 40	
Bognor Regis	d		07 00		07 26		08 00			08 31		09 00					09 31		10 00	10 06			10 31
Barnham	a		07 06		07 32		08 06			08 37		09 06					09 37		10 06	10 13			10 37
Barnham	d	06 08	07 07	07 39		08 02	08 07	08 31	08 44		09 02	09 07	09 23	09 31		09 44		10 02	10 07		10 31	10 44	
Ford	d	06 12	07 11	07 43		08 06	08 11	08 35	08 48		09 06	09 11	09 27			09 48		10 06	10 11		10 35	10 48	
Littlehampton	a	06 17	07 16				08 16					09 16							10 16				
Angmering	a					08 13		08 42			09 13		09 34					10 13			10 42		
Goring-by-Sea	a					08 18		08 47			09 18		09 39					10 18			10 47		
Durrington-on-Sea	a					08 20		08 49			09 20		09 41					10 20			10 49		
West Worthing	a					08 23		08 52			09 23		09 44					10 23			10 52		
Worthing	a	06 36				08 25		08 54			09 25		09 46	09 49	←			10 25			10 54		
Lancing	a	06 41				08 31		09 00			09 31		10 00		10 00			10 31			11 00		
Shoreham-by-Sea	a	06 45				08 35		09 04			09 35		→	09 56	10 04			10 35			11 04		
Southwick	a	06 48				08 39		09 08			09 39				10 08			10 39			11 08		
Portslade	a	06 52				08 43		09 12			09 43				10 12			10 43			11 12		
Hove	a	06 55				08 47		09 16			09 47			10 03	10 16			10 47			11 16		
Brighton	a	07 00				08 52		09 22			09 52			10 08	10 22			10 52			11 22		
Arundel	d			07 49					08 54							09 54						10 54	
Amberley	d			07 53					08 58							09 58						10 58	
Pulborough	d			07 59					09 04							10 04						11 04	
Billingshurst	d			08 06					09 11							10 11						11 11	
Christs Hospital	d			08 12					09 17							10 17						11 17	
Horsham	a			08 16					09 21							10 21						11 21	
	d			08 17					09 21							10 21						11 21	
Crawley	a			08 25					09 30							10 30						11 30	
Three Bridges	a			08 30					09 35							10 35						11 35	
	d			08 31					09 35							10 35						11 35	
Gatwick Airport	a			08 35					09 40							10 40						11 40	
East Croydon	a			08 58					10 03							11 03						12 03	
East Croydon	d																						
London Bridge	a																						
East Croydon	d			08 59					10 04							11 04						12 04	
Clapham Junction	a			09 08					10 14							11 14						12 14	
London Victoria	a			09 15					10 21							11 21						12 21	

Table T186-R

Sundays
15 December to 10 May

Bognor Regis, Chichester, Portsmouth and Southampton - London, Gatwick Airport, Arun Valley and Brighton

		SN	SN	SN	SN ■	SN ■	SN ■	SN	SN	SN ■	SN ■	SN ■	SN	SN	SN ■	SN ■	SN ■	SN	GW ◇	SN	SN	SN ■
Southampton Central	d				10 30					11 30					12 30				13 04			13 30
Swanwick	d				10 47					11 47					12 47							13 47
Fareham	d				10 54					11 54					12 54				13 30			13 54
Portchester	d																					
Cosham	d				11 03					12 03					13 03				13 38			14 03
Portsmouth Harbour	d	10 14				11 01		11 14			12 01		12 13			13 01		13 14				
Portsmouth & Southsea	d	10 18				11 05		11 18			12 05		12 17			13 05		13 18				
Fratton	d	10 22				11 09		11 22			12 09		12 21			13 09		13 22				
Hilsea	d																					
Bedhampton	d	10 30						11 30					12 29					13 30				
Havant	d	10 33			11 10	11 18		11 33		12 10	12 18		12 33		13 10	13 18		13 33	13 46			14 10
Warblington	d	10 35						11 35					12 35					13 35				
Emsworth	d	10 38			11 14	11 21		11 38		12 14	12 21		12 38		13 14	13 21		13 38				14 14
Southbourne	d	10 41				11 24		11 41			12 24		12 41			13 24		13 41				
Nutbourne	d	10 44						11 44					12 44					13 44				
Bosham	d	10 47						11 47					12 47					13 47				
Fishbourne (Sussex)	d	10 50						11 50					12 50					13 50				
Chichester	a	10 53			11 22	11 31		11 53		12 22	12 31		12 53		13 22	13 31		13 53	13 57			14 22
	d	10 53			11 22	11 32		11 53		12 22	12 32		12 53		13 22	13 32		13 53	13 58			14 22
Barnham	a	11 01			11 30	11 40		12 01		12 30	12 40		13 01		13 30	13 40		14 01	14 08			14 30
Bognor Regis	d		11 00	11 06			11 31		12 00			12 31		13 00			13 31				14 05	
Barnham	a		11 06	11 13			11 37		12 06			12 37		13 06			13 37				14 12	
Barnham	d	11 02	11 07		11 31	11 44		12 02	12 07	12 31	12 44		13 02	13 07	13 31	13 44		14 02	14 08		14 12	14 31
Ford	d	11 06	11 11		11 35	11 48		12 06	12 11	12 35	12 48		13 06	13 11	13 35	13 48		14 06			14 20	14 35
Littlehampton	a		11 16						12 16					13 16							14 25	
Angmering	a	11 13			11 42			12 13		12 42			13 13		13 42			14 13				14 42
Goring-by-Sea	a	11 18			11 47			12 18		12 47			13 18		13 47			14 18				14 47
Durrington-on-Sea	a	11 20			11 49			12 20		12 49			13 20		13 49			14 20				14 49
West Worthing	a	11 23			11 52			12 23		12 52			13 23		13 52			14 23				14 52
Worthing	a	11 25			11 54			12 25		12 54			13 25		13 54			14 25	14 30	←		14 54
Lancing	a	11 31			12 00			12 31		13 00			13 31		14 00			14 44		14 44		15 00
Shoreham-by-Sea	a	11 35			12 04			12 35		13 04			13 35		14 04			→	14 36	14 48		15 04
Southwick	a	11 39			12 08			12 39		13 08			13 39		14 08					14 52		15 08
Portslade	a	11 43			12 12			12 43		13 12			13 43		14 12					14 56		15 12
Hove	a	11 47			12 16			12 47		13 16			13 47		14 16				14 43	15 00		15 16
Brighton	a	11 52			12 22			12 52		13 22			13 52		14 22				14 49	15 05		15 22
Arundel	d					11 54					12 54					13 54						
Amberley	d					11 58					12 58					13 58						
Pulborough	d					12 04					13 04					14 04						
Billingshurst	d					12 11					13 11					14 11						
Christs Hospital	d					12 17					13 17					14 17						
Horsham	a					12 21					13 21					14 21						
	d					12 21					13 21					14 21						
Crawley	a					12 30					13 30					14 30						
Three Bridges	a					12 35					13 35					14 35						
	d					12 35					13 35					14 35						
Gatwick Airport	a					12 40					13 40					14 40						
East Croydon	a					13 06					14 03					15 03						
East Croydon	d																					
London Bridge	a																					
East Croydon	d					13 06					14 04					15 04						
Clapham Junction	a					13 16					14 14					15 14						
London Victoria	a					13 23					14 21					15 21						

Table T186-R

Sundays
15 December to 10 May

Bognor Regis, Chichester, Portsmouth and Southampton - London, Gatwick Airport, Arun Valley and Brighton

		SN 1	SN 1	SN	SN		SN 1	SN 1	SN 1	SN	GW ◇	SN	SN	SN 1	SN 1	SN 1		SN	SN	SN 1	SN 1	SN 1	SN	SN	SN 1
Southampton Central	d						14 30				15 06			15 30						16 30					17 30
Swanwick	d						14 47							15 47						16 47					17 47
Fareham	d						14 54				15 28			15 54						16 54					17 54
Portchester	d																								
Cosham	d						15 03				15 36			16 03						17 03					18 03
Portsmouth Harbour	d	14 01		14 14				15 01		15 14					16 01			16 14			17 01				
Portsmouth & Southsea	d	14 05		14 18				15 05		15 18					16 05			16 18			17 05				
Fratton	d	14 09		14 22				15 09		15 22					16 09			16 22			17 09		17 22		
Hilsea	d																								
Bedhampton	d			14 30						15 30								16 30					17 30		
Havant	d	14 18		14 33			15 10	15 18		15 33	15 43			16 10	16 18			16 33		17 10	17 18		17 33		18 10
Warblington	d			14 35						15 35								16 35					17 35		
Emsworth	d	14 21		14 38			15 14	15 21		15 38				16 14	16 21			16 38		17 14	17 21		17 38		18 14
Southbourne	d	14 24		14 41				15 24		15 41					16 24			16 41			17 24		17 41		
Nutbourne	d			14 44						15 44								16 44					17 44		
Bosham	d			14 47						15 47								16 47					17 47		
Fishbourne (Sussex)	d			14 50						15 50								16 50					17 50		
Chichester	a	14 31		14 53			15 22	15 31		15 53	15 57			16 22	16 31			16 53		17 22	17 31		17 53		18 22
	d	14 32		14 53			15 22	15 32		15 53	15 58			16 22	16 32			16 53		17 22	17 32		17 53		18 22
Barnham	a	14 40		15 01			15 30	15 40		16 01	16 05			16 30	16 40			17 01		17 30	17 40		18 01		18 30
Bognor Regis	d		14 31		15 00				15 31			16 02				16 31			17 00			17 31		18 00	
Barnham	a		14 37		15 06				15 37			16 09	←			16 37			17 06			17 37		18 06	
Barnham	d	14 44		15 02	15 07		15 31	15 44		16 14	16 06	16 09	16 14	16 31	16 44			17 02	17 07	17 31	17 44		18 02	18 07	18 31
Ford	d	14 48		15 06	15 11		15 35	15 48		→		16 14	16 18	16 35	16 48			17 06	17 11	17 35	17 48		18 06	18 11	18 35
Littlehampton	a				15 16							16 19							17 16					18 16	
Angmering	a			15 13			15 42						16 27	16 42				17 13		17 42			18 13		18 42
Goring-by-Sea	a			15 18			15 47						16 31	16 47				17 18		17 47			18 18		18 47
Durrington-on-Sea	a			15 20			15 49						16 33	16 49				17 20		17 49			18 20		18 49
West Worthing	a			15 23			15 52						16 36	16 52				17 23		17 52			18 23		18 52
Worthing	a			15 25			15 54				16 23		16 38	16 54				17 25		17 54			18 25		18 54
Lancing	a			15 31			16 00						16 44	17 00				17 31		18 00			18 31		19 00
Shoreham-by-Sea	a			15 35			16 04				16 31		16 48	17 04				17 35		18 04			18 35		19 04
Southwick	a			15 39			16 08						16 51	17 08				17 39		18 08			18 39		19 08
Portslade	a			15 43			16 12						16 55	17 12				17 43		18 12			18 43		19 12
Hove	a			15 47			16 16				16 37		17 00	17 16				17 47		18 16			18 47		19 16
Brighton	a			15 52			16 22				16 44		17 04	17 22				17 52		18 22			18 52		19 22
Arundel	d	14 54						15 54							16 54						17 54				
Amberley	d	14 58						15 58							16 58						17 58				
Pulborough	d	15 04						16 04							17 04						18 04				
Billingshurst	d	15 11						16 11							17 11						18 11				
Christs Hospital	d	15 17						16 17							17 17						18 17				
Horsham	a	15 21						16 21							17 21						18 21				
	d	15 21						16 21							17 21						18 21				
Crawley	a	15 30						16 30							17 30						18 30				
Three Bridges	a	15 35						16 35							17 35						18 35				
	d	15 35						16 35							17 35						18 35				
Gatwick Airport	a	15 40						16 40							17 40						18 40				
East Croydon	a	16 06						17 06							18 03						19 03				
East Croydon	d																								
London Bridge	a																								
East Croydon	d	16 06						17 06							18 04						19 04				
Clapham Junction	a	16 16						17 16							18 14						19 14				
London Victoria	a	16 23						17 23							18 21						19 21				

NRT DECEMBER 19 EDITION

Table T186-R

Sundays
15 December to 10 May

Bognor Regis, Chichester, Portsmouth and Southampton - London, Gatwick Airport, Arun Valley and Brighton

		SN 1	SN 1		SN	SN	SN 1	SN 1	SN 1	SN	SN	SN 1	GW ◇		SN 1	SN 1	SN 1	SN	SN	SN 1	SN 1	SN 1	SN		SN
Southampton Central	d						18 30					19 23	19 28							20 28					
Swanwick	d						18 47					19 41								20 46					
Fareham	d						18 54					19 49	19 54							20 53					
Portchester	d																								
Cosham	d						19 03					19 57	20 02							21 03					
Portsmouth Harbour	d	18 01			18 14			19 01								20 01		20 14			21 01		21 14		
Portsmouth & Southsea	d	18 05			18 18			19 05								20 05		20 18			21 05		21 18		
Fratton	d	18 09			18 22			19 09		19 22						20 09		20 22			21 09		21 22		
Hilsea	d																								
Bedhampton	d				18 30					19 30								20 30					21 30		
Havant	d	18 18			18 33		19 10	19 18		19 33		20 04	20 11			20 18		20 33		21 10	21 18		21 33		
Warblington	d				18 35					19 35								20 35					21 35		
Emsworth	d	18 21			18 38		19 14	19 21		19 38		20 07				20 21		20 38		21 14	21 21		21 38		
Southbourne	d	18 24			18 41			19 24		19 41						20 24		20 41			21 24		21 41		
Nutbourne	d				18 44					19 44								20 44					21 44		
Bosham	d				18 47					19 47								20 47					21 47		
Fishbourne (Sussex)	d				18 50					19 50								20 50					21 50		
Chichester	a	18 31			18 53		19 22	19 31		19 53		20 15	20 21			20 31		20 53		21 22	21 31		21 53		
	d	18 32			18 53		19 22	19 32		19 53		20 16	20 22			20 32		20 53		21 22	21 32		21 53		
Barnham	a	18 40			19 01		19 30	19 40		20 01		20 23	20 29			20 40		21 01		21 30	21 40		22 01		
Bognor Regis	d		18 31			19 00			19 31		20 00						20 31		21 00			21 31			22 00
Barnham	a		18 37			19 06			19 37		20 06						20 37		21 06			21 37			22 06
Barnham	d	18 44			19 02	19 07	19 31	19 44		20 02	20 07	20 24	20 30			20 44		21 02	21 07	21 31	21 44		22 02		22 07
Ford	d	18 48			19 06	19 11	19 35	19 48		20 06	20 11	20 28				20 48		21 06	21 11	21 35	21 48		22 06		22 11
Littlehampton	a					19 16					20 16							21 11	21 16	21 40					22 16
Angmering	a				19 13		19 42			20 13		20 35						21 25		21 55			22 13		
Goring-by-Sea	a				19 18		19 47			20 18		20 40						21 29		21 59			22 18		
Durrington-on-Sea	a				19 20		19 49			20 20		20 42						21 32		22 02			22 20		
West Worthing	a				19 23		19 52			20 23		20 45						21 34		22 04			22 23		
Worthing	a				19 25		19 54			20 25		20 47	20 50		←			21 37		22 07			22 25		
Lancing	a				19 31		20 00			20 31		21 02			21 02			21 43		22 13			22 31		
Shoreham-by-Sea	a				19 35		20 04			20 35		→	20 57		21 06			21 47		22 17			22 35		
Southwick	a				19 39		20 08			20 39					21 09			21 50		22 20			22 39		
Portslade	a				19 43		20 12			20 43					21 13			21 54		22 24			22 43		
Hove	a				19 47		20 16			20 47			21 05		21 18			21 59		22 29			22 47		
Brighton	a				19 52		20 22			20 52			21 10		21 22			22 04		22 34			22 52		
Arundel	d	18 54						19 54								20 54					21 54				
Amberley	d	18 58						19 58								20 58					21 58				
Pulborough	d	19 04						20 04								21 04					22 04				
Billingshurst	d	19 11						20 11								21 11					22 11				
Christs Hospital	d	19 17						20 17								21 17					22 17				
Horsham	a	19 21						20 21								21 21					22 21				
	d	19 21						20 21								21 21					22 21				
Crawley	a	19 30						20 30								21 30					22 30				
Three Bridges	a	19 35						20 35								21 35					22 35				
	d	19 35						20 35								21 35					22 35				
Gatwick Airport	a	19 40						20 40								21 40					22 40				
East Croydon	a	20 03						21 03								22 03					23 03				
East Croydon	d																								
London Bridge	a																								
East Croydon	d	20 04						21 04								22 04					23 04				
Clapham Junction	a	20 14						21 14								22 14					23 14				
London Victoria	a	20 21						21 21								22 21					23 21				

Table T186-R

Sundays

15 December to 10 May

Bognor Regis, Chichester, Portsmouth and Southampton - London, Gatwick Airport, Arun Valley and Brighton

		SN [1]	SN	SN	SN	SN	SN	SN
Southampton Central	d	21 30				22 30		22 58
Swanwick	d	21 47				22 47		23 15
Fareham	d	21 54				22 54		23 22
Portchester	d							
Cosham	d	22 03				23 04		23 31
Portsmouth Harbour	d		22 01		22 14		23 01	
Portsmouth & Southsea	d		22 05		22 18		23 05	
Fratton	d		22 09		22 22		23 09	
Hilsea	d							
Bedhampton	d							
Havant	d	22 10	22 17		22 31	23 12	23 18	23 38
Warblington	d				22 33			
Emsworth	d	22 14	22 21		22 36		23 22	23 42
Southbourne	d		22 24		22 39		23 25	
Nutbourne	d							
Bosham	d				22 43			
Fishbourne (Sussex)	d				22 46			
Chichester	a	22 22	22 31		22 49	23 22	23 32	23 50
	d	22 22	22 32		22 50	23 22	23 32	23 50
Barnham	a	22 30	22 39		22 57	23 30	23 40	23 58
Bognor Regis	d			22 28				
Barnham	a			22 34				
Barnham	d	22 31	22 40	22 43	22 58	23 30	23 40	23 59
Ford	d	22 35	22 44	22 47	23 02		23 45	00 03
Littlehampton	a		22 50	22 54	23 07	23 40	23 50	00 09
Angmering	a	22 42	23 04					
Goring-by-Sea	a	22 47	23 09					
Durrington-on-Sea	a	22 49	23 11					
West Worthing	a	22 52	23 14					
Worthing	a	22 54	23 16					
Lancing	a	23 00	23 22					
Shoreham-by-Sea	a	23 04	23 26					
Southwick	a	23 08	23 30					
Portslade	a	23 12	23 34					
Hove	a	23 16	23 38					
Brighton	a	23 22	23 43					
Arundel	d							
Amberley	d							
Pulborough	d							
Billingshurst	d							
Christs Hospital	d							
Horsham	a							
	d							
Crawley	a							
Three Bridges	a							
	d							
Gatwick Airport	a							
East Croydon	a							
East Croydon	d							
London Bridge	a							
East Croydon	d							
Clapham Junction	a							
London Victoria	a							

Table T188-F

Mondays to Fridays

16 December to 15 May

London - Gatwick Airport and Brighton - Worthing - Southampton Central

		SN MX [1] A	SN MX	SN MO	SN MX	SN MO [1] A	SN MX [1] A	SN MX [1]	SN MX [1] A	SN	SN [1]	SN	SN	SN	SN	SN	SN [1]	SN	SN	SN	SN	SN	SN [1]
London Victoria [15]	d							00 02															
Clapham Junction [10]	d							00 09															
East Croydon	a							00 23															
St Pancras International	d																						
Farringdon	d																						
City Thameslink	d																						
London Blackfriars	d																						
London Bridge	d																						
East Croydon	a																						
East Croydon	d							00 24															
Gatwick Airport [10]	d							00 44															
Haywards Heath [3]	d					00 08	00 09	01 02															
Preston Park	d					00 19	00 22																
Brighton [10]	d		00 04	00 10	00 12			01s16		05 00	05 27	05 39	05 51	06 02	06 11	06 21	06 32	06 41	06 47	06 59	07 11	07 20	07 32
Hove [2]	a		00 08	00 14	00 17	00 23	00 26	01s25		05 04	05 31	05 44	05 55	06 06	06 16	06 25	06 36	06 45	06 51	07 03	07 15	07 24	07 36
	d		00 09			00 23	00 26			05 05	05 32		05 55	06 06		06 25	06 36	06 45	06 51	07 03	07 15	07 24	07 36
Aldrington	d		00 11								05 34		05 57			06 27			06 53			07 26	
Portslade	d		00 14			00 26	00 29	01s28		05 08	05 37		06 00	06 09		06 30	06 39	06 48	06 56	07 06	07 18	07 29	07 39
Fishersgate	d		00 16								05 39		06 02			06 32			06 58			07 31	
Southwick	d		00 18			00 29	00 32	01s31		05 11	05 41		06 04	06 12		06 34	06 42	06 51	07 00	07 09	07 21	07 33	07 42
Shoreham-by-Sea	d	00 02	00 22			00 32	00 36	01s34		05 14	05 44		06 08	06 16		06 38	06 46	06 55	07 04	07 13	07 25	07 37	07 46
Lancing	d	00 06	00 26			00 36	00 40	01s38		05 18	05 48		06 12	06 20		06 42	06 50	06 59	07 08	07 17	07 29	07 41	07 50
East Worthing	d		00 29								05 51		06 15			06 45			07 11			07 44	
Worthing [4]	a	00 11	00 31			00 40	00 45	01 43		05 22	05 54		06 18	06 24		06 48	06 54	07 03	07 13	07 21	07 33	07 47	07 54
	d		00 32							05 22	05 54		06 18	06 24		06 48	06 55	07 04	07 14	07 22	07 34	07 47	07 55
West Worthing	d		00a34							05 24	05 56		06a21	06 27		06 50	06 57	07a06	07 16		07a36	07 49	07 57
Durrington-on-Sea	d									05 27	05 59			06 29		06 53	06 59		07 18			07 52	07 59
Goring-by-Sea	d									05 29	06 01			06 32		06 55	07 02		07 21			07 54	08 02
Angmering [3]	d									05 33	06 05			06 36		06 59	07 06		07 25	07 28		07 58	08 06
Littlehampton [4]	a															07 11			07 38			08 08	
Barnham	a									05 44	06 17			06 47			07 18			07 39			08 18
Barnham	d								00 12														
Bognor Regis	a								00 19														
Barnham	d									05 45	06 19			06 48			07 19			07 40			08 19
Chichester [4]	a									05 52	06 26			06 56			07 26			07 48			08 26
Havant	a									06 06	06 40			07 10			07 38			08 03			08 38
Havant	d									06 07				07 11						08 03			
Portsmouth & Southsea	a									06 20				07 25						08 16			
Portsmouth Harbour	a									06 24										08 22			
Havant	d										06 42						07 39						08 39
Fareham	a										06 59						07 56						08 54
Southampton Central	a										07 25						08 20						09 20

		SN	SN	SN	SN	SN	SN [1]	SN	SN [1]	SN	GW ◇ B	SN	SN	TL [1] C	SN	SN [1]	SN	SN [1]	SN	SN	SN	SN [1]	SN
London Victoria [15]	d								07 46									08 46				09 16	
Clapham Junction [10]	d								07 53									08 53				09 23	
East Croydon	a								08 03									09 02				09 32	
St Pancras International	d													08 10									
Farringdon	d													08 14									
City Thameslink	d													08 16									
London Blackfriars	d													08 19									
London Bridge	d													08 25									
East Croydon	a													08 38									
East Croydon	d								08 03					08 38				09 03				09 33	
Gatwick Airport [10]	d								08 20									09 20				09 50	
Haywards Heath [3]	d								08 38					09 07				09 38				10 05	
Preston Park	d													09 18								10 18	
Brighton [10]	d	07 41	07 51	08 00	08 14	08 22	08 32	08 40		08 51	09 00	09 05	09 09		09 21	09 32	09 39		09 51	10 02	10 09		10 21
Hove [2]	a	07 45	07 55	08 04	08 18	08 26	08 36	08 45	08 52	08 55	09 03	09 09	09 14	09 23	09 26	09 36	09 44	09 52	09 55	10 06	10 14	10 22	10 25
	d	07 45	07 55	08 04	08 19	08 26	08 36		08 53	08 56	09 04	09 09		09 23	09 26	09 36		09 52	09 55	10 06		10 22	10 25
Aldrington	d		07 57			08 28				08 58					09 28				09 57				10 27
Portslade	d	07 48	08 00	08 07	08 22	08 31	08 39		08 56	09 00		09 12		09 27	09 31	09 39		09 55	10 00	10 09		10 25	10 30
Fishersgate	d		08 02			08 33				09 02					09 33				10 02				10 32
Southwick	d	07 51	08 04	08 10	08 25	08 35	08 42			09 04		09 16			09 35	09 42			10 04	10 12			10 34
Shoreham-by-Sea	d	07 55	08 08	08 14	08 29	08 39	08 46		09 01	09 08	09 13	09 20		09 32	09 39	09 46		10 00	10 08	10 16		10 30	10 38
Lancing	d	07 59	08 12	08 18	08 33	08 43	08 50		09 05	09 12		09 24		09 36	09 43	09 50		10 04	10 12	10 20			10 42
East Worthing	d		08 15			08 46				09 15					09 46				10 15				10 45
Worthing [4]	a	08 03	08 18	08 22	08 37	08 49	08 54		09 09	09 17	09 20	09 28		09 40	09 48	09 54		10 08	10 18	10 24		10 36	10 48
	d	08 04	08 18	08 25	08 38	08 49	08 55		09 09	09 18	09 22	09 29		09 40	09 49	09 55		10 09	10 18	10 25		10 39	10 48
West Worthing	d	08 06	08a21	08 27	08 40	08a52	08 57		09 11	09a20				09 43	09a51	09 57		10 11	10a21			10 41	10a51
Durrington-on-Sea	d	08 08		08 29	08 43		08 59		09 14					09 46		09 59		10 13				10 43	
Goring-by-Sea	d	08 11		08 32	08 45		09 02		09 16					09 49		10 02		10 16				10 46	
Angmering [3]	d	08 15		08 36	08 50		09 06		09 20			09 35		09 53		10 06		10 20		10 32		10 50	
Littlehampton [4]	a				09 00				09 31					10 03				10 31				11 01	
Barnham	a	08 28		08 47			09 18				09 38	09 47				10 18				10 43			
Barnham	d																						
Bognor Regis	a																						
Barnham	d	08 28		08 48			09 19				09 38	09 48				10 19				10 44			
Chichester [4]	a	08 36		08 55			09 26				09 46	09 55				10 26				10 51			
Havant	a	08 46		09 09			09 39				09 57	10 09				10 38				11 05			
Havant	d	08 47		09 10								10 10								11 06			
Portsmouth & Southsea	a	08 59		09 23								10 23								11 18			
Portsmouth Harbour	a	09 04																		11 22			
Havant	d						09 40				09 57					10 39							
Fareham	a						09 55				10 12					10 54							
Southampton Central	a						10 19				10 40					11 19							

A From London Victoria

B To Great Malvern

C From Bedford

Table T188-F

Mondays to Fridays
16 December to 15 May

London - Gatwick Airport and Brighton - Worthing - Southampton Central

		SN 1	SN	SN 1	SN	SN	SN	SN 1	SN	SN 1	SN	SN 1	SN	SN	SN	SN 1	SN	SN 1	SN	SN 1	SN	SN
London Victoria	d			09 46				10 16				10 46				11 16				11 46		
Clapham Junction	d			09 53				10 23				10 53				11 23				11 53		
East Croydon	a			10 02				10 32				11 02				11 32				12 02		
St Pancras International	d																					
Farringdon	d																					
City Thameslink	d																					
London Blackfriars	d																					
London Bridge	d																					
East Croydon	a																					
East Croydon	d			10 03				10 33				11 03				11 33				12 03		
Gatwick Airport	d			10 20				10 50				11 20				11 50				12 20		
Haywards Heath	d			10 38				11 05				11 38				12 05				12 38		
Preston Park	d							11 18								12 18						
Brighton	d	10 32	10 39		10 51	11 02	11 09		11 21	11 32	11 39		11 51	12 02	12 09		12 21	12 32	12 39		12 51	13 02
Hove	a	10 36	10 44	10 52	10 55	11 06	11 14	11 22	11 25	11 36	11 44	11 52	11 55	12 06	12 14	12 22	12 25	12 36	12 44	12 52	12 55	13 06
	d	10 36		10 52	10 55	11 06		11 22	11 25	11 36		11 52	11 55	12 06		12 22	12 25	12 36		12 52	12 56	13 06
Aldrington	d				10 57				11 27				11 57				12 27				12 58	
Portslade	d	10 39		10 55	11 00	11 09		11 25	11 30	11 39		11 55	12 00	12 09		12 25	12 30	12 39		12 55	13 01	13 09
Fishersgate	d				11 02				11 32				12 02				12 32				13 03	
Southwick	d	10 42			11 04	11 12			11 34	11 42			12 04	12 12			12 34	12 42			13 05	13 12
Shoreham-by-Sea	d	10 46		11 00	11 08	11 16		11 30	11 38	11 46		12 00	12 08	12 16		12 30	12 38	12 46		13 00	13 09	13 16
Lancing	d	10 50		11 04	11 12	11 20			11 42	11 50		12 04	12 12	12 20			12 42	12 50		13 04	13 13	13 20
East Worthing	d				11 15				11 45				12 15				12 45				13 16	
Worthing	a	10 54		11 08	11 18	11 24		11 36	11 48	11 54		12 08	12 18	12 24		12 36	12 48	12 54		13 08	13 18	13 24
	d	10 55		11 09	11 18	11 25		11 39	11 48	11 55		12 09	12 18	12 25		12 39	12 48	12 55		13 09	13 19	13 25
West Worthing	d	10 57		11 11	11a21			11 41	11a51	11 57		12 11	12a21			12 41	12a51	12 57		13 11	13a21	
Durrington-on-Sea	d	10 59		11 13				11 43		11 59		12 13				12 43		12 59		13 13		
Goring-by-Sea	d	11 02		11 16				11 46		12 02		12 16				12 46		13 02		13 16		
Angmering	d	11 06		11 20		11 32		11 50		12 06		12 20		12 32		12 50		13 06		13 20		13 32
Littlehampton	a			11 31				12 01				12 31				13 01				13 31		
Barnham	a	11 18				11 43				12 18				12 43				13 18				13 43
Barnham	d																					
Bognor Regis	a																					
Barnham	d	11 19				11 44				12 19				12 44				13 19				13 44
Chichester	a	11 26				11 51				12 26				12 51				13 26				13 51
Havant	a	11 38				12 05				12 38				13 05				13 38				14 05
Havant	d					12 06								13 06								14 06
Portsmouth & Southsea	a					12 18								13 18								14 18
Portsmouth Harbour	a					12 22								13 22								14 22
Havant	d	11 39								12 39								13 39				
Fareham	a	11 54								12 56								13 54				
Southampton Central	a	12 19								13 20								14 19				

		SN	SN 1	SN	SN 1	SN	SN 1	SN	SN	SN	SN 1	SN	SN 1	SN	SN 1	SN	SN	SN	SN 1	SN	SN 1	SN	SN 1
London Victoria	d		12 16				12 46				13 16				13 46				14 16				14 46
Clapham Junction	d		12 23				12 53				13 23				13 53				14 23				14 53
East Croydon	a		12 32				13 02				13 32				14 02				14 32				15 02
St Pancras International	d																						
Farringdon	d																						
City Thameslink	d																						
London Blackfriars	d																						
London Bridge	d																						
East Croydon	a																						
East Croydon	d		12 33				13 03				13 33				14 03				14 33				15 03
Gatwick Airport	d		12 50				13 20				13 50				14 20				14 50				15 20
Haywards Heath	d		13 05				13 38				14 05				14 38				15 05				15 38
Preston Park	d		13 18								14 18								15 18				
Brighton	d	13 09		13 21	13 32	13 39		13 51	14 02	14 09		14 21	14 32	14 39		14 51	15 02	15 09		15 21	15 32	15 39	
Hove	a	13 14	13 22	13 25	13 36	13 44	13 52	13 55	14 06	14 14	14 22	14 25	14 36	14 44	14 52	14 55	15 06	15 14	15 22	15 25	15 36	15 44	15 52
	d		13 22	13 26	13 36		13 52	13 55	14 06		14 22	14 25	14 36		14 52	14 55	15 06		15 22	15 25	15 36		15 52
Aldrington	d			13 28				13 57				14 27				14 57				15 27			
Portslade	d		13 25	13 31	13 39		13 55	14 00	14 09		14 25	14 30	14 39		14 55	15 00	15 09		15 25	15 30	15 39		15 55
Fishersgate	d			13 33				14 02				14 32				15 02				15 32			
Southwick	d			13 35	13 42			14 04	14 12			14 34	14 42			15 04	15 12			15 34	15 42		
Shoreham-by-Sea	d		13 30	13 39	13 46		14 00	14 08	14 16		14 30	14 38	14 46		15 00	15 08	15 16		15 30	15 38	15 46		16 00
Lancing	d			13 43	13 50		14 04	14 12	14 20			14 42	14 50		15 04	15 12	15 20		15 34	15 42	15 50		16 04
East Worthing	d			13 46				14 15				14 45				15 15			15 37	15 46			
Worthing	a		13 36	13 48	13 54		14 08	14 18	14 24		14 36	14 48	14 54		15 08	15 18	15 24		15 40	15 49	15 54		16 08
	d		13 39	13 49	13 55		14 09	14 18	14 25		14 39	14 48	14 55		15 09	15 18	15 26		15 40	15 50	15 55		16 09
West Worthing	d		13 41	13a51	13 57		14 11	14a21			14 41	14a51	14 57		15 11	15 20			15 42	15 52	15 57		16 11
Durrington-on-Sea	d		13 43		13 59		14 13				14 43		14 59		15 13	15 23			15 45	15 55	15 59		16 13
Goring-by-Sea	d		13 46		14 02		14 16				14 46		15 02		15 16	15 25			15 47	15 58	16 02		16 16
Angmering	d		13 50		14 06		14 20		14 32		14 50		15 06		15 20	15 29	15 34		15 51	16 03	16 06		16 20
Littlehampton	a		14 01				14 31				15 01				15 31	15 41			16 01	16 13			16 31
Barnham	a				14 18				14 43				15 18				15 47				16 18		
Barnham	d																						
Bognor Regis	a																						
Barnham	d				14 19				14 44				15 19				15 48				16 19		
Chichester	a				14 26				14 51				15 26				15 55				16 26		
Havant	a				14 38				15 05				15 38				16 09				16 38		
Havant	d								15 06								16 10						
Portsmouth & Southsea	a								15 18								16 23						
Portsmouth Harbour	a								15 22														
Havant	d				14 39								15 39								16 39		
Fareham	a				14 54								15 54								16 54		
Southampton Central	a				15 19								16 20								17 19		

NRT DECEMBER 19 EDITION

Table T188-F

Mondays to Fridays
16 December to 15 May

London - Gatwick Airport and Brighton - Worthing - Southampton Central

		SN	SN	SN	SN 1	SN	SN 1	SN	SN 1	SN	GW ◇ A	SN	SN	SN 1	SN	SN 1	SN	TL 1 B	SN	SN 1	SN	SN
London Victoria	d				15 16				15 46					16 16						16 54		
Clapham Junction	d				15 23				15 53					16 23						17 02		
East Croydon	a				15 32				16 02					16 32						17 11		
St Pancras International	d																	16 40				
Farringdon	d																	16 44				
City Thameslink	d																	16 46				
London Blackfriars	d																	16 49				
London Bridge	d																	16 55				
East Croydon	a																	17 08				
East Croydon	d				15 33				16 03					16 33				17 08		17 11		
Gatwick Airport	d				15 50				16 20					16 50						17 27		
Haywards Heath	d				16 06				16 38					17 05				17 37		17 40		
Preston Park	d				16 18									17 20				17 50		17 55		
Brighton	d	15 51	16 02	16 09		16 21	16 32	16 39		16 51	17 02	17 05	17 12		17 21	17 32	17 42		17 52		18 02	18 10
Hove	a	15 55	16 06	16 14	16 22	16 25	16 36	16 44	16 52	16 55	17 05	17 10	17 16	17 24	17 25	17 36	17 46	17 54	17 58	18 00	18 06	18 14
	d	15 55	16 06		16 22	16 25	16 36		16 52	16 55	17 06	17 10	17 16	17 27		17 37	17 46	17 54		18 01	18 07	18 14
Aldrington	d	15 57				16 27				16 57			17 18				17 48					18 16
Portslade	d	16 00	16 09		16 25	16 30	16 39		16 55	17 00		17 13	17 21	17 30		17 40	17 51	17 58		18 04	18 10	18 19
Fishersgate	d	16 02				16 32				17 02			17 23				17 53					18 21
Southwick	d	16 04	16 12			16 34	16 42			17 04		17 16	17 25			17 43	17 55				18 13	18 23
Shoreham-by-Sea	d	16 08	16 16		16 30	16 38	16 46		17 00	17 08	17 12	17 20	17 29	17 35		17 47	17 59	18 03		18 09	18 16	18 27
Lancing	d	16 12	16 20			16 42	16 50		17 04	17 12		17 24	17 33	17 39		17 51	18 03	18 07		18 14	18 20	18 31
East Worthing	d	16 15				16 45				17 15			17 36				18 06					18 34
Worthing	a	16 18	16 25		16 36	16 48	16 54		17 08	17 18	17 23	17 28	17 39	17 43		17 55	18 08	18 11		18 18	18 24	18 36
	d	16 18	16 27		16 39	16 48	16 55		17 09	17 18	17 23	17 28	17 39	17 43		17 56	18 09	18 12		18 18	18 25	18 37
West Worthing	d	16 21			16 41	16 51	16 57		17 11	17 21		17 30	17 42	17 45		17 58		18 15		18 21	18 27	18a39
Durrington-on-Sea	d	16 23			16 43		16 59		17 13			17 33	17 44	17 48		18 00		18 18		18 24	18 29	
Goring-by-Sea	d	16 26			16 46		17 02		17 16			17 35	17 47	17 50		18 03		18 21		18 27	18 32	
Angmering	d	16 30	16 35		16 50		17 06		17 20			17 39	17 51	17 55		18 07		18 25		18 31	18 36	
Littlehampton	a	16 41			17 01	17 05			17 31	17 35			18 01	18 05			18 30	18 37		18 43		
Barnham	a		16 46				17 18				17 38	17 52				18 19					18 48	
Barnham	d																					
Bognor Regis	a																					
Barnham	d		16 47				17 19				17 39	17 52				18 19					18 49	
Chichester	a		16 54				17 26				17 46	18 00				18 27					18 56	
Havant	a		17 08				17 38				17 57	18 14				18 39					19 10	
Havant	d		17 09									18 14									19 11	
Portsmouth & Southsea	a		17 23									18 28									19 23	
Portsmouth Harbour	a																					
Havant	d						17 39				17 58					18 40						
Fareham	a						17 54				18 12					18 54						
Southampton Central	a						18 19				18 41					19 20						

		SN	SN 1	SN 1	SN	TL 1 B	SN	SN 1	SN	SN	SN	SN 1	SN 1	SN	SN	SN 1	SN	SN	SN 1	SN	SN 1	SN	SN 1
London Victoria	d		17 24					17 54				18 24				18 54			19 16				19 46
Clapham Junction	d		17 32					18 02				18 32				19 02			19 23				19 53
East Croydon	a		17 41					18 11				18 41				19 11			19 32				20 02
St Pancras International	d					17 40																	
Farringdon	d					17 44																	
City Thameslink	d					17 46																	
London Blackfriars	d					17 49																	
London Bridge	d					17 55																	
East Croydon	a					18 08																	
East Croydon	d		17 41			18 08		18 11				18 41				19 11			19 33				20 03
Gatwick Airport	d		17 57					18 27				18 57				19 27			19 50				20 20
Haywards Heath	d		18 09			18 37		18 40				19 10				19 40			20 05				20 38
Preston Park	d		18 26			18 50		18 55				19 25				19 55			20 18				
Brighton	d	18 22		18 32	18 40		18 52		19 02	19 10	19 22		19 32	19 40	19 52		20 02	20 10		20 21	20 32	20 39	
Hove	a	18 27	18 30	18 36	18 44	18 54	18 57	19 00	19 06	19 14	19 27	19 30	19 36	19 44	19 57	19 59	20 06	20 14	20 22	20 25	20 36	20 44	20 52
	d		18 31	18 37	18 44	18 54		19 01	19 07	19 14		19 31	19 37	19 44		20 02	20 07		20 22	20 25	20 36		20 52
Aldrington	d				18 46					19 16				19 46						20 27			
Portslade	d		18 34	18 40	18 49	18 58		19 04	19 10	19 19		19 34	19 40	19 49		20 05	20 10		20 25	20 30	20 39		20 55
Fishersgate	d				18 51					19 21				19 51						20 32			
Southwick	d			18 43	18 53				19 13	19 23			19 43	19 53			20 13			20 34	20 42		20 58
Shoreham-by-Sea	d		18 39	18 47	18 57	19 03		19 09	19 16	19 27		19 39	19 47	19 57		20 10	20 16		20 30	20 38	20 46		21 02
Lancing	d		18 44	18 51	19 01	19 07		19 14	19 20	19 31		19 44	19 51	20 01		20 14	20 20		20 34	20 42	20 50		21 06
East Worthing	d				19 04					19 34				20 04						20 45			
Worthing	a		18 48	18 55	19 06	19 11		19 18	19 24	19 36		19 48	19 55	20 06		20 18	20 24		20 38	20 48	20 54		21 10
	d		18 48	18 56	19 07	19 12		19 18	19 25	19 37		19 48	19 56	20 07		20 19	20 25		20 39	20 48	20 55		21 11
West Worthing	d		18 51	18 58	19a09	19 15		19 21		19a39		19 51	19 58	20a09		20 21	20 27		20 41	20a51	20 57		21 13
Durrington-on-Sea	d		18 54	19 00		19 18		19 24	19 29			19 54	20 00			20 24	20 29		20 43		20 59		21 15
Goring-by-Sea	d		18 57	19 03		19 21		19 27	19 31			19 57	20 03			20 27	20 32		20 46		21 02		21 18
Angmering	d		19 01	19 07		19 25		19 31	19 35			20 01	20 07			20 31	20 36		20 50		21 06		21 22
Littlehampton	a		19 13			19 37		19 43				20 13				20 43			21 01				21 32
Barnham	a			19 19					19 47				20 19				20 48				21 18		
Barnham	d																						
Bognor Regis	a																						
Barnham	d			19 20					19 48				20 20				20 49				21 19		
Chichester	a			19 27					19 56				20 27				20 56				21 26		
Havant	a			19 39					20 10				20 39				21 10				21 38		
Havant	d								20 10								21 11						
Portsmouth & Southsea	a								20 23								21 23						
Portsmouth Harbour	a																						
Havant	d			19 40									20 40								21 39		
Fareham	a			19 54									20 54								21 55		
Southampton Central	a			20 19									21 20								22 23		

A To Bristol Parkway
B From Bedford

Table T188-F

Mondays to Fridays
16 December to 15 May

London - Gatwick Airport and Brighton - Worthing - Southampton Central

		SN	SN	SN	SN ■	SN	SN	SN	SN ■	SN	SN	SN	SN ■	SN	SN	SN ■	SN	SN	SN ■	SN	SN ■	SN ■
London Victoria 15 ⊖	d				20 16				20 46				21 16			21 46			22 16		22 46	23 16
Clapham Junction 10	d				20 23				20 53				21 23			21 53			22 23		22 53	23 23
East Croydon	a				20 32				21 02				21 32			22 02			22 32		23 02	23 32
St Pancras International	d																					
Farringdon	d																					
City Thameslink	d																					
London Blackfriars	d																					
London Bridge	d																					
East Croydon	a																					
East Croydon	d				20 33				21 03				21 33			22 03			22 33		23 03	23 33
Gatwick Airport 10 ✈	d				20 50				21 20				21 50			22 20			22 50		23 20	23 56
Haywards Heath 3	d				21 05				21 38				22 05			22 38			23 05		23 38	00 09
Preston Park	d				21 18								22 18						23 18			00 22
Brighton 10	d	20 51	21 02	21 09		21 21	21 32	21 39		21 51	22 02	22 09		22 32	22 39		22 57	23 09		23 42		
Hove 2	a	20 55	21 06	21 14	21 22	21 25	21 36	21 44	21 52	21 55	22 06	22 14	22 22	22 36	22 44	22 52	23 01	23 14	23 22	23 48	23 52	00 26
	d	20 55	21 07		21 22	21 25	21 37		21 52	21 55	22 07		22 22	22 37		22 52	23 01		23 22		23 52	00 26
Aldrington	d	20 57				21 27				21 57				22 39			23 03					
Portslade	d	21 00	21 10		21 25	21 30	21 40		21 55	22 00	22 10		22 25	22 41		22 55	23 06		23 25		23 55	00 29
Fishersgate	d	21 02				21 32				22 02				22 43			23 08					
Southwick	d	21 04	21 13		21 28	21 34	21 43		21 58	22 04	22 13		22 28	22 45		22 58	23 10		23 28		23 58	00 32
Shoreham-by-Sea	d	21 08	21 16		21 32	21 38	21 46		22 02	22 08	22 16		22 32	22 49		23 02	23 14		23 32		00 02	00 36
Lancing	d	21 12	21 20		21 36	21 42	21 50		22 06	22 12	22 20		22 36	22 53		23 06	23 18		23 36		00 06	00 40
East Worthing	d	21 15				21 45				22 15				22 56			23 21					
Worthing 4	a	21 18	21 24		21 40	21 48	21 54		22 10	22 18	22 24		22 40	22 58		23 10	23 24		23 40		00 11	00 45
	d	21 18	21 25		21 41	21 48	21 55		22 11	22 18	22 25		22 41	22 59		23 11	23 24		23 41			
West Worthing	d	21a21	21 27		21 43	21a51	21 57		22 13	22a21	22 27		22 43	23 01		23 13	23a27		23 43			
Durrington-on-Sea	d		21 29		21 45		21 59		22 15		22 29		22 45	23 03		23 15			23 45			
Goring-by-Sea	d		21 32		21 48		22 02		22 18		22 32		22 48	23 06		23 18			23 48			
Angmering 3	d		21 36		21 52		22 06		22 22		22 36		22 52	23 10		23 22			23 52			
Littlehampton 4	a				22 02				22 32				23 02			23 32						
Barnham	a		21 48				22 18				22 48			23 22					00 04			
Barnham	d																		00 12			
Bognor Regis	a																		00 19			
Barnham	d		21 49				22 19				22 49			23 22								
Chichester 4	a		21 56				22 27				22 56			23 30								
Havant	a		22 10								23 10			23 41								
Havant	d		22 11								23 11											
Portsmouth & Southsea	a		22 23								23 23											
Portsmouth Harbour ⛴	a		22 27								23 28											
Havant	d																					
Fareham	a																					
Southampton Central ⛴	a																					

Saturdays
21 December to 16 May

		SN ■ A	SN	SN	SN ■ A	SN ■ B	SN ■ A	SN ■	SN ■	SN	SN	SN	SN	SN	SN ■	SN	SN ■	SN	SN	SN	SN	SN ■	SN
London Victoria 15 ⊖	d					00 02																	
Clapham Junction 10	d					00 09																	
East Croydon	a					00 23																	
St Pancras International	d																						
Farringdon	d																						
City Thameslink	d																						
London Blackfriars	d																						
London Bridge	d																						
East Croydon	a																						
East Croydon	d					00 24																	
Gatwick Airport 10 ✈	d					00 44																	
Haywards Heath 3	d				00 09	01 02																	
Preston Park	d				00 22																		
Brighton 10	d		00 04	00 12		01s16		05 14	05 32	05 39	05 51	06 02	06 09	06 21	06 32	06 39	06 47	06 51	07 02	07 09	07 21	07 32	07 39
Hove 2	a		00 08	00 17	00 26	01s25		05 18	05 36	05 44	05 55	06 06	06 14	06 25	06 36	06 44	06 51	06 55	07 06	07 14	07 25	07 36	07 44
	d		00 09		00 26			05 20	05 36		05 55	06 06		06 25	06 36		06 52	06 55	07 06		07 25	07 36	
Aldrington	d		00 11								05 57			06 27				06 57			07 27		
Portslade	d		00 14		00 29	01s28		05 23	05 39		06 00	06 09		06 30	06 39		06 55	07 00	07 09		07 30	07 39	
Fishersgate	d		00 16								06 02			06 32				07 02			07 32		
Southwick	d		00 18		00 32	01s31		05 26	05 42		06 04	06 12		06 34	06 42			07 04	07 12		07 34	07 42	
Shoreham-by-Sea	d	00 02	00 22		00 36	01s34		05 29	05 46		06 08	06 16		06 38	06 46		07 00	07 08	07 16		07 38	07 46	
Lancing	d	00 06	00 26		00 40	01s38		05 33	05 50		06 12	06 20		06 42	06 50		07 04	07 12	07 20		07 42	07 50	
East Worthing	d		00 29								06 15			06 45				07 15			07 45		
Worthing 4	a	00 11	00 31		00 45	01 43		05 37	05 54		06 18	06 24		06 48	06 54		07 08	07 18	07 24		07 48	07 54	
	d		00 32					05 37	05 55		06 18	06 25		06 48	06 55		07 09	07 18	07 25		07 48	07 55	
West Worthing	d		00a34					05 39	05 57		06a21			06a51	06 57		07 11	07a21			07a51	07 57	
Durrington-on-Sea	d							05 42	05 59						06 59		07 13					07 59	
Goring-by-Sea	d							05 44	06 02						07 02		07 16					08 02	
Angmering 3	d							05 48	06 06			06 32			07 06		07 20		07 32			08 06	
Littlehampton 4	a																07 31						
Barnham	a							06 00	06 18			06 43			07 18				07 43			08 18	
Barnham	d						00 12																
Bognor Regis	a						00 19																
Barnham	d							06 01	06 19			06 44			07 19				07 44			08 19	
Chichester 4	a							06 08	06 26			06 51			07 26				07 51			08 26	
Havant	a							06 20	06 38			07 05			07 38				08 05			08 38	
Havant	d											07 06							08 06				
Portsmouth & Southsea	a											07 18							08 20				
Portsmouth Harbour ⛴	a											07 22							08 24				
Havant	d							06 21	06 39						07 39							08 39	
Fareham	a							06 36	06 54						07 54							08 54	
Southampton Central ⛴	a							07 00	07 18						08 19							09 19	

A From London Victoria
B not 16 May

Table T188-F

Saturdays
21 December to 16 May

London - Gatwick Airport and Brighton - Worthing - Southampton Central

		SN ■	SN	SN	SN	SN	SN ■	SN	SN ■	SN	GW ◇ A	SN	SN	SN ■	SN	SN ■	SN	SN ■	SN	SN	SN	SN ■	SN
London Victoria 15 ⊖	d								07 46					08 16				08 46				09 16	
Clapham Junction 10	d								07 53					08 23				08 53				09 23	
East Croydon	a								08 02					08 32				09 02				09 32	
St Pancras International	d																						
Farringdon	d																						
City Thameslink	d																						
London Blackfriars	d																						
London Bridge	d																						
East Croydon	a																						
East Croydon	d								08 03					08 33				09 03				09 33	
Gatwick Airport 10 ✈	d								08 20					08 50				09 20				09 50	
Haywards Heath 3	d	07 38							08 38					09 05				09 38				10 05	
Preston Park	d													09 18								10 18	
Brighton 10	d		07 51	08 02	08 09	08 21	08 33	08 39		08 51	09 00	09 04	09 09		09 21	09 32	09 39		09 51	10 02	10 09		10 21
Hove 2	a	07 52	07 55	08 06	08 14	08 25	08 37	08 44	08 52	08 55	09 03	09 08	09 14	09 22	09 25	09 36	09 44	09 52	09 55	10 06	10 14	10 22	10 25
	d	07 52	07 55	08 06		08 25	08 37		08 52	08 55	09 04	09 08		09 22	09 25	09 36		09 52	09 55	10 06		10 22	10 25
Aldrington	d		07 57			08 27				08 57					09 27				09 57				10 27
Portslade	d	07 55	08 00	08 09		08 30	08 40		08 55	09 00		09 11		09 25	09 30	09 39		09 55	10 00	10 09		10 25	10 30
Fishersgate	d		08 02			08 32				09 02					09 32				10 02				10 32
Southwick	d		08 04	08 12		08 34	08 43			09 04		09 14			09 34	09 42			10 04	10 12			10 34
Shoreham-by-Sea	d	08 00	08 08	08 16		08 38	08 47		09 00	09 08	09 13	09 18		09 30	09 38	09 46		10 00	10 08	10 16		10 30	10 38
Lancing	d	08 04	08 12	08 20		08 42	08 51		09 04	09 12		09 22			09 42	09 50		10 04	10 12	10 20			10 42
East Worthing	d		08 15			08 45				09 15					09 45				10 15				10 45
Worthing 4	a	08 08	08 18	08 24		08 48	08 55		09 08	09 18	09 22	09 26		09 36	09 48	09 54		10 08	10 18	10 24		10 36	10 48
	d	08 09	08 18	08 25		08 48	08 56		09 09	09 18	09 23	09 27		09 39	09 48	09 55		10 09	10 18	10 25		10 39	10 48
West Worthing	d	08 11	08a21			08a51	08 58		09 11	09a21				09 41	09a51	09 57		10 11	10a21			10 41	10a51
Durrington-on-Sea	d	08 13					09 00		09 13					09 43		09 59		10 13				10 43	
Goring-by-Sea	d	08 16					09 03		09 16					09 46		10 02		10 16				10 46	
Angmering 3	d	08 20		08 32			09 07		09 20			09 35		09 50		10 06		10 20		10 32		10 50	
Littlehampton 4	a	08 31							09 31					10 01				10 31				11 01	
Barnham	a			08 43			09 18				09 42	09 46				10 18				10 43			
Barnham	d																						
Bognor Regis	a																						
Barnham	d			08 44			09 19				09 43	09 47				10 19				10 44			
Chichester 4	a			08 51			09 26				09 50	09 55				10 26				10 51			
Havant	a			09 05			09 38				10 01	10 09				10 38				11 05			
Havant	d			09 06								10 09								11 06			
Portsmouth & Southsea	a			09 18								10 21								11 18			
Portsmouth Harbour ⛴	a			09 22								10 25								11 22			
Havant	d						09 39				10 03					10 39							
Fareham	a						09 54				10 19					10 54							
Southampton Central ⛴	a						10 19				10 41					11 19							

		SN ■	SN	SN ■	SN	SN	SN	SN ■	SN	SN ■	SN	SN ■	SN	SN	SN	SN ■	SN	SN ■	SN	SN ■	SN	SN
London Victoria 15 ⊖	d			09 46				10 16				10 46				11 16				11 46		
Clapham Junction 10	d			09 53				10 23				10 53				11 23				11 53		
East Croydon	a			10 02				10 32				11 02				11 32				12 02		
St Pancras International	d																					
Farringdon	d																					
City Thameslink	d																					
London Blackfriars	d																					
London Bridge	d																					
East Croydon	a																					
East Croydon	d			10 03				10 33				11 03				11 33				12 03		
Gatwick Airport 10 ✈	d			10 20				10 50				11 20				11 50				12 20		
Haywards Heath 3	d			10 38				11 05				11 38				12 05				12 38		
Preston Park	d							11 18								12 18						
Brighton 10	d	10 32	10 39		10 51	11 02	11 09		11 21	11 32	11 39		11 51	12 02	12 09		12 21	12 32	12 39		12 51	13 02
Hove 2	a	10 36	10 44	10 52	10 55	11 06	11 14	11 22	11 25	11 36	11 44	11 52	11 55	12 06	12 14	12 22	12 25	12 36	12 44	12 52	12 55	13 06
	d	10 36		10 52	10 55	11 06		11 22	11 25	11 36		11 52	11 55	12 06		12 22	12 25	12 36		12 52	12 55	13 06
Aldrington	d				10 57				11 27				11 57				12 27				12 57	
Portslade	d	10 39		10 55	11 00	11 09		11 25	11 30	11 39		11 55	12 00	12 09		12 25	12 30	12 39		12 55	13 00	13 09
Fishersgate	d				11 02				11 32				12 02				12 32				13 02	
Southwick	d	10 42			11 04	11 12			11 34	11 42			12 04	12 12			12 34	12 42			13 04	13 12
Shoreham-by-Sea	d	10 46		11 00	11 08	11 16		11 30	11 38	11 46		12 00	12 08	12 16		12 30	12 38	12 46		13 00	13 08	13 16
Lancing	d	10 50		11 04	11 12	11 20			11 42	11 50		12 04	12 12	12 20			12 42	12 50		13 04	13 12	13 20
East Worthing	d				11 15				11 45				12 15				12 45				13 15	
Worthing 4	a	10 54		11 08	11 18	11 24		11 36	11 48	11 54		12 08	12 18	12 24		12 36	12 48	12 54		13 08	13 18	13 24
	d	10 55		11 09	11 18	11 25		11 39	11 48	11 55		12 09	12 18	12 25		12 39	12 48	12 55		13 09	13 18	13 25
West Worthing	d	10 57		11 11	11a21			11 41	11a51	11 57		12 11	12a21			12 41	12a51	12 57		13 11	13a21	
Durrington-on-Sea	d	10 59		11 13				11 43		11 59		12 13				12 43		12 59		13 13		
Goring-by-Sea	d	11 02		11 16				11 46		12 02		12 16				12 46		13 02		13 16		
Angmering 3	d	11 06		11 20		11 32		11 50		12 06		12 20		12 32		12 50		13 06		13 20		13 32
Littlehampton 4	a			11 31				12 01				12 31				13 01				13 31		
Barnham	a	11 18				11 43				12 18				12 43				13 18				13 43
Barnham	d																					
Bognor Regis	a																					
Barnham	d	11 19				11 44				12 19				12 44				13 19				13 44
Chichester 4	a	11 26				11 51				12 26				12 51				13 26				13 51
Havant	a	11 38				12 05				12 38				13 05				13 38				14 05
Havant	d					12 06								13 06								14 06
Portsmouth & Southsea	a					12 18								13 18								14 18
Portsmouth Harbour ⛴	a					12 22								13 22								14 22
Havant	d	11 39								12 39								13 39				
Fareham	a	11 54								12 54								13 54				
Southampton Central ⛴	a	12 19								13 19								14 19				

A To Great Malvern

Table T188-F

Saturdays

21 December to 16 May

London - Gatwick Airport and Brighton - Worthing - Southampton Central

		SN	SN 1	SN	SN 1	SN	SN 1	SN	SN	SN	SN 1	SN	SN 1	SN	SN 1	SN	SN	SN	SN 1	SN	SN 1	SN	SN 1
London Victoria 15 ⊖	d		12 16				12 46				13 16				13 46				14 16				14 46
Clapham Junction 10	d		12 23				12 53				13 23				13 53				14 23				14 53
East Croydon	a		12 32				13 02				13 32				14 02				14 32				15 02
St Pancras International	d																						
Farringdon	d																						
City Thameslink	d																						
London Blackfriars	d																						
London Bridge	d																						
East Croydon	a																						
East Croydon	d		12 33				13 03				13 33				14 03				14 33				15 03
Gatwick Airport 10 ✈	d		12 50				13 20				13 50				14 20				14 50				15 20
Haywards Heath 3	d		13 05				13 38				14 05				14 38				15 05				15 38
Preston Park	d		13 18								14 18								15 18				
Brighton 10	d	13 09		13 21	13 32	13 39		13 51	14 02	14 09		14 21	14 32	14 39		14 51	15 02	15 09		15 21	15 32	15 39	
Hove 2	a	13 14	13 22	13 25	13 36	13 44	13 52	13 56	14 06	14 14	14 22	14 25	14 36	14 44	14 52	14 55	15 06	15 14	15 22	15 25	15 36	15 44	15 52
	d		13 22	13 25	13 36		13 52	13 56	14 06		14 22	14 25	14 36		14 52	14 55	15 06		15 22	15 25	15 36		15 52
Aldrington	d			13 27				13 58				14 27				14 57				15 27			
Portslade	d		13 25	13 30	13 39		13 55	14 01	14 09		14 25	14 30	14 39		14 55	15 00	15 09		15 25	15 30	15 39		15 55
Fishersgate	d			13 32				14 03				14 32				15 02				15 32			
Southwick	d			13 34	13 42			14 05	14 12			14 34	14 42			15 04	15 12			15 34	15 42		
Shoreham-by-Sea	d		13 30	13 38	13 46		14 00	14 09	14 16		14 30	14 38	14 46		15 00	15 08	15 16		15 30	15 38	15 46		16 00
Lancing	d			13 42	13 50		14 04	14 13	14 20			14 42	14 50		15 04	15 12	15 20			15 42	15 50		16 04
East Worthing	d			13 45				14 16				14 45				15 15				15 45			
Worthing 4	a		13 36	13 48	13 54		14 08	14 19	14 24		14 36	14 48	14 54		15 08	15 18	15 24		15 36	15 48	15 54		16 08
	d		13 39	13 48	13 55		14 09	14 19	14 25		14 39	14 48	14 55		15 09	15 18	15 25		15 39	15 48	15 55		16 09
West Worthing	d		13 41	13a51	13 57		14 11	14a22			14 41	14a51	14 57		15 11	15a21			15 41	15a51	15 57		16 11
Durrington-on-Sea	d		13 43		13 59		14 13				14 43		14 59		15 13				15 43		15 59		16 13
Goring-by-Sea	d		13 46		14 02		14 16				14 46		15 02		15 16				15 46		16 02		16 16
Angmering 3	d		13 50		14 06		14 20		14 32		14 50		15 06		15 20		15 32		15 50		16 06		16 20
Littlehampton 4	a		14 02				14 31				15 01				15 31				16 01				16 31
Barnham	a				14 18				14 43				15 18				15 43				16 18		
Barnham	d																						
Bognor Regis	a																						
Barnham	d				14 19				14 44				15 19				15 44				16 19		
Chichester 4	a				14 26				14 51				15 26				15 51				16 26		
Havant	a				14 38				15 05				15 38				16 05				16 38		
Havant	d								15 06								16 06						
Portsmouth & Southsea	a								15 18								16 18						
Portsmouth Harbour ⛴	a								15 22								16 22						
Havant	d				14 39								15 39								16 39		
Fareham	a				14 54								15 54								16 54		
Southampton Central ⛴	a				15 19								16 19								17 19		

		SN	SN	SN	SN 1	SN	SN 1	SN	SN 1	SN	GW ◇ A	SN	SN	SN 1	SN	SN 1	SN	SN 1	SN	SN	SN	SN 1
London Victoria 15 ⊖	d				15 16				15 46					16 16				16 46				17 16
Clapham Junction 10	d				15 23				15 53					16 23				16 53				17 23
East Croydon	a				15 32				16 02					16 32				17 02				17 32
St Pancras International	d																					
Farringdon	d																					
City Thameslink	d																					
London Blackfriars	d																					
London Bridge	d																					
East Croydon	a																					
East Croydon	d				15 33				16 03					16 33				17 03				17 33
Gatwick Airport 10 ✈	d				15 50				16 20					16 50				17 20				17 50
Haywards Heath 3	d				16 05				16 38					17 05				17 38				18 05
Preston Park	d				16 18									17 18								18 18
Brighton 10	d	15 51	16 02	16 08		16 21	16 32	16 39		16 51	17 00	17 04	17 09		17 21	17 32	17 39		17 51	18 02	18 09	
Hove 2	a	15 55	16 06	16 12	16 22	16 25	16 36	16 44	16 52	16 55	17 03	17 08	17 14	17 22	17 25	17 36	17 44	17 52	17 55	18 06	18 14	18 22
	d	15 55	16 06		16 22	16 25	16 36		16 52	16 55	17 04	17 08		17 22	17 25	17 36		17 52	17 55	18 06		18 22
Aldrington	d	15 57				16 27				16 57					17 27				17 57			
Portslade	d	16 00	16 09		16 25	16 30	16 39		16 55	17 00		17 11		17 25	17 30	17 39		17 55	18 00	18 09		18 25
Fishersgate	d	16 02				16 32				17 02					17 32				18 02			
Southwick	d	16 04	16 12			16 34	16 42			17 04		17 14			17 34	17 42			18 04	18 12		
Shoreham-by-Sea	d	16 08	16 16		16 30	16 38	16 46		17 00	17 08	17 13	17 18		17 30	17 38	17 46		18 00	18 08	18 16		18 30
Lancing	d	16 12	16 20			16 42	16 50		17 04	17 12		17 22			17 42	17 50		18 04	18 12	18 20		
East Worthing	d	16 15				16 45				17 15					17 45				18 15			
Worthing 4	a	16 18	16 24		16 36	16 48	16 54		17 08	17 18	17 23	17 26		17 36	17 48	17 54		18 08	18 18	18 24		18 36
	d	16 18	16 25		16 39	16 48	16 55		17 09	17 18	17 23	17 27		17 39	17 48	17 55		18 09	18 18	18 25		18 39
West Worthing	d	16a21			16 41	16a51	16 57		17 11	17a21				17 41	17a51	17 57		18 11	18a21			18 41
Durrington-on-Sea	d				16 43		16 59		17 13					17 43		17 59		18 13				18 43
Goring-by-Sea	d				16 46		17 02		17 16					17 46		18 02		18 16				18 46
Angmering 3	d		16 32		16 50		17 06		17 20			17 34		17 50		18 06		18 20		18 32		18 50
Littlehampton 4	a				17 01				17 31					18 01				18 31				19 01
Barnham	a		16 43				17 18				17 42	17 46				18 18				18 43		
Barnham	d																					
Bognor Regis	a																					
Barnham	d		16 44				17 19				17 42	17 47				18 19				18 44		
Chichester 4	a		16 51				17 26				17 50	17 55				18 26				18 51		
Havant	a		17 05				17 38				18 05	18 09				18 38				19 05		
Havant	d		17 06									18 09								19 06		
Portsmouth & Southsea	a		17 18									18 21								19 18		
Portsmouth Harbour ⛴	a		17 22									18 25								19 22		
Havant	d						17 39				18 05					18 39						
Fareham	a						17 54				18 20					18 54						
Southampton Central ⛴	a						18 20				18 43					19 19						

A To Bristol Temple Meads

NRT DECEMBER 19 EDITION

Table T188-F

Saturdays

21 December to 16 May

London - Gatwick Airport and Brighton - Worthing - Southampton Central

		SN	SN 1	SN	SN 1	SN	SN	SN	SN 1	SN	SN 1	SN	SN 1	SN	SN	SN	SN 1	SN	SN 1	SN	SN 1	SN	SN
London Victoria 15 ⊖	d				17 46				18 16				18 46				19 16				19 46		
Clapham Junction 10	d				17 53				18 23				18 53				19 23				19 53		
East Croydon	a				18 02				18 32				19 02				19 32				20 02		
St Pancras International	d																						
Farringdon	d																						
City Thameslink	d																						
London Blackfriars	d																						
London Bridge	d																						
East Croydon	a																						
East Croydon	d				18 03				18 33				19 03				19 33				20 03		
Gatwick Airport 10 ✈	d				18 20				18 50				19 20				19 50				20 20		
Haywards Heath 3	d				18 38				19 05				19 38				20 05				20 38		
Preston Park	d								19 18								20 18						
Brighton 10	d	18 21	18 32	18 39		18 51	19 02	19 09		19 21	19 32	19 39		19 51	20 02	20 09		20 21	20 32	20 39		20 51	21 02
Hove 2	a	18 25	18 36	18 44	18 52	18 55	19 06	19 14	19 22	19 25	19 36	19 45	19 52	19 55	20 06	20 14	20 22	20 25	20 36	20 44	20 52	20 55	21 06
	d	18 25	18 36		18 52	18 55	19 06		19 22	19 25	19 36		19 52	19 55	20 06		20 22	20 25	20 36		20 52	20 55	21 06
Aldrington	d	18 27				18 57				19 27				19 57				20 27				20 57	
Portslade	d	18 30	18 39		18 55	19 00	19 09		19 25	19 30	19 39		19 55	20 00	20 09		20 25	20 30	20 39		20 55	21 00	21 09
Fishersgate	d	18 32				19 02				19 32				20 02				20 32				21 02	
Southwick	d	18 34	18 42			19 04	19 12			19 34	19 42			20 04	20 12			20 34	20 42		20 58	21 04	21 12
Shoreham-by-Sea	d	18 38	18 46		19 00	19 08	19 16		19 30	19 38	19 46		20 00	20 08	20 16		20 30	20 38	20 46		21 02	21 08	21 16
Lancing	d	18 42	18 50		19 04	19 12	19 20			19 42	19 50		20 04	20 12	20 20			20 42	20 50		21 06	21 12	21 20
East Worthing	d	18 45				19 15				19 45				20 15				20 45				21 15	
Worthing 4	a	18 48	18 54		19 08	19 18	19 24		19 36	19 48	19 54		20 08	20 18	20 24		20 36	20 48	20 54		21 10	21 18	21 24
	d	18 48	18 55		19 09	19 18	19 25		19 39	19 48	19 55		20 09	20 18	20 25		20 39	20 48	20 55		21 11	21 18	21 25
West Worthing	d	18a51	18 57		19 11	19a21			19 41	19a51	19 57		20 11	20a21			20 41	20a51	20 57		21 13	21a21	
Durrington-on-Sea	d		18 59		19 13				19 43		19 59		20 13				20 43		20 59		21 15		
Goring-by-Sea	d		19 02		19 16				19 46		20 02		20 16				20 46		21 02		21 18		
Angmering 3	d		19 06		19 20		19 32		19 50		20 06		20 20		20 32		20 50		21 06		21 22		21 32
Littlehampton 4	a				19 31				20 01				20 31				21 01				21 32		
Barnham	a		19 18				19 43				20 18				20 43				21 18				21 43
Barnham	d																						
Bognor Regis	a																						
Barnham	d		19 19				19 44				20 19				20 44				21 19				21 44
Chichester 4	a		19 26				19 51				20 26				20 51				21 26				21 51
Havant	a		19 38				20 05				20 38				21 05				21 38				22 05
Havant	d						20 06								21 06								22 06
Portsmouth & Southsea	a						20 18								21 18								22 18
Portsmouth Harbour ⛴	a						20 22								21 22								22 22
Havant	d		19 39								20 39								21 39				
Fareham	a		19 54								20 54								21 55				
Southampton Central ⛴	a		20 19								21 19								22 20				

		SN	SN 1	SN	SN	SN	SN 1	SN	SN	SN	SN 1	SN	SN	SN 1	SN	SN	SN 1	SN	SN 1	SN 1
London Victoria 15 ⊖	d		20 16				20 46				21 16			21 46			22 16		22 46	23 16
Clapham Junction 10	d		20 23				20 53				21 23			21 53			22 23		22 53	23 23
East Croydon	a		20 32				21 02				21 32			22 02			22 32		23 02	23 32
St Pancras International	d																			
Farringdon	d																			
City Thameslink	d																			
London Blackfriars	d																			
London Bridge	d																			
East Croydon	a																			
East Croydon	d		20 33				21 03				21 33			22 03			22 33		23 03	23 33
Gatwick Airport 10 ✈	d		20 50				21 20				21 50			22 20			22 50		23 20	23 54
Haywards Heath 3	d		21 05				21 38				22 05			22 38			23 05		23 38	00 09
Preston Park	d		21 18								22 18						23 18			00 21
Brighton 10	d	21 09		21 21	21 32	21 39		21 51	22 02	22 09		22 32	22 39		23 02	23 09		23 39		
Hove 2	a	21 14	21 22	21 25	21 36	21 44	21 52	21 55	22 06	22 14	22 22	22 36	22 44	22 52	23 07	23 14	23 22	23 44	23 52	00 25
	d		21 22	21 25	21 36		21 52	21 55	22 06		22 22	22 37		22 52	23 07		23 22		23 52	00 25
Aldrington	d			21 27				21 57				22 39			23 09					
Portslade	d		21 25	21 30	21 39		21 55	22 00	22 09		22 25	22 41		22 55	23 12		23 25		23 55	00 28
Fishersgate	d			21 32				22 02				22 43			23 14					
Southwick	d		21 28	21 34	21 42		21 58	22 04	22 12		22 28	22 45		22 58	23 16		23 28		23 58	00 31
Shoreham-by-Sea	d		21 32	21 38	21 46		22 02	22 08	22 16		22 32	22 49		23 02	23 20		23 32		00 02	00 35
Lancing	d		21 36	21 42	21 50		22 06	22 12	22 20		22 36	22 53		23 06	23 24		23 36		00 06	00 39
East Worthing	d			21 45				22 15				22 56			23 27					
Worthing 4	a		21 40	21 48	21 54		22 10	22 18	22 24		22 40	22 58		23 10	23 30		23 40		00 11	00 43
	d		21 41	21 48	21 55		22 11	22 18	22 25		22 41	22 59		23 11	23 30		23 41			00 43
West Worthing	d		21 43	21a51			22 13	22a21			22 43	23 01		23 13	23a33		23 43			00 45
Durrington-on-Sea	d		21 45				22 15				22 45	23 03		23 15			23 45			00 48
Goring-by-Sea	d		21 48				22 18				22 48	23 06		23 18			23 48			00 50
Angmering 3	d		21 52		22 02		22 22		22 32		22 52	23 10		23 22			23 52			00 54
Littlehampton 4	a		22 02				22 33				23 02			23 32						
Barnham	a				22 16				22 43			23 22					00 04			01 06
Barnham	d																00 12			
Bognor Regis	a																00 19			
Barnham	d				22 17				22 44			23 24								01 08
Chichester 4	a				22 24				22 51			23 31								01 15
Havant	a				22 38				23 05											
Havant	d				22 39				23 06											
Portsmouth & Southsea	a				22 52				23 18											
Portsmouth Harbour ⛴	a				22 56				23 22											
Havant	d																			
Fareham	a																			
Southampton Central ⛴	a																			

Table T188-F

Sundays

15 December to 10 May

London - Gatwick Airport and Brighton - Worthing - Southampton Central

Station		SN ■ A	SN	SN ■ A	SN ■ A	SN ■	SN	SN	SN	SN ■	SN	SN	SN	SN ■	SN	SN ■	SN	SN ■	SN	SN ■	SN	SN ■	GW ◇ B
London Victoria [15] ⊖	d					00 02										08 14				09 16			
Clapham Junction [10]	d					00 09										08 21				09 23			
East Croydon	a					00 23										08 39				09 32			
St Pancras International	d																						
Farringdon	d																						
City Thameslink	d																						
London Blackfriars	d																						
London Bridge	d																						
East Croydon	a																						
East Croydon	d					00 24										08 40				09 33			
Gatwick Airport [10] ✈	d					00 44										08 59				09 50			
Haywards Heath [3]	d				00 09	01 02										09 10				10 02			
Preston Park	d				00 21											09 22				10 14			
Brighton [10]	d		00 04			01s16	07 15	07 30	07 46	08 00	08 09	08 20	08 30	09 00	09 09		09 30	10 00	10 09		10 30	11 00	11 10
Hove [2]	a		00 08		00 25	01s25	07 19	07 34	07 50	08 04	08 13	08 24	08 34	09 04	09 13	09 25	09 34	10 04	10 13	10 17	10 34	11 04	11 13
	d		00 09		00 25		07 19	07 34		08 04		08 24	08 34	09 04		09 26	09 34	10 04		10 19	10 34	11 04	11 14
Aldrington	d		00 11					07 36		08 06			08 36	09 06			09 36	10 06			10 36	11 06	
Portslade	d		00 14		00 28	01s28		07 39		08 09			08 39	09 09		09 29	09 39	10 09		10 22	10 39	11 09	
Fishersgate	d		00 16					07 41		08 11			08 41	09 11			09 41	10 11			10 41	11 11	
Southwick	d		00 18		00 31	01s31		07 43		08 13			08 43	09 13			09 43	10 13			10 43	11 13	
Shoreham-by-Sea	d	00 02	00 22		00 35	01s34	07 26	07 47		08 17		08 31	08 47	09 17		09 34	09 47	10 17		10 27	10 47	11 17	11 21
Lancing	d	00 06	00 26		00 39	01s38		07 51		08 21			08 51	09 21		09 38	09 51	10 21		10 31	10 51	11 21	
East Worthing	d		00 29					07 54		08 24			08 54	09 24			09 54	10 24			10 54	11 24	
Worthing [4]	a	00 11	00 31		00 43	01 43	07 32	07 56		08 26		08 37	08 56	09 26		09 42	09 56	10 26		10 35	10 56	11 26	11 31
	d		00 32		00 43		07 33	07 57		08 27		08 38	08 57	09 27		09 42	09 57	10 27		10 35	10 57	11 27	11 31
West Worthing	d		00a34		00 45			07 59		08 29			08 59	09 29		09 44	09 59	10 29		10 37	10 59	11 29	
Durrington-on-Sea	d				00 48			08 01		08 31			09 01	09 31		09 47	10 01	10 31		10 40	11 01	11 31	
Goring-by-Sea	d				00 50			08 04		08 34			09 04	09 34		09 49	10 04	10 34		10 42	11 04	11 34	
Angmering [3]	d				00 54		07 40	08 08		08 38		08 45	09 08	09 38		09 53	10 08	10 38		10 46	11 08	11 38	
Littlehampton [4]	a															10 03				10 56			
Barnham	a				01 06		07 53	08 20		08 50		08 57	09 21	09 50			10 20	10 50			11 20	11 50	11 55
Barnham	d			00 12																			
Bognor Regis	a			00 19																			
Barnham	d				01 08		07 54	08 21		08 51		08 57	09 22	09 51			10 21	10 51			11 21	11 51	11 56
Chichester [4]	a				01 15		08 02	08 28		08 58		09 05	09 29	09 58			10 28	10 58			11 28	11 58	12 03
Havant	a						08 16	08 49		09 10		09 19	09 50	10 10			10 49	11 10			11 49	12 10	12 15
Havant	d						08 16	08 50				09 19	09 51				10 50				11 50		
Portsmouth & Southsea	a						08 28	09 03				09 31	10 04				11 03				12 03		
Portsmouth Harbour ⛴	a						08 32	09 07				09 35	10 08				11 07				12 07		
Havant	d									09 11				10 11				11 11				12 11	12 15
Fareham	a									09 25				10 25				11 25				12 25	12 33
Southampton Central ⛴	a									09 50				10 50				11 50				12 50	12 55

Station		SN	SN ■	SN	SN ■	SN	SN ■	SN	SN ■	SN	SN ■	SN	SN ■	SN	SN ■	SN	SN ■	SN	SN ■	SN C	GW ◇ D	SN ■	SN
London Victoria [15] ⊖	d		10 16				11 16				12 16				13 16				14 16				
Clapham Junction [10]	d		10 23				11 23				12 23				13 23				14 23				
East Croydon	a		10 32				11 32				12 32				13 32				14 32				
St Pancras International	d																						
Farringdon	d																						
City Thameslink	d																						
London Blackfriars	d																						
London Bridge	d																						
East Croydon	a																						
East Croydon	d		10 33				11 33				12 33				13 33				14 33				
Gatwick Airport [10] ✈	d		10 50				11 50				12 50				13 50				14 50				
Haywards Heath [3]	d		11 02				12 02				13 02				14 02				15 02				
Preston Park	d		11 14				12 14				13 14				14 14				15 14				
Brighton [10]	d	11 13		11 30	12 00	12 09		12 30	13 00	13 09		13 30	14 00	14 09		14 30	15 00	15 09		15 30	15 47	16 00	16 09
Hove [2]	a	11 17	11 20	11 34	12 04	12 13	12 17	12 34	13 04	13 13	13 17	13 34	14 04	14 13	14 17	14 34	15 04	15 13	15 17	15 34	15 50	16 04	16 13
	d		11 21	11 34	12 04		12 19	12 34	13 04		13 19	13 34	14 04		14 19	14 34	15 04		15 19	15 34	15 51	16 04	
Aldrington	d			11 36	12 06			12 36	13 06			13 36	14 06			14 36	15 06			15 36		16 06	
Portslade	d		11 24	11 39	12 09		12 22	12 39	13 09		13 22	13 39	14 09		14 22	14 39	15 09		15 22	15 39		16 09	
Fishersgate	d			11 41	12 11			12 41	13 11			13 41	14 11			14 41	15 11			15 41		16 11	
Southwick	d			11 43	12 13			12 43	13 13			13 43	14 13			14 43	15 13			15 43		16 13	
Shoreham-by-Sea	d		11 29	11 47	12 17		12 27	12 47	13 17		13 27	13 47	14 17		14 27	14 47	15 17		15 27	15 47	15 57	16 17	
Lancing	d		11 33	11 51	12 21		12 31	12 51	13 21		13 31	13 51	14 21		14 31	14 51	15 21		15 31	15 51		16 21	
East Worthing	d			11 54	12 24			12 54	13 24			13 54	14 24			14 54	15 24			15 54		16 24	
Worthing [4]	a		11 37	11 56	12 26		12 35	12 56	13 26		13 35	13 56	14 26		14 35	14 56	15 26		15 35	15 56	16 04	16 26	
	d		11 37	11 57	12 27		12 35	12 57	13 27		13 35	13 57	14 27		14 35	14 57	15 27		15 35	15 57	16 09	16 27	
West Worthing	d		11 39	11 59	12 29		12 37	12 59	13 29		13 37	13 59	14 29		14 37	14 59	15 29		15 37	15 59		16 29	
Durrington-on-Sea	d		11 42	12 01	12 31		12 40	13 01	13 31		13 40	14 01	14 31		14 40	15 01	15 31		15 40	16 01		16 31	
Goring-by-Sea	d		11 44	12 04	12 34		12 42	13 04	13 34		13 42	14 04	14 34		14 42	15 04	15 34		15 42	16 04		16 34	
Angmering [3]	d		11 48	12 08	12 38		12 46	13 08	13 38		13 46	14 08	14 38		14 46	15 08	15 38		15 46	16 08		16 38	
Littlehampton [4]	a		11 58				12 56				13 56				14 56				15 56				
Barnham	a			12 20	12 50			13 20	13 50			14 20	14 50			15 20	15 50			16 20	16 26	16 50	
Barnham	d																						
Bognor Regis	a																						
Barnham	d			12 21	12 51			13 21	13 51			14 21	14 51			15 21	15 51			16 31	16 27	16 51	
Chichester [4]	a			12 28	12 58			13 28	13 58			14 28	14 58			15 28	15 58			16 38	16 34	16 58	
Havant	a			12 49	13 10			13 49	14 10			14 49	15 10			15 49	16 10			16 59	16 44	17 10	
Havant	d			12 50				13 50				14 50				15 50							
Portsmouth & Southsea	a			13 03				14 03				15 03				16 03							
Portsmouth Harbour ⛴	a			13 07				14 07				15 07				16 07							
Havant	d				13 11				14 11				15 11				16 11				16 44	17 11	
Fareham	a				13 25				14 25				15 25				16 25				16 59	17 25	
Southampton Central ⛴	a				13 50				14 50				15 50				16 50				17 20	17 50	

A not 15 December. From London Victoria
B To Cardiff Central
C To Fratton
D To Bristol Temple Meads

Table T188-F

Sundays

15 December to 10 May

London - Gatwick Airport and Brighton - Worthing - Southampton Central

Station		SN ■	SN	SN ■	SN	SN ■	SN A	GW ◇ B	SN ■	SN	SN ■	SN	SN ■	SN	SN ■	SN	SN ■	SN	SN ■	SN	SN ■	SN
London Victoria [15] ⊖	d	15 16				16 16					17 16				18 16				19 16			
Clapham Junction [10]	d	15 23				16 23					17 23				18 23				19 23			
East Croydon	a	15 32				16 32					17 32				18 32				19 32			
St Pancras International	d																					
Farringdon	d																					
City Thameslink	d																					
London Blackfriars	d																					
London Bridge	d																					
East Croydon	a																					
East Croydon	d	15 33				16 33					17 33				18 33				19 33			
Gatwick Airport [10] ✈	d	15 50				16 50					17 50				18 50				19 50			
Haywards Heath [3]	d	16 02				17 02					18 02				19 02				20 02			
Preston Park	d	16 14				17 14					18 14				19 14				20 14			
Brighton [10]	d		16 30	17 00	17 09		17 30	17 46	18 00	18 09		18 30	19 00	19 09		19 30	20 00	20 09		20 30	21 00	21 10
Hove [2]	a	16 17	16 34	17 04	17 13	17 17	17 34	17 49	18 04	18 13	18 17	18 34	19 04	19 13	19 17	19 34	20 04	20 13	20 17	20 34	21 04	21 14
	d	16 19	16 34	17 04		17 19	17 34	17 50	18 04		18 19	18 34	19 04		19 19	19 34	20 04		20 19	20 34	21 04	
Aldrington	d		16 36	17 06			17 36		18 06			18 36	19 06			19 36	20 06			20 36	21 06	
Portslade	d	16 22	16 39	17 09		17 22	17 39		18 09		18 22	18 39	19 09		19 22	19 39	20 09		20 22	20 39	21 09	
Fishersgate	d		16 41	17 11			17 41		18 11			18 41	19 11			19 41	20 11			20 41	21 11	
Southwick	d		16 43	17 13			17 43		18 13			18 43	19 13			19 43	20 13			20 43	21 13	
Shoreham-by-Sea	d	16 27	16 47	17 17		17 27	17 47	17 56	18 17		18 27	18 47	19 17		19 27	19 47	20 17		20 27	20 47	21 17	
Lancing	d	16 31	16 51	17 21		17 31	17 51		18 21		18 31	18 51	19 21		19 31	19 51	20 21		20 31	20 51	21 21	
East Worthing	d		16 54	17 24			17 54		18 24			18 54	19 24			19 54	20 24			20 54	21 24	
Worthing [4]	a	16 35	16 56	17 26		17 35	17 56	18 03	18 26		18 35	18 56	19 26		19 35	19 56	20 26		20 35	20 56	21 26	
	d	16 35	16 57	17 27		17 35	17 57	18 08	18 27		18 35	18 57	19 27		19 35	19 57	20 27		20 35	20 57	21 27	
West Worthing	d	16 37	16 59	17 29		17 37	17 59		18 29		18 37	18 59	19 29		19 37	19 59	20 29		20 37	20 59	21 29	
Durrington-on-Sea	d	16 40	17 01	17 31		17 40	18 01		18 31		18 40	19 01	19 31		19 40	20 01	20 31		20 40	21 01	21 31	
Goring-by-Sea	d	16 42	17 04	17 34		17 42	18 04		18 34		18 42	19 04	19 34		19 42	20 04	20 34		20 42	21 04	21 34	
Angmering [3]	d	16 46	17 08	17 38		17 46	18 08		18 38		18 46	19 08	19 38		19 46	20 08	20 38		20 46	21 08	21 38	
Littlehampton [4]	a	16 56				17 56					18 56				19 56				20 56			
Barnham	a		17 20	17 50			18 20	18 26	18 50			19 20	19 50			20 20	20 50			21 20	21 50	
Barnham	d																					
Bognor Regis	a																					
Barnham	d		17 21	17 51			18 31	18 27	18 51			19 21	19 51			20 21	20 51			21 21	21 51	
Chichester [4]	a		17 28	17 58			18 38	18 34	18 58			19 28	19 58			20 28	20 58			21 28	21 58	
Havant	a		17 49	18 10			18 59	18 50	19 10			19 49	20 10			20 49	21 11			21 49	22 10	
Havant	d		17 50									19 50				20 50				21 50		
Portsmouth & Southsea	a		18 03									20 03				21 03				22 03		
Portsmouth Harbour ⛴	a		18 07									20 07				21 07				22 07		
Havant	d			18 11				18 50	19 11				20 11				21 12				22 11	
Fareham	a			18 25				19 04	19 25				20 25				21 26				22 25	
Southampton Central ⛴	a			18 50				19 26	19 50				20 50				21 51				22 50	

Station		SN ■	SN	GW	SN	SN	SN ■		SN	SN	SN ■	SN ■
London Victoria [15] ⊖	d	20 16					21 16				22 16	23 16
Clapham Junction [10]	d	20 23					21 23				22 23	23 23
East Croydon	a	20 32					21 32				22 32	23 32
St Pancras International	d											
Farringdon	d											
City Thameslink	d											
London Blackfriars	d											
London Bridge	d											
East Croydon	a											
East Croydon	d	20 33					21 33				22 33	23 33
Gatwick Airport [10] ✈	d	20 50					21 50				22 50	23 55
Haywards Heath [3]	d	21 02					22 04	22 07			23 02	00 08
Preston Park	d	21 14						22 18			23 14	00 19
Brighton [10]	d		21 30	21 46	21 55	22 10			22 47	23 05		
Hove [2]	a	21 17	21 34	21 49	21 59	22 14	22 18	22 22	22 51	23 09	23 17	00 23
	d	21 19	21 34	21 50	22 00		22 19	22 22	22 52		23 19	00 23
Aldrington	d		21 36		22 02			22 24	22 54			
Portslade	d	21 22	21 39		22 04			22 27	22 56		23 22	00 26
Fishersgate	d		21 41		22 06			22 29	22 58			
Southwick	d		21 43		22 08			22 31	23 00		23 25	00 29
Shoreham-by-Sea	d	21 27	21 47	21 56	22 12		22 25	22 34	23 04		23 28	00 32
Lancing	d	21 31	21 51		22 16			22 38	23 08		23 32	00 36
East Worthing	d		21 54		22 19			22 41	23 11			
Worthing [4]	a	21 35	21 56	22 02	22 22		22 31	22 44	23 14		23 37	00 40
	d	21 35	21 57	22 03	22 22		22 35	22 45	23 14			
West Worthing	d	21 37	21 59		22 24			22 47	23 16			
Durrington-on-Sea	d	21 40	22 01		22 27			22 50	23 19			
Goring-by-Sea	d	21 42	22 04		22 29			22 53	23 21			
Angmering [3]	d	21 46	22 08		22 34			22 58	23 26			
Littlehampton [4]	a	21 56			22 44			23 11	23 36			
Barnham	a		22 20	22 24			22 51		23 51			
Barnham	d											
Bognor Regis	a											
Barnham	d		22 29	22 24			22 52		23 52			
Chichester [4]	a		22 36	22 32			22 59		23 59			
Havant	a		22 57	22 45			23 17					
Havant	d		22 58	22 46			23 17					
Portsmouth & Southsea	a		23 15	23 02			23 29					
Portsmouth Harbour ⛴	a		23 20	23 07			23 33					
Havant	d											
Fareham	a											
Southampton Central ⛴	a											

A To Fratton
B To Bristol Temple Meads

Table T188-R

Mondays to Fridays

16 December to 15 May

Southampton Central - Worthing - Brighton and Gatwick Airport - London

Station		SN MX A	SN	SN 1	SN	SN	SN 1	TL 1 B	SN	SN	SN 1	SN	SN	SN 1	SN	TL 1 B	SN 1	SN	SN 1	SN	SN	SN	SN 1
Southampton Central	d																05 46						
Fareham	d																06 11						
Havant	a																06 27						
Portsmouth Harbour	d																			06 32			
Portsmouth & Southsea	d																			06 36			
Havant	a																			06 50			
Havant	d																06 28			06 51			
Chichester 4	d		04 54			05 25				05 50		06 16					06 44			07 05			
Barnham	a		05 01			05 32				05 57		06 24					06 52			07 12			
Bognor Regis	d																						
Barnham	a																						
Barnham	d		05 03			05 33				05 58		06 24					06 55			07 13			
Littlehampton 4	d			05 14			05 44	05 52			06 16			06 47		06 52			07 12		07 22		07 42
Angmering 3	d		05 14	05 23		05 44	05 54	06 01		06 10	06 26	06 36		06 56		07 01	07 07		07 21	07 25	07 31		07 53
Goring-by-Sea	d		05 18	05 27		05 48	05 58	06 06		06 14	06 31	06 40		07 01		07 06	07 11		07 26	07 30	07 36		07 57
Durrington-on-Sea	d		05 21	05 30		05 51	06 00	06 09		06 16	06 34	06 43		07 04		07 09	07 13		07 29	07 33	07 39		08 00
West Worthing	d	00 01	05 23	05 32		05 53	06 03	06 12		06 19	06 37	06 46	06 52	07 06		07 12	07 16	07 22	07 32	07 36	07 42	07 52	08 03
Worthing 4	a	00 04	05 26	05 35		05 56	06 05	06 14		06 21	06 39	06 49	06 55	07 09		07 14	07 18	07 25	07 34	07 38	07 44	07 55	08 06
	d	00 04	05 26	05 35		05 56	06 06	06 15		06 22	06 40	06 49	06 55	07 09		07 15	07 19	07 25	07 35	07 39	07 45	07 55	08 06
East Worthing	d	00 07	05 29			05 59				06 24			06 58					07 28			07 48	07 58	
Lancing	d	00 10	05 32	05 40		06 02	06 10	06 19		06 27	06 44	06 53	07 01	07 14		07 19	07 23	07 31	07 39	07 43	07 51	08 01	08 11
Shoreham-by-Sea	d	00 14	05 36	05 44		06 06	06 15	06 24		06 32	06 49	06 58	07 06	07 18		07 24	07 27	07 36	07 44	07 48	07 56	08 06	08 15
Southwick	d	00 17	05 39			06 09				06 35		07 01	07 09				07 30	07 39		07 51	07 59	08 09	
Fishersgate	d	00 19	05 41			06 11				06 37		07 03	07 11					07 41				08 11	
Portslade	d	00 21	05 44	05 49		06 14	06 20	06 29		06 40	06 54	07 05	07 14	07 23		07 29	07 34	07 44	07 49	07 55	08 03	08 14	08 20
Aldrington	d	00 23	05 46			06 16				06 42			07 16					07 46				08 16	
Hove 2	a	00 25	05 48	05 52		06 18	06 23	06 32		06 44	06 57	07 08	07 18	07 26		07 32	07 37	07 48	07 52	07 58	08 06	08 18	08 23
	d	00 26	05 49	05 53	06 01	06 19	06 23	06 32	06 36	06 45	06 57	07 09	07 19	07 27	07 30	07 33	07 39	07 49	07 52	07 59	08 07	08 19	08 24
Brighton 10	a	00 30	05 54		06 05	06 24			06 40	06 49		07 14	07 23		07 35		07 44	07 54		08 03	08 11	08 25	
Preston Park	a			05 58			06 28	06 37			07 02			07 32		07 38			07 57				08 29
Haywards Heath 3	a			06 13			06 44	06 50			07 19			07 47		07 50			08 14				08 44
Gatwick Airport 10	a			06 31			07 02				07 36			08 02					08 31				09 01
East Croydon	a			06 48			07 18	07 20			07 52			08 18		08 20			08 48				09 18
East Croydon	d							07 21								08 21							
London Bridge	a							07 34								08 34							
London Blackfriars	a							07 41								08 41							
City Thameslink	a							07 43								08 43							
Farringdon	a							07 46								08 46							
St Pancras International	a							07 50								08 50							
East Croydon	d			06 49			07 19				07 52			08 20					08 50				09 19
Clapham Junction 10	a			06 58			07 28				08 01			08 30					09 00				09 28
London Victoria 15	a			07 05			07 35				08 09			08 37					09 08				09 35

Station		GW	SN	SN	SN 1	SN	SN	SN 1	SN 1	SN	SN	SN	SN 1	SN	SN	SN 1	SN 1	SN	SN	SN	TL 1	SN	SN
Southampton Central	d							07 33								08 28							
Fareham	d							07 57								08 56							
Havant	a							08 12								09 10							
Portsmouth Harbour	d	07 09		07 18								08 29											
Portsmouth & Southsea	d	07 13		07 22								08 33								09 33			
Havant	a	07 25		07 38								08 45								09 45			
Havant	d	07 27		07 38				08 12				08 46				09 11				09 46			
Chichester 4	d	07 43		07 58				08 23				09 00				09 23				10 00			
Barnham	a	07 51		08 06				08 31				09 08				09 30				10 07			
Bognor Regis	d																						
Barnham	a																						
Barnham	d	07 52		08 06				08 31				09 09				09 31				10 09			
Littlehampton 4	d		07 59		08 14				08 44				09 14				09 44				10 14		
Angmering 3	d	08 02	08 08	08 18	08 23			08 44	08 53			09 19	09 23			09 43	09 53			10 19	10 23		
Goring-by-Sea	d		08 12		08 27			08 48	08 57				09 27			09 47	09 57				10 27		
Durrington-on-Sea	d		08 14		08 30			08 51	08 59				09 29			09 50	09 59				10 29		
West Worthing	d		08 17		08 32		08 38	08 53	09 02		09 12		09 32		09 42	09 52	10 02		10 12		10 32		10 42
Worthing 4	a	08 09	08 19	08 25	08 35		08 41	08 56	09 04		09 15	09 26	09 34		09 45	09 55	10 04		10 15	10 26	10 34		10 45
	d	08 10	08 20	08 25	08 35		08 41	08 56	09 05		09 15	09 26	09 35		09 45	09 56	10 05		10 15	10 26	10 35		10 45
East Worthing	d		08 23	08 28			08 44				09 18				09 48				10 18				10 48
Lancing	d		08 26	08 31	08 39		08 47	09 00			09 21	09 30	09 39		09 51	10 00			10 21	10 30	10 39		10 51
Shoreham-by-Sea	d	08 18	08 30	08 36	08 44		08 52	09 05	09 12		09 26	09 35	09 43		09 56	10 05	10 12		10 26	10 35	10 43		10 56
Southwick	d		08 33	08 39			08 55	09 08			09 29	09 38			09 59	10 08			10 29	10 38			10 59
Fishersgate	d			08 41			08 57				09 31				10 01				10 31				11 01
Portslade	d	08 23	08 37	08 43	08 48		09 00	09 12	09 17		09 34	09 42	09 48		10 04	10 11	10 17		10 34	10 42	10 48		11 04
Aldrington	d			08 46			09 02				09 36				10 06				10 36				11 06
Hove 2	a	08 26	08 40	08 48	08 51		09 04	09 16	09 20		09 38	09 45	09 51		10 08	10 15	10 20		10 38	10 45	10 51		11 08
	d	08 26	08 41	08 48	08 52	09 00	09 07	09 16	09 21	09 26	09 39	09 46	09 51	09 56	10 09	10 16	10 21	10 26	10 39	10 46	10 51	10 56	11 09
Brighton 10	a	08 30	08 45	08 54		09 04	09 12	09 21		09 30	09 44	09 51		10 01	10 14	10 21		10 31	10 44	10 51		11 01	11 14
Preston Park	a				08 57								09 56								10 56		
Haywards Heath 3	a				09 11				09 36				10 10				10 36				11 09		
Gatwick Airport 10	a				09 27				09 56				10 26				10 56						
East Croydon	a				09 42				10 11				10 41				11 11						
East Croydon	d																						
London Bridge	a																						
London Blackfriars	a																						
City Thameslink	a																						
Farringdon	a																						
St Pancras International	a																						
East Croydon	d				09 43				10 12				10 42				11 12						
Clapham Junction 10	a				09 52				10 21				10 51				11 21						
London Victoria 15	a				09 59				10 29				10 59				11 29						

A From Portsmouth Harbour B To Bedford

NRT DECEMBER 19 EDITION

Table T188-R

Mondays to Fridays

16 December to 15 May

Southampton Central - Worthing - Brighton and Gatwick Airport - London

Station		SN 1	SN 1	SN	SN	SN	SN 1	SN	SN	SN 1	SN 1	SN	SN	SN	SN 1	SN	SN	SN 1	SN 1	SN	SN	SN
Southampton Central	d	09 26								10 28								11 26				
Fareham	d									10 53												
Havant	a	10 10								11 09								12 09				
Portsmouth Harbour	d													11 29								12 29
Portsmouth & Southsea	d					10 33								11 33								12 33
Havant	a					10 45								11 45								12 45
Havant	d	10 10				10 46				11 10				11 46				12 10				12 46
Chichester 4	d	10 23				11 00				11 22				12 00				12 22				13 00
Barnham	a	10 30				11 07				11 30				12 07				12 30				13 07
Bognor Regis	d																					
Barnham	a																					
Barnham	d	10 31				11 09				11 31				12 09				12 31				13 09
Littlehampton 4	d		10 44				11 14				11 44				12 14				12 44			
Angmering 3	d	10 43	10 53			11 19	11 23			11 43	11 53			12 19	12 23			12 43	12 53			13 19
Goring-by-Sea	d	10 47	10 57				11 27			11 47	11 57				12 27			12 47	12 57			
Durrington-on-Sea	d	10 50	10 59				11 29			11 50	11 59				12 29			12 50	12 59			
West Worthing	d	10 52	11 02		11 12		11 32		11 42	11 52	12 02		12 12		12 32		12 42	12 52	13 02		13 12	
Worthing 4	a	10 55	11 04		11 15	11 26	11 34		11 45	11 55	12 04		12 15	12 26	12 34		12 45	12 55	13 04		13 15	13 26
	d	10 56	11 05		11 15	11 26	11 35		11 45	11 56	12 05		12 15	12 26	12 35		12 45	12 56	13 05		13 15	13 26
East Worthing	d				11 18				11 48				12 18				12 48				13 18	
Lancing	d	11 00			11 21	11 30	11 39		11 51	12 00			12 21	12 30	12 39		12 51	13 00			13 21	13 30
Shoreham-by-Sea	d	11 05	11 12		11 26	11 35	11 43		11 56	12 05	12 12		12 26	12 35	12 43		12 56	13 05	13 12		13 26	13 35
Southwick	d	11 08			11 29	11 38			11 59	12 08			12 29	12 38			12 59	13 08			13 29	13 38
Fishersgate	d				11 31				12 01				12 31				13 01				13 31	
Portslade	d	11 11	11 17		11 34	11 42	11 48		12 04	12 11	12 17		12 34	12 42	12 48		13 04	13 11	13 17		13 34	13 42
Aldrington	d				11 36				12 06				12 36				13 06				13 36	
Hove 2	a	11 15	11 20		11 38	11 45	11 51		12 08	12 15	12 20		12 38	12 45	12 51		13 08	13 15	13 20		13 38	13 45
	d	11 16	11 21	11 26	11 39	11 46	11 51	11 56	12 09	12 16	12 21	12 26	12 39	12 46	12 51	12 56	13 09	13 16	13 21	13 26	13 39	13 46
Brighton 10	a	11 21		11 31	11 44	11 51		12 01	12 14	12 21		12 31	12 44	12 51		13 01	13 14	13 21		13 31	13 44	13 51
Preston Park	a						11 56								12 56							
Haywards Heath 3	a		11 36				12 10				12 36				13 10				13 36			
Gatwick Airport 10	a		11 56				12 26				12 56				13 26				13 56			
East Croydon	a		12 11				12 41				13 11				13 41				14 11			
East Croydon	d																					
London Bridge	a																					
London Blackfriars	a																					
City Thameslink	a																					
Farringdon	a																					
St Pancras International	a																					
East Croydon	d		12 12				12 42				13 12				13 42				14 12			
Clapham Junction 10	a		12 22				12 51				13 21				13 51				14 21			
London Victoria 15	a		12 29				12 59				13 29				13 59				14 29			

Station		SN 1	SN	SN	SN 1	SN 1	SN	SN	SN	SN 1	SN	SN	SN 1	SN 1	SN	SN	SN	SN 1	SN	SN	SN 1 A	GW ◇ B	SN 1 C
Southampton Central	d				12 28								13 28								14 28	14 34	
Fareham	d				12 53								13 53								14 53	14 57	
Havant	a				13 09								14 09								15 07	15 11	
Portsmouth Harbour	d								13 29								14 29						
Portsmouth & Southsea	d								13 33								14 33						
Havant	a								13 45								14 45						
Havant	d				13 10				13 46				14 10				14 46				15 08	15 12	
Chichester 4	d				13 22				14 00				14 22				15 00				15 18	15 26	
Barnham	a				13 30				14 07				14 30				15 07				15 26	15 36	
Bognor Regis	d																						
Barnham	a																						
Barnham	d				13 31				14 09				14 31				15 09				15 26	15 37	
Littlehampton 4	d	13 14				13 44				14 14				14 44				15 13					
Angmering 3	d	13 23			13 43	13 53			14 19	14 23			14 43	14 53			15 19	15 22			15 38		
Goring-by-Sea	d	13 27			13 47	13 57				14 27			14 47	14 57				15 26			15 42		
Durrington-on-Sea	d	13 29			13 50	13 59				14 29			14 50	14 59				15 28			15 45		
West Worthing	d	13 32		13 42	13 52	14 02		14 12		14 32		14 42	14 52	15 02		15 12		15 31		15 39	15 48		←
Worthing 4	a	13 34		13 45	13 55	14 04		14 15	14 26	14 34		14 45	14 55	15 04		15 15	15 26	15 33		15 42	15 51	15 54	15 51
	d	13 35		13 45	13 56	14 05		14 15	14 26	14 35		14 45	14 56	15 05		15 15	15 26	15 34		15 42	15 59	15 54	15 59
East Worthing	d			13 48				14 18				14 48				15 18		15 37		15 45	→		
Lancing	d	13 39		13 51	14 00			14 21	14 30	14 39		14 51	15 00			15 21	15 30	15 40		15 48			16 03
Shoreham-by-Sea	d	13 43		13 56	14 05	14 12		14 26	14 35	14 43		14 56	15 05	15 12		15 26	15 35	15 44		15 53		16 01	16 07
Southwick	d			13 59	14 08			14 29	14 38			14 59	15 08			15 29	15 38			15 56			16 10
Fishersgate	d			14 01				14 31				15 01				15 31				15 58			
Portslade	d	13 48		14 04	14 11	14 17		14 34	14 42	14 48		15 04	15 11	15 17		15 34	15 42	15 49		16 01			16 14
Aldrington	d			14 06				14 36				15 06				15 36				16 03			
Hove 2	a	13 51		14 08	14 15	14 20		14 38	14 45	14 51		15 08	15 15	15 20		15 38	15 45	15 52		16 05		16 09	16 17
	d	13 51	13 56	14 09	14 16	14 21	14 26	14 39	14 46	14 51	14 56	15 09	15 16	15 21	15 26	15 39	15 46	15 52	15 56	16 06		16 09	16 17
Brighton 10	a		14 01	14 14	14 21		14 31	14 44	14 51		15 01	15 14	15 21		15 31	15 44	15 51		16 01	16 10		16 13	16 24
Preston Park	a	13 56								14 56								15 57					
Haywards Heath 3	a	14 10				14 36				15 10				15 36				16 10					
Gatwick Airport 10	a	14 26				14 56				15 26				15 56				16 26					
East Croydon	a	14 41				15 11				15 41				16 11				16 42					
East Croydon	d																						
London Bridge	a																						
London Blackfriars	a																						
City Thameslink	a																						
Farringdon	a																						
St Pancras International	a																						
East Croydon	d	14 42				15 12				15 42				16 12				16 42					
Clapham Junction 10	a	14 51				15 21				15 51				16 21				16 51					
London Victoria 15	a	14 59				15 29				16 00				16 29				16 59					

A To Brighton B From Great Malvern C From Southampton Central

Table T188-R

Mondays to Fridays
16 December to 15 May

Southampton Central - Worthing - Brighton and Gatwick Airport - London

		SN ■	SN	SN		SN	SN ■	SN	SN	SN ■	SN ■	SN	SN	SN		SN ■	SN	SN	SN ■	SN ■	SN	SN	SN	SN ■
Southampton Central ⛴	d									15 28									16 28					
Fareham	d									15 53									16 53					
Havant	a									16 09									17 09					
Portsmouth Harbour ⛴	d					15 29																		
Portsmouth & Southsea	d					15 33								16 33									17 33	
Havant	a					15 45								16 45									17 45	
Havant	d					15 46				16 10				16 46					17 10				17 46	
Chichester 4	d					16 00				16 22				17 00					17 22				18 00	
Barnham	a					16 07				16 30				17 07					17 30				18 07	
Bognor Regis	d																							
Barnham	a																							
Barnham	d					16 09				16 31				17 09					17 31				18 09	
Littlehampton 4	d	15 44		15 51			16 14		16 23		16 44		16 51			17 14		17 21		17 44		17 51		18 14
Angmering 3	d	15 53		16 02		16 19	16 23		16 32	16 43	16 53		17 02	17 19		17 23		17 32	17 43	17 53		18 02	18 19	18 24
Goring-by-Sea	d	15 57		16 06			16 27		16 36	16 47	16 57		17 06			17 27		17 36	17 47	17 57		18 06		18 28
Durrington-on-Sea	d	15 59		16 09			16 29		16 39	16 50	16 59		17 09			17 29		17 39	17 50	17 59		18 09		18 31
West Worthing	d	16 02		16 12			16 32		16 42	16 52	17 02		17 12			17 32		17 42	17 52	18 02		18 12		18 33
Worthing 4	a	16 04		16 15		16 26	16 34		16 45	16 55	17 04		17 15	17 26		17 34		17 45	17 55	18 04		18 15	18 26	18 36
	d	16 05		16 15		16 26	16 35		16 45	16 56	17 05		17 15	17 26		17 35		17 45	17 56	18 05		18 15	18 26	18 36
East Worthing	d			16 18					16 48				17 18					17 48				18 18		
Lancing	d			16 21		16 30	16 39		16 51	17 00			17 21	17 30		17 39		17 51	18 00			18 21	18 30	18 40
Shoreham-by-Sea	d	16 12		16 26		16 35	16 43		16 56	17 05	17 12		17 26	17 35		17 43		17 56	18 05	18 12		18 26	18 35	18 45
Southwick	d			16 29		16 38			16 59	17 08			17 29	17 38				17 59	18 08			18 29	18 38	
Fishersgate	d			16 31					17 01				17 31					18 01				18 31		
Portslade	d	16 17		16 34		16 42	16 48		17 04	17 11	17 17		17 34	17 42		17 48		18 04	18 11	18 17		18 34	18 42	18 49
Aldrington	d			16 36					17 06				17 36					18 06				18 36		
Hove 2	a	16 20		16 38		16 45	16 51		17 08	17 15	17 20		17 38	17 45		17 51		18 08	18 15	18 20		18 38	18 45	18 52
	d	16 21	16 26	16 39		16 46	16 51	17 01	17 09	17 16	17 21	17 31	17 39	17 46		17 51	18 02	18 09	18 16	18 21	18 31	18 39	18 46	18 53
Brighton 10	a		16 31	16 44		16 51		17 05	17 15	17 21		17 36	17 45	17 51			18 06	18 14	18 21		18 35	18 44	18 51	
Preston Park	a						16 56									17 56								18 58
Haywards Heath 3	a	16 36					17 11				17 36					18 11				18 36				19 11
Gatwick Airport 10 ✈	a	16 56					17 26				17 56					18 26				18 56				19 26
East Croydon	a	17 12					17 42				18 12					18 42				19 11				19 42
East Croydon	d																							
London Bridge	a																							
London Blackfriars	a																							
City Thameslink	a																							
Farringdon	a																							
St Pancras International	a																							
East Croydon 🚊	d	17 12					17 42				18 12					18 42				19 12				19 42
Clapham Junction 10	a	17 21					17 51				18 21					18 51				19 21				19 51
London Victoria 15 ⊖	a	17 30					17 59				18 29					18 59				19 29				19 59

		SN	SN	SN ■	SN ■	SN	SN	SN	SN ■	SN		SN	SN ■	SN ■	SN	SN	SN	SN ■	SN	SN		SN ■	SN ■	SN	SN
Southampton Central ⛴	d			17 28									18 28									19 28			
Fareham	d			17 53									18 53									19 53			
Havant	a			18 09									19 09									20 09			
Portsmouth Harbour ⛴	d																								
Portsmouth & Southsea	d							18 33									19 33								
Havant	a							18 46									19 45								
Havant	d			18 10				18 47					19 10				19 46					20 10			
Chichester 4	d			18 22				19 01					19 22				20 00					20 22			
Barnham	a			18 30				19 08					19 30				20 07					20 30			
Bognor Regis	d																								
Barnham	a																								
Barnham	d			18 31				19 09					19 31				20 09					20 31			
Littlehampton 4	d		18 27		18 40				19 10					19 40				20 10					20 40		
Angmering 3	d		18 36	18 43	18 53			19 19	19 24				19 43	19 53			20 19	20 23				20 43	20 53		
Goring-by-Sea	d			18 47	18 57				19 28				19 47	19 57				20 27				20 47	20 57		
Durrington-on-Sea	d			18 50	18 59				19 30				19 50	19 59				20 29				20 50	20 59		
West Worthing	d		18 42	18 52	19 02		19 12		19 33			19 42	19 52	20 02		20 12		20 32		20 42		20 52	21 02		21 12
Worthing 4	a		18 45	18 55	19 04		19 15	19 26	19 35			19 45	19 55	20 04		20 15	20 26	20 34		20 45		20 55	21 04		21 15
	d		18 45	18 56	19 05		19 15	19 26	19 36			19 45	19 56	20 05		20 15	20 26	20 35		20 45		20 56	21 05		21 15
East Worthing	d		18 48				19 18					19 48				20 18				20 48					21 18
Lancing	d		18 51	19 00			19 21	19 30	19 40			19 51	20 00			20 21	20 30	20 39		20 51		21 00			21 21
Shoreham-by-Sea	d		18 56	19 05	19 12		19 26	19 35	19 44			19 56	20 05	20 12		20 26	20 35	20 43		20 56		21 05	21 12		21 26
Southwick	d		18 59	19 08			19 29	19 38				19 59	20 08			20 29	20 38			20 59		21 08			21 29
Fishersgate	d		19 01				19 31					20 01				20 31				21 01					21 31
Portslade	d		19 04	19 11	19 17		19 34	19 42	19 49			20 04	20 11	20 17		20 34	20 42	20 48		21 04		21 11	21 17		21 34
Aldrington	d		19 06				19 36					20 06				20 36				21 06					21 36
Hove 2	a		19 08	19 15	19 20		19 38	19 45	19 52			20 08	20 15	20 20		20 38	20 45	20 51		21 08		21 15	21 20		21 38
	d	19 01	19 09	19 16	19 21	19 31	19 39	19 46	19 52	20 02		20 10	20 16	20 21	20 26	20 40	20 46	20 51	20 56	21 10		21 16	21 21	21 26	21 40
Brighton 10	a	19 05	19 14	19 21		19 35	19 44	19 51		20 06		20 15	20 21		20 31	20 45	20 51		21 01	21 15		21 21		21 31	21 45
Preston Park	a								19 57									20 56							
Haywards Heath 3	a				19 36				20 11					20 37				21 10					21 36		
Gatwick Airport 10 ✈	a				19 56				20 27					20 56				21 26					21 56		
East Croydon	a				20 11				20 42					21 11				21 41					22 12		
East Croydon	d																								
London Bridge	a																								
London Blackfriars	a																								
City Thameslink	a																								
Farringdon	a																								
St Pancras International	a																								
East Croydon 🚊	d				20 12				20 43					21 12				21 42					22 12		
Clapham Junction 10	a				20 21				20 52					21 21				21 51					22 21		
London Victoria 15 ⊖	a				20 30				20 59					21 29				21 59					22 29		

Table T188-R

Mondays to Fridays
16 December to 15 May

Southampton Central - Worthing - Brighton and Gatwick Airport - London

		SN	SN ■	SN	SN	SN ■		SN ■	SN	SN	SN	SN ■	SN	SN ■	SN	SN		SN	SN
Southampton Central ⛴	d					20 28								21 13					
Fareham	d					20 54								21 40					
Havant	a					21 09								21 55					
Portsmouth Harbour ⛴	d															22 15			22 40
Portsmouth & Southsea	d	20 33									21 33					22 19			22 44
Havant	a	20 45									21 46					22 34			22 59
Havant	d	20 46				21 10					21 47			21 56		22 35			23 00
Chichester 4	d	21 00				21 22					22 01			22 07		22 49			23 10
Barnham	a	21 07				21 30					22 08			22 14		22 56			23 18
Bognor Regis	d																		
Barnham	a																		
Barnham	d	21 09				21 31					22 09			22 16		22 58			23 19
Littlehampton 4	d		21 14					21 44				22 14		22 33					23 43
Angmering 3	d	21 19	21 23			21 43		21 53			22 19	22 23		22 43		23 09			23 52
Goring-by-Sea	d		21 27			21 47		21 57				22 27		22 47		23 13			23 56
Durrington-on-Sea	d		21 29			21 50		21 59				22 29		22 49		23 16			23 59
West Worthing	d		21 32		21 42	21 52		22 02		22 12		22 32		22 52		23 18			00 01
Worthing 4	a	21 26	21 34		21 45	21 55		22 04		22 15	22 26	22 34		22 54		23 21			00 04
	d	21 26	21 35		21 45	21 56		22 05		22 15	22 26	22 35		22 55		23 21			00 04
East Worthing	d				21 48					22 18				22 57		23 24			00 07
Lancing	d	21 30	21 39		21 51	22 00				22 21	22 30	22 39		23 00		23 27			00 10
Shoreham-by-Sea	d	21 35	21 43		21 56	22 05		22 12		22 26	22 35	22 43		23 04		23 32			00 14
Southwick	d	21 38			21 59	22 08				22 29	22 38			23 07		23 35			00 17
Fishersgate	d				22 01					22 31				23 09		23 37			00 19
Portslade	d	21 42	21 48		22 04	22 12		22 17		22 34	22 42	22 48		23 11		23 39			00 21
Aldrington	d				22 06					22 36	22 44			23 14		23 42			00 23
Hove 2	a	21 45	21 51		22 08	22 15		22 20		22 38	22 46	22 51		23 16		23 44			00 25
	d	21 46	21 51	21 56	22 10	22 16		22 21	22 26	22 40	22 47	22 51	22 56	23 16	23 26	23 44		23 56	00 26
Brighton 10	a	21 51		22 01	22 15	22 21			22 31	22 45	22 51		23 01	23 20	23 31	23 49		00 01	00 30
Preston Park	a		21 56									22 56							
Haywards Heath 3	a		22 11					22 36				23 10							
Gatwick Airport 10 ✈	a		22 26					22 56				23 26							
East Croydon	a		22 42					23 11				23 42							
East Croydon	d																		
London Bridge	a																		
London Blackfriars	a																		
City Thameslink	a																		
Farringdon	a																		
St Pancras International	a																		
East Croydon 🚊	d		22 43					23 12				23 42							
Clapham Junction 10	a		22 52					23 21				23 57							
London Victoria 15 ⊖	a		23 00					23 30				00 05							

Saturdays
21 December to 16 May

		SN A	SN ■	SN ■	SN	SN ■	SN	SN	SN ■	SN		SN	SN ■	SN ■	SN	SN	SN	SN ■	SN	SN		GW	SN ■	SN ■	SN
Southampton Central ⛴	d																						06 25		
Fareham	d																						06 52		
Havant	a																						07 10		
Portsmouth Harbour ⛴	d																06 29					06 50			
Portsmouth & Southsea	d			04 55													06 33					06 54			
Havant	a			05 07													06 45					07 07			
Havant	d			05 07													06 46					07 08	07 11		
Chichester 4	d			05 18									06 23				07 00					07 19	07 24		
Barnham	a			05 26									06 30				07 07					07 27	07 32		
Bognor Regis	d							05 37																	
Barnham	a							05 43																	
Barnham	d		04 48	05 26				05 45					06 31				07 08					07 27	07 32		
Littlehampton 4	d		05 04			05 44			06 14					06 44				07 14						07 44	
Angmering 3	d		05 14			05 53		05 57	06 23				06 43	06 53			07 19	07 23					07 44	07 53	
Goring-by-Sea	d		05 18			05 57		06 01	06 27				06 47	06 57				07 27					07 48	07 57	
Durrington-on-Sea	d		05 20			05 59		06 03	06 29				06 50	06 59				07 29					07 51	07 59	
West Worthing	d	00 01	05 23			06 02		06 06	06 32			06 42	06 52	07 02		07 12		07 32		07 42			07 53	08 02	
Worthing 4	a	00 04	05 25	05 41		06 04		06 08	06 34			06 45	06 55	07 04		07 15	07 26	07 34		07 45		07 49	07 56	08 04	
	d	00 04	05 26	05 42		06 05		06 09	06 35			06 45	06 56	07 05		07 15	07 26	07 35		07 45		07 50	07 57	08 05	
East Worthing	d	00 07	05 29					06 11				06 48				07 18				07 48					
Lancing	d	00 10	05 32					06 14	06 39			06 51	07 00			07 21	07 30	07 39		07 51			08 01		
Shoreham-by-Sea	d	00 14	05 37	05 48		06 12		06 19	06 43			06 56	07 05	07 12		07 26	07 35	07 43		07 56		08 01	08 06	08 12	
Southwick	d	00 17	05 40					06 22				06 59	07 08			07 29	07 38			07 59			08 09		
Fishersgate	d	00 19	05 42					06 24				07 01				07 31				08 01					
Portslade	d	00 21	05 44			06 17		06 26	06 48			07 04	07 11	07 17		07 34	07 42	07 48		08 04			08 12	08 17	
Aldrington	d	00 23	05 46					06 29				07 06				07 36				08 06					
Hove 2	a	00 25	05 48	05 54		06 20		06 31	06 51			07 08	07 15	07 20		07 38	07 45	07 51		08 08		08 12	08 16	08 20	
	d	00 26	05 49	05 55	05 58	06 21	06 26	06 32	06 51	06 56		07 09	07 16	07 21	07 26	07 39	07 46	07 51	07 56	08 09		08 13	08 17	08 21	08 27
Brighton 10	a	00 30	05 54		06 02		06 31	06 36		07 01		07 14	07 21		07 31	07 44	07 51		08 01	08 14		08 18	08 24		08 32
Preston Park	a								06 56									07 56							
Haywards Heath 3	a			06 10		06 36			07 10					07 36				08 10						08 36	
Gatwick Airport 10 ✈	a			06 26		06 56			07 26					07 56				08 26						08 56	
East Croydon	a			06 41		07 11			07 41					08 11				08 41						09 11	
East Croydon	d																								
London Bridge	a																								
London Blackfriars	a																								
City Thameslink	a																								
Farringdon	a																								
St Pancras International	a																								
East Croydon 🚊	d			06 42		07 12			07 42					08 12				08 42						09 12	
Clapham Junction 10	a			06 51		07 21			07 51					08 21				08 51						09 21	
London Victoria 15 ⊖	a			06 59		07 29			07 59					08 29				08 59						09 29	

A From Portsmouth Harbour

Table T188-R

Saturdays

21 December to 16 May

Southampton Central - Worthing - Brighton and Gatwick Airport - London

Station		SN	SN	SN 1	SN	SN	SN 1	SN 1	SN	SN	SN	SN 1	SN	SN	SN 1	SN 1	SN	SN	SN	SN 1	SN	SN	SN 1
Southampton Central	d						07 28								08 28								09 28
Fareham	d						07 53								08 54								09 53
Havant	a						08 09								09 09								10 09
Portsmouth Harbour	d		07 29								08 29								09 29				
Portsmouth & Southsea	d		07 33								08 33								09 33				
Havant	a		07 45								08 45								09 45				
Havant	d		07 46				08 10				08 46				09 10				09 46				10 10
Chichester 4	d		08 00				08 22				09 00				09 22				10 00				10 22
Barnham	a		08 07				08 30				09 07				09 30				10 07				10 30
Bognor Regis	d																						
Barnham	a																						
Barnham	d		08 09				08 31				09 09				09 31				10 09				10 31
Littlehampton 4	d			08 14				08 44				09 14				09 44				10 14			
Angmering 3	d		08 19	08 23			08 43	08 53			09 19	09 23			09 43	09 53			10 19	10 23			10 43
Goring-by-Sea	d			08 27			08 47	08 57				09 27			09 47	09 57				10 27			10 47
Durrington-on-Sea	d			08 29			08 50	08 59				09 29			09 50	09 59				10 29			10 50
West Worthing	d	08 12		08 32		08 42	08 52	09 02		09 12		09 32		09 42	09 52	10 02		10 12		10 32		10 42	10 52
Worthing 4	a	08 17	08 26	08 34		08 45	08 55	09 04		09 15	09 26	09 34		09 45	09 55	10 04		10 15	10 26	10 34		10 45	10 55
	d	08 17	08 26	08 35		08 45	08 56	09 05		09 15	09 26	09 35		09 45	09 56	10 05		10 15	10 26	10 35		10 45	10 56
East Worthing	d	08 20				08 48				09 18				09 48				10 18				10 48	
Lancing	d	08 23	08 30	08 39		08 51	09 00			09 21	09 30	09 39		09 51	10 00			10 21	10 30	10 39		10 51	11 00
Shoreham-by-Sea	d	08 28	08 35	08 43		08 56	09 05	09 12		09 26	09 35	09 43		09 56	10 05	10 12		10 26	10 35	10 43		10 56	11 05
Southwick	d	08 31	08 38			08 59	09 08			09 29	09 38			09 59	10 08			10 29	10 38			10 59	11 08
Fishersgate	d	08 33				09 01				09 31				10 01				10 31				11 01	
Portslade	d	08 36	08 42	08 48		09 04	09 11	09 17		09 34	09 42	09 48		10 04	10 11	10 17		10 34	10 42	10 48		11 04	11 11
Aldrington	d	08 38				09 06				09 36				10 06				10 36				11 06	
Hove 2	a	08 40	08 45	08 51		09 08	09 15	09 20		09 38	09 45	09 51		10 08	10 15	10 20		10 38	10 45	10 51		11 08	11 15
	d	08 41	08 46	08 51	08 58	09 09	09 16	09 21	09 26	09 39	09 46	09 51	09 56	10 09	10 16	10 21	10 26	10 39	10 46	10 51	10 56	11 09	11 16
Brighton 10	a	08 46	08 51		09 03	09 14	09 21		09 31	09 44	09 51		10 01	10 14	10 21		10 31	10 44	10 51		11 01	11 14	11 21
Preston Park	a			08 56								09 56								10 56			
Haywards Heath 3	a			09 10				09 36				10 10				10 36				11 10			
Gatwick Airport 10	a			09 26				09 56				10 26				10 56				11 26			
East Croydon	a			09 41				10 11				10 41				11 11				11 41			
East Croydon	d																						
London Bridge	a																						
London Blackfriars	a																						
City Thameslink	a																						
Farringdon	a																						
St Pancras International	a																						
East Croydon	d			09 42				10 12				10 42				11 12				11 42			
Clapham Junction 10	a			09 51				10 21				10 51				11 21				11 51			
London Victoria 15	a			09 59				10 29				10 59				11 29				11 59			

Station		SN 1	SN	SN	SN	SN 1	SN	SN	SN 1	SN 1	SN	SN	SN	SN 1	SN	SN	SN 1	SN 1	SN	SN	SN	SN 1
Southampton Central	d								10 28								11 28					
Fareham	d								10 53								11 53					
Havant	a								11 09								12 09					
Portsmouth Harbour	d				10 29								11 29								12 29	
Portsmouth & Southsea	d				10 33								11 33								12 33	
Havant	a				10 45								11 45								12 45	
Havant	d				10 46				11 10				11 46				12 10				12 46	
Chichester 4	d				11 00				11 22				12 00				12 22				13 00	
Barnham	a				11 07				11 30				12 07				12 30				13 07	
Bognor Regis	d																					
Barnham	a																					
Barnham	d				11 09				11 31				12 09				12 31				13 09	
Littlehampton 4	d	10 44				11 14				11 44				12 14				12 44				13 14
Angmering 3	d	10 53			11 19	11 23			11 43	11 53			12 19	12 23			12 43	12 53			13 19	13 23
Goring-by-Sea	d	10 57				11 27			11 47	11 57				12 27			12 47	12 57				13 27
Durrington-on-Sea	d	10 59				11 29			11 50	11 59				12 29			12 50	12 59				13 29
West Worthing	d	11 02		11 12		11 32		11 42	11 52	12 02		12 12		12 32		12 42	12 52	13 02		13 12		13 32
Worthing 4	a	11 04		11 15	11 26	11 34		11 45	11 55	12 04		12 15	12 26	12 34		12 45	12 55	13 04		13 15	13 26	13 34
	d	11 05		11 15	11 26	11 35		11 45	11 56	12 05		12 15	12 26	12 35		12 45	12 56	13 05		13 15	13 26	13 35
East Worthing	d			11 18				11 48				12 18				12 48				13 18		
Lancing	d			11 21	11 30	11 39		11 51	12 00			12 21	12 30	12 39		12 51	13 00			13 21	13 30	13 39
Shoreham-by-Sea	d	11 12		11 26	11 35	11 43		11 56	12 05	12 12		12 26	12 35	12 43		12 56	13 05	13 12		13 26	13 35	13 43
Southwick	d			11 29	11 38			11 59	12 08			12 29	12 38			12 59	13 08			13 29	13 38	
Fishersgate	d			11 31				12 01				12 31				13 01				13 31		
Portslade	d	11 17		11 34	11 42	11 48		12 04	12 11	12 17		12 34	12 42	12 48		13 04	13 11	13 17		13 34	13 42	13 48
Aldrington	d			11 36				12 06				12 36				13 06				13 36		
Hove 2	a	11 20		11 38	11 45	11 51		12 08	12 15	12 20		12 38	12 45	12 51		13 08	13 15	13 20		13 38	13 45	13 51
	d	11 21	11 26	11 39	11 46	11 51	11 56	12 09	12 16	12 21	12 26	12 39	12 46	12 51	12 56	13 09	13 16	13 21	13 26	13 39	13 46	13 51
Brighton 10	a		11 31	11 44	11 51		12 01	12 14	12 21		12 31	12 44	12 51		13 01	13 14	13 21		13 31	13 44	13 51	
Preston Park	a					11 56								12 56								13 56
Haywards Heath 3	a	11 36				12 10				12 36				13 10				13 36				14 10
Gatwick Airport 10	a	11 56				12 26				12 56				13 26				13 56				14 26
East Croydon	a	12 11				12 41				13 11				13 41				14 11				14 41
East Croydon	d																					
London Bridge	a																					
London Blackfriars	a																					
City Thameslink	a																					
Farringdon	a																					
St Pancras International	a																					
East Croydon	d	12 12				12 42				13 12				13 42				14 12				14 42
Clapham Junction 10	a	12 21				12 51				13 21				13 51				14 21				14 51
London Victoria 15	a	12 29				12 59				13 29				13 59				14 30				14 59

Table T188-R

Saturdays

21 December to 16 May

Southampton Central - Worthing - Brighton and Gatwick Airport - London

Station		SN	SN	SN 1	SN 1	SN	SN	SN	SN 1	SN	SN	SN 1	SN 1	SN	SN	SN	SN 1	SN	SN	GW ◇ A	SN 1	SN 1	SN
Southampton Central	d			12 28								13 28								14 34	14 26		
Fareham	d			12 53								13 53								14 56	15 00		
Havant	a			13 09								14 09								15 10	15 13		
Portsmouth Harbour	d							13 29								14 29							
Portsmouth & Southsea	d							13 33								14 33							
Havant	a							13 45								14 45							
Havant	d			13 10				13 46				14 10				14 46				15 10	15 13		
Chichester 4	d			13 22				14 00				14 22				15 00				15 21	15 25		
Barnham	a			13 30				14 07				14 30				15 07				15 29	15 33		
Bognor Regis	d																						
Barnham	a																						
Barnham	d			13 31				14 09				14 31				15 09				15 29	15 33		
Littlehampton 4	d				13 44				14 14				14 44				15 14					15 44	
Angmering 3	d			13 43	13 53			14 19	14 23			14 43	14 53			15 19	15 23				15 45	15 53	
Goring-by-Sea	d			13 47	13 57				14 27			14 47	14 57				15 27				15 49	15 57	
Durrington-on-Sea	d			13 50	13 59				14 29			14 50	14 59				15 29				15 52	15 59	
West Worthing	d		13 42	13 52	14 02		14 12		14 32		14 42	14 52	15 02		15 12		15 32		15 42		15 54	16 02	
Worthing 4	a		13 45	13 55	14 04		14 15	14 26	14 34		14 45	14 55	15 04		15 15	15 26	15 34		15 45	15 49	15 57	16 04	
	d		13 45	13 56	14 05		14 15	14 26	14 35		14 45	14 56	15 05		15 15	15 26	15 35		15 45	15 50	15 57	16 05	
East Worthing	d		13 48				14 18				14 48				15 18				15 48				
Lancing	d		13 51	14 00			14 21	14 30	14 39		14 51	15 00			15 21	15 30	15 39		15 51		16 01		
Shoreham-by-Sea	d		13 56	14 05	14 12		14 26	14 35	14 43		14 56	15 05	15 12		15 26	15 35	15 43		15 56	16 00	16 06	16 12	
Southwick	d		13 59	14 08			14 29	14 38			14 59	15 08			15 29	15 38			15 59		16 09		
Fishersgate	d		14 01				14 31				15 01				15 31				16 01				
Portslade	d		14 04	14 11	14 17		14 34	14 42	14 48		15 04	15 11	15 17		15 34	15 42	15 48		16 04		16 12	16 17	
Aldrington	d		14 06				14 36				15 06				15 36				16 06				
Hove 2	a		14 08	14 15	14 20		14 38	14 45	14 51		15 08	15 15	15 20		15 38	15 45	15 51		16 08	16 12	16 15	16 20	
	d	13 56	14 09	14 16	14 21	14 26	14 39	14 46	14 51	14 56	15 09	15 16	15 21	15 26	15 39	15 46	15 51	15 56	16 09	16 13	16 16	16 21	16 26
Brighton 10	a	14 01	14 14	14 21		14 31	14 44	14 51		15 01	15 14	15 21		15 31	15 44	15 51		16 01	16 14	16 18	16 24		16 31
Preston Park	a								14 56								15 56						
Haywards Heath 3	a				14 36				15 10				15 36				16 10					16 36	
Gatwick Airport 10	a				14 56				15 26				15 56				16 26					16 56	
East Croydon	a				15 11				15 41				16 11				16 41					17 11	
East Croydon	d																						
London Bridge	a																						
London Blackfriars	a																						
City Thameslink	a																						
Farringdon	a																						
St Pancras International	a																						
East Croydon	d				15 12				15 42				16 12				16 42					17 12	
Clapham Junction 10	a				15 21				15 51				16 21				16 51					17 21	
London Victoria 15	a				15 29				15 59				16 29				16 59					17 29	

Station		SN	SN	SN 1	SN	SN	SN 1	SN 1	SN	SN	SN	SN 1	SN	SN	SN 1	SN 1	SN	SN	SN	SN 1	SN	SN
Southampton Central	d						15 28								16 28							
Fareham	d						15 53								16 53							
Havant	a						16 09								17 09							
Portsmouth Harbour	d		15 29								16 29								17 29			
Portsmouth & Southsea	d		15 33								16 33								17 33			
Havant	a		15 45								16 45								17 45			
Havant	d		15 46				16 10				16 46				17 10				17 46			
Chichester 4	d		16 00				16 22				17 00				17 22				18 00			
Barnham	a		16 07				16 30				17 07				17 30				18 07			
Bognor Regis	d																					
Barnham	a																					
Barnham	d		16 09				16 31				17 09				17 31				18 09			
Littlehampton 4	d			16 14				16 44				17 14				17 44				18 14		
Angmering 3	d		16 19	16 23			16 43	16 53			17 19	17 23			17 43	17 53			18 19	18 23		
Goring-by-Sea	d			16 27			16 47	16 57				17 27			17 47	17 57				18 27		
Durrington-on-Sea	d			16 29			16 50	16 59				17 29			17 50	17 59				18 29		
West Worthing	d	16 12		16 32		16 42	16 52	17 02		17 12		17 32		17 42	17 52	18 02		18 12		18 32		18 43
Worthing 4	a	16 15	16 26	16 34		16 45	16 55	17 04		17 15	17 26	17 34		17 45	17 55	18 04		18 15	18 26	18 34		18 46
	d	16 15	16 26	16 35		16 45	16 56	17 05		17 15	17 26	17 35		17 45	17 56	18 05		18 15	18 26	18 35		18 46
East Worthing	d	16 18				16 48				17 18				17 48				18 18				18 49
Lancing	d	16 21	16 30	16 39		16 51	17 00			17 21	17 30	17 39		17 51	18 00			18 21	18 30	18 39		18 52
Shoreham-by-Sea	d	16 26	16 35	16 43		16 56	17 05	17 12		17 26	17 35	17 43		17 56	18 05	18 12		18 26	18 35	18 43		18 56
Southwick	d	16 29	16 38			16 59	17 08			17 29	17 38			17 59	18 08			18 29	18 38			19 00
Fishersgate	d	16 31				17 01				17 31				18 01				18 31				19 02
Portslade	d	16 34	16 42	16 48		17 04	17 11	17 17		17 34	17 42	17 48		18 04	18 11	18 17		18 34	18 42	18 48		19 04
Aldrington	d	16 36				17 06				17 36				18 06				18 36				19 07
Hove 2	a	16 38	16 45	16 51		17 08	17 15	17 20		17 38	17 45	17 51		18 08	18 15	18 20		18 38	18 45	18 51		19 09
	d	16 39	16 46	16 51	16 58	17 09	17 16	17 21	17 26	17 39	17 46	17 51	17 56	18 09	18 16	18 21	18 26	18 39	18 46	18 51	18 56	19 09
Brighton 10	a	16 44	16 51		17 03	17 14	17 21		17 31	17 44	17 51		18 01	18 14	18 21		18 31	18 44	18 51		19 01	19 14
Preston Park	a			16 56								17 56								18 56		
Haywards Heath 3	a			17 10				17 36				18 10				18 36				19 10		
Gatwick Airport 10	a			17 26				17 56				18 26				18 56				19 26		
East Croydon	a			17 41				18 11				18 41				19 11				19 41		
East Croydon	d																					
London Bridge	a																					
London Blackfriars	a																					
City Thameslink	a																					
Farringdon	a																					
St Pancras International	a																					
East Croydon	d			17 42				18 12				18 42				19 12				19 42		
Clapham Junction 10	a			17 51				18 21				18 51				19 21				19 51		
London Victoria 15	a			17 59				18 29				18 59				19 29				19 59		

A From Great Malvern

Table T188-R

Saturdays

21 December to 16 May

Southampton Central - Worthing - Brighton and Gatwick Airport - London

		SN 1	SN 1	SN	SN	SN	SN 1	SN	SN	SN 1		SN 1	SN	SN	SN	SN 1	SN	SN	SN 1	SN 1		SN	SN	SN	SN 1
Southampton Central	d	17 28								18 28									19 28						
Fareham	d	17 53								18 53									19 53						
Havant	a	18 09								19 09									20 09						
Portsmouth Harbour	d					18 29									19 29									20 29	
Portsmouth & Southsea	d					18 33									19 33									20 33	
Havant	a					18 45									19 45									20 45	
Havant	d	18 10				18 46				19 10					19 46				20 10					20 46	
Chichester 4	d	18 22				19 00				19 22					20 00				20 22					21 00	
Barnham	a	18 30				19 07				19 30					20 07				20 30					21 07	
Bognor Regis	d																								
Barnham	a																								
Barnham	d	18 31				19 09				19 31					20 09				20 31					21 09	
Littlehampton 4	d		18 44				19 14					19 44				20 14				20 44					21 14
Angmering 3	d	18 43	18 53			19 19	19 23			19 43		19 53			20 19	20 23			20 43	20 53				21 19	21 23
Goring-by-Sea	d	18 47	18 57				19 27			19 47		19 57				20 27			20 47	20 57					21 27
Durrington-on-Sea	d	18 50	18 59				19 29			19 50		19 59				20 29			20 50	20 59					21 29
West Worthing	d	18 52	19 02		19 12		19 32		19 42	19 52		20 02		20 12		20 32		20 42	20 52	21 02			21 12		21 32
Worthing 4	a	18 55	19 04		19 15	19 26	19 34		19 45	19 55		20 04		20 15	20 26	20 34		20 45	20 55	21 04			21 15	21 26	21 34
	d	18 56	19 05		19 15	19 26	19 35		19 45	19 56		20 05		20 15	20 26	20 35		20 45	20 56	21 05			21 15	21 26	21 35
East Worthing	d				19 18				19 48					20 18				20 48					21 18		
Lancing	d	19 00			19 21	19 30	19 39		19 51	20 00				20 21	20 30	20 39		20 51	21 00				21 21	21 30	21 39
Shoreham-by-Sea	d	19 05	19 12		19 26	19 35	19 43		19 56	20 05		20 12		20 26	20 35	20 43		20 56	21 05	21 12			21 26	21 35	21 43
Southwick	d	19 08			19 29	19 38			19 59	20 08				20 29	20 38			20 59	21 08				21 29	21 38	
Fishersgate	d				19 31				20 01					20 31				21 01					21 31		
Portslade	d	19 11	19 17		19 34	19 42	19 48		20 04	20 11		20 17		20 34	20 42	20 48		21 04	21 11	21 17			21 34	21 42	21 48
Aldrington	d				19 36				20 06					20 36				21 06					21 36		
Hove 2	a	19 15	19 20		19 39	19 45	19 51		20 08	20 15		20 20		20 38	20 45	20 51		21 08	21 15	21 20			21 38	21 45	21 51
	d	19 16	19 21	19 26	19 39	19 46	19 51	19 56	20 09	20 16		20 21	20 26	20 39	20 46	20 51	20 56	21 09	21 16	21 21		21 26	21 39	21 46	21 51
Brighton 10	a	19 21		19 31	19 44	19 51		20 01	20 14	20 21			20 31	20 44	20 51		21 01	21 14	21 21			21 31	21 44	21 51	
Preston Park	a						19 56									20 56									21 56
Haywards Heath 3	a		19 36				20 10					20 36				21 10				21 36					22 10
Gatwick Airport 10 ✈	a		19 56				20 26					20 56				21 26				21 56					22 27
East Croydon	a		20 11				20 41					21 11				21 41				22 12					22 42
East Croydon	d																								
London Bridge	a																								
London Blackfriars	a																								
City Thameslink	a																								
Farringdon	a																								
St Pancras International	a																								
East Croydon	d		20 12				20 42					21 12				21 42				22 12					22 43
Clapham Junction 10	a		20 21				20 51					21 21				21 51				22 21					22 52
London Victoria 15 ⊖	a		20 29				20 59					21 29				21 59				22 28					23 00

		SN	SN	SN 1	SN 1	SN		SN	SN	SN	SN 1	SN	SN	SN	SN
Southampton Central	d			20 28							21 13				
Fareham	d			20 53							21 40				
Havant	a			21 09							21 55				
Portsmouth Harbour	d												22 15		22 40
Portsmouth & Southsea	d												22 19		22 44
Havant	a												22 35		22 59
Havant	d			21 10							21 56		22 35		23 00
Chichester 4	d			21 22							22 07		22 49		23 10
Barnham	a			21 30							22 14		22 57		23 18
Bognor Regis	d														
Barnham	a														
Barnham	d			21 31							22 16		22 58		23 19
Littlehampton 4	d				21 44						22 33				23 42
Angmering 3	d			21 43	21 53						22 42		23 09		23 51
Goring-by-Sea	d			21 47	21 57						22 46		23 13		23 55
Durrington-on-Sea	d			21 50	21 59						22 49		23 16		23 57
West Worthing	d		21 42	21 52	22 02			22 12		22 42	22 51		23 18		23 59
Worthing 4	a		21 45	21 55	22 04			22 15		22 45	22 54		23 21		00 02
	d		21 45	21 56	22 05			22 15		22 45	22 54		23 21		00 03
East Worthing	d		21 48					22 18		22 48	22 57		23 24		00 06
Lancing	d		21 51	22 00				22 21		22 51	23 00		23 27		00 09
Shoreham-by-Sea	d		21 56	22 05	22 12			22 26		22 56	23 04		23 32		00 13
Southwick	d		21 59	22 08				22 29		22 59	23 07		23 35		00 16
Fishersgate	d		22 01					22 31		23 01	23 09		23 37		00 18
Portslade	d		22 04	22 11	22 17			22 34		23 04	23 11		23 39		00 21
Aldrington	d		22 06					22 36		23 06	23 13		23 42		00 23
Hove 2	a		22 08	22 15	22 20			22 38		23 08	23 15		23 44		00 25
	d	21 56	22 09	22 16	22 21	22 26		22 39	22 56	23 09	23 16	23 26	23 44	23 56	00 26
Brighton 10	a	22 01	22 14	22 21		22 31		22 44	23 01	23 14	23 20	23 31	23 49	00 01	00 30
Preston Park	a														
Haywards Heath 3	a				22 36										
Gatwick Airport 10 ✈	a				22 56										
East Croydon	a				23 11										
East Croydon	d														
London Bridge	a														
London Blackfriars	a														
City Thameslink	a														
Farringdon	a														
St Pancras International	a														
East Croydon	d				23 12										
Clapham Junction 10	a				23 21										
London Victoria 15 ⊖	a				23 29										

Table T188-R

Sundays

15 December to 10 May

Southampton Central - Worthing - Brighton and Gatwick Airport - London

		SN A	SN	SN 1	SN	SN	SN	SN 1	SN	SN 1		SN	SN 1	SN	SN 1 B	GW C	SN 1 D	SN	SN 1	SN		SN 1	SN	SN 1	SN
Southampton Central	d									07 30					08 21	08 31						09 30			
Fareham	d									07 54					08 47	08 54						09 54			
Havant	a									08 10					09 02	09 13						10 10			
Portsmouth Harbour	d						07 14					08 14						09 14					10 14		
Portsmouth & Southsea	d						07 18					08 18						09 18					10 18		
Havant	a						07 33					08 33						09 33					10 33		
Havant	d						07 33			08 10		08 33			09 02	09 13		09 33				10 10	10 33		
Chichester 4	d						07 53			08 22		08 53			09 14	09 24		09 53				10 22	10 53		
Barnham	a						08 01			08 30		09 01			09 22	09 31		10 01				10 30	11 01		
Bognor Regis	d																								
Barnham	a																								
Barnham	d		06 08				08 02			08 31		09 02			09 23	09 31		10 02				10 31	11 02		
Littlehampton 4	d		06 22	07 12		07 35		08 14					09 14						10 14					11 14	
Angmering 3	d			07 21		07 44	08 14	08 23		08 43		09 14	09 23		09 35			10 14	10 23			10 43	11 14	11 23	
Goring-by-Sea	d			07 25		07 48	08 18	08 27		08 47		09 18	09 27		09 39			10 18	10 27			10 47	11 18	11 27	
Durrington-on-Sea	d			07 27		07 51	08 20	08 29		08 49		09 20	09 29		09 41			10 20	10 29			10 49	11 20	11 29	
West Worthing	d			07 30		07 53	08 23	08 32		08 52		09 23	09 32		09 44		←	10 23	10 32			10 52	11 23	11 32	
Worthing 4	a		06 36	07 32		07 56	08 25	08 34		08 54		09 25	09 34		09 46	09 49	09 46	10 25	10 34			10 54	11 25	11 34	
	d	00 03	06 37	07 33		07 56	08 26	08 35		08 55		09 26	09 35		09 55	09 50	09 55	10 26	10 35			10 55	11 26	11 35	
East Worthing	d	00 06				07 59	08 28			08 57		09 28			→		09 57	10 28				10 57	11 28		
Lancing	d	00 09	06 41	07 37		08 02	08 31	08 39		09 00		09 31	09 39				10 00	10 31	10 39			11 00	11 31	11 39	
Shoreham-by-Sea	d	00 13	06 45	07 41		08 06	08 36	08 43		09 05		09 36	09 43			09 56	10 05	10 36	10 43			11 05	11 36	11 43	
Southwick	d	00 16	06 48	07 44		08 09	08 39			09 08		09 39					10 08	10 39				11 08	11 39		
Fishersgate	d	00 18				08 11	08 41			09 10		09 41					10 10	10 41				11 10	11 41		
Portslade	d	00 21	06 52	07 48		08 13	08 43	08 48		09 12		09 43	09 48				10 12	10 43	10 48			11 12	11 43	11 48	
Aldrington	d	00 23				08 16	08 45			09 14		09 45					10 14	10 45				11 14	11 45		
Hove 2	a	00 25	06 55	07 51		08 18	08 47	08 51		09 16		09 47	09 51			10 03	10 16	10 47	10 51			11 16	11 47	11 51	
	d	00 26	06 56	07 52	07 59	08 20	08 48	08 52	08 59	09 18		09 48	09 52	09 59		10 04	10 18	10 48	10 52	10 59		11 18	11 48	11 52	11 59
Brighton 10	a	00 30	07 00		08 03	08 24	08 52		09 03	09 22		09 52		10 03		10 08	10 22	10 52		11 03		11 22	11 52		12 03
Preston Park	a			07 57				08 57					09 57						10 57					11 57	
Haywards Heath 3	a			08 09				09 08					10 08						11 08					12 08	
Gatwick Airport 10 ✈	a			08 24				09 24					10 24						11 23					12 24	
East Croydon	a			08 45				09 40					10 40						11 39					12 40	
East Croydon	d																								
London Bridge	a																								
London Blackfriars	a																								
City Thameslink	a																								
Farringdon	a																								
St Pancras International	a																								
East Croydon	d			08 46				09 41					10 41						11 40					12 41	
Clapham Junction 10	a			08 55				09 50					10 50						11 50					12 50	
London Victoria 15 ⊖	a			09 02				09 58					10 58						11 58					12 58	

		SN 1	SN	SN 1	SN	SN 1		SN	SN 1	SN	SN 1	SN B	GW ◇ E	SN	SN 1	SN F		SN 1	SN	SN 1	SN	SN 1	GW ◇ E	SN	SN 1
Southampton Central	d	10 30				11 30					12 30		13 04					13 30				14 30	15 06		
Fareham	d	10 54				11 54					12 54		13 30					13 54				14 54	15 28		
Havant	a	11 10				12 10					13 10		13 45					14 10				15 10	15 42		
Portsmouth Harbour	d		11 14					12 13				13 14							14 14						
Portsmouth & Southsea	d		11 18					12 17				13 18							14 18						
Havant	a		11 33					12 32				13 33							14 33						
Havant	d	11 10	11 33			12 10		12 33			13 10	13 33	13 46					14 10	14 33			15 10	15 43		
Chichester 4	d	11 22	11 53			12 22		12 53			13 22	13 53	13 58					14 22	14 53			15 22	15 58		
Barnham	a	11 30	12 01			12 30		13 01			13 30	14 01	14 08					14 30	15 01			15 30	16 05		
Bognor Regis	d																								
Barnham	a																								
Barnham	d	11 31	12 02			12 31		13 02			13 31	14 02	14 08					14 31	15 02			15 31	16 06		
Littlehampton 4	d			12 14					13 14						14 14					15 14					16 14
Angmering 3	d	11 43	12 14	12 23		12 43		13 14	13 23		13 43	14 14			14 23			14 43	15 14	15 23		15 43			16 23
Goring-by-Sea	d	11 47	12 18	12 27		12 47		13 18	13 27		13 47	14 18			14 27			14 47	15 18	15 27		15 47			16 27
Durrington-on-Sea	d	11 49	12 20	12 29		12 49		13 20	13 29		13 49	14 20			14 29			14 49	15 20	15 29		15 49			16 29
West Worthing	d	11 52	12 23	12 32		12 52		13 23	13 32		13 52	14 23			14 32	←		14 52	15 23	15 32		15 52			16 32
Worthing 4	a	11 54	12 25	12 34		12 54		13 25	13 34		13 54	14 25	14 30		14 34	14 25		14 54	15 25	15 34		15 54	16 23		16 34
	d	11 55	12 26	12 35		12 55		13 26	13 35		13 55	14 39	14 30		14 35	14 39		14 55	15 26	15 35		15 55	16 24		16 35
East Worthing	d	11 57	12 28			12 57		13 28			13 57	→				14 41		14 57	15 28			15 57			
Lancing	d	12 00	12 31	12 39		13 00		13 31	13 39		14 00				14 39	14 44		15 00	15 31	15 39		16 00			16 39
Shoreham-by-Sea	d	12 05	12 36	12 43		13 05		13 36	13 43		14 05		14 37		14 43	14 49		15 05	15 36	15 43		16 05	16 31		16 43
Southwick	d	12 08	12 39			13 08		13 39			14 08					14 52		15 08	15 39			16 08			
Fishersgate	d	12 10	12 41			13 10		13 41			14 10					14 54		15 10	15 41			16 10			
Portslade	d	12 12	12 43	12 48		13 12		13 43	13 48		14 12				14 48	14 56		15 12	15 43	15 48		16 12			16 48
Aldrington	d	12 14	12 45			13 14		13 45			14 14					14 58		15 14	15 45			16 14			
Hove 2	a	12 16	12 47	12 51		13 16		13 47	13 51		14 16		14 43		14 51	15 00		15 16	15 47	15 51		16 16	16 37		16 51
	d	12 18	12 48	12 52	12 59	13 18		13 48	13 52	13 59	14 18		14 43	14 48	14 52	15 01		15 18	15 48	15 52	15 59	16 18	16 39	16 48	16 52
Brighton 10	a	12 22	12 52		13 03	13 22		13 52		14 03	14 22		14 49	14 52		15 05		15 22	15 52		16 03	16 22	16 44	16 52	
Preston Park	a			12 57					13 57						14 57					15 57					16 57
Haywards Heath 3	a			13 08					14 08						15 08					16 08					17 08
Gatwick Airport 10 ✈	a			13 24					14 24						15 24					16 24					17 24
East Croydon	a			13 40					14 40						15 40					16 40					17 40
East Croydon	d																								
London Bridge	a																								
London Blackfriars	a																								
City Thameslink	a																								
Farringdon	a																								
St Pancras International	a																								
East Croydon	d			13 41					14 41						15 41					16 41					17 41
Clapham Junction 10	a			13 50					14 50						15 50					16 50					17 50
London Victoria 15 ⊖	a			13 58					14 58						15 58					16 58					17 58

A not 15 December. From Portsmouth Harbour
B To Brighton
C From Romsey
D From Southampton Central
E From Cardiff Central
F From Portsmouth Harbour

Table T188-R

Sundays

15 December to 10 May

Southampton Central - Worthing - Brighton and Gatwick Airport - London

		SN		SN 1	SN	SN 1	SN	SN 1	SN A	SN 1	SN	SN 1		SN	SN 1	SN	SN 1	SN A	SN 1	SN	SN 1 B	GW ◇ C		SN 1 D	SN
Southampton Central	d			15 30				16 30				17 30					18 30				19 23	19 28			
Fareham	d			15 54				16 54				17 54					18 54				19 49	19 54			
Havant	a			16 10				17 10				18 10					19 10				20 03	20 10			
Portsmouth Harbour	d	15 14			16 14									18 14											20 14
Portsmouth & Southsea	d	15 18			16 18									18 18											20 18
Havant	a	15 33			16 33									18 33											20 33
Havant	d	15 33		16 10	16 33			17 10	17 33			18 10		18 33			19 10	19 33			20 04	20 11			20 33
Chichester 4	d	15 53		16 22	16 53			17 22	17 53			18 22		18 53			19 22	19 53			20 16	20 22			20 53
Barnham	a	16 01		16 30	17 01			17 30	18 01			18 30		19 01			19 30	20 01			20 23	20 29			21 01
Bognor Regis	d																								
Barnham	a																								
Barnham	d	16 14		16 31	17 02			17 31	18 02			18 31		19 02			19 31	20 02			20 24	20 30			21 02
Littlehampton 4	d					17 14				18 14					19 14				20 14						21 15
Angmering 3	d	16 27		16 43	17 14	17 23		17 43	18 14	18 23		18 43		19 14	19 23		19 43	20 14	20 23		20 36				21 25
Goring-by-Sea	d	16 31		16 47	17 18	17 27		17 47	18 18	18 27		18 47		19 18	19 27		19 47	20 18	20 27		20 40				21 29
Durrington-on-Sea	d	16 33		16 49	17 20	17 29		17 49	18 20	18 29		18 49		19 20	19 29		19 49	20 20	20 29		20 42				21 32
West Worthing	d	16 36		16 52	17 23	17 32		17 52	18 23	18 32		18 52		19 23	19 32		19 52	20 23	20 32		20 45			←	21 34
Worthing 4	a	16 38		16 54	17 25	17 34		17 54	18 25	18 34		18 54		19 25	19 34		19 54	20 25	20 34		20 47	20 50		20 47	21 37
	d	16 39		16 55	17 26	17 35		17 55	18 26	18 35		18 55		19 26	19 35		19 55	20 26	20 35		20 56	20 51		20 56	21 37
East Worthing	d	16 41		16 57	17 28			17 57	18 28			18 57		19 28			19 57	20 28			→			20 59	21 40
Lancing	d	16 44		17 00	17 31	17 39		18 00	18 31	18 39		19 00		19 31	19 39		20 00	20 31	20 39					21 02	21 43
Shoreham-by-Sea	d	16 48		17 05	17 36	17 43		18 05	18 36	18 43		19 05		19 36	19 43		20 05	20 36	20 43			20 57		21 06	21 47
Southwick	d	16 51		17 08	17 39			18 08	18 39			19 08		19 39			20 08	20 39						21 09	21 50
Fishersgate	d	16 53		17 10	17 41			18 10	18 41			19 10		19 41			20 10	20 41						21 11	21 52
Portslade	d	16 55		17 12	17 43	17 48		18 12	18 43	18 48		19 12		19 43	19 48		20 12	20 43	20 48					21 13	21 54
Aldrington	d	16 58		17 14	17 45			18 14	18 45			19 14		19 45			20 14	20 45						21 16	21 57
Hove 2	a	17 00		17 16	17 47	17 51		18 16	18 47	18 51		19 16		19 47	19 51		20 16	20 47	20 51			21 05		21 18	21 59
	d	17 00		17 18	17 48	17 52	17 59	18 18	18 48	18 52	18 59	19 18		19 48	19 52	19 59	20 18	20 48	20 52	20 59		21 06		21 18	22 00
Brighton 10	a	17 04		17 22	17 52		18 03	18 22	18 52		19 03	19 22		19 52		20 03	20 22	20 52		21 03		21 10		21 22	22 04
Preston Park	a					17 57				18 57					19 57				20 57						
Haywards Heath 5	a					18 08				19 08					20 08				21 08						
Gatwick Airport 10	a					18 24				19 24					20 24				21 24						
East Croydon	a					18 40				19 40					20 40				21 40						
East Croydon	d																								
London Bridge	a																								
London Blackfriars	a																								
City Thameslink	a																								
Farringdon	a																								
St Pancras International	a																								
East Croydon	d					18 41				19 41					20 41				21 41						
Clapham Junction 10	a					18 50				19 50					20 50				21 50						
London Victoria 15	a					18 58				19 58					20 58				21 58						

		SN 1	SN	SN 1	SN
Southampton Central	d	20 28		21 30	
Fareham	d	20 53		21 54	
Havant	a	21 10		22 10	
Portsmouth Harbour	d		21 14		22 01
Portsmouth & Southsea	d		21 18		22 05
Havant	a		21 33		22 17
Havant	d	21 10	21 33	22 10	22 17
Chichester 4	d	21 22	21 53	22 22	22 32
Barnham	a	21 30	22 01	22 30	22 39
Bognor Regis	d				
Barnham	a				
Barnham	d	21 31	22 02	22 31	22 40
Littlehampton 4	d	21 45			22 55
Angmering 3	d	21 55	22 14	22 43	23 05
Goring-by-Sea	d	21 59	22 18	22 47	23 09
Durrington-on-Sea	d	22 02	22 20	22 49	23 11
West Worthing	d	22 04	22 23	22 52	23 14
Worthing 4	a	22 07	22 25	22 54	23 16
	d	22 07	22 26	22 55	23 17
East Worthing	d	22 10	22 28	22 57	23 19
Lancing	d	22 13	22 31	23 00	23 22
Shoreham-by-Sea	d	22 17	22 36	23 05	23 27
Southwick	d	22 20	22 39	23 08	23 30
Fishersgate	d	22 22	22 41	23 10	23 32
Portslade	d	22 24	22 43	23 12	23 34
Aldrington	d	22 27	22 45	23 14	23 36
Hove 2	a	22 29	22 47	23 16	23 38
	d	22 30	22 48	23 18	23 39
Brighton 10	a	22 34	22 52	23 22	23 43
Preston Park	a				
Haywards Heath 5	a				
Gatwick Airport 10	a				
East Croydon	a				
East Croydon	d				
London Bridge	a				
London Blackfriars	a				
City Thameslink	a				
Farringdon	a				
St Pancras International	a				
East Croydon	d				
Clapham Junction 10	a				
London Victoria 15	a				

A From Fratton
B To Brighton
C From Cardiff Central
D From Southampton Central

Table T189-F

Mondays to Fridays

16 December to 15 May

Brighton - Falmer - Lewes - Newhaven - Seaford with London connections

Miles			TL MO 1	SN MX 1	SN MX	SN 1	SN	SN 1	SN	SN	SN 1		SN	SN 1	SN	SN 1	SN	SN	SN 1	SN	SN 1		SN	SN 1	SN
0	Brighton	d				05 00	05 21	05 31	05 41	05 47	05 58		06 07		06 21	06 31	06 41	06 51	07 01	07 11			07 21	07 31	07 41
0¾	London Road (Brighton)	d					05 24		05 44	05 50			06 10		06 24		06 44	06 54		07 14			07 24		07 44
1¾	Moulsecoomb	d					05 27		05 47	05 53			06 13		06 27		06 47	06 57		07 17			07 27	07 35	07 47
3½	Falmer	d					05 31	05 38	05 51	05 57	06 05		06 17		06 31	06 38	06 51	07 01	07 08	07 21			07 31	07 40	07 51
8	Lewes 4	a				05 12	05 38	05 45	05 58	06 04	06 12		06 24		06 38	06 45	06 58	07 08	07 15	07 28			07 38	07 47	07 58
—	London Victoria	d		00 02										05 32							06 46				
—	Clapham Junction	d		00 09										05 42							06 53				
—	East Croydon	a		00 23										05 51							07 02				
—	London Bridge	d																							
—	East Croydon	a																							
—	East Croydon	d	00 01	00 24										05 52							07 03				
—	Gatwick Airport	a	00 29	00 43										06 17							07 17				
—	Haywards Heath	a		00 58										06 32							07 33				
—	Lewes	a		01 23										06 53							07 54				
—	Lewes	d							06 01				06 25				06 59			07 29					07 59
11½	Southease	d			00 06																				
14¼	Newhaven Town	d			00 11				06 12				06 35				07 09			07 39					08 09
14½	Newhaven Harbour	d			00 12				06 13				06 36				07 10			07 40					08 10
16	Bishopstone	d			00 15				06 16				06 39				07 13			07 43					08 13
17	Seaford	a			00 19				06 20				06 43				07 17			07 47					08 17

		SN 1	SN	SN 1	SN	SN 1	SN		SN 1	SN	SN 1	SN	SN 1	SN	SN 1	SN	SN 1		SN	SN 1	SN	SN 1	SN	SN 1	SN
Brighton	d		07 51	08 01	08 11		08 21		08 31	08 41		08 51	09 01	09 11		09 21	09 31		09 41		09 51	10 01	10 11		10 21
London Road (Brighton)	d		07 54		08 14		08 24			08 44		08 54		09 14		09 24			09 44		09 54		10 14		10 24
Moulsecoomb	d		07 57		08 17		08 27		08 35	08 47		08 57		09 17		09 27	09 35		09 47		09 57		10 17		10 27
Falmer	d		08 01	08 08	08 21		08 31		08 40	08 51		09 01	09 08	09 21		09 31	09 40		09 51		10 01	10 08	10 21		10 31
Lewes 4	a		08 08	08 15	08 28		08 38		08 47	08 59		09 08	09 15	09 28		09 38	09 47		09 58		10 08	10 15	10 28		10 38
London Victoria	d	07 16				07 46					08 16				08 46					09 16				09 46	
Clapham Junction	d	07 23				07 53					08 23				08 53					09 23				09 53	
East Croydon	a	07 32				08 03					08 33				09 02					09 32				10 02	
London Bridge	d																								
East Croydon	a																								
East Croydon	d	07 33				08 03					08 33				09 03					09 33				10 03	
Gatwick Airport	a	07 47				08 18					08 48				09 17					09 47				10 17	
Haywards Heath	a	08 01				08 31					09 02				09 31					10 01				10 31	
Lewes	a	08 22				08 53					09 22				09 53					10 25				10 53	
Lewes	d				08 29					08 59				09 29					09 59				10 29		
Southease	d									09 07									10 06						
Newhaven Town	d				08 39					09 11				09 39					10 11				10 39		
Newhaven Harbour	d				08 40					09 12				09 40					10 12				10 40		
Bishopstone	d				08 43					09 15				09 43					10 15				10 43		
Seaford	a				08 47					09 19				09 47					10 19				10 47		

		SN 1	SN		SN 1	TL 1	SN	SN 1	SN	SN 1	SN	SN 1	SN	SN 1		SN	SN 1	SN	SN 1	SN	SN 1	SN	SN 1
Brighton	d	10 31	10 41				10 51	11 01	11 11		11 21	11 31	11 41			13 51	14 01	14 11		14 21	14 31	14 41	
London Road (Brighton)	d		10 44				10 54		11 14		11 24		11 44			13 54		14 14		14 24		14 44	
Moulsecoomb	d	10 35	10 47				10 57		11 17		11 27	11 35	11 47			13 57		14 17		14 27	14 35	14 47	
Falmer	d	10 40	10 51				11 01	11 08	11 21		11 31	11 40	11 51			14 01	14 08	14 21		14 31	14 40	14 51	
Lewes 4	a	10 47	10 58				11 08	11 15	11 28		11 38	11 47	11 58			14 08	14 15	14 28		14 38	14 47	14 58	
London Victoria	d				10 16					10 46				11 16	and at				13 46				14 16
Clapham Junction	d				10 23					10 53				11 23	the same				13 53				14 23
East Croydon	a				10 32					11 02				11 32	minutes				14 02				14 32
London Bridge	d					10 22									past								
East Croydon	a					10 38									each								
East Croydon	d				10 33	10 38				11 03				11 33	hour until				14 03				14 33
Gatwick Airport	a				10 47	10 53				11 17				11 47					14 17				14 47
Haywards Heath	a				11 01					11 31				12 01					14 31				15 01
Lewes	a				11 25					11 53				12 25					14 53				15 25
Lewes	d		10 59						11 29				11 59					14 29				14 59	
Southease	d		11 06										12 06									15 06	
Newhaven Town	d		11 11						11 39				12 11					14 39				15 11	
Newhaven Harbour	d		11 12						11 40				12 12					14 40				15 12	
Bishopstone	d		11 15						11 43				12 15					14 43				15 15	
Seaford	a		11 19						11 47				12 19					14 47				15 19	

		SN	SN 1	SN	SN 1	SN	SN 1	SN	SN 1	SN		SN 1	SN	SN 1	SN	SN 1	SN	SN 1	SN	SN 1		SN	SN 1	SN	SN 1
Brighton	d	14 51	15 01	15 11		15 21	15 31	15 41		15 51		16 01	16 11		16 21	16 31	16 41		16 51	17 01		17 11		17 21	17 31
London Road (Brighton)	d	14 54		15 14		15 24		15 44		15 54			16 14		16 24		16 44		16 54			17 14		17 24	
Moulsecoomb	d	14 57		15 17		15 27	15 35	15 47		15 57		16 05	16 17		16 27	16 35	16 47		16 57	17 05		17 17		17 27	17 35
Falmer	d	15 01	15 08	15 21		15 31	15 40	15 51		16 01		16 10	16 21		16 31	16 40	16 51		17 01	17 10		17 21		17 31	17 40
Lewes 4	a	15 08	15 15	15 28		15 38	15 47	15 58		16 08		16 17	16 29		16 38	16 47	16 58		17 08	17 17		17 28		17 38	17 47
London Victoria	d				14 46				15 16					15 46				16 16					16 45		
Clapham Junction	d				14 53				15 23					15 53				16 23					16 52		
East Croydon	a				15 02				15 32					16 02				16 32					17 01		
London Bridge	d																								
East Croydon	a																								
East Croydon	d				15 03				15 33					16 03				16 33					17 02		
Gatwick Airport	a				15 17				15 47					16 17				16 47					17 19		
Haywards Heath	a				15 31				16 02					16 31				17 01					17 32		
Lewes	a				15 53				16 26					16 53				17 25					17 52		
Lewes	d			15 29				15 59					16 30				16 59					17 29			
Southease	d							16 06					16 37				17 06					17 36			
Newhaven Town	d			15 39				16 11					16 42				17 11					17 41			
Newhaven Harbour	d			15 40				16 12					16 43				17 12					17 42			
Bishopstone	d			15 43				16 15					16 46				17 15					17 45			
Seaford	a			15 47				16 19					16 50				17 19					17 49			

Table T189-F

Brighton - Falmer - Lewes - Newhaven - Seaford with London connections

Mondays to Fridays
16 December to 15 May

		SN	SN ■	SN	SN ■	SN	SN ■	SN	SN ■	SN ■ A	SN	SN ■	SN	SN ■	SN	SN ■	SN ■	SN	SN ■	SN	SN ■	SN	SN ■
Brighton	d	17 41		17 51	18 01	18 11		18 21	18 31		18 38		18 51	19 01	19 11			19 21	19 32	19 41		19 51	20 01
London Road (Brighton)	d	17 44		17 54		18 14		18 24			18 41		18 54		19 14			19 24		19 44		19 54	
Moulsecoomb	d	17 47		17 57	18 05	18 17		18 27	18 35		18 44		18 57		19 17			19 27	19 36	19 47		19 57	
Falmer	d	17 51		18 01	18 10	18 21		18 31	18 40		18 48		19 01	19 08	19 21			19 31	19 41	19 51		20 01	20 08
Lewes ■	a	17 58		18 08	18 17	18 28		18 38	18 47		18 55		19 08	19 15	19 28			19 39	19 48	19 58		20 08	20 15
London Victoria	d		17 15							17 45		18 15					18 45				19 16		
Clapham Junction	d		17 22							17 52		18 22					18 52				19 23		
East Croydon	a		17 31							18 01		18 31					19 01				19 32		
London Bridge	d						17 32									18 32							
East Croydon	a						17 46									18 46							
East Croydon	d		17 32				17 47			18 02		18 32				18 47	19 02				19 33		
Gatwick Airport	a		17 49				18 02			18 19		18 49				19 02	19 19				19 47		
Haywards Heath	a		18 02				18 15			18 32		19 02				19 15	19 32				20 01		
Lewes	a		18 22				18 38			18 52		19 22				19 38	19 52				20 25		
Lewes	d	17 59				18 29				18 59	19 05				19 29					19 59			
Southease	d	18 06				18 37					19 12									20 06			
Newhaven Town ⛴	d	18 11				18 42				19 09	19 17				19 39					20 11			
Newhaven Harbour	d	18 12				18 43				19 10	19a18				19 40					20 12			
Bishopstone	d	18 15				18 46				19 13					19 43					20 15			
Seaford	a	18 19				18 50				19 17					19 47					20 19			

		SN	SN ■	SN	SN ■	SN	SN ■	TL ■	SN	SN ■	SN	SN ■	TL ■	SN	SN ■	SN	SN ■	TL ■	SN	SN ■	SN	SN ■
Brighton	d	20 11		20 21	20 31	20 41			20 51	21 01	21 11			21 21	21 31	21 41			21 51	22 01	22 11	
London Road (Brighton)	d	20 14		20 24		20 44			20 54		21 14			21 24		21 44			21 54		22 14	
Moulsecoomb	d	20 17		20 27	20 35	20 47			20 57		21 17			21 27	21 35	21 47			21 57		22 17	
Falmer	d	20 21		20 31	20 40	20 51			21 01	21 08	21 21			21 31	21 40	21 51			22 01	22 08	22 21	
Lewes ■	a	20 28		20 38	20 47	20 58			21 08	21 15	21 28			21 38	21 47	21 58			22 08	22 15	22 28	
London Victoria	d		19 46				20 16					20 46					21 16					21 46
Clapham Junction	d		19 53				20 23					20 53					21 23					21 53
East Croydon	a		20 02				20 32					21 02					21 32					22 02
London Bridge	d							20 22					20 52					21 22				
East Croydon	a							20 38					21 08					21 38				
East Croydon	d		20 03				20 33	20 38				21 03	21 08				21 33	21 38				22 03
Gatwick Airport	a		20 17				20 47	20 53				21 17	21 23				21 47	21 53				22 17
Haywards Heath	a		20 31				21 01					21 31					22 01					22 31
Lewes	a		20 53				21 25					21 53					22 25					22 53
Lewes	d	20 29				20 59					21 29					21 59					22 29	
Southease	d					21 06										22 06						
Newhaven Town ⛴	d	20 39				21 11					21 39					22 11					22 39	
Newhaven Harbour	d	20 40				21 12					21 40					22 12					22 40	
Bishopstone	d	20 43				21 15					21 43					22 15					22 43	
Seaford	a	20 47				21 19					21 47					22 19					22 47	

		SN	SN ■	SN	SN ■	SN	SN ■	SN	SN ■	SN	SN ■	SN
Brighton	d	22 21	22 32	22 41		22 51	23 02	23 11		23 21	23 32	23 41
London Road (Brighton)	d	22 24		22 44		22 54		23 14		23 24		23 44
Moulsecoomb	d	22 27		22 47		22 57		23 17		23 27		23 47
Falmer	d	22 31	22 39	22 51		23 01	23 09	23 21		23 31	23 39	23 51
Lewes ■	a	22 38	22 46	22 58		23 08	23 16	23 28		23 38	23 46	23 58
London Victoria	d				22 16				22 46			
Clapham Junction	d				22 23				22 53			
East Croydon	a				22 32				23 02			
London Bridge	d											
East Croydon	a											
East Croydon	d				22 33				23 03			
Gatwick Airport	a				22 47				23 17			
Haywards Heath	a				23 01				23 31			
Lewes	a				23 25				23 55			
Lewes	d			22 59				23 29				23 59
Southease	d			23 06								00 06
Newhaven Town ⛴	d			23 11				23 40				00 11
Newhaven Harbour	d			23 12				23 41				00 12
Bishopstone	d			23 15				23 44				00 15
Seaford	a			23 19				23 48				00 19

Saturdays
21 December to 16 May

		SN ■ B	SN	SN ■	SN	SN	SN	SN ■	SN	SN	SN ■	SN	SN	SN ■	SN	SN	SN ■	SN	SN ■	SN	SN ■	SN
Brighton	d			05 10	05 41	06 11	06 21	06 31	06 41	06 51	07 01	07 11	07 21	07 31	07 41	07 51	08 01	08 11		08 21	08 31	08 41
London Road (Brighton)	d				05 44	06 14	06 24		06 44	06 54		07 14	07 24		07 44	07 54		08 14		08 24		08 44
Moulsecoomb	d				05 47	06 17	06 27	06 35	06 47	06 57		07 17	07 27	07 35	07 47	07 57		08 17		08 27	08 35	08 47
Falmer	d				05 51	06 21	06 31	06 40	06 51	07 01	07 08	07 21	07 31	07 40	07 51	08 01	08 08	08 21		08 31	08 40	08 51
Lewes ■	a			05 22	05 58	06 28	06 38	06 47	06 58	07 08	07 15	07 28	07 38	07 47	07 58	08 08	08 15	08 28		08 38	08 47	08 58
London Victoria	d	00 02																	07 46			
Clapham Junction	d	00 09																	07 53			
East Croydon	a	00 23																	08 02			
London Bridge	d																					
East Croydon	a																					
East Croydon	d	00 24																	08 03			
Gatwick Airport	a	00 43																	08 18			
Haywards Heath	a	00 58																	08 31			
Lewes	a	01 23																	08 53			
Lewes	d				05 59	06 29			06 59			07 29			07 59			08 29				08 59
Southease	d		00 06						07 06						08 06							09 06
Newhaven Town ⛴	d		00 11		06 09	06 39			07 11			07 39			08 11			08 39				09 11
Newhaven Harbour	d		00 12		06 10	06 40			07 12			07 40			08 12			08 40				09 12
Bishopstone	d		00 15		06 13	06 43			07 15			07 43			08 15			08 43				09 15
Seaford	a		00 19		06 17	06 47			07 19			07 47			08 19			08 47				09 19

A ■ to Lewes   B not 16 May

Table T189-F

Brighton - Falmer - Lewes - Newhaven - Seaford with London connections

Saturdays
21 December to 16 May

		SN ■		SN	SN ■	SN	SN ■	SN	SN ■	SN	SN ■	SN	SN ■	SN	SN ■	SN	SN ■	SN	SN ■	SN	SN ■	SN
Brighton	d			18 51	19 01	19 11		19 21	19 31	19 41		19 51	20 01	20 11		20 21	20 31	20 41		20 51	21 01	21 11
London Road (Brighton)	d			18 54		19 14		19 24		19 44		19 54		20 14		20 24		20 44		20 54		21 14
Moulsecoomb	d			18 57		19 17		19 27	19 35	19 47		19 57		20 17		20 27	20 35	20 47		20 57		21 17
Falmer	d			19 01	19 08	19 21		19 31	19 40	19 51		20 01	20 08	20 21		20 31	20 40	20 51		21 01	21 08	21 21
Lewes ■	a			19 08	19 15	19 28		19 38	19 47	19 58		20 08	20 15	20 29		20 38	20 47	20 58		21 08	21 15	21 28
London Victoria	d	08 16	and at				18 46				19 16				19 46				20 16			
Clapham Junction	d	08 23	the same				18 53				19 23				19 53				20 23			
East Croydon	a	08 32	minutes				19 02				19 32				20 02				20 32			
London Bridge	d		past																			
East Croydon	a		each																			
East Croydon	d	08 33	hour until				19 03				19 33				20 03				20 33			
Gatwick Airport	a	08 47					19 18				19 47				20 18				20 47			
Haywards Heath	a	09 01					19 31				20 01				20 31				21 01			
Lewes	a	09 25					19 53				20 25				20 53				21 25			
Lewes	d					19 29				19 59				20 29				20 59				21 29
Southease	d									20 06								21 06				
Newhaven Town ⛴	d					19 39				20 11				20 39				21 11				21 39
Newhaven Harbour	d					19 40				20 12				20 40				21 12				21 40
Bishopstone	d					19 43				20 15				20 43				21 15				21 43
Seaford	a					19 47				20 19				20 47				21 19				21 47

		SN ■	SN	SN ■	SN	SN ■	SN	SN ■	SN	SN ■	SN	SN ■	SN	SN ■	SN	SN ■	SN	SN ■	SN	SN ■	SN	SN ■ A
Brighton	d		21 21	21 31	21 41		21 51	22 01	22 11		22 21	22 32	22 41		22 51	23 02	23 11		23 21	23 32	23 41	
London Road (Brighton)	d		21 24		21 44		21 54		22 14		22 24		22 44		22 54		23 14		23 24		23 44	
Moulsecoomb	d		21 27	21 35	21 47		21 57		22 17		22 27		22 47		22 57		23 17		23 27		23 47	
Falmer	d		21 31	21 40	21 51		22 01	22 08	22 21		22 31	22 39	22 51		23 01	23 09	23 21		23 31	23 39	23 51	
Lewes ■	a		21 38	21 47	21 58		22 08	22 15	22 28		22 38	22 46	22 58		23 08	23 16	23 28		23 38	23 46	23 58	
London Victoria	d	20 46				21 16				21 46				22 16				22 46				23 16
Clapham Junction	d	20 53				21 23				21 53				22 23				22 53				23 23
East Croydon	a	21 02				21 32				22 02				22 32				23 02				23 32
London Bridge	d																					
East Croydon	a																					
East Croydon	d	21 03				21 33				22 03				22 33				23 03				23 33
Gatwick Airport	a	21 18				21 47				22 18				22 47				23 18				23 52
Haywards Heath	a	21 31				22 01				22 31				23 01				23 31				00 05
Lewes	a	21 53				22 25				22 53				23 25				23 55				00 27
Lewes	d				21 59				22 29				22 59				23 30				23 59	
Southease	d				22 06								23 06								00 06	
Newhaven Town ⛴	d				22 11				22 39				23 11				23 39				00 11	
Newhaven Harbour	d				22 12				22 40				23 12				23 41				00 12	
Bishopstone	d				22 15				22 43				23 15				23 44				00 15	
Seaford	a				22 19				22 47				23 19				23 48				00 19	

Sundays
15 December to 10 May

		SN ■	SN B	SN	SN ■	TL ■	SN	TL ■	SN ■	TL ■	SN	SN ■	TL ■	SN	TL ■	SN ■	TL ■	SN	SN ■	SN	SN ■	TL ■	TL ■
Brighton	d			06 55	07 05		07 15		07 35		07 47	08 05		08 17		08 35		08 47	09 05	09 17			
London Road (Brighton)	d			06 58			07 18		07 38		07 50			08 20		08 38		08 50		09 20			
Moulsecoomb	d			07 01			07 21		07 41		07 53			08 23		08 41		08 53		09 23			
Falmer	d			07 05	07 12		07 25		07 45		07 57	08 12		08 27		08 45		08 57	09 12	09 27			
Lewes ■	a			07 12	07 19		07 32		07 52		08 04	08 19		08 34		08 52		09 04	09 19	09 34			
London Victoria	d	00 02																			08 46		
Clapham Junction	d	00 09																			08 53		
East Croydon	a	00 23																			09 02		
London Bridge	d					07 11		07 19		07 41			08 11		08 19		08 41					09 11	09 19
East Croydon	a					07 24		07 35		07 54			08 24		08 35		08 54					09 24	09 37
East Croydon	d	00 24				07 25		07 35		07 55			08 25		08 37		08 55				09 03	09 25	09 37
Gatwick Airport	a	00 43				07 43		08 06		08 14			08 43		09 07		09 09				09 18	09 39	10 02
Haywards Heath	a	00 58				08 00				08 31			09 00				09 26				09 30	09 54	
Lewes	a	01s23																			09 49		
Lewes	d						07 33				08 05			08 35				09 05		09 35			
Southease	d		00 06								08 12							09 12					
Newhaven Town ⛴	d		00 11				07 42				08 16			08 44				09 16		09 44			
Newhaven Harbour	d		00 12				07 44				08 17			08 45				09 17		09 45			
Bishopstone	d		00 15				07 47				08 20			08 48				09 20		09 48			
Seaford	a		00 19				07 51				08 24			08 52				09 24		09 52			

A not 16 May. ■ to Haywards Heath   B not 15 December

Table T189-F

Sundays

15 December to 10 May

Brighton - Falmer - Lewes - Newhaven - Seaford with London connections

		TL 1	SN	SN 1	SN	SN 1	TL 1		SN	SN 1	SN	SN 1	TL 1	SN	SN 1	SN	SN 1	TL 1	SN	SN 1	SN 1	SN
Brighton	d		09 47	10 05	10 17			and at the same minutes past each hour until	20 47	21 05	21 17			21 47	22 10	22 17			22 47		23 20	23 35
London Road (Brighton)	d		09 50		10 20				20 50		21 20			21 50		22 20			22 50			23 38
Moulsecoomb	d		09 53		10 23				20 53		21 23			21 53		22 23			22 53			23 41
Falmer	d		09 57	10 12	10 27				20 57	21 12	21 27			21 57	22 17	22 27			22 57		23 27	23 45
Lewes 4	a		10 04	10 19	10 34				21 04	21 19	21 34			22 04	22 24	22 34			23 04		23 34	23 53
London Victoria	d					09 46						20 46					21 46			22 46		
Clapham Junction	d					09 53						20 53					21 53			22 53		
East Croydon	a					10 02						21 02					22 02			23 02		
London Bridge	d	09 27					10 21						21 21					22 21				
East Croydon	a	09 41					10 37						21 37					22 37				
East Croydon	d	09 41				10 03	10 37					21 03	21 37				22 03	22 37		23 03		
Gatwick Airport	a	10 09				10 18	11 02					21 18	22 02				22 18	23 02		23 18		
Haywards Heath	a					10 30						21 30					22 30			23 30		
Lewes	a					10 49						21 49					22 49			23 49		
Lewes	d		10 05		10 35				21 05		21 35			22 05		22 35			23 05			
Southease	d		10 12						21 12					22 12					23 12			
Newhaven Town	d		10 16		10 44				21 16		21 44			22 16		22 44			23 16			
Newhaven Harbour	d		10 17		10 45				21 17		21 45			22 18		22 45			23 17			
Bishopstone	d		10 20		10 48				21 20		21 48			22 21		22 48			23 20			
Seaford	a		10 24		10 52				21 24		21 52			22 25		22 52			23 24			

		TL 1
Brighton	d	
London Road (Brighton)	d	
Moulsecoomb	d	
Falmer	d	
Lewes 4	a	
London Victoria	d	
Clapham Junction	d	
East Croydon	a	
London Bridge	d	23 45
East Croydon	a	23 59
East Croydon	d	00 01
Gatwick Airport	a	00 29
Haywards Heath	a	
Lewes	a	
Lewes	d	
Southease	d	
Newhaven Town	d	
Newhaven Harbour	d	
Bishopstone	d	
Seaford	a	

Table T189-R

Mondays to Fridays

16 December to 15 May

Seaford with London connections - Newhaven - Lewes - Falmer - Brighton

Miles			SN MX	SN MX	SN MX 1	SN	SN 1	SN		SN 1	SN	SN 1	SN 1	SN	SN 1	SN	SN	SN 1		SN	SN 1	SN 1	SN 1	SN	SN 1
0	**Seaford**	d				04 50		05 25						05 55			06 25						06 50		
1	**Bishopstone**	d				04 52		05 27						05 57			06 27						06 52		
2½	**Newhaven Harbour**	d				04 56		05 31						06 01			06 31						06 56	07 03	
2¾	**Newhaven Town**	d		00 02		04 58		05 33						06 03			06 33						06 57	07 05	
5½	**Southease**	d		00 06																				07 09	
9	**Lewes**	a		00 12		05 07		05 42						06 12			06 42						07 07	07 15	
—	Lewes	d					05 11			05 46		06 00			06 16			06 46				07 02	07 16		07 16
—	Haywards Heath	a					05 31			06 07		06 24			06 37			07 06				07 26	07 36		07 36
—	Gatwick Airport	a					05 53			06 31		06 39			07 02			07 19				07 40	07 49		07 49
—	East Croydon	a					06 08			06 48		06 56			07 18			07 37				07 57	08 07		08 07
—	East Croydon	d										06 57										07 57			
—	London Bridge	a										07 13										08 13			
—	East Croydon	d					06 09			06 49					07 19			07 38					08 08		08 08
—	Clapham Junction	d					06 20			06 59					07 29			07 48					08 18		08 18
—	London Victoria	a					06 27			07 05					07 35			07 54					08 24		08 24
—	**Lewes 4**	d		00 13	00 27	05 15		05 42			05 53		06 07	06 13		06 23	06 42			06 53	07 00			07 16	
13½	**Falmer**	d	00 01	00 20	00 35	05 22		05 50			06 00		06 14	06 20		06 30	06 50			07 00	07 07			07 23	
15¼	**Moulsecoomb**	d	00 05	00 24	00 39	05 26		05 54			06 04		06 18	06 24		06 34	06 54			07 04	07 12			07 27	
16¼	**London Road (Brighton)**	d	00 07	00 27	00 41	05 29		05 56			06 07		06 21	06 27		06 37	06 56			07 07				07 30	
17	**Brighton**	a	00 12	00 30	00 45	05 33		06 00			06 10		06 24	06 30		06 40	07 00			07 10	07 17			07 33	

		SN	SN 1	SN		SN 1	SN	SN 1	SN	SN 1	SN	SN 1	SN	SN 1		SN	SN 1	SN	SN 1	SN	SN 1	SN	SN 1	SN	
Seaford	d			07 23					07 53				08 23					08 53				09 25			
Bishopstone	d			07 25					07 55				08 25					08 55				09 27			
Newhaven Harbour	d			07 29					07 59				08 29					08 59				09 31			
Newhaven Town	d			07 31					08 01				08 31					09 01				09 33			
Southease	d			07 35									08 35					09 05							
Lewes	a			07 41					08 10				08 41					09 11				09 41			
Lewes	d					07 46				08 14				08 46					09 21				09 45		
Haywards Heath	a					08 06				08 38				09 07					09 40				10 06		
Gatwick Airport	a					08 19				08 50				09 27					09 56				10 26		
East Croydon	a					08 37				09 09				09 42					10 11				10 41		
East Croydon	d																								
London Bridge	a																								
East Croydon	d					08 38				09 09				09 43					10 12				10 42		
Clapham Junction	d					08 48				09 19				09 53					10 22				10 52		
London Victoria	a					08 54				09 26				09 59					10 29				10 59		
Lewes 4	d	07 23	07 33	07 43			07 53	08 03	08 13		08 23	08 33	08 43			08 53	09 03	09 13		09 23	09 33	09 43		09 53	
Falmer	d	07 30	07 40	07 50			08 00	08 11	08 20		08 30	08 40	08 50			09 00	09 11	09 20		09 30	09 41	09 50		10 00	
Moulsecoomb	d	07 34	07 44	07 54			08 04	08 15	08 24		08 34	08 44	08 54			09 04	09 15	09 24		09 34	09 45	09 54		10 04	
London Road (Brighton)	d	07 37		07 57			08 07		08 27		08 37		08 57			09 07		09 27		09 37		09 57		10 07	
Brighton	a	07 40	07 49	08 00			08 10	08 20	08 30		08 40	08 49	09 00			09 10	09 20	09 30		09 40	09 49	10 00		10 10	

		SN 1	SN	SN 1	SN	SN 1	SN	SN 1	SN	SN 1		SN	SN 1	SN	SN 1	SN	SN 1	SN	SN 1	SN		SN 1	SN	SN 1	SN
Seaford	d		09 53				10 25					10 53				11 25				11 53					12 25
Bishopstone	d		09 55				10 27					10 55				11 27				11 55					12 27
Newhaven Harbour	d		09 59				10 31					10 59				11 31				11 59					12 31
Newhaven Town	d		10 01				10 33					11 01				11 33				12 01					12 33
Southease	d		10 05									11 05								12 05					
Lewes	a		10 11				10 41					11 11				11 41				12 11					12 41
Lewes	d			10 21				10 45					11 21				11 45					12 21			
Haywards Heath	a			10 40				11 06					11 40				12 06					12 40			
Gatwick Airport	a			10 56				11 26					11 56				12 26					12 56			
East Croydon	a			11 11				11 41					12 11				12 41					13 11			
East Croydon	d																								
London Bridge	a																								
East Croydon	d			11 12				11 42					12 12				12 42					13 12			
Clapham Junction	d			11 22				11 52					12 23				12 53					13 22			
London Victoria	a			11 29				11 59					12 29				12 59					13 29			
Lewes 4	d	10 03	10 13		10 23	10 33	10 43		10 53	11 03		11 13		11 23	11 33	11 43		11 53	12 03	12 13			12 23	12 33	12 43
Falmer	d	10 11	10 20		10 30	10 41	10 50		11 00	11 10		11 20		11 30	11 41	11 50		12 00	12 10	12 20			12 30	12 41	12 50
Moulsecoomb	d	10 15	10 24		10 34		10 54		11 04	11 14		11 24		11 34		11 54		12 04	12 14	12 24			12 34		12 54
London Road (Brighton)	d		10 27		10 37		10 57		11 07			11 27		11 37		11 57		12 07		12 27			12 37		12 57
Brighton	a	10 20	10 30		10 40	10 48	11 00		11 10	11 19		11 30		11 40	11 48	12 00		12 10	12 19	12 30			12 40	12 48	13 00

		SN 1	SN	SN 1	SN	SN 1		SN	SN 1	SN	SN 1	SN	SN 1	SN	SN 1	SN		SN 1	SN	SN 1	SN	SN 1	SN	SN 1	SN
Seaford	d				12 53					13 25				13 53					14 25				14 53		
Bishopstone	d				12 55					13 27				13 55					14 27				14 55		
Newhaven Harbour	d				12 59					13 31				13 59					14 31				14 59		
Newhaven Town	d				13 01					13 33				14 01					14 33				15 01		
Southease	d				13 05									14 05									15 05		
Lewes	a				13 11					13 41				14 11					14 41				15 11		
Lewes	d	12 45				13 21					13 45				14 21					14 45				15 21	
Haywards Heath	a	13 06				13 40					14 06				14 40					15 06				15 40	
Gatwick Airport	a	13 26				13 56					14 26				14 56					15 26				15 56	
East Croydon	a	13 41				14 11					14 41				15 11					15 41				16 11	
East Croydon	d																								
London Bridge	a																								
East Croydon	d	13 42				14 12					14 42				15 12					15 42				16 12	
Clapham Junction	d	13 52				14 22					14 52				15 22					15 52				16 22	
London Victoria	a	13 59				14 29					14 59				15 29					16 00				16 29	
Lewes 4	d		12 53	13 03	13 13			13 23	13 33	13 43		13 53	14 03	14 13		14 23		14 33	14 43		14 53	15 03	15 13		15 23
Falmer	d		13 00	13 10	13 20			13 30	13 41	13 50		14 00	14 10	14 20		14 30		14 41	14 50		15 00	15 10	15 20		15 30
Moulsecoomb	d		13 04	13 14	13 24			13 34		13 54		14 04	14 14	14 24		14 34			14 54		15 04	15 14	15 24		15 34
London Road (Brighton)	d		13 07		13 27			13 37		13 57		14 07		14 27		14 37			14 57		15 07		15 27		15 37
Brighton	a		13 10	13 19	13 30			13 40	13 48	14 00		14 10	14 19	14 30		14 40		14 48	15 00		15 10	15 19	15 30		15 40

Table T189-R

Mondays to Fridays

16 December to 15 May

Seaford with London connections - Newhaven - Lewes - Falmer - Brighton

		SN [1]		SN	SN [1]	SN	SN [1]	SN	SN [1]	SN	SN [1]	SN		SN [1]	SN	SN [1]	SN	SN [1]	SN	SN [1]	SN	SN [1]		SN	SN [1]
Seaford	d			15 25				15 53				16 25					16 55				17 25				
Bishopstone	d			15 27				15 55				16 27					16 57				17 27				
Newhaven Harbour	d			15 31				15 59				16 31					17 01				17 31				
Newhaven Town	d			15 33				16 01				16 33					17 03				17 33				
Southease	d							16 05									17 07								
Lewes	a			15 41				16 11				16 41					17 13				17 41				
Lewes	d				15 45				16 21					16 45				17 21				17 45			
Haywards Heath	a				16 06				16 40					17 07				17 40				18 07			
Gatwick Airport	a				16 26				16 56					17 26				17 56				18 26			
East Croydon	a				16 42				17 12					17 42				18 12				18 42			
East Croydon	d																								
London Bridge	a																								
East Croydon	d				16 42				17 12					17 42				18 12				18 42			
Clapham Junction	d				16 52				17 23					17 52				18 22				18 52			
London Victoria	a				16 59				17 30					17 59				18 29				18 59			
Lewes [4]	d	15 33		15 43		15 53	16 03	16 13		16 23	16 33	16 43			16 53	17 03	17 14		17 23	17 33	17 43			17 53	18 03
Falmer	d	15 41		15 50		16 00	16 10	16 20		16 30	16 41	16 50			17 00	17 10	17 21		17 30	17 41	17 50			18 00	18 10
Moulsecoomb	d			15 54		16 04	16 14	16 24		16 34		16 54			17 04	17 14	17 25		17 34		17 54			18 04	18 14
London Road (Brighton)	d			15 57		16 07		16 27		16 37		16 57			17 07		17 28		17 37		17 57			18 07	
Brighton	a	15 48		16 00		16 10	16 19	16 30		16 40	16 48	17 00			17 10	17 19	17 31		17 40	17 48	18 00			18 10	18 19

		SN	SN [1]	SN	SN [1]	SN	SN [1]	SN		SN [1]	SN	SN [1]	SN	SN [1]	SN	SN [1]	SN	SN [1]		SN	SN [1]	SN	SN [1]	SN	SN [1]
Seaford	d	17 55				18 25					18 55				19 25					19 53				20 25	
Bishopstone	d	17 57				18 27					18 57				19 27					19 55				20 27	
Newhaven Harbour	d	18 01				18 31					19 01				19 31					19 59				20 31	
Newhaven Town	d	18 03				18 33					19 03				19 33					20 01				20 33	
Southease	d	18 07									19 07									20 05					
Lewes	a	18 13				18 41					19 13				19 42					20 11				20 43	
Lewes	d		18 21				18 45					19 21				19 46					20 21				20 48
Haywards Heath	a		18 40				19 07					19 40				20 07					20 40				21 06
Gatwick Airport	a		18 56				19 26					19 56				20 27					20 56				21 26
East Croydon	a		19 11				19 42					20 11				20 42					21 11				21 41
East Croydon	d																								
London Bridge	a																								
East Croydon	d		19 12				19 42					20 12				20 43					21 12				21 42
Clapham Junction	d		19 22				19 52					20 22				20 52					21 22				21 52
London Victoria	a		19 29				19 59					20 30				20 59					21 29				21 59
Lewes [4]	d	18 14		18 23	18 34	18 43		18 53		19 03	19 14		19 23	19 36	19 43		19 53	20 03		20 13		20 23	20 39	20 46	
Falmer	d	18 21		18 30	18 42	18 50		19 00		19 10	19 21		19 30	19 43	19 50		20 01	20 10		20 20		20 30	20 46	20 53	
Moulsecoomb	d	18 25		18 35		18 54		19 04		19 14	19 25		19 34		19 54		20 05	20 14		20 24		20 34		20 57	
London Road (Brighton)	d	18 28		18 38		18 57		19 07			19 28		19 37		19 57		20 08			20 27		20 37		21 00	
Brighton	a	18 31		18 42	18 49	19 00		19 10		19 19	19 31		19 40	19 51	20 00		20 12	20 19		20 31		20 40	20 54	21 04	

		SN	SN [1]	SN		SN [1]	SN	SN [1]	SN	SN [1]	SN	SN [1]	SN	SN [1]		SN	SN [1]	SN	SN [1]	SN	SN [1]	SN	SN	SN [1]	
Seaford	d			20 53					21 25				21 53					22 25				22 53			
Bishopstone	d			20 55					21 27				21 55					22 27				22 55			
Newhaven Harbour	d			20 59					21 31				21 59					22 31				22 59			
Newhaven Town	d			21 01					21 33				22 01					22 33				23 01			
Southease	d			21 05									22 05									23 05			
Lewes	a			21 11					21 41				22 11					22 41				23 11			
Lewes	d					21 21				21 45				22 21					22 45						
Haywards Heath	a					21 40				22 08				22 40					23 06						
Gatwick Airport	a					21 56				22 26				22 56					23 26						
East Croydon	a					22 12				22 42				23 11					23 42						
East Croydon	d																								
London Bridge	a																								
East Croydon	d					22 12				22 43				23 12					23 42						
Clapham Junction	d					22 22				22 53				23 22					23 57						
London Victoria	a					22 29				23 00				23 30					00 05						
Lewes [4]	d	20 53	21 05	21 13			21 23	21 33	21 43		21 53	22 03	22 13			22 23	22 33	22 43		22 53	23 03	23 13	23 23	23 35	
Falmer	d	21 00	21 12	21 20			21 30	21 41	21 50		22 00	22 10	22 20			22 30	22 41	22 50		23 00	23 10	23 20	23 30	23 42	
Moulsecoomb	d	21 04	21 17	21 24			21 34		21 54		22 04	22 14	22 24			22 34		22 54		23 04	23 14	23 24	23 34		
London Road (Brighton)	d	21 07		21 27			21 37		21 57		22 07		22 27			22 37		22 57		23 07		23 27	23 37		
Brighton	a	21 10	21 24	21 30			21 40	21 48	22 00		22 10	22 19	22 30			22 40	22 48	23 00		23 10	23 19	23 30	23 40	23 50	

		SN [1]	SN	SN
Seaford	d	23 25		23 53
Bishopstone	d	23 27		23 55
Newhaven Harbour	d	23 31		23 59
Newhaven Town	d	23 33		00 02
Southease	d			00 06
Lewes	a	23 42		00 12
Lewes	d			
Haywards Heath	a			
Gatwick Airport	a			
East Croydon	a			
East Croydon	d			
London Bridge	a			
East Croydon	d			
Clapham Junction	d			
London Victoria	a			
Lewes [4]	d	23 43	23 53	00 13
Falmer	d	23 50	00 01	00 20
Moulsecoomb	d	23 54	00 05	00 24
London Road (Brighton)	d	23 57	00 07	00 27
Brighton	a	00 01	00 12	00 30

Table T189-R

Saturdays

21 December to 16 May

Seaford with London connections - Newhaven - Lewes - Falmer - Brighton

		SN	SN	SN [1]	SN	SN [1]	SN [1]	SN [1]	SN	SN [1]	SN	SN [1]	SN	SN [1]	SN	SN [1]		SN	SN [1]	SN	SN [1]	SN	SN [1]	SN
Seaford	d				05 04				06 25				06 53					10 25				10 53		
Bishopstone	d				05 06				06 27				06 55					10 27				10 55		
Newhaven Harbour	d				05 10				06 31				06 59					10 31				10 59		
Newhaven Town	d		00 02		05 11				06 33				07 01					10 33				11 01		
Southease	d		00 06										07 05									11 05		
Lewes	a		00 12		05 20				06 41				07 11					10 41				11 11		
Lewes	d					05 24		06 21		06 45				07 21			and at the same minutes past each hour until		10 45				11 21	
Haywards Heath	a					05 40		06 40		07 06				07 40					11 06				11 40	
Gatwick Airport	a					06 00		06 56		07 26				07 56					11 26				11 56	
East Croydon	a							07 11		07 41				08 11					11 41				12 11	
East Croydon	d																							
London Bridge	a																							
East Croydon	d							07 12		07 42				08 12					11 42				12 12	
Clapham Junction	d							07 22		07 52				08 22					11 52				12 22	
London Victoria	a							07 29		07 59				08 29					11 59				12 29	
Lewes [4]	d		00 13	00 27	05 27		06 08		06 43		06 53	07 03	07 13		07 23	07 33		10 43		10 53	11 03	11 13		11 23
Falmer	d	00 01	00 20	00 35	05 34		06 15		06 50		07 00	07 10	07 20		07 30	07 41		10 50		11 00	11 10	11 20		11 30
Moulsecoomb	d	00 05	00 24	00 39	05 38		06 19		06 54		07 04	07 14	07 24		07 34			10 54		11 04	11 14	11 24		11 34
London Road (Brighton)	d	00 07	00 27	00 41	05 41		06 22		06 57		07 07		07 27		07 37			10 57		11 07		11 27		11 37
Brighton	a	00 12	00 30	00 45	05 44		06 25		07 00		07 10	07 19	07 30		07 40	07 48		11 00		11 10	11 19	11 30		11 40

		SN [1]		SN	SN [1]	SN	SN [1]	SN	SN [1]	SN	SN [1]	SN		SN [1]	SN	SN [1]	SN	SN [1]	SN	SN [1]	SN	SN [1]	SN	SN [1]	SN
Seaford	d			11 25				11 53				12 25					12 53				13 25				13 53
Bishopstone	d			11 27				11 55				12 27					12 55				13 27				13 55
Newhaven Harbour	d			11 31				11 59				12 31					12 59				13 31				13 59
Newhaven Town	d			11 33				12 01				12 33					13 01				13 33				14 01
Southease	d							12 05									13 05								14 05
Lewes	a			11 41				12 11				12 41					13 11				13 41				14 11
Lewes	d				11 45				12 21					12 45				13 21				13 45			
Haywards Heath	a				12 06				12 40					13 06				13 40				14 06			
Gatwick Airport	a				12 26				12 56					13 26				13 56				14 26			
East Croydon	a				12 41				13 11					13 41				14 11				14 41			
East Croydon	d																								
London Bridge	a																								
East Croydon	d				12 42				13 12					13 42				14 12				14 42			
Clapham Junction	d				12 52				13 22					13 52				14 22				14 52			
London Victoria	a				12 59				13 29					13 59				14 30				14 59			
Lewes [4]	d	11 33		11 43		11 53	12 03	12 13		12 23	12 33	12 43			12 53	13 03	13 13		13 23	13 33	13 43		13 53	14 03	14 13
Falmer	d	11 41		11 50		12 00	12 10	12 20		12 30	12 41	12 50			13 00	13 10	13 20		13 30	13 41	13 50		14 00	14 10	14 20
Moulsecoomb	d			11 54		12 04	12 14	12 24		12 34		12 54			13 04	13 14	13 24		13 34		13 54		14 04	14 14	14 24
London Road (Brighton)	d			11 57		12 07		12 27		12 37		12 57			13 07		13 27		13 37		13 57		14 07		14 27
Brighton	a	11 48		12 00		12 11	12 19	12 30		12 40	12 48	13 00			13 10	13 19	13 30		13 40	13 48	14 00		14 10	14 19	14 30

		SN [1]		SN	SN [1]	SN	SN [1]	SN	SN [1]	SN	SN [1]		SN	SN [1]	SN	SN [1]	SN	SN [1]	SN	SN [1]	SN		SN [1]	SN
Seaford	d					19 25				19 53					20 25				20 53					21 25
Bishopstone	d					19 27				19 55					20 27				20 55					21 27
Newhaven Harbour	d					19 31				19 59					20 31				20 59					21 31
Newhaven Town	d					19 33				20 01					20 33				21 01					21 33
Southease	d									20 05									21 05					
Lewes	a					19 41				20 11					20 41				21 11					21 41
Lewes	d	14 21	and at the same minutes past each hour until				19 45				20 21					20 45				21 21				
Haywards Heath	a	14 40					20 06				20 40					21 06				21 40				
Gatwick Airport	a	14 56					20 26				20 56					21 26				21 56				
East Croydon	a	15 11					20 41				21 11					21 41				22 12				
East Croydon	d																							
London Bridge	a																							
East Croydon	d	15 12					20 42				21 12					21 42				22 12				
Clapham Junction	d	15 22					20 52				21 22					21 52				22 22				
London Victoria	a	15 29					20 59				21 29					21 59				22 28				
Lewes [4]	d			19 23	19 33	19 43		19 53	20 03	20 13			20 23	20 33	20 43		20 53	21 03	21 13		21 23		21 33	21 43
Falmer	d			19 30	19 41	19 50		20 00	20 10	20 20			20 30	20 41	20 50		21 00	21 10	21 20		21 30		21 41	21 50
Moulsecoomb	d			19 34		19 54		20 04	20 14	20 24			20 34		20 54		21 04	21 14	21 24		21 34			21 54
London Road (Brighton)	d			19 37		19 57		20 07		20 27			20 37		20 57		21 07		21 27		21 37			21 57
Brighton	a			19 40	19 48	20 00		20 10	20 19	20 30			20 40	20 48	21 00		21 10	21 19	21 30		21 40		21 48	22 00

		SN [1]	SN	SN [1]	SN	SN [1]	SN	SN [1]		SN	SN	SN [1]	SN	SN	SN [1]	SN	SN	SN
Seaford	d				21 53					22 25			22 53			23 25		23 53
Bishopstone	d				21 55					22 27			22 55			23 27		23 55
Newhaven Harbour	d				21 59					22 31			22 59			23 31		23 59
Newhaven Town	d				22 01					22 33			23 01			23 33		00 02
Southease	d				22 05								23 05					00 06
Lewes	a				22 11					22 42			23 11			23 42		00 12
Lewes	d	21 45				22 21												
Haywards Heath	a	22 06				22 40												
Gatwick Airport	a	22 27				22 56												
East Croydon	a	22 42				23 11												
East Croydon	d																	
London Bridge	a																	
East Croydon	d	22 43				23 12												
Clapham Junction	d	22 53				23 22												
London Victoria	a	23 00				23 29												
Lewes [4]	d		21 53	22 03	22 13		22 23	22 33		22 43	22 53	23 03	23 13	23 23	23 35	23 43	23 53	00 13
Falmer	d		22 00	22 10	22 20		22 30	22 41		22 50	23 00	23 10	23 20	23 30	23 42	23 50	00 01	00 20
Moulsecoomb	d		22 04	22 14	22 24		22 34			22 54	23 04	23 14	23 24	23 34		23 54	00 05	00 24
London Road (Brighton)	d		22 07		22 27		22 37			22 57	23 07		23 27	23 37		23 57	00 08	00 27
Brighton	a		22 10	22 20	22 30		22 40	22 49		23 00	23 10	23 19	23 30	23 40	23 50	00 01	00 11	00 30

Table T189-R

Sundays

15 December to 10 May

Seaford with London connections - Newhaven - Lewes - Falmer - Brighton

		SN A	SN A	SN ■ A	SN ■	SN	SN ■	SN	SN ■	SN ■	SN	SN	SN ■	SN ■	SN	SN ■	SN	SN ■	SN	SN ■	SN	SN ■	SN
Seaford	d							07 57			08 29	08 59			09 29		09 59		10 29		10 59		11 29
Bishopstone	d							07 59			08 31	09 01			09 31		10 01		10 31		11 01		11 31
Newhaven Harbour	d							08 03			08 35	09 05			09 35		10 05		10 35		11 05		11 35
Newhaven Town ⛴	d		00 02					08 04			08 36	09 06			09 36		10 06		10 36		11 06		11 36
Southease	d		00 06					08 08				09 10					10 10				11 10		
Lewes	a		00 12					08 14			08 45	09 17			09 45		10 17		10 45		11 17		11 45
Lewes	d				07 19				08 18				09 21					10 21				11 21	
Haywards Heath	a				07 38				08 39				09 41					10 41				11 41	
Gatwick Airport	a				07 53				08 52				09 53					10 53				11 54	
East Croydon	a				08 22				09 10				10 10					11 10				12 10	
East Croydon	d																						
London Bridge	a																						
East Croydon	d				08 23				09 11				10 11					11 11				12 11	
Clapham Junction	d				08 39				09 21				10 21					11 21				12 21	
London Victoria	a				08 46				09 28				10 28					11 28				12 28	
Lewes ■	d		00 13	00 27		07 23	07 38	08 23		08 38	08 46	09 24		09 36	09 46	10 09	10 24		10 46	11 07	11 24		11 46
Falmer	d	00 01	00 20	00 35		07 30	07 45	08 30		08 45	08 53	09 31		09 44	09 53	10 16	10 31		10 53	11 14	11 31		11 53
Moulsecoomb	d	00 05	00 24	00 39		07 34	07 49	08 34		08 49	08 57	09 35			09 57		10 35		10 57		11 35		11 57
London Road (Brighton)	d	00 08	00 27	00 41		07 37	07 52	08 37		08 52	09 00	09 38			10 00		10 38		11 00		11 38		12 00
Brighton	a	00 11	00 30	00 45		07 40	07 56	08 41		08 56	09 04	09 41		09 51	10 04	10 24	10 41		11 04	11 22	11 41		12 04

		SN ■	SN	SN ■	SN	SN ■	SN	SN ■	SN	SN ■	SN	SN ■	SN	SN ■	SN	SN ■	SN	SN ■	SN	SN ■	SN	SN ■	SN
Seaford	d		11 59		12 29		12 59		13 29		13 59		14 29		14 59		15 29		15 59		16 29		16 59
Bishopstone	d		12 01		12 31		13 01		13 31		14 01		14 31		15 01		15 31		16 01		16 31		17 01
Newhaven Harbour	d		12 05		12 35		13 05		13 35		14 05		14 35		15 05		15 35		16 05		16 35		17 05
Newhaven Town ⛴	d		12 06		12 36		13 06		13 36		14 06		14 36		15 06		15 36		16 06		16 36		17 06
Southease	d		12 10				13 10				14 10				15 10				16 10				17 10
Lewes	a		12 17		12 45		13 17		13 45		14 17		14 45		15 17		15 45		16 17		16 45		17 17
Lewes	d			12 21				13 21				14 21				15 21				16 21			
Haywards Heath	a			12 41				13 41				14 41				15 41				16 41			
Gatwick Airport	a			12 54				13 53				14 53				15 54				16 54			
East Croydon	a			13 10				14 10				15 10				16 10				17 10			
East Croydon	d																						
London Bridge	a																						
East Croydon	d			13 11				14 11				15 11				16 11				17 11			
Clapham Junction	d			13 23				14 21				15 21				16 23				17 23			
London Victoria	a			13 30				14 28				15 28				16 30				17 30			
Lewes ■	d	12 07	12 24		12 46	13 07	13 24		13 46	14 07	14 24		14 46	15 07	15 24		15 46	16 07	16 24		16 46	17 07	17 24
Falmer	d	12 14	12 31		12 53	13 14	13 31		13 53	14 14	14 31		14 53	15 14	15 31		15 53	16 14	16 31		16 53	17 14	17 31
Moulsecoomb	d		12 35		12 57		13 35		13 57		14 35		14 57		15 35		15 57		16 35		16 57		17 35
London Road (Brighton)	d		12 38		13 00		13 38		14 00		14 38		15 00		15 38		16 00		16 38		17 00		17 38
Brighton	a	12 22	12 41		13 04	13 22	13 41		14 04	14 22	14 41		15 04	15 22	15 41		16 04	16 22	16 41		17 04	17 22	17 41

		SN ■	SN	SN ■	SN	SN ■		SN	SN ■	SN	SN ■	SN	SN ■	SN	SN	SN	SN ■	SN	SN
Seaford	d		17 29		17 59			20 29		20 59		21 29		21 57		22 29		22 57	
Bishopstone	d		17 31		18 01			20 31		21 01		21 31		21 59		22 31		22 59	
Newhaven Harbour	d		17 35		18 05			20 35		21 05		21 35		22 03		22 35		23 03	
Newhaven Town ⛴	d		17 36		18 06			20 36		21 06		21 36		22 04		22 36		23 04	
Southease	d				18 10					21 10				22 08				23 08	
Lewes	a		17 45		18 17		and at the same minutes past each hour until	20 45		21 17		21 45		22 15		22 45		23 15	
Lewes	d	17 21				18 21					21 21								
Haywards Heath	a	17 41				18 41					21 41								
Gatwick Airport	a	17 54				18 53					21 53								
East Croydon	a	18 10				19 10					22 10								
East Croydon	d																		
London Bridge	a																		
East Croydon	d	18 11				19 11					22 11								
Clapham Junction	d	18 21				19 21					22 21								
London Victoria	a	18 28				19 28					22 28								
Lewes ■	d		17 46	18 07	18 24			20 46	21 07	21 24		21 46	22 07	22 15	22 23	22 46	23 07	23 15	23 23
Falmer	d		17 53	18 14	18 31			20 53	21 14	21 31		21 53	22 14	22 23	22 30	22 53	23 14	23 23	23 30
Moulsecoomb	d		17 57		18 35			20 57		21 35		21 57		22 27	22 34	22 57		23 27	23 34
London Road (Brighton)	d		18 00		18 38			21 00		21 38		22 00		22 29	22 37	23 00		23 29	23 37
Brighton	a		18 04	18 22	18 41			21 04	21 22	21 41		22 04	22 22	22 33	22 41	23 04	23 23	23 33	23 41

A not 15 December

Table T190-F

Mondays to Fridays

16 December to 15 May

London and Brighton - Eastbourne - Bexhill - Hastings

Miles	Miles			SN MX ■	SN MX ■	SN MO ■	SN MX ■	SN	SN ■	SN ■	SN	SN ■	SN ■	SN ■	SN	SN ■	SN ■	SN ■	SN	SN ■	SN ■	SN ■	SN ■
—	—	London Victoria ■ ⊖	d				00 02										05 32				06 46		07 16
—	—	Clapham Junction ■	d				00 09										05 42				06 53		07 23
—	—	East Croydon	a				00 23										05 51				07 02		07 32
—	—	London Bridge ■ ⊖	d																				
—	—	East Croydon	a																				
—	—	East Croydon	d				00 24										05 52				07 03		07 33
—	—	Gatwick Airport ■ ✈	d				00 44										06 18				07 20		07 50
—	0	Haywards Heath ■	d				01 08										06 33				07 34		08 03
—	3	Wivelsfield ■	d														06 37						08 08
—	6¾	**Plumpton**	d														06 44				07 44		
—	9½	**Cooksbridge**	d														06 48				07 49		08 17
—	—	**Lewes**	a				01 23										06 53				07 54		08 22
0	—	Brighton ■	d							05 00		05 31		05 58		06 31		07 01		07 31		08 01	
0¾	—	London Road (Brighton)	d																				
1¾	—	Moulsecoomb	d																	07 35			
3½	—	Falmer	d									05 38		06 05		06 38		07 08		07 40		08 08	
8	12¼	Lewes ■	a							05 12		05 45		06 12		06 45		07 15		07 47		08 15	
—	—	**Lewes**	d				01 23			05 12		05 46		06 12		06 46	06 54	07 15		07 47	07 54	08 15	08 26
11	—	**Glynde**	d											06 18			06 59	07 21				08 21	
15½	—	**Berwick**	d		00 05	00 07						05 55				06 55	07 05			07 56			
19¾	—	**Polegate**	d	00 02	00 10	00 13	01s35			05 24		06 00		06 27		07 00	07 10	07 30		08 02	08 07	08 30	08 38
21¾	—	Hampden Park ■	d	00 06	00 14	00 17	01s40			05 29		06 05				07 05	07 15			08 06			08 43
23¾	—	Eastbourne ■	a	00 11	00 19	00 22	01 44			05 33		06 09		06 35		07 09	07 19	07 38		08 11	08 15	08 38	08 48
—	—		d		00 25			04 53	05 10	05 37	05 44	06 14	06 29	06 41	06 46	07 15	07 25	07 43	07 49	08 16	08 21	08 44	
25¾	—	Hampden Park ■	d						05 14	05 42		06 18		06 45	06 50	07 19	07 29	07 47	07 53		08 25	08 48	
28¾	—	**Pevensey & Westham**	d		00 32				05 19	05 47				06 51	06 56		07 34	07 52	07 59	08 24	08 30	08 53	
29½	—	**Pevensey Bay**	d																08 01				
31½	—	**Normans Bay**	d							05 52					07 01				08 05		08 35		
33¼	—	**Cooden Beach**	d		00 39						05 58	06 28			07 05		07 41	07 59	08 10	08 30	08 39	09 00	
34¾	—	**Collington**	d		00 42						06 01	06 32			07 09		07 44	08 02	08 13	08 34	08 43	09 03	
35½	—	**Bexhill** ■	d		00 45			05 10	05 28	05 58	06 04	06 34	06 43	07 02	07 13	07 31	07 48	08 09	08 16	08 37	08 45	09 06	
39¼	—	St Leonards Warrior Sq ■	d		00 51			05 16	05 34	06 05	06 11	06 41	06 50	07 09	07 19	07 39	07 55	08 15	08 23	08 43	08 52	09 12	
40	0	Hastings ■	a		00 54			05 21	05 37	06 08	06 14	06 44	06 53	07 12	07 23	07 42	07 58	08 18	08 26	08 46	08 55	09 15	
—	1	Ore	a					05 28		06 12	06 18		06 57	07 17	07 27		08 02	08 22	08 30		08 59	09 19	
—	11¼	Rye	a					05 44			06 36				07 44				08 47				
—	26½	Ashford International	a					06 07			07 00				08 10				09 10				

		SN	SN ■	SN ■	SN ■	SN ■	SN	SN ■	SN ■	SN ■	SN ■	SN	SN ■	SN ■	SN ■	SN ■	SN	SN ■	SN ■	SN ■	SN ■	SN	SN ■
London Victoria ■ ⊖	d			07 46		08 16			08 46		09 16			09 46		10 16			10 46		11 16		
Clapham Junction ■	d			07 53		08 23			08 53		09 23			09 53		10 23			10 53		11 23		
East Croydon	a			08 03		08 33			09 02		09 32			10 02		10 32			11 02		11 32		
London Bridge ■ ⊖	d																						
East Croydon	a																						
East Croydon	d			08 03		08 33			09 03		09 33			10 03		10 33			11 03		11 33		
Gatwick Airport ■ ✈	d			08 20		08 49			09 20		09 50			10 20		10 50			11 20		11 50		
Haywards Heath ■	d			08 35		09 03			09 35		10 07			10 35		11 07			11 35		12 07		
Wivelsfield ■	d					09 08					10 11					11 11					12 11		
Plumpton	d			08 45					09 45					10 45					11 45				
Cooksbridge	d					09 17					10 20					11 20					12 20		
Lewes	a			08 53		09 22			09 53		10 25			10 53		11 25			11 53		12 25		
Brighton ■	d		08 31		09 01			09 31		10 01			10 31		11 01			11 31		12 01			12 31
London Road (Brighton)	d																						
Moulsecoomb	d		08 35					09 35					10 35					11 35					12 35
Falmer	d		08 40		09 08			09 40		10 08			10 40		11 08			11 40		12 08			12 40
Lewes ■	a		08 47		09 15			09 47		10 15			10 47		11 15			11 47		12 15			12 47
Lewes	d		08 47	08 53	09 15	09 24		09 47	09 54	10 15	10 26		10 47	10 54	11 15	11 26		11 47	11 54	12 15	12 26		12 47
Glynde	d				09 21					10 21					11 21					12 21			
Berwick	d		08 56					09 56					10 56					11 56					12 56
Polegate	d		09 02	09 06	09 30	09 37		10 02	10 06	10 30	10 38		11 02	11 06	11 30	11 38		12 02	12 06	12 30	12 38		13 02
Hampden Park ■	d		09 06			09 42		10 06			10 43		11 06			11 43		12 06			12 43		13 06
Eastbourne ■	a		09 11	09 14	09 38	09 47		10 11	10 14	10 38	10 48		11 11	11 14	11 38	11 48		12 11	12 14	12 38	12 48		13 11
	d	08 49	09 16	09 20	09 44		09 49	10 16	10 20	10 44		10 49	11 16	11 20	11 44		11 49	12 16	12 20	12 44		12 49	13 16
Hampden Park ■	d	08 53		09 24	09 48		09 53		10 24	10 48		10 53		11 24	11 48		11 53		12 24	12 48		12 53	
Pevensey & Westham	d	08 59		09 29	09 53		09 59		10 29	10 53		10 59		11 29	11 53		11 59		12 29	12 53		12 59	
Pevensey Bay	d	09 01																					
Normans Bay	d	09 05					10 04					11 04					12 04					13 04	
Cooden Beach	d	09 10		09 36	10 00		10 08		10 36			11 08		11 36			12 08		12 36			13 08	
Collington	d	09 13		09 39	10 03		10 12		10 39			11 12		11 39			12 12		12 39			13 12	
Bexhill ■	d	09 16	09 34	09 42	10 06		10 15	10 30	10 42	11 02		11 15	11 30	11 42	12 02		12 15	12 30	12 42	13 02		13 15	13 30
St Leonards Warrior Sq ■	d	09 23	09 40	09 49	10 12		10 22	10 37	10 49	11 08		11 22	11 37	11 50	12 08		12 22	12 37	12 49	13 08		13 22	13 37
Hastings ■	a	09 26	09 43	09 53	10 15		10 26	10 40	10 53	11 11		11 25	11 40	11 53	12 11		12 25	12 40	12 53	13 11		13 25	13 40
Ore	a	09 31		09 57	10 19		10 30		10 57	11 15		11 29		11 57	12 15		12 29		12 57	13 15		13 29	
Rye	a	09 47					10 47					11 45					12 46					13 45	
Ashford International	a	10 10					11 11					12 10					13 10					14 10	

For complete service between Eastbourne and Hampden park, see Table T191

Table T190-F

Mondays to Fridays
16 December to 15 May

London and Brighton - Eastbourne - Bexhill - Hastings

Station		SN 1	SN 1	SN 1	SN	SN 1	SN 1	SN 1	SN 1	SN	SN 1	SN 1	SN 1	SN 1	SN	SN 1	SN 1	SN 1	SN 1	SN	SN 1	SN 1
London Victoria 15 ⊖	d	11 46		12 16			12 46		13 16			13 46		14 16			14 46		15 16			15 46
Clapham Junction 10	d	11 53		12 23			12 53		13 23			13 53		14 23			14 53		15 23			15 53
East Croydon	a	12 02		12 32			13 02		13 32			14 02		14 32			15 02		15 32			16 02
London Bridge 4 ⊖	d																					
East Croydon	a																					
East Croydon	d	12 03		12 33			13 03		13 33			14 03		14 33			15 03		15 33			16 03
Gatwick Airport 10 ✈	d	12 20		12 50			13 20		13 50			14 20		14 50			15 20		15 50			16 20
Haywards Heath 3	d	12 35		13 07			13 35		14 07			14 35		15 07			15 35		16 08			16 35
Wivelsfield 4	d			13 11					14 11					15 11					16 12			
Plumpton	d	12 45					13 45					14 45					15 45					16 45
Cooksbridge	d			13 20					14 20					15 20					16 21			
Lewes	a	12 53		13 25			13 53		14 25			14 53		15 25			15 53		16 26			16 53
Brighton 10	d		13 01			13 31		14 01			14 31		15 01			15 31		16 01			16 31	
London Road (Brighton)	d																					
Moulsecoomb	d					13 35					14 35					15 35		16 05			16 35	
Falmer	d		13 08			13 40		14 08			14 40		15 08			15 40		16 10			16 40	
Lewes 4	a		13 15			13 47		14 15			14 47		15 15			15 47		16 17			16 47	
Lewes	d	12 54	13 15	13 26		13 47	13 54	14 15	14 26		14 47	14 54	15 15	15 26		15 47	15 54	16 17	16 27		16 47	16 54
Glynde	d		13 21					14 21					15 21					16 23				
Berwick	d					13 56					14 56					15 56					16 56	
Polegate	d	13 06	13 30	13 38		14 02	14 06	14 30	14 38		15 02	15 06	15 30	15 38		16 02	16 06	16 32	16 39		17 02	17 06
Hampden Park 4	d			13 43		14 06			14 43		15 06			15 43		16 06		16 37	16 44		17 07	
Eastbourne 4	a	13 14	13 38	13 48		14 11	14 14	14 38	14 48		15 11	15 14	15 38	15 48		16 11	16 14	16 41	16 49		17 11	17 14
	d	13 20	13 44		13 49	14 16	14 20	14 44		14 49	15 16	15 20	15 44		15 49	16 16	16 20	16 46		16 52	17 16	17 20
Hampden Park 4	d	13 24	13 48		13 53		14 24	14 48		14 53		15 24	15 48		15 53		16 24			16 56		17 24
Pevensey & Westham	d	13 29	13 53		13 59		14 29	14 53		14 59		15 29	15 53		15 59		16 29	16 54		17 02		17 29
Pevensey Bay	d														16 01			16 56				
Normans Bay	d				14 04					15 04					16 05			17 00				
Cooden Beach	d	13 36			14 08		14 36			15 08		15 36	15 59		16 10		16 36	17 05		17 10		17 36
Collington	d	13 39			14 12		14 39			15 12		15 39	16 03		16 13		16 39	17 09		17 13		17 39
Bexhill 4	d	13 42	14 02		14 15	14 30	14 42	15 02		15 15	15 30	15 42	16 05		16 16	16 31	16 42	17 11		17 17	17 32	17 42
St Leonards Warrior Sq 4	d	13 49	14 08		14 22	14 37	14 49	15 08		15 22	15 37	15 49	16 12		16 23	16 37	16 49	17 18		17 23	17 38	17 49
Hastings 4	a	13 53	14 11		14 25	14 40	14 53	15 11		15 25	15 40	15 53	16 15		16 26	16 40	16 53	17 21		17 27	17 43	17 53
Ore	a	13 57	14 15		14 29		14 57	15 15		15 29		15 57	16 19		16 30		16 57	17 25		17 31		17 57
Rye	a				14 46					15 45					16 47					17 46		
Ashford International	a				15 10					16 10					17 10					18 10		

Station		SN 1	SN 1	SN	SN 1	SN 1	SN 1	SN 1	SN	SN 1	SN 1	SN 1	SN 1	SN 1	SN 1	SN	SN 1	SN 1	SN 1	SN 1	SN	SN 1	SN 1
London Victoria 15 ⊖	d		16 16			16 45		17 15				17 45	17 45		18 15				18 45			19 16	
Clapham Junction 10	d		16 23			16 52		17 22				17 52	17 52		18 22				18 52			19 23	
East Croydon	a		16 32			17 01		17 31				18 01	18 01		18 31				19 01			19 32	
London Bridge 4 ⊖	d									17 32							18 32						
East Croydon	a									17 46							18 46						
East Croydon	d		16 33			17 02		17 32		17 47		18 02	18 02		18 32		18 47		19 02			19 33	
Gatwick Airport 10 ✈	d		16 50			17 20		17 50		18 03		18 20	18 20		18 50		19 03		19 20			19 50	
Haywards Heath 3	d		17 07			17 33		18 03		18 16		18 33	18 33		19 03		19 16		19 33			20 07	
Wivelsfield 4	d		17 11			17 37		18 07		18 21		18 37	18 37		19 07		19 21		19 37			20 11	
Plumpton	d					17 45				18 28		18 45	18 45				19 28		19 45				
Cooksbridge	d		17 20					18 17		18 33					19 17		19 33					20 20	
Lewes	a		17 25			17 52		18 22		18 38		18 52	18 52		19 22		19 38		19 52			20 25	
Brighton 10	d	17 01			17 31		18 01				18 31			19 01				19 32		20 01			20 31
London Road (Brighton)	d																						
Moulsecoomb	d	17 05			17 35		18 05				18 35							19 36					20 35
Falmer	d	17 10			17 40		18 10				18 40			19 08				19 41		20 08			20 40
Lewes 4	a	17 17			17 47		18 17				18 47			19 15				19 48		20 15			20 47
Lewes	d	17 17	17 26		17 47	17 53	18 17	18 22		18 39	18 47		18 56	19 15	19 22		19 39	19 48	19 53	20 15		20 26	20 47
Glynde	d	17 23					18 23	18 28		18 45				19 21	19 28		19 45			20 21			
Berwick	d				17 56			18 33		18 51	18 56				19 33		19 51	19 57				20 35	20 57
Polegate	d	17 32	17 38		18 02	18 06	18 32	18 39		18 56	19 02		19 08	19 30	19 39		19 56	20 03	20 07	20 30		20 40	21 02
Hampden Park 4	d	17 37	17 43		18 08	18 11	18 37	18 45		19 01	19 08		19 13		19 44		20 01	20 08	20 12			20 45	21 07
Eastbourne 4	a	17 41	17 49		18 12	18 15	18 41	18 49		19 06	19 12		19 20	19 38	19 48		20 06	20 12	20 17	20 38		20 50	21 11
	d	17 46		17 52	18 17	18 21	18 46		18 52		19 17		19 27	19 44		19 49		20 17	20 23	20 43	20 49		21 16
Hampden Park 4	d			17 56		18 25			18 56				19 31	19 48		19 53			20 27	20 47	20 53		
Pevensey & Westham	d	17 53		18 02		18 30	18 53		19 02				19 36	19 53		19 59			20 33	20 52	21 00		
Pevensey Bay	d			18 04																			
Normans Bay	d	17 58					18 58									20 04					21 05		
Cooden Beach	d	18 03		18 10		18 37	19 03		19 10				19 43			20 08			20 40		21 10		
Collington	d	18 06		18 13		18 40	19 06		19 13				19 46			20 12			20 43		21 13		
Bexhill 4	d	18 09		18 17	18 35	18 44	19 09		19 19		19 34		19 49	20 02		20 15		20 31	20 46	21 02	21 16		21 31
St Leonards Warrior Sq 4	d	18 15		18 24	18 41	18 50	19 15		19 26		19 41		19 55	20 08		20 22		20 37	20 52	21 08	21 22		21 37
Hastings 4	a	18 18		18 27	18 45	18 53	19 18		19 29		19 44		19 58	20 11		20 25		20 40	20 55	21 11	21 25		21 40
Ore	a	18 22		18 31		18 57	19 23		19 33				20 02	20 17		20 29			20 59	21 15	21 29		
Rye	a			18 48					19 48							20 46					21 45		
Ashford International	a			19 10					20 11							21 10					22 10		

For complete service between Eastbourne and Hampden park, see Table T191

Table T190-F

Mondays to Fridays
16 December to 15 May

London and Brighton - Eastbourne - Bexhill - Hastings

Station		SN 1	SN 1	SN	SN 1	SN 1	SN 1	SN 1	SN 1	SN 1	SN 1	SN 1	SN 1	SN 1	SN 1
London Victoria 15 ⊖	d	19 46			20 16		20 46		21 16		21 46		22 16		22 46
Clapham Junction 10	d	19 53			20 23		20 53		21 23		21 53		22 23		22 53
East Croydon	a	20 02			20 32		21 02		21 32		22 02		22 32		23 02
London Bridge 4 ⊖	d														
East Croydon	a														
East Croydon	d	20 03			20 33		21 03		21 33		22 03		22 33		23 03
Gatwick Airport 10 ✈	d	20 20			20 50		21 20		21 50		22 20		22 50		23 20
Haywards Heath 3	d	20 35			21 07		21 35		22 07		22 35		23 07		23 35
Wivelsfield 4	d				21 11				22 11				23 11		23 39
Plumpton	d	20 45					21 45				22 45				23 46
Cooksbridge	d				21 20				22 20				23 20		23 50
Lewes	a	20 53			21 25		21 53		22 25		22 53		23 25		23 55
Brighton 10	d		21 01			21 31		22 01		22 32		23 02		23 32	
London Road (Brighton)	d														
Moulsecoomb	d					21 35									
Falmer	d		21 08			21 40		22 08		22 39		23 09		23 39	
Lewes 4	a		21 15			21 47		22 15		22 46		23 16		23 46	
Lewes	d	20 54	21 15		21 26	21 47	21 54	22 15	22 26	22 48	22 54	23 16	23 26	23 48	23 56
Glynde	d		21 21					22 21				23 22			
Berwick	d				21 35	21 56						23 27			00 05
Polegate	d	21 06	21 30		21 40	22 02	22 06	22 30	22 38	23 01	23 06	23 33	23 38	00 02	00 10
Hampden Park 4	d				21 45	22 06			22 43	23 06		23 37	23 43	00 06	00 14
Eastbourne 4	a	21 14	21 38		21 50	22 11	22 14	22 38	22 48	23 11	23 14	23 42	23 48	00 11	00 19
	d	21 20	21 44	21 49		22 16	22 20	22 44			23 20				00 25
Hampden Park 4	d	21 24	21 48	21 53			22 24	22 48			23 24				
Pevensey & Westham	d	21 29	21 53	21 59			22 29	22 53			23 29				00 32
Pevensey Bay	d														
Normans Bay	d			22 04											
Cooden Beach	d	21 36		22 08			22 36				23 36				00 39
Collington	d	21 39		22 12			22 39				23 39				00 42
Bexhill 4	d	21 42	22 02	22 15		22 31	22 42	23 03			23 42				00 45
St Leonards Warrior Sq 4	d	21 49	22 08	22 21		22 37	22 49	23 09			23 49				00 51
Hastings 4	a	21 53	22 11	22 25		22 40	22 53	23 13			23 53				00 54
Ore	a	21 57	22 15	22 29											
Rye	a			22 48											
Ashford International	a			23 10											

Saturdays
21 December to 16 May

Station		SN 1	SN 1	SN 1 A	SN 1	SN 1	SN 1	SN	SN 1	SN	SN 1	SN 1	SN 1	SN	SN 1	SN 1	SN 1	SN	SN 1	SN 1	SN 1	SN 1	SN
London Victoria 15 ⊖	d			00 02																07 46		08 16	
Clapham Junction 10	d			00 09																07 53		08 23	
East Croydon	a			00 23																08 02		08 32	
London Bridge 4 ⊖	d																						
East Croydon	a																						
East Croydon	d			00 24																08 03		08 33	
Gatwick Airport 10 ✈	d			00 44								06 13								08 20		08 50	
Haywards Heath 3	d			01 08								06 31				07 35				08 35		09 07	
Wivelsfield 4	d																					09 11	
Plumpton	d											06 42				07 46				08 46			
Cooksbridge	d																					09 20	
Lewes	a			01 23								06 49				07 53				08 53		09 25	
Brighton 10	d					05 10					06 31		07 01		07 31		08 01		08 31		09 01		
London Road (Brighton)	d																						
Moulsecoomb	d										06 35				07 35				08 35				
Falmer	d										06 40		07 08		07 40		08 08		08 40		09 08		
Lewes 4	a					05 22					06 47		07 15		07 47		08 15		08 47		09 15		
Lewes	d			01 23		05 24					06 47	06 50	07 15		07 47	07 54	08 15		08 47	08 54	09 15	09 26	
Glynde	d												07 21				08 21				09 21		
Berwick	d		00 05									06 59			07 56				08 56				
Polegate	d	00 02	00 10	01s35		05 36					07 00	07 05	07 30		08 02	08 06	08 30		09 02	09 06	09 30	09 38	
Hampden Park 4	d	00 06	00 14	01s40		05 41					07 04	07 10			08 06	08 11			09 06			09 43	
Eastbourne 4	a	00 11	00 19	01 44		05 45					07 09	07 14	07 38		08 11	08 15	08 38		09 11	09 14	09 38	09 48	
	d		00 25		05 30		05 46	05 49	06 43	06 49	07 15	07 21	07 43	07 49	08 16	08 21	08 43	08 49	09 16	09 20	09 43		09 49
Hampden Park 4	d						05 50	05 53	06 47	06 53	07 19	07 25	07 47	07 53		08 25	08 47	08 53		09 24	09 47		09 53
Pevensey & Westham	d		00 32				05 55	05 59	06 52	06 59		07 31	07 52	07 59		08 31	08 52	08 59		09 29	09 52		09 59
Pevensey Bay	d																						
Normans Bay	d							06 04		07 04				08 04				09 04					10 04
Cooden Beach	d		00 39					06 09		07 08		07 38	07 59	08 08	08 29	08 38	08 58	09 08		09 36	09 58		10 08
Collington	d		00 42					06 12		07 12		07 41	08 02	08 12	08 32	08 41	09 02	09 12		09 39	10 02		10 12
Bexhill 4	d		00 45		05 44		06 07	06 16	07 02	07 15	07 30	07 44	08 05	08 15	08 35	08 44	09 04	09 15	09 30	09 42	10 04		10 15
St Leonards Warrior Sq 4	d		00 51		05 51		06 14	06 22	07 08	07 22	07 37	07 50	08 11	08 22	08 42	08 50	09 11	09 22	09 37	09 49	10 11		10 22
Hastings 4	a		00 54		05 54		06 17	06 26	07 11	07 25	07 40	07 53	08 14	08 25	08 45	08 53	09 14	09 25	09 40	09 53	10 14		10 25
Ore	a				05 58		06 21	06 30	07 15	07 29		07 57	08 18	08 29		08 57	09 18	09 29		09 57	10 18		10 29
Rye	a							06 47		07 45				08 46				09 45					10 46
Ashford International	a							07 09		08 10				09 10				10 10					11 10

A not 16 May

For complete service between Eastbourne and Hampden park, see Table T191

Table T190-F

Saturdays

21 December to 16 May

London and Brighton - Eastbourne - Bexhill - Hastings

		SN ■	SN ■	SN ■	SN ■	SN		SN ■	SN ■	SN ■	SN ■	SN	SN ■	SN ■	SN ■	SN ■		SN	SN ■	SN ■	SN ■	SN ■	SN	SN ■	SN ■
London Victoria 15 ⊖	d		08 46		09 16				09 46		10 16			10 46		11 16				11 46		12 16			12 46
Clapham Junction 10	d		08 53		09 23				09 53		10 23			10 53		11 23				11 53		12 23			12 53
East Croydon	a		09 02		09 32				10 02		10 32			11 02		11 32				12 02		12 32			13 02
London Bridge 4 ⊖	d																								
East Croydon	a																								
East Croydon	d		09 03		09 33				10 03		10 33			11 03		11 33				12 03		12 33			13 03
Gatwick Airport 10 ✈	d		09 20		09 50				10 20		10 50			11 20		11 50				12 20		12 50			13 20
Haywards Heath 3	d		09 35		10 07				10 35		11 07			11 35		12 07				12 35		13 07			13 35
Wivelsfield 4	d				10 11						11 11					12 11						13 11			
Plumpton	d		09 46						10 46					11 46						12 46					13 46
Cooksbridge	d				10 20						11 20					12 20						13 20			
Lewes	a		09 53		10 25				10 53		11 25			11 53		12 25				12 53		13 25			13 53
Brighton 10	d	09 31		10 01				10 31		11 01			11 31		12 01				12 31		13 01			13 31	
London Road (Brighton)	d																								
Moulsecoomb	d	09 35						10 35					11 35						12 35					13 35	
Falmer	d	09 40		10 08				10 40		11 08			11 40		12 08				12 40		13 08			13 40	
Lewes 4	a	09 47		10 15				10 47		11 15			11 47		12 15				12 47		13 15			13 47	
Lewes	d	09 47	09 54	10 15	10 26			10 47	10 54	11 15	11 26		11 47	11 54	12 15	12 26			12 47	12 54	13 15	13 26		13 47	13 54
Glynde	d			10 21						11 21					12 21						13 21				
Berwick	d	09 56						10 56					11 56						12 56					13 56	
Polegate	d	10 02	10 06	10 30	10 38			11 02	11 06	11 30	11 38		12 02	12 06	12 30	12 38			13 02	13 06	13 30	13 38		14 02	14 06
Hampden Park 4	d	10 06			10 43			11 06			11 43		12 06			12 43			13 06			13 43		14 06	
Eastbourne 4	a	10 11	10 14	10 38	10 48			11 11	11 14	11 38	11 48		12 11	12 14	12 38	12 48			13 11	13 14	13 38	13 48		14 11	14 14
	d	10 16	10 20	10 43		10 49		11 16	11 20	11 43		11 49	12 16	12 20	12 43			12 49	13 16	13 20	13 43		13 49	14 16	14 20
Hampden Park 4	d		10 24	10 47		10 53			11 24	11 47		11 53		12 24	12 47			12 53		13 24	13 47		13 53		14 24
Pevensey & Westham	d		10 29	10 52		10 59			11 29	11 52		11 59		12 29	12 52			12 59		13 29	13 52		13 59		14 29
Pevensey Bay	d																								
Normans Bay	d					11 04						12 04						13 04					14 04		
Cooden Beach	d		10 36			11 08			11 36			12 08		12 36				13 08		13 36			14 08		14 36
Collington	d		10 39			11 12			11 39			12 12		12 39				13 12		13 39			14 12		14 39
Bexhill 4	d	10 30	10 42	11 02		11 15		11 30	11 42	12 02		12 15	12 30	12 42	13 02			13 15	13 30	13 42	14 02		14 15	14 30	14 42
St Leonards Warrior Sq 4	d	10 37	10 49	11 09		11 22		11 37	11 49	12 08		12 22	12 37	12 49	13 08			13 22	13 37	13 49	14 08		14 22	14 37	14 49
Hastings 4	a	10 40	10 53	11 12		11 25		11 40	11 53	12 11		12 25	12 40	12 53	13 11			13 25	13 40	13 53	14 11		14 25	14 40	14 53
Ore	a		10 57	11 16		11 29			11 57	12 15		12 29		12 57	13 15			13 29		13 57	14 15		14 29		14 57
Rye	a					11 45						12 46						13 45					14 46		
Ashford International	a					12 10						13 10						14 10					15 10		

		SN ■		SN ■	SN	SN ■	SN ■	SN ■	SN ■	SN	SN ■	SN ■		SN ■	SN ■	SN	SN ■	SN ■	SN ■	SN ■	SN	SN ■		SN ■	SN ■
London Victoria 15 ⊖	d			13 16			13 46		14 16			14 46			15 16			15 46		16 16				16 46	
Clapham Junction 10	d			13 23			13 53		14 23			14 53			15 23			15 53		16 23				16 53	
East Croydon	a			13 32			14 02		14 32			15 02			15 32			16 02		16 32				17 02	
London Bridge 4 ⊖	d																								
East Croydon	a																								
East Croydon	d			13 33			14 03		14 33			15 03			15 33			16 03		16 33				17 03	
Gatwick Airport 10 ✈	d			13 50			14 20		14 50			15 20			15 50			16 20		16 50				17 20	
Haywards Heath 3	d			14 07			14 35		15 07			15 35			16 07			16 35		17 07				17 35	
Wivelsfield 4	d			14 11					15 11						16 11					17 11					
Plumpton	d						14 46					15 46						16 46						17 46	
Cooksbridge	d			14 20					15 20						16 20					17 20					
Lewes	a			14 25			14 53		15 25			15 53			16 25			16 53		17 25				17 53	
Brighton 10	d	14 01				14 31		15 01			15 31			16 01			16 31		17 01			17 31			18 01
London Road (Brighton)	d																								
Moulsecoomb	d					14 35					15 35						16 35					17 35			
Falmer	d	14 08				14 40		15 08			15 40			16 08			16 40		17 08			17 40			18 08
Lewes 4	a	14 15				14 47		15 15			15 47			16 15			16 47		17 15			17 47			18 15
Lewes	d	14 15		14 26		14 47	14 54	15 15	15 26		15 47	15 54		16 15	16 26		16 47	16 54	17 15	17 26		17 47		17 54	18 15
Glynde	d	14 21						15 21						16 21					17 21						18 21
Berwick	d					14 56					15 56						16 56					17 56			
Polegate	d	14 30		14 38		15 02	15 06	15 30	15 38		16 02	16 06		16 30	16 38		17 02	17 06	17 30	17 38		18 02		18 06	18 30
Hampden Park 4	d			14 43		15 06			15 43		16 06				16 43		17 06			17 43		18 06			
Eastbourne 4	a	14 38		14 48		15 11	15 14	15 38	15 48		16 11	16 14		16 38	16 48		17 11	17 14	17 38	17 48		18 11		18 14	18 38
	d	14 43			14 49	15 16	15 20	15 43		15 49	16 16	16 20		16 43		16 49	17 16	17 20	17 43		17 49	18 16		18 20	18 43
Hampden Park 4	d	14 47			14 53		15 24	15 47		15 53		16 24		16 47		16 53		17 24	17 47		17 53			18 24	18 47
Pevensey & Westham	d	14 52			14 59		15 29	15 52		15 59		16 29		16 52		16 59		17 29	17 52		17 59			18 29	18 52
Pevensey Bay	d																								
Normans Bay	d				15 04					16 04						17 04					18 04				
Cooden Beach	d				15 08		15 36	15 58		16 08		16 36		16 58		17 08		17 36	17 58		18 08			18 36	18 58
Collington	d				15 12		15 39	16 02		16 12		16 39		17 02		17 12		17 39	18 02		18 12			18 39	19 02
Bexhill 4	d	15 02			15 15	15 30	15 42	16 04		16 15	16 30	16 42		17 04		17 15	17 30	17 42	18 04		18 15	18 30		18 42	19 04
St Leonards Warrior Sq 4	d	15 08			15 22	15 37	15 49	16 11		16 22	16 37	16 49		17 11		17 22	17 37	17 49	18 11		18 22	18 37		18 49	19 11
Hastings 4	a	15 11			15 25	15 40	15 53	16 14		16 25	16 40	16 53		17 14		17 25	17 40	17 53	18 14		18 25	18 40		18 53	19 14
Ore	a	15 15			15 29		15 57	16 18		16 29		16 57		17 18		17 29		17 57	18 18		18 29			18 57	19 18
Rye	a				15 45					16 46						17 45					18 46				
Ashford International	a				16 10					17 10						18 10					19 10				

For complete service between Eastbourne and Hampden park, see Table T191

NRT DECEMBER 19 EDITION

Table T190-F

Saturdays

21 December to 16 May

London and Brighton - Eastbourne - Bexhill - Hastings

		SN ■	SN	SN ■	SN ■	SN ■	SN ■	SN		SN ■	SN ■	SN ■	SN ■	SN	SN ■	SN ■	SN ■	SN ■		SN	SN ■	SN ■	SN ■	SN ■	SN ■
London Victoria 15 ⊖	d	17 16			17 46		18 16				18 46		19 16			19 46		20 16				20 46		21 16	
Clapham Junction 10	d	17 23			17 53		18 23				18 53		19 23			19 53		20 23				20 53		21 23	
East Croydon	a	17 32			18 02		18 32				19 02		19 32			20 02		20 32				21 02		21 32	
London Bridge 4 ⊖	d																								
East Croydon	a																								
East Croydon	d	17 33			18 03		18 33				19 03		19 33			20 03		20 33				21 03		21 33	
Gatwick Airport 10 ✈	d	17 50			18 20		18 50				19 20		19 50			20 20		20 50				21 20		21 50	
Haywards Heath 3	d	18 07			18 35		19 07				19 35		20 07			20 35		21 07				21 35		22 07	
Wivelsfield 4	d	18 11					19 11						20 11					21 11						22 11	
Plumpton	d				18 46						19 46					20 46						21 46			
Cooksbridge	d	18 20					19 20						20 20					21 20						22 20	
Lewes	a	18 25			18 53		19 25				19 53		20 25			20 53		21 25				21 53		22 25	
Brighton 10	d			18 31		19 01				19 31		20 01			20 31		21 01				21 31		22 01		22 32
London Road (Brighton)	d																								
Moulsecoomb	d			18 35						19 35					20 35						21 35				
Falmer	d			18 40		19 08				19 40		20 08			20 40		21 08				21 40		22 08		22 39
Lewes 4	a			18 47		19 15				19 47		20 15			20 47		21 15				21 47		22 15		22 46
Lewes	d	18 26		18 47	18 54	19 15	19 26			19 47	19 54	20 15	20 26		20 47	20 54	21 15	21 26			21 47	21 54	22 15	22 26	22 47
Glynde	d					19 21						20 21					21 21						22 21		
Berwick	d			18 56						19 56					20 56						21 56				
Polegate	d	18 38		19 02	19 06	19 30	19 38			20 02	20 06	20 30	20 38		21 02	21 06	21 30	21 38			22 02	22 06	22 30	22 38	23 00
Hampden Park 4	d	18 43		19 06			19 43			20 06			20 43		21 06			21 43			22 06			22 43	
Eastbourne 4	a	18 48		19 11	19 14	19 38	19 48			20 11	20 14	20 38	20 48		21 11	21 14	21 38	21 48			22 11	22 14	22 38	22 48	23 08
	d		18 49	19 16	19 20	19 43		19 49		20 16	20 20	20 43		20 49	21 16	21 20	21 43			21 49	22 16	22 20	22 43		23 15
Hampden Park 4	d		18 53		19 24	19 47		19 53			20 24	20 47		20 53		21 24	21 47			21 53		22 24	22 47		
Pevensey & Westham	d		18 59		19 29	19 52		19 59			20 29	20 52		20 59		21 29	21 52			21 59		22 29	22 52		
Pevensey Bay	d																								
Normans Bay	d		19 04					20 04						21 04						22 04					
Cooden Beach	d		19 08		19 36			20 08			20 36			21 08		21 36				22 08		22 36			
Collington	d		19 12		19 39			20 12			20 39			21 12		21 39				22 12		22 39			
Bexhill 4	d		19 15	19 30	19 42	20 02		20 15		20 30	20 42	21 02		21 15	21 30	21 42	22 02			22 15	22 30	22 42	23 02		23 29
St Leonards Warrior Sq 4	d		19 22	19 37	19 49	20 08		20 22		20 37	20 49	21 08		21 22	21 37	21 49	22 08			22 21	22 37	22 49	23 08		23 36
Hastings 4	a		19 25	19 40	19 53	20 11		20 25		20 40	20 53	21 11		21 26	21 40	21 53	22 11			22 25	22 40	22 53	23 11		23 39
Ore	a		19 29		19 57	20 15		20 29			20 57	21 15		21 30		21 57	22 15			22 29			23 15		
Rye	a		19 45					20 46						21 45						22 48					
Ashford International	a		20 10					21 10						22 10						23 10					

		SN ■	SN ■	SN ■		SN ■	SN ■	SN ■ A
London Victoria 15 ⊖	d	21 46		22 16			22 46	23 16
Clapham Junction 10	d	21 53		22 23			22 53	23 23
East Croydon	a	22 02		22 32			23 02	23 32
London Bridge 4 ⊖	d							
East Croydon	a							
East Croydon	d	22 03		22 33			23 03	23 33
Gatwick Airport 10 ✈	d	22 20		22 50			23 20	23 54
Haywards Heath 3	d	22 35		23 07			23 35	00 11
Wivelsfield 4	d			23 11				00 15
Plumpton	d	22 46					23 46	
Cooksbridge	d			23 20			23 50	
Lewes	a	22 53		23 25			23 55	00 27
Brighton 10	d		23 02			23 32		
London Road (Brighton)	d							
Moulsecoomb	d							
Falmer	d		23 09			23 39		
Lewes 4	a		23 16			23 46		
Lewes	d	22 54	23 16	23 26		23 48	23 56	00 27
Glynde	d		23 22					
Berwick	d		23 27				00 05	
Polegate	d	23 06	23 33	23 38		00 01	00 10	00s39
Hampden Park 4	d		23 37	23 43		00 06	00 15	00s44
Eastbourne 4	a	23 14	23 42	23 49		00 10	00 19	00 48
	d	23 20					00 24	
Hampden Park 4	d	23 24						
Pevensey & Westham	d	23 29					00 32	
Pevensey Bay	d							
Normans Bay	d							
Cooden Beach	d	23 36					00 38	
Collington	d	23 39					00 42	
Bexhill 4	d	23 42					00 44	
St Leonards Warrior Sq 4	d	23 49					00 51	
Hastings 4	a	23 53					00 54	
Ore	a							
Rye	a							
Ashford International	a							

A not 16 May. ■ to Haywards Heath

For complete service between Eastbourne and Hampden park, see Table T191

Table T190-F

Sundays
15 December to 10 May

London and Brighton - Eastbourne - Bexhill - Hastings

Station		SN 1 A	SN 1 A	SN	SN 1	SN 1	SN 1	SN	SN 1	SN 1		SN	SN 1	SN 1	SN	SN 1	SN 1	SN	SN 1	SN 1	SN	and at the same minutes past each hour until
London Victoria 15 ⊖	d				00 02											08 46			09 46			
Clapham Junction 10	d				00 09											08 53			09 53			
East Croydon	a				00 23											09 02			10 02			
London Bridge 4 ⊖	d																					
East Croydon	a																					
East Croydon	d				00 24											09 03			10 03			
Gatwick Airport 10 ✈	d				00 44											09 20			10 20			
Haywards Heath 3	d			00 11	01 08											09 31			10 31			
Wivelsfield 4	d			00 15												09 35			10 35			
Plumpton	d															09 42			10 42			
Cooksbridge	d																					
Lewes	a			00 27	01s23											09 49			10 49			
Brighton 10	d						07 05		07 35	08 05			08 35	09 05			10 05			11 05		
London Road (Brighton)	d								07 38				08 38									
Moulsecoomb	d								07 41				08 41									
Falmer	d						07 12		07 45	08 12			08 45	09 12			10 12			11 12		
Lewes 4	a						07 19		07 52	08 19			08 52	09 19			10 19			11 19		
Lewes	d			00 27			07 21		07 55	08 21			08 55	09 21		09 50	10 21		10 50	11 21		
Glynde	d						07 26			08 26				09 26			10 26			11 26		
Berwick	d		00 05				07 32			08 32				09 32			10 32			11 32		
Polegate	d	00 01	00 10	00s39	01s35		07 37		08 07	08 37			09 07	09 37		10 02	10 37		11 02	11 37		
Hampden Park 4	d	00 06	00 15	00s44	01s40		07 42			08 42				09 42			10 42			11 42		
Eastbourne 4	a	00 10	00 19	00 48	01 44		07 47		08 15	08 47			09 15	09 46		10 10	10 47		11 10	11 47		
	d		00 24			07 26		07 59	08 23			08 56	09 23		09 56	10 17		10 56	11 17		11 56	
Hampden Park 4	d					07 30			08 27				09 27			10 21			11 21			
Pevensey & Westham	d		00 32			07 35			08 32				09 32			10 26			11 26			
Pevensey Bay	d																					
Normans Bay	d								08 37				09 37			10 31			11 31			
Cooden Beach	d		00 38			07 42			08 42				09 42			10 36			11 36			
Collington	d		00 42			07 45			08 45				09 45			10 39			11 39			
Bexhill 4	d		00 44			07 48		08 16	08 48			09 14	09 55		10 14	10 43		11 14	11 43		12 14	
St Leonards Warrior Sq 4	d		00 51			07 54		08 22	08 55			09 21	10 01		10 21	10 50		11 21	11 50		12 21	
Hastings 4	a		00 54			07 57		08 26	08 58			09 24	10 04		10 24	10 53		11 25	11 53		12 24	
Ore	a					08 01		08 30	09 02			09 29	10 08		10 29	10 57		11 29	11 57		12 29	
Rye	a							08 47				09 46			10 46			11 46			12 46	
Ashford International	a							09 10				10 10			11 10			12 10			13 10	

Station		SN 1	SN 1	SN		SN 1	SN 1	SN	SN 1	SN 1	SN 1	SN 1	SN 1	SN 1		SN 1
London Victoria 15 ⊖	d	17 46				18 46			19 46		20 46		21 46			22 46
Clapham Junction 10	d	17 53				18 53			19 53		20 53		21 53			22 53
East Croydon	a	18 02				19 02			20 02		21 02		22 02			23 02
London Bridge 4 ⊖	d															
East Croydon	a															
East Croydon	d	18 03				19 03			20 03		21 03		22 03			23 03
Gatwick Airport 10 ✈	d	18 20				19 20			20 20		21 20		22 20			23 20
Haywards Heath 3	d	18 31				19 31			20 31		21 31		22 31			23 31
Wivelsfield 4	d	18 35				19 35			20 35		21 35		22 35			23 35
Plumpton	d	18 42				19 42			20 42		21 42		22 42			23 42
Cooksbridge	d															
Lewes	a	18 49				19 49			20 49		21 49		22 49			23 49
Brighton 10	d		19 05				20 05			21 05		22 10		23 20		
London Road (Brighton)	d															
Moulsecoomb	d															
Falmer	d		19 12				20 12			21 12		22 17		23 27		
Lewes 4	a		19 19				20 19			21 19		22 24		23 34		
Lewes	d	18 50	19 21			19 50	20 21		20 50	21 21	21 50	22 25	22 50	23 35		23 58
Glynde	d		19 26				20 26			21 26		22 30		23 40		
Berwick	d		19 32				20 32			21 32		22 36		23 46		00 07
Polegate	d	19 02	19 37			20 02	20 37		21 02	21 37	22 02	22 41	23 02	23 51		00 13
Hampden Park 4	d		19 42				20 42			21 42				23 56		00 17
Eastbourne 4	a	19 10	19 47			20 10	20 47		21 10	21 46	22 10	22 49	23 10	00 01		00 22
	d	19 17		19 56		20 17		20 56	21 17	21 51	22 17	22 55	23 17			
Hampden Park 4	d	19 21				20 21			21 21	21 55	22 21	22 59	23 21			
Pevensey & Westham	d	19 26				20 26			21 26		22 26		23 26			
Pevensey Bay	d															
Normans Bay	d	19 31														
Cooden Beach	d	19 36				20 32			21 32		22 32		23 32			
Collington	d	19 39				20 36			21 36		22 36		23 36			
Bexhill 4	d	19 43		20 14		20 38		21 14	21 38	22 06	22 38	23 10	23 38			
St Leonards Warrior Sq 4	d	19 50		20 21		20 45		21 21	21 45	22 13	22 45	23 17	23 45			
Hastings 4	a	19 53		20 24		20 48		21 24	21 48	22 16	22 48	23 20	23 48			
Ore	a	19 57		20 29		20 52		21 28	21 52	22 20						
Rye	a			20 46				21 47								
Ashford International	a			21 10				22 10								

A not 15 December

For complete service between Eastbourne and Hampden park, see Table T191

Table T190-R

Mondays to Fridays
16 December to 15 May

Hastings - Bexhill - Eastbourne - Brighton and London

Miles	Miles	Station		SN MX 1	SN 1	SN 1	SN 1	SN 1	SN 1	SN 1	SN 1	SN 1		SN 1	SN 1	SN 1	SN 1	SN	SN 1	SN 1	SN 1	SN 1		SN	SN 1
—	0	Ashford International	d															06 15						07 22	
—	15¼	Rye	d															06 39						07 45	
—	25½	Ore	d												06 33			06 59	07 12	07 35				08 04	08 18
0	26½	Hastings 4	d						05 08		05 53			06 10	06 37		06 49	07 09	07 15	07 39		07 53		08 08	08 22
0¾	—	St Leonards Warrior Sq 4	d						05 11		05 56			06 13	06 40		06 52	07 12	07 19	07 42		07 56		08 11	08 25
4½	—	**Bexhill 4**	d						05 18		06 03			06 20	06 47		06 59	07 20	07 26	07 49		08 03		08 19	08 33
5¼	—	**Collington**	d						05 21		06 06			06 23			07 02	07 22	07 28			08 06		08 22	08 35
6¾	—	**Cooden Beach**	d						05 24		06 09			06 26			07 06	07 25	07 31			08 09		08 25	08 38
8½	—	**Normans Bay**	d														07 10					08 13			
10½	—	**Pevensey Bay**	d																			08 16			
11¾	—	**Pevensey & Westham**	d						05 31		06 16			06 32			07 15	07 32	07 38			08 19		08 32	08 45
14¼	—	Hampden Park 4	d						05 36		06 21			06 37			07 20	07 38				08 24		08 38	08 50
16¼	—	Eastbourne 4	a						05 40		06 25			06 42	07 03		07 24	07 42	07 46	08 04		08 28		08 43	08 54
—	—		d	00 06	04 49	05 20	05 34	05 40	05 54	06 20	06 32	06 36		06 49	07 09	07 20	07 37		07 52	08 09	08 24	08 37			09 00
18¼	—	Hampden Park 4	d	00 10	04 53	05 24	05 39	05 45	05 58	06 24	06 36	06 40		06 53		07 24	07 42		07 56		08 28	08 42			
20¼	—	**Polegate**	d	00 14	04 58	05 29	05 44	05 50	06 03	06 29	06 41	06 45		06 58	07 16	07 29	07 47		08 01	08 16	08 33	08 47			09 07
24¼	—	**Berwick**	d			05 34	05 49	05 55		06 34	06 46	06 50			07 21	07 34	07 52			08 21		08 52			
29	—	**Glynde**	d			05 40	05 54	06 00		06 40	06 51	06 56			07 27	07 40	07 57			08 27		08 57			
32	9	**Lewes 4**	a	00 27	05 11	05 45	06 00	06 06	06 16	06 45	06 57	07 01		07 12	07 32	07 45	08 03		08 14	08 32	08 46	09 03			09 20
—	—	Lewes	d	00 27				06 07			07 00				07 33		08 03			08 33		09 03			
36½	—	Falmer	d	00 35				06 14			07 07				07 40		08 11			08 40		09 11			
38¼	—	Moulsecoomb	d	00 39				06 18			07 12				07 44		08 15			08 44		09 15			
39¼	—	London Road (Brighton)	d	00 41				06 21																	
40	—	Brighton 10	a	00 45				06 24			07 17				07 49		08 20			08 49		09 20			
—	—	**Lewes**	d		05 11	05 46	06 00		06 16	06 46		07 02		07 16		07 46			08 14		08 46				09 21
—	11¾	**Cooksbridge**	d				06 06		06 22			07 07		07 21					08 20		08 52				
—	14½	**Plumpton**	d		05 20	05 54	06 12			06 54		07 13				07 54			08 25						09 29
—	18¼	Wivelsfield 4	d			06 02	06 20		06 33	07 02		07 21		07 32		08 02			08 33		09 03				
—	21¼	Haywards Heath 3	d		05 39	06 17	06 25		06 49	07 07		07 26		07 37		08 07			08 38		09 15				09 44
—	—	Gatwick Airport 10 ✈	d		05 54	06 33	06 41		07 03	07 20		07 41		07 50		08 20			08 51		09 28				09 57
—	—	East Croydon	a		06 08	06 48	06 56		07 18	07 37		07 57		08 07		08 37			09 09		09 42				10 11
—	—	East Croydon	d				06 57					07 57													
—	—	London Bridge 4 ⊖	a				07 13					08 13													
—	—	East Croydon	d		06 09	06 49			07 19	07 38				08 08		08 38			09 09		09 43				10 12
—	—	Clapham Junction 10	d		06 20	06 59			07 29	07 48				08 18		08 48			09 19		09 53				10 22
—	—	London Victoria 15 ⊖	a		06 27	07 05			07 35	07 54				08 24		08 54			09 26		09 59				10 29

Station		SN 1	SN 1	SN 1	SN	SN 1	SN 1	SN 1		SN 1	SN	SN 1	SN 1	SN 1	SN 1	SN	SN 1	SN 1		SN 1	SN 1	SN	SN 1	SN 1	SN 1
Ashford International	d				08 25						09 25					10 25						11 25			
Rye	d				08 48						09 47					10 47						11 47			
Ore	d	08 36			09 05	09 18	09 33				10 03	10 18	10 33			11 03	11 18	11 33				12 03	12 18	12 33	
Hastings 4	d	08 40		08 53	09 09	09 22	09 37			10 00	10 07	10 22	10 37		11 00	11 07	11 22	11 37			12 00	12 07	12 22	12 37	
St Leonards Warrior Sq 4	d	08 43		08 56	09 12	09 25	09 40			10 04	10 10	10 25	10 40		11 04	11 10	11 25	11 40			12 04	12 10	12 25	12 40	
Bexhill 4	d	08 50		09 03	09 20	09 33	09 47			10 11	10 18	10 33	10 47		11 11	11 18	11 33	11 47			12 11	12 18	12 33	12 47	
Collington	d			09 06	09 22	09 35					10 20	10 35				11 20	11 35					12 20	12 35		
Cooden Beach	d			09 09	09 25	09 38					10 23	10 38				11 23	11 38					12 23	12 38		
Normans Bay	d			09 13							10 27					11 27						12 27			
Pevensey Bay	d			09 16																					
Pevensey & Westham	d			09 19	09 32	09 45				10 19	10 32	10 45			11 19	11 32	11 45				12 19	12 32	12 45		
Hampden Park 4	d			09 24	09 38	09 50				10 25	10 38	10 50			11 25	11 38	11 50				12 25	12 38	12 50		
Eastbourne 4	a	09 05		09 28	09 43	09 54	10 03			10 29	10 44	10 54	11 03		11 29	11 44	11 54	12 03			12 29	12 44	12 54	13 03	
	d	09 10	09 24	09 38		10 00	10 10	10 24		10 40		11 00	11 10	11 24	11 40		12 00	12 10		12 24	12 40		13 00	13 10	13 24
Hampden Park 4	d		09 28	09 42				10 28		10 44				11 28	11 44					12 28	12 44				13 28
Polegate	d	09 17	09 32	09 47		10 07	10 17	10 32		10 49		11 07	11 17	11 32	11 49		12 07	12 17		12 32	12 49		13 07	13 17	13 32
Berwick	d			09 52						10 54					11 54						12 54				
Glynde	d	09 26		09 57			10 26						11 26					12 26						13 26	
Lewes 4	a	09 32	09 45	10 03		10 20	10 32	10 45		11 02		11 20	11 32	11 45	12 02		12 20	12 32		12 45	13 02		13 20	13 32	13 45
Lewes	d	09 33		10 03			10 33			11 03			11 33		12 03			12 33			13 03			13 33	
Falmer	d	09 41		10 11			10 41			11 10			11 41		12 10			12 41			13 10			13 41	
Moulsecoomb	d	09 45		10 15						11 14					12 14						13 14				
London Road (Brighton)	d																								
Brighton 10	a	09 49		10 20			10 48			11 19			11 48		12 19			12 48			13 19			13 48	
Lewes	d		09 45			10 21		10 45				11 21		11 45			12 21			12 45			13 21		13 45
Cooksbridge	d		09 51					10 51						11 51						12 51					13 51
Plumpton	d					10 29						11 29					12 29						13 29		
Wivelsfield 4	d		10 01					11 01						12 01						13 01					14 01
Haywards Heath 3	d		10 14			10 44		11 14				11 44		12 14			12 44			13 14			13 44		14 14
Gatwick Airport 10 ✈	d		10 27			10 57		11 27				11 57		12 27			12 57			13 27			13 57		14 27
East Croydon	a		10 41			11 11		11 41				12 11		12 41			13 11			13 41			14 11		14 41
East Croydon	d																								
London Bridge 4 ⊖	a																								
East Croydon	d		10 42			11 12		11 42				12 12		12 42			13 12			13 42			14 12		14 42
Clapham Junction 10	d		10 52			11 22		11 52				12 23		12 53			13 22			13 52			14 22		14 52
London Victoria 15 ⊖	a		10 59			11 29		11 59				12 29		12 59			13 29			13 59			14 29		14 59

For complete service between Eastbourne and Hampden park, see Table T191

Table T190-R

Mondays to Fridays
16 December to 15 May

Hastings - Bexhill - Eastbourne - Brighton and London

		SN [1]	SN	SN [1]	SN [1]	SN [1]	SN [1]	SN	SN [1]	SN [1]	SN [1]	SN [1]	SN	SN [1]	SN [1]	SN [1]	SN [1]	SN	SN [1]	SN [1]	SN [1]	SN [1]
Ashford International	d		12 25					13 25					14 25					15 25				
Rye	d		12 47					13 47					14 47					15 47				
Ore	d		13 03	13 18	13 33			14 03	14 18	14 33			15 03	15 18	15 33			16 03	16 11	16 33		
Hastings [4]	d	13 00	13 07	13 22	13 37		14 00	14 07	14 22	14 37		14 55	15 07	15 22	15 37		15 54	16 07	16 15	16 37		16 54
St Leonards Warrior Sq [4]	d	13 04	13 10	13 25	13 40		14 04	14 10	14 25	14 40		14 58	15 10	15 25	15 40		15 57	16 10	16 18	16 40		16 57
Bexhill [4]	d	13 11	13 18	13 33	13 47		14 11	14 18	14 33	14 47		15 05	15 18	15 32	15 47		16 04	16 20	16 29	16 47		17 04
Collington	d		13 20	13 35				14 20	14 35			15 08	15 20	15 35			16 07	16 23	16 32			17 07
Cooden Beach	d		13 23	13 38				14 23	14 38			15 11	15 23	15 38			16 10	16 26	16 35			17 10
Normans Bay	d		13 27					14 27				15 15		15 42			16 14					17 14
Pevensey Bay	d											15 18					16 17					
Pevensey & Westham	d	13 19	13 32	13 45			14 19	14 32	14 45			15 21	15 32	15 46			16 20	16 33	16 42			17 19
Hampden Park [4]	d	13 25	13 38	13 50			14 25	14 38	14 50			15 26	15 38	15 51			16 25	16 40	16 48			17 24
Eastbourne [4]	a	13 29	13 44	13 54	14 03		14 29	14 44	14 54	15 03		15 30	15 44	15 55	16 04		16 29	16 44	16 52	17 03		17 28
	d	13 40		14 00	14 10	14 24	14 40		15 00	15 10	15 24	15 40		16 01	16 10	16 24	16 40		17 00	17 10	17 24	17 40
Hampden Park [4]	d	13 44				14 28	14 44				15 28	15 44				16 28	16 44		17 04		17 28	17 44
Polegate	d	13 49		14 07	14 17	14 32	14 49		15 07	15 17	15 32	15 49		16 08	16 17	16 32	16 49		17 08	17 17	17 32	17 49
Berwick	d	13 54					14 54					15 54					16 54					17 54
Glynde	d				14 26					15 26					16 26					17 26		
Lewes [4]	a	14 02		14 20	14 32	14 45	15 02		15 20	15 32	15 45	16 02		16 20	16 32	16 45	17 02		17 21	17 32	17 45	18 02
Lewes	d	14 03			14 33		15 03			15 33		16 03			16 33		17 03			17 33		18 03
Falmer	d	14 10			14 41		15 10			15 41		16 10			16 41		17 10			17 41		18 10
Moulsecoomb	d	14 14					15 14					16 14					17 14					18 14
London Road (Brighton)	d																					
Brighton [10]	a	14 19			14 48		15 19			15 48		16 19			16 48		17 19			17 48		18 19
Lewes	d			14 21		14 45			15 21		15 45			16 21		16 45			17 21		17 45	
Cooksbridge	d					14 51					15 51					16 51					17 51	
Plumpton	d			14 29					15 29					16 29					17 29			
Wivelsfield [4]	d					15 01					16 01					17 02					18 02	
Haywards Heath [3]	d			14 44		15 14			15 44		16 14			16 44		17 15			17 44		18 15	
Gatwick Airport [10]	d			14 57		15 27			15 57		16 27			16 57		17 27			17 57		18 27	
East Croydon	a			15 11		15 41			16 11		16 42			17 12		17 42			18 12		18 42	
East Croydon	d																					
London Bridge [4]	a																					
East Croydon	d			15 12		15 42			16 12		16 42			17 12		17 42			18 12		18 42	
Clapham Junction [10]	d			15 22		15 52			16 22		16 52			17 23		17 52			18 22		18 52	
London Victoria [15]	a			15 29		16 00			16 29		16 59			17 30		17 59			18 29		18 59	

		SN	SN [1]	SN [1]	SN [1]	SN [1]	SN	SN [1]	SN [1]	SN [1]	SN [1]	SN	SN [1]	SN [1]	SN [1]	SN [1]	SN	SN [1]	SN [1]	SN [1]	SN [1]	SN	SN [1]
Ashford International	d	16 25					17 25					18 25					19 25					20 25	
Rye	d	16 48					17 48					18 48					19 48					20 47	
Ore	d	17 05	17 13	17 36			18 04	18 11	18 37			19 03	19 18	19 37			20 04	20 18	20 35			21 03	21 18
Hastings [4]	d	17 09	17 17	17 40		17 55	18 08	18 15	18 41		18 54	19 07	19 22	19 41		20 00	20 08	20 22	20 40		21 01	21 07	21 22
St Leonards Warrior Sq [4]	d	17 12	17 20	17 43		17 58	18 11	18 18	18 44		18 57	19 10	19 25	19 44		20 04	20 11	20 25	20 43		21 05	21 10	21 25
Bexhill [4]	d	17 20	17 29	17 50		18 05	18 20	18 29	18 52		19 04	19 18	19 33	19 52		20 11	20 19	20 33	20 50		21 12	21 18	21 33
Collington	d	17 23	17 32	17 53		18 08	18 23	18 32			19 07	19 20	19 35				20 21	20 35				21 20	21 35
Cooden Beach	d	17 26	17 35			18 11	18 26	18 35			19 10	19 23	19 38				20 24	20 38				21 23	21 38
Normans Bay	d					18 15					19 14						20 28					21 27	
Pevensey Bay	d																						
Pevensey & Westham	d	17 33	17 42			18 20	18 33	18 42			19 19	19 32	19 45			20 19	20 33	20 45			21 20	21 32	21 45
Hampden Park [4]	d	17 40	17 47			18 25	18 40	18 47			19 24	19 38	19 50			20 25	20 39	20 50			21 26	21 38	21 50
Eastbourne [4]	a	17 44	17 52	18 08		18 29	18 44	18 51	19 09		19 30	19 43	19 54	20 09		20 30	20 43	20 54	21 05		21 30	21 43	21 54
	d		18 00	18 12	18 24	18 40		19 00	19 14	19 24	19 40		20 00	20 14	20 27	20 40		21 00	21 10	21 24	21 40		22 00
Hampden Park [4]	d		18 04		18 28	18 44		19 04		19 28	19 44				20 31	20 44				21 28	21 44		
Polegate	d		18 08	18 19	18 32	18 49		19 08	19 21	19 33	19 49		20 07	20 21	20 35	20 49		21 07	21 17	21 32	21 49		22 07
Berwick	d					18 54					19 54					20 54					21 54		
Glynde	d			18 28					19 30					20 30					21 26				
Lewes [4]	a		18 21	18 34	18 45	19 02		19 21	19 35	19 45	20 02		20 20	20 37	20 48	21 03		21 20	21 32	21 45	22 02		22 20
Lewes	d			18 34		19 03			19 36		20 03			20 39		21 05			21 33		22 03		
Falmer	d			18 42		19 10			19 43		20 10			20 46		21 12			21 41		22 10		
Moulsecoomb	d					19 14					20 14					21 17					22 14		
London Road (Brighton)	d																						
Brighton [10]	a			18 49		19 19			19 51		20 19			20 54		21 24			21 48		22 19		
Lewes	d		18 21		18 45			19 21		19 46			20 21		20 48			21 21		21 45			22 21
Cooksbridge	d				18 51					19 52										21 51			
Plumpton	d		18 29					19 29					20 29					21 29					22 29
Wivelsfield [4]	d				19 02					20 02					21 02					22 03			
Haywards Heath [3]	d		18 44		19 15			19 44		20 15			20 44		21 14			21 44		22 15			22 44
Gatwick Airport [10]	d		18 57		19 27			19 57		20 28			20 57		21 27			21 57		22 27			22 57
East Croydon	a		19 11		19 42			20 11		20 42			21 11		21 41			22 12		22 42			23 11
East Croydon	d																						
London Bridge [4]	a																						
East Croydon	d		19 12		19 42			20 12		20 43			21 12		21 42			22 12		22 43			23 12
Clapham Junction [10]	d		19 22		19 52			20 22		20 52			21 22		21 52			22 22		22 53			23 22
London Victoria [15]	a		19 29		19 59			20 30		20 59			21 29		21 59			22 29		23 00			23 30

For complete service between Eastbourne and Hampden park, see Table T191

NRT DECEMBER 19 EDITION

Table T190-R

Mondays to Fridays
16 December to 15 May

Hastings - Bexhill - Eastbourne - Brighton and London

		SN [1]	SN [1]	SN [1]	SN [1] A	SN [1]	SN [1]	SN [1]
Ashford International	d				21 25			
Rye	d				21 48			
Ore	d	21 35			22 05	22 15	22 27	
Hastings [4]	d	21 39		22 00	22 09	22 19	22 30	23 29
St Leonards Warrior Sq [4]	d	21 42		22 04	22 12	22 22	22 34	23 32
Bexhill [4]	d	21 49		22 11	22 20	22 29	22 41	23 39
Collington	d				22 22	22 32	22 43	23 42
Cooden Beach	d				22 25	22 35	22 46	23 45
Normans Bay	d				22 29		22 50	
Pevensey Bay	d							
Pevensey & Westham	d			22 19	22 34	22 42	22 55	23 52
Hampden Park [4]	d			22 25	22 40	22 47	23 00	23 57
Eastbourne [4]	a	22 04		22 29	22 44	22 52	23 04	00 01
	d	22 10	22 24	22 40			23 10	00 06
Hampden Park [4]	d		22 28	22 44			23 14	00 10
Polegate	d	22 17	22 32	22 49			23 18	00 14
Berwick	d			22 54			23 23	
Glynde	d	22 26					23 29	
Lewes [4]	a	22 32	22 45	23 02			23 34	00 27
Lewes	d	22 33		23 03			23 35	00 27
Falmer	d	22 41		23 10			23 42	00 35
Moulsecoomb	d			23 14				00 39
London Road (Brighton)	d							00 41
Brighton [10]	a	22 48		23 19			23 50	00 45
Lewes	d		22 45					
Cooksbridge	d		22 51					
Plumpton	d							
Wivelsfield [4]	d		23 01					
Haywards Heath [3]	d		23 14					
Gatwick Airport [10]	d		23 27					
East Croydon	a		23 42					
East Croydon	d							
London Bridge [4]	a							
East Croydon	d		23 42					
Clapham Junction [10]	d		23 57					
London Victoria [15]	a		00 05					

Saturdays
21 December to 16 May

		SN [1]	SN [1]	SN [1]	SN [1]	SN [1]	SN [1]	SN [1]	SN [1]	SN [1]	SN [1]	SN	SN [1]	SN [1]	SN [1]	SN [1]	SN	SN [1]	SN [1]	SN [1]	SN [1]	SN	SN [1]
Ashford International	d											06 25					07 25					08 25	
Rye	d											06 47					07 47					08 47	
Ore	d							06 20	06 33			07 07	07 20	07 33			08 03	08 20	08 33			09 03	09 18
Hastings [4]	d						06 00	06 24	06 37		07 00	07 11	07 24	07 37		08 00	08 07	08 24	08 37		09 00	09 07	09 22
St Leonards Warrior Sq [4]	d						06 04	06 27	06 40		07 04	07 14	07 27	07 40		08 04	08 10	08 27	08 40		09 04	09 10	09 25
Bexhill [4]	d						06 11	06 34	06 47		07 11	07 23	07 34	07 47		08 11	08 18	08 34	08 47		09 11	09 18	09 33
Collington	d						06 13	06 37			07 13		07 37			08 13	08 20	08 37			09 13	09 20	09 35
Cooden Beach	d						06 16	06 40			07 16		07 40			08 16	08 23	08 40			09 16	09 23	09 38
Normans Bay	d																08 27					09 27	
Pevensey Bay	d																						
Pevensey & Westham	d						06 23	06 46			07 23	07 31	07 46			08 23	08 32	08 46			09 23	09 32	09 45
Hampden Park [4]	d						06 28	06 51			07 28	07 38	07 51			08 28	08 38	08 51			09 28	09 38	09 50
Eastbourne [4]	a						06 32	06 55	07 04		07 32	07 43	07 55	08 04		08 32	08 43	08 55	09 04		09 32	09 43	09 54
	d	00 06	05 02	05 42	05 58	06 24	06 40	07 01	07 10	07 24	07 40		08 01	08 10	08 24	08 40		09 01	09 10	09 24	09 40		10 00
Hampden Park [4]	d	00 10	05 06	05 46	06 02	06 28	06 44			07 28	07 44				08 28	08 44				09 28	09 44		
Polegate	d	00 14	05 11	05 51	06 07	06 32	06 49	07 08	07 17	07 32	07 49		08 08	08 17	08 32	08 49		09 08	09 17	09 32	09 49		10 07
Berwick	d			05 56			06 54				07 54					08 54					09 54		
Glynde	d			06 02					07 26					08 26					09 26				
Lewes [4]	a	00 27	05 23	06 07	06 20	06 45	07 02	07 20	07 32	07 45	08 02		08 20	08 32	08 45	09 02		09 20	09 32	09 45	10 02		10 20
Lewes	d	00 27		06 08			07 03		07 33		08 03			08 33		09 03			09 33		10 03		
Falmer	d	00 35		06 15			07 10		07 41		08 10			08 41		09 10			09 41		10 10		
Moulsecoomb	d	00 39		06 19			07 14				08 14					09 14					10 14		
London Road (Brighton)	d	00 41		06 22																			
Brighton [10]	a	00 45		06 25			07 19		07 48		08 19			08 48		09 19			09 48		10 19		
Lewes	d		05 24		06 21	06 45		07 21		07 45			08 21		08 45			09 21		09 45			10 21
Cooksbridge	d					06 51				07 51					08 51					09 51			
Plumpton	d				06 29			07 29					08 29					09 29					10 29
Wivelsfield [4]	d					07 01				08 01					09 01					10 01			
Haywards Heath [3]	d		05 43		06 44	07 14		07 44		08 14			08 44		09 14			09 44		10 14			10 44
Gatwick Airport [10]	d		06a00		06 57	07 27		07 57		08 27			08 57		09 27			09 57		10 27			10 57
East Croydon	a				07 11	07 41		08 11		08 41			09 11		09 41			10 11		10 41			11 11
East Croydon	d																						
London Bridge [4]	a																						
East Croydon	d				07 12	07 42		08 12		08 42			09 12		09 42			10 12		10 42			11 12
Clapham Junction [10]	d				07 22	07 52		08 22		08 52			09 22		09 52			10 22		10 52			11 22
London Victoria [15]	a				07 29	07 59		08 29		08 59			09 29		09 59			10 29		10 59			11 29

A [1] from Hastings

For complete service between Eastbourne and Hampden park, see Table T191

Table T190-R

Saturdays
21 December to 16 May

Hastings - Bexhill - Eastbourne - Brighton and London

		SN 1	SN 1	SN 1	SN	SN 1	SN 1	SN 1	SN 1	SN	SN 1	SN 1	SN 1	SN 1	SN	SN 1	SN 1	SN 1	SN 1	SN	SN 1	SN 1	SN 1
Ashford International	d				09 25					10 25					11 25					12 25			
Rye	d				09 47					10 47					11 47					12 47			
Ore	d	09 33			10 03	10 18	10 33			11 03	11 18	11 33			12 03	12 18	12 33			13 03	13 18	13 33	
Hastings [4]	d	09 37		10 00	10 07	10 22	10 37		11 00	11 07	11 22	11 37		12 00	12 07	12 22	12 37		13 00	13 07	13 22	13 37	
St Leonards Warrior Sq [4]	d	09 40		10 04	10 10	10 25	10 40		11 04	11 10	11 25	11 40		12 04	12 10	12 25	12 40		13 04	13 10	13 25	13 40	
Bexhill [4]	d	09 47		10 11	10 18	10 33	10 47		11 11	11 18	11 33	11 47		12 11	12 18	12 33	12 47		13 11	13 18	13 33	13 47	
Collington	d				10 20	10 35				11 20	11 35				12 20	12 35				13 20	13 35		
Cooden Beach	d				10 23	10 38				11 23	11 38				12 23	12 38				13 23	13 38		
Normans Bay	d				10 27					11 27					12 27					13 27			
Pevensey Bay	d																						
Pevensey & Westham	d			10 19	10 32	10 45			11 19	11 32	11 45			12 19	12 32	12 45			13 19	13 32	13 45		
Hampden Park [4]	d			10 25	10 38	10 50			11 25	11 38	11 50			12 25	12 38	12 50			13 25	13 38	13 50		
Eastbourne [4]	a	10 03		10 29	10 43	10 54	11 03		11 29	11 43	11 54	12 03		12 29	12 43	12 54	13 03		13 29	13 43	13 54	14 03	
	d	10 10	10 24	10 40		11 00	11 10	11 24	11 40		12 00	12 10	12 24	12 40		13 00	13 10	13 24	13 40		14 00	14 10	14 24
Hampden Park [4]	d		10 28	10 44				11 28	11 44				12 28	12 44				13 28	13 44				14 28
Polegate	d	10 17	10 32	10 49		11 07	11 17	11 32	11 49		12 07	12 17	12 32	12 49		13 07	13 17	13 32	13 49		14 07	14 17	14 32
Berwick	d			10 54					11 54					12 54					13 54				
Glynde	d	10 26					11 26					12 26					13 26					14 26	
Lewes [4]	a	10 32	10 45	11 02		11 20	11 32	11 45	12 02		12 20	12 32	12 45	13 02		13 20	13 32	13 45	14 02		14 20	14 32	14 45
Lewes	d	10 33		11 03			11 33		12 03			12 33		13 03			13 33		14 03			14 33	
Falmer	d	10 41		11 10			11 41		12 10			12 41		13 10			13 41		14 10			14 41	
Moulsecoomb	d			11 14					12 14					13 14					14 14				
London Road (Brighton)	d																						
Brighton [10]	a	10 48		11 19			11 48		12 19			12 48		13 19			13 48		14 19			14 48	
Lewes	d		10 45			11 21		11 45			12 21		12 45			13 21		13 45			14 21		14 45
Cooksbridge	d		10 51					11 51					12 51					13 51					14 51
Plumpton	d					11 29					12 29					13 29					14 29		
Wivelsfield [4]	d		11 01					12 01					13 01					14 01					15 01
Haywards Heath [3]	d		11 14			11 44		12 14			12 44		13 14			13 44		14 14			14 44		15 14
Gatwick Airport [10]	d		11 27			11 57		12 27			12 57		13 27			13 57		14 27			14 57		15 27
East Croydon	a		11 41			12 11		12 41			13 11		13 41			14 11		14 41			15 11		15 41
East Croydon	d																						
London Bridge [4]	a																						
East Croydon	d		11 42			12 12		12 42			13 12		13 42			14 12		14 42			15 12		15 42
Clapham Junction [10]	d		11 52			12 22		12 52			13 22		13 52			14 22		14 52			15 22		15 52
London Victoria [15]	a		11 59			12 29		12 59			13 29		13 59			14 30		14 59			15 29		15 59

		SN 1	SN	SN 1	SN 1	SN 1	SN 1	SN	SN 1	SN 1	SN 1	SN 1	SN	SN 1	SN 1	SN 1	SN 1	SN	SN 1	SN 1	SN 1	SN 1
Ashford International	d		13 25					14 25					15 25					16 25				
Rye	d		13 47					14 47					15 47					16 47				
Ore	d		14 03	14 18	14 33			15 03	15 18	15 33			16 03	16 18	16 33			17 03	17 20	17 33		
Hastings [4]	d	14 00	14 07	14 22	14 37		15 00	15 07	15 22	15 37		16 00	16 07	16 22	16 37		16 55	17 07	17 24	17 37		18 00
St Leonards Warrior Sq [4]	d	14 04	14 10	14 25	14 40		15 04	15 10	15 25	15 40		16 04	16 10	16 25	16 40		16 59	17 10	17 27	17 40		18 04
Bexhill [4]	d	14 11	14 18	14 33	14 47		15 11	15 18	15 33	15 47		16 11	16 18	16 33	16 47		17 11	17 18	17 34	17 47		18 11
Collington	d		14 20	14 35			15 13	15 20	15 35			16 13	16 20	16 35			17 13	17 20	17 37			18 13
Cooden Beach	d		14 23	14 38			15 16	15 23	15 38			16 16	16 23	16 38			17 16	17 23	17 40			18 16
Normans Bay	d		14 27					15 27					16 27					17 27				
Pevensey Bay	d																					
Pevensey & Westham	d	14 19	14 32	14 45			15 23	15 32	15 45			16 23	16 32	16 45			17 23	17 32	17 46			18 23
Hampden Park [4]	d	14 25	14 38	14 50			15 28	15 38	15 50			16 28	16 38	16 50			17 28	17 38	17 51			18 28
Eastbourne [4]	a	14 29	14 43	14 54	15 03		15 32	15 43	15 54	16 03		16 32	16 43	16 54	17 03		17 32	17 43	17 55	18 04		18 32
	d	14 40		15 00	15 10	15 24	15 40		16 00	16 10	16 24	16 40		17 00	17 10	17 24	17 40		18 01	18 10	18 24	18 40
Hampden Park [4]	d	14 44				15 28	15 44				16 28	16 44				17 28	17 44				18 28	18 44
Polegate	d	14 49		15 07	15 17	15 32	15 49		16 07	16 17	16 32	16 49		17 07	17 17	17 32	17 49		18 08	18 17	18 32	18 49
Berwick	d	14 54					15 54					16 54					17 54					18 54
Glynde	d				15 26					16 26					17 26					18 26		
Lewes [4]	a	15 02		15 20	15 32	15 45	16 02		16 20	16 32	16 45	17 02		17 20	17 32	17 45	18 02		18 20	18 32	18 45	19 02
Lewes	d	15 03			15 33		16 03			16 33		17 03			17 33		18 03			18 33		19 03
Falmer	d	15 10			15 41		16 10			16 41		17 10			17 41		18 10			18 41		19 10
Moulsecoomb	d	15 14					16 14					17 14					18 14					19 14
London Road (Brighton)	d																					
Brighton [10]	a	15 19			15 48		16 19			16 48		17 19			17 48		18 19			18 48		19 19
Lewes	d			15 21		15 45			16 21		16 45			17 21		17 45			18 21		18 45	
Cooksbridge	d					15 51					16 51					17 51					18 51	
Plumpton	d			15 29					16 29					17 29					18 29			
Wivelsfield [4]	d					16 01					17 01					18 01					19 01	
Haywards Heath [3]	d			15 44		16 14			16 44		17 14			17 44		18 14			18 44		19 14	
Gatwick Airport [10]	d			15 57		16 27			16 57		17 27			17 57		18 27			18 57		19 27	
East Croydon	a			16 11		16 41			17 11		17 41			18 11		18 41			19 11		19 41	
East Croydon	d																					
London Bridge [4]	a																					
East Croydon	d			16 12		16 42			17 12		17 42			18 12		18 42			19 12		19 42	
Clapham Junction [10]	d			16 22		16 52			17 22		17 52			18 22		18 52			19 22		19 52	
London Victoria [15]	a			16 29		16 59			17 29		17 59			18 29		18 59			19 29		19 59	

For complete service between Eastbourne and Hampden park, see Table T191

Table T190-R

Saturdays
21 December to 16 May

Hastings - Bexhill - Eastbourne - Brighton and London

		SN	SN 1	SN 1	SN 1	SN 1	SN	SN 1	SN 1	SN 1	SN 1	SN	SN 1	SN 1	SN 1	SN 1	SN	SN 1	SN 1	SN 1	SN	SN 1	SN 1
Ashford International	d	17 25					18 25					19 25					20 25				21 25		
Rye	d	17 47					18 47					19 47					20 47				21 47		
Ore	d	18 03	18 20	18 33			19 03	19 18	19 33			20 03	20 18	20 33			21 03	21 18	21 34		22 03	22 15	22 27
Hastings [4]	d	18 07	18 24	18 37		19 00	19 07	19 22	19 37		20 00	20 07	20 22	20 37		21 00	21 07	21 22	21 38	22 00	22 07	22 19	22 30
St Leonards Warrior Sq [4]	d	18 10	18 27	18 40		19 04	19 10	19 25	19 40		20 04	20 10	20 25	20 40		21 04	21 10	21 25	21 41	22 04	22 10	22 22	22 34
Bexhill [4]	d	18 18	18 34	18 47		19 11	19 18	19 33	19 47		20 11	20 18	20 33	20 47		21 11	21 18	21 33	21 48	22 11	22 18	22 29	22 41
Collington	d	18 20	18 37				19 20	19 35				20 20	20 35				21 20	21 35			22 20	22 32	22 43
Cooden Beach	d	18 23	18 40				19 23	19 38				20 23	20 38				21 23	21 38			22 23	22 35	22 46
Normans Bay	d	18 27					19 27					20 27					21 27				22 27		22 50
Pevensey Bay	d																						
Pevensey & Westham	d	18 32	18 46			19 19	19 32	19 45			20 19	20 32	20 45			21 19	21 32	21 45		22 19	22 32	22 42	22 55
Hampden Park [4]	d	18 38	18 51			19 26	19 38	19 50			20 25	20 38	20 50			21 25	21 38	21 50		22 25	22 38	22 47	23 00
Eastbourne [4]	a	18 43	18 55	19 04		19 30	19 43	19 54	20 03		20 29	20 43	20 54	21 03		21 29	21 43	21 54	22 03	22 29	22 43	22 51	23 04
	d		19 01	19 10	19 24	19 40		20 00	20 10	20 24	20 40		21 00	21 10	21 24	21 40		22 00	22 10	22 40			23 09
Hampden Park [4]	d				19 28	19 44				20 28	20 44				21 28	21 44				22 44			23 13
Polegate	d		19 08	19 17	19 32	19 49		20 07	20 17	20 32	20 49		21 07	21 17	21 32	21 49		22 07	22 17	22 49			23 18
Berwick	d					19 54					20 54					21 54				22 54			23 23
Glynde	d			19 26					20 26					21 26					22 26				23 28
Lewes [4]	a		19 20	19 32	19 45	20 02		20 20	20 32	20 45	21 02		21 20	21 32	21 45	22 02		22 20	22 32	23 02			23 34
Lewes	d			19 33		20 03			20 33		21 03			21 33		22 03			22 33	23 03			23 35
Falmer	d			19 41		20 10			20 41		21 10			21 41		22 10			22 41	23 10			23 42
Moulsecoomb	d					20 14					21 14					22 14				23 14			
London Road (Brighton)	d																						
Brighton [10]	a			19 48		20 19			20 48		21 19			21 48		22 20			22 49	23 19			23 50
Lewes	d		19 21		19 45			20 21		20 45			21 21		21 45			22 21					
Cooksbridge	d				19 51					20 51					21 51								
Plumpton	d		19 29					20 29					21 29					22 29					
Wivelsfield [4]	d				20 01					21 01					22 01								
Haywards Heath [3]	d		19 44		20 14			20 44		21 14			21 44		22 14			22 44					
Gatwick Airport [10]	d		19 57		20 27			20 57		21 27			21 57		22 28			22 57					
East Croydon	a		20 11		20 41			21 11		21 41			22 12		22 42			23 11					
East Croydon	d																						
London Bridge [4]	a																						
East Croydon	d		20 12		20 42			21 12		21 42			22 12		22 43			23 12					
Clapham Junction [10]	d		20 22		20 52			21 22		21 52			22 22		22 53			23 22					
London Victoria [15]	a		20 29		20 59			21 29		21 59			22 28		23 00			23 29					

		SN 1 A	SN 1
Ashford International	d	22 25	
Rye	d	22 48	
Ore	d	23 03	23 26
Hastings [4]	d	23 07	23 29
St Leonards Warrior Sq [4]	d	23 10	23 33
Bexhill [4]	d	23 18	23 40
Collington	d	23 20	23 42
Cooden Beach	d	23 23	23 45
Normans Bay	d	23 27	
Pevensey Bay	d		
Pevensey & Westham	d	23 34	23 52
Hampden Park [4]	d	23 40	23 57
Eastbourne [4]	a	23 45	00 01
	d		00 06
Hampden Park [4]	d		00 10
Polegate	d		00 14
Berwick	d		
Glynde	d		
Lewes [4]	a		00 27
Lewes	d		00 27
Falmer	d		00 35
Moulsecoomb	d		00 39
London Road (Brighton)	d		00 41
Brighton [10]	a		00 45
Lewes	d		
Cooksbridge	d		
Plumpton	d		
Wivelsfield [4]	d		
Haywards Heath [3]	d		
Gatwick Airport [10]	d		
East Croydon	a		
East Croydon	d		
London Bridge [4]	a		
East Croydon	d		
Clapham Junction [10]	d		
London Victoria [15]	a		

A 1 from Hastings

For complete service between Eastbourne and Hampden park, see Table T191

Table T190-R

Sundays

15 December to 10 May

Hastings - Bexhill - Eastbourne - Brighton and London

		SN 1 A	SN 1	SN 1	SN 1	SN 1	SN 1	SN 1	SN	SN 1
Ashford International	d								08 25	
Rye	d								08 48	
Ore	d						08 15	08 35	09 07	
Hastings 4	d						08 19	08 38	09 11	
St Leonards Warrior Sq 4	d						08 22	08 42	09 14	
Bexhill 4	d						08 30	08 49	09 22	
Collington	d						08 32			
Cooden Beach	d						08 35			
Normans Bay	d						08 39			
Pevensey Bay	d									
Pevensey & Westham	d						08 44			
Hampden Park 4	d						08 49	09 00		
Eastbourne 4	a						08 54	09 05	09 39	
	d	00 06	06 57	07 12	07 55	08 12	09 00	09 11		09 43
Hampden Park 4	d	00 10	07 01	07 16	07 59	08 16		09 15		09 47
Polegate	d	00 14	07 06	07 21	08 05	08 21	09 07	09 20		09 52
Berwick	d			07 26		08 26		09 25		09 57
Glynde	d			07 31		08 31		09 30		10 02
Lewes 4	a	00 27	07 18	07 37	08 18	08 37	09 20	09 36		10 08
Lewes	d	00 27		07 38		08 38		09 36		10 09
Falmer	d	00 35		07 45		08 45		09 44		10 16
Moulsecoomb	d	00 39		07 49		08 49				
London Road (Brighton)	d	00 41		07 52		08 52				
Brighton 10	a	00 45		07 56		08 56		09 51		10 24
Lewes	d		07 19		08 18		09 21			
Cooksbridge	d									
Plumpton	d		07 27		08 27		09 29			
Wivelsfield 4	d				08 35		09 36			
Haywards Heath 3	d		07 42		08 41		09 41			
Gatwick Airport 10	d		07 54		08 56		09 56			
East Croydon	a		08 22		09 10		10 10			
East Croydon	d									
London Bridge 4	a									
East Croydon	d		08 23		09 11		10 11			
Clapham Junction 10	d		08 39		09 21		10 21			
London Victoria 15	a		08 46		09 28		10 28			

		SN 1	SN	SN 1	SN 1	SN	SN 1	SN 1	SN	SN 1	SN 1	SN	SN 1	SN 1
Ashford International	d		09 25			10 25			11 25			12 25		
Rye	d		09 48			10 48			11 48			12 48		
Ore	d	09 15	10 04		10 19	11 04		11 15	12 04		12 15	13 04		13 15
Hastings 4	d	09 19	10 08		10 22	11 08		11 19	12 08		12 19	13 08		13 19
St Leonards Warrior Sq 4	d	09 22	10 11		10 25	11 11		11 22	12 11		12 22	13 11		13 22
Bexhill 4	d	09 30	10 19		10 32	11 19		11 30	12 19		12 30	13 19		13 30
Collington	d	09 32			10 35			11 32			12 32			13 32
Cooden Beach	d	09 35			10 38			11 35			12 35			13 35
Normans Bay	d	09 39			10 42			11 39			12 39			13 39
Pevensey Bay	d													
Pevensey & Westham	d	09 44			10 46			11 44			12 44			13 44
Hampden Park 4	d	09 49			10 51			11 49			12 49			13 49
Eastbourne 4	a	09 54	10 36		10 55	11 36		11 54	12 36		12 54	13 36		13 54
	d	10 00		10 41	11 00		11 41	12 00		12 41	13 00		13 41	14 00
Hampden Park 4	d			10 45			11 45			12 45			13 45	
Polegate	d	10 07		10 50	11 07		11 50	12 07		12 50	13 07		13 50	14 07
Berwick	d			10 55			11 55			12 55			13 55	
Glynde	d			11 00			12 00			13 00			14 00	
Lewes 4	a	10 20		11 06	11 20		12 06	12 20		13 06	13 20		14 06	14 20
Lewes	d			11 07			12 07			13 07			14 07	
Falmer	d			11 14			12 14			13 14			14 14	
Moulsecoomb	d													
London Road (Brighton)	d													
Brighton 10	a			11 22			12 22			13 22			14 22	
Lewes	d	10 21			11 21			12 21			13 21			14 21
Cooksbridge	d													
Plumpton	d	10 29			11 29			12 29			13 29			14 29
Wivelsfield 4	d	10 36			11 36			12 36			13 36			14 36
Haywards Heath 3	d	10 41			11 41			12 41			13 41			14 41
Gatwick Airport 10	d	10 56			11 56			12 56			13 56			14 56
East Croydon	a	11 10			12 10			13 10			14 10			15 10
East Croydon	d													
London Bridge 4	a													
East Croydon	d	11 11			12 11			13 11			14 11			15 11
Clapham Junction 10	d	11 21			12 21			13 23			14 21			15 21
London Victoria 15	a	11 28			12 28			13 30			14 28			15 28

		SN	SN 1	SN 1	SN	SN 1	SN 1	SN	SN 1	SN 1	
Ashford International	d	13 25			14 25			15 25			
Rye	d	13 48			14 48			15 48			
Ore	d	14 04		14 15	15 04		15 15	16 04		16 15	
Hastings 4	d	14 08		14 19	15 08		15 19	16 08		16 19	
St Leonards Warrior Sq 4	d	14 11		14 22	15 11		15 22	16 11		16 22	
Bexhill 4	d	14 19		14 30	15 19		15 30	16 19		16 30	
Collington	d			14 32			15 32			16 32	
Cooden Beach	d			14 35			15 35			16 35	
Normans Bay	d			14 39			15 39			16 39	
Pevensey Bay	d										
Pevensey & Westham	d			14 44			15 44			16 44	
Hampden Park 4	d			14 49			15 49			16 49	
Eastbourne 4	a	14 36		14 54	15 36		15 54	16 36		16 54	
	d		14 41	15 00		15 41	16 00		16 41	17 00	and at
Hampden Park 4	d		14 45			15 45			16 45		the same
Polegate	d		14 50	15 07		15 50	16 07		16 50	17 07	minutes
Berwick	d		14 55			15 55			16 55		past
Glynde	d		15 00			16 00			17 00		each
Lewes 4	a		15 06	15 20		16 06	16 20		17 06	17 20	hour until
Lewes	d		15 07			16 07			17 07		
Falmer	d		15 14			16 14			17 14		
Moulsecoomb	d										
London Road (Brighton)	d										
Brighton 10	a		15 22			16 22			17 22		
Lewes	d			15 21			16 21			17 21	
Cooksbridge	d										
Plumpton	d			15 29			16 29			17 29	
Wivelsfield 4	d			15 36			16 36			17 36	
Haywards Heath 3	d			15 41			16 41			17 41	
Gatwick Airport 10	d			15 56			16 56			17 56	
East Croydon	a			16 10			17 10			18 10	
East Croydon	d										
London Bridge 4	a										
East Croydon	d			16 11			17 11			18 11	
Clapham Junction 10	d			16 23			17 23			18 21	
London Victoria 15	a			16 30			17 30			18 28	

		SN	SN 1	SN 1	SN	SN 1	SN 1	SN	SN 1	SN	SN	SN 1
Ashford International	d	18 25			19 25			20 25			21 25	
Rye	d	18 48			19 48			20 48			21 48	
Ore	d	19 04		19 15	20 04		20 18	21 04		21 14	22 04	
Hastings 4	d	19 08		19 19	20 08		20 22	21 08		21 17	22 08	
St Leonards Warrior Sq 4	d	19 11		19 22	20 11		20 25	21 11		21 21	22 11	
Bexhill 4	d	19 19		19 30	20 19		20 33	21 19		21 28	22 19	
Collington	d			19 32			20 35			21 30		
Cooden Beach	d			19 35			20 38			21 33		
Normans Bay	d			19 39								
Pevensey Bay	d											
Pevensey & Westham	d			19 44			20 45			21 40		
Hampden Park 4	d			19 49			20 49			21 44		
Eastbourne 4	a	19 36		19 54	20 36		20 54	21 36		21 49	22 36	
	d		19 41	20 00		20 41	21 00		21 41	21 59		22 41
Hampden Park 4	d		19 45			20 45			21 45			22 45
Polegate	d		19 50	20 07		20 50	21 07		21 50	22 06		22 50
Berwick	d		19 55			20 55			21 55			22 55
Glynde	d		20 00			21 00			22 00			23 00
Lewes 4	a		20 06	20 20		21 06	21 20		22 06	22 19		23 06
Lewes	d		20 07			21 07			22 07	22 23		23 07
Falmer	d		20 14			21 14			22 14	22 30		23 14
Moulsecoomb	d									22 34		
London Road (Brighton)	d									22 37		
Brighton 10	a		20 22			21 22			22 22	22 41		23 23
Lewes	d			20 21			21 21					
Cooksbridge	d											
Plumpton	d			20 29			21 29					
Wivelsfield 4	d			20 36			21 36					
Haywards Heath 3	d			20 41			21 41					
Gatwick Airport 10	d			20 56			21 56					
East Croydon	a			21 10			22 10					
East Croydon	d											
London Bridge 4	a											
East Croydon	d			21 11			22 11					
Clapham Junction 10	d			21 21			22 21					
London Victoria 15	a			21 28			22 28					

A not 15 December

For complete service between Eastbourne and Hampden park, see Table T191

NRT DECEMBER 19 EDITION

Table T190-R

Sundays

15 December to 10 May

Hastings - Bexhill - Eastbourne - Brighton and London

		SN	SN 1	SN 1
Ashford International	d			
Rye	d			
Ore	d	22 14	22 35	
Hastings 4	d	22 17	22 38	23 25
St Leonards Warrior Sq 4	d	22 21	22 42	23 28
Bexhill 4	d	22 30	22 49	23 35
Collington	d	22 32		23 38
Cooden Beach	d	22 35		23 41
Normans Bay	d			
Pevensey Bay	d			
Pevensey & Westham	d	22 43		23 48
Hampden Park 4	d	22 49	23 00	23 52
Eastbourne 4	a	22 53	23 05	23 57
	d	22 59		
Hampden Park 4	d			
Polegate	d	23 06		
Berwick	d			
Glynde	d			
Lewes 4	a	23 19		
Lewes	d	23 23		
Falmer	d	23 30		
Moulsecoomb	d	23 34		
London Road (Brighton)	d	23 37		
Brighton 10	a	23 41		
Lewes	d			
Cooksbridge	d			
Plumpton	d			
Wivelsfield 4	d			
Haywards Heath 3	d			
Gatwick Airport 10	d			
East Croydon	a			
East Croydon	d			
London Bridge 4	a			
East Croydon	d			
Clapham Junction 10	d			
London Victoria 15	a			

For complete service between Eastbourne and Hampden park, see Table T191

Table T191-F

Eastbourne - Hampden Park

Mondays to Fridays
16 December to 15 May

Miles			SN MX 1	SN 1	SN 1	SN 1	SN 1	SN 1	SN 1	SN 1	SN 1		SN 1	SN 1	SN 1	SN 1	SN	SN 1	SN 1	SN 1	SN 1		SN 1	SN 1	SN
0	Eastbourne	d	00 06	04 49	05 10	05 20	05 34	05 37	05 40	05 54	06 14	.....	06 20	06 32	06 36	06 41	06 46	06 49	07 15	07 20	07 25	.....	07 37	07 43	07 49
2	Hampden Park	a	00 10	04 53	05 14	05 24	05 38	05 41	05 44	05 58	06 18	.	06 24	06 36	06 40	06 45	06 50	06 53	07 19	07 24	07 29	.	07 41	07 47	07 53

		SN 1	SN 1	SN 1	SN 1	SN 1	SN		SN 1	SN 1	SN 1	SN 1	SN	SN 1	SN 1	SN 1	and at the same minutes past each hour until	SN 1	SN	SN 1	SN 1	SN 1		SN
Eastbourne	d	07 52	08 21	08 24	08 37	08 44	08 49	.....	09 20	09 24	09 38	09 44	09 49	10 20	10 24	10 40		15 44	15 49	16 20	16 24	16 40	.....	16 52
Hampden Park	a	07 56	08 25	08 28	08 41	08 48	08 53	.	09 24	09 28	09 42	09 48	09 53	10 24	10 28	10 44		15 48	15 53	16 24	16 28	16 44	.	16 56

		SN 1	SN 1	SN 1	SN 1	SN	SN 1	SN 1	SN 1		SN 1	SN	SN 1	SN 1	SN 1	SN 1	SN 1	SN	SN 1		SN 1	SN 1	SN 1	SN	SN 1
Eastbourne	d	17 00	17 20	17 24	17 40	17 52	18 00	18 21	18 24	.....	18 40	18 52	19 00	19 24	19 27	19 40	19 44	19 49	20 23	.....	20 27	20 40	20 43	20 49	21 20
Hampden Park	a	17 04	17 24	17 28	17 44	17 56	18 04	18 25	18 28	.	18 44	18 56	19 04	19 28	19 31	19 44	19 48	19 53	20 27	.	20 31	20 44	20 47	20 53	21 24

		SN 1	SN 1	SN 1	SN		SN 1	SN 1	SN 1	SN 1	SN 1	SN 1
Eastbourne	d	21 24	21 40	21 44	21 49	.....	22 20	22 24	22 40	22 44	23 10	23 20
Hampden Park	a	21 28	21 44	21 48	21 53	.	22 24	22 28	22 44	22 48	23 14	23 24

Saturdays
21 December to 16 May

		SN 1	SN 1	SN 1	SN 1	SN	SN 1	SN 1	SN 1	SN 1		SN	SN 1	SN 1	SN 1	SN 1	SN 1	SN	SN 1	SN 1	SN 1	SN 1	SN
Eastbourne	d	00 06	05 02	05 42	05 46	05 49	05 58	06 24	06 40	06 43	.....	06 49	07 15	07 21	07 24	07 40	07 43	07 49	08 21	08 24	08 40	08 43	08 49
Hampden Park	a	00 10	05 06	05 46	05 50	05 53	06 02	06 28	06 44	06 47	.	06 53	07 19	07 25	07 28	07 44	07 47	07 53	08 25	08 28	08 44	08 47	08 53

		SN 1	and at the same minutes past each hour until	SN 1	SN 1	SN 1	SN	SN 1		SN 1	SN 1	SN 1	SN 1
Eastbourne	d	09 20		21 24	21 40	21 43	21 49	22 20	.....	22 40	22 43	23 09	23 20
Hampden Park	a	09 24		21 28	21 44	21 47	21 53	22 24	.	22 44	22 47	23 13	23 24

Sundays
15 December to 10 May

		SN 1 A	SN 1	SN 1	SN 1	SN 1	SN 1	SN 1	SN 1	SN 1		SN 1	SN 1	SN 1	and at the same minutes past each hour until	SN 1	SN 1	SN 1	SN 1	SN 1		SN 1	SN 1
Eastbourne	d	00 06	06 57	07 12	07 26	07 55	08 12	08 23	09 11	09 23	.....	09 43	10 17	10 41		21 17	21 41	21 51	22 17	22 41	.....	22 55	23 17
Hampden Park	a	00 10	07 01	07 16	07 30	07 59	08 16	08 27	09 15	09 27	.	09 47	10 21	10 45		21 21	21 45	21 55	22 21	22 45	.	22 59	23 21

A not 15 December

Table T191-R

Hampden Park - Eastbourne

Mondays to Fridays
16 December to 15 May

Miles			SN MX 1	SN MX 1	SN MO 1	SN 1	SN 1	SN 1		SN 1	SN 1	SN 1	SN 1	SN 1	SN	SN 1	SN 1	SN		SN 1	SN 1	SN 1	SN 1	SN	SN 1
0	Hampden Park	d	00 06	00 14	00 17	05 29	05 36	06 05	.....	06 21	06 37	07 05	07 15	07 20	07 38	08 06	08 24	08 38	.....	08 43	08 50	09 06	09 24	09 38	09 42
2	Eastbourne	a	00 11	00 19	00 22	05 33	05 40	06 09	.	06 25	06 42	07 09	07 19	07 24	07 42	08 11	08 28	08 43	.	08 48	08 54	09 11	09 28	09 43	09 47

		SN 1	SN 1	SN 1	SN	SN 1	and at the same minutes past each hour until	SN 1	SN 1	SN 1	SN	SN 1		SN 1	SN 1	SN 1	SN	SN 1	SN 1	SN 1	SN 1	SN 1		SN
Hampden Park	d	09 50	10 06	10 25	10 38	10 43		13 50	14 06	14 25	14 38	14 43	.....	14 50	15 06	15 26	15 38	15 43	15 51	16 06	16 25	16 37	.....	16 40
Eastbourne	a	09 54	10 11	10 29	10 44	10 48		13 54	14 11	14 29	14 44	14 48	.	14 54	15 11	15 30	15 44	15 48	15 55	16 11	16 29	16 41	.	16 44

		SN 1	SN 1	SN 1	SN 1	SN 1	SN	SN 1	SN 1		SN 1	SN 1	SN 1	SN 1	SN	SN 1	SN 1	SN 1	SN 1		SN 1	SN 1	SN	SN 1	SN 1
Hampden Park	d	16 44	16 48	17 07	17 24	17 37	17 40	17 43	17 47	.....	18 08	18 11	18 25	18 37	18 40	18 45	18 47	19 01	19 08	.....	19 13	19 24	19 38	19 44	19 50
Eastbourne	a	16 49	16 52	17 11	17 28	17 41	17 44	17 49	17 52	.	18 12	18 15	18 29	18 41	18 44	18 49	18 51	19 06	19 12	.	19 20	19 30	19 43	19 48	19 54

		SN 1	SN 1	SN 1	SN 1		SN	SN 1	SN 1	SN 1	SN 1	SN	SN 1	SN 1	SN 1		SN 1	SN 1	SN 1	SN 1	SN 1	SN 1	SN 1	SN 1	SN 1
Hampden Park	d	20 01	20 08	20 12	20 25	.....	20 39	20 45	20 50	21 07	21 26	21 38	21 45	21 50	22 06	.....	22 25	22 40	22 43	22 47	23 00	23 06	23 37	23 43	23 57
Eastbourne	a	20 06	20 12	20 17	20 30	.	20 43	20 50	20 54	21 11	21 30	21 43	21 50	21 54	22 11	.	22 29	22 44	22 48	22 52	23 04	23 11	23 42	23 48	00 01

Saturdays
21 December to 16 May

		SN 1	SN 1	SN 1	SN 1	SN 1	SN 1	SN 1	SN 1	SN		SN 1	SN 1	SN 1	SN 1	SN	SN 1	SN 1	SN 1	SN	SN 1	SN 1	SN 1
Hampden Park	d	00 06	00 14	05 41	06 28	06 51	07 04	07 10	07 28	07 38	.....	07 51	08 06	08 11	08 28	08 38	08 51	09 06	09 28	09 38	09 43	09 50	10 06
Eastbourne	a	00 11	00 19	05 45	06 32	06 55	07 09	07 14	07 32	07 43	.	07 55	08 11	08 15	08 32	08 43	08 55	09 11	09 32	09 43	09 48	09 54	10 11

		SN 1	and at the same minutes past each hour until	SN	SN 1	SN 1	SN 1	SN 1		SN	SN 1	SN 1	SN 1	SN 1	SN	SN 1	SN 1	SN 1		SN 1	SN	SN 1	SN 1	SN 1
Hampden Park	d	10 25		13 38	13 43	13 50	14 06	14 25	.....	14 38	14 43	14 50	15 06	15 28	15 38	15 43	15 50	16 06	.....	16 28	16 38	16 43	16 50	17 06
Eastbourne	a	10 29		13 43	13 48	13 54	14 11	14 29	.	14 43	14 48	14 54	15 11	15 32	15 43	15 48	15 54	16 11	.	16 32	16 43	16 48	16 54	17 11

		SN 1	SN	SN 1	SN 1		SN 1	SN 1	SN	SN 1	SN 1	SN 1	SN 1	SN	SN 1		SN 1	SN 1	SN 1	SN	SN 1	SN 1	SN 1	SN 1	SN
Hampden Park	d	17 28	17 38	17 43	17 51	.....	18 06	18 28	18 38	18 43	18 51	19 06	19 26	19 38	19 43	.....	19 50	20 06	20 25	20 38	20 43	20 50	21 06	21 25	21 38
Eastbourne	a	17 32	17 43	17 48	17 55	.	18 11	18 32	18 43	18 48	18 55	19 11	19 30	19 43	19 48	.	19 54	20 11	20 29	20 43	20 48	20 54	21 11	21 29	21 43

			SN 1	SN 1	SN 1	SN 1	SN	SN 1	SN 1	SN 1	SN 1		SN 1	SN 1	SN 1
Hampden Park	d	.....	21 43	21 50	22 06	22 25	22 38	22 43	22 47	23 00	23 37	.....	23 40	23 43	23 57
Eastbourne	a	.	21 48	21 54	22 11	22 29	22 43	22 48	22 51	23 04	23 42	.	23 45	23 49	00 01

Sundays
15 December to 10 May

		SN 1 A	SN 1 A	SN 1	SN 1	SN 1	SN 1	SN 1	SN 1	SN 1		SN 1	SN 1	SN 1	and at the same minutes past each hour until	SN 1	SN 1	SN 1	SN	SN		SN 1	SN 1	SN 1
Hampden Park	d	00 06	00 15	07 42	08 42	08 49	09 00	09 42	09 49	10 42	.....	10 51	11 42	11 49		20 42	20 49	21 42	21 44	22 49	.....	23 00	23 52	23 56
Eastbourne	a	00 10	00 19	07 47	08 47	08 54	09 05	09 46	09 54	10 47	.	10 55	11 47	11 54		20 47	20 54	21 46	21 49	22 53	.	23 05	23 57	00 01

A not 15 December

Table T192-F

Eastbourne - Hastings - Rye - Ashford with Brighton and London connect

Mondays to Fridays

16 December to 15 May

		SE	SE	SN	SE	SN	SE	SE	SN	SE		SE	SN	SE	SE	SE	SN	SE	SE	SN		SE	SN	SE	SE
		◇	◇		◇		◇	◇		◇		◇		◇	◇	◇		◇	◇			◇		◇	◇
Brighton	d																								
Lewes	d																								
Eastbourne	a																								
Eastbourne	d			04 53					05 44								06 46						07 49		
Hampden Park	d																06 50						07 53		
Pevensey & Westham	d																06 56						07 59		
Pevensey Bay	d																						08 01		
Normans Bay	d																07 01						08 05		
Cooden Beach	d								05 58								07 05						08 10		
Collington	d								06 01								07 09						08 13		
Bexhill	d			05 10					06 04								07 13						08 16		
St Leonards Warrior Sq	d			05 16					06 11								07 19						08 23		
Hastings	d			05 25		05 45			06 15								07 23						08 27		
Ore	d			05 29		05 49			06 19								07 27						08 31		
Three Oaks	d					05 55			06 25								07 33						08 37		
Doleham	d					05 58																			
Winchelsea	d					06 04			06 33								07 41								
Rye	a			05 44		06 07			06 36								07 44						08 47		
	d			05 45		06 08			06 38				07 06				07 47			08 16			08 48		
Appledore (Kent)	d			05 54		06 17			06 47				07 15				07 56			08 25			08 57		
Ham Street	a			05 59		06 22			06 52				07 20				08 01			08 30			09 02		
Ashford International	a			06 07		06 30			07 00				07 28				08 10			08 38			09 10		
Ashford International	d	05 13	05 43		06 13		06 36	06 46		07 06		07 16		07 36	07 44	08 06		08 15	08 16			08 43		09 15	09 16
Ebbsfleet International	a	05 32	06 02		06 32		06 55	07 05		07 25		07 35						10 46	08 35			09 02		11 46	09 35
Stratford International	a	05 44	06 14		06 44		07 07	07 17		07 37		07 47		08 04	08 12	08 34		10 58	08 47			09 14		11 58	09 47
St Pancras International	a	05 51	06 21		06 51		07 14	07 25		07 45		07 54		08 12	08 20	08 42		11 06	08 54			09 21		12 06	09 54

		SE	SN	SE	SE	SE		SE	SN	SE	SE	SE	SN	SE	SE	SE		SN	SE	SE	SE	SN	SE	SE	SE
		◇		◇	◇	◇		◇		◇	◇	◇		◇	◇	◇			◇	◇	◇		◇	◇	◇
Brighton	d																								
Lewes	d																								
Eastbourne	a																								
Eastbourne	d		08 49						09 49				10 49					11 49				12 49			
Hampden Park	d		08 53						09 53				10 53					11 53				12 53			
Pevensey & Westham	d		08 59						09 59				10 59					11 59				12 59			
Pevensey Bay	d		09 01																						
Normans Bay	d		09 05						10 04				11 04					12 04				13 04			
Cooden Beach	d		09 10						10 08				11 08					12 08				13 08			
Collington	d		09 13						10 12				11 12					12 12				13 12			
Bexhill	d		09 16						10 15				11 15					12 15				13 15			
St Leonards Warrior Sq	d		09 23						10 22				11 22					12 22				13 22			
Hastings	d		09 28						10 27				11 26					12 26				13 26			
Ore	d		09 32						10 31				11 30					12 30				13 30			
Three Oaks	d								10 37									12 36							
Doleham	d																								
Winchelsea	d		09 43										11 42									13 42			
Rye	a		09 47						10 47				11 45					12 46				13 45			
	d		09 48						10 48				11 47					12 47				13 47			
Appledore (Kent)	d		09 57						10 57				11 56					12 56				13 56			
Ham Street	a		10 02						11 02				12 01					13 01				14 01			
Ashford International	a		10 10						11 11				12 10					13 10				14 10			
Ashford International	d	09 43		10 11	10 15	10 16		10 43		11 15	11 16	11 43		12 15	12 16	12 43			13 15	13 16	13 43		14 15	14 16	14 43
Ebbsfleet International	a	10 02			12 46	10 35		11 02		13 46	11 35	12 02		14 46	12 35	13 02			15 46	13 35	14 02		16 46	14 35	15 02
Stratford International	a	10 14		10 39	12 58	10 47		11 14		14 02	11 47	12 14		14 58	12 47	13 14			16 02	13 47	14 14		17 02	14 47	15 14
St Pancras International	a	10 21		10 47	13 06	10 55		11 21		14 10	11 54	12 21		15 06	12 55	13 21			16 10	13 54	14 21		17 10	14 54	15 21

		SN		SE	SE	SE	SN	SE	SE	SE	SN	SE		SE	SN	SN	SE	SE	SN	SN	SE	SE		SN	SN
				◇	◇	◇		◇	◇	◇		◇		◇			◇	◇			◇	◇			
Brighton	d																								
Lewes	d																								
Eastbourne	a																								
Eastbourne	d	13 49					14 49				15 49					16 52				17 52					18 52
Hampden Park	d	13 53					14 53				15 53					16 56				17 56					18 56
Pevensey & Westham	d	13 59					14 59				15 59					17 02				18 02					19 02
Pevensey Bay	d										16 01									18 04					
Normans Bay	d	14 04					15 04				16 05														
Cooden Beach	d	14 08					15 08				16 10					17 10				18 10					19 10
Collington	d	14 12					15 12				16 13					17 13				18 13					19 13
Bexhill	d	14 15					15 15				16 16					17 17				18 17					19 19
St Leonards Warrior Sq	d	14 22					15 22				16 23					17 23				18 24					19 26
Hastings	d	14 26					15 26				16 27				17 05	17 27				18 28					19 30
Ore	d	14 30					15 30				16 31				17 09	17 31				18 31					19 33
Three Oaks	d	14 36									16 37				17 15					18 37					
Doleham	d														17 18										
Winchelsea	d						15 42								17 24	17 43									19 45
Rye	a	14 46					15 45				16 47				17 27	17 46				18 48					19 48
	d	14 47					15 47				16 48				17 28	17 48			18 26	18 48				19 26	19 49
Appledore (Kent)	d	14 56					15 56				16 57				17 37	17 57			18 35	18 57				19 35	19 58
Ham Street	a	15 01					16 01				17 02				17 42	18 02			18 40	19 02				19 40	20 03
Ashford International	a	15 10					16 10				17 10				17 50	18 10			18 48	19 10				19 48	20 11
Ashford International	d			15 15	15 19	15 43		16 15	16 16	16 45		17 16		17 43			18 16	18 43			19 16	19 43			
Ebbsfleet International	a			17 46	15 38	16 02		18 49	16 35	17 04		17 35		18 02			18 35	19 02			19 35	20 02			
Stratford International	a			18 03	15 50	16 14		19 01	16 47	17 16		17 47		18 14			18 47	19 14			19 47	20 14			
St Pancras International	a			18 10	15 58	16 21		19 09	16 54	17 23		17 54		18 23			18 54	19 21			19 54	20 21			

NRT DECEMBER 19 EDITION

Table T192-F

Eastbourne - Hastings - Rye - Ashford with Brighton and London connect

Mondays to Fridays

16 December to 15 May

		SE	SE	SE	SN	SE	SE	SN		SE	SE	SN	SE
		◇	◇	◇		◇	◇			◇	◇		◇
Brighton	d												
Lewes	d												
Eastbourne	a												
Eastbourne	d				19 49			20 49				21 49	
Hampden Park	d				19 53			20 53				21 53	
Pevensey & Westham	d				19 59			21 00				21 59	
Pevensey Bay	d												
Normans Bay	d				20 04			21 05				22 04	
Cooden Beach	d				20 08			21 10				22 08	
Collington	d				20 12			21 13				22 12	
Bexhill	d				20 15			21 16				22 15	
St Leonards Warrior Sq	d				20 22			21 22				22 21	
Hastings	d				20 26			21 26				22 26	
Ore	d				20 30			21 30				22 29	
Three Oaks	d				20 36							22 35	
Doleham	d											22 38	
Winchelsea	d							21 42				22 44	
Rye	a				20 46			21 45				22 48	
	d				20 47			21 47				22 48	
Appledore (Kent)	d				20 56			21 56				22 57	
Ham Street	a				21 01			22 01				23 02	
Ashford International	a				21 10			22 10				23 10	
Ashford International	d	20 15	20 16	20 43		21 16	21 43			22 16	22 43		23 16
Ebbsfleet International	a	22 46	20 35	21 02		21 35	22 02			22 35	23 02		23 35
Stratford International	a	22 58	20 47	21 14		21 47	22 14			22 47	23 14		23 47
St Pancras International	a	23 06	20 54	21 21		21 54	22 21			22 54	23 21		23 54

Saturdays

21 December to 16 May

		SE	SN	SE	SE	SE	SN	SE	SE	SE		SN	SE	SE	SE	SN	SE	SE	SE	SN		SE	SE	SE	SN
		◇		◇	◇	◇		◇	◇	◇			◇	◇	◇		◇	◇	◇			◇	◇	◇	
Brighton	d																								
Lewes	d																								
Eastbourne	a																								
Eastbourne	d						05 49					06 49				07 49				08 49					09 49
Hampden Park	d						05 53					06 53				07 53				08 53					09 53
Pevensey & Westham	d						05 59					06 59				07 59				08 59					09 59
Pevensey Bay	d																								
Normans Bay	d						06 04					07 04				08 04				09 04					10 04
Cooden Beach	d						06 09					07 08				08 08				09 08					10 08
Collington	d						06 12					07 12				08 12				09 12					10 12
Bexhill	d						06 16					07 15				08 15				09 15					10 15
St Leonards Warrior Sq	d						06 22					07 22				08 22				09 22					10 22
Hastings	d		05 20				06 26					07 26				08 26				09 26					10 26
Ore	d		05 24				06 30					07 30				08 30				09 30					10 30
Three Oaks	d		05 30				06 36									08 36									10 36
Doleham	d		05 33																						
Winchelsea	d		05 39									07 42								09 42					
Rye	a		05 42				06 47					07 45				08 46				09 45					10 46
	d		05 44				06 47					07 47				08 47				09 47					10 47
Appledore (Kent)	d		05 53				06 56					07 56				08 56				09 56					10 56
Ham Street	a		05 58				07 01					08 01				09 01				10 01					11 01
Ashford International	a		06 06				07 09					08 10				09 10				10 10					11 10
Ashford International	d	05 43		06 15	06 16	06 43		07 15	07 16	07 43			08 15	08 16	08 43		09 15	09 16	09 43			10 15	10 19	10 43	
Ebbsfleet International	a	06 02		08 46	06 35	07 02		09 46	07 35	08 02			10 46	08 35	09 02		11 46	09 35	10 02			12 46	10 38	11 02	
Stratford International	a	06 14		08 58	06 47	07 14		10 02	07 47	08 14			10 58	08 47	09 14		11 58	09 47	10 14			12 58	10 50	11 14	
St Pancras International	a	06 21		09 06	06 54	07 21		10 10	07 54	08 21			11 06	08 54	09 21		12 06	09 54	10 21			13 06	10 57	11 21	

		SE	SE	SE	SN	SE		SE	SE	SN	SE	SE	SE	SN	SE	SE		SE	SN	SE	SE	SE	SN	SE	SE
		◇	◇	◇		◇		◇	◇		◇	◇	◇		◇	◇		◇		◇	◇	◇		◇	◇
Brighton	d																								
Lewes	d																								
Eastbourne	a																								
Eastbourne	d				10 49					11 49				12 49					13 49				14 49		
Hampden Park	d				10 53					11 53				12 53					13 53				14 53		
Pevensey & Westham	d				10 59					11 59				12 59					13 59				14 59		
Pevensey Bay	d																								
Normans Bay	d				11 04					12 04				13 04					14 04				15 04		
Cooden Beach	d				11 08					12 08				13 08					14 08				15 08		
Collington	d				11 12					12 12				13 12					14 12				15 12		
Bexhill	d				11 15					12 15				13 15					14 15				15 15		
St Leonards Warrior Sq	d				11 22					12 22				13 22					14 22				15 22		
Hastings	d				11 26					12 26				13 26					14 26				15 26		
Ore	d				11 30					12 30				13 30					14 30				15 30		
Three Oaks	d									12 36									14 36						
Doleham	d																								
Winchelsea	d				11 42									13 42									15 42		
Rye	a				11 45					12 46				13 45					14 46				15 45		
	d				11 47					12 47				13 47					14 47				15 47		
Appledore (Kent)	d				11 56					12 56				13 56					14 56				15 56		
Ham Street	a				12 01					13 01				14 01					15 01				16 01		
Ashford International	a				12 10					13 10				14 10					15 10				16 10		
Ashford International	d	11 15	11 19	11 43		12 15		12 16	12 43		13 16	13 18	13 45		14 15	14 16		14 45		15 15	15 16	15 46		16 15	16 16
Ebbsfleet International	a	13 46	11 38	12 02		14 46		12 35	13 02		13 35	15 46	14 04		16 46	14 35		15 04		17 46	15 35	16 05		18 46	16 35
Stratford International	a	14 02	11 50	12 14		14 58		12 47	13 14		13 47	16 02	14 16		17 02	14 47		15 16		18 02	15 47	16 17		18 58	16 47
St Pancras International	a	14 10	11 58	12 21		15 06		12 55	13 21		13 54	16 10	14 23		17 10	14 54		15 23		18 10	15 54	16 24		19 06	16 54

Table T192-F

Eastbourne - Hastings - Rye - Ashford with Brighton and London connect

Saturdays
21 December to 16 May

		SE ◇		SN	SE ◇	SE ◇	SE ◇	SN	SE ◇	SE ◇	SE ◇	SN		SE ◇	SE ◇	SE ◇	SN	SE ◇	SE ◇	SE ◇	SN	SE ◇		SE ◇	SN
Brighton	d																								
Lewes	d																								
Eastbourne	a																								
Eastbourne	d			15 49				16 49				17 49					18 49				19 49				20 49
Hampden Park	d			15 53				16 53				17 53					18 53				19 53				20 53
Pevensey & Westham	d			15 59				16 59				17 59					18 59				19 59				20 59
Pevensey Bay	d																								
Normans Bay	d			16 04				17 04				18 04					19 04				20 04				21 04
Cooden Beach	d			16 08				17 08				18 08					19 08				20 08				21 08
Collington	d			16 12				17 12				18 12					19 12				20 12				21 12
Bexhill	d			16 15				17 15				18 15					19 15				20 15				21 15
St Leonards Warrior Sq	d			16 22				17 22				18 22					19 22				20 22				21 22
Hastings	d			16 26				17 26				18 26					19 26				20 26				21 26
Ore	d			16 30				17 30				18 30					19 30				20 30				21 30
Three Oaks	d			16 36								18 36									20 36				
Doleham	d																								
Winchelsea	d							17 42									19 42								21 41
Rye	a			16 46				17 45				18 46					19 45				20 46				21 45
	d			16 47				17 47				18 47					19 47				20 47				21 47
Appledore (Kent)	d			16 56				17 56				18 56					19 56				20 56				21 56
Ham Street	a			17 01				18 01				19 01					20 01				21 01				22 01
Ashford International	a			17 10				18 10				19 10					20 10				21 10				22 10
Ashford International	d	16 43			17 15	17 19	17 43		18 15	18 19	18 43			19 15	19 16	19 43		20 15	20 16	20 45		21 16		21 43	
Ebbsfleet International	a	17 02			19 46	17 38	18 02		20 46	18 38	19 02			21 46	19 35	20 02		22 46	20 35	21 04		21 35		22 02	
Stratford International	a	17 14			19 58	17 50	18 14		20 58	18 50	19 14			21 58	19 47	20 14		22 58	20 47	21 16		21 47		22 14	
St Pancras International	a	17 21			20 06	17 58	18 21		21 06	18 58	19 21			22 06	19 54	20 21		23 06	20 54	21 23		21 54		22 21	

		SE ◇	SE ◇	SN	SE ◇
Brighton	d				
Lewes	d				
Eastbourne	a				
Eastbourne	d			21 49	
Hampden Park	d			21 53	
Pevensey & Westham	d			21 59	
Pevensey Bay	d				
Normans Bay	d			22 04	
Cooden Beach	d			22 08	
Collington	d			22 12	
Bexhill	d			22 15	
St Leonards Warrior Sq	d			22 21	
Hastings	d			22 26	
Ore	d			22 29	
Three Oaks	d			22 35	
Doleham	d			22 38	
Winchelsea	d			22 44	
Rye	a			22 48	
	d			22 48	
Appledore (Kent)	d			22 57	
Ham Street	a			23 02	
Ashford International	a			23 10	
Ashford International	d	22 16	22 43		23 16
Ebbsfleet International	a	22 35	23 02		23 35
Stratford International	a	22 47	23 14		23 47
St Pancras International	a	22 54	23 21		23 54

Sundays
15 December to 10 May

		SE ◇	SN	SE ◇	SE ◇	SE ◇	SN	SE ◇	SE ◇	SE ◇		SN	SE ◇	SE ◇	SE ◇	SN	SE ◇	SE ◇	SE ◇	SN		SE ◇	SE ◇	SE ◇	SN
Brighton	d																								
Lewes	d																								
Eastbourne	a																								
Eastbourne	d						07 59					08 56				09 56				10 56					11 56
Hampden Park	d																								
Pevensey & Westham	d																								
Pevensey Bay	d																								
Normans Bay	d																								
Cooden Beach	d																								
Collington	d																								
Bexhill	d						08 16					09 14				10 14				11 14					12 14
St Leonards Warrior Sq	d						08 22					09 21				10 21				11 21					12 21
Hastings	d		07 24				08 26					09 26				10 26				11 26					12 26
Ore	d		07 28				08 30					09 30				10 30				11 30					12 30
Three Oaks	d		07 34				08 36									10 36									12 36
Doleham	d		07 37																						
Winchelsea	d		07 43									09 42								11 42					
Rye	a		07 46				08 47					09 46				10 46				11 46					12 46
	d		07 48				08 48					09 48				10 48				11 48					12 48
Appledore (Kent)	d		07 57				08 57					09 57				10 57				11 57					12 57
Ham Street	a		08 02				09 02					10 02				11 02				12 02					13 02
Ashford International	a		08 10				09 10					10 10				11 10				12 10					13 10
Ashford International	d	07 43		08 15	08 16	08 43		09 15	09 16	09 43			10 15	10 16	10 43		11 15	11 16	11 43			12 15	12 16	12 43	
Ebbsfleet International	a	08 02		10 46	08 35	09 02		11 46	09 35	10 02			12 46	10 35	11 02		13 46	11 35	12 02			14 46	12 35	13 02	
Stratford International	a	08 14		10 58	08 47	09 14		11 58	09 47	10 14			12 58	10 47	11 14		13 58	11 47	12 14			14 59	12 47	13 14	
St Pancras International	a	08 21		11 06	08 54	09 21		12 06	09 54	10 21			13 06	10 54	11 21		14 06	11 54	12 21			15 07	12 54	13 21	

Table T192-F

Eastbourne - Hastings - Rye - Ashford with Brighton and London connect

Sundays
15 December to 10 May

		SE ◇	SE ◇	SE ◇	SN	SE ◇		SE ◇	SE ◇	SN	SE ◇	SE ◇	SE ◇	SN	SE ◇	SE ◇		SE ◇	SN	SE ◇	SE ◇	SE ◇	SN	SE ◇	SE ◇
Brighton	d																								
Lewes	d																								
Eastbourne	a																								
Eastbourne	d				12 56					13 56				14 56					15 56				16 56		
Hampden Park	d																								
Pevensey & Westham	d																								
Pevensey Bay	d																								
Normans Bay	d																								
Cooden Beach	d																								
Collington	d																								
Bexhill	d				13 14					14 14				15 14					16 14				17 14		
St Leonards Warrior Sq	d				13 21					14 21				15 21					16 21				17 21		
Hastings	d				13 26					14 26				15 26					16 26				17 26		
Ore	d				13 30					14 30				15 30					16 30				17 30		
Three Oaks	d									14 36									16 36						
Doleham	d																								
Winchelsea	d				13 42									15 42									17 42		
Rye	a				13 46					14 46				15 46					16 46				17 46		
	d				13 48					14 48				15 48					16 48				17 48		
Appledore (Kent)	d				13 57					14 57				15 57					16 57				17 57		
Ham Street	a				14 02					15 02				16 02					17 02				18 02		
Ashford International	a				14 10					15 10				16 10					17 10				18 10		
Ashford International	d	13 15	13 16	13 43		14 15		14 16	14 43		15 15	15 16	15 43		16 15	16 16		16 43		17 15	17 16	17 43		18 15	18 16
Ebbsfleet International	a	15 46	13 35	14 02		16 46		14 35	15 02		17 46	15 35	16 02		18 46	16 35		17 02		19 46	17 35	18 02		20 46	18 35
Stratford International	a	16 02	13 47	14 14		17 02		14 47	15 14		18 02	15 47	16 14		18 59	16 47		17 14		19 58	17 47	18 14		20 58	18 47
St Pancras International	a	16 10	13 54	14 21		17 10		14 54	15 21		18 10	15 54	16 21		19 07	16 54		17 21		20 06	17 54	18 21		21 06	18 54

		SE ◇		SN	SE ◇	SE ◇	SE ◇	SN	SE ◇	SE ◇	SE ◇	SN		SE ◇	SE ◇	SN	SE ◇	SE ◇
Brighton	d																	
Lewes	d																	
Eastbourne	a																	
Eastbourne	d			17 56				18 56				19 56				20 56		
Hampden Park	d																	
Pevensey & Westham	d																	
Pevensey Bay	d																	
Normans Bay	d																	
Cooden Beach	d																	
Collington	d																	
Bexhill	d			18 14				19 14				20 14				21 14		
St Leonards Warrior Sq	d			18 21				19 21				20 21				21 21		
Hastings	d			18 26				19 26				20 26				21 25		
Ore	d			18 30				19 30				20 30				21 29		
Three Oaks	d			18 36								20 36				21 35		
Doleham	d															21 38		
Winchelsea	d							19 42								21 44		
Rye	a			18 46				19 46				20 46				21 47		
	d			18 48				19 48				20 48				21 48		
Appledore (Kent)	d			18 57				19 57				20 57				21 57		
Ham Street	a			19 02				20 02				21 02				22 02		
Ashford International	a			19 10				20 10				21 10				22 10		
Ashford International	d	18 43			19 15	19 16	19 43		20 15	20 16	20 43			21 16	21 43		22 16	22 43
Ebbsfleet International	a	19 02			21 46	19 35	20 02		22 46	20 35	21 02			21 35	22 02		22 35	23 02
Stratford International	a	19 14			21 59	19 47	20 14		22 58	20 47	21 14			21 47	22 14		22 47	23 14
St Pancras International	a	19 21			22 07	19 54	20 21		23 06	20 54	21 21			21 54	22 21		22 54	23 21

Table T192-R

Mondays to Fridays

16 December to 15 May

London connect and Brighton with Ashford - Rye - Hastings - Eastbourne

		SE MX ◇	SN	SN	SE ◇	SN		SE ◇	SN	SE ◇	SE ◇	SN	SN	SE ◇	SE ◇	SN		SE ◇	SE ◇	SE ◇	SN	SE ◇	SE ◇	SE ◇	SN
St Pancras International	d	00 12			06 40			07 05		07 25	07 37			08 12	08 37			09 09	09 37	07 22		10 09	10 37	08 25	
Stratford International	d	00 19			06 47			07 12		07 32	07 44			08 19	08 44			09 16	09 44	07 29		10 16	10 44	08 32	
Ebbsfleet International	d	00 30			06 59			07 23		07 43	07 55			08 30	08 55			09 27	09 55	07 40		10 27	10 55	08 43	
Ashford International	a	00 50			07 19			07 42		08 02	08 14			08 50	09 14			09 47	10 14	10 15		10 47	11 14	11 15	
Ashford International	d		06 15	06 35		07 22			07 45			08 25	08 45			09 25					10 25				11 25
Ham Street	d		06 23	06 43		07 30			07 53			08 33	08 53			09 33					10 33				11 33
Appledore (Kent)	d		06 27	06 47		07 34			07 57			08 37	08 58			09 37					10 37				11 37
Rye	a		06 36	06 56		07 43			08 06			08 46	09 07			09 46					10 46				11 46
	d		06 39			07 45						08 48	09 08			09 47					10 47				11 47
Winchelsea	d		06 43			07 48						08 51	09 11								10 50				
Doleham	d		06 49			07 55							09 18												
Three Oaks	d		06 53			07 58						08 59	09 21			09 58									11 57
Ore	d		06 59			08 04						09 05	09 28			10 03					11 03				12 03
Hastings	d		07 09			08 08						09 09	09a31			10 07					11 07				12 07
St Leonards Warrior Sq	d		07 12			08 11						09 12				10 10					11 10				12 10
Bexhill	d		07 20			08 19						09 20				10 18					11 18				12 18
Collington	d		07 22			08 22						09 22				10 20					11 20				12 20
Cooden Beach	d		07 25			08 25						09 25				10 23					11 23				12 23
Normans Bay	d															10 27					11 27				12 27
Pevensey Bay	d																								
Pevensey & Westham	d		07 32			08 32						09 32				10 32					11 32				12 32
Hampden Park	d		07 38			08 38						09 38				10 38					11 38				12 38
Eastbourne	a		07 42			08 43						09 43				10 44					11 44				12 44
Eastbourne	d																								
Lewes	d																								
Brighton	a																								

		SE ◇		SE ◇	SE ◇	SN	SE ◇	SE ◇	SE ◇	SN	SE ◇	SE ◇		SE ◇	SN	SE ◇	SE ◇	SE ◇	SN	SE ◇	SE ◇	SE ◇		SN	SE ◇
St Pancras International	d	11 12		11 37	09 25		12 12	12 37	10 27		13 12	13 37		11 25		14 10	14 37	12 27		15 12	15 37	13 25			16 10
Stratford International	d	11 19		11 44	09 32		12 19	12 44	10 34		13 19	13 44		11 32		14 17	14 44	12 34		15 19	15 44	13 32			16 17
Ebbsfleet International	d	11 30		11 55	09 44		12 30	12 55	10 45		13 30	13 55		11 43		14 28	14 55	12 45		15 30	15 55	13 43			16 28
Ashford International	a	11 50		12 14	12 15		12 50	13 14	13 15		13 50	14 14		14 15		14 48	15 14	15 15		15 50	16 14	16 15			16 48
Ashford International	d					12 25				13 25					14 25				15 25					16 25	
Ham Street	d					12 33				13 33					14 33				15 33					16 33	
Appledore (Kent)	d					12 37				13 37					14 37				15 37					16 37	
Rye	a					12 46				13 46					14 46				15 46					16 46	
	d					12 47				13 47					14 47				15 47					16 48	
Winchelsea	d					12 50									14 50									16 51	
Doleham	d																								
Three Oaks	d									13 57									15 57					16 59	
Ore	d					13 03				14 03					15 03				16 03					17 05	
Hastings	d					13 07				14 07					15 07				16 07					17 09	
St Leonards Warrior Sq	d					13 10				14 10					15 10				16 10					17 12	
Bexhill	d					13 18				14 18					15 18				16 20					17 20	
Collington	d					13 20				14 20					15 20				16 23					17 23	
Cooden Beach	d					13 23				14 23					15 23				16 26					17 26	
Normans Bay	d					13 27				14 27															
Pevensey Bay	d																								
Pevensey & Westham	d					13 32				14 32					15 32				16 33					17 33	
Hampden Park	d					13 38				14 38					15 38				16 40					17 40	
Eastbourne	a					13 44				14 44					15 44				16 44					17 44	
Eastbourne	d																								
Lewes	d																								
Brighton	a																								

		SE ◇	SE ◇	SE ◇	SN	SE ◇	SE ◇	SN		SE ◇	SE ◇	SE ◇	SN	SE ◇	SE ◇	SN	SE ◇	SE ◇		SN	SE ◇	SN	SE ◇	SE ◇	SN
St Pancras International	d	16 37	14 25	16 50		17 07	17 20			15 25	17 37	17 50		18 07	18 20		18 37	18 50			19 07		19 20	19 37	
Stratford International	d	16 44	14 32	16 57		17 14	17 27			15 32	17 44	17 57		18 14	18 27		18 45	18 57			19 14		19 27	19 44	
Ebbsfleet International	d	16 55	14 43			17 25				15 43	17 56			18 26			18 56				19 26			19 55	
Ashford International	a	17 14	17 15	17 24		17 44	17 54			18 15	18 15	18 24		18 45	18 54		19 15	19 25			19 45		19 54	20 14	
Ashford International	d				17 25			17 55					18 25			18 55				19 25		19 52			20 25
Ham Street	d				17 33			18 03					18 33			19 03				19 33		20 00			20 33
Appledore (Kent)	d				17 38			18 07					18 37			19 07				19 37		20 04			20 37
Rye	a				17 47			18 16					18 46			19 16				19 46		20 13			20 46
	d				17 48								18 48							19 48		20 14			20 47
Winchelsea	d												18 52												20 50
Doleham	d																								
Three Oaks	d				17 58															19 59					
Ore	d				18 04								19 03							20 04		20 30			21 03
Hastings	d				18 08								19 07							20 08		20a33			21 07
St Leonards Warrior Sq	d				18 11								19 10							20 11					21 10
Bexhill	d				18 20								19 18							20 19					21 18
Collington	d				18 23								19 20							20 21					21 20
Cooden Beach	d				18 26								19 23							20 24					21 23
Normans Bay	d																			20 28					21 27
Pevensey Bay	d																								
Pevensey & Westham	d				18 33								19 32							20 33					21 32
Hampden Park	d				18 40								19 38							20 39					21 38
Eastbourne	a				18 44								19 43							20 43					21 43
Eastbourne	d																								
Lewes	d																								
Brighton	a																								

Table T192-R

Mondays to Fridays

16 December to 15 May

London connect and Brighton with Ashford - Rye - Hastings - Eastbourne

		SE ◇	SE ◇	SN ■1 A		SE ◇	SE ◇	SN	SE ◇	SE ◇	SN	SE ◇	SE ◇
St Pancras International	d	20 12	20 37			21 12	21 37		22 12	22 37		23 12	23 37
Stratford International	d	20 19	20 44			21 19	21 44		22 19	22 44		23 19	23 44
Ebbsfleet International	d	20 30	20 55			21 30	21 55		22 30	22 55		23 30	23 55
Ashford International	a	20 50	21 14			21 50	22 14		22 50	23 14		23 50	00 14
Ashford International	d			21 25				22 25			23 25		
Ham Street	d			21 33				22 33			23 33		
Appledore (Kent)	d			21 37				22 37			23 37		
Rye	a			21 46				22 46			23 46		
	d			21 48				22 49			23 47		
Winchelsea	d			21 51				22 53			23 50		
Doleham	d							22 59					
Three Oaks	d			21 59				23 03			23 58		
Ore	d			22 05				23 09			00 04		
Hastings	d			22 09				23a12			00a08		
St Leonards Warrior Sq	d			22 12									
Bexhill	d			22 20									
Collington	d			22 22									
Cooden Beach	d			22 25									
Normans Bay	d			22 29									
Pevensey Bay	d												
Pevensey & Westham	d			22 34									
Hampden Park	d			22 40									
Eastbourne	a			22 44									
Eastbourne	d												
Lewes	d												
Brighton	a												

Saturdays

21 December to 16 May

		SE ◇	SN	SE ◇	SN	SE ◇	SE ◇	SN	SE ◇	SE ◇		SN	SE ◇	SE ◇	SE ◇	SN	SE ◇	SE ◇	SE ◇	SN		SE ◇	SE ◇	SN	SE ◇
St Pancras International	d	00 12		06 37		07 07	07 37		08 12	08 37			09 09	09 34	07 25		10 09	10 37	08 25			11 37	09 25		12 37
Stratford International	d	00 19		06 44		07 14	07 44		08 19	08 44			09 16	09 41	07 32		10 16	10 44	08 32			11 44	09 32		12 44
Ebbsfleet International	d	00 30		06 55		07 25	07 55		08 30	08 55			09 27	09 52	07 43		10 27	10 55	08 43			11 55	09 44		12 55
Ashford International	a	00 50		07 14		07 44	08 14		08 50	09 14			09 47	10 11	10 15		10 47	11 14	11 15			12 14	12 15		13 14
Ashford International	d		06 25		07 25			08 25				09 25				10 25				11 25				12 25	
Ham Street	d		06 33		07 33			08 33				09 33				10 33				11 33				12 33	
Appledore (Kent)	d		06 37		07 37			08 37				09 37				10 37				11 37				12 37	
Rye	a		06 46		07 46			08 46				09 46				10 46				11 46				12 46	
	d		06 47		07 47			08 47				09 47				10 47				11 47				12 47	
Winchelsea	d		06 51					08 50								10 50								12 50	
Doleham	d		06 57																						
Three Oaks	d		07 01		07 57							09 57								11 57					
Ore	d		07 07		08 03			09 03				10 03				11 03				12 03				13 03	
Hastings	d		07 11		08 07			09 07				10 07				11 07				12 07				13 07	
St Leonards Warrior Sq	d		07 14		08 10			09 10				10 10				11 10				12 10				13 10	
Bexhill	d		07 23		08 18			09 18				10 18				11 18				12 18				13 18	
Collington	d				08 20			09 20				10 20				11 20				12 20				13 20	
Cooden Beach	d				08 23			09 23				10 23				11 23				12 23				13 23	
Normans Bay	d				08 27			09 27				10 27				11 27				12 27				13 27	
Pevensey Bay	d																								
Pevensey & Westham	d		07 31		08 32			09 32				10 32				11 32				12 32				13 32	
Hampden Park	d		07 38		08 38			09 38				10 38				11 38				12 38				13 38	
Eastbourne	a		07 43		08 43			09 43				10 43				11 43				12 43				13 43	
Eastbourne	d																								
Lewes	d																								
Brighton	a																								

		SE ◇	SN	SE ◇	SE ◇	SE ◇		SN	SE ◇	SE ◇	SN	SE ◇	SE ◇	SE ◇	SN	SE ◇		SE ◇	SE ◇	SN	SE ◇	SE ◇	SE ◇	SN	SE ◇
St Pancras International	d	10 25		13 12	13 37	11 25			14 37	12 27		15 12	15 37	13 25		16 10		16 37	14 25		17 12	17 37	15 25		18 37
Stratford International	d	10 32		13 19	13 44	11 32			14 44	12 34		15 19	15 44	13 32		16 17		16 44	14 32		17 19	17 44	15 32		18 44
Ebbsfleet International	d	10 43		13 30	13 55	11 43			14 55	12 45		15 30	15 55	13 43		16 28		16 55	14 43		17 30	17 55	15 43		18 55
Ashford International	a	13 15		13 50	14 14	14 15			15 14	15 15		15 50	16 14	16 15		16 48		17 14	17 15		17 50	18 14	18 15		19 14
Ashford International	d		13 25					14 25			15 25				16 25					17 25				18 25	
Ham Street	d		13 33					14 33			15 33				16 33					17 33				18 33	
Appledore (Kent)	d		13 37					14 37			15 37				16 37					17 37				18 37	
Rye	a		13 46					14 46			15 46				16 46					17 46				18 46	
	d		13 47					14 47			15 47				16 47					17 47				18 47	
Winchelsea	d							14 50							16 50									18 50	
Doleham	d																								
Three Oaks	d		13 57								15 57									17 57					
Ore	d		14 03					15 03			16 03				17 03					18 03				19 03	
Hastings	d		14 07					15 07			16 07				17 07					18 07				19 07	
St Leonards Warrior Sq	d		14 10					15 10			16 10				17 10					18 10				19 10	
Bexhill	d		14 18					15 18			16 18				17 18					18 18				19 18	
Collington	d		14 20					15 20			16 20				17 20					18 20				19 20	
Cooden Beach	d		14 23					15 23			16 23				17 23					18 23				19 23	
Normans Bay	d		14 27					15 27			16 27				17 27					18 27				19 27	
Pevensey Bay	d																								
Pevensey & Westham	d		14 32					15 32			16 32				17 32					18 32				19 32	
Hampden Park	d		14 38					15 38			16 38				17 38					18 38				19 38	
Eastbourne	a		14 43					15 43			16 43				17 43					18 43				19 43	
Eastbourne	d																								
Lewes	d																								
Brighton	a																								

A ■1 from Hastings

Table T192-R

Saturdays
21 December to 16 May

London connect and Brighton with Ashford - Rye - Hastings - Eastbourne

		SE	SN	SE	SE	SN	SE	SE	SE	SN	SE	SE	SE	SN	SE	SE	SE	SN	SE	SE	SE
		◇		◇	◇		◇	◇	◇		◇	◇	◇	1 A	◇	◇	◇		◇	◇	◇
St Pancras International	d	16 25		19 37	17 25		20 12	20 37	18 25		21 12	21 37	19 25		22 12	22 37	20 25		23 12	23 37	21 25
Stratford International	d	16 32		19 44	17 32		20 19	20 44	18 32		21 19	21 44	19 32		22 19	22 44	20 32		23 19	23 44	21 32
Ebbsfleet International	d	16 43		19 55	17 43		20 30	20 55	18 43		21 30	21 55	19 43		22 30	22 55	20 43		23 30	23 55	21 43
Ashford International	a	19 15		20 14	20 15		20 50	21 14	21 15		21 50	22 14	22 15		22 50	23 14	23 15		23 50	00 14	00 21
Ashford International	d		19 25			20 25				21 25				22 25				23 25			
Ham Street	d		19 33			20 33				21 33				22 33				23 33			
Appledore (Kent)	d		19 37			20 37				21 37				22 37				23 37			
Rye	a		19 46			20 46				21 46				22 46				23 46			
	d		19 47			20 47				21 47				22 48				23 47			
Winchelsea	d					20 50								22 52				23 50			
Doleham	d																	23 57			
Three Oaks	d		19 57							21 57								00 01			
Ore	d		20 03			21 03				22 03				23 03				00 07			
Hastings	d		20 07			21 07				22 07				23 07				00a10			
St Leonards Warrior Sq	d		20 10			21 10				22 10				23 10							
Bexhill	d		20 18			21 18				22 18				23 18							
Collington	d		20 20			21 20				22 20				23 20							
Cooden Beach	d		20 23			21 23				22 23				23 23							
Normans Bay	d		20 27			21 27				22 27				23 27							
Pevensey Bay	d																				
Pevensey & Westham	d		20 32			21 32				22 32				23 34							
Hampden Park	d		20 38			21 38				22 38				23 40							
Eastbourne	a		20 43			21 43				22 43				23 45							
Eastbourne	d																				
Lewes	d																				
Brighton	a																				

Sundays
15 December to 10 May

		SE	SN	SE	SN	SE	SE	SN	SE	SE	SE	SN	SE	SE	SE	SN	SE	SE	SE	SN	SE	SE	SE
		◇		◇		◇	◇		◇	◇	◇		◇	◇	◇		◇	◇	◇		◇	◇	◇
St Pancras International	d	00 12		08 37		09 09	09 37		10 09	10 37	08 25		11 12	11 37	09 25		12 12	12 37	10 27		13 12	13 37	11 25
Stratford International	d	00 19		08 44		09 16	09 44		10 16	10 44	08 32		11 19	11 44	09 32		12 19	12 44	10 34		13 19	13 44	11 32
Ebbsfleet International	d	00 30		08 55		09 27	09 55		10 27	10 55	08 43		11 30	11 55	09 44		12 30	12 55	10 45		13 30	13 55	11 43
Ashford International	a	00 50		09 14		09 47	10 14		10 47	11 14	11 15		11 50	12 14	12 15		12 50	13 14	13 15		13 50	14 14	14 15
Ashford International	d		08 25		09 25			10 25				11 25				12 25				13 25			
Ham Street	d		08 33		09 33			10 33				11 33				12 33				13 33			
Appledore (Kent)	d		08 37		09 37			10 37				11 37				12 37				13 37			
Rye	a		08 46		09 46			10 46				11 46				12 46				13 46			
	d		08 48		09 48			10 48				11 48				12 48				13 48			
Winchelsea	d		08 51					10 51								12 51							
Doleham	d		08 58																				
Three Oaks	d		09 01		09 58							11 58								13 58			
Ore	d		09 07		10 04			11 04				12 04				13 04				14 04			
Hastings	d		09 11		10 08			11 08				12 08				13 08				14 08			
St Leonards Warrior Sq	d		09 14		10 11			11 11				12 11				13 11				14 11			
Bexhill	d		09 22		10 19			11 19				12 19				13 19				14 19			
Collington	d																						
Cooden Beach	d																						
Normans Bay	d																						
Pevensey Bay	d																						
Pevensey & Westham	d																						
Hampden Park	d																						
Eastbourne	a		09 39		10 36			11 36				12 36				13 36				14 36			
Eastbourne	d																						
Lewes	d																						
Brighton	a																						

		SN	SE	SE	SE	SN	SE	SE	SE	SN	SE	SE	SE	SN	SE	SE	SE	SN	SE	SE	SE	SN	SE
			◇	◇	◇		◇	◇	◇		◇	◇	◇		◇	◇	◇		◇	◇	◇		◇
St Pancras International	d		14 10	14 37	12 27		15 12	15 37	13 25		16 12	16 37	14 25		17 07	17 37	15 25		18 12	18 37	16 25		19 12
Stratford International	d		14 17	14 44	12 34		15 19	15 44	13 32		16 19	16 44	14 32		17 14	17 44	15 32		18 19	18 44	16 32		19 19
Ebbsfleet International	d		14 28	14 55	12 45		15 30	15 55	13 43		16 30	16 55	14 43		17 25	17 55	15 43		18 30	18 55	16 43		19 30
Ashford International	a		14 48	15 14	15 15		15 50	16 14	16 15		16 50	17 14	17 15		17 44	18 14	18 15		18 50	19 14	19 15		19 50
Ashford International	d	14 25				15 25				16 25				17 25				18 25				19 25	
Ham Street	d	14 33				15 33				16 33				17 33				18 33				19 33	
Appledore (Kent)	d	14 37				15 37				16 37				17 37				18 37				19 37	
Rye	a	14 46				15 46				16 46				17 46				18 46				19 46	
	d	14 48				15 48				16 48				17 48				18 48				19 48	
Winchelsea	d	14 51								16 51								18 51					
Doleham	d																						
Three Oaks	d					15 58								17 58								19 58	
Ore	d	15 04				16 04				17 04				18 04				19 04				20 04	
Hastings	d	15 08				16 08				17 08				18 08				19 08				20 08	
St Leonards Warrior Sq	d	15 11				16 11				17 11				18 11				19 11				20 11	
Bexhill	d	15 19				16 19				17 19				18 19				19 19				20 19	
Collington	d																						
Cooden Beach	d																						
Normans Bay	d																						
Pevensey Bay	d																						
Pevensey & Westham	d																						
Hampden Park	d																						
Eastbourne	a	15 36				16 36				17 36				18 36				19 36				20 36	
Eastbourne	d																						
Lewes	d																						
Brighton	a																						

A 1 from Hastings

Table T192-R

Sundays
15 December to 10 May

London connect and Brighton with Ashford - Rye - Hastings - Eastbourne

		SE	SE	SN	SE	SE	SE	SN	SE	SE	SE	SN	SE	SE	SE	SE	SE
		◇	◇		◇	◇	◇		◇	◇	◇		◇	◇	◇	◇	◇
St Pancras International	d	19 37	17 25		20 12	20 37	18 25		21 12	21 37	19 25		22 12	22 37	20 25	23 12	23 37
Stratford International	d	19 44	17 32		20 19	20 44	18 32		21 19	21 44	19 32		22 19	22 44	20 32	23 19	23 44
Ebbsfleet International	d	19 55	17 43		20 30	20 55	18 43		21 30	21 55	19 43		22 30	22 55	20 43	23 30	23 55
Ashford International	a	20 14	20 15		20 50	21 14	21 15		21 50	22 14	22 15		22 50	23 14	23 15	23 50	00 15
Ashford International	d			20 25				21 25				22 34					
Ham Street	d			20 33				21 33				22 42					
Appledore (Kent)	d			20 37				21 37				22 46					
Rye	a			20 46				21 46				22 55					
	d			20 48				21 48				22 56					
Winchelsea	d			20 51								22 59					
Doleham	d											23 06					
Three Oaks	d							21 58				23 09					
Ore	d			21 04				22 04				23 15					
Hastings	d			21 08				22 08				23a19					
St Leonards Warrior Sq	d			21 11				22 11									
Bexhill	d			21 19				22 19									
Collington	d																
Cooden Beach	d																
Normans Bay	d																
Pevensey Bay	d																
Pevensey & Westham	d																
Hampden Park	d																
Eastbourne	a			21 36				22 36									
Eastbourne	d																
Lewes	d																
Brighton	a																

AVAILABLE FROM MP Middleton Press

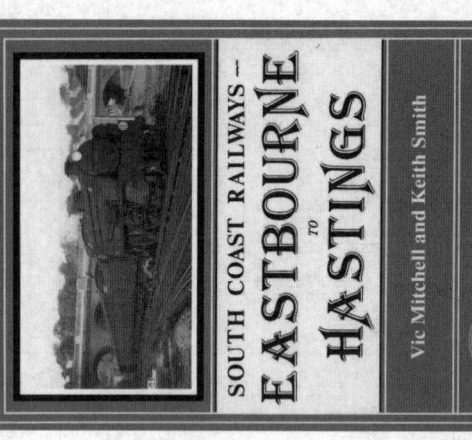

SOUTH COAST RAILWAYS –
EASTBOURNE
TO
HASTINGS
Vic Mitchell and Keith Smith
SOUTHERN MP CLASSICS
Middleton Press

Table T194-F

Mondays to Fridays

16 December to 15 May

St Pancras International - Kent High Speed Domestic Services

Miles	Miles	Miles	Miles			SE MX ◇ A	SE MO ◇ A	SE MX ◇ A	SE TThFO ◇ A	SE MX ◇1 B	SE MO ◇1 B	SE WO C 🚌	SE MO ◇ A	SE WO ◇ A	SE ThFO ◇ A	SE WO C 🚌	SE WO 🚌	SE TO ◇ A	SE WO C 🚌	SE TO D 🚌	SE WO C 🚌	SE WO C 🚌	SE TO D 🚌	SE MX ◇ A
0	0	0	0	**St Pancras International** 15 ⊖	d																			
6	6	6	6	**Stratford International** ⊖	d			00 02																
22¾	22¾	22¾	22¾	**Ebbsfleet International**	a			00 12																
—	—	—	—		d			00 13																
24¾	—	—	24¾	Gravesend 4	d			00 18																
32	—	—	32	Strood 4	d			00 29																
—	—	—	44¼	Maidstone West	d																			
33	—	—	—	Rochester 4	d	00 02	00 02	00 32																
33½	—	—	—	Chatham 4	d	00 06	00 06	00 36																
35¼	—	—	—	Gillingham (Kent) 4	d	00 10	00 10	00 40																
38¼	—	—	—	Rainham (Kent)	d	00 15	00 15	00 45																
44	—	—	—	Sittingbourne 4	d	00 23	00 23	00 53																
51¼	—	—	—	**Faversham** 2	a	00 31	00 32	01 03																
58¾	—	—	—	Whitstable	d																00 19			
62½	—	—	—	Herne Bay	d														00 14		00 35			
70½	—	—	—	Birchington-on-Sea	d														00 34		00 55			
73½	—	—	—	Margate 4	d				00 04			00 22				00 43			00 45		01 06	01 22		
76¾	—	—	—	**Broadstairs**	a				00 09			00 32				00 53			00 55		01 16	01 32		
—	—	—	—	Ramsgate	d				00a16			00a43				01a04			01a06		01a27	01a43		
—	56	56	—	**Ashford International**	a																			
—	—	—	—		d					00 04	00 05													00 15
—	69¼	—	—	Folkestone West	d					00 21	00 21													00 28
—	70	—	—	Folkestone Central	d					00 24	00 24													00 31
—	77¼	—	—	**Dover Priory** 4	d					00a35	00a35													00 43
—	—	—	—	Deal	a																			01s01
—	—	—	—	Sandwich	a																			01s07
—	—	—	—	Dover Priory	a																			
—	—	70¼	—	**Canterbury West** 4	a																			
—	—	—	—		d								00 07	00 07	00 08					00 19			00 34	
—	—	87¾	—	Ramsgate 4	d								00 27	00a31	00 30		00 36	00 44		01a02			01s12	01a23
—	—	87¾	—	Broadstairs	d								00s32		00s35		00s45	00s49					01s21	
—	—	91	—	**Margate** 4	a								00 38		00 40		00 55	00 57					01 31	
—	—	—	—	St Pancras International	a																			

		SE WThFO ◇1 B		SE TO ◇1 B	SE TO 🚌	SE MX ◇	SE MX ◇1 B	SE WO C 🚌	SE WThFO ◇	SE TO 🚌	SE ◇1 E	SE ◇1 F	TL G		SE ◇ H	SE ◇1 I	TL G	SE ◇1 J	SE ◇1 E	TL K	SE ◇1 I	SE ◇ H	TL K	SE ◇	
St Pancras International 15 ⊖	d					00 12																		06 25	
Stratford International ⊖	d					00 19																		06 32	
Ebbsfleet International	a					00 30																		06 42	
	d					00 30																		06 43	
Gravesend 4	d												04 59				05 29			05 59			06 30	06 48	
Strood 4	d																							07 02	
Maidstone West	d																							07a16	
Rochester 4	d																								
Chatham 4	d																								
Gillingham (Kent) 4	d																								
Rainham (Kent)	d																								
Sittingbourne 4	d																								
Faversham 2	a																								
Whitstable	d							00 58																	
Herne Bay	d							01 14																	
Birchington-on-Sea	d							01 34																	
Margate 4	d							01 45																	
Broadstairs	a							01 55																	
Ramsgate	d							02a06				04 51				05 20									
Ashford International	a					00 50																			
	d	00 34		00 34	00 40		01 05		01 07	01 10															
Folkestone West	d						01s22																		
Folkestone Central	d						01s24																		
Dover Priory 4	d						01a38																		
Deal	a																								
Sandwich	a											05 05				05 33									
Dover Priory	a											05 29				05 57									
Canterbury West 4	a	00 55			01 19				01 30	01 49															
	d	00 56			01 19																				
Ramsgate 4	d	01a20		01a29	02a02						04 25				05 12				05 56						
Broadstairs	d										04 31				05 18			05 42	06 02		06 23	06 29			
Margate 4	a										04 36				05 23			05 46	06 07		06 27	06 33			
St Pancras International	a												06 13				06 43			07 13			07 43		

A From St Pancras International
B From London Charing Cross
C From Faversham
D From Ashford International
E To London Victoria
F To London Charing Cross
G From Gillingham (Kent) to Luton
H To St Pancras International
I To London Cannon Street
J To London Blackfriars
K From Rainham (Kent) to Luton

NRT DECEMBER 19 EDITION

Table T194-F

Mondays to Fridays

16 December to 15 May

St Pancras International - Kent High Speed Domestic Services

		SE ◇1 A	SE 1	SE ◇ B	SE ◇1 C	SE 1 D	SE ◇1 E	SE ◇ F	SE ◇ B	SE ◇1 G	SE 1		SE 1 H	SE	TL I	SE ◇1 G	SE ◇1 A	SE ◇1 J	SE K	SE ◇	SE	SE ◇1 A		SE ◇	SE ◇
St Pancras International 15 ⊖	d																			06 40				06 55	07 05
Stratford International ⊖	d																			06 47				07 02	07 12
Ebbsfleet International	a																			06 58				07 12	07 22
	d																			06 59				07 15	07 23
Gravesend 4	d														06 59									07 20	
Strood 4	d																							07 31	
Maidstone West	d																								
Rochester 4	d																							07 34	
Chatham 4	d																							07 38	
Gillingham (Kent) 4	d																							07 43	
Rainham (Kent)	d																							07 47	
Sittingbourne 4	d																							07 55	
Faversham 2	a																							08 03	
Whitstable	d							06 30					07 01												
Herne Bay	d							06 37					07 08												
Birchington-on-Sea	d							06 45					07 16												
Margate 4	d							06 53					07 24												
Broadstairs	a							06 58					07 29												
Ramsgate	d			06 14	06 50			07 08					07a36												
Ashford International	a																			07 19					07 42
	d		05 25			06 05					06 28			06 30				07 00	07 05		07 22				07 44
Folkestone West	d		05 42								06 45							07 17							
Folkestone Central	d		05 45								06 48							07 20							
Dover Priory 4	d		05 57								07 10							07 34							
Deal	a		06 14	06 32							07 27							07 52							
Sandwich	a		06 20		07 02			07 20			07 33							07 59							
Dover Priory	a			06 47	07 24			07 43																	
Canterbury West 4	a					06 26								06 51					07 26		07 43				07 58
	d					06 28								06 52							07 44				08 00
Ramsgate 4	d	06 30	06a36			06a52				06 55	07a46			07 14		07 19	07 40	08a16			08a05	08 10			08 23
Broadstairs	d	06 36					06 41		06 58	07 02				07 20		07 25	07 46					08 16			08 28
Margate 4	a	06 40					06 46		07 02	07 06				07 26		07 30	07 51					08 21			08 34
St Pancras International	a														08 13										

		TL L	SE ◇1 C	SE ◇1 C	SE 1 H	SE ◇1 M	SE ◇1 A	SE 1 H	SE ◇ B		SE ◇	SE ◇ B	TL L	SE ◇	TL I	SE ◇1 J	SE ◇1 J	SE ◇	SE ◇1 J	SE ◇1 A		SE ◇ B	TL I	SE ◇1 J	SE ◇ B
St Pancras International 15 ⊖	d								07 22		07 25	07 37		08 04				08 12				08 25			08 37
Stratford International ⊖	d								07 29		07 32	07 44		08 11				08 19				08 32			08 44
Ebbsfleet International	a								07 39		07 42	07 54		08 22				08 30				08 42			08 54
	d								07 40		07 43	07 55		08 23				08 30				08 43			08 55
Gravesend 4	d	07 29							07 44				07 59	08 29	08 30							08 48	08 59		
Strood 4	d								07 56					08 40								08 59			
Maidstone West	d																								
Rochester 4	d								07 59					08 44								09 02			
Chatham 4	d								08 02					08 47								09 06			
Gillingham (Kent) 4	d								08 07					08 53								09 10			
Rainham (Kent)	d								08 11					08 58								09 15			
Sittingbourne 4	d								08 19					09 05								09 23			
Faversham 2	a								08 27					09 14								09 31			
Whitstable	d				07 32			08 01	08 35													09 40			
Herne Bay	d				07 39			08 08	08 42													09 45			
Birchington-on-Sea	d				07 47			08 16	08 51													09 54			
Margate 4	d				07 59			08 24	08 59													09 59			
Broadstairs	a				08 04			08 29	09 04													10 05			
Ramsgate	d		07 42	07 58	08a11			08a37	09 12													10 12			
Ashford International	a										08 02	08 14						08 50							09 14
	d					07 58					08 07	08 15				08 33	08 38	08 52	09 05					09 08	09 15
Folkestone West	d										08 23	08 28					08 55		09 21						09 28
Folkestone Central	d										08 26	08 31					08 58		09 24						09 31
Dover Priory 4	d										08a37	08 42					09a11		09a38						09 43
Deal	a											09 00													10 00
Sandwich	a		08 01	08 17					09 24			09 07										10 24			10 07
Dover Priory	a		08 24	08 45					09 47													10 47			
Canterbury West 4	a					08 19										08 54		09 06						09 30	
	d					08 20										08 54		09 08							
Ramsgate 4	d					08a45	08 53					09 20				09a18		09 31		09 53					10 20
Broadstairs	d						08 59					09 25						09 36		09 59					10 25
Margate 4	a						09 04					09 29						09 42		10 04					10 29
St Pancras International	a	08 43											09 13		09 43								10 13		

A To London Victoria
B To St Pancras International
C To London Charing Cross
D From Tonbridge
E From Dumpton Park to London Cannon Street
F From Faversham to St Pancras International
G To London Cannon Street
H From Faversham
I From Rainham (Kent) to Luton
J From London Charing Cross
K From Maidstone East to Minster
L From Rainham (Kent) to West Hampstead Thameslink
M From London Cannon Street

Table T194-F

Mondays to Fridays

16 December to 15 May

St Pancras International - Kent High Speed Domestic Services

		SE ◇	TL A	SE ◇■ B	SE ◇	SE ◇■ B	SE ◇■ C	SE ◇ D	SE ◇ D	TL A	SE ◇	TL A	SE ◇■ B	SE ◇	SE ◇■ B	SE ◇■ C	SE ◇ D	SE ◇ D	TL A	SE ◇	TL A	SE ◇■ B	SE ◇
St Pancras International ⊖	d	08 57			09 09			09 25	09 37		09 55			10 09			10 27	10 37		10 52			11 12
Stratford International ⊖	d	09 04			09 16			09 32	09 44		10 02			10 16			10 34	10 44		10 59			11 19
Ebbsfleet International	a	09 14			09 27			09 43	09 54		10 12			10 26			10 44	10 54		11 09			11 30
	d	09 15			09 27			09 44	09 55		10 13			10 27			10 45	10 55		11 13			11 30
Gravesend	d	09 19	09 29					09 48		09 59	10 18	10 29					10 49		10 59	11 18	11 29		
Strood	d	09 30						09 59			10 29						10 59			11 29			
Maidstone West	d																						
Rochester	d	09 33						10 02			10 32						11 02			11 32			
Chatham	d	09 37						10 06			10 36						11 06			11 36			
Gillingham (Kent)	d	09 41						10 10			10 40						11 10			11 40			
Rainham (Kent)	d	09 46						10 15			10 45						11 15			11 45			
Sittingbourne	d	09 54						10 23			10 54						11 23			11 54			
Faversham	a	10 05						10 31			11 05						11 31			12 05			
Whitstable	d							10 40									11 40						
Herne Bay	d							10 45									11 45						
Birchington-on-Sea	d							10 54									11 54						
Margate	d							10 59									11 59						
Broadstairs	a							11 05									12 05						
Ramsgate	d							11 12									12 12						
Ashford International	a				09 47				10 14					10 47				11 14					11 50
	d			09 35	09 52	10 05			10 15				10 35	10 52	11 02			11 15				11 35	11 52
Folkestone West	d					10 22			10 28						11 19			11 28					
Folkestone Central	d					10 25			10 31						11 22			11 31					
Dover Priory	d					10a38			10 42						11a33			11 42					
Deal	a								11 00									12 00					
Sandwich	a							11 24	11 07								12 24	12 07					
Dover Priory	a							11 47									12 47						
Canterbury West	a			09 53	10 06								10 53	11 06								11 53	12 06
	d			09 54	10 08								10 54	11 08								11 54	12 08
Ramsgate	d			10a18	10 28		10 53		11 20				11a19	11 28		11 53		12 20				12a16	12 28
Broadstairs	d				10 33		10 59		11 25					11 33		11 59		12 25					12 33
Margate	a				10 38		11 04		11 29					11 38		12 04		12 29					12 38
St Pancras International	a		10 43							11 13		11 43							12 13		12 43		

		SE ◇■ B	SE ◇■ C	SE ◇ D	SE ◇ D	TL A	SE ◇	TL A	SE ◇■ B	SE ◇	SE ◇■ B	SE ◇■ C	SE ◇ D	SE ◇ D	TL A	SE ◇	TL A	SE ◇■ B	SE ◇	SE ◇■ B	SE ◇■ C	SE ◇ D	SE ◇ D
St Pancras International ⊖	d			11 25	11 37		11 55			12 12			12 27	12 37		12 52			13 12			13 25	13 37
Stratford International ⊖	d			11 32	11 44		12 02			12 19			12 34	12 44		12 59			13 19			13 32	13 44
Ebbsfleet International	a			11 42	11 54		12 12			12 30			12 44	12 54		13 09			13 30			13 42	13 54
	d			11 43	11 55		12 13			12 30			12 45	12 55		13 13			13 30			13 43	13 55
Gravesend	d			11 48		11 59	12 18	12 29					12 49		12 59	13 18	13 29					13 48	
Strood	d			11 59			12 29						12 59			13 29						13 59	
Maidstone West	d																						
Rochester	d			12 02			12 32						13 02			13 32						14 02	
Chatham	d			12 06			12 36						13 06			13 36						14 06	
Gillingham (Kent)	d			12 10			12 40						13 10			13 40						14 10	
Rainham (Kent)	d			12 15			12 45						13 15			13 45						14 15	
Sittingbourne	d			12 23			12 54						13 23			13 54						14 23	
Faversham	a			12 31			13 05						13 31			14 05						14 31	
Whitstable	d			12 40									13 40									14 40	
Herne Bay	d			12 45									13 45									14 45	
Birchington-on-Sea	d			12 54									13 54									14 54	
Margate	d			12 59									13 59									14 59	
Broadstairs	a			13 05									14 05									15 05	
Ramsgate	d			13 12									14 12									15 12	
Ashford International	a				12 14					12 50				13 14					13 50				14 14
	d	12 02			12 15				12 35	12 52	13 02			13 15				13 35	13 52	14 02			14 15
Folkestone West	d	12 19			12 28						13 19			13 28						14 19			14 28
Folkestone Central	d	12 22			12 31						13 22			13 31						14 22			14 31
Dover Priory	d	12a33			12 42						13a33			13 42						14a33			14 42
Deal	a				13 00									14 00									15 00
Sandwich	a			13 24	13 07								14 24	14 07								15 24	15 07
Dover Priory	a			13 47									14 47									15 47	
Canterbury West	a								12 53	13 06								13 53	14 06				
	d								12 54	13 08								13 54	14 08				
Ramsgate	d		12 53		13 20				13a16	13 28		13 53		14 20				14a16	14 28		14 49		15 20
Broadstairs	d		12 59		13 25					13 33		13 59		14 25					14 33		14 55		15 25
Margate	a		13 04		13 29					13 38		14 04		14 29					14 38		14 59		15 29
St Pancras International	a					13 13		13 43							14 13		14 43						

A From Rainham (Kent) to Luton
B From London Charing Cross
C To London Victoria
D To St Pancras International

Table T194-F

Mondays to Fridays

16 December to 15 May

St Pancras International - Kent High Speed Domestic Services

		TL A	SE ◇	TL A	SE ◇■ B	SE ◇■ C	SE ◇■ B	SE ◇	SE ◇■ B	SE ◇■ D	SE ◇■ C	SE ◇ E	TL A	SE ■ F	SE ◇ E	SE ◇	TL A	SE ◇■ B	SE ■ B	SE ◇	SE ◇■ B	SE ◇■ C	SE ◇■ D
St Pancras International ⊖	d		13 55					14 10				14 25			14 37	14 55				15 12			
Stratford International ⊖	d		14 02					14 17				14 32			14 44	15 02				15 19			
Ebbsfleet International	a		14 12					14 28				14 42			14 54	15 12				15 30			
	d		14 13					14 28				14 43			14 55	15 13				15 30			
Gravesend	d	13 59	14 18	14 29								14 48	14 59			15 18	15 29						
Strood	d		14 29									14 59				15 29							
Maidstone West	d																						
Rochester	d		14 32									15 02				15 32							
Chatham	d		14 36									15 05				15 36							
Gillingham (Kent)	d		14 40									15 10				15 40							
Rainham (Kent)	d		14 45									15 14				15 45							
Sittingbourne	d		14 54									15 22				15 54							
Faversham	a		15 05									15 30				16 05							
Whitstable	d											15 39											
Herne Bay	d											15 46											
Birchington-on-Sea	d											15 54											
Margate	d											16 02											
Broadstairs	a											16 07											
Ramsgate	d					15 21					15 50	16 13										16 50	
Ashford International	a							14 48							15 14					15 50			
	d				14 35		14 38	14 52	15 02						15 15			15 35	15 38	15 52	16 02		
Folkestone West	d						14 55		15 19						15 28				15 55		16 19		
Folkestone Central	d						14 58		15 22						15 31				15 58		16 22		
Dover Priory	d						15 25		15a33						15 42				16 10		16a33		
Deal	a						15 42								16 00				16 27				
Sandwich	a					15 33	15 48				16 02	16 25			16 07				16 34			17 02	
Dover Priory	a					15 58					16 24	16 48										17 24	
Canterbury West	a				14 53			15 06										15 53		16 06			
	d				14 54			15 08										15 54		16 08			
Ramsgate	d				15a16		16a13	15 28		15 42				16 05	16 20			16a16	16a54	16 28			16 52
Broadstairs	d							15 33		15 48				16 11	16 25					16 33			16 58
Margate	a							15 38		15 53				16 16	16 29					16 38			17 03
St Pancras International	a	15 13		15 43									16 13				16 43						

		SE ◇ E	TL A	SE ◇■ D	SE ◇ E	SE ◇	TL A	SE ◇■ B	SE ◇■ B	SE ◇	SE ◇■ B	SE ◇	TL A	SE ◇■ D	SE ◇	SE ◇■ C	SE ◇ F	SE ◇	TL A	SE ◇■ B	SE ◇■ B	SE ◇
St Pancras International ⊖	d	15 25			15 37	15 55				16 10		16 25			16 50		16 37	16 55				17 07
Stratford International ⊖	d	15 32			15 44	16 02				16 17		16 32			16 57		16 44	17 02				17 14
Ebbsfleet International	a	15 42			15 54	16 12				16 28		16 42					16 54	17 12				17 24
	d	15 43			15 55	16 13				16 28		16 43					16 55	17 13				17 25
Gravesend	d	15 48	15 59			16 18	16 29					16 48	16 59					17 18	17 29			
Strood	d	15 59				16 29						16 59						17 28				
Maidstone West	d																					
Rochester	d	16 02				16 32						17 02						17 32				
Chatham	d	16 05				16 36						17 06						17 35				
Gillingham (Kent)	d	16 10				16 40						17 10						17 41				
Rainham (Kent)	d	16 14				16 45						17 15						17 46				
Sittingbourne	d	16 22				16 53						17 23						17 54				
Faversham	a	16 30				17 01						17 31						18 02				
Whitstable	d	16 39																				
Herne Bay	d	16 46																				
Birchington-on-Sea	d	16 54																				
Margate	d	17 02																				
Broadstairs	a	17 07																				
Ramsgate	d	17 13														17 50						
Ashford International	a				16 14					16 48					17 24		17 14					17 44
	d				16 15			16 35	16 38	16 52	17 02				17 26		17 18			17 35	17 38	17 46
Folkestone West	d				16 28				16 55		17 19						17 30				17 55	17 59
Folkestone Central	d				16 31				16 58		17 22						17 33				17 58	18 02
Dover Priory	d				16 42				17 11		17a33						17 45				18 12	18a14
Deal	a				17 00				17 28								18 03				18 29	
Sandwich	a	17 25			17 07				17 34							18 02	18 09				18 36	
Dover Priory	a	17 48														18 24						
Canterbury West	a							16 56		17 06					17 40					17 56		
	d							16 57		17 09					17 44					17 57		
Ramsgate	d			17 05	17 20			17a24	17a49	17 32				17 48	18 03		18 26			18a21	18a53	
Broadstairs	d			17 11	17 25					17 37				17 54	18 08		18 32					
Margate	a			17 16	17 29					17 42				17 59	18 15		18 37					
St Pancras International	a		17 13				17 43						18 13						18 43			

A From Rainham (Kent) to Luton
B From London Charing Cross
C To London Charing Cross
D To London Victoria
E To St Pancras International
F To Faversham

Table T194-F

Mondays to Fridays

16 December to 15 May

St Pancras International - Kent High Speed Domestic Services

		SE ◇	SE ◇	SE ◇1 A	SE ◇	TL B	SE ◇1 C	SE ◇1 C	SE ◇	SE ◇	SE ◇1 C	SE ◇	SE ◇ D	SE ◇	TL B	SE ◇1 C	SE ◇	SE ◇	TL B	SE ◇1 E	SE ◇1 F	SE ◇	SE ◇
St Pancras International 15 ⊖	d	17 12	17 20		17 25				17 37	17 46		17 50		17 55			18 07	18 16				18 20	18 25
Stratford International ⊖	d	17 19	17 27		17 32				17 44	17 53		17 57		18 02			18 14	18 23				18 27	18 32
Ebbsfleet International	a	17 29			17 42				17 55	18 03				18 12			18 25	18 33					18 42
	d	17 31			17 43				17 56	18 05				18 13			18 26	18 35					18 43
Gravesend 4	d	17 35				17 59				18 09				18 18	18 30			18 39	18 59				
Strood 4	d	17 46								18 20				18 31				18 51					
Maidstone West	d	18a04								18a38								19a09					
Rochester 4	d				17 58									18 36									19 01
Chatham 4	d				18 02									18 40									19 05
Gillingham (Kent) 4	d				18 07									18 45									19 10
Rainham (Kent)	d				18 12									18 50									19 15
Sittingbourne 4	d				18 20									18 58									19 25
Faversham 2	a				18 29									19 06									19 33
Whitstable	d				18 38									19 15									19 42
Herne Bay	d				18 44									19 21									19 48
Birchington-on-Sea	d				18 52									19 30									19 57
Margate 4	d				18 58									19 36									20 02
Broadstairs	a				19 03									19 45									20 10
Ramsgate	d				19a13															19 23			
Ashford International	a		17 54						18 15			18 24					18 45					18 54	
	d		17 56				18 03	18 05	18 17		18 20	18 26				18 33	18 47				18 51	18 56	
Folkestone West	d							18 22	18 30		18 38						19 00				19 09		
Folkestone Central	d							18 25	18 35		18a43						19 03				19 12		
Dover Priory 4	d							18a39	18 46								19a15				19 25		
Deal	a								19 04												19 43		
Sandwich	a								19 10											19 35	19 50		
Dover Priory	a																			19 57			
Canterbury West 4	a		18 10				18 24					18 40				18 55						19 10	
	d		18 11				18 25					18 41				18 56						19 11	
Ramsgate 4	d		18 31	18 48			18a49		19a25			19 01	19 20			19a21					20a08	19 31	
Broadstairs	d		18 36	18 54								19 06	19 25									19 36	
Margate 4	a		18 44	18 59								19 14	19 29									19 44	
St Pancras International	a					19 13									19 43				20 13				

		SE ◇1 C	SE ◇1 A	SE ◇1 F	SE ◇	SE ◇1 C	SE ◇	SE ◇1 F	SE ◇ D	SE ◇1 E	SE ◇1 F	SE ◇	SE ◇	TL B	SE ◇1 F	SE ◇	SE ◇ D	SE ◇1 A	SE ◇	TL B	SE ◇1 C	SE ◇ D	SE ◇
St Pancras International 15 ⊖	d				18 37		18 50					18 55	19 07			19 20			19 25			19 37	19 55
Stratford International ⊖	d				18 45		18 57					19 02	19 14			19 27			19 32			19 44	20 02
Ebbsfleet International	a				18 55							19 12	19 25						19 42			19 54	20 12
	d				18 56							19 13	19 26						19 43			19 55	20 13
Gravesend 4	d											19 18		19 29					19 48	19 59			20 18
Strood 4	d											19 30							19 59				20 29
Maidstone West	d																						
Rochester 4	d										19 26	19 35							20 02				20 32
Chatham 4	d										19 30	19 39							20 06				20 36
Gillingham (Kent) 4	d										19 35	19 44							20 11				20 40
Rainham (Kent)	d										19 40	19 49							20 16				20 45
Sittingbourne 4	d										19 49	19 56							20 23				20 54
Faversham 2	a										20 00	20 05							20 31				21 05
Whitstable	d										20 09								20 40				
Herne Bay	d										20 16								20 47				
Birchington-on-Sea	d										20 25								20 56				
Margate 4	d										20 33						21 00		21 04				
Broadstairs	a										20 38						21 05		21 09				
Ramsgate	d									20 23	20a48						21 12		21a17				
Ashford International	a				19 15		19 25						19 45			19 54						20 14	
	d	19 02		19 06	19 17	19 22	19 27	19 32					19 47		19 52	19 56					20 07	20 15	
Folkestone West	d			19 23	19 31	19 40							20 00		20 09							20 28	
Folkestone Central	d			19a28	19 35	19 43							20 03		20 12							20 31	
Dover Priory 4	d				19 47	19 55							20a14		20a27							20 42	
Deal	a				20 05	20 14																20 59	
Sandwich	a				20 14	20 21				20 35							21 24					21 06	
Dover Priory	a									20 57							21 47						
Canterbury West 4	a	19 24					19 41	19 54								20 10					20 29		
	d	19 25					19 42	19 55								20 11					20 30		
Ramsgate 4	d	19a52	19 53			20a39	20 02	20a20	20 20							20 31		20 53			20a55	21 20	
Broadstairs	d		19 59				20 07		20 25							20 36		20 59				21 25	
Margate 4	a		20 04				20 15		20 29							20 44		21 04				21 29	
St Pancras International	a													20 43						21 13			

A To London Victoria
B From Rainham (Kent) to Luton
C From London Charing Cross
D To St Pancras International
E To London Charing Cross
F From London Cannon Street

NRT DECEMBER 19 EDITION

Table T194-F

Mondays to Fridays

16 December to 15 May

St Pancras International - Kent High Speed Domestic Services

		TL A	SE ◇1 B	SE ◇1 B	SE ◇	SE ◇1 B	SE ◇1 C	SE ◇ D	SE ◇	SE ◇	TL E	SE ◇	TL E	SE ◇1 B	SE ◇	SE ◇1 B	SE TO 1 F	SE 1 G	SE TX 1 H	SE TO H bus	SE ◇	SE ◇	TL E
St Pancras International 15 ⊖	d				20 12				20 25	20 37		20 55			21 12						21 25	21 37	
Stratford International ⊖	d				20 19				20 32	20 44		21 02			21 19						21 32	21 44	
Ebbsfleet International	a				20 30				20 42	20 54		21 12			21 30						21 42	21 54	
	d				20 30				20 43	20 55		21 13			21 30						21 43	21 55	
Gravesend 4	d	20 29							20 48		20 59	21 18	21 29								21 48		21 59
Strood 4	d								20 59			21 29									21 59		
Maidstone West	d																						
Rochester 4	d								21 02			21 32									22 02		
Chatham 4	d								21 06			21 36									22 06		
Gillingham (Kent) 4	d								21 10			21 40									22 10		
Rainham (Kent)	d								21 15			21 45									22 15		
Sittingbourne 4	d								21 23			21 53									22 23		
Faversham 2	a								21 31			22 01									22 31		
Whitstable	d								21 40												22 40		
Herne Bay	d								21 47												22 47		
Birchington-on-Sea	d								21 56												22 56		
Margate 4	d								22 04												23 04		
Broadstairs	a								22 09												23 09		
Ramsgate	d							22 12	22a19									23 12			23a18		
Ashford International	a				20 50					21 14					21 50							22 14	
	d		20 35	20 38	20 52	21 05				21 15				21 32	21 52	22 04						22 15	
Folkestone West	d			20 55		21 21				21 28						22 21						22 28	
Folkestone Central	d			20 58		21 24				21 31						22 24						22 31	
Dover Priory 4	d			21 10		21a37				21 42						22a35						22 42	
Deal	a			21 27						22 00												23 00	
Sandwich	a			21 33				22 24		22 07								23 24				23 07	
Dover Priory	a							22 47										23 47					
Canterbury West 4	a		20 56		21 06									21 53	22 06								
	d		20 57		21 09									21 54	22 08								
Ramsgate 4	d		21a23	21a50	21 32		21 53			22a19				22a17	22 28		22 48		23 15	23 15		23a22	
Broadstairs	d				21 38		21 59								22 33		22 54		23 21	23 26			
Margate 4	a				21 43		22 04								22 38		22 59		23 26	23 36			
St Pancras International	a	21 43									22 13		22 43										23 13

		SE ◇	TL E	SE ◇1 B	SE TO ◇	SE TX ◇	SE ◇1 B	SE TO bus	SE TX ◇	SE TO ◇	SE ◇	SE ◇	SE MX ◇1 B	SE MO ◇1 B	SE MO bus	SE TO ◇	SE WTh FO ◇	SE TO I bus	SE MO ◇	SE MO bus	SE ◇	SE ◇	SE ◇
St Pancras International 15 ⊖	d	21 55			22 12	22 12			22 25	22 25	22 37	22 55				23 12	23 12		23 12		23 25	23 37	23 55
Stratford International ⊖	d	22 02			22 19	22 19			22 32	22 32	22 44	23 02				23 19	23 19		23 19		23 32	23 44	00 02
Ebbsfleet International	a	22 12			22 30	22 30			22 42	22 42	22 54	23 12				23 30	23 30		23 30		23 42	23 54	00 12
	d	22 13			22 30	22 30			22 43	22 43	22 55	23 13				23 30	23 30		23 30		23 43	23 55	00 13
Gravesend 4	d	22 18	22 29						22 48	22 48		23 18									23 48		00 18
Strood 4	d	22 29							22 59	22 59		23 29									23 59		00 29
Maidstone West	d																						
Rochester 4	d	22 32							23 02	23 02		23 32									00 02		00 32
Chatham 4	d	22 36							23 06	23 06		23 36									00 06		00 36
Gillingham (Kent) 4	d	22 40							23 10	23 10		23 40									00 10		00 40
Rainham (Kent)	d	22 45							23 15	23 15		23 45									00 15		00 45
Sittingbourne 4	d	22 53							23 23	23 23		23 53									00 23		00 53
Faversham 2	a	23 01							23 31	23 31		00 01									00 31		01 03
Whitstable	d								23 40									23 58					
Herne Bay	d								23 47									00 14					
Birchington-on-Sea	d								23 56									00 34					
Margate 4	d								00 04									00 45					
Broadstairs	a								00 09									00 55					
Ramsgate	d								00a16	00a39								01a06					
Ashford International	a				22 50	22 50					23 14					23 50	23 50		23 50			00 14	
	d			22 34	22 52	22 52	23 04				23 15		23 34	23 34	23 40	23 52	23 52		23 52	23 59		00 15	
Folkestone West	d						23 21				23 28											00 28	
Folkestone Central	d						23 24				23 31											00 31	
Dover Priory 4	d						23a35				23 43											00 43	
Deal	a										00 01											01s01	
Sandwich	a										00 08											01s07	
Dover Priory	a																						
Canterbury West 4	a			22 55	23 06	23 06							23 55		00 19	00 06	00 06			00 34			
	d			22 55	23 08	23 08							23 56		00 19	00 07	00 08			00 34			
Ramsgate 4	d			23a17	23a29	23 29		23 36			00a21		00a18	00a29	01a02	00a31	00 30		00 44	01s12		01a23	
Broadstairs	d					23 34		23 45									00s35		00s49	01s21			
Margate 4	a					23 40		23 55									00 40		00 57	01 31			
St Pancras International	a		23 43																				

A From Rainham (Kent) to Luton
B From London Charing Cross
C To London Victoria
D To St Pancras International
E From Rainham (Kent) to West Hampstead Thameslink
F To Faversham
G To Ashford International
H To Gillingham (Kent)
I From Faversham

Table T194-F

Saturdays

21 December to 16 May

St Pancras International - Kent High Speed Domestic Services

		SE	SE	SE	SE	SE	SE	SE	SE	SE	SE		SE	TL	TL	SE	TL	SE	SE	TL	SE	SE		SE	SE
		◇	◇	◇	◇■	◇	◇	◇■	◇	◇■	◇		◇■			◇■		◇	◇		◇■			◇	◇
		A	A	A	B	A	A	B		B			C	D	E	C	F	G	G	F	C			G	H
St Pancras International ⊖	d								00 12																
Stratford International ⊖	d		00 02						00 19																
Ebbsfleet International	a		00 12						00 30																
	d		00 13						00 30																
Gravesend	d		00 18											04 59	05 29		05 59			06 29					
Strood	d		00 29																						
Maidstone West	d																								
Rochester	d	00 02	00 32																						
Chatham	d	00 06	00 36																						
Gillingham (Kent)	d	00 10	00 40																						
Rainham (Kent)	d	00 15	00 45																						
Sittingbourne	d	00 23	00 53																						
Faversham	a	00 31	01 03																						
Whitstable	d																								06 32
Herne Bay	d																								06 39
Birchington-on-Sea	d																								06 48
Margate	d			00 04																					06 57
Broadstairs	a			00 09																					07 02
Ramsgate	d			00a16														06 12							07 12
Ashford International	a								00 50																
	d				00 04		00 15	00 34		01 05	01 07											06 35		06 15	
Folkestone West	d				00 21		00 28			01s22														06 28	
Folkestone Central	d				00 24		00 31			01s24														06 31	
Dover Priory	d				00a35		00 43			01a38														06 42	
Deal	a						01s01																	07 00	
Sandwich	a						01s07											06 24						07 07	07 24
Dover Priory	a																	06 47							07 47
Canterbury West	a							00 55			01 30											06 53			
	d					00 08		00 56														06 54			
Ramsgate	d					00 30	01a23	01a20					04 30			05 53			06 20		06 53	07 16		07 20	
Broadstairs	d					00s35							04 35			05 59			06 25		06 59	07 21		07 25	
Margate	a					00 40							04 40			06 04			06 29		07 04	07 26		07 29	
St Pancras International	a													06 13	06 43		07 13			07 43					

		TL	SE	SE	SE	SE	SE	TL	SE		SE	SE	SE	SE	SE	SE	SE	TL	SE	TL		SE	SE	SE	SE
			■	■	◇■	■	◇		◇		■	◇■	◇	■	◇■	◇	◇		◇			◇■	◇	◇■	◇■
		F	I	J	C	K	G	F	G			B		I	C	G	G	F		F		B		B	C
St Pancras International ⊖	d						06 37						07 07			07 25	07 37		07 55				08 12		
Stratford International ⊖	d						06 44						07 14			07 32	07 44		08 02				08 19		
Ebbsfleet International	a						06 54						07 24			07 42	07 54		08 12				08 30		
	d						06 55						07 25			07 43	07 55		08 13				08 30		
Gravesend	d	06 59						07 29								07 48		07 59	08 18	08 29					
Strood	d															07 59			08 29						
Maidstone West	d																								
Rochester	d															08 02			08 32						
Chatham	d															08 06			08 36						
Gillingham (Kent)	d										07 28					08 10			08 40						
Rainham (Kent)	d										07 33					08 15			08 45						
Sittingbourne	d										07 42					08 23			08 54						
Faversham	a										07 52					08 31			09 05						
Whitstable	d					07 25					08 02					08 40									
Herne Bay	d					07 32					08 09					08 45									
Birchington-on-Sea	d					07 41					08 18					08 54									
Margate	d					07 49					08 25					08 59									
Broadstairs	a					07 54					08 31					09 05									
Ramsgate	d					08a02			08 12		08a38					09 12									
Ashford International	a						07 14						07 44				08 14						08 50		
	d		07 02	07 05			07 15					07 35	07 52	08 02			08 15					08 35	08 52	09 02	
Folkestone West	d		07 19				07 28							08 19			08 28							09 19	
Folkestone Central	d		07 22				07 31							08 22			08 31							09 22	
Dover Priory	d		07a33				07 42							08a33			08 42							09a33	
Deal	a						08 00										09 00								
Sandwich	a						08 07		08 24							09 24	09 07								
Dover Priory	a								08 47							09 47									
Canterbury West	a			07 27								07 53	08 06									08 53	09 06		
	d											07 54	08 08									08 54	09 08		
Ramsgate	d				07 53		08 20					08a16	08 28		08 53		09 20					09a16	09 28		09 53
Broadstairs	d				07 59		08 25						08 33		08 59		09 25						09 33		09 59
Margate	a				08 04		08 29						08 38		09 04		09 29						09 38		10 04
St Pancras International	a	08 13						08 43										09 13		09 43					

A From St Pancras International
B From London Charing Cross
C To London Victoria
D From Gillingham (Kent) to St Albans City
E From Gillingham (Kent) to Kentish Town
F From Rainham (Kent) to Kentish Town
G To St Pancras International
H From Faversham to St Pancras International
I From Tonbridge
J From Maidstone East
K From Faversham

Table T194-F

Saturdays

21 December to 16 May

St Pancras International - Kent High Speed Domestic Services

		SE	SE	TL	SE	TL	SE		SE	SE	SE	SE	SE	TL	SE	TL	SE	SE		SE	SE	SE	SE	TL	SE
		◇	◇		◇		◇■		◇	◇■	◇■	◇	◇		◇		◇■	◇		◇■	◇■	◇	◇		◇
		A	A	B		B	C			C	D	A	A	B		B	C			C	D	A	A	B	
St Pancras International ⊖	d	08 25	08 37		08 57				09 09			09 25	09 34		09 55			10 09				10 25	10 37		10 52
Stratford International ⊖	d	08 32	08 44		09 04				09 16			09 32	09 41		10 02			10 16				10 32	10 44		10 59
Ebbsfleet International	a	08 42	08 54		09 14				09 27			09 43	09 51		10 12			10 27				10 42	10 54		11 09
	d	08 43	08 55		09 15				09 27			09 44	09 52		10 13			10 27				10 43	10 55		11 13
Gravesend	d	08 48		08 59	09 19	09 29						09 48		09 59	10 18	10 29						10 48		10 59	11 18
Strood	d	08 59			09 30							09 59			10 29							10 59			11 29
Maidstone West	d																								
Rochester	d	09 02			09 33							10 02			10 32							11 02			11 32
Chatham	d	09 06			09 37							10 06			10 36							11 06			11 36
Gillingham (Kent)	d	09 10			09 41							10 10			10 40							11 10			11 40
Rainham (Kent)	d	09 15			09 46							10 15			10 45							11 15			11 45
Sittingbourne	d	09 23			09 54							10 23			10 54							11 23			11 54
Faversham	a	09 31			10 05							10 31			11 05							11 31			12 05
Whitstable	d	09 40										10 40										11 40			
Herne Bay	d	09 45										10 45										11 45			
Birchington-on-Sea	d	09 54										10 54										11 54			
Margate	d	09 59										10 59										11 59			
Broadstairs	a	10 05										11 05										12 05			
Ramsgate	d	10 12										11 12										12 12			
Ashford International	a		09 14						09 47				10 11					10 47					11 14		
	d		09 15				09 35		09 52	10 02			10 15				10 35	10 52		11 02			11 15		
Folkestone West	d		09 28							10 19			10 28							11 19			11 28		
Folkestone Central	d		09 31							10 22			10 31							11 22			11 31		
Dover Priory	d		09 42							10a33			10 42							11a33			11 42		
Deal	a		10 00										11 00										12 00		
Sandwich	a	10 24	10 07									11 24	11 07									12 24	12 07		
Dover Priory	a	10 47										11 47										12 47			
Canterbury West	a						09 53		10 06								10 53	11 06							
	d						09 54		10 08								10 54	11 08							
Ramsgate	d		10 20				10a16		10 28		10 53		11 20				11a16	11 28			11 53		12 20		
Broadstairs	d		10 25						10 33		10 59		11 25					11 33			11 59		12 25		
Margate	a		10 29						10 38		11 04		11 29					11 38			12 04		12 29		
St Pancras International	a			10 13		10 43								11 13		11 43								12 13	

		TL	SE	SE	SE		SE	TL	SE	SE	SE	TL	SE	SE	SE	SE		TL	SE	SE	SE	TL	SE	SE	SE
			◇■	◇	◇■		◇		◇■	◇	◇		◇■	◇	◇■	◇			◇■	◇	◇		◇■	◇	◇■
		B	C		D		A	B	C	A		B	C		D	A		B	C	A		B	C		C
St Pancras International ⊖	d			11 12			11 25			11 37	11 55			12 12		12 27				12 37	12 52			13 12	
Stratford International ⊖	d			11 19			11 32			11 44	12 02			12 19		12 34				12 44	12 59			13 19	
Ebbsfleet International	a			11 30			11 42			11 54	12 12			12 30		12 44				12 54	13 09			13 30	
	d			11 30			11 43			11 55	12 13			12 30		12 45				12 55	13 13			13 30	
Gravesend	d	11 29					11 48	11 59			12 18	12 29				12 49		12 59			13 18	13 29			
Strood	d						11 59				12 29					12 59					13 29				
Maidstone West	d																								
Rochester	d						12 02				12 32					13 02					13 32				
Chatham	d						12 06				12 36					13 06					13 36				
Gillingham (Kent)	d						12 10				12 40					13 10					13 40				
Rainham (Kent)	d						12 15				12 45					13 15					13 45				
Sittingbourne	d						12 23				12 54					13 23					13 54				
Faversham	a						12 31				13 05					13 31					14 05				
Whitstable	d						12 40									13 40									
Herne Bay	d						12 45									13 45									
Birchington-on-Sea	d						12 54									13 54									
Margate	d						12 59									13 59									
Broadstairs	a						13 05									14 05									
Ramsgate	d						13 12									14 12									
Ashford International	a									12 14										13 14				13 50	
	d		11 35						12 02	12 15			12 35						13 02	13 18			13 35	13 52	14 02
Folkestone West	d								12 19	12 28									13 19	13 30					14 19
Folkestone Central	d								12 22	12 31									13 22	13 33					14 22
Dover Priory	d								12a33	12 42									13a33	13 44					14a33
Deal	a									13 00										14 01					
Sandwich	a						13 24			13 07						14 24				14 07					
Dover Priory	a						13 47									14 47									
Canterbury West	a		11 53	12 06									12 53	13 06									13 53	14 06	
	d		11 54	12 08									12 54	13 08									13 54	14 08	
Ramsgate	d		12a16	12 28	12 53					13 20			13a16	13 28	13 53					14 20			14a16	14 28	
Broadstairs	d			12 33	12 59					13 25				13 33	13 59					14 25				14 33	
Margate	a			12 38	13 04					13 29				13 38	14 04					14 29				14 38	
St Pancras International	a	12 43						13 13				13 43						14 13				14 43			

A To St Pancras International
B From Rainham (Kent) to Kentish Town
C From London Charing Cross
D To London Victoria

Table T194-F

Saturdays
21 December to 16 May

St Pancras International - Kent High Speed Domestic Services

Station		SE ◇1 A	SE ◇ B	SE ◇ B	TL C	SE ◇	TL C	SE ◇1 D	SE ◇	SE ◇1 A	SE ◇ B	TL C	SE ◇1 D	SE ◇ B	SE ◇	TL C	SE ◇1 D	SE ◇	SE ◇1 D	SE ◇1 A	SE ◇ B	SE ◇ B	TL C
St Pancras International 15 ⊖	d		13 25	13 37		13 55			14 10		14 25			14 37	14 55			15 12			15 25	15 37	
Stratford International ⊖	d		13 32	13 44		14 02			14 17		14 32			14 44	15 02			15 19			15 32	15 44	
Ebbsfleet International	a		13 42	13 54		14 12			14 28		14 42			14 54	15 12			15 30			15 42	15 54	
	d		13 43	13 55		14 13			14 28		14 43			14 55	15 13			15 30			15 43	15 55	
Gravesend 4	d		13 48		13 59	14 18	14 29				14 48	14 59			15 18	15 29					15 48		15 59
Strood 4	d		13 59			14 29					14 59				15 29						15 59		
Maidstone West	d																						
Rochester 4	d		14 02			14 32					15 02				15 32						16 02		
Chatham 4	d		14 06			14 36					15 06				15 36						16 06		
Gillingham (Kent) 4	d		14 10			14 40					15 10				15 40						16 10		
Rainham (Kent)	d		14 15			14 45					15 15				15 45						16 15		
Sittingbourne 4	d		14 23			14 54					15 23				15 54						16 23		
Faversham 2	a		14 31			15 05					15 31				16 05						16 31		
Whitstable	d		14 40								15 40										16 40		
Herne Bay	d		14 45								15 45										16 45		
Birchington-on-Sea	d		14 54								15 54										16 54		
Margate 4	d		14 59								15 59										16 59		
Broadstairs	a		15 05								16 05										17 05		
Ramsgate	d		15 12								16 12										17 12		
Ashford International	a			14 14										15 14				15 50				16 14	
	d			14 15				14 35					15 02	15 15			15 35	15 52	16 02			16 15	
Folkestone West	d			14 28									15 19	15 28					16 19			16 28	
Folkestone Central	d			14 31									15 22	15 31					16 22			16 31	
Dover Priory 4	d			14 42									15a33	15 42					16a33			16 42	
Deal	a			15 00										16 00								17 00	
Sandwich	a		15 24	15 07							16 24			16 07							17 24	17 07	
Dover Priory	a		15 47								16 47										17 47		
Canterbury West 4	a							14 53	15 06								15 53	16 06					
	d							14 54	15 08								15 54	16 08					
Ramsgate 4	d	14 53		15 20				15a16	15 28	15 53				16 20			16a16	16 28		16 53		17 20	
Broadstairs	d	14 59		15 25					15 33	15 59				16 25				16 33		16 59		17 25	
Margate 4	a	15 04		15 29					15 38	16 04				16 29				16 38		17 04		17 29	
St Pancras International	a				15 13		15 43					16 13				16 43							17 13

Station		SE ◇	TL C	SE ◇1 D	SE ◇	SE ◇1 D	SE ◇1 A	SE ◇ B	SE ◇ B	TL C	SE ◇	TL C	SE ◇1 D	SE ◇	SE ◇1 D	SE ◇1 A	SE ◇ B	SE ◇ B	TL C	SE ◇	TL C	SE ◇1 D
St Pancras International 15 ⊖	d	15 55			16 10			16 25	16 37		16 55			17 12			17 25	17 37		17 55		
Stratford International ⊖	d	16 02			16 17			16 32	16 44		17 02			17 19			17 32	17 44		18 02		
Ebbsfleet International	a	16 12			16 28			16 42	16 54		17 12			17 30			17 42	17 54		18 12		
	d	16 13			16 28			16 43	16 55		17 13			17 30			17 43	17 55		18 13		
Gravesend 4	d	16 18	16 29					16 48		16 59	17 18	17 29					17 48		17 59	18 18	18 29	
Strood 4	d	16 29						16 59			17 29						17 59			18 29		
Maidstone West	d																					
Rochester 4	d	16 32						17 02			17 32						18 02			18 32		
Chatham 4	d	16 36						17 06			17 36						18 06			18 36		
Gillingham (Kent) 4	d	16 40						17 10			17 40						18 10			18 40		
Rainham (Kent)	d	16 45						17 15			17 45						18 15			18 45		
Sittingbourne 4	d	16 54						17 23			17 54						18 23			18 54		
Faversham 2	a	17 05						17 31			18 05						18 31			19 05		
Whitstable	d							17 40									18 40					
Herne Bay	d							17 45									18 45					
Birchington-on-Sea	d							17 54									18 54					
Margate 4	d							17 59									18 59					
Broadstairs	a							18 05									19 05					
Ramsgate	d							18 12									19 14					
Ashford International	a				16 48				17 14					17 50				18 14				
	d			16 35	16 52	17 02			17 15				17 35	17 52	18 02			18 15				18 35
Folkestone West	d					17 19			17 28						18 19			18 28				
Folkestone Central	d					17 22			17 31						18 22			18 31				
Dover Priory 4	d					17a33			17 42						18a33			18 42				
Deal	a								18 00									19 00				
Sandwich	a							18 24	18 07								19 26	19 07				
Dover Priory	a							18 47									19 48					
Canterbury West 4	a			16 53	17 06								17 53	18 06								18 53
	d			16 54	17 08								17 54	18 08								18 54
Ramsgate 4	d			17a16	17 28		17 53		18 20				18a16	18 28		18 53		19 20				19a16
Broadstairs	d				17 33		17 59		18 25					18 33		18 59		19 25				
Margate 4	a				17 38		18 04		18 29					18 38		19 04		19 29				
St Pancras International	a		17 43							18 13		18 43							19 13		19 43	

A To London Victoria
B To St Pancras International
C From Rainham (Kent) to Kentish Town
D From London Charing Cross

NRT DECEMBER 19 EDITION

Table T194-F

Saturdays
21 December to 16 May

St Pancras International - Kent High Speed Domestic Services

Station		SE ◇	SE ◇1 A	SE ◇ B	TL C	SE ◇1 D	SE ◇ B	SE ◇	TL C	SE ◇1 D	SE ◇	SE ◇1 A	SE ◇ B	TL C	SE ◇1 D	SE ◇ B	SE ◇	TL C	SE ◇1 D	SE ◇	SE ◇1 D	SE ◇1 A	SE ◇ B
St Pancras International 15 ⊖	d	18 12		18 25			18 37	18 55			19 12		19 25			19 37	19 55			20 12			20 25
Stratford International ⊖	d	18 19		18 32			18 44	19 02			19 19		19 32			19 44	20 02			20 19			20 32
Ebbsfleet International	a	18 30		18 42			18 54	19 12			19 30		19 42			19 54	20 12			20 30			20 42
	d	18 30		18 43			18 55	19 13			19 30		19 43			19 55	20 13			20 30			20 43
Gravesend 4	d			18 48	18 59			19 18	19 29				19 48	19 59			20 18	20 29					20 48
Strood 4	d			18 59				19 29					19 59				20 29						20 59
Maidstone West	d																						
Rochester 4	d			19 02				19 32					20 02				20 32						21 02
Chatham 4	d			19 06				19 36					20 06				20 36						21 06
Gillingham (Kent) 4	d			19 10				19 40					20 10				20 40						21 10
Rainham (Kent)	d			19 15				19 45					20 15				20 45						21 15
Sittingbourne 4	d			19 23				19 54					20 23				20 54						21 23
Faversham 2	a			19 31				20 05					20 31				21 05						21 31
Whitstable	d			19 40									20 40										21 40
Herne Bay	d			19 45									20 45										21 45
Birchington-on-Sea	d			19 54									20 54										21 54
Margate 4	d			19 59									20 59										21 59
Broadstairs	a			20 05									21 05										22 05
Ramsgate	d			20 12									21 12										22 12
Ashford International	a						19 14									20 14				20 50			
	d					19 02	19 15			19 35					20 02	20 15			20 32	20 52	21 02		
Folkestone West	d					19 19	19 28								20 19	20 28					21 19		
Folkestone Central	d					19 22	19 31								20 22	20 31					21 22		
Dover Priory 4	d					19a33	19 42								20a33	20 42					21a33		
Deal	a						20 00									21 00							
Sandwich	a			20 24			20 07						21 24			21 07							22 24
Dover Priory	a			20 47									21 47										22 47
Canterbury West 4	a	19 06								19 53	20 06								20 53	21 06			
	d	19 08								19 54	20 08								20 54	21 08			
Ramsgate 4	d	19 28	19 53				20 20			20a16	20 28	20 53				21 20			21a16	21 28		21 53	
Broadstairs	d	19 33	19 59				20 25				20 33	20 59				21 25				21 33		21 59	
Margate 4	a	19 38	20 04				20 29				20 38	21 04				21 29				21 38		22 04	
St Pancras International	a				20 13				20 43					21 13				21 43					

Station		SE ◇	TL C	SE ◇	TL E	SE ◇1 D	SE ◇	SE ◇1 D	SE ◇ F	TL E	SE 1 G	SE ◇	SE ◇	TL E	SE ◇1 D	SE ◇	SE ◇1 D	SE ◇	SE ◇	SE ◇	SE ◇1 D	SE ◇	SE ◇
St Pancras International 15 ⊖	d	20 37		20 55			21 12		21 25			21 37	21 55			22 12		22 25	22 37	22 55		23 12	23 25
Stratford International ⊖	d	20 44		21 02			21 19		21 32			21 44	22 02			22 19		22 32	22 44	23 02		23 19	23 32
Ebbsfleet International	a	20 54		21 12			21 30		21 42			21 54	22 12			22 30		22 42	22 54	23 12		23 30	23 42
	d	20 55		21 13			21 30		21 43			21 55	22 13			22 30		22 43	22 55	23 13		23 30	23 43
Gravesend 4	d		20 59	21 18	21 29				21 48	21 59			22 18	22 29				22 48		23 18			23 48
Strood 4	d			21 29					21 59				22 29					22 59		23 29			23 59
Maidstone West	d																						
Rochester 4	d			21 32					22 02				22 32					23 02		23 32			00 02
Chatham 4	d			21 36					22 06				22 36					23 06		23 36			00 06
Gillingham (Kent) 4	d			21 40					22 10				22 40					23 10		23 40			00 10
Rainham (Kent)	d			21 45					22 15				22 45					23 15		23 45			00 15
Sittingbourne 4	d			21 53					22 23				22 53					23 23		23 53			00 23
Faversham 2	a			22 01					22 31				23 01					23 31		00 01			00 31
Whitstable	d								22 40									23 40					
Herne Bay	d								22 45									23 45					
Birchington-on-Sea	d								22 54									23 54					
Margate 4	d								22 59									23 59					
Broadstairs	a								23 05									00 05					
Ramsgate	d								23 12									00a11					
Ashford International	a	21 14					21 50					22 14				22 50			23 14			23 50	
	d	21 15				21 32	21 52	22 02				22 15			22 34	22 52	23 04		23 15		23 34	23 52	
Folkestone West	d	21 28						22 19				22 28					23 21		23 28				
Folkestone Central	d	21 31						22 22				22 31					23 24		23 31				
Dover Priory 4	d	21 42						22a33				22 42					23a35		23 42				
Deal	a	22 00										23 00							00 01				
Sandwich	a	22 07							23 24			23 07							00 07				
Dover Priory	a								23 47														
Canterbury West 4	a					21 53	22 06								22 55	23 06					23 55	00 06	
	d					21 54	22 08								22 56	23 08					23 56	00 08	
Ramsgate 4	d	22a19				22a16	22 27				23 15	23a21			23a18	23 29			00a21		00a18	00 29	
Broadstairs	d						22 33				23 21					23 35						00s34	
Margate 4	a						22 37				23 26					23 40						00 40	
St Pancras International	a		22 13		22 43					23 13				23 43									

A To London Victoria
B To St Pancras International
C From Rainham (Kent) to Kentish Town
D From London Charing Cross
E From Rainham (Kent) to West Hampstead Thameslink
F To Ashford International
G To Gillingham (Kent)

Table T194-F

Saturdays
21 December to 16 May

St Pancras International - Kent High Speed Domestic Services

		SE	SE
		◇	◇
St Pancras International 15 ⊖	d	23 37	23 55
Stratford International ⊖	d	23 44	00 02
Ebbsfleet International	a	23 54	00 12
	d	23 55	00 13
Gravesend 4	d		00 18
Strood 4	d		00 29
Maidstone West	d		
Rochester 4	d		00 32
Chatham 4	d		00 36
Gillingham (Kent) 4	d		00 40
Rainham (Kent)	d		00 45
Sittingbourne 4	d		00 53
Faversham 2	a		01 01
Whitstable	d		
Herne Bay	d		
Birchington-on-Sea	d		
Margate 4	d		
Broadstairs	a		
Ramsgate	d		
Ashford International	a	00 14	
	d	00 15	
Folkestone West	d	00 28	
Folkestone Central	d	00 31	
Dover Priory 4	d	00 42	
Deal	a	01s00	
Sandwich	a	01s07	
Dover Priory	a		
Canterbury West 4	a		
	d		
Ramsgate 4	d	01a23	
Broadstairs	d		
Margate 4	a		
St Pancras International	a		

Sundays
15 December to 10 May

		SE	SE	SE	SE	SE	SE	SE	SE	SE	SE	SE	SE	SE	SE	SE	SE	SE	SE	SE	SE	SE	TL
		◇	◇	◇■	◇	◇	◇■	◇	◇■	◇	◇■	◇	◇■	■	◇	◇	◇■	◇	◇	■	◇■	◇	
		A	A	B	A	A	B		B		C	D	C		D	D	C	D	D		C	D	E
St Pancras International 15 ⊖	d							00 12														08 25	
Stratford International ⊖	d		00 02					00 19														08 32	
Ebbsfleet International	a		00 12					00 30														08 42	
	d		00 13					00 30														08 43	
Gravesend 4	d		00 18																			08 48	08 59
Strood 4	d		00 29																			08 59	
Maidstone West	d																						
Rochester 4	d	00 02	00 32																			09 02	
Chatham 4	d	00 06	00 36																			09 06	
Gillingham (Kent) 4	d	00 10	00 40																			09 10	
Rainham (Kent)	d	00 15	00 45																			09 15	
Sittingbourne 4	d	00 23	00 53																			09 23	
Faversham 2	a	00 31	01 01																			09 31	
Whitstable	d																					09 40	
Herne Bay	d																					09 45	
Birchington-on-Sea	d																					09 54	
Margate 4	d																					09 59	
Broadstairs	a																					10 05	
Ramsgate	d											07 12			08 12				09 12			10 12	
Ashford International	a							00 50															
	d			00 04		00 15	00 34		01 05	01 07				08 08				08 15		08 32			
Folkestone West	d			00 21		00 28			01s22									08 28					
Folkestone Central	d			00 24		00 31			01s24									08 31					
Dover Priory 4	d			00a35		00 42			01a38									08 42					
Deal	a					01s00												09 00					
Sandwich	a					01s07						07 24			08 24			09 07	09 24			10 24	
Dover Priory	a											07 47			08 47				09 47			10 47	
Canterbury West 4	a						00 55			01 30				08 30						08 50			
	d				00 08		00 56													08 51			
Ramsgate 4	d				00 29	01a23	01a20				07 05		08 05			08 20	09 05	09 20		09a15	10 05		
Broadstairs	d				00s34						07 11		08 11			08 25	09 11	09 25			10 11		
Margate 4	a				00 40						07 15		08 15			08 29	09 15	09 29			10 15		
St Pancras International	a																						10 13

A not 15 December. From St Pancras International
B not 15 December. From London Charing Cross
C To Faversham
D To St Pancras International
E From Rainham (Kent) to Kentish Town

Table T194-F

Sundays
15 December to 10 May

St Pancras International - Kent High Speed Domestic Services

		SE	SE	TL	SE	SE	SE	SE	TL	TL	SE	SE	SE	SE	SE	SE	TL	TL	SE	SE	SE	SE	SE
		■	◇		◇■	◇	◇■	◇			◇■	◇	◇■	◇	◇■	◇			◇■	◇	◇■	◇	◇■
		A	B	C	D		D	B	C	C	E	B	D		D	B	C	C	E	B	D		D
St Pancras International 15 ⊖	d		08 37			09 09		09 25				09 37		10 09		10 27				10 37		11 12	
Stratford International ⊖	d		08 44			09 16		09 32				09 44		10 16		10 34				10 44		11 19	
Ebbsfleet International	a		08 54			09 27		09 43				09 54		10 26		10 44				10 54		11 30	
	d		08 55			09 27		09 44				09 55		10 27		10 45				10 55		11 30	
Gravesend 4	d			09 29				09 48	09 59	10 29						10 49	10 59	11 29					
Strood 4	d							09 59								10 59							
Maidstone West	d																						
Rochester 4	d							10 02								11 03							
Chatham 4	d							10 06								11 06							
Gillingham (Kent) 4	d							10 10								11 11							
Rainham (Kent)	d							10 15								11 15							
Sittingbourne 4	d							10 23								11 23							
Faversham 2	a							10 31								11 31							
Whitstable	d							10 40								11 40							
Herne Bay	d							10 45								11 45							
Birchington-on-Sea	d							10 54								11 54							
Margate 4	d							10 59								11 59							
Broadstairs	a							11 05								12 05							
Ramsgate	d							11 12								12 12							
Ashford International	a		09 14			09 47						10 14		10 47						11 14		11 50	
	d	09 05	09 15		09 32	09 52	10 05					10 15	10 32	10 52	11 05					11 15	11 32	11 52	12 05
Folkestone West	d	09 21	09 28				10 21					10 28			11 21					11 28			12 21
Folkestone Central	d	09 24	09 31				10 24					10 31			11 24					11 31			12 24
Dover Priory 4	d	09a35	09 42				10a35					10 42			11a35					11 42			12a35
Deal	a		10 00									11 00								12 00			
Sandwich	a		10 07					11 24				11 07				12 24				12 07			
Dover Priory	a							11 47								12 47							
Canterbury West 4	a				09 50	10 06							10 50	11 06							11 50	12 06	
	d				09 51	10 07							10 51	11 07							11 51	12 07	
Ramsgate 4	d		10 20		10a15	10 27					11 05	11 20	11a15	11 27					12 05	12 20	12a15	12 27	
Broadstairs	d		10 25			10 32					11 11	11 25		11 32					12 11	12 25		12 32	
Margate 4	a		10 29			10 38					11 15	11 29		11 38					12 15	12 29		12 38	
St Pancras International	a			10 43					11 13	11 43							12 13	12 43					

		SE	TL	TL	SE	SE	SE	SE	SE	SE	TL	SE	SE	SE	TL	SE	SE	SE	SE	TL	SE	SE	SE
		◇			◇■	◇	◇■	◇	◇■	◇		◇■	◇	◇		◇■	◇	◇■	◇		◇■	◇	◇
		B	C	C	E	B	D		D	B	C	E	B		C	D		D	B	C	E	B	
St Pancras International 15 ⊖	d	11 25				11 37		12 12		12 27			12 37	12 52			13 12		13 25			13 37	13 55
Stratford International ⊖	d	11 32				11 44		12 19		12 34			12 44	12 59			13 19		13 32			13 44	14 02
Ebbsfleet International	a	11 42				11 54		12 30		12 44			12 54	13 09			13 30		13 42			13 54	14 12
	d	11 43				11 55		12 30		12 45			12 55	13 13			13 30		13 43			13 55	14 13
Gravesend 4	d	11 48	11 59	12 29						12 49	12 59			13 18	13 29				13 48	13 59			14 18
Strood 4	d	11 59								12 59				13 29					13 59				14 29
Maidstone West	d																						
Rochester 4	d	12 02								13 03				13 32					14 02				14 32
Chatham 4	d	12 06								13 06				13 36					14 06				14 36
Gillingham (Kent) 4	d	12 10								13 11				13 40					14 10				14 40
Rainham (Kent)	d	12 15								13 15				13 45					14 15				14 45
Sittingbourne 4	d	12 23								13 23				13 53					14 23				14 53
Faversham 2	a	12 31								13 31				14 03					14 31				15 03
Whitstable	d	12 40								13 40									14 40				
Herne Bay	d	12 45								13 45									14 45				
Birchington-on-Sea	d	12 54								13 54									14 54				
Margate 4	d	12 59								13 59									14 59				
Broadstairs	a	13 05								14 05									15 05				
Ramsgate	d	13 12								14 12									15 12				
Ashford International	a					12 14		12 50					13 14				13 50					14 14	
	d					12 15	12 32	12 52	13 05				13 15			13 32	13 52	14 05				14 15	
Folkestone West	d					12 28			13 21				13 28					14 21				14 28	
Folkestone Central	d					12 31			13 24				13 31					14 24				14 31	
Dover Priory 4	d					12 42			13a35				13 42					14a35				14 42	
Deal	a					13 00							14 00									15 00	
Sandwich	a	13 24				13 07				14 24			14 07						15 24			15 07	
Dover Priory	a	13 47								14 47									15 47				
Canterbury West 4	a						12 50	13 06								13 50	14 06						
	d						12 51	13 07								13 51	14 07						
Ramsgate 4	d				13 05	13 20	13a15	13 27				14 05	14 20			14a15	14 27				15 05	15 20	
Broadstairs	d				13 11	13 25		13 32				14 11	14 25				14 32				15 11	15 25	
Margate 4	a				13 15	13 29		13 38				14 15	14 29				14 38				15 15	15 29	
St Pancras International	a		13 13	13 43							14 13				14 43					15 13			

A From Tonbridge
B To St Pancras International
C From Rainham (Kent) to Kentish Town
D From London Charing Cross
E To Faversham

Table T194-F

Sundays

15 December to 10 May

St Pancras International - Kent
High Speed Domestic Services

Station		TL	SE	SE	SE	SE	TL	SE	SE	SE	TL	SE	SE	SE	SE	TL	SE	SE	SE	TL	SE	SE	SE
		A	◇1 B	◇	◇1 B	◇ C	A	◇1 D	◇ C	◇	A	◇1 B	◇	◇1 B	◇ C	A	◇1 D	◇ C	◇	A	◇1 B	◇	◇1 B
St Pancras International 15 ⊖	d			14 10		14 25			14 37	14 55			15 12		15 25			15 37	15 55			16 12	
Stratford International ⊖	d			14 17		14 32			14 44	15 02			15 19		15 32			15 44	16 02			16 19	
Ebbsfleet International	a			14 28		14 42			14 54	15 12			15 30		15 42			15 54	16 12			16 30	
	d			14 28		14 43			14 55	15 13			15 30		15 43			15 55	16 13			16 30	
Gravesend 4	d	14 29				14 48	14 59			15 18	15 29				15 48	15 59			16 18	16 29			
Strood 4	d					14 59				15 29					15 59				16 29				
Maidstone West	d																						
Rochester 4	d					15 02				15 32					16 02				16 32				
Chatham 4	d					15 06				15 36					16 06				16 36				
Gillingham (Kent) 4	d					15 10				15 40					16 10				16 40				
Rainham (Kent)	d					15 15				15 45					16 15				16 45				
Sittingbourne 4	d					15 23				15 53					16 23				16 53				
Faversham 2	a					15 31				16 03					16 31				17 03				
Whitstable	d					15 40									16 40								
Herne Bay	d					15 45									16 45								
Birchington-on-Sea	d					15 54									16 54								
Margate 4	d					15 59									16 59								
Broadstairs	a					16 05									17 05								
Ramsgate	d					16 12									17 12								
Ashford International	a			14 48					15 14				15 50					16 14				16 50	
	d		14 32	14 52	15 07				15 15			15 32	15 52	16 05				16 15			16 32	16 52	17 05
Folkestone West	d				15 23				15 28					16 21				16 28					17 21
Folkestone Central	d				15 26				15 31					16 24				16 31					17 24
Dover Priory 4	d				15a37				15 42					16a35				16 42					17a35
Deal	a								16 00									17 00					
Sandwich	a					16 24			16 07						17 24			17 07					
Dover Priory	a					16 47									17 47								
Canterbury West 4	a		14 50	15 06								15 50	16 06								16 50	17 06	
	d		14 51	15 07								15 51	16 07								16 51	17 07	
Ramsgate 4	d		15a15	15 27				16 05	16 20			16a15	16 27				17 05	17 20			17a15	17 27	
Broadstairs	d			15 32				16 11	16 25				16 32				17 11	17 25				17 32	
Margate 4	a			15 38				16 15	16 29				16 38				17 15	17 29				17 38	
St Pancras International	a	15 43					16 13				16 43					17 13				17 43			

Station		SE	TL	SE	SE	SE	TL	SE	SE	SE	SE	TL	SE	SE	SE	TL	SE	SE	SE	SE	TL	SE	SE
		◇ C	A	◇1 D	◇ C	◇	A	◇1 B	◇	◇1 B	◇ C	A	◇1 D	◇ C	◇	A	◇1 B	◇	◇1 B	◇ C	A	◇1 D	◇ C
St Pancras International 15 ⊖	d	16 25			16 37	16 55			17 07		17 25			17 37	17 57			18 12		18 25			18 37
Stratford International ⊖	d	16 32			16 44	17 02			17 14		17 32			17 44	18 04			18 19		18 32			18 44
Ebbsfleet International	a	16 42			16 54	17 12			17 24		17 42			17 54	18 14			18 30		18 42			18 54
	d	16 43			16 55	17 13			17 25		17 43			17 55	18 15			18 30		18 43			18 55
Gravesend 4	d	16 48	16 59			17 18	17 29				17 48	17 59			18 19	18 29				18 48	18 59		
Strood 4	d	16 59				17 29					17 59				18 29					18 59			
Maidstone West	d																						
Rochester 4	d	17 02				17 32					18 02				18 32					19 02			
Chatham 4	d	17 06				17 36					18 06				18 36					19 06			
Gillingham (Kent) 4	d	17 10				17 40					18 10				18 40					19 10			
Rainham (Kent)	d	17 15				17 45					18 15				18 45					19 15			
Sittingbourne 4	d	17 23				17 53					18 23				18 53					19 23			
Faversham 2	a	17 31				18 03					18 31				19 03					19 31			
Whitstable	d	17 40									18 40									19 40			
Herne Bay	d	17 45									18 45									19 45			
Birchington-on-Sea	d	17 54									18 54									19 54			
Margate 4	d	17 59									18 59									19 59			
Broadstairs	a	18 05									19 05									20 05			
Ramsgate	d	18 12									19 12									20 12			
Ashford International	a				17 14				17 44					18 14				18 50					19 14
	d				17 15			17 32	17 52	18 05				18 15			18 32	18 52	19 05				19 15
Folkestone West	d				17 28					18 21				18 28					19 21				19 28
Folkestone Central	d				17 31					18 24				18 31					19 24				19 31
Dover Priory 4	d				17 42					18a35				18 42					19a35				19 42
Deal	a				18 00									19 00									20 00
Sandwich	a	18 24			18 07						19 24			19 07						20 24			20 07
Dover Priory	a	18 47									19 47									20 47			
Canterbury West 4	a							17 50	18 06								18 53	19 06					
	d							17 51	18 07								18 54	19 07					
Ramsgate 4	d			18 05	18 20			18a15	18 27				19 05	19 20			19a15	19 27				20 05	20 20
Broadstairs	d			18 11	18 25				18 32				19 11	19 25				19 32				20 11	20 25
Margate 4	a			18 15	18 29				18 38				19 15	19 29				19 38				20 15	20 29
St Pancras International	a		18 13				18 43					19 13				19 43					20 13		

A From Rainham (Kent) to Kentish Town
B From London Charing Cross
C To St Pancras International
D To Faversham

Table T194-F

Sundays

15 December to 10 May

St Pancras International - Kent
High Speed Domestic Services

Station		SE	TL	SE	SE	SE	SE	TL	SE	SE	SE	TL	SE	SE	SE	SE	SE	TL	SE	TL	SE	SE
		◇	A	◇1 B	◇	◇1 B	◇ C	A	◇1 D	◇ C	◇	A	◇1 B	◇	◇1 B	◇ E	◇	A	◇	A	◇1 B	◇
St Pancras International 15 ⊖	d	18 55			19 12		19 25			19 37	19 55			20 12		20 25	20 37		20 55			21 12
Stratford International ⊖	d	19 02			19 19		19 32			19 44	20 02			20 19		20 32	20 44		21 02			21 19
Ebbsfleet International	a	19 12			19 30		19 42			19 54	20 12			20 30		20 42	20 54		21 12			21 30
	d	19 13			19 30		19 43			19 55	20 13			20 30		20 43	20 55		21 13			21 30
Gravesend 4	d	19 18	19 29				19 48	19 59			20 18	20 29				20 48		20 59	21 18	21 29		
Strood 4	d	19 29					19 59				20 29					20 59			21 29			
Maidstone West	d																					
Rochester 4	d	19 32					20 02				20 32					21 02			21 32			
Chatham 4	d	19 36					20 06				20 36					21 06			21 36			
Gillingham (Kent) 4	d	19 40					20 10				20 40					21 10			21 40			
Rainham (Kent)	d	19 45					20 15				20 45					21 15			21 45			
Sittingbourne 4	d	19 53					20 23				20 53					21 23			21 53			
Faversham 2	a	20 03					20 31				21 03					21 31			22 03			
Whitstable	d						20 40									21 40						
Herne Bay	d						20 45									21 45						
Birchington-on-Sea	d						20 54									21 54						
Margate 4	d						20 59									21 59						
Broadstairs	a						21 05									22 05						
Ramsgate	d						21 12									22 12						
Ashford International	a				19 50					20 14				20 50			21 14					21 50
	d			19 32	19 52	20 05				20 15			20 32	20 52	21 05		21 15				21 32	21 52
Folkestone West	d					20 21				20 28					21 21		21 28					
Folkestone Central	d					20 24				20 31					21 24		21 31					
Dover Priory 4	d					20a35				20 42					21a35		21 42					
Deal	a									21 00							22 00					
Sandwich	a						21 24			21 07						22 24	22 07					
Dover Priory	a						21 47									22 47						
Canterbury West 4	a			19 53	20 06								20 53	21 06							21 53	22 06
	d			19 54	20 07								20 54	21 07							21 54	22 07
Ramsgate 4	d			20a15	20 27				21 05	21 20			21a15	21 27			22a19				22a15	22 27
Broadstairs	d				20 32				21 11	21 25				21 32								22 32
Margate 4	a				20 38				21 15	21 29				21 38								22 38
St Pancras International	a		20 43					21 13				21 43						22 13		22 43		

Station		SE	SE	SE	SE	TL	SE	TL	SE	SE	SE	SE	SE	SE	SE	SE	SE	SE
		◇1 B	◇1 F	◇	◇	G	◇	H	◇1 B	◇	◇1 B	◇	◇	◇	◇1 B	◇	◇	◇
St Pancras International 15 ⊖	d			21 25	21 37		21 55			22 12		22 25	22 37	22 55		23 12	23 25	23 37
Stratford International ⊖	d			21 32	21 44		22 02			22 19		22 32	22 44	23 02		23 19	23 32	23 44
Ebbsfleet International	a			21 42	21 54		22 12			22 30		22 42	22 54	23 12		23 30	23 42	23 54
	d			21 43	21 55		22 13			22 30		22 43	22 55	23 13		23 30	23 43	23 55
Gravesend 4	d			21 48		21 59	22 18	22 29				22 48		23 18			23 48	
Strood 4	d			21 59			22 29					22 59		23 29			23 59	
Maidstone West	d																	
Rochester 4	d			22 02			22 32					23 02		23 32			00 02	
Chatham 4	d			22 06			22 36					23 06		23 36			00 06	
Gillingham (Kent) 4	d			22 10			22 40					23 10		23 40			00 10	
Rainham (Kent)	d			22 15			22 45					23 15		23 45			00 15	
Sittingbourne 4	d			22 23			22 53					23 23		23 53			00 23	
Faversham 2	a			22 31			23 03					23 31		00 01			00 32	
Whitstable	d			22 40								23 40						
Herne Bay	d			22 45								23 45						
Birchington-on-Sea	d			22 54								23 54						
Margate 4	d			22 59								23 59						
Broadstairs	a			23 05								00 05						
Ramsgate	d			23a11								00a11						
Ashford International	a				22 14					22 50			23 14			23 50		00 15
	d	22 05			22 15				22 32	22 52	23 05		23 15		23 32	23 52		
Folkestone West	d	22 21			22 28						23 21		23 28					
Folkestone Central	d	22 24			22 31						23 24		23 31					
Dover Priory 4	d	22a35			22 42						23a35		23 42					
Deal	a				23 00								00 01					
Sandwich	a				23 07								00 07					
Dover Priory	a																	
Canterbury West 4	a								22 53	23 06					23 53	00 06		
	d								22 54	23 07					23 54	00 07		
Ramsgate 4	d		22 35		23a19				23a15	23 27			00a19		00a15	00 27		
Broadstairs	d		22 41							23 32						00s32		
Margate 4	a		22 45							23 38						00 38		
St Pancras International	a					23 13		23 45										

A From Rainham (Kent) to Kentish Town
B From London Charing Cross
C To St Pancras International
D To Faversham
E To Ashford International
F To London Victoria
G From Rainham (Kent) to West Hampstead Thameslink
H From Rainham (Kent) to Bedford

Table T194-R

Mondays to Fridays

16 December to 15 May

Kent - St Pancras International High Speed Domestic Services

Miles	Miles	Miles	Miles			SE	SE	SE	SE	SE	SE	SE	SE	SE	SE	SE	SE	SE	SE	SE	SE	SE	SE	SE
						MX	MO	TTh FO	MO	MX	MO	MX	ThFO	WO	TTh FO	MO	TO	MX	MX	TO	WO	WO	WO	TTh FO
						1	◇	◇	◇	◇	◇	◇	◇	bus	◇1	◇1	◇	◇1	◇	bus	bus	bus	bus	◇1
—	—	—	—	St Pancras International	d							00 12												
—	—	0	—	**Margate** 4	d			00 04						00 22	00 25	00 26					00 43	00 45	01 06	01 08
—	—	3¼	—	Broadstairs	d		00 05	00 10						00 32	00 31	00 32					00 53	00 55	01 16	01 14
—	—	5½	—	Ramsgate 4	d		00a11	00a16						00a43	00a38	00a39					01a04	01a06	01a27	01a21
—	—	20¾	—	**Canterbury West**	a																			
—	—	—	—		d																			
—	—	—	—	Dover Priory	d														00 43					
—	—	—	—	Sandwich	d				00 07	00 08									01s07					
—	—	—	—	Deal	d																			
—	0	—	—	**Dover Priory**	d																			
—	7¼	—	—	Folkestone Central	d																			
—	8	—	—	Folkestone West	d	00 02																		
—	21¼	—	—	**Ashford International**	a	00 20																		
					d													00 34		00 40				
—	—	—	—	Ramsgate	d				00a19	00a21	00 27		00 30				00 44	01a20	01a23	02a02				
0	—	—	—	**Broadstairs**	d						00s32		00s35				00s49							
3¼	—	—	—	Margate 4	d						00a38		00a40				00a57							
6¼	—	—	—	Birchington-on-Sea	d																			
14¼	—	—	—	Herne Bay	d																			
18¾	—	—	—	Whitstable	d																			
25	—	—	—	**Faversham** 2	a																			
					d																			
32¾	—	—	—	Sittingbourne 4	d																			
38½	—	—	—	Rainham (Kent)	d																			
41½	—	—	—	Gillingham (Kent) 4	d																			
43¼	—	—	—	Chatham 4	d																			
43¾	—	—	—	Rochester 4	d																			
—	—	—	0	Maidstone West	d																			
44¾	—	—	12¼	Strood 4	d																			
52	—	—	19½	Gravesend	d																			
54	54½	68¼	21½	**Ebbsfleet International**	a																			
—	—	—	—		d																			
70¾	71¼	85	38¼	**Stratford International** ⊖	a							00 18												
76¾	77¼	91	44¼	**St Pancras International** 4 ⊖	a																			

		SE	SE	SE	SE	SE	SE	SE	SE	SE	SE	SE	SE	SE	SE	SE	SE	SE	SE	SE	SE	SE
		WO	WO																			
		bus	bus	◇1	◇	◇	◇	◇1	1	◇	◇	◇	◇1	◇1	◇	◇		◇	◇	◇	◇1	◇1
St Pancras International	d										06 25				06 40			06 55				
Margate 4	d	01 22	01 45																05 48			
Broadstairs	d	01 32	01 55																05 54			
Ramsgate 4	d	01a43	02a06				04 55	04 51					05 38	05 20					06 00		06 10	
Canterbury West	a						05 17						06 00						06 19		06 33	
	d						05 18						06 01						06 19		06 34	
Dover Priory	d																					
Sandwich	d							05 06						05 34						05 54		06 05
Deal	d							05 12						05 40						06 00		06 11
Dover Priory	d			04 27				05 30				05 45		05 59						06 18		06 30
Folkestone Central	d			04 38				05 41				05 56		06 10						06 29		06 42
Folkestone West	d			04 40				05 43				05 58		06 12						06 31		06 44
Ashford International	a			04 57			05 41	06 01				06 11	06 23	06 30					06 34	06 44	06 55	07 01
	d				05 13		05 43		06 05			06 13					06 30		06 36	06 46		
Ramsgate	d								06a52							05 12	07 14					
Broadstairs	d															05 18	07 20					
Margate 4	d															05 23	07a26					
Birchington-on-Sea	d															05 31						
Herne Bay	d															05 40						
Whitstable	d															05 47						
Faversham 2	a															05 55						
	d					04 58				05 28						05 56						
Sittingbourne 4	d					05 07				05 37						06 04						
Rainham (Kent)	d					05 15				05 45						06 11						
Gillingham (Kent) 4	d					05 20				05 50						06 17						
Chatham 4	d					05 24				05 54						06 21						
Rochester 4	d					05 28				05 58						06 25						
Maidstone West	d																					
Strood 4	d					05 31				06 01						06 28						
Gravesend	d					05 41				06 11						06 39						
Ebbsfleet International	a				05 32	05 45	06 02			06 15		06 32				06 42			06 55	07 05		
	d				05 32	05 46	06 02			06 16		06 32				06 43			06 55	07 06		
Stratford International ⊖	a				05 44	05 57	06 14			06 27	06 31	06 44			06 46	06 55		07 01	07 07	07 17		
St Pancras International 4 ⊖	a				05 51	06 05	06 21			06 35		06 51				07 02			07 14	07 25		

Table T194-R

Mondays to Fridays

16 December to 15 May

Kent - St Pancras International High Speed Domestic Services

		SE	SE	SE	SE	SE	SE	SE	SE	SE	SE	SE	SE	SE	SE	SE	SE	SE	SE	SE	SE	SE	SE
		1	◇	◇	◇	◇		◇	◇1	◇1	◇	◇	◇	◇	◇	◇	◇1	◇1	◇	◇1	◇	1	1
St Pancras International	d															07 05							
Margate 4	d				06 18						06 48								06 53		07 18		07 24
Broadstairs	d				06 24						06 54								06 59		07 24		07 30
Ramsgate 4	d				06 30	06 14					07 00						06 50		07 08	07 12	07 30		07a36
Canterbury West	a				06 49						07 19									07 34	07 49		
	d				06 49				07 03		07 19									07 36	07 49		
Dover Priory	d	05 57																				07 10	
Sandwich	d	06 21				06 26							06 50				07 02		07 20			07 34	
Deal	d					06 32							06 56				07 08		07 26				
Dover Priory	d					06 48							07 13				07 25		→				
Folkestone Central	d					06 59				07 11			07 24				07 36						
Folkestone West	d					07 01				07 14			07 27				07 38						
Ashford International	a				07 04	07 14			07 25	07 31	07 34		07 40			07 42	07 55			07 58	08 04		
	d				07 06	07 16	07 22				07 36		07 44			07 44		07 58			08 06		
Ramsgate	d	06a36					08a05									08 23		08a45				07a46	
Broadstairs	d							06 29							06 58	08 28							
Margate 4	d							06 34							07 03	08a34							
Birchington-on-Sea	d							06 39							07 08								
Herne Bay	d							06 48							07 17								
Whitstable	d							06 53							07 23								
Faversham 2	a							07 01							07 31								
	d		06 28					07 02							07 31								
Sittingbourne 4	d		06 36					07 10							07 39								
Rainham (Kent)	d		06 44					07 17							07 47								
Gillingham (Kent) 4	d		06 49					07 22							07 52								
Chatham 4	d		06 53					07 27							07 56								
Rochester 4	d		06 57					07 30							08 00								
Maidstone West	d			06 52								07 25											
Strood 4	d			07 09				07 34				07 43			08 03								
Gravesend	d			07 19				07 44				07 53			08 14								
Ebbsfleet International	a		07 11		07 25	07 35		07 48				07 56			08 17								
	d		07 12		07 26	07 36		07 49				07 57		08 09	08 18								
Stratford International ⊖	a		07 24	07 33	07 37	07 47		08 00			08 04	08 09	08 12	08 20	08 30						08 34		
St Pancras International 4 ⊖	a		07 31	07 41	07 45	07 54		08 08			08 12	08 16	08 20	08 28	08 38						08 42		

		SE	SE	SE	SE	SE	SE	SE	SE	SE	SE	SE	SE	SE	SE	SE	SE	SE	SE	SE	SE	SE	SE
		◇1	◇	◇	◇1	◇1	◇	◇	◇	◇1	◇1	◇	◇	◇1	◇1	1	1	◇	◇	◇	◇1	◇1	◇
St Pancras International	d								08 12											09 09			
Margate 4	d							07 55								07 59	08 24		08 51				
Broadstairs	d							08 01								08 05	08 30		08 57				
Ramsgate 4	d							08 07		07 42	08 14			07 58		08a11	08a37		09 03			09 08	
Canterbury West	a							08 26			08 35								09 22			09 35	
	d							08 26			08 36								09 23			09 36	
Dover Priory	d	07 34																					
Sandwich	d	08 01		←						08 02				08 22									
Deal	d			07 26						08 08				08 28									
Dover Priory	d			07 44	07 58					08 25			08 49	08 58							09 25		
Folkestone Central	d			07 55	08 09					08 36			09 00	09 09							09 36		
Folkestone West	d			07 57	08 11					08 38			09 02	09 11							09 38		
Ashford International	a			08 11	08 28			08 41	08 50	08 55	08 58		09 15	09 28					09 38	09 47	09 55	09 58	
	d			08 16		08 33		08 43	08 52				09 16		09 35				09 43	09 52			
Ramsgate	d	08a16				09a18			09 31						10a18					10 28			
Broadstairs	d								09 36											10 33			
Margate 4	d								09a42											10a38			
Birchington-on-Sea	d																						
Herne Bay	d																						
Whitstable	d																						
Faversham 2	a																						
	d						07 59					08 28						08 59					09 30
Sittingbourne 4	d						08 07					08 38						09 08					09 38
Rainham (Kent)	d						08 14					08 46						09 16					09 46
Gillingham (Kent) 4	d						08 19					08 51						09 21					09 51
Chatham 4	d						08 24					08 55						09 25					09 55
Rochester 4	d						08 27					08 59						09 29					09 59
Maidstone West	d		07 53																				
Strood 4	d		08 11				08 32					09 02						09 32					10 02
Gravesend	d		08 21				08 43					09 12						09 42					10 12
Ebbsfleet International	a		08 25	08 35			08 46	09 02				09 16	09 35					09 46	10 02				10 16
	d		08 26	08 36			08 48	09 02				09 17	09 35					09 51	10 02				10 22
Stratford International ⊖	a		08 39	08 47			08 59	09 14				09 28	09 47					10 02	10 14				10 33
St Pancras International 4 ⊖	a		08 46	08 54			09 07	09 21				09 36	09 54					10 10	10 21				10 41

Table T194-R

Mondays to Fridays

16 December to 15 May

Kent - St Pancras International High Speed Domestic Services

		SE ◇	SE ◇	SE ◇	SE ◇	SE ◇	SE ◇1	SE ◇1	SE ◇1	SE ◇	SE ◇	SE ◇1	SE ◇	SE ◇	SE ◇	SE ◇	SE ◇1	SE ◇1	SE ◇1	SE ◇	SE ◇	SE ◇1	SE ◇
St Pancras International	d		07 22	07 25	07 37	08 04					10 09			08 25	08 37	08 57					11 12		
Margate 4	d		08 59				09 31			09 55				09 59			10 25			10 55			
Broadstairs	d		09 05				09 37			10 01				10 05			10 31			11 01			
Ramsgate 4	d	09 36	09 12				09a45			10 07		10 19		10 12			10a38			11 07		11 19	
Canterbury West	a	09 55								10 26		10 41								11 26		11 41	
	d	09 55								10 26		10 42								11 26		11 42	
Dover Priory	d				08 42										09 43								
Sandwich	d		09 25		09 07									10 25	10 07								
Deal	d		09 31											10 31									
Dover Priory	d		09 49					09 58						10 49				10 58					
Folkestone Central	d		10 00					10 09						11 00				11 09					
Folkestone West	d		10 02					10 11						11 02				11 11					
Ashford International	a	10 10	10 15					10 28		10 41	10 47	11 00		11 15				11 28		11 41	11 50	12 00	
	d	10 11	10 16						10 35	10 43	10 52			11 16					11 35	11 43	11 52		
Ramsgate	d				09 20				11a19		11 28				10 20				12a16		12 28		
Broadstairs	d				09 25						11 33				10 25						12 33		
Margate 4	d				09 30						11a38				10 30						12a38		
Birchington-on-Sea	d				09 35										10 35								
Herne Bay	d				09 44										10 44								
Whitstable	d				09 49										10 49								
Faversham 2	a				09 57										10 57								
	d				09 58								10 30		10 58								11 30
Sittingbourne 4	d				10 08								10 38		11 08								11 38
Rainham (Kent)	d				10 16								10 46		11 16								11 46
Gillingham (Kent) 4	d				10 21								10 51		11 21								11 51
Chatham 4	d				10 25								10 55		11 25								11 55
Rochester 4	d				10 29								10 59		11 29								11 59
Maidstone West	d																						
Strood 4	d				10 32								11 02		11 32								12 02
Gravesend	d				10 42								11 12		11 42								12 12
Ebbsfleet International	a		10 35		10 46					11 02			11 16	11 35	11 46					12 02			12 16
	d		10 35		10 47					11 02			11 18	11 36	11 47					12 02			12 17
Stratford International ⊖	a	10 39	10 47	07 31	10 58	08 10				11 14			11 29	11 47	11 58	09 04				12 14			12 28
St Pancras International 4 ⊖	a	10 47	10 55		11 06					11 21			11 40	11 54	12 06					12 21			12 36

		SE ◇	SE ◇	SE ◇	SE ◇1	SE ◇1	SE ◇1	SE ◇	SE ◇	SE ◇1	SE ◇	SE ◇	SE ◇	SE ◇	SE ◇1	SE ◇1	SE ◇1	SE ◇	SE ◇	SE ◇1	SE ◇	SE ◇	SE ◇
St Pancras International	d	09 25	09 37	09 55					12 12			10 27	10 37	10 52					13 12			11 25	11 37
Margate 4	d	10 59			11 25			11 55				11 59			12 25			12 55				12 59	
Broadstairs	d	11 05			11 31			12 01				12 05			12 31			13 01				13 05	
Ramsgate 4	d	11 12			11a38			12 07		12 19		12 12			12a38			13 07		13 19		13 12	
Canterbury West	a							12 26		12 41								13 26		13 41			
	d							12 26		12 42								13 26		13 42			
Dover Priory	d		10 42										11 42										12 42
Sandwich	d	11 25	11 07									12 25	12 07									13 25	13 07
Deal	d	11 31										12 31										13 31	
Dover Priory	d	11 49				11 58						12 49				12 58						13 49	
Folkestone Central	d	12 00				12 09						13 00				13 09						14 00	
Folkestone West	d	12 02				12 11						13 02				13 11						14 02	
Ashford International	a	12 15				12 28		12 41	12 50	13 00		13 15				13 28		13 41	13 50	14 00		14 15	
	d	12 16					12 35	12 43	12 52			13 16					13 35	13 43	13 52			14 16	
Ramsgate	d		11 20				13a16		13 28				12 20				14a16		14 28				13 20
Broadstairs	d		11 25						13 33				12 25						14 33				13 25
Margate 4	d		11 30						13a38				12 30						14a38				13 30
Birchington-on-Sea	d		11 35										12 35										13 35
Herne Bay	d		11 44										12 44										13 44
Whitstable	d		11 49										12 49										13 49
Faversham 2	a		11 57										12 57										13 57
	d		11 58								12 30		12 58								13 30		13 58
Sittingbourne 4	d		12 08								12 38		13 08								13 38		14 08
Rainham (Kent)	d		12 16								12 46		13 16								13 46		14 16
Gillingham (Kent) 4	d		12 21								12 51		13 21								13 51		14 21
Chatham 4	d		12 25								12 55		13 25								13 55		14 25
Rochester 4	d		12 29								12 59		13 29								13 59		14 29
Maidstone West	d																						
Strood 4	d		12 32								13 02		13 32								14 02		14 32
Gravesend	d		12 42								13 12		13 42								14 12		14 42
Ebbsfleet International	a	12 35	12 46					13 02			13 16	13 35	13 46					14 02			14 16	14 35	14 46
	d	12 35	12 47					13 02			13 18	13 35	13 51					14 02			14 17	14 35	14 47
Stratford International ⊖	a	12 47	12 58	10 01				13 14			13 29	13 47	14 02	10 58				14 14			14 28	14 47	14 58
St Pancras International 4 ⊖	a	12 55	13 06					13 21			13 37	13 54	14 10					14 21			14 36	14 54	15 06

NRT DECEMBER 19 EDITION

Table T194-R

Mondays to Fridays

16 December to 15 May

Kent - St Pancras International High Speed Domestic Services

		SE ◇	SE ◇1	SE ◇1	SE ◇1	SE ◇	SE ◇	SE ◇1	SE ◇	SE ◇	SE ◇	SE ◇	SE ◇1	SE ◇1	SE ◇1	SE ◇	SE ◇	SE ◇1	SE ◇	SE ◇	SE ◇	SE ◇	SE ◇1
St Pancras International	d	11 55					14 10			12 27	12 37	12 52					15 12			13 25	13 37	13 55	
Margate 4	d		13 25			13 55				13 59			14 25			14 55				14 59			
Broadstairs	d		13 31			14 01				14 05			14 31			15 01				15 05			
Ramsgate 4	d		13a38			14 07		14 19		14 12			14a38			15 07		15 17		15 12			15 21
Canterbury West	a					14 26		14 41								15 26		15 40					
	d					14 26		14 42								15 26		15 42					
Dover Priory	d										13 42										14 42		
Sandwich	d									14 25	14 07									15 25	15 07		15 35
Deal	d									14 31										15 31			15 42
Dover Priory	d			13 58						14 49				14 58						15 49			15 59
Folkestone Central	d			14 09						15 00				15 09						16 00			16 10
Folkestone West	d			14 11						15 02				15 11						16 02			16 12
Ashford International	a			14 28		14 41	14 48	15 00		15 15				15 28		15 41	15 50	16 00		16 15			16 30
	d				14 35	14 43	14 52			15 19					15 35	15 43	15 52			16 16			
Ramsgate	d				15a16		15 28				14 20				16a16		16 28				15 20		
Broadstairs	d						15 33				14 25						16 33				15 25		
Margate 4	d						15a38				14 30						16a38				15 30		
Birchington-on-Sea	d										14 35										15 35		
Herne Bay	d										14 44										15 44		
Whitstable	d										14 49										15 49		
Faversham 2	a										14 57										15 57		
	d								14 30		14 58								15 28		15 58		
Sittingbourne 4	d								14 38		15 08								15 38		16 08		
Rainham (Kent)	d								14 46		15 16								15 46		16 16		
Gillingham (Kent) 4	d								14 51		15 21								15 51		16 21		
Chatham 4	d								14 55		15 25								15 55		16 25		
Rochester 4	d								14 59		15 29								15 59		16 29		
Maidstone West	d																						
Strood 4	d								15 02		15 32								16 02		16 32		
Gravesend	d								15 12		15 42								16 12		16 42		
Ebbsfleet International	a					15 02			15 16	15 38	15 46					16 02			16 16	16 35	16 46		
	d					15 02			15 17	15 38	15 51					16 02			16 17	16 35	16 51		
Stratford International ⊖	a	12 01				15 14			15 28	15 50	16 02	12 58				16 14			16 28	16 47	17 02	14 01	
St Pancras International 4 ⊖	a					15 21			15 36	15 58	16 10					16 21			16 36	16 54	17 10		

		SE ◇1	SE ◇1	SE ◇1	SE ◇	SE ◇	SE ◇1	SE ◇1	SE ◇	SE ◇	SE ◇	SE ◇	SE 1	SE ◇1	SE ◇	SE ◇1	SE ◇1	SE ◇	SE ◇	SE ◇1	SE ◇1	SE ◇1
St Pancras International	d					16 10				14 25	14 37	14 55			16 50				17 20			
Margate 4	d		15 25		15 55					16 02				16 28				16 55				
Broadstairs	d		15 31		16 01					16 08				16 34				17 01				
Ramsgate 4	d		15a38		16 07		15 50	16 17		16 13				16a40				17 07		16 50	17 18	
Canterbury West	a				16 26			16 39										17 26			17 39	
	d				16 26			16 40										17 26			17 40	
Dover Priory	d	15 25									15 42		16 10									
Sandwich	d	15 50					16 02			16 26	16 07		16 36							17 02		
Deal	d						16 08			16 32										17 08		
Dover Priory	d						16 25			16 49						16 58				17 25		
Folkestone Central	d						16 36			17 00						17 09				17 36		
Folkestone West	d						16 38			17 02						17 11				17 38		
Ashford International	a				16 41	16 48	16 55	16 58		17 15					17 24	17 28		17 41	17 54	17 55	17 58	
	d			16 35	16 45	16 52				17 16					17 26		17 35	17 43	17 56			18 03
Ramsgate	d	16a13		17a24		17 32					16 20		16a54		18 03		18a21		18 31			18a49
Broadstairs	d					17 37					16 25				18 08				18 36			
Margate 4	d					17a42					16 30				18a15				18a44			
Birchington-on-Sea	d										16 35											
Herne Bay	d										16 44											
Whitstable	d										16 49											
Faversham 2	a										16 57											
	d								16 25		16 58											
Sittingbourne 4	d								16 37		17 08											
Rainham (Kent)	d								16 46		17 16											
Gillingham (Kent) 4	d								16 51		17 21											
Chatham 4	d								16 55		17 25											
Rochester 4	d								16 59		17 29											
Maidstone West	d																					
Strood 4	d								17 02		17 32											
Gravesend	d								17 12		17 42											
Ebbsfleet International	a				17 04				17 16	17 35	17 46							18 02				
	d				17 04				17 17	17 35	17 51							18 02				
Stratford International ⊖	a				17 16				17 28	17 47	18 03	15 01						18 14				
St Pancras International 4 ⊖	a				17 23				17 36	17 54	18 10							18 23				

Table T194-R

Mondays to Fridays
16 December to 15 May

Kent - St Pancras International High Speed Domestic Services

		SE	SE	SE	SE	SE	SE	SE	SE	SE	SE	SE	SE	SE	SE	SE	SE	SE	SE	SE	SE	SE	SE
		◇	◇	◇	◇	◇	◇1	◇1	◇	◇	◇	◇	◇	◇1	◇1	◇	◇	◇1	◇1	◇1	◇	◇	◇
St Pancras International	d		15 25	15 37	15 55	16 25			16 37	16 55	17 07	17 12	17 50				18 20						
Margate 4	d		17 02					17 32								17 55							
Broadstairs	d		17 08					17 38								18 01							
Ramsgate 4	d		17 13					17a46								18 07		17 50	18 10				
Canterbury West	a															18 26			18 35				
	d															18 26			18 36				
Dover Priory	d			16 42			17 11		17 45														
Sandwich	d		17 26	17 07			17 35		18 11									18 02					
Deal	d		17 32															18 08					
Dover Priory	d		17 49											17 58				18 25					18 49
Folkestone Central	d		18 00											18 09				18 36					19 00
Folkestone West	d		18 02											18 11				18 38					19 02
Ashford International	a		18 15										18 24	18 28		18 41	18 54	18 55	18 58				19 15
	d		18 16										18 26		18 33	18 43	18 56			19 02			19 16
Ramsgate	d			17 20			17a49		18 26				19 01		19a21		19 31			19a52			
Broadstairs	d			17 25					18 32				19 06				19 36						
Margate 4	d			17 30					18 38				19a14				19a44						
Birchington-on-Sea	d			17 35					18 45														
Herne Bay	d			17 44					18 54														
Whitstable	d			17 49					19 01														
Faversham 2	a			17 57					19 10														
	d	17 28		17 58																		18 28	
Sittingbourne 4	d	17 38		18 08																		18 38	
Rainham (Kent)	d	17 46		18 16																		18 46	
Gillingham (Kent) 4	d	17 51		18 21																		18 51	
Chatham 4	d	17 55		18 25																		18 55	
Rochester 4	d	17 59		18 29																		18 59	
Maidstone West	d																				18 42		
Strood 4	d	18 03		18 35																	18 58	19 02	
Gravesend	d	18 13		18 45																	19 08	19 12	
Ebbsfleet International	a	18 17	18 35	18 49												19 02					19 12	19 16	19 35
	d	18 18	18 35	18 50												19 02					19 13	19 17	19 35
Stratford International ⊖	a	18 29	18 47	19 01	16 01	16 32				17 01	17 13	17 18				19 14					19 24	19 28	19 47
St Pancras International 4 ⊖	a	18 37	18 54	19 09												19 21					19 31	19 36	19 54

		SE	SE	SE	SE	SE	SE	SE	SE	SE	SE	SE	SE	SE	SE	SE	SE	SE	SE	SE	SE	SE	SE
		◇	◇	◇1	◇1	◇1	◇1	◇	◇	◇	◇	◇1	◇1	◇	◇	◇	◇	◇1	◇1	◇	◇	◇	◇1
St Pancras International	d		18 50						17 25	17 37	17 46			17 55	18 07	18 16	19 20						
Margate 4	d			18 08		18 26		18 53	18 58			19 26	19 30	19 36									
Broadstairs	d			18 14		18 32		18 59	19 04			19 32	19a39	19a45									
Ramsgate 4	d			18 23		18a41		19 07	19a13			19a39						19 16					19 23
Canterbury West	a							19 26										19 38					
	d							19 26										19 39					
Dover Priory	d				18 12					18 46													
Sandwich	d			18 35	18 37					19 11													19 35
Deal	d			18 41																			19 41
Dover Priory	d			18 58																	19 49		19 58
Folkestone Central	d			19 09																	20 00		20 09
Folkestone West	d			19 11																	20 02		20 11
Ashford International	a		19 25	19 28				19 41									19 54	20 00			20 15		20 28
	d		19 27				19 32	19 43									19 56		20 07		20 16		
Ramsgate	d		20 02		18a53		20a20			19a25							20 31		20a55			19 20	
Broadstairs	d		20 07														20 36					19 25	
Margate 4	d	18 25	20a15														20a44					19 30	
Birchington-on-Sea	d	18 33																				19 35	
Herne Bay	d	18 42																				19 44	
Whitstable	d	18 49																				19 49	
Faversham 2	a	18 57																				19 57	
	d	18 58																		19 30		19 58	
Sittingbourne 4	d	19 08																		19 38		20 08	
Rainham (Kent)	d	19 16																		19 46		20 16	
Gillingham (Kent) 4	d	19 21																		19 51		20 21	
Chatham 4	d	19 25																		19 55		20 25	
Rochester 4	d	19 29																		19 59		20 29	
Maidstone West	d																						
Strood 4	d	19 32																		20 02		20 32	
Gravesend	d	19 42																		20 12		20 42	
Ebbsfleet International	a	19 46						20 02												20 16	20 35	20 46	
	d	19 47						20 02												20 17	20 35	20 47	
Stratford International ⊖	a	19 58						20 14			17 52				18 14	18 22				20 28	20 47	20 59	
St Pancras International 4 ⊖	a	20 06						20 21												20 36	20 54	21 06	

Table T194-R

Mondays to Fridays
16 December to 15 May

Kent - St Pancras International High Speed Domestic Services

		SE	SE	SE	SE	SE	SE	SE	SE	SE	SE	SE	SE	SE	SE	SE	SE	SE	SE	SE	SE	SE	SE
		◇1	◇1	◇	◇1	◇	◇	◇	◇	◇	◇1	◇	◇	◇	◇1	◇1	◇1	◇1	◇	◇	◇1	◇	◇
St Pancras International	d					18 25	18 37	18 55	19 07	20 12										21 12			
Margate 4	d			19 53	19 57	20 02												20 33	20 53				21 00
Broadstairs	d			19 59	20 03	20a10												20 39	20 59				21 06
Ramsgate 4	d			20 05	20a12						20 16					20 23		20a48	21 05		21 16		21 12
Canterbury West	a			20 24							20 38								21 24		21 38		
	d			20 26							20 39								21 26		21 39		
Dover Priory	d	19 25													19 55								
Sandwich	d	19 52													20 23	20 35							21 25
Deal	d															20 41							21 31
Dover Priory	d												20 49			20 58							21 49
Folkestone Central	d												21 00			21 09							22 00
Folkestone West	d												21 02			21 11							22 02
Ashford International	a			20 41						20 50	21 00		21 15			21 28			21 41	21 50	22 00		22 15
	d		20 35	20 43						20 52			21 16				21 32		21 43	21 52			22 16
Ramsgate	d	20a08	21a23							21 32				20 20	20a39		22a17			22 28			
Broadstairs	d									21 38				20 25						22 33			
Margate 4	d									21a43				20 30						22a38			
Birchington-on-Sea	d													20 35									
Herne Bay	d													20 44									
Whitstable	d													20 49									
Faversham 2	a													20 57									
	d											20 30		20 58								21 30	
Sittingbourne 4	d											20 38		21 08								21 38	
Rainham (Kent)	d											20 46		21 16								21 46	
Gillingham (Kent) 4	d											20 52		21 21								21 51	
Chatham 4	d											20 56		21 25								21 55	
Rochester 4	d											21 00		21 29								21 59	
Maidstone West	d																						
Strood 4	d											21 03		21 32								22 02	
Gravesend	d											21 13		21 42								22 12	
Ebbsfleet International	a			21 02								21 18	21 35	21 46					22 02			22 16	22 35
	d			21 02								21 21	21 35	21 48					22 02			22 17	22 35
Stratford International ⊖	a			21 14			18 44	19 01	19 13			21 32	21 47	21 59					22 14			22 28	22 47
St Pancras International 4 ⊖	a			21 21								21 40	21 54	22 07					22 21			22 36	22 54

		SE	SE	SE	SE	SE	SE	SE	SE	SE	SE	SE	SE	SE	SE	SE	SE	SE	SE	SE	SE	SE	SE
													TX					MO					TO
		◇	◇	◇	◇1	◇1	◇1	◇1	◇	◇	◇	◇	◇	1	◇	◇1	◇1	🚌		◇	◇	◇	◇
St Pancras International	d	19 25	19 37	19 55						20 25	20 37	20 55	22 12							21 25	21 37	21 55	22 12
Margate 4	d	21 04				21 28			21 55	22 04							22 25		22 55	23 04			
Broadstairs	d	21 10				21 34			22 01	22 10							22 31		23 01	23 10			
Ramsgate 4	d	21a17				21a42			22 07	22a19				22 17	22 12		22a38		23 07	23a18			
Canterbury West	a								22 26					22 39					23 26				
	d								22 26					22 40					23 26				
Dover Priory	d		20 42		21 10						21 42										22 42		
Sandwich	d		21 06		21 34						22 07				22 25						23 07		
Deal	d														22 31								
Dover Priory	d						21 58								22 49								
Folkestone Central	d						22 09								23 00								
Folkestone West	d						22 11								23 02								
Ashford International	a						22 28		22 41				22 50	23 00	23 15				23 41				
	d							22 34	22 43				22 52		23 16	23 34		23 40					
Ramsgate	d		21 20		21a50			23a17			22a19		23 29			00a18		01a02			23a22		
Broadstairs	d		21 25										23 34										
Margate 4	d		21 30										23a40										
Birchington-on-Sea	d		21 35																				
Herne Bay	d		21 44																				
Whitstable	d		21 49																				
Faversham 2	a		21 57																				
	d		21 58																				
Sittingbourne 4	d		22 08																				
Rainham (Kent)	d		22 16																				
Gillingham (Kent) 4	d		22 21																				
Chatham 4	d		22 25																				
Rochester 4	d		22 29																				
Maidstone West	d																						
Strood 4	d		22 32																				
Gravesend	d		22 42																				
Ebbsfleet International	a		22 46						23 02						23 35								
	d		22 47						23 02						23 35								
Stratford International ⊖	a		22 58	20 01					23 14			21 01			23 47							22 01	22 18
St Pancras International 4 ⊖	a		23 06						23 21						23 54								

Table T194-R

Mondays to Fridays
16 December to 15 May

Kent - St Pancras International High Speed Domestic Services

		SE		SE	SE	SE	SE	SE	SE	SE	SE	SE	SE		SE	SE
		TO			TX			TO	WThFO	MO		MO				
		◇		◇[1]	◇	◇	◇	◇	◇	◇	◇	🚌	[1]		◇	◇
St Pancras International	d	22 25			22 25	22 37	22 55	23 12	23 12	23 12	23 25				23 37	23 55
Margate [4]	d			23 25	00 04											
Broadstairs	d			23 31	00 10											
Ramsgate [4]	d			23a38	00a16								23 12			
Canterbury West	a															
	d															
Dover Priory	d					23 43									00 43	
Sandwich	d					00 08							23 25		01s07	
Deal	d												23 31			
Dover Priory	d												23 49			
Folkestone Central	d												23 59			
Folkestone West	d												00 02			
Ashford International	a								23 50	23 50			00 20			
	d								23 52	23 52		23 59				
Ramsgate	d					00a21			00 30	00 44		01s12			01a23	
Broadstairs	d								00s35	00s49		01s21				
Margate [4]	d								00a40	00a57		01a31				
Birchington-on-Sea	d															
Herne Bay	d															
Whitstable	d															
Faversham [2]	a															
	d															
Sittingbourne [4]	d															
Rainham (Kent)	d															
Gillingham (Kent) [4]	d															
Chatham [4]	d															
Rochester [4]	d															
Maidstone West	d															
Strood [4]	d															
Gravesend	d															
Ebbsfleet International	a															
	d															
Stratford International ⊖	a	22 31					23 01	23 18			23 31					00 01
St Pancras International [4] ⊖	a															

Saturdays
21 December to 16 May

		SE	SE	SE	SE	SE	SE	SE	SE	SE	SE		SE	SE	SE	SE	SE	SE	SE	SE	SE	SE		SE	SE
		[1]	◇	◇	◇	◇	◇[1]	◇[1]	◇	◇[1]	◇[1]		◇	◇[1]	◇	◇	◇[1]		◇	◇[1]	◇	◇		◇	◇[1]
St Pancras International	d					00 12																			
Margate [4]	d		00 04				00 25			01 08									05 53						
Broadstairs	d		00 10				00 31			01 14									05 59						
Ramsgate [4]	d		00a16				00a38			01a21			05 05	05 15					06 05	06 15		06 12			
Canterbury West	a												05 24	05 36					06 24	06 36					
	d												05 26	05 37					06 26	06 37					
Dover Priory	d								00 43																
Sandwich	d			00 08					01s07													06 25			
Deal	d																					06 31			
Dover Priory	d										04 58					05 49	05 58					06 49			06 58
Folkestone Central	d										05 09					06 00	06 09					07 00			07 09
Folkestone West	d	00 02									05 11					06 02	06 11					07 02			07 11
Ashford International	a	00 20									05 28		05 41	05 58		06 15	06 28		06 41	06 58		07 15			07 28
	d							00 34					05 43			06 16		06 35	06 43			07 16			
Ramsgate	d			00a21	00 30			01a20	01a23									07 16						06 20	
Broadstairs	d				00s35													07 21						06 25	
Margate [4]	d				00a40													07a26						06 30	
Birchington-on-Sea	d																							06 35	
Herne Bay	d																							06 44	
Whitstable	d																							06 49	
Faversham [2]	a																							06 57	
	d														05 30						06 30			06 58	
Sittingbourne [4]	d														05 38						06 38			07 08	
Rainham (Kent)	d														05 46						06 46			07 16	
Gillingham (Kent) [4]	d														05 51						06 51			07 21	
Chatham [4]	d														05 55						06 55			07 25	
Rochester [4]	d														05 59						06 59			07 29	
Maidstone West	d																								
Strood [4]	d														06 02						07 02			07 32	
Gravesend	d														06 12						07 12			07 42	
Ebbsfleet International	a												06 02		06 16	06 35			07 02		07 16	07 35		07 46	
	d												06 02		06 17	06 35			07 02		07 17	07 35		07 47	
Stratford International ⊖	a					00 18							06 14		06 28	06 47			07 14		07 28	07 47		07 58	
St Pancras International [4] ⊖	a												06 21		06 36	06 54			07 21		07 36	07 54		08 06	

Table T194-R

Saturdays
21 December to 16 May

Kent - St Pancras International High Speed Domestic Services

		SE	SE	SE	SE	SE	SE	SE	SE		SE	SE	SE	SE	SE	SE	SE	SE	SE	SE		SE	SE	SE	SE
		◇[1]	◇	◇	◇[1]	◇	◇	◇	[1]		◇[1]	◇[1]	◇	◇	◇[1]	◇	◇	◇	[1]	◇[1]		◇[1]	◇	◇	◇[1]
St Pancras International	d			07 07										08 12				06 37						09 09	
Margate [4]	d		06 53				06 57		07 49				07 55						08 25				08 55		
Broadstairs	d		06 59				07 03		07 55				08 01						08 31				09 01		
Ramsgate [4]	d		07 05		07 15		07 12		08a02				08 07		08 17		08 12		08a38				09 07		09 17
Canterbury West	a		07 24		07 36								08 26		08 39								09 26		09 39
	d		07 26		07 37								08 26		08 40								09 26		09 40
Dover Priory	d							06 42										07 42							
Sandwich	d						07 25	07 07									08 25	08 07							
Deal	d						07 31										08 31								
Dover Priory	d						07 49				07 58						08 49			08 58					
Folkestone Central	d						08 00				08 09						09 00			09 09					
Folkestone West	d						08 02				08 11						09 02			09 11					
Ashford International	a		07 41	07 44	07 58		08 15				08 30		08 41	08 50	08 58		09 15			09 30			09 41	09 47	09 58
	d	07 35	07 43	07 52			08 16					08 35	08 43	08 52			09 16					09 35	09 43	09 52	
Ramsgate	d	08a16		08 28				07 20				09a16		09 28				08 20				10a16		10 28	
Broadstairs	d			08 33				07 25						09 33				08 25						10 33	
Margate [4]	d			08a38				07 30						09a38				08 30						10a38	
Birchington-on-Sea	d							07 35										08 35							
Herne Bay	d							07 44										08 44							
Whitstable	d							07 49										08 49							
Faversham [2]	a							07 57										08 57							
	d					07 30		07 58								08 30		08 58							
Sittingbourne [4]	d					07 38		08 08								08 38		09 08							
Rainham (Kent)	d					07 46		08 16								08 46		09 16							
Gillingham (Kent) [4]	d					07 51		08 21								08 51		09 21							
Chatham [4]	d					07 55		08 25								08 55		09 25							
Rochester [4]	d					07 59		08 29								08 59		09 29							
Maidstone West	d																								
Strood [4]	d					08 02		08 32								09 02		09 32							
Gravesend	d					08 12		08 42								09 12		09 42							
Ebbsfleet International	a		08 02			08 16	08 35	08 46					09 02			09 16	09 35	09 46					10 02		
	d		08 02			08 18	08 35	08 47					09 02			09 18	09 35	09 51					10 02		
Stratford International ⊖	a		08 14			08 29	08 47	08 58					09 14			09 29	09 47	10 02					10 14		
St Pancras International [4] ⊖	a		08 21			08 37	08 54	09 06					09 21			09 37	09 54	10 10					10 21		

		SE	SE	SE	SE	SE	SE		SE	SE	SE	SE	SE	SE	SE	SE	SE	SE		SE	SE	SE	SE	SE	SE
		◇	◇	◇	◇	◇[1]	◇[1]		◇[1]	◇	◇	◇[1]	◇	◇	◇	◇	◇[1]	◇[1]		◇[1]	◇	◇[1]	◇	◇	◇
St Pancras International	d		07 25	07 37	07 55						10 09			08 25	08 37	08 57								09 25	09 34
Margate [4]	d		08 59			09 25				09 55				09 59			10 25				10 55			10 59	
Broadstairs	d		09 05			09 31				10 01				10 05			10 31				11 01			11 05	
Ramsgate [4]	d		09 12			09a38				10 07		10 19		10 12			10a38				11 07	11 19		11 12	
Canterbury West	a									10 26		10 41									11 26	11 41			
	d									10 26		10 42									11 26	11 42			
Dover Priory	d			08 42											09 42										10 42
Sandwich	d		09 25	09 07										10 25	10 07									11 25	11 07
Deal	d		09 31											10 31										11 31	
Dover Priory	d		09 49				09 58							10 49				10 58						11 49	
Folkestone Central	d		10 00				10 09							11 00				11 09						12 00	
Folkestone West	d		10 02				10 11							11 02				11 11						12 02	
Ashford International	a		10 15				10 30			10 41	10 47	11 00		11 15				11 28			11 41	12 00		12 15	
	d		10 19						10 35	10 43	10 52			11 19						11 35	11 43			12 16	
Ramsgate	d			09 20					11a16		11 28				10 20					12a16					11 20
Broadstairs	d			09 25							11 33				10 25										11 25
Margate [4]	d			09 30							11a38				10 30										11 30
Birchington-on-Sea	d			09 35											10 35										11 35
Herne Bay	d			09 44											10 44										11 44
Whitstable	d			09 49											10 49										11 49
Faversham [2]	a			09 57											10 57										11 57
	d	09 30		09 58									10 30		10 58								11 30		11 58
Sittingbourne [4]	d	09 38		10 08									10 38		11 08								11 38		12 08
Rainham (Kent)	d	09 46		10 16									10 46		11 16								11 46		12 16
Gillingham (Kent) [4]	d	09 51		10 21									10 51		11 21								11 51		12 21
Chatham [4]	d	09 55		10 25									10 55		11 25								11 55		12 25
Rochester [4]	d	09 59		10 29									10 59		11 29								11 59		12 29
Maidstone West	d																								
Strood [4]	d	10 02		10 32									11 02		11 32								12 02		12 32
Gravesend	d	10 12		10 42									11 12		11 42								12 12		12 42
Ebbsfleet International	a	10 16	10 38	10 46						11 02			11 16	11 38	11 46						12 02		12 16	12 35	12 46
	d	10 22	10 38	10 47						11 02			11 18	11 38	11 47						12 02		12 17	12 35	12 47
Stratford International ⊖	a	10 33	10 50	10 58	08 02					11 14			11 29	11 50	11 58	09 04					12 14		12 28	12 47	12 58
St Pancras International [4] ⊖	a	10 41	10 57	11 06						11 21			11 37	11 58	12 06						12 21		12 36	12 55	13 06

Table T194-R

Saturdays
21 December to 16 May

Kent - St Pancras International High Speed Domestic Services

		SE	SE	SE	SE		SE	SE	SE	SE	SE	SE	SE	SE	SE	SE		SE	SE	SE	SE	SE	SE	SE	SE
		◇	◇■	◇■	◇■		◇	◇■	◇	◇	◇	◇	◇■	◇	◇■	◇■		◇	◇	◇■	◇	◇	◇	◇	◇■
St Pancras International	d	09 55								10 25	10 37	10 52		11 12					13 12			11 25	11 37	11 55	
Margate 4	d		11 25				11 55			11 59			12 25					12 55				12 59			13 25
Broadstairs	d		11 31				12 01			12 05			12 31					13 01				13 05			13 31
Ramsgate 4	d		11a38				12 07	12 19		12 12			12a38					13 07		13 19		13 12			13a38
Canterbury West	a						12 26	12 41						12 06				13 26		13 41					
	d						12 26	12 42						12 08				13 26		13 42					
Dover Priory	d										11 42												12 42		
Sandwich	d									12 25	12 07											13 25	13 07		
Deal	d									12 31												13 31			
Dover Priory	d			11 58						12 49					12 58							13 49			
Folkestone Central	d			12 09						13 00					13 09							14 00			
Folkestone West	d			12 11						13 02					13 11							14 02			
Ashford International	a			12 29			12 41	13 00		13 15					13 28			13 41	13 50	14 00		14 15			
	d				12 35		12 43			13 16						13 35		13 45	13 52			14 16			
Ramsgate	d				13a16						12 20			12 28		14a16			14 28				13 20		
Broadstairs	d										12 25			12 33					14 33				13 25		
Margate 4	d										12 30			12a38					14a38				13 30		
Birchington-on-Sea	d										12 35												13 35		
Herne Bay	d										12 44												13 44		
Whitstable	d										12 49												13 49		
Faversham 2	a										12 57												13 57		
	d								12 30		12 58										13 30		13 58		
Sittingbourne 4	d								12 38		13 08										13 38		14 08		
Rainham (Kent)	d								12 46		13 16										13 46		14 16		
Gillingham (Kent) 4	d								12 51		13 21										13 51		14 21		
Chatham 4	d								12 55		13 25										13 55		14 25		
Rochester 4	d								12 59		13 29										13 59		14 29		
Maidstone West	d																								
Strood 4	d								13 02		13 32										14 02		14 32		
Gravesend	d								13 12		13 42										14 12		14 42		
Ebbsfleet International	a						13 02		13 16	13 35	13 46							14 04			14 16	14 35	14 46		
	d						13 02		13 18	13 35	13 51							14 04			14 17	14 35	14 47		
Stratford International ⊖	a	10 01					13 14		13 29	13 47	14 02	10 58						14 16			14 28	14 47	14 58	12 01	
St Pancras International 4 ⊖	a						13 21		13 37	13 54	14 10							14 23			14 36	14 54	15 06		

		SE	SE		SE	SE	SE	SE	SE	SE	SE	SE	SE	SE		SE	SE	SE	SE	SE	SE	SE	SE	SE	SE
		◇	◇■		◇■	◇	◇■	◇	◇	◇	◇	◇■	◇■	◇■		◇	◇	◇■	◇	◇	◇	◇	◇■	◇	◇■
St Pancras International	d	12 12							12 27	12 37	12 52						15 12			13 25	13 37	13 55		14 10	
Margate 4	d					13 55			13 59			14 25				14 55				14 59			15 25		
Broadstairs	d					14 01			14 05			14 31				15 01				15 05			15 31		
Ramsgate 4	d					14 07	14 19		14 12			14a38				15 07		15 19		15 12			15a38		
Canterbury West	a	13 06				14 26	14 41									15 26		15 41						15 06	
	d	13 08				14 26	14 42									15 26		15 42						15 08	
Dover Priory	d									13 44											14 42				
Sandwich	d								14 25	14 08										15 25	15 07				
Deal	d								14 31											15 31					
Dover Priory	d		13 58						14 49				14 58							15 49					15 58
Folkestone Central	d		14 09						15 00				15 09							16 00					16 09
Folkestone West	d		14 11						15 02				15 11							16 02					16 11
Ashford International	a		14 28			14 41	15 00		15 15				15 28			15 41	15 50	16 00		16 15					16 28
	d				14 35	14 45			15 16					15 35		15 46	15 52			16 16					
Ramsgate	d	13 28			15a16					14 20				16a16			16 28				15 20			15 28	
Broadstairs	d	13 33								14 25							16 33				15 25			15 33	
Margate 4	d	13a38								14 30							16a38				15 30			15a38	
Birchington-on-Sea	d									14 35											15 35				
Herne Bay	d									14 44											15 44				
Whitstable	d									14 49											15 49				
Faversham 2	a									14 57											15 57				
	d							14 30		14 58									15 30		15 58				
Sittingbourne 4	d							14 38		15 08									15 38		16 08				
Rainham (Kent)	d							14 46		15 16									15 46		16 16				
Gillingham (Kent) 4	d							14 51		15 21									15 51		16 21				
Chatham 4	d							14 55		15 25									15 55		16 25				
Rochester 4	d							14 59		15 29									15 59		16 29				
Maidstone West	d																								
Strood 4	d							15 02		15 32									16 02		16 32				
Gravesend	d							15 12		15 42									16 12		16 42				
Ebbsfleet International	a					15 04		15 16	15 35	15 46						16 05			16 16	16 35	16 46				
	d					15 04		15 17	15 35	15 51						16 06			16 17	16 35	16 51				
Stratford International ⊖	a					15 16		15 28	15 47	16 02	12 58					16 17			16 28	16 47	17 02	14 01			
St Pancras International 4 ⊖	a					15 23		15 36	15 54	16 10						16 24			16 36	16 54	17 10				

Table T194-R

Saturdays
21 December to 16 May

Kent - St Pancras International High Speed Domestic Services

			SE	SE	SE	SE	SE	SE	SE	SE	SE	SE		SE	SE	SE	SE	SE	SE	SE	SE	SE	SE		SE
			◇■	◇	◇	◇■	◇	◇	◇	◇	◇■	◇■		◇■	◇	◇	◇■	◇	◇	◇	◇	◇■	◇■		◇■
St Pancras International	d				16 10			14 25	14 37	14 55						17 12			15 25	15 37	15 55				
Margate 4	d			15 55				15 59			16 25				16 55				16 59			17 25			
Broadstairs	d			16 01				16 05			16 31				17 01				17 05			17 31			
Ramsgate 4	d			16 07		16 19		16 12			16a38				17 07		17 19		17 12			17a38			
Canterbury West	a			16 26		16 41									17 26		17 41								
	d			16 26		16 42									17 26		17 42								
Dover Priory	d								15 42											16 42					
Sandwich	d							16 25	16 07										17 25	17 07					
Deal	d							16 31											17 31						
Dover Priory	d							16 49				16 58							17 49				17 58		
Folkestone Central	d							17 00				17 09							18 00				18 09		
Folkestone West	d							17 02				17 11							18 02				18 11		
Ashford International	a			16 41	16 48	17 00		17 15				17 28			17 41	17 50	18 00		18 15				18 28		
	d		16 35	16 43	16 52			17 19						17 35	17 43	17 52			18 19						18 35
Ramsgate	d		17a16		17 28				16 20					18a16		18 28				17 20					19a16
Broadstairs	d				17 33				16 25							18 33				17 25					
Margate 4	d				17a38				16 30							18a38				17 30					
Birchington-on-Sea	d								16 35											17 35					
Herne Bay	d								16 44											17 44					
Whitstable	d								16 49											17 49					
Faversham 2	a								16 57											17 57					
	d						16 30		16 58									17 30		17 58					
Sittingbourne 4	d						16 38		17 08									17 38		18 08					
Rainham (Kent)	d						16 46		17 16									17 46		18 16					
Gillingham (Kent) 4	d						16 51		17 21									17 51		18 21					
Chatham 4	d						16 55		17 25									17 55		18 25					
Rochester 4	d						16 59		17 29									17 59		18 29					
Maidstone West	d																								
Strood 4	d						17 02		17 32									18 02		18 32					
Gravesend	d						17 12		17 42									18 12		18 42					
Ebbsfleet International	a			17 02			17 16	17 38	17 46						18 02			18 16	18 38	18 46					
	d			17 02			17 17	17 38	17 51						18 02			18 18	18 38	18 47					
Stratford International ⊖	a			17 14			17 28	17 50	18 02	15 01					18 14			18 29	18 50	18 58	16 01				
St Pancras International 4 ⊖	a			17 21			17 36	17 58	18 10						18 21			18 37	18 58	19 06					

		SE	SE	SE	SE	SE	SE	SE	SE	SE		SE	SE	SE	SE	SE	SE	SE	SE	SE	SE		SE	SE	SE
		◇	◇■	◇	◇	◇	◇	◇■	◇■	◇■		◇	◇■	◇	◇	◇	◇	◇■	◇	◇■	◇■		◇	◇	◇■
St Pancras International	d				16 25	16 37	16 55								17 25	17 37	17 55		18 12					20 12	
Margate 4	d	17 55			17 59			18 25				18 55			18 59			19 25					19 55		
Broadstairs	d	18 01			18 05			18 31				19 01			19 05			19 31					20 01		
Ramsgate 4	d	18 07	18 19		18 12			18a38				19 07	19 19		19 14			19a38					20 07		20 19
Canterbury West	a	18 26	18 41									19 26	19 41						19 06				20 26		20 41
	d	18 26	18 42									19 26	19 42						19 08				20 26		20 42
Dover Priory	d					17 42										18 42									
Sandwich	d				18 25	18 07									19 27	19 07									
Deal	d				18 31										19 33										
Dover Priory	d				18 49				18 58						19 49					19 58					
Folkestone Central	d				19 00				19 09						20 00					20 09					
Folkestone West	d				19 02				19 11						20 02					20 11					
Ashford International	a	18 41	19 00		19 15				19 28			19 41	20 00		20 15					20 28			20 41	20 50	21 00
	d	18 43			19 16					19 35		19 43			20 16						20 32		20 45	20 52	
Ramsgate	d					18 20				20a16						19 20			19 28		21a16			21 28	
Broadstairs	d					18 25										19 25			19 33					21 33	
Margate 4	d					18 30										19 30			19a38					21a38	
Birchington-on-Sea	d					18 35										19 35									
Herne Bay	d					18 44										19 44									
Whitstable	d					18 49										19 49									
Faversham 2	a					18 57										19 57									
	d			18 30		18 58								19 30		19 58									
Sittingbourne 4	d			18 38		19 08								19 38		20 08									
Rainham (Kent)	d			18 46		19 16								19 46		20 16									
Gillingham (Kent) 4	d			18 51		19 21								19 51		20 21									
Chatham 4	d			18 55		19 25								19 55		20 25									
Rochester 4	d			18 59		19 29								19 59		20 29									
Maidstone West	d																								
Strood 4	d			19 02		19 32								20 02		20 32									
Gravesend	d			19 12		19 42								20 12		20 42									
Ebbsfleet International	a	19 02		19 16	19 35	19 46						20 02		20 16	20 35	20 46							21 04		
	d	19 02		19 17	19 35	19 47						20 02		20 17	20 35	20 47							21 04		
Stratford International ⊖	a	19 14		19 28	19 47	19 58	17 01					20 14		20 28	20 47	20 58	18 01						21 16		
St Pancras International 4 ⊖	a	19 21		19 36	19 54	20 06						20 21		20 36	20 54	21 06							21 23		

Table T194-R

Saturdays

21 December to 16 May

Kent - St Pancras International High Speed Domestic Services

		SE	SE	SE	SE	SE	SE	SE	SE	SE	SE	SE	SE	SE	SE	SE	SE	SE	SE	SE	SE	SE	SE
		◇	◇	◇	◇	◇1	◇	◇1	◇1	◇	◇	◇1	◇	◇	◇	◇	◇1	1	◇1	◇	◇	1	◇
St Pancras International	d		18 25	18 37	18 55		19 12				21 12			19 25	19 37	19 55					22 12		20 25
Margate 4	d		19 59			20 25				20 55				20 59			21 25			21 55			21 59
Broadstairs	d		20 05			20 31				21 01				21 05			21 31			22 01			22 05
Ramsgate 4	d		20 12			20a38				21 07		21 16		21 12			21a38			22 07		22 16	22 12
Canterbury West	a						20 06			21 26		21 38								22 26		22 38	
	d						20 08			21 26		21 39								22 26		22 39	
Dover Priory	d			19 42											20 42								
Sandwich	d		20 25	20 07										21 25	21 07								22 25
Deal	d		20 31											21 31									22 31
Dover Priory	d		20 49					20 58						21 49				21 58					22 49
Folkestone Central	d		21 00					21 09						22 00				22 09					23 00
Folkestone West	d		21 02					21 11						22 02				22 11					23 02
Ashford International	a		21 15					21 28		21 41	21 50	22 00		22 15				22 28		22 41	22 50	23 00	23 15
	d		21 16						21 32	21 43	21 52			22 16					22 34	22 43	22 52		23 16
Ramsgate	d			20 20			20 28		22a16		22 27				21 20				23a18		23 29		
Broadstairs	d			20 25			20 33				22 33				21 25						23 35		
Margate 4	d			20 30			20a38				22a37				21 30						23a40		
Birchington-on-Sea	d			20 35											21 35								
Herne Bay	d			20 44											21 44								
Whitstable	d			20 49											21 49								
Faversham 2	a			20 57											21 57								
	d	20 30		20 58									21 30		21 58								
Sittingbourne 4	d	20 38		21 08									21 38		22 08								
Rainham (Kent)	d	20 46		21 16									21 46		22 16								
Gillingham (Kent) 4	d	20 51		21 21									21 51		22 21								
Chatham 4	d	20 55		21 25									21 55		22 25								
Rochester 4	d	20 59		21 29									21 59		22 29								
Maidstone West	d																						
Strood 4	d	21 02		21 32									22 02		22 32								
Gravesend	d	21 12		21 42									22 12		22 42								
Ebbsfleet International	a	21 16	21 35	21 46						22 02			22 16	22 35	22 46					23 02			23 35
	d	21 21	21 35	21 47						22 02			22 17	22 35	22 47					23 02			23 35
Stratford International ⊖	a	21 32	21 47	21 58	19 01					22 14			22 28	22 47	22 58	20 01				23 14			23 47
St Pancras International 4 ⊖	a	21 40	21 54	22 06						22 21			22 36	22 54	23 06					23 21			23 54

		SE	SE	SE	SE	SE	SE	SE	SE	SE	SE	SE	SE	SE	SE	SE	SE	SE
		◇	◇	◇1		◇1		◇	◇	◇	◇	◇1	◇	◇	◇	◇	◇	◇
St Pancras International	d	20 37	20 55					23 12	21 25	21 37	21 55		22 25	22 37	22 55	23 25	23 37	23 55
Margate 4	d			22 25			22 55		22 59			23 25	23 59					
Broadstairs	d			22 31			23 01		23 05			23 31	00 05					
Ramsgate 4	d			22a38			23 07		23 12			23a38	00a11					
Canterbury West	a						23 26											
	d						23 26											
Dover Priory	d	21 42								22 42				23 42			00 42	
Sandwich	d	22 07							23 25	23 07				00 07			01s07	
Deal	d								23 31									
Dover Priory	d				22 58				23 49									
Folkestone Central	d				23 09				23 59									
Folkestone West	d				23 11				00 02									
Ashford International	a				23 29		23 41	23 50	00 21									
	d					23 34		23 52										
Ramsgate	d	22a19				00a18		00 29		23a21				00a21			01a23	
Broadstairs	d							00s34										
Margate 4	d							00a40										
Birchington-on-Sea	d																	
Herne Bay	d																	
Whitstable	d																	
Faversham 2	a																	
	d																	
Sittingbourne 4	d																	
Rainham (Kent)	d																	
Gillingham (Kent) 4	d																	
Chatham 4	d																	
Rochester 4	d																	
Maidstone West	d																	
Strood 4	d																	
Gravesend	d																	
Ebbsfleet International	a																	
	d																	
Stratford International ⊖	a		21 01								22 01				23 01	23 31		00 02
St Pancras International 4 ⊖	a																	

NRT DECEMBER 19 EDITION

Table T194-R

Sundays

15 December to 10 May

Kent - St Pancras International High Speed Domestic Services

		SE	SE	SE	SE	SE	SE	SE	SE	SE	SE	SE	SE	SE	SE	SE	SE	SE	SE	SE	SE	SE	SE
		◇	◇	◇	◇	◇	◇1	◇1	◇	◇1	◇	◇	◇1	◇	◇1	1	◇	◇	◇1	◇	◇	◇1	◇1
		A	A	A	A		A	A	A	A													
St Pancras International	d					00 12																	
Margate 4	d						00 25			01 07								07 55					
Broadstairs	d		00 05				00 31			01 13								08 01					
Ramsgate 4	d		00a11				00a38			01a20			07 16	07 12				08 07	08 16	08 12			
Canterbury West	a												07 38					08 26	08 38				
	d												07 40					08 26	08 40				
Dover Priory	d								00 42														
Sandwich	d			00 07					01s07					07 25						08 25			
Deal	d													07 31						08 31			
Dover Priory	d													07 49	07 58					08 49		08 58	
Folkestone Central	d													08 00	08 09					09 00		09 09	
Folkestone West	d	00 02												08 02	08 11					09 02		09 11	
Ashford International	a	00 21											08 02	08 15	08 28			08 41	09 02	09 15		09 28	
	d							00 34				07 43		08 16		08 32		08 43		09 16			09 32
Ramsgate	d			00a21	00 29			01a20	01a23							09a15					08 20		10a15
Broadstairs	d				00s34																08 25		
Margate 4	d				00a40																08 30		
Birchington-on-Sea	d																				08 35		
Herne Bay	d																				08 44		
Whitstable	d																				08 49		
Faversham 2	a																				08 57		
	d										07 00						08 00				08 58		
Sittingbourne 4	d										07 08						08 08				09 08		
Rainham (Kent)	d										07 16						08 16				09 16		
Gillingham (Kent) 4	d										07 21						08 21				09 21		
Chatham 4	d										07 25						08 25				09 25		
Rochester 4	d										07 29						08 29				09 29		
Maidstone West	d																						
Strood 4	d										07 32						08 32				09 32		
Gravesend	d										07 42						08 42				09 42		
Ebbsfleet International	a										07 46	08 02		08 35			08 46	09 02		09 35	09 46		
	d										07 47	08 02		08 35			08 47	09 02		09 35	09 51		
Stratford International ⊖	a					00 18					07 58	08 14		08 47			08 58	09 14		09 47	10 02		
St Pancras International 4 ⊖	a										08 06	08 21		08 54			09 06	09 21		09 54	10 10		

		SE	SE	SE	SE	SE	SE	SE	SE	SE	SE	SE	SE	SE	SE	SE	SE	SE	SE	SE	SE	SE	SE
		◇	◇	◇1	◇	◇	◇1	◇1	◇1	◇	◇	◇1	◇	◇	◇1	◇1	◇1	◇	◇	◇1	◇	◇	◇
St Pancras International	d		09 09								10 09		08 25	08 37					11 12			09 25	09 37
Margate 4	d	08 55					09 24			09 55			09 59		10 24			10 55				10 59	
Broadstairs	d	09 01					09 30			10 01			10 05		10 30			11 01				11 05	
Ramsgate 4	d	09 07		09 20	09 12		09a37			10 07		10 20	10 12		10a37			11 07		11 20		11 12	
Canterbury West	a	09 26		09 42						10 26		10 42						11 26		11 42			
	d	09 26		09 43						10 26		10 43						11 26		11 43			
Dover Priory	d					08 42								09 42									10 42
Sandwich	d				09 25	09 07							10 25	10 07								11 25	11 07
Deal	d				09 31								10 31									11 31	
Dover Priory	d				09 49			09 58					10 49			10 58						11 49	
Folkestone Central	d				10 00			10 09					11 00			11 09						12 00	
Folkestone West	d				10 02			10 11					11 02			11 11						12 02	
Ashford International	a	09 41	09 47	10 02	10 15			10 28		10 41	10 47	11 02	11 15			11 28		11 41	11 50	12 02		12 15	
	d	09 43	09 52		10 16				10 32	10 43	10 52		11 16				11 32	11 43	11 52			12 16	
Ramsgate	d		10 27			09 20			11a15		11 27			10 20			12a15		12 27				11 20
Broadstairs	d		10 32			09 25					11 32			10 25					12 32				11 25
Margate 4	d		10a38			09 30					11a38			10 30					12a38				11 30
Birchington-on-Sea	d					09 35								10 35									11 35
Herne Bay	d					09 44								10 44									11 44
Whitstable	d					09 49								10 49									11 49
Faversham 2	a					09 57								10 57									11 57
	d					09 58								10 58							11 30		11 58
Sittingbourne 4	d					10 08								11 08							11 38		12 08
Rainham (Kent)	d					10 16								11 16							11 46		12 16
Gillingham (Kent) 4	d					10 21								11 21							11 51		12 21
Chatham 4	d					10 25								11 25							11 55		12 25
Rochester 4	d					10 29								11 29							11 59		12 29
Maidstone West	d																						
Strood 4	d					10 32								11 32							12 02		12 32
Gravesend	d					10 42								11 42							12 12		12 42
Ebbsfleet International	a	10 02			10 35	10 46				11 02			11 35	11 46				12 02			12 16	12 35	12 46
	d	10 02			10 35	10 47				11 02			11 35	11 47				12 02			12 17	12 35	12 47
Stratford International ⊖	a	10 14			10 47	10 58				11 14			11 47	11 58				12 14			12 28	12 47	12 58
St Pancras International 4 ⊖	a	10 21			10 54	11 06				11 21			11 54	12 06				12 21			12 36	12 54	13 06

A not 15 December

Table T194-R

Sundays

15 December to 10 May

Kent - St Pancras International High Speed Domestic Services

		SE ◇1	SE ◇1	SE ◇1	SE ◇	SE ◇	SE ◇1		SE ◇	SE ◇	SE ◇	SE ◇1	SE ◇1	SE ◇1	SE ◇	SE ◇	SE ◇1	SE ◇		SE ◇	SE ◇	SE ◇1	SE ◇1	SE ◇1	SE ◇
St Pancras International	d					12 12				10 27	10 37					13 12				11 25	11 37				
Margate 4	d	11 24			11 55					11 59		12 24			12 55					12 59		13 24			13 55
Broadstairs	d	11 30			12 01					12 05		12 30			13 01					13 05		13 30			14 01
Ramsgate 4	d	11a37			12 07		12 20			12 12		12a37			13 07		13 20			13 12		13a37			14 07
Canterbury West	a				12 26		12 42								13 26		13 42								14 26
	d				12 26		12 43								13 26		13 43								14 26
Dover Priory	d										11 42										12 42				
Sandwich	d									12 25	12 07									13 25	13 07				
Deal	d									12 31										13 31					
Dover Priory	d		11 58							12 49			12 58							13 49			13 58		
Folkestone Central	d		12 09							13 00			13 09							14 00			14 09		
Folkestone West	d		12 11							13 02			13 11							14 02			14 11		
Ashford International	a		12 28		12 41	12 50	13 02			13 15			13 28		13 41	13 50	14 02			14 15			14 28		14 41
	d			12 32	12 43	12 52				13 16				13 32	13 43	13 52				14 16				14 32	14 43
Ramsgate	d			13a15		13 27					12 20			14a15		14 27					13 20			15a15	
Broadstairs	d					13 32					12 25					14 32					13 25				
Margate 4	d					13a38					12 30					14a38					13 30				
Birchington-on-Sea	d										12 35										13 35				
Herne Bay	d										12 44										13 44				
Whitstable	d										12 49										13 49				
Faversham 2	a										12 57										13 57				
	d								12 30		12 58							13 30			13 58				
Sittingbourne 4	d								12 38		13 08							13 38			14 08				
Rainham (Kent)	d								12 46		13 16							13 46			14 16				
Gillingham (Kent) 4	d								12 51		13 21							13 51			14 21				
Chatham 4	d								12 55		13 25							13 55			14 25				
Rochester 4	d								12 59		13 29							13 59			14 29				
Maidstone West	d																								
Strood 4	d								13 02		13 32							14 02			14 32				
Gravesend	d								13 12		13 42							14 12			14 42				
Ebbsfleet International	a				13 02				13 16	13 35	13 46				14 02			14 16		14 35	14 46				15 02
	d				13 03				13 18	13 35	13 47				14 02			14 17		14 35	14 48				15 02
Stratford International ⊖	a				13 14				13 29	13 47	13 58				14 14			14 28		14 47	14 59				15 14
St Pancras International 4 ⊖	a				13 21				13 37	13 54	14 06				14 21			14 36		14 54	15 07				15 21

		SE ◇	SE ◇1	SE ◇	SE ◇		SE ◇	SE ◇	SE ◇1	SE ◇1	SE ◇1	SE ◇	SE ◇	SE ◇1	SE ◇	SE ◇		SE ◇	SE ◇	SE ◇1	SE ◇1	SE ◇1	SE ◇	SE ◇	SE ◇1
St Pancras International	d	14 10			12 27		12 37	12 52					15 12			13 25		13 37	13 55					16 12	
Margate 4	d				13 59				14 24			14 55				14 59				15 24			15 55		
Broadstairs	d				14 05				14 30			15 01				15 05				15 30			16 01		
Ramsgate 4	d		14 20		14 12				14a37			15 07		15 20		15 12				15a37			16 07		16 20
Canterbury West	a		14 42									15 26		15 42									16 26		16 42
	d		14 43									15 26		15 43									16 26		16 43
Dover Priory	d						13 42											14 42							
Sandwich	d				14 25		14 07									15 25		15 07							
Deal	d				14 31											15 31									
Dover Priory	d				14 49					14 58						15 49					15 58				
Folkestone Central	d				15 00					15 09						16 00					16 09				
Folkestone West	d				15 02					15 11						16 02					16 11				
Ashford International	a	14 48	15 02		15 15					15 28		15 41	15 50	16 02		16 15					16 28		16 41	16 50	17 02
	d	14 52			15 16						15 32	15 43	15 52			16 16						16 32	16 43	16 52	
Ramsgate	d	15 27					14 20				16a15		16 27					15 20				17a15		17 27	
Broadstairs	d	15 32					14 25						16 32					15 25						17 32	
Margate 4	d	15a38					14 30						16a38					15 30						17a38	
Birchington-on-Sea	d						14 35											15 35							
Herne Bay	d						14 44											15 44							
Whitstable	d						14 49											15 49							
Faversham 2	a						14 57											15 57							
	d			14 30			14 58								15 30			15 58							
Sittingbourne 4	d			14 38			15 08								15 38			16 08							
Rainham (Kent)	d			14 46			15 16								15 46			16 16							
Gillingham (Kent) 4	d			14 51			15 21								15 51			16 21							
Chatham 4	d			14 55			15 25								15 55			16 25							
Rochester 4	d			14 59			15 29								15 59			16 29							
Maidstone West	d																								
Strood 4	d			15 02			15 32								16 02			16 32							
Gravesend	d			15 12			15 42								16 12			16 42							
Ebbsfleet International	a			15 16	15 35		15 46					16 02			16 16	16 35		16 46					17 02		
	d			15 17	15 35		15 51					16 02			16 17	16 35		16 51					17 02		
Stratford International ⊖	a			15 28	15 47		16 02	12 58				16 14			16 28	16 47		17 02	14 01				17 14		
St Pancras International 4 ⊖	a			15 36	15 54		16 10					16 21			16 36	16 54		17 10					17 21		

Table T194-R

Sundays

15 December to 10 May

Kent - St Pancras International High Speed Domestic Services

		SE ◇	SE ◇		SE ◇	SE ◇	SE ◇1	SE ◇1	SE ◇1	SE ◇	SE ◇	SE ◇1	SE ◇	SE ◇		SE ◇	SE ◇	SE ◇1	SE ◇1	SE ◇1	SE ◇	SE ◇	SE ◇1	SE ◇	SE ◇
St Pancras International	d		14 25		14 37	14 55					17 07			15 25		15 37	15 55					18 12			16 25
Margate 4	d		15 59				16 24			16 55				16 59				17 24			17 55				17 59
Broadstairs	d		16 05				16 30			17 01				17 05				17 30			18 01				18 05
Ramsgate 4	d		16 12				16a37			17 07		17 20		17 12				17a37			18 07		18 20		18 12
Canterbury West	a									17 26		17 42									18 26		18 42		
	d									17 26		17 43									18 26		18 43		
Dover Priory	d				15 42											16 42									
Sandwich	d		16 25		16 07									17 25		17 07									18 25
Deal	d		16 31											17 31											18 31
Dover Priory	d		16 49					16 58						17 49					17 58						18 49
Folkestone Central	d		17 00					17 09						18 00					18 09						19 00
Folkestone West	d		17 02					17 11						18 02					18 11						19 02
Ashford International	a		17 15					17 28		17 41	17 44	18 02		18 15					18 28		18 41	18 50	19 02		19 15
	d		17 16						17 32	17 43	17 52			18 16						18 32	18 43	18 52			19 16
Ramsgate	d				16 20				18a15		18 27					17 20				19a15		19 27			
Broadstairs	d				16 25						18 32					17 25						19 32			
Margate 4	d				16 30						18a38					17 30						19a38			
Birchington-on-Sea	d				16 35											17 35									
Herne Bay	d				16 44											17 44									
Whitstable	d				16 49											17 49									
Faversham 2	a				16 57											17 57									
	d	16 30			16 58								17 30			17 58								18 30	
Sittingbourne 4	d	16 38			17 08								17 38			18 08								18 38	
Rainham (Kent)	d	16 46			17 16								17 46			18 16								18 46	
Gillingham (Kent) 4	d	16 51			17 21								17 51			18 21								18 51	
Chatham 4	d	16 55			17 25								17 55			18 25								18 55	
Rochester 4	d	16 59			17 29								17 59			18 29								18 59	
Maidstone West	d																								
Strood 4	d	17 02			17 32								18 02			18 32								19 02	
Gravesend	d	17 12			17 42								18 12			18 42								19 12	
Ebbsfleet International	a	17 16	17 35		17 46					18 02			18 16	18 35		18 46					19 02			19 16	19 35
	d	17 17	17 35		17 51					18 02			18 17	18 35		18 48					19 02			19 17	19 35
Stratford International ⊖	a	17 28	17 47		18 02	15 01				18 14			18 28	18 47		18 59	16 01				19 14			19 28	19 47
St Pancras International 4 ⊖	a	17 36	17 54		18 10					18 21			18 36	18 54		19 07					19 21			19 36	19 54

			SE ◇	SE ◇	SE ◇1	SE ◇1	SE ◇1	SE ◇	SE ◇	SE ◇1	SE ◇	SE ◇		SE ◇	SE ◇	SE ◇1	SE ◇1	SE ◇1	SE ◇	SE ◇	SE ◇1	SE ◇	SE ◇		SE ◇
St Pancras International	d		16 37	16 55					19 12			17 25		17 37	17 57					20 12			18 25		18 37
Margate 4	d				18 24			18 55				18 59				19 24			19 55				19 59		
Broadstairs	d				18 30			19 01				19 05				19 30			20 01				20 05		
Ramsgate 4	d				18a37			19 07		19 16		19 12				19a37			20 07		20 16		20 12		
Canterbury West	a							19 26		19 38									20 26		20 38				
	d							19 26		19 40									20 26		20 40				
Dover Priory	d		17 42											18 42											19 42
Sandwich	d		18 07									19 25		19 07									20 25		20 07
Deal	d											19 31											20 31		
Dover Priory	d					18 58						19 49					19 58						20 49		
Folkestone Central	d					19 09						20 00					20 09						21 00		
Folkestone West	d					19 11						20 02					20 11						21 02		
Ashford International	a					19 28		19 41	19 50	20 02		20 15					20 28		20 41	20 50	21 02		21 15		
	d						19 32	19 43	19 52			20 16						20 32	20 43	20 52			21 16		
Ramsgate	d		18 20				20a15		20 27					19 20				21a15		21 27					20 20
Broadstairs	d		18 25						20 32					19 25						21 32					20 25
Margate 4	d		18 30						20a38					19 30						21a38					20 30
Birchington-on-Sea	d		18 35											19 35											20 35
Herne Bay	d		18 44											19 44											20 44
Whitstable	d		18 49											19 49											20 49
Faversham 2	a		18 57											19 57											20 57
	d		18 58								19 30			19 58								20 30			20 58
Sittingbourne 4	d		19 08								19 38			20 08								20 38			21 08
Rainham (Kent)	d		19 16								19 46			20 16								20 46			21 16
Gillingham (Kent) 4	d		19 21								19 51			20 21								20 51			21 21
Chatham 4	d		19 25								19 55			20 25								20 55			21 25
Rochester 4	d		19 29								19 59			20 29								20 59			21 29
Maidstone West	d																								
Strood 4	d		19 32								20 02			20 32								21 02			21 32
Gravesend	d		19 42								20 12			20 42								21 12			21 42
Ebbsfleet International	a		19 46					20 02			20 16	20 35		20 46					21 02			21 16	21 35		21 46
	d		19 47					20 02			20 17	20 35		20 47					21 02			21 21	21 35		21 48
Stratford International ⊖	a		19 58	17 01				20 14			20 28	20 47		20 58	18 04				21 14			21 32	21 47		21 59
St Pancras International 4 ⊖	a		20 06					20 21			20 36	20 54		21 06					21 21			21 40	21 54		22 07

Table T194-R

Sundays

15 December to 10 May

Kent - St Pancras International High Speed Domestic Services

		SE ◇	SE ◇1	SE ◇1	SE ◇1	SE ◇	SE ◇	SE ◇1	SE ◇	SE ◇	SE ◇	SE ◇	SE ◇1	SE 1	SE ◇1	SE ◇	SE ◇	SE 1	SE ◇	SE ◇	SE ◇	SE ◇1	SE ◇1
St Pancras International	d	18 55					21 12			19 25	19 37	19 55					22 12		20 25	20 37	20 55		
Margate 4	d		20 24			20 55				20 59			21 24			21 55			21 59			22 24	
Broadstairs	d		20 30			21 01				21 05			21 30			22 01			22 05			22 30	
Ramsgate 4	d		20a37			21 07		21 16		21 12			21a37			22 07		22 16	22 12			22a37	
Canterbury West	a					21 26		21 38								22 26		22 38					
	d					21 26		21 40								22 26		22 40					
Dover Priory	d										20 42									21 42			
Sandwich	d									21 25	21 07								22 25	22 07			
Deal	d									21 31									22 31				
Dover Priory	d			20 58						21 49				21 58					22 49				
Folkestone Central	d			21 09						22 00				22 09					23 00				
Folkestone West	d			21 11						22 02				22 11					23 02				
Ashford International	a			21 28		21 41	21 50	22 02		22 15				22 28		22 41	22 50	23 02	23 15				
	d				21 32	21 43	21 52			22 16					22 32	22 43	22 52						23 32
Ramsgate	d				22a15		22 27				21 20				23a15		23 27			22a19			00a15
Broadstairs	d						22 32				21 25						23 32						
Margate 4	d						22a38				21 30						23a38						
Birchington-on-Sea	d										21 35												
Herne Bay	d										21 44												
Whitstable	d										21 49												
Faversham 2	a										21 57												
	d								21 30		21 58												
Sittingbourne 4	d								21 38		22 08												
Rainham (Kent)	d								21 46		22 16												
Gillingham (Kent) 4	d								21 51		22 21												
Chatham 4	d								21 55		22 25												
Rochester 4	d								21 59		22 29												
Maidstone West	d																						
Strood 4	d								22 02		22 32												
Gravesend	d								22 12		22 42												
Ebbsfleet International	a					22 02			22 16	22 35	22 46					23 02							
	d					22 02			22 17	22 35	22 47					23 02							
Stratford International ⊖	a	19 01				22 14			22 28	22 47	22 58	20 01				23 14					21 01		
St Pancras International 4 ⊖	a					22 21			22 36	22 54	23 06					23 21							

		SE	SE ◇	SE ◇	SE ◇	SE ◇1	SE ◇	SE ◇	SE ◇	SE ◇	SE ◇	SE ◇
St Pancras International	d		21 25	21 37	21 55		22 25	22 37	22 55	23 12	23 25	23 37
Margate 4	d	22 55	22 59			23 24	23 59					
Broadstairs	d	23 01	23 05			23 30	00 05					
Ramsgate 4	d	23 07	23a11			23a37	00a11					
Canterbury West	a	23 26										
	d	23 26										
Dover Priory	d			22 42				23 42				
Sandwich	d			23 07				00 07				
Deal	d											
Dover Priory	d											
Folkestone Central	d											
Folkestone West	d											
Ashford International	a	23 41								23 50		
	d									23 52		
Ramsgate	d			23a19				00a19		00 27		
Broadstairs	d									00s32		
Margate 4	d									00a38		
Birchington-on-Sea	d											
Herne Bay	d											
Whitstable	d											
Faversham 2	a											
	d											
Sittingbourne 4	d											
Rainham (Kent)	d											
Gillingham (Kent) 4	d											
Chatham 4	d											
Rochester 4	d											
Maidstone West	d											
Strood 4	d											
Gravesend	d											
Ebbsfleet International	a											
	d											
Stratford International ⊖	a				22 01				23 01		23 31	23 43
St Pancras International 4 ⊖	a											

NRT DECEMBER 19 EDITION

Table T195-F

Mondays to Fridays

16 December to 15 May

London - Catford, Beckenham Junction, Bromley South, Orpington, Otford and Sevenoaks

Miles	Miles	Miles			TL MX A	TL MO B	TL MX B	SE MO ◇1 C	SE MX D	SE MX 1 E	SE MX F	SE MX ◇1 G	SE MO D	TL MO B	TL MX B	SE MX H	SE MO F	SE MX F	SE MX ◇1 I	SE MX ◇1 J	SE MX	SE ◇ K	TL
—	—	—	**London Victoria** 15 ⊖	d												00 04			00 10	00 25	00 28	00 40	
3¼	—	—	Brixton ⊖	d													00 05	00 05			00 35		
—	—	—	Kentish Town ⊖	d																			
—	—	—	St Pancras International 15 ⊖	d																			
—	—	—	Farringdon ⊖	d																			
—	—	—	City Thameslink 3	d																			
—	—	—	**London Blackfriars** 3 ⊖	d																			04 56
—	—	—	Elephant & Castle ⊖	d																			05 00
—	—	—	Loughborough Jn	d	00 02																		
—	—	—	Herne Hill 4	d	00a06												00 08	00 08			00 38		
5	—	—	West Dulwich	d													00 10	00 11			00 40		
5¾	—	—	Sydenham Hill	d													00 12	00 13			00 42		
7¼	—	—	Penge East	d							00 01						00 16	00 16			00 46		
7¾	—	—	Kent House 4	d							00 03						00 18	00 18			00 48		
8¾	—	—	**Beckenham Junction** 4	d							00 05						00 20	00 20			00 50		
—	3¾	4¼	Denmark Hill 4	d												00 14							05 08
—	4½	5	Peckham Rye 4	d											00 01	00 17							05 11
—	5¼	5¾	Nunhead 4	d											00 04	00 19							05 14
—	—	7½	Lewisham 4	a												00 26							
—	6½	—	Crofton Park	d										00 02	00 07								05 17
—	7½	—	Catford	d										00 05	00 10								05 20
—	8¼	—	Bellingham	d										00 08	00 13								05 23
—	9	—	Beckenham Hill	d										00 10	00 15								05 25
—	9¾	—	Ravensbourne	d										00 13	00 18								05 27
10	10½	—	Shortlands 4	d							00 09			00 15	00 20		00 23	00 23			00 53		05 30
11	11½	—	**Bromley South** 4	d						00 07	00a12	00 13		00 18	00 23		00 26	00 26	00s31	00 42	00 56	00 57	05 33
12	12½	—	Bickley 4	d										00 21	00 26		00 29	00 29			00 59		05 36
13¾	—	—	Petts Wood 4	d					00 06				00 23				00 33	00 33			01 03		05 40
15	—	—	**Orpington** 4	a					00 12				00 27				00 38	00 38			01 08		05 44
—	14¾	—	St Mary Cray	d			00 01	00 02		00 12		00 19		00 25	00 31					00 48		01s02	
—	17½	—	**Swanley** 4	d			00 06	00a06		00a16		00 23		00 30	00 36					00 52		01s07	
—	20½	—	Eynsford	d		00 05	00 11							00 35	00 41								
—	22¾	—	Shoreham (Kent)	d		00 09	00 15							00 39	00 45								
—	24	—	Otford 4	d		00 12	00 18					00a31		00 42	00 48					01a00			
—	25¾	—	Bat & Ball	d		00 15	00 21							00 45	00 51								
—	27	—	**Sevenoaks** 4	a		00 19	00 25		00 27				00 42	00 49	00 55								

		SE ◇1 L	TL	TL A	SE	SE D	TL	TL M	SE ◇1 L	SE ◇1 J	TL	TL A	SE	SE D	TL N	TL O	SE ◇1 L	SE	SE H	SE ◇1 P	TL	TL A	SE
London Victoria 15 ⊖	d	05 12			05 28				05 42	05 50			05 58				06 12	06 13	06 15	06 25			06 28
Brixton ⊖	d				05 35								06 05					06 20					06 35
Kentish Town ⊖	d			05 04				05 21				05 36			05 41	05 51						06 04	
St Pancras International 15 ⊖	d			05 12				05 27				05 42			05 47	05 57						06 12	
Farringdon ⊖	d			05 17				05 32				05 47			05 52	06 02						06 17	
City Thameslink 3	d			05 19				05 34				05 49			05 54	06 04						06 19	
London Blackfriars 3 ⊖	d		05 16	05 21			05 26	05 36			05 46	05 51			05 56	06 06					06 16	06 21	
Elephant & Castle ⊖	d		05 20	05 25			05 30	05 40			05 50	05 55			06 00	06 10					06 20	06 25	
Loughborough Jn	d			05 30				05 45				06 00				06 15						06 30	
Herne Hill 4	d			05a34	05 38			05a49				06a04	06 08			06a19		06 23				06a34	06 38
West Dulwich	d				05 40								06 10					06 25					06 40
Sydenham Hill	d				05 42								06 12					06 27					06 42
Penge East	d				05 46								06 16					06 30					06 46
Kent House 4	d				05 48								06 18					06 32					06 48
Beckenham Junction 4	d				05 50								06 20					06 35					06 50
Denmark Hill 4	d	05 22	05 28				05 38		05 52		05 58				06 08		06 22		06 25		06 28		
Peckham Rye 4	d		05 31				05 41				06 01				06 11				06 28		06 31		
Nunhead 4	d		05 34				05 44				06 04				06 14				06 30		06 34		
Lewisham 4	a																		06 36				
Crofton Park	d		05 37				05 47				06 07				06 17						06 37		
Catford	d		05 40				05 50				06 10				06 20						06 40		
Bellingham	d		05 43				05 53				06 13				06 23						06 43		
Beckenham Hill	d		05 45				05 55				06 15				06 25						06 45		
Ravensbourne	d		05 47				05 58				06 17				06 27						06 47		
Shortlands 4	d		05 50		05 53		06 00				06 20		06 23		06 30			06 38			06 50		06 53
Bromley South 4	d	05 35	05 53		05 56		06 03		06 05	06 12	06 23		06 26		06 33		06 36	06a42		06 42	06 53		06 56
Bickley 4	d		05 56		05 59		06 06				06 26		06 29		06 36						06 56		06 59
Petts Wood 4	d				06 03	06 06	06 10						06 33	06 37	06 40								07 03
Orpington 4	a				06 08	06 11	06 14						06 38	06 40	06 44								07 08
St Mary Cray	d	05 40	06 01						06 10	06 18	06 31						06 41			06 48	07 01		
Swanley 4	d	05a44	06 06						06a14	06 22	06 36						06a45			06 52	07 06		
Eynsford	d		06 11								06 41										07 11		
Shoreham (Kent)	d		06 15								06 45										07 15		
Otford 4	d		06 18							06a30	06 48									07a00	07 20		
Bat & Ball	d		06 21								06 51										07 23		
Sevenoaks 4	a		06 25			06 27					06 55			07 00							07 27		

A From Luton to Sutton (Surrey)
B From London Blackfriars
C From London Victoria to Faversham
D From London Charing Cross
E From London Victoria to Gillingham (Kent)
F From London Victoria
G From London Victoria to Ashford International
H To Dartford
I To Ramsgate
J To Ashford International
K To Gillingham (Kent)
L To Dover Priory
M From West Hampstead Thameslink to Sutton (Surrey)
N From West Hampstead Thameslink
O To Sutton (Surrey)
P To Canterbury West

Table T195-F

Mondays to Fridays
16 December to 15 May

London - Catford, Beckenham Junction, Bromley South, Orpington, Otford and Sevenoaks

	SE ◇1 A	SE B	TL C	TL D		SE E	SE	SE ◇1 F	TL	TL G	SE	SE E	SE B	TL H		TL G	SE ◇1 I	SE	TL J	TL G	SE ◇1 K	TL L	SE	SE ◇1 M
London Victoria 15 ⊖ d	06 40					06 42	06 43	06 55			06 58	07 08					07 10	07 13					07 27	07 40
Brixton ⊖ d							06 50				07 05							07 20					07 34	
Kentish Town ⊖ d			06 11	06 21						06 36						06 51				07 06				
St Pancras International 15 ⊖ d			06 17	06 27						06 42				06 47		06 57				07 12				
Farringdon ⊖ d			06 22	06 32						06 47				06 52		07 02				07 17				
City Thameslink 3 d			06 24	06 34						06 49				06 54		07 04				07 19				
London Blackfriars 3 ⊖ d			06 26	06 36					06 46	06 51				06 56		07 06			07 16	07 21	07 23			
Elephant & Castle ⊖ d			06 30	06 40					06 50	06 55				07 00		07 10			07 20	07 25	07 27			
Loughborough Jn. d				06 45						07 00						07 15				07 30				
Herne Hill 4 d				06a49			06 53			07a04	07 08					07a19		07 23		07a34			07 37	
West Dulwich d							06 55				07 10							07 25					07 39	
Sydenham Hill d							06 57				07 12							07 27					07 41	
Penge East d							07 01				07 16							07 31					07 45	
Kent House 4 d							07 03				07 18							07 33					07 47	
Beckenham Junction 4 d							07 05				07 20							07 35					07 51	
Denmark Hill 4 d			06 38			06 52			06 58					07 08			07 20		07 28		07 36	←		
Peckham Rye 4 d			06 41			06 55			07 01					07 11					07 31			07 31		
Nunhead 4 d			06 44						07 04					07 14					→			07 34		
Lewisham 4 a						07 01						07 25												
Crofton Park d			06 47						07 07					07 17								07 37		
Catford d			06 50						07 10					07 20								07 40		
Bellingham d			06 53						07 13					07 23								07 43		
Beckenham Hill d			06 55						07 15					07 25								07 45		
Ravensbourne d			06 57						07 17					07 27								07 47		
Shortlands 4 d			07 00				07 09		07 20		07 23			07 30				07 38				07 50	07 55	
Bromley South 4 d	06 58		07 03				07a12	07 13	07 23		07 26			07 33			07 33	07a42			07 53	07 53	07 58	07a58
Bickley 4 d			07 06						07 26		07 29			07 36								07 56	08 00	
Petts Wood 4 d		07 07	07 10								07 34		07 38	07 41									08 05	
Orpington 4 a		07 10	07 14								07 39		07 41	07 45									08 10	
St Mary Cray d	07 04							07 19	07 32								07 39				07 59	08 02		
Swanley 4 d	07a08							07 23	07 37								07a43				08 04	08 08		
Eynsford d									07 42													08 13		
Shoreham (Kent) d									07 46													08 17		
Otford 4 d								07a31	07 49												08a12	08 20		
Bat & Ball d									07 52													08 23		
Sevenoaks 4 a		07 25							07 56				08 02									08 26		

		SE B	TL N	SE	TL G	SE ◇1 A	TL H	SE	SE O	SE ◇1 F		TL	TL G	SE	SE B	TL H	SE	TL G	SE O	SE ◇1 A		SE 1 P	SE	SE ◇1 Q
London Victoria 15 ⊖ d						07 42		07 43	07 45	07 55				07 58					08 07	08 10		08 12	08 13	08 25
Brixton ⊖ d								07 50						08 05									08 20	
Kentish Town ⊖ d					07 21								07 36					07 51						
St Pancras International 15 ⊖ d			07 17		07 27								07 42			07 47		07 57						
Farringdon ⊖ d			07 22		07 32								07 47			07 52		08 02						
City Thameslink 3 d			07 24		07 34								07 49			07 54		08 04						
London Blackfriars 3 ⊖ d			07 26	07 34	07 36							07 46	07 51			07 56	08 04	08 06						
Elephant & Castle ⊖ d			07 30		07 40							07 50	07 55			08 00		08 10						
Loughborough Jn. d					07 45								08 00					08 15						
Herne Hill 4 d				07 43	07a49			07 53					08a04	08 08			08 13	08a19					08 23	
West Dulwich d								07 55						08 10									08 25	
Sydenham Hill d								07 57						08 12									08 27	
Penge East d								08 01						08 15									08 31	
Kent House 4 d								08 03						08 17									08 33	
Beckenham Junction 4 d				07a54				08 05						08 20			08a24						08 35	
Denmark Hill 4 d			07 39			07 52	←		07 55			07 58				08 08			08 17			08 22		
Peckham Rye 4 d			07 42				07 42		07 58			08 01				08 11			08 20					
Nunhead 4 d			→				07 45		08 00			08 04				08 14			08 22					
Lewisham 4 a									08 06										08 28					
Crofton Park d							07 48					08 07				08 17								
Catford d							07 51					08 10				08 20								
Bellingham d							07 54					08 13				08 23								
Beckenham Hill d							07 56					08 15				08 25								
Ravensbourne d							07 58					08 17				08 27								
Shortlands 4 d							08 01	08 08				08 20		08 23		08 30							08 38	
Bromley South 4 d						08 05	08 07	08a12		08 12		08 23		08 26		08 33				08a28		08 36	08a42	08 42
Bickley 4 d							08 10					08 26		08 28		08 36								
Petts Wood 4 d		08 08					08 15							08 33	08 40	08 43								
Orpington 4 a		08 12					08 18							08 38	08 45	08 47								
St Mary Cray d						08 10				08 18		08 31										08 41		
Swanley 4 d						08a14				08 22		08 36										08a45		08 50
Eynsford d												08 41												
Shoreham (Kent) d												08 45												
Otford 4 d										08a30		08 48												08a58
Bat & Ball d												08 51												
Sevenoaks 4 a		08 29										08 55			09 01									

A To Dover Priory
B From London Charing Cross
C From West Hampstead Thameslink
D From Luton to Sutton (Surrey)
E To Dartford
F To Ashford International
G From St Albans City to Sutton (Surrey)
H From Luton
I To Gillingham (Kent)
J To Sevenoaks
K To Maidstone East
L From London Blackfriars
M To Ramsgate
N From Luton to Orpington
O To Gravesend
P To Rochester
Q To Canterbury West

Table T195-F

Mondays to Fridays
16 December to 15 May

London - Catford, Beckenham Junction, Bromley South, Orpington, Otford and Sevenoaks

	TL	TL A	SE	SE B	TL C	SE		TL A	SE D	SE ◇1 E	SE ◇1 F	SE	SE ◇1 G	TL	TL A	SE		SE B	TL C	TL A	SE D	SE ◇1 F	SE	SE ◇1 H
London Victoria 15 ⊖ d			08 28						08 38	08 40	08 42	08 43	08 55			08 58					09 04	09 10	09 13	09 25
Brixton ⊖ d			08 35									08 50				09 05							09 20	
Kentish Town ⊖ d		08 06						08 21							08 36					08 51				
St Pancras International 15 ⊖ d		08 12			08 17			08 27							08 42				08 47	08 57				
Farringdon ⊖ d		08 17			08 22			08 32							08 47				08 52	09 02				
City Thameslink 3 d		08 19			08 24			08 34							08 49				08 54	09 04				
London Blackfriars 3 ⊖ d	08 16	08 21			08 26	08 34		08 36						08 46	08 51				08 56	09 06				
Elephant & Castle ⊖ d	08 20	08 25			08 30			08 40						08 50	08 55				09 00	09 10				
Loughborough Jn. d		08 30						08 45							09 00					09 15				
Herne Hill 4 d		08a34	08 38			08 43		08a49				08 53			09a04	09 08				09a19			09 23	
West Dulwich d			08 40									08 55				09 10							09 25	
Sydenham Hill d			08 42									08 57				09 12							09 27	
Penge East d			08 46									09 01				09 16							09 31	
Kent House 4 d			08 48									09 03				09 18							09 33	
Beckenham Junction 4 d			08 50			08a54						09 05				09 20							09 35	
Denmark Hill 4 d	08 28				08 38				08 47		08 52			08 58					09 08		09 14			
Peckham Rye 4 d	08 31				08 41				08 50					09 01					09 12		09 17			
Nunhead 4 d	08 34				08 44				08 53					09 04					09 15		09 20			
Lewisham 4 a									09 00												09 26			
Crofton Park d	08 37				08 47									09 07					09 18					
Catford d	08 40				08 50									09 10					09 21					
Bellingham d	08 43				08 53									09 13					09 24					
Beckenham Hill d	08 45				08 55									09 15					09 26					
Ravensbourne d	08 47				08 57									09 17					09 28					
Shortlands 4 d	08 50		08 54		09 00							09 08		09 20		09 23			09 31				09 38	
Bromley South 4 d	08 53		08 57		09 03					08a58	09 05	09a12	09 12	09 23		09 26			09 34			09a26	09a42	09 42
Bickley 4 d	08 56		08 59		09 06									09 26		09 29			09 37					
Petts Wood 4 d			09 03	09 08	09 12											09 33		09 36	09 42					
Orpington 4 a			09 09	09 13	09 16											09 38		09 40	09 46					
St Mary Cray d	09 01										09 10		09 18	09 32										
Swanley 4 d	09 06										09a14		09 22	09 37										09 50
Eynsford d	09 11													09 42										
Shoreham (Kent) d	09 15													09 46										
Otford 4 d	09 18												09a30	09 49										09a58
Bat & Ball d	09 21													09 52										
Sevenoaks 4 a	09 25			09 30										09 56				09 59						

	TL	TL A		SE	SE B	TL C	TL A	SE D	SE ◇1 E	SE ◇1 F	SE	SE ◇1 G		TL	TL A	SE	SE B	TL C	TL A	SE D	SE ◇1 F	SE		SE ◇1 H
London Victoria 15 ⊖ d				09 28				09 34	09 40	09 42	09 43	09 55				09 58				10 04	10 10	10 13		10 25
Brixton ⊖ d				09 35							09 50					10 05						10 20		
Kentish Town ⊖ d		09 06					09 21								09 36				09 51					
St Pancras International 15 ⊖ d		09 12				09 17	09 27								09 42			09 47	09 57					
Farringdon ⊖ d		09 17				09 22	09 32								09 47			09 52	10 02					
City Thameslink 3 d		09 19				09 24	09 34								09 49			09 54	10 04					
London Blackfriars 3 ⊖ d	09 16	09 21				09 26	09 36							09 46	09 51			09 56	10 06					
Elephant & Castle ⊖ d	09 20	09 25				09 30	09 40							09 50	09 55			10 00	10 10					
Loughborough Jn. d		09 30					09 45								10 00				10 15					
Herne Hill 4 d		09a34		09 38			09a49				09 53				10a04	10 08			10a19			10 23		
West Dulwich d				09 40							09 55					10 10						10 25		
Sydenham Hill d				09 42							09 57					10 12						10 27		
Penge East d				09 46							10 01					10 16						10 31		
Kent House 4 d				09 48							10 03					10 18						10 33		
Beckenham Junction 4 d				09 50							10 05					10 20						10 35		
Denmark Hill 4 d	09 28					09 38		09 44		09 52				09 58				10 08		10 14				
Peckham Rye 4 d	09 31					09 41		09 47						10 01				10 11		10 17				
Nunhead 4 d	09 34					09 44		09 50						10 04				10 14		10 19				
Lewisham 4 a								09 56												10 25				
Crofton Park d	09 37					09 47								10 07				10 17						
Catford d	09 40					09 50								10 10				10 20						
Bellingham d	09 43					09 53								10 13				10 23						
Beckenham Hill d	09 45					09 55								10 15				10 25						
Ravensbourne d	09 47					09 57								10 17				10 27						
Shortlands 4 d	09 50			09 53		10 00					10 08			10 20		10 23		10 30				10 38		
Bromley South 4 d	09 53			09 56		10 03			09a56	10 05	10a12	10 12		10 23		10 26		10 33			10a26	10a42		10 42
Bickley 4 d	09 56			09 59		10 06								10 26		10 29		10 37						
Petts Wood 4 d				10 03	10 06	10 10										10 33	10 36	10 42						
Orpington 4 a				10 08	10 10	10 14										10 38	10 40	10 45						
St Mary Cray d	10 01									10 10		10 18		10 31										
Swanley 4 d	10 06									10a14		10 22		10 36										10 50
Eynsford d	10 11													10 41										
Shoreham (Kent) d	10 15													10 45										
Otford 4 d	10 18											10a30		10 48										10a58
Bat & Ball d	10 21													10 51										
Sevenoaks 4 a	10 25				10 29									10 55			10 57							

A From St Albans City to Sutton (Surrey)
B From London Charing Cross
C From Luton
D To Gravesend
E To Ramsgate
F To Dover Priory
G To Ashford International
H To Canterbury West

Table T195-F

Mondays to Fridays

16 December to 15 May

London - Catford, Beckenham Junction, Bromley South, Orpington, Otford and Sevenoaks

		TL	TL	SE	SE	TL	TL	SE	SE	SE	SE	SE	TL	TL	SE	SE	TL	TL	SE	SE	SE	SE	TL
			A		B		A	C	◇1 D	◇1 E		◇1 F		A		B		A	C	◇1 E		◇1 G	
London Victoria 15	⊖ d			10 28				10 34	10 40	10 42	10 43	10 55			10 58				11 04	11 10	11 13	11 25	
Brixton	⊖ d			10 35							10 50				11 05						11 20		
Kentish Town	⊖ d		10 06			10 11	10 21							10 36			10 41	10 51					
St Pancras International 15	⊖ d		10 12			10 17	10 27							10 42			10 47	10 57					
Farringdon	⊖ d		10 17			10 22	10 32							10 47			10 52	11 02					
City Thameslink 3	d		10 19			10 24	10 34							10 49			10 54	11 04					
London Blackfriars 3	⊖ d	10 16	10 21			10 26	10 36						10 46	10 51			10 56	11 06					11 16
Elephant & Castle	⊖ d	10 20	10 25			10 30	10 40						10 50	10 55			11 00	11 10					11 20
Loughborough Jn.	d		10 30				10 45							11 00				11 15					
Herne Hill 4	d		10a34	10 38			10a49				10 53			11a04	11 08			11a19			11 23		
West Dulwich	d			10 40							10 55				11 10						11 25		
Sydenham Hill	d			10 42							10 57				11 12						11 27		
Penge East	d			10 46							11 01				11 16						11 31		
Kent House 4	d			10 48							11 03				11 18						11 33		
Beckenham Junction 4	d			10 50							11 05				11 20						11 35		
Denmark Hill 4	d	10 28				10 38		10 44		10 52			10 58				11 08		11 14				11 28
Peckham Rye 4	d	10 31				10 41		10 47					11 01				11 11		11 17				11 31
Nunhead 4	d	10 34				10 44		10 49					11 04				11 14		11 19				11 34
Lewisham 4	a							10 55											11 25				
Crofton Park	d	10 37				10 47							11 07				11 17						11 37
Catford	d	10 40				10 50							11 10				11 20						11 40
Bellingham	d	10 43				10 53							11 13				11 23						11 43
Beckenham Hill	d	10 45				10 55							11 15				11 25						11 45
Ravensbourne	d	10 47				10 57							11 17				11 27						11 47
Shortlands 4	d	10 50		10 53		11 00					11 08		11 20		11 23		11 30				11 38		11 50
Bromley South 4	d	10 53		10 56		11 03			10a56	11 05	11a12	11 12	11 23		11 26		11 33			11a26	11a42	11 42	11 53
Bickley 4	d	10 56		10 59		11 06							11 26		11 29		11 36						11 56
Petts Wood 4	d			11 03	11 06	11 10									11 33	11 36	11 40						
Orpington 4	a			11 08	11 10	11 14									11 39	11 40	11 44						
St Mary Cray	d	11 01								11 10		11 18	11 31										12 01
Swanley 4	d	11 06								11a14		11 22	11 36									11 50	12 06
Eynsford	d	11 11											11 41										12 11
Shoreham (Kent)	d	11 15											11 45										12 15
Otford 4	d	11 18										11a30	11 48									11a58	12 18
Bat & Ball	d	11 21											11 51										12 21
Sevenoaks 4	a	11 25			11 27								11 55			11 57							12 25

		TL	SE	SE	TL	TL	SE	SE	SE	SE	SE	TL	TL	SE	SE	TL	TL	SE	SE	SE	SE	TL	TL
		A		B		A	C	◇1 D	◇1 E		◇1 F		A		B		A	C	◇1 E		◇1 G		A
London Victoria 15	⊖ d		11 28				11 34	11 40	11 42	11 43	11 55			11 58				12 04	12 10	12 13	12 25		
Brixton	⊖ d		11 35							11 50				12 05						12 20			
Kentish Town	⊖ d	11 06			11 12	11 21							11 36			11 41	11 51						12 06
St Pancras International 15	⊖ d	11 12			11 17	11 27							11 42			11 47	11 57						12 12
Farringdon	⊖ d	11 17			11 22	11 32							11 47			11 52	12 02						12 17
City Thameslink 3	d	11 19			11 24	11 34							11 49			11 54	12 04						12 19
London Blackfriars 3	⊖ d	11 21			11 26	11 36						11 46	11 51			11 56	12 06					12 16	12 21
Elephant & Castle	⊖ d	11 25			11 30	11 40						11 50	11 55			12 00	12 10					12 20	12 25
Loughborough Jn.	d	11 30				11 45							12 00				12 15						12 30
Herne Hill 4	d	11a34	11 38			11a49				11 53			12a04	12 08			12a19			12 23			12a34
West Dulwich	d		11 40							11 55				12 10						12 25			
Sydenham Hill	d		11 42							11 57				12 12						12 27			
Penge East	d		11 46							12 01				12 16						12 31			
Kent House 4	d		11 48							12 03				12 18						12 33			
Beckenham Junction 4	d		11 50							12 05				12 20						12 35			
Denmark Hill 4	d				11 38		11 44		11 52			11 58				12 08		12 14				12 28	
Peckham Rye 4	d				11 41		11 47					12 01				12 11		12 17				12 31	
Nunhead 4	d				11 44		11 49					12 04				12 14		12 19				12 34	
Lewisham 4	a						11 55											12 25					
Crofton Park	d				11 47							12 07				12 17						12 37	
Catford	d				11 50							12 10				12 20						12 40	
Bellingham	d				11 53							12 13				12 23						12 43	
Beckenham Hill	d				11 55							12 15				12 25						12 45	
Ravensbourne	d				11 57							12 17				12 27						12 47	
Shortlands 4	d		11 53		12 00					12 08		12 20		12 23		12 30				12 38		12 50	
Bromley South 4	d		11 56		12 03			11a56	12 05	12a12	12 12	12 23		12 26		12 33			12a26	12a42	12 42	12 53	
Bickley 4	d		11 59		12 06							12 26		12 29		12 36						12 56	
Petts Wood 4	d		12 03	12 06	12 10									12 33	12 36	12 40							
Orpington 4	a		12 08	12 10	12 14									12 38	12 40	12 44							
St Mary Cray	d								12 10		12 18	12 31										13 01	
Swanley 4	d								12a14		12 22	12 36									12 50	13 06	
Eynsford	d											12 41										13 11	
Shoreham (Kent)	d											12 45										13 15	
Otford 4	d										12a30	12 48									12a58	13 18	
Bat & Ball	d											12 51										13 21	
Sevenoaks 4	a			12 27								12 55			12 57							13 25	

A From St Albans City to Sutton (Surrey)
B From London Charing Cross
C To Gravesend
D To Ramsgate
E To Dover Priory
F To Ashford International
G To Canterbury West

Table T195-F

Mondays to Fridays

16 December to 15 May

London - Catford, Beckenham Junction, Bromley South, Orpington, Otford and Sevenoaks

		SE	SE	TL	TL	SE	SE	SE	SE	SE	TL	TL	SE	SE	TL	TL	SE	SE	SE	SE	TL	TL
			A		B	C	◇1 D	◇1 E		◇1 F		B		A		B	C	◇1 E		◇1 G		B
London Victoria 15	⊖ d	12 28				12 34	12 40	12 42	12 43	12 55			12 58				13 04	13 10	13 13	13 25		
Brixton	⊖ d	12 35							12 50				13 05						13 20			
Kentish Town	⊖ d			12 11	12 21							12 36			12 41	12 51						13 06
St Pancras International 15	⊖ d			12 17	12 27							12 42			12 47	12 57						13 12
Farringdon	⊖ d			12 22	12 32							12 47			12 52	13 02						13 17
City Thameslink 3	d			12 24	12 34							12 49			12 54	13 04						13 19
London Blackfriars 3	⊖ d			12 26	12 36						12 46	12 51			12 56	13 06					13 16	13 21
Elephant & Castle	⊖ d			12 30	12 40						12 50	12 55			13 00	13 10					13 20	13 25
Loughborough Jn.	d				12 45							13 00				13 15						13 30
Herne Hill 4	d	12 38			12a49				12 53			13a04	13 08			13a19			13 23			13a34
West Dulwich	d	12 40							12 55				13 10						13 25			
Sydenham Hill	d	12 42							12 57				13 12						13 27			
Penge East	d	12 46							13 01				13 16						13 31			
Kent House 4	d	12 48							13 03				13 18						13 33			
Beckenham Junction 4	d	12 50							13 05				13 20						13 35			
Denmark Hill 4	d			12 38		12 44		12 52			12 58				13 08		13 14				13 28	
Peckham Rye 4	d			12 41		12 47					13 01				13 11		13 17				13 31	
Nunhead 4	d			12 44		12 49					13 04				13 14		13 19				13 34	
Lewisham 4	a					12 55											13 25					
Crofton Park	d			12 47							13 07				13 17						13 37	
Catford	d			12 50							13 10				13 20						13 40	
Bellingham	d			12 53							13 13				13 23						13 43	
Beckenham Hill	d			12 55							13 15				13 25						13 45	
Ravensbourne	d			12 57							13 17				13 27						13 47	
Shortlands 4	d	12 53		13 00					13 08		13 20		13 23		13 30				13 38		13 50	
Bromley South 4	d	12 56		13 03			12a56	13 05	13a12	13 12	13 23		13 26		13 33			13a26	13a42	13 42	13 53	
Bickley 4	d	12 59		13 06							13 26		13 29		13 36						13 56	
Petts Wood 4	d	13 03	13 06	13 10									13 33	13 36	13 40							
Orpington 4	a	13 08	13 10	13 14									13 38	13 40	13 44							
St Mary Cray	d							13 10		13 18	13 31										14 01	
Swanley 4	d							13a14		13 22	13 36									13 50	14 06	
Eynsford	d										13 41										14 11	
Shoreham (Kent)	d										13 45										14 15	
Otford 4	d									13a30	13 48									13a58	14 18	
Bat & Ball	d										13 51										14 21	
Sevenoaks 4	a		13 27								13 55			13 57							14 25	

		SE	SE	TL	TL	SE	SE	SE	SE	SE	TL	TL	SE	SE	TL	TL	SE	SE	SE	SE	TL	TL	SE
			A		B	C	◇1 D	◇1 E		◇1 F		B		A		B	C	◇1 E		◇1 G		B	
London Victoria 15	⊖ d	13 28				13 34	13 40	13 42	13 43	13 55			13 58				14 04	14 10	14 13	14 25			14 28
Brixton	⊖ d	13 35							13 50				14 05						14 20				14 35
Kentish Town	⊖ d			13 11	13 21							13 36			13 41	13 51						14 06	
St Pancras International 15	⊖ d			13 17	13 27							13 42			13 47	13 57						14 12	
Farringdon	⊖ d			13 22	13 32							13 47			13 52	14 02						14 17	
City Thameslink 3	d			13 24	13 34							13 49			13 54	14 04						14 19	
London Blackfriars 3	⊖ d			13 26	13 36						13 46	13 51			13 56	14 06					14 16	14 21	
Elephant & Castle	⊖ d			13 30	13 40						13 50	13 55			14 00	14 10					14 20	14 25	
Loughborough Jn.	d				13 45							14 00				14 15						14 30	
Herne Hill 4	d	13 38			13a49				13 53			14a04	14 08			14a19			14 23			14a34	14 38
West Dulwich	d	13 40							13 55				14 10						14 25				14 40
Sydenham Hill	d	13 42							13 57				14 12						14 27				14 42
Penge East	d	13 46							14 01				14 16						14 31				14 46
Kent House 4	d	13 48							14 03				14 18						14 33				14 48
Beckenham Junction 4	d	13 50							14 05				14 20						14 35				14 50
Denmark Hill 4	d			13 38		13 44		13 52			13 58				14 08		14 14				14 28		
Peckham Rye 4	d			13 41		13 47					14 01				14 11		14 17				14 31		
Nunhead 4	d			13 44		13 49					14 04				14 14		14 19				14 34		
Lewisham 4	a					13 55											14 25						
Crofton Park	d			13 47							14 07				14 17						14 37		
Catford	d			13 50							14 10				14 20						14 40		
Bellingham	d			13 53							14 13				14 23						14 43		
Beckenham Hill	d			13 55							14 15				14 25						14 45		
Ravensbourne	d			13 57							14 17				14 27						14 47		
Shortlands 4	d	13 53		14 00					14 08		14 20		14 23		14 30				14 38		14 50		14 53
Bromley South 4	d	13 56		14 03			13a56	14 05	14a12	14 12	14 23		14 26		14 33			14a26	14a42	14 42	14 53		14 56
Bickley 4	d	13 59		14 06							14 26		14 29		14 36						14 56		14 59
Petts Wood 4	d	14 03	14 06	14 10									14 33	14 36	14 40								15 03
Orpington 4	a	14 08	14 10	14 14									14 38	14 40	14 44								15 08
St Mary Cray	d							14 10		14 18	14 31										15 01		
Swanley 4	d							14a14		14 22	14 36									14 50	15 06		
Eynsford	d										14 41										15 11		
Shoreham (Kent)	d										14 45										15 15		
Otford 4	d									14a30	14 48									14a58	15 18		
Bat & Ball	d										14 51										15 21		
Sevenoaks 4	a		14 27								14 55			14 57							15 25		

A From London Charing Cross
B From St Albans City to Sutton (Surrey)
C To Gravesend
D To Ramsgate
E To Dover Priory
F To Ashford International
G To Canterbury West

Table T195-F

Mondays to Fridays

16 December to 15 May

London - Catford, Beckenham Junction, Bromley South, Orpington, Otford and Sevenoaks

		SE	TL	TL	SE	SE	SE	SE	SE	TL	TL	SE	SE	TL	TL	SE	SE	SE	SE	TL	TL	SE
						◇1	◇1		◇1								◇1		◇1			
		A		B	C	D	E		F		B		A		B	C	G		H		B	
London Victoria 15 ⊖	d				14 34	14 40	14 42	14 43	14 55			14 58				15 04	15 10	15 13	15 25			15 28
Brixton ⊖	d							14 50				15 05						15 20				15 35
Kentish Town ⊖	d		14 11	14 21							14 36			14 41	14 51						15 06	
St Pancras International 15 ⊖	d		14 17	14 27							14 42			14 47	14 57						15 12	
Farringdon ⊖	d		14 22	14 32							14 47			14 52	15 02						15 17	
City Thameslink 3	d		14 24	14 34							14 49			14 54	15 04						15 19	
London Blackfriars 3 ⊖	d		14 26	14 36						14 46	14 51			14 56	15 06					15 16	15 21	
Elephant & Castle ⊖	d		14 30	14 40						14 50	14 55			15 00	15 10					15 20	15 25	
Loughborough Jn.	d			14 45							15 00				15 15						15 30	
Herne Hill 4	d			14a49				14 53			15a04	15 08			15a19			15 23			15a34	15 38
West Dulwich	d							14 55				15 10						15 25				15 40
Sydenham Hill	d							14 57				15 12						15 27				15 42
Penge East	d							15 01				15 16						15 31				15 46
Kent House 4	d							15 03				15 18						15 33				15 48
Beckenham Junction 4	d							15 05				15 20						15 35				15 50
Denmark Hill 4	d		14 38		14 44		14 52			14 58				15 08		15 14				15 28		
Peckham Rye 4	d		14 41		14 47					15 01				15 11		15 17				15 31		
Nunhead 4	d		14 44		14 49					15 04				15 14		15 19				15 34		
Lewisham 4	a				14 55											15 25						
Crofton Park	d		14 47							15 07				15 17						15 37		
Catford	d		14 50							15 10				15 20						15 40		
Bellingham	d		14 53							15 13				15 23						15 43		
Beckenham Hill	d		14 55							15 15				15 25						15 45		
Ravensbourne	d		14 57							15 17				15 27						15 47		
Shortlands 4	d		15 00					15 08		15 20		15 23		15 30				15 38		15 50		15 53
Bromley South 4	d		15 03			14a56	15 05	15a12	15 12	15 23		15 26		15 33			15a26	15a42	15 42	15 53		15 56
Bickley 4	d		15 06							15 26		15 29		15 36						15 56		15 59
Petts Wood 4	d	15 06	15 10									15 33	15 36	15 40								16 03
Orpington 4	a	15 10	15 14									15 38	15 40	15 44								16 08
St Mary Cray	d						15 10		15 18	15 31										16 01		
Swanley 4	d						15a14		15 22	15 36									15 50	16 06		
Eynsford	d									15 41										16 11		
Shoreham (Kent)	d									15 45										16 15		
Otford 4	d								15a30	15 48									15a58	16 18		
Bat & Ball	d									15 51										16 21		
Sevenoaks 4	a	15 27								15 55			15 57							16 25		

		SE	TL	TL	SE	SE	SE	SE	SE	TL	TL	SE	SE	TL	TL	SE	SE	TL	SE	SE	SE	TL	TL
						◇1	◇1		◇1								◇1		1		◇1		
		A		B	C	G	E		F		B		A	I	B	C	J	K	E		F		B
London Victoria 15 ⊖	d				15 34	15 40	15 42	15 43	15 55			15 58				16 04	16 10		16 12	16 13	16 25		
Brixton ⊖	d							15 50				16 05								16 20			
Kentish Town ⊖	d		15 11	15 21							15 36			15 41	15 51								16 06
St Pancras International 15 ⊖	d		15 17	15 27							15 42			15 47	15 57								16 12
Farringdon ⊖	d		15 22	15 32							15 47			15 52	16 02								16 17
City Thameslink 3	d		15 24	15 34							15 49			15 54	16 04								16 19
London Blackfriars 3 ⊖	d		15 26	15 36						15 46	15 51			15 56	16 06							16 16	16 21
Elephant & Castle ⊖	d		15 30	15 40						15 50	15 55			16 00	16 10							16 20	16 25
Loughborough Jn.	d			15 45							16 00				16 15								16 30
Herne Hill 4	d			15a49				15 53			16a04	16 08			16a19					16 23			16a34
West Dulwich	d							15 55				16 10								16 25			
Sydenham Hill	d							15 57				16 12								16 27			
Penge East	d							16 01				16 16								16 31			
Kent House 4	d							16 03				16 18								16 33			
Beckenham Junction 4	d							16 05				16 20								16 35			
Denmark Hill 4	d		15 38		15 44		15 52			15 58				16 08		16 14			16 22			16 28	
Peckham Rye 4	d		15 41		15 47					16 01				16 11		16 17						16 31	
Nunhead 4	d		15 44		15 49					16 04				16 14		16 19						16 34	
Lewisham 4	a				15 55											16 25		←					
Crofton Park	d		15 47							16 07				16 17				16 17				16 37	
Catford	d		15 50							16 10				→				16 20				16 40	
Bellingham	d		15 53							16 13								16 23				16 43	
Beckenham Hill	d		15 55							16 15								16 25				16 45	
Ravensbourne	d		15 58							16 17								16 27				16 47	
Shortlands 4	d		16 00					16 08		16 20		16 23						16 30		16 38		16 50	
Bromley South 4	d		16 03			15a56	16 05	16a12	16 12	16 23		16 26					16 27	16 33	16 35	16a43	16 42	16 53	
Bickley 4	d		16 06							16 26		16 29						16 36				16 56	
Petts Wood 4	d	16 06	16 11									16 33	16 36					16 40					
Orpington 4	a	16 10	16 14									16 38	16 40					16 44					
St Mary Cray	d						16 10		16 18	16 31									16 40			17 01	
Swanley 4	d						16a14		16 22	16 36									16a44		16 50	17 06	
Eynsford	d									16 41												17 11	
Shoreham (Kent)	d									16 45												17 15	
Otford 4	d								16a30	16 48											16a58	17 18	
Bat & Ball	d									16 51												17 21	
Sevenoaks 4	a	16 27								16 55			17 00				20 18					17 25	

A From London Charing Cross
B From St Albans City to Sutton (Surrey)
C To Gravesend
D To Ramsgate
E To Gillingham (Kent)
F To Ashford International
G To Dover Priory
H To Canterbury West
I To Orpington
J To London Charing Cross
K From Kentish Town

Table T195-F

Mondays to Fridays

16 December to 15 May

London - Catford, Beckenham Junction, Bromley South, Orpington, Otford and Sevenoaks

		SE	SE	TL	TL	SE	SE	SE	SE	SE	SE	TL	SE	TL	SE	TL	SE	SE	TL	SE	SE	TL	SE
							◇1	◇1		◇1								◇1		1	◇1		◇1
		A			B	C	D	E		F	G			B		H	C	E	B	I	J	K	L
London Victoria 15 ⊖	d		16 28			16 34	16 40	16 42	16 43	16 52					16 57		17 04			17 09	17 10		17 12
Brixton ⊖	d		16 35						16 50						17 04								
Kentish Town ⊖	d			16 11	16 22									16 37		16 41			16 52				
St Pancras International 15 ⊖	d			16 17	16 27									16 42		16 47			16 57				
Farringdon ⊖	d			16 22	16 32									16 47		16 52			17 02				
City Thameslink 3	d			16 24	16 34									16 49		16 54			17 04				
London Blackfriars 3 ⊖	d			16 26	16 36							16 46	16 49	16 51		16 56		17 05	17 06				
Elephant & Castle ⊖	d			16 30	16 40							16 50	16 53	16 55		17 00		17 09	17 10				
Loughborough Jn.	d				16 45								16 57	17 00					17 15				
Herne Hill 4	d		16 38		16a49				16 53				17 01	17a04	17 07				17a19				
West Dulwich	d		16 40						16 55				17 04		17 10								
Sydenham Hill	d		16 42						16 57				17 06		17 12								
Penge East	d		16 46						17 01				17 09		17 16								
Kent House 4	d		16 48						17 03				17 12		17 18								
Beckenham Junction 4	d		16 50						17 05				17a16		17 20								
Denmark Hill 4	d			16 38		16 44		16 52				16 58				17 08	17 14						17 22
Peckham Rye 4	d			16 41		16 47						17 01				17 11	17 17						
Nunhead 4	d			16 44		16 49						17 04				17 14	17 20						
Lewisham 4	a					16 56											17 26						
Crofton Park	d			16 47								17 07				17 17							
Catford	d			16 50								17 10				17 20							
Bellingham	d			16 53								17 13				17 23							
Beckenham Hill	d			16 55								17 15				17 25							
Ravensbourne	d			16 57								17 17				17 27							
Shortlands 4	d		16 53	17 00					17 08			17 20			17 23	17 30						←	
Bromley South 4	d		16 56	17 03			16a56	17 05	17a13	17 12		17 23			17 26	17 33		17 29		17 34	17a29	17 33	17 37
Bickley 4	d		16 59	17 06								17 26			17 29	→						17 36	
Petts Wood 4	d	17 02	17 05	17 10							17 24				17 33							17 42	
Orpington 4	a	17 06	17 11	17 14							17 27				17 38							17 45	
St Mary Cray	d							17 11		17 18		17 31						17 36					17 43
Swanley 4	d							17a15		17 22		17 36						17a40					17a47
Eynsford	d											17 41											
Shoreham (Kent)	d											17 45											
Otford 4	d									17a30		17 48								17a51			
Bat & Ball	d											17 51											
Sevenoaks 4	a	17 26									17 44	17 55											

		SE	SE	SE	TL	SE	TL	SE	SE	TL	TL	SE	SE	SE	SE	SE	SE	SE	TL	SE	TL	SE
			◇1										◇1	◇1	◇1		◇1					
			F	G			B	A		K	B	C	D	F	E		F	G			B	C
London Victoria 15 ⊖	d	17 12	17 22						17 27			17 35	17 40		17 42	17 42	17 52					17 55
Brixton ⊖	d	17 19							17 34							17 49						
Kentish Town ⊖	d						17 07			17 11	17 22										17 37	
St Pancras International 15 ⊖	d						17 12			17 17	17 27										17 42	
Farringdon ⊖	d						17 17			17 22	17 32										17 47	
City Thameslink 3	d						17 19			17 24	17 34										17 49	
London Blackfriars 3 ⊖	d				17 16	17 19	17 21			17 26	17 36			17 38					17 46	17 49	17 51	
Elephant & Castle ⊖	d				17 20	17 23	17 25			17 30	17 40			17 42					17 50	17 53	17 55	
Loughborough Jn.	d					17 27	17 30				17 45									17 57	18 00	
Herne Hill 4	d	17 22				17 31	17a34		17 37		17a49					17 52				18 01	18a04	
West Dulwich	d	17 25				17 34			17 40							17 55				18 04		
Sydenham Hill	d	17 27				17 36			17 42							17 57				18 06		
Penge East	d	17 31				17 39			17 46							18 01				18 09		
Kent House 4	d	17 33				17 42			17 48							18 03				18 12		
Beckenham Junction 4	d	17 35				17a46			17 50							18 05				18a16		
Denmark Hill 4	d				17 28					17 38		17 45			17 52				17 58			18 05
Peckham Rye 4	d				17 31					17 41		17 48							18 01			18 08
Nunhead 4	d				17 34					17 44		17 51							18 04			18 11
Lewisham 4	a											17 59										18 18
Crofton Park	d				17 37					17 47									18 07			
Catford	d				17 40					17 50									18 10			
Bellingham	d				17 43					17 53									18 13			
Beckenham Hill	d				17 45					17 55									18 15			
Ravensbourne	d				17 47					17 57									18 17			
Shortlands 4	d	17 38			17 50				17 53	18 00						18 08			18 20			
Bromley South 4	d	17a43	17 42		17 53				17 56	18 03			17a56	18 03	18 07	18a13	18 12		18 23			
Bickley 4	d				17 56				17 59	18 06									18 26			
Petts Wood 4	d			17 46				18 03	18 06	18 12								18 31				
Orpington 4	a			17 49				18 09	18 12	18 16								18 34				
St Mary Cray	d				18 01									18 10	18 14		18 18		18 30			
Swanley 4	d		17 51		18 06									18 14	18a18		18 22		18 35			
Eynsford	d				18 11														18 40			
Shoreham (Kent)	d				18 15														18 44			
Otford 4	d		17a59		18 18									18a22			18a30		18 47			
Bat & Ball	d				18 21														18 50			
Sevenoaks 4	a			18 07	18 25			18 29										18 51	18 55			

A From London Charing Cross
B From St Albans City to Sutton (Surrey)
C To Dartford
D To Ramsgate
E To Rochester
F To Ashford International
G From London Cannon Street
H From West Hampstead Thameslink to Orpington
I To Maidstone East
J To Dover Priory
K From West Hampstead Thameslink
L To Sheerness-on-Sea

Table T195-F

Mondays to Fridays
16 December to 15 May

London - Catford, Beckenham Junction, Bromley South, Orpington, Otford and Sevenoaks

	SE	SE ■ A	SE ◇1 B	TL C	SE ◇1 D	SE ■ E	TL F	TL G	SE ◇1 H	SE	SE I	TL J	SE	TL G	SE K	SE ◇1 L	TL M	SE	TL N	TL G	SE ◇1 D	SE ◇1 O
London Victoria 15 ⊖ d	17 57	18 07	18 10						18 12	18 12					18 21	18 22		18 27			18 39	18 40
Brixton ⊖ d	18 04									18 19								18 34				
Kentish Town ⊖ d				17 41				17 52						18 06					18 11	18 22		
St Pancras International 15 ⊖ d				17 47				17 57						18 12					18 17	18 27		
Farringdon ⊖ d				17 52				18 02						18 17					18 22	18 32		
City Thameslink 3 d				17 54				18 04						18 19					18 24	18 34		
London Blackfriars 3 ⊖ d				17 56	18 05			18 06				18 16	18 19	18 21					18 26	18 36		
Elephant & Castle ⊖ d				18 00	18 09			18 10				18 20	18 23	18 25					18 30	18 40		
Loughborough Jn. d								18 15					18 27	18 30						18 45		
Herne Hill 4 d	18 07							18a19		18 22			18 31	18a34				18 37		18a49		
West Dulwich d	18 10									18 25			18 34					18 40				
Sydenham Hill d	18 12									18 27			18 36					18 42				
Penge East d	18 16									18 31			18 39					18 46				
Kent House 4 d	18 18									18 33			18 42					18 48				
Beckenham Junction 4 d	18 20						←			18 35			18a46					18 50				
Denmark Hill 4 d				18 08			18 08		18 22			18 28			18 31				18 38		18 49	
Peckham Rye 4 d				→			18 11					18 31			18 34				18 41			
Nunhead 4 d							18 14					18 34			18 37				18 44			
Lewisham 4 a															18 43		←					
Crofton Park d							18 17					18 37					18 37		18 47			
Catford d							18 20					→					18 40		18 50			
Bellingham d							18 23										18 43		18 53			
Beckenham Hill d							18 25										18 45		18 55			
Ravensbourne d							18 27										18 47		18 57			
Shortlands 4 d	18 23					←	18 30			18 38							18 50	18 53	19 00			
Bromley South 4 d	18 26	18 33	18a29		18 29	18 33	18 33		18 37	18a43						18 42	18 53	18 56	19 03		19 04	18a56
Bickley 4 d	18 29	→					18 36										18 56	18 59	19 06			
Petts Wood 4 d	18 34						18 44				18 56							19 06	19 10			
Orpington 4 a	18 40						18 48				18 59							19 11	19 14			
St Mary Cray d					18 36				18 43								19 01				19 10	
Swanley 4 d					18a40				18a47							18 51	19 07				19a14	
Eynsford d																	19 12					
Shoreham (Kent) d																	19 16					
Otford 4 d						18a52										18a59	19 19					
Bat & Ball d																	19 22					
Sevenoaks 4 a											19 16						19 25					

	SE	SE K	SE ◇1 L	TL	SE	TL G	SE	SE P	TL Q	SE R	SE ◇1 A	TL G	SE ◇1 O	TL N	SE ■ S	SE	SE ◇1 T	TL	TL G	SE	SE P
London Victoria 15 ⊖ d	18 42	18 42	18 52				18 57			19 04			19 10		19 12	19 13	19 25			19 28	
Brixton ⊖ d	18 49						19 04									19 20				19 35	
Kentish Town ⊖ d						18 36			18 41			18 52							19 05		
St Pancras International 15 ⊖ d						18 42			18 47			18 57							19 12		
Farringdon ⊖ d						18 47			18 52			19 02							19 17		
City Thameslink 3 d						18 49			18 54			19 04							19 19		
London Blackfriars 3 ⊖ d				18 46	18 49	18 51			18 56		19 05	19 06						19 16	19 21		
Elephant & Castle ⊖ d				18 50	18 53	18 55			19 00		19 09	19 10						19 20	19 25		
Loughborough Jn. d					18 57	19 00						19 15							19 30		
Herne Hill 4 d	18 52				19 01	19a04	19 07					19a19				19 23			19a34	19 38	
West Dulwich d	18 55				19 04		19 10									19 25				19 40	
Sydenham Hill d	18 57				19 06		19 12									19 27				19 42	
Penge East d	19 01				19 09		19 16									19 31				19 46	
Kent House 4 d	19 03				19 12		19 18									19 33				19 48	
Beckenham Junction 4 d	19 05				19a16		19 20									19 35				19 50	
Denmark Hill 4 d		18 52		18 58					19 08	19 14					19 22			19 28			
Peckham Rye 4 d		18 55		19 01					19 11	19 17								19 31			
Nunhead 4 d		18 58		19 04					19 14	19 19								19 34			
Lewisham 4 a		19 05								19 25				←							
Crofton Park d				19 07					19 17					19 17				19 37			
Catford d				19 10					→					19 20				19 40			
Bellingham d				19 13										19 23				19 43			
Beckenham Hill d				19 15										19 25				19 45			
Ravensbourne d				19 17										19 27				19 47			
Shortlands 4 d	19 08			19 20			19 23							19 30		19 38		19 50		19 53	
Bromley South 4 d	19a13		19 12	19 23			19 26				19 27		19a29	19 33	19 35	19a42	19 42	19 53		19 56	
Bickley 4 d				19 26			19 29							19 36				19 56		19 59	
Petts Wood 4 d							19 33	19 36						19 40						20 03	20 06
Orpington 4 a							19 39	19 40						19 44						20 08	20 10
St Mary Cray d			19 18	19 31							19 34				19 41			20 01			
Swanley 4 d			19 22	19 36							19 40				19a46		19 50	20 06			
Eynsford d				19 41														20 11			
Shoreham (Kent) d				19 45														20 15			
Otford 4 d			19a30	19 48							19a51						19a58	20 18			
Bat & Ball d				19 51														20 21			
Sevenoaks 4 a				19 55				19 59										20 25			20 27

A To Maidstone East
B To Ramsgate
C From West Hampstead Thameslink to Orpington
D To Rochester
E From London Victoria to Maidstone East
F From West Hampstead Thameslink
G From St Albans City to Sutton (Surrey)
H To Sheerness-on-Sea
I From London Cannon Street
J To Sevenoaks
K To Dartford
L To Ashford International
M From London Blackfriars
N From Luton
O To Dover Priory
P From London Charing Cross
Q From Luton to Orpington
R To Gravesend
S To Gillingham (Kent)
T To Canterbury West

Table T195-F

Mondays to Fridays
16 December to 15 May

London - Catford, Beckenham Junction, Bromley South, Orpington, Otford and Sevenoaks

	TL A	TL B	SE C	SE ◇1 D	SE ◇ E	SE	SE ◇1 F	TL	TL B	SE	SE G	TL A	TL B	SE C	SE ◇1 H	SE ◇1 E	SE	SE ◇1 F	TL	TL B	SE	SE G
London Victoria 15 ⊖ d			19 34	19 40	19 42	19 43	19 55			19 58				20 04	20 10	20 12	20 13	20 25			20 28	
Brixton ⊖ d						19 50				20 05							20 20				20 35	
Kentish Town ⊖ d	19 11	19 21							19 36			19 41	19 51							20 06		
St Pancras International 15 ⊖ d	19 17	19 27							19 42			19 47	19 57							20 12		
Farringdon ⊖ d	19 22	19 32							19 47			19 52	20 02							20 17		
City Thameslink 3 d	19 24	19 34							19 49			19 54	20 04							20 19		
London Blackfriars 3 ⊖ d	19 26	19 36						19 46	19 51			19 56	20 06						20 16	20 21		
Elephant & Castle ⊖ d	19 30	19 40						19 50	19 55			20 00	20 10						20 20	20 25		
Loughborough Jn. d		19 45							20 00				20 15							20 30		
Herne Hill 4 d		19a49				19 53			20a04	20 08			20a19				20 23			20a34	20 38	
West Dulwich d						19 55				20 10							20 25				20 40	
Sydenham Hill d						19 57				20 12							20 27				20 42	
Penge East d						20 01				20 16							20 31				20 46	
Kent House 4 d						20 03				20 18							20 33				20 48	
Beckenham Junction 4 d						20 05				20 20							20 35				20 50	
Denmark Hill 4 d	19 38		19 44		19 52			19 58				20 08		20 14		20 22			20 28			
Peckham Rye 4 d	19 40		19 47					20 01				20 11		20 17					20 31			
Nunhead 4 d	19 43		19 49					20 04				20 14		20 19					20 34			
Lewisham 4 a			19 55											20 25								
Crofton Park d	19 46							20 07				20 17							20 37			
Catford d	19 49							20 10				20 20							20 40			
Bellingham d	19 52							20 13				20 23							20 43			
Beckenham Hill d	19 54							20 15				20 25							20 45			
Ravensbourne d	19 57							20 17				20 27							20 47			
Shortlands 4 d	20 01					20 08		20 20		20 23		20 30					20 38		20 50		20 53	
Bromley South 4 d	20 04			19a56	20 05	20a12	20 12	20 23		20 26		20 33			20a26	20 37	20a42	20 42	20 53		20 56	
Bickley 4 d	20 06							20 26		20 29		20 36							20 56		20 59	
Petts Wood 4 d	20 11									20 33	20 36	20 40									21 03	21 06
Orpington 4 a	20 14									20 38	20 40	20 44									21 08	21 10
St Mary Cray d					20 10		20 18	20 31								20 42			21 01			
Swanley 4 d					20a14		20 22	20 36								20a46		20 51	21 06			
Eynsford d								20 41											21 11			
Shoreham (Kent) d								20 45											21 15			
Otford 4 d							20a30	20 48										20a59	21 18			
Bat & Ball d								20 51											21 21			
Sevenoaks 4 a								20 55			20 57								21 25			21 27

	TL A	TL B	SE C	SE ◇1 D	SE ◇1 I	SE	SE ◇1 F	TL	TL B	SE	SE G	TL	TL B	SE C	SE ◇1 H	SE	SE ◇1 F	TL	TL B	SE	SE G	TL
London Victoria 15 ⊖ d			20 34	20 40	20 42	20 43	20 55			20 58				21 04	21 10	21 13	21 25			21 28		
Brixton ⊖ d						20 50				21 05						21 20				21 35		
Kentish Town ⊖ d	20 11	20 21							20 36			20 41	20 51						21 06			21 11
St Pancras International 15 ⊖ d	20 17	20 27							20 42			20 47	20 57						21 12			21 17
Farringdon ⊖ d	20 22	20 32							20 47			20 52	21 02						21 17			21 22
City Thameslink 3 d	20 24	20 34							20 49			20 54	21 04						21 19			21 24
London Blackfriars 3 ⊖ d	20 26	20 36						20 46	20 51			20 56	21 06					21 16	21 21			21 26
Elephant & Castle ⊖ d	20 30	20 40						20 50	20 55			21 00	21 10					21 20	21 25			21 30
Loughborough Jn. d		20 45							21 00				21 15						21 30			
Herne Hill 4 d		20a49				20 53			21a04	21 08			21a19			21 23			21a34	21 38		
West Dulwich d						20 55				21 10						21 25				21 40		
Sydenham Hill d						20 57				21 12						21 27				21 42		
Penge East d						21 01				21 16						21 31				21 46		
Kent House 4 d						21 03				21 18						21 33				21 48		
Beckenham Junction 4 d						21 05				21 20						21 35				21 50		
Denmark Hill 4 d	20 38		20 44		20 52			20 58				21 08		21 14				21 28				21 38
Peckham Rye 4 d	20 41		20 47					21 01				21 11		21 17				21 31				21 41
Nunhead 4 d	20 44		20 49					21 04				21 14		21 19				21 34				21 44
Lewisham 4 a			20 55											21 25								
Crofton Park d	20 47							21 07				21 17						21 37				21 47
Catford d	20 50							21 10				21 20						21 40				21 50
Bellingham d	20 53							21 13				21 23						21 43				21 53
Beckenham Hill d	20 55							21 15				21 25						21 45				21 55
Ravensbourne d	20 57							21 17				21 27						21 47				21 57
Shortlands 4 d	21 00					21 08		21 20		21 23		21 30				21 38		21 50		21 53		22 00
Bromley South 4 d	21 03			20a56	21 05	21a12	21 12	21 23		21 26		21 33			21a26	21a42	21 42	21 53		21 56		22 03
Bickley 4 d	21 06							21 26		21 29		21 36						21 56		21 59		22 06
Petts Wood 4 d	21 10									21 33	21 36	21 40								22 03	22 06	22 10
Orpington 4 a	21 14									21 38	21 40	21 44								22 08	22 10	22 14
St Mary Cray d					21 10		21 18	21 31										22 01				
Swanley 4 d					21a14		21 22	21 36									21 50	22 06				
Eynsford d								21 41										22 11				
Shoreham (Kent) d								21 45										22 15				
Otford 4 d							21a30	21 48									21a58	22 18				
Bat & Ball d								21 51										22 21				
Sevenoaks 4 a								21 55			21 57							22 25			22 27	

A From Luton
B From St Albans City to Sutton (Surrey)
C To Gravesend
D To Ramsgate
E To Gillingham (Kent)
F To Ashford International
G From London Charing Cross
H To Dover Priory
I To Canterbury East

Table T195-F

Mondays to Fridays
16 December to 15 May

London - Catford, Beckenham Junction, Bromley South, Orpington, Otford and Sevenoaks

		TL	SE	SE	SE	SE	SE	TL	TL	SE		SE	TL	TL	SE	SE	SE	SE	TL	TL		SE	SE	TL
				◇1	◇1		◇1									◇1		◇1						
		A	B	C	D		E		A			F		A	B	G		E		A			F	
London Victoria 15	⊖ d		21 34	21 40	21 42	21 43	21 55			21 58					22 04	22 10	22 13	22 25				22 28		
Brixton	⊖ d					21 50				22 05							22 20					22 35		
Kentish Town	⊖ d	21 21							21 36				21 41	21 51						22 06				22 11
St Pancras International 15	⊖ d	21 27							21 42				21 47	21 57						22 12				22 17
Farringdon	⊖ d	21 32							21 47				21 52	22 02						22 17				22 22
City Thameslink 3	d	21 34							21 49				21 54	22 04						22 19				22 24
London Blackfriars 3	⊖ d	21 36						21 46	21 51				21 56	22 06					22 16	22 21				22 26
Elephant & Castle	⊖ d	21 40						21 50	21 55				22 00	22 10					22 20	22 25				22 30
Loughborough Jn.	d	21 45							22 00					22 15						22 30				
Herne Hill 4	d	21a49				21 53			22a04	22 08				22a19			22 23			22a34		22 38		
West Dulwich	d					21 55				22 10							22 25					22 40		
Sydenham Hill	d					21 57				22 12							22 27					22 42		
Penge East	d					22 01				22 16							22 31					22 46		
Kent House 4	d					22 03				22 18							22 33					22 48		
Beckenham Junction 4	d					22 05				22 20							22 35					22 50		
Denmark Hill 4	d		21 44		21 52			21 58					22 08		22 14				22 28					22 38
Peckham Rye 4	d		21 47					22 01					22 11		22 17				22 31					22 41
Nunhead 4	d		21 49					22 04					22 14		22 19				22 34					22 44
Lewisham 4	a		21 55												22 25									
Crofton Park	d							22 07					22 17						22 37					22 47
Catford	d							22 10					22 20						22 40					22 50
Bellingham	d							22 13					22 23						22 43					22 53
Beckenham Hill	d							22 15					22 25						22 45					22 55
Ravensbourne	d							22 17					22 27						22 47					22 57
Shortlands 4	d					22 08		22 20		22 23			22 30				22 38		22 50			22 53		23 00
Bromley South 4	d			21a56	22 05	22a12	22 12	22 23		22 26			22 33			22a26	22a42	22 42	22 53			22 56		23 03
Bickley 4	d							22 26		22 29			22 36						22 56			22 59		23 06
Petts Wood 4	d									22 33		22 36	22 40									23 03	23 06	23 10
Orpington 4	a									22 38		22 40	22 44									23 08	23 10	23 14
St Mary Cray	d				22 10		22 18	22 31											23 01					
Swanley 4	d				22a14		22 22	22 36										22 50	23 06					
Eynsford	d							22 41											23 11					
Shoreham (Kent)	d							22 45											23 15					
Otford 4	d						22a30	22 48										22a58	23 18					
Bat & Ball	d							22 51											23 21					
Sevenoaks 4	a							22 55				22 57							23 25				23 27	

		TL	SE	SE	SE	SE	SE		TL	TL	SE	SE	TL	TL	SE	SE	SE		SE	TL	TL	SE	SE	SE	SE
				◇1	◇1		◇1									◇1			◇1					1	
		A	B	C	H		E			A		F		A	I	C			E		A		I	H	
London Victoria 15	⊖ d		22 34	22 40	22 42	22 43	22 55				22 58				23 04	23 10	23 13		23 25			23 28	23 34	23 42	23 43
Brixton	⊖ d					22 50					23 05						23 20					23 35			23 50
Kentish Town	⊖ d	22 21								22 36			22 41	22 51							23 06				
St Pancras International 15	⊖ d	22 27								22 42			22 47	22 57							23 12				
Farringdon	⊖ d	22 32								22 47			22 52	23 02							23 17				
City Thameslink 3	d	22 34								22 49			22 54												
London Blackfriars 3	⊖ d	22 36							22 46	22 51			22 56	23 06						23 16	23 21				
Elephant & Castle	⊖ d	22 40							22 50	22 55			23 00	23 10						23 20	23 25				
Loughborough Jn.	d	22 45								23 00				23 15							23 30				
Herne Hill 4	d	22a49				22 53				23a04	23 08			23a19			23 23				23a34	23 38			23 53
West Dulwich	d					22 55					23 10						23 25					23 40			23 55
Sydenham Hill	d					22 57					23 12						23 27					23 42			23 57
Penge East	d					23 01					23 16						23 31					23 46			00 01
Kent House 4	d					23 03					23 18						23 33					23 48			00 03
Beckenham Junction 4	d					23 05					23 20						23 35					23 50			00 05
Denmark Hill 4	d		22 44		22 52				22 58				23 08		23 14					23 28			23 44	23 51	
Peckham Rye 4	d		22 47						23 01				23 11		23 17					23 31			23 47		
Nunhead 4	d		22 49						23 04				23 14		23 19					23 34			23 49		
Lewisham 4	a		22 55												23 25								23 55		
Crofton Park	d								23 07				23 17							23 37					
Catford	d								23 10				23 20							23 40					
Bellingham	d								23 13				23 23							23 43					
Beckenham Hill	d								23 15				23 25							23 45					
Ravensbourne	d								23 17				23 27							23 47					
Shortlands 4	d					23 08			23 20		23 23		23 30				23 38			23 50		23 53			00 09
Bromley South 4	d			22a56	23 05	23a12	23 12		23 23		23 26		23 33			23a26	23a42		23 42	23 53		23 56		00 07	00a12
Bickley 4	d								23 26		23 29		23 36							23 56		23 59			
Petts Wood 4	d										23 33	23 36	23 40									00 03			
Orpington 4	a										23 38	23 40	23 44									00 08			
St Mary Cray	d				23 10		23 18		23 31											00 01				00 12	
Swanley 4	d				23a14		23 22		23 36										23 50	00 06				00a16	
Eynsford	d								23 41											00 11					
Shoreham (Kent)	d								23 45											00 15					
Otford 4	d						23a30		23 48										23a58	00 18					
Bat & Ball	d								23 51											00 21					
Sevenoaks 4	a								23 55			23 57								00 25					

A From St Albans City to Sutton (Surrey)
B To Gravesend
C To Ramsgate
D To Canterbury East
E To Ashford International
F From London Charing Cross
G To Dover Priory
H To Gillingham (Kent)
I To Dartford

Table T195-F

Mondays to Fridays
16 December to 15 May

London - Catford, Beckenham Junction, Bromley South, Orpington, Otford and Sevenoaks

		SE	TL		TL	SE
		◇1				
		A			B	
London Victoria 15	⊖ d	23 55				23 58
Brixton	⊖ d					00 05
Kentish Town	⊖ d				23 38	
St Pancras International 15	⊖ d				23 44	
Farringdon	⊖ d				23 49	
City Thameslink 3	d					
London Blackfriars 3	⊖ d		23 46		23 53	
Elephant & Castle	⊖ d		23 50		23 57	
Loughborough Jn.	d				00 02	
Herne Hill 4	d				00a06	00 08
West Dulwich	d					00 11
Sydenham Hill	d					00 13
Penge East	d					00 16
Kent House 4	d					00 18
Beckenham Junction 4	d					00 20
Denmark Hill 4	d		23 58			
Peckham Rye 4	d		00 01			
Nunhead 4	d		00 04			
Lewisham 4	a					
Crofton Park	d		00 07			
Catford	d		00 10			
Bellingham	d		00 13			
Beckenham Hill	d		00 15			
Ravensbourne	d		00 18			
Shortlands 4	d		00 20			00 23
Bromley South 4	d	00 13	00 23			00 26
Bickley 4	d		00 26			00 29
Petts Wood 4	d					00 33
Orpington 4	a					00 38
St Mary Cray	d	00 19	00 31			
Swanley 4	d	00 23	00 36			
Eynsford	d		00 41			
Shoreham (Kent)	d		00 45			
Otford 4	d	00a31	00 48			
Bat & Ball	d		00 51			
Sevenoaks 4	a		00 55			

Saturdays
21 December to 16 May

		TL	TL	SE	SE	SE	SE	TL	SE	SE		SE	SE	SE	SE	TL	TL	SE	TL	SE		SE	SE	TL	TL
					1		◇1					◇1	◇1		◇					◇1					
		C	B	D	E	F	G	C	H	F		I	A		J		B		K	L			D		B
London Victoria 15	⊖ d								00 04			00 10	00 25	00 28	00 40			05 28		05 42		05 43			
Brixton	⊖ d									00 05				00 35				05 35				05 50			
Kentish Town	⊖ d																05 04		05 21						05 34
St Pancras International 15	⊖ d																05 12		05 27						05 42
Farringdon	⊖ d																05 17		05 32						05 47
City Thameslink 3	d																								
London Blackfriars 3	⊖ d															05 16	05 21		05 36					05 46	05 51
Elephant & Castle	⊖ d															05 20	05 25		05 40					05 50	05 55
Loughborough Jn.	d		00 02														05 30		05 45						06 00
Herne Hill 4	d		00a06							00 08				00 38			05a34	05 38	05a49			05 53			06a04
West Dulwich	d									00 11				00 40				05 40				05 55			
Sydenham Hill	d									00 13				00 42				05 42				05 57			
Penge East	d					00 01				00 16				00 46				05 46				06 01			
Kent House 4	d					00 03				00 18				00 48				05 48				06 03			
Beckenham Junction 4	d					00 05				00 20				00 50				05 50				06 05			
Denmark Hill 4	d								00 14							05 28				05 52				05 58	
Peckham Rye 4	d							00 01	00 17							05 31								06 01	
Nunhead 4	d							00 04	00 19							05 34								06 04	
Lewisham 4	a								00 25																
Crofton Park	d							00 07								05 37								06 07	
Catford	d							00 10								05 40								06 10	
Bellingham	d							00 13								05 43								06 13	
Beckenham Hill	d							00 15								05 45								06 15	
Ravensbourne	d							00 18								05 47								06 17	
Shortlands 4	d					00 09		00 20		00 23				00 53		05 50		05 53				06 08		06 20	
Bromley South 4	d				00 07	00a12	00 13	00 23		00 26		00s31	00 42	00 56	00 57	05 53		05 56		06 05		06a11		06 23	
Bickley 4	d							00 26		00 29				00 59		05 56		05 59						06 26	
Petts Wood 4	d			00 06						00 33				01 03				06 03					06 06		
Orpington 4	a			00 12						00 38				01 08				06 08					06 10		
St Mary Cray	d	00 01			00 12		00 19	00 31					00 48		01s02	06 01				06 10				06 31	
Swanley 4	d	00 06			00a16		00 23	00 36					00 52		01s07	06 06				06a14				06 36	
Eynsford	d	00 11						00 41								06 11								06 41	
Shoreham (Kent)	d	00 15						00 45								06 15								06 45	
Otford 4	d	00 18					00a31	00 48					01a00			06 18								06 48	
Bat & Ball	d	00 21						00 51								06 21								06 51	
Sevenoaks 4	a	00 25		00 27				00 55								06 25							06 27	06 55	

A To Ashford International
B From Luton to Sutton (Surrey)
C From London Blackfriars
D From London Charing Cross
E From London Victoria to Gillingham (Kent)
F From London Victoria
G From London Victoria to Ashford International
H To Dartford
I To Ramsgate
J To Gillingham (Kent)
K From West Hampstead Thameslink to Sutton (Surrey)
L To Dover Priory

Table T195-F

Saturdays
21 December to 16 May

London - Catford, Beckenham Junction, Bromley South, Orpington, Otford and Sevenoaks

Station		SE	TL A	SE	SE ◇1 B	SE C	TL	TL D	SE	TL D	SE ◇1 E	SE	SE C	TL	TL F	SE	TL F	SE G	SE ◇1 E	SE	SE ◇1 B	SE C	TL
London Victoria	d	05 58		06 13	06 25				06 28		06 42	06 43				06 58		07 04	07 10	07 13	07 25		
Brixton	d	06 05		06 20					06 35			06 50				07 05				07 20			
Kentish Town	d		05 51					06 04		06 21					06 36		06 51						
St Pancras International	d		05 57					06 12		06 27					06 42		06 57						
Farringdon	d		06 02					06 17		06 32					06 47		07 02						
City Thameslink	d																						
London Blackfriars	d		06 06				06 16	06 21		06 36				06 46	06 51		07 06						07 16
Elephant & Castle	d		06 10				06 20	06 25		06 40				06 50	06 55		07 10						07 20
Loughborough Jn.	d		06 15					06 30		06 45					07 00		07 15						
Herne Hill	d	06 08	06a19	06 23				06a34	06 38	06a49		06 53			07a04	07 08	07a19			07 23			
West Dulwich	d	06 10		06 25					06 40			06 55				07 10				07 25			
Sydenham Hill	d	06 12		06 27					06 42			06 57				07 12				07 27			
Penge East	d	06 16		06 31					06 46			07 01				07 16				07 31			
Kent House	d	06 18		06 33					06 48			07 03				07 18				07 33			
Beckenham Junction	d	06 20		06 35					06 50			07 05				07 20				07 35			
Denmark Hill	d						06 28				06 52			06 58				07 14					07 28
Peckham Rye	d						06 31							07 01				07 17					07 31
Nunhead	d						06 34							07 04				07 19					07 34
Lewisham	a																	07 25					
Crofton Park	d						06 37							07 07									07 37
Catford	d						06 40							07 10									07 40
Bellingham	d						06 43							07 13									07 43
Beckenham Hill	d						06 45							07 15									07 45
Ravensbourne	d						06 47							07 17									07 47
Shortlands	d	06 23		06 38			06 50		06 53			07 08		07 20		07 23				07 38			07 50
Bromley South	d	06 26		06a41	06 42		06 53		06 56		07 05	07a11		07 23		07 26			07a26	07a41	07 42		07 53
Bickley	d	06 29					06 56		06 59					07 26		07 29							07 56
Petts Wood	d	06 33				06 36			07 03				07 06			07 33						07 36	
Orpington	a	06 38				06 40			07 08				07 10			07 38						07 40	
St Mary Cray	d				06 48		07 01				07 10			07 31							07 48		08 01
Swanley	d				06 52		07 06				07a14			07 36							07 52		08 06
Eynsford	d						07 11							07 41									08 11
Shoreham (Kent)	d						07 15							07 45									08 15
Otford	d				07a00		07 18							07 48							08a00		08 18
Bat & Ball	d						07 21							07 51									08 21
Sevenoaks	a					06 57	07 25						07 27	07 55								07 57	08 25

Station		TL H	SE	TL F	SE G	SE ◇1 I	SE ◇1 E	SE	SE ◇1 J	SE C	TL	TL F	SE	TL F	SE G	SE ◇1 E	SE	SE ◇1 B	SE C	TL	TL F	SE
London Victoria	d		07 28		07 34	07 40	07 42	07 43	07 55				07 58		08 04	08 10	08 13	08 25				08 28
Brixton	d		07 35					07 50					08 05				08 20					08 35
Kentish Town	d	07 06		07 21								07 36		07 51							08 06	
St Pancras International	d	07 12		07 27								07 42		07 57							08 12	
Farringdon	d	07 17		07 32								07 47		08 02							08 17	
City Thameslink	d																					
London Blackfriars	d	07 21		07 36							07 46	07 51		08 06						08 16	08 21	
Elephant & Castle	d	07 25		07 40							07 50	07 55		08 10						08 20	08 25	
Loughborough Jn.	d	07 30		07 45								08 00		08 15							08 30	
Herne Hill	d	07a34	07 38	07a49				07 53				08a04	08 08	08a19			08 23				08a34	08 38
West Dulwich	d		07 40					07 55					08 10				08 25					08 40
Sydenham Hill	d		07 42					07 57					08 12				08 27					08 42
Penge East	d		07 46					08 01					08 16				08 31					08 46
Kent House	d		07 48					08 03					08 18				08 33					08 48
Beckenham Junction	d		07 50					08 05					08 20				08 35					08 50
Denmark Hill	d				07 44		07 52				07 58				08 14					08 28		
Peckham Rye	d				07 47						08 01				08 17					08 31		
Nunhead	d				07 49						08 04				08 19					08 34		
Lewisham	a				07 55										08 25							
Crofton Park	d										08 07									08 37		
Catford	d										08 10									08 40		
Bellingham	d										08 13									08 43		
Beckenham Hill	d										08 15									08 45		
Ravensbourne	d										08 17									08 47		
Shortlands	d		07 53					08 08			08 20		08 23				08 38			08 50		08 53
Bromley South	d		07 56			07a56	08 05	08a11	08 12		08 23		08 26			08a26	08a41	08 42		08 53		08 56
Bickley	d		07 59								08 26		08 29							08 56		08 59
Petts Wood	d		08 03							08 06			08 33						08 36			09 03
Orpington	a		08 08							08 10			08 38						08 40			09 08
St Mary Cray	d						08 10		08 18		08 31									09 01		
Swanley	d						08a14		08 22		08 36							08 50		09 06		
Eynsford	d										08 41									09 11		
Shoreham (Kent)	d										08 45									09 15		
Otford	d								08a30		08 48							08a58		09 18		
Bat & Ball	d										08 51									09 21		
Sevenoaks	a									08 27	08 55								08 57	09 25		

A From West Hampstead Thameslink to Sutton (Surrey)
B To Canterbury West
C From London Charing Cross
D From Luton to Sutton (Surrey)
E To Dover Priory
F From St Albans City to Sutton (Surrey)
G To Gravesend
H From Bedford to Sutton (Surrey)
I To Ramsgate
J To Ashford International

Table T195-F

Saturdays
21 December to 16 May

London - Catford, Beckenham Junction, Bromley South, Orpington, Otford and Sevenoaks

Station		TL A	SE B	SE ◇1 C	SE ◇1 D	SE	SE ◇1 E	SE F	TL	TL A	SE	TL A	SE B	SE ◇1 D	SE	SE ◇1 G	SE F	TL	TL A	SE	TL A	SE B	SE ◇1 C	SE ◇1 D
London Victoria	d		08 34	08 40	08 42	08 43	08 55				08 58		09 04	09 10	09 13	09 25				09 28		09 34	09 40	09 42
Brixton	d					08 50					09 05				09 20					09 35				
Kentish Town	d	08 21								08 36		08 51							09 06		09 21			
St Pancras International	d	08 27								08 42		08 57							09 12		09 27			
Farringdon	d	08 32								08 47		09 02							09 17		09 32			
City Thameslink	d											09 04							09 19		09 34			
London Blackfriars	d	08 36							08 46	08 51		09 06						09 16	09 21		09 36			
Elephant & Castle	d	08 40							08 50	08 55		09 10						09 20	09 25		09 40			
Loughborough Jn.	d	08 45								09 00		09 15							09 30		09 45			
Herne Hill	d	08a49				08 53				09a04	09 08	09a19			09 23				09a34	09 38	09a49			
West Dulwich	d					08 55					09 10				09 25					09 40				
Sydenham Hill	d					08 57					09 12				09 27					09 42				
Penge East	d					09 01					09 16				09 31					09 46				
Kent House	d					09 03					09 18				09 33					09 48				
Beckenham Junction	d					09 05					09 20				09 35					09 50				
Denmark Hill	d		08 44		08 52				08 58				09 14					09 28				09 44		09 52
Peckham Rye	d		08 47						09 01				09 17					09 31				09 47		
Nunhead	d		08 49						09 04				09 19					09 34				09 49		
Lewisham	a		08 55										09 25									09 55		
Crofton Park	d								09 07									09 37						
Catford	d								09 10									09 40						
Bellingham	d								09 13									09 43						
Beckenham Hill	d								09 15									09 45						
Ravensbourne	d								09 17									09 47						
Shortlands	d					09 08			09 20		09 23				09 38			09 50		09 53				
Bromley South	d			08a56	09 05	09a11	09 12		09 23		09 26			09a26	09a41	09 42		09 53		09 56			09a56	10 05
Bickley	d								09 26		09 29							09 56		09 59				
Petts Wood	d							09 06			09 33						09 36			10 03				
Orpington	a							09 10			09 38						09 40			10 08				
St Mary Cray	d				09 10		09 18		09 31									10 01						10 10
Swanley	d				09a14		09 22		09 36							09 50		10 06						10a14
Eynsford	d								09 41									10 11						
Shoreham (Kent)	d								09 45									10 15						
Otford	d						09a30		09 48							09a58		10 18						
Bat & Ball	d								09 51									10 21						
Sevenoaks	a							09 27	09 55								09 57	10 25						

Station		SE	SE ◇1 E	SE F	TL	TL A		SE	TL A	SE B	SE ◇1 D	SE	SE ◇1 G	SE F	TL	TL A	SE	TL A	SE B	SE ◇1 C	SE ◇1 D	SE	SE ◇1 E	SE F
London Victoria	d	09 43	09 55					14 58		15 04	15 10	15 13	15 25				15 28		15 34	15 40	15 42	15 43	15 55	
Brixton	d	09 50						15 05				15 20					15 35					15 50		
Kentish Town	d					09 36			14 51							15 06		15 21						
St Pancras International	d					09 42			14 57							15 12		15 27						
Farringdon	d					09 47			15 02							15 17		15 32						
City Thameslink	d					09 49			15 04							15 19		15 34						
London Blackfriars	d				09 46	09 51			15 06						15 16	15 21		15 36						
Elephant & Castle	d				09 50	09 55			15 10						15 20	15 25		15 40						
Loughborough Jn.	d					10 00			15 15							15 30		15 45						
Herne Hill	d	09 53				10a04		15 08	15a19			15 23				15a34	15 38	15a49				15 53		
West Dulwich	d	09 55						15 10				15 25					15 40					15 55		
Sydenham Hill	d	09 57						15 12				15 27					15 42					15 57		
Penge East	d	10 01						15 16				15 31					15 46					16 01		
Kent House	d	10 03					and at the same minutes past each hour until	15 18				15 33					15 48					16 03		
Beckenham Junction	d	10 05						15 20				15 35					15 50					16 05		
Denmark Hill	d				09 58					15 14					15 28				15 44		15 52			
Peckham Rye	d				10 01					15 17					15 31				15 47					
Nunhead	d				10 04					15 19					15 34				15 49					
Lewisham	a									15 25									15 55					
Crofton Park	d				10 07										15 37									
Catford	d				10 10										15 40									
Bellingham	d				10 13										15 43									
Beckenham Hill	d				10 15										15 45									
Ravensbourne	d				10 17										15 47									
Shortlands	d	10 08			10 20			15 23				15 38			15 50		15 53					16 08		
Bromley South	d	10a11	10 12		10 23			15 26			15a26	15a41	15 42		15 53		15 56			15a56	16 05	16a11	16 12	
Bickley	d				10 26			15 29							15 56		15 59							
Petts Wood	d			10 06				15 33						15 36			16 03							16 06
Orpington	a			10 10				15 38						15 40			16 08							16 10
St Mary Cray	d		10 18		10 31										16 01						16 10		16 18	
Swanley	d		10 22		10 36								15 50		16 06						16a14		16 22	
Eynsford	d				10 41										16 11									
Shoreham (Kent)	d				10 45										16 15									
Otford	d		10a30		10 48								15a58		16 18								16a30	
Bat & Ball	d				10 51										16 21									
Sevenoaks	a			10 27	10 55									15 57	16 25									16 27

A From St Albans City to Sutton (Surrey)
B To Gravesend
C To Ramsgate
D To Dover Priory
E To Ashford International
F From London Charing Cross
G To Canterbury West

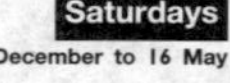

Table T195-F

Saturdays

21 December to 16 May

London - Catford, Beckenham Junction, Bromley South, Orpington, Otford and Sevenoaks

Station		TL	TL A		SE	TL A	SE B	SE ◇1 C	SE	SE ◇1 D	SE E	TL	TL A		SE	TL A	SE B	SE ◇1 F	SE ◇1 C	SE	SE ◇1 G	SE E
London Victoria 15 ⊖	d				15 58		16 04	16 10	16 13	16 25					16 28		16 34	16 40	16 42	16 43	16 55	
Brixton ⊖	d				16 05				16 20						16 35					16 50		
Kentish Town ⊖	d		15 36			15 51							16 06			16 21						
St Pancras International 15 ⊖	d		15 42			15 57							16 12			16 27						
Farringdon ⊖	d		15 47			16 02							16 17			16 32						
City Thameslink 3	d		15 49			16 04							16 19			16 34						
London Blackfriars 3 ⊖	d	15 46	15 51			16 06						16 16	16 21			16 36						
Elephant & Castle ⊖	d	15 50	15 55			16 10						16 20	16 25			16 40						
Loughborough Jn.	d		16 00			16 15							16 30			16 45						
Herne Hill 4	d		16a04		16 08	16a19			16 23				16a34		16 38	16a49				16 53		
West Dulwich	d				16 10				16 25						16 40					16 55		
Sydenham Hill	d				16 12				16 27						16 42					16 57		
Penge East	d				16 16				16 31						16 46					17 01		
Kent House 4	d				16 18				16 33						16 48					17 03		
Beckenham Junction 4	d				16 20				16 35						16 50					17 05		
Denmark Hill 4	d	15 58					16 14					16 28					16 44		16 52			
Peckham Rye 4	d	16 01					16 17					16 31					16 47					
Nunhead 4	d	16 04					16 19					16 34					16 49					
Lewisham 4	a						16 25										16 55					
Crofton Park	d	16 07										16 37										
Catford	d	16 10										16 40										
Bellingham	d	16 13										16 43										
Beckenham Hill	d	16 15										16 45										
Ravensbourne	d	16 17										16 47										
Shortlands 4	d	16 20			16 23				16 38			16 50			16 53					17 08		
Bromley South 4	d	16 23			16 26			16a26	16a41	16 42		16 53			16 56			16a56	17 05	17a11	17 12	
Bickley 4	d	16 26			16 29							16 56			16 59							
Petts Wood 4	d				16 33						16 36				17 03							17 06
Orpington 4	a				16 38						16 40				17 08							17 09
St Mary Cray	d	16 31										17 01							17 10		17 18	
Swanley 4	d	16 36								16 50		17 06							17a14		17 22	
Eynsford	d	16 41										17 11										
Shoreham (Kent)	d	16 45										17 15										
Otford 4	d	16 48								16a58		17 18									17a30	
Bat & Ball	d	16 51										17 21										
Sevenoaks 4	a	16 55									16 57	17 25										17 27

Station		TL	TL A	SE	TL A	SE B	SE ◇1 C	SE	SE ◇1 D	SE E	TL	TL A	SE	TL A	SE B	SE ◇1 F	SE ◇1 C	SE	SE ◇1 G	SE E	
London Victoria 15 ⊖	d			16 58		17 04	17 10	17 13	17 25				17 28		17 34	17 40	17 42	17 43	17 55		
Brixton ⊖	d			17 05				17 20					17 35					17 50			
Kentish Town ⊖	d		16 36		16 51							17 06		17 21							
St Pancras International 15 ⊖	d		16 42		16 57							17 12		17 27							
Farringdon ⊖	d		16 47		17 02							17 17		17 32							
City Thameslink 3	d		16 49		17 04							17 19		17 34							
London Blackfriars 3 ⊖	d	16 46	16 51		17 06						17 16	17 21		17 36							
Elephant & Castle ⊖	d	16 50	16 55		17 10						17 20	17 25		17 40							
Loughborough Jn.	d		17 00		17 15							17 30		17 45							
Herne Hill 4	d		17a04	17 08	17a19			17 23				17a34	17 38	17a49				17 53			
West Dulwich	d			17 10				17 25					17 40					17 55			
Sydenham Hill	d			17 12				17 27					17 42					17 57			
Penge East	d			17 16				17 31					17 46					18 01			
Kent House 4	d			17 18				17 33					17 48					18 03			and at the same minutes past each hour until
Beckenham Junction 4	d			17 20				17 35					17 50					18 05			
Denmark Hill 4	d	16 58				17 14					17 28				17 44		17 52				
Peckham Rye 4	d	17 01				17 17					17 31				17 47						
Nunhead 4	d	17 04				17 19					17 34				17 49						
Lewisham 4	a					17 25									17 55						
Crofton Park	d	17 07									17 37										
Catford	d	17 10									17 40										
Bellingham	d	17 13									17 43										
Beckenham Hill	d	17 15									17 45										
Ravensbourne	d	17 17									17 47										
Shortlands 4	d	17 20		17 23				17 38			17 50		17 53					18 08			
Bromley South 4	d	17 23		17 26			17a26	17a41	17 42		17 53		17 56			17a56	18 05	18a11	18 12		
Bickley 4	d	17 26		17 29							17 56		17 59								
Petts Wood 4	d			17 33						17 36			18 03							18 06	
Orpington 4	a			17 38						17 40			18 08							18 10	
St Mary Cray	d	17 31									18 01						18 10		18 18		
Swanley 4	d	17 36							17 50		18 06						18a14		18 22		
Eynsford	d	17 41									18 11										
Shoreham (Kent)	d	17 45									18 15										
Otford 4	d	17 48							17a58		18 18								18a30		
Bat & Ball	d	17 51									18 21										
Sevenoaks 4	a	17 55								17 57	18 25									18 27	

A From St Albans City to Sutton (Surrey)
B To Gravesend
C To Dover Priory
D To Canterbury West
E From London Charing Cross
F To Ramsgate
G To Ashford International

Table T195-F

Saturdays

21 December to 16 May

London - Catford, Beckenham Junction, Bromley South, Orpington, Otford and Sevenoaks

Station		TL	TL A	SE	TL A	SE B	SE ◇1 C	SE	SE ◇1 D	SE E	TL	TL A	SE	TL A	SE B	SE ◇1 F	SE ◇1 G	SE	SE ◇1 D	SE E		TL	TL A	SE	TL A
London Victoria 15 ⊖	d			19 58		20 04	20 10	20 13	20 25				20 28		20 34	20 40	20 42	20 43	20 55					20 58	
Brixton ⊖	d			20 05				20 20					20 35					20 50						21 05	
Kentish Town ⊖	d		19 36		19 51							20 06		20 21									20 36		20 51
St Pancras International 15 ⊖	d		19 42		19 57							20 12		20 27									20 42		20 57
Farringdon ⊖	d		19 47		20 02							20 17		20 32									20 47		21 02
City Thameslink 3	d		19 49		20 04							20 19		20 34									20 49		
London Blackfriars 3 ⊖	d	19 46	19 51		20 06						20 16	20 21		20 36								20 46	20 51		21 06
Elephant & Castle ⊖	d	19 50	19 55		20 10						20 20	20 25		20 40								20 50	20 55		21 10
Loughborough Jn.	d		20 00		20 15							20 30		20 45									21 00		21 15
Herne Hill 4	d		20a04	20 08	20a19			20 23				20a34	20 38	20a49				20 53					21a04	21 08	21a19
West Dulwich	d			20 10				20 25					20 40					20 55						21 10	
Sydenham Hill	d			20 12				20 27					20 42					20 57						21 12	
Penge East	d			20 16				20 31					20 46					21 01						21 16	
Kent House 4	d			20 18				20 33					20 48					21 03						21 18	
Beckenham Junction 4	d			20 20				20 35					20 50					21 05						21 20	
Denmark Hill 4	d	19 58				20 14					20 28				20 44		20 52					20 58			
Peckham Rye 4	d	20 01				20 17					20 31				20 47							21 01			
Nunhead 4	d	20 04				20 19					20 34				20 49							21 04			
Lewisham 4	a					20 25									20 55										
Crofton Park	d	20 07									20 37											21 07			
Catford	d	20 10									20 40											21 10			
Bellingham	d	20 13									20 43											21 13			
Beckenham Hill	d	20 15									20 45											21 15			
Ravensbourne	d	20 17									20 47											21 17			
Shortlands 4	d	20 20		20 23				20 38			20 50		20 53					21 08				21 20		21 23	
Bromley South 4	d	20 23		20 26			20a26	20a41	20 42		20 53		20 56			20a56	21 05	21a11	21 12			21 23		21 26	
Bickley 4	d	20 26		20 29							20 56		20 59									21 26		21 29	
Petts Wood 4	d			20 33						20 36			21 03							21 06				21 33	
Orpington 4	a			20 38						20 40			21 08							21 10				21 38	
St Mary Cray	d	20 31									21 01						21 10		21 18			21 31			
Swanley 4	d	20 36							20 50		21 06						21a14		21 22			21 36			
Eynsford	d	20 41									21 11											21 41			
Shoreham (Kent)	d	20 45									21 15											21 45			
Otford 4	d	20 48							20a58		21 18								21a30			21 48			
Bat & Ball	d	20 51									21 21											21 51			
Sevenoaks 4	a	20 55								20 57	21 25									21 27		21 55			

Station		SE B	SE ◇1 C	SE	SE ◇1 D	SE E		TL	TL A	SE	TL A	SE B	SE ◇1 F	SE ◇1 G	SE	SE ◇1 D		SE E	TL	TL A	SE	TL A	SE B	SE ◇1 C	SE
London Victoria 15 ⊖	d	21 04	21 10	21 13	21 25					21 28		21 34	21 40	21 42	21 43	21 55					21 58		22 04	22 10	22 13
Brixton ⊖	d			21 20						21 35					21 50						22 05				22 20
Kentish Town ⊖	d								21 06		21 21									21 36		21 51			
St Pancras International 15 ⊖	d								21 12		21 27									21 42		21 57			
Farringdon ⊖	d								21 17		21 32									21 47		22 02			
City Thameslink 3	d																								
London Blackfriars 3 ⊖	d							21 16	21 21		21 36								21 46	21 51		22 06			
Elephant & Castle ⊖	d							21 20	21 25		21 40								21 50	21 55		22 10			
Loughborough Jn.	d								21 30		21 45									22 00		22 15			
Herne Hill 4	d			21 23					21a34	21 38	21a49				21 53					22a04	22 08	22a19			22 23
West Dulwich	d			21 25						21 40					21 55						22 10				22 25
Sydenham Hill	d			21 27						21 42					21 57						22 12				22 27
Penge East	d			21 31						21 46					22 01						22 16				22 31
Kent House 4	d			21 33						21 48					22 03						22 18				22 33
Beckenham Junction 4	d			21 35						21 50					22 05						22 20				22 35
Denmark Hill 4	d	21 14						21 28				21 44		21 52					21 58				22 14		
Peckham Rye 4	d	21 17						21 31				21 47							22 01				22 17		
Nunhead 4	d	21 19						21 34				21 49							22 04				22 19		
Lewisham 4	a	21 25										21 55											22 25		
Crofton Park	d							21 37											22 07						
Catford	d							21 40											22 10						
Bellingham	d							21 43											22 13						
Beckenham Hill	d							21 45											22 15						
Ravensbourne	d							21 47											22 17						
Shortlands 4	d			21 38				21 50		21 53					22 08				22 20		22 23				22 38
Bromley South 4	d		21a26	21a41	21 42			21 53		21 56			21a56	22 05	22a11	22 12			22 23		22 26			22a26	22a41
Bickley 4	d							21 56		21 59									22 26		22 29				
Petts Wood 4	d					21 36				22 03								22 06			22 33				
Orpington 4	a					21 40				22 08								22 10			22 38				
St Mary Cray	d							22 01						22 10		22 18			22 31						
Swanley 4	d				21 50			22 06						22a14		22 22			22 36						
Eynsford	d							22 11											22 41						
Shoreham (Kent)	d							22 15											22 45						
Otford 4	d				21a58			22 18								22a30			22 48						
Bat & Ball	d							22 21											22 51						
Sevenoaks 4	a					21 57		22 25										22 27	22 55						

A From St Albans City to Sutton (Surrey)
B To Gravesend
C To Dover Priory
D To Ashford International
E From London Charing Cross
F To Ramsgate
G To Canterbury East

Table T195-F

Saturdays

21 December to 16 May

London - Catford, Beckenham Junction, Bromley South, Orpington, Otford and Sevenoaks

		SE		SE	TL	TL	SE	TL	SE	SE	SE	SE		SE	SE	TL	TL	SE	TL	SE	SE	SE		SE	SE
		◇1								◇1	◇1			◇1							◇1			◇1	
		A		B		C		C	D	E	F			A	B		C		C	G	E			A	B
London Victoria ⊖	d	22 25					22 28		22 34	22 40	22 42	22 43		22 55				22 58		23 04	23 10	23 13		23 25	
Brixton ⊖	d						22 35					22 50						23 05				23 20			
Kentish Town ⊖	d					22 06		22 21									22 36		22 51						
St Pancras International ⊖	d					22 12		22 27									22 42		22 57						
Farringdon ⊖	d					22 17		22 32									22 47		23 02						
City Thameslink	d																								
London Blackfriars ⊖	d				22 16	22 21		22 36								22 46	22 51		23 06						
Elephant & Castle ⊖	d				22 20	22 25		22 40								22 50	22 55		23 10						
Loughborough Jn.	d					22 30		22 45									23 00		23 15						
Herne Hill	d					22a34	22 38	22a49				22 53					23a04	23 08	23a19			23 23			
West Dulwich	d						22 40					22 55						23 10				23 25			
Sydenham Hill	d						22 42					22 57						23 12				23 27			
Penge East	d						22 46					23 01						23 16				23 31			
Kent House	d						22 48					23 03						23 18				23 33			
Beckenham Junction	d						22 50					23 05						23 20				23 35			
Denmark Hill	d				22 28				22 44		22 52					22 58				23 14					
Peckham Rye	d				22 31				22 47							23 01				23 17					
Nunhead	d				22 34				22 49							23 04				23 19					
Lewisham	a								22 55											23 25					
Crofton Park	d				22 37											23 07									
Catford	d				22 40											23 10									
Bellingham	d				22 43											23 13									
Beckenham Hill	d				22 45											23 15									
Ravensbourne	d				22 47											23 17									
Shortlands	d				22 50		22 53					23 08				23 20		23 23				23 38			
Bromley South	d	22 42			22 53		22 56			22a56	23 05	23a11		23 12		23 23		23 26			23a26	23a41		23 42	
Bickley	d				22 56		22 59									23 26		23 29							
Petts Wood	d			22 36			23 03								23 06			23 33							23 36
Orpington	a			22 40			23 08								23 09			23 38							23 40
St Mary Cray	d				23 01						23 10			23 18		23 31									
Swanley	d	22 50			23 06						23a14			23 22		23 36								23 50	
Eynsford	d				23 11											23 41									
Shoreham (Kent)	d				23 15											23 45									
Otford	d	22a58			23 18									23a30		23 48								23a58	
Bat & Ball	d				23 21											23 51									
Sevenoaks	a			22 57	23 25										23 27	23 55									23 57

		TL	TL	SE	SE	SE	SE	SE		TL	TL	SE
						◇1		◇1				
			C		G	F		A			H	
London Victoria ⊖	d			23 28	23 34	23 42	23 43	23 55				23 58
Brixton ⊖	d			23 35			23 50					00 05
Kentish Town ⊖	d		23 06								23 38	
St Pancras International ⊖	d		23 12								23 44	
Farringdon ⊖	d		23 17								23 49	
City Thameslink	d											
London Blackfriars ⊖	d	23 16	23 21							23 46	23 53	
Elephant & Castle ⊖	d	23 20	23 25							23 50	23 57	
Loughborough Jn.	d		23 30								00 02	
Herne Hill	d		23a34	23 38			23 53				00a06	00 08
West Dulwich	d			23 40			23 55					00 11
Sydenham Hill	d			23 42			23 57					00 13
Penge East	d			23 46			23 59					00 16
Kent House	d			23 48			00 02					00 18
Beckenham Junction	d			23 50			00 05					00 20
Denmark Hill	d	23 28			23 44	23 52				23 58		
Peckham Rye	d	23 31			23 47					00 01		
Nunhead	d	23 34			23 49					00 04		
Lewisham	a				23 55							
Crofton Park	d	23 37								00 07		
Catford	d	23 40								00 10		
Bellingham	d	23 43								00 13		
Beckenham Hill	d	23 45								00 15		
Ravensbourne	d	23 47								00 17		
Shortlands	d	23 50		23 53			00 08			00 20		00 23
Bromley South	d	23 53		23 56		00 05	00a11	00 12		00 23		00 26
Bickley	d	23 56		23 59						00 26		00 29
Petts Wood	d			00 03								00 33
Orpington	a			00 07								00 38
St Mary Cray	d	00 01				00 10		00 18		00 31		
Swanley	d	00 06				00a14		00 22		00 36		
Eynsford	d	00 11								00 41		
Shoreham (Kent)	d	00 15								00 45		
Otford	d	00 18						00a30		00 48		
Bat & Ball	d	00 21								00 51		
Sevenoaks	a	00 25								00 55		

A To Ashford International
B From London Charing Cross
C From St Albans City to Sutton (Surrey)
D To Gravesend
E To Ramsgate
F To Gillingham (Kent)
G To Dartford
H From Luton to Sutton (Surrey)

Table T195-F

Sundays

15 December to 10 May

London - Catford, Beckenham Junction, Bromley South, Orpington, Otford and Sevenoaks

		TL	TL	SE	SE	SE	SE	TL	SE	SE		SE	SE	SE	SE	TL	SE	TL	SE	SE		SE	SE	TL	SE
				◇1		◇1						◇1	◇1				◇1					◇1			
		A	B	C	D	E	F	A	G	D		H	I		J	K	L	M		G		H	N		
London Victoria ⊖	d								00 04			00 10	00 25	00 28	00 40	07 12	07 25		07 28	07 34		07 40		07 44	07 58
Brixton ⊖	d									00 05				00 35					07 35						08 05
Kentish Town ⊖	d																								
St Pancras International ⊖	d																								
Farringdon ⊖	d																								
City Thameslink	d																								
London Blackfriars ⊖	d																								
Elephant & Castle ⊖	d																								
Loughborough Jn.	d		00 02																						
Herne Hill	d		00a06							00 08				00 38					07 38						08 08
West Dulwich	d									00 11				00 40					07 40						08 10
Sydenham Hill	d									00 13				00 42					07 42						08 12
Penge East	d									00 16				00 46					07 46						08 16
Kent House	d				00 02					00 18				00 48					07 48						08 18
Beckenham Junction	d				00 05					00 20				00 50				←	07 50						08 20
Denmark Hill	d								00 14							07 23		07 23		07 44				07 53	
Peckham Rye	d							00 01	00 17							→		07 26		07 47				07 56	
Nunhead	d							00 04	00 19									07 29		07 49				07 59	
Lewisham	a								00 25											07 55					
Crofton Park	d							00 07										07 32						08 02	
Catford	d							00 10										07 35						08 05	
Bellingham	d							00 13										07 38						08 08	
Beckenham Hill	d							00 15										07 40						08 10	
Ravensbourne	d							00 17										07 43						08 13	
Shortlands	d				00 08			00 20		00 23				00 53				07 45	07 53					08 15	08 23
Bromley South	d			00 05	00a11	00 12		00 23		00 26		00s31	00 42	00 56	00 57		07 42	07 48	07 56			07a56		08 18	08 26
Bickley	d							00 26		00 29				00 59				07 51	07 59					08 21	08 29
Petts Wood	d						00 06			00 33				01 03					08 03				08 23		08 33
Orpington	a						00 10			00 38				01 09					08 08				08 27		08 38
St Mary Cray	d	00 01		00 10		00 18		00 31					00 48		01s02		07 48	07 55						08 25	
Swanley	d	00 06		00a14		00 22		00 36					00 52		01s07		07 52	08 00						08 30	
Eynsford	d	00 11						00 41										08 05						08 35	
Shoreham (Kent)	d	00 15						00 45										08 09						08 39	
Otford	d	00 18				00a30		00 48					01a00				08a00	08 12						08 42	
Bat & Ball	d	00 21						00 51										08 15						08 45	
Sevenoaks	a	00 25					00 27	00 55										08 19					08 42	08 49	

		SE	SE	SE	TL	SE		TL	SE	SE	SE	SE	TL	SE	SE	SE		SE	TL	SE	TL	SE	TL	SE	SE
			◇1			◇1					◇1					◇1				◇1					◇1
		G	O	N	K	L		M		G	H	N			G	O		N	K	L	M		P	G	H
London Victoria ⊖	d	08 04	08 10		08 14	08 25			08 28	08 34	08 40		08 44	08 58	09 04	09 10			09 14	09 25		09 28		09 34	09 40
Brixton ⊖	d								08 35					09 05								09 35			
Kentish Town ⊖	d																								
St Pancras International ⊖	d																								
Farringdon ⊖	d																								
City Thameslink	d																								
London Blackfriars ⊖	d																						09 30		
Elephant & Castle ⊖	d																						09 34		
Loughborough Jn.	d																						09 39		
Herne Hill	d								08 38					09 08								09 38	09a42		
West Dulwich	d								08 40					09 10								09 40			
Sydenham Hill	d								08 42					09 12								09 42			
Penge East	d								08 46					09 16								09 46			
Kent House	d								08 48					09 18								09 48			
Beckenham Junction	d							←	08 50					09 20							←	09 50			
Denmark Hill	d	08 14	08 20		08 23			08 23		08 44			08 53		09 14	09 20			09 23		09 23			09 44	
Peckham Rye	d	08 17			→			08 26		08 47			08 56		09 17				→		09 26			09 47	
Nunhead	d	08 19						08 29		08 49			08 59		09 19						09 29			09 49	
Lewisham	a	08 25								08 55					09 25									09 55	
Crofton Park	d							08 32					09 02								09 32				
Catford	d							08 35					09 05								09 35				
Bellingham	d							08 38					09 08								09 38				
Beckenham Hill	d							08 40					09 10								09 40				
Ravensbourne	d							08 43					09 13								09 43				
Shortlands	d							08 45	08 53				09 15	09 23							09 45	09 53			
Bromley South	d		08 33			08 42		08 48	08 56		08a56		09 18	09 26		09 33				09 42	09 48	09 56			09a56
Bickley	d							08 51	08 59				09 21	09 29							09 51	09 59			
Petts Wood	d			08 53					09 03			09 23		09 33				09 53				10 03			
Orpington	a			08 57					09 08			09 27		09 38				09 57				10 08			
St Mary Cray	d		08 38			08 48		08 55					09 25			09 38				09 48	09 55				
Swanley	d		08a42			08 52		09 00					09 30			09a42				09 52	10 00				
Eynsford	d							09 05					09 35								10 05				
Shoreham (Kent)	d							09 09					09 39								10 09				
Otford	d					09a00		09 12					09 42							10a00	10 12				
Bat & Ball	d							09 15					09 45								10 15				
Sevenoaks	a			09 12				09 19				09 42	09 49					10 12			10 19				

A not 15 December. From London Blackfriars
B not 15 December. From Luton to Sutton (Surrey)
C not 15 December. From London Victoria to Gillingham (Kent)
D not 15 December. From London Victoria
E not 15 December. From London Victoria to Ashford International
F not 15 December. From London Charing Cross
G To Dartford
H To Ramsgate
I To Ashford International
J To Gillingham (Kent)
K To Sevenoaks
L To Canterbury West
M From London Victoria
N From London Charing Cross
O To Canterbury East
P To Sutton (Surrey)

Table T195-F

Sundays
15 December to 10 May

London - Catford, Beckenham Junction, Bromley South, Orpington, Otford and Sevenoaks

	SE	TL	TL	SE	TL	SE	SE	SE	SE	TL	TL	SE	TL	SE	SE	SE	TL	TL	SE	TL	SE
							◇1	◇1							◇1						
	A		B		C	D	E	F	A		B		C	D	G	A		B		C	D
London Victoria 15 ⊖ d				09 58		10 04	10 10	10 25				10 28		10 34	10 40				10 58		11 04
Brixton ⊖ d				10 05								10 35							11 05		
Kentish Town ⊖ d			09 31								10 01							10 31			
St Pancras International 15 ⊖ d			09 38								10 08							10 38			
Farringdon ⊖ d			09 42								10 12							10 42			
City Thameslink 3 d																					
London Blackfriars 3 ⊖ d		09 42	09 47		10 00					10 12	10 17		10 30				10 42	10 47		11 00	
Elephant & Castle ⊖ d		09 46	09 51		10 04					10 16	10 21		10 34				10 46	10 51		11 04	
Loughborough Jn. d			09 56		10 09						10 26		10 39					10 56		11 09	
Herne Hill 4 d			09a59	10 08	10a12						10a29	10 38	10a42					10a59	11 08	11a12	
West Dulwich d				10 10								10 40							11 10		
Sydenham Hill d				10 12								10 42							11 12		
Penge East d				10 16								10 46							11 16		
Kent House 4 d				10 18								10 48							11 18		
Beckenham Junction 4 d				10 20								10 50							11 20		
Denmark Hill 4 d		09 53				10 14	10 20			10 23				10 44			10 53				11 14
Peckham Rye 4 d		09 56				10 17				10 26				10 47			10 56				11 17
Nunhead 4 d		09 59				10 19				10 29				10 49			10 59				11 19
Lewisham 4 a						10 25								10 55							11 25
Crofton Park d		10 02								10 32							11 02				
Catford d		10 05								10 35							11 05				
Bellingham d		10 08								10 38							11 08				
Beckenham Hill d		10 10								10 40							11 10				
Ravensbourne d		10 13								10 43							11 13				
Shortlands 4 d		10 15		10 23						10 45		10 53					11 15		11 23		
Bromley South 4 d		10 18		10 26			10 33	10 42		10 48		10 56			10a56		11 18		11 26		
Bickley 4 d		10 21		10 29						10 51		10 59					11 21		11 29		
Petts Wood 4 d	10 23			10 33					10 53			11 03				11 23			11 33		
Orpington 4 a	10 27			10 38					10 57			11 08				11 27			11 38		
St Mary Cray d		10 25					10 38	10 48		10 55							11 25				
Swanley 4 d		10 30					10a42	10 52		11 00							11 30				
Eynsford d		10 35								11 05							11 35				
Shoreham (Kent) d		10 39								11 09							11 39				
Otford 4 d		10 42						11a00		11 12							11 42				
Bat & Ball d		10 45								11 15							11 45				
Sevenoaks 4 a	10 42	10 49							11 12	11 19						11 42	11 49				

	SE	SE	SE	TL	TL	SE	TL	SE	SE	SE	TL	TL	SE	TL	SE	SE	SE	SE	TL	TL	SE	TL
	◇1	◇1							◇1							◇1	◇1					
	E	F	A		B		C	D	G	A		B		C	D	E	F	A		B		C
London Victoria 15 ⊖ d	11 10	11 25				11 28		11 34	11 40				11 58		12 04	12 10	12 25				12 28	
Brixton ⊖ d						11 35							12 05								12 35	
Kentish Town ⊖ d					11 01							11 31								12 01		
St Pancras International 15 ⊖ d					11 08							11 38								12 08		12 21
Farringdon ⊖ d					11 12							11 42								12 12		12 25
City Thameslink 3 d																						
London Blackfriars 3 ⊖ d				11 12	11 17		11 30				11 42	11 47		12 00					12 12	12 17		12 30
Elephant & Castle ⊖ d				11 16	11 21		11 34				11 46	11 51		12 04					12 16	12 21		12 34
Loughborough Jn. d					11 26		11 39					11 56		12 09						12 26		12 39
Herne Hill 4 d					11a29	11 38	11a42					11a59	12 08	12a12						12a29	12 38	12a42
West Dulwich d						11 40							12 10								12 40	
Sydenham Hill d						11 42							12 12								12 42	
Penge East d						11 46							12 16								12 46	
Kent House 4 d						11 48							12 18								12 48	
Beckenham Junction 4 d						11 50							12 20								12 50	
Denmark Hill 4 d	11 20			11 23				11 44			11 53				12 14	12 20			12 23			
Peckham Rye 4 d				11 26				11 47			11 56				12 17				12 26			
Nunhead 4 d				11 29				11 49			11 59				12 19				12 29			
Lewisham 4 a								11 55							12 25							
Crofton Park d				11 32							12 02								12 32			
Catford d				11 35							12 05								12 35			
Bellingham d				11 38							12 08								12 38			
Beckenham Hill d				11 40							12 10								12 40			
Ravensbourne d				11 43							12 13								12 43			
Shortlands 4 d				11 45		11 53					12 15		12 23						12 45		12 53	
Bromley South 4 d	11 33	11 42		11 48		11 56			11a56		12 18		12 26			12 33	12 42		12 48		12 56	
Bickley 4 d				11 51		11 59					12 21		12 29						12 51		12 59	
Petts Wood 4 d			11 53			12 03				12 23			12 33					12 53			13 03	
Orpington 4 a			11 57			12 08				12 27			12 38					12 57			13 08	
St Mary Cray d	11 38	11 48		11 55							12 25					12 38	12 48		12 55			
Swanley 4 d	11a42	11 52		12 00							12 30					12a42	12 52		13 00			
Eynsford d				12 05							12 35								13 05			
Shoreham (Kent) d				12 09							12 39								13 09			
Otford 4 d		12a00		12 12							12 42						13a00		13 12			
Bat & Ball d				12 15							12 45								13 15			
Sevenoaks 4 a			12 12	12 19						12 42	12 49							13 12	13 19			

A From London Charing Cross
B From Luton to Sutton (Surrey)
C To Sutton (Surrey)
D To Dartford
E To Canterbury East
F To Canterbury West
G To Ramsgate

Table T195-F

Sundays
15 December to 10 May

London - Catford, Beckenham Junction, Bromley South, Orpington, Otford and Sevenoaks

	SE	SE	SE	TL	TL	SE	TL	SE	SE	SE	SE	TL	TL	SE	TL	SE	SE	SE	TL	TL	
		◇1							◇1	◇1							◇1				
	A	B	C		D		D	A	E	F	C		D		G	A	B	C		D	and at the same minutes past each hour until
London Victoria 15 ⊖ d	12 34	12 40				12 58		13 04	13 10	13 25				13 28		13 34	13 40				
Brixton ⊖ d						13 05								13 35							
Kentish Town ⊖ d					12 31		12 44								13 14						
St Pancras International 15 ⊖ d					12 38		12 51						13 08		13 21					13 38	
Farringdon ⊖ d					12 42		12 55						13 12		13 25					13 42	
City Thameslink 3 d																					
London Blackfriars 3 ⊖ d				12 42	12 47		13 00					13 12	13 17		13 30				13 42	13 47	
Elephant & Castle ⊖ d				12 46	12 51		13 04					13 16	13 21		13 34				13 46	13 51	
Loughborough Jn. d					12 56		13 09						13 26		13 39					13 56	
Herne Hill 4 d					12a59	13 08	13a12						13a29	13 38	13a42					13a59	
West Dulwich d						13 10								13 40							
Sydenham Hill d						13 12								13 42							
Penge East d						13 16								13 46							
Kent House 4 d						13 18								13 48							
Beckenham Junction 4 d						13 20								13 50							
Denmark Hill 4 d	12 44			12 53				13 14	13 20			13 23				13 44			13 53		
Peckham Rye 4 d	12 47			12 56				13 17				13 26				13 47			13 56		
Nunhead 4 d	12 49			12 59				13 19				13 29				13 49			13 59		
Lewisham 4 a	12 55							13 25								13 55					
Crofton Park d				13 02								13 32							14 02		
Catford d				13 05								13 35							14 05		
Bellingham d				13 08								13 38							14 08		
Beckenham Hill d				13 10								13 40							14 10		
Ravensbourne d				13 13								13 43							14 13		
Shortlands 4 d				13 15		13 23						13 45		13 53					14 15		
Bromley South 4 d		12a56		13 18		13 26			13 33	13 42		13 48		13 56			13a56		14 18		
Bickley 4 d				13 21		13 29						13 51		13 59					14 21		
Petts Wood 4 d			13 23			13 33					13 53			14 03				14 23			
Orpington 4 a			13 27			13 38					13 57			14 08				14 27			
St Mary Cray d				13 25					13 38	13 48		13 55							14 25		
Swanley 4 d				13 30					13a42	13 52		14 00							14 30		
Eynsford d				13 35								14 05							14 35		
Shoreham (Kent) d				13 39								14 09							14 39		
Otford 4 d				13 42						14a00		14 12							14 42		
Bat & Ball d				13 45								14 15							14 45		
Sevenoaks 4 a			13 42	13 49							14 12	14 19						14 42	14 49		

	SE	TL	SE	SE	SE	SE	TL	TL	SE	TL	SE	SE	SE	TL	TL	SE	TL	SE	SE	SE	SE	TL	TL
				◇1	◇1							◇1							◇1	◇1			
		G	A	E	H	C		D		G	A	B	C		D		G	A	E	H	C		D
London Victoria 15 ⊖ d	18 58		19 04	19 10	19 25				19 28		19 34	19 40				19 58		20 04	20 10	20 25			
Brixton ⊖ d	19 05								19 35							20 05							
Kentish Town ⊖ d		18 44								19 14							19 44						
St Pancras International 15 ⊖ d		18 51						19 08		19 21					19 38		19 51						20 08
Farringdon ⊖ d		18 55						19 12		19 25					19 42		19 55						20 12
City Thameslink 3 d																							
London Blackfriars 3 ⊖ d		19 00					19 12	19 17		19 30				19 42	19 47		20 00					20 12	20 17
Elephant & Castle ⊖ d		19 04					19 16	19 21		19 34				19 46	19 51		20 04					20 16	20 21
Loughborough Jn. d		19 09						19 26		19 39					19 56		20 09						20 26
Herne Hill 4 d	19 08	19a12						19a29	19 38	19a42					19a59	20 08	20a12						20a29
West Dulwich d	19 10								19 40							20 10							
Sydenham Hill d	19 12								19 42							20 12							
Penge East d	19 16								19 46							20 16							
Kent House 4 d	19 18								19 48							20 18							
Beckenham Junction 4 d	19 20								19 50							20 20							
Denmark Hill 4 d			19 14	19 20			19 23				19 44			19 53				20 14	20 20			20 23	
Peckham Rye 4 d			19 17				19 26				19 47			19 56				20 17				20 26	
Nunhead 4 d			19 19				19 29				19 49			19 59				20 19				20 29	
Lewisham 4 a			19 25								19 55							20 25					
Crofton Park d							19 32							20 02								20 32	
Catford d							19 35							20 05								20 35	
Bellingham d							19 38							20 08								20 38	
Beckenham Hill d							19 40							20 10								20 40	
Ravensbourne d							19 43							20 13								20 43	
Shortlands 4 d	19 23						19 45		19 53					20 15		20 23						20 45	
Bromley South 4 d	19 26			19 33	19 42		19 48		19 56			19a56		20 18		20 26			20 33	20 42		20 48	
Bickley 4 d	19 29						19 51		19 59					20 21		20 29						20 51	
Petts Wood 4 d	19 33					19 53			20 03				20 23			20 33					20 53		
Orpington 4 a	19 38					19 57			20 08				20 27			20 38					20 57		
St Mary Cray d				19 38	19 48		19 55							20 25					20 38	20 48		20 55	
Swanley 4 d				19a42	19 52		20 00							20 30					20a42	20 52		21 00	
Eynsford d							20 05							20 35								21 05	
Shoreham (Kent) d							20 09							20 39								21 09	
Otford 4 d					20a00		20 12							20 42						21a00		21 12	
Bat & Ball d							20 15							20 45								21 15	
Sevenoaks 4 a						20 12	20 19						20 42	20 49							21 12	21 20	

A To Dartford
B To Ramsgate
C From London Charing Cross
D From Luton to Sutton (Surrey)
E To Canterbury East
F To Canterbury West
G From St Albans City to Sutton (Surrey)
H To Ashford International

Table T195-F

Sundays
15 December to 10 May

London - Catford, Beckenham Junction, Bromley South, Orpington, Otford and Sevenoaks

	SE		TL	SE	SE	SE	TL	TL	SE	TL	SE		SE	SE	SE	TL	TL	SE	TL	SE	SE		SE	TL
					◇1								◇1	◇1							◇1			
			A	B	C	D		E		A	B		F	G	D		E		A	B	C		D	
London Victoria 15 ⊖ d	20 28			20 34	20 40				20 58		21 04		21 10	21 25				21 28		21 34	21 40			
Brixton ⊖ d	20 35								21 05									21 35						
Kentish Town ⊖ d			20 14							20 44									21 14					
St Pancras International 15 ⊖ d			20 21					20 38		20 51							21 08		21 21					
Farringdon ⊖ d			20 25					20 42		20 55							21 12		21 25					
City Thameslink 3 d																								
London Blackfriars 3 ⊖ d			20 30				20 42	20 47		21 00						21 12	21 17		21 30					21 42
Elephant & Castle ⊖ d			20 34				20 46	20 51		21 04						21 16	21 21		21 34					21 46
Loughborough Jn. d			20 39					20 56		21 09							21 26		21 39					
Herne Hill 4 d	20 38		20a42					20a59	21 08	21a12							21a29	21 38	21a42					
West Dulwich d	20 40								21 10									21 40						
Sydenham Hill d	20 42								21 12									21 42						
Penge East d	20 46								21 16									21 46						
Kent House 4 d	20 48								21 18									21 48						
Beckenham Junction 4 d	20 50								21 20									21 50						
Denmark Hill 4 d				20 44			20 53				21 14		21 20			21 23				21 44				21 53
Peckham Rye 4 d				20 47			20 56				21 17					21 26				21 47				21 56
Nunhead 4 d				20 49			20 59				21 19					21 29				21 49				21 59
Lewisham 4 a				20 55							21 25									21 55				
Crofton Park d							21 02									21 32								22 02
Catford d							21 05									21 35								22 05
Bellingham d							21 08									21 38								22 08
Beckenham Hill d							21 10									21 40								22 10
Ravensbourne d							21 13									21 43								22 13
Shortlands 4 d	20 53						21 15		21 23							21 45		21 53						22 15
Bromley South 4 d	20 56				20a56		21 18		21 26				21 33	21 42		21 48		21 56			21a56			22 18
Bickley 4 d	20 59						21 21		21 29							21 51		21 59						22 21
Petts Wood 4 d	21 03					21 23			21 33						21 53			22 03					22 23	
Orpington 4 a	21 08					21 27			21 38						21 57			22 08					22 27	
St Mary Cray d							21 25						21 38	21 48		21 55								22 25
Swanley 4 d							21 30						21a42	21 52		22 00								22 30
Eynsford d							21 35									22 05								22 35
Shoreham (Kent) d							21 39									22 09								22 39
Otford 4 d							21 42							22a00		22 12								22 42
Bat & Ball d							21 45									22 15								22 45
Sevenoaks 4 a						21 42	21 49								22 12	22 19							22 42	22 49

	TL	SE	SE	SE	SE	SE	TL		SE	SE	SE	SE	TL	SE	SE	SE	SE		SE	TL	SE	SE	SE	TL
				◇1	◇1						◇1					◇1	◇1						◇1	
	E		B	F	G	D				B	C	D			B	H	G		D			B	F	
London Victoria 15 ⊖ d		21 58	22 04	22 10	22 25				22 28	22 34	22 40			22 58	23 04	23 10	23 25				23 28	23 34	23 40	
Brixton ⊖ d		22 05							22 35					23 05							23 35			
Kentish Town ⊖ d																								
St Pancras International 15 ⊖ d	21 38																							
Farringdon ⊖ d	21 42																							
City Thameslink 3 d																								
London Blackfriars 3 ⊖ d	21 47						22 12						22 42							23 12				23 42
Elephant & Castle ⊖ d	21 51						22 16						22 46							23 16				23 46
Loughborough Jn. d	21 56																							
Herne Hill 4 d	21a59	22 08							22 38					23 08							23 38			
West Dulwich d		22 10							22 40					23 10							23 40			
Sydenham Hill d		22 12							22 42					23 12							23 42			
Penge East d		22 16							22 46					23 16							23 46			
Kent House 4 d		22 18							22 48					23 18							23 48			
Beckenham Junction 4 d		22 20							22 50					23 20							23 50			
Denmark Hill 4 d			22 14	22 20			22 23			22 44			22 53		23 14	23 20				23 23		23 44		23 53
Peckham Rye 4 d			22 17				22 26			22 47			22 56		23 17					23 26		23 47		23 56
Nunhead 4 d			22 19				22 29			22 49			22 59		23 19					23 29		23 49		23 59
Lewisham 4 a			22 25							22 55					23 25							23 55		
Crofton Park d							22 32						23 02							23 32				00 02
Catford d							22 35						23 05							23 35				00 05
Bellingham d							22 38						23 08							23 38				00 08
Beckenham Hill d							22 40						23 10							23 40				00 10
Ravensbourne d							22 43						23 13							23 43				00 13
Shortlands 4 d		22 23					22 45		22 53				23 15	23 23						23 45	23 53			00 15
Bromley South 4 d		22 26		22 33	22 42		22 48		22 56		22a56		23 18	23 26		23 33	23 42			23 48	23 56		23 57	00 18
Bickley 4 d		22 29					22 51		22 59				23 21	23 29						23 51	23 59			00 21
Petts Wood 4 d		22 33				22 53			23 03			23 23		23 33					23 53		00 04			
Orpington 4 a		22 38				22 57			23 08			23 27		23 38					23 57		00 09			
St Mary Cray d				22 38	22 48		22 55						23 25			23 38	23 48			23 55			00 02	00 25
Swanley 4 d				22a42	22 52		23 00						23 30			23a42	23 52			23 59			00a06	00 30
Eynsford d							23 05						23 35							00 05				00 35
Shoreham (Kent) d							23 09						23 39							00 09				00 39
Otford 4 d					23a00		23 12						23 42				23a59			00 12				00 42
Bat & Ball d							23 15						23 45							00 15				00 45
Sevenoaks 4 a						23 12	23 19					23 42	23 49						00 12	00 19				00 49

A From St Albans City to Sutton (Surrey)
B To Dartford
C To Ramsgate
D From London Charing Cross
E From Luton to Sutton (Surrey)
F To Faversham
G To Ashford International
H To Gillingham (Kent)

Table T195-F

Sundays
15 December to 10 May

London - Catford, Beckenham Junction, Bromley South, Orpington, Otford and Sevenoaks

	SE
London Victoria 15 ⊖ d	23 58
Brixton ⊖ d	00 05
Kentish Town ⊖ d	
St Pancras International 15 ⊖ d	
Farringdon ⊖ d	
City Thameslink 3 d	
London Blackfriars 3 ⊖ d	
Elephant & Castle ⊖ d	
Loughborough Jn. d	
Herne Hill 4 d	00 08
West Dulwich d	00 10
Sydenham Hill d	00 12
Penge East d	00 16
Kent House 4 d	00 18
Beckenham Junction 4 d	00 20
Denmark Hill 4 d	
Peckham Rye 4 d	
Nunhead 4 d	
Lewisham 4 a	
Crofton Park d	
Catford d	
Bellingham d	
Beckenham Hill d	
Ravensbourne d	
Shortlands 4 d	00 23
Bromley South 4 d	00 26
Bickley 4 d	00 29
Petts Wood 4 d	00 33
Orpington 4 a	00 38
St Mary Cray d	
Swanley 4 d	
Eynsford d	
Shoreham (Kent) d	
Otford 4 d	
Bat & Ball d	
Sevenoaks 4 a	

Table T195-R

Mondays to Fridays

16 December to 15 May

Sevenoaks and Otford, Orpington, Bromley South, Beckenham Junction, Catford - London

Miles	Miles	Miles			TL	SE	SE	TL	TL	SE	SE	TL	TL	TL	TL	TL	TL	TL	TL	TL	TL	TL	TL
					MX	MX	MX	MO	MX	MX	MO	MX	MX	MO	MX	MX	MX	MO					
						◇1		1			◇1	1		1	1	1	1	1	1	1	1	1	1
					A	B	C	D	A		E	D	F	D	G	D	D	D	D	H	H	H	H
—	0	—	**Sevenoaks**	d																			
—	1¼	—	Bat & Ball	d																			
—	3	—	Otford	d																			
—	4¼	—	Shoreham (Kent)	d																			
—	6½	—	Eynsford	d																			
—	9½	—	**Swanley**	d																			
—	12¼	—	St Mary Cray	d																			
0	—	—	**Orpington**	d																			
1¼	—	—	Petts Wood	d																			
3	14½	—	Bickley	d			00 01																
4	15½	—	**Bromley South**	d		00 04	00 04			00 19	00 20												
5	16½	—	Shortlands	d			00 07																
—	17¼	—	Ravensbourne	d																			
—	18	—	Beckenham Hill	d									00 01										
—	18¾	—	Bellingham	d									00 03										
—	19½	—	Catford	d									00 06										
—	20½	—	Crofton Park	d									00 09										
—	—	0	Lewisham	a																			
—	—	—		d																			
—	21¾	1¾	Nunhead	d									00 11										
—	22½	2½	Peckham Rye	d									00 14										
—	23¼	3¼	Denmark Hill	d									00 17										
6¼	—	—	**Beckenham Junction**	d			00 10																
7¼	—	—	Kent House	d			00 12																
7¾	—	—	Penge East	d			00 14																
9¼	—	—	Sydenham Hill	d			00 18																
10	—	—	West Dulwich	d			00 20																
11	—	—	Herne Hill	d			00 23																
—	—	—	Loughborough Jn	d																			
—	25¾	—	Elephant & Castle ⊖	d					00 04				00 24										
—	27	—	**London Blackfriars** ⊖	d	00 02			00 06	00 09			00 22	00a29	00 36	00 37	00 50	01 06	01 06	01 36	02 36	03 06	03 36	04 06
—	—	—	City Thameslink	a																			
—	—	—	Farringdon ⊖	a	00 06			00 10	00 13			00 26			00 41								
—	—	—	St Pancras International ⊖	a	00 10			00 15	00 17			00 30		00 45	00 45	00 59	01 13	01 15	01 43	02 43	03 13	03 43	04 13
—	—	—	Kentish Town ⊖	a				00 20	00 22					00 50		01 05			01 48	02 48		03 48	
11¾	—	—	Brixton ⊖	d			00 26																
15	—	7½	**London Victoria** ⊖	a		00 24	00 34			00 39	00 36												

		TL	TL	TL	SE	SE	TL	TL	SE	SE	TL	TL	TL	TL	TL	TL	TL	TL	SE	SE	SE	SE	TL
		1	1				1				1			1		1			1	◇1			1
		H	H	I			D	I		J	H	K	I	L	M	H		K	N	E		O	G
Sevenoaks	d									05 17							05 22						
Bat & Ball	d																05 25						
Otford	d																05 29						
Shoreham (Kent)	d																05 32						
Eynsford	d																05 36						
Swanley	d				04 38												05 41		05 47				
St Mary Cray	d				04 42												05 45		05 52				
Orpington	d			04 33		04 54		05 03	05 24	05 33			05 33								05 52		
Petts Wood	d			04 36		04 57		05 06	05 27	05 36			05 36								05 55		
Bickley	d			04 40	04 46	05 01		05 10	05 31				05 40				05 50				06 00		
Bromley South	d			04 43	04 49	05 04		05 13	05 34				05 43				05 53		05 59	06 02	06 04		
Shortlands	d			04 45	04 52	05 07		05 15	05 37				05 45				05 55				06 07		
Ravensbourne	d			04 48				05 18					05 48				05 58						
Beckenham Hill	d			04 50				05 20					05 50				06 00						
Bellingham	d			04 52				05 22					05 52				06 02						
Catford	d			04 55				05 25					05 55				06 05						
Crofton Park	d			04 58				05 28					05 58				06 08						
Lewisham	a									05 53													
	d																					06 11	
Nunhead	d			05 01				05 31					06 01				06 11					06 17	
Peckham Rye	d			05 04				05 34					06 04				06 14					06 20	
Denmark Hill	d			05 07				05 37					06 07				06 17					06 24	
Beckenham Junction	d				04 55	05 10			05 40												06 10		
Kent House	d				04 57	05 12			05 42												06 12		
Penge East	d				04 59	05 14			05 44												06 14		
Sydenham Hill	d				05 03	05 18			05 48												06 18		
West Dulwich	d				05 05	05 20			05 50												06 20		
Herne Hill	d				05 08	05 23			05 53						06 12						06 23		
Loughborough Jn	d														06 15								
Elephant & Castle ⊖	d			05 14				05 44					06 14		06 19		06 24						
London Blackfriars ⊖	d	04 36	05 06	05 19			05 31	05 49			06 01	06 04	06 19	06 22	06 24	06 27	06a29	06 34					06 37
City Thameslink	a		05 08	05 21			05 33	05 51			06 03	06 06	06 21	06 23	06 26	06 28		06 36					06 38
Farringdon ⊖	a		05 10	05 23			05 35	05 53			06 05	06 08	06 23	06 26	06 28	06 31		06 38					06 41
St Pancras International ⊖	a	04 43	05 15	05 28			05 40	05 58			06 10	06 13	06 28	06 30	06 33	06 35		06 43					06 45
Kentish Town ⊖	a	04 48		05 33				06 03				06 18			06 38								
Brixton ⊖	d				05 11	05 26			05 56												06 26		
London Victoria ⊖	a				05 20	05 35			06 05										06 20	06 23	06 35	06 37	

A From Sutton (Surrey) to Bedford
B From Dover Priory
C From Orpington
D From Brighton to Bedford
E From Ramsgate
F From Sevenoaks
G From Horsham to Peterborough
H From Three Bridges to Bedford
I To Luton
J To London Charing Cross
K From Gillingham (Kent) to Luton
L From Brighton to Cambridge
M From Sutton (Surrey) to St Albans City
N From Gillingham (Kent)
O From Dartford

Table T195-R

Mondays to Fridays

16 December to 15 May

Sevenoaks and Otford, Orpington, Bromley South, Beckenham Junction, Catford - London

		TL	TL	TL	TL	SE	TL	TL	TL	TL	TL	SE	SE	SE	SE	SE	SE	TL	SE	TL	TL	TL
			◇1	1			1		1		1		◇1				◇1		◇1	1		1
		A	B	C	D		E	A	F		B	G	H	G	I		J	K	J	L	A	C
Sevenoaks	d									05 52					06 01							
Bat & Ball	d									05 55												
Otford	d									05 59							06 17		06 25			
Shoreham (Kent)	d									06 02												
Eynsford	d									06 05												
Swanley	d									06 11		06 19					06 26		06 34			
St Mary Cray	d									06 15		06 23										
Orpington	d				06 03										06 18	06 24						
Petts Wood	d				06 06										06 21	06 28						
Bickley	d				06 10					06 20						06 32						
Bromley South	d				06 13	06 16				06 23		06 30	06 33			06 35	06 36		06 42			
Shortlands	d				06 15	06 19				06 25						06 38						
Ravensbourne	d				06 18					06 28												
Beckenham Hill	d				06 20					06 30												
Bellingham	d				06 22					06 32												
Catford	d				06 25					06 35												
Crofton Park	d				06 28					06 38												
Lewisham	a														06 40							
	d													06 36								
Nunhead	d				06 31					06 41				06 44								
Peckham Rye	d				06 34					06 44				06 47								
Denmark Hill	d				06 37					06 47				06 50								
Beckenham Junction	d					06 22										06 42						
Kent House	d					06 24										06 44						
Penge East	d					06 26										06 46						
Sydenham Hill	d					06 30										06 50						
West Dulwich	d					06 32										06 52						
Herne Hill	d	06 27				06 35		06 42								06 55					06 57	
Loughborough Jn	d	06 30						06 45													07 00	
Elephant & Castle ⊖	d	06 34			06 44			06 49		06 54									06 59		07 04	
London Blackfriars ⊖	d	06 39	06 42	06 47	06 49		06 52	06 54	06 57	06a59	07 02							07 04	07a05	07 07	07 09	07 12
City Thameslink	a	06 41	06 43	06 48	06 51		06 53	06 56	06 58		07 03							07 06		07 08	07 11	07 13
Farringdon ⊖	a	06 43	06 46	06 51	06 53		06 56	06 58	07 01		07 06							07 08		07 11	07 13	07 16
St Pancras International ⊖	a	06 48	06 50	06 55	06 58		07 00	07 03	07 05		07 10							07 13		07 15	07 18	07 20
Kentish Town ⊖	a	06 53						07 08													07 23	
Brixton ⊖	d					06 38										06 58						
London Victoria ⊖	a					06 47						06 50	06 53	07 02		07 07	06 55					

		TL	SE	TL	TL	TL	SE	TL	TL	SE	SE	SE	SE	SE	SE	TL	TL	TL	TL	TL	SE	TL	TL
				1		1			1		◇1		1		◇1		1		1		◇1	1	
		D		M	A	N			B	O	J		G	P	H	K	Q	A	R	D	S	C	T
Sevenoaks	d							06 22		06 34													
Bat & Ball	d							06 25															
Otford	d							06 29			06 48												
Shoreham (Kent)	d							06 32															
Eynsford	d							06 35															
Swanley	d							06 41					06 56										
St Mary Cray	d							06 45					07 00										
Orpington	d	06 30								06 49		06 54								06 59			
Petts Wood	d	06 33								06a52		06 57								07 02			
Bickley	d	06 40						06 50				07 01								07 06			
Bromley South	d	06 43	06 49					06 53			07 04	07 04	07 07		07 12					07 13	07 16		←
Shortlands	d	06 45	06 52					06 55				07 07								07 15			07 15
Ravensbourne	d	06 48						06 58												→			07 18
Beckenham Hill	d	06 50						07 00															07 20
Bellingham	d	06 52						07 02															07 22
Catford	d	06 55						07 05															07 25
Crofton Park	d	06 58						07 08															07 28
Lewisham	a																						
	d													07 15									
Nunhead	d	07 01						07 11					07 16										07 31
Peckham Rye	d	07 04						07 14						07 21									07 34
Denmark Hill	d	07 07						07 17					07 22	07 25									07 37
Beckenham Junction	d		06 55				07 01					07 10											
Kent House	d		06 57				07 04					07 13											
Penge East	d		06 59				07 06					07 15											
Sydenham Hill	d		07 03				07 10				07 14												
West Dulwich	d		07 05				07 12					07 20											
Herne Hill	d		07 08		07 12		07 15					07 23						07 27					
Loughborough Jn	d				07 15		07 19											07 30					
Elephant & Castle ⊖	d	07 14			07 19		07 23	07 24										07 34			07 37		07 44
London Blackfriars ⊖	d	07 19		07 22	07 24	07 27	07a29	07a29	07 32							07 34	07 37	07 39	07 42		07a44	07 47	07 49
City Thameslink	a	07 21		07 23	07 26	07 28			07 33							07 36	07 38	07 41	07 43			07 48	07 51
Farringdon ⊖	a	07 23		07 26	07 28	07 31			07 36							07 38	07 41	07 43	07 46			07 51	07 53
St Pancras International ⊖	a	07 28		07 30	07 33	07 35			07 40							07 43	07 45	07 48	07 50			07 55	07 58
Kentish Town ⊖	a	07 33														07 48							08 03
Brixton ⊖	d		07 11									07 26											
London Victoria ⊖	a		07 20								07 28	07 35	07 34	07 37	07 38								

A From Sutton (Surrey) to St Albans City
B From Brighton to Bedford
C From East Grinstead to Bedford
D To Luton
E From Brighton to Cambridge
F From Three Bridges to Bedford
G From Gillingham (Kent)
H From Dover Priory
I To London Charing Cross
J From Ashford International
K From Rainham (Kent) to Luton
L From Three Bridges to Peterborough
M From Brighton to Royston
N From Horsham to Bedford
O To London Cannon Street
P From Barnehurst
Q From Horsham to Peterborough
R From Littlehampton to Bedford
S From Broadstairs
T From Orpington to Luton

Table T195-R

Mondays to Fridays

16 December to 15 May

Sevenoaks and Otford, Orpington, Bromley South, Beckenham Junction, Catford - London

Station		TL ■ A	TL B	SE C	SE ◇■ D	SE		TL E	TL ■ F	SE	TL G	TL ■ H	SE ◇■ D	SE	SE ◇■ I	SE ◇■ J		SE K	TL L	TL ■ M	SE ◇■ D	TL E	TL ■ N	TL O	SE C
Sevenoaks ■	d		06 45	06 57																					07 17
Bat & Ball	d		06 48																						
Otford ■	d		06 52		06 58								07 16								07 22				
Shoreham (Kent)	d		06 55																						
Eynsford	d		06 58																						
Swanley ■	d		07 04		07 07										07 27						07 32				
St Mary Cray	d		07 08		07 11										07 32										
Orpington ■	d			07 12										07 23										07 30	07 33
Petts Wood ■	d			07a15							←			07 27										07 33	07a36
Bickley ■	d		07 13								07 13			07 31										07 40	
Bromley South ■	d		→		07 19	07 19					07 23		07 33	07 34	07 39	07 40					07 43			07 43	
Shortlands ■	d					07 22					07 25			07 36										07 45	
Ravensbourne	d										07 28													07 48	
Beckenham Hill	d										07 30													07 50	
Bellingham	d										07 32													07 52	
Catford	d										07 35													07 55	
Crofton Park	d										07 38				07 46									07 58	
Lewisham ■	a																								
	d																	07 46							
Nunhead ■	d										07 41							07 54						08 01	
Peckham Rye ■	d										07 44							07 57						08 04	
Denmark Hill ■	d										07 47				07 55			08 00						08 07	
Beckenham Junction ■ ⇌	d					07 25				07 31				07 40											
Kent House ■	d					07 28				07 34				07 45											
Penge East	d					07 30				07 36			07 39												
Sydenham Hill	d					07 34				07 40				07 49											
West Dulwich	d				07 29					07 42				07 52											
Herne Hill ■	d					07 38		07 42		07 45				07 55								07 57			
Loughborough Jn	d							07 45		07 49												08 00			
Elephant & Castle	⊖ d							07 49		07 53	07 54										08 02	08 04		08 14	
London Blackfriars ■	⊖ d	07 52						07 54	07 57	07a59	07a59	08 02							08 04	08 07	08a09	08 09	08 17	08 19	
City Thameslink ■	a	07 53						07 56	07 58			08 03							08 06	08 08		08 11	08 18	08 21	
Farringdon	⊖ a	07 56						07 58	08 01			08 06							08 08	08 11		08 13	08 21	08 23	
St Pancras International ■	⊖ a	08 00						08 03	08 05			08 10							08 13	08 15		08 18	08 25	08 28	
Kentish Town	⊖ a							08 08											08 18			08 23		08 33	
Brixton	⊖ d					07 41								07 58											
London Victoria ■	⊖ a				07 43	07 50							07 58	08 07	08 07	08 03		08 13							

Station		SE		TL ■ A	TL E	TL ■ F	TL B	SE ◇■ D	SE ■ P	SE	TL G	TL ■ H		SE	SE C	SE K	TL Q	SE ■ R	TL ■ M	SE ◇■ I	SE ◇■ J	TL E		TL ■ S	TL ■ N
Sevenoaks ■	d						07 18								07 37										
Bat & Ball	d						07 21																		
Otford ■	d						07 25	07 34																	
Shoreham (Kent)	d						07 28																		
Eynsford	d						07 31																		
Swanley ■	d						07 37		07 41									07 54		07 58					
St Mary Cray	d						07 41		07 45									07 59		08 02					
Orpington ■	d													07 48	07 51										
Petts Wood ■	d										←			07 51	07a54										
Bickley ■	d						07 46				07 46			07 55											
Bromley South ■	d	07 49					→	07 50	07 53		07 53			07 59				08 06		08 09	08 13				
Shortlands ■	d	07 52									07 55			08 01											
Ravensbourne	d										07 58														
Beckenham Hill	d										08 00														
Bellingham	d								07 58		08 02														
Catford	d										08 05														
Crofton Park	d										08 08									08 18					
Lewisham ■	a																								
	d															08 06									
Nunhead ■	d										08 11					08 14									
Peckham Rye ■	d										08 14					08 17									
Denmark Hill ■	d								08 10		08 17					08 21		08 23							
Beckenham Junction ■ ⇌	d	07 56								08 01				08 05											
Kent House ■	d							07 55		08 04				08 07											
Penge East	d	08 00								08 06				08 10											
Sydenham Hill	d	08 03								08 10				08 13											
West Dulwich	d	08 06								08 12				08 16											
Herne Hill ■	d	08 09			08 12					08 15				08 19								08 27			
Loughborough Jn	d				08 15					08 19												08 30			
Elephant & Castle	⊖ d				08 19					08 23	08 24							08 31				08 34			
London Blackfriars ■	⊖ d			08 22	08 24	08 27				08a29	08a29	08 32					08 34	08a37	08 37			08 39		08 42	08 47
City Thameslink ■	a			08 23	08 26	08 28						08 33					08 36		08 38			08 41		08 43	08 48
Farringdon	⊖ a			08 26	08 28	08 31						08 36					08 38		08 41			08 43		08 46	08 51
St Pancras International ■	⊖ a			08 30	08 33	08 35						08 40					08 43		08 45			08 48		08 50	08 55
Kentish Town	⊖ a																08 48								
Brixton	⊖ d	08 12												08 22											
London Victoria ■	⊖ a	08 21						08 11	08 24					08 32		08 33				08 36	08 35				

A From Brighton to Cambridge
B To London Blackfriars
C To London Cannon Street
D From Ashford International
E From Sutton (Surrey) to St Albans City
F From Horsham to Bedford
G From Sevenoaks
H From Brighton to Bedford
I From Sheerness-on-Sea
J From Ramsgate
K From Dartford
L From Rainham (Kent) to Luton
M From Gatwick Airport to Peterborough
N From East Grinstead to Bedford
O To Luton
P From Rochester
Q From Rainham (Kent) to West Hampstead Thameslink
R From Sole Street
S From Littlehampton to Bedford

NRT DECEMBER 19 EDITION

Table T195-R

Mondays to Fridays

16 December to 15 May

Sevenoaks and Otford, Orpington, Bromley South, Beckenham Junction, Catford - London

Station		TL A	TL ■ B	TL C	SE D	SE ◇■ E	SE	TL F		SE G	TL ■ H	SE	TL I	TL J	SE ■ K	SE	SE L	TL ■ M		TL F	TL ■ N	TL ■ O	TL A	SE D	SE ◇■ E
Sevenoaks ■	d			07 45	07 57																			08 17	
Bat & Ball	d			07 48																					
Otford ■	d			07 52		07 59																			08 26
Shoreham (Kent)	d			07 55																					
Eynsford	d			07 58																					
Swanley ■	d			08 04		08 08							←		08 23										08 35
St Mary Cray	d			08 08									08 08		08 27										08 39
Orpington ■	d	08 03		→	08 12											08 24							08 29	08 34	
Petts Wood ■	d	08 06			08a15											08 27							08 32	08a37	
Bickley ■	d	08 10											08 15			08 31							08 36		
Bromley South ■	d	08 13				08 17	08 19						08 23		08 34	08 34							08 43		08 46
Shortlands ■	d	08 15					08 22						08 25			08 36							08 45		
Ravensbourne	d	08 18											08 28										08 48		
Beckenham Hill	d	08 20											08 30										08 50		
Bellingham	d	08 22											08 32		08 40								08 52		
Catford	d	08 25											08 35										08 55		
Crofton Park	d	08 28											08 38										08 58		
Lewisham ■	a																								
	d									08 27							08 46								
Nunhead ■	d	08 31								08 34			08 41				08 52						09 01		
Peckham Rye ■	d	08 34								08 37			08 44				08 55						09 04		
Denmark Hill ■	d	08 37								08 42			08 47		08 50		08 59						09 07		
Beckenham Junction ■ ⇌	d						08 25					08 31				08 40									
Kent House ■	d						08 28					08 34				08 42									
Penge East	d						08 30					08 36				08 44									
Sydenham Hill	d					08 24						08 40				08 47									
West Dulwich	d						08 35					08 42				08 50									
Herne Hill ■	d						08 38	08 42				08 45				08 53				08 57					
Loughborough Jn	d							08 45				08 49								09 00					
Elephant & Castle	⊖ d	08 44						08 49				08 53	08 54							09 04			09 14		
London Blackfriars ■	⊖ d	08 49	08 52					08 54			08 57	08a59	08a59	09 04				09 07		09 09	09 12	09 17	09 19		
City Thameslink ■	a	08 51	08 53					08 56			08 58			09 06				09 08		09 11	09 13	09 18	09 21		
Farringdon	⊖ a	08 53	08 56					08 58			09 01			09 08				09 11		09 13	09 16	09 21	09 23		
St Pancras International ■	⊖ a	08 58	09 00					09 03			09 05			09 13				09 15		09 18	09 20	09 25	09 28		
Kentish Town	⊖ a	09 03												09 18									09 33		
Brixton	⊖ d						08 41									08 56									
London Victoria ■	⊖ a					08 38	08 51			08 55					09 03	09 05	09 11								09 08

Station		SE ◇■ P	SE	TL ■ B		TL F	TL ■ H	SE	TL	TL Q	SE R	SE	SE	SE G		SE ■ S	TL ■ M	TL F	TL ■ N	TL ■ O	TL	SE ◇ E	SE	SE T	
Sevenoaks ■	d								08 22		08 37														
Bat & Ball	d								08 25																
Otford ■	d								08 29													08 56			
Shoreham (Kent)	d								08 32																
Eynsford	d								08 35																
Swanley ■	d								08 41			08 51				09 01						09 05			
St Mary Cray	d								08 45			08 56				09 06						09 09			
Orpington ■	d										08 52		08 55								09 03				
Petts Wood ■	d										08a55		08 58								09 06				
Bickley ■	d								08 50				09 02								09 10				
Bromley South ■	d	08 49	08 49						08 53			09 03	09 05			09 12					09 13	09 17	09 19		
Shortlands ■	d		08 52						08 55				09 07								09 15		09 22		
Ravensbourne	d								08 58												09 18				
Beckenham Hill	d								09 00												09 20				
Bellingham	d								09 02							09 18					09 22				
Catford	d								09 05												09 25				
Crofton Park	d								09 08							09 22					09 28				
Lewisham ■	a																								
	d													09 07										09 32	
Nunhead ■	d								09 11					09 14							09 31			09 37	
Peckham Rye ■	d								09 14					09 17							09 34			09 40	
Denmark Hill ■	d								09 17					09 22		09 28					09 37			09 44	
Beckenham Junction ■ ⇌	d		08 55					09 01				09 07	09 11										09 25		
Kent House ■	d		08 57					09 04					09 13										09 27		
Penge East	d		08 59					09 06				09 11											09 29		
Sydenham Hill	d		09 03					09 10					09 17										09 33		
West Dulwich	d		09 05					09 12					09 20										09 35		
Herne Hill ■	d		09 08			09 12		09 15					09 23					09 27					09 38		
Loughborough Jn	d					09 15		09 19										09 30							
Elephant & Castle	⊖ d					09 19		09 23	09 24									09 34			09 44				
London Blackfriars ■	⊖ d			09 22		09 24	09 27	09a29	09a29	09 34							09 37	09 39	09 42	09 47	09 49				
City Thameslink ■	a			09 23		09 26	09 28			09 36							09 38	09 41	09 43	09 48	09 51				
Farringdon	⊖ a			09 26		09 28	09 31			09 38							09 41	09 43	09 46	09 51	09 53				
St Pancras International ■	⊖ a			09 30		09 33	09 35			09 43							09 45	09 48	09 50	09 55	09 58				
Kentish Town	⊖ a									09 48								09 53			10 03				
Brixton	⊖ d		09 11										09 26										09 41		
London Victoria ■	⊖ a	09 11	09 21									09 28	09 35	09 35		09 41						09 38	09 50	09 57	

A To Luton
B From Brighton to Cambridge
C To London Blackfriars
D To London Cannon Street
E From Ashford International
F From Sutton (Surrey) to St Albans City
G From Dartford
H From Horsham to Bedford
I From Sevenoaks
J From Rainham (Kent) to West Hampstead Thameslink
K From Rochester
L From Barnehurst
M From Gatwick Airport to Peterborough
N From Brighton to Bedford
O From East Grinstead to Bedford
P From Dover Priory
Q From Rainham (Kent) to Luton
R To London Charing Cross
S From Gillingham (Kent)
T From Gravesend

Table T195-R

Mondays to Fridays

16 December to 15 May

Sevenoaks and Otford, Orpington, Bromley South, Beckenham Junction, Catford - London

		TL ■ A	TL B	TL ■ C	TL D	SE E	SE ◇■ F	SE	SE ◇■ G	TL H	TL I	TL ■ J	TL B	TL ■ K	TL	SE ◇■ L	SE	SE M	TL ■ A	TL B	TL ■ N	TL	TL I
Sevenoaks 4	d				08 52	09 06																09 22	
Bat & Ball	d				08 55																	09 25	
Otford 4	d				08 59				09 15							09 26						09 29	
Shoreham (Kent)	d				09 02																	09 32	
Eynsford	d				09 05																	09 35	
Swanley 4	d				09 11				09 24							09 35						09 41	
St Mary Cray	d				09 15				09 29							09 39						09 45	
Orpington 4	d					09 21		09 24							09 33								
Petts Wood 4	d					09a24		09 28							09 36								
Bickley 4	d				09 20			09 32							09 40							09 50	
Bromley South 4	d				09 23		09 33	09 35	09 36						09 43	09 47	09 49					09 53	
Shortlands 4	d				09 25			09 37		←					09 45		09 52					09 55	
Ravensbourne	d				09 28					09 28					09 48							09 58	
Beckenham Hill	d				→					09 30					09 50							10 00	
Bellingham	d									09 32					09 52							10 02	
Catford	d									09 35					09 55							10 05	
Crofton Park	d									09 38					09 58							10 08	
Lewisham 4	a																						
	d																	10 02					
Nunhead 4	d									09 41					10 01			10 07				10 11	
Peckham Rye 4	d									09 44					10 04			10 10				10 14	
Denmark Hill 4	d									09 47					10 07			10 14				10 17	
Beckenham Junction 4 ⇌	d							09 42									09 55						
Kent House 4	d							09 44									09 57						
Penge East	d							09 46									09 59						
Sydenham Hill	d							09 49									10 03						
West Dulwich	d							09 51									10 05						
Herne Hill 4	d		09 42					09 54					09 57				10 08			10 12			
Loughborough Jn.	d		09 45										10 00							10 15			
Elephant & Castle ⊖	d		09 49						09 52	09 54			10 04		10 14					10 19		10 24	
London Blackfriars 3 ⊖	d	09 52	09 54	09 57					09a59	09a59	10 04	10 07	10 09	10 12	10 19				10 22	10 24	10 27	10a29	10 34
City Thameslink 3	a	09 53	09 56	09 58							10 06	10 08	10 11	10 13	10 21				10 23	10 26	10 28		10 36
Farringdon ⊖	a	09 56	09 58	10 01							10 08	10 11	10 13	10 16	10 23				10 26	10 28	10 31		10 38
St Pancras International 15 ⊖	a	10 00	10 03	10 05							10 13	10 15	10 18	10 20	10 28				10 30	10 33	10 35		10 43
Kentish Town ⊖	a		10 08										10 23		10 33					10 38			
Brixton ⊖	d							09 57									10 11						
London Victoria 15 ⊖	a						09 53	10 04								10 07	10 20	10 25					

		SE E	SE ■ O	SE ◇■ F	SE	TL ■ J	TL B	TL ■ K	TL	SE ◇■ P	SE	SE M	TL ■ A	TL B	TL ■ N	TL	TL I	SE E	SE ◇■ Q	SE ◇■ F	SE	TL ■ J	TL B
Sevenoaks 4	d	09 35														09 52		10 05					
Bat & Ball	d															09 55							
Otford 4	d									09 56						09 59							
Shoreham (Kent)	d															10 02							
Eynsford	d															10 05							
Swanley 4	d		09 47							10 05						10 11			10 17				
St Mary Cray	d		09 52							10 09						10 15			10 22				
Orpington 4	d	09 50			09 54				10 03									10 20			10 24		
Petts Wood 4	d	09a53			09 57				10 06									10a23			10 27		
Bickley 4	d				10 01				10 10							10 20					10 31		
Bromley South 4	d		10 00	10 03	10 04				10 13	10 17	10 19					10 23			10 30	10 33	10 34		
Shortlands 4	d				10 07				10 15		10 22					10 25					10 37		
Ravensbourne	d								10 18							10 28							
Beckenham Hill	d								10 20							10 30							
Bellingham	d								10 22							10 32							
Catford	d								10 25							10 35							
Crofton Park	d								10 28							10 38							
Lewisham 4	a																						
	d											10 32											
Nunhead 4	d								10 31			10 37				10 41							
Peckham Rye 4	d								10 34			10 40				10 44							
Denmark Hill 4	d		10 20						10 37			10 44				10 47			10 50				
Beckenham Junction 4 ⇌	d				10 10						10 25										10 40		
Kent House 4	d				10 12						10 27										10 42		
Penge East	d				10 14						10 29										10 44		
Sydenham Hill	d				10 18						10 33										10 48		
West Dulwich	d				10 20						10 35										10 50		
Herne Hill 4	d				10 23		10 27				10 38			10 42							10 53		10 57
Loughborough Jn.	d						10 30							10 45									11 00
Elephant & Castle ⊖	d						10 34		10 44					10 49		10 54							11 04
London Blackfriars 3 ⊖	d					10 37	10 39	10 42	10 49				10 52	10 54	10 57	10a59	11 04					11 07	11 09
City Thameslink 3	a					10 38	10 41	10 43	10 51				10 53	10 56	10 58		11 06					11 08	11 11
Farringdon ⊖	a					10 41	10 43	10 46	10 53				10 56	10 58	11 01		11 08					11 11	11 13
St Pancras International 15 ⊖	a					10 45	10 48	10 50	10 58				11 00	11 03	11 05		11 13					11 15	11 18
Kentish Town ⊖	a						10 53		11 03					11 08									11 23
Brixton ⊖	d				10 26						10 41										10 56		
London Victoria 15 ⊖	a		10 32	10 23	10 33					10 36	10 48	10 55							11 00	10 51	11 03		

A From Brighton to Cambridge
B From Sutton (Surrey) to St Albans City
C From Horsham to Bedford
D To London Blackfriars
E To London Charing Cross
F From Ramsgate
G From Maidstone East
H From Sevenoaks
I From Rainham (Kent) to Luton
J From Horsham to Peterborough
K From Brighton to Bedford
L From Minster
M From Gravesend
N From Gatwick Airport to Bedford
O From Rochester
P From Ashford International
Q From Dover Priory

Table T195-R

Mondays to Fridays

16 December to 15 May

Sevenoaks and Otford, Orpington, Bromley South, Beckenham Junction, Catford - London

		TL ■ A	TL	SE ◇■ B	SE	SE C	TL ■ D	TL E	TL ■ F	TL	TL G	SE H	SE ◇■ I	SE	TL ■ J	TL E	TL ■ A	TL	SE ◇■ K	SE	SE C	TL ■ D
Sevenoaks 4	d									10 22		10 35										
Bat & Ball	d									10 25												
Otford 4	d			10 26						10 29									10 56			
Shoreham (Kent)	d									10 32												
Eynsford	d									10 35												
Swanley 4	d			10 37						10 41									11 05			
St Mary Cray	d									10 45									11 09			
Orpington 4	d		10 33									10 50		10 54				11 03				
Petts Wood 4	d		10 36									10a53		10 57				11 06				
Bickley 4	d		10 40							10 50				11 01				11 10				
Bromley South 4	d		10 43	10 47	10 49					10 53			11 03	11 04				11 13	11 17	11 19		
Shortlands 4	d		10 45		10 52					10 55				11 07				11 15		11 22		
Ravensbourne	d		10 48							10 58								11 18				
Beckenham Hill	d		10 50							11 00								11 20				
Bellingham	d		10 52							11 02								11 22				
Catford	d		10 55							11 05								11 25				
Crofton Park	d		10 58							11 08								11 28				
Lewisham 4	a																					
	d					11 02															11 32	
Nunhead 4	d		11 01			11 07				11 11								11 31			11 37	
Peckham Rye 4	d		11 04			11 10				11 14								11 34			11 40	
Denmark Hill 4	d		11 07			11 14				11 17								11 37			11 44	
Beckenham Junction 4 ⇌	d				10 55									11 10						11 25		
Kent House 4	d				10 57									11 12						11 27		
Penge East	d				10 59									11 14						11 29		
Sydenham Hill	d				11 03									11 18						11 33		
West Dulwich	d				11 05									11 20						11 35		
Herne Hill 4	d				11 08			11 12						11 23		11 27				11 38		
Loughborough Jn.	d							11 15								11 30						
Elephant & Castle ⊖	d		11 14					11 19		11 24						11 34		11 44				
London Blackfriars 3 ⊖	d	11 12	11 19				11 22	11 24	11 27	11a29	11 34				11 37	11 39	11 42	11 49				11 52
City Thameslink 3	a	11 13	11 21				11 23	11 26	11 28		11 36				11 38	11 41	11 43	11 51				11 53
Farringdon ⊖	a	11 16	11 23				11 26	11 28	11 31		11 38				11 41	11 43	11 46	11 53				11 56
St Pancras International 15 ⊖	a	11 20	11 28				11 30	11 33	11 35		11 43				11 45	11 48	11 50	11 58				12 00
Kentish Town ⊖	a		11 33					11 38								11 53		12 03				
Brixton ⊖	d				11 11									11 26						11 41		
London Victoria 15 ⊖	a			11 06	11 18	11 25							11 21	11 33					11 36	11 48	11 55	

		TL E	TL ■ F	TL	TL G	SE H	SE ◇■ I	SE ◇■ L	SE	TL ■ J	TL E	TL ■ A	TL	SE ◇■ B	SE	SE C	TL ■ D	TL E	TL ■ F	TL	TL G	SE H	SE ◇■ I
Sevenoaks 4	d			10 52		11 05														11 22		11 35	
Bat & Ball	d			10 55																11 25			
Otford 4	d			10 59										11 26						11 29			
Shoreham (Kent)	d			11 02																11 32			
Eynsford	d			11 05																11 35			
Swanley 4	d			11 11			11 17							11 37						11 41			
St Mary Cray	d			11 15			11 22													11 45			
Orpington 4	d					11 20			11 24				11 33									11 50	
Petts Wood 4	d					11a23			11 27				11 36									11a53	
Bickley 4	d			11 20					11 31				11 40							11 50			
Bromley South 4	d			11 23			11 30	11 33	11 34				11 43	11 47	11 49					11 53			12 03
Shortlands 4	d			11 25					11 37				11 45		11 52					11 55			
Ravensbourne	d			11 28									11 48							11 58			
Beckenham Hill	d			11 30									11 50							12 00			
Bellingham	d			11 32									11 52							12 02			
Catford	d			11 35									11 55							12 05			
Crofton Park	d			11 38									11 58							12 08			
Lewisham 4	a																						
	d															12 02							
Nunhead 4	d			11 41									12 01			12 07				12 11			
Peckham Rye 4	d			11 44									12 04			12 10				12 14			
Denmark Hill 4	d			11 47			11 50						12 07			12 14				12 17			
Beckenham Junction 4 ⇌	d								11 40						11 55								
Kent House 4	d								11 42						11 57								
Penge East	d								11 44						11 59								
Sydenham Hill	d								11 48						12 03								
West Dulwich	d								11 50						12 05								
Herne Hill 4	d	11 42							11 53		11 57				12 08			12 12					
Loughborough Jn.	d	11 45									12 00							12 15					
Elephant & Castle ⊖	d	11 49		11 54							12 04		12 14					12 19		12 24			
London Blackfriars 3 ⊖	d	11 54	11 57	11a59	12 04					12 07	12 09	12 12	12 19				12 22	12 24	12 27	12a29	12 34		
City Thameslink 3	a	11 56	11 58		12 06					12 08	12 11	12 13	12 21				12 23	12 26	12 28		12 36		
Farringdon ⊖	a	11 58	12 01		12 08					12 11	12 13	12 16	12 23				12 26	12 28	12 31		12 38		
St Pancras International 15 ⊖	a	12 03	12 05		12 13					12 15	12 18	12 20	12 28				12 30	12 33	12 35		12 43		
Kentish Town ⊖	a	12 08									12 23		12 33					12 38					
Brixton ⊖	d								11 56						12 11								
London Victoria 15 ⊖	a						12 00	11 51	12 03					12 06	12 18	12 25							12 21

A From Brighton to Bedford
B From Canterbury West
C From Gravesend
D From Brighton to Cambridge
E From Sutton (Surrey) to St Albans City
F From Gatwick Airport to Bedford
G From Rainham (Kent) to Luton
H To London Charing Cross
I From Dover Priory
J From Horsham to Peterborough
K From Ashford International
L From Ramsgate

Table T195-R

Mondays to Fridays

16 December to 15 May

Sevenoaks and Otford, Orpington, Bromley South, Beckenham Junction, Catford - London

Station		SE	TL 1 A	TL B	TL 1 C	TL	SE ◇1 D	SE	SE E	TL 1 F	TL B	TL 1 G	TL	TL H	SE I	SE ◇1 J	SE ◇1 K	SE	TL 1 A	TL B	TL 1 C	TL
Sevenoaks 4	d												11 52		12 05							
Bat & Ball	d												11 55									
Otford 4	d						11 56						11 59									
Shoreham (Kent)	d												12 02									
Eynsford	d												12 05									
Swanley 4	d						12 05						12 11			12 17						
St Mary Cray	d						12 09						12 15			12 22						
Orpington 4	d	11 54				12 03									12 20			12 24				12 33
Petts Wood 4	d	11 57				12 06									12a23			12 27				12 36
Bickley 4	d	12 01				12 10							12 20					12 31				12 40
Bromley South 4	d	12 04				12 13	12 17	12 19					12 23			12 30	12 33	12 34				12 43
Shortlands 4	d	12 07				12 15		12 22					12 25					12 37				12 45
Ravensbourne	d					12 18							12 28									12 48
Beckenham Hill	d					12 20							12 30									12 50
Bellingham	d					12 22							12 32									12 52
Catford	d					12 25							12 35									12 55
Crofton Park	d					12 28							12 38									12 58
Lewisham 4	a																					
	d								12 32													
Nunhead 4	d					12 31			12 37				12 41									13 01
Peckham Rye 4	d					12 34			12 40				12 44									13 04
Denmark Hill 4	d					12 37			12 44				12 47			12 50						13 07
Beckenham Junction 4	d	12 10						12 25										12 40				
Kent House 4	d	12 12						12 27										12 42				
Penge East	d	12 14						12 29										12 44				
Sydenham Hill	d	12 18						12 33										12 48				
West Dulwich	d	12 20						12 35										12 50				
Herne Hill 4	d	12 23		12 27				12 38			12 42							12 53		12 57		
Loughborough Jn.	d			12 30							12 45									13 00		
Elephant & Castle ⊖	d			12 34		12 44					12 49		12 54							13 04		13 14
London Blackfriars 3 ⊖	d		12 37	12 39	12 42	12 49				12 52	12 54	12 57	12a59	13 04					13 07	13 09	13 12	13 19
City Thameslink 3	a		12 38	12 41	12 43	12 51				12 53	12 56	12 58		13 06					13 08	13 11	13 13	13 21
Farringdon ⊖	a		12 41	12 43	12 46	12 53				12 56	12 58	13 01		13 08					13 11	13 13	13 16	13 23
St Pancras International 15 ⊖	a		12 45	12 48	12 50	12 58				13 00	13 03	13 05		13 13					13 15	13 18	13 20	13 28
Kentish Town ⊖	a			12 53		13 03					13 08									13 23		13 33
Brixton ⊖	d	12 26						12 41										12 56				
London Victoria 15 ⊖	a	12 33					12 36	12 48	12 55							13 00	12 51	13 03				

Station		SE ◇1 L	SE	SE E	TL 1 F	TL B	TL 1 G	TL	TL H	SE I	SE ◇1 J	SE	TL 1 A	TL B	TL 1 C	TL	SE ◇1 D	SE	SE E	TL 1 F	TL B	TL 1 G	TL
Sevenoaks 4	d							12 22		12 35													12 52
Bat & Ball	d							12 25															12 55
Otford 4	d	12 26						12 29									12 56						12 59
Shoreham (Kent)	d							12 32															13 02
Eynsford	d							12 35															13 05
Swanley 4	d	12 37						12 41									13 05						13 11
St Mary Cray	d							12 45									13 09						13 15
Orpington 4	d									12 50		12 54				13 03							
Petts Wood 4	d									12a53		12 57				13 06							
Bickley 4	d							12 50				13 01				13 10							13 20
Bromley South 4	d	12 47	12 49					12 53			13 03	13 04				13 13	13 17	13 19					13 23
Shortlands 4	d		12 52					12 55				13 07				13 15		13 22					13 25
Ravensbourne	d							12 58								13 18							13 28
Beckenham Hill	d							13 00								13 20							13 30
Bellingham	d							13 02								13 22							13 32
Catford	d							13 05								13 25							13 35
Crofton Park	d							13 08								13 28							13 38
Lewisham 4	a																						
	d			13 02															13 32				
Nunhead 4	d			13 07				13 11								13 31			13 37				13 41
Peckham Rye 4	d			13 10				13 14								13 34			13 40				13 44
Denmark Hill 4	d			13 14				13 17								13 37			13 44				13 47
Beckenham Junction 4	d		12 55									13 10						13 25					
Kent House 4	d		12 57									13 12						13 27					
Penge East	d		12 59									13 14						13 29					
Sydenham Hill	d		13 03									13 18						13 33					
West Dulwich	d		13 05									13 20						13 35					
Herne Hill 4	d		13 08			13 12						13 23		13 27				13 38			13 42		
Loughborough Jn.	d					13 15								13 30							13 45		
Elephant & Castle ⊖	d					13 19		13 24						13 34		13 44					13 49		13 54
London Blackfriars 3 ⊖	d				13 22	13 24	13 27	13a29	13 34				13 37	13 39	13 42	13 49				13 52	13 54	13 57	13a59
City Thameslink 3	a				13 23	13 26	13 28		13 36				13 38	13 41	13 43	13 51				13 53	13 56	13 58	
Farringdon ⊖	a				13 26	13 28	13 31		13 38				13 41	13 43	13 46	13 53				13 56	13 58	14 01	
St Pancras International 15 ⊖	a				13 30	13 33	13 35		13 43				13 45	13 48	13 50	13 58				14 00	14 03	14 05	
Kentish Town ⊖	a					13 38								13 53		14 03					14 08		
Brixton ⊖	d		13 11									13 26						13 41					
London Victoria 15 ⊖	a	13 06	13 18	13 25							13 21	13 33					13 36	13 48	13 55				

A From Horsham to Peterborough
B From Sutton (Surrey) to St Albans City
C From Brighton to Bedford
D From Ashford International
E From Gravesend
F From Brighton to Cambridge
G From Gatwick Airport to Bedford
H From Rainham (Kent) to Luton
I To London Charing Cross
J From Dover Priory
K From Ramsgate
L From Canterbury West

NRT DECEMBER 19 EDITION

Table T195-R

Mondays to Fridays

16 December to 15 May

Sevenoaks and Otford, Orpington, Bromley South, Beckenham Junction, Catford - London

Station		TL A	SE B	SE ◇1 C	SE ◇1 D	SE	TL 1 E	TL F	TL 1 G	TL	SE ◇1 H	SE	SE I	TL 1 J	TL F	TL 1 K	TL	TL A	SE B	SE ◇1 C	SE	TL 1 E	TL F
Sevenoaks 4	d		13 05														13 22		13 35				
Bat & Ball	d																13 25						
Otford 4	d										13 26						13 29						
Shoreham (Kent)	d																13 32						
Eynsford	d																13 35						
Swanley 4	d			13 17							13 37						13 41						
St Mary Cray	d			13 22													13 45						
Orpington 4	d		13 20			13 24				13 33									13 50		13 54		
Petts Wood 4	d		13a23			13 27				13 36									13a53		13 57		
Bickley 4	d					13 31				13 40							13 50				14 01		
Bromley South 4	d			13 30	13 33	13 34				13 43	13 47	13 49					13 53			14 03	14 04		
Shortlands 4	d					13 37				13 45		13 52					13 55				14 07		
Ravensbourne	d									13 48							13 58						
Beckenham Hill	d									13 50							14 00						
Bellingham	d									13 52							14 02						
Catford	d									13 55							14 05						
Crofton Park	d									13 58							14 08						
Lewisham 4	a																						
	d												14 02										
Nunhead 4	d									14 01			14 07				14 11						
Peckham Rye 4	d									14 04			14 10				14 14						
Denmark Hill 4	d			13 50						14 07			14 14				14 17						
Beckenham Junction 4	d					13 40						13 55									14 10		
Kent House 4	d					13 42						13 57									14 12		
Penge East	d					13 44						13 59									14 14		
Sydenham Hill	d					13 48						14 03									14 18		
West Dulwich	d					13 50						14 05									14 20		
Herne Hill 4	d					13 53		13 57				14 08			14 12						14 23		14 27
Loughborough Jn.	d							14 00							14 15								14 30
Elephant & Castle ⊖	d							14 04		14 14					14 19		14 24						14 34
London Blackfriars 3 ⊖	d	14 04					14 07	14 09	14 12	14 19				14 22	14 24	14 27	14a29	14 34				14 37	14 39
City Thameslink 3	a	14 06					14 08	14 11	14 13	14 21				14 23	14 26	14 28		14 36				14 38	14 41
Farringdon ⊖	a	14 08					14 11	14 13	14 16	14 23				14 26	14 28	14 31		14 38				14 41	14 43
St Pancras International 15 ⊖	a	14 13					14 15	14 18	14 20	14 28				14 30	14 33	14 35		14 43				14 45	14 48
Kentish Town ⊖	a							14 23		14 33					14 38								14 53
Brixton ⊖	d					13 56						14 11									14 26		
London Victoria 15 ⊖	a			14 01	13 51	14 03					14 06	14 18	14 25							14 21	14 33		

Station		TL 1 G	TL	SE ◇1 L	SE	SE I	TL 1 J	TL F	TL 1 K	TL	TL A	SE B	SE ◇1 C	SE ◇1 D	SE	TL 1 E	TL F	TL 1 G	TL	SE ◇1 H	SE	SE I
Sevenoaks 4	d									13 52		14 05										
Bat & Ball	d									13 55												
Otford 4	d			13 56						13 59										14 26		
Shoreham (Kent)	d									14 02												
Eynsford	d									14 05												
Swanley 4	d			14 05						14 11			14 17							14 37		
St Mary Cray	d			14 09						14 15			14 22									
Orpington 4	d		14 03									14 20			14 24				14 33			
Petts Wood 4	d		14 06									14a23			14 27				14 36			
Bickley 4	d		14 10							14 20					14 31				14 40			
Bromley South 4	d		14 13	14 17	14 19					14 23			14 30	14 33	14 34				14 43	14 47	14 49	
Shortlands 4	d		14 15		14 22					14 25					14 37				14 45		14 52	
Ravensbourne	d		14 18							14 28									14 48			
Beckenham Hill	d		14 20							14 30									14 50			
Bellingham	d		14 22							14 32									14 52			
Catford	d		14 25							14 35									14 55			
Crofton Park	d		14 28							14 38									14 58			
Lewisham 4	a																					
	d					14 32																15 02
Nunhead 4	d		14 31			14 37				14 41									15 01			15 07
Peckham Rye 4	d		14 34			14 40				14 44									15 04			15 10
Denmark Hill 4	d		14 37			14 44				14 47			14 50						15 07			15 14
Beckenham Junction 4	d				14 25										14 40						14 55	
Kent House 4	d				14 27										14 42						14 57	
Penge East	d				14 29										14 44						14 59	
Sydenham Hill	d				14 33										14 48						15 03	
West Dulwich	d				14 35										14 50						15 05	
Herne Hill 4	d				14 38			14 42							14 53		14 57				15 08	
Loughborough Jn.	d							14 45									15 00					
Elephant & Castle ⊖	d		14 44					14 49		14 54							15 04		15 14			
London Blackfriars 3 ⊖	d	14 42	14 49				14 52	14 54	14 57	14a59	15 04					15 07	15 09	15 12	15 19			
City Thameslink 3	a	14 43	14 51				14 53	14 56	14 58		15 06					15 08	15 11	15 13	15 21			
Farringdon ⊖	a	14 46	14 53				14 56	14 58	15 01		15 08					15 11	15 13	15 16	15 23			
St Pancras International 15 ⊖	a	14 50	14 58				15 00	15 03	15 05		15 13					15 15	15 18	15 20	15 28			
Kentish Town ⊖	a		15 03					15 08									15 23		15 33			
Brixton ⊖	d				14 41										14 56						15 11	
London Victoria 15 ⊖	a			14 36	14 48	14 55						15 00	14 51		15 03					15 06	15 18	15 25

A From Rainham (Kent) to Luton
B To London Charing Cross
C From Dover Priory
D From Ramsgate
E From Horsham to Peterborough
F From Sutton (Surrey) to St Albans City
G From Brighton to Bedford
H From Canterbury West
I From Gravesend
J From Brighton to Cambridge
K From Gatwick Airport to Bedford
L From Ashford International

Table T195-R

Mondays to Fridays
16 December to 15 May

Sevenoaks and Otford, Orpington, Bromley South, Beckenham Junction, Catford - London

		TL ■ A	TL B	TL ■ C	TL	TL D	SE E	SE ◇■ F	SE	TL ■ G	TL B	TL ■ H	TL	SE ◇■ I	SE	SE J	TL ■ A	TL B	TL ■ C	TL	TL D	SE E	SE ◇■ F
Sevenoaks ■	d				14 22		14 35													14 52		15 05	
Bat & Ball	d				14 25															14 55			
Otford ■	d				14 29									14 56						14 59			
Shoreham (Kent)	d				14 32															15 02			
Eynsford	d				14 35															15 05			
Swanley ■	d				14 41									15 05						15 11			15 17
St Mary Cray	d				14 45									15 09						15 15			15 22
Orpington ■	d						14 50		14 54				15 03									15 20	
Petts Wood ■	d						14a53		14 57				15 06									15a23	
Bickley ■	d				14 50				15 01				15 10							15 20			
Bromley South ■	d				14 53			15 03	15 04				15 13	15 17	15 19					15 23			15 30
Shortlands ■	d				14 55				15 07				15 15		15 22					15 25			
Ravensbourne	d				14 58								15 18							15 28			
Beckenham Hill	d				15 00								15 20							15 30			
Bellingham	d				15 02								15 22							15 32			
Catford	d				15 05								15 25							15 35			
Crofton Park	d				15 08								15 28							15 38			
Lewisham ■	a																						
	d															15 32							
Nunhead ■	d				15 11								15 31			15 37				15 41			
Peckham Rye ■	d				15 14								15 34			15 40				15 44			
Denmark Hill ■	d				15 17								15 37			15 44				15 47			15 50
Beckenham Junction ■	d								15 10						15 25								
Kent House ■	d								15 12						15 27								
Penge East	d								15 14						15 29								
Sydenham Hill	d								15 18						15 33								
West Dulwich	d								15 20						15 35								
Herne Hill ■	d		15 12						15 23		15 27				15 38			15 42					
Loughborough Jn.	d		15 15								15 30							15 45					
Elephant & Castle	d		15 19		15 24						15 34		15 44					15 49		15 54			
London Blackfriars ■	d	15 22	15 24	15 27	15a29	15 34				15 37	15 39	15 42	15 49				15 52	15 54	15 57	15a59	16 04		
City Thameslink ■	a	15 23	15 26	15 28		15 36				15 38	15 41	15 43	15 51				15 53	15 56	15 58		16 06		
Farringdon	a	15 26	15 28	15 31		15 38				15 41	15 43	15 46	15 53				15 56	15 58	16 01		16 08		
St Pancras International ■	a	15 30	15 33	15 35		15 43				15 45	15 48	15 50	15 58				16 00	16 03	16 05		16 13		
Kentish Town	a		15 38								15 53		16 03					16 08			16 18		
Brixton	d								15 26						15 41								
London Victoria ■	a							15 21	15 33					15 36	15 48	15 55							16 01

		SE ◇■ K	SE	TL ■ G	TL B	TL ■ H	TL ■ C	TL L	SE ◇■ M	SE	SE J	TL ■ A	TL B	TL ■ C	TL	TL D	SE E	SE ◇■ F	SE	TL ■ G	TL B	TL ■ H
Sevenoaks ■	d														15 22		15 35					
Bat & Ball	d														15 25							
Otford ■	d								15 26						15 29							
Shoreham (Kent)	d														15 32							
Eynsford	d														15 35							
Swanley ■	d								15 35						15 41							
St Mary Cray	d								15 39						15 45							
Orpington ■	d		15 24					15 33									15 50		15 54			
Petts Wood ■	d		15 27					15 36									15a53		15 57			
Bickley ■	d		15 31					15 40							15 50				16 01			
Bromley South ■	d	15 33	15 34					15 43	15 47	15 49					15 53			16 03	16 04			
Shortlands ■	d		15 37					15 45		15 52					15 55				16 07			
Ravensbourne	d							15 48							15 58							
Beckenham Hill	d							15 50							16 00							
Bellingham	d							15 52							16 02							
Catford	d							15 55							16 05							
Crofton Park	d							15 58							16 08							
Lewisham ■	a																					
	d										16 02											
Nunhead ■	d							16 01			16 08				16 11							
Peckham Rye ■	d							16 04			16 11				16 14							
Denmark Hill ■	d							16 07			16 14				16 17							
Beckenham Junction ■	d		15 40							15 55									16 10			
Kent House ■	d		15 42							15 57									16 12			
Penge East	d		15 44							15 59									16 14			
Sydenham Hill	d		15 48							16 03									16 18			
West Dulwich	d		15 50							16 05									16 20			
Herne Hill ■	d		15 53		15 57					16 08			16 12						16 23		16 27	
Loughborough Jn.	d				16 00								16 15								16 30	
Elephant & Castle	d				16 04			16 14					16 19		16 24						16 34	
London Blackfriars ■	d			16 07	16 09	16 12	16 17	16 19				16 22	16 24	16 27	16a29	16 34				16 37	16 39	16 42
City Thameslink ■	a			16 08	16 11	16 13	16 18	16 21				16 23	16 26	16 28		16 36				16 38	16 41	16 43
Farringdon	a			16 11	16 13	16 16	16 21	16 23				16 26	16 28	16 31		16 38				16 41	16 43	16 46
St Pancras International ■	a			16 15	16 18	16 20	16 25	16 28				16 30	16 33	16 35		16 43				16 45	16 48	16 50
Kentish Town	a							16 33								16 48						
Brixton	d		15 56							16 11									16 26			
London Victoria ■	a	15 51	16 03						16 06	16 18	16 25							16 21	16 33			

A From Brighton to Cambridge
B From Sutton (Surrey) to St Albans City
C From Gatwick Airport to Bedford
D From Rainham (Kent) to Luton
E To London Charing Cross
F From Dover Priory
G From Horsham to Peterborough
H From Brighton to Bedford
I From Ashford International
J From Gravesend
K From Ramsgate
L To Luton
M From Canterbury West

Table T195-R

Mondays to Fridays
16 December to 15 May

Sevenoaks and Otford, Orpington, Bromley South, Beckenham Junction, Catford - London

		TL ■ A	TL B	SE ◇■ C	SE	SE D	TL ■ E	TL F	TL ■ A	TL	TL ■ G	SE H	SE ◇ I	SE ◇■ J	SE	TL K	TL ■ L	TL F	TL ■ M	TL ■ A	TL B	SE ◇■ N	SE
Sevenoaks ■	d									15 52		16 05											
Bat & Ball	d									15 55													
Otford ■	d			15 56						15 59												16 26	
Shoreham (Kent)	d									16 02													
Eynsford	d									16 05													
Swanley ■	d			16 05						16 11			16 17									16 35	
St Mary Cray	d			16 09						16 15			16 22									16 39	
Orpington ■	d		16 03									16 20			16 24						16 33		
Petts Wood ■	d		16 06									16a23			16 27						16 36		
Bickley ■	d		16 10							16 20					16 31						16 40		
Bromley South ■	d		16 13	16 17	16 19					16 23			16 30	16 33	16 34						16 43	16 47	16 49
Shortlands ■	d		16 15		16 22					16 25					16 37						16 45		16 52
Ravensbourne	d		16 18							16 28											16 48		
Beckenham Hill	d		16 20							16 30											16 50		
Bellingham	d		16 22							16 32											16 52		
Catford	d		16 25							16 35											16 55		
Crofton Park	d		16 28							16 38											16 58		
Lewisham ■	a																						
	d					16 32																	
Nunhead ■	d		16 31			16 37				16 41											17 01		
Peckham Rye ■	d		16 34			16 40				16 44											17 04		
Denmark Hill ■	d		16 37			16 44				16 47			16 50								17 07		
Beckenham Junction ■	d				16 25										16 40								16 55
Kent House ■	d				16 27										16 42								16 57
Penge East	d				16 29										16 44								16 59
Sydenham Hill	d				16 33										16 48								17 03
West Dulwich	d				16 35										16 50								17 05
Herne Hill ■	d				16 38			16 42							16 53			16 57					17 08
Loughborough Jn.	d							16 45										17 00					
Elephant & Castle	d		16 44					16 49		16 54								17 04			17 14		
London Blackfriars ■	d	16 47	16 49				16 52	16 54	16 57	16a59	17 02					17 04	17 07	17 09	17 12	17 17	17 19		
City Thameslink ■	a	16 48	16 51				16 53	16 56	16 58		17 03					17 06	17 08	17 11	17 13	17 18	17 21		
Farringdon	a	16 51	16 53				16 56	16 58	17 01		17 06					17 08	17 11	17 13	17 16	17 21	17 23		
St Pancras International ■	a	16 55	16 58				17 00	17 03	17 05		17 10					17 13	17 15	17 18	17 20	17 25	17 28		
Kentish Town	a		17 03													17 18					17 33		
Brixton	d				16 41										16 56								17 11
London Victoria ■	a			16 36	16 48	16 55							17 01	16 51	17 03							17 06	17 18

		SE D	TL ■ E	TL F	TL ■ A	TL	TL ■ G	SE H	SE ◇■ I	SE	TL K	TL ■ L	TL F	TL ■ M	SE	TL ■ A	TL B	SE ◇■ C	SE	SE D	TL ■ E	TL F	TL ■ A
Sevenoaks ■	d					16 22		16 35															
Bat & Ball	d					16 25																	
Otford ■	d					16 29												16 56					
Shoreham (Kent)	d					16 32																	
Eynsford	d					16 35																	
Swanley ■	d					16 41												17 05					
St Mary Cray	d					16 45												17 09					
Orpington ■	d							16 50		16 54							17 03						
Petts Wood ■	d							16a53		16 57							17 06						
Bickley ■	d					16 50				17 01							17 10						
Bromley South ■	d					16 53			17 03	17 04							17 13	17 17	17 19				
Shortlands ■	d					16 55				17 07							17 15		17 22				
Ravensbourne	d					16 58											17 18						
Beckenham Hill	d					17 00											17 20						
Bellingham	d					17 02											17 22						
Catford	d					17 05											17 25						
Crofton Park	d					17 08											17 28						
Lewisham ■	a																						
	d	17 02																		17 32			
Nunhead ■	d	17 07				17 11											17 31			17 37			
Peckham Rye ■	d	17 10				17 14											17 34			17 40			
Denmark Hill ■	d	17 14				17 17											17 37			17 44			
Beckenham Junction ■	d									17 10					17 24				17 25				
Kent House ■	d									17 12									17 27				
Penge East	d									17 14									17 29				
Sydenham Hill	d									17 18									17 33				
West Dulwich	d									17 20									17 35				
Herne Hill ■	d			17 12						17 23			17 27		17 32				17 38			17 42	
Loughborough Jn.	d			17 15									17 30									17 45	
Elephant & Castle	d			17 19		17 24							17 34				17 44					17 49	
London Blackfriars ■	d		17 22	17 24	17 27	17a29	17 32				17 34	17 37	17 39	17 42	17a43	17 47	17 49				17 52	17 54	17 57
City Thameslink ■	a		17 23	17 26	17 28		17 33				17 36	17 38	17 41	17 43		17 48	17 51				17 53	17 56	17 58
Farringdon	a		17 26	17 28	17 31		17 36				17 38	17 41	17 43	17 46		17 51	17 53				17 56	17 58	18 01
St Pancras International ■	a		17 30	17 33	17 35		17 40				17 43	17 45	17 48	17 50		17 55	17 58				18 00	18 03	18 05
Kentish Town	a										17 48						18 03						
Brixton	d									17 26									17 41				
London Victoria ■	a	17 25							17 21	17 33								17 36	17 48	17 55			

A From Gatwick Airport to Bedford
B To Luton
C From Ashford International
D From Gravesend
E From Brighton to Cambridge
F From Sutton (Surrey) to St Albans City
G From Three Bridges to Bedford
H To London Charing Cross
I From Dover Priory
J From Ramsgate
K From Rainham (Kent) to Luton
L From Horsham to Peterborough
M From Brighton to Bedford
N From Canterbury West

Table T195-R

Mondays to Fridays
16 December to 15 May

Sevenoaks and Otford, Orpington, Bromley South, Beckenham Junction, Catford - London

		TL	TL ■ A	SE B	SE ■ C	SE ◇■ D	SE	TL E	TL ■ F	TL G	TL ■ H	SE	TL ■ I	TL J	SE ◇■ K	SE	SE L	TL ■ M	TL G	TL ■ I	TL	TL E
Sevenoaks	d	16 52		17 06																	17 22	
Bat & Ball	d	16 55																			17 25	
Otford	d	16 59													17 26						17 29	
Shoreham (Kent)	d	17 02																			17 32	
Eynsford	d	17 05																			17 35	
Swanley	d	17 11			17 17										17 35						17 41	
St Mary Cray	d	17 15			17 22										17 39						17 45	
Orpington	d			17 19			17 24							17 33								
Petts Wood	d			17a22			17 27							17 36								
Bickley	d	17 20					17 31							17 40							17 50	
Bromley South	d	17 23			17 30	17 34	17 34							17 43	17 47	17 49					17 53	
Shortlands	d	17 25					17 37							17 45		17 52					17 55	
Ravensbourne	d	17 28												17 48							17 58	
Beckenham Hill	d	17 30												17 50							18 00	
Bellingham	d	17 32												17 52							18 02	
Catford	d	17 35												17 55							18 05	
Crofton Park	d	17 38												17 58							18 08	
Lewisham	a																					
	d																18 00					
Nunhead	d	17 41												18 01			18 07				18 11	
Peckham Rye	d	17 44												18 04			18 10				18 14	
Denmark Hill	d	17 47			17 50									18 07			18 14				18 17	
Beckenham Junction	d						17 40					17 54				17 55						
Kent House	d						17 42									17 57						
Penge East	d						17 44									17 59						
Sydenham Hill	d						17 48									18 03						
West Dulwich	d						17 50									18 05						
Herne Hill	d						17 53			17 57		18 02				18 08			18 12			
Loughborough Jn.	d									18 00									18 15			
Elephant & Castle ⊖	d	17 54								18 04				18 14					18 19		18 24	
London Blackfriars ⊖	d	17a59	18 02					18 04	18 07	18 09	18 12	18a13	18 17	18 19				18 22	18 24	18 27	18a29	18 34
City Thameslink	a		18 03					18 06	18 08	18 11	18 13		18 18	18 21				18 23	18 26	18 28		18 36
Farringdon ⊖	a		18 06					18 08	18 11	18 13	18 16		18 21	18 23				18 26	18 28	18 31		18 38
St Pancras International ⊖	a		18 10					18 13	18 15	18 18	18 20		18 25	18 28				18 30	18 33	18 35		18 43
Kentish Town ⊖	a							18 18						18 33								18 48
Brixton ⊖	d						17 56									18 11						
London Victoria ⊖	a				18 00	17 54	18 03								18 06	18 18	18 25					

		SE B	SE ■ C	SE ◇■ N	SE	TL ■ F	TL G	TL ■ H	SE	TL ■ O	TL J	SE ◇■ P	SE	SE Q	TL ■ M	TL G	TL ■ I	TL	TL E	SE B	SE ■ C	SE ◇■ D	SE
Sevenoaks	d	17 34																17 52		18 02			
Bat & Ball	d																	17 55					
Otford	d											17 56						17 59					
Shoreham (Kent)	d																	18 02					
Eynsford	d																	18 05					
Swanley	d		17 47									18 05						18 11			18 17		
St Mary Cray	d		17 52									18 09						18 15			18 22		
Orpington	d	17 49			17 54						18 02									18 19			18 22
Petts Wood	d	17a52			17 57						18 05									18a22			18 26
Bickley	d				18 01						18 10							18 20					18 30
Bromley South	d		18 00	18 03	18 04						18 13	18 17	18 19					18 23			18 30	18 33	18 34
Shortlands	d				18 07						18 15		18 22					18 25					18 37
Ravensbourne	d										18 18							18 28					
Beckenham Hill	d										18 20							18 30					
Bellingham	d										18 22							18 32					
Catford	d										18 25							18 35					
Crofton Park	d										18 28							18 38					
Lewisham	a																						
	d													18 32									
Nunhead	d										18 31			18 37				18 41					
Peckham Rye	d										18 34			18 40				18 44					
Denmark Hill	d		18 20								18 37			18 44				18 47			18 50		
Beckenham Junction	d				18 10				18 24				18 25										18 40
Kent House	d				18 12								18 27										18 42
Penge East	d				18 14								18 29										18 44
Sydenham Hill	d				18 18								18 33										18 48
West Dulwich	d				18 20								18 35										18 50
Herne Hill	d				18 23		18 27		18 32				18 38			18 42							18 53
Loughborough Jn.	d						18 30									18 45							
Elephant & Castle ⊖	d						18 34				18 44					18 49		18 54					
London Blackfriars ⊖	d					18 37	18 39	18 42	18a43	18 47	18 49				18 52	18 54	18 57	18a59	19 04				
City Thameslink	a					18 38	18 41	18 43		18 48	18 51				18 53	18 56	18 58		19 06				
Farringdon ⊖	a					18 41	18 43	18 46		18 51	18 53				18 56	18 58	19 01		19 08				
St Pancras International ⊖	a					18 45	18 48	18 50		18 55	18 58				19 00	19 03	19 05		19 13				
Kentish Town ⊖	a										19 03								19 18				
Brixton ⊖	d				18 26								18 41										18 56
London Victoria ⊖	a		18 30	18 21	18 33							18 36	18 48	18 57							19 00	18 52	19 03

A From Three Bridges to Bedford
B To London Charing Cross
C From Gillingham (Kent)
D From Ramsgate
E From Rainham (Kent) to Luton
F From Horsham to Peterborough
G From Sutton (Surrey) to St Albans City
H From Brighton to Bedford
I From Gatwick Airport to Bedford
J To Luton
K From Canterbury West
L From Gravesend
M From Brighton to Cambridge
N From Dover Priory
O From East Grinstead to Bedford
P From Ashford International
Q From Dartford

Table T195-R

Mondays to Fridays
16 December to 15 May

Sevenoaks and Otford, Orpington, Bromley South, Beckenham Junction, Catford - London

		TL ■ A	TL B	TL ■ C	TL ■ D	TL E	SE ◇■ F	SE	SE	SE G	TL ■ H	TL B	TL ■ I	TL	TL J	SE K	SE ◇■ L	SE M	SE	TL ■ A	TL B	TL ■ C
Sevenoaks	d													18 22		18 35						
Bat & Ball	d													18 25								
Otford	d						18 26							18 29								
Shoreham (Kent)	d													18 32								
Eynsford	d													18 35								
Swanley	d						18 35							18 41								
St Mary Cray	d						18 39							18 45								
Orpington	d					18 33										18 50			18 54			
Petts Wood	d					18 36										18a53			18 57			
Bickley	d					18 40								18 50					19 01			
Bromley South	d					18 43	18 47	18 49						18 53			19 04		19 04			
Shortlands	d					18 45		18 52						18 55					19 07			
Ravensbourne	d					18 48								18 58								
Beckenham Hill	d					18 50								19 00								
Bellingham	d					18 52								19 02								
Catford	d					18 55								19 05								
Crofton Park	d					18 58								19 08								
Lewisham	a																					
	d									19 00								19 14				
Nunhead	d					19 01				19 07				19 11								
Peckham Rye	d					19 04				19 10				19 14								
Denmark Hill	d					19 07				19 14				19 17								
Beckenham Junction	d							18 55	19 01										19 10			
Kent House	d							18 57											19 12			
Penge East	d							18 59											19 14			
Sydenham Hill	d							19 03											19 18			
West Dulwich	d							19 05											19 20			
Herne Hill	d		18 57					19 08				19 12							19 23		19 27	
Loughborough Jn.	d		19 00									19 15									19 30	
Elephant & Castle ⊖	d		19 04			19 14						19 19		19 24							19 34	
London Blackfriars ⊖	d	19 07	19 09	19 12	19 17	19 19					19 22	19 24	19 27	19a29	19 34					19 37	19 39	19 42
City Thameslink	a	19 08	19 11	19 13	19 18	19 21					19 23	19 26	19 28		19 36					19 38	19 41	19 43
Farringdon ⊖	a	19 11	19 13	19 16	19 21	19 23					19 26	19 28	19 31		19 38					19 41	19 43	19 46
St Pancras International ⊖	a	19 15	19 18	19 20	19 25	19 28					19 30	19 33	19 35		19 43					19 45	19 48	19 50
Kentish Town ⊖	a											19 38									19 53	
Brixton ⊖	d							19 11											19 26			
London Victoria ⊖	a						19 06	19 18	19 24	19 27							19 24	19 33	19 34			

		TL ■ D	TL E	SE ◇■ N	SE	SE	SE G	TL ■ H	TL B	TL ■ I	TL	TL J	SE K	SE O	SE ◇■ L	SE	TL ■ A	TL B	TL ■ C	TL	SE ◇■ F	SE	SE P
Sevenoaks	d										18 52		19 05										
Bat & Ball	d										18 55												
Otford	d			18 56							18 59										19 26		
Shoreham (Kent)	d										19 02												
Eynsford	d										19 05												
Swanley	d			19 05							19 11			19 18							19 35		
St Mary Cray	d			19 09							19 15			19 23							19 39		
Orpington	d		19 03										19 20			19 24				19 33			
Petts Wood	d		19 06										19a23			19 27				19 36			
Bickley	d		19 10								19 20					19 31				19 40			
Bromley South	d		19 13	19 17	19 19						19 23			19 30	19 33	19 34				19 43	19 47	19 49	
Shortlands	d		19 15		19 22						19 25					19 37				19 45		19 52	
Ravensbourne	d		19 18								19 28									19 48			
Beckenham Hill	d		19 20								19 30									19 50			
Bellingham	d		19 22								19 32									19 52			
Catford	d		19 25								19 35									19 55			
Crofton Park	d		19 28								19 38									19 58			
Lewisham	a																						
	d						19 32																20 02
Nunhead	d		19 31				19 37				19 41									20 01			20 07
Peckham Rye	d		19 34				19 40				19 44									20 04			20 10
Denmark Hill	d		19 37				19 44				19 47			19 50						20 07			20 14
Beckenham Junction	d				19 25	19 31										19 40						19 55	
Kent House	d				19 27											19 42						19 57	
Penge East	d				19 29											19 44						19 59	
Sydenham Hill	d				19 33											19 48						20 03	
West Dulwich	d				19 35											19 50						20 05	
Herne Hill	d				19 38				19 42							19 53		19 57				20 08	
Loughborough Jn.	d								19 45									20 00					
Elephant & Castle ⊖	d		19 44						19 49		19 54							20 04		20 14			
London Blackfriars ⊖	d	19 47	19 49					19 52	19 54	19 57	19a59	20 04					20 07	20 09	20 12	20 19			
City Thameslink	a	19 48	19 51					19 53	19 56	19 58		20 06					20 08	20 11	20 13	20 21			
Farringdon ⊖	a	19 51	19 53					19 56	19 58	20 01		20 08					20 11	20 13	20 16	20 23			
St Pancras International ⊖	a	19 55	19 58					20 00	20 03	20 05		20 13					20 15	20 18	20 20	20 28			
Kentish Town ⊖	a								20 08									20 23		20 33			
Brixton ⊖	d				19 41											19 56						20 11	
London Victoria ⊖	a			19 37	19 48	19 54	19 55							20 00	19 54	20 03					20 06	20 18	20 25

A From Horsham to Peterborough
B From Sutton (Surrey) to St Albans City
C From Brighton to Bedford
D From East Grinstead to Bedford
E To West Hampstead Thameslink
F From Canterbury West
G From Dartford
H From Brighton to Cambridge
I From Gatwick Airport to Bedford
J From Rainham (Kent) to Luton
K To London Charing Cross
L From Ramsgate
M From London Charing Cross
N From Ashford International
O From Rochester
P From Gravesend

Table T195-R

Mondays to Fridays

16 December to 15 May

Sevenoaks and Otford, Orpington, Bromley South, Beckenham Junction, Catford - London

		TL	TL	TL	TL	TL		SE	SE	SE	TL	TL	TL	TL	SE	SE		TL	SE	TL	TL	TL	SE	SE	SE
		■		■					◇■		■	■	■		◇■					■				■	◇■
		A	B	C		D		E	F		G	B	H		I			B	J	C		D	E	K	L
Sevenoaks	d				19 22			19 35													19 52		20 05		
Bat & Ball	d				19 25																19 55				
Otford	d				19 29										19 56						19 59				
Shoreham (Kent)	d				19 32																20 02				
Eynsford	d				19 35																20 05				
Swanley	d				19 41										20 05						20 11			20 18	
St Mary Cray	d				19 45										20 09						20 15			20 23	
Orpington	d							19 50		19 54				20 03									20 20		
Petts Wood	d							19a53		19 57				20 06									20a23		
Bickley	d				19 50					20 01				20 10							20 20				
Bromley South	d				19 53				20 03	20 04				20 13	20 17	20 19					20 23			20 30	20 33
Shortlands	d				19 55					20 07				20 15		20 22					20 25				
Ravensbourne	d				19 58									20 18							20 28				
Beckenham Hill	d				20 00									20 20							20 30				
Bellingham	d				20 02									20 22							20 32				
Catford	d				20 05									20 25							20 35				
Crofton Park	d				20 08									20 28							20 38				
Lewisham	a																								
	d																		20 32						
Nunhead	d				20 11									20 31					20 37		20 41				
Peckham Rye	d				20 14									20 34					20 40		20 44				
Denmark Hill	d				20 17									20 37					20 44		20 47			20 50	
Beckenham Junction	d									20 10						20 25									
Kent House	d									20 12						20 27									
Penge East	d									20 14						20 29									
Sydenham Hill	d									20 18						20 33									
West Dulwich	d									20 20						20 35									
Herne Hill	d		20 12							20 23		20 27				20 38		20 42							
Loughborough Jn.	d		20 15									20 30						20 45							
Elephant & Castle	d		20 19		20 24							20 34		20 44				20 49			20 54				
London Blackfriars	d	20 22	20 24	20 27	20a29	20 34					20 37	20 39	20 42	20 49				20 54		20 57	20a59	21 04			
City Thameslink	a	20 23	20 26	20 28		20 36					20 38	20 41	20 43	20 51				20 56		20 58		21 06			
Farringdon	a	20 26	20 28	20 31		20 38					20 41	20 43	20 46	20 53				20 58		21 01		21 08			
St Pancras International	a	20 30	20 33	20 35		20 43					20 45	20 48	20 50	20 58				21 03		21 05		21 13			
Kentish Town	a		20 38									20 53		21 03				21 08				21 18			
Brixton	d									20 26						20 41									
London Victoria	a								20 21	20 33					20 36	20 48			20 55					21 00	20 51

		SE		TL	TL	TL	TL	SE	SE	SE	TL	TL		TL	TL	TL	SE	SE	SE	TL	TL	TL		TL	SE
				■	■			◇■			■			■				◇■		■		■			◇■
				G	H	B		I		M	A	B		C		D	E	F		G	B	H			I
Sevenoaks	d														20 22		20 35								
Bat & Ball	d														20 25										
Otford	d							20 26							20 29										20 56
Shoreham (Kent)	d														20 32										
Eynsford	d														20 35										
Swanley	d							20 37							20 41										21 05
St Mary Cray	d														20 45										21 09
Orpington	d	20 24					20 33										20 50		20 54					21 03	
Petts Wood	d	20 27					20 36										20a53		20 57					21 06	
Bickley	d	20 31					20 40								20 50				21 01					21 10	
Bromley South	d	20 34					20 43	20 47	20 49						20 53			21 03	21 04					21 13	21 17
Shortlands	d	20 37					20 45		20 52						20 55				21 07					21 15	
Ravensbourne	d						20 48								20 58									21 18	
Beckenham Hill	d						20 50								21 00									21 20	
Bellingham	d						20 52								21 02									21 22	
Catford	d						20 55								21 05									21 25	
Crofton Park	d						20 58								21 08									21 28	
Lewisham	a																								
	d									21 02															
Nunhead	d						21 01			21 07					21 11									21 31	
Peckham Rye	d						21 04			21 10					21 14									21 34	
Denmark Hill	d						21 07			21 14					21 17									21 37	
Beckenham Junction	d	20 40							20 55										21 10						
Kent House	d	20 42							20 57										21 12						
Penge East	d	20 44							20 59										21 14						
Sydenham Hill	d	20 48							21 03										21 18						
West Dulwich	d	20 50							21 05										21 20						
Herne Hill	d	20 53				21 04			21 08			21 12							21 23		21 27				
Loughborough Jn.	d					21 07						21 15									21 30				
Elephant & Castle	d					21 11	21 14					21 19			21 24						21 34			21 44	
London Blackfriars	d			21 07	21 12	21 17	21 19				21 22	21 24		21 27	21a29	21 34				21 37	21 39	21 42		21 49	
City Thameslink	a			21 08	21 13	21 18	21 21				21 23	21 26		21 28		21 36				21 38	21 41	21 43		21 51	
Farringdon	a			21 11	21 16	21 21	21 23				21 26	21 28		21 31		21 38				21 41	21 43	21 46		21 53	
St Pancras International	a			21 15	21 20	21 25	21 28				21 30	21 33		21 35		21 43				21 45	21 48	21 50		21 58	
Kentish Town	a						21 33					21 38									21 53			22 03	
Brixton	d	20 56							21 11										21 26						
London Victoria	a	21 03						21 07	21 18	21 25								21 22	21 33						21 36

A From Brighton to Cambridge
B From Sutton (Surrey) to St Albans City
C From Gatwick Airport to Bedford
D From Rainham (Kent) to Luton
E To London Charing Cross
F From Dover Priory
G From Horsham to Peterborough
H From Brighton to Bedford
I From Ashford International
J From Dartford
K From Rochester
L From Ramsgate
M From Gravesend

Table T195-R

Mondays to Fridays

16 December to 15 May

Sevenoaks and Otford, Orpington, Bromley South, Beckenham Junction, Catford - London

		SE	TL	SE	TL	TL	TL	SE		SE	SE	SE	TL	TL	TL	TL	SE	SE		SE	TL	TL	TL	TL	TL
					■					■	◇■		■		■		◇■				■		■		
			A	B	C		D	E		F	G		H	I	J		K			B	L	I	C		D
Sevenoaks	d					20 52		21 05																21 22	
Bat & Ball	d					20 55																		21 25	
Otford	d					20 59											21 26							21 29	
Shoreham (Kent)	d					21 02																		21 32	
Eynsford	d					21 05																		21 35	
Swanley	d					21 11				21 17							21 37							21 41	
St Mary Cray	d					21 15				21 22														21 45	
Orpington	d							21 20				21 24				21 33									
Petts Wood	d							21a23				21 27				21 36									
Bickley	d					21 20						21 31				21 40								21 50	
Bromley South	d	21 19				21 23				21 30	21 33	21 34				21 43	21 47	21 49						21 53	
Shortlands	d	21 22				21 25						21 37				21 45		21 52						21 55	
Ravensbourne	d					21 28										21 48								21 58	
Beckenham Hill	d					21 30										21 50								22 00	
Bellingham	d					21 32										21 52								22 02	
Catford	d					21 35										21 55								22 05	
Crofton Park	d					21 38										21 58								22 08	
Lewisham	a																								
	d			21 32																22 02					
Nunhead	d			21 37		21 41										22 01				22 07				22 11	
Peckham Rye	d			21 40		21 44										22 04				22 10				22 14	
Denmark Hill	d			21 44		21 47				21 50						22 07				22 14				22 17	
Beckenham Junction	d	21 25										21 40						21 55							
Kent House	d	21 27										21 42						21 57							
Penge East	d	21 29										21 44						21 59							
Sydenham Hill	d	21 33										21 48						22 03							
West Dulwich	d	21 35										21 50						22 05							
Herne Hill	d	21 38	21 42									21 53		21 57				22 08				22 12			
Loughborough Jn.	d		21 45											22 00								22 15			
Elephant & Castle	d		21 49			21 54								22 04		22 14						22 19		22 24	
London Blackfriars	d		21 54		21 57	21a59	22 04						22 07	22 09	22 12	22 19					22 22	22 24	22 27	22a29	22 34
City Thameslink	a		21 56		21 58		22 06						22 08	22 11	22 13	22 21					22 23	22 26	22 28		22 36
Farringdon	a		21 58		22 01		22 08						22 11	22 13	22 16	22 23					22 26	22 28	22 31		22 38
St Pancras International	a		22 03		22 05		22 13						22 15	22 18	22 20	22 28					22 30	22 33	22 35		22 43
Kentish Town	a		22 08											22 23		22 33						22 38			
Brixton	d	21 41										21 56						22 11							
London Victoria	a	21 49		21 55						22 00	21 51	22 03					22 06	22 18		22 25					

		SE	SE	SE		TL	TL	TL	TL	SE	SE	TL	SE	TL		TL	SE	SE	SE	SE	TL	TL	TL	TL	
			◇■			■		■		◇■								◇■	◇■		■	■			
		E	M			H	I	J	N	K		I	B			D	E	F	G		H	J	I		
Sevenoaks	d	21 35												21 52			22 05								
Bat & Ball	d													21 55											
Otford	d									21 56				21 59											
Shoreham (Kent)	d													22 02											
Eynsford	d													22 05											
Swanley	d									22 05				22 11				22 17							
St Mary Cray	d									22 09				22 15				22 22							
Orpington	d	21 50		21 54					22 03								22 20			22 24				22 33	
Petts Wood	d	21a53		21 57					22 06								22a23			22 27				22 36	
Bickley	d			22 01					22 10					22 20						22 31				22 40	
Bromley South	d		22 03	22 04					22 13	22 17	22 19			22 23				22 30	22 33	22 34				22 43	
Shortlands	d			22 07					22 15		22 22			22 25						22 37				22 45	
Ravensbourne	d								22 18					22 28										22 48	
Beckenham Hill	d								22 20					22 30										22 50	
Bellingham	d								22 22					22 32										22 52	
Catford	d								22 25					22 35										22 55	
Crofton Park	d								22 28					22 38										22 58	
Lewisham	a																								
	d												22 32												
Nunhead	d								22 31				22 37	22 41										23 01	
Peckham Rye	d								22 34				22 40	22 44										23 04	
Denmark Hill	d								22 37				22 44	22 47				22 50						23 07	
Beckenham Junction	d			22 10							22 25									22 40					
Kent House	d			22 12							22 27									22 42					
Penge East	d			22 14							22 29									22 44					
Sydenham Hill	d			22 18							22 33									22 48					
West Dulwich	d			22 20							22 35									22 50					
Herne Hill	d			22 23			22 27				22 38	22 44								22 53			23 04		
Loughborough Jn.	d						22 30					22 47											23 07		
Elephant & Castle	d						22 34		22 44			22 51		22 54									23 11	23 14	
London Blackfriars	d					22 37	22 39	22 42	22 49			22 59		22a59		23 04					23 07	23 12	23 17	23a19	
City Thameslink	a					22 38	22 41	22 43	22 51																
Farringdon	a					22 41	22 43	22 46	22 53			23 03				23 08					23 11	23 16	23 21		
St Pancras International	a					22 45	22 48	22 50	22 58			23 08				23 13					23 15	23 20	23 25		
Kentish Town	a						22 53					23 13											23 30		
Brixton	d			22 26							22 41									22 56					
London Victoria	a		22 22	22 33						22 36	22 48		22 55					23 00	22 51	23 03					

A From Sutton (Surrey) to St Albans City
B From Gravesend
C From Gatwick Airport to Bedford
D From Rainham (Kent) to West Hampstead Thameslink
E To London Charing Cross
F From Gillingham (Kent)
G From Ramsgate
H From Horsham to Peterborough
I From Sutton (Surrey) to Bedford
J From Brighton to Bedford
K From Ashford International
L From Brighton to Cambridge
M From Dover Priory
N To West Hampstead Thameslink

Table T195-R

Mondays to Fridays

16 December to 15 May

Sevenoaks and Otford, Orpington, Bromley South, Beckenham Junction, Catford - London

		TL	SE	SE	TL	SE	TL	TL	SE	SE		SE	TL	TL	TL	TL	SE	SE	SE	TL		SE MTO	SE WThFO	SE	TL
		1	◇1							◇1			1	1			◇1							◇1	
		A	B		C	D		E	F	G			H	I	C		B		D			J	F	K	C
Sevenoaks	d						22 22		22 35											22 52		23 05	23 05		
Bat & Ball	d						22 25													22 55					
Otford	d		22 27				22 29										22 56			22 59					
Shoreham (Kent)	d						22 32													23 02					
Eynsford	d						22 35													23 05					
Swanley	d		22 37				22 41			22 47							23 05			23 11					
St Mary Cray	d						22 45			22 52							23 09			23 15					
Orpington	d								22 50			22 54				23 03						23 20	23 20		
Petts Wood	d								22a53			22 57				23 06						23 23	23a23		
Bickley	d						22 50					23 01				23 10				23 20					
Bromley South	d		22 47	22 49			22 53			23 00		23 04				23 13	23 17	23 19		23 23				23 33	
Shortlands	d			22 52			22 55					23 07				23 15		23 22		23 25					
Ravensbourne	d						22 58									23 18				23 28					
Beckenham Hill	d						23 00									23 20				23 30					
Bellingham	d						23 02									23 22				23 32					
Catford	d						23 05									23 25				23 35					
Crofton Park	d						23 08									23 28				23 38					
Lewisham	a																					23 40			
	d					23 02													23 32						
Nunhead	d					23 07	23 11									23 31			23 37	23 41					
Peckham Rye	d					23 10	23 14									23 34			23 40	23 44					
Denmark Hill	d					23 14	23 17			23 20						23 37			23 44	23 47					
Beckenham Junction	d			22 55								23 10						23 25							
Kent House	d			22 57								23 12						23 27							
Penge East	d			22 59								23 14						23 29							
Sydenham Hill	d			23 03								23 18						23 33							
West Dulwich	d			23 05								23 20						23 35							
Herne Hill	d			23 08	23 14							23 23			23 34			23 38							23 44
Loughborough Jn.	d				23 17										23 37										23 47
Elephant & Castle	d				23 21		23 24								23 41	23 44				23 54					23 54
London Blackfriars	d	23 22			23 29		23a29	23 34					23 37	23 42	23 49	23a49				23a59					00 02
City Thameslink	a																								
Farringdon	a	23 26			23 33			23 38					23 41	23 46	23 53										00 06
St Pancras International	a	23 30			23 37			23 43					23 45	23 50	23 57										00 10
Kentish Town	a				23 42										00 01										
Brixton	d			23 11								23 26						23 41							
London Victoria	a		23 06	23 18		23 25				23 31		23 33					23 37	23 48	23 55					00 03	

		SE	TL	TL	SE WThFO	SE MTO		SE	SE	SE
								◇1	◇1	
			C		F	J		L	G	
Sevenoaks	d			23 22	23 35	23 35				
Bat & Ball	d			23 25						
Otford	d			23 29				23 36		
Shoreham (Kent)	d			23 32						
Eynsford	d			23 35						
Swanley	d			23 41				23 45	23 53	
St Mary Cray	d			23 45				23 50	23 57	
Orpington	d	23 24			23 50	23 50				23 54
Petts Wood	d	23 27			23 53	23 53				23 57
Bickley	d	23 31		23 50						00 01
Bromley South	d	23 34		23 53				23 57	00 04	00 04
Shortlands	d	23 37		23 55						00 07
Ravensbourne	d			23 58						
Beckenham Hill	d			00 01						
Bellingham	d			00 03						
Catford	d			00 06						
Crofton Park	d			00 09						
Lewisham	a				00 10	00 12				
	d									
Nunhead	d			00 11						
Peckham Rye	d			00 14						
Denmark Hill	d			00 17						
Beckenham Junction	d	23 40								00 10
Kent House	d	23 42								00 12
Penge East	d	23 44								00 14
Sydenham Hill	d	23 48								00 18
West Dulwich	d	23 50								00 20
Herne Hill	d	23 53	23 57							00 23
Loughborough Jn.	d									
Elephant & Castle	d		00 04	00 24						
London Blackfriars	d		00 09	00a29						
City Thameslink	a									
Farringdon	a		00 13							
St Pancras International	a		00 17							
Kentish Town	a		00 22							
Brixton	d	23 56								00 26
London Victoria	a	00 03						00 18	00 24	00 34

A From Brighton to Cambridge
B From Ashford International
C From Sutton (Surrey) to Bedford
D From Gravesend
E From Rainham (Kent) to West Hampstead Thameslink
F To London Charing Cross
G From Dover Priory
H From Horsham to Peterborough
I From Brighton to Bedford
J To London Cannon Street
K From Ramsgate
L From Canterbury West

Table T195-R

Saturdays

21 December to 16 May

Sevenoaks and Otford, Orpington, Bromley South, Beckenham Junction, Catford - London

		TL	SE	SE	TL	SE	TL	TL	TL	TL		TL	TL	TL	TL	TL	TL	TL	SE	TL		SE	TL	TL	TL
			◇1				1		1	1		1	1	1	1	1	1	1		1				1	1
		A	B	C	A		D	E	F	D		D	D	G	G	G	G	G		G			H	D	G
Sevenoaks	d																								
Bat & Ball	d																								
Otford	d																								
Shoreham (Kent)	d																								
Eynsford	d																								
Swanley	d																		04 37						
St Mary Cray	d																		04 41						
Orpington	d																					05 24			
Petts Wood	d																					05 27			
Bickley	d			00 01															04 45			05 31			
Bromley South	d		00 04	00 04		00 19													04 49			05 34			
Shortlands	d			00 07															04 52			05 37			
Ravensbourne	d																								
Beckenham Hill	d							00 01																	
Bellingham	d							00 03																	
Catford	d							00 06																	
Crofton Park	d							00 09																	
Lewisham	a																								
	d																								
Nunhead	d							00 11																	
Peckham Rye	d							00 14																	
Denmark Hill	d							00 17																	
Beckenham Junction	d			00 10															04 55			05 40			
Kent House	d			00 12															04 57			05 42			
Penge East	d			00 14															04 59			05 44			
Sydenham Hill	d			00 18															05 03			05 48			
West Dulwich	d			00 20															05 05			05 50			
Herne Hill	d			00 23															05 08			05 53			
Loughborough Jn.	d																								
Elephant & Castle	d				00 04			00 24																	
London Blackfriars	d	00 02			00 09		00 22	00a29	00 37	00 50		01 06	01 36	02 36	03 06	03 36	04 06	04 36		05 06			05 27	05 32	06 02
City Thameslink	a																								
Farringdon	a	00 06			00 13		00 26		00 41											05 10			05 31	05 36	06 06
St Pancras International	a	00 10			00 17		00 30		00 45	00 59		01 13	01 43	02 43	03 13	03 43	04 13	04 43		05 15			05 35	05 40	06 10
Kentish Town	a				00 22					01 05			01 48	02 48		03 48	04 18	04 48					05 40		
Brixton	d			00 26															05 11			05 56			
London Victoria	a		00 24	00 34		00 39													05 18			06 03			

		TL	TL	TL	TL	TL		TL	SE	SE	SE	TL	TL	SE	TL	TL		TL	TL	TL	SE	SE	SE	TL	TL
			1		1						◇1	1			1			1					◇1	1	
		I	J	K	G			L	M		N	F	K		D	K		O		P	M		Q	F	K
Sevenoaks	d					05 22			05 35										05 52		06 05				
Bat & Ball	d					05 25													05 55						
Otford	d					05 29													05 59				06 26		
Shoreham (Kent)	d					05 32													06 02						
Eynsford	d					05 36													06 05						
Swanley	d					05 41					06 03								06 11				06 35		
St Mary Cray	d					05 45					06 08								06 15				06 39		
Orpington	d								05 50	05 54											06 20	06 24			
Petts Wood	d								05a53	05 57											06a23	06 27			
Bickley	d					05 50				06 01									06 20			06 31			
Bromley South	d					05 53				06 04	06 16			06 19					06 23			06 34	06 47		
Shortlands	d					05 55				06 07				06 22					06 25			06 37			
Ravensbourne	d					05 58													06 28						
Beckenham Hill	d					06 00													06 30						
Bellingham	d					06 02													06 32						
Catford	d					06 05													06 35						
Crofton Park	d					06 08													06 38						
Lewisham	a																								
	d																								
Nunhead	d					06 11													06 41						
Peckham Rye	d					06 14													06 44						
Denmark Hill	d					06 17					06 27								06 47						
Beckenham Junction	d									06 10				06 25								06 40			
Kent House	d									06 12				06 27								06 42			
Penge East	d									06 14				06 29								06 44			
Sydenham Hill	d									06 18				06 33								06 48			
West Dulwich	d									06 20				06 35								06 50			
Herne Hill	d			06 12						06 23			06 27	06 38		06 42						06 53			06 57
Loughborough Jn.	d			06 15									06 30			06 45									07 00
Elephant & Castle	d			06 19		06 24							06 34			06 49			06 54						07 04
London Blackfriars	d	06 04	06 22	06 24	06 27	06a29		06 34				06 37	06 39		06 42	06 54		06 57	06a59	07 04				07 07	07 09
City Thameslink	a																								
Farringdon	a	06 08	06 26	06 28	06 31			06 38				06 41	06 43		06 46	06 58		07 01		07 08				07 11	07 13
St Pancras International	a	06 13	06 30	06 33	06 35			06 43				06 45	06 48		06 50	07 03		07 05		07 13				07 15	07 18
Kentish Town	a	06 18		06 38				06 48					06 53			07 08				07 18					07 23
Brixton	d									06 26				06 41								06 56			
London Victoria	a									06 33	06 38			06 48								07 03	07 06		

A From Sutton (Surrey) to Bedford
B From Dover Priory
C From Orpington
D From Brighton to Bedford
E From Sevenoaks
F From Horsham to Peterborough
G From Three Bridges to Bedford
H To St Albans City
I From Gillingham (Kent) to St Albans City
J From Brighton to Cambridge
K From Sutton (Surrey) to St Albans City
L From Gillingham (Kent)
M To London Charing Cross
N From Ramsgate
O From Gatwick Airport to Bedford
P From Rainham (Kent)
Q From Ashford International

Table T195-R

Saturdays

21 December to 16 May

Sevenoaks and Otford, Orpington, Bromley South, Beckenham Junction, Catford - London

		SE	SE A	TL ■ B	TL ■ C	TL D	TL ■ E	TL	TL F	SE G	SE ◇■ H	SE	SE ◇■ I	TL ■ J	TL D	SE	SE K	TL ■ B	TL D	TL ■ E	TL	TL F
Sevenoaks	d							06 22		06 35											06 52	
Bat & Ball	d							06 25													06 55	
Otford	d							06 29					06 56								06 59	
Shoreham (Kent)	d							06 32													07 02	
Eynsford	d							06 35													07 05	
Swanley	d							06 41					07 05								07 11	
St Mary Cray	d							06 45					07 09								07 15	
Orpington	d									06 50		06 54										
Petts Wood	d									06a53		06 57										
Bickley	d							06 50				07 01									07 20	
Bromley South	d	06 49						06 53			07 03	07 04	07 17			07 19					07 23	
Shortlands	d	06 52						06 55				07 07				07 22					07 25	
Ravensbourne	d							06 58													07 28	
Beckenham Hill	d							07 00													07 30	
Bellingham	d							07 02													07 32	
Catford	d							07 05													07 35	
Crofton Park	d							07 08													07 38	
Lewisham	a																					
	d		07 02														07 32					
Nunhead	d		07 07					07 11									07 37				07 41	
Peckham Rye	d		07 10					07 14									07 40				07 44	
Denmark Hill	d		07 14					07 17									07 44				07 47	
Beckenham Junction	d	06 55										07 10				07 25						
Kent House	d	06 57										07 12				07 27						
Penge East	d	06 59										07 14				07 29						
Sydenham Hill	d	07 03										07 18				07 33						
West Dulwich	d	07 05										07 20				07 35						
Herne Hill	d	07 08				07 12						07 23			07 27	07 38			07 42			
Loughborough Jn.	d					07 15									07 30				07 45			
Elephant & Castle	d					07 19		07 24							07 34				07 49		07 54	
London Blackfriars	d			07 12	07 22	07 24	07 27	07a29	07 34					07 37	07 39			07 42	07 54	07 57	07a59	08 04
City Thameslink	a																					
Farringdon	a			07 16	07 26	07 28	07 31		07 38					07 41	07 43			07 46	07 58	08 01		08 08
St Pancras International	a			07 20	07 30	07 33	07 35		07 43					07 45	07 48			07 50	08 03	08 05		08 13
Kentish Town	a					07 38			07 48						07 53				08 08			08 18
Brixton	d	07 11										07 26				07 41						
London Victoria	a	07 18	07 25								07 21	07 33	07 36			07 48	07 55					

		SE G	SE ◇■ L	SE ◇■ M	SE	SE ◇■ I	TL ■ J	TL D	SE	SE K	TL ■ B	TL ■ C	TL D	TL ■ E	TL	TL F	SE G	SE ◇■ H	SE	SE ◇■ I	TL ■ J	TL D	SE
Sevenoaks	d	07 05													07 22		07 35						
Bat & Ball	d														07 25								
Otford	d					07 26									07 29					07 56			
Shoreham (Kent)	d														07 32								
Eynsford	d														07 35								
Swanley	d		07 17			07 37									07 41					08 05			
St Mary Cray	d		07 22												07 45					08 09			
Orpington	d	07 20			07 24												07 50		07 54				
Petts Wood	d	07a23			07 27												07a53		07 57				
Bickley	d				07 31										07 50				08 01				
Bromley South	d		07 30	07 33	07 34	07 47			07 49						07 53			08 03	08 04	08 17			08 19
Shortlands	d				07 37				07 52						07 55				08 07				08 22
Ravensbourne	d														07 58								
Beckenham Hill	d														08 00								
Bellingham	d														08 02								
Catford	d														08 05								
Crofton Park	d														08 08								
Lewisham	a																						
	d									08 02													
Nunhead	d									08 07					08 11								
Peckham Rye	d									08 10					08 14								
Denmark Hill	d		07 50							08 14					08 17								
Beckenham Junction	d				07 40				07 55										08 10				08 25
Kent House	d				07 42				07 57										08 12				08 27
Penge East	d				07 44				07 59										08 14				08 29
Sydenham Hill	d				07 48				08 03										08 18				08 33
West Dulwich	d				07 50				08 05										08 20				08 35
Herne Hill	d				07 53			07 57	08 08				08 12						08 23			08 27	08 38
Loughborough Jn.	d							08 00					08 15									08 30	
Elephant & Castle	d							08 04					08 19		08 24							08 34	
London Blackfriars	d						08 07	08 09			08 12	08 22	08 24	08 27	08a29	08 34					08 37	08 39	
City Thameslink	a																						
Farringdon	a						08 11	08 13			08 16	08 26	08 28	08 31		08 38					08 41	08 43	
St Pancras International	a						08 15	08 18			08 20	08 30	08 33	08 35		08 43					08 45	08 48	
Kentish Town	a							08 23					08 38			08 48						08 53	
Brixton	d				07 56				08 11										08 26				08 41
London Victoria	a		08 00	07 51	08 03	08 06			08 18	08 25								08 21	08 33	08 36			08 48

A From Dartford
B From Brighton to Bedford
C From Brighton to Cambridge
D From Sutton (Surrey) to St Albans City
E From Gatwick Airport to Bedford
F From Rainham (Kent)
G To London Charing Cross
H From Dover Priory
I From Ashford International
J From Horsham to Peterborough
K From Gravesend
L From Gillingham (Kent)
M From Ramsgate

Table T195-R

Saturdays

21 December to 16 May

Sevenoaks and Otford, Orpington, Bromley South, Beckenham Junction, Catford - London

		SE A	TL ■ B	TL C	TL ■ D	TL	TL E	SE F	SE ◇■ G	SE ◇■ H	SE	SE ◇■ I	TL ■ J	TL C	SE	SE A	TL ■ B	TL ■ K	TL C	TL ■ D	TL	TL E
Sevenoaks	d					07 52		08 05													08 22	
Bat & Ball	d					07 55															08 25	
Otford	d					07 59						08 26									08 29	
Shoreham (Kent)	d					08 02															08 32	
Eynsford	d					08 05															08 35	
Swanley	d					08 11			08 17			08 37									08 41	
St Mary Cray	d					08 15			08 22												08 45	
Orpington	d							08 20			08 24											
Petts Wood	d							08a23			08 27											
Bickley	d					08 20					08 31										08 50	
Bromley South	d					08 23			08 30	08 33	08 34	08 47			08 49						08 53	
Shortlands	d					08 25					08 37				08 52						08 55	
Ravensbourne	d					08 28															08 58	
Beckenham Hill	d					08 30															09 00	
Bellingham	d					08 32															09 02	
Catford	d					08 35															09 05	
Crofton Park	d					08 38															09 08	
Lewisham	a																					
	d	08 32														09 02						
Nunhead	d	08 37				08 41										09 07					09 11	
Peckham Rye	d	08 40				08 44										09 10					09 14	
Denmark Hill	d	08 44				08 47			08 50							09 14					09 17	
Beckenham Junction	d										08 40				08 55							
Kent House	d										08 42				08 57							
Penge East	d										08 44				08 59							
Sydenham Hill	d										08 48				09 03							
West Dulwich	d										08 50				09 05							
Herne Hill	d			08 42							08 53			08 57	09 08				09 12			
Loughborough Jn.	d			08 45										09 00					09 15			
Elephant & Castle	d			08 49		08 54								09 04					09 19		09 24	
London Blackfriars	d		08 42	08 54	08 57	08a59	09 04						09 07	09 09			09 12	09 22	09 24	09 27	09a29	09 34
City Thameslink	a						09 06						09 08	09 11			09 13	09 23	09 26	09 28		09 36
Farringdon	a		08 46	08 58	09 01		09 08						09 11	09 13			09 16	09 26	09 28	09 31		09 38
St Pancras International	a		08 50	09 03	09 05		09 13						09 15	09 18			09 20	09 30	09 33	09 35		09 43
Kentish Town	a			09 08			09 18							09 23					09 38			09 48
Brixton	d										08 56				09 11							
London Victoria	a	08 55							09 00	08 51	09 03	09 06			09 18	09 25						

		SE F	SE ◇■ G	SE	SE ◇■ I	TL ■ J	TL C	SE	SE A	TL ■ B	TL C	TL ■ D	TL	TL E	SE F	SE ◇■ G	SE ◇■ H	SE	SE ◇■ L	TL ■ J	TL C	SE	SE A
Sevenoaks	d	08 35											08 52		09 05								
Bat & Ball	d												08 55										
Otford	d				08 56								08 59						09 26				
Shoreham (Kent)	d												09 02										
Eynsford	d												09 05										
Swanley	d				09 05								09 11			09 17			09 37				
St Mary Cray	d				09 09								09 15			09 22							
Orpington	d	08 50		08 54											09 20			09 24					
Petts Wood	d	08a53		08 57											09a23			09 27					
Bickley	d			09 01									09 20					09 31					
Bromley South	d		09 03	09 04	09 17			09 19					09 23			09 30	09 33	09 34	09 47			09 49	
Shortlands	d			09 07				09 22					09 25					09 37				09 52	
Ravensbourne	d												09 28										
Beckenham Hill	d												09 30										
Bellingham	d												09 32										
Catford	d												09 35										
Crofton Park	d												09 38										
Lewisham	a																						
	d								09 32														10 02
Nunhead	d								09 37				09 41										10 07
Peckham Rye	d								09 40				09 44										10 10
Denmark Hill	d								09 44				09 47			09 50							10 14
Beckenham Junction	d			09 10				09 25										09 40				09 55	
Kent House	d			09 12				09 27										09 42				09 57	
Penge East	d			09 14				09 29										09 44				09 59	
Sydenham Hill	d			09 18				09 33										09 48				10 03	
West Dulwich	d			09 20				09 35										09 50				10 05	
Herne Hill	d			09 23			09 27	09 38			09 42							09 53			09 57	10 08	
Loughborough Jn.	d						09 30				09 45										10 00		
Elephant & Castle	d						09 34				09 49		09 54								10 04		
London Blackfriars	d					09 37	09 39			09 42	09 54	09 57	09a59	10 04						10 07	10 09		
City Thameslink	a					09 38	09 41			09 43	09 56	09 58		10 06						10 08	10 11		
Farringdon	a					09 41	09 43			09 46	09 58	10 01		10 08						10 11	10 13		
St Pancras International	a					09 45	09 48			09 50	10 03	10 05		10 13						10 15	10 18		
Kentish Town	a						09 53				10 08			10 18							10 23		
Brixton	d			09 26				09 41										09 56				10 11	
London Victoria	a		09 21	09 33	09 36			09 48	09 55							10 00	09 51	10 03	10 06			10 18	10 25

A From Gravesend
B From Brighton to Bedford
C From Sutton (Surrey) to St Albans City
D From Gatwick Airport to Bedford
E From Rainham (Kent)
F To London Charing Cross
G From Dover Priory
H From Ramsgate
I From Ashford International
J From Horsham to Peterborough
K From Brighton to Cambridge
L From Canterbury West

Table T195-R

Saturdays

21 December to 16 May

Sevenoaks and Otford, Orpington, Bromley South, Beckenham Junction, Catford - London

		TL 1 A	TL 1 B	TL C	TL 1 D	TL		TL E	SE F	SE ◇1 G	SE	SE ◇1 H	TL 1 I	TL C	SE	SE J		TL 1 A	TL C	TL 1 D	TL	TL E	SE F	SE ◇1 G	SE ◇1 K
Sevenoaks 4	d					09 22			09 35												09 52		10 05		
Bat & Ball	d					09 25															09 55				
Otford 4	d					09 29						09 56									09 59				
Shoreham (Kent)	d					09 32															10 02				
Eynsford	d					09 35															10 05				
Swanley 4	d					09 41						10 05									10 11			10 17	
St Mary Cray	d					09 45						10 09									10 15			10 22	
Orpington 4	d								09 50		09 54												10 20		
Petts Wood 4	d								09a53		09 57												10a23		
Bickley 4	d					09 50					10 01										10 20				
Bromley South 4	d					09 53				10 03	10 04	10 17			10 19						10 23			10 30	10 33
Shortlands 4	d					09 55					10 07				10 22						10 25				
Ravensbourne	d					09 58															10 28				
Beckenham Hill	d					10 00															10 30				
Bellingham	d					10 02															10 32				
Catford	d					10 05															10 35				
Crofton Park	d					10 08															10 38				
Lewisham 4	a																								
	d															10 32									
Nunhead 4	d					10 11										10 37					10 41				
Peckham Rye 4	d					10 14										10 40					10 44				
Denmark Hill 4	d					10 17										10 44					10 47			10 50	
Beckenham Junction 4	d										10 10				10 25										
Kent House 4	d										10 12				10 27										
Penge East	d										10 14				10 29										
Sydenham Hill	d										10 18				10 33										
West Dulwich	d										10 20				10 35										
Herne Hill 4	d			10 12							10 23			10 27	10 38				10 42						
Loughborough Jn.	d			10 15										10 30					10 45						
Elephant & Castle	⊖ d			10 19		10 24								10 34					10 49		10 54				
London Blackfriars 3	⊖ d	10 12	10 22	10 24	10 27	10a29		10 34					10 37	10 39				10 42	10 54	10 57	10a59	11 04			
City Thameslink 3	a	10 13	10 23	10 26	10 28			10 36					10 38	10 41				10 43	10 56	10 58		11 06			
Farringdon	⊖ a	10 16	10 26	10 28	10 31			10 38					10 41	10 43				10 46	10 58	11 01		11 08			
St Pancras International 15	⊖ a	10 20	10 30	10 33	10 35			10 43					10 45	10 48				10 50	11 03	11 05		11 13			
Kentish Town	⊖ a			10 38				10 48						10 53					11 08			11 18			
Brixton	⊖ d										10 26				10 41										
London Victoria 15	⊖ a									10 21	10 33	10 36			10 48	10 55								11 00	10 51

		SE		SE ◇1 L	TL 1 I	TL C	SE	SE J	TL 1 A	TL 1 B	TL C	TL 1 D		TL	TL E	SE F	SE ◇1 G	SE	SE ◇1 H	TL 1 I	TL C	SE		SE J	TL 1 A
Sevenoaks 4	d													10 22		10 35									
Bat & Ball	d													10 25											
Otford 4	d			10 26										10 29					10 56						
Shoreham (Kent)	d													10 32											
Eynsford	d													10 35											
Swanley 4	d			10 37										10 41					11 05						
St Mary Cray	d													10 45					11 09						
Orpington 4	d	10 24														10 50		10 54							
Petts Wood 4	d	10 27														10a53		10 57							
Bickley 4	d	10 31												10 50				11 01							
Bromley South 4	d	10 34		10 47			10 49							10 53			11 03	11 04	11 17			11 19			
Shortlands 4	d	10 37					10 52							10 55				11 07				11 22			
Ravensbourne	d													10 58											
Beckenham Hill	d													11 00											
Bellingham	d													11 02											
Catford	d													11 05											
Crofton Park	d													11 08											
Lewisham 4	a																								
	d							11 02																11 32	
Nunhead 4	d							11 07						11 11										11 37	
Peckham Rye 4	d							11 10						11 14										11 40	
Denmark Hill 4	d							11 14						11 17										11 44	
Beckenham Junction 4	d	10 40					10 55											11 10				11 25			
Kent House 4	d	10 42					10 57											11 12				11 27			
Penge East	d	10 44					10 59											11 14				11 29			
Sydenham Hill	d	10 48					11 03											11 18				11 33			
West Dulwich	d	10 50					11 05											11 20				11 35			
Herne Hill 4	d	10 53				10 57	11 08				11 12							11 23			11 27	11 38			
Loughborough Jn.	d					11 00					11 15										11 30				
Elephant & Castle	⊖ d					11 04					11 19			11 24							11 34				
London Blackfriars 3	⊖ d				11 07	11 09			11 12	11 22	11 24	11 27		11a29	11 34					11 37	11 39				11 42
City Thameslink 3	a				11 08	11 11			11 13	11 23	11 26	11 28			11 36					11 38	11 41				11 43
Farringdon	⊖ a				11 11	11 13			11 16	11 26	11 28	11 31			11 38					11 41	11 43				11 46
St Pancras International 15	⊖ a				11 15	11 18			11 20	11 30	11 33	11 35			11 43					11 45	11 48				11 50
Kentish Town	⊖ a					11 23					11 38				11 48						11 53				
Brixton	⊖ d	10 56					11 11											11 26				11 41			
London Victoria 15	⊖ a	11 03		11 06			11 18	11 25									11 21	11 33	11 36			11 48		11 55	

A From Brighton to Bedford
B From Brighton to Cambridge
C From Sutton (Surrey) to St Albans City
D From Gatwick Airport to Bedford
E From Rainham (Kent)
F To London Charing Cross
G From Dover Priory
H From Ashford International
I From Horsham to Peterborough
J From Gravesend
K From Ramsgate
L From Canterbury West

NRT DECEMBER 19 EDITION

Table T195-R

Saturdays

21 December to 16 May

Sevenoaks and Otford, Orpington, Bromley South, Beckenham Junction, Catford - London

		TL A	TL 1 B	TL	TL C	SE D	SE ◇1 E	SE ◇1 F		SE	SE ◇1 G	TL 1 H	TL A	SE	SE I	TL 1 J	TL 1 K	TL A		TL 1 B	TL	TL C	SE D	SE ◇1 E	SE
Sevenoaks 4	d			10 52		11 05															11 22		11 35		
Bat & Ball	d			10 55																	11 25				
Otford 4	d			10 59							11 26										11 29				
Shoreham (Kent)	d			11 02																	11 32				
Eynsford	d			11 05																	11 35				
Swanley 4	d			11 11			11 17				11 37										11 41				
St Mary Cray	d			11 15			11 22														11 45				
Orpington 4	d					11 20				11 24													11 50		11 54
Petts Wood 4	d					11a23				11 27													11a53		11 57
Bickley 4	d			11 20						11 31											11 50				12 01
Bromley South 4	d			11 23			11 30	11 33		11 34	11 47			11 49							11 53			12 03	12 04
Shortlands 4	d			11 25						11 37				11 52							11 55				12 07
Ravensbourne	d			11 28																	11 58				
Beckenham Hill	d			11 30																	12 00				
Bellingham	d			11 32																	12 02				
Catford	d			11 35																	12 05				
Crofton Park	d			11 38																	12 08				
Lewisham 4	a																								
	d														12 02										
Nunhead 4	d			11 41											12 07						12 11				
Peckham Rye 4	d			11 44											12 10						12 14				
Denmark Hill 4	d			11 47			11 50								12 14						12 17				
Beckenham Junction 4	d									11 40				11 55											12 10
Kent House 4	d									11 42				11 57											12 12
Penge East	d									11 44				11 59											12 14
Sydenham Hill	d									11 48				12 03											12 18
West Dulwich	d									11 50				12 05											12 20
Herne Hill 4	d	11 42								11 53			11 57	12 08				12 12							12 23
Loughborough Jn.	d	11 45											12 00					12 15							
Elephant & Castle	⊖ d	11 49		11 54									12 04					12 19			12 24				
London Blackfriars 3	⊖ d	11 54	11 57	11a59	12 04							12 07	12 09			12 12	12 22	12 24		12 27	12a29	12 34			
City Thameslink 3	a	11 56	11 58		12 06							12 08	12 11			12 13	12 23	12 26		12 28		12 36			
Farringdon	⊖ a	11 58	12 01		12 08							12 11	12 13			12 16	12 26	12 28		12 31		12 38			
St Pancras International 15	⊖ a	12 03	12 05		12 13							12 15	12 18			12 20	12 30	12 33		12 35		12 43			
Kentish Town	⊖ a	12 08			12 18								12 23					12 38				12 48			
Brixton	⊖ d									11 56				12 11											12 26
London Victoria 15	⊖ a						12 00	11 51		12 03	12 06			12 18	12 25									12 21	12 33

		SE ◇1 L	TL 1 H	TL A		SE	SE I	TL 1 J	TL A	TL 1 B	TL	TL C	SE D	SE ◇1 E		SE ◇1 F	SE	SE ◇1 G	TL 1 H	TL A	SE	SE I	TL 1 J	TL 1 K	
Sevenoaks 4	d										11 52		12 05												
Bat & Ball	d										11 55														
Otford 4	d	11 56									11 59							12 26							
Shoreham (Kent)	d										12 02														
Eynsford	d										12 05														
Swanley 4	d	12 05									12 11			12 17				12 37							
St Mary Cray	d	12 09									12 15			12 22											
Orpington 4	d												12 20				12 24								
Petts Wood 4	d												12a23				12 27								
Bickley 4	d										12 20						12 31								
Bromley South 4	d	12 17				12 19					12 23			12 30		12 33	12 34	12 47			12 49				
Shortlands 4	d					12 22					12 25						12 37				12 52				
Ravensbourne	d										12 28														
Beckenham Hill	d										12 30														
Bellingham	d										12 32														
Catford	d										12 35														
Crofton Park	d										12 38														
Lewisham 4	a																								
	d						12 32															13 02			
Nunhead 4	d						12 37				12 41											13 07			
Peckham Rye 4	d						12 40				12 44											13 10			
Denmark Hill 4	d						12 44				12 47			12 50								13 14			
Beckenham Junction 4	d					12 25											12 40				12 55				
Kent House 4	d					12 27											12 42				12 57				
Penge East	d					12 29											12 44				12 59				
Sydenham Hill	d					12 33											12 48				13 03				
West Dulwich	d					12 35											12 50				13 05				
Herne Hill 4	d			12 27		12 38			12 42								12 53			12 57	13 08				
Loughborough Jn.	d			12 30					12 45											13 00					
Elephant & Castle	⊖ d			12 34					12 49		12 54									13 04					
London Blackfriars 3	⊖ d		12 37	12 39				12 42	12 54	12 57	12a59	13 04							13 07	13 09			13 12	13 22	
City Thameslink 3	a		12 38	12 41				12 43	12 56	12 58		13 06							13 08	13 11			13 13	13 23	
Farringdon	⊖ a		12 41	12 43				12 46	12 58	13 01		13 08							13 11	13 13			13 16	13 26	
St Pancras International 15	⊖ a		12 45	12 48				12 50	13 03	13 05		13 13							13 15	13 18			13 20	13 30	
Kentish Town	⊖ a			12 53					13 08			13 18								13 23					
Brixton	⊖ d					12 41											12 56				13 11				
London Victoria 15	⊖ a	12 36				12 48	12 55							13 00		12 51	13 03	13 06			13 18	13 25			

A From Sutton (Surrey) to St Albans City
B From Gatwick Airport to Bedford
C From Rainham (Kent)
D To London Charing Cross
E From Dover Priory
F From Ramsgate
G From Canterbury West
H From Horsham to Peterborough
I From Gravesend
J From Brighton to Bedford
K From Brighton to Cambridge
L From Ashford International

Table T195-R

Saturdays

21 December to 16 May

Sevenoaks and Otford, Orpington, Bromley South, Beckenham Junction, Catford - London

Station		TL	TL	TL	TL	SE	SE	SE	SE	TL		TL	SE	SE	TL	TL	TL	TL	TL	SE		SE	SE	SE	SE
			■1				◇■1		◇■1	■1					■1		■1					◇■1	◇■1		◇■1
		A	B		C	D	E		F	G		A		H	I	A	B		C	D		E	J		K
Sevenoaks	d			12 22		12 35												12 52		13 05					
Bat & Ball	d			12 25														12 55							
Otford	d			12 29					12 56									12 59							13 26
Shoreham (Kent)	d			12 32														13 02							
Eynsford	d			12 35														13 05							
Swanley	d			12 41					13 05									13 11				13 17			13 37
St Mary Cray	d			12 45					13 09									13 15				13 22			
Orpington	d					12 50		12 54												13 20				13 24	
Petts Wood	d					12a53		12 57												13a23				13 27	
Bickley	d			12 50				13 01										13 20						13 31	
Bromley South	d			12 53			13 03	13 04	13 17				13 19					13 23				13 30	13 33	13 34	13 47
Shortlands	d			12 55				13 07					13 22					13 25						13 37	
Ravensbourne	d			12 58														13 28							
Beckenham Hill	d			13 00														13 30							
Bellingham	d			13 02														13 32							
Catford	d			13 05														13 35							
Crofton Park	d			13 08														13 38							
Lewisham	a																								
	d													13 32											
Nunhead	d			13 11										13 37				13 41							
Peckham Rye	d			13 14										13 40				13 44							
Denmark Hill	d			13 17										13 44				13 47				13 50			
Beckenham Junction	d							13 10					13 25											13 40	
Kent House	d							13 12					13 27											13 42	
Penge East	d							13 14					13 29											13 44	
Sydenham Hill	d							13 18					13 33											13 48	
West Dulwich	d							13 20					13 35											13 50	
Herne Hill	d	13 12						13 23				13 27	13 38			13 42								13 53	
Loughborough Jn.	d	13 15										13 30				13 45									
Elephant & Castle ⊖	d	13 19		13 24								13 34				13 49		13 54							
London Blackfriars ⊖	d	13 24	13 27	13a29	13 34					13 37		13 39			13 42	13 54	13 57	13a59	14 04						
City Thameslink	a	13 26	13 28		13 36					13 38		13 41			13 43	13 56	13 58		14 06						
Farringdon ⊖	a	13 28	13 31		13 38					13 41		13 43			13 46	13 58	14 01		14 08						
St Pancras International ⊖	a	13 33	13 35		13 43					13 45		13 48			13 50	14 03	14 05		14 13						
Kentish Town ⊖	a	13 38			13 48							13 53				14 08			14 18						
Brixton ⊖	d							13 26					13 41											13 56	
London Victoria ⊖	a						13 21	13 33	13 36				13 48	13 55								14 00	13 51	14 03	14 06

Station		TL	TL	SE	SE	TL		TL	TL	TL	TL	TL	SE	SE	SE	SE		TL	TL	SE	SE	TL	TL	TL	TL
		■1				■1		■1		■1				◇■1		◇■1		■1				■1		■1	
		G	A		H	I		L	A	B		C	D	E		F		G	A		H	I	A	B	
Sevenoaks	d										13 22		13 35												13 52
Bat & Ball	d										13 25														13 55
Otford	d										13 29					13 56									13 59
Shoreham (Kent)	d										13 32														14 02
Eynsford	d										13 35														14 05
Swanley	d										13 41					14 05									14 11
St Mary Cray	d										13 45					14 09									14 15
Orpington	d												13 50		13 54										
Petts Wood	d												13a53		13 57										
Bickley	d										13 50				14 01										14 20
Bromley South	d			13 49							13 53			14 03	14 04	14 17				14 19					14 23
Shortlands	d			13 52							13 55				14 07					14 22					14 25
Ravensbourne	d										13 58														14 28
Beckenham Hill	d										14 00														14 30
Bellingham	d										14 02														14 32
Catford	d										14 05														14 35
Crofton Park	d										14 08														14 38
Lewisham	a																								
	d				14 02																14 32				
Nunhead	d				14 07						14 11										14 37				14 41
Peckham Rye	d				14 10						14 14										14 40				14 44
Denmark Hill	d				14 14						14 17										14 44				14 47
Beckenham Junction	d			13 55											14 10					14 25					
Kent House	d			13 57											14 12					14 27					
Penge East	d			13 59											14 14					14 29					
Sydenham Hill	d			14 03											14 18					14 33					
West Dulwich	d			14 05											14 20					14 35					
Herne Hill	d		13 57	14 08					14 12						14 23				14 27	14 38			14 42		
Loughborough Jn.	d		14 00						14 15										14 30				14 45		
Elephant & Castle ⊖	d		14 04						14 19		14 24								14 34				14 49		14 54
London Blackfriars ⊖	d	14 07	14 09			14 12		14 22	14 24	14 27	14a29	14 34						14 37	14 39			14 42	14 54	14 57	14a59
City Thameslink	a	14 08	14 11			14 13		14 23	14 26	14 28		14 36						14 38	14 41			14 43	14 56	14 58	
Farringdon ⊖	a	14 11	14 13			14 16		14 26	14 28	14 31		14 38						14 41	14 43			14 46	14 58	15 01	
St Pancras International ⊖	a	14 15	14 18			14 20		14 30	14 33	14 35		14 43						14 45	14 48			14 50	15 03	15 05	
Kentish Town ⊖	a		14 23						14 38			14 48							14 53				15 08		
Brixton ⊖	d			14 11											14 26					14 41					
London Victoria ⊖	a			14 18	14 25									14 21	14 33	14 36				14 48	14 55				

A From Sutton (Surrey) to St Albans City
B From Gatwick Airport to Bedford
C From Rainham (Kent)
D To London Charing Cross
E From Dover Priory
F From Ashford International
G From Horsham to Peterborough
H From Gravesend
I From Brighton to Bedford
J From Ramsgate
K From Canterbury West
L From Brighton to Cambridge

Table T195-R

Saturdays

21 December to 16 May

Sevenoaks and Otford, Orpington, Bromley South, Beckenham Junction, Catford - London

Station		TL		SE	SE	SE	SE	SE	TL	TL	SE	SE		TL	TL	TL	TL	TL	TL	SE	SE	SE		SE	TL
					◇■1	◇■1		◇■1	■1					■1	■1		■1				◇■1			◇■1	■1
		A		B	C	D		E	F	G		H		I	J	G	K		A	B	C			L	F
Sevenoaks	d			14 05														14 22		14 35					
Bat & Ball	d																	14 25							
Otford	d							14 26										14 29						14 56	
Shoreham (Kent)	d																	14 32							
Eynsford	d																	14 35							
Swanley	d				14 17			14 37										14 41						15 05	
St Mary Cray	d				14 22													14 45						15 09	
Orpington	d			14 20			14 24													14 50		14 54			
Petts Wood	d			14a23			14 27													14a53		14 57			
Bickley	d						14 31											14 50				15 01			
Bromley South	d				14 30	14 33	14 34	14 47			14 49							14 53			15 03	15 04		15 17	
Shortlands	d						14 37				14 52							14 55				15 07			
Ravensbourne	d																	14 58							
Beckenham Hill	d																	15 00							
Bellingham	d																	15 02							
Catford	d																	15 05							
Crofton Park	d																	15 08							
Lewisham	a																								
	d											15 02													
Nunhead	d											15 07						15 11							
Peckham Rye	d											15 10						15 14							
Denmark Hill	d				14 50							15 14						15 17							
Beckenham Junction	d						14 40				14 55											15 10			
Kent House	d						14 42				14 57											15 12			
Penge East	d						14 44				14 59											15 14			
Sydenham Hill	d						14 48				15 03											15 18			
West Dulwich	d						14 50				15 05											15 20			
Herne Hill	d						14 53			14 57	15 08					15 12						15 23			
Loughborough Jn.	d									15 00						15 15									
Elephant & Castle ⊖	d									15 04						15 19		15 24							
London Blackfriars ⊖	d	15 04							15 07	15 09				15 12	15 22	15 24	15 27	15a29	15 34						15 37
City Thameslink	a	15 06							15 08	15 11				15 13	15 23	15 26	15 28		15 36						15 38
Farringdon ⊖	a	15 08							15 11	15 13				15 16	15 26	15 28	15 31		15 38						15 41
St Pancras International ⊖	a	15 13							15 15	15 18				15 20	15 30	15 33	15 35		15 43						15 45
Kentish Town ⊖	a	15 18								15 23						15 38			15 48						
Brixton ⊖	d						14 56				15 11											15 26			
London Victoria ⊖	a				15 00	14 51	15 03	15 06			15 18	15 25									15 21	15 33		15 36	

Station		TL	SE	SE	TL	TL	TL	TL		TL	SE	SE	SE	SE	SE	TL	TL	SE		SE	TL	TL	TL	TL	TL
					■1		■1					◇■1	◇■1		◇■1	■1					■1	■1		■1	
		G		H	I	G	K			A	B	C	D		E	F	G			H	I	J	G	K	
Sevenoaks	d							14 52			15 05														15 22
Bat & Ball	d							14 55																	15 25
Otford	d							14 59							15 26										15 29
Shoreham (Kent)	d							15 02																	15 32
Eynsford	d							15 05																	15 35
Swanley	d							15 11				15 17			15 37										15 41
St Mary Cray	d							15 15				15 22													15 45
Orpington	d										15 20			15 24											
Petts Wood	d										15a23			15 27											
Bickley	d							15 20						15 31											15 50
Bromley South	d		15 19					15 23				15 30	15 33	15 34	15 47			15 49							15 53
Shortlands	d		15 22					15 25						15 37				15 52							15 55
Ravensbourne	d							15 28																	15 58
Beckenham Hill	d							15 30																	16 00
Bellingham	d							15 32																	16 02
Catford	d							15 35																	16 05
Crofton Park	d							15 38																	16 08
Lewisham	a																								
	d			15 32																16 02					
Nunhead	d			15 37				15 41												16 07					16 11
Peckham Rye	d			15 40				15 44												16 10					16 14
Denmark Hill	d			15 44				15 47				15 50								16 14					16 17
Beckenham Junction	d		15 25											15 40				15 55							
Kent House	d		15 27											15 42				15 57							
Penge East	d		15 29											15 44				15 59							
Sydenham Hill	d		15 33											15 48				16 03							
West Dulwich	d		15 35											15 50				16 05							
Herne Hill	d	15 27	15 38			15 42								15 53			15 57	16 08					16 12		
Loughborough Jn.	d	15 30				15 45											16 00						16 15		
Elephant & Castle ⊖	d	15 34				15 49		15 54									16 04						16 19		16 24
London Blackfriars ⊖	d	15 39			15 42	15 54	15 57	15a59		16 04						16 07	16 09				16 12	16 22	16 24	16 27	16a29
City Thameslink	a	15 41			15 43	15 56	15 58			16 06						16 08	16 11				16 13	16 23	16 26	16 28	
Farringdon ⊖	a	15 43			15 46	15 58	16 01			16 08						16 11	16 13				16 16	16 26	16 28	16 31	
St Pancras International ⊖	a	15 48			15 50	16 03	16 05			16 13						16 15	16 18				16 20	16 30	16 33	16 35	
Kentish Town ⊖	a	15 53				16 08				16 18							16 23						16 38		
Brixton ⊖	d		15 41											15 56				16 11							
London Victoria ⊖	a		15 48	15 55								16 00	15 51	16 03	16 06			16 18		16 25					

A From Rainham (Kent)
B To London Charing Cross
C From Dover Priory
D From Ramsgate
E From Canterbury West
F From Horsham to Peterborough
G From Sutton (Surrey) to St Albans City
H From Gravesend
I From Brighton to Bedford
J From Brighton to Cambridge
K From Gatwick Airport to Bedford
L From Ashford International

Table T195-R

Saturdays

21 December to 16 May

Sevenoaks and Otford, Orpington, Bromley South, Beckenham Junction, Catford - London

		TL	SE	SE	SE	SE	TL	TL	SE	SE	TL	TL	TL	TL	TL	SE	SE	SE	SE	SE	TL	TL
				◇1		◇1	1				1		1				◇1	◇1		◇1	1	
		A	B	C		D	E	F		G	H	F	I		A	B	C	J		K	E	F
Sevenoaks 4	d		15 35											15 52		16 05						
Bat & Ball	d													15 55								
Otford 4	d					15 56								15 59						16 26		
Shoreham (Kent)	d													16 02								
Eynsford	d													16 05								
Swanley 4	d					16 05								16 11			16 17			16 37		
St Mary Cray	d					16 09								16 15			16 22					
Orpington 4	d		15 50		15 54											16 20			16 24			
Petts Wood 4	d		15a53		15 57											16a23			16 27			
Bickley 4	d				16 01									16 20					16 31			
Bromley South 4	d			16 03	16 04	16 17			16 19					16 23			16 30	16 33	16 34	16 47		
Shortlands 4	d				16 07				16 22					16 25					16 37			
Ravensbourne	d													16 28								
Beckenham Hill	d													16 30								
Bellingham	d													16 32								
Catford	d													16 35								
Crofton Park	d													16 38								
Lewisham 4	a																					
	d									16 32												
Nunhead 4	d									16 37				16 41								
Peckham Rye 4	d									16 40				16 44								
Denmark Hill 4	d									16 44				16 47			16 50					
Beckenham Junction 4	d				16 10				16 25										16 40			
Kent House 4	d				16 12				16 27										16 42			
Penge East	d				16 14				16 29										16 44			
Sydenham Hill	d				16 18				16 33										16 48			
West Dulwich	d				16 20				16 35										16 50			
Herne Hill 4	d				16 23			16 27	16 38			16 42							16 53			16 57
Loughborough Jn.	d							16 30				16 45										17 00
Elephant & Castle ⊖	d							16 34				16 49		16 54								17 04
London Blackfriars 3 ⊖	d	16 34					16 37	16 39			16 42	16 54	16 57	16a59	17 04						17 07	17 09
City Thameslink 3	a	16 36					16 38	16 41			16 43	16 56	16 58		17 06						17 08	17 11
Farringdon ⊖	a	16 38					16 41	16 43			16 46	16 58	17 01		17 08						17 11	17 13
St Pancras International 15 ⊖	a	16 43					16 45	16 48			16 50	17 03	17 05		17 13						17 15	17 18
Kentish Town ⊖	a	16 48						16 53				17 08			17 18							17 23
Brixton ⊖	d				16 26				16 41										16 56			
London Victoria 15 ⊖	a			16 21	16 33	16 36			16 48	16 55							17 00	16 51	17 03	17 06		

		SE	SE	TL	TL	TL	TL	TL	TL	SE	SE	SE	SE	TL	TL	SE	SE	TL	TL	TL	TL	TL	SE
				1	1		1				◇1		◇1	1				1		1			
			G	H	L	F	I		A	B	C		D	E	F		G	H	F	I		A	B
Sevenoaks 4	d							16 22		16 35											16 52		17 05
Bat & Ball	d							16 25													16 55		
Otford 4	d							16 29					16 56								16 59		
Shoreham (Kent)	d							16 32													17 02		
Eynsford	d							16 35													17 05		
Swanley 4	d							16 41					17 05								17 11		
St Mary Cray	d							16 45					17 09								17 15		
Orpington 4	d									16 50		16 54											17 20
Petts Wood 4	d									16a53		16 57											17a23
Bickley 4	d							16 50				17 01									17 20		
Bromley South 4	d	16 49						16 53			17 03	17 04	17 17			17 19					17 23		
Shortlands 4	d	16 52						16 55				17 07				17 22					17 25		
Ravensbourne	d							16 58													17 28		
Beckenham Hill	d							17 00													17 30		
Bellingham	d							17 02													17 32		
Catford	d							17 05													17 35		
Crofton Park	d							17 08													17 38		
Lewisham 4	a																						
	d		17 02														17 32						
Nunhead 4	d		17 07					17 11									17 37				17 41		
Peckham Rye 4	d		17 10					17 14									17 40				17 44		
Denmark Hill 4	d		17 14					17 17									17 44				17 47		
Beckenham Junction 4	d	16 55										17 10				17 25							
Kent House 4	d	16 57										17 12				17 27							
Penge East	d	16 59										17 14				17 29							
Sydenham Hill	d	17 03										17 18				17 33							
West Dulwich	d	17 05										17 20				17 35							
Herne Hill 4	d	17 08				17 12						17 23			17 27	17 38			17 42				
Loughborough Jn.	d					17 15									17 30				17 45				
Elephant & Castle ⊖	d					17 19		17 24							17 34				17 49		17 54		
London Blackfriars 3 ⊖	d			17 12	17 22	17 24	17 27	17a29	17 34					17 37	17 39			17 42	17 54	17 57	17a59	18 04	
City Thameslink 3	a			17 13	17 23	17 26	17 28		17 36					17 38	17 41			17 43	17 56	17 58		18 06	
Farringdon ⊖	a			17 16	17 26	17 28	17 31		17 38					17 41	17 43			17 46	17 58	18 01		18 08	
St Pancras International 15 ⊖	a			17 20	17 30	17 33	17 35		17 43					17 45	17 48			17 50	18 03	18 05		18 13	
Kentish Town ⊖	a					17 38			17 48						17 53				18 08			18 18	
Brixton ⊖	d	17 11										17 26				17 41							
London Victoria 15 ⊖	a	17 18	17 25								17 21	17 33	17 36			17 48	17 55						

A From Rainham (Kent)
B To London Charing Cross
C From Dover Priory
D From Ashford International
E From Horsham to Peterborough
F From Sutton (Surrey) to St Albans City
G From Gravesend
H From Brighton to Bedford
I From Gatwick Airport to Bedford
J From Ramsgate
K From Canterbury West
L From Brighton to Cambridge

Table T195-R

Saturdays

21 December to 16 May

Sevenoaks and Otford, Orpington, Bromley South, Beckenham Junction, Catford - London

		SE	SE	SE	SE	TL	TL	SE	SE	TL	TL	TL	TL	TL	TL	SE	SE	SE	SE	TL	TL	SE	SE
		◇1	◇1		◇1	1				1	1		1				◇1		◇1	1			
		A	B		C	D	E		F	G	H	E	I		J	K	A		L	D	E		F
Sevenoaks 4	d													17 22		17 35							
Bat & Ball	d													17 25									
Otford 4	d				17 26									17 29					17 56				
Shoreham (Kent)	d													17 32									
Eynsford	d													17 35									
Swanley 4	d	17 17			17 37									17 41					18 05				
St Mary Cray	d	17 22												17 45					18 09				
Orpington 4	d			17 24												17 50		17 54					
Petts Wood 4	d			17 27												17a53		17 57					
Bickley 4	d			17 31										17 50				18 01					
Bromley South 4	d	17 30	17 33	17 34	17 47			17 49						17 53			18 03	18 04	18 17			18 19	
Shortlands 4	d			17 37				17 52						17 55				18 07				18 22	
Ravensbourne	d													17 58									
Beckenham Hill	d													18 00									
Bellingham	d													18 02									
Catford	d													18 05									
Crofton Park	d													18 08									
Lewisham 4	a																						
	d								18 02														18 32
Nunhead 4	d								18 07					18 11									18 37
Peckham Rye 4	d								18 10					18 14									18 40
Denmark Hill 4	d	17 50							18 14					18 17									18 44
Beckenham Junction 4	d			17 40				17 55										18 10				18 25	
Kent House 4	d			17 42				17 57										18 12				18 27	
Penge East	d			17 44				17 59										18 14				18 29	
Sydenham Hill	d			17 48				18 03										18 18				18 33	
West Dulwich	d			17 50				18 05										18 20				18 35	
Herne Hill 4	d			17 53			17 57	18 08				18 12						18 23			18 27	18 38	
Loughborough Jn.	d						18 00					18 15									18 30		
Elephant & Castle ⊖	d						18 04					18 19		18 24							18 34		
London Blackfriars 3 ⊖	d					18 07	18 09			18 12	18 22	18 24	18 27	18a29	18 34					18 37	18 39		
City Thameslink 3	a					18 08	18 11			18 13	18 23	18 26	18 28		18 36					18 38	18 41		
Farringdon ⊖	a					18 11	18 13			18 16	18 26	18 28	18 31		18 38					18 41	18 43		
St Pancras International 15 ⊖	a					18 15	18 18			18 20	18 30	18 33	18 35		18 43					18 45	18 48		
Kentish Town ⊖	a						18 23					18 38			18 48						18 53		
Brixton ⊖	d			17 56				18 11										18 26				18 41	
London Victoria 15 ⊖	a	18 00	17 51	18 03	18 06			18 18	18 25								18 21	18 33	18 36			18 48	18 55

		TL	TL	TL	TL	TL	SE	SE	SE	SE	SE	TL	TL	SE	SE	TL	TL	TL	TL	TL	TL	SE
		1		1				◇1	◇1		◇1	1				1	1		1			
		G	E	I		J	K	A	B		C	D	E		F	G	H	E	I		J	K
Sevenoaks 4	d				17 52		18 05													18 22		18 35
Bat & Ball	d				17 55															18 25		
Otford 4	d				17 59						18 26									18 29		
Shoreham (Kent)	d				18 02															18 32		
Eynsford	d				18 05															18 35		
Swanley 4	d				18 11			18 17			18 37									18 41		
St Mary Cray	d				18 15			18 22												18 45		
Orpington 4	d						18 20			18 24												18 50
Petts Wood 4	d						18a23			18 27												18a53
Bickley 4	d				18 20					18 31										18 50		
Bromley South 4	d				18 23			18 30	18 33	18 34	18 47			18 49						18 53		
Shortlands 4	d				18 25					18 37				18 52						18 55		
Ravensbourne	d				18 28															18 58		
Beckenham Hill	d				18 30															19 00		
Bellingham	d				18 32															19 02		
Catford	d				18 35															19 05		
Crofton Park	d				18 38															19 08		
Lewisham 4	a																					
	d														19 02							
Nunhead 4	d				18 41										19 07					19 11		
Peckham Rye 4	d				18 44										19 10					19 14		
Denmark Hill 4	d				18 47			18 50							19 14					19 17		
Beckenham Junction 4	d									18 40				18 55								
Kent House 4	d									18 42				18 57								
Penge East	d									18 44				18 59								
Sydenham Hill	d									18 48				19 03								
West Dulwich	d									18 50				19 05								
Herne Hill 4	d		18 42							18 53			18 57	19 08				19 12				
Loughborough Jn.	d		18 45										19 00					19 15				
Elephant & Castle ⊖	d		18 49		18 54								19 04					19 19		19 24		
London Blackfriars 3 ⊖	d	18 42	18 54	18 57	18a59	19 04						19 07	19 09			19 12	19 22	19 24	19 27	19a29	19 34	
City Thameslink 3	a	18 43	18 56	18 58		19 06						19 08	19 11			19 13	19 23	19 26	19 28		19 36	
Farringdon ⊖	a	18 46	18 58	19 01		19 08						19 11	19 13			19 16	19 26	19 28	19 31		19 38	
St Pancras International 15 ⊖	a	18 50	19 03	19 05		19 13						19 15	19 18			19 20	19 30	19 33	19 35		19 43	
Kentish Town ⊖	a		19 08			19 18							19 23					19 38			19 48	
Brixton ⊖	d									18 56				19 11								
London Victoria 15 ⊖	a							19 00	18 51	19 03	19 06			19 18	19 25							

A From Dover Priory
B From Ramsgate
C From Canterbury West
D From Horsham to Peterborough
E From Sutton (Surrey) to St Albans City
F From Gravesend
G From Brighton to Bedford
H From Brighton to Cambridge
I From Gatwick Airport to Bedford
J From Rainham (Kent)
K To London Charing Cross
L From Ashford International

Table T195-R

Saturdays

21 December to 16 May

Sevenoaks and Otford, Orpington, Bromley South, Beckenham Junction, Catford - London

		SE ◇■ A	SE	SE ◇■ B	TL ■ C	TL D	SE	SE E		TL ■ F	TL D	TL ■ G	TL	TL H	SE I	SE ◇■ A	SE ◇■ J	SE		SE ◇■ K	TL ■ C	TL D	SE	SE E	TL ■ F
Sevenoaks	d												18 52		19 05										
Bat & Ball	d												18 55												
Otford	d			18 56									18 59							19 26					
Shoreham (Kent)	d												19 02												
Eynsford	d												19 05												
Swanley	d			19 05									19 11			19 17				19 37					
St Mary Cray	d			19 09									19 15			19 22									
Orpington	d		18 54												19 20			19 24							
Petts Wood	d		18 57												19a23			19 27							
Bickley	d		19 01										19 20					19 31							
Bromley South	d	19 03	19 04	19 17			19 19						19 23			19 30	19 33	19 34		19 47			19 49		
Shortlands	d		19 07				19 22						19 25					19 37					19 52		
Ravensbourne	d												19 28												
Beckenham Hill	d												19 30												
Bellingham	d												19 32												
Catford	d												19 35												
Crofton Park	d												19 38												
Lewisham	a																								
	d							19 32																20 02	
Nunhead	d							19 37					19 41											20 07	
Peckham Rye	d							19 40					19 44											20 10	
Denmark Hill	d							19 44					19 47			19 50								20 14	
Beckenham Junction	d		19 10				19 25											19 40					19 55		
Kent House	d		19 12				19 27											19 42					19 57		
Penge East	d		19 14				19 29											19 44					19 59		
Sydenham Hill	d		19 18				19 33											19 48					20 03		
West Dulwich	d		19 20				19 35											19 50					20 05		
Herne Hill	d		19 23			19 27	19 38				19 42							19 53				19 57	20 08		
Loughborough Jn.	d					19 30					19 45											20 00			
Elephant & Castle	d					19 34					19 49		19 54									20 04			
London Blackfriars	d				19 37	19 39				19 42	19 54	19 57	19a59	20 04							20 07	20 09			20 12
City Thameslink	a				19 38	19 41				19 43	19 56	19 58		20 06							20 08	20 11			20 13
Farringdon	a				19 41	19 43				19 46	19 58	20 01		20 08							20 11	20 13			20 16
St Pancras International	a				19 45	19 48				19 50	20 03	20 05		20 13							20 15	20 18			20 20
Kentish Town	a					19 53					20 08			20 18								20 23			
Brixton	d		19 26				19 41											19 56					20 11		
London Victoria	a	19 21	19 33	19 36			19 48	19 55								20 00	19 51	20 03		20 06			20 18	20 25	

		TL ■ L	TL D	TL ■ G		TL	TL H	SE I	SE ◇■ A	SE	SE ◇■ B	TL ■ C	TL D	SE		SE E	TL ■ F	TL D	TL ■ G	TL	TL H	SE I	SE ◇■ A	SE ◇■ J	
Sevenoaks	d					19 22		19 35												19 52		20 05			
Bat & Ball	d					19 25														19 55					
Otford	d					19 29					19 56									19 59					
Shoreham (Kent)	d					19 32														20 02					
Eynsford	d					19 35														20 05					
Swanley	d					19 41					20 05									20 11			20 17		
St Mary Cray	d					19 45					20 09									20 15			20 22		
Orpington	d							19 50		19 54												20 20			
Petts Wood	d							19a53		19 57												20a23			
Bickley	d					19 50				20 01										20 20					
Bromley South	d					19 53			20 03	20 04	20 17			20 19						20 23			20 30	20 33	
Shortlands	d					19 55				20 07				20 22						20 25					
Ravensbourne	d					19 58														20 28					
Beckenham Hill	d					20 00														20 30					
Bellingham	d					20 02														20 32					
Catford	d					20 05														20 35					
Crofton Park	d					20 08														20 38					
Lewisham	a																								
	d															20 32									
Nunhead	d					20 11										20 37				20 41					
Peckham Rye	d					20 14										20 40				20 44					
Denmark Hill	d					20 17										20 44				20 47			20 50		
Beckenham Junction	d									20 10				20 25											
Kent House	d									20 12				20 27											
Penge East	d									20 14				20 29											
Sydenham Hill	d									20 18				20 33											
West Dulwich	d									20 20				20 35											
Herne Hill	d		20 12							20 23			20 27	20 38				20 42							
Loughborough Jn.	d		20 15										20 30					20 45							
Elephant & Castle	d		20 19			20 24							20 34					20 49		20 54					
London Blackfriars	d	20 22	20 24	20 27		20a29	20 34					20 37	20 39				20 42	20 54	20 57	20a59	21 04				
City Thameslink	a	20 23	20 26	20 28			20 36					20 38	20 41				20 43	20 56	20 58						
Farringdon	a	20 26	20 28	20 31			20 38					20 41	20 43				20 46	20 58	21 01		21 08				
St Pancras International	a	20 30	20 33	20 35			20 43					20 45	20 48				20 50	21 03	21 05		21 13				
Kentish Town	a		20 38				20 48						20 53					21 08			21 18				
Brixton	d									20 26				20 41											
London Victoria	a								20 21	20 33	20 36			20 48		20 55							21 00	20 51	

A From Dover Priory
B From Ashford International
C From Horsham to Peterborough
D From Sutton (Surrey) to St Albans City
E From Gravesend
F From Brighton to Bedford
G From Gatwick Airport to Bedford
H From Rainham (Kent)
I To London Charing Cross
J From Ramsgate
K From Canterbury West
L From Brighton to Cambridge

Table T195-R

Saturdays

21 December to 16 May

Sevenoaks and Otford, Orpington, Bromley South, Beckenham Junction, Catford - London

		SE	SE ◇■ A	TL ■ B	TL C	SE	SE D	TL ■ E	TL ■ F	TL C		TL ■ G	TL	TL H	SE I	SE ◇■ J	SE	SE ◇■ K	TL ■ B	TL C		SE	SE D	TL ■ E	TL C
Sevenoaks	d												20 22		20 35										
Bat & Ball	d												20 25												
Otford	d		20 26										20 29					20 56							
Shoreham (Kent)	d												20 32												
Eynsford	d												20 35												
Swanley	d		20 37										20 41					21 05							
St Mary Cray	d												20 45					21 09							
Orpington	d	20 24													20 50		20 54								
Petts Wood	d	20 27													20a53		20 57								
Bickley	d	20 31											20 50				21 01								
Bromley South	d	20 34	20 47			20 49							20 53			21 03	21 04	21 17				21 19			
Shortlands	d	20 37				20 52							20 55				21 07					21 22			
Ravensbourne	d												20 58												
Beckenham Hill	d												21 00												
Bellingham	d												21 02												
Catford	d												21 05												
Crofton Park	d												21 08												
Lewisham	a																								
	d						21 02																21 32		
Nunhead	d						21 07						21 11										21 37		
Peckham Rye	d						21 10						21 14										21 40		
Denmark Hill	d						21 14						21 17										21 44		
Beckenham Junction	d	20 40				20 55											21 10					21 25			
Kent House	d	20 42				20 57											21 12					21 27			
Penge East	d	20 44				20 59											21 14					21 29			
Sydenham Hill	d	20 48				21 03											21 18					21 33			
West Dulwich	d	20 50				21 05											21 20					21 35			
Herne Hill	d	20 53			20 57	21 08				21 12							21 23			21 27		21 38			21 42
Loughborough Jn.	d				21 00					21 15										21 30					21 45
Elephant & Castle	d				21 04					21 19			21 24							21 34					21 49
London Blackfriars	d			21 07	21 09			21 12	21 22	21 24		21 27	21a29	21 34					21 37	21 39				21 42	21 54
City Thameslink	a																								
Farringdon	a			21 11	21 13			21 16	21 26	21 28		21 31		21 38					21 41	21 43				21 46	21 58
St Pancras International	a			21 15	21 18			21 20	21 30	21 33		21 35		21 43					21 45	21 48				21 50	22 03
Kentish Town	a				21 23					21 38				21 48						21 53					22 08
Brixton	d	20 56				21 11											21 26					21 41			
London Victoria	a	21 03	21 06			21 18	21 25									21 21	21 33	21 36				21 48	21 55		

		TL ■ G	TL	TL H	SE I	SE ◇■ J		SE ◇■ L	SE	SE ◇■ A	TL ■ B	TL M	SE	SE D	TL ■ E	TL ■ F		TL M	TL ■ G	TL	TL N	SE I	SE ◇■ J	SE	SE ◇■ K
Sevenoaks	d		20 52		21 05															21 22		21 35			
Bat & Ball	d		20 55																	21 25					
Otford	d		20 59							21 26										21 29					21 56
Shoreham (Kent)	d		21 02																	21 32					
Eynsford	d		21 05																	21 35					
Swanley	d		21 11			21 17				21 37										21 41					22 05
St Mary Cray	d		21 15			21 22														21 45					22 09
Orpington	d				21 20				21 24													21 50		21 54	
Petts Wood	d				21a23				21 27													21a53		21 57	
Bickley	d		21 20						21 31											21 50				22 01	
Bromley South	d		21 23			21 30		21 33	21 34	21 47			21 49							21 53			22 03	22 04	22 17
Shortlands	d		21 25						21 37				21 52							21 55				22 07	
Ravensbourne	d		21 28																	21 58					
Beckenham Hill	d		21 30																	22 00					
Bellingham	d		21 32																	22 02					
Catford	d		21 35																	22 05					
Crofton Park	d		21 38																	22 08					
Lewisham	a																								
	d													22 02											
Nunhead	d		21 41											22 07						22 11					
Peckham Rye	d		21 44											22 10						22 14					
Denmark Hill	d		21 47			21 50								22 14						22 17					
Beckenham Junction	d								21 40				21 55											22 10	
Kent House	d								21 42				21 57											22 12	
Penge East	d								21 44				21 59											22 14	
Sydenham Hill	d								21 48				22 03											22 18	
West Dulwich	d								21 50				22 05											22 20	
Herne Hill	d								21 53			21 57	22 08					22 12						22 23	
Loughborough Jn.	d											22 00						22 15							
Elephant & Castle	d		21 54									22 04						22 19		22 24					
London Blackfriars	d	21 57	21a59	22 04							22 07	22 09			22 12	22 22		22 24	22 27	22a29	22 34				
City Thameslink	a																								
Farringdon	a	22 01		22 08							22 11	22 13			22 16	22 26		22 28	22 31		22 38				
St Pancras International	a	22 05		22 13							22 15	22 18			22 20	22 30		22 33	22 35		22 43				
Kentish Town	a			22 18								22 23						22 38							
Brixton	d								21 56				22 11											22 26	
London Victoria	a					22 00		21 51	22 03	22 06			22 18	22 25									22 21	22 33	22 36

A From Canterbury West
B From Horsham to Peterborough
C From Sutton (Surrey) to St Albans City
D From Gravesend
E From Brighton to Bedford
F From Brighton to Cambridge
G From Gatwick Airport to Bedford
H From Rainham (Kent)
I To London Charing Cross
J From Dover Priory
K From Ashford International
L From Ramsgate
M From Sutton (Surrey) to Bedford
N From Rainham (Kent) to West Hampstead Thameslink

Table T195-R

Saturdays
21 December to 16 May

Sevenoaks and Otford, Orpington, Bromley South, Beckenham Junction, Catford - London

	TL ■ A	TL B	SE	SE C	TL ■ D	TL B	TL	TL E	SE F	SE ◇■ G	SE	SE ◇■ H	TL ■ A	TL ■ D	TL B	SE	SE C	TL ■ I	TL B	TL	TL E
Sevenoaks d							21 52		22 05											22 22	
Bat & Ball d							21 55													22 25	
Otford d							21 59					22 26								22 29	
Shoreham (Kent) d							22 02													22 32	
Eynsford d							22 05													22 35	
Swanley d							22 11					22 37								22 41	
St Mary Cray d							22 15													22 45	
Orpington d									22 20		22 24										
Petts Wood d									22a23		22 27										
Bickley d							22 20				22 31									22 50	
Bromley South d			22 19				22 23			22 33	22 34	22 47				22 49				22 53	
Shortlands d			22 22				22 25				22 37					22 52				22 55	
Ravensbourne d							22 28													22 58	
Beckenham Hill d							22 30													23 00	
Bellingham d							22 32													23 02	
Catford d							22 35													23 05	
Crofton Park d							22 38													23 08	
Lewisham a																					
Lewisham d				22 32													23 02				
Nunhead d				22 37			22 41										23 07			23 11	
Peckham Rye d				22 40			22 44										23 10			23 14	
Denmark Hill d				22 44			22 47										23 14			23 17	
Beckenham Junction d			22 25								22 40					22 55					
Kent House d			22 27								22 42					22 57					
Penge East d			22 29								22 44					22 59					
Sydenham Hill d			22 33								22 48					23 03					
West Dulwich d			22 35								22 50					23 05					
Herne Hill d		22 27	22 38			22 44					22 53				23 04	23 08			23 14		
Loughborough Jn. d		22 30				22 47									23 07				23 17		
Elephant & Castle d		22 34				22 51	22 54								23 11				23 21	23 24	
London Blackfriars d	22 37	22 39			22 42	22 59	22a59	23 04					23 07	23 12	23 17			23 22	23 27	23a29	23 34
City Thameslink a																					
Farringdon a	22 41	22 43			22 46	23 03		23 08					23 11	23 16	23 21			23 26	23 31		23 38
St Pancras International a	22 45	22 48			22 50	23 08		23 13					23 15	23 20	23 25			23 30	23 35		23 43
Kentish Town a		22 53				23 13									23 30				23 40		
Brixton d			22 41								22 56					23 11					
London Victoria a			22 48	22 55						22 51	23 03	23 06				23 18	23 25				

	SE F	SE ◇■ J	SE	SE ◇■ K	TL ■ A	TL ■ D	TL B	SE	TL B	SE C	TL	SE F	SE ◇■ G	SE	TL B	TL	SE F	SE ◇■ K	SE ◇■ J	SE
Sevenoaks d	22 35										22 52	23 05				23 22	23 35			
Bat & Ball d											22 55					23 25				
Otford d				22 56							22 59					23 29		23 36		
Shoreham (Kent) d											23 02					23 32				
Eynsford d											23 05					23 35				
Swanley d		22 47		23 05							23 11					23 41		23 45	23 53	
St Mary Cray d		22 52		23 09							23 15					23 45		23 49	23 57	
Orpington d	22 50		22 54									23 20		23 24			23 50			23 54
Petts Wood d	22a53		22 57									23a23		23 27			23 53			23 57
Bickley d			23 01								23 20			23 31		23 50				00 01
Bromley South d		23 00	23 04	23 17				23 19			23 23		23 33	23 34		23 53		23 56	00 04	00 04
Shortlands d			23 07					23 22			23 25			23 37		23 55				00 07
Ravensbourne d											23 28					23 58				
Beckenham Hill d											23 30					00 01				
Bellingham d											23 32					00 03				
Catford d											23 35					00 06				
Crofton Park d											23 38					00 09				
Lewisham a																	00 10			
Lewisham d										23 32										
Nunhead d										23 37	23 41					00 11				
Peckham Rye d										23 40	23 44					00 14				
Denmark Hill d		23 20								23 44	23 47					00 17				
Beckenham Junction d			23 10					23 25						23 40						00 10
Kent House d			23 12					23 27						23 42						00 12
Penge East d			23 14					23 29						23 44						00 14
Sydenham Hill d			23 18					23 33						23 48						00 18
West Dulwich d			23 20					23 35						23 50						00 20
Herne Hill d			23 23				23 34	23 38	23 44					23 53	23 57					00 23
Loughborough Jn. d							23 37		23 47											
Elephant & Castle d							23 41		23 54		23 55				00 04	00 24				
London Blackfriars d					23 37	23 42	23 49		00 02		23a59				00 09	00a29				
City Thameslink a																				
Farringdon a					23 41	23 46	23 53		00 06						00 13					
St Pancras International a					23 45	23 50	23 57		00 10						00 17					
Kentish Town a							00 01								00 22					
Brixton d			23 26					23 41						23 56						00 26
London Victoria a		23 30	23 33	23 36				23 48		23 55			23 51	00 03				00 15	00 23	00 33

A From Horsham to Peterborough
B From Sutton (Surrey) to Bedford
C From Gravesend
D From Brighton to Bedford
E From Rainham (Kent) to West Hampstead Thameslink
F To London Charing Cross
G From Ramsgate
H From Canterbury West
I From Brighton to Cambridge
J From Dover Priory
K From Ashford International

NRT DECEMBER 19 EDITION

Table T195-R

Sundays
15 December to 10 May

Sevenoaks and Otford, Orpington, Bromley South, Beckenham Junction, Catford - London

	TL A	SE ◇■ B	SE C	TL A	SE	TL ■ D	TL E	TL ■ F	TL ■ D	TL ■ D	TL ■ G	SE H	TL	SE	SE ◇■ I	SE J	TL	SE K	SE	SE ◇■ L	SE ◇■ M	SE J
Sevenoaks d																		07 04				
Bat & Ball d																						
Otford d																					07 29	
Shoreham (Kent) d																						
Eynsford d																						
Swanley d															07 13						07 42	
St Mary Cray d															07 18						07 46	
Orpington d													06 46	06 54			07 16	07 19	07 24			
Petts Wood d													06 49	06 57			07 19	07 22	07 27			
Bickley d			00 01										06 57	07 01			07 26		07 31			
Bromley South d		00 04	00 04		00 19								07 01	07 04	07 26		07 29		07 34	07 48	07 54	
Shortlands d			00 07										07 03	07 07			07 31		07 37			
Ravensbourne d													07 06				07 34					
Beckenham Hill d							00 01						07 08				07 36					
Bellingham d							00 03						07 10				07 38					
Catford d							00 06						07 13				07 41					
Crofton Park d							00 09						07 16				07 44					
Lewisham a																		07 39				
Lewisham d												07 02				07 32						08 02
Nunhead d							00 11					07 07	07 19			07 37	07 47					08 07
Peckham Rye d							00 14					07 10	07 22			07 40	07 50					08 10
Denmark Hill d							00 17					07 14	07 25		07 38	07 44	07 53					08 14
Beckenham Junction d			00 10											07 10					07 40			
Kent House d			00 12											07 12					07 42			
Penge East d			00 14											07 14					07 44			
Sydenham Hill d			00 18											07 18					07 48			
West Dulwich d			00 20											07 20					07 50			
Herne Hill d			00 23											07 23					07 53			
Loughborough Jn. d																						
Elephant & Castle d				00 04			00 24															
London Blackfriars d	00 02			00 09		00 22	00a29	00 37	00 50	01 06	01 36											
City Thameslink a																						
Farringdon a	00 06			00 13		00 26		00 41														
St Pancras International a	00 10			00 17		00 30		00 45	00 59	01 15	01 43											
Kentish Town a				00 22					01 05		01 48											
Brixton d			00 26											07 26					07 56			
London Victoria a		00 23	00 33		00 37							07 25	07 36	07 34	07 48	07 56	08 06		08 04	08 09	08 12	08 25

	TL	SE K	SE	SE ◇■ L	SE J	TL	SE K	SE	SE ◇■ N	SE ◇■ M	SE J	TL ■ O	TL	TL ■ P	SE K	SE	SE ◇■ L	SE J	TL ■ G	TL Q	TL	TL R
Sevenoaks d	07 28	07 34				07 58	08 04						08 28		08 34						08 58	
Bat & Ball d	07 31					08 01							08 31								09 01	
Otford d	07 35					08 05				08 32			08 35								09 05	
Shoreham (Kent) d	07 38					08 08							08 38								09 08	
Eynsford d	07 41					08 11							08 41								09 11	
Swanley d	07 47			08 13		08 17				08 42			08 47				09 13				09 17	
St Mary Cray d	07 51			08 18		08 21				08 46			08 51				09 18				09 21	
Orpington d		07 49	07 54				08 19	08 24							08 49	08 54						
Petts Wood d		07 52	07 57				08 22	08 27							08 52	08 57						
Bickley d	07 56		08 01			08 26		08 31					08 56			09 01					09 26	
Bromley South d	07 59		08 04	08 26		08 29		08 34	08 48	08 54			08 59			09 04	09 26				09 29	
Shortlands d	08 01		08 07			08 31		08 37					09 01			09 07					09 31	
Ravensbourne d	08 04					08 34							09 04								09 34	
Beckenham Hill d	08 06					08 36							09 06								09 36	
Bellingham d	08 08					08 38							09 08								09 38	
Catford d	08 11					08 41							09 11								09 41	
Crofton Park d	08 14					08 44							09 14								09 44	
Lewisham a		08 09					08 39								09 09							
Lewisham d					08 32						09 02							09 32				
Nunhead d	08 17				08 37	08 47					09 07		09 17					09 37			09 47	
Peckham Rye d	08 20				08 40	08 50					09 10		09 20					09 40			09 50	
Denmark Hill d	08 23			08 38	08 44	08 53					09 14		09 23				09 38	09 44			09 53	
Beckenham Junction d			08 10					08 40								09 10						
Kent House d			08 12					08 42								09 12						
Penge East d			08 14					08 44								09 14						
Sydenham Hill d			08 18					08 48								09 18						
West Dulwich d			08 20					08 50								09 20						
Herne Hill d			08 23					08 53								09 23				09 45		
Loughborough Jn. d																				09 48		
Elephant & Castle d													09 30							09 53	10 00	
London Blackfriars d												09 31	09a34	09 39					09 55	09 58	10a04	10 05
City Thameslink a																						
Farringdon a												09 35		09 43					09 59	10 02		10 09
St Pancras International a												09 39		09 47					10 03	10 06		10 13
Kentish Town a																				10 11		10 18
Brixton d			08 26					08 56								09 26						
London Victoria a	08 36		08 34	08 48	08 56	09 06		09 04	09 09	09 12	09 25					09 34	09 48	09 56				

A not 15 December. From Sutton (Surrey) to Bedford
B not 15 December. From Dover Priory
C not 15 December. From Orpington
D not 15 December. From Brighton to Bedford
E not 15 December. From Sevenoaks
F not 15 December. From Horsham to Hitchin
G From Brighton to Bedford
H From Barnehurst
I From Gillingham (Kent)
J From Dartford
K To London Charing Cross
L From Faversham
M From Ashford International
N From Dover Priory
O From Gatwick Airport to Cambridge
P From Three Bridges to Bedford
Q From Sutton (Surrey) to Luton
R From Rainham (Kent)

Table T195-R

Sundays

15 December to 10 May

Sevenoaks and Otford, Orpington, Bromley South, Beckenham Junction, Catford - London

		SE A		SE	SE ◇1 B	SE ◇1 C	SE D	TL 1 E	TL 1 F	TL G	TL 1 H	TL		TL I	SE A	SE	SE ◇1 J	SE D	TL 1 E	TL 1 F	TL G	TL		TL I	SE A
Sevenoaks 4	d	09 04										09 28			09 34							09 58			10 04
Bat & Ball	d											09 31										10 01			
Otford 4	d					09 32						09 35										10 05			
Shoreham (Kent)	d											09 38										10 08			
Eynsford	d											09 41										10 11			
Swanley 4	d					09 42						09 47					10 13					10 17			
St Mary Cray	d					09 46						09 51					10 18					10 21			
Orpington 4	d	09 19		09 24											09 49	09 54									10 19
Petts Wood 4	d	09 22		09 27											09 52	09 57									10 22
Bickley 4	d			09 31								09 56				10 01						10 26			
Bromley South 4	d			09 34	09 48	09 54						09 59				10 04	10 26					10 29			
Shortlands 4	d			09 37								10 01				10 07						10 31			
Ravensbourne	d											10 04										10 34			
Beckenham Hill	d											10 06										10 36			
Bellingham	d											10 08										10 38			
Catford	d											10 11										10 41			
Crofton Park	d											10 14										10 44			
Lewisham 4	a	09 39													10 09										10 39
	d						10 02											10 32							
Nunhead 4	d						10 07					10 17						10 37				10 47			
Peckham Rye 4	d						10 10					10 20						10 40				10 50			
Denmark Hill 4	d						10 14					10 23					10 38	10 44				10 53			
Beckenham Junction 4	d			09 40												10 10									
Kent House 4	d			09 42												10 12									
Penge East	d			09 44												10 14									
Sydenham Hill	d			09 48												10 18									
West Dulwich	d			09 50												10 20									
Herne Hill 4	d			09 53						10 15						10 23					10 45				
Loughborough Jn.	d									10 18											10 48				
Elephant & Castle ⊖	d									10 23		10 30									10 53	11 00			
London Blackfriars 3 ⊖	d							10 09	10 25	10 28	10 31	10a34		10 35					10 39	10 55	10 58	11a04		11 05	
City Thameslink 3	a																								
Farringdon ⊖	a							10 13	10 29	10 32	10 35			10 39					10 43	10 59	11 02			11 09	
St Pancras International 15 ⊖	a							10 17	10 33	10 36	10 39			10 43					10 47	11 03	11 06			11 13	
Kentish Town ⊖	a									10 41				10 48							11 11			11 18	
Brixton ⊖	d			09 56												10 26									
London Victoria 15 ⊖	a			10 04	10 06	10 12	10 25									10 34	10 48	10 56							

		SE	SE ◇1 B	SE ◇1 K	SE D	TL 1 L	TL 1 F	TL G		TL 1 H	TL	TL I	SE A	SE	SE ◇1 J	SE D	TL 1 E	TL 1 F		TL M	TL	TL I	SE A	SE	SE ◇1 B
Sevenoaks 4	d										10 28		10 34								10 58		11 04		
Bat & Ball	d										10 31										11 01				
Otford 4	d			10 32							10 35										11 05				
Shoreham (Kent)	d										10 38										11 08				
Eynsford	d										10 41										11 11				
Swanley 4	d			10 42							10 47				11 13						11 17				
St Mary Cray	d			10 46							10 51				11 18						11 21				
Orpington 4	d	10 24											10 49	10 54									11 19	11 24	
Petts Wood 4	d	10 27											10 52	10 57									11 22	11 27	
Bickley 4	d	10 31									10 56			11 01							11 26			11 31	
Bromley South 4	d	10 34	10 48	10 54							10 59			11 04	11 26						11 29			11 34	11 48
Shortlands 4	d	10 37									11 01			11 07							11 31			11 37	
Ravensbourne	d										11 04										11 34				
Beckenham Hill	d										11 06										11 36				
Bellingham	d										11 08										11 38				
Catford	d										11 11										11 41				
Crofton Park	d										11 14										11 44				
Lewisham 4	a												11 09										11 39		
	d				11 02											11 32									
Nunhead 4	d				11 07						11 17					11 37					11 47				
Peckham Rye 4	d				11 10						11 20					11 40					11 50				
Denmark Hill 4	d				11 14						11 23				11 38	11 44					11 53				
Beckenham Junction 4	d	10 40												11 10										11 40	
Kent House 4	d	10 42												11 12										11 42	
Penge East	d	10 44												11 14										11 44	
Sydenham Hill	d	10 48												11 18										11 48	
West Dulwich	d	10 50												11 20										11 50	
Herne Hill 4	d	10 53						11 15						11 23						11 45				11 53	
Loughborough Jn.	d							11 18												11 48					
Elephant & Castle ⊖	d							11 23			11 30									11 53	12 00				
London Blackfriars 3 ⊖	d					11 09	11 25	11 28		11 31	11a34	11 35					11 39	11 55		11 58	12a04	12 05			
City Thameslink 3	a																								
Farringdon ⊖	a					11 13	11 29	11 32		11 35		11 39					11 43	11 59		12 02		12 09			
St Pancras International 15 ⊖	a					11 17	11 33	11 36		11 39		11 43					11 47	12 03		12 06		12 13			
Kentish Town ⊖	a							11 41				11 48								12 11		12 18			
Brixton ⊖	d	10 56												11 26										11 56	
London Victoria 15 ⊖	a	11 04	11 06	11 12	11 25									11 34	11 48	11 56								12 04	12 06

A To London Charing Cross
B From Dover Priory
C From Ashford International
D From Dartford
E From Three Bridges to Bedford
F From Brighton to Bedford
G From Sutton (Surrey) to Luton
H From Gatwick Airport to Cambridge
I From Rainham (Kent)
J From Canterbury East
K From Canterbury West
L From Gatwick Airport to Bedford
M From Sutton (Surrey) to St Albans City

Table T195-R

Sundays

15 December to 10 May

Sevenoaks and Otford, Orpington, Bromley South, Beckenham Junction, Catford - London

		SE ◇1 A	SE B	TL 1 C		TL D	TL 1 E	TL F	TL 1 G	TL	TL H	SE I	SE	SE ◇1 J		SE B	TL 1 K	TL D	TL 1 E	TL F	TL	TL H	SE I	SE	SE ◇1 L
Sevenoaks 4	d									11 28		11 34									11 58		12 04		
Bat & Ball	d									11 31											12 01				
Otford 4	d	11 32								11 35											12 05				
Shoreham (Kent)	d									11 38											12 08				
Eynsford	d									11 41											12 11				
Swanley 4	d	11 42								11 47				12 13							12 17				
St Mary Cray	d	11 46								11 51				12 18							12 21				
Orpington 4	d											11 49	11 54										12 19	12 24	
Petts Wood 4	d											11 52	11 57										12 22	12 27	
Bickley 4	d									11 56			12 01								12 26			12 31	
Bromley South 4	d	11 54								11 59			12 04	12 26							12 29			12 34	12 48
Shortlands 4	d									12 01			12 07								12 31			12 37	
Ravensbourne	d									12 04											12 34				
Beckenham Hill	d									12 06											12 36				
Bellingham	d									12 08											12 38				
Catford	d									12 11											12 41				
Crofton Park	d									12 14											12 44				
Lewisham 4	a											12 09											12 39		
	d		12 02													12 32									
Nunhead 4	d		12 07							12 17						12 37					12 47				
Peckham Rye 4	d		12 10							12 20						12 40					12 50				
Denmark Hill 4	d		12 14							12 23				12 38		12 44					12 53				
Beckenham Junction 4	d												12 10											12 40	
Kent House 4	d												12 12											12 42	
Penge East	d												12 14											12 44	
Sydenham Hill	d												12 18											12 48	
West Dulwich	d												12 20											12 50	
Herne Hill 4	d					12 03		12 15					12 23					12 33		12 45				12 53	
Loughborough Jn.	d					12 06		12 18										12 36		12 48					
Elephant & Castle ⊖	d					12 11		12 23		12 30								12 41		12 53	13 00				
London Blackfriars 3 ⊖	d			12 09		12 16	12 25	12 28	12 31	12a34	12 35						12 41	12 46	12 55	12 58	13a04	13 05			
City Thameslink 3	a																								
Farringdon ⊖	a			12 13		12 20	12 29	12 32	12 35		12 39						12 45	12 50	12 59	13 02		13 09			
St Pancras International 15 ⊖	a			12 17		12 24	12 33	12 36	12 39		12 43						12 49	12 54	13 03	13 06		13 13			
Kentish Town ⊖	a							12 41			12 48									13 11		13 18			
Brixton ⊖	d												12 26											12 56	
London Victoria 15 ⊖	a	12 12	12 24										12 34	12 48		12 54								13 04	13 06

		SE ◇1 A	SE B	TL 1 C	TL D	TL 1 E	TL F	TL 1 G	TL	TL H	SE I	SE	SE ◇1 J	SE B	TL 1 K		TL D	TL 1 E	TL F	TL	TL H	SE I	SE	SE ◇1 L
Sevenoaks 4	d								12 28		12 34									18 58		19 04		
Bat & Ball	d								12 31											19 01				
Otford 4	d	12 32							12 35											19 05				
Shoreham (Kent)	d								12 38											19 08				
Eynsford	d								12 41											19 11				
Swanley 4	d	12 42							12 47				13 13							19 17				
St Mary Cray	d	12 46							12 51				13 18							19 21				
Orpington 4	d										12 49	12 54										19 19	19 24	
Petts Wood 4	d										12 52	12 57										19 22	19 27	
Bickley 4	d								12 56			13 01								19 26			19 31	
Bromley South 4	d	12 54							12 59			13 04	13 26							19 29			19 34	19 48
Shortlands 4	d								13 01			13 07								19 31			19 37	
Ravensbourne	d								13 04											19 34				
Beckenham Hill	d								13 06							and at the same minutes past each hour until				19 36				
Bellingham	d								13 08											19 38				
Catford	d								13 11											19 41				
Crofton Park	d								13 14											19 44				
Lewisham 4	a										13 09											19 39		
	d		13 02											13 32										
Nunhead 4	d		13 07						13 17					13 37						19 47				
Peckham Rye 4	d		13 10						13 20					13 40						19 50				
Denmark Hill 4	d		13 14						13 23				13 38	13 44						19 53				
Beckenham Junction 4	d											13 10											19 40	
Kent House 4	d											13 12											19 42	
Penge East	d											13 14											19 44	
Sydenham Hill	d											13 18											19 48	
West Dulwich	d											13 20											19 50	
Herne Hill 4	d				13 03		13 15					13 23					19 33		19 45				19 53	
Loughborough Jn.	d				13 06		13 18										19 36		19 48					
Elephant & Castle ⊖	d				13 11		13 23		13 30								19 41		19 53	20 00				
London Blackfriars 3 ⊖	d			13 09	13 16	13 25	13 28	13 31	13a34	13 35					13 39		19 46	19 55	19 58	20a04	20 05			
City Thameslink 3	a																							
Farringdon ⊖	a			13 13	13 20	13 29	13 32	13 35		13 39					13 43		19 50	19 59	20 02		20 09			
St Pancras International 15 ⊖	a			13 17	13 24	13 33	13 36	13 39		13 43					13 47		19 54	20 03	20 06		20 13			
Kentish Town ⊖	a						13 41			13 48									20 11		20 18			
Brixton ⊖	d											13 26											19 56	
London Victoria 15 ⊖	a	13 12	13 24									13 34	13 48	13 54									20 04	20 06

A From Canterbury West
B From Dartford
C From Gatwick Airport to Bedford
D From Sutton (Surrey) to Luton
E From Brighton to Bedford
F From Sutton (Surrey) to St Albans City
G From Gatwick Airport to Cambridge
H From Rainham (Kent)
I To London Charing Cross
J From Canterbury East
K From Three Bridges to Bedford
L From Dover Priory

Table T195-R

Sundays

15 December to 10 May

Sevenoaks and Otford, Orpington, Bromley South, Beckenham Junction, Catford - London

		SE	SE	TL	TL	TL	TL	TL	TL	TL	SE	SE	SE	SE	TL		TL	TL	TL	TL	TL	SE	SE	SE	SE
		◇1		1		1		1					◇1		1			1						◇1	◇1
		A	B	C	D	E	F	G		H	I		J	B	K		D	E	F		H	I		L	A
Sevenoaks 4	d								19 28		19 34									19 58		20 04			
Bat & Ball	d								19 31											20 01					
Otford 4	d	19 32							19 35											20 05					20 32
Shoreham (Kent)	d								19 38											20 08					
Eynsford	d								19 41											20 11					
Swanley 4	d	19 42							19 47				20 13							20 17					20 42
St Mary Cray	d	19 46							19 51				20 18							20 21					20 46
Orpington 4	d										19 49	19 54										20 19	20 24		
Petts Wood 4	d										19 52	19 57										20 22	20 27		
Bickley 4	d								19 56			20 01								20 26			20 31		
Bromley South 4	d	19 54							19 59			20 04	20 26							20 29			20 34	20 48	20 54
Shortlands 4	d								20 01			20 07								20 31			20 37		
Ravensbourne	d								20 04											20 34					
Beckenham Hill	d								20 06											20 36					
Bellingham	d								20 08											20 38					
Catford	d								20 11											20 41					
Crofton Park	d								20 14											20 44					
Lewisham 4	a										20 09											20 39			
	d		20 02											20 32											
Nunhead 4	d		20 07						20 17					20 37						20 47					
Peckham Rye 4	d		20 10						20 20					20 40						20 50					
Denmark Hill 4	d		20 14						20 23				20 38	20 44						20 53					
Beckenham Junction 4	d											20 10											20 40		
Kent House 4	d											20 12											20 42		
Penge East	d											20 14											20 44		
Sydenham Hill	d											20 18											20 48		
West Dulwich	d											20 20											20 50		
Herne Hill 4	d				20 03		20 15					20 23					20 33		20 45				20 53		
Loughborough Jn.	d				20 06		20 18										20 36		20 48						
Elephant & Castle ⊖	d				20 11		20 23		20 30								20 41		20 53	21 00					
London Blackfriars 3 ⊖	d			20 09	20 16	20 25	20 28	20 31	20a34	20 35					20 39		20 46	20 55	20 58	21a04	21 05				
City Thameslink 3	a																								
Farringdon ⊖	a			20 13	20 20	20 29	20 32	20 35		20 39					20 43		20 50	20 59	21 02		21 09				
St Pancras International 15 ⊖	a			20 17	20 24	20 33	20 36	20 39		20 43					20 47		20 54	21 03	21 06		21 13				
Kentish Town ⊖	a						20 41			20 48									21 11		21 18				
Brixton ⊖	d											20 26											20 56		
London Victoria 15 ⊖	a	20 12	20 24									20 34	20 48	20 54									21 04	21 06	21 10

			SE	TL	TL	TL	TL	TL	TL	TL	SE		SE	SE	SE	TL	TL	TL	TL	TL	TL		SE	SE	SE
				1		1		1						◇1		1		1							◇1
			B	C	D	E	F	G		H	I			J	B	K	D	E	M		H		I		L
Sevenoaks 4	d								20 28		20 34									20 58			21 04		
Bat & Ball	d								20 31											21 01					
Otford 4	d								20 35											21 05					
Shoreham (Kent)	d								20 38											21 08					
Eynsford	d								20 41											21 11					
Swanley 4	d								20 47					21 13						21 17					
St Mary Cray	d								20 51					21 18						21 21					
Orpington 4	d										20 49		20 54										21 19	21 24	
Petts Wood 4	d										20 52		20 57										21 22	21 27	
Bickley 4	d								20 56				21 01							21 26				21 31	
Bromley South 4	d								20 59				21 04	21 26						21 29				21 34	21 48
Shortlands 4	d								21 01				21 07							21 31				21 37	
Ravensbourne	d								21 04											21 34					
Beckenham Hill	d								21 06											21 36					
Bellingham	d								21 08											21 38					
Catford	d								21 11											21 41					
Crofton Park	d								21 14											21 44					
Lewisham 4	a										21 09												21 39		
	d		21 02												21 32										
Nunhead 4	d		21 07						21 17						21 37					21 47					
Peckham Rye 4	d		21 10						21 20						21 40					21 50					
Denmark Hill 4	d		21 14						21 23					21 38	21 44					21 53					
Beckenham Junction 4	d												21 10											21 40	
Kent House 4	d												21 12											21 42	
Penge East	d												21 14											21 44	
Sydenham Hill	d												21 18											21 48	
West Dulwich	d												21 20											21 50	
Herne Hill 4	d				21 03		21 15						21 23				21 33		21 45					21 53	
Loughborough Jn.	d				21 06		21 18										21 36		21 48						
Elephant & Castle ⊖	d				21 11		21 23		21 30								21 41		21 53	22 00					
London Blackfriars 3 ⊖	d			21 09	21 16	21 25	21 28	21 31	21a34	21 35						21 39	21 46	21 55	21 58	22a04	22 05				
City Thameslink 3	a																								
Farringdon ⊖	a			21 13	21 20	21 29	21 32	21 35		21 39						21 43	21 50	21 59	22 02		22 09				
St Pancras International 15 ⊖	a			21 17	21 24	21 33	21 36	21 39		21 43						21 47	21 54	22 03	22 06		22 13				
Kentish Town ⊖	a						21 41			21 48									22 11		22 18				
Brixton ⊖	d												21 26											21 56	
London Victoria 15 ⊖	a		21 24										21 34	21 48	21 54									22 04	22 06

A From Canterbury West
B From Dartford
C From Gatwick Airport to Bedford
D From Sutton (Surrey) to Luton
E From Brighton to Bedford
F From Sutton (Surrey) to St Albans City
G From Gatwick Airport to Cambridge
H From Rainham (Kent)
I To London Charing Cross
J From Canterbury East
K From Three Bridges to Bedford
L From Dover Priory
M From Sutton (Surrey) to Bedford

Table T195-R

Sundays

15 December to 10 May

Sevenoaks and Otford, Orpington, Bromley South, Beckenham Junction, Catford - London

		SE	SE	TL	TL	TL	TL		TL	TL	TL	SE	SE	SE	SE	TL	TL		TL	TL	SE	SE	TL	SE	SE
		◇1		1		1			1					◇1		1								◇1	◇1
		A	B	C	D	E	F		G		H	I		J	B	E	K			L	I		K	M	A
Sevenoaks 4	d									21 28		21 34							21 58		22 04				
Bat & Ball	d									21 31									22 01						
Otford 4	d	21 32								21 35									22 05						22 32
Shoreham (Kent)	d									21 38									22 08						
Eynsford	d									21 41									22 11						
Swanley 4	d	21 42								21 47				22 13					22 17						22 42
St Mary Cray	d	21 46								21 51				22 18					22 21						22 46
Orpington 4	d											21 49	21 54								22 19	22 24			
Petts Wood 4	d											21 52	21 57								22 22	22 27			
Bickley 4	d									21 56			22 01						22 26			22 31			
Bromley South 4	d	21 54								21 59			22 04	22 26					22 29			22 34		22 48	22 54
Shortlands 4	d									22 01			22 07						22 31			22 37			
Ravensbourne	d									22 04									22 34						
Beckenham Hill	d									22 06									22 36						
Bellingham	d									22 08									22 38						
Catford	d									22 11									22 41						
Crofton Park	d									22 14									22 44						
Lewisham 4	a											22 09									22 39				
	d		22 02												22 32										
Nunhead 4	d		22 07							22 17					22 37				22 47						
Peckham Rye 4	d		22 10							22 20					22 40				22 50						
Denmark Hill 4	d		22 14							22 23				22 38	22 44				22 53						
Beckenham Junction 4	d												22 10									22 40			
Kent House 4	d												22 12									22 42			
Penge East	d												22 14									22 44			
Sydenham Hill	d												22 18									22 48			
West Dulwich	d												22 20									22 50			
Herne Hill 4	d				22 03		22 15						22 23				22 45					22 53	23 03		
Loughborough Jn.	d				22 06		22 18										22 48						23 06		
Elephant & Castle ⊖	d				22 11		22 23			22 30							22 53		23 00				23 11		
London Blackfriars 3 ⊖	d			22 09	22 16	22 25	22 28		22 31	22a34	22 35					22 55	22 58		23a04	23 05			23 16		
City Thameslink 3	a																								
Farringdon ⊖	a			22 13	22 20	22 29	22 32		22 35		22 39					22 59	23 02			23 09			23 20		
St Pancras International 15 ⊖	a			22 17	22 24	22 33	22 36		22 39		22 43					23 03	23 06			23 13			23 24		
Kentish Town ⊖	a						22 41				22 48						23 11			23 18			23 29		
Brixton ⊖	d												22 26									22 56			
London Victoria 15 ⊖	a	22 11	22 24										22 34	22 48	22 54							23 04		23 06	23 11

		SE	TL		TL	TL	SE	SE	SE	SE	SE	SE
			1							◇1		
		B	E			N	I		I	J		I
Sevenoaks 4	d				22 28		22 34		23 04			23 34
Bat & Ball	d				22 31							
Otford 4	d				22 35							
Shoreham (Kent)	d				22 38							
Eynsford	d				22 41							
Swanley 4	d				22 47					23 13		
St Mary Cray	d				22 51					23 18		
Orpington 4	d						22 49	22 54	23 19		23 24	23 49
Petts Wood 4	d						22 52	22 57	23 22		23 27	23 52
Bickley 4	d				22 56			23 01			23 31	
Bromley South 4	d				22 59			23 04		23 26	23 34	
Shortlands 4	d				23 01			23 07			23 37	
Ravensbourne	d				23 04							
Beckenham Hill	d				23 06							
Bellingham	d				23 08							
Catford	d				23 11							
Crofton Park	d				23 14							
Lewisham 4	a						23 09		23 39			00 09
	d	23 02										
Nunhead 4	d	23 07			23 17							
Peckham Rye 4	d	23 10			23 20							
Denmark Hill 4	d	23 14			23 23					23 38		
Beckenham Junction 4	d							23 10			23 40	
Kent House 4	d							23 12			23 42	
Penge East	d							23 14			23 44	
Sydenham Hill	d							23 18			23 48	
West Dulwich	d							23 20			23 50	
Herne Hill 4	d							23 23			23 53	
Loughborough Jn.	d											
Elephant & Castle ⊖	d				23 30							
London Blackfriars 3 ⊖	d		23 27		23a34	23 37						
City Thameslink 3	a											
Farringdon ⊖	a		23 31			23 41						
St Pancras International 15 ⊖	a		23 35			23 45						
Kentish Town ⊖	a					23 50						
Brixton ⊖	d							23 26			23 56	
London Victoria 15 ⊖	a	23 24						23 34		23 48	00 04	

A From Ashford International
B From Dartford
C From Gatwick Airport to Bedford
D From Sutton (Surrey) to West Hampstead Thameslink
E From Brighton to Bedford
F From Sutton (Surrey) to Luton
G From Gatwick Airport to Cambridge
H From Rainham (Kent)
I To London Charing Cross
J From Canterbury East
K From Sutton (Surrey) to Bedford
L From Rainham (Kent) to West Hampstead Thameslink
M From Dover Priory
N From Rainham (Kent) to Bedford

Table T196-F

Mondays to Fridays

16 December to 15 May

Cambridge, Kentish Town and London Thameslink-Denmark Hill-Catford-Bromley South-Orpington and Swanley-Otford and Sevenoaks

		TL	TL	TL	TL	TL	TL	TL	TL	TL		TL	SE ◇1	TL	TL	TL	TL	TL	TL	TL		TL	TL	TL	TL
Cambridge	d																								
Stevenage	d																								
Welwyn Garden City	d																								
Finsbury Park	d																								
Kentish Town	d					05 41		06 11																	
St Pancras International	d					05 47		06 17		06 47					07 17		07 47		08 17			08 47		09 17	
Farringdon	d					05 52		06 22		06 52					07 22		07 52		08 22			08 52		09 22	
City Thameslink	d					05 54		06 24		06 54					07 24		07 54		08 24			08 54		09 24	
London Blackfriars	d	04 56	05 16	05 26	05 46	05 56	06 16	06 26	06 46	06 56		07 16	07 23		07 26	07 46	07 56	08 16	08 26	08 46		08 56	09 16	09 26	09 46
London Bridge	a																								
Elephant & Castle	d	05 00	05 20	05 30	05 50	06 00	06 20	06 30	06 50	07 00		07 20	07 27		07 30	07 50	08 00	08 20	08 30	08 50		09 00	09 20	09 30	09 50
Denmark Hill	d	05 08	05 28	05 38	05 58	06 08	06 28	06 38	06 58	07 08		07 28	07 36	←	07 39	07 58	08 08	08 28	08 38	08 58		09 08	09 28	09 38	09 58
Peckham Rye	d	05 11	05 31	05 41	06 01	06 11	06 31	06 41	07 01	07 11		07 31		07 31	07 42	08 01	08 11	08 31	08 41	09 01		09 12	09 31	09 41	10 01
Nunhead	d	05 14	05 34	05 44	06 04	06 14	06 34	06 44	07 04	07 14		→		07 34	07 45	08 04	08 14	08 34	08 44	09 04		09 15	09 34	09 44	10 04
Crofton Park	d	05 17	05 37	05 47	06 07	06 17	06 37	06 47	07 07	07 17				07 37	07 48	08 07	08 17	08 37	08 47	09 07		09 18	09 37	09 47	10 07
Catford	d	05 20	05 40	05 50	06 10	06 20	06 40	06 50	07 10	07 20				07 40	07 51	08 10	08 20	08 40	08 50	09 10		09 21	09 40	09 50	10 10
Bellingham	d	05 23	05 43	05 53	06 13	06 23	06 43	06 53	07 13	07 23				07 43	07 54	08 13	08 23	08 43	08 53	09 13		09 24	09 43	09 53	10 13
Beckenham Hill	d	05 25	05 45	05 55	06 15	06 25	06 45	06 55	07 15	07 25				07 45	07 56	08 15	08 25	08 45	08 55	09 15		09 26	09 45	09 55	10 15
Ravensbourne	d	05 27	05 47	05 58	06 17	06 27	06 47	06 57	07 17	07 27				07 47	07 58	08 17	08 27	08 47	08 57	09 17		09 28	09 47	09 57	10 17
Shortlands	d	05 30	05 50	06 00	06 20	06 30	06 50	07 00	07 20	07 30				07 50	08 01	08 20	08 30	08 50	09 00	09 20		09 31	09 50	10 00	10 20
Bromley South	d	05 33	05 53	06 03	06 23	06 33	06 53	07 03	07 23	07 33			07 53	07 53	08 07	08 23	08 33	08 53	09 03	09 23		09 34	09 53	10 03	10 23
Bickley	d	05 36	05 56	06 06	06 26	06 36	06 56	07 06	07 26	07 36				07 56	08 10	08 26	08 36	08 56	09 06	09 26		09 37	09 56	10 06	10 26
Petts Wood	d	05 40		06 10		06 40		07 10		07 41					08 15		08 43		09 12			09 42		10 10	
Orpington	a	05 44		06 14		06 44		07 14		07 45					08 18		08 47		09 16			09 46		10 14	
St Mary Cray	d		06 01		06 31		07 01		07 32				07 59	08 02		08 31		09 01		09 32			10 01		10 31
Swanley	d		06 06		06 36		07 06		07 37				08 04	08 08		08 36		09 06		09 37			10 06		10 36
Eynsford	d		06 11		06 41		07 11		07 42					08 13		08 41		09 11		09 42			10 11		10 41
Shoreham (Kent)	d		06 15		06 45		07 15		07 46					08 17		08 45		09 15		09 46			10 15		10 45
Otford	d		06 18		06 48		07 20		07 49				08 12	08 20		08 48		09 18		09 49			10 18		10 48
Bat & Ball	d		06 21		06 51		07 23		07 52					08 23		08 51		09 21		09 52			10 21		10 51
Sevenoaks	a		06 25		06 55		07 27		07 56					08 26		08 55		09 25		09 56			10 25		10 55
Borough Green & Wrotham	d												08 22												
West Malling	d												08 28												
Maidstone East	a												08 42												
Bearsted	a																								
Ashford International	a																								

		TL	TL	TL	TL	TL		TL	TL	TL	TL	TL	TL	TL	TL	TL		TL	TL	TL	TL	TL	TL	TL	TL
Cambridge	d																								
Stevenage	d																								
Welwyn Garden City	d																								
Finsbury Park	d																								
Kentish Town	d			10 11		10 41			11 12		11 41		12 11		12 41			13 11		13 41		14 11		14 41	
St Pancras International	d	09 47		10 17		10 47			11 17		11 47		12 17		12 47			13 17		13 47		14 17		14 47	
Farringdon	d	09 52		10 22		10 52			11 22		11 52		12 22		12 52			13 22		13 52		14 22		14 52	
City Thameslink	d	09 54		10 24		10 54			11 24		11 54		12 24		12 54			13 24		13 54		14 24		14 54	
London Blackfriars	d	09 56	10 16	10 26	10 46	10 56		11 16	11 26	11 46	11 56	12 16	12 26	12 46	12 56	13 16		13 26	13 46	13 56	14 16	14 26	14 46	14 56	15 16
London Bridge	a																								
Elephant & Castle	d	10 00	10 20	10 30	10 50	11 00		11 20	11 30	11 50	12 00	12 20	12 30	12 50	13 00	13 20		13 30	13 50	14 00	14 20	14 30	14 50	15 00	15 20
Denmark Hill	d	10 08	10 28	10 38	10 58	11 08		11 28	11 38	11 58	12 08	12 28	12 38	12 58	13 08	13 28		13 38	13 58	14 08	14 28	14 38	14 58	15 08	15 28
Peckham Rye	d	10 11	10 31	10 41	11 01	11 11		11 31	11 41	12 01	12 11	12 31	12 41	13 01	13 11	13 31		13 41	14 01	14 11	14 31	14 41	15 01	15 11	15 31
Nunhead	d	10 14	10 34	10 44	11 04	11 14		11 34	11 44	12 04	12 14	12 34	12 44	13 04	13 14	13 34		13 44	14 04	14 14	14 34	14 44	15 04	15 14	15 34
Crofton Park	d	10 17	10 37	10 47	11 07	11 17		11 37	11 47	12 07	12 17	12 37	12 47	13 07	13 17	13 37		13 47	14 07	14 17	14 37	14 47	15 07	15 17	15 37
Catford	d	10 20	10 40	10 50	11 10	11 20		11 40	11 50	12 10	12 20	12 40	12 50	13 10	13 20	13 40		13 50	14 10	14 20	14 40	14 50	15 10	15 20	15 40
Bellingham	d	10 23	10 43	10 53	11 13	11 23		11 43	11 53	12 13	12 23	12 43	12 53	13 13	13 23	13 43		13 53	14 13	14 23	14 43	14 53	15 13	15 23	15 43
Beckenham Hill	d	10 25	10 45	10 55	11 15	11 25		11 45	11 55	12 15	12 25	12 45	12 55	13 15	13 25	13 45		13 55	14 15	14 25	14 45	14 55	15 15	15 25	15 45
Ravensbourne	d	10 27	10 47	10 57	11 17	11 27		11 47	11 57	12 17	12 27	12 47	12 57	13 17	13 27	13 47		13 57	14 17	14 27	14 47	14 57	15 17	15 27	15 47
Shortlands	d	10 30	10 50	11 00	11 20	11 30		11 50	12 00	12 20	12 30	12 50	13 00	13 20	13 30	13 50		14 00	14 20	14 30	14 50	15 00	15 20	15 30	15 50
Bromley South	d	10 33	10 53	11 03	11 23	11 33		11 53	12 03	12 23	12 33	12 53	13 03	13 23	13 33	13 53		14 03	14 23	14 33	14 53	15 03	15 23	15 33	15 53
Bickley	d	10 37	10 56	11 06	11 26	11 36		11 56	12 06	12 26	12 36	12 56	13 06	13 26	13 36	13 56		14 06	14 26	14 36	14 56	15 06	15 26	15 36	15 56
Petts Wood	d	10 42		11 10		11 40			12 10		12 40		13 10		13 40			14 10		14 40		15 10		15 40	
Orpington	a	10 45		11 14		11 44			12 14		12 44		13 14		13 44			14 14		14 44		15 14		15 44	
St Mary Cray	d		11 01		11 31			12 01		12 31		13 01		13 31		14 01			14 31		15 01		15 31		16 01
Swanley	d		11 06		11 36			12 06		12 36		13 06		13 36		14 06			14 36		15 06		15 36		16 06
Eynsford	d		11 11		11 41			12 11		12 41		13 11		13 41		14 11			14 41		15 11		15 41		16 11
Shoreham (Kent)	d		11 15		11 45			12 15		12 45		13 15		13 45		14 15			14 45		15 15		15 45		16 15
Otford	d		11 18		11 48			12 18		12 48		13 18		13 48		14 18			14 48		15 18		15 48		16 18
Bat & Ball	d		11 21		11 51			12 21		12 51		13 21		13 51		14 21			14 51		15 21		15 51		16 21
Sevenoaks	a		11 25		11 55			12 25		12 55		13 25		13 55		14 25			14 55		15 25		15 55		16 25
Borough Green & Wrotham	d																								
West Malling	d																								
Maidstone East	a																								
Bearsted	a																								
Ashford International	a																								

Table T196-F

Mondays to Fridays

16 December to 15 May

Cambridge, Kentish Town and London Thameslink-Denmark Hill-Catford-Bromley South-Orpington and Swanley-Otford and Sevenoaks

		TL		TL	TL	TL	TL	TL	TL	TL	TL	SE ◇1		TL	TL	TL	TL	TL	TL	SE ◇1	TL	TL		TL	TL
Cambridge	d																								
Stevenage	d																								
Welwyn Garden City	d																								
Finsbury Park	d																								
Kentish Town	d	15 11			15 41		16 11		16 41		17 11				17 41		18 11		18 41					19 11	
St Pancras International	d	15 17			15 47		16 17		16 47		17 17				17 47		18 17		18 47					19 17	
Farringdon	d	15 22			15 52		16 22		16 52		17 22				17 52		18 22		18 52					19 22	
City Thameslink	d	15 24			15 54		16 24		16 54		17 24				17 54		18 24		18 54					19 24	
London Blackfriars	d	15 26		15 46	15 56	16 16	16 26	16 46	16 56	17 16	17 26	17 38		17 46	17 56	18 16	18 26	18 46	18 56	19 05		19 16		19 26	19 46
London Bridge	a																								
Elephant & Castle	d	15 30		15 50	16 00	16 20	16 30	16 50	17 00	17 20	17 30	17 42		17 50	18 00	18 20	18 30	18 50	19 00	19 09	←	19 20		19 30	19 50
Denmark Hill	d	15 38		15 58	16 08	16 28	16 38	16 58	17 08	17 28	17 38			17 58	18 08	18 28	18 38	18 58	19 08		19 08	19 28		19 38	19 58
Peckham Rye	d	15 41		16 01	16 11	16 31	16 41	17 01	17 11	17 31	17 41			18 01	18 11	18 31	18 41	19 01	→		19 11	19 31		19 40	20 01
Nunhead	d	15 44		16 04	16 14	16 34	16 44	17 04	17 14	17 34	17 44			18 04	18 14	18 34	18 44	19 04			19 14	19 34		19 43	20 04
Crofton Park	d	15 47		16 07	16 17	16 37	16 47	17 07	17 17	17 37	17 47			18 07	18 17	18 37	18 47	19 07			19 17	19 37		19 46	20 07
Catford	d	15 50		16 10	16 20	16 40	16 50	17 10	17 20	17 40	17 50			18 10	18 20	18 40	18 50	19 10			19 20	19 40		19 49	20 10
Bellingham	d	15 53		16 13	16 23	16 43	16 53	17 13	17 23	17 43	17 53			18 13	18 23	18 43	18 53	19 13			19 23	19 43		19 52	20 13
Beckenham Hill	d	15 55		16 15	16 25	16 45	16 55	17 15	17 25	17 45	17 55			18 15	18 25	18 45	18 55	19 15			19 25	19 45		19 54	20 15
Ravensbourne	d	15 58		16 17	16 27	16 47	16 57	17 17	17 27	17 47	17 57			18 17	18 27	18 47	18 57	19 17			19 27	19 47		19 57	20 17
Shortlands	d	16 00		16 20	16 30	16 50	17 00	17 20	17 30	17 50	18 00			18 20	18 30	18 50	19 00	19 20			19 30	19 50		20 01	20 20
Bromley South	d	16 03		16 23	16 33	16 53	17 03	17 23	17 33	17 53	18 03	18 03		18 23	18 33	18 53	19 03	19 23		19 27	19 33	19 53		20 04	20 23
Bickley	d	16 06		16 26	16 36	16 56	17 06	17 26	17 36	17 56	18 06			18 26	18 36	18 56	19 06	19 26			19 36	19 56		20 06	20 26
Petts Wood	d	16 11			16 40		17 10		17 42		18 12				18 44		19 10				19 40			20 11	
Orpington	a	16 14			16 44		17 14		17 45		18 16				18 48		19 14				19 44			20 14	
St Mary Cray	d			16 31		17 01		17 31		18 01		18 10		18 30		19 01		19 31		19 34		20 01			20 31
Swanley	d			16 36		17 06		17 36		18 06		18 14		18 35		19 07		19 36		19 40		20 06			20 36
Eynsford	d			16 41		17 11		17 41		18 11				18 40		19 12		19 41				20 11			20 41
Shoreham (Kent)	d			16 45		17 15		17 45		18 15				18 44		19 16		19 45				20 15			20 45
Otford	d			16 48		17 18		17 48		18 18		18 23		18 47		19 19		19 48		19 52		20 18			20 48
Bat & Ball	d			16 51		17 21		17 51		18 21				18 50		19 22		19 51				20 21			20 51
Sevenoaks	a			16 55		17 25		17 55		18 25				18 55		19 25		19 55				20 25			20 55
Borough Green & Wrotham	d											18 33								19 59					
West Malling	d											18 39								20 06					
Maidstone East	a											18 50								20 16					
Bearsted	a											18 56													
Ashford International	a											19 24													

		TL	TL	TL	TL	TL	TL	TL		TL	TL	TL	TL	TL	TL	TL	TL
Cambridge	d																
Stevenage	d																
Welwyn Garden City	d																
Finsbury Park	d																
Kentish Town	d	19 41		20 11		20 41		21 11			21 41		22 11		22 41		
St Pancras International	d	19 47		20 17		20 47		21 17			21 47		22 17		22 47		
Farringdon	d	19 52		20 22		20 52		21 22			21 52		22 22		22 52		
City Thameslink	d	19 54		20 24		20 54		21 24			21 54		22 24		22 54		
London Blackfriars	d	19 56	20 16	20 26	20 46	20 56	21 16	21 26		21 46	21 56	22 16	22 26	22 46	22 56	23 16	23 46
London Bridge	a																
Elephant & Castle	d	20 00	20 20	20 30	20 50	21 00	21 20	21 30		21 50	22 00	22 20	22 30	22 50	23 00	23 20	23 50
Denmark Hill	d	20 08	20 28	20 38	20 58	21 08	21 28	21 38		21 58	22 08	22 28	22 38	22 58	23 08	23 28	23 58
Peckham Rye	d	20 11	20 31	20 41	21 01	21 11	21 31	21 41		22 01	22 11	22 31	22 41	23 01	23 11	23 31	00 01
Nunhead	d	20 14	20 34	20 44	21 04	21 14	21 34	21 44		22 04	22 14	22 34	22 44	23 04	23 14	23 34	00 04
Crofton Park	d	20 17	20 37	20 47	21 07	21 17	21 37	21 47		22 07	22 17	22 37	22 47	23 07	23 17	23 37	00 07
Catford	d	20 20	20 40	20 50	21 10	21 20	21 40	21 50		22 10	22 20	22 40	22 50	23 10	23 20	23 40	00 10
Bellingham	d	20 23	20 43	20 53	21 13	21 23	21 43	21 53		22 13	22 23	22 43	22 53	23 13	23 23	23 43	00 13
Beckenham Hill	d	20 25	20 45	20 55	21 15	21 25	21 45	21 55		22 15	22 25	22 45	22 55	23 15	23 25	23 45	00 15
Ravensbourne	d	20 27	20 47	20 57	21 17	21 27	21 47	21 57		22 17	22 27	22 47	22 57	23 17	23 27	23 47	00 18
Shortlands	d	20 30	20 50	21 00	21 20	21 30	21 50	22 00		22 20	22 30	22 50	23 00	23 20	23 30	23 50	00 20
Bromley South	d	20 33	20 53	21 03	21 23	21 33	21 53	22 03		22 23	22 33	22 53	23 03	23 23	23 33	23 53	00 23
Bickley	d	20 36	20 56	21 06	21 26	21 36	21 56	22 06		22 26	22 36	22 56	23 06	23 26	23 36	23 56	00 26
Petts Wood	d	20 40		21 10		21 40		22 10			22 40		23 10		23 40		
Orpington	a	20 44		21 14		21 44		22 14			22 44		23 14		23 44		
St Mary Cray	d		21 01		21 31		22 01			22 31		23 01		23 31		00 01	00 31
Swanley	d		21 06		21 36		22 06			22 36		23 06		23 36		00 06	00 36
Eynsford	d		21 11		21 41		22 11			22 41		23 11		23 41		00 11	00 41
Shoreham (Kent)	d		21 15		21 45		22 15			22 45		23 15		23 45		00 15	00 45
Otford	d		21 18		21 48		22 18			22 48		23 18		23 48		00 18	00 48
Bat & Ball	d		21 21		21 51		22 21			22 51		23 21		23 51		00 21	00 51
Sevenoaks	a		21 25		21 55		22 25			22 55		23 25		23 55		00 25	00 55
Borough Green & Wrotham	d																
West Malling	d																
Maidstone East	a																
Bearsted	a																
Ashford International	a																

Table T196-F

Saturdays
21 December to 16 May

Cambridge, Kentish Town and London Thameslink-Denmark Hill-Catford-Bromley South-Orpington and Swanley-Otford and Sevenoaks

Station		TL		TL
Cambridge	d			
Stevenage	d			
Welwyn Garden City	d			
Finsbury Park	d			
Kentish Town	d			
St Pancras International	d			
Farringdon	d			
City Thameslink	d			
London Blackfriars	d	05 16		23 46
London Bridge	a			
Elephant & Castle	d	05 20		23 50
Denmark Hill	d	05 28		23 58
Peckham Rye	d	05 31		00 01
Nunhead	d	05 34		00 04
Crofton Park	d	05 37		00 07
Catford	d	05 40	and every 30 minutes until	00 10
Bellingham	d	05 43		00 13
Beckenham Hill	d	05 45		00 15
Ravensbourne	d	05 47		00 17
Shortlands	d	05 50		00 20
Bromley South	d	05 53		00 23
Bickley	d	05 56		00 26
Petts Wood	d			
Orpington	a			
St Mary Cray	d	06 01		00 31
Swanley	d	06 06		00 36
Eynsford	d	06 11		00 41
Shoreham (Kent)	d	06 15		00 45
Otford	d	06 18		00 48
Bat & Ball	d	06 21		00 51
Sevenoaks	a	06 25		00 55
Borough Green & Wrotham	d			
West Malling	d			
Maidstone East	a			
Bearsted	a			
Ashford International	a			

Sundays
15 December to 10 May

Station		TL		TL	TL	TL		TL	TL	TL
Cambridge	d									
Stevenage	d									
Welwyn Garden City	d									
Finsbury Park	d									
Kentish Town	d									
St Pancras International	d									
Farringdon	d									
City Thameslink	d									
London Blackfriars	d	09 42		19 42	20 12	20 42		22 42	23 12	23 42
London Bridge	a									
Elephant & Castle	d	09 46		19 46	20 16	20 46		22 46	23 16	23 46
Denmark Hill	d	09 53		19 53	20 23	20 53		22 53	23 23	23 53
Peckham Rye	d	09 56		19 56	20 26	20 56		22 56	23 26	23 56
Nunhead	d	09 59		19 59	20 29	20 59		22 59	23 29	23 59
Crofton Park	d	10 02		20 02	20 32	21 02		23 02	23 32	00 02
Catford	d	10 05	and every 30 minutes until	20 05	20 35	21 05	and every 30 minutes until	23 05	23 35	00 05
Bellingham	d	10 08		20 08	20 38	21 08		23 08	23 38	00 08
Beckenham Hill	d	10 10		20 10	20 40	21 10		23 10	23 40	00 10
Ravensbourne	d	10 13		20 13	20 43	21 13		23 13	23 43	00 13
Shortlands	d	10 15		20 15	20 45	21 15		23 15	23 45	00 15
Bromley South	d	10 18		20 18	20 48	21 18		23 18	23 48	00 18
Bickley	d	10 21		20 21	20 51	21 21		23 21	23 51	00 21
Petts Wood	d									
Orpington	a									
St Mary Cray	d	10 25		20 25	20 55	21 25		23 25	23 55	00 25
Swanley	d	10 30		20 30	21 00	21 30		23 30	23 59	00 30
Eynsford	d	10 35		20 35	21 05	21 35		23 35	00 05	00 35
Shoreham (Kent)	d	10 39		20 39	21 09	21 39		23 39	00 09	00 39
Otford	d	10 42		20 42	21 12	21 42		23 42	00 12	00 42
Bat & Ball	d	10 45		20 45	21 15	21 45		23 45	00 15	00 45
Sevenoaks	a	10 49		20 49	21 20	21 49		23 49	00 19	00 49
Borough Green & Wrotham	d									
West Malling	d									
Maidstone East	a									
Bearsted	a									
Ashford International	a									

Table T196-R

Mondays to Fridays
16 December to 15 May

Sevenoaks and Otford-Swanley and Orpington-Bromley South-Catford-Denmark Hill-London Thameslink and Kentish Town, Cambridge

Station		TL	TL	TL	TL	TL	TL	SE ◇1	TL	TL		TL	TL	SE ◇1	TL	TL	TL	TL	TL	TL		TL	TL	SE ◇1	TL
Ashford International	d							05 30						06 22											
Bearsted	d							05 55						06 48											
Maidstone East	d							06 02						06 54										08 53	
West Malling	d							06 09						07 05										09 00	
Borough Green & Wrotham	d							06 16						07 12										09 07	
Sevenoaks	d				05 22		05 52			06 22			06 45			07 18		07 45		08 22			08 52		
Bat & Ball	d				05 25		05 55			06 25			06 48			07 21		07 48		08 25			08 55		
Otford	d				05 29		05 59	06 25		06 29			06 52	07 22		07 25		07 52		08 29			08 59	09 15	
Shoreham (Kent)	d				05 32		06 02			06 32			06 55			07 28		07 55		08 32			09 02		
Eynsford	d				05 36		06 05			06 35			06 58			07 31		07 58		08 35			09 05		
Swanley	d				05 41		06 11	06 34		06 41			07 04	07 32		07 37		08 04		08 41			09 11	09 24	
St Mary Cray	d				05 45		06 15			06 45			07 08			07 41		08 08		08 45			09 15	09 29	
Orpington	d	04 33	05 03	05 33		06 03			06 30			06 59			07 30		08 03		08 29			09 03			
Petts Wood	d	04 36	05 06	05 36		06 06			06 33			07 02			07 33		08 06		08 32			09 06			
Bickley	d	04 40	05 10	05 40	05 50	06 10	06 20		06 40	06 50		07 06	07 13		07 40	07 46	08 10	08 15	08 36	08 50		09 10	09 20		
Bromley South	d	04 43	05 13	05 43	05 53	06 13	06 23	06 42	06 43	06 53		07 13	07 23	07 43	07 43	07 53	08 13	08 23	08 43	08 53		09 13	09 23	09 36	←
Shortlands	d	04 45	05 15	05 45	05 55	06 15	06 25		06 45	06 55		07 15	07 25		07 45	07 55	08 15	08 25	08 45	08 55		09 15	09 25		09 25
Ravensbourne	d	04 48	05 18	05 48	05 58	06 18	06 28		06 48	06 58		07 18	07 28		07 48	07 58	08 18	08 28	08 48	08 58		09 18	→		09 28
Beckenham Hill	d	04 50	05 20	05 50	06 00	06 20	06 30		06 50	07 00		07 20	07 30		07 50	08 00	08 20	08 30	08 50	09 00		09 20			09 30
Bellingham	d	04 52	05 22	05 52	06 02	06 22	06 32		06 52	07 02		07 22	07 32		07 52	08 02	08 22	08 32	08 52	09 02		09 22			09 32
Catford	d	04 55	05 25	05 55	06 05	06 25	06 35		06 55	07 05		07 25	07 35		07 55	08 05	08 25	08 35	08 55	09 05		09 25			09 35
Crofton Park	d	04 58	05 28	05 58	06 08	06 28	06 38		06 58	07 08		07 28	07 38		07 58	08 08	08 28	08 38	08 58	09 08		09 28			09 38
Nunhead	d	05 01	05 31	06 01	06 11	06 31	06 41		07 01	07 11		07 31	07 41		08 01	08 11	08 31	08 41	09 01	09 11		09 31			09 41
Peckham Rye	d	05 04	05 34	06 04	06 14	06 34	06 44		07 04	07 14		07 34	07 44		08 04	08 14	08 34	08 44	09 04	09 14		09 34			09 44
Denmark Hill	d	05 07	05 37	06 07	06 17	06 37	06 47		07 07	07 17		07 37	07 47		08 07	08 17	08 37	08 47	09 07	09 17		09 37			09 47
Elephant & Castle	a	05 14	05 44	06 14	06 24	06 44	06 54	06 58	07 14	07 24		07 44	07 54	08 01	08 14	08 24	08 44	08 54	09 14	09 24		09 44		09 52	09 54
London Bridge	a																								
London Blackfriars	a	05 19	05 49	06 19	06 29	06 49	06 59	07 05	07 19	07 29		07 49	07 59	08 09	08 19	08 29	08 49	08 59	09 19	09 29		09 49		09 59	09 59
City Thameslink	a	05 21	05 51	06 21		06 51			07 21			07 51			08 21		08 51		09 21			09 51			
Farringdon	a	05 23	05 53	06 23		06 53			07 23			07 53			08 23		08 53		09 23			09 53			
St Pancras International	a	05 28	05 58	06 28		06 58			07 28			07 58			08 28		08 58		09 28			09 58			
Kentish Town	a	05 33	06 03						07 33			08 03			08 33		09 03		09 33			10 03			
Finsbury Park	a																								
Welwyn Garden City	a																								
Stevenage	a																								
Cambridge	a																								

Station		TL	TL	TL	TL		TL	TL	TL	TL		TL	TL	TL	TL	TL	TL	TL	TL	TL		TL	TL	TL
Ashford International	d																							
Bearsted	d																							
Maidstone East	d																							
West Malling	d																							
Borough Green & Wrotham	d																							
Sevenoaks	d		09 22		09 52			16 22		16 52			17 22		17 52		18 22		18 52			19 22		19 52
Bat & Ball	d		09 25		09 55			16 25		16 55			17 25		17 55		18 25		18 55			19 25		19 55
Otford	d		09 29		09 59			16 29		16 59			17 29		17 59		18 29		18 59			19 29		19 59
Shoreham (Kent)	d		09 32		10 02			16 32		17 02			17 32		18 02		18 32		19 02			19 32		20 02
Eynsford	d		09 35		10 05			16 35		17 05			17 35		18 05		18 35		19 05			19 35		20 05
Swanley	d		09 41		10 11			16 41		17 11			17 41		18 11		18 41		19 11			19 41		20 11
St Mary Cray	d		09 45		10 15			16 45		17 15			17 45		18 15		18 45		19 15			19 45		20 15
Orpington	d	09 33		10 03			16 33		17 03			17 33		18 02		18 33		19 03		19 33			20 03	
Petts Wood	d	09 36		10 06			16 36		17 06			17 36		18 05		18 36		19 06		19 36			20 06	
Bickley	d	09 40	09 50	10 10	10 20	and at the same minutes past each hour until	16 40	16 50	17 10	17 20		17 40	17 50	18 10	18 20	18 40	18 50	19 10	19 20	19 40		19 50	20 10	20 20
Bromley South	d	09 43	09 53	10 13	10 23		16 43	16 53	17 13	17 23		17 43	17 53	18 13	18 23	18 43	18 53	19 13	19 23	19 43		19 53	20 13	20 23
Shortlands	d	09 45	09 55	10 15	10 25		16 45	16 55	17 15	17 25		17 45	17 55	18 15	18 25	18 45	18 55	19 15	19 25	19 45		19 55	20 15	20 25
Ravensbourne	d	09 48	09 58	10 18	10 28		16 48	16 58	17 18	17 28		17 48	17 58	18 18	18 28	18 48	18 58	19 18	19 28	19 48		19 58	20 18	20 28
Beckenham Hill	d	09 50	10 00	10 20	10 30		16 50	17 00	17 20	17 30		17 50	18 00	18 20	18 30	18 50	19 00	19 20	19 30	19 50		20 00	20 20	20 30
Bellingham	d	09 52	10 02	10 22	10 32		16 52	17 02	17 22	17 32		17 52	18 02	18 22	18 32	18 52	19 02	19 22	19 32	19 52		20 02	20 22	20 32
Catford	d	09 55	10 05	10 25	10 35		16 55	17 05	17 25	17 35		17 55	18 05	18 25	18 35	18 55	19 05	19 25	19 35	19 55		20 05	20 25	20 35
Crofton Park	d	09 58	10 08	10 28	10 38		16 58	17 08	17 28	17 38		17 58	18 08	18 28	18 38	18 58	19 08	19 28	19 38	19 58		20 08	20 28	20 38
Nunhead	d	10 01	10 11	10 31	10 41		17 01	17 11	17 31	17 41		18 01	18 11	18 31	18 41	19 01	19 11	19 31	19 41	20 01		20 11	20 31	20 41
Peckham Rye	d	10 04	10 14	10 34	10 44		17 04	17 14	17 34	17 44		18 04	18 14	18 34	18 44	19 04	19 14	19 34	19 44	20 04		20 14	20 34	20 44
Denmark Hill	d	10 07	10 17	10 37	10 47		17 07	17 17	17 37	17 47		18 07	18 17	18 37	18 47	19 07	19 17	19 37	19 47	20 07		20 17	20 37	20 47
Elephant & Castle	a	10 14	10 24	10 44	10 54		17 14	17 24	17 44	17 54		18 14	18 24	18 44	18 54	19 14	19 24	19 44	19 54	20 14		20 24	20 44	20 54
London Bridge	a																							
London Blackfriars	a	10 19	10 29	10 49	10 59		17 19	17 29	17 49	17 59		18 19	18 29	18 49	18 59	19 19	19 29	19 49	19 59	20 19		20 29	20 49	20 59
City Thameslink	a	10 21		10 51			17 21		17 51			18 21		18 51		19 21		19 51		20 21			20 51	
Farringdon	a	10 23		10 53			17 23		17 53			18 23		18 53		19 23		19 53		20 23			20 53	
St Pancras International	a	10 28		10 58			17 28		17 58			18 28		18 58		19 28		19 58		20 28			20 58	
Kentish Town	a	10 33		11 03			17 33		18 03			18 33		19 03						20 33			21 03	
Finsbury Park	a																							
Welwyn Garden City	a																							
Stevenage	a																							
Cambridge	a																							

Table T196-R

Mondays to Fridays
16 December to 15 May

Sevenoaks and Otford-Swanley and Orpington-Bromley South-Catford-Denmark Hill-London Thameslink and Kentish Town, Cambridge

		TL	TL	TL	TL	TL	TL	TL	TL	TL	TL	TL	TL	TL
Ashford International	d													
Bearsted	d													
Maidstone East	d													
West Malling	d													
Borough Green & Wrotham	d													
Sevenoaks	d		20 22		20 52		21 22		21 52		22 22		22 52	23 22
Bat & Ball	d		20 25		20 55		21 25		21 55		22 25		22 55	23 25
Otford	d		20 29		20 59		21 29		21 59		22 29		22 59	23 29
Shoreham (Kent)	d		20 32		21 02		21 32		22 02		22 32		23 02	23 32
Eynsford	d		20 35		21 05		21 35		22 05		22 35		23 05	23 35
Swanley	d		20 41		21 11		21 41		22 11		22 41		23 11	23 41
St Mary Cray	d		20 45		21 15		21 45		22 15		22 45		23 15	23 45
Orpington	d	20 33		21 03		21 33		22 03		22 33		23 03		
Petts Wood	d	20 36		21 06		21 36		22 06		22 36		23 06		
Bickley	d	20 40	20 50	21 10	21 20	21 40	21 50	22 10	22 20	22 40	22 50	23 10	23 20	23 50
Bromley South	d	20 43	20 53	21 13	21 23	21 43	21 53	22 13	22 23	22 43	22 53	23 13	23 23	23 53
Shortlands	d	20 45	20 55	21 15	21 25	21 45	21 55	22 15	22 25	22 45	22 55	23 15	23 25	23 55
Ravensbourne	d	20 48	20 58	21 18	21 28	21 48	21 58	22 18	22 28	22 48	22 58	23 18	23 28	23 58
Beckenham Hill	d	20 50	21 00	21 20	21 30	21 50	22 00	22 20	22 30	22 50	23 00	23 20	23 30	00 01
Bellingham	d	20 52	21 02	21 22	21 32	21 52	22 02	22 22	22 32	22 52	23 02	23 22	23 32	00 03
Catford	d	20 55	21 05	21 25	21 35	21 55	22 05	22 25	22 35	22 55	23 05	23 25	23 35	00 06
Crofton Park	d	20 58	21 08	21 28	21 38	21 58	22 08	22 28	22 38	22 58	23 08	23 28	23 38	00 09
Nunhead	d	21 01	21 11	21 31	21 41	22 01	22 11	22 31	22 41	23 01	23 11	23 31	23 41	00 11
Peckham Rye	d	21 04	21 14	21 34	21 44	22 04	22 14	22 34	22 44	23 04	23 14	23 34	23 44	00 14
Denmark Hill	d	21 07	21 17	21 37	21 47	22 07	22 17	22 37	22 47	23 07	23 17	23 37	23 47	00 17
Elephant & Castle	a	21 14	21 24	21 44	21 54	22 14	22 24	22 44	22 54	23 14	23 24	23 44	23 54	00 24
London Bridge	a													
London Blackfriars	a	21 19	21 29	21 49	21 59	22 19	22 29	22 49	22 59	23 19	23 29	23 49	23 59	00 29
City Thameslink	a	21 21		21 51		22 21		22 51						
Farringdon	a	21 23		21 53		22 23		22 53						
St Pancras International	a	21 28		21 58		22 28		22 58						
Kentish Town	a	21 33		22 03		22 33								
Finsbury Park	a													
Welwyn Garden City	a													
Stevenage	a													
Cambridge	a													

Saturdays
21 December to 16 May

		TL	TL		TL	TL
Ashford International	d					
Bearsted	d					
Maidstone East	d					
West Malling	d					
Borough Green & Wrotham	d					
Sevenoaks	d	05 22	05 52		22 52	23 22
Bat & Ball	d	05 25	05 55		22 55	23 25
Otford	d	05 29	05 59		22 59	23 29
Shoreham (Kent)	d	05 32	06 02		23 02	23 32
Eynsford	d	05 36	06 05		23 05	23 35
Swanley	d	05 41	06 11		23 11	23 41
St Mary Cray	d	05 45	06 15		23 15	23 45
Orpington	d					
Petts Wood	d					
Bickley	d	05 50	06 20		23 20	23 50
Bromley South	d	05 53	06 23	and	23 23	23 53
Shortlands	d	05 55	06 25	every 30	23 25	23 55
Ravensbourne	d	05 58	06 28	minutes	23 28	23 58
Beckenham Hill	d	06 00	06 30	until	23 30	00 01
Bellingham	d	06 02	06 32		23 32	00 03
Catford	d	06 05	06 35		23 35	00 06
Crofton Park	d	06 08	06 38		23 38	00 09
Nunhead	d	06 11	06 41		23 41	00 11
Peckham Rye	d	06 14	06 44		23 44	00 14
Denmark Hill	d	06 17	06 47		23 47	00 17
Elephant & Castle	a	06 24	06 54		23 54	00 24
London Bridge	a					
London Blackfriars	a	06 29	06 59		23 59	00 29
City Thameslink	a					
Farringdon	a					
St Pancras International	a					
Kentish Town	a					
Finsbury Park	a					
Welwyn Garden City	a					
Stevenage	a					
Cambridge	a					

Table T196-R

Sundays
15 December to 10 May

Sevenoaks and Otford-Swanley and Orpington-Bromley South-Catford-Denmark Hill-London Thameslink and Kentish Town, Cambridge

		TL		TL
Ashford International	d			
Bearsted	d			
Maidstone East	d			
West Malling	d			
Borough Green & Wrotham	d			
Sevenoaks	d	08 28		22 28
Bat & Ball	d	08 31		22 31
Otford	d	08 35		22 35
Shoreham (Kent)	d	08 38		22 38
Eynsford	d	08 41		22 41
Swanley	d	08 47		22 47
St Mary Cray	d	08 51		22 51
Orpington	d			
Petts Wood	d			
Bickley	d	08 56		22 56
Bromley South	d	08 59	and	22 59
Shortlands	d	09 01	every 30	23 01
Ravensbourne	d	09 04	minutes	23 04
Beckenham Hill	d	09 06	until	23 06
Bellingham	d	09 08		23 08
Catford	d	09 11		23 11
Crofton Park	d	09 14		23 14
Nunhead	d	09 17		23 17
Peckham Rye	d	09 20		23 20
Denmark Hill	d	09 23		23 23
Elephant & Castle	a	09 29		23 29
London Bridge	a			
London Blackfriars	a	09 34		23 34
City Thameslink	a			
Farringdon	a			
St Pancras International	a			
Kentish Town	a			
Finsbury Park	a			
Welwyn Garden City	a			
Stevenage	a			
Cambridge	a			

Mondays to Fridays
16 December to 15 May

London - Maidstone East, Ashford International and Canterbury West

Miles	Miles			SE MX ◇1 A	SE MX ◇1 A	SE MO ◇1 A	SE MX ◇1 A	SE MX ◇1	SE B	SE ◇1	SE ◇1	SE ◇1	SE ◇1	SE ◇1	SE ◇1	SE ◇1		SE ◇1	SE ◇1	SE ◇1	SE ◇1	SE ◇1
—	—	**London Victoria**	d					00 25		05 50	06 25	06 55		07 55	08 25	08 55	and at the same minutes past each hour until	13 25	13 55	14 25	14 55	15 25
—	—	St Pancras International	d																			
—	—	Farringdon	d																			
—	—	City Thameslink	d																			
—	—	**London Blackfriars**	d										07 23									
—	—	**Bromley South**	d				00 13	00 42		06 12	06 42	07 13	07 53	08 12	08 42	09 12		13 42	14 12	14 42	15 12	15 42
14¾	—	St Mary Cray 195	d				00 19	00 48		06 18	06 48	07 19	07 59	08 18		09 18			14 18		15 18	
17½	—	Swanley 4 195	d				00 23	00 52		06 22	06 52	07 23	08 04	08 22	08 50	09 22		13 50	14 22	14 50	15 22	15 50
24	—	Otford 4 195	d				00 31	01 00		06 30	07 00	07 31	08 12	08 30	08 58	09 30		13 58	14 30	14 58	15 30	15 58
27	—	Kemsing	d				00s36			06 35	07 05	07 36	08 17	08 35		09 35			14 35		15 35	
29½	—	Borough Green & Wrotham	d		00 06	00 08	00s41	01s08		06 40	07 10	07 41	08 22	08 40	09 06	09 40		14 06	14 40	15 06	15 40	16 06
34¾	—	West Malling	d		00 12	00 14	00s47	01s14		06 46	07 16	07 47	08 28	08 46	09 12	09 46		14 12	14 46	15 12	15 46	16 12
35¾	—	East Malling	d			00 17	00s50	01s17		06 49	07 19	07 50	08 31	08 49		09 49			14 49		15 49	
37½	—	Barming	d			00 21	00s54	01s21		06 53	07 23	07 54	08 35	08 53		09 53			14 53		15 53	
40	—	Maidstone East 4	a		00 20	00 25	00 58	01 25		06 57	07 27	07 58	08 42	08 57	09 20	09 57		14 20	14 57	15 20	15 57	16 20
—	—	Maidstone East	d		00 22	00 26	01 00	01 27	06 22	06 59	07 29	07 59		08 59	09 22	09 59		14 22	14 59	15 22	15 59	16 22
42¾	—	Bearsted	d	00 04	00s27	00s31	01s05	01s32	06 27	07 04	07 34	08 04		09 04	09 27	10 04		14 27	15 04	15 27	16 04	16 27
45	—	Hollingbourne	d	00 08	00s31	00s35		01s36	06 31	07 08	07 38	08 08		09 08	09 31			14 31		15 31	16 08	16 31
47½	—	Harrietsham	d	00 11	00s34	00s38		01s39	06 35	07 12	07 42	08 12		09 12	09 34			14 34		15 34	16 11	16 34
49¼	—	Lenham	d	00 15	00s38	00s42		01s43	06 39	07 16	07 46	08 16		09 16	09 38			14 38		15 38	16 15	16 38
53¼	—	Charing	d	00 20	00s43	00s47		01s48	06 44	07 21	07 51	08 21		09 21	09 43			14 43		15 43	16 20	16 43
—	0	**Ashford International**	a	00 29	00 53	00 56	01 24	02 01	06 53	07 31	08 01	08 31		09 30	09 53	10 23		14 53	15 23	15 53	16 29	16 53
—	4	Wye	a						07 11		08 11					10 11		15 11		16 11		17 11
—	9	Chilham	a						07 17		08 17					10 17		15 17		16 17		17 17
—	11	Chartham	a						07 21		08 21					10 21		15 21		16 21		17 21
—	14	**Canterbury West**	a						07 26		08 29					10 27		15 27		16 27		17 27

		SE ◇1	SE ◇1	SE ◇1	SE 1	SE ◇1	SE ◇1	SE ◇1	SE 1	SE ◇1	SE ◇1	SE ◇1	SE ◇1	SE ◇1	SE ◇1	SE ◇1	SE ◇1	SE ◇1	SE ◇1	SE ◇1	SE ◇1	SE ◇1
London Victoria	d	15 55	16 25	16 52	17 09	17 22		17 52	18 07	18 22	18 52		19 25	19 55	20 25	20 55	21 25	21 55	22 25	22 55	23 25	23 55
St Pancras International	d																					
Farringdon	d																					
City Thameslink	d																					
London Blackfriars	d						17 38					19 05										
Bromley South	d	16 12	16 42	17 12	17 34	17 42	18 03	18 12	18 33	18 42	19 12	19 27	19 42	20 12	20 42	21 12	21 42	22 12	22 42	23 12	23 42	00 13
St Mary Cray 195	d	16 18		17 18			18 10	18 18			19 18	19 34		20 18		21 18		22 18		23 18		00 19
Swanley 4 195	d	16 22	16 50	17 22		17 51	18 14	18 22		18 51	19 22	19 40	19 50	20 22	20 51	21 22	21 50	22 22	22 50	23 22	23 50	00 23
Otford 4 195	d	16 30	16 59	17 31	17 52	17 59	18 23	18 31	18 52	18 59	19 31	19 52	19 58	20 30	20 59	21 30	21 58	22 30	22 58	23 30	23 58	00 31
Kemsing	d	16 35		17 36			18 28	18 36			19 36			20 35		21 35		22 35		23 35		00s36
Borough Green & Wrotham	d	16 40	17 07	17 41	18 00	18 07	18 33	18 41	19 00	19 07	19 41	19 59	20 06	20 40	21 06	21 40	22 06	22 40	23 06	23 40	00 06	00s41
West Malling	d	16 46	17 13	17 47	18 06	18 14	18 39	18 47	19 06	19 14	19 47	20 06	20 12	20 46	21 13	21 46	22 12	22 46	23 12	23 46	00 12	00s47
East Malling	d	16 49		17 50	18 09		18 42	18 50	19 09		19 50		20 15	20 49		21 49		22 49		23 49		00s50
Barming	d	16 53		17 54	18 13		18 46	18 54	19 13		19 54		20 19	20 53		21 53		22 53		23 53		00s54
Maidstone East 4	a	16 57	17 21	17 58	18 20	18 22	18 50	18 58	19 20	19 22	19 58	20 16	20 24	20 57	21 21	21 57	22 20	22 57	23 20	23 57	00 20	00 58
Maidstone East	d	16 59	17 23	18 00		18 23	18 51	18 59		19 23	20 00		20 25	20 59	21 23	21 59	22 22	22 59	23 22	23 59	00 22	01 00
Bearsted	d	17 04	17 28	18 05		18 28	18 56	19 05		19 28	20 05		20 30	21 04	21 28	22 04	22 27	23 04	23 27	00 04	00s27	01s05
Hollingbourne	d	17 08	17 32	18 09		18 32	19 00	19 08		19 32	20 09		20 34	21 08	21 32	22 08	22 31	23 08	23 31	00 08	00s31	
Harrietsham	d	17 11	17 35	18 12		18 36	19 04	19 12		19 36	20 12		20 37	21 11	21 35	22 11	22 34	23 11	23 34	00 11	00s34	
Lenham	d	17 15	17 39	18 16		18 40	19 07	19 16		19 40	20 16		20 41	21 15	21 39	22 15	22 38	23 15	23 38	00 15	00s38	
Charing	d	17 20	17 44	18 21		18 45	19 13	19 21		19 45	20 21		20 46	21 20	21 45	22 20	22 43	23 20	23 43	00 20	00s43	
Ashford International	a	17 29	17 56	18 32		18 59	19 24	19 34		19 57	20 32		20 56	21 29	21 54	22 29	22 53	23 29	23 53	00 29	00 53	01 24
Wye	a												21 11									
Chilham	a												21 17									
Chartham	a												21 21									
Canterbury West	a												21 27									

Saturdays
21 December to 16 May

		SE ◇1 A	SE ◇1 A	SE ◇1 A	SE ◇1	SE 1	SE ◇1	SE ◇1	SE ◇1	SE ◇1		SE ◇1	SE ◇1	SE ◇1	SE ◇1	SE ◇1	SE ◇1	SE ◇1	SE ◇1		SE ◇1	SE ◇1
London Victoria	d				00 25		06 25	07 25	07 55	08 25	and at the same minutes past each hour until	10 55	11 25	11 55	12 25	12 55	13 25	13 55	14 25	and at the same minutes past each hour until	17 55	18 25
St Pancras International	d																					
Farringdon	d																					
City Thameslink	d																					
London Blackfriars	d																					
Bromley South	d			00 13	00 42		06 42	07 42	08 12	08 42		11 12	11 42	12 12	12 42	13 12	13 42	14 12	14 42		18 12	18 42
St Mary Cray 195	d			00 19	00 48		06 48	07 48	08 18			11 18		12 18		13 18		14 18			18 18	
Swanley 4 195	d			00 23	00 52		06 52	07 52	08 22	08 50		11 22	11 50	12 22	12 50	13 22	13 50	14 22	14 50		18 22	18 50
Otford 4 195	d			00 31	01 00		07 00	08 00	08 30	08 58		11 30	11 58	12 30	12 58	13 30	13 58	14 30	14 58		18 30	18 58
Kemsing	d			00s36			07 05	08 05	08 35			11 35		12 35		13 35		14 35			18 35	
Borough Green & Wrotham	d		00 06	00s41	01s08		07 10	08 10	08 40	09 06		11 40	12 06	12 40	13 06	13 40	14 06	14 40	15 06		18 40	19 06
West Malling	d		00 12	00s47	01s14		07 16	08 16	08 46	09 12		11 46	12 12	12 46	13 12	13 46	14 12	14 46	15 12		18 46	19 12
East Malling	d			00s50	01s17		07 19	08 19	08 49			11 49		12 49		13 49		14 49			18 49	
Barming	d			00s54	01s21		07 23	08 23	08 53			11 53		12 53		13 53		14 53			18 53	
Maidstone East 4	a		00 20	00 58	01 25		07 27	08 27	08 57	09 20		11 57	12 20	12 57	13 20	13 57	14 20	14 57	15 20		18 57	19 20
Maidstone East	d		00 22	01 00	01 27	06 22	07 28	08 28	08 59	09 22		11 59	12 22	12 59	13 22	13 59	14 22	14 59	15 22		18 59	19 22
Bearsted	d	00 04	00s27	01s05	01s32	06 27	07 34	08 34	09 04	09 27		12 04	12 27	13 04	13 27	14 04	14 27	15 04	15 27		19 04	19 27
Hollingbourne	d	00 08	00s31		01s36	06 31	07 37	08 37		09 31			12 31		13 31		14 31		15 31			19 31
Harrietsham	d	00 11	00s34		01s39	06 34	07 41	08 41		09 34			12 34		13 34		14 34		15 34			19 34
Lenham	d	00 15	00s38		01s43	06 38	07 45	08 45		09 38			12 38		13 38		14 38		15 38			19 38
Charing	d	00 20	00s43		01s48	06 43	07 50	08 50		09 43			12 43		13 43		14 43		15 43			19 43
Ashford International	a	00 29	00 53	01 24	02 01	06 53	07 58	08 58	09 23	09 53		12 23	12 53	13 23	13 55	14 23	14 55	15 23	15 53		19 23	19 53
Wye	a					07 11	08 11	09 11		10 11			13 11		14 11		15 11		16 11			20 11
Chilham	a					07 17	08 17	09 17		10 17			13 17		14 17		15 17		16 17			20 17
Chartham	a					07 21	08 21	09 21		10 21			13 21		14 21		15 21		16 21			20 21
Canterbury West	a					07 27	08 27	09 27		10 27			13 27		14 27		15 27		16 27			20 27

A From London Victoria

B To Minster

NRT DECEMBER 19 EDITION

Saturdays
21 December to 16 May

London - Maidstone East, Ashford International and Canterbury West

		SE ◇1	SE ◇1	SE ◇1	SE ◇1	SE ◇1	SE ◇1	SE ◇1	SE ◇1	SE ◇1	SE ◇1	SE ◇1
London Victoria	d	18 55	19 25	19 55	20 25	20 55	21 25	21 55	22 25	22 55	23 25	23 55
St Pancras International	d											
Farringdon	d											
City Thameslink	d											
London Blackfriars	d											
Bromley South	d	19 12	19 42	20 12	20 42	21 12	21 42	22 12	22 42	23 12	23 42	00 12
St Mary Cray 195	d	19 18		20 18		21 18		22 18		23 18		00 18
Swanley 4 195	d	19 22	19 50	20 22	20 50	21 22	21 50	22 22	22 50	23 22	23 50	00 22
Otford 4 195	d	19 30	19 58	20 30	20 58	21 30	21 58	22 30	22 58	23 30	23 58	00 30
Kemsing	d	19 35		20 35		21 35		22 35		23 35		00s35
Borough Green & Wrotham	d	19 40	20 06	20 40	21 06	21 40	22 06	22 40	23 06	23 40	00 06	00s40
West Malling	d	19 46	20 12	20 46	21 12	21 46	22 12	22 46	23 12	23 46	00 12	00s46
East Malling	d	19 49		20 49		21 49		22 49		23 49		00s49
Barming	d	19 53		20 53		21 53		22 53		23 53		00s53
Maidstone East 4	a	19 57	20 20	20 57	21 20	21 57	22 20	22 57	23 20	23 57	00 20	00 57
Maidstone East	d	19 59	20 22	20 59	21 22	21 59	22 22	22 59	23 22	23 59	00 22	00 59
Bearsted	d	20 04	20 27	21 04	21 27	22 04	22 27	23 04	23 27	00 04	00s27	01s04
Hollingbourne	d		20 31		21 31		22 31		23 31		00s31	
Harrietsham	d		20 34		21 34		22 34		23 34		00s34	
Lenham	d		20 38		21 38		22 38		23 38		00s38	
Charing	d		20 43		21 43		22 43		23 43		00s43	
Ashford International	a	20 23	20 53	21 23	21 53	22 23	22 53	23 23	23 55	00 23	00 53	01 23
Wye	a											
Chilham	a											
Chartham	a											
Canterbury West	a											

Sundays
15 December to 10 May

		SE ◇1 A	SE ◇1 A	SE ◇1 A	SE ◇1	SE ◇1		SE ◇1	SE ◇1		SE ◇1	SE ◇1
London Victoria	d				00 25	07 25	and hourly until	16 25	17 25	and hourly until	22 25	23 25
St Pancras International	d											
Farringdon	d											
City Thameslink	d											
London Blackfriars	d											
Bromley South	d			00 12	00 42	07 42		16 42	17 42		22 42	23 42
St Mary Cray 195	d			00 18	00 48	07 48		16 48	17 48		22 48	23 48
Swanley 4 195	d			00 22	00 52	07 52		16 52	17 52		22 52	23 52
Otford 4 195	d			00 30	01 00	08 00		17 00	18 00		23 00	23 59
Kemsing	d			00s35								
Borough Green & Wrotham	d		00 06	00s40	01s08	08 08		17 08	18 08		23 08	00 08
West Malling	d		00 12	00s46	01s14	08 14		17 14	18 14		23 14	00 14
East Malling	d			00s49	01s17	08 17		17 17	18 17		23 17	00 17
Barming	d			00s53	01s21	08 21		17 21	18 21		23 21	00 21
Maidstone East 4	a		00 20	00 57	01 25	08 25		17 25	18 25		23 25	00 25
Maidstone East	d		00 22	00 59	01 27	08 27		17 27	18 27		23 27	00 26
Bearsted	d	00 04	00s27	01s04	01s32	08 32		17 32	18 32		23 32	00s31
Hollingbourne	d		00s31		01s36	08 36		17 36	18 36		23 36	00s35
Harrietsham	d		00s34		01s39	08 39		17 39	18 39		23 39	00s38
Lenham	d		00s38		01s43	08 43		17 43	18 43		23 43	00s42
Charing	d		00s43		01s48	08 48		17 48	18 48		23 48	00s47
Ashford International	a	00 23	00 53	01 23	02 01	08 58		17 58	18 57		23 57	00 56
Wye	a					09 14		18 14				
Chilham	a					09 20		18 20				
Chartham	a					09 24		18 24				
Canterbury West	a					09 30		18 30				

A not 15 December. From London Victoria

Mondays to Fridays
16 December to 15 May

Canterbury West - Ashford International - Maidstone East - London

Miles			SE	SE	SE	SE	SE	SE	SE	SE	SE	SE	SE	SE	SE	SE		SE	SE	SE	SE	SE
			◇1	◇1	◇1	◇1	◇1	◇1	◇1	◇1	◇1	◇	◇1	◇1	◇1	◇1		◇1	◇1	◇1	◇1	◇1
			A	A	A	A	A	A	A	A	A	A		B	A			A		A		A
0	**Canterbury West**	d												08 04		09 05	and at the same minutes past each hour until		13 05		14 05	
3	Chartham	d												08 09		09 10			13 10		14 10	
5	Chilham	d												08 12		09 13			13 13		14 13	
10	Wye	d												08 19		09 20			13 20		14 20	
14	**Ashford International**	a												08 26		09 27			13 27		14 27	
—	Charing	d	05 27	05 39	05 56	06 11	06 25	06 31	06 48	07 07	07 35	08 05		08 38		09 41			13 41		14 41	
—	Lenham	d	05 32	05 44	06 01	06 16	06 30	06 36	06 53	07 12	07 40	08 10		08 43		09 46			13 46		14 46	
—	Harrietsham	d	05 35	05 47	06 04	06 19	06 33	06 40	06 56	07 15	07 44	08 14		08 47		09 50			13 50		14 50	
—	Hollingbourne	d	05 39	05 51	06 08	06 23	06 37	06 44	07 00	07 19	07 48	08 18		08 51		09 54			13 54		14 54	
—	Bearsted	a	05 43	05 55	06 12	06 27	06 41	06 47	07 04	07 23	07 51	08 21		08 54		09 57			13 57		14 57	
—	Maidstone East	a	05 49	06 01	06 18	06 33	06 47	06 53	07 10	07 29	07 58	08 28		09 00		10 03			14 03		15 03	
—	Maidstone East 4	d	05 50	06 02	06 19	06 34	06 48	06 54	07 11	07 30	07 59	08 29	08 53	09 00	09 29	10 04		13 29	14 04	14 29	15 04	15 29
—	Barming	d	05 54		06 23		06 52	06 59		07 34	08 03	08 33		09 05	09 33			13 33		14 33		15 33
—	East Malling	d	05 58		06 27		06 56	07 02		07 38	08 07	08 37		09 08	09 37			13 37		14 37		15 37
—	West Malling	d	06 01	06 09	06 30	06 41	06 59	07 05	07 18	07 41	08 10	08 40	09 00	09 11	09 40	10 11		13 40	14 11	14 40	15 11	15 40
—	Borough Green & Wrotham	d	06 08	06 16	06 37	06 48	07 06	07 12	07 25	07 48	08 16	08 46	09 07	09 18	09 46	10 18		13 46	14 18	14 46	15 18	15 46
—	Kemsing	d			06 41		07 10	07 16		07 52	08 20	08 50			09 50			13 50		14 50		15 50
—	Otford 4	195 d	06 17	06 25	06 48	06 58	07 16	07 22	07 34	07 59	08 26	08 56	09 15	09 26	09 56	10 26		13 56	14 26	14 56	15 26	15 56
—	Swanley 4	195 d	06 26	06 34		07 07		07 32		08 08	08 35	09 05	09 24	09 35	10 05	10 37		14 05	14 37	15 05	15 35	16 05
—	St Mary Cray	195 d				07 11					08 39	09 09	09 29	09 39	10 09			14 09		15 09	15 39	16 09
—	**Bromley South**	a	06 35	06 42	07 03	07 18	07 31	07 42	07 49	08 16	08 45	09 16	09 35	09 46	10 16	10 45		14 16	14 45	15 16	15 46	16 16
—	London Bridge	d																				
—	**London Blackfriars**	d		07a05				08a09					09a59									
—	City Thameslink	d																				
—	Farringdon	d																				
—	St Pancras International	d																				
—	**London Victoria**	a	06 55		07 28	07 43	07 58		08 11	08 38	09 08	09 38		10 07	10 36	11 06		14 36	15 06	15 36	16 06	16 36

		SE	SE	SE	SE	SE	SE	SE	SE	SE	SE	SE	SE	SE	SE	SE
		◇1	◇1	◇1	◇1	◇1	◇1	◇1	◇1	◇1	◇1	◇1	◇1	◇1	◇1	◇1
			A		A		A		A	A	A	A	A	A	A	
Canterbury West	d	15 05		16 05		17 05		18 05								22 08
Chartham	d	15 10		16 10		17 10		18 10								
Chilham	d	15 13		16 13		17 13		18 13								
Wye	d	15 20		16 20		17 20		18 20								
Ashford International	a	15 27		16 27		17 28		18 27								22 27
Charing	d	15 41	16 05	16 41	17 05	17 41	18 05	18 41	19 05	19 43		20 43		21 43		22 48
Lenham	d	15 46	16 10	16 46	17 10	17 46	18 10	18 46	19 10	19 48		20 48		21 48		22 53
Harrietsham	d	15 50	16 14	16 50	17 14	17 50	18 14	18 50	19 14	19 51		20 51		21 51		22 57
Hollingbourne	d	15 54	16 18	16 54	17 18	17 54	18 18	18 54	19 18	19 55		20 55		21 55		23 01
Bearsted	a	15 57	16 21	16 57	17 21	17 57	18 21	18 57	19 21	19 59		20 59		21 59		23 04
Maidstone East	a	16 03	16 28	17 03	17 28	18 03	18 28	19 03	19 28	20 04		21 04		22 04		23 10
Maidstone East 4	d	16 04	16 29	17 04	17 29	18 04	18 29	19 04	19 29	20 05	20 29	21 05	21 29	22 05	22 29	23 11
Barming	d		16 33		17 33		18 33		19 33		20 33		21 33		22 33	23 15
East Malling	d		16 37		17 37		18 37		19 37		20 37		21 37		22 37	23 19
West Malling	d	16 11	16 40	17 11	17 40	18 11	18 40	19 11	19 40	20 12	20 40	21 12	21 40	22 12	22 40	23 22
Borough Green & Wrotham	d	16 18	16 46	17 18	17 46	18 18	18 46	19 18	19 46	20 18	20 46	21 18	21 46	22 19	22 46	23 28
Kemsing	d		16 50		17 50		18 50		19 50		20 50		21 50		22 50	
Otford 4	195 d	16 26	16 56	17 26	17 56	18 26	18 56	19 26	19 56	20 26	20 56	21 26	21 56	22 27	22 56	23 36
Swanley 4	195 d	16 35	17 05	17 35	18 05	18 35	19 05	19 35	20 05	20 37	21 05	21 37	22 05	22 37	23 05	23 45
St Mary Cray	195 d	16 39	17 09	17 39	18 09	18 39	19 09	19 39	20 09		21 09		22 09		23 09	23 50
Bromley South	a	16 46	17 16	17 46	18 16	18 46	19 16	19 46	20 16	20 45	21 16	21 45	22 16	22 45	23 16	23 56
London Bridge	d															
London Blackfriars	d															
City Thameslink	d															
Farringdon	d															
St Pancras International	d															
London Victoria	a	17 06	17 36	18 06	18 36	19 06	19 37	20 06	20 36	21 07	21 36	22 06	22 36	23 06	23 37	00 18

Saturdays
21 December to 16 May

		SE	SE	SE	SE	SE	SE	SE		SE	SE	SE	SE
		◇1	◇1	◇1	◇1	◇1	◇1	◇1		◇1	◇1	◇1	◇1
		A	A	A	A	A	A			A		A	A
Canterbury West	d							08 05	and at the same minutes past each hour until		21 05		
Chartham	d							08 10			21 10		
Chilham	d							08 13			21 13		
Wye	d							08 20			21 20		
Ashford International	a							08 27			21 27		
Charing	d	05 36		06 41		07 41		08 41			21 41		22 48
Lenham	d	05 41		06 46		07 46		08 46			21 46		22 53
Harrietsham	d	05 44		06 50		07 50		08 50			21 50		22 57
Hollingbourne	d	05 48		06 54		07 54		08 54			21 54		23 01
Bearsted	a	05 53		06 57		07 57		08 57			21 57		23 04
Maidstone East	a	05 58		07 03		08 03		09 03			22 03		23 10
Maidstone East 4	d	05 59	06 29	07 04	07 29	08 04	08 29	09 04		21 29	22 04	22 29	23 11
Barming	d	06 03	06 33		07 33		08 33			21 33		22 33	23 15
East Malling	d	06 07	06 37		07 37		08 37			21 37		22 37	23 19
West Malling	d	06 10	06 40	07 11	07 40	08 11	08 40	09 11		21 40	22 11	22 40	23 22
Borough Green & Wrotham	d	06 16	06 46	07 18	07 46	08 18	08 46	09 18		21 46	22 18	22 46	23 28
Kemsing	d	06 20	06 50		07 50		08 50			21 50		22 50	
Otford 4	195 d	06 26	06 56	07 26	07 56	08 26	08 56	09 26		21 56	22 26	22 56	23 36
Swanley 4	195 d	06 35	07 05	07 37	08 05	08 37	09 05	09 37		22 05	22 37	23 05	23 45
St Mary Cray	195 d	06 39	07 09		08 09		09 09			22 09		23 09	23 49
Bromley South	a	06 46	07 16	07 45	08 16	08 45	09 16	09 45		22 16	22 45	23 16	23 56
London Bridge	d												
London Blackfriars	d												
City Thameslink	d												
Farringdon	d												
St Pancras International	d												
London Victoria	a	07 06	07 36	08 06	08 36	09 06	09 36	10 06		22 36	23 06	23 36	00 15

A From Ashford International
B From Minster

Sundays
15 December to 10 May

Canterbury West - Ashford International - Maidstone East - London

		SE	SE	SE	SE		SE	SE	SE	SE
		◇1	◇1	◇1	◇1		◇1	◇1	◇1	◇1
		A	A	A					A	A
Canterbury West	d				09 04	and hourly until	18 04	19 04		
Chartham	d				09 09		18 09	19 09		
Chilham	d				09 12		18 12	19 12		
Wye	d				09 19		18 19	19 19		
Ashford International	a				09 26		18 26	19 26		
Charing	d	06 41	07 44	08 44	09 44		18 44	19 44	20 44	21 44
Lenham	d	06 46	07 49	08 49	09 49		18 49	19 49	20 49	21 49
Harrietsham	d	06 49	07 52	08 52	09 52		18 52	19 52	20 52	21 52
Hollingbourne	d	06 53	07 56	08 56	09 56		18 56	19 56	20 56	21 56
Bearsted	a	06 56	07 59	08 59	09 59		18 59	19 59	20 59	21 59
Maidstone East	a	07 02	08 05	09 05	10 05		19 05	20 05	21 05	22 05
Maidstone East 4	d	07 03	08 06	09 06	10 06		19 06	20 06	21 06	22 06
Barming	d	07 08	08 11	09 11	10 11		19 11	20 11	21 11	22 11
East Malling	d	07 11	08 14	09 14	10 14		19 14	20 14	21 14	22 14
West Malling	d	07 14	08 17	09 17	10 17		19 17	20 17	21 17	22 17
Borough Green & Wrotham	d	07 21	08 24	09 24	10 24		19 24	20 24	21 24	22 24
Kemsing	d									
Otford 4	195 d	07 29	08 32	09 32	10 32		19 32	20 32	21 32	22 32
Swanley 4	195 d	07 42	08 42	09 42	10 42		19 42	20 42	21 42	22 42
St Mary Cray	195 d	07 46	08 46	09 46	10 46		19 46	20 46	21 46	22 46
Bromley South	a	07 53	08 53	09 53	10 53		19 53	20 53	21 53	22 53
London Bridge	d									
London Blackfriars	d									
City Thameslink	d									
Farringdon	d									
St Pancras International	d									
London Victoria	a	08 12	09 12	10 12	11 12		20 12	21 10	22 11	23 11

A From Ashford International

AVAILABLE FROM MP Middleton Press

London Suburban Railways
SOUTH LONDON LINE
London Bridge to Victoria
Vic Mitchell and Keith Smith
MP Middleton Press
EVOLVING THE ULTIMATE RAIL ENCYCLOPEDIA

Table T199-F

Mondays to Fridays
16 December to 15 May

London - Lewisham, Hither Green, Petts Wood and Orpington (Summary of Services)

	SE TWO	SE MX	SE MO	SE ThFO	SE ThFO	SE ThFO	SE MX	SE MO	SE ThFO		SE ThFO ◇	SE TWO	SE MO	SE ThFO	SE ThFO	SE TWO	SE TWO	SE ThFO	SE MX		SE ThFO	SE TWO	SE ThFO	SE MO
London Charing Cross 4 ⊖ d				00 02	00 04	00 07		00 12	00 12		00 15		00 16	00 18				00 26			00 32		00 42	00 46
London Waterloo (East) 4 ⊖ d				00 05	00 07	00 10		00 15	00 15		00 18		00 19	00 21				00 29			00 35		00 45	00 49
London Cannon Street 4 ⊖ d												00 20			00 20	00 25	00 27					00 46		
London Blackfriars 3 ⊖ d																								
London Bridge 4 ⊖ d		00 01	00 01	00 11	00 13	00 16		00 21	00 21		00 24	00 24	00 25	00 28	00 28	00 29	00 32	00 35			00 41	00 51	00 51	00 55
London Victoria 15 ⊖ d							00 04												00 28					
New Cross 4 ⊖ d												00 30			00 42		00 38							
St Johns d	00 02											00 32			00 47		00 40							
Lewisham 4 a	00 04	00 09				00 24	00 26	00 30	00 31			00 34	00 34	00 36	00 54		00 42	00 44			00 49	00 58	00 59	01 03
Hither Green 4 a	00 09		00 12	00 21	00 23							00 39	00 39	00 41							00 54			01 09
Petts Wood 4 a	00 22				00 36							00 52	00 52	00 54					01 03					01 22
Orpington 4 a	00 26				00 43						00 50	00 58	00 57	01 00		00 49			01 08					01 29

	SE TWO	SE ThFO	SE TWO	SE TWO	SE MThFO		SE TWO	TL	SE WX	SE WO	SE	SE ◇1	SE	SE	SE		TL	SE	TL	SE	SE	SE	SE	SE
London Charing Cross 4 ⊖ d		00 50			04 50				05 20		05 26	05 30			05 32					05 42	05 48		05 52	05 54
London Waterloo (East) 4 ⊖ d		00 53			04 53				05 23		05 29	05 33			05 35					05 45	05 51		05 55	05 57
London Cannon Street 4 ⊖ d	00 52		01 02	01 10										05 35				05 39				05 55		
London Blackfriars 3 ⊖ d								04 56									05 26		05 39					
London Bridge 4 ⊖ d	00 57	00 59	01 07	01 15	04 59		04 59		05 29	05 29	05 35	05 39		05 39	05 41			05 43	05a45	05 51	05 57	05 59	06 01	06 03
London Victoria 15 ⊖ d													05 28											
New Cross 4 ⊖ d														06a58				05 49				07a21		
St Johns d																		05 51						
Lewisham 4 a	01 04	01 07	01 14	01 22	05 07		05 07		05 37	05 37	05 43				05 49			05 53		06 00	06 08			06 11
Hither Green 4 a	01 09	01 12		01 27	05 12		05 12		05 42	05 42					05 54			05 58					06 12	
Petts Wood 4 a		01 25		01 40				05 40					06 03		06 06		06 10							
Orpington 4 a		01 32		01 47				05 44				05 55	06 08		06 11		06 14							

	SE ◇1		SE	SE	SE	TL	TL	SE	SE	SE	SE		SE	SE	SE	SE ◇1	SE	SE	SE	TL	SE		TL	SE
London Charing Cross 4 ⊖ d	05 56				06 05				06 12				06 23		06 25	06 28			06 34					06 41
London Waterloo (East) 4 ⊖ d	05 59				06 08				06 15				06 26		06 28	06 31			06 37					06 44
London Cannon Street 4 ⊖ d				06 09				06 16			06 25			06 28				06 35			06 39			
London Blackfriars 3 ⊖ d						05 56	06 11													06 26			06 41	
London Bridge 4 ⊖ d	06 05			06 13	06 14		06a17	06 20	06 21		06 29		06 32	06 32	06 35	06 37		06 39	06 43		06 43		06a47	06 50
London Victoria 15 ⊖ d			05 58							06 15							06 28							
New Cross 4 ⊖ d				06 19				06 26			07a38			06 38				08a05			06 49			
St Johns d				06 21				06 28						06 40							06 51			
Lewisham 4 a				06 23				06 31	06 29	06 36				06 42	06 44						06 53			06 58
Hither Green 4 a				06 28	06 23			06 36					06 43						06 52		06 58			
Petts Wood 4 a			06 33		06 37	06 40		06 48									07 03		07 07	07 10				
Orpington 4 a	06 21		06 38		06 40	06 44		06 55								06 53	07 08		07 10	07 14				

	SE	SE	SE	SE	SE	SE	SE ◇1		SE	SE	SE	TL	SE	SE	TL	SE	SE		SE	SE ◇1	SE	SE	SE	SE
London Charing Cross 4 ⊖ d				06 53		06 56	07 00				07 06						07 12			07 15				07 21
London Waterloo (East) 4 ⊖ d				06 56		06 59	07 03				07 09						07 15			07 18				07 24
London Cannon Street 4 ⊖ d		06 49	06 55		07 00					07 05				07 11		07 15			07 19		07 22	07 22	07 25	
London Blackfriars 3 ⊖ d												06 56			07 11									
London Bridge 4 ⊖ d		06 53	06 59	07 02	07 04	07 05	07 09			07 09	07 15			07 15	07a17	07 19	07 21		07 23	07 24	07 26	07 26	07 29	07 30
London Victoria 15 ⊖ d	06 42								06 58				07 08											
New Cross 4 ⊖ d		06 59	08a20		07 10									07 21		07 26			07 29		07 32	07 32	08a39	
St Johns d		07 01			07 12									07 23					07 31		07 34	07 34		
Lewisham 4 a	07 01	07 03			07 17	07 13							07 25	07 27			07 29		07 33		07 36	07 36		
Hither Green 4 a		07 08		07 13						08 26	07 25			07 34		07 31						08 31		07 40
Petts Wood 4 a		07 20							07 34		07 38	07 41				07 44								
Orpington 4 a		07 25					07 25		07 39		07 41	07 45				07 50				07 40				

	SE	SE ◇1	SE		SE	SE	SE	SE ◇1	TL	TL	SE	SE	SE		SE	SE	SE	SE	SE	SE ◇1	SE	SE	TL	
London Charing Cross 4 ⊖ d	07 25	07 27				07 33					07 39		07 46			07 52		07 56		08 00		08 06		
London Waterloo (East) 4 ⊖ d	07 28	07 30				07 36					07 42		07 49			07 56		07 59		08 05		08 09		
London Cannon Street 4 ⊖ d					07 36		07 40	07 42							07 53		08 00		08 05					
London Blackfriars 3 ⊖ d									07 26	07 41													07 56	
London Bridge 4 ⊖ d	07 34	07 36			07 40	07 42		07 46		07a47	07 48		07 55		07 57	08 02		08 05	08 09	08 11		08 15		
London Victoria 15 ⊖ d			07 27									07 45									07 58			
New Cross 4 ⊖ d					09a01		07 50								08 03				09a33					
St Johns d							07 52								08 05									
Lewisham 4 a	07 43						07 54				07 59	08 06			08 08		08 10	08 17						
Hither Green 4 a						07 53	08 00								08 14	08 12						08 27		
Petts Wood 4 a			08 05			08 08			08 15						08 27						08 33	08 40	08 43	
Orpington 4 a		07 55	08 10			08 12		08 07	08 18				08 17		08 34					08 29	08 38	08 45	08 47	

Table T199-F

Mondays to Fridays
16 December to 15 May

London - Lewisham, Hither Green, Petts Wood and Orpington (Summary of Services)

	SE	TL	SE	SE	SE		SE	SE	SE ◇1	SE	SE	SE	SE	SE	SE		SE	SE ◇1	SE	SE	SE	SE	SE ◇1	TL
London Charing Cross 4 ⊖ d				08 10	08 12			08 14	08 18				08 20	08 22	08 24		08 26	08 28			08 32			
London Waterloo (East) 4 ⊖ d				08 13	08 15			08 17	08 21				08 23	08 25	08 27		08 29	08 31			08 35			
London Cannon Street 4 ⊖ d			08 14				08 17			08 19	08 22	08 24								08 34		08 37	08 40	
London Blackfriars 3 ⊖ d		08 11																						08 26
London Bridge 4 ⊖ d		08a17	08 18	08 19	08 21		08 21	08 23	08 27			08 28	08 29	08 31	08 33		08 35	08 37		08 38	08 41	08 41	08 44	
London Victoria 15 ⊖ d	08 07																		08 28					
New Cross 4 ⊖ d							08 28			08 31	08 34	09a46								10a01		08 47		
St Johns d							08 30			08 33	08 36											08 49		
Lewisham 4 a	08 28				08 31		08 33			08 35	08 38						08 43					08 54		
Hither Green 4 a			08 29				08 38	08 33						08 41							08 52	08 59		
Petts Wood 4 a							08 51												09 03		09 06			09 10
Orpington 4 a				08 42			08 58		08 43				08 52		08 55			08 56	09 09		09 13		09 05	09 16

	SE		SE	TL	SE	SE	SE	SE	SE	SE	SE		SE ◇1	SE	SE ◇1	SE	SE	SE	SE	TL	TL		SE ◇1	SE
London Charing Cross 4 ⊖ d	08 38				08 42	08 44		08 46	08 50				08 58		09 02				09 06					09 12
London Waterloo (East) 4 ⊖ d	08 41				08 45	08 47		08 49	08 53				09 01		09 05				09 09					09 15
London Cannon Street 4 ⊖ d							08 52			08 54	08 58			09 05			09 08						09 14	
London Blackfriars 3 ⊖ d				08 41																08 56	09 11			
London Bridge 4 ⊖ d	08 47			08a47	08 51	08 53	08 56	08 57	08 59	08 59	09 02		09 07	09 09	09 11		09 13		09 15		09a17		09 18	09 21
London Victoria 15 ⊖ d			08 38													08 58		09 04						
New Cross 4 ⊖ d							09 02			10a16	09 08			10a33			09 19							
St Johns d							09 04				09 10						09 21							
Lewisham 4 a	08 57		09 00		09 03		09 06		09 09		09 12						09 23	09 26						09 31
Hither Green 4 a							09 12	09 10									09 29							
Petts Wood 4 a							09 25									09 33			09 36	09 42				
Orpington 4 a						09 16	09 32						09 24		09 30	09 38			09 40	09 46			09 38	

	SE	SE	SE	SE	SE ◇1	SE	SE ◇1		SE	SE	SE	SE	TL	SE	SE	TL	SE		SE	SE ◇1	SE	SE	SE	SE
London Charing Cross 4 ⊖ d				09 20	09 22		09 24		09 26			09 34					09 40			09 45		09 48		
London Waterloo (East) 4 ⊖ d				09 23	09 25		09 27		09 29			09 37					09 45			09 48		09 51		
London Cannon Street 4 ⊖ d	09 17	09 20	09 24			09 27					09 35			09 38					09 47		09 50		09 54	09 57
London Blackfriars 3 ⊖ d													09 26			09 41								
London Bridge 4 ⊖ d	09 21	09 24	09 28	09 29	09 31	09 31	09 33		09 35		09 39	09 43		09 43		09a47	09 51		09 51	09 54	09 54	09 57	09 58	10 01
London Victoria 15 ⊖ d										09 28					09 34									
New Cross 4 ⊖ d	09 28	09 31	10a46			09 37					11a03			09 49					09 57		10 00		11a16	10 07
St Johns d	09 30	09 33				09 39								09 51					09 59		10 02			10 09
Lewisham 4 a	09 34	09 36				09 41			09 44					09 53	09 56		09 59		10 02		10 04			10 11
Hither Green 4 a		09 41		09 38								09 52		09 58							10 09	10 07		
Petts Wood 4 a		09 54								10 03		10 06	10 10								10 22			
Orpington 4 a		10 00			09 48		09 53			10 08		10 10	10 14							10 09	10 28			

	SE	SE ◇1	SE		SE	SE	TL	SE	SE	TL	SE	SE	SE ◇1		SE	SE	SE	SE	SE	SE ◇1	SE	SE	SE	
London Charing Cross 4 ⊖ d	09 54	10 00				10 04					10 12		10 15			10 18			10 24	10 30			10 34	
London Waterloo (East) 4 ⊖ d	09 58	10 03				10 07					10 15		10 18			10 21			10 28	10 33			10 37	
London Cannon Street 4 ⊖ d					10 05			10 08				10 17			10 20		10 24	10 27				10 35		
London Blackfriars 3 ⊖ d							09 56			10 11														
London Bridge 4 ⊖ d	10 05	10 09			10 09	10 13		10 13		10a17	10 21	10 21	10 24		10 24	10 27	10 28	10 31	10 35	10 39		10 39	10 43	
London Victoria 15 ⊖ d			09 58						10 04												10 28			
New Cross 4 ⊖ d					11a31			10 19				10 27			10 30		11a46	10 37				12a01		
St Johns d								10 21				10 29			10 32			10 39						
Lewisham 4 a	10 14							10 23	10 25		10 29	10 32			10 34			10 41	10 44					
Hither Green 4 a						10 23		10 28							10 39	10 36							10 53	
Petts Wood 4 a			10 33			10 36	10 42								10 52						11 03		11 06	
Orpington 4 a		10 25	10 38			10 40	10 45						10 39		10 57					10 55	11 08		11 10	

	TL	SE	SE	TL	SE	SE	SE ◇1	SE	SE		SE	SE	SE	SE ◇1	SE	SE	SE	TL	SE		SE	TL	SE	SE
London Charing Cross 4 ⊖ d					10 42		10 45		10 48				10 54	11 00			11 04						11 12	
London Waterloo (East) 4 ⊖ d					10 45		10 48		10 51				10 58	11 03			11 07						11 15	
London Cannon Street 4 ⊖ d		10 38				10 47		10 50			10 54	10 57				11 05			11 08					11 17
London Blackfriars 3 ⊖ d	10 26			10 41														10 56				11 11		
London Bridge 4 ⊖ d		10 43		10a47	10 51	10 51	10 54	10 54	10 57		10 58	11 01	11 05	11 09		11 09	11 13		11 13			11a17	11 21	11 21
London Victoria 15 ⊖ d			10 34												10 58						11 04			
New Cross 4 ⊖ d		10 49				10 57		11 00			12a16	11 07				12a31			11 19					11 27
St Johns d		10 51				10 59		11 02				11 09							11 21					11 29
Lewisham 4 a		10 53	10 55		10 59	11 02		11 04				11 11	11 14						11 23		11 25		11 29	11 32
Hither Green 4 a		10 58						11 09	11 06								11 23		11 28					
Petts Wood 4 a	11 10							11 22							11 33		11 36	11 40						
Orpington 4 a	11 14						11 09	11 26						11 25	11 39		11 40	11 44						

	SE ◇1	SE	SE	SE	SE		SE	SE ◇1	SE	SE	SE	TL	SE	SE	TL		SE	SE	SE ◇1	SE	SE	SE	SE	SE
London Charing Cross 4 ⊖ d	11 15		11 18				11 24	11 30			11 34						11 42		11 45		11 48			11 54
London Waterloo (East) 4 ⊖ d	11 18		11 21				11 28	11 33			11 37						11 45		11 48		11 51			11 58
London Cannon Street 4 ⊖ d		11 20		11 24	11 27					11 35			11 38					11 47		11 50		11 54	11 57	
London Blackfriars 3 ⊖ d												11 26			11 41									
London Bridge 4 ⊖ d	11 24	11 24	11 27	11 28	11 31		11 35	11 39		11 39	11 43		11 43		11a47		11 51	11 51	11 54	11 54	11 57	11 58	12 01	12 05
London Victoria 15 ⊖ d									11 28					11 34										
New Cross 4 ⊖ d		11 30		12a46	11 37					13a01			11 49					11 57		12 00		13a16	12 07	
St Johns d		11 32			11 39								11 51					11 59		12 02			12 09	
Lewisham 4 a		11 34			11 41		11 44						11 53	11 55			11 59	12 02		12 04			12 11	12 14
Hither Green 4 a		11 39	11 36								11 53		11 58							12 09	12 06			
Petts Wood 4 a		11 52							12 03		12 06	12 10								12 22				
Orpington 4 a	11 39	11 57						11 55	12 08		12 10	12 14							12 09	12 26				

London - Lewisham, Hither Green, Petts Wood and Orpington (Summary of Services)

		SE ◇1	SE	SE	SE	TL	SE	SE		TL	SE	SE	SE ◇1	SE	SE	SE	SE	SE		SE ◇1	SE	SE	SE	TL	SE
London Charing Cross 4 ⊖	d	12 00			12 04						12 12		12 15		12 18			12 24		12 30			12 34		
London Waterloo (East) 4 ⊖	d	12 03			12 07						12 15		12 18		12 21			12 28		12 33			12 37		
London Cannon Street 4 ⊖	d			12 05			12 08					12 17		12 20		12 24	12 27					12 35			12 38
London Blackfriars 3 ⊖	d					11 56				12 11														12 26	
London Bridge 4 ⊖	d	12 09		12 09	12 13		12 13			12a17	12 21	12 21	12 24	12 24	12 27	12 28	12 31	12 35		12 39		12 39	12 43		12 43
London Victoria 15 ⊖	d		11 58					12 04													12 28				
New Cross 4 ⊖	d			13a31			12 19					12 27		12 30		13a46	12 37					14a01			12 49
St Johns	d						12 21					12 29		12 32			12 39								12 51
Lewisham 4	a						12 23	12 25			12 29	12 32		12 34			12 41	12 44							12 53
Hither Green 4	a				12 23		12 28							12 39	12 36								12 53		12 58
Petts Wood 4	a		12 33		12 36	12 40								12 52							13 03		13 06	13 10	
Orpington 4	a	12 25	12 38		12 40	12 44							12 39	12 56						12 55	13 08		13 10	13 14	

		SE	TL	SE		SE	SE ◇1	SE	SE	SE	SE	SE	SE ◇1	SE		SE	SE	TL	SE	SE	TL	SE	SE	SE ◇1	
London Charing Cross 4 ⊖	d			12 42			12 45		12 48			12 54	13 00				13 04					13 12		13 15	
London Waterloo (East) 4 ⊖	d			12 45			12 48		12 51			12 58	13 03				13 07					13 15		13 18	
London Cannon Street 4 ⊖	d					12 47		12 50		12 54	12 57					13 05			13 08				13 17		
London Blackfriars 3 ⊖	d		12 41															12 56			13 11				
London Bridge 4 ⊖	d		12a47	12 51		12 51	12 54	12 54	12 57	12 58	13 01	13 05	13 09			13 09	13 13		13 13		13a17	13 21	13 21	13 24	
London Victoria 15 ⊖	d	12 34												12 58						13 04					
New Cross 4 ⊖	d					12 57		13 00		14a16	13 07					14a31			13 19				13 27		
St Johns	d					12 59		13 02			13 09								13 21				13 29		
Lewisham 4	a	12 55		12 59		13 02		13 04			13 11	13 14							13 23	13 25		13 29	13 32		
Hither Green 4	a							13 09	13 06								13 23		13 28						
Petts Wood 4	a							13 22						13 33			13 36	13 40							
Orpington 4	a						13 09	13 26					13 25	13 38			13 40	13 44						13 39	

		SE	SE	SE	SE	SE	SE ◇1	SE	SE	SE		TL	SE	SE	TL	SE	SE	SE ◇1	SE	SE		SE	SE	SE	SE ◇1
London Charing Cross 4 ⊖	d		13 18			13 24	13 30			13 34						13 42		13 45		13 48				13 54	14 00
London Waterloo (East) 4 ⊖	d		13 21			13 28	13 33			13 37						13 45		13 48		13 51				13 58	14 03
London Cannon Street 4 ⊖	d	13 20		13 24	13 27				13 35				13 38				13 47		13 50			13 54	13 57		
London Blackfriars 3 ⊖	d											13 26			13 41										
London Bridge 4 ⊖	d	13 24	13 27	13 28	13 31	13 35	13 39		13 39	13 43			13 43		13a47	13 51	13 51	13 54	13 54	13 57		13 58	14 01	14 05	14 09
London Victoria 15 ⊖	d							13 28						13 34											
New Cross 4 ⊖	d	13 30		14a46	13 37				15a01				13 49				13 57		14 00			15a16	14 07		
St Johns	d	13 32			13 39								13 51				13 59		14 02				14 09		
Lewisham 4	a	13 34			13 41	13 44							13 53	13 55		13 59	14 02		14 04				14 11	14 14	
Hither Green 4	a	13 39	13 36							13 53			13 58						14 09	14 06					
Petts Wood 4	a	13 52						14 03		14 06		14 10							14 22						
Orpington 4	a	13 56					13 55	14 08		14 10		14 14						14 09	14 26						14 25

		SE	SE	SE	TL	SE		SE	TL	SE	SE	SE ◇1	SE	SE	SE	SE		SE	SE ◇1	SE	SE	SE	TL	SE	SE
London Charing Cross 4 ⊖	d			14 04						14 12		14 15		14 18				14 24	14 30			14 34			
London Waterloo (East) 4 ⊖	d			14 07						14 15		14 18		14 21				14 28	14 33			14 37			
London Cannon Street 4 ⊖	d		14 05			14 08					14 17		14 20		14 24	14 27					14 35			14 38	
London Blackfriars 3 ⊖	d				13 56				14 11														14 26		
London Bridge 4 ⊖	d		14 09	14 13		14 13			14a17	14 21	14 21	14 24	14 24	14 27	14 28	14 31		14 35	14 39		14 39	14 43		14 43	
London Victoria 15 ⊖	d	13 58						14 04												14 28					14 34
New Cross 4 ⊖	d		15a31			14 19					14 27		14 30		15a46	14 37					16a02			14 49	
St Johns	d					14 21					14 29		14 32			14 39								14 51	
Lewisham 4	a					14 23		14 25		14 29	14 32		14 34			14 41		14 44						14 53	14 55
Hither Green 4	a			14 23		14 28							14 39	14 36								14 53		14 58	
Petts Wood 4	a	14 33		14 36	14 40								14 52							15 03		15 06	15 10		
Orpington 4	a	14 38		14 40	14 44							14 39	14 56						14 55	15 08		15 10	15 14		

		TL		SE	SE	SE ◇1	SE	SE	SE	SE	SE	SE ◇1		SE	SE	SE	TL	SE	SE	TL	SE	SE		SE ◇1	SE
London Charing Cross 4 ⊖	d			14 42		14 45		14 48			14 54	15 00				15 04					15 12			15 15	
London Waterloo (East) 4 ⊖	d			14 45		14 48		14 51			14 58	15 03				15 07					15 15			15 18	
London Cannon Street 4 ⊖	d				14 47		14 50		14 54	14 57					15 05			15 08				15 17			15 20
London Blackfriars 3 ⊖	d	14 41															14 56			15 11					
London Bridge 4 ⊖	d	14a47		14 51	14 51	14 54	14 54	14 57	14 58	15 01	15 05	15 09			15 09	15 13		15 13		15a17	15 21	15 21		15 24	15 24
London Victoria 15 ⊖	d													14 58					15 04						
New Cross 4 ⊖	d				14 57		15 00		16a16	15 07					16a31			15 19				15 27			15 30
St Johns	d				14 59		15 02			15 09								15 21				15 29			15 32
Lewisham 4	a			14 59	15 02		15 04			15 11	15 14							15 23	15 25		15 29	15 32			15 34
Hither Green 4	a						15 09	15 07								15 23		15 28							15 39
Petts Wood 4	a						15 22							15 33		15 36	15 40								15 52
Orpington 4	a					15 09	15 27					15 25		15 38		15 40	15 44							15 39	15 56

		SE	SE	SE	SE	SE ◇1	SE	SE		SE	TL	SE	SE	TL	SE	SE	SE ◇1	SE		SE	SE	SE	SE	SE ◇1	SE
London Charing Cross 4 ⊖	d	15 18			15 24	15 30				15 34					15 42		15 45			15 48			15 54	16 00	
London Waterloo (East) 4 ⊖	d	15 21			15 28	15 33				15 37					15 45		15 48			15 51			15 58	16 03	
London Cannon Street 4 ⊖	d		15 24	15 27				15 35				15 38				15 47		15 50			15 54	15 57			
London Blackfriars 3 ⊖	d										15 26			15 41											
London Bridge 4 ⊖	d	15 27	15 28	15 31	15 35	15 39		15 39		15 43		15 43		15a47	15 51	15 51	15 54	15 54		15 57	15 58	16 01	16 05	16 09	
London Victoria 15 ⊖	d						15 28						15 34												15 58
New Cross 4 ⊖	d		16a41	15 37				17a04				15 49				15 57		16 01			17a13	16 07			
St Johns	d			15 39								15 51				15 59		16 03				16 09			
Lewisham 4	a			15 41	15 44							15 53	15 55		16 00	16 03		16 05				16 11	16 14		
Hither Green 4	a	15 36								15 53		15 58						16 10		16 06					
Petts Wood 4	a						16 03			16 06	16 11							16 23							16 33
Orpington 4	a					15 55	16 08			16 10	16 14						16 10	16 30						16 25	16 38

		SE	SE	TL	SE	SE	TL	SE	SE	SE ◇1		SE	SE	SE	SE	SE	SE ◇1	SE	SE	TL		SE	SE	SE	TL
London Charing Cross 4 ⊖	d		16 04						16 12	16 14			16 18			16 24	16 28	16 30							
London Waterloo (East) 4 ⊖	d		16 07						16 15	16 17			16 21			16 28	16 31	16 33							
London Cannon Street 4 ⊖	d	16 05			16 08			16 15				16 18		16 25	16 27							16 37	16 39		
London Blackfriars 3 ⊖	d			15 56			16 11													16 26					16 41
London Bridge 4 ⊖	d	16 10	16 13		16 13		16a17	16 20	16 21	16 23		16 23	16 27	16 30	16 32	16 35	16 37	16 39				16 42	16 44		16a47
London Victoria 15 ⊖	d					16 04													16 28					16 34	
New Cross 4 ⊖	d	17a33			16 19			16 26				16 29		16 36	17a41							17a58	16 50		
St Johns	d				16 21			16 28				16 31		16 38									16 52		
Lewisham 4	a				16 23	16 25		16 32	16 29			16 34		16 40		16 44							16 54	16 56	
Hither Green 4	a		16 23		16 28							16 41	16 38					16 48					16 59		
Petts Wood 4	a		16 36	16 40								16 54						17 02	17 05	17 10					
Orpington 4	a		16 40	16 44						16 39		17 00					16 54	17 06	17 11	17 14					

		SE	SE	SE	SE	SE		SE	SE ◇1	SE	SE	SE	SE	SE	SE	TL		SE	SE	SE	TL	SE	SE	SE	SE
London Charing Cross 4 ⊖	d	16 41		16 45		16 48			16 51	16 53					17 03			17 06				17 09		17 13	
London Waterloo (East) 4 ⊖	d	16 44		16 48		16 51			16 54	16 56					17 06			17 09				17 12		17 16	
London Cannon Street 4 ⊖	d		16 45		16 50			16 52				16 58	17 03	17 05						17 11			17 16		17 19
London Blackfriars 3 ⊖	d															16 56					17 11				
London Bridge 4 ⊖	d	16 50	16 50	16 54	16 55	16 57		16 57	17 00	17 02		17 03	17 08	17 10	17 12			17 15		17 16	17a17	17 18	17 21	17 22	17 24
London Victoria 15 ⊖	d										16 57								17 04						
New Cross 4 ⊖	d		16 56		17 01			17 04				17 09	17 15	18a36						17 22					17 30
St Johns	d		16 58		17 03							17 11								17 24					17 32
Lewisham 4	a	16 59	17 00	17 03	17 05					17 11		17 13	17 18		17 20			17 23	17 26	17 28				17 30	17 34
Hither Green 4	a	17 04				17 07		17 09				17 19			17 25							17 28	17 31		17 40
Petts Wood 4	a	17 18						17 23			17 33				17 38	17 41							17 45		
Orpington 4	a	17 25						17 27	17 17		17 38				17 45	17 45							17 49		

		SE		SE	SE	SE	SE	SE	SE	SE	TL	SE		SE	SE	TL	SE	SE	SE	SE	SE	SE		SE	SE
London Charing Cross 4 ⊖	d	17 17			17 26		17 28		17 34			17 36					17 41		17 47	17 51		17 53			17 55
London Waterloo (East) 4 ⊖	d	17 20			17 29		17 31		17 37			17 39					17 44		17 50	17 54		17 56			17 58
London Cannon Street 4 ⊖	d			17 27				17 32		17 39				17 41				17 47			17 55			17 58	
London Blackfriars 3 ⊖	d										17 26					17 41									
London Bridge 4 ⊖	d	17 26		17 32	17 35		17 37	17 37	17 43	17 44		17 45		17 46		17a47	17 50	17 52	17 56	18 00	18 00	18 02		18 03	18 04
London Victoria 15 ⊖	d					17 27									17 35										
New Cross 4 ⊖	d			17 37				17 43		17 50				17 53				17 58			18 06			18 09	
St Johns	d							17 45						17 55							18 08				
Lewisham 4	a			17 41	17 43			17 47	17 51			17 54		17 57	17 59			18 02	18 04	18 09	18 11				18 13
Hither Green 4	a	17 36			17 49		17 47		18 57	17 55				18 03			18 00					18 12		18 14	
Petts Wood 4	a				18 02	18 05				18 09	18 12								18 22					18 30	
Orpington 4	a				18 09	18 12				18 15	18 16								18 29					18 34	

		SE	SE	SE	TL	SE	SE	SE		TL	SE	SE	SE	SE	SE	SE	SE	SE		SE	SE	SE ◇1	SE	TL	SE
London Charing Cross 4 ⊖	d					17 59					18 09	18 11		18 15		18 17				18 29		18 31			
London Waterloo (East) 4 ⊖	d					18 02					18 12	18 14		18 18		18 20				18 32		18 34			
London Cannon Street 4 ⊖	d	18 00					18 04	18 09					18 15		18 20		18 22				18 33				18 35
London Blackfriars 3 ⊖	d				17 56					18 11														18 26	
London Bridge 4 ⊖	d	18 05				18 08	18 09	18 14		18a17	18 18	18 20	18 20	18 24	18 25	18 26	18 27			18 38	18 38	18 40			18 40
London Victoria 15 ⊖	d		17 55	17 57														18 21					18 27		
New Cross 4 ⊖	d	18 11					19a31	18 20					18 26		18 31		18 34				18 44				20a01
St Johns	d	18 13											18 28				18 36				18 46				
Lewisham 4	a	18 16	18 18					18 23				18 28	18 30		18 36	18 34	18 39	18 43			18 48				
Hither Green 4	a	18 21				18 18								18 35	18 41		18 46			18 48					
Petts Wood 4	a			18 33	18 43						18 40				18 55					19 02			19 05	19 10	
Orpington 4	a			18 40	18 48						18 47				18 59					19 09		18 56	19 11	19 14	

		SE	SE	SE		SE	TL	SE ◇1	SE	SE	SE	SE	SE	SE		SE	SE	SE ◇1	SE	SE	SE	SE	TL	SE	
London Charing Cross 4 ⊖	d		18 36			18 38		18 41	18 43			18 48					18 56	19 00			19 02	19 04			
London Waterloo (East) 4 ⊖	d		18 39			18 41		18 44	18 46			18 51					18 59	19 03			19 05	19 07			
London Cannon Street 4 ⊖	d	18 38		18 41						18 48			18 53	18 55		18 57				19 05				19 08	
London Blackfriars 3 ⊖	d						18 41																18 56		
London Bridge 4 ⊖	d	18 43	18 45	18 46		18 47	18a47	18 50	18 52	18 53		18 57	18 58	19 00		19 02	19 05	19 09		19 09	19 11	19 13		19 13	
London Victoria 15 ⊖	d										18 42								18 57						
New Cross 4 ⊖	d	18 49		18 52						18 59			19 04	20a16		19 08				20a31				19 19	
St Johns	d	18 51		18 54						19 01			19 06			19 10								19 21	
Lewisham 4	a	18 53		18 57		18 55			19 00	19 03	19 05		19 08			19 12	19 14							19 23	
Hither Green 4	a		18 55	19 03						19 09		19 06									19 21	19 23		19 28	
Petts Wood 4	a									19 24		19 20							19 33			19 36	19 40		
Orpington 4	a							19 06		19 31		19 27						19 26	19 39			19 40	19 44		

		SE	TL	SE	SE	SE ◇1	SE	SE	SE	SE		SE	SE ◇1	SE	SE	SE	TL	SE	SE	TL		SE	SE	SE ◇1	SE
London Charing Cross 4 ⊖	d				19 12	19 15		19 18				19 24	19 30			19 34						19 42		19 45	
London Waterloo (East) 4 ⊖	d				19 15	19 18		19 21				19 28	19 33			19 37						19 45		19 48	
London Cannon Street 4 ⊖	d			19 16			19 22		19 24	19 27					19 35			19 38					19 47		19 50
London Blackfriars 3 ⊖	d		19 11														19 26			19 41					
London Bridge 4 ⊖	d		19a17	19 20	19 21	19 24	19 26	19 27	19 28	19 31		19 35	19 39		19 39	19 43		19 43		19a47		19 51	19 51	19 54	19 54
London Victoria 15 ⊖	d	19 04												19 28					19 34						
New Cross 4 ⊖	d			19 26			19 32		20a46	19 37					21a01			19 49					19 57		20 00
St Johns	d			19 28			19 34			19 39								19 51					19 59		20 02
Lewisham 4	a	19 25		19 32	19 29		19 36			19 41		19 44						19 53	19 55			19 59	20 02		20 04
Hither Green 4	a						19 41	19 38								19 53		19 58							20 09
Petts Wood 4	a						19 54							20 03		20 06	20 11								20 22
Orpington 4	a					19 39	20 00						19 55	20 08		20 10	20 14							20 09	20 27

Table T199-F

Mondays to Fridays
16 December to 15 May

London - Lewisham, Hither Green, Petts Wood and Orpington (Summary of Services)

		SE		SE	SE	SE ◇1	SE	SE	SE	TL	SE	SE		TL	SE	SE	SE ◇1	SE	SE	SE	SE	SE ◇1		SE	SE
London Charing Cross 4 ⊖	d	19 48			19 54	20 00			20 04						20 12		20 15		20 18		20 24	20 30			
London Waterloo (East) 4 ⊖	d	19 51			19 58	20 03			20 07						20 15		20 18		20 21		20 28	20 33			
London Cannon Street 4 ⊖	d			19 57				20 05			20 08					20 17		20 20		20 27					20 35
London Blackfriars 3 ⊖	d									19 56				20 11											
London Bridge 4 ⊖	d	19 57		20 01	20 05	20 09		20 09	20 13		20 13			20a17	20 21	20 21	20 24	20 24	20 27	20 31	20 35	20 39			20 39
London Victoria 15 ⊖	d						19 58					20 04												20 28	
New Cross 4 ⊖	d			20 07				21a31			20 19					20 27		20 30		20 37					22a01
St Johns	d			20 09							20 21					20 29		20 32		20 39					
Lewisham 4	a			20 11	20 14						20 23	20 25			20 29	20 32		20 34		20 41	20 44				
Hither Green 4	a	20 06							20 23		20 28							20 39	20 36						
Petts Wood 4	a						20 33		20 36	20 40								20 52						21 03	
Orpington 4	a					20 25	20 38		20 40	20 44							20 39	20 56				20 55		21 08	

		SE	TL	SE	SE	TL	SE	SE		SE ◇1	SE	SE	SE	SE	SE ◇1	SE	SE	SE		TL	SE	SE	TL	SE ◇1	SE
London Charing Cross 4 ⊖	d	20 34					20 42			20 45		20 48		20 54	21 00			21 04						21 10	21 12
London Waterloo (East) 4 ⊖	d	20 37					20 45			20 48		20 51		20 58	21 03			21 07						21 13	21 15
London Cannon Street 4 ⊖	d			20 38				20 47			20 50		20 57				21 05				21 08				
London Blackfriars 3 ⊖	d		20 26			20 41														20 56			21 11		
London Bridge 4 ⊖	d	20 43		20 43		20a47	20 51	20 51		20 54	20 54	20 57	21 01	21 05	21 09		21 09	21 13			21 13		21a17	21 19	21 21
London Victoria 15 ⊖	d				20 34											20 58						21 04			
New Cross 4 ⊖	d			20 49				20 57			21 00		21 07				22a31				21 19				
St Johns	d			20 51				20 59			21 02		21 09								21 21				
Lewisham 4	a			20 53	20 55		20 59	21 02			21 04		21 11	21 14							21 23	21 25			21 29
Hither Green 4	a	20 53		20 58							21 09	21 06						21 23			21 28				
Petts Wood 4	a	21 06	21 10								21 22					21 33		21 36		21 40					
Orpington 4	a	21 10	21 14							21 09	21 26				21 25	21 38		21 40		21 44				21 35	

		SE	SE	SE		SE	SE	SE ◇1	SE	SE	TL	SE	SE	TL		SE	SE ◇1	SE	SE	SE	SE	SE	SE ◇1	SE	
London Charing Cross 4 ⊖	d		21 18			21 24		21 30		21 34						21 42	21 45		21 48		21 54		22 00		
London Waterloo (East) 4 ⊖	d		21 21			21 28		21 33		21 37						21 45	21 48		21 51		21 58		22 03		
London Cannon Street 4 ⊖	d	21 20		21 27			21 32					21 38						21 50		21 57		22 02			
London Blackfriars 3 ⊖	d										21 26			21 41											
London Bridge 4 ⊖	d	21 24	21 27	21 31		21 35	21 36	21 39		21 43		21 43		21a47		21 51	21 54	21 54	21 57	22 01	22 05	22 06	22 09		
London Victoria 15 ⊖	d								21 28				21 34											21 58	
New Cross 4 ⊖	d	21 30		21 37			23a01					21 49						22 00		22 07		23a31			
St Johns	d	21 32		21 39								21 51						22 02		22 09					
Lewisham 4	a	21 34		21 41		21 44						21 53	21 55			21 59		22 04		22 11	22 14				
Hither Green 4	a	21 39	21 36							21 53		21 58						22 09	22 06						
Petts Wood 4	a	21 52							22 03	22 06	22 10							22 22						22 33	
Orpington 4	a	21 56						21 55	22 08	22 10	22 14						22 09	22 26					22 25	22 38	

		SE	TL	SE	SE	TL	SE ◇1	SE	SE	SE		SE	SE	SE W ThO	SE MT FO	SE ◇1	SE	SE	TL	SE		SE	TL	SE	SE ◇1
London Charing Cross 4 ⊖	d	22 04					22 10	22 12		22 18			22 24			22 30		22 34						22 42	22 45
London Waterloo (East) 4 ⊖	d	22 07					22 13	22 15		22 21			22 28			22 33		22 37						22 45	22 48
London Cannon Street 4 ⊖	d			22 08					22 20			22 27		22 32	22 32					22 38					
London Blackfriars 3 ⊖	d		21 56			22 11													22 26				22 41		
London Bridge 4 ⊖	d	22 13		22 13		22a17	22 19	22 21	22 24	22 27		22 31	22 35	22 36	22 36	22 39		22 43		22 43			22a47	22 51	22 54
London Victoria 15 ⊖	d				22 04												22 28					22 34			
New Cross 4 ⊖	d			22 19					22 30			22 37			00a01					22 49					
St Johns	d			22 21					22 32			22 39								22 51					
Lewisham 4	a			22 23	22 25			22 29	22 34			22 41	22 44	23 56						22 53		22 55		22 59	
Hither Green 4	a	22 23		22 28					22 39	22 36								22 53		22 58					
Petts Wood 4	a	22 36	22 40						22 52								23 03	23 06	23 10						
Orpington 4	a	22 40	22 44				22 35		22 56							22 55	23 08	23 10	23 14						23 09

		SE W ThO	SE MT FO	SE	SE	SE		SE ◇1	SE	SE	SE	SE	TL	TL	SE ◇1	SE		SE	SE	SE	SE	SE ◇1	SE	SE	SE
London Charing Cross 4 ⊖	d			22 48		22 54		23 00		23 02		23 04			23 10	23 12			23 20		23 24	23 30		23 32	
London Waterloo (East) 4 ⊖	d			22 51		22 58		23 03		23 05		23 07			23 13	23 15			23 23		23 28	23 33		23 35	
London Cannon Street 4 ⊖	d	22 50	22 50		22 57													23 20		23 27					
London Blackfriars 3 ⊖	d												22 56	23 11											
London Bridge 4 ⊖	d	22 54	22 54	22 57	23 01	23 05		23 09		23 11		23 13		23a17	23 19	23 21		23 24	23 29	23 31	23 35	23 39		23 41	
London Victoria 15 ⊖	d								22 58		23 04												23 28		23 34
New Cross 4 ⊖	d	23 00	23 00		23 07													23 30		23 37					
St Johns	d	23 02	23 02		23 09													23 32		23 39					
Lewisham 4	a	23 04	23 04		23 11	23 14					23 25					23 29		23 34	23 37	23 41	23 44				23 55
Hither Green 4	a	23 09	23 09	23 06						23 21		23 23						23 39	23 42					23 51	
Petts Wood 4	a	23 22	23 22						23 33			23 36	23 40					23 52					00 03		
Orpington 4	a	23 27	23 29					23 25	23 38			23 40	23 44		23 35			23 57				23 55	00 08		

NRT DECEMBER 19 EDITION

Table T199-F

Mondays to Fridays
16 December to 15 May

London - Lewisham, Hither Green, Petts Wood and Orpington (Summary of Services)

		SE		SE W ThO	SE	SE ◇1	SE MT FO	SE	SE	SE FO	SE
London Charing Cross 4 ⊖	d	23 34			23 42	23 45		23 50	23 52		
London Waterloo (East) 4 ⊖	d	23 37			23 45	23 48		23 53	23 55		
London Cannon Street 4 ⊖	d			23 45			23 50			23 57	
London Blackfriars 3 ⊖	d										
London Bridge 4 ⊖	d	23 43		23 49	23 51	23 54	23 54	23 59	00 01	00 01	
London Victoria 15 ⊖	d										23 58
New Cross 4 ⊖	d			23 54			23 59			00 07	
St Johns	d			23 57			00 02			00 09	
Lewisham 4	a			00 01	23 59		00 04	00 07	00 09	00 11	
Hither Green 4	a	23 53		00 09			00 09	00 12			
Petts Wood 4	a	00 06		00 22			00 22				00 33
Orpington 4	a	00 12		00 26		00 09	00 26				00 38

Saturdays
21 December to 16 May

		SE	SE	SE	SE	SE	SE	SE	SE ◇	SE		SE	SE	SE	SE	SE	SE	SE	SE	SE		SE	SE	SE	SE
London Charing Cross 4 ⊖	d				00 02	00 04		00 12	00 15			00 26		00 32	00 42	00 50	04 50		05 20	05 24				05 34	05 37
London Waterloo (East) 4 ⊖	d				00 05	00 07		00 15	00 18			00 29		00 35	00 45	00 53	04 53		05 23	05 28				05 37	05 40
London Cannon Street 4 ⊖	d									00 20								05 05					05 35		
London Blackfriars 3 ⊖	d																								
London Bridge 4 ⊖	d		00 01	00 01	00 11	00 13		00 21	00 24	00 24		00 35		00 41	00 51	00 59	04 59	05 09	05 29	05 35			05 39	05 43	05 46
London Victoria 15 ⊖	d						00 04						00 28									05 28			
New Cross 4 ⊖	d			00 07						00 30								06a31					07a01		
St Johns	d	00 02		00 09						00 32															
Lewisham 4	a	00 04	00 09	00 11			00 25	00 33		00 35		00 44		00 49	00 59	01 07	05 07		05 37	05 44					05 56
Hither Green 4	a	00 09			00 21	00 23				00 39				00 54		01 12	05 14		05 44					05 53	
Petts Wood 4	a	00 22				00 36				00 52			01 03			01 25						06 03		06 06	
Orpington 4	a	00 26				00 43			00 50	00 58			01 08			01 32						06 08		06 10	

		TL	SE	SE	SE	SE ◇1		SE	SE	SE	SE	SE	TL	SE	SE	SE		SE	SE	SE	SE	SE	SE	TL	SE
London Charing Cross 4 ⊖	d			05 50	05 54	06 00				06 04		06 07		06 12		06 18		06 24			06 34		06 37		06 42
London Waterloo (East) 4 ⊖	d			05 53	05 58	06 03				06 07		06 10		06 15		06 21		06 28			06 37		06 40		06 45
London Cannon Street 4 ⊖	d		05 50						06 05		06 08				06 20					06 35		06 38			
London Blackfriars 3 ⊖	d	05 41											06 11											06 41	
London Bridge 4 ⊖	d	05a47	05 54	05 59	06 05	06 09			06 09	06 13	06 13	06 16	06a17	06 21	06 24	06 27		06 35		06 39	06 43	06 43	06 46	06a47	06 51
London Victoria 15 ⊖	d							05 58											06 28						
New Cross 4 ⊖	d		06 00						07a31		06 19				06 30					08a01		06 49			
St Johns	d		06 02								06 21				06 32							06 51			
Lewisham 4	a		06 04	06 07	06 14						06 23	06 26		06 29	06 34			06 44				06 53	06 56		06 59
Hither Green 4	a		06 09	06 14						06 23	06 28				06 39	06 36					06 53	06 58			
Petts Wood 4	a		06 22					06 33		06 36					06 52				07 03		07 06				
Orpington 4	a		06 26			06 25		06 38		06 40					06 56				07 08		07 10				

		SE		SE	SE	SE	SE	SE	SE	SE	SE	TL		SE	SE	SE ◇1	SE	SE	SE	SE	SE	SE		SE	SE
London Charing Cross 4 ⊖	d			06 48		06 54			07 04					07 12		07 15		07 18		07 24				07 34	
London Waterloo (East) 4 ⊖	d			06 51		06 58			07 07					07 15		07 18		07 21		07 28				07 37	
London Cannon Street 4 ⊖	d	06 50			06 57			07 05		07 08					07 17		07 20		07 27			07 35			07 38
London Blackfriars 3 ⊖	d											07 11													
London Bridge 4 ⊖	d	06 54		06 57	07 01	07 05		07 09	07 13	07 13		07a17		07 21	07 21	07 24	07 24	07 27	07 31	07 35		07 39		07 43	07 43
London Victoria 15 ⊖	d						06 58				07 04										07 28				
New Cross 4 ⊖	d	07 00			07 07			08a31		07 19					07 27		07 30		07 37			09a01			07 49
St Johns	d	07 02			07 09					07 21					07 29		07 32		07 39						07 51
Lewisham 4	a	07 04			07 11	07 14				07 23	07 25			07 29	07 32		07 34		07 41	07 44					07 53
Hither Green 4	a	07 09		07 06					07 23	07 28							07 39	07 36						07 53	07 58
Petts Wood 4	a	07 22					07 33		07 36								07 52				08 03			08 06	
Orpington 4	a	07 26					07 38		07 40							07 39	07 56				08 08			08 10	

		SE	TL	SE	SE	SE ◇1	SE	SE		SE	SE	SE	SE	SE	SE	SE	SE	TL	SE	SE	SE ◇1	SE	SE	SE	SE
London Charing Cross 4 ⊖	d			07 42		07 45		07 48				07 54			08 04				08 12		08 15		08 18		
London Waterloo (East) 4 ⊖	d			07 45		07 48		07 51				07 58			08 07				08 15		08 18		08 21		
London Cannon Street 4 ⊖	d				07 47		07 50			07 54	07 57			08 05		08 08				08 17		08 20		08 24	08 27
London Blackfriars 3 ⊖	d		07 41															08 11							
London Bridge 4 ⊖	d		07a47	07 51	07 51	07 54	07 54	07 57		07 58	08 01	08 05		08 09	08 13	08 13		08a17	08 21	08 21	08 24	08 24	08 27	08 28	08 31
London Victoria 15 ⊖	d	07 34											07 58				08 04								
New Cross 4 ⊖	d				07 57		08 00			09a16	08 07			09a31		08 19				08 27		08 30		09a46	08 37
St Johns	d				07 59		08 02				08 09					08 21				08 29		08 32			08 39
Lewisham 4	a	07 55		07 59	08 02		08 04				08 11	08 14				08 23	08 25		08 29	08 32		08 34			08 41
Hither Green 4	a						08 09	08 06							08 23	08 28						08 39	08 36		
Petts Wood 4	a						08 22						08 33		08 36							08 52			
Orpington 4	a					08 09	08 26						08 38		08 40						08 39	08 56			

London - Lewisham, Hither Green, Petts Wood and Orpington (Summary of Services)

	SE	SE	SE	SE	SE	SE	SE	TL	SE	SE	SE	SE	SE	SE	SE	SE	SE	and at the same minutes past each hour until	SE	SE	SE	SE	SE
		◇1									◇1						◇1						
London Charing Cross 4 ⊖ d	08 24	08 30			08 34				08 42		08 45		08 48			08 54	09 00				13 04		
London Waterloo (East) 4 ⊖ d	08 28	08 33			08 37				08 45		08 48		08 51			08 58	09 03				13 07		
London Cannon Street 4 ⊖ d				08 35		08 38				08 47		08 50		08 54	08 57					13 05		13 08	
London Blackfriars 3 ⊖ d								08 41															
London Bridge 4 ⊖ d	08 35	08 39		08 39	08 43	08 43		08a47	08 51	08 51	08 54	08 54	08 57	08 58	09 01	09 05	09 09			13 09	13 13	13 13	
London Victoria 15 ⊖ d			08 28				08 34												12 58				13 04
New Cross 4 ⊖ d				10a01		08 49				08 57		09 00		10a16	09 07					14a31		13 19	
St Johns d						08 51				08 59		09 02			09 09							13 21	
Lewisham 4 a	08 44					08 53	08 55		08 59	09 02		09 04			09 11	09 14						13 23	13 25
Hither Green 4 a					08 53	08 58						09 09	09 06								13 23	13 28	
Petts Wood 4 a			09 03		09 06							09 22							13 33		13 36		
Orpington 4 a		08 55	09 08		09 10						09 09	09 26					09 25		13 38		13 40		

	TL	SE	SE	SE	SE	SE	SE	SE	SE	SE	SE	SE	SE	SE	SE	TL	SE	SE	SE	SE	SE	SE	SE	SE
				◇1						◇1									◇1					
London Charing Cross 4 ⊖ d		13 12		13 15		13 18			13 24	13 30			13 34				13 42		13 45		13 48			13 54
London Waterloo (East) 4 ⊖ d		13 15		13 18		13 21			13 28	13 33			13 37				13 45		13 48		13 51			13 58
London Cannon Street 4 ⊖ d			13 17		13 20		13 24	13 27				13 35		13 38				13 47		13 50		13 54	13 57	
London Blackfriars 3 ⊖ d	13 11															13 41								
London Bridge 4 ⊖ d	13a17	13 21	13 21	13 24	13 24	13 27	13 28	13 31	13 35	13 39		13 39	13 43	13 43		13a47	13 51	13 51	13 54	13 54	13 57	13 58	14 01	14 05
London Victoria 15 ⊖ d											13 28				13 34									
New Cross 4 ⊖ d			13 27		13 30		14a46	13 37				15a01		13 49				13 57		14 00		15a16	14 07	
St Johns d			13 29		13 32			13 39						13 51				13 59		14 02			14 09	
Lewisham 4 a		13 29	13 32		13 34			13 41	13 44					13 53	13 55		13 59	14 02		14 04			14 11	14 14
Hither Green 4 a					13 39	13 36							13 53	13 58						14 09	14 06			
Petts Wood 4 a					13 52						14 03		14 06							14 22				
Orpington 4 a				13 39	13 56					13 55	14 08		14 10						14 09	14 26				

	SE		SE	SE	SE	SE	SE	TL	SE	SE	SE		SE	SE	SE	SE	SE	SE	SE	SE	SE		SE	SE
	◇1										◇1							◇1						
London Charing Cross 4 ⊖ d	14 00				14 04				14 12		14 15			14 18			14 24	14 30			14 34			
London Waterloo (East) 4 ⊖ d	14 03				14 07				14 15		14 18			14 21			14 28	14 33			14 37			
London Cannon Street 4 ⊖ d				14 05		14 08				14 17			14 20		14 24	14 27				14 35			14 38	
London Blackfriars 3 ⊖ d								14 11																
London Bridge 4 ⊖ d	14 09			14 09	14 13	14 13		14a17	14 21	14 21	14 24		14 24	14 27	14 28	14 31	14 35	14 39		14 39	14 43		14 43	
London Victoria 15 ⊖ d			13 58				14 04												14 28					14 34
New Cross 4 ⊖ d				15a31		14 19				14 27			14 30		15a46	14 37				16a01			14 49	
St Johns d						14 21				14 29			14 32			14 39							14 51	
Lewisham 4 a						14 23	14 25		14 29	14 32			14 34			14 41	14 44						14 53	14 55
Hither Green 4 a					14 23	14 30							14 39	14 36							14 53		14 58	
Petts Wood 4 a			14 33		14 36								14 52						15 03		15 06			
Orpington 4 a	14 25		14 38		14 40						14 39		14 56					14 55	15 08		15 10			

	TL	SE	SE	SE	SE	SE	SE		SE	SE	SE	SE	SE	SE	SE	SE	TL		SE	SE	SE	SE	SE	SE
				◇1							◇1										◇1			
London Charing Cross 4 ⊖ d		14 42		14 45		14 48				14 54	15 00			15 04					15 12		15 15		15 18	
London Waterloo (East) 4 ⊖ d		14 45		14 48		14 51				14 58	15 03			15 07					15 15		15 18		15 21	
London Cannon Street 4 ⊖ d			14 47		14 50		14 54		14 57				15 05		15 08					15 17		15 20		15 24
London Blackfriars 3 ⊖ d	14 41																15 11							
London Bridge 4 ⊖ d	14a47	14 51	14 51	14 54	14 54	14 57	14 58		15 01	15 05	15 09		15 09	15 13	15 13		15a17		15 21	15 21	15 24	15 24	15 27	15 28
London Victoria 15 ⊖ d												14 58				15 04								
New Cross 4 ⊖ d			14 57		15 00		16a16		15 07				16a31		15 19					15 27		15 30		16a46
St Johns d			14 59		15 02				15 09						15 21					15 29		15 32		
Lewisham 4 a		14 59	15 02		15 04				15 11	15 14					15 23	15 25			15 29	15 32		15 34		
Hither Green 4 a					15 09	15 06								15 23	15 28							15 39	15 36	
Petts Wood 4 a					15 22							15 33		15 36								15 52		
Orpington 4 a				15 09	15 26						15 25	15 38		15 40							15 39	15 56		

	SE	SE	SE		SE	SE	SE	SE	SE	TL	SE	SE	SE		SE	SE	SE	SE	SE	SE	SE	SE	SE	
			◇1										◇1							◇1				
London Charing Cross 4 ⊖ d		15 24	15 30				15 34				15 42		15 45			15 48			15 54	16 00			16 04	
London Waterloo (East) 4 ⊖ d		15 28	15 33				15 37				15 45		15 48			15 51			15 58	16 03			16 07	
London Cannon Street 4 ⊖ d	15 27					15 35		15 38				15 47			15 50		15 54	15 57				16 05		
London Blackfriars 3 ⊖ d										15 41														
London Bridge 4 ⊖ d	15 31	15 35	15 39			15 39	15 43	15 43		15a47	15 51	15 51	15 54		15 54	15 57	15 58	16 01	16 05	16 09		16 09	16 13	
London Victoria 15 ⊖ d					15 28				15 34												15 58			
New Cross 4 ⊖ d	15 37					17a01		15 49				15 57			16 00		17a16	16 07				17a31		
St Johns d	15 39							15 51				15 59			16 02			16 09						
Lewisham 4 a	15 41	15 44						15 53	15 55		15 59	16 02			16 04			16 11	16 14					
Hither Green 4 a							15 53	15 58							16 09	16 06							16 23	
Petts Wood 4 a					16 03		16 06								16 22						16 33		16 36	
Orpington 4 a			15 55		16 08		16 10						16 09		16 26					16 25	16 38		16 40	

	SE	SE	TL	SE	SE	SE	SE	SE	SE		SE	SE	SE	SE	SE	SE	SE	SE	TL		SE	SE	SE	SE
						◇1							◇1										◇1	
London Charing Cross 4 ⊖ d				16 12		16 15		16 18				16 24	16 30			16 34					16 42		16 45	
London Waterloo (East) 4 ⊖ d				16 15		16 18		16 21				16 28	16 33			16 37					16 45		16 48	
London Cannon Street 4 ⊖ d	16 08				16 17		16 20		16 24		16 27				16 35		16 38					16 47		16 50
London Blackfriars 3 ⊖ d			16 11																16 41					
London Bridge 4 ⊖ d	16 13		16a17	16 21	16 21	16 24	16 24	16 27	16 28		16 31	16 35	16 39		16 39	16 43	16 43		16a47		16 51	16 51	16 54	16 54
London Victoria 15 ⊖ d		16 04												16 28				16 34						
New Cross 4 ⊖ d	16 19				16 27		16 30		17a46		16 37				18a01		16 49					16 57		17 00
St Johns d	16 21				16 29		16 32				16 39						16 51					16 59		17 02
Lewisham 4 a	16 23	16 25		16 29	16 32		16 34				16 41	16 44					16 53	16 55			16 59	17 02		17 04
Hither Green 4 a	16 28						16 39	16 36								16 53	16 58							17 09
Petts Wood 4 a							16 52							17 03		17 06								17 22
Orpington 4 a						16 39	16 56						16 55	17 08		17 09							17 09	17 26

Table T199-F

Saturdays

21 December to 16 May

London - Lewisham, Hither Green, Petts Wood and Orpington (Summary of Services)

	SE		SE	SE	SE	SE	SE	SE	SE	SE	SE		TL	SE	SE	SE	SE	SE	SE	SE	SE		SE	SE
						◇1										◇1							◇1	
London Charing Cross 4 ⊖ d	16 48				16 54	17 00			17 04					17 12		17 15		17 18			17 24		17 30	
London Waterloo (East) 4 ⊖ d	16 51				16 58	17 03			17 07					17 15		17 18		17 21			17 28		17 33	
London Cannon Street 4 ⊖ d			16 54	16 57				17 05		17 08					17 17		17 20		17 24	17 27				
London Blackfriars 3 ⊖ d													17 11											
London Bridge 4 ⊖ d	16 57		16 58	17 01	17 05	17 09		17 09	17 13	17 13			17a17	17 21	17 21	17 24	17 24	17 27	17 28	17 31	17 35		17 39	
London Victoria 15 ⊖ d							16 58				17 04													17 28
New Cross 4 ⊖ d			18a16	17 07				18a31		17 19					17 27		17 30		18a46	17 37				
St Johns d				17 09						17 21					17 29		17 32			17 39				
Lewisham 4 a				17 11	17 14					17 23	17 25			17 29	17 32		17 34			17 41	17 44			
Hither Green 4 a	17 06								17 23	17 28							17 39	17 36						
Petts Wood 4 a							17 33		17 36								17 52							18 03
Orpington 4 a						17 25	17 38		17 40							17 39	17 56						17 55	18 08

	SE	SE	SE	SE	TL	SE	SE		SE	SE	SE	SE	SE	SE	SE	SE	SE		SE	SE	SE	TL	SE	SE
									◇1						◇1									
London Charing Cross 4 ⊖ d		17 34				17 42			17 45		17 48			17 54	18 00				18 04				18 12	
London Waterloo (East) 4 ⊖ d		17 37				17 45			17 48		17 51			17 58	18 03				18 07				18 15	
London Cannon Street 4 ⊖ d	17 35		17 38				17 47			17 50		17 54	17 57				18 05			18 08				18 17
London Blackfriars 3 ⊖ d					17 41																	18 11		
London Bridge 4 ⊖ d	17 39	17 43	17 43		17a47	17 51	17 51		17 54	17 54	17 57	17 58	18 01	18 05	18 09		18 09		18 13	18 13		18a17	18 21	18 21
London Victoria 15 ⊖ d				17 34												17 58					18 04			
New Cross 4 ⊖ d	19a01		17 49				17 57			18 00		19a16	18 07				19a31			18 19				18 27
St Johns d			17 51				17 59			18 02			18 09							18 21				18 29
Lewisham 4 a			17 53	17 55		17 59	18 02			18 04			18 11	18 14						18 23	18 25		18 29	18 32
Hither Green 4 a		17 53	17 58							18 09	18 06								18 23	18 28				
Petts Wood 4 a		18 06								18 22						18 33			18 36					
Orpington 4 a		18 10							18 09	18 26					18 25	18 38			18 40					

	SE	SE	SE		SE	SE	SE	SE	SE	SE	SE	SE	SE		TL	SE	SE	SE	SE	SE	SE	SE	SE	
	◇1							◇1										◇1						
London Charing Cross 4 ⊖ d	18 15		18 18				18 24	18 30			18 34					18 42		18 45		18 48			18 54	
London Waterloo (East) 4 ⊖ d	18 18		18 21				18 28	18 33			18 37					18 45		18 48		18 51			18 58	
London Cannon Street 4 ⊖ d		18 20			18 24	18 27				18 35		18 38					18 47		18 50		18 54	18 57		
London Blackfriars 3 ⊖ d															18 41									
London Bridge 4 ⊖ d	18 24	18 24	18 27		18 28	18 31	18 35	18 39		18 39	18 43	18 43			18a47	18 51	18 51	18 54	18 54	18 57	18 58	19 01	19 05	
London Victoria 15 ⊖ d									18 28				18 34											
New Cross 4 ⊖ d		18 30			19a46	18 37				20a01		18 49					18 57		19 00		20a16	19 07		
St Johns d		18 32				18 39						18 51					18 59		19 02			19 09		
Lewisham 4 a		18 34				18 41	18 44					18 53	18 55			18 59	19 02		19 04			19 11	19 14	
Hither Green 4 a		18 39	18 36								18 53	18 58							19 09	19 06				
Petts Wood 4 a		18 52							19 03		19 06								19 22					
Orpington 4 a	18 39	18 56						18 55	19 08		19 10							19 09	19 26					

	SE	SE	SE	SE	SE	SE	TL	SE	SE		SE	SE	SE	SE	SE	SE	SE	SE	SE		SE	SE	SE	TL
	◇1										◇1						◇1							
London Charing Cross 4 ⊖ d	19 00			19 04				19 12			19 15		19 18			19 24	19 30				19 34			
London Waterloo (East) 4 ⊖ d	19 03			19 07				19 15			19 18		19 21			19 28	19 33				19 37			
London Cannon Street 4 ⊖ d			19 05		19 08				19 17			19 20		19 24	19 27				19 35			19 38		
London Blackfriars 3 ⊖ d							19 11																	19 41
London Bridge 4 ⊖ d	19 09		19 09	19 13	19 13		19a17	19 21	19 21		19 24	19 24	19 27	19 28	19 31	19 35	19 39		19 39		19 43	19 43		19a47
London Victoria 15 ⊖ d		18 58				19 04												19 28					19 34	
New Cross 4 ⊖ d			20a31		19 19				19 27			19 30		20a46	19 37				21a01			19 49		
St Johns d					19 21				19 29			19 32			19 39							19 51		
Lewisham 4 a					19 23	19 25		19 29	19 32			19 34			19 41	19 44						19 53	19 55	
Hither Green 4 a				19 23	19 28							19 39	19 36								19 53	19 58		
Petts Wood 4 a		19 33		19 36								19 52						20 03			20 06			
Orpington 4 a	19 25	19 38		19 40							19 39	19 56					19 55	20 08			20 10			

	SE	SE	SE	SE	SE		SE	SE	SE	SE	SE	SE	SE	SE	TL		SE	SE	SE	SE	SE	SE	SE	SE
			◇1						◇1										◇1					
London Charing Cross 4 ⊖ d	19 42		19 45		19 48			19 54	20 00			20 04					20 12		20 15		20 18		20 24	
London Waterloo (East) 4 ⊖ d	19 45		19 48		19 51			19 58	20 03			20 07					20 15		20 18		20 21		20 28	
London Cannon Street 4 ⊖ d		19 47		19 50			19 57				20 05		20 08					20 17		20 20		20 27		20 32
London Blackfriars 3 ⊖ d															20 11									
London Bridge 4 ⊖ d	19 51	19 51	19 54	19 54	19 57		20 01	20 05	20 09		20 09	20 13	20 13		20a17		20 21	20 21	20 24	20 24	20 27	20 31	20 35	20 36
London Victoria 15 ⊖ d										19 58				20 04										
New Cross 4 ⊖ d		19 57		20 00			20 07				21a31		20 19					20 27		20 30		20 37		22a01
St Johns d		19 59		20 02			20 09						20 21					20 29		20 32		20 39		
Lewisham 4 a	19 59	20 02		20 04			20 11	20 14					20 23	20 25			20 29	20 32		20 34		20 41	20 44	
Hither Green 4 a				20 09	20 06							20 23	20 28							20 39	20 36			
Petts Wood 4 a				20 22						20 33		20 36								20 52				
Orpington 4 a			20 09	20 26					20 25	20 38		20 40							20 39	20 56				

	SE		SE	SE	SE	SE	TL	SE	SE	SE	SE		SE	SE	SE	SE	SE	SE	SE	SE	SE		TL	SE
	◇1									◇1							◇1							◇1
London Charing Cross 4 ⊖ d	20 30			20 34				20 42		20 45			20 48		20 54		21 00		21 04					21 10
London Waterloo (East) 4 ⊖ d	20 33			20 37				20 45		20 48			20 51		20 58		21 03		21 07					21 13
London Cannon Street 4 ⊖ d					20 38				20 47		20 50			20 57		21 02				21 08				
London Blackfriars 3 ⊖ d							20 41																21 11	
London Bridge 4 ⊖ d	20 39			20 43	20 43		20a47	20 51	20 51	20 54	20 54		20 57	21 01	21 05	21 06	21 09		21 13	21 13			21a17	21 19
London Victoria 15 ⊖ d			20 28			20 34												20 58			21 04			
New Cross 4 ⊖ d					20 49				20 57		21 00			21 07		22a31				21 19				
St Johns d					20 51				20 59		21 02			21 09						21 21				
Lewisham 4 a					20 53	20 55		20 59	21 02		21 04			21 11	21 14					21 23	21 25			
Hither Green 4 a				20 53	20 58						21 09		21 06						21 23	21 28				
Petts Wood 4 a			21 03	21 06							21 22							21 33	21 36					
Orpington 4 a	20 55		21 08	21 10						[illegible]	[illegible]							[illegible]	[illegible]					

Table T199-F

Saturdays
21 December to 16 May

London - Lewisham, Hither Green, Petts Wood and Orpington (Summary of Services)

	SE	SE	SE		SE	SE	SE	SE	SE	SE	SE	SE	TL		SE	SE	SE	SE	SE	SE	SE	SE	SE	
								◇1								◇1						◇1		
London Charing Cross 4 ⊖ d	21 12		21 18			21 24		21 30		21 34					21 42	21 45		21 48		21 54		22 00		
London Waterloo (East) 4 ⊖ d	21 15		21 21			21 28		21 33		21 37					21 45	21 48		21 51		21 58		22 03		
London Cannon Street 4 ⊖ d		21 20			21 27		21 32				21 38						21 50		21 57		22 02			
London Blackfriars 3 ⊖ d													21 41											
London Bridge 4 ⊖ d	21 21	21 24	21 27		21 31	21 35	21 36	21 39		21 43	21 43		21a47		21 51	21 54	21 54	21 57	22 01	22 05	22 06	22 09		
London Victoria 15 ⊖ d									21 28			21 34											21 58	
New Cross 4 ⊖ d		21 30			21 37		23a01				21 49						22 00		22 07		23a31			
St Johns d		21 32			21 39						21 51						22 02		22 09					
Lewisham 4 a	21 29	21 34			21 41	21 44					21 53	21 55			21 59		22 04		22 11	22 14				
Hither Green 4 a		21 39	21 36							21 53	21 58						22 09	22 06						
Petts Wood 4 a		21 52							22 03	22 06							22 22						22 33	
Orpington 4 a		21 56						21 55	22 08	22 10						22 09	22 26					22 25	22 38	

	SE	SE	SE	TL	SE	SE	SE	SE	SE		SE	SE	SE	SE	SE	SE	SE	TL	SE		SE	SE	SE	SE
					◇1								◇1								◇1			
London Charing Cross 4 ⊖ d	22 04				22 10	22 12		22 18			22 24		22 30		22 34				22 42		22 45		22 48	
London Waterloo (East) 4 ⊖ d	22 07				22 13	22 15		22 21			22 28		22 33		22 37				22 45		22 48		22 51	
London Cannon Street 4 ⊖ d		22 08					22 20		22 27			22 32				22 38						22 50		22 57
London Blackfriars 3 ⊖ d				22 11														22 41						
London Bridge 4 ⊖ d	22 13	22 13		22a17	22 19	22 21	22 24	22 27	22 31		22 35	22 36	22 39		22 43	22 43		22a47	22 51		22 54	22 54	22 57	23 01
London Victoria 15 ⊖ d			22 04											22 28			22 34							
New Cross 4 ⊖ d		22 19					22 30		22 37			00a02				22 49						23 00		23 07
St Johns d		22 21					22 32		22 39							22 51						23 02		23 10
Lewisham 4 a		22 23	22 25			22 29	22 34		22 41		22 44					22 53	22 55		22 59			23 04		23 12
Hither Green 4 a	22 23	22 28					22 39	22 37							22 53	22 58						23 09	23 06	
Petts Wood 4 a	22 36						22 52							23 03	23 06							23 22		
Orpington 4 a	22 40				22 35		22 56						22 55	23 08	23 09						23 09	23 26		

	SE	SE	SE	SE	SE		SE	TL	SE	SE	SE	SE	SE	SE	SE		SE	SE	SE	SE	SE	SE	SE	SE
		◇1							◇1						◇1							◇1		
London Charing Cross 4 ⊖ d	22 54	23 00		23 02	23 04				23 10	23 12		23 20		23 24	23 30			23 32		23 34	23 42	23 45		23 50
London Waterloo (East) 4 ⊖ d	22 58	23 03		23 05	23 07				23 13	23 15		23 23		23 28	23 33			23 35		23 37	23 45	23 48		23 53
London Cannon Street 4 ⊖ d											23 20		23 27										23 50	
London Blackfriars 3 ⊖ d								23 11																
London Bridge 4 ⊖ d	23 05	23 09		23 11	23 13			23a17	23 19	23 21	23 24	23 29	23 31	23 35	23 39			23 41		23 43	23 51	23 54	23 54	23 59
London Victoria 15 ⊖ d			22 58				23 04										23 28		23 34					
New Cross 4 ⊖ d											23 30		23 37										23 59	
St Johns d											23 32		23 40										00 02	
Lewisham 4 a	23 14						23 25			23 29	23 34	23 37	23 42	23 44					23 55		23 59		00 04	00 07
Hither Green 4 a				23 21	23 23						23 39	23 42						23 51		23 53			00 09	00 12
Petts Wood 4 a			23 33		23 36						23 52						00 03			00 06			00 22	
Orpington 4 a		23 25	23 38		23 40				23 35		23 56				23 55		00 07			00 10		00 09	00 26	

	SE		SE	SE
London Charing Cross 4 ⊖ d			23 54	
London Waterloo (East) 4 ⊖ d			23 58	
London Cannon Street 4 ⊖ d	23 57			
London Blackfriars 3 ⊖ d				
London Bridge 4 ⊖ d	00 01		00 05	
London Victoria 15 ⊖ d				23 58
New Cross 4 ⊖ d	00 07			
St Johns d	00 09			
Lewisham 4 a	00 11		00 14	
Hither Green 4 a				
Petts Wood 4 a				00 33
Orpington 4 a				00 38

Sundays
15 December to 10 May

	SE	SE	SE	SE	SE	SE	SE	SE	SE		SE	SE	SE	SE	SE	SE	SE	SE	SE		SE	SE	SE	SE
	A	A	A					◇																
London Charing Cross 4 ⊖ d				00 02	00 04		00 12	00 15			00 26		00 32	00 42	00 50							07 42	07 46	07 52
London Waterloo (East) 4 ⊖ d				00 05	00 07		00 15	00 18			00 29		00 35	00 45	00 53							07 45	07 49	07 55
London Cannon Street 4 ⊖ d									00 20								07 29	07 33			07 42			
London Blackfriars 3 ⊖ d																								
London Bridge 4 ⊖ d		00 01	00 05	00 11	00 13		00 21	00 24	00 24		00 36		00 41	00 51	00 59		07 33	07 37			07 46	07 51	07 55	08 01
London Victoria 15 ⊖ d						00 04						00 28				07 28			07 34					
New Cross 4 ⊖ d		00 07							00 30								08a52	07 43			07 52			
St Johns d	00 02	00 09							00 32									07 45			07 54			
Lewisham 4 a	00 04	00 11	00 14			00 25	00 29		00 35		00 44		00 49	00 59	01 07			07 47	07 55		07 58	08 00	08 04	
Hither Green 4 a	00 09			00 21	00 23				00 39				00 54		01 12						08 03		08 09	08 12
Petts Wood 4 a	00 22				00 37				00 52			01 03			01 25	08 03							08 22	
Orpington 4 a	00 26				00 43			00 49	00 56			01 09			01 32	08 08							08 27	

A not 15 December

Table T199-F

Sundays
15 December to 10 May

London - Lewisham, Hither Green, Petts Wood and Orpington (Summary of Services)

	SE		SE	SE	SE	SE	SE	SE	SE	SE	SE		SE	SE	SE	SE	SE	SE	SE	SE	SE		SE	SE
							◇1						◇1					◇1						◇1
London Charing Cross 4 ⊖ d							08 10	08 12	08 16	08 22			08 25					08 40	08 42	08 46	08 52			08 55
London Waterloo (East) 4 ⊖ d							08 13	08 15	08 19	08 25			08 28					08 43	08 45	08 49	08 55			08 58
London Cannon Street 4 ⊖ d			07 59	08 03		08 12					08 29				08 33		08 42						08 59	
London Blackfriars 3 ⊖ d																								
London Bridge 4 ⊖ d			08 03	08 07		08 16	08 19	08 21	08 25	08 31	08 33		08 34		08 37		08 46	08 49	08 51	08 55	09 01		09 03	09 04
London Victoria 15 ⊖ d	07 58				08 04									08 28		08 34								
New Cross 4 ⊖ d			09a22	08 13		08 22					09a52				08 43		08 52						10a22	
St Johns d				08 15		08 24									08 45		08 54							
Lewisham 4 a				08 17	08 25	08 28		08 30	08 34						08 47	08 55	08 58		09 00	09 04				
Hither Green 4 a						08 33			08 39	08 42							09 03			09 09	09 12			
Petts Wood 4 a	08 33								08 52					09 03						09 22				
Orpington 4 a	08 38						08 35		08 57				08 50	09 08				09 05		09 27				09 20

	SE	SE	SE	SE	SE	SE	SE	SE	SE	SE	SE	SE	SE	TL	SE	SE	SE	SE	SE	SE	SE	SE	SE	SE
					◇1					◇1						◇1					◇1			
London Charing Cross 4 ⊖ d					09 10	09 12	09 16	09 22		09 25						09 40	09 42	09 46	09 52		09 55			
London Waterloo (East) 4 ⊖ d					09 13	09 15	09 19	09 25		09 28						09 43	09 45	09 49	09 55		09 58			
London Cannon Street 4 ⊖ d		09 03		09 12					09 29			09 33			09 42					09 59			10 03	
London Blackfriars 3 ⊖ d														09 41										
London Bridge 4 ⊖ d		09 07		09 16	09 19	09 21	09 25	09 31	09 33	09 34		09 37		09a46	09 46	09 49	09 51	09 55	10 01	10 03	10 04		10 07	
London Victoria 15 ⊖ d	08 58		09 04								09 28		09 34									09 58		10 04
New Cross 4 ⊖ d		09 13		09 22					10a52			09 43			09 52					11a22			10 13	
St Johns d		09 15		09 24								09 45			09 54								10 15	
Lewisham 4 a		09 17	09 25	09 28		09 30	09 34					09 47	09 55		09 58		10 00	10 04					10 17	10 25
Hither Green 4 a				09 33			09 39	09 42							10 03			10 09	10 12					
Petts Wood 4 a	09 33						09 52				10 03							10 22				10 33		
Orpington 4 a	09 38				09 35		09 57			09 50	10 08					10 05		10 27			10 20	10 38		

	TL			SE	SE	SE	SE	SE	SE	SE	SE	SE	SE	TL	SE	SE	SE	SE	SE	SE	SE	SE	SE	SE
					◇1					◇1						◇1					◇1			
London Charing Cross 4 ⊖ d		and at the same minutes past each hour until			19 10	19 12	19 16	19 22		19 25						19 40	19 42	19 46	19 52		19 55			
London Waterloo (East) 4 ⊖ d					19 13	19 15	19 19	19 25		19 28						19 43	19 45	19 49	19 55		19 58			
London Cannon Street 4 ⊖ d				19 12					19 29			19 33			19 42					19 59			20 03	
London Blackfriars 3 ⊖ d	10 11													19 41										
London Bridge 4 ⊖ d	10a16			19 16	19 19	19 21	19 25	19 31	19 33	19 34		19 37		19a46	19 46	19 49	19 51	19 55	20 01	20 03	20 04		20 07	
London Victoria 15 ⊖ d											19 28		19 34									19 58		20 04
New Cross 4 ⊖ d				19 22					20a52			19 43			19 52					21a22			20 13	
St Johns d				19 24								19 45			19 54								20 15	
Lewisham 4 a				19 28		19 30	19 34					19 47	19 55		19 58		20 00	20 04					20 17	20 25
Hither Green 4 a				19 33			19 39	19 42							20 03			20 09	20 12					
Petts Wood 4 a							19 52				20 03							20 22				20 33		
Orpington 4 a					19 35		19 57			19 50	20 08					20 05		20 27			20 20	20 38		

	TL		SE	SE	SE	SE	SE	SE	SE	SE	SE		SE	TL	SE	SE	SE	SE	SE	SE	SE		SE	SE
				◇1					◇1							◇1								
London Charing Cross 4 ⊖ d				20 10	20 12	20 16	20 22		20 25							20 40	20 42	20 46	20 52					
London Waterloo (East) 4 ⊖ d				20 13	20 15	20 19	20 25		20 28							20 43	20 45	20 49	20 55					
London Cannon Street 4 ⊖ d			20 12					20 29			20 33				20 42						20 59		21 03	
London Blackfriars 3 ⊖ d	20 11													20 41										
London Bridge 4 ⊖ d	20a16		20 16	20 19	20 21	20 25	20 31	20 33	20 34		20 37			20a46	20 46	20 49	20 51	20 55	21 01		21 03		21 07	
London Victoria 15 ⊖ d										20 28			20 34							20 58				21 04
New Cross 4 ⊖ d			20 22					21a52			20 43				20 52						22a22		21 13	
St Johns d			20 24								20 45				20 54								21 15	
Lewisham 4 a			20 28		20 30	20 34					20 47		20 55		20 58		21 00	21 04					21 17	21 25
Hither Green 4 a			20 33			20 39	20 42								21 03			21 09	21 12					
Petts Wood 4 a						20 52				21 03								21 22		21 33				
Orpington 4 a				20 35		20 57			20 50	21 08						21 05		21 27		21 38				

	TL	SE	SE	SE	SE	SE	SE		SE	SE	SE	SE	TL	SE	SE	SE	SE		SE	SE	SE	SE	SE	TL
			◇1						◇1						◇1									
London Charing Cross 4 ⊖ d			21 10	21 12	21 16	21 22			21 25						21 40	21 42	21 46		21 52					
London Waterloo (East) 4 ⊖ d			21 13	21 15	21 19	21 25			21 28						21 43	21 45	21 49		21 55					
London Cannon Street 4 ⊖ d		21 12					21 29				21 33			21 42							21 59	22 03		
London Blackfriars 3 ⊖ d	21 11												21 41											22 11
London Bridge 4 ⊖ d	21a16	21 16	21 19	21 21	21 25	21 31	21 33		21 34		21 37		21a46	21 46	21 49	21 51	21 55		22 01		22 03	22 07		22a16
London Victoria 15 ⊖ d										21 28		21 34								21 58			22 04	
New Cross 4 ⊖ d		21 22					22a52				21 43			21 52							23a22	22 13		
St Johns d		21 24									21 45			21 54								22 15		
Lewisham 4 a		21 28		21 30	21 34						21 47	21 55		21 58		22 00	22 04					22 17	22 25	
Hither Green 4 a		21 33			21 39	21 42								22 03			22 09		22 12					
Petts Wood 4 a					21 52					22 03							22 22			22 33				
Orpington 4 a			21 35		21 57				21 50	22 08					22 05		22 27			22 38				

	SE	SE	SE		SE	SE	SE	SE	SE	SE	SE	TL	SE		SE	SE	SE	SE	SE	SE	SE	TL	SE	
		◇1						◇1							◇1									
London Charing Cross 4 ⊖ d		22 10	22 12		22 16	22 22		22 25							22 40	22 42	22 46	22 52						
London Waterloo (East) 4 ⊖ d		22 13	22 15		22 19	22 25		22 28							22 43	22 45	22 49	22 55						
London Cannon Street 4 ⊖ d	22 12						22 29			22 33			22 42							23 03			23 12	
London Blackfriars 3 ⊖ d												22 41										23 11		
London Bridge 4 ⊖ d	22 16	22 19	22 21		22 25	22 31	22 33	22 34		22 37		22a46	22 46		22 49	22 51	22 55	23 01		23 07		23a16	23 16	
London Victoria 15 ⊖ d									22 28		22 34								22 58		23 04			
New Cross 4 ⊖ d	22 22						23a52			22 43			22 52							23 13			23 22	
St Johns d	22 24									22 45			22 54							23 15			23 24	
Lewisham 4 a	22 28		22 30		22 34					22 47	22 55		22 58			23 00	23 04			23 17	23 25		23 28	
Hither Green 4 a	22 33				22 39	22 42							23 03				23 09	23 12					23 33	
Petts Wood 4 a					22 52				23 03								23 22		23 33					
Orpington 4 a		22 35			22 57			22 50	23 08						23 05		23 27		23 38					

Table T199-F

Sundays 15 December to 10 May

London - Lewisham, Hither Green, Petts Wood and Orpington (Summary of Services)

		SE ◇1	SE	SE	SE	SE ◇1		SE	SE ◇1	SE	SE	SE	SE	SE	SE
London Charing Cross	⊖ d	23 10	23 12	23 16	23 22	23 25			23 40			23 42	23 46	23 52	
London Waterloo (East)	⊖ d	23 13	23 15	23 19	23 25	23 28			23 43			23 45	23 49	23 55	
London Cannon Street	⊖ d							23 33							
London Blackfriars	⊖ d														
London Bridge	⊖ d	23 19	23 21	23 25	23 31	23 34		23 37	23 49			23 51	23 55	00 01	
London Victoria	⊖ d									23 28	23 34				23 58
New Cross	⊖ d							23 43							
St Johns	d							23 45							
Lewisham	a		23 30	23 34				23 47			23 55	00 01	00 04		
Hither Green	a			23 39	23 42								00 09	00 12	
Petts Wood	a			23 52						00 04			00 22		00 33
Orpington	a	23 35		23 57		23 50			00 05	00 09			00 27		00 38

Vic Mitchell and Keith Smith

MP Middleton Press
EVOLVING THE ULTIMATE RAIL ENCYCLOPEDIA

Table T199-R

Mondays to Fridays 16 December to 15 May

Orpington, Petts Wood, Hither Green and Lewisham - London (Summary of Services)

		SE TWO	SE MO	SE ThFO	SE TWO	SE TWO		SE MO	SE ThFO	SE TWO	SE TWO	SE ThFO	SE TWO	SE ThFO	TL	SE		SE	SE	TL	SE 1 A	SE	SE	SE	SE
Orpington	d														04 33	04 54			04 59	05 03	05 09		05 24		
Petts Wood	d														04 36	04 57			05 03	05 06			05 27		
Hither Green	d							00 05	00 06	00 06			00 16	00 16				05 10	05 16			05 22			05 37
Lewisham	d					00 05		00 11	00 11	00 13	00 15	00 16						05 16	05 21			05 27		05 35	05 43
St Johns	d				00 02																	05 29			
New Cross	⊖ d	00 01	00 02	00 02	00 05																	05 31			
London Victoria	⊖ a															05 35							06 05		
London Bridge	⊖ d	00 09	00 09	00 17	00 12	00a13		00 21	00 21	00 21	00 25	00 26	00a29	00 29				05 26	05 30		05 37	05 38		05 45	05 53
London Blackfriars	⊖ a														05 19					05 49					
London Cannon Street	⊖ a	00 13	00 13	00 25	00 18					00 27	00 33											05 44			
London Waterloo (East)	⊖ d							00 26	00 26			00 31		00 34				05 31	05 36		05 42			05 50	05 58
London Charing Cross	⊖ a							00 29	00 31			00 35		00 39				05 37	05 41		05 48			05 57	06 03

		TL		TL	SE	SE	SE	SE	SE ◇1	SE	SE	SE		SE	SE	SE	SE	SE	SE	SE ◇1	TL	SE		TL	SE
Orpington	d			05 33			05 33		05 51		05 52								05 55	05 59		05 59		06 03	
Petts Wood	d			05 36			05 36				05 55								05 58			06 03		06 06	
Hither Green	d				05 42		05 49			05 52							05 58	06 08	06 11			06 16			
Lewisham	d				05 47	05 50	05 54	05 56		05 58		06 03		06 09	06 11	06 19	07 08					06 21			06 26
St Johns	d				05 49					06 00		06 05		06 11								06 23			
New Cross	⊖ d				05 52					06 02		06 07		06 13								06 25			
London Victoria	⊖ a										06 35				06 37										
London Bridge	⊖ d	05 58			06 00	05 59	06 03	06 06	06 08	06 09		06 14		06 20		06 29	07 18	06 19	06 22	06 18	06 28	06 33			06 35
London Blackfriars	⊖ a	06 04		06 19																	06 34			06 49	
London Cannon Street	⊖ a				06 06					06 15		06 20		06 26						06 24		06 39			
London Waterloo (East)	⊖ d					06 05	06 08	06 11	06 13							06 35	07 23	06 24	06 27						06 40
London Charing Cross	⊖ a					06 10	06 14	06 16	06 19							06 40	07 29	06 30	06 33						06 46

		SE	SE	SE	SE	SE	SE	SE		SE ◇1	SE	SE ◇1	TL	SE	SE	SE	SE	SE		SE	SE ◇1	TL	SE	SE	SE
Orpington	d							06 18		06 21	06 24	06 27	06 30							06 33	06 40				06 41
Petts Wood	d							06 21			06 28		06 33							06 37					06 45
Hither Green	d	06 25	06 29				06 30	06 36										06 48		06 50			06 56		06 58
Lewisham	d	06 31		06 33	06 36	06 38	07 40	06 41						06 44		06 48	06 50	06 54						06 59	07 04
St Johns	d			06 35												06 50		06 56						07 01	
New Cross	⊖ d	06 36		06 37						06 33					06 49	06 52		06 58		06 56				07 03	
London Victoria	⊖ a				07 02						07 07														
London Bridge	⊖ d	06 42	06 41	06 44		06 47	07 53	06 52		06 39		06 45		06 54	08 17	07 00	07 00	07 05		07 03	06 57	06 58	07 07	07 10	07 14
London Blackfriars	⊖ a												07 19									07 04			
London Cannon Street	⊖ a	06 48		06 50						06 46					08 21	07 06		07 11		07 09				07 16	
London Waterloo (East)	⊖ d		06 46			06 53	07 58	06 57				06 50		06 59			07 05				07 02		07 12		07 19
London Charing Cross	⊖ a		06 52			06 58	08 04	07 03				06 56		07 05			07 12				07 08		07 18		07 25

		SE	SE ◇1	SE		TL	SE	SE	SE	SE	SE	SE	SE	SE		SE ◇1	TL	SE	SE ◇1	SE	SE	SE	SE	SE	
Orpington	d	06 49	06 53	06 54		06 59								07 02		07 04		07 12	07 15					07 20	
Petts Wood	d	06 52		06 57		07 02								07 05				07 15						07 24	
Hither Green	d	07 06								07 11	07 16			07 19				07 29				07 31	07 36	07 38	
Lewisham	d						07 12	07 15		07 17		07 21	07 23	07 25						07 31	07 35	07 38		07 44	
St Johns	d									07 19			07 25									07 40			
New Cross	⊖ d	07 12							07 21	07 22		07 24	07 28					07 34			07 38	07 43			
London Victoria	⊖ a			07 35				07 37																	
London Bridge	⊖ d	07 19	07 10				07 22		08 39	07 30	07 27	07 32	07 35	07 35		07 25	07 28	07 42	07 32	07 41	07 45	07 50	07 47	07 55	
London Blackfriars	⊖ a					07 49											07 34								
London Cannon Street	⊖ a	07 25							08 45	07 35		07 38	07 41			07 31		07 48			07 51	07 56			
London Waterloo (East)	⊖ d		07 15				07 27				07 32			07 40					07 37	07 47			07 52	08 00	
London Charing Cross	⊖ a		07 21				07 33				07 38			07 46					07 44	07 53			07 58	08 06	

		TL	SE	TL	SE	SE	SE	SE	SE	SE		SE	SE	SE	SE	SE	SE	SE	SE	SE		SE	SE	SE	SE
Orpington	d		07 23	07 30					07 33						07 42	07 48		07 51		07 56					
Petts Wood	d		07 27	07 33					07 36						07 46	07 51		07 54		08 00					
Hither Green	d								07 50			07 53			08 00		08 02							08 11	08 15
Lewisham	d				07 46		07 48	07 51		07 55		08 00	08 02	08 06	08 08				08 11			08 13	08 15	08 19	
St Johns	d						07 50			07 57		08 03										08 15	08 18	08 21	
New Cross	⊖ d					07 50	07 53		07 56	08 00		08 06						08 11				08 18	08 21	08 24	
London Victoria	⊖ a		08 07		08 13									08 33		08 32									
London Bridge	⊖ d	07 58				09 08	08 00	08 02	08 03	08 07		08 13	08 13		08 19		08 15	08 19	08 21	08 23		08 25	08 30	08 32	08 27
London Blackfriars	⊖ a	08 04		08 19																					
London Cannon Street	⊖ a					09 14	08 06		08 09	08 13		08 19						08 25				08 31	08 36	08 38	
London Waterloo (East)	⊖ d							08 07					08 18		08 24		08 20		08 26	08 28					08 32
London Charing Cross	⊖ a							08 13					08 24		08 30		08 26		08 32	08 33					08 38

		TL	SE	SE	SE	TL		SE	SE	SE	SE	SE	SE	SE	SE	SE		SE	SE	SE	TL	TL	SE	SE	SE
Orpington	d			07 59		08 03						08 12						08 21	08 24			08 29			
Petts Wood	d			08 03		08 06						08 15						08 24	08 27			08 32			
Hither Green	d			08 18				08 27				08 30		08 30	08 32	08 35		08 38		08 42					
Lewisham	d		08 22	08 24	08 27					08 29	08 31		08 36		08 39			08 44					08 46		08 48
St Johns	d									08 31					08 41										08 50
New Cross	⊖ d								08 31	08 34		08 37	08 39		08 44									08 47	08 53
London Victoria	⊖ a				08 55														09 05				09 11		
London Bridge	⊖ d	08 28	08 33	08 35				08 39	09 47	08 41	08 43	08 44	08 47	09 38	08 51	08 47		08 54		08 56	08 58			10 07	09 00
London Blackfriars	⊖ a	08 34				08 49															09 04	09 19			
London Cannon Street	⊖ a								09 55	08 47		08 50	08 53	09 44	08 57									10 13	09 07
London Waterloo (East)	⊖ d		08 38	08 40				08 44			08 48					08 52		09 00		09 02					
London Charing Cross	⊖ a		08 43	08 46				08 50			08 54					08 58		09 05		09 07					

Orpington, Petts Wood, Hither Green and Lewisham - London (Summary of Services)

Station		SE	SE	SE	SE 1	SE	SE	SE		SE	SE	SE	SE ◇	SE	SE	SE	TL	SE ◇1		SE	TL	SE	SE	SE	SE
Orpington 4	d			08 34							08 41		08 46		08 52	08 55	09 03	09 05							
Petts Wood 4	d			08 37							08 45				08 55	08 58	09 06								
Hither Green 4	d		08 50	08 52		08 55					08 59			09 03	09 09							09 16			
Lewisham 4	d	08 51	08 55		08 56		09 01	09 04		09 04	09 05	09 07		09 10						09 15				09 17	09 26
St Johns	d		08 59					09 06						09 12										09 20	
New Cross 4	d		09 01	08 58				09 08						09 15									09 19	09 22	
London Victoria 15	a											09 35				09 35									
London Bridge 4	d	09 01	09 10	09 06	09 06	09 08	09 11	09 15		10 17	09 15		09 04	09 22	09 20			09 22		09 25	09 28	09 29	10 37	09 30	09 36
London Blackfriars 3	a																09 49				09 34				
London Cannon Street 4	a		09 16	09 12				09 21		10 21				09 28									10 41	09 36	
London Waterloo (East) 4	d	09 06			09 12	09 14	09 16				09 20		09 09		09 25			09 27		09 30		09 34			09 42
London Charing Cross 4	a	09 12			09 18	09 20	09 22				09 27		09 15		09 31			09 33		09 37		09 40			09 47

Station		SE	SE	SE		SE	SE	SE	SE ◇1	SE	TL	SE	SE	SE		SE ◇1	SE	TL	SE	SE	SE	SE	SE	SE	
Orpington 4	d					09 10		09 21	09 24	09 24	09 33					09 38								09 41	
Petts Wood 4	d					09 14		09 24		09 28	09 36													09 45	
Hither Green 4	d		09 22			09 27	09 34	09 37					09 42									09 52		09 58	
Lewisham 4	d		09 29	09 32		09 34						09 39		09 42			09 46		09 55			09 57	10 02	10 04	
St Johns	d		09 31			09 36						09 41		09 44								09 59		10 06	
New Cross 4	d	09 28	09 33			09 38						09 44		09 47						09 49	09 57	10 01		10 08	
London Victoria 15	a			09 57						10 04													10 25		
London Bridge 4	d	10 47	09 40			09 45	09 45	09 48	09 41			09 51	09 53	09 54		09 55	09 57	09 58	10 05	11 07	11 17	10 09		10 14	
London Blackfriars 3	a										10 19							10 04							
London Cannon Street 4	a	10 51	09 46			09 51						09 57		10 02						11 11	11 21	10 15		10 18	
London Waterloo (East) 4	d						09 50	09 53	09 46				09 58			10 00	10 02		10 10						
London Charing Cross 4	a						09 56	09 59	09 52				10 03			10 06	10 05		10 15						

Station		SE	SE	SE ◇1	SE	TL	SE	SE	SE ◇1	SE		TL	SE	SE	SE	SE	SE	SE	SE	SE		SE ◇1	SE	TL	SE
Orpington 4	d		09 50	09 52	09 54	10 03			10 08									10 11		10 20		10 22	10 24	10 33	
Petts Wood 4	d		09 53		09 57	10 06												10 15		10 23			10 27	10 36	
Hither Green 4	d	10 03	10 06													10 22		10 28	10 33	10 36					
Lewisham 4	d						10 09	10 12		10 16			10 25			10 27	10 32	10 34							10 39
St Johns	d						10 11	10 14								10 31		10 36							10 41
New Cross 4	d						10 14	10 17						10 19	10 27	10 33		10 38							10 44
London Victoria 15	a				10 33												10 55							11 03	
London Bridge 4	d	10 15	10 17	10 09			10 20	10 24	10 25	10 27		10 28	10 35	11 37	11 47	10 39		10 44	10 45	10 47		10 39			10 50
London Blackfriars 3	a					10 49						10 34												11 19	
London Cannon Street 4	a						10 24	10 30						11 41	11 51	10 43		10 48							10 54
London Waterloo (East) 4	d	10 20	10 22	10 14					10 30	10 32			10 40						10 50	10 52		10 44			
London Charing Cross 4	a	10 23	10 27	10 20					10 36	10 35			10 43						10 53	10 57		10 48			

Station		SE	SE ◇1	SE	TL	SE		SE	SE	SE	SE	SE	SE	SE	SE ◇1	SE		TL	SE	SE	SE ◇1	SE	TL	SE	SE
Orpington 4	d		10 38									10 41		10 50	10 52	10 54		11 03			11 08				
Petts Wood 4	d											10 45		10 53		10 57		11 06							
Hither Green 4	d									10 52		10 58	11 03	11 06											
Lewisham 4	d	10 42		10 46		10 55				10 57	11 02	11 04							11 09	11 12		11 16		11 25	
St Johns	d	10 44								11 01		11 06							11 11	11 14					
New Cross 4	d	10 47						10 49	10 57	11 03		11 08							11 14	11 17					11 19
London Victoria 15	a										11 25					11 33									
London Bridge 4	d	10 54	10 55	10 57	10 58	11 05		12 07	12 17	11 09		11 14	11 15	11 17	11 09				11 20	11 24	11 25	11 27	11 28	11 35	12 37
London Blackfriars 3	a				11 04													11 49					11 34		
London Cannon Street 4	a	11 00						12 11	12 21	11 13		11 18							11 24	11 30					12 41
London Waterloo (East) 4	d		11 00	11 02		11 10							11 20	11 22	11 14						11 30	11 32		11 40	
London Charing Cross 4	a		11 04	11 05		11 13							11 23	11 27	11 18						11 34	11 35		11 43	

Station		SE		SE	SE	SE	SE	SE	SE ◇1	SE	TL	SE		SE	SE ◇1	SE	TL	SE	SE	SE	SE	SE		SE	SE
Orpington 4	d					11 11		11 20	11 22	11 24	11 33				11 38									11 41	
Petts Wood 4	d					11 15		11 23		11 27	11 36													11 45	
Hither Green 4	d			11 22		11 28	11 33	11 36													11 51			11 58	12 03
Lewisham 4	d			11 27	11 32	11 34						11 39		11 42		11 46		11 55			11 57	12 02		12 04	
St Johns	d			11 29		11 36						11 41		11 44							11 59			12 06	
New Cross 4	d	11 27		11 32		11 38						11 44		11 47					11 49	11 57	12 01			12 08	
London Victoria 15	a				11 55					12 03												12 25			
London Bridge 4	d	12 47		11 39		11 44	11 45	11 47	11 39			11 50		11 54	11 55	11 57	11 58	12 05	13 07	13 17	12 09			12 14	12 15
London Blackfriars 3	a										12 19						12 04								
London Cannon Street 4	a	12 51		11 43		11 48						11 54		12 00					13 11	13 21	12 13			12 18	
London Waterloo (East) 4	d						11 50	11 52	11 44						12 00	12 02		12 10							12 20
London Charing Cross 4	a						11 53	11 57	11 48						12 04	12 05		12 13							12 23

Station		SE	SE ◇1	SE	TL	SE	SE	SE ◇1		SE	TL	SE	SE	SE	SE	SE	SE	SE		SE	SE ◇1	SE	TL	SE	SE
Orpington 4	d	11 50	11 52	11 54	12 03			12 08									12 11			12 20	12 22	12 24	12 33		
Petts Wood 4	d	11 53		11 57	12 06												12 15			12 23		12 27	12 36		
Hither Green 4	d	12 06													12 21		12 28	12 33		12 36					
Lewisham 4	d					12 09	12 12			12 16		12 25			12 27	12 32	12 34							12 39	12 42
St Johns	d					12 11	12 14								12 29		12 36							12 41	12 44
New Cross 4	d					12 14	12 17						12 19	12 27	12 31		12 38							12 44	12 47
London Victoria 15	a			12 33												12 55						13 03			
London Bridge 4	d	12 17	12 09			12 20	12 24	12 25		12 27	12 28	12 35	13 37	13 47	12 39		12 44	12 45		12 47	12 39			12 50	12 54
London Blackfriars 3	a				12 49						12 34												13 19		
London Cannon Street 4	a					12 24	12 30						13 41	13 51	12 43		12 48							12 54	13 00
London Waterloo (East) 4	d	12 22	12 14					12 30		12 32		12 40						12 50		12 52	12 44				
London Charing Cross 4	a	12 27	12 18					12 34		12 35		12 43						12 53		12 57	12 48				

Station		SE ◇1	SE	TL	SE	SE	SE	SE	SE	SE		SE	SE	SE ◇1	SE	TL	SE	SE	SE ◇1	SE		TL	SE	SE	SE
Orpington 4	d	12 38								12 41			12 50	12 52	12 54	13 03			13 08						
Petts Wood 4	d									12 45			12 53		12 57	13 06									
Hither Green 4	d							12 51		12 58		13 03	13 06												
Lewisham 4	d		12 46		12 55			12 57	13 02	13 04							13 09	13 12		13 16			13 25		
St Johns	d							12 59		13 06							13 11	13 14							
New Cross 4	d					12 49	12 57	13 01		13 08							13 14	13 17						13 19	13 27
London Victoria 15	a								13 25						13 33										
London Bridge 4	d	12 55	12 57	12 58	13 05	14 07	14 17	13 09		13 14		13 15	13 17	13 09			13 20	13 24	13 25	13 27		13 28	13 35	14 37	14 47
London Blackfriars 3	a			13 04												13 49						13 34			
London Cannon Street 4	a					14 11	14 21	13 13		13 18							13 24	13 30						14 41	14 51
London Waterloo (East) 4	d	13 00	13 02		13 10							13 20	13 22	13 14					13 30	13 32			13 40		
London Charing Cross 4	a	13 04	13 05		13 13							13 23	13 27	13 18					13 34	13 35			13 43		

Station		SE	SE	SE	SE	SE		SE ◇1	SE	TL	SE	SE	SE ◇1	SE	TL	SE		SE	SE	SE	SE	SE	SE	SE	SE ◇1
Orpington 4	d			13 11		13 20		13 22	13 24	13 33			13 38									13 41		13 50	13 52
Petts Wood 4	d			13 15		13 23			13 27	13 36												13 45		13 53	
Hither Green 4	d	13 21		13 28	13 33	13 36														13 51		13 58	14 03	14 06	
Lewisham 4	d	13 27	13 32	13 34							13 39	13 42		13 46		13 55				13 57	14 02	14 04			
St Johns	d	13 29		13 36							13 41	13 44								13 59		14 06			
New Cross 4	d	13 31		13 38							13 44	13 47						13 49	13 57	14 01		14 08			
London Victoria 15	a		13 55						14 03												14 25				
London Bridge 4	d	13 39		13 44	13 45	13 47		13 39			13 50	13 54	13 55	13 57	13 58	14 05		15 07	15 17	14 09		14 14	14 15	14 17	14 09
London Blackfriars 3	a									14 19					14 04										
London Cannon Street 4	a	13 43		13 48							13 54	14 00						15 11	15 21	14 13		14 18			
London Waterloo (East) 4	d				13 50	13 52		13 44					14 00	14 02		14 10							14 20	14 22	14 14
London Charing Cross 4	a				13 53	13 57		13 48					14 04	14 05		14 13							14 23	14 27	14 18

Station		SE		TL	SE	SE	SE ◇1	SE	TL	SE	SE	SE		SE	SE	SE	SE	SE	SE ◇1	SE	TL	SE		SE	SE ◇1
Orpington 4	d	13 54		14 03			14 08									14 11		14 20	14 22	14 24	14 33				14 38
Petts Wood 4	d	13 57		14 06												14 15		14 23		14 27	14 36				
Hither Green 4	d													14 21		14 28	14 33	14 36							
Lewisham 4	d				14 09	14 12		14 16		14 25				14 27	14 32	14 34						14 39		14 42	
St Johns	d				14 11	14 14								14 29		14 36						14 41		14 44	
New Cross 4	d				14 14	14 17					14 19	14 27		14 31		14 38						14 44		14 47	
London Victoria 15	a	14 33													14 55					15 03					
London Bridge 4	d				14 20	14 24	14 25	14 27	14 28	14 35	15 37	15 47		14 39		14 44	14 45	14 47	14 39			14 50		14 54	14 55
London Blackfriars 3	a			14 49					14 34												15 19				
London Cannon Street 4	a				14 24	14 30					15 41	15 51		14 43		14 48						14 55		15 00	
London Waterloo (East) 4	d						14 30	14 32		14 40							14 50	14 52	14 44						15 00
London Charing Cross 4	a						14 34	14 35		14 43							14 53	14 57	14 48						15 04

Station		SE	TL	SE	SE	SE	SE	SE		SE	SE	SE	SE ◇1	SE	TL	SE	SE	SE ◇1		SE	TL	SE	SE	SE	SE
Orpington 4	d									14 41		14 50	14 52	14 54	15 03			15 08							
Petts Wood 4	d									14 45		14 53		14 57	15 06										
Hither Green 4	d						14 51			14 58	15 03	15 06													15 21
Lewisham 4	d	14 46		14 55			14 57	15 02		15 04						15 09	15 12			15 16		15 25			15 27
St Johns	d						14 59			15 06						15 11	15 14								15 29
New Cross 4	d				14 49	14 57	15 01			15 08						15 14	15 17						15 19	15 27	15 31
London Victoria 15	a							15 25						15 33											
London Bridge 4	d	14 57	14 58	15 05	16 06	16 17	15 09			15 14	15 15	15 17	15 09			15 20	15 24	15 25		15 27	15 28	15 35	16 34	16 47	15 39
London Blackfriars 3	a		15 04												15 49						15 34				
London Cannon Street 4	a				16 12	16 23	15 13			15 18						15 24	15 30						16 40	16 53	15 43
London Waterloo (East) 4	d	15 02		15 10							15 20	15 22	15 14					15 30		15 32		15 40			
London Charing Cross 4	a	15 05		15 13							15 23	15 27	15 18					15 34		15 35		15 43			

Station		SE	SE	SE		SE	SE ◇1	SE	TL	SE	SE	SE ◇1	SE	TL		SE	SE	SE	SE	SE	SE	SE	SE ◇1	SE	
Orpington 4	d		15 11			15 20	15 22	15 24	15 33			15 38								15 41		15 50	15 52	15 54	
Petts Wood 4	d		15 15			15 23		15 27	15 36											15 45		15 53		15 57	
Hither Green 4	d		15 28	15 33		15 36												15 51		15 58	16 03	16 06			
Lewisham 4	d	15 32	15 34							15 39	15 42		15 46			15 56		15 58	16 02	16 04					
St Johns	d		15 36							15 41	15 44							16 00		16 06					
New Cross 4	d		15 38							15 44	15 47						15 49	16 02		16 08					
London Victoria 15	a	15 55						16 03											16 25					16 33	
London Bridge 4	d		15 44	15 45		15 47	15 39			15 50	15 54	15 55	15 57	15 58		16 05	17 08	16 09		16 14	16 15	16 17	16 09		
London Blackfriars 3	a								16 19					16 04											
London Cannon Street 4	a		15 48							15 54	16 00						17 14	16 15		16 20					
London Waterloo (East) 4	d			15 50		15 52	15 44					16 00	16 02			16 10					16 20	16 24	16 14		
London Charing Cross 4	a			15 53		15 57	15 48					16 04	16 05			16 15					16 23	16 27	16 18		

Station		TL	SE	SE	SE ◇1	SE	TL	SE 1	SE	SE		SE	SE	SE	SE	SE	SE	SE ◇1	SE	TL		SE	SE ◇1	SE	SE
Orpington 4	d	16 03			16 08			16 11							16 11		16 20	16 24	16 24	16 33			16 38		
Petts Wood 4	d	16 06													16 15		16 23		16 27	16 36					
Hither Green 4	d												16 21		16 28	16 33	16 36								
Lewisham 4	d		16 09	16 12		16 16			16 25				16 27	16 32	16 34							16 37		16 42	16 46
St Johns	d		16 11	16 14									16 29		16 36							16 39		16 46	
New Cross 4	d		16 14	16 17						16 19		16 26	16 31		16 38							16 42		16 48	
London Victoria 15	a													16 55					17 03						
London Bridge 4	d		16 20	16 23	16 25	16 27	16 28	16 29	16 35	17 34		17 40	16 38		16 44	16 45	16 47	16 41				16 50	16 55	16 55	16 57
London Blackfriars 3	a	16 49					16 34													17 19					
London Cannon Street 4	a		16 24	16 29						17 41		17 46	16 44		16 50							16 56		17 02	
London Waterloo (East) 4	d				16 30	16 32		16 34	16 41							16 52	16 53	16 46					17 00		17 02
London Charing Cross 4	a				16 34	16 36		16 38	16 46							16 57	16 58	16 51					17 07		17 06

Orpington, Petts Wood, Hither Green and Lewisham - London (Summary of Services)

		TL		SE	SE	SE	SE	SE	SE	SE	SE	SE		SE	SE	SE	SE	SE	SE	SE	TL	TL		SE	SE
														◇1		◇1								◇1	
Orpington 4	d									16 41		16 50		16 52	16 54	16 59						17 03		17 09	
Petts Wood 4	d									16 45		16 53			16 57							17 06			
Hither Green 4	d							16 53				16 58	17 02	17 09											
Lewisham 4	⇌ d			16 55			17 00	17 02		17 05							17 09		17 13	17 15					17 25
St Johns	d						17 02										17 11		17 16						
New Cross 4	⊖ d				16 50	16 56	17 05		17 09	17 10							17 14	17 15	17 19						
London Victoria 15	⊖ a							17 25							17 33										
London Bridge 4	⊖ d	16 58		17 05	18 04	18 18	17 11		18 31	17 16	17 15	17 20		17 11		17 18	17 21	18 38	17 26	17 25	17 28			17 31	17 35
London Blackfriars 3	⊖ a	17 04																			17 34	17 49			
London Cannon Street 4	⊖ a				18 10	18 24	17 17		18 37	17 22							17 27	18 44	17 32					17 37	
London Waterloo (East) 4	⊖ d			17 10							17 20	17 28		17 16		17 25				17 32					17 40
London Charing Cross 4	⊖ a			17 16							17 25	17 31		17 21		17 30				17 39					17 46

		SE	SE	SE	SE	SE	SE	SE		SE	SE	SE	SE	SE	TL	TL	SE	SE		SE	SE	SE	SE	SE	SE
								◇1																	
Orpington 4	d			17 11	17 15		17 19	17 23		17 24	17 28					17 33									
Petts Wood 4	d			17 15			17 24			17 27						17 36									
Hither Green 4	d	17 26		17 29		17 31	17 40																17 52		
Lewisham 4	⇌ d		17 32	17 34								17 38	17 41	17 45			17 48	17 53		17 55				17 56	18 00
St Johns	d	17 31		17 37									17 44										17 56		
New Cross 4	⊖ d	17 34		17 39								17 41	17 47								17 53	17 58	17 59		
London Victoria 15	⊖ a		17 55							18 03															18 25
London Bridge 4	⊖ d			17 45	17 37	17 42	17 50	17 40			17 46	17 48	17 53	17 54	17 58		17 58	18 02		18 05	19 25	19 20	18 07	19 09	
London Blackfriars 3	⊖ a														18 04	18 19									
London Cannon Street 4	⊖ a	17 48		17 51								17 54	18 00								19 30	19 26	18 13	19 15	
London Waterloo (East) 4	⊖ d				17 43	17 47	17 55	17 45			17 51			17 59			18 03	18 07		18 11					
London Charing Cross 4	⊖ a				17 48	17 52	18 00	17 50			17 54			18 05			18 08	18 12		18 17					

		SE	SE	SE		SE	SE	TL	SE	SE	SE	SE	TL	SE		SE	SE	SE	SE	SE	SE	SE	SE	SE	
			◇1						◇1			◇1													
Orpington 4	d	17 40	17 41			17 49	17 54	18 02	18 03			18 09										18 10			
Petts Wood 4	d	17 44				17 52	17 57	18 05														18 14			
Hither Green 4	d	17 57		18 03		18 05												18 13		18 24		18 27	18 33	18 36	
Lewisham 4	⇌ d	18 02		18 09							18 14			18 17		18 19	18 23	19 14		18 30	18 32	18 35			
St Johns	d	18 07														18 22				18 34		18 41			
New Cross 4	⊖ d	18 09								18 11	18 17					18 26			18 34	18 37		18 44			
London Victoria 15	⊖ a						18 33											19 33			18 57				
London Bridge 4	⊖ d		18 00	18 19		18 17			18 21	19 37	18 23	18 26	18 28	18 28		18 34	18 33		20 07	18 44		18 52	18 45	19 47	
London Blackfriars 3	⊖ a							18 49					18 34												
London Cannon Street 4	⊖ a	18 20								19 43	18 27					18 40			20 11	18 50		18 56		19 51	
London Waterloo (East) 4	⊖ d		18 06	18 25		18 22			18 27			18 31		18 33			18 38						18 50		
London Charing Cross 4	⊖ a		18 12	18 30		18 27			18 32			18 37		18 38			18 41						18 55		

		SE	SE	SE	SE	TL	SE	SE	SE	SE		SE	SE	SE	SE	TL	SE	SE	SE	SE		SE	SE	TL	SE
			◇1												◇1					◇1					◇1
Orpington 4	d	18 19	18 22	18 22	18 29	18 33								18 40	18 41				18 50	18 52			18 54	19 03	19 10
Petts Wood 4	d	18 22		18 26		18 36								18 44					18 53				18 57	19 06	
Hither Green 4	d	18 39												18 57			18 59	19 02	19 06						
Lewisham 4	⇌ d						18 41	18 48	18 50	18 55		18 57	19 00	19 03			19 07					19 14			
St Johns	d						18 44		18 52					19 06			19 09								
New Cross 4	⊖ d						18 47		18 54					19 08			19 11								
London Victoria 15	⊖ a			19 03									19 27									19 33	19 34		
London Bridge 4	⊖ d	18 50	18 41		18 47		18 55	19 00	19 01	19 05		20 17		19 14	18 57	18 58	19 17	19 13	19 19	19 10					19 26
London Blackfriars 3	⊖ a					19 19										19 04								19 49	
London Cannon Street 4	⊖ a		18 47				19 01		19 05			20 21		19 19			19 21								
London Waterloo (East) 4	⊖ d	18 55			18 54			19 06		19 10					19 02			19 20	19 24	19 15					19 31
London Charing Cross 4	⊖ a	19 02			18 57			19 09		19 13					19 05			19 23	19 27	19 19					19 35

		TL	SE	SE	SE	SE		SE	SE	SE	SE	SE	SE	SE	SE	TL		SE	SE	SE	SE	TL	SE	SE	SE
														◇1						◇1					
Orpington 4	d										19 11		19 20	19 23	19 24	19 33				19 38					
Petts Wood 4	d										19 15		19 23		19 27	19 36									
Hither Green 4	d								19 21		19 27	19 34	19 36												19 51
Lewisham 4	⇌ d			19 16	19 18	19 25			19 27	19 32	19 34							19 39	19 42		19 46		19 55		19 57
St Johns	d			19 19					19 29		19 36							19 41	19 44						19 59
New Cross 4	⊖ d		19 19	19 22				19 26	19 32		19 38							19 44	19 47					19 49	20 01
London Victoria 15	⊖ a									19 55					20 03										
London Bridge 4	⊖ d	19 28	20 37	19 29	19 28	19 35		20 47	19 40		19 44	19 45	19 47	19 40				19 50	19 54	19 55	19 57	19 58	20 05	21 07	20 09
London Blackfriars 3	⊖ a	19 34														20 19						20 04			
London Cannon Street 4	⊖ a		20 41	19 33				20 51	19 46		19 48							19 54	19 58					21 11	20 15
London Waterloo (East) 4	⊖ d				19 33	19 40						19 50	19 52	19 45						20 00	20 02		20 10		
London Charing Cross 4	⊖ a				19 36	19 43						19 53	19 57	19 49						20 04	20 05		20 13		

		SE		SE	SE	SE	SE	SE	TL	SE	SE	SE		SE	TL	SE	SE	SE	SE	SE	SE	SE		SE	SE
							◇1					◇1												◇1	
Orpington 4	d			19 41		19 50	19 52	19 54	20 03			20 08								20 11		20 20		20 22	20 24
Petts Wood 4	d			19 45		19 53		19 57	20 06											20 15		20 23			20 27
Hither Green 4	d			19 58	20 03	20 06												20 21		20 28	20 33	20 36			
Lewisham 4	⇌ d	20 02		20 04						20 09	20 12			20 17		20 25		20 27	20 32	20 34					
St Johns	d			20 06						20 11	20 14							20 29		20 36					
New Cross 4	⊖ d			20 08						20 14	20 17						20 19	20 31		20 38					
London Victoria 15	⊖ a	20 25						20 33											20 55						21 03
London Bridge 4	⊖ d			20 14	20 15	20 17	20 09			20 20	20 24	20 25		20 27	20 28	20 35	21 37	20 39		20 44	20 45	20 47		20 39	
London Blackfriars 3	⊖ a								20 49						20 34										
London Cannon Street 4	⊖ a			20 18						20 24	20 30						21 41	20 43		20 48					
London Waterloo (East) 4	⊖ d				20 20	20 22	20 14					20 30		20 32		20 40					20 50	20 52		20 44	
London Charing Cross 4	⊖ a				20 23	20 27	20 18					20 34		20 35		20 43					20 53	20 57		20 48	

Table T199-R

Mondays to Fridays

16 December to 15 May

Orpington, Petts Wood, Hither Green and Lewisham - London (Summary of Services)

		SE	SE	SE		TL	TL	SE	SE	SE	SE	SE	SE	SE		SE	SE	TL	SE	SE	SE	TL	SE	SE	
																◇1				◇1					
Orpington 4	d						20 33					20 41		20 50		20 52	20 54	21 03		21 08					
Petts Wood 4	d						20 36					20 45		20 53			20 57	21 06							
Hither Green 4	d									20 51		20 58	21 03	21 06											
Lewisham 4	⇌ d	20 39	20 42	20 46				20 55		20 57	21 02	21 04							21 09		21 16		21 25		
St Johns	d	20 41	20 44							20 59		21 06							21 11						
New Cross 4	⊖ d	20 44	20 47						20 49	21 01		21 08							21 14					21 19	
London Victoria 15	⊖ a										21 25						21 33								
London Bridge 4	⊖ d	20 50	20 54	20 57		20 58		21 05	22 07	21 09		21 14	21 15	21 17		21 09			21 20	21 25	21 27	21 28	21 35	22 37	
London Blackfriars 3	⊖ a					21 04	21 19											21 49				21 34			
London Cannon Street 4	⊖ a	20 54	21 00						22 11	21 13		21 18							21 25					22 41	
London Waterloo (East) 4	⊖ d			21 02				21 10					21 20	21 22		21 14				21 30	21 32		21 40		
London Charing Cross 4	⊖ a			21 05				21 13					21 23	21 27		21 18				21 34	21 35		21 43		

		SE	SE	SE	SE	SE	SE	SE	SE	SE		TL	TL	SE	SE	SE	SE	SE	SE	SE		SE	SE	TL	SE
							◇1															◇1			
Orpington 4	d			21 11		21 20	21 22	21 24					21 33					21 41		21 50		21 53	21 54	22 03	
Petts Wood 4	d			21 15		21 23		21 27					21 36					21 45		21 53			21 57	22 06	
Hither Green 4	d	21 21		21 28	21 33	21 36										21 51		21 58	22 03	22 06					
Lewisham 4	⇌ d	21 27	21 32	21 34					21 39	21 46				21 55		21 57	22 02	22 04							22 09
St Johns	d	21 29		21 36					21 41							21 59		22 06							22 11
New Cross 4	⊖ d	21 31		21 38					21 44						21 49	22 01		22 08							22 14
London Victoria 15	⊖ a		21 55					22 03									22 25						22 33		
London Bridge 4	⊖ d	21 39		21 44	21 45	21 47	21 39		21 50	21 57		21 58		22 05	23 07	22 09		22 14	22 15	22 17		22 09			22 20
London Blackfriars 3	⊖ a											22 04	22 19											22 49	
London Cannon Street 4	⊖ a	21 43		21 48					21 54						23 11	22 13		22 18							22 24
London Waterloo (East) 4	⊖ d				21 50	21 52	21 44			22 02				22 10					22 20	22 22		22 14			
London Charing Cross 4	⊖ a				21 53	21 57	21 48			22 05				22 13					22 23	22 27		22 18			

		SE	SE	TL	SE	SE		SE	SE	SE	SE	SE	SE	SE	SE	SE		TL	TL	SE	TL	SE	SE	SE	SE
																						MT FO			
		◇1											◇1												
Orpington 4	d	22 08								22 11		22 20	22 22	22 24					22 33						22 41
Petts Wood 4	d									22 15		22 23		22 27					22 36						22 45
Hither Green 4	d							22 21		22 28	22 33	22 36											22 51		22 58
Lewisham 4	⇌ d		22 16		22 25			22 27	22 32	22 34					22 39	22 46				22 55			22 57	23 02	23 04
St Johns	d							22 29		22 36					22 41								22 59		23 06
New Cross 4	⊖ d					22 19		22 31		22 38					22 44							22 49	23 01		23 08
London Victoria 15	⊖ a								22 55					23 03										23 25	
London Bridge 4	⊖ d	22 25	22 27	22 28	22 35	23 37		22 39		22 44	22 45	22 47	22 39		22 50	22 57		22 58		23 05	23 28	00 07	23 09		23 14
London Blackfriars 3	⊖ a			22 34														23 04	23 19		23 34				
London Cannon Street 4	⊖ a					23 41		22 43		22 48					22 54							00 11	23 13		23 18
London Waterloo (East) 4	⊖ d	22 30	22 32		22 40						22 50	22 52	22 44			23 02				23 10					
London Charing Cross 4	⊖ a	22 34	22 35		22 43						22 53	22 57	22 48			23 05				23 13					

		SE		SE	SE	SE	TL	SE	SE	SE	SE	SE		SE	SE	SE	SE	SE	SE	SE	SE	SE		SE	SE
											WTh FO	MTO		MT FO	W ThO		MT FO	WTh FO	WTh FO	FO	W ThO	MTO			WTh FO
					◇1				◇1																◇1
Orpington 4	d			22 50	22 52	22 54	23 03		23 08								23 11		23 20			23 20		23 24	23 36
Petts Wood 4	d			22 53		22 57	23 06										23 15		23 23			23 23		23 27	
Hither Green 4	d	23 03		23 06										23 21	23 21		23 28	23 33	23 36			23 36			
Lewisham 4	⇌ d							23 09		23 16	23 25	23 25		23 27	23 27	23 32	23 34			23 39	23 40	23 41			
St Johns	d							23 11						23 29	23 29		23 36			23 41		23 43			
New Cross 4	⊖ d							23 14						23 31	23 31		23 38			23 44		23 45			
London Victoria 15	⊖ a					23 33										23 55								00 03	
London Bridge 4	⊖ d	23 15		23 17	23 09			23 20	23 25	23 27	23 35	23 35		23 39	23a41		23 44	23 45	23 47	23 50	23 50	23 52			23 54
London Blackfriars 3	⊖ a						23 49																		
London Cannon Street 4	⊖ a							23 24						23 43			23 48			23 54		23 58			
London Waterloo (East) 4	⊖ d	23 20		23 22	23 14				23 30	23 32	23 40	23 40						23 50	23 52		23 55				23 59
London Charing Cross 4	⊖ a	23 23		23 27	23 18				23 34	23 35	23 43	23 44						23 53	23 57		00 01				00 03

		SE	SE	SE	SE	SE	SE	SE		SE	SE	SE
		MTO		W ThO	WTh FO	MT FO	W ThO	MTO		WTh FO	MTO	
		◇1										
Orpington 4	d	23 36								23 50	23 50	23 54
Petts Wood 4	d									23 53	23 53	23 57
Hither Green 4	d					23 51	23 51			00 06	00 06	
Lewisham 4	⇌ d		23 46	23 50	23 55	23 57	23 58	23 59		00 11	00 13	
St Johns	d			23 57		23 59		00 02				
New Cross 4	⊖ d			00 02		00 01		00 05				
London Victoria 15	⊖ a											00 34
London Bridge 4	⊖ d	23 56	23 57	00 17	00 05	00 09	00a08	00 12		00 21	00 21	
London Blackfriars 3	⊖ a											
London Cannon Street 4	⊖ a	00 03		00 25		00 13		00 18			00 27	
London Waterloo (East) 4	⊖ d		00 02		00 10					00 26		
London Charing Cross 4	⊖ a		00 05		00 13					00 31		

Table T199-R

Saturdays

21 December to 16 May

Orpington, Petts Wood, Hither Green and Lewisham - London (Summary of Services)

	SE	SE	SE	SE	SE		SE	SE	SE	SE	SE	TL	SE	SE	SE		SE	SE	SE	SE	SE	TL	SE	SE
Orpington d										05 20			05 24				05 41		05 50	05 54				
Petts Wood d										05 23			05 27				05 45		05 53	05 57				
Hither Green d		00 06		00 16	05 10		05 25	05 30	05 33	05 36	05 40			05 44			05 58	06 03	06 06					
Lewisham d		00 11	00 16		05 16		05 31	05 35			05 46			05 49	05 55		06 04				06 16		06 20	
St Johns d								05 37						05 51			06 06							
New Cross ⊖ d	00 01							05 39						05 53			06 08							06 19
London Victoria ⊖ a													06 03							06 33				
London Bridge ⊖ d	00 09	00 21	00 26	00 29	05 26		05 41	05 45	05 45	05 47	05 56	05 58		06 00	06 05		06 14	06 15	06 17		06 27	06 28	06 30	07 37
London Blackfriars ⊖ a												06 04										06 34		
London Cannon Street ⊖ a	00 13							05 49						06 04			06 18							07 41
London Waterloo (East) ⊖ d		00 26	00 31	00 34	05 31		05 46		05 50	05 53	06 01				06 10			06 20	06 22		06 32		06 35	
London Charing Cross ⊖ a		00 31	00 35	00 39	05 35		05 49		05 53	05 57	06 04				06 13			06 23	06 27		06 35		06 39	

	SE		SE	SE	SE	SE	SE	SE ◇1	SE	SE	TL		SE	SE	SE	SE	SE	SE	SE	SE	SE		SE	SE ◇1
Orpington d					06 11		06 20	06 22	06 24										06 41		06 50		06 54	07 08
Petts Wood d					06 15		06 23		06 27										06 45		06 53		06 57	
Hither Green d	06 17			06 21	06 28	06 33	06 36								06 47		06 51		06 58	07 03	07 06			
Lewisham d			06 25	06 27	06 34					06 46			06 50			06 55	06 57	07 02	07 04					
St Johns d	06 21			06 29	06 36										06 51		06 59		07 06					
New Cross ⊖ d	06 23			06 31	06 38									06 49	06 53		07 01		07 08					
London Victoria ⊖ a									07 03									07 25					07 33	
London Bridge ⊖ d	06 30		06 35	06 39	06 44	06 45	06 47	06 39		06 57	06 58		07 00	08 07	07 00	07 05	07 09		07 14	07 15	07 17			07 25
London Blackfriars ⊖ a											07 04													
London Cannon Street ⊖ a	06 34			06 43	06 48									08 11	07 04		07 13		07 18					
London Waterloo (East) ⊖ d			06 40			06 50	06 52	06 44		07 02			07 05			07 10				07 20	07 22			07 30
London Charing Cross ⊖ a			06 43			06 53	06 57	06 48		07 05			07 09			07 13				07 23	07 27			07 34

	SE	TL	SE	SE	SE	SE	SE		SE	SE	SE	SE	SE	SE	SE	SE ◇1	SE	TL	SE	SE	SE	SE	SE	SE
Orpington d											07 11		07 20	07 24		07 38								07 41
Petts Wood d											07 15		07 23	07 27										07 45
Hither Green d					07 17				07 21		07 28	07 33	07 36									07 51		07 58
Lewisham d	07 16		07 20			07 25			07 27	07 32	07 34				07 39		07 46		07 55			07 57	08 02	08 04
St Johns d					07 21				07 29		07 36				07 41							07 59		08 06
New Cross ⊖ d				07 19	07 23		07 27		07 31		07 38				07 44					07 49	07 57	08 01		08 08
London Victoria ⊖ a										07 55				08 03									08 25	
London Bridge ⊖ d	07 27	07 28	07 30	08 37	07 30	07 35	08 47		07 39		07 44	07 45	07 47		07 50	07 55	07 57	07 58	08 05	09 07	09 17	08 09		08 14
London Blackfriars ⊖ a		07 34																08 04						
London Cannon Street ⊖ a				08 41	07 34		08 51		07 43		07 48				07 54					09 11	09 21	08 13		08 18
London Waterloo (East) ⊖ d	07 32		07 35			07 40						07 50	07 52			08 00	08 02		08 10					
London Charing Cross ⊖ a	07 35		07 39			07 43						07 53	07 57			08 04	08 05		08 13					

	SE	SE	SE ◇1	SE	SE	SE	SE ◇1	SE	TL	SE	SE	SE	SE	SE	SE	SE	SE	SE ◇1	SE	SE	SE		
Orpington d		07 50	07 52	07 54			08 08								08 11		08 20	08 22	08 24			and at the same minutes past each hour until	
Petts Wood d		07 53		07 57											08 15		08 23		08 27				
Hither Green d	08 03	08 06											08 21		08 28	08 33	08 36						
Lewisham d					08 09	08 12		08 16		08 25			08 27	08 32	08 34					08 39	08 42		
St Johns d					08 11	08 14							08 29		08 36					08 41	08 44		
New Cross ⊖ d					08 14	08 17					08 19	08 27	08 31		08 38					08 44	08 47		
London Victoria ⊖ a				08 33										08 55					09 03				
London Bridge ⊖ d	08 15	08 17	08 09		08 20	08 24	08 25	08 27	08 28	08 35	09 37	09 47	08 39		08 44	08 45	08 47	08 39		08 50	08 54		
London Blackfriars ⊖ a									08 34														
London Cannon Street ⊖ a					08 24	08 30					09 41	09 51	08 43		08 48					08 54	09 00		
London Waterloo (East) ⊖ d	08 20	08 22	08 14				08 30	08 32		08 40						08 50	08 52	08 44					
London Charing Cross ⊖ a	08 23	08 27	08 18				08 34	08 35		08 43						08 53	08 57	08 48					

	SE ◇1	SE	TL	SE	SE	SE	SE	SE	SE	SE	SE	SE ◇1	SE	SE	SE	SE ◇1	SE	TL	SE	SE	SE	SE	SE	SE
Orpington d	11 38								11 41		11 50	11 52	11 54			12 08								12 11
Petts Wood d									11 45		11 53		11 57											12 15
Hither Green d							11 51		11 58	12 03	12 06											12 21		12 28
Lewisham d		11 46		11 55			11 57	12 02	12 04					12 09	12 12		12 16		12 25			12 27	12 32	12 34
St Johns d							11 59		12 06					12 11	12 14							12 29		12 36
New Cross ⊖ d					11 49	11 57	12 01		12 08					12 14	12 17					12 19	12 27	12 31		12 38
London Victoria ⊖ a								12 25					12 33										12 55	
London Bridge ⊖ d	11 55	11 57	11 58	12 05	13 07	13 17	12 09		12 14	12 15	12 17	12 09		12 20	12 24	12 25	12 27	12 28	12 35	13 37	13 47	12 39		12 44
London Blackfriars ⊖ a			12 04															12 34						
London Cannon Street ⊖ a					13 11	13 21	12 13		12 18					12 24	12 30					13 41	13 51	12 43		12 48
London Waterloo (East) ⊖ d	12 00	12 02		12 10						12 20	12 22	12 14				12 30	12 32		12 40					
London Charing Cross ⊖ a	12 04	12 05		12 13						12 23	12 27	12 18				12 34	12 35		12 43					

	SE	SE	SE ◇1	SE	SE	SE		SE ◇1	SE	TL	SE	SE	SE	SE	SE	SE	SE	SE	SE ◇1	SE	SE	SE	SE ◇1	SE
Orpington d		12 20	12 22	12 24				12 38								12 41		12 50	12 52	12 54			13 08	
Petts Wood d		12 23		12 27												12 45		12 53		12 57				
Hither Green d	12 33	12 36												12 51		12 58	13 03	13 06						
Lewisham d					12 39	12 42			12 45		12 55			12 57	13 02	13 04					13 09	13 12		13 16
St Johns d					12 41	12 44								12 59		13 06					13 11	13 14		
New Cross ⊖ d					12 44	12 47						12 49	12 57	13 01		13 08					13 14	13 17		
London Victoria ⊖ a				13 03											13 25					13 33				
London Bridge ⊖ d	12 45	12 47	12 39		12 50	12 54		12 55	12 57	12 58	13 05	14 07	14 17	13 09		13 14	13 15	13 17	13 09		13 20	13 24	13 25	13 27
London Blackfriars ⊖ a										13 04														
London Cannon Street ⊖ a					12 54	13 00						14 11	14 21	13 13		13 18					13 24	13 30		
London Waterloo (East) ⊖ d	12 50	12 52	12 44					13 00	13 02		13 10						13 20	13 22	13 14				13 30	13 32
London Charing Cross ⊖ a	12 53	12 57	12 48					13 04	13 05		13 13						13 23	13 27	13 18				13 34	13 35

Table T199-R

Saturdays

21 December to 16 May

Orpington, Petts Wood, Hither Green and Lewisham - London (Summary of Services)

	TL	SE	SE	SE	SE	SE	SE	SE	SE	SE ◇1	SE	SE	SE	SE ◇1	SE		TL	SE	SE	SE	SE	SE	SE
Orpington d							13 11		13 20	13 22	13 24			13 38		and at the same minutes past each hour until							17 41
Petts Wood d							13 15		13 23		13 27												17 45
Hither Green d					13 21		13 28	13 33	13 36												17 51		17 58
Lewisham d		13 25			13 27	13 32	13 34					13 39	13 42		13 46			17 55			17 57	18 02	18 04
St Johns d					13 29		13 36					13 41	13 44								17 59		18 06
New Cross ⊖ d			13 19	13 27	13 31		13 38					13 44	13 47						17 49	17 57	18 01		18 08
London Victoria ⊖ a						13 55					14 03											18 25	
London Bridge ⊖ d	13 28	13 35	14 37	14 47	13 39		13 44	13 45	13 47	13 39		13 50	13 54	13 55	13 57		17 58	18 05	19 07	19 17	18 09		18 14
London Blackfriars ⊖ a	13 34																18 04						
London Cannon Street ⊖ a			14 41	14 51	13 43		13 48					13 54	14 00						19 11	19 21	18 13		18 18
London Waterloo (East) ⊖ d		13 40						13 50	13 52	13 44				14 00	14 02			18 10					
London Charing Cross ⊖ a		13 43						13 53	13 57	13 48				14 04	14 05			18 13					

	SE	SE	SE ◇1	SE	SE	SE	SE ◇1	SE	TL	SE	SE	SE	SE	SE	SE	SE	SE	SE ◇1	SE	SE	SE	SE ◇1	SE
Orpington d		17 50	17 52	17 54			18 08								18 11		18 20	18 22	18 24			18 38	
Petts Wood d		17 53		17 57											18 15		18 23		18 27				
Hither Green d	18 03	18 06											18 21		18 28	18 33	18 36						
Lewisham d					18 09	18 12		18 16		18 25			18 27	18 32	18 34					18 39	18 42		18 46
St Johns d					18 11	18 14							18 29		18 36					18 41	18 44		
New Cross ⊖ d					18 14	18 17					18 19	18 27	18 31		18 38					18 44	18 47		
London Victoria ⊖ a				18 33										18 55					19 03				
London Bridge ⊖ d	18 15	18 17	18 09		18 20	18 24	18 25	18 27	18 28	18 35	19 37	19 47	18 39		18 44	18 45	18 47	18 39		18 50	18 54	18 55	18 57
London Blackfriars ⊖ a									18 34														
London Cannon Street ⊖ a					18 24	18 30					19 41	19 51	18 43		18 48					18 54	19 00		
London Waterloo (East) ⊖ d	18 20	18 22	18 14				18 30	18 32		18 40						18 50	18 52	18 44				19 00	19 02
London Charing Cross ⊖ a	18 23	18 27	18 18				18 34	18 35		18 43						18 53	18 57	18 48				19 04	19 05

	TL	SE	SE	SE	SE	SE	SE	SE	SE ◇1		SE	SE	SE	SE ◇1	SE	TL	SE	SE	SE		SE	SE	SE	SE
Orpington d						18 41		18 50	18 52		18 54			19 08								19 11		19 20
Petts Wood d						18 45		18 53			18 57											19 15		19 23
Hither Green d				18 51		18 58	19 03	19 06											19 21			19 28	19 33	19 36
Lewisham d		18 55		18 57	19 02	19 04						19 09	19 12		19 16		19 25		19 27		19 32	19 34		
St Johns d				18 59		19 06						19 11	19 14						19 29			19 36		
New Cross ⊖ d			18 49	19 01		19 08						19 14	19 17					19 19	19 31			19 38		
London Victoria ⊖ a					19 25						19 33										19 55			
London Bridge ⊖ d	18 58	19 05	20 07	19 09		19 14	19 15	19 17	19 09			19 20	19 24	19 25	19 27	19 28	19 35	20 37	19 39			19 44	19 45	19 47
London Blackfriars ⊖ a	19 04															19 34								
London Cannon Street ⊖ a			20 11	19 13		19 18						19 24	19 30					20 41	19 43			19 48		
London Waterloo (East) ⊖ d		19 10					19 20	19 22	19 14					19 30	19 32		19 40						19 50	19 52
London Charing Cross ⊖ a		19 13					19 23	19 27	19 18					19 34	19 35		19 43						19 53	19 57

	SE ◇1	SE	SE	SE	SE ◇1		SE	TL	SE	SE	SE	SE	SE	SE	SE		SE ◇1	SE	SE	SE	SE ◇1	SE	TL	SE
Orpington d	19 22	19 24			19 38								19 41		19 50		19 52	19 54			20 08			
Petts Wood d		19 27											19 45		19 53			19 57						
Hither Green d											19 51		19 58	20 03	20 06									
Lewisham d			19 39	19 42			19 46		19 55		19 57	20 02	20 04						20 09	20 12		20 16		20 25
St Johns d			19 41	19 44							19 59		20 06						20 11	20 14				
New Cross ⊖ d			19 44	19 47						19 49	20 01		20 08						20 14	20 17				
London Victoria ⊖ a		20 03										20 25						20 33						
London Bridge ⊖ d	19 39		19 50	19 54	19 55		19 57	19 58	20 05	21 07	20 09		20 14	20 15	20 17		20 09		20 20	20 24	20 25	20 27	20 28	20 35
London Blackfriars ⊖ a								20 04															20 34	
London Cannon Street ⊖ a			19 54	20 00						21 11	20 13		20 18						20 24	20 30				
London Waterloo (East) ⊖ d	19 44				20 00		20 02		20 10					20 20	20 22		20 14				20 30	20 32		20 40
London Charing Cross ⊖ a	19 48				20 04		20 05		20 13					20 23	20 27		20 18				20 34	20 35		20 43

	SE		SE	SE	SE	SE	SE	SE ◇1	SE	SE	SE		SE	TL	SE	SE	SE	SE	SE	SE	SE		SE ◇1	SE
Orpington d					20 11		20 20	20 22	20 24										20 41		20 50		20 52	20 54
Petts Wood d					20 15		20 23		20 27										20 45		20 53			20 57
Hither Green d			20 21		20 28	20 33	20 36										20 51		20 58	21 03	21 06			
Lewisham d			20 27	20 32	20 34					20 39	20 42		20 46		20 55		20 57	21 02	21 04					
St Johns d			20 29		20 36					20 41	20 44						20 59		21 06					
New Cross ⊖ d	20 19		20 31		20 38					20 44	20 47					20 49	21 01		21 08					
London Victoria ⊖ a				20 55					21 03									21 25						21 33
London Bridge ⊖ d	21 37		20 39		20 44	20 45	20 47	20 39		20 50	20 54		20 57	20 58	21 05	22 07	21 09		21 14	21 15	21 17		21 09	
London Blackfriars ⊖ a														21 04										
London Cannon Street ⊖ a	21 41		20 43		20 48					20 54	21 00					22 11	21 13		21 18					
London Waterloo (East) ⊖ d						20 50	20 52	20 44					21 02		21 10					21 20	21 22		21 14	
London Charing Cross ⊖ a						20 53	20 57	20 48					21 05		21 13					21 23	21 27		21 18	

	SE	SE ◇1	SE	TL	SE	SE	SE		SE	SE	SE	SE	SE ◇1	SE	SE	SE	TL		SE	SE	SE	SE	SE	SE
Orpington d		21 08								21 11		21 20	21 22	21 24									21 41	
Petts Wood d										21 15		21 23		21 27									21 45	
Hither Green d							21 21			21 28	21 33	21 36									21 51		21 58	22 03
Lewisham d	21 09		21 16		21 25		21 27		21 32	21 34					21 39	21 46			21 55		21 57	22 02	22 04	
St Johns d	21 11						21 29			21 36					21 41						21 59		22 06	
New Cross ⊖ d	21 14					21 19	21 31			21 38					21 44					21 49	22 01		22 08	
London Victoria ⊖ a									21 55					22 03								22 25		
London Bridge ⊖ d	21 20	21 25	21 27	21 28	21 35	22 37	21 39			21 44	21 45	21 47	21 39		21 50	21 57	21 58		22 05	23 07	22 09		22 14	22 15
London Blackfriars ⊖ a				21 34													22 04							
London Cannon Street ⊖ a	21 24					22 41	21 43			21 48					21 54					23 11	22 13		22 18	
London Waterloo (East) ⊖ d		21 30	21 32		21 40						21 50	21 52	21 44			22 02			22 10					22 20
London Charing Cross ⊖ a		21 34	21 35		21 43						21 53	21 57	21 48			22 05			22 13					22 23

Table T199-R

Orpington, Petts Wood, Hither Green and Lewisham - London (Summary of Services)

Saturdays
21 December to 16 May

	SE	SE ◇1	SE	SE	SE ◇1	SE	TL	SE	SE		SE	SE	SE	SE	SE	SE ◇1	SE	SE	SE		TL	SE	SE	SE
Orpington d	21 50	21 52	21 54		22 08								22 11		22 20	22 22	22 24							
Petts Wood d	21 53		21 57										22 15		22 23		22 27							
Hither Green d	22 06										22 21		22 28	22 33	22 36									22 51
Lewisham d				22 09		22 16		22 25			22 27	22 32	22 34					22 39	22 46			22 55		22 57
St Johns d				22 11							22 29		22 36					22 41						22 59
New Cross d				22 14					22 19		22 31		22 38					22 44					22 49	23 01
London Victoria a			22 33									22 55					23 03							
London Bridge d	22 17	22 09		22 20	22 25	22 27	22 28	22 35	23 37		22 39		22 44	22 45	22 47	22 39		22 50	22 57		22 58	23 05	00 07	23 09
London Blackfriars a							22 34														23 04			
London Cannon Street a				22 24					23 41		22 43		22 48					22 54					00 11	23 13
London Waterloo (East) d	22 22	22 14			22 30	22 32		22 40						22 50	22 52	22 44			23 02			23 10		
London Charing Cross a	22 27	22 18			22 34	22 35		22 43						22 53	22 57	22 48			23 05			23 13		

	SE	SE	SE	SE	SE ◇1		SE	SE	SE ◇1	SE	TL	SE	SE	SE	SE		SE	SE	SE	SE	SE ◇1	SE	SE	SE
Orpington d		22 41		22 50	22 52		22 54		23 08						23 11			23 20	23 24		23 36			
Petts Wood d		22 45		22 53			22 57								23 15			23 23	23 27					
Hither Green d		22 58	23 03	23 06									23 21		23 28		23 33	23 36						23 51
Lewisham d	23 02	23 04						23 09		23 16		23 25	23 27	23 32	23 34					23 39		23 46	23 55	23 57
St Johns d		23 06						23 11					23 29		23 36					23 41				23 59
New Cross d		23 08						23 14					23 31		23 38					23 44				00 02
London Victoria a	23 25						23 33							23 55					00 03					
London Bridge d		23 14	23 15	23 17	23 09			23 20	23 25	23 27	23 28	23 35	23 39		23 44		23 45	23 47		23 50	23 54	23 56	00 05	00 09
London Blackfriars a											23 34													
London Cannon Street a		23 18						23 24					23 43		23 48					23 54				00 13
London Waterloo (East) d			23 20	23 22	23 14				23 30	23 32		23 40					23 50	23 52			23 59	00 02	00 10	
London Charing Cross a			23 23	23 27	23 18				23 34	23 35		23 43					23 53	23 57			00 03	00 06	00 13	

	SE	SE
Orpington d	23 50	23 54
Petts Wood d	23 53	23 57
Hither Green d	00 06	
Lewisham d	00 12	
St Johns d		
New Cross d		
London Victoria a		00 33
London Bridge d	00 22	
London Blackfriars a		
London Cannon Street a		
London Waterloo (East) d	00 27	
London Charing Cross a	00 32	

Sundays
15 December to 10 May

	SE A	SE A	SE A	SE A	SE	TL	SE	SE	SE		SE	SE	SE	TL	SE	SE	SE ◇1	SE ◇1	SE		SE	SE	SE	SE
Orpington d						06 46	06 48	06 54						07 16	07 19	07 24	07 28	07 40						
Petts Wood d						06 49	06 52	06 57						07 19	07 22	07 27								
Hither Green d		00 06		00 16			07 05		07 12			07 29			07 35						07 42			07 59
Lewisham d		00 12	00 16		07 02		07 11		07 18		07 25		07 32		07 41						07 48	07 55	07 58	
St Johns d									07 20												07 50		08 00	
New Cross d	00 02								07 23										07 52		07 53		08 02	
London Victoria a					07 25	07 36		07 34					07 56	08 06		08 04								
London Bridge d	00 09	00 22	00 26	00 28			07 21		07 30		07 35	07 41			07 51		07 45	07 57	09 13		08 00	08 05	08 09	08 11
London Blackfriars a																								
London Cannon Street a	00 13								07 34										09 17		08 04		08 13	
London Waterloo (East) d		00 27	00 31	00 34			07 26				07 40	07 46			07 56		07 50	08 02				08 10		08 16
London Charing Cross a		00 32	00 35	00 38			07 29				07 43	07 49			07 59		07 54	08 06				08 15		08 19

	SE	SE	SE	SE ◇1	SE ◇1		SE	SE	SE	SE	SE	SE	SE	SE	SE ◇1		SE ◇1	SE	SE	SE	SE	SE	SE	SE
Orpington d		07 49	07 54	07 58	08 10								08 19	08 24	08 28		08 40							08 49
Petts Wood d		07 52	07 57										08 22	08 27										08 52
Hither Green d		08 05						08 12			08 29		08 35						08 42			08 59		09 05
Lewisham d	08 02	08 11						08 18	08 25	08 28		08 32	08 41						08 48	08 55	08 58		09 02	09 11
St Johns d								08 20		08 30									08 50		09 00			
New Cross d							08 22	08 23		08 32								08 52	08 53		09 02			
London Victoria a	08 25		08 34									08 56		09 04									09 25	
London Bridge d		08 21		08 15	08 27		09 43	08 30	08 35	08 39	08 41		08 51		08 45		08 57	10 13	09 00	09 05	09 09	09 11		09 21
London Blackfriars a																								
London Cannon Street a							09 47	08 34		08 43								10 17	09 04		09 13			
London Waterloo (East) d		08 26		08 20	08 32				08 40		08 46		08 56		08 50		09 02			09 10		09 16		09 26
London Charing Cross a		08 29		08 24	08 36				08 44		08 49		08 59		08 54		09 06			09 13		09 19		09 29

A not 15 December

Table T199-R

Orpington, Petts Wood, Hither Green and Lewisham - London (Summary of Services)

Sundays
15 December to 10 May

	SE	SE ◇1	SE ◇1	SE	SE	SE	SE		SE	SE	SE	SE	SE ◇1	SE ◇1	TL	SE	SE		SE	SE	SE	SE	SE	SE
Orpington d	08 54	08 58	09 10								09 19	09 24	09 28	09 40									09 49	09 54
Petts Wood d	08 57										09 22	09 27											09 52	09 57
Hither Green d					09 12				09 29		09 35						09 42				09 59		10 05	
Lewisham d					09 18	09 25	09 28			09 32	09 41						09 48		09 55	09 58		10 02	10 11	
St Johns d					09 20		09 30										09 50			10 00				
New Cross d				09 22	09 23		09 32									09 52	09 53			10 02				
London Victoria a	09 34									09 56		10 04										10 25		10 34
London Bridge d		09 15	09 27	10 43	09 30	09 35	09 39		09 41		09 51		09 45	09 57	09 58	11 13	10 00		10 05	10 09	10 11		10 21	
London Blackfriars a															10 04									
London Cannon Street a				10 47	09 34		09 43									11 17	10 04			10 13				
London Waterloo (East) d		09 20	09 32			09 40			09 46		09 56		09 50	10 02					10 10		10 16		10 26	
London Charing Cross a		09 24	09 36			09 43			09 49		09 59		09 54	10 06					10 13		10 19		10 29	

	SE ◇1	SE ◇1	TL		SE	SE	SE	SE	SE	SE	SE	SE	SE ◇1		SE ◇1	TL	SE	SE	SE	SE	SE	SE	SE	
Orpington d	09 58	10 10									10 19	10 24	10 28		10 40								10 49	
Petts Wood d											10 22	10 27											10 52	
Hither Green d						10 12			10 29		10 35							10 42			10 59		11 05	
Lewisham d						10 18	10 25	10 28		10 32	10 41							10 48	10 55	10 58		11 02	11 11	
St Johns d						10 20		10 30										10 50		11 00				
New Cross d					10 22	10 23		10 32									10 52	10 53		11 02				
London Victoria a										10 56		11 04										11 25		
London Bridge d	10 15	10 27	10 28		11 43	10 30	10 35	10 39	10 41		10 51		10 45		10 57	10 58	12 13	11 00	11 05	11 09	11 11		11 21	
London Blackfriars a			10 34													11 04								
London Cannon Street a					11 47	10 34		10 43									12 17	11 04		11 13				
London Waterloo (East) d	10 20	10 32					10 40		10 46		10 56		10 50		11 02				11 10		11 16		11 26	
London Charing Cross a	10 24	10 36					10 43		10 49		10 59		10 54		11 06				11 13		11 19		11 29	

	SE	SE ◇1	SE ◇1	TL	SE	SE	SE	SE	SE		SE	SE	SE	SE ◇1	SE ◇1	TL	SE	SE	SE	SE	SE	SE	SE	SE
Orpington d	10 54	10 58	11 10									11 19	11 24	11 28	11 40								11 49	11 54
Petts Wood d	10 57											11 22	11 27										11 52	11 57
Hither Green d						11 12			11 29			11 35						11 42			11 59		12 05	
Lewisham d						11 18	11 25	11 28			11 32	11 41						11 48	11 55	11 58		12 02	12 11	
St Johns d						11 20		11 30										11 50		12 00				
New Cross d					11 22	11 23		11 32									11 52	11 53		12 02				
London Victoria a	11 34										11 56		12 04									12 24		12 34
London Bridge d		11 15	11 27	11 28	12 43	11 30	11 35	11 39	11 41			11 51		11 45	11 57	11 58	13 13	12 00	12 05	12 09	12 11		12 21	
London Blackfriars a				11 34												12 04								
London Cannon Street a					12 47	11 34		11 43									13 17	12 04		12 13				
London Waterloo (East) d		11 20	11 32				11 40		11 46			11 56		11 50	12 02				12 10		12 16		12 26	
London Charing Cross a		11 24	11 36				11 43		11 49			11 59		11 54	12 06				12 13		12 19		12 29	

	SE ◇1	SE ◇1	TL	SE	SE	SE	SE	SE	SE		SE	SE	SE ◇1	SE ◇1	TL	SE	SE	SE	SE	SE	SE	SE	SE
Orpington d	11 58	12 10									19 19	19 24	19 28	19 40								19 49	19 54
Petts Wood d										and at	19 22	19 27										19 52	19 57
Hither Green d					12 12			12 29		the same	19 35						19 42			19 59		20 05	
Lewisham d					12 18	12 25	12 28		12 32	minutes	19 41						19 48	19 55	19 58		20 02	20 11	
St Johns d					12 20		12 30			past							19 50		20 00				
New Cross d				12 22	12 23		12 32			each						19 52	19 53		20 02				
London Victoria a									12 54	hour until		20 04									20 24		20 34
London Bridge d	12 15	12 27	12 28	13 43	12 30	12 35	12 39	12 41			19 51		19 45	19 57	19 58	21 13	20 00	20 05	20 09	20 11		20 21	
London Blackfriars a			12 34												20 04								
London Cannon Street a				13 47	12 34		12 43									21 17	20 04		20 13				
London Waterloo (East) d	12 20	12 32				12 40		12 46			19 56		19 50	20 02				20 10		20 16		20 26	
London Charing Cross a	12 24	12 36				12 43		12 49			19 59		19 54	20 06				20 13		20 19		20 29	

	SE ◇1	SE ◇1	TL	SE	SE	SE	SE	SE	SE		SE	SE	SE ◇1	TL	SE	SE	SE	SE	SE		SE	SE	SE	SE ◇1
Orpington d	19 58	20 10									20 19	20 24	20 28									20 49	20 54	20 58
Petts Wood d											20 22	20 27										20 52	20 57	
Hither Green d					20 12			20 29			20 35					20 42			20 59			21 05		
Lewisham d					20 18	20 25	20 28		20 32		20 41					20 48	20 55	20 58			21 02	21 11		
St Johns d					20 20		20 30									20 50		21 00						
New Cross d				20 22	20 23		20 32								20 52	20 53		21 02						
London Victoria a									20 54			21 04									21 24		21 34	
London Bridge d	20 15	20 27	20 28	21 43	20 30	20 35	20 39	20 41			20 51		20 45	20 58	22 13	21 00	21 05	21 09	21 11			21 21		21 15
London Blackfriars a			20 34											21 04										
London Cannon Street a				21 47	20 34		20 43								22 17	21 04		21 13						
London Waterloo (East) d	20 20	20 32				20 40		20 46			20 56		20 50				21 10		21 16			21 26		21 20
London Charing Cross a	20 24	20 36				20 43		20 49			20 59		20 54				21 13		21 19			21 29		21 24

	SE ◇1	TL	SE	SE	SE		SE	SE	SE	SE	SE	SE ◇1	TL	SE	SE		SE	SE	SE	SE	SE	SE	SE ◇1	SE ◇1
Orpington d	21 10									21 19	21 24	21 28									21 49	21 54	21 58	22 10
Petts Wood d										21 22	21 27										21 52	21 57		
Hither Green d				21 12				21 29		21 35					21 42				21 59		22 05			
Lewisham d				21 18	21 25		21 28		21 32	21 41					21 48		21 55	21 58		22 02	22 11			
St Johns d				21 20			21 30								21 50			22 00						
New Cross d			21 22	21 23			21 32							21 52	21 53			22 02						
London Victoria a									21 54		22 04									22 24		22 34		
London Bridge d	21 27	21 28	22 43	21 30	21 35		21 39	21 41		21 51		21 45	21 58	23 13	22 00		22 05	22 09	22 11		22 21		22 15	22 27
London Blackfriars a		21 34											22 04											
London Cannon Street a			22 47	21 34			21 43							23 17	22 04			22 13						
London Waterloo (East) d	21 32				21 40			21 46		21 56		21 50					22 10		22 16		22 26		22 20	22 32
London Charing Cross a	21 36				21 43			21 49		21 59		21 54					[illegible]		[illegible]		[illegible]		[illegible]	[illegible]

Table T199-R

Sundays
15 December to 10 May

Orpington, Petts Wood, Hither Green and Lewisham - London (Summary of Services)

		TL	SE	SE	SE	SE	SE	SE		SE	SE	SE ◇[1]	TL	SE	SE	SE	SE	SE		SE	SE	SE ◇[1]	SE ◇[1]	TL	SE
Orpington [4]	d									22 19	22 24	22 28								22 49	22 54	22 58	23 10		
Petts Wood [4]	d									22 22	22 27									22 52	22 57				
Hither Green [4]	d			22 12			22 29			22 35				22 42			22 59			23 05					23 12
Lewisham [4] ⛴	d			22 18	22 25	22 28		22 32		22 41				22 48	22 55	22 58		23 02		23 11					23 18
St Johns	d			22 20		22 30								22 50		23 00									23 20
New Cross [4] ⊖	d		22 22	22 23		22 32								22 53		23 02									23 23
London Victoria [15] ⊖	a							22 54			23 04							23 24			23 34				
London Bridge [4] ⊖	d	22 28	23 43	22 30	22 35	22 39	22 41			22 51		22 45	22 58	23 00	23 05	23 09	23 11			23 21		23 15	23 27	23 28	23 30
London Blackfriars [3] ⊖	a	22 34											23 04											23 34	
London Cannon Street [4] ⊖	a		23 47	22 34		22 43								23 04		23 13									23 34
London Waterloo (East) [4] ⊖	d				22 40		22 46			22 56		22 50			23 10		23 16			23 26		23 20	23 32		
London Charing Cross [4] ⊖	a				22 43		22 49			22 59		22 54			23 13		23 19			23 29		23 24	23 36		

		SE	SE	SE		SE	SE	SE	SE	SE	SE	SE
Orpington [4]	d					23 19	23 24					23 49
Petts Wood [4]	d					23 22	23 27					23 52
Hither Green [4]	d			23 29		23 35		23 42			23 59	00 05
Lewisham [4] ⛴	d	23 25	23 28			23 41		23 48	23 55	23 58		00 11
St Johns	d		23 30					23 50		23 59		
New Cross [4] ⊖	d		23 32					23 53		00 02		
London Victoria [15] ⊖	a						00 04					
London Bridge [4] ⊖	d	23 35	23 39	23 41		23 51		23 59	00 05	00 09	00 11	00 21
London Blackfriars [3] ⊖	a											
London Cannon Street [4] ⊖	a		23 43					00 04		00 13		
London Waterloo (East) [4] ⊖	d	23 40		23 46		23 56			00 10		00 16	00 26
London Charing Cross [4] ⊖	a	23 43		23 49		23 59			00 13		00 19	00 29

AVAILABLE FROM MP Middleton Press

NARROW GAUGE
BRANCH LINES
KENT
NARROW GAUGE
Vic
Mitchell
and
Keith
Smith
MP Middleton Press

Table T200-F

Mondays to Fridays
16 December to 15 May

London - Dartford and Gillingham

Miles	Miles	Miles	Miles	Miles			SE MO	TL	SE ◇	TL MO	TL MX	SE MX ◇	SE MX	SE MO	SE MX	SE MO	SE MX	SE MX	SE	TL MX	SE MO		SE MX	SE MO	SE TWO
—	—	—	—	0	St Pancras Int'l [15] ⊖	d																			
—	—	—	—	6	Stratford International ⊖ ⛴	d						00 02													
—	—	—	—	22¾	Ebbsfleet International	d						00 13													
0	—	0	0	—	London Charing Cross [4] ⊖	d																			
0¾	—	0¾	0¾	—	London Waterloo (East) [4] ⊖	d																			
—	0	—	—	—	London Cannon Street [4] ⊖	d																		00 01	
1¾	1¾	1¾	1¾	—	London Bridge [4] ⊖	d																			
—	3¾	—	—	—	Deptford	d																			
—	4¼	—	—	—	Greenwich [4] ⛴	d																			
—	5¼	—	—	—	Maze Hill	d																			
—	5¾	—	—	—	Westcombe Park	d																			
—	—	—	—	0	London Victoria [15] ⊖	d																			
—	—	—	—	4¼	Denmark Hill [4]	d																			
—	—	—	—	5	Peckham Rye [4]	d																			
—	—	—	—	5¾	Nunhead [4]	d																			
—	—	4¾	4¾	—	New Cross [4] ⊖	d																			
—	—	5½	5½	—	St Johns	d																			
6	—	6	6	7½	Lewisham [4] ⛴	d															00 01				00 08
7	—	7	—	8½	Blackheath [4]	d															00 03		00 03		
—	—	8	—	9½	Kidbrooke	d													00 02						
—	—	9	—	10½	Eltham	d													00 05						
—	—	10¼	—	11¾	Falconwood	d													00 08						
—	—	11¼	—	12¾	Welling	d													00 11						
—	—	12¾	—	14¼	Bexleyheath	d									00 03				00 14						
—	—	14	—	15½	Barnehurst [4]	d									00 06				00 17						
—	—	—	7¼	—	Hither Green [4]	d																		00 13	00 13
—	—	—	8	—	Lee	d																		00 15	00 15
—	—	—	9½	—	Mottingham	d																		00 18	00 18
—	—	—	10½	—	New Eltham	d																		00 21	00 21
—	—	—	12	—	Sidcup [4]	d											00 03							00 24	00 24
—	—	—	13	—	Albany Park	d											00 06							00 27	00 27
—	—	—	14	—	Bexley	d											00 08							00 29	00 29
—	—	—	15½	—	Crayford	d							00 03	00 03			00 12							00 33	00 33
9	6½	—	—	—	Charlton [4]	d															00 08		00 08		
10	7½	—	—	—	Woolwich Dockyard	d															00 11		00 11		
10¾	8¼	—	—	—	Woolwich Arsenal [4] ⛴	d															00 14		00 14		
11¼	8¾	—	—	—	Plumstead	d															00 16		00 16		
12¾	10¼	—	—	—	Abbey Wood	d												00 03			00 20		00 20		
14¼	11¾	—	—	—	Belvedere	d										00 03		00 06			00 23		00 23		
15½	13	—	—	—	Erith	d										00 06		00 09			00 25		00 25		
16¾	14¼	—	—	—	Slade Green [4]	d	00 01									00 10		00 14			00 31		00 31		
18¾	16¼	17	17¼	18½	Dartford [4]	a	00 06						00 08	00 08	00 14	00 15	00 17	00 22	00 24		00 36		00 36	00 38	00 38
—	—	—	—	—		d								00 09			00 18			00 28				00 39	00 39
20¾	—	—	19¼	—	Stone Crossing	d				00 02	00 02			00 13			00 22			00 32				00s43	00 43
21½	—	—	20	—	Greenhithe for Bluewater	d				00 04	00 04			00 15			00 24			00 34				00s45	00 45
22¾	—	—	21¼	—	Swanscombe	d				00 07	00 07			00 18			00 27			00 37				00s48	00s48
23½	—	—	22	—	Northfleet	d				00 09	00 09			00 20			00 29			00 39				00s50	00s50
25½	—	—	24	24¾	Gravesend [4]	d				00 13	00 13	00 18		00a25			00a36			00 43				00a55	00a57
30	—	—	28½	29¼	Higham	d				00 19	00 19									00 49					
32¾	—	—	31¼	32	Strood [4]	d				00 25	00 25	00 29								00 56					
—	—	—	—	—	Maidstone West	d																			
33¾	—	—	32¼	33	Rochester [4]	d			00 02	00 28	00 28	00 32								00 59					
34½	—	—	32¾	33½	Chatham [4]	d		00 02	00 06	00 31	00 32	00 36								01 03					
36	—	—	34½	35¼	Gillingham (Kent) [4]	a		00 06	00 10	00 36	00 36	00 40								01 07					
—	—	—	—	—	Rainham (Kent)	a			00 15			00 45													

Table T200-F

London - Dartford and Gillingham

Mondays to Fridays

16 December to 15 May

Station		SE ThFO	SE MX	SE MO	TL MO	SE TWO	SE ThFO	SE MX	SE MO	SE ThFO	SE ThFO	SE TWO	SE ThFO (bus)	SE ThFO	TL MX	SE TWO	SE ThFO	SE TWO	SE TWO	TL	SE TWO	SE MTh FO	SE	TL
St Pancras Int'l 15 ⊖	d																							
Stratford International ⊖ ⛴	d																							
Ebbsfleet International	d																							
London Charing Cross 4 ⊖	d						00 02		00 12	00 12	00 26			00 32			00 42					04 50		
London Waterloo (East) 4 ⊖	d						00 05		00 15	00 15	00 29			00 35			00 45					04 53		
London Cannon Street 4 ⊖	d					00 02						00 32	00 32			00 46		00 52	01 02				05 05	
London Bridge 4 ⊖	d		00 01	00 03		00 06	00 11		00 21	00 21	00 35	00 36	00 40	00 41		00 51	00 51	00 57	01 07		04 59	04 59	05 09	
Deptford	d			00 09		00 12						00 42	00 54										05 15	
Greenwich 4 ⛴	d			00 11		00 14						00 44	00 59										05 17	
Maze Hill	d			00 14		00 17						00 47	01 06										05 20	
Westcombe Park	d			00 16		00 19						00 49	01 11										05 22	
London Victoria 15 ⊖	d							00 04																
Denmark Hill 4	d							00 14																
Peckham Rye 4	d							00 17																
Nunhead 4	d							00 19																
New Cross 4 ⊖	d																							
St Johns	d																							
Lewisham 4 ⛴	d	00 08	00 10					00 26	00 31	00 31	00 45			00 50		00 59	01 00	01 05	01 15		05 08	05 08		
Blackheath 4	d		00 13					00 29	00 33	00 35	00 48					01 02	01 03		01 18					
Kidbrooke	d		00 16					00 32			00 51					01 05								
Eltham	d		00 19					00 35			00 54					01 08								
Falconwood	d		00 22					00 38			00 57					01 11								
Welling	d		00 25					00 41			01 00					01 14								
Bexleyheath	d		00 28					00 44			01 03					01 17								
Barnehurst 4	d		00 31					00 47			01 06					01 20								
Hither Green 4	d	00 13					00 22							00 55				01 10			05 13	05 13		
Lee	d	00 15					00 24							00 57				01 12			05 15	05 15		
Mottingham	d	00 18					00 27							01 00				01 15			05 18	05 18		
New Eltham	d	00 21					00 30							01 03				01 18			05 20	05 20		
Sidcup 4	d	00 24					00 33							01 06				01 21			05 24	05 24		
Albany Park	d	00 27					00 36							01 09				01 24			05 26	05 26		
Bexley	d	00 29					00 38							01 11				01 26			05 29	05 29		
Crayford	d	00 33					00 42							01 15				01 30			05 32	05 33		
Charlton 4	d			00 19		00 22			00 38	00 40		00 52	01s18				01 08		01 23				05 25	
Woolwich Dockyard	d			00 22		00 25			00 41	00 43		00 55	01s23				01 11		01 26				05 28	
Woolwich Arsenal 4 ⛴	d			00 25		00 28			00 44	00 46		00 58	01s29				01 14		01 29				05 31	
Plumstead	d			00 27		00 30			00 46	00 48		01 00	01s33				01 16		01 31				05 33	
Abbey Wood	d			00 30		00 33			00 50	00 52		01 03	01s39				01 20		01 34				05 36	
Belvedere	d			00 33		00 36			00 53	00 55		01 06	01s43				01 23		01 37				05 39	
Erith	d			00 36		00 39			00 55	00 57		01 09	01s48				01 25		01 40				05 42	
Slade Green 4	d			00 40		00 44			01 01	01 02		01 12	01s54				01 30		01 44				05 47	
Dartford 4	a	00 38	00 41	00 45		00 49	00 47	00 56	01 06	01 07	01 16	01 20	02 05	01 19		01 31	01 37	01 34	01 52		05 38	05 38	05 52	
	d				00 46		00 48							01 20	01 24			01 35		04 58	05 39	05 39		05 58
Stone Crossing	d				00s50		00 52								01s28					05 02	05 43	05 43		06 02
Greenhithe for Bluewater	d				00s52		00 54							01s25	01s30			01 41		05 04	05 45	05 45		06 04
Swanscombe	d				00s55		00s57								01s33					05 07	05 48	05 48		06 07
Northfleet	d				00s57		00s59								01s35					05 09	05 50	05 50		06 09
Gravesend 4	d				01 01		01a07							01a35	01 39			01a50		05 13	05a56	05a56		06 13
Higham	d				01s07										01s45					05 19				06 19
Strood 4	d				01s12										01s50					05 25				06 25
Maidstone West	d																							
Rochester 4	d				01s15										01s53					05 28				06 28
Chatham 4	d				01s19										01s57					05 31				06 31
Gillingham (Kent) 4	a				01 24										02 02					05 35				06 35
Rainham (Kent)	a																			05 41				06 41

Table T200-F

London - Dartford and Gillingham

Mondays to Fridays

16 December to 15 May

Station		SE WX	SE WO	SE	SE	SE	SE	TL	SE	SE	SE	SE	SE	SE	SE ◇	TL	SE	SE	SE	SE ◇	SE	SE	SE
St Pancras Int'l 15 ⊖	d														06 25					06 55			
Stratford International ⊖ ⛴	d														06 32					07 02			
Ebbsfleet International	d														06 43					07 15			
London Charing Cross 4 ⊖	d	05 20		05 26					05 42		05 52	05 54					06 12				06 23	06 25	
London Waterloo (East) 4 ⊖	d	05 23		05 29					05 45		05 55	05 57					06 15				06 26	06 28	
London Cannon Street 4 ⊖	d				05 35	05 39	05 39			05 55			06 09	06 09					06 25				06 35
London Bridge 4 ⊖	d	05 29	05 29	05 35	05 39	05 43	05 43	05 46	05 51	05 59	06 01	06 03	06 13	06 13		06 18	06 21		06 29		06 32	06 35	06 39
Deptford	d				05 45			05 53		06 05						06 25			06 35				06 45
Greenwich 4 ⛴	d				05 47			05 55		06 07						06 27			06 37				06 47
Maze Hill	d				05 50			05 58		06 10						06 30			06 40				06 50
Westcombe Park	d				05 52			06 00		06 12						06 32			06 42				06 52
London Victoria 15 ⊖	d																	06 15					
Denmark Hill 4	d																	06 25					
Peckham Rye 4	d																	06 28					
Nunhead 4	d																	06 30					
New Cross 4 ⊖	d					05 49	05 49						06 19	06 19									
St Johns	d					05 51	05 51						06 21	06 21									
Lewisham 4 ⛴	d	05 38	05 38	05 44		05 54	05 54		06 01			06 14	06 24	06 24			06 30	06 37				06 45	
Blackheath 4	d			05 47					06 03			06 17					06 33	06 40				06 48	
Kidbrooke	d			05 50								06 20						06 43				06 51	
Eltham	d			05 53								06 23						06 46				06 54	
Falconwood	d			05 56								06 26						06 49				06 57	
Welling	d			05 59								06 29						06 52				07 00	
Bexleyheath	d			06 02								06 32						06 55				07 03	
Barnehurst 4	d			06 05								06 35						06 58				07 08	
Hither Green 4	d	05 43	05 43			05 58	05 58				06 13		06 30	06 30							06 43		
Lee	d	05 45	05 45			06 00	06 00				06 15		06 32	06 32							06 45		
Mottingham	d	05 48	05 48			06 03	06 03				06 18		06 35	06 35							06 48		
New Eltham	d	05 50	05 50			06 06	06 06				06 20		06 38	06 38							06 51		
Sidcup 4	d	05 54	05 54			06 09	06 09				06 24		06 41	06 41							06 54		
Albany Park	d	05 56	05 56			06 12	06 12				06 26		06 44	06 44							06 57		
Bexley	d	05 59	05 59			06 15	06 15				06 29		06 47	06 47							06 59		
Crayford	d	06 03	06 03			06 22	06 22				06 32		06 53	06 53							07 03		
Charlton 4	d				05 55		06a59	06 03	06 08	06 15				07a30		06 35	06 38		06 45				06 55
Woolwich Dockyard	d				05 58				06 11	06 18							06 41		06 48				06 58
Woolwich Arsenal 4 ⛴	d				06 01			06 08	06 14	06 21						06 40	06 44		06 51				07 01
Plumstead	d				06 03			06 11	06 16	06 23						06 43	06 46		06 53				07 03
Abbey Wood	d				06 06			06 14	06 19	06 26						06 46	06 49		06 56				07 06
Belvedere	d				06 09				06 22	06 29							06 52		06 59				07 09
Erith	d				06 12				06 25	06 32							06 55		07 02				07 12
Slade Green 4	d				06a15	06a34		06 20	06 28	06a35			07a07			06 52	06 58		07a05				07a16
Dartford 4	a	06 08	06 08	06 14				06 25	06 34		06 37	06 44				06 57	07 05	07 05			07 07	07 18	
	d	06 09	06 09					06 26								06 58					07 09		
Stone Crossing	d	06 13	06 13					06 30								07 02					07 13		
Greenhithe for Bluewater	d	06 15	06 15					06 32								07 04					07 15		
Swanscombe	d	06 18	06 18					06 35								07 07					07 18		
Northfleet	d	06 20	06 20					06 37								07 09					07 20		
Gravesend 4	d	06a25	06a25					06 41							06 48	07 15				07 20	07a27		
Higham	d							06 47								07 21							
Strood 4	d							06 53							07 02	07 28				07 31			
Maidstone West	d														07a16								
Rochester 4	d							06 56								07 31				07 34			
Chatham 4	d							06 59								07 34				07 38			
Gillingham (Kent) 4	a							07 03								07 38				07 42			
Rainham (Kent)	a							07 09								07 44				07 47			

Table T200-F

Mondays to Fridays

16 December to 15 May

London - Dartford and Gillingham

		SE	SE ◇	TL	SE	SE	SE	SE	SE	SE	SE	SE	TL		SE	SE	SE	SE	SE	SE	SE	SE	SE	SE ◇	SE
St Pancras Int'l 15	d		07 22																					08 04	
Stratford International	d		07 29																					08 11	
Ebbsfleet International	d		07 40																					08 23	
London Charing Cross 4	d				06 41			06 53	06 56						07 12				07 21	07 25			07 39		
London Waterloo (East) 4	d				06 44			06 56	06 59						07 15				07 24	07 28			07 42		
London Cannon Street 4	d	06 39					06 55			07 05		07 11				07 22	07 22	07 25			07 36	07 40			
London Bridge 4	d	06 43		06 48	06 50		06 59	07 02	07 05	07 09		07 15	07 18		07 21	07 26	07 26	07 29	07 30	07 34	07 40		07 48		
Deptford	d			06 55			07 05			07 15			07 25					07 35			07 46				
Greenwich 4	d			06 57			07 07			07 17			07 27					07 37			07 48				
Maze Hill	d			07 00			07 10			07 20			07 30					07 40			07 51				
Westcombe Park	d			07 02			07 12			07 22			07 32					07 42			07 53				
London Victoria 15	d					06 42					07 08														07 45
Denmark Hill 4	d					06 52																			07 55
Peckham Rye 4	d					06 55																			07 58
Nunhead 4	d																								08 00
New Cross 4	d	06 49										07 21				07 32	07 32					07 50			
St Johns	d	06 51										07 23				07 34	07 34					07 52			
Lewisham 4	d	06 54			06 59	07 02			07 15		07 26	07 28			07 30	07 37	07 37			07 45		07 56	08 00		08 07
Blackheath 4	d				07 02	07 05			07 18		07 29				07 33	07 40	07 40			07 48			08 03		
Kidbrooke	d					07 08			07 21							07 43	07 43			07 51					
Eltham	d					07 11			07 24							07 46	07 46			07 54					
Falconwood	d								07 27							07 49	07 49			07 57					
Welling	d								07 30							07 52	07 52			08 00					
Bexleyheath	d					07 17			07 33							07 55	07 55			08 03					
Barnehurst 4	d					07 20			07 36							07 58	07 58			08 06					
Hither Green 4	d	06 59						07 13				07 34					08a31		07 41			08 01			
Lee	d	07 01						07 15											07 43			08 03			
Mottingham	d	07 04						07 18											07 46			08 06			
New Eltham	d	07 07						07 21				07 39							07 49			08 08			
Sidcup 4	d	07 10						07 24				07 43							07 52			08 12			
Albany Park	d	07 13						07 27				07 45							07 55			08 14			
Bexley	d	07 16						07 29				07 48							07 57			08 17			
Crayford	d	07 25						07 33				07 51				08a09			08 01			08 21			
Charlton 4	d	07a57		07 05	07 08		07 15			07 25		08a19	07 35		07 38			07 45			07 56	08a50	08 08		
Woolwich Dockyard	d				07 11		07 18			07 28					07 41						07 59		08 11		
Woolwich Arsenal 4	d			07 10	07 14		07 21			07 31			07 40		07 44			07 50			08 02		08 14		
Plumstead	d			07 13	07 16		07 23			07 33			07 43		07 46						08 04		08 16		
Abbey Wood	d			07 16	07 20		07 26			07 36			07 46		07 50			07 55			08 07		08 20		
Belvedere	d				07 23		07 29			07 39					07 53						08 10		08 23		
Erith	d				07 25		07 32			07 42					07 55						08 13		08 25		
Slade Green 4	d			07 22	07 29		07a36			07a46			07 52		07 59			08a02			08a16		08 29		
Dartford 4	a			07 29	07 38	07 29		07 37	07 46		07 50		07 57		08 06				08 06	08 16			08 37		08 24
	d			07 30				07 39					08 01						08 09						08 24
Stone Crossing	d			07 34				07 43					08 05						08 13						
Greenhithe for Bluewater	d			07 36				07 45					08 07						08 15						08 30
Swanscombe	d			07 39				07 48					08 10						08 18						
Northfleet	d			07 41				07 50					08 12						08 20						
Gravesend 4	d		07 44	07 47				07a56					08 19						08a27					08 29	08a41
Higham	d			07 53									08 25												
Strood 4	d		07 56	07 59									08 31											08 40	
Maidstone West	d																								
Rochester 4	d		07 59	08 02									08 34											08 44	
Chatham 4	d		08 02	08 06									08 37											08 47	
Gillingham (Kent) 4	a		08 06	08 10									08 41											08 51	
Rainham (Kent)	a		08 11	08 21									08 49											08 57	

Table T200-F

Mondays to Fridays

16 December to 15 May

London - Dartford and Gillingham

		TL	SE	SE	SE		SE ◇	SE	SE	SE	SE	TL	SE	SE	SE	SE	SE	SE ◇	SE	SE	SE		SE	SE	SE
St Pancras Int'l 15	d						08 25											08 57							
Stratford International	d						08 32											09 04							
Ebbsfleet International	d						08 43											09 15							
London Charing Cross 4	d							07 52	07 56					08 12	08 14				08 22	08 26				08 38	
London Waterloo (East) 4	d							07 56	07 59					08 15	08 17				08 25	08 29				08 41	
London Cannon Street 4	d		07 47	07 57	08 00					08 05			08 14			08 19	08 24				08 34		08 37		
London Bridge 4	d	07 48		08 01				08 02	08 05	08 09		08 18	08 18	08 21	08 23		08 28		08 31	08 35	08 38		08 41	08 47	
Deptford	d	07 55		08 07						08 15		08 25					08 35				08 45				
Greenwich 4	d	07 57		08 09						08 17		08 27					08 37				08 47				
Maze Hill	d	08 00		08 12						08 20		08 30					08 40				08 50				
Westcombe Park	d	08 02		08 14						08 22		08 32					08 42				08 52				
London Victoria 15	d										08 07														08 38
Denmark Hill 4	d										08 17														08 47
Peckham Rye 4	d										08 20														08 50
Nunhead 4	d										08 22														08 53
New Cross 4	d															08 31							08 47		
St Johns	d															08 33							08 49		
Lewisham 4	d				08 11				08 18		08 29			08 32		08 36				08 45			08 55	08 58	09 01
Blackheath 4	d				08 14				08 21		08 32			08 35		08 39				08 48				09 01	09 04
Kidbrooke	d				08 17				08 24		08 35					08 42				08 51					
Eltham	d		08 04		08 20				08 27		08 38					08 45				08 54					09 10
Falconwood	d				08 24				08 30							08 48				08 57					
Welling	d		08 08		08 26				08 33							08 51				09 00					
Bexleyheath	d		08 11		08 30				08 36		08 44					08 54				09 03					09 16
Barnehurst 4	d		08 14		08 35				08 39		08 47					09 00				09 06					
Hither Green 4	d							08 14					08 30		08 34				08 42				09 00		
Lee	d							08 16					08 32		08 36				08 44				09 02		
Mottingham	d							08 19					08 35		08 39				08 47				09 05		
New Eltham	d							08 21					08 38		08 42				08 50				09 08		
Sidcup 4	d							08 25					08 41		08 45				08 53				09 11		
Albany Park	d							08 27					08 44		08 48				08 56				09 14		
Bexley	d							08 30					08 46		08 51				08 58				09 16		
Crayford	d							08 33					08 50		08 55				09 02				09 21		
Charlton 4	d	08 05		08 17						08 25		08 35	09a19	08 43			08 46				08 55		09a49	09 08	
Woolwich Dockyard	d			08 20						08 28				08 46			08 49				08 58			09 11	
Woolwich Arsenal 4	d	08 10		08 23						08 31		08 40		08 49			08 52				09 01			09 14	
Plumstead	d	08 13		08 25						08 33		08 43		08 51			08 54				09 03			09 16	
Abbey Wood	d	08 16		08 28						08 36		08 46		08 54			08 58				09 06			09 19	
Belvedere	d			08 31						08 39				08 57			09 01				09 09			09 22	
Erith	d			08 34						08 42				09 00			09 03				09 12			09 25	
Slade Green 4	d	08 22	08a24	08 37	08a44					08a45		08 52		09 04		09a07	09a07				09a15			09 30	
Dartford 4	a	08 27		08 45				08 38	08 48		08 54	08 57		09 12	09 03				09 07	09 17				09 40	09 24
	d	08 28						08 39			08 54	08 58							09 08						09 24
Stone Crossing	d	08 32						08 43				09 02							09 12						
Greenhithe for Bluewater	d	08 34						08 45			09 00	09 04							09 15						09 30
Swanscombe	d	08 37						08 48				09 07							09 18						
Northfleet	d	08 39						08 50				09 09							09 20						
Gravesend 4	d	08 43					08 48	08a57			09a09	09 13						09 19	09a26						09a41
Higham	d	08 49										09 19													
Strood 4	d	08 55					08 59					09 25						09 30							
Maidstone West	d																								
Rochester 4	d	08 58					09 02					09 28						09 33							
Chatham 4	d	09 01					09 06					09 31						09 37							
Gillingham (Kent) 4	a	09 05					09 10					09 35						09 41							
Rainham (Kent)	a	09 11					09 15					09 41						09 46							

Table T200-F

London - Dartford and Gillingham

Mondays to Fridays

16 December to 15 May

		TL	SE	SE	SE	SE	SE	SE ◇	SE	SE	SE	TL	SE	SE	SE	SE	SE	SE ◇	SE	SE	SE	SE	TL	SE
St Pancras Int'l ⊖	d							09 25										09 55						
Stratford International ⊖	d							09 32										10 02						
Ebbsfleet International	d							09 44										10 13						
London Charing Cross ⊖	d		08 42	08 46	08 50				09 00				09 12			09 20	09 26		09 28					09 40
London Waterloo (East) ⊖	d		08 45	08 49	08 53				09 03				09 15			09 23	09 29		09 31					09 45
London Cannon Street ⊖	d					08 54	09 05			09 08				09 17	09 24					09 35	09 38			
London Bridge ⊖	d	08 48	08 51	08 57	08 59	08 59	09 09		09 09	09 13		09 18	09 21	09 21	09 28	09 29	09 35		09 37	09 39	09 43		09 48	09 51
Deptford	d	08 55				09 05	09 15					09 25			09 35					09 45			09 55	
Greenwich	d	08 57				09 07	09 17					09 27			09 37					09 47			09 57	
Maze Hill	d	09 00				09 10	09 20					09 30			09 40					09 50			10 00	
Westcombe Park	d	09 02				09 12	09 22					09 32			09 42					09 52			10 02	
London Victoria ⊖	d										09 04											09 34		
Denmark Hill	d										09 14											09 44		
Peckham Rye	d										09 17											09 47		
Nunhead	d										09 20											09 50		
New Cross ⊖	d									09 19				09 28							09 49			
St Johns	d									09 21				09 30							09 51			
Lewisham	d		09 04		09 12					09 24	09 26		09 32	09 35			09 45				09 54	09 56		10 00
Blackheath	d		09 07		09 15						09 29		09 35	09 38			09 48					09 59		10 03
Kidbrooke	d		09 10		09 18						09 32			09 41			09 51					10 02		
Eltham	d		09 13		09 22						09 35			09 44			09 54					10 05		
Falconwood	d		09 16		09 25						09 38			09 47			09 57					10 08		
Welling	d		09 19		09 27						09 41			09 50			10 00					10 11		
Bexleyheath	d		09 22		09 31						09 44			09 53			10 03					10 14		
Barnehurst	d		09 30		09 35						09 47			09 59			10 06					10 17		
Hither Green	d			09 11						09 30						09 39					09 58			
Lee	d									09 32						09 41					10 01			
Mottingham	d									09 35						09 44					10 04			
New Eltham	d			09 16					09 25	09 38						09 46			09 55		10 07			
Sidcup	d			09 20					09 29	09 41						09 50			09 58		10 10			
Albany Park	d									09 44						09 52					10 13			
Bexley	d			09 23					09 32	09 46						09 55			10 02		10 15			
Crayford	d			09 27					09 36	09 51						09 58			10 05		10 21			
Charlton	d	09 05				09 16	09 25			10a19		09 35	09 40		09 45					09 55	10a49		10 05	10 08
Woolwich Dockyard	d					09 19	09 28						09 43		09 48					09 58				10 11
Woolwich Arsenal	d	09 10				09 22	09 31					09 40	09 46		09 51					10 01			10 10	10 14
Plumstead	d	09 13				09 24	09 33					09 43	09 48		09 53					10 03			10 13	10 16
Abbey Wood	d	09 16				09 27	09 36					09 46	09 51		09 56					10 06			10 16	10 20
Belvedere	d					09 30	09 39						09 54		09 59					10 09				10 23
Erith	d					09 33	09 42						09 57		10 02					10 12				10 25
Slade Green	d	09 22	09a39			09a36	09a46					09 52	10 03	10a05	10a06					10a15			10 22	10 31
Dartford	a	09 27		09 34	09 46				09 40		09 54	09 57	10 08			10 05	10 14		10 10			10 24	10 27	10 38
	d	09 28							09 41		09 54	09 58							10 11			10 24	10 28	
Stone Crossing	d	09 32							09 45			10 02							10 15				10 32	
Greenhithe for Bluewater	d	09 34							09 47		10 00	10 04							10 17			10 30	10 34	
Swanscombe	d	09 37							09 50			10 07							10 20				10 37	
Northfleet	d	09 39							09 52			10 09							10 22				10 39	
Gravesend	d	09 43						09 48	09a56		10a09	10 13						10 18	10a26			10a38	10 43	
Higham	d	09 49										10 19											10 49	
Strood	d	09 55						09 59				10 25						10 29					10 55	
Maidstone West	d																							
Rochester	d	09 58						10 02				10 28						10 32					10 58	
Chatham	d	10 01						10 06				10 31						10 36					11 01	
Gillingham (Kent)	a	10 05						10 10				10 35						10 40					11 05	
Rainham (Kent)	a	10 11						10 15				10 41						10 45					11 11	

Table T200-F

London - Dartford and Gillingham

Mondays to Fridays

16 December to 15 May

		SE	SE	SE	SE	SE	SE ◇	SE	SE	SE	TL	SE	SE	SE	SE	SE	SE	SE ◇	SE	SE	SE	TL	SE
St Pancras Int'l ⊖	d						10 27											10 52					
Stratford International ⊖	d						10 34											10 59					
Ebbsfleet International	d						10 45											11 13					
London Charing Cross ⊖	d		09 48		09 54			10 02				10 12		10 18		10 24			10 32				10 42
London Waterloo (East) ⊖	d		09 51		09 58			10 05				10 15		10 21		10 28			10 35				10 45
London Cannon Street ⊖	d	09 47		09 54		10 05			10 08				10 17		10 24		10 35			10 38			
London Bridge ⊖	d	09 51	09 57	09 58	10 05	10 09		10 11	10 13		10 18	10 21	10 21	10 27	10 28	10 35	10 39		10 41	10 43		10 48	10 51
Deptford	d			10 05		10 15					10 25				10 35		10 45					10 55	
Greenwich	d			10 07		10 17					10 27				10 37		10 47					10 57	
Maze Hill	d			10 10		10 20					10 30				10 40		10 50					11 00	
Westcombe Park	d			10 12		10 22					10 32				10 42		10 52					11 02	
London Victoria ⊖	d									10 04											10 34		
Denmark Hill	d									10 14											10 44		
Peckham Rye	d									10 17											10 47		
Nunhead	d									10 19											10 49		
New Cross ⊖	d	09 57							10 19				10 27							10 49			
St Johns	d	09 59							10 21				10 29							10 51			
Lewisham	d	10 04			10 15				10 24	10 26		10 30	10 34			10 45				10 54	10 56		11 00
Blackheath	d	10 07			10 18					10 29		10 33	10 37			10 48					10 59		11 03
Kidbrooke	d	10 10			10 21					10 32			10 40			10 51					11 02		
Eltham	d	10 13			10 24					10 35			10 43			10 54					11 05		
Falconwood	d	10 16			10 27					10 38			10 46			10 57					11 08		
Welling	d	10 19			10 30					10 41			10 49			11 00					11 11		
Bexleyheath	d	10 22			10 33					10 44			10 52			11 03					11 14		
Barnehurst	d	10 28			10 36					10 47			10 58			11 06					11 17		
Hither Green	d		10 07						10 29					10 37						10 59			
Lee	d		10 09						10 31					10 39						11 01			
Mottingham	d		10 12						10 34					10 42						11 04			
New Eltham	d		10 15					10 25	10 37					10 45					10 55	11 07			
Sidcup	d		10 19					10 28	10 40					10 48					10 58	11 10			
Albany Park	d		10 21						10 43					10 51						11 13			
Bexley	d		10 24					10 32	10 45					10 53					11 02	11 15			
Crayford	d		10 27					10 35	10 51					10 57					11 05	11 21			
Charlton	d			10 15		10 25			11a19		10 35	10 38			10 45		10 55			11a49		11 05	11 08
Woolwich Dockyard	d			10 18		10 28						10 41			10 48		10 58						11 11
Woolwich Arsenal	d			10 21		10 31					10 40	10 44			10 51		11 01					11 10	11 14
Plumstead	d			10 23		10 33					10 43	10 46			10 53		11 03					11 13	11 16
Abbey Wood	d			10 26		10 36					10 46	10 50			10 56		11 06					11 16	11 20
Belvedere	d			10 29		10 39						10 53			10 59		11 09						11 23
Erith	d			10 32		10 42						10 55			11 02		11 12						11 25
Slade Green	d	10a35		10a36		10a45					10 52	11 01	11a05		11a06		11a15					11 22	11 31
Dartford	a		10 32		10 44			10 40		10 54	10 57	11 08		11 02		11 14			11 10		11 24	11 27	11 38
	d							10 41		10 54	10 58								11 11		11 24	11 28	
Stone Crossing	d							10 45			11 02								11 15			11 32	
Greenhithe for Bluewater	d							10 47		11 00	11 04								11 17		11 30	11 34	
Swanscombe	d							10 50			11 07								11 20			11 37	
Northfleet	d							10 52			11 09								11 22			11 39	
Gravesend	d						10 49	10a56		11a09	11 13							11 18	11a26		11a39	11 43	
Higham	d										11 19											11 49	
Strood	d						10 59				11 25							11 29				11 55	
Maidstone West	d																						
Rochester	d						11 02				11 28							11 32				11 58	
Chatham	d						11 06				11 31							11 36				12 01	
Gillingham (Kent)	a						11 10				11 35							11 40				12 05	
Rainham (Kent)	a						11 15				11 41							11 45				12 11	

Table T200-F

Mondays to Fridays

16 December to 15 May

London - Dartford and Gillingham

	SE	SE	SE	SE	SE	SE ◇	SE	SE	SE	TL	SE	SE		SE	SE	SE	SE	SE ◇	SE	SE	SE	TL	SE	SE
St Pancras Int'l 15 ⊖ d						11 25												11 55						
Stratford International ⊖ d						11 32												12 02						
Ebbsfleet International d						11 43												12 13						
London Charing Cross 4 ⊖ d		10 48		10 54			11 02				11 12			11 18		11 24			11 32				11 42	
London Waterloo (East) 4 ⊖ d		10 51		10 58			11 05				11 15			11 21		11 28			11 35				11 45	
London Cannon Street 4 ⊖ d	10 47		10 54		11 05			11 08				11 17			11 24		11 35			11 38				11 47
London Bridge 4 ⊖ d	10 51	10 57	10 58	11 05	11 09		11 11	11 13		11 18	11 21	11 21		11 27	11 28	11 35	11 39		11 41	11 43		11 48	11 51	11 51
Deptford d			11 05		11 15					11 25					11 35		11 45					11 55		
Greenwich 4 d			11 07		11 17					11 27					11 37		11 47					11 57		
Maze Hill d			11 10		11 20					11 30					11 40		11 50					12 00		
Westcombe Park d			11 12		11 22					11 32					11 42		11 52					12 02		
London Victoria 15 ⊖ d									11 04												11 34			
Denmark Hill 4 d									11 14												11 44			
Peckham Rye 4 d									11 17												11 47			
Nunhead 4 d									11 19												11 49			
New Cross 4 ⊖ d	10 57							11 19				11 27								11 49				11 57
St Johns d	10 59							11 21				11 29								11 51				11 59
Lewisham 4 d	11 04			11 15				11 24	11 26		11 30	11 34				11 45				11 54	11 56		12 00	12 04
Blackheath 4 d	11 07			11 18					11 29		11 33	11 37				11 48					11 59		12 03	12 07
Kidbrooke d	11 10			11 21					11 32			11 40				11 51					12 02			12 10
Eltham d	11 13			11 24					11 35			11 43				11 54					12 05			12 13
Falconwood d	11 16			11 27					11 38			11 46				11 57					12 08			12 16
Welling d	11 19			11 30					11 41			11 49				12 00					12 11			12 19
Bexleyheath d	11 22			11 33					11 44			11 52				12 03					12 14			12 22
Barnehurst 4 d	11 28			11 36					11 47			11 58				12 06					12 17			12 28
Hither Green 4 d		11 07						11 29						11 37						11 59				
Lee d		11 09						11 31						11 39						12 01				
Mottingham d		11 12						11 34						11 42						12 04				
New Eltham d		11 15					11 25	11 37						11 45					11 55	12 07				
Sidcup 4 d		11 18					11 28	11 40						11 48					11 58	12 10				
Albany Park d		11 21						11 43						11 51						12 13				
Bexley d		11 23					11 32	11 45						11 53					12 02	12 15				
Crayford d		11 27					11 35	11 51						11 57					12 05	12 21				
Charlton 4 d			11 15		11 25			12a19		11 35	11 38				11 45		11 55			12a49		12 05	12 08	
Woolwich Dockyard d			11 18		11 28						11 41				11 48		11 58						12 11	
Woolwich Arsenal 4 d			11 21		11 31					11 40	11 44				11 51		12 01					12 10	12 14	
Plumstead d			11 23		11 33					11 43	11 46				11 53		12 03					12 13	12 16	
Abbey Wood d			11 26		11 36					11 46	11 50				11 56		12 06					12 16	12 20	
Belvedere d			11 29		11 39						11 53				11 59		12 09						12 23	
Erith d			11 32		11 42						11 55				12 02		12 12						12 25	
Slade Green 4 d	11a35		11a36		11a45					11 52	12 01	12a05			12a06		12a15					12 22	12 31	12a35
Dartford 4 a		11 32		11 44			11 40		11 54	11 57	12 08			12 02		12 14			12 10		12 24	12 27	12 38	
d							11 41		11 54	11 58									12 11		12 24	12 28		
Stone Crossing d							11 45			12 02									12 15			12 32		
Greenhithe for Bluewater d							11 47		12 00	12 04									12 17		12 30	12 34		
Swanscombe d							11 50			12 07									12 20			12 37		
Northfleet d							11 52			12 09									12 22			12 39		
Gravesend 4 d						11 48	11a56		12a09	12 13								12 18	12a26		12a39	12 43		
Higham d										12 19												12 49		
Strood 4 d						11 59				12 25								12 29				12 55		
Maidstone West d																								
Rochester 4 d						12 02				12 28								12 32				12 58		
Chatham 4 d						12 06				12 31								12 36				13 01		
Gillingham (Kent) 4 a						12 10				12 35								12 40				13 05		
Rainham (Kent) a						12 15				12 41								12 45				13 11		

Table T200-F

Mondays to Fridays

16 December to 15 May

London - Dartford and Gillingham

	SE	SE	SE	SE		SE ◇	SE	SE	SE	TL	SE	SE	SE	SE	SE	SE	SE ◇	SE	SE	SE		TL	SE	SE
St Pancras Int'l 15 ⊖ d						12 27											12 52							
Stratford International ⊖ d						12 34											12 59							
Ebbsfleet International d						12 45											13 13							
London Charing Cross 4 ⊖ d	11 48		11 54				12 02				12 12		12 18		12 24			12 32					12 42	
London Waterloo (East) 4 ⊖ d	11 51		11 58				12 05				12 15		12 21		12 28			12 35					12 45	
London Cannon Street 4 ⊖ d		11 54		12 05				12 08				12 17		12 24		12 35			12 38					12 47
London Bridge 4 ⊖ d	11 57	11 58	12 05	12 09			12 11	12 13		12 18	12 21	12 21	12 27	12 28	12 35	12 39		12 41	12 43			12 48	12 51	12 51
Deptford d		12 05		12 15						12 25				12 35		12 45						12 55		
Greenwich 4 d		12 07		12 17						12 27				12 37		12 47						12 57		
Maze Hill d		12 10		12 20						12 30				12 40		12 50						13 00		
Westcombe Park d		12 12		12 22						12 32				12 42		12 52						13 02		
London Victoria 15 ⊖ d									12 04											12 34				
Denmark Hill 4 d									12 14											12 44				
Peckham Rye 4 d									12 17											12 47				
Nunhead 4 d									12 19											12 49				
New Cross 4 ⊖ d								12 19				12 27							12 49					12 57
St Johns d								12 21				12 29							12 51					12 59
Lewisham 4 d			12 15					12 24	12 26		12 30	12 34			12 45				12 54	12 56			13 00	13 04
Blackheath 4 d			12 18						12 29		12 33	12 37			12 48					12 59			13 03	13 07
Kidbrooke d			12 21						12 32			12 40			12 51					13 02				13 10
Eltham d			12 24						12 35			12 43			12 54					13 05				13 13
Falconwood d			12 27						12 38			12 46			12 57					13 08				13 16
Welling d			12 30						12 41			12 49			13 00					13 11				13 19
Bexleyheath d			12 33						12 44			12 52			13 03					13 14				13 22
Barnehurst 4 d			12 36						12 47			12 58			13 06					13 17				13 28
Hither Green 4 d	12 07							12 29					12 37						12 59					
Lee d	12 09							12 31					12 39						13 01					
Mottingham d	12 12							12 34					12 42						13 04					
New Eltham d	12 15						12 25	12 37					12 45					12 55	13 07					
Sidcup 4 d	12 18						12 28	12 40					12 48					12 58	13 10					
Albany Park d	12 21							12 43					12 51						13 13					
Bexley d	12 23						12 32	12 45					12 53					13 02	13 15					
Crayford d	12 27						12 35	12 51					12 57					13 05	13 21					
Charlton 4 d		12 15		12 25				13a19		12 35	12 38			12 45		12 55			13a49			13 05	13 08	
Woolwich Dockyard d		12 18		12 28							12 41			12 48		12 58							13 11	
Woolwich Arsenal 4 d		12 21		12 31						12 40	12 44			12 51		13 01						13 10	13 14	
Plumstead d		12 23		12 33						12 43	12 46			12 53		13 03						13 13	13 16	
Abbey Wood d		12 26		12 36						12 46	12 50			12 56		13 06						13 16	13 20	
Belvedere d		12 29		12 39							12 53			12 59		13 09							13 23	
Erith d		12 32		12 42							12 55			13 02		13 12							13 25	
Slade Green 4 d		12a36		12a45						12 52	13 01	13a05		13a06		13a15						13 22	13 31	13a35
Dartford 4 a	12 32		12 44				12 40		12 54	12 57	13 08		13 03		13 14			13 10		13 24		13 27	13 38	
d							12 41		12 54	12 58								13 11		13 24		13 28		
Stone Crossing d							12 45			13 02								13 15				13 32		
Greenhithe for Bluewater d							12 47		13 00	13 04								13 17		13 30		13 34		
Swanscombe d							12 50			13 07								13 20				13 37		
Northfleet d							12 52			13 09								13 22				13 39		
Gravesend 4 d						12 49	12a56		13a09	13 13							13 18	13a26		13a39		13 43		
Higham d										13 19												13 49		
Strood 4 d						12 59				13 25							13 29					13 55		
Maidstone West d																								
Rochester 4 d						13 02				13 28							13 32					13 58		
Chatham 4 d						13 06				13 31							13 36					14 01		
Gillingham (Kent) 4 a						13 10				13 35							13 40					14 05		
Rainham (Kent) a						13 15				13 41							13 45					14 11		

Table T200-F

Mondays to Fridays

16 December to 15 May

London - Dartford and Gillingham

		SE	SE	SE	SE	SE ◇	SE	SE	SE	TL	SE	SE	SE		SE	SE	SE	SE ◇	SE	SE	SE	TL	SE	SE	SE
St Pancras Int'l ⊖	d					13 25												13 55							
Stratford International ⊖	d					13 32												14 02							
Ebbsfleet International	d					13 43												14 13							
London Charing Cross ⊖	d	12 48		12 54			13 02				13 12		13 18			13 24			13 32				13 42		13 48
London Waterloo (East) ⊖	d	12 51		12 58			13 05				13 15		13 21			13 28			13 35				13 45		13 51
London Cannon Street ⊖	d		12 54		13 05			13 08				13 17			13 24		13 35			13 38				13 47	
London Bridge ⊖	d	12 57	12 58	13 05	13 09		13 11	13 13		13 18	13 21	13 21	13 27		13 28	13 35	13 39		13 41	13 43		13 48	13 51	13 51	13 57
Deptford	d		13 05		13 15					13 25					13 35		13 45					13 55			
Greenwich	d		13 07		13 17					13 27					13 37		13 47					13 57			
Maze Hill	d		13 10		13 20					13 30					13 40		13 50					14 00			
Westcombe Park	d		13 12		13 22					13 32					13 42		13 52					14 02			
London Victoria ⊖	d								13 04												13 34				
Denmark Hill	d								13 14												13 44				
Peckham Rye	d								13 17												13 47				
Nunhead	d								13 19												13 49				
New Cross ⊖	d							13 19				13 27								13 49				13 57	
St Johns	d							13 21				13 29								13 51				13 59	
Lewisham	d			13 15				13 24	13 26		13 30	13 34				13 45				13 54	13 56		14 00	14 04	
Blackheath	d			13 18					13 29		13 33	13 37				13 48					13 59		14 03	14 07	
Kidbrooke	d			13 21					13 32			13 40				13 51					14 02			14 10	
Eltham	d			13 24					13 35			13 43				13 54					14 05			14 13	
Falconwood	d			13 27					13 38			13 46				13 57					14 08			14 16	
Welling	d			13 30					13 41			13 49				14 00					14 11			14 19	
Bexleyheath	d			13 33					13 44			13 52				14 03					14 14			14 22	
Barnehurst	d			13 36					13 47			13 58				14 06					14 17			14 28	
Hither Green	d	13 07						13 29					13 37							13 59					14 07
Lee	d	13 09						13 31					13 39							14 01					14 09
Mottingham	d	13 12						13 34					13 42							14 04					14 12
New Eltham	d	13 15					13 25	13 37					13 45						13 55	14 07					14 15
Sidcup	d	13 18					13 28	13 40					13 48						13 58	14 10					14 18
Albany Park	d	13 21						13 43					13 51							14 13					14 21
Bexley	d	13 23					13 32	13 45					13 53						14 02	14 15					14 23
Crayford	d	13 27					13 35	13 51					13 57						14 05	14 21					14 27
Charlton	d		13 15		13 25			14a19		13 35	13 38				13 45		13 55			14a49		14 05	14 08		
Woolwich Dockyard	d		13 18		13 28						13 41				13 48		13 58						14 11		
Woolwich Arsenal	d		13 21		13 31					13 40	13 44				13 51		14 01					14 10	14 14		
Plumstead	d		13 23		13 33					13 43	13 46				13 53		14 03					14 13	14 16		
Abbey Wood	d		13 26		13 36					13 46	13 50				13 56		14 06					14 16	14 20		
Belvedere	d		13 29		13 39						13 53				13 59		14 09						14 23		
Erith	d		13 32		13 42						13 55				14 02		14 12						14 25		
Slade Green	d		13a36		13a45					13 52	14 01	14a05			14a06		14a15					14 22	14 31	14a35	
Dartford	a	13 32		13 44			13 40		13 54	13 57	14 08		14 02			14 14			14 10		14 24	14 27	14 38		14 32
	d						13 41		13 54	13 58									14 11		14 24	14 28			
Stone Crossing	d						13 45			14 02									14 15			14 32			
Greenhithe for Bluewater	d						13 47		14 00	14 04									14 17		14 30	14 34			
Swanscombe	d						13 50			14 07									14 20			14 37			
Northfleet	d						13 52			14 09									14 22			14 39			
Gravesend	d					13 48	13a56		14a09	14 13								14 18	14a26		14a39	14 43			
Higham	d									14 19												14 49			
Strood	d					13 59				14 25								14 29				14 55			
Maidstone West	d																								
Rochester	d					14 02				14 28								14 32				14 58			
Chatham	d					14 06				14 31								14 36				15 01			
Gillingham (Kent)	a					14 10				14 35								14 40				15 05			
Rainham (Kent)	a					14 15				14 41								14 45				15 11			

Table T200-F

Mondays to Fridays

16 December to 15 May

London - Dartford and Gillingham

		SE	SE	SE	SE ◇		SE	SE	SE	TL	SE	SE	SE	SE	SE	SE	SE ◇	SE	SE	SE	TL		SE	SE	SE
St Pancras Int'l ⊖	d				14 25												14 55								
Stratford International ⊖	d				14 32												15 02								
Ebbsfleet International	d				14 43												15 13								
London Charing Cross ⊖	d		13 54				14 02				14 12		14 18		14 24			14 32					14 42		14 48
London Waterloo (East) ⊖	d		13 58				14 05				14 15		14 21		14 28			14 35					14 45		14 51
London Cannon Street ⊖	d	13 54		14 05				14 08				14 17		14 24		14 35			14 38					14 47	
London Bridge ⊖	d	13 58	14 05	14 09			14 11	14 13		14 18	14 21	14 21	14 27	14 28	14 35	14 39		14 41	14 43		14 48		14 51	14 51	14 57
Deptford	d	14 05		14 15						14 25				14 35		14 45					14 55				
Greenwich	d	14 07		14 17						14 27				14 37		14 47					14 57				
Maze Hill	d	14 10		14 20						14 30				14 40		14 50					15 00				
Westcombe Park	d	14 12		14 22						14 32				14 42		14 52					15 02				
London Victoria ⊖	d								14 04											14 34					
Denmark Hill	d								14 14											14 44					
Peckham Rye	d								14 17											14 47					
Nunhead	d								14 19											14 49					
New Cross ⊖	d							14 19				14 27							14 49					14 57	
St Johns	d							14 21				14 29							14 51					14 59	
Lewisham	d		14 15					14 24	14 26		14 30	14 34			14 45				14 54	14 56			15 00	15 04	
Blackheath	d		14 18						14 29		14 33	14 37			14 48					14 59			15 03	15 07	
Kidbrooke	d		14 21						14 32			14 40			14 51					15 02				15 10	
Eltham	d		14 24						14 35			14 43			14 54					15 05				15 13	
Falconwood	d		14 27						14 38			14 46			14 57					15 08				15 16	
Welling	d		14 30						14 41			14 49			15 00					15 11				15 19	
Bexleyheath	d		14 33						14 44			14 52			15 03					15 14				15 22	
Barnehurst	d		14 36						14 47			14 58			15 06					15 17				15 28	
Hither Green	d							14 29					14 37						14 59						15 07
Lee	d							14 31					14 39						15 01						15 09
Mottingham	d							14 34					14 42						15 04						15 12
New Eltham	d						14 25	14 37					14 45					14 55	15 07						15 15
Sidcup	d						14 28	14 40					14 48					14 58	15 10						15 18
Albany Park	d							14 43					14 51						15 13						15 21
Bexley	d						14 32	14 45					14 53					15 02	15 15						15 23
Crayford	d						14 35	14 51					14 57					15 05	15 21						15 27
Charlton	d	14 15		14 25				15a19		14 35	14 38			14 45		14 55			15a49		15 05		15 08		
Woolwich Dockyard	d	14 18		14 28							14 41			14 48		14 58							15 11		
Woolwich Arsenal	d	14 21		14 31						14 40	14 44			14 51		15 01					15 10		15 14		
Plumstead	d	14 23		14 33						14 43	14 46			14 53		15 03					15 13		15 16		
Abbey Wood	d	14 26		14 36						14 46	14 50			14 56		15 06					15 16		15 20		
Belvedere	d	14 29		14 39							14 53			14 59		15 09							15 23		
Erith	d	14 32		14 42							14 55			15 02		15 12							15 25		
Slade Green	d	14a36		14a45						14 52	15 01	15a05		15a06		15a15					15 22		15 31	15a35	
Dartford	a		14 44				14 40		14 54	14 57	15 08		15 02		15 14			15 10		15 24	15 27		15 38		15 32
	d						14 41		14 54	14 58								15 11		15 24	15 28				
Stone Crossing	d						14 45			15 02								15 15			15 32				
Greenhithe for Bluewater	d						14 47		15 00	15 04								15 17		15 30	15 34				
Swanscombe	d						14 50			15 07								15 20			15 37				
Northfleet	d						14 52			15 09								15 22			15 39				
Gravesend	d				14 48		14a56		15a09	15 13							15 18	15a26		15a39	15 43				
Higham	d									15 19											15 49				
Strood	d				14 59					15 25							15 29				15 55				
Maidstone West	d																								
Rochester	d				15 02					15 28							15 32				15 58				
Chatham	d				15 05					15 31							15 36				16 01				
Gillingham (Kent)	a				15 09					15 35							15 40				16 05				
Rainham (Kent)	a				15 14					15 41							15 45				16 11				

Table T200-F

Mondays to Fridays

16 December to 15 May

London - Dartford and Gillingham

Station		SE	SE	SE	SE ◇	SE	SE	SE	TL	SE	SE	SE	SE		SE	SE	SE ◇	SE	SE	SE	TL	SE	SE	SE	SE
St Pancras Int'l ⊖	d				15 25												15 55								
Stratford International ⊖ ⛴	d				15 32												16 02								
Ebbsfleet International	d				15 43												16 13								
London Charing Cross ⊖	d		14 54			15 02				15 12		15 18			15 24			15 32				15 42		15 48	
London Waterloo (East) ⊖	d		14 58			15 05				15 15		15 21			15 28			15 35				15 45		15 51	
London Cannon Street ⊖	d	14 54		15 05			15 08				15 17		15 24			15 35			15 38				15 47		15 54
London Bridge ⊖	d	14 58	15 05	15 09		15 11	15 13		15 18	15 21	15 21	15 27	15 28		15 35	15 39		15 41	15 43		15 48	15 51	15 51	15 57	15 58
Deptford	d	15 05		15 15					15 25				15 35			15 45					15 55				16 05
Greenwich ⛴	d	15 07		15 17					15 27				15 37			15 47					15 57				16 07
Maze Hill	d	15 10		15 20					15 30				15 40			15 50					16 00				16 10
Westcombe Park	d	15 12		15 22					15 32				15 42			15 52					16 02				16 12
London Victoria ⊖	d							15 04												15 34					
Denmark Hill	d							15 14												15 44					
Peckham Rye	d							15 17												15 47					
Nunhead	d							15 19												15 49					
New Cross ⊖	d						15 19				15 27								15 49				15 57		
St Johns	d						15 21				15 29								15 51				15 59		
Lewisham ⛴	d		15 15				15 24	15 26		15 30	15 34				15 45				15 54	15 56		16 01	16 04		
Blackheath	d		15 18					15 29		15 33	15 37				15 48					15 59		16 03	16 07		
Kidbrooke	d		15 21					15 32			15 40				15 51					16 02			16 10		
Eltham	d		15 24					15 35			15 43				15 54					16 05			16 13		
Falconwood	d		15 27					15 38			15 46				15 57					16 08			16 16		
Welling	d		15 30					15 41			15 49				16 00					16 11			16 19		
Bexleyheath	d		15 33					15 44			15 52				16 03					16 14			16 22		
Barnehurst	d		15 36					15 47			15 58				16 06					16 17			16 28		
Hither Green	d						15 29					15 37							15 59					16 07	
Lee	d						15 31					15 39							16 01					16 09	
Mottingham	d						15 34					15 42							16 04					16 12	
New Eltham	d					15 25	15 37					15 45						15 55	16 07					16 15	
Sidcup	d					15 28	15 40					15 48						15 58	16 10					16 18	
Albany Park	d						15 43					15 51							16 13					16 21	
Bexley	d					15 32	15 45					15 53						16 02	16 15					16 23	
Crayford	d					15 35	15 51					15 57						16 05	16 21					16 27	
Charlton	d	15 15		15 25			16a17		15 35	15 38			15 45			15 55			16a50		16 05	16 08			16 15
Woolwich Dockyard	d	15 18		15 28						15 41			15 48			15 58						16 11			16 18
Woolwich Arsenal ⛴	d	15 21		15 31					15 40	15 44			15 51			16 01					16 10	16 14			16 21
Plumstead	d	15 23		15 33					15 43	15 46			15 53			16 03					16 13	16 16			16 23
Abbey Wood	d	15 26		15 36					15 46	15 50			15 56			16 06					16 16	16 20			16 26
Belvedere	d	15 29		15 39						15 53			15 59			16 09						16 23			16 29
Erith	d	15 32		15 42						15 55			16 02			16 12						16 25			16 32
Slade Green	d	15a36		15a45					15 52	16 01	16a05		16a06			16a15					16 22	16 32	16a35		16a36
Dartford	a		15 44			15 40		15 54	15 57	16 08		16 02			16 14			16 10		16 24	16 27	16 38		16 32	
	d					15 41		15 54	15 58									16 11		16 24	16 28				
Stone Crossing	d					15 45			16 02									16 15			16 32				
Greenhithe for Bluewater	d					15 47		16 00	16 04									16 17		16 30	16 34				
Swanscombe	d					15 50			16 07									16 20			16 37				
Northfleet	d					15 52			16 09									16 22			16 39				
Gravesend	d				15 48	15a56		16a09	16 13								16 18	16a26		16a39	16 43				
Higham	d								16 19												16 49				
Strood	d				15 59				16 25								16 29				16 55				
Maidstone West	d																								
Rochester	d				16 02				16 28								16 32				16 58				
Chatham	d				16 05				16 31								16 36				17 01				
Gillingham (Kent)	a				16 09				16 35								16 40				17 05				
Rainham (Kent)	a				16 14				16 41								16 45				17 11				

Table T200-F

Mondays to Fridays

16 December to 15 May

London - Dartford and Gillingham

Station		SE	SE	SE ◇	SE		SE	SE	TL	SE ◇	SE	SE	SE	SE	SE	SE	SE	SE	SE	SE ◇	TL		SE	SE	SE
St Pancras Int'l ⊖	d			16 25						16 55										17 12					
Stratford International ⊖ ⛴	d			16 32						17 02										17 19					
Ebbsfleet International	d			16 43						17 13										17 31					
London Charing Cross ⊖	d	15 54			16 02							16 12		16 18		16 24	16 33								16 45
London Waterloo (East) ⊖	d	15 58			16 05							16 15		16 21		16 28	16 36								16 48
London Cannon Street ⊖	d		16 05				16 08				16 15				16 27			16 37	16 39					16 45	
London Bridge ⊖	d	16 05	16 10		16 11		16 13		16 18		16 20	16 21		16 27	16 32	16 35	16 42	16 42	16 44		16 48			16 50	16 54
Deptford	d		16 16						16 25						16 38			16 48			16 55				
Greenwich ⛴	d		16 18						16 27						16 40			16 50			16 57				
Maze Hill	d		16 21						16 30						16 43			16 53			17 00				
Westcombe Park	d		16 23						16 32						16 45			16 55			17 02				
London Victoria ⊖	d							16 04															16 34		
Denmark Hill	d							16 14															16 44		
Peckham Rye	d							16 17															16 47		
Nunhead	d							16 19					←										16 49		
New Cross ⊖	d						16 19				16 26		16 26						16 50					16 56	
St Johns	d						16 21				→		16 28						16 52					16 58	
Lewisham ⛴	d	16 15					16 24	16 26				16 30	16 33			16 45			16 55				16 57	17 01	17 04
Blackheath	d	16 18						16 29				16 33	16 36			16 48							17 00	17 04	17 07
Kidbrooke	d	16 21						16 32					16 39			16 51							17 03	17 07	
Eltham	d	16 24						16 35					16 42			16 54							17 07	17 11	
Falconwood	d	16 27						16 38					16 45			16 57							17 10	17 14	
Welling	d	16 30						16 41					16 48			17 00							17 13	17 17	
Bexleyheath	d	16 33						16 44					16 51			17 03							17 16	17 20	
Barnehurst	d	16 36						16 47					16 54			17 06							17 19	17 28	
Hither Green	d						16 29							16 39					17 00						
Lee	d						16 31							16 41					17 02						
Mottingham	d						16 34							16 44					17 05						
New Eltham	d				16 25		16 37							16 47			16 55		17 08						
Sidcup	d				16 28		16 40							16 50			16 58		17 12						
Albany Park	d						16 43							16 53					17 14						
Bexley	d				16 32		16 45							16 55			17 02		17 17						
Crayford	d				16 35		16 50							16 59			17 05		17 22						
Charlton	d		16 26				17a18		16 35			16 38			16 48			16 58	17a47		17 05				17 13
Woolwich Dockyard	d		16 29									16 41			16 51			17 01							17 16
Woolwich Arsenal ⛴	d		16 32						16 40			16 44			16 54			17 04			17 10				17 19
Plumstead	d		16 34						16 43			16 46			16 56			17 06			17 13				17 21
Abbey Wood	d		16 37						16 46			16 50			16 59			17 09			17 16				17 24
Belvedere	d		16 40									16 53			17 02			17 12							17 27
Erith	d		16 43									16 55			17 05			17 15							17 30
Slade Green	d		16a46						16 52			17 01	17a00		17a09			17a18			17 22			17a38	17a33
Dartford	a	16 44			16 40			16 54	16 57			17 10		17 04		17 16	17 10				17 27		17 32		
	d				16 41			16 54	16 58								17 11				17 32				
Stone Crossing	d				16 45				17 02								17 15				17 36				
Greenhithe for Bluewater	d				16 47			17 00	17 04								17 17				17 38				
Swanscombe	d				16 50				17 07								17 20				17 41				
Northfleet	d				16 52				17 09								17 22				17 44				
Gravesend	d			16 48	16a58			17a09	17 13	17 18							17a28			17 35	17 50				
Higham	d								17 19												17 56				
Strood	d			16 59					17 25	17 28										17 46	18 01				
Maidstone West	d																			18a04					
Rochester	d			17 02					17 28	17 32											18 05				
Chatham	d			17 06					17 32	17 35											18 08				
Gillingham (Kent)	a			17 10					17 36	17 40											18 12				
Rainham (Kent)	a			17 15					17 42	17 46											18 19				

Table T200-F

London - Dartford and Gillingham

Mondays to Fridays

16 December to 15 May

Station		SE	SE	SE	SE	SE	SE	SE	SE	SE ◇	TL	SE	SE		SE	SE ◇	SE	SE	SE	SE	SE	SE	SE	SE	SE
St Pancras Int'l 15 ⊖	d									17 46						18 55									
Stratford International ⊖ ⛴	d									17 53						18 02									
Ebbsfleet International	d									18 05						18 13									
London Charing Cross 4 ⊖	d	16 48		16 53				17 06	17 09				17 13				17 17			17 28		17 32	17 34	17 36	
London Waterloo (East) 4 ⊖	d	16 51		16 56				17 09	17 12				17 16				17 20			17 31		17 35	17 37	17 39	
London Cannon Street 4 ⊖	d		16 54		16 58	17 03	17 05								17 19			17 25	17 27		17 34				17 41
London Bridge 4 ⊖	d	16 57	16 59	17 02	17 03	17 08	17 10	17 15	17 18		17 18		17 22		17 24		17 26	17 30	17 32	17 37	17 39	17 41	17 43	17 45	17 46
Deptford	d		17 05				17 16				17 25							17 36			17 45				
Greenwich 4 ⛴	d		17 08				17 19				17 27							17 39			17 48				
Maze Hill	d		17 11				17 22				17 30							17 43			17 51				
Westcombe Park	d		17 14				17 24				17 32							17 45			17 54				
London Victoria 15 ⊖	d											17 04													
Denmark Hill 4	d											17 14													
Peckham Rye 4	d											17 17													
Nunhead 4	d											17 20													
New Cross 4 ⊖	d				17 09	17 15									17 30				17 37						17 53
St Johns	d				17 11										17 32										17 55
Lewisham 4 ⛴	d			17 12	17 15	17 19		17 24				17 28	17 31		17 36				17 43				17 52	17 56	17 59
Blackheath 4	d			17 15		17 22		17 27				17 31	17 34						17 46			17 52	17 55	17 59	
Kidbrooke	d			17 18		17 25		17 30				17 34							17 49			17 56		18 02	
Eltham	d			17 21		17 29		17 34				17 38							17 53			17 59		18 06	
Falconwood	d			17 24		17 32		17 37				17 41							17 56			18 03		18 09	
Welling	d			17 27		17 35		17 40				17 44							17 59			18 06		18 12	
Bexleyheath	d			17 31		17 38		17 44				17 48							18 03			18 09		18 15	
Barnehurst 4	d			17 34		17 43		17 47				17 51							18 08			18 12		18 19	
Hither Green 4	d	17 08			17 20				17 28						17 41		17 37			17 48					18 04
Lee	d	17 10			17 22				17 31						17 43					17 50					18 06
Mottingham	d	17 14			17 26				17 34						17 47					17 54					18 10
New Eltham	d	17 17			17 29				17 37						17 50		17 43			17 57					18 13
Sidcup 4	d	17 21			17 32				17a42						17 53		17 47			18a03					18 16
Albany Park	d	17 24			17 35										17 56		17 50								18 19
Bexley	d	17 27			17 38										17 59		17 53								18 22
Crayford	d	17 30			17 45										18 03		17 56								18 28
Charlton 4	d		17 17		18a14		17 26				17 35		17 39					17 48			17 56		18 00		19a03
Woolwich Dockyard	d		17 20				17 29						17 42								17 59		18 03		
Woolwich Arsenal 4 ⛴	d		17 23				17 32				17 40		17 45					17 53			18 02		18 06		
Plumstead	d		17 25				17 34				17 43		17 47								18 04		18 09		
Abbey Wood	d		17 29				17 38				17 46		17 50					17 58			18 08		18 12		
Belvedere	d		17 32				17 41						17 53								18 11		18 15		
Erith	d		17 35				17 43						17 56								18 13		18 18		
Slade Green 4	d		17 39			17a58	17a46				17 52		17a59						18a16		18 17		18a21	18a28	
Dartford 4	a	17 36	17 50	17 44				17 58			17 57	18 02			18 13		18 01	18 08			18 26	18 22			
	d	17 37									17 58						18 03	18 09							
Stone Crossing	d	17 41									18 02						18 07	18 13							
Greenhithe for Bluewater	d	17 43									18 04						18 09	18 15							
Swanscombe	d	17 46									18 07						18 12								
Northfleet	d	17 49									18 09						18 15								
Gravesend 4	d	17a56								18 09	18 13					18 18	18 22	18a25							
Higham	d										18 19						18 28								
Strood 4	d									18 20	18 25					18 31	18a36								
Maidstone West	d									18a38															
Rochester 4	d										18 28					18 36									
Chatham 4	d										18 32					18 40									
Gillingham (Kent) 4	a										18 36					18 44									
Rainham (Kent)	a										18 42					18 50									

Table T200-F

London - Dartford and Gillingham

Mondays to Fridays

16 December to 15 May

Station		TL	SE ◇	SE	TL		SE	SE	SE	SE	SE	SE	SE	SE	SE	SE	SE	SE	TL	SE	SE		SE	SE	SE ◇
St Pancras Int'l 15 ⊖	d		18 16																						18 55
Stratford International ⊖ ⛴	d		18 23																						19 02
Ebbsfleet International	d		18 35																						19 13
London Charing Cross 4 ⊖	d			17 41						17 49	17 51	17 53	17 55		17 59					18 11	18 15		18 17		
London Waterloo (East) 4 ⊖	d			17 44						17 52	17 54	17 56	17 58		18 02					18 14	18 18		18 20		
London Cannon Street 4 ⊖	d							17 47	17 49					18 00			18 04	18 09						18 22	
London Bridge 4 ⊖	d	17 48		17 50	←			17 52	17 54	17 58	18 00	18 02	18 04	18 05	18 08		18 09	18 14	18 18	18 20	18 24		18 26	18 27	
Deptford	d	17 55			17 55				18 00								18 15		18 25						
Greenwich 4 ⛴	d	→			17 57				18 03								18 18		18 27						
Maze Hill	d				18 00				18 06								18 21		18 30						
Westcombe Park	d				18 02				18 09								18 24		18 32						
London Victoria 15 ⊖	d						17 35									17 55									
Denmark Hill 4	d						17 45									18 05									
Peckham Rye 4	d						17 48									18 08									
Nunhead 4	d						17 51									18 11									
New Cross 4 ⊖	d							17 58						18 11				18 20						18 34	
St Johns	d													18 13										18 36	
Lewisham 4 ⛴	d						18 00	18 03			18 10		18 14	18 17		18 19		18 24		18 30			18 35	18 41	
Blackheath 4	d						18 03	18 06		18 09	18 13		18 17			18 22		18 27		18 33			18 39		
Kidbrooke	d						18 06	18 09		18 12			18 20			18 25		18 31					18 42		
Eltham	d						18 10	18 13		18 16			18 24			18 29		18 34					18 46		
Falconwood	d						18 13	18 16		18 19			18 27			18 32		18 38					18 49		
Welling	d						18 16	18 19		18 22			18 30			18 34		18 41					18 52		
Bexleyheath	d						18 20	18 23		18 26			18 33			18 38		18 44					18 56		
Barnehurst 4	d						18 23	18 26		18a31			18 37			18 41		18 54					19 02		
Hither Green 4	d			18 00								18 13		18 22	18 19						18 36			18 47	
Lee	d											18 16		18 25							18 38			18 49	
Mottingham	d											18 19		18 28							18 41			18 53	
New Eltham	d			18 06								18 22		18 31	18 26						18 44			18 56	
Sidcup 4	d			18 10								18 26		18 35	18 30						18 47			18 59	
Albany Park	d			18 13										18 38	18 33						18 50			19 02	
Bexley	d			18 16								18 30		18 41	18 36						18 53			19 05	
Crayford	d			18 19								18a33		18 48	18 39						18 57			19 14	
Charlton 4	d				18 05				18 11		18 18			19a19			18 26		18 35	18 38	19a29			19a49	
Woolwich Dockyard	d								18 14		18 21						18 29			18 41					
Woolwich Arsenal 4 ⛴	d				18 10				18 17		18 24						18 32		18 40	18 44					
Plumstead	d				18 13				18 20		18 26						18 35		18 43	18 46					
Abbey Wood	d				18 16				18 23		18 30						18 38		18 46	18 50					
Belvedere	d								18 27		18 33						18 41			18 53					
Erith	d								18 30		18 36						18 44			18 56					
Slade Green 4	d				18 24			18a33	18 34		18a42						18a47	19a12	18 52	18a59					
Dartford 4	a			18 24	18 29		18 33		18 39				18 48		18 44	18 51			18 57				19 12		
	d			18 25	18 32				18 40						18 46				18 58						
Stone Crossing	d			18 29	18 36														19 02						
Greenhithe for Bluewater	d			18 31	18 38				18 45						18 51				19 04						
Swanscombe	d			18 34	18 41														19 07						
Northfleet	d			18 37	18 44														19 09						
Gravesend 4	d		18 39	18a43	18 50				18a57						19 00				19 13						19 18
Higham	d				18 56										19 06				19 19						
Strood 4	d		18 51		19 01										19a14				19 27						19 30
Maidstone West	d		19a09																						
Rochester 4	d				19 05														19 30						19 35
Chatham 4	d				19 08														19 34						19 39
Gillingham (Kent) 4	a				19 12														19 38						19 43
Rainham (Kent)	a				19 19														19 44						19 48

Table T200-F

Mondays to Fridays
16 December to 15 May

London - Dartford and Gillingham

Station		SE	SE	SE	SE	SE	SE	SE	SE	SE	TL	SE	SE	SE	SE	SE	SE ◇	SE	SE	SE	SE	SE	SE	TL
St Pancras Int'l ⊖	d																19 25							
Stratford International ⊖	d																19 32							
Ebbsfleet International	d																19 43							
London Charing Cross ⊖	d		18 25					18 36		18 38			18 43					18 54	18 56		19 02			
London Waterloo (East) ⊖	d		18 28					18 39		18 41			18 46					18 57	18 59		19 05			
London Cannon Street ⊖	d	18 24				18 33	18 35		18 41						18 53	18 55				19 05		19 08		
London Bridge ⊖	d	18 29	18 34	←		18 38	18 40	18 45	18 46	18 47	18 48		18 52		18 58	19 00		19 03	19 05	19 09	19 11	19 13		19 18
Deptford	d	18 35		18 35			18 46				18 55					19 06				19 15				19 25
Greenwich	d	→		18 38			18 49				18 57					19 09				19 17				19 27
Maze Hill	d			18 42			18 52				19 00					19 12				19 20				19 30
Westcombe Park	d			18 44			18 55				19 02					19 15				19 22				19 32
London Victoria ⊖	d				18 21									18 42									19 04	
Denmark Hill	d				18 31									18 52									19 14	
Peckham Rye	d				18 34									18 55									19 17	
Nunhead	d				18 37							←		18 58									19 19	
New Cross ⊖	d					18 44			18 52			18 52			19 04							19 19		
St Johns	d					18 46			→			18 54			19 06							19 21		
Lewisham	d				18 44	18 49				18 57		18 59	19 01	19 06	19 10				19 15			19 24	19 26	
Blackheath	d				18 47	18 52				19 00			19 04	19 09	19 13				19 18				19 29	
Kidbrooke	d				18 50	18 55				19 03				19 12	19 16				19 21				19 32	
Eltham	d				18 54	18 59				19 07				19 16	19 20				19 25				19 35	
Falconwood	d				18 57	19 02				19 10				19 19	19 23				19 28				19 38	
Welling	d				19 00	19 05				19 13				19 22	19 26				19 31				19 41	
Bexleyheath	d				19 03	19 09				19 17				19 25	19 29				19 35				19 44	
Barnehurst	d				19 06	19a15				19 23				19 28	19 32				19 38				19 47	
Hither Green	d							18 56				19 04									19 22	19 29		
Lee	d							18 58				19 06									19 24	19 31		
Mottingham	d							19 02				19 09									19 28	19 34		
New Eltham	d		18 48					19 05				19 12						19 17			19 31	19 37		
Sidcup	d		18 51					19 09				19 16						19 21			19 34	19 40		
Albany Park	d		18 54					19 12				19 18									19 37	19 43		
Bexley	d		18 57					19 15				19 21						19 25			19 40	19 45		
Crayford	d		19 01					19 18				19 25			19a44			19 29			19 47	19 51		
Charlton	d			18 47			18 57				19 05		19 09			19 17				19 25		20a19		19 35
Woolwich Dockyard	d						19 00						19 12			19 20				19 28				
Woolwich Arsenal	d			18 52			19 03				19 10		19 15			19 23				19 31				19 40
Plumstead	d						19 06				19 13		19 17			19 25				19 33				19 43
Abbey Wood	d			18 57			19 09				19 16		19 21			19 29				19 36				19 46
Belvedere	d						19 13						19 24			19 32				19 39				
Erith	d						19 16						19 27			19 35				19 42				
Slade Green	d						19a19			19a36	19 22		19a33			19a39				19a45				19 52
Dartford	a		19 06	19 08	19 16			19 26			19 27	19 33		19 40				19 34	19 48		19 56		19 54	19 57
	d		19 07	19 10							19 28							19 35					19 54	19 58
Stone Crossing	d		19 11	19 14							19 32							19 39						20 02
Greenhithe for Bluewater	d		19 13	19 16							19 34							19 41					20 00	20 04
Swanscombe	d			19 19							19 37							19 44						20 07
Northfleet	d			19 21							19 39							19 46						20 09
Gravesend	d		19a23	19 26							19 43						19 48	19a55					20a09	20 13
Higham	d			19 32							19 49													20 19
Strood	d			19a40							19 55						19 59							20 25
Maidstone West	d																							
Rochester	d										19 58						20 02							20 28
Chatham	d										20 02						20 06							20 31
Gillingham (Kent)	a										20 06						20 10							20 35
Rainham (Kent)	a										20 12						20 15							20 41

NRT DECEMBER 19 EDITION

Table T200-F

Mondays to Fridays
16 December to 15 May

London - Dartford and Gillingham

Station		SE ◇	SE	SE	SE	SE	SE	SE	SE	SE	SE	SE	TL	SE	SE	SE	SE	SE	SE	SE ◇	SE	SE	SE
St Pancras Int'l ⊖	d	19 55																		20 25			
Stratford International ⊖	d	20 02																		20 32			
Ebbsfleet International	d	20 13																		20 43			
London Charing Cross ⊖	d			19 12		19 18		19 24		19 32				19 42		19 48		19 54			20 02		
London Waterloo (East) ⊖	d			19 15		19 21		19 28		19 35				19 45		19 51		19 58			20 05		
London Cannon Street ⊖	d		19 16				19 24		19 35		19 38				19 47		19 54		20 05			20 08	
London Bridge ⊖	d		19 20	19 21		19 27	19 28	19 35	19 39	19 41	19 43		19 48	19 51	19 51	19 57	19 58	20 05	20 09		20 11	20 13	
Deptford	d						19 35		19 45				19 55				20 05		20 15				
Greenwich	d						19 37		19 47				19 57				20 07		20 17				
Maze Hill	d						19 40		19 50				20 00				20 10		20 20				
Westcombe Park	d						19 42		19 52				20 02				20 12		20 22				
London Victoria ⊖	d											19 34											20 04
Denmark Hill	d											19 44											20 14
Peckham Rye	d											19 47											20 17
Nunhead	d				←							19 49											20 19
New Cross ⊖	d		19 26		19 26						19 49				19 57							20 19	
St Johns	d		→		19 28						19 51				19 59							20 21	
Lewisham	d			19 30	19 34			19 45			19 54	19 56		20 00	20 04			20 15				20 24	20 26
Blackheath	d			19 33	19 37			19 48				19 59		20 03	20 07			20 18					20 29
Kidbrooke	d				19 40			19 51				20 02			20 10			20 21					20 32
Eltham	d				19 43			19 55				20 05			20 13			20 24					20 35
Falconwood	d				19 46			19 58				20 08			20 16			20 27					20 38
Welling	d				19 49			20 01				20 11			20 19			20 30					20 41
Bexleyheath	d				19 52			20 05				20 14			20 22			20 33					20 44
Barnehurst	d				19 58			20 08				20 17			20a26			20 36					20 47
Hither Green	d					19 38					19 59					20 07						20 29	
Lee	d					19 41					20 01					20 09						20 31	
Mottingham	d					19 44					20 04					20 12						20 34	
New Eltham	d					19 47				19 55	20 07					20 15					20 25	20 37	
Sidcup	d					19 50				19 58	20 10					20 18					20 28	20 40	
Albany Park	d					19 53					20 13					20 21						20 43	
Bexley	d					19 55				20 02	20 15					20 23					20 32	20 45	
Crayford	d					19 59				20 05	20 21					20 27					20 35	20 51	
Charlton	d			19 38			19 45		19 55		20a49		20 05	20 08			20 15		20 25			21a19	
Woolwich Dockyard	d			19 41			19 48		19 58					20 11			20 18		20 28				
Woolwich Arsenal	d			19 44			19 51		20 01				20 10	20 14			20 21		20 31				
Plumstead	d			19 46			19 53		20 03				20 13	20 16			20 23		20 33				
Abbey Wood	d			19 50			19 56		20 06				20 16	20 20			20 26		20 36				
Belvedere	d			19 53			19 59		20 09					20 23			20 29		20 39				
Erith	d			19 55			20 02		20 12					20 25			20 32		20 42				
Slade Green	d			20 01	20a05		20a06		20a15				20 22	20 31			20a38		20a45				
Dartford	a			20 08		20 06		20 18		20 10		20 24	20 27	20 38		20 34		20 44			20 40		20 54
	d									20 11		20 24	20 28								20 41		20 54
Stone Crossing	d									20 15			20 32								20 45		
Greenhithe for Bluewater	d									20 17		20 30	20 34								20 47		21 00
Swanscombe	d									20 20			20 37								20 50		
Northfleet	d									20 22			20 39								20 52		
Gravesend	d	20 18								20a26		20a39	20 43							20 48	20a56		21a09
Higham	d												20 49										
Strood	d	20 29											20 55							20 59			
Maidstone West	d																						
Rochester	d	20 32											20 58							21 02			
Chatham	d	20 36											21 01							21 06			
Gillingham (Kent)	a	20 40											21 05							21 10			
Rainham (Kent)	a	20 45											21 11							21 15			

Table T200-F

Mondays to Fridays

16 December to 15 May

London - Dartford and Gillingham

		TL	SE	SE	SE	SE	SE	SE	SE ◇	SE	SE	SE	TL		SE	SE	SE	SE	SE	SE	SE ◇	SE	SE	SE	TL
St Pancras Int'l ⊖	d								20 55												21 25				
Stratford International ⊖	d								21 02												21 32				
Ebbsfleet International	d								21 13												21 43				
London Charing Cross ⊖	d		20 12		20 18		20 24			20 32					20 42		20 48		20 54			21 02			
London Waterloo (East) ⊖	d		20 15		20 21		20 28			20 35					20 45		20 51		20 58			21 05			
London Cannon Street ⊖	d			20 17		20 24		20 35			20 38					20 47		20 54		21 05			21 08		
London Bridge ⊖	d	20 18	20 21	20 21	20 27	20 28	20 35	20 39		20 41	20 43		20 48		20 51	20 51	20 57	20 58	21 05	21 09		21 11	21 13		21 18
Deptford	d	20 25				20 35		20 45					20 55					21 05		21 15					21 25
Greenwich	d	20 27				20 37		20 47					20 57					21 07		21 17					21 27
Maze Hill	d	20 30				20 40		20 50					21 00					21 10		21 20					21 30
Westcombe Park	d	20 32				20 42		20 52					21 02					21 12		21 22					21 32
London Victoria ⊖	d											20 34												21 04	
Denmark Hill	d											20 44												21 14	
Peckham Rye	d											20 47												21 17	
Nunhead	d											20 49												21 19	
New Cross ⊖	d			20 27							20 49					20 57							21 19		
St Johns	d			20 29							20 51					20 59							21 21		
Lewisham	d		20 30	20 34			20 45				20 54	20 56			21 00	21 04			21 15				21 24	21 26	
Blackheath	d		20 33	20 37			20 48					20 59			21 03	21 07			21 18					21 29	
Kidbrooke	d			20 40			20 51					21 02				21 10			21 21					21 32	
Eltham	d			20 43			20 54					21 05				21 13			21 24					21 35	
Falconwood	d			20 46			20 57					21 08				21 16			21 27					21 38	
Welling	d			20 49			21 00					21 11				21 19			21 30					21 41	
Bexleyheath	d			20 52			21 03					21 14				21 22			21 33					21 44	
Barnehurst	d			20a56			21 06					21 17				21a26			21 36					21 47	
Hither Green	d				20 37						20 59						21 07						21 29		
Lee	d				20 39						21 01						21 09						21 31		
Mottingham	d				20 42						21 04						21 12						21 34		
New Eltham	d				20 45					20 55	21 07						21 15					21 25	21 37		
Sidcup	d				20 48					20 58	21 10						21 18					21 28	21 40		
Albany Park	d				20 51						21 13						21 21						21 43		
Bexley	d				20 53					21 02	21 15						21 23					21 32	21 45		
Crayford	d				20 57					21 05	21 21						21 27					21 35	21 51		
Charlton	d	20 35	20 38			20 45		20 55			21a49		21 05		21 08			21 15		21 25			22a19		21 35
Woolwich Dockyard	d		20 41			20 48		20 58							21 11			21 18		21 28					
Woolwich Arsenal	d	20 40	20 44			20 51		21 01					21 10		21 14			21 21		21 31					21 40
Plumstead	d	20 43	20 46			20 53		21 03					21 13		21 16			21 23		21 33					21 43
Abbey Wood	d	20 46	20 50			20 56		21 06					21 16		21 20			21 26		21 36					21 46
Belvedere	d		20 53			20 59		21 09							21 23			21 29		21 39					
Erith	d		20 55			21 02		21 12							21 25			21 32		21 42					
Slade Green	d	20 52	21 01			21a06		21a15					21 22		21 31			21a36		21a45					21 52
Dartford	a	20 57	21 08		21 02		21 14			21 10		21 24	21 27		21 38		21 32		21 44			21 40		21 54	21 57
	d	20 58								21 11		21 24	21 28									21 41		21 54	21 58
Stone Crossing	d	21 02								21 15			21 32									21 45			22 02
Greenhithe for Bluewater	d	21 04								21 17		21 30	21 34									21 47		22 00	22 04
Swanscombe	d	21 07								21 20			21 37									21 50			22 07
Northfleet	d	21 09								21 22			21 39									21 52			22 09
Gravesend	d	21 13							21 18	21a26		21a39	21 43								21 48	21a56		22a09	22 13
Higham	d	21 19											21 49												22 19
Strood	d	21 25							21 29				21 55								21 59				22 25
Maidstone West	d																								
Rochester	d	21 28							21 32				21 58								22 02				22 28
Chatham	d	21 31							21 36				22 01								22 06				22 31
Gillingham (Kent)	a	21 35							21 40				22 05								22 10				22 35
Rainham (Kent)	a	21 41							21 45				22 12								22 15				22 41

Table T200-F

Mondays to Fridays

16 December to 15 May

London - Dartford and Gillingham

		SE	SE	SE	SE		SE ◇	SE	SE	SE	TL	SE	SE	SE	SE	SE ◇	SE	SE	SE	TL	SE		SE	SE	SE
St Pancras Int'l ⊖	d						21 55									22 25									
Stratford International ⊖	d						22 02									22 32									
Ebbsfleet International	d						22 13									22 43									
London Charing Cross ⊖	d	21 12	21 18	21 24				21 32				21 42	21 48	21 54			22 02				22 12		22 18	22 24	
London Waterloo (East) ⊖	d	21 15	21 21	21 28				21 35				21 45	21 51	21 58			22 05				22 15		22 21	22 28	
London Cannon Street ⊖	d				21 32				21 38						22 02			22 08							22 32
London Bridge ⊖	d	21 21	21 27	21 35	21 36			21 41	21 43		21 48	21 51	21 57	22 05	22 06		22 11	22 13		22 18	22 21		22 27	22 35	22 36
Deptford	d				21 42						21 55				22 12					22 25					22 42
Greenwich	d				21 44						21 57				22 14					22 27					22 44
Maze Hill	d				21 47						22 00				22 17					22 30					22 47
Westcombe Park	d				21 49						22 02				22 19					22 32					22 49
London Victoria ⊖	d									21 34									22 04						
Denmark Hill	d									21 44									22 14						
Peckham Rye	d									21 47									22 17						
Nunhead	d									21 49									22 19						
New Cross ⊖	d								21 49									22 19							
St Johns	d								21 51									22 21							
Lewisham	d	21 30		21 45					21 54	21 56		22 00		22 15				22 24	22 26		22 30			22 45	
Blackheath	d	21 33		21 48						21 59		22 03		22 18					22 29		22 33			22 48	
Kidbrooke	d			21 51						22 02				22 21					22 32					22 51	
Eltham	d			21 54						22 05				22 24					22 35					22 54	
Falconwood	d			21 57						22 08				22 27					22 38					22 57	
Welling	d			22 00						22 11				22 30					22 41					23 00	
Bexleyheath	d			22 03						22 14				22 33					22 44					23 03	
Barnehurst	d			22 06						22 16				22 36					22 47					23 06	
Hither Green	d		21 37						21 59				22 07					22 29					22 37		
Lee	d		21 39						22 01				22 09					22 31					22 39		
Mottingham	d		21 42						22 04				22 12					22 34					22 42		
New Eltham	d		21 45					21 55	22 07				22 15				22 25	22 37					22 45		
Sidcup	d		21 48					21 58	22 10				22 18				22 28	22 40					22 48		
Albany Park	d		21 51						22 13				22 21					22 43					22 51		
Bexley	d		21 53					22 02	22 15				22 23				22 32	22 45					22 53		
Crayford	d		21 57					22 05	22 21				22 27				22 35	22 51					22 57		
Charlton	d	21 38			21 52				22a49		22 05	22 08			22 22			23a19		22 35	22 38				22 52
Woolwich Dockyard	d	21 41			21 55							22 11			22 25						22 41				22 55
Woolwich Arsenal	d	21 44			21 58						22 10	22 14			22 28					22 40	22 44				22 58
Plumstead	d	21 46			22 00						22 13	22 16			22 30					22 43	22 46				23 00
Abbey Wood	d	21 50			22 03						22 16	22 20			22 33					22 46	22 50				23 03
Belvedere	d	21 53			22 06							22 23			22 36						22 53				23 06
Erith	d	21 55			22 09							22 25			22 39						22 55				23 09
Slade Green	d	22 01			22a13						22 22	22 31			22a43					22 52	23 01				23a13
Dartford	a	22 08	22 02	22 14				22 10		22 23	22 27	22 38	22 32	22 44			22 40		22 54	22 57	23 08		23 02	23 14	
	d							22 11		22 24	22 28						22 41		22 54	22 58					
Stone Crossing	d							22 15			22 32						22 45			23 02					
Greenhithe for Bluewater	d							22 17		22 30	22 34						22 47		23 00	23 04					
Swanscombe	d							22 20			22 37						22 50			23 07					
Northfleet	d							22 22			22 39						22 52			23 09					
Gravesend	d						22 18	22a26		22a39	22 43					22 48	22a56		23a09	23 13					
Higham	d										22 49									23 19					
Strood	d						22 29				22 55					22 59				23 25					
Maidstone West	d																								
Rochester	d						22 32				22 58					23 02				23 28					
Chatham	d						22 36				23 01					23 06				23 31					
Gillingham (Kent)	a						22 40				23 05					23 10				23 35					
Rainham (Kent)	a						22 45				23 11					23 15				23 41					

Table T200-F

Mondays to Fridays

16 December to 15 May

London - Dartford and Gillingham

		SE ◇	SE	SE MT FO	SE W ThO	SE	TL	SE	SE	SE	SE	SE ◇	SE	SE	TL	SE	SE	SE	SE	SE ◇	SE	SE	SE	SE WTh FO	SE MTO	SE
St Pancras Int'l	d	22 55										23 25								23 55						
Stratford International	d	23 02										23 32								00 02						
Ebbsfleet International	d	23 13										23 43								00 13						
London Charing Cross	d		22 32					22 42	22 48	22 54			23 02			23 12	23 20	23 24			23 32		23 42	23 50	23 50	23 52
London Waterloo (East)	d		22 35					22 45	22 51	22 58			23 05			23 15	23 23	23 28			23 35		23 45	23 53	23 53	23 55
London Cannon Street	d			22 38	22 38						23 02								23 32							
London Bridge	d		22 41	22 43	22 43		22 48	22 51	22 57	23 05	23 06		23 11		23 18	23 21	23 29	23 35	23 36		23 41		23 51	23 59	23 59	00 01
Deptford	d						22 55				23 12				23 25				23 42							
Greenwich	d						22 57				23 14				23 27				23 44							
Maze Hill	d						23 00				23 17				23 30				23 47							
Westcombe Park	d						23 02				23 19				23 32				23 49							
London Victoria	d					22 34								23 04								23 34				
Denmark Hill	d					22 44								23 14								23 44				
Peckham Rye	d					22 47								23 17								23 47				
Nunhead	d					22 49								23 19								23 49				
New Cross	d			22 49	22 49																					
St Johns	d			22 51	22 51																					
Lewisham	d			22 54	22 54	22 56		23 00		23 15				23 26		23 30	23 38	23 45				23 56	23 59	00 08	00 08	00 10
Blackheath	d					22 59		23 03		23 18				23 29		23 33		23 48				23 59	00 03			00 13
Kidbrooke	d					23 02				23 21				23 32				23 51				00 02				00 16
Eltham	d					23 05				23 24				23 35				23 54				00 05				00 19
Falconwood	d					23 08				23 27				23 38				23 57				00 08				00 22
Welling	d					23 11				23 30				23 41				23 59				00 11				00 25
Bexleyheath	d					23 14				23 33				23 44				00 03				00 14				00 28
Barnehurst	d					23 17				23 36				23 47				00 06				00 17				00 31
Hither Green	d			22 59	22 59				23 07				23 22				23 43				23 52			00 13	00 13	
Lee	d			23 01	23 01				23 09				23 24				23 45				23 54			00 15	00 15	
Mottingham	d			23 04	23 04				23 12				23 27				23 48				23 57			00 18	00 18	
New Eltham	d		22 55	23 07	23 07				23 15				23 30				23 51				23 59			00 21	00 21	
Sidcup	d		22 58	23 10	23 10				23 18				23 33				23 54				00 03			00 24	00 24	
Albany Park	d			23 13	23 13				23 21				23 36				23 57				00 06			00 27	00 27	
Bexley	d		23 02	23 15	23 15				23 23				23 38				23 59				00 08			00 29	00 29	
Crayford	d		23 05	23 21	23 21				23 27				23 42				00 03				00 12			00 33	00 33	
Charlton	d			23a49			23 05	23 08			23 22				23 35	23 38			23 52				00 08			
Woolwich Dockyard	d							23 11			23 25					23 41			23 55				00 11			
Woolwich Arsenal	d						23 10	23 14			23 28				23 40	23 44			23 58				00 14			
Plumstead	d						23 13	23 16			23 30				23 43	23 46			23 59				00 16			
Abbey Wood	d						23 16	23 20			23 33				23 46	23 50			00 03				00 20			
Belvedere	d							23 23			23 36					23 53			00 06				00 23			
Erith	d							23 25			23 39					23 55			00 09				00 25			
Slade Green	d						23 22	23 31			23 44				23 52	23 59			00 14				00 31			
Dartford	a		23 10		23 28	23 24	23 27	23 38	23 32	23 44	23 51		23 47	23 54	23 57	00 05	00 08	00 14	00 22		00 17	00 24	00 36	00 38	00 38	00 41
	d		23 11			23 24	23 28						23 48		23 58						00 18				00 39	
Stone Crossing	d		23 15				23 32						23 52		00 02						00 22				00 43	
Greenhithe for Bluewater	d		23 17			23 30	23 34						23 54		00 04						00 24				00 45	
Swanscombe	d		23 20				23 37						23 57		00 07						00 27				00s48	
Northfleet	d		23 22				23 39						23 59		00 09						00 29				00s50	
Gravesend	d	23 18	23a26			23a39	23 43					23 48	00a06		00 13					00 18	00a36				00a57	
Higham	d						23 49								00 19											
Strood	d	23 29					23 55					23 59			00 25					00 29						
Maidstone West	d																									
Rochester	d	23 32					23 58					00 02			00 28					00 32						
Chatham	d	23 36					00 02					00 06			00 32					00 36						
Gillingham (Kent)	a	23 40					00 06					00 10			00 36					00 40						
Rainham (Kent)	a	23 45										00 15								00 45						

Table T200-F

Saturdays

21 December to 16 May

London - Dartford and Gillingham

		TL	SE ◇	TL	SE ◇	SE	SE	SE	SE	SE	TL	SE	SE	SE	SE	SE	SE	SE	SE	SE	SE	TL	SE	TL
St Pancras Int'l	d																							
Stratford International	d				00 02																			
Ebbsfleet International	d				00 13																			
London Charing Cross	d															00 02		00 12	00 26		00 32		00 42	
London Waterloo (East)	d															00 05		00 15	00 29		00 35		00 45	
London Cannon Street	d														00 02					00 32				
London Bridge	d													00 01	00 06	00 11		00 21	00 35	00 36	00 41		00 51	
Deptford	d														00 12					00 42				
Greenwich	d														00 14					00 44				
Maze Hill	d														00 17					00 47				
Westcombe Park	d														00 19					00 49				
London Victoria	d																00 04							
Denmark Hill	d																00 14							
Peckham Rye	d																00 17							
Nunhead	d																00 19							
New Cross	d																							
St Johns	d																							
Lewisham	d												00 08	00 10			00 26	00 34	00 45		00 50		01 00	
Blackheath	d											00 03		00 13			00 29	00 37	00 48				01 03	
Kidbrooke	d									00 02				00 16			00 32		00 51					
Eltham	d									00 05				00 19			00 35		00 54					
Falconwood	d									00 08				00 22			00 38		00 57					
Welling	d									00 11				00 25			00 41		01 00					
Bexleyheath	d						00 03			00 14				00 28			00 44		01 03					
Barnehurst	d						00 06			00 17				00 31			00 47		01 06					
Hither Green	d												00 13			00 22					00 55			
Lee	d												00 15			00 24					00 57			
Mottingham	d												00 18			00 27					01 00			
New Eltham	d												00 21			00 30					01 03			
Sidcup	d							00 03					00 24			00 33					01 06			
Albany Park	d							00 06					00 27			00 36					01 09			
Bexley	d							00 08					00 29			00 38					01 11			
Crayford	d					00 03		00 12					00 33			00 42					01 15			
Charlton	d											00 08			00 22			00 41		00 52			01 08	
Woolwich Dockyard	d											00 11			00 25			00 44		00 55			01 11	
Woolwich Arsenal	d											00 14			00 28			00 47		00 58			01 14	
Plumstead	d											00 16			00 30			00 49		01 00			01 16	
Abbey Wood	d								00 03			00 20			00 33			00 53		01 03			01 20	
Belvedere	d								00 06			00 23			00 36			00 56		01 06			01 23	
Erith	d								00 09			00 25			00 39			00 58		01 09			01 25	
Slade Green	d								00 14			00 31			00 44			01 02		01 12			01 30	
Dartford	a					00 08	00 14	00 17	00 22	00 24		00 36	00 38	00 41	00 51	00 47	00 56	01 07	01 16	01 20	01 19		01 37	
	d							00 18			00 28					00 48					01 20	01 24		04 58
Stone Crossing	d			00 02				00 22			00 32					00 52						01s28		05 02
Greenhithe for Bluewater	d			00 04				00 24			00 34					00 54					01s25	01s30		05 04
Swanscombe	d			00 07				00 27			00 37					00s57						01s33		05 07
Northfleet	d			00 09				00 29			00 39					00s59						01s35		05 09
Gravesend	d			00 13	00 18			00a36			00 43					01a07					01a35	01 39		05 13
Higham	d			00 19							00 49											01s45		05 19
Strood	d			00 25	00 29						00 56											01s50		05 25
Maidstone West	d																							
Rochester	d		00 02	00 28	00 32						00 59											01s53		05 28
Chatham	d	00 02	00 06	00 32	00 36						01 03											01s57		05 31
Gillingham (Kent)	a	00 06	00 10	00 36	00 40						01 07											02 02		05 35
Rainham (Kent)	a		00 15		00 45																			05 42

Table T200-F

London - Dartford and Gillingham

Saturdays
21 December to 16 May

		SE	SE	TL	SE	SE	SE	TL	SE	SE	SE	SE	TL	SE	SE	SE	SE	SE	TL	SE	SE ◇	SE	SE
St Pancras Int'l ⊖	d																				07 25		
Stratford International ⊖	d																				07 32		
Ebbsfleet International	d																				07 43		
London Charing Cross ⊖	d	04 50			05 20	05 24			05 50	05 54				06 12	06 18	06 24				06 42		06 48	06 54
London Waterloo (East) ⊖	d	04 53			05 23	05 28			05 53	05 58				06 15	06 21	06 28				06 45		06 51	06 58
London Cannon Street ⊖	d		05 05				05 35				06 05	06 08					06 35	06 38					
London Bridge ⊖	d	04 59	05 09		05 29	05 35	05 39	05 48	05 59	06 05	06 09	06 13	06 18	06 21	06 27	06 35	06 39	06 43	06 48	06 51		06 57	07 05
Deptford	d		05 15				05 45	05 55			06 15		06 25				06 45		06 55				
Greenwich	d		05 17				05 47	05 57			06 17		06 27				06 47		06 57				
Maze Hill	d		05 20				05 50	06 00			06 20		06 30				06 50		07 00				
Westcombe Park	d		05 22				05 52	06 02			06 22		06 32				06 52		07 02				
London Victoria ⊖	d																						
Denmark Hill	d																						
Peckham Rye	d																						
Nunhead	d																						
New Cross ⊖	d											06 19						06 49					
St Johns	d											06 21						06 51					
Lewisham	d	05 10			05 40	05 45			06 10	06 15		06 24		06 30		06 45		06 54		07 00			07 15
Blackheath	d					05 48				06 18				06 33		06 48				07 03			07 18
Kidbrooke	d					05 51				06 21						06 51							07 21
Eltham	d					05 54				06 24						06 54							07 24
Falconwood	d					05 57				06 27						06 57							07 27
Welling	d					06 00				06 30						07 00							07 30
Bexleyheath	d					06 03				06 33						07 03							07 33
Barnehurst	d					06 06				06 36						07 06							07 36
Hither Green	d	05 15			05 45				06 15			06 29			06 37			06 59				07 07	
Lee	d	05 17			05 47				06 17			06 31			06 39			07 01				07 09	
Mottingham	d	05 20			05 50				06 20			06 34			06 42			07 04				07 12	
New Eltham	d	05 23			05 53				06 23			06 37			06 45			07 07				07 15	
Sidcup	d	05 26			05 56				06 26			06 40			06 48			07 10				07 18	
Albany Park	d	05 29			05 59				06 29			06 43			06 51			07 13				07 21	
Bexley	d	05 31			06 01				06 31			06 45			06 53			07 15				07 23	
Crayford	d	05 35			06 05				06 35			06 51			06 57			07 21				07 27	
Charlton	d		05 25				05 55	06 05			06 25	07a19	06 35	06 38			06 55	07a49	07 05	07 08			
Woolwich Dockyard	d		05 28				05 58				06 28			06 41			06 58			07 11			
Woolwich Arsenal	d		05 31				06 01	06 10			06 31		06 40	06 44			07 01		07 10	07 14			
Plumstead	d		05 33				06 03	06 13			06 33		06 43	06 46			07 03		07 13	07 16			
Abbey Wood	d		05 36				06 06	06 16			06 36		06 46	06 50			07 06		07 16	07 20			
Belvedere	d		05 39				06 09				06 39			06 53			07 09			07 23			
Erith	d		05 42				06 12				06 42			06 55			07 12			07 25			
Slade Green	d		05a45				06a15	06 22			06a45		06 52	07 01			07a15		07 22	07 31			
Dartford	a	05 40			06 10	06 14		06 27	06 40	06 44			06 57	07 08	07 02	07 14			07 27	07 38		07 32	07 44
	d	05 41		05 58	06 11			06 28	06 41				06 58		07 04				07 28			07 34	
Stone Crossing	d	05 45		06 02	06 15			06 32	06 45				07 02		07 08				07 32			07 38	
Greenhithe for Bluewater	d	05 47		06 04	06 17			06 34	06 47				07 04		07 11				07 34			07 41	
Swanscombe	d	05 50		06 07	06 20			06 37	06 50				07 07		07 14				07 37			07 44	
Northfleet	d	05 52		06 09	06 22			06 39	06 52				07 09		07 17				07 39			07 47	
Gravesend	d	05a56		06 13	06a26			06 43	06a56				07 13		07a23				07 43		07 48	07a53	
Higham	d			06 19				06 49					07 19						07 49				
Strood	d			06 25				06 55					07 25						07 55		07 59		
Maidstone West	d																						
Rochester	d			06 28				06 58					07 28						07 58		08 02		
Chatham	d			06 31				07 01					07 31						08 01		08 06		
Gillingham (Kent)	a			06 35				07 05					07 35						08 05		08 10		
Rainham (Kent)	a			06 41				07 11					07 41						08 11		08 15		

Table T200-F

London - Dartford and Gillingham

Saturdays
21 December to 16 May

		SE	SE	SE	TL	SE	SE	SE	SE	SE	SE ◇	SE	SE	SE	TL	SE	SE	SE	SE	SE	SE	SE ◇	SE	SE
St Pancras Int'l ⊖	d										07 55											08 25		
Stratford International ⊖	d										08 02											08 32		
Ebbsfleet International	d										08 13											08 43		
London Charing Cross ⊖	d					07 12		07 18	07 24			07 32				07 42		07 48		07 54			08 02	
London Waterloo (East) ⊖	d					07 15		07 21	07 28			07 35				07 45		07 51		07 58			08 05	
London Cannon Street ⊖	d	07 05	07 08				07 17			07 35			07 38				07 47		07 54		08 05			08 08
London Bridge ⊖	d	07 09	07 13		07 18	07 21	07 21	07 27	07 35	07 39		07 41	07 43		07 48	07 51	07 51	07 57	07 58	08 05	08 09		08 11	08 13
Deptford	d	07 15			07 25					07 45					07 55				08 05		08 15			
Greenwich	d	07 17			07 27					07 47					07 57				08 07		08 17			
Maze Hill	d	07 20			07 30					07 50					08 00				08 10		08 20			
Westcombe Park	d	07 22			07 32					07 52					08 02				08 12		08 22			
London Victoria ⊖	d			07 04										07 34										
Denmark Hill	d			07 14										07 44										
Peckham Rye	d			07 17										07 47										
Nunhead	d			07 19										07 49										
New Cross ⊖	d		07 19				07 27						07 49				07 57							08 19
St Johns	d		07 21				07 29						07 51				07 59							08 21
Lewisham	d		07 24	07 26		07 30	07 34		07 45				07 54	07 56		08 00	08 04			08 15				08 24
Blackheath	d			07 29		07 33	07 37		07 48					07 59		08 03	08 07			08 18				
Kidbrooke	d			07 32			07 40		07 51					08 02			08 10			08 21				
Eltham	d			07 35			07 43		07 54					08 05			08 13			08 24				
Falconwood	d			07 38			07 46		07 57					08 08			08 16			08 27				
Welling	d			07 41			07 49		08 00					08 11			08 19			08 30				
Bexleyheath	d			07 44			07 52		08 03					08 14			08 22			08 33				
Barnehurst	d			07 47			07 58		08 06					08 17			08 28			08 36				
Hither Green	d		07 29					07 37					07 59					08 07						08 29
Lee	d		07 31					07 39					08 01					08 09						08 31
Mottingham	d		07 34					07 42					08 04					08 12						08 34
New Eltham	d		07 37					07 45				07 55	08 07					08 15					08 25	08 37
Sidcup	d		07 40					07 48				07 58	08 10					08 18					08 28	08 40
Albany Park	d		07 43					07 51					08 13					08 21						08 43
Bexley	d		07 45					07 53				08 02	08 15					08 23					08 32	08 45
Crayford	d		07 51					07 57				08 05	08 21					08 27					08 35	08 51
Charlton	d	07 25	08a19		07 35	07 38				07 55			08a49		08 05	08 08			08 15		08 25			09a19
Woolwich Dockyard	d	07 28				07 41				07 58						08 11			08 18		08 28			
Woolwich Arsenal	d	07 31			07 40	07 44				08 01					08 10	08 14			08 21		08 31			
Plumstead	d	07 33			07 43	07 46				08 03					08 13	08 16			08 23		08 33			
Abbey Wood	d	07 36			07 46	07 50				08 06					08 16	08 20			08 26		08 36			
Belvedere	d	07 39				07 53				08 09						08 23			08 29		08 39			
Erith	d	07 42				07 55				08 12						08 25			08 32		08 42			
Slade Green	d	07a45			07 52	08 01	08a05			08a15					08 22	08 31	08a35		08a36		08a45			
Dartford	a			07 54	07 57	08 08		08 02	08 14			08 10		08 24	08 27	08 38		08 32		08 44			08 40	
	d			07 54	07 58							08 11		08 24	08 28								08 41	
Stone Crossing	d				08 02							08 15			08 32								08 45	
Greenhithe for Bluewater	d			08 00	08 04							08 17		08 30	08 34								08 47	
Swanscombe	d				08 07							08 20			08 37								08 50	
Northfleet	d				08 09							08 22			08 39								08 52	
Gravesend	d			08a09	08 13						08 18	08a26		08a39	08 43							08 48	08a56	
Higham	d				08 19										08 49									
Strood	d				08 25						08 29				08 55							08 59		
Maidstone West	d																							
Rochester	d				08 28						08 32				08 58							09 02		
Chatham	d				08 31						08 36				09 01							09 06		
Gillingham (Kent)	a				08 35						08 40				09 05							09 10		
Rainham (Kent)	a				08 41						08 45				09 11							09 15		

Table T200-F

Saturdays

21 December to 16 May

London - Dartford and Gillingham

Station		SE	TL	SE	SE	SE	SE	SE		SE	SE ◇	SE	SE	SE	TL	SE	SE	SE	SE	SE	SE	SE ◇	SE	SE
St Pancras Int'l ⊖	d										08 57											09 25		
Stratford International ⊖	d										09 04											09 32		
Ebbsfleet International	d										09 15											09 44		
London Charing Cross ⊖	d			08 12		08 18		08 24				08 32				08 42		08 48		08 54			09 02	
London Waterloo (East) ⊖	d			08 15		08 21		08 28				08 35				08 45		08 51		08 58			09 05	
London Cannon Street ⊖	d				08 17		08 24			08 35			08 38				08 47		08 54		09 05			09 08
London Bridge ⊖	d		08 18	08 21	08 21	08 27	08 28	08 35		08 39		08 41	08 43		08 48	08 51	08 51	08 57	08 58	09 05	09 09		09 11	09 13
Deptford	d		08 25				08 35			08 45					08 55				09 05		09 15			
Greenwich	d		08 27				08 37			08 47					08 57				09 07		09 17			
Maze Hill	d		08 30				08 40			08 50					09 00				09 10		09 20			
Westcombe Park	d		08 32				08 42			08 52					09 02				09 12		09 22			
London Victoria ⊖	d	08 04												08 34										
Denmark Hill	d	08 14												08 44										
Peckham Rye	d	08 17												08 47										
Nunhead	d	08 19												08 49										
New Cross ⊖	d				08 27								08 49				08 57							09 19
St Johns	d				08 29								08 51				08 59							09 21
Lewisham	d	08 26		08 30	08 34			08 45					08 54	08 56		09 00	09 04			09 15				09 24
Blackheath	d	08 29		08 33	08 37			08 48						08 59		09 03	09 07			09 18				
Kidbrooke	d	08 32			08 40			08 51						09 02			09 10			09 21				
Eltham	d	08 35			08 43			08 54						09 05			09 13			09 24				
Falconwood	d	08 38			08 46			08 57						09 08			09 16			09 27				
Welling	d	08 41			08 49			09 00						09 11			09 19			09 30				
Bexleyheath	d	08 44			08 52			09 03						09 14			09 22			09 33				
Barnehurst	d	08 47			08 58			09 06						09 17			09 28			09 36				
Hither Green	d					08 37							08 59					09 07						09 29
Lee	d					08 39							09 01					09 09						09 31
Mottingham	d					08 42							09 04					09 12						09 34
New Eltham	d					08 45						08 55	09 07					09 15					09 25	09 37
Sidcup	d					08 48						08 58	09 10					09 18					09 28	09 40
Albany Park	d					08 51							09 13					09 21						09 43
Bexley	d					08 53						09 02	09 15					09 23					09 32	09 45
Crayford	d					08 57						09 05	09 21					09 27					09 35	09 51
Charlton	d		08 35	08 38			08 45			08 55			09a49		09 05	09 08			09 15		09 25			10a19
Woolwich Dockyard	d			08 41			08 48			08 58						09 11			09 18		09 28			
Woolwich Arsenal	d		08 40	08 44			08 51			09 01					09 10	09 14			09 21		09 31			
Plumstead	d		08 43	08 46			08 53			09 03					09 13	09 16			09 23		09 33			
Abbey Wood	d		08 46	08 50			08 56			09 06					09 16	09 20			09 26		09 36			
Belvedere	d			08 53			08 59			09 09						09 23			09 29		09 39			
Erith	d			08 55			09 02			09 12						09 25			09 32		09 42			
Slade Green	d		08 52	09 01	09a05		09a06			09a15					09 22	09 31	09a35		09a36		09a45			
Dartford	a	08 54	08 57	09 08		09 02		09 14				09 10		09 24	09 27	09 38		09 32		09 44			09 40	
	d	08 54	08 58									09 11		09 24	09 28								09 41	
Stone Crossing	d		09 02									09 15			09 32								09 45	
Greenhithe for Bluewater	d	09 00	09 04									09 17		09 30	09 34								09 47	
Swanscombe	d		09 07									09 20			09 37								09 50	
Northfleet	d		09 09									09 22			09 39								09 52	
Gravesend	d	09a09	09 13								09 19	09a26		09a39	09 43							09 48	09a56	
Higham	d		09 19												09 49									
Strood	d		09 25								09 30				09 55							09 59		
Maidstone West	d																							
Rochester	d		09 28								09 33				09 58							10 02		
Chatham	d		09 31								09 37				10 01							10 06		
Gillingham (Kent)	a		09 35								09 41				10 05							10 10		
Rainham (Kent)	a		09 41								09 46				10 11							10 15		

NRT DECEMBER 19 EDITION

Table T200-F

Saturdays

21 December to 16 May

London - Dartford and Gillingham

Station		SE	TL	SE	SE	SE	SE	SE	SE	SE ◇	SE	SE	SE	TL	SE	SE		SE	SE	SE	SE	SE ◇	SE	SE	SE
St Pancras Int'l ⊖	d									09 55												10 25			
Stratford International ⊖	d									10 02												10 32			
Ebbsfleet International	d									10 13												10 43			
London Charing Cross ⊖	d			09 12		09 18		09 24			09 32				09 42			09 48		09 54			10 02		
London Waterloo (East) ⊖	d			09 15		09 21		09 28			09 35				09 45			09 51		09 58			10 05		
London Cannon Street ⊖	d				09 17		09 24		09 35			09 38				09 47			09 54		10 05			10 08	
London Bridge ⊖	d		09 18	09 21	09 21	09 27	09 28	09 35	09 39		09 41	09 43		09 48	09 51	09 51		09 57	09 58	10 05	10 09		10 11	10 13	
Deptford	d		09 25				09 35		09 45					09 55					10 05		10 15				
Greenwich	d		09 27				09 37		09 47					09 57					10 07		10 17				
Maze Hill	d		09 30				09 40		09 50					10 00					10 10		10 20				
Westcombe Park	d		09 32				09 42		09 52					10 02					10 12		10 22				
London Victoria ⊖	d	09 04											09 34												10 04
Denmark Hill	d	09 14											09 44												10 14
Peckham Rye	d	09 17											09 47												10 17
Nunhead	d	09 19											09 49												10 19
New Cross ⊖	d				09 27							09 49				09 57								10 19	
St Johns	d				09 29							09 51				09 59								10 21	
Lewisham	d	09 26		09 30	09 34			09 45				09 54	09 56		10 00	10 04				10 15				10 24	10 26
Blackheath	d	09 29		09 33	09 37			09 48					09 59		10 03	10 07				10 18					10 29
Kidbrooke	d	09 32			09 40			09 51					10 02			10 10				10 21					10 32
Eltham	d	09 35			09 43			09 54					10 05			10 13				10 24					10 35
Falconwood	d	09 38			09 46			09 57					10 08			10 16				10 27					10 38
Welling	d	09 41			09 49			10 00					10 11			10 19				10 30					10 41
Bexleyheath	d	09 44			09 52			10 03					10 14			10 22				10 33					10 44
Barnehurst	d	09 47			09 58			10 06					10 17			10 28				10 36					10 47
Hither Green	d					09 37						09 59						10 07						10 29	
Lee	d					09 39						10 01						10 09						10 31	
Mottingham	d					09 42						10 04						10 12						10 34	
New Eltham	d					09 45					09 55	10 07						10 15					10 25	10 37	
Sidcup	d					09 48					09 58	10 10						10 18					10 28	10 40	
Albany Park	d					09 51						10 13						10 21						10 43	
Bexley	d					09 53					10 02	10 15						10 23					10 32	10 45	
Crayford	d					09 57					10 05	10 21						10 27					10 35	10 51	
Charlton	d		09 35	09 38			09 45		09 55			10a49		10 05	10 08				10 15		10 25			11a19	
Woolwich Dockyard	d			09 41			09 48		09 58						10 11				10 18		10 28				
Woolwich Arsenal	d		09 40	09 44			09 51		10 01					10 10	10 14				10 21		10 31				
Plumstead	d		09 43	09 46			09 53		10 03					10 13	10 16				10 23		10 33				
Abbey Wood	d		09 46	09 50			09 56		10 06					10 16	10 20				10 26		10 36				
Belvedere	d			09 53			09 59		10 09						10 23				10 29		10 39				
Erith	d			09 55			10 02		10 12						10 25				10 32		10 42				
Slade Green	d		09 52	10 01	10a05		10a06		10a15					10 22	10 31	10a35			10a36		10a45				
Dartford	a	09 54	09 57	10 08		10 02		10 14			10 10		10 24	10 27	10 38			10 32		10 44			10 40		10 54
	d	09 54	09 58								10 11		10 24	10 28									10 41		10 54
Stone Crossing	d		10 02								10 15			10 32									10 45		
Greenhithe for Bluewater	d	10 00	10 04								10 17		10 30	10 34									10 47		11 00
Swanscombe	d		10 07								10 20			10 37									10 50		
Northfleet	d		10 09								10 22			10 39									10 52		
Gravesend	d	10a09	10 13							10 18	10a26		10a39	10 43								10 48	10a56		11a09
Higham	d		10 19											10 49											
Strood	d		10 25							10 29				10 55								10 59			
Maidstone West	d																								
Rochester	d		10 28							10 32				10 58								11 02			
Chatham	d		10 31							10 36				11 01								11 06			
Gillingham (Kent)	a		10 35							10 40				11 05								11 10			
Rainham (Kent)	a		10 41							10 45				11 11								11 15			

Table T200-F

London - Dartford and Gillingham

Saturdays

21 December to 16 May

		TL	SE	SE	SE	SE	SE	SE		SE ◇	SE	SE	SE	TL	SE	SE	SE	SE	SE	SE	SE ◇	SE	SE	SE	
St Pancras Int'l ⊖	d									10 52											11 25				
Stratford International ⊖	d									10 59											11 32				
Ebbsfleet International	d									11 13											11 43				
London Charing Cross ⊖	d		10 12		10 18		10 24				10 32				10 42		10 48		10 54			11 02			
London Waterloo (East) ⊖	d		10 15		10 21		10 28				10 35				10 45		10 51		10 58			11 05			
London Cannon Street ⊖	d			10 17		10 24		10 35				10 38				10 47		10 54		11 05			11 08		
London Bridge ⊖	d	10 18	10 21	10 21	10 27	10 28	10 35	10 39			10 41	10 43		10 48	10 51	10 51	10 57	10 58	11 05	11 09		11 11	11 13		
Deptford	d	10 25				10 35		10 45						10 55				11 05		11 15					
Greenwich	d	10 27				10 37		10 47						10 57				11 07		11 17					
Maze Hill	d	10 30				10 40		10 50						11 00				11 10		11 20					
Westcombe Park	d	10 32				10 42		10 52						11 02				11 12		11 22					
London Victoria ⊖	d												10 34											11 04	
Denmark Hill	d												10 44											11 14	
Peckham Rye	d												10 47											11 17	
Nunhead	d												10 49											11 19	
New Cross ⊖	d			10 27								10 49				10 57							11 19		
St Johns	d			10 29								10 51				10 59							11 21		
Lewisham	d		10 30	10 34			10 45					10 54	10 56		11 00	11 04			11 15				11 24	11 26	
Blackheath	d		10 33	10 37			10 48						10 59		11 03	11 07			11 18					11 29	
Kidbrooke	d			10 40			10 51						11 02			11 10			11 21					11 32	
Eltham	d			10 43			10 54						11 05			11 13			11 24					11 35	
Falconwood	d			10 46			10 57						11 08			11 16			11 27					11 38	
Welling	d			10 49			11 00						11 11			11 19			11 30					11 41	
Bexleyheath	d			10 52			11 03						11 14			11 22			11 33					11 44	
Barnehurst	d			10 58			11 06						11 17			11 28			11 36					11 47	
Hither Green	d				10 37							10 59					11 07						11 29		
Lee	d				10 39							11 01					11 09						11 31		
Mottingham	d				10 42							11 04					11 12						11 34		
New Eltham	d				10 45						10 55	11 07					11 15					11 25	11 37		
Sidcup	d				10 48						10 58	11 10					11 18					11 28	11 40		
Albany Park	d				10 51							11 13					11 21						11 43		
Bexley	d				10 53						11 02	11 15					11 23					11 32	11 45		
Crayford	d				10 57						11 05	11 21					11 27					11 35	11 51		
Charlton	d	10 35	10 38			10 45		10 55				11a49		11 05	11 08			11 15		11 25			12a19		
Woolwich Dockyard	d		10 41			10 48		10 58							11 11			11 18		11 28					
Woolwich Arsenal	d	10 40	10 44			10 51		11 01						11 10	11 14			11 21		11 31					
Plumstead	d	10 43	10 46			10 53		11 03						11 13	11 16			11 23		11 33					
Abbey Wood	d	10 46	10 50			10 56		11 06						11 16	11 20			11 26		11 36					
Belvedere	d		10 53			10 59		11 09							11 23			11 29		11 39					
Erith	d		10 55			11 02		11 12							11 25			11 32		11 42					
Slade Green	d	10 52	11 01	11a05		11a06		11a15						11 22	11 31	11a35		11a36		11a45					
Dartford	a	10 57	11 08		11 02		11 14				11 10		11 24	11 27	11 38		11 32		11 44			11 40		11 54	
	d	10 58									11 11		11 24	11 28								11 41		11 54	
Stone Crossing	d	11 02									11 15			11 32								11 45			
Greenhithe for Bluewater	d	11 04									11 17		11 30	11 34								11 47		12 00	
Swanscombe	d	11 07									11 20			11 37								11 50			
Northfleet	d	11 09									11 22			11 39								11 52			
Gravesend	d	11 13								11 18	11a26		11a39	11 43							11 48	11a56		12a09	
Higham	d	11 19												11 49											
Strood	d	11 25								11 29				11 55							11 59				
Maidstone West	d																								
Rochester	d	11 28								11 32				11 58							12 02				
Chatham	d	11 31								11 36				12 01							12 06				
Gillingham (Kent)	a	11 35								11 40				12 05							12 10				
Rainham (Kent)	a	11 41								11 45				12 11							12 15				

Table T200-F

London - Dartford and Gillingham

Saturdays

21 December to 16 May

		TL	SE	SE	SE	SE	SE	SE	SE ◇	SE	SE	SE	TL	SE	SE	SE		SE	SE	SE	SE ◇	SE	SE	SE	TL
St Pancras Int'l ⊖	d								11 55												12 27				
Stratford International ⊖	d								12 02												12 34				
Ebbsfleet International	d								12 13												12 45				
London Charing Cross ⊖	d		11 12		11 18		11 24			11 32				11 42		11 48			11 54			12 02			
London Waterloo (East) ⊖	d		11 15		11 21		11 28			11 35				11 45		11 51			11 58			12 05			
London Cannon Street ⊖	d			11 17		11 24		11 35			11 38				11 47			11 54		12 05			12 08		
London Bridge ⊖	d	11 18	11 21	11 21	11 27	11 28	11 35	11 39		11 41	11 43		11 48	11 51	11 51	11 57		11 58	12 05	12 09		12 11	12 13		12 18
Deptford	d	11 25				11 35		11 45					11 55					12 05		12 15					12 25
Greenwich	d	11 27				11 37		11 47					11 57					12 07		12 17					12 27
Maze Hill	d	11 30				11 40		11 50					12 00					12 10		12 20					12 30
Westcombe Park	d	11 32				11 42		11 52					12 02					12 12		12 22					12 32
London Victoria ⊖	d											11 34												12 04	
Denmark Hill	d											11 44												12 14	
Peckham Rye	d											11 47												12 17	
Nunhead	d											11 49												12 19	
New Cross ⊖	d			11 27							11 49				11 57								12 19		
St Johns	d			11 29							11 51				11 59								12 21		
Lewisham	d		11 30	11 34			11 45				11 54	11 56		12 00	12 04				12 15				12 24	12 26	
Blackheath	d		11 33	11 37			11 48					11 59		12 03	12 07				12 18					12 29	
Kidbrooke	d			11 40			11 51					12 02			12 10				12 21					12 32	
Eltham	d			11 43			11 54					12 05			12 13				12 24					12 35	
Falconwood	d			11 46			11 57					12 08			12 16				12 27					12 38	
Welling	d			11 49			12 00					12 11			12 19				12 30					12 41	
Bexleyheath	d			11 52			12 03					12 14			12 22				12 33					12 44	
Barnehurst	d			11 58			12 06					12 17			12 28				12 36					12 47	
Hither Green	d				11 37						11 59					12 07							12 29		
Lee	d				11 39						12 01					12 09							12 31		
Mottingham	d				11 42						12 04					12 12							12 34		
New Eltham	d				11 45					11 55	12 07					12 15						12 25	12 37		
Sidcup	d				11 48					11 58	12 10					12 18						12 28	12 40		
Albany Park	d				11 51						12 13					12 21							12 43		
Bexley	d				11 53					12 02	12 15					12 23						12 32	12 45		
Crayford	d				11 57					12 05	12 21					12 27						12 35	12 51		
Charlton	d	11 35	11 38			11 45		11 55			12a49		12 05	12 08				12 15		12 25			13a19		12 35
Woolwich Dockyard	d		11 41			11 48		11 58						12 11				12 18		12 28					
Woolwich Arsenal	d	11 40	11 44			11 51		12 01					12 10	12 14				12 21		12 31					12 40
Plumstead	d	11 43	11 46			11 53		12 03					12 13	12 16				12 23		12 33					12 43
Abbey Wood	d	11 46	11 50			11 56		12 06					12 16	12 20				12 26		12 36					12 46
Belvedere	d		11 53			11 59		12 09						12 23				12 29		12 39					
Erith	d		11 55			12 02		12 12						12 25				12 32		12 42					
Slade Green	d	11 52	12 01	12a05		12a06		12a15					12 22	12 31	12a35			12a36		12a45					12 52
Dartford	a	11 57	12 08		12 02		12 14			12 10		12 24	12 27	12 38		12 32			12 44			12 40		12 54	12 57
	d	11 58								12 11		12 24	12 28									12 41		12 54	12 58
Stone Crossing	d	12 02								12 15			12 32									12 45			13 02
Greenhithe for Bluewater	d	12 04								12 17		12 30	12 34									12 47		13 00	13 04
Swanscombe	d	12 07								12 20			12 37									12 50			13 07
Northfleet	d	12 09								12 22			12 39									12 52			13 09
Gravesend	d	12 13							12 18	12a26		12a39	12 43								12 49	12a56		13a09	13 13
Higham	d	12 19											12 49												13 19
Strood	d	12 25							12 29				12 55								12 59				13 25
Maidstone West	d																								
Rochester	d	12 28							12 32				12 58								13 02				13 28
Chatham	d	12 31							12 36				13 01								13 06				13 31
Gillingham (Kent)	a	12 35							12 40				13 05								13 10				13 35
Rainham (Kent)	a	12 41							12 45				13 11								13 15				13 41

Table T200-F

Saturdays

21 December to 16 May

London - Dartford and Gillingham

		SE	SE	SE	SE	SE	SE	SE ◇		SE	SE	SE	TL	SE	SE	SE	SE	SE	SE	SE ◇	SE	SE	SE	TL	
St Pancras Int'l ⊖	d							12 52												13 25					
Stratford International ⊖	d							12 59												13 32					
Ebbsfleet International	d							13 13												13 43					
London Charing Cross ⊖	d	12 12		12 18		12 24				12 32				12 42		12 48		12 54			13 02				
London Waterloo (East) ⊖	d	12 15		12 21		12 28				12 35				12 45		12 51		12 58			13 05				
London Cannon Street ⊖	d		12 17		12 24		12 35				12 38				12 47		12 54		13 05			13 08			
London Bridge ⊖	d	12 21	12 21	12 27	12 28	12 35	12 39			12 41	12 43		12 48	12 51	12 51	12 57	12 58	13 05	13 09		13 11	13 13		13 18	
Deptford	d				12 35		12 45						12 55				13 05		13 15					13 25	
Greenwich	d				12 37		12 47						12 57				13 07		13 17					13 27	
Maze Hill	d				12 40		12 50						13 00				13 10		13 20					13 30	
Westcombe Park	d				12 42		12 52						13 02				13 12		13 22					13 32	
London Victoria ⊖	d											12 34											13 04		
Denmark Hill	d											12 44											13 14		
Peckham Rye	d											12 47											13 17		
Nunhead	d											12 49											13 19		
New Cross ⊖	d		12 27								12 49				12 57							13 19			
St Johns	d		12 29								12 51				12 59							13 21			
Lewisham	d	12 30	12 34			12 45					12 54	12 56		13 00	13 04			13 15				13 24	13 26		
Blackheath	d	12 33	12 37			12 48						12 59		13 03	13 07			13 18					13 29		
Kidbrooke	d		12 40			12 51						13 02			13 10			13 21					13 32		
Eltham	d		12 43			12 54						13 05			13 13			13 24					13 35		
Falconwood	d		12 46			12 57						13 08			13 16			13 27					13 38		
Welling	d		12 49			13 00						13 11			13 19			13 30					13 41		
Bexleyheath	d		12 52			13 03						13 14			13 22			13 33					13 44		
Barnehurst	d		12 58			13 06						13 17			13 28			13 36					13 47		
Hither Green	d			12 37							12 59					13 07						13 29			
Lee	d			12 39							13 01					13 09						13 31			
Mottingham	d			12 42							13 04					13 12						13 34			
New Eltham	d			12 45						12 55	13 07					13 15					13 25	13 37			
Sidcup	d			12 48						12 58	13 10					13 18					13 28	13 40			
Albany Park	d			12 51							13 13					13 21						13 43			
Bexley	d			12 53						13 02	13 15					13 23					13 32	13 45			
Crayford	d			12 57						13 05	13 21					13 27					13 35	13 51			
Charlton	d	12 38			12 45		12 55				13a49		13 05	13 08			13 15		13 25			14a19		13 35	
Woolwich Dockyard	d	12 41			12 48		12 58							13 11			13 18		13 28						
Woolwich Arsenal	d	12 44			12 51		13 01						13 10	13 14			13 21		13 31					13 40	
Plumstead	d	12 46			12 53		13 03						13 13	13 16			13 23		13 33					13 43	
Abbey Wood	d	12 50			12 56		13 06						13 16	13 20			13 26		13 36					13 46	
Belvedere	d	12 53			12 59		13 09							13 23			13 29		13 39						
Erith	d	12 55			13 02		13 12							13 25			13 32		13 42						
Slade Green	d	13 01	13a05		13a06		13a15						13 22	13 31	13a35		13a36		13a45					13 52	
Dartford	a	13 08		13 02		13 14				13 10		13 24	13 27	13 38		13 32		13 44			13 40		13 54	13 57	
	d									13 11		13 24	13 28								13 41		13 54	13 58	
Stone Crossing	d									13 15			13 32								13 45			14 02	
Greenhithe for Bluewater	d									13 17		13 30	13 34								13 47		14 00	14 04	
Swanscombe	d									13 20			13 37								13 50			14 07	
Northfleet	d									13 22			13 39								13 52			14 09	
Gravesend	d							13 18		13a26		13a39	13 43							13 48	13a56		14a09	14 13	
Higham	d												13 49											14 19	
Strood	d							13 29					13 55							13 59				14 25	
Maidstone West	d																								
Rochester	d							13 32					13 58							14 02				14 28	
Chatham	d							13 36					14 01							14 06				14 31	
Gillingham (Kent)	a							13 40					14 05							14 10				14 35	
Rainham (Kent)	a							13 45					14 11							14 15				14 41	

NRT DECEMBER 19 EDITION

Table T200-F

Saturdays

21 December to 16 May

London - Dartford and Gillingham

		SE	SE	SE	SE	SE	SE	SE ◇	SE	SE	SE	TL	SE	SE	SE	SE		SE	SE	SE ◇	SE	SE	SE	TL	SE
St Pancras Int'l ⊖	d							13 55												14 25					
Stratford International ⊖	d							14 02												14 32					
Ebbsfleet International	d							14 13												14 43					
London Charing Cross ⊖	d	13 12		13 18		13 24			13 32				13 42		13 48			13 54			14 02				14 12
London Waterloo (East) ⊖	d	13 15		13 21		13 28			13 35				13 45		13 51			13 58			14 05				14 15
London Cannon Street ⊖	d		13 17		13 24		13 35			13 38				13 47		13 54			14 05			14 08			
London Bridge ⊖	d	13 21	13 21	13 27	13 28	13 35	13 39		13 41	13 43		13 48	13 51	13 51	13 57	13 58		14 05	14 09		14 11	14 13		14 18	14 21
Deptford	d				13 35		13 45					13 55				14 05			14 15					14 25	
Greenwich	d				13 37		13 47					13 57				14 07			14 17					14 27	
Maze Hill	d				13 40		13 50					14 00				14 10			14 20					14 30	
Westcombe Park	d				13 42		13 52					14 02				14 12			14 22					14 32	
London Victoria ⊖	d										13 34												14 04		
Denmark Hill	d										13 44												14 14		
Peckham Rye	d										13 47												14 17		
Nunhead	d										13 49												14 19		
New Cross ⊖	d		13 27							13 49				13 57								14 19			
St Johns	d		13 29							13 51				13 59								14 21			
Lewisham	d	13 30	13 34			13 45				13 54	13 56		14 00	14 04				14 15				14 24	14 26		14 30
Blackheath	d	13 33	13 37			13 48					13 59		14 03	14 07				14 18					14 29		14 33
Kidbrooke	d		13 40			13 51					14 02			14 10				14 21					14 32		
Eltham	d		13 43			13 54					14 05			14 13				14 24					14 35		
Falconwood	d		13 46			13 57					14 08			14 16				14 27					14 38		
Welling	d		13 49			14 00					14 11			14 19				14 30					14 41		
Bexleyheath	d		13 52			14 03					14 14			14 22				14 33					14 44		
Barnehurst	d		13 58			14 06					14 17			14 28				14 36					14 47		
Hither Green	d			13 37						13 59					14 07							14 31			
Lee	d			13 39						14 01					14 09							14 33			
Mottingham	d			13 42						14 04					14 12							14 36			
New Eltham	d			13 45					13 55	14 07					14 15						14 25	14 39			
Sidcup	d			13 48					13 58	14 10					14 18						14 28	14 42			
Albany Park	d			13 51						14 13					14 21							14 45			
Bexley	d			13 53					14 02	14 15					14 23						14 32	14 47			
Crayford	d			13 57					14 05	14 21					14 27						14 35	14 52			
Charlton	d	13 38			13 45		13 55			14a49		14 05	14 08			14 15			14 25			15a19		14 35	14 38
Woolwich Dockyard	d	13 41			13 48		13 58						14 11			14 18			14 28						14 41
Woolwich Arsenal	d	13 44			13 51		14 01					14 10	14 14			14 21			14 31					14 40	14 44
Plumstead	d	13 46			13 53		14 03					14 13	14 16			14 23			14 33					14 43	14 46
Abbey Wood	d	13 50			13 56		14 06					14 16	14 20			14 26			14 36					14 46	14 50
Belvedere	d	13 53			13 59		14 09						14 23			14 29			14 39						14 53
Erith	d	13 55			14 02		14 12						14 25			14 32			14 42						14 55
Slade Green	d	14 01	14a05		14a06		14a15					14 22	14 31	14a35		14a36			14a45					14 52	15 01
Dartford	a	14 08		14 02		14 14			14 10		14 24	14 27	14 38		14 32			14 44			14 40		14 54	14 57	15 08
	d								14 11		14 24	14 28									14 41		14 54	14 58	
Stone Crossing	d								14 15			14 32									14 45			15 02	
Greenhithe for Bluewater	d								14 17		14 30	14 34									14 47		15 00	15 04	
Swanscombe	d								14 20			14 37									14 50			15 07	
Northfleet	d								14 22			14 39									14 52			15 09	
Gravesend	d							14 18	14a26		14a39	14 43								14 48	14a56		15a09	15 13	
Higham	d											14 49												15 19	
Strood	d							14 29				14 55								14 59				15 25	
Maidstone West	d																								
Rochester	d							14 32				14 58								15 02				15 28	
Chatham	d							14 36				15 01								15 06				15 31	
Gillingham (Kent)	a							14 40				15 05								15 10				15 35	
Rainham (Kent)	a							14 45				15 11								15 15				15 41	

Table T200-F

Saturdays

21 December to 16 May

London - Dartford and Gillingham

		SE	SE	SE	SE	SE	SE ◇	SE		SE	SE	TL	SE	SE	SE	SE	SE	SE	SE ◇	SE	SE	SE	TL	SE	
St Pancras Int'l 15 ⊖	d						14 55												15 25						
Stratford International ⊖ ⛴	d						15 02												15 32						
Ebbsfleet International	d						15 13												15 43						
London Charing Cross 4 ⊖	d		14 18		14 24			14 32					14 42		14 48		14 54			15 02				15 12	
London Waterloo (East) 4 ⊖	d		14 21		14 28			14 35					14 45		14 51		14 58			15 05				15 15	
London Cannon Street 4 ⊖	d	14 17		14 24		14 35				14 38				14 47		14 54		15 05			15 08				
London Bridge 4 ⊖	d	14 21	14 27	14 28	14 35	14 39		14 41		14 43		14 48	14 51	14 51	14 57	14 58	15 05	15 09		15 11	15 13		15 18	15 21	
Deptford	d			14 35		14 45						14 55				15 05		15 15					15 25		
Greenwich 4 ⛴	d			14 37		14 47						14 57				15 07		15 17					15 27		
Maze Hill	d			14 40		14 50						15 00				15 10		15 20					15 30		
Westcombe Park	d			14 42		14 52						15 02				15 12		15 22					15 32		
London Victoria 15 ⊖	d										14 34											15 04			
Denmark Hill 4	d										14 44											15 14			
Peckham Rye 4	d										14 47											15 17			
Nunhead 4	d										14 49											15 19			
New Cross 4 ⊖	d	14 27								14 49				14 57							15 19				
St Johns	d	14 29								14 51				14 59							15 21				
Lewisham 4 ⛴	d	14 34			14 45					14 54	14 56		15 00	15 04			15 15				15 24	15 26		15 30	
Blackheath 4	d	14 37			14 48						14 59		15 03	15 07			15 18					15 29		15 33	
Kidbrooke	d	14 40			14 51						15 02			15 10			15 21					15 32			
Eltham	d	14 43			14 54						15 05			15 13			15 24					15 35			
Falconwood	d	14 46			14 57						15 08			15 16			15 27					15 38			
Welling	d	14 49			15 00						15 11			15 19			15 30					15 41			
Bexleyheath	d	14 52			15 03						15 14			15 22			15 33					15 44			
Barnehurst 4	d	14 58			15 06						15 17			15 28			15 36					15 47			
Hither Green 4	d		14 37							14 59					15 07						15 29				
Lee	d		14 39							15 01					15 09						15 31				
Mottingham	d		14 42							15 04					15 12						15 34				
New Eltham	d		14 45					14 55		15 07					15 15					15 25	15 37				
Sidcup 4	d		14 48					14 58		15 10					15 18					15 28	15 40				
Albany Park	d		14 51							15 13					15 21						15 43				
Bexley	d		14 53					15 02		15 15					15 23					15 32	15 45				
Crayford	d		14 57					15 05		15 21					15 27					15 35	15 51				
Charlton 4	d			14 45		14 55				15a49		15 05	15 08			15 15		15 25			16a19		15 35	15 38	
Woolwich Dockyard	d			14 48		14 58							15 11			15 18		15 28						15 41	
Woolwich Arsenal 4 ⛴	d			14 51		15 01						15 10	15 14			15 21		15 31					15 40	15 44	
Plumstead	d			14 53		15 03						15 13	15 16			15 23		15 33					15 43	15 46	
Abbey Wood	d			14 56		15 06						15 16	15 20			15 26		15 36					15 46	15 50	
Belvedere	d			14 59		15 09							15 23			15 29		15 39						15 53	
Erith	d			15 02		15 12							15 25			15 32		15 42						15 55	
Slade Green 4	d	15a05		15a06		15a15						15 22	15 31	15a35		15a36		15a45					15 52	16 01	
Dartford 4	a		15 02		15 14			15 10			15 24	15 27	15 38		15 32		15 44			15 40		15 54	15 57	16 08	
	d							15 11			15 24	15 28								15 41		15 54	15 58		
Stone Crossing	d							15 15				15 32								15 45			16 02		
Greenhithe for Bluewater	d							15 17			15 30	15 34								15 47		16 00	16 04		
Swanscombe	d							15 20				15 37								15 50			16 07		
Northfleet	d							15 22				15 39								15 52			16 09		
Gravesend 4	d						15 18	15a26			15a39	15 43							15 48	15a56		16a09	16 13		
Higham	d											15 49											16 19		
Strood 4	d						15 29					15 55							15 59				16 25		
Maidstone West	d																								
Rochester 4	d						15 32					15 58							16 02				16 28		
Chatham 4	d						15 36					16 01							16 06				16 31		
Gillingham (Kent) 4	a						15 40					16 05							16 10				16 35		
Rainham (Kent)	a						15 45					16 11							16 15				16 41		

Table T200-F

Saturdays

21 December to 16 May

London - Dartford and Gillingham

		SE	SE	SE	SE	SE	SE ◇	SE	SE	SE	TL	SE	SE	SE	SE	SE		SE	SE ◇	SE	SE	SE	TL	SE	SE
St Pancras Int'l 15 ⊖	d						15 55												16 25						
Stratford International ⊖ ⛴	d						16 02												16 32						
Ebbsfleet International	d						16 13												16 43						
London Charing Cross 4 ⊖	d		15 18		15 24			15 32				15 42		15 48		15 54				16 02				16 12	
London Waterloo (East) 4 ⊖	d		15 21		15 28			15 35				15 45		15 51		15 58				16 05				16 15	
London Cannon Street 4 ⊖	d	15 17		15 24		15 35			15 38				15 47		15 54			16 05			16 08				16 17
London Bridge 4 ⊖	d	15 21	15 27	15 28	15 35	15 39		15 41	15 43		15 48	15 51	15 51	15 57	15 58	16 05		16 09		16 11	16 13		16 18	16 21	16 21
Deptford	d			15 35		15 45					15 55				16 05			16 15					16 25		
Greenwich 4 ⛴	d			15 37		15 47					15 57				16 07			16 17					16 27		
Maze Hill	d			15 40		15 50					16 00				16 10			16 20					16 30		
Westcombe Park	d			15 42		15 52					16 02				16 12			16 22					16 32		
London Victoria 15 ⊖	d									15 34												16 04			
Denmark Hill 4	d									15 44												16 14			
Peckham Rye 4	d									15 47												16 17			
Nunhead 4	d									15 49												16 19			
New Cross 4 ⊖	d	15 27							15 49				15 57								16 19				16 27
St Johns	d	15 29							15 51				15 59								16 21				16 29
Lewisham 4 ⛴	d	15 34			15 45				15 54	15 56		16 00	16 04			16 15					16 24	16 26		16 30	16 34
Blackheath 4	d	15 37			15 48					15 59		16 03	16 07			16 18						16 29		16 33	16 37
Kidbrooke	d	15 40			15 51					16 02			16 10			16 21						16 32			16 40
Eltham	d	15 43			15 54					16 05			16 13			16 24						16 35			16 43
Falconwood	d	15 46			15 57					16 08			16 16			16 27						16 38			16 46
Welling	d	15 49			16 00					16 11			16 19			16 30						16 41			16 49
Bexleyheath	d	15 52			16 03					16 14			16 22			16 33						16 44			16 52
Barnehurst 4	d	15 58			16 06					16 17			16 28			16 36						16 47			16 58
Hither Green 4	d		15 37						15 59					16 07							16 29				
Lee	d		15 39						16 01					16 09							16 31				
Mottingham	d		15 42						16 04					16 12							16 34				
New Eltham	d		15 45					15 55	16 07					16 15						16 25	16 37				
Sidcup 4	d		15 48					15 58	16 10					16 18						16 28	16 40				
Albany Park	d		15 51						16 13					16 21							16 43				
Bexley	d		15 53					16 02	16 15					16 23						16 32	16 45				
Crayford	d		15 57					16 05	16 21					16 27						16 35	16 51				
Charlton 4	d			15 45		15 55			16a49		16 05	16 08			16 15			16 25			17a19		16 35	16 38	
Woolwich Dockyard	d			15 48		15 58						16 11			16 18			16 28						16 41	
Woolwich Arsenal 4 ⛴	d			15 51		16 01					16 10	16 14			16 21			16 31					16 40	16 44	
Plumstead	d			15 53		16 03					16 13	16 16			16 23			16 33					16 43	16 46	
Abbey Wood	d			15 56		16 06					16 16	16 20			16 26			16 36					16 46	16 50	
Belvedere	d			15 59		16 09						16 23			16 29			16 39						16 53	
Erith	d			16 02		16 12						16 25			16 32			16 42						16 55	
Slade Green 4	d	16a05		16a06		16a15					16 22	16 31	16a35		16a36			16a45					16 52	17 01	17a05
Dartford 4	a		16 02		16 14			16 10		16 24	16 27	16 38		16 32		16 44				16 40		16 54	16 57	17 08	
	d							16 11		16 24	16 28									16 41		16 54	16 58		
Stone Crossing	d							16 15			16 32									16 45			17 02		
Greenhithe for Bluewater	d							16 17		16 30	16 34									16 47		17 00	17 04		
Swanscombe	d							16 20			16 37									16 50			17 07		
Northfleet	d							16 22			16 39									16 52			17 09		
Gravesend 4	d						16 18	16a26		16a39	16 43								16 48	16a56		17a09	17 13		
Higham	d										16 49												17 19		
Strood 4	d						16 29				16 55								16 59				17 25		
Maidstone West	d																								
Rochester 4	d						16 32				16 58								17 02				17 28		
Chatham 4	d						16 36				17 01								17 06				17 31		
Gillingham (Kent) 4	a						16 40				17 05								17 10				17 35		
Rainham (Kent)	a						16 45				17 11								17 15				17 41		

Table T200-F

Saturdays

21 December to 16 May

London - Dartford and Gillingham

		SE	SE	SE	SE	SE ◇	SE	SE	SE	TL	SE	SE	SE	SE	SE	SE	SE ◇	SE	SE	SE	TL	SE	SE
St Pancras Int'l 15	d					16 55											17 25						
Stratford International	d					17 02											17 32						
Ebbsfleet International	d					17 13											17 43						
London Charing Cross 4	d	16 18		16 24			16 32				16 42		16 48		16 54			17 02				17 12	
London Waterloo (East) 4	d	16 21		16 28			16 35				16 45		16 51		16 58			17 05				17 15	
London Cannon Street 4	d		16 24		16 35			16 38				16 47		16 54		17 05			17 08				17 17
London Bridge 4	d	16 27	16 28	16 35	16 39		16 41	16 43		16 48	16 51	16 51	16 57	16 58	17 05	17 09		17 11	17 13		17 18	17 21	17 21
Deptford	d		16 35		16 45					16 55				17 05		17 15					17 25		
Greenwich 4	d		16 37		16 47					16 57				17 07		17 17					17 27		
Maze Hill	d		16 40		16 50					17 00				17 10		17 20					17 30		
Westcombe Park	d		16 42		16 52					17 02				17 12		17 22					17 32		
London Victoria 15	d								16 34											17 04			
Denmark Hill 4	d								16 44											17 14			
Peckham Rye 4	d								16 47											17 17			
Nunhead 4	d								16 49											17 19			
New Cross 4	d							16 49				16 57							17 19				17 27
St Johns	d							16 51				16 59							17 21				17 29
Lewisham 4	d			16 45				16 54	16 56		17 00	17 04			17 15				17 24	17 26		17 30	17 34
Blackheath 4	d			16 48					16 59		17 03	17 07			17 18					17 29		17 33	17 37
Kidbrooke	d			16 51					17 02			17 10			17 21					17 32			17 40
Eltham	d			16 54					17 05			17 13			17 24					17 35			17 43
Falconwood	d			16 57					17 08			17 16			17 27					17 38			17 46
Welling	d			17 00					17 11			17 19			17 30					17 41			17 49
Bexleyheath	d			17 03					17 14			17 22			17 33					17 44			17 52
Barnehurst 4	d			17 06					17 17			17 28			17 36					17 47			17 58
Hither Green 4	d	16 37						16 59					17 07						17 29				
Lee	d	16 39						17 01					17 09						17 31				
Mottingham	d	16 42						17 04					17 12						17 34				
New Eltham	d	16 45					16 55	17 07					17 15					17 25	17 37				
Sidcup 4	d	16 48					16 58	17 10					17 18					17 28	17 40				
Albany Park	d	16 51						17 13					17 21						17 43				
Bexley	d	16 53					17 02	17 15					17 23					17 32	17 45				
Crayford	d	16 57					17 05	17 21					17 27					17 35	17 51				
Charlton 4	d		16 45		16 55			17a49		17 05	17 08			17 15		17 25			18a19		17 35	17 38	
Woolwich Dockyard	d		16 48		16 58						17 11			17 18		17 28						17 41	
Woolwich Arsenal 4	d		16 51		17 01					17 10	17 14			17 21		17 31					17 40	17 44	
Plumstead	d		16 53		17 03					17 13	17 16			17 23		17 33					17 43	17 46	
Abbey Wood	d		16 56		17 06					17 16	17 20			17 26		17 36					17 46	17 50	
Belvedere	d		16 59		17 09						17 23			17 29		17 39						17 53	
Erith	d		17 02		17 12						17 25			17 32		17 42						17 55	
Slade Green 4	d		17a06		17a15					17 22	17 31	17a35		17a36		17a45					17 52	18 01	18a05
Dartford 4	a	17 02		17 14			17 10		17 24	17 27	17 38		17 32		17 44			17 40		17 54	17 57	18 08	
	d						17 11		17 24	17 28								17 41		17 54	17 58		
Stone Crossing	d						17 15			17 32								17 45			18 02		
Greenhithe for Bluewater	d						17 17		17 30	17 34								17 47		18 00	18 04		
Swanscombe	d						17 20			17 37								17 50			18 07		
Northfleet	d						17 22			17 39								17 52			18 09		
Gravesend 4	d					17 18	17a26		17a39	17 43							17 48	17a56		18a09	18 13		
Higham	d									17 49											18 19		
Strood 4	d					17 29				17 55							17 59				18 25		
Maidstone West	d																						
Rochester 4	d					17 32				17 58							18 02				18 28		
Chatham 4	d					17 36				18 01							18 06				18 31		
Gillingham (Kent) 4	a					17 40				18 05							18 10				18 35		
Rainham (Kent)	a					17 45				18 11							18 15				18 41		

Table T200-F

Saturdays

21 December to 16 May

London - Dartford and Gillingham

		SE	SE	SE	SE	SE ◇	SE	SE	SE	TL	SE	SE	SE	SE	SE	SE	SE ◇	SE	SE	SE	TL	SE	SE	SE
St Pancras Int'l 15	d					17 55											18 25							
Stratford International	d					18 02											18 32							
Ebbsfleet International	d					18 13											18 43							
London Charing Cross 4	d	17 18		17 24			17 32				17 42		17 48		17 54			18 02				18 12		18 18
London Waterloo (East) 4	d	17 21		17 28			17 35				17 45		17 51		17 58			18 05				18 15		18 21
London Cannon Street 4	d		17 24		17 35			17 38				17 47		17 54		18 05			18 08				18 17	
London Bridge 4	d	17 27	17 28	17 35	17 39		17 41	17 43		17 48	17 51	17 51	17 57	17 58	18 05	18 09		18 11	18 13		18 18	18 21	18 21	18 27
Deptford	d		17 35		17 45					17 55				18 05		18 15					18 25			
Greenwich 4	d		17 37		17 47					17 57				18 07		18 17					18 27			
Maze Hill	d		17 40		17 50					18 00				18 10		18 20					18 30			
Westcombe Park	d		17 42		17 52					18 02				18 12		18 22					18 32			
London Victoria 15	d								17 34											18 04				
Denmark Hill 4	d								17 44											18 14				
Peckham Rye 4	d								17 47											18 17				
Nunhead 4	d								17 49											18 19				
New Cross 4	d							17 49				17 57							18 19				18 27	
St Johns	d							17 51				17 59							18 21				18 29	
Lewisham 4	d			17 45				17 54	17 56		18 00	18 04			18 15				18 24	18 26		18 30	18 34	
Blackheath 4	d			17 48					17 59		18 03	18 07			18 18					18 29		18 33	18 37	
Kidbrooke	d			17 51					18 02			18 10			18 21					18 32			18 40	
Eltham	d			17 54					18 05			18 13			18 24					18 35			18 43	
Falconwood	d			17 57					18 08			18 16			18 27					18 38			18 46	
Welling	d			18 00					18 11			18 19			18 30					18 41			18 49	
Bexleyheath	d			18 03					18 14			18 22			18 33					18 44			18 52	
Barnehurst 4	d			18 06					18 17			18 28			18 36					18 47			18 58	
Hither Green 4	d	17 37						17 59					18 07						18 29					18 37
Lee	d	17 39						18 01					18 09						18 31					18 39
Mottingham	d	17 42						18 04					18 12						18 34					18 42
New Eltham	d	17 45					17 55	18 07					18 15					18 25	18 37					18 45
Sidcup 4	d	17 48					17 58	18 10					18 18					18 28	18 40					18 48
Albany Park	d	17 51						18 13					18 21						18 43					18 51
Bexley	d	17 53					18 02	18 15					18 23					18 32	18 45					18 53
Crayford	d	17 57					18 05	18 21					18 27					18 35	18 51					18 57
Charlton 4	d		17 45		17 55			18a49		18 05	18 08			18 15		18 25			19a19		18 35	18 38		
Woolwich Dockyard	d		17 48		17 58						18 11			18 18		18 28						18 41		
Woolwich Arsenal 4	d		17 51		18 01					18 10	18 14			18 21		18 31					18 40	18 44		
Plumstead	d		17 53		18 03					18 13	18 16			18 23		18 33					18 43	18 46		
Abbey Wood	d		17 56		18 06					18 16	18 20			18 26		18 36					18 46	18 50		
Belvedere	d		17 59		18 09						18 23			18 29		18 39						18 53		
Erith	d		18 02		18 12						18 25			18 32		18 42						18 55		
Slade Green 4	d		18a06		18a15					18 22	18 31	18a35		18a36		18a45					18 52	19 01	19a05	
Dartford 4	a	18 02		18 14			18 10		18 24	18 27	18 38		18 32		18 44			18 40		18 54	18 57	19 08		19 02
	d						18 11		18 24	18 28								18 41		18 54	18 58			
Stone Crossing	d						18 15			18 32								18 45			19 02			
Greenhithe for Bluewater	d						18 17		18 30	18 34								18 47		19 00	19 04			
Swanscombe	d						18 20			18 37								18 50			19 07			
Northfleet	d						18 22			18 39								18 52			19 09			
Gravesend 4	d					18 18	18a26		18a39	18 43							18 48	18a56		19a09	19 13			
Higham	d									18 49											19 19			
Strood 4	d					18 29				18 55							18 59				19 25			
Maidstone West	d																							
Rochester 4	d					18 32				18 58							19 02				19 28			
Chatham 4	d					18 36				19 01							19 06				19 31			
Gillingham (Kent) 4	a					18 40				19 05							19 10				19 35			
Rainham (Kent)	a					18 45				19 11							19 15				19 41			

Table T200-F

Saturdays

21 December to 16 May

London - Dartford and Gillingham

Station	d/a	SE	SE	SE	SE ◇	SE	SE	SE		TL	SE	SE	SE	SE	SE	SE	SE ◇	SE	SE	SE	TL	SE	SE	SE
St Pancras Int'l	d				18 55												19 25							
Stratford International	d				19 02												19 32							
Ebbsfleet International	d				19 13												19 43							
London Charing Cross	d		18 24			18 32					18 42		18 48		18 54			19 02				19 12		19 18
London Waterloo (East)	d		18 28			18 35					18 45		18 51		18 58			19 05				19 15		19 21
London Cannon Street	d	18 24		18 35			18 38					18 47		18 54		19 05			19 08				19 17	
London Bridge	d	18 28	18 35	18 39		18 41	18 43			18 48	18 51	18 51	18 57	18 58	19 05	19 09		19 11	19 13		19 18	19 21	19 21	19 27
Deptford	d	18 35		18 45						18 55				19 05		19 15					19 25			
Greenwich	d	18 37		18 47						18 57				19 07		19 17					19 27			
Maze Hill	d	18 40		18 50						19 00				19 10		19 20					19 30			
Westcombe Park	d	18 42		18 52						19 02				19 12		19 22					19 32			
London Victoria	d							18 34												19 04				
Denmark Hill	d							18 44												19 14				
Peckham Rye	d							18 47												19 17				
Nunhead	d							18 49												19 19				
New Cross	d						18 49					18 57							19 19				19 27	
St Johns	d						18 51					18 59							19 21				19 29	
Lewisham	d		18 45				18 54	18 56			19 00	19 04			19 15				19 24	19 26		19 30	19 34	
Blackheath	d		18 48					18 59			19 03	19 07			19 18					19 29		19 33	19 37	
Kidbrooke	d		18 51					19 02				19 10			19 21					19 32			19 40	
Eltham	d		18 54					19 05				19 13			19 24					19 35			19 43	
Falconwood	d		18 57					19 08				19 16			19 27					19 38			19 46	
Welling	d		19 00					19 11				19 19			19 30					19 41			19 49	
Bexleyheath	d		19 03					19 14				19 22			19 33					19 44			19 52	
Barnehurst	d		19 06					19 17				19a25			19 36					19 47			19a55	
Hither Green	d						18 59						19 07						19 29					19 37
Lee	d						19 01						19 09						19 31					19 39
Mottingham	d						19 04						19 12						19 34					19 42
New Eltham	d					18 55	19 07						19 15					19 25	19 37					19 45
Sidcup	d					18 58	19 10						19 18					19 28	19 40					19 48
Albany Park	d						19 13						19 21						19 43					19 51
Bexley	d					19 02	19 15						19 23					19 32	19 45					19 53
Crayford	d					19 05	19 21						19 27					19 35	19 51					19 57
Charlton	d	18 45		18 55			19a49			19 05	19 08			19 15		19 25			20a19		19 35	19 38		
Woolwich Dockyard	d	18 48		18 58							19 11			19 18		19 28						19 41		
Woolwich Arsenal	d	18 51		19 01						19 10	19 14			19 21		19 31					19 40	19 44		
Plumstead	d	18 53		19 03						19 13	19 16			19 23		19 33					19 43	19 46		
Abbey Wood	d	18 56		19 06						19 16	19 20			19 26		19 36					19 46	19 50		
Belvedere	d	18 59		19 09							19 23			19 29		19 39						19 53		
Erith	d	19 02		19 12							19 25			19 32		19 42						19 55		
Slade Green	d	19a06		19a15						19 22	19 31			19a36		19a45					19 52	20 01		
Dartford	a		19 14			19 10		19 24		19 27	19 38		19 32		19 44			19 40		19 54	19 57	20 08		20 02
	d					19 11		19 24		19 28								19 41		19 54	19 58			
Stone Crossing	d					19 15				19 32								19 45			20 02			
Greenhithe for Bluewater	d					19 17		19 30		19 34								19 47		20 00	20 04			
Swanscombe	d					19 20				19 37								19 50			20 07			
Northfleet	d					19 22				19 39								19 52			20 09			
Gravesend	d				19 18	19a26		19a39		19 43							19 48	19a56		20a09	20 13			
Higham	d									19 49											20 19			
Strood	d				19 29					19 55							19 59				20 25			
Maidstone West	d																							
Rochester	d				19 32					19 58							20 02				20 28			
Chatham	d				19 36					20 01							20 06				20 31			
Gillingham (Kent)	a				19 40					20 05							20 10				20 35			
Rainham (Kent)	a				19 45					20 11							20 15				20 41			

Table T200-F

Saturdays

21 December to 16 May

London - Dartford and Gillingham

Station	d/a	SE	SE	SE	SE ◇	SE	SE	SE	TL	SE	SE	SE	SE	SE	SE	SE ◇		SE	SE	SE	TL	SE	SE	SE	SE
St Pancras Int'l	d				19 55											20 25									
Stratford International	d				20 02											20 32									
Ebbsfleet International	d				20 13											20 43									
London Charing Cross	d		19 24			19 32				19 42		19 48		19 54				20 02				20 12		20 18	20 24
London Waterloo (East)	d		19 28			19 35				19 45		19 51		19 58				20 05				20 15		20 21	20 28
London Cannon Street	d	19 24		19 35			19 38				19 47		19 54		20 05				20 08				20 17		
London Bridge	d	19 28	19 35	19 39		19 41	19 43		19 48	19 51	19 51	19 57	19 58	20 05	20 09			20 11	20 13		20 18	20 21	20 21	20 27	20 35
Deptford	d	19 35		19 45					19 55				20 05		20 15						20 25				
Greenwich	d	19 37		19 47					19 57				20 07		20 17						20 27				
Maze Hill	d	19 40		19 50					20 00				20 10		20 20						20 30				
Westcombe Park	d	19 42		19 52					20 02				20 12		20 22						20 32				
London Victoria	d							19 34												20 04					
Denmark Hill	d							19 44												20 14					
Peckham Rye	d							19 47												20 17					
Nunhead	d							19 49												20 19					
New Cross	d						19 49				19 57								20 19				20 27		
St Johns	d						19 51				19 59								20 21				20 29		
Lewisham	d		19 45				19 54	19 56		20 00	20 04			20 15					20 24	20 26		20 30	20 34		20 45
Blackheath	d		19 48					19 59		20 03	20 07			20 18						20 29		20 33	20 37		20 48
Kidbrooke	d		19 51					20 02			20 10			20 21						20 32			20 40		20 51
Eltham	d		19 54					20 05			20 13			20 24						20 35			20 43		20 54
Falconwood	d		19 57					20 08			20 16			20 27						20 38			20 46		20 57
Welling	d		20 00					20 11			20 19			20 30						20 41			20 49		21 00
Bexleyheath	d		20 03					20 14			20 22			20 33						20 44			20 52		21 03
Barnehurst	d		20 06					20 17			20a25			20 36						20 47			20a55		21 06
Hither Green	d						19 59					20 07							20 29					20 37	
Lee	d						20 01					20 09							20 31					20 39	
Mottingham	d						20 04					20 12							20 34					20 42	
New Eltham	d					19 55	20 07					20 15						20 25	20 37					20 45	
Sidcup	d					19 58	20 10					20 18						20 28	20 40					20 48	
Albany Park	d						20 13					20 21							20 43					20 51	
Bexley	d					20 02	20 15					20 23						20 32	20 45					20 53	
Crayford	d					20 05	20 21					20 27						20 35	20 51					20 57	
Charlton	d	19 45		19 55			20a49		20 05	20 08			20 15		20 25				21a19		20 35	20 38			
Woolwich Dockyard	d	19 48		19 58						20 11			20 18		20 28							20 41			
Woolwich Arsenal	d	19 51		20 01					20 10	20 14			20 21		20 31						20 40	20 44			
Plumstead	d	19 53		20 03					20 13	20 16			20 23		20 33						20 43	20 46			
Abbey Wood	d	19 56		20 06					20 16	20 20			20 26		20 36						20 46	20 50			
Belvedere	d	19 59		20 09						20 23			20 29		20 39							20 53			
Erith	d	20 02		20 12						20 25			20 32		20 42							20 55			
Slade Green	d	20a06		20a15					20 22	20 31			20a36		20a45						20 52	21 01			
Dartford	a		20 14			20 10		20 24	20 27	20 38		20 32		20 44				20 40		20 54	20 57	21 08		21 02	21 14
	d					20 11		20 24	20 28									20 41		20 54	20 58				
Stone Crossing	d					20 15			20 32									20 45			21 02				
Greenhithe for Bluewater	d					20 17		20 30	20 34									20 47		21 00	21 04				
Swanscombe	d					20 20			20 37									20 50			21 07				
Northfleet	d					20 22			20 39									20 52			21 09				
Gravesend	d				20 18	20a26		20a39	20 43							20 48		20a56		21a09	21 13				
Higham	d								20 49												21 19				
Strood	d				20 29				20 55							20 59					21 25				
Maidstone West	d																								
Rochester	d				20 32				20 58							21 02					21 28				
Chatham	d				20 36				21 01							21 06					21 31				
Gillingham (Kent)	a				20 40				21 05							21 10					21 35				
Rainham (Kent)	a				20 45				21 11							21 15					21 41				

Table T200-F

Saturdays

21 December to 16 May

London - Dartford and Gillingham

Station		SE	SE ◇	SE	SE	SE	TL	SE		SE	SE	SE	SE	SE ◇	SE	SE	SE	TL	SE	SE	SE	SE	SE ◇	SE
St Pancras Int'l 15 ⊖	d		20 55											21 25									21 55	
Stratford International ⊖	d		21 02											21 32									22 02	
Ebbsfleet International	d		21 13											21 43									22 13	
London Charing Cross 4 ⊖	d			20 32				20 42			20 48	20 54			21 02				21 12	21 18	21 24			21 32
London Waterloo (East) 4 ⊖	d			20 35				20 45			20 51	20 58			21 05				21 15	21 21	21 28			21 35
London Cannon Street 4 ⊖	d	20 32			20 38					20 47			21 02			21 08						21 32		
London Bridge 4 ⊖	d	20 36		20 41	20 43		20 48	20 51		20 51	20 57	21 05	21 06		21 11	21 13		21 18	21 21	21 27	21 35	21 36		21 41
Deptford	d	20 42					20 55						21 12					21 25				21 42		
Greenwich 4	d	20 44					20 57						21 14					21 27				21 44		
Maze Hill	d	20 47					21 00						21 17					21 30				21 47		
Westcombe Park	d	20 49					21 02						21 19					21 32				21 49		
London Victoria 15 ⊖	d					20 34											21 04							
Denmark Hill 4	d					20 44											21 14							
Peckham Rye 4	d					20 47											21 17							
Nunhead 4	d					20 49											21 19							
New Cross 4 ⊖	d				20 49					20 57						21 19								
St Johns	d				20 51					20 59						21 21								
Lewisham 4	d				20 54	20 56		21 00		21 04		21 15				21 24	21 26		21 30		21 45			
Blackheath 4	d					20 59		21 03		21 07		21 18					21 29		21 33		21 48			
Kidbrooke	d					21 02				21 10		21 21					21 32				21 51			
Eltham	d					21 05				21 13		21 24					21 35				21 54			
Falconwood	d					21 08				21 16		21 27					21 38				21 57			
Welling	d					21 11				21 19		21 30					21 41				22 00			
Bexleyheath	d					21 14				21 22		21 33					21 44				22 03			
Barnehurst 4	d					21 17				21a25		21 36					21 47				22 06			
Hither Green 4	d				20 59						21 07					21 29				21 37				
Lee	d				21 01						21 09					21 31				21 39				
Mottingham	d				21 04						21 12					21 34				21 42				
New Eltham	d			20 55	21 07						21 15				21 25	21 37				21 45				21 55
Sidcup 4	d			20 58	21 10						21 18				21 28	21 40				21 48				21 58
Albany Park	d				21 13						21 21					21 43				21 51				
Bexley	d			21 02	21 15						21 23				21 32	21 45				21 53				22 02
Crayford	d			21 05	21 21						21 27				21 35	21 51				21 57				22 05
Charlton 4	d	20 52			21a49		21 05	21 08					21 22			22a19		21 35	21 38			21 52		
Woolwich Dockyard	d	20 55						21 11					21 25						21 41			21 55		
Woolwich Arsenal 4	d	20 58					21 10	21 14					21 28					21 40	21 44			21 58		
Plumstead	d	21 00					21 13	21 16					21 30					21 43	21 46			22 00		
Abbey Wood	d	21 03					21 16	21 20					21 33					21 46	21 50			22 03		
Belvedere	d	21 06						21 23					21 36						21 53			22 06		
Erith	d	21 09						21 25					21 39						21 55			22 09		
Slade Green 4	d	21a13					21 22	21 31					21a43					21 52	22 01			22a13		
Dartford 4	a			21 10		21 24	21 27	21 38			21 32	21 44			21 40		21 54	21 57	22 08	22 02	22 14			22 10
	d			21 11		21 24	21 28								21 41		21 54	21 58						22 11
Stone Crossing	d			21 15			21 32								21 45			22 02						22 15
Greenhithe for Bluewater	d			21 17		21 30	21 34								21 47		22 00	22 04						22 17
Swanscombe	d			21 20			21 37								21 50			22 07						22 20
Northfleet	d			21 22			21 39								21 52			22 09						22 22
Gravesend 4	d		21 18	21a26		21a39	21 43							21 48	21a56		22a09	22 13					22 18	22a26
Higham	d						21 49											22 19						
Strood 4	d		21 29				21 55							21 59				22 25					22 29	
Maidstone West	d																							
Rochester 4	d		21 32				21 58							22 02				22 28					22 32	
Chatham 4	d		21 36				22 01							22 06				22 31					22 36	
Gillingham (Kent) 4	a		21 40				22 05							22 10				22 35					22 40	
Rainham (Kent)	a		21 45				22 11							22 15				22 41					22 45	

Table T200-F

Saturdays

21 December to 16 May

London - Dartford and Gillingham

Station		SE	SE	TL	SE	SE	SE	SE	SE ◇	SE	SE	SE	TL	SE	SE	SE		SE	SE ◇	SE	SE	SE	TL	SE	SE
St Pancras Int'l 15 ⊖	d								22 25										22 55						
Stratford International ⊖	d								22 32										23 02						
Ebbsfleet International	d								22 43										23 13						
London Charing Cross 4 ⊖	d				21 42	21 48	21 54			22 02				22 12	22 18	22 24				22 32				22 42	22 48
London Waterloo (East) 4 ⊖	d				21 45	21 51	21 58			22 05				22 15	22 21	22 28				22 35				22 45	22 51
London Cannon Street 4 ⊖	d	21 38						22 02			22 08							22 32			22 38				
London Bridge 4 ⊖	d	21 43		21 48	21 51	21 57	22 05	22 06		22 11	22 13		22 18	22 21	22 27	22 35		22 36		22 41	22 43		22 48	22 51	22 57
Deptford	d			21 55				22 12					22 25					22 42					22 55		
Greenwich 4	d			21 57				22 14					22 27					22 44					22 57		
Maze Hill	d			22 00				22 17					22 30					22 47					23 00		
Westcombe Park	d			22 02				22 19					22 32					22 49					23 02		
London Victoria 15 ⊖	d		21 34									22 04										22 34			
Denmark Hill 4	d		21 44									22 14										22 44			
Peckham Rye 4	d		21 47									22 17										22 47			
Nunhead 4	d		21 49									22 19										22 49			
New Cross 4 ⊖	d	21 49									22 19										22 49				
St Johns	d	21 51									22 21										22 51				
Lewisham 4	d	21 54	21 56		22 00		22 15				22 24	22 26		22 30		22 45					22 54	22 56		23 00	
Blackheath 4	d		21 59		22 03		22 18					22 29		22 33		22 48						22 59		23 03	
Kidbrooke	d		22 02				22 21					22 32				22 51						23 02			
Eltham	d		22 05				22 24					22 35				22 54						23 05			
Falconwood	d		22 08				22 27					22 38				22 57						23 08			
Welling	d		22 11				22 30					22 41				23 00						23 11			
Bexleyheath	d		22 14				22 33					22 44				23 03						23 14			
Barnehurst 4	d		22 17				22 36					22 47				23 06						23 17			
Hither Green 4	d	21 59				22 07					22 29				22 37						22 59				23 07
Lee	d	22 01				22 09					22 31				22 39						23 01				23 09
Mottingham	d	22 04				22 12					22 34				22 42						23 04				23 12
New Eltham	d	22 07				22 15				22 25	22 37				22 45					22 55	23 07				23 15
Sidcup 4	d	22 10				22 18				22 28	22 40				22 48					22 58	23 10				23 18
Albany Park	d	22 13				22 21					22 43				22 51						23 13				23 21
Bexley	d	22 15				22 23				22 32	22 45				22 53					23 02	23 15				23 23
Crayford	d	22 21				22 27				22 35	22 51				22 57					23 05	23 21				23 27
Charlton 4	d	22a49		22 05	22 08			22 22			23a19		22 35	22 38				22 52			23a49		23 05	23 08	
Woolwich Dockyard	d				22 11			22 25						22 41				22 55						23 11	
Woolwich Arsenal 4	d			22 10	22 14			22 28					22 40	22 44				22 58					23 10	23 14	
Plumstead	d			22 13	22 16			22 30					22 43	22 46				23 00					23 13	23 16	
Abbey Wood	d			22 16	22 20			22 33					22 46	22 50				23 03					23 16	23 20	
Belvedere	d				22 23			22 36						22 53				23 06						23 23	
Erith	d				22 25			22 39						22 55				23 09						23 25	
Slade Green 4	d			22 22	22 31			22a43					22 52	23 01				23a13					23 22	23 31	
Dartford 4	a		22 24	22 27	22 38	22 32	22 44			22 40		22 54	22 57	23 08	23 02	23 14				23 10		23 24	23 27	23 38	23 32
	d		22 24	22 28						22 41		22 54	22 58							23 11		23 24	23 28		
Stone Crossing	d			22 32						22 45			23 02							23 15			23 32		
Greenhithe for Bluewater	d		22 30	22 34						22 47		23 00	23 04							23 17		23 30	23 34		
Swanscombe	d			22 37						22 50			23 07							23 20			23 37		
Northfleet	d			22 39						22 52			23 09							23 22			23 39		
Gravesend 4	d		22a39	22 43					22 48	22a56		23a09	23 13						23 18	23a26		23a39	23 43		
Higham	d			22 49									23 19										23 49		
Strood 4	d			22 55					22 59				23 25						23 29				23 55		
Maidstone West	d																								
Rochester 4	d			22 58					23 02				23 28						23 32				23 58		
Chatham 4	d			23 01					23 06				23 31						23 36				00 02		
Gillingham (Kent) 4	a			23 05					23 10				23 35						23 40				00 06		
Rainham (Kent)	a			23 11					23 15				23 41						23 45						

Table T200-F

Saturdays

21 December to 16 May

London - Dartford and Gillingham

		SE	SE	SE ◇	SE	TL	SE	SE	SE	SE	SE	SE ◇	SE	SE	SE	SE	SE
St Pancras Int'l	d			23 25								23 55					
Stratford International	d			23 32								00 02					
Ebbsfleet International	d			23 43								00 13					
London Charing Cross	d	22 54			23 02			23 12	23 20	23 24			23 32		23 42	23 50	23 54
London Waterloo (East)	d	22 58			23 05			23 15	23 23	23 28			23 35		23 45	23 53	23 58
London Cannon Street	d		23 02								23 32						
London Bridge	d	23 05	23 06		23 11	23 18		23 21	23 29	23 35	23 36		23 41		23 51	23 59	00 05
Deptford	d		23 12			23 25					23 42						
Greenwich	d		23 14			23 27					23 44						
Maze Hill	d		23 17			23 30					23 47						
Westcombe Park	d		23 19			23 32					23 49						
London Victoria	d						23 04							23 34			
Denmark Hill	d						23 14							23 44			
Peckham Rye	d						23 17							23 47			
Nunhead	d						23 19							23 49			
New Cross	d																
St Johns	d																
Lewisham	d	23 15					23 26	23 30	23 38	23 45				23 56	23 59	00 08	00 15
Blackheath	d	23 18					23 29	23 33		23 48				23 59	00 03		00 18
Kidbrooke	d	23 21					23 32			23 51				00 02			00 21
Eltham	d	23 24					23 35			23 54				00 05			00 24
Falconwood	d	23 27					23 38			23 57				00 08			00 27
Welling	d	23 30					23 41			23 59				00 11			00 30
Bexleyheath	d	23 33					23 44			00 03				00 14			00 33
Barnehurst	d	23 36					23 47			00 06				00 17			00 36
Hither Green	d				23 22				23 43				23 52			00 13	
Lee	d				23 24				23 45				23 54			00 15	
Mottingham	d				23 27				23 48				23 57			00 18	
New Eltham	d				23 30				23 51				23 59			00 21	
Sidcup	d				23 33				23 54				00 03			00 24	
Albany Park	d				23 36				23 57				00 06			00 27	
Bexley	d				23 38				23 59				00 08			00 29	
Crayford	d				23 42				00 03				00 12			00 33	
Charlton	d		23 22			23 35		23 38			23 52				00 08		
Woolwich Dockyard	d		23 25					23 41			23 55				00 11		
Woolwich Arsenal	d		23 28			23 40		23 44			23 58				00 14		
Plumstead	d		23 30			23 43		23 46			23 59				00 16		
Abbey Wood	d		23 33			23 46		23 50			00 03				00 20		
Belvedere	d		23 36					23 53			00 06				00 23		
Erith	d		23 39					23 55			00 09				00 25		
Slade Green	d		23 44			23 52		00 01			00 14				00 31		
Dartford	a	23 44	23 50		23 47	23 57	23 57	00 06	00 08	00 14	00 20		00 18	00 24	00 36	00 38	00 44
	d				23 48	23 58							00 19				
Stone Crossing	d				23 52	00 02							00 23				
Greenhithe for Bluewater	d				23 54	00 04							00 25				
Swanscombe	d				23 57	00 07							00 28				
Northfleet	d				23 59	00 09							00 30				
Gravesend	d			23 48	00a04	00 13						00 18	00a34				
Higham	d					00 19											
Strood	d			23 59		00 25						00 29					
Maidstone West	d																
Rochester	d			00 02		00 28						00 32					
Chatham	d			00 06		00 32						00 36					
Gillingham (Kent)	a			00 10		00 36						00 40					
Rainham (Kent)	a			00 15								00 45					

Table T200-F

Sundays

15 December to 10 May

London - Dartford and Gillingham

		SE A	TL A	SE ◇ A	TL A	SE ◇ A	SE A	SE A	SE A	SE A	SE A	TL	SE A	SE A	SE A	SE	SE	SE	SE	SE	SE	SE	TL	SE
St Pancras Int'l	d																							
Stratford International	d					00 02																		
Ebbsfleet International	d					00 13																		
London Charing Cross	d																00 02		00 12	00 26		00 32		00 42
London Waterloo (East)	d																00 05		00 15	00 29		00 35		00 45
London Cannon Street	d															00 02					00 32			
London Bridge	d														00 05	00 06	00 11		00 21	00 36	00 36	00 41		00 51
Deptford	d															00 12					00 42			
Greenwich	d															00 14					00 44			
Maze Hill	d															00 17					00 47			
Westcombe Park	d															00 19					00 49			
London Victoria	d																	00 04						
Denmark Hill	d																	00 14						
Peckham Rye	d																	00 17						
Nunhead	d																	00 19						
New Cross	d																							
St Johns	d																							
Lewisham	d													00 08	00 15			00 26	00 30	00 45		00 50		01 00
Blackheath	d												00 03		00 18			00 29	00 33	00 48				01 03
Kidbrooke	d										00 02				00 21			00 32		00 51				
Eltham	d										00 05				00 24			00 35		00 54				
Falconwood	d										00 08				00 27			00 38		00 57				
Welling	d										00 11				00 30			00 41		01 00				
Bexleyheath	d							00 03			00 14				00 33			00 44		01 03				
Barnehurst	d							00 06			00 17				00 36			00 47		01 06				
Hither Green	d													00 13			00 22					00 55		
Lee	d													00 15			00 24					00 57		
Mottingham	d													00 18			00 27					01 00		
New Eltham	d													00 21			00 30					01 03		
Sidcup	d								00 03					00 24			00 33					01 06		
Albany Park	d								00 06					00 27			00 36					01 09		
Bexley	d								00 08					00 29			00 38					01 11		
Crayford	d						00 03		00 12					00 33			00 42					01 15		
Charlton	d												00 08			00 22			00 38		00 52			01 08
Woolwich Dockyard	d												00 11			00 25			00 41		00 55			01 11
Woolwich Arsenal	d												00 14			00 28			00 44		00 58			01 14
Plumstead	d												00 16			00 30			00 46		01 00			01 16
Abbey Wood	d									00 03			00 20			00 33			00 50		01 03			01 20
Belvedere	d									00 06			00 23			00 36			00 53		01 06			01 23
Erith	d									00 09			00 25			00 39			00 55		01 09			01 25
Slade Green	d	00 01								00 14			00 31			00 44			01 01		01 12			01 30
Dartford	a	00 06					00 08	00 14	00 18	00 20	00 24		00 36	00 38	00 44	00 49	00 47	00 56	01 07	01 16	01 20	01 19		01 37
	d								00 19			00 28					00 48					01 20	01 24	
Stone Crossing	d				00 02				00 23			00 32					00 52						01s28	
Greenhithe for Bluewater	d				00 04				00 25			00 34					00 54					01s25	01s30	
Swanscombe	d				00 07				00 28			00 37					00s57						01s33	
Northfleet	d				00 09				00 30			00 39					00s59						01s35	
Gravesend	d				00 13	00 18			00a34			00 43					01a05					01a35	01 39	
Higham	d				00 19							00 49											01s45	
Strood	d				00 25	00 29						00 55											01s50	
Maidstone West	d																							
Rochester	d			00 02	00 28	00 32						00 58											01s53	
Chatham	d		00 02	00 06	00 32	00 36						01 02											01s57	
Gillingham (Kent)	a		00 06	00 10	00 36	00 40						01 06											02 02	
Rainham (Kent)	a			00 15		00 45																		

A not 15 December

Table T200-F

Sundays

15 December to 10 May

London - Dartford and Gillingham

Station		SE	TL	SE	SE	TL	SE	SE		SE ◇	SE	SE	SE	SE	TL	SE	SE	SE	SE	SE	TL	SE	SE ◇	SE
St Pancras Int'l 15 ⊖	d									08 25													09 25	
Stratford International ⊖ ⛴	d									08 32													09 32	
Ebbsfleet International	d									08 43													09 44	
London Charing Cross 4 ⊖	d							07 42			07 52					08 12	08 22					08 42		08 52
London Waterloo (East) 4 ⊖	d							07 45			07 55					08 15	08 25					08 45		08 55
London Cannon Street 4 ⊖	d	07 29					07 42					07 59		08 12				08 29		08 42				
London Bridge 4 ⊖	d	07 33					07 46	07 51			08 01	08 03		08 16	08 18	08 21	08 31	08 33		08 46	08 48	08 51		09 01
Deptford	d	07 39										08 09			08 25			08 39			08 55			
Greenwich 4 ⛴	d	07 41										08 11			08 27			08 41			08 57			
Maze Hill	d	07 44										08 14			08 30			08 44			09 00			
Westcombe Park	d	07 46										08 16			08 32			08 46			09 02			
London Victoria 15 ⊖	d				07 34								08 04						08 34					
Denmark Hill 4	d				07 44								08 14						08 44					
Peckham Rye 4	d				07 47								08 17						08 47					
Nunhead 4	d				07 49								08 19						08 49					
New Cross 4 ⊖	d						07 52							08 22						08 52				
St Johns	d						07 54							08 24						08 54				
Lewisham 4 ⛴	d				07 56		07 59	08 01					08 26	08 29		08 31			08 56	08 59		09 01		
Blackheath 4	d				07 59			08 03					08 29			08 33			08 59			09 03		
Kidbrooke	d				08 02								08 32						09 02					
Eltham	d				08 05								08 35						09 05					
Falconwood	d				08 08								08 38						09 08					
Welling	d				08 11								08 41						09 11					
Bexleyheath	d				08 14								08 44						09 14					
Barnehurst 4	d				08 17								08 47						09 17					
Hither Green 4	d						08 04				08 13			08 34			08 43			09 04				09 13
Lee	d						08 06				08 15			08 36			08 45			09 06				09 15
Mottingham	d						08 09				08 18			08 39			08 48			09 09				09 18
New Eltham	d						08 12				08 21			08 42			08 51			09 12				09 21
Sidcup 4	d						08 16				08 24			08 46			08 54			09 16				09 24
Albany Park	d						08 18				08 27			08 48			08 57			09 18				09 27
Bexley	d						08 21				08 29			08 51			08 59			09 21				09 29
Crayford	d						08 25				08 33			08 55			09 03			09 25				09 33
Charlton 4	d	07 49					08a55	08 08				08 19		09a25	08 35	08 38		08 49		09a55	09 05	09 08		
Woolwich Dockyard	d	07 52						08 11				08 22				08 41		08 52				09 11		
Woolwich Arsenal 4 ⛴	d	07 55						08 14				08 25			08 40	08 44		08 55			09 10	09 14		
Plumstead	d	07 57						08 16				08 27			08 43	08 46		08 57			09 13	09 16		
Abbey Wood	d	08 00						08 20				08 30			08 46	08 50		09 00			09 16	09 20		
Belvedere	d	08 03						08 23				08 33				08 53		09 03				09 23		
Erith	d	08 06						08 25				08 36				08 55		09 06				09 25		
Slade Green 4	d	08a09						08 31				08a39			08 52	09 01		09a09			09 22	09 31		
Dartford 4	a				08 24			08 36			08 38		08 54		08 57	09 06	09 08		09 24		09 27	09 36		09 38
	d		07 58	08 09		08 28					08 39				08 58		09 09				09 28			09 39
Stone Crossing	d		08 02	08 13		08 32					08 43				09 02		09 13				09 32			09 43
Greenhithe for Bluewater	d		08 04	08 15		08 34					08 45				09 04		09 15				09 34			09 45
Swanscombe	d		08 07	08 18		08 37					08 48				09 07		09 18				09 37			09 48
Northfleet	d		08 09	08 20		08 39					08 50				09 09		09 20				09 39			09 50
Gravesend 4	d		08 13	08a25		08 43				08 48	08a55				09 13		09a25				09 43		09 48	09a55
Higham	d		08 19			08 49									09 19						09 49			
Strood 4	d		08 25			08 55				08 59					09 25						09 55		09 59	
Maidstone West	d																							
Rochester 4	d		08 28			08 58				09 02					09 28						09 58		10 02	
Chatham 4	d		08 31			09 01				09 06					09 31						10 01		10 06	
Gillingham (Kent) 4	a		08 35			09 05				09 10					09 35						10 05		10 10	
Rainham (Kent)	a		08 41			09 11				09 15					09 41						10 11		10 15	

Table T200-F

Sundays

15 December to 10 May

London - Dartford and Gillingham

Station		SE	SE	SE	TL	SE	SE	SE	SE	SE	TL	SE	SE ◇	SE	SE	SE		SE	TL	SE	SE	SE	SE	SE	TL
St Pancras Int'l 15 ⊖	d												10 27												
Stratford International ⊖ ⛴	d												10 34												
Ebbsfleet International	d												10 45												
London Charing Cross 4 ⊖	d					09 12	09 22					09 42		09 52						10 12	10 22				
London Waterloo (East) 4 ⊖	d					09 15	09 25					09 45		09 55						10 15	10 25				
London Cannon Street 4 ⊖	d	08 59		09 12				09 29		09 42					09 59			10 12				10 29		10 42	
London Bridge 4 ⊖	d	09 03		09 16	09 18	09 21	09 31	09 33		09 46	09 48	09 51		10 01	10 03			10 16	10 18	10 21	10 31	10 33		10 46	10 48
Deptford	d	09 09			09 25			09 39			09 55				10 09				10 25			10 39			10 55
Greenwich 4 ⛴	d	09 11			09 27			09 41			09 57				10 11				10 27			10 41			10 57
Maze Hill	d	09 14			09 30			09 44			10 00				10 14				10 30			10 44			11 00
Westcombe Park	d	09 16			09 32			09 46			10 02				10 16				10 32			10 46			11 02
London Victoria 15 ⊖	d		09 04						09 34							10 04							10 34		
Denmark Hill 4	d		09 14						09 44							10 14							10 44		
Peckham Rye 4	d		09 17						09 47							10 17							10 47		
Nunhead 4	d		09 19						09 49							10 19							10 49		
New Cross 4 ⊖	d			09 22						09 52								10 22						10 52	
St Johns	d			09 24						09 54								10 24						10 54	
Lewisham 4 ⛴	d		09 26	09 29		09 31			09 56	09 59		10 01				10 26		10 29		10 31			10 56	10 59	
Blackheath 4	d		09 29			09 33			09 59			10 03				10 29				10 33			10 59		
Kidbrooke	d		09 32						10 02							10 32							11 02		
Eltham	d		09 35						10 05							10 35							11 05		
Falconwood	d		09 38						10 08							10 38							11 08		
Welling	d		09 41						10 11							10 41							11 11		
Bexleyheath	d		09 44						10 14							10 44							11 14		
Barnehurst 4	d		09 47						10 17							10 47							11 17		
Hither Green 4	d			09 34			09 43			10 04				10 13				10 34			10 43			11 04	
Lee	d			09 36			09 45			10 06				10 15				10 36			10 45			11 06	
Mottingham	d			09 39			09 48			10 09				10 18				10 39			10 48			11 09	
New Eltham	d			09 42			09 51			10 12				10 21				10 42			10 51			11 12	
Sidcup 4	d			09 46			09 54			10 16				10 24				10 46			10 54			11 16	
Albany Park	d			09 48			09 57			10 18				10 27				10 48			10 57			11 18	
Bexley	d			09 51			09 59			10 21				10 29				10 51			10 59			11 21	
Crayford	d			09 55			10 03			10 25				10 33				10 55			11 03			11 25	
Charlton 4	d	09 19		10a25	09 35	09 38		09 49		10a55	10 05	10 08			10 19			11a25	10 35	10 38		10 49		11a55	11 05
Woolwich Dockyard	d	09 22				09 41		09 52				10 11			10 22					10 41		10 52			
Woolwich Arsenal 4 ⛴	d	09 25			09 40	09 44		09 55			10 10	10 14			10 25				10 40	10 44		10 55			11 10
Plumstead	d	09 27			09 43	09 46		09 57			10 13	10 16			10 27				10 43	10 46		10 57			11 13
Abbey Wood	d	09 30			09 46	09 50		10 00			10 16	10 20			10 30				10 46	10 50		11 00			11 16
Belvedere	d	09 33				09 53		10 03				10 23			10 33					10 53		11 03			
Erith	d	09 36				09 55		10 06				10 25			10 36					10 55		11 06			
Slade Green 4	d	09a39			09 52	10 01		10a09			10 22	10 31			10a39				10 52	11 01		11a09			11 22
Dartford 4	a		09 54		09 57	10 06	10 08		10 24		10 27	10 36		10 38		10 54			10 57	11 06	11 08		11 24		11 27
	d				09 58		10 09				10 28			10 39					10 58		11 09				11 28
Stone Crossing	d				10 02		10 13				10 32			10 43					11 02		11 13				11 32
Greenhithe for Bluewater	d				10 04		10 15				10 34			10 45					11 04		11 15				11 34
Swanscombe	d				10 07		10 18				10 37			10 48					11 07		11 18				11 37
Northfleet	d				10 09		10 20				10 39			10 50					11 09		11 20				11 39
Gravesend 4	d				10 13		10a25				10 43		10 49	10a55					11 13		11a25				11 43
Higham	d				10 19						10 49								11 19						11 49
Strood 4	d				10 25						10 55		10 59						11 25						11 55
Maidstone West	d																								
Rochester 4	d				10 28						10 58		11 03						11 28						11 58
Chatham 4	d				10 31						11 01		11 06						11 31						12 01
Gillingham (Kent) 4	a				10 35						11 05		11 10						11 35						12 05
Rainham (Kent)	a				10 41						11 11		11 15						11 41						12 11

Table T200-F

Sundays

15 December to 10 May

London - Dartford and Gillingham

		SE	SE ◇	SE	SE	SE	SE	TL	SE	SE	SE	SE	SE	TL	SE	SE ◇	SE	SE	SE	SE	TL	SE	SE ◇
St Pancras Int'l 15 ⊖	d		11 25													12 27							12 52
Stratford International ⊖	d		11 32													12 34							12 59
Ebbsfleet International	d		11 43													12 45							13 13
London Charing Cross 4 ⊖	d	10 42		10 52					11 12	11 22					11 42		11 52					12 12	
London Waterloo (East) 4 ⊖	d	10 45		10 55					11 15	11 25					11 45		11 55					12 15	
London Cannon Street 4 ⊖	d				10 59		11 12				11 29		11 42					11 59		12 12			
London Bridge 4 ⊖	d	10 51		11 01	11 03		11 16	11 18	11 21	11 31	11 33		11 46	11 48	11 51		12 01	12 03		12 16	12 18	12 21	
Deptford	d				11 09			11 25			11 39			11 55				12 09			12 25		
Greenwich 4	d				11 11			11 27			11 41			11 57				12 11			12 27		
Maze Hill	d				11 14			11 30			11 44			12 00				12 14			12 30		
Westcombe Park	d				11 16			11 32			11 46			12 02				12 16			12 32		
London Victoria 15 ⊖	d					11 04						11 34							12 04				
Denmark Hill 4	d					11 14						11 44							12 14				
Peckham Rye 4	d					11 17						11 47							12 17				
Nunhead 4	d					11 19						11 49							12 19				
New Cross 4 ⊖	d						11 22						11 52							12 22			
St Johns	d						11 24						11 54							12 24			
Lewisham 4	d	11 01				11 26	11 29		11 31			11 56	11 59		12 01				12 26	12 29		12 31	
Blackheath 4	d	11 03				11 29			11 33			11 59			12 03				12 29			12 33	
Kidbrooke	d					11 32						12 02							12 32				
Eltham	d					11 35						12 05							12 35				
Falconwood	d					11 38						12 08							12 38				
Welling	d					11 41						12 11							12 41				
Bexleyheath	d					11 44						12 14							12 44				
Barnehurst 4	d					11 47						12 17							12 47				
Hither Green 4	d			11 13			11 34			11 43			12 04				12 13			12 34			
Lee	d			11 15			11 36			11 45			12 06				12 15			12 36			
Mottingham	d			11 18			11 39			11 48			12 09				12 18			12 39			
New Eltham	d			11 21			11 42			11 51			12 12				12 21			12 42			
Sidcup 4	d			11 24			11 46			11 54			12 16				12 24			12 46			
Albany Park	d			11 27			11 48			11 57			12 18				12 27			12 48			
Bexley	d			11 29			11 51			11 59			12 21				12 29			12 51			
Crayford	d			11 33			11 55			12 03			12 25				12 33			12 55			
Charlton 4	d	11 08			11 19		12a25	11 35	11 38		11 49		12a55	12 05	12 08			12 19		13a25	12 35	12 38	
Woolwich Dockyard	d	11 11			11 22				11 41		11 52				12 11			12 22				12 41	
Woolwich Arsenal 4	d	11 14			11 25			11 40	11 44		11 55			12 10	12 14			12 25			12 40	12 44	
Plumstead	d	11 16			11 27			11 43	11 46		11 57			12 13	12 16			12 27			12 43	12 46	
Abbey Wood	d	11 20			11 30			11 46	11 50		12 00			12 16	12 20			12 30			12 46	12 50	
Belvedere	d	11 23			11 33				11 53		12 03				12 23			12 33				12 53	
Erith	d	11 25			11 36				11 55		12 06				12 25			12 36				12 55	
Slade Green 4	d	11 31			11a39			11 52	12 01		12a09			12 22	12 31			12a39			12 52	13 01	
Dartford 4	a	11 36		11 38		11 54		11 57	12 06	12 08		12 24		12 27	12 36		12 38		12 54		12 57	13 06	
	d			11 39				11 58		12 09				12 28			12 39				12 58		
Stone Crossing	d			11 43				12 02		12 13				12 32			12 43				13 02		
Greenhithe for Bluewater	d			11 45				12 04		12 15				12 34			12 45				13 04		
Swanscombe	d			11 48				12 07		12 18				12 37			12 48				13 07		
Northfleet	d			11 50				12 09		12 20				12 39			12 50				13 09		
Gravesend 4	d		11 48	11a55				12 13		12a25				12 43		12 49	12a55				13 13		13 18
Higham	d							12 19						12 49							13 19		
Strood 4	d		11 59					12 25						12 55		12 59					13 25		13 29
Maidstone West	d																						
Rochester 4	d		12 02					12 28						12 58		13 03					13 28		13 32
Chatham 4	d		12 06					12 31						13 01		13 06					13 31		13 36
Gillingham (Kent) 4	a		12 10					12 35						13 05		13 10					13 35		13 40
Rainham (Kent)	a		12 15					12 41						13 11		13 15					13 41		13 45

Table T200-F

Sundays

15 December to 10 May

London - Dartford and Gillingham

		SE	SE	SE	SE	TL	SE	SE ◇	SE	SE	SE	SE	TL	SE	SE ◇	SE	SE	SE	SE	TL	SE	SE ◇	SE	SE
St Pancras Int'l 15 ⊖	d							13 25							13 55							14 25		
Stratford International ⊖	d							13 32							14 02							14 32		
Ebbsfleet International	d							13 43							14 13							14 43		
London Charing Cross 4 ⊖	d	12 22					12 42		12 52					13 12		13 22					13 42		13 52	
London Waterloo (East) 4 ⊖	d	12 25					12 45		12 55					13 15		13 25					13 45		13 55	
London Cannon Street 4 ⊖	d		12 29		12 42					12 59		13 12					13 29		13 42					13 59
London Bridge 4 ⊖	d	12 31	12 33		12 46	12 48	12 51		13 01	13 03		13 16	13 18	13 21		13 31	13 33		13 46	13 48	13 51		14 01	14 03
Deptford	d		12 39			12 55				13 09			13 25				13 39			13 55				14 09
Greenwich 4	d		12 41			12 57				13 11			13 27				13 41			13 57				14 11
Maze Hill	d		12 44			13 00				13 14			13 30				13 44			14 00				14 14
Westcombe Park	d		12 46			13 02				13 16			13 32				13 46			14 02				14 16
London Victoria 15 ⊖	d			12 34							13 04							13 34						
Denmark Hill 4	d			12 44							13 14							13 44						
Peckham Rye 4	d			12 47							13 17							13 47						
Nunhead 4	d			12 49							13 19							13 49						
New Cross 4 ⊖	d				12 52							13 22							13 52					
St Johns	d				12 54							13 24							13 54					
Lewisham 4	d			12 56	12 59		13 01				13 26	13 29		13 31				13 56	13 59		14 01			
Blackheath 4	d			12 59			13 03				13 29			13 33				13 59			14 03			
Kidbrooke	d			13 02							13 32							14 02						
Eltham	d			13 05							13 35							14 05						
Falconwood	d			13 08							13 38							14 08						
Welling	d			13 11							13 41							14 11						
Bexleyheath	d			13 14							13 44							14 14						
Barnehurst 4	d			13 17							13 47							14 17						
Hither Green 4	d	12 43			13 04				13 13			13 34				13 43			14 04				14 13	
Lee	d	12 45			13 06				13 15			13 36				13 45			14 06				14 15	
Mottingham	d	12 48			13 09				13 18			13 39				13 48			14 09				14 18	
New Eltham	d	12 51			13 12				13 21			13 42				13 51			14 12				14 21	
Sidcup 4	d	12 54			13 16				13 24			13 46				13 54			14 16				14 24	
Albany Park	d	12 57			13 18				13 27			13 48				13 57			14 18				14 27	
Bexley	d	12 59			13 21				13 29			13 51				13 59			14 21				14 29	
Crayford	d	13 03			13 25				13 33			13 55				14 03			14 25				14 33	
Charlton 4	d		12 49		13a55	13 05	13 08			13 19		14a25	13 35	13 38			13 49		14a55	14 05	14 08			14 19
Woolwich Dockyard	d		12 52				13 11			13 22				13 41			13 52				14 11			14 22
Woolwich Arsenal 4	d		12 55			13 10	13 14			13 25			13 40	13 44			13 55			14 10	14 14			14 25
Plumstead	d		12 57			13 13	13 16			13 27			13 43	13 46			13 57			14 13	14 16			14 27
Abbey Wood	d		13 00			13 16	13 20			13 30			13 46	13 50			14 00			14 16	14 20			14 30
Belvedere	d		13 03				13 23			13 33				13 53			14 03				14 23			14 33
Erith	d		13 06				13 25			13 36				13 55			14 06				14 25			14 36
Slade Green 4	d		13a09			13 22	13 31			13a39			13 52	14 01			14a09			14 22	14 31			14a39
Dartford 4	a	13 08		13 24		13 27	13 36		13 38		13 54		13 57	14 06		14 08		14 24		14 27	14 36		14 38	
	d	13 09				13 28			13 39				13 58			14 09				14 28			14 39	
Stone Crossing	d	13 13				13 32			13 43				14 02			14 13				14 32			14 43	
Greenhithe for Bluewater	d	13 15				13 34			13 45				14 04			14 15				14 34			14 45	
Swanscombe	d	13 18				13 37			13 48				14 07			14 18				14 37			14 48	
Northfleet	d	13 20				13 39			13 50				14 09			14 20				14 39			14 50	
Gravesend 4	d	13a25				13 43		13 48	13a55				14 13		14 18	14a25				14 43		14 48	14a55	
Higham	d					13 49							14 19							14 49				
Strood 4	d					13 55		13 59					14 25		14 29					14 55		14 59		
Maidstone West	d																							
Rochester 4	d					13 58		14 02					14 28		14 32					14 58		15 02		
Chatham 4	d					14 01		14 06					14 31		14 36					15 01		15 06		
Gillingham (Kent) 4	a					14 05		14 10					14 35		14 40					15 05		15 10		
Rainham (Kent)	a					14 11		14 15					14 41		14 45					15 11		15 15		

Table T200-F

Sundays

15 December to 10 May

London - Dartford and Gillingham

		SE	SE	TL	SE	SE	SE	SE	SE	SE	TL	SE	SE	SE	SE	SE	SE	TL	SE	SE	SE	SE	SE
						◇							◇							◇			
St Pancras Int'l	d					14 55							15 25							15 55			
Stratford International	d					15 02							15 32							16 02			
Ebbsfleet International	d					15 13							15 43							16 13			
London Charing Cross	d				14 12		14 22					14 42		14 52					15 12		15 22		
London Waterloo (East)	d				14 15		14 25					14 45		14 55					15 15		15 25		
London Cannon Street	d		14 12					14 29		14 42					14 59		15 12					15 29	
London Bridge	d		14 16	14 18	14 21		14 31	14 33		14 46	14 48	14 51		15 01	15 03		15 16	15 18	15 21		15 31	15 33	
Deptford	d			14 25				14 39			14 55				15 09			15 25				15 39	
Greenwich	d			14 27				14 41			14 57				15 11			15 27				15 41	
Maze Hill	d			14 30				14 44			15 00				15 14			15 30				15 44	
Westcombe Park	d			14 32				14 46			15 02				15 16			15 32				15 46	
London Victoria	d	14 04							14 34							15 04							15 34
Denmark Hill	d	14 14							14 44							15 14							15 44
Peckham Rye	d	14 17							14 47							15 17							15 47
Nunhead	d	14 19							14 49							15 19							15 49
New Cross	d		14 22							14 52							15 22						
St Johns	d		14 24							14 54							15 24						
Lewisham	d	14 26	14 29		14 31				14 56	14 59		15 01				15 26	15 29		15 31				15 56
Blackheath	d	14 29			14 33				14 59			15 03				15 29			15 33				15 59
Kidbrooke	d	14 32							15 02							15 32							16 02
Eltham	d	14 35							15 05							15 35							16 05
Falconwood	d	14 38							15 08							15 38							16 08
Welling	d	14 41							15 11							15 41							16 11
Bexleyheath	d	14 44							15 14							15 44							16 14
Barnehurst	d	14 47							15 17							15 47							16 17
Hither Green	d		14 34				14 43			15 04				15 13			15 34				15 43		
Lee	d		14 36				14 45			15 06				15 15			15 36				15 45		
Mottingham	d		14 39				14 48			15 09				15 18			15 39				15 48		
New Eltham	d		14 42				14 51			15 12				15 21			15 42				15 51		
Sidcup	d		14 46				14 54			15 16				15 24			15 46				15 54		
Albany Park	d		14 48				14 57			15 18				15 27			15 48				15 57		
Bexley	d		14 51				14 59			15 21				15 29			15 51				15 59		
Crayford	d		14 55				15 03			15 25				15 33			15 55				16 03		
Charlton	d		15a25	14 35	14 38			14 49		15a55	15 05	15 08			15 19		16a25	15 35	15 38			15 49	
Woolwich Dockyard	d				14 41			14 52				15 11			15 22				15 41			15 52	
Woolwich Arsenal	d			14 40	14 44			14 55			15 10	15 14			15 25			15 40	15 44			15 55	
Plumstead	d			14 43	14 46			14 57			15 13	15 16			15 27			15 43	15 46			15 57	
Abbey Wood	d			14 46	14 50			15 00			15 16	15 20			15 30			15 46	15 50			16 00	
Belvedere	d				14 53			15 03				15 23			15 33				15 53			16 03	
Erith	d				14 55			15 06				15 25			15 36				15 55			16 06	
Slade Green	d			14 52	15 01			15a09			15 22	15 31			15a39			15 52	16 01			16a09	
Dartford	a	14 54		14 57	15 06		15 08		15 24		15 27	15 36		15 38		15 54		15 57	16 06		16 08		16 24
	d			14 58			15 09				15 28			15 39				15 58			16 09		
Stone Crossing	d			15 02			15 13				15 32			15 43				16 02			16 13		
Greenhithe for Bluewater	d			15 04			15 15				15 34			15 45				16 04			16 15		
Swanscombe	d			15 07			15 18				15 37			15 48				16 07			16 18		
Northfleet	d			15 09			15 20				15 39			15 50				16 09			16 20		
Gravesend	d			15 13		15 18	15a25				15 43		15 48	15a55				16 13		16 18	16a25		
Higham	d			15 19							15 49							16 19					
Strood	d			15 25		15 29					15 55		15 59					16 25		16 29			
Maidstone West	d																						
Rochester	d			15 28		15 32					15 58		16 02					16 28		16 32			
Chatham	d			15 31		15 36					16 01		16 06					16 31		16 36			
Gillingham (Kent)	a			15 35		15 40					16 05		16 10					16 35		16 40			
Rainham (Kent)	a			15 41		15 45					16 11		16 15					16 41		16 45			

Table T200-F

Sundays

15 December to 10 May

London - Dartford and Gillingham

		SE	TL	SE	SE	SE	SE	SE	SE	TL	SE	SE	SE	SE	SE	SE	TL	SE	SE	SE	SE	SE	SE	TL
					◇							◇							◇					
St Pancras Int'l	d				16 25							16 55							17 25					
Stratford International	d				16 32							17 02							17 32					
Ebbsfleet International	d				16 43							17 13							17 43					
London Charing Cross	d			15 42		15 52					16 12		16 22					16 42		16 52				
London Waterloo (East)	d			15 45		15 55					16 15		16 25					16 45		16 55				
London Cannon Street	d	15 42					15 59		16 12					16 29		16 42					16 59		17 12	
London Bridge	d	15 46	15 48	15 51		16 01	16 03		16 16	16 18	16 21		16 31	16 33		16 46	16 48	16 51		17 01	17 03		17 16	17 18
Deptford	d		15 55				16 09			16 25				16 39			16 55				17 09			17 25
Greenwich	d		15 57				16 11			16 27				16 41			16 57				17 11			17 27
Maze Hill	d		16 00				16 14			16 30				16 44			17 00				17 14			17 30
Westcombe Park	d		16 02				16 16			16 32				16 46			17 02				17 16			17 32
London Victoria	d							16 04							16 34							17 04		
Denmark Hill	d							16 14							16 44							17 14		
Peckham Rye	d							16 17							16 47							17 17		
Nunhead	d							16 19							16 49							17 19		
New Cross	d	15 52							16 22							16 52							17 22	
St Johns	d	15 54							16 24							16 54							17 24	
Lewisham	d	15 59		16 01				16 26	16 29		16 31				16 56	16 59		17 01				17 26	17 29	
Blackheath	d			16 03				16 29			16 33				16 59			17 03				17 29		
Kidbrooke	d							16 32							17 02							17 32		
Eltham	d							16 35							17 05							17 35		
Falconwood	d							16 38							17 08							17 38		
Welling	d							16 41							17 11							17 41		
Bexleyheath	d							16 44							17 14							17 44		
Barnehurst	d							16 47							17 17							17 47		
Hither Green	d	16 04				16 13			16 34				16 43			17 04				17 13			17 34	
Lee	d	16 06				16 15			16 36				16 45			17 06				17 15			17 36	
Mottingham	d	16 09				16 18			16 39				16 48			17 09				17 18			17 39	
New Eltham	d	16 12				16 21			16 42				16 51			17 12				17 21			17 42	
Sidcup	d	16 16				16 24			16 46				16 54			17 16				17 24			17 46	
Albany Park	d	16 18				16 27			16 48				16 57			17 18				17 27			17 48	
Bexley	d	16 21				16 29			16 51				16 59			17 21				17 29			17 51	
Crayford	d	16 25				16 33			16 55				17 03			17 25				17 33			17 55	
Charlton	d	16a55	16 05	16 08			16 19		17a25	16 35	16 38			16 49		17a55	17 05	17 08			17 19		18a25	17 35
Woolwich Dockyard	d			16 11			16 22				16 41			16 52				17 11			17 22			
Woolwich Arsenal	d		16 10	16 14			16 25			16 40	16 44			16 55			17 10	17 14			17 25			17 40
Plumstead	d		16 13	16 16			16 27			16 43	16 46			16 57			17 13	17 16			17 27			17 43
Abbey Wood	d		16 16	16 20			16 30			16 46	16 50			17 00			17 16	17 20			17 30			17 46
Belvedere	d			16 23			16 33				16 53			17 03				17 23			17 33			
Erith	d			16 25			16 36				16 55			17 06				17 25			17 36			
Slade Green	d		16 22	16 31			16a39			16 52	17 01			17a09			17 22	17 31			17a39			17 52
Dartford	a		16 27	16 36		16 38		16 54		16 57	17 06		17 08		17 24		17 27	17 36		17 38		17 54		17 57
	d		16 28			16 39				16 58			17 09				17 28			17 39				17 58
Stone Crossing	d		16 32			16 43				17 02			17 13				17 32			17 43				18 02
Greenhithe for Bluewater	d		16 34			16 45				17 04			17 15				17 34			17 45				18 04
Swanscombe	d		16 37			16 48				17 07			17 18				17 37			17 48				18 07
Northfleet	d		16 39			16 50				17 09			17 20				17 39			17 50				18 09
Gravesend	d		16 43		16 48	16a55				17 13		17 18	17a25				17 43		17 48	17a55				18 13
Higham	d		16 49							17 19							17 49							18 19
Strood	d		16 55		16 59					17 25		17 29					17 55		17 59					18 25
Maidstone West	d																							
Rochester	d		16 58		17 02					17 28		17 32					17 58		18 02					18 28
Chatham	d		17 01		17 06					17 31		17 36					18 01		18 06					18 31
Gillingham (Kent)	a		17 05		17 10					17 35		17 40					18 05		18 10					18 35
Rainham (Kent)	a		17 11		17 15					17 41		17 45					18 11		18 15					18 41

Table T200-F

Sundays
15 December to 10 May

London - Dartford and Gillingham

		SE	SE ◇	SE	SE	SE	SE	TL	SE	SE ◇	SE	SE	SE	SE	TL	SE	SE ◇	SE	SE	SE	SE	TL	SE
St Pancras Int'l 15 ⊖	d		17 57							18 25							18 55						
Stratford International ⊖ ⛴	d		18 04							18 32							19 02						
Ebbsfleet International	d		18 15							18 43							19 13						
London Charing Cross 4 ⊖	d	17 12		17 22					17 42		17 52					18 12		18 22					18 42
London Waterloo (East) 4 ⊖	d	17 15		17 25					17 45		17 55					18 15		18 25					18 45
London Cannon Street 4 ⊖	d				17 29		17 42					17 59		18 12					18 29		18 42		
London Bridge 4 ⊖	d	17 21		17 31	17 33		17 46	17 48	17 51		18 01	18 03		18 16	18 18	18 21		18 31	18 33		18 46	18 48	18 51
Deptford	d				17 39			17 55				18 09			18 25				18 39			18 55	
Greenwich 4 ⛴	d				17 41			17 57				18 11			18 27				18 41			18 57	
Maze Hill	d				17 44			18 00				18 14			18 30				18 44			19 00	
Westcombe Park	d				17 46			18 02				18 16			18 32				18 46			19 02	
London Victoria 15 ⊖	d					17 34							18 04							18 34			
Denmark Hill 4	d					17 44							18 14							18 44			
Peckham Rye 4	d					17 47							18 17							18 47			
Nunhead 4	d					17 49							18 19							18 49			
New Cross 4 ⊖	d						17 52							18 22							18 52		
St Johns	d						17 54							18 24							18 54		
Lewisham 4 ⛴	d	17 31				17 56	17 59		18 01				18 26	18 29		18 31				18 56	18 59		19 01
Blackheath 4	d	17 33				17 59			18 03				18 29			18 33				18 59			19 03
Kidbrooke	d					18 02							18 32							19 02			
Eltham	d					18 05							18 35							19 05			
Falconwood	d					18 08							18 38							19 08			
Welling	d					18 11							18 41							19 11			
Bexleyheath	d					18 14							18 44							19 14			
Barnehurst 4	d					18 17							18 47							19 17			
Hither Green 4	d			17 43			18 04				18 13			18 34				18 43			19 04		
Lee	d			17 45			18 06				18 15			18 36				18 45			19 06		
Mottingham	d			17 48			18 09				18 18			18 39				18 48			19 09		
New Eltham	d			17 51			18 12				18 21			18 42				18 51			19 12		
Sidcup 4	d			17 54			18 16				18 24			18 46				18 54			19 16		
Albany Park	d			17 57			18 18				18 27			18 48				18 57			19 18		
Bexley	d			17 59			18 21				18 29			18 51				18 59			19 21		
Crayford	d			18 03			18 25				18 33			18 55				19 03			19 25		
Charlton 4	d	17 38			17 49		18a55	18 05	18 08			18 19		19a25	18 35	18 38			18 49		19a55	19 05	19 08
Woolwich Dockyard	d	17 41			17 52				18 11			18 22				18 41			18 52				19 11
Woolwich Arsenal 4 ⛴	d	17 44			17 55			18 10	18 14			18 25			18 40	18 44			18 55			19 10	19 14
Plumstead	d	17 46			17 57			18 13	18 16			18 27			18 43	18 46			18 57			19 13	19 16
Abbey Wood	d	17 50			18 00			18 16	18 20			18 30			18 46	18 50			19 00			19 16	19 20
Belvedere	d	17 53			18 03				18 23			18 33				18 53			19 03				19 23
Erith	d	17 55			18 06				18 25			18 36				18 55			19 06				19 25
Slade Green 4	d	18 01			18a09			18 22	18 31			18a39			18 52	19 01			19a09			19 22	19 31
Dartford 4	a	18 06		18 08		18 24		18 27	18 36		18 38		18 54		18 57	19 06		19 08		19 24		19 27	19 36
	d			18 09				18 28			18 39				18 58			19 09				19 28	
Stone Crossing	d			18 13				18 32			18 43				19 02			19 13				19 32	
Greenhithe for Bluewater	d			18 15				18 34			18 45				19 04			19 15				19 34	
Swanscombe	d			18 18				18 37			18 48				19 07			19 18				19 37	
Northfleet	d			18 20				18 39			18 50				19 09			19 20				19 39	
Gravesend 4	d		18 19	18a25				18 43		18 48	18a55				19 13		19 18	19a25				19 43	
Higham	d							18 49							19 19							19 49	
Strood 4	d		18 29					18 55		18 59					19 25		19 29					19 55	
Maidstone West	d																						
Rochester 4	d		18 32					18 58		19 02					19 28		19 32					19 58	
Chatham 4	d		18 36					19 01		19 06					19 31		19 36					20 01	
Gillingham (Kent) 4	a		18 40					19 05		19 10					19 35		19 40					20 05	
Rainham (Kent)	a		18 45					19 11		19 15					19 41		19 45					20 11	

Table T200-F

Sundays
15 December to 10 May

London - Dartford and Gillingham

		SE ◇	SE	SE	SE	SE	TL	SE	SE ◇	SE	SE	SE	SE	TL	SE	SE ◇	SE	SE	SE	SE	TL	SE	SE ◇	SE
St Pancras Int'l 15 ⊖	d	19 25							19 55							20 25							20 55	
Stratford International ⊖ ⛴	d	19 32							20 02							20 32							21 02	
Ebbsfleet International	d	19 43							20 13							20 43							21 13	
London Charing Cross 4 ⊖	d		18 52					19 12		19 22					19 42		19 52					20 12		20 22
London Waterloo (East) 4 ⊖	d		18 55					19 15		19 25					19 45		19 55					20 15		20 25
London Cannon Street 4 ⊖	d			18 59		19 12					19 29		19 42					19 59		20 12				
London Bridge 4 ⊖	d		19 01	19 03		19 16	19 18	19 21		19 31	19 33		19 46	19 48	19 51		20 01	20 03		20 16	20 18	20 21		20 31
Deptford	d			19 09			19 25				19 39			19 55				20 09			20 25			
Greenwich 4 ⛴	d			19 11			19 27				19 41			19 57				20 11			20 27			
Maze Hill	d			19 14			19 30				19 44			20 00				20 14			20 30			
Westcombe Park	d			19 16			19 32				19 46			20 02				20 16			20 32			
London Victoria 15 ⊖	d				19 04							19 34							20 04					
Denmark Hill 4	d				19 14							19 44							20 14					
Peckham Rye 4	d				19 17							19 47							20 17					
Nunhead 4	d				19 19							19 49							20 19					
New Cross 4 ⊖	d					19 22							19 52							20 22				
St Johns	d					19 24							19 54							20 24				
Lewisham 4 ⛴	d				19 26	19 29		19 31				19 56	19 59		20 01				20 26	20 29		20 31		
Blackheath 4	d				19 29			19 33				19 59			20 03				20 29			20 33		
Kidbrooke	d				19 32							20 02							20 32					
Eltham	d				19 35							20 05							20 35					
Falconwood	d				19 38							20 08							20 38					
Welling	d				19 41							20 11							20 41					
Bexleyheath	d				19 44							20 14							20 44					
Barnehurst 4	d				19 47							20 17							20 47					
Hither Green 4	d		19 13			19 34				19 43			20 04				20 13			20 34				20 43
Lee	d		19 15			19 36				19 45			20 06				20 15			20 36				20 45
Mottingham	d		19 18			19 39				19 48			20 09				20 18			20 39				20 48
New Eltham	d		19 21			19 42				19 51			20 12				20 21			20 42				20 51
Sidcup 4	d		19 24			19 46				19 54			20 16				20 24			20 46				20 54
Albany Park	d		19 27			19 48				19 57			20 18				20 27			20 48				20 57
Bexley	d		19 29			19 51				19 59			20 21				20 29			20 51				20 59
Crayford	d		19 33			19 55				20 03			20 25				20 33			20 55				21 03
Charlton 4	d			19 19		20a25	19 35	19 38			19 49		20a55	20 05	20 08			20 19		21a25	20 35	20 38		
Woolwich Dockyard	d			19 22				19 41			19 52				20 11			20 22				20 41		
Woolwich Arsenal 4 ⛴	d			19 25			19 40	19 44			19 55			20 10	20 14			20 25			20 40	20 44		
Plumstead	d			19 27			19 43	19 46			19 57			20 13	20 16			20 27			20 43	20 46		
Abbey Wood	d			19 30			19 46	19 50			20 00			20 16	20 20			20 30			20 46	20 50		
Belvedere	d			19 33				19 53			20 03				20 23			20 33				20 53		
Erith	d			19 36				19 55			20 06				20 25			20 36				20 55		
Slade Green 4	d			19a39			19 52	20 01			20a09			20 22	20 31			20a39			20 52	21 01		
Dartford 4	a		19 38		19 54		19 57	20 06		20 08		20 24		20 27	20 36		20 38		20 54		20 57	21 06		21 08
	d		19 39				19 58			20 09				20 28			20 39				20 58			21 09
Stone Crossing	d		19 43				20 02			20 13				20 32			20 43				21 02			21 13
Greenhithe for Bluewater	d		19 45				20 04			20 15				20 34			20 45				21 04			21 15
Swanscombe	d		19 48				20 07			20 18				20 37			20 48				21 07			21 18
Northfleet	d		19 50				20 09			20 20				20 39			20 50				21 09			21 20
Gravesend 4	d	19 48	19a55				20 13		20 18	20a25				20 43		20 48	20a55				21 13		21 18	21a25
Higham	d						20 19							20 49							21 19			
Strood 4	d	19 59					20 25		20 29					20 55		20 59					21 25		21 29	
Maidstone West	d																							
Rochester 4	d	20 02					20 28		20 32					20 58		21 02					21 28		21 32	
Chatham 4	d	20 06					20 31		20 36					21 01		21 06					21 31		21 36	
Gillingham (Kent) 4	a	20 10					20 35		20 40					21 05		21 10					21 35		21 40	
Rainham (Kent)	a	20 15					20 41		20 45					21 11		21 15					21 41		21 45	

Table T200-F

Sundays

15 December to 10 May

London - Dartford and Gillingham

		SE	SE	SE	TL	SE	SE ◇	SE		SE	SE	SE	TL	SE	SE ◇	SE	SE	SE	SE	TL	SE	SE ◇	SE	SE
St Pancras Int'l	d						21 25								21 55							22 25		
Stratford International	d						21 32								22 02							22 32		
Ebbsfleet International	d						21 43								22 13							22 43		
London Charing Cross	d					20 42		20 52						21 12		21 22					21 42		21 52	
London Waterloo (East)	d					20 45		20 55						21 15		21 25					21 45		21 55	
London Cannon Street	d	20 29		20 42						20 59		21 12					21 29		21 42					21 59
London Bridge	d	20 33		20 46	20 48	20 51		21 01		21 03		21 16	21 18	21 21		21 31	21 33		21 46	21 48	21 51		22 01	22 03
Deptford	d	20 39			20 55					21 09			21 25				21 39			21 55				22 09
Greenwich	d	20 41			20 57					21 11			21 27				21 41			21 57				22 11
Maze Hill	d	20 44			21 00					21 14			21 30				21 44			22 00				22 14
Westcombe Park	d	20 46			21 02					21 16			21 32				21 46			22 02				22 16
London Victoria	d		20 34								21 04							21 34						
Denmark Hill	d		20 44								21 14							21 44						
Peckham Rye	d		20 47								21 17							21 47						
Nunhead	d		20 49								21 19							21 49						
New Cross	d			20 52								21 22							21 52					
St Johns	d			20 54								21 24							21 54					
Lewisham	d		20 56	20 59		21 01					21 26	21 29		21 31				21 56	21 59		22 01			
Blackheath	d		20 59			21 03					21 29			21 33				21 59			22 03			
Kidbrooke	d		21 02								21 32							22 02						
Eltham	d		21 05								21 35							22 05						
Falconwood	d		21 08								21 38							22 08						
Welling	d		21 11								21 41							22 11						
Bexleyheath	d		21 14								21 44							22 14						
Barnehurst	d		21 17								21 47							22 17						
Hither Green	d			21 04				21 13				21 34				21 43			22 04				22 13	
Lee	d			21 06				21 15				21 36				21 45			22 06				22 15	
Mottingham	d			21 09				21 18				21 39				21 48			22 09				22 18	
New Eltham	d			21 12				21 21				21 42				21 51			22 12				22 21	
Sidcup	d			21 16				21 24				21 46				21 54			22 16				22 24	
Albany Park	d			21 18				21 27				21 48				21 57			22 18				22 27	
Bexley	d			21 21				21 29				21 51				21 59			22 21				22 29	
Crayford	d			21 25				21 33				21 55				22 03			22 25				22 33	
Charlton	d	20 49		21a55	21 05	21 08				21 19		22a25	21 35	21 38			21 49		22a55	22 05	22 08			22 19
Woolwich Dockyard	d	20 52				21 11				21 22				21 41			21 52				22 11			22 22
Woolwich Arsenal	d	20 55			21 10	21 14				21 25			21 40	21 44			21 55			22 10	22 14			22 25
Plumstead	d	20 57			21 13	21 16				21 27			21 43	21 46			21 57			22 13	22 16			22 27
Abbey Wood	d	21 00			21 16	21 20				21 30			21 46	21 50			22 00			22 16	22 20			22 30
Belvedere	d	21 03				21 23				21 33				21 53			22 03				22 23			22 33
Erith	d	21 06				21 25				21 36				21 55			22 06				22 25			22 36
Slade Green	d	21a09			21 22	21 31				21a39			21 52	22 01			22a09			22 22	22 31			22a39
Dartford	a		21 24		21 27	21 36		21 38			21 54		21 57	22 06		22 08		22 24		22 27	22 36		22 38	
	d				21 28			21 39					21 58			22 09				22 28			22 39	
Stone Crossing	d				21 32			21 43					22 02			22 13				22 32			22 43	
Greenhithe for Bluewater	d				21 34			21 45					22 04			22 15				22 34			22 45	
Swanscombe	d				21 37			21 48					22 07			22 18				22 37			22 48	
Northfleet	d				21 39			21 50					22 09			22 20				22 39			22 50	
Gravesend	d				21 43		21 48	21a55					22 13		22 18	22a25				22 43		22 48	22a55	
Higham	d				21 49								22 19							22 49				
Strood	d				21 55		21 59						22 25		22 29					22 55		22 59		
Maidstone West	d																							
Rochester	d				21 58		22 02						22 28		22 32					22 58		23 02		
Chatham	d				22 01		22 06						22 31		22 36					23 01		23 06		
Gillingham (Kent)	a				22 05		22 10						22 35		22 40					23 05		23 10		
Rainham (Kent)	a				22 11		22 15						22 41		22 45					23 11		23 15		

Table T200-F

Sundays

15 December to 10 May

London - Dartford and Gillingham

		SE	SE	TL	SE	SE ◇	SE	SE	SE	SE	TL	SE	SE ◇	SE	SE	SE		SE	TL	SE	SE	SE	SE	SE	SE	SE
St Pancras Int'l	d					22 55							23 25													
Stratford International	d					23 02							23 32													
Ebbsfleet International	d					23 13							23 43													
London Charing Cross	d				22 12		22 22					22 42		22 52						23 12	23 22			23 42	23 52	
London Waterloo (East)	d				22 15		22 25					22 45		22 55						23 15	23 25			23 45	23 55	
London Cannon Street	d		22 12					22 29		22 42					22 59			23 12				23 29				23 59
London Bridge	d		22 16	22 18	22 21		22 31	22 33		22 46	22 48	22 51		23 01	23 03			23 16	23 18	23 21	23 31	23 33		23 51	00 01	00 03
Deptford	d			22 25				22 39			22 55				23 09				23 25			23 39				00 09
Greenwich	d			22 27				22 41			22 57				23 11				23 27			23 41				00 11
Maze Hill	d			22 30				22 44			23 00				23 14				23 30			23 44				00 14
Westcombe Park	d			22 32				22 46			23 02				23 16				23 32			23 46				00 16
London Victoria	d	22 04							22 34							23 04							23 34			
Denmark Hill	d	22 14							22 44							23 14							23 44			
Peckham Rye	d	22 17							22 47							23 17							23 47			
Nunhead	d	22 19							22 49							23 19							23 49			
New Cross	d		22 22							22 52								23 22								
St Johns	d		22 24							22 54								23 24								
Lewisham	d	22 26	22 29		22 31				22 56	22 59		23 01				23 26		23 29		23 31			23 56	00 01		
Blackheath	d	22 29			22 33				22 59			23 03				23 29				23 33			23 59	00 03		
Kidbrooke	d	22 32							23 02							23 32							00 02			
Eltham	d	22 35							23 05							23 35							00 05			
Falconwood	d	22 38							23 08							23 38							00 08			
Welling	d	22 41							23 11							23 41							00 11			
Bexleyheath	d	22 44							23 14							23 44							00 14			
Barnehurst	d	22 47							23 17							23 47							00 17			
Hither Green	d		22 34				22 43			23 03				23 13				23 33			23 43				00 13	
Lee	d		22 36				22 45			23 06				23 15				23 36			23 45				00 15	
Mottingham	d		22 39				22 48			23 09				23 18				23 39			23 48				00 18	
New Eltham	d		22 42				22 51			23 12				23 21				23 42			23 51				00 21	
Sidcup	d		22 46				22 54			23 15				23 24				23 45			23 54				00 24	
Albany Park	d		22 48				22 57			23 18				23 27				23 48			23 57				00 27	
Bexley	d		22 51				22 59			23 20				23 29				23 50			23 59				00 29	
Crayford	d		22 55				23 03			23 24				23 33				23 54			00 03				00 33	
Charlton	d		23a25	22 35	22 38			22 49			23 05	23 08			23 19				23 35	23 38		23 49		00 08		00 19
Woolwich Dockyard	d				22 41			22 52				23 11			23 22					23 41		23 52		00 11		00 22
Woolwich Arsenal	d			22 40	22 44			22 55			23 10	23 14			23 25				23 40	23 44		23 55		00 14		00 25
Plumstead	d			22 43	22 46			22 57			23 13	23 16			23 27				23 43	23 46		23 57		00 16		00 27
Abbey Wood	d			22 46	22 50			23 00			23 16	23 20			23 30				23 46	23 50		23 59		00 20		00 30
Belvedere	d				22 53			23 03				23 23			23 33					23 53		00 03		00 23		00 33
Erith	d				22 55			23 06				23 25			23 36					23 55		00 06		00 25		00 36
Slade Green	d			22 52	23 01			23a09			23 22	23 31			23 40				23 52	00 01		00 10		00 31		00 40
Dartford	a	22 54		22 57	23 06		23 08		23 24	23 29	23 27	23 36		23 38	23 45	23 54		23 59	23 57	00 06	00 08	00 15	00 24	00 36	00 38	00 45
	d			22 58			23 09				23 28			23 39					23 58		00 09				00 39	
Stone Crossing	d			23 02			23 13				23 32			23 43					00 02		00 13				00s43	
Greenhithe for Bluewater	d			23 04			23 15				23 34			23 45					00 04		00 15				00s45	
Swanscombe	d			23 07			23 18				23 37			23 48					00 07		00 18				00s48	
Northfleet	d			23 09			23 20				23 39			23 50					00 09		00 20				00s50	
Gravesend	d			23 13		23 18	23a25				23 43		23 48	23a55					00 13		00a25				00a55	
Higham	d			23 19							23 49								00 19							
Strood	d			23 25		23 29					23 55		23 59						00 25							
Maidstone West	d																									
Rochester	d			23 28		23 32					23 58		00 02						00 28							
Chatham	d			23 31		23 36					00 02		00 06						00 31							
Gillingham (Kent)	a			23 35		23 40					00 06		00 10						00 36							
Rainham (Kent)	a			23 41		23 45							00 15													

16 December to 15 May

Gillingham and Dartford - London

Miles	Miles	Miles	Miles	Miles			SE TWO	SE MO	SE TWO	TL	SE TWO	SE ThFO	SE TWO	SE ThFO	SE ThFO	SE TWO	SE ThFO	TL	SE	SE	SE		TL	SE	SE
—	—	—	—	—	Rainham (Kent)	d																			
0	—	—	0	0	**Gillingham (Kent)**	d												04 00					04 36		
1¾	—	—	1¾	1¾	**Chatham**	d												04 04					04 40		
2¼	—	—	2¼	2¼	Rochester	d												04 08					04 44		
—	—	—	—	—	Maidstone West	d																			
3¼	—	—	3¼	3¼	Strood	d												04 11					04 47		
6	—	—	6	6	Higham	d												04 16					04 52		
10½	—	—	10½	10½	**Gravesend**	d												04 23	04 32		04 55		04 59		
12½	—	—	12½	—	Northfleet	d				00 03								04 27			04 59		05 03		
13¼	—	—	13¼	—	Swanscombe	d				00 05								04 29			05 01		05 05		
14½	—	—	14½	—	Greenhithe for Bluewater	d				00 08								04 32	04 38		05 04		05 08		
15¼	—	—	15¼	—	Stone Crossing	d				00 10								04 34			05 06		05 10		
17¼	0	0	17¼	0	**Dartford**	a				00 15								04 39	04 44		05 11		05 14		
—	—	—	—	—		d													04 45	05 03	05 12		05 15	05 18	
19¼	2	—	—	—	Slade Green	d														05 08			05 21		05 26
20½	3¼	—	—	—	Erith	d														05 11					05 29
21¼	4½	—	—	—	Belvedere	d														05 13					05 31
23¼	6	—	—	—	Abbey Wood	d														05 17			05 28		05 35
24¾	7½	—	—	—	Plumstead	d														05 20			05 31		05 38
25¼	8	—	—	—	**Woolwich Arsenal**	d														05 23			05 34		05 41
26	8¾	—	—	—	Woolwich Dockyard	d							00 03	00 03						05 25					
27	9¾	—	—	—	Charlton	d							00 06	00 06			00 13			05 29			05 40		05 47
—	—	—	19	—	Crayford	d													04 50		05 17				
—	—	—	20½	—	Bexley	d													04 53		05 20				
—	—	—	21½	—	Albany Park	d									00 01	00 01			04 55		05 22				
—	—	—	22½	—	Sidcup	d									00 04	00 04			04 58		05 25				
—	—	—	24	—	New Eltham	d									00 08	00 08			05 02		05 29				
—	—	—	25	—	Mottingham	d									00 10	00 10			05 04		05 31				
—	—	—	26½	—	Lee	d									00 13	00 13			05 07		05 34				
—	—	—	27¼	—	Hither Green	d									00 16	00 16			05 10		05 37				
—	—	3	—	3	Barnehurst	d																		05 27	
—	—	4¼	—	4¼	Bexleyheath	d																		05 30	
—	—	5¾	—	5¾	Welling	d																		05 33	
—	—	6¾	—	6¾	Falconwood	d																		05 35	
—	—	8	—	8	Eltham	d																		05 38	
—	—	9	—	9	Kidbrooke	d																		05 42	
29	—	10	—	10	Blackheath	d							00 11	00 11										05 46	05 52
30	—	11	28½	11	Lewisham	d					00 05		00 15	00 16					05 16		05 43			05 50	05 56
—	—	11½	29	—	St Johns	d			00 02																
—	—	12¼	29¾	—	New Cross	d	00 01	00 02	00 05			00 02													
—	—	—	—	12¾	Nunhead	d																			
—	—	—	—	13½	Peckham Rye	d																			
—	—	—	—	14¼	Denmark Hill	d																			
—	—	—	—	18½	**London Victoria**	a																			
—	10½	—	—	—	Westcombe Park	d											00 20			05 31			05 42		
—	11	—	—	—	Maze Hill	d											00 25			05 33			05 44		
—	12	—	—	—	Greenwich	d											00 32			05 36			05 47		
—	12½	—	—	—	**Deptford**	a											00 37			05 38			05 49		
34¼	15½	15¼	32¾	—	London Bridge	a	00 07	00 07	00 10		00 13	00 17	00 23	00 24	00 27	00 29	00 51		05 24	05 44	05 51		05 57	05 58	06 04
—	16¼	—	—	—	**London Cannon Street**	a	00 13	00 13	00 18			00 25	00 33							05 52					
35¼	—	16¼	33¾	—	**London Waterloo (East)**	a								00 30	00 33				05 30		05 57			06 04	06 10
—	—	—	—	—	**London Charing Cross**	a								00 35	00 39				05 37		06 03			06 10	06 16
—	—	—	—	12½	**Ebbsfleet International**	a																			
—	—	—	—	29¼	**Stratford International**	a																			
—	—	—	—	35¼	**St Pancras Int'l**	a																			

16 December to 15 May

Gillingham and Dartford - London

		SE	SE	SE	SE	SE	SE ◇■	TL	SE ◇	SE	SE	SE ◇■	SE		SE	SE	SE	SE	SE	SE	TL	SE ◇	SE	SE	SE
Rainham (Kent)	d								05 15												05 30	05 45			
Gillingham (Kent)	d						05 40	05 06	05 20										05 26		05 36	05 50			
Chatham	d						05 44	05 10	05 24										05 30		05 40	05 54			
Rochester	d						05 48	05 14	05 28										05 34		05 44	05 58			
Maidstone West	d																								
Strood	d							05 17	05 31										05 38		05 47	06 01			
Higham	d							05 22											05 43		05 52				
Gravesend	d					05 25		05 29	05 41						05 46				05 51		05 59	06 11			06 13
Northfleet	d					05 29		05 33							05 50						06 03				
Swanscombe	d					05 31		05 35							05 52						06 05				
Greenhithe for Bluewater	d					05 34		05 38							05 55				05 59		06 08				06 19
Stone Crossing	d					05 36		05 40							05 57						06 10				06 21
Dartford	a					05 41		05 44							06 01				06 05		06 14				06 26
	d			05 33	05 40	05 42		05 45		05 48			06 01		06 03				06 06		06 15		06 20		06 27
Slade Green	d			05 38				05 51			05 56		06 07							06 14	06 21				
Erith	d			05 41							05 59		06 10							06 17					
Belvedere	d			05 43							06 01		06 12							06 19					
Abbey Wood	d			05 47				05 58			06 05		06 16							06 23	06 28				06 37
Plumstead	d			05 50				06 01			06 08		06 19							06 26	06 31				
Woolwich Arsenal	d			05 53				06 04			06 11		06 22							06 29	06 34				06 41
Woolwich Dockyard	d			05 55							06 13		06 25					←		06 31					
Charlton	d			05 59				06 10			06 17		06 28					06 28		06 35	06 40			05 55	06 47
Crayford	d	05 32				05 47							→		06 08	06 04								06 26	
Bexley	d	05 35				05 50									06 11	06 07								06 29	
Albany Park	d	05 37				05 52									06 14	06 10								06 32	
Sidcup	d	05 40				05 55									06 17	06 13								06 35	
New Eltham	d	05 43				05 59									06 20	06 16								06 38	
Mottingham	d	05 46				06 01									06 23	06 19								06 41	
Lee	d	05 49				06 05									06 26	06 22								06 44	
Hither Green	d	05 52				06 08									06 29	06 25								06 48	
Barnehurst	d		05 42		05 48					05 56							06 10		06 14				06 28		
Bexleyheath	d		05 44		05 51					05 59							06 13		06 17				06 31		
Welling	d		05 47		05 54					06 02							06 16		06 20				06 34		
Falconwood	d		05 50		05 56					06 04							06 18		06 22				06 36		
Eltham	d		05 53		05 59					06 07							06 21		06 25				06 39		
Kidbrooke	d		05 56		06 02					06 11							06 25		06 28				06 42		
Blackheath	d		05 59		06 06					06 15	06 22						06 29		06 32	06 40			06 46		
Lewisham	d	05 58	06 03		06 11					06 19	06 26					06 31	06 33		06 36	06 44			06 50	06 54	
St Johns	d	06 00	06 05														06 35							06 56	
New Cross	d	06 02	06 07									06 33				06 36	06 37							06 58	
Nunhead	d				06 17														06 44						
Peckham Rye	d				06 20														06 47						
Denmark Hill	d				06 24														06 50						
London Victoria	a				06 37														07 02						
Westcombe Park	d			06 01				06 12										06 31			06 42				06 49
Maze Hill	d			06 03				06 14										06 33			06 44				06 52
Greenwich	d			06 06				06 17										06 37			06 47				06 56
Deptford	a			06 08				06 19										06 39			06 49				06 58
London Bridge	a	06 07	06 13	06 14		06 17	06 25	06 27		06 27	06 34	06 38			06 39	06 41	06 43	06 46		06 52	06 57		06 58	07 04	07 05
London Cannon Street	a	06 15	06 20	06 22			06 33					06 46				06 48	06 50	06 54						07 11	07 13
London Waterloo (East)	a					06 23				06 34	06 40				06 45					06 58			07 04		
London Charing Cross	a					06 30				06 40	06 46				06 52					07 05			07 12		
Ebbsfleet International	a								05 45													06 15			
Stratford International	a								05 57													06 27			
St Pancras Int'l	a								06 05													06 35			

Table T200-R

Mondays to Fridays

16 December to 15 May

Gillingham and Dartford - London

Station		SE	SE	SE	SE ◇1		SE	SE	SE	TL	SE	SE ◇	SE	SE	SE	SE	SE	SE	SE	SE	SE		SE	SE	TL
Rainham (Kent)	d				06 28					06 00		06 11													06 30
Gillingham (Kent)	d				06 33					06 06		06 17													06 36
Chatham	d				06 37					06 10		06 21													06 40
Rochester	d				06 41					06 14		06 25													06 44
Maidstone West	d																								
Strood	d									06 18	06 23	06 28									06 44				06 47
Higham	d									06 23	06 28										06 49				06 52
Gravesend	d									06 30	06 35	06 39							06 50		06 56				06 59
Northfleet	d									06 33									06 54						07 03
Swanscombe	d									06 35									06 56						07 05
Greenhithe for Bluewater	d									06 39	06 42								06 59		07 03				07 08
Stone Crossing	d									06 41	06 44								07 01		07 05				07 10
Dartford	a									06 45	06 48								07 06		07 10				07 14
	d	06 30					06 38	06 41		06 46	06 49					06 55	06 59		07 07		07 11			07 13	07 15
Slade Green	d			06 38			06 43			06 51						07 00		07 06					07 10		07 21
Erith	d			06 41			06 46									07 03							07 12		
Belvedere	d			06 43			06 48									07 05							07 15		
Abbey Wood	d			06 47			06 52			06 58						07 09					07 23		07 18		07 28
Plumstead	d			06 50			06 55			07 01						07 12							07 21		07 31
Woolwich Arsenal	d			06 53			06 58			07 04						07 15					07 28		07 24		07 34
Woolwich Dockyard	d			06 56			07 01		←							07 17							07 27		
Charlton	d			06 59			07 04		07 04	07 10				06 15		07 21					07 33		07 30		07 40
Crayford	d	06 35					→				06 54			06 49					07 12	07 08					
Bexley	d	06 38									06 57			06 52					07 16	07 11					
Albany Park	d	06 40									07 00			06 55					07 19	07 14					
Sidcup	d	06 43									07 03			06 58					07 22	07 18					
New Eltham	d	06 47									07 06			07 01					07 26	07 21					
Mottingham	d	06 49									07 09			07 04					07 29	07 24					
Lee	d	06 53									07 12			07 07					07 32	07 28					
Hither Green	d	06 56									07 16			07 11					07 36	07 31					
Barnehurst	d		06 36					06 49					06 53		07 00		07 07	07 12						07 21	
Bexleyheath	d		06 39					06 52					06 56		07 03		07 10	07 15						07 24	
Welling	d		06 42					06 55					06 59		07 06		07 13	07 18						07 28	
Falconwood	d		06 44					06 57					07 01		07 08		07 16	07 20						07 31	
Eltham	d		06 47					07 00					07 04		07 11		07 19	07 23						07 34	
Kidbrooke	d		06 51					07 04					07 07		07 15		07 23	07 27						07 37	
Blackheath	d		06 55	07 04				07 08					07 11		07 19		07 27	07 31					07 36	07 42	
Lewisham	d		06 59	07 08				07 12					07 15	07 17	07 23		07 31	07 35		07 38			07 40	07 46	
St Johns	d		07 01											07 19	07 25					07 40					
New Cross	d		07 03											07 22	07 28			07 38		07 43					
Nunhead	d																							07 54	
Peckham Rye	d												07 21											07 57	
Denmark Hill	d												07 25											08 00	
London Victoria	a												07 37											08 13	
Westcombe Park	d								07 07	07 12						07 23					07 36				07 42
Maze Hill	d								07 09	07 14						07 26					07 38				07 44
Greenwich	d								07 13	07 17						07 30					07 42				07 47
Deptford	a								07 15	07 19						07 32					07 44				07 49
London Bridge	a	07 05	07 09	07 16	07 19			07 20	07 21	07 27	07 25			07 28	07 33	07 38	07 39	07 44	07 45	07 48	07 50		07 51		07 57
London Cannon Street	a		07 16		07 27				07 29					07 35	07 41	07 46		07 51		07 56	07 58				
London Waterloo (East)	a	07 11		07 22				07 26			07 31						07 46		07 51				07 57		
London Charing Cross	a	07 18		07 29				07 33			07 38						07 53		07 58				08 04		
Ebbsfleet International	a											06 42													
Stratford International	a											06 55													
St Pancras Int'l	a											07 02													

NRT DECEMBER 19 EDITION

Table T200-R

Mondays to Fridays

16 December to 15 May

Gillingham and Dartford - London

Station		SE	SE	SE	SE	SE	SE	SE ◇	SE ◇1	SE	SE	SE	SE		SE	SE	SE	SE	TL	SE	SE ◇	SE	SE	SE	SE
Rainham (Kent)	d								07 13										06 56		07 17				
Gillingham (Kent)	d								07 18										07 03		07 22				
Chatham	d								07 22										07 07		07 27				
Rochester	d								07 26										07 11		07 30				
Maidstone West	d							06 52																	
Strood	d						07 03	07 09											07 17		07 34				
Higham	d						07 08												07 22						
Gravesend	d						07 15	07 19											07 29	07 39	07 44				
Northfleet	d						07 18												07 32						
Swanscombe	d						07 20												07 34						
Greenhithe for Bluewater	d						07 24												07 38	07 45					
Stone Crossing	d						07 26												07 40						
Dartford	a						07 30												07 44	07 50					
	d	07 19				07 28	07 31						07 35					07 39	07 45	07 51					
Slade Green	d		07 25			07 33										07 36			07 50				07 37		07 54
Erith	d		07 28			07 35										07 39									07 56
Belvedere	d		07 30			07 38										07 41									07 59
Abbey Wood	d		07 34			07 41										07 45			07 57						08 02
Plumstead	d		07 37			07 44										07 48			08 01						08 05
Woolwich Arsenal	d		07 40			07 47										07 51			08 04						08 08
Woolwich Dockyard	d		07 43									←				07 54									
Charlton	d		07 46		06 55	07 53						07 53				07 57			08 10						08 13
Crayford	d				07 31	→	07 36								07 40					07 56				07 49	
Bexley	d				07 34		07 39								07 43					07 59				07 52	
Albany Park	d				07 37		07 42								07 46					08 02				07 55	
Sidcup	d				07 40		07 45								07 49					08 05				07 58	
New Eltham	d				07 43		07 49				←				07 52					08 09				08 01	
Mottingham	d				07 46						07 46				07 55									08 04	
Lee	d				→						07 49				07 59									08 08	
Hither Green	d										07 53				08 02					08 15				08 11	
Barnehurst	d	07 27		07 32						07 36			07 43					07 47				07 56	07 52		
Bexleyheath	d	07 30		07 35						07 39			07 46					07 50				07 59	07 55		
Welling	d	07 34		07 38						07 42			07 49					07 54				08 02	07 58		
Falconwood	d	07 36		07 40						07 44			07 51					07 56				08 04	08 00		
Eltham	d	07 39		07 43						07 47			07 54					07 59				08 07	08 03		
Kidbrooke	d	07 43		07 47						07 51			07 57					08 03				08 11	08 07		
Blackheath	d	07 47		07 51						07 55		07 58	08 02					08 07				08 15	08 11		08 18
Lewisham	d	07 51		07 55							08 00	08 02	08 06					08 11					08 15	08 19	08 22
St Johns	d			07 57							08 03												08 18	08 21	
New Cross	d			08 00							08 06						08 11						08 21	08 24	
Nunhead	d												08 14												
Peckham Rye	d												08 17												
Denmark Hill	d												08 21												
London Victoria	a												08 33												
Westcombe Park	d		07 49													08 00			08 12						
Maze Hill	d		07 51													08 02			08 14						
Greenwich	d		07 55													08 06			08 17						
Deptford	a		07 57													08 08			08 19						
London Bridge	a	08 00	08 03	08 05			08 05		08 07	08 07	08 11	08 11			08 13	08 16	08 17	08 19	08 27	08 25		08 27	08 28	08 30	08 31
London Cannon Street	a		08 11	08 13					08 15		08 19					08 21	08 25						08 36	08 38	
London Waterloo (East)	a	08 06					08 11			08 13		08 17			08 19			08 25		08 31		08 33			08 37
London Charing Cross	a	08 13					08 18			08 20		08 24			08 26			08 32		08 38		08 40			08 43
Ebbsfleet International	a																				07 48				
Stratford International	a							07 33													08 00				
St Pancras Int'l	a							07 41													08 08				

Table T200-R

Mondays to Fridays

16 December to 15 May

Gillingham and Dartford - London

		SE ◇1	SE	SE	SE		SE	SE	SE	SE	SE	SE	SE ◇	SE	SE ◇1	SE	SE	TL	SE	SE	SE 1		SE	SE ◇	SE ◇
Rainham (Kent)	d	07 39													07 57			07 30						07 47	
Gillingham (Kent) 4	d	07 44													08 03			07 36						07 52	
Chatham 4	d	07 49													08 07			07 40						07 56	
Rochester 4	d	07 52													08 11			07 44						08 00	
Maidstone West	d												07 25												07 53
Strood 4	d										07 38		07 43					07 47						08 03	08 11
Higham	d										07 43							07 52							
Gravesend 4	d										07 50		07 53					07 59					08 11	08 14	08 21
Northfleet	d										07 55							08 03					08 15		
Swanscombe	d										07 57							08 05					08 17		
Greenhithe for Bluewater	d										08 01							08 08					08 20		
Stone Crossing	d										08 03							08 10					08 22		
Dartford 4	a										08 08							08 14					08 27		
	d				07 56			07 59		08 04	08 09							08 15	08 20				08 28		
Slade Green 4	d						07 59		08 03	08 09								08 21			08 26				
Erith	d						08 02			08 12											08 29				
Belvedere	d						08 04			08 14											08 31				
Abbey Wood	d						08 08			08 18								08 28			08 35				
Plumstead	d						08 11			08 21								08 31			08 38				
Woolwich Arsenal 4 ⛴	d						08 14			08 24								08 34			08 41				
Woolwich Dockyard	d						08 16			08 26		←									08 44				
Charlton 4	d		07 25				08 20			08 30		08 30						08 40		07 56	08 47				
Crayford	d		08 04	08 04						→	08 14			08 10						08 28			08 33		
Bexley	d		08 07	08 07							08 17			08 13						08 31			08 36		
Albany Park	d		08 10	08 10							08 20			08 16						08 34			08 39		
Sidcup 4	d		08 13	08 13							08 24			08 19			08 29			08 37			08 42		
New Eltham	d		08 17	08 17							08 28			08 22			08 32			08 40			08 45		
Mottingham	d		08 20	08 20										08 25			08 35			08 43			08 48		
Lee	d		08 23	08 23										08 29			08 38			08 46			08 51		
Hither Green 4	d		08 27	08 27							08 35			08 32			08 42			08 50			08 55		
Barnehurst 4	d				08 04			08 07	08 12							08 23			08 28						
Bexleyheath	d				08 07			08 10	08 15							08 26			08 31						
Welling	d				08 10			08 13	08 18							08 29			08 34						
Falconwood	d				08 12			08 16	08 21							08 31			08 36						
Eltham	d				08 15			08 19	08 24							08 34			08 39						
Kidbrooke	d				08 19			08 23	08 28							08 37			08 43						
Blackheath 4	d				08 23			08 27	08 32							08 42			08 47		08 52				
Lewisham 4 ⛴	d				08 27			08 31	08 36					08 39		08 46			08 51	08 55	08 56				
St Johns	d													08 41						08 59					
New Cross 4 ⊖	d								08 39					08 44						→					
Nunhead 4	d				08 34											08 52									
Peckham Rye 4	d				08 37											08 55									
Denmark Hill 4	d				08 42											08 59									
London Victoria 15 ⊖	a				08 55											09 11									
Westcombe Park	d						08 22					08 32						08 42							
Maze Hill	d						08 25					08 35						08 44							
Greenwich 4 ⛴	d						08 28					08 38						08 47							
Deptford	a						08 30					08 40						08 49							
London Bridge 4 ⊖	a	08 32	08 37	08 37			08 37	08 41	08 45		08 45	08 47		08 49	08 51		08 54	08 57	08 59		09 04		09 06		
London Cannon Street 4 ⊖	a	08 40					08 45		08 53			08 55		08 57	08 59										
London Waterloo (East) 4 ⊖	a		08 43	08 43				08 47			08 51						09 01		09 05		09 11		09 13		
London Charing Cross 4 ⊖	a		08 50	08 50				08 54			08 58						09 07		09 12		09 18		09 20		
Ebbsfleet International	a												07 56											08 17	08 25
Stratford International ⊖ ⛴	a												08 09											08 30	08 39
St Pancras Int'l 15 ⊖	a												08 16											08 38	08 46

Table T200-R

Mondays to Fridays

16 December to 15 May

Gillingham and Dartford - London

		SE	SE	SE ◇1	SE	SE	SE	SE	SE	TL	SE	SE ◇	SE		SE	SE	SE	SE	SE	SE	SE	TL	SE	SE	SE
Rainham (Kent)	d			08 18						08 01		08 14										08 30			
Gillingham (Kent) 4	d			08 24						08 07		08 19										08 36			
Chatham 4	d			08 28						08 11		08 24										08 40			
Rochester 4	d			08 32						08 15		08 27										08 44			
Maidstone West	d																								
Strood 4	d									08 18		08 32										08 47			
Higham	d									08 23												08 52			
Gravesend 4	d									08 30	08 34	08 43					08 50					08 59	09 05		
Northfleet	d									08 34	08 38											09 03	09 08		
Swanscombe	d									08 36	08 40											09 05	09 10		
Greenhithe for Bluewater	d									08 39	08 43						08 56					09 08	09 14		
Stone Crossing	d									08 41	08 45											09 10	09 16		
Dartford 4	a									08 45	08 49						09 01					09 14	09 20		
	d					08 32	08 37			08 46	08 50		08 54				09 02	09 05			09 11	09 15	09 21		
Slade Green 4	d	08 30				08 39			08 45	08 51					08 59				09 07	09 09	09 16	09 21			
Erith	d	08 32				08 42			08 48						09 02					09 12	09 18				
Belvedere	d	08 35				08 44			08 50						09 04					09 14	09 21				
Abbey Wood	d	08 38				08 48			08 54	08 58					09 08					09 18	09 24	09 28			
Plumstead	d	08 41				08 51			08 57	09 01					09 11					09 21	09 27	09 31			
Woolwich Arsenal 4 ⛴	d	08 44				08 54			09 00	09 04					09 14					09 24	09 30	09 34			
Woolwich Dockyard	d	08 47				08 57			09 02						09 16					09 26	09 33				
Charlton 4	d	08 50				09 00			09 06	09 10					09 20	08 25				09 30	09 36	09 40			
Crayford	d										08 55					09 00		09 12					09 26		
Bexley	d										08 58					09 03		09 15					09 29		
Albany Park	d										09 01					09 06		09 17							
Sidcup 4	d							08 50			09 04					09 09		09 20					09 33		
New Eltham	d							08 53			09 07					09 12		09 24					09 36		
Mottingham	d							08 56			09 10					09 15		09 27							
Lee	d							08 59			09 13					09 18		09 30							
Hither Green 4	d							09 03			09 16					09 22		09 34					09 42		
Barnehurst 4	d				08 41		08 45						09 02				09 09		09 20						
Bexleyheath	d				08 44		08 47						09 05				09 12		09 23						
Welling	d				08 47		08 50						09 08				09 15		09 26						
Falconwood	d				08 49		08 53						09 11				09 18		09 28						
Eltham	d				08 52		08 56						09 14				09 21		09 31						
Kidbrooke	d				08 56		08 59						09 18				09 24		09 34						
Blackheath 4	d				09 00		09 03		09 11				09 22				09 28		09 38		09 41				
Lewisham 4 ⛴	d		←		09 04		09 07	09 10	09 15				09 26			09 29	09 32		09 42		09 46				
St Johns	d		08 59		09 06			09 12								09 31			09 44						
New Cross 4 ⊖	d		09 01		09 08			09 15								09 33			09 47						
Nunhead 4	d						09 14										09 37								
Peckham Rye 4	d						09 17										09 40								
Denmark Hill 4	d						09 22										09 44								
London Victoria 15 ⊖	a						09 35										09 57								
Westcombe Park	d	08 52				09 03				09 12					09 22					09 32		09 42			
Maze Hill	d	08 54				09 05				09 14					09 24					09 34		09 44			
Greenwich 4 ⛴	d	08 58				09 09				09 17					09 28					09 37		09 47			
Deptford	a	09 00				09 11				09 19					09 30					09 39		09 49		←	←
London Bridge 4 ⊖	a	09 06	09 08	09 10	09 14	09 18		09 20	09 23	09 27	09 27		09 34		09 36	09 39		09 43	09 52	09 45	09 55	09 57	09 51	09 52	09 55
London Cannon Street 4 ⊖	a	09 14	09 16	09 18	09 21	09 26		09 28							09 44	09 46			→	09 55	→			10 02	
London Waterloo (East) 4 ⊖	a								09 29		09 33		09 42					09 49					09 57		10 01
London Charing Cross 4 ⊖	a								09 37		09 40		09 47					09 56					10 03		10 05
Ebbsfleet International	a											08 46													
Stratford International ⊖ ⛴	a											08 59													
St Pancras Int'l 15 ⊖	a											09 07													

Table T200-R

Mondays to Fridays

16 December to 15 May

Gillingham and Dartford - London

		SE	SE	SE	SE		SE	SE	SE	SE	SE	TL	SE	SE	SE	SE	SE	SE	SE	SE	SE		SE	SE	SE
		◇														◇									
Rainham (Kent)	d	08 46										09 00				09 16									
Gillingham (Kent) 4	d	08 51										09 06				09 21									
Chatham 4	d	08 55										09 10				09 25									
Rochester 4	d	08 59										09 14				09 29									
Maidstone West	d																								
Strood 4	d	09 02										09 17				09 32									
Higham	d											09 22													
Gravesend 4	d	09 12					09 20					09 29	09 35			09 42				09 50					
Northfleet	d											09 33	09 38												
Swanscombe	d											09 35	09 40												
Greenhithe for Bluewater	d						09 26					09 38	09 44							09 56					
Stone Crossing	d											09 40	09 46												
Dartford 4	a						09 31					09 44	09 50							10 01					
	d		09 25				09 32	09 35			09 41	09 45	09 51				09 55			10 02	10 05				10 11
Slade Green 4	d			09 29					09 37	09 39	09 46	09 51						09 59					10 07	10 09	10 16
Erith	d			09 32						09 42	09 48							10 02						10 12	10 18
Belvedere	d			09 34						09 44	09 51							10 04						10 14	10 21
Abbey Wood	d			09 38						09 48	09 54	09 58						10 08						10 18	10 24
Plumstead	d			09 41						09 51	09 57	10 01						10 11						10 21	10 27
Woolwich Arsenal 4 ⛴	d			09 44						09 54	10 00	10 04						10 14						10 24	10 30
Woolwich Dockyard	d			09 46						09 56	10 03							10 16						10 26	10 33
Charlton 4	d			09 50	08 55					10 00	10 06	10 10						10 20	09 25					10 30	10 36
Crayford	d				09 31			09 42					09 56						10 02		10 12				
Bexley	d				09 34			09 45					09 59						10 05		10 15				
Albany Park	d				09 36			09 47											10 07		10 17				
Sidcup 4	d				09 39			09 50					10 03						10 10		10 20				
New Eltham	d				09 43			09 54					10 06						10 14		10 24				
Mottingham	d				09 45			09 56											10 16		10 26				
Lee	d				09 48			09 59											10 19		10 29				
Hither Green 4	d				09 52			10 03											10 22		10 33				
Barnehurst 4	d		09 33				09 39		09 50								10 03			10 09			10 20		
Bexleyheath	d		09 36				09 42		09 53								10 06			10 12			10 23		
Welling	d		09 39				09 45		09 56								10 09			10 15			10 26		
Falconwood	d		09 41				09 48		09 58								10 11			10 18			10 28		
Eltham	d		09 44				09 51		10 01								10 14			10 21			10 31		
Kidbrooke	d		09 47				09 54		10 04								10 17			10 24			10 34		
Blackheath 4	d		09 51				09 58		10 08		10 11						10 21			10 28			10 38		10 41
Lewisham 4 ⛴	d		09 55		09 57		10 02		10 12		10 16						10 25		10 27	10 32			10 42		10 46
St Johns	d				09 59				10 14										10 31				10 44		
New Cross 4 ⊖	d				10 01				10 17										10 33				10 47		
Nunhead 4	d						10 07													10 37					
Peckham Rye 4	d						10 10													10 40					
Denmark Hill 4	d						10 14													10 44					
London Victoria 15 ⊖	a						10 25													10 55					
Westcombe Park	d			09 52						10 02		10 12						10 22						10 32	
Maze Hill	d			09 54						10 04		10 14						10 24						10 34	
Greenwich 4 ⛴	d			09 57						10 07		10 17						10 27						10 37	
Deptford	a			09 59						10 09		10 19		←	←			10 29						10 39	
London Bridge 4 ⊖	a		10 03	10 05	10 07			10 13	10 22	10 15	10 25	10 27	10 20	10 22	10 25		10 33	10 35	10 39		10 43		10 52	10 45	10 55
London Cannon Street 4 ⊖	a			10 13	10 15				→	10 21	→			10 30				10 41	10 43				→	10 51	→
London Waterloo (East) 4 ⊖	a		10 09					10 19					10 26		10 31		10 39				10 49				
London Charing Cross 4 ⊖	a		10 15					10 23					10 30		10 35		10 43				10 53				
Ebbsfleet International	a	09 16														09 46									
Stratford International ⊖ ⛴	a	09 28														10 02									
St Pancras Int'l 15 ⊖	a	09 36														10 10									

Table T200-R

Mondays to Fridays

16 December to 15 May

Gillingham and Dartford - London

		TL	SE	SE	SE	SE	SE	SE	SE	SE	SE	SE	SE		SE	TL	SE	SE	SE	SE	SE	SE	SE	SE	SE
						◇														◇					
Rainham (Kent)	d	09 28				09 46										09 58				10 16					
Gillingham (Kent) 4	d	09 34				09 51										10 04				10 21					
Chatham 4	d	09 38				09 55										10 08				10 25					
Rochester 4	d	09 42				09 59										10 12				10 29					
Maidstone West	d																								
Strood 4	d	09 45				10 02										10 15				10 32					
Higham	d	09 50														10 20									
Gravesend 4	d	09 59	10 05			10 12				10 20						10 29	10 35			10 42				10 50	
Northfleet	d	10 02	10 08													10 32	10 38								
Swanscombe	d	10 04	10 10													10 34	10 40								
Greenhithe for Bluewater	d	10 08	10 14							10 26						10 38	10 44							10 56	
Stone Crossing	d	10 10	10 16													10 40	10 46								
Dartford 4	a	10 14	10 20							10 31						10 44	10 50							11 01	
	d	10 15	10 21				10 25			10 32	10 35				10 41	10 45	10 51				10 55			11 02	11 05
Slade Green 4	d	10 21						10 29				10 37	10 39		10 46	10 51						10 59			
Erith	d							10 32					10 42		10 48							11 02			
Belvedere	d							10 34					10 44		10 51							11 04			
Abbey Wood	d	10 28						10 38					10 48		10 54	10 58						11 08			
Plumstead	d	10 31						10 41					10 51		10 57	11 01						11 11			
Woolwich Arsenal 4 ⛴	d	10 34						10 44					10 54		11 00	11 04						11 14			
Woolwich Dockyard	d							10 46					10 56		11 03							11 16			
Charlton 4	d	10 40						10 50	09 55				11 00		11 06	11 10						11 20	10 25		
Crayford	d		10 26						10 32		10 42						10 56						11 02		11 12
Bexley	d		10 29						10 35		10 45						10 59						11 05		11 15
Albany Park	d								10 37		10 47												11 07		11 17
Sidcup 4	d		10 33						10 40		10 50						11 03						11 10		11 20
New Eltham	d		10 36						10 44		10 54						11 06						11 14		11 24
Mottingham	d								10 46		10 56												11 16		11 26
Lee	d								10 49		10 59												11 19		11 29
Hither Green 4	d								10 52		11 03												11 22		11 33
Barnehurst 4	d						10 33			10 39		10 50									11 03			11 09	
Bexleyheath	d						10 36			10 42		10 53									11 06			11 12	
Welling	d						10 39			10 45		10 56									11 09			11 15	
Falconwood	d						10 41			10 48		10 58									11 11			11 18	
Eltham	d						10 44			10 51		11 01									11 14			11 21	
Kidbrooke	d						10 47			10 54		11 04									11 17			11 24	
Blackheath 4	d						10 51			10 58		11 08			11 11						11 21			11 28	
Lewisham 4 ⛴	d						10 55		10 57	11 02		11 12			11 16						11 25		11 27	11 32	
St Johns	d								11 01			11 14											11 29		
New Cross 4 ⊖	d								11 03			11 17											11 32		
Nunhead 4	d									11 07														11 37	
Peckham Rye 4	d									11 10														11 40	
Denmark Hill 4	d									11 14														11 44	
London Victoria 15 ⊖	a									11 25														11 55	
Westcombe Park	d	10 42						10 52					11 02			11 12						11 22			
Maze Hill	d	10 44						10 54					11 04			11 14						11 24			
Greenwich 4 ⛴	d	10 47						10 57					11 07			11 17						11 27			
Deptford	a	10 49		←	←			10 59					11 09			11 19		←	←			11 29			
London Bridge 4 ⊖	a	10 57	10 50	10 52	10 55		11 03	11 05	11 09		11 13	11 22	11 15		11 25	11 27	11 20	11 22	11 25		11 33	11 35	11 38		11 43
London Cannon Street 4 ⊖	a			11 00				11 11	11 13			→	11 21		→			11 30				11 41	11 43		
London Waterloo (East) 4 ⊖	a		10 56		11 01		11 09				11 19						11 26		11 31		11 39				11 49
London Charing Cross 4 ⊖	a		11 00		11 05		11 13				11 23						11 30		11 35		11 43				11 53
Ebbsfleet International	a					10 16														10 46					
Stratford International ⊖ ⛴	a					10 33														10 58					
St Pancras Int'l 15 ⊖	a					10 41														11 06					

Table T200-R

Mondays to Fridays
16 December to 15 May

Gillingham and Dartford - London

		SE	SE	SE	TL		SE	SE	SE	SE ◇	SE	SE	SE	SE	SE	SE	SE	SE	TL	SE	SE		SE	SE ◇	SE
Rainham (Kent)	d				10 28					10 46									10 58					11 16	
Gillingham (Kent)	d				10 34					10 51									11 04					11 21	
Chatham	d				10 38					10 55									11 08					11 25	
Rochester	d				10 42					10 59									11 12					11 29	
Maidstone West	d																								
Strood	d				10 45					11 02									11 15					11 32	
Higham	d				10 50														11 20						
Gravesend	d				10 59		11 05			11 12				11 20					11 29	11 35				11 42	
Northfleet	d				11 02		11 08												11 32	11 38					
Swanscombe	d				11 04		11 10												11 34	11 40					
Greenhithe for Bluewater	d				11 08		11 14							11 26					11 38	11 44					
Stone Crossing	d				11 10		11 16												11 40	11 46					
Dartford	a				11 14		11 20							11 31					11 44	11 50					
	d			11 11	11 15		11 21				11 25			11 32	11 35			11 41	11 45	11 51					11 55
Slade Green	d	11 07	11 09	11 16	11 21							11 29				11 37	11 39	11 46	11 51						
Erith	d		11 12	11 18								11 32					11 42	11 48							
Belvedere	d		11 14	11 21								11 34					11 44	11 51							
Abbey Wood	d		11 18	11 24	11 28							11 38					11 48	11 54	11 58						
Plumstead	d		11 21	11 27	11 31							11 41					11 51	11 57	12 01						
Woolwich Arsenal	d		11 24	11 30	11 34							11 44					11 54	12 00	12 04						
Woolwich Dockyard	d		11 26	11 33								11 46					11 56	12 03							
Charlton	d		11 30	11 36	11 40							11 50	10 55				12 00	12 06	12 10						
Crayford	d						11 26						11 31		11 42					11 56					
Bexley	d						11 29						11 34		11 45					11 59					
Albany Park	d												11 36		11 47										
Sidcup	d						11 33						11 39		11 50					12 03					
New Eltham	d						11 36						11 43		11 54					12 06					
Mottingham	d												11 45		11 56										
Lee	d												11 48		11 59										
Hither Green	d												11 51		12 03										
Barnehurst	d	11 20									11 33			11 39		11 50									12 03
Bexleyheath	d	11 23									11 36			11 42		11 53									12 06
Welling	d	11 26									11 39			11 45		11 56									12 09
Falconwood	d	11 28									11 41			11 48		11 58									12 11
Eltham	d	11 31									11 44			11 51		12 01									12 14
Kidbrooke	d	11 34									11 47			11 54		12 04									12 17
Blackheath	d	11 38		11 41							11 51			11 58		12 08		12 11							12 21
Lewisham	d	11 42		11 46							11 55		11 57	12 02		12 12		12 16							12 25
St Johns	d	11 44											11 59			12 14									
New Cross	d	11 47											12 01			12 17									
Nunhead	d													12 07											
Peckham Rye	d													12 10											
Denmark Hill	d													12 14											
London Victoria	a													12 25											
Westcombe Park	d		11 32		11 42							11 52					12 02		12 12						
Maze Hill	d		11 34		11 44							11 54					12 04		12 14						
Greenwich	d		11 37		11 47							11 57					12 07		12 17						
Deptford	a		11 39		11 49			←	←			11 59					12 09		12 19		←		←		
London Bridge	a	11 52	11 45	11 55	11 57		11 50	11 52	11 55		12 03	12 05	12 07		12 13	12 22	12 15	12 25	12 27	12 20	12 22		12 25		12 33
London Cannon Street	a	→	11 51	→				12 00				12 11	12 13			→	12 21	→			12 30				
London Waterloo (East)	a						11 56		12 01		12 09				12 19					12 26			12 31		12 39
London Charing Cross	a						12 00		12 05		12 13				12 23					12 30			12 35		12 43
Ebbsfleet International	a									11 16														11 46	
Stratford International	a									11 29														11 58	
St Pancras Int'l	a									11 40														12 06	

Table T200-R

Mondays to Fridays
16 December to 15 May

Gillingham and Dartford - London

		SE	SE	SE	SE	SE	SE	SE	TL	SE	SE	SE	SE ◇		SE	SE	SE	SE	SE	SE	SE	SE	TL	SE	SE
Rainham (Kent)	d								11 28				11 46										11 58		
Gillingham (Kent)	d								11 34				11 51										12 04		
Chatham	d								11 38				11 55										12 08		
Rochester	d								11 42				11 59										12 12		
Maidstone West	d																								
Strood	d								11 45				12 02										12 15		
Higham	d								11 50														12 20		
Gravesend	d			11 50					11 59	12 05			12 12					12 20					12 29	12 35	
Northfleet	d								12 02	12 08													12 32	12 38	
Swanscombe	d								12 04	12 10													12 34	12 40	
Greenhithe for Bluewater	d			11 56					12 08	12 14								12 26					12 38	12 44	
Stone Crossing	d								12 10	12 16													12 40	12 46	
Dartford	a			12 01					12 14	12 20								12 31					12 44	12 50	
	d			12 02	12 05			12 11	12 15	12 21					12 25			12 32	12 35			12 41	12 45	12 51	
Slade Green	d	11 59				12 07	12 09	12 16	12 21							12 29				12 37	12 39	12 46	12 51		
Erith	d	12 02					12 12	12 18								12 32					12 42	12 48			
Belvedere	d	12 04					12 14	12 21								12 34					12 44	12 51			
Abbey Wood	d	12 08					12 18	12 24	12 28							12 38					12 48	12 54	12 58		
Plumstead	d	12 11					12 21	12 27	12 31							12 41					12 51	12 57	13 01		
Woolwich Arsenal	d	12 14					12 24	12 30	12 34							12 44					12 54	13 00	13 04		
Woolwich Dockyard	d	12 16					12 26	12 33								12 46					12 56	13 03			
Charlton	d	12 20	11 25				12 30	12 36	12 40							12 50	11 55				13 00	13 06	13 10		
Crayford	d		12 01		12 12					12 26							12 31		12 42					12 56	
Bexley	d		12 04		12 15					12 29							12 34		12 45					12 59	
Albany Park	d		12 06		12 17												12 36		12 47						
Sidcup	d		12 09		12 20					12 33							12 39		12 50					13 03	
New Eltham	d		12 13		12 24					12 36							12 43		12 54					13 06	
Mottingham	d		12 15		12 26												12 45		12 56						
Lee	d		12 18		12 29												12 48		12 59						
Hither Green	d		12 21		12 33												12 51		13 03						
Barnehurst	d			12 09		12 20									12 33			12 39		12 50					
Bexleyheath	d			12 12		12 23									12 36			12 42		12 53					
Welling	d			12 15		12 26									12 39			12 45		12 56					
Falconwood	d			12 18		12 28									12 41			12 48		12 58					
Eltham	d			12 21		12 31									12 44			12 51		13 01					
Kidbrooke	d			12 24		12 34									12 47			12 54		13 04					
Blackheath	d			12 28		12 38		12 41							12 51			12 58		13 08		13 11			
Lewisham	d		12 27	12 32		12 42		12 46							12 55		12 57	13 02		13 12		13 16			
St Johns	d		12 29			12 44											12 59			13 14					
New Cross	d		12 31			12 47											13 01			13 17					
Nunhead	d			12 37														13 07							
Peckham Rye	d			12 40														13 10							
Denmark Hill	d			12 44														13 14							
London Victoria	a			12 55														13 25							
Westcombe Park	d	12 22					12 32		12 42							12 52					13 02		13 12		
Maze Hill	d	12 24					12 34		12 44							12 54					13 04		13 14		
Greenwich	d	12 27					12 37		12 47							12 57					13 07		13 17		
Deptford	a	12 29					12 39		12 49		←	←				12 59					13 09		13 19		←
London Bridge	a	12 35	12 37		12 43	12 52	12 45	12 55	12 57	12 50	12 52	12 55			13 03	13 05	13 07		13 13	13 22	13 15	13 25	13 27	13 20	13 22
London Cannon Street	a	12 41	12 43			→	12 51	→			13 00					13 11	13 13			→	13 21	→			13 30
London Waterloo (East)	a				12 49					12 56		13 01			13 09				13 19					13 26	
London Charing Cross	a				12 53					13 00		13 05			13 13				13 23					13 30	
Ebbsfleet International	a												12 16												
Stratford International	a												12 28												
St Pancras Int'l	a												12 36												

Table T200-R

Mondays to Fridays
16 December to 15 May

Gillingham and Dartford - London

		SE	SE	SE	SE		SE	SE	SE	SE	SE	SE	TL	SE	SE	SE	SE	SE	SE	SE	SE		SE	SE	SE
			◇														◇								
Rainham (Kent)	d		12 16										12 28				12 46								
Gillingham (Kent)	d		12 21										12 34				12 51								
Chatham	d		12 25										12 38				12 55								
Rochester	d		12 29										12 42				12 59								
Maidstone West	d																								
Strood	d		12 32										12 45				13 02								
Higham	d												12 50												
Gravesend	d		12 42					12 50					12 59	13 05			13 12				13 20				
Northfleet	d												13 02	13 08											
Swanscombe	d												13 04	13 10											
Greenhithe for Bluewater	d							12 56					13 08	13 14							13 26				
Stone Crossing	d												13 10	13 16											
Dartford	a							13 01					13 14	13 20							13 31				
	d			12 55				13 02	13 05			13 11	13 15	13 21				13 25			13 32		13 35		
Slade Green	d				12 59					13 07	13 09	13 16	13 21						13 29					13 37	13 39
Erith	d				13 02						13 12	13 18							13 32						13 42
Belvedere	d				13 04						13 14	13 21							13 34						13 44
Abbey Wood	d				13 08						13 18	13 24	13 28						13 38						13 48
Plumstead	d				13 11						13 21	13 27	13 31						13 41						13 51
Woolwich Arsenal	d				13 14						13 24	13 30	13 34						13 44						13 54
Woolwich Dockyard	d				13 16						13 26	13 33							13 46						13 56
Charlton	d				13 20		12 25				13 30	13 36	13 40						13 50	12 55					14 00
Crayford	d						13 01		13 12					13 26						13 31			13 42		
Bexley	d						13 04		13 15					13 29						13 34			13 45		
Albany Park	d						13 06		13 17											13 36			13 47		
Sidcup	d						13 09		13 20					13 33						13 39			13 50		
New Eltham	d						13 13		13 24					13 36						13 43			13 54		
Mottingham	d						13 15		13 26											13 45			13 56		
Lee	d						13 18		13 29											13 48			13 59		
Hither Green	d						13 21		13 33											13 51			14 03		
Barnehurst	d			13 03				13 09		13 20								13 33			13 39			13 50	
Bexleyheath	d			13 06				13 12		13 23								13 36			13 42			13 53	
Welling	d			13 09				13 15		13 26								13 39			13 45			13 56	
Falconwood	d			13 11				13 18		13 28								13 41			13 48			13 58	
Eltham	d			13 14				13 21		13 31								13 44			13 51			14 01	
Kidbrooke	d			13 17				13 24		13 34								13 47			13 54			14 04	
Blackheath	d			13 21				13 28		13 38		13 41						13 51			13 58			14 08	
Lewisham	d			13 25			13 27	13 32		13 42		13 46						13 55		13 57	14 02			14 12	
St Johns	d						13 29			13 44										13 59				14 14	
New Cross ⊖	d						13 31			13 47										14 01				14 17	
Nunhead	d							13 37													14 07				
Peckham Rye	d							13 40													14 10				
Denmark Hill	d							13 44													14 14				
London Victoria ⊖	a							13 55													14 25				
Westcombe Park	d				13 22						13 32		13 42						13 52						14 02
Maze Hill	d				13 24						13 34		13 44						13 54						14 04
Greenwich	d				13 27						13 37		13 47						13 57						14 07
Deptford	a	←			13 29						13 39		13 49		←	←			13 59						14 09
London Bridge ⊖	a	13 25		13 33	13 35		13 37		13 43	13 52	13 45	13 55	13 57	13 50	13 52	13 55		14 03	14 05	14 07			14 13	14 22	14 15
London Cannon Street ⊖	a				13 41		13 43			→	13 51	→			14 00				14 11	14 13				→	14 21
London Waterloo (East) ⊖	a	13 31		13 39					13 49					13 56		14 01		14 09					14 19		
London Charing Cross ⊖	a	13 35		13 43					13 53					14 00		14 05		14 13					14 23		
Ebbsfleet International	a		12 46														13 16								
Stratford International ⊖	a		12 58														13 29								
St Pancras Int'l ⊖	a		13 06														13 37								

NRT DECEMBER 19 EDITION

Table T200-R

Mondays to Fridays
16 December to 15 May

Gillingham and Dartford - London

		SE	TL	SE	SE	SE	SE	SE	SE	SE	SE	SE	SE		SE	SE	TL	SE	SE	SE	SE	SE	SE	SE	SE
							◇														◇				
Rainham (Kent)	d		12 58				13 16										13 28				13 46				
Gillingham (Kent)	d		13 04				13 21										13 34				13 51				
Chatham	d		13 08				13 25										13 38				13 55				
Rochester	d		13 12				13 29										13 42				13 59				
Maidstone West	d																								
Strood	d		13 15				13 32										13 45				14 02				
Higham	d		13 20														13 50								
Gravesend	d		13 29	13 35			13 42				13 50						13 59	14 05			14 12				14 20
Northfleet	d		13 32	13 38													14 02	14 08							
Swanscombe	d		13 34	13 40													14 04	14 10							
Greenhithe for Bluewater	d		13 38	13 44							13 56						14 08	14 14							14 26
Stone Crossing	d		13 40	13 46													14 10	14 16							
Dartford	a		13 44	13 50							14 01						14 14	14 20							14 31
	d	13 41	13 45	13 51				13 55			14 02	14 05				14 11	14 15	14 21				14 25			14 32
Slade Green	d	13 46	13 51						13 59				14 07		14 09	14 16	14 21						14 29		
Erith	d	13 48							14 02						14 12	14 18							14 32		
Belvedere	d	13 51							14 04						14 14	14 21							14 34		
Abbey Wood	d	13 54	13 58						14 08						14 18	14 24	14 28						14 38		
Plumstead	d	13 57	14 01						14 11						14 21	14 27	14 31						14 41		
Woolwich Arsenal	d	14 00	14 04						14 14						14 24	14 30	14 34						14 44		
Woolwich Dockyard	d	14 03							14 16						14 26	14 33							14 46		
Charlton	d	14 06	14 10						14 20	13 25					14 30	14 36	14 40						14 50	13 55	
Crayford	d			13 56						14 01		14 12						14 26						14 31	
Bexley	d			13 59						14 04		14 15						14 29						14 34	
Albany Park	d									14 06		14 17												14 36	
Sidcup	d			14 03						14 09		14 20						14 33						14 39	
New Eltham	d			14 06						14 13		14 24						14 36						14 43	
Mottingham	d									14 15		14 26												14 45	
Lee	d									14 18		14 29												14 48	
Hither Green	d									14 21		14 33												14 51	
Barnehurst	d							14 03			14 09		14 20									14 33			14 39
Bexleyheath	d							14 06			14 12		14 23									14 36			14 42
Welling	d							14 09			14 15		14 26									14 39			14 45
Falconwood	d							14 11			14 18		14 28									14 41			14 48
Eltham	d							14 14			14 21		14 31									14 44			14 51
Kidbrooke	d							14 17			14 24		14 34									14 47			14 54
Blackheath	d	14 11						14 21			14 28		14 38			14 41						14 51			14 58
Lewisham	d	14 16						14 25		14 27	14 32		14 42			14 46						14 55		14 57	15 02
St Johns	d									14 29			14 44											14 59	
New Cross ⊖	d									14 31			14 47											15 01	
Nunhead	d										14 37														15 07
Peckham Rye	d										14 40														15 10
Denmark Hill	d										14 44														15 14
London Victoria ⊖	a										14 55														15 25
Westcombe Park	d		14 12						14 22						14 32		14 42						14 52		
Maze Hill	d		14 14						14 24						14 34		14 44						14 54		
Greenwich	d		14 17						14 27						14 37		14 47						14 57		
Deptford	a		14 19		←	←			14 29						14 39		14 49		←	←			14 59		
London Bridge ⊖	a	14 25	14 27	14 20	14 22	14 25		14 33	14 35	14 37		14 43	14 53		14 46	14 55	14 57	14 50	14 53	14 55		15 03	15 05	15 07	
London Cannon Street ⊖	a	→			14 30				14 41	14 43			→		14 51	→			15 00				15 11	15 13	
London Waterloo (East) ⊖	a			14 26		14 31		14 39				14 49						14 56		15 01		15 09			
London Charing Cross ⊖	a			14 30		14 35		14 43				14 53						15 00		15 05		15 13			
Ebbsfleet International	a						13 46														14 16				
Stratford International ⊖	a						14 02														14 28				
St Pancras Int'l ⊖	a						14 10														14 36				

Table T200-R

Mondays to Fridays

16 December to 15 May

Gillingham and Dartford - London

		SE	SE	SE	SE		TL	SE	SE	SE	SE ◇	SE	SE	SE	SE	SE	SE	SE	SE	TL	SE		SE	SE	SE ◇
Rainham (Kent)	d						13 58				14 16									14 28					14 46
Gillingham (Kent)	d						14 04				14 21									14 34					14 51
Chatham	d						14 08				14 25									14 38					14 55
Rochester	d						14 12				14 29									14 42					14 59
Maidstone West	d																								
Strood	d						14 15				14 32									14 45					15 02
Higham	d						14 20													14 50					
Gravesend	d						14 29	14 35			14 42				14 50					14 59	15 05				15 12
Northfleet	d						14 32	14 38												15 02	15 08				
Swanscombe	d						14 34	14 40												15 04	15 10				
Greenhithe for Bluewater	d						14 38	14 44							14 56					15 08	15 14				
Stone Crossing	d						14 40	14 46												15 10	15 16				
Dartford	a						14 44	14 50							15 01					15 14	15 20				
	d	14 35			14 41		14 45	14 51				14 55			15 02	15 05			15 11	15 15	15 21				
Slade Green	d		14 37	14 39	14 46		14 51						14 59				15 07	15 09	15 16	15 21					
Erith	d			14 42	14 48								15 02					15 12	15 18						
Belvedere	d			14 44	14 51								15 04					15 14	15 21						
Abbey Wood	d			14 48	14 54		14 58						15 08					15 18	15 24	15 28					
Plumstead	d			14 51	14 57		15 01						15 11					15 21	15 27	15 31					
Woolwich Arsenal	d			14 54	15 00		15 04						15 14					15 24	15 30	15 34					
Woolwich Dockyard	d			14 56	15 03								15 16					15 26	15 33						
Charlton	d			15 00	15 06		15 10						15 20	14 25				15 30	15 36	15 40					
Crayford	d	14 42						14 56						15 01		15 12					15 26				
Bexley	d	14 45						14 59						15 04		15 15					15 29				
Albany Park	d	14 47												15 06		15 17									
Sidcup	d	14 50						15 03						15 09		15 20					15 33				
New Eltham	d	14 54						15 06						15 13		15 24					15 36				
Mottingham	d	14 56												15 15		15 26									
Lee	d	14 59												15 18		15 29									
Hither Green	d	15 03												15 21		15 33									
Barnehurst	d		14 50									15 03			15 09		15 20								
Bexleyheath	d		14 53									15 06			15 12		15 23								
Welling	d		14 56									15 09			15 15		15 26								
Falconwood	d		14 58									15 11			15 18		15 28								
Eltham	d		15 01									15 14			15 21		15 31								
Kidbrooke	d		15 04									15 17			15 24		15 34								
Blackheath	d		15 08		15 11							15 21			15 28		15 38		15 41						
Lewisham	d		15 12		15 16							15 25		15 27	15 32		15 42		15 46						
St Johns	d		15 14											15 29			15 44								
New Cross	d		15 17											15 31			15 47								
Nunhead	d														15 37										
Peckham Rye	d														15 40										
Denmark Hill	d														15 44										
London Victoria	a														15 55										
Westcombe Park	d			15 02			15 12						15 22					15 32		15 42					
Maze Hill	d			15 04			15 14						15 24					15 34		15 44					
Greenwich	d			15 07			15 17						15 27					15 37		15 47					
Deptford	a			15 09			15 19		←	←			15 29					15 39		15 49			←	←	
London Bridge	a	15 13	15 22	15 15	15 25		15 27	15 20	15 22	15 25		15 33	15 35	15 37		15 43	15 52	15 45	15 55	15 57	15 50		15 52	15 55	
London Cannon Street	a		→	15 21	→				15 30				15 41	15 43			→	15 51	→				16 00		
London Waterloo (East)	a	15 19						15 26		15 31		15 39				15 49					15 56			16 01	
London Charing Cross	a	15 23						15 30		15 35		15 43				15 53					16 00			16 05	
Ebbsfleet International	a										14 46														15 16
Stratford International	a										14 58														15 28
St Pancras Int'l	a										15 06														15 36

Table T200-R

Mondays to Fridays

16 December to 15 May

Gillingham and Dartford - London

		SE	SE	SE	SE	SE	SE	SE	SE	TL	SE	SE	SE		SE ◇	SE	SE	SE	SE	SE	SE	SE	SE	TL	SE
Rainham (Kent)	d									14 58					15 16									15 28	
Gillingham (Kent)	d									15 04					15 21									15 34	
Chatham	d									15 08					15 25									15 38	
Rochester	d									15 12					15 29									15 42	
Maidstone West	d																								
Strood	d									15 15					15 32									15 45	
Higham	d									15 20														15 50	
Gravesend	d				15 20					15 29	15 35				15 42				15 50					15 59	16 03
Northfleet	d									15 32	15 38													16 02	16 06
Swanscombe	d									15 34	15 40													16 04	16 08
Greenhithe for Bluewater	d				15 26					15 38	15 44								15 56					16 08	16 12
Stone Crossing	d									15 40	15 46													16 10	16 14
Dartford	a				15 31					15 44	15 50								16 01					16 14	16 18
	d	15 25			15 32	15 35			15 41	15 45	15 51					15 55			16 02	16 05			16 11	16 15	16 19
Slade Green	d		15 29				15 37	15 39	15 46	15 51							15 57				16 09	16 07	16 16	16 21	
Erith	d		15 32					15 42	15 48								16 00				16 12		16 18		
Belvedere	d		15 34					15 44	15 51								16 02				16 14		16 21		
Abbey Wood	d		15 38					15 48	15 54	15 58							16 06				16 18		16 24	16 28	
Plumstead	d		15 41					15 51	15 57	16 01							16 09				16 21		16 27	16 31	
Woolwich Arsenal	d		15 44					15 54	16 00	16 04							16 12				16 24		16 30	16 34	
Woolwich Dockyard	d		15 46					15 56	16 03								16 14				16 26		16 33		
Charlton	d		15 50	14 55				16 00	16 06	16 10							16 18	15 25			16 30		16 36	16 40	
Crayford	d			15 31		15 42					15 56							16 01		16 12					16 24
Bexley	d			15 34		15 45					15 59							16 04		16 15					16 27
Albany Park	d			15 36		15 47												16 06		16 17					
Sidcup	d			15 39		15 50					16 03							16 09		16 20					16 31
New Eltham	d			15 43		15 54					16 06							16 13		16 24					16 34
Mottingham	d			15 45		15 56												16 15		16 26					
Lee	d			15 48		15 59												16 18		16 29					
Hither Green	d			15 51		16 03												16 21		16 33					
Barnehurst	d	15 33			15 39		15 50									16 03			16 09			16 15			
Bexleyheath	d	15 36			15 42		15 53									16 06			16 12			16 18			
Welling	d	15 39			15 45		15 56									16 09			16 15			16 21			
Falconwood	d	15 41			15 48		15 58									16 11			16 18			16 23			
Eltham	d	15 44			15 51		16 01									16 14			16 21			16 26			
Kidbrooke	d	15 47			15 54		16 04									16 17			16 24			16 29			
Blackheath	d	15 51			15 58		16 08		16 11							16 21			16 28			16 33	16 41		
Lewisham	d	15 56		15 58	16 02		16 12		16 16							16 25		16 27	16 32			16 37	16 46		
St Johns	d			16 00			16 14											16 29				16 39			
New Cross	d			16 02			16 17											16 31				16 42			
Nunhead	d				16 08														16 37						
Peckham Rye	d				16 11														16 40						
Denmark Hill	d				16 14														16 44						
London Victoria	a				16 25														16 55						
Westcombe Park	d		15 52					16 02		16 12							16 20				16 32			16 42	
Maze Hill	d		15 54					16 04		16 14							16 22				16 34			16 44	
Greenwich	d		15 57					16 07		16 17							16 25				16 37			16 47	
Deptford	a		15 59					16 09		16 19		←	←				16 27				16 39			16 49	
London Bridge	a	16 04	16 05	16 08		16 13	16 22	16 16	16 25	16 27	16 20	16 22	16 25			16 33	16 33	16 37		16 43	16 46	16 49	16 55	16 57	16 49
London Cannon Street	a		16 12	16 15			→	16 23	→			16 29					16 40	16 44			16 53	16 56	→		
London Waterloo (East)	a	16 10				16 19					16 26		16 31			16 40				16 51					16 55
London Charing Cross	a	16 15				16 23					16 30		16 36			16 46				16 57					17 01
Ebbsfleet International	a														15 46										
Stratford International	a														16 02										
St Pancras Int'l	a														16 10										

Table T200-R

Mondays to Fridays

16 December to 15 May

Gillingham and Dartford - London

		SE	SE ◇	SE	SE		SE	SE	SE	SE	SE	SE	SE	TL	SE	SE	SE ◇	SE	SE	SE	SE		SE	SE	SE
Rainham (Kent)	d		15 46											16 00			16 16								
Gillingham (Kent)	d		15 51											16 06			16 21								
Chatham	d		15 55											16 10			16 25								
Rochester	d		15 59											16 14			16 29								
Maidstone West	d																								
Strood	d		16 02											16 17			16 32								
Higham	d													16 22											
Gravesend	d		16 12					16 20						16 29	16 35		16 42		16 50						
Northfleet	d													16 33	16 38										
Swanscombe	d													16 35	16 40										
Greenhithe for Bluewater	d							16 26						16 38	16 44				16 56						
Stone Crossing	d													16 40	16 46										
Dartford	a							16 31						16 44	16 50				17 01						
	d			16 25				16 32	16 35				16 41	16 45	16 51			16 55	17 02				17 05		17 11
Slade Green	d				16 30					16 37		16 39	16 46	16 51						16 58	17 02			17 10	17 16
Erith	d				16 32							16 42	16 48							17 00	17 04				17 18
Belvedere	d				16 35							16 44	16 51							17 03	17 07				17 21
Abbey Wood	d				16 38							16 48	16 54	16 58						17 06	17 10				17 24
Plumstead	d				16 41							16 51	16 57	17 01						17 09	17 13				17 27
Woolwich Arsenal	d				16 44							16 54	17 00	17 04						17 12	17 16				17 30
Woolwich Dockyard	d				16 47							16 56	17 03							17 15	17 19				17 33
Charlton	d				16 50		15 55				16 26	17 00	17 06	17 10						17 18	17 22				17 36
Crayford	d						16 32		16 41		17 04				16 56								17 10		
Bexley	d						16 35		16 44		17 07				16 59								17 13		
Albany Park	d						16 37		16 46		17 09												17 15		
Sidcup	d						16 40		16 49		17 12				17 03								17 18		
New Eltham	d						16 44		16 53		17 16				17 06								17 22		
Mottingham	d						16 46		16 55		17 18												17 24		
Lee	d						16 49		16 58		17 21												17 27		
Hither Green	d						16 53		17 02		17 26												17 31		
Barnehurst	d			16 33				16 40		16 47								17 03	17 09					17 18	
Bexleyheath	d			16 36				16 43		16 50								17 06	17 12					17 21	
Welling	d			16 39				16 46		16 53								17 09	17 15						
Falconwood	d			16 41				16 48		16 55								17 11	17 18						
Eltham	d			16 44				16 51		16 58								17 14	17 21					17 27	
Kidbrooke	d			16 47				16 54		17 01								17 17	17 24					17 30	
Blackheath	d			16 51				16 58		17 05			17 11					17 21	17 28					17 34	17 41
Lewisham	d			16 55			17 00	17 02		17 09			17 15					17 25	17 32					17 38	17 45
St Johns	d						17 02			17 11	17 31														
New Cross	d						17 05			17 14	17 34													17 41	
Nunhead	d							17 07											17 37						
Peckham Rye	d							17 10											17 40						
Denmark Hill	d							17 14											17 44						
London Victoria	a							17 25											17 55						
Westcombe Park	d				16 52							17 02		17 12						17 20	17 24				
Maze Hill	d				16 54							17 04		17 14						17 22	17 26				
Greenwich	d				16 58							17 08		17 17						17 26	17 30				
Deptford	a	←			17 00							17 10		17 19		←				17 28	17 32				
London Bridge	a	16 55		17 03	17 07		17 10		17 13	17 20			17 23	17 27	17 20	17 23		17 34		17 34	17 38		17 40	17 47	17 53
London Cannon Street	a				17 14		17 17			17 27	17 48	17 25	→							17 41	17 46			17 54	→
London Waterloo (East)	a	17 01		17 09					17 20						17 28	17 30		17 39					17 46		
London Charing Cross	a	17 06		17 16					17 25						17 34	17 39		17 46					17 52		
Ebbsfleet International	a		16 16														16 46								
Stratford International	a		16 28														17 02								
St Pancras Int'l	a		16 36														17 10								

NRT DECEMBER 19 EDITION

Table T200-R

Mondays to Fridays

16 December to 15 May

Gillingham and Dartford - London

		TL	SE	SE	SE ◇	SE	SE	SE	SE	SE	SE	SE	SE		SE	SE	TL	SE	SE	SE ◇	SE	SE	SE	SE	SE
Rainham (Kent)	d	16 30			16 46												17 00			17 16					
Gillingham (Kent)	d	16 36			16 51												17 06			17 21					
Chatham	d	16 40			16 55												17 10			17 25					
Rochester	d	16 44			16 59												17 14			17 29					
Maidstone West	d																								
Strood	d	16 47			17 02												17 17			17 32					
Higham	d	16 52															17 22								
Gravesend	d	16 59	17 05		17 12			17 18									17 29	17 35		17 42					
Northfleet	d	17 03	17 08														17 33	17 38							
Swanscombe	d	17 05	17 10														17 35	17 40							
Greenhithe for Bluewater	d	17 08	17 14					17 24									17 38	17 44							
Stone Crossing	d	17 10	17 16														17 40	17 46							
Dartford	a	17 14	17 20					17 29									17 44	17 50							
	d	17 15	17 21				17 25	17 30			17 35					17 39	17 45	17 51				17 53			
Slade Green	d	17 21							17 29			17 40	17 34			17 46	17 51				17 54		18 00		18 00
Erith	d								17 32			17 43				17 48					17 57		18 03		
Belvedere	d								17 34			17 45				17 51					17 59		18 05		
Abbey Wood	d	17 28							17 38			17 49				17 54	17 58				18 03		18 09		
Plumstead	d	17 31										17 52				17 57	18 01				18 06		18 12		
Woolwich Arsenal	d	17 34							17 42			17 55				18 00	18 04				18 09		18 15		
Woolwich Dockyard	d											17 57				18 03					18 11		18 17		
Charlton	d	17 40							17 48	16 58		18 01				18 06	18 10				18 15		18 21	17 26	
Crayford	d		17 26							17 31	17 42							17 56						18 03	
Bexley	d		17 29							17 34	17 45							17 59						18 06	
Albany Park	d									17 36	17 47													18 08	
Sidcup	d		17 33							17 39	17 50							18 03						18 11	
New Eltham	d		17 36							17 43	17 54							18 06						18 15	
Mottingham	d									17 45	17 56													18 17	
Lee	d									17 48	17 59													18 20	
Hither Green	d									17 52	18 03													18 24	
Barnehurst	d					17 25	17 34	17 38					17 50		17 50							18 01			18a18
Bexleyheath	d					17 28	17 36	17 41					17 53		17 53							18 04			
Welling	d					17 31	17 39	17 44					17 56		17 56							18 07			
Falconwood	d					17 33	17 42	17 46					17 58		17 58							18 09			
Eltham	d					17 36	17 44	17 49					18 01		18 01							18 12			
Kidbrooke	d					17 40	17 47	17 52					18 04		18 04							18 15			
Blackheath	d					17 44	17 51	17 56					18 08		18 08	18 13						18 19			
Lewisham	d					17 48	17 55	18 00			18 09		18 14		18 14	18 17						18 23		18 30	
St Johns	d									17 56														18 34	
New Cross	d									17 59			18 17		18 17									18 37	
Nunhead	d							18 07																	
Peckham Rye	d							18 10																	
Denmark Hill	d							18 14																	
London Victoria	a							18 25																	
Westcombe Park	d	17 42							17 50			18 03					18 12				18 17		18 23		
Maze Hill	d	17 44							17 52			18 05					18 14				18 19		18 25		
Greenwich	d	17 47							17 55			18 08					18 17				18 22		18 28		
Deptford	a	17 49		←					17 57			18 10					18 19		←		18 24		18 30		
London Bridge	a	17 57	17 51	17 53		17 56	18 03		18 03	18 06	18 17	18 17	18 22		18 22	18 26	18 27	18 22	18 26		18 30	18 31	18 37	18 43	
London Cannon Street	a								18 10	18 13		18 24	18 27		18 27	→					18 37		18 44	18 50	
London Waterloo (East)	a		17 56	17 58		18 02	18 09				18 24							18 28	18 32			18 37			
London Charing Cross	a		18 03	18 05		18 08	18 17				18 30							18 34	18 38			18 41			
Ebbsfleet International	a				17 16															17 46					
Stratford International	a				17 28															18 03					
St Pancras Int'l	a				17 36															18 10					

Table T200-R

Mondays to Fridays

16 December to 15 May

Gillingham and Dartford - London

		SE	SE	SE	SE		TL	SE	SE ◇	SE	SE	SE	SE	SE	SE	SE	SE	SE	SE	SE	SE		SE	TL	SE
Rainham (Kent)	d						17 28		17 46															18 00	
Gillingham (Kent)	d						17 34		17 51															18 06	
Chatham	d						17 38		17 55															18 10	
Rochester	d						17 42		17 59															18 14	
Maidstone West	d																								
Strood	d						17 47		18 03															18 18	
Higham	d						17 52																	18 23	
Gravesend	d						17 59	18 05	18 13															18 30	18 35
Northfleet	d						18 03	18 08																18 33	18 38
Swanscombe	d						18 05	18 10																18 35	18 40
Greenhithe for Bluewater	d						18 08	18 14																18 39	18 44
Stone Crossing	d						18 10	18 16																18 41	18 46
Dartford	a						18 14	18 20																18 45	18 51
	d	18 02	18 06		18 08		18 15	18 21					18 25		18 35	18 38							18 42	18 46	18 52
Slade Green	d	18 09					18 21			18 00		18 16		18 29							18 37		18 48	18 51	
Erith	d	18 11										18 18		18 32							18 42		18 50		
Belvedere	d	18 14										18 21		18 34							18 44		18 53		
Abbey Wood	d	18 17					18 28					18 24		18 38							18 48		18 56	18 59	
Plumstead	d	18 20					18 31					18 27		18 41							18 51		18 59	19 02	
Woolwich Arsenal	d	18 23					18 34					18 30		18 44							18 54		19 02	19 05	
Woolwich Dockyard	d	18 26		←								18 33		18 46							18 56		19 04		
Charlton	d	18 29		18 29			18 40					18 36		18 50			18 00				19 00		19 07	19 10	
Crayford	d	→	18 12					18 26							18 41		18 37	18 37					→		18 56
Bexley	d		18 15					18 29							18 44		18 40	18 40							18 59
Albany Park	d		18 17												18 46		18 42	18 42							
Sidcup	d		18 20					18 33							18 49		18 45	18 45							19 03
New Eltham	d		18 24					18 36							18 53		18 49	18 49							19 06
Mottingham	d		18 26												18 55		18 51	18 51							
Lee	d		18 30												18 59		18 54	18 54							
Hither Green	d		18 33												19 02		18 59	18 59	18 13						
Barnehurst	d									18 19	18 19		18 33						18 52	18 52					
Bexleyheath	d				18 16					18 22	18 22		18 36						18 55	18 55					
Welling	d									18 25	18 25		18 39						18 58	18 58					
Falconwood	d									18 27	18 27		18 41						19 00	19 00					
Eltham	d				18 23					18 30	18 30		18 44						19 03	19 03					
Kidbrooke	d									18 33	18 33		18 47						19 06	19 06					
Blackheath	d				18 28					18 37	18 37	18 42	18 51			18 55			19 10	19 10					
Lewisham	d				18 32					18 41	18 41	18 48	18 55			19 00	19 07	19 07	19 14	19 14					
St Johns	d									18 44	18 44						19 09	19 09							
New Cross	d									18 47	18 47						19 11	19 11							
Nunhead	d				18 37											19 07									
Peckham Rye	d				18 40											19 10									
Denmark Hill	d				18 44											19 14									
London Victoria	a				18 57											19 27			19 33	19 33					
Westcombe Park	d			18 31			18 42							18 52							19 02			19 12	
Maze Hill	d			18 33			18 44							18 54							19 04			19 14	
Greenwich	d			18 37			18 47							18 57							19 08			19 18	
Deptford	a			18 39			18 49							18 59							19 10			19 20	
London Bridge	a		18 44	18 48			18 57	18 52		18 54	18 54	18 58	19 03	19 08	19 11		19 16	19 16			19 19			19 27	19 20
London Cannon Street	a			18 54						19 01	19 01			19 15			19 21	19 21			19 26				
London Waterloo (East)	a		18 50					18 57				19 05	19 09		19 19										19 27
London Charing Cross	a		18 55					19 02				19 09	19 13		19 23										19 31
Ebbsfleet International	a								18 17																
Stratford International	a								18 29																
St Pancras Int'l	a								18 37																

Table T200-R

Mondays to Fridays

16 December to 15 May

Gillingham and Dartford - London

		SE ◇	SE	SE	SE	SE	SE	SE	SE	SE	TL	SE	SE ◇		SE ◇	SE	SE	SE	SE	SE	SE	SE	SE	SE	SE
Rainham (Kent)	d	18 16									18 30				18 46										
Gillingham (Kent)	d	18 21									18 36				18 51										
Chatham	d	18 25									18 40				18 55										
Rochester	d	18 29									18 44				18 59										
Maidstone West	d												18 42												
Strood	d	18 35									18 47		18 58		19 02										
Higham	d										18 52														
Gravesend	d	18 45							18 51		18 59	19 05	19 08		19 12							19 18			
Northfleet	d										19 03	19 08													
Swanscombe	d										19 05	19 10													
Greenhithe for Bluewater	d								18 58		19 08	19 14										19 26			
Stone Crossing	d										19 10	19 16													
Dartford	a								19 03		19 14	19 20										19 31			
	d				18 55			19 02	19 07		19 15	19 21							19 25			19 32	19 35		
Slade Green	d		18 43			18 59				19 09	19 21					19 01		19 16		19 29				19 39	
Erith	d		18 46			19 02				19 12								19 18		19 32				19 42	
Belvedere	d		18 48			19 04				19 14								19 21		19 34				19 44	
Abbey Wood	d		18 52			19 08				19 18	19 28							19 24		19 38				19 48	
Plumstead	d		18 55			19 11				19 21	19 31							19 27		19 41				19 51	
Woolwich Arsenal	d		18 58			19 14				19 24	19 34							19 30		19 44				19 54	
Woolwich Dockyard	d		19 00	←		19 16				19 26								19 33		19 46				19 56	
Charlton	d		19 04	19 07		19 20	18 26			19 30	19 40							19 36		19 50	18 57			20 00	
Crayford	d						19 01		19 12			19 26									19 31		19 42		19 45
Bexley	d						19 04		19 15			19 29									19 34		19 45		
Albany Park	d						19 06		19 17												19 36		19 47		
Sidcup	d						19 09		19 20			19 33									19 39		19 50		19a55
New Eltham	d						19 13		19 24			19 36									19 43		19 54		
Mottingham	d						19 15		19 26												19 45		19 56		
Lee	d						19 18		19 29												19 48		19 59		
Hither Green	d						19 21		19 34												19 51		20 03		
Barnehurst	d				19 03			19 09								19 20	19 20		19 33			19 39			
Bexleyheath	d				19 06			19 12								19 23	19 23		19 36			19 42			
Welling	d				19 09			19 15								19 26	19 26		19 39			19 45			
Falconwood	d				19 11			19 18								19 28	19 28		19 41			19 48			
Eltham	d				19 14			19 21								19 31	19 31		19 44			19 51			
Kidbrooke	d				19 17			19 24								19 34	19 34		19 47			19 54			
Blackheath	d			19 13	19 21			19 28								19 38	19 38	19 41	19 51			19 58			
Lewisham	d			19 18	19 25		19 27	19 32								19 42	19 42	19 46	19 55		19 57	20 02			
St Johns	d						19 29									19 44	19 44				19 59				
New Cross	d						19 32									19 47	19 47				20 01				
Nunhead	d							19 37														20 07			
Peckham Rye	d							19 40														20 10			
Denmark Hill	d							19 44														20 14			
London Victoria	a							19 55														20 25			
Westcombe Park	d		19 06			19 22				19 32	19 42									19 52				20 02	
Maze Hill	d		19 09			19 24				19 34	19 44									19 54				20 04	
Greenwich	d		19 13			19 27				19 37	19 47									19 57				20 07	
Deptford	a		19 15			19 29				19 39	19 49									19 59				20 09	
London Bridge	a		19 23	19 27	19 33	19 36	19 39		19 43	19 46	19 57	19 51				19 52	19 52	19 55	20 03	20 05	20 07		20 13	20 15	
London Cannon Street	a		19 30			19 43	19 46			19 51						19 58	19 58			20 11	20 15			20 21	
London Waterloo (East)	a			19 32	19 39				19 49			19 57						20 01	20 09				20 19		
London Charing Cross	a			19 36	19 43				19 53			20 01						20 05	20 13				20 23		
Ebbsfleet International	a	18 49											19 12		19 16										
Stratford International	a	19 01											19 24		19 28										
St Pancras Int'l	a	19 09											19 31		19 36										

Table T200-R

Mondays to Fridays

16 December to 15 May

Gillingham and Dartford - London

		SE	SE	TL	SE		SE	SE	SE ◇	SE	SE	SE	SE	SE	SE	SE	SE	TL	SE	SE	SE		SE ◇	SE	SE
Rainham (Kent)	d			18 58					19 16									19 28					19 46		
Gillingham (Kent)	d			19 04					19 21									19 34					19 51		
Chatham	d			19 08					19 25									19 38					19 55		
Rochester	d			19 12					19 29									19 42					19 59		
Maidstone West	d																								
Strood	d			19 15					19 32									19 45					20 02		
Higham	d			19 20														19 50							
Gravesend	d			19 29	19 35				19 42									19 59	20 05				20 12		
Northfleet	d			19 32	19 38													20 02	20 08						
Swanscombe	d			19 34	19 40													20 04	20 10						
Greenhithe for Bluewater	d			19 38	19 44													20 08	20 14						
Stone Crossing	d			19 40	19 46													20 10	20 16						
Dartford	a			19 44	19 50													20 14	20 20						
	d		19 41	19 45	19 51					19 55			20 02	20 05			20 11	20 15	20 21					20 25	
Slade Green	d	19 40	19 46	19 51							19 59				20 07	20 09	20 16	20 21							20 29
Erith	d		19 48								20 02					20 12	20 18								20 32
Belvedere	d		19 51								20 04					20 14	20 21								20 34
Abbey Wood	d		19 54	19 58							20 08					20 18	20 24	20 28							20 38
Plumstead	d		19 57	20 01							20 11					20 21	20 27	20 31							20 41
Woolwich Arsenal	d		20 00	20 04							20 14					20 24	20 30	20 34							20 44
Woolwich Dockyard	d		20 03								20 16					20 26	20 33								20 46
Charlton	d		20 06	20 10							20 20	19 25				20 30	20 36	20 40							20 50
Crayford	d				19 56							20 01		20 12					20 26						
Bexley	d				19 59							20 04		20 15					20 29						
Albany Park	d											20 06		20 17											
Sidcup	d				20 03							20 09		20 20					20 33						
New Eltham	d				20 06							20 13		20 24					20 36						
Mottingham	d											20 15		20 26											
Lee	d											20 18		20 29											
Hither Green	d											20 21		20 33											
Barnehurst	d	19 50								20 03			20 09		20 20									20 33	
Bexleyheath	d	19 53								20 06			20 12		20 23									20 36	
Welling	d	19 56								20 09			20 15		20 26									20 39	
Falconwood	d	19 58								20 11			20 18		20 28									20 41	
Eltham	d	20 01								20 14			20 21		20 31									20 44	
Kidbrooke	d	20 04								20 17			20 24		20 34									20 47	
Blackheath	d	20 08	20 11							20 21			20 28		20 38		20 41							20 51	
Lewisham	d	20 12	20 17							20 25		20 27	20 32		20 42		20 46							20 55	
St Johns	d	20 14										20 29			20 44										
New Cross ⊖	d	20 17										20 31			20 47										
Nunhead	d												20 37												
Peckham Rye	d												20 40												
Denmark Hill	d												20 44												
London Victoria ⊖	a												20 55												
Westcombe Park	d			20 12							20 22					20 32		20 42							20 52
Maze Hill	d			20 14							20 24					20 34		20 44							20 54
Greenwich	d			20 17							20 27					20 37		20 47							20 57
Deptford	a			20 19			←	←			20 29					20 39		20 49		←	←				20 59
London Bridge ⊖	a	20 22	20 25	20 27	20 20		20 22	20 25		20 33	20 35	20 37		20 43	20 52	20 45	20 55	20 57	20 50	20 52	20 55			21 03	21 05
London Cannon Street ⊖	a	→	→				20 30				20 41	20 43			→	20 51	→			21 00					21 11
London Waterloo (East) ⊖	a				20 26			20 31		20 39				20 49					20 56		21 01			21 09	
London Charing Cross ⊖	a				20 30			20 35		20 43				20 53					21 00		21 05			21 13	
Ebbsfleet International	a								19 46														20 16		
Stratford International ⊖	a								19 58														20 28		
St Pancras Int'l ⊖	a								20 06														20 36		

Table T200-R

Mondays to Fridays

16 December to 15 May

Gillingham and Dartford - London

		SE	SE	SE	SE	TL	SE	SE	SE ◇	SE	SE	SE	SE		SE	SE	TL	SE	SE	SE ◇	SE	SE	SE	SE	SE
Rainham (Kent)	d					19 58			20 16								20 28			20 46					
Gillingham (Kent)	d					20 04			20 21								20 34			20 52					
Chatham	d					20 08			20 25								20 38			20 56					
Rochester	d					20 12			20 29								20 42			21 00					
Maidstone West	d																								
Strood	d					20 15			20 32								20 45			21 03					
Higham	d					20 20											20 50								
Gravesend	d		20 20			20 29	20 35		20 42				20 50				20 59	21 05		21 13				21 20	
Northfleet	d					20 32	20 38										21 02	21 08							
Swanscombe	d					20 34	20 40										21 04	21 10							
Greenhithe for Bluewater	d		20 26			20 38	20 44						20 56				21 08	21 14						21 26	
Stone Crossing	d					20 40	20 46										21 10	21 16							
Dartford	a		20 31			20 44	20 50						21 01				21 14	21 20						21 31	
	d		20 32	20 35	20 41	20 45	20 51			20 55			21 02		21 05	21 11	21 15	21 21			21 25			21 32	21 35
Slade Green	d				20 46	20 51					20 59					21 16	21 21					21 29			
Erith	d				20 48						21 02					21 18						21 32			
Belvedere	d				20 51						21 04					21 21						21 34			
Abbey Wood	d				20 54	20 58					21 08					21 24	21 28					21 38			
Plumstead	d				20 57	21 01					21 11					21 27	21 31					21 41			
Woolwich Arsenal	d				21 00	21 04					21 14					21 30	21 34					21 44			
Woolwich Dockyard	d				21 03						21 16					21 33						21 46			
Charlton	d	19 55			21 06	21 10					21 20	20 25				21 36	21 40					21 50	20 55		
Crayford	d	20 31		20 43			20 56					21 01			21 12			21 26					21 31		21 42
Bexley	d	20 34		20 46			20 59					21 04			21 15			21 29					21 34		21 45
Albany Park	d	20 36		20 48								21 06			21 17								21 36		21 47
Sidcup	d	20 39		20 51			21 03					21 09			21 20			21 33					21 39		21 50
New Eltham	d	20 43		20 54			21 06					21 13			21 24			21 36					21 43		21 54
Mottingham	d	20 45		20 57								21 15			21 26								21 45		21 56
Lee	d	20 48		21 00								21 18			21 29								21 48		21 59
Hither Green	d	20 51		21 03								21 21			21 33								21 51		22 03
Barnehurst	d		20 39							21 03			21 09								21 33			21 39	
Bexleyheath	d		20 42							21 06			21 12								21 36			21 42	
Welling	d		20 45							21 09			21 15								21 39			21 45	
Falconwood	d		20 48							21 11			21 18								21 41			21 48	
Eltham	d		20 51							21 14			21 21								21 44			21 51	
Kidbrooke	d		20 54							21 17			21 24								21 47			21 54	
Blackheath	d		20 58		21 11					21 21			21 28			21 41					21 51			21 58	
Lewisham	d	20 57	21 02		21 16					21 25		21 27	21 32			21 46					21 55		21 57	22 02	
St Johns	d	20 59										21 29											21 59		
New Cross ⊖	d	21 01										21 31											22 01		
Nunhead	d		21 07										21 37											22 07	
Peckham Rye	d		21 10										21 40											22 10	
Denmark Hill	d		21 14										21 44											22 14	
London Victoria ⊖	a		21 25										21 55											22 25	
Westcombe Park	d					21 12					21 22						21 42					21 52			
Maze Hill	d					21 14					21 24						21 44					21 54			
Greenwich	d					21 17					21 27						21 47					21 57			
Deptford	a					21 19		←			21 29						21 49		←			21 59			
London Bridge ⊖	a	21 07		21 13	21 25	21 27	21 20	21 25		21 33	21 35	21 37			21 43	21 55	21 57	21 50	21 55		22 03	22 05	22 07		22 13
London Cannon Street ⊖	a	21 13			→						21 41	21 43				→						22 11	22 13		
London Waterloo (East) ⊖	a			21 19			21 26	21 31		21 39					21 49			21 56	22 01		22 09				22 19
London Charing Cross ⊖	a			21 23			21 30	21 35		21 43					21 53			22 00	22 05		22 13				22 23
Ebbsfleet International	a								20 46											21 18					
Stratford International ⊖	a								20 59											21 32					
St Pancras Int'l ⊖	a								21 06											21 40					

Table T200-R

Mondays to Fridays

16 December to 15 May

Gillingham and Dartford - London

Station		SE	TL	SE	SE		SE ◇	SE	SE	SE	SE	SE	SE	TL	SE	SE	SE ◇	SE	SE	SE	SE		SE	SE	TL
Rainham (Kent)	d		20 58				21 16							21 28			21 46								22 00
Gillingham (Kent) [4]	d		21 04				21 21							21 34			21 51								22 06
Chatham [4]	d		21 08				21 25							21 38			21 55								22 10
Rochester [4]	d		21 12				21 29							21 42			21 59								22 14
Maidstone West	d																								
Strood [4]	d		21 15				21 32							21 45			22 02								22 17
Higham	d		21 20											21 50											22 22
Gravesend [4]	d		21 29	21 35			21 42				21 50			21 59	22 05		22 12				22 20				22 29
Northfleet	d		21 32	21 38										22 02	22 08										22 33
Swanscombe	d		21 34	21 40										22 04	22 10										22 35
Greenhithe for Bluewater	d		21 38	21 44							21 56			22 08	22 14						22 26				22 38
Stone Crossing	d		21 40	21 46										22 10	22 16										22 40
Dartford [4]	a		21 44	21 50							22 01			22 14	22 20						22 31				22 44
	d	21 41	21 45	21 51				21 55			22 02	22 05	22 11	22 15	22 21			22 25			22 32		22 35	22 41	22 45
Slade Green [4]	d	21 46	21 51						21 59				22 16	22 21					22 29					22 46	22 51
Erith	d	21 48							22 02				22 18						22 32					22 48	
Belvedere	d	21 51							22 04				22 21						22 34					22 51	
Abbey Wood	d	21 54	21 58						22 08				22 24	22 28					22 38					22 54	22 58
Plumstead	d	21 57	22 01						22 11				22 27	22 31					22 41					22 57	23 01
Woolwich Arsenal [4] ⛴	d	22 00	22 04						22 14				22 30	22 34					22 44					23 00	23 04
Woolwich Dockyard	d	22 03							22 16				22 33						22 46					23 03	
Charlton [4]	d	22 06	22 10						22 20	21 25			22 36	22 40					22 50	21 52				23 06	23 10
Crayford	d			21 56						22 01		22 12			22 26					22 31			22 42		
Bexley	d			21 59						22 04		22 15			22 29					22 34			22 45		
Albany Park	d									22 06		22 17								22 36			22 47		
Sidcup [4]	d			22 03						22 09		22 20			22 33					22 39			22 50		
New Eltham	d			22 06						22 13		22 24			22 36					22 43			22 54		
Mottingham	d									22 15		22 26								22 45			22 56		
Lee	d									22 18		22 29								22 48			22 59		
Hither Green [4]	d									22 21		22 33								22 51			23 03		
Barnehurst [4]	d							22 03			22 09							22 33			22 39				
Bexleyheath	d							22 06			22 12							22 36			22 42				
Welling	d							22 09			22 15							22 39			22 45				
Falconwood	d							22 11			22 18							22 41			22 48				
Eltham	d							22 14			22 21							22 44			22 51				
Kidbrooke	d							22 17			22 24							22 47			22 54				
Blackheath [4]	d	22 11						22 21			22 28		22 41					22 51			22 58			23 11	
Lewisham [4] ⛴	d	22 16						22 25		22 27	22 32		22 46					22 55		22 57	23 02			23 16	
St Johns	d									22 29										22 59					
New Cross [4] ⊖	d									22 31										23 01					
Nunhead [4]	d										22 37										23 07				
Peckham Rye [4]	d										22 40										23 10				
Denmark Hill [4]	d										22 44										23 14				
London Victoria [15] ⊖	a										22 55										23 25				
Westcombe Park	d		22 12						22 22					22 42					22 52						23 12
Maze Hill	d		22 14						22 24					22 44					22 54						23 14
Greenwich [4] ⛴	d		22 17						22 27					22 47					22 57						23 17
Deptford	a		22 19		←				22 29					22 49		←			22 59						23 19
London Bridge [4] ⊖	a	22 25	22 27	22 20	22 25			22 33	22 35	22 37		22 43	22 55	22 57	22 50	22 55		23 03	23 05	23 07			23 13	23 25	23 27
London Cannon Street [4] ⊖	a	→							22 41	22 43			→						23 11	23 13				→	
London Waterloo (East) [4] ⊖	a			22 26	22 31			22 39				22 49			22 56	23 01		23 09					23 19		
London Charing Cross [4] ⊖	a			22 30	22 35			22 43				22 53			23 00	23 05		23 13					23 23		
Ebbsfleet International	a						21 46										22 16								
Stratford International ⊖ ⛴	a						21 59										22 28								
St Pancras Int'l [15] ⊖	a						22 07										22 36								

Table T200-R

Mondays to Fridays

16 December to 15 May

Gillingham and Dartford - London

Station		SE	SE	SE ◇	SE WTh FO	SE MTO	SE	SE MT FO	SE W ThO	SE	SE WTh FO	SE	TL		SE	SE	SE WTh FO	SE MT FO	SE MT FO	SE W ThO	SE W ThO	SE MTO	SE MTO	SE WTh FO	TL	SE WTh FO	SE MTO	TL	
Rainham (Kent)	d			22 16									22 30												23 00			23 30	
Gillingham (Kent) [4]	d			22 21									22 36												23 06			23 36	
Chatham [4]	d			22 25									22 40												23 10			23 40	
Rochester [4]	d			22 29									22 44												23 14			23 44	
Maidstone West	d																												
Strood [4]	d			22 32									22 47												23 17			23 47	
Higham	d												22 52												23 22			23 52	
Gravesend [4]	d	22 35		22 42						22 50			22 59		23 05										23 29	23 35	23 35	23 59	
Northfleet	d	22 38											23 03		23 08										23 33	23 38	23 38	00 03	
Swanscombe	d	22 40											23 05		23 10										23 35	23 40	23 40	00 05	
Greenhithe for Bluewater	d	22 44								22 56			23 08		23 14										23 38	23 44	23 44	00 08	
Stone Crossing	d	22 46											23 10		23 16										23 40	23 46	23 46	00 10	
Dartford [4]	a	22 50								23 01			23 15		23 20										23 45	23 50	23 50	00 15	
	d	22 51			22 55	22 55				23 02	23 05	23 11			23 21		23 25					23 25	23 41	23 41		23 51	23 51		
Slade Green [4]	d						22 59					23 16						23 29					23 46	23 46					
Erith	d						23 02					23 18						23 32					23 48	23 48					
Belvedere	d						23 04					23 21						23 34					23 51	23 51					
Abbey Wood	d						23 08					23 24						23 38					23 54	23 54					
Plumstead	d						23 11					23 27						23 41					23 57	23 57					
Woolwich Arsenal [4] ⛴	d						23 14					23 30						23 44					23 59	23 59					
Woolwich Dockyard	d						23 16					23 33				←		23 46					00 03	00 03					
Charlton [4]	d						23 20	22 22	22 22			23 36				23 36		23 50	22 52	22 52			00 06	00 06					
Crayford	d	22 56						23 01	23 01		23 12	→			23 26				23 31	23 31	23 31					23 56	23 56		
Bexley	d	22 59						23 04	23 04		23 15				23 29				23 34	23 34	23 34					23 59	23 59		
Albany Park	d							23 06	23 06		23 17								23 36	23 36	23 36					00 01	00 01		
Sidcup [4]	d	23 03						23 09	23 09		23 20				23 33				23 39	23 39	23 39					00 04	00 04		
New Eltham	d	23 06						23 13	23 13		23 24				23 36				23 43	23 43	23 43					00 08	00 08		
Mottingham	d							23 15	23 15		23 26								23 45	23 45	23 45					00 10	00 10		
Lee	d							23 18	23 18		23 29								23 48	23 48	23 48					00 13	00 13		
Hither Green [4]	d							23 21	23 21		23 33								23 51	23 51	23 51					00 16	00 16		
Barnehurst [4]	d				23 03	23 03				23 09							23 33					23 33							
Bexleyheath	d				23 06	23 06				23 12							23 36					23 36							
Welling	d				23 09	23 09				23 15							23 39					23 39							
Falconwood	d				23 11	23 11				23 18							23 41					23 41							
Eltham	d				23 14	23 14				23 21							23 44					23 44							
Kidbrooke	d				23 17	23 17				23 24							23 47					23 47							
Blackheath [4]	d				23 21	23 21				23 28						23 41	23 51					23 51	00 11	00 11					
Lewisham [4] ⛴	d				23 25	23 25		23 27	23 27	23 32						23 46	23 55		23 57	23 58	23 58	00 05	00 15	00 16					
St Johns	d							23 29	23 29										23 59										
New Cross [4] ⊖	d							23 31	23 31										00 01										
Nunhead [4]	d									23 37																			
Peckham Rye [4]	d									23 40																			
Denmark Hill [4]	d									23 44																			
London Victoria [15] ⊖	a									23 55																			
Westcombe Park	d						23 22											23 52											
Maze Hill	d						23 24											23 54											
Greenwich [4] ⛴	d						23 27											23 57											
Deptford	a		←				23 29											23 59											
London Bridge [4] ⊖	a	23 20	23 25		23 33	23 33	23 35	23 37	23 41		23 43				23 50	23 55	00 03	00 05	00 07	00 08	00 08	00 13	00 23	00 24		00 27	00 29		
London Cannon Street [4] ⊖	a						23 41	23 43										00 11	00 13				00 33						
London Waterloo (East) [4] ⊖	a	23 26	23 31		23 39	23 39					23 49				23 56	00 01	00 09							00 30		00 33			
London Charing Cross [4] ⊖	a	23 30	23 35		23 43	23 44					23 53				00 01	00 05	00 13							00 35		00 39			
Ebbsfleet International	a			22 46																									
Stratford International ⊖ ⛴	a			22 58																									
St Pancras Int'l [15] ⊖	a			23 06																									

Table T200-R

Saturdays

21 December to 16 May

Gillingham and Dartford - London

		SE	TL	SE	SE	TL	SE	SE	SE	TL	SE	SE	SE	SE	TL	SE		SE	SE	SE	SE	TL	SE ◇	SE	SE
Rainham (Kent)	d																					05 28	05 46		
Gillingham (Kent) 4	d					04 06				04 36					05 06							05 34	05 51		
Chatham 4	d					04 10				04 40					05 10							05 38	05 55		
Rochester 4	d					04 14				04 44					05 14							05 42	05 59		
Maidstone West	d																								
Strood 4	d					04 17				04 47					05 17							05 45	06 02		
Higham	d					04 22				04 52					05 22							05 50			
Gravesend 4	d					04 29				04 59		05 18			05 29				05 48			05 59	06 12		
Northfleet	d		00 03			04 33				05 03		05 22			05 33				05 52			06 02			
Swanscombe	d		00 05			04 35				05 05		05 24			05 35				05 54			06 04			
Greenhithe for Bluewater	d		00 08			04 38				05 08		05 27			05 38				05 57			06 08			
Stone Crossing	d		00 10			04 40				05 10		05 29			05 40				05 59			06 10			
Dartford 4	a		00 15			04 45				05 14		05 34			05 44				06 03			06 14			
	d						05 03	05 05		05 15	05 25	05 35		05 41	05 45	05 55			06 05		06 11	06 15		06 25	
Slade Green 4	d						05 09			05 21			05 39	05 46	05 51					06 09	06 16	06 21			
Erith	d						05 12						05 42	05 48						06 12	06 18				
Belvedere	d						05 14						05 44	05 51						06 14	06 21				
Abbey Wood	d						05 18			05 28			05 48	05 54	05 58					06 18	06 24	06 28			
Plumstead	d						05 21			05 31			05 51	05 57	06 01					06 21	06 27	06 31			
Woolwich Arsenal 4	d						05 24			05 34			05 54	06 00	06 04					06 24	06 30	06 34			
Woolwich Dockyard	d			00 03			05 26		←				05 56	06 03						06 26	06 33				
Charlton 4	d			00 06			05 30		05 30	05 40			06 00	06 06	06 10			05 25		06 30	06 36	06 40			05 55
Crayford	d						→	05 12				05 42						06 01	06 12						06 31
Bexley	d							05 15				05 45						06 04	06 15						06 34
Albany Park	d				00 01			05 17				05 47						06 06	06 17						06 36
Sidcup 4	d				00 04			05 20				05 50						06 09	06 20						06 39
New Eltham	d				00 08			05 24				05 54						06 13	06 24						06 43
Mottingham	d				00 10			05 26				05 56						06 15	06 26						06 45
Lee	d				00 13			05 29				05 59						06 18	06 29						06 48
Hither Green 4	d				00 16			05 33				06 03						06 21	06 33						06 51
Barnehurst 4	d										05 33					06 03								06 33	
Bexleyheath	d										05 36					06 06								06 36	
Welling	d										05 39					06 09								06 39	
Falconwood	d										05 41					06 11								06 41	
Eltham	d										05 44					06 14								06 44	
Kidbrooke	d										05 47					06 17								06 47	
Blackheath 4	d			00 11							05 51			06 11		06 21					06 41			06 51	
Lewisham 4	d			00 16							05 55			06 16		06 25		06 27			06 46			06 55	06 57
St Johns	d																	06 29							06 59
New Cross 4	d	00 01																06 31							07 01
Nunhead 4	d																								
Peckham Rye 4	d																								
Denmark Hill 4	d																								
London Victoria 15	a																								
Westcombe Park	d								05 32	05 42			06 02		06 12					06 32		06 42			
Maze Hill	d								05 34	05 44			06 04		06 14					06 34		06 44			
Greenwich 4	d								05 37	05 47			06 07		06 17					06 37		06 47			
Deptford	a								05 39	05 49			06 09		06 19					06 39		06 49			
London Bridge 4	a	00 07		00 24	00 27			05 43	05 45	05 57	06 03	06 13	06 15	06 25	06 27	06 33		06 37	06 43	06 45	06 55	06 57		07 03	07 07
London Cannon Street 4	a	00 13							05 51				06 21					06 43		06 51					07 13
London Waterloo (East) 4	a			00 30	00 33			05 49			06 09	06 19		06 31		06 39			06 49		07 01			07 09	
London Charing Cross 4	a			00 35	00 39			05 53			06 13	06 23		06 35		06 43			06 53		07 05			07 13	
Ebbsfleet International	a																						06 16		
Stratford International	a																						06 28		
St Pancras Int'l 15	a																						06 36		

Table T200-R

Saturdays

21 December to 16 May

Gillingham and Dartford - London

		SE	SE	SE	SE	TL	SE	SE		SE	SE	SE	SE	SE	SE	SE	TL	SE	SE	SE ◇	SE	SE	SE	SE
Rainham (Kent)	d					05 58											06 28			06 46				
Gillingham (Kent) 4	d					06 04											06 34			06 51				
Chatham 4	d					06 08											06 38			06 55				
Rochester 4	d					06 12											06 42			06 59				
Maidstone West	d																							
Strood 4	d					06 15											06 45			07 02				
Higham	d					06 20											06 50							
Gravesend 4	d		06 18			06 29	06 35						06 50				06 59	07 05		07 12				07 20
Northfleet	d		06 22			06 32	06 38										07 02	07 08						
Swanscombe	d		06 24			06 34	06 40										07 04	07 10						
Greenhithe for Bluewater	d		06 27			06 38	06 44						06 56				07 08	07 14						07 26
Stone Crossing	d		06 29			06 40	06 46										07 10	07 16						
Dartford 4	a		06 34			06 44	06 50						07 01				07 14	07 20						07 31
	d	06 32	06 35		06 41	06 45	06 51			06 55			07 02	07 05		07 11	07 15	07 21			07 25			07 32
Slade Green 4	d			06 39	06 46	06 51					06 59				07 09	07 16	07 21					07 29		
Erith	d			06 42	06 48						07 02				07 12	07 18						07 32		
Belvedere	d			06 44	06 51						07 04				07 14	07 21						07 34		
Abbey Wood	d			06 48	06 54	06 58					07 08				07 18	07 24	07 28					07 38		
Plumstead	d			06 51	06 57	07 01					07 11				07 21	07 27	07 31					07 41		
Woolwich Arsenal 4	d			06 54	07 00	07 04					07 14				07 24	07 30	07 34					07 44		
Woolwich Dockyard	d			06 56	07 03						07 16				07 26	07 33						07 46		
Charlton 4	d			07 00	07 06	07 10					07 20	06 25			07 30	07 36	07 40					07 50	06 55	
Crayford	d		06 42				06 56					07 01		07 12				07 26					07 31	
Bexley	d		06 45				06 59					07 04		07 15				07 29					07 34	
Albany Park	d		06 47									07 06		07 17									07 36	
Sidcup 4	d		06 50				07 03					07 09		07 20				07 33					07 39	
New Eltham	d		06 54				07 06					07 13		07 24				07 36					07 43	
Mottingham	d		06 56									07 15		07 26									07 45	
Lee	d		06 59									07 18		07 29									07 48	
Hither Green 4	d		07 03									07 21		07 33									07 51	
Barnehurst 4	d	06 39								07 03			07 09								07 33			07 39
Bexleyheath	d	06 42								07 06			07 12								07 36			07 42
Welling	d	06 45								07 09			07 15								07 39			07 45
Falconwood	d	06 48								07 11			07 18								07 41			07 48
Eltham	d	06 51								07 14			07 21								07 44			07 51
Kidbrooke	d	06 54								07 17			07 24								07 47			07 54
Blackheath 4	d	06 58			07 11					07 21			07 28			07 41					07 51			07 58
Lewisham 4	d	07 02			07 16					07 25		07 27	07 32			07 46					07 55		07 57	08 02
St Johns	d											07 29											07 59	
New Cross 4	d											07 31											08 01	
Nunhead 4	d	07 07											07 37											08 07
Peckham Rye 4	d	07 10											07 40											08 10
Denmark Hill 4	d	07 14											07 44											08 14
London Victoria 15	a	07 25											07 55											08 25
Westcombe Park	d			07 02		07 12					07 22				07 32		07 42					07 52		
Maze Hill	d			07 04		07 14					07 24				07 34		07 44					07 54		
Greenwich 4	d			07 07		07 17					07 27				07 37		07 47					07 57		
Deptford	a			07 09		07 19		←			07 29				07 39		07 49		←			07 59		
London Bridge 4	a		07 13	07 15	07 25	07 27	07 20	07 25		07 33	07 35	07 37		07 43	07 45	07 55	07 57	07 50	07 55		08 03	08 05	08 07	
London Cannon Street 4	a			07 21	→						07 41	07 43			07 51	→						08 11	08 13	
London Waterloo (East) 4	a		07 19				07 26	07 31		07 39				07 49				07 56	08 01		08 09			
London Charing Cross 4	a		07 23				07 30	07 35		07 43				07 53				08 00	08 05		08 13			
Ebbsfleet International	a																			07 16				
Stratford International	a																			07 28				
St Pancras Int'l 15	a																			07 36				

Table T200-R

Saturdays

21 December to 16 May

Gillingham and Dartford - London

		SE	SE	SE	SE	TL	SE	SE	SE	SE	SE	SE	SE	SE	SE	SE		SE	SE	TL	SE	SE	SE	SE	SE
										◇														◇	
Rainham (Kent)	d					06 58				07 16										07 28				07 46	
Gillingham (Kent)	d					07 04				07 21										07 34				07 51	
Chatham	d					07 08				07 25										07 38				07 55	
Rochester	d					07 12				07 29										07 42				07 59	
Maidstone West	d																								
Strood	d					07 15				07 32										07 45				08 02	
Higham	d					07 20														07 50					
Gravesend	d					07 29	07 35			07 42				07 50						07 59	08 05			08 12	
Northfleet	d					07 32	07 38													08 02	08 08				
Swanscombe	d					07 34	07 40													08 04	08 10				
Greenhithe for Bluewater	d					07 38	07 44							07 56						08 08	08 14				
Stone Crossing	d					07 40	07 46													08 10	08 16				
Dartford	a					07 44	07 50							08 01						08 14	08 20				
	d	07 35			07 41	07 45	07 51				07 55			08 02	08 05				08 11	08 15	08 21				08 25
Slade Green	d		07 39		07 46	07 51						07 59				08 09			08 16	08 21					
Erith	d		07 42		07 48							08 02				08 12			08 18						
Belvedere	d		07 44		07 51							08 04				08 14			08 21						
Abbey Wood	d		07 48		07 54	07 58						08 08				08 18			08 24	08 28					
Plumstead	d		07 51		07 57	08 01						08 11				08 21			08 27	08 31					
Woolwich Arsenal	d		07 54		08 00	08 04						08 14				08 24			08 30	08 34					
Woolwich Dockyard	d		07 56		08 03							08 16				08 26			08 33						
Charlton	d		08 00		08 06	08 10						08 20	07 25			08 30			08 36	08 40					
Crayford	d	07 42					07 56						08 01		08 12						08 26				
Bexley	d	07 45					07 59						08 04		08 15						08 29				
Albany Park	d	07 47											08 06		08 17										
Sidcup	d	07 50					08 03						08 09		08 20						08 33				
New Eltham	d	07 54					08 06						08 13		08 24						08 36				
Mottingham	d	07 56											08 15		08 26										
Lee	d	07 59											08 18		08 29										
Hither Green	d	08 03											08 21		08 33										
Barnehurst	d			07 50							08 03			08 09				08 20							08 33
Bexleyheath	d			07 53							08 06			08 12				08 23							08 36
Welling	d			07 56							08 09			08 15				08 26							08 39
Falconwood	d			07 58							08 11			08 18				08 28							08 41
Eltham	d			08 01							08 14			08 21				08 31							08 44
Kidbrooke	d			08 04							08 17			08 24				08 34							08 47
Blackheath	d			08 08	08 11						08 21			08 28				08 38	08 41						08 51
Lewisham	d			08 12	08 16						08 25		08 27	08 32				08 42	08 46						08 55
St Johns	d			08 14									08 29					08 44							
New Cross	d			08 17									08 31					08 47							
Nunhead	d													08 37											
Peckham Rye	d													08 40											
Denmark Hill	d													08 44											
London Victoria	a													08 55											
Westcombe Park	d		08 02			08 12						08 22				08 32				08 42					
Maze Hill	d		08 04			08 14						08 24				08 34				08 44					
Greenwich	d		08 07			08 17						08 27				08 37				08 47					
Deptford	a		08 09			08 19		←	←			08 29				08 39				08 49		←	←		
London Bridge	a	08 13	08 15	08 22	08 25	08 27	08 20	08 22	08 25		08 33	08 35	08 37		08 43	08 45		08 52	08 55	08 57	08 50	08 52	08 55		09 03
London Cannon Street	a		08 21	→	→			08 30				08 41	08 43			08 51		→	→			09 00			
London Waterloo (East)	a	08 19					08 26		08 31		08 39				08 49						08 56		09 01		09 09
London Charing Cross	a	08 23					08 30		08 35		08 43				08 53						09 00		09 05		09 13
Ebbsfleet International	a									07 46														08 16	
Stratford International	a									07 58														08 29	
St Pancras Int'l	a									08 06														08 37	

Table T200-R

Saturdays

21 December to 16 May

Gillingham and Dartford - London

		SE	SE	SE	SE	SE	SE	SE		TL	SE	SE	SE	SE	SE	SE	SE	SE	SE	SE	SE	SE	TL	SE	
														◇											
Rainham (Kent)	d									07 58				08 16									08 28		
Gillingham (Kent)	d									08 04				08 21									08 34		
Chatham	d									08 08				08 25									08 38		
Rochester	d									08 12				08 29									08 42		
Maidstone West	d																								
Strood	d									08 15				08 32									08 45		
Higham	d									08 20													08 50		
Gravesend	d			08 20						08 29	08 35			08 42				08 50					08 59	09 05	
Northfleet	d									08 32	08 38												09 02	09 08	
Swanscombe	d									08 34	08 40												09 04	09 10	
Greenhithe for Bluewater	d			08 26						08 38	08 44							08 56					09 08	09 14	
Stone Crossing	d									08 40	08 46												09 10	09 16	
Dartford	a			08 31						08 44	08 50							09 01					09 14	09 20	
	d			08 32	08 35			08 41		08 45	08 51				08 55			09 02	09 05			09 11	09 15	09 21	
Slade Green	d	08 29				08 37	08 39	08 46		08 51						08 59				09 07	09 09	09 16	09 21		
Erith	d	08 32					08 42	08 48								09 02					09 12	09 18			
Belvedere	d	08 34					08 44	08 51								09 04					09 14	09 21			
Abbey Wood	d	08 38					08 48	08 54		08 58						09 08					09 18	09 24	09 28		
Plumstead	d	08 41					08 51	08 57		09 01						09 11					09 21	09 27	09 31		
Woolwich Arsenal	d	08 44					08 54	09 00		09 04						09 14					09 24	09 30	09 34		
Woolwich Dockyard	d	08 46					08 56	09 03								09 16					09 26	09 33			
Charlton	d	08 50	07 55				09 00	09 06		09 10						09 20	08 25				09 30	09 36	09 40		
Crayford	d		08 31		08 42						08 56						09 01		09 12					09 26	
Bexley	d		08 34		08 45						08 59						09 04		09 15					09 29	
Albany Park	d		08 36		08 47												09 06		09 17						
Sidcup	d		08 39		08 50						09 03						09 09		09 20					09 33	
New Eltham	d		08 43		08 54						09 06						09 13		09 24					09 36	
Mottingham	d		08 45		08 56												09 15		09 26						
Lee	d		08 48		08 59												09 18		09 29						
Hither Green	d		08 51		09 03												09 21		09 33						
Barnehurst	d			08 39		08 50									09 03			09 09		09 20					
Bexleyheath	d			08 42		08 53									09 06			09 12		09 23					
Welling	d			08 45		08 56									09 09			09 15		09 26					
Falconwood	d			08 48		08 58									09 11			09 18		09 28					
Eltham	d			08 51		09 01									09 14			09 21		09 31					
Kidbrooke	d			08 54		09 04									09 17			09 24		09 34					
Blackheath	d			08 58		09 08		09 11							09 21			09 28		09 38		09 41			
Lewisham	d		08 57	09 02		09 12		09 16							09 25		09 27	09 32		09 42		09 46			
St Johns	d		08 59			09 14											09 29			09 44					
New Cross	d		09 01			09 17											09 31			09 47					
Nunhead	d			09 07														09 37							
Peckham Rye	d			09 10														09 40							
Denmark Hill	d			09 14														09 44							
London Victoria	a			09 25														09 55							
Westcombe Park	d	08 52					09 02			09 12						09 22					09 32		09 42		
Maze Hill	d	08 54					09 04			09 14						09 24					09 34		09 44		
Greenwich	d	08 57					09 07			09 17						09 27					09 37		09 47		
Deptford	a	08 59					09 09			09 19		←	←			09 29					09 39		09 49		
London Bridge	a	09 05	09 07		09 13	09 22	09 15	09 25		09 27	09 20	09 22	09 25		09 33	09 35	09 37		09 43	09 52	09 45	09 55	09 57	09 50	
London Cannon Street	a	09 11	09 13			→	09 21	→				09 30				09 41	09 43			→	09 51	→			
London Waterloo (East)	a				09 19						09 26		09 31		09 39				09 49					09 56	
London Charing Cross	a				09 23						09 30		09 35		09 43				09 53					10 00	
Ebbsfleet International	a													08 46											
Stratford International	a													08 58											
St Pancras Int'l	a													09 06											

Table T200-R

Saturdays

21 December to 16 May

Gillingham and Dartford - London

		SE	SE	SE	SE	SE	SE	SE	SE	SE	SE	SE	TL	SE	SE	SE	SE	SE	SE	SE	SE	SE	SE	SE
				◇													◇							
Rainham (Kent)	d			08 46									08 58				09 16							
Gillingham (Kent)	d			08 51									09 04				09 21							
Chatham	d			08 55									09 08				09 25							
Rochester	d			08 59									09 12				09 29							
Maidstone West	d																							
Strood	d			09 02									09 15				09 32							
Higham	d												09 20											
Gravesend	d			09 12				09 20					09 29	09 35			09 42				09 50			
Northfleet	d												09 32	09 38										
Swanscombe	d												09 34	09 40										
Greenhithe for Bluewater	d							09 26					09 38	09 44							09 56			
Stone Crossing	d												09 40	09 46										
Dartford	a							09 31					09 44	09 50							10 01			
	d				09 25			09 32	09 35			09 41	09 45	09 51				09 55			10 02	10 05		
Slade Green	d					09 29				09 37	09 39	09 46	09 51						09 59				10 07	10 09
Erith	d					09 32					09 42	09 48							10 02					10 12
Belvedere	d					09 34					09 44	09 51							10 04					10 14
Abbey Wood	d					09 38					09 48	09 54	09 58						10 08					10 18
Plumstead	d					09 41					09 51	09 57	10 01						10 11					10 21
Woolwich Arsenal	d					09 44					09 54	10 00	10 04						10 14					10 24
Woolwich Dockyard	d					09 46					09 56	10 03							10 16					10 26
Charlton	d					09 50	08 55				10 00	10 06	10 10						10 20	09 25				10 30
Crayford	d						09 31		09 42					09 56						10 01		10 12		
Bexley	d						09 34		09 45					09 59						10 04		10 15		
Albany Park	d						09 36		09 47											10 06		10 17		
Sidcup	d						09 39		09 50					10 03						10 09		10 20		
New Eltham	d						09 43		09 54					10 06						10 13		10 24		
Mottingham	d						09 45		09 56											10 15		10 26		
Lee	d						09 48		09 59											10 18		10 29		
Hither Green	d						09 51		10 03											10 21		10 33		
Barnehurst	d				09 33			09 39		09 50								10 03			10 09		10 20	
Bexleyheath	d				09 36			09 42		09 53								10 06			10 12		10 23	
Welling	d				09 39			09 45		09 56								10 09			10 15		10 26	
Falconwood	d				09 41			09 48		09 58								10 11			10 18		10 28	
Eltham	d				09 44			09 51		10 01								10 14			10 21		10 31	
Kidbrooke	d				09 47			09 54		10 04								10 17			10 24		10 34	
Blackheath	d				09 51			09 58		10 08		10 11						10 21			10 28		10 38	
Lewisham	d				09 55		09 57	10 02		10 12		10 16						10 25		10 27	10 32		10 42	
St Johns	d						09 59			10 14										10 29			10 44	
New Cross	d						10 01			10 17										10 31			10 47	
Nunhead	d							10 07													10 37			
Peckham Rye	d							10 10													10 40			
Denmark Hill	d							10 14													10 44			
London Victoria	a							10 25													10 55			
Westcombe Park	d					09 52					10 02		10 12						10 22					10 32
Maze Hill	d					09 54					10 04		10 14						10 24					10 34
Greenwich	d					09 57					10 07		10 17						10 27					10 37
Deptford	a	←	←			09 59					10 09		10 19		←	←			10 29					10 39
London Bridge	a	09 52	09 55		10 03	10 05	10 07		10 13	10 22	10 15	10 25	10 27	10 20	10 22	10 25		10 33	10 35	10 37		10 43	10 52	10 45
London Cannon Street	a	10 00				10 11	10 13			→	10 21	→			10 30				10 41	10 43			→	10 51
London Waterloo (East)	a		10 01		10 09				10 19					10 26		10 31		10 39				10 49		
London Charing Cross	a		10 05		10 13				10 23					10 30		10 35		10 43				10 53		
Ebbsfleet International	a			09 16													09 46							
Stratford International	a			09 29													10 02							
St Pancras Int'l	a			09 37													10 10							

Table T200-R

Saturdays

21 December to 16 May

Gillingham and Dartford - London

		SE	TL	SE	SE	SE	SE	SE	SE	SE	SE	SE	SE	SE	SE	TL	SE	SE	SE	SE	SE	SE	SE
							◇													◇			
Rainham (Kent)	d		09 28				09 46									09 58				10 16			
Gillingham (Kent)	d		09 34				09 51									10 04				10 21			
Chatham	d		09 38				09 55									10 08				10 25			
Rochester	d		09 42				09 59									10 12				10 29			
Maidstone West	d																						
Strood	d		09 45				10 02									10 15				10 32			
Higham	d		09 50													10 20							
Gravesend	d		09 59	10 05			10 12				10 20					10 29	10 35			10 42			
Northfleet	d		10 02	10 08												10 32	10 38						
Swanscombe	d		10 04	10 10												10 34	10 40						
Greenhithe for Bluewater	d		10 08	10 14							10 26					10 38	10 44						
Stone Crossing	d		10 10	10 16												10 40	10 46						
Dartford	a		10 14	10 20							10 31					10 44	10 50						
	d	10 11	10 15	10 21				10 25			10 32	10 35			10 41	10 45	10 51				10 55		
Slade Green	d	10 16	10 21						10 29				10 37	10 39	10 46	10 51						10 59	
Erith	d	10 18							10 32					10 42	10 48							11 02	
Belvedere	d	10 21							10 34					10 44	10 51							11 04	
Abbey Wood	d	10 24	10 28						10 38					10 48	10 54	10 58						11 08	
Plumstead	d	10 27	10 31						10 41					10 51	10 57	11 01						11 11	
Woolwich Arsenal	d	10 30	10 34						10 44					10 54	11 00	11 04						11 14	
Woolwich Dockyard	d	10 33							10 46					10 56	11 03							11 16	
Charlton	d	10 36	10 40						10 50	09 55				11 00	11 06	11 10						11 20	10 25
Crayford	d			10 26						10 31		10 42					10 56						11 01
Bexley	d			10 29						10 34		10 45					10 59						11 04
Albany Park	d									10 36		10 47											11 06
Sidcup	d			10 33						10 39		10 50					11 03						11 09
New Eltham	d			10 36						10 43		10 54					11 06						11 13
Mottingham	d									10 45		10 56											11 15
Lee	d									10 48		10 59											11 18
Hither Green	d									10 51		11 03											11 21
Barnehurst	d							10 33			10 39		10 50								11 03		
Bexleyheath	d							10 36			10 42		10 53								11 06		
Welling	d							10 39			10 45		10 56								11 09		
Falconwood	d							10 41			10 48		10 58								11 11		
Eltham	d							10 44			10 51		11 01								11 14		
Kidbrooke	d							10 47			10 54		11 04								11 17		
Blackheath	d	10 41						10 51			10 58		11 08		11 11						11 21		
Lewisham	d	10 46						10 55		10 57	11 02		11 12		11 16						11 25		11 27
St Johns	d									10 59			11 14										11 29
New Cross	d									11 01			11 17										11 31
Nunhead	d										11 07												
Peckham Rye	d										11 10												
Denmark Hill	d										11 14												
London Victoria	a										11 25												
Westcombe Park	d		10 42						10 52					11 02		11 12						11 22	
Maze Hill	d		10 44						10 54					11 04		11 14						11 24	
Greenwich	d		10 47						10 57					11 07		11 17						11 27	
Deptford	a		10 49		←	←			10 59					11 09		11 19		←	←			11 29	
London Bridge	a	10 55	10 57	10 50	10 52	10 55		11 03	11 05	11 07		11 13	11 22	11 15	11 25	11 27	11 20	11 22	11 25		11 33	11 35	11 37
London Cannon Street	a	→			11 00				11 11	11 13			→	11 21	→			11 30				11 41	11 43
London Waterloo (East)	a			10 56		11 01		11 09				11 19					11 26		11 31		11 39		
London Charing Cross	a			11 00		11 05		11 13				11 23					11 30		11 35		11 43		
Ebbsfleet International	a						10 16													10 46			
Stratford International	a						10 33													10 58			
St Pancras Int'l	a						10 41													11 06			

Table T200-R

Saturdays

21 December to 16 May

Gillingham and Dartford - London

		SE	SE	SE	SE	SE	TL	SE	SE	SE	SE	SE	SE	SE	SE	SE	SE	SE	SE	TL	SE	SE	SE	SE
											◇													◇
Rainham (Kent)	d						10 28				10 46									10 58				11 16
Gillingham (Kent) 4	d						10 34				10 51									11 04				11 21
Chatham 4	d						10 38				10 55									11 08				11 25
Rochester 4	d						10 42				10 59									11 12				11 29
Maidstone West	d																							
Strood 4	d						10 45				11 02									11 15				11 32
Higham	d						10 50													11 20				
Gravesend 4	d	10 50					10 59	11 05			11 12				11 20					11 29	11 35			11 42
Northfleet	d						11 02	11 08												11 32	11 38			
Swanscombe	d						11 04	11 10												11 34	11 40			
Greenhithe for Bluewater	d	10 56					11 08	11 14							11 26					11 38	11 44			
Stone Crossing	d						11 10	11 16												11 40	11 46			
Dartford 4	a	11 01					11 14	11 20							11 31					11 44	11 50			
	d	11 02	11 05			11 11	11 15	11 21				11 25			11 32	11 35			11 41	11 45	11 51			
Slade Green 4	d			11 07	11 09	11 16	11 21						11 29				11 37	11 39	11 46	11 51				
Erith	d				11 12	11 18							11 32					11 42	11 48					
Belvedere	d				11 14	11 21							11 34					11 44	11 51					
Abbey Wood	d				11 18	11 24	11 28						11 38					11 48	11 54	11 58				
Plumstead	d				11 21	11 27	11 31						11 41					11 51	11 57	12 01				
Woolwich Arsenal 4	d				11 24	11 30	11 34						11 44					11 54	12 00	12 04				
Woolwich Dockyard	d				11 26	11 33							11 46					11 56	12 03					
Charlton 4	d				11 30	11 36	11 40						11 50	10 55				12 00	12 06	12 10				
Crayford	d		11 12					11 26						11 31		11 42					11 56			
Bexley	d		11 15					11 29						11 34		11 45					11 59			
Albany Park	d		11 17											11 36		11 47								
Sidcup 4	d		11 20					11 33						11 39		11 50					12 03			
New Eltham	d		11 24					11 36						11 43		11 54					12 06			
Mottingham	d		11 26											11 45		11 56								
Lee	d		11 29											11 48		11 59								
Hither Green 4	d		11 33											11 51		12 03								
Barnehurst 4	d	11 09		11 20								11 33			11 39		11 50							
Bexleyheath	d	11 12		11 23								11 36			11 42		11 53							
Welling	d	11 15		11 26								11 39			11 45		11 56							
Falconwood	d	11 18		11 28								11 41			11 48		11 58							
Eltham	d	11 21		11 31								11 44			11 51		12 01							
Kidbrooke	d	11 24		11 34								11 47			11 54		12 04							
Blackheath 4	d	11 28		11 38		11 41						11 51			11 58		12 08		12 11					
Lewisham 4	d	11 32		11 42		11 46						11 55		11 57	12 02		12 12		12 16					
St Johns	d			11 44										11 59			12 14							
New Cross 4 ⊖	d			11 47										12 01			12 17							
Nunhead 4	d	11 37													12 07									
Peckham Rye 4	d	11 40													12 10									
Denmark Hill 4	d	11 44													12 14									
London Victoria 15 ⊖	a	11 55													12 25									
Westcombe Park	d				11 32		11 42						11 52					12 02		12 12				
Maze Hill	d				11 34		11 44						11 54					12 04		12 14				
Greenwich 4	d				11 37		11 47						11 57					12 07		12 17				
Deptford	a				11 39		11 49		←	←			11 59					12 09		12 19		←	←	
London Bridge 4 ⊖	a		11 43	11 52	11 45	11 55	11 57	11 50	11 52	11 55		12 03	12 05	12 07		12 13	12 22	12 15	12 25	12 27	12 20	12 22	12 25	
London Cannon Street 4 ⊖	a			→	11 51	→			12 00				12 11	12 13			→	12 21	→			12 30		
London Waterloo (East) 4 ⊖	a		11 49					11 56		12 01		12 09				12 19					12 26		12 31	
London Charing Cross 4 ⊖	a		11 53					12 00		12 05		12 13				12 23					12 30		12 35	
Ebbsfleet International	a										11 16													11 46
Stratford International ⊖	a										11 29													11 58
St Pancras Int'l 15 ⊖	a										11 37													12 06

Table T200-R

Saturdays

21 December to 16 May

Gillingham and Dartford - London

		SE	SE	SE	SE	SE	SE	SE	SE	TL	SE	SE	SE	SE	SE	SE	SE	SE	SE	SE	SE	SE	TL
														◇									
Rainham (Kent)	d									11 28				11 46									11 58
Gillingham (Kent) 4	d									11 34				11 51									12 04
Chatham 4	d									11 38				11 55									12 08
Rochester 4	d									11 42				11 59									12 12
Maidstone West	d																						
Strood 4	d									11 45				12 02									12 15
Higham	d									11 50													12 20
Gravesend 4	d				11 50					11 59	12 05			12 12				12 20					12 29
Northfleet	d									12 02	12 08												12 32
Swanscombe	d									12 04	12 10												12 34
Greenhithe for Bluewater	d				11 56					12 08	12 14							12 26					12 38
Stone Crossing	d									12 10	12 16												12 40
Dartford 4	a				12 01					12 14	12 20							12 31					12 44
	d	11 55			12 02	12 05			12 11	12 15	12 21				12 25			12 32	12 35			12 41	12 45
Slade Green 4	d		11 59				12 07	12 09	12 16	12 21						12 29				12 37	12 39	12 46	12 51
Erith	d		12 02					12 12	12 18							12 32					12 42	12 48	
Belvedere	d		12 04					12 14	12 21							12 34					12 44	12 51	
Abbey Wood	d		12 08					12 18	12 24	12 28						12 38					12 48	12 54	12 58
Plumstead	d		12 11					12 21	12 27	12 31						12 41					12 51	12 57	13 01
Woolwich Arsenal 4	d		12 14					12 24	12 30	12 34						12 44					12 54	13 00	13 04
Woolwich Dockyard	d		12 16					12 26	12 33							12 46					12 56	13 03	
Charlton 4	d		12 20	11 25				12 30	12 36	12 40						12 50	11 55				13 00	13 06	13 10
Crayford	d			12 01		12 12					12 26						12 31		12 42				
Bexley	d			12 04		12 15					12 29						12 34		12 45				
Albany Park	d			12 06		12 17											12 36		12 47				
Sidcup 4	d			12 09		12 20					12 33						12 39		12 50				
New Eltham	d			12 13		12 24					12 36						12 43		12 54				
Mottingham	d			12 15		12 26											12 45		12 56				
Lee	d			12 18		12 29											12 48		12 59				
Hither Green 4	d			12 21		12 33											12 51		13 03				
Barnehurst 4	d	12 03			12 09		12 20								12 33			12 39		12 50			
Bexleyheath	d	12 06			12 12		12 23								12 36			12 42		12 53			
Welling	d	12 09			12 15		12 26								12 39			12 45		12 56			
Falconwood	d	12 11			12 18		12 28								12 41			12 48		12 58			
Eltham	d	12 14			12 21		12 31								12 44			12 51		13 01			
Kidbrooke	d	12 17			12 24		12 34								12 47			12 54		13 04			
Blackheath 4	d	12 21			12 28		12 38		12 41						12 51			12 58		13 08		13 11	
Lewisham 4	d	12 25		12 27	12 32		12 42		12 45						12 55		12 57	13 02		13 12		13 16	
St Johns	d			12 29			12 44										12 59			13 14			
New Cross 4 ⊖	d			12 31			12 47										13 01			13 17			
Nunhead 4	d				12 37													13 07					
Peckham Rye 4	d				12 40													13 10					
Denmark Hill 4	d				12 44													13 14					
London Victoria 15 ⊖	a				12 55													13 25					
Westcombe Park	d		12 22					12 32		12 42						12 52					13 02		13 12
Maze Hill	d		12 24					12 34		12 44						12 54					13 04		13 14
Greenwich 4	d		12 27					12 37		12 47						12 57					13 07		13 17
Deptford	a		12 29					12 39		12 49		←	←			12 59					13 09		13 19
London Bridge 4 ⊖	a	12 33	12 35	12 37		12 43	12 52	12 45	12 55	12 57	12 50	12 52	12 55		13 03	13 05	13 07		13 13	13 22	13 15	13 25	13 27
London Cannon Street 4 ⊖	a		12 41	12 43			→	12 51	→			13 00				13 11	13 13			→	13 21	→	
London Waterloo (East) 4 ⊖	a	12 39				12 49					12 56		13 01		13 09				13 19				
London Charing Cross 4 ⊖	a	12 43				12 53					13 00		13 05		13 13				13 23				
Ebbsfleet International	a													12 16									
Stratford International ⊖	a													12 28									
St Pancras Int'l 15 ⊖	a													12 36									

Table T200-R

Saturdays

21 December to 16 May

Gillingham and Dartford - London

		SE	SE	SE	SE ◇	SE	SE	SE	SE	SE	SE	SE	SE	TL	SE	SE		SE	SE ◇	SE	SE	SE	SE	SE	SE
Rainham (Kent)	d				12 16									12 28					12 46						
Gillingham (Kent)	d				12 21									12 34					12 51						
Chatham	d				12 25									12 38					12 55						
Rochester	d				12 29									12 42					12 59						
Maidstone West	d																								
Strood	d				12 32									12 45					13 02						
Higham	d													12 50											
Gravesend	d	12 35			12 42				12 50					12 59	13 05				13 12				13 20		
Northfleet	d	12 38												13 02	13 08										
Swanscombe	d	12 40												13 04	13 10										
Greenhithe for Bluewater	d	12 44							12 56					13 08	13 14								13 26		
Stone Crossing	d	12 46												13 10	13 16										
Dartford	a	12 50							13 01					13 14	13 20								13 31		
	d	12 51				12 55			13 02	13 05			13 11	13 15	13 21					13 25			13 32	13 35	
Slade Green	d						12 59				13 07	13 09	13 16	13 21							13 29				13 37
Erith	d						13 02					13 12	13 18								13 32				
Belvedere	d						13 04					13 14	13 21								13 34				
Abbey Wood	d						13 08					13 18	13 24	13 28							13 38				
Plumstead	d						13 11					13 21	13 27	13 31							13 41				
Woolwich Arsenal	d						13 14					13 24	13 30	13 34							13 44				
Woolwich Dockyard	d						13 16					13 26	13 33								13 46				
Charlton	d						13 20	12 25				13 30	13 36	13 40							13 50	12 55			
Crayford	d	12 56						13 01		13 12					13 26							13 31		13 42	
Bexley	d	12 59						13 04		13 15					13 29							13 34		13 45	
Albany Park	d							13 06		13 17												13 36		13 47	
Sidcup	d	13 03						13 09		13 20					13 33							13 39		13 50	
New Eltham	d	13 06						13 13		13 24					13 36							13 43		13 54	
Mottingham	d							13 15		13 26												13 45		13 56	
Lee	d							13 18		13 29												13 48		13 59	
Hither Green	d							13 21		13 33												13 51		14 03	
Barnehurst	d					13 03			13 09		13 20									13 33			13 39		13 50
Bexleyheath	d					13 06			13 12		13 23									13 36			13 42		13 53
Welling	d					13 09			13 15		13 26									13 39			13 45		13 56
Falconwood	d					13 11			13 18		13 28									13 41			13 48		13 58
Eltham	d					13 14			13 21		13 31									13 44			13 51		14 01
Kidbrooke	d					13 17			13 24		13 34									13 47			13 54		14 04
Blackheath	d					13 21			13 28		13 38		13 41							13 51			13 58		14 08
Lewisham	d					13 25		13 27	13 32		13 42		13 46							13 55		13 57	14 02		14 12
St Johns	d							13 29			13 44											13 59			14 14
New Cross	d							13 31			13 47											14 01			14 17
Nunhead	d								13 37														14 07		
Peckham Rye	d								13 40														14 10		
Denmark Hill	d								13 44														14 14		
London Victoria	a								13 55														14 25		
Westcombe Park	d						13 22					13 32		13 42							13 52				
Maze Hill	d						13 24					13 34		13 44							13 54				
Greenwich	d						13 27					13 37		13 47							13 57				
Deptford	a		←	←			13 29					13 39		13 49		←		←			13 59				
London Bridge	a	13 20	13 22	13 25		13 33	13 35	13 37		13 43	13 52	13 45	13 55	13 57	13 50	13 52		13 55		14 03	14 05	14 07		14 13	14 22
London Cannon Street	a		13 30				13 41	13 43			→	13 51	→			14 00					14 11	14 13			→
London Waterloo (East)	a	13 26		13 31		13 39				13 49					13 56			14 01		14 09				14 19	
London Charing Cross	a	13 30		13 35		13 43				13 53					14 00			14 05		14 13				14 23	
Ebbsfleet International	a				12 46														13 16						
Stratford International	a				12 58														13 29						
St Pancras Int'l	a				13 06														13 37						

NRT DECEMBER 19 EDITION

Table T200-R

Saturdays

21 December to 16 May

Gillingham and Dartford - London

		SE	SE	TL	SE	SE	SE	SE ◇		SE	SE	SE	SE	SE	SE	SE	SE	TL	SE	SE	SE	SE ◇	SE	SE
Rainham (Kent)	d			12 58				13 16										13 28				13 46		
Gillingham (Kent)	d			13 04				13 21										13 34				13 51		
Chatham	d			13 08				13 25										13 38				13 55		
Rochester	d			13 12				13 29										13 42				13 59		
Maidstone West	d																							
Strood	d			13 15				13 32										13 45				14 02		
Higham	d			13 20														13 50						
Gravesend	d			13 29	13 35			13 42					13 50					13 59	14 05			14 12		
Northfleet	d			13 32	13 38													14 02	14 08					
Swanscombe	d			13 34	13 40													14 04	14 10					
Greenhithe for Bluewater	d			13 38	13 44								13 56					14 08	14 14					
Stone Crossing	d			13 40	13 46													14 10	14 16					
Dartford	a			13 44	13 50								14 01					14 14	14 20					
	d		13 41	13 45	13 51					13 55			14 02	14 05			14 11	14 15	14 21				14 25	
Slade Green	d	13 39	13 46	13 51							13 59				14 07	14 09	14 16	14 21						14 29
Erith	d	13 42	13 48								14 02					14 12	14 18							14 32
Belvedere	d	13 44	13 51								14 04					14 14	14 21							14 34
Abbey Wood	d	13 48	13 54	13 58							14 08					14 18	14 24	14 28						14 38
Plumstead	d	13 51	13 57	14 01							14 11					14 21	14 27	14 31						14 41
Woolwich Arsenal	d	13 54	14 00	14 04							14 14					14 24	14 30	14 34						14 44
Woolwich Dockyard	d	13 56	14 03								14 16					14 26	14 33							14 46
Charlton	d	14 00	14 06	14 10							14 20	13 25				14 30	14 36	14 40						14 50
Crayford	d				13 56							14 01		14 12					14 26					
Bexley	d				13 59							14 04		14 15					14 29					
Albany Park	d											14 06		14 17										
Sidcup	d				14 03							14 09		14 20					14 33					
New Eltham	d				14 06							14 13		14 24					14 36					
Mottingham	d											14 15		14 26										
Lee	d											14 18		14 29										
Hither Green	d											14 21		14 33										
Barnehurst	d									14 03			14 09		14 20								14 33	
Bexleyheath	d									14 06			14 12		14 23								14 36	
Welling	d									14 09			14 15		14 26								14 39	
Falconwood	d									14 11			14 18		14 28								14 41	
Eltham	d									14 14			14 21		14 31								14 44	
Kidbrooke	d									14 17			14 24		14 34								14 47	
Blackheath	d		14 11							14 21			14 28		14 38		14 41						14 51	
Lewisham	d		14 16							14 25		14 27	14 32		14 42		14 46						14 55	
St Johns	d											14 29			14 44									
New Cross	d											14 31			14 47									
Nunhead	d												14 37											
Peckham Rye	d												14 40											
Denmark Hill	d												14 44											
London Victoria	a												14 55											
Westcombe Park	d	14 02		14 12							14 22					14 32		14 42						14 52
Maze Hill	d	14 04		14 14							14 24					14 34		14 44						14 54
Greenwich	d	14 07		14 17							14 27					14 37		14 47						14 57
Deptford	a	14 09		14 19		←	←				14 29					14 39		14 49		←	←			14 59
London Bridge	a	14 15	14 25	14 27	14 20	14 22	14 25			14 33	14 35	14 37		14 43	14 52	14 45	14 55	14 57	14 50	14 52	14 55		15 03	15 05
London Cannon Street	a	14 21	→			14 30					14 41	14 43			→	14 51	→			15 00				15 11
London Waterloo (East)	a				14 26		14 31			14 39				14 49					14 56		15 01		15 09	
London Charing Cross	a				14 30		14 35			14 43				14 53					15 00		15 05		15 13	
Ebbsfleet International	a							13 46														14 16		
Stratford International	a							14 02														14 28		
St Pancras Int'l	a							14 10														14 36		

Table T200-R

Saturdays

21 December to 16 May

Gillingham and Dartford - London

		SE	SE	SE	SE	SE	SE	TL	SE	SE	SE	SE ◇	SE	SE	SE	SE		SE	SE	SE	SE	TL	SE	SE	SE
Rainham (Kent)	d							13 58				14 16										14 28			
Gillingham (Kent)	d							14 04				14 21										14 34			
Chatham	d							14 08				14 25										14 38			
Rochester	d							14 12				14 29										14 42			
Maidstone West	d																								
Strood	d							14 15				14 32										14 45			
Higham	d							14 20														14 50			
Gravesend	d		14 20					14 29	14 35			14 42				14 50						14 59	15 05		
Northfleet	d							14 32	14 38													15 02	15 08		
Swanscombe	d							14 34	14 40													15 04	15 10		
Greenhithe for Bluewater	d		14 26					14 38	14 44							14 56						15 08	15 14		
Stone Crossing	d							14 40	14 46													15 10	15 16		
Dartford	a		14 31					14 44	14 50							15 01						15 14	15 20		
	d		14 32	14 35			14 41	14 45	14 51				14 55			15 02		15 05			15 11	15 15	15 21		
Slade Green	d				14 37	14 39	14 46	14 51						14 59					15 07	15 09	15 16	15 21			
Erith	d					14 42	14 48							15 02						15 12	15 18				
Belvedere	d					14 44	14 51							15 04						15 14	15 21				
Abbey Wood	d					14 48	14 54	14 58						15 08						15 18	15 24	15 28			
Plumstead	d					14 51	14 57	15 01						15 11						15 21	15 27	15 31			
Woolwich Arsenal	d					14 54	15 00	15 04						15 14						15 24	15 30	15 34			
Woolwich Dockyard	d					14 56	15 03							15 16						15 26	15 33				
Charlton	d	13 55				15 00	15 06	15 10						15 20	14 25					15 30	15 36	15 40			
Crayford	d	14 31		14 42					14 56						15 01			15 12					15 26		
Bexley	d	14 34		14 45					14 59						15 04			15 15					15 29		
Albany Park	d	14 36		14 47											15 06			15 17							
Sidcup	d	14 39		14 50					15 03						15 09			15 20					15 33		
New Eltham	d	14 43		14 54					15 06						15 13			15 24					15 36		
Mottingham	d	14 45		14 56											15 15			15 26							
Lee	d	14 48		14 59											15 18			15 29							
Hither Green	d	14 51		15 03											15 21			15 33							
Barnehurst	d		14 39		14 50								15 03			15 09			15 20						
Bexleyheath	d		14 42		14 53								15 06			15 12			15 23						
Welling	d		14 45		14 56								15 09			15 15			15 26						
Falconwood	d		14 48		14 58								15 11			15 18			15 28						
Eltham	d		14 51		15 01								15 14			15 21			15 31						
Kidbrooke	d		14 54		15 04								15 17			15 24			15 34						
Blackheath	d		14 58		15 08		15 11						15 21			15 28			15 38		15 41				
Lewisham	d	14 57	15 02		15 12		15 16						15 25		15 27	15 32			15 42		15 46				
St Johns	d	14 59			15 14										15 29				15 44						
New Cross	d	15 01			15 17										15 31				15 47						
Nunhead	d		15 07													15 37									
Peckham Rye	d		15 10													15 40									
Denmark Hill	d		15 14													15 44									
London Victoria	a		15 25													15 55									
Westcombe Park	d					15 02		15 12						15 22						15 32		15 42			
Maze Hill	d					15 04		15 14						15 24						15 34		15 44			
Greenwich	d					15 07		15 17						15 27						15 37		15 47			
Deptford	a					15 09		15 19		←	←			15 29						15 39		15 49		←	←
London Bridge	a	15 07		15 13	15 22	15 15	15 25	15 27	15 20	15 22	15 25		15 33	15 35	15 37			15 43	15 52	15 45	15 55	15 57	15 50	15 52	15 55
London Cannon Street	a	15 13			→	15 21	→			15 30				15 41	15 43				→	15 51	→			16 00	
London Waterloo (East)	a			15 19					15 26		15 31		15 39					15 49					15 56		16 01
London Charing Cross	a			15 23					15 30		15 35		15 43					15 53					16 00		16 05
Ebbsfleet International	a											14 46													
Stratford International	a											14 58													
St Pancras Int'l	a											15 06													

Table T200-R

Saturdays

21 December to 16 May

Gillingham and Dartford - London

		SE ◇	SE	SE	SE	SE	SE	SE		SE	SE	TL	SE	SE	SE	SE ◇	SE	SE	SE	SE	SE	SE	SE	SE
Rainham (Kent)	d	14 46										14 58				15 16								
Gillingham (Kent)	d	14 51										15 04				15 21								
Chatham	d	14 55										15 08				15 25								
Rochester	d	14 59										15 12				15 29								
Maidstone West	d																							
Strood	d	15 02										15 15				15 32								
Higham	d											15 20												
Gravesend	d	15 12				15 20						15 29	15 35			15 42				15 50				
Northfleet	d											15 32	15 38											
Swanscombe	d											15 34	15 40											
Greenhithe for Bluewater	d					15 26						15 38	15 44							15 56				
Stone Crossing	d											15 40	15 46											
Dartford	a					15 31						15 44	15 50							16 01				
	d		15 25			15 32	15 35				15 41	15 45	15 51				15 55			16 02	16 05			16 11
Slade Green	d			15 29				15 37		15 39	15 46	15 51						15 59				16 07	16 09	16 16
Erith	d			15 32						15 42	15 48							16 02					16 12	16 18
Belvedere	d			15 34						15 44	15 51							16 04					16 14	16 21
Abbey Wood	d			15 38						15 48	15 54	15 58						16 08					16 18	16 24
Plumstead	d			15 41						15 51	15 57	16 01						16 11					16 21	16 27
Woolwich Arsenal	d			15 44						15 54	16 00	16 04						16 14					16 24	16 30
Woolwich Dockyard	d			15 46						15 56	16 03							16 16					16 26	16 33
Charlton	d			15 50	14 55					16 00	16 06	16 10						16 20	15 25				16 30	16 36
Crayford	d				15 31		15 42						15 56						16 01		16 12			
Bexley	d				15 34		15 45						15 59						16 04		16 15			
Albany Park	d				15 36		15 47												16 06		16 17			
Sidcup	d				15 39		15 50						16 03						16 09		16 20			
New Eltham	d				15 43		15 54						16 06						16 13		16 24			
Mottingham	d				15 45		15 56												16 15		16 26			
Lee	d				15 48		15 59												16 18		16 29			
Hither Green	d				15 51		16 03												16 21		16 33			
Barnehurst	d		15 33			15 39		15 50									16 03			16 09		16 20		
Bexleyheath	d		15 36			15 42		15 53									16 06			16 12		16 23		
Welling	d		15 39			15 45		15 56									16 09			16 15		16 26		
Falconwood	d		15 41			15 48		15 58									16 11			16 18		16 28		
Eltham	d		15 44			15 51		16 01									16 14			16 21		16 31		
Kidbrooke	d		15 47			15 54		16 04									16 17			16 24		16 34		
Blackheath	d		15 51			15 58		16 08			16 11						16 21			16 28		16 38		16 41
Lewisham	d		15 55		15 57	16 02		16 12			16 16						16 25		16 27	16 32		16 42		16 46
St Johns	d				15 59			16 14											16 29			16 44		
New Cross	d				16 01			16 17											16 31			16 47		
Nunhead	d					16 07														16 37				
Peckham Rye	d					16 10														16 40				
Denmark Hill	d					16 14														16 44				
London Victoria	a					16 25														16 55				
Westcombe Park	d			15 52						16 02		16 12						16 22					16 32	
Maze Hill	d			15 54						16 04		16 14						16 24					16 34	
Greenwich	d			15 57						16 07		16 17						16 27					16 37	
Deptford	a			15 59						16 09		16 19		←	←			16 29					16 39	
London Bridge	a		16 03	16 05	16 07		16 13	16 22		16 15	16 25	16 27	16 20	16 22	16 25		16 33	16 35	16 37		16 43	16 52	16 45	16 55
London Cannon Street	a			16 11	16 13			→		16 21	→			16 30				16 41	16 43			→	16 51	→
London Waterloo (East)	a		16 09				16 19						16 26		16 31		16 39				16 49			
London Charing Cross	a		16 13				16 23						16 30		16 35		16 43				16 53			
Ebbsfleet International	a	15 16														15 46								
Stratford International	a	15 28														16 02								
St Pancras Int'l	a	15 36														16 10								

Table T200-R

Saturdays

21 December to 16 May

Gillingham and Dartford - London

		TL	SE	SE	SE	SE ◇	SE	SE	SE	SE	SE	SE	SE	SE	TL	SE		SE	SE	SE ◇	SE	SE	SE	SE	SE
Rainham (Kent)	d	15 28				15 46									15 58					16 16					
Gillingham (Kent)	d	15 34				15 51									16 04					16 21					
Chatham	d	15 38				15 55									16 08					16 25					
Rochester	d	15 42				15 59									16 12					16 29					
Maidstone West	d																								
Strood	d	15 45				16 02									16 16					16 32					
Higham	d	15 50													16 21										
Gravesend	d	15 59	16 05			16 12				16 20					16 29	16 35				16 42				16 50	
Northfleet	d	16 02	16 08												16 32	16 38									
Swanscombe	d	16 04	16 10												16 34	16 40									
Greenhithe for Bluewater	d	16 08	16 14							16 26					16 38	16 44								16 56	
Stone Crossing	d	16 10	16 16												16 40	16 46									
Dartford	a	16 14	16 20							16 31					16 44	16 50								17 01	
	d	16 15	16 21				16 25			16 32	16 35			16 41	16 45	16 51					16 55			17 02	17 05
Slade Green	d	16 21						16 29				16 37	16 39	16 46	16 51							16 59			
Erith	d							16 32					16 42	16 48								17 02			
Belvedere	d							16 34					16 44	16 51								17 04			
Abbey Wood	d	16 28						16 38					16 48	16 54	16 58							17 08			
Plumstead	d	16 31						16 41					16 51	16 57	17 01							17 11			
Woolwich Arsenal	d	16 34						16 44					16 54	17 00	17 04							17 14			
Woolwich Dockyard	d							16 46					16 56	17 03								17 16			
Charlton	d	16 40						16 50	15 55				17 00	17 06	17 10							17 20	16 25		
Crayford	d		16 26						16 31		16 42					16 56							17 01		17 12
Bexley	d		16 29						16 34		16 45					16 59							17 04		17 15
Albany Park	d								16 36		16 47												17 06		17 17
Sidcup	d		16 33						16 39		16 50					17 03							17 09		17 20
New Eltham	d		16 36						16 43		16 54					17 06							17 13		17 24
Mottingham	d								16 45		16 56												17 15		17 26
Lee	d								16 48		16 59												17 18		17 29
Hither Green	d								16 51		17 03												17 21		17 33
Barnehurst	d						16 33			16 39		16 50									17 03			17 09	
Bexleyheath	d						16 36			16 42		16 53									17 06			17 12	
Welling	d						16 39			16 45		16 56									17 09			17 15	
Falconwood	d						16 41			16 48		16 58									17 11			17 18	
Eltham	d						16 44			16 51		17 01									17 14			17 21	
Kidbrooke	d						16 47			16 54		17 04									17 17			17 24	
Blackheath	d						16 51			16 58		17 08		17 11							17 21			17 28	
Lewisham	d						16 55		16 57	17 02		17 12		17 16							17 25		17 27	17 32	
St Johns	d								16 59			17 14											17 29		
New Cross ⊖	d								17 01			17 17											17 31		
Nunhead	d									17 07														17 37	
Peckham Rye	d									17 10														17 40	
Denmark Hill	d									17 14														17 44	
London Victoria ⊖	a									17 25														17 55	
Westcombe Park	d	16 42						16 52					17 02		17 12							17 22			
Maze Hill	d	16 44						16 54					17 04		17 14							17 24			
Greenwich	d	16 47						16 57					17 07		17 17							17 27			
Deptford	a	16 49		←	←			16 59					17 09		17 19			←	←			17 29			
London Bridge ⊖	a	16 57	16 50	16 52	16 55		17 03	17 05	17 07		17 13	17 22	17 15	17 25	17 27	17 20		17 22	17 25		17 33	17 35	17 37		17 43
London Cannon Street ⊖	a			17 00				17 11	17 13			→	17 21	→				17 30				17 41	17 43		
London Waterloo (East) ⊖	a		16 56		17 01		17 09				17 19					17 26			17 31		17 39				17 49
London Charing Cross ⊖	a		17 00		17 05		17 13				17 23					17 30			17 35		17 43				17 53
Ebbsfleet International	a					16 16														16 46					
Stratford International ⊖	a					16 28														17 02					
St Pancras Int'l ⊖	a					16 36														17 10					

NRT DECEMBER 19 EDITION

Table T200-R

Saturdays

21 December to 16 May

Gillingham and Dartford - London

		SE	SE	SE	TL	SE	SE	SE		SE ◇	SE	SE	SE	SE	SE	SE	SE	SE	TL	SE	SE	SE	SE ◇	SE
Rainham (Kent)	d				16 28					16 46									16 58				17 16	
Gillingham (Kent)	d				16 34					16 51									17 04				17 21	
Chatham	d				16 38					16 55									17 08				17 25	
Rochester	d				16 42					16 59									17 12				17 29	
Maidstone West	d																							
Strood	d				16 45					17 02									17 15				17 32	
Higham	d				16 50														17 20					
Gravesend	d				16 59	17 05				17 12				17 20					17 29	17 35			17 42	
Northfleet	d				17 02	17 08													17 32	17 38				
Swanscombe	d				17 04	17 10													17 34	17 40				
Greenhithe for Bluewater	d				17 08	17 14								17 26					17 38	17 44				
Stone Crossing	d				17 10	17 16													17 40	17 46				
Dartford	a				17 14	17 20								17 31					17 44	17 50				
	d			17 11	17 15	17 21					17 25			17 32	17 35			17 41	17 45	17 51				17 55
Slade Green	d	17 07	17 09	17 16	17 21							17 29				17 37	17 39	17 46	17 51					
Erith	d		17 12	17 18								17 32					17 42	17 48						
Belvedere	d		17 14	17 21								17 34					17 44	17 51						
Abbey Wood	d		17 18	17 24	17 28							17 38					17 48	17 54	17 58					
Plumstead	d		17 21	17 27	17 31							17 41					17 51	17 57	18 01					
Woolwich Arsenal	d		17 24	17 30	17 34							17 44					17 54	18 00	18 04					
Woolwich Dockyard	d		17 26	17 33								17 46					17 56	18 03						
Charlton	d		17 30	17 36	17 40							17 50	16 55				18 00	18 06	18 10					
Crayford	d					17 26							17 31		17 42					17 56				
Bexley	d					17 29							17 34		17 45					17 59				
Albany Park	d												17 36		17 47									
Sidcup	d					17 33							17 39		17 50					18 03				
New Eltham	d					17 36							17 43		17 54					18 06				
Mottingham	d												17 45		17 56									
Lee	d												17 48		17 59									
Hither Green	d												17 51		18 03									
Barnehurst	d	17 20									17 33			17 39		17 50								18 03
Bexleyheath	d	17 23									17 36			17 42		17 53								18 06
Welling	d	17 26									17 39			17 45		17 56								18 09
Falconwood	d	17 28									17 41			17 48		17 58								18 11
Eltham	d	17 31									17 44			17 51		18 01								18 14
Kidbrooke	d	17 34									17 47			17 54		18 04								18 17
Blackheath	d	17 38		17 41							17 51			17 58		18 08		18 11						18 21
Lewisham	d	17 42		17 46							17 55		17 57	18 02		18 12		18 16						18 25
St Johns	d	17 44											17 59			18 14								
New Cross ⊖	d	17 47											18 01			18 17								
Nunhead	d													18 07										
Peckham Rye	d													18 10										
Denmark Hill	d													18 14										
London Victoria ⊖	a													18 25										
Westcombe Park	d		17 32		17 42							17 52					18 02		18 12					
Maze Hill	d		17 34		17 44							17 54					18 04		18 14					
Greenwich	d		17 37		17 47							17 57					18 07		18 17					
Deptford	a		17 39		17 49		←	←				17 59					18 09		18 19		←	←		
London Bridge ⊖	a	17 52	17 45	17 55	17 57	17 50	17 52	17 55			18 03	18 05	18 07		18 13	18 22	18 15	18 25	18 27	18 20	18 22	18 25		18 33
London Cannon Street ⊖	a	→	17 51	→			18 00					18 11	18 13			→	18 21	→			18 30			
London Waterloo (East) ⊖	a					17 56		18 01			18 09				18 19					18 26		18 31		18 39
London Charing Cross ⊖	a					18 00		18 05			18 13				18 23					18 30		18 35		18 43
Ebbsfleet International	a									17 16													17 46	
Stratford International ⊖	a									17 28													18 02	
St Pancras Int'l ⊖	a									17 36													18 10	

Table T200-R

Saturdays

21 December to 16 May

Gillingham and Dartford - London

		SE	SE	SE	SE	SE	SE	SE	TL	SE	SE	SE	SE	SE	SE	SE	SE	SE	SE	SE	SE	TL	SE	SE
													◇											
Rainham (Kent)	d								17 28				17 46									17 58		
Gillingham (Kent)	d								17 34				17 51									18 04		
Chatham	d								17 38				17 55									18 08		
Rochester	d								17 42				17 59									18 12		
Maidstone West	d																							
Strood	d								17 45				18 02									18 15		
Higham	d								17 50													18 20		
Gravesend	d			17 50					17 59	18 05			18 12				18 20					18 29	18 35	
Northfleet	d								18 02	18 08												18 32	18 38	
Swanscombe	d								18 04	18 10												18 34	18 40	
Greenhithe for Bluewater	d			17 56					18 08	18 14							18 26					18 38	18 44	
Stone Crossing	d								18 10	18 16												18 40	18 46	
Dartford	a			18 01					18 14	18 20							18 31					18 44	18 50	
	d			18 02	18 05			18 11	18 15	18 21				18 25			18 32	18 35			18 41	18 45	18 51	
Slade Green	d	17 59				18 07	18 09	18 16	18 21						18 29				18 37	18 39	18 46	18 51		
Erith	d	18 02					18 12	18 18							18 32					18 42	18 48			
Belvedere	d	18 04					18 14	18 21							18 34					18 44	18 51			
Abbey Wood	d	18 08					18 18	18 24	18 28						18 38					18 48	18 54	18 58		
Plumstead	d	18 11					18 21	18 27	18 31						18 41					18 51	18 57	19 01		
Woolwich Arsenal	d	18 14					18 24	18 30	18 34						18 44					18 54	19 00	19 04		
Woolwich Dockyard	d	18 16					18 26	18 33							18 46					18 56	19 03			
Charlton	d	18 20	17 25				18 30	18 36	18 40						18 50	17 55				19 00	19 06	19 10		
Crayford	d		18 01		18 12					18 26						18 31		18 42					18 56	
Bexley	d		18 04		18 15					18 29						18 34		18 45					18 59	
Albany Park	d		18 06		18 17											18 36		18 47						
Sidcup	d		18 09		18 20					18 33						18 39		18 50					19 03	
New Eltham	d		18 13		18 24					18 36						18 43		18 54					19 06	
Mottingham	d		18 15		18 26											18 45		18 56						
Lee	d		18 18		18 29											18 48		18 59						
Hither Green	d		18 21		18 33											18 51		19 03						
Barnehurst	d			18 09		18 20								18 33			18 39		18 50					
Bexleyheath	d			18 12		18 23								18 36			18 42		18 53					
Welling	d			18 15		18 26								18 39			18 45		18 56					
Falconwood	d			18 18		18 28								18 41			18 48		18 58					
Eltham	d			18 21		18 31								18 44			18 51		19 01					
Kidbrooke	d			18 24		18 34								18 47			18 54		19 04					
Blackheath	d			18 28		18 38		18 41						18 51			18 58		19 08		19 11			
Lewisham	d		18 27	18 32		18 42		18 46						18 55		18 57	19 02		19 12		19 16			
St Johns	d		18 29			18 44										18 59			19 14					
New Cross	d		18 31			18 47										19 01			19 17					
Nunhead	d			18 37													19 07							
Peckham Rye	d			18 40													19 10							
Denmark Hill	d			18 44													19 14							
London Victoria	a			18 55													19 25							
Westcombe Park	d	18 22					18 32		18 42						18 52					19 02		19 12		
Maze Hill	d	18 24					18 34		18 44						18 54					19 04		19 14		
Greenwich	d	18 27					18 37		18 47						18 57					19 07		19 17		
Deptford	a	18 29					18 39		18 49		←	←			18 59					19 09		19 19		←
London Bridge	a	18 35	18 37		18 43	18 52	18 45	18 55	18 57	18 50	18 52	18 55		19 03	19 05	19 07		19 13	19 22	19 15	19 25	19 27	19 20	19 22
London Cannon Street	a	18 41	18 43			→	18 51	→			19 00				19 11	19 13			→	19 21	→			19 30
London Waterloo (East)	a				18 49					18 56		19 01		19 09				19 19					19 26	
London Charing Cross	a				18 53					19 00		19 05		19 13				19 23					19 30	
Ebbsfleet International	a												18 16											
Stratford International	a												18 29											
St Pancras Int'l	a												18 37											

Table T200-R

Saturdays

21 December to 16 May

Gillingham and Dartford - London

		SE	SE	SE	SE	SE	SE	SE	SE	SE	SE	TL	SE	SE	SE	SE	SE	SE	SE	SE	SE	SE	SE
			◇													◇							
Rainham (Kent)	d		18 16									18 28				18 46							
Gillingham (Kent)	d		18 21									18 34				18 51							
Chatham	d		18 25									18 38				18 55							
Rochester	d		18 29									18 42				18 59							
Maidstone West	d																						
Strood	d		18 32									18 45				19 02							
Higham	d											18 50											
Gravesend	d		18 42				18 50					18 59	19 05			19 12				19 20			
Northfleet	d											19 02	19 08										
Swanscombe	d											19 04	19 10										
Greenhithe for Bluewater	d						18 56					19 08	19 14							19 26			
Stone Crossing	d											19 10	19 16										
Dartford	a						19 01					19 14	19 20							19 31			
	d			18 55			19 02	19 05			19 11	19 15	19 21				19 25			19 32	19 35		19 41
Slade Green	d				18 59				19 07	19 09	19 16	19 21						19 29				19 37	19 46
Erith	d				19 02					19 12	19 18							19 32					19 48
Belvedere	d				19 04					19 14	19 21							19 34					19 51
Abbey Wood	d				19 08					19 18	19 24	19 28						19 38					19 54
Plumstead	d				19 11					19 21	19 27	19 31						19 41					19 57
Woolwich Arsenal	d				19 14					19 24	19 30	19 34						19 44					20 00
Woolwich Dockyard	d				19 16					19 26	19 33							19 46					20 03
Charlton	d				19 20	18 25				19 30	19 36	19 40						19 50	18 55				20 06
Crayford	d					19 01		19 12					19 26						19 31		19 42		
Bexley	d					19 04		19 15					19 29						19 34		19 45		
Albany Park	d					19 06		19 17											19 36		19 47		
Sidcup	d					19 09		19 20					19 33						19 39		19 50		
New Eltham	d					19 13		19 24					19 36						19 43		19 54		
Mottingham	d					19 15		19 26											19 45		19 56		
Lee	d					19 18		19 29											19 48		19 59		
Hither Green	d					19 21		19 33											19 51		20 03		
Barnehurst	d			19 03			19 09		19 20								19 33			19 39		19 50	
Bexleyheath	d			19 06			19 12		19 23								19 36			19 42		19 53	
Welling	d			19 09			19 15		19 26								19 39			19 45		19 56	
Falconwood	d			19 11			19 18		19 28								19 41			19 48		19 58	
Eltham	d			19 14			19 21		19 31								19 44			19 51		20 01	
Kidbrooke	d			19 17			19 24		19 34								19 47			19 54		20 04	
Blackheath	d			19 21			19 28		19 38		19 41						19 51			19 58		20 08	20 11
Lewisham	d			19 25		19 27	19 32		19 42		19 46						19 55		19 57	20 02		20 12	20 16
St Johns	d					19 29			19 44										19 59			20 14	
New Cross	d					19 31			19 47										20 01			20 17	
Nunhead	d						19 37													20 07			
Peckham Rye	d						19 40													20 10			
Denmark Hill	d						19 44													20 14			
London Victoria	a						19 55													20 25			
Westcombe Park	d				19 22					19 32		19 42						19 52					
Maze Hill	d				19 24					19 34		19 44						19 54					
Greenwich	d				19 27					19 37		19 47						19 57					
Deptford	a	←			19 29					19 39		19 49		←	←			19 59					
London Bridge	a	19 25		19 33	19 35	19 37		19 43	19 52	19 45	19 55	19 57	19 50	19 52	19 55		20 03	20 05	20 07		20 13	20 22	20 25
London Cannon Street	a				19 41	19 43			→	19 51	→			20 00				20 11	20 13			→	→
London Waterloo (East)	a	19 31		19 39				19 49					19 56		20 01		20 09				20 19		
London Charing Cross	a	19 35		19 43				19 53					20 00		20 05		20 13				20 23		
Ebbsfleet International	a		18 46													19 16							
Stratford International	a		18 58													19 28							
St Pancras Int'l	a		19 06													19 36							

Table T200-R

Saturdays

21 December to 16 May

Gillingham and Dartford - London

		TL	SE	SE	SE	SE ◇	SE	SE	SE	SE	SE	SE	SE	TL	SE	SE		SE	SE ◇	SE	SE	SE	SE	SE	SE
Rainham (Kent)	d	18 58				19 16								19 28					19 46						
Gillingham (Kent) 4	d	19 04				19 21								19 34					19 51						
Chatham 4	d	19 08				19 25								19 38					19 55						
Rochester 4	d	19 12				19 29								19 42					19 59						
Maidstone West	d																								
Strood 4	d	19 15				19 32								19 45					20 02						
Higham	d	19 20												19 50											
Gravesend 4	d	19 29	19 35			19 42				19 50				19 59	20 05				20 12				20 20		
Northfleet	d	19 32	19 38											20 02	20 08										
Swanscombe	d	19 34	19 40											20 04	20 10										
Greenhithe for Bluewater	d	19 38	19 44							19 56				20 08	20 14								20 26		
Stone Crossing	d	19 40	19 46											20 10	20 16										
Dartford 4	a	19 44	19 50							20 01				20 14	20 20								20 31		
	d	19 45	19 51				19 55			20 02	20 05		20 11	20 15	20 21					20 25			20 32	20 35	20 41
Slade Green 4	d	19 51						19 59				20 07	20 16	20 21							20 29				20 46
Erith	d							20 02					20 18								20 32				20 48
Belvedere	d							20 04					20 21								20 34				20 51
Abbey Wood	d	19 58						20 08					20 24	20 28							20 38				20 54
Plumstead	d	20 01						20 11					20 27	20 31							20 41				20 57
Woolwich Arsenal 4	d	20 04						20 14					20 30	20 34							20 44				21 00
Woolwich Dockyard	d							20 16					20 33								20 46				21 03
Charlton 4	d	20 10						20 20	19 25				20 36	20 40							20 50	19 55			21 06
Crayford	d		19 56						20 01		20 12				20 26							20 31		20 42	
Bexley	d		19 59						20 04		20 15				20 29							20 34		20 45	
Albany Park	d								20 06		20 17											20 36		20 47	
Sidcup 4	d		20 03						20 09		20 20				20 33							20 39		20 50	
New Eltham	d		20 06						20 13		20 24				20 36							20 43		20 54	
Mottingham	d								20 15		20 26											20 45		20 56	
Lee	d								20 18		20 29											20 48		20 59	
Hither Green 4	d								20 21		20 33											20 51		21 03	
Barnehurst 4	d						20 03			20 09		20 20								20 33			20 39		
Bexleyheath	d						20 06			20 12		20 23								20 36			20 42		
Welling	d						20 09			20 15		20 26								20 39			20 45		
Falconwood	d						20 11			20 18		20 28								20 41			20 48		
Eltham	d						20 14			20 21		20 31								20 44			20 51		
Kidbrooke	d						20 17			20 24		20 34								20 47			20 54		
Blackheath 4	d						20 21			20 28		20 38	20 41							20 51			20 58		21 11
Lewisham 4	d						20 25		20 27	20 32		20 42	20 46							20 55		20 57	21 02		21 16
St Johns	d								20 29			20 44										20 59			
New Cross 4 ⊖	d								20 31			20 47										21 01			
Nunhead 4	d									20 37													21 07		
Peckham Rye 4	d									20 40													21 10		
Denmark Hill 4	d									20 44													21 14		
London Victoria 15 ⊖	a									20 55													21 25		
Westcombe Park	d	20 12						20 22						20 42							20 52				
Maze Hill	d	20 14						20 24						20 44							20 54				
Greenwich 4	d	20 17						20 27						20 47							20 57				
Deptford	a	20 19		←	←			20 29						20 49		←		←			20 59				
London Bridge 4 ⊖	a	20 27	20 20	20 22	20 25		20 33	20 35	20 37		20 43	20 52	20 55	20 57	20 50	20 52		20 55		21 03	21 05	21 07		21 13	21 25
London Cannon Street 4 ⊖	a			20 30				20 41	20 43			→	→			21 00					21 11	21 13			→
London Waterloo (East) 4 ⊖	a		20 26		20 31		20 39				20 49				20 56			21 01		21 09				21 19	
London Charing Cross 4 ⊖	a		20 30		20 35		20 43				20 53				21 00			21 05		21 13				21 23	
Ebbsfleet International	a					19 46													20 16						
Stratford International ⊖	a					19 58													20 28						
St Pancras Int'l 15 ⊖	a					20 06													20 36						

Table T200-R

Saturdays

21 December to 16 May

Gillingham and Dartford - London

		TL	SE	SE	SE ◇	SE	SE	SE		SE	SE	SE	TL	SE	SE	SE ◇	SE	SE	SE	SE	SE	SE	TL	SE	
Rainham (Kent)	d	19 58			20 16								20 28			20 46							20 58		
Gillingham (Kent) 4	d	20 04			20 21								20 34			20 51							21 04		
Chatham 4	d	20 08			20 25								20 38			20 55							21 08		
Rochester 4	d	20 12			20 29								20 42			20 59							21 12		
Maidstone West	d																								
Strood 4	d	20 15			20 32								20 45			21 02							21 15		
Higham	d	20 20											20 50										21 20		
Gravesend 4	d	20 29	20 35		20 42					20 50			20 59	21 05		21 12				21 20			21 29	21 35	
Northfleet	d	20 32	20 38										21 02	21 08									21 32	21 38	
Swanscombe	d	20 34	20 40										21 04	21 10									21 34	21 40	
Greenhithe for Bluewater	d	20 38	20 44							20 56			21 08	21 14						21 26			21 38	21 44	
Stone Crossing	d	20 40	20 46										21 10	21 16									21 40	21 46	
Dartford 4	a	20 44	20 50							21 01			21 14	21 20						21 31			21 44	21 50	
	d	20 45	20 51			20 55				21 02	21 05	21 11	21 15	21 21			21 25			21 32	21 35	21 41	21 45	21 51	
Slade Green 4	d	20 51					20 59					21 16	21 21					21 29				21 46	21 51		
Erith	d						21 02					21 18						21 32				21 48			
Belvedere	d						21 04					21 21						21 34				21 51			
Abbey Wood	d	20 58					21 08					21 24	21 28					21 38				21 54	21 58		
Plumstead	d	21 01					21 11					21 27	21 31					21 41				21 57	22 01		
Woolwich Arsenal 4	d	21 04					21 14					21 30	21 34					21 44				22 00	22 04		
Woolwich Dockyard	d						21 16					21 33						21 46				22 03			
Charlton 4	d	21 10					21 20	20 25				21 36	21 40					21 50	20 52			22 06	22 10		
Crayford	d		20 56					21 01			21 12			21 26					21 31		21 42			21 56	
Bexley	d		20 59					21 04			21 15			21 29					21 34		21 45			21 59	
Albany Park	d							21 06			21 17								21 36		21 47				
Sidcup 4	d		21 03					21 09			21 20			21 33					21 39		21 50			22 03	
New Eltham	d		21 06					21 13			21 24			21 36					21 43		21 54			22 06	
Mottingham	d							21 15			21 26								21 45		21 56				
Lee	d							21 18			21 29								21 48		21 59				
Hither Green 4	d							21 21			21 33								21 51		22 03				
Barnehurst 4	d					21 03				21 09							21 33			21 39					
Bexleyheath	d					21 06				21 12							21 36			21 42					
Welling	d					21 09				21 15							21 39			21 45					
Falconwood	d					21 11				21 18							21 41			21 48					
Eltham	d					21 14				21 21							21 44			21 51					
Kidbrooke	d					21 17				21 24							21 47			21 54					
Blackheath 4	d					21 21				21 28		21 41					21 51			21 58		22 11			
Lewisham 4	d					21 25		21 27		21 32		21 46					21 55		21 57	22 02		22 16			
St Johns	d							21 29											21 59						
New Cross 4 ⊖	d							21 31											22 01						
Nunhead 4	d									21 37										22 07					
Peckham Rye 4	d									21 40										22 10					
Denmark Hill 4	d									21 44										22 14					
London Victoria 15 ⊖	a									21 55										22 25					
Westcombe Park	d	21 12					21 22						21 42					21 52					22 12		
Maze Hill	d	21 14					21 24						21 44					21 54					22 14		
Greenwich 4	d	21 17					21 27						21 47					21 57					22 17		
Deptford	a	21 19		←			21 29						21 49		←			21 59					22 19		
London Bridge 4 ⊖	a	21 27	21 20	21 25		21 33	21 35	21 37			21 43	21 55	21 57	21 50	21 55		22 03	22 05	22 07		22 13	22 25	22 27	22 20	
London Cannon Street 4 ⊖	a						21 41	21 43				→						22 11	22 13			→			
London Waterloo (East) 4 ⊖	a		21 26	21 31		21 39					21 49			21 56	22 01		22 09				22 19			22 26	
London Charing Cross 4 ⊖	a		21 30	21 35		21 43					21 53			22 00	22 05		22 13				22 23			22 30	
Ebbsfleet International	a				20 46											21 16									
Stratford International ⊖	a				20 58											21 32									
St Pancras Int'l 15 ⊖	a				21 06											21 40									

Table T200-R

Saturdays

21 December to 16 May

Gillingham and Dartford - London

		SE	SE ◇	SE	SE	SE	SE	SE	SE	TL	SE	SE	SE ◇	SE	SE	SE		SE	SE	SE	TL	SE	SE	SE ◇	SE
Rainham (Kent)	d		21 16							21 28			21 46								21 58			22 16	
Gillingham (Kent) 4	d		21 21							21 34			21 51								22 04			22 21	
Chatham 4	d		21 25							21 38			21 55								22 08			22 25	
Rochester 4	d		21 29							21 42			21 59								22 12			22 29	
Maidstone West	d																								
Strood 4	d		21 32							21 45			22 02								22 15			22 32	
Higham	d									21 50											22 20				
Gravesend 4	d		21 42				21 50			21 59	22 05		22 12					22 20			22 29	22 35		22 42	
Northfleet	d									22 02	22 08										22 32	22 38			
Swanscombe	d									22 04	22 10										22 34	22 40			
Greenhithe for Bluewater	d						21 56			22 08	22 14							22 26			22 38	22 44			
Stone Crossing	d									22 10	22 16										22 40	22 46			
Dartford 4	a						22 01			22 14	22 20							22 31			22 44	22 50			
	d			21 55			22 02	22 05	22 11	22 15	22 21			22 25				22 32	22 35	22 41	22 45	22 51			22 55
Slade Green 4	d				21 59				22 16	22 21					22 29					22 46	22 51				
Erith	d				22 02				22 18						22 32					22 48					
Belvedere	d				22 04				22 21						22 34					22 51					
Abbey Wood	d				22 08				22 24	22 28					22 38					22 54	22 58				
Plumstead	d				22 11				22 27	22 31					22 41					22 57	23 01				
Woolwich Arsenal 4 ⛴	d				22 14				22 30	22 34					22 44					23 00	23 04				
Woolwich Dockyard	d				22 16				22 33						22 46					23 03					
Charlton 4	d				22 20	21 22			22 36	22 40					22 50	21 52				23 06	23 10				
Crayford	d					22 01		22 12			22 26					22 31			22 42			22 56			
Bexley	d					22 04		22 15			22 29					22 34			22 45			22 59			
Albany Park	d					22 06		22 17								22 36			22 47						
Sidcup 4	d					22 09		22 20			22 33					22 39			22 50			23 03			
New Eltham	d					22 13		22 24			22 36					22 43			22 54			23 06			
Mottingham	d					22 15		22 26								22 45			22 56						
Lee	d					22 18		22 29								22 48			22 59						
Hither Green 4	d					22 21		22 33								22 51			23 03						
Barnehurst 4	d			22 03			22 09							22 33				22 39							23 03
Bexleyheath	d			22 06			22 12							22 36				22 42							23 06
Welling	d			22 09			22 15							22 39				22 45							23 09
Falconwood	d			22 11			22 18							22 41				22 48							23 11
Eltham	d			22 14			22 21							22 44				22 51							23 14
Kidbrooke	d			22 17			22 24							22 47				22 54							23 17
Blackheath 4	d			22 21			22 28		22 41					22 51				22 58		23 11					23 21
Lewisham 4 ⛴	d			22 25		22 27	22 32		22 46					22 55		22 57		23 02		23 16					23 25
St Johns	d					22 29										22 59									
New Cross 4 ⊖	d					22 31										23 01									
Nunhead 4	d						22 37											23 07							
Peckham Rye 4	d						22 40											23 10							
Denmark Hill 4	d						22 44											23 14							
London Victoria 15 ⊖	a						22 55											23 25							
Westcombe Park	d				22 22					22 42					22 52						23 12				
Maze Hill	d				22 24					22 44					22 54						23 14				
Greenwich 4 ⛴	d				22 27					22 47					22 57						23 17				
Deptford	a	←			22 29					22 49		←			22 59						23 19		←		
London Bridge 4 ⊖	a	22 25		22 33	22 35	22 37		22 43	22 55	22 57	22 50	22 55		23 03	23 05	23 07			23 13	23 25	23 27	23 20	23 25		23 33
London Cannon Street 4 ⊖	a				22 41	22 43			→						23 11	23 13				→					
London Waterloo (East) 4 ⊖	a	22 31		22 39				22 49			22 56	23 01		23 09					23 19			23 26	23 31		23 39
London Charing Cross 4 ⊖	a	22 35		22 43				22 53			23 00	23 05		23 13					23 23			23 30	23 35		23 43
Ebbsfleet International	a		21 46										22 16											22 46	
Stratford International ⊖ ⛴	a		21 58										22 28											22 58	
St Pancras Int'l 15 ⊖	a		22 06										22 36											23 06	

Table T200-R

Saturdays

21 December to 16 May

Gillingham and Dartford - London

		SE	SE	SE	SE	SE	TL	SE		SE	SE	SE	SE	SE	TL	SE	TL
Rainham (Kent)	d						22 28								22 58		23 28
Gillingham (Kent) 4	d						22 34								23 04		23 34
Chatham 4	d						22 38								23 08		23 38
Rochester 4	d						22 42								23 12		23 42
Maidstone West	d																
Strood 4	d						22 45								23 15		23 45
Higham	d						22 50								23 20		23 50
Gravesend 4	d			22 50			22 59	23 05							23 27	23 35	23 57
Northfleet	d						23 02	23 08							23 31	23 38	00 01
Swanscombe	d						23 04	23 10							23 33	23 40	00 03
Greenhithe for Bluewater	d			22 56			23 08	23 14							23 36	23 44	00 06
Stone Crossing	d						23 10	23 16							23 38	23 46	00 08
Dartford 4	a			23 01			23 14	23 20							23 43	23 50	00 13
	d			23 02	23 05	23 11		23 21			23 25			23 41		23 51	
Slade Green 4	d	22 59				23 16						23 29		23 46			
Erith	d	23 02				23 18						23 32		23 48			
Belvedere	d	23 04				23 21						23 34		23 51			
Abbey Wood	d	23 08				23 24						23 38		23 54			
Plumstead	d	23 11				23 27						23 41		23 57			
Woolwich Arsenal 4 ⛴	d	23 14				23 30						23 44		23 59			
Woolwich Dockyard	d	23 16				23 33				←		23 46		00 03			
Charlton 4	d	23 20	22 22			23 36				23 36		23 50	22 52	00 06			
Crayford	d		23 01		23 12	→		23 26					23 31			23 56	
Bexley	d		23 04		23 15			23 29					23 34			23 59	
Albany Park	d		23 06		23 17								23 36			00 01	
Sidcup 4	d		23 09		23 20			23 33					23 39			00 04	
New Eltham	d		23 13		23 24			23 36					23 43			00 08	
Mottingham	d		23 15		23 26								23 45			00 10	
Lee	d		23 18		23 29								23 48			00 13	
Hither Green 4	d		23 21		23 33								23 51			00 16	
Barnehurst 4	d			23 09							23 33						
Bexleyheath	d			23 12							23 36						
Welling	d			23 15							23 39						
Falconwood	d			23 18							23 41						
Eltham	d			23 21							23 44						
Kidbrooke	d			23 24							23 47						
Blackheath 4	d			23 28						23 41	23 51			00 11			
Lewisham 4 ⛴	d		23 27	23 32						23 46	23 55		23 57	00 16			
St Johns	d		23 29										23 59				
New Cross 4 ⊖	d		23 31										00 02				
Nunhead 4	d			23 37													
Peckham Rye 4	d			23 40													
Denmark Hill 4	d			23 44													
London Victoria 15 ⊖	a			23 55													
Westcombe Park	d	23 22										23 52					
Maze Hill	d	23 24										23 54					
Greenwich 4 ⛴	d	23 27										23 57					
Deptford	a	23 29										23 59					
London Bridge 4 ⊖	a	23 35	23 37		23 43			23 50		23 54	00 03	00 05	00 07	00 24		00 26	
London Cannon Street 4 ⊖	a	23 41	23 43									00 11	00 13				
London Waterloo (East) 4 ⊖	a				23 49			23 56		00 01	00 09			00 30		00 33	
London Charing Cross 4 ⊖	a				23 53			00 01		00 06	00 13			00 35		00 38	
Ebbsfleet International	a																
Stratford International ⊖ ⛴	a																
St Pancras Int'l 15 ⊖	a																

Table T200-R

Sundays

15 December to 10 May

Gillingham and Dartford - London

		TL	SE	SE	SE	SE	SE	SE	SE	SE	SE	SE	TL	SE	SE	SE		SE	SE	TL	SE ◇	SE	SE	SE	SE
		A	A	A	A																				
Rainham (Kent)	d																				07 16				
Gillingham (Kent)	d												06 36							07 06	07 21				
Chatham	d												06 40							07 10	07 25				
Rochester	d												06 44							07 14	07 29				
Maidstone West	d																								
Strood	d												06 47							07 17	07 32				
Higham	d												06 52							07 22					
Gravesend	d												06 59					07 18		07 29	07 42				07 48
Northfleet	d	00 01											07 03					07 21		07 33					07 51
Swanscombe	d	00 03											07 05					07 23		07 35					07 53
Greenhithe for Bluewater	d	00 06											07 08					07 27		07 38					07 57
Stone Crossing	d	00 08											07 10					07 29		07 40					07 59
Dartford	a	00 13											07 14					07 33		07 44					08 03
	d								06 50	07 02	07 04		07 15		07 20	07 32		07 34		07 45			07 50	08 02	08 04
Slade Green	d					06 35			06 55			07 05	07 21		07 25				07 35	07 51			07 55		
Erith	d					06 37			06 57			07 07			07 27				07 37				07 57		
Belvedere	d					06 40			07 00			07 10			07 30				07 40				08 00		
Abbey Wood	d					06 43			07 03			07 13	07 28		07 33				07 43	07 58			08 03		
Plumstead	d					06 46			07 06			07 16	07 31		07 36				07 46	08 01			08 06		
Woolwich Arsenal	d					06 49			07 09			07 19	07 34		07 39				07 49	08 04			08 09		
Woolwich Dockyard	d			00 03		06 52			07 12			07 22			07 42				07 52				08 12		
Charlton	d			00 06		06 55			07 15			07 25	07 40		07 45				07 55	08 10			08 15		
Crayford	d							06 52			07 09			07 22				07 39				07 52			08 09
Bexley	d							06 55			07 12			07 25				07 42				07 55			08 12
Albany Park	d				00 01			06 57			07 14			07 27				07 44				07 57			08 14
Sidcup	d				00 04			07 00			07 17			07 30				07 47				08 00			08 17
New Eltham	d				00 08			07 04			07 21			07 34				07 51				08 04			08 21
Mottingham	d				00 10			07 06			07 23			07 36				07 53				08 06			08 23
Lee	d				00 13			07 09			07 26			07 39				07 56				08 09			08 26
Hither Green	d				00 16			07 12			07 29			07 42				07 59				08 12			08 29
Barnehurst	d						06 39			07 09						07 39								08 09	
Bexleyheath	d						06 42			07 12						07 42								08 12	
Welling	d						06 45			07 15						07 45								08 15	
Falconwood	d						06 48			07 18						07 48								08 18	
Eltham	d						06 51			07 21						07 51								08 21	
Kidbrooke	d						06 54			07 24						07 54								08 24	
Blackheath	d			00 11			06 58		07 20	07 28					07 50	07 58							08 20	08 28	
Lewisham	d			00 16			07 02	07 18	07 25	07 32				07 48	07 55	08 02						08 18	08 25	08 32	
St Johns	d							07 20						07 50								08 20			
New Cross	d		00 02					07 23						07 53								08 23			
Nunhead	d						07 07			07 37						08 07								08 37	
Peckham Rye	d						07 10			07 40						08 10								08 40	
Denmark Hill	d						07 14			07 44						08 14								08 44	
London Victoria	a						07 25			07 56						08 25								08 56	
Westcombe Park	d					06 57						07 27	07 42						07 57	08 12					
Maze Hill	d					06 59						07 29	07 44						07 59	08 14					
Greenwich	d					07 03						07 33	07 47						08 03	08 17					
Deptford	a					07 05						07 35	07 49						08 05	08 19					
London Bridge	a		00 07	00 24	00 26	07 11		07 28	07 33		07 39	07 41	07 57	07 58	08 03			08 09	08 11	08 27		08 28	08 33		08 39
London Cannon Street	a		00 13			07 17		07 34				07 47		08 04					08 17			08 34			
London Waterloo (East)	a			00 30	00 33				07 39		07 45				08 09			08 15					08 39		08 45
London Charing Cross	a			00 35	00 38				07 43		07 49				08 15			08 19					08 44		08 49
Ebbsfleet International	a																				07 46				
Stratford International	a																				07 58				
St Pancras Int'l	a																				08 06				

A not 15 December

NRT DECEMBER 19 EDITION

Table T200-R

Sundays

15 December to 10 May

Gillingham and Dartford - London

		SE	TL	SE	SE	SE	SE	SE ◇		SE	SE	SE	SE	SE	SE	TL	SE	SE	SE	SE	SE	TL	SE	SE ◇
Rainham (Kent)	d		07 30					08 16								08 30						09 00		09 16
Gillingham (Kent)	d		07 36					08 21								08 36						09 06		09 21
Chatham	d		07 40					08 25								08 40						09 10		09 25
Rochester	d		07 44					08 29								08 44						09 14		09 29
Maidstone West	d																							
Strood	d		07 47					08 32								08 47						09 17		09 32
Higham	d		07 52													08 52						09 22		
Gravesend	d		07 59				08 18	08 42						08 48		08 59				09 18		09 29		09 42
Northfleet	d		08 03				08 21							08 51		09 03				09 21		09 33		
Swanscombe	d		08 05				08 23							08 53		09 05				09 23		09 35		
Greenhithe for Bluewater	d		08 08				08 27							08 57		09 08				09 27		09 38		
Stone Crossing	d		08 10				08 29							08 59		09 10				09 29		09 40		
Dartford	a		08 14				08 33							09 03		09 14				09 33		09 44		
	d		08 15		08 20	08 32	08 34					08 50	09 02	09 04		09 15		09 20	09 32	09 34		09 45		
Slade Green	d	08 05	08 21		08 25					08 35		08 55			09 05	09 21		09 25			09 35	09 51		
Erith	d	08 07			08 27					08 37		08 57			09 07			09 27			09 37			
Belvedere	d	08 10			08 30					08 40		09 00			09 10			09 30			09 40			
Abbey Wood	d	08 13	08 28		08 33					08 43		09 03			09 13	09 28		09 33			09 43	09 58		
Plumstead	d	08 16	08 31		08 36					08 46		09 06			09 16	09 31		09 36			09 46	10 01		
Woolwich Arsenal	d	08 19	08 34		08 39					08 49		09 09			09 19	09 34		09 39			09 49	10 04		
Woolwich Dockyard	d	08 22			08 42					08 52		09 12			09 22			09 42			09 52			
Charlton	d	08 25	08 40	07 49	08 45					08 55	08 19	09 15			09 25	09 40	08 49	09 45			09 55	10 10	09 19	
Crayford	d			08 22			08 39				08 52			09 09			09 22			09 39			09 52	
Bexley	d			08 25			08 42				08 55			09 12			09 25			09 42			09 55	
Albany Park	d			08 27			08 44				08 57			09 14			09 27			09 44			09 57	
Sidcup	d			08 30			08 47				09 00			09 17			09 30			09 47			10 00	
New Eltham	d			08 34			08 51				09 04			09 21			09 34			09 51			10 04	
Mottingham	d			08 36			08 53				09 06			09 23			09 36			09 53			10 06	
Lee	d			08 39			08 56				09 09			09 26			09 39			09 56			10 09	
Hither Green	d			08 42			08 59				09 12			09 29			09 42			09 59			10 12	
Barnehurst	d					08 39							09 09						09 39					
Bexleyheath	d					08 42							09 12						09 42					
Welling	d					08 45							09 15						09 45					
Falconwood	d					08 48							09 18						09 48					
Eltham	d					08 51							09 21						09 51					
Kidbrooke	d					08 54							09 24						09 54					
Blackheath	d				08 50	08 58						09 20	09 28					09 50	09 58					
Lewisham	d			08 48	08 55	09 02					09 18	09 25	09 32				09 48	09 55	10 02				10 18	
St Johns	d			08 50							09 20						09 50						10 20	
New Cross	d			08 53							09 23						09 53						10 23	
Nunhead	d					09 07							09 37						10 07					
Peckham Rye	d					09 10							09 40						10 10					
Denmark Hill	d					09 14							09 44						10 14					
London Victoria	a					09 25							09 56						10 25					
Westcombe Park	d	08 27	08 42							08 57					09 27	09 42					09 57	10 12		
Maze Hill	d	08 29	08 44							08 59					09 29	09 44					09 59	10 14		
Greenwich	d	08 33	08 47							09 03					09 33	09 47					10 03	10 17		
Deptford	a	08 35	08 49							09 05					09 35	09 49					10 05	10 19		
London Bridge	a	08 41	08 57	08 58	09 03		09 09			09 11	09 28	09 33		09 39	09 41	09 57	09 58	10 03		10 09	10 11	10 27	10 28	
London Cannon Street	a	08 47		09 04						09 17	09 34				09 47		10 04				10 17		10 34	
London Waterloo (East)	a				09 09		09 15					09 39		09 45				10 09		10 15				
London Charing Cross	a				09 13		09 19					09 43		09 49				10 13		10 19				
Ebbsfleet International	a							08 46																09 46
Stratford International	a							08 58																10 02
St Pancras Int'l	a							09 06																10 10

Table T200-R

Sundays
15 December to 10 May

Gillingham and Dartford - London

		SE	SE	SE	SE	TL	SE	SE	SE	SE	SE	TL	SE	SE ◇	SE	SE		SE	SE	TL	SE	SE	SE	SE	SE
Rainham (Kent)	d					09 30						10 00		10 16						10 30					
Gillingham (Kent)	d					09 36						10 06		10 21						10 36					
Chatham	d					09 40						10 10		10 25						10 40					
Rochester	d					09 44						10 14		10 29						10 44					
Maidstone West	d																								
Strood	d					09 47						10 17		10 32						10 47					
Higham	d					09 52						10 22								10 52					
Gravesend	d			09 48		09 59				10 18		10 29		10 42				10 48		10 59				11 18	
Northfleet	d			09 51		10 03				10 21		10 33						10 51		11 03				11 21	
Swanscombe	d			09 53		10 05				10 23		10 35						10 53		11 05				11 23	
Greenhithe for Bluewater	d			09 57		10 08				10 27		10 38						10 57		11 08				11 27	
Stone Crossing	d			09 59		10 10				10 29		10 40						10 59		11 10				11 29	
Dartford	a			10 03		10 14				10 33		10 44						11 03		11 14				11 33	
	d	09 50	10 02	10 04		10 15		10 20	10 32	10 34		10 46			10 50	11 02		11 04		11 15		11 20	11 32	11 34	
Slade Green	d	09 55			10 05	10 21		10 25			10 35	10 51			10 55				11 05	11 21		11 25			11 35
Erith	d	09 57			10 07			10 27			10 37				10 57				11 07			11 27			11 37
Belvedere	d	10 00			10 10			10 30			10 40				11 00				11 10			11 30			11 40
Abbey Wood	d	10 03			10 13	10 28		10 33			10 43	10 58			11 03				11 13	11 28		11 33			11 43
Plumstead	d	10 06			10 16	10 31		10 36			10 46	11 01			11 06				11 16	11 31		11 36			11 46
Woolwich Arsenal	d	10 09			10 19	10 34		10 39			10 49	11 04			11 09				11 19	11 34		11 39			11 49
Woolwich Dockyard	d	10 12			10 22			10 42			10 52				11 12				11 22			11 42			11 52
Charlton	d	10 15			10 25	10 40	09 49	10 45			10 55	11 10	10 19		11 15				11 25	11 40	10 49	11 45			11 55
Crayford	d			10 09			10 22			10 39			10 52					11 09			11 22			11 39	
Bexley	d			10 12			10 25			10 42			10 55					11 12			11 25			11 42	
Albany Park	d			10 14			10 27			10 44			10 57					11 14			11 27			11 44	
Sidcup	d			10 17			10 30			10 47			11 00					11 17			11 30			11 47	
New Eltham	d			10 21			10 34			10 51			11 04					11 21			11 34			11 51	
Mottingham	d			10 23			10 36			10 53			11 06					11 23			11 36			11 53	
Lee	d			10 26			10 39			10 56			11 09					11 26			11 39			11 56	
Hither Green	d			10 29			10 42			10 59			11 12					11 29			11 42			11 59	
Barnehurst	d		10 09						10 39							11 09							11 39		
Bexleyheath	d		10 12						10 42							11 12							11 42		
Welling	d		10 15						10 45							11 15							11 45		
Falconwood	d		10 18						10 48							11 18							11 48		
Eltham	d		10 21						10 51							11 21							11 51		
Kidbrooke	d		10 24						10 54							11 24							11 54		
Blackheath	d	10 20	10 28					10 50	10 58						11 20	11 28						11 50	11 58		
Lewisham	d	10 25	10 32				10 48	10 55	11 02				11 18		11 25	11 32					11 48	11 55	12 02		
St Johns	d						10 50						11 20								11 50				
New Cross	d						10 53						11 23								11 53				
Nunhead	d		10 37						11 07							11 37							12 07		
Peckham Rye	d		10 40						11 10							11 40							12 10		
Denmark Hill	d		10 44						11 14							11 44							12 14		
London Victoria	a		10 56						11 25							11 56							12 24		
Westcombe Park	d				10 27	10 42					10 57	11 12							11 27	11 42					11 57
Maze Hill	d				10 29	10 44					10 59	11 14							11 29	11 44					11 59
Greenwich	d				10 33	10 47					11 03	11 17							11 33	11 47					12 03
Deptford	a				10 35	10 49					11 05	11 19							11 35	11 49					12 05
London Bridge	a	10 33		10 39	10 41	10 57	10 58	11 03		11 09	11 11	11 27	11 28		11 33			11 39	11 41	11 57	11 58	12 03		12 09	12 11
London Cannon Street	a				10 47		11 04				11 17		11 34						11 47		12 04				12 17
London Waterloo (East)	a	10 39		10 45				11 09		11 15					11 39			11 45				12 09		12 15	
London Charing Cross	a	10 43		10 49				11 13		11 19					11 43			11 49				12 13		12 19	
Ebbsfleet International	a													10 46											
Stratford International	a													10 58											
St Pancras Int'l	a													11 06											

Table T200-R

Sundays
15 December to 10 May

Gillingham and Dartford - London

		TL	SE	SE ◇	SE	SE	SE	SE		TL	SE	SE ◇	SE	SE	SE	SE	TL	SE	SE ◇	SE	SE	SE	SE	TL	
Rainham (Kent)	d	11 00		11 16						11 30		11 46					12 00		12 16					12 30	
Gillingham (Kent)	d	11 06		11 21						11 36		11 51					12 06		12 21					12 36	
Chatham	d	11 10		11 25						11 40		11 55					12 10		12 25					12 40	
Rochester	d	11 14		11 29						11 44		11 59					12 14		12 29					12 44	
Maidstone West	d																								
Strood	d	11 17		11 32						11 47		12 02					12 17		12 32					12 47	
Higham	d	11 22								11 52							12 22							12 52	
Gravesend	d	11 29		11 42			11 48			11 59		12 12			12 18		12 29		12 42			12 48		12 59	
Northfleet	d	11 33					11 51			12 03					12 21		12 33					12 51		13 03	
Swanscombe	d	11 35					11 53			12 05					12 23		12 35					12 53		13 05	
Greenhithe for Bluewater	d	11 38					11 57			12 08					12 27		12 38					12 57		13 08	
Stone Crossing	d	11 40					11 59			12 10					12 29		12 40					12 59		13 10	
Dartford	a	11 44					12 03			12 14					12 33		12 44					13 03		13 14	
	d	11 45			11 50	12 02	12 04			12 15			12 20	12 32	12 34		12 45			12 50	13 02	13 04		13 15	
Slade Green	d	11 51			11 55			12 05		12 21			12 25			12 35	12 51			12 55			13 05	13 21	
Erith	d				11 57			12 07					12 27			12 37				12 57			13 07		
Belvedere	d				12 00			12 10					12 30			12 40				13 00			13 10		
Abbey Wood	d	11 58			12 03			12 13		12 28			12 33			12 43	12 58			13 03			13 13	13 28	
Plumstead	d	12 01			12 06			12 16		12 31			12 36			12 46	13 01			13 06			13 16	13 31	
Woolwich Arsenal	d	12 04			12 09			12 19		12 34			12 39			12 49	13 04			13 09			13 19	13 34	
Woolwich Dockyard	d				12 12			12 22					12 42			12 52				13 12			13 22		
Charlton	d	12 10	11 19		12 15			12 25		12 40	11 49		12 45			12 55	13 10	12 19		13 15			13 25	13 40	
Crayford	d		11 52				12 09				12 22				12 39			12 52				13 09			
Bexley	d		11 55				12 12				12 25				12 42			12 55				13 12			
Albany Park	d		11 57				12 14				12 27				12 44			12 57				13 14			
Sidcup	d		12 00				12 17				12 30				12 47			13 00				13 17			
New Eltham	d		12 04				12 21				12 34				12 51			13 04				13 21			
Mottingham	d		12 06				12 23				12 36				12 53			13 06				13 23			
Lee	d		12 09				12 26				12 39				12 56			13 09				13 26			
Hither Green	d		12 12				12 29				12 42				12 59			13 12				13 29			
Barnehurst	d					12 09								12 39							13 09				
Bexleyheath	d					12 12								12 42							13 12				
Welling	d					12 15								12 45							13 15				
Falconwood	d					12 18								12 48							13 18				
Eltham	d					12 21								12 51							13 21				
Kidbrooke	d					12 24								12 54							13 24				
Blackheath	d				12 20	12 28							12 50	12 58						13 20	13 28				
Lewisham	d		12 18		12 25	12 32					12 48		12 55	13 02				13 18		13 25	13 32				
St Johns	d		12 20								12 50							13 20							
New Cross	d		12 23								12 53							13 23							
Nunhead	d					12 37								13 07							13 37				
Peckham Rye	d					12 40								13 10							13 40				
Denmark Hill	d					12 44								13 14							13 44				
London Victoria	a					12 54								13 24							13 54				
Westcombe Park	d	12 12						12 27		12 42						12 57	13 12						13 27	13 42	
Maze Hill	d	12 14						12 29		12 44						12 59	13 14						13 29	13 44	
Greenwich	d	12 17						12 33		12 47						13 03	13 17						13 33	13 47	
Deptford	a	12 19						12 35		12 49						13 05	13 19						13 35	13 49	
London Bridge	a	12 27	12 28		12 33		12 39	12 41		12 57	12 58		13 03		13 09	13 11	13 27	13 28		13 33		13 39	13 41	13 57	
London Cannon Street	a		12 34					12 47			13 04					13 17		13 34					13 47		
London Waterloo (East)	a				12 39		12 45						13 09		13 15					13 39		13 45			
London Charing Cross	a				12 43		12 49						13 13		13 19					13 43		13 49			
Ebbsfleet International	a			11 46								12 16							12 46						
Stratford International	a			11 58								12 28							12 58						
St Pancras Int'l	a			12 06								12 36							13 06						

Table T200-R

Sundays

15 December to 10 May

Gillingham and Dartford - London

		SE	SE ◇	SE	SE	SE	SE	TL	SE	SE ◇	SE	SE	SE	SE	TL	SE		SE ◇	SE	SE	SE	SE	TL	SE	SE ◇
Rainham (Kent)	d		12 46					13 00		13 16					13 30			13 46					14 00		14 16
Gillingham (Kent) 4	d		12 51					13 06		13 21					13 36			13 51					14 06		14 21
Chatham 4	d		12 55					13 10		13 25					13 40			13 55					14 10		14 25
Rochester 4	d		12 59					13 14		13 29					13 44			13 59					14 14		14 29
Maidstone West	d																								
Strood 4	d		13 02					13 17		13 32					13 47			14 02					14 17		14 32
Higham	d							13 22							13 52								14 22		
Gravesend 4	d		13 12			13 18		13 29		13 42			13 48		13 59			14 12			14 18		14 29		14 42
Northfleet	d					13 21		13 33					13 51		14 03						14 21		14 33		
Swanscombe	d					13 23		13 35					13 53		14 05						14 23		14 35		
Greenhithe for Bluewater	d					13 27		13 38					13 57		14 08						14 27		14 38		
Stone Crossing	d					13 29		13 40					13 59		14 10						14 29		14 40		
Dartford 4	a					13 33		13 44					14 03		14 14						14 33		14 44		
	d			13 20	13 32	13 34		13 45			13 50	14 02	14 04		14 15				14 20	14 32	14 34		14 45		
Slade Green 4	d			13 25			13 35	13 51			13 55			14 05	14 21				14 25			14 35	14 51		
Erith	d			13 27			13 37				13 57			14 07					14 27			14 37			
Belvedere	d			13 30			13 40				14 00			14 10					14 30			14 40			
Abbey Wood	d			13 33			13 43	13 58			14 03			14 13	14 28				14 33			14 43	14 58		
Plumstead	d			13 36			13 46	14 01			14 06			14 16	14 31				14 36			14 46	15 01		
Woolwich Arsenal 4	d			13 39			13 49	14 04			14 09			14 19	14 34				14 39			14 49	15 04		
Woolwich Dockyard	d			13 42			13 52				14 12			14 22					14 42			14 52			
Charlton 4	d	12 49		13 45			13 55	14 10	13 19		14 15			14 25	14 40	13 49			14 45			14 55	15 10	14 19	
Crayford	d	13 22				13 39			13 52				14 09			14 22					14 39			14 52	
Bexley	d	13 25				13 42			13 55				14 12			14 25					14 42			14 55	
Albany Park	d	13 27				13 44			13 57				14 14			14 27					14 44			14 57	
Sidcup 4	d	13 30				13 47			14 00				14 17			14 30					14 47			15 00	
New Eltham	d	13 34				13 51			14 04				14 21			14 34					14 51			15 04	
Mottingham	d	13 36				13 53			14 06				14 23			14 36					14 53			15 06	
Lee	d	13 39				13 56			14 09				14 26			14 39					14 56			15 09	
Hither Green 4	d	13 42				13 59			14 12				14 29			14 42					14 59			15 12	
Barnehurst 4	d				13 39							14 09								14 39					
Bexleyheath	d				13 42							14 12								14 42					
Welling	d				13 45							14 15								14 45					
Falconwood	d				13 48							14 18								14 48					
Eltham	d				13 51							14 21								14 51					
Kidbrooke	d				13 54							14 24								14 54					
Blackheath 4	d			13 50	13 58						14 20	14 28							14 50	14 58					
Lewisham 4	d	13 48		13 55	14 02				14 18		14 25	14 32				14 48			14 55	15 02				15 18	
St Johns	d	13 50							14 20							14 50								15 20	
New Cross 4	d	13 53							14 23							14 53								15 23	
Nunhead 4	d				14 07							14 37								15 07					
Peckham Rye 4	d				14 10							14 40								15 10					
Denmark Hill 4	d				14 14							14 44								15 14					
London Victoria 15	a				14 24							14 54								15 24					
Westcombe Park	d						13 57	14 12						14 27	14 42							14 57	15 12		
Maze Hill	d						13 59	14 14						14 29	14 44							14 59	15 14		
Greenwich 4	d						14 03	14 17						14 33	14 47							15 03	15 17		
Deptford	a						14 05	14 19						14 35	14 49							15 05	15 19		
London Bridge 4	a	13 58		14 03		14 09	14 11	14 27	14 28		14 33		14 39	14 41	14 57	14 58			15 03		15 09	15 11	15 27	15 28	
London Cannon Street 4	a	14 04					14 17		14 34					14 47		15 04						15 17		15 34	
London Waterloo (East) 4	a			14 09		14 15					14 39		14 45						15 09		15 15				
London Charing Cross 4	a			14 13		14 19					14 43		14 49						15 13		15 19				
Ebbsfleet International	a		13 16							13 46								14 16							14 46
Stratford International	a		13 29							13 58								14 28							14 59
St Pancras Int'l 15	a		13 37							14 06								14 36							15 07

Table T200-R

Sundays

15 December to 10 May

Gillingham and Dartford - London

		SE	SE	SE	SE	TL	SE	SE ◇		SE	SE	SE	SE	TL	SE	SE ◇	SE	SE	SE	SE	TL	SE	SE ◇	SE
Rainham (Kent)	d					14 30		14 46						15 00		15 16					15 30		15 46	
Gillingham (Kent) 4	d					14 36		14 51						15 06		15 21					15 36		15 51	
Chatham 4	d					14 40		14 55						15 10		15 25					15 40		15 55	
Rochester 4	d					14 44		14 59						15 14		15 29					15 44		15 59	
Maidstone West	d																							
Strood 4	d					14 47		15 02						15 17		15 32					15 47		16 02	
Higham	d					14 52								15 22							15 52			
Gravesend 4	d			14 48		14 59		15 12				15 18		15 29		15 42			15 48		15 59		16 12	
Northfleet	d			14 51		15 03						15 21		15 33					15 51		16 03			
Swanscombe	d			14 53		15 05						15 23		15 35					15 53		16 05			
Greenhithe for Bluewater	d			14 57		15 08						15 27		15 38					15 57		16 08			
Stone Crossing	d			14 59		15 10						15 29		15 40					15 59		16 10			
Dartford 4	a			15 03		15 14						15 33		15 44					16 03		16 14			
	d	14 50	15 02	15 04		15 15				15 20	15 32	15 34		15 45			15 50	16 02	16 04		16 15			16 20
Slade Green 4	d	14 55			15 05	15 21				15 25			15 35	15 51			15 55			16 05	16 21			16 25
Erith	d	14 57			15 07					15 27			15 37				15 57			16 07				16 27
Belvedere	d	15 00			15 10					15 30			15 40				16 00			16 10				16 30
Abbey Wood	d	15 03			15 13	15 28				15 33			15 43	15 58			16 03			16 13	16 28			16 33
Plumstead	d	15 06			15 16	15 31				15 36			15 46	16 01			16 06			16 16	16 31			16 36
Woolwich Arsenal 4	d	15 09			15 19	15 34				15 39			15 49	16 04			16 09			16 19	16 34			16 39
Woolwich Dockyard	d	15 12			15 22					15 42			15 52				16 12			16 22				16 42
Charlton 4	d	15 15			15 25	15 40	14 49			15 45			15 55	16 10	15 19		16 15			16 25	16 40	15 49		16 45
Crayford	d			15 09			15 22					15 39			15 52				16 09			16 22		
Bexley	d			15 12			15 25					15 42			15 55				16 12			16 25		
Albany Park	d			15 14			15 27					15 44			15 57				16 14			16 27		
Sidcup 4	d			15 17			15 30					15 47			16 00				16 17			16 30		
New Eltham	d			15 21			15 34					15 51			16 04				16 21			16 34		
Mottingham	d			15 23			15 36					15 53			16 06				16 23			16 36		
Lee	d			15 26			15 39					15 56			16 09				16 26			16 39		
Hither Green 4	d			15 29			15 42					15 59			16 12				16 29			16 42		
Barnehurst 4	d		15 09								15 39							16 09						
Bexleyheath	d		15 12								15 42							16 12						
Welling	d		15 15								15 45							16 15						
Falconwood	d		15 18								15 48							16 18						
Eltham	d		15 21								15 51							16 21						
Kidbrooke	d		15 24								15 54							16 24						
Blackheath 4	d	15 20	15 28							15 50	15 58						16 20	16 28						16 50
Lewisham 4	d	15 25	15 32				15 48			15 55	16 02				16 18		16 25	16 32				16 48		16 55
St Johns	d						15 50								16 20							16 50		
New Cross 4	d						15 53								16 23							16 53		
Nunhead 4	d		15 37								16 07							16 37						
Peckham Rye 4	d		15 40								16 10							16 40						
Denmark Hill 4	d		15 44								16 14							16 44						
London Victoria 15	a		15 54								16 24							16 54						
Westcombe Park	d				15 27	15 42							15 57	16 12						16 27	16 42			
Maze Hill	d				15 29	15 44							15 59	16 14						16 29	16 44			
Greenwich 4	d				15 33	15 47							16 03	16 17						16 33	16 47			
Deptford	a				15 35	15 49							16 05	16 19						16 35	16 49			
London Bridge 4	a	15 33		15 39	15 41	15 57	15 58			16 03		16 09	16 11	16 27	16 28		16 33		16 39	16 41	16 57	16 58		17 03
London Cannon Street 4	a				15 47		16 04						16 17		16 34					16 47		17 04		
London Waterloo (East) 4	a	15 39		15 45						16 09		16 15					16 39		16 45					17 09
London Charing Cross 4	a	15 43		15 49						16 13		16 19					16 43		16 49					17 13
Ebbsfleet International	a							15 16								15 46							16 16	
Stratford International	a							15 28								16 02							16 28	
St Pancras Int'l 15	a							15 36								16 10							16 36	

Table T200-R

Sundays

15 December to 10 May

Gillingham and Dartford - London

Station		SE	SE	SE	TL	SE	SE ◇	SE	SE	SE	SE	TL	SE	SE ◇	SE	SE		SE	SE	TL	SE	SE ◇	SE	SE	SE
Rainham (Kent)	d				16 00		16 16					16 30		16 46						17 00		17 16			
Gillingham (Kent) 4	d				16 06		16 21					16 36		16 51						17 06		17 21			
Chatham 4	d				16 10		16 25					16 40		16 55						17 10		17 25			
Rochester 4	d				16 14		16 29					16 44		16 59						17 14		17 29			
Maidstone West	d																								
Strood 4	d				16 17		16 32					16 47		17 02						17 17		17 32			
Higham	d				16 22							16 52								17 22					
Gravesend 4	d		16 18		16 29		16 42			16 48		16 59		17 12				17 18		17 29		17 42			17 48
Northfleet	d		16 21		16 33					16 51		17 03						17 21		17 33					17 51
Swanscombe	d		16 23		16 35					16 53		17 05						17 23		17 35					17 53
Greenhithe for Bluewater	d		16 27		16 38					16 57		17 08						17 27		17 38					17 57
Stone Crossing	d		16 29		16 40					16 59		17 10						17 29		17 40					17 59
Dartford 4	a		16 33		16 44					17 03		17 14						17 33		17 44					18 03
	d	16 32	16 34		16 45			16 50	17 02	17 04		17 15			17 20	17 32		17 34		17 45			17 50	18 02	18 04
Slade Green 4	d			16 35	16 51			16 55			17 05	17 21			17 25				17 35	17 51			17 55		
Erith	d			16 37				16 57			17 07				17 27				17 37				17 57		
Belvedere	d			16 40				17 00			17 10				17 30				17 40				18 00		
Abbey Wood	d			16 43	16 58			17 03			17 13	17 28			17 33				17 43	17 58			18 03		
Plumstead	d			16 46	17 01			17 06			17 16	17 31			17 36				17 46	18 01			18 06		
Woolwich Arsenal 4	d			16 49	17 04			17 09			17 19	17 34			17 39				17 49	18 04			18 09		
Woolwich Dockyard	d			16 52				17 12			17 22				17 42				17 52				18 12		
Charlton 4	d			16 55	17 10	16 19		17 15			17 25	17 40	16 49		17 45				17 55	18 10	17 19		18 15		
Crayford	d		16 39			16 52				17 09			17 22					17 39			17 52				18 09
Bexley	d		16 42			16 55				17 12			17 25					17 42			17 55				18 12
Albany Park	d		16 44			16 57				17 14			17 27					17 44			17 57				18 14
Sidcup 4	d		16 47			17 00				17 17			17 30					17 47			18 00				18 17
New Eltham	d		16 51			17 04				17 21			17 34					17 51			18 04				18 21
Mottingham	d		16 53			17 06				17 23			17 36					17 53			18 06				18 23
Lee	d		16 56			17 09				17 26			17 39					17 56			18 09				18 26
Hither Green 4	d		16 59			17 12				17 29			17 42					17 59			18 12				18 29
Barnehurst 4	d	16 39							17 09							17 39								18 09	
Bexleyheath	d	16 42							17 12							17 42								18 12	
Welling	d	16 45							17 15							17 45								18 15	
Falconwood	d	16 48							17 18							17 48								18 18	
Eltham	d	16 51							17 21							17 51								18 21	
Kidbrooke	d	16 54							17 24							17 54								18 24	
Blackheath 4	d	16 58						17 20	17 28						17 50	17 58							18 20	18 28	
Lewisham 4	d	17 02				17 18		17 25	17 32				17 48		17 55	18 02					18 18		18 25	18 32	
St Johns	d					17 20							17 50								18 20				
New Cross 4 ⊖	d					17 23							17 53								18 23				
Nunhead 4	d	17 07							17 37							18 07								18 37	
Peckham Rye 4	d	17 10							17 40							18 10								18 40	
Denmark Hill 4	d	17 14							17 44							18 14								18 44	
London Victoria 15 ⊖	a	17 24							17 54							18 24								18 54	
Westcombe Park	d			16 57	17 12						17 27	17 42							17 57	18 12					
Maze Hill	d			16 59	17 14						17 29	17 44							17 59	18 14					
Greenwich 4	d			17 03	17 17						17 33	17 47							18 03	18 17					
Deptford	a			17 05	17 19						17 35	17 49							18 05	18 19					
London Bridge 4 ⊖	a		17 09	17 11	17 27	17 28		17 33		17 39	17 41	17 57	17 58		18 03			18 09	18 11	18 27	18 28		18 33		18 39
London Cannon Street 4 ⊖	a			17 17		17 34					17 47		18 04						18 17		18 34				
London Waterloo (East) 4 ⊖	a		17 15					17 39		17 45					18 09			18 15					18 39		18 45
London Charing Cross 4 ⊖	a		17 19					17 43		17 49					18 13			18 19					18 43		18 49
Ebbsfleet International	a						16 46							17 16								17 46			
Stratford International ⊖	a						17 02							17 28								18 02			
St Pancras Int'l 15 ⊖	a						17 10							17 36								18 10			

Table T200-R

Sundays

15 December to 10 May

Gillingham and Dartford - London

Station		SE	TL	SE	SE ◇	SE	SE	SE		SE	TL	SE	SE ◇	SE	SE	SE	SE	TL	SE	SE ◇	SE	SE	SE	SE	
Rainham (Kent)	d		17 30		17 46						18 00		18 16					18 30		18 46					
Gillingham (Kent) 4	d		17 36		17 51						18 06		18 21					18 36		18 51					
Chatham 4	d		17 40		17 55						18 10		18 25					18 40		18 55					
Rochester 4	d		17 44		17 59						18 14		18 29					18 44		18 59					
Maidstone West	d																								
Strood 4	d		17 47		18 02						18 17		18 32					18 47		19 02					
Higham	d		17 52								18 22							18 52							
Gravesend 4	d		17 59		18 12			18 18			18 29		18 42			18 48		18 59		19 12			19 18		
Northfleet	d		18 03					18 21			18 33					18 51		19 03					19 21		
Swanscombe	d		18 05					18 23			18 35					18 53		19 05					19 23		
Greenhithe for Bluewater	d		18 08					18 27			18 38					18 57		19 08					19 27		
Stone Crossing	d		18 10					18 29			18 40					18 59		19 10					19 29		
Dartford 4	a		18 14					18 33			18 44					19 03		19 14					19 33		
	d		18 15			18 20	18 32	18 34			18 45			18 50	19 02	19 04		19 15			19 20	19 32	19 34		
Slade Green 4	d	18 05	18 21			18 25				18 35	18 51			18 55			19 05	19 21			19 25			19 35	
Erith	d	18 07				18 27				18 37				18 57			19 07				19 27			19 37	
Belvedere	d	18 10				18 30				18 40				19 00			19 10				19 30			19 40	
Abbey Wood	d	18 13	18 28			18 33				18 43	18 58			19 03			19 13	19 28			19 33			19 43	
Plumstead	d	18 16	18 31			18 36				18 46	19 01			19 06			19 16	19 31			19 36			19 46	
Woolwich Arsenal 4	d	18 19	18 34			18 39				18 49	19 04			19 09			19 19	19 34			19 39			19 49	
Woolwich Dockyard	d	18 22				18 42				18 52				19 12			19 22				19 42			19 52	
Charlton 4	d	18 25	18 40	17 49		18 45				18 55	19 10	18 19		19 15			19 25	19 40	18 49		19 45			19 55	
Crayford	d			18 22				18 39				18 52				19 09			19 22				19 39		
Bexley	d			18 25				18 42				18 55				19 12			19 25				19 42		
Albany Park	d			18 27				18 44				18 57				19 14			19 27				19 44		
Sidcup 4	d			18 30				18 47				19 00				19 17			19 30				19 47		
New Eltham	d			18 34				18 51				19 04				19 21			19 34				19 51		
Mottingham	d			18 36				18 53				19 06				19 23			19 36				19 53		
Lee	d			18 39				18 56				19 09				19 26			19 39				19 56		
Hither Green 4	d			18 42				18 59				19 12				19 29			19 42				19 59		
Barnehurst 4	d						18 39								19 09							19 39			
Bexleyheath	d						18 42								19 12							19 42			
Welling	d						18 45								19 15							19 45			
Falconwood	d						18 48								19 18							19 48			
Eltham	d						18 51								19 21							19 51			
Kidbrooke	d						18 54								19 24							19 54			
Blackheath 4	d					18 50	18 58							19 20	19 28						19 50	19 58			
Lewisham 4	d			18 48		18 55	19 02					19 18		19 25	19 32				19 48		19 55	20 02			
St Johns	d			18 50								19 20							19 50						
New Cross 4 ⊖	d			18 53								19 23							19 53						
Nunhead 4	d						19 07								19 37							20 07			
Peckham Rye 4	d						19 10								19 40							20 10			
Denmark Hill 4	d						19 14								19 44							20 14			
London Victoria 15 ⊖	a						19 24								19 54							20 24			
Westcombe Park	d	18 27	18 42							18 57	19 12						19 27	19 42						19 57	
Maze Hill	d	18 29	18 44							18 59	19 14						19 29	19 44						19 59	
Greenwich 4	d	18 33	18 47							19 03	19 17						19 33	19 47						20 03	
Deptford	a	18 35	18 49							19 05	19 19						19 35	19 49						20 05	
London Bridge 4 ⊖	a	18 41	18 57	18 58		19 03		19 09		19 11	19 27	19 28		19 33		19 39	19 41	19 57	19 58		20 03		20 09	20 11	
London Cannon Street 4 ⊖	a	18 47		19 04						19 17		19 34					19 47		20 04					20 17	
London Waterloo (East) 4 ⊖	a					19 09		19 15						19 39		19 45					20 09		20 15		
London Charing Cross 4 ⊖	a					19 13		19 19						19 43		19 49					20 13		20 19		
Ebbsfleet International	a				18 16								18 46							19 16					
Stratford International ⊖	a				18 28								18 59							19 28					
St Pancras Int'l 15 ⊖	a				18 36								19 07							19 36					

Table T200-R

Sundays

15 December to 10 May

Gillingham and Dartford - London

		TL	SE	SE	SE	SE	SE	SE	TL	SE	SE	SE	SE	SE	SE	TL		SE	SE	SE	SE	SE	SE	TL	SE
				◇							◇								◇						
Rainham (Kent)	d	19 00		19 16					19 30		19 46					20 00			20 16					20 30	
Gillingham (Kent)	d	19 06		19 21					19 36		19 51					20 06			20 21					20 36	
Chatham	d	19 10		19 25					19 40		19 55					20 10			20 25					20 40	
Rochester	d	19 14		19 29					19 44		19 59					20 14			20 29					20 44	
Maidstone West	d																								
Strood	d	19 17		19 32					19 47		20 02					20 17			20 32					20 47	
Higham	d	19 22							19 52							20 22								20 52	
Gravesend	d	19 29		19 42			19 48		19 59		20 12			20 18		20 29			20 42			20 48		20 59	
Northfleet	d	19 33					19 51		20 03					20 21		20 33						20 51		21 03	
Swanscombe	d	19 35					19 53		20 05					20 23		20 35						20 53		21 05	
Greenhithe for Bluewater	d	19 38					19 57		20 08					20 27		20 38						20 57		21 08	
Stone Crossing	d	19 40					19 59		20 10					20 29		20 40						20 59		21 10	
Dartford	a	19 44					20 03		20 14					20 33		20 44						21 03		21 14	
	d	19 45			19 50	20 02	20 04		20 15			20 20	20 32	20 34		20 45				20 50	21 02	21 04		21 15	
Slade Green	d	19 51			19 55			20 05	20 21			20 25			20 35	20 51				20 55			21 05	21 21	
Erith	d				19 57			20 07				20 27			20 37					20 57			21 07		
Belvedere	d				20 00			20 10				20 30			20 40					21 00			21 10		
Abbey Wood	d	19 58			20 03			20 13	20 28			20 33			20 43	20 58				21 03			21 13	21 28	
Plumstead	d	20 01			20 06			20 16	20 31			20 36			20 46	21 01				21 06			21 16	21 31	
Woolwich Arsenal	d	20 04			20 09			20 19	20 34			20 39			20 49	21 04				21 09			21 19	21 34	
Woolwich Dockyard	d				20 12			20 22				20 42			20 52					21 12			21 22		
Charlton	d	20 10	19 19		20 15			20 25	20 40	19 49		20 45			20 55	21 10		20 19		21 15			21 25	21 40	20 49
Crayford	d		19 52				20 09			20 22				20 39				20 52				21 09			21 22
Bexley	d		19 55				20 12			20 25				20 42				20 55				21 12			21 25
Albany Park	d		19 57				20 14			20 27				20 44				20 57				21 14			21 27
Sidcup	d		20 00				20 17			20 30				20 47				21 00				21 17			21 30
New Eltham	d		20 04				20 21			20 34				20 51				21 04				21 21			21 34
Mottingham	d		20 06				20 23			20 36				20 53				21 06				21 23			21 36
Lee	d		20 09				20 26			20 39				20 56				21 09				21 26			21 39
Hither Green	d		20 12				20 29			20 42				20 59				21 12				21 29			21 42
Barnehurst	d					20 09							20 39								21 09				
Bexleyheath	d					20 12							20 42								21 12				
Welling	d					20 15							20 45								21 15				
Falconwood	d					20 18							20 48								21 18				
Eltham	d					20 21							20 51								21 21				
Kidbrooke	d					20 24							20 54								21 24				
Blackheath	d				20 20	20 28						20 50	20 58							21 20	21 28				
Lewisham	d		20 18		20 25	20 32				20 48		20 55	21 02					21 18		21 25	21 32				21 48
St Johns	d		20 20							20 50								21 20							21 50
New Cross	d		20 23							20 53								21 23							21 53
Nunhead	d					20 37							21 07								21 37				
Peckham Rye	d					20 40							21 10								21 40				
Denmark Hill	d					20 44							21 14								21 44				
London Victoria	a					20 54							21 24								21 54				
Westcombe Park	d	20 12						20 27	20 42						20 57	21 12							21 27	21 42	
Maze Hill	d	20 14						20 29	20 44						20 59	21 14							21 29	21 44	
Greenwich	d	20 17						20 33	20 47						21 03	21 17							21 33	21 47	
Deptford	a	20 19						20 35	20 49						21 05	21 19							21 35	21 49	
London Bridge	a	20 27	20 28		20 33		20 39	20 41	20 57	20 58		21 03		21 09	21 11	21 27		21 28		21 33		21 39	21 41	21 57	21 58
London Cannon Street	a		20 34					20 47		21 04					21 17			21 34					21 47		22 04
London Waterloo (East)	a				20 39		20 45					21 09		21 15						21 39		21 45			
London Charing Cross	a				20 43		20 49					21 13		21 19						21 43		21 49			
Ebbsfleet International	a			19 46							20 16								20 46						
Stratford International	a			19 58							20 28								20 58						
St Pancras Int'l	a			20 06							20 36								21 06						

Table T200-R

Sundays

15 December to 10 May

Gillingham and Dartford - London

		SE	SE	SE	SE	SE	TL	SE		SE	SE	SE	SE	SE	TL	SE	SE	SE	SE	SE	SE	TL	SE	SE	
		◇								◇							◇							◇	
Rainham (Kent)	d	20 46					21 00			21 16					21 30		21 46					22 00		22 16	
Gillingham (Kent)	d	20 51					21 06			21 21					21 36		21 51					22 06		22 21	
Chatham	d	20 55					21 10			21 25					21 40		21 55					22 10		22 25	
Rochester	d	20 59					21 14			21 29					21 44		21 59					22 14		22 29	
Maidstone West	d																								
Strood	d	21 02					21 17			21 32					21 47		22 02					22 17		22 32	
Higham	d						21 22								21 52							22 22			
Gravesend	d	21 12			21 18		21 29			21 42			21 48		21 59		22 12			22 18		22 29		22 42	
Northfleet	d				21 21		21 33						21 51		22 03					22 21		22 33			
Swanscombe	d				21 23		21 35						21 53		22 05					22 23		22 35			
Greenhithe for Bluewater	d				21 27		21 38						21 57		22 08					22 27		22 38			
Stone Crossing	d				21 29		21 40						21 59		22 10					22 29		22 40			
Dartford	a				21 33		21 44						22 03		22 14					22 33		22 44			
	d		21 20	21 32	21 34		21 45				21 50	22 02	22 04		22 15			22 20	22 32	22 34		22 45			
Slade Green	d		21 25			21 35	21 51				21 55			22 05	22 21			22 25			22 35	22 51			
Erith	d		21 27			21 37					21 57			22 07				22 27			22 37				
Belvedere	d		21 30			21 40					22 00			22 10				22 30			22 40				
Abbey Wood	d		21 33			21 43	21 58				22 03			22 13	22 28			22 33			22 43	22 58			
Plumstead	d		21 36			21 46	22 01				22 06			22 16	22 31			22 36			22 46	23 01			
Woolwich Arsenal	d		21 39			21 49	22 04				22 09			22 19	22 34			22 39			22 49	23 04			
Woolwich Dockyard	d		21 42			21 52					22 12			22 22				22 42			22 52				
Charlton	d		21 45			21 55	22 10	21 19			22 15			22 25	22 40	21 49		22 45			22 55	23 10	22 19		
Crayford	d				21 39			21 52					22 09			22 22				22 39			22 52		
Bexley	d				21 42			21 55					22 12			22 25				22 42			22 55		
Albany Park	d				21 44			21 57					22 14			22 27				22 44			22 57		
Sidcup	d				21 47			22 00					22 17			22 30				22 47			23 00		
New Eltham	d				21 51			22 04					22 21			22 34				22 51			23 04		
Mottingham	d				21 53			22 06					22 23			22 36				22 53			23 06		
Lee	d				21 56			22 09					22 26			22 39				22 56			23 09		
Hither Green	d				21 59			22 12					22 29			22 42				22 59			23 12		
Barnehurst	d			21 39								22 09							22 39						
Bexleyheath	d			21 42								22 12							22 42						
Welling	d			21 45								22 15							22 45						
Falconwood	d			21 48								22 18							22 48						
Eltham	d			21 51								22 21							22 51						
Kidbrooke	d			21 54								22 24							22 54						
Blackheath	d		21 50	21 58							22 20	22 28						22 50	22 58						
Lewisham	d		21 55	22 02				22 18			22 25	22 32				22 48		22 55	23 02				23 18		
St Johns	d							22 20								22 50							23 20		
New Cross	d							22 23								22 53							23 23		
Nunhead	d			22 07								22 37							23 07						
Peckham Rye	d			22 10								22 40							23 10						
Denmark Hill	d			22 14								22 44							23 14						
London Victoria	a			22 24								22 54							23 24						
Westcombe Park	d					21 57	22 12							22 27	22 42						22 57	23 12			
Maze Hill	d					21 59	22 14							22 29	22 44						22 59	23 14			
Greenwich	d					22 03	22 17							22 33	22 47						23 03	23 17			
Deptford	a					22 05	22 19							22 35	22 49						23 05	23 19			
London Bridge	a		22 03		22 09	22 11	22 27	22 28			22 33		22 39	22 41	22 57	22 58		23 03		23 09	23 11	23 27	23 28		
London Cannon Street	a					22 17		22 34						22 47		23 04					23 17		23 34		
London Waterloo (East)	a		22 09		22 15						22 39		22 45					23 09		23 15					
London Charing Cross	a		22 13		22 19						22 43		22 49					23 13		23 19					
Ebbsfleet International	a	21 16								21 46							22 16							22 46	
Stratford International	a	21 32								21 59							22 28							22 58	
St Pancras Int'l	a	21 40								22 07							22 36							23 06	

Table T200-R

Sundays

15 December to 10 May

Gillingham and Dartford - London

		SE	SE	TL	SE	SE	SE	SE	TL	TL
Rainham (Kent)	d			22 30					23 00	23 30
Gillingham (Kent)	d			22 36					23 06	23 36
Chatham	d			22 40					23 10	23 40
Rochester	d			22 44					23 14	23 44
Maidstone West	d									
Strood	d			22 47					23 17	23 47
Higham	d			22 52					23 22	23 52
Gravesend	d		22 48	22 59				23 18	23 29	23 59
Northfleet	d		22 51	23 03				23 21	23 33	00 03
Swanscombe	d		22 53	23 05				23 23	23 35	00 05
Greenhithe for Bluewater	d		22 57	23 08				23 27	23 38	00 08
Stone Crossing	d		22 59	23 10				23 29	23 40	00 10
Dartford	a		23 03	23 15				23 33	23 45	00 15
	d	22 50	23 04				23 20	23 34		
Slade Green	d	22 55			23 05		23 25			
Erith	d	22 57			23 07		23 27			
Belvedere	d	23 00			23 10		23 30			
Abbey Wood	d	23 03			23 13		23 33			
Plumstead	d	23 06			23 16		23 36			
Woolwich Arsenal	d	23 09			23 19		23 39			
Woolwich Dockyard	d	23 12			23 22		23 42			
Charlton	d	23 15			23 25	22 49	23 45			
Crayford	d		23 09			23 22		23 39		
Bexley	d		23 12			23 25		23 42		
Albany Park	d		23 14			23 27		23 44		
Sidcup	d		23 17			23 30		23 47		
New Eltham	d		23 21			23 34		23 51		
Mottingham	d		23 23			23 36		23 53		
Lee	d		23 26			23 39		23 56		
Hither Green	d		23 29			23 42		23 59		
Barnehurst	d									
Bexleyheath	d									
Welling	d									
Falconwood	d									
Eltham	d									
Kidbrooke	d									
Blackheath	d	23 20					23 50			
Lewisham	d	23 25				23 48	23 55			
St Johns	d					23 50				
New Cross	d					23 53				
Nunhead	d									
Peckham Rye	d									
Denmark Hill	d									
London Victoria	a									
Westcombe Park	d				23 27					
Maze Hill	d				23 29					
Greenwich	d				23 33					
Deptford	a				23 35					
London Bridge	a	23 33	23 39		23 41	23 58	00 04	00 09		
London Cannon Street	a				23 47	00 04				
London Waterloo (East)	a	23 39	23 45				00 09	00 15		
London Charing Cross	a	23 43	23 49				00 13	00 19		
Ebbsfleet International	a									
Stratford International	a									
St Pancras Int'l	a									

Table T201-F

Mondays to Fridays

16 December to 15 May

London Thameslink - Greenwich - Woolwich - Medway

		TL MX	TL MO	SE TWO	SE ThFO	SE ThFO	SE MO	SE ThFO	SE TWO	TL MX		SE ThFO	SE ThFO	SE TWO	SE TWO	TL	SE MTh FO	SE TWO	SE	TL		SE WX	SE WO	SE	TL
Luton	d																								
Luton Airport Parkway	d																								
St Albans	d																								
West Hampstead Thameslink	d																								05 20
St Pancras International	d																								05 30
Farringdon	d																								05 35
City Thameslink	d																								05 37
London Blackfriars	a																								05 39
London Charing Cross	d					00 02	00 12	00 12					00 42				04 50					05 20			
Waterloo East	a					00 04	00 14	00 14					00 44				04 52					05 22			
London Cannon Street	d			00 02	00 02				00 32			00 32		00 52	01 02				05 05					05 35	
London Bridge	d			00 06	00 10	00 11	00 21	00 21	00 36			00 40	00 51	00 57	01 07		04 59	04 59	05 09			05 29	05 29	05 39	05 46
London Victoria	d																								
Deptford	d			00 12	00 24				00 42			00 54							05 15					05 45	05 53
Greenwich	d			00 14	00 29				00 44			00 59							05 17					05 47	05 55
Maze Hill	d			00 17	00 36				00 47			01 06							05 20					05 50	05 58
Westcombe Park	d			00 19	00 41				00 49			01 11							05 22					05 52	06 00
Charlton	d			00 22	00a53		00 38	00 40	00 52			01s18	01 08		01 23				05 25					05 55	06 03
Woolwich Dockyard	d			00 25			00 41	00 43	00 55			01s23	01 11		01 26				05 28					05 58	
Woolwich Arsenal	d			00 28			00 44	00 46	00 58			01s29	01 14		01 29				05 31					06 01	06 08
Plumstead	d			00 30			00 46	00 48	01 00			01s33	01 16		01 31				05 33					06 03	06 11
Abbey Wood	d			00 33			00 50	00 52	01 03			01s39	01 20		01 34				05 36					06 06	06 14
Belvedere	d			00 36			00 53	00 55	01 06			01s43	01 23		01 37				05 39					06 09	
Erith	d			00 39			00 55	00 57	01 09			01s48	01 25		01 40				05 42					06 12	
Slade Green	d			00 44			01 01	01 02	01 12			01s54	01 30		01 44				05 47					06a15	06 20
Dartford	d	00 28	00 46	00a49		00 48	01a06	01a07	01a20	01 24		02a05	01a37	01 35	01a52	04 58	05 39	05 39	05a52	05 58		06 09	06 09		06 26
Stone Crossing	d	00 32	00s50			00 52				01s28						05 02	05 43	05 43		06 02		06 13	06 13		06 30
Greenhithe	d	00 34	00s52			00 54				01s30				01 41		05 04	05 45	05 45		06 04		06 15	06 15		06 32
Swanscombe	d	00 37	00s55			00s57				01s33						05 07	05 48	05 48		06 07		06 18	06 18		06 35
Northfleet	d	00 39	00s57			00s59				01s35						05 09	05 50	05 50		06 09		06 20	06 20		06 37
Gravesend	d	00 43	01 01			01a07				01 39				01a50		05 13	05a56	05a56		06 13		06a25	06a25		06 41
Higham	d	00 49	01s07							01s45						05 19				06 19					06 47
Strood	d	00 56	01s12							01s50						05 25				06 25					06 53
Rochester	d	00 59	01s15							01s53						05 28				06 28					06 56
Chatham	d	01 03	01s19							01s57						05 31				06 31					06 59
Gillingham	d	01a07	01a24							02a02						05 36				06 36					07 04
Rainham (Kent)	a															05 41				06 41					07 09

		SE	SE	SE ◇	TL	SE		SE	SE ◇	SE	SE	SE ◇	TL	SE	SE	SE		SE	TL	SE	SE	SE	SE	SE ◇	SE
Luton	d																		06 25						
Luton Airport Parkway	d																		06 28						
St Albans	d																		06 38						
West Hampstead Thameslink	d				05 52								06 21												
St Pancras International	d			06 25	06 02				06 55			07 22	06 32						07 02					08 04	
Farringdon	d				06 07								06 37						07 07						
City Thameslink	d				06 09								06 39						07 09						
London Blackfriars	a				06 11								06 41						07 11						
London Charing Cross	d	05 42				06 12				06 23				06 41		06 53				07 12		07 21			
Waterloo East	a	05 44				06 14				06 25				06 43		06 55				07 14		07 23			
London Cannon Street	d		05 55					06 25			06 35				06 55			07 05			07 25		07 36		
London Bridge	d	05 51	05 59		06 18	06 21		06 29		06 32	06 39		06 48	06 50	06 59	07 02		07 09	07 18	07 21	07 29	07 30	07 40		
London Victoria	d																								07 45
Deptford	d		06 05		06 25			06 35			06 45		06 55		07 05			07 15	07 25		07 35		07 46		
Greenwich	d		06 07		06 27			06 37			06 47		06 57		07 07			07 17	07 27		07 37		07 48		
Maze Hill	d		06 10		06 30			06 40			06 50		07 00		07 10			07 20	07 30		07 40		07 51		
Westcombe Park	d		06 12		06 32			06 42			06 52		07 02		07 12			07 22	07 32		07 42		07 53		
Charlton	d	06 08	06 15		06 35	06 38		06 45			06 55		07 05	07 08	07 15			07 25	07 35	07 38	07 45		07 56		
Woolwich Dockyard	d	06 11	06 18			06 41		06 48			06 58			07 11	07 18			07 28		07 41			07 59		
Woolwich Arsenal	d	06 14	06 21		06 40	06 44		06 51			07 01		07 10	07 14	07 21			07 31	07 40	07 44	07 50		08 02		
Plumstead	d	06 16	06 23		06 43	06 46		06 53			07 03		07 13	07 16	07 23			07 33	07 43	07 46			08 04		
Abbey Wood	d	06 19	06 26		06 46	06 49		06 56			07 06		07 16	07 20	07 26			07 36	07 46	07 50	07 55		08 07		
Belvedere	d	06 22	06 29			06 52		06 59			07 09			07 23	07 29			07 39		07 53			08 10		
Erith	d	06 25	06 32			06 55		07 02			07 12			07 25	07 32			07 42		07 55			08 13		
Slade Green	d	06 28	06a35		06 52	06 58		07a05			07a16		07 22	07 29	07a36			07a46	07 52	07 59	08a02		08a16		
Dartford	d	06a34			06 58	07a05				07 09			07 30	07a38		07 39			08 01	08a06		08 09			08 24
Stone Crossing	d				07 02					07 13			07 34			07 43			08 05			08 13			
Greenhithe	d				07 04					07 15			07 36			07 45			08 07			08 15			08 30
Swanscombe	d				07 07					07 18			07 39			07 48			08 10			08 18			
Northfleet	d				07 09					07 20			07 41			07 50			08 12			08 20			
Gravesend	d			06 48	07 15				07 20	07a27		07 44	07 47			07a56			08 19			08a27		08 29	08a41
Higham	d				07 21								07 53						08 25						
Strood	d			06a58	07 28				07 31			07 56	07 59						08 31					08 40	
Rochester	d				07 31				07 34			07 59	08 02						08 34					08 44	
Chatham	d				07 34				07 38			08 02	08 06						08 37					08 47	
Gillingham	d				07 39				07 43			08 07	08 16						08 44					08 53	
Rainham (Kent)	a				07 44				07 47			08 11	08 21						08 49					08 57	

Table T201-F

Mondays to Fridays

16 December to 15 May

London Thameslink - Greenwich - Woolwich - Medway

		TL		SE	SE	SE ◇	SE	SE	SE	TL	SE	SE		SE ◇	SE	SE	SE	SE	TL	SE	SE	SE		SE ◇	SE
Luton	d	06 55								07 16									07 46						
Luton Airport Parkway	d	06 58								07 19									07 49						
St Albans	d	07 10								07 30									08 00						
West Hampstead Thameslink	d									07 51									08 21						
St Pancras International	d	07 32				08 25				08 02				08 57					08 32					09 25	
Farringdon	d	07 37								08 07									08 37						
City Thameslink	d	07 39								08 09									08 39						
London Blackfriars	a	07 41								08 11									08 41						
London Charing Cross	d			07 39			07 52				08 12				08 22			08 38							09 00
Waterloo East	a			07 41			07 54				08 14				08 24			08 40							09 02
London Cannon Street	d				07 57			08 05				08 24				08 34					08 54	09 05			
London Bridge	d	07 48		07 48	08 01		08 02	08 09		08 18	08 21	08 28			08 31	08 38		08 47	08 48		08 59	09 09			09 09
London Victoria	d								08 07								08 38								
Deptford	d	07 55			08 07			08 15		08 25		08 35				08 45			08 55		09 05	09 15			
Greenwich	d	07 57			08 09			08 17		08 27		08 37				08 47			08 57		09 07	09 17			
Maze Hill	d	08 00			08 12			08 20		08 30		08 40				08 50			09 00		09 10	09 20			
Westcombe Park	d	08 02			08 14			08 22		08 32		08 42				08 52			09 02	←	09 12	09 22			
Charlton	d	08 05		08 08	08 17			08 25		08 35	08 43	08 46				08 55		09 08	09 05	09 08	09 16	09 25			
Woolwich Dockyard	d			08 11	08 20			08 28			08 46	08 49				08 58		→		09 11	09 19	09 28			
Woolwich Arsenal	d	08 10		08 14	08 23			08 31		08 40	08 49	08 52				09 01			09 10	09 14	09 22	09 31			
Plumstead	d	08 13		08 16	08 25			08 33		08 43	08 51	08 54				09 03			09 13	09 16	09 24	09 33			
Abbey Wood	d	08 16		08 20	08 28			08 36		08 46	08 54	08 58				09 06			09 16	09 19	09 27	09 36			
Belvedere	d			08 23	08 31			08 39			08 57	09 01				09 09				09 22	09 30	09 39			
Erith	d			08 25	08 34			08 42			09 00	09 03				09 12				09 25	09 33	09 42			
Slade Green	d	08 22		08 29	08 37			08a45		08 52	09 04	09a07				09a15			09 22	09 30	09a36	09a46			
Dartford	d	08 28		08a37	08a45		08 39		08 54	08 58	09a12				09 08		09 24		09 28	09a40					09 41
Stone Crossing	d	08 32					08 43			09 02					09 12				09 32						09 45
Greenhithe	d	08 34					08 45		09 00	09 04					09 15		09 30		09 34						09 47
Swanscombe	d	08 37					08 48			09 07					09 18				09 37						09 50
Northfleet	d	08 39					08 50			09 09					09 20				09 39						09 52
Gravesend	d	08 43				08 48	08a57		09a09	09 13				09 19	09a26		09a41		09 43					09 48	09a56
Higham	d	08 49								09 19									09 49						
Strood	d	08 55				08 59				09 25				09 30					09 55					09 59	
Rochester	d	08 58				09 02				09 28				09 33					09 58					10 02	
Chatham	d	09 01				09 06				09 31				09 37					10 01					10 06	
Gillingham	d	09 06				09 10				09 36				09 41					10 06					10 10	
Rainham (Kent)	a	09 11				09 15				09 41				09 46					10 11					10 15	

		SE	TL	SE	SE	SE ◇	SE	SE		SE	TL	SE	SE	SE	SE ◇	SE	SE	TL		SE	SE	SE	SE ◇	SE	SE
Luton	d		08 16								08 46							09 17							
Luton Airport Parkway	d		08 19								08 49							09 20							
St Albans	d		08 30								09 00							09 30							
West Hampstead Thameslink	d		08 51								09 21							09 51							
St Pancras International	d		09 02			09 55					09 32				10 27			10 02					10 52		
Farringdon	d		09 07								09 37							10 07							
City Thameslink	d		09 09								09 39							10 09							
London Blackfriars	a		09 11								09 41							10 11							
London Charing Cross	d			09 12			09 28					09 40				10 02				10 12				10 32	
Waterloo East	a			09 14			09 30					09 42				10 04				10 14				10 34	
London Cannon Street	d				09 24					09 35			09 54	10 05							10 24	10 35			
London Bridge	d		09 18	09 21	09 28		09 37			09 39	09 48	09 51	09 58	10 09		10 11		10 18		10 21	10 28	10 39		10 41	
London Victoria	d	09 04						09 34									10 04								10 34
Deptford	d		09 25		09 35					09 45	09 55		10 05	10 15				10 25			10 35	10 45			
Greenwich	d		09 27		09 37					09 47	09 57		10 07	10 17				10 27			10 37	10 47			
Maze Hill	d		09 30		09 40					09 50	10 00		10 10	10 20				10 30			10 40	10 50			
Westcombe Park	d		09 32		09 42					09 52	10 02		10 12	10 22				10 32			10 42	10 52			
Charlton	d		09 35	09 40	09 45					09 55	10 05	10 08	10 15	10 25				10 35		10 38	10 45	10 55			
Woolwich Dockyard	d			09 43	09 48					09 58		10 11	10 18	10 28						10 41	10 48	10 58			
Woolwich Arsenal	d		09 40	09 46	09 51					10 01	10 10	10 14	10 21	10 31				10 40		10 44	10 51	11 01			
Plumstead	d		09 43	09 48	09 53					10 03	10 13	10 16	10 23	10 33				10 43		10 46	10 53	11 03			
Abbey Wood	d		09 46	09 51	09 56					10 06	10 16	10 20	10 26	10 36				10 46		10 50	10 56	11 06			
Belvedere	d			09 54	09 59					10 09		10 23	10 29	10 39						10 53	10 59	11 09			
Erith	d			09 57	10 02					10 12		10 25	10 32	10 42						10 55	11 02	11 12			
Slade Green	d		09 52	10 03	10a06					10a15	10 22	10 31	10a36	10a45				10 52		11 01	11a06	11a15			
Dartford	d	09 54	09 58	10a08			10 11	10 24			10 28	10a38				10 41	10 54	10 58		11a08				11 11	11 24
Stone Crossing	d		10 02				10 15				10 32					10 45		11 02						11 15	
Greenhithe	d	10 00	10 04				10 17	10 30			10 34					10 47	11 00	11 04						11 17	11 30
Swanscombe	d		10 07				10 20				10 37					10 50		11 07						11 20	
Northfleet	d		10 09				10 22				10 39					10 52		11 09						11 22	
Gravesend	d	10a09	10 13			10 18	10a26	10a38			10 43				10 49	10a56	11a09	11 13					11 18	11a26	11a39
Higham	d		10 19								10 49							11 19							
Strood	d		10 25			10 29					10 55				10 59			11 25					11 29		
Rochester	d		10 28			10 32					10 58				11 02			11 28					11 32		
Chatham	d		10 31			10 36					11 01				11 06			11 31					11 36		
Gillingham	d		10 36			10 40					11 06				11 10			11 36					11 40		
Rainham (Kent)	a		10 41			10 45					11 11				11 15			11 41					11 45		

Table T201-F

Mondays to Fridays

16 December to 15 May

London Thameslink - Greenwich - Woolwich - Medway

		TL	SE	SE		SE	SE ◇	SE	SE	TL	SE	SE	SE	SE ◇		SE	SE	TL	SE	SE	SE	SE ◇	SE	SE	
Luton	d	09 46								10 16								10 48							
Luton Airport Parkway	d	09 51								10 21								10 51							
St Albans	d	10 01								10 31								11 01							
West Hampstead Thameslink	d	10 21								10 51								11 21							
St Pancras International	d	10 32					11 25			11 02				11 55				11 32				12 27			
Farringdon	d	10 37								11 07								11 37							
City Thameslink	d	10 39								11 09								11 39							
London Blackfriars	a	10 41								11 11								11 41							
London Charing Cross	d		10 42					11 02			11 12					11 32			11 42				12 02		
Waterloo East	a		10 44					11 04			11 14					11 34			11 44				12 04		
London Cannon Street	d			10 54		11 05						11 24	11 35							11 54	12 05				
London Bridge	d	10 48	10 51	10 58		11 09		11 11		11 18	11 21	11 28	11 39			11 41		11 48	11 51	11 58	12 09		12 11		
London Victoria	d								11 04								11 34							12 04	
Deptford	d	10 55		11 05		11 15				11 25		11 35	11 45					11 55		12 05	12 15				
Greenwich	d	10 57		11 07		11 17				11 27		11 37	11 47					11 57		12 07	12 17				
Maze Hill	d	11 00		11 10		11 20				11 30		11 40	11 50					12 00		12 10	12 20				
Westcombe Park	d	11 02		11 12		11 22				11 32		11 42	11 52					12 02		12 12	12 22				
Charlton	d	11 05	11 08	11 15		11 25				11 35	11 38	11 45	11 55					12 05	12 08	12 15	12 25				
Woolwich Dockyard	d		11 11	11 18		11 28					11 41	11 48	11 58						12 11	12 18	12 28				
Woolwich Arsenal	d	11 10	11 14	11 21		11 31				11 40	11 44	11 51	12 01					12 10	12 14	12 21	12 31				
Plumstead	d	11 13	11 16	11 23		11 33				11 43	11 46	11 53	12 03					12 13	12 16	12 23	12 33				
Abbey Wood	d	11 16	11 20	11 26		11 36				11 46	11 50	11 56	12 06					12 16	12 20	12 26	12 36				
Belvedere	d		11 23	11 29		11 39					11 53	11 59	12 09						12 23	12 29	12 39				
Erith	d		11 25	11 32		11 42					11 55	12 02	12 12						12 25	12 32	12 42				
Slade Green	d	11 22	11 31	11a36		11a45				11 52	12 01	12a06	12a15					12 22	12 31	12a36	12a45				
Dartford	d	11 28	11a38					11 41	11 54	11 58	12a08					12 11	12 24	12 28	12a38				12 41	12 54	
Stone Crossing	d	11 32						11 45		12 02						12 15		12 32					12 45		
Greenhithe	d	11 34						11 47	12 00	12 04						12 17	12 30	12 34					12 47	13 00	
Swanscombe	d	11 37						11 50		12 07						12 20		12 37					12 50		
Northfleet	d	11 39						11 52		12 09						12 22		12 39					12 52		
Gravesend	d	11 43					11 48	11a56	12a09	12 13				12 18		12a26	12a39	12 43				12 49	12a56	13a09	
Higham	d	11 49								12 19								12 49							
Strood	d	11 55					11 59			12 25				12 29				12 55				12 59			
Rochester	d	11 58					12 02			12 28				12 32				12 58				13 02			
Chatham	d	12 01					12 06			12 31				12 36				13 01				13 06			
Gillingham	d	12 06					12 10			12 36				12 40				13 06				13 10			
Rainham (Kent)	a	12 11					12 15			12 41				12 45				13 11				13 15			

		TL	SE	SE	SE	SE ◇	SE	SE	TL	SE		SE	SE	SE ◇	SE	SE	TL	SE	SE	SE		SE ◇	SE	SE	TL
Luton	d	11 18							11 48								12 18								12 48
Luton Airport Parkway	d	11 21							11 51								12 21								12 51
St Albans	d	11 31							12 01								12 31								13 01
West Hampstead Thameslink	d	11 51							12 21								12 51								13 21
St Pancras International	d	12 02				12 52			12 32					13 25			13 02					13 55			13 32
Farringdon	d	12 07							12 37								13 07								13 37
City Thameslink	d	12 09							12 39								13 09								13 39
London Blackfriars	a	12 11							12 41								13 11								13 41
London Charing Cross	d		12 12				12 32			12 42					13 02			13 12					13 32		
Waterloo East	a		12 14				12 34			12 44					13 04			13 14					13 34		
London Cannon Street	d			12 24	12 35							12 54	13 05						13 24	13 35					
London Bridge	d	12 18	12 21	12 28	12 39		12 41		12 48	12 51		12 58	13 09		13 11		13 18	13 21	13 28	13 39			13 41		13 48
London Victoria	d							12 34								13 04								13 34	
Deptford	d	12 25		12 35	12 45				12 55			13 05	13 15				13 25		13 35	13 45					13 55
Greenwich	d	12 27		12 37	12 47				12 57			13 07	13 17				13 27		13 37	13 47					13 57
Maze Hill	d	12 30		12 40	12 50				13 00			13 10	13 20				13 30		13 40	13 50					14 00
Westcombe Park	d	12 32		12 42	12 52				13 02			13 12	13 22				13 32		13 42	13 52					14 02
Charlton	d	12 35	12 38	12 45	12 55				13 05	13 08		13 15	13 25				13 35	13 38	13 45	13 55					14 05
Woolwich Dockyard	d		12 41	12 48	12 58					13 11		13 18	13 28					13 41	13 48	13 58					
Woolwich Arsenal	d	12 40	12 44	12 51	13 01				13 10	13 14		13 21	13 31				13 40	13 44	13 51	14 01					14 10
Plumstead	d	12 43	12 46	12 53	13 03				13 13	13 16		13 23	13 33				13 43	13 46	13 53	14 03					14 13
Abbey Wood	d	12 46	12 50	12 56	13 06				13 16	13 20		13 26	13 36				13 46	13 50	13 56	14 06					14 16
Belvedere	d		12 53	12 59	13 09					13 23		13 29	13 39					13 53	13 59	14 09					
Erith	d		12 55	13 02	13 12					13 25		13 32	13 42					13 55	14 02	14 12					
Slade Green	d	12 52	13 01	13a06	13a15				13 22	13 31		13a36	13a45				13 52	14 01	14a06	14a15					14 22
Dartford	d	12 58	13a08				13 11	13 24	13 28	13a38					13 41	13 54	13 58	14a08					14 11	14 24	14 28
Stone Crossing	d	13 02					13 15		13 32						13 45		14 02						14 15		14 32
Greenhithe	d	13 04					13 17	13 30	13 34						13 47	14 00	14 04						14 17	14 30	14 34
Swanscombe	d	13 07					13 20		13 37						13 50		14 07						14 20		14 37
Northfleet	d	13 09					13 22		13 39						13 52		14 09						14 22		14 39
Gravesend	d	13 13				13 18	13a26	13a39	13 43					13 48	13a56	14a09	14 13					14 18	14a26	14a39	14 43
Higham	d	13 19							13 49								14 19								14 49
Strood	d	13 25				13 29			13 55					13 59			14 25					14 29			14 55
Rochester	d	13 28				13 32			13 58					14 02			14 28					14 32			14 58
Chatham	d	13 31				13 36			14 01					14 06			14 31					14 36			15 01
Gillingham	d	13 36				13 40			14 06					14 10			14 36					14 40			15 06
Rainham (Kent)	a	13 41				13 45			14 11					14 15			14 41					14 45			15 11

Table T201-F

Mondays to Fridays

16 December to 15 May

London Thameslink - Greenwich - Woolwich - Medway

		SE	SE	SE	SE ◇	SE		SE	TL	SE	SE	SE	SE ◇	SE	SE	TL		SE	SE	SE	SE ◇	SE	SE	TL	SE
Luton	d								13 18							13 48								14 18	
Luton Airport Parkway	d								13 21							13 51								14 21	
St Albans	d								13 31							14 01								14 31	
West Hampstead Thameslink	d								13 51							14 21								14 51	
St Pancras International	d				14 25				14 02				14 55			14 32					15 25			15 02	
Farringdon	d								14 07							14 37								15 07	
City Thameslink	d								14 09							14 39								15 09	
London Blackfriars	a								14 11							14 41								15 11	
London Charing Cross	d	13 42				14 02				14 12				14 32				14 42				15 02			15 12
Waterloo East	a	13 44				14 04				14 14				14 34				14 44				15 04			15 14
London Cannon Street	d		13 54	14 05							14 24	14 35							14 54	15 05					
London Bridge	d	13 51	13 58	14 09		14 11			14 18	14 21	14 28	14 39		14 41		14 48		14 51	14 58	15 09		15 11		15 18	15 21
London Victoria	d							14 04							14 34								15 04		
Deptford	d		14 05	14 15					14 25		14 35	14 45				14 55			15 05	15 15				15 25	
Greenwich	d		14 07	14 17					14 27		14 37	14 47				14 57			15 07	15 17				15 27	
Maze Hill	d		14 10	14 20					14 30		14 40	14 50				15 00			15 10	15 20				15 30	
Westcombe Park	d		14 12	14 22					14 32		14 42	14 52				15 02			15 12	15 22				15 32	
Charlton	d	14 08	14 15	14 25					14 35	14 38	14 45	14 55				15 05		15 08	15 15	15 25				15 35	15 38
Woolwich Dockyard	d	14 11	14 18	14 28						14 41	14 48	14 58						15 11	15 18	15 28					15 41
Woolwich Arsenal	d	14 14	14 21	14 31					14 40	14 44	14 51	15 01				15 10		15 14	15 21	15 31				15 40	15 44
Plumstead	d	14 16	14 23	14 33					14 43	14 46	14 53	15 03				15 13		15 16	15 23	15 33				15 43	15 46
Abbey Wood	d	14 20	14 26	14 36					14 46	14 50	14 56	15 06				15 16		15 20	15 26	15 36				15 46	15 50
Belvedere	d	14 23	14 29	14 39						14 53	14 59	15 09						15 23	15 29	15 39					15 53
Erith	d	14 25	14 32	14 42						14 55	15 02	15 12						15 25	15 32	15 42					15 55
Slade Green	d	14 31	14a36	14a45					14 52	15 01	15a06	15a15				15 22		15 31	15a36	15a45				15 52	16 01
Dartford	d	14a38				14 41		14 54	14 58	15a08				15 11	15 24	15 28		15a38				15 41	15 54	15 58	16a08
Stone Crossing	d					14 45			15 02					15 15		15 32						15 45		16 02	
Greenhithe	d					14 47		15 00	15 04					15 17	15 30	15 34						15 47	16 00	16 04	
Swanscombe	d					14 50			15 07					15 20		15 37						15 50		16 07	
Northfleet	d					14 52			15 09					15 22		15 39						15 52		16 09	
Gravesend	d				14 48	14a56		15a09	15 13				15 18	15a26	15a39	15 43					15 48	15a56	16a09	16 13	
Higham	d								15 19							15 49								16 19	
Strood	d				14 59				15 25				15 29			15 55					15 59			16 25	
Rochester	d				15 02				15 28				15 32			15 58					16 02			16 28	
Chatham	d				15 05				15 31				15 36			16 01					16 05			16 31	
Gillingham	d				15 10				15 36				15 40			16 06					16 10			16 36	
Rainham (Kent)	a				15 14				15 41				15 45			16 11					16 14			16 41	

		SE		SE	SE ◇	SE	SE	TL	SE	SE	SE	SE ◇		SE	SE	TL	SE	SE	SE	SE ◇	SE	SE ◇		TL	SE
Luton	d							14 48								15 18								15 48	
Luton Airport Parkway	d							14 51								15 21								15 51	
St Albans	d							15 01								15 31								16 01	
West Hampstead Thameslink	d							15 21								15 51								16 21	
St Pancras International	d				15 55			15 32				16 25				16 02				16 55		17 12		16 32	
Farringdon	d							15 37								16 07								16 37	
City Thameslink	d							15 39								16 09								16 39	
London Blackfriars	a							15 41								16 11								16 41	
London Charing Cross	d					15 32			15 42					16 02			16 12				16 33				16 45
Waterloo East	a					15 34			15 44					16 04			16 14				16 35				16 47
London Cannon Street	d	15 24		15 35						15 54	16 05							16 27	16 37						
London Bridge	d	15 28		15 39		15 41		15 48	15 51	15 58	16 10			16 11		16 18	16 21	16 32	16 42		16 42			16 48	16 54
London Victoria	d						15 34								16 04										
Deptford	d	15 35		15 45				15 55		16 05	16 16					16 25		16 38	16 48					16 55	
Greenwich	d	15 37		15 47				15 57		16 07	16 18					16 27		16 40	16 50					16 57	
Maze Hill	d	15 40		15 50				16 00		16 10	16 21					16 30		16 43	16 53					17 00	
Westcombe Park	d	15 42		15 52				16 02		16 12	16 23					16 32		16 45	16 55					17 02	
Charlton	d	15 45		15 55				16 05	16 08	16 15	16 26					16 35	16 38	16 48	16 58					17 05	17 13
Woolwich Dockyard	d	15 48		15 58					16 11	16 18	16 29						16 41	16 51	17 01						17 16
Woolwich Arsenal	d	15 51		16 01				16 10	16 14	16 21	16 32					16 40	16 44	16 54	17 04					17 10	17 19
Plumstead	d	15 53		16 03				16 13	16 16	16 23	16 34					16 43	16 46	16 56	17 06					17 13	17 21
Abbey Wood	d	15 56		16 06				16 16	16 20	16 26	16 37					16 46	16 50	16 59	17 09					17 16	17 24
Belvedere	d	15 59		16 09					16 23	16 29	16 40						16 53	17 02	17 12						17 27
Erith	d	16 02		16 12					16 25	16 32	16 43						16 55	17 05	17 15						17 30
Slade Green	d	16a06		16a15				16 22	16 32	16a36	16a46					16 52	17 01	17a09	17a18					17 22	17a33
Dartford	d					16 11	16 24	16 28	16a38					16 41	16 54	16 58	17a10				17 11			17 32	
Stone Crossing	d					16 15		16 32						16 45		17 02					17 15			17 36	
Greenhithe	d					16 17	16 30	16 34						16 47	17 00	17 04					17 17			17 38	
Swanscombe	d					16 20		16 37						16 50		17 07					17 20			17 41	
Northfleet	d					16 22		16 39						16 52		17 09					17 22			17 44	
Gravesend	d				16 18	16a26	16a39	16 43				16 48		16a58	17a09	17 13				17 18	17a28	17 35		17 50	
Higham	d							16 49								17 19								17 56	
Strood	d				16 29			16 55				16 59				17 25				17 28		17a45		18 01	
Rochester	d				16 32			16 58				17 02				17 28				17 32				18 05	
Chatham	d				16 36			17 01				17 06				17 32				17 35				18 08	
Gillingham	d				16 40			17 06				17 10				17 37				17 41				18 13	
Rainham (Kent)	a				16 45			17 11				17 15				17 42				17 46				18 19	

Table T201-F

Mondays to Fridays

16 December to 15 May

London Thameslink - Greenwich - Woolwich - Medway

		SE	SE	SE	SE ◇	TL	SE	SE ◇		SE	SE	SE	SE	SE ◇	TL	SE	TL	SE		SE	SE	SE	TL	SE	SE ◇
Luton	d					16 18									16 46								17 17		
Luton Airport Parkway	d					16 21									16 49								17 20		
St Albans	d					16 31									17 00								17 30		
West Hampstead Thameslink	d					16 51									17 21								17 51		
St Pancras International	d				17 46	17 02		17 55						18 16	17 32								18 02		18 55
Farringdon	d					17 07									17 37								18 07		
City Thameslink	d					17 09									17 39								18 09		
London Blackfriars	a					17 11									17 41								18 11		
London Charing Cross	d	16 48					17 13			17 17			17 34			17 41				17 51	17 59			18 11	
Waterloo East	a	16 50					17 15			17 19			17 36			17 43				17 53	18 01			18 13	
London Cannon Street	d		16 54	17 05							17 25	17 34						17 49				18 04			
London Bridge	d	16 57	16 59	17 10		17 18	17 22			17 26	17 30	17 39	17 43		17 48	17 50		17 54		18 00	18 08	18 09	18 18	18 20	
London Victoria	d																←								
Deptford	d		17 05	17 16		17 25					17 36	17 45			17 55		17 55	18 00				18 15	18 25		
Greenwich	d		17 08	17 19		17 27					17 39	17 48			→		17 57	18 03				18 18	18 27		
Maze Hill	d		17 11	17 22		17 30					17 43	17 51					18 00	18 06				18 21	18 30		
Westcombe Park	d		17 14	17 24		17 32					17 45	17 54					18 02	18 09				18 24	18 32		
Charlton	d		17 17	17 26		17 35	17 39				17 48	17 56	18 00				18 05	18 11		18 18		18 26	18 35	18 38	
Woolwich Dockyard	d		17 20	17 29			17 42					17 59	18 03					18 14		18 21		18 29		18 41	
Woolwich Arsenal	d		17 23	17 32		17 40	17 45				17 53	18 02	18 06				18 10	18 17		18 24		18 32	18 40	18 44	
Plumstead	d		17 25	17 34		17 43	17 47					18 04	18 09				18 13	18 20		18 26		18 35	18 43	18 46	
Abbey Wood	d		17 29	17 38		17 46	17 50				17 58	18 08	18 12				18 16	18 23		18 30		18 38	18 46	18 50	
Belvedere	d		17 32	17 41			17 53					18 11	18 15					18 27		18 33		18 41		18 53	
Erith	d		17 35	17 43			17 56					18 13	18 18					18 30		18 36		18 44		18 56	
Slade Green	d		17 39	17a46		17 52	17a59					18 17	18a21				18 24	18 34		18a42		18a47	18 52	18a59	
Dartford	d	17 37	17a50			17 58				18 03	18 09	18a26				18 25	18 32	18 40			18 46		18 58		
Stone Crossing	d	17 41				18 02				18 07	18 13					18 29	18 36						19 02		
Greenhithe	d	17 43				18 04				18 09	18 15					18 31	18 38	18 45			18 51		19 04		
Swanscombe	d	17 46				18 07				18 12						18 34	18 41						19 07		
Northfleet	d	17 49				18 09				18 15						18 37	18 44						19 09		
Gravesend	d	17a56			18 09	18 13		18 18		18 22	18a25			18 39		18a43	18 50	18a57			19 00		19 13		19 18
Higham	d					18 19				18 28							18 56				19 06		19 19		
Strood	d				18a19	18 25		18 31		18a36				18a49			19 01				19a14		19 27		19 30
Rochester	d					18 28		18 36									19 05						19 30		19 35
Chatham	d					18 32		18 40									19 08						19 34		19 39
Gillingham	d					18 37		18 45									19 13						19 39		19 44
Rainham (Kent)	a					18 42		18 50									19 19						19 44		19 48

		SE	SE	SE		SE	TL	SE	SE	SE ◇	SE	SE	SE	TL		SE	SE	SE	SE ◇	SE	SE	TL	SE	SE	
Luton	d						17 46							18 16								18 46			
Luton Airport Parkway	d						17 49							18 19								18 49			
St Albans	d						18 00							18 30								19 00			
West Hampstead Thameslink	d						18 21							18 51								19 21			
St Pancras International	d						18 32			19 25				19 02					19 55			19 32			
Farringdon	d						18 37							19 07								19 37			
City Thameslink	d						18 39							19 09								19 39			
London Blackfriars	a						18 41							19 11								19 41			
London Charing Cross	d		18 25					18 43			18 54					19 12				19 32			19 42		
Waterloo East	a		18 27					18 45			18 56					19 14				19 34			19 44		
London Cannon Street	d	18 24				18 35			18 55				19 05				19 24	19 35						19 54	
London Bridge	d	18 29	18 34			18 40	18 48	18 52	19 00		19 03		19 09	19 18		19 21	19 28	19 39		19 41		19 48	19 51	19 58	
London Victoria	d			←								19 04									19 34				
Deptford	d	18 35		18 35		18 46	18 55		19 06				19 15	19 25			19 35	19 45				19 55		20 05	
Greenwich	d	→		18 38		18 49	18 57		19 09				19 17	19 27			19 37	19 47				19 57		20 07	
Maze Hill	d			18 42		18 52	19 00		19 12				19 20	19 30			19 40	19 50				20 00		20 10	
Westcombe Park	d			18 44		18 55	19 02		19 15				19 22	19 32			19 42	19 52				20 02		20 12	
Charlton	d			18 47		18 57	19 05	19 09	19 17				19 25	19 35		19 38	19 45	19 55				20 05	20 08	20 15	
Woolwich Dockyard	d					19 00		19 12	19 20				19 28			19 41	19 48	19 58					20 11	20 18	
Woolwich Arsenal	d			18 52		19 03	19 10	19 15	19 23				19 31	19 40		19 44	19 51	20 01				20 10	20 14	20 21	
Plumstead	d					19 06	19 13	19 17	19 25				19 33	19 43		19 46	19 53	20 03				20 13	20 16	20 23	
Abbey Wood	d			18 57		19 09	19 16	19 21	19 29				19 36	19 46		19 50	19 56	20 06				20 16	20 20	20 26	
Belvedere	d					19 13		19 24	19 32				19 39			19 53	19 59	20 09					20 23	20 29	
Erith	d					19 16		19 27	19 35				19 42			19 55	20 02	20 12					20 25	20 32	
Slade Green	d					19a19	19 22	19a33	19a39				19a45	19 52		20 01	20a06	20a15				20 22	20 31	20a38	
Dartford	d		19 07	19 10			19 28				19 35	19 54		19 58		20a08				20 11	20 24	20 28	20a38		
Stone Crossing	d		19 11	19 14			19 32				19 39			20 02						20 15		20 32			
Greenhithe	d		19 13	19 16			19 34				19 41	20 00		20 04						20 17	20 30	20 34			
Swanscombe	d			19 19			19 37				19 44			20 07						20 20		20 37			
Northfleet	d			19 21			19 39				19 46			20 09						20 22		20 39			
Gravesend	d		19a23	19 26			19 43			19 48	19a55	20a09		20 13					20 18	20a26	20a39	20 43			
Higham	d			19 32			19 49							20 19								20 49			
Strood	d			19a40			19 55			19 59				20 25					20 29			20 55			
Rochester	d						19 58			20 02				20 28					20 32			20 58			
Chatham	d						20 02			20 06				20 31					20 36			21 01			
Gillingham	d						20 07			20 11				20 36					20 40			21 06			
Rainham (Kent)	a						20 12			20 15				20 41					20 45			21 11			

Table T201-F

Mondays to Fridays
16 December to 15 May

London Thameslink - Greenwich - Woolwich - Medway

		SE	SE ◇	SE	SE	TL	SE	SE	SE	SE ◇		SE	SE	TL	SE	SE	SE	SE ◇	SE	SE		TL	SE	SE	SE ◇
Luton	d					19 18								19 48								20 18			
Luton Airport Parkway	d					19 21								19 51								20 21			
St Albans	d					19 31								20 01								20 31			
West Hampstead Thameslink	d					19 51								20 21								20 51			
St Pancras International	d		20 25			20 02				20 55				20 32				21 25				21 02			21 55
Farringdon	d					20 07								20 37								21 07			
City Thameslink	d					20 09								20 39								21 09			
London Blackfriars	a					20 11								20 41								21 11			
London Charing Cross	d			20 02			20 12					20 32			20 42				21 02				21 12		
Waterloo East	a			20 04			20 14					20 34			20 44				21 04				21 14		
London Cannon Street	d	20 05						20 24	20 35							20 54	21 05							21 32	
London Bridge	d	20 09		20 11		20 18	20 21	20 28	20 39			20 41		20 48	20 51	20 58	21 09		21 11			21 18	21 21	21 36	
London Victoria	d				20 04								20 34							21 04					
Deptford	d	20 15				20 25		20 35	20 45					20 55		21 05	21 15					21 25		21 42	
Greenwich	d	20 17				20 27		20 37	20 47					20 57		21 07	21 17					21 27		21 44	
Maze Hill	d	20 20				20 30		20 40	20 50					21 00		21 10	21 20					21 30		21 47	
Westcombe Park	d	20 22				20 32		20 42	20 52					21 02		21 12	21 22					21 32		21 49	
Charlton	d	20 25				20 35	20 38	20 45	20 55					21 05	21 08	21 15	21 25					21 35	21 38	21 52	
Woolwich Dockyard	d	20 28					20 41	20 48	20 58						21 11	21 18	21 28						21 41	21 55	
Woolwich Arsenal	d	20 31				20 40	20 44	20 51	21 01					21 10	21 14	21 21	21 31					21 40	21 44	21 58	
Plumstead	d	20 33				20 43	20 46	20 53	21 03					21 13	21 16	21 23	21 33					21 43	21 46	22 00	
Abbey Wood	d	20 36				20 46	20 50	20 56	21 06					21 16	21 20	21 26	21 36					21 46	21 50	22 03	
Belvedere	d	20 39					20 53	20 59	21 09						21 23	21 29	21 39						21 53	22 06	
Erith	d	20 42					20 55	21 02	21 12						21 25	21 32	21 42						21 55	22 09	
Slade Green	d	20a45				20 52	21 01	21a06	21a15					21 22	21 31	21a36	21a45					21 52	22 01	22a13	
Dartford	d			20 41	20 54	20 58	21a08					21 11	21 24	21 28	21a38				21 41	21 54		21 58	22a08		
Stone Crossing	d			20 45		21 02						21 15		21 32					21 45			22 02			
Greenhithe	d			20 47	21 00	21 04						21 17	21 30	21 34					21 47	22 00		22 04			
Swanscombe	d			20 50		21 07						21 20		21 37					21 50			22 07			
Northfleet	d			20 52		21 09						21 22		21 39					21 52			22 09			
Gravesend	d		20 48	20a56	21a09	21 13				21 18		21a26	21a39	21 43				21 48	21a56	22a09		22 13			22 18
Higham	d					21 19								21 49								22 19			
Strood	d		20 59			21 25				21 29				21 55				21 59				22 25			22 29
Rochester	d		21 02			21 28				21 32				21 58				22 02				22 28			22 32
Chatham	d		21 06			21 31				21 36				22 01				22 06				22 31			22 36
Gillingham	d		21 10			21 36				21 40				22 06				22 10				22 36			22 40
Rainham (Kent)	a		21 15			21 41				21 45				22 12				22 15				22 41			22 45

		SE	SE	TL	SE	SE		SE ◇	SE	SE	TL	SE	SE	SE ◇	SE	SE		TL	SE	SE	SE ◇	SE	TL	SE	SE
Luton	d			20 48							21 18							21 48					22 18		
Luton Airport Parkway	d			20 51							21 21							21 51					22 21		
St Albans	d			21 01							21 31							22 01					22 31		
West Hampstead Thameslink	d			21 21							21 51							22 21					22 51		
St Pancras International	d			21 32				22 25			22 02			22 55				22 32			23 25		23 02		
Farringdon	d			21 37							22 07							22 37					23 07		
City Thameslink	d			21 39							22 09							22 39							
London Blackfriars	a			21 41							22 11							22 41					23 11		
London Charing Cross	d	21 32			21 42				22 02			22 12			22 32				22 42			23 02		23 12	
Waterloo East	a	21 34			21 44				22 04			22 14			22 34				22 44			23 04		23 14	
London Cannon Street	d					22 02							22 32							23 02					23 32
London Bridge	d	21 41		21 48	21 51	22 06			22 11		22 18	22 21	22 36		22 41			22 48	22 51	23 06		23 11	23 18	23 21	23 36
London Victoria	d		21 34							22 04						22 34									
Deptford	d			21 55		22 12					22 25		22 42					22 55		23 12			23 25		23 42
Greenwich	d			21 57		22 14					22 27		22 44					22 57		23 14			23 27		23 44
Maze Hill	d			22 00		22 17					22 30		22 47					23 00		23 17			23 30		23 47
Westcombe Park	d			22 02		22 19					22 32		22 49					23 02		23 19			23 32		23 49
Charlton	d			22 05	22 08	22 22					22 35	22 38	22 52					23 05	23 08	23 22			23 35	23 38	23 52
Woolwich Dockyard	d				22 11	22 25						22 41	22 55						23 11	23 25				23 41	23 55
Woolwich Arsenal	d			22 10	22 14	22 28					22 40	22 44	22 58					23 10	23 14	23 28			23 40	23 44	23 58
Plumstead	d			22 13	22 16	22 30					22 43	22 46	23 00					23 13	23 16	23 30			23 43	23 46	23 59
Abbey Wood	d			22 16	22 20	22 33					22 46	22 50	23 03					23 16	23 20	23 33			23 46	23 50	00 03
Belvedere	d				22 23	22 36						22 53	23 06						23 23	23 36				23 53	00 06
Erith	d				22 25	22 39						22 55	23 09						23 25	23 39				23 55	00 09
Slade Green	d			22 22	22 31	22a43					22 52	23 01	23a13					23 22	23 31	23 44			23 52	23 59	00 14
Dartford	d	22 11	22 24	22 28	22a38				22 41	22 54	22 58	23a08			23 11	23 24		23 28	23a38	23a51		23 48	23 58	00a05	00a22
Stone Crossing	d	22 15		22 32					22 45		23 02				23 15			23 32				23 52	00 02		
Greenhithe	d	22 17	22 30	22 34					22 47	23 00	23 04				23 17	23 30		23 34				23 54	00 04		
Swanscombe	d	22 20		22 37					22 50		23 07				23 20			23 37				23 57	00 07		
Northfleet	d	22 22		22 39					22 52		23 09				23 22			23 39				23 59	00 09		
Gravesend	d	22a26	22a39	22 43				22 48	22a56	23a09	23 13			23 18	23a26	23a39		23 43			23 48	00a06	00 13		
Higham	d			22 49							23 19							23 49					00 19		
Strood	d			22 55				22 59			23 25			23 29				23 55			23 59		00 25		
Rochester	d			22 58				23 02			23 28			23 32				23 58			00 02		00 28		
Chatham	d			23 01				23 06			23 31			23 36				00 02			00 06		00 32		
Gillingham	d			23 06				23 10			23 36			23 40				00a06			00 10		00a36		
Rainham (Kent)	a			23 11				23 15			23 41			23 45							00 15				

NRT DECEMBER 19 EDITION

Table T201-F

Mondays to Fridays
16 December to 15 May

London Thameslink - Greenwich - Woolwich - Medway

		SE ◇		SE	SE	SE MTO
Luton	d					
Luton Airport Parkway	d					
St Albans	d					
West Hampstead Thameslink	d					
St Pancras International	d	23 55				
Farringdon	d					
City Thameslink	d					
London Blackfriars	a					
London Charing Cross	d			23 32	23 42	23 50
Waterloo East	a			23 34	23 44	23 52
London Cannon Street	d					
London Bridge	d			23 41	23 51	23 59
London Victoria	d					
Deptford	d					
Greenwich	d					
Maze Hill	d					
Westcombe Park	d					
Charlton	d				00 08	
Woolwich Dockyard	d				00 11	
Woolwich Arsenal	d				00 14	
Plumstead	d				00 16	
Abbey Wood	d				00 20	
Belvedere	d				00 23	
Erith	d				00 25	
Slade Green	d				00 31	
Dartford	d			00 18	00a36	00 39
Stone Crossing	d			00 22		00 43
Greenhithe	d			00 24		00 45
Swanscombe	d			00 27		00s48
Northfleet	d			00 29		00s50
Gravesend	d	00 18		00a36		00a57
Higham	d					
Strood	d	00 29				
Rochester	d	00 32				
Chatham	d	00 36				
Gillingham	d	00 40				
Rainham (Kent)	a	00 45				

Saturdays
21 December to 16 May

		TL	SE	SE	SE	SE	TL	SE	TL	SE		SE	TL	SE	SE	TL	SE	SE	TL	SE		SE	SE	TL	SE
Luton	d																								
Luton Airport Parkway	d																								
St Albans	d																								
West Hampstead Thameslink	d															05 22			05 52					06 22	
St Pancras International	d															05 32			06 02					06 32	
Farringdon	d															05 37			06 07					06 37	
City Thameslink	d																								
London Blackfriars	a															05 41			06 11					06 41	
London Charing Cross	d			00 02	00 12			00 42		04 50				05 20			05 50			06 12		06 18			06 42
Waterloo East	a			00 04	00 14			00 44		04 52				05 22			05 52			06 14		06 20			06 44
London Cannon Street	d		00 02			00 32						05 05			05 35			06 05					06 35		
London Bridge	d		00 06	00 11	00 21	00 36		00 51		04 59		05 09		05 29	05 39	05 48	05 59	06 09	06 18	06 21		06 27	06 39	06 48	06 51
London Victoria	d																								
Deptford	d		00 12			00 42						05 15			05 45	05 55		06 15	06 25				06 45	06 55	
Greenwich	d		00 14			00 44						05 17			05 47	05 57		06 17	06 27				06 47	06 57	
Maze Hill	d		00 17			00 47						05 20			05 50	06 00		06 20	06 30				06 50	07 00	
Westcombe Park	d		00 19			00 49						05 22			05 52	06 02		06 22	06 32				06 52	07 02	
Charlton	d		00 22		00 41	00 52		01 08				05 25			05 55	06 05		06 25	06 35	06 38			06 55	07 05	07 08
Woolwich Dockyard	d		00 25		00 44	00 55		01 11				05 28			05 58			06 28		06 41			06 58		07 11
Woolwich Arsenal	d		00 28		00 47	00 58		01 14				05 31			06 01	06 10		06 31	06 40	06 44			07 01	07 10	07 14
Plumstead	d		00 30		00 49	01 00		01 16				05 33			06 03	06 13		06 33	06 43	06 46			07 03	07 13	07 16
Abbey Wood	d		00 33		00 53	01 03		01 20				05 36			06 06	06 16		06 36	06 46	06 50			07 06	07 16	07 20
Belvedere	d		00 36		00 56	01 06		01 23				05 39			06 09			06 39		06 53			07 09		07 23
Erith	d		00 39		00 58	01 09		01 25				05 42			06 12			06 42		06 55			07 12		07 25
Slade Green	d		00 44		01 02	01 12		01 30				05a45			06a15	06 22		06a45	06 52	07 01			07a15	07 22	07 31
Dartford	d	00 28	00a51	00 48	01a07	01a20	01 24	01a37	04 58	05 41			05 58	06 11		06 28	06 41		06 58	07a08		07 04		07 28	07a38
Stone Crossing	d	00 32		00 52			01s28		05 02	05 45			06 02	06 15		06 32	06 45		07 02			07 08		07 32	
Greenhithe	d	00 34		00 54			01s30		05 04	05 47			06 04	06 17		06 34	06 47		07 04			07 11		07 34	
Swanscombe	d	00 37		00s57			01s33		05 07	05 50			06 07	06 20		06 37	06 50		07 07			07 14		07 37	
Northfleet	d	00 39		00s59			01s35		05 09	05 52			06 09	06 22		06 39	06 52		07 09			07 17		07 39	
Gravesend	d	00 43		01a07			01 39		05 13	05a56			06 13	06a26		06 43	06a56		07 13			07a23		07 43	
Higham	d	00 49					01s45		05 19				06 19			06 49			07 19					07 49	
Strood	d	00 56					01s50		05 25				06 25			06 55			07 25					07 55	
Rochester	d	00 59					01s53		05 28				06 28			06 58			07 28					07 58	
Chatham	d	01 03					01s57		05 31				06 31			07 01			07 31					08 01	
Gillingham	d	01a07					02a02		05 36				06 36			07 06			07 36					08 06	
Rainham (Kent)	a								05 42				06 41			07 11			07 41					08 11	

Table T201-F

Saturdays

21 December to 16 May

London Thameslink - Greenwich - Woolwich - Medway

		SE	SE	SE	SE	TL		SE	SE	SE	SE	SE	TL	SE	SE	SE		SE	SE	SE	TL	SE	SE	SE	SE
		◇								◇								◇							◇
Luton	d																								
Luton Airport Parkway	d																								
St Albans	d																								
West Hampstead Thameslink	d																								
St Pancras International	d	07 25				07 02				07 55			07 32					08 25			08 02				08 57
Farringdon	d					07 07							07 37								08 07				
City Thameslink	d																								
London Blackfriars	a					07 11							07 41								08 11				
London Charing Cross	d		06 48					07 12			07 32			07 42					08 02			08 12			
Waterloo East	a		06 50					07 14			07 34			07 44					08 04			08 14			
London Cannon Street	d				07 05				07 35						07 54	08 05							08 24	08 35	
London Bridge	d		06 57		07 09	07 18		07 21	07 39		07 41		07 48	07 51	07 58	08 09			08 11		08 18	08 21	08 28	08 39	
London Victoria	d			07 04								07 34								08 04					
Deptford	d				07 15	07 25			07 45				07 55		08 05	08 15					08 25		08 35	08 45	
Greenwich	d				07 17	07 27			07 47				07 57		08 07	08 17					08 27		08 37	08 47	
Maze Hill	d				07 20	07 30			07 50				08 00		08 10	08 20					08 30		08 40	08 50	
Westcombe Park	d				07 22	07 32			07 52				08 02		08 12	08 22					08 32		08 42	08 52	
Charlton	d				07 25	07 35		07 38	07 55				08 05	08 08	08 15	08 25					08 35	08 38	08 45	08 55	
Woolwich Dockyard	d				07 28			07 41	07 58					08 11	08 18	08 28						08 41	08 48	08 58	
Woolwich Arsenal	d				07 31	07 40		07 44	08 01				08 10	08 14	08 21	08 31					08 40	08 44	08 51	09 01	
Plumstead	d				07 33	07 43		07 46	08 03				08 13	08 16	08 23	08 33					08 43	08 46	08 53	09 03	
Abbey Wood	d				07 36	07 46		07 50	08 06				08 16	08 20	08 26	08 36					08 46	08 50	08 56	09 06	
Belvedere	d				07 39			07 53	08 09					08 23	08 29	08 39						08 53	08 59	09 09	
Erith	d				07 42			07 55	08 12					08 25	08 32	08 42						08 55	09 02	09 12	
Slade Green	d				07a45	07 52		08 01	08a15				08 22	08 31	08a36	08a45					08 52	09 01	09a06	09a15	
Dartford	d		07 34	07 54		07 58		08a08			08 11	08 24	08 28	08a38					08 41	08 54	08 58	09a08			
Stone Crossing	d		07 38			08 02					08 15		08 32						08 45		09 02				
Greenhithe	d		07 41	08 00		08 04					08 17	08 30	08 34						08 47	09 00	09 04				
Swanscombe	d		07 44			08 07					08 20		08 37						08 50		09 07				
Northfleet	d		07 47			08 09					08 22		08 39						08 52		09 09				
Gravesend	d	07 48	07a53	08a09		08 13				08 18	08a26	08a39	08 43					08 48	08a56	09a09	09 13				09 19
Higham	d					08 19							08 49								09 19				
Strood	d	07 59				08 25				08 29			08 55					08 59			09 25				09 30
Rochester	d	08 02				08 28				08 32			08 58					09 02			09 28				09 33
Chatham	d	08 06				08 31				08 36			09 01					09 06			09 31				09 37
Gillingham	d	08 10				08 36				08 40			09 06					09 10			09 36				09 41
Rainham (Kent)	a	08 15				08 41				08 45			09 11					09 15			09 41				09 46

		SE		SE	TL	SE	SE	SE	SE	SE	SE	TL		SE	SE	SE	SE	SE	SE	TL	SE	SE		SE	SE
									◇								◇								◇
Luton	d																								
Luton Airport Parkway	d																								
St Albans	d																								
West Hampstead Thameslink	d																								
St Pancras International	d				08 32				09 25			09 02					09 55			09 32					10 25
Farringdon	d				08 37							09 07								09 37					
City Thameslink	d											09 09								09 39					
London Blackfriars	a				08 41							09 11								09 41					
London Charing Cross	d	08 32				08 42				09 02				09 12				09 32			09 42				
Waterloo East	a	08 34				08 44				09 04				09 14				09 34			09 44				
London Cannon Street	d						08 54	09 05							09 24	09 35						09 54		10 05	
London Bridge	d	08 41			08 48	08 51	08 58	09 09		09 11		09 18		09 21	09 28	09 39		09 41		09 48	09 51	09 58		10 09	
London Victoria	d			08 34							09 04								09 34						
Deptford	d				08 55		09 05	09 15				09 25			09 35	09 45				09 55		10 05		10 15	
Greenwich	d				08 57		09 07	09 17				09 27			09 37	09 47				09 57		10 07		10 17	
Maze Hill	d				09 00		09 10	09 20				09 30			09 40	09 50				10 00		10 10		10 20	
Westcombe Park	d				09 02		09 12	09 22				09 32			09 42	09 52				10 02		10 12		10 22	
Charlton	d				09 05	09 08	09 15	09 25				09 35		09 38	09 45	09 55				10 05	10 08	10 15		10 25	
Woolwich Dockyard	d					09 11	09 18	09 28						09 41	09 48	09 58					10 11	10 18		10 28	
Woolwich Arsenal	d				09 10	09 14	09 21	09 31				09 40		09 44	09 51	10 01				10 10	10 14	10 21		10 31	
Plumstead	d				09 13	09 16	09 23	09 33				09 43		09 46	09 53	10 03				10 13	10 16	10 23		10 33	
Abbey Wood	d				09 16	09 20	09 26	09 36				09 46		09 50	09 56	10 06				10 16	10 20	10 26		10 36	
Belvedere	d					09 23	09 29	09 39						09 53	09 59	10 09					10 23	10 29		10 39	
Erith	d					09 25	09 32	09 42						09 55	10 02	10 12					10 25	10 32		10 42	
Slade Green	d				09 22	09 31	09a36	09a45				09 52		10 01	10a06	10a15				10 22	10 31	10a36		10a45	
Dartford	d	09 11		09 24	09 28	09a38				09 41	09 54	09 58		10a08				10 11	10 24	10 28	10a38				
Stone Crossing	d	09 15			09 32					09 45		10 02						10 15		10 32					
Greenhithe	d	09 17		09 30	09 34					09 47	10 00	10 04						10 17	10 30	10 34					
Swanscombe	d	09 20			09 37					09 50		10 07						10 20		10 37					
Northfleet	d	09 22			09 39					09 52		10 09						10 22		10 39					
Gravesend	d	09a26		09a39	09 43				09 48	09a56	10a09	10 13					10 18	10a26	10a39	10 43					10 48
Higham	d				09 49							10 19								10 49					
Strood	d				09 55				09 59			10 25					10 29			10 55					10 59
Rochester	d				09 58				10 02			10 28					10 32			10 58					11 02
Chatham	d				10 01				10 06			10 31					10 36			11 01					11 06
Gillingham	d				10 06				10 10			10 36					10 40			11 06					11 10
Rainham (Kent)	a				10 11				10 15			10 41					10 45			11 11					11 15

Table T201-F

Saturdays

21 December to 16 May

London Thameslink - Greenwich - Woolwich - Medway

		SE	SE	TL	SE	SE	SE	SE		SE	SE	TL	SE	SE	SE	SE	SE	SE		TL	SE	SE	SE	SE	SE
								◇								◇								◇	
Luton	d																								
Luton Airport Parkway	d																								
St Albans	d																								
West Hampstead Thameslink	d																								
St Pancras International	d			10 02				10 52				10 32				11 25				11 02				11 55	
Farringdon	d			10 07								10 37								11 07					
City Thameslink	d			10 09								10 39								11 09					
London Blackfriars	a			10 11								10 41								11 11					
London Charing Cross	d	10 02			10 12					10 32			10 42				11 02				11 12				11 32
Waterloo East	a	10 04			10 14					10 34			10 44				11 04				11 14				11 34
London Cannon Street	d					10 24	10 35							10 54	11 05							11 24	11 35		
London Bridge	d	10 11		10 18	10 21	10 28	10 39			10 41		10 48	10 51	10 58	11 09		11 11			11 18	11 21	11 28	11 39		11 41
London Victoria	d		10 04								10 34							11 04							
Deptford	d			10 25		10 35	10 45					10 55		11 05	11 15					11 25		11 35	11 45		
Greenwich	d			10 27		10 37	10 47					10 57		11 07	11 17					11 27		11 37	11 47		
Maze Hill	d			10 30		10 40	10 50					11 00		11 10	11 20					11 30		11 40	11 50		
Westcombe Park	d			10 32		10 42	10 52					11 02		11 12	11 22					11 32		11 42	11 52		
Charlton	d			10 35	10 38	10 45	10 55					11 05	11 08	11 15	11 25					11 35	11 38	11 45	11 55		
Woolwich Dockyard	d				10 41	10 48	10 58						11 11	11 18	11 28						11 41	11 48	11 58		
Woolwich Arsenal	d			10 40	10 44	10 51	11 01					11 10	11 14	11 21	11 31					11 40	11 44	11 51	12 01		
Plumstead	d			10 43	10 46	10 53	11 03					11 13	11 16	11 23	11 33					11 43	11 46	11 53	12 03		
Abbey Wood	d			10 46	10 50	10 56	11 06					11 16	11 20	11 26	11 36					11 46	11 50	11 56	12 06		
Belvedere	d				10 53	10 59	11 09						11 23	11 29	11 39						11 53	11 59	12 09		
Erith	d				10 55	11 02	11 12						11 25	11 32	11 42						11 55	12 02	12 12		
Slade Green	d			10 52	11 01	11a06	11a15					11 22	11 31	11a36	11a45					11 52	12 01	12a06	12a15		
Dartford	d	10 41	10 54	10 58	11a08					11 11	11 24	11 28	11a38				11 41	11 54		11 58	12a08				12 11
Stone Crossing	d	10 45		11 02						11 15		11 32					11 45			12 02					12 15
Greenhithe	d	10 47	11 00	11 04						11 17	11 30	11 34					11 47	12 00		12 04					12 17
Swanscombe	d	10 50		11 07						11 20		11 37					11 50			12 07					12 20
Northfleet	d	10 52		11 09						11 22		11 39					11 52			12 09					12 22
Gravesend	d	10a56	11a09	11 13				11 18		11a26	11a39	11 43				11 48	11a56	12a09		12 13				12 18	12a26
Higham	d			11 19								11 49								12 19					
Strood	d			11 25				11 29				11 55				11 59				12 25				12 29	
Rochester	d			11 28				11 32				11 58				12 02				12 28				12 32	
Chatham	d			11 31				11 36				12 01				12 06				12 31				12 36	
Gillingham	d			11 36				11 40				12 06				12 10				12 36				12 40	
Rainham (Kent)	a			11 41				11 45				12 11				12 15				12 41				12 45	

		SE	TL	SE		SE	SE	SE	SE	SE	TL	SE	SE	SE		SE	SE	SE	TL	SE	SE	SE	SE	SE	
								◇								◇							◇		
Luton	d																								
Luton Airport Parkway	d																								
St Albans	d																								
West Hampstead Thameslink	d																								
St Pancras International	d		11 32					12 27			12 02					12 52			12 32				13 25		
Farringdon	d		11 37								12 07								12 37						
City Thameslink	d		11 39								12 09								12 39						
London Blackfriars	a		11 41								12 11								12 41						
London Charing Cross	d			11 42					12 02			12 12					12 32			12 42				13 02	
Waterloo East	a			11 44					12 04			12 14					12 34			12 44				13 04	
London Cannon Street	d					11 54	12 05						12 24	12 35							12 54	13 05			
London Bridge	d		11 48	11 51		11 58	12 09		12 11		12 18	12 21	12 28	12 39			12 41		12 48	12 51	12 58	13 09		13 11	
London Victoria	d	11 34								12 04								12 34							
Deptford	d		11 55			12 05	12 15				12 25		12 35	12 45					12 55		13 05	13 15			
Greenwich	d		11 57			12 07	12 17				12 27		12 37	12 47					12 57		13 07	13 17			
Maze Hill	d		12 00			12 10	12 20				12 30		12 40	12 50					13 00		13 10	13 20			
Westcombe Park	d		12 02			12 12	12 22				12 32		12 42	12 52					13 02		13 12	13 22			
Charlton	d		12 05	12 08		12 15	12 25				12 35	12 38	12 45	12 55					13 05	13 08	13 15	13 25			
Woolwich Dockyard	d			12 11		12 18	12 28					12 41	12 48	12 58						13 11	13 18	13 28			
Woolwich Arsenal	d		12 10	12 14		12 21	12 31				12 40	12 44	12 51	13 01					13 10	13 14	13 21	13 31			
Plumstead	d		12 13	12 16		12 23	12 33				12 43	12 46	12 53	13 03					13 13	13 16	13 23	13 33			
Abbey Wood	d		12 16	12 20		12 26	12 36				12 46	12 50	12 56	13 06					13 16	13 20	13 26	13 36			
Belvedere	d			12 23		12 29	12 39					12 53	12 59	13 09						13 23	13 29	13 39			
Erith	d			12 25		12 32	12 42					12 55	13 02	13 12						13 25	13 32	13 42			
Slade Green	d		12 22	12 31		12a36	12a45				12 52	13 01	13a06	13a15					13 22	13 31	13a36	13a45			
Dartford	d	12 24	12 28	12a38					12 41	12 54	12 58	13a08					13 11	13 24	13 28	13a38				13 41	
Stone Crossing	d		12 32						12 45		13 02						13 15		13 32					13 45	
Greenhithe	d	12 30	12 34						12 47	13 00	13 04						13 17	13 30	13 34					13 47	
Swanscombe	d		12 37						12 50		13 07						13 20		13 37					13 50	
Northfleet	d		12 39						12 52		13 09						13 22		13 39					13 52	
Gravesend	d	12a39	12 43					12 49	12a56	13a09	13 13					13 18	13a26	13a39	13 43				13 48	13a56	
Higham	d		12 49								13 19								13 49						
Strood	d		12 55					12 59			13 25					13 29			13 55				13 59		
Rochester	d		12 58					13 02			13 28					13 32			13 58				14 02		
Chatham	d		13 01					13 06			13 31					13 36			14 01				14 06		
Gillingham	d		13 06					13 10			13 36					13 40			14 06				14 10		
Rainham (Kent)	a		13 11					13 15			13 41					13 45			14 11				14 15		

Table T201-F

Saturdays
21 December to 16 May

London Thameslink - Greenwich - Woolwich - Medway

		SE	TL	SE	SE	SE	SE ◇	SE	SE	TL		SE	SE	SE	SE ◇	SE	SE	TL	SE	SE		SE	SE ◇	SE	SE
Luton	d																								
Luton Airport Parkway	d																								
St Albans	d																								
West Hampstead Thameslink	d																								
St Pancras International	d		13 02				13 55			13 32					14 25			14 02					14 55		
Farringdon	d		13 07							13 37								14 07							
City Thameslink	d		13 09							13 39								14 09							
London Blackfriars	a		13 11							13 41								14 11							
London Charing Cross	d			13 12				13 32				13 42				14 02			14 12					14 32	
Waterloo East	a			13 14				13 34				13 44				14 04			14 14					14 34	
London Cannon Street	d				13 24	13 35							13 54	14 05						14 24		14 35			
London Bridge	d		13 18	13 21	13 28	13 39		13 41		13 48		13 51	13 58	14 09		14 11		14 18	14 21	14 28		14 39		14 41	
London Victoria	d	13 04							13 34								14 04								14 34
Deptford	d		13 25		13 35	13 45				13 55			14 05	14 15				14 25		14 35		14 45			
Greenwich	d		13 27		13 37	13 47				13 57			14 07	14 17				14 27		14 37		14 47			
Maze Hill	d		13 30		13 40	13 50				14 00			14 10	14 20				14 30		14 40		14 50			
Westcombe Park	d		13 32		13 42	13 52				14 02			14 12	14 22				14 32		14 42		14 52			
Charlton	d		13 35	13 38	13 45	13 55				14 05		14 08	14 15	14 25				14 35	14 38	14 45		14 55			
Woolwich Dockyard	d			13 41	13 48	13 58						14 11	14 18	14 28					14 41	14 48		14 58			
Woolwich Arsenal	d		13 40	13 44	13 51	14 01				14 10		14 14	14 21	14 31				14 40	14 44	14 51		15 01			
Plumstead	d		13 43	13 46	13 53	14 03				14 13		14 16	14 23	14 33				14 43	14 46	14 53		15 03			
Abbey Wood	d		13 46	13 50	13 56	14 06				14 16		14 20	14 26	14 36				14 46	14 50	14 56		15 06			
Belvedere	d			13 53	13 59	14 09						14 23	14 29	14 39					14 53	14 59		15 09			
Erith	d			13 55	14 02	14 12						14 25	14 32	14 42					14 55	15 02		15 12			
Slade Green	d		13 52	14 01	14a06	14a15				14 22		14 31	14a36	14a45				14 52	15 01	15a06		15a15			
Dartford	d	13 54	13 58	14a08				14 11	14 24	14 28		14a38				14 41	14 54	14 58	15a08					15 11	15 24
Stone Crossing	d		14 02					14 15		14 32						14 45		15 02						15 15	
Greenhithe	d	14 00	14 04					14 17	14 30	14 34						14 47	15 00	15 04						15 17	15 30
Swanscombe	d		14 07					14 20		14 37						14 50		15 07						15 20	
Northfleet	d		14 09					14 22		14 39						14 52		15 09						15 22	
Gravesend	d	14a09	14 13				14 18	14a26	14a39	14 43					14 48	14a56	15a09	15 13					15 18	15a26	15a39
Higham	d		14 19							14 49								15 19							
Strood	d		14 25				14 29			14 55					14 59			15 25					15 29		
Rochester	d		14 28				14 32			14 58					15 02			15 28					15 32		
Chatham	d		14 31				14 36			15 01					15 06			15 31					15 36		
Gillingham	d		14 36				14 40			15 06					15 10			15 36					15 40		
Rainham (Kent)	a		14 41				14 45			15 11					15 15			15 41					15 45		

		TL	SE	SE	SE	SE ◇		SE	SE	TL	SE	SE	SE	SE ◇	SE	SE		TL	SE	SE	SE	SE ◇	SE	SE	TL
Luton	d																								
Luton Airport Parkway	d																								
St Albans	d																								
West Hampstead Thameslink	d																								
St Pancras International	d	14 32				15 25				15 02				15 55				15 32				16 25			16 02
Farringdon	d	14 37								15 07								15 37							16 07
City Thameslink	d	14 39								15 09								15 39							16 09
London Blackfriars	a	14 41								15 11								15 41							16 11
London Charing Cross	d		14 42					15 02			15 12				15 32				15 42				16 02		
Waterloo East	a		14 44					15 04			15 14				15 34				15 44				16 04		
London Cannon Street	d			14 54	15 05							15 24	15 35							15 54	16 05				
London Bridge	d	14 48	14 51	14 58	15 09			15 11		15 18	15 21	15 28	15 39		15 41			15 48	15 51	15 58	16 09		16 11		16 18
London Victoria	d								15 04							15 34								16 04	
Deptford	d	14 55		15 05	15 15					15 25		15 35	15 45					15 55		16 05	16 15				16 25
Greenwich	d	14 57		15 07	15 17					15 27		15 37	15 47					15 57		16 07	16 17				16 27
Maze Hill	d	15 00		15 10	15 20					15 30		15 40	15 50					16 00		16 10	16 20				16 30
Westcombe Park	d	15 02		15 12	15 22					15 32		15 42	15 52					16 02		16 12	16 22				16 32
Charlton	d	15 05	15 08	15 15	15 25					15 35	15 38	15 45	15 55					16 05	16 08	16 15	16 25				16 35
Woolwich Dockyard	d		15 11	15 18	15 28						15 41	15 48	15 58						16 11	16 18	16 28				
Woolwich Arsenal	d	15 10	15 14	15 21	15 31					15 40	15 44	15 51	16 01					16 10	16 14	16 21	16 31				16 40
Plumstead	d	15 13	15 16	15 23	15 33					15 43	15 46	15 53	16 03					16 13	16 16	16 23	16 33				16 43
Abbey Wood	d	15 16	15 20	15 26	15 36					15 46	15 50	15 56	16 06					16 16	16 20	16 26	16 36				16 46
Belvedere	d		15 23	15 29	15 39						15 53	15 59	16 09						16 23	16 29	16 39				
Erith	d		15 25	15 32	15 42						15 55	16 02	16 12						16 25	16 32	16 42				
Slade Green	d	15 22	15 31	15a36	15a45					15 52	16 01	16a06	16a15					16 22	16 31	16a36	16a45				16 52
Dartford	d	15 28	15a38					15 41	15 54	15 58	16a08				16 11	16 24		16 28	16a38				16 41	16 54	16 58
Stone Crossing	d	15 32						15 45		16 02					16 15			16 32					16 45		17 02
Greenhithe	d	15 34						15 47	16 00	16 04					16 17	16 30		16 34					16 47	17 00	17 04
Swanscombe	d	15 37						15 50		16 07					16 20			16 37					16 50		17 07
Northfleet	d	15 39						15 52		16 09					16 22			16 39					16 52		17 09
Gravesend	d	15 43				15 48		15a56	16a09	16 13				16 18	16a26	16a39		16 43				16 48	16a56	17a09	17 13
Higham	d	15 49								16 19								16 49							17 19
Strood	d	15 55				15 59				16 25				16 29				16 55				16 59			17 25
Rochester	d	15 58				16 02				16 28				16 32				16 58				17 02			17 28
Chatham	d	16 01				16 06				16 31				16 36				17 01				17 06			17 31
Gillingham	d	16 06				16 10				16 36				16 40				17 06				17 10			17 36
Rainham (Kent)	a	16 11				16 15				16 41				16 45				17 11				17 15			17 41

Table T201-F

Saturdays
21 December to 16 May

London Thameslink - Greenwich - Woolwich - Medway

		SE		SE	SE	SE ◇	SE	SE	TL	SE	SE	SE		SE ◇	SE	SE	TL	SE	SE	SE	SE ◇	SE		SE	TL
Luton	d																								
Luton Airport Parkway	d																								
St Albans	d																								
West Hampstead Thameslink	d																								
St Pancras International	d					16 55			16 32					17 25			17 02				17 55				17 32
Farringdon	d								16 37								17 07								17 37
City Thameslink	d								16 39								17 09								17 39
London Blackfriars	a								16 41								17 11								17 41
London Charing Cross	d	16 12					16 32			16 42					17 02			17 12				17 32			
Waterloo East	a	16 14					16 34			16 44					17 04			17 14				17 34			
London Cannon Street	d			16 24	16 35						16 54	17 05							17 24	17 35					
London Bridge	d	16 21		16 28	16 39		16 41		16 48	16 51	16 58	17 09			17 11		17 18	17 21	17 28	17 39		17 41			17 48
London Victoria	d							16 34								17 04								17 34	
Deptford	d			16 35	16 45				16 55		17 05	17 15					17 25		17 35	17 45					17 55
Greenwich	d			16 37	16 47				16 57		17 07	17 17					17 27		17 37	17 47					17 57
Maze Hill	d			16 40	16 50				17 00		17 10	17 20					17 30		17 40	17 50					18 00
Westcombe Park	d			16 42	16 52				17 02		17 12	17 22					17 32		17 42	17 52					18 02
Charlton	d	16 38		16 45	16 55				17 05	17 08	17 15	17 25					17 35	17 38	17 45	17 55					18 05
Woolwich Dockyard	d	16 41		16 48	16 58					17 11	17 18	17 28						17 41	17 48	17 58					
Woolwich Arsenal	d	16 44		16 51	17 01				17 10	17 14	17 21	17 31					17 40	17 44	17 51	18 01					18 10
Plumstead	d	16 46		16 53	17 03				17 13	17 16	17 23	17 33					17 43	17 46	17 53	18 03					18 13
Abbey Wood	d	16 50		16 56	17 06				17 16	17 20	17 26	17 36					17 46	17 50	17 56	18 06					18 16
Belvedere	d	16 53		16 59	17 09					17 23	17 29	17 39						17 53	17 59	18 09					
Erith	d	16 55		17 02	17 12					17 25	17 32	17 42						17 55	18 02	18 12					
Slade Green	d	17 01		17a06	17a15				17 22	17 31	17a36	17a45					17 52	18 01	18a06	18a15					18 22
Dartford	d	17a08					17 11	17 24	17 28	17a38					17 41	17 54	17 58	18a08				18 11		18 24	18 28
Stone Crossing	d						17 15		17 32						17 45		18 02					18 15			18 32
Greenhithe	d						17 17	17 30	17 34						17 47	18 00	18 04					18 17		18 30	18 34
Swanscombe	d						17 20		17 37						17 50		18 07					18 20			18 37
Northfleet	d						17 22		17 39						17 52		18 09					18 22			18 39
Gravesend	d					17 18	17a26	17a39	17 43					17 48	17a56	18a09	18 13				18 18	18a26		18a39	18 43
Higham	d								17 49								18 19								18 49
Strood	d					17 29			17 55					17 59			18 25				18 29				18 55
Rochester	d					17 32			17 58					18 02			18 28				18 32				18 58
Chatham	d					17 36			18 01					18 06			18 31				18 36				19 01
Gillingham	d					17 40			18 06					18 10			18 36				18 40				19 06
Rainham (Kent)	a					17 45			18 11					18 15			18 41				18 45				19 11

		SE	SE	SE	SE ◇	SE	SE	TL		SE	SE	SE	SE ◇	SE	SE	TL	SE	SE		SE	SE ◇	SE	SE	TL	SE
Luton	d																								
Luton Airport Parkway	d																								
St Albans	d																								
West Hampstead Thameslink	d																								
St Pancras International	d				18 25			18 02					18 55			18 32					19 25			19 02	
Farringdon	d							18 07								18 37								19 07	
City Thameslink	d							18 09								18 39								19 09	
London Blackfriars	a							18 11								18 41								19 11	
London Charing Cross	d	17 42				18 02				18 12				18 32			18 42					19 02			19 12
Waterloo East	a	17 44				18 04				18 14				18 34			18 44					19 04			19 14
London Cannon Street	d		17 54	18 05							18 24	18 35						18 54		19 05					
London Bridge	d	17 51	17 58	18 09		18 11		18 18		18 21	18 28	18 39		18 41		18 48	18 51	18 58		19 09		19 11		19 18	19 21
London Victoria	d						18 04								18 34								19 04		
Deptford	d		18 05	18 15				18 25			18 35	18 45				18 55		19 05		19 15				19 25	
Greenwich	d		18 07	18 17				18 27			18 37	18 47				18 57		19 07		19 17				19 27	
Maze Hill	d		18 10	18 20				18 30			18 40	18 50				19 00		19 10		19 20				19 30	
Westcombe Park	d		18 12	18 22				18 32			18 42	18 52				19 02		19 12		19 22				19 32	
Charlton	d	18 08	18 15	18 25				18 35		18 38	18 45	18 55				19 05	19 08	19 15		19 25				19 35	19 38
Woolwich Dockyard	d	18 11	18 18	18 28						18 41	18 48	18 58					19 11	19 18		19 28					19 41
Woolwich Arsenal	d	18 14	18 21	18 31				18 40		18 44	18 51	19 01				19 10	19 14	19 21		19 31				19 40	19 44
Plumstead	d	18 16	18 23	18 33				18 43		18 46	18 53	19 03				19 13	19 16	19 23		19 33				19 43	19 46
Abbey Wood	d	18 20	18 26	18 36				18 46		18 50	18 56	19 06				19 16	19 20	19 26		19 36				19 46	19 50
Belvedere	d	18 23	18 29	18 39						18 53	18 59	19 09					19 23	19 29		19 39					19 53
Erith	d	18 25	18 32	18 42						18 55	19 02	19 12					19 25	19 32		19 42					19 55
Slade Green	d	18 31	18a36	18a45				18 52		19 01	19a06	19a15				19 22	19 31	19a36		19a45				19 52	20 01
Dartford	d	18a38				18 41	18 54	18 58		19a08				19 11	19 24	19 28	19a38					19 41	19 54	19 58	20a08
Stone Crossing	d					18 45		19 02						19 15		19 32						19 45		20 02	
Greenhithe	d					18 47	19 00	19 04						19 17	19 30	19 34						19 47	20 00	20 04	
Swanscombe	d					18 50		19 07						19 20		19 37						19 50		20 07	
Northfleet	d					18 52		19 09						19 22		19 39						19 52		20 09	
Gravesend	d				18 48	18a56	19a09	19 13					19 18	19a26	19a39	19 43					19 48	19a56	20a09	20 13	
Higham	d							19 19								19 49								20 19	
Strood	d				18 59			19 25					19 29			19 55					19 59			20 25	
Rochester	d				19 02			19 28					19 32			19 58					20 02			20 28	
Chatham	d				19 06			19 31					19 36			20 01					20 06			20 31	
Gillingham	d				19 10			19 36					19 40			20 06					20 10			20 36	
Rainham (Kent)	a				19 15			19 41					19 45			20 11					20 15			20 41	

Table T201-F

21 December to 16 May

London Thameslink - Greenwich - Woolwich - Medway

		SE	SE	SE ◇	SE	SE	TL	SE	SE	SE	SE ◇	SE	SE	TL	SE	SE	SE ◇	SE	SE	TL	SE	SE
Luton	d																					
Luton Airport Parkway	d																					
St Albans	d																					
West Hampstead Thameslink	d																					
St Pancras International	d			19 55			19 32				20 25			20 02			20 55			20 32		
Farringdon	d						19 37							20 07						20 37		
City Thameslink	d						19 39							20 09						20 39		
London Blackfriars	a						19 41							20 11						20 41		
London Charing Cross	d				19 32			19 42				20 02			20 12			20 32			20 42	
Waterloo East	a				19 34			19 44				20 04			20 14			20 34			20 44	
London Cannon Street	d	19 24	19 35						19 54	20 05						20 32						21 02
London Bridge	d	19 28	19 39		19 41		19 48	19 51	19 58	20 09		20 11		20 18	20 21	20 36		20 41		20 48	20 51	21 06
London Victoria	d					19 34							20 04						20 34			
Deptford	d	19 35	19 45				19 55		20 05	20 15				20 25		20 42				20 55		21 12
Greenwich	d	19 37	19 47				19 57		20 07	20 17				20 27		20 44				20 57		21 14
Maze Hill	d	19 40	19 50				20 00		20 10	20 20				20 30		20 47				21 00		21 17
Westcombe Park	d	19 42	19 52				20 02		20 12	20 22				20 32		20 49				21 02		21 19
Charlton	d	19 45	19 55				20 05	20 08	20 15	20 25				20 35	20 38	20 52				21 05	21 08	21 22
Woolwich Dockyard	d	19 48	19 58					20 11	20 18	20 28					20 41	20 55					21 11	21 25
Woolwich Arsenal	d	19 51	20 01				20 10	20 14	20 21	20 31				20 40	20 44	20 58				21 10	21 14	21 28
Plumstead	d	19 53	20 03				20 13	20 16	20 23	20 33				20 43	20 46	21 00				21 13	21 16	21 30
Abbey Wood	d	19 56	20 06				20 16	20 20	20 26	20 36				20 46	20 50	21 03				21 16	21 20	21 33
Belvedere	d	19 59	20 09					20 23	20 29	20 39					20 53	21 06					21 23	21 36
Erith	d	20 02	20 12					20 25	20 32	20 42					20 55	21 09					21 25	21 39
Slade Green	d	20a06	20a15				20 22	20 31	20a36	20a45				20 52	21 01	21a13				21 22	21 31	21a43
Dartford	d				20 11	20 24	20 28	20a38				20 41	20 54	20 58	21a08			21 11	21 24	21 28	21a38	
Stone Crossing	d				20 15		20 32					20 45		21 02				21 15		21 32		
Greenhithe	d				20 17	20 30	20 34					20 47	21 00	21 04				21 17	21 30	21 34		
Swanscombe	d				20 20		20 37					20 50		21 07				21 20		21 37		
Northfleet	d				20 22		20 39					20 52		21 09				21 22		21 39		
Gravesend	d			20 18	20a26	20a39	20 43				20 48	20a56	21a09	21 13			21 18	21a26	21a39	21 43		
Higham	d						20 49							21 19						21 49		
Strood	d			20 29			20 55				20 59			21 25			21 29			21 55		
Rochester	d			20 32			20 58				21 02			21 28			21 32			21 58		
Chatham	d			20 36			21 01				21 06			21 31			21 36			22 01		
Gillingham	d			20 40			21 06				21 10			21 36			21 40			22 06		
Rainham (Kent)	a			20 45			21 11				21 15			21 41			21 45			22 11		

		SE ◇	SE	SE	TL	SE	SE	SE ◇	SE	SE	TL	SE	SE	SE ◇	SE	SE	TL	SE	SE	SE ◇	SE	SE	TL
Luton	d																						
Luton Airport Parkway	d																						
St Albans	d																						
West Hampstead Thameslink	d																						
St Pancras International	d	21 25			21 02			21 55			21 32			22 25			22 02			22 55			22 32
Farringdon	d				21 07						21 37						22 07						22 37
City Thameslink	d																						
London Blackfriars	a				21 11						21 41						22 11						22 41
London Charing Cross	d		21 02			21 12			21 32			21 42			22 02			22 12			22 32		
Waterloo East	a		21 04			21 14			21 34			21 44			22 04			22 14			22 34		
London Cannon Street	d						21 32						22 02						22 32				
London Bridge	d		21 11		21 18	21 21	21 36		21 41		21 48	21 51	22 06		22 11		22 18	22 21	22 36		22 41		22 48
London Victoria	d			21 04						21 34						22 04						22 34	
Deptford	d				21 25		21 42				21 55		22 12				22 25		22 42				22 55
Greenwich	d				21 27		21 44				21 57		22 14				22 27		22 44				22 57
Maze Hill	d				21 30		21 47				22 00		22 17				22 30		22 47				23 00
Westcombe Park	d				21 32		21 49				22 02		22 19				22 32		22 49				23 02
Charlton	d				21 35	21 38	21 52				22 05	22 08	22 22				22 35	22 38	22 52				23 05
Woolwich Dockyard	d					21 41	21 55					22 11	22 25					22 41	22 55				
Woolwich Arsenal	d				21 40	21 44	21 58				22 10	22 14	22 28				22 40	22 44	22 58				23 10
Plumstead	d				21 43	21 46	22 00				22 13	22 16	22 30				22 43	22 46	23 00				23 13
Abbey Wood	d				21 46	21 50	22 03				22 16	22 20	22 33				22 46	22 50	23 03				23 16
Belvedere	d					21 53	22 06					22 23	22 36					22 53	23 06				
Erith	d					21 55	22 09					22 25	22 39					22 55	23 09				
Slade Green	d				21 52	22 01	22a13				22 22	22 31	22a43				22 52	23 01	23a13				23 22
Dartford	d		21 41	21 54	21 58	22a08			22 11	22 24	22 28	22a38			22 41	22 54	22 58	23a08			23 11	23 24	23 28
Stone Crossing	d		21 45		22 02				22 15		22 32				22 45		23 02				23 15		23 32
Greenhithe	d		21 47	22 00	22 04				22 17	22 30	22 34				22 47	23 00	23 04				23 17	23 30	23 34
Swanscombe	d		21 50		22 07				22 20		22 37				22 50		23 07				23 20		23 37
Northfleet	d		21 52		22 09				22 22		22 39				22 52		23 09				23 22		23 39
Gravesend	d	21 48	21a56	22a09	22 13			22 18	22a26	22a39	22 43			22 48	22a56	23a09	23 13			23 18	23a26	23a39	23 43
Higham	d				22 19						22 49						23 19						23 49
Strood	d	21 59			22 25			22 29			22 55			22 59			23 25			23 29			23 55
Rochester	d	22 02			22 28			22 32			22 58			23 02			23 28			23 32			23 58
Chatham	d	22 06			22 31			22 36			23 01			23 06			23 31			23 36			00 02
Gillingham	d	22 10			22 36			22 40			23 06			23 10			23 36			23 40			00a06
Rainham (Kent)	a	22 15			22 41			22 45			23 11			23 15			23 41			23 45			

Table T201-F

21 December to 16 May

London Thameslink - Greenwich - Woolwich - Medway

		SE	SE	SE ◇	SE	TL	SE	SE	SE ◇	SE	SE
Luton	d										
Luton Airport Parkway	d										
St Albans	d										
West Hampstead Thameslink	d										
St Pancras International	d			23 25		23 02			23 55		
Farringdon	d					23 07					
City Thameslink	d										
London Blackfriars	a					23 11					
London Charing Cross	d	22 42			23 02		23 12			23 32	23 42
Waterloo East	a	22 44			23 04		23 14			23 34	23 44
London Cannon Street	d		23 02					23 32			
London Bridge	d	22 51	23 06		23 11	23 18	23 21	23 36		23 41	23 51
London Victoria	d										
Deptford	d		23 12			23 25		23 42			
Greenwich	d		23 14			23 27		23 44			
Maze Hill	d		23 17			23 30		23 47			
Westcombe Park	d		23 19			23 32		23 49			
Charlton	d	23 08	23 22			23 35	23 38	23 52			00 08
Woolwich Dockyard	d	23 11	23 25				23 41	23 55			00 11
Woolwich Arsenal	d	23 14	23 28			23 40	23 44	23 58			00 14
Plumstead	d	23 16	23 30			23 43	23 46	23 59			00 16
Abbey Wood	d	23 20	23 33			23 46	23 50	00 03			00 20
Belvedere	d	23 23	23 36				23 53	00 06			00 23
Erith	d	23 25	23 39				23 55	00 09			00 25
Slade Green	d	23 31	23 44			23 52	00 01	00 14			00 31
Dartford	d	23a38	23a50		23 48	23 58	00a06	00a20		00 19	00a36
Stone Crossing	d				23 52	00 02				00 23	
Greenhithe	d				23 54	00 04				00 25	
Swanscombe	d				23 57	00 07				00 28	
Northfleet	d				23 59	00 09				00 30	
Gravesend	d			23 48	00a04	00 13			00 18	00a34	
Higham	d					00 19					
Strood	d			23 59		00 25			00 29		
Rochester	d			00 02		00 28			00 32		
Chatham	d			00 06		00 32			00 36		
Gillingham	d			00 10		00a36			00 40		
Rainham (Kent)	a			00 15					00 45		

15 December to 10 May

		TL	SE	SE	SE	SE	TL	SE	SE	TL	SE	TL	SE	SE ◇	SE	SE	TL	SE	SE	SE	TL	SE	SE ◇
Luton	d																						
Luton Airport Parkway	d																						
St Albans	d																						
West Hampstead Thameslink	d																						
St Pancras International	d													08 25									09 25
Farringdon	d																						
City Thameslink	d																						
London Blackfriars	a																						
London Charing Cross	d			00 02	00 12			00 42					07 42		07 52			08 12	08 22			08 42	
Waterloo East	a			00 04	00 14			00 44					07 44		07 54			08 14	08 24			08 44	
London Cannon Street	d		00 02			00 32			07 29							07 59				08 29			
London Bridge	d		00 06	00 11	00 21	00 36		00 51	07 33				07 51		08 01	08 03	08 18	08 21	08 31	08 33	08 48	08 51	
London Victoria	d																						
Deptford	d		00 12			00 42			07 39							08 09	08 25			08 39	08 55		
Greenwich	d		00 14			00 44			07 41							08 11	08 27			08 41	08 57		
Maze Hill	d		00 17			00 47			07 44							08 14	08 30			08 44	09 00		
Westcombe Park	d		00 19			00 49			07 46							08 16	08 32			08 46	09 02		
Charlton	d		00 22		00 38	00 52		01 08	07 49				08 08			08 19	08 35	08 38		08 49	09 05	09 08	
Woolwich Dockyard	d		00 25		00 41	00 55		01 11	07 52				08 11			08 22		08 41		08 52		09 11	
Woolwich Arsenal	d		00 28		00 44	00 58		01 14	07 55				08 14			08 25	08 40	08 44		08 55	09 10	09 14	
Plumstead	d		00 30		00 46	01 00		01 16	07 57				08 16			08 27	08 43	08 46		08 57	09 13	09 16	
Abbey Wood	d		00 33		00 50	01 03		01 20	08 00				08 20			08 30	08 46	08 50		09 00	09 16	09 20	
Belvedere	d		00 36		00 53	01 06		01 23	08 03				08 23			08 33		08 53		09 03		09 23	
Erith	d		00 39		00 55	01 09		01 25	08 06				08 25			08 36		08 55		09 06		09 25	
Slade Green	d		00 44		01 01	01 12		01 30	08a09				08 31			08a39	08 52	09 01		09a09	09 22	09 31	
Dartford	d	00 28	00a49	00 48	01a07	01a20	01 24	01a37		07 58	08 09	08 28	08a36		08 39		08 58	09a06	09 09		09 28	09a36	
Stone Crossing	d	00 32		00 52			01s28			08 02	08 13	08 32			08 43		09 02		09 13		09 32		
Greenhithe	d	00 34		00 54			01s30			08 04	08 15	08 34			08 45		09 04		09 15		09 34		
Swanscombe	d	00 37		00s57			01s33			08 07	08 18	08 37			08 48		09 07		09 18		09 37		
Northfleet	d	00 39		00s59			01s35			08 09	08 20	08 39			08 50		09 09		09 20		09 39		
Gravesend	d	00 43		01a05			01 39			08 13	08a25	08 43		08 48	08a55		09 13		09a25		09 43		09 48
Higham	d	00 49					01s45			08 19		08 49					09 19				09 49		
Strood	d	00 55					01s50			08 25		08 55		08 59			09 25				09 55		09 59
Rochester	d	00 58					01s53			08 28		08 58		09 02			09 28				09 58		10 02
Chatham	d	01 02					01s57			08 31		09 01		09 06			09 31				10 01		10 06
Gillingham	d	01a06					02a02			08 36		09 06		09 10			09 36				10 06		10 10
Rainham (Kent)	a									08 41		09 11		09 15			09 41				10 11		10 15

Table T201-F

Sundays
15 December to 10 May

London Thameslink - Greenwich - Woolwich - Medway

		SE	SE	TL	SE	SE	SE	TL	SE	SE ◇	SE	SE	TL	SE	SE	SE	TL	SE	SE ◇	SE	SE	TL	SE
Luton	d																						
Luton Airport Parkway	d																						
St Albans	d																						
West Hampstead Thameslink	d							09 20					09 50										
St Pancras International	d							09 32		10 27			10 02				10 32		11 25			11 02	
Farringdon	d							09 36					10 06				10 36					11 06	
City Thameslink	d																						
London Blackfriars	a							09 40					10 10				10 40					11 10	
London Charing Cross	d	08 52			09 12	09 22			09 42		09 52			10 12	10 22			10 42		10 52			11 12
Waterloo East	a	08 54			09 14	09 24			09 44		09 54			10 14	10 24			10 44		10 54			11 14
London Cannon Street	d		08 59				09 29					09 59				10 29					10 59		
London Bridge	d	09 01	09 03	09 18	09 21	09 31	09 33	09 48	09 51		10 01	10 03	10 18	10 21	10 31	10 33	10 48	10 51		11 01	11 03	11 18	11 21
London Victoria	d																						
Deptford	d		09 09	09 25			09 39	09 55				10 09	10 25			10 39	10 55				11 09	11 25	
Greenwich	d		09 11	09 27			09 41	09 57				10 11	10 27			10 41	10 57				11 11	11 27	
Maze Hill	d		09 14	09 30			09 44	10 00				10 14	10 30			10 44	11 00				11 14	11 30	
Westcombe Park	d		09 16	09 32			09 46	10 02				10 16	10 32			10 46	11 02				11 16	11 32	
Charlton	d		09 19	09 35	09 38		09 49	10 05	10 08			10 19	10 35	10 38		10 49	11 05	11 08			11 19	11 35	11 38
Woolwich Dockyard	d		09 22		09 41		09 52		10 11			10 22		10 41		10 52		11 11			11 22		11 41
Woolwich Arsenal	d		09 25	09 40	09 44		09 55	10 10	10 14			10 25	10 40	10 44		10 55	11 10	11 14			11 25	11 40	11 44
Plumstead	d		09 27	09 43	09 46		09 57	10 13	10 16			10 27	10 43	10 46		10 57	11 13	11 16			11 27	11 43	11 46
Abbey Wood	d		09 30	09 46	09 50		10 00	10 16	10 20			10 30	10 46	10 50		11 00	11 16	11 20			11 30	11 46	11 50
Belvedere	d		09 33		09 53		10 03		10 23			10 33		10 53		11 03		11 23			11 33		11 53
Erith	d		09 36		09 55		10 06		10 25			10 36		10 55		11 06		11 25			11 36		11 55
Slade Green	d		09a39	09 52	10 01		10a09	10 22	10 31			10a39	10 52	11 01		11a09	11 22	11 31			11a39	11 52	12 01
Dartford	d	09 39		09 58	10a06	10 09		10 28	10a36		10 39		10 58	11a06	11 09		11 28	11a36		11 39		11 58	12a06
Stone Crossing	d	09 43		10 02		10 13		10 32			10 43		11 02		11 13		11 32			11 43		12 02	
Greenhithe	d	09 45		10 04		10 15		10 34			10 45		11 04		11 15		11 34			11 45		12 04	
Swanscombe	d	09 48		10 07		10 18		10 37			10 48		11 07		11 18		11 37			11 48		12 07	
Northfleet	d	09 50		10 09		10 20		10 39			10 50		11 09		11 20		11 39			11 50		12 09	
Gravesend	d	09a55		10 13		10a25		10 43		10 49	10a55		11 13		11a25		11 43		11 48	11a55		12 13	
Higham	d			10 19				10 49					11 19				11 49					12 19	
Strood	d			10 25				10 55		10 59			11 25				11 55		11 59			12 25	
Rochester	d			10 28				10 58		11 03			11 28				11 58		12 02			12 28	
Chatham	d			10 31				11 01		11 06			11 31				12 01		12 06			12 31	
Gillingham	d			10 36				11 06		11 11			11 36				12 06		12 10			12 36	
Rainham (Kent)	a			10 41				11 11		11 15			11 41				12 11		12 15			12 41	

		SE	SE	TL	SE	SE ◇	SE	SE	TL	SE	SE ◇	SE	SE	TL	SE	SE ◇	SE	SE	TL	SE	SE ◇	
Luton	d																					
Luton Airport Parkway	d																					
St Albans	d																					
West Hampstead Thameslink	d																					
St Pancras International	d			11 32		12 27			12 02		12 52			12 32		13 25			13 02		13 55	
Farringdon	d			11 36					12 06					12 36					13 06			
City Thameslink	d																					
London Blackfriars	a			11 40					12 10					12 40					13 10			
London Charing Cross	d	11 22			11 42		11 52			12 12		12 22			12 42		12 52			13 12		
Waterloo East	a	11 24			11 44		11 54			12 14		12 24			12 44		12 54			13 14		
London Cannon Street	d		11 29					11 59					12 29					12 59				
London Bridge	d	11 31	11 33	11 48	11 51		12 01	12 03	12 18	12 21		12 31	12 33	12 48	12 51		13 01	13 03	13 18	13 21		
London Victoria	d																					
Deptford	d		11 39	11 55				12 09	12 25				12 39	12 55				13 09	13 25			and at the same minutes past each hour until
Greenwich	d		11 41	11 57				12 11	12 27				12 41	12 57				13 11	13 27			
Maze Hill	d		11 44	12 00				12 14	12 30				12 44	13 00				13 14	13 30			
Westcombe Park	d		11 46	12 02				12 16	12 32				12 46	13 02				13 16	13 32			
Charlton	d		11 49	12 05	12 08			12 19	12 35	12 38			12 49	13 05	13 08			13 19	13 35	13 38		
Woolwich Dockyard	d		11 52		12 11			12 22		12 41			12 52		13 11			13 22		13 41		
Woolwich Arsenal	d		11 55	12 10	12 14			12 25	12 40	12 44			12 55	13 10	13 14			13 25	13 40	13 44		
Plumstead	d		11 57	12 13	12 16			12 27	12 43	12 46			12 57	13 13	13 16			13 27	13 43	13 46		
Abbey Wood	d		12 00	12 16	12 20			12 30	12 46	12 50			13 00	13 16	13 20			13 30	13 46	13 50		
Belvedere	d		12 03		12 23			12 33		12 53			13 03		13 23			13 33		13 53		
Erith	d		12 06		12 25			12 36		12 55			13 06		13 25			13 36		13 55		
Slade Green	d		12a09	12 22	12 31			12a39	12 52	13 01			13a09	13 22	13 31			13a39	13 52	14 01		
Dartford	d	12 09		12 28	12a36		12 39		12 58	13a06		13 09		13 28	13a36		13 39		13 58	14a06		
Stone Crossing	d	12 13		12 32			12 43		13 02			13 13		13 32			13 43		14 02			
Greenhithe	d	12 15		12 34			12 45		13 04			13 15		13 34			13 45		14 04			
Swanscombe	d	12 18		12 37			12 48		13 07			13 18		13 37			13 48		14 07			
Northfleet	d	12 20		12 39			12 50		13 09			13 20		13 39			13 50		14 09			
Gravesend	d	12a25		12 43		12 49	12a55		13 13		13 18	13a25		13 43		13 48	13a55		14 13		14 18	
Higham	d			12 49					13 19					13 49					14 19			
Strood	d			12 55		12 59			13 25		13 29			13 55		13 59			14 25		14 29	
Rochester	d			12 58		13 03			13 28		13 32			13 58		14 02			14 28		14 32	
Chatham	d			13 01		13 06			13 31		13 36			14 01		14 06			14 31		14 36	
Gillingham	d			13 06		13 11			13 36		13 40			14 06		14 10			14 36		14 40	
Rainham (Kent)	a			13 11		13 15			13 41		13 45			14 11		14 15			14 41		14 45	

NRT DECEMBER 19 EDITION

Table T201-F

Sundays
15 December to 10 May

London Thameslink - Greenwich - Woolwich - Medway

		SE	SE	TL	SE	SE ◇	SE	SE	TL	SE	SE ◇	SE	SE	TL	SE	SE ◇	SE	SE	TL	SE	SE ◇
Luton	d																				
Luton Airport Parkway	d																				
St Albans	d																				
West Hampstead Thameslink	d																				
St Pancras International	d			15 32		16 25			16 02		16 55			16 32		17 25			17 02		17 5
Farringdon	d			15 36					16 06					16 36					17 06		
City Thameslink	d																				
London Blackfriars	a			15 40					16 10					16 40					17 10		
London Charing Cross	d	15 22			15 42		15 52			16 12		16 22			16 42		16 52			17 12	
Waterloo East	a	15 24			15 44		15 54			16 14		16 24			16 44		16 54			17 14	
London Cannon Street	d		15 29					15 59					16 29					16 59			
London Bridge	d	15 31	15 33	15 48	15 51		16 01	16 03	16 18	16 21		16 31	16 33	16 48	16 51		17 01	17 03	17 18	17 21	
London Victoria	d																				
Deptford	d		15 39	15 55				16 09	16 25				16 39	16 55				17 09	17 25		
Greenwich	d		15 41	15 57				16 11	16 27				16 41	16 57				17 11	17 27		
Maze Hill	d		15 44	16 00				16 14	16 30				16 44	17 00				17 14	17 30		
Westcombe Park	d		15 46	16 02				16 16	16 32				16 46	17 02				17 16	17 32		
Charlton	d		15 49	16 05	16 08			16 19	16 35	16 38			16 49	17 05	17 08			17 19	17 35	17 38	
Woolwich Dockyard	d		15 52		16 11			16 22		16 41			16 52		17 11			17 22		17 41	
Woolwich Arsenal	d		15 55	16 10	16 14			16 25	16 40	16 44			16 55	17 10	17 14			17 25	17 40	17 44	
Plumstead	d		15 57	16 13	16 16			16 27	16 43	16 46			16 57	17 13	17 16			17 27	17 43	17 46	
Abbey Wood	d		16 00	16 16	16 20			16 30	16 46	16 50			17 00	17 16	17 20			17 30	17 46	17 50	
Belvedere	d		16 03		16 23			16 33		16 53			17 03		17 23			17 33		17 53	
Erith	d		16 06		16 25			16 36		16 55			17 06		17 25			17 36		17 55	
Slade Green	d		16a09	16 22	16 31			16a39	16 52	17 01			17a09	17 22	17 31			17a39	17 52	18 01	
Dartford	d	16 09		16 28	16a36		16 39		16 58	17a06		17 09		17 28	17a36		17 39		17 58	18a06	
Stone Crossing	d	16 13		16 32			16 43		17 02			17 13		17 32			17 43		18 02		
Greenhithe	d	16 15		16 34			16 45		17 04			17 15		17 34			17 45		18 04		
Swanscombe	d	16 18		16 37			16 48		17 07			17 18		17 37			17 48		18 07		
Northfleet	d	16 20		16 39			16 50		17 09			17 20		17 39			17 50		18 09		
Gravesend	d	16a25		16 43		16 48	16a55		17 13		17 18	17a25		17 43		17 48	17a55		18 13		18 1
Higham	d			16 49					17 19					17 49					18 19		
Strood	d			16 55		16 59			17 25		17 29			17 55		17 59			18 25		18 2
Rochester	d			16 58		17 02			17 28		17 32			17 58		18 02			18 28		18 3
Chatham	d			17 01		17 06			17 31		17 36			18 01		18 06			18 31		18 3
Gillingham	d			17 06		17 10			17 36		17 40			18 06		18 10			18 36		18 4
Rainham (Kent)	a			17 11		17 15			17 41		17 45			18 11		18 15			18 41		18 4

		SE	SE	TL	SE	SE ◇	SE	SE	TL	SE	SE ◇		SE	SE	TL	SE	SE ◇	SE	SE	TL	SE	SE ◇	SE
Luton	d																						
Luton Airport Parkway	d																						
St Albans	d																						
West Hampstead Thameslink	d																						
St Pancras International	d			17 32		18 25			18 02		18 55				20 32		21 25			21 02		21 5	
Farringdon	d			17 36					18 06						20 36					21 06			
City Thameslink	d																						
London Blackfriars	a			17 40					18 10						20 40					21 10			
London Charing Cross	d	17 22			17 42		17 52			18 12			20 22			20 42		20 52			21 12		21 22
Waterloo East	a	17 24			17 44		17 54			18 14			20 24			20 44		20 54			21 14		21 24
London Cannon Street	d		17 29					17 59						20 29					20 59				
London Bridge	d	17 31	17 33	17 48	17 51		18 01	18 03	18 18	18 21			20 31	20 33	20 48	20 51		21 01	21 03	21 18	21 21		21 31
London Victoria	d																						
Deptford	d		17 39	17 55				18 09	18 25			and at the same minutes past each hour until		20 39	20 55				21 09	21 25			
Greenwich	d		17 41	17 57				18 11	18 27					20 41	20 57				21 11	21 27			
Maze Hill	d		17 44	18 00				18 14	18 30					20 44	21 00				21 14	21 30			
Westcombe Park	d		17 46	18 02				18 16	18 32					20 46	21 02				21 16	21 32			
Charlton	d		17 49	18 05	18 08			18 19	18 35	18 38				20 49	21 05	21 08			21 19	21 35	21 38		
Woolwich Dockyard	d		17 52		18 11			18 22		18 41				20 52		21 11			21 22		21 41		
Woolwich Arsenal	d		17 55	18 10	18 14			18 25	18 40	18 44				20 55	21 10	21 14			21 25	21 40	21 44		
Plumstead	d		17 57	18 13	18 16			18 27	18 43	18 46				20 57	21 13	21 16			21 27	21 43	21 46		
Abbey Wood	d		18 00	18 16	18 20			18 30	18 46	18 50				21 00	21 16	21 20			21 30	21 46	21 50		
Belvedere	d		18 03		18 23			18 33		18 53				21 03		21 23			21 33		21 53		
Erith	d		18 06		18 25			18 36		18 55				21 06		21 25			21 36		21 55		
Slade Green	d		18a09	18 22	18 31			18a39	18 52	19 01				21a09	21 22	21 31			21a39	21 52	22 01		
Dartford	d	18 09		18 28	18a36		18 39		18 58	19a06			21 09		21 28	21a36		21 39		21 58	22a06		22 09
Stone Crossing	d	18 13		18 32			18 43		19 02				21 13		21 32			21 43		22 02			22 13
Greenhithe	d	18 15		18 34			18 45		19 04				21 15		21 34			21 45		22 04			22 15
Swanscombe	d	18 18		18 37			18 48		19 07				21 18		21 37			21 48		22 07			22 18
Northfleet	d	18 20		18 39			18 50		19 09				21 20		21 39			21 50		22 09			22 20
Gravesend	d	18a25		18 43		18 48	18a55		19 13		19 18		21a25		21 43		21 48	21a55		22 13		22 18	22a25
Higham	d			18 49					19 19						21 49					22 19			
Strood	d			18 55		18 59			19 25		19 29				21 55		21 59			22 25		22 29	
Rochester	d			18 58		19 02			19 28		19 32				21 58		22 02			22 28		22 32	
Chatham	d			19 01		19 06			19 31		19 36				22 01		22 06			22 31		22 36	
Gillingham	d			19 06		19 10			19 36		19 40				22 06		22 10			22 36		22 40	
Rainham (Kent)	a			19 11		19 15			19 41		19 45				22 11		22 15			22 41		22 45	

Table T201-F

Sundays
15 December to 10 May

London Thameslink - Greenwich - Woolwich - Medway

		SE	TL	SE	SE ◇	SE	SE	TL	SE		SE ◇	SE	SE	TL	SE	SE ◇	SE	SE	TL		SE	SE	SE	SE	SE
Luton	d																								
Luton Airport Parkway	d																								
St Albans	d							21 27						21 57					22 27						
West Hampstead Thameslink	d							21 50						22 20					22 50						
St Pancras International	d		21 32		22 25			22 02			22 55			22 32		23 25			23 02						
Farringdon	d		21 36					22 06						22 36					23 06						
City Thameslink	d																								
London Blackfriars	a		21 40					22 10						22 40					23 10						
London Charing Cross	d			21 42		21 52			22 12			22 22			22 42		22 52				23 12	23 22		23 42	
Waterloo East	a			21 44		21 54			22 14			22 24			22 44		22 54				23 14	23 24		23 44	
London Cannon Street	d	21 29					21 59						22 29					22 59					23 29		23 59
London Bridge	d	21 33	21 48	21 51		22 01	22 03	22 18	22 21			22 31	22 33	22 48	22 51		23 01	23 03	23 18		23 21	23 31	23 33	23 51	00 03
London Victoria	d																								
Deptford	d	21 39	21 55				22 09	22 25					22 39	22 55				23 09	23 25				23 39		00 09
Greenwich	d	21 41	21 57				22 11	22 27					22 41	22 57				23 11	23 27				23 41		00 11
Maze Hill	d	21 44	22 00				22 14	22 30					22 44	23 00				23 14	23 30				23 44		00 14
Westcombe Park	d	21 46	22 02				22 16	22 32					22 46	23 02				23 16	23 32				23 46		00 16
Charlton	d	21 49	22 05	22 08			22 19	22 35	22 38				22 49	23 05	23 08			23 19	23 35		23 38		23 49	00 08	00 19
Woolwich Dockyard	d	21 52		22 11			22 22		22 41				22 52		23 11			23 22			23 41		23 52	00 11	00 22
Woolwich Arsenal	d	21 55	22 10	22 14			22 25	22 40	22 44				22 55	23 10	23 14			23 25	23 40		23 44		23 55	00 14	00 25
Plumstead	d	21 57	22 13	22 16			22 27	22 43	22 46				22 57	23 13	23 16			23 27	23 43		23 46		23 57	00 16	00 27
Abbey Wood	d	22 00	22 16	22 20			22 30	22 46	22 50				23 00	23 16	23 20			23 30	23 46		23 50		23 59	00 20	00 30
Belvedere	d	22 03		22 23			22 33		22 53				23 03		23 23			23 33			23 53		00 03	00 23	00 33
Erith	d	22 06		22 25			22 36		22 55				23 06		23 25			23 36			23 55		00 06	00 25	00 36
Slade Green	d	22a09	22 22	22 31			22a39	22 52	23 01				23a09	23 22	23 31			23 40	23 52		00 01		00 10	00 31	00 40
Dartford	d		22 28	22a36		22 39		22 58	23a06			23 09		23 28	23a36		23 39	23a45	23 58		00a06	00 09	00a15	00a36	00a45
Stone Crossing	d		22 32			22 43		23 02				23 13		23 32			23 43		00 02			00 13			
Greenhithe	d		22 34			22 45		23 04				23 15		23 34			23 45		00 04			00 15			
Swanscombe	d		22 37			22 48		23 07				23 18		23 37			23 48		00 07			00 18			
Northfleet	d		22 39			22 50		23 09				23 20		23 39			23 50		00 09			00 20			
Gravesend	d		22 43		22 48	22a55		23 13			23 18	23a25		23 43		23 48	23a55		00 13			00a25			
Higham	d		22 49					23 19						23 49					00 19						
Strood	d		22 55		22 59			23 25			23 29			23 55		23 59			00 25						
Rochester	d		22 58		23 02			23 28			23 32			23 58		00 02			00 28						
Chatham	d		23 01		23 06			23 31			23 36			00 02		00 06			00 31						
Gillingham	d		23 06		23 10			23 36			23 40			00a06		00 10			00a36						
Rainham (Kent)	a		23 11		23 15			23 41			23 45					00 15									

Table T201-R

Mondays to Fridays
16 December to 15 May

Medway - Woolwich - Greenwich - London Thameslink

		SE ThFO	TL	SE	SE	SE		TL	SE	SE	SE	SE	SE	TL	SE	SE ◇		SE	SE	SE	SE	SE	TL	SE	SE ◇
Rainham (Kent)	d															05 15							05 30		05 45
Gillingham	d		04 00					04 36						05 06		05 20					05 26		05 36		05 50
Chatham	d		04 04					04 40						05 10		05 24					05 30		05 40		05 54
Rochester	d		04 08					04 44						05 14		05 28					05 34		05 44		05 58
Strood	d		04 11					04 47						05 17		05 31					05 38		05 47		06 01
Higham	d		04 16					04 52						05 22							05 43		05 52		
Gravesend	d		04 23	04 32		04 55		04 59				05 25		05 29		05 41			05 46		05 51		05 59		06 11
Northfleet	d		04 27			04 59		05 03				05 29		05 33					05 50				06 03		
Swanscombe	d		04 29			05 01		05 05				05 31		05 35					05 52				06 05		
Greenhithe	d		04 32	04 38		05 04		05 08				05 34		05 38					05 55		05 59		06 08		
Stone Crossing	d		04 34			05 06		05 10				05 36		05 40					05 57				06 10		
Dartford	d		04a39	04 45	05 03	05 12		05 15			05 33	05 42		05 45				06 01	06 03	←	06 06		06 15		
Slade Green	d				05 08			05 21	05 26		05 38			05 51	05 56			06 07		06 07		06 14	06 21		
Erith	d				05 11				05 29		05 41				05 59			→		06 10		06 17			
Belvedere	d				05 13				05 31		05 43				06 01					06 12		06 19			
Abbey Wood	d				05 17			05 28	05 35		05 47			05 58	06 05					06 16		06 23	06 28		
Plumstead	d				05 20			05 31	05 38		05 50			06 01	06 08					06 19		06 26	06 31		
Woolwich Arsenal	d				05 23			05 34	05 41		05 53			06 04	06 11					06 22		06 29	06 34		
Woolwich Dockyard	d				05 25						05 55				06 13					06 25		06 31			
Charlton	d	00 13			05 29			05 40	05 47		05 59			06 10	06 17					06 28		06 35	06 40		
Westcombe Park	d	00 20			05 31			05 42			06 01			06 12						06 31			06 42		
Maze Hill	d	00 25			05 33			05 44			06 03			06 14						06 33			06 44		
Greenwich	d	00 32			05 36			05 47		05 47	06 06		06 07	06 17						06 37			06 47		
Deptford	a	00 37			05 38			05 49			06 08			06 19						06 39			06 49		
London Victoria	d																				07a02			←	
London Bridge	d	00a51		05 26	05 46	05 53		05 58	06 06	07 05	06 16	06 19	07 30	06 28	06 35				06 41	06 48		06 54	06 58	07 05	
London Cannon Street	d				05a52					→	06a22		→							06a54				07a11	
Waterloo East	d			05 31		05 58			06 11			06 24			06 40				06 46			06 59			
London Charing Cross	a			05 37		06 03			06 16			06 30			06 46				06 52			07 05			
London Blackfriars	d							06 04						06 34									07 04		
City Thameslink	d							06 06						06 36									07 06		
Farringdon	d							06 09						06 39									07 09		
St Pancras International	d							06 13						06 43		06a05							07 13		06a35
West Hampstead Thameslink	d							06 22						06 52									07 22		
St Albans	d							06 49						07 17									07 47		
Luton Airport Parkway	d							07 02						07 32									08 02		
Luton	a							07 06						07 36									08 06		

		SE		SE	SE	SE	TL	SE	TL	SE	SE ◇	SE		SE	SE	SE	SE	SE	SE	TL	SE	SE		SE	SE
Rainham (Kent)	d						06 00				06 11									06 30					
Gillingham	d						06 06				06 17									06 36					
Chatham	d						06 10				06 21									06 40					
Rochester	d						06 14				06 25									06 44					
Strood	d						06 18	06 23			06 28							06 44		06 47					07 03
Higham	d						06 23	06 28										06 49		06 52					07 08
Gravesend	d			06 13			06 30	06 35			06 39					06 50		06 56		06 59					07 15
Northfleet	d						06 33									06 54				07 03					07 18
Swanscombe	d						06 35									06 56				07 05					07 20
Greenhithe	d			06 19			06 39	06 42								06 59		07 03		07 08					07 24
Stone Crossing	d			06 21			06 41	06 44								07 01		07 05		07 10					07 26
Dartford	d			06 27		06 38	06 46	06 49	←					06 55		07 07		07 11		07 15				07 28	07 31
Slade Green	d				06 38	06 43	06 51		06 51					07 00	07 06		07 10			07 21		07 25		07 33	
Erith	d				06 41	06 46	→							07 03			07 12					07 28		→	
Belvedere	d				06 43	06 48								07 05			07 15					07 30			
Abbey Wood	d			06 37	06 47	06 52			06 58					07 09			07 18	07 23		07 28		07 34			
Plumstead	d				06 50	06 55			07 01					07 12			07 21			07 31		07 37			
Woolwich Arsenal	d			06 41	06 53	06 58			07 04					07 15			07 24	07 28		07 34		07 40			
Woolwich Dockyard	d				06 56	07 01								07 17			07 27					07 43			
Charlton	d			06 47	06 59	07 04			07 10					07 21			07 30	07 33		07 40		07 46			
Westcombe Park	d			06 49		07 07			07 12					07 23				07 36		07 42		07 49			
Maze Hill	d			06 52		07 09			07 14					07 26				07 38		07 44		07 51			
Greenwich	d	06 47		06 56		07 13			07 17			07 17		07 30				07 42		07 47	07 48	07 55			
Deptford	a			06 58		07 15			07 19					07 32				07 44		07 49		07 57			
London Victoria	d									←									←						
London Bridge	d	08 13		07 07	07 18	07 23		07 27	07 28	07 30		08 39		07 40	07 45	07 47	07 53	07 52	07 53	07 58	09 10	08 05			08 07
London Cannon Street	d	→		07a13		07a29				07a35		→		07a46	07a51		→	07a58			→	08a11			
Waterloo East	d				07 23			07 32								07 52			07 58						08 12
London Charing Cross	a				07 29			07 38								07 58			08 04						08 18
London Blackfriars	d								07 34											08 04					
City Thameslink	d								07 36											08 06					
Farringdon	d								07 39											08 09					
St Pancras International	d								07 43		07a02									08 13					
West Hampstead Thameslink	d								07 52											08 22					
St Albans	d								08 17											08 47					
Luton Airport Parkway	d								08 30											09 01					
Luton	a								08 34											09 04					

Table T201-R

Mondays to Fridays
16 December to 15 May

Medway - Woolwich - Greenwich - London Thameslink

		SE	SE	SE ◇	SE	SE	TL	SE		TL	SE	SE ◇	SE	SE	SE	SE	SE	SE		SE	SE	SE ◇	TL	SE 1	SE ◇
Rainham (Kent)	d						06 56					07 17											07 30		
Gillingham	d						07 03					07 22											07 36		
Chatham	d						07 07					07 27											07 40		
Rochester	d						07 11					07 30											07 44		
Strood	d			07 09			07 17					07 34								07 38		07 43	07 47		07 56
Higham	d						07 22													07 43			07 52		
Gravesend	d			07 19			07 29	07 39				07 44								07 50		07 53	07 59		
Northfleet	d						07 32													07 55			08 03		
Swanscombe	d						07 34													07 57			08 05		
Greenhithe	d						07 38	07 45												08 01			08 08		
Stone Crossing	d						07 40													08 03			08 10		
Dartford	d		←				07 45	07 51		←								08 04		08 09	←		08 15		
Slade Green	d		07 33		07 36	07 37	07 50			07 50			07 54			07 59	08 03	08 09			08 09		08 21	08 26	
Erith	d		07 35		07 39		→						07 56			08 02		→			08 12			08 29	
Belvedere	d		07 38		07 41								07 59			08 04					08 14			08 31	
Abbey Wood	d		07 41		07 45					07 57			08 02			08 08					08 18		08 28	08 35	
Plumstead	d		07 44		07 48					08 01			08 05			08 11					08 21		08 31	08 38	
Woolwich Arsenal	d		07 47		07 51					08 04			08 08			08 14					08 24		08 34	08 41	
Woolwich Dockyard	d				07 54											08 16					08 26			08 44	
Charlton	d		07 53		07 57					08 10			08 13			08 20					08 30		08 40	08 47	
Westcombe Park	d				08 00					08 12						08 22					08 32		08 42		
Maze Hill	d				08 02					08 14						08 25					08 35		08 44		
Greenwich	d				08 06					08 17					08 17	08 28					08 38		08 47		
Deptford	a				08 08					08 19						08 30					08 40		08 49		
London Victoria	d	←									←			←											
London Bridge	d	08 13	08 13		08 17	08 30		08 27		08 28	08 30		08 33	08 39	09 40	08 39	08 47			08 47	08 49		08 58	09 06	
London Cannon Street	d	08a19			08a21	→					08a36				→	08a45	08a53				08a55				
Waterloo East	d		08 18					08 32					08 38	08 44						08 52				09 12	
London Charing Cross	a		08 24					08 38					08 43	08 50						08 58				09 18	
London Blackfriars	d									08 34													09 04		
City Thameslink	d									08 36													09 06		
Farringdon	d									08 39													09 09		
St Pancras International	d			07a41						08 43		08a08										08a16	09 13		10a55
West Hampstead Thameslink	d									08a52													09a22		
St Albans	d																								
Luton Airport Parkway	d																								
Luton	a																								

		SE	SE ◇	SE ◇		SE	SE	SE	SE	SE	TL	SE	SE ◇	SE		SE	SE	SE	SE	SE	SE	TL	SE ◇	SE	
Rainham (Kent)	d		07 47								08 01		08 14									08 30			
Gillingham	d		07 52								08 07		08 19									08 36			
Chatham	d		07 56								08 11		08 24									08 40			
Rochester	d		08 00								08 15		08 27									08 44			
Strood	d		08 03	08 11							08 18		08 32									08 47	08 59		
Higham	d										08 23											08 52			
Gravesend	d	08 11	08 14	08 21							08 30	08 34	08 43	08 50								08 59		09 05	
Northfleet	d	08 15									08 34	08 38										09 03		09 08	
Swanscombe	d	08 17									08 36	08 40										09 05		09 10	
Greenhithe	d	08 20									08 39	08 43		08 56								09 08		09 14	
Stone Crossing	d	08 22									08 41	08 45										09 10		09 16	
Dartford	d	08 28							08 32		08 46	08 50		09 02							09 11	09 15		09 21	
Slade Green	d						08 30		08 39	08 45	08 51						08 59		09 07	09 09	09 16	09 21			
Erith	d						08 32		08 42	08 48							09 02			09 12	09 18	→			
Belvedere	d						08 35		08 44	08 50							09 04			09 14	→				
Abbey Wood	d						08 38		08 48	08 54	08 58						09 08			09 18					
Plumstead	d						08 41		08 51	08 57	09 01						09 11			09 21					
Woolwich Arsenal	d						08 44		08 54	09 00	09 04						09 14			09 24					
Woolwich Dockyard	d						08 47		08 57	09 02							09 16			09 26					
Charlton	d						08 50		09 00	09 06	09 10						09 20			09 30					
Westcombe Park	d						08 52		09 03		09 12						09 22			09 32					
Maze Hill	d						08 54		09 05		09 14						09 24			09 34					
Greenwich	d					08 47	08 58		09 09		09 17					09 17	09 28			09 37					
Deptford	a						09 00		09 11		09 19						09 30			09 39					
London Victoria	d							←						09a57				←							
London Bridge	d	09 08				10 09	09 08	09 10	09 20	09 25	09 28	09 29				10 39	09 38	09 40	09 54	09 47				09 53	
London Cannon Street	d					→	09a14	09a16	09a26							→	09a44	09a46	→	09a55					
Waterloo East	d	09 14								09 30		09 34												09 58	
London Charing Cross	a	09 20								09 37		09 40												10 03	
London Blackfriars	d										09 34														
City Thameslink	d										09 36														
Farringdon	d										09 39														
St Pancras International	d		08a38	08a46							09 43		09a07										11a54		
West Hampstead Thameslink	d										09 52														
St Albans	d										10 20														
Luton Airport Parkway	d										10 32														
Luton	a										10 36														

Table T201-R

Mondays to Fridays
16 December to 15 May

Medway - Woolwich - Greenwich - London Thameslink

		SE	SE	TL	SE ◇	SE	SE	SE	SE	SE		SE	SE	TL	SE	SE	SE	TL	SE ◇	SE		SE	SE	SE	SE
Rainham (Kent)	d				08 46									09 00					09 16						
Gillingham	d				08 51									09 06					09 21						
Chatham	d				08 55									09 10					09 25						
Rochester	d				08 59									09 14					09 29						
Strood	d				09 02									09 17					09 32						
Higham	d													09 22											
Gravesend	d				09 12	09 20								09 29	09 35				09 42	09 50					
Northfleet	d													09 33	09 38										
Swanscombe	d													09 35	09 40										
Greenhithe	d					09 26								09 38	09 44					09 56					
Stone Crossing	d													09 40	09 46										
Dartford	d			←		09 32							09 41	09 45	09 51			←		10 02					
Slade Green	d		←	09 21				09 29		09 37		09 39	09 46	09 51			←	09 51					09 59		10 07
Erith	d		09 18					09 32				09 42	09 48	→			09 48						10 02		
Belvedere	d		09 21					09 34				09 44	→				09 51						10 04		
Abbey Wood	d		09 24	09 28				09 38				09 48					09 54	09 58					10 08		
Plumstead	d		09 27	09 31				09 41				09 51					09 57	10 01					10 11		
Woolwich Arsenal	d		09 30	09 34				09 44				09 54					10 00	10 04					10 14		
Woolwich Dockyard	d		09 33					09 46				09 56					10 03						10 16		
Charlton	d		09 36	09 40				09 50				10 00					10 06	10 10					10 20		
Westcombe Park	d			09 42				09 52				10 02						10 12					10 22		
Maze Hill	d			09 44				09 54				10 04						10 14					10 24		
Greenwich	d			09 47			09 47	09 57				10 07						10 17				10 17	10 27		
Deptford	a			09 49				09 59				10 09						10 19					10 29		
London Victoria	d	←				10a25			←							←				10a55				←	
London Bridge	d	09 54	09 57	09 58			11 09	10 07	10 09	10 24		10 17			10 22	10 24	10 27	10 28				11 39	10 37	10 39	10 54
London Cannon Street	d	10a02					→	10a13	10a15	→		10a21				10a30						→	10a41	10a43	→
Waterloo East	d		10 02												10 27		10 32								
London Charing Cross	a		10 05												10 30		10 35								
London Blackfriars	d			10 04														10 34							
City Thameslink	d			10 06														10 36							
Farringdon	d			10 09														10 39							
St Pancras International	d			10 13	09a36													10 43	10a10						
West Hampstead Thameslink	d			10 22														10 52							
St Albans	d			10 45														11 15							
Luton Airport Parkway	d			10 57														11 27							
Luton	a			11 01														11 31							

		SE	SE	TL	SE ◇	SE		SE	SE	TL	SE ◇	SE	SE	SE	SE	SE		SE	SE	TL	SE	SE	SE	TL	SE ◇
Rainham (Kent)	d			09 28							09 46									09 58					10 16
Gillingham	d			09 34							09 51									10 04					10 21
Chatham	d			09 38							09 55									10 08					10 25
Rochester	d			09 42							09 59									10 12					10 29
Strood	d			09 45	09 59						10 02									10 15					10 32
Higham	d			09 50																10 20					
Gravesend	d			09 59		10 05					10 12	10 20								10 29	10 35				10 42
Northfleet	d			10 02		10 08														10 32	10 33				
Swanscombe	d			10 04		10 10														10 34	10 40				
Greenhithe	d			10 08		10 14						10 26								10 38	10 44				
Stone Crossing	d			10 10		10 16														10 40	10 46				
Dartford	d		10 11	10 15		10 21				←		10 32							10 41	10 45	10 51			←	
Slade Green	d	10 09	10 16	10 21					←	10 21				10 29		10 37		10 39	10 46	10 51			←	10 51	
Erith	d	10 12	10 18	→					10 18					10 32				10 42	10 48	→			10 48		
Belvedere	d	10 14	→						10 21					10 34				10 44	→				10 51		
Abbey Wood	d	10 18							10 24	10 28				10 38				10 48					10 54	10 58	
Plumstead	d	10 21							10 27	10 31				10 41				10 51					10 57	11 01	
Woolwich Arsenal	d	10 24							10 30	10 34				10 44				10 54					11 00	11 04	
Woolwich Dockyard	d	10 26							10 33					10 46				10 56					11 03		
Charlton	d	10 30							10 36	10 40				10 50				11 00					11 06	11 10	
Westcombe Park	d	10 32								10 42				10 52				11 02						11 12	
Maze Hill	d	10 34								10 44				10 54				11 04						11 14	
Greenwich	d	10 37								10 47			10 47	10 57				11 07						11 17	
Deptford	a	10 39								10 49				10 59				11 09						11 19	
London Victoria	d							←				11a25			←							←			
London Bridge	d	10 47				10 52		10 54	10 57	10 58			12 09	11 07	11 09	11 24		11 17			11 22	11 24	11 27	11 28	
London Cannon Street	d	10a51						11a00					→	11a11	11a13	→		11a21				11a30			
Waterloo East	d					10 57			11 02												11 27		11 32		
London Charing Cross	a					11 00			11 05												11 30		11 35		
London Blackfriars	d									11 04														11 34	
City Thameslink	d									11 06														11 36	
Farringdon	d									11 09														11 39	
St Pancras International	d				12a55					11 13	10a41													11 43	11a06
West Hampstead Thameslink	d									11 22														11 52	
St Albans	d									11 45														12 15	
Luton Airport Parkway	d									11 57														12 27	
Luton	a									12 01														12 31	

Table T201-R

Mondays to Fridays

16 December to 15 May

Medway - Woolwich - Greenwich - London Thameslink

		SE		SE	SE	SE	SE	SE	SE	TL	SE ◇	SE		SE	SE	TL	SE ◇	SE	SE	SE	SE	SE		SE	SE
Rainham (Kent)	d									10 28							10 46								
Gillingham	d									10 34							10 51								
Chatham	d									10 38							10 55								
Rochester	d									10 42							10 59								
Strood	d									10 45	10 59						11 02								
Higham	d									10 50															
Gravesend	d	10 50								10 59		11 05					11 12	11 20							
Northfleet	d									11 02		11 08													
Swanscombe	d									11 04		11 10													
Greenhithe	d	10 56								11 08		11 14						11 26							
Stone Crossing	d									11 10		11 16													
Dartford	d	11 02							11 11	11 15		11 21				←		11 32							11 41
Slade Green	d				10 59		11 07	11 09	11 16	11 21					←	11 21				11 29		11 37		11 39	11 46
Erith	d				11 02			11 12	11 18	→					11 18					11 32				11 42	11 48
Belvedere	d				11 04			11 14	→						11 21					11 34				11 44	→
Abbey Wood	d				11 08			11 18							11 24	11 28				11 38				11 48	
Plumstead	d				11 11			11 21							11 27	11 31				11 41				11 51	
Woolwich Arsenal	d				11 14			11 24							11 30	11 34				11 44				11 54	
Woolwich Dockyard	d				11 16			11 26							11 33					11 46				11 56	
Charlton	d				11 20			11 30							11 36	11 40				11 50				12 00	
Westcombe Park	d				11 22			11 32								11 42				11 52				12 02	
Maze Hill	d				11 24			11 34								11 44				11 54				12 04	
Greenwich	d			11 17	11 27			11 37								11 47			11 47	11 57				12 07	
Deptford	a				11 29			11 39								11 49				11 59				12 09	
London Victoria	d	11a55				←								←				12a25			←				
London Bridge	d			12 39	11 37	11 39	11 54	11 47				11 52		11 54	11 57	11 58			13 09	12 07	12 09	12 24		12 17	
London Cannon Street	d			→	11a41	11a43	→	11a51						12a00					→	12a11	12a13	→		12a21	
Waterloo East	d											11 57			12 02										
London Charing Cross	a											12 00			12 05										
London Blackfriars	d															12 04									
City Thameslink	d															12 06									
Farringdon	d															12 09									
St Pancras International	d										13a54					12 13	11a40								
West Hampstead Thameslink	d															12 22									
St Albans	d															12 45									
Luton Airport Parkway	d															12 57									
Luton	a															13 01									

		TL	SE	SE	SE	TL	SE ◇	SE		SE	SE	SE	SE	SE	SE	TL	SE ◇	SE		SE	SE	TL	SE ◇	SE	SE
Rainham (Kent)	d	10 58					11 16									11 28							11 46		
Gillingham	d	11 04					11 21									11 34							11 51		
Chatham	d	11 08					11 25									11 38							11 55		
Rochester	d	11 12					11 29									11 42							11 59		
Strood	d	11 15					11 32									11 45	11 59						12 02		
Higham	d	11 20														11 50									
Gravesend	d	11 29	11 35				11 42	11 50								11 59		12 05					12 12	12 20	
Northfleet	d	11 32	11 38													12 02		12 08							
Swanscombe	d	11 34	11 40													12 04		12 10							
Greenhithe	d	11 38	11 44					11 56								12 08		12 14						12 26	
Stone Crossing	d	11 40	11 46													12 10		12 16							
Dartford	d	11 45	11 51			←		12 02							12 11	12 15		12 21				←		12 32	
Slade Green	d	11 51			←	11 51					11 59		12 07	12 09	12 16	12 21					←	12 21			
Erith	d	→			11 48						12 02			12 12	12 18	→					12 18				
Belvedere	d				11 51						12 04			12 14	→						12 21				
Abbey Wood	d				11 54	11 58					12 08			12 18							12 24	12 28			
Plumstead	d				11 57	12 01					12 11			12 21							12 27	12 31			
Woolwich Arsenal	d				12 00	12 04					12 14			12 24							12 30	12 34			
Woolwich Dockyard	d				12 03						12 16			12 26							12 33				
Charlton	d				12 06	12 10					12 20			12 30							12 36	12 40			
Westcombe Park	d					12 12					12 22			12 32								12 42			
Maze Hill	d					12 14					12 24			12 34								12 44			
Greenwich	d					12 17				12 17	12 27			12 37								12 47			12 47
Deptford	a					12 19					12 29			12 39								12 49			
London Victoria	d			←				12a55				←								←				13a25	
London Bridge	d		12 22	12 24	12 27	12 28				13 39	12 37	12 39	12 54	12 47				12 52		12 54	12 57	12 58			14 09
London Cannon Street	d			12a30						→	12a41	12a43	→	12a51						13a00					→
Waterloo East	d		12 27		12 32													12 57			13 02				
London Charing Cross	a		12 30		12 35													13 00			13 05				
London Blackfriars	d					12 34																13 04			
City Thameslink	d					12 36																13 06			
Farringdon	d					12 39																13 09			
St Pancras International	d					12 43	12a06										14a54					13 13	12a36		
West Hampstead Thameslink	d					12 52																13 22			
St Albans	d					13 15																13 45			
Luton Airport Parkway	d					13 27																13 57			
Luton	a					13 31																14 01			

Table T201-R

Mondays to Fridays

16 December to 15 May

Medway - Woolwich - Greenwich - London Thameslink

		SE	SE	SE		SE	SE	TL	SE	SE	SE	TL	SE ◇	SE		SE	SE	SE	SE	SE	SE	TL	SE ◇	SE	
Rainham (Kent)	d							11 58					12 16									12 28			
Gillingham	d							12 04					12 21									12 34			
Chatham	d							12 08					12 25									12 38			
Rochester	d							12 12					12 29									12 42			
Strood	d							12 15					12 32									12 45	12 59		
Higham	d							12 20														12 50			
Gravesend	d							12 29	12 35				12 42	12 50								12 59		13 05	
Northfleet	d							12 32	12 38													13 02		13 08	
Swanscombe	d							12 34	12 40													13 04		13 10	
Greenhithe	d							12 38	12 44					12 56								13 08		13 14	
Stone Crossing	d							12 40	12 46													13 10		13 16	
Dartford	d						12 41	12 45	12 51			←		13 02							13 11	13 15		13 21	
Slade Green	d	12 29		12 37		12 39	12 46	12 51			←	12 51					12 59		13 07	13 09	13 16	13 21			
Erith	d	12 32				12 42	12 48	→			12 48						13 02			13 12	13 18	→			
Belvedere	d	12 34				12 44	→				12 51						13 04			13 14	→				
Abbey Wood	d	12 38				12 48					12 54	12 58					13 08			13 18					
Plumstead	d	12 41				12 51					12 57	13 01					13 11			13 21					
Woolwich Arsenal	d	12 44				12 54					13 00	13 04					13 14			13 24					
Woolwich Dockyard	d	12 46				12 56					13 03						13 16			13 26					
Charlton	d	12 50				13 00					13 06	13 10					13 20			13 30					
Westcombe Park	d	12 52				13 02						13 12					13 22			13 32					
Maze Hill	d	12 54				13 04						13 14					13 24			13 34					
Greenwich	d	12 57				13 07						13 17				13 17	13 27			13 37					
Deptford	a	12 59				13 09						13 19					13 29			13 39					
London Victoria	d		←							←				13a55				←							
London Bridge	d	13 07	13 09	13 24		13 17			13 22	13 24	13 27	13 28				14 39	13 37	13 39	13 54	13 47				13 52	
London Cannon Street	d	13a11	13a13	→		13a21				13a30						→	13a41	13a43	→	13a51					
Waterloo East	d								13 27		13 32													13 57	
London Charing Cross	a								13 30		13 35													14 00	
London Blackfriars	d											13 34													
City Thameslink	d											13 36													
Farringdon	d											13 39													
St Pancras International	d											13 43	13a06										15a58		
West Hampstead Thameslink	d											13 52													
St Albans	d											14 15													
Luton Airport Parkway	d											14 27													
Luton	a											14 31													

		SE	SE	TL	SE ◇	SE	SE	SE	SE	SE		SE	SE	TL	SE	SE	SE	TL	SE ◇	SE		SE	SE	SE	SE
Rainham (Kent)	d				12 46									12 58					13 16						
Gillingham	d				12 51									13 04					13 21						
Chatham	d				12 55									13 08					13 25						
Rochester	d				12 59									13 12					13 29						
Strood	d				13 02									13 15					13 32						
Higham	d													13 20											
Gravesend	d				13 12	13 20								13 29	13 35				13 42	13 50					
Northfleet	d													13 32	13 38										
Swanscombe	d													13 34	13 40										
Greenhithe	d					13 26								13 38	13 44					13 56					
Stone Crossing	d													13 40	13 46										
Dartford	d			←		13 32							13 41	13 45	13 51			←		14 02					
Slade Green	d		←	13 21				13 29		13 37		13 39	13 46	13 51			←	13 51					13 59		14 07
Erith	d		13 18					13 32				13 42	13 48	→			13 48						14 02		
Belvedere	d		13 21					13 34				13 44	→				13 51						14 04		
Abbey Wood	d		13 24	13 28				13 38				13 48					13 54	13 58					14 08		
Plumstead	d		13 27	13 31				13 41				13 51					13 57	14 01					14 11		
Woolwich Arsenal	d		13 30	13 34				13 44				13 54					14 00	14 04					14 14		
Woolwich Dockyard	d		13 33					13 46				13 56					14 03						14 16		
Charlton	d		13 36	13 40				13 50				14 00					14 06	14 10					14 20		
Westcombe Park	d			13 42				13 52				14 02						14 12					14 22		
Maze Hill	d			13 44				13 54				14 04						14 14					14 24		
Greenwich	d			13 47			13 47	13 57				14 07						14 17				14 17	14 27		
Deptford	a			13 49				13 59				14 09						14 19					14 29		
London Victoria	d	←				14a25			←							←				14a55				←	
London Bridge	d	13 54	13 57	13 58			15 09	14 07	14 09	14 24		14 17			14 22	14 24	14 27	14 28				15 39	14 37	14 39	14 54
London Cannon Street	d	14a00					→	14a11	14a13	→		14a21				14a30						→	14a41	14a43	→
Waterloo East	d		14 02												14 27		14 32								
London Charing Cross	a		14 05												14 30		14 35								
London Blackfriars	d			14 04														14 34							
City Thameslink	d			14 06														14 36							
Farringdon	d			14 09														14 39							
St Pancras International	d			14 13	13a37													14 43	14a10						
West Hampstead Thameslink	d			14 22														14 52							
St Albans	d			14 45														15 15							
Luton Airport Parkway	d			14 57														15 27							
Luton	a			15 01														15 31							

Table T201-R

Mondays to Fridays

16 December to 15 May

Medway - Woolwich - Greenwich - London Thameslink

		SE	SE	TL	SE	SE		SE	SE	TL	SE	SE	SE	SE	SE	SE		SE	SE	TL	SE	SE	SE	TL	SE
					◇						◇														◇
Rainham (Kent)	d			13 28							13 46									13 58					14 16
Gillingham	d			13 34							13 51									14 04					14 21
Chatham	d			13 38							13 55									14 08					14 25
Rochester	d			13 42							13 59									14 12					14 29
Strood	d			13 45	13 59						14 02									14 15					14 32
Higham	d			13 50																14 20					
Gravesend	d			13 59		14 05					14 12	14 20								14 29	14 35				14 42
Northfleet	d			14 02		14 08														14 32	14 38				
Swanscombe	d			14 04		14 10														14 34	14 40				
Greenhithe	d			14 08		14 14						14 26								14 38	14 44				
Stone Crossing	d			14 10		14 16														14 40	14 46				
Dartford	d		14 11	14 15		14 21				←		14 32							14 41	14 45	14 51			←	
Slade Green	d	14 09	14 16	14 21					←	14 21				14 29		14 37		14 39	14 46	14 51			←	14 51	
Erith	d	14 12	14 18	→					14 18					14 32				14 42	14 48	→			14 48		
Belvedere	d	14 14	→						14 21					14 34				14 44	→				14 51		
Abbey Wood	d	14 18							14 24	14 28				14 38				14 48					14 54	14 58	
Plumstead	d	14 21							14 27	14 31				14 41				14 51					14 57	15 01	
Woolwich Arsenal	d	14 24							14 30	14 34				14 44				14 54					15 00	15 04	
Woolwich Dockyard	d	14 26							14 33					14 46				14 56					15 03		
Charlton	d	14 30							14 36	14 40				14 50				15 00					15 06	15 10	
Westcombe Park	d	14 32								14 42				14 52				15 02						15 12	
Maze Hill	d	14 34								14 44				14 54				15 04						15 14	
Greenwich	d	14 37								14 47			14 47	14 57				15 07						15 17	
Deptford	a	14 39								14 49				14 59				15 09						15 19	
London Victoria	d							←				15a25			←							←			
London Bridge	d	14 47				14 52		14 54	14 57	14 58			16 09	15 07	15 09	15 24		15 17			15 22	15 24	15 27	15 28	
London Cannon Street	d	14a51						15a00					→	15a11	15a13	→		15a21				15a30			
Waterloo East	d					14 57			15 02												15 27		15 32		
London Charing Cross	a					15 00			15 05												15 30		15 35		
London Blackfriars	d									15 04														15 34	
City Thameslink	d									15 06														15 36	
Farringdon	d									15 09														15 39	
St Pancras International	d				16a54					15 13	14a36													15 43	15a06
West Hampstead Thameslink	d									15 22														15 52	
St Albans	d									15 45														16 19	
Luton Airport Parkway	d									15 57														16 32	
Luton	a									16 01														16 36	

		SE		SE	SE	SE	SE	SE	SE	TL	SE	SE		SE	SE	TL	SE	SE	SE	SE	SE	SE		SE	SE
											◇						◇								
Rainham (Kent)	d									14 28							14 46								
Gillingham	d									14 34							14 51								
Chatham	d									14 38							14 55								
Rochester	d									14 42							14 59								
Strood	d									14 45	14 59						15 02								
Higham	d									14 50															
Gravesend	d	14 50								14 59		15 05					15 12	15 20							
Northfleet	d									15 02		15 08													
Swanscombe	d									15 04		15 10													
Greenhithe	d	14 56								15 08		15 14						15 26							
Stone Crossing	d									15 10		15 16													
Dartford	d	15 02							15 11	15 15		15 21				←		15 32							15 41
Slade Green	d				14 59		15 07	15 09	15 16	15 21					←	15 21				15 29		15 37		15 39	15 46
Erith	d				15 02			15 12	15 18	→					15 18					15 32				15 42	15 48
Belvedere	d				15 04			15 14	→						15 21					15 34				15 44	→
Abbey Wood	d				15 08			15 18							15 24	15 28				15 38				15 48	
Plumstead	d				15 11			15 21							15 27	15 31				15 41				15 51	
Woolwich Arsenal	d				15 14			15 24							15 30	15 34				15 44				15 54	
Woolwich Dockyard	d				15 16			15 26							15 33					15 46				15 56	
Charlton	d				15 20			15 30							15 36	15 40				15 50				16 00	
Westcombe Park	d				15 22			15 32								15 42				15 52				16 02	
Maze Hill	d				15 24			15 34								15 44				15 54				16 04	
Greenwich	d			15 17	15 27			15 37								15 47			15 47	15 57				16 07	
Deptford	a				15 29			15 39								15 49				15 59				16 09	
London Victoria	d	15a55				←								←				16a25			←				
London Bridge	d			16 38	15 37	15 39	15 54	15 47				15 52		15 54	15 57	15 58			17 11	16 06	16 09	16 23		16 17	
London Cannon Street	d			→	15a41	15a43	→	15a51						16a00					→	16a12	16a15	→		16a23	
Waterloo East	d											15 57			16 02										
London Charing Cross	a											16 00			16 05										
London Blackfriars	d															16 04									
City Thameslink	d															16 06									
Farringdon	d															16 09									
St Pancras International	d										17a54					16 13	15a36								
West Hampstead Thameslink	d															16 22									
St Albans	d															16 47									
Luton Airport Parkway	d															17 01									
Luton	a															17 05									

NRT DECEMBER 19 EDITION

Table T201-R

Mondays to Fridays

16 December to 15 May

Medway - Woolwich - Greenwich - London Thameslink

		TL	SE	SE	SE	TL	SE	SE		SE	SE	SE	SE	SE	SE	TL	SE	SE		SE	TL	SE	SE	SE	SE
							◇										◇					◇			
Rainham (Kent)	d	14 58					15 16									15 28						15 46			
Gillingham	d	15 04					15 21									15 34						15 51			
Chatham	d	15 08					15 25									15 38						15 55			
Rochester	d	15 12					15 29									15 42						15 59			
Strood	d	15 15					15 32									15 45	15 59					16 02			
Higham	d	15 20														15 50									
Gravesend	d	15 29	15 35				15 42	15 50								15 59		16 03				16 12	16 20		
Northfleet	d	15 32	15 38													16 02		16 06							
Swanscombe	d	15 34	15 40													16 04		16 08							
Greenhithe	d	15 38	15 44					15 56								16 08		16 12					16 26		
Stone Crossing	d	15 40	15 46													16 10		16 14							
Dartford	d	15 45	15 51			←		16 02							16 11	16 15		16 19			←		16 32		
Slade Green	d	15 51			←	15 51				15 57		16 07	16 09		16 16	16 21				←	16 21			16 30	
Erith	d	→			15 48					16 00			16 12		16 18	→				16 18				16 32	
Belvedere	d				15 51					16 02			16 14		→					16 21				16 35	
Abbey Wood	d				15 54	15 58				16 06			16 18							16 24	16 28			16 38	
Plumstead	d				15 57	16 01				16 09			16 21							16 27	16 31			16 41	
Woolwich Arsenal	d				16 00	16 04				16 12			16 24							16 30	16 34			16 44	
Woolwich Dockyard	d				16 03					16 14			16 26							16 33				16 47	
Charlton	d				16 06	16 10				16 18			16 30							16 36	16 40			16 50	
Westcombe Park	d					16 12				16 20			16 32								16 42			16 52	
Maze Hill	d					16 14				16 22			16 34								16 44			16 54	
Greenwich	d					16 17				16 25			16 37								16 47			16 58	
Deptford	a					16 19				16 27			16 39								16 49			17 00	
London Victoria	d			←				16a55			←			←									17a25		←
London Bridge	d		16 21	16 23	16 27	16 28				16 34	16 38	16 50	16 47	16 50				16 51		16 57	16 58			17 08	17 11
London Cannon Street	d			16a29						16a40	16a44	→	16a53	16a56										17a14	17a17
Waterloo East	d		16 27		16 32													16 56		17 02					
London Charing Cross	a		16 30		16 36													17 01		17 06					
London Blackfriars	d					16 34															17 04				
City Thameslink	d					16 36															17 06				
Farringdon	d					16 39															17 09				
St Pancras International	d					16 43	16a10										18a54				17 13	16a36			
West Hampstead Thameslink	d					16 52															17 22				
St Albans	d					17 17															17 47				
Luton Airport Parkway	d					17 32															18 01				
Luton	a					17 36															18 05				

		SE	SE	SE		SE	TL	SE	SE	TL	SE	SE	SE	SE		SE	SE	SE	SE	TL	SE	SE	TL	SE	
											◇													◇	
Rainham (Kent)	d						16 00				16 16									16 30				16 46	
Gillingham	d						16 06				16 21									16 36				16 51	
Chatham	d						16 10				16 25									16 40				16 55	
Rochester	d						16 14				16 29									16 44				16 59	
Strood	d						16 17				16 32									16 47				17 02	
Higham	d						16 22													16 52					
Gravesend	d						16 29	16 35			16 42	16 50								16 59	17 05			17 12	
Northfleet	d						16 33	16 38												17 03	17 08				
Swanscombe	d						16 35	16 40												17 05	17 10				
Greenhithe	d						16 38	16 44				16 56								17 08	17 14				
Stone Crossing	d						16 40	16 46												17 10	17 16				
Dartford	d			16 41			16 45	16 51		←		17 02						17 11		17 15	17 21		←		
Slade Green	d	16 37	16 39	16 46		16 47	16 51		←	16 51				16 58		17 02	17 10	17 16	17 19	17 21			17 21		
Erith	d		16 42	16 48			→		16 48					17 00		17 04		17 18		→					
Belvedere	d		16 44	→					16 51					17 03		17 07		17 21							
Abbey Wood	d		16 48						16 54	16 58				17 06		17 10		17 24					17 28		
Plumstead	d		16 51						16 57	17 01				17 09		17 13		17 27					17 31		
Woolwich Arsenal	d		16 54						17 00	17 04				17 12		17 16		17 30					17 34		
Woolwich Dockyard	d		16 56						17 03					17 15		17 19		17 33							
Charlton	d		17 00						17 06	17 10				17 18		17 22		17 36					17 40		
Westcombe Park	d		17 02							17 12				17 20		17 24							17 42		
Maze Hill	d		17 04							17 14				17 22		17 26							17 44		
Greenwich	d		17 08							17 17			17 19	17 26		17 30							17 47		
Deptford	a		17 10							17 19				17 28		17 32							17 49		
London Victoria	d											17a55										←			
London Bridge	d	17 21						17 22	17 25	17 28			18 44	17 34		17 40	17 48	17 54	18 07		17 52	17 54	17 58		
London Cannon Street	d	17a27	17a25			17a48							→	17a41		17a46	17a54	→	→						
Waterloo East	d							17 29	17 32												17 57	17 59			
London Charing Cross	a							17 34	17 39												18 03	18 05			
London Blackfriars	d									17 34													18 04		
City Thameslink	d									17 36													18 06		
Farringdon	d									17 39													18 09		
St Pancras International	d									17 43	17a10												18 13	17a36	
West Hampstead Thameslink	d									17 52													18 22		
St Albans	d									18 20													18 47		
Luton Airport Parkway	d									18 31													19 01		
Luton	a									18 35													19 05		

Table T201-R

Mondays to Fridays

16 December to 15 May

Medway - Woolwich - Greenwich - London Thameslink

		SE	SE	SE	SE	SE	SE	SE	TL	SE		SE	TL	SE ◇	SE	SE	SE	SE	SE	SE		SE	TL	SE	SE
Rainham (Kent)	d								17 00					17 16									17 28		
Gillingham	d								17 06					17 21									17 34		
Chatham	d								17 10					17 25									17 38		
Rochester	d								17 14					17 29									17 42		
Strood	d								17 17					17 32									17 47		
Higham	d								17 22														17 52		
Gravesend	d	17 18							17 29	17 35				17 42									17 59	18 05	
Northfleet	d								17 33	17 38													18 03	18 08	
Swanscombe	d								17 35	17 40													18 05	18 10	
Greenhithe	d	17 24							17 38	17 44													18 08	18 14	
Stone Crossing	d								17 40	17 46													18 10	18 16	
Dartford	d	17 30						17 39	17 45	17 51			←							18 02			18 15	18 21	
Slade Green	d		17 29		17 34	17 40		17 46	17 51			←	17 51			17 54	18 00		18 00	18 09		18 16	18 21		
Erith	d		17 32			17 43		17 48	→			17 48				17 57	18 03			18 11		18 18	→		
Belvedere	d		17 34			17 45		→				17 51				17 59	18 05			18 14		18 21			
Abbey Wood	d		17 38			17 49						17 54	17 58			18 03	18 09			18 17		18 24			
Plumstead	d					17 52						17 57	18 01			18 06	18 12			18 20		18 27			
Woolwich Arsenal	d		17 42			17 55						18 00	18 04			18 09	18 15			18 23		18 30			
Woolwich Dockyard	d					17 57						18 03				18 11	18 17			18 26		18 33			
Charlton	d		17 48			18 01						18 06	18 10			18 15	18 21			18 29		18 36			
Westcombe Park	d		17 50			18 03							18 12			18 17	18 23			18 31					
Maze Hill	d		17 52			18 05							18 14			18 19	18 25			18 33					
Greenwich	d		17 55			18 08							18 17		18 18	18 22	18 28			18 37					
Deptford	a		17 57			18 10							18 19			18 24	18 30			18 39					
London Victoria	d	18a25		←			←											←							←
London Bridge	d		18 04	18 07	18 23	18 18	18 23			18 24		18 28	18 28		19 40	18 31	18 38	18 44	18 55	18 49		19 00		18 53	18 55
London Cannon Street	d		18a10	18a13	→	18a24	18a27								→	18a37	18a44	18a50	→	18a54		→			19a01
Waterloo East	d									18 29		18 33												18 58	
London Charing Cross	a									18 34		18 38												19 02	
London Blackfriars	d												18 34												
City Thameslink	d												18 36												
Farringdon	d												18 39												
St Pancras International	d												18 43	18a10											
West Hampstead Thameslink	d												18 52												
St Albans	d												19 17												
Luton Airport Parkway	d												19 32												
Luton	a												19 36												

		TL	SE	SE ◇	SE	SE		SE	SE	SE	SE	SE	SE	TL	SE	SE		SE	TL	SE ◇	SE	SE	SE	SE	SE
Rainham (Kent)	d			17 46										18 00						18 16					
Gillingham	d			17 51										18 06						18 21					
Chatham	d			17 55										18 10						18 25					
Rochester	d			17 59										18 14						18 29					
Strood	d			18 03										18 18						18 35					
Higham	d													18 23											
Gravesend	d			18 13										18 30	18 35					18 45			18 51		
Northfleet	d													18 33	18 38										
Swanscombe	d													18 35	18 40										
Greenhithe	d													18 39	18 44								18 58		
Stone Crossing	d													18 41	18 46										
Dartford	d	←										18 42		18 46	18 52				←				19 07		
Slade Green	d	18 21			18 22			18 29		18 37	18 43	18 48		18 51					18 51		18 59			19 01	19 09
Erith	d							18 32		18 42	18 46	18 50		→							19 02				19 12
Belvedere	d							18 34		18 44	18 48	18 53									19 04				19 14
Abbey Wood	d	18 28						18 38		18 48	18 52	18 56							18 59		19 08				19 18
Plumstead	d	18 31						18 41		18 51	18 55	18 59							19 02		19 11				19 21
Woolwich Arsenal	d	18 34						18 44		18 54	18 58	19 02							19 05		19 14				19 24
Woolwich Dockyard	d							18 46		18 56	19 00	19 04									19 16				19 26
Charlton	d	18 40						18 50		19 00	19 04	19 07							19 10		19 20				19 30
Westcombe Park	d	18 42						18 52		19 02	19 06								19 12		19 22				19 32
Maze Hill	d	18 44						18 54		19 04	19 09								19 14		19 24				19 34
Greenwich	d	18 47				18 49		18 57		19 08	19 13		19 17						19 18		19 27				19 37
Deptford	a	18 49						18 59		19 10	19 15								19 20		19 29				19 39
London Victoria	d		←						←							←		←				←			
London Bridge	d	18 58	19 00		19 17	20 09		19 09	19 17	19 20	19 25	19 28	20 39		19 23	19 25		19 28	19 28		19 37	19 40	19 45	19 54	19 47
London Cannon Street	d				→	→		19a15	19a21	19a26	→	→	→			19a30					19a43	19a46		→	19a51
Waterloo East	d		19 06												19 28			19 33					19 50		
London Charing Cross	a		19 09												19 31			19 36					19 53		
London Blackfriars	d	19 04																	19 34						
City Thameslink	d	19 06																	19 36						
Farringdon	d	19 09																	19 39						
St Pancras International	d	19 13		18a37															19 43	19a09					
West Hampstead Thameslink	d	19 22																	19 52						
St Albans	d	19 50																	20 17						
Luton Airport Parkway	d	20 02																	20 32						
Luton	a	20 06																	20 36						

Table T201-R

Mondays to Fridays

16 December to 15 May

Medway - Woolwich - Greenwich - London Thameslink

		SE		TL	SE	SE	SE	TL	SE ◇	SE ◇	SE	SE		SE	SE	SE	SE	SE	TL	SE	SE	SE		TL	SE ◇
Rainham (Kent)	d			18 30						18 46									18 58						19 16
Gillingham	d			18 36						18 51									19 04						19 21
Chatham	d			18 40						18 55									19 08						19 25
Rochester	d			18 44						18 59									19 12						19 29
Strood	d			18 47					18 58	19 02									19 15						19 32
Higham	d			18 52															19 20						
Gravesend	d			18 59	19 05				19 08	19 12	19 18								19 29	19 35					19 42
Northfleet	d			19 03	19 08														19 32	19 38					
Swanscombe	d			19 05	19 10														19 34	19 40					
Greenhithe	d			19 08	19 14						19 26								19 38	19 44					
Stone Crossing	d			19 10	19 16														19 40	19 46					
Dartford	d			19 15	19 21			←			19 32							19 41	19 45	19 51				←	
Slade Green	d	19 16		19 21			←	19 21						19 29		19 39	19 40	19 46	19 51			←		19 51	
Erith	d	19 18		→			19 18							19 32		19 42		19 48	→			19 48			
Belvedere	d	→					19 21							19 34		19 44		→				19 51			
Abbey Wood	d						19 24	19 28						19 38		19 48						19 54		19 58	
Plumstead	d						19 27	19 31						19 41		19 51						19 57		20 01	
Woolwich Arsenal	d						19 30	19 34						19 44		19 54						20 00		20 04	
Woolwich Dockyard	d						19 33							19 46		19 56						20 03			
Charlton	d						19 36	19 40						19 50		20 00						20 06		20 10	
Westcombe Park	d							19 42						19 52		20 02								20 12	
Maze Hill	d							19 44						19 54		20 04								20 14	
Greenwich	d							19 47				19 47		19 57		20 07								20 17	
Deptford	a							19 49						19 59		20 09								20 19	
London Victoria	d					←					20a25				←						←				
London Bridge	d				19 53	19 54	19 57	19 58				21 09		20 07	20 09	20 17	20 24			20 22	20 24	20 27		20 28	
London Cannon Street	d					19a58						→		20a11	20a15	20a21	→				20a30				
Waterloo East	d				19 58		20 02													20 27		20 32			
London Charing Cross	a				20 01		20 05													20 30		20 35			
London Blackfriars	d							20 04																20 34	
City Thameslink	d							20 06																20 36	
Farringdon	d							20 09																20 39	
St Pancras International	d							20 13	19a31	19a36														20 43	20a06
West Hampstead Thameslink	d							20 22																20 52	
St Albans	d							20 45																21 15	
Luton Airport Parkway	d							20 57																21 27	
Luton	a							21 01																21 31	

		SE	SE	SE	SE	SE	SE	TL		SE	SE	SE	TL	SE ◇	SE	SE	SE	SE		SE	TL	SE	SE	TL	SE ◇
Rainham (Kent)	d							19 28						19 46							19 58				20 16
Gillingham	d							19 34						19 51							20 04				20 21
Chatham	d							19 38						19 55							20 08				20 25
Rochester	d							19 42						19 59							20 12				20 29
Strood	d							19 45						20 02							20 15				20 32
Higham	d							19 50													20 20				
Gravesend	d							19 59		20 05				20 12	20 20						20 29	20 35			20 42
Northfleet	d							20 02		20 08											20 32	20 38			
Swanscombe	d							20 04		20 10											20 34	20 40			
Greenhithe	d							20 08		20 14					20 26						20 38	20 44			
Stone Crossing	d							20 10		20 16											20 40	20 46			
Dartford	d						20 11	20 15		20 21			←		20 32					20 41	20 45	20 51		←	
Slade Green	d		19 59		20 07	20 09	20 16	20 21				←	20 21				20 29			20 46	20 51		←	20 51	
Erith	d		20 02			20 12	20 18	→				20 18					20 32			20 48	→		20 48		
Belvedere	d		20 04			20 14	→					20 21					20 34			→			20 51		
Abbey Wood	d		20 08			20 18						20 24	20 28				20 38						20 54	20 58	
Plumstead	d		20 11			20 21						20 27	20 31				20 41						20 57	21 01	
Woolwich Arsenal	d		20 14			20 24						20 30	20 34				20 44						21 00	21 04	
Woolwich Dockyard	d		20 16			20 26						20 33					20 46						21 03		
Charlton	d		20 20			20 30						20 36	20 40				20 50						21 06	21 10	
Westcombe Park	d		20 22			20 32							20 42				20 52							21 12	
Maze Hill	d		20 24			20 34							20 44				20 54							21 14	
Greenwich	d	20 17	20 27			20 37							20 47			20 47	20 57							21 17	
Deptford	a		20 29			20 39							20 49				20 59							21 19	
London Victoria	d			←							←				21a25			←							
London Bridge	d	21 39	20 37	20 39	20 54	20 47				20 52	20 54	20 57	20 58			22 09	21 07	21 09				21 22	21 27	21 28	
London Cannon Street	d	→	20a41	20a43	→	20a51					21a00					→	21a11	21a13							
Waterloo East	d									20 57		21 02										21 27	21 32		
London Charing Cross	a									21 00		21 05										21 30	21 35		
London Blackfriars	d												21 04											21 34	
City Thameslink	d												21 06											21 36	
Farringdon	d												21 09											21 39	
St Pancras International	d												21 13	20a36										21 43	21a06
West Hampstead Thameslink	d												21 24											21 52	
St Albans	d												21 48											22 15	
Luton Airport Parkway	d												22 02											22 27	
Luton	a												22 06											22 31	

Table T201-R

Mondays to Fridays

16 December to 15 May

Medway - Woolwich - Greenwich - London Thameslink

		SE	SE	SE		SE	SE	SE	TL	SE	SE	TL	SE	SE		SE	SE	SE	SE MT FO	TL	SE	SE	TL	SE
													◇											◇
Rainham (Kent)	d								20 28				20 46							20 58				21 16
Gillingham	d								20 34				20 52							21 04				21 21
Chatham	d								20 38				20 56							21 08				21 25
Rochester	d								20 42				21 00							21 12				21 29
Strood	d								20 45				21 03							21 15				21 32
Higham	d								20 50											21 20				
Gravesend	d	20 50							20 59	21 05			21 13	21 20						21 29	21 35			21 42
Northfleet	d								21 02	21 08										21 32	21 38			
Swanscombe	d								21 04	21 10										21 34	21 40			
Greenhithe	d	20 56							21 08	21 14				21 26						21 38	21 44			
Stone Crossing	d								21 10	21 16										21 40	21 46			
Dartford	d	21 02					21 11		21 15	21 21		←		21 32				21 41		21 45	21 51		←	
Slade Green	d			20 59			21 16		21 21			21 21				21 29		21 46		21 51			21 51	
Erith	d			21 02			21 18		→							21 32		21 48		→				
Belvedere	d			21 04			21 21									21 34		21 51						
Abbey Wood	d			21 08			21 24					21 28				21 38		21 54					21 58	
Plumstead	d			21 11			21 27					21 31				21 41		21 57					22 01	
Woolwich Arsenal	d			21 14			21 30					21 34				21 44		22 00					22 04	
Woolwich Dockyard	d			21 16			21 33									21 46		22 03						
Charlton	d			21 20			21 36					21 40				21 50		22 06					22 10	
Westcombe Park	d			21 22								21 42				21 52							22 12	
Maze Hill	d			21 24								21 44				21 54							22 14	
Greenwich	d		21 17	21 27				21 44				21 47				21 57			22 14				22 17	
Deptford	a			21 29								21 49				21 59							22 19	
London Victoria	d	21a55				←					←			22a25			←					←		
London Bridge	d		22 39	21 37		21 39	21 57	23 09		21 52	21 57	21 58				22 07	22 09	22 27	23 39		22 22	22 27	22 28	
London Cannon Street	d		→	21a41		21a43	→	→								22a11	22a13	→	→					
Waterloo East	d									21 57	22 02										22 27	22 32		
London Charing Cross	a									22 00	22 05										22 30	22 35		
London Blackfriars	d											22 04											22 34	
City Thameslink	d											22 06											22 36	
Farringdon	d											22 09											22 39	
St Pancras International	d											22 13	21a40										22 43	22a07
West Hampstead Thameslink	d											22a21											22a51	
St Albans	d																							
Luton Airport Parkway	d																							
Luton	a																							

		SE	SE	SE	SE	SE MT FO	TL	SE	SE	TL		SE	SE	SE	SE	SE	SE W ThO	TL	SE	SE		TL	SE	SE	SE
												◇											◇		
Rainham (Kent)	d						21 28					21 46						22 00					22 16		
Gillingham	d						21 34					21 51						22 06					22 21		
Chatham	d						21 38					21 55						22 10					22 25		
Rochester	d						21 42					21 59						22 14					22 29		
Strood	d						21 45					22 02						22 17					22 32		
Higham	d						21 50											22 22							
Gravesend	d	21 50					21 59	22 05				22 12	22 20					22 29	22 35				22 42	22 50	
Northfleet	d						22 02	22 08										22 33	22 38						
Swanscombe	d						22 04	22 10										22 35	22 40						
Greenhithe	d	21 56					22 08	22 14					22 26					22 38	22 44					22 56	
Stone Crossing	d						22 10	22 16										22 40	22 46						
Dartford	d	22 02			22 11		22 15	22 21		←			22 32			22 41		22 45	22 51			←		23 02	
Slade Green	d		21 59		22 16		22 21			22 21				22 29		22 46	22 46	22 51		←		22 51			22 59
Erith	d		22 02		22 18		→							22 32		22 48		→		22 48					23 02
Belvedere	d		22 04		22 21									22 34		→				22 51					23 04
Abbey Wood	d		22 08		22 24					22 28				22 38						22 54		22 58			23 08
Plumstead	d		22 11		22 27					22 31				22 41						22 57		23 01			23 11
Woolwich Arsenal	d		22 14		22 30					22 34				22 44						23 00		23 04			23 14
Woolwich Dockyard	d		22 16		22 33									22 46						23 03					23 16
Charlton	d		22 20		22 36					22 40				22 50						23 06		23 10			23 20
Westcombe Park	d		22 22							22 42				22 52								23 12			23 22
Maze Hill	d		22 24							22 44				22 54								23 14			23 24
Greenwich	d		22 27			22 44				22 47				22 57								23 17			23 27
Deptford	a		22 29							22 49				22 59								23 19			23 29
London Victoria	d	22a55		←					←				23a25		←									23a55	
London Bridge	d		22 37	22 39	22 57	00 09		22 52	22 57	22 58				23 07	23 09		23a41		23 22	23 27		23 28			23 37
London Cannon Street	d		22a41	22a43	→	→								23a11	23a13										23a41
Waterloo East	d							22 57	23 02										23 27	23 32					
London Charing Cross	a							23 00	23 05										23 30	23 35					
London Blackfriars	d									23 04												23 34			
City Thameslink	d																								
Farringdon	d									23 09												23 39			
St Pancras International	d									23 13		22a36										23 43	23a06		
West Hampstead Thameslink	d									23a21												23a51			
St Albans	d																								
Luton Airport Parkway	d																								
Luton	a																								

NRT DECEMBER 19 EDITION

Table T201-R

Mondays to Fridays

16 December to 15 May

Medway - Woolwich - Greenwich - London Thameslink

		SE MT FO	SE	TL	SE	SE		SE W ThO	SE MT FO	SE MT FO	SE MTO	SE WTh FO	TL	SE MTO	SE WTh FO	TL
Rainham (Kent)	d			22 30									23 00			23 30
Gillingham	d			22 36									23 06			23 36
Chatham	d			22 40									23 10			23 40
Rochester	d			22 44									23 14			23 44
Strood	d			22 47									23 17			23 47
Higham	d			22 52									23 22			23 52
Gravesend	d			22 59	23 05								23 29	23 35	23 35	23 59
Northfleet	d			23 03	23 08								23 33	23 38	23 38	00 03
Swanscombe	d			23 05	23 10								23 35	23 40	23 40	00 05
Greenhithe	d			23 08	23 14								23 38	23 44	23 44	00 08
Stone Crossing	d			23 10	23 16								23 40	23 46	23 46	00 10
Dartford	d		23 11	23a15	23 21	←					23 41	23 41	23a45	23 51	23 51	00a15
Slade Green	d		23 16			23 16		23 16	23 29		23 46	23 46				
Erith	d		→			23 18			23 32		23 48	23 48				
Belvedere	d					23 21			23 34		23 51	23 51				
Abbey Wood	d					23 24			23 38		23 54	23 54				
Plumstead	d					23 27			23 41		23 57	23 57				
Woolwich Arsenal	d					23 30			23 44		23 59	23 59				
Woolwich Dockyard	d					23 33			23 46		00 03	00 03				
Charlton	d					23 36			23 50		00 06	00 06				
Westcombe Park	d								23 52							
Maze Hill	d								23 54							
Greenwich	d								23 57							
Deptford	a								23 59							
London Victoria	d	←								←						
London Bridge	d	23 39			23 52	23 57		00a08	00 07	00 09	00 25	00 26		00a29	00 29	
London Cannon Street	d	23a43							00a11	00a13	00a33					
Waterloo East	d				23 57	00 02						00 31			00 34	
London Charing Cross	a				00 01	00 05						00 35			00 39	
London Blackfriars	d															
City Thameslink	d															
Farringdon	d															
St Pancras International	d															
West Hampstead Thameslink	d															
St Albans	d															
Luton Airport Parkway	d															
Luton	a															

Saturdays

21 December to 16 May

		TL	SE	SE	TL	SE	SE	SE	SE	TL		SE	SE	SE	SE	SE	TL	SE	SE	SE		SE	SE	SE	TL
																			◇						
Rainham (Kent)	d																05 28		05 46						05 58
Gillingham	d	04 06			04 36					05 06							05 34		05 51						06 04
Chatham	d	04 10			04 40					05 10							05 38		05 55						06 08
Rochester	d	04 14			04 44					05 14							05 42		05 59						06 12
Strood	d	04 17			04 47					05 17							05 45		06 02						06 15
Higham	d	04 22			04 52					05 22							05 50								06 20
Gravesend	d	04 29			04 59	05 18				05 29			05 48				05 59		06 12	06 18					06 29
Northfleet	d	04 33			05 03	05 22				05 33			05 52				06 02			06 22					06 32
Swanscombe	d	04 35			05 05	05 24				05 35			05 54				06 04			06 24					06 34
Greenhithe	d	04 38			05 08	05 27				05 38			05 57				06 08			06 27					06 38
Stone Crossing	d	04 40			05 10	05 29				05 40			05 59				06 10			06 29					06 40
Dartford	d	04a45		05 03	05 15	05 35			05 41	05 45			06 05			06 11	06 15			06 35				06 41	06 45
Slade Green	d			05 09	05 21			05 39	05 46	05 51					06 09	06 16	06 21						06 39	06 46	06 51
Erith	d			05 12				05 42	05 48						06 12	06 18							06 42	06 48	→
Belvedere	d			05 14				05 44	05 51						06 14	06 21							06 44	→	
Abbey Wood	d			05 18	05 28			05 48	05 54	05 58					06 18	06 24	06 28						06 48		
Plumstead	d			05 21	05 31			05 51	05 57	06 01					06 21	06 27	06 31						06 51		
Woolwich Arsenal	d			05 24	05 34			05 54	06 00	06 04					06 24	06 30	06 34						06 54		
Woolwich Dockyard	d			05 26				05 56	06 03						06 26	06 33							06 56		
Charlton	d			05 30	05 40			06 00	06 06	06 10					06 30	06 36	06 40						07 00		
Westcombe Park	d			05 32	05 42			06 02		06 12					06 32		06 42						07 02		
Maze Hill	d			05 34	05 44			06 04		06 14					06 34		06 44						07 04		
Greenwich	d		05 17	05 37	05 47		05 47	06 07		06 17				06 17	06 37		06 47					06 47	07 07		
Deptford	a			05 39	05 49			06 09		06 19					06 39		06 49						07 09		
London Victoria	d											←						←							
London Bridge	d		06 39	05 47	05 58	06 15	07 09	06 17	06 27	06 28		06 39	06 45	07 39	06 47	06 57	06 58	07 09		07 15		08 09	07 17		
London Cannon Street	d		→	05a51			→	06a21				06a43		→	06a51			07a13				→	07a21		
Waterloo East	d					06 20			06 32				06 50			07 02				07 20					
London Charing Cross	a					06 23			06 35				06 53			07 05				07 23					
London Blackfriars	d				06 04					06 34							07 04								
City Thameslink	d																								
Farringdon	d				06 09					06 39							07 09								
St Pancras International	d				06 13					06a43							07a13		06a36						
West Hampstead Thameslink	d				06 22																				
St Albans	d				06a46																				
Luton Airport Parkway	d																								
Luton	a																								

Table T201-R

Saturdays

21 December to 16 May

Medway - Woolwich - Greenwich - London Thameslink

		SE	SE	TL	SE	SE		SE	SE	SE	SE	TL	SE	SE	TL	SE ◇		SE	SE	SE	SE	SE	SE	TL	SE
Rainham (Kent)	d											06 28				06 46								06 58	
Gillingham	d											06 34				06 51								07 04	
Chatham	d											06 38				06 55								07 08	
Rochester	d											06 42				06 59								07 12	
Strood	d											06 45				07 02								07 15	
Higham	d											06 50												07 20	
Gravesend	d	06 35			06 50							06 59	07 05			07 12		07 20						07 29	07 35
Northfleet	d	06 38										07 02	07 08											07 32	07 38
Swanscombe	d	06 40										07 04	07 10											07 34	07 40
Greenhithe	d	06 44			06 56							07 08	07 14					07 26						07 38	07 44
Stone Crossing	d	06 46										07 10	07 16											07 40	07 46
Dartford	d	06 51		←	07 02						07 11	07 15	07 21		←			07 32					07 41	07 45	07 51
Slade Green	d		←	06 51				06 59		07 09	07 16	07 21		←	07 21					07 29		07 39	07 46	07 51	
Erith	d		06 48					07 02		07 12	07 18	→		07 18						07 32		07 42	07 48	→	
Belvedere	d		06 51					07 04		07 14	→			07 21						07 34		07 44	→		
Abbey Wood	d		06 54	06 58				07 08		07 18				07 24	07 28					07 38		07 48			
Plumstead	d		06 57	07 01				07 11		07 21				07 27	07 31					07 41		07 51			
Woolwich Arsenal	d		07 00	07 04				07 14		07 24				07 30	07 34					07 44		07 54			
Woolwich Dockyard	d		07 03					07 16		07 26				07 33						07 46		07 56			
Charlton	d		07 06	07 10				07 20		07 30				07 36	07 40					07 50		08 00			
Westcombe Park	d			07 12				07 22		07 32					07 42					07 52		08 02			
Maze Hill	d			07 14				07 24		07 34					07 44					07 54		08 04			
Greenwich	d			07 17		07 17		07 27		07 37					07 47				07 47	07 57		08 07			
Deptford	a			07 19				07 29		07 39					07 49					07 59		08 09			
London Victoria	d				07a55				←									08a25			←				
London Bridge	d	07 22	07 27	07 28		08 39		07 37	07 39	07 47			07 52	07 57	07 58				09 09	08 07	08 09	08 17			08 22
London Cannon Street	d					→		07a41	07a43	07a51									→	08a11	08a13	08a21			
Waterloo East	d	07 27	07 32										07 57	08 02											08 27
London Charing Cross	a	07 30	07 35										08 00	08 05											08 30
London Blackfriars	d			07 34											08 04										
City Thameslink	d																								
Farringdon	d			07 39											08 09										
St Pancras International	d			07a43											08a13	07a36									
West Hampstead Thameslink	d																								
St Albans	d																								
Luton Airport Parkway	d																								
Luton	a																								

		SE		TL	SE ◇	SE	SE	SE	SE	SE	SE	TL		SE ◇	SE	SE	TL	SE ◇	SE	SE	SE	SE		SE	SE
Rainham (Kent)	d				07 16							07 28						07 46							
Gillingham	d				07 21							07 34						07 51							
Chatham	d				07 25							07 38						07 55							
Rochester	d				07 29							07 42						07 59							
Strood	d				07 32							07 45		07 59				08 02							
Higham	d											07 50													
Gravesend	d				07 42	07 50						07 59			08 05			08 12	08 20						
Northfleet	d											08 02			08 08										
Swanscombe	d											08 04			08 10										
Greenhithe	d					07 56						08 08			08 14				08 26						
Stone Crossing	d											08 10			08 16										
Dartford	d			←		08 02					08 11	08 15			08 21		←		08 32						
Slade Green	d	←		07 51				07 59		08 09	08 16	08 21				←	08 21				08 29			08 37	08 39
Erith	d	07 48						08 02		08 12	08 18	→				08 18					08 32				08 42
Belvedere	d	07 51						08 04		08 14	→					08 21					08 34				08 44
Abbey Wood	d	07 54		07 58				08 08		08 18						08 24	08 28				08 38				08 48
Plumstead	d	07 57		08 01				08 11		08 21						08 27	08 31				08 41				08 51
Woolwich Arsenal	d	08 00		08 04				08 14		08 24						08 30	08 34				08 44				08 54
Woolwich Dockyard	d	08 03						08 16		08 26						08 33					08 46				08 56
Charlton	d	08 06		08 10				08 20		08 30						08 36	08 40				08 50				09 00
Westcombe Park	d			08 12				08 22		08 32							08 42				08 52				09 02
Maze Hill	d			08 14				08 24		08 34							08 44				08 54				09 04
Greenwich	d			08 17			08 17	08 27		08 37							08 47			08 47	08 57				09 07
Deptford	a			08 19				08 29		08 39							08 49				08 59				09 09
London Victoria	d					08a55			←										09a25			←			
London Bridge	d	08 27		08 28			09 39	08 37	08 39	08 47					08 52	08 57	08 58			10 09	09 07	09 09		09 24	09 17
London Cannon Street	d						→	08a41	08a43	08a51										→	09a11	09a13		→	09a21
Waterloo East	d	08 32													08 57	09 02									
London Charing Cross	a	08 35													09 00	09 05									
London Blackfriars	d			08 34													09 04								
City Thameslink	d																09 06								
Farringdon	d			08 39													09 09								
St Pancras International	d			08a43	08a06									10a57			09a13	08a37							
West Hampstead Thameslink	d																								
St Albans	d																								
Luton Airport Parkway	d																								
Luton	a																								

Table T201-R

Saturdays

21 December to 16 May

Medway - Woolwich - Greenwich - London Thameslink

		SE	TL	SE	SE	SE	TL	SE ◇		SE	SE	SE	SE	SE	SE	SE	TL	SE ◇		SE	SE	SE	TL	SE ◇	SE
Rainham (Kent)	d		07 58					08 16									08 28							08 46	
Gillingham	d		08 04					08 21									08 34							08 51	
Chatham	d		08 08					08 25									08 38							08 55	
Rochester	d		08 12					08 29									08 42							08 59	
Strood	d		08 15					08 32									08 45	08 59						09 02	
Higham	d		08 20														08 50								
Gravesend	d		08 29	08 35				08 42		08 50							08 59			09 05				09 12	09 20
Northfleet	d		08 32	08 38													09 02			09 08					
Swanscombe	d		08 34	08 40													09 04			09 10					
Greenhithe	d		08 38	08 44						08 56							09 08			09 14					09 26
Stone Crossing	d		08 40	08 46													09 10			09 16					
Dartford	d	08 41	08 45	08 51			←			09 02						09 11	09 15			09 21			←		09 32
Slade Green	d	08 46	08 51			←	08 51					08 59		09 07	09 09	09 16	09 21					←	09 21		
Erith	d	08 48	→			08 48						09 02			09 12	09 18	→					09 18			
Belvedere	d	→				08 51						09 04			09 14	→						09 21			
Abbey Wood	d					08 54	08 58					09 08			09 18							09 24	09 28		
Plumstead	d					08 57	09 01					09 11			09 21							09 27	09 31		
Woolwich Arsenal	d					09 00	09 04					09 14			09 24							09 30	09 34		
Woolwich Dockyard	d					09 03						09 16			09 26							09 33			
Charlton	d					09 06	09 10					09 20			09 30							09 36	09 40		
Westcombe Park	d						09 12					09 22			09 32								09 42		
Maze Hill	d						09 14					09 24			09 34								09 44		
Greenwich	d						09 17				09 17	09 27			09 37								09 47		
Deptford	a						09 19					09 29			09 39								09 49		
London Victoria	d				←					09a55			←								←				10a25
London Bridge	d			09 22	09 24	09 27	09 28				10 39	09 37	09 39	09 54	09 47					09 52	09 54	09 57	09 58		
London Cannon Street	d				09a30						→	09a41	09a43	→	09a51						10a00				
Waterloo East	d			09 27		09 32														09 57		10 02			
London Charing Cross	a			09 30		09 35														10 00		10 05			
London Blackfriars	d						09 34																10 04		
City Thameslink	d						09 36																10 06		
Farringdon	d						09 39																10 09		
St Pancras International	d						09a43	09a06										11a58					10a13	09a37	
West Hampstead Thameslink	d																								
St Albans	d																								
Luton Airport Parkway	d																								
Luton	a																								

		SE	SE	SE		SE	SE	SE	TL	SE	SE	SE	TL	SE ◇		SE	SE	SE	SE	SE	SE	SE	TL	SE ◇	
Rainham (Kent)	d								08 58					09 16									09 28		
Gillingham	d								09 04					09 21									09 34		
Chatham	d								09 08					09 25									09 38		
Rochester	d								09 12					09 29									09 42		
Strood	d								09 15					09 32									09 45	09 59	
Higham	d								09 20														09 50		
Gravesend	d								09 29	09 35				09 42		09 50							09 59		
Northfleet	d								09 32	09 38													10 02		
Swanscombe	d								09 34	09 40													10 04		
Greenhithe	d								09 38	09 44						09 56							10 08		
Stone Crossing	d								09 40	09 46													10 10		
Dartford	d							09 41	09 45	09 51			←			10 02						10 11	10 15		
Slade Green	d		09 29			09 37	09 39	09 46	09 51			←	09 51					09 59		10 07	10 09	10 16	10 21		
Erith	d		09 32				09 42	09 48	→			09 48						10 02			10 12	10 18	→		
Belvedere	d		09 34				09 44	→				09 51						10 04			10 14	→			
Abbey Wood	d		09 38				09 48					09 54	09 58					10 08			10 18				
Plumstead	d		09 41				09 51					09 57	10 01					10 11			10 21				
Woolwich Arsenal	d		09 44				09 54					10 00	10 04					10 14			10 24				
Woolwich Dockyard	d		09 46				09 56					10 03						10 16			10 26				
Charlton	d		09 50				10 00					10 06	10 10					10 20			10 30				
Westcombe Park	d		09 52				10 02						10 12					10 22			10 32				
Maze Hill	d		09 54				10 04						10 14					10 24			10 34				
Greenwich	d	09 47	09 57				10 07						10 17				10 17	10 27			10 37				
Deptford	a		09 59				10 09						10 19					10 29			10 39				
London Victoria	d			←							←					10a55			←						
London Bridge	d	11 09	10 07	10 09		10 24	10 17			10 22	10 24	10 27	10 28				11 39	10 37	10 39	10 54	10 47				
London Cannon Street	d	→	10a11	10a13		→	10a21				10a30						→	10a41	10a43	→	10a51				
Waterloo East	d									10 27		10 32													
London Charing Cross	a									10 30		10 35													
London Blackfriars	d												10 34												
City Thameslink	d												10 36												
Farringdon	d												10 39												
St Pancras International	d												10a43	10a10										12a55	
West Hampstead Thameslink	d																								
St Albans	d																								
Luton Airport Parkway	d																								
Luton	a																								

Table T201-R

Saturdays

21 December to 16 May

Medway - Woolwich - Greenwich - London Thameslink

		SE	SE	SE	TL	SE ◇	SE	SE	SE	SE		SE	SE	SE	TL	SE	SE	SE	TL	SE ◇		SE	SE	SE	SE
Rainham (Kent)	d					09 46									09 58					10 16					
Gillingham	d					09 51									10 04					10 21					
Chatham	d					09 55									10 08					10 25					
Rochester	d					09 59									10 12					10 29					
Strood	d					10 02									10 15					10 32					
Higham	d														10 20										
Gravesend	d	10 05				10 12	10 20								10 29	10 35				10 42		10 50			
Northfleet	d	10 08													10 32	10 38									
Swanscombe	d	10 10													10 34	10 40									
Greenhithe	d	10 14					10 26								10 38	10 44						10 56			
Stone Crossing	d	10 16													10 40	10 46									
Dartford	d	10 21			←		10 32							10 41	10 45	10 51			←			11 02			
Slade Green	d			←	10 21				10 29			10 37	10 39	10 46	10 51			←	10 51					10 59	
Erith	d			10 18					10 32				10 42	10 48	→			10 48						11 02	
Belvedere	d			10 21					10 34				10 44	→				10 51						11 04	
Abbey Wood	d			10 24	10 28				10 38				10 48					10 54	10 58					11 08	
Plumstead	d			10 27	10 31				10 41				10 51					10 57	11 01					11 11	
Woolwich Arsenal	d			10 30	10 34				10 44				10 54					11 00	11 04					11 14	
Woolwich Dockyard	d			10 33					10 46				10 56					11 03						11 16	
Charlton	d			10 36	10 40				10 50				11 00					11 06	11 10					11 20	
Westcombe Park	d				10 42				10 52				11 02						11 12					11 22	
Maze Hill	d				10 44				10 54				11 04						11 14					11 24	
Greenwich	d				10 47			10 47	10 57				11 07						11 17				11 17	11 27	
Deptford	a				10 49				10 59				11 09						11 19					11 29	
London Victoria	d		←				11a25			←							←					11a55			←
London Bridge	d	10 52	10 54	10 57	10 58			12 09	11 07	11 09		11 24	11 17			11 22	11 24	11 27	11 28				12 39	11 37	11 39
London Cannon Street	d		11a00					→	11a11	11a13		→	11a21				11a30						→	11a41	11a43
Waterloo East	d	10 57		11 02												11 27		11 32							
London Charing Cross	a	11 00		11 05												11 30		11 35							
London Blackfriars	d				11 04														11 34						
City Thameslink	d				11 06														11 36						
Farringdon	d				11 09														11 39						
St Pancras International	d				11a13	10a41													11a43	11a06					
West Hampstead Thameslink	d																								
St Albans	d																								
Luton Airport Parkway	d																								
Luton	a																								

		SE	SE	SE	TL	SE ◇		SE	SE	SE	TL	SE ◇	SE	SE	SE	SE		SE	SE	SE	TL	SE	SE	SE	TL
Rainham (Kent)	d				10 28							10 46									10 58				
Gillingham	d				10 34							10 51									11 04				
Chatham	d				10 38							10 55									11 08				
Rochester	d				10 42							10 59									11 12				
Strood	d				10 45	10 59						11 02									11 15				
Higham	d				10 50																11 20				
Gravesend	d				10 59			11 05				11 12	11 20								11 29	11 35			
Northfleet	d				11 02			11 08													11 32	11 38			
Swanscombe	d				11 04			11 10													11 34	11 40			
Greenhithe	d				11 08			11 14					11 26								11 38	11 44			
Stone Crossing	d				11 10			11 16													11 40	11 46			
Dartford	d			11 11	11 15			11 21			←		11 32							11 41	11 45	11 51			←
Slade Green	d	11 07	11 09	11 16	11 21					←	11 21				11 29			11 37	11 39	11 46	11 51			←	11 51
Erith	d		11 12	11 18	→					11 18					11 32				11 42	11 48	→			11 48	
Belvedere	d		11 14	→						11 21					11 34				11 44	→				11 51	
Abbey Wood	d		11 18							11 24	11 28				11 38				11 48					11 54	11 58
Plumstead	d		11 21							11 27	11 31				11 41				11 51					11 57	12 01
Woolwich Arsenal	d		11 24							11 30	11 34				11 44				11 54					12 00	12 04
Woolwich Dockyard	d		11 26							11 33					11 46				11 56					12 03	
Charlton	d		11 30							11 36	11 40				11 50				12 00					12 06	12 10
Westcombe Park	d		11 32								11 42				11 52				12 02						12 12
Maze Hill	d		11 34								11 44				11 54				12 04						12 14
Greenwich	d		11 37								11 47			11 47	11 57				12 07						12 17
Deptford	a		11 39								11 49				11 59				12 09						12 19
London Victoria	d								←				12a25			←							←		
London Bridge	d	11 54	11 47					11 52	11 54	11 57	11 58			13 09	12 07	12 09		12 24	12 17			12 22	12 24	12 27	12 28
London Cannon Street	d	→	11a51						12a00					→	12a11	12a13		→	12a21				12a30		
Waterloo East	d							11 57		12 02												12 27		12 32	
London Charing Cross	a							12 00		12 05												12 30		12 35	
London Blackfriars	d										12 04														12 34
City Thameslink	d										12 06														12 36
Farringdon	d										12 09														12 39
St Pancras International	d					13a54					12a13	11a37													12a43
West Hampstead Thameslink	d																								
St Albans	d																								
Luton Airport Parkway	d																								
Luton	a																								

NRT DECEMBER 19 EDITION

Table T201-R

Saturdays

21 December to 16 May

Medway - Woolwich - Greenwich - London Thameslink

		SE ◇		SE	SE	SE	SE	SE	SE	SE	TL	SE ◇		SE	SE	SE	TL	SE ◇	SE	SE	SE	SE		SE	SE
Rainham (Kent)	d	11 16									11 28							11 46							
Gillingham	d	11 21									11 34							11 51							
Chatham	d	11 25									11 38							11 55							
Rochester	d	11 29									11 42							11 59							
Strood	d	11 32									11 45	11 59						12 02							
Higham	d										11 50														
Gravesend	d	11 42		11 50							11 59			12 05				12 12	12 20						
Northfleet	d										12 02			12 08											
Swanscombe	d										12 04			12 10											
Greenhithe	d			11 56							12 08			12 14					12 26						
Stone Crossing	d										12 10			12 16											
Dartford	d			12 02						12 11	12 15			12 21			←		12 32						
Slade Green	d					11 59		12 07	12 09	12 16	12 21					←	12 21				12 29			12 37	12 39
Erith	d					12 02			12 12	12 18	→					12 18					12 32				12 42
Belvedere	d					12 04			12 14	→						12 21					12 34				12 44
Abbey Wood	d					12 08			12 18							12 24	12 28				12 38				12 48
Plumstead	d					12 11			12 21							12 27	12 31				12 41				12 51
Woolwich Arsenal	d					12 14			12 24							12 30	12 34				12 44				12 54
Woolwich Dockyard	d					12 16			12 26							12 33					12 46				12 56
Charlton	d					12 20			12 30							12 36	12 40				12 50				13 00
Westcombe Park	d					12 22			12 32								12 42				12 52				13 02
Maze Hill	d					12 24			12 34								12 44				12 54				13 04
Greenwich	d				12 17	12 27			12 37								12 47			12 47	12 57				13 07
Deptford	a					12 29			12 39								12 49				12 59				13 09
London Victoria	d			12a55			←								←				13a25			←			
London Bridge	d				13 39	12 37	12 39	12 54	12 47					12 52	12 54	12 57	12 58			14 09	13 07	13 09		13 24	13 17
London Cannon Street	d				→	12a41	12a43	→	12a51						13a00					→	13a11	13a13		→	13a21
Waterloo East	d													12 57		13 02									
London Charing Cross	a													13 00		13 05									
London Blackfriars	d																13 04								
City Thameslink	d																13 06								
Farringdon	d																13 09								
St Pancras International	d	12a06										14a54					13a13	12a36							
West Hampstead Thameslink	d																								
St Albans	d																								
Luton Airport Parkway	d																								
Luton	a																								

		SE	TL	SE	SE	SE	TL	SE ◇		SE	SE	SE	SE	SE	SE	SE	TL	SE ◇		SE	SE	SE	TL	SE ◇	SE
Rainham (Kent)	d		11 58					12 16									12 28							12 46	
Gillingham	d		12 04					12 21									12 34							12 51	
Chatham	d		12 08					12 25									12 38							12 55	
Rochester	d		12 12					12 29									12 42							12 59	
Strood	d		12 15					12 32									12 45	12 59						13 02	
Higham	d		12 20														12 50								
Gravesend	d		12 29	12 35				12 42		12 50							12 59			13 05				13 12	13 20
Northfleet	d		12 32	12 38													13 02			13 08					
Swanscombe	d		12 34	12 40													13 04			13 10					
Greenhithe	d		12 38	12 44						12 56							13 08			13 14					13 26
Stone Crossing	d		12 40	12 46													13 10			13 16					
Dartford	d	12 41	12 45	12 51			←			13 02						13 11	13 15			13 21			←		13 32
Slade Green	d	12 46	12 51			←	12 51					12 59		13 07	13 09	13 16	13 21					←	13 21		
Erith	d	12 48	→			12 48						13 02			13 12	13 18	→					13 18			
Belvedere	d	→				12 51						13 04			13 14	→						13 21			
Abbey Wood	d					12 54	12 58					13 08			13 18							13 24	13 28		
Plumstead	d					12 57	13 01					13 11			13 21							13 27	13 31		
Woolwich Arsenal	d					13 00	13 04					13 14			13 24							13 30	13 34		
Woolwich Dockyard	d					13 03						13 16			13 26							13 33			
Charlton	d					13 06	13 10					13 20			13 30							13 36	13 40		
Westcombe Park	d						13 12					13 22			13 32								13 42		
Maze Hill	d						13 14					13 24			13 34								13 44		
Greenwich	d						13 17				13 17	13 27			13 37								13 47		
Deptford	a						13 19					13 29			13 39								13 49		
London Victoria	d				←					13a55			←								←				14a25
London Bridge	d			13 22	13 24	13 27	13 28				14 39	13 37	13 39	13 54	13 47					13 52	13 54	13 57	13 58		
London Cannon Street	d				13a30						→	13a41	13a43	→	13a51						14a00				
Waterloo East	d			13 27		13 32														13 57		14 02			
London Charing Cross	a			13 30		13 35														14 00		14 05			
London Blackfriars	d						13 34																14 04		
City Thameslink	d						13 36																14 06		
Farringdon	d						13 39																14 09		
St Pancras International	d						13a43	13a06										15a54					14a13	13a37	
West Hampstead Thameslink	d																								
St Albans	d																								
Luton Airport Parkway	d																								
Luton	a																								

Table T201-R

Medway - Woolwich - Greenwich - London Thameslink

Saturdays
21 December to 16 May

		SE	SE	SE		SE	SE	SE	TL	SE	SE	SE	TL	SE ◇		SE	SE	SE	SE	SE	SE	SE	TL	SE ◇	
Rainham (Kent)	d								12 58					13 16									13 28		
Gillingham	d								13 04					13 21									13 34		
Chatham	d								13 08					13 25									13 38		
Rochester	d								13 12					13 29									13 42		
Strood	d								13 15					13 32									13 45	13 59	
Higham	d								13 20														13 50		
Gravesend	d								13 29	13 35				13 42		13 50							13 59		
Northfleet	d								13 32	13 38													14 02		
Swanscombe	d								13 34	13 40													14 04		
Greenhithe	d								13 38	13 44						13 56							14 08		
Stone Crossing	d								13 40	13 46													14 10		
Dartford	d							13 41	13 45	13 51			←			14 02						14 11	14 15		
Slade Green	d		13 29			13 37	13 39	13 46	13 51			←	13 51					13 59		14 07	14 09	14 16	14 21		
Erith	d		13 32				13 42	13 48	→			13 48						14 02			14 12	14 18	→		
Belvedere	d		13 34				13 44	→				13 51						14 04			14 14	→			
Abbey Wood	d		13 38				13 48					13 54	13 58					14 08			14 18				
Plumstead	d		13 41				13 51					13 57	14 01					14 11			14 21				
Woolwich Arsenal	d		13 44				13 54					14 00	14 04					14 14			14 24				
Woolwich Dockyard	d		13 46				13 56					14 03						14 16			14 26				
Charlton	d		13 50				14 00					14 06	14 10					14 20			14 30				
Westcombe Park	d		13 52				14 02						14 12					14 22			14 32				
Maze Hill	d		13 54				14 04						14 14					14 24			14 34				
Greenwich	d	13 47	13 57				14 07						14 17				14 17	14 27			14 37				
Deptford	a		13 59				14 09						14 19					14 29			14 39				
London Victoria	d			←							←					14a55			←						
London Bridge	d	15 09	14 07	14 09		14 24	14 17			14 22	14 24	14 27	14 28				15 39	14 37	14 39	14 54	14 47				
London Cannon Street	d	→	14a11	14a13		→	14a21				14a30						→	14a41	14a43	→	14a51				
Waterloo East	d									14 27		14 32													
London Charing Cross	a									14 30		14 35													
London Blackfriars	d												14 34												
City Thameslink	d												14 36												
Farringdon	d												14 39												
St Pancras International	d												14a43	14a10										16a54	
West Hampstead Thameslink	d																								
St Albans	d																								
Luton Airport Parkway	d																								
Luton	a																								

		SE	SE	SE	TL	SE ◇	SE	SE	SE	SE		SE	SE	SE	TL	SE	SE	SE	TL	SE ◇		SE	SE	SE	SE
Rainham (Kent)	d					13 46									13 58					14 16					
Gillingham	d					13 51									14 04					14 21					
Chatham	d					13 55									14 08					14 25					
Rochester	d					13 59									14 12					14 29					
Strood	d					14 02									14 15					14 32					
Higham	d														14 20										
Gravesend	d	14 05				14 12	14 20								14 29	14 35				14 42		14 50			
Northfleet	d	14 08													14 32	14 38									
Swanscombe	d	14 10													14 34	14 40									
Greenhithe	d	14 14					14 26								14 38	14 44						14 56			
Stone Crossing	d	14 16													14 40	14 46									
Dartford	d	14 21			←		14 32							14 41	14 45	14 51			←			15 02			
Slade Green	d			←	14 21				14 29			14 37	14 39	14 46	14 51			←	14 51					14 59	←
Erith	d			14 18					14 32				14 42	14 48	→			14 48						15 02	
Belvedere	d			14 21					14 34				14 44	→				14 51						15 04	
Abbey Wood	d			14 24	14 28				14 38				14 48					14 54	14 58					15 08	
Plumstead	d			14 27	14 31				14 41				14 51					14 57	15 01					15 11	
Woolwich Arsenal	d			14 30	14 34				14 44				14 54					15 00	15 04					15 14	
Woolwich Dockyard	d			14 33					14 46				14 56					15 03						15 16	
Charlton	d			14 36	14 40				14 50				15 00					15 06	15 10					15 20	
Westcombe Park	d				14 42				14 52				15 02						15 12					15 22	
Maze Hill	d				14 44				14 54				15 04						15 14					15 24	
Greenwich	d				14 47			14 47	14 57				15 07						15 17				15 17	15 27	
Deptford	a				14 49				14 59				15 09						15 19					15 29	
London Victoria	d		←				15a25			←							←					15a55			←
London Bridge	d	14 52	14 54	14 57	14 58			16 09	15 07	15 09		15 24	15 17			15 22	15 24	15 27	15 28				16 39	15 37	15 39
London Cannon Street	d		15a00					→	15a11	15a13		→	15a21				15a30						→	15a41	15a43
Waterloo East	d	14 57		15 02												15 27		15 32							
London Charing Cross	a	15 00		15 05												15 30		15 35							
London Blackfriars	d				15 04														15 34						
City Thameslink	d				15 06														15 36						
Farringdon	d				15 09														15 39						
St Pancras International	d				15a13	14a36													15a43	15a06					
West Hampstead Thameslink	d																								
St Albans	d																								
Luton Airport Parkway	d																								
Luton	a																								

Table T201-R

Medway - Woolwich - Greenwich - London Thameslink

Saturdays
21 December to 16 May

		SE	SE	SE	TL	SE ◇		SE	SE	SE	TL	SE ◇	SE	SE	SE	SE		SE	SE	SE	TL	SE	SE	SE	TL
Rainham (Kent)	d				14 28							14 46									14 58				
Gillingham	d				14 34							14 51									15 04				
Chatham	d				14 38							14 55									15 08				
Rochester	d				14 42							14 59									15 12				
Strood	d				14 45	14 59						15 02									15 15				
Higham	d				14 50																15 20				
Gravesend	d				14 59			15 05				15 12	15 20								15 29	15 35			
Northfleet	d				15 02			15 08													15 32	15 38			
Swanscombe	d				15 04			15 10													15 34	15 40			
Greenhithe	d				15 08			15 14					15 26								15 38	15 44			
Stone Crossing	d				15 10			15 16													15 40	15 46			
Dartford	d			15 11	15 15			15 21			←		15 32							15 41	15 45	15 51			←
Slade Green	d	15 07	15 09	15 16	15 21					←	15 21				15 29			15 37	15 39	15 46	15 51			←	15 51
Erith	d		15 12	15 18	→					15 18					15 32				15 42	15 48	→			15 48	
Belvedere	d		15 14	→						15 21					15 34				15 44	→				15 51	
Abbey Wood	d		15 18							15 24	15 28				15 38				15 48					15 54	15 58
Plumstead	d		15 21							15 27	15 31				15 41				15 51					15 57	16 01
Woolwich Arsenal	d		15 24							15 30	15 34				15 44				15 54					16 00	16 04
Woolwich Dockyard	d		15 26							15 33					15 46				15 56					16 03	
Charlton	d		15 30							15 36	15 40				15 50				16 00					16 06	16 10
Westcombe Park	d		15 32								15 42				15 52				16 02						16 12
Maze Hill	d		15 34								15 44				15 54				16 04						16 14
Greenwich	d		15 37								15 47			15 47	15 57				16 07						16 17
Deptford	a		15 39								15 49				15 59				16 09						16 19
London Victoria	d								←				16a25			←							←		
London Bridge	d	15 54	15 47					15 52	15 54	15 57	15 58			17 09	16 07	16 09		16 24	16 17			16 22	16 24	16 27	16 28
London Cannon Street	d	→	15a51						16a00					→	16a11	16a13		→	16a21				16a30		
Waterloo East	d							15 57		16 02												16 27		16 32	
London Charing Cross	a							16 00		16 05												16 30		16 35	
London Blackfriars	d										16 04														16 34
City Thameslink	d										16 06														16 36
Farringdon	d										16 09														16 39
St Pancras International	d					17a58					16a13	15a36													16a43
West Hampstead Thameslink	d																								
St Albans	d																								
Luton Airport Parkway	d																								
Luton	a																								

		SE ◇		SE	SE	SE	SE	SE	SE	SE	TL	SE ◇		SE	SE	SE	TL	SE ◇	SE	SE	SE	SE		SE	SE
Rainham (Kent)	d	15 16									15 28							15 46							
Gillingham	d	15 21									15 34							15 51							
Chatham	d	15 25									15 38							15 55							
Rochester	d	15 29									15 42							15 59							
Strood	d	15 32									15 45	15 59						16 02							
Higham	d										15 50														
Gravesend	d	15 42		15 50							15 59			16 05				16 12	16 20						
Northfleet	d										16 02			16 08											
Swanscombe	d										16 04			16 10											
Greenhithe	d			15 56							16 08			16 14					16 26						
Stone Crossing	d										16 10			16 16											
Dartford	d			16 02						16 11	16 15			16 21			←		16 32						
Slade Green	d					15 59		16 07	16 09	16 16	16 21					←	16 21				16 29			16 37	16 39
Erith	d					16 02			16 12	16 18	→					16 18					16 32				16 42
Belvedere	d					16 04			16 14	→						16 21					16 34				16 44
Abbey Wood	d					16 08			16 18							16 24	16 28				16 38				16 48
Plumstead	d					16 11			16 21							16 27	16 31				16 41				16 51
Woolwich Arsenal	d					16 14			16 24							16 30	16 34				16 44				16 54
Woolwich Dockyard	d					16 16			16 26							16 33					16 46				16 56
Charlton	d					16 20			16 30							16 36	16 40				16 50				17 00
Westcombe Park	d					16 22			16 32								16 42				16 52				17 02
Maze Hill	d					16 24			16 34								16 44				16 54				17 04
Greenwich	d				16 17	16 27			16 37								16 47			16 47	16 57				17 07
Deptford	a					16 29			16 39								16 49				16 59				17 09
London Victoria	d			16a55			←								←				17a25			←			
London Bridge	d				17 39	16 37	16 39	16 54	16 47					16 52	16 54	16 57	16 58			18 09	17 07	17 09		17 24	17 17
London Cannon Street	d				→	16a41	16a43	→	16a51						17a00					→	17a11	17a13		→	17a21
Waterloo East	d													16 57		17 02									
London Charing Cross	a													17 00		17 05									
London Blackfriars	d																17 04								
City Thameslink	d																17 06								
Farringdon	d																17 09								
St Pancras International	d	16a10										18a58					17a13	16a36							
West Hampstead Thameslink	d																								
St Albans	d																								
Luton Airport Parkway	d																								
Luton	a																								

Table T201-R

Saturdays
21 December to 16 May

Medway - Woolwich - Greenwich - London Thameslink

		SE	TL	SE	SE	SE	TL	SE ◇		SE	SE	SE	SE	SE	SE	SE	TL	SE ◇		SE	SE	SE	TL	SE ◇	SE
Rainham (Kent)	d		15 58					16 16									16 28							16 46	
Gillingham	d		16 04					16 21									16 34							16 51	
Chatham	d		16 08					16 25									16 38							16 55	
Rochester	d		16 12					16 29									16 42							16 59	
Strood	d		16 16					16 32									16 45	16 59						17 02	
Higham	d		16 21														16 50								
Gravesend	d		16 29	16 35				16 42		16 50							16 59			17 05				17 12	17 20
Northfleet	d		16 32	16 38													17 02			17 08					
Swanscombe	d		16 34	16 40													17 04			17 10					
Greenhithe	d		16 38	16 44						16 56							17 08			17 14					17 26
Stone Crossing	d		16 40	16 46													17 10			17 16					
Dartford	d	16 41	16 45	16 51			←			17 02						17 11	17 15			17 21			←		17 32
Slade Green	d	16 46	16 51			←	16 51					16 59		17 07	17 09	17 16	17 21					←	17 21		
Erith	d	16 48	→			16 48						17 02			17 12	17 18	→					17 18			
Belvedere	d	→				16 51						17 04			17 14	→						17 21			
Abbey Wood	d					16 54	16 58					17 08			17 18							17 24	17 28		
Plumstead	d					16 57	17 01					17 11			17 21							17 27	17 31		
Woolwich Arsenal	d					17 00	17 04					17 14			17 24							17 30	17 34		
Woolwich Dockyard	d					17 03						17 16			17 26							17 33			
Charlton	d					17 06	17 10					17 20			17 30							17 36	17 40		
Westcombe Park	d						17 12					17 22			17 32								17 42		
Maze Hill	d						17 14					17 24			17 34								17 44		
Greenwich	d						17 17				17 17	17 27			17 37								17 47		
Deptford	a						17 19					17 29			17 39								17 49		
London Victoria	d				←					17a55		←									←				18a25
London Bridge	d			17 22	17 24	17 27	17 28				18 39	17 37	17 39	17 54	17 47					17 52	17 54	17 57	17 58		
London Cannon Street	d				17a30						→	17a41	17a43	→	17a51						18a00				
Waterloo East	d			17 27		17 32														17 57		18 02			
London Charing Cross	a			17 30		17 35														18 00		18 05			
London Blackfriars	d						17 34																18 04		
City Thameslink	d						17 36																18 06		
Farringdon	d						17 39																18 09		
St Pancras International	d						17a43	17a10										19a54					18a13	17a36	
West Hampstead Thameslink	d																								
St Albans	d																								
Luton Airport Parkway	d																								
Luton	a																								

		SE	SE	SE		SE	SE	SE	TL	SE	SE	SE	TL	SE ◇		SE	SE	SE	SE	SE	SE	SE	TL	SE ◇	
Rainham (Kent)	d								16 58					17 16									17 28		
Gillingham	d								17 04					17 21									17 34		
Chatham	d								17 08					17 25									17 38		
Rochester	d								17 12					17 29									17 42		
Strood	d								17 15					17 32									17 45	17 59	
Higham	d								17 20														17 50		
Gravesend	d								17 29	17 35				17 42		17 50							17 59		
Northfleet	d								17 32	17 38													18 02		
Swanscombe	d								17 34	17 40													18 04		
Greenhithe	d								17 38	17 44						17 56							18 08		
Stone Crossing	d								17 40	17 46													18 10		
Dartford	d							17 41	17 45	17 51			←			18 02						18 11	18 15		
Slade Green	d		17 29			17 37	17 39	17 46	17 51			←	17 51					17 59		18 07	18 09	18 16	18 21		
Erith	d		17 32				17 42	17 48	→			17 48						18 02			18 12	18 18	→		
Belvedere	d		17 34				17 44	→				17 51						18 04			18 14	→			
Abbey Wood	d		17 38				17 48					17 54	17 58					18 08			18 18				
Plumstead	d		17 41				17 51					17 57	18 01					18 11			18 21				
Woolwich Arsenal	d		17 44				17 54					18 00	18 04					18 14			18 24				
Woolwich Dockyard	d		17 46				17 56					18 03						18 16			18 26				
Charlton	d		17 50				18 00					18 06	18 10					18 20			18 30				
Westcombe Park	d		17 52				18 02						18 12					18 22			18 32				
Maze Hill	d		17 54				18 04						18 14					18 24			18 34				
Greenwich	d	17 47	17 57				18 07						18 17				18 17	18 27			18 37				
Deptford	a		17 59				18 09						18 19					18 29			18 39				
London Victoria	d			←							←					18a55			←						
London Bridge	d	19 09	18 07	18 09		18 24	18 17			18 22	18 24	18 27	18 28				19 39	18 37	18 39	18 54	18 47				
London Cannon Street	d	→	18a11	18a13		→	18a21				18a30						→	18a41	18a43	→	18a51				
Waterloo East	d									18 27		18 32													
London Charing Cross	a									18 30		18 35													
London Blackfriars	d												18 34												
City Thameslink	d												18 36												
Farringdon	d												18 39												
St Pancras International	d												18a43	18a10										20a54	
West Hampstead Thameslink	d																								
St Albans	d																								
Luton Airport Parkway	d																								
Luton	a																								

NRT DECEMBER 19 EDITION

Table T201-R

Saturdays
21 December to 16 May

Medway - Woolwich - Greenwich - London Thameslink

		SE	SE	SE	TL	SE ◇	SE	SE	SE	SE		SE	SE	SE	TL	SE	SE	SE	TL	SE ◇		SE	SE	SE	SE
Rainham (Kent)	d					17 46									17 58					18 16					
Gillingham	d					17 51									18 04					18 21					
Chatham	d					17 55									18 08					18 25					
Rochester	d					17 59									18 12					18 29					
Strood	d					18 02									18 15					18 32					
Higham	d														18 20										
Gravesend	d	18 05				18 12	18 20								18 29	18 35				18 42		18 50			
Northfleet	d	18 08													18 32	18 38									
Swanscombe	d	18 10													18 34	18 40									
Greenhithe	d	18 14					18 26								18 38	18 44						18 56			
Stone Crossing	d	18 16													18 40	18 46									
Dartford	d	18 21			←		18 32							18 41	18 45	18 51			←			19 02			
Slade Green	d			←	18 21				18 29			18 37	18 39	18 46	18 51			←	18 51					18 59	
Erith	d			18 18					18 32				18 42	18 48	→			18 48						19 02	
Belvedere	d			18 21					18 34				18 44	→				18 51						19 04	
Abbey Wood	d			18 24	18 28				18 38				18 48					18 54	18 58					19 08	
Plumstead	d			18 27	18 31				18 41				18 51					18 57	19 01					19 11	
Woolwich Arsenal	d			18 30	18 34				18 44				18 54					19 00	19 04					19 14	
Woolwich Dockyard	d			18 33					18 46				18 56					19 03						19 16	
Charlton	d			18 36	18 40				18 50				19 00					19 06	19 10					19 20	
Westcombe Park	d				18 42				18 52				19 02						19 12					19 22	
Maze Hill	d				18 44				18 54				19 04						19 14					19 24	
Greenwich	d				18 47			18 47	18 57				19 07						19 17				19 17	19 27	
Deptford	a				18 49				18 59				19 09						19 19					19 29	
London Victoria	d		←				19a25			←							←					19a55			←
London Bridge	d	18 52	18 54	18 57	18 58			20 09	19 07	19 09		19 24	19 17			19 22	19 24	19 27	19 28				20 39	19 37	19 39
London Cannon Street	d		19a00					→	19a11	19a13		→	19a21				19a30						→	19a41	19a43
Waterloo East	d	18 57		19 02												19 27		19 32							
London Charing Cross	a	19 00		19 05												19 30		19 35							
London Blackfriars	d				19 04														19 34						
City Thameslink	d				19 06														19 36						
Farringdon	d				19 09														19 39						
St Pancras International	d				19a13	18a37													19a43	19a06					
West Hampstead Thameslink	d																								
St Albans	d																								
Luton Airport Parkway	d																								
Luton	a																								

		SE	SE	SE	TL	SE ◇		SE	SE	SE	TL	SE ◇	SE	SE	SE	SE		SE	SE	TL	SE	SE	SE	TL	SE ◇
Rainham (Kent)	d				18 28							18 46								18 58					19 16
Gillingham	d				18 34							18 51								19 04					19 21
Chatham	d				18 38							18 55								19 08					19 25
Rochester	d				18 42							18 59								19 12					19 29
Strood	d				18 45	18 59						19 02								19 15					19 32
Higham	d				18 50															19 20					
Gravesend	d				18 59			19 05				19 12	19 20							19 29	19 35				19 42
Northfleet	d				19 02			19 08												19 32	19 38				
Swanscombe	d				19 04			19 10												19 34	19 40				
Greenhithe	d				19 08			19 14					19 26							19 38	19 44				
Stone Crossing	d				19 10			19 16												19 40	19 46				
Dartford	d			19 11	19 15			19 21			←		19 32						19 41	19 45	19 51			←	
Slade Green	d	19 07	19 09	19 16	19 21					←	19 21				19 29			19 37	19 46	19 51			←	19 51	
Erith	d		19 12	19 18	→					19 18					19 32				19 48	→			19 48		
Belvedere	d		19 14	→						19 21					19 34				→				19 51		
Abbey Wood	d		19 18							19 24	19 28				19 38								19 54	19 58	
Plumstead	d		19 21							19 27	19 31				19 41								19 57	20 01	
Woolwich Arsenal	d		19 24							19 30	19 34				19 44								20 00	20 04	
Woolwich Dockyard	d		19 26							19 33					19 46								20 03		
Charlton	d		19 30							19 36	19 40				19 50								20 06	20 10	
Westcombe Park	d		19 32								19 42				19 52									20 12	
Maze Hill	d		19 34								19 44				19 54									20 14	
Greenwich	d		19 37								19 47			19 47	19 57									20 17	
Deptford	a		19 39								19 49				19 59									20 19	
London Victoria	d								←				20a25			←						←			
London Bridge	d	19 54	19 47					19 52	19 54	19 57	19 58			21 09	20 07	20 09		20 24			20 22	20 24	20 27	20 28	
London Cannon Street	d	→	19a51						20a00					→	20a11	20a13		→				20a30			
Waterloo East	d							19 57		20 02											20 27		20 32		
London Charing Cross	a							20 00		20 05											20 30		20 35		
London Blackfriars	d										20 04													20 34	
City Thameslink	d										20 06													20 36	
Farringdon	d										20 09													20 39	
St Pancras International	d					21a54					20a13	19a36												20a43	20a06
West Hampstead Thameslink	d																								
St Albans	d																								
Luton Airport Parkway	d																								
Luton	a																								

Table T201-R

Saturdays

21 December to 16 May

Medway - Woolwich - Greenwich - London Thameslink

		SE		SE	SE	SE	SE	SE	SE	TL	SE	SE		SE	SE	TL	SE	SE	SE	SE	SE	SE		TL	SE
											◇						◇								
Rainham (Kent)	d									19 28							19 46							19 58	
Gillingham	d									19 34							19 51							20 04	
Chatham	d									19 38							19 55							20 08	
Rochester	d									19 42							19 59							20 12	
Strood	d									19 45	19 59						20 02							20 15	
Higham	d									19 50														20 20	
Gravesend	d	19 50								19 59		20 05					20 12	20 20						20 29	20 35
Northfleet	d									20 02		20 08												20 32	20 38
Swanscombe	d									20 04		20 10												20 34	20 40
Greenhithe	d	19 56								20 08		20 14						20 26						20 38	20 44
Stone Crossing	d									20 10		20 16												20 40	20 46
Dartford	d	20 02						20 11		20 15		20 21				←		20 32			20 41			20 45	20 51
Slade Green	d				19 59		20 07	20 16		20 21						20 21			20 29		20 46			20 51	
Erith	d				20 02			20 18		→									20 32		20 48			→	
Belvedere	d				20 04			20 21											20 34		20 51				
Abbey Wood	d				20 08			20 24								20 28			20 38		20 54				
Plumstead	d				20 11			20 27								20 31			20 41		20 57				
Woolwich Arsenal	d				20 14			20 30								20 34			20 44		21 00				
Woolwich Dockyard	d				20 16			20 33											20 46		21 03				
Charlton	d				20 20			20 36								20 40			20 50		21 06				
Westcombe Park	d				20 22											20 42			20 52						
Maze Hill	d				20 24											20 44			20 54						
Greenwich	d			20 17	20 27				20 44							20 47			20 57			21 14			
Deptford	a				20 29											20 49			20 59						
London Victoria	d	20a55				←								←	←			21a25		←					
London Bridge	d			21 39	20 37	20 39	20 54	20 57	22 09			20 52		20 54	20 57	20 58			21 07	21 09	21 27	22 39			21 22
London Cannon Street	d			→	20a41	20a43	→	→	→					21a00					21a11	21a13	→	→			
Waterloo East	d											20 57			21 02										21 27
London Charing Cross	a											21 00			21 05										21 30
London Blackfriars	d															21 04									
City Thameslink	d																								
Farringdon	d															21 09									
St Pancras International	d										22a54					21a13	20a36								
West Hampstead Thameslink	d																								
St Albans	d																								
Luton Airport Parkway	d																								
Luton	a																								

		SE	TL	SE	SE	SE	SE	SE		SE	TL	SE	SE	SE	TL	SE	SE	SE		SE	SE	SE	TL	SE	SE
				◇								◇				◇									
Rainham (Kent)	d			20 16							20 28					20 46							20 58		
Gillingham	d			20 21							20 34					20 51							21 04		
Chatham	d			20 25							20 38					20 55							21 08		
Rochester	d			20 29							20 42					20 59							21 12		
Strood	d			20 32							20 45	20 59				21 02							21 15		
Higham	d										20 50												21 20		
Gravesend	d			20 42	20 50						20 59		21 05			21 12	21 20						21 29	21 35	
Northfleet	d										21 02		21 08										21 32	21 38	
Swanscombe	d										21 04		21 10										21 34	21 40	
Greenhithe	d				20 56						21 08		21 14				21 26						21 38	21 44	
Stone Crossing	d										21 10		21 16										21 40	21 46	
Dartford	d		←		21 02			21 11			21 15		21 21		←		21 32				21 41		21 45	21 51	
Slade Green	d		20 51			20 59		21 16			21 21				21 21			21 29			21 46		21 51		
Erith	d					21 02		21 18			→							21 32			21 48		→		
Belvedere	d					21 04		21 21										21 34			21 51				
Abbey Wood	d		20 58			21 08		21 24							21 28			21 38			21 54				
Plumstead	d		21 01			21 11		21 27							21 31			21 41			21 57				
Woolwich Arsenal	d		21 04			21 14		21 30							21 34			21 44			22 00				
Woolwich Dockyard	d					21 16		21 33										21 46			22 03				
Charlton	d		21 10			21 20		21 36							21 40			21 50			22 06				
Westcombe Park	d		21 12			21 22									21 42			21 52							
Maze Hill	d		21 14			21 24									21 44			21 54							
Greenwich	d		21 17			21 27				21 44					21 47			21 57				22 14			
Deptford	a		21 19			21 29									21 49			21 59							
London Victoria	d	←			21a55		←							←			22a25			←					←
London Bridge	d	21 27	21 28			21 37	21 39	21 57		23 09			21 52	21 57	21 58			22 07		22 09	22 27	23 39		22 22	22 27
London Cannon Street	d					21a41	21a43	→		→								22a11		22a13	→	→			
Waterloo East	d	21 32											21 57	22 02										22 27	22 32
London Charing Cross	a	21 35											22 00	22 05										22 30	22 35
London Blackfriars	d		21 34												22 04										
City Thameslink	d																								
Farringdon	d		21 39												22 09										
St Pancras International	d		21a43	21a06								23a54			22a13	21a40									
West Hampstead Thameslink	d																								
St Albans	d																								
Luton Airport Parkway	d																								
Luton	a																								

Table T201-R

Saturdays

21 December to 16 May

Medway - Woolwich - Greenwich - London Thameslink

		TL	SE	SE		SE	SE	SE	SE	TL	SE	SE	TL	SE		SE	SE	SE	SE	TL	SE	SE	TL	SE
			◇											◇										◇
Rainham (Kent)	d		21 16							21 28				21 46						21 58				22 16
Gillingham	d		21 21							21 34				21 51						22 04				22 21
Chatham	d		21 25							21 38				21 55						22 08				22 25
Rochester	d		21 29							21 42				21 59						22 12				22 29
Strood	d		21 32							21 45				22 02						22 15				22 32
Higham	d									21 50										22 20				
Gravesend	d		21 42	21 50						21 59	22 05			22 12		22 20				22 29	22 35			22 42
Northfleet	d									22 02	22 08									22 32	22 38			
Swanscombe	d									22 04	22 10									22 34	22 40			
Greenhithe	d			21 56						22 08	22 14					22 26				22 38	22 44			
Stone Crossing	d									22 10	22 16									22 40	22 46			
Dartford	d	←		22 02				22 11		22 15	22 21		←			22 32			22 41	22 45	22 51		←	
Slade Green	d	21 51				21 59		22 16		22 21			22 21				22 29		22 46	22 51		←	22 51	
Erith	d					22 02		22 18		→							22 32		22 48	→		22 48		
Belvedere	d					22 04		22 21									22 34		→			22 51		
Abbey Wood	d	21 58				22 08		22 24					22 28				22 38					22 54	22 58	
Plumstead	d	22 01				22 11		22 27					22 31				22 41					22 57	23 01	
Woolwich Arsenal	d	22 04				22 14		22 30					22 34				22 44					23 00	23 04	
Woolwich Dockyard	d					22 16		22 33									22 46					23 03		
Charlton	d	22 10				22 20		22 36					22 40				22 50					23 06	23 10	
Westcombe Park	d	22 12				22 22							22 42				22 52						23 12	
Maze Hill	d	22 14				22 24							22 44				22 54						23 14	
Greenwich	d	22 17				22 27			22 44				22 47				22 57						23 17	
Deptford	a	22 19				22 29							22 49				22 59						23 19	
London Victoria	d			22a55			←					←				23a25		←						
London Bridge	d	22 28				22 37	22 39	22 57	00 09		22 52	22 57	22 58				23 07	23 09			23 22	23 27	23 28	
London Cannon Street	d					22a41	22a43	→	→								23a11	23a13						
Waterloo East	d										22 57	23 02									23 27	23 32		
London Charing Cross	a										23 00	23 05									23 30	23 35		
London Blackfriars	d	22 34											23 04										23 34	
City Thameslink	d																							
Farringdon	d	22 39											23 09										23 39	
St Pancras International	d	22 43	22a06										23 13	22a36									23 43	23a06
West Hampstead Thameslink	d	22a51											23a21										23a51	
St Albans	d																							
Luton Airport Parkway	d																							
Luton	a																							

		SE	SE	SE	SE	TL	SE	SE	SE	SE		SE	TL	SE	TL
Rainham (Kent)	d					22 28							22 58		23 28
Gillingham	d					22 34							23 04		23 34
Chatham	d					22 38							23 08		23 38
Rochester	d					22 42							23 12		23 42
Strood	d					22 45							23 15		23 45
Higham	d					22 50							23 20		23 50
Gravesend	d	22 50				22 59	23 05						23 27	23 35	23 57
Northfleet	d					23 02	23 08						23 31	23 38	00 01
Swanscombe	d					23 04	23 10						23 33	23 40	00 03
Greenhithe	d	22 56				23 08	23 14						23 36	23 44	00 06
Stone Crossing	d					23 10	23 16						23 38	23 46	00 08
Dartford	d	23 02			23 11	23a14	23 21	←				23 41	23a43	23 51	00a13
Slade Green	d		22 59		23 16			23 16	23 29			23 46			
Erith	d		23 02		→			23 18	23 32			23 48			
Belvedere	d		23 04					23 21	23 34			23 51			
Abbey Wood	d		23 08					23 24	23 38			23 54			
Plumstead	d		23 11					23 27	23 41			23 57			
Woolwich Arsenal	d		23 14					23 30	23 44			23 59			
Woolwich Dockyard	d		23 16					23 33	23 46			00 03			
Charlton	d		23 20					23 36	23 50			00 06			
Westcombe Park	d		23 22						23 52						
Maze Hill	d		23 24						23 54						
Greenwich	d		23 27						23 57						
Deptford	a		23 29						23 59						
London Victoria	d	23a55		←						←					
London Bridge	d		23 37	23 39			23 52	23 56	00 07	00 09		00 26		00 28	
London Cannon Street	d		23a41	23a43					00a11	00a13					
Waterloo East	d						23 57	00 02				00 31		00 34	
London Charing Cross	a						00 01	00 06				00 35		00 38	
London Blackfriars	d														
City Thameslink	d														
Farringdon	d														
St Pancras International	d														
West Hampstead Thameslink	d														
St Albans	d														
Luton Airport Parkway	d														
Luton	a														

Table T201-R

Sundays
15 December to 10 May

Medway - Woolwich - Greenwich - London Thameslink

		SE	SE	SE	SE	TL	SE	SE	SE	SE		TL	SE ◇	SE	SE	SE	SE	TL	SE	SE		SE	SE ◇	SE	SE
Rainham (Kent)	d												07 16					07 30					08 16		
Gillingham	d					06 36						07 06	07 21					07 36					08 21		
Chatham	d					06 40						07 10	07 25					07 40					08 25		
Rochester	d					06 44						07 14	07 29					07 44					08 29		
Strood	d					06 47						07 17	07 32					07 47					08 32		
Higham	d					06 52						07 22						07 52							
Gravesend	d					06 59		07 18				07 29	07 42		07 48			07 59				08 18	08 42		
Northfleet	d					07 03		07 21				07 33			07 51			08 03				08 21			
Swanscombe	d					07 05		07 23				07 35			07 53			08 05				08 23			
Greenhithe	d					07 08		07 27				07 38			07 57			08 08				08 27			
Stone Crossing	d					07 10		07 29				07 40			07 59			08 10				08 29			
Dartford	d		06 50			07 15	07 20	07 34				07 45		07 50	08 04			08 15		08 20		08 34			
Slade Green	d	06 35	06 55	07 05		07 21	07 25		07 35			07 51		07 55		08 05		08 21		08 25				08 35	
Erith	d	06 37	06 57	07 07			07 27		07 37					07 57		08 07				08 27				08 37	
Belvedere	d	06 40	07 00	07 10			07 30		07 40					08 00		08 10				08 30				08 40	
Abbey Wood	d	06 43	07 03	07 13		07 28	07 33		07 43			07 58		08 03		08 13		08 28		08 33				08 43	
Plumstead	d	06 46	07 06	07 16		07 31	07 36		07 46			08 01		08 06		08 16		08 31		08 36				08 46	
Woolwich Arsenal	d	06 49	07 09	07 19		07 34	07 39		07 49			08 04		08 09		08 19		08 34		08 39				08 49	
Woolwich Dockyard	d	06 52	07 12	07 22			07 42		07 52					08 12		08 22				08 42				08 52	
Charlton	d	06 55	07 15	07 25		07 40	07 45		07 55			08 10		08 15		08 25		08 40		08 45				08 55	
Westcombe Park	d	06 57		07 27		07 42			07 57			08 12				08 27		08 42						08 57	
Maze Hill	d	06 59		07 29		07 44			07 59			08 14				08 29		08 44						08 59	
Greenwich	d	07 03		07 33	07 41	07 47			08 03	08 11		08 17				08 33	08 41	08 47						09 03	
Deptford	a	07 05		07 35		07 49			08 05			08 19				08 35		08 49						09 05	
London Victoria	d																		←						←
London Bridge	d	07 13	07 35	07 43	09 00	07a57	08 05	08 11	08 13	09 30		08a27		08 35	08 41	08 43	10 00	08a57	09 00	09 05		09 11		09 13	09 30
London Cannon Street	d	07a17		07a47	→				08a17	→						08a47	→		09a04					09a17	09a34
Waterloo East	d		07 40				08 10	08 16						08 40	08 46					09 10		09 16			
London Charing Cross	a		07 43				08 15	08 19						08 44	08 49					09 13		09 19			
London Blackfriars	d																								
City Thameslink	d																								
Farringdon	d																								
St Pancras International	d												08a06										09a06		
West Hampstead Thameslink	d																								
St Albans	d																								
Luton Airport Parkway	d																								
Luton	a																								

		SE	SE	SE	SE	SE		TL	SE	SE ◇	SE	SE	SE	SE	TL	SE		SE ◇	SE	SE	SE	SE	TL	SE	SE ◇
Rainham (Kent)	d							08 30							09 00			09 16					09 30		
Gillingham	d							08 36							09 06			09 21					09 36		
Chatham	d							08 40							09 10			09 25					09 40		
Rochester	d							08 44							09 14			09 29					09 44		
Strood	d							08 47		08 59					09 17			09 32					09 47		09 59
Higham	d							08 52							09 22								09 52		
Gravesend	d		08 48					08 59				09 18			09 29			09 42		09 48			09 59		
Northfleet	d		08 51					09 03				09 21			09 33					09 51			10 03		
Swanscombe	d		08 53					09 05				09 23			09 35					09 53			10 05		
Greenhithe	d		08 57					09 08				09 27			09 38					09 57			10 08		
Stone Crossing	d		08 59					09 10				09 29			09 40					09 59			10 10		
Dartford	d	08 50	09 04					09 15			09 20	09 34			09 45				09 50	10 04			10 15		
Slade Green	d	08 55			09 05			09 21			09 25		09 35		09 51				09 55		10 05		10 21		
Erith	d	08 57			09 07						09 27		09 37						09 57		10 07				
Belvedere	d	09 00			09 10						09 30		09 40						10 00		10 10				
Abbey Wood	d	09 03			09 13			09 28			09 33		09 43		09 58				10 03		10 13		10 28		
Plumstead	d	09 06			09 16			09 31			09 36		09 46		10 01				10 06		10 16		10 31		
Woolwich Arsenal	d	09 09			09 19			09 34			09 39		09 49		10 04				10 09		10 19		10 34		
Woolwich Dockyard	d	09 12			09 22						09 42		09 52						10 12		10 22				
Charlton	d	09 15			09 25			09 40			09 45		09 55		10 10				10 15		10 25		10 40		
Westcombe Park	d				09 27			09 42					09 57		10 12						10 27		10 42		
Maze Hill	d				09 29			09 44					09 59		10 14						10 29		10 44		
Greenwich	d			09 11	09 33	09 41		09 47					10 03	10 11	10 17						10 33	10 41	10 47		
Deptford	a				09 35			09 49					10 05		10 19						10 35		10 49		
London Victoria	d								←							←								←	
London Bridge	d	09 35	09 41	10 30	09 43	11 00		09 58	10 00		10 05	10 11	10 13	11 30	10 28	10 30			10 35	10 41	10 43	12 00	10 58	11 00	
London Cannon Street	d			→	09a47	→			10a04				10a17	→		10a34					10a47	→		11a04	
Waterloo East	d	09 40	09 46								10 10	10 16							10 40	10 46					
London Charing Cross	a	09 43	09 49								10 13	10 19							10 43	10 49					
London Blackfriars	d							10 05							10 35								11 05		
City Thameslink	d																								
Farringdon	d							10 09							10 39								11 09		
St Pancras International	d							10a13		11a54					10a43			10a10					11a13		12a54
West Hampstead Thameslink	d																								
St Albans	d																								
Luton Airport Parkway	d																								
Luton	a																								

NRT DECEMBER 19 EDITION

Table T201-R

Sundays
15 December to 10 May

Medway - Woolwich - Greenwich - London Thameslink

		SE		SE	SE	SE	TL	SE	SE ◇	SE	SE	SE		SE	TL	SE	SE ◇	SE	SE	SE	SE	TL		SE	SE ◇
Rainham (Kent)	d						10 00		10 16						10 30							11 00			11 16
Gillingham	d						10 06		10 21						10 36							11 06			11 21
Chatham	d						10 10		10 25						10 40							11 10			11 25
Rochester	d						10 14		10 29						10 44							11 14			11 29
Strood	d						10 17		10 32						10 47		10 59					11 17			11 32
Higham	d						10 22								10 52							11 22			
Gravesend	d			10 18			10 29		10 42		10 48				10 59				11 18			11 29			11 42
Northfleet	d			10 21			10 33				10 51				11 03				11 21			11 33			
Swanscombe	d			10 23			10 35				10 53				11 05				11 23			11 35			
Greenhithe	d			10 27			10 38				10 57				11 08				11 27			11 38			
Stone Crossing	d			10 29			10 40				10 59				11 10				11 29			11 40			
Dartford	d	10 20		10 34			10 46			10 50	11 04				11 15			11 20	11 34			11 45			
Slade Green	d	10 25			10 35		10 51			10 55		11 05			11 21			11 25		11 35		11 51			
Erith	d	10 27			10 37					10 57		11 07						11 27		11 37					
Belvedere	d	10 30			10 40					11 00		11 10						11 30		11 40					
Abbey Wood	d	10 33			10 43		10 58			11 03		11 13			11 28			11 33		11 43		11 58			
Plumstead	d	10 36			10 46		11 01			11 06		11 16			11 31			11 36		11 46		12 01			
Woolwich Arsenal	d	10 39			10 49		11 04			11 09		11 19			11 34			11 39		11 49		12 04			
Woolwich Dockyard	d	10 42			10 52					11 12		11 22						11 42		11 52					
Charlton	d	10 45			10 55		11 10			11 15		11 25			11 40			11 45		11 55		12 10			
Westcombe Park	d				10 57		11 12					11 27			11 42					11 57		12 12			
Maze Hill	d				10 59		11 14					11 29			11 44					11 59		12 14			
Greenwich	d				11 03	11 11	11 17					11 33		11 41	11 47					12 03	12 11	12 17			
Deptford	a				11 05		11 19					11 35			11 49					12 05		12 19			
London Victoria	d							←								←								←	
London Bridge	d	11 05		11 11	11 13	12 30	11 28	11 30		11 35	11 41	11 43		13 00	11 58	12 00		12 05	12 11	12 13	13 30	12 28		12 30	
London Cannon Street	d				11a17	→		11a34				11a47		→		12a04				12a17	→			12a34	
Waterloo East	d	11 10		11 16						11 40	11 46							12 10	12 16						
London Charing Cross	a	11 13		11 19						11 43	11 49							12 13	12 19						
London Blackfriars	d						11 35								12 05							12 35			
City Thameslink	d																								
Farringdon	d						11 39								12 09							12 39			
St Pancras International	d						11a43		11a06						12a13		13a54					12a43			12a06
West Hampstead Thameslink	d																								
St Albans	d																								
Luton Airport Parkway	d																								
Luton	a																								

		SE	SE	SE	SE	TL	SE	SE ◇		SE ◇	SE	SE	SE	SE	TL	SE	SE ◇	SE		SE	SE	SE	TL	SE	SE ◇
Rainham (Kent)	d					11 30				11 46					12 00		12 16						12 30		
Gillingham	d					11 36				11 51					12 06		12 21						12 36		
Chatham	d					11 40				11 55					12 10		12 25						12 40		
Rochester	d					11 44				11 59					12 14		12 29						12 44		
Strood	d					11 47		11 59		12 02					12 17		12 32						12 47		12 59
Higham	d					11 52									12 22								12 52		
Gravesend	d		11 48			11 59				12 12		12 18			12 29		12 42			12 48			12 59		
Northfleet	d		11 51			12 03						12 21			12 33					12 51			13 03		
Swanscombe	d		11 53			12 05						12 23			12 35					12 53			13 05		
Greenhithe	d		11 57			12 08						12 27			12 38					12 57			13 08		
Stone Crossing	d		11 59			12 10						12 29			12 40					12 59			13 10		
Dartford	d	11 50	12 04			12 15					12 20	12 34			12 45			12 50		13 04			13 15		
Slade Green	d	11 55		12 05		12 21					12 25		12 35		12 51			12 55			13 05		13 21		
Erith	d	11 57		12 07							12 27		12 37					12 57			13 07				
Belvedere	d	12 00		12 10							12 30		12 40					13 00			13 10				
Abbey Wood	d	12 03		12 13		12 28					12 33		12 43		12 58			13 03			13 13		13 28		
Plumstead	d	12 06		12 16		12 31					12 36		12 46		13 01			13 06			13 16		13 31		
Woolwich Arsenal	d	12 09		12 19		12 34					12 39		12 49		13 04			13 09			13 19		13 34		
Woolwich Dockyard	d	12 12		12 22							12 42		12 52					13 12			13 22				
Charlton	d	12 15		12 25		12 40					12 45		12 55		13 10			13 15			13 25		13 40		
Westcombe Park	d			12 27		12 42							12 57		13 12						13 27		13 42		
Maze Hill	d			12 29		12 44							12 59		13 14						13 29		13 44		
Greenwich	d			12 33	12 41	12 47							13 03	13 11	13 17						13 33	13 41	13 47		
Deptford	a			12 35		12 49							13 05		13 19						13 35		13 49		
London Victoria	d						←									←								←	
London Bridge	d	12 35	12 41	12 43	14 00	12 58	13 00				13 05	13 11	13 13	14 30	13 28	13 30		13 35		13 41	13 43	15 00	13 58	14 00	
London Cannon Street	d			12a47	→		13a04						13a17	→		13a34					13a47	→		14a04	
Waterloo East	d	12 40	12 46								13 10	13 16						13 40		13 46					
London Charing Cross	a	12 43	12 49								13 13	13 19						13 43		13 49					
London Blackfriars	d					13 05									13 35								14 05		
City Thameslink	d																								
Farringdon	d					13 09									13 39								14 09		
St Pancras International	d					13a13		14a54		12a36					13a43		13a06						14a13		15a54
West Hampstead Thameslink	d																								
St Albans	d																								
Luton Airport Parkway	d																								
Luton	a																								

Table T201-R

Sundays

15 December to 10 May

Medway - Woolwich - Greenwich - London Thameslink

Station		SE ◇	SE	SE	SE	SE	TL	SE	SE ◇	SE	SE	SE	SE	TL	SE	SE ◇	SE ◇	SE	SE	SE	SE	TL
Rainham (Kent)	d	12 46					13 00		13 16					13 30			13 46					14 00
Gillingham	d	12 51					13 06		13 21					13 36			13 51					14 06
Chatham	d	12 55					13 10		13 25					13 40			13 55					14 10
Rochester	d	12 59					13 14		13 29					13 44			13 59					14 14
Strood	d	13 02					13 17		13 32					13 47		13 59	14 02					14 17
Higham	d						13 22							13 52								14 22
Gravesend	d	13 12		13 18			13 29		13 42		13 48			13 59			14 12		14 18			14 29
Northfleet	d			13 21			13 33				13 51			14 03					14 21			14 33
Swanscombe	d			13 23			13 35				13 53			14 05					14 23			14 35
Greenhithe	d			13 27			13 38				13 57			14 08					14 27			14 38
Stone Crossing	d			13 29			13 40				13 59			14 10					14 29			14 40
Dartford	d		13 20	13 34			13 45			13 50	14 04			14 15				14 20	14 34			14 45
Slade Green	d		13 25		13 35		13 51			13 55		14 05		14 21				14 25		14 35		14 51
Erith	d		13 27		13 37					13 57		14 07						14 27		14 37		
Belvedere	d		13 30		13 40					14 00		14 10						14 30		14 40		
Abbey Wood	d		13 33		13 43		13 58			14 03		14 13		14 28				14 33		14 43		14 58
Plumstead	d		13 36		13 46		14 01			14 06		14 16		14 31				14 36		14 46		15 01
Woolwich Arsenal	d		13 39		13 49		14 04			14 09		14 19		14 34				14 39		14 49		15 04
Woolwich Dockyard	d		13 42		13 52					14 12		14 22						14 42		14 52		
Charlton	d		13 45		13 55		14 10			14 15		14 25		14 40				14 45		14 55		15 10
Westcombe Park	d				13 57		14 12					14 27		14 42						14 57		15 12
Maze Hill	d				13 59		14 14					14 29		14 44						14 59		15 14
Greenwich	d				14 03	14 11	14 17					14 33	14 41	14 47						15 03	15 11	15 17
Deptford	a				14 05		14 19					14 35		14 49						15 05		15 19
London Victoria	d							←							←							
London Bridge	d		14 05	14 11	14 13	15 30	14 28	14 30		14 35	14 41	14 43	16 00	14 58	15 00			15 05	15 11	15 13	16 30	15 28
London Cannon Street	d				14a17	→		14a34				14a47	→		15a04					15a17	→	
Waterloo East	d		14 10	14 16						14 40	14 46							15 10	15 16			
London Charing Cross	a		14 13	14 19						14 43	14 49							15 13	15 19			
London Blackfriars	d						14 35							15 05								15 35
City Thameslink	d																					
Farringdon	d						14 39							15 09								15 39
St Pancras International	d	13a37					14a43		14a06					15a13		16a54	14a36					15a43
West Hampstead Thameslink	d																					
St Albans	d																					
Luton Airport Parkway	d																					
Luton	a																					

Station		SE	SE ◇	SE	SE	SE	SE	TL	SE	SE ◇	SE ◇	SE	SE	SE	SE	TL	SE	SE ◇	SE	SE	SE	SE	TL
Rainham (Kent)	d		14 16					14 30			14 46					15 00		15 16					15 30
Gillingham	d		14 21					14 36			14 51					15 06		15 21					15 36
Chatham	d		14 25					14 40			14 55					15 10		15 25					15 40
Rochester	d		14 29					14 44			14 59					15 14		15 29					15 44
Strood	d		14 32					14 47		14 59	15 02					15 17		15 32					15 47
Higham	d							14 52								15 22							15 52
Gravesend	d		14 42		14 48			14 59			15 12		15 18			15 29		15 42		15 48			15 59
Northfleet	d				14 51			15 03					15 21			15 33				15 51			16 03
Swanscombe	d				14 53			15 05					15 23			15 35				15 53			16 05
Greenhithe	d				14 57			15 08					15 27			15 38				15 57			16 08
Stone Crossing	d				14 59			15 10					15 29			15 40				15 59			16 10
Dartford	d			14 50	15 04			15 15				15 20	15 34			15 45			15 50	16 04			16 15
Slade Green	d			14 55		15 05		15 21				15 25		15 35		15 51			15 55		16 05		16 21
Erith	d			14 57		15 07						15 27		15 37					15 57		16 07		
Belvedere	d			15 00		15 10						15 30		15 40					16 00		16 10		
Abbey Wood	d			15 03		15 13		15 28				15 33		15 43		15 58			16 03		16 13		16 28
Plumstead	d			15 06		15 16		15 31				15 36		15 46		16 01			16 06		16 16		16 31
Woolwich Arsenal	d			15 09		15 19		15 34				15 39		15 49		16 04			16 09		16 19		16 34
Woolwich Dockyard	d			15 12		15 22						15 42		15 52					16 12		16 22		
Charlton	d			15 15		15 25		15 40				15 45		15 55		16 10			16 15		16 25		16 40
Westcombe Park	d					15 27		15 42						15 57		16 12					16 27		16 42
Maze Hill	d					15 29		15 44						15 59		16 14					16 29		16 44
Greenwich	d					15 33	15 41	15 47						16 03	16 11	16 17					16 33	16 41	16 47
Deptford	a					15 35		15 49						16 05		16 19					16 35		16 49
London Victoria	d	←							←								←						
London Bridge	d	15 30		15 35	15 41	15 43	17 00	15 58	16 00			16 05	16 11	16 13	17 30	16 28	16 30		16 35	16 41	16 43	18 00	16 58
London Cannon Street	d	15a34				15a47	→		16a04					16a17	→		16a34				16a47	→	
Waterloo East	d			15 40	15 46							16 10	16 16						16 40	16 46			
London Charing Cross	a			15 43	15 49							16 13	16 19						16 43	16 49			
London Blackfriars	d							16 05								16 35							17 05
City Thameslink	d																						
Farringdon	d							16 09								16 39							17 09
St Pancras International	d		15a07					16a13		17a54	15a36					16a43		16a10					17a13
West Hampstead Thameslink	d																						
St Albans	d																						
Luton Airport Parkway	d																						
Luton	a																						

Table T201-R

Sundays

15 December to 10 May

Medway - Woolwich - Greenwich - London Thameslink

Station		SE	SE ◇	SE ◇	SE	SE	SE	SE	TL	SE	SE ◇	SE	SE	SE	SE	TL	SE	SE ◇	SE ◇	SE	SE	SE	SE
Rainham (Kent)	d			15 46					16 00		16 16					16 30			16 46				
Gillingham	d			15 51					16 06		16 21					16 36			16 51				
Chatham	d			15 55					16 10		16 25					16 40			16 55				
Rochester	d			15 59					16 14		16 29					16 44			16 59				
Strood	d		15 59	16 02					16 17		16 32					16 47		16 59	17 02				
Higham	d								16 22							16 52							
Gravesend	d			16 12		16 18			16 29		16 42		16 48			16 59			17 12		17 18		
Northfleet	d					16 21			16 33				16 51			17 03					17 21		
Swanscombe	d					16 23			16 35				16 53			17 05					17 23		
Greenhithe	d					16 27			16 38				16 57			17 08					17 27		
Stone Crossing	d					16 29			16 40				16 59			17 10					17 29		
Dartford	d				16 20	16 34			16 45			16 50	17 04			17 15				17 20	17 34		
Slade Green	d				16 25		16 35		16 51			16 55		17 05		17 21				17 25		17 35	
Erith	d				16 27		16 37					16 57		17 07						17 27		17 37	
Belvedere	d				16 30		16 40					17 00		17 10						17 30		17 40	
Abbey Wood	d				16 33		16 43		16 58			17 03		17 13		17 28				17 33		17 43	
Plumstead	d				16 36		16 46		17 01			17 06		17 16		17 31				17 36		17 46	
Woolwich Arsenal	d				16 39		16 49		17 04			17 09		17 19		17 34				17 39		17 49	
Woolwich Dockyard	d				16 42		16 52					17 12		17 22						17 42		17 52	
Charlton	d				16 45		16 55		17 10			17 15		17 25		17 40				17 45		17 55	
Westcombe Park	d						16 57		17 12					17 27		17 42						17 57	
Maze Hill	d						16 59		17 14					17 29		17 44						17 59	
Greenwich	d						17 03	17 11	17 17					17 33	17 41	17 47						18 03	18 11
Deptford	a						17 05		17 19					17 35		17 49						18 05	
London Victoria	d	←								←							←						
London Bridge	d	17 00			17 05	17 11	17 13	18 30	17 28	17 30		17 35	17 41	17 43	19 00	17 58	18 00			18 05	18 11	18 13	19 30
London Cannon Street	d	17a04					17a17	→		17a34				17a47	→		18a04					18a17	→
Waterloo East	d				17 10	17 16						17 40	17 46							18 10	18 16		
London Charing Cross	a				17 13	17 19						17 43	17 49							18 13	18 19		
London Blackfriars	d								17 35							18 05							
City Thameslink	d																						
Farringdon	d								17 39							18 09							
St Pancras International	d		18a54	16a36					17a43		17a10					18a13		19a54	17a36				
West Hampstead Thameslink	d																						
St Albans	d																						
Luton Airport Parkway	d																						
Luton	a																						

Station		TL	SE	SE ◇	SE	SE	SE	SE	TL	SE	SE ◇	SE ◇	SE	SE	SE	SE	TL	SE	SE ◇	SE	SE	SE
Rainham (Kent)	d	17 00		17 16					17 30			17 46					18 00		18 16			
Gillingham	d	17 06		17 21					17 36			17 51					18 06		18 21			
Chatham	d	17 10		17 25					17 40			17 55					18 10		18 25			
Rochester	d	17 14		17 29					17 44			17 59					18 14		18 29			
Strood	d	17 17		17 32					17 47		17 59	18 02					18 17		18 32			
Higham	d	17 22							17 52								18 22					
Gravesend	d	17 29		17 42		17 48			17 59			18 12		18 18			18 29		18 42		18 48	
Northfleet	d	17 33				17 51			18 03					18 21			18 33				18 51	
Swanscombe	d	17 35				17 53			18 05					18 23			18 35				18 53	
Greenhithe	d	17 38				17 57			18 08					18 27			18 38				18 57	
Stone Crossing	d	17 40				17 59			18 10					18 29			18 40				18 59	
Dartford	d	17 45			17 50	18 04			18 15				18 20	18 34			18 45			18 50	19 04	
Slade Green	d	17 51			17 55		18 05		18 21				18 25		18 35		18 51			18 55		19 05
Erith	d				17 57		18 07						18 27		18 37					18 57		19 07
Belvedere	d				18 00		18 10						18 30		18 40					19 00		19 10
Abbey Wood	d	17 58			18 03		18 13		18 28				18 33		18 43		18 58			19 03		19 13
Plumstead	d	18 01			18 06		18 16		18 31				18 36		18 46		19 01			19 06		19 16
Woolwich Arsenal	d	18 04			18 09		18 19		18 34				18 39		18 49		19 04			19 09		19 19
Woolwich Dockyard	d				18 12		18 22						18 42		18 52					19 12		19 22
Charlton	d	18 10			18 15		18 25		18 40				18 45		18 55		19 10			19 15		19 25
Westcombe Park	d	18 12					18 27		18 42						18 57		19 12					19 27
Maze Hill	d	18 14					18 29		18 44						18 59		19 14					19 29
Greenwich	d	18 17					18 33	18 41	18 47						19 03	19 11	19 17					19 33
Deptford	a	18 19					18 35		18 49						19 05		19 19					19 35
London Victoria	d		←							←								←				
London Bridge	d	18 28	18 30		18 35	18 41	18 43	20 00	18 58	19 00			19 05	19 11	19 13	20 30	19 28	19 30		19 35	19 41	19 43
London Cannon Street	d		18a34				18a47	→		19a04					19a17	→		19a34				19a47
Waterloo East	d				18 40	18 46							19 10	19 16						19 40	19 46	
London Charing Cross	a				18 43	18 49							19 13	19 19						19 43	19 49	
London Blackfriars	d	18 35							19 05								19 35					
City Thameslink	d																					
Farringdon	d	18 39							19 09								19 39					
St Pancras International	d	18a43		18a10					19a13		20a54	18a36					19a43		19a07			
West Hampstead Thameslink	d																					
St Albans	d																					
Luton Airport Parkway	d																					
Luton	a																					

Table T201-R

Sundays
15 December to 10 May

Medway - Woolwich - Greenwich - London Thameslink

		SE	TL	SE	SE	SE	SE	SE	SE	SE	TL	SE	SE	SE	SE	SE	SE	TL	SE	SE	SE	SE	SE
					◇	◇							◇							◇	◇		
Rainham (Kent)	d		18 30			18 46					19 00		19 16					19 30			19 46		
Gillingham	d		18 36			18 51					19 06		19 21					19 36			19 51		
Chatham	d		18 40			18 55					19 10		19 25					19 40			19 55		
Rochester	d		18 44			18 59					19 14		19 29					19 44			19 59		
Strood	d		18 47		18 59	19 02					19 17		19 32					19 47		19 59	20 02		
Higham	d		18 52								19 22							19 52					
Gravesend	d		18 59			19 12		19 18			19 29		19 42		19 48			19 59			20 12		20 18
Northfleet	d		19 03					19 21			19 33				19 51			20 03					20 21
Swanscombe	d		19 05					19 23			19 35				19 53			20 05					20 23
Greenhithe	d		19 08					19 27			19 38				19 57			20 08					20 27
Stone Crossing	d		19 10					19 29			19 40				19 59			20 10					20 29
Dartford	d		19 15				19 20	19 34			19 45			19 50	20 04			20 15				20 20	20 34
Slade Green	d		19 21				19 25		19 35		19 51			19 55		20 05		20 21				20 25	
Erith	d						19 27		19 37					19 57		20 07						20 27	
Belvedere	d						19 30		19 40					20 00		20 10						20 30	
Abbey Wood	d		19 28				19 33		19 43		19 58			20 03		20 13		20 28				20 33	
Plumstead	d		19 31				19 36		19 46		20 01			20 06		20 16		20 31				20 36	
Woolwich Arsenal	d		19 34				19 39		19 49		20 04			20 09		20 19		20 34				20 39	
Woolwich Dockyard	d						19 42		19 52					20 12		20 22						20 42	
Charlton	d		19 40				19 45		19 55		20 10			20 15		20 25		20 40				20 45	
Westcombe Park	d		19 42						19 57		20 12					20 27		20 42					
Maze Hill	d		19 44						19 59		20 14					20 29		20 44					
Greenwich	d	19 41	19 47						20 03	20 11	20 17					20 33	20 41	20 47					
Deptford	a		19 49						20 05		20 19					20 35		20 49					
London Victoria	d			←								←							←				
London Bridge	d	21 00	19 58	20 00			20 05	20 11	20 13	21 30	20 28	20 30		20 35	20 41	20 43	22 00	20 58	21 00			21 05	21 11
London Cannon Street	d	→		20a04					20a17	→		20a34				20a47	→		21a04				
Waterloo East	d						20 10	20 16						20 40	20 46							21 10	21 16
London Charing Cross	a						20 13	20 19						20 43	20 49							21 13	21 19
London Blackfriars	d		20 05								20 35							21 05					
City Thameslink	d																						
Farringdon	d		20 09								20 39							21 09					
St Pancras International	d		20a13		21a54	19a36					20a43		20a06					21a13		22a54	20a36		
West Hampstead Thameslink	d																						
St Albans	d																						
Luton Airport Parkway	d																						
Luton	a																						

		SE	SE	TL	SE	SE	SE	SE	SE	SE	TL	SE	SE	SE	SE	SE	SE	TL	SE	SE	SE	SE
						◇							◇							◇		
Rainham (Kent)	d			20 00		20 16					20 30		20 46					21 00		21 16		
Gillingham	d			20 06		20 21					20 36		20 51					21 06		21 21		
Chatham	d			20 10		20 25					20 40		20 55					21 10		21 25		
Rochester	d			20 14		20 29					20 44		20 59					21 14		21 29		
Strood	d			20 17		20 32					20 47		21 02					21 17		21 32		
Higham	d			20 22							20 52							21 22				
Gravesend	d			20 29		20 42		20 48			20 59		21 12		21 18			21 29		21 42		21 48
Northfleet	d			20 33				20 51			21 03				21 21			21 33				21 51
Swanscombe	d			20 35				20 53			21 05				21 23			21 35				21 53
Greenhithe	d			20 38				20 57			21 08				21 27			21 38				21 57
Stone Crossing	d			20 40				20 59			21 10				21 29			21 40				21 59
Dartford	d			20 45			20 50	21 04			21 15			21 20	21 34			21 45			21 50	22 04
Slade Green	d	20 35		20 51			20 55		21 05		21 21			21 25		21 35		21 51			21 55	
Erith	d	20 37					20 57		21 07					21 27		21 37					21 57	
Belvedere	d	20 40					21 00		21 10					21 30		21 40					22 00	
Abbey Wood	d	20 43		20 58			21 03		21 13		21 28			21 33		21 43		21 58			22 03	
Plumstead	d	20 46		21 01			21 06		21 16		21 31			21 36		21 46		22 01			22 06	
Woolwich Arsenal	d	20 49		21 04			21 09		21 19		21 34			21 39		21 49		22 04			22 09	
Woolwich Dockyard	d	20 52					21 12		21 22					21 42		21 52					22 12	
Charlton	d	20 55		21 10			21 15		21 25		21 40			21 45		21 55		22 10			22 15	
Westcombe Park	d	20 57		21 12					21 27		21 42					21 57		22 12				
Maze Hill	d	20 59		21 14					21 29		21 44					21 59		22 14				
Greenwich	d	21 03	21 11	21 17					21 33	21 41	21 47					22 03	22 11	22 17				
Deptford	a	21 05		21 19					21 35		21 49					22 05		22 19				
London Victoria	d				←							←							←			
London Bridge	d	21 13	22 30	21 28	21 30		21 35	21 41	21 43	23 00	21 58	22 00		22 05	22 11	22 13	23 30	22 28	22 30		22 35	22 41
London Cannon Street	d	21a17	→		21a34				21a47	→		22a04				22a17	→		22a34			
Waterloo East	d						21 40	21 46						22 10	22 16						22 40	22 46
London Charing Cross	a						21 43	21 49						22 13	22 19						22 43	22 49
London Blackfriars	d			21 35							22 05							22 35				
City Thameslink	d																					
Farringdon	d			21 39							22 09							22 39				
St Pancras International	d			21a43		21a06					22a13		21a40					22a43		22a07		
West Hampstead Thameslink	d																					
St Albans	d																					
Luton Airport Parkway	d																					
Luton	a																					

NRT DECEMBER 19 EDITION

Table T201-R

Sundays
15 December to 10 May

Medway - Woolwich - Greenwich - London Thameslink

		SE	SE	TL	SE	SE	SE	SE	SE	TL	SE	SE	SE	SE	TL	SE	SE	SE	SE	TL	TL
						◇						◇									
Rainham (Kent)	d			21 30		21 46				22 00		22 16			22 30					23 00	23 30
Gillingham	d			21 36		21 51				22 06		22 21			22 36					23 06	23 36
Chatham	d			21 40		21 55				22 10		22 25			22 40					23 10	23 40
Rochester	d			21 44		21 59				22 14		22 29			22 44					23 14	23 44
Strood	d			21 47		22 02				22 17		22 32			22 47					23 17	23 47
Higham	d			21 52						22 22					22 52					23 22	23 52
Gravesend	d			21 59		22 12		22 18		22 29		22 42		22 48	22 59				23 18	23 29	23 59
Northfleet	d			22 03				22 21		22 33				22 51	23 03				23 21	23 33	00 03
Swanscombe	d			22 05				22 23		22 35				22 53	23 05				23 23	23 35	00 05
Greenhithe	d			22 08				22 27		22 38				22 57	23 08				23 27	23 38	00 08
Stone Crossing	d			22 10				22 29		22 40				22 59	23 10				23 29	23 40	00 10
Dartford	d			22 15			22 20	22 34		22 45			22 50	23 04	23a15			23 20	23 34	23a45	00a15
Slade Green	d	22 05		22 21			22 25		22 35	22 51			22 55			23 05		23 25			
Erith	d	22 07					22 27		22 37				22 57			23 07		23 27			
Belvedere	d	22 10					22 30		22 40				23 00			23 10		23 30			
Abbey Wood	d	22 13		22 28			22 33		22 43	22 58			23 03			23 13		23 33			
Plumstead	d	22 16		22 31			22 36		22 46	23 01			23 06			23 16		23 36			
Woolwich Arsenal	d	22 19		22 34			22 39		22 49	23 04			23 09			23 19		23 39			
Woolwich Dockyard	d	22 22					22 42		22 52				23 12			23 22		23 42			
Charlton	d	22 25		22 40			22 45		22 55	23 10			23 15			23 25		23 45			
Westcombe Park	d	22 27		22 42					22 57	23 12						23 27					
Maze Hill	d	22 29		22 44					22 59	23 14						23 29					
Greenwich	d	22 33	22 41	22 47					23 03	23 17						23 33					
Deptford	a	22 35		22 49					23 05	23 19						23 35					
London Victoria	d				←						←						←				
London Bridge	d	22 43	23 59	22 58	23 00		23 05	23 11	23 13	23 28	23 30		23 35	23 41		23 43	23 59	00 05	00 11		
London Cannon Street	d	22a47	→		23a04				23a17		23a34					23a47	00a04				
Waterloo East	d						23 10	23 16					23 40	23 46				00 10	00 16		
London Charing Cross	a						23 13	23 19					23 43	23 49				00 13	00 19		
London Blackfriars	d			23 05						23 37											
City Thameslink	d																				
Farringdon	d			23 09						23 41											
St Pancras International	d			23 14		22a36				23 46		23a06									
West Hampstead Thameslink	d			23a22						23 54											
St Albans	d									00 21											
Luton Airport Parkway	d									00 32											
Luton	a									00 36											

AVAILABLE FROM MP Middleton Press

Table T203-F

Mondays to Fridays

16 December to 15 May

London - Hayes via Catford Bridge

Miles	Miles	Station		SE MX	SE MO	SE MX	SE ThFO	SE TWO	SE	SE	SE	SE	SE	SE	SE	SE	SE	SE	SE	SE	SE	SE
0	—	**London Charing Cross** 4	⊖ d				00 07		05 48	06 17		06 47			07 31	07 43	08 00	08 04		08 36		09 07
0¾	—	**London Waterloo (East)** 4	⊖ d				00 10		05 51	06 20		06 50			07 34	07 46	08 03	08 07		08 39		09 10
—	0	**London Cannon Street** 4	⊖ d					00 27			06 28		07 00	07 19					08 22		08 58	
1¾	0¾	**London Bridge** 4	⊖ d				00 16	00 32	05 57	06 26	06 32	06 56	07 04	07 23	07 40	07 52	08 09	08 13		08 45	09 02	09 17
4¾	—	New Cross 4	⊖ d					00 38			06 38		07 10	07 29					08 34		09 08	
5½	—	St Johns	d					00 40			06 40		07 12	07 31					08 36		09 10	
6	—	**Lewisham** 4	d				00 25	00 43	06 08		06 43		07 18	07 36					08 39		09 13	
6¾	—	Ladywell	d				00 28	00 46	06 11	06 37	06 46	07 05	07 21	07 39	07 51	08 02	08 18	08 25	08 42	08 55	09 16	09 26
7½	—	**Catford Bridge**	d				00 30	00 48	06 14	06 39	06 48	07 08	07 23	07 42	07 54	08 05	08 21	08 27	08 44	08 58	09 18	09 29
9	—	Lower Sydenham	d			00 01	00 33	00 51	06 17	06 42	06 51	07 11	07 26	07 45	07 57	08 08	08 24	08 30	08 47	09 01	09 21	09 32
9½	—	New Beckenham 4	d			00 03	00 35	00 53	06 19	06 44	06 53	07 13	07 28	07 47	07 59	08 10	08 26	08 32	08 49	09 03	09 23	09 34
10¼	—	Clock House	d		00 02	00 05	00 38	00 56	06 21	06 47	06 56	07 15	07 31	07 49	08 01	08 12	08 28	08 35	08 52	09 05	09 26	09 36
11	—	Elmers End 4	d		00 05	00 08	00 41	00 59	06 24	06 50	06 59	07 18	07 34	07 52	08 04	08 15	08 31	08 38	08 55	09 08	09 29	09 39
12½	—	Eden Park	d	00 02	00 08	00 12	00 44	01 02	06 28	06 53	07 02	07 22	07 37	07 56		08 19		08 41	08 58	09 12	09 32	09 43
13½	—	West Wickham	d	00 05	00 11	00 14	00 47	01 05	06 30	06 56	07 05	07 24	07 40	07 58		08 21		08 44	09 01	09 14	09 35	09 45
14½	—	**Hayes**	a	00 08	00 15	00 18	00 53	01 10	06 35	07 01	07 11	07 30	07 46	08 06	08 13	08 28	08 40	08 50	09 07	09 21	09 40	09 49

Station		SE	SE	SE	SE		SE	SE	SE	SE	SE	SE	SE	SE	SE	SE	SE	SE	SE	SE	SE	SE
London Charing Cross 4	⊖ d		09 37		10 07			14 37		15 07		15 37		16 07		16 35		16 58		17 21		17 43
London Waterloo (East) 4	⊖ d		09 40		10 10			14 40		15 10		15 40		16 10		16 38		17 01		17 24		17 46
London Cannon Street 4	⊖ d	09 27		09 57			14 27		14 57		15 27		15 57		16 25		16 50		17 11		17 32	
London Bridge 4	⊖ d	09 31	09 46	10 01	10 16	and at	14 31	14 46	15 01	15 16	15 31	15 46	16 01	16 16	16 30	16 44	16 55	17 07	17 16	17 30	17 37	17 52
New Cross 4	⊖ d	09 37		10 07		the same	14 37		15 07		15 37		16 07		16 36		17 01		17 22		17 43	
St Johns	d	09 39		10 09		minutes	14 39		15 09		15 39		16 09		16 38		17 03		17 24		17 45	
Lewisham 4	d	09 43		10 13		past	14 43		15 13		15 43		16 13		16 42		17 07		17 29		17 49	
Ladywell	d	09 46	09 55	10 16	10 25	each	14 46	14 55	15 16	15 25	15 46	15 55	16 16	16 26	16 45	16 55	17 10	17 18	17 32	17 42	17 52	18 02
Catford Bridge	d	09 48	09 58	10 18	10 28	hour until	14 48	14 58	15 18	15 28	15 48	15 58	16 18	16 29	16 48	16 57	17 13	17 20	17 35	17 44	17 55	18 04
Lower Sydenham	d	09 51	10 01	10 21	10 31		14 51	15 01	15 21	15 31	15 51	16 01	16 21	16 32	16 51	17 00	17 16	17 23	17 38	17 47	17 58	18 08
New Beckenham 4	d	09 53	10 03	10 23	10 33		14 53	15 03	15 23	15 33	15 53	16 03	16 23	16 34	16 53	17 03	17 18	17 26	17 40	17 50	18 00	18 10
Clock House	d	09 56	10 05	10 26	10 35		14 56	15 05	15 26	15 35	15 56	16 05	16 26	16 37	16 56	17 06	17 21	17 28	17 43	17 52	18 03	18 13
Elmers End 4	d	09 59	10 08	10 29	10 38		14 59	15 08	15 29	15 38	15 59	16 08	16 29	16 40	16 59	17 09	17 24	17 31	17 46	17 55	18 06	18 16
Eden Park	d	10 02	10 12	10 32	10 42		15 02	15 12	15 32	15 42	16 02	16 12	16 32	16 43	17 02	17 12	17 27	17 35	17 49	17 59	18 09	18 20
West Wickham	d	10 05	10 14	10 35	10 44		15 05	15 14	15 35	15 44	16 05	16 14	16 35	16 46	17 05	17 15	17 30	17 37	17 52	18 01	18 12	18 22
Hayes	a	10 08	10 18	10 38	10 48		15 08	15 18	15 38	15 48	16 08	16 18	16 38	16 51	17 11	17 21	17 36	17 44	17 57	18 08	18 18	18 30

Station		SE	SE	SE	SE	SE	SE	SE	SE	SE	SE	SE	SE		SE	SE	SE	SE	SE	SE	SE FO
London Charing Cross 4	⊖ d		18 04		18 27		18 52		19 07		19 37		20 07			22 37		23 07		23 37	
London Waterloo (East) 4	⊖ d		18 07		18 30		18 55		19 10		19 40		20 10			22 40		23 10		23 40	
London Cannon Street 4	⊖ d	17 55		18 15		18 38		18 57		19 27		19 57			22 27		22 57		23 27		23 57
London Bridge 4	⊖ d	18 00	18 13	18 20	18 36	18 43	19 01	19 02	19 16	19 31	19 46	20 01	20 16	and at	22 31	22 46	23 01	23 16	23 31	23 46	00 01
New Cross 4	⊖ d	18 06		18 26		18 49		19 08		19 37		20 07		the same	22 37		23 07		23 37		00 07
St Johns	d	18 08		18 28		18 51		19 10		19 39		20 09		minutes	22 39		23 09		23 39		00 09
Lewisham 4	d	18 13		18 32		18 55		19 14		19 43		20 13		past	22 43		23 13		23 43		00 13
Ladywell	d	18 16	18 23	18 35	18 46	18 58	19 11	19 17	19 26	19 46	19 55	20 16	20 25	each	22 46	22 55	23 16	23 25	23 46	23 55	00 16
Catford Bridge	d	18 19	18 26	18 38	18 48	19 01	19 13	19 20	19 28	19 48	19 58	20 18	20 28	hour until	22 48	22 58	23 18	23 28	23 48	23 58	00 18
Lower Sydenham	d	18 22	18 29	18 41	18 52	19 04	19 17	19 23	19 31	19 51	20 01	20 21	20 31		22 51	23 01	23 21	23 31	23 51	00 01	00 21
New Beckenham 4	d	18 24	18 32	18 43	18 54	19 06	19 19	19 25	19 34	19 53	20 03	20 23	20 33		22 53	23 03	23 23	23 33	23 53	00 03	00 23
Clock House	d	18 27	18 35	18 46	18 57	19 09	19 22	19 28	19 36	19 56	20 05	20 26	20 35		22 56	23 05	23 26	23 35	23 56	00 05	00 26
Elmers End 4	d	18 30	18 38	18 49	19 00	19 12	19 25	19 31	19 39	19 59	20 08	20 29	20 38		22 59	23 08	23 29	23 38	23 59	00 08	00 29
Eden Park	d	18 33	18 41	18 52	19 04	19 15	19 29	19 34	19 43	20 02	20 12	20 32	20 42		23 02	23 12	23 32	23 42	00 02	00 12	00 32
West Wickham	d	18 36	18 44	18 55	19 06	19 18	19 31	19 37	19 45	20 05	20 14	20 35	20 44		23 05	23 14	23 35	23 44	00 05	00 14	00 35
Hayes	a	18 42	18 50	19 01	19 13	19 24	19 37	19 43	19 51	20 08	20 18	20 38	20 48		23 08	23 18	23 38	23 48	00 08	00 18	00 40

Saturdays

21 December to 16 May

Station		SE	SE	SE	SE	SE	SE	SE	SE	SE	SE	SE		SE	SE	SE	SE	SE	SE	SE	SE	SE
London Charing Cross 4	⊖ d				00 07	05 37	06 07	06 37		07 07		07 37			22 07		22 37		23 07		23 37	
London Waterloo (East) 4	⊖ d				00 10	05 40	06 10	06 40		07 10		07 40			22 10		22 40		23 10		23 40	
London Cannon Street 4	⊖ d								06 57		07 27			21 57		22 27		22 57		23 27		23 57
London Bridge 4	⊖ d			00 01	00 16	05 46	06 16	06 46	07 01	07 16	07 31	07 46	and at	22 01	22 16	22 31	22 46	23 01	23 16	23 31	23 46	00 01
New Cross 4	⊖ d			00 07					07 07		07 37		the same	22 07		22 37		23 07		23 37		00 07
St Johns	d			00 09					07 09		07 39		minutes	22 09		22 39		23 10		23 40		00 09
Lewisham 4	d			00 13		05 57	06 27	06 58	07 13		07 43		past	22 13		22 43		23 13		23 43		00 13
Ladywell	d			00 16	00 25	06 00	06 30	07 01	07 16	07 25	07 46	07 55	each	22 16	22 25	22 46	22 55	23 16	23 25	23 46	23 55	00 16
Catford Bridge	d			00 18	00 28	06 02	06 32	07 03	07 18	07 28	07 48	07 58	hour until	22 18	22 28	22 48	22 58	23 18	23 28	23 48	23 58	00 18
Lower Sydenham	d		00 01	00 21	00 31	06 05	06 35	07 06	07 21	07 31	07 51	08 01		22 21	22 31	22 51	23 01	23 21	23 31	23 51	00 01	00 21
New Beckenham 4	d		00 03	00 23	00 33	06 07	06 37	07 08	07 23	07 33	07 53	08 03		22 23	22 33	22 53	23 03	23 23	23 33	23 53	00 03	00 23
Clock House	d		00 05	00 26	00 35	06 10	06 40	07 11	07 26	07 35	07 56	08 05		22 26	22 35	22 56	23 05	23 26	23 35	23 56	00 05	00 26
Elmers End 4	d		00 08	00 29	00 38	06 13	06 43	07 14	07 29	07 38	07 59	08 08		22 29	22 38	22 59	23 08	23 29	23 38	23 59	00 08	00 29
Eden Park	d	00 02	00 12	00 32	00 42	06 16	06 46	07 17	07 32	07 42	08 02	08 12		22 32	22 42	23 02	23 12	23 32	23 42	00 02	00 12	00 32
West Wickham	d	00 05	00 14	00 35	00 44	06 19	06 49	07 20	07 35	07 44	08 05	08 14		22 35	22 44	23 05	23 14	23 35	23 44	00 05	00 14	00 35
Hayes	a	00 08	00 18	00 40	00 48	06 22	06 52	07 23	07 38	07 48	08 08	08 18		22 38	22 48	23 08	23 18	23 38	23 48	00 08	00 18	00 38

Table T203-F

Sundays

15 December to 10 May

London - Hayes via Catford Bridge

Station		SE A	SE A	SE A	SE	SE		SE
London Charing Cross 4	⊖ d				00 07			
London Waterloo (East) 4	⊖ d				00 10			
London Cannon Street 4	⊖ d					07 33		23 33
London Bridge 4	⊖ d			00 01	00 16	07 37		23 37
New Cross 4	⊖ d			00 07		07 43	and	23 43
St Johns	d			00 09		07 45	every 30	23 45
Lewisham 4	d			00 13		07 49	minutes	23 49
Ladywell	d			00 16	00 25	07 52	until	23 52
Catford Bridge	d			00 18	00 28	07 54		23 54
Lower Sydenham	d		00 01	00 21	00 31	07 57		23 57
New Beckenham 4	d		00 03	00 23	00 33	07 59		23 59
Clock House	d		00 05	00 26	00 35	08 02		00 02
Elmers End 4	d		00 08	00 29	00 38	08 05		00 05
Eden Park	d	00 02	00 12	00 32	00 42	08 08		00 08
West Wickham	d	00 05	00 14	00 35	00 44	08 11		00 11
Hayes	a	00 08	00 18	00 38	00 48	08 15		00 15

A not 15 December

SUNDAY RETURN TIMES

NRT DECEMBER 19 EDITION

Table T203-R

Sundays

15 December to 10 May

Hayes - London via Catford Bridge

Station		SE		SE	SE
Hayes	d	07 32		23 02	23 32
West Wickham	d	07 35		23 05	23 35
Eden Park	d	07 37		23 07	23 37
Elmers End 4	d	07 41		23 11	23 41
Clock House	d	07 43		23 13	23 43
New Beckenham 4	d	07 46	and	23 16	23 46
Lower Sydenham	d	07 48	every 30	23 18	23 48
Catford Bridge	d	07 51	minutes	23 21	23 51
Ladywell	d	07 53	until	23 23	23 53
Lewisham 4	d	07 58		23 28	23 58
St Johns	a	08 00		23 30	23 59
New Cross 4	⊖ a	08 02		23 32	00 02
London Bridge 4	⊖ a	08 07		23 37	00 07
London Cannon Street 4	⊖ a	08 13		23 43	00 13
London Waterloo (East) 4	⊖ a				
London Charing Cross 4	⊖ a				

Table T203-R

Mondays to Fridays
16 December to 15 May

Hayes - London via Catford Bridge

Miles	Miles	Station		SE	SE	SE	SE	SE	SE	SE	SE	SE	SE	SE	SE	SE	SE	SE	SE	SE	SE
0	—	**Hayes**	d	05 10	05 44	06 11	06 23	06 38	06 54	07 11	07 21	07 31	07 45	07 51	08 01	08 11	08 21	08 34	08 50	09 02	09 13
1¼	—	West Wickham	d	05 13	05 47	06 14	06 26	06 41	06 57	07 14	07 24	07 34	07 48	07 54	08 04	08 14	08 24	08 37	08 53	09 05	09 16
2	—	Eden Park	d	05 15	05 49	06 16	06 28	06 43	06 59	07 16	07 26	07 36	07 50	07 56	08 06	08 16	08 26	08 39	08 55	09 07	09 18
3½	—	Elmers End [4]	d	05 19	05 53	06 20	06 32	06 47	07 03	07 20	07 30	07 40	07 54	08 00	08 10	08 20	08 30	08 43	08 59	09 11	09 22
4¼	—	Clock House	d	05 21	05 55	06 22	06 34	06 50	07 06	07 23	07 33	07 43	07 57	08 03	08 13	08 23	08 33	08 46	09 02	09 13	09 24
5	—	New Beckenham [4]	d	05 24	05 58	06 25	06 37	06 53	07 09	07 26	07 36	07 46	08 00	08 06	08 16	08 26	08 36	08 49	09 05	09 16	09 27
5½	—	Lower Sydenham	d	05 26	06 00	06 27	06 39	06 55	07 11	07 28	07 38	07 48	08 02	08 08	08 18	08 28	08 38	08 51	09 07	09 18	09 30
7	—	**Catford Bridge**	d	05 29	06 03	06 31	06 42	06 59	07 15	07 32	07 42	07 52	08 06	08 12	08 22	08 32	08 42	08 55	09 11	09 21	09 33
7¾	—	Ladywell	d	05 31	06 05	06 33	06 44	07 01	07 17	07 34	07 44	07 54	08 09	08 14	08 24	08 34	08 44	08 57	09 13	09 23	09 36
8½	—	**Lewisham** [4]	d	05 35	06 09	06 38	06 48		07 21		07 48		08 13		08 29		08 48	09 01	09 17		09 39
9	—	St Johns	a		06 11		06 50				07 50		08 15		08 31		08 50		09 19		09 41
9¾	—	New Cross [4]	a		06 13		06 52		07 24		07 52		08 17		08 33		08 52		09 22		09 43
12¾	0	**London Bridge** [4]	a	05 43	06 19	06 46	06 58	07 10	07 30	07 43	07 58	08 03	08 23	08 23	08 39	08 43	08 58	09 09	09 28	09 32	09 49
—	0¾	**London Cannon Street** [4]	a		06 26		07 06		07 38		08 06		08 31		08 47		09 07		09 36		09 57
13¾	—	**London Waterloo (East)** [4]	a	05 49		06 52		07 16		07 49		08 09		08 29		08 49		09 15		09 38	
14½	—	**London Charing Cross** [4]	a	05 57		06 58		07 23		07 56		08 16		08 36		08 56		09 22		09 45	

Station		SE	SE	SE	SE		SE	SE	SE	SE	SE	SE	SE	SE	SE	SE	SE	SE	SE	SE	SE	SE
Hayes	d	09 30	09 45	10 00	10 15	and at the same minutes past each hour until	12 30	12 45	13 00	13 15	13 30	13 45	14 00	14 15	14 30	14 45	15 00	15 15	15 30	15 45	16 00	16 17
West Wickham	d	09 33	09 48	10 03	10 18		12 33	12 48	13 03	13 18	13 33	13 48	14 03	14 18	14 33	14 48	15 03	15 18	15 33	15 48	16 03	16 20
Eden Park	d	09 35	09 50	10 05	10 20		12 35	12 50	13 05	13 20	13 35	13 50	14 05	14 20	14 35	14 50	15 05	15 20	15 35	15 50	16 05	16 22
Elmers End [4]	d	09 39	09 54	10 09	10 24		12 39	12 54	13 09	13 24	13 39	13 54	14 09	14 24	14 39	14 54	15 09	15 24	15 39	15 54	16 09	16 26
Clock House	d	09 41	09 56	10 11	10 26		12 41	12 56	13 11	13 26	13 41	13 56	14 11	14 26	14 41	14 56	15 11	15 26	15 41	15 56	16 11	16 28
New Beckenham [4]	d	09 44	09 59	10 14	10 29		12 44	12 59	13 14	13 29	13 44	13 59	14 14	14 29	14 44	14 59	15 14	15 29	15 44	15 59	16 14	16 31
Lower Sydenham	d	09 46	10 01	10 16	10 31		12 46	13 01	13 16	13 31	13 46	14 01	14 16	14 31	14 46	15 01	15 16	15 31	15 46	16 01	16 16	16 33
Catford Bridge	d	09 49	10 04	10 19	10 34		12 49	13 04	13 19	13 34	13 49	14 04	14 19	14 34	14 49	15 04	15 19	15 34	15 49	16 04	16 19	16 36
Ladywell	d	09 51	10 06	10 21	10 36		12 51	13 06	13 21	13 36	13 51	14 06	14 21	14 36	14 51	15 06	15 21	15 36	15 51	16 06	16 21	16 38
Lewisham [4]	d		10 09		10 39			13 09		13 39		14 09		14 39		15 09		15 39		16 09		16 42
St Johns	a		10 11		10 41			13 11		13 41		14 11		14 41		15 11		15 41		16 11		16 45
New Cross [4]	a		10 13		10 43			13 13		13 43		14 13		14 43		15 13		15 43		16 13		16 48
London Bridge [4]	a	10 00	10 19	10 30	10 49		13 00	13 19	13 30	13 49	14 00	14 19	14 30	14 49	15 00	15 19	15 30	15 49	16 00	16 19	16 30	16 54
London Cannon Street [4]	a		10 24		10 54			13 24		13 54		14 24		14 55		15 24		15 54		16 24		17 02
London Waterloo (East) [4]	a	10 06		10 36			13 06		13 36		14 06		14 36		15 06		15 36		16 06		16 37	
London Charing Cross [4]	a	10 10		10 40			13 10		13 40		14 10		14 40		15 10		15 40		16 10		16 42	

Station		SE	SE	SE	SE	SE	SE	SE	SE	SE	SE	SE	SE	SE	SE	SE	SE	SE	SE	SE	SE	SE	SE
Hayes	d	16 29	16 47	16 59	17 16	17 28	17 52	18 03	18 25	18 35	18 50	19 00	19 15	19 30	19 45	20 00	20 15	20 30	20 45	21 00	21 15	21 30	21 45
West Wickham	d	16 32	16 50	17 02	17 19	17 31	17 55	18 06	18 28	18 38	18 53	19 03	19 18	19 33	19 48	20 03	20 18	20 33	20 48	21 03	21 18	21 33	21 48
Eden Park	d	16 34	16 52	17 04	17 21	17 33	17 57	18 08	18 30	18 40	18 55	19 05	19 20	19 35	19 50	20 05	20 20	20 35	20 50	21 05	21 20	21 35	21 50
Elmers End [4]	d	16 38	16 56	17 08	17 25	17 37	18 01	18 12	18 34	18 44	18 59	19 09	19 24	19 39	19 54	20 09	20 24	20 39	20 54	21 09	21 24	21 39	21 54
Clock House	d	16 40	16 58	17 10	17 27	17 39	18 03	18 14	18 36	18 46	19 01	19 11	19 26	19 41	19 56	20 11	20 26	20 41	20 56	21 11	21 26	21 41	21 56
New Beckenham [4]	d	16 43	17 01	17 13	17 30	17 42	18 06	18 17	18 39	18 49	19 04	19 14	19 29	19 44	19 59	20 14	20 29	20 44	20 59	21 14	21 29	21 44	21 59
Lower Sydenham	d	16 45	17 03	17 15	17 32	17 44	18 08	18 19	18 41	18 51	19 06	19 16	19 31	19 46	20 01	20 16	20 31	20 46	21 01	21 16	21 31	21 46	22 01
Catford Bridge	d	16 48	17 07	17 18	17 35	17 47	18 12	18 22	18 44	18 54	19 09	19 19	19 34	19 49	20 04	20 19	20 34	20 49	21 04	21 19	21 34	21 49	22 04
Ladywell	d	16 50	17 09	17 20	17 37	17 49	18 14	18 24	18 46	18 56	19 11	19 21	19 36	19 51	20 06	20 21	20 36	20 51	21 06	21 21	21 36	21 51	22 06
Lewisham [4]	d		17 13		17 41	17 53	18 19		18 50		19 16		19 39		20 09		20 39		21 09		21 39		22 09
St Johns	a		17 16		17 44		18 21		18 52		19 19		19 41		20 11		20 41		21 11		21 41		22 11
New Cross [4]	a		17 18		17 46		18 24		18 54		19 21		19 43		20 13		20 43		21 13		21 43		22 13
London Bridge [4]	a	16 59	17 25	17 29	17 52	18 01	18 33	18 34	19 00	19 06	19 28	19 30	19 49	20 00	20 19	20 30	20 49	21 00	21 19	21 30	21 49	22 00	22 19
London Cannon Street [4]	a		17 32		18 00		18 40		19 05		19 33		19 54		20 24		20 54		21 25		21 54		22 24
London Waterloo (East) [4]	a	17 05		17 35		18 06		18 40		19 11		19 36		20 06		20 36		21 06		21 36		22 06	
London Charing Cross [4]	a	17 10		17 44		18 12		18 46		19 14		19 43		20 10		20 40		21 10		21 40		22 10	

Station		SE	SE	SE	SE	SE	SE FO	SE W ThO	SE FO	SE MTO	SE WTh FO	SE MTO
Hayes	d	22 00	22 15	22 30	22 45	23 00	23 15	23 15		23 18	23 30	23 35
West Wickham	d	22 03	22 18	22 33	22 48	23 03	23 18	23 18		23 21	23 33	23 38
Eden Park	d	22 05	22 20	22 35	22 50	23 05	23 20	23 20		23 23	23 35	23 40
Elmers End [4]	d	22 09	22 24	22 39	22 54	23 09	23 24	23 24		23 27	23 39	23 44
Clock House	d	22 11	22 26	22 41	22 56	23 11	23 26	23 26		23 29	23 41	23 46
New Beckenham [4]	d	22 14	22 29	22 44	22 59	23 14	23 29	23 29		23 32	23 44	23 49
Lower Sydenham	d	22 16	22 31	22 46	23 01	23 16	23 31	23 31		23 34	23 46	23 51
Catford Bridge	d	22 19	22 34	22 49	23 04	23 19	23 34	23 34		23 37	23 49	23 54
Ladywell	d	22 21	22 36	22 51	23 06	23 21	23 36	23 36		23 40	23 51	23 56
Lewisham [4]	d		22 39		23 09		23 39	23 40	←	23a43		23 59
St Johns	a		22 41		23 11		23 41		23 41			00 02
New Cross [4]	a		22 43		23 13		→		23 43			00 04
London Bridge [4]	a	22 30	22 49	23 00	23 19	23 30		23 48	23 49		00 01	00 10
London Cannon Street [4]	a		22 54		23 24				23 54			00 18
London Waterloo (East) [4]	a	22 36		23 06		23 36		23 54			00 06	
London Charing Cross [4]	a	22 40		23 10		23 40		00 01			00 10	

Saturdays
21 December to 16 May

Station		SE	SE	SE	SE	SE	SE	SE		SE	SE	SE	SE	SE	SE
Hayes	d	05 54	06 24	06 54	07 15	07 30	07 45	08 00	and at the same minutes past each hour until	22 15	22 30	22 45	23 00	23 15	23 30
West Wickham	d	05 57	06 27	06 57	07 18	07 33	07 48	08 03		22 18	22 33	22 48	23 03	23 18	23 33
Eden Park	d	05 59	06 29	06 59	07 20	07 35	07 50	08 05		22 20	22 35	22 50	23 05	23 20	23 35
Elmers End [4]	d	06 03	06 33	07 03	07 24	07 39	07 54	08 09		22 24	22 39	22 54	23 09	23 24	23 39
Clock House	d	06 05	06 35	07 05	07 26	07 41	07 56	08 11		22 26	22 41	22 56	23 11	23 26	23 41
New Beckenham [4]	d	06 08	06 38	07 08	07 29	07 44	07 59	08 14		22 29	22 44	22 59	23 14	23 29	23 44
Lower Sydenham	d	06 10	06 40	07 10	07 31	07 46	08 01	08 16		22 31	22 46	23 01	23 16	23 31	23 46
Catford Bridge	d	06 13	06 43	07 13	07 34	07 49	08 04	08 19		22 34	22 49	23 04	23 19	23 34	23 49
Ladywell	d	06 15	06 45	07 15	07 36	07 51	08 06	08 21		22 36	22 51	23 06	23 21	23 36	23 51
Lewisham [4]	d	06 20	06 50	07 20	07 39		08 09			22 39		23 09		23 39	
St Johns	a				07 41		08 11			22 41		23 11		23 41	
New Cross [4]	a				07 43		08 13			22 43		23 13		23 43	
London Bridge [4]	a	06 28	06 58	07 28	07 49	08 00	08 19	08 30		22 49	23 00	23 19	23 30	23 49	00 01
London Cannon Street [4]	a				07 54		08 24			22 54		23 24		23 54	
London Waterloo (East) [4]	a	06 34	07 04	07 34		08 06		08 36			23 06		23 36		00 07
London Charing Cross [4]	a	06 39	07 09	07 39		08 10		08 40			23 10		23 40		00 11

See opposite page for Sunday times.

Table T204-F

Mondays to Fridays
16 December to 15 May

London Charing Cross/Cannon Street - Grove Park, Orpington, Sevenoaks and Tonbridge, Grove Park - Bromley North

Miles	Miles	Miles	Station		SE MO ◇1	SE MX ◇1	SE MO	SE MX ◇1	SE MO ◇1	SE MX ◇1	SE MX	SE TWO	SE ThFO	SE MO	SE MX	SE ThFO	SE MX	SE TWO	SE ThFO ◇	SE TWO	SE MO	SE ThFO	SE MX
0	—	—	**London Charing Cross** [4]	d												00 04			00 15		00 16	00 18	
0¾	—	—	**London Waterloo (East)** [4]	d												00 07			00 18		00 19	00 21	
—	0	—	**London Cannon Street** [4]	d														00 25		00 20			
1¾	0¾	—	**London Bridge** [4]	d												00 13		00 29	00 24	00 24	00 25	00 28	
4¾	—	—	New Cross [4]	d																00 30			
5½	—	—	St Johns	d								00 02								00 32			
6	—	—	**Lewisham** [4]	d								00 05	00 05	00 05						00 35	00 35	00 37	
7¼	—	—	Hither Green [4]	d								00 09	00 09	00 10		00 23				00 39	00 40	00 41	
9	—	0	**Grove Park** [4]	d								00 13	00 13	00 14	00 15	00 27	00 35			00 43	00 44	00 45	00 55
—	—	1¼	Sundridge Park	d											00 18		00 38						00 58
—	—	1¾	**Bromley North**	a											00 20		00 40						01 00
10¼	—	—	Elmstead Woods	d								00 16	00 16	00 17		00 30				00 46	00 47	00 48	
11¼	—	—	Chislehurst	d							00 03	00 19	00 19	00 19		00 33				00 49	00 49	00 51	
12¾	—	—	Petts Wood [4]	d							00 06	00 22	00 22	00 23		00 36				00 52	00 53	00 54	
13¾	—	—	**Orpington** [4]	a							00 12	00 26	00 26	00 27		00 43		00 49	00 50	00 58	00 57	01 00	
—	—	—		d					00 06	00 10	00 13			00 28				00 50	00 51				
15¼	—	—	Chelsfield [3]	d			00 01				00 16			00s31				00 54	00 54				
16½	—	—	Knockholt	d			00 04				00 19			00s34									
20½	—	—	Dunton Green	d			00 09				00 24			00s39				01 00	01 00				
22	—	—	**Sevenoaks** [4]	a			00 12		00 15	00 19	00 27			00 42				01 03	01 03				
—	—	—		d		00 06		00 13	00 16	00 20								01 04	01 04				
27	—	—	Hildenborough	d	00 06	00 12												01 10	01s10				
29½	—	—	**Tonbridge** [4]	a	00 10	00 16		00 21	00 24	00 28								01 14	01 14				

Station		SE MO	SE ThFO	SE TWO	SE	SE ◇1	SE	SE	SE	SE ◇1	SE	SE	SE ◇1	SE	SE	SE ◇1	SE	SE	SE	SE	SE ◇1	SE	SE
London Charing Cross [4]	d	00 46	00 50			05 30		05 32		05 56	06 05		06 28				06 34				07 00		07 06
London Waterloo (East) [4]	d	00 49	00 53			05 33		05 35		05 59	06 08		06 31				06 37				07 03		07 09
London Cannon Street [4]	d			01 10										06 16		06 32			06 49				
London Bridge [4]	d	00 55	00 59	01 15		05 39		05 41		06 05	06 14		06 37	06 20		06 36	06 43		06 53		07 09		07 15
New Cross [4]	d													06 26					06 59				
St Johns	d													06 28					07 01				
Lewisham [4]	d	01 05	01 08	01 23				05 50						06 32					07 04				
Hither Green [4]	d	01 10	01 13	01 28				05 54			06 24			06 36			06 53		07 08				07 26
Grove Park [4]	d	01 14	01 17	01 32	05 24		05 44	05 58	06 04		06 28	06 28		06 40	06 45		06 58	06 59	07 12	07 12		07 26	07 30
Sundridge Park	d				05 27		05 47		06 07			06 31			06 48					07 15			
Bromley North	a				05 29		05 49		06 09			06 33			06 50			07 03		07 17		07 30	
Elmstead Woods	d	01 17	01 20	01 35				06 01			06 31			06 43			07 01		07 15				07 33
Chislehurst	d	01 19	01 22	01 37				06 03			06 34			06 45			07 04		07 17				07 35
Petts Wood [4]	d	01 23	01 25	01 40				06 06			06 37			06 48			07 07		07 20				07 38
Orpington [4]	a	01 29	01 32	01 47		05 55		06 11		06 21	06 40		06 53	06 55			07 10		07 25		07 25		→
	d					05 55		06 13		06 22	06 43		06 53				07 11				07 26		
Chelsfield [3]	d					05 58		06 16			06 46						07 14						
Knockholt	d							06 19			06 49						07 17						
Dunton Green	d							06 24			06 54						07 22						
Sevenoaks [4]	a					06 06		06 27		06 31	07 00		07 02			07 06	07 25				07 35		
	d					06 06				06 31			07 03			07 06					07 36		
Hildenborough	d					06 13				06 37						07 12					07 42		
Tonbridge [4]	a					06 18				06 41			07 11			07 16					07 46		

Station		SE ◇1	SE ◇1	SE	SE	SE	SE ◇1	SE ◇1	SE	SE	SE	SE ◇1	SE	SE ◇1	SE ◇1	SE	SE	SE	SE	SE ◇1	SE ◇1	SE	SE
London Charing Cross [4]	d	07 09	07 15				07 27			07 33		07 37	07 46	07 57	08 00			08 06	08 10	08 16	08 18		08 20
London Waterloo (East) [4]	d	07 12	07 18				07 30			07 36		07 40	07 49	08 01	08 05			08 09	08 13	08 19	08 21		08 23
London Cannon Street [4]	d				07 15			07 42								07 53							
London Bridge [4]	d	07 18	07 24		07 19		07 36	07 46		07 42		07 46	07 55	08 07	08 11	07 57		08 15	08 19	08 25	08 27		08 29
New Cross [4]	d				07 26											08 03							
St Johns	d															08 05							
Lewisham [4]	d															08 10							
Hither Green [4]	d				07 31					07 53						08 15		08 27					
Grove Park [4]	d				07 35	07 39			07 53	07 58	08 08					08 19	08 23	08 31					
Sundridge Park	d					07 42			07 56								08 26						
Bromley North	a					07 44			07 58		08 12						08 28						
Elmstead Woods	d				07 38					08 01						08 22		08 34					
Chislehurst	d			←	07 41					08 04						08 24		08 37				←	
Petts Wood [4]	d			07 38	07 44					08 08						08 27		08 40				08 40	
Orpington [4]	a		07 40	07 41	07 50		07 55	08 07		08 12			08 17		08 29	08 34		→	08 42		08 43	08 45	08 52
	d		07 40	07 44			07 55	08 08		08 13					08 32						08 44	08 46	
Chelsfield [3]	d			07 47			07 58			08 16													
Knockholt	d			07 50						08 19												08 50	
Dunton Green	d			07 55						08 24												08 55	
Sevenoaks [4]	a	07 41	07 49	08 02			08 06	08 17		08 29		08 12			08 41					08 49	08 53	09 01	
	d	07 42	07 50				08 06	08 18				08 13			08 41					08 49	08 53		
Hildenborough	d						08 12								08 47								
Tonbridge [4]	a	07 50	07 58				08 16	08 26				08 21		08 36	08 51					08 57	09 01		

Table T204-F

Mondays to Fridays

16 December to 15 May

London Charing Cross/Cannon Street - Grove Park, Orpington, Sevenoaks and Tonbridge, Grove Park - Bromley North

		SE	SE	SE	SE	SE	SE	SE	SE	SE	SE	SE	SE	SE	SE	SE	SE	SE	SE	SE	SE	SE	SE
			◇1			◇1			◇1		◇1	◇1			◇1			◇1	◇1				
London Charing Cross 4 ⊖	d	08 24	08 28				08 32		08 34	08 44	08 58	09 02				09 06		09 22	09 24			09 34	
London Waterloo (East) 4 ⊖	d	08 27	08 31				08 35		08 37	08 47	09 01	09 05				09 09		09 25	09 27			09 37	
London Cannon Street 4 ⊖	d			08 17		08 40								08 52	09 14						09 20		
London Bridge 4 ⊖	d	08 33	08 37	08 21		08 44	08 41		08 43	08 53	09 07	09 11		08 56	09 18	09 15		09 31	09 33		09 24	09 43	
New Cross 4 ⊖	d			08 28										09 02							09 31		
St Johns	d			08 30										09 04							09 33		
Lewisham 4 ⛴	d			08 34										09 07							09 37		
Hither Green 4	d			08 38			08 54							09 13							09 41	09 53	
Grove Park 4	d			08 42	08 46		08 58	09 00					09 14	09 17		09 27	09 29			09 43	09 45	09 57	09 58
Sundridge Park	d				08 49			09 03					09 17				09 32			09 46			10 01
Bromley North	a				08 51			09 05					09 19				09 34			09 48			10 03
Elmstead Woods	d			08 45			09 01							09 20		09 30					09 48	10 00	
Chislehurst	d			08 48			09 03							09 22		09 33					09 51	10 03	
Petts Wood 4	d			08 51			09 08							09 25		09 36					09 54	10 06	
Orpington 4	a	08 55	08 56	08 58		09 05	09 13			09 16	09 24	09 30		09 32	09 38	09 40		09 48	09 53		10 00	→	
	d		08 56			09 07	09 14				09 26	09 31			09 40	09 43		09 50	09 56				
Chelsfield 3	d		08 59				09 17									09 46							
Knockholt	d						09 20									09 49							
Dunton Green	d						09 25									09 54							
Sevenoaks 4	a		09 07			09 17	09 30		09 10		09 35	09 40			09 49	09 59		10 01	10 05				
	d		09 07			09 20			09 13		09 36	09 41			09 50			10 02	10 06				
Hildenborough	d		09 13								09 42								10 12				
Tonbridge 4	a		09 17			09 28			09 21		09 46	09 50			09 58			10 10	10 16				

		SE	SE	SE	SE	SE	SE	SE	SE	SE	SE	SE	SE	SE	SE	SE	SE	SE	SE	SE	SE	SE
		◇1	◇1		◇1					◇1	◇1		◇1				◇1	◇1		◇1		
London Charing Cross 4 ⊖	d	09 40	09 45		10 00			10 04		10 10	10 15		10 30			10 34	10 40	10 45		11 00		
London Waterloo (East) 4 ⊖	d	09 43	09 48		10 03			10 07		10 13	10 18		10 33			10 37	10 43	10 48		11 03		
London Cannon Street 4 ⊖	d						09 50							10 20							10 50	
London Bridge 4 ⊖	d	09 49	09 54		10 09		09 54	10 13		10 19	10 24		10 39	10 24		10 43	10 49	10 54		11 09	10 54	
New Cross 4 ⊖	d						10 00							10 30							11 00	
St Johns	d						10 02							10 32							11 02	
Lewisham 4 ⛴	d						10 05							10 35							11 05	
Hither Green 4	d						10 09	10 23						10 39		10 53					11 09	
Grove Park 4	d					10 12	10 13	10 27	10 28					10 43	10 50	10 57					11 13	11 15
Sundridge Park	d					10 15			10 31						10 53							11 18
Bromley North	a					10 17			10 33						10 55							11 20
Elmstead Woods	d						10 16	10 30						10 46		11 00					11 16	
Chislehurst	d			←			10 19	10 33				←		10 49		11 03			←		11 19	
Petts Wood 4	d			10 06			10 22	10 36				10 36		10 52		11 06			11 06		11 22	
Orpington 4	a		10 09	10 10	10 25		10 28	→			10 39	10 40	10 55	10 57		→		11 09	11 10	11 25	11 26	
	d		10 10	10 13	10 26						10 39	10 43	10 56					11 10	11 13	11 26		
Chelsfield 3	d			10 16								10 46							11 16			
Knockholt	d			10 19								10 49							11 19			
Dunton Green	d			10 24								10 54							11 24			
Sevenoaks 4	a	10 12	10 19	10 29	10 35					10 42	10 49	10 57	11 05				11 12	11 19	11 27	11 35		
	d	10 13	10 20		10 36					10 43	10 50		11 06				11 13	11 20		11 36		
Hildenborough	d				10 42								11 12							11 42		
Tonbridge 4	a	10 21	10 28		10 46					10 51	10 58		11 16				11 21	11 28		11 46		

		SE	SE	SE	SE	SE	SE	SE	SE	SE	SE	SE	SE	SE	SE	SE	SE	SE	SE	SE	SE	SE	SE
				◇1	◇1		◇1				◇1	◇1		◇1					◇1	◇1		◇1	
London Charing Cross 4 ⊖	d	11 04		11 10	11 15		11 30			11 34	11 40	11 45		12 00			12 04		12 10	12 15		12 30	
London Waterloo (East) 4 ⊖	d	11 07		11 13	11 18		11 33			11 37	11 43	11 48		12 03			12 07		12 13	12 18		12 33	
London Cannon Street 4 ⊖	d							11 20							11 50								12 20
London Bridge 4 ⊖	d	11 13		11 19	11 24		11 39	11 24		11 43	11 49	11 54		12 09	11 54		12 13		12 19	12 24		12 39	12 24
New Cross 4 ⊖	d							11 30							12 00								12 30
St Johns	d							11 32							12 02								12 32
Lewisham 4 ⛴	d							11 35							12 05								12 35
Hither Green 4	d	11 23						11 39		11 53					12 09		12 23						12 39
Grove Park 4	d	11 27	11 35					11 43	11 55	11 57					12 13	12 15	12 27	12 35					12 43
Sundridge Park	d		11 38						11 58							12 18		12 38					
Bromley North	a		11 40						12 00							12 20		12 40					
Elmstead Woods	d	11 30						11 46		12 00					12 16		12 30						12 46
Chislehurst	d	11 33				←		11 49		12 03			←		12 19		12 33				←		12 49
Petts Wood 4	d	11 36				11 36		11 52		12 06			12 06		12 22		12 36				12 36		12 52
Orpington 4	a	→			11 39	11 40	11 55	11 57		→		12 09	12 10	12 25	12 26		→			12 39	12 40	12 55	12 56
	d				11 39	11 43	11 56					12 10	12 13	12 26						12 39	12 43	12 56	
Chelsfield 3	d					11 46							12 16								12 46		
Knockholt	d					11 49							12 19								12 49		
Dunton Green	d					11 54							12 24								12 54		
Sevenoaks 4	a			11 42	11 49	11 57	12 05				12 12	12 19	12 27	12 35					12 42	12 49	12 57	13 05	
	d			11 43	11 50		12 06				12 13	12 20		12 36					12 43	12 50		13 06	
Hildenborough	d						12 12							12 42								13 12	
Tonbridge 4	a			11 51	11 58		12 16				12 21	12 28		12 46					12 51	12 58		13 16	

Table T204-F

Mondays to Fridays

16 December to 15 May

London Charing Cross/Cannon Street - Grove Park, Orpington, Sevenoaks and Tonbridge, Grove Park - Bromley North

		SE	SE	SE	SE	SE	SE	SE	SE	SE	SE	SE	SE	SE	SE	SE	SE	SE	SE	SE	SE	SE
				◇1	◇1		◇1					◇1	◇1		◇1				◇1	◇1		◇1
London Charing Cross 4 ⊖	d		12 34	12 40	12 45		13 00			13 04		13 10	13 15		13 30			13 34	13 40	13 45		14 00
London Waterloo (East) 4 ⊖	d		12 37	12 43	12 48		13 03			13 07		13 13	13 18		13 33			13 37	13 43	13 48		14 03
London Cannon Street 4 ⊖	d							12 50								13 20						
London Bridge 4 ⊖	d		12 43	12 49	12 54		13 09	12 54		13 13		13 19	13 24		13 39	13 24		13 43	13 49	13 54		14 09
New Cross 4 ⊖	d							13 00								13 30						
St Johns	d							13 02								13 32						
Lewisham 4 ⛴	d							13 05								13 35						
Hither Green 4	d		12 53					13 09		13 23						13 39		13 53				
Grove Park 4	d	12 55	12 57					13 13	13 15	13 27	13 35					13 43	13 55	13 57				
Sundridge Park	d	12 58							13 18		13 38						13 58					
Bromley North	a	13 00							13 20		13 40						14 00					
Elmstead Woods	d		13 00					13 16		13 30						13 46		14 00				
Chislehurst	d		13 03			←		13 19		13 33				←		13 49		14 03			←	
Petts Wood 4	d		13 06			13 06		13 22		13 36				13 36		13 52		14 06			14 06	
Orpington 4	a		→		13 09	13 10	13 25	13 26		→			13 39	13 40	13 55	13 56		→		14 09	14 10	14 25
	d				13 10	13 13	13 26						13 39	13 43	13 56					14 10	14 13	14 26
Chelsfield 3	d					13 16								13 46							14 16	
Knockholt	d					13 19								13 49							14 19	
Dunton Green	d					13 24								13 54							14 24	
Sevenoaks 4	a			13 12	13 19	13 27	13 35					13 42	13 49	13 57	14 05				14 12	14 19	14 27	14 35
	d			13 13	13 20		13 36					13 43	13 50		14 06				14 13	14 20		14 36
Hildenborough	d						13 42								14 12							14 42
Tonbridge 4	a			13 21	13 28		13 46					13 51	13 58		14 17				14 21	14 28		14 46

		SE	SE	SE	SE	SE	SE	SE	SE	SE	SE	SE	SE	SE	SE	SE	SE	SE	SE	SE	SE	SE	SE
						◇1	◇1		◇1				◇1	◇1		◇1					◇1	◇1	
London Charing Cross 4 ⊖	d			14 04		14 10	14 15		14 30			14 34	14 40	14 45		15 00			15 04		15 10	15 15	
London Waterloo (East) 4 ⊖	d			14 07		14 13	14 18		14 33			14 37	14 43	14 48		15 03			15 07		15 13	15 18	
London Cannon Street 4 ⊖	d	13 50								14 20							14 50						
London Bridge 4 ⊖	d	13 54		14 13		14 19	14 24		14 39	14 24		14 43	14 49	14 54		15 09	14 54		15 13		15 19	15 24	
New Cross 4 ⊖	d	14 00								14 30							15 00						
St Johns	d	14 02								14 32							15 02						
Lewisham 4 ⛴	d	14 05								14 35							15 05						
Hither Green 4	d	14 09		14 23						14 39		14 53					15 09		15 23				
Grove Park 4	d	14 13	14 15	14 27	14 35					14 43	14 55	14 57					15 13	15 15	15 27	15 35			
Sundridge Park	d		14 18		14 38						14 58							15 18		15 38			
Bromley North	a		14 20		14 40						15 00							15 20		15 40			
Elmstead Woods	d	14 16		14 30						14 46		15 00					15 16		15 30				
Chislehurst	d	14 19		14 33				←		14 49		15 03			←		15 19		15 33				←
Petts Wood 4	d	14 22		14 36				14 36		14 52		15 06			15 06		15 22		15 36				15 36
Orpington 4	a	14 26		→			14 39	14 40	14 55	14 56		→		15 09	15 10	15 25	15 27		→			15 39	15 40
	d						14 39	14 43	14 56					15 10	15 13	15 26						15 39	15 43
Chelsfield 3	d							14 46							15 16								15 46
Knockholt	d							14 49							15 19								15 49
Dunton Green	d							14 54							15 24								15 54
Sevenoaks 4	a					14 42	14 49	14 57	15 05				15 12	15 19	15 27	15 35					15 42	15 49	15 57
	d					14 43	14 50		15 06				15 13	15 20		15 36					15 43	15 50	
Hildenborough	d								15 12							15 42							
Tonbridge 4	a					14 51	14 58		15 16				15 21	15 28		15 46					15 51	15 58	

		SE	SE	SE	SE	SE	SE	SE	SE	SE	SE	SE	SE	SE	SE	SE	SE	SE	SE	SE	SE	SE
		◇1				◇1	◇1		◇1					◇1	◇1		◇1					◇1
London Charing Cross 4 ⊖	d	15 30			15 34	15 40	15 45		16 00			16 04		16 10	16 14		16 28			16 30		16 39
London Waterloo (East) 4 ⊖	d	15 33			15 37	15 43	15 48		16 03			16 07		16 13	16 17		16 31			16 33		16 42
London Cannon Street 4 ⊖	d		15 20							15 50								16 18				
London Bridge 4 ⊖	d	15 39	15 24		15 43	15 49	15 54		16 09	15 54		16 13		16 19	16 23		16 37	16 23		16 39		16 48
New Cross 4 ⊖	d		15 30							16 01								16 29				
St Johns	d		15 32							16 03								16 31				
Lewisham 4 ⛴	d		15 35							16 06								16 36				
Hither Green 4	d		15 39		15 53					16 10		16 23						16 42		16 49		
Grove Park 4	d		15 43	15 55	15 57					16 14	16 18	16 27	16 34					16 46	16 49	16 53	17 02	
Sundridge Park	d			15 58							16 21		16 37						16 52		17 05	
Bromley North	a			16 00							16 23		16 39						16 54		17 07	
Elmstead Woods	d		15 46		16 00					16 17		16 30						16 49		16 56		
Chislehurst	d		15 49		16 03			←		16 20		16 33				←		16 51		16 59		
Petts Wood 4	d		15 52		16 06			16 06		16 23		16 36				16 36		16 54		17 02		
Orpington 4	a	15 55	15 56		→		16 10	16 10	16 25	16 30		→			16 39	16 40	16 54	17 00		17 06		
	d	15 56					16 10	16 13	16 26						16 39	16 44	16 55			17 10		
Chelsfield 3	d							16 16								16 47				17 13		
Knockholt	d							16 19								16 50				17 16		
Dunton Green	d							16 24								16 55				17 21		
Sevenoaks 4	a	16 05				16 12	16 19	16 27	16 35					16 42	16 48	17 00	17 04			17 26		17 11
	d	16 06				16 13	16 20		16 36					16 43	16 49		17 05					17 12
Hildenborough	d	16 12							16 42								17 11					
Tonbridge 4	a	16 16				16 21	16 28		16 46					16 51	16 58		17 15					17 20

Table T204-F

Mondays to Fridays

16 December to 15 May

London Charing Cross/Cannon Street - Grove Park, Orpington, Sevenoaks and Tonbridge, Grove Park - Bromley North

		SE	SE	SE	SE		SE	SE	SE	SE	SE	SE	SE	SE	SE		SE	SE	SE	SE	SE	SE	SE	SE	SE
			◇1	◇1				◇1	◇1		◇1			◇1	◇1						◇1	◇1	◇1		
London Charing Cross 4 ⊖	d	16 41	16 43	16 51					17 01	17 03	17 11				17 24		17 26				17 39		17 44	17 47	
London Waterloo (East) 4 ⊖	d	16 44	16 46	16 54					17 04	17 06	17 14				17 27		17 29				17 42		17 48	17 50	
London Cannon Street 4 ⊖	d				16 52			17 01				17 16		17 23					17 39			17 45			17 58
London Bridge 4 ⊖	d	16 50	16 52	17 00	16 57			17 06	17 10	17 12	17 20	17 21		17 28	17 33		17 35		17 44		17 48	17 50	17 54	17 56	18 03
New Cross 4 ⊖	d				17 04														17 50						18 09
St Johns	d																								
Lewisham 4	d	17 00								17 21							17 45							18 06	
Hither Green 4	d	17 05			17 10					17 26		17 32					17 49		17 55						18 15
Grove Park 4	d	17 09			17 14		17 19			17 30		17 36	17 40				17 53	17 56	18 00	18 09				18 13	18 20
Sundridge Park	d						17 22						17 43					17 59		18 12					
Bromley North	a						17 24						17 45					18 01		18 14					
Elmstead Woods	d	17 12			17 17					17 33		17 39					17 56		18 03					18 16	18 23
Chislehurst	d	17 15			17 20					17 35		17 42					17 59		18 06					18 19	18 26
Petts Wood 4	d	17 18			17 24					17 39		17 46					18 03		18 09					18 23	18 31
Orpington 4	a	17 25		17 17	17 27					17 45		17 49					18 09		18 15					18 29	18 34
	d			17 18	17 28							17 51					18 13								18 35
Chelsfield 3	d				17 31				17 28			17 54			17 51		18 16						18 12		18 38
Knockholt	d				17 34							17 57					18 19								18 41
Dunton Green	d				17 39							18 02					18 24								18 46
Sevenoaks 4	a		17 15	17 27	17 44			17 31	17 35		17 45	18 07		17 53	17 59		18 29				18 11	18 15	18 20		18 51
	d		17 16	17 28				17 32	17 36		17 46			17 54	18 00						18 12	18 16	18 21		
Hildenborough	d								17 42					18 01	18 06								18 27		
Tonbridge 4	a		17 24	17 36				17 40	17 46		17 54			18 05	18 10						18 20	18 24	18 31		

			SE	SE	SE	SE	SE	SE	SE	SE	SE		SE	SE	SE	SE	SE	SE	SE	SE	SE		SE	SE	SE
				◇1	◇1	◇1				◇1	◇1				◇1		◇1	◇1		◇1				◇1	
London Charing Cross 4 ⊖	d			18 01		18 07	18 09			18 19			18 29		18 31		18 41	18 46	18 48	19 00					19 04
London Waterloo (East) 4 ⊖	d			18 04		18 10	18 12			18 22			18 32		18 34		18 44	18 49	18 51	19 03					19 07
London Cannon Street 4 ⊖	d				18 07				18 20		18 31										18 48			19 02	
London Bridge 4 ⊖	d			18 10	18 12	18 16	18 18		18 25	18 28	18 36		18 38		18 40		18 50	18 55	18 57	19 09	18 53			19 07	19 13
New Cross 4 ⊖	d								18 31												18 59				
St Johns	d																				19 01				
Lewisham 4	d								18 37												19 05				
Hither Green 4	d								18 41				18 49						19 07		19 11				19 23
Grove Park 4	d		18 23				18 31	18 38	18 46				18 53	18 57					19 11		19 15		19 18		19 27
Sundridge Park	d		18 26					18 41						19 00									19 21		
Bromley North	a		18 28					18 43						19 02									19 23		
Elmstead Woods	d						18 34		18 49				18 56						19 14		19 18				19 30
Chislehurst	d						18 37		18 52				18 59						19 17		19 21				19 33
Petts Wood 4	d						18 41		18 56				19 03			←			19 20		19 24				19 36
Orpington 4	a						18 47		18 59				19 09		18 56	18 59	19 06		19 27	19 26	19 31				→
	d								19 00						18 58	19 00	19 07			19 26					
Chelsfield 3	d					18 34			→							19 03		19 13		19 29					
Knockholt	d															19 06									
Dunton Green	d															19 11									
Sevenoaks 4	a			18 33	18 37	18 42				18 52	18 59				19 07	19 16	19 17	19 20		19 37				19 30	
	d			18 34	18 38	18 43				18 53	19 00				19 08		19 18	19 22		19 38				19 31	
Hildenborough	d				18 44	18 49									19 14					19 44				19 37	
Tonbridge 4	a			18 42	18 48	18 53				19 01	19 08				19 18		19 26	19 30		19 48				19 41	

		SE	SE	SE	SE	SE	SE		SE	SE	SE	SE	SE	SE	SE	SE	SE		SE	SE	SE	SE	SE	SE	SE
			◇1	◇1		◇1						◇1	◇1		◇1						◇1	◇1		◇1	
London Charing Cross 4 ⊖	d		19 10	19 15		19 30				19 34		19 40	19 45		20 00				20 04		20 10	20 15		20 30	
London Waterloo (East) 4 ⊖	d		19 13	19 18		19 33				19 37		19 43	19 48		20 03				20 07		20 13	20 18		20 33	
London Cannon Street 4 ⊖	d						19 22									19 50									20 20
London Bridge 4 ⊖	d		19 19	19 24		19 39	19 26			19 43		19 49	19 54		20 09	19 54			20 13		20 19	20 24		20 39	20 24
New Cross 4 ⊖	d						19 32									20 00									20 30
St Johns	d						19 34									20 02									20 32
Lewisham 4	d						19 37									20 05									20 35
Hither Green 4	d						19 41			19 53						20 09			20 23						20 39
Grove Park 4	d	19 33					19 45		19 49	19 57	20 03					20 13	20 17		20 27	20 33					20 43
Sundridge Park	d	19 36							19 52		20 06						20 20			20 36					
Bromley North	a	19 38							19 54		20 08						20 22			20 38					
Elmstead Woods	d						19 48			20 00						20 16			20 30						20 46
Chislehurst	d				←		19 51			20 03				←		20 19			20 33				←		20 49
Petts Wood 4	d				19 36		19 54			20 06				20 06		20 22			20 36				20 36		20 52
Orpington 4	a			19 39	19 40	19 55	20 00			→			20 09	20 10	20 25	20 27			→			20 39	20 40	20 55	20 56
	d			19 40	19 43	19 56							20 10	20 13	20 26							20 40	20 43	20 56	
Chelsfield 3	d				19 46									20 16									20 46		
Knockholt	d				19 49									20 19									20 49		
Dunton Green	d				19 54									20 24									20 54		
Sevenoaks 4	a		19 42	19 49	19 59	20 05						20 12	20 19	20 27	20 35						20 42	20 49	20 57	21 05	
	d		19 43	19 50		20 06						20 13	20 20		20 36						20 43	20 50		21 06	
Hildenborough	d					20 12									20 42									21 12	
Tonbridge 4	a		19 51	19 58		20 16						20 21	20 28		20 46						20 51	20 58		21 16	

NRT DECEMBER 19 EDITION

Table T204-F

Mondays to Fridays

16 December to 15 May

London Charing Cross/Cannon Street - Grove Park, Orpington, Sevenoaks and Tonbridge, Grove Park - Bromley North

		SE	SE	SE	SE	SE	SE	SE	SE		SE	SE	SE	SE	SE	SE	SE	SE	SE		SE	SE	SE	SE	SE
					◇1	◇1		◇1					◇1		◇1				◇1		◇1		◇1		
London Charing Cross 4 ⊖	d		20 34		20 40	20 45		21 00			21 04		21 10		21 30			21 34	21 40		21 45		22 00		
London Waterloo (East) 4 ⊖	d		20 37		20 43	20 48		21 03			21 07		21 13		21 33			21 37	21 43		21 48		22 03		
London Cannon Street 4 ⊖	d								20 50							21 20								21 50	
London Bridge 4 ⊖	d		20 43		20 49	20 54		21 09	20 54		21 13		21 19		21 39	21 24		21 43	21 49		21 54		22 09	21 54	
New Cross 4 ⊖	d								21 00							21 30								22 00	
St Johns	d								21 02							21 32								22 02	
Lewisham 4	d								21 05							21 35								22 05	
Hither Green 4	d		20 53						21 09		21 23					21 39		21 53						22 09	
Grove Park 4	d	20 47	20 57	21 05					21 13		21 27	21 35				21 43	21 55	21 57						22 13	22 15
Sundridge Park	d	20 50		21 08								21 38					21 58								22 18
Bromley North	a	20 52		21 10								21 40					22 00								22 20
Elmstead Woods	d		21 00						21 16		21 30					21 46		22 00						22 16	
Chislehurst	d		21 03				←		21 19		21 33			←		21 49		22 03				←		22 19	
Petts Wood 4	d		21 06				21 06		21 22		21 36			21 36		21 52		22 06				22 06		22 22	
Orpington 4	a		→			21 09	21 10	21 25	21 26		→		21 35	21 40	21 55	21 56		→			22 09	22 10	22 25	22 26	
	d					21 10	21 13	21 26					21 35	21 43	21 56						22 10	22 13	22 26		
Chelsfield 3	d						21 16							21 46								22 16			
Knockholt	d						21 19							21 49								22 19			
Dunton Green	d						21 24							21 54								22 24			
Sevenoaks 4	a				21 12	21 19	21 27	21 35					21 44	21 57	22 05				22 12		22 19	22 27	22 35		
	d				21 13	21 20		21 36					21 45		22 06				22 13		22 20		22 36		
Hildenborough	d							21 42							22 12								22 42		
Tonbridge 4	a				21 21	21 28		21 46					21 53		22 16				22 21		22 28		22 46		

		SE	SE	SE	SE		SE	SE	SE	SE	SE	SE	SE	SE	SE W ThO		SE MT FO	SE	SE	SE	SE	SE	SE	SE	SE
				◇1			◇1				◇1	◇1		◇1							◇1		◇1		
London Charing Cross 4 ⊖	d	22 04		22 10			22 30			22 34	22 40	22 45		23 00					23 04		23 10		23 30		
London Waterloo (East) 4 ⊖	d	22 07		22 13			22 33			22 37	22 43	22 48		23 03					23 07		23 13		23 33		
London Cannon Street 4 ⊖	d							22 20							22 50		22 50							23 20	
London Bridge 4 ⊖	d	22 13		22 19			22 39	22 24		22 43	22 49	22 54		23 09	22 54		22 54		23 13		23 19		23 39	23 24	
New Cross 4 ⊖	d							22 30							23 00		23 00							23 30	
St Johns	d							22 32							23 02		23 02							23 32	
Lewisham 4	d							22 35							23 05		23 05							23 35	
Hither Green 4	d	22 23						22 39		22 53					23 09		23 09		23 23					23 39	
Grove Park 4	d	22 27	22 35					22 43	22 55	22 57					23 13		23 13	23 15	23 27	23 35				23 43	23 55
Sundridge Park	d		22 38						22 58									23 18		23 38					23 58
Bromley North	a		22 40						23 00									23 20		23 40					00 01
Elmstead Woods	d	22 30						22 46		23 00					23 16		23 16		23 30					23 46	
Chislehurst	d	22 33			←			22 49		23 03			←		23 19		23 19		23 33			←		23 49	
Petts Wood 4	d	22 36			22 36			22 52		23 06			23 06		23 22		23 22		23 36			23 36		23 52	
Orpington 4	a	→		22 35	22 40		22 55	22 56		→		23 09	23 10	23 25	23 27		23 29		→		23 35	23 40	23 55	23 57	
	d			22 35	22 43		22 56					23 10	23 13	23 26							23 35	23 43	23 56		
Chelsfield 3	d				22 46								23 16									23 46			
Knockholt	d				22 49								23 19									23 49			
Dunton Green	d				22 54								23 24									23 54			
Sevenoaks 4	a			22 44	22 57		23 05				23 13	23 19	23 27	23 35							23 45	23 57	00 05		
	d			22 45			23 06				23 13	23 20		23 36							23 45		00 06		
Hildenborough	d						23 12							23 42									00 12		
Tonbridge 4	a			22 53			23 16				23 21	23 28		23 46							23 53		00 16		

			SE	SE	SE	SE	SE W ThO	SE MT FO
				◇1	◇1			
London Charing Cross 4 ⊖	d		23 34	23 40	23 45			
London Waterloo (East) 4 ⊖	d		23 37	23 43	23 48			
London Cannon Street 4 ⊖	d						23 45	23 50
London Bridge 4 ⊖	d		23 43	23 49	23 54		23 49	23 54
New Cross 4 ⊖	d						23 54	23 59
St Johns	d						23 57	00 02
Lewisham 4	d						00 05	00 05
Hither Green 4	d		23 53				00 09	00 09
Grove Park 4	d		23 57				00 13	00 13
Sundridge Park	d							
Bromley North	a							
Elmstead Woods	d		23 59				00 16	00 16
Chislehurst	d		00 03			←	00 19	00 19
Petts Wood 4	d		00 06			00 06	00 22	00 22
Orpington 4	a		→		00 09	00 12	00 26	00 26
	d				00 10	00 13		
Chelsfield 3	d					00 16		
Knockholt	d					00 19		
Dunton Green	d					00 24		
Sevenoaks 4	a			00 12	00 19	00 27		
	d			00 13	00 20			
Hildenborough	d							
Tonbridge 4	a			00 21	00 28			

Table T204-F

Saturdays

21 December to 16 May

London Charing Cross/Cannon Street - Grove Park, Orpington, Sevenoaks and Tonbridge, Grove Park - Bromley North

		SE	SE	SE	SE	SE		SE	SE	SE	SE	SE	SE	SE	SE	SE		SE	SE	SE	SE	SE	SE	SE	SE
		◇1	◇1	◇1							◇								◇1						
London Charing Cross 4 ⊖	d								00 04		00 15			00 50				05 34	06 00			06 04			
London Waterloo (East) 4 ⊖	d								00 07		00 18			00 53				05 37	06 03			06 07			
London Cannon Street 4 ⊖	d											00 20								05 50				06 20	
London Bridge 4 ⊖	d								00 13		00 24	00 24		00 59				05 43	06 09	05 54		06 13		06 24	
New Cross 4 ⊖	d											00 30								06 00				06 30	
St Johns	d					00 02						00 32								06 02				06 32	
Lewisham 4	d					00 05						00 35		01 08						06 05				06 35	
Hither Green 4	d					00 09			00 23			00 39		01 13				05 53		06 09		06 23		06 39	
Grove Park 4	d					00 13		00 15	00 27	00 35		00 43	00 55	01 17	05 35	05 55		05 57		06 13	06 15	06 27	06 35	06 43	06 55
Sundridge Park	d							00 18		00 38			00 58		05 38	05 58					06 18		06 38		06 58
Bromley North	a							00 20		00 40			01 00		05 40	06 00					06 20		06 40		07 00
Elmstead Woods	d					00 16			00 30			00 46		01 20				06 00		06 16		06 30		06 46	
Chislehurst	d				00 03	00 19			00 33			00 49		01 22				06 03		06 19		06 33		06 49	
Petts Wood 4	d				00 06	00 22			00 36			00 52		01 25				06 06		06 22		06 36		06 52	
Orpington 4	a				00 12	00 26			00 43		00 50	00 58		01 32				06 10	06 25	06 26		06 40		06 56	
	d			00 10	00 13						00 51							06 13	06 26			06 43			
Chelsfield 3	d				00 16						00 54							06 16				06 46			
Knockholt	d				00 19													06 19				06 49			
Dunton Green	d				00 24						01 00							06 24				06 54			
Sevenoaks 4	a			00 19	00 27						01 03							06 27	06 35			06 57			
	d	00 06	00 13	00 20							01 04								06 36						
Hildenborough	d	00 12									01s10								06 42						
Tonbridge 4	a	00 16	00 21	00 28							01 14								06 46						

		SE		SE	SE	SE	SE	SE	SE	SE	SE	SE		SE	SE	SE	SE	SE	SE	SE	SE	SE		SE	SE
								◇1	◇1						◇1	◇1						◇1		◇1	
London Charing Cross 4 ⊖	d	06 34				07 04		07 10	07 15					07 34	07 40	07 45				08 04		08 10		08 15	
London Waterloo (East) 4 ⊖	d	06 37				07 07		07 13	07 18					07 37	07 43	07 48				08 07		08 13		08 18	
London Cannon Street 4 ⊖	d			06 50							07 20							07 50							
London Bridge 4 ⊖	d	06 43		06 54		07 13		07 19	07 24		07 24			07 43	07 49	07 54		07 54		08 13		08 19		08 24	
New Cross 4 ⊖	d			07 00							07 30							08 00							
St Johns	d			07 02							07 32							08 02							
Lewisham 4	d			07 05							07 35							08 05							
Hither Green 4	d	06 53		07 09		07 23					07 39			07 53				08 09		08 23					
Grove Park 4	d	06 57		07 13	07 15	07 27	07 35				07 43	07 55		07 57				08 13	08 15	08 27	08 35				
Sundridge Park	d				07 18		07 38					07 58							08 18		08 38				
Bromley North	a				07 20		07 40					08 00							08 20		08 40				
Elmstead Woods	d	07 00		07 16		07 30					07 46			08 00				08 16		08 30					
Chislehurst	d	07 03		07 19		07 33				←	07 49			08 03			←	08 19		08 33					←
Petts Wood 4	d	07 06		07 22		07 36				07 36	07 52			08 06			08 06	08 22		08 36					08 36
Orpington 4	a	07 10		07 26		→			07 39	07 40	07 56			→		08 09	08 10	08 26		→				08 39	08 40
	d	07 13							07 40	07 43						08 10	08 13							08 40	08 43
Chelsfield 3	d	07 16								07 46							08 16								08 46
Knockholt	d	07 19								07 49							08 19								08 49
Dunton Green	d	07 24								07 54							08 24								08 54
Sevenoaks 4	a	07 27						07 42	07 49	07 57					08 12	08 19	08 27					08 42		08 49	08 57
	d							07 43	07 49						08 13	08 19						08 43		08 50	
Hildenborough	d								07 55							08 25									
Tonbridge 4	a							07 51	07 59						08 21	08 29						08 51		08 58	

		SE	SE	SE	SE	SE	SE	SE		SE	SE	SE	SE	SE	SE	SE	SE	SE		SE	SE	SE	SE	SE	SE
		◇1				◇1	◇1			◇1					◇1	◇1		◇1					◇1	◇1	
London Charing Cross 4 ⊖	d	08 30			08 34	08 40	08 45			09 00			09 04		09 10	09 15		09 30				09 34	09 40	09 45	
London Waterloo (East) 4 ⊖	d	08 33			08 37	08 43	08 48			09 03			09 07		09 13	09 18		09 33				09 37	09 43	09 48	
London Cannon Street 4 ⊖	d		08 20								08 50									09 20					
London Bridge 4 ⊖	d	08 39	08 24		08 43	08 49	08 54			09 09	08 54		09 13		09 19	09 24		09 39		09 24		09 43	09 49	09 54	
New Cross 4 ⊖	d		08 30								09 00									09 30					
St Johns	d		08 32								09 02									09 32					
Lewisham 4	d		08 35								09 05									09 35					
Hither Green 4	d		08 39		08 53						09 09		09 23							09 39		09 53			
Grove Park 4	d		08 43	08 55	08 57						09 13	09 15	09 27	09 35						09 43	09 55	09 57			
Sundridge Park	d			08 58								09 18		09 38							09 58				
Bromley North	a			09 00								09 20		09 40							10 00				
Elmstead Woods	d		08 46		09 00						09 16		09 30							09 46		10 00			
Chislehurst	d		08 49		09 03			←			09 19		09 33				←			09 49		10 03			←
Petts Wood 4	d		08 52		09 06			09 06			09 22		09 36				09 36			09 52		10 06			10 06
Orpington 4	a	08 55	08 56		→		09 09	09 10		09 25	09 26		→			09 39	09 40	09 55		09 56		→		10 09	10 10
	d	08 56					09 10	09 13		09 26						09 40	09 43	09 56						10 10	10 13
Chelsfield 3	d							09 16									09 46								10 16
Knockholt	d							09 19									09 49								10 19
Dunton Green	d							09 24									09 54								10 24
Sevenoaks 4	a	09 05				09 12	09 19	09 27		09 35					09 42	09 49	09 57	10 05					10 12	10 19	10 27
	d	09 06				09 13	09 20			09 36					09 43	09 50		10 06					10 13	10 20	
Hildenborough	d	09 12								09 42								10 12							
Tonbridge 4	a	09 16				09 21	09 28			09 47					09 51	09 58		10 16					10 21	10 28	

Table T204-F

Saturdays

21 December to 16 May

London Charing Cross/Cannon Street - Grove Park, Orpington, Sevenoaks and Tonbridge, Grove Park - Bromley North

		SE	SE	SE	SE	SE	SE	SE	SE	SE		SE	SE	SE	SE	SE	SE	SE	SE	SE		SE	SE	SE	SE
		◇1					◇1	◇1		◇1					◇1	◇1		◇1						◇1	◇1
London Charing Cross 4 ⊖	d	10 00			10 04		10 10	10 15		10 30				10 34	10 40	10 45		11 00				11 04		11 10	11 15
London Waterloo (East) 4 ⊖	d	10 03			10 07		10 13	10 18		10 33				10 37	10 43	10 48		11 03				11 07		11 13	11 18
London Cannon Street 4 ⊖	d		09 50									10 20							10 50						
London Bridge 4 ⊖	d	10 09	09 54		10 13		10 19	10 24		10 39		10 24		10 43	10 49	10 54		11 09	10 54			11 13		11 19	11 24
New Cross 4 ⊖	d		10 00									10 30							11 00						
St Johns	d		10 02									10 32							11 02						
Lewisham 4	d		10 05									10 35							11 05						
Hither Green 4	d		10 09		10 23							10 39		10 53					11 09			11 23			
Grove Park 4	d		10 13	10 15	10 27	10 35						10 43	10 55	10 57					11 13	11 15		11 27	11 35		
Sundridge Park	d			10 18		10 38							10 58							11 18			11 38		
Bromley North	a			10 20		10 40							11 00							11 20			11 40		
Elmstead Woods	d		10 16		10 30							10 46		11 00					11 16			11 30			
Chislehurst	d		10 19		10 33				←			10 49		11 03			←		11 19			11 33			
Petts Wood 4	d		10 22		10 36				10 36			10 52		11 06			11 06		11 22			11 36			
Orpington 4	a	10 25	10 26		→			10 39	10 40	10 55		10 56		→		11 09	11 10	11 25	11 26			→			11 39
	d	10 26						10 40	10 43	10 56						11 10	11 13	11 26							11 40
Chelsfield 3	d								10 46								11 16								
Knockholt	d								10 49								11 19								
Dunton Green	d								10 54								11 24								
Sevenoaks 4	a	10 35					10 42	10 49	10 57	11 05					11 12	11 19	11 27	11 35						11 42	11 49
	d	10 36					10 43	10 50		11 06					11 13	11 20		11 36						11 43	11 50
Hildenborough	d	10 42								11 12								11 42							
Tonbridge 4	a	10 46					10 51	10 58		11 16					11 21	11 28		11 46						11 51	11 58

		SE	SE	SE	SE	SE		SE	SE	SE	SE	SE	SE	SE	SE	SE		SE	SE	SE	SE	SE	SE	SE	SE
			◇1					◇1	◇1		◇1					◇1		◇1		◇1				◇1	◇1
London Charing Cross 4 ⊖	d		11 30			11 34		11 40	11 45		12 00			12 04		12 10		12 15		12 30			12 34	12 40	12 45
London Waterloo (East) 4 ⊖	d		11 33			11 37		11 43	11 48		12 03			12 07		12 13		12 18		12 33			12 37	12 43	12 48
London Cannon Street 4 ⊖	d			11 20								11 50									12 20				
London Bridge 4 ⊖	d		11 39	11 24		11 43		11 49	11 54		12 09	11 54		12 13		12 19		12 24		12 39	12 24		12 43	12 49	12 54
New Cross 4 ⊖	d			11 30								12 00									12 30				
St Johns	d			11 32								12 02									12 32				
Lewisham 4	d			11 35								12 05									12 35				
Hither Green 4	d			11 39		11 53						12 09		12 23							12 39		12 53		
Grove Park 4	d			11 43	11 55	11 57						12 13	12 15	12 27	12 35						12 43	12 55	12 57		
Sundridge Park	d				11 58								12 18		12 38							12 58			
Bromley North	a				12 00								12 20		12 40							13 00			
Elmstead Woods	d			11 46		12 00						12 16		12 30							12 46		13 00		
Chislehurst	d	←		11 49		12 03				←		12 19		12 33					←		12 49		13 03		
Petts Wood 4	d	11 36		11 52		12 06				12 06		12 22		12 36					12 36		12 52		13 06		
Orpington 4	a	11 40	11 55	11 56		→			12 09	12 10	12 25	12 26		→				12 39	12 40	12 55	12 56		→		13 09
	d	11 43	11 56						12 10	12 13	12 26							12 40	12 43	12 56					13 10
Chelsfield 3	d	11 46								12 16									12 46						
Knockholt	d	11 49								12 19									12 49						
Dunton Green	d	11 54								12 24									12 54						
Sevenoaks 4	a	11 57	12 05					12 12	12 19	12 27	12 35					12 42		12 49	12 57	13 05				13 12	13 19
	d		12 06					12 13	12 20		12 36					12 43		12 50		13 06				13 13	13 20
Hildenborough	d		12 12								12 42									13 12					
Tonbridge 4	a		12 16					12 21	12 28		12 46					12 51		12 58		13 16				13 21	13 28

		SE		SE	SE	SE	SE	SE	SE	SE	SE	SE		SE	SE	SE	SE	SE	SE	SE	SE	SE		SE	SE
				◇1					◇1	◇1		◇1					◇1	◇1		◇1					
London Charing Cross 4 ⊖	d			13 00			13 04		13 10	13 15		13 30				13 34	13 40	13 45		14 00				14 04	
London Waterloo (East) 4 ⊖	d			13 03			13 07		13 13	13 18		13 33				13 37	13 43	13 48		14 03				14 07	
London Cannon Street 4 ⊖	d				12 50									13 20							13 50				
London Bridge 4 ⊖	d			13 09	12 54		13 13		13 19	13 24		13 39		13 24		13 43	13 49	13 54		14 09	13 54			14 13	
New Cross 4 ⊖	d				13 00									13 30							14 00				
St Johns	d				13 02									13 32							14 02				
Lewisham 4	d				13 05									13 35							14 05				
Hither Green 4	d				13 09		13 23							13 39		13 53					14 09			14 23	
Grove Park 4	d				13 13	13 15	13 27	13 35						13 43	13 55	13 57					14 13	14 15		14 27	14 35
Sundridge Park	d					13 18		13 38							13 58							14 18			14 38
Bromley North	a					13 20		13 40							14 00							14 20			14 40
Elmstead Woods	d				13 16		13 30							13 46		14 00					14 16			14 30	
Chislehurst	d	←			13 19		13 33				←			13 49		14 03			←		14 19			14 33	
Petts Wood 4	d	13 06			13 22		13 36				13 36			13 52		14 06			14 06		14 22			14 36	
Orpington 4	a	13 10		13 25	13 26		→			13 39	13 40	13 55		13 56		→		14 09	14 10	14 25	14 26			→	
	d	13 13		13 26						13 40	13 43	13 56						14 10	14 13	14 26					
Chelsfield 3	d	13 16									13 46								14 16						
Knockholt	d	13 19									13 49								14 19						
Dunton Green	d	13 24									13 54								14 24						
Sevenoaks 4	a	13 27		13 35					13 42	13 49	13 57	14 05					14 12	14 19	14 27	14 35					
	d			13 36					13 43	13 50		14 06					14 13	14 20		14 36					
Hildenborough	d			13 42								14 12								14 42					
Tonbridge 4	a			13 46					13 51	13 58		14 16					14 21	14 28		14 46					

Table T204-F

Saturdays

21 December to 16 May

London Charing Cross/Cannon Street - Grove Park, Orpington, Sevenoaks and Tonbridge, Grove Park - Bromley North

		SE ◇1	SE ◇1	SE	SE ◇1	SE	SE	SE	SE ◇1	SE ◇1	SE	SE ◇1	SE	SE	SE	SE	SE ◇1	SE ◇1	SE	SE ◇1	SE	SE
London Charing Cross 4 ⊖	d	14 10	14 15		14 30			14 34	14 40	14 45		15 00			15 04		15 10	15 15		15 30		
London Waterloo (East) 4 ⊖	d	14 13	14 18		14 33			14 37	14 43	14 48		15 03			15 07		15 13	15 18		15 33		
London Cannon Street 4 ⊖	d					14 20							14 50								15 20	
London Bridge 4 ⊖	d	14 19	14 24		14 39	14 24		14 43	14 49	14 54		15 09	14 54		15 13		15 19	15 24		15 39	15 24	
New Cross 4 ⊖	d					14 30							15 00								15 30	
St Johns	d					14 32							15 02								15 32	
Lewisham 4	d					14 35							15 05								15 35	
Hither Green 4	d					14 39		14 53					15 09		15 23						15 39	
Grove Park 4	d					14 43	14 55	14 57					15 13	15 15	15 27	15 35					15 43	15 55
Sundridge Park	d						14 58							15 18		15 38						15 58
Bromley North	a						15 00							15 20		15 40						16 00
Elmstead Woods	d					14 46		15 00					15 16		15 30						15 46	
Chislehurst	d			←		14 49		15 03			←		15 19		15 33				←		15 49	
Petts Wood 4	d			14 36		14 52		15 06			15 06		15 22		15 36				15 36		15 52	
Orpington 4	a		14 39	14 40	14 55	14 56		→		15 09	15 10	15 25	15 26		→			15 39	15 40	15 55	15 56	
	d		14 40	14 43	14 56					15 10	15 13	15 26						15 40	15 43	15 56		
Chelsfield 3	d			14 46							15 16								15 46			
Knockholt	d			14 49							15 19								15 49			
Dunton Green	d			14 54							15 24								15 54			
Sevenoaks 4	a	14 42	14 49	14 57	15 05				15 12	15 19	15 27	15 35					15 42	15 49	15 57	16 05		
	d	14 43	14 50		15 06				15 13	15 20		15 36					15 43	15 50		16 06		
Hildenborough	d				15 12							15 42								16 12		
Tonbridge 4	a	14 51	14 59		15 16				15 21	15 28		15 46					15 51	15 58		16 16		

		SE	SE ◇1	SE ◇1	SE	SE ◇1	SE	SE	SE	SE	SE ◇1	SE ◇1	SE	SE ◇1	SE	SE	SE	SE ◇1	SE ◇1	SE	SE ◇1	SE	SE
London Charing Cross 4 ⊖	d	15 34	15 40	15 45		16 00			16 04		16 10	16 15		16 30			16 34	16 40	16 45		17 00		
London Waterloo (East) 4 ⊖	d	15 37	15 43	15 48		16 03			16 07		16 13	16 18		16 33			16 37	16 43	16 48		17 03		
London Cannon Street 4 ⊖	d						15 50								16 20							16 50	
London Bridge 4 ⊖	d	15 43	15 49	15 54		16 09	15 54		16 13		16 19	16 24		16 39	16 24		16 43	16 49	16 54		17 09	16 54	
New Cross 4 ⊖	d						16 00								16 30							17 00	
St Johns	d						16 02								16 32							17 02	
Lewisham 4	d						16 05								16 35							17 05	
Hither Green 4	d	15 53					16 09		16 23						16 39		16 53					17 09	
Grove Park 4	d	15 57					16 13	16 15	16 27	16 35					16 43	16 55	16 57					17 13	17 15
Sundridge Park	d							16 18		16 38						16 58							17 18
Bromley North	a							16 20		16 40						17 00							17 20
Elmstead Woods	d	16 00					16 16		16 30						16 46		17 00					17 16	
Chislehurst	d	16 03			←		16 19		16 33				←		16 49		17 03			←		17 19	
Petts Wood 4	d	16 06			16 06		16 22		16 36				16 36		16 52		17 06			17 06		17 22	
Orpington 4	a	→		16 09	16 10	16 25	16 26		→			16 39	16 40	16 55	16 56		→		17 09	17 09	17 25	17 26	
	d			16 10	16 13	16 26						16 40	16 43	16 56					17 10	17 13	17 26		
Chelsfield 3	d				16 16								16 46							17 16			
Knockholt	d				16 19								16 49							17 19			
Dunton Green	d				16 24								16 54							17 24			
Sevenoaks 4	a		16 12	16 19	16 27	16 35					16 42	16 49	16 57	17 05				17 12	17 19	17 27	17 35		
	d		16 13	16 20		16 36					16 43	16 50		17 06				17 13	17 20		17 36		
Hildenborough	d					16 42								17 12							17 42		
Tonbridge 4	a		16 21	16 28		16 46					16 51	16 58		17 16				17 21	17 28		17 46		

		SE	SE	SE ◇1	SE ◇1	SE	SE ◇1	SE	SE	SE	SE ◇1	SE ◇1	SE	SE ◇1	SE	SE	SE	SE	SE ◇1	SE ◇1	SE	SE ◇1	SE
London Charing Cross 4 ⊖	d	17 04		17 10	17 15		17 30			17 34	17 40	17 45		18 00			18 04		18 10	18 15		18 30	
London Waterloo (East) 4 ⊖	d	17 07		17 13	17 18		17 33			17 37	17 43	17 48		18 03			18 07		18 13	18 18		18 33	
London Cannon Street 4 ⊖	d							17 20							17 50								18 20
London Bridge 4 ⊖	d	17 13		17 19	17 24		17 39	17 24		17 43	17 49	17 54		18 09	17 54		18 13		18 19	18 24		18 39	18 24
New Cross 4 ⊖	d							17 30							18 00								18 30
St Johns	d							17 32							18 02								18 32
Lewisham 4	d							17 35							18 05								18 35
Hither Green 4	d	17 23						17 39		17 53					18 09		18 23						18 39
Grove Park 4	d	17 27	17 35					17 43	17 55	17 57					18 13	18 15	18 27	18 35					18 43
Sundridge Park	d		17 38						17 58							18 18		18 38					
Bromley North	a		17 40						18 00							18 20		18 40					
Elmstead Woods	d	17 30						17 46		18 00					18 16		18 30						18 46
Chislehurst	d	17 33				←		17 49		18 03			←		18 19		18 33				←		18 49
Petts Wood 4	d	17 36				17 36		17 52		18 06			18 06		18 22		18 36				18 36		18 52
Orpington 4	a	→			17 39	17 40	17 55	17 56		→		18 09	18 10	18 25	18 26		→			18 39	18 40	18 55	18 56
	d				17 40	17 43	17 56					18 10	18 13	18 26						18 40	18 43	18 56	
Chelsfield 3	d					17 46							18 16								18 46		
Knockholt	d					17 49							18 19								18 49		
Dunton Green	d					17 54							18 24								18 54		
Sevenoaks 4	a			17 42	17 49	17 57	18 05				18 12	18 19	18 27	18 35					18 42	18 49	18 57	19 05	
	d			17 43	17 50		18 06				18 13	18 20		18 36					18 43	18 50		19 06	
Hildenborough	d						18 12							18 42								19 12	
Tonbridge 4	a			17 51	17 58		18 16				18 21	18 28		18 46					18 51	18 58		19 16	

Table T204-F

Saturdays

21 December to 16 May

London Charing Cross/Cannon Street - Grove Park, Orpington, Sevenoaks and Tonbridge, Grove Park - Bromley North

		SE	SE	SE ◇1	SE ◇1	SE	SE ◇1	SE	SE	SE	SE	SE ◇1	SE ◇1	SE	SE ◇1	SE	SE	SE	SE ◇1	SE ◇1	SE	SE ◇1	SE
London Charing Cross 4 ⊖	d		18 34	18 40	18 45		19 00			19 04		19 10	19 15		19 30			19 34	19 40	19 45		20 00	
London Waterloo (East) 4 ⊖	d		18 37	18 43	18 48		19 03			19 07		19 13	19 18		19 33			19 37	19 43	19 48		20 03	
London Cannon Street 4 ⊖	d							18 50								19 20							19 50
London Bridge 4 ⊖	d		18 43	18 49	18 54		19 09	18 54		19 13		19 19	19 24		19 39	19 24		19 43	19 49	19 54		20 09	19 54
New Cross 4 ⊖	d							19 00								19 30							20 00
St Johns	d							19 02								19 32							20 02
Lewisham 4	d							19 05								19 35							20 05
Hither Green 4	d		18 53					19 09		19 23						19 39		19 53					20 09
Grove Park 4	d	18 55	18 57					19 13	19 15	19 27	19 35					19 43	19 55	19 57					20 13
Sundridge Park	d	18 58							19 18		19 38						19 58						
Bromley North	a	19 00							19 20		19 40						20 00						
Elmstead Woods	d		19 00					19 16		19 30						19 46		20 00					20 16
Chislehurst	d		19 03			←		19 19		19 33				←		19 49		20 03			←		20 19
Petts Wood 4	d		19 06			19 06		19 22		19 36				19 36		19 52		20 06			20 06		20 22
Orpington 4	a		→		19 09	19 10	19 25	19 26		→			19 39	19 40	19 55	19 56		→		20 09	20 10	20 25	20 26
	d				19 10	19 13	19 26						19 40	19 43	19 56					20 10	20 13	20 26	
Chelsfield 3	d					19 16								19 46							20 16		
Knockholt	d					19 19								19 49							20 19		
Dunton Green	d					19 24								19 54							20 24		
Sevenoaks 4	a			19 12	19 19	19 27	19 35					19 42	19 49	19 57	20 05				20 12	20 19	20 27	20 35	
	d			19 13	19 20		19 36					19 43	19 50		20 06				20 13	20 20		20 36	
Hildenborough	d						19 42								20 12							20 42	
Tonbridge 4	a			19 21	19 28		19 46					19 51	19 58		20 16				20 21	20 28		20 46	

		SE	SE	SE	SE ◇1	SE ◇1	SE	SE ◇1	SE	SE	SE	SE ◇1	SE ◇1	SE	SE ◇1	SE	SE	SE	SE	SE ◇1	SE	SE ◇1
London Charing Cross 4 ⊖	d		20 04		20 10	20 15		20 30			20 34	20 40	20 45		21 00			21 04		21 10		21 30
London Waterloo (East) 4 ⊖	d		20 07		20 13	20 18		20 33			20 37	20 43	20 48		21 03			21 07		21 13		21 33
London Cannon Street 4 ⊖	d								20 20							20 50						
London Bridge 4 ⊖	d		20 13		20 19	20 24		20 39	20 24		20 43	20 49	20 54		21 09	20 54		21 13		21 19		21 39
New Cross 4 ⊖	d								20 30							21 00						
St Johns	d								20 32							21 02						
Lewisham 4	d								20 35							21 05						
Hither Green 4	d		20 23						20 39		20 53					21 09		21 23				
Grove Park 4	d	20 15	20 27	20 35					20 43	20 55	20 57					21 13	21 15	21 27	21 35			
Sundridge Park	d	20 18		20 38						20 58							21 18		21 38			
Bromley North	a	20 20		20 40						21 00							21 20		21 40			
Elmstead Woods	d		20 30						20 46		21 00					21 16		21 30				
Chislehurst	d		20 33				←		20 49		21 03			←		21 19		21 33			←	
Petts Wood 4	d		20 36				20 36		20 52		21 06			21 06		21 22		21 36			21 36	
Orpington 4	a		→			20 39	20 40	20 55	20 56		→		21 09	21 10	21 25	21 26		→		21 35	21 40	21 55
	d					20 40	20 43	20 56					21 10	21 13	21 26					21 35	21 43	21 56
Chelsfield 3	d						20 46							21 16							21 46	
Knockholt	d						20 49							21 19							21 49	
Dunton Green	d						20 54							21 24							21 54	
Sevenoaks 4	a				20 42	20 49	20 57	21 05				21 12	21 19	21 27	21 35					21 44	21 57	22 05
	d				20 43	20 50		21 06				21 13	21 20		21 36					21 45		22 06
Hildenborough	d							21 12							21 42							22 12
Tonbridge 4	a				20 51	20 58		21 16				21 21	21 28		21 46					21 53		22 16

		SE	SE	SE	SE ◇1	SE ◇1	SE	SE ◇1	SE	SE	SE	SE	SE ◇1	SE	SE ◇1	SE	SE	SE	SE ◇1	SE ◇1	SE	SE ◇1	SE
London Charing Cross 4 ⊖	d			21 34	21 40	21 45		22 00			22 04		22 10		22 30			22 34	22 40	22 45		23 00	
London Waterloo (East) 4 ⊖	d			21 37	21 43	21 48		22 03			22 07		22 13		22 33			22 37	22 43	22 48		23 03	
London Cannon Street 4 ⊖	d	21 20							21 50							22 20							22 50
London Bridge 4 ⊖	d	21 24		21 43	21 49	21 54		22 09	21 54		22 13		22 19		22 39	22 24		22 43	22 49	22 54		23 09	22 54
New Cross 4 ⊖	d	21 30							22 00							22 30							23 00
St Johns	d	21 32							22 02							22 32							23 02
Lewisham 4	d	21 35							22 05							22 35							23 05
Hither Green 4	d	21 39		21 53					22 09		22 23					22 39		22 53					23 09
Grove Park 4	d	21 43	21 55	21 57					22 13	22 15	22 27	22 35				22 43	22 55	22 57					23 13
Sundridge Park	d		21 58							22 18		22 38					22 58						
Bromley North	a		22 00							22 20		22 40					23 00						
Elmstead Woods	d	21 46		22 00					22 16		22 30					22 46		23 00					23 16
Chislehurst	d	21 49		22 03			←		22 19		22 33			←		22 49		23 03			←		23 19
Petts Wood 4	d	21 52		22 06			22 06		22 22		22 36			22 36		22 52		23 06			23 06		23 22
Orpington 4	a	21 56		→		22 09	22 10	22 25	22 26		→		22 35	22 40	22 55	22 56		→		23 09	23 09	23 25	23 26
	d					22 10	22 13	22 26					22 35	22 43	22 56					23 10	23 13	23 26	
Chelsfield 3	d						22 16							22 46							23 16		
Knockholt	d						22 19							22 49							23 19		
Dunton Green	d						22 24							22 54							23 24		
Sevenoaks 4	a				22 12	22 19	22 27	22 35					22 44	22 57	23 05				23 12	23 19	23 27	23 35	
	d				22 13	22 20		22 36					22 45		23 06				23 13	23 20		23 36	
Hildenborough	d							22 42							23 12							23 42	
Tonbridge 4	a				22 21	22 28		22 46					22 53		23 16				23 21	23 28		23 46	

Table T204-F

Saturdays
21 December to 16 May

London Charing Cross/Cannon Street - Grove Park, Orpington, Sevenoaks and Tonbridge, Grove Park - Bromley North

		SE		SE	SE	SE ◇1	SE	SE ◇1	SE	SE	SE	SE ◇1		SE ◇1	SE	SE
London Charing Cross 4 ⊖	d			23 04		23 10		23 30			23 34	23 40		23 45		
London Waterloo (East) 4 ⊖	d			23 07		23 13		23 33			23 37	23 43		23 48		
London Cannon Street 4 ⊖	d								23 20							23 50
London Bridge 4 ⊖	d			23 13		23 19		23 39	23 24		23 43	23 49		23 54		23 54
New Cross 4 ⊖	d								23 30							23 59
St Johns	d								23 32							00 02
Lewisham 4	d								23 35							00 05
Hither Green 4	d			23 23					23 39		23 53					00 09
Grove Park 4	d	23 15		23 27	23 35				23 43	23 55	23 57					00 13
Sundridge Park	d	23 18			23 38					23 58						
Bromley North	a	23 20			23 40					00 01						
Elmstead Woods	d			23 30					23 46		23 59					00 16
Chislehurst	d			23 33			←		23 49		00 03				←	00 19
Petts Wood 4	d			23 36			23 36		23 52		00 06				00 06	00 22
Orpington 4	a			→		23 35	23 40	23 55	23 56		→			00 09	00 10	00 26
	d					23 35	23 43	23 56						00 10	00 13	
Chelsfield 3	d						23 46								00 16	
Knockholt	d						23 49								00 19	
Dunton Green	d						23 54								00 24	
Sevenoaks 4	a					23 46	23 57	00 05				00 12		00 19	00 27	
	d					23 46		00 06				00 13		00 20		
Hildenborough	d							00 12								
Tonbridge 4	a					23 54		00 16				00 21		00 28		

Sundays
15 December to 10 May

		SE ◇1 A	SE ◇1 A	SE ◇1 A	SE A	SE A	SE	SE	SE	SE ◇		SE	SE	SE	SE	SE ◇1	SE	SE ◇1	SE	SE ◇1	SE	SE ◇1	SE	
London Charing Cross 4 ⊖	d							00 04		00 15				00 50	07 46	08 10	08 16	08 25		08 40	08 46	08 55		
London Waterloo (East) 4 ⊖	d							00 07		00 18				00 53	07 49	08 13	08 19	08 28		08 43	08 49	08 58		
London Cannon Street 4 ⊖	d											00 20												
London Bridge 4 ⊖	d							00 13		00 24		00 24		00 59	07 55	08 19	08 25	08 34		08 49	08 55	09 04		
New Cross 4 ⊖	d											00 30												
St Johns	d					00 02						00 32												
Lewisham 4	d					00 05						00 35		01 08	08 05		08 35				09 05			and at
Hither Green 4	d					00 09		00 23				00 39		01 13	08 10		08 40				09 10			the same
Grove Park 4	d					00 13	00 15	00 27	00 35			00 43	00 55	01 17	08 14		08 44				09 14			minutes
Sundridge Park	d						00 18		00 38				00 58											past
Bromley North	a						00 20		00 40				01 00											each
Elmstead Woods	d					00 16		00 30				00 46		01 20	08 17		08 47				09 17			hour until
Chislehurst	d				00 03	00 19		00 33				00 49		01 22	08 19		08 49		←		09 19		←	
Petts Wood 4	d				00 06	00 22		00 37				00 52		01 25	08 23		08 53		08 53		09 23		09 23	
Orpington 4	a				00 10	00 26		00 43		00 49		00 56		01 32	08 27	08 35	→	08 50	08 57	09 05	→	09 20	09 27	
	d			00 10	00 13					00 51					08 28	08 36		08 50	08 58	09 06		09 20	09 28	
Chelsfield 3	d				00 16					00 54					08 31				09 01				09 31	
Knockholt	d				00 19										08 34				09 04				09 34	
Dunton Green	d				00 24					01 00					08 39				09 09				09 39	
Sevenoaks 4	a			00 19	00 27					01 03					08 42	08 45		08 59	09 12	09 15		09 29	09 42	
	d	00 06	00 13	00 20						01 04						08 46		09 00		09 16		09 30		
Hildenborough	d	00 12								01s10												09 36		
Tonbridge 4	a	00 16	00 21	00 28						01 14						08 54		09 08		09 24		09 40		

		SE ◇1	SE	SE ◇1	SE	SE ◇1	SE	SE ◇1	SE		SE ◇1	SE	SE ◇1	SE	SE ◇1	SE	SE ◇1	SE	SE ◇1		SE	SE ◇1	SE	SE ◇1	SE
London Charing Cross 4 ⊖	d	19 10	19 16	19 25		19 40	19 46	19 55			20 10	20 16	20 25		20 40	20 46	21 10	21 16	21 25			21 40	21 46	22 10	22 16
London Waterloo (East) 4 ⊖	d	19 13	19 19	19 28		19 43	19 49	19 58			20 13	20 19	20 28		20 43	20 49	21 13	21 19	21 28			21 43	21 49	22 13	22 19
London Cannon Street 4 ⊖	d																								
London Bridge 4 ⊖	d	19 19	19 25	19 34		19 49	19 55	20 04			20 19	20 25	20 34		20 49	20 55	21 19	21 25	21 34			21 49	21 55	22 19	22 25
New Cross 4 ⊖	d																								
St Johns	d																								
Lewisham 4	d		19 35				20 05					20 35				21 05		21 35					22 05		22 35
Hither Green 4	d		19 40				20 10					20 40				21 10		21 40					22 10		22 40
Grove Park 4	d		19 44				20 14					20 44				21 14		21 44					22 14		22 44
Sundridge Park	d																								
Bromley North	a																								
Elmstead Woods	d		19 47				20 17					20 47				21 17		21 47					22 17		22 47
Chislehurst	d		19 49		←		20 19		←			20 49		←		21 19		21 49			←		22 19		22 49
Petts Wood 4	d		19 53		19 53		20 23		20 23			20 53		20 53		21 23		21 53			21 53		22 23		22 53
Orpington 4	a	19 35	→	19 50	19 57	20 05	→	20 20	20 27		20 35	→	20 50	20 57	21 05	21 27	21 35	→	21 50		21 57	22 05	22 27	22 35	→
	d	19 36		19 50	19 58	20 06		20 20	20 28		20 36		20 50	20 58	21 06	21 28	21 36		21 50		21 58	22 06	22 28	22 36	
Chelsfield 3	d				20 01				20 31					21 01		21 31					22 01		22 31		
Knockholt	d				20 04				20 34					21 04		21 34					22 04		22 34		
Dunton Green	d				20 09				20 39					21 09		21 39					22 09		22 39		
Sevenoaks 4	a	19 45		19 59	20 12	20 15		20 29	20 42		20 45		20 59	21 12	21 15	21 42	21 45		21 59		22 12	22 15	22 42	22 45	
	d	19 46		20 00		20 16		20 30			20 46		21 00		21 16		21 46		22 00			22 16		22 46	
Hildenborough	d							20 36					21 06						22 06						
Tonbridge 4	a	19 54		20 08		20 24		20 40			20 54		21 10		21 24		21 54		22 10			22 24		22 54	

A not 15 December

Table T204-F

Sundays
15 December to 10 May

London Charing Cross/Cannon Street - Grove Park, Orpington, Sevenoaks and Tonbridge, Grove Park - Bromley North

		SE ◇1	SE	SE ◇1		SE	SE ◇1	SE	SE ◇1	SE	SE ◇1	SE
London Charing Cross 4 ⊖	d	22 25		22 40		22 46	23 10	23 16	23 25		23 40	23 46
London Waterloo (East) 4 ⊖	d	22 28		22 43		22 49	23 13	23 19	23 28		23 43	23 49
London Cannon Street 4 ⊖	d											
London Bridge 4 ⊖	d	22 34		22 49		22 55	23 19	23 25	23 34		23 49	23 55
New Cross 4 ⊖	d											
St Johns	d											
Lewisham 4	d					23 05		23 35				00 05
Hither Green 4	d					23 10		23 40				00 10
Grove Park 4	d					23 14		23 44				00 14
Sundridge Park	d											
Bromley North	a											
Elmstead Woods	d					23 17		23 47				00 17
Chislehurst	d		←			23 19		23 49		←		00 19
Petts Wood 4	d		22 53			23 23		23 53		23 53		00 23
Orpington 4	a	22 50	22 57	23 05		23 27	23 35	→	23 50	23 57	00 05	00 27
	d	22 50	22 58	23 06		23 28	23 36		23 50	23 58	00 06	00 28
Chelsfield 3	d		23 01			23 31				00 01		00s31
Knockholt	d		23 04			23 34				00 04		00s34
Dunton Green	d		23 09			23 39				00 09		00s39
Sevenoaks 4	a	23 00	23 12	23 15		23 42	23 45		23 59	00 12	00 15	00 42
	d	23 00		23 16			23 46		23 59		00 16	
Hildenborough	d	23 06							00 06			
Tonbridge 4	a	23 10		23 24			23 54		00 10		00 24	

AVAILABLE FROM MP Middleton Press

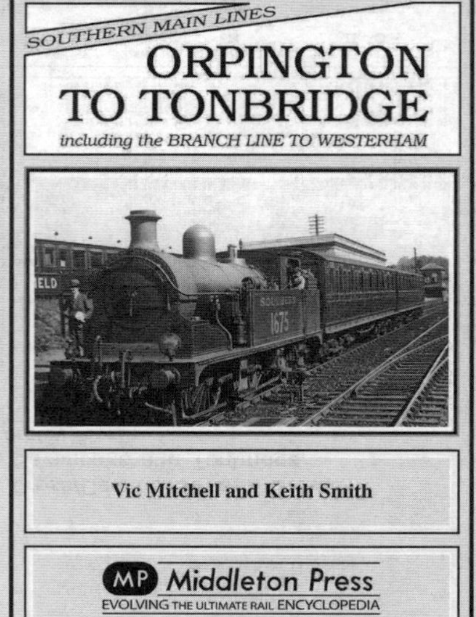

Table T204-R

Mondays to Fridays

16 December to 15 May

Bromley North to Grove Park, Tonbridge, Sevenoaks, Orpington and Grove Park - London Cannon Street/Charing Cross

Miles	Miles	Miles			SE MO	SE ThFO	SE TWO	SE MX	SE MX	SE MX	SE	SE 1 A	SE	SE	SE ◇1	SE	SE	SE ◇1	SE	SE	SE	SE ◇1	SE ◇1
0	—	—	Tonbridge 4	d								04 45			05 28			05 37				05 58	06 07
2½	—	—	Hildenborough	d								04 50			05 32							06 02	
7½	—	—	Sevenoaks 4	a								04 56			05 39			05 49				06 09	06 16
—	—	—		d								04 57		05 17	05 40			05 50			06 01	06 09	06 17
1½	—	—	Dunton Green	d										05 20							06 04		
5½	—	—	Knockholt	d										05 25							06 09		
6¾	—	—	Chelsfield 3	d								05 05		05 28	05 47						06 12	06 17	
8¼	—	—	Orpington 4	a								05 08		05 31	05 50			05 58			06 16	06 20	06 25
—	—	—		d							04 59	05 09		05 33	05 51		05 55	05 59	05 59		06 18	06 21	06 27
9¼	—	—	Petts Wood 4	d							05 03			05 36			05 58		06 03		06 21		
10¾	—	—	Chislehurst	d							05 06			05 39			06 01		06 06		06 25		
11¾	—	—	Elmstead Woods	d							05 08			05 41			06 04		06 08		06 28		
—	—	0	Bromley North	d				00 04	00 24	00 44			05 34			05 54				06 19			
—	—	0½	Sundridge Park	d				00 06	00 26	00 46			05 36			05 56				06 21			
13	—	1¾	Grove Park 4	d	00 01	00 02	00 02	00a09	00a29	00a49	05 12		05a39	05 45		05a59	06 07		06 12	06a24	06 31		
14¾	—	—	Hither Green 4	d	00 05	00 06	00 06				05 16			05 49			06 11		06 16		06 36		
16	—	—	Lewisham 4	d	00 11	00 11	00 13				05 21			05 54					06 21		06 41		
16½	—	—	St Johns	a															06 23				
17¼	—	—	New Cross 4	a															06 25			06 32	
20¼	0	—	London Bridge 4	a	00 19	00 19	00 20				05 29	05 35		06 02	06 07		06 20	06 16	06 31		06 50	06 38	06 43
—	0¾	—	London Cannon Street 4	a			00 27											06 24	06 39			06 46	
21¼	—	—	London Waterloo (East) 4	a	00 25	00 25					05 35	05 41		06 07	06 12		06 26				06 56		06 49
22	—	—	London Charing Cross 4	a	00 29	00 31					05 41	05 48		06 14	06 19		06 33				07 03		06 56

		SE	SE	SE ◇1	SE	SE	SE	SE ◇1	SE ◇1	SE	SE	SE ◇1	SE	SE	SE ◇1	SE ◇1	SE ◇1	SE	SE	SE	SE ◇1	SE ◇1	SE ◇1
Tonbridge 4	d			06 19				06 29	06 39			06 44			06 51	07 03	07 10				07 16	07 23	07 31
Hildenborough	d			06 23				06 33							06 56		07 14				07 21		07 36
Sevenoaks 4	a			06 30				06 40	06 48			06 53			07 02	07 11	07 22				07 27	07 31	07 43
	d			06 31			06 34	06 41	06 49			06 54		06 57	07 03	07 12	07 23			07 17	07 28	07 32	07 43
Dunton Green	d						06 37							07 00						07 20			
Knockholt	d						06 42							07 05						07 25			
Chelsfield 3	d						06 45	06 49						07 08	07 11		07 31			07 28			07 52
Orpington 4	a			06 39			06 48	06 52				07 02		07 11	07 14					07 31			
	d		06 33	06 40	06 41		06 49	06 53			07 02	07 04		07 12	07 15			07 20		07 33			
Petts Wood 4	d		06 37		06 45		06 52				07 05			07 15				07 24		07 36			
Chislehurst	d		06 40		06 48		06 56				07 09			07 18				07 27		07 40			
Elmstead Woods	d		06 43		06 51		06 58				07 11			07 21				07 30		07 43			
Bromley North	d	06 35				06 52				07 05			07 19						07 32				
Sundridge Park	d	06 37				06 54				07 07			07 21						07 34				
Grove Park 4	d	06a40	06 46		06 54	06a57	07 02			07a10	07 15		07a24	07 25				07 34	07a37	07 46			
Hither Green 4	d		06 50		06 58		07 06				07 19			07 29				07 38		07 50			
Lewisham 4	d				07 04						07 25							07 44					
St Johns	a																						
New Cross 4	a		06 55				07 11							07 34						07 55			
London Bridge 4	a		07 01	06 55	07 12		07 17	07 08	07 14		07 33	07 23		07 40	07 30	07 35	07 49	07 53		08 01	07 52	07 55	08 09
London Cannon Street 4	a		07 09				07 25					07 31		07 48						08 09	08 00		
London Waterloo (East) 4	a			07 01	07 18			07 14	07 21		07 39				07 36	07 42	07 55	07 59				08 01	08 15
London Charing Cross 4	a			07 08	07 25			07 21	07 27		07 46				07 44	07 49	08 02	08 06				08 09	08 22

		SE ◇1	SE ◇1	SE	SE	SE	SE	SE	SE ◇1	SE	SE	SE	SE ◇1	SE ◇1	SE ◇1	SE	SE	SE	SE ◇1	SE ◇1	SE	SE ◇
Tonbridge 4	d	07 35	07 42						07 50				07 58	08 03	08 10				08 14	08 21		
Hildenborough	d	07 39							07 55						08 15				08 19			
Sevenoaks 4	a	07 46	07 50						08 02				08 07	08 11	08 22				08 26	08 30		
	d	07 47	07 51			07 37			08 03			07 57	08 08	08 12	08 23			08 17	08 27	08 31		
Dunton Green	d					07 40						08 00						08 20				
Knockholt	d					07 45						08 05						08 25				
Chelsfield 3	d					07 48			08 11			08 08			08 32			08 28				
Orpington 4	a					07 51						08 11						08 31				
	d				07 42	07 51		07 56		07 59		08 12				08 21		08 34			08 41	08 46
Petts Wood 4	d				07 46	07 54		08 00		08 03		08 15				08 24		08 37			08 45	
Chislehurst	d				07 49	07 58		08 03		08 07		08 19				08 28		08 41			08 48	
Elmstead Woods	d				07 52	08 00		08 06		08 10		08 22				08 30		08 44			08 51	
Bromley North	d			07 46			08 01				08 14						08 35					
Sundridge Park	d			07 48			08 03				08 16						08 37					
Grove Park 4	d			07a51	07 56	08 04	08a06	08 10		08 14	08a19	08 25				08 34	08a40	08 48			08 55	
Hither Green 4	d				08 00					08 18		08 30				08 38		08 52			08 59	
Lewisham 4	d				08 08					08 24						08 44					09 05	
St Johns	a																					
New Cross 4	a					08 11						08 36						08 58				
London Bridge 4	a	08 13	08 15		08 17	08 17		08 21	08 29	08 33		08 42	08 34	08 35	08 50	08 52		09 04	08 54	08 56	09 13	09 02
London Cannon Street 4	a	08 21				08 25						08 50	08 42					09 12	09 02			
London Waterloo (East) 4	a		08 21		08 23			08 27	08 35	08 39				08 41	08 56	08 59				09 03	09 19	09 08
London Charing Cross 4	a		08 28		08 30			08 33	08 42	08 46				08 48	09 03	09 05				09 10	09 27	09 15

A not 16 December

Table T204-R

Mondays to Fridays

16 December to 15 May

Bromley North to Grove Park, Tonbridge, Sevenoaks, Orpington and Grove Park - London Cannon Street/Charing Cross

		SE ◇1	SE ◇1	SE	SE	SE ◇1	SE	SE	SE	SE	SE ◇1	SE ◇1	SE ◇1	SE	SE	SE	SE	SE ◇1	SE ◇1	SE ◇1	SE	SE	SE
Tonbridge 4	d	08 36	08 40			08 47					09 01	09 09	09 19					09 31	09 39	09 49			
Hildenborough	d	08 40									09 05							09 35					
Sevenoaks 4	a	08 46	08 50			08 55					09 12	09 18	09 28					09 42	09 48	09 58			
	d	08 47	08 51		08 37	08 56				09 06	09 13	09 19	09 29				09 35	09 43	09 49	09 59			
Dunton Green	d				08 40					09 09							09 38						
Knockholt	d				08 45					09 14							09 43						
Chelsfield 3	d	08 55			08 48					09 17							09 46						
Orpington 4	a				08 51	09 04				09 20	09 23		09 37				09 49	09 51		10 07			
	d				08 52	09 05		09 10		09 21	09 24		09 38		09 41		09 50	09 52		10 08		10 11	
Petts Wood 4	d				08 55			09 14		09 24					09 45		09 53					10 15	
Chislehurst	d				08 58			09 17		09 27					09 48		09 56					10 18	
Elmstead Woods	d				09 01			09 19		09 29					09 50		09 58					10 20	
Bromley North	d			08 53			09 07		09 22					09 36		09 50					10 05		10 20
Sundridge Park	d			08 55			09 09		09 24					09 38		09 52					10 07		10 22
Grove Park 4	d			08a58	09 05		09a12	09 23	09a27	09 33				09a41	09 54	09a55	10 02				10a10	10 24	10a25
Hither Green 4	d				09 09			09 27		09 37					09 58		10 06					10 28	
Lewisham 4	d							09 34							10 04							10 34	
St Johns	a							09 36							10 06							10 36	
New Cross 4	a							09 38							10 08							10 38	
London Bridge 4	a	09 11	09 15		09 18	09 20		09 43		09 46	09 39	09 41	09 53		10 13		10 15	10 07	10 11	10 23		10 43	
London Cannon Street 4	a							09 51							10 18							10 48	
London Waterloo (East) 4	a	09 17	09 21		09 24	09 26				09 52	09 45	09 49	09 59				10 21	10 13	10 17	10 29			
London Charing Cross 4	a	09 26	09 29		09 31	09 33				09 59	09 52	09 56	10 06				10 27	10 20	10 24	10 36			

		SE	SE ◇1	SE ◇1	SE ◇1	SE	SE	SE	SE ◇1	SE ◇1	SE ◇1	SE	SE	SE	SE	SE ◇1	SE ◇1	SE ◇1	SE	SE	SE	SE ◇1
Tonbridge 4	d		10 01	10 09	10 19				10 31	10 39	10 49					11 01	11 09	11 19				11 31
Hildenborough	d		10 05						10 35							11 05						11 35
Sevenoaks 4	a		10 12	10 18	10 28				10 42	10 48	10 58					11 12	11 18	11 28				11 42
	d	10 05	10 13	10 19	10 29			10 35	10 43	10 49	10 59				11 05	11 13	11 19	11 29			11 35	11 43
Dunton Green	d	10 08						10 38							11 08						11 38	
Knockholt	d	10 13						10 43							11 13						11 43	
Chelsfield 3	d	10 16						10 46							11 16						11 46	
Orpington 4	a	10 19	10 21		10 37			10 49	10 51		11 07				11 19	11 21		11 37			11 49	11 51
	d	10 20	10 22		10 38		10 41	10 50	10 52		11 08		11 11		11 20	11 22		11 38		11 41	11 50	11 52
Petts Wood 4	d	10 23					10 45	10 53					11 15		11 23					11 45	11 53	
Chislehurst	d	10 26					10 48	10 56					11 18		11 26					11 48	11 56	
Elmstead Woods	d	10 28					10 50	10 58					11 20		11 28					11 50	11 58	
Bromley North	d					10 40						11 05		11 24					11 44			
Sundridge Park	d					10 42						11 07		11 26					11 46			
Grove Park 4	d	10 32				10a45	10 54	11 02				11a10	11 24	11a29	11 32				11a49	11 54	12 02	
Hither Green 4	d	10 36					10 58	11 06					11 28		11 36					11 58	12 06	
Lewisham 4	d						11 04						11 34							12 04		
St Johns	a						11 06						11 36							12 06		
New Cross 4	a						11 08						11 38							12 08		
London Bridge 4	a	10 45	10 37	10 41	10 53		11 13	11 15	11 07	11 11	11 23		11 43		11 45	11 37	11 41	11 53		12 13	12 15	12 07
London Cannon Street 4	a						11 18						11 48							12 18		
London Waterloo (East) 4	a	10 51	10 43	10 47	10 59			11 21	11 13	11 17	11 29				11 51	11 43	11 47	11 59			12 21	12 13
London Charing Cross 4	a	10 57	10 48	10 52	11 04			11 27	11 18	11 22	11 34				11 57	11 48	11 52	12 04			12 27	12 18

		SE ◇1	SE ◇1	SE	SE	SE	SE	SE ◇1	SE ◇1	SE ◇1	SE	SE	SE	SE ◇1	SE ◇1	SE ◇1	SE	SE	SE	SE	SE ◇1	SE ◇1	SE ◇1
Tonbridge 4	d	11 39	11 49					12 01	12 09	12 19				12 31	12 39	12 49					13 01	13 09	13 19
Hildenborough	d							12 05						12 35							13 05		
Sevenoaks 4	a	11 48	11 58					12 12	12 18	12 28				12 42	12 48	12 58					13 12	13 18	13 28
	d	11 49	11 59				12 05	12 13	12 19	12 29			12 35	12 43	12 49	12 59				13 05	13 13	13 19	13 29
Dunton Green	d						12 08						12 38							13 08			
Knockholt	d						12 13						12 43							13 13			
Chelsfield 3	d						12 16						12 46							13 16			
Orpington 4	a		12 07				12 19	12 21		12 37			12 49	12 51		13 07				13 19	13 21		13 37
	d		12 08		12 11		12 20	12 22		12 38		12 41	12 50	12 52		13 08		13 11		13 20	13 22		13 38
Petts Wood 4	d				12 15		12 23					12 45	12 53					13 15		13 23			
Chislehurst	d				12 18		12 26					12 48	12 56					13 18		13 26			
Elmstead Woods	d				12 20		12 28					12 50	12 58					13 20		13 28			
Bromley North	d			12 04		12 24					12 44						13 04		13 24				
Sundridge Park	d			12 06		12 26					12 46						13 06		13 26				
Grove Park 4	d			12a09	12 24	12a29	12 32				12a49	12 54	13 02				13a09	13 24	13a29	13 32			
Hither Green 4	d				12 28		12 36					12 58	13 06					13 28		13 36			
Lewisham 4	d				12 34							13 04						13 34					
St Johns	a				12 36							13 06						13 36					
New Cross 4	a				12 38							13 08						13 38					
London Bridge 4	a	12 11	12 23		12 43		12 45	12 37	12 41	12 53		13 13	13 15	13 07	13 11	13 23		13 43		13 45	13 37	13 41	13 53
London Cannon Street 4	a				12 48							13 18						13 48					
London Waterloo (East) 4	a	12 17	12 29				12 51	12 43	12 47	12 59			13 21	13 13	13 17	13 29				13 51	13 43	13 47	13 59
London Charing Cross 4	a	12 22	12 34				12 57	12 48	12 52	13 04			13 27	13 18	13 22	13 34				13 57	13 48	13 52	14 04

Table T204-R

Mondays to Fridays

16 December to 15 May

Bromley North to Grove Park, Tonbridge, Sevenoaks, Orpington and Grove Park - London Cannon Street/Charing Cross

		SE	SE	SE	SE ◇1	SE ◇1	SE ◇1	SE	SE	SE	SE	SE ◇1	SE ◇1	SE ◇1	SE	SE	SE	SE ◇1	SE ◇1	SE ◇1	SE	SE	SE
Tonbridge 4	d				13 31	13 39	13 49					14 01	14 09	14 19				14 31	14 39	14 49			
Hildenborough	d				13 35							14 05						14 35					
Sevenoaks 4	a				13 42	13 48	13 58					14 12	14 18	14 28				14 42	14 48	14 58			
	d			13 35	13 43	13 49	13 59				14 05	14 13	14 19	14 29			14 35	14 43	14 49	14 59			
Dunton Green	d			13 38							14 08						14 38						
Knockholt	d			13 43							14 13						14 43						
Chelsfield 3	d			13 46							14 16						14 46						
Orpington 4	a			13 49	13 51		14 07				14 19	14 21		14 37			14 49	14 51		15 07			
	d		13 41	13 50	13 52		14 08		14 11		14 20	14 22		14 38		14 41	14 50	14 52		15 08		15 11	
Petts Wood 4	d		13 45	13 53					14 15		14 23					14 45	14 53					15 15	
Chislehurst	d		13 48	13 56					14 18		14 26					14 48	14 56					15 18	
Elmstead Woods	d		13 50	13 58					14 20		14 28					14 50	14 58					15 20	
Bromley North	d	13 44						14 04		14 24					14 44						15 04		15 24
Sundridge Park	d	13 46						14 06		14 26					14 46						15 06		15 26
Grove Park 4	d	13a49	13 54	14 02				14a09	14 24	14a29	14 32				14a49	14 54	15 02				15a09	15 24	15a29
Hither Green 4	d		13 58	14 06					14 28		14 36					14 58	15 06					15 28	
Lewisham 4	d		14 04						14 34							15 04						15 34	
St Johns	a		14 06						14 36							15 06						15 36	
New Cross 4	a		14 08						14 38							15 08						15 38	
London Bridge 4	a		14 13	14 15	14 07	14 11	14 23		14 43		14 45	14 37	14 41	14 53		15 13	15 15	15 07	15 11	15 23		15 43	
London Cannon Street 4	a		14 18						14 48							15 18						15 48	
London Waterloo (East) 4	a			14 21	14 13	14 17	14 29				14 51	14 43	14 47	14 59			15 21	15 13	15 17	15 29			
London Charing Cross 4	a			14 27	14 18	14 22	14 34				14 57	14 48	14 52	15 04			15 27	15 18	15 22	15 34			

		SE	SE ◇1	SE ◇1	SE ◇1	SE	SE	SE	SE ◇1	SE ◇1	SE ◇1	SE	SE 1	SE	SE	SE ◇1	SE ◇1	SE ◇1	SE	SE	SE	SE	SE
Tonbridge 4	d		15 01	15 09	15 19				15 31	15 39	15 49					16 01	16 09	16 19					
Hildenborough	d		15 05						15 35							16 05							
Sevenoaks 4	a		15 12	15 18	15 28				15 42	15 48	15 58					16 12	16 18	16 28					
	d	15 05	15 13	15 19	15 29			15 35	15 43	15 49	15 59				16 05	16 13	16 19	16 29					16 35
Dunton Green	d	15 08						15 38							16 08								16 38
Knockholt	d	15 13						15 43							16 13								16 43
Chelsfield 3	d	15 16						15 46							16 16	16 20							16 46
Orpington 4	a	15 19	15 21		15 37			15 49	15 51		16 07				16 19	16 23		16 37					16 49
	d	15 20	15 22		15 38		15 41	15 50	15 52		16 08		16 11	16 11	16 20	16 24		16 38			16 41		16 50
Petts Wood 4	d	15 23					15 45	15 53						16 15	16 23						16 45		16 53
Chislehurst	d	15 26					15 48	15 56						16 18	16 26						16 48		16 56
Elmstead Woods	d	15 28					15 50	15 58						16 20	16 28						16 50		16 58
Bromley North	d					15 44						16 04							16 27	16 41		16 56	
Sundridge Park	d					15 46						16 06							16 29	16 43			
Grove Park 4	d	15 32				15a49	15 54	16 02				16a09		16 24	16 32				16a32	16a46	16 54	17a00	17 05
Hither Green 4	d	15 36					15 58	16 06						16 28	16 36						16 58		17 09
Lewisham 4	d						16 04							16 34							17 05		
St Johns	a						16 06							16 36									
New Cross 4	a						16 08							16 38							17 10		
London Bridge 4	a	15 45	15 37	15 41	15 53		16 13	16 15	16 07	16 11	16 23		16 27	16 43	16 45	16 39	16 41	16 53			17 15		17 18
London Cannon Street 4	a						16 20							16 50							17 22		
London Waterloo (East) 4	a	15 51	15 43	15 47	15 59			16 23	16 13	16 17	16 29		16 33		16 52	16 45	16 48	16 59					17 27
London Charing Cross 4	a	15 57	15 48	15 52	16 04			16 27	16 18	16 22	16 34		16 38		16 58	16 51	16 54	17 07					17 31

		SE ◇1	SE ◇1	SE ◇1	SE	SE	SE	SE	SE	SE ◇1	SE ◇1	SE	SE	SE	SE ◇1	SE ◇1	SE	SE ◇1	SE ◇1	SE	SE ◇1	SE
Tonbridge 4	d	16 31	16 41	16 49						17 00	17 09				17 23	17 33		17 39	17 49		18 09	
Hildenborough	d	16 35								17 04								17 43				
Sevenoaks 4	a	16 42	16 49	16 58						17 10	17 17				17 31	17 41		17 49	17 58		18 18	
	d	16 43	16 50	16 59					17 06	17 11	17 18				17 32	17 42	17 34	17 50	17 59		18 19	
Dunton Green	d								17 09								17 37					
Knockholt	d									17 17							17 42					
Chelsfield 3	d								17 15									17 58				
Orpington 4	a	16 51	16 58	17 07					17 18	17 22					17 40		17 47	18 02	18 07			
	d	16 52	16 59	17 09		17 11	17 15		17 19	17 23		17 28		17 40	17 41		17 49	18 03	18 09			
Petts Wood 4	d					17 15			17 24					17 44			17 52					
Chislehurst	d					17 18			17 27					17 47			17 55					
Elmstead Woods	d					17 20			17 29					17 49			17 57					
Bromley North	d				17 10			17 26					17 47							18 03		18 16
Sundridge Park	d				17 12			17 28					17 49									18 18
Grove Park 4	d				17a15	17 24		17a31	17 35				17a52	17 53			18 01			18a07		18a21
Hither Green 4	d					17 29			17 40					17 57			18 05					
Lewisham 4	d					17 34								18 02								
St Johns	a					17 37								18 07								
New Cross 4	a					17 39								18 09								
London Bridge 4	a	17 09	17 16	17 30		17 44	17 36		17 49	17 38	17 42	17 44			17 59	18 06	18 15	18 19	18 24		18 42	
London Cannon Street 4	a			17 37		17 51								18 20								
London Waterloo (East) 4	a	17 15	17 24				17 41		17 54	17 44	17 48	17 50			18 05	18 12	18 21	18 26	18 30		18 48	
London Charing Cross 4	a	17 21	17 30				17 48		18 00	17 50	17 54	17 54			18 12	18 20	18 27	18 32	18 37		18 57	

Table T204-R

Mondays to Fridays

16 December to 15 May

Bromley North to Grove Park, Tonbridge, Sevenoaks, Orpington and Grove Park - London Cannon Street/Charing Cross

		SE	SE	SE ◇1	SE	SE	SE	SE	SE ◇1	SE	SE ◇1	SE ◇1	SE ◇1	SE	SE	SE	SE	SE ◇1	SE ◇1	SE ◇1	SE	SE
Tonbridge 4	d			18 01					18 23		18 31	18 42	18 52					19 02	19 09	19 19		
Hildenborough	d			18 05							18 35							19 06				
Sevenoaks 4	a			18 12					18 31		18 42	18 50	19 00					19 13	19 18	19 28		
	d		18 02	18 13					18 32	18 35	18 43	18 51	19 01				19 05	19 14	19 19	19 29		
Dunton Green	d		18 05							18 38							19 08					
Knockholt	d		18 10							18 43							19 13					
Chelsfield 3	d		18 13							18 46							19 16					
Orpington 4	a		18 16	18 21					18 40	18 49	18 51		19 09				19 19	19 22		19 37		
	d	18 10	18 19	18 22	18 29			18 40	18 41	18 50	18 52		19 10		19 11		19 20	19 23		19 38		19 41
Petts Wood 4	d	18 14	18 22					18 44		18 53					19 15		19 23					19 45
Chislehurst	d	18 17	18 25					18 47		18 56					19 18		19 26					19 48
Elmstead Woods	d	18 19	18 29					18 49		18 58					19 20		19 28					19 50
Bromley North	d					18 31	18 46							19 06		19 25					19 40	
Sundridge Park	d					18 33	18 48							19 08		19 27					19 42	
Grove Park 4	d	18 23	18 34			18a36	18a51	18 53		19 02				19a11	19 24	19a30	19 32				19a45	19 54
Hither Green 4	d	18 27	18 39					18 57		19 06					19 27		19 36					19 58
Lewisham 4	d	18 35						19 03							19 34							20 04
St Johns	a	18 40						19 05							19 36							20 06
New Cross 4	a	18 43						19 08							19 38							20 08
London Bridge 4	a	18 51	18 48	18 40	18 46			19 13	18 56	19 17	19 08	19 13	19 25		19 43		19 45	19 38	19 41	19 53		20 13
London Cannon Street 4	a	18 56		18 47				19 19							19 48							20 18
London Waterloo (East) 4	a		18 54		18 53				19 01	19 24	19 14	19 21	19 30				19 51	19 44	19 47	19 59		
London Charing Cross 4	a		19 02		18 57				19 05	19 27	19 19	19 24	19 35				19 57	19 49	19 52	20 04		

		SE	SE	SE ◇1	SE ◇1	SE ◇1	SE	SE	SE	SE	SE ◇1	SE ◇1	SE	SE	SE	SE	SE ◇1	SE ◇1	SE ◇1	SE	SE	SE	SE ◇1
Tonbridge 4	d			19 31	19 39	19 49					20 01	20 09					20 31	20 39	20 50				21 01
Hildenborough	d			19 35							20 05						20 35						21 05
Sevenoaks 4	a			19 42	19 48	19 58					20 12	20 18					20 42	20 48	20 58				21 12
	d		19 35	19 43	19 49	19 59				20 05	20 13	20 19				20 35	20 43	20 49	20 59			21 05	21 13
Dunton Green	d		19 38							20 08						20 38						21 08	
Knockholt	d		19 43							20 13						20 43						21 13	
Chelsfield 3	d		19 46							20 16						20 46						21 16	
Orpington 4	a		19 49	19 51		20 07				20 19	20 21					20 49	20 51		21 07			21 19	21 21
	d		19 50	19 52		20 08		20 11		20 20	20 22			20 41		20 50	20 52		21 08		21 11	21 20	21 22
Petts Wood 4	d		19 53					20 15		20 23				20 45		20 53					21 15	21 23	
Chislehurst	d		19 56					20 18		20 26				20 48		20 56					21 18	21 26	
Elmstead Woods	d		19 58					20 20		20 28				20 50		20 58					21 20	21 28	
Bromley North	d	19 56					20 10		20 24				20 40		20 54					21 15			
Sundridge Park	d	19 58					20 12		20 26				20 42		20 56					21 17			
Grove Park 4	d	20a01	20 02				20a15	20 24	20a29	20 32			20a45	20 54	20a59	21 02				21a20	21 24	21 32	
Hither Green 4	d		20 06					20 28		20 36				20 58		21 06					21 28	21 36	
Lewisham 4	d							20 34						21 04							21 34		
St Johns	a							20 36						21 06							21 36		
New Cross 4	a							20 38						21 08							21 38		
London Bridge 4	a		20 15	20 07	20 11	20 23		20 43		20 45	20 37	20 41		21 13		21 15	21 07	21 11	21 23		21 44	21 45	21 37
London Cannon Street 4	a							20 48						21 18							21 48		
London Waterloo (East) 4	a		20 21	20 13	20 17	20 29				20 51	20 43	20 47				21 21	21 13	21 17	21 29			21 51	21 43
London Charing Cross 4	a		20 27	20 18	20 22	20 34				20 57	20 48	20 52				21 27	21 18	21 22	21 34			21 57	21 48

		SE ◇1	SE	SE	SE	SE ◇1	SE ◇1	SE ◇1	SE	SE	SE	SE	SE ◇1	SE ◇1	SE	SE	SE	SE ◇1	SE ◇1	SE ◇1	SE	SE MT FO	SE
Tonbridge 4	d	21 09				21 31	21 39	21 49					22 01	22 09				22 31	22 39	22 49			
Hildenborough	d					21 35							22 05					22 35					
Sevenoaks 4	a	21 18				21 42	21 48	21 58					22 12	22 18				22 42	22 48	22 58			
	d	21 19			21 35	21 43	21 49	21 59				22 05	22 13	22 19			22 35	22 43	22 49	22 59			
Dunton Green	d				21 38							22 08					22 38						
Knockholt	d				21 43							22 13					22 43						
Chelsfield 3	d				21 46							22 16					22 46						
Orpington 4	a				21 49	21 51		22 07				22 19	22 21				22 49	22 51		23 07			
	d			21 41	21 50	21 53		22 08		22 11		22 20	22 22			22 41	22 50	22 52		23 08		23 11	
Petts Wood 4	d			21 45	21 53					22 15		22 23				22 45	22 53					23 15	
Chislehurst	d			21 48	21 56					22 18		22 26				22 48	22 56					23 18	
Elmstead Woods	d			21 50	21 58					22 20		22 28				22 50	22 58					23 20	
Bromley North	d		21 44						22 04		22 24				22 44						23 04		23 24
Sundridge Park	d		21 46						22 06		22 26				22 46						23 06		23 26
Grove Park 4	d		21a49	21 54	22 02				22a09	22 24	22a29	22 32			22a49	22 54	23 02				23a09	23 24	23a29
Hither Green 4	d			21 58	22 06					22 28		22 36				22 58	23 06					23 28	
Lewisham 4	d			22 04						22 34						23 04						23 34	
St Johns	a			22 06						22 36						23 06						23 36	
New Cross 4	a			22 08						22 38						23 08						23 38	
London Bridge 4	a	21 41		22 13	22 15	22 08	22 11	22 23		22 44		22 45	22 37	22 41		23 13	23 15	23 07	23 11	23 23		23 43	
London Cannon Street 4	a			22 18						22 48						23 18						23 48	
London Waterloo (East) 4	a	21 47			22 21	22 13	22 17	22 29				22 51	22 43	22 47			23 21	23 13	23 17	23 29			
London Charing Cross 4	a	21 52			22 27	22 18	22 22	22 34				22 57	22 48	22 52			23 27	23 18	23 22	23 34			

Table T204-R

Mondays to Fridays

16 December to 15 May

Bromley North to Grove Park, Tonbridge, Sevenoaks, Orpington and Grove Park - London Cannon Street/Charing Cross

		SE WTh FO	SE MTO	SE WTh FO ◇1		SE MTO ◇1	SE	SE WTh FO	SE MTO
Tonbridge 4	d			23 15		23 15			
Hildenborough	d			23 19		23 19			
Sevenoaks 4	a			23 26		23 26			
	d	23 05	23 05	23 27		23 27		23 35	23 35
Dunton Green	d	23 08	23 08					23 38	23 38
Knockholt	d	23 13	23 13					23 43	23 43
Chelsfield 3	d	23 16	23 16					23 46	23 46
Orpington 4	a	23 19	23 19	23 35		23 35		23 49	23 49
	d	23 20	23 20	23 36		23 36		23 50	23 50
Petts Wood 4	d	23 23	23 23					23 53	23 53
Chislehurst	d	23 26	23 26					23 56	23 56
Elmstead Woods	d	23 28	23 28					23 58	23 58
Bromley North	d						23 44		
Sundridge Park	d						23 46		
Grove Park 4	d	23 32	23 32				23a49	00 02	00 02
Hither Green 4	d	23 36	23 36					00 06	00 06
Lewisham 4	d		23 41					00 11	00 13
St Johns	a		23 43						
New Cross 4	a		23 45						
London Bridge 4	a	23 45	23 51	23 52		23 54		00 19	00 20
London Cannon Street 4	a		23 58			00 03			00 27
London Waterloo (East) 4	a	23 51		23 58				00 25	
London Charing Cross 4	a	23 57		00 03				00 31	

Saturdays

21 December to 16 May

		SE	SE	SE	SE	SE	SE	SE	SE	SE		SE	SE	SE	SE	SE ◇1	SE ◇1	SE ◇1	SE	SE		SE	SE ◇1	SE	SE ◇1
Tonbridge 4	d															06 01	06 09	06 39					06 47		07 09
Hildenborough	d															06 05							06 51		
Sevenoaks 4	a															06 12	06 18	06 48					06 58		07 18
	d									05 35					06 05	06 13	06 19	06 49				06 35	06 59		07 19
Dunton Green	d									05 38					06 08							06 38			
Knockholt	d									05 43					06 13							06 43			
Chelsfield 3	d									05 46					06 16							06 46			
Orpington 4	a									05 49					06 19	06 21						06 49	07 07		
	d						05 20		05 41	05 50			06 11		06 20	06 22				06 41		06 50	07 08		
Petts Wood 4	d						05 23		05 45	05 53			06 15		06 23					06 45		06 53			
Chislehurst	d						05 26		05 48	05 56			06 18		06 26					06 48		06 56			
Elmstead Woods	d						05 28		05 50	05 58			06 20		06 28					06 50		06 58			
Bromley North	d		00 04	00 24	00 44	05 22		05 44				06 04		06 24					06 44					07 04	
Sundridge Park	d		00 06	00 26	00 46	05 24		05 46				06 06		06 26					06 46					07 06	
Grove Park 4	d	00 02	00a09	00a29	00a49	05a27	05 32	05a49	05 54	06 02		06a09	06 24	06a29	06 32				06a49	06 54		07 02		07a09	
Hither Green 4	d	00 06					05 36		05 58	06 06			06 28		06 36					06 58		07 06			
Lewisham 4	d	00 11							06 04				06 34							07 04					
St Johns	a								06 06				06 36							07 06					
New Cross 4	a								06 08				06 38							07 08					
London Bridge 4	a	00 19					05 45		06 13	06 15			06 43		06 45	06 37	06 41	07 11		07 13		07 15	07 23		07 41
London Cannon Street 4	a								06 18				06 48							07 18					
London Waterloo (East) 4	a	00 25					05 52			06 21					06 51	06 43	06 47	07 17				07 21	07 29		07 47
London Charing Cross 4	a	00 31					05 57			06 27					06 57	06 48	06 52	07 22				07 27	07 34		07 52

		SE	SE	SE	SE ◇1	SE		SE	SE	SE ◇1	SE ◇1	SE ◇1	SE	SE	SE	SE		SE ◇1	SE ◇1	SE ◇1	SE	SE	SE	SE ◇1	SE ◇1
Tonbridge 4	d				07 19					07 31	07 39	07 49						08 01	08 09	08 19				08 31	08 39
Hildenborough	d									07 35								08 05						08 35	
Sevenoaks 4	a				07 28					07 42	07 48	07 58						08 12	08 18	08 28				08 42	08 48
	d			07 05	07 29				07 35	07 43	07 49	07 59				08 05		08 13	08 19	08 29			08 35	08 43	08 49
Dunton Green	d			07 08					07 38							08 08							08 38		
Knockholt	d			07 13					07 43							08 13							08 43		
Chelsfield 3	d			07 16					07 46							08 16							08 46		
Orpington 4	a			07 19	07 37				07 49	07 51		08 07				08 19		08 21		08 37			08 49	08 51	
	d	07 11		07 20	07 38			07 41	07 50	07 52		08 08		08 11		08 20		08 22		08 38		08 41	08 50	08 52	
Petts Wood 4	d	07 15		07 23				07 45	07 53					08 15		08 23						08 45	08 53		
Chislehurst	d	07 18		07 26				07 48	07 56					08 18		08 26						08 48	08 56		
Elmstead Woods	d	07 20		07 28				07 50	07 58					08 20		08 28						08 50	08 58		
Bromley North	d		07 24			07 44							08 04		08 24						08 44				
Sundridge Park	d		07 26			07 46							08 06		08 26						08 46				
Grove Park 4	d	07 24	07a29	07 32		07a49		07 54	08 02				08a09	08 24	08a29	08 32					08a49	08 54	09 02		
Hither Green 4	d	07 28		07 36				07 58	08 06					08 28		08 36						08 58	09 06		
Lewisham 4	d	07 34						08 04						08 34								09 04			
St Johns	a	07 36						08 06						08 36								09 06			
New Cross 4	a	07 38						08 08						08 38								09 08			
London Bridge 4	a	07 43		07 45	07 53			08 13	08 15	08 07	08 11	08 23		08 43		08 45		08 37	08 41	08 53		09 13	09 15	09 07	09 11
London Cannon Street 4	a	07 48						08 18						08 48								09 18			
London Waterloo (East) 4	a			07 51	07 59				08 21	08 13	08 17	08 29				08 51		08 43	08 47	08 59			09 21	09 13	09 17
London Charing Cross 4	a			07 57	08 04				08 27	08 18	08 22	08 34				08 57		08 48	08 52	09 04			09 27	09 18	09 22

Table T204-R

Saturdays

21 December to 16 May

Bromley North to Grove Park, Tonbridge, Sevenoaks, Orpington and Grove Park - London Cannon Street/Charing Cross

		SE ◇1	SE	SE	SE	SE	SE ◇1	SE ◇1		SE ◇1	SE	SE	SE	SE ◇1	SE ◇1	SE ◇1	SE	SE		SE	SE	SE ◇1	SE ◇1	SE ◇1	SE
Tonbridge 4	d	08 49					09 01	09 09		09 19				09 31	09 39	09 49						10 01	10 10	10 19	
Hildenborough	d						09 05							09 35								10 05			
Sevenoaks 4	a	08 58					09 12	09 18		09 28				09 42	09 48	09 58						10 12	10 18	10 28	
	d	08 59				09 05	09 13	09 19		09 29			09 35	09 43	09 49	09 59					10 05	10 13	10 19	10 29	
Dunton Green	d					09 08							09 38								10 08				
Knockholt	d					09 13							09 43								10 13				
Chelsfield 3	d					09 16							09 46								10 16				
Orpington 4	a	09 07				09 19	09 21			09 37			09 49	09 51		10 07					10 19	10 21		10 37	
	d	09 08		09 11		09 20	09 22			09 38		09 41	09 50	09 52		10 08		10 11			10 20	10 22		10 38	
Petts Wood 4	d			09 15		09 23						09 45	09 53					10 15			10 23				
Chislehurst	d			09 18		09 26						09 48	09 56					10 18			10 26				
Elmstead Woods	d			09 20		09 28						09 50	09 58					10 20			10 28				
Bromley North	d		09 04		09 24						09 44						10 04			10 24					10 44
Sundridge Park	d		09 06		09 26						09 46						10 06			10 26					10 46
Grove Park 4	d		09a09	09 24	09a29	09 32					09a49	09 54	10 02				10a09	10 24		10a29	10 32				10a49
Hither Green 4	d			09 28		09 36						09 58	10 06					10 28			10 36				
Lewisham 4	d			09 34								10 04						10 34							
St Johns	a			09 36								10 06						10 36							
New Cross 4	a			09 38								10 08						10 38							
London Bridge 4	a	09 23		09 43		09 45	09 37	09 41		09 53		10 13	10 15	10 07	10 11	10 23		10 43			10 45	10 37	10 41	10 53	
London Cannon Street 4	a			09 48								10 18						10 48							
London Waterloo (East) 4	a	09 29				09 51	09 43	09 47		09 59			10 21	10 13	10 17	10 29					10 51	10 43	10 47	10 59	
London Charing Cross 4	a	09 34				09 57	09 48	09 52		10 04			10 27	10 18	10 22	10 34					10 57	10 48	10 52	11 04	

		SE	SE	SE ◇1		SE ◇1	SE ◇1	SE	SE	SE	SE	SE ◇1	SE ◇1	SE ◇1		SE	SE	SE	SE ◇1	SE ◇1	SE ◇1	SE	SE	SE	
Tonbridge 4	d			10 31		10 39	10 49					11 01	11 09	11 19					11 31	11 39	11 49				
Hildenborough	d			10 35								11 05							11 35						
Sevenoaks 4	a			10 42		10 48	10 58					11 12	11 18	11 28					11 42	11 48	11 58				
	d		10 35	10 43		10 49	10 59				11 05	11 13	11 19	11 29				11 35	11 43	11 49	11 59				
Dunton Green	d		10 38								11 08							11 38							
Knockholt	d		10 43								11 13							11 43							
Chelsfield 3	d		10 46								11 16							11 46							
Orpington 4	a		10 49	10 51			11 07				11 19	11 21		11 37				11 49	11 51		12 07				
	d	10 41	10 50	10 52			11 08		11 11		11 20	11 22		11 38			11 41	11 50	11 52		12 08		12 11		
Petts Wood 4	d	10 45	10 53						11 15		11 23						11 45	11 53					12 15		
Chislehurst	d	10 48	10 56						11 18		11 26						11 48	11 56					12 18		
Elmstead Woods	d	10 50	10 58						11 20		11 28						11 50	11 58					12 20		
Bromley North	d							11 04		11 24						11 44						12 04		12 24	
Sundridge Park	d							11 06		11 26						11 46						12 06		12 26	
Grove Park 4	d	10 54	11 02					11a09	11 24	11a29	11 32					11a49	11 54	12 02				12a09	12 24	12a29	
Hither Green 4	d	10 58	11 06						11 28		11 36						11 58	12 06					12 28		
Lewisham 4	d	11 04							11 34								12 04						12 34		
St Johns	a	11 06							11 36								12 06						12 36		
New Cross 4	a	11 08							11 38								12 08						12 38		
London Bridge 4	a	11 13	11 15	11 07		11 11	11 23		11 43		11 45	11 37	11 41	11 53			12 13	12 15	12 07	12 11	12 23		12 43		
London Cannon Street 4	a	11 18							11 48								12 18						12 48		
London Waterloo (East) 4	a		11 21	11 13		11 17	11 29				11 51	11 43	11 47	11 59				12 21	12 13	12 17	12 29				
London Charing Cross 4	a		11 27	11 18		11 22	11 34				11 57	11 48	11 52	12 04				12 27	12 18	12 22	12 34				

		SE	SE ◇1	SE ◇1	SE ◇1	SE	SE	SE	SE ◇1	SE ◇1		SE ◇1	SE	SE	SE	SE	SE ◇1	SE ◇1	SE ◇1	SE		SE	SE	SE ◇1	SE ◇1
Tonbridge 4	d		12 01	12 09	12 19				12 31	12 39		12 49					13 01	13 09	13 19					13 31	13 39
Hildenborough	d		12 05						12 35								13 05							13 35	
Sevenoaks 4	a		12 12	12 18	12 28				12 42	12 48		12 58					13 12	13 18	13 28					13 42	13 48
	d	12 05	12 13	12 19	12 29			12 35	12 43	12 49		12 59				13 05	13 13	13 19	13 29				13 35	13 43	13 49
Dunton Green	d	12 08						12 38								13 08							13 38		
Knockholt	d	12 13						12 43								13 13							13 43		
Chelsfield 3	d	12 16						12 46								13 16							13 46		
Orpington 4	a	12 19	12 21		12 37			12 49	12 51			13 07				13 19	13 21		13 37				13 49	13 51	
	d	12 20	12 22		12 38		12 41	12 50	12 52			13 08		13 11		13 20	13 22		13 38			13 41	13 50	13 52	
Petts Wood 4	d	12 23					12 45	12 53						13 15		13 23						13 45	13 53		
Chislehurst	d	12 26					12 48	12 56						13 18		13 26						13 48	13 56		
Elmstead Woods	d	12 28					12 50	12 58						13 20		13 28						13 50	13 58		
Bromley North	d					12 44							13 04		13 24					13 44					
Sundridge Park	d					12 46							13 06		13 26					13 46					
Grove Park 4	d	12 32				12a49	12 54	13 02					13a09	13 24	13a29	13 32				13a49		13 54	14 02		
Hither Green 4	d	12 36					12 58	13 06						13 28		13 36						13 58	14 06		
Lewisham 4	d						13 04							13 34								14 04			
St Johns	a						13 06							13 36								14 06			
New Cross 4	a						13 08							13 38								14 08			
London Bridge 4	a	12 45	12 37	12 41	12 53		13 13	13 15	13 07	13 11		13 23		13 43		13 45	13 37	13 41	13 53			14 13	14 15	14 07	14 11
London Cannon Street 4	a						13 18							13 48								14 18			
London Waterloo (East) 4	a	12 51	12 43	12 47	12 59			13 21	13 13	13 17		13 29				13 51	13 43	13 47	13 59				14 21	14 13	14 17
London Charing Cross 4	a	12 57	12 48	12 52	13 04			13 27	13 18	13 22		13 34				13 57	13 48	13 52	14 04				14 27	14 18	14 22

Table T204-R

Saturdays

21 December to 16 May

Bromley North to Grove Park, Tonbridge, Sevenoaks, Orpington and Grove Park - London Cannon Street/Charing Cross

		SE ◇1		SE	SE	SE	SE	SE ◇1	SE ◇1	SE ◇1	SE	SE		SE	SE ◇1	SE ◇1	SE ◇1	SE	SE	SE	SE	SE ◇1		SE ◇1	SE ◇1
Tonbridge	d	13 49						14 01	14 09	14 19					14 31	14 39	14 49					15 01		15 09	15 19
Hildenborough	d							14 05							14 35							15 05			
Sevenoaks	a	13 58						14 12	14 18	14 28					14 42	14 48	14 58					15 12		15 18	15 28
	d	13 59					14 05	14 13	14 19	14 29				14 35	14 43	14 49	14 59				15 05	15 13		15 19	15 29
Dunton Green	d						14 08							14 38							15 08				
Knockholt	d						14 13							14 43							15 13				
Chelsfield	d						14 16							14 46							15 16				
Orpington	a	14 07					14 19	14 21		14 37				14 49	14 51		15 07				15 19	15 21			15 37
	d	14 08			14 11		14 20	14 22		14 38		14 41		14 50	14 52		15 08		15 11		15 20	15 22			15 38
Petts Wood	d				14 15		14 23					14 45		14 53					15 15		15 23				
Chislehurst	d				14 18		14 26					14 48		14 56					15 18		15 26				
Elmstead Woods	d				14 20		14 28					14 50		14 58					15 20		15 28				
Bromley North	d			14 04		14 24					14 44							15 04		15 24					
Sundridge Park	d			14 06		14 26					14 46							15 06		15 26					
Grove Park	d			14a09	14 24	14a29	14 32				14a49	14 54		15 02				15a09	15 24	15a29	15 32				
Hither Green	d				14 28		14 36					14 58		15 06					15 28		15 36				
Lewisham	d				14 34							15 04							15 34						
St Johns	a				14 36							15 06							15 36						
New Cross	a				14 38							15 08							15 38						
London Bridge	a	14 23			14 43		14 45	14 37	14 41	14 53		15 13		15 15	15 07	15 11	15 23		15 43		15 45	15 37		15 41	15 53
London Cannon Street	a				14 48							15 18							15 48						
London Waterloo (East)	a	14 29					14 51	14 43	14 47	14 59				15 21	15 13	15 17	15 29				15 51	15 43		15 47	15 59
London Charing Cross	a	14 34					14 57	14 48	14 52	15 04				15 27	15 18	15 22	15 34				15 57	15 48		15 52	16 04

		SE	SE	SE	SE ◇1	SE ◇1	SE ◇1	SE		SE	SE	SE	SE ◇1	SE ◇1	SE ◇1	SE	SE	SE		SE ◇1	SE ◇1	SE ◇1	SE	SE	SE
Tonbridge	d				15 31	15 39	15 49						16 01	16 09	16 19					16 31	16 39	16 49			
Hildenborough	d				15 35								16 05							16 35					
Sevenoaks	a				15 42	15 48	15 58						16 12	16 18	16 28					16 42	16 48	16 58			
	d			15 35	15 43	15 49	15 59					16 05	16 13	16 19	16 29			16 35		16 43	16 49	16 59			
Dunton Green	d			15 38								16 08						16 38							
Knockholt	d			15 43								16 13						16 43							
Chelsfield	d			15 46								16 16						16 46							
Orpington	a			15 49	15 51		16 07					16 19	16 21		16 37			16 49		16 51		17 07			
	d		15 41	15 50	15 52		16 08			16 11		16 20	16 22		16 38		16 41	16 50		16 52		17 08		17 11	
Petts Wood	d		15 45	15 53						16 15		16 23					16 45	16 53						17 15	
Chislehurst	d		15 48	15 56						16 18		16 26					16 48	16 56						17 18	
Elmstead Woods	d		15 50	15 58						16 20		16 28					16 50	16 58						17 20	
Bromley North	d	15 44						16 04			16 24					16 44							17 04		17 24
Sundridge Park	d	15 46						16 06			16 26					16 46							17 06		17 26
Grove Park	d	15a49	15 54	16 02				16a09		16 24	16a29	16 32				16a49	16 54	17 02					17a09	17 24	17a29
Hither Green	d		15 58	16 06						16 28		16 36					16 58	17 06						17 28	
Lewisham	d		16 04							16 34							17 04							17 34	
St Johns	a		16 06							16 36							17 06							17 36	
New Cross	a		16 08							16 38							17 08							17 38	
London Bridge	a		16 13	16 15	16 07	16 11	16 23			16 43		16 45	16 37	16 41	16 53		17 13	17 15		17 07	17 11	17 23		17 43	
London Cannon Street	a		16 18							16 48							17 18							17 48	
London Waterloo (East)	a			16 21	16 13	16 17	16 29					16 51	16 43	16 47	16 59			17 21		17 13	17 17	17 29			
London Charing Cross	a			16 27	16 18	16 22	16 34					16 57	16 48	16 52	17 04			17 27		17 18	17 22	17 34			

		SE	SE ◇1	SE ◇1		SE ◇1	SE	SE	SE	SE ◇1	SE ◇1	SE ◇1	SE	SE		SE	SE	SE ◇1	SE ◇1	SE ◇1	SE	SE	SE	SE ◇1	
Tonbridge	d		17 01	17 09		17 19				17 31	17 39	17 49						18 01	18 09	18 19				18 31	
Hildenborough	d		17 05							17 35								18 05						18 35	
Sevenoaks	a		17 12	17 18		17 28				17 42	17 48	17 58						18 12	18 18	18 28				18 42	
	d	17 05	17 13	17 19		17 29			17 35	17 43	17 49	17 59					18 05	18 13	18 19	18 29			18 35	18 43	
Dunton Green	d	17 08							17 38								18 08						18 38		
Knockholt	d	17 13							17 43								18 13						18 43		
Chelsfield	d	17 16							17 46								18 16						18 46		
Orpington	a	17 19	17 21			17 37			17 49	17 51		18 07					18 19	18 21		18 37			18 49	18 51	
	d	17 20	17 22			17 38		17 41	17 50	17 52		18 08		18 11			18 20	18 22		18 38		18 41	18 50	18 52	
Petts Wood	d	17 23						17 45	17 53					18 15			18 23					18 45	18 53		
Chislehurst	d	17 26						17 48	17 56					18 18			18 26					18 48	18 56		
Elmstead Woods	d	17 28						17 50	17 58					18 20			18 28					18 50	18 58		
Bromley North	d						17 44						18 04			18 24					18 44				
Sundridge Park	d						17 46						18 06			18 26					18 46				
Grove Park	d	17 32					17a49	17 54	18 02				18a09	18 24		18a29	18 32				18a49	18 54	19 02		
Hither Green	d	17 36						17 58	18 06					18 28			18 36					18 58	19 06		
Lewisham	d							18 04						18 34								19 04			
St Johns	a							18 06						18 36								19 06			
New Cross	a							18 08						18 38								19 08			
London Bridge	a	17 45	17 37	17 41		17 53		18 13	18 15	18 07	18 11	18 23		18 43			18 45	18 37	18 41	18 53		19 13	19 15	19 07	
London Cannon Street	a							18 18						18 48								19 18			
London Waterloo (East)	a	17 51	17 43	17 47		17 59			18 21	18 13	18 17	18 29					18 51	18 43	18 47	18 59			19 21	19 13	
London Charing Cross	a	17 57	17 48	17 52		18 04			18 27	18 18	18 22	18 34					18 57	18 48	18 52	19 04			19 27	19 18	

Table T204-R

Saturdays

21 December to 16 May

Bromley North to Grove Park, Tonbridge, Sevenoaks, Orpington and Grove Park - London Cannon Street/Charing Cross

		SE ◇1	SE ◇1	SE	SE	SE		SE	SE ◇1	SE ◇1	SE ◇1	SE	SE	SE	SE ◇1	SE ◇1		SE ◇1	SE	SE	SE	SE	SE ◇1	SE ◇1	SE
Tonbridge	d	18 39	18 49						19 01	19 09	19 19				19 31	19 39		19 49					20 01	20 09	
Hildenborough	d								19 05						19 35								20 05		
Sevenoaks	a	18 48	18 58						19 12	19 18	19 28				19 42	19 48		19 58					20 12	20 18	
	d	18 49	18 59					19 05	19 13	19 19	19 29			19 35	19 43	19 49		19 59				20 05	20 13	20 19	
Dunton Green	d							19 08						19 38								20 08			
Knockholt	d							19 13						19 43								20 13			
Chelsfield	d							19 16						19 46								20 16			
Orpington	a		19 07					19 19	19 21		19 37			19 49	19 51			20 07				20 19	20 21		
	d		19 08		19 11			19 20	19 22		19 38		19 41	19 50	19 52			20 08		20 11		20 20	20 22		
Petts Wood	d				19 15			19 23					19 45	19 53						20 15		20 23			
Chislehurst	d				19 18			19 26					19 48	19 56						20 18		20 26			
Elmstead Woods	d				19 20			19 28					19 50	19 58						20 20		20 28			
Bromley North	d			19 04		19 24						19 44							20 04		20 24				20 44
Sundridge Park	d			19 06		19 26						19 46							20 06		20 26				20 46
Grove Park	d			19a09	19 24	19a29		19 32				19a49	19 54	20 02					20a09	20 24	20a29	20 32			20a49
Hither Green	d				19 28			19 36					19 58	20 06						20 28		20 36			
Lewisham	d				19 34								20 04							20 34					
St Johns	a				19 36								20 06							20 36					
New Cross	a				19 38								20 08							20 38					
London Bridge	a	19 11	19 23		19 43			19 45	19 37	19 41	19 53		20 13	20 15	20 07	20 11		20 23		20 43		20 45	20 37	20 41	
London Cannon Street	a				19 48								20 18							20 48					
London Waterloo (East)	a	19 17	19 29					19 51	19 43	19 47	19 59			20 21	20 13	20 17		20 29				20 51	20 43	20 47	
London Charing Cross	a	19 22	19 34					19 57	19 48	19 52	20 04			20 27	20 18	20 22		20 34				20 57	20 48	20 52	

		SE		SE	SE ◇1	SE ◇1	SE ◇1	SE	SE	SE	SE	SE ◇1		SE ◇1	SE	SE	SE	SE ◇1	SE ◇1	SE ◇1	SE	SE		SE	SE
Tonbridge	d				20 31	20 39	20 49					21 01		21 09				21 31	21 39	21 49					
Hildenborough	d				20 35							21 05						21 35							
Sevenoaks	a				20 42	20 48	20 58					21 12		21 18				21 42	21 48	21 58					
	d			20 35	20 43	20 49	20 59				21 05	21 13		21 19			21 35	21 43	21 49	21 59					22 05
Dunton Green	d			20 38							21 08						21 38								22 08
Knockholt	d			20 43							21 13						21 43								22 13
Chelsfield	d			20 46							21 16						21 46								22 16
Orpington	a			20 49	20 51		21 07				21 19	21 21					21 49	21 51		22 07					22 19
	d	20 41		20 50	20 52		21 08		21 11		21 20	21 22				21 41	21 50	21 52		22 08		22 11			22 20
Petts Wood	d	20 45		20 53					21 15		21 23					21 45	21 53					22 15			22 23
Chislehurst	d	20 48		20 56					21 18		21 26					21 48	21 56					22 18			22 26
Elmstead Woods	d	20 50		20 58					21 20		21 28					21 50	21 58					22 20			22 28
Bromley North	d							21 04		21 24					21 44						22 04			22 24	
Sundridge Park	d							21 06		21 26					21 46						22 06			22 26	
Grove Park	d	20 54		21 02				21a09	21 24	21a29	21 32				21a49	21 54	22 02				22a09	22 24		22a29	22 32
Hither Green	d	20 58		21 06					21 28		21 36					21 58	22 06					22 28			22 36
Lewisham	d	21 04							21 34							22 04						22 34			
St Johns	a	21 06							21 36							22 06						22 36			
New Cross	a	21 08							21 38							22 08						22 38			
London Bridge	a	21 13		21 15	21 07	21 11	21 23		21 43		21 45	21 37		21 41		22 13	22 15	22 07	22 11	22 23		22 43			22 45
London Cannon Street	a	21 18							21 48							22 18						22 48			
London Waterloo (East)	a			21 21	21 13	21 17	21 29				21 51	21 43		21 47			22 21	22 13	22 17	22 29					22 51
London Charing Cross	a			21 27	21 18	21 22	21 34				21 57	21 48		21 52			22 27	22 18	22 22	22 34					22 57

		SE ◇1	SE ◇1	SE	SE	SE	SE ◇1	SE ◇1		SE ◇1	SE	SE	SE	SE	SE ◇1	SE	SE
Tonbridge	d	22 01	22 09				22 31	22 39		22 49					23 15		
Hildenborough	d	22 05					22 35								23 19		
Sevenoaks	a	22 12	22 18				22 42	22 48		22 58					23 26		
	d	22 13	22 19			22 35	22 43	22 49		22 59				23 05	23 27		23 35
Dunton Green	d					22 38								23 08			23 38
Knockholt	d					22 43								23 13			23 43
Chelsfield	d					22 46								23 16			23 46
Orpington	a	22 21				22 49	22 51			23 07				23 19	23 35		23 49
	d	22 22			22 41	22 50	22 52			23 08		23 11		23 20	23 36		23 50
Petts Wood	d				22 45	22 53						23 15		23 23			23 53
Chislehurst	d				22 48	22 56						23 18		23 26			23 56
Elmstead Woods	d				22 50	22 58						23 20		23 28			23 58
Bromley North	d			22 44							23 04		23 24			23 44	
Sundridge Park	d			22 46							23 06		23 26			23 46	
Grove Park	d			22a49	22 54	23 02					23a09	23 24	23a29	23 32		23a49	00 02
Hither Green	d				22 58	23 06						23 28		23 36			00 06
Lewisham	d				23 04							23 34					00 12
St Johns	a				23 06							23 36					
New Cross	a				23 08							23 38					
London Bridge	a	22 37	22 41		23 13	23 15	23 07	23 11		23 23		23 43		23 45	23 52		00 20
London Cannon Street	a				23 18							23 48					
London Waterloo (East)	a	22 43	22 47			23 21	23 13	23 17		23 29				23 51	23 58		00 26
London Charing Cross	a	22 48	22 52			23 27	23 18	23 22		23 34				23 57	00 03		00 32

Table T204-R

Sundays

15 December to 10 May

Bromley North to Grove Park, Tonbridge, Sevenoaks, Orpington and Grove Park - London Cannon Street/Charing Cross

		SE	SE	SE	SE	SE	SE	SE	SE	SE	SE	SE		SE	SE	SE	SE	SE	SE		SE	SE	SE	SE
		A						◇1	◇1		◇1	◇1			◇1	◇1		◇1	◇1			◇1	◇1	
Tonbridge [4]	d							07 09	07 21		07 39	07 49			12 09	12 21		12 39	12 49			13 09	13 21	
Hildenborough	d											07 53							12 53					
Sevenoaks [4]	a							07 18	07 30		07 48	08 00			12 18	12 30		12 48	13 00			13 18	13 30	
	d						07 04	07 19	07 31	07 34	07 49	08 01		12 04	12 19	12 31	12 34	12 49	13 01		13 04	13 19	13 31	13 34
Dunton Green	d						07 07			07 37				12 07			12 37				13 07			13 37
Knockholt	d						07 12			07 42				12 12			12 42				13 12			13 42
Chelsfield [3]	d						07 15			07 45			and at the same minutes past each hour until	12 15			12 45				13 15			13 45
Orpington [4]	a						07 18	07 27	07 39	07 48	07 57	08 09		12 18	12 27	12 39	12 48	12 57	13 09		13 18	13 27	13 39	13 48
	d					06 48	07 19	07 28	07 40	07 49	07 58	08 10		12 19	12 28	12 40	12 49	12 58	13 10		13 19	13 28	13 40	13 49
Petts Wood [4]	d					06 52	07 22			07 52				12 22			12 52				13 22			13 52
Chislehurst	d					06 55	07 25			07 55				12 25			12 55				13 25			13 55
Elmstead Woods	d					06 57	07 27			07 57				12 27			12 57				13 27			13 57
Bromley North	d		00 04	00 24	00 44																			
Sundridge Park	d		00 06	00 26	00 46																			
Grove Park [4]	d	00 02	00a09	00a29	00a49	07 01	07 31			08 01				12 31			13 01				13 31			14 01
Hither Green [4]	d	00 06				07 05	07 35			08 05				12 35			13 05				13 35			14 05
Lewisham [4]	d	00 12				07 11	07 41			08 11				12 41			13 11				13 41			14 11
St Johns	a																							
New Cross [4] ⊖	a																							
London Bridge [4] ⊖	a	00 20				07 19	07 49	07 43	07 55	08 19	08 13	08 25		12 49	12 43	12 55	13 19	13 13	13 25		13 49	13 43	13 55	14 19
London Cannon Street [4] ⊖	a																							
London Waterloo (East) [4] ⊖	a	00 26				07 25	07 55	07 49	08 01	08 25	08 19	08 31		12 55	12 49	13 01	13 25	13 19	13 31		13 55	13 49	14 01	14 25
London Charing Cross [4] ⊖	a	00 32				07 29	07 59	07 54	08 06	08 29	08 24	08 36		12 59	12 54	13 06	13 29	13 24	13 36		13 59	13 54	14 06	14 29

		SE	SE	SE	SE	SE	SE	SE	SE		SE	SE	SE	SE	SE	SE		SE	SE	SE	SE	SE	SE	SE
		◇1	◇1		◇1	◇1		◇1	◇1			◇1	◇1		◇1	◇1			◇1		◇1	◇1		◇1
Tonbridge [4]	d	13 39	13 50		14 09	14 21		14 39	14 49			19 09	19 21		19 39	19 49			20 09		20 39	20 49		21 09
Hildenborough	d		13 54						14 53							19 53						20 53		
Sevenoaks [4]	a	13 48	14 00		14 18	14 30		14 48	15 00			19 18	19 30		19 48	20 00			20 18		20 48	21 00		21 18
	d	13 49	14 01	14 04	14 19	14 31	14 34	14 49	15 01		19 04	19 19	19 31	19 34	19 49	20 01		20 04	20 19	20 34	20 49	21 01	21 04	21 19
Dunton Green	d			14 07			14 37				19 07			19 37				20 07		20 37			21 07	
Knockholt	d			14 12			14 42				19 12			19 42				20 12		20 42			21 12	
Chelsfield [3]	d			14 15			14 45			and at the same minutes past each hour until	19 15			19 45				20 15		20 45			21 15	
Orpington [4]	a	13 57	14 09	14 18	14 27	14 39	14 48	14 57	15 09		19 18	19 27	19 39	19 48	19 57	20 09		20 18	20 27	20 48	20 57	21 09	21 18	21 27
	d	13 58	14 10	14 19	14 28	14 40	14 49	14 58	15 10		19 19	19 28	19 40	19 49	19 58	20 10		20 19	20 28	20 49	20 58	21 10	21 19	21 28
Petts Wood [4]	d			14 22			14 52				19 22			19 52				20 22		20 52			21 22	
Chislehurst	d			14 25			14 55				19 25			19 55				20 25		20 55			21 25	
Elmstead Woods	d			14 27			14 57				19 27			19 57				20 27		20 57			21 27	
Bromley North	d																							
Sundridge Park	d																							
Grove Park [4]	d			14 31			15 01				19 31			20 01				20 31		21 01			21 31	
Hither Green [4]	d			14 35			15 05				19 35			20 05				20 35		21 05			21 35	
Lewisham [4]	d			14 41			15 11				19 41			20 11				20 41		21 11			21 41	
St Johns	a																							
New Cross [4] ⊖	a																							
London Bridge [4] ⊖	a	14 13	14 25	14 49	14 43	14 55	15 19	15 13	15 25		19 49	19 43	19 55	20 19	20 13	20 25		20 49	20 43	21 19	21 13	21 25	21 49	21 43
London Cannon Street [4] ⊖	a																							
London Waterloo (East) [4] ⊖	a	14 19	14 31	14 55	14 49	15 01	15 25	15 19	15 31		19 55	19 49	20 01	20 25	20 19	20 31		20 55	20 49	21 25	21 19	21 31	21 55	21 49
London Charing Cross [4] ⊖	a	14 24	14 36	14 59	14 54	15 06	15 29	15 24	15 36		19 59	19 54	20 06	20 29	20 24	20 36		20 59	20 54	21 29	21 24	21 36	21 59	21 54

		SE	SE		SE	SE	SE	SE	SE	SE	SE	SE
			◇1		◇1		◇1		◇1	◇1		
Tonbridge [4]	d		21 39		21 49		22 09		22 39	22 49		
Hildenborough	d				21 53					22 53		
Sevenoaks [4]	a		21 48		22 00		22 18		22 48	23 00		
	d	21 34	21 49		22 01	22 04	22 19	22 34	22 49	23 01	23 04	23 34
Dunton Green	d	21 37				22 07		22 37			23 07	23 37
Knockholt	d	21 42				22 12		22 42			23 12	23 42
Chelsfield [3]	d	21 45				22 15		22 45			23 15	23 45
Orpington [4]	a	21 48	21 57		22 09	22 18	22 27	22 48	22 57	23 09	23 18	23 48
	d	21 49	21 58		22 10	22 19	22 28	22 49	22 58	23 10	23 19	23 49
Petts Wood [4]	d	21 52				22 22		22 52			23 22	23 52
Chislehurst	d	21 55				22 25		22 55			23 25	23 55
Elmstead Woods	d	21 57				22 27		22 57			23 27	23 57
Bromley North	d											
Sundridge Park	d											
Grove Park [4]	d	22 01				22 31		23 01			23 31	00 01
Hither Green [4]	d	22 05				22 35		23 05			23 35	00 05
Lewisham [4]	d	22 11				22 41		23 11			23 41	00 11
St Johns	a											
New Cross [4] ⊖	a											
London Bridge [4] ⊖	a	22 19	22 13		22 25	22 49	22 43	23 19	23 13	23 25	23 49	00 19
London Cannon Street [4] ⊖	a											
London Waterloo (East) [4] ⊖	a	22 25	22 19		22 31	22 55	22 49	23 25	23 19	23 31	23 55	00 25
London Charing Cross [4] ⊖	a	22 29	22 24		22 36	22 59	22 54	23 29	23 24	23 36	23 59	00 29

A not 15 December

Table T206-F

Mondays to Fridays

16 December to 15 May

London and Tonbridge - Tunbridge Wells and Hastings

Miles	Miles			SE	SE	SE	SE	SE	SE	SE	SE	SE		SE	SE	SE	SE	SE	SE	SE	SE	SE		SE	SE
				MO	MX	MO	MX	MX	TWO	ThFO															
				◇1	◇1	◇1	◇1	◇1		◇	1	1		1	1	1	◇1	1	◇1	◇1	◇1	◇1		◇1	◇1
0	—	**London Charing Cross** [4] ⊖	d							00 15							05 56		06 28	07 00	07 15	07 27			08 00
0¾	—	**London Waterloo (East)** [4] ⊖	d							00 18							05 59		06 31	07 03	07 18	07 30			08 05
—	0	**London Cannon Street** [4] ⊖	d						00 25															07 42	
1¾	0¾	**London Bridge** [4] ⊖	d						00 29	00 24							06 05		06 37	07 09	07 24	07 36		07 46	08 11
13¾	—	Orpington [4]	d					00 10	00 50	00 51							06 22		06 53	07 26	07 40	07 55		08 08	08 32
15¼	—	Chelsfield	d						00 54	00 54												07 58			
22	—	Sevenoaks [4]	d				00 06	00 20	01 04	01 04							06 31		07 03	07 36	07 50	08 06		08 18	08 41
27	—	Hildenborough	d			00 06	00 12		01 10	01s10							06 37			07 42		08 12			08 47
29½	—	**Tonbridge** [4]	a			00 10	00 16	00 28	01 14	01 14							06 41		07 11	07 46	07 58	08 16		08 26	08 51
—	—		d			00 11	00 17	00 29	01 15	01 15	05 00	05 30		06 07	06 20	06 35	06 42	06 56	07 12	07 47	07 59	08 17		08 27	08 52
33	—	High Brooms	d			00 16	00 24	00 35	01 20	01s20	05 06	05 36		06 12	06 26	06 40	06 48	07 02	07 17	07 55	08 05	08 24		08 34	08 57
34½	—	**Tunbridge Wells** [4]	a			00 20	00 28	00 40	01 25	01 27	05 10	05 40		06 16	06 30	06 45	06 54	07 06	07 21	08 03	08 09	08 33		08 41	09 01
—	—		d			00 21		00 41						06 17		06 45			07 22		08 15			08 49	
36¾	—	Frant	d			00s25		00s45						06 21		06 51			07 27		08 19				
39¼	—	Wadhurst	d			00s30		00s50						06 26		06 57			07 32		08 24			08 56	
43¼	—	Stonegate	d			00s36		00s56						06 32		07 03			07 38		08 30				
47½	—	Etchingham	d			00s41		01s01						06 37		07 08			07 43		08 35			09 05	
49¼	—	Robertsbridge	d		00 03	00s44		01s05						06 41		07 12			07 47		08 39			09 09	
55½	—	Battle	d		00 11	00s52		01s13						06 49		07 20			07 55		08 47			09 17	
57½	—	Crowhurst	d		00s15	00s56		01s17						06 52		07 24			07 58		08 50			09 21	
60¾	—	West St Leonards	d	00 02	00 21	01s02		01s22						06 58		07 30			08 04		08 56			09 27	
61¾	—	St Leonards Warrior Sq [4]	d	00 05	00 24	01s05		01s26						07 02		07 33			08 08		09 00			09 30	
62½	—	**Hastings** [4]	a	00 09	00 28	01 09		01 33						07 06		07 36			08 11		09 06			09 35	
63½	—	Ore	a																						

		SE	SE	SE	SE	SE	SE	SE		SE	SE	SE	SE	SE	SE	SE	SE	SE		SE	SE	SE	SE	SE	SE
		◇1	◇1	◇1	◇1	◇1	◇1	◇1		◇1	◇1	◇1	◇1	◇1	◇1	◇1	◇1	◇1		◇1	◇1	◇1	◇1	◇1	◇1
London Charing Cross [4] ⊖	d	08 18	08 28		08 58		09 24	09 45		10 00	10 15	10 30	10 45	11 00	11 15	11 30	11 45	12 00		12 15	12 30	12 45	13 00	13 15	13 30
London Waterloo (East) [4] ⊖	d	08 21	08 31		09 01		09 27	09 48		10 03	10 18	10 33	10 48	11 03	11 18	11 33	11 48	12 03		12 18	12 33	12 48	13 03	13 18	13 33
London Cannon Street [4] ⊖	d			08 40		09 14																			
London Bridge [4] ⊖	d	08 27	08 37	08 44	09 07	09 18	09 33	09 54		10 09	10 24	10 39	10 54	11 09	11 24	11 39	11 54	12 09		12 24	12 39	12 54	13 09	13 24	13 39
Orpington [4]	d	08 44	08 56	09 07	09 26	09 40	09 56	10 10		10 26	10 39	10 56	11 10	11 26	11 39	11 56	12 10	12 26		12 39	12 56	13 10	13 26	13 39	13 56
Chelsfield	d		08 59																						
Sevenoaks [4]	d	08 53	09 07	09 20	09 36	09 50	10 06	10 20		10 36	10 50	11 06	11 20	11 36	11 50	12 06	12 20	12 36		12 50	13 06	13 20	13 36	13 50	14 06
Hildenborough	d		09 13		09 42		10 12			10 42		11 12		11 42		12 12		12 42			13 12		13 42		14 12
Tonbridge [4]	a	09 01	09 17	09 28	09 46	09 58	10 16	10 28		10 46	10 58	11 16	11 28	11 46	11 58	12 16	12 28	12 46		12 58	13 16	13 28	13 46	13 58	14 17
	d	09 02	09 18	09 29	09 47	09 59	10 17	10 29		10 47	10 59	11 17	11 29	11 47	11 59	12 17	12 29	12 47		12 59	13 17	13 29	13 47	13 59	14 18
High Brooms	d	09 08	09 24	09 35	09 54	10 05	10 23	10 35		10 54	11 05	11 24	11 35	11 54	12 05	12 24	12 35	12 54		13 05	13 24	13 35	13 54	14 05	14 24
Tunbridge Wells [4]	a	09 12	09 30	09 38	09 58	10 08	10 28	10 38		10 58	11 08	11 28	11 38	11 58	12 08	12 28	12 38	12 58		13 08	13 28	13 38	13 58	14 08	14 28
	d	09 20		09 43		10 10		10 40			11 10		11 40		12 10		12 40			13 10		13 43		14 10	
Frant	d	09 25				10 14					11 14				12 14					13 14				14 14	
Wadhurst	d	09 30		09 50		10 19		10 47			11 19		11 47		12 19		12 47			13 19		13 50		14 19	
Stonegate	d	09 36				10 25					11 25				12 25					13 25				14 25	
Etchingham	d	09 41				10 30					11 30				12 30					13 30				14 30	
Robertsbridge	d	09 45				10 33					11 33				12 33					13 33				14 33	
Battle	d	09 54		10 06		10 41		11 02			11 41		12 02		12 41		13 02			13 41		14 05		14 41	
Crowhurst	d	09 57				10 45					11 45				12 45					13 45				14 45	
West St Leonards	d	10 03				10 52					11 52				12 52					13 52				14 52	
St Leonards Warrior Sq [4]	d	10 07		10 18		10 55		11 13			11 55		12 13		12 55		13 14			13 55		14 15		14 55	
Hastings [4]	a	10 12		10 24		11 02		11 17			12 00		12 17		13 00		13 17			14 00		14 19		15 00	
Ore	a																								

		SE	SE	SE		SE	SE	SE	SE	SE	SE	SE	SE	SE		SE	SE	SE	SE	SE	SE	SE		SE
		◇1	◇1	◇1		◇1	◇1	◇1	◇1	◇1	◇1	◇1	◇1	◇1		◇1	◇1	◇1	◇1	◇1	◇1	◇1		◇1
London Charing Cross [4] ⊖	d	13 45	14 00	14 15		14 30	14 45	15 00	15 15	15 30	15 45	16 00		16 14		16 28	16 43		17 01	17 15	17 24			17 44
London Waterloo (East) [4] ⊖	d	13 48	14 03	14 18		14 33	14 48	15 03	15 18	15 33	15 48	16 03		16 17		16 31	16 46		17 04	17 18	17 27			17 48
London Cannon Street [4] ⊖	d												16 22					17 01				17 37		
London Bridge [4] ⊖	d	13 54	14 09	14 24		14 39	14 54	15 09	15 24	15 39	15 54	16 09	16 27	16 23		16 37	16 52	17 06	17 10	17 24	17 33	17 41		17 54
Orpington [4]	d	14 10	14 26	14 39		14 56	15 10	15 26	15 39	15 56	16 10	16 26		16 39		16 55								
Chelsfield	d																		17 28		17 51			18 12
Sevenoaks [4]	d	14 20	14 36	14 50		15 06	15 20	15 36	15 50	16 06	16 20	16 36		16 49		17 05	17 16	17 32	17 36		18 00			18 21
Hildenborough	d		14 42			15 12		15 42		16 12		16 42				17 11			17 42		18 06			18 27
Tonbridge [4]	a	14 28	14 46	14 58		15 16	15 28	15 46	15 58	16 16	16 28	16 46		16 58		17 15	17 24	17 40	17 46		18 10			18 31
	d	14 29	14 47	14 59		15 17	15 29	15 47	15 59	16 17	16 29	16 47		17 04		17 16	17 25	17 40	17 48		18 11			18 32
High Brooms	d	14 35	14 54	15 05		15 24	15 35	15 54	16 05	16 24	16 35	16 53	17 06	17 10		17 22	17 31	17 46	17 54	18 04	18 17	18 21		18 38
Tunbridge Wells [4]	a	14 38	14 58	15 08		15 28	15 38	15 58	16 09	16 28	16 38	16 58	17 10	17 14		17 28	17 35	17 50	18 01	18 07	18 24	18 25		18 44
	d	14 40		15 10			15 40		16 13		16 40		17 11	17 15			17 40	17 51		18 08		18 30	18 34	
Frant	d			15 14					16 18		16 44			17 20				17 56		18 13			18 38	
Wadhurst	d	14 47		15 19			15 47		16 24		16 49			17 25			17 47	18 01		18 18		18 37	18 43	
Stonegate	d			15 25					16 30		16 55			17 31				18 07		18 24			18 49	
Etchingham	d			15 30					16 35		17 00			17 36			17 56	18 12		18 28		18 46	18 54	
Robertsbridge	d			15 35					16 39		17 04			17 40			18 00	18 15		18 32			18 58	
Battle	d	15 02		15 43			16 02		16 47		17 14		17 33	17 51			18 08	18 23		18 40		18 56	19 06	
Crowhurst	d			15 46					16 51		17 17			17 54				18 27		18 44			19 10	
West St Leonards	d			15 53			16 12		16 56		17 23			18 00				18 33		18 52			19 17	
St Leonards Warrior Sq [4]	d	15 13		15 56			16 16		16 59		17 28		17 44	18 03			18 20	18 36		18 55		19 07	19 20	
Hastings [4]	a	15 17		16 00			16 21		17 05		17 33		17 50	18 08			18 25	18 42		19 01		19 10	19 23	
Ore	a																							

Table T206-F

Mondays to Fridays
16 December to 15 May

London and Tonbridge - Tunbridge Wells and Hastings

		SE	SE	SE	SE	SE	SE	SE	SE	SE	SE	SE	SE	SE	SE	SE	SE	SE	SE	SE	SE	SE	SE
		◇■	◇■	◇■	◇■	◇■	◇■	◇■	◇■	◇■	◇■	◇■	◇■	◇■	◇■	◇■	◇■	◇■	◇■	◇■	◇■	◇■	◇■
London Charing Cross ■ ⊖	d	17 57	18 07		18 31	18 46		19 00	19 15	19 30	19 45	20 00	20 15	20 30	20 45	21 00	21 30	21 45	22 00	22 30	22 45	23 00	23 30
London Waterloo (East) ■ ⊖	d	18 00	18 10		18 34	18 49		19 03	19 18	19 33	19 48	20 03	20 18	20 33	20 48	21 03	21 33	21 48	22 03	22 33	22 48	23 03	23 33
London Cannon Street ■ ⊖	d			18 26			19 02																
London Bridge ■ ⊖	d	18 06	18 16	18 31	18 40	18 55	19 07	19 09	19 24	19 39	19 54	20 09	20 24	20 39	20 54	21 09	21 39	21 54	22 09	22 39	22 54	23 09	23 39
Orpington ■	d				18 58			19 26	19 40	19 56	20 10	20 26	20 40	20 56	21 10	21 26	21 56	22 10	22 26	22 56	23 10	23 26	23 56
Chelsfield	d		18 34			19 13		19 29															
Sevenoaks ■	d		18 43		19 08	19 22	19 31	19 38	19 50	20 06	20 20	20 36	20 50	21 06	21 20	21 36	22 06	22 20	22 36	23 06	23 20	23 36	00 06
Hildenborough	d		18 49		19 14		19 37	19 44		20 12		20 42		21 12		21 42	22 12		22 42	23 12		23 42	00 12
Tonbridge ■	a		18 53		19 18	19 30	19 41	19 48	19 58	20 16	20 28	20 46	20 58	21 16	21 28	21 46	22 16	22 28	22 46	23 16	23 28	23 46	00 16
	d		18 53		19 19	19 31	19 42	19 49	19 59	20 17	20 29	20 47	20 59	21 17	21 29	21 47	22 17	22 29	22 47	23 17	23 29	23 47	00 17
High Brooms	d	18 43	19 00	19 09	19 25	19 37	19 48	19 55	20 05	20 24	20 35	20 54	21 05	21 24	21 35	21 54	22 24	22 35	22 54	23 24	23 35	23 54	00 24
Tunbridge Wells ■	a	18 47	19 06	19 13	19 32	19 40	19 51	20 02	20 08	20 28	20 38	20 58	21 08	21 28	21 38	21 58	22 28	22 38	22 58	23 28	23 38	23 58	00 28
	d	18 49		19 18		19 42	19 53		20 10		20 40		21 10		21 40			22 40			23 40		
Frant	d	18 54		19 22		19 46	19 57		20 14		20 44		21 14		21 44			22 44			23 44		
Wadhurst	d	18 59		19 27		19 51	20 02		20 19		20 49		21 19		21 49			22 49			23 49		
Stonegate	d	19 05		19 33		19 57	20 08		20 25		20 55		21 25		21 55			22 55			23 55		
Etchingham	d	19 10		19 38		20 02	20 13		20 30		21 00		21 30		22 00			23 00			23 59		
Robertsbridge	d	19 14		19 42		20 06	20 17		20 34		21 04		21 33		22 03			23 03			00 03		
Battle	d	19 22		19 50		20 14	20 25		20 42		21 12		21 41		22 11			23 11			00 11		
Crowhurst	d	19 25		19 53			20 29		20 46		21 16		21 45		22 15			23 15			00s15		
West St Leonards	d	19 31		19 59		20 23	20 38		20 53		21 23		21 51		22 22			23 21			00 21		
St Leonards Warrior Sq ■	d	19 35		20 02		20 26	20 42		20 56		21 27		21 54		22 26			23 24			00 24		
Hastings ■	a	19 41		20 05		20 32	20 47		21 02		21 31		21 58		22 30			23 28			00 28		
Ore	a			20 13																			

		SE
		◇■
London Charing Cross ■ ⊖	d	23 45
London Waterloo (East) ■ ⊖	d	23 48
London Cannon Street ■ ⊖	d	
London Bridge ■ ⊖	d	23 54
Orpington ■	d	00 10
Chelsfield	d	
Sevenoaks ■	d	00 20
Hildenborough	d	
Tonbridge ■	a	00 28
	d	00 29
High Brooms	d	00 35
Tunbridge Wells ■	a	00 40
	d	00 41
Frant	d	00s45
Wadhurst	d	00s50
Stonegate	d	00s56
Etchingham	d	01s01
Robertsbridge	d	01s05
Battle	d	01s13
Crowhurst	d	01s17
West St Leonards	d	01s22
St Leonards Warrior Sq ■	d	01s26
Hastings ■	a	01 33
Ore	a	

Saturdays
21 December to 16 May

		SE	SE	SE	SE	SE	SE	SE	SE	SE	SE	SE	SE	SE	SE	SE	SE	SE	SE	SE	SE	SE	
		◇■	◇■	◇■	◇	■	■	■	■	■	◇■	■	◇■	■	◇■	◇■	◇■	◇■	◇■	◇■	◇■	◇■	
London Charing Cross ■ ⊖	d				00 15						07 15		07 45		08 15	08 30	08 45	09 00	09 15	09 30	09 45	10 00	
London Waterloo (East) ■ ⊖	d				00 18						07 18		07 48		08 18	08 33	08 48	09 03	09 18	09 33	09 48	10 03	
London Cannon Street ■ ⊖	d																						
London Bridge ■ ⊖	d				00 24						07 24		07 54		08 24	08 39	08 54	09 09	09 24	09 39	09 54	10 09	
Orpington ■	d			00 10	00 51						07 40		08 10		08 40	08 56	09 10	09 26	09 40	09 56	10 10	10 26	
Chelsfield	d				00 54																		
Sevenoaks ■	d		00 06	00 20	01 04						07 49		08 19		08 50	09 06	09 20	09 36	09 50	10 06	10 20	10 36	and at
Hildenborough	d		00 12		01s10						07 55		08 25			09 12		09 42		10 12		10 42	the same
Tonbridge ■	a		00 16	00 28	01 14						07 59		08 29		08 58	09 16	09 28	09 47	09 58	10 16	10 28	10 46	minutes
	d		00 17	00 29	01 15	05 29	06 29	06 59	07 29	07 47	08 00	08 15	08 30	08 50	08 59	09 17	09 29	09 48	09 59	10 17	10 29	10 47	past
High Brooms	d		00 24	00 35	01s20	05 35	06 35	07 05	07 35	07 54	08 06	08 24	08 36	08 56	09 05	09 24	09 35	09 54	10 05	10 24	10 35	10 54	each
Tunbridge Wells ■	a		00 28	00 40	01 27	05 39	06 39	07 09	07 39	07 58	08 10	08 28	08 40	09 00	09 09	09 28	09 39	09 58	10 09	10 28	10 39	10 58	hour until
	d			00 41				07 10			08 10		08 40		09 10		09 40		10 10		10 40		
Frant	d			00s45				07 15			08 15				09 15				10 15				
Wadhurst	d			00s50				07 20			08 20		08 48		09 20		09 48		10 20		10 48		
Stonegate	d			00s56				07 26			08 26				09 26				10 26				
Etchingham	d			01s01				07 30			08 30				09 30				10 30				
Robertsbridge	d	00 03		01s05				07 34			08 34				09 34				10 34				
Battle	d	00 11		01s13				07 42			08 42		09 04		09 42		10 04		10 42		11 04		
Crowhurst	d	00s15		01s17				07 46			08 46				09 46				10 46				
West St Leonards	d	00 21		01s22				07 52			08 52				09 52				10 52				
St Leonards Warrior Sq ■	d	00 24		01s26				07 55			08 55		09 16		09 55		10 15		10 55		11 15		
Hastings ■	a	00 28		01 33				07 59			08 59		09 19		09 59		10 19		10 59		11 19		
Ore	a																						

Table T206-F

Saturdays
21 December to 16 May

London and Tonbridge - Tunbridge Wells and Hastings

		SE	SE	SE	SE	SE	SE	SE	SE	SE	SE	SE	SE	SE	SE	SE	SE	SE	SE	SE	SE	SE	SE
		◇■	◇■	◇■	◇■	◇■	◇■	◇■	◇■	◇■	◇■	◇■	◇■	◇■	◇■	◇■	◇■	◇■	◇■	◇■	◇■	◇■	◇■
London Charing Cross ■ ⊖	d	13 15	13 30	13 45	14 00	14 15	14 30	14 45	15 00	15 15	15 30	15 45	16 00	16 15	16 30	16 45	17 00	17 15	17 30	17 45	18 00	18 15	18 30
London Waterloo (East) ■ ⊖	d	13 18	13 33	13 48	14 03	14 18	14 33	14 48	15 03	15 18	15 33	15 48	16 03	16 18	16 33	16 48	17 03	17 18	17 33	17 48	18 03	18 18	18 33
London Cannon Street ■ ⊖	d																						
London Bridge ■ ⊖	d	13 24	13 39	13 54	14 09	14 24	14 39	14 54	15 09	15 24	15 39	15 54	16 09	16 24	16 39	16 54	17 09	17 24	17 39	17 54	18 09	18 24	18 39
Orpington ■	d	13 40	13 56	14 10	14 26	14 40	14 56	15 10	15 26	15 40	15 56	16 10	16 26	16 40	16 56	17 10	17 26	17 40	17 56	18 10	18 26	18 40	18 56
Chelsfield	d																						
Sevenoaks ■	d	13 50	14 06	14 20	14 36	14 50	15 06	15 20	15 36	15 50	16 06	16 20	16 36	16 50	17 06	17 20	17 36	17 50	18 06	18 20	18 36	18 50	19 06
Hildenborough	d		14 12		14 42		15 12		15 42		16 12		16 42		17 12		17 42		18 12		18 42		19 12
Tonbridge ■	a	13 58	14 16	14 28	14 46	14 59	15 16	15 28	15 46	15 58	16 16	16 28	16 46	16 58	17 16	17 28	17 46	17 58	18 16	18 28	18 46	18 58	19 16
	d	13 59	14 17	14 29	14 47	15 01	15 17	15 29	15 47	15 59	16 17	16 29	16 47	16 59	17 17	17 29	17 47	17 59	18 17	18 29	18 47	18 59	19 17
High Brooms	d	14 05	14 24	14 35	14 54	15 06	15 24	15 35	15 54	16 05	16 24	16 35	16 54	17 05	17 24	17 35	17 54	18 05	18 24	18 35	18 54	19 05	19 24
Tunbridge Wells ■	a	14 09	14 28	14 39	14 58	15 10	15 28	15 39	15 58	16 09	16 28	16 39	16 58	17 09	17 28	17 39	17 58	18 09	18 28	18 39	18 58	19 09	19 28
	d	14 10		14 40		15 10		15 40		16 10		16 40		17 10		17 40		18 10		18 40		19 10	
Frant	d	14 15				15 15				16 15				17 15				18 15				19 15	
Wadhurst	d	14 20		14 48		15 20		15 48		16 20		16 48		17 20		17 48		18 20		18 48		19 20	
Stonegate	d	14 26				15 26				16 26				17 26				18 26				19 26	
Etchingham	d	14 30				15 30				16 30				17 30				18 30				19 30	
Robertsbridge	d	14 34				15 34				16 34				17 34				18 34				19 34	
Battle	d	14 42		15 04		15 42		16 04		16 42		17 04		17 42		18 04		18 42		19 04		19 42	
Crowhurst	d	14 46				15 46				16 46				17 46				18 46				19 46	
West St Leonards	d	14 52				15 52				16 52				17 52				18 52				19 52	
St Leonards Warrior Sq ■	d	14 55		15 15		15 55		16 16		16 55		17 16		17 55		18 16		18 55		19 16		19 55	
Hastings ■	a	14 59		15 19		15 59		16 19		16 59		17 21		17 59		18 21		18 59		19 19		19 59	
Ore	a																						

		SE	SE	SE	SE	SE	SE	SE	SE	SE	SE	SE	SE	SE	SE	SE	SE	SE	SE
		◇■	◇■	◇■	◇■	◇■	◇■	◇■	◇■	◇■	◇■	◇■	◇■	◇■	◇■	◇■	◇■	◇■	◇■
London Charing Cross ■ ⊖	d	18 45	19 00	19 15	19 30	19 45	20 00	20 15	20 30	20 45	21 00	21 30	21 45	22 00	22 30	22 45	23 00	23 30	23 45
London Waterloo (East) ■ ⊖	d	18 48	19 03	19 18	19 33	19 48	20 03	20 18	20 33	20 48	21 03	21 33	21 48	22 03	22 33	22 48	23 03	23 33	23 48
London Cannon Street ■ ⊖	d																		
London Bridge ■ ⊖	d	18 54	19 09	19 24	19 39	19 54	20 09	20 24	20 39	20 54	21 09	21 39	21 54	22 09	22 39	22 54	23 09	23 39	23 54
Orpington ■	d	19 10	19 26	19 40	19 56	20 10	20 26	20 40	20 56	21 10	21 26	21 56	22 10	22 26	22 56	23 10	23 26	23 56	00 10
Chelsfield	d																		
Sevenoaks ■	d	19 20	19 36	19 50	20 06	20 20	20 36	20 50	21 06	21 20	21 36	22 06	22 20	22 36	23 06	23 20	23 36	00 06	00 20
Hildenborough	d		19 42		20 12		20 42		21 12		21 42	22 12		22 42	23 12		23 42	00 12	
Tonbridge ■	a	19 28	19 46	19 58	20 16	20 28	20 46	20 58	21 16	21 28	21 46	22 16	22 28	22 46	23 16	23 28	23 46	00 16	00 28
	d	19 29	19 47	19 59	20 17	20 29	20 47	20 59	21 17	21 29	21 47	22 17	22 29	22 47	23 17	23 29	23 47	00 17	00 29
High Brooms	d	19 35	19 54	20 05	20 24	20 35	20 54	21 05	21 24	21 35	21 54	22 24	22 35	22 54	23 24	23 35	23 54	00 24	00 35
Tunbridge Wells ■	a	19 39	19 58	20 09	20 28	20 39	20 58	21 09	21 28	21 39	21 58	22 28	22 39	22 58	23 28	23 39	23 58	00 28	00 40
	d	19 40		20 10		20 40		21 10		21 40			22 40			23 40			00 41
Frant	d			20 15				21 15		21 45			22 45			23 45			00s46
Wadhurst	d	19 48		20 20		20 48		21 20		21 50			22 50			23 50			00s50
Stonegate	d			20 26				21 26		21 56			22 56			23 56			00s57
Etchingham	d			20 30				21 30		22 00			23 00			23 59			01s01
Robertsbridge	d			20 34				21 34		22 04			23 04			00 04			01s05
Battle	d	20 04		20 42		21 04		21 42		22 12			23 12			00 12			01s13
Crowhurst	d			20 46				21 46		22 16			23 16			00s16			01s17
West St Leonards	d			20 52				21 52		22 21			23 21			00 21			01s22
St Leonards Warrior Sq ■	d	20 15		20 55		21 15		21 55		22 25			23 25			00 25			01s25
Hastings ■	a	20 19		20 59		21 19		21 59		22 29			23 29			00 29			01 33
Ore	a																		

Sundays
15 December to 10 May

		SE	SE	SE	SE	SE	SE	SE	SE		SE	SE	SE	SE	SE	SE
		◇■	◇■	◇■	◇	■	■	◇■	◇■		◇■	◇■	◇■	◇■	◇■	◇■
		A	A	A												
London Charing Cross ■ ⊖	d				00 15			08 25	08 55		19 25	19 55	20 25	21 25	22 25	23 25
London Waterloo (East) ■ ⊖	d				00 18			08 28	08 58		19 28	19 58	20 28	21 28	22 28	23 28
London Cannon Street ■ ⊖	d															
London Bridge ■ ⊖	d				00 24			08 34	09 04		19 34	20 04	20 34	21 34	22 34	23 34
Orpington ■	d			00 10	00 51			08 50	09 20		19 50	20 20	20 50	21 50	22 50	23 50
Chelsfield	d				00 54											
Sevenoaks ■	d		00 06	00 20	01 04			09 00	09 30		20 00	20 30	21 00	22 00	23 00	23 59
Hildenborough	d		00 12		01s10				09 36	and at		20 36	21 06	22 06	23 06	00 06
Tonbridge ■	a		00 16	00 28	01 14			09 08	09 40	the same	20 08	20 40	21 10	22 10	23 10	00 10
	d		00 17	00 29	01 15	07 41	08 41	09 11	09 41	minutes	20 11	20 41	21 11	22 11	23 11	00 11
High Brooms	d		00 24	00 35	01s20	07 46	08 46	09 16	09 46	past	20 16	20 46	21 16	22 16	23 17	00 16
Tunbridge Wells ■	a		00 28	00 40	01 27	07 50	08 50	09 20	09 50	each	20 20	20 50	21 20	22 20	23 20	00 20
	d			00 41		07 51	08 51	09 21	09 51	hour until	20 21	20 51	21 21	22 21	23 21	00 21
Frant	d			00s46		07 55	08 55		09 55			20 55	21 25	22 25	23 25	00s25
Wadhurst	d			00s50		08 00	09 00	09 29	10 00		20 29	21 00	21 30	22 30	23 30	00s30
Stonegate	d			00s57		08 06	09 06		10 06			21 06	21 36	22 36	23 36	00s36
Etchingham	d			01s01		08 11	09 11		10 11			21 11	21 41	22 41	23 41	00s41
Robertsbridge	d	00 04		01s05		08 15	09 15		10 15			21 15	21 45	22 45	23 45	00s44
Battle	d	00 12		01s13		08 23	09 23	09 45	10 23		20 45	21 23	21 53	22 53	23 53	00s52
Crowhurst	d	00s16		01s17		08 26	09 26		10 26			21 26	21 56	22 56	23s56	00s56
West St Leonards	d	00 21		01s22		08 32	09 32		10 32			21 32	22 02	23 02	00 02	01s02
St Leonards Warrior Sq ■	d	00 25		01s25		08 35	09 35	09 55	10 35		20 55	21 35	22 05	23 05	00 05	01s05
Hastings ■	a	00 29		01 33		08 39	09 39	09 59	10 39		20 59	21 39	22 09	23 09	00 09	01 09
Ore	a															

A not 15 December

Table T206-R

Mondays to Fridays
16 December to 15 May

Hastings and Tunbridge Wells - Tonbridge and London

Miles	Miles			SE MX ■1	SE MX ■1	SE ◇■1	SE ◇■1	SE ◇■1	SE ◇■1	SE ◇■1	SE ◇■1	SE ◇■1	SE ◇■1	SE ◇■1	SE ◇■1	SE ◇■1	SE ◇■1	SE ◇■1	SE ◇■1	SE ◇■1	SE ◇■1	SE ◇■1	SE ◇■1
0	—	Ore	d												06 16			06 40					
1	—	**Hastings** ■4	d					05 18		05 38	05 48		06 05		06 20	06 27		06 44		07 03		07 26	
1¾	—	St Leonards Warrior Sq ■4	d					05 21		05 41	05 51		06 08		06 24	06 30		06 47		07 06		07 29	
2¾	—	West St Leonards	d					05 25		05 44			06 12			06 35		06 51		07 10		07 33	
6	—	Crowhurst	d					05 31		05 50			06 18			06 41		06 57		07 16		07 39	
8	—	Battle	d					05 35		05 54	06 02		06 22		06 35	06 45		07 01		07 20		07 43	
14¼	—	Robertsbridge	d					05 42		06 01			06 29		06 42			07 09		07 27		07 50	
16	—	Etchingham	d					05 46		06 05	06 11		06 33		06 46	06 54		07 13		07 31		07 54	
19¾	—	Stonegate	d					05 51		06 10			06 38		06 51			07 18		07 37		07 59	
24¼	—	Wadhurst	d					05 58		06 16	06 21		06 45		06 57	07 04		07 25		07 44		08 06	
26¾	—	Frant	d					06 02		06 20			06 49		07 01			07 29		07 48		08 10	
29	—	**Tunbridge Wells** ■4	a					06 06		06 25	06 29		06 53		07 06	07 12		07 33		07 52		08 14	
—	—		d	00 05	00 35	05 17	05 48	06 08	06 18	06 34		06 39	06 55	06 59	07 16		07 20	07 35	07 39	07 55	07 59	08 16	08 24
30½	—	High Brooms	d	00 08	00 38	05 20	05 51	06 11	06 22	06 37		06 43	06 59	07 03	07 20		07 24	07 39	07 43	07 59	08 04	08 20	08 28
34	—	**Tonbridge** ■4	a	00 15	00 45	05 26	05 57	06 17	06 28	06 43		06 50		07 09			07 30		07 49		08 10	08 26	08 35
36½	—	Hildenborough	d			05 32	06 02	06 23	06 33			06 56		07 14			07 36		07 55		08 15		08 40
41½	—	Sevenoaks ■4	a			05 39	06 09	06 30	06 40	06 53		07 02		07 22			07 43		08 02		08 22		08 46
48¼	—	Chelsfield	d			05 47	06 17		06 49			07 11		07 31			07 52		08 11		08 32		08 55
49¾	—	Orpington ■4	a			05 50	06 20	06 39	06 52	07 02		07 14											
61¼	0	**London Bridge** ■4 ⊖	a			06 07	06 38	06 55	07 08	07 23		07 30	07 37	07 49	07 58		08 09	08 19	08 29	08 39	08 50	09 00	09 11
—	0¾	**London Cannon Street** ■4 ⊖	a				06 46			07 31								08 27				09 09	
62¾	—	**London Waterloo (East)** ■4 ⊖	a			06 12		07 01	07 14			07 36	07 44	07 55	08 04		08 15		08 35	08 45	08 56		09 17
63½	—	**London Charing Cross** ■4 ⊖	a			06 19		07 08	07 21			07 44	07 51	08 02	08 11		08 22		08 42	08 52	09 03		09 26

		SE ◇■1	SE ◇■1	SE ◇■1	SE ◇■1	SE ◇■1	SE ◇■1	SE ◇■1	SE ◇■1	SE ◇■1	SE ◇■1	SE ◇■1	SE ◇■1	SE ◇■1	SE ◇■1		SE ◇■1	SE ◇■1	SE ◇■1	SE ◇■1	SE ◇■1	SE ◇■1
Ore	d																					
Hastings ■4	d	07 44	08 04		08 17		08 47		09 27		09 47		10 31		10 50			14 31		14 50		15 31
St Leonards Warrior Sq ■4	d	07 47	08 07		08 20		08 50		09 30		09 50		10 34		10 53			14 34		14 53		15 34
West St Leonards	d	07 51			08 24		08 53				09 54				10 57					14 57		
Crowhurst	d	07 57			08 30		08 59				10 00				11 03					15 03		
Battle	d	08 01	08 18		08 34		09 03		09 41		10 04		10 44		11 07	and at		14 44		15 07		15 44
Robertsbridge	d	08 08			08 41		09 10				10 11				11 14	the same				15 14		
Etchingham	d	08 12			08 45		09 13				10 15				11 18	minutes				15 18		
Stonegate	d	08 17			08 50		09 18				10 20				11 23	past				15 23		
Wadhurst	d	08 23			08 56		09 24		09 57		10 26		11 00		11 29	each		15 00		15 29		16 00
Frant	d	08 27			09 00		09 28				10 30				11 33	hour until				15 33		
Tunbridge Wells ■4	a	08 32	08 41		09 05		09 34		10 05		10 35		11 08		11 38			15 08		15 38		16 08
	d	08 36	08 43	08 51	09 09	09 21	09 39	09 51	10 09	10 21	10 39	10 51	11 09	11 21	11 39		14 51	15 09	15 21	15 39	15 51	16 09
High Brooms	d	08 39	08 47	08 54	09 12	09 24	09 42	09 54	10 12	10 24	10 42	10 54	11 12	11 24	11 42		14 54	15 12	15 24	15 42	15 54	16 12
Tonbridge ■4	a	08 46		09 00	09 18	09 30	09 48	10 00	10 18	10 30	10 48	11 00	11 18	11 30	11 48		15 00	15 18	15 30	15 48	16 00	16 19
Hildenborough	d			09 05		09 35		10 05		10 35		11 05		11 35			15 05		15 35		16 05	
Sevenoaks ■4	a	08 55		09 12	09 28	09 42	09 58	10 12	10 28	10 42	10 58	11 12	11 28	11 42	11 58		15 12	15 28	15 42	15 58	16 12	16 28
Chelsfield	d																				16 20	
Orpington ■4	a	09 04		09 23	09 37	09 51	10 07	10 21	10 37	10 51	11 07	11 21	11 37	11 51	12 07		15 21	15 37	15 51	16 07	16 23	16 37
London Bridge ■4 ⊖	a	09 20	09 23	09 39	09 53	10 07	10 23	10 37	10 53	11 07	11 23	11 37	11 53	12 07	12 23		15 37	15 53	16 07	16 23	16 39	16 53
London Cannon Street ■4 ⊖	a		09 32																			
London Waterloo (East) ■4 ⊖	a	09 26		09 45	09 59	10 13	10 29	10 43	10 59	11 13	11 29	11 43	11 59	12 13	12 29		15 43	15 59	16 13	16 29	16 45	16 59
London Charing Cross ■4 ⊖	a	09 33		09 52	10 06	10 20	10 36	10 48	11 04	11 18	11 34	11 48	12 04	12 18	12 34		15 48	16 04	16 18	16 34	16 51	17 07

		SE ◇■1	SE ◇■1	SE ◇■1	SE ◇■1	SE ◇■1	SE ◇■1	SE ◇■1	SE ◇■1	SE ◇■1	SE ◇■1	SE ◇■1	SE ◇■1	SE ◇■1	SE ◇■1	SE ◇■1	SE ■1	SE ◇■1	SE ◇■1	SE ◇■1	SE ◇■1	SE ◇■1	SE ◇■1
Ore	d																						
Hastings ■4	d		15 45		16 20		16 45		17 21		17 50		18 20		18 46		19 30		19 50			20 50	
St Leonards Warrior Sq ■4	d		15 48		16 23		16 48		17 24		17 53		18 23		18 49		19 33		19 53			20 53	
West St Leonards	d		15 52		16 26		16 51		17 28		17 57		18 27		18 53		19 36		19 57			20 57	
Crowhurst	d		15 58		16 32		16 57		17 34		18 03		18 33		18 59				20 03			21 03	
Battle	d		16 02		16 36		17 01		17 38		18 07		18 37		19 03		19 44		20 07			21 07	
Robertsbridge	d		16 09		16 43		17 08		17 45		18 14		18 44		19 10				20 16			21 14	
Etchingham	d		16 13		16 47		17 12		17 48		18 18		18 47		19 13				20 20			21 18	
Stonegate	d		16 18		16 52		17 17		17 53		18 23		18 52		19 18				20 25			21 23	
Wadhurst	d		16 24		16 59		17 24		18 00		18 29		18 59		19 25		20 00		20 31			21 29	
Frant	d		16 28		17 03		17 28		18 04		18 33		19 03		19 29				20 35			21 33	
Tunbridge Wells ■4	a		16 33		17 08		17 33		18 08		18 41		19 07		19 34		20 08		20 39			21 38	
	d	16 21	16 39	16 49	17 12	17 21	17 38	17 49	18 12	18 18	18 42	18 52	19 08	19 21	19 39	19 51	20 09	20 21	20 40	20 51	21 21	21 39	21 51
High Brooms	d	16 24	16 42	16 52	17 16	17 25	17 41	17 53	18 16	18 24	18 46	18 55	19 11	19 24	19 42	19 54	20 12	20 24	20 43	20 54	21 24	21 42	21 54
Tonbridge ■4	a	16 30	16 48	16 58	17 23	17 33	17 48	17 59	18 23	18 30	18 52	19 01	19 17	19 30	19 49	20 00	20 19	20 30	20 49	21 00	21 30	21 48	22 00
Hildenborough	d	16 35		17 04				18 05		18 35		19 06		19 35		20 05		20 35		21 05	21 35		22 05
Sevenoaks ■4	a	16 42	16 58	17 10	17 31	17 41	17 58	18 12	18 31	18 42	19 00	19 13	19 28	19 42	19 58	20 12		20 42	20 58	21 12	21 42	21 58	22 12
Chelsfield	d																						
Orpington ■4	a	16 51	17 07	17 22	17 40		18 07	18 21	18 40	18 51	19 09	19 22	19 37	19 51	20 07	20 21		20 51	21 07	21 21	21 51	22 07	22 21
London Bridge ■4 ⊖	a	17 09	17 30	17 38	17 59	18 06	18 24	18 40	18 56	19 08	19 25	19 38	19 53	20 07	20 23	20 37		21 07	21 23	21 37	22 08	22 23	22 37
London Cannon Street ■4 ⊖	a		17 37					18 47															
London Waterloo (East) ■4 ⊖	a	17 15		17 44	18 05	18 12	18 30		19 01	19 14	19 30	19 44	19 59	20 13	20 29	20 43		21 13	21 29	21 43	22 13	22 29	22 43
London Charing Cross ■4 ⊖	a	17 21		17 50	18 12	18 20	18 37		19 05	19 19	19 35	19 49	20 04	20 18	20 34	20 48		21 18	21 34	21 48	22 18	22 34	22 48

NRT DECEMBER 19 EDITION

Table T206-R

Mondays to Fridays
16 December to 15 May

Hastings and Tunbridge Wells - Tonbridge and London

		SE ◇■1	SE ◇■1	SE WThFO ◇■1	SE MTO ◇■1	SE ■1
Ore	d					
Hastings ■4	d		21 50			22 50
St Leonards Warrior Sq ■4	d		21 53			22 53
West St Leonards	d		21 57			22 57
Crowhurst	d		22 03			23 03
Battle	d		22 07			23 07
Robertsbridge	d		22 14			23 14
Etchingham	d		22 18			23 18
Stonegate	d		22 23			23 23
Wadhurst	d		22 29			23 29
Frant	d		22 33			23 33
Tunbridge Wells ■4	a		22 38			23 37
	d	22 21	22 39	23 05	23 05	23 39
High Brooms	d	22 24	22 42	23 08	23 08	23 42
Tonbridge ■4	a	22 30	22 48	23 14	23 14	23 49
Hildenborough	d	22 35		23 19	23 19	
Sevenoaks ■4	a	22 42	22 58	23 26	23 26	
Chelsfield	d					
Orpington ■4	a	22 51	23 07	23 35	23 35	
London Bridge ■4 ⊖	a	23 07	23 23	23 52	23 54	
London Cannon Street ■4 ⊖	a				00 03	
London Waterloo (East) ■4 ⊖	a	23 13	23 29	23 58		
London Charing Cross ■4 ⊖	a	23 18	23 34	00 03		

Saturdays
21 December to 16 May

		SE ■1	SE ■1	SE ◇■1	SE ◇■1	SE ◇■1	SE ◇■1	SE ◇■1	SE ◇■1	SE ◇■1	SE ◇■1	SE ◇■1	SE ◇■1	SE ◇■1	SE ◇■1	SE ◇■1	SE ◇■1	SE ◇■1		SE ◇■1	SE ◇■1	SE ◇■1	SE ◇■1
Ore	d																						
Hastings ■4	d				05 48	06 19		06 50		07 19		07 50		08 19		08 50		09 31			15 50		16 31
St Leonards Warrior Sq ■4	d				05 51	06 22		06 53		07 22		07 53		08 22		08 53		09 34			15 53		16 34
West St Leonards	d				05 55	06 26		06 57		07 26		07 57		08 26		08 57					15 57		
Crowhurst	d				06 01	06 33		07 03		07 33		08 03		08 33		09 03					16 03		
Battle	d				06 05	06 37		07 07		07 37		08 07		08 37		09 07		09 44			16 07		16 44
Robertsbridge	d				06 12	06 44		07 14		07 44		08 14		08 44		09 14			and at		16 14		
Etchingham	d				06 16	06 48		07 18		07 48		08 18		08 48		09 18			the same		16 18		
Stonegate	d				06 21	06 53		07 23		07 53		08 23		08 53		09 23			minutes		16 23		
Wadhurst	d				06 27	06 59		07 29		07 59		08 29		08 59		09 29		10 00	past		16 29		17 00
Frant	d				06 31	07 03		07 33		08 03		08 33		09 03		09 33			each		16 33		
Tunbridge Wells ■4	a				06 35	07 08		07 38		08 08		08 38		09 08		09 38		10 08	hour until		16 38		17 08
	d	00 05	00 35	05 51	06 37	07 09	07 21	07 39	07 51	08 09	08 21	08 39	08 51	09 09	09 21	09 39	09 51	10 09		16 21	16 39	16 51	17 09
High Brooms	d	00 08	00 38	05 54	06 40	07 12	07 24	07 42	07 54	08 12	08 24	08 42	08 54	09 12	09 24	09 42	09 54	10 12		16 24	16 42	16 54	17 12
Tonbridge ■4	a	00 15	00 45	06 00	06 46	07 18	07 30	07 48	08 00	08 18	08 30	08 48	09 00	09 18	09 30	09 48	10 00	10 18		16 30	16 48	17 00	17 18
Hildenborough	d			06 05	06 51		07 35		08 05		08 35		09 05		09 35		10 05			16 35		17 05	
Sevenoaks ■4	a			06 12	06 58	07 28	07 42	07 58	08 12	08 28	08 42	08 58	09 12	09 28	09 42	09 58	10 12	10 28		16 42	16 58	17 12	17 28
Chelsfield	d																						
Orpington ■4	a			06 21	07 07	07 37	07 51	08 07	08 21	08 37	08 51	09 07	09 21	09 37	09 51	10 07	10 21	10 37		16 51	17 07	17 21	17 37
London Bridge ■4 ⊖	a			06 37	07 23	07 53	08 07	08 23	08 37	08 53	09 07	09 23	09 37	09 53	10 07	10 23	10 37	10 53		17 07	17 23	17 37	17 53
London Cannon Street ■4 ⊖	a																						
London Waterloo (East) ■4 ⊖	a			06 43	07 29	07 59	08 13	08 29	08 43	08 59	09 13	09 29	09 43	09 59	10 13	10 29	10 43	10 59		17 13	17 29	17 43	17 59
London Charing Cross ■4 ⊖	a			06 48	07 34	08 04	08 18	08 34	08 48	09 04	09 18	09 34	09 48	10 04	10 18	10 34	10 48	11 04		17 18	17 34	17 48	18 04

		SE ◇■1	SE ◇■1	SE ◇■1	SE ◇■1	SE ◇■1	SE ◇■1	SE ◇■1	SE ◇■1	SE ◇■1	SE ◇■1	SE ◇■1	SE ◇■1	SE ◇■1	SE ◇■1	SE ◇■1	SE ◇■1	SE ◇■1	SE ◇■1	SE ◇■1	SE ◇■1	SE ■1
Ore	d																					
Hastings ■4	d		16 50		17 18		17 50		18 18		18 50			19 50			20 50			21 50		22 50
St Leonards Warrior Sq ■4	d		16 53		17 21		17 53		18 21		18 53			19 53			20 53			21 53		22 53
West St Leonards	d		16 57		17 26		17 57		18 26		18 57			19 57			20 57			21 57		22 57
Crowhurst	d		17 03		17 33		18 03		18 33		19 03			20 03			21 03			22 03		23 03
Battle	d		17 07		17 37		18 07		18 37		19 07			20 07			21 07			22 07		23 07
Robertsbridge	d		17 14		17 44		18 14		18 44		19 14			20 14			21 14			22 14		23 14
Etchingham	d		17 18		17 48		18 18		18 48		19 18			20 18			21 18			22 18		23 18
Stonegate	d		17 23		17 53		18 23		18 53		19 23			20 23			21 23			22 23		23 23
Wadhurst	d		17 29		17 59		18 29		18 59		19 29			20 29			21 29			22 29		23 29
Frant	d		17 33		18 03		18 33		19 03		19 33			20 33			21 33			22 33		23 33
Tunbridge Wells ■4	a		17 38		18 08		18 38		19 08		19 38			20 38			21 38			22 38		23 38
	d	17 21	17 39	17 51	18 09	18 21	18 39	18 51	19 09	19 21	19 39	19 51	20 21	20 39	20 51	21 21	21 39	21 51	22 21	22 39	23 05	23 39
High Brooms	d	17 24	17 42	17 54	18 12	18 24	18 42	18 54	19 12	19 24	19 42	19 54	20 24	20 42	20 54	21 24	21 42	21 54	22 24	22 42	23 08	23 42
Tonbridge ■4	a	17 30	17 48	18 00	18 18	18 30	18 48	19 00	19 18	19 30	19 48	20 00	20 30	20 48	21 00	21 30	21 48	22 00	22 30	22 48	23 14	23 49
Hildenborough	d	17 35		18 05		18 35		19 05		19 35		20 05	20 35		21 05	21 35		22 05	22 35		23 19	
Sevenoaks ■4	a	17 42	17 58	18 12	18 28	18 42	18 58	19 12	19 28	19 42	19 58	20 12	20 42	20 58	21 12	21 42	21 58	22 12	22 42	22 58	23 26	
Chelsfield	d																					
Orpington ■4	a	17 51	18 07	18 21	18 37	18 51	19 07	19 21	19 37	19 51	20 07	20 21	20 51	21 07	21 21	21 51	22 07	22 21	22 51	23 07	23 35	
London Bridge ■4 ⊖	a	18 07	18 23	18 37	18 53	19 07	19 23	19 37	19 53	20 07	20 23	20 37	21 07	21 23	21 37	22 07	22 23	22 37	23 07	23 23	23 52	
London Cannon Street ■4 ⊖	a																					
London Waterloo (East) ■4 ⊖	a	18 13	18 29	18 43	18 59	19 13	19 29	19 43	19 59	20 13	20 29	20 43	21 13	21 29	21 43	22 13	22 29	22 43	23 13	23 29	23 58	
London Charing Cross ■4 ⊖	a	18 18	18 34	18 48	19 04	19 18	19 34	19 48	20 04	20 18	20 34	20 48	21 18	21 34	21 48	22 18	22 34	22 48	23 18	23 34	00 03	

Table T206-R

Sundays

15 December to 10 May

Hastings and Tunbridge Wells - Tonbridge and London

		SE 1	SE 1	SE ◇1	SE ◇1		SE ◇1	SE ◇1	SE ◇1	SE ◇1	SE ◇1		SE ◇1	SE ◇1	SE ◇1	SE ◇1	SE ◇1	SE ◇1
Ore	d					and at the same minutes past each hour until						and at the same minutes past each hour until						
Hastings 4	d			06 50	07 31		11 50	12 31	12 50	13 31	13 50		18 31	18 50	19 50	20 50	21 50	22 50
St Leonards Warrior Sq 4	d			06 53	07 34		11 53	12 34	12 53	13 34	13 53		18 34	18 53	19 53	20 53	21 53	22 53
West St Leonards	d			06 57			11 57		12 57		13 57			18 57	19 57	20 57	21 57	22 57
Crowhurst	d			07 03			12 03		13 03		14 03			19 03	20 03	21 03	22 03	23 03
Battle	d			07 07	07 44		12 07	12 44	13 07	13 44	14 07		18 44	19 07	20 07	21 07	22 07	23 07
Robertsbridge	d			07 14			12 14		13 14		14 14			19 14	20 14	21 14	22 14	23 14
Etchingham	d			07 18			12 18		13 18		14 18			19 18	20 18	21 18	22 18	23 18
Stonegate	d			07 23			12 23		13 23		14 23			19 23	20 23	21 23	22 23	23 23
Wadhurst	d			07 29	08 00		12 29	13 00	13 29	14 00	14 29		19 00	19 29	20 29	21 29	22 29	23 29
Frant	d			07 33			12 33		13 33		14 33			19 33	20 33	21 33	22 33	23 33
Tunbridge Wells 4	a			07 38	08 08		12 38	13 08	13 38	14 08	14 38		19 08	19 38	20 38	21 38	22 38	23 38
	d	00 05	00 35	07 39	08 09		12 39	13 09	13 39	14 09	14 39		19 09	19 39	20 39	21 39	22 39	23 39
High Brooms	d	00 08	00 38	07 42	08 12		12 42	13 12	13 42	14 12	14 42		19 12	19 42	20 42	21 42	22 42	23 42
Tonbridge 4	a	00 15	00 45	07 49	08 19		12 49	13 19	13 49	14 19	14 49		19 19	19 49	20 49	21 49	22 49	23 49
Hildenborough	d			07 53			12 53		13 54		14 53			19 53	20 53	21 53	22 53	
Sevenoaks 4	a			08 00	08 30		13 00	13 30	14 00	14 30	15 00		19 30	20 00	21 00	22 00	23 00	
Chelsfield	d																	
Orpington 4	a			08 09	08 39		13 09	13 39	14 09	14 39	15 09		19 39	20 09	21 09	22 09	23 09	
London Bridge 4 ⊖	a			08 25	08 55		13 25	13 55	14 25	14 55	15 25		19 55	20 25	21 25	22 25	23 25	
London Cannon Street 4 ⊖	a																	
London Waterloo (East) 4 ⊖	a			08 31	09 01		13 31	14 01	14 31	15 01	15 31		20 01	20 31	21 31	22 31	23 31	
London Charing Cross 4 ⊖	a			08 36	09 06		13 36	14 06	14 36	15 06	15 36		20 06	20 36	21 36	22 36	23 36	

AVAILABLE FROM MP Middleton Press

Table T207-F

Mondays to Fridays

16 December to 15 May

London and Tonbridge - Ashford International, Folkestone, Dover, Canterbury West, Ramsgate and Margate

Miles	Miles	Miles	Miles	Miles			SE MX ◇1	SE MO ◇1	SE MO ◇1	SE WTh FO ◇1	SE MO ◇	SE MX ◇	SE MO ◇	SE WO ◇	SE ThFO ◇	SE TO 🚌	SE TO 🚌	SE MX ◇	SE WTh FO ◇1	SE TO ◇1	SE MO ◇1	SE TO 🚌	SE MX ◇	SE MX ◇1
—	—	—	0	—	**St Pancras Intl.** 15 ⊖	d																	00 12	
—	—	—	6	—	Stratford International ⊖	d																	00 19	
—	—	—	22¼	—	Ebbsfleet International	d																	00 30	
0	—	—	—	—	**London Charing Cross** 4 ⊖	d																		
0¾	—	—	—	—	**London Waterloo (East)** 4 ⊖	d																		
—	—	—	—	0	**London Cannon Street** 4 ⊖	d																		
1¾	—	—	—	0¾	**London Bridge** 4 ⊖	d																		
13¾	—	—	—	—	Orpington 4	d																		
22	—	—	—	—	Sevenoaks 4	d																		00 13
27	—	—	—	—	Hildenborough	d																		
29½	—	—	—	—	**Tonbridge** 4	a																		00 21
—	—	—	—	—		d																		00 22
34¾	—	—	—	—	Paddock Wood 4	d													00 01	00 01	00 02			00 29
—	—	—	—	—	Maidstone West 4 208	a																		
39½	—	—	—	—	Marden	d													00 07	00 07	00 08			00 34
41¾	—	—	—	—	Staplehurst	d													00 11	00 11	00 12			00 38
45¼	—	—	—	—	Headcorn	d													00 17	00 17	00 18			00 44
50½	—	—	—	—	Pluckley	d													00 23	00 23				00s50
56	0	—	56	—	**Ashford International**	a													00 33	00 33	00 30		00 50	01 00
—	—	—	—	—		d	00 04	00 05										00 15	00 34	00 34		00 40		01 05
—	4¼	—	—	—	Wye	d													00s40			00 52		
—	9	—	—	—	Chilham	d										00 01			00s47			01 01		
—	11	—	—	—	Chartham	d										00 07			00s50			01 07		
—	14¼	—	—	—	**Canterbury West** 4	d							00 07	00 07	00 08	00 19	00 34		00 56			01 19		
—	16½	—	—	—	Sturry	d										00 29			01s01			01s29		
64¾	—	—	—	—	Westenhanger	d	00 12	00 13																01s13
65½	—	—	—	—	Sandling	d	00 15	00 16																01s16
69¼	—	—	—	—	Folkestone West	d	00 21	00 21										00 28						01s22
70	—	—	—	—	**Folkestone Central**	d	00 24	00 24										00 31						01s24
77¼	—	—	—	—	**Dover Priory** 4	a	00 35	00 35										00 41						01 38
—	—	—	—	—		d												00 43						
82¼	—	—	—	—	Martin Mill	d												00s52						
85	—	—	—	—	Walmer	d												00s56						
86½	—	—	—	—	**Deal**	d					00 01	00 02						01s01						
90¾	—	0	—	—	Sandwich	d					00 07	00 08						01s07						
—	25½	4¾	—	—	Minster 4	d			00 09	00 11						00 49			01s12			01s49		
99	29½	—	—	—	**Ramsgate** 4	a			00 15	00 18	00 19	00 21	00 26	00 31	00 29	01 02	01s12	01 23	01 20	01 29		02 02		
101¼	31¾	—	—	—	Broadstairs	a							00s32		00s35		01s21							
104½	35	—	—	—	**Margate** 4	a							00 38		00 40		01 31							

		SE WTh FO ◇1 A	SE MO ◇1	SE TO 🚌	SE	SE 1	SE	SE 1	SE	SE 1	SE	SE ◇1	SE	SE	SE ◇	SE ◇	SE	SE ◇	SE ◇1	SE	SE ◇	SE ◇1
St Pancras Intl. 15 ⊖	d														06 25	06 40		07 05			07 22	
Stratford International ⊖	d														06 32	06 47		07 12			07 29	
Ebbsfleet International	d														06 43	06 59		07 23			07 40	
London Charing Cross 4 ⊖	d											05 30										
London Waterloo (East) 4 ⊖	d											05 33										
London Cannon Street 4 ⊖	d																		06 32			
London Bridge 4 ⊖	d											05 39							06 36			
Orpington 4	d		00 06									05 55										
Sevenoaks 4	d	00 13	00 16									06 06							07 06			
Hildenborough	d											06 13							07 12			
Tonbridge 4	a	00 21	00 24									06 18							07 16			
	d	00 22	00 25		05 06			05 22				06 22							07 17			
Paddock Wood 4	d	00 29	00 32		05 13		05 28	05 29	06 18			06 29		06 48					07 24	07 41		
Maidstone West 4 208	a				05 28		05 49		06 39					07 09	07 16					08 02		
Marden	d	00 34	00 38					05 34				06 34							07 29			
Staplehurst	d	00 38	00 42					05 38				06 38							07 33			
Headcorn	d	00 44	00 48					05 44				06 44							07 39			
Pluckley	d	00s50	00s54					05 50				06 50							07 45			
Ashford International	a	01 00	01 04					06 00				06 59				07 19		07 42	07 54			
	d	01 07		01 10		05 25		06 05		06 28	06 30	07 00	07 05				07 22	07 44	07 58			08 05
Wye	d	01s13		01s22				06 11			06 36		07 11				07 28		08 04			08 11
Chilham	d	01s19		01s31				06 17			06 42		07 17				07 34		08 10			08 17
Chartham	d	01s23		01s37				06 21			06 46		07 21				07 38		08 14			08 21
Canterbury West 4	d	01a30		01a49				06 28			06 52		07 26				07 44	08 00	08 20			08a29
Sturry	d							06 33			06 56						07 48		08 25			
Westenhanger	d					05 33				06 36		07 08										
Sandling	d					05 36				06 39		07 11										
Folkestone West	d					05 42				06 45		07 17										
Folkestone Central	d					05 45				06 48		07 20										
Dover Priory 4	a					05 55				06 58		07 33										
	d					05 57				07 10		07 34										
Martin Mill	d					06 06				07 19		07 43										
Walmer	d					06 10				07 23		07 48										
Deal	d					06 14				07 27		07 53										
Sandwich	d					06 21				07 34		08 01										
Minster 4	d							06 44			07 08		07a41				08 00		08 36			
Ramsgate 4	a					06 36		06 52		07 46	07 13	08 16					08 05	08 22	08 45			
Broadstairs	a										07 19							08 28				
Margate 4	a										07 26							08 34			08 58	

A 1 to Ashford International

Table T207-F

Mondays to Fridays

16 December to 15 May

London and Tonbridge - Ashford International, Folkestone, Dover, Canterbury West, Ramsgate and Margate

		SE ◇	SE ◇	SE ◇1		SE	SE ◇		SE ◇1		SE ◇	SE ◇	SE ◇1	SE ◇1	SE	SE ◇	SE ◇1		SE ◇1	SE ◇	SE ◇	SE ◇1	SE	SE ◇1	SE ◇
St Pancras Intl. 15 ⊖	d	07 25	07 37				08 12				08 25	08 37				09 09				09 25	09 37				10 09
Stratford International ⊖	d	07 32	07 44				08 19				08 32	08 44				09 16				09 32	09 44				10 16
Ebbsfleet International	d	07 43	07 55				08 30				08 43	08 55				09 27				09 44	09 55				10 27
London Charing Cross 4 ⊖	d			07 09					07 37				07 57	08 16					08 34			09 02		09 22	
London Waterloo (East) 4 ⊖	d			07 12					07 40				08 01	08 19					08 37			09 05		09 25	
London Cannon Street 4 ⊖	d																								
London Bridge 4 ⊖	d			07 18					07 46				08 07	08 25					08 43			09 11		09 31	
Orpington 4	d																					09 31		09 50	
Sevenoaks 4	d			07 42					08 13					08 49					09 13			09 41		10 02	
Hildenborough	d																								
Tonbridge 4	a			07 50					08 21				08 36	08 57					09 21			09 50		10 10	
	d			07 51					08 22				08 38	08 58	09 05				09 22			09 52	10 04	10 11	
Paddock Wood 4	d			07 57		08 11			08 29				08 45	09 05	09 12				09 29			09 59	10 11		
Maidstone West 4 208	a					08 32									09 32								10 31		
Marden	d			08 03					08 34				08 51	09 11					09 34			10 04			
Staplehurst	d			08 07					08 38				08 55	09 15					09 38			10 08			
Headcorn	d			08 13					08 44				09 01	09 21					09 44			10 14			
Pluckley	d			08 19					08 50				09 07						09 50			10 20			
Ashford International	a	08 02	08 14	08 28			08 50		09 00			09 14	09 19	09 33		09 47			10 00		10 14	10 30		10 41	10 47
	d	08 07	08 15	08 33	08 38		08 52		09 05	09 08		09 15		09 35		09 52	10 05		10 05		10 15	10 35			10 52
Wye	d			08 39						09 14				09 41			10 11					10 41			
Chilham	d			08 45						09 20							10 17								
Chartham	d			08 49						09 24							10 21								
Canterbury West 4	d			08 54			09 08			09a30				09 54		10 08	10a27					10 54			11 08
Sturry	d			08 59										09 58								10 58			
Westenhanger	d	08 15			08 46				09 13										10 13						
Sandling	d	08 18			08 49				09 16										10 16						
Folkestone West	d	08 23	08 28		08 55				09 21			09 28							10 22		10 28				
Folkestone Central	d	08 26	08 31		08 58				09 24			09 31							10 25		10 31				
Dover Priory 4	a	08 37	08 41		09 11				09 38			09 41							10 38		10 41				
	d		08 42									09 43									10 42				
Martin Mill	d		08 52									09 52									10 52				
Walmer	d		08 56									09 56									10 56				
Deal	d		09 01									10 01									11 01				
Sandwich	d		09 07									10 07									11 07				
Minster 4	d			09 10										10 09								11 09			
Ramsgate 4	a		09 19	09 18			09 27					10 19		10 18		10 27					11 19	11 19			11 27
Broadstairs	a		09 25				09 36					10 25				10 33					11 25				11 33
Margate 4	a		09 29				09 42				09 59	10 29				10 38				10 59	11 29				11 38

		SE ◇1	SE ◇1		SE ◇	SE ◇	SE ◇1	SE	SE ◇	SE ◇1	SE ◇1	SE ◇	SE ◇		SE ◇1	SE	SE ◇	SE ◇1	SE ◇1	SE ◇	SE ◇	SE ◇1	SE		SE ◇
St Pancras Intl. 15 ⊖	d				10 27	10 37			11 12			11 25	11 37				12 12			12 27	12 37				13 12
Stratford International ⊖	d				10 34	10 44			11 19			11 32	11 44				12 19			12 34	12 44				13 19
Ebbsfleet International	d				10 45	10 55			11 30			11 43	11 55				12 30			12 45	12 55				13 30
London Charing Cross 4 ⊖	d	09 40					10 10			10 40					11 10			11 40				12 10			
London Waterloo (East) 4 ⊖	d	09 43					10 13			10 43					11 13			11 43				12 13			
London Cannon Street 4 ⊖	d																								
London Bridge 4 ⊖	d	09 49					10 19			10 49					11 19			11 49				12 19			
Orpington 4	d																								
Sevenoaks 4	d	10 13					10 43			11 13					11 43			12 13				12 43			
Hildenborough	d																								
Tonbridge 4	a	10 21					10 51			11 21					11 51			12 21				12 51			
	d	10 22					10 52	11 04		11 22					11 52	12 04		12 22				12 52	13 04		
Paddock Wood 4	d	10 29					10 59	11 11		11 29					11 59	12 11		12 29				12 59	13 11		
Maidstone West 4 208	a							11 31								12 31							13 31		
Marden	d	10 34					11 04			11 34					12 04			12 34				13 04			
Staplehurst	d	10 38					11 08			11 38					12 08			12 38				13 08			
Headcorn	d	10 44					11 14			11 44					12 14			12 44				13 14			
Pluckley	d	10 50					11 20			11 50					12 20			12 50				13 20			
Ashford International	a	11 00				11 14	11 30		11 50	12 00			12 14		12 30		12 50	13 00			13 14	13 30			13 50
	d	11 02	11 05			11 15	11 35		11 52	12 02	12 05		12 15		12 35		12 52	13 02	13 05		13 15	13 35			13 52
Wye	d		11 11				11 41				12 11				12 41				13 11			13 41			
Chilham	d		11 17								12 17								13 17						
Chartham	d		11 21								12 21								13 21						
Canterbury West 4	d		11a27				11 54		12 08		12a27				12 54		13 08		13a27			13 54			14 08
Sturry	d						11 58								12 58							13 58			
Westenhanger	d	11 10								12 10								13 10							
Sandling	d	11 13								12 13								13 13							
Folkestone West	d	11 19				11 28				12 19			12 28					13 19			13 28				
Folkestone Central	d	11 22				11 31				12 22			12 31					13 22			13 31				
Dover Priory 4	a	11 33				11 41				12 33			12 41					13 33			13 41				
	d					11 42							12 42								13 42				
Martin Mill	d					11 52							12 52								13 52				
Walmer	d					11 56							12 56								13 56				
Deal	d					12 01							13 01								14 01				
Sandwich	d					12 07							13 07								14 07				
Minster 4	d						12 09								13 09							14 09			
Ramsgate 4	a					12 19	12 16		12 27				13 19		13 16		13 27				14 19	14 16			14 27
Broadstairs	a					12 25			12 33				13 25				13 33				14 25				14 33
Margate 4	a				11 59	12 29			12 38			12 59	13 29				13 38			13 59	14 29				14 38

Table T207-F

Mondays to Fridays

16 December to 15 May

London and Tonbridge - Ashford International, Folkestone, Dover, Canterbury West, Ramsgate and Margate

		SE ◇1	SE ◇1	SE ◇	SE ◇	SE ◇1		SE	SE ◇		SE ◇1	SE ◇1	SE ◇	SE ◇	SE ◇1		SE	SE ◇	SE ◇1		SE ◇1	SE ◇	SE ◇	SE ◇1	
St Pancras Intl. 15 ⊖	d			13 25	13 37				14 10				14 25	14 37				15 12				15 25	15 37		
Stratford International ⊖	d			13 32	13 44				14 17				14 32	14 44				15 19				15 32	15 44		
Ebbsfleet International	d			13 43	13 55				14 28				14 43	14 55				15 30				15 43	15 55		
London Charing Cross 4 ⊖	d	12 40				13 10					13 40				14 10				14 40					15 10	
London Waterloo (East) 4 ⊖	d	12 43				13 13					13 43				14 13				14 43					15 13	
London Cannon Street 4 ⊖	d																								
London Bridge 4 ⊖	d	12 49				13 19					13 49				14 19				14 49					15 19	
Orpington 4	d																								
Sevenoaks 4	d	13 13				13 43					14 13				14 43				15 13					15 43	
Hildenborough	d																								
Tonbridge 4	a	13 21				13 51					14 21				14 51				15 21					15 51	
	d	13 22				13 52		14 04			14 22				14 52		15 04		15 22					15 52	
Paddock Wood 4	d	13 29				13 59		14 11			14 29				14 59		15 11		15 29					15 59	
Maidstone West 4 208	a							14 31									15 31								
Marden	d	13 34				14 04					14 34				15 04				15 34					16 04	
Staplehurst	d	13 38				14 08					14 38				15 08				15 38					16 08	
Headcorn	d	13 44				14 14					14 44				15 14				15 44					16 14	
Pluckley	d	13 50				14 20					14 50				15 20				15 50					16 20	
Ashford International	a	14 00			14 14	14 29			14 48		15 00			15 14	15 30			15 50	16 00				16 14	16 30	
	d	14 02	14 05		14 15	14 35	14 38		14 52		15 02	15 05		15 15	15 35	15 38		15 52	16 02		16 05		16 15	16 35	16 38
Wye	d		14 11			14 41						15 11			15 41						16 11			16 41	
Chilham	d		14 17									15 17									16 17			16 47	
Chartham	d		14 21									15 21									16 21			16 51	
Canterbury West 4	d		14a27			14 54			15 08			15a27			15 54			16 08			16a27			16 57	
Sturry	d					14 58									15 58									17 01	
Westenhanger	d	14 10					14 46				15 10					15 46			16 10						16 46
Sandling	d	14 13					14 49				15 13					15 49			16 13						16 49
Folkestone West	d	14 19			14 28		14 55				15 19			15 28		15 55			16 19				16 28		16 55
Folkestone Central	d	14 22			14 31		14 58				15 22			15 31		15 58			16 22				16 31		16 58
Dover Priory 4	a	14 33			14 41		15 09				15 33			15 41		16 09			16 33				16 41		17 09
	d				14 42		15 25							15 42		16 10							16 42		17 11
Martin Mill	d				14 52		15 34							15 52		16 19							16 52		17 20
Walmer	d				14 56		15 38							15 56		16 23							16 56		17 24
Deal	d				15 01		15 42							16 01		16 28							17 01		17 28
Sandwich	d				15 07		15 50							16 07		16 36							17 07		17 35
Minster 4	d					15 09	16 02								16 09	16 48								17 16	
Ramsgate 4	a				15 19	15 16	16 13		15 27					16 19	16 16	16 54		16 27					17 19	17 24	17 49
Broadstairs	a				15 25				15 33					16 25				16 33					17 25		
Margate 4	a			14 59	15 29				15 38				16 01	16 29				16 38				17 01	17 29		

		SE	SE ◇	SE ◇1	SE ◇1		SE ◇	SE ◇	SE ◇1		SE	SE ◇	SE ◇1	SE ◇	SE ◇		SE ◇1		SE	SE ◇	SE ◇	SE ◇1	SE	SE ◇1	SE ◇
St Pancras Intl. 15 ⊖	d		16 10				16 37	16 50				17 07		17 12	17 20					17 25	17 37				17 46
Stratford International ⊖	d		16 17				16 44	16 57				17 14		17 19	17 27					17 32	17 44				17 53
Ebbsfleet International	d		16 28				16 55					17 25		17 31						17 43	17 56				18 05
London Charing Cross 4 ⊖	d			15 40					16 10								16 39					16 51			
London Waterloo (East) 4 ⊖	d			15 43					16 13								16 42					16 54			
London Cannon Street 4 ⊖	d												16 30											17 09	
London Bridge 4 ⊖	d			15 49					16 19				16 35				16 48					17 00		17 14	
Orpington 4	d																					17 18			
Sevenoaks 4	d			16 13					16 43								17 12					17 28			
Hildenborough	d																								
Tonbridge 4	a			16 21					16 51								17 20					17 36			
	d	16 04		16 22					16 52								17 21					17 37			
Paddock Wood 4	d	16 11		16 29					16 59		17 04						17 28		17 34			17 44	17 52		
Maidstone West 4 208	a	16 31									17 25			18 04					17 55				18 15		18 38
Marden	d			16 34					17 04								17 34					17 50			
Staplehurst	d			16 38					17 08								17 38					17 54			
Headcorn	d			16 44					17 14								17 44					18 00			
Pluckley	d			16 50					17 20								17 50					18 06			
Ashford International	a		16 48	17 00			17 14	17 24	17 30			17 44			17 54		17 59				18 15	18 15			
	d		16 52	17 02	17 05		17 18	17 26	17 35	17 38		17 46			17 56		18 03	18 05			18 17	18 20			
Wye	d				17 11				17 41								18 09								
Chilham	d				17 17				17 47								18 15								
Chartham	d				17 21				17 51								18 19								
Canterbury West 4	d		17 09		17a27			17 44	17 57						18 11		18 25								
Sturry	d								18 01								18 29								
Westenhanger	d			17 10						17 46								18 13				18 29			
Sandling	d			17 13						17 49								18 16				18 32			
Folkestone West	d			17 19			17 30			17 55		17 59						18 22			18 30	18 38			
Folkestone Central	d			17 22			17 33			17 58		18 02						18 25			18 35	18a43			
Dover Priory 4	a			17 33			17 44			18 09		18 14	18 43					18 39			18 45				
	d						17 45			18 12											18 46				
Martin Mill	d						17 54			18 21											18 55				
Walmer	d						17 59			18 25											19 00				
Deal	d						18 03			18 30											19 04				
Sandwich	d						18 11			18 37											19 11				
Minster 4	d								18 13								18 41								
Ramsgate 4	a		17 31				18 25	18 02	18 21	18 53					18 30		18 49				19 25				
Broadstairs	a		17 37				18 32	18 08							18 36										
Margate 4	a		17 42				18 37	18 15							18 44					18 57				18 56	

Table T207-F

Mondays to Fridays
16 December to 15 May

London and Tonbridge - Ashford International, Folkestone, Dover, Canterbury West, Ramsgate and Margate

		SE	SE	SE	SE	SE	SE	SE	SE	SE	SE	SE	SE	SE	SE	SE	SE	SE	SE	SE	SE	SE
		◇	◇1	◇	◇	◇1	◇1	◇	◇	◇1	◇1		◇1	◇	◇	◇1	◇	◇1	◇1	◇1		◇
St Pancras Intl. 15 ⊖	d	17 50		17 55	18 07			18 16	18 20					18 25	18 37		18 50					19 07
Stratford International ⊖	d	17 57		18 02	18 14			18 23	18 27					18 32	18 45		18 57					19 14
Ebbsfleet International	d			18 13	18 26			18 35						18 43	18 56							19 26
London Charing Cross 4 ⊖	d		17 11							17 39						18 01				18 19		
London Waterloo (East) 4 ⊖	d		17 14							17 42						18 04				18 22		
London Cannon Street 4 ⊖	d					17 23	17 30				17 45		17 52					18 07	18 11			
London Bridge 4 ⊖	d		17 20			17 28	17 35			17 48	17 50		17 57			18 10		18 12	18 16	18 28		
Orpington 4	d																					
Sevenoaks 4	d		17 46			17 54				18 12	18 16					18 34		18 38		18 53		
Hildenborough	d					18 01												18 44				
Tonbridge 4	a		17 54			18 05				18 20	18 24					18 42		18 48		19 01		
	d		17 55			18 06				18 21	18 25					18 44		18 49		19 02		
Paddock Wood 4	d		18 03			18 13				18 28	18 32	18 43				18 51		18 56		19 10	19 13	
Maidstone West 4 208	a							19 09				19 04									19 34	
Marden	d		18 09			18 19					18 38					18 57		19 02		19 16		
Staplehurst	d		18 13			18 23				18 36	18 42					19 01		19 06		19 20		
Headcorn	d		18 19			18 29				18 42	18 48					19 07		19 12		19 26		
Pluckley	d					18 35				18 48	18 54							19 18		19 32		
Ashford International	a	18 24	18 31		18 45	18 45			18 54	18 59	19 04				19 15	19 20	19 25	19 30		19 45		19 45
	d	18 26	18 33		18 47	18 51			18 56	19 02	19 06				19 17	19 22	19 27	19 32				19 47
Wye	d		18 39							19 08								19 38				
Chilham	d		18 46							19 15								19 45				
Chartham	d		18 50							19 19								19 49				
Canterbury West 4	d	18 41	18 56						19 11	19 25							19 42	19 55				
Sturry	d		19 01							19 30								20 00				
Westenhanger	d					19 00					19 15					19 31						
Sandling	d					19 03					19 18					19 34						
Folkestone West	d				19 00	19 09					19 23				19 31	19 40						20 00
Folkestone Central	d				19 03	19 12					19a28				19 35	19 43						20 03
Dover Priory 4	a				19 15	19 23	19 42								19 46	19 53			20 14			20 14
	d					19 25									19 47	19 55						
Martin Mill	d					19 34									19 56	20 05						
Walmer	d					19 39									20 01	20 10						
Deal	d					19 44									20 05	20 15						
Sandwich	d					19 52									20a14	20 23						
Minster 4	d		19 12							19 42								20 11				
Ramsgate 4	a	19 00	19 21			20 08			19 30	19 52						20 39	20 01	20 20				
Broadstairs	a	19 06							19 36								20 07					
Margate 4	a	19 14		19 35					19 44				19 30	20 02			20 15					

		SE	SE	SE	SE	SE	SE	SE	SE		SE	SE	SE	SE	SE	SE	SE	SE	SE	SE	SE	SE	SE
		◇1	◇1	◇	◇1		◇	◇	◇1		◇	◇1	◇1	◇		◇	◇1	◇	◇1	◇		◇	◇1
St Pancras Intl. 15 ⊖	d			19 20			19 25	19 37			20 12			20 25		20 37		21 12		21 25		21 37	
Stratford International ⊖	d			19 27			19 32	19 44			20 19			20 32		20 44		21 19		21 32		21 44	
Ebbsfleet International	d						19 43	19 55			20 30			20 43		20 55		21 30		21 43		21 55	
London Charing Cross 4 ⊖	d				18 41				19 10				19 40				20 10		20 40				21 10
London Waterloo (East) 4 ⊖	d				18 44				19 13				19 43				20 13		20 43				21 13
London Cannon Street 4 ⊖	d	18 31	18 45																				
London Bridge 4 ⊖	d	18 36	18 50		18 50				19 19				19 49				20 19		20 49				21 19
Orpington 4	d				19 07																		21 35
Sevenoaks 4	d	19 00			19 18				19 43				20 13				20 43		21 13				21 45
Hildenborough	d																						
Tonbridge 4	a	19 08			19 26				19 51				20 21				20 51		21 21				21 53
	d	19 10			19 27				19 53				20 22		20 34		20 52		21 22		21 34		21 54
Paddock Wood 4	d	19 17			19 34	19 42			19 59				20 29		20 41		20 59		21 29		21 41		22 01
Maidstone West 4 208	a					20 03									21 01						22 01		
Marden	d	19 23			19 40				20 05				20 34				21 04		21 34				22 06
Staplehurst	d	19 27			19 44				20 09				20 38				21 08		21 38				22 10
Headcorn	d	19 33			19 50				20 15				20 44				21 14		21 44				22 16
Pluckley	d	19 39			19 56				20 21				20 50				21 20		21 50				22 22
Ashford International	a	19 50		19 54	20 05			20 14	20 31		20 50		20 59			21 14	21 30	21 50	22 00			22 14	22 32
	d	19 52		19 56	20 07			20 15	20 35	20 38	20 52	21 05	21 05			21 15	21 32	21 52	22 04			22 15	22 34
Wye	d				20 13				20 41			21 11					21 38						22 40
Chilham	d				20 20				20 47			21 17					21 44						22 46
Chartham	d				20 24				20 51			21 21					21 48						22 50
Canterbury West 4	d			20 11	20 30				20 57		21 09	21a27					21 54	22 08					22 55
Sturry	d				20 35				21 01								21 58						23 00
Westenhanger	d	20 01								20 46			21 13						22 12				
Sandling	d	20 04								20 49			21 16						22 15				
Folkestone West	d	20 09						20 28		20 55			21 21			21 28			22 21			22 28	
Folkestone Central	d	20 12						20 31		20 58			21 24			21 31			22 24			22 31	
Dover Priory 4	a	20 27						20 41		21 09			21 37			21 41			22 35			22 41	
	d							20 42		21 10						21 42						22 42	
Martin Mill	d							20 51		21 19						21 52						22 52	
Walmer	d							20 55		21 23						21 56						22 56	
Deal	d							21 00		21 27						22 01						23 01	
Sandwich	d							21 06		21 34						22 07						23 07	
Minster 4	d				20 46				21 15								22 09						23 11
Ramsgate 4	a			20 30	20 55			21 18	21 23	21 50	21 32					22 19	22 17	22 27				23 22	23 17
Broadstairs	a			20 36				21 25			21 37							22 33					
Margate 4	a		20 32	20 44			21 03	21 29			21 43			22 03				22 38		23 03			

Table T207-F

Mondays to Fridays
16 December to 15 May

London and Tonbridge - Ashford International, Folkestone, Dover, Canterbury West, Ramsgate and Margate

		SE TX	SE TO	SE	SE TX	SE TO	SE	SE	SE MX	SE MO	SE MO	SE TO	SE WThFO	SE MO	SE MO	SE	SE	SE MX	SE MO	SE	SE TWThO
		◇	◇	◇1	◇	◇		◇	◇1	◇1	Bus	◇	◇	◇	Bus	◇1	◇	◇1	◇1	◇1	◇1 A
St Pancras Intl. 15 ⊖	d	22 12	22 12		22 25	22 25		22 37				23 12	23 12	23 12			23 37				
Stratford International ⊖	d	22 19	22 19		22 32	22 32		22 44				23 19	23 19	23 19			23 44				
Ebbsfleet International	d	22 30	22 30		22 43	22 43		22 55				23 30	23 30	23 30			23 55				
London Charing Cross 4 ⊖	d			21 40					22 10	22 10						22 40		23 10	23 10	23 40	23 40
London Waterloo (East) 4 ⊖	d			21 43					22 13	22 13						22 43		23 13	23 13	23 43	23 43
London Cannon Street 4 ⊖	d																				
London Bridge 4 ⊖	d			21 49					22 19	22 19						22 49		23 19	23 19	23 49	23 49
Orpington 4	d								22 35	22 35								23 35	23 35		
Sevenoaks 4	d			22 13					22 45	22 45						23 13		23 45	23 45	00 13	00 13
Hildenborough	d																				
Tonbridge 4	a			22 21					22 53	22 53						23 21		23 53	23 53	00 21	00 21
	d			22 22			22 34		22 54	22 54						23 22		23 54	23 54	00 22	00 22
Paddock Wood 4	d			22 29			22 41		23 01	23 01						23 29		00 01	00 01	00 29	00 29
Maidstone West 4 208	a						23 01														
Marden	d			22 34					23 06	23 06						23 34		00 07	00 07	00 34	00 34
Staplehurst	d			22 38					23 10	23 10						23 38		00 11	00 11	00 38	00 38
Headcorn	d			22 44					23 16	23 16						23 44		00 17	00 17	00 44	00 44
Pluckley	d			22 50					23 22	23 22						23 50		00 23	00 23	00s50	00s50
Ashford International	a	22 50	22 50	23 00				23 14	23 32	23 32		23 50	23 50	23 50		23 59	00 14	00 33	00 33	01 00	01 00
	d	22 52	22 52	23 04				23 15	23 34	23 34	23 40	23 52	23 52	23 52	23 59	00 04	00 15	00 34	00 34	01 05	01 07
Wye	d								23 40		23 52							00s40			01s13
Chilham	d								23 46		00 01							00s47			01s19
Chartham	d								23 50		00 07							00s50			01s23
Canterbury West 4	d	23 08	23 08						23 56		00 19	00 07	00 08		00 34			00 56			01a30
Sturry	d								23 59		00 29							01s01			
Westenhanger	d			23 12												00 12				01s13	
Sandling	d			23 15												00 15				01s16	
Folkestone West	d			23 21				23 28								00 21	00 28			01s22	
Folkestone Central	d			23 24				23 31								00 24	00 31			01s24	
Dover Priory 4	a			23 35				23 43								00 35	00 41			01 38	
	d							23 43									00 43				
Martin Mill	d							23 53									00s52				
Walmer	d							23 57									00s56				
Deal	d							00 02									01s01				
Sandwich	d							00 08									01s07				
Minster 4	d								00 11		00 49							01s12			
Ramsgate 4	a	23 28	23 29			00 39		00 21	00 18	00 29	01 02	00 31	00 29	00 43	01s12		01 23	01 20	01 29		
Broadstairs	a	23 34											00s35	00s49	01s21						
Margate 4	a	23 40			00 03								00 40	00 57	01 31						

Saturdays
21 December to 16 May

		SE	SE	SE	SE	SE	SE	SE	SE	SE	SE	SE	SE	SE	SE	SE	SE	SE	SE	SE	SE	SE	SE
		◇1	◇1	◇	◇	◇	◇1	◇	◇1	◇		◇		1	1	◇	◇1		◇	1	◇1	◇	◇
St Pancras Intl. 15 ⊖	d							00 12								06 37			07 07			07 25	07 37
Stratford International ⊖	d							00 19								06 44			07 14			07 32	07 44
Ebbsfleet International	d							00 30								06 55			07 25			07 43	07 55
London Charing Cross 4 ⊖	d																06 00						
London Waterloo (East) 4 ⊖	d																06 03						
London Cannon Street 4 ⊖	d																						
London Bridge 4 ⊖	d																06 09						
Orpington 4	d																06 26						
Sevenoaks 4	d								00 13								06 36						
Hildenborough	d																06 42						
Tonbridge 4	a								00 21								06 46						
	d								00 22		06 04			06 22			06 52	07 04		07 22			
Paddock Wood 4	d						00 01		00 29		06 11			06 29			06 59	07 11		07 29			
Maidstone West 4 208	a										06 31							07 31					
Marden	d						00 07		00 34					06 34			07 04			07 34			
Staplehurst	d						00 11		00 38					06 38			07 08			07 38			
Headcorn	d						00 17		00 44					06 44			07 14			07 44			
Pluckley	d						00 23		00s50					06 50			07 20			07 50			
Ashford International	a						00 33	00 50	01 00					07 00		07 14	07 30		07 44	08 00			08 14
	d	00 04				00 15	00 34		01 05	01 07		06 15	06 35	07 02	07 05	07 15	07 35		07 52	08 02	08 05		08 15
Wye	d						00s40			01s13			06 41		07 11		07 41				08 11		
Chilham	d						00s47			01s19					07 17						08 17		
Chartham	d						00s50			01s23					07 21						08 21		
Canterbury West 4	d				00 08		00 56			01a30			06 54		07a27		07 54		08 08		08a27		
Sturry	d						01s01						06 58				07 58						
Westenhanger	d	00 12							01s13					07 10						08 10			
Sandling	d	00 15							01s16					07 13						08 13			
Folkestone West	d	00 21				00 28			01s22			06 28		07 19		07 28				08 19			08 28
Folkestone Central	d	00 24				00 31			01s24			06 31		07 22		07 31				08 22			08 31
Dover Priory 4	a	00 35				00 41			01 38			06 41		07 33		07 41				08 33			08 41
	d					00 43						06 42				07 42							08 42
Martin Mill	d					00s52						06 52				07 52							08 52
Walmer	d					00s56						06 56				07 56							08 56
Deal	d			00 02		01s01						07 01				08 01							09 01
Sandwich	d			00 08		01s07						07 07				08 07							09 07
Minster 4	d		00 11				01s12						07 09				08 09						
Ramsgate 4	a		00 18	00 21	00 29	01 23	01 20					07 19	07 15			08 19	08 16		08 27				09 19
Broadstairs	a				00s35							07 25	07 21			08 25			08 33				09 25
Margate 4	a				00 40							07 29	07 26			08 29			08 38			08 59	09 29

A 1 to Ashford International

Table T207-F

Saturdays

21 December to 16 May

London and Tonbridge - Ashford International, Folkestone, Dover, Canterbury West, Ramsgate and Margate

		SE ◇1	SE	SE ◇	SE ◇1	SE ◇1		SE ◇	SE ◇	SE ◇1	SE	SE ◇	SE ◇1	SE ◇1	SE ◇	SE ◇		SE ◇1	SE	SE ◇	SE ◇1	SE ◇1	SE ◇	SE ◇	SE ◇1
St Pancras Intl. 15 ⊖	d			08 12				08 25	08 37			09 09			09 25	09 34				10 09			10 25	10 37	
Stratford International ⊖	d			08 19				08 32	08 44			09 16			09 32	09 41				10 16			10 32	10 44	
Ebbsfleet International	d			08 30				08 43	08 55			09 27			09 44	09 52				10 27			10 43	10 55	
London Charing Cross 4 ⊖	d	07 10			07 40					08 10			08 40					09 10			09 40				10 10
London Waterloo (East) 4 ⊖	d	07 13			07 43					08 13			08 43					09 13			09 43				10 13
London Cannon Street 4 ⊖	d																								
London Bridge 4 ⊖	d	07 19			07 49					08 19			08 49					09 19			09 49				10 19
Orpington 4	d																								
Sevenoaks 4	d	07 43			08 13					08 43			09 13					09 43			10 13				10 43
Hildenborough	d																								
Tonbridge 4	a	07 51			08 21					08 51			09 21					09 51			10 21				10 51
	d	07 52	08 04		08 22					08 52	09 04		09 22					09 52	10 04		10 22				10 52
Paddock Wood 4	d	07 59	08 11		08 29					08 59	09 11		09 29					09 59	10 11		10 29				10 59
Maidstone West 4 208	a		08 31								09 31								10 31						
Marden	d	08 04			08 34					09 04			09 34					10 04			10 34				11 04
Staplehurst	d	08 08			08 38					09 08			09 38					10 08			10 38				11 08
Headcorn	d	08 14			08 44					09 14			09 44					10 14			10 44				11 14
Pluckley	d	08 20			08 50					09 20			09 50					10 20			10 50				11 20
Ashford International	a	08 30		08 50	09 00				09 14	09 30		09 47	10 00			10 11		10 30		10 47	11 00			11 14	11 30
	d	08 35		08 52	09 02	09 05			09 15	09 35		09 52	10 02	10 05		10 15		10 35		10 52	11 02	11 05		11 15	11 35
Wye	d	08 41				09 11				09 41				10 11				10 41				11 11			11 41
Chilham	d					09 17								10 17								11 17			
Chartham	d					09 21								10 21								11 21			
Canterbury West 4	d	08 54		09 08		09a27				09 54		10 08		10a27				10 54		11 08		11a27			11 54
Sturry	d	08 58								09 58								10 58							11 58
Westenhanger	d				09 10								10 10								11 10				
Sandling	d				09 13								10 13								11 13				
Folkestone West	d				09 19				09 28				10 19			10 28					11 19			11 28	
Folkestone Central	d				09 22				09 31				10 22			10 31					11 22			11 31	
Dover Priory 4	a				09 33				09 41				10 33			10 41					11 33			11 41	
	d								09 42							10 42								11 42	
Martin Mill	d								09 52							10 52								11 52	
Walmer	d								09 56							10 56								11 56	
Deal	d								10 01							11 01								12 01	
Sandwich	d								10 07							11 07								12 07	
Minster 4	d	09 09								10 09								11 09							12 09
Ramsgate 4	a	09 16		09 27					10 19	10 16		10 27				11 19		11 16		11 27				12 19	12 16
Broadstairs	a			09 33					10 25			10 33				11 25				11 33				12 25	
Margate 4	a			09 38				09 59	10 29			10 38			10 59	11 29				11 38			11 59	12 29	

		SE		SE ◇1	SE ◇	SE ◇	SE ◇1	SE ◇	SE ◇1	SE	SE ◇1	SE ◇		SE ◇	SE ◇1	SE ◇	SE ◇1	SE	SE ◇	SE ◇1	SE ◇1	SE ◇		SE ◇	SE ◇1
St Pancras Intl. 15 ⊖	d				11 12	11 25		11 37				12 12		12 27		12 37			13 12			13 25		13 37	
Stratford International ⊖	d				11 19	11 32		11 44				12 19		12 34		12 44			13 19			13 32		13 44	
Ebbsfleet International	d				11 30	11 43		11 55				12 30		12 45		12 55			13 30			13 43		13 55	
London Charing Cross 4 ⊖	d			10 40					11 10		11 40						12 10			12 40					13 10
London Waterloo (East) 4 ⊖	d			10 43					11 13		11 43						12 13			12 43					13 13
London Cannon Street 4 ⊖	d																								
London Bridge 4 ⊖	d			10 49					11 19		11 49						12 19			12 49					13 19
Orpington 4	d																								
Sevenoaks 4	d			11 13					11 43		12 13						12 43			13 13					13 43
Hildenborough	d																								
Tonbridge 4	a			11 21					11 51		12 21						12 51			13 21					13 51
	d	11 04		11 22					11 52	12 04	12 22						12 52	13 04		13 22					13 52
Paddock Wood 4	d	11 11		11 29					11 59	12 11	12 29						12 59	13 11		13 29					13 59
Maidstone West 4 208	a	11 31								12 31								13 31							
Marden	d			11 34					12 04		12 34						13 04			13 34					14 04
Staplehurst	d			11 38					12 08		12 38						13 08			13 38					14 08
Headcorn	d			11 44					12 14		12 44						13 14			13 44					14 14
Pluckley	d			11 50					12 20		12 50						13 20			13 50					14 20
Ashford International	a			12 00				12 14	12 30		13 00					13 14	13 30		13 50	14 00				14 14	14 30
	d			12 02			12 05	12 15	12 35		13 02				13 05	13 18	13 35		13 52	14 02	14 05			14 15	14 35
Wye	d						12 11		12 41						13 11		13 41				14 11				14 41
Chilham	d						12 17								13 17						14 17				
Chartham	d						12 21								13 21						14 21				
Canterbury West 4	d				12 08		12a27		12 54			13 08			13a27		13 54		14 08		14a27				14 54
Sturry	d								12 58								13 58								14 58
Westenhanger	d			12 10							13 10									14 10					
Sandling	d			12 13							13 13									14 13					
Folkestone West	d			12 19				12 28			13 19					13 30				14 19				14 28	
Folkestone Central	d			12 22				12 31			13 22					13 33				14 22				14 31	
Dover Priory 4	a			12 33				12 41			13 33					13 43				14 33				14 41	
	d							12 42								13 44								14 42	
Martin Mill	d							12 52								13 53								14 52	
Walmer	d							12 56								13 57								14 56	
Deal	d							13 01								14 01								15 01	
Sandwich	d							13 07								14 08								15 07	
Minster 4	d								13 09								14 09								15 09
Ramsgate 4	a				12 27			13 19	13 16			13 27				14 19	14 16		14 27					15 19	15 16
Broadstairs	a				12 33			13 25				13 33				14 25			14 33					15 25	
Margate 4	a				12 38	12 59		13 29				13 38		13 59		14 29			14 38			14 59		15 29	

NRT DECEMBER 19 EDITION

Table T207-F

Saturdays

21 December to 16 May

London and Tonbridge - Ashford International, Folkestone, Dover, Canterbury West, Ramsgate and Margate

		SE	SE ◇1	SE ◇	SE ◇	SE ◇1	SE ◇	SE ◇1		SE	SE ◇	SE ◇1	SE ◇1	SE ◇	SE ◇	SE ◇1	SE	SE ◇		SE ◇1	SE ◇1	SE ◇	SE ◇	SE ◇1	SE
St Pancras Intl. 15 ⊖	d			14 10	14 25		14 37				15 12			15 25	15 37			16 10				16 25	16 37		
Stratford International ⊖	d			14 17	14 32		14 44				15 19			15 32	15 44			16 17				16 32	16 44		
Ebbsfleet International	d			14 28	14 43		14 55				15 30			15 43	15 55			16 28				16 43	16 55		
London Charing Cross 4 ⊖	d		13 40					14 10				14 40				15 10				15 40				16 10	
London Waterloo (East) 4 ⊖	d		13 43					14 13				14 43				15 13				15 43				16 13	
London Cannon Street 4 ⊖	d																								
London Bridge 4 ⊖	d		13 49					14 19				14 49				15 19				15 49				16 19	
Orpington 4	d																								
Sevenoaks 4	d		14 13					14 43				15 13				15 43				16 13				16 43	
Hildenborough	d																								
Tonbridge 4	a		14 21					14 51				15 21				15 51				16 21				16 51	
	d	14 04	14 22					14 52		15 04		15 22				15 52	16 04			16 22				16 52	17 04
Paddock Wood 4	d	14 11	14 29					14 59		15 11		15 29				15 59	16 11			16 29				16 59	17 11
Maidstone West 4 208	a	14 31								15 31							16 31								17 31
Marden	d		14 34					15 04				15 34				16 04				16 34				17 04	
Staplehurst	d		14 38					15 08				15 38				16 08				16 38				17 08	
Headcorn	d		14 44					15 14				15 44				16 14				16 44				17 14	
Pluckley	d		14 50					15 20				15 50				16 20				16 50				17 20	
Ashford International	a		15 00				15 14	15 30			15 50	16 00			16 14	16 30		16 48		17 00			17 14	17 30	
	d		15 02			15 05	15 15	15 35			15 52	16 02	16 05		16 15	16 35		16 52		17 02	17 05		17 15	17 35	
Wye	d					15 11		15 41					16 11			16 41					17 11			17 41	
Chilham	d					15 17							16 17								17 17				
Chartham	d					15 21							16 21								17 21				
Canterbury West 4	d			15 08		15a27		15 54			16 08		16a27			16 54		17 08			17a27			17 54	
Sturry	d							15 58								16 58								17 58	
Westenhanger	d		15 10									16 10								17 10					
Sandling	d		15 13									16 13								17 13					
Folkestone West	d		15 19				15 28					16 19			16 28					17 19			17 28		
Folkestone Central	d		15 22				15 31					16 22			16 31					17 22			17 31		
Dover Priory 4	a		15 33				15 41					16 33			16 41					17 33			17 41		
	d						15 42								16 42								17 42		
Martin Mill	d						15 52								16 52								17 52		
Walmer	d						15 56								16 56								17 56		
Deal	d						16 01								17 01								18 01		
Sandwich	d						16 07								17 07								18 07		
Minster 4	d							16 09								17 09								18 09	
Ramsgate 4	a			15 27			16 19	16 16			16 27				17 19	17 16		17 27					18 19	18 16	
Broadstairs	a			15 33			16 25				16 33				17 25			17 33					18 25		
Margate 4	a			15 38	15 59		16 29				16 38			16 59	17 29			17 38				17 59	18 29		

		SE ◇	SE ◇1	SE ◇1		SE ◇	SE ◇	SE ◇1	SE	SE ◇1	SE ◇	SE ◇	SE ◇1	SE ◇		SE ◇1	SE	SE ◇1	SE ◇	SE ◇	SE ◇1	SE ◇	SE ◇1	SE	
St Pancras Intl. 15 ⊖	d	17 12				17 25	17 37				18 12	18 25		18 37					19 12	19 25		19 37			
Stratford International ⊖	d	17 19				17 32	17 44				18 19	18 32		18 44					19 19	19 32		19 44			
Ebbsfleet International	d	17 30				17 43	17 55				18 30	18 43		18 55					19 30	19 43		19 55			
London Charing Cross 4 ⊖	d		16 40					17 10		17 40						18 10		18 40					19 10		
London Waterloo (East) 4 ⊖	d		16 43					17 13		17 43						18 13		18 43					19 13		
London Cannon Street 4 ⊖	d																								
London Bridge 4 ⊖	d		16 49					17 19		17 49						18 19		18 49					19 19		
Orpington 4	d																								
Sevenoaks 4	d		17 13					17 43		18 13						18 43		19 13					19 43		
Hildenborough	d																								
Tonbridge 4	a		17 21					17 51		18 21						18 51		19 21					19 51		
	d		17 22					17 52	18 04	18 22						18 52	19 04	19 22					19 52	20 04	
Paddock Wood 4	d		17 29					17 59	18 11	18 29						18 59	19 11	19 29					19 59	20 11	
Maidstone West 4 208	a								18 31								19 31							20 31	
Marden	d		17 34					18 04		18 34						19 04		19 34					20 04		
Staplehurst	d		17 38					18 08		18 38						19 08		19 38					20 08		
Headcorn	d		17 44					18 14		18 44						19 14		19 44					20 14		
Pluckley	d		17 50					18 20		18 50						19 20		19 50					20 20		
Ashford International	a	17 50	18 00				18 14	18 30		19 00				19 14		19 30		20 00				20 14	20 30		
	d	17 52	18 02	18 05			18 15	18 35		19 02			19 05	19 15		19 35		20 02			20 05	20 15	20 32		
Wye	d			18 11				18 41					19 11			19 41					20 11		20 38		
Chilham	d			18 17									19 17								20 17		20 44		
Chartham	d			18 21									19 21								20 21		20 48		
Canterbury West 4	d	18 08		18a27				18 54			19 08		19a27			19 54			20 08		20a27		20 54		
Sturry	d							18 58								19 58							20 58		
Westenhanger	d		18 10							19 10								20 10							
Sandling	d		18 13							19 13								20 13							
Folkestone West	d		18 19				18 28			19 19				19 28				20 19				20 28			
Folkestone Central	d		18 22				18 31			19 22				19 31				20 22				20 31			
Dover Priory 4	a		18 33				18 41			19 33				19 41				20 33				20 41			
	d						18 42							19 42								20 42			
Martin Mill	d						18 52							19 52								20 52			
Walmer	d						18 56							19 56								20 56			
Deal	d						19 01							20 01								21 01			
Sandwich	d						19 07							20 07								21 07			
Minster 4	d							19 09								20 09							21 09		
Ramsgate 4	a	18 27					19 19	19 16			19 27			20 19		20 16			20 27			21 19	21 16		
Broadstairs	a	18 33					19 25				19 33			20 25					20 33			21 25			
Margate 4	a	18 38				18 59	19 29				19 38	19 59		20 29					20 38	20 59		21 29			

Table T207-F

London and Tonbridge - Ashford International, Folkestone, Dover, Canterbury West, Ramsgate and Margate

Saturdays
21 December to 16 May

		SE	SE	SE	SE	SE	SE	SE	SE	SE	SE	SE	SE	SE	SE	SE	SE	SE	SE	SE	SE	SE	SE
		◇	◇■	◇	◇	◇■		◇	◇■	◇	◇	◇■		◇	◇■	◇	◇	◇■	◇	◇■	◇	◇■	◇■
St Pancras Intl. 15 ⊖	d	20 12		20 25	20 37			21 12		21 25	21 37			22 12		22 25	22 37		23 12		23 37		
Stratford International ⊖	d	20 19		20 32	20 44			21 19		21 32	21 44			22 19		22 32	22 44		23 19		23 44		
Ebbsfleet International	d	20 30		20 43	20 55			21 30		21 43	21 55			22 30		22 43	22 55		23 30		23 55		
London Charing Cross 4 ⊖	d		19 40			20 10			20 40			21 10			21 40			22 10		22 40		23 10	23 40
London Waterloo (East) 4 ⊖	d		19 43			20 13			20 43			21 13			21 43			22 13		22 43		23 13	23 43
London Cannon Street 4 ⊖	d																						
London Bridge 4 ⊖	d		19 49			20 19			20 49			21 19			21 49			22 19		22 49		23 19	23 49
Orpington 4	d											21 35						22 35				23 35	
Sevenoaks 4	d		20 13			20 43			21 13			21 45			22 13			22 45		23 13		23 46	00 13
Hildenborough	d																						
Tonbridge 4	a		20 21			20 51			21 21			21 53			22 21			22 53		23 21		23 54	00 21
	d		20 22			20 52	21 04		21 22			21 54	22 04		22 22			22 54		23 22		23 55	00 22
Paddock Wood 4	d		20 29			20 59	21 11		21 29			22 01	22 11		22 29			23 01		23 29		00 01	00 29
Maidstone West 4 208	a						21 31						22 31										
Marden	d		20 34			21 04			21 34			22 06			22 34			23 06		23 34		00 07	00 34
Staplehurst	d		20 38			21 08			21 38			22 10			22 38			23 10		23 38		00 11	00 38
Headcorn	d		20 44			21 14			21 44			22 16			22 44			23 16		23 44		00 17	00 44
Pluckley	d		20 50			21 20			21 50			22 22			22 50			23 22		23 50		00 23	00s50
Ashford International	a	20 50	21 00		21 14	21 30		21 50	22 00		22 14	22 32		22 50	23 00		23 14	23 32	23 50	23 59	00 14	00 33	01 00
	d	20 52	21 02		21 15	21 32		21 52	22 02		22 15	22 34		22 52	23 04		23 15	23 34	23 52	00 04	00 15	00 34	01 05
Wye	d					21 38						22 40						23 40				00s40	
Chilham	d					21 44						22 46						23 46				00s47	
Chartham	d					21 48						22 50						23 50				00s50	
Canterbury West 4	d	21 08				21 54		22 08				22 56		23 08				23 56	00 08			00 56	
Sturry	d					21 58						23 00						23 59				01s01	
Westenhanger	d		21 10						22 10						23 12					00 12			01s13
Sandling	d		21 13						22 13						23 15					00 15			01s16
Folkestone West	d		21 19		21 28				22 19		22 28				23 21		23 28			00 21	00 28		01s22
Folkestone Central	d		21 22		21 31				22 22		22 31				23 24		23 31			00 24	00 31		01s24
Dover Priory 4	a		21 33		21 41				22 33		22 41				23 35		23 41			00 35	00 41		01 38
	d				21 42						22 42						23 42				00 42		
Martin Mill	d				21 52						22 52						23 52				00s51		
Walmer	d				21 56						22 56						23 56				00s56		
Deal	d				22 01						23 01						00 01				01s00		
Sandwich	d				22 07						23 07						00 07				01s07		
Minster 4	d					22 09						23 11						00 11				01s12	
Ramsgate 4	a	21 27			22 19	22 16		22 27			23 21	23 18		23 29			00 21	00 18	00 29		01 23	01 20	
Broadstairs	a	21 33						22 32						23 34					00s34				
Margate 4	a	21 38		21 59				22 37		22 59				23 40		23 59			00 40				

Sundays
15 December to 10 May

		SE	SE	SE	SE	SE	SE	SE	SE	SE	SE	SE	SE	SE	SE	SE	SE	SE	SE	SE	SE	SE	SE
		◇■	◇■	◇	◇	◇	◇■	◇	◇■	◇			■	◇	◇	■	■	◇■		◇	◇■	◇	◇■
		A	A	A	A	A	A		A														
St Pancras Intl. 15 ⊖	d							00 12							08 25					08 37		09 09	
Stratford International ⊖	d							00 19							08 32					08 44		09 16	
Ebbsfleet International	d							00 30							08 43					08 55		09 27	
London Charing Cross 4 ⊖	d																				08 10		08 40
London Waterloo (East) 4 ⊖	d																				08 13		08 43
London Cannon Street 4 ⊖	d																						
London Bridge 4 ⊖	d																				08 19		08 49
Orpington 4	d																				08 36		09 06
Sevenoaks 4	d								00 13												08 46		09 16
Hildenborough	d																						
Tonbridge 4	a								00 21												08 54		09 24
	d								00 22		06 33	07 33					08 25		08 33		08 55		09 25
Paddock Wood 4	d						00 01		00 29		06 40	07 40					08 32		08 40		09 02		09 32
Maidstone West 4 208	a										07 00	08 00							09 00				
Marden	d						00 07		00 34								08 38				09 08		09 38
Staplehurst	d						00 11		00 38								08 42				09 12		09 42
Headcorn	d						00 17		00 44								08 48				09 18		09 48
Pluckley	d						00 23		00s50								08 54						09 54
Ashford International	a						00 33	00 50	01 00								09 03			09 14	09 30	09 47	10 03
	d	00 04				00 15	00 34		01 05	01 07			08 08	08 15		08 32	09 05	09 08		09 15	09 32	09 52	10 05
Wye	d						00s40			01s13			08 14			08 38		09 14			09 38		
Chilham	d						00s47			01s19			08 20					09 20					
Chartham	d						00s50			01s23			08 24					09 24					
Canterbury West 4	d				00 08		00 56			01a30			08a30			08 51		09a30			09 51	10 07	
Sturry	d						01s01									08 55					09 55		
Westenhanger	d	00 12							01s13								09 13						10 13
Sandling	d	00 15							01s16								09 16						10 16
Folkestone West	d	00 21				00 28			01s22					08 28			09 21			09 28			10 21
Folkestone Central	d	00 24				00 31			01s24					08 31			09 24			09 31			10 24
Dover Priory 4	a	00 35				00 41			01 38					08 41			09 35			09 41			10 35
	d					00 42								08 42						09 42			
Martin Mill	d					00s51								08 52						09 52			
Walmer	d					00s56								08 56						09 56			
Deal	d			00 01		01s00								09 01						10 01			
Sandwich	d			00 07		01s07								09 07						10 07			
Minster 4	d		00 11				01s12									09 07					10 07		
Ramsgate 4	a		00 18	00 21	00 29	01 23	01 20							09 19		09 15				10 19	10 15	10 26	
Broadstairs	a				00s34									09 25						10 25		10 32	
Margate 4	a				00 40									09 29	09 59					10 29		10 38	

A not 15 December

Table T207-F

London and Tonbridge - Ashford International, Folkestone, Dover, Canterbury West, Ramsgate and Margate

Sundays
15 December to 10 May

		SE	SE	SE	SE	SE	SE	SE	SE	SE	SE	SE	SE	SE	SE	SE	SE	SE	SE	SE	SE	SE	SE
		◇■	◇		◇	◇■	◇	◇■	◇■	◇		◇	◇■	◇	◇■	◇■	◇		◇	◇■	◇	◇■	◇■
St Pancras Intl. 15 ⊖	d		09 25		09 37		10 09			10 27		10 37		11 12			11 25		11 37		12 12		
Stratford International ⊖	d		09 32		09 44		10 16			10 34		10 44		11 19			11 32		11 44		12 19		
Ebbsfleet International	d		09 44		09 55		10 27			10 45		10 55		11 30			11 43		11 55		12 30		
London Charing Cross 4 ⊖	d					09 10		09 40					10 10		10 40					11 10		11 40	
London Waterloo (East) 4 ⊖	d					09 13		09 43					10 13		10 43					11 13		11 43	
London Cannon Street 4 ⊖	d																						
London Bridge 4 ⊖	d					09 19		09 49					10 19		10 49					11 19		11 49	
Orpington 4	d					09 36		10 06					10 36		11 06					11 36		12 06	
Sevenoaks 4	d					09 46		10 16					10 46		11 16					11 46		12 16	
Hildenborough	d																						
Tonbridge 4	a					09 54		10 24					10 54		11 24					11 54		12 24	
	d			09 33		09 55		10 25			10 33		10 55		11 25			11 33		11 55		12 25	
Paddock Wood 4	d			09 40		10 02		10 32			10 40		11 02		11 32			11 40		12 02		12 32	
Maidstone West 4 208	a			10 00							11 00							12 00					
Marden	d					10 08		10 38					11 08		11 38					12 08		12 38	
Staplehurst	d					10 12		10 42					11 12		11 42					12 12		12 42	
Headcorn	d					10 18		10 48					11 18		11 48					12 18		12 48	
Pluckley	d							10 54							11 54							12 54	
Ashford International	a				10 14	10 30	10 47	11 03				11 14	11 30	11 50	12 03				12 14	12 30	12 50	13 03	
	d	10 08			10 15	10 32	10 52	11 05	11 08			11 15	11 32	11 52	12 05	12 08			12 15	12 32	12 52	13 05	13 08
Wye	d	10 14				10 38			11 14				11 38			12 14				12 38			13 14
Chilham	d	10 20							11 20							12 20							13 20
Chartham	d	10 24							11 24							12 24							13 24
Canterbury West 4	d	10a30				10 51	11 07		11a30				11 51	12 07		12a30				12 51	13 07		13a30
Sturry	d					10 55							11 55							12 55			
Westenhanger	d							11 13							12 13							13 13	
Sandling	d							11 16							12 16							13 16	
Folkestone West	d				10 28			11 21				11 28			12 21				12 28			13 21	
Folkestone Central	d				10 31			11 24				11 31			12 24				12 31			13 24	
Dover Priory 4	a				10 41			11 35				11 41			12 35				12 41			13 35	
	d				10 42							11 42							12 42				
Martin Mill	d				10 52							11 52							12 52				
Walmer	d				10 56							11 56							12 56				
Deal	d				11 01							12 01							13 01				
Sandwich	d				11 07							12 07							13 07				
Minster 4	d					11 07							12 07							13 07			
Ramsgate 4	a				11 19	11 15	11 26					12 19	12 15	12 26					13 19	13 15	13 26		
Broadstairs	a				11 25		11 32					12 25		12 32					13 25		13 32		
Margate 4	a		10 59		11 29		11 38			11 59		12 29		12 38			12 59		13 29		13 38		

		SE	SE	SE	SE	SE	SE	SE	SE	SE	SE	SE	SE	SE	SE	SE	SE	SE	SE	SE	SE	SE
		◇		◇	◇■	◇	◇■	◇■	◇		◇	◇■	◇	◇■	◇■	◇		◇	◇■	◇	◇■	◇■
St Pancras Intl. 15 ⊖	d	12 27		12 37		13 12			13 25		13 37		14 10			14 25		14 37		15 12		
Stratford International ⊖	d	12 34		12 44		13 19			13 32		13 44		14 17			14 32		14 44		15 19		
Ebbsfleet International	d	12 45		12 55		13 30			13 43		13 55		14 28			14 43		14 55		15 30		
London Charing Cross 4 ⊖	d				12 10		12 40					13 10		13 40					14 10		14 40	
London Waterloo (East) 4 ⊖	d				12 13		12 43					13 13		13 43					14 13		14 43	
London Cannon Street 4 ⊖	d																					
London Bridge 4 ⊖	d				12 19		12 49					13 19		13 49					14 19		14 49	
Orpington 4	d				12 36		13 06					13 36		14 06					14 36		15 06	
Sevenoaks 4	d				12 46		13 16					13 46		14 16					14 46		15 16	
Hildenborough	d																					
Tonbridge 4	a				12 54		13 24					13 54		14 24					14 54		15 24	
	d		12 33		12 55		13 25			13 33		13 55		14 25			14 33		14 55		15 25	
Paddock Wood 4	d		12 40		13 02		13 32			13 40		14 02		14 32			14 40		15 02		15 32	
Maidstone West 4 208	a		13 00							14 00							15 00					
Marden	d				13 08		13 38					14 08		14 38					15 08		15 38	
Staplehurst	d				13 12		13 42					14 12		14 42					15 12		15 42	
Headcorn	d				13 18		13 48					14 18		14 48					15 18		15 48	
Pluckley	d						13 54							14 54							15 54	
Ashford International	a			13 14	13 30	13 50	14 03				14 14	14 30	14 48	15 05				15 14	15 30	15 50	16 03	
	d			13 15	13 32	13 52	14 05	14 08			14 15	14 32	14 52	15 07	15 08			15 15	15 32	15 52	16 05	16 08
Wye	d				13 38			14 14				14 38			15 14				15 38			16 14
Chilham	d							14 20							15 20							16 20
Chartham	d							14 24							15 24							16 24
Canterbury West 4	d				13 51	14 07		14a30				14 51	15 07		15a30				15 51	16 07		16a30
Sturry	d				13 55							14 55							15 55			
Westenhanger	d						14 13							15 15							16 13	
Sandling	d						14 16							15 18							16 16	
Folkestone West	d			13 28			14 21				14 28			15 23				15 28			16 21	
Folkestone Central	d			13 31			14 24				14 31			15 26				15 31			16 24	
Dover Priory 4	a			13 41			14 35				14 41			15 37				15 41			16 35	
	d			13 42							14 42							15 42				
Martin Mill	d			13 52							14 52							15 52				
Walmer	d			13 56							14 56							15 56				
Deal	d			14 01							15 01							16 01				
Sandwich	d			14 07							15 07							16 07				
Minster 4	d				14 07							15 07							16 07			
Ramsgate 4	a			14 19	14 15	14 26					15 19	15 15	15 26					16 19	16 15	16 26		
Broadstairs	a			14 25		14 32					15 25		15 32					16 25		16 32		
Margate 4	a	13 59		14 29		14 38			14 59		15 29		15 38			15 59		16 29		16 38		

Table T207-F

Sundays

15 December to 10 May

London and Tonbridge - Ashford International, Folkestone, Dover, Canterbury West, Ramsgate and Margate

		SE ◇	SE	SE ◇	SE ◇1	SE ◇	SE ◇1	SE ◇1		SE ◇	SE	SE ◇	SE ◇1	SE ◇	SE ◇1	SE ◇1	SE ◇	SE		SE ◇	SE ◇1	SE ◇	SE ◇1	SE ◇	SE
St Pancras Intl. 15 ⊖	d	15 25		15 37		16 12				16 25		16 37		17 07			17 25			17 37		18 12		18 25	
Stratford International ⊖	d	15 32		15 44		16 19				16 32		16 44		17 14			17 32			17 44		18 19		18 32	
Ebbsfleet International	d	15 43		15 55		16 30				16 43		16 55		17 25			17 43			17 55		18 30		18 43	
London Charing Cross 4 ⊖	d				15 10		15 40						16 10		16 40						17 10		17 40		
London Waterloo (East) 4 ⊖	d				15 13		15 43						16 13		16 43						17 13		17 43		
London Cannon Street 4 ⊖	d																								
London Bridge 4 ⊖	d				15 19		15 49						16 19		16 49						17 19		17 49		
Orpington 4	d				15 36		16 06						16 36		17 06						17 36		18 06		
Sevenoaks 4	d				15 46		16 16						16 46		17 16						17 46		18 16		
Hildenborough	d																								
Tonbridge 4	a				15 54		16 24						16 54		17 24						17 54		18 24		
	d		15 33		15 55		16 25				16 33		16 55		17 25			17 33			17 55		18 25		18 33
Paddock Wood 4	d		15 40		16 02		16 32				16 40		17 02		17 32			17 40			18 02		18 32		18 40
Maidstone West 4 208	a		16 00								17 00							18 00							19 00
Marden	d				16 08		16 38						17 08		17 38						18 08		18 38		
Staplehurst	d				16 12		16 42						17 12		17 42						18 12		18 42		
Headcorn	d				16 18		16 48						17 18		17 48						18 18		18 48		
Pluckley	d						16 54								17 54								18 54		
Ashford International	a			16 14	16 30	16 50	17 03					17 14	17 30	17 44	18 03					18 14	18 30	18 50	19 03		
	d			16 15	16 32	16 52	17 05	17 08				17 15	17 32	17 52	18 05	18 08				18 15	18 32	18 52	19 05		
Wye	d				16 38			17 14					17 38			18 14					18 38				
Chilham	d							17 20								18 20					18 44				
Chartham	d							17 24								18 24					18 48				
Canterbury West 4	d				16 51	17 07		17a30					17 51	18 07		18a30					18 54	19 07			
Sturry	d				16 55								17 55								18 58				
Westenhanger	d						17 13								18 13								19 13		
Sandling	d						17 16								18 16								19 16		
Folkestone West	d			16 28			17 21					17 28			18 21					18 28			19 21		
Folkestone Central	d			16 31			17 24					17 31			18 24					18 31			19 24		
Dover Priory 4	a			16 41			17 35					17 41			18 35					18 41			19 35		
	d			16 42								17 42								18 42					
Martin Mill	d			16 52								17 52								18 52					
Walmer	d			16 56								17 56								18 56					
Deal	d			17 01								18 01								19 01					
Sandwich	d			17 07								18 07								19 07					
Minster 4	d				17 07								18 07								19 09				
Ramsgate 4	a			17 19	17 15	17 26						18 19	18 15	18 26						19 19	19 15	19 26			
Broadstairs	a			17 25		17 32						18 25		18 32						19 25		19 32			
Margate 4	a	16 59		17 29		17 38				17 59		18 29		18 38			18 59			19 29		19 38		19 59	

		SE ◇	SE ◇1	SE ◇		SE ◇1	SE ◇	SE	SE ◇	SE ◇1	SE ◇	SE ◇1	SE ◇	SE		SE ◇	SE ◇1	SE ◇	SE ◇1	SE ◇	SE	SE ◇	SE ◇1	SE ◇
St Pancras Intl. 15 ⊖	d	18 37		19 12			19 25		19 37		20 12		20 25			20 37		21 12		21 25		21 37		22 12
Stratford International ⊖	d	18 44		19 19			19 32		19 44		20 19		20 32			20 44		21 19		21 32		21 44		22 19
Ebbsfleet International	d	18 55		19 30			19 43		19 55		20 30		20 43			20 55		21 30		21 43		21 55		22 30
London Charing Cross 4 ⊖	d		18 10			18 40				19 10		19 40					20 10		20 40				21 10	
London Waterloo (East) 4 ⊖	d		18 13			18 43				19 13		19 43					20 13		20 43				21 13	
London Cannon Street 4 ⊖	d																							
London Bridge 4 ⊖	d		18 19			18 49				19 19		19 49					20 19		20 49				21 19	
Orpington 4	d		18 36			19 06				19 36		20 06					20 36		21 06				21 36	
Sevenoaks 4	d		18 46			19 16				19 46		20 16					20 46		21 16				21 46	
Hildenborough	d																							
Tonbridge 4	a		18 54			19 24				19 54		20 24					20 54		21 24				21 54	
	d		18 55			19 25		19 33		19 55		20 25		20 33			20 55		21 25		21 33		21 55	
Paddock Wood 4	d		19 02			19 32		19 40		20 02		20 32		20 40			21 02		21 32		21 40		22 02	
Maidstone West 4 208	a							20 00						21 00							22 00			
Marden	d		19 08			19 38				20 08		20 38					21 08		21 38				22 08	
Staplehurst	d		19 12			19 42				20 12		20 42					21 12		21 42				22 12	
Headcorn	d		19 18			19 48				20 18		20 48					21 18		21 48				22 18	
Pluckley	d					19 54						20 54							21 54					
Ashford International	a	19 14	19 30	19 50		20 03			20 14	20 30	20 50	21 03				21 14	21 30	21 50	22 03			22 14	22 30	22 50
	d	19 15	19 32	19 52		20 05			20 15	20 32	20 52	21 05				21 15	21 32	21 52	22 05			22 15	22 32	22 52
Wye	d		19 38							20 38							21 38						22 38	
Chilham	d		19 44							20 44							21 44						22 44	
Chartham	d		19 48							20 48							21 48						22 48	
Canterbury West 4	d		19 54	20 07						20 54	21 07						21 54	22 07					22 54	23 07
Sturry	d		19 58							20 58							21 58						22 58	
Westenhanger	d					20 13						21 13							22 13					
Sandling	d					20 16						21 16							22 16					
Folkestone West	d	19 28				20 21			20 28			21 21				21 28			22 21			22 28		
Folkestone Central	d	19 31				20 24			20 31			21 24				21 31			22 24			22 31		
Dover Priory 4	a	19 41				20 35			20 41			21 35				21 41			22 35			22 41		
	d	19 42							20 42							21 42						22 42		
Martin Mill	d	19 52							20 52							21 52						22 52		
Walmer	d	19 56							20 56							21 56						22 56		
Deal	d	20 01							21 01							22 01						23 01		
Sandwich	d	20 07							21 07							22 07						23 07		
Minster 4	d		20 09							21 09							22 09						23 09	
Ramsgate 4	a	20 19	20 15	20 26					21 19	21 15	21 26					22 19	22 15	22 26				23 19	23 15	23 26
Broadstairs	a	20 25		20 32					21 25		21 32							22 32						23 32
Margate 4	a	20 29		20 38			20 59		21 29		21 38		21 59					22 38		22 59				23 38

NRT DECEMBER 19 EDITION

Table T207-F

Sundays

15 December to 10 May

London and Tonbridge - Ashford International, Folkestone, Dover, Canterbury West, Ramsgate and Margate

		SE ◇1	SE ◇	SE	SE ◇	SE ◇1	SE ◇	SE ◇1	SE ◇	SE ◇1		SE ◇1
St Pancras Intl. 15 ⊖	d		22 25		22 37		23 12		23 37			
Stratford International ⊖	d		22 32		22 44		23 19		23 44			
Ebbsfleet International	d		22 43		22 55		23 30		23 55			
London Charing Cross 4 ⊖	d	21 40				22 10		22 40		23 10		23 40
London Waterloo (East) 4 ⊖	d	21 43				22 13		22 43		23 13		23 43
London Cannon Street 4 ⊖	d											
London Bridge 4 ⊖	d	21 49				22 19		22 49		23 19		23 49
Orpington 4	d	22 06				22 36		23 06		23 36		00 06
Sevenoaks 4	d	22 16				22 46		23 16		23 46		00 16
Hildenborough	d											
Tonbridge 4	a	22 24				22 54		23 24		23 54		00 24
	d	22 25		22 33		22 55		23 25		23 55		00 25
Paddock Wood 4	d	22 32		22 40		23 02		23 32		00 02		00 32
Maidstone West 4 208	a			23 00								
Marden	d	22 38				23 08		23 38		00 08		00 38
Staplehurst	d	22 42				23 12		23 42		00 12		00 42
Headcorn	d	22 48				23 18		23 48		00 18		00 48
Pluckley	d	22 54						23 54				00s54
Ashford International	a	23 03			23 14	23 30	23 50	00 03	00 15	00 30		01 04
	d	23 05			23 15	23 32	23 52	00 05				
Wye	d					23 38						
Chilham	d					23 44						
Chartham	d					23 48						
Canterbury West 4	d					23 54	00 07					
Sturry	d					23 58						
Westenhanger	d	23 13						00 13				
Sandling	d	23 16						00 16				
Folkestone West	d	23 21			23 28			00 21				
Folkestone Central	d	23 24			23 31			00 24				
Dover Priory 4	a	23 35			23 41			00 35				
	d				23 42							
Martin Mill	d				23 52							
Walmer	d				23 56							
Deal	d				00 01							
Sandwich	d				00 07							
Minster 4	d					00 09						
Ramsgate 4	a				00 19	00 15	00 26					
Broadstairs	a						00s32					
Margate 4	a		23 58				00 38					

Table T207-R

Mondays to Fridays

16 December to 15 May

Margate, Ramsgate, Canterbury West, Dover, Folkestone, Ashford International - Tonbridge and London

Miles	Miles	Miles	Miles	Miles			SE MX 1	SE	SE ◇1	SE ◇	SE ◇1	SE ◇	SE	SE ◇1	SE ◇	SE ◇	SE	SE ◇1	SE ◇1	SE ◇	SE ◇1	SE ◇1	SE ◇
0	0	—	—	—	Margate [4]	d														05 48			
3¼	3¼	—	—	—	Broadstairs	d														05 54			
5½	5½	—	—	—	Ramsgate [4]	d						04 55		04 51		05 12		05 38	05 20	06 00			
—	9½	0	—	—	Minster [4]	d						05 01						05 44					
13¾	—	4¾	—	—	Sandwich	d								05 06					05 34				05 54
18	—	—	—	—	Deal	d								05 12					05 40				06 00
19¾	—	—	—	—	Walmer	d								05 15					05 43				06 03
22¼	—	—	—	—	Martin Mill	d								05 20					05 48				06 08
27¼	—	—	—	—	Dover Priory [4]	a								05 29					05 57				06 17
—	—	—	—	—		d			04 27					05 30	05 45				05 59				06 18
34½	—	—	—	—	Folkestone Central	d			04 38					05 41	05 56				06 10				06 29
35¼	—	—	—	—	Folkestone West	d	00 02		04 40					05 43	05 58				06 12				06 31
39	—	—	—	—	Sandling	d	00 07		04 45					05 48					06 18				
40¼	—	—	—	—	Westenhanger	d	00 10		04 48					05 51					06 21				
—	18½	—	—	—	Sturry	d						05 13						05 56					
—	20¼	—	—	—	Canterbury West [4]	d						05 18						06 01		06 19			
—	24	—	—	—	Chartham	d						05 24						06 06					
—	26	—	—	—	Chilham	d						05 28						06 10					
—	30¼	—	—	—	Wye	d						05 34						06 17			←		
48½	35	—	0	—	Ashford International	a	00 20		04 57			05 41		06 01	06 11			06 23	06 30	06 34	06 30		06 44
—	—	—	—	—		d			04 59	05 13	05 29	05 43		06 02	06 13			06 25	06 37	06 36	06 37	06 45	06 46
54	—	—	—	—	Pluckley	d			05 05		05 36			06 09				06 32	→		06 44	06 52	
59¾	—	—	—	—	Headcorn	d			05 12		05 43			06 16				06 39			06 51	06 59	
62¾	—	—	—	—	Staplehurst	d			05 17		05 48			06 21				06 44			06 56	07 04	
65	—	—	—	—	Marden	d			05 22		05 52			06 25				06 48			07 00	07 08	
—	—	—	—	—	Maidstone West [4] 208	d		05 00					05 54				06 24						
69¾	—	—	—	—	Paddock Wood [4]	d		05a20	05 28		05 58		06a13	06 31			06a43	06 54			07 06	07 14	
75	—	—	—	—	Tonbridge [4]	a			05 35		06 05			06 38				07 02			07 15	07 23	
—	—	—	—	—		d			05 37		06 07			06 39				07 03			07 16	07 23	
77½	—	—	—	—	Hildenborough	a															07 20		
82¾	—	—	—	—	Sevenoaks [4]	a			05 49		06 16			06 48				07 11			07 27	07 31	
90¾	—	—	—	—	Orpington [4]	a			05 58		06 25												
102¾	—	—	—	0	London Bridge [4]	⊖ a			06 16		06 43			07 14				07 35			07 52	07 55	
—	—	—	—	0¾	London Cannon Street [4]	⊖ a			06 24												08 00		
103¾	—	—	—	—	London Waterloo (East) [4]	⊖ a					06 49			07 21				07 42				08 01	
104¾	—	—	—	—	London Charing Cross [4]	⊖ a					06 56			07 27				07 49				08 09	
—	—	—	33¾	—	Ebbsfleet International	a				05 32		06 02			06 32	06 42				06 55			07 05
—	—	—	50	—	Stratford International	⊖ a				05 44		06 14			06 44	06 55				07 07			07 17
—	—	—	56	—	St Pancras Intl. [15]	⊖ a				05 51		06 21			06 51	07 02				07 14			07 25

		SE ◇	SE	SE ◇1	SE ◇1	SE ◇	SE ◇	SE ◇1	SE ◇1	SE ◇	SE	SE ◇1	SE ◇	SE ◇1	SE ◇	SE ◇1	SE ◇1	SE ◇1	SE ◇	SE ◇	SE ◇	SE ◇1
Margate [4]	d					06 18							06 48						07 18		06 53	
Broadstairs	d					06 24							06 54						07 24		06 59	
Ramsgate [4]	d			06 10		06 30	06 14						07 00			06 55	06 50	07 12	07 30		07 08	07 19
Minster [4]	d			06 17					06 46									07 18				
Sandwich	d				06 05		06 26								06 50		07 02				07 20	
Deal	d				06 11		06 32								06 56		07 08				07 26	
Walmer	d				06 14										06 59		07 11				07 30	
Martin Mill	d				06 19										07 04		07 16				07 35	
Dover Priory [4]	a				06 28		06 47								07 12		07 24				07 43	
	d				06 30		06 48								07 13		07 25				07 44	
Folkestone Central	d				06 42		06 59					07 11			07 24		07 36				07 55	
Folkestone West	d				06 44		07 01					07 14			07 27		07 38				07 57	
Sandling	d				06 49							07 19					07 43					
Westenhanger	d				06 52							07 22					07 46					
Sturry	d			06 29					06 58									07 30				
Canterbury West [4]	d			06 34		06 49			07 03				07 19					07 36	07 49			
Chartham	d			06 39					07 08									07 41				
Chilham	d			06 42					07 12									07 44				
Wye	d			06 49					07 19									07 51				
Ashford International	a			06 55	07 01	07 04	07 14		07 25			07 31	07 34		07 40		07 55	07 58	08 04		08 11	
	d			06 57	07 03	07 06	07 16	07 19	07 27			07 36	07 36	07 43	07 44		08 03		08 06		08 16	
Pluckley	d			07 04	07 09			07 26				07 43		07 50			08 09					
Headcorn	d			07 11	07 16			07 33	07 38			07 50		07 57			08 16					
Staplehurst	d			07 16	07 22			07 38	07 43			07 55		08 02			08 21					
Marden	d			07 20	07 26			07 42	07 48			07 59		08 06			08 25					
Maidstone West [4] 208	d	06 52	07 00							07 25	07 36									07 53		
Paddock Wood [4]	d		07a19	07 26	07 33			07 48	07 54		07a56	08 05		08 12			08 31					
Tonbridge [4]	a			07 34	07 40			07 56	08 02			08 13		08 20			08 39					
	d			07 35	07 42			07 58	08 03			08 14		08 21			08 40					
Hildenborough	a			07 39								08 18										
Sevenoaks [4]	a			07 46	07 50			08 07	08 11			08 26		08 30			08 50					
Orpington [4]	a																					
London Bridge [4]	⊖ a			08 13	08 15			08 34	08 35			08 54		08 56		08 51	09 15					09 10
London Cannon Street [4]	⊖ a			08 21				08 42				09 02				08 59						09 18
London Waterloo (East) [4]	⊖ a				08 21				08 41					09 03			09 21					
London Charing Cross [4]	⊖ a				08 28				08 48					09 10			09 29					
Ebbsfleet International	a					07 25	07 35			07 56										08 25	08 35	
Stratford International	⊖ a	07 33				07 37	07 47			08 09			08 04		08 12				08 34	08 39	08 47	
St Pancras Intl. [15]	⊖ a	07 41				07 45	07 54			08 16			08 12		08 20				08 42	08 46	08 54	

Table T207-R

Mondays to Fridays

16 December to 15 May

Margate, Ramsgate, Canterbury West, Dover, Folkestone, Ashford International - Tonbridge and London

		SE ◇1	SE	SE ◇1	SE ◇	SE ◇1	SE ◇1	SE ◇	SE ◇1	SE	SE ◇1	SE ◇	SE ◇1	SE ◇1	SE ◇	SE ◇	SE ◇	SE ◇1	SE	SE ◇1	SE ◇	SE ◇1	SE ◇
Margate [4]	d				07 55							08 51				08 59					09 55		09 59
Broadstairs	d				08 01							08 57				09 05					10 01		10 05
Ramsgate [4]	d				08 07	07 42	08 14				07 58	09 03		09 08	09 36	09 12	09 20				10 07	10 19	10 12
Minster [4]	d	07 46				07 54	08 20				08 09			09 19								10 25	
Sandwich	d					08 02					08 22					09 25							10 25
Deal	d					08 08					08 28					09 31							10 31
Walmer	d					08 11					08 31					09 34							10 34
Martin Mill	d					08 16					08 36					09 39							10 39
Dover Priory [4]	a					08 24					08 45					09 47							10 47
	d			07 58		08 25		08 49			08 58		09 25			09 49				09 58			10 49
Folkestone Central	d			08 09		08 36		09 00			09 09		09 36			10 00				10 09			11 00
Folkestone West	d			08 11		08 38		09 02			09 11		09 38			10 02				10 11			11 02
Sandling	d			08 16		08 43					09 16		09 43							10 16			
Westenhanger	d			08 19		08 46					09 19		09 46							10 19			
Sturry	d	07 58					08 31							09 31								10 37	
Canterbury West [4]	d	08 04			08 26		08 36		09 05			09 23		09 36	09 55			10 05			10 26	10 42	
Chartham	d	08 09					08 41		09 10					09 41				10 10					
Chilham	d	08 12					08 44		09 13					09 44				10 13					
Wye	d	08 19					08 51		09 20					09 51				10 20				10 54	
Ashford International	a	08 26		08 28	08 41	08 55	08 58	09 15	09 27		09 28	09 38	09 55	09 58	10 10	10 15		10 27		10 28	10 41	11 00	11 15
	d			08 32	08 43	09 02		09 16			09 32	09 43	10 02		10 11	10 16				10 32	10 43	11 02	11 16
Pluckley	d			08 38		09 08					09 38		10 08							10 38		11 08	
Headcorn	d			08 45		09 15					09 45		10 15							10 45		11 15	
Staplehurst	d			08 50		09 20					09 50		10 20							10 50		11 20	
Marden	d			08 54		09 24					09 54		10 24							10 54		11 24	
Maidstone West [4] 208	d		08 16							09 28									10 28				
Paddock Wood [4]	d		08 35	09 00		09 30				09 47	10 00		10 30						10 47	11 00		11 30	
Tonbridge [4]	a		08 43	09 08		09 37				09 55	10 07		10 38						10 55	11 08		11 38	
	d			09 09		09 39					10 09		10 39							11 09		11 39	
Hildenborough	a																						
Sevenoaks [4]	a			09 18		09 48					10 18		10 48							11 18		11 48	
Orpington [4]	a																						
London Bridge [4]	⊖ a			09 41		10 11					10 41		11 11							11 41		12 11	
London Cannon Street [4]	⊖ a																						
London Waterloo (East) [4]	⊖ a			09 49		10 17					10 47		11 17							11 47		12 17	
London Charing Cross [4]	⊖ a			09 56		10 24					10 52		11 22							11 52		12 22	
Ebbsfleet International	a				09 02			09 35				10 02				10 35	10 46				11 02		11 35
Stratford International	⊖ a				09 14			09 47				10 14			10 39	10 47	10 58				11 14		11 47
St Pancras Intl. [15]	⊖ a				09 21			09 54				10 21			10 47	10 55	11 06				11 21		11 54

		SE ◇	SE ◇1	SE	SE ◇1	SE ◇	SE ◇1	SE ◇	SE ◇	SE ◇1	SE	SE ◇1	SE ◇	SE ◇1	SE ◇	SE ◇	SE ◇1	SE	SE ◇1	SE ◇	SE ◇1	SE ◇
Margate [4]	d					10 55		10 59					11 55		11 59					12 55		12 59
Broadstairs	d					11 01		11 05					12 01		12 05					13 01		13 05
Ramsgate [4]	d	10 20				11 07	11 19	11 12	11 20				12 07	12 19	12 12	12 20				13 07	13 19	13 12
Minster [4]	d						11 25							12 25							13 25	
Sandwich	d							11 25							12 25							13 25
Deal	d							11 31							12 31							13 31
Walmer	d							11 34							12 34							13 34
Martin Mill	d							11 39							12 39							13 39
Dover Priory [4]	a							11 47							12 47							13 47
	d				10 58			11 49				11 58			12 49				12 58			13 49
Folkestone Central	d				11 09			12 00				12 09			13 00				13 09			14 00
Folkestone West	d				11 11			12 02				12 11			13 02				13 11			14 02
Sandling	d				11 16							12 16							13 16			
Westenhanger	d				11 19							12 19							13 19			
Sturry	d						11 37							12 37							13 37	
Canterbury West [4]	d		11 05			11 26	11 42			12 05			12 26	12 42			13 05			13 26	13 42	
Chartham	d		11 10							12 10							13 10					
Chilham	d		11 13							12 13							13 13					
Wye	d		11 20				11 54			12 20				12 54			13 20				13 54	
Ashford International	a		11 27		11 28	11 41	12 00	12 15		12 27		12 28	12 41	13 00	13 15		13 27		13 28	13 41	14 00	14 15
	d				11 32	11 43	12 02	12 16				12 32	12 43	13 02	13 16				13 32	13 43	14 02	14 16
Pluckley	d				11 38		12 08					12 38		13 08					13 38		14 08	
Headcorn	d				11 45		12 15					12 45		13 15					13 45		14 15	
Staplehurst	d				11 50		12 20					12 50		13 20					13 50		14 20	
Marden	d				11 54		12 24					12 54		13 24					13 54		14 24	
Maidstone West [4] 208	d			11 28							12 28							13 28				
Paddock Wood [4]	d			11 47	12 00		12 30				12 47	13 00		13 30				13 47	14 00		14 30	
Tonbridge [4]	a			11 55	12 08		12 38				12 55	13 08		13 38				13 55	14 08		14 38	
	d				12 09		12 39					13 09		13 39					14 09		14 39	
Hildenborough	a																					
Sevenoaks [4]	a				12 18		12 48					13 18		13 48					14 18		14 48	
Orpington [4]	a																					
London Bridge [4]	⊖ a				12 41		13 11					13 41		14 11					14 41		15 11	
London Cannon Street [4]	⊖ a																					
London Waterloo (East) [4]	⊖ a				12 47		13 17					13 47		14 17					14 47		15 17	
London Charing Cross [4]	⊖ a				12 52		13 22					13 52		14 22					14 52		15 22	
Ebbsfleet International	a	11 46				12 02		12 35	12 46				13 02		13 35	13 46				14 02		14 35
Stratford International	⊖ a	11 58				12 14		12 47	12 58				13 14		13 47	14 02				14 14		14 47
St Pancras Intl. [15]	⊖ a	12 06				12 21		12 55	13 06				13 21		13 54	14 10				14 21		14 54

Table T207-R

Mondays to Fridays
16 December to 15 May

Margate, Ramsgate, Canterbury West, Dover, Folkestone, Ashford International - Tonbridge and London

		SE ◇	SE ◇[1]	SE	SE ◇[1]	SE ◇	SE ◇[1]	SE ◇	SE ◇	SE ◇[1]	SE	SE ◇[1]	SE ◇	SE ◇[1]	SE ◇	SE ◇	SE ◇[1]	SE	SE ◇[1]	SE ◇	SE	SE ◇[1]	SE ◇[1]
Margate [4]	d					13 55		13 59					14 55		14 59					15 55			
Broadstairs	d					14 01		14 05					15 01		15 05					16 01			
Ramsgate [4]	d	13 20				14 07	14 19	14 12	14 20				15 07	15 17	15 12	15 20			15 21	16 07		15 50	16 17
Minster [4]	d						14 25							15 24									16 24
Sandwich	d							14 25							15 25				15 35			16 02	
Deal	d							14 31							15 31				15 42			16 08	
Walmer	d							14 34							15 34				15 45			16 11	
Martin Mill	d							14 39							15 39				15 50			16 16	
Dover Priory [4]	a							14 47							15 47				15 58			16 24	
	d				13 58			14 49				14 58			15 49				15 59			16 25	
Folkestone Central	d				14 09			15 00				15 09			16 00				16 10			16 36	
Folkestone West	d				14 11			15 02				15 11			16 02				16 12			16 38	
Sandling	d				14 16							15 16							16 18			16 43	
Westenhanger	d				14 19							15 19							16 21			16 46	
Sturry	d						14 37							15 36									16 35
Canterbury West [4]	d		14 05			14 26	14 42			15 05			15 26	15 42			16 05			16 26			16 40
Chartham	d		14 10							15 10							16 10						
Chilham	d		14 13							15 13							16 13						
Wye	d		14 20				14 54			15 20				15 54			16 20						16 52
Ashford International	a		14 27		14 28	14 41	15 00	15 15		15 27		15 28	15 41	16 00	16 15		16 27		16 30	16 41		16 55	16 58
	d				14 32	14 43	15 02	15 19				15 32	15 43	16 02	16 16				16 32	16 45			17 02
Pluckley	d				14 38		15 08					15 38		16 08					16 38				17 08
Headcorn	d				14 45		15 15					15 45		16 15					16 45				17 15
Staplehurst	d				14 50		15 20					15 50		16 20					16 50				17 20
Marden	d				14 54		15 24					15 54		16 24					16 54				17 24
Maidstone West [4] 208	d			14 28							15 28							16 28			16 58		
Paddock Wood [4]	d			14 47	15 00		15 30				15 47	16 00		16 30				16a47	17 00		17a17		17 30
Tonbridge [4]	a			14 55	15 08		15 38				15 55	16 08		16 40					17 07				17 38
	d				15 09		15 39					16 09		16 41					17 09				17 39
Hildenborough	a																						17 43
Sevenoaks [4]	a				15 18		15 48					16 18		16 49					17 17				17 49
Orpington [4]	a													16 58									18 02
London Bridge [4] ⊖	a				15 41		16 11					16 41		17 16					17 42				18 19
London Cannon Street [4] ⊖	a																						
London Waterloo (East) [4] ⊖	a				15 47		16 17					16 48		17 24					17 48				18 26
London Charing Cross [4] ⊖	a				15 52		16 22					16 54		17 30					17 54				18 32
Ebbsfleet International	a	14 46				15 02		15 38	15 46				16 02		16 35	16 46				17 04			
Stratford International ⊖	a	14 58				15 14		15 50	16 02				16 14		16 47	17 02				17 16			
St Pancras Intl. [15] ⊖	a	15 06				15 21		15 58	16 10				16 21		16 54	17 10				17 23			

		SE ◇	SE ◇	SE ◇[1]	SE	SE ◇[1]	SE ◇	SE ◇[1]	SE ◇[1]	SE ◇	SE ◇	SE ◇[1]	SE	SE ◇[1]	SE ◇	SE ◇	SE	SE ◇[1]	SE ◇[1]	SE ◇	SE	SE ◇[1]	SE ◇
Margate [4]	d	16 02					16 55			17 02					17 55							18 08	18 53
Broadstairs	d	16 08					17 01			17 08					18 01							18 14	18 59
Ramsgate [4]	d	16 13	16 20				17 07	16 50	17 18	17 13	17 20				18 07			17 50	18 10			18 23	19 07
Minster [4]	d								17 24										18 20				
Sandwich	d	16 26						17 02		17 26								18 02				18 35	
Deal	d	16 32						17 08		17 32								18 08				18 41	
Walmer	d	16 35						17 11		17 35								18 11				18 44	
Martin Mill	d	16 39						17 16		17 39								18 16				18 49	
Dover Priory [4]	a	16 48						17 24		17 48								18 24				18 57	
	d	16 49				16 58		17 25		17 49				17 58				18 25		18 49		18 58	
Folkestone Central	d	17 00				17 09		17 36		18 00				18 09				18 36		19 00		19 09	
Folkestone West	d	17 02				17 11		17 38		18 02				18 11				18 38		19 02		19 11	
Sandling	d					17 16		17 43						18 16				18 43				19 16	
Westenhanger	d					17 19		17 46						18 19				18 46				19 19	
Sturry	d								17 35										18 31				
Canterbury West [4]	d			17 05			17 26		17 40			18 05			18 26				18 36				19 26
Chartham	d			17 10								18 10							18 41				
Chilham	d			17 13								18 13							18 44				
Wye	d			17 20					17 52			18 20							18 51				
Ashford International	a	17 15		17 28		17 28	17 41	17 55	17 58	18 15		18 27		18 28	18 41			18 55	18 58	19 15		19 28	19 41
	d	17 16				17 32	17 43		18 02	18 16				18 32	18 43				19 02	19 16		19 32	19 43
Pluckley	d					17 38			18 08					18 38					19 08			19 38	
Headcorn	d					17 45			18 15					18 45					19 15			19 45	
Staplehurst	d					17 50			18 20					18 50					19 20			19 50	
Marden	d					17 54			18 24					18 54					19 24			19 54	
Maidstone West [4] 208	d				17 28								18 19			18 42	18 48				19 18		
Paddock Wood [4]	d				17a47	18 00			18 30				18a38	19 00			19a07		19 30		19a37	20 00	
Tonbridge [4]	a					18 08			18 40					19 08					19 38			20 08	
	d					18 09			18 42					19 09					19 39			20 09	
Hildenborough	a																						
Sevenoaks [4]	a					18 18			18 50					19 18					19 48			20 18	
Orpington [4]	a																						
London Bridge [4] ⊖	a					18 42			19 13					19 41					20 11			20 41	
London Cannon Street [4] ⊖	a																						
London Waterloo (East) [4] ⊖	a					18 48			19 21					19 47					20 17			20 47	
London Charing Cross [4] ⊖	a					18 57			19 24					19 52					20 22			20 52	
Ebbsfleet International	a	17 35	17 46				18 02			18 35	18 49				19 02	19 12				19 35			20 02
Stratford International ⊖	a	17 47	18 03				18 14			18 47	19 01				19 14	19 24				19 47			20 14
St Pancras Intl. [15] ⊖	a	17 54	18 10				18 23			18 54	19 09				19 21	19 31				19 54			20 21

NRT DECEMBER 19 EDITION

Table T207-R

Mondays to Fridays
16 December to 15 May

Margate, Ramsgate, Canterbury West, Dover, Folkestone, Ashford International - Tonbridge and London

		SE	SE ◇[1]	SE ◇	SE ◇	SE ◇[1]	SE ◇	SE	SE ◇[1]	SE ◇	SE ◇	SE ◇[1]	SE ◇	SE	SE ◇[1]	SE ◇	SE ◇	SE ◇[1]	SE ◇[1]	SE ◇	SE	SE [1]
Margate [4]	d						19 53						20 53			21 00				21 55		
Broadstairs	d						19 59						20 59			21 06				22 01		
Ramsgate [4]	d		19 16		19 20	19 23	20 05		20 16		20 20	20 23	21 05		21 16	21 12	21 20			22 07		22 17
Minster [4]	d		19 22						20 22						21 22							22 24
Sandwich	d					19 35						20 35				21 25						
Deal	d					19 41						20 41				21 31						
Walmer	d					19 44						20 44				21 34						
Martin Mill	d					19 49						20 49				21 39						
Dover Priory [4]	a					19 57						20 57				21 47						
	d			19 49		19 58				20 49		20 58				21 49			21 58			
Folkestone Central	d			20 00		20 09				21 00		21 09				22 00			22 09			
Folkestone West	d			20 02		20 11				21 02		21 11				22 02			22 11			
Sandling	d					20 16						21 16							22 16			
Westenhanger	d					20 19						21 19							22 19			
Sturry	d		19 34						20 34						21 34							22 35
Canterbury West [4]	d		19 39				20 26		20 39				21 26		21 39			22 08		22 26		22 40
Chartham	d		19 44						20 44						21 44							22 45
Chilham	d		19 47						20 47						21 47							22 48
Wye	d		19 54						20 54						21 54							22 54
Ashford International	a		20 00	20 15		20 28	20 41		21 00	21 15		21 28	21 41		22 00	22 15		22 27	22 28	22 41		23 00
	d		20 02	20 16		20 32	20 43		21 02	21 16		21 32	21 43		22 02	22 16			22 32	22 43		23 02
Pluckley	d		20 08			20 38			21 08			21 38			22 08				22 38			23 08
Headcorn	d		20 15			20 45			21 15			21 45			22 15				22 45			23 15
Staplehurst	d		20 20			20 50			21 20			21 50			22 20				22 50			23 20
Marden	d		20 24			20 54			21 24			21 54			22 24				22 54			23 24
Maidstone West [4] 208	d	19 58						20 58						21 58							22 58	
Paddock Wood [4]	d	20 17	20 30			21 00		21 17	21 30			22 00		22 17	22 30				23 00		23 17	23 30
Tonbridge [4]	a	20 25	20 38			21 08		21 25	21 38			22 08		22 25	22 38				23 08		23 25	23 39
	d		20 39			21 09			21 39			22 09			22 39							
Hildenborough	a																					
Sevenoaks [4]	a		20 48			21 18			21 48			22 18			22 48							
Orpington [4]	a																					
London Bridge [4] ⊖	a		21 11			21 41			22 11			22 41			23 11							
London Cannon Street [4] ⊖	a																					
London Waterloo (East) [4] ⊖	a		21 17			21 47			22 17			22 47			23 17							
London Charing Cross [4] ⊖	a		21 22			21 52			22 22			22 52			23 22							
Ebbsfleet International	a			20 35	20 46		21 02			21 35	21 46		22 02			22 35	22 46			23 02		
Stratford International ⊖	a			20 47	20 59		21 14			21 47	21 59		22 14			22 47	22 58			23 14		
St Pancras Intl. [15] ⊖	a			20 54	21 06		21 21			21 54	22 07		22 21			22 54	23 06			23 21		

		SE ◇	SE	SE [1]
Margate [4]	d		22 55	
Broadstairs	d		23 01	
Ramsgate [4]	d	22 12	23 07	23 12
Minster [4]	d			
Sandwich	d	22 25		23 25
Deal	d	22 31		23 31
Walmer	d	22 34		23 34
Martin Mill	d	22 38		23 39
Dover Priory [4]	a	22 47		23 47
	d	22 49		23 49
Folkestone Central	d	23 00		23 59
Folkestone West	d	23 02		00 02
Sandling	d			00 07
Westenhanger	d			00 10
Sturry	d			
Canterbury West [4]	d		23 26	
Chartham	d			
Chilham	d			
Wye	d			
Ashford International	a	23 15	23 41	00 20
	d	23 16		
Pluckley	d			
Headcorn	d			
Staplehurst	d			
Marden	d			
Maidstone West [4] 208	d			
Paddock Wood [4]	d			
Tonbridge [4]	a			
	d			
Hildenborough	a			
Sevenoaks [4]	a			
Orpington [4]	a			
London Bridge [4] ⊖	a			
London Cannon Street [4] ⊖	a			
London Waterloo (East) [4] ⊖	a			
London Charing Cross [4] ⊖	a			
Ebbsfleet International	a	23 35		
Stratford International ⊖	a	23 47		
St Pancras Intl. [15] ⊖	a	23 54		

Table T207-R

Saturdays

21 December to 16 May

Margate, Ramsgate, Canterbury West, Dover, Folkestone, Ashford International - Tonbridge and London

		SE 1	SE ◇1	SE ◇	SE ◇1	SE ◇	SE	SE ◇1	SE ◇	SE ◇1		SE ◇	SE ◇	SE	SE ◇1	SE ◇	SE ◇1	SE ◇	SE ◇	SE ◇1		SE	SE ◇1	SE ◇	SE ◇1
Margate 4	d								05 53							06 53		06 57						07 55	
Broadstairs	d								05 59							06 59		07 03						08 01	
Ramsgate 4	d			05 05	05 15				06 05	06 15		06 12	06 20			07 05	07 15	07 12	07 20					08 07	08 17
Minster 4	d				05 21					06 21							07 21								08 23
Sandwich	d											06 25						07 25							
Deal	d											06 31						07 31							
Walmer	d											06 34						07 34							
Martin Mill	d											06 39						07 39							
Dover Priory 4	a											06 47						07 47							
	d		04 58			05 49		05 58				06 49			06 58			07 49					07 58		
Folkestone Central	d		05 09			06 00		06 09				07 00			07 09			08 00					08 09		
Folkestone West	d	00 02	05 11			06 02		06 11				07 02			07 11			08 02					08 11		
Sandling	d	00 07	05 16					06 16							07 16								08 16		
Westenhanger	d	00 10	05 19					06 19							07 19								08 19		
Sturry	d				05 32					06 32							07 32								08 35
Canterbury West 4	d			05 26	05 37				06 26	06 37						07 26	07 37			08 05				08 26	08 40
Chartham	d				05 42					06 42							07 42			08 10					
Chilham	d				05 45					06 45							07 45			08 13					
Wye	d				05 52					06 52							07 52			08 20					08 52
Ashford International	a	00 20	05 28	05 41	05 58	06 15		06 28	06 41	06 58		07 15			07 28	07 41	07 58	08 15		08 27			08 30	08 41	08 58
	d		05 32	05 43	06 02	06 16		06 32	06 43	07 02		07 16			07 32	07 43	08 02	08 16					08 32	08 43	09 02
Pluckley	d		05 38		06 08			06 38		07 08					07 38		08 08						08 38		09 08
Headcorn	d		05 45		06 15			06 45		07 15					07 45		08 15						08 45		09 15
Staplehurst	d		05 50		06 20			06 50		07 20					07 50		08 20						08 50		09 20
Marden	d		05 54		06 24			06 54		07 24					07 54		08 24						08 54		09 24
Maidstone West 4 208	d						06 28							07 28								08 28			
Paddock Wood 4	d		06 00		06 30		06 47	07 00		07 30				07 47	08 00		08 30					08 47	09 00		09 30
Tonbridge 4	a		06 08		06 38		06 55	07 08		07 38				07 55	08 08		08 38					08 55	09 08		09 38
	d		06 09		06 39			07 09		07 39					08 09		08 39						09 09		09 39
Hildenborough	a																								
Sevenoaks 4	a		06 18		06 48			07 18		07 48					08 18		08 48						09 18		09 48
Orpington 4	a																								
London Bridge 4 ⊖	a		06 41		07 11			07 41		08 11					08 41		09 11						09 41		10 11
London Cannon Street 4 ⊖	a																								
London Waterloo (East) 4 ⊖	a		06 47		07 17			07 47		08 17					08 47		09 17						09 47		10 17
London Charing Cross 4 ⊖	a		06 52		07 22			07 52		08 22					08 52		09 22						09 52		10 22
Ebbsfleet International	a			06 02		06 35			07 02			07 35	07 46			08 02		08 35	08 46					09 02	
Stratford International ⊖	a			06 14		06 47			07 14			07 47	07 58			08 14		08 47	08 58					09 14	
St Pancras Intl. 15 ⊖	a			06 21		06 54			07 21			07 54	08 06			08 21		08 54	09 06					09 21	

		SE ◇	SE ◇	SE ◇1	SE	SE ◇1		SE ◇	SE ◇1	SE ◇	SE ◇	SE ◇1	SE	SE ◇1	SE ◇	SE ◇1		SE ◇	SE ◇	SE ◇1	SE	SE ◇1	SE ◇	SE ◇1	SE ◇
Margate 4	d							08 55		08 59					09 55			09 59					10 55		10 59
Broadstairs	d							09 01		09 05					10 01			10 05					11 01		11 05
Ramsgate 4	d	08 12	08 20					09 07	09 17	09 12	09 20				10 07	10 19		10 12	10 20				11 07	11 19	11 12
Minster 4	d								09 23							10 25								11 25	
Sandwich	d	08 25								09 25								10 25							11 25
Deal	d	08 31								09 31								10 31							11 31
Walmer	d	08 34								09 34								10 34							11 34
Martin Mill	d	08 39								09 39								10 39							11 39
Dover Priory 4	a	08 47								09 47								10 47							11 47
	d	08 49				08 58				09 49				09 58				10 49				10 58			11 49
Folkestone Central	d	09 00				09 09				10 00				10 09				11 00				11 09			12 00
Folkestone West	d	09 02				09 11				10 02				10 11				11 02				11 11			12 02
Sandling	d					09 16								10 16								11 16			
Westenhanger	d					09 19								10 19								11 19			
Sturry	d								09 35							10 37								11 37	
Canterbury West 4	d			09 05				09 26	09 40			10 05			10 26	10 42				11 05			11 26	11 42	
Chartham	d			09 10								10 10								11 10					
Chilham	d			09 13								10 13								11 13					
Wye	d			09 20					09 52			10 20				10 54				11 20				11 54	
Ashford International	a	09 15		09 27		09 30		09 41	09 58	10 15		10 27		10 30	10 41	11 00		11 15		11 27		11 28	11 41	12 00	12 15
	d	09 16				09 32		09 43	10 02	10 19				10 32	10 43	11 02		11 19				11 32	11 43	12 02	12 16
Pluckley	d					09 38			10 08					10 38		11 08						11 38		12 08	
Headcorn	d					09 45			10 15					10 45		11 15						11 45		12 15	
Staplehurst	d					09 50			10 20					10 50		11 20						11 50		12 20	
Marden	d					09 54			10 24					10 54		11 24						11 54		12 24	
Maidstone West 4 208	d				09 28								10 28								11 28				
Paddock Wood 4	d				09 47	10 00			10 30				10 47	11 00		11 30					11 47	12 00		12 30	
Tonbridge 4	a				09 55	10 09			10 38				10 55	11 08		11 38					11 55	12 08		12 38	
	d					10 10			10 39					11 09		11 39						12 09		12 39	
Hildenborough	a																								
Sevenoaks 4	a					10 18			10 48					11 18		11 48						12 18		12 48	
Orpington 4	a																								
London Bridge 4 ⊖	a					10 41			11 11					11 41		12 11						12 41		13 11	
London Cannon Street 4 ⊖	a																								
London Waterloo (East) 4 ⊖	a					10 47			11 17					11 47		12 17						12 47		13 17	
London Charing Cross 4 ⊖	a					10 52			11 22					11 52		12 22						12 52		13 22	
Ebbsfleet International	a	09 35	09 46					10 02		10 38	10 46				11 02			11 38	11 46				12 02		12 35
Stratford International ⊖	a	09 47	10 02					10 14		10 50	10 58				11 14			11 50	11 58				12 14		12 47
St Pancras Intl. 15 ⊖	a	09 54	10 10					10 21		10 57	11 06				11 21			11 58	12 06				12 21		12 55

Table T207-R

Saturdays

21 December to 16 May

Margate, Ramsgate, Canterbury West, Dover, Folkestone, Ashford International - Tonbridge and London

		SE ◇		SE ◇1	SE	SE ◇1	SE ◇	SE ◇1	SE ◇	SE ◇	SE ◇1	SE		SE ◇1	SE ◇	SE ◇1	SE ◇	SE ◇	SE ◇1	SE	SE ◇1	SE ◇		SE ◇1	SE ◇
Margate 4	d						11 55		11 59						12 55		12 59					13 55			13 59
Broadstairs	d						12 01		12 05						13 01		13 05					14 01			14 05
Ramsgate 4	d	11 20					12 07	12 19	12 12	12 20					13 07	13 19	13 12	13 20				14 07		14 19	14 12
Minster 4	d							12 25								13 25								14 25	
Sandwich	d								12 25								13 25								14 25
Deal	d								12 31								13 31								14 31
Walmer	d								12 34								13 34								14 34
Martin Mill	d								12 39								13 39								14 39
Dover Priory 4	a								12 47								13 47								14 47
	d					11 58			12 49					12 58			13 49				13 58				14 49
Folkestone Central	d					12 09			13 00					13 09			14 00				14 09				15 00
Folkestone West	d					12 11			13 02					13 11			14 02				14 11				15 02
Sandling	d					12 16								13 16							14 16				
Westenhanger	d					12 19								13 19							14 19				
Sturry	d							12 37								13 37								14 37	
Canterbury West 4	d			12 05			12 26	12 42			13 05				13 26	13 42			14 05			14 26		14 42	
Chartham	d			12 10							13 10								14 10						
Chilham	d			12 13							13 13								14 13						
Wye	d			12 20				12 54			13 20					13 54			14 20					14 54	
Ashford International	a			12 27		12 29	12 41	13 00	13 15		13 27			13 28	13 41	14 00	14 15		14 27		14 28	14 41		15 00	15 15
	d					12 32	12 43	13 02	13 16					13 32	13 45	14 02	14 16				14 32	14 45		15 02	15 16
Pluckley	d					12 38		13 08						13 38		14 08					14 38			15 08	
Headcorn	d					12 45		13 15						13 45		14 15					14 45			15 15	
Staplehurst	d					12 50		13 20						13 50		14 20					14 50			15 20	
Marden	d					12 54		13 24						13 54		14 24					14 54			15 24	
Maidstone West 4 208	d				12 28							13 28								14 28					
Paddock Wood 4	d				12 47	13 00		13 30				13 47		14 00		14 30				14 47	15 00			15 30	
Tonbridge 4	a				12 55	13 08		13 38				13 55		14 08		14 38				14 55	15 08			15 38	
	d					13 09		13 39						14 09		14 39					15 09			15 39	
Hildenborough	a																								
Sevenoaks 4	a					13 18		13 48						14 18		14 48					15 18			15 48	
Orpington 4	a																								
London Bridge 4 ⊖	a					13 41		14 11						14 41		15 11					15 41			16 11	
London Cannon Street 4 ⊖	a																								
London Waterloo (East) 4 ⊖	a					13 47		14 17						14 47		15 17					15 47			16 17	
London Charing Cross 4 ⊖	a					13 52		14 22						14 52		15 22					15 52			16 22	
Ebbsfleet International	a	12 46					13 02		13 35	13 46					14 04		14 35	14 46				15 04			15 35
Stratford International ⊖	a	12 58					13 14		13 47	14 02					14 16		14 47	14 58				15 16			15 47
St Pancras Intl. 15 ⊖	a	13 06					13 21		13 54	14 10					14 23		14 54	15 06				15 23			15 54

		SE ◇	SE ◇1	SE	SE ◇1	SE ◇	SE ◇1	SE ◇		SE ◇	SE ◇1	SE	SE ◇1	SE ◇	SE ◇1	SE ◇	SE ◇	SE ◇1		SE	SE ◇1	SE ◇	SE ◇1	SE ◇	SE ◇
Margate 4	d					14 55		14 59						15 55		15 59						16 55		16 59	
Broadstairs	d					15 01		15 05						16 01		16 05						17 01		17 05	
Ramsgate 4	d	14 20				15 07	15 19	15 12		15 20				16 07	16 19	16 12	16 20					17 07	17 19	17 12	17 20
Minster 4	d						15 25								16 25								17 25		
Sandwich	d							15 25								16 25								17 25	
Deal	d							15 31								16 31								17 31	
Walmer	d							15 34								16 34								17 34	
Martin Mill	d							15 39								16 39								17 39	
Dover Priory 4	a							15 47								16 47								17 47	
	d				14 58			15 49					15 58			16 49					16 58			17 49	
Folkestone Central	d				15 09			16 00					16 09			17 00					17 09			18 00	
Folkestone West	d				15 11			16 02					16 11			17 02					17 11			18 02	
Sandling	d				15 16								16 16								17 16				
Westenhanger	d				15 19								16 19								17 19				
Sturry	d						15 37								16 37								17 37		
Canterbury West 4	d		15 05			15 26	15 42				16 05			16 26	16 42			17 05				17 26	17 42		
Chartham	d		15 10								16 10							17 10							
Chilham	d		15 13								16 13							17 13							
Wye	d		15 20				15 54				16 20				16 54			17 20					17 54		
Ashford International	a		15 27		15 28	15 41	16 00	16 15			16 27		16 28	16 41	17 00	17 15		17 27			17 28	17 41	18 00	18 15	
	d				15 32	15 46	16 02	16 16					16 32	16 43	17 02	17 19					17 32	17 43	18 02	18 19	
Pluckley	d				15 38		16 08						16 38		17 08						17 38		18 08		
Headcorn	d				15 45		16 15						16 45		17 15						17 45		18 15		
Staplehurst	d				15 50		16 20						16 50		17 20						17 50		18 20		
Marden	d				15 54		16 24						16 54		17 24						17 54		18 24		
Maidstone West 4 208	d			15 28								16 28								17 28					
Paddock Wood 4	d			15 47	16 00		16 30					16 47	17 00		17 30					17 47	18 00		18 30		
Tonbridge 4	a			15 55	16 08		16 38					16 55	17 08		17 38					17 55	18 08		18 38		
	d				16 09		16 39						17 09		17 39						18 09		18 39		
Hildenborough	a																								
Sevenoaks 4	a				16 18		16 48						17 18		17 48						18 18		18 48		
Orpington 4	a																								
London Bridge 4 ⊖	a				16 41		17 11						17 41		18 11						18 41		19 11		
London Cannon Street 4 ⊖	a																								
London Waterloo (East) 4 ⊖	a				16 47		17 17						17 47		18 17						18 47		19 17		
London Charing Cross 4 ⊖	a				16 52		17 22						17 52		18 22						18 52		19 22		
Ebbsfleet International	a	15 46				16 05		16 35		16 46				17 02		17 38	17 46					18 02		18 38	18 46
Stratford International ⊖	a	16 02				16 17		16 47		17 02				17 14		17 50	18 02					18 14		18 50	18 58
St Pancras Intl. 15 ⊖	a	16 10				16 24		16 54		17 10				17 21		17 58	18 10					18 21		18 58	19 06

Table T207-R

Saturdays

21 December to 16 May

Margate, Ramsgate, Canterbury West, Dover, Folkestone, Ashford International - Tonbridge and London

		SE ◇■	SE	SE ◇■	SE ◇	SE ◇■	SE ◇	SE ◇	SE ◇■	SE	SE ◇■	SE ◇	SE ◇■	SE ◇	SE ◇	SE ◇■	SE	SE ◇■	SE ◇	SE ◇■	SE ◇	SE ◇
Margate ■	d				17 55		17 59					18 55		18 59					19 55		19 59	
Broadstairs	d				18 01		18 05					19 01		19 05					20 01		20 05	
Ramsgate ■	d				18 07	18 19	18 12	18 20				19 07	19 19	19 14	19 20				20 07	20 19	20 12	20 20
Minster ■	d					18 25							19 25							20 25		
Sandwich	d						18 25							19 27							20 25	
Deal	d						18 31							19 33							20 31	
Walmer	d						18 34							19 36							20 34	
Martin Mill	d						18 39							19 40							20 39	
Dover Priory ■	a						18 47							19 48							20 47	
	d			17 58			18 49				18 58			19 49				19 58			20 49	
Folkestone Central	d			18 09			19 00				19 09			20 00				20 09			21 00	
Folkestone West	d			18 11			19 02				19 11			20 02				20 11			21 02	
Sandling	d			18 16							19 16							20 16				
Westenhanger	d			18 19							19 19							20 19				
Sturry	d					18 37							19 37							20 37		
Canterbury West ■	d	18 05			18 26	18 42			19 05			19 26	19 42			20 05			20 26	20 42		
Chartham	d	18 10							19 10							20 10						
Chilham	d	18 13							19 13							20 13						
Wye	d	18 20				18 54			19 20				19 54			20 20				20 54		
Ashford International	a	18 27		18 28	18 41	19 00	19 15		19 27		19 28	19 41	20 00	20 15		20 27		20 28	20 41	21 00	21 15	
	d			18 32	18 43	19 02	19 16				19 32	19 43	20 02	20 16				20 32	20 45	21 02	21 16	
Pluckley	d			18 38		19 08					19 38		20 08					20 38		21 08		
Headcorn	d			18 45		19 15					19 45		20 15					20 45		21 15		
Staplehurst	d			18 50		19 20					19 50		20 20					20 50		21 20		
Marden	d			18 54		19 24					19 54		20 24					20 54		21 24		
Maidstone West ■ 208	d		18 28							19 28							20 28					
Paddock Wood ■	d		18 47	19 00		19 30				19 47	20 00		20 30				20 47	21 00		21 30		
Tonbridge ■	a		18 55	19 08		19 38				19 55	20 08		20 38				20 55	21 08		21 38		
	d			19 09		19 39					20 09		20 39					21 09		21 39		
Hildenborough	a																					
Sevenoaks ■	a			19 18		19 48					20 18		20 48					21 18		21 48		
Orpington ■	a																					
London Bridge ■ ⊖	a			19 41		20 11					20 41		21 11					21 41		22 11		
London Cannon Street ■ ⊖	a																					
London Waterloo (East) ■ ⊖	a			19 47		20 17					20 47		21 17					21 47		22 17		
London Charing Cross ■ ⊖	a			19 52		20 22					20 52		21 22					21 52		22 22		
Ebbsfleet International	a				19 02		19 35	19 46				20 02		20 35	20 46				21 04		21 35	21 46
Stratford International ⊖	a				19 14		19 47	19 58				20 14		20 47	20 58				21 16		21 47	21 58
St Pancras Intl. ■ ⊖	a				19 21		19 54	20 06				20 21		20 54	21 06				21 23		21 54	22 06

		SE ◇■	SE	SE ◇■	SE ◇	SE ◇■	SE ◇	SE ◇	SE	SE ■	SE ◇	SE ■	SE ◇	SE	SE	SE ◇
Margate ■	d				20 55		20 59				21 55		21 59		22 55	22 59
Broadstairs	d				21 01		21 05				22 01		22 05		23 01	23 05
Ramsgate ■	d				21 07	21 16	21 12	21 20			22 07	22 16	22 12		23 07	23 12
Minster ■	d					21 22						22 22				
Sandwich	d						21 25						22 25			23 25
Deal	d						21 31						22 31			23 31
Walmer	d						21 34						22 34			23 34
Martin Mill	d						21 39						22 39			23 39
Dover Priory ■	a						21 47						22 47			23 47
	d			20 58			21 49			21 58			22 49	22 58		23 49
Folkestone Central	d			21 09			22 00			22 09			23 00	23 09		23 59
Folkestone West	d			21 11			22 02			22 11			23 02	23 11		00 02
Sandling	d			21 16						22 16				23 16		00 07
Westenhanger	d			21 19						22 19				23 19		00 10
Sturry	d					21 34						22 34				
Canterbury West ■	d	21 05			21 26	21 39					22 26	22 39			23 26	
Chartham	d	21 10				21 44						22 44				
Chilham	d	21 13				21 47						22 47				
Wye	d	21 20				21 54						22 54				
Ashford International	a	21 27		21 28	21 41	22 00	22 15			22 28	22 41	23 00	23 15	23 29	23 41	00 21
	d			21 32	21 43	22 02	22 16			22 32	22 43	23 02	23 16			
Pluckley	d			21 38		22 08				22 38		23 08				
Headcorn	d			21 45		22 15				22 45		23 15				
Staplehurst	d			21 50		22 20				22 50		23 20				
Marden	d			21 54		22 24				22 54		23 24				
Maidstone West ■ 208	d		21 28						22 28							
Paddock Wood ■	d		21 47	22 00		22 30			22 47	23 00		23 30				
Tonbridge ■	a		21 56	22 08		22 38			22 55	23 08		23 39				
	d			22 09		22 39										
Hildenborough	a															
Sevenoaks ■	a			22 18		22 48										
Orpington ■	a															
London Bridge ■ ⊖	a			22 41		23 11										
London Cannon Street ■ ⊖	a															
London Waterloo (East) ■ ⊖	a			22 47		23 17										
London Charing Cross ■ ⊖	a			22 52		23 22										
Ebbsfleet International	a				22 02		22 35	22 46			23 02		23 35			
Stratford International ⊖	a				22 14		22 47	22 58			23 14		23 47			
St Pancras Intl. ■ ⊖	a				22 21		22 54	23 06			23 21		23 54			

NRT DECEMBER 19 EDITION

Table T207-R

Sundays

15 December to 10 May

Margate, Ramsgate, Canterbury West, Dover, Folkestone, Ashford International - Tonbridge and London

		SE ◇ A	SE ◇■	SE	SE ◇■	SE ◇■	SE ◇	SE	SE ◇■	SE ◇	SE ◇■	SE ◇	SE	SE ◇■	SE ◇	SE ◇	SE ◇■	SE ◇■	SE ◇	SE	SE ◇■	SE ◇
Margate ■	d											07 55							08 55			
Broadstairs	d											08 01							09 01			
Ramsgate ■	d								07 16	07 12		08 07		08 16	08 12	08 20			09 07		09 20	09 12
Minster ■	d								07 22					08 22							09 26	
Sandwich	d									07 25					08 25							09 25
Deal	d									07 31					08 31							09 31
Walmer	d									07 34					08 34							09 34
Martin Mill	d									07 39					08 39							09 39
Dover Priory ■	a									07 47					08 47							09 47
	d									07 49	07 58				08 49			08 58				09 49
Folkestone Central	d									08 00	08 09				09 00			09 09				10 00
Folkestone West	d	00 02								08 02	08 11				09 02			09 11				10 02
Sandling	d	00 07									08 16							09 16				
Westenhanger	d	00 10									08 19							09 19				
Sturry	d								07 34					08 34							09 38	
Canterbury West ■	d								07 40			08 26		08 40			09 04		09 26		09 43	
Chartham	d								07 45					08 45			09 09					
Chilham	d								07 48					08 48			09 12					
Wye	d								07 55					08 55			09 19				09 55	
Ashford International	a	00 21							08 02	08 15	08 28	08 41		09 02	09 15		09 26	09 28	09 41		10 02	10 15
	d		06 32		07 04	07 32	07 43		08 04	08 16	08 32	08 43		09 04	09 16			09 32	09 43		10 04	10 16
Pluckley	d		06 38			07 38					08 38							09 38				
Headcorn	d		06 45		07 15	07 45			08 15		08 45			09 15				09 45			10 15	
Staplehurst	d		06 50		07 20	07 50			08 20		08 50			09 20				09 50			10 20	
Marden	d		06 54		07 24	07 54			08 24		08 54			09 24				09 54			10 24	
Maidstone West ■ 208	d			07 00				08 00					09 00							10 00		
Paddock Wood ■	d		07 00	07 19	07 30	08 00		08 19	08 30		09 00		09 19	09 30				10 00		10 19	10 30	
Tonbridge ■	a		07 07	07 27	07 37	08 07		08 27	08 37		09 07		09 27	09 37				10 07		10 27	10 37	
	d		07 09		07 39	08 09			08 39		09 09			09 39				10 09			10 39	
Hildenborough	a																					
Sevenoaks ■	a		07 18		07 48	08 18			08 48		09 18			09 48				10 18			10 48	
Orpington ■	a		07 27		07 57	08 27			08 57		09 27			09 57				10 27			10 57	
London Bridge ■ ⊖	a		07 43		08 13	08 43			09 13		09 43			10 13				10 43			11 13	
London Cannon Street ■ ⊖	a																					
London Waterloo (East) ■ ⊖	a		07 49		08 19	08 49			09 19		09 49			10 19				10 49			11 19	
London Charing Cross ■ ⊖	a		07 54		08 24	08 54			09 24		09 54			10 24				10 54			11 24	
Ebbsfleet International	a						08 02			08 35		09 02			09 35	09 46			10 02			10 35
Stratford International ⊖	a						08 14			08 47		09 14			09 47	10 02			10 14			10 47
St Pancras Intl. ■ ⊖	a						08 21			08 54		09 21			09 54	10 10			10 21			10 54

		SE ◇	SE ◇■	SE ◇■	SE ◇	SE	SE ◇■	SE ◇	and at the same minutes past each hour until	SE ◇	SE ◇■	SE ◇■	SE ◇	SE	SE ◇■	SE ◇	SE ◇	SE ◇■	SE ◇■	SE ◇	SE	SE ◇■	SE ◇
Margate ■	d				09 55			09 59					12 55			12 59				13 55			13 59
Broadstairs	d				10 01			10 05					13 01			13 05				14 01			14 05
Ramsgate ■	d	09 20			10 07		10 20	10 12		12 20			13 07		13 20	13 12	13 20			14 07		14 20	14 12
Minster ■	d						10 26								13 26							14 26	
Sandwich	d							10 25								13 25							14 25
Deal	d							10 31								13 31							14 31
Walmer	d							10 34								13 34							14 34
Martin Mill	d							10 39								13 39							14 39
Dover Priory ■	a							10 47								13 47							14 47
	d			09 58				10 49				12 58				13 49			13 58				14 49
Folkestone Central	d			10 09				11 00				13 09				14 00			14 09				15 00
Folkestone West	d			10 11				11 02				13 11				14 02			14 11				15 02
Sandling	d			10 16								13 16							14 16				
Westenhanger	d			10 19								13 19							14 19				
Sturry	d						10 38								13 38							14 38	
Canterbury West ■	d		10 04		10 26		10 43				13 04		13 26		13 43			14 04		14 26		14 43	
Chartham	d		10 09								13 09							14 09					
Chilham	d		10 12								13 12							14 12					
Wye	d		10 19				10 55				13 19				13 55			14 19				14 55	
Ashford International	a		10 26	10 28	10 41		11 02	11 15			13 26	13 28	13 41		14 02	14 15		14 26	14 28	14 41		15 02	15 15
	d			10 32	10 43		11 04	11 16				13 32	13 43		14 04	14 16			14 32	14 43		15 04	15 16
Pluckley	d			10 38								13 38							14 38				
Headcorn	d			10 45			11 15					13 45			14 15				14 45			15 15	
Staplehurst	d			10 50			11 20					13 50			14 20				14 50			15 20	
Marden	d			10 54			11 24					13 54			14 24				14 54			15 24	
Maidstone West ■ 208	d					11 00								14 00							15 00		
Paddock Wood ■	d			11 00		11 19	11 30					14 00		14 19	14 30				15 00		15 19	15 30	
Tonbridge ■	a			11 07		11 27	11 37					14 07		14 27	14 37				15 07		15 27	15 37	
	d			11 09			11 39					14 09			14 39				15 09			15 39	
Hildenborough	a																						
Sevenoaks ■	a			11 18			11 48					14 18			14 48				15 18			15 48	
Orpington ■	a			11 27			11 57					14 27			14 57				15 27			15 57	
London Bridge ■ ⊖	a			11 43			12 13					14 43			15 13				15 43			16 13	
London Cannon Street ■ ⊖	a																						
London Waterloo (East) ■ ⊖	a			11 49			12 19					14 49			15 19				15 49			16 19	
London Charing Cross ■ ⊖	a			11 54			12 24					14 54			15 24				15 54			16 24	
Ebbsfleet International	a	10 46			11 02			11 35		13 46			14 02			14 35	14 46			15 02			15 35
Stratford International ⊖	a	10 58			11 14			11 47		13 58			14 14			14 47	14 59			15 14			15 47
St Pancras Intl. ■ ⊖	a	11 06			11 21			11 54		14 06			14 21			14 54	15 07			15 21			15 54

A not 15 December

Table T207-R

Sundays
15 December to 10 May

Margate, Ramsgate, Canterbury West, Dover, Folkestone, Ashford International - Tonbridge and London

		SE	SE	SE	SE	SE	SE	SE	SE	SE	SE	SE	SE	SE	SE	SE	SE	SE	SE	SE	SE	SE
		◇	◇[1]	◇[1]	◇		◇[1]	◇	◇	◇[1]	◇[1]	◇		◇[1]	◇	◇	◇[1]	◇[1]	◇		◇[1]	◇
Margate [4]	d				14 55			14 59				15 55			15 59				16 55			16 59
Broadstairs	d				15 01			15 05				16 01			16 05				17 01			17 05
Ramsgate [4]	d	14 20			15 07		15 20	15 12	15 20			16 07		16 20	16 12	16 20			17 07		17 20	17 12
Minster [4]	d						15 26							16 26							17 26	
Sandwich	d							15 25							16 25							17 25
Deal	d							15 31							16 31							17 31
Walmer	d							15 34							16 34							17 34
Martin Mill	d							15 39							16 39							17 39
Dover Priory [4]	a							15 47							16 47							17 47
	d			14 58				15 49			15 58				16 49			16 58				17 49
Folkestone Central	d			15 09				16 00			16 09				17 00			17 09				18 00
Folkestone West	d			15 11				16 02			16 11				17 02			17 11				18 02
Sandling	d			15 16							16 16							17 16				
Westenhanger	d			15 19							16 19							17 19				
Sturry	d						15 38							16 38							17 38	
Canterbury West [4]	d		15 04		15 26		15 43			16 04		16 26		16 43			17 04		17 26		17 43	
Chartham	d		15 09							16 09							17 09					
Chilham	d		15 12							16 12							17 12					
Wye	d		15 19				15 55			16 19				16 55			17 19				17 55	
Ashford International	a		15 26	15 28	15 41		16 02	16 15		16 26	16 28	16 41		17 02	17 15		17 26	17 28	17 41		18 02	18 15
	d			15 32	15 43		16 04	16 16			16 32	16 43		17 04	17 16			17 32	17 43		18 04	18 16
Pluckley	d			15 38							16 38							17 38				
Headcorn	d			15 45			16 15				16 45			17 15				17 45			18 15	
Staplehurst	d			15 50			16 20				16 50			17 20				17 50			18 20	
Marden	d			15 54			16 24				16 54			17 24				17 54			18 24	
Maidstone West [4] 208	d					16 00							17 00							18 00		
Paddock Wood [4]	d			16 00		16 19	16 30				17 00		17 19	17 30				18 00		18 19	18 30	
Tonbridge [4]	a			16 07		16 27	16 37				17 07		17 27	17 37				18 07		18 27	18 37	
	d			16 09			16 39				17 09			17 39				18 09			18 39	
Hildenborough	a																					
Sevenoaks [4]	a			16 18			16 48				17 18			17 48				18 18			18 48	
Orpington [4]	a			16 27			16 57				17 27			17 57				18 27			18 57	
London Bridge [4] ⊖	a			16 43			17 13				17 43			18 13				18 43			19 13	
London Cannon Street [4] ⊖	a																					
London Waterloo (East) [4] ⊖	a			16 49			17 19				17 49			18 19				18 49			19 19	
London Charing Cross [4] ⊖	a			16 54			17 24				17 54			18 24				18 54			19 24	
Ebbsfleet International	a	15 46			16 02			16 35	16 46			17 02			17 35	17 46			18 02			18 35
Stratford International ⊖	a	16 02			16 14			16 47	17 02			17 14			17 47	18 02			18 14			18 47
St Pancras Intl. [15] ⊖	a	16 10			16 21			16 54	17 10			17 21			17 54	18 10			18 21			18 54

		SE	SE	SE	SE	SE	SE	SE	SE	SE	SE	SE	SE	SE	SE	SE	SE	SE	SE	SE	SE	SE	SE
		◇	◇[1]	◇[1]	◇		◇[1]	◇	◇	◇[1]	◇[1]	◇		◇[1]	◇	◇	◇[1]	◇		◇[1]	◇	◇	◇[1]
Margate [4]	d				17 55			17 59				18 55			18 59			19 55			19 59		
Broadstairs	d				18 01			18 05				19 01			19 05			20 01			20 05		
Ramsgate [4]	d	17 20			18 07		18 20	18 12	18 20			19 07		19 16	19 12	19 20		20 07		20 16	20 12	20 20	
Minster [4]	d						18 26							19 22						20 22			
Sandwich	d							18 25							19 25						20 25		
Deal	d							18 31							19 31						20 31		
Walmer	d							18 34							19 34						20 34		
Martin Mill	d							18 39							19 39						20 39		
Dover Priory [4]	a							18 47							19 47						20 47		
	d			17 58				18 49			18 58				19 49		19 58				20 49		20 58
Folkestone Central	d			18 09				19 00			19 09				20 00		20 09				21 00		21 09
Folkestone West	d			18 11				19 02			19 11				20 02		20 11				21 02		21 11
Sandling	d			18 16							19 16						20 16						21 16
Westenhanger	d			18 19							19 19						20 19						21 19
Sturry	d						18 38							19 34						20 34			
Canterbury West [4]	d		18 04		18 26		18 43			19 04		19 26		19 40				20 26		20 40			
Chartham	d		18 09							19 09				19 45						20 45			
Chilham	d		18 12							19 12				19 48						20 48			
Wye	d		18 19				18 55			19 19				19 55						20 55			
Ashford International	a		18 26	18 28	18 41		19 02	19 15		19 26	19 28	19 41		20 02	20 15		20 28	20 41		21 02	21 15		21 28
	d			18 32	18 43		19 04	19 16			19 32	19 43		20 04	20 16		20 32	20 43		21 04	21 16		21 32
Pluckley	d			18 38							19 38						20 38						21 38
Headcorn	d			18 45			19 15				19 45			20 15			20 45			21 15			21 45
Staplehurst	d			18 50			19 20				19 50			20 20			20 50			21 20			21 50
Marden	d			18 54			19 24				19 54			20 24			20 54			21 24			21 54
Maidstone West [4] 208	d					19 00							20 00						21 00				
Paddock Wood [4]	d			19 00		19 19	19 30				20 00		20 19	20 30			21 00		21 19	21 30			22 00
Tonbridge [4]	a			19 07		19 27	19 37				20 07		20 27	20 37			21 07		21 27	21 37			22 07
	d			19 09			19 39				20 09			20 39			21 09			21 39			22 09
Hildenborough	a																						
Sevenoaks [4]	a			19 18			19 48				20 18			20 48			21 18			21 48			22 18
Orpington [4]	a			19 27			19 57				20 27			20 57			21 27			21 57			22 27
London Bridge [4] ⊖	a			19 43			20 13				20 43			21 13			21 43			22 13			22 43
London Cannon Street [4] ⊖	a																						
London Waterloo (East) [4] ⊖	a			19 49			20 19				20 49			21 19			21 49			22 19			22 49
London Charing Cross [4] ⊖	a			19 54			20 24				20 54			21 24			21 54			22 24			22 54
Ebbsfleet International	a	18 46			19 02			19 35	19 46			20 02			20 35	20 46		21 02			21 35	21 46	
Stratford International ⊖	a	18 59			19 14			19 47	19 58			20 14			20 47	20 58		21 14			21 47	21 59	
St Pancras Intl. [15] ⊖	a	19 07			19 21			19 54	20 06			20 21			20 54	21 06		21 21			21 54	22 07	

Table T207-R

Sundays
15 December to 10 May

Margate, Ramsgate, Canterbury West, Dover, Folkestone, Ashford International - Tonbridge and London

		SE	SE	SE	SE	SE	SE	SE	SE	SE	SE	SE
		◇		◇[1]	◇	◇	[1]	◇		[1]	◇	
Margate [4]	d	20 55			20 59			21 55			21 59	22 55
Broadstairs	d	21 01			21 05			22 01			22 05	23 01
Ramsgate [4]	d	21 07		21 16	21 12	21 20		22 07		22 16	22 12	23 07
Minster [4]	d			21 22						22 22		
Sandwich	d				21 25						22 25	
Deal	d				21 31						22 31	
Walmer	d				21 34						22 34	
Martin Mill	d				21 39						22 39	
Dover Priory [4]	a				21 47						22 47	
	d				21 49		21 58				22 49	
Folkestone Central	d				22 00		22 09				23 00	
Folkestone West	d				22 02		22 11				23 02	
Sandling	d						22 16					
Westenhanger	d						22 19					
Sturry	d			21 34						22 34		
Canterbury West [4]	d	21 26		21 40				22 26		22 40		23 26
Chartham	d			21 45						22 45		
Chilham	d			21 48						22 48		
Wye	d			21 55						22 55		
Ashford International	a	21 41		22 02	22 15		22 28	22 41		23 02	23 15	23 41
	d	21 43		22 04	22 16			22 43		23 04		
Pluckley	d									23 10		
Headcorn	d			22 15						23 17		
Staplehurst	d			22 20						23 22		
Marden	d			22 24						23 26		
Maidstone West [4] 208	d		22 00						23 00			
Paddock Wood [4]	d		22 19	22 30					23 19	23 32		
Tonbridge [4]	a		22 27	22 37					23 27	23 40		
	d			22 39								
Hildenborough	a											
Sevenoaks [4]	a			22 48								
Orpington [4]	a			22 57								
London Bridge [4] ⊖	a			23 13								
London Cannon Street [4] ⊖	a											
London Waterloo (East) [4] ⊖	a			23 19								
London Charing Cross [4] ⊖	a			23 24								
Ebbsfleet International	a	22 02			22 35	22 46		23 02				
Stratford International ⊖	a	22 14			22 47	22 58		23 14				
St Pancras Intl. [15] ⊖	a	22 21			22 54	23 06		23 21				

Table T208-F

Mondays to Fridays
16 December to 15 May

Strood - Maidstone West and Paddock Wood

Miles			SE	SE	SE	SE	SE	SE	SE	SE	SE		SE	SE	SE	SE	SE	SE	SE	SE	SE	SE	SE
							◇												◇		◇		◇
0	St Pancras International	d					06 25											17 12		17 46		18 16
5¼	Stratford International	d					06 32											17 19		17 53		18 23
22	Ebbsfleet International	d					06 43											17 31		18 05		18 35
25	Gravesend	d					06 48											17 35		18 09		18 39
33	**Strood [4]**	d	04 35	05 25	06 00	06 35	07 02	07 10	07 52	08 34	09 04	and at the same minutes past each hour until	14 34	15 04	15 34	16 04	16 34	17 04	17 46	17 55	18 20	18 24	18 51
35¼	Cuxton	d	04 39	05 29	06 04	06 39		07 14	07 56	08 38	09 08		14 38	15 08	15 38	16 08	16 38	17 08		17 59		18 28	
37	Halling	d	04 43	05 33	06 08	06 43		07 18	08 00	08 42	09 12		14 42	15 12	15 42	16 12	16 42	17 12		18 03		18 32	
38½	Snodland	d	04 46	05 36	06 11	06 46		07 21	08 03	08 45	09 15		14 45	15 15	15 45	16 15	16 45	17 15	17 54	18 06	18 28	18 35	18 59
39¾	New Hythe	d	04 48	05 38	06 13	06 48		07 23	08 05	08 47	09 17		14 47	15 17	15 47	16 17	16 47	17 17		18 08		18 37	
40¾	Aylesford	d	04 51	05 41	06 16	06 51		07 26	08 08	08 50	09 20		14 50	15 20	15 50	16 20	16 50	17 20		18 11		18 40	
43¾	Maidstone Barracks	d	04 56	05 46	06 21	06 56		07 31	08 13	08 55	09 25		14 55	15 25	15 55	16 25	16 55	17 25		18 16		18 45	
44¼	**Maidstone West [4]** 207	a	04 58	05 48	06 23	06 58	07 16	07 33	08 15	08 57	09 27		14 57	15 27	15 57	16 27	16 57	17 27	18 04	18 18	18 38	18 47	19 09
—		d	05 00	05 54	06 24	07 00		07 36	08 16		09 28			15 28		16 28	16 58	17 28		18 19		18 48	
46	East Farleigh	d	05 03	05 57	06 27	07 03		07 39	08 19		09 31			15 31		16 31	17 01	17 31		18 22		18 51	
49	Wateringbury	d	05 08	06 02	06 32	07 08		07 44	08 24		09 36			15 36		16 36	17 06	17 36		18 27		18 56	
50¾	Yalding	d	05 12	06 06	06 36	07 12		07 48	08 28		09 40			15 40		16 40	17 10	17 40		18 31		19 00	
52¼	Beltring	d	05 15	06 09	06 39	07 15		07 51	08 31		09 43			15 43		16 43	17 13	17 43		18 34		19 03	
54¼	**Paddock Wood [4]**	a	05 20	06 13	06 43	07 19		07 56	08 35		09 47			15 47		16 47	17 17	17 47		18 38		19 07	
59½	Tonbridge [4]	a							08 43		09 55			15 55									

		SE	SE	SE	SE	SE	SE	SE	SE
St Pancras International	d								
Stratford International	d								
Ebbsfleet International	d								
Gravesend	d								
Strood [4]	d	18 54	19 34	20 04	20 34	21 04	21 34	22 04	22 34
Cuxton	d	18 58	19 38	20 08	20 38	21 08	21 38	22 08	22 38
Halling	d	19 02	19 42	20 12	20 42	21 12	21 42	22 12	22 42
Snodland	d	19 05	19 45	20 15	20 45	21 15	21 45	22 15	22 45
New Hythe	d	19 07	19 47	20 17	20 47	21 17	21 47	22 17	22 47
Aylesford	d	19 10	19 50	20 20	20 50	21 20	21 50	22 20	22 50
Maidstone Barracks	d	19 15	19 55	20 25	20 55	21 25	21 55	22 25	22 55
Maidstone West [4] 207	a	19 17	19 57	20 29	20 57	21 27	21 57	22 27	22 57
	d	19 18	19 58		20 58		21 58		22 58
East Farleigh	d	19 21	20 01		21 01		22 01		23 01
Wateringbury	d	19 26	20 06		21 06		22 06		23 06
Yalding	d	19 30	20 10		21 10		22 10		23 10
Beltring	d	19 33	20 13		21 13		22 13		23 13
Paddock Wood [4]	a	19 37	20 17		21 17		22 17		23 17
Tonbridge [4]	a		20 25		21 25		22 25		23 25

Saturdays
21 December to 16 May

		SE	SE		SE	SE	SE	SE	SE	SE
St Pancras International	d									
Stratford International	d									
Ebbsfleet International	d									
Gravesend	d									
Strood [4]	d	06 04	06 34	and at the same minutes past each hour until	20 04	20 34	21 04	21 34	22 04	22 34
Cuxton	d	06 08	06 38		20 08	20 38	21 08	21 38	22 08	22 38
Halling	d	06 12	06 42		20 12	20 42	21 12	21 42	22 12	22 42
Snodland	d	06 15	06 45		20 15	20 45	21 15	21 45	22 15	22 45
New Hythe	d	06 17	06 47		20 17	20 47	21 17	21 47	22 17	22 47
Aylesford	d	06 20	06 50		20 20	20 50	21 20	21 50	22 20	22 50
Maidstone Barracks	d	06 25	06 55		20 25	20 55	21 25	21 55	22 25	22 55
Maidstone West [4] 207	a	06 27	06 57		20 27	20 57	21 27	21 57	22 27	22 57
	d	06 28			20 28		21 28		22 28	
East Farleigh	d	06 31			20 31		21 31		22 31	
Wateringbury	d	06 36			20 36		21 36		22 36	
Yalding	d	06 40			20 40		21 40		22 40	
Beltring	d	06 43			20 43		21 43		22 43	
Paddock Wood [4]	a	06 47			20 47		21 47		22 47	
Tonbridge [4]	a	06 55			20 55		21 56		22 55	

Sundays
15 December to 10 May

		SE		SE
St Pancras International	d			
Stratford International	d			
Ebbsfleet International	d			
Gravesend	d			
Strood [4]	d	06 35	and hourly until	22 35
Cuxton	d	06 39		22 39
Halling	d	06 43		22 43
Snodland	d	06 46		22 46
New Hythe	d	06 48		22 48
Aylesford	d	06 51		22 51
Maidstone Barracks	d	06 56		22 56
Maidstone West [4] 207	a	06 58		22 58
	d	07 00		23 00
East Farleigh	d	07 03		23 03
Wateringbury	d	07 08		23 08
Yalding	d	07 12		23 12
Beltring	d	07 15		23 15
Paddock Wood [4]	a	07 19		23 19
Tonbridge [4]	a	07 27		23 27

Table T208-R

Mondays to Fridays
16 December to 15 May

Paddock Wood and Maidstone West - Strood

Miles			SE	SE	SE	SE	SE	SE	SE	SE	SE	SE	SE	SE	SE		SE	SE	SE	SE	SE	SE
						◇		◇	◇													◇
0	Tonbridge [4]	d	05 06										09 05		10 04			16 04				
5¼	**Paddock Wood [4]**	d	05 13	05 28	06 18		06 48			07 41	08 11		09 12		10 11	and at the same minutes past each hour until		16 11	17 04	17 34	17 52	
7	Beltring	d		05 32	06 22		06 52			07 45	08 15		09 16		10 15			16 15	17 08	17 38	17 56	
8¾	Yalding	d		05 36	06 26		06 56			07 49	08 19		09 19		10 18			16 18	17 12	17 42	18 00	
10¾	Wateringbury	d		05 39	06 29		06 59			07 52	08 22		09 23		10 22			16 22	17 15	17 45	18 03	
13½	East Farleigh	d		05 44	06 34		07 04			07 57	08 27		09 28		10 27			16 27	17 20	17 50	18 08	
15¼	**Maidstone West [4]** 207	a	05 28	05 49	06 39		07 09			08 02	08 32		09 32		10 31			16 31	17 25	17 55	18 15	
—		d	05 29	05 50	06 40	06 52	07 10	07 25	07 53	08 03	08 33	09 03	09 33	10 03	10 33		16 03	16 33	17 26	17 56	18 16	18 42
15½	Maidstone Barracks	d	05 31	05 52	06 42		07 12			08 05	08 35	09 05	09 35	10 05	10 35		16 05	16 35	17 28	17 58	18 18	
18¼	Aylesford	d	05 36	05 57	06 47		07 17			08 10	08 40	09 10	09 40	10 10	10 40		16 10	16 40	17 33	18 03	18 23	
19½	New Hythe	d	05 39	05 59	06 49		07 19			08 12	08 42	09 12	09 43	10 12	10 42		16 12	16 42	17 35	18 05	18 25	
21	Snodland	d	05 42	06 02	06 52	07 00	07 22	07 33	08 01	08 15	08 45	09 15	09 46	10 15	10 45		16 15	16 45	17 38	18 08	18 28	
22½	Halling	d	05 45	06 05	06 55		07 25			08 18	08 48	09 18	09 49	10 18	10 48		16 18	16 48	17 41	18 11	18 31	
24¼	Cuxton	d	05 49	06 09	06 59		07 29			08 22	08 52	09 22	09 52	10 22	10 52		16 22	16 52	17 45	18 15	18 35	
26½	**Strood [4]**	a	05 54	06 13	07 03	07 08	07 33	07 42	08 10	08 26	08 56	09 26	09 57	10 26	10 56		16 26	16 56	17 49	18 19	18 39	18 57
34½	Gravesend	d				07 19		07 53	08 21													19 08
37½	Ebbsfleet International	d						07 57	08 26													19 13
54¼	Stratford International	d				07 34		08 09	08 39													19 24
59½	St Pancras International	a				07 41		08 16	08 46													19 31

		SE	SE	SE	SE	SE	SE	SE	SE	SE
Tonbridge [4]	d					20 34		21 34		22 34
Paddock Wood [4]	d	18 43	19 13	19 42		20 41		21 41		22 41
Beltring	d	18 47	19 17	19 46		20 45		21 45		22 45
Yalding	d	18 51	19 21	19 50		20 48		21 48		22 48
Wateringbury	d	18 54	19 24	19 53		20 52		21 52		22 52
East Farleigh	d	18 59	19 29	19 58		20 57		21 57		22 57
Maidstone West [4] 207	a	19 04	19 34	20 03		21 01		22 01		23 01
	d	19 05	19 35	20 04	20 33	21 03	21 33	22 03	22 33	23 03
Maidstone Barracks	d	19 07	19 37	20 06	20 35	21 05	21 35	22 05	22 35	23 05
Aylesford	d	19 12	19 42	20 11	20 40	21 10	21 40	22 10	22 40	23 10
New Hythe	d	19 14	19 44	20 13	20 42	21 12	21 42	22 12	22 42	23 12
Snodland	d	19 17	19 47	20 16	20 45	21 15	21 45	22 15	22 45	23 15
Halling	d	19 20	19 50	20 19	20 48	21 18	21 48	22 18	22 48	23 18
Cuxton	d	19 24	19 54	20 23	20 52	21 22	21 52	22 22	22 52	23 22
Strood [4]	a	19 29	19 58	20 27	20 56	21 26	21 56	22 26	22 56	23 26
Gravesend	d									
Ebbsfleet International	d									
Stratford International	d									
St Pancras International	a									

Saturdays
21 December to 16 May

		SE	SE		SE	SE
Tonbridge [4]	d	06 04		and at the same minutes past each hour until	22 04	
Paddock Wood [4]	d	06 11			22 11	
Beltring	d	06 15			22 15	
Yalding	d	06 18			22 18	
Wateringbury	d	06 22			22 22	
East Farleigh	d	06 27			22 27	
Maidstone West [4] 207	a	06 31			22 31	
	d	06 33	07 03		22 33	23 03
Maidstone Barracks	d	06 35	07 05		22 35	23 05
Aylesford	d	06 40	07 10		22 40	23 10
New Hythe	d	06 42	07 12		22 42	23 12
Snodland	d	06 45	07 15		22 45	23 15
Halling	d	06 48	07 18		22 48	23 18
Cuxton	d	06 52	07 22		22 52	23 22
Strood [4]	a	06 56	07 26		22 56	23 26
Gravesend	d					
Ebbsfleet International	d					
Stratford International	d					
St Pancras International	a					

Sundays
15 December to 10 May

		SE		SE
Tonbridge [4]	d	06 33	and hourly until	22 33
Paddock Wood [4]	d	06 40		22 40
Beltring	d	06 44		22 44
Yalding	d	06 47		22 47
Wateringbury	d	06 51		22 51
East Farleigh	d	06 56		22 56
Maidstone West [4] 207	a	07 00		23 00
	d	07 01		23 01
Maidstone Barracks	d	07 03		23 03
Aylesford	d	07 08		23 08
New Hythe	d	07 11		23 11
Snodland	d	07 14		23 14
Halling	d	07 17		23 17
Cuxton	d	07 20		23 20
Strood [4]	a	07 25		23 25
Gravesend	d			
Ebbsfleet International	d			
Stratford International	d			
St Pancras International	a			

Table T212-F

London - Medway, Sheerness-on-Sea, Dover and Ramsgate

Mondays to Fridays

16 December to 15 May

Miles	Miles	Miles	Miles	Miles	Station		SE MO ◇ A	SE TTh FO ◇ A	SE WO B (bus)	SE TTh FO ◇1 C	SE MO ◇1 C	SE WO B (bus)	SE WO B (bus)	SE WO B (bus)	SE WO ◇1 C	SE TTh FO ◇1 C	SE MX ◇ A	SE MO ◇ A	SE WO (bus)	SE MO ◇1 C	SE MX	SE WO (bus)	SE MO ◇1 C	SE MX ◇ A
—	—	—	—	0	**St Pancras Intl.** [15] ⊖	d																		
—	—	—	—	6	Stratford International ⊖	d																		00 02
—	—	—	—	22¾	Ebbsfleet International	d																		00 13
—	—	—	—	—	**London Blackfriars** [3] ⊖	d																		
—	—	—	—	—	Elephant & Castle ⊖	d																		
0	0	—	—	—	**London Victoria** [15] ⊖	d																		
11	11	—	—	—	Bromley South [4]	d																		
14¾	14¾	—	—	—	St Mary Cray	d																	00 02	
17½	17½	—	—	—	Swanley [4]	d																	00 07	
20½	20½	—	—	—	Farningham Road	d																	00s12	
23½	23½	—	—	—	Longfield	d																	00s16	
26	26	—	—	—	Meopham	d																	00s20	
27	27	—	—	—	Sole Street	d																	00s23	
—	—	—	0	—	**London Charing Cross** [4] ⊖	d																		
—	—	—	0¾	—	**London Waterloo (East)** [4] ⊖	d																		
—	—	—	—	—	**London Cannon Street** [4] ⊖	d																		
—	—	—	1¾	—	**London Bridge** [4] ⊖	d																		
—	—	—	18¾	—	Dartford [4]	d																		
—	—	—	21½	—	Greenhithe for Bluewater	d																		
—	—	—	25½	24¾	Gravesend [4]	d																		00 18
—	—	—	32¾	32	Strood [4]	d																		00 29
33¾	33¾	—	33¾	33	Rochester [4]	d											00 02	00 02		00 08			00 32	00 32
34¼	34¼	—	34¾	33½	**Chatham** [4]	d											00 06	00 06		00 11			00 35	00 36
36	36	—	36	35¼	**Gillingham (Kent)** [4]	d									00 01	00 01	00 10	00 10		00a17			00 40	00 40
39	39	—	—	38¼	Rainham (Kent)	d									00 06	00 06	00 15	00 15					00 45	00 45
41½	41½	—	—	40¾	Newington	d									00 10	00 10							00s49	
44¾	44¾	0	—	44	**Sittingbourne** [4]	a									00 15	00 15	00 22	00 22					00 54	00 52
—	—	—	—	—		d									00 15	00 15	00 23	00 23			00 26		00 54	00 53
—	—	2	—	—	Kemsley	d															00s30			
—	—	4	—	—	Swale	d															00s34			
—	—	6	—	—	Queenborough	d															00s38			
—	—	8	—	—	**Sheerness-on-Sea**	a															00 44			
47½	47½	—	—	46¾	Teynham	d									00 20	00 20							00s59	
52	52	—	—	51¾	**Faversham** [2]	a									00 26	00 26	00 31	00 32					01 06	01 03
—	—	—	—	—		d									00 28	00 36			00 37			00 38		
—	55¼	—	—	—	Selling	d																		
—	61¾	—	—	—	**Canterbury East** [4]	d																		
—	64¾	—	—	—	Bekesbourne	d																		
—	67¾	—	—	—	Adisham	d																		
—	68¾	—	—	—	Aylesham	d																		
—	69¾	—	—	—	Snowdown	d																		
—	71¾	—	—	—	Shepherds Well	d																		
—	75	—	—	—	Kearsney	d																		
—	77¼	—	—	—	**Dover Priory** [4]	a																		
59	—	—	—	—	Whitstable	d				00 02	00 03			00 19		00 44						00 58		
60½	—	—	—	—	Chestfield & Swalecliffe	d				00 05	00 06		00 06	00 27		00 47						01 06		
62¾	—	—	—	—	**Herne Bay**	d				00 09	00 09		00 14	00 35		00 51						01 14		
70¾	—	—	—	—	Birchington-on-Sea	d				00 18	00 18		00 34	00 55		01 00						01 34		
72½	—	—	—	—	Westgate-on-Sea	d				00 21	00 22		00 39	01 00		01 04						01 39		
73¾	—	—	—	—	**Margate** [4]	d		00 04	00 22	00 25	00 26	00 43	00 45	01 06		01 08			01 22			01 45		
77	—	—	—	—	Broadstairs	d	00 05	00 10	00 32	00 31	00 32	00 53	00 55	01 16		01 14			01 32			01 55		
78¼	—	—	—	—	Dumpton Park	d		00 13	00 37	00 34	00 35	00 58	01 00	01 21		01 17			01 37			02 00		
79¼	—	—	—	—	**Ramsgate** [4]	a	00 11	00 16	00 43	00 38	00 39	01 04	01 06	01 27	01 35	01 21			01 43			02 06		

A From St Pancras International
B From Faversham
C From London Victoria

For further services between St Pancras International, London Blackfriars and Elephant & Castle and Bromley South, St Mary Cray and Swanley refer to table T52

Table T212-F

London - Medway, Sheerness-on-Sea, Dover and Ramsgate

Mondays to Fridays

16 December to 15 May

Station		SE MX 1 A	SE TTh FO ◇1	SE WO ◇1	SE WO (bus)	SE MX ◇ B	SE WO (bus)	SE	SE	SE 1	SE ◇ C	SE	SE ◇ C	SE ◇ D	SE ◇ B	SE ◇ C	SE ◇ C	SE 1	SE	SE ◇1	SE	SE ◇ C
St Pancras Intl. [15] ⊖	d					00 12								06 25	06 40							
Stratford International ⊖	d					00 19								06 32	06 47							
Ebbsfleet International	d					00a30								06 43	06a58							
London Blackfriars [3] ⊖	d																					
Elephant & Castle ⊖	d																					
London Victoria [15] ⊖	d		00 10	00 10																05 12		
Bromley South [4]	d	00 07	00s31	00s31																05 35		
St Mary Cray	d	00 12																		05 40		
Swanley [4]	d	00 17																		05 45		
Farningham Road	d	00 22																		05 50		
Longfield	d	00 26																		05 54		
Meopham	d	00 30																		05 58		
Sole Street	d	00s33																		06 01		
London Charing Cross [4] ⊖	d																					
London Waterloo (East) [4] ⊖	d																					
London Cannon Street [4] ⊖	d																					
London Bridge [4] ⊖	d																					
Dartford [4]	d																					
Greenhithe for Bluewater	d																					
Gravesend [4]	d													06 48								
Strood [4]	d													06a58								
Rochester [4]	d	00 42	00 54	00 54																06 10		
Chatham [4]	d	00 45	00 58	00 58																06 13		
Gillingham (Kent) [4]	d	00a49	01 02	01 02				04 56										05 50		06 20		
Rainham (Kent)	d		01 07	01 07				05 01										05 55		06 25		
Newington	d		01s11	01s11				05 05										05 59		06 29		
Sittingbourne [4]	a		01 16	01 16														06 03		06 33		
	d		01 16	01 16					05 22			05 56						06 04	06 22	06 34	07 00	
Kemsley	d							05 12	05 27			06 02							06 32		07 08	
Swale	d							05 16	05 30			06 07							06 36		07 12	
Queenborough	d							05 20	05 38			06 12							06 42		07 16	
Sheerness-on-Sea	a							05 26	05 43			06 17							06 47		07 21	
Teynham	d		01s21	01s21														06 08		06 38		
Faversham [2]	a		01 26	01 26														06 14		06 44		
	d		01 27	01 27	01 35		01 36			05 26							06 21	06 26		06 48		
Selling	d									05 30								06 30		06 52		
Canterbury East [4]	d									05 40								06 40		07 02		
Bekesbourne	d									05 44								06 44		07 06		
Adisham	d									05 48								06 48		07 10		
Aylesham	d									05 51								06 51		07 13		
Snowdown	d									05 54								06 54		07 16		
Shepherds Well	d									05 58								06 58		07 20		
Kearsney	d									06 02								07 02		07 24		
Dover Priory [4]	a									06 08								07 08		07 30		
Whitstable	d		01s35				01s56										06 30					
Chestfield & Swalecliffe	d		01s38				02s04										06 33					
Herne Bay	d		01s42				02s12										06 37					
Birchington-on-Sea	d		01s51				02s32										06 45					
Westgate-on-Sea	d		01s55				02a37										06 49					
Margate [4]	d		01s58		02s20						05 48		06 18			06 48	06 53					07 18
Broadstairs	d		02s04		02s30						05 54		06 24			06 54	06 59					07 24
Dumpton Park	d		02s08		02s35												07 02					
Ramsgate [4]	a		02 15	02 33	02 41						05 59		06 29			06 59	07 06					07 29

A From London Victoria
B To Ashford International
C To St Pancras International
D To Maidstone West

For further services between St Pancras International, London Blackfriars and Elephant & Castle and Bromley South, St Mary Cray and Swanley refer to table T52

Table T212-F

Mondays to Fridays
16 December to 15 May

London - Medway, Sheerness-on-Sea, Dover and Ramsgate

Station		SE 1	SE ◇1	SE	SE ◇ A	SE 1	SE ◇1		SE	SE 1	SE ◇	SE ◇1	SE ◇ A	SE ◇ A	SE	SE ◇1	SE ◇1		SE	SE ◇1	SE ◇	SE ◇1	SE ◇ A	SE ◇ A	SE
St Pancras Intl. ⊖	d										06 55			07 22							08 04			08 25	
Stratford International ⊖	d										07 02			07 29							08 11			08 32	
Ebbsfleet International	d										07 15			07 40							08 23			08 43	
London Blackfriars ⊖	d																								
Elephant & Castle ⊖	d																								
London Victoria ⊖	d		05 42				06 12					06 40				07 10	07 40			07 42		08 10			
Bromley South	d		06 05				06 36					06 58				07 33	07 59			08 05		08 28			
St Mary Cray	d		06 10				06 41					07 04				07 39				08 10					
Swanley	d		06 15				06 46					07 08				07 43				08 15					
Farningham Road	d		06 20				06 51					07 13				07 48				08 20					
Longfield	d		06 24				06 55					07 17				07 53	08 11			08 24		08 40			
Meopham	d		06 28				06 59					07 21				07 57	08 15			08 28		08 44			
Sole Street	d		06 31				07 02					07 24				07 59				08 31					
London Charing Cross ⊖	d																								
London Waterloo (East) ⊖	d																								
London Cannon Street ⊖	d																								
London Bridge ⊖	d																								
Dartford	d																								
Greenhithe for Bluewater	d																								
Gravesend	d										07 20			07 44							08 29			08 48	
Strood	d										07 31			07 56							08 40			08 59	
Rochester	d		06 40				07 11				07 34	07 38		07 59		08 08	08 25			08 40	08 44	08 54		09 02	
Chatham	d		06 43				07 14				07 38	07 42		08 02		08 12	08 29			08 43	08 47	08 58		09 06	
Gillingham (Kent)	d		06 50				07 20				07 43	07 50		08 07		08a18	08 33			08 48	08 53	09 02		09 10	
Rainham (Kent)	d		06 55				07 25				07 47	07 55		08 11			08 38			08 53	08 58	09 07		09 15	
Newington	d		06 59				07 29					07 59					08 42					09 11			
Sittingbourne	a		07 05				07 33				07 54	08 03		08 18			08 47			09 00	09 05	09 16		09 22	
	d		07 06	07 15			07 34		07 55		07 55	08 04		08 19	08 25		08 47		08 55	09 01	09 05	09 16		09 23	09 25
Kemsley	d			07 20					08 00						08 30				09 00						09 30
Swale	d			07 23					08 03						08 33				09 03						09 33
Queenborough	d			07 32					08 08						08 38				09 08						09 38
Sheerness-on-Sea	a			07 37					08 13						08 43				09 13						09 43
Teynham	d		07 10				07 38					08 08					08 52					09 21			
Faversham	a		07 16				07 44				08 03	08 14		08 27			08 57			09 09	09 14	09 26		09 31	
	d	06 52	07 18			07 23	07 48			07 52		08 18		08 27			08 59			09 10		09 27		09 31	
Selling	d		07 22				07 52					08 22										09 31			
Canterbury East	d		07 32				08 03					08 33								09 22		09 40			
Bekesbourne	d		07 36				08 07					08 37										09 45			
Adisham	d		07 40				08 11					08 41										09 49			
Aylesham	d		07 43				08 14					08 44										09 52			
Snowdown	d		07 46				08 17					08 47										09 54			
Shepherds Well	d		07 50				08 21					08 51								09 32		09 58			
Kearsney	d		07 54				08 25					08 55								09 37		10 03			
Dover Priory	a		08 02				08 33					09 00								09 42		10 08			
Whitstable	d	07 01				07 32				08 01				08 35			09 07							09 40	
Chestfield & Swalecliffe	d	07 04				07 35				08 04				08 38			09 10								
Herne Bay	d	07 08				07 39				08 08				08 42			09 14							09 45	
Birchington-on-Sea	d	07 16				07 47				08 16				08 51			09 23							09 54	
Westgate-on-Sea	d	07 20				07 51				08 20				08 55			09 27								
Margate	d	07 24			07 55	07 59				08 24			08 51	08 59			09 31						09 55	09 59	
Broadstairs	d	07 30			08 01	08 05				08 30			08 57	09 05			09 37						10 01	10 05	
Dumpton Park	d	07 33				08 08				08 33				09 08			09 40								
Ramsgate	a	07 36			08 06	08 11				08 37			09 02	09 11			09 45						10 06	10 11	

A To St Pancras International

For further services between St Pancras International, London Blackfriars and Elephant & Castle and Bromley South, St Mary Cray and Swanley refer to table T52

NRT DECEMBER 19 EDITION

Table T212-F

Mondays to Fridays
16 December to 15 May

London - Medway, Sheerness-on-Sea, Dover and Ramsgate

Station		SE ◇1	SE ◇		SE	SE ◇1	SE ◇1	SE ◇ A	SE ◇ A	SE	SE ◇1	SE ◇	SE		SE ◇1	SE ◇1	SE ◇ A	SE ◇ A	SE	SE ◇1	SE ◇	SE	SE ◇1		SE ◇1
St Pancras Intl. ⊖	d		08 57						09 25			09 55						10 27			10 52				
Stratford International ⊖	d		09 04						09 32			10 02						10 34			10 59				
Ebbsfleet International	d		09 15						09 44			10 13						10 45			11 13				
London Blackfriars ⊖	d																								
Elephant & Castle ⊖	d																								
London Victoria ⊖	d	08 40				08 42	09 10				09 40				09 42	10 10				10 40			10 42		11 10
Bromley South	d	08 58				09 05	09 27				09 57				10 05	10 27				10 57			11 05		11 27
St Mary Cray	d					09 10									10 10								11 10		
Swanley	d					09 15									10 15								11 15		
Farningham Road	d					09 20									10 20								11 20		
Longfield	d	09 10				09 24	09 39				10 09				10 24	10 39				11 09			11 24		11 39
Meopham	d	09 14				09 28	09 43				10 13				10 28	10 43				11 13			11 28		11 43
Sole Street	d					09 31									10 31								11 31		
London Charing Cross ⊖	d																								
London Waterloo (East) ⊖	d																								
London Cannon Street ⊖	d																								
London Bridge ⊖	d																								
Dartford	d																								
Greenhithe for Bluewater	d																								
Gravesend	d		09 19						09 48			10 18						10 49			11 18				
Strood	d		09 30						09 59			10 29						10 59			11 29				
Rochester	d	09 24	09 33			09 40	09 53		10 02		10 23	10 32			10 40	10 53		11 02		11 23	11 32		11 40		11 53
Chatham	d	09 27	09 37			09 43	09 57		10 06		10 27	10 36			10 43	10 57		11 06		11 27	11 36		11 43		11 57
Gillingham (Kent)	d	09 32	09 41			09 48	10 01		10 10		10 31	10 40			10 48	11 01		11 10		11 31	11 40		11 48		12 01
Rainham (Kent)	d	09 37	09 46			09 53	10 06		10 15		10 36	10 45			10 53	11 06		11 15		11 36	11 45		11 53		12 06
Newington	d						10 10									11 10									12 10
Sittingbourne	a	09 44	09 53			10 00	10 15		10 22		10 43	10 52			11 00	11 15		11 22		11 43	11 52		12 00		12 15
	d	09 44	09 54		09 55	10 01	10 15		10 23	10 25	10 44	10 54	10 55		11 01	11 15		11 23	11 25	11 44	11 54	11 55	12 01		12 15
Kemsley	d				10 00					10 30			11 00						11 30			12 00			
Swale	d				10 03					10 33			11 03						11 33			12 03			
Queenborough	d				10 08					10 38			11 08						11 38			12 08			
Sheerness-on-Sea	a				10 13					10 43			11 13						11 43			12 13			
Teynham	d						10 20									11 20									12 20
Faversham	a	09 52	10 05			10 09	10 25		10 31		10 52	11 05			11 09	11 25		11 31		11 52	12 05		12 09		12 25
	d	09 53				10 10	10 26		10 31		10 53				11 10	11 26		11 31		11 53			12 10		12 26
Selling	d						10 31									11 31									12 31
Canterbury East	d					10 22	10 40								11 22	11 40							12 22		12 40
Bekesbourne	d						10 45									11 45									12 45
Adisham	d						10 49									11 49									12 49
Aylesham	d						10 52									11 52									12 52
Snowdown	d						10 54									11 54									12 54
Shepherds Well	d						10 58									11 58									12 58
Kearsney	d						11 03									12 03									13 03
Dover Priory	a					10 39	11 08								11 39	12 08							12 39		13 08
Whitstable	d	10 02							10 40		11 02							11 40		12 02					
Chestfield & Swalecliffe	d	10 05									11 05									12 05					
Herne Bay	d	10 09							10 45		11 09							11 45		12 09					
Birchington-on-Sea	d	10 18							10 54		11 18							11 54		12 18					
Westgate-on-Sea	d	10 21									11 21									12 21					
Margate	d	10 25						10 55	10 59		11 25						11 55	11 59		12 25					
Broadstairs	d	10 31						11 01	11 05		11 31						12 01	12 05		12 31					
Dumpton Park	d	10 34									11 34									12 34					
Ramsgate	a	10 38						11 06	11 11		11 38						12 06	12 11		12 38					

A To St Pancras International

For further services between St Pancras International, London Blackfriars and Elephant & Castle and Bromley South, St Mary Cray and Swanley refer to table T52

Table T212-F

Mondays to Fridays
16 December to 15 May

London - Medway, Sheerness-on-Sea, Dover and Ramsgate

		SE	SE	SE	SE	SE	SE	SE	SE	SE	SE	SE	SE	SE	SE	SE	SE	SE	SE	SE	SE	SE	SE
		◇	◇		◇ 1	◇		◇ 1	◇ 1	◇	◇		◇ 1	◇		◇ 1	◇ 1	◇	◇		◇ 1	◇	
		A	A							A	A							A	A				
St Pancras Intl. 15 ⊖	d		11 25			11 55					12 27			12 52					13 25			13 55	
Stratford International ⊖	d		11 32			12 02					12 34			12 59					13 32			14 02	
Ebbsfleet International	d		11 43			12 13					12 45			13 13					13 43			14 13	
London Blackfriars 3 ⊖	d																						
Elephant & Castle ⊖	d																						
London Victoria 15 ⊖	d				11 40			11 42	12 10				12 40			12 42	13 10				13 40		
Bromley South 4	d				11 57			12 05	12 27				12 57			13 05	13 27				13 57		
St Mary Cray	d							12 10								13 10							
Swanley 4	d							12 15								13 15							
Farningham Road	d							12 20								13 20							
Longfield	d				12 09			12 24	12 39				13 09			13 24	13 39				14 09		
Meopham	d				12 13			12 28	12 43				13 13			13 28	13 43				14 13		
Sole Street	d							12 31								13 31							
London Charing Cross 4 ⊖	d																						
London Waterloo (East) 4 ⊖	d																						
London Cannon Street 4 ⊖	d																						
London Bridge 4 ⊖	d																						
Dartford 4	d																						
Greenhithe for Bluewater	d																						
Gravesend 4	d		11 48			12 18					12 49			13 18					13 48			14 18	
Strood 4	d		11 59			12 29					12 59			13 29					13 59			14 29	
Rochester 4	d		12 02		12 23	12 32		12 40	12 53		13 02		13 23	13 32		13 40	13 53		14 02		14 23	14 32	
Chatham 4	d		12 06		12 27	12 36		12 43	12 57		13 06		13 27	13 36		13 43	13 57		14 06		14 27	14 36	
Gillingham (Kent) 4	d		12 10		12 31	12 40		12 48	13 01		13 10		13 31	13 40		13 48	14 01		14 10		14 31	14 40	
Rainham (Kent)	d		12 15		12 36	12 45		12 53	13 06		13 15		13 36	13 45		13 53	14 06		14 15		14 36	14 45	
Newington	d								13 10								14 10						
Sittingbourne 4	a		12 22		12 43	12 52		13 00	13 15		13 22		13 43	13 52		14 00	14 15		14 22		14 43	14 52	
	d		12 23	12 25	12 44	12 54	12 55	13 01	13 15		13 23	13 25	13 44	13 54	13 55	14 01	14 15		14 23	14 25	14 44	14 54	14 55
Kemsley	d			12 30			13 00					13 30			14 00					14 30			15 00
Swale	d			12 33			13 03					13 33			14 03					14 33			15 03
Queenborough	d			12 38			13 08					13 38			14 08					14 38			15 08
Sheerness-on-Sea	a			12 43			13 13					13 43			14 13					14 43			15 13
Teynham	d								13 20								14 20						
Faversham 2	a		12 31		12 52	13 05		13 09	13 25		13 31		13 52	14 05		14 09	14 25		14 31		14 52	15 05	
	d		12 31		12 53			13 10	13 26		13 31		13 53			14 10	14 26		14 31		14 53		
Selling	d								13 31								14 31						
Canterbury East 4	d							13 22	13 40							14 22	14 40						
Bekesbourne	d								13 45								14 45						
Adisham	d								13 49								14 49						
Aylesham	d								13 52								14 52						
Snowdown	d								13 54								14 54						
Shepherds Well	d								13 58								14 58						
Kearsney	d								14 03								15 03						
Dover Priory 4	a							13 39	14 08							14 39	15 08						
Whitstable	d		12 40		13 02						13 40		14 02						14 40		15 02		
Chestfield & Swalecliffe	d				13 05								14 05								15 05		
Herne Bay	d		12 45		13 09						13 45		14 09						14 45		15 09		
Birchington-on-Sea	d		12 54		13 18						13 54		14 18						14 54		15 18		
Westgate-on-Sea	d				13 21								14 21								15 21		
Margate 4	d	12 55	12 59		13 25					13 55	13 59		14 25					14 55	14 59		15 25		
Broadstairs	d	13 01	13 05		13 31					14 01	14 05		14 31					15 01	15 05		15 31		
Dumpton Park	d				13 34								14 34								15 34		
Ramsgate 4	a	13 06	13 11		13 38					14 06	14 11		14 38					15 06	15 11		15 38		

A To St Pancras International

For further services between St Pancras International, London Blackfriars and Elephant & Castle and Bromley South, St Mary Cray and Swanley refer to table T52

Table T212-F

Mondays to Fridays
16 December to 15 May

London - Medway, Sheerness-on-Sea, Dover and Ramsgate

		SE	SE	SE	SE	SE	SE		SE	SE	SE	SE	SE	SE	SE	SE		SE	SE	SE	SE	SE	
		◇ 1	◇ 1	◇	◇		◇ 1		◇		◇ 1	◇ 1	◇	◇		◇ 1		◇		◇ 1	◇	◇ 1	
				A	A								A	A							A		
St Pancras Intl. 15 ⊖	d				14 25				14 55					15 25				15 55					
Stratford International ⊖	d				14 32				15 02					15 32				16 02					
Ebbsfleet International	d				14 43				15 13					15 43				16 13					
London Blackfriars 3 ⊖	d																						
Elephant & Castle ⊖	d																						
London Victoria 15 ⊖	d	13 42	14 10				14 40				14 42	15 10				15 40				15 42		16 10	
Bromley South 4	d	14 05	14 27				14 57				15 05	15 27				15 57				16 05		16 27	
St Mary Cray	d	14 10									15 10									16 10			
Swanley 4	d	14 15									15 15									16 15			
Farningham Road	d	14 20									15 20									16 20			
Longfield	d	14 24	14 39				15 09				15 24	15 39				16 09				16 24		16 39	
Meopham	d	14 28	14 43				15 13				15 28	15 43				16 13				16 28		16 43	
Sole Street	d	14 31									15 31									16 31			
London Charing Cross 4 ⊖	d																						
London Waterloo (East) 4 ⊖	d																						
London Cannon Street 4 ⊖	d																						
London Bridge 4 ⊖	d																						
Dartford 4	d																						
Greenhithe for Bluewater	d																						
Gravesend 4	d				14 48				15 18					15 48				16 18					
Strood 4	d				14 59				15 29					15 59				16 29					
Rochester 4	d	14 40	14 53		15 02		15 23		15 32		15 40	15 53		16 02		16 23		16 32		16 40		16 53	
Chatham 4	d	14 43	14 57		15 05		15 27		15 36		15 43	15 57		16 05		16 27		16 36		16 43		16 57	
Gillingham (Kent) 4	d	14 48	15 01		15 10		15 31		15 40		15a48	16 01		16 10		16 31		16 40		16a50		17 02	
Rainham (Kent)	d	14 53	15 06		15 14		15 36		15 45			16 06		16 14		16 36		16 45				17 07	
Newington	d		15 10									16 10				16 40						17 11	
Sittingbourne 4	a	15 00	15 15		15 21		15 43		15 52			16 15		16 21		16 45		16 52				17 15	
	d	15 01	15 15		15 22	15 25	15 44		15 54	15 55		16 15		16 22	16 25	16 45		16 53	16 55			17 16	
Kemsley	d					15 30				16 00					16 30				17 00				
Swale	d					15 33				16 03					16 33				17 03				
Queenborough	d					15 38				16 08					16 38				17 08				
Sheerness-on-Sea	a					15 43				16 13					16 43				17 13				
Teynham	d		15 20									16 20				16 50						17 20	
Faversham 2	a	15 09	15 25		15 30		15 52		16 05			16 25		16 30		16 56		17 01				17 26	
	d	15 10	15 26		15 30		15 56	15 58				16 30		16 30		17 00	17 02					17 30	17 36
Selling	d		15 31					16 02				16 34					17 06					17 34	
Canterbury East 4	d	15 22	15 40					16 12				16 43					17 16					17 43	
Bekesbourne	d		15 45					16 16				16 48					17 20					17 48	
Adisham	d		15 49					16 20				16 52					17 24					17 52	
Aylesham	d		15 52					16 23				16 54					17 27					17 54	
Snowdown	d		15 54					16 26				16 57					17 30					17 57	
Shepherds Well	d		15 58					16 30				17 01					17 34					18 01	
Kearsney	d		16 03					16 34				17 05					17 38					18 05	
Dover Priory 4	a	15 39	16 08					16 42				17 12					17 45					18 13	
Whitstable	d				15 39		16 04							16 39		17 08							17 44
Chestfield & Swalecliffe	d				15 42		16 07							16 42		17 11							17 47
Herne Bay	d				15 46		16 11							16 46		17 15							17 51
Birchington-on-Sea	d				15 54		16 20							16 54		17 24							18 00
Westgate-on-Sea	d				15 58		16 24							16 58		17 28							18 04
Margate 4	d			15 55	16 02		16 28						16 55	17 02		17 32					17 55		18 08
Broadstairs	d			16 01	16 08		16 34						17 01	17 08		17 38					18 01		18 14
Dumpton Park	d						16 37									17 41							18 17
Ramsgate 4	a			16 06	16 13		16 40						17 06	17 13		17 46					18 06		18 20

A To St Pancras International

For further services between St Pancras International, London Blackfriars and Elephant & Castle and Bromley South, St Mary Cray and Swanley refer to table T52

Table T212-F

Mondays to Fridays

16 December to 15 May

London - Medway, Sheerness-on-Sea, Dover and Ramsgate

	SE ◇	SE	SE 1	SE ◇1 A	SE ◇1	SE ◇1 B	SE ◇	SE	SE ◇ C	SE ◇ D	SE ◇1	SE ◇1	SE ◇	SE	SE ◇1	SE ◇ C	SE	SE ◇1 A	SE ◇1	SE ◇1 B	SE ◇1
St Pancras Intl. 15 ⊖ d	16 25						16 55		17 12				17 25			17 46					
Stratford International ⊖ d	16 32						17 02		17 19				17 32			17 53					
Ebbsfleet International d	16 43						17 13		17 31				17 43			18 05					
London Blackfriars 3 ⊖ d																					
Elephant & Castle ⊖ d																					
London Victoria 15 ⊖ d			16 12		16 40							17 10			17 12				17 40		
Bromley South 4 d			16 35		16 57							17 30			17 37				17 57		
St Mary Cray d			16 40												17 43						
Swanley 4 d			16 45												17 48						
Farningham Road d			16 50												17 53						
Longfield d			16 54												17 57						
Meopham d			16 58												18 01						
Sole Street d			17 01												18 04						
London Charing Cross 4 ⊖ d																	17 17				
London Waterloo (East) 4 ⊖ d																	17 20				
London Cannon Street 4 ⊖ d				16 30							17 09							17 30			17 52
London Bridge 4 ⊖ d				16 35							17 14						17 26	17 35			17 57
Dartford 4 d																	18 03				
Greenhithe for Bluewater d																	18 09				
Gravesend 4 d	16 48						17 18		17 35							18 09	18 22				
Strood 4 d	16 59						17 28		17a45							18a19	18a36				
Rochester 4 d	17 02		17 10	17 15	17 19		17 32				17 48	17 53	17 58		18 13			18 17	18 21		18 31
Chatham 4 d	17 06		17 13	17 18	17 23		17 35				17 52	17 57	18 02		18 16			18 21	18 25		18 35
Gillingham (Kent) 4 d	17 10		17a20	17 23	17 28		17 41				17 57	18 02	18 07		18 21			18 26	18 30		18 41
Rainham (Kent) d	17 15			17 28	17 33		17 46				18 02	18 07	18 12		18 26			18 31	18 35		18 46
Newington d					17 37						18 06	18 11							18 39		
Sittingbourne 4 a	17 22			17 35	17 41		17 53				18 10	18 15	18 19					18 39	18 44		18 53
d	17 23	17 28		17 36	17 42		17 54	17 55			18 11	18 16	18 20	18 24				18 39	18 44		18 53
Kemsley d		17 33						18 00						18 29	18 37						
Swale d		17 36						18 03						18 32							
Queenborough d		17 41						18 08						18 37	18 44						
Sheerness-on-Sea a		17 46						18 15						18 42	18 52						
Teynham d					17 46	←					18 15	18 20						18 44		←	
Faversham 2 a	17 31			17 44	17 52	17 44	18 02				18 21	18 26	18 29					18 49	18 53	18 49	19 01
d				17 58	17 54	17 58					18 22	18 28	18 30					18 58	18 54	18 58	19 02
Selling d				→		18 02						18 32						→		19 02	
Canterbury East 4 d						18 12						18 42								19 12	
Bekesbourne d						18 16						18 46								19 16	
Adisham d						18 21						18 50								19 21	
Aylesham d						18 24						18 53								19 24	
Snowdown d						18 26						18 56								19 26	
Shepherds Well d						18 30						19 00								19 30	
Kearsney d						18 35						19 05								19 35	
Dover Priory 4 a						18 43						19 13								19 42	
Whitstable d					18 02						18 31		18 38						19 02		19 10
Chestfield & Swalecliffe d					18 05						18 34								19 05		
Herne Bay d					18 09						18 38		18 44						19 09		19 16
Birchington-on-Sea d					18 18						18 46		18 52						19 18		19 25
Westgate-on-Sea d					18 22						18 50								19 22		
Margate 4 d					18 26					18 53	18a56		18 58						19 26		19 30
Broadstairs d					18 32					18 59			19 04						19 32		19a39
Dumpton Park d					18 35								19 07						19 35		
Ramsgate 4 a					18 41					19 04			19 13						19 39		

A To Dover Priory
B From London Cannon Street
C To Maidstone West
D To St Pancras International

For further services between St Pancras International, London Blackfriars and Elephant & Castle and Bromley South, St Mary Cray and Swanley refer to table T52

Table T212-F

Mondays to Fridays

16 December to 15 May

London - Medway, Sheerness-on-Sea, Dover and Ramsgate

	SE ◇	SE	SE ◇ A	SE	SE ◇ B	SE ◇1	SE ◇1	SE	SE	SE ◇	SE ◇1	SE ◇1	SE ◇1	SE	SE ◇	SE ◇1	SE	SE ◇ B	SE ◇ B	SE ◇	SE ◇1	SE 1
St Pancras Intl. 15 ⊖ d	17 55		18 16							18 25					18 55					19 25		
Stratford International ⊖ d	18 02		18 23							18 32					19 02					19 32		
Ebbsfleet International d	18 13		18 35							18 43					19 13					19 43		
London Blackfriars 3 ⊖ d																						
Elephant & Castle ⊖ d																						
London Victoria 15 ⊖ d						18 10					18 12	18 40				19 10						19 12
Bromley South 4 d						18 29					18 37	18 57				19 30						19 35
St Mary Cray d											18 43											19 41
Swanley 4 d											18 47											19 47
Farningham Road d											18 52											19 52
Longfield d											18 57											19 56
Meopham d											19 01											20 01
Sole Street d											19 04											20 03
London Charing Cross 4 ⊖ d				17 59																		
London Waterloo (East) 4 ⊖ d				18 02																		
London Cannon Street 4 ⊖ d							18 11		18 24				18 45								19 20	
London Bridge 4 ⊖ d				18 08			18 16		18 29				18 50								19 25	
Dartford 4 d				18 46					19 10													
Greenhithe for Bluewater d				18 51					19 16													
Gravesend 4 d	18 18		18 39	19 00					19 26						19 18					19 48		
Strood 4 d	18 31		18a49	19a14					19a40						19 30					19 59		
Rochester 4 d	18 36					18 52	18 56			19 01	19 13	19 21	19 26		19 35	19 52				20 02	20 06	20 12
Chatham 4 d	18 40					18 56	19 00			19 05	19 17	19 25	19 30		19 39	19 56				20 06	20 10	20 16
Gillingham (Kent) 4 d	18 45					19 01	19 05			19 10	19 22	19 30	19 35		19 44	20 00				20 11	20 15	20a25
Rainham (Kent) d	18 50					19 06	19 10			19 15	19 27	19 35	19 40		19 49	20 05				20 16	20 20	
Newington d							19 14					19 39	19 44			20 09					20 24	
Sittingbourne 4 a	18 57					19 13	19 18			19 24		19 44	19 49		19 56	20 14				20 23	20 29	
d	18 58	19 00				19 13	19 19	19 25		19 25		19 44	19 49	19 53	19 56	20 14	20 19			20 23	20 29	
Kemsley d		19 05						19 30			19 38			20 02			20 29					
Swale d		19 08						19 34						20 06			20 32					
Queenborough d		19 13						19 38			19 45			20 10			20 37					
Sheerness-on-Sea a		19 19						19 43			19 53			20 15			20 42					
Teynham d						19 18						19 49	19 54			20 19					20 34	
Faversham 2 a	19 06					19 24	19 27			19 33		19 55	20 00		20 05	20 24				20 31	20 43	
d	19 07					19 25	19 28			19 34		19 58	20 01			20 25				20 32		
Selling d							19 33					20 03				20 30						
Canterbury East 4 d							19 42					20 12				20 39						
Bekesbourne d							19 47					20 17				20 44						
Adisham d							19 51					20 21				20 48						
Aylesham d							19 54					20 24				20 51						
Snowdown d							19 57					20 27				20 53						
Shepherds Well d							20 01					20 31				20 57						
Kearsney d							20 06					20 36				21 02						
Dover Priory 4 a							20 14					20 44				21 10						
Whitstable d	19 15					19 33				19 42			20 09							20 40		
Chestfield & Swalecliffe d						19 36							20 12							20 43		
Herne Bay d	19 21					19 40				19 48			20 16							20 47		
Birchington-on-Sea d	19 30					19 49				19 57			20 25							20 56		
Westgate-on-Sea d						19 53							20 29							21 00		
Margate 4 d	19 36				19 53	19 57				20 02			20 33					20 53	21 00	21 04		
Broadstairs d	19a45				19 59	20 03				20a10			20 39					20 59	21 06	21 10		
Dumpton Park d						20 06							20 42							21 13		
Ramsgate 4 a					20 04	20 12							20 48					21 04	21 11	21 17		

A To Maidstone West
B To St Pancras International

For further services between St Pancras International, London Blackfriars and Elephant & Castle and Bromley South, St Mary Cray and Swanley refer to table T52

Table T212-F

Mondays to Fridays

16 December to 15 May

London - Medway, Sheerness-on-Sea, Dover and Ramsgate

		SE ◇1		SE ◇	SE	SE ◇	SE ◇1	SE ◇ A	SE ◇	SE	SE ◇1	SE ◇1	SE ◇	SE	SE ◇1	SE ◇1	SE B	SE ◇	SE	SE ◇1	SE ◇	SE ◇1
St Pancras Intl. 15 ⊖	d			19 55					20 25				20 55					21 25			21 55	
Stratford International ⊖	d			20 02					20 32				21 02					21 32			22 02	
Ebbsfleet International	d			20 13					20 43				21 13					21 43			22 13	
London Blackfriars 8 ⊖	d																					
Elephant & Castle ⊖	d																					
London Victoria 15 ⊖	d	19 40				19 42	20 10				20 12	20 40			20 42	21 10				21 40		21 42
Bromley South 4	d	19 57				20 05	20 27				20 37	20 57			21 05	21 27				21 57		22 05
St Mary Cray	d					20 10					20 42				21 10							22 10
Swanley 4	d					20 15					20 47				21 15							22 15
Farningham Road	d					20 20					20 52				21 20							22 20
Longfield	d	20 09				20 24	20 39				20 56	21 09			21 24	21 39				22 09		22 24
Meopham	d	20 13				20 28	20 43				21 00	21 13			21 28	21 43				22 13		22 28
Sole Street	d					20 31					21 03				21 31							22 31
London Charing Cross 4 ⊖	d																					
London Waterloo (East) 4 ⊖	d																					
London Cannon Street 4 ⊖	d																					
London Bridge 4 ⊖	d																					
Dartford 4	d																					
Greenhithe for Bluewater	d																					
Gravesend 4	d			20 18					20 48				21 18					21 48			22 18	
Strood 4	d			20 29					20 59				21 29					21 59			22 29	
Rochester 4	d	20 23		20 32		20 40	20 53		21 02		21 12	21 23	21 32		21 40	21 53		22 02		22 23	22 32	22 40
Chatham 4	d	20 27		20 36		20 43	20 57		21 06		21 16	21 27	21 36		21 43	21 57		22 06		22 27	22 36	22 43
Gillingham (Kent) 4	d	20 31		20 40		20a48	21 01		21 10		21a23	21 31	21 40		21 48	22 01		22 10		22 31	22 40	22 48
Rainham (Kent)	d	20 36		20 45			21 06		21 15			21 36	21 45		21 53	22 06		22 15		22 36	22 45	22 53
Newington	d						21 10									22 10						
Sittingbourne 4	a	20 43		20 52			21 15		21 22			21 43	21 52		22 00	22 15		22 22		22 43	22 52	23 00
	d	20 44		20 54	20 55		21 15		21 23	21 25		21 44	21 53	21 55	22 01	22 15		22 23	22 25	22 44	22 53	23 01
Kemsley	d				21 00					21 30				22 00					22 30			
Swale	d				21 03					21 33				22 03					22 33			
Queenborough	d				21 08					21 38				22 08					22 38			
Sheerness-on-Sea	a				21 13					21 43				22 13					22 43			
Teynham	d						21 20									22 20						
Faversham 2	a	20 52		21 05			21 25		21 31			21 52	22 01		22 09	22 25		22 31		22 52	23 01	23 09
	d	20 56	20 58				21 26		21 32			21 53			22 10	22 26		22 32		22 53		23 10
Selling	d		21 02				21 31									22 31						
Canterbury East 4	d		21 12				21 40								22a23	22 40						23a23
Bekesbourne	d		21 16				21 45									22 45						
Adisham	d		21 20				21 49									22 49						
Aylesham	d		21 23				21 52									22 52						
Snowdown	d		21 26				21 54									22 54						
Shepherds Well	d		21 30				21 58									22 58						
Kearsney	d		21 34				22 03									23 03						
Dover Priory 4	a		21 40				22 08									23 08						
Whitstable	d	21 04							21 40			22 02						22 40		23 02		
Chestfield & Swalecliffe	d	21 07							21 43			22 05						22 43		23 05		
Herne Bay	d	21 11							21 47			22 09						22 47		23 09		
Birchington-on-Sea	d	21 20							21 56			22 18						22 56		23 18		
Westgate-on-Sea	d	21 24							22 00			22 21						23 00		23 21		
Margate 4	d	21 28						21 55	22 04			22 25					22 55	23 04		23 25		
Broadstairs	d	21 34						22 01	22 10			22 31					23 01	23 10		23 31		
Dumpton Park	d	21 37							22 13			22 34						23 13		23 34		
Ramsgate 4	a	21 42						22 06	22 19			22 38					23 06	23 18		23 38		

A To St Pancras International **B** To Ashford International

For further services between St Pancras International, London Blackfriars and Elephant & Castle and Bromley South, St Mary Cray and Swanley refer to table T52

Table T212-F

Mondays to Fridays

16 December to 15 May

London - Medway, Sheerness-on-Sea, Dover and Ramsgate

		SE TX ◇1 A	SE TO ◇1 A	SE TX ◇	SE TO ◇	SE TX ◇1 B	SE	SE TO Bus	SE TO Bus	SE TO ◇1 B	SE TX ◇1	SE TO ◇1	SE TO Bus	SE TO Bus	SE ◇	SE ◇1	SE TO ◇1	SE TX ◇1	SE ◇	SE ◇	SE 1
St Pancras Intl. 15 ⊖	d			22 25	22 25										22 55				23 25	23 55	
Stratford International ⊖	d			22 32	22 32										23 02				23 32	00 02	
Ebbsfleet International	d			22 43	22 43										23 13				23 43	00 13	
London Blackfriars 8 ⊖	d																				
Elephant & Castle ⊖	d																				
London Victoria 15 ⊖	d	22 10	22 10								22 40	22 40				22 42	23 10	23 10			23 42
Bromley South 4	d	22 27	22 27								22 57	22 57				23 05	23 27	23 27			00 07
St Mary Cray	d															23 10					00 12
Swanley 4	d															23 15					00 17
Farningham Road	d															23 20					00 22
Longfield	d	22 39	22 39								23 09	23 09				23 24	23 39	23 39			00 26
Meopham	d	22 43	22 43								23 13	23 13				23 28	23 43	23 43			00 30
Sole Street	d															23 31					00s33
London Charing Cross 4 ⊖	d																				
London Waterloo (East) 4 ⊖	d																				
London Cannon Street 4 ⊖	d																				
London Bridge 4 ⊖	d																				
Dartford 4	d																				
Greenhithe for Bluewater	d																				
Gravesend 4	d			22 48	22 48										23 18				23 48	00 18	
Strood 4	d			22 59	22 59										23 29				23 59	00 29	
Rochester 4	d	22 53	22 53	23 02	23 02						23 23	23 23			23 32	23 40	23 53	23 53	00 02	00 32	00 42
Chatham 4	d	22 57	22 57	23 06	23 06						23 27	23 27			23 36	23 43	23 57	23 57	00 06	00 36	00 45
Gillingham (Kent) 4	d	23 01	23 01	23 10	23 10						23 31	23 31			23 40	23a48	00 01	00 01	00 10	00 40	00a49
Rainham (Kent)	d	23 06	23 06	23 15	23 15						23 36	23 36			23 45		00 06	00 06	00 15	00 45	
Newington	d	23 10	23 10														00 10	00 10			
Sittingbourne 4	a	23 15	23 15	23 22	23 22						23 43	23 43			23 52		00 15	00 15	00 22	00 52	
	d	23 15	23 15	23 23	23 23		23 25				23 44	23 44			23 53		00 15	00 15	00 23	00 53	
Kemsley	d						23 30														
Swale	d						23 33														
Queenborough	d						23 38														
Sheerness-on-Sea	a						23 43														
Teynham	d	23 20	23 20			←				←							00 20	00 20			
Faversham 2	a	23 25	23 25	23 31	23 31	23 25				23 25	23 52	23 52			00 01		00 26	00 26	00 31	01 03	
	d	23 34	23 40	23 32	23 32	23 34		23 37	23 38	23 40	23 53	23 56	23 58	23 59			00 28	00 36			
Selling	d	→	→			23s38				23s44											
Canterbury East 4	d					23 48				23 54											
Bekesbourne	d					23s52				23s58											
Adisham	d					23s56				00s02											
Aylesham	d					23s59				00s05											
Snowdown	d					00s01				00s07											
Shepherds Well	d					00s05				00s11											
Kearsney	d					00s10				00s16											
Dover Priory 4	a					00 16				00 23											
Whitstable	d			23 40					23 58		00 02			00 19				00 44			
Chestfield & Swalecliffe	d			23 43					00 06		00 05			00 27				00 47			
Herne Bay	d			23 47					00 14		00 09			00 35				00 51			
Birchington-on-Sea	d			23 56					00 34		00 18			00 55				01 00			
Westgate-on-Sea	d			23 59					00 39		00 21			01 00				01 04			
Margate 4	d			00 04				00 22	00 45		00 25		00 43	01 06				01 08			
Broadstairs	d			00 10				00 32	00 55		00 31		00 53	01 16				01 14			
Dumpton Park	d			00 13				00 37	01 00		00 34		00 58	01 21				01 17			
Ramsgate 4	a			00 16	00 39			00 43	01 06		00 38	01 10	01 04	01 27			01 35	01 21			

A To Dover Priory **B** From London Victoria

For further services between St Pancras International, London Blackfriars and Elephant & Castle and Bromley South, St Mary Cray and Swanley refer to table T52

Table T212-F

Saturdays

21 December to 16 May

London - Medway, Sheerness-on-Sea, Dover and Ramsgate

		SE	SE	SE	SE	SE	SE	SE	SE	SE		SE	SE	SE	SE	SE	SE	SE	SE	SE		SE	SE	SE	SE
		◇	◇1	◇1	◇		◇	1	◇1	◇		◇	◇	◇	1			◇1		1		1	◇	1	
		A	B	B	A		A	B		C		D	D	D									D		
St Pancras Intl. 15 ⊖	d									00 12															
Stratford International ⊖	d						00 02			00 19															
Ebbsfleet International	d						00 13			00a30															
London Blackfriars 3 ⊖	d																								
Elephant & Castle ⊖	d																								
London Victoria 15 ⊖	d								00 10									05 42							
Bromley South 4	d							00 07	00s31									06 05							
St Mary Cray	d							00 12										06 10							
Swanley 4	d							00 17										06 15							
Farningham Road	d							00 22										06 20							
Longfield	d							00 26										06 24							
Meopham	d							00 30										06 28							
Sole Street	d							00s33										06 31							
London Charing Cross 4 ⊖	d																								
London Waterloo (East) 4 ⊖	d																								
London Cannon Street 4 ⊖	d																								
London Bridge 4 ⊖	d																								
Dartford 4	d																								
Greenhithe for Bluewater	d																								
Gravesend 4	d						00 18																		
Strood 4	d						00 29																		
Rochester 4	d				00 02		00 32	00 42	00 54									06 40							
Chatham 4	d				00 06		00 36	00 45	00 58									06 43							
Gillingham (Kent) 4	d			00 01	00 10		00 40	00a49	01 02						05 53			06 48						07 28	
Rainham (Kent)	d			00 06	00 15		00 45		01 07						05 58			06 53						07 33	
Newington	d			00 10					01s11						06 02			06 57						07 37	
Sittingbourne 4	a			00 15	00 22		00 52		01 16						06 06			07 01						07 41	
	d			00 15	00 23	00 26	00 53		01 16						06 07	06 25	06 55	07 02	07 25					07 42	07 55
Kemsley	d					00s30										06 30	07 00		07 30						08 00
Swale	d					00s34										06 33	07 03		07 33						08 03
Queenborough	d					00s38										06 38	07 08		07 38						08 08
Sheerness-on-Sea	a					00 44										06 43	07 13		07 43						08 13
Teynham	d			00 20					01s21						06 11			07 06						07 46	
Faversham 2	a			00 26	00 31		01 03		01 26						06 17			07 12						07 52	
	d			00 36					01 27					06 24	06 26			07 13		07 17		07 26		07 53	
Selling	d														06 31							07 31			
Canterbury East 4	d														06 40			07 25				07 40			
Bekesbourne	d														06 45							07 45			
Adisham	d														06 49							07 49			
Aylesham	d														06 52							07 52			
Snowdown	d														06 54							07 54			
Shepherds Well	d														06 58							07 58			
Kearsney	d														07 03							08 03			
Dover Priory 4	a														07 08			07 41				08 08			
Whitstable	d		00 02	00 44					01s35					06 32						07 25				08 02	
Chestfield & Swalecliffe	d		00 05	00 47					01s38					06 35						07 28				08 05	
Herne Bay	d		00 09	00 51					01s42					06 39						07 32				08 09	
Birchington-on-Sea	d		00 18	01 00					01s51					06 48						07 41				08 18	
Westgate-on-Sea	d		00 21	01 04					01s55					06 52						07 45				08 21	
Margate 4	d	00 04	00 25	01 08					01s58			05 53	06 53	06 57						07 49			07 55	08 25	
Broadstairs	d	00 10	00 31	01 14					02s04			05 59	06 59	07 03						07 55			08 01	08 31	
Dumpton Park	d	00 13	00 34	01 17					02s08					07 06						07 58				08 34	
Ramsgate 4	a	00 16	00 38	01 21					02 15			06 04	07 04	07 09						08 02			08 06	08 38	

A From St Pancras International
B From London Victoria
C To Ashford International
D To St Pancras International

For further services between St Pancras International, London Blackfriars and Elephant & Castle and Bromley South, St Mary Cray and Swanley refer to table T52

Table T212-F

Saturdays

21 December to 16 May

London - Medway, Sheerness-on-Sea, Dover and Ramsgate

		SE	SE	SE	SE	SE		SE	SE	SE	SE	SE	SE	SE	SE	SE		SE	SE	SE	SE	SE	SE	SE	SE
		◇1	◇1	◇	◇			◇1	◇		◇1	◇1	◇	◇		◇1		◇		◇1	◇1	◇	◇		◇1
				A	A								A	A								A	A		
St Pancras Intl. 15 ⊖	d				07 25				07 55					08 25				08 57					09 25		
Stratford International ⊖	d				07 32				08 02					08 32				09 04					09 32		
Ebbsfleet International	d				07 43				08 13					08 43				09 15					09 44		
London Blackfriars 3 ⊖	d																								
Elephant & Castle ⊖	d																								
London Victoria 15 ⊖	d	06 42	07 10					07 40			07 42	08 10				08 40				08 42	09 10				09 40
Bromley South 4	d	07 05	07 27					07 57			08 05	08 27				08 57				09 05	09 27				09 57
St Mary Cray	d	07 10									08 10									09 10					
Swanley 4	d	07 15									08 15									09 15					
Farningham Road	d	07 20									08 20									09 20					
Longfield	d	07 24	07 39					08 09			08 24	08 39				09 09				09 24	09 39				10 09
Meopham	d	07 28	07 43					08 13			08 28	08 43				09 13				09 28	09 43				10 13
Sole Street	d	07 31									08 31									09 31					
London Charing Cross 4 ⊖	d																								
London Waterloo (East) 4 ⊖	d																								
London Cannon Street 4 ⊖	d																								
London Bridge 4 ⊖	d																								
Dartford 4	d																								
Greenhithe for Bluewater	d																								
Gravesend 4	d				07 48				08 18					08 48				09 19					09 48		
Strood 4	d				07 59				08 29					08 59				09 30					09 59		
Rochester 4	d	07 40	07 53		08 02			08 23	08 32		08 40	08 53		09 02		09 23		09 33		09 40	09 53		10 02		10 23
Chatham 4	d	07 43	07 57		08 06			08 27	08 36		08 43	08 57		09 06		09 27		09 37		09 43	09 57		10 06		10 27
Gillingham (Kent) 4	d	07 48	08 01		08 10			08 31	08 40		08 48	09 01		09 10		09 31		09 41		09 48	10 01		10 10		10 31
Rainham (Kent)	d	07 53	08 06		08 15			08 36	08 45		08 53	09 06		09 15		09 36		09 46		09 53	10 06		10 15		10 36
Newington	d		08 10									09 10									10 10				
Sittingbourne 4	a	08 00	08 15		08 22			08 43	08 52		09 00	09 15		09 22		09 43		09 53		10 00	10 15		10 22		10 43
	d	08 01	08 15		08 23	08 25		08 44	08 54	08 55	09 01	09 15		09 23	09 25	09 44		09 54	09 55	10 01	10 15		10 23	10 25	10 44
Kemsley	d					08 30				09 00					09 30				10 00					10 30	
Swale	d					08 33				09 03					09 33				10 03					10 33	
Queenborough	d					08 38				09 08					09 38				10 08					10 38	
Sheerness-on-Sea	a					08 43				09 13					09 43				10 13					10 43	
Teynham	d		08 20									09 20									10 20				
Faversham 2	a	08 09	08 25		08 31			08 52	09 05		09 09	09 25		09 31		09 52		10 05		10 09	10 25		10 31		10 52
	d	08 10	08 26		08 31			08 53			09 10	09 26		09 31		09 53				10 10	10 26		10 31		10 53
Selling	d		08 31									09 31									10 31				
Canterbury East 4	d	08 22	08 40								09 22	09 40								10 22	10 40				
Bekesbourne	d		08 45									09 45									10 45				
Adisham	d		08 49									09 49									10 49				
Aylesham	d		08 52									09 52									10 52				
Snowdown	d		08 54									09 54									10 54				
Shepherds Well	d		08 58									09 58									10 58				
Kearsney	d		09 03									10 03									11 03				
Dover Priory 4	a	08 39	09 08								09 39	10 08								10 39	11 08				
Whitstable	d				08 40			09 02						09 40		10 02							10 40		11 02
Chestfield & Swalecliffe	d							09 05								10 05									11 05
Herne Bay	d				08 45			09 09						09 45		10 09							10 45		11 09
Birchington-on-Sea	d				08 54			09 18						09 54		10 18							10 54		11 18
Westgate-on-Sea	d							09 21								10 21									11 21
Margate 4	d			08 55	08 59			09 25					09 55	09 59		10 25						10 55	10 59		11 25
Broadstairs	d			09 01	09 05			09 31					10 01	10 05		10 31						11 01	11 05		11 31
Dumpton Park	d							09 34								10 34									11 34
Ramsgate 4	a			09 06	09 11			09 38					10 06	10 11		10 38						11 06	11 11		11 38

A To St Pancras International

For further services between St Pancras International, London Blackfriars and Elephant & Castle and Bromley South, St Mary Cray and Swanley refer to table T52

Table T212-F

Saturdays

21 December to 16 May

London - Medway, Sheerness-on-Sea, Dover and Ramsgate

	SE ◇		SE	SE ◇1	SE ◇1	SE ◇ A	SE ◇ A	SE	SE ◇1	SE ◇	SE		SE ◇1	SE ◇1	SE ◇ B	SE ◇ A	SE ◇ A	SE	SE ◇1	SE ◇	SE		SE ◇1	SE ◇1
St Pancras Intl. 15 ⊖ d	09 55						10 25			10 52					11 12		11 25			11 55				
Stratford International ⊖ d	10 02						10 32			10 59					11 19		11 32			12 02				
Ebbsfleet International d	10 13						10 43			11 13					11 30		11 43			12 13				
London Blackfriars 3 ⊖ d																								
Elephant & Castle ⊖ d																								
London Victoria 15 ⊖ d				09 42	10 10				10 40				10 42	11 10					11 40				11 42	12 10
Bromley South 4 d				10 05	10 27				10 57				11 05	11 27					11 57				12 05	12 27
St Mary Cray d				10 10									11 10										12 10	
Swanley 4 d				10 15									11 15										12 15	
Farningham Road d				10 20									11 20										12 20	
Longfield d				10 24	10 39				11 09				11 24	11 39					12 09				12 24	12 39
Meopham d				10 28	10 43				11 13				11 28	11 43					12 13				12 28	12 43
Sole Street d				10 31									11 31										12 31	
London Charing Cross 4 ⊖ d																								
London Waterloo (East) 4 ⊖ d																								
London Cannon Street 4 ⊖ d																								
London Bridge 4 ⊖ d																								
Dartford 4 d																								
Greenhithe for Bluewater d																								
Gravesend 4 d	10 18						10 48			11 18							11 48			12 18				
Strood 4 d	10 29						10 59			11 29							11 59			12 29				
Rochester 4 d	10 32			10 40	10 53		11 02		11 23	11 32			11 40	11 53			12 02		12 23	12 32			12 40	12 53
Chatham 4 d	10 36			10 43	10 57		11 06		11 27	11 36			11 43	11 57			12 06		12 27	12 36			12 43	12 57
Gillingham (Kent) 4 d	10 40			10 48	11 01		11 10		11 31	11 40			11 48	12 01			12 10		12 31	12 40			12 48	13 01
Rainham (Kent) d	10 45			10 53	11 06		11 15		11 36	11 45			11 53	12 06			12 15		12 36	12 45			12 53	13 06
Newington d					11 10									12 10										13 10
Sittingbourne 4 a	10 52			11 00	11 15		11 22		11 43	11 52			12 00	12 15			12 22		12 43	12 52			13 00	13 15
d	10 54		10 55	11 01	11 15		11 23	11 25	11 44	11 54	11 55		12 01	12 15			12 23	12 25	12 44	12 54	12 55		13 01	13 15
Kemsley d			11 00					11 30			12 00							12 30			13 00			
Swale d			11 03					11 33			12 03							12 33			13 03			
Queenborough d			11 08					11 38			12 08							12 38			13 08			
Sheerness-on-Sea a			11 13					11 43			12 13							12 43			13 13			
Teynham d					11 20									12 20										13 20
Faversham 2 a	11 05			11 09	11 25		11 31		11 52	12 05			12 09	12 25			12 31		12 52	13 05			13 09	13 25
d				11 10	11 26		11 31		11 53				12 10	12 26			12 31		12 53				13 10	13 26
Selling d					11 31									12 31										13 31
Canterbury East 4 d				11 22	11 40								12 22	12 40									13 22	13 40
Bekesbourne d					11 45									12 45										13 45
Adisham d					11 49									12 49										13 49
Aylesham d					11 52									12 52										13 52
Snowdown d					11 54									12 54										13 54
Shepherds Well d					11 58									12 58										13 58
Kearsney d					12 03									13 03										14 03
Dover Priory 4 a				11 39	12 08								12 39	13 08									13 39	14 08
Whitstable d							11 40		12 02								12 40		13 02					
Chestfield & Swalecliffe d									12 05										13 05					
Herne Bay d							11 45		12 09								12 45		13 09					
Birchington-on-Sea d							11 54		12 18								12 54		13 18					
Westgate-on-Sea d									12 21										13 21					
Margate 4 d						11 55	11 59		12 25							12 55	12 59		13 25					
Broadstairs d						12 01	12 05		12 31							13 01	13 05		13 31					
Dumpton Park d									12 34										13 34					
Ramsgate 4 a						12 06	12 11		12 38						12 27	13 06	13 11		13 38					

A To St Pancras International

B To Margate

For further services between St Pancras International, London Blackfriars and Elephant & Castle and Bromley South, St Mary Cray and Swanley refer to table T52

Table T212-F

Saturdays

21 December to 16 May

London - Medway, Sheerness-on-Sea, Dover and Ramsgate

	SE ◇ A	SE ◇ B	SE ◇ B	SE	SE ◇1	SE ◇	SE		SE ◇1	SE ◇1	SE ◇ B	SE ◇ B	SE	SE ◇1	SE ◇	SE	SE ◇1		SE ◇ A	SE ◇1	SE ◇ B	SE ◇ B	SE	SE ◇1
St Pancras Intl. 15 ⊖ d	12 12		12 27			12 52						13 25			13 55				14 10			14 25		
Stratford International ⊖ d	12 19		12 34			12 59						13 32			14 02				14 17			14 32		
Ebbsfleet International d	12 30		12 45			13 13						13 43			14 13				14 28			14 43		
London Blackfriars 3 ⊖ d																								
Elephant & Castle ⊖ d																								
London Victoria 15 ⊖ d					12 40				12 42	13 10				13 40			13 42			14 10				14 40
Bromley South 4 d					12 57				13 05	13 27				13 57			14 05			14 27				14 57
St Mary Cray d									13 10								14 10							
Swanley 4 d									13 15								14 15							
Farningham Road d									13 20								14 20							
Longfield d					13 09				13 24	13 39				14 09			14 24			14 39				15 09
Meopham d					13 13				13 28	13 43				14 13			14 28			14 43				15 13
Sole Street d									13 31								14 31							
London Charing Cross 4 ⊖ d																								
London Waterloo (East) 4 ⊖ d																								
London Cannon Street 4 ⊖ d																								
London Bridge 4 ⊖ d																								
Dartford 4 d																								
Greenhithe for Bluewater d																								
Gravesend 4 d			12 49			13 18						13 48			14 18							14 48		
Strood 4 d			12 59			13 29						13 59			14 29							14 59		
Rochester 4 d			13 02		13 23	13 32			13 40	13 53		14 02		14 23	14 32		14 40			14 53		15 02		15 23
Chatham 4 d			13 06		13 27	13 36			13 43	13 57		14 06		14 27	14 36		14 43			14 57		15 06		15 27
Gillingham (Kent) 4 d			13 10		13 31	13 40			13 48	14 01		14 10		14 31	14 40		14 48			15 01		15 10		15 31
Rainham (Kent) d			13 15		13 36	13 45			13 53	14 06		14 15		14 36	14 45		14 53			15 06		15 15		15 36
Newington d										14 10										15 10				
Sittingbourne 4 a			13 22		13 43	13 52			14 00	14 15		14 22		14 43	14 52		15 00			15 15		15 22		15 43
d			13 23	13 25	13 44	13 54	13 55		14 01	14 15		14 23	14 25	14 44	14 54	14 55	15 01			15 15		15 23	15 25	15 44
Kemsley d				13 30			14 00						14 30			15 00							15 30	
Swale d				13 33			14 03						14 33			15 03							15 33	
Queenborough d				13 38			14 08						14 38			15 08							15 38	
Sheerness-on-Sea a				13 43			14 13						14 43			15 13							15 43	
Teynham d										14 20										15 20				
Faversham 2 a			13 31		13 52	14 05			14 09	14 25		14 31		14 52	15 05		15 09			15 25		15 31		15 52
d			13 31		13 53				14 10	14 26		14 31		14 53			15 10			15 26		15 31		15 53
Selling d										14 31										15 31				
Canterbury East 4 d									14 22	14 40							15 22			15 40				
Bekesbourne d										14 45										15 45				
Adisham d										14 49										15 49				
Aylesham d										14 52										15 52				
Snowdown d										14 54										15 54				
Shepherds Well d										14 58										15 58				
Kearsney d										15 03										16 03				
Dover Priory 4 a									14 39	15 08							15 39			16 08				
Whitstable d			13 40		14 02							14 40		15 02								15 40		16 02
Chestfield & Swalecliffe d					14 05									15 05										16 05
Herne Bay d			13 45		14 09							14 45		15 09								15 45		16 09
Birchington-on-Sea d			13 54		14 18							14 54		15 18								15 54		16 18
Westgate-on-Sea d					14 21									15 21										16 21
Margate 4 d		13 55	13 59		14 25						14 55	14 59		15 25							15 55	15 59		16 25
Broadstairs d		14 01	14 05		14 31						15 01	15 05		15 31							16 01	16 05		16 31
Dumpton Park d					14 34									15 34										16 34
Ramsgate 4 a	13 27	14 06	14 11		14 38						15 06	15 11		15 38					15 27		16 06	16 11		16 38

A To Margate

B To St Pancras International

For further services between St Pancras International, London Blackfriars and Elephant & Castle and Bromley South, St Mary Cray and Swanley refer to table T52

Table T212-F

Saturdays
21 December to 16 May

London - Medway, Sheerness-on-Sea, Dover and Ramsgate

		SE	SE	SE	SE	SE	SE	SE	SE	SE	SE	SE	SE	SE	SE	SE	SE	SE	SE	SE	SE	SE
		◇		◇1	◇1	◇ A	◇ A		◇1	◇		◇1	◇1	◇ A	◇ A		◇1	◇		◇1	◇1	◇ A
St Pancras Intl. 15 ⊖	d	14 55					15 25			15 55					16 25			16 55				
Stratford International ⊖	d	15 02					15 32			16 02					16 32			17 02				
Ebbsfleet International	d	15 13					15 43			16 13					16 43			17 13				
London Blackfriars 3 ⊖	d																					
Elephant & Castle ⊖	d																					
London Victoria 15 ⊖	d			14 42	15 10				15 40			15 42	16 10				16 40			16 42	17 10	
Bromley South 4	d			15 05	15 27				15 57			16 05	16 27				16 57			17 05	17 27	
St Mary Cray	d			15 10								16 10								17 10		
Swanley 4	d			15 15								16 15								17 15		
Farningham Road	d			15 20								16 20								17 20		
Longfield	d			15 24	15 39				16 09			16 24	16 39				17 09			17 24	17 39	
Meopham	d			15 28	15 43				16 13			16 28	16 43				17 13			17 28	17 43	
Sole Street	d			15 31								16 31								17 31		
London Charing Cross 4 ⊖	d																					
London Waterloo (East) 4 ⊖	d																					
London Cannon Street 4 ⊖	d																					
London Bridge 4 ⊖	d																					
Dartford 4	d																					
Greenhithe for Bluewater	d																					
Gravesend 4	d	15 18					15 48			16 18					16 48			17 18				
Strood 4	d	15 29					15 59			16 29					16 59			17 29				
Rochester 4	d	15 32		15 40	15 53		16 02		16 23	16 32		16 40	16 53		17 02		17 23	17 32		17 40	17 53	
Chatham 4	d	15 36		15 43	15 57		16 06		16 27	16 36		16 43	16 57		17 06		17 27	17 36		17 43	17 57	
Gillingham (Kent) 4	d	15 40		15 48	16 01		16 10		16 31	16 40		16 48	17 01		17 10		17 31	17 40		17 48	18 01	
Rainham (Kent)	d	15 45		15 53	16 06		16 15		16 36	16 45		16 53	17 06		17 15		17 36	17 45		17 53	18 06	
Newington	d				16 10								17 10								18 10	
Sittingbourne 4	a	15 52		16 00	16 15		16 22		16 43	16 52		17 00	17 15		17 22		17 43	17 52		18 00	18 15	
	d	15 54	15 55	16 01	16 15		16 23	16 25	16 44	16 54	16 55	17 01	17 15		17 23	17 25	17 44	17 54	17 55	18 01	18 15	
Kemsley	d		16 00					16 30			17 00					17 30			18 00			
Swale	d		16 03					16 33			17 03					17 33			18 03			
Queenborough	d		16 08					16 38			17 08					17 38			18 08			
Sheerness-on-Sea	a		16 13					16 43			17 13					17 43			18 13			
Teynham	d				16 20								17 20								18 20	
Faversham 2	a	16 05		16 09	16 25		16 31		16 52	17 05		17 09	17 25		17 31		17 52	18 05		18 09	18 25	
	d			16 10	16 26		16 31		16 53			17 10	17 26		17 31		17 53			18 10	18 26	
Selling	d				16 31								17 31								18 31	
Canterbury East 4	d			16 22	16 40							17 22	17 40							18 22	18 40	
Bekesbourne	d				16 45								17 45								18 45	
Adisham	d				16 49								17 49								18 49	
Aylesham	d				16 52								17 52								18 52	
Snowdown	d				16 54								17 54								18 54	
Shepherds Well	d				16 58								17 58								18 58	
Kearsney	d				17 03								18 03								19 03	
Dover Priory 4	a			16 39	17 08							17 39	18 08							18 39	19 08	
Whitstable	d						16 40		17 02						17 40		18 02					
Chestfield & Swalecliffe	d								17 05								18 05					
Herne Bay	d						16 45		17 09						17 45		18 09					
Birchington-on-Sea	d						16 54		17 18						17 54		18 18					
Westgate-on-Sea	d								17 21								18 21					
Margate 4	d					16 55	16 59		17 25					17 55	17 59		18 25					18 55
Broadstairs	d					17 01	17 05		17 31					18 01	18 05		18 31					19 01
Dumpton Park	d								17 34								18 34					
Ramsgate 4	a					17 06	17 11		17 38					18 06	18 11		18 38					19 06

A To St Pancras International

For further services between St Pancras International, London Blackfriars and Elephant & Castle and Bromley South, St Mary Cray and Swanley refer to table T52

NRT DECEMBER 19 EDITION

Table T212-F

Saturdays
21 December to 16 May

London - Medway, Sheerness-on-Sea, Dover and Ramsgate

		SE	SE	SE	SE	SE	SE	SE	SE	SE	SE	SE	SE	SE	SE	SE	SE	SE	SE	SE	SE	SE	SE
		◇ A		◇1	◇		◇1	◇1	◇ B	◇ A	◇ A		◇1	◇		◇1	◇1	◇ B	◇ A	◇ A		◇1	◇
St Pancras Intl. 15 ⊖	d	17 25			17 55				18 12		18 25			18 55				19 12		19 25			19 55
Stratford International ⊖	d	17 32			18 02				18 19		18 32			19 02				19 19		19 32			20 02
Ebbsfleet International	d	17 43			18 13				18 30		18 43			19 13				19 30		19 43			20 13
London Blackfriars 3 ⊖	d																						
Elephant & Castle ⊖	d																						
London Victoria 15 ⊖	d			17 40			17 42	18 10					18 40			18 42	19 10					19 40	
Bromley South 4	d			17 57			18 05	18 27					18 57			19 05	19 27					19 57	
St Mary Cray	d						18 10									19 10							
Swanley 4	d						18 15									19 15							
Farningham Road	d						18 20									19 20							
Longfield	d			18 09			18 24	18 39					19 09			19 24	19 39					20 09	
Meopham	d			18 13			18 28	18 43					19 13			19 28	19 43					20 13	
Sole Street	d						18 31									19 31							
London Charing Cross 4 ⊖	d																						
London Waterloo (East) 4 ⊖	d																						
London Cannon Street 4 ⊖	d																						
London Bridge 4 ⊖	d																						
Dartford 4	d																						
Greenhithe for Bluewater	d																						
Gravesend 4	d	17 48			18 18						18 48			19 18						19 48			20 18
Strood 4	d	17 59			18 29						18 59			19 29						19 59			20 29
Rochester 4	d	18 02		18 23	18 32		18 40	18 53			19 02		19 23	19 32		19 40	19 53			20 02		20 23	20 32
Chatham 4	d	18 06		18 27	18 36		18 43	18 57			19 06		19 27	19 36		19 43	19 57			20 06		20 27	20 36
Gillingham (Kent) 4	d	18 10		18 31	18 40		18 48	19 01			19 10		19 31	19 40		19 48	20 01			20 10		20 31	20 40
Rainham (Kent)	d	18 15		18 36	18 45		18 53	19 06			19 15		19 36	19 45		19 53	20 06			20 15		20 36	20 45
Newington	d							19 10									20 10						
Sittingbourne 4	a	18 22		18 43	18 52		19 00	19 15			19 22		19 43	19 52		20 00	20 15			20 22		20 43	20 52
	d	18 23	18 25	18 44	18 54	18 55	19 01	19 15			19 23	19 25	19 44	19 54	19 55	20 01	20 15			20 23	20 25	20 44	20 54
Kemsley	d		18 30			19 00						19 30			20 00						20 30		
Swale	d		18 33			19 03						19 33			20 03						20 33		
Queenborough	d		18 38			19 08						19 38			20 08						20 38		
Sheerness-on-Sea	a		18 43			19 13						19 43			20 13						20 43		
Teynham	d							19 20									20 20						
Faversham 2	a	18 31		18 52	19 05		19 09	19 25			19 31		19 52	20 05		20 09	20 25			20 31		20 52	21 05
	d	18 31		18 53			19 10	19 26			19 31		19 53			20 10	20 26			20 31		20 53	
Selling	d							19 31									20 31						
Canterbury East 4	d						19 22	19 40								20 22	20 40						
Bekesbourne	d							19 45									20 45						
Adisham	d							19 49									20 49						
Aylesham	d							19 52									20 52						
Snowdown	d							19 54									20 54						
Shepherds Well	d							19 58									20 58						
Kearsney	d							20 03									21 03						
Dover Priory 4	a						19 39	20 08								20 39	21 08						
Whitstable	d	18 40		19 02							19 40		20 02							20 40		21 02	
Chestfield & Swalecliffe	d			19 05									20 05									21 05	
Herne Bay	d	18 45		19 09							19 45		20 09							20 45		21 09	
Birchington-on-Sea	d	18 54		19 18							19 54		20 18							20 54		21 18	
Westgate-on-Sea	d			19 21									20 21									21 21	
Margate 4	d	18 59		19 25						19 55	19 59		20 25						20 55	20 59		21 25	
Broadstairs	d	19 05		19 31						20 01	20 05		20 31						21 01	21 05		21 31	
Dumpton Park	d			19 34									20 34									21 34	
Ramsgate 4	a	19 10		19 38					19 27	20 06	20 11		20 38					20 27	21 06	21 11		21 38	

A To St Pancras International B To Margate

For further services between St Pancras International, London Blackfriars and Elephant & Castle and Bromley South, St Mary Cray and Swanley refer to table T52

Table T212-F

Saturdays

21 December to 16 May

London - Medway, Sheerness-on-Sea, Dover and Ramsgate

		SE	SE	SE	SE	SE		SE	SE	SE	SE	SE	SE	SE	SE	SE		SE	SE	SE	SE	SE	SE	SE	SE
			◇1	◇1	◇	◇			◇1	◇		◇1	◇1		◇			◇1	◇	◇1	◇1	◇		◇1	◇
					A	A								B	B										
St Pancras Intl. 15 ⊖	d					20 25				20 55					21 25				21 55			22 25			22 55
Stratford International ⊖	d					20 32				21 02					21 32				22 02			22 32			23 02
Ebbsfleet International	d					20 43				21 13					21 43				22 13			22 43			23 13
London Blackfriars 3 ⊖	d																								
Elephant & Castle ⊖	d																								
London Victoria 15 ⊖	d		19 42	20 10					20 40			20 42	21 10					21 40		21 42	22 10			22 40	
Bromley South 4	d		20 05	20 27					20 57			21 05	21 27					21 57		22 05	22 27			22 57	
St Mary Cray	d		20 10									21 10								22 10					
Swanley 4	d		20 15									21 15								22 15					
Farningham Road	d		20 20									21 20								22 20					
Longfield	d		20 24	20 39					21 09			21 24	21 39					22 09		22 24	22 39			23 09	
Meopham	d		20 28	20 43					21 13			21 28	21 43					22 13		22 28	22 43			23 13	
Sole Street	d		20 31									21 31								22 31					
London Charing Cross 4 ⊖	d																								
London Waterloo (East) 4 ⊖	d																								
London Cannon Street 4 ⊖	d																								
London Bridge 4 ⊖	d																								
Dartford 4	d																								
Greenhithe for Bluewater	d																								
Gravesend 4	d					20 48				21 18					21 48				22 18			22 48			23 18
Strood 4	d					20 59				21 29					21 59				22 29			22 59			23 29
Rochester 4	d		20 40	20 53		21 02			21 23	21 32		21 40	21 53		22 02			22 23	22 32	22 40	22 53	23 02		23 23	23 32
Chatham 4	d		20 43	20 57		21 06			21 27	21 36		21 43	21 57		22 06			22 27	22 36	22 43	22 57	23 06		23 27	23 36
Gillingham (Kent) 4	d		20 48	21 01		21 10			21 31	21 40		21 48	22 01		22 10			22 31	22 40	22 48	23 01	23 10		23 31	23 40
Rainham (Kent)	d		20 53	21 06		21 15			21 36	21 45		21 53	22 06		22 15			22 36	22 45	22 53	23 06	23 15		23 36	23 45
Newington	d			21 10									22 10								23 10				
Sittingbourne 4	a		21 00	21 15		21 22			21 43	21 52		22 00	22 15		22 22			22 43	22 52	23 00	23 15	23 22		23 43	23 52
	d	20 55	21 01	21 15		21 23		21 25	21 44	21 53	21 55	22 01	22 15		22 23	22 25		22 44	22 53	23 01	23 15	23 23	23 25	23 44	23 53
Kemsley	d	21 00						21 30			22 00					22 30							23 30		
Swale	d	21 03						21 33			22 03					22 33							23 33		
Queenborough	d	21 08						21 38			22 08					22 38							23 38		
Sheerness-on-Sea	a	21 13						21 43			22 13					22 43							23 43		
Teynham	d			21 20									22 20								23 20				
Faversham 2	a		21 09	21 25		21 31			21 52	22 01		22 09	22 25		22 31			22 52	23 01	23 09		23 31		23 52	00 01
	d		21 10	21 26		21 31			21 53			22 10	22 26		22 31			22 54		23 10		23 31		23 54	
Selling	d			21 31									22 31								23s38				
Canterbury East 4	d		21 22	21 40								22a23	22 40							23a23	23 48				
Bekesbourne	d			21 45									22 45								23s52				
Adisham	d			21 49									22 49								23s56				
Aylesham	d			21 52									22 52								23s59				
Snowdown	d			21 54									22 54								00s02				
Shepherds Well	d			21 58									22 58								00s05				
Kearsney	d			22 03									23 03								00s10				
Dover Priory 4	a		21 39	22 08									23 08								00 15				
Whitstable	d					21 40			22 02						22 40			23 02				23 40		00 02	
Chestfield & Swalecliffe	d								22 05									23 05						00 05	
Herne Bay	d					21 45			22 09						22 45			23 09				23 45		00 09	
Birchington-on-Sea	d					21 54			22 18						22 54			23 18				23 54		00 18	
Westgate-on-Sea	d								22 21									23 21						00 21	
Margate 4	d				21 55	21 59			22 25					22 55	22 59			23 25				23 59		00 25	
Broadstairs	d				22 01	22 05			22 31					23 01	23 05			23 31				00 05		00 31	
Dumpton Park	d								22 34									23 34						00 34	
Ramsgate 4	a				22 06	22 11			22 38					23 06	23 11			23 38				00 11		00 38	

A To St Pancras International

B To Ashford International

For further services between St Pancras International, London Blackfriars and Elephant & Castle and Bromley South, St Mary Cray and Swanley refer to table T52

Table T212-F

Saturdays

21 December to 16 May

London - Medway, Sheerness-on-Sea, Dover and Ramsgate

		SE		SE	SE	SE	SE
		◇1		◇1	◇	◇	◇1
St Pancras Intl. 15 ⊖	d				23 25	23 55	
Stratford International ⊖	d				23 32	00 02	
Ebbsfleet International	d				23 43	00 13	
London Blackfriars 3 ⊖	d						
Elephant & Castle ⊖	d						
London Victoria 15 ⊖	d	22 42		23 10			23 42
Bromley South 4	d	23 05		23 27			00 05
St Mary Cray	d	23 10					00 10
Swanley 4	d	23 15					00 15
Farningham Road	d	23 20					00 20
Longfield	d	23 24		23 39			00 24
Meopham	d	23 28		23 43			00 28
Sole Street	d	23 31					00s31
London Charing Cross 4 ⊖	d						
London Waterloo (East) 4 ⊖	d						
London Cannon Street 4 ⊖	d						
London Bridge 4 ⊖	d						
Dartford 4	d						
Greenhithe for Bluewater	d						
Gravesend 4	d				23 48	00 18	
Strood 4	d				23 59	00 29	
Rochester 4	d	23 40		23 53	00 02	00 32	00 40
Chatham 4	d	23 43		23 57	00 06	00 36	00 43
Gillingham (Kent) 4	d	23a48		00 01	00 10	00 40	00a48
Rainham (Kent)	d			00 06	00 15	00 45	
Newington	d			00 10			
Sittingbourne 4	a			00 15	00 22	00 52	
	d			00 15	00 23	00 53	
Kemsley	d						
Swale	d						
Queenborough	d						
Sheerness-on-Sea	a						
Teynham	d			00 20			
Faversham 2	a			00 26	00 31	01 01	
	d			00 35			
Selling	d						
Canterbury East 4	d						
Bekesbourne	d						
Adisham	d						
Aylesham	d						
Snowdown	d						
Shepherds Well	d						
Kearsney	d						
Dover Priory 4	a						
Whitstable	d			00 43			
Chestfield & Swalecliffe	d			00 46			
Herne Bay	d			00 50			
Birchington-on-Sea	d			00 59			
Westgate-on-Sea	d			01 03			
Margate 4	d			01 07			
Broadstairs	d			01 13			
Dumpton Park	d			01 16			
Ramsgate 4	a			01 20			

For further services between St Pancras International, London Blackfriars and Elephant & Castle and Bromley South, St Mary Cray and Swanley refer to table T52

Table T212-F

Sundays

15 December to 10 May

London - Medway, Sheerness-on-Sea, Dover and Ramsgate

		SE ◇ A	SE ◇1 B	SE ◇1 B	SE ◇ A	SE	SE ◇ A	SE ◇1 B	SE ◇1	SE ◇ C		SE ◇ D	SE	SE	SE ◇ D	SE ◇1		SE ◇ D	SE ◇ D	SE ◇1		SE	SE ◇1		SE ◇ D
St Pancras Intl. 15 ⊖	d									00 12									08 25						
Stratford International ⊖	d						00 02			00 19									08 32						
Ebbsfleet International	d						00 13			00a30									08 43						
London Blackfriars 3 ⊖	d																								
Elephant & Castle ⊖	d																								
London Victoria 15 ⊖	d								00 10							07 40				08 10			08 40		
Bromley South 4	d							00 05	00s31							07 57				08 33			08 57		
St Mary Cray	d							00 10												08 38					
Swanley 4	d							00 15												08 43					
Farningham Road	d							00 20												08 48					
Longfield	d							00 24												08 52					
Meopham	d							00 28												08 56					
Sole Street	d							00s31												08 59					
London Charing Cross 4 ⊖	d																								
London Waterloo (East) 4 ⊖	d																								
London Cannon Street 4 ⊖	d																								
London Bridge 4 ⊖	d																								
Dartford 4	d																								
Greenhithe for Bluewater	d																								
Gravesend 4	d						00 18												08 48						
Strood 4	d						00 29												08 59						
Rochester 4	d				00 02		00 32	00 40	00 54							08 19			09 02	09 08			09 19		
Chatham 4	d				00 06		00 36	00 43	00 58							08 23			09 06	09 11			09 23		
Gillingham (Kent) 4	d			00 01	00 10		00 40	00a48	01 02				08 17			08 27			09 10	09 16			09 27		
Rainham (Kent)	d			00 06	00 15		00 45		01 07				08 21			08 32			09 15	09 21			09 32		
Newington	d			00 10					01s11				08 25							09 25					
Sittingbourne 4	a			00 15	00 22		00 52		01 16				08 30			08 39			09 22	09 30			09 39		
	d			00 15	00 23	00 26	00 53		01 16				08 30	08 34		08 40			09 23	09 30		09 34	09 40		
Kemsley	d					00s30								08 39								09 39			
Swale	d					00s34								08 42								09 42			
Queenborough	d					00s38								08 47								09 47			
Sheerness-on-Sea	a					00 44								08 52								09 52			
Teynham	d			00 20					01s21				08 35							09 35					
Faversham 2	a			00 26	00 31		01 01		01 26				08 40			08 48			09 31	09 40			09 48		
	d			00 35					01 27				08 41			08 52	08 54		09 31	09 41			09 52	09 54	
Selling	d																08 58							09 58	
Canterbury East 4	d												08a53				09 08			09a53				10 08	
Bekesbourne	d																09 12							10 12	
Adisham	d																09 16							10 16	
Aylesham	d																09 19							10 19	
Snowdown	d																09 22							10 22	
Shepherds Well	d																09 26							10 26	
Kearsney	d																09 30							10 30	
Dover Priory 4	a																09 38							10 38	
Whitstable	d		00 02	00 43					01s35							09 00			09 40				10 00		
Chestfield & Swalecliffe	d		00 05	00 46					01s38							09 03							10 03		
Herne Bay	d		00 09	00 50					01s42							09 07			09 45				10 07		
Birchington-on-Sea	d		00 18	00 59					01s51							09 16			09 54				10 16		
Westgate-on-Sea	d		00 21	01 03					01s55							09 20							10 20		
Margate 4	d		00 25	01 07					01s58			07 55			08 55	09 24		09 55	09 59				10 24		10 55
Broadstairs	d	00 05	00 31	01 13					02s04			08 01			09 01	09 30		10 01	10 05				10 30		11 01
Dumpton Park	d		00 34	01 16					02s08							09 33							10 33		
Ramsgate 4	a	00 11	00 38	01 20					02 15			08 06			09 06	09 37		10 06	10 11				10 37		11 06

A not 15 December. From St Pancras International
B not 15 December. From London Victoria
C To Ashford International
D To St Pancras International

For further services between St Pancras International, London Blackfriars and Elephant & Castle and Bromley South, St Mary Cray and Swanley refer to table T52

NRT DECEMBER 19 EDITION

Table T212-F

Sundays

15 December to 10 May

London - Medway, Sheerness-on-Sea, Dover and Ramsgate

		SE ◇ A	SE ◇1	SE	SE ◇1			SE ◇ A	SE ◇ A	SE ◇1	SE	SE ◇1		SE ◇ A	SE ◇ A	SE ◇1		SE	SE ◇1		SE ◇ A	SE ◇ A	SE ◇1	SE	
St Pancras Intl. 15 ⊖	d	09 25							10 27						11 25							12 27			
Stratford International ⊖	d	09 32							10 34						11 32							12 34			
Ebbsfleet International	d	09 44							10 45						11 43							12 45			
London Blackfriars 3 ⊖	d																								
Elephant & Castle ⊖	d																								
London Victoria 15 ⊖	d		09 10		09 40					10 10		10 40				11 10			11 40				12 10		
Bromley South 4	d		09 33		09 57					10 33		10 57				11 33			11 57				12 33		
St Mary Cray	d		09 38							10 38						11 38							12 38		
Swanley 4	d		09 43							10 43						11 43							12 43		
Farningham Road	d		09 48							10 48						11 48							12 48		
Longfield	d		09 52							10 52						11 52							12 52		
Meopham	d		09 56							10 56						11 56							12 56		
Sole Street	d		09 59							10 59						11 59							12 59		
London Charing Cross 4 ⊖	d																								
London Waterloo (East) 4 ⊖	d																								
London Cannon Street 4 ⊖	d																								
London Bridge 4 ⊖	d																								
Dartford 4	d																								
Greenhithe for Bluewater	d																								
Gravesend 4	d	09 48							10 49						11 48							12 49			
Strood 4	d	09 59							10 59						11 59							12 59			
Rochester 4	d	10 02	10 08		10 19				11 03	11 08		11 19			12 02	12 08			12 19			13 03	13 08		
Chatham 4	d	10 06	10 11		10 23				11 06	11 11		11 23			12 06	12 11			12 23			13 06	13 11		
Gillingham (Kent) 4	d	10 10	10 16		10 27				11 11	11 16		11 27			12 10	12 16			12 27			13 11	13 16		
Rainham (Kent)	d	10 15	10 21		10 32				11 15	11 21		11 32			12 15	12 21			12 32			13 15	13 21		
Newington	d		10 25							11 25						12 25							13 25		
Sittingbourne 4	a	10 22	10 30		10 39				11 22	11 30		11 39			12 22	12 30			12 39			13 22	13 30		
	d	10 23	10 30	10 34	10 40				11 23	11 30	11 34	11 40			12 23	12 30		12 34	12 40			13 23	13 30	13 34	
Kemsley	d			10 39							11 39							12 39						13 39	
Swale	d			10 42							11 42							12 42						13 42	
Queenborough	d			10 47							11 47							12 47						13 47	
Sheerness-on-Sea	a			10 52							11 52							12 52						13 52	
Teynham	d		10 35							11 35						12 35							13 35		
Faversham 2	a	10 31	10 40		10 48				11 31	11 40		11 48			12 31	12 40			12 48			13 31	13 40		
	d	10 31	10 41		10 52	10 54			11 31	11 41		11 52	11 54		12 31	12 41			12 52	12 54		13 31	13 41		
Selling	d					10 58							11 58							12 58					
Canterbury East 4	d		10a53			11 08				11a53			12 08			12a53				13 08			13a53		
Bekesbourne	d					11 12							12 12							13 12					
Adisham	d					11 16							12 16							13 16					
Aylesham	d					11 19							12 19							13 19					
Snowdown	d					11 22							12 22							13 22					
Shepherds Well	d					11 26							12 26							13 26					
Kearsney	d					11 30							12 30							13 30					
Dover Priory 4	a					11 38							12 38							13 38					
Whitstable	d	10 40			11 00				11 40			12 00			12 40				13 00			13 40			
Chestfield & Swalecliffe	d				11 03							12 03							13 03						
Herne Bay	d	10 45			11 07				11 45			12 07			12 45				13 07			13 45			
Birchington-on-Sea	d	10 54			11 16				11 54			12 16			12 54				13 16			13 54			
Westgate-on-Sea	d				11 20							12 20							13 20						
Margate 4	d	10 59			11 24			11 55	11 59			12 24		12 55	12 59				13 24		13 55	13 59			
Broadstairs	d	11 05			11 30			12 01	12 05			12 30		13 01	13 05				13 30		14 01	14 05			
Dumpton Park	d				11 33							12 33							13 33						
Ramsgate 4	a	11 11			11 37			12 06	12 11			12 37		13 06	13 11				13 37		14 06	14 11			

A To St Pancras International

For further services between St Pancras International, London Blackfriars and Elephant & Castle and Bromley South, St Mary Cray and Swanley refer to table T52

Table T212-F

Sundays

15 December to 10 May

London - Medway, Sheerness-on-Sea, Dover and Ramsgate

		SE ◇1			SE ◇	SE ◇ A	SE ◇ A	SE ◇1	SE	SE ◇1		SE ◇		SE ◇ A	SE ◇ A	SE ◇1	SE	SE ◇1		SE ◇		SE ◇ A	SE ◇ A	SE ◇1
St Pancras Intl. 15 ⊖	d				12 52		13 25					13 55			16 25					16 55			17 25	
Stratford International ⊖	d				12 59		13 32					14 02			16 32					17 02			17 32	
Ebbsfleet International	d				13 13		13 43					14 13			16 43					17 13			17 43	
London Blackfriars 3 ⊖	d																							
Elephant & Castle ⊖	d																							
London Victoria 15 ⊖	d	12 40						13 10		13 40						16 10		16 40						17 10
Bromley South 4	d	12 57						13 33		13 57						16 33		16 57						17 33
St Mary Cray	d							13 38								16 38								17 38
Swanley 4	d							13 43								16 43								17 43
Farningham Road	d							13 48								16 48								17 48
Longfield	d							13 52								16 52								17 52
Meopham	d							13 56								16 56								17 56
Sole Street	d							13 59								16 59								17 59
London Charing Cross 4 ⊖	d																							
London Waterloo (East) 4 ⊖	d																							
London Cannon Street 4 ⊖	d																							
London Bridge 4 ⊖	d																							
Dartford 4	d																							
Greenhithe for Bluewater	d																							
Gravesend 4	d				13 18		13 48					14 18			16 48					17 18			17 48	
Strood 4	d				13 29		13 59					14 29			16 59					17 29			17 59	
Rochester 4	d	13 19			13 32		14 02	14 08		14 19		14 32	and at the same minutes past each hour until		17 02	17 08		17 19		17 32			18 02	18 08
Chatham 4	d	13 23			13 36		14 06	14 11		14 23		14 36			17 06	17 11		17 23		17 36			18 06	18 11
Gillingham (Kent) 4	d	13 27			13 40		14 10	14 16		14 27		14 40			17 10	17 16		17 27		17 40			18 10	18 16
Rainham (Kent)	d	13 32			13 45		14 15	14 21		14 32		14 45			17 15	17 21		17 32		17 45			18 15	18 21
Newington	d							14 25								17 25								18 25
Sittingbourne 4	a	13 39			13 52		14 22	14 30		14 39		14 52			17 22	17 30		17 39		17 52			18 22	18 30
	d	13 40			13 53		14 23	14 30	14 34	14 40		14 53			17 23	17 30	17 34	17 40		17 53			18 23	18 30
Kemsley	d								14 39								17 39							
Swale	d								14 42								17 42							
Queenborough	d								14 47								17 47							
Sheerness-on-Sea	a								14 52								17 52							
Teynham	d							14 35								17 35								18 35
Faversham 2	a	13 48			14 03		14 31	14 40		14 48		15 03			17 31	17 40		17 48		18 03			18 31	18 40
	d	13 52	13 54				14 31	14 41		14 52	14 54				17 31	17 41		17 52	17 54				18 31	18 41
Selling	d		13 58								14 58								17 58					
Canterbury East 4	d		14 08					14a53			15 08					17a53			18 08					18a53
Bekesbourne	d		14 12								15 12								18 12					
Adisham	d		14 16								15 16								18 16					
Aylesham	d		14 19								15 19								18 19					
Snowdown	d		14 22								15 22								18 22					
Shepherds Well	d		14 26								15 26								18 26					
Kearsney	d		14 30								15 30								18 30					
Dover Priory 4	a		14 38								15 38								18 38					
Whitstable	d	14 00					14 40			15 00					17 40			18 00					18 40	
Chestfield & Swalecliffe	d	14 03								15 03								18 03						
Herne Bay	d	14 07					14 45			15 07					17 45			18 07					18 45	
Birchington-on-Sea	d	14 16					14 54			15 16					17 54			18 16					18 54	
Westgate-on-Sea	d	14 20								15 20								18 20						
Margate 4	d	14 24				14 55	14 59			15 24				17 55	17 59			18 24				18 55	18 59	
Broadstairs	d	14 30				15 01	15 05			15 30				18 01	18 05			18 30				19 01	19 05	
Dumpton Park	d	14 33								15 33								18 33						
Ramsgate 4	a	14 37				15 06	15 11			15 37				18 06	18 11			18 37				19 06	19 11	

A To St Pancras International

For further services between St Pancras International, London Blackfriars and Elephant & Castle and Bromley South, St Mary Cray and Swanley refer to table T52

Table T212-F

Sundays

15 December to 10 May

London - Medway, Sheerness-on-Sea, Dover and Ramsgate

		SE	SE ◇1		SE ◇	SE ◇ A	SE ◇ A		SE ◇1	SE	SE ◇1		SE ◇	SE ◇ A	SE ◇ A	SE ◇1	SE		SE ◇1		SE ◇	SE ◇ A	SE ◇ B	SE ◇1	SE
St Pancras Intl. 15 ⊖	d				17 57		18 25						18 55		19 25						19 55		20 25		
Stratford International ⊖	d				18 04		18 32						19 02		19 32						20 02		20 32		
Ebbsfleet International	d				18 15		18 43						19 13		19 43						20 13		20 43		
London Blackfriars 3 ⊖	d																								
Elephant & Castle ⊖	d																								
London Victoria 15 ⊖	d		17 40						18 10		18 40					19 10			19 40					20 10	
Bromley South 4	d		17 57						18 33		18 57					19 33			19 57					20 33	
St Mary Cray	d								18 38							19 38								20 38	
Swanley 4	d								18 43							19 43								20 43	
Farningham Road	d								18 48							19 48								20 48	
Longfield	d								18 52							19 52								20 52	
Meopham	d								18 56							19 56								20 56	
Sole Street	d								18 59							19 59								20 59	
London Charing Cross 4 ⊖	d																								
London Waterloo (East) 4 ⊖	d																								
London Cannon Street 4 ⊖	d																								
London Bridge 4 ⊖	d																								
Dartford 4	d																								
Greenhithe for Bluewater	d																								
Gravesend 4	d				18 19		18 48						19 18		19 48						20 18		20 48		
Strood 4	d				18 29		18 59						19 29		19 59						20 29		20 59		
Rochester 4	d		18 19		18 32		19 02		19 08		19 19		19 32		20 02	20 08			20 19		20 32		21 02	21 08	
Chatham 4	d		18 23		18 36		19 06		19 11		19 23		19 36		20 06	20 11			20 23		20 36		21 06	21 11	
Gillingham (Kent) 4	d		18 27		18 40		19 10		19 16		19 27		19 40		20 10	20 16			20 27		20 40		21 10	21 16	
Rainham (Kent)	d		18 32		18 45		19 15		19 21		19 32		19 45		20 15	20 21			20 32		20 45		21 15	21 21	
Newington	d								19 25							20 25								21 25	
Sittingbourne 4	a		18 39		18 52		19 22		19 30		19 39		19 52		20 22	20 30			20 39		20 52		21 22	21 30	
	d	18 34	18 40		18 53		19 23		19 30	19 34	19 40		19 53		20 23	20 30	20 34		20 40		20 53		21 23	21 30	21 34
Kemsley	d	18 39								19 39							20 39								21 39
Swale	d	18 42								19 42							20 42								21 42
Queenborough	d	18 47								19 47							20 47								21 47
Sheerness-on-Sea	a	18 52								19 52							20 52								21 52
Teynham	d								19 35							20 35								21 35	
Faversham 2	a		18 48		19 03		19 31		19 40		19 48		20 03		20 31	20 40			20 48		21 03		21 31	21 40	
	d		18 52	18 54			19 31		19 41		19 52	19 54			20 31	20 41			20 52	20 54			21 31	21 41	
Selling	d			18 58								19 58								20 58					
Canterbury East 4	d			19 08					19a53			20 08				20a53				21 08				21a53	
Bekesbourne	d			19 12								20 12								21 12					
Adisham	d			19 16								20 16								21 16					
Aylesham	d			19 19								20 19								21 19					
Snowdown	d			19 22								20 22								21 22					
Shepherds Well	d			19 26								20 26								21 26					
Kearsney	d			19 30								20 30								21 30					
Dover Priory 4	a			19 38								20 38								21 38					
Whitstable	d		19 00				19 40				20 00				20 40				21 00				21 40		
Chestfield & Swalecliffe	d		19 03								20 03								21 03						
Herne Bay	d		19 07				19 45				20 07				20 45				21 07				21 45		
Birchington-on-Sea	d		19 16				19 54				20 16				20 54				21 16				21 54		
Westgate-on-Sea	d		19 20								20 20								21 20						
Margate 4	d		19 24			19 55	19 59				20 24			20 55	20 59				21 24			21 55	21 59		
Broadstairs	d		19 30			20 01	20 05				20 30			21 01	21 05				21 30			22 01	22 05		
Dumpton Park	d		19 33								20 33								21 33						
Ramsgate 4	a		19 37			20 06	20 11				20 37			21 06	21 11				21 37			22 06	22 11		

A To St Pancras International

B To Ashford International

For further services between St Pancras International, London Blackfriars and Elephant & Castle and Bromley South, St Mary Cray and Swanley refer to table T52

Table T212-F

Sundays

15 December to 10 May

London - Medway, Sheerness-on-Sea, Dover and Ramsgate

Station		SE ◇■1		SE ◇	SE A	SE ◇	SE	SE ◇■1		SE ◇	SE ◇	SE	SE ◇■1	SE ◇	SE ◇	SE ◇■1	SE ◇ A
St Pancras Intl. ■15 ⊖	d			20 55		21 25				21 55	22 25			22 55	23 25		23 37
Stratford International ⊖	d			21 02		21 32				22 02	22 32			23 02	23 32		23 44
Ebbsfleet International	d			21 13		21 43				22 13	22 43			23 13	23 43		23a54
London Blackfriars ■3 ⊖	d																
Elephant & Castle ⊖	d																
London Victoria ■15 ⊖	d	20 40						21 40					22 40			23 10	
Bromley South ■4	d	20 57						21 57					22 57			23 33	
St Mary Cray	d															23 38	
Swanley ■4	d															23 43	
Farningham Road	d															23 48	
Longfield	d															23 52	
Meopham	d															23 56	
Sole Street	d															23s59	
London Charing Cross ■4 ⊖	d																
London Waterloo (East) ■4 ⊖	d																
London Cannon Street ■4 ⊖	d																
London Bridge ■4 ⊖	d																
Dartford ■4	d																
Greenhithe for Bluewater	d																
Gravesend ■4	d			21 18		21 48				22 18	22 48			23 18	23 48		
Strood ■4	d			21 29		21 59				22 29	22 59			23 29	23 59		
Rochester ■4	d	21 19		21 32		22 02		22 19		22 32	23 02		23 19	23 32	00 02	00 08	
Chatham ■4	d	21 23		21 36		22 06		22 23		22 36	23 06		23 23	23 36	00 06	00 11	
Gillingham (Kent) ■4	d	21 27		21 40		22 10		22 27		22 40	23 10		23 27	23 40	00 10	00a17	
Rainham (Kent)	d	21 32		21 45		22 15		22 32		22 45	23 15		23 32	23 45	00 15		
Newington	d												23 36				
Sittingbourne ■4	a	21 39		21 52		22 22		22 39		22 52	23 22		23 42	23 52	00 22		
	d	21 40		21 53		22 23	22 34	22 40		22 53	23 23	23 36	23 43	23 53	00 23		
Kemsley	d						22 39					23 41					
Swale	d						22 42					23 44					
Queenborough	d						22 47					23 49					
Sheerness-on-Sea	a						22 52					23 54					
Teynham	d												23 47				
Faversham ■2	a	21 48		22 03		22 31		22 48		23 03	23 31		23 53	00 01	00 32		
	d	21 52	21 54			22 31		22 52	22 54		23 31		23 54				
Selling	d		21 58						22 58								
Canterbury East ■4	d		22 08						23 08								
Bekesbourne	d		22 12						23 12								
Adisham	d		22 16						23 16								
Aylesham	d		22 19						23 19								
Snowdown	d		22 22						23 22								
Shepherds Well	d		22 26						23 26								
Kearsney	d		22 30						23 30								
Dover Priory ■4	a		22 38						23 38								
Whitstable	d	22 00				22 40		23 00			23 40		00 03				
Chestfield & Swalecliffe	d	22 03						23 03					00 06				
Herne Bay	d	22 07				22 45		23 07			23 45		00 09				
Birchington-on-Sea	d	22 16				22 54		23 16			23 54		00 18				
Westgate-on-Sea	d	22 20						23 20					00 22				
Margate ■4	d	22 24			22 55	22 59		23 24			23 59		00 26				
Broadstairs	d	22 30			23 01	23 05		23 30			00 05		00 32				
Dumpton Park	d	22 33						23 33					00 35				
Ramsgate ■4	a	22 37			23 06	23 11		23 37			00 11		00 39				

A To Ashford International

For further services between St Pancras International, London Blackfriars and Elephant & Castle and Bromley South, St Mary Cray and Swanley refer to table T52

NRT DECEMBER 19 EDITION

Table T212-R

Mondays to Fridays

16 December to 15 May

Ramsgate, Dover, Sheerness-on-Sea and Medway - London

Miles	Miles	Miles	Miles	Miles	Station		SE MX ■1 A	SE WO B (bus)	SE MO ◇ C	SE ThFO ◇ C	SE WO (bus)	SE TO ◇ C	SE ■1	SE ◇	SE	SE ◇■1	SE ◇■1	SE	SE ◇	SE ◇■1	SE	SE ◇	SE	SE ■1
0	—	—	—	—	**Ramsgate** ■4	d			00 27	00 30	00 36	00 44				04 25						05 12		
1	—	—	—	—	Dumpton Park	d										04 28						05 15		
2¼	—	—	—	—	Broadstairs	d			00s32	00s35	00s45	00s49				04 31						05 18		
5½	—	—	—	—	**Margate** ■4	d			00a38	00a40	00a55	00a57				04 36						05 23		
6¾	—	—	—	—	Westgate-on-Sea	d										04 40						05 27		
8½	—	—	—	—	Birchington-on-Sea	d										04 43						05 31		
16¼	—	—	—	—	**Herne Bay**	d		00 07								04 52						05 40		
18½	—	—	—	—	Chestfield & Swalecliffe	d		00 15								04 56						05 43		
20½	—	—	—	—	Whitstable	d		00 23								04 59						05 47		
—	0	—	—	—	**Dover Priory** ■4	d														04 48				
—	2¼	—	—	—	Kearsney	d														04 53				
—	5½	—	—	—	Shepherds Well	d														04 58				
—	7½	—	—	—	Snowdown	d														05 02				
—	8½	—	—	—	Aylesham	d														05 05				
—	9½	—	—	—	Adisham	d														05 07				
—	12½	—	—	—	Bekesbourne	d														05 12				
—	15½	—	—	—	**Canterbury East** ■4	d														05 17				
—	22	—	—	—	Selling	d														05 27				
27¼	25¼	—	—	0	**Faversham** ■2	a		00s43								05 07				05 31		05 55		
—	—	—	—	—		d	00 02							04 58		05 09			05 28	05 33		05 56		
31¾	29¾	—	—	4½	Teynham	d	00 08	00s58												05 39				
—	—	0	—	—	**Sheerness-on-Sea**	d															05 32		05 55	
—	—	2	—	—	Queenborough	d															05 37		06 00	
—	—	4	—	—	Swale	d															05 41		06 04	
—	—	6	—	—	Kemsley	d															05 45		06 08	
34½	32½	8	—	7¼	**Sittingbourne** ■4	a	00 12	01s08						05 06		05 16			05 36	05 44	05 50	06 03	06 13	
—	—	—	—	—		d	00 13							05 07		05 17			05 37	05 44		06 04		
37¾	35¾	—	—	10½	Newington	d	00 18	01s20												05 50				
40¼	38¼	—	—	13	Rainham (Kent)	d	00 22	01s30						05 15		05 24			05 45	05 54		06 11		
43¼	41¼	—	0	16	**Gillingham (Kent)** ■4	d	00a29	01a45					05 14	05 20	05 26	05 30	05 40	05 45	05 50	06 00		06 17		06 21
45	43	—	1¾	17¾	**Chatham** ■4	d							05 18	05 24	05 30	05 34	05 44	05 49	05 54	06 04		06 21		06 25
45½	43½	—	2¼	18¼	Rochester ■4	d							05 22	05 28	05 34	05 38	05 48	05 53	05 58	06 08		06 25		06 29
—	—	—	3¼	19¼	Strood ■4	a								05 31	05 37				06 01			06 28		
—	—	—	10½	26½	Gravesend ■4	a								05 41	05 49				06 11			06 38		
—	—	—	14½	—	Greenhithe for Bluewater	a									05 58									
—	—	—	17¼	—	Dartford ■4	a									06 05									
—	—	—	34¼	—	**London Bridge** ■4 ⊖	a											06 25							
—	—	—	—	—	**London Cannon Street** ■4 ⊖	a											06 33							
—	—	—	35¼	—	**London Waterloo (East)** ■4 ⊖	a																		
—	—	—	36	—	**London Charing Cross** ■4 ⊖	a																		
52¼	50¼	—	—	—	Sole Street	d							05 31					06 02						06 38
53¼	51¼	—	—	—	Meopham	d							05 34					06 05						06 41
55¾	53¾	—	—	—	Longfield	d							05 38					06 10						06 46
58¾	56¾	—	—	—	Farningham Road	d							05 42					06 14						06 50
61¾	59¾	—	—	—	Swanley ■4	a							05 47					06 18						06 55
64½	62½	—	—	—	St Mary Cray	a							05 51					06 23						07 00
68¼	66¼	—	—	—	Bromley South ■4	a							05 58			06 01		06 29		06 32				07 06
79¼	77¼	—	—	—	**London Victoria** ■15 ⊖	a							06 20		07 02	06 23		06 50		06 53				07 34
—	—	—	—	—	Elephant & Castle ⊖	a																		
—	—	—	—	—	**London Blackfriars** ■3 ⊖	a																		
—	—	—	—	28½	Ebbsfleet International	a								05 45					06 15			06 42		
—	—	—	—	45¼	Stratford International ⊖	a								05 57					06 27			06 55		
—	—	—	—	51¾	**St Pancras International**	a								06 05					06 35			07 02		

A From Dover Priory **B** From Ramsgate **C** From St Pancras International

For further services between St Pancras International, London Blackfriars and Elephant & Castle and Bromley South, St Mary Cray and Swanley refer to table T52

Table T212-R

Mondays to Fridays

16 December to 15 May

Ramsgate, Dover, Sheerness-on-Sea and Medway - London

		SE	SE	SE	SE	SE	SE	SE	SE	SE	SE	SE	SE	SE	SE	SE	SE	SE	SE	SE	SE	SE
		◇1	◇1	◇1	◇	◇1	◇1	1	1		◇1	◇	1		◇1	◇1	◇1	1	◇		◇1	◇1
Ramsgate [4]	d						05 56									06 30					06 55	
Dumpton Park	d						05 59									06 33	06 38				06 58	
Broadstairs	d			05 42			06 02				06 23	06 29				06 36	06 41		06 58		07 02	
Margate [4]	d			05 48			06 07				06 28	06 34				06 41	06 50		07 03		07 07	
Westgate-on-Sea	d			05 52			06 11									06 44	06 54				07 10	
Birchington-on-Sea	d			05 56			06 14				06 33	06 39				06 48	06 58		07 08		07 14	
Herne Bay	d			06 05			06 23				06 42	06 48				06 57	07 07		07 17		07 23	
Chestfield & Swalecliffe	d			06 09			06 27									07 00	07 11				07 26	
Whitstable	d			06 12			06 30				06 48	06 53				07 04	07 14		07 23		07 30	
Dover Priory [4]	d		05 32						06 02				06 24									07 04
Kearsney	d		05 36						06 06				06 28									07 08
Shepherds Well	d		05 42						06 12				06 34									07 14
Snowdown	d		05 45						06 15				06 37									07 17
Aylesham	d		05 48						06 18				06 40									07 20
Adisham	d		05 51						06 21				06 43									07 23
Bekesbourne	d		05 55						06 25				06 47									07 27
Canterbury East [4]	d		06 02						06 31				06 53									07 33
Selling	d		06 11						06 40				07 02									07 42
Faversham [2]	a		06 16	06 21			06 38		06 46		06 56	07 01	07 07			07 12	07 22		07 31		07 38	07 46
	d	06 07	06 18	06 23	06 28		06 39				06 57	07 02				07 13	07 23		07 31		07 39	07 47
Teynham	d	06 13					06 46									07 19						07 53
Sheerness-on-Sea	d					06 24				06 36				06 52	07 00					07 26		
Queenborough	d					06 29				06 42				06 56	07 05					07 30		
Swale	d									06 46				07 00						07 34		
Kemsley	d					06 37				06 50				07 04	07 12					07 38		
Sittingbourne [4]	a	06 17	06 25	06 30	06 36		06 50			06 55	07 04	07 09		07 09		07 23	07 31		07 39	07 42	07 46	07 58
	d	06 18	06 26	06 31	06 36		06 51				07 05	07 10				07 24	07 31		07 39		07 47	07 58
Newington	d	06 23					06 56									07 29					07 52	08 03
Rainham (Kent)	d	06 28	06 34	06 38	06 44	06 48	07 01				07 13	07 17			07 22	07 34	07 39		07 47		07 57	08 08
Gillingham (Kent) [4]	d	06 33	06 39	06 44	06 49	06 53	07 06				07 18	07 22			07 27	07 39	07 44		07 52		08 03	08 13
Chatham [4]	d	06 37	06 43	06 48	06 53	06 58	07 10				07 22	07 27			07 32	07 44	07 49		07 56		08 07	08 17
Rochester [4]	d	06 41	06 47	06 52	06 57	07 01	07 14	07 17			07 26	07 30			07 35	07 48	07 52	07 56	08 00		08 11	08 21
Strood [4]	a											07 33							08 03			
Gravesend [4]	a											07 43							08 13			
Greenhithe for Bluewater	a																					
Dartford [4]	a																					
London Bridge [4] ⊖	a	07 19									08 07						08 32				08 51	
London Cannon Street [4] ⊖	a	07 27									08 15						08 40				08 59	
London Waterloo (East) [4] ⊖	a																					
London Charing Cross [4] ⊖	a																					
Sole Street	d					07 11		07 27										08 06				
Meopham	d					07 13		07 30							07 46			08 09				08 32
Longfield	d					07 18	07 27								07 51			08 13				08 36
Farningham Road	d					07 22		07 36										08 18				
Swanley [4]	a					07 27		07 40							07 57			08 22				
St Mary Cray	a					07 31		07 45							08 02			08 27				
Bromley South [4]	a		07 10	07 15		07 38	07 39	07 52							08 08	08 11		08 33				08 48
London Victoria [15] ⊖	a		07 38			08 07	08 03	08 24							08 36	08 35		09 03				09 11
Elephant & Castle ⊖	a			07 37																		
London Blackfriars [3] ⊖	a			07 44																		
Ebbsfleet International	a				07 11							07 48							08 17			
Stratford International ⊖	a				07 24							08 00							08 30			
St Pancras International	a				07 31							08 08							08 38			

For further services between St Pancras International, London Blackfriars and Elephant & Castle and Bromley South, St Mary Cray and Swanley refer to table T52

Table T212-R

Mondays to Fridays

16 December to 15 May

Ramsgate, Dover, Sheerness-on-Sea and Medway - London

		SE	SE	SE	SE	SE	SE	SE	SE	SE	SE	SE	SE	SE	SE	SE	SE	SE	SE	SE	SE	SE	SE
				◇	◇1		1	◇	◇1	◇1	1	◇		◇1	◇1	◇	◇1		◇	◇1	◇	◇	
		A														B					B	B	
Ramsgate [4]	d	07 14			07 19				07 40					08 10		08 23				08 53	09 20	09 31	
Dumpton Park	d				07 22				07 43					08 13						08 56			
Broadstairs	d	07 20			07 25				07 46					08 16		08 28				08 59	09 25	09 36	
Margate [4]	d	07a26			07 30				07 52					08 21		08a34				09 04	09 30	09a42	
Westgate-on-Sea	d				07 34				07 55					08 25						09 08			
Birchington-on-Sea	d				07 37				07 59					08 28						09 11	09 35		
Herne Bay	d				07 46				08 08					08 37						09 20	09 44		
Chestfield & Swalecliffe	d				07 50				08 11					08 41						09 24			
Whitstable	d				07 53				08 15					08 44						09 27	09 49		
Dover Priory [4]	d									07 40					08 15		08 52						
Kearsney	d									07 44					08 19								
Shepherds Well	d									07 50					08 25								
Snowdown	d									07 53					08 28								
Aylesham	d									07 56					08 31								
Adisham	d									07 59					08 34								
Bekesbourne	d									08 03					08 38								
Canterbury East [4]	d									08 11					08 44		09 09						
Selling	d									08 20					08 53								
Faversham [2]	a				08 01				08 23	08 25				08 53	08 58		09 20			09 35	09 57		
	d			07 59	08 03			08 28	08 32			08 59		09 02			09 22		09 30	09 37	09 58		
Teynham	d								08 38					09 08									
Sheerness-on-Sea	d		07 42			08 18							08 50					09 18					09 48
Queenborough	d		07 47			08 23							08 55					09 23					09 53
Swale	d		07 51			08 27							08 59					09 27					09 57
Kemsley	d		07 55			08 31							09 03					09 31					10 01
Sittingbourne [4]	a		07 59	08 06	08 10	08 35		08 36	08 42			09 07	09 09	09 12			09 29	09 36	09 38	09 44	10 05		10 06
	d			08 07	08 11			08 38	08 43			09 08		09 13			09 30		09 38	09 45	10 08		
Newington	d								08 48					09 18									
Rainham (Kent)	d			08 14	08 18			08 46	08 52			09 16		09 22			09 37		09 46	09 52	10 16		
Gillingham (Kent) [4]	d			08 19	08 24		08 28	08 51	08 57			09 21		09 27			09 44		09 51	09 57	10 21		
Chatham [4]	d			08 24	08 28		08 32	08 55	09 02			09 25		09 32			09 48		09 55	10 02	10 25		
Rochester [4]	d			08 27	08 32		08 36	08 59	09 05		09 20	09 29		09 35			09 52		09 59	10 05	10 29		
Strood [4]	a			08 31				09 02				09 32							10 02		10 32		
Gravesend [4]	a			08 41				09 12				09 42							10 12		10 42		
Greenhithe for Bluewater	a																						
Dartford [4]	a																						
London Bridge [4] ⊖	a				09 10																		
London Cannon Street [4] ⊖	a				09 18																		
London Waterloo (East) [4] ⊖	a																						
London Charing Cross [4] ⊖	a																						
Sole Street	d						08 45				09 31						10 01						
Meopham	d						08 48		09 16		09 34			09 46			10 04			10 16			
Longfield	d						08 52		09 20		09 38			09 50			10 08			10 20			
Farningham Road	d						08 56				09 42						10 12						
Swanley [4]	a						09 01				09 47						10 17						
St Mary Cray	a						09 05				09 51						10 21						
Bromley South [4]	a						09 12		09 32		09 59			10 02			10 29			10 32			
London Victoria [15] ⊖	a						09 41		09 53		10 32			10 23			11 00			10 51			
Elephant & Castle ⊖	a																						
London Blackfriars [3] ⊖	a																						
Ebbsfleet International	a			08 46				09 16				09 46							10 16		10 46		
Stratford International ⊖	a			08 59				09 28				10 02							10 33		10 58		
St Pancras International	a			09 07				09 36				10 10							10 41		11 06		

A From Ashford International

B From St Pancras International

For further services between St Pancras International, London Blackfriars and Elephant & Castle and Bromley South, St Mary Cray and Swanley refer to table T52

Table T212-R

Mondays to Fridays
16 December to 15 May

Ramsgate, Dover, Sheerness-on-Sea and Medway - London

		SE ◇1	SE ◇1	SE	SE ◇	SE ◇1	SE ◇ A	SE ◇ A	SE	SE ◇1	SE ◇1	SE	SE ◇	SE ◇1	SE ◇ A	SE ◇ A	SE	SE ◇1	SE ◇1	SE	SE ◇	SE ◇1
Ramsgate	d					09 53	10 20	10 28						10 53	11 20	11 28						11 53
Dumpton Park	d					09 56								10 56								11 56
Broadstairs	d					09 59	10 25	10 33						10 59	11 25	11 33						11 59
Margate	d					10 04	10 30	10a38						11 04	11 30	11a38						12 04
Westgate-on-Sea	d					10 08								11 08								12 08
Birchington-on-Sea	d					10 11	10 35							11 11	11 35							12 11
Herne Bay	d					10 20	10 44							11 20	11 44							12 20
Chestfield & Swalecliffe	d					10 24								11 24								12 24
Whitstable	d					10 27	10 49							11 27	11 49							12 27
Dover Priory	d	09 15	09 52							10 18	10 52							11 18	11 52			
Kearsney	d	09 19								10 22								11 22				
Shepherds Well	d	09 25								10 28								11 28				
Snowdown	d	09 28								10 31								11 31				
Aylesham	d	09 31								10 34								11 34				
Adisham	d	09 34								10 37								11 37				
Bekesbourne	d	09 38								10 41								11 41				
Canterbury East	d	09 44	10 09							10 47	11 09							11 47	12 09			
Selling	d	09 53								10 56								11 56				
Faversham	a	09 58	10 20			10 35	10 57			11 01	11 20			11 35	11 57			12 01	12 20			12 35
	d	10 02	10 22		10 30	10 37	10 58			11 02	11 22		11 30	11 37	11 58			12 02	12 22		12 30	12 37
Teynham	d	10 08								11 08								12 08				
Sheerness-on-Sea	d			10 18					10 48			11 18					11 48			12 18		
Queenborough	d			10 23					10 53			11 23					11 53			12 23		
Swale	d			10 27					10 57			11 27					11 57			12 27		
Kemsley	d			10 31					11 01			11 31					12 01			12 31		
Sittingbourne	a	10 12	10 29	10 36	10 38	10 44	11 05		11 06	11 12	11 29	11 36	11 38	11 44	12 05		12 06	12 12	12 29	12 36	12 38	12 44
	d	10 13	10 30		10 38	10 45	11 08			11 13	11 30		11 38	11 45	12 08			12 13	12 30		12 38	12 45
Newington	d	10 18								11 18								12 18				
Rainham (Kent)	d	10 22	10 37		10 46	10 52	11 16			11 22	11 37		11 46	11 52	12 16			12 22	12 37		12 46	12 52
Gillingham (Kent)	d	10 27	10 44		10 51	10 57	11 21			11 27	11 44		11 51	11 57	12 21			12 27	12 44		12 51	12 57
Chatham	d	10 32	10 48		10 55	11 02	11 25			11 32	11 48		11 55	12 02	12 25			12 32	12 48		12 55	13 02
Rochester	d	10 35	10 52		10 59	11 05	11 29			11 35	11 52		11 59	12 05	12 29			12 35	12 52		12 59	13 05
Strood	a				11 02		11 32						12 02		12 32						13 02	
Gravesend	a				11 12		11 42						12 12		12 42						13 12	
Greenhithe for Bluewater	a																					
Dartford	a																					
London Bridge ⊖	a																					
London Cannon Street ⊖	a																					
London Waterloo (East) ⊖	a																					
London Charing Cross ⊖	a																					
Sole Street	d		11 01								12 01								13 01			
Meopham	d	10 46	11 04			11 16				11 46	12 04			12 16				12 46	13 04			13 16
Longfield	d	10 50	11 08			11 20				11 50	12 08			12 20				12 50	13 08			13 20
Farningham Road	d		11 12								12 12								13 12			
Swanley	a		11 17								12 17								13 17			
St Mary Cray	a		11 21								12 21								13 21			
Bromley South	a	11 02	11 29			11 32				12 02	12 29			12 32				13 02	13 29			13 32
London Victoria ⊖	a	11 21	12 00			11 51				12 21	13 00			12 51				13 21	14 01			13 51
Elephant & Castle ⊖	a																					
London Blackfriars ⊖	a																					
Ebbsfleet International	a				11 16		11 46						12 16		12 46						13 16	
Stratford International ⊖	a				11 29		11 58						12 28		12 58						13 29	
St Pancras International	a				11 40		12 06						12 36		13 06						13 37	

A From St Pancras International

For further services between St Pancras International, London Blackfriars and Elephant & Castle and Bromley South, St Mary Cray and Swanley refer to table T52

Table T212-R

Mondays to Fridays
16 December to 15 May

Ramsgate, Dover, Sheerness-on-Sea and Medway - London

		SE ◇ A	SE ◇ A	SE	SE ◇1	SE ◇1	SE	SE ◇	SE ◇1	SE ◇ A	SE ◇ A	SE	SE ◇1	SE ◇1	SE	SE ◇	SE ◇1	SE ◇ A	SE ◇ A	SE	SE ◇1	SE ◇	SE
Ramsgate	d	12 20	12 28						12 53	13 20	13 28						13 53	14 20	14 28				
Dumpton Park	d								12 56								13 56						
Broadstairs	d	12 25	12 33						12 59	13 25	13 33						13 59	14 25	14 33				
Margate	d	12 30	12a38						13 04	13 30	13a38						14 04	14 30	14a38				
Westgate-on-Sea	d								13 08								14 08						
Birchington-on-Sea	d	12 35							13 11	13 35							14 11	14 35					
Herne Bay	d	12 44							13 20	13 44							14 20	14 44					
Chestfield & Swalecliffe	d								13 24								14 24						
Whitstable	d	12 49							13 27	13 49							14 27	14 49					
Dover Priory	d				12 18	12 52							13 18	13 52							14 18	14 52	
Kearsney	d				12 22								13 22								14 22		
Shepherds Well	d				12 28								13 28								14 28		
Snowdown	d				12 31								13 31								14 31		
Aylesham	d				12 34								13 34								14 34		
Adisham	d				12 37								13 37								14 37		
Bekesbourne	d				12 41								13 41								14 41		
Canterbury East	d				12 47	13 09							13 47	14 09							14 47	15 09	
Selling	d				12 56								13 56								14 56		
Faversham	a	12 57			13 01	13 20			13 35	13 57			14 01	14 20			14 35	14 57			15 01	15 20	
	d	12 58			13 02	13 22		13 30	13 37	13 58			14 02	14 22		14 30	14 37	14 58			15 02	15 22	
Teynham	d				13 08								14 08								15 08		
Sheerness-on-Sea	d			12 48			13 18					13 48			14 18					14 48			15 18
Queenborough	d			12 53			13 23					13 53			14 23					14 53			15 23
Swale	d			12 57			13 27					13 57			14 27					14 57			15 27
Kemsley	d			13 01			13 31					14 01			14 31					15 01			15 31
Sittingbourne	a	13 05		13 06	13 12	13 29	13 37	13 38	13 44	14 05		14 06	14 12	14 29	14 36	14 38	14 44	15 05		15 06	15 12	15 29	15 36
	d	13 08			13 13	13 30		13 38	13 45	14 08			14 13	14 30		14 38	14 45	15 08			15 13	15 30	
Newington	d				13 18								14 18								15 18		
Rainham (Kent)	d	13 16			13 22	13 37		13 46	13 52	14 16			14 22	14 37		14 46	14 52	15 16			15 22	15 37	
Gillingham (Kent)	d	13 21			13 27	13 44		13 51	13 57	14 21			14 27	14 44		14 51	14 57	15 21			15 27	15 44	
Chatham	d	13 25			13 32	13 48		13 55	14 02	14 25			14 32	14 48		14 55	15 02	15 25			15 32	15 48	
Rochester	d	13 29			13 35	13 52		13 59	14 05	14 29			14 35	14 52		14 59	15 05	15 29			15 35	15 52	
Strood	a	13 32						14 02		14 32						15 02		15 32					
Gravesend	a	13 42						14 12		14 42						15 12		15 42					
Greenhithe for Bluewater	a																						
Dartford	a																						
London Bridge ⊖	a																						
London Cannon Street ⊖	a																						
London Waterloo (East) ⊖	a																						
London Charing Cross ⊖	a																						
Sole Street	d					14 01								15 01								16 01	
Meopham	d				13 46	14 04			14 16				14 46	15 04			15 16				15 46	16 04	
Longfield	d				13 50	14 08			14 20				14 50	15 08			15 20				15 50	16 08	
Farningham Road	d					14 12								15 12								16 12	
Swanley	a					14 17								15 17								16 17	
St Mary Cray	a					14 21								15 21								16 21	
Bromley South	a				14 02	14 29			14 32				15 02	15 29			15 32				16 02	16 29	
London Victoria ⊖	a				14 21	15 00			14 51				15 21	16 01			15 51				16 21	17 01	
Elephant & Castle ⊖	a																						
London Blackfriars ⊖	a																						
Ebbsfleet International	a	13 46						14 16		14 46						15 16		15 46					
Stratford International ⊖	a	14 02						14 28		14 58						15 28		16 02					
St Pancras International	a	14 10						14 36		15 06						15 36		16 10					

A From St Pancras International

For further services between St Pancras International, London Blackfriars and Elephant & Castle and Bromley South, St Mary Cray and Swanley refer to table T52

Table T212-R

Mondays to Fridays

16 December to 15 May

Ramsgate, Dover, Sheerness-on-Sea and Medway - London

		SE	SE	SE	SE	SE	SE	SE	SE	SE	SE	SE	SE	SE	SE	SE	SE	SE	SE	SE	SE	SE	SE
		◇	◇1	◇	◇		◇1	1	◇		◇1	◇1	1	1	◇	◇		◇1	1	◇		◇1	◇1
				A	A										A	A							
Ramsgate 4	d		14 49	15 20	15 28						15 42		16 05		16 20	16 28						16 52	
Dumpton Park	d		14 52								15 45		16 08									16 55	
Broadstairs	d		14 55	15 25	15 33						15 48		16 11		16 25	16 33						16 58	
Margate 4	d		15 00	15 30	15a38						15 55		16 16		16 30	16a38						17 03	
Westgate-on-Sea	d		15 03								15 59		16 20									17 07	
Birchington-on-Sea	d		15 07	15 35							16 03		16 23		16 35							17 10	
Herne Bay	d		15 16	15 44							16 12		16 32		16 44							17 19	
Chestfield & Swalecliffe	d		15 19								16 15		16 36									17 23	
Whitstable	d		15 23	15 49							16 19		16 39		16 49							17 26	
Dover Priory 4	d						15 18					15 48						16 20					16 55
Kearsney	d						15 22					15 52						16 24					16 59
Shepherds Well	d						15 28					15 58						16 29					17 05
Snowdown	d						15 31					16 01											17 08
Aylesham	d						15 34					16 04						16 34					17 11
Adisham	d						15 37											16 36					
Bekesbourne	d						15 41					16 09											17 17
Canterbury East 4	d						15 47					16 15						16 44					17 23
Selling	d						15 56					16 24						16 53					17 32
Faversham 2	a		15 31	15 57			16 01				16 27	16 29	16 48		16 57			16 58				17 35	17 37
	d	15 28	15 32	15 58			16 02		16 25		16 33				16 58			17 02		17 28		17 41	
Teynham	d		15 38				16 08				16 39							17 08					
Sheerness-on-Sea	d					15 51				16 18							16 48				17 21		
Queenborough	d					15 56				16 23							16 53				17 25		
Swale	d					16 00				16 27							16 57				17 29		
Kemsley	d					16 04				16 31							17 01				17 33		
Sittingbourne 4	a	15 36	15 42	16 05		16 09	16 12		16 33	16 36	16 43				17 05		17 06	17 12		17 36	17 38	17 48	
	d	15 38	15 43	16 08			16 13		16 37		16 44				17 08			17 13		17 38		17 49	
Newington	d		15 48				16 18				16 49							17 18					
Rainham (Kent)	d	15 46	15 52	16 16			16 22		16 46		16 53				17 16			17 22		17 46		17 56	
Gillingham (Kent) 4	d	15 51	15 57	16 21			16 27	16 44	16 51		16 58			17 14	17 21			17 27	17 44	17 51		18 01	
Chatham 4	d	15 55	16 02	16 25			16 32	16 48	16 55		17 03			17 18	17 25			17 32	17 48	17 55		18 05	
Rochester 4	d	15 59	16 05	16 29			16 35	16 52	16 59		17 06			17 22	17 29			17 35	17 52	17 59		18 09	
Strood 4	a	16 02		16 32					17 02						17 32					18 02			
Gravesend 4	a	16 12		16 42					17 12						17 42					18 13			
Greenhithe for Bluewater	a																						
Dartford 4	a																						
London Bridge 4 ⊖	a																						
London Cannon Street 4 ⊖	a																						
London Waterloo (East) 4 ⊖	a																						
London Charing Cross 4 ⊖	a																						
Sole Street	d							17 01						17 31					18 01				
Meopham	d		16 16				16 46	17 04			17 17			17 34				17 46	18 04				
Longfield	d		16 20				16 50	17 08			17 21			17 38				17 50	18 08				
Farningham Road	d							17 12						17 42					18 12				
Swanley 4	a							17 17						17 47					18 17				
St Mary Cray	a							17 21						17 51					18 21				
Bromley South 4	a		16 32				17 02	17 29			17 33			17 59				18 02	18 29			18 32	
London Victoria 15 ⊖	a		16 51				17 21	18 00			17 54			18 30				18 21	19 00			18 52	
Elephant & Castle ⊖	a																						
London Blackfriars 3 ⊖	a																						
Ebbsfleet International	a	16 16		16 46					17 16						17 46					18 17			
Stratford International ⊖	a	16 28		17 02					17 28						18 03					18 29			
St Pancras International	a	16 36		17 10					17 36						18 10					18 37			

A From St Pancras International

For further services between St Pancras International, London Blackfriars and Elephant & Castle and Bromley South, St Mary Cray and Swanley refer to table T52

Table T212-R

Mondays to Fridays

16 December to 15 May

Ramsgate, Dover, Sheerness-on-Sea and Medway - London

		SE	SE	SE	SE	SE	SE	SE	SE	SE	SE	SE	SE	SE	SE	SE	SE	SE	SE	SE	SE	SE
		◇	◇		◇1	◇1			◇	◇1	◇1	◇	◇		◇1	1	◇	◇	◇		◇1	◇1
		A	A									A					A		A			
Ramsgate 4	d	17 20	17 32		17 05					17 48		18 03					18 26		18 31		18 48	
Dumpton Park	d				17 08					17 51							18 29				18 51	
Broadstairs	d	17 25	17 37		17 11					17 54		18 08					18 32		18 36		18 54	
Margate 4	d	17 30	17a42		17 16					17 59		18a15	18 25				18 38		18a44		18 59	
Westgate-on-Sea	d				17 20					18 03			18 29				18 41				19 03	
Birchington-on-Sea	d	17 35			17 23					18 06			18 33				18 45				19 06	
Herne Bay	d	17 44			17 32					18 15			18 42				18 54				19 15	
Chestfield & Swalecliffe	d				17 36					18 19			18 45				18 58				19 19	
Whitstable	d	17 49			17 39					18 22			18 49				19 01				19 22	
Dover Priory 4	d					17 20					17 52				18 20							18 52
Kearsney	d					17 24					17 56				18 24							18 56
Shepherds Well	d					17 29					18 02				18 29							19 02
Snowdown	d										18 05											19 05
Aylesham	d					17 34					18 08				18 34							19 08
Adisham	d					17 36									18 36							
Bekesbourne	d										18 14											19 14
Canterbury East 4	d					17 44					18 19				18 44							19 19
Selling	d					17 53					18 28				18 53							19 28
Faversham 2	a	17 57			17 48	17 58				18 31	18 33		18 57		18 58		19 10				19 31	19 33
	d	17 58			18 03				18 28	18 37			18 58		19 02			19 30			19 37	
Teynham	d				18 09										19 08							
Sheerness-on-Sea	d			17 51				18 18						18 52						19 22		
Queenborough	d			17 55				18 23						18 56						19 26		
Swale	d			17 59				18 27						19 00						19 30		
Kemsley	d			18 03				18 30						19 04						19 34		
Sittingbourne 4	a	18 05		18 08	18 13			18 35	18 36	18 44			19 05	19 08	19 12			19 38		19 38	19 44	
	d	18 08			18 14				18 38	18 45			19 08		19 13			19 38			19 45	
Newington	d				18 19										19 18							
Rainham (Kent)	d	18 16			18 23				18 46	18 52			19 16		19 22			19 46			19 52	
Gillingham (Kent) 4	d	18 21			18 28				18 51	18 57			19 21		19 27			19 51			19 57	
Chatham 4	d	18 25			18 33				18 55	19 02			19 25		19 32			19 55			20 02	
Rochester 4	d	18 29			18 36		18 53		18 59	19 05			19 29		19 35	19 53		19 59			20 05	
Strood 4	a	18 34							19 02				19 32					20 02				
Gravesend 4	a	18 44							19 12				19 42					20 12				
Greenhithe for Bluewater	a																					
Dartford 4	a																					
London Bridge 4 ⊖	a																					
London Cannon Street 4 ⊖	a																					
London Waterloo (East) 4 ⊖	a																					
London Charing Cross 4 ⊖	a																					
Sole Street	d						19 02									20 02						
Meopham	d				18 47		19 05			19 16					19 46	20 05					20 16	
Longfield	d				18 51		19 09			19 20					19 50	20 09					20 20	
Farningham Road	d						19 13									20 13						
Swanley 4	a						19 18									20 18						
St Mary Cray	a						19 22									20 22						
Bromley South 4	a				19 03		19 29			19 32					20 02	20 29					20 32	
London Victoria 15 ⊖	a				19 24		20 00			19 54					20 21	21 00					20 51	
Elephant & Castle ⊖	a																					
London Blackfriars 3 ⊖	a																					
Ebbsfleet International	a	18 49							19 16				19 46					20 16				
Stratford International ⊖	a	19 01							19 28				19 58					20 28				
St Pancras International	a	19 09							19 36				20 06					20 36				

A From St Pancras International

For further services between St Pancras International, London Blackfriars and Elephant & Castle and Bromley South, St Mary Cray and Swanley refer to table T52

Table T212-R

Mondays to Fridays

16 December to 15 May

Ramsgate, Dover, Sheerness-on-Sea and Medway - London

		SE ◇ A	SE ◇	SE ◇ A	SE	SE ◇1	SE	SE 1	SE ◇	SE 1	SE ◇1	SE ◇ A	SE ◇	SE ◇ A	SE	SE ◇1	SE	SE ◇1	SE ◇	SE ◇1	SE ◇1	SE ◇ A	SE ◇ A
Ramsgate 4	d	19 01	19 20	19 31							19 53	20 02	20 20	20 31						20 53		21 20	21 32
Dumpton Park	d										19 56									20 56			
Broadstairs	d	19 06	19 25	19 36							19 59	20 07	20 25	20 36						20 59		21 25	21 38
Margate 4	d	19a14	19 30	19a44							20 04	20a15	20 30	20a44						21 04		21 30	21a43
Westgate-on-Sea	d										20 08									21 08			
Birchington-on-Sea	d		19 35								20 11		20 35							21 11		21 35	
Herne Bay	d		19 44								20 20		20 44							21 20		21 44	
Chestfield & Swalecliffe	d										20 24									21 24			
Whitstable	d		19 49								20 27		20 49							21 27		21 49	
Dover Priory 4	d					19 22				19 50						20 22					21 05		
Kearsney	d					19 26				19 54						20 26					21 09		
Shepherds Well	d					19 32				20 00						20 32					21 15		
Snowdown	d									20 03											21 18		
Aylesham	d					19 36				20 06						20 36					21 21		
Adisham	d					19 39										20 39					21 24		
Bekesbourne	d									20 12											21 28		
Canterbury East 4	d					19 47				20 19						20 47					21 33		
Selling	d					19 56				20 28						20 56					21 42		
Faversham 2	a		19 57			20 01				20 33	20 35		20 57			21 01				21 35	21 47	21 57	
	d		19 58			20 02			20 30		20 37		20 58			21 02			21 30	21 37	21 47	21 58	
Teynham	d					20 08										21 08					21 53		
Sheerness-on-Sea	d				19 52		20 20								20 48		21 18						
Queenborough	d				19 56		20 25								20 53		21 23						
Swale	d				20 00		20 29								20 57		21 27						
Kemsley	d				20 04		20 33								21 01		21 31						
Sittingbourne 4	a		20 05		20 09	20 12	20 37		20 38		20 44		21 05		21 06	21 12	21 36		21 38	21 44	21 58	22 06	
	d		20 08			20 13			20 38		20 45		21 08			21 13			21 38	21 45	21 58	22 08	
Newington	d					20 18										21 18					22 03		
Rainham (Kent)	d		20 16			20 22			20 46		20 52		21 16			21 22			21 46	21 52	22 08	22 16	
Gillingham (Kent) 4	d		20 21			20 27		20 44	20 52		20 57		21 21			21 27		21 44	21 51	21 57	22 14	22 21	
Chatham 4	d		20 25			20 32		20 48	20 56		21 02		21 25			21 32		21 48	21 55	22 02	22 18	22 25	
Rochester 4	d		20 29			20 35		20 52	21 00		21 05		21 29			21 35		21 52	21 59	22 05	22 22	22 29	
Strood 4	a		20 32						21 03				21 32						22 02			22 32	
Gravesend 4	a		20 42						21 13				21 42						22 12			22 42	
Greenhithe for Bluewater	a																						
Dartford 4	a																						
London Bridge 4 ⊖	a																						
London Cannon Street 4 ⊖	a																						
London Waterloo (East) 4 ⊖	a																						
London Charing Cross 4 ⊖	a																						
Sole Street	d							21 01										22 01			22 31		
Meopham	d					20 46		21 04			21 16					21 46		22 04		22 16	22 34		
Longfield	d					20 50		21 08			21 20					21 50		22 08		22 20	22 38		
Farningham Road	d							21 12										22 12			22 42		
Swanley 4	a							21 17										22 17			22 47		
St Mary Cray	a							21 21										22 21			22 51		
Bromley South 4	a					21 02		21 29			21 32					22 02		22 29		22 32	22 59		
London Victoria 15 ⊖	a					21 22		22 00			21 51					22 22		23 00		22 51	23 31		
Elephant & Castle ⊖	a																						
London Blackfriars 3 ⊖	a																						
Ebbsfleet International	a		20 46						21 18				21 46						22 16			22 46	
Stratford International ⊖	a		20 59						21 32				21 59						22 28			22 58	
St Pancras International	a		21 06						21 40				22 07						22 36			23 06	

A From St Pancras International

For further services between St Pancras International, London Blackfriars and Elephant & Castle and Bromley South, St Mary Cray and Swanley refer to table T52

Table T212-R

Mondays to Fridays

16 December to 15 May

Ramsgate, Dover, Sheerness-on-Sea and Medway - London

		SE	SE	SE ◇1	SE ◇1	SE ◇ A	SE	SE TO 1	SE	SE TO 1	SE TX 1	SE TX 1	SE TO 🚌	SE TX ◇ A	SE TO 🚌
Ramsgate 4	d			21 53		22 28		22 48				23 15	23 15	23 29	23 36
Dumpton Park	d			21 56				22 51				23 18	23 21		
Broadstairs	d			21 59		22 33		22 54				23 21	23 26	23 34	23 45
Margate 4	d			22 04		22a38		22 59				23 26	23 36	23a40	23a55
Westgate-on-Sea	d			22 08				23 03				23 30	23 42		
Birchington-on-Sea	d			22 11				23 06				23 33	23 47		
Herne Bay	d			22 20				23 15				23 42	00 07		
Chestfield & Swalecliffe	d			22 24				23 19				23 46	00 15		
Whitstable	d			22 27				23 22				23 49	00 23		
Dover Priory 4	d				22 05					23 10	23 10				
Kearsney	d				22 09					23 14	23 14				
Shepherds Well	d				22 15					23 20	23 20				
Snowdown	d				22 18					23 23	23 23				
Aylesham	d				22 21					23 26	23 26				
Adisham	d				22 24					23 29	23 29				
Bekesbourne	d				22 28					23 33	23 33				
Canterbury East 4	d				22 39					23 39	23 39				
Selling	d				22 48					23 48	23 48				
Faversham 2	a			22 35	22 53			23 31		23 53	23 54	23 58	00s43		
	d			22 37	22 54					00 02		00 02			
Teynham	d				23 00					00 08		00 08	00s58		
Sheerness-on-Sea	d	21 48	22 18				22 48		23 48						
Queenborough	d	21 53	22 23				22 53		23 53						
Swale	d	21 57	22 27				22 57		23 57						
Kemsley	d	22 01	22 31				23 01		23 59						
Sittingbourne 4	a	22 06	22 36	22 44	23 04		23 06		00 06	00 12		00 12	01s08		
	d			22 45	23 05					00 13		00 13			
Newington	d				23 10					00 18		00 18	01s20		
Rainham (Kent)	d			22 52	23 14					00 22		00 22	01s30		
Gillingham (Kent) 4	d			22 57	23 20					00a29		00a29	01a45		
Chatham 4	d			23 02	23 24										
Rochester 4	d			23 05	23 28										
Strood 4	a														
Gravesend 4	a														
Greenhithe for Bluewater	a														
Dartford 4	a														
London Bridge 4 ⊖	a														
London Cannon Street 4 ⊖	a														
London Waterloo (East) 4 ⊖	a														
London Charing Cross 4 ⊖	a														
Sole Street	d				23 37										
Meopham	d			23 16	23 40										
Longfield	d			23 20	23 44										
Farningham Road	d				23 48										
Swanley 4	a				23 53										
St Mary Cray	a				23 57										
Bromley South 4	a			23 32	00 03										
London Victoria 15 ⊖	a			00 03	00 24										
Elephant & Castle ⊖	a														
London Blackfriars 3 ⊖	a														
Ebbsfleet International	a														
Stratford International ⊖	a														
St Pancras International	a														

A From St Pancras International

For further services between St Pancras International, London Blackfriars and Elephant & Castle and Bromley South, St Mary Cray and Swanley refer to table T52

Table T212-R

Saturdays

21 December to 16 May

Ramsgate, Dover, Sheerness-on-Sea and Medway - London

Station		SE	SE	SE	SE	SE	SE	SE	SE	SE	SE	SE	SE	SE	SE	SE	SE	SE	SE	SE	SE	SE	SE
		■1	◇	◇■1	◇	◇■1		◇■1	◇	◇■1	◇		◇■1	◇■1		◇	◇■1		◇		◇■1	◇■1	
		A	B															C	C				
Ramsgate ■4	d		00 30	04 30						05 53	06 20						06 53	07 16	07 20				
Dumpton Park	d									05 56							06 56						
Broadstairs	d		00s35	04 35						05 59	06 25						06 59	07 21	07 25				
Margate ■4	d		00a40	04 40						06 04	06 30						07 04	07a26	07 30				
Westgate-on-Sea	d									06 08							07 08						
Birchington-on-Sea	d			04 45						06 11	06 35						07 11		07 35				
Herne Bay	d			04 54						06 20	06 44						07 20		07 44				
Chestfield & Swalecliffe	d									06 24							07 24						
Whitstable	d			05 00						06 27	06 49						07 27		07 49				
Dover Priory ■4	d					05 18							06 18	06 52							07 18	07 52	
Kearsney	d					05 22							06 22								07 22		
Shepherds Well	d					05 28							06 28								07 28		
Snowdown	d					05 31							06 31								07 31		
Aylesham	d					05 34							06 34								07 34		
Adisham	d					05 37							06 37								07 37		
Bekesbourne	d					05 41							06 41								07 41		
Canterbury East ■4	d					05 47							06 47	07 09							07 47	08 09	
Selling	d					05 56							06 56								07 56		
Faversham ■2	a			05 08		06 01				06 35	06 57		07 01	07 20			07 35		07 57		08 01	08 20	
	d	00 02		05 09	05 30	06 02			06 30	06 37	06 58		07 02	07 22		07 30	07 37		07 58		08 02	08 22	
Teynham	d	00 08				06 08							07 08								08 08		
Sheerness-on-Sea	d						06 18					06 48			07 18					07 48			08 18
Queenborough	d						06 23					06 53			07 23					07 53			08 23
Swale	d						06 27					06 57			07 27					07 57			08 27
Kemsley	d						06 31					07 01			07 31					08 01			08 31
Sittingbourne ■4	a	00 12		05 16	05 38	06 12	06 36		06 38	06 44	07 05	07 06	07 12	07 29	07 36	07 38	07 44		08 05	08 06	08 12	08 29	08 36
	d	00 13		05 17	05 38	06 13			06 38	06 45	07 08		07 13	07 30		07 38	07 45		08 08		08 13	08 30	
Newington	d	00 18				06 18							07 18								08 18		
Rainham (Kent)	d	00 22		05 24	05 46	06 22			06 46	06 52	07 16		07 22	07 37		07 46	07 52		08 16		08 22	08 37	
Gillingham (Kent) ■4	d	00a29		05 30	05 51	06 27		06 44	06 51	06 57	07 21		07 27	07 44		07 51	07 57		08 21		08 27	08 44	
Chatham ■4	d			05 34	05 55	06 32		06 48	06 55	07 02	07 25		07 32	07 48		07 55	08 02		08 25		08 32	08 48	
Rochester ■4	d			05 38	05 59	06 35		06 52	06 59	07 05	07 29		07 35	07 52		07 59	08 05		08 29		08 35	08 52	
Strood ■4	a				06 02				07 02		07 32					08 02			08 32				
Gravesend ■4	a				06 12				07 12		07 42					08 12			08 42				
Greenhithe for Bluewater	a																						
Dartford ■4	a																						
London Bridge ■4 ⊖	a																						
London Cannon Street ■4 ⊖	a																						
London Waterloo (East) ■4 ⊖	a																						
London Charing Cross ■4 ⊖	a																						
Sole Street	d			05 47				07 01						08 01								09 01	
Meopham	d			05 50		06 46		07 04		07 16			07 46	08 04			08 16				08 46	09 04	
Longfield	d			05 54		06 50		07 08		07 20			07 50	08 08			08 20				08 50	09 08	
Farningham Road	d			05 58				07 12						08 12								09 12	
Swanley ■4	a			06 03				07 17						08 17								09 17	
St Mary Cray	a			06 07				07 21						08 21								09 21	
Bromley South ■4	a			06 15		07 02		07 29		07 32			08 02	08 29			08 32				09 02	09 29	
London Victoria ■15 ⊖	a			06 38		07 21		08 00		07 51			08 21	09 00			08 51				09 21	10 00	
Elephant & Castle ⊖	a																						
London Blackfriars ■3 ⊖	a																						
Ebbsfleet International	a				06 16				07 16		07 46					08 16			08 46				
Stratford International ⊖	a				06 28				07 28		07 58					08 29			08 58				
St Pancras International	a				06 36				07 36		08 06					08 37			09 06				

A From Ramsgate B From St Pancras International C From Ashford International

For further services between St Pancras International, London Blackfriars and Elephant & Castle and Bromley South, St Mary Cray and Swanley refer to table T52

Table T212-R

Saturdays

21 December to 16 May

Ramsgate, Dover, Sheerness-on-Sea and Medway - London

Station		SE	SE	SE	SE	SE	SE	SE	SE	SE	SE	SE	SE	SE	SE	SE	SE	SE	SE	SE	SE	SE	SE
		◇	◇■1	◇	◇		◇■1	◇■1		◇	◇■1	◇	◇		◇■1	◇■1		◇	◇■1	◇	◇		◇■1
				A	A							A	A							A	A		
Ramsgate ■4	d		07 53	08 20	08 28						08 53	09 20	09 28						09 53	10 20	10 28		
Dumpton Park	d		07 56								08 56								09 56				
Broadstairs	d		07 59	08 25	08 33						08 59	09 25	09 33						09 59	10 25	10 33		
Margate ■4	d		08 04	08 30	08a38						09 04	09 30	09a38						10 04	10 30	10a38		
Westgate-on-Sea	d		08 08								09 08								10 08				
Birchington-on-Sea	d		08 11	08 35							09 11	09 35							10 11	10 35			
Herne Bay	d		08 20	08 44							09 20	09 44							10 20	10 44			
Chestfield & Swalecliffe	d		08 24								09 24								10 24				
Whitstable	d		08 27	08 49							09 27	09 49							10 27	10 49			
Dover Priory ■4	d						08 18	08 52							09 18	09 52							10 18
Kearsney	d						08 22								09 22								10 22
Shepherds Well	d						08 28								09 28								10 28
Snowdown	d						08 31								09 31								10 31
Aylesham	d						08 34								09 34								10 34
Adisham	d						08 37								09 37								10 37
Bekesbourne	d						08 41								09 41								10 41
Canterbury East ■4	d						08 47	09 09							09 47	10 09							10 47
Selling	d						08 56								09 56								10 56
Faversham ■2	a		08 35	08 57			09 01	09 20			09 35	09 57			10 01	10 20			10 35	10 57			11 01
	d	08 30	08 37	08 58			09 02	09 22		09 30	09 37	09 58			10 02	10 22		10 30	10 37	10 58			11 02
Teynham	d						09 08								10 08								11 08
Sheerness-on-Sea	d					08 48			09 18					09 48			10 18					10 48	
Queenborough	d					08 53			09 23					09 53			10 23					10 53	
Swale	d					08 57			09 27					09 57			10 27					10 57	
Kemsley	d					09 01			09 31					10 01			10 31					11 01	
Sittingbourne ■4	a	08 38	08 44	09 05		09 06	09 12	09 29	09 36	09 38	09 44	10 05		10 06	10 12	10 29	10 36	10 38	10 44	11 05		11 06	11 12
	d	08 38	08 45	09 08			09 13	09 30		09 38	09 45	10 08			10 13	10 30		10 38	10 45	11 08			11 13
Newington	d						09 18								10 18								11 18
Rainham (Kent)	d	08 46	08 52	09 16			09 22	09 37		09 46	09 52	10 16			10 22	10 37		10 46	10 52	11 16			11 22
Gillingham (Kent) ■4	d	08 51	08 57	09 21			09 27	09 44		09 51	09 57	10 21			10 27	10 44		10 51	10 57	11 21			11 27
Chatham ■4	d	08 55	09 02	09 25			09 32	09 48		09 55	10 02	10 25			10 32	10 48		10 55	11 02	11 25			11 32
Rochester ■4	d	08 59	09 05	09 29			09 35	09 52		09 59	10 05	10 29			10 35	10 52		10 59	11 05	11 29			11 35
Strood ■4	a	09 02		09 32						10 02		10 32						11 02		11 32			
Gravesend ■4	a	09 12		09 42						10 12		10 42						11 12		11 42			
Greenhithe for Bluewater	a																						
Dartford ■4	a																						
London Bridge ■4 ⊖	a																						
London Cannon Street ■4 ⊖	a																						
London Waterloo (East) ■4 ⊖	a																						
London Charing Cross ■4 ⊖	a																						
Sole Street	d							10 01								11 01							
Meopham	d		09 16				09 46	10 04			10 16				10 46	11 04			11 16				11 46
Longfield	d		09 20				09 50	10 08			10 20				10 50	11 08			11 20				11 50
Farningham Road	d							10 12								11 12							
Swanley ■4	a							10 17								11 17							
St Mary Cray	a							10 21								11 21							
Bromley South ■4	a		09 32				10 02	10 29			10 32				11 02	11 29			11 32				12 02
London Victoria ■15 ⊖	a		09 51				10 21	11 00			10 51				11 21	12 00			11 51				12 21
Elephant & Castle ⊖	a																						
London Blackfriars ■3 ⊖	a																						
Ebbsfleet International	a	09 16		09 46						10 16		10 46						11 16		11 46			
Stratford International ⊖	a	09 29		10 02						10 33		10 58						11 29		11 58			
St Pancras International	a	09 37		10 10						10 41		11 06						11 37		12 06			

A From St Pancras International

For further services between St Pancras International, London Blackfriars and Elephant & Castle and Bromley South, St Mary Cray and Swanley refer to table T52

Table T212-R

Saturdays

21 December to 16 May

Ramsgate, Dover, Sheerness-on-Sea and Medway - London

		SE ◇1		SE	SE ◇	SE ◇1	SE ◇ A	SE ◇ A	SE	SE ◇1	SE ◇1	SE		SE ◇	SE ◇1	SE ◇ A	SE ◇ A	SE	SE ◇1	SE ◇1	SE	SE ◇		SE ◇1	SE ◇ A
Ramsgate 4	d					10 53	11 20	11 28							11 53	12 20	12 28							12 53	13 20
Dumpton Park	d					10 56									11 56									12 56	
Broadstairs	d					10 59	11 25	11 33							11 59	12 25	12 33							12 59	13 25
Margate 4	d					11 04	11 30	11a38							12 04	12 30	12a38							13 04	13 30
Westgate-on-Sea	d					11 08									12 08									13 08	
Birchington-on-Sea	d					11 11	11 35								12 11	12 35								13 11	13 35
Herne Bay	d					11 20	11 44								12 20	12 44								13 20	13 44
Chestfield & Swalecliffe	d					11 24									12 24									13 24	
Whitstable	d					11 27	11 49								12 27	12 49								13 27	13 49
Dover Priory 4	d	10 52								11 18	11 52								12 18	12 52					
Kearsney	d									11 22									12 22						
Shepherds Well	d									11 28									12 28						
Snowdown	d									11 31									12 31						
Aylesham	d									11 34									12 34						
Adisham	d									11 37									12 37						
Bekesbourne	d									11 41									12 41						
Canterbury East 4	d	11 09								11 47	12 09								12 47	13 09					
Selling	d									11 56									12 56						
Faversham 2	a	11 20				11 35	11 57			12 01	12 20				12 35	12 57			13 01	13 20				13 35	13 57
	d	11 22			11 30	11 37	11 58			12 02	12 22			12 30	12 37	12 58			13 02	13 22		13 30		13 37	13 58
Teynham	d									12 08									13 08						
Sheerness-on-Sea	d			11 18					11 48			12 18						12 48			13 18				
Queenborough	d			11 23					11 53			12 23						12 53			13 23				
Swale	d			11 27					11 57			12 27						12 57			13 27				
Kemsley	d			11 31					12 01			12 31						13 01			13 31				
Sittingbourne 4	a	11 29		11 36	11 38	11 44	12 05		12 06	12 12	12 29	12 36		12 38	12 44	13 05		13 06	13 12	13 29	13 36	13 38		13 44	14 05
	d	11 30			11 38	11 45	12 08			12 13	12 30			12 38	12 45	13 08			13 13	13 30		13 38		13 45	14 08
Newington	d									12 18									13 18						
Rainham (Kent)	d	11 37			11 46	11 52	12 16			12 22	12 37			12 46	12 52	13 16			13 22	13 37		13 46		13 52	14 16
Gillingham (Kent) 4	d	11 44			11 51	11 57	12 21			12 27	12 44			12 51	12 57	13 21			13 27	13 44		13 51		13 57	14 21
Chatham 4	d	11 48			11 55	12 02	12 25			12 32	12 48			12 55	13 02	13 25			13 32	13 48		13 55		14 02	14 25
Rochester 4	d	11 52			11 59	12 05	12 29			12 35	12 52			12 59	13 05	13 29			13 35	13 52		13 59		14 05	14 29
Strood 4	a				12 02		12 32							13 02		13 32						14 02			14 32
Gravesend 4	a				12 12		12 42							13 12		13 42						14 12			14 42
Greenhithe for Bluewater	a																								
Dartford 4	a																								
London Bridge 4 ⊖	a																								
London Cannon Street 4 ⊖	a																								
London Waterloo (East) 4 ⊖	a																								
London Charing Cross 4 ⊖	a																								
Sole Street	d	12 01									13 01									14 01					
Meopham	d	12 04				12 16				12 46	13 04				13 16				13 46	14 04				14 16	
Longfield	d	12 08				12 20				12 50	13 08				13 20				13 50	14 08				14 20	
Farningham Road	d	12 12									13 12									14 12					
Swanley 4	a	12 17									13 17									14 17					
St Mary Cray	a	12 21									13 21									14 21					
Bromley South 4	a	12 29				12 32				13 02	13 29				13 32				14 02	14 29				14 32	
London Victoria 15 ⊖	a	13 00				12 51				13 21	14 00				13 51				14 21	15 00				14 51	
Elephant & Castle ⊖	a																								
London Blackfriars 3 ⊖	a																								
Ebbsfleet International	a				12 16		12 46							13 16		13 46						14 16			14 46
Stratford International ⊖	a				12 28		12 58							13 29		14 02						14 28			14 58
St Pancras International	a				12 36		13 06							13 37		14 10						14 36			15 06

A From St Pancras International

For further services between St Pancras International, London Blackfriars and Elephant & Castle and Bromley South, St Mary Cray and Swanley refer to table T52

Table T212-R

Saturdays

21 December to 16 May

Ramsgate, Dover, Sheerness-on-Sea and Medway - London

		SE ◇ A	SE	SE ◇1	SE ◇1	SE	SE ◇	SE ◇1		SE ◇ A	SE ◇ A	SE	SE ◇1	SE ◇1	SE	SE ◇	SE ◇1	SE ◇ A		SE ◇ A	SE	SE ◇1	SE ◇1	SE	SE ◇
Ramsgate 4	d	13 28						13 53		14 20	14 28						14 53	15 20		15 28					
Dumpton Park	d							13 56									14 56								
Broadstairs	d	13 33						13 59		14 25	14 33						14 59	15 25		15 33					
Margate 4	d	13a38						14 04		14 30	14a38						15 04	15 30		15a38					
Westgate-on-Sea	d							14 08									15 08								
Birchington-on-Sea	d							14 11		14 35							15 11	15 35							
Herne Bay	d							14 20		14 44							15 20	15 44							
Chestfield & Swalecliffe	d							14 24									15 24								
Whitstable	d							14 27		14 49							15 27	15 49							
Dover Priory 4	d			13 18	13 52								14 18	14 52								15 18	15 52		
Kearsney	d			13 22									14 22									15 22			
Shepherds Well	d			13 28									14 28									15 28			
Snowdown	d			13 31									14 31									15 31			
Aylesham	d			13 34									14 34									15 34			
Adisham	d			13 37									14 37									15 37			
Bekesbourne	d			13 41									14 41									15 41			
Canterbury East 4	d			13 47	14 09								14 47	15 09								15 47	16 09		
Selling	d			13 56									14 56									15 56			
Faversham 2	a			14 01	14 20			14 35		14 57			15 01	15 20			15 35	15 57				16 01	16 20		
	d			14 02	14 22		14 30	14 37		14 58			15 02	15 22		15 30	15 37	15 58				16 02	16 22		16 30
Teynham	d			14 08									15 08									16 08			
Sheerness-on-Sea	d		13 48			14 18						14 48			15 18						15 48			16 18	
Queenborough	d		13 53			14 23						14 53			15 23						15 53			16 23	
Swale	d		13 57			14 27						14 57			15 27						15 57			16 27	
Kemsley	d		14 01			14 31						15 01			15 31						16 01			16 31	
Sittingbourne 4	a		14 06	14 12	14 29	14 36	14 38	14 44		15 05		15 06	15 12	15 29	15 36	15 38	15 44	16 05			16 06	16 12	16 29	16 36	16 38
	d			14 13	14 30		14 38	14 45		15 08			15 13	15 30		15 38	15 45	16 08				16 13	16 30		16 38
Newington	d			14 18									15 18									16 18			
Rainham (Kent)	d			14 22	14 37		14 46	14 52		15 16			15 22	15 37		15 46	15 52	16 16				16 22	16 37		16 46
Gillingham (Kent) 4	d			14 27	14 44		14 51	14 57		15 21			15 27	15 44		15 51	15 57	16 21				16 27	16 44		16 51
Chatham 4	d			14 32	14 48		14 55	15 02		15 25			15 32	15 48		15 55	16 02	16 25				16 32	16 48		16 55
Rochester 4	d			14 35	14 52		14 59	15 05		15 29			15 35	15 52		15 59	16 05	16 29				16 35	16 52		16 59
Strood 4	a						15 02			15 32						16 02		16 32							17 02
Gravesend 4	a						15 12			15 42						16 12		16 42							17 12
Greenhithe for Bluewater	a																								
Dartford 4	a																								
London Bridge 4 ⊖	a																								
London Cannon Street 4 ⊖	a																								
London Waterloo (East) 4 ⊖	a																								
London Charing Cross 4 ⊖	a																								
Sole Street	d				15 01									16 01									17 01		
Meopham	d			14 46	15 04			15 16					15 46	16 04			16 16					16 46	17 04		
Longfield	d			14 50	15 08			15 20					15 50	16 08			16 20					16 50	17 08		
Farningham Road	d				15 12									16 12									17 12		
Swanley 4	a				15 17									16 17									17 17		
St Mary Cray	a				15 21									16 21									17 21		
Bromley South 4	a			15 02	15 29			15 32					16 02	16 29			16 32					17 02	17 29		
London Victoria 15 ⊖	a			15 21	16 00			15 51					16 21	17 00			16 51					17 21	18 00		
Elephant & Castle ⊖	a																								
London Blackfriars 3 ⊖	a																								
Ebbsfleet International	a						15 16			15 46						16 16		16 46							17 16
Stratford International ⊖	a						15 28			16 02						16 28		17 02							17 28
St Pancras International	a						15 36			16 10						16 36		17 10							17 36

A From St Pancras International

For further services between St Pancras International, London Blackfriars and Elephant & Castle and Bromley South, St Mary Cray and Swanley refer to table T52

Table T212-R

Saturdays
21 December to 16 May

Ramsgate, Dover, Sheerness-on-Sea and Medway - London

		SE ◇1	SE ◇ A	SE ◇ A	SE	SE ◇1	SE ◇1	SE	SE ◇	SE ◇1	SE ◇ A	SE ◇ A	SE	SE ◇1	SE ◇1	SE	SE ◇	SE ◇1	SE ◇ A	SE ◇ A	SE	SE ◇1
Ramsgate 4	d	15 53	16 20	16 28						16 53	17 20	17 28						17 53	18 20	18 28		
Dumpton Park	d	15 56								16 56								17 56				
Broadstairs	d	15 59	16 25	16 33						16 59	17 25	17 33						17 59	18 25	18 33		
Margate 4	d	16 04	16 30	16a38						17 04	17 30	17a38						18 04	18 30	18a38		
Westgate-on-Sea	d	16 08								17 08								18 08				
Birchington-on-Sea	d	16 11	16 35							17 11	17 35							18 11	18 35			
Herne Bay	d	16 20	16 44							17 20	17 44							18 20	18 44			
Chestfield & Swalecliffe	d	16 24								17 24								18 24				
Whitstable	d	16 27	16 49							17 27	17 49							18 27	18 49			
Dover Priory 4	d					16 18	16 52							17 18	17 52							18 18
Kearsney	d					16 22								17 22								18 22
Shepherds Well	d					16 28								17 28								18 28
Snowdown	d					16 31								17 31								18 31
Aylesham	d					16 34								17 34								18 34
Adisham	d					16 37								17 37								18 37
Bekesbourne	d					16 41								17 41								18 41
Canterbury East 4	d					16 47	17 09							17 47	18 09							18 47
Selling	d					16 56								17 56								18 56
Faversham 2	a	16 35	16 57			17 01	17 20			17 35	17 57			18 01	18 20			18 35	18 57			19 01
	d	16 37	16 58			17 02	17 22		17 30	17 37	17 58			18 02	18 22		18 30	18 37	18 58			19 02
Teynham	d					17 08								18 08								19 08
Sheerness-on-Sea	d				16 48			17 18					17 48			18 18					18 48	
Queenborough	d				16 53			17 23					17 53			18 23					18 53	
Swale	d				16 57			17 27					17 57			18 27					18 57	
Kemsley	d				17 01			17 31					18 01			18 31					19 01	
Sittingbourne 4	a	16 44	17 05		17 06	17 12	17 29	17 36	17 38	17 44	18 05		18 06	18 12	18 29	18 36	18 38	18 44	19 05		19 06	19 12
	d	16 45	17 08			17 13	17 30		17 38	17 45	18 08			18 13	18 30		18 38	18 45	19 08			19 13
Newington	d					17 18								18 18								19 18
Rainham (Kent)	d	16 52	17 16			17 22	17 37		17 46	17 52	18 16			18 22	18 37		18 46	18 52	19 16			19 22
Gillingham (Kent) 4	d	16 57	17 21			17 27	17 44		17 51	17 57	18 21			18 27	18 44		18 51	18 57	19 21			19 27
Chatham 4	d	17 02	17 25			17 32	17 48		17 55	18 02	18 25			18 32	18 48		18 55	19 02	19 25			19 32
Rochester 4	d	17 05	17 29			17 35	17 52		17 59	18 05	18 29			18 35	18 52		18 59	19 05	19 29			19 35
Strood 4	a		17 32						18 02		18 32						19 02		19 32			
Gravesend 4	a		17 42						18 12		18 42						19 12		19 42			
Greenhithe for Bluewater	a																					
Dartford 4	a																					
London Bridge 4 ⊖	a																					
London Cannon Street 4 ⊖	a																					
London Waterloo (East) 4 ⊖	a																					
London Charing Cross 4 ⊖	a																					
Sole Street	d						18 01								19 01							
Meopham	d	17 16				17 46	18 04			18 16				18 46	19 04			19 16				19 46
Longfield	d	17 20				17 50	18 08			18 20				18 50	19 08			19 20				19 50
Farningham Road	d						18 12								19 12							
Swanley 4	a						18 17								19 17							
St Mary Cray	a						18 21								19 21							
Bromley South 4	a	17 32				18 02	18 29			18 32				19 02	19 29			19 32				20 02
London Victoria 15 ⊖	a	17 51				18 21	19 00			18 51				19 21	20 00			19 51				20 21
Elephant & Castle ⊖	a																					
London Blackfriars 3 ⊖	a																					
Ebbsfleet International	a		17 46						18 16		18 46						19 16		19 46			
Stratford International ⊖	a		18 02						18 29		18 58						19 28		19 58			
St Pancras International	a		18 10						18 37		19 06						19 36		20 06			

A From St Pancras International

For further services between St Pancras International, London Blackfriars and Elephant & Castle and Bromley South, St Mary Cray and Swanley refer to table T52

Table T212-R

Saturdays
21 December to 16 May

Ramsgate, Dover, Sheerness-on-Sea and Medway - London

		SE ◇1	SE	SE ◇	SE ◇1	SE ◇ A	SE ◇ A	SE	SE ◇1	SE ◇1	SE	SE ◇	SE ◇1	SE ◇ A	SE ◇ A	SE	SE ◇1	SE	SE ◇	SE ◇1	SE ◇1	SE ◇ A	SE ◇ A
Ramsgate 4	d				18 53	19 20	19 28						19 53	20 20	20 28					20 53		21 20	21 28
Dumpton Park	d				18 56								19 56							20 56			
Broadstairs	d				18 59	19 25	19 33						19 59	20 25	20 33					20 59		21 25	21 33
Margate 4	d				19 04	19 30	19a38						20 04	20 30	20a38					21 04		21 30	21a38
Westgate-on-Sea	d				19 08								20 08							21 08			
Birchington-on-Sea	d				19 11	19 35							20 11	20 35						21 11		21 35	
Herne Bay	d				19 20	19 44							20 20	20 44						21 20		21 44	
Chestfield & Swalecliffe	d				19 24								20 24							21 24			
Whitstable	d				19 27	19 49							20 27	20 49						21 27		21 49	
Dover Priory 4	d	18 52							19 18	19 52							20 18				21 05		
Kearsney	d								19 22								20 22				21 09		
Shepherds Well	d								19 28								20 28				21 15		
Snowdown	d								19 31								20 31				21 18		
Aylesham	d								19 34								20 34				21 21		
Adisham	d								19 37								20 37				21 24		
Bekesbourne	d								19 41								20 41				21 28		
Canterbury East 4	d	19 09							19 47	20 09							20 47				21 33		
Selling	d								19 56								20 56				21 42		
Faversham 2	a	19 20			19 35	19 57			20 01	20 20			20 35	20 57			21 01			21 35	21 47	21 57	
	d	19 22		19 30	19 37	19 58			20 02	20 22		20 30	20 37	20 58			21 02		21 30	21 37	21 47	21 58	
Teynham	d								20 08								21 08				21 53		
Sheerness-on-Sea	d		19 18					19 48			20 18					20 48		21 18					
Queenborough	d		19 23					19 53			20 23					20 53		21 23					
Swale	d		19 27					19 57			20 27					20 57		21 27					
Kemsley	d		19 31					20 01			20 31					21 01		21 31					
Sittingbourne 4	a	19 29	19 36	19 38	19 44	20 05		20 06	20 12	20 29	20 36	20 38	20 44	21 05		21 06	21 12	21 36	21 38	21 44	21 58	22 05	
	d	19 30		19 38	19 45	20 08			20 13	20 30		20 38	20 45	21 08			21 13		21 38	21 45	21 58	22 08	
Newington	d								20 18								21 18				22 03		
Rainham (Kent)	d	19 37		19 46	19 52	20 16			20 22	20 37		20 46	20 52	21 16			21 22		21 46	21 52	22 08	22 16	
Gillingham (Kent) 4	d	19 44		19 51	19 57	20 21			20 27	20 44		20 51	20 57	21 21			21 27		21 51	21 57	22 14	22 21	
Chatham 4	d	19 48		19 55	20 02	20 25			20 32	20 48		20 55	21 02	21 25			21 32		21 55	22 02	22 18	22 25	
Rochester 4	d	19 52		19 59	20 05	20 29			20 35	20 52		20 59	21 05	21 29			21 35		21 59	22 05	22 22	22 29	
Strood 4	a			20 02		20 32						21 02		21 32					22 02			22 32	
Gravesend 4	a			20 12		20 42						21 12		21 42					22 12			22 42	
Greenhithe for Bluewater	a																						
Dartford 4	a																						
London Bridge 4 ⊖	a																						
London Cannon Street 4 ⊖	a																						
London Waterloo (East) 4 ⊖	a																						
London Charing Cross 4 ⊖	a																						
Sole Street	d	20 01								21 01											22 31		
Meopham	d	20 04			20 16				20 46	21 04			21 16				21 46			22 16	22 34		
Longfield	d	20 08			20 20				20 50	21 08			21 20				21 50			22 20	22 38		
Farningham Road	d	20 12								21 12											22 42		
Swanley 4	a	20 17								21 17											22 47		
St Mary Cray	a	20 21								21 21											22 51		
Bromley South 4	a	20 29			20 32				21 02	21 29			21 32				22 02			22 32	22 59		
London Victoria 15 ⊖	a	21 00			20 51				21 21	22 00			21 51				22 21			22 51	23 30		
Elephant & Castle ⊖	a																						
London Blackfriars 3 ⊖	a																						
Ebbsfleet International	a			20 16		20 46						21 16		21 46					22 16			22 46	
Stratford International ⊖	a			20 28		20 58						21 32		21 58					22 28			22 58	
St Pancras International	a			20 36		21 06						21 40		22 06					22 36			23 06	

A From St Pancras International

For further services between St Pancras International, London Blackfriars and Elephant & Castle and Bromley South, St Mary Cray and Swanley refer to table T52

Table T212-R

Saturdays

21 December to 16 May

Ramsgate, Dover, Sheerness-on-Sea and Medway - London

		SE	SE	SE	SE	SE	SE	SE	SE	SE	SE
				◇1	◇1	◇		1		1	◇
						A					A
Ramsgate 4	d			21 53		22 27				23 15	23 29
Dumpton Park	d			21 56						23 18	
Broadstairs	d			21 59		22 33				23 21	23 35
Margate 4	d			22 04		22a37				23 26	23a40
Westgate-on-Sea	d			22 08						23 30	
Birchington-on-Sea	d			22 11						23 33	
Herne Bay	d			22 20						23 42	
Chestfield & Swalecliffe	d			22 24						23 46	
Whitstable	d			22 27						23 49	
Dover Priory 4	d				22 05			23 10			
Kearsney	d				22 09			23 14			
Shepherds Well	d				22 15			23 20			
Snowdown	d				22 18			23 23			
Aylesham	d				22 21			23 26			
Adisham	d				22 24			23 29			
Bekesbourne	d				22 28			23 33			
Canterbury East 4	d				22 39			23 39			
Selling	d				22 48			23 48			
Faversham 2	a			22 35	22 53			23 54		23 58	
	d			22 37	22 54					00 02	
Teynham	d				23 00					00 08	
Sheerness-on-Sea	d	21 48	22 18				22 48		23 48		
Queenborough	d	21 53	22 23				22 53		23 53		
Swale	d	21 57	22 27				22 57		23 57		
Kemsley	d	22 01	22 31				23 01		23 59		
Sittingbourne 4	a	22 06	22 36	22 44	23 04		23 06		00 06	00 12	
	d			22 45	23 05					00 13	
Newington	d				23 10					00 18	
Rainham (Kent)	d			22 52	23 14					00 22	
Gillingham (Kent) 4	d			22 57	23 20					00a27	
Chatham 4	d			23 02	23 24						
Rochester 4	d			23 05	23 28						
Strood 4	a										
Gravesend 4	a										
Greenhithe for Bluewater	a										
Dartford 4	a										
London Bridge 4 ⊖	a										
London Cannon Street 4 ⊖	a										
London Waterloo (East) 4 ⊖	a										
London Charing Cross 4 ⊖	a										
Sole Street	d				23 37						
Meopham	d			23 16	23 40						
Longfield	d			23 20	23 44						
Farningham Road	d				23 48						
Swanley 4	a				23 53						
St Mary Cray	a				23 57						
Bromley South 4	a			23 32	00 03						
London Victoria 15 ⊖	a			23 51	00 23						
Elephant & Castle ⊖	a										
London Blackfriars 3 ⊖	a										
Ebbsfleet International	a										
Stratford International ⊖	a										
St Pancras International	a										

A From St Pancras International

For further services between St Pancras International, London Blackfriars and Elephant & Castle and Bromley South, St Mary Cray and Swanley refer to table T52

Table T212-R

Sundays

15 December to 10 May

Ramsgate, Dover, Sheerness-on-Sea and Medway - London

		SE	SE	SE	SE	SE	SE	SE	SE	SE	SE	SE	SE	SE	SE	SE	SE	SE	SE	SE	SE	SE	SE
		1	◇	◇1	◇	◇1	◇1	◇		◇1	◇1	◇		◇1	◇1	◇1	◇		◇1	◇1	◇1	◇	◇
		A	B														C					D	D
Ramsgate 4	d		00 29				07 05				08 05	08 20				09 05	09 20				10 05	10 20	10 27
Dumpton Park	d						07 08				08 08					09 08					10 08		
Broadstairs	d		00s34				07 11				08 11	08 25				09 11	09 25				10 11	10 25	10 32
Margate 4	d		00a40				07 16				08 16	08 30				09 16	09 30				10 16	10 30	10a38
Westgate-on-Sea	d						07 20				08 20					09 20					10 20		
Birchington-on-Sea	d						07 24				08 24	08 35				09 24	09 35				10 24	10 35	
Herne Bay	d						07 33				08 33	08 44				09 33	09 44				10 33	10 44	
Chestfield & Swalecliffe	d						07 36				08 36					09 36					10 36		
Whitstable	d						07 40				08 40	08 49				09 40	09 49				10 40	10 49	
Dover Priory 4	d					07 03				08 03					09 03					10 03			
Kearsney	d					07 07				08 07					09 07					10 07			
Shepherds Well	d					07 13				08 13					09 13					10 13			
Snowdown	d					07 16				08 16					09 16					10 16			
Aylesham	d					07 19				08 19					09 19					10 19			
Adisham	d					07 22				08 22					09 22					10 22			
Bekesbourne	d					07 26				08 26					09 26					10 26			
Canterbury East 4	d					07 32				08 32				09 02	09 32				10 02	10 32			
Selling	d					07 41				08 41					09 41					10 41			
Faversham 2	a					07 46	07 48			08 46	08 48	08 57		09 13	09 46	09 48	09 57		10 13	10 46	10 48	10 57	
	d	00 02			07 00		07 52	08 00			08 52	08 58		09 14		09 52	09 58		10 14		10 52	10 58	
Teynham	d	00 08												09 20					10 20				
Sheerness-on-Sea	d								08 00				09 00					10 00					
Queenborough	d								08 04				09 04					10 04					
Swale	d								08 08				09 08					10 08					
Kemsley	d								08 12				09 12					10 12					
Sittingbourne 4	a	00 12			07 08		07 59	08 08	08 17		08 59	09 05	09 17	09 24		09 59	10 05	10 17	10 24		10 59	11 05	
	d	00 13			07 08		08 00	08 08			09 00	09 08		09 25		10 00	10 08		10 25		11 00	11 08	
Newington	d	00 18												09 30					10 30				
Rainham (Kent)	d	00 22			07 16		08 07	08 16			09 07	09 16		09 34		10 07	10 16		10 34		11 07	11 16	
Gillingham (Kent) 4	d	00a27		06 40	07 21		08 13	08 21			09 13	09 21		09 40		10 13	10 21		10 40		11 13	11 21	
Chatham 4	d			06 44	07 25		08 18	08 25			09 18	09 25		09 44		10 18	10 25		10 44		11 18	11 25	
Rochester 4	d			06 48	07 29		08 21	08 29			09 21	09 29		09 48		10 21	10 29		10 48		11 21	11 29	
Strood 4	a				07 32			08 32				09 32					10 32					11 32	
Gravesend 4	a				07 42			08 42				09 42					10 42					11 42	
Greenhithe for Bluewater	a																						
Dartford 4	a																						
London Bridge 4 ⊖	a																						
London Cannon Street 4 ⊖	a																						
London Waterloo (East) 4 ⊖	a																						
London Charing Cross 4 ⊖	a																						
Sole Street	d			06 57										09 57					10 57				
Meopham	d			07 00										10 00					11 00				
Longfield	d			07 04										10 04					11 04				
Farningham Road	d			07 08										10 08					11 08				
Swanley 4	a			07 13										10 13					11 13				
St Mary Cray	a			07 17										10 17					11 17				
Bromley South 4	a			07 25			08 46				09 46			10 25		10 46			11 25		11 46		
London Victoria 15 ⊖	a			07 48			09 09				10 06			10 48		11 06			11 48		12 06		
Elephant & Castle ⊖	a																						
London Blackfriars 3 ⊖	a																						
Ebbsfleet International	a				07 46			08 46				09 46					10 46					11 46	
Stratford International ⊖	a				07 58			08 58				10 02					10 58					11 58	
St Pancras International	a				08 06			09 06				10 10					11 06					12 06	

A not 15 December. From Ramsgate
B not 15 December. From St Pancras International
C From Ashford International
D From St Pancras International

For further services between St Pancras International, London Blackfriars and Elephant & Castle and Bromley South, St Mary Cray and Swanley refer to table T52

Table T212-R

Sundays

15 December to 10 May

Ramsgate, Dover, Sheerness-on-Sea and Medway - London

		SE	SE ◇■	SE ◇	SE ◇■	SE ◇■	SE ◇ A	SE ◇ A	SE	SE ◇■	SE ◇	SE ◇■	SE ◇■	SE ◇ A	SE ◇ A	SE	SE ◇■	SE ◇	SE ◇■	SE ◇■	SE ◇ A	SE ◇ A	SE
Ramsgate ■	d					11 05	11 20	11 27					12 05	12 20	12 27					13 05	13 20	13 27	
Dumpton Park	d					11 08							12 08							13 08			
Broadstairs	d					11 11	11 25	11 32					12 11	12 25	12 32					13 11	13 25	13 32	
Margate ■	d					11 16	11 30	11a38					12 16	12 30	12a38					13 16	13 30	13a38	
Westgate-on-Sea	d					11 20							12 20							13 20			
Birchington-on-Sea	d					11 24	11 35						12 24	12 35						13 24	13 35		
Herne Bay	d					11 33	11 44						12 33	12 44						13 33	13 44		
Chestfield & Swalecliffe	d					11 36							12 36							13 36			
Whitstable	d					11 40	11 49						12 40	12 49						13 40	13 49		
Dover Priory ■	d				11 03							12 03							13 03				
Kearsney	d				11 07							12 07							13 07				
Shepherds Well	d				11 13							12 13							13 13				
Snowdown	d				11 16							12 16							13 16				
Aylesham	d				11 19							12 19							13 19				
Adisham	d				11 22							12 22							13 22				
Bekesbourne	d				11 26							12 26							13 26				
Canterbury East ■	d		11 02		11 32					12 02		12 32					13 02		13 32				
Selling	d				11 41							12 41							13 41				
Faversham ■	a		11 13		11 46	11 48	11 57			12 13		12 46	12 48	12 57			13 13		13 46	13 48	13 57		
	d		11 14	11 30	11 52		11 58			12 14	12 30	12 52		12 58			13 14	13 30	13 52		13 58		
Teynham	d		11 20							12 20							13 20						
Sheerness-on-Sea	d	11 00							12 00							13 00							14 00
Queenborough	d	11 04							12 04							13 04							14 04
Swale	d	11 08							12 08							13 08							14 08
Kemsley	d	11 12							12 12							13 12							14 12
Sittingbourne ■	a	11 17	11 24	11 38	11 59		12 05		12 17	12 24	12 38	12 59		13 05		13 17	13 24	13 38	13 59		14 05		14 17
	d		11 25	11 38	12 00		12 08			12 25	12 38	13 00		13 08			13 25	13 38	14 00		14 08		
Newington	d		11 30							12 30							13 30						
Rainham (Kent)	d		11 34	11 46	12 07		12 16			12 34	12 46	13 07		13 16			13 34	13 46	14 07		14 16		
Gillingham (Kent) ■	d		11 40	11 51	12 13		12 21			12 40	12 51	13 13		13 21			13 40	13 51	14 13		14 21		
Chatham ■	d		11 44	11 55	12 18		12 25			12 44	12 55	13 18		13 25			13 44	13 55	14 18		14 25		
Rochester ■	d		11 48	11 59	12 21		12 29			12 48	12 59	13 21		13 29			13 48	13 59	14 21		14 29		
Strood ■	a			12 02			12 32				13 02			13 32				14 02			14 32		
Gravesend ■	a			12 12			12 42				13 12			13 42				14 12			14 42		
Greenhithe for Bluewater	a																						
Dartford ■	a																						
London Bridge ■ ⊖	a																						
London Cannon Street ■ ⊖	a																						
London Waterloo (East) ■ ⊖	a																						
London Charing Cross ■ ⊖	a																						
Sole Street	d		11 57							12 57							13 57						
Meopham	d		12 00							13 00							14 00						
Longfield	d		12 04							13 04							14 04						
Farningham Road	d		12 08							13 08							14 08						
Swanley ■	a		12 13							13 13							14 13						
St Mary Cray	a		12 17							13 17							14 17						
Bromley South ■	a		12 25		12 46					13 25		13 46					14 25		14 46				
London Victoria ■ ⊖	a		12 48		13 06					13 48		14 06					14 48		15 06				
Elephant & Castle ⊖	a																						
London Blackfriars ■ ⊖	a																						
Ebbsfleet International	a			12 16			12 46				13 16			13 46				14 16			14 46		
Stratford International ⊖	a			12 28			12 58				13 29			13 58				14 28			14 59		
St Pancras International	a			12 36			13 06				13 37			14 06				14 36			15 07		

A From St Pancras International

For further services between St Pancras International, London Blackfriars and Elephant & Castle and Bromley South, St Mary Cray and Swanley refer to table T52

Table T212-R

Sundays

15 December to 10 May

Ramsgate, Dover, Sheerness-on-Sea and Medway - London

		SE ◇■	SE ◇	SE ◇■	SE ◇■	SE ◇ A	SE ◇ A	SE	SE ◇■	SE ◇	SE ◇■	SE ◇■	SE ◇ A	SE ◇ A	SE	SE ◇■	SE ◇	SE ◇■	SE ◇■	SE ◇ A	SE ◇ A	SE	SE ◇■
Ramsgate ■	d				14 05	14 20	14 27					15 05	15 20	15 27					16 05	16 20	16 27		
Dumpton Park	d				14 08							15 08							16 08				
Broadstairs	d				14 11	14 25	14 32					15 11	15 25	15 32					16 11	16 25	16 32		
Margate ■	d				14 16	14 30	14a38					15 16	15 30	15a38					16 16	16 30	16a38		
Westgate-on-Sea	d				14 20							15 20							16 20				
Birchington-on-Sea	d				14 24	14 35						15 24	15 35						16 24	16 35			
Herne Bay	d				14 33	14 44						15 33	15 44						16 33	16 44			
Chestfield & Swalecliffe	d				14 36							15 36							16 36				
Whitstable	d				14 40	14 49						15 40	15 49						16 40	16 49			
Dover Priory ■	d			14 03							15 03							16 03					
Kearsney	d			14 07							15 07							16 07					
Shepherds Well	d			14 13							15 13							16 13					
Snowdown	d			14 16							15 16							16 16					
Aylesham	d			14 19							15 19							16 19					
Adisham	d			14 22							15 22							16 22					
Bekesbourne	d			14 26							15 26							16 26					
Canterbury East ■	d	14 02		14 32					15 02		15 32					16 02		16 32					17 02
Selling	d			14 41							15 41							16 41					
Faversham ■	a	14 13		14 46	14 48	14 57			15 13		15 46	15 48	15 57			16 13		16 46	16 48	16 57			17 13
	d	14 14	14 30	14 52		14 58			15 14	15 30	15 52		15 58			16 14	16 30	16 52		16 58			17 14
Teynham	d	14 20							15 20							16 20							17 20
Sheerness-on-Sea	d							15 00							16 00							17 00	
Queenborough	d							15 04							16 04							17 04	
Swale	d							15 08							16 08							17 08	
Kemsley	d							15 12							16 12							17 12	
Sittingbourne ■	a	14 24	14 38	14 59		15 05		15 17	15 24	15 38	15 59		16 05		16 17	16 24	16 38	16 59		17 05		17 17	17 24
	d	14 25	14 38	15 00		15 08			15 25	15 38	16 00		16 08			16 25	16 38	17 00		17 08			17 25
Newington	d	14 30							15 30							16 30							17 30
Rainham (Kent)	d	14 34	14 46	15 07		15 16			15 34	15 46	16 07		16 16			16 34	16 46	17 07		17 16			17 34
Gillingham (Kent) ■	d	14 40	14 51	15 13		15 21			15 40	15 51	16 13		16 21			16 40	16 51	17 13		17 21			17 40
Chatham ■	d	14 44	14 55	15 18		15 25			15 44	15 55	16 18		16 25			16 44	16 55	17 18		17 25			17 44
Rochester ■	d	14 48	14 59	15 21		15 29			15 48	15 59	16 21		16 29			16 48	16 59	17 21		17 29			17 48
Strood ■	a		15 02			15 32				16 02			16 32				17 02			17 32			
Gravesend ■	a		15 12			15 42				16 12			16 42				17 12			17 42			
Greenhithe for Bluewater	a																						
Dartford ■	a																						
London Bridge ■ ⊖	a																						
London Cannon Street ■ ⊖	a																						
London Waterloo (East) ■ ⊖	a																						
London Charing Cross ■ ⊖	a																						
Sole Street	d	14 57							15 57							16 57							17 57
Meopham	d	15 00							16 00							17 00							18 00
Longfield	d	15 04							16 04							17 04							18 04
Farningham Road	d	15 08							16 08							17 08							18 08
Swanley ■	a	15 13							16 13							17 13							18 13
St Mary Cray	a	15 17							16 17							17 17							18 17
Bromley South ■	a	15 25		15 46					16 25		16 46					17 25		17 46					18 25
London Victoria ■ ⊖	a	15 48		16 06					16 48		17 06					17 48		18 06					18 48
Elephant & Castle ⊖	a																						
London Blackfriars ■ ⊖	a																						
Ebbsfleet International	a		15 16			15 46				16 16			16 46				17 16			17 46			
Stratford International ⊖	a		15 28			16 02				16 28			17 02				17 28			18 02			
St Pancras International	a		15 36			16 10				16 36			17 10				17 36			18 10			

A From St Pancras International

For further services between St Pancras International, London Blackfriars and Elephant & Castle and Bromley South, St Mary Cray and Swanley refer to table T52

Table T212-R

Sundays

15 December to 10 May

Ramsgate, Dover, Sheerness-on-Sea and Medway - London

		SE	SE	SE	SE	SE	SE	SE	SE	SE	SE	SE	SE	SE	SE	SE	SE	SE	SE	SE	SE	SE
		◇	◇[1]	◇[1]	◇ A	◇ A		◇[1]	◇	◇[1]	◇[1]	◇ A	◇ A		◇[1]	◇	◇[1]	◇[1]	◇ A	◇ A		◇[1]
Ramsgate [4]	d			17 05	17 20	17 27					18 05	18 20	18 27					19 05	19 20	19 27		
Dumpton Park	d			17 08							18 08							19 08				
Broadstairs	d			17 11	17 25	17 32					18 11	18 25	18 32					19 11	19 25	19 32		
Margate [4]	d			17 16	17 30	17a38					18 16	18 30	18a38					19 16	19 30	19a38		
Westgate-on-Sea	d			17 20							18 20							19 20				
Birchington-on-Sea	d			17 24	17 35						18 24	18 35						19 24	19 35			
Herne Bay	d			17 33	17 44						18 33	18 44						19 33	19 44			
Chestfield & Swalecliffe	d			17 36							18 36							19 36				
Whitstable	d			17 40	17 49						18 40	18 49						19 40	19 49			
Dover Priory [4]	d		17 03							18 03							19 03					
Kearsney	d		17 07							18 07							19 07					
Shepherds Well	d		17 13							18 13							19 13					
Snowdown	d		17 16							18 16							19 16					
Aylesham	d		17 19							18 19							19 19					
Adisham	d		17 22							18 22							19 22					
Bekesbourne	d		17 26							18 26							19 26					
Canterbury East [4]	d		17 32					18 02		18 32					19 02		19 32					20 02
Selling	d		17 41							18 41							19 41					
Faversham [2]	a		17 46	17 48	17 57			18 13		18 46	18 48	18 57			19 13		19 46	19 48	19 57			20 13
	d	17 30	17 52		17 58			18 14	18 30	18 52		18 58			19 14	19 30	19 52		19 58			20 14
Teynham	d							18 20							19 20							20 20
Sheerness-on-Sea	d						18 00							19 00							20 00	
Queenborough	d						18 04							19 04							20 04	
Swale	d						18 08							19 08							20 08	
Kemsley	d						18 12							19 12							20 12	
Sittingbourne [4]	a	17 38	17 59		18 05		18 17	18 24	18 38	18 59		19 05		19 17	19 24	19 38	19 59		20 05		20 17	20 24
	d	17 38	18 00		18 08			18 25	18 38	19 00		19 08			19 25	19 38	20 00		20 08			20 25
Newington	d							18 30							19 30							20 30
Rainham (Kent)	d	17 46	18 07		18 16			18 34	18 46	19 07		19 16			19 34	19 46	20 07		20 16			20 34
Gillingham (Kent) [4]	d	17 51	18 13		18 21			18 40	18 51	19 13		19 21			19 40	19 51	20 13		20 21			20 40
Chatham [4]	d	17 55	18 18		18 25			18 44	18 55	19 18		19 25			19 44	19 55	20 18		20 25			20 44
Rochester [4]	d	17 59	18 21		18 29			18 48	18 59	19 21		19 29			19 48	19 59	20 21		20 29			20 48
Strood [4]	a	18 02			18 32				19 02			19 32				20 02			20 32			
Gravesend [4]	a	18 12			18 42				19 12			19 42				20 12			20 42			
Greenhithe for Bluewater	a																					
Dartford [4]	a																					
London Bridge [4] ⊖	a																					
London Cannon Street [4] ⊖	a																					
London Waterloo (East) [4] ⊖	a																					
London Charing Cross [4] ⊖	a																					
Sole Street	d							18 57							19 57							20 57
Meopham	d							19 00							20 00							21 00
Longfield	d							19 04							20 04							21 04
Farningham Road	d							19 08							20 08							21 08
Swanley [4]	a							19 13							20 13							21 13
St Mary Cray	a							19 17							20 17							21 17
Bromley South [4]	a		18 46					19 25		19 46					20 25		20 46					21 25
London Victoria [15] ⊖	a		19 06					19 48		20 06					20 48		21 06					21 48
Elephant & Castle ⊖	a																					
London Blackfriars [3] ⊖	a																					
Ebbsfleet International	a	18 16			18 46				19 16			19 46				20 16			20 46			
Stratford International ⊖	a	18 28			18 59				19 28			19 58				20 28			20 58			
St Pancras International	a	18 36			19 07				19 36			20 06				20 36			21 06			

A From St Pancras International

For further services between St Pancras International, London Blackfriars and Elephant & Castle and Bromley South, St Mary Cray and Swanley refer to table T52

Table T212-R

Sundays

15 December to 10 May

Ramsgate, Dover, Sheerness-on-Sea and Medway - London

		SE	SE	SE	SE	SE	SE	SE	SE	SE	SE	SE	SE	SE	SE	SE	SE	SE	SE	SE
		◇	◇[1]	◇[1]	◇ A	◇ A		◇[1]	◇	◇[1]	◇[1]	◇ A	◇ A		◇[1]	◇ A	◇[1]		◇[1]	◇ A
Ramsgate [4]	d			20 05	20 20	20 27					21 05	21 20	21 27			22 27			22 35	23 27
Dumpton Park	d			20 08							21 08								22 38	
Broadstairs	d			20 11	20 25	20 32					21 11	21 25	21 32			22 32			22 41	23 32
Margate [4]	d			20 16	20 30	20a38					21 16	21 30	21a38			22a38			22 46	23a38
Westgate-on-Sea	d			20 20							21 20								22 50	
Birchington-on-Sea	d			20 24	20 35						21 24	21 35							22 54	
Herne Bay	d			20 33	20 44						21 33	21 44							23 03	
Chestfield & Swalecliffe	d			20 36							21 36								23 06	
Whitstable	d			20 40	20 49						21 40	21 49							23 10	
Dover Priory [4]	d		20 03							21 03							22 33			
Kearsney	d		20 07							21 07							22 37			
Shepherds Well	d		20 13							21 13							22 43			
Snowdown	d		20 16							21 16							22 46			
Aylesham	d		20 19							21 19							22 49			
Adisham	d		20 22							21 22							22 52			
Bekesbourne	d		20 26							21 26							22 56			
Canterbury East [4]	d		20 32					21 02		21 32					22 02		23 02			
Selling	d		20 41							21 41							23 11			
Faversham [2]	a		20 46	20 48	20 57			21 13		21 46	21 48	21 57			22 13		23 16		23 18	
	d	20 30	20 52		20 58			21 14	21 30	21 52		21 58			22 14				23 22	
Teynham	d							21 20							22 20				23 28	
Sheerness-on-Sea	d						21 00							22 00				23 00		
Queenborough	d						21 04							22 04				23 04		
Swale	d						21 08							22 08				23 08		
Kemsley	d						21 12							22 12				23 12		
Sittingbourne [4]	a	20 38	20 59		21 05		21 17	21 24	21 38	21 59		22 05		22 17	22 24			23 17	23 32	
	d	20 38	21 00		21 08			21 25	21 38	22 00		22 08			22 25				23 33	
Newington	d							21 30							22 30				23 38	
Rainham (Kent)	d	20 46	21 07		21 16			21 34	21 46	22 07		22 16			22 34				23 43	
Gillingham (Kent) [4]	d	20 51	21 13		21 21			21 40	21 51	22 13		22 21			22 40				23 48	
Chatham [4]	d	20 55	21 18		21 25			21 44	21 55	22 18		22 25			22 44				23 52	
Rochester [4]	d	20 59	21 21		21 29			21 48	21 59	22 21		22 29			22 48				23 55	
Strood [4]	a	21 02			21 32				22 02			22 32								
Gravesend [4]	a	21 12			21 42				22 12			22 42								
Greenhithe for Bluewater	a																			
Dartford [4]	a																			
London Bridge [4] ⊖	a																			
London Cannon Street [4] ⊖	a																			
London Waterloo (East) [4] ⊖	a																			
London Charing Cross [4] ⊖	a																			
Sole Street	d							21 57							22 57					
Meopham	d							22 00							23 00					
Longfield	d							22 04							23 04					
Farningham Road	d							22 08							23 08					
Swanley [4]	a							22 13							23 13					
St Mary Cray	a							22 17							23 17					
Bromley South [4]	a		21 46					22 25		22 46					23 25				00 19	
London Victoria [15] ⊖	a		22 06					22 48		23 06					23 48				00 36	
Elephant & Castle ⊖	a																			
London Blackfriars [3] ⊖	a																			
Ebbsfleet International	a	21 16			21 46				22 16			22 46								
Stratford International ⊖	a	21 32			21 59				22 28			22 58								
St Pancras International	a	21 40			22 07				22 36			23 06								

A From St Pancras International

For further services between St Pancras International, London Blackfriars and Elephant & Castle and Bromley South, St Mary Cray and Swanley refer to table T52

Table T216-F

Mondays to Fridays

16 December to 15 May

Carlisle and Dumfries - Kilmarnock and Glasgow Central

Miles			SR	SR	SR	SR 🍴	SR 🍴	SR	SR 🍴	SR	SR 🍴		SR	SR 🍴	SR	SR	SR 🍴	SR 🍴	SR	SR 🍴	SR
—	Newcastle [8]	48 d																			
0	**Carlisle [8]**	65 d			05 31	06 08	08 08	09 58	11 12	12 20	13 08		14 30	15 05	16 20	17 27	17 58	19 20	20 31	21 12	23 10
9¾	Gretna Green	d			05 42	06 19	08 19	10 09	11 23	12 32	13 20		14 41	15 17	16 31	17 41	18 11	19 31	20 42	21 24	23 21
17½	Annan	d			05 53	06 27	08 27	10 17	11 31	12 40	13 28		14 49	15 26	16 39	17 51	18 20	19 39	20 50	21 32	23 29
33	**Dumfries**	d	05 13	05 45	06a10	06 46	08 47	10a35	11 50	12a58	13 47		15a07	15 50	16a57	18a08	18 38	19 58	21a08	21 51	23a47
59¼	Sanquhar	d	05 39	06 12		07 12	09 13		12 16		14 13			16 16			19 04	20 24		22 17	
62½	Kirkconnel	d	05 44	06 17		07 17	09 18		12 21		14 18			16 21			19 09	20 29		22 22	
69¾	New Cumnock	d	05 53	06 26		07 26	09 27		12 30		14 27			16 30			19 18	20 38		22 31	
77¼	Auchinleck	d	06 01	06 34		07 34	09 35		12 38		14 35			16 38			19 27	20 46		22 39	
91	**Kilmarnock [3]**	218,222 a	06 18	06 51		07 52	09 55		12 55		14 52			16 55			19 44	21 03		22 56	
—		d	06 20	06 52		07 55	10 00		12 59		14 59			16 56			19 57	21 04		22 57	
107¾	Barrhead	222 d	06 44	07 17		08 22	10 24							17 21			20 21	21 28		23 22	
115¼	**Glasgow Central [15]**	65,222 a	07 07	07 31		08 37	10 38		13 35		15 37			17 37			20 37	21 42		23 36	

Saturdays

21 December to 16 May

		SR	SR	SR	SR 🍴	SR 🍴	SR	SR 🍴	SR	SR 🍴		SR	SR 🍴	SR	SR	SR 🍴	SR 🍴	SR	SR 🍴	SR
Newcastle [8]	48 d																			
Carlisle [8]	65 d			05 31	06 08	08 06	09 58	11 12	12 20	13 08		14 30	15 05	16 20	17 21	17 57	19 20	20 22	21 09	23 10
Gretna Green	d			05 42	06 19	08 17	10 09	11 23	12 32	13 20		14 41	15 17	16 31	17 32	18 08	19 31	20 33	21 20	23 21
Annan	d			05 53	06 27	08 25	10 17	11 31	12 40	13 28		14 49	15 26	16 39	17 40	18 17	19 39	20 41	21 28	23 29
Dumfries	d	05 13	05 45	06a10	06 46	08 44	10a35	11 50	12a58	13 47		15a07	15 50	16a57	17a58	18 35	19 58	20a59	21 51	23a47
Sanquhar	d	05 39	06 12		07 12	09 10		12 16		14 13			16 16			19 01	20 24		22 17	
Kirkconnel	d	05 44	06 17		07 17	09 15		12 21		14 18			16 21			19 06	20 29		22 22	
New Cumnock	d	05 53	06 26		07 26	09 24		12 30		14 27			16 30			19 15	20 38		22 31	
Auchinleck	d	06 01	06 34		07 34	09 32		12 38		14 35			16 38			19 24	20 46		22 39	
Kilmarnock [3]	218,222 a	06 18	06 51		07 52	09 49		12 55		14 52			16 55			19 41	21 03		22 56	
	d	06 20	06 52		07 55	09 50		12 59		14 59			16 56			19 57	21 04		22 57	
Barrhead	222 d	06 44	07 18		08 21	10 15							17 21			20 21	21 28		23 22	
Glasgow Central [15]	65,222 a	07 11	07 32		08 34	10 33		13 35		15 37			17 37			20 37	21 42		23 36	

Sundays

15 December to 10 May

		SR 🍴	SR	SR	SR 🍴	SR
Newcastle [8]	48 d					
Carlisle [8]	65 d	13 12	15 12	17 12	19 12	21 26
Gretna Green	d	13 23	15 23	17 23	19 23	21 37
Annan	d	13 31	15 31	17 31	19 31	21 45
Dumfries	d	13 50	15a49	17a49	19 50	22a03
Sanquhar	d	14 16			20 16	
Kirkconnel	d	14 21			20 21	
New Cumnock	d	14 30			20 30	
Auchinleck	d	14 38			20 38	
Kilmarnock [3]	218,222 a	14 55			20 55	
	d	14 57			20 57	
Barrhead	222 d	15 22			21 21	
Glasgow Central [15]	65,222 a	15 43			21 35	

For connections from London Euston please refer to Table T65

Some through services between Glasgow Central and Newcastle and vice versa are jointly operated with Northern Rail.

Table T216-R

Mondays to Fridays

16 December to 15 May

Glasgow Central and Kilmarnock - Dumfries and Carlisle

Miles			SR MX	SR MO 🍴	SR	SR	SR	SR		SR 🍴	SR 🍴	SR	SR 🍴	SR	SR 🍴	SR 🍴	SR	SR		SR A 🍴	SR	SR 🍴	SR 🍴	SR	SR 🍴
0	**Glasgow Central [15]**	65,222 d								07 09	08 38		10 13		12 13	13 13				16 13		17 42	19 13	20 13	21 13
7½	Barrhead	222 d								07 22	08 51									16 25		17 55	19 25	20 25	21 29
24¼	**Kilmarnock [3]**	218,222 a								07 49	09 18		10 51		12 50	13 50				16 52		18 22	19 52	20 52	21 56
—		d	00 02							07 54	09 18		10 51		12 50	13 50				16 52		18 25	19 52	20 58	21 56
38	Auchinleck	d	00 20							08 11	09 35		11 08		13 07	14 07				17 09		18 42	20 09	21 25	22 13
45½	New Cumnock	d	00 30							08 19	09 43		11 16		13 15	14 15				17 17		18 51	20 17	21 37	22 21
52¾	Kirkconnel	d	00 44							08 28	09 52		11 25		13 24	14 24				17 26		18 59	20 26	21 50	22 30
56	Sanquhar	d	00 49							08 33	09 57		11 30		13 29	14 29				17 31		19 04	20 31	21 55	22 35
82¼	**Dumfries**	d	01a15		04 58	06 18	07 14	07 41		09 01	10 25	11 02	11 58	13 04	13 57	15 00	16 02	17 07		17 59	18 41	19 33	21 00	22a22	23 03
97¾	Annan	d		00 11	05 13	06 33	07 29	07 56		09 16	10 40	11 17	12 13	13 19	14 13	15 15	16 17	17 22		18 14	18 56	19 48	21 15		23 18
105½	Gretna Green	d		00 20	05 22	06 42	07 38	08 05		09 29	10 49	11 26	12 22	13 28	14 21	15 24	16 26	17 31		18 23	19 05	19 57	21 24		23 27
115½	**Carlisle [8]**	65 a		00 33	05 35	06 55	07 53	08 18		09 42	11 01	11 39	12 35	13 41	14 35	15 38	16 42	17 44		18 37	19 18	20 12	21 39		23 43
—	Newcastle [8]	48 a				08 35		09 54												20 07					

		SR
Glasgow Central [15]	65,222 d	23 13
Barrhead	222 d	23 35
Kilmarnock [3]	218,222 a	00 01
	d	00 02
Auchinleck	d	00 20
New Cumnock	d	00 30
Kirkconnel	d	00 44
Sanquhar	d	00 49
Dumfries	d	01a15
Annan	d	
Gretna Green	d	
Carlisle [8]	65 a	
Newcastle [8]	48 a	

Saturdays

21 December to 16 May

		SR	SR	SR	SR	SR 🍴	SR 🍴	SR	SR 🍴	SR		SR 🍴	SR 🍴	SR	SR	SR B 🍴	SR	SR 🍴	SR 🍴	SR		SR	SR 🍴
Glasgow Central [15]	65,222 d					07 07	08 37		10 13			12 13	13 13			16 13		17 43	19 13	20 13			22 13
Barrhead	222 d					07 22	08 51									16 25		17 55	19 25	20 25			22 25
Kilmarnock [3]	218,222 a					07 49	09 18		10 51			12 50	13 50			16 52		18 22	19 52	20 52			22 52
	d	00 02				07 54	09 18		10 51			12 50	13 50			16 52		18 25	19 52	20 58			22 53
Auchinleck	d	00 20				08 11	09 35		11 08			13 07	14 07			17 09		18 42	20 09	21 14			23 09
New Cumnock	d	00 30				08 19	09 43		11 16			13 15	14 15			17 17		18 51	20 17	21 23			23 18
Kirkconnel	d	00 44				08 28	09 52		11 25			13 24	14 24			17 26		18 59	20 26	21 38			23 26
Sanquhar	d	00 49				08 33	09 57		11 30			13 29	14 29			17 31		19 04	20 31	21 43			23 31
Dumfries	d	01a15	04 58	06 18	07 41	09 05	10 25	11 02	11 58	13 04		13 57	14 58	16 02	17 07	17 59	18 40	19 33	21 00	22a10		22 20	23 59
Annan	d		05 13	06 33	07 56	09 20	10 40	11 17	12 13	13 19		14 13	15 13	16 17	17 22	18 15	18 55	19 48	21 15			22 35	00 14
Gretna Green	d		05 22	06 42	08 05	09 29	10 49	11 26	12 22	13 28		14 21	15 25	16 26	17 31	18 25	19 04	19 57	21 24			22 44	00 23
Carlisle [8]	65 a		05 35	06 55	08 18	09 42	11 02	11 39	12 35	13 41		14 35	15 40	16 42	17 44		19 17	20 11	21 37			22 57	00 36
Newcastle [8]	48 a		08 35													20 16							

Sundays

15 December to 10 May

		SR C 🍴	SR	SR	SR 🍴	SR	SR 🍴
Glasgow Central [15]	65,222 d				15 03		22 12
Barrhead	222 d				15 24		22 24
Kilmarnock [3]	218,222 a				15 50		22 48
	d				15 51		22 49
Auchinleck	d				16 08		23 06
New Cumnock	d				16 16		23 14
Kirkconnel	d				16 25		23 23
Sanquhar	d				16 30		23 28
Dumfries	d		13 01	15 01	17 01	19 01	23 56
Annan	d	00 14	13 16	15 16	17 16	19 16	00 11
Gretna Green	d	00 23	13 25	15 26	17 26	19 26	00 20
Carlisle [8]	65 a	00 36	13 38	15 39	17 39	19 39	00 33
Newcastle [8]	48 a						

A 🍴 to Carlisle B 🍴 to Gretna Green C not 15 December

For connections to London Euston refer to Table T65

Some through services between Glasgow Central and Newcastle and vice versa are jointly operated with Northern Rail.

Table T217-F

Mondays to Saturdays
16 December to 16 May

Glasgow Central - Paisley Canal

Miles			SR SO	SR		SR
0	**Glasgow Central** 15	d	00 12	06 12	and every 30 minutes until	23 12
1¾	Dumbreck	d	00 17	06 17		23 17
3¼	Corkerhill	d	00 20	06 20		23 20
3¾	Mosspark	d	00 22	06 22		23 22
4½	Crookston	d	00 24	06 24		23 24
6½	Hawkhead	d	00 27	06 27		23 27
7	**Paisley Canal**	a	00 30	06 30		23 30

Sundays
15 December to 10 May

		SR		SR
Glasgow Central 15	d	09 12	and hourly until	18 12
Dumbreck	d	09 17		18 17
Corkerhill	d	09 20		18 20
Mosspark	d	09 22		18 22
Crookston	d	09 24		18 24
Hawkhead	d	09 27		18 27
Paisley Canal	a	09 30		18 30

Table T217-R

Mondays to Saturdays
16 December to 16 May

Paisley Canal - Glasgow Central

Miles			SR SO	SR SX	SR	SR SO	SR SX	SR SX	SR SO	SR	SR	SR	SR SO	SR SX	SR	SR	SR	SR SO	SR SX	SR	SR	SR SO	SR SX
0	**Paisley Canal**	d	06 35	06 35	07 05	07 35	07 35	08 05	08 05	08 35	09 05	09 35	10 05	10 05	10 35	11 05	11 35	12 05	12 05	12 35	13 05	13 35	13 35
0½	Hawkhead	d	06 37	06 37	07 07	07 37	07 37	08 07	08 07	08 37	09 07	09 37	10 07	10 07	10 37	11 07	11 37	12 07	12 07	12 37	13 07	13 37	13 37
2½	Crookston	d	06 40	06 40	07 10	07 40	07 40	08 10	08 10	08 40	09 10	09 40	10 10	10 10	10 40	11 10	11 40	12 10	12 10	12 40	13 10	13 40	13 40
3¼	Mosspark	d	06 43	06 43	07 13	07 43	07 43	08 13	08 13	08 43	09 13	09 43	10 13	10 13	10 43	11 13	11 43	12 13	12 13	12 43	13 13	13 43	13 43
3¾	Corkerhill	d	06 45	06 45	07 15	07 45	07 45	08 15	08 15	08 45	09 15	09 45	10 15	10 15	10 45	11 15	11 45	12 15	12 15	12 45	13 15	13 45	13 45
5¼	Dumbreck	d	06 48	06 51	07 18	07 48	07 48	08 18	08 18	08 48	09 18	09 48	10 18	10 18	10 48	11 18	11 48	12 18	12 18	12 48	13 18	13 48	13 48
7	**Glasgow Central** 15	a	06 56	06 56	07 26	07 53	07 57	08 23	08 24	08 54	09 24	09 54	10 23	10 24	10 54	11 24	11 54	12 24	12 25	12 54	13 24	13 53	13 54

		SR	SR	SR SO	SR SX	SR	SR	SR	SR SX	SR SO	SR	SR	SR	SR SX	SR SO	SR SX	SR SO	SR	SR	SR	SR	SR FX
Paisley Canal	d	14 05	14 35	15 05	15 05	15 35	16 05	16 35	17 05	17 05	17 35	18 05	18 35	19 05	19 05	19 35	19 35	20 05	20 35	21 05	21 35	22 05
Hawkhead	d	14 07	14 37	15 07	15 07	15 37	16 07	16 37	17 07	17 07	17 37	18 07	18 37	19 07	19 07	19 37	19 37	20 07	20 37	21 07	21 37	22 07
Crookston	d	14 10	14 40	15 10	15 10	15 40	16 10	16 40	17 10	17 10	17 40	18 10	18 40	19 10	19 10	19 40	19 40	20 10	20 40	21 10	21 40	22 10
Mosspark	d	14 13	14 43	15 13	15 13	15 43	16 13	16 43	17 13	17 13	17 43	18 13	18 43	19 13	19 13	19 43	19 43	20 13	20 43	21 13	21 43	22 13
Corkerhill	d	14 15	14 45	15 15	15 15	15 45	16 15	16 45	17 15	17 15	17 45	18 15	18 45	19 15	19 15	19 45	19 45	20 15	20 45	21 15	21 45	22 15
Dumbreck	d	14 18	14 48	15 18	15 18	15 48	16 18	16 48	17 18	17 18	17 48	18 18	18 48	19 18	19 18	19 48	19 48	20 18	20 48	21 18	21 48	22 18
Glasgow Central 15	a	14 24	14 54	15 24	15 26	15 54	16 25	16 54	17 24	17 25	17 54	18 24	18 54	19 23	19 27	19 55	19 56	20 24	20 56	21 26	21 56	22 26

		SR	SR SO	SR SX
Paisley Canal	d	22 35	23 05	23 05
Hawkhead	d	22 37	23 07	23 07
Crookston	d	22 40	23 10	23 10
Mosspark	d	22 43	23 13	23 13
Corkerhill	d	22 45	23 15	23 15
Dumbreck	d	22 48	23 18	23 20
Glasgow Central 15	a	22 56	23 25	23 27

Sundays
15 December to 10 May

		SR		SR
Paisley Canal	d	09 35	and hourly until	18 35
Hawkhead	d	09 37		18 37
Crookston	d	09 40		18 40
Mosspark	d	09 43		18 43
Corkerhill	d	09 45		18 45
Dumbreck	d	09 48		18 48
Glasgow Central 15	a	09 54		18 54

Table T218-F

Mondays to Saturdays
16 December to 16 May

Glasgow Central and Kilmarnock - Girvan, Stranraer

Miles	Miles			SR MX ◇	SR	SR	SR	SR	SR SO ◇	SR SX ◇	SR	SR	SR	SR	SR	SR ◇	SR	SR	SR	SR	SR	SR	SR
0	—	**Glasgow Cen.** 15 219,221,222	d						08 08	08 08						14 13			17 13	18 13			
7¼	—	Paisley Gilmour St. 219,221 ✈	d																				
26¾	—	Kilwinning 4 221	d																				
—	0	**Kilmarnock** 3 222	a						08 48	08 49						14 50			17 52	18 52			
—	—		d					08 01	09 00	09 00		11 04		13 03		14 57		17 00	18 03	19 04		21 08	
35	10¾	Troon 221	d					08 14	09 12	09 12		11 16		13 15		15 10		17 12	18 16	19 16		21 20	
37¾	11¾	Prestwick Int. Airport 221 ✈	d																				
38¼	12½	Prestwick Town 221	d					08 20				11 21		13 21		15 16			18 21				
41½	15½	**Ayr** 221	a					08 27	09 23	09 23		11 29		13 28		15 24		17 23	18 28	19 27		21 31	
—	—		d		05 25	06 21	07 17	08 28	09 23	09 23	10 28	11 31	12 26	13 29	14 24	15 25	16 25	17 23	18 29	19 27	20 32	21 32	22 30
50½	24½	Maybole	d		05 36	06 32	07 28	08 39	09 35	09 35	10 39	11 42	12 37	13 40	14 35	15 36	16 36	17 35	18 40	19 39	20 43	21 43	22 41
62¾	36½	**Girvan**	d	00 01	05a52	06a48	07 56	08a55	09 54	09 54	10a55	12 01	12a53	13 59	14a51	15 55	16a52	17 54	18a56	19 58	20a59	21a57	22a57
75	51¼	Barrhill	d	00 20			08 16		10 13	10 13		12 20		14 18		16 14		18 13		20 17			
101	77¼	**Stranraer**	a	00 56			08 52		10 49	10 49		12 56		14 54		16 50		18 49		20 53			

		SR SX ◇	SR SO
Glasgow Cen. 15 219,221,222	d	22 13	
Paisley Gilmour St. 219,221 ✈	d		
Kilwinning 4 221	d		
Kilmarnock 3 222	a	22 52	
	d	23 07	23 07
Troon 221	d	23 19	23 19
Prestwick Int. Airport 221 ✈	d		
Prestwick Town 221	d	23 25	23 25
Ayr 221	a	23 32	23 32
	d	23 33	23 33
Maybole	d	23 44	23 44
Girvan	d	00 01	00 01
Barrhill	d	00 20	00 20
Stranraer	a	00 56	00 56

Sundays
15 December to 10 May

		SR A	SR	SR	SR	SR	SR
Glasgow Cen. 15 219,221,222	d						
Paisley Gilmour St. 219,221 ✈	d						
Kilwinning 4 221	d						
Kilmarnock 3 222	a						
	d						
Troon 221	d						
Prestwick Int. Airport 221 ✈	d						
Prestwick Town 221	d						
Ayr 221	a						
	d		11 06	12 27	15 05	18 05	19 27
Maybole	d		11 17	12 38	15 16	18 16	19 38
Girvan	d	00 01	11 36	12 53	15 35	18 35	19 53
Barrhill	d	00 20	11 55	13 18	15 54	18 54	20 17
Stranraer	a	00 56	12 31	13 54	16 30	19 30	20 53

A not 15 December

Table T218-R

Mondays to Saturdays

16 December to 16 May

Stranraer and Girvan - Kilmarnock and Glasgow Central

Miles	Miles			SR	SR	SR SO ◇	SR SX ◇	SR	SR	SR	SR	SR	SR	SR	SR	SR	SR ◇	SR	SR	SR	SR	SR	SR
0	—	**Stranraer**	d			07 00	07 00		08 59		11 06		13 04		15 00		16 59		19 03		21 03		
26	—	Barrhill	d			07 34	07 34		09 33		11 40		13 38		15 34		17 33		19 37		21 37		
38¾	—	**Girvan**	d	05 57	06 53	07 52	07 52	09 00	09 51	11 00	11 59	13 00	13 57	15 01	15 53	16 59	17 51	19 01	19 56	21 04	21 59	22 29	23 02
50½	—	Maybole	d	06 13	07 09	08 08	08 08	09 16	10 07	11 16	12 16	13 16	14 13	15 17	16 09	17 15	18 07	19 17	20 12	21 20	22 15	22 56	23 18
59¼	—	**Ayr** 221	a	06 25	07 21	08 21	08 21	09 28	10 20	11 28	12 29	13 28	14 28	15 29	16 23	17 28	18 20	19 29	20 26	21 32	22 27	23 08	23 30
—	—		d		07 22	08 22	08 22		10 21		12 29		14 30		16 27	17 28	18 21		20 27		22 28		
62½	—	Prestwick Town 221	a		07 27	08 27	08 29						14 35		16 32	17 34			20 32		22 33		
63	—	Prestwick Int. Airport 221 ✈	a																		22 36		
63¾	0	Troon 221	a		07 32	08 32	08 34		10 29		12 38		14 41		16 38	17 39	18 29		20 38		22 41		
—	10¾	**Kilmarnock** 3	a		07 49	08 52	08 52		10 44		12 54		14 56		16 53	17 56	18 44		20 55		23 02		
—	—		d			08 56	08 56										18 57						
74¼	—	Kilwinning 4 221	a																				
93¾	—	Paisley Gilmour St. 219,221 ✈	a																				
101	—	**Glasgow Cen.** 15 219,221,222	a			09 37	09 37										19 37						

Sundays

15 December to 10 May

		SR	SR	SR	SR	SR
Stranraer	d	10 41	12 41	14 40	17 40	19 40
Barrhill	d	11 16	13 16	15 14	18 14	20 15
Girvan	d	11 34	13 34	15 33	18 33	20 33
Maybole	d	11 50	13 50	15 49	18 49	20 49
Ayr 221	a	12 02	14 02	16 01	19 01	21 01
	d					
Prestwick Town 221	a					
Prestwick Int. Airport 221 ✈	a					
Troon 221	a					
Kilmarnock 3	a					
	d					
Kilwinning 4 221	a					
Paisley Gilmour St. 219,221 ✈	a					
Glasgow Cen. 15 219,221,222	a					

Table T219-F

Mondays to Saturdays

16 December to 16 May

Glasgow Central - Wemyss Bay and Gourock

Miles	Miles			SR MO	SR MX	SR MX	SR	SR SO	SR SX	SR	SR	SR	SR	SR	SR	SR	SR SX	SR SO	SR	SR SO	SR SX	SR	SR
0	0	**Glasgow Central** 15 221	d				05 55	06 03	06 05	06 25	06 32	06 56	07 07	07 22	07 40	07 50	08 04	08 05	08 28	08 40	08 40	08 55	09 06
3¾	3¾	Cardonald	d								06 39		07 14	07 29	07 47		08 11	08 12		08 47	08 47		
4½	4½	Hillington East	d					06 12	06 12		06 41		07 16	07 31	07 49		08 13	08 14		08 49	08 49		
5	5	Hillington West	d			00 01	06 03	06 14	06 14		06 43	07 04	07 18	07 33	07 51	07 59	08 15	08 16		08 51	08 51		
7¼	7¼	Paisley Gilmour Street 221 ✈	a			00 05	06 08	06 18	06 18	06 37	06 47	07 08	07 22	07 38	07 55	08 03	08 20	08 20	08 38	08 55	08 56	09 07	09 17
—	—		d			00 05	06 08	06 19	06 19	06 37	06 47	07 08	07 22	07 38	07 55	08 04	08 21	08 21	08 38	08 56	08 56	09 07	09 18
8	8	Paisley St James	d			00 07				06 39			07 24		07 57		08 23	08 23		08 58	08 58		
12¼	12¼	Bishopton	d			00 12	06 14	06 24	06 24	06 44	06 53	07 14	07 29	07 44	08 02	08 10	08 28	08 28	08 44	09 03	09 03	09 13	09 23
16¾	16¾	Langbank	d			00 18				06 49			07 35		08 08		08 33	08 33		09 09	09 09		
19	19	Woodhall	d			00 22		06 32	06 32	06 53	07 00		07 39	07 51	08 12		08 37	08 37		09 13	09 13		
20¼	20¼	Port Glasgow	d			00 25	06 23	06 35	06 35	06 56	07 05	07 23	07 42	07 54	08 15	08 19	08 40	08 40	08 53	09 17	09 17	09 22	09 32
—	22½	Whinhill	d					06 39	06 39		07 09					08 23						09 26	
—	23	Drumfrochar	d					06 41	06 41		07 11					08 26						09 28	
—	24¾	Branchton	d					06 44	06 44		07 14					08 29						09 31	
—	25½	I.B.M.	d																				
—	28¾	Inverkip	d					06 52	06 52		07 27					08 36						09 39	
—	31	**Wemyss Bay**	a					06 57	06 57		07 32					08 42						09 44	
21¼	—	Bogston	d			00 27				06 58		07 25	07 44	07 56	08 17		08 42	08 42		09 19	09 19		
22	—	Cartsdyke	d			00 29	06 26			07 01		07 27	07 46	07 59	08 19		08 45	08 45		09 22	09 22		
23	—	Greenock Central	d	00 01	00 02	00 31	06 28			07 03		07 29	07 48	08 01	08 21		08 47	08 47	08 57	09 24	09 24		09 37
23¾	—	Greenock West	d	00 03	00 04	00 33	06 30			07 05		07 31	07 50	08 03	08 23		08 49	08 49	08 59	09 26	09 26		09 39
25	—	Fort Matilda	d	00 06	00 07	00 36				07 08		07 34	07 53	08 06	08 26		08 52	08 52	09 02	09 29	09 29		09 42
26¼	—	**Gourock**	a	00 10	00 11	00 40	06 35			07 11		07 38	07 57	08 09	08 30		08 55	08 55	09 06	09 32	09 32		09 45

		SR SX	SR SO	SR	SR	SR	SR	SR	SR	SR	SR	SR	SR	SR	SR	SR	SR	SR	SR	SR	SR	SR	SR
Glasgow Central 15 221	d	09 08	09 09	09 25	09 36	09 55	09 57	10 06	10 25	10 36	10 55	10 57	11 06	11 25	11 36	11 55	11 57	12 06	12 25	12 36	12 55	12 57	13 06
Cardonald	d	09 16	09 16		09 43			10 13		10 43			11 13		11 43			12 14		12 43			13 14
Hillington East	d	09 18	09 18		09 45			10 15		10 45			11 15		11 45			12 16		12 45			13 16
Hillington West	d	09 20	09 20		09 47			10 17		10 47			11 17		11 47			12 18		12 47			13 18
Paisley Gilmour Street 221 ✈	a	09 24	09 24	09 35	09 53	10 05	10 08	10 21	10 35	10 51	11 05	11 08	11 24	11 36	11 51	12 05	12 08	12 22	12 37	12 51	13 05	13 08	13 24
	d	09 24	09 24	09 36	09 53	10 06	10 10	10 22	10 36	10 51	11 05	11 10	11 24	11 37	11 51	12 05	12 10	12 22	12 37	12 52	13 05	13 10	13 25
Paisley St James	d	09 26	09 26		09 55			10 24		10 53			11 26		11 53			12 24		12 54			13 27
Bishopton	d	09 31	09 31	09 41	10 00	10 11	10 16	10 29	10 41	10 58	11 11	11 16	11 31	11 42	11 58	12 11	12 16	12 29	12 43	12 59	13 11	13 16	13 32
Langbank	d	09 37	09 37		10 06			10 34		11 04			11 37		12 04			12 35		13 04			13 37
Woodhall	d	09 41	09 41		10 10			10 39		11 08			11 41		12 08			12 39		13 08			13 41
Port Glasgow	d	09 44	09 44	09 50	10 13	10 20	10 25	10 42	10 50	11 11	11 20	11 25	11 44	11 51	12 11	12 20	12 25	12 42	12 52	13 11	13 20	13 25	13 44
Whinhill	d						10 29					11 29					12 29					13 29	
Drumfrochar	d						10 31					11 31					12 31					13 31	
Branchton	d						10 34					11 34					12 34					13 34	
I.B.M.	d																						
Inverkip	d						10 42					11 42					12 42					13 42	
Wemyss Bay	a						10 47					11 47					12 47					13 47	
Bogston	d	09 46	09 46		10 15			10 44		11 13			11 46		12 13			12 44		13 13			13 46
Cartsdyke	d	09 48	09 48		10 17			10 46		11 15			11 48		12 15			12 46		13 16			13 49
Greenock Central	d	09 50	09 50	09 55	10 19	10 25		10 48	10 55	11 17	11 24		11 50	11 56	12 17	12 24		12 48	12 56	13 18	13 24		13 51
Greenock West	d	09 52	09 52	09 57	10 21	10 27		10 50	10 57	11 19	11 26		11 52	11 58	12 19	12 26		12 50	12 58	13 20	13 26		13 53
Fort Matilda	d	09 55	09 55	10 00	10 24	10 30		10 53	11 00	11 22	11 29		11 55	12 01	12 22	12 29		12 53	13 01	13 23	13 29		13 56
Gourock	a	09 59	09 59	10 03	10 28	10 33		10 58	11 03	11 26	11 33		11 59	12 04	12 26	12 33		12 57	13 05	13 26	13 33		13 59

		SR	SR	SR	SR	SR	SR	SR	SR	SR	SR	SR	SR	SR	SR SO	SR	SR	SR	SR	SR	SR	SR
Glasgow Central 15 221	d	13 25	13 36	13 55	13 57	14 07	14 25	14 36	14 55	14 57	15 06	15 25	15 36	15 50	15 55	16 06	16 18	16 35	16 52	17 07	17 18	17 25
Cardonald	d		13 43			14 14		14 43			15 13		15 44			16 13	16 26	16 42		17 14	17 26	
Hillington East	d		13 45			14 16		14 45			15 15		15 46			16 15	16 28	16 44		17 16	17 28	
Hillington West	d		13 47			14 18		14 47			15 17		15 48	15 58		16 17	16 30	16 46	17 00	17 18		
Paisley Gilmour Street 221 ✈	a	13 36	13 51	14 05	14 09	14 23	14 35	14 51	15 05	15 08	15 24	15 36	15 52	16 03	16 07	16 22	16 34	16 50	17 04	17 22	17 32	17 36
	d	13 37	13 51	14 06	14 11	14 23	14 36	14 52	15 06	15 10	15 24	15 37	15 52	16 03	16 08	16 22	16 34	16 50	17 04	17 22	17 33	17 37
Paisley St James	d		13 53			14 25		14 54			15 26		15 54			16 24	16 36			17 24		
Bishopton	d	13 42	13 58	14 11	14 17	14 30	14 41	14 59	15 11	15 16	15 31	15 42	15 59	16 09	16 13	16 29	16 41	16 56	17 10	17 29	17 38	
Langbank	d		14 04			14 36		15 05			15 37		16 05			16 35	16 47		17 15	17 35		
Woodhall	d		14 08			14 40		15 09			15 41		16 09			16 39	16 51		17 19	17 39		
Port Glasgow	d	13 51	14 11	14 20	14 26	14 43	14 50	15 12	15 20	15 25	15 44	15 51	16 12	16 18	16 22	16 42	16 54	17 06	17 22	17 42	17 47	17 52
Whinhill	d				14 30					15 29				16 22				17 10			17 51	
Drumfrochar	d				14 32					15 31				16 24				17 12			17 54	
Branchton	d				14 35					15 34				16 27				17 15			17 57	
I.B.M.	d																					
Inverkip	d				14 43					15 42				16 35				17 21			18 03	
Wemyss Bay	a				14 48					15 47				16 40				17 26			18 08	
Bogston	d		14 13			14 45		15 14			15 46		16 14			16 44	16 56		17 24	17 44		
Cartsdyke	d		14 15			14 47		15 16			15 48		16 16			16 46	16 58		17 27	17 46		
Greenock Central	d	13 56	14 17	14 25		14 49	14 55	15 18	15 25		15 50	15 56	16 18		16 27	16 48	17 00		17 29	17 48		17 56
Greenock West	d	13 58	14 19	14 27		14 51	14 57	15 20	15 27		15 52	15 58	16 20		16 29	16 50	17 02		17 31	17 50		17 58
Fort Matilda	d	14 01	14 22	14 30		14 54	15 00	15 23	15 30		15 55	16 01	16 23		16 32	16 53	17 05		17 34	17 53		18 01
Gourock	a	14 04	14 26	14 33		14 58	15 03	15 27	15 33		15 59	16 04	16 27		16 35	16 58	17 09		17 37	17 57		18 05

Table T219-F

Mondays to Saturdays
16 December to 16 May

Glasgow Central - Wemyss Bay and Gourock

		SR	SR	SR	SR	SR	SR	SR	SR	SR	SR	SR	SR	SR	SR	SR	SR	SR	SR	SR	SR	SR
Glasgow Central 15 221	d	17 38	17 56	18 06	18 26	18 40	18 55	19 06	19 25	19 36	19 50	20 06	20 36	20 50	21 06	21 36	21 50	22 06	22 36	22 52	23 21	23 50
Cardonald	d	17 45		18 13		18 47		19 13		19 43		20 13	20 43		21 13	21 43		22 13	22 43		23 28	23 57
Hillington East	d	17 47		18 15		18 49		19 15		19 45		20 15	20 45		21 15	21 45		22 15	22 45		23 30	23 59
Hillington West	d	17 49		18 17		18 51		19 17		19 47		20 17	20 47		21 17	21 47		22 17	22 47		23 32	00 01
Paisley Gilmour Street 221	a	17 53	18 06	18 21	18 37	18 55	19 05	19 22	19 35	19 52	20 01	20 22	20 51	21 00	21 22	21 51	22 00	22 21	22 51	23 02	23 36	00 05
	d	17 53	18 06	18 21	18 38	18 55	19 05	19 23	19 36	19 52	20 01	20 22	20 51	21 01	21 22	21 51	22 01	22 22	22 51	23 03	23 36	00 05
Paisley St James	d	17 55		18 23		18 57		19 25		19 54		20 24	20 53		21 24	21 53		22 24	22 53		23 38	00 07
Bishopton	d	18 00	18 12	18 28	18 43	19 02	19 11	19 30	19 41	19 59	20 07	20 29	20 58	21 06	21 29	21 58	22 06	22 29	22 58	23 08	23 43	00 12
Langbank	d	18 06		18 34		19 08		19 35		20 05		20 35	21 04		21 35	22 04		22 34	23 04		23 49	00 18
Woodhall	d	18 10		18 38		19 12		19 39		20 09		20 39	21 08		21 39	22 08		22 38	23 08		23 53	00 22
Port Glasgow	d	18 13	18 21	18 41	18 52	19 15	19 20	19 42	19 50	20 12	20 17	20 42	21 11	21 16	21 42	22 11	22 16	22 41	23 11	23 17	23 56	00 25
Whinhill	d		18 25			19 19				20 16			21 15			22 15			23 15			
Drumfrochar	d		18 27			19 22				20 18			21 17			22 17			23 17			
Branchton	d		18 30			19 25				20 21			21 20			22 20			23 20			
I.B.M.	d																					
Inverkip	d		18 38			19 32				20 30			21 28			22 28			23 28			
Wemyss Bay	a		18 44			19 38				20 34			21 33			22 33			23 33			
Bogston	d	18 15		18 43			19 22	19 44				20 44			21 44			22 43			23 58	00 27
Cartsdyke	d	18 17		18 45			19 24	19 47			20 20	20 47		21 19	21 46		22 19	22 46		23 20	23 59	00 29
Greenock Central	d	18 19		18 47	18 57		19 26	19 49	19 55		20 22	20 49		21 21	21 48		22 21	22 48		23 22	00 02	00 31
Greenock West	d	18 21		18 49	18 59		19 28	19 51	19 57		20 24	20 51		21 23	21 50		22 23	22 50		23 24	00 04	00 33
Fort Matilda	d	18 24		18 52	19 02		19 31	19 54	20 00		20 27	20 54		21 26	21 53		22 26	22 53		23 27	00 07	00 36
Gourock	a	18 28		18 56	19 05		19 35	19 57	20 03		20 30	20 57		21 29	21 57		22 29	22 56		23 31	00 11	00 40

Sundays
15 December to 10 May

		SR A	SR A	SR	SR	SR		SR	SR	SR	SR	SR	SR	SR	SR	SR	SR	SR	SR	SR	SR	SR
Glasgow Central 15 221	d			07 20	07 50	08 20	and at the same minutes past each hour until	11 50	12 20	12 50	13 20	13 50	14 20	14 50	15 20	15 50	16 20	16 50	17 20	17 50	18 20	18 50
Cardonald	d			07 27		08 27			12 27		13 27		14 27		15 27		16 27		17 27		18 27	
Hillington East	d			07 29	07 57	08 29		11 57	12 29	12 57	13 29	13 57	14 29	14 57	15 29	15 57	16 29	16 57	17 29	17 57	18 29	18 57
Hillington West	d		00 01	07 31		08 31			12 31	12 59	13 31		14 31		15 31		16 31		17 31		18 31	
Paisley Gilmour Street 221	a		00 05	07 35	08 02	08 35		12 02	12 35	13 03	13 35	14 02	14 35	15 03	15 35	16 02	16 35	17 02	17 35	18 02	18 36	19 02
	d		00 05	07 35	08 02	08 35		12 02	12 35	13 04	13 35	14 02	14 35	15 03	15 35	16 02	16 35	17 02	17 35	18 02	18 36	19 02
Paisley St James	d		00 07			08 37			12 37		13 37		14 37		15 37		16 37		17 37		18 38	
Bishopton	d		00 12	07 41	08 08	08 42		12 08	12 42	13 09	13 42	14 08	14 42	15 09	15 42	16 08	16 42	17 08	17 42	18 08	18 43	19 08
Langbank	d		00 18			08 48			12 48		13 48		14 48		15 48		16 48		17 48		18 49	
Woodhall	d		00 22	07 48		08 52			12 52		13 52		14 52		15 52		16 52		17 52		18 53	
Port Glasgow	d		00 25	07 51	08 17	08 55		12 17	12 55	13 18	13 55	14 17	14 55	15 18	15 55	16 17	16 55	17 17	17 55	18 17	18 56	19 17
Whinhill	d				08 21			12 21		13 22		14 21		15 22		16 21		17 21		18 21		19 21
Drumfrochar	d				08 23			12 23		13 25		14 23		15 24		16 23		17 23		18 23		19 23
Branchton	d				08 26			12 26		13 28		14 26		15 27		16 26		17 26		18 26		19 26
I.B.M.	d																					
Inverkip	d				08 34			12 34		13 35		14 34		15 35		16 34		17 34		18 38		19 34
Wemyss Bay	a				08 39			12 39		13 40		14 39		15 40		16 39		17 39		18 44		19 39
Bogston	d		00 27	07 53		08 57			12 57		13 57		14 57		15 57		16 57		17 57		18 58	
Cartsdyke	d		00 29	07 56		08 59			12 59		13 59		14 59		15 59		16 59		17 59		19 00	
Greenock Central	d	00 02	00 31	07 58		09 01			13 01		14 01		15 01		16 01		17 01		18 01		19 02	
Greenock West	d	00 04	00 33	08 00		09 03			13 03		14 03		15 03		16 03		17 03		18 03		19 04	
Fort Matilda	d	00 07	00 36			09 06			13 06		14 06		15 06		16 06		17 06		18 06		19 07	
Gourock	a	00 11	00 40	08 05		09 10			13 10		14 10		15 10		16 10		17 10		18 10		19 11	

		SR	SR	SR	SR	SR	SR	SR
Glasgow Central 15 221	d	19 20	19 50	20 20	20 50	21 21	22 20	23 20
Cardonald	d	19 27		20 27		21 28	22 27	23 27
Hillington East	d	19 29	19 57	20 29	20 57	21 30	22 29	23 29
Hillington West	d	19 31		20 31		21 32	22 31	23 31
Paisley Gilmour Street 221	a	19 35	20 02	20 35	21 02	21 36	22 35	23 35
	d	19 35	20 02	20 35	21 02	21 36	22 35	23 35
Paisley St James	d	19 37		20 37		21 38	22 37	23 37
Bishopton	d	19 42	20 08	20 42	21 08	21 43	22 42	23 42
Langbank	d	19 48		20 48		21 49	22 48	23 48
Woodhall	d	19 52		20 52		21 53	22 52	23 52
Port Glasgow	d	19 55	20 17	20 55	21 17	21 56	22 55	23 55
Whinhill	d		20 21		21 21			
Drumfrochar	d		20 23		21 23			
Branchton	d		20 26		21 26			
I.B.M.	d							
Inverkip	d		20 34		21 34			
Wemyss Bay	a		20 39		21 39			
Bogston	d	19 57		20 57		21 58	22 57	23 57
Cartsdyke	d	19 59		20 59		22 00	22 59	23 59
Greenock Central	d	20 01		21 01		22 02	23 01	00 01
Greenock West	d	20 03		21 03		22 04	23 03	00 03
Fort Matilda	d	20 06		21 06		22 07	23 06	00 06
Gourock	a	20 10		21 10		22 11	23 10	00 10

A not 15 December

Table T219-R

Mondays to Saturdays
16 December to 16 May

Gourock and Wemyss Bay - Glasgow Central

Miles	Miles			SR MX	SR	SR	SR SX	SR SX	SR SO	SR SX	SR SX	SR SO	SR	SR SX	SR SO	SR SX	SR SX	SR SO	SR	SR SX	SR	SR	SR
0	—	**Gourock**	d		05 20	06 05		06 25	06 38	06 47	07 07	07 07		07 28	07 38	07 46	07 50	07 50		08 11	08 23	08 38	
1¼	—	Fort Matilda	d		05 23	06 08		06 28	06 41	06 50	07 10	07 10		07 31	07 41		07 53	07 53		08 14	08 26	08 41	
2¼	—	Greenock West	d		05 26	06 11		06 31	06 44	06 53	07 13	07 13		07 34	07 44	07 51	07 56	07 56		08 17	08 29	08 44	
3¼	—	Greenock Central	d		05 28	06 13		06 33	06 46	06 55	07 15	07 15		07 36	07 46	07 53	07 58	07 58		08 19	08 31	08 46	
4¼	—	Cartsdyke	d		05 31	06 16		06 36	06 49	06 58	07 18	07 18		07 39	07 49		08 01	08 01			08 34	08 49	
5	—	Bogston	d		05 33			06 38	06 51	07 00	07 20	07 20		07 41	07 51		08 03	08 03			08 36	08 51	
—	0	**Wemyss Bay**	d				06 12						07 15						07 54				08 57
—	2¼	Inverkip	d				06 16						07 19						07 58				09 01
—	4¾	I.B.M.	d																				
—	6¼	Branchton	d				06 23						07 27						08 05				09 08
—	8	Drumfrochar	d				06 26						07 29						08 08				09 11
—	8½	Whinhill	d				06 28						07 32						08 10				09 13
6	10¾	Port Glasgow	d		05 35	06 19	06 33	06 40	06 53	07 02	07 22	07 22	07 36	07 43	07 53	07 58	08 05	08 05	08 15	08 24	08 38	08 53	09 18
7¼	12	Woodhall	d		05 38			06 43	06 56	07 05		07 25	07 39	07 46	07 56		08 08	08 08	08 17		08 41	08 56	
10	14¾	Langbank	d		05 42			06 47	07 00	07 09		07 29		07 50	08 00				08 21		08 45	09 00	
14	18¾	Bishopton	d		05 47	06 28	06 42	06 52	07 05	07 14	07 31	07 34	07 46	07 55	08 05	08 07	08 15	08 15	08 27	08 33	08 50	09 05	09 27
18¼	23	Paisley St James	d		05 52	06 33		06 57	07 10	07 19		07 39		08 00	08 10				08 32		08 55	09 10	
19	23¾	Paisley Gilmour Street 221	a		05 55	06 36	06 48	07 00	07 13	07 22	07 37	07 43	07 52	08 03	08 13	08 14	08 21	08 21	08 34	08 39	08 58	09 13	09 33
—	—		d		05 55	06 36	06 48	07 00	07 13	07 22	07 38	07 43	07 53	08 04	08 14	08 14	08 22	08 22	08 35	08 39	08 58	09 13	09 33
21¼	26	Hillington West	d	00 03	05 59	06 40		07 04	07 17	07 26	07 41	07 47	07 56	08 07	08 18	08 18	08 25	08 25			09 02	09 17	
21¾	26½	Hillington East	d	00 05	06 01	06 42		07 06	07 19	07 28	07 43	07 49	07 58	08 09	08 20	08 20	08 27	08 27			09 04	09 19	
22½	27¼	Cardonald	d	00 07	06 03	06 44		07 08	07 21	07 30	07 45	07 51	08 00	08 11	08 22	08 22	08 29	08 29			09 06	09 21	
26½	31	**Glasgow Central** 15 221	a	00 14	06 11	06 52	07 02	07 16	07 29	07 38	07 54	07 58	08 08	08 18	08 29	08 30	08 37	08 38	08 46	08 50	09 14	09 29	09 44

		SR	SR	SR	SR	SR	SR	SR	SR	SR	SR	SR	SR	SR	SR	SR	SR	SR	SR	SR	SR	SR	SR
Gourock	d	09 08	09 24	09 39	09 54		10 08	10 24	10 38	10 54		11 08	11 24	11 38	11 54		12 08	12 24	12 38	12 54		13 08	13 24
Fort Matilda	d	09 11	09 27	09 42	09 57		10 11	10 27	10 41	10 57		11 11	11 27	11 41	11 57		12 11	12 27	12 41	12 57		13 11	13 27
Greenock West	d	09 14	09 30	09 45	10 00		10 14	10 30	10 44	11 00		11 14	11 30	11 44	12 00		12 14	12 30	12 44	13 00		13 14	13 30
Greenock Central	d	09 16	09 32	09 47	10 02		10 16	10 32	10 46	11 02		11 16	11 32	11 46	12 02		12 16	12 32	12 46	13 02		13 16	13 32
Cartsdyke	d	09 19		09 50			10 19		10 49			11 19		11 49			12 19		12 49			13 19	
Bogston	d	09 21		09 52			10 21		10 51			11 21		11 51			12 21		12 51			13 21	
Wemyss Bay	d					09 57					10 57					11 57					12 57		
Inverkip	d					10 01					11 01					12 01					13 01		
I.B.M.	d																						
Branchton	d					10 08					11 08					12 08					13 08		
Drumfrochar	d					10 11					11 11					12 11					13 11		
Whinhill	d					10 13					11 13					12 13					13 13		
Port Glasgow	d	09 23	09 37	09 54	10 07	10 18	10 23	10 37	10 53	11 07	11 18	11 23	11 37	11 53	12 07	12 18	12 23	12 37	12 53	13 07	13 18	13 23	13 37
Woodhall	d	09 26		09 57			10 26		10 56			11 26		11 56			12 26		12 56			13 26	
Langbank	d	09 30		10 01			10 30		11 00			11 30		12 00			12 30		13 00			13 30	
Bishopton	d	09 35	09 46	10 06	10 16	10 27	10 35	10 46	11 05	11 16	11 27	11 35	11 46	12 05	12 16	12 27	12 35	12 46	13 05	13 16	13 27	13 35	13 46
Paisley St James	d	09 40		10 11			10 40		11 10			11 40		12 10			12 40		13 10			13 40	
Paisley Gilmour Street 221	a	09 43	09 52	10 14	10 22	10 33	10 43	10 52	11 13	11 22	11 33	11 43	11 52	12 13	12 22	12 33	12 43	12 52	13 13	13 22	13 33	13 43	13 52
	d	09 43	09 52	10 14	10 22	10 34	10 43	10 52	11 13	11 22	11 33	11 43	11 52	12 13	12 22	12 33	12 43	12 52	13 13	13 25	13 33	13 43	13 52
Hillington West	d	09 47		10 18			10 47		11 17			11 47		12 17			12 47		13 17			13 47	
Hillington East	d	09 49		10 20			10 49		11 19			11 49		12 19			12 49		13 19			13 49	
Cardonald	d	09 51		10 22			10 51		11 21			11 51		12 21			12 51		13 21			13 51	
Glasgow Central 15 221	a	09 59	10 03	10 29	10 32	10 44	10 59	11 03	11 29	11 33	11 44	11 59	12 03	12 29	12 33	12 44	12 59	13 03	13 29	13 35	13 44	13 59	14 03

		SR	SR	SR SO	SR SX	SR	SR	SR	SR	SR SO	SR SX	SR	SR SO	SR SX	SR	SR	SR	SR	SR	SR	SR	SR SO
Gourock	d	13 38	13 54			14 08	14 24	14 38	14 54			15 08	15 24	15 24	15 38	15 50		16 08	16 27	16 38		16 54
Fort Matilda	d	13 41	13 57			14 11	14 27	14 41	14 57			15 11	15 27	15 27	15 41	15 53		16 11	16 30	16 41		16 57
Greenock West	d	13 44	14 00			14 14	14 30	14 44	15 00			15 14	15 30	15 30	15 44	15 56		16 14	16 33	16 44		17 00
Greenock Central	d	13 46	14 02			14 16	14 32	14 46	15 02			15 16	15 32	15 32	15 46	15 58		16 16	16 35	16 46		17 02
Cartsdyke	d	13 49				14 19		14 49				15 19			15 49			16 19		16 49		17 05
Bogston	d	13 51				14 21		14 51				15 21			15 51			16 21		16 51		17 07
Wemyss Bay	d			13 57	13 57					14 57	14 57						15 57				16 45	
Inverkip	d			14 01	14 01					15 01	15 01						16 01				16 49	
I.B.M.	d																					
Branchton	d			14 08	14 08					15 08	15 08						16 08				16 56	
Drumfrochar	d			14 11	14 11					15 11	15 11						16 11				16 59	
Whinhill	d			14 13	14 13					15 13	15 13						16 13				17 01	
Port Glasgow	d	13 53	14 07	14 18	14 18	14 23	14 37	14 53	15 07	15 18	15 18	15 23	15 37	15 37	15 53	16 03	16 18	16 23	16 40	16 53	17 06	17 10
Woodhall	d	13 56				14 26		14 56				15 26			15 56			16 26		16 56		
Langbank	d	14 00				14 30		15 00				15 30			16 00			16 30		17 00		
Bishopton	d	14 05	14 16	14 27	14 27	14 35	14 46	15 05	15 16	15 27	15 27	15 35	15 46	15 46	16 05	16 12	16 27	16 35	16 49	17 05	17 15	17 20
Paisley St James	d	14 10				14 40		15 10				15 40			16 10			16 40		17 10		
Paisley Gilmour Street 221	a	14 13	14 22	14 33	14 33	14 43	14 52	15 13	15 22	15 33	15 33	15 43	15 52	15 52	16 13	16 18	16 33	16 43	16 55	17 13	17 21	17 26
	d	14 13	14 22	14 33	14 33	14 43	14 52	15 13	15 22	15 33	15 33	15 43	15 52	15 52	16 13	16 18	16 33	16 43	16 55	17 13	17 21	17 26
Hillington West	d	14 17				14 47		15 17				15 47	15 56	15 56	16 17			16 47	16 59	17 17		
Hillington East	d	14 19				14 49		15 19				15 49			16 19			16 49		17 19		
Cardonald	d	14 21				14 51		15 21				15 51			16 21			16 51		17 21		
Glasgow Central 15 221	a	14 29	14 33	14 44	14 46	14 59	15 03	15 29	15 33	15 44	15 46	15 59	16 06	16 07	16 30	16 28	16 46	16 59	17 08	17 30	17 33	17 36

Table T219-R

Gourock and Wemyss Bay - Glasgow Central

Mondays to Saturdays
16 December to 16 May

		SR	SR	SR SO	SR SX	SR	SR	SR	SR	SR	SR	SR
Gourock	d	17 08	17 24	17 43	17 45		18 08	18 24		18 39		19 08
Fort Matilda	d	17 11	17 27	17 46	17 48		18 11	18 27		18 42		19 11
Greenock West	d	17 14	17 30	17 49	17 51		18 14	18 30		18 45		19 14
Greenock Central	d	17 16	17 32	17 51	17 53		18 16	18 32		18 47		19 16
Cartsdyke	d	17 19		17 54	17 56		18 19			18 50		19 19
Bogston	d	17 21		17 56	17 58		18 21			18 52		19 21
Wemyss Bay	d					17 50			18 25		18 55	
Inverkip	d					17 54			18 29		18 59	
I.B.M.	d											
Branchton	d					18 06			18 41		19 06	
Drumfrochar	d					18 08			18 44		19 09	
Whinhill	d					18 11			18 46		19 11	
Port Glasgow	d	17 23	17 37	17 58	18 00	18 18	18 23	18 37	18 51	18 55	19 16	19 23
Woodhall	d	17 26		18 01	18 03		18 26			18 57		19 26
Langbank	d	17 30		18 05	18 07		18 30			19 01		19 30
Bishopton	d	17 35	17 46	18 10	18 12	18 27	18 35	18 46	19 00	19 07	19 25	19 35
Paisley St James	d	17 40		18 15	18 17		18 40			19 12		19 40
Paisley Gilmour Street 221	a	17 43	17 52	18 18	18 20	18 33	18 43	18 52	19 06	19 14	19 31	19 43
	d	17 43	17 52	18 18	18 20	18 34	18 43	18 52	19 07	19 15	19 31	19 43
Hillington West	d	17 47		18 22	18 24		18 47			19 18		19 47
Hillington East	d	17 49		18 24	18 26		18 49			19 20		19 49
Cardonald	d	17 51		18 26	18 28		18 51			19 22		19 51
Glasgow Central 221	a	17 59	18 04	18 33	18 35	18 44	18 59	19 02	19 17	19 29	19 42	19 59

		SR	SR	SR	SR	SR	SR	SR	SR	SR SX	SR SO
Gourock	d	19 24	19 48		20 24	20 48		21 24	21 48		
Fort Matilda	d	19 27	19 51		20 27	20 51		21 27	21 51		
Greenock West	d	19 30	19 54		20 30	20 54		21 30	21 54		
Greenock Central	d	19 32	19 56		20 32	20 56		21 32	21 56		
Cartsdyke	d	19 35	19 59		20 35	20 59		21 35	21 59		
Bogston	d	19 37			20 37			21 37			
Wemyss Bay	d			19 48			20 47			21 47	21 47
Inverkip	d			19 52			20 51			21 51	21 51
I.B.M.	d										
Branchton	d			19 59			20 58			21 58	21 58
Drumfrochar	d			20 02			21 01			22 01	22 01
Whinhill	d			20 04			21 03			22 03	22 03
Port Glasgow	d	19 39	20 02	20 09	20 39	21 02	21 08	21 39	22 02	22 08	22 08
Woodhall	d	19 42		20 11	20 42		21 10	21 42		22 10	22 10
Langbank	d	19 46		20 15	20 46		21 14	21 46		22 14	22 14
Bishopton	d	19 51	20 11	20 21	20 51	21 11	21 20	21 51	22 11	22 20	22 20
Paisley St James	d	19 56		20 26	20 56		21 25	21 56		22 25	22 25
Paisley Gilmour Street 221	a	19 59	20 17	20 28	20 59	21 17	21 27	21 59	22 17	22 27	22 27
	d	19 59	20 18	20 29	20 59	21 18	21 28	21 59	22 18	22 28	22 28
Hillington West	d	20 03		20 32	21 03		21 31	22 03		22 31	22 31
Hillington East	d	20 05		20 34	21 05		21 33	22 05		22 33	22 33
Cardonald	d	20 07		20 36	21 07		21 35	22 07		22 35	22 35
Glasgow Central 221	a	20 14	20 29	20 43	21 16	21 28	21 44	22 15	22 29	22 43	22 46

		SR	SR	SR	SR SO
Gourock	d	22 24		23 24	
Fort Matilda	d	22 27		23 27	
Greenock West	d	22 30		23 30	
Greenock Central	d	22 32		23 32	
Cartsdyke	d	22 35		23 35	
Bogston	d	22 37		23 37	
Wemyss Bay	d		22 47		23 39
Inverkip	d		22 51		23 43
I.B.M.	d				
Branchton	d		22 58		23 50
Drumfrochar	d		23 01		23 53
Whinhill	d		23 03		23 55
Port Glasgow	d	22 39	23 08	23 39	00 02
Woodhall	d	22 42	23 10	23 42	
Langbank	d	22 46	23 14	23 46	
Bishopton	d	22 51	23 20	23 51	00 10
Paisley St James	d	22 56	23 25	23 56	
Paisley Gilmour Street 221	a	22 59	23 27	23 59	00 16
	d	22 59	23 28	23 59	00 17
Hillington West	d	23 03	23 31	00 03	
Hillington East	d	23 05	23 33	00 05	
Cardonald	d	23 07	23 35	00 07	
Glasgow Central 221	a	23 16	23 43	00 14	00 27

Sundays
15 December to 10 May

		SR A	SR A	SR	SR	SR	SR	SR	SR	SR	SR
Gourock	d			08 23		09 23		10 23		11 23	
Fort Matilda	d			08 26		09 26		10 26		11 26	
Greenock West	d			08 29		09 29		10 29		11 29	
Greenock Central	d			08 31		09 31		10 31		11 31	
Cartsdyke	d			08 34		09 34		10 34		11 34	
Bogston	d			08 36		09 36		10 36		11 36	
Wemyss Bay	d				08 50		09 50		10 55		11 50
Inverkip	d				08 54		09 54		10 59		11 54
I.B.M.	d										
Branchton	d				09 01		10 01		11 06		12 01
Drumfrochar	d				09 04		10 04		11 09		12 04
Whinhill	d				09 06		10 06		11 11		12 06
Port Glasgow	d		00 02	08 38	09 11	09 38	10 11	10 38	11 16	11 38	12 11
Woodhall	d			08 41		09 41		10 41		11 41	
Langbank	d			08 45		09 45		10 45		11 45	
Bishopton	d		00 10	08 50	09 20	09 50	10 20	10 50	11 25	11 50	12 20
Paisley St James	d			08 55		09 55		10 55		11 55	
Paisley Gilmour Street 221	a		00 16	08 58	09 26	09 58	10 26	10 58	11 31	11 58	12 26
	d		00 17	08 58	09 26	09 58	10 26	10 58	11 31	11 58	12 26
Hillington West	d	00 03		09 02		10 02		11 02		12 02	
Hillington East	d	00 05		09 04	09 30	10 04	10 30	11 04	11 35	12 04	12 30
Cardonald	d	00 07		09 06		10 06		11 06		12 06	
Glasgow Central 221	a	00 14	00 27	09 13	09 39	10 13	10 39	11 13	11 43	12 13	12 39

and at the same minutes past each hour until

		SR	SR	SR	SR	SR	SR	SR	SR	SR	SR	SR
Gourock	d	14 23		15 23		16 23		17 23		18 23		19 23
Fort Matilda	d	14 26		15 26		16 26		17 26		18 26		19 26
Greenock West	d	14 29		15 29		16 29		17 29		18 29		19 29
Greenock Central	d	14 31		15 31		16 31		17 31		18 31		19 31
Cartsdyke	d	14 34		15 34		16 34		17 34		18 34		19 34
Bogston	d	14 36		15 36		16 36		17 36		18 36		19 36
Wemyss Bay	d		14 50		15 55		16 50		17 50		18 55	
Inverkip	d		14 54		15 59		16 54		17 54		18 59	
I.B.M.	d											
Branchton	d		15 01		16 06		17 01		18 01		19 06	
Drumfrochar	d		15 04		16 09		17 04		18 04		19 09	
Whinhill	d		15 06		16 11		17 06		18 06		19 11	
Port Glasgow	d	14 38	15 11	15 38	16 16	16 38	17 11	17 38	18 11	18 38	19 16	19 38
Woodhall	d	14 41		15 41		16 41		17 41		18 41		19 41
Langbank	d	14 45		15 45		16 45		17 45		18 45		19 45
Bishopton	d	14 50	15 20	15 50	16 25	16 50	17 20	17 50	18 20	18 50	19 25	19 50
Paisley St James	d	14 55		15 55		16 55		17 55		18 55		19 55
Paisley Gilmour Street 221	a	14 58	15 26	15 58	16 31	16 58	17 26	17 58	18 26	18 58	19 31	19 58
	d	14 58	15 26	15 58	16 31	16 58	17 26	17 58	18 26	18 58	19 31	19 58
Hillington West	d	15 02		16 02		17 02		18 02		19 02		20 02
Hillington East	d	15 04	15 30	16 04	16 35	17 04	17 30	18 04	18 30	19 04	19 35	20 04
Cardonald	d	15 06		16 06		17 06		18 06		19 06		20 06
Glasgow Central 221	a	15 13	15 39	16 13	16 43	17 13	17 39	18 13	18 39	19 14	19 44	20 13

A not 15 December

Table T219-R

Gourock and Wemyss Bay - Glasgow Central

Sundays
15 December to 10 May

		SR	SR	SR	SR	SR
Gourock	d		20 23		21 23	22 23
Fort Matilda	d		20 26		21 26	22 26
Greenock West	d		20 29		21 29	22 29
Greenock Central	d		20 31		21 31	22 31
Cartsdyke	d		20 34		21 34	22 34
Bogston	d		20 36		21 36	22 36
Wemyss Bay	d	19 50		20 50		
Inverkip	d	19 54		20 54		
I.B.M.	d					
Branchton	d	20 01		21 01		
Drumfrochar	d	20 04		21 04		
Whinhill	d	20 06		21 06		
Port Glasgow	d	20 11	20 38	21 11	21 38	22 38
Woodhall	d		20 41		21 41	22 41
Langbank	d		20 45		21 45	22 45
Bishopton	d	20 20	20 50	21 20	21 50	22 50
Paisley St James	d		20 55		21 55	22 55
Paisley Gilmour Street 221	a	20 26	20 58	21 26	21 58	22 58
	d	20 26	20 58	21 26	21 58	22 58
Hillington West	d		21 02		22 02	23 02
Hillington East	d	20 30	21 04	21 30	22 04	23 04
Cardonald	d		21 06		22 06	23 06
Glasgow Central 221	a	20 39	21 15	21 39	22 13	23 13

AVAILABLE FROM MP Middleton Press

Table T221-F

Mondays to Fridays
16 December to 15 May

Glasgow Central - Ardrossan, Largs and Ayr

Miles	Miles	Miles			SR MX A	SR MX A	SR MX A	SR MX	SR	SR	SR	SR	SR	SR	SR	SR B	SR	SR	SR ◇ C	SR	SR D	SR ◇ E	SR
0	0	0	Glasgow Central 15 219	d				00 15	06 00	06 15	06 30	06 45	07 00	07 15	07 30		07 46	08 00	08 08	08 15	08 30		08 33
7¼	7¼	7¼	Paisley Gilmour Street 219	a				00 25	06 12	06 24	06 39	06 54	07 11	07 24	07 40		07 58	08 10		08 26			08 43
—	—	—		d				00 25	06 12	06 25	06 40	06 55	07 11	07 25	07 41		07 58	08 11		08 27			08 44
10¾	10¾	10¾	Johnstone	d			00 02	00 29	06 16	06 29	06 44	06 59	07 15	07 29	07 45		08 02	08 15		08 31			08 48
11½	11½	11½	Milliken Park	d			00 04			06 32		07 02		07 32			08 05			08 34			
13	13	13	Howwood	d			00 06			06 34		07 04		07 34			08 08			08 36			
16½	16½	16½	Lochwinnoch	d			00 10			06 38		07 08		07 38			08 12			08 40			
20½	20½	20½	Glengarnock	d			00 15			06 43		07 13		07 43			08 16	08 23					
23¼	23¼	23¼	Dalry	d			00 19			06 47		07 17		07 47			08 20	08 27					
26¾	26¾	26¾	Kilwinning 4	d			00 23	00 45	06 30	06 51	06 57	07 21	07 29	07 51	07 58		08 24	08 31		08 49	08 54		09 03
—	29	29	Stevenston	d			00 27			06 55		07 25		07 55						08 53			09 07
—	30¼	30¼	Saltcoats	d			00 30			07 01		07 28		08 01						08 56			09 12
—	31¼	31¼	Ardrossan South Beach	d	00 01		00a32			07 03		07 30		08 03						08 58			09 14
—	—	31¾	Ardrossan Town	d								07 33								09a01			09 17
—	—	32¼	**Ardrossan Harbour**	a								07 35											09 20
—	35¾	—	West Kilbride	d	00 07					07 09				08 09									
—	39½	—	Fairlie	d	00 13					07 15				08 15									
—	42¾	—	**Largs**	a	00 18					07 20				08 20									
30	—	—	Irvine	d		00 01		00 50	06 34		07 01		07 33		08 02		08 28	08 35			08 58		
33¾	—	—	Barassie	d		00 06		00 54	06 38		07 06		07 38		08 07			08 42				←	
35	—	—	Troon	d		00 09		00 57	06 41		07 09		07 41		08 10	08 14	08 35	08 45	09 12		09 05	09 12	
37¾	—	—	Prestwick Int. Airport ✈	d		00 13		01 01	06 45		07 13		07 45		08 14		08 39	08 49	→		09 09		
38½	—	—	Prestwick Town	d		00 14		01 03	06 47		07 14		07 47		08 15	08 20	08 40	08 50			09 10		
40¼	—	—	Newton-on-Ayr	d		00 18		01 06	06 50		07 18		07 50		08 19			08 54					
41½	—	—	**Ayr**	a		00 21		01 10	06 54		07 21		07 55		08 22	08 27	08 46	08 57			09 16	09 23	

		SR	SR	SR	SR	SR	SR	SR	SR	SR	SR	SR	SR	SR F	SR	SR	SR	SR	SR	SR	SR	SR	SR
Glasgow Central 15 219	d	08 38	08 48	09 00	09 04	09 18	09 32	09 34	09 48	10 00	10 04	10 18	10 30		10 34	10 48	11 00	11 04	11 18	11 29	11 34	11 48	12 00
Paisley Gilmour Street 219	a	08 47	08 59		09 13	09 27		09 44	09 57		10 13	10 29			10 43	10 57		11 13	11 27		11 43	11 57	
	d	08 48	08 59		09 14	09 28		09 45	09 58		10 14	10 29			10 44	10 58		11 14	11 28		11 44	11 58	
Johnstone	d	08 52	09 03		09 18	09 32		09 49	10 02		10 18	10 33			10 48	11 02		11 18	11 32		11 48	12 02	
Milliken Park	d	08 55			09 21			09 52			10 21				10 51			11 21			11 51		
Howwood	d	08 57			09 23			09 54			10 23				10 53			11 23			11 53		
Lochwinnoch	d	09 01			09 27			09 58			10 27				10 57			11 27			11 57		
Glengarnock	d	09 06	09 12		09 32			10 03	10 10		10 32				11 02	11 10		11 32			12 02	12 10	
Dalry	d	09 10			09 36	09 43		10 07			10 36	10 46			11 06			11 36	11 46		12 06		
Kilwinning 4	d	09 14	09 18	09 26	09 40	09 48	09 56	10 11	10 17	10 26	10 40	10 50	10 55		11 10	11 17	11 25	11 40	11 51	11 55	12 10	12 18	12 25
Stevenston	d		09 22			09 52			10 21			10 54				11 21			11 55			12 22	
Saltcoats	d		09 25			09 55			10 24			10 57				11 24			11 58			12 25	
Ardrossan South Beach	d		09 27			09 57			10 26			10 59				11 26			12 00			12 27	
Ardrossan Town	d					10 00						11 02							12 03				
Ardrossan Harbour	a					10 03						11 04							12 05				
West Kilbride	d		09 33						10 32							11 32						12 33	
Fairlie	d		09 39						10 38							11 38						12 39	
Largs	a		09 45						10 43							11 43						12 44	
Irvine	d	09 18		09 30	09 46		10 00	10 15		10 30	10 44		10 59		11 14		11 29	11 44		11 59	12 14		12 29
Barassie	d	09 22		09 35	09 50			10 20		10 35	10 48				11 18		11 35	11 48			12 18		12 33
Troon	d	09 25		09 38	09 53		10 07	10 23		10 38	10 51		11 06	11 16	11 21		11 38	11 51		12 07	12 21		12 36
Prestwick Int. Airport ✈	d	09 29		09 42	09 57		10 11	10 27		10 42	10 55		11 10		11 25		11 42	11 55		12 11	12 25		12 40
Prestwick Town	d	09 31		09 43	09 59		10 12	10 28		10 43	10 57		11 11	11 21	11 27		11 43	11 57		12 12	12 27		12 42
Newton-on-Ayr	d	09 34		09 47	10 02			10 32		10 47	11 00				11 30		11 47	12 00			12 30		12 48
Ayr	a	09 40		09 50	10 07		10 18	10 35		10 50	11 05		11 17	11 29	11 35		11 50	12 05		12 20	12 35		12 54

		SR	SR	SR	SR F	SR	SR	SR	SR	SR	SR	SR G	SR	SR	SR	SR ◇ C	SR	SR	SR ◇ E	SR	SR	SR	SR
Glasgow Central 15 219	d	12 04	12 18	12 30		12 34	12 48	13 00	13 04	13 18	13 30	13 34	13 49	14 00	14 04	14 13	14 18	14 30		14 34	14 48	15 00	15 04
Paisley Gilmour Street 219	a	12 15	12 27			12 43	12 57		13 13	13 27		13 43	13 59		14 13		14 27			14 43	14 58		15 13
	d	12 16	12 28			12 44	12 58		13 14	13 28		13 44	13 59		14 14		14 28			14 44	14 59		15 14
Johnstone	d	12 20	12 32			12 48	13 02		13 18	13 32		13 48	14 03		14 18		14 32			14 48	15 03		15 18
Milliken Park	d	12 23				12 51			13 21			13 51			14 21					14 51			15 21
Howwood	d	12 26				12 53			13 23			13 53			14 23					14 53			15 23
Lochwinnoch	d	12 30				12 57			13 27			13 57			14 27					14 57			15 27
Glengarnock	d	12 34				13 02	13 10		13 32			14 02	14 12		14 32					15 02	15 11		15 32
Dalry	d	12 38	12 45			13 06			13 36	13 44		14 06			14 36		14 43			15 06			15 36
Kilwinning 4	d	12 42	12 50	12 55		13 10	13 17	13 25	13 40	13 49	13 55	14 10	14 18	14 28	14 40		14 49	14 55		15 10	15 18	15 26	15 40
Stevenston	d		12 54				13 21			13 53			14 22				14 53				15 22		
Saltcoats	d		12 57				13 24			13 56			14 25				14 56				15 25		
Ardrossan South Beach	d		12 59				13 26			13 59			14 27				14 58				15 27		
Ardrossan Town	d		13 02							14 02							15 01						
Ardrossan Harbour	a		13 04							14 04							15 04						
West Kilbride	d						13 32						14 33								15 33		
Fairlie	d						13 38						14 39								15 39		
Largs	a						13 43						14 45								15 44		
Irvine	d	12 46		12 59		13 14		13 29	13 44		13 59	14 14		14 32	14 44			14 59		15 14		15 30	15 44
Barassie	d	12 51				13 18		13 35	13 48			14 18		14 37	14 48				←	15 18		15 34	15 48
Troon	d	12 54		13 06	13 15	13 21		13 39	13 51		14 06	14 21		14 40	14 51	15 10		15 05	15 10	15 21		15 37	15 51
Prestwick Int. Airport ✈	d	12 58		13 10		13 25		13 43	13 55		14 10	14 25		14 44	14 55	→		15 09		15 25		15 41	15 55
Prestwick Town	d	12 59		13 11	13 21	13 27		13 44	13 57		14 11	14 27		14 45	14 57			15 11	15 16	15 27		15 43	15 57
Newton-on-Ayr	d	13 03				13 30		13 48	14 00			14 30		14 49	15 00					15 30		15 46	16 00
Ayr	a	13 09		13 19	13 28	13 34		13 54	14 05		14 19	14 34		14 54	15 04			15 18	15 24	15 34		15 51	16 05

A From Glasgow Central
B From Kilmarnock to Girvan
C To Stranraer
D To Glasgow Central
E From Glasgow Central to Stranraer
F From Kilmarnock to Stranraer
G From Edinburgh

Table T221-F

Mondays to Fridays
16 December to 15 May

Glasgow Central - Ardrossan, Largs and Ayr

		SR	SR A	SR	SR	SR	SR	SR	SR	SR	SR B	SR	SR	SR	SR	SR C	SR	SR	SR	SR D	SR	SR
Glasgow Central 15 219	d	15 18	15 30	15 34	15 48	16 00	16 04	16 14	16 28	16 30		16 40	16 50	17 01	17 05	17 13	17 16	17 23	17 32		17 36	17 47
Paisley Gilmour Street 219	a	15 27		15 47	15 57		16 13	16 24		16 40		16 52	16 59		17 14		17 26	17 34			17 46	17 56
	d	15 28		15 48	15 58		16 14	16 24		16 41		16 52	17 00		17 15		17 27	17 35			17 47	17 57
Johnstone	d	15 32		15 52	16 02		16 18	16 28		16 45		16 56	17 04		17 19		17 31	17 39			17 51	
Milliken Park	d			15 55			16 21					16 59			17 22			17 42			17 54	
Howwood	d			15 57			16 23					17 02			17 24		17 35				17 56	
Lochwinnoch	d			16 01			16 27					17 06			17 28						18 00	
Glengarnock	d			16 06	16 10		16 32	16 37				17 10	17 14		17 33		17 41				18 05	
Dalry	d	15 43		16 10			16 36	16 41				17 14	17 18		17 37		17 46				18 09	
Kilwinning 4	d	15 48	15 56	16 14	16 17	16 26	16 40	16 46	16 52	16 58		17 18	17 22	17 26	17 41		17 50	17 54	17 57		18 13	
Stevenston	d	15 52			16 21			16 50		17 02			17 26					17 58			18 17	
Saltcoats	d	15 55			16 24			16 53		17 07			17 29					18 01			18 20	
Ardrossan South Beach	d	15 57			16 26			16 55		17 09			17 31					18 03			18 22	
Ardrossan Town	d	16 00						16 58					17 34								18 25	
Ardrossan Harbour	a	16 03						17 01					17 36								18 27	
West Kilbride	d				16 32					17 15								18 09				
Fairlie	d				16 38					17 21								18 15				
Largs	a				16 43					17 26								18 21				
Irvine	d		16 00	16 18		16 30	16a44		16 56			17 22		17 30	17 45		17 54		18 02			18 18
Barassie	d			16 22		16 35			17 01					17 36			17 59		18 06	←		18 23
Troon	d		16 07	16 25		16 38			17 04		17 12	17 29		17 39	17 51	18 16	18 02		18 10	18 16		18 26
Prestwick Int. Airport ✈	d		16 11	16 29		16 42			17 08			17 33		17 43	17 55	→	18 06		18 14			18 30
Prestwick Town	d		16 12	16 31		16 43			17 09			17 34		17 44	17 57		18 07		18 16	18 21		18 31
Newton-on-Ayr	d			16 34		16 47			17 13					17 48			18 11		18 19			18 35
Ayr	a		16 20	16 39		16 50			17 17		17 23	17 42		17 51	18 03		18 14		18 24	18 28		18 38

		SR	SR	SR	SR ◇ E	SR	SR	SR ◇ F	SR	SR	SR A	SR	SR	SR	SR A	SR	SR	SR	SR G	SR	SR	SR	SR
Glasgow Central 15 219	d	17 49	18 00	18 04	18 13	18 18	18 30		18 34	18 50	19 01	19 15	19 30	19 45	20 00	20 15	20 30	20 45		21 00	21 15	21 30	21 45
Paisley Gilmour Street 219	a	17 59		18 13		18 27			18 43	18 59	19 10	19 24	19 39	19 55	20 10	20 27	20 39	20 54		21 09	21 24	21 39	21 54
	d	18 00		18 14		18 28			18 44	19 00	19 11	19 25	19 40	19 55	20 10	20 28	20 40	20 55		21 10	21 25	21 40	21 55
Johnstone	d	18 04		18 18		18 32			18 48	19 04	19 15	19 29	19 44	19 59	20 14	20 32	20 44	20 59		21 14	21 29	21 44	21 59
Milliken Park	d			18 21					18 51			19 32		20 02		20 35		21 02			21 32		22 02
Howwood	d			18 23					18 53			19 34				20 37					21 34		
Lochwinnoch	d			18 27					18 57			19 38				20 41					21 38		
Glengarnock	d	18 12		18 32					19 02	19 12		19 43		20 10		20 46		21 09			21 43		22 09
Dalry	d			18 36		18 43			19 06			19 47		20 14		20 50		21 13			21 47		22 13
Kilwinning 4	d	18 19	18 26	18 40		18 48	18 59		19 10	19 19	19 28	19 51	19 58	20 18	20 28	20 54	20 57	21 17		21 27	21 51	21 57	22 17
Stevenston	d	18 23				18 52				19 23		19 55		20 22		20 58		21 21			21 55		22 21
Saltcoats	d	18 26				18 55				19 26		19 58		20 25		21 01		21 24			21 58		22 24
Ardrossan South Beach	d	18 28				18 57				19 28		20 00		20 27		21 03		21 26			22 00		22 26
Ardrossan Town	d					19 00						20 03				21 06					22 03		
Ardrossan Harbour	a					19 03						20 05				21 08					22 05		
West Kilbride	d	18 34								19 34				20 33				21 32					22 32
Fairlie	d	18 40								19 40				20 39				21 38					22 38
Largs	a	18 45								19 46				20 44				21 44					22 44
Irvine	d		18 30	18 44			19 03		19 14		19 32		20 02		20 32		21 01			21 31		22 01	
Barassie	d		18 36	18 48				←	19 18		19 37				20 37					21 36			
Troon	d		18 39	18 51	19 16		19 09	19 16	19 21		19 40		20 08		20 40		21 08		21 20	21 39		22 08	
Prestwick Int. Airport ✈	d		18 43	18 55	→		19 13		19 25		19 44		20 12		20 44		21 12			21 43		22 12	
Prestwick Town	d		18 44	18 57			19 15		19 27		19 45		20 14		20 45		21 13			21 44		22 13	
Newton-on-Ayr	d		18 48	19 00					19 30		19 49				20 49					21 48			
Ayr	a		18 53	19 05			19 21		19 27	19 35		19 52		20 21		20 52		21 21		21 31	21 51		22 21	

		SR	SR ◇ E	SR	SR	SR ◇ F	SR	SR	SR FO	SR FX	SR	SR FO	SR FX
Glasgow Central 15 219	d	22 00	22 13	22 16	22 30		22 45	23 00	23 15	23 15	23 30	23 47	23 47
Paisley Gilmour Street 219	a	22 09		22 25	22 39		22 54	23 09	23 24	23 24	23 39	23 56	23 56
	d	22 10		22 26	22 40		22 55	23 10	23 25	23 25	23 40	23 57	23 57
Johnstone	d	22 14		22 30	22 44		22 59	23 14	23 29	23 29	23 44	00 01	00 02
Milliken Park	d			22 33			23 02		23 32	23 32		00 04	00 04
Howwood	d			22 35					23 34	23 34		00 06	00 06
Lochwinnoch	d			22 39					23 38	23 38		00 10	00 10
Glengarnock	d			22 44			23 09		23 43	23 43		00 15	00 15
Dalry	d			22 48			23 13		23 47	23 47		00 19	00 19
Kilwinning 4	d	22 27		22 52	22 57		23 17	23 27	23 51	23 51	23 57	00 23	00 23
Stevenston	d			22 56			23 21		23 55	23 55		00 27	00 27
Saltcoats	d			22 59			23 24		23 58	23 58		00 30	00 30
Ardrossan South Beach	d			23 02			23 26		00 01	00 01		00 32	00a32
Ardrossan Town	d			23a04					00a03				
Ardrossan Harbour	a												
West Kilbride	d						23 35			00 07		00 38	
Fairlie	d						23 41			00 13		00 43	
Largs	a						23 46			00 18		00 50	
Irvine	d	22 31			23 01			23 31			00 01		
Barassie	d	22 36				←		23 36			00 06		
Troon	d	22 39	23 19		23 10	23 19		23 39			00 09		
Prestwick Int. Airport ✈	d	22 43	→		23 14			23 43			00 13		
Prestwick Town	d	22 45			23 15	23 25		23 44			00 14		
Newton-on-Ayr	d	22 48						23 48			00 18		
Ayr	a	22 53			23 21	23 32		23 51			00 21		

A From Edinburgh
B From Kilmarnock to Stranraer
C To Girvan
D From Glasgow Central to Girvan
E To Stranraer
F From Glasgow Central to Stranraer
G From Kilmarnock to Girvan

Table T221-F

Saturdays

21 December to 16 May

Glasgow Central - Ardrossan, Largs and Ayr

		SR A	SR A	SR A	SR	SR	SR	SR	SR	SR	SR	SR B	SR C	SR	SR	SR ◇ D	SR	SR ◇ E	SR	SR	SR	SR	SR
Glasgow Central 15	219 d				00 15	06 00	06 15	06 30	06 45	07 00	07 15	07 30		07 46	08 00	08 08	08 30		08 34	08 38	08 48	09 00	09 04
Paisley Gilmour Street	219 a				00 25	06 12	06 24	06 39	06 54	07 11	07 24	07 40		07 58	08 10				08 43	08 47	08 59		09 13
	d				00 25	06 12	06 25	06 40	06 55	07 11	07 25	07 41		07 58	08 11				08 44	08 48	08 59		09 14
Johnstone	d			00 01	00 29	06 16	06 29	06 44	06 59	07 15	07 29	07 45		08 02	08 15				08 48	08 52	09 03		09 18
Milliken Park	d			00 04			06 32		07 02		07 32			08 05						08 55			09 21
Howwood	d			00 06			06 34		07 04		07 34			08 08						08 57			09 23
Lochwinnoch	d			00 10			06 38		07 08		07 38			08 12						09 01			09 27
Glengarnock	d			00 15			06 43		07 13		07 43			08 16	08 23					09 06	09 12		09 32
Dalry	d			00 19			06 47		07 17		07 47			08 20	08 27					09 10			09 36
Kilwinning 4	d			00 23	00 45	06 30	06 51	06 57	07 21	07 29	07 51	07 58		08 24	08 31		08 54		09 03	09 14	09 18	09 26	09 40
Stevenston	d			00 27			06 55		07 25		07 55								09 07		09 22		
Saltcoats	d			00 30			07 01		07 28		08 01								09 12		09 25		
Ardrossan South Beach	d	00 01		00 32			07 03		07 30		08 03								09 14		09 27		
Ardrossan Town	d	00a03							07 33										09 17				
Ardrossan Harbour	a								07 35										09 20				
West Kilbride	d			00 38			07 09				08 09										09 33		
Fairlie	d			00 43			07 15				08 15										09 39		
Largs	a			00 50			07 20				08 20										09 45		
Irvine	d		00 01		00 50	06 34		07 01		07 33		08 02		08 28	08 35		08 58			09 18		09 30	09 46
Barassie	d		00 06		00 54	06 38		07 06		07 38		08 07			08 42			←		09 22		09 35	09 50
Troon	d		00 09		00 57	06 41		07 09		07 41		08 10	08 14	08 35	08 45	09 12	09 05	09 12		09 25		09 38	09 53
Prestwick Int. Airport	✈ d		00 13		01 01	06 45		07 13		07 45		08 14		08 39	08 49	→	09 09			09 29		09 42	09 57
Prestwick Town	d		00 14		01 03	06 47		07 14		07 47		08 15	08 20	08 40	08 50		09 10			09 31		09 43	09 59
Newton-on-Ayr	d		00 18		01 06	06 50		07 18		07 50		08 19			08 54					09 34		09 47	10 02
Ayr	a		00 21		01 10	06 54		07 21		07 55		08 22	08 27	08 46	08 57		09 16	09 23		09 40		09 50	10 07

		SR	SR F	SR	SR	SR	SR	SR	SR	SR G	SR	SR	SR	SR	SR	SR	SR	SR	SR	SR	SR	SR	SR G
Glasgow Central 15	219 d	09 18	09 32	09 34	09 48	10 00	10 04	10 18	10 30		10 34	10 48	11 00	11 04	11 18	11 30	11 34	11 48	12 00	12 04	12 18	12 30	
Paisley Gilmour Street	219 a	09 27		09 44	09 57		10 13	10 29			10 43	10 57		11 13	11 27		11 43	11 57		12 15	12 27		
	d	09 28		09 45	09 58		10 14	10 29			10 44	10 58		11 14	11 28		11 44	11 58		12 16	12 28		
Johnstone	d	09 32		09 49	10 02		10 18	10 33			10 48	11 02		11 18	11 32		11 48	12 02		12 20	12 32		
Milliken Park	d			09 52			10 21				10 51			11 21			11 51			12 23			
Howwood	d			09 54			10 23				10 53			11 23			11 53			12 26			
Lochwinnoch	d			09 58			10 27				10 57			11 27			11 57			12 30			
Glengarnock	d			10 03	10 10		10 32				11 02	11 10		11 32			12 02	12 10		12 34			
Dalry	d	09 43		10 07			10 36	10 46			11 06			11 36	11 46		12 06			12 38	12 45		
Kilwinning 4	d	09 48	09 56	10 11	10 17	10 26	10 40	10 50	10 55		11 10	11 17	11 25	11 40	11 51	11 55	12 10	12 18	12 25	12 42	12 50	12 55	
Stevenston	d	09 52			10 21			10 54				11 21			11 55			12 22			12 54		
Saltcoats	d	09 55			10 24			10 57				11 24			11 58			12 25			12 57		
Ardrossan South Beach	d	09 57			10 26			10 59				11 26			12 00			12 27			12 59		
Ardrossan Town	d	10 00						11 02							12 03						13 02		
Ardrossan Harbour	a	10 03						11 04							12 05						13 04		
West Kilbride	d				10 32							11 32						12 33					
Fairlie	d				10 38							11 38						12 39					
Largs	a				10 43							11 43						12 44					
Irvine	d		10 00	10 15		10 30	10 44		10 59		11 14		11 29	11 44		11 59	12 14		12 29	12 46		12 59	
Barassie	d			10 20		10 35	10 48				11 18		11 35	11 48			12 18		12 33	12 51			
Troon	d		10 07	10 23		10 38	10 51		11 06	11 16	11 21		11 38	11 51		12 07	12 21		12 36	12 54		13 06	13 15
Prestwick Int. Airport	✈ d		10 11	10 27		10 42	10 55		11 10		11 25		11 42	11 55		12 11	12 25		12 40	12 58		13 10	
Prestwick Town	d		10 12	10 28		10 43	10 57		11 11	11 21	11 27		11 43	11 57		12 12	12 27		12 42	12 59		13 11	13 21
Newton-on-Ayr	d			10 32		10 47	11 00				11 30		11 47	12 00			12 30		12 48	13 03			
Ayr	a		10 18	10 35		10 50	11 05		11 17	11 29	11 34		11 50	12 05		12 20	12 34		12 54	13 09		13 17	13 28

		SR	SR	SR	SR	SR	SR	SR F	SR	SR	SR	SR ◇ D	SR	SR	SR ◇ E	SR	SR	SR	SR	SR	SR F	SR
Glasgow Central 15	219 d	12 34	12 48	13 00	13 04	13 18	13 30	13 34	13 49	14 00	14 04	14 13	14 18	14 30		14 34	14 48	15 00	15 04	15 18	15 30	15 34
Paisley Gilmour Street	219 a	12 43	12 57		13 13	13 27		13 43	13 59		14 13		14 27			14 43	14 58		15 13	15 27		15 47
	d	12 44	12 58		13 14	13 28		13 44	13 59		14 14		14 28			14 44	14 59		15 14	15 28		15 48
Johnstone	d	12 48	13 02		13 18	13 32		13 48	14 03		14 18		14 32			14 48	15 03		15 18	15 32		15 52
Milliken Park	d	12 51			13 21			13 51			14 21					14 51			15 21			15 55
Howwood	d	12 53			13 23			13 53			14 23					14 53			15 23			15 57
Lochwinnoch	d	12 57			13 27			13 57			14 27					14 57			15 27			16 01
Glengarnock	d	13 02	13 10		13 32			14 02	14 12		14 32					15 02	15 11		15 32			16 06
Dalry	d	13 06			13 36	13 44		14 06			14 36		14 43			15 06			15 36	15 43		16 10
Kilwinning 4	d	13 10	13 17	13 25	13 40	13 49	13 55	14 10	14 18	14 28	14 40		14 49	14 55		15 10	15 18	15 26	15 40	15 48	15 56	16 14
Stevenston	d		13 21			13 53			14 22				14 53				15 22			15 52		
Saltcoats	d		13 24			13 56			14 25				14 56				15 25			15 55		
Ardrossan South Beach	d		13 26			13 59			14 27				14 58				15 27			15 57		
Ardrossan Town	d					14 02							15 01							16 00		
Ardrossan Harbour	a					14 04							15 04							16 03		
West Kilbride	d		13 32						14 33								15 33					
Fairlie	d		13 38						14 39								15 39					
Largs	a		13 43						14 45								15 44					
Irvine	d	13 14		13 29	13 44		13 59	14 14		14 32	14 44			14 59		15 14		15 30	15 44		16 00	16 18
Barassie	d	13 18		13 35	13 48			14 18		14 37	14 48				←	15 18		15 34	15 48			16 22
Troon	d	13 21		13 39	13 51		14 06	14 21		14 40	14 51	15 10		15 05	15 10	15 21		15 37	15 51		16 07	16 25
Prestwick Int. Airport	✈ d	13 25		13 43	13 55		14 10	14 25		14 44	14 55	→		15 09		15 25		15 41	15 55		16 11	16 29
Prestwick Town	d	13 27		13 44	13 57		14 11	14 27		14 45	14 57			15 11	15 16	15 27		15 43	15 57		16 12	16 31
Newton-on-Ayr	d	13 30		13 48	14 00			14 30		14 49	15 00					15 30		15 46	16 00			16 34
Ayr	a	13 34		13 54	14 04		14 19	14 34		14 54	15 05			15 17	15 24	15 34		15 51	16 05		16 20	16 38

A From Glasgow Central
B To Edinburgh
C From Kilmarnock to Girvan
D To Stranraer
E From Glasgow Central to Stranraer
F From Edinburgh
G From Kilmarnock to Stranraer

Table T221-F

Saturdays

21 December to 16 May

Glasgow Central - Ardrossan, Largs and Ayr

		SR	SR	SR	SR	SR	SR	SR A	SR	SR	SR	SR	SR B	SR	SR C	SR D	SR	SR	SR	SR	SR E	SR	SR
Glasgow Central 15	219 d	15 48	16 00	16 04	16 14	16 28	16 30		16 40	16 50	17 01	17 05	17 13	17 14	17 32		17 36	17 49	18 00	18 04	18 13	18 18	18 30
Paisley Gilmour Street	219 a	15 57		16 13	16 24		16 40		16 52	16 59		17 14		17 25	17 41		17 46	17 59		18 13		18 27	
	d	15 58		16 14	16 24		16 41		16 52	17 00		17 15		17 25	17 42		17 47	18 00		18 14		18 28	
Johnstone	d	16 02		16 18	16 28		16 45		16 56	17 04		17 19		17 29			17 51	18 04		18 18		18 32	
Milliken Park	d			16 21					16 59			17 22		17 32			17 54			18 21			
Howwood	d			16 23					17 02			17 24		17 35			17 56			18 23			
Lochwinnoch	d			16 27					17 06			17 28					18 00			18 27			
Glengarnock	d	16 10		16 32	16 37				17 10	17 14		17 33		17 41			18 05	18 12		18 32			
Dalry	d			16 36	16 41				17 14	17 18		17 37		17 45			18 09			18 36		18 43	
Kilwinning 4	d	16 17	16 26	16 40	16 46	16 52	16 58		17 18	17 22	17 26	17 41		17 52	17 57		18 13	18 19	18 26	18 40		18 48	18 59
Stevenston	d	16 21			16 50		17 02			17 26				17 56			18 17	18 23				18 52	
Saltcoats	d	16 24			16 53		17 07			17 29				17 59			18 20	18 26				18 55	
Ardrossan South Beach	d	16 26			16 55		17 09			17 31				18 01			18 22	18 28				18 57	
Ardrossan Town	d				16 58					17 34							18 25					19 00	
Ardrossan Harbour	a				17 01					17 36							18 27					19 03	
West Kilbride	d	16 32					17 15							18 07				18 34					
Fairlie	d	16 38					17 21							18 13				18 40					
Largs	a	16 43					17 26							18 18				18 45					
Irvine	d		16 30	16 44		16 56			17 22		17 30	17 45			18 02				18 30	18 44			19 03
Barassie	d		16 35	16 48		17 01					17 36				18 06	←			18 36	18 48			
Troon	d		16 38	16 51		17 04		17 12	17 29		17 39	17 51	18 16		18 10	18 16			18 39	18 51	19 16		19 09
Prestwick Int. Airport	✈ d		16 42	16 55		17 08			17 33		17 43	17 55	→		18 14				18 43	18 55	→		19 13
Prestwick Town	d		16 43	16 57		17 09			17 34		17 44	17 57			18 16	18 21			18 44	18 57			19 15
Newton-on-Ayr	d		16 47	17 00		17 13					17 48				18 19				18 48	19 00			
Ayr	a		16 50	17 05		17 17		17 23	17 40		17 51	18 04			18 24	18 28			18 53	19 05			19 21

		SR F	SR	SR	SR C	SR	SR	SR	SR C	SR	SR	SR	SR G	SR	SR	SR	SR	SR	SR	SR	SR	SR A
Glasgow Central 15	219 d		18 34	18 50	19 01	19 15	19 30	19 45	20 00	20 15	20 30	20 45		21 00	21 15	21 30	21 45	22 00	22 16	22 30	22 45	
Paisley Gilmour Street	219 a		18 43	18 59	19 10	19 24	19 39	19 55	20 10	20 27	20 39	20 54		21 09	21 24	21 39	21 54	22 09	22 25	22 39	22 54	
	d		18 44	19 00	19 11	19 25	19 40	19 55	20 10	20 28	20 40	20 55		21 10	21 25	21 40	21 55	22 10	22 26	22 40	22 55	
Johnstone	d		18 48	19 04	19 15	19 29	19 44	19 59	20 14	20 32	20 44	20 59		21 14	21 29	21 44	21 59	22 14	22 30	22 44	22 59	
Milliken Park	d		18 51			19 32		20 02		20 35		21 02			21 32		22 02		22 33		23 02	
Howwood	d		18 53			19 34				20 37					21 34				22 35			
Lochwinnoch	d		18 57			19 38				20 41					21 38				22 39			
Glengarnock	d		19 02	19 12		19 43		20 10		20 46		21 09			21 43		22 09		22 44		23 09	
Dalry	d		19 06			19 47		20 14		20 50		21 13			21 47		22 13		22 48		23 13	
Kilwinning 4	d		19 10	19 19	19 28	19 51	19 58	20 18	20 28	20 54	20 57	21 17		21 27	21 51	21 57	22 17	22 27	22 52	22 57	23 17	
Stevenston	d			19 23		19 55		20 22		20 58		21 21			21 55		22 21		22 56		23 21	
Saltcoats	d			19 26		19 58		20 25		21 01		21 24			21 58		22 24		22 59		23 24	
Ardrossan South Beach	d			19 28		20 00		20 27		21 03		21 26			22 00		22 26		23 02		23 26	
Ardrossan Town	d					20 03				21 06					22 03				23a04			
Ardrossan Harbour	a					20 06				21 08					22 05							
West Kilbride	d			19 34				20 33				21 32					22 32				23 35	
Fairlie	d			19 40				20 39				21 38					22 38				23 41	
Largs	a			19 46				20 44				21 44					22 44				23 46	
Irvine	d		19 14		19 32		20 02		20 32		21 01			21 31		22 01		22 31		23 01		
Barassie	d	←	19 18		19 37				20 37					21 36				22 36				
Troon	d	19 16	19 21		19 40		20 08		20 40		21 08		21 20	21 39		22 08		22 39		23 10		23 19
Prestwick Int. Airport	✈ d		19 25		19 44		20 12		20 44		21 12			21 43		22 12		22 43		23 14		
Prestwick Town	d		19 27		19 45		20 14		20 45		21 13			21 44		22 13		22 45		23 15		23 25
Newton-on-Ayr	d		19 30		19 49				20 49					21 48				22 48				
Ayr	a	19 27	19 35		19 52		20 21		20 52		21 21		21 31	21 51		22 19		22 53		23 21		23 32

		SR	SR	SR
Glasgow Central 15	219 d	23 00	23 15	23 30
Paisley Gilmour Street	219 a	23 09	23 24	23 39
	d	23 10	23 25	23 40
Johnstone	d	23 14	23 29	23 44
Milliken Park	d		23 32	
Howwood	d		23 34	
Lochwinnoch	d		23 38	
Glengarnock	d		23 43	
Dalry	d		23 47	
Kilwinning 4	d	23 27	23 51	23 57
Stevenston	d		23 55	
Saltcoats	d		23 58	
Ardrossan South Beach	d		00 01	
Ardrossan Town	d			
Ardrossan Harbour	a			
West Kilbride	d		00 07	
Fairlie	d		00 13	
Largs	a		00 18	
Irvine	d	23 31		00 01
Barassie	d	23 36		00 06
Troon	d	23 39		00 09
Prestwick Int. Airport	✈ d	23 43		00 13
Prestwick Town	d	23 44		00 14
Newton-on-Ayr	d	23 48		00 18
Ayr	a	23 51		00 21

A From Kilmarnock to Stranraer
B To Girvan
C From Edinburgh
D From Glasgow Central to Girvan
E To Stranraer
F From Glasgow Central to Stranraer
G From Kilmarnock to Girvan

Table T221-F

Sundays

15 December to 10 May

Glasgow Central - Ardrossan, Largs and Ayr

Station		SR A	SR A	SR	SR	SR	SR	SR	SR	SR	SR	SR	SR	SR	SR	SR	SR	SR	SR	SR	SR	SR	SR
Glasgow Central 15	219 d			08 40	09 00	09 30	09 40	10 00	10 30	10 40	11 00	11 15	11 30	11 40	12 00	12 30	12 33	12 40	13 00	13 30	13 40	14 00	14 05
Paisley Gilmour Street	219 a			08 49	09 09	09 39	09 49	10 09	10 39	10 49	11 09	11 24	11 39	11 49	12 09	12 39	12 42	12 49	13 09	13 39	13 49	14 09	14 14
	d			08 50	09 10	09 40	09 50	10 10	10 40	10 50	11 10	11 25	11 40	11 50	12 10	12 40	12 43	12 50	13 10	13 40	13 50	14 10	14 15
Johnstone	d			08 54	09 14	09 44	09 54	10 14	10 44	10 54	11 14	11 29	11 44	11 54	12 14	12 44	12 47	12 54	13 14	13 44	13 54	14 14	14 19
Milliken Park	d			08 57			09 57			10 57		11 32		11 57			12 50	12 57			13 57		14 22
Howwood	d						09 59			10 59				11 59				12 59			13 59		
Lochwinnoch	d						10 03			11 03				12 03				13 03			14 03		
Glengarnock	d			09 04			10 08			11 08				12 08				13 08			14 08		
Dalry	d			09 08			10 12			11 12				12 12				13 12			14 12		
Kilwinning 4	d			09 13	09 28	09 58	10 16	10 28	10 58	11 16	11 28	11 45	11 58	12 16	12 28	12 58	13 03	13 16	13 28	13 58	14 16	14 28	14 35
Stevenston	d			09 17			10 20			11 20		11 49		12 20			13 08	13 20			14 20		14 39
Saltcoats	d			09 20			10 23			11 23		11 52		12 23			13 13	13 23			14 23		14 42
Ardrossan South Beach	d	00 01		09 22			10 25			11 25		11 54		12 25			13 15	13 25			14 25		14 44
Ardrossan Town	d			09 25								11 57					13 18						14 47
Ardrossan Harbour	a			09 28								12 00					13 20						14 50
West Kilbride	d	00 07					10 31			11 31				12 31				13 31			14 31		
Fairlie	d	00 13					10 37			11 37				12 37				13 37			14 37		
Largs	a	00 18					10 43			11 43				12 43				13 43			14 43		
Irvine	d		00 01		09 32	10 02		10 32	11 02		11 32		12 02		12 32	13 02			13 32	14 02		14 32	
Barassie	d		00 06		09 36			10 36			11 36				12 36				13 36			14 36	
Troon	d		00 09		09 39	10 08		10 39	11 08		11 39		12 08		12 39	13 08			13 39	14 08		14 39	
Prestwick Int. Airport ✈	d		00 13		09 43	10 12		10 43	11 12		11 43		12 12		12 43	13 12			13 43	14 12		14 43	
Prestwick Town	d		00 14		09 45	10 14		10 45	11 14		11 45		12 14		12 45	13 14			13 45	14 14		14 45	
Newton-on-Ayr	d		00 18		09 48			10 48			11 48				12 48				13 48			14 48	
Ayr	a		00 21		09 52	10 20		10 53	11 20		11 53		12 21		12 52	13 21			13 53	14 21		14 53	

Station		SR	SR	SR	SR	SR	SR	SR	SR	SR	SR	SR	SR	SR	SR	SR	SR	SR	SR	SR	SR	SR	SR
Glasgow Central 15	219 d	14 30	14 40	15 00	15 30	15 40	16 00	16 30	16 40	16 55	17 00	17 30	17 40	18 00	18 30	18 40	19 00	19 40	20 00	20 40	21 00	21 40	22 00
Paisley Gilmour Street	219 a	14 39	14 49	15 09	15 39	15 49	16 09	16 39	16 49	17 04	17 09	17 39	17 49	18 09	18 39	18 49	19 09	19 49	20 09	20 49	21 09	21 49	22 09
	d	14 40	14 50	15 10	15 40	15 50	16 10	16 40	16 50	17 05	17 10	17 40	17 50	18 10	18 40	18 50	19 10	19 50	20 10	20 50	21 10	21 50	22 10
Johnstone	d	14 44	14 54	15 14	15 44	15 54	16 14	16 44	16 54	17 09	17 14	17 44	17 54	18 14	18 44	18 54	19 14	19 54	20 14	20 54	21 14	21 54	22 14
Milliken Park	d		14 57			15 57			16 57	17 12			17 57			18 57		19 57		20 57		21 57	
Howwood	d		14 59			15 59			16 59				17 59			18 59		19 59		20 59		21 59	
Lochwinnoch	d		15 03			16 03			17 03				18 03			19 03		20 03		21 03		22 03	
Glengarnock	d		15 08			16 08			17 08				18 08			19 08		20 08		21 08		22 08	
Dalry	d		15 12			16 12			17 12				18 12			19 12		20 12		21 12		22 12	
Kilwinning 4	d	14 58	15 16	15 28	15 58	16 16	16 28	16 58	17 16	17 25	17 29	17 58	18 16	18 28	18 58	19 16	19 28	20 16	20 28	21 16	21 28	22 16	22 28
Stevenston	d		15 20			16 20			17 20	17 29			18 20			19 20		20 20		21 20		22 20	
Saltcoats	d		15 23			16 23			17 23	17 32			18 23			19 23		20 23		21 23		22 23	
Ardrossan South Beach	d		15 25			16 25			17 25	17 34			18 25			19 25		20 25		21 25		22 25	
Ardrossan Town	d									17 37													
Ardrossan Harbour	a									17 40													
West Kilbride	d		15 31			16 31			17 31				18 31			19 31		20 31		21 31		22 31	
Fairlie	d		15 37			16 37			17 37				18 37			19 37		20 37		21 37		22 37	
Largs	a		15 43			16 43			17 43				18 43			19 43		20 43		21 43		22 43	
Irvine	d	15 02		15 32	16 02		16 32	17 02			17 33	18 02		18 32	19 02		19 32		20 32		21 32		22 32
Barassie	d			15 36			16 36				17 37			18 36			19 36		20 36		21 36		22 36
Troon	d	15 08		15 39	16 08		16 39	17 08			17 40	18 08		18 39	19 08		19 39		20 39		21 39		22 39
Prestwick Int. Airport ✈	d	15 12		15 43	16 12		16 43	17 12			17 44	18 12		18 43	19 12		19 43		20 43		21 43		22 43
Prestwick Town	d	15 14		15 45	16 14		16 45	17 14			17 46	18 14		18 45	19 14		19 45		20 45		21 45		22 45
Newton-on-Ayr	d			15 48			16 48				17 49			18 48			19 48		20 48		21 48		22 48
Ayr	a	15 20		15 53	16 21		16 53	17 21			17 54	18 20		18 53	19 21		19 53		20 53		21 52		22 52

Station		SR	SR
Glasgow Central 15	219 d	22 42	23 00
Paisley Gilmour Street	219 a	22 51	23 09
	d	22 52	23 10
Johnstone	d	22 56	23 14
Milliken Park	d	22 59	
Howwood	d	23 01	
Lochwinnoch	d	23 05	
Glengarnock	d	23 10	
Dalry	d	23 14	
Kilwinning 4	d	23 26	23 30
Stevenston	d	23 30	
Saltcoats	d	23 33	
Ardrossan South Beach	d	23 35	
Ardrossan Town	d		
Ardrossan Harbour	a		
West Kilbride	d	23 41	
Fairlie	d	23 47	
Largs	a	23 52	
Irvine	d		23 34
Barassie	d		23 38
Troon	d		23 41
Prestwick Int. Airport ✈	d		23 45
Prestwick Town	d		23 47
Newton-on-Ayr	d		23 50
Ayr	a		23 54

A not 15 December. From Glasgow Central

Table T221-R

Mondays to Fridays

16 December to 15 May

Ayr, Largs and Ardrossan - Glasgow Central

Miles	Miles	Miles	Station		SR	SR	SR	SR	SR	SR	SR	SR	SR	SR	SR A	SR	SR	SR	SR	SR	SR	SR	SR ◇ B
0	—	—	**Ayr**	d	05 13	05 40	06 02	06 20		06 33		06 50	07 05	07 17	07 22		07 34	07 41			08 05		08 22
1¼	—	—	Newton-on-Ayr	d	05 15	05 42	06 04			06 35		06 52	07 07	07 19				07 43			08 07		
3¼	—	—	Prestwick Town	d	05 18	05 45	06 07	06 25		06 38		06 55	07 10	07 22	07 27		07 39	07 47			08 10		08 29
3¾	—	—	Prestwick Int. Airport ✈	d	05 20	05 47	06 09	06 26		06 40		06 57	07 12	07 24			07 41	07 48			08 12		
6½	—	—	Troon	d	05 24	05 51	06 13	06 30		06 44		07 01	07 16	07 28	07a32		07 45	07 52			08 16		08 36
7¾	—	—	Barassie	d	05 26	05 54	06 15			06 49		07 03	07 18	07 30				07 55			08 18		
11½	—	—	Irvine	d	05 31	05 58	06 20	06 36		06 53		07 08	07 23	07 37			07 51	07 59			08 23		
—	0	—	**Largs**	d							06 42					07 22			07 42				
—	3	—	Fairlie	d							06 47					07 27			07 47				
—	7	—	West Kilbride	d							06 52					07 32			07 52				
—	—	0	**Ardrossan Harbour**	d					06 34													08 19	
—	—	0½	Ardrossan Town	d					06 36													08 21	
—	11½	1	Ardrossan South Beach	d					06 38		06 59					07 39			07 59			08 24	
—	12½	2	Saltcoats	d					06 40		07 01					07 41			08 01			08 26	
—	13¾	3¼	Stevenston	d					06 43		07 03					07 43			08 03			08 28	
14¾	16	5½	Kilwinning 4	d	05 35	06 02	06 24	06 40	06 46	06 57	07 07	07 12	07 27	07 41		07 49	07 55	08 03	08 07	08 14	08 27	08 32	
18½	19¾	9¼	Dalry	d	05 39	06 07	06 28		06 51	07 02	07 11		07 31	07 46						08 18		08 37	
21	22¼	11¾	Glengarnock	d	05 43	06 11	06 32			07 06	07 15		07 35	07 50		07 55				08 22		08 41	
25	26¼	15½	Lochwinnoch	d	05 48	06 15	06 37			07 10			07 40				08 04			08 27		08 45	
28½	29¾	19¼	Howwood	d	05 52	06 19	06 41			07 14			07 44				08 08			08 31		08 49	
30	31¼	20¾	Milliken Park	d	05 54	06 22	06 43			07 17		07 26	07 46				08 11			08 33		08 52	
30¾	32	21½	Johnstone	d	05 57	06 25	06 46		07 01	07 20	07 24	07 29	07 49	07 59		08 04		08 17	08 21	08 36	08 41	08 55	
34¼	35½	25	Paisley Gilmour Street 219	a	06 02	06 29	06 51	06 55	07 05	07 24	07 28	07 33	07 54	08 03		08 08	08 16	08 21	08 25	08 41	08 45	08 59	
—	—	—		d	06 02	06 29	06 52	06 56	07 06	07 24	07 28	07 33	07 54	08 03		08 10	08 16	08 21	08 25	08 41	08 46	08 59	
41½	42¾	32¼	**Glasgow Central 15** 219	a	06 13	06 39	07 03	07 06	07 19	07 36	07 40	07 44	08 04	08 13		08 21	08 28	08 32	08 35	08 52	08 58	09 11	09 37

Station		SR C	SR	SR	SR	SR	SR D	SR	SR	SR	SR	SR	SR E	SR	SR	SR	SR C	SR	SR	SR	SR	SR	SR
Ayr	d	08 29		08 51		09 06	09 24		09 36	09 50		10 07	10 21	10 25		10 36	10 51		11 08	11 24		11 36	11 52
Newton-on-Ayr	d	08 31		08 54		09 08			09 38	09 52		10 09				10 38	10 53		11 10			11 38	11 54
Prestwick Town	d	08 34		08 57		09 11	09 29		09 41	09 55		10 12		10 30		10 41	10 56		11 13	11 29		11 41	11 57
Prestwick Int. Airport ✈	d	08 36		08 58		09 13	09 30		09 43	09 57		10 14		10 31		10 43	10 58		11 15	11 30		11 43	11 59
Troon	d	08 40		09 02		09 17	09 34		09 47	10 01		10 18	10a29	10 35		10 47	11 02		11 19	11 34		11 47	12 03
Barassie	d	08 43		09 05		09 19			09 49	10 03		10 20				10 49	11 04		11 21			11 49	12 05
Irvine	d	08 48		09 09		09 24	09 40		09 54	10 08		10 25		10 41		10 54	11 09		11 26	11 40		11 54	12 10
Largs	d		08 33								09 53							10 53					
Fairlie	d		08 38								09 58							10 58					
West Kilbride	d		08 43								10 03							11 03					
Ardrossan Harbour	d							09 36							10 36						11 36		
Ardrossan Town	d				09 07			09 39							10 38						11 38		
Ardrossan South Beach	d		08 50		09 10			09 42			10 10				10 41			11 10			11 41		
Saltcoats	d		08 52		09 13			09 44			10 13				10 43			11 13			11 43		
Stevenston	d		08 54		09 15			09 46			10 15				10 45			11 15			11 45		
Kilwinning 4	d	08 52	08 58	09 13	09 19	09 28	09 44	09 50	09 58	10 12	10 19	10 29		10 45	10 49	10 58	11 13	11 19	11 30	11 45	11 51	11 58	12 14
Dalry	d		09 02			09 32		09 54	10 03			10 33			10 53	11 02			11 34		11 56	12 02	
Glengarnock	d		09 06		09 25	09 36			10 07		10 25	10 37				11 06		11 25	11 38			12 06	
Lochwinnoch	d		09 11			09 41			10 11			10 42				11 12			11 43			12 11	
Howwood	d		09 15			09 45			10 15			10 46				11 16			11 47			12 15	
Milliken Park	d		09 17			09 47			10 18			10 48				11 19			11 49			12 17	
Johnstone	d	09 07	09 20		09 34	09 50		10 05	10 21		10 34	10 51			11 05	11 22		11 34	11 52		12 06	12 20	
Paisley Gilmour Street 219	a	09 11	09 24		09 38	09 55		10 09	10 25		10 39	10 55			11 12	11 26		11 39	11 56		12 10	12 24	
	d	09 12	09 25		09 39	09 55		10 10	10 25		10 39	10 56			11 12	11 26		11 40	11 57		12 11	12 25	
Glasgow Central 15 219	a	09 24	09 36	09 40	09 51	10 06	10 09	10 21	10 36	10 38	10 50	11 06		11 10	11 22	11 36	11 40	11 50	12 07	12 11	12 23	12 35	12 40

Station		SR	SR	SR	SR E	SR	SR C	SR	SR	SR	SR	SR	SR	SR	SR	SR	SR	SR E	SR	SR	SR C	SR	SR
Ayr	d		12 06	12 23	12 29		12 37	12 50		13 06	13 25		13 36	13 50		14 06	14 26	14 30		14 36	14 50		15 06
Newton-on-Ayr	d		12 08				12 39	12 52		13 08			13 38	13 52		14 08				14 38	14 52		15 08
Prestwick Town	d		12 11	12 28			12 42	12 55		13 11	13 30		13 41	13 55		14 11	14 31	14 36		14 41	14 55		15 11
Prestwick Int. Airport ✈	d		12 13	12 29			12 44	12 57		13 13	13 31		13 43	13 57		14 13	14 32			14 43	14 57		15 13
Troon	d		12 17	12 33	12a38		12 48	13 01		13 17	13 35		13 47	14 01		14 17	14 36	14a41		14 47	15 01		15 17
Barassie	d		12 19				12 50	13 04		13 19			13 49	14 03		14 19				14 49	15 03		15 19
Irvine	d		12 24	12 39			12 55	13 09		13 24	13 42		13 54	14 08		14 24	14 42			14 54	15 08		15 24
Largs	d	11 53							12 53						13 53							14 53	
Fairlie	d	11 58							12 58						13 58							14 58	
West Kilbride	d	12 03							13 03						14 03							15 03	
Ardrossan Harbour	d					12 36						13 36							14 36				
Ardrossan Town	d					12 38						13 38							14 38				
Ardrossan South Beach	d	12 10				12 41			13 10			13 40			14 10				14 41			15 10	
Saltcoats	d	12 13				12 43			13 13			13 43			14 13				14 43			15 13	
Stevenston	d	12 15				12 45			13 15			13 45			14 15				14 45			15 15	
Kilwinning 4	d	12 19	12 28	12 43		12 49	12 59	13 13	13 19	13 28	13 46	13 49	13 58	14 12	14 19	14 28	14 46		14 49	14 58	15 12	15 19	15 28
Dalry	d		12 32			12 54	13 03			13 33		13 53	14 02			14 33			14 53	15 03			15 33
Glengarnock	d	12 25	12 36				13 07		13 25	13 37			14 06		14 26	14 37				15 07		15 25	15 37
Lochwinnoch	d		12 41				13 12			13 41			14 11			14 41				15 12			15 41
Howwood	d		12 45				13 16			13 45			14 15			14 45				15 16			15 45
Milliken Park	d		12 47				13 19			13 48			14 17			14 48				15 19			15 48
Johnstone	d	12 34	12 50			13 04	13 22		13 34	13 51		14 04	14 20		14 37	14 51			15 04	15 22		15 34	15 51
Paisley Gilmour Street 219	a	12 38	12 55			13 10	13 26		13 38	13 55		14 08	14 24		14 41	14 55			15 08	15 26		15 38	15 55
	d	12 39	12 55			13 11	13 26		13 39	13 55		14 09	14 25		14 42	14 56			15 09	15 26		15 38	15 55
Glasgow Central 15 219	a	12 50	13 05	13 09		13 21	13 39	13 42	13 50	14 05	14 10	14 19	14 35	14 40	14 52	15 07	15 11		15 22	15 39	15 42	15 52	16 08

A From Girvan to Kilmarnock
B From Stranraer
C To Edinburgh
D From Glasgow Central
E From Stranraer to Kilmarnock

Table T221-R

Ayr, Largs and Ardrossan - Glasgow Central

Mondays to Fridays
16 December to 15 May

		SR	SR	SR	SR	SR	SR	SR	SR A	SR	SR	SR	SR	SR	SR	SR	SR B	SR	SR	SR	SR	SR ◇ C
Ayr	d	15 25		15 37	15 48		16 00	16 23	16 27				16 54	17 06		17 24	17 28		17 53		18 05	18 21
Newton-on-Ayr	d			15 39	15 50		16 02						16 56	17 08		17 26			17 55		18 07	
Prestwick Town	d	15 30		15 42	15 53		16 06	16 28	16 33				16 59	17 11		17 29	17 34		17 58		18 10	
Prestwick Int. Airport ✈	d	15 31		15 44	15 55		16 08	16 29					17 01	17 13		17 31			18 00		18 12	
Troon	d	15 35		15 48	15 59		16 13	16 33	16a38				17 05	17 17		17 35	17a39		18 04		18 16	18 29
Barassie	d			15 50	16 01		16 15						17 07	17 19		17 37			18 06		18 18	
Irvine	d	15 41		15 55	16 06		16 20	16 39			16 58		17 12	17 24		17 42			18 11		18 23	
Largs	d					15 53						16 48						17 33				
Fairlie	d					15 58						16 53						17 38				
West Kilbride	d					16 03						16 58						17 43				
Ardrossan Harbour	d		15 36							16 36					17 21					18 07		
Ardrossan Town	d		15 38							16 38					17 23					18 09		
Ardrossan South Beach	d		15 41			16 10				16 41		17 05			17 26			17 50		18 12		
Saltcoats	d		15 43			16 13				16 43		17 07			17 30			17 52		18 14		
Stevenston	d		15 45			16 15				16 45		17 09			17 32			17 54		18 16		
Kilwinning	d	15 45	15 49	15 59	16 10	16 19	16 25	16 43		16 49	17 02	17 13	17 17	17 28	17 41	17 46		17 58	18 15	18 20	18 27	
Dalry	d		15 53	16 04			16 29			16 53	17 06		17 21	17 32		17 51		18 02			18 31	
Glengarnock	d			16 08		16 25	16 33				17 10		17 25	17 36	17 48			18 06		18 26	18 35	
Lochwinnoch	d			16 12			16 38				17 15			17 41				18 11			18 40	
Howwood	d			16 16			16 42				17 19			17 45				18 15			18 44	
Milliken Park	d			16 19			16 44				17 21			17 47				18 17			18 46	
Johnstone	d		16 04	16 22		16 34	16 47			17 04	17 24		17 36	17 50		18 01		18 20		18 35	18 49	
Paisley Gilmour Street 219	a		16 08	16 26		16 39	16 51			17 11	17 28	17 32	17 40	17 54	17 58	18 05		18 24	18 30	18 39	18 54	
	d		16 09	16 26		16 40	16 52			17 11	17 29	17 33	17 41	17 55	18 00	18 06		18 25	18 31	18 39	18 55	
Glasgow Central 15 219	a	16 11	16 21	16 37	16 39	16 52	17 05	17 11		17 22	17 39	17 45	17 52	18 06	18 10	18 17		18 37	18 41	18 50	19 05	19 37

		SR	SR	SR D	SR	SR	SR	SR	SR	SR	SR	SR A	SR	SR	SR	SR	SR	SR FX	SR FO	SR	SR	SR A	SR
Ayr	d	18 25		18 39	18 50		19 15		19 45		20 15	20 27		20 45		21 15		21 45	21 45		22 15	22 28	
Newton-on-Ayr	d			18 41	18 52				19 47					20 47				21 47	21 47		22 17		
Prestwick Town	d	18 30		18 44	18 55		19 20		19 50		20 20	20 32		20 50		21 20		21 50	21 50		22 20	22 33	
Prestwick Int. Airport ✈	d	18 31		18 46	18 57		19 21		19 52		20 21			20 52		21 21		21 52	21 52		22 22	22 36	
Troon	d	18 35		18 50	19 01		19 25		19 56		20 25	20a38		20 56		21 26		21 56	21 56		22 26	22a41	
Barassie	d			18 52	19 03				19 59					20 58				21 58	21 58		22 28		
Irvine	d	18 41		18 57	19 09		19 31		20 04		20 31			21 03		21 32		22 03	22 03		22 33		
Largs	d					18 52				19 54					20 52					21 52			22 52
Fairlie	d					18 57				19 59					20 57					21 57			22 57
West Kilbride	d					19 02				20 04					21 02					22 02			23 02
Ardrossan Harbour	d		18 36					19 31					20 31				21 31						
Ardrossan Town	d		18 38					19 33					20 34				21 33						
Ardrossan South Beach	d		18 41			19 09		19 36		20 11			20 36		21 09		21 36			22 09			23 09
Saltcoats	d		18 43			19 11		19 38		20 13			20 38		21 11		21 38			22 11			23 11
Stevenston	d		18 45			19 13		19 40		20 15			20 41		21 13		21 40			22 13			23 13
Kilwinning	d	18 45	18 49	19 01	19 13	19 17	19 35	19 44	20 08	20 19	20 35		20 44	21 07	21 17	21 36	21 44	22 08	22 08	22 17	22 37		23 17
Dalry	d		18 53	19 05		19 21		19 48		20 23			20 52		21 22		21 48			22 21			
Glengarnock	d			19 09		19 25		19 52		20 27			20 56		21 26		21 52			22 25			
Lochwinnoch	d			19 14				19 57					21 00				21 57						
Howwood	d			19 18				20 01					21 04				22 01						
Milliken Park	d			19 20		19 33		20 03		20 35			21 07		21 35		22 03			22 33			
Johnstone	d		19 04	19 23		19 36	19 48	20 06	20 22	20 38	20 48		21 10	21 21	21 38	21 49	22 06	22 21	22 21	22 36	22 50		23 30
Paisley Gilmour Street 219	a	19 00	19 08	19 27	19 32	19 40	19 52	20 10	20 26	20 42	20 52		21 14	21 25	21 42	21 53	22 10	22 25	22 25	22 41	22 55		23 35
	d	19 01	19 09	19 28	19 35	19 40	19 53	20 11	20 27	20 42	20 53		21 14	21 25	21 42	21 54	22 11	22 26	22 26	22 42	22 55		23 36
Glasgow Central 15 219	a	19 13	19 19	19 40	19 46	19 51	20 04	20 21	20 37	20 53	21 05		21 24	21 35	21 54	22 04	22 22	22 36	22 37	22 54	23 06		23 46

		SR
Ayr	d	23 00
Newton-on-Ayr	d	23 02
Prestwick Town	d	23 05
Prestwick Int. Airport ✈	d	23 07
Troon	d	23 11
Barassie	d	23 13
Irvine	d	23 18
Largs	d	
Fairlie	d	
West Kilbride	d	
Ardrossan Harbour	d	
Ardrossan Town	d	
Ardrossan South Beach	d	
Saltcoats	d	
Stevenston	d	
Kilwinning	d	23 22
Dalry	d	23 26
Glengarnock	d	23 30
Lochwinnoch	d	23 35
Howwood	d	23 39
Milliken Park	d	23 41
Johnstone	d	23 44
Paisley Gilmour Street 219	a	23 49
	d	23 49
Glasgow Central 15 219	a	00 01

A From Stranraer to Kilmarnock
B From Girvan to Kilmarnock
C From Stranraer
D To Edinburgh

Table T221-R

Ayr, Largs and Ardrossan - Glasgow Central

Saturdays
21 December to 16 May

		SR	SR	SR	SR	SR	SR	SR	SR	SR	SR A	SR	SR	SR	SR ◇ B	SR C	SR	SR	SR	SR	SR	SR	SR
Ayr	d	05 13	05 40	06 02		06 33		06 50	07 05	07 17	07 22	07 41		08 05	08 22	08 29		08 51		09 06	09 24		09 36
Newton-on-Ayr	d	05 15	05 42	06 04		06 35		06 52	07 07	07 19		07 43		08 07		08 31		08 54		09 08			09 38
Prestwick Town	d	05 18	05 45	06 07		06 38		06 55	07 10	07 22	07 27	07 47		08 10	08 27	08 34		08 57		09 11	09 29		09 41
Prestwick Int. Airport ✈	d	05 20	05 47	06 09		06 40		06 57	07 12	07 24		07 48		08 12		08 36		08 58		09 13	09 30		09 43
Troon	d	05 24	05 51	06 13		06 44		07 01	07 16	07 28	07a32	07 52		08 16	08 36	08 40		09 02		09 17	09 34		09 47
Barassie	d	05 26	05 54	06 15		06 49		07 03	07 18	07 30		07 55		08 18		08 43		09 05		09 19			09 49
Irvine	d	05 31	05 58	06 20		06 53		07 08	07 23	07 37		07 59		08 23		08 48		09 09		09 24	09 40		09 54
Largs	d						06 42						07 42						08 53				
Fairlie	d						06 47						07 47						08 58				
West Kilbride	d						06 52						07 52						09 03				
Ardrossan Harbour	d				06 34												08 45					09 36	
Ardrossan Town	d				06 36												08 47					09 39	
Ardrossan South Beach	d				06 38		06 59						07 59				08 50		09 10			09 42	
Saltcoats	d				06 40		07 01						08 01				08 52		09 13			09 44	
Stevenston	d				06 43		07 03						08 03				08 54		09 15			09 46	
Kilwinning	d	05 35	06 02	06 24	06 46	06 57	07 07	07 12	07 27	07 41		08 03	08 07	08 27		08 52	08 58	09 13	09 19	09 28	09 44	09 50	09 58
Dalry	d	05 39	06 07	06 28	06 51	07 02	07 11		07 31	07 46			08 12	08 31			09 02			09 32		09 54	10 03
Glengarnock	d	05 43	06 11	06 32		07 06	07 15		07 35	07 50			08 16	08 35			09 06		09 25	09 36			10 07
Lochwinnoch	d	05 48	06 15	06 37		07 10			07 40				08 20	08 40			09 11			09 41			10 11
Howwood	d	05 52	06 19	06 41		07 14			07 44				08 24	08 44			09 15			09 45			10 15
Milliken Park	d	05 54	06 22	06 43		07 17		07 26	07 46				08 27	08 46			09 17			09 47			10 18
Johnstone	d	05 57	06 25	06 46	07 01	07 20	07 24	07 29	07 49	07 59		08 17	08 30	08 49		09 07	09 20		09 34	09 50		10 05	10 21
Paisley Gilmour Street 219	a	06 02	06 29	06 51	07 05	07 24	07 28	07 33	07 54	08 03		08 21	08 34	08 53		09 11	09 24		09 38	09 55		10 09	10 25
	d	06 02	06 29	06 52	07 06	07 24	07 28	07 33	07 54	08 03		08 21	08 35	08 55		09 12	09 25		09 39	09 55		10 10	10 25
Glasgow Central 15 219	a	06 13	06 39	07 03	07 18	07 34	07 40	07 44	08 04	08 13		08 33	08 48	09 05	09 37	09 22	09 35	09 40	09 52	10 06	10 09	10 21	10 36

		SR	SR	SR	SR D	SR	SR	SR	SR E	SR	SR	SR	SR	SR	SR	SR	SR	SR	SR D	SR	SR E	SR	SR
Ayr	d	09 50		10 07	10 21	10 25		10 36	10 51		11 08	11 24		11 36	11 52		12 06	12 23	12 29		12 37	12 50	
Newton-on-Ayr	d	09 52		10 09				10 38	10 53		11 10			11 38	11 54		12 08				12 39	12 52	
Prestwick Town	d	09 55		10 12		10 30		10 41	10 56		11 13	11 29		11 41	11 57		12 11	12 28			12 42	12 55	
Prestwick Int. Airport ✈	d	09 57		10 14		10 31		10 43	10 58		11 15	11 30		11 43	11 59		12 13	12 29			12 44	12 57	
Troon	d	10 01		10 18	10a29	10 35		10 47	11 02		11 19	11 34		11 47	12 03		12 17	12 33	12a38		12 48	13 01	
Barassie	d	10 03		10 20				10 49	11 04		11 21			11 49	12 05		12 19				12 50	13 04	
Irvine	d	10 08		10 25		10 41		10 54	11 09		11 26	11 40		11 54	12 10		12 24	12 39			12 55	13 09	
Largs	d		09 53							10 53						11 53							12 53
Fairlie	d		09 58							10 58						11 58							12 58
West Kilbride	d		10 03							11 03						12 03							13 03
Ardrossan Harbour	d						10 36						11 36							12 36			
Ardrossan Town	d						10 38						11 38							12 38			
Ardrossan South Beach	d		10 10				10 41			11 10			11 41			12 10				12 41			13 10
Saltcoats	d		10 13				10 43			11 13			11 43			12 13				12 43			13 13
Stevenston	d		10 15				10 45			11 15			11 45			12 15				12 45			13 15
Kilwinning	d	10 12	10 19	10 29		10 45	10 49	10 58	11 13	11 19	11 30	11 45	11 51	11 58	12 14	12 19	12 28	12 43		12 49	12 59	13 13	13 19
Dalry	d			10 33			10 53	11 02			11 34		11 56	12 02			12 32			12 54	13 03		
Glengarnock	d		10 25	10 37				11 06		11 25	11 38			12 06		12 25	12 36				13 07		13 25
Lochwinnoch	d			10 42				11 12			11 43			12 11			12 41				13 12		
Howwood	d			10 46				11 16			11 47			12 15			12 45				13 16		
Milliken Park	d			10 48				11 19			11 49			12 17			12 47				13 19		
Johnstone	d		10 34	10 51			11 05	11 22		11 34	11 52		12 06	12 20		12 34	12 50			13 04	13 22		13 34
Paisley Gilmour Street 219	a		10 39	10 55			11 12	11 26		11 39	11 56		12 10	12 24		12 38	12 55			13 10	13 26		13 38
	d		10 39	10 56			11 12	11 26		11 40	11 57		12 11	12 25		12 39	12 55			13 11	13 26		13 39
Glasgow Central 15 219	a	10 38	10 52	11 06		11 10	11 22	11 36	11 40	11 52	12 09	12 11	12 22	12 35	12 40	12 50	13 05	13 09		13 21	13 40	13 42	13 50

		SR	SR	SR	SR	SR	SR	SR	SR	SR D	SR	SR	SR E	SR	SR	SR	SR	SR	SR	SR	SR	SR
Ayr	d	13 06	13 25		13 36	13 50		14 06	14 26	14 30		14 36	14 50		15 06	15 25		15 37	15 48		16 00	16 23
Newton-on-Ayr	d	13 08			13 38	13 52		14 08				14 38	14 52		15 08			15 39	15 50		16 02	
Prestwick Town	d	13 11	13 30		13 41	13 55		14 11	14 31	14 36		14 41	14 55		15 11	15 30		15 42	15 53		16 06	16 28
Prestwick Int. Airport ✈	d	13 13	13 31		13 43	13 57		14 13	14 32			14 43	14 57		15 13	15 31		15 44	15 55		16 08	16 29
Troon	d	13 17	13 35		13 47	14 01		14 17	14 36	14a41		14 47	15 01		15 17	15 35		15 48	15 59		16 13	16 33
Barassie	d	13 19			13 49	14 03		14 19				14 49	15 03		15 19			15 50	16 01		16 15	
Irvine	d	13 24	13 42		13 54	14 08		14 24	14 42			14 54	15 08		15 24	15 41		15 55	16 06		16 20	16 39
Largs	d						13 53							14 53						15 53		
Fairlie	d						13 58							14 58						15 58		
West Kilbride	d						14 03							15 03						16 03		
Ardrossan Harbour	d			13 36							14 36						15 36					
Ardrossan Town	d			13 38							14 38						15 38					
Ardrossan South Beach	d			13 40			14 10				14 41			15 10			15 41			16 10		
Saltcoats	d			13 43			14 13				14 43			15 13			15 43			16 13		
Stevenston	d			13 45			14 15				14 45			15 15			15 45			16 15		
Kilwinning	d	13 28	13 46	13 49	13 58	14 12	14 19	14 28	14 46		14 49	14 58	15 12	15 19	15 28	15 45	15 49	15 59	16 10	16 19	16 25	16 43
Dalry	d	13 33		13 53	14 02			14 33			14 53	15 03			15 33		15 53	16 04			16 29	
Glengarnock	d	13 37			14 06		14 26	14 37				15 07		15 25	15 37			16 08		16 25	16 33	
Lochwinnoch	d	13 41			14 11			14 41				15 12			15 41			16 12			16 38	
Howwood	d	13 45			14 15			14 45				15 16			15 45			16 16			16 42	
Milliken Park	d	13 48			14 17			14 48				15 19			15 48			16 19			16 44	
Johnstone	d	13 51		14 04	14 20		14 37	14 51			15 04	15 22		15 34	15 51		16 04	16 22		16 34	16 47	
Paisley Gilmour Street 219	a	13 55		14 08	14 24		14 41	14 55			15 08	15 26		15 38	15 55		16 08	16 26		16 39	16 51	
	d	13 55		14 09	14 25		14 42	14 56			15 09	15 26		15 38	15 55		16 09	16 26		16 40	16 52	
Glasgow Central 15 219	a	14 05	14 10	14 19	14 35	14 38	14 52	15 09	15 11		15 22	15 39	15 42	15 52	16 08	16 11	16 21	16 37	16 39	16 51	17 04	17 11

A From Girvan to Kilmarnock
B From Stranraer
C From Glasgow Central to Edinburgh
D From Stranraer to Kilmarnock
E To Edinburgh

Table T221-R

Saturdays

21 December to 16 May

Ayr, Largs and Ardrossan - Glasgow Central

		SR	SR	SR	SR	SR	SR	SR		SR	SR	SR	SR	SR	SR	SR	SR	SR		SR	SR	SR	SR	SR	SR
		A									B					◇ C				D					
Ayr	d	16 27		16 40		16 54	17 06			17 24	17 28		17 53		18 05	18 21	18 25			18 39	18 50		19 15		19 34
Newton-on-Ayr	d			16 42		16 56	17 08			17 26			17 55		18 07					18 41	18 52				19 36
Prestwick Town	d	16 33		16 45		16 59	17 11			17 29	17 34		17 58		18 10		18 30			18 44	18 55		19 20		19 39
Prestwick Int. Airport ✈	d			16 47		17 01	17 13			17 31			18 00		18 12		18 31			18 46	18 57		19 21		19 41
Troon	d	16a38		16 51		17 05	17 17			17 35	17a39		18 04		18 16	18 29	18 35			18 50	19 01		19 25		19 45
Barassie	d			16 53		17 07	17 19			17 37			18 06		18 18					18 52	19 03				19 47
Irvine	d			16 58		17 12	17 24			17 42			18 11		18 23		18 41			18 57	19 09		19 31		19 52
Largs	d				16 48							17 33										18 52			
Fairlie	d				16 53							17 38										18 57			
West Kilbride	d				16 58							17 43										19 02			
Ardrossan Harbour	d		16 36					17 21						18 07				18 36						19 31	
Ardrossan Town	d		16 38					17 23						18 09				18 38						19 33	
Ardrossan South Beach	d		16 41		17 05			17 26				17 50		18 12				18 41				19 09		19 36	
Saltcoats	d		16 43		17 07			17 30				17 52		18 14				18 43				19 11		19 38	
Stevenston	d		16 45		17 09			17 32				17 54		18 16				18 45				19 13		19 40	
Kilwinning 4	d		16 49	17 02	17 13	17 17	17 28	17 41		17 46		17 58	18 15	18 20	18 27		18 45	18 49		19 01	19 13	19 17	19 35	19 44	19 56
Dalry	d		16 53	17 06		17 21	17 32			17 51		18 02			18 31			18 53		19 05		19 21		19 48	20 00
Glengarnock	d			17 10		17 25	17 36	17 48				18 06		18 26	18 35					19 09		19 25		19 52	20 04
Lochwinnoch	d			17 15			17 41					18 11			18 40					19 14				19 57	20 09
Howwood	d			17 19			17 45					18 15			18 44					19 18				20 01	20 13
Milliken Park	d			17 21			17 47					18 17			18 46					19 20		19 33		20 03	20 15
Johnstone	d		17 04	17 24		17 36	17 50			18 01		18 20		18 35	18 49			19 04		19 23		19 36	19 48	20 06	20 18
Paisley Gilmour Street 219	a		17 11	17 28	17 32	17 40	17 54	17 58		18 05		18 24	18 30	18 39	18 54		19 00	19 08		19 27	19 32	19 40	19 52	20 10	20 22
	d		17 11	17 29	17 33	17 41	17 55	18 00		18 06		18 25	18 31	18 39	18 55		19 01	19 09		19 28	19 35	19 40	19 53	20 11	20 23
Glasgow Central 15 219	a		17 22	17 39	17 45	17 52	18 06	18 10		18 17		18 36	18 41	18 49	19 05	19 37	19 13	19 20		19 39	19 46	19 51	20 04	20 21	20 33

		SR	SR	SR		SR	SR	SR	SR	SR	SR	SR	SR	SR		SR	SR	SR
						A										A		
Ayr	d	19 45		20 15		20 27		20 45		21 15		21 45		22 15		22 28		23 00
Newton-on-Ayr	d	19 47						20 47				21 47		22 17				23 02
Prestwick Town	d	19 50		20 20		20 32		20 50		21 20		21 50		22 20		22 33		23 05
Prestwick Int. Airport ✈	d	19 52		20 21				20 52		21 21		21 52		22 22		22 36		23 07
Troon	d	19 56		20 25		20a38		20 56		21 26		21 56		22 26		22a41		23 11
Barassie	d	19 59						20 58				21 58		22 28				23 13
Irvine	d	20 04		20 31				21 03		21 32		22 03		22 33				23 18
Largs	d		19 54						20 52				21 52				22 52	
Fairlie	d		19 59						20 57				21 57				22 57	
West Kilbride	d		20 04						21 02				22 02				23 02	
Ardrossan Harbour	d						20 31				21 31							
Ardrossan Town	d						20 34				21 33							
Ardrossan South Beach	d		20 11				20 36		21 09		21 36		22 09				23 09	
Saltcoats	d		20 13				20 38		21 11		21 38		22 11				23 11	
Stevenston	d		20 15				20 41		21 13		21 40		22 13				23 13	
Kilwinning 4	d	20 08	20 19	20 35			20 44	21 07	21 17	21 36	21 44	22 08	22 17	22 37			23 17	23 22
Dalry	d		20 23				20 52		21 22		21 48		22 21					23 26
Glengarnock	d		20 27				20 56		21 26		21 52		22 25					23 30
Lochwinnoch	d						21 00				21 57							23 35
Howwood	d						21 04				22 01							23 39
Milliken Park	d		20 35				21 07		21 35		22 03		22 33					23 41
Johnstone	d	20 22	20 38	20 48			21 10	21 21	21 38	21 49	22 06	22 21	22 36	22 50			23 30	23 44
Paisley Gilmour Street 219	a	20 26	20 42	20 52			21 14	21 25	21 42	21 53	22 10	22 25	22 41	22 55			23 35	23 49
	d	20 27	20 42	20 53			21 14	21 25	21 42	21 54	22 11	22 26	22 42	22 55			23 36	23 49
Glasgow Central 15 219	a	20 37	20 54	21 05			21 24	21 35	21 54	22 04	22 22	22 36	22 54	23 06			23 46	00 01

Sundays

15 December to 10 May

		SR	SR	SR	SR	SR	SR	SR	SR	SR		SR	SR	SR	SR	SR	SR	SR	SR	SR		SR	SR	SR	SR
Ayr	d	08 45		09 15		09 45		10 15	10 45			11 15	11 45		12 15		12 45		13 15	13 45			14 15	14 45	
Newton-on-Ayr	d	08 47				09 47			10 47				11 47				12 47			13 47				14 47	
Prestwick Town	d	08 50		09 20		09 50		10 20	10 50			11 20	11 50		12 20		12 50		13 20	13 50			14 20	14 50	
Prestwick Int. Airport ✈	d	08 52		09 21		09 52		10 21	10 52			11 21	11 52		12 21		12 52		13 21	13 52			14 21	14 52	
Troon	d	08 56		09 25		09 56		10 25	10 56			11 25	11 56		12 25		12 56		13 25	13 56			14 25	14 56	
Barassie	d	08 58				09 58			10 58				11 58				12 58			13 58				14 58	
Irvine	d	09 03		09 31		10 03		10 31	11 03			11 31	12 03		12 31		13 03		13 31	14 03			14 31	15 03	
Largs	d		08 54				09 54			10 54				11 54				12 54				13 54			
Fairlie	d		08 59				09 59			10 59				11 59				12 59				13 59			
West Kilbride	d		09 04				10 04			11 04				12 04				13 04				14 04			
Ardrossan Harbour	d				09 35											12 35									15 02
Ardrossan Town	d				09 37											12 37									15 04
Ardrossan South Beach	d		09 11		09 39		10 11			11 11				12 11		12 39		13 11				14 11			15 06
Saltcoats	d		09 13		09 41		10 13			11 13				12 13		12 41		13 13				14 13			15 08
Stevenston	d		09 15		09 44		10 15			11 15				12 15		12 44		13 15				14 15			15 11
Kilwinning 4	d	09 07	09 19	09 35	09 48	10 07	10 19	10 35	11 07	11 19		11 35	12 07	12 19	12 35	12 47	13 07	13 19	13 36	14 07		14 19	14 38	15 07	15 14
Dalry	d		09 24				10 24			11 24				12 24				13 24				14 24			
Glengarnock	d		09 28				10 28			11 28				12 28				13 28				14 28			
Lochwinnoch	d		09 32				10 32			11 32				12 32				13 32				14 32			
Howwood	d		09 36				10 36			11 36				12 36				13 36				14 36			
Milliken Park	d		09 39				10 39			11 39				12 39		13 00		13 39				14 39			15 27
Johnstone	d	09 21	09 42	09 49	10 01	10 21	10 42	10 49	11 21	11 42		11 49	12 21	12 42	12 49	13 03	13 21	13 42	13 50	14 21		14 42	14 52	15 21	15 30
Paisley Gilmour Street 219	a	09 25	09 46	09 53	10 05	10 25	10 46	10 53	11 25	11 46		11 53	12 25	12 46	12 53	13 07	13 25	13 46	13 54	14 25		14 46	14 56	15 25	15 34
	d	09 25	09 46	09 53	10 06	10 25	10 46	10 53	11 25	11 46		11 53	12 25	12 46	12 53	13 07	13 25	13 46	13 54	14 25		14 46	14 56	15 25	15 35
Glasgow Central 15 219	a	09 36	09 57	10 04	10 17	10 36	10 57	11 04	11 36	11 57		12 04	12 36	12 57	13 04	13 18	13 36	13 57	14 04	14 36		14 57	15 06	15 36	15 45

A From Stranraer to Kilmarnock
B From Girvan to Kilmarnock
C From Stranraer
D To Edinburgh

Table T221-R

Sundays

15 December to 10 May

Ayr, Largs and Ardrossan - Glasgow Central

		SR	SR	SR	SR	SR		SR	SR	SR	SR	SR	SR	SR	SR	SR		SR	SR	SR	SR	SR	SR	SR	SR
Ayr	d		15 15	15 45		16 15		16 45		17 15	17 45			18 15	18 45			19 15	19 45			20 45		21 45	
Newton-on-Ayr	d			15 47				16 47			17 47				18 47				19 47			20 47		21 47	
Prestwick Town	d		15 20	15 50		16 20		16 50		17 20	17 50			18 20	18 50			19 20	19 50			20 50		21 50	
Prestwick Int. Airport ✈	d		15 21	15 52		16 21		16 52		17 21	17 52			18 21	18 52			19 21	19 52			20 52		21 52	
Troon	d		15 25	15 56		16 25		16 56		17 25	17 56			18 25	18 56			19 25	19 56			20 56		21 56	
Barassie	d			15 58				16 58			17 58				18 58				19 58			20 58		21 58	
Irvine	d		15 31	16 03		16 31		17 03		17 31	18 03			18 31	19 03			19 31	20 03			21 03		22 03	
Largs	d	14 54			15 54				16 54				17 54			18 54				19 54			20 54		21 54
Fairlie	d	14 59			15 59				16 59				17 59			18 59				19 59			20 59		21 59
West Kilbride	d	15 04			16 04				17 04				18 04			19 04				20 04			21 04		22 04
Ardrossan Harbour	d											18 00									20 30				
Ardrossan Town	d											18 02									20 32				
Ardrossan South Beach	d	15 11			16 11				17 11			18 04	18 11			19 11				20 11	20 34		21 11		22 11
Saltcoats	d	15 13			16 13				17 13			18 06	18 13			19 13				20 13	20 36		21 13		22 13
Stevenston	d	15 15			16 15				17 15			18 09	18 15			19 15				20 15	20 39		21 15		22 15
Kilwinning 4	d	15 19	15 35	16 07	16 19	16 35		17 07	17 19	17 35	18 07	18 12	18 19	18 35	19 07	19 19		19 35	20 07	20 19	20 42	21 07	21 19	22 07	22 19
Dalry	d	15 24			16 24				17 24				18 24			19 24				20 24			21 24		22 24
Glengarnock	d	15 28			16 28				17 28				18 28			19 28				20 28			21 28		22 28
Lochwinnoch	d	15 32			16 32				17 32				18 32			19 32				20 32			21 32		22 32
Howwood	d	15 36			16 36				17 36				18 36			19 36				20 36			21 36		22 36
Milliken Park	d	15 39			16 39				17 39			18 25	18 39			19 39				20 39	20 55		21 39		22 39
Johnstone	d	15 42	15 49	16 21	16 42	16 49		17 21	17 42	17 49	18 21	18 28	18 42	18 49	19 21	19 42		19 49	20 21	20 42	20 58	21 21	21 42	22 21	22 42
Paisley Gilmour Street 219	a	15 46	15 53	16 25	16 46	16 53		17 25	17 46	17 53	18 25	18 32	18 46	18 53	19 25	19 46		19 53	20 25	20 46	21 02	21 25	21 46	22 25	22 46
	d	15 46	15 53	16 25	16 46	16 53		17 25	17 46	17 53	18 25	18 34	18 46	18 53	19 25	19 46		19 53	20 25	20 46	21 02	21 25	21 46	22 25	22 46
Glasgow Central 15 219	a	15 57	16 04	16 36	16 57	17 04		17 36	17 58	18 04	18 36	18 44	18 57	19 04	19 36	19 57		20 04	20 36	20 56	21 13	21 36	21 57	22 36	22 57

		SR		SR
Ayr	d	23 00		
Newton-on-Ayr	d	23 02		
Prestwick Town	d	23 05		
Prestwick Int. Airport ✈	d	23 07		
Troon	d	23 11		
Barassie	d	23 13		
Irvine	d	23 18		
Largs	d			23 00
Fairlie	d			23 05
West Kilbride	d			23 10
Ardrossan Harbour	d			
Ardrossan Town	d			
Ardrossan South Beach	d			23 17
Saltcoats	d			23 19
Stevenston	d			23 21
Kilwinning 4	d	23 22		23 26
Dalry	d			23 30
Glengarnock	d			23 34
Lochwinnoch	d			23 39
Howwood	d			23 43
Milliken Park	d			23 45
Johnstone	d	23 36		23 48
Paisley Gilmour Street 219	a	23 40		23 52
	d	23 40		23 53
Glasgow Central 15 219	a	23 51		00 04

Table T222-F

Kilmarnock, Barrhead and East Kilbride - Glasgow Central

Mondays to Fridays
16 December to 15 May

Miles	Miles			SR A	SR	SR	SR B	SR	SR B	SR	SR	SR	SR	SR	SR	SR C ⚲	SR	SR	SR	SR	SR	SR	SR ◇ D
0	—	**Kilmarnock 3**	d		05 22		06 20		06 52			07 21				07 55				08 23			08 56
2¼	—	Kilmaurs	d		05 26		06 24		06 56			07 25				07 59				08 27			09 00
5½	—	Stewarton	d		05 31		06 29		07 02			07 32				08 05				08 32			09 06
7¾	—	Dunlop	d		05 36		06 34		07 06			07 37				08 10				08 37			09 10
16¾	—	**Barrhead**	d		05 46		06 44		07 17	07 26		07 50		07 55		08 22		08 31		08 50	08 56		09 22
18½	—	Nitshill	d		05 49		06 47			07 29				07 59				08 35			09 00		
19½	—	Priesthill & Darnley	d		05 52		06 50			07 31				08 01				08 37			09 02		
20	—	Kennishead	d		05 54		06 52			07 33				08 03				08 39			09 04		
—	0	**East Kilbride**	d			06 18		06 51			07 25		07 43		07 59		08 11		08 26			08 57	
—	1½	Hairmyres	d	00 02		06 22		06 55			07 29		07 47		08 03		08 19		08 30			09 01	
—	3	Thorntonhall	d	00 05		06 25		06 58			07 32				08 06				08 33			09 04	
—	4¼	Busby	d	00 08		06 28		07 01			07 36				08 10		08 24		08 36			09 07	
—	5	Clarkston	d	00 11		06 31		07 04			07 39		07 54		08 13		08 27		08 39			09 10	
—	6¼	Giffnock	d	00 14		06 35		07 08			07 42				08 16		08 30		08 43			09 14	
—	7¼	Thornliebank	d	00 17		06 37		07 10			07 46				08 19		08 34		08 46			09 16	
21¼	8¼	Pollokshaws West	d	00 20	05 57	06 40	06 55	07 13		07 37	07 49			08 07	08 22		08 37	08 43	08 49		09 08	09 19	
22¼	9¼	Crossmyloof	d	00 23	06 00	06 43	06 58	07 16		07 40	07 52			08 10	08 24		08 40	08 46	08 51		09 11	09 22	
24¼	11½	**Glasgow Central 15**	a	00 30	06 09	06 49	07 07	07 24	07 31	07 46	07 58	08 03	08 09	08 16	08 31	08 37	08 46	08 52	08 58	09 01	09 17	09 28	09 37

		SR	SR	SR	SR	SR	SR C ⚲	SR	SR	SR	SR	SR	SR E	SR	SR	SR	SR	SR	SR	SR	SR	SR	SR
Kilmarnock 3	d			09 27			10 00			10 28			11 00			11 27			11 58			12 27	
Kilmaurs	d			09 31			10 04			10 32			11 04			11 31			12 02			12 31	
Stewarton	d			09 36			10 09			10 37			11 09			11 36			12 07			12 36	
Dunlop	d			09 41			10 14			10 42			11 14			11 41			12 12			12 41	
Barrhead	d	09 26		09 53	09 56		10 24	10 27		10 52	10 56			11 26		11 52	11 56			12 26		12 52	12 56
Nitshill	d	09 30			10 00			10 31			11 00			11 30			12 00			12 30			13 00
Priesthill & Darnley	d	09 32			10 02			10 34			11 02			11 32			12 02			12 32			13 02
Kennishead	d	09 34			10 04			10 36			11 04			11 34			12 04			12 34			13 04
East Kilbride	d		09 28			09 57			10 28			10 57			11 28			11 57			12 28		
Hairmyres	d		09 32			10 01			10 32			11 01			11 32			12 01			12 32		
Thorntonhall	d					10 04						11 04						12 04					
Busby	d		09 37			10 07			10 37			11 07			11 37			12 07			12 37		
Clarkston	d		09 40			10 10			10 40			11 10			11 40			12 10			12 40		
Giffnock	d		09 43			10 14			10 43			11 14			11 43			12 14			12 43		
Thornliebank	d		09 46			10 16			10 46			11 16			11 46			12 16			12 46		
Pollokshaws West	d	09 38	09 49		10 08	10 20		10 39	10 49		11 08	11 20		11 38	11 49		12 08	12 20		12 38	12 49		13 08
Crossmyloof	d	09 41	09 52		10 11	10 23		10 42	10 52		11 11	11 23		11 41	11 52		12 11	12 23		12 41	12 52		13 11
Glasgow Central 15	a	09 47	09 59	10 06	10 17	10 29	10 38	10 48	10 59	11 06	11 17	11 29	11 37	11 47	11 59	12 06	12 19	12 29	12 34	12 47	12 59	13 05	13 17

		SR	SR C ⚲	SR	SR	SR	SR	SR	SR	SR	SR	SR	SR	SR	SR C ⚲	SR	SR	SR	SR	SR	SR	SR
Kilmarnock 3	d		12 59			13 28			13 58			14 28			14 59			15 27			16 00	
Kilmaurs	d		13 03			13 32			14 02			14 32			15 03			15 31			16 04	
Stewarton	d		13 08			13 37			14 07			14 37			15 09			15 36			16 10	
Dunlop	d		13 13			13 42			14 12			14 42			15 13			15 41			16 14	
Barrhead	d			13 26		13 52	13 56			14 26		14 52	14 56			15 26		15 53	15 56			16 27
Nitshill	d			13 30			14 00			14 30			15 00			15 30			16 00			16 31
Priesthill & Darnley	d			13 32			14 03			14 32			15 02			15 32			16 02			16 33
Kennishead	d			13 34			14 05			14 34			15 04			15 34			16 04			16 35
East Kilbride	d	12 57			13 28			13 57			14 28			14 57			15 28			15 57		
Hairmyres	d	13 01			13 32			14 01			14 32			15 01			15 32			16 01		
Thorntonhall	d	13 04						14 04						15 04						16 04		
Busby	d	13 07			13 37			14 07			14 37			15 07			15 37			16 07		
Clarkston	d	13 10			13 40			14 10			14 40			15 10			15 40			16 10		
Giffnock	d	13 14			13 43			14 14			14 43			15 14			15 43			16 14		
Thornliebank	d	13 16			13 46			14 16			14 46			15 16			15 46			16 16		
Pollokshaws West	d	13 20		13 38	13 49		14 08	14 20		14 38	14 49		15 08	15 20		15 38	15 49		16 08	16 20		16 39
Crossmyloof	d	13 23		13 41	13 52		14 11	14 23		14 41	14 52		15 11	15 23		15 41	15 52		16 11	16 23		16 41
Glasgow Central 15	a	13 29	13 35	13 47	13 59	14 07	14 17	14 29	14 34	14 47	14 59	15 06	15 17	15 29	15 37	15 47	16 01	16 09	16 17	16 29	16 36	16 48

		SR	SR	SR	SR	SR C ⚲	SR	SR	SR	SR	SR	SR	SR	SR	SR	SR	SR	SR ◇ D	SR	SR	SR	SR	SR C ⚲
Kilmarnock 3	d		16 28			16 56			17 27			17 59			18 29			18 57			19 27		19 57
Kilmaurs	d		16 32			17 00			17 31			18 03			18 33			19 01			19 31		20 01
Stewarton	d		16 37			17 06			17 36			18 09			18 39			19 06			19 36		20 06
Dunlop	d		16 42			17 10			17 41			18 13			18 43			19 11			19 41		20 11
Barrhead	d		16 52	16 58		17 21	17 26		17 52	17 56		18 24	18 27		18 54	18 57		19 22	19 26		19 51		20 21
Nitshill	d			17 02			17 30			18 00			18 31			19 01			19 30		19 54		
Priesthill & Darnley	d			17 04			17 32			18 02			18 33			19 04			19 32		19 57		
Kennishead	d			17 06			17 34			18 04			18 35			19 06			19 34		19 59		
East Kilbride	d	16 28			16 57			17 25			17 57			18 29			18 57			19 28		19 57	
Hairmyres	d	16 32			17 01			17 32			18 05			18 37			19 01			19 32		20 01	
Thorntonhall	d				17 04						18 09						19 04					20 04	
Busby	d	16 37			17 07			17 37			18 12			18 43			19 07			19 37		20 07	
Clarkston	d	16 40			17 10			17 40			18 15			18 46			19 10			19 40		20 10	
Giffnock	d	16 43			17 14			17 44			18 18			18 50			19 14			19 43		20 14	
Thornliebank	d	16 46			17 16			17 46			18 21			18 52			19 16			19 46		20 16	
Pollokshaws West	d	16 49		17 10	17 20		17 38	17 49		18 08	18 24		18 39	18 55		19 09	19 20		19 38	19 49	20 02	20 20	
Crossmyloof	d	16 52		17 13	17 23		17 40	17 52		18 11	18 26		18 41	18 58		19 12	19 23		19 41	19 52	20 05	20 23	
Glasgow Central 15	a	17 01	17 06	17 19	17 29	17 37	17 47	17 58	18 05	18 17	18 33	18 37	18 48	19 04	19 07	19 19	19 29	19 37	19 48	19 59	20 13	20 29	20 37

A From East Kilbride
B From Dumfries
C From Carlisle
D From Stranraer
E From Auchinleck

Table T222-F

Kilmarnock, Barrhead and East Kilbride - Glasgow Central

Mondays to Fridays
16 December to 15 May

		SR	SR	SR	SR A ⚲	SR	SR	SR	SR	SR	SR	SR	SR A ⚲	SR	SR FO	SR FX
Kilmarnock 3	d		20 27		21 04		21 29		21 57		22 26		22 57			
Kilmaurs	d		20 31		21 08		21 33		22 01		22 30		23 01			
Stewarton	d		20 36		21 13		21 38		22 07		22 35		23 06			
Dunlop	d		20 41		21 18		21 43		22 11		22 40		23 11			
Barrhead	d		20 51		21 28		21 53		22 22		22 50		23 22			
Nitshill	d		20 54				21 56				22 53					
Priesthill & Darnley	d		20 57				21 59				22 56					
Kennishead	d		20 59				22 01				22 58					
East Kilbride	d	20 28		20 57		21 28		21 57		22 28		22 57		23 28	23 57	23 57
Hairmyres	d	20 32		21 01		21 32		22 01		22 32		23 01		23 32	00 02	00 02
Thorntonhall	d			21 04				22 04				23 04			00 04	00 05
Busby	d	20 37		21 07		21 37		22 07		22 37		23 07		23 37	00 07	00 08
Clarkston	d	20 40		21 10		21 40		22 10		22 40		23 10		23 40	00 10	00 11
Giffnock	d	20 43		21 14		21 43		22 14		22 43		23 14		23 43	00 14	00 14
Thornliebank	d	20 46		21 16		21 46		22 16		22 46		23 16		23 46	00 16	00 17
Pollokshaws West	d	20 49	21 02	21 20		21 49	22 04	22 20		22 49	23 01	23 20		23 49	00 19	00 20
Crossmyloof	d	20 52	21 05	21 23		21 52	22 07	22 23		22 52	23 04	23 23		23 52	00 22	00 23
Glasgow Central 15	a	20 59	21 13	21 29	21 42	21 59	22 15	22 29	22 37	22 59	23 12	23 29	23 36	23 59	00 28	00 30

Saturdays
21 December to 16 May

		SR B	SR	SR C	SR	SR C	SR	SR	SR	SR	SR A ⚲	SR	SR	SR	SR	SR	SR ◇ D	SR	SR	SR	SR	SR	SR A ⚲
Kilmarnock 3	d		05 22	06 20		06 52			07 22		07 55			08 23			08 56			09 27			09 50
Kilmaurs	d		05 26	06 24		06 56			07 26		07 59			08 27			09 00			09 31			09 54
Stewarton	d		05 31	06 29		07 02			07 31		08 05			08 32			09 06			09 36			10 00
Dunlop	d		05 36	06 34		07 06			07 36		08 10			08 37			09 10			09 41			10 04
Barrhead	d		05 46	06 44		07 18	07 26		07 47		08 21	08 26		08 50	08 56		09 22	09 26		09 53	09 56		10 15
Nitshill	d		05 49	06 47			07 29		07 50			08 30			09 00			09 30			10 00		
Priesthill & Darnley	d		05 52	06 50			07 31		07 53			08 32			09 02			09 32			10 02		
Kennishead	d		05 54	06 52			07 33		07 55			08 34			09 04			09 34			10 04		
East Kilbride	d				06 54			07 27		07 57			08 27			08 57			09 28			09 57	
Hairmyres	d	00 02			06 58			07 31		08 01			08 31			09 01			09 32			10 01	
Thorntonhall	d	00 04			07 01			07 34		08 04			08 34			09 04						10 04	
Busby	d	00 07			07 04			07 37		08 07			08 37			09 07			09 37			10 07	
Clarkston	d	00 10			07 07			07 40		08 10			08 40			09 10			09 40			10 10	
Giffnock	d	00 14			07 11			07 44		08 14			08 44			09 14			09 43			10 14	
Thornliebank	d	00 16			07 13			07 47		08 16			08 46			09 16			09 46			10 16	
Pollokshaws West	d	00 19	05 57	06 55	07 17		07 37	07 50	07 58	08 20		08 38	08 50		09 08	09 20		09 38	09 49		10 08	10 20	
Crossmyloof	d	00 22	06 00	06 58	07 19		07 40	07 53	08 01	08 23		08 41	08 53		09 11	09 23		09 41	09 52		10 11	10 23	
Glasgow Central 15	a	00 28	06 09	07 11	07 26	07 32	07 46	07 59	08 09	08 29	08 34	08 47	08 59	09 03	09 17	09 29	09 37	09 47	09 59	10 06	10 17	10 29	10 33

		SR	SR	SR	SR	SR	SR E	SR	SR	SR	SR	SR	SR	SR	SR	SR	SR	SR	SR A ⚲	SR	SR	SR	SR
Kilmarnock 3	d			10 28			11 00			11 27			11 58			12 27			12 59			13 28	
Kilmaurs	d			10 32			11 04			11 31			12 02			12 31			13 03			13 32	
Stewarton	d			10 37			11 09			11 36			12 07			12 36			13 08			13 37	
Dunlop	d			10 42			11 14			11 41			12 12			12 41			13 13			13 42	
Barrhead	d	10 26		10 52	10 56			11 26		11 52	11 56			12 26		12 52	12 56			13 26		13 52	13 56
Nitshill	d	10 30			11 00			11 30			12 00			12 30			13 00			13 30			14 00
Priesthill & Darnley	d	10 33			11 02			11 32			12 02			12 32			13 02			13 32			14 03
Kennishead	d	10 35			11 04			11 34			12 04			12 34			13 04			13 34			14 05
East Kilbride	d		10 28			10 57			11 28			11 57			12 28			12 57			13 28		
Hairmyres	d		10 32			11 01			11 32			12 01			12 32			13 01			13 32		
Thorntonhall	d					11 04						12 04						13 04					
Busby	d		10 37			11 07			11 37			12 07			12 37			13 07			13 37		
Clarkston	d		10 40			11 10			11 40			12 10			12 40			13 10			13 40		
Giffnock	d		10 43			11 14			11 43			12 14			12 43			13 14			13 43		
Thornliebank	d		10 46			11 16			11 46			12 16			12 46			13 16			13 46		
Pollokshaws West	d	10 38	10 49		11 08	11 20		11 38	11 49		12 08	12 20		12 38	12 49		13 08	13 20		13 38	13 49		14 08
Crossmyloof	d	10 41	10 52		11 11	11 23		11 41	11 52		12 11	12 23		12 41	12 52		13 11	13 23		13 41	13 52		14 11
Glasgow Central 15	a	10 47	10 59	11 06	11 17	11 29	11 36	11 47	12 01	12 05	12 17	12 29	12 34	12 47	12 59	13 05	13 17	13 29	13 35	13 47	13 59	14 07	14 17

		SR	SR	SR	SR	SR	SR	SR	SR A ⚲	SR	SR	SR	SR	SR	SR	SR	SR	SR	SR	SR	SR A ⚲	SR
Kilmarnock 3	d		13 58			14 28			14 59			15 27			16 00			16 28			16 56	
Kilmaurs	d		14 02			14 32			15 03			15 31			16 04			16 32			17 00	
Stewarton	d		14 07			14 37			15 09			15 36			16 10			16 37			17 06	
Dunlop	d		14 12			14 42			15 13			15 41			16 14			16 42			17 10	
Barrhead	d			14 26		14 52	14 56			15 26		15 53	15 56			16 27		16 52	16 58		17 21	17 26
Nitshill	d			14 30			15 00			15 30			16 00			16 31			17 02			17 30
Priesthill & Darnley	d			14 32			15 02			15 32			16 02			16 33			17 04			17 32
Kennishead	d			14 34			15 04			15 34			16 04			16 35			17 06			17 34
East Kilbride	d	13 57			14 28			14 57			15 28			15 57			16 29			16 57		
Hairmyres	d	14 01			14 32			15 01			15 32			16 01			16 33			17 01		
Thorntonhall	d	14 04						15 04						16 04						17 04		
Busby	d	14 07			14 37			15 07			15 37			16 07			16 38			17 07		
Clarkston	d	14 10			14 40			15 10			15 40			16 10			16 41			17 10		
Giffnock	d	14 14			14 43			15 14			15 43			16 14			16 44			17 14		
Thornliebank	d	14 16			14 46			15 16			15 46			16 16			16 47			17 16		
Pollokshaws West	d	14 20		14 38	14 49		15 08	15 20		15 38	15 49		16 08	16 20		16 39	16 50		17 10	17 20		17 38
Crossmyloof	d	14 23		14 41	14 52		15 11	15 23		15 41	15 52		16 11	16 23		16 41	16 53		17 12	17 23		17 41
Glasgow Central 15	a	14 29	14 34	14 47	14 59	15 06	15 17	15 29	15 37	15 47	15 59	16 06	16 17	16 29	16 36	16 48	17 00	17 05	17 20	17 29	17 37	17 47

A From Carlisle
B From East Kilbride
C From Dumfries
D From Stranraer
E From Auchinleck

Table T222-F

21 December to 16 May

Kilmarnock, Barrhead and East Kilbride - Glasgow Central

		SR	SR	SR		SR	SR	SR	SR	SR	SR	SR	SR ◇ A	SR		SR	SR	SR	SR B 🍴	SR	SR	SR	SR B 🍴	SR
Kilmarnock 3	d		17 27				17 59			18 29			18 57				19 27		19 57		20 27		21 04	
Kilmaurs	d		17 31				18 03			18 33			19 01				19 31		20 01		20 31		21 08	
Stewarton	d		17 36				18 09			18 39			19 06				19 36		20 06		20 36		21 13	
Dunlop	d		17 41				18 13			18 43			19 11				19 41		20 11		20 41		21 18	
Barrhead	d		17 52	17 56			18 24	18 27		18 54	18 57		19 22	19 26			19 51		20 21		20 51		21 28	
Nitshill	d			18 00				18 31			19 01			19 30			19 54				20 54			
Priesthill & Darnley	d			18 02				18 33			19 04			19 32			19 57				20 57			
Kennishead	d			18 04				18 35			19 06			19 34			19 59				20 59			
East Kilbride	d	17 28				17 57			18 28			18 57				19 28		19 57		20 28		20 57		21 28
Hairmyres	d	17 32				18 01			18 32			19 01				19 32		20 01		20 32		21 01		21 32
Thorntonhall	d					18 04						19 04						20 04				21 04		
Busby	d	17 37				18 07			18 37			19 07				19 37		20 07		20 37		21 07		21 37
Clarkston	d	17 40				18 10			18 40			19 10				19 40		20 10		20 40		21 10		21 40
Giffnock	d	17 43				18 14			18 43			19 14				19 43		20 14		20 43		21 14		21 43
Thornliebank	d	17 46				18 16			18 46			19 16				19 46		20 16		20 46		21 16		21 46
Pollokshaws West	d	17 49		18 08		18 20		18 39	18 49		19 09	19 20		19 38		19 49	20 02	20 20		20 49	21 02	21 20		21 49
Crossmyloof	d	17 52		18 11		18 23		18 41	18 52		19 12	19 23		19 41		19 52	20 05	20 23		20 52	21 05	21 23		21 52
Glasgow Central 15	a	17 59	18 06	18 17		18 29	18 37	18 48	18 59	19 07	19 18	19 29	19 37	19 47		19 59	20 13	20 29	20 37	20 59	21 13	21 29	21 42	21 59

		SR	SR	SR	SR	SR	SR	SR B 🍴	SR	SR
Kilmarnock 3	d	21 31		22 00		22 29		22 57		
Kilmaurs	d	21 35		22 04		22 33		23 01		
Stewarton	d	21 41		22 09		22 38		23 06		
Dunlop	d	21 45		22 14		22 43		23 11		
Barrhead	d	21 56		22 24		22 53		23 22		
Nitshill	d	21 59				22 56				
Priesthill & Darnley	d	22 01				22 59				
Kennishead	d	22 03				23 01				
East Kilbride	d		21 57		22 28		22 57		23 28	23 57
Hairmyres	d		22 01		22 32		23 01		23 32	00 02
Thorntonhall	d		22 04				23 04			00 04
Busby	d		22 07		22 37		23 07		23 37	00 07
Clarkston	d		22 10		22 40		23 10		23 40	00 10
Giffnock	d		22 14		22 43		23 14		23 43	00 14
Thornliebank	d		22 16		22 46		23 16		23 46	00 16
Pollokshaws West	d	22 07	22 20		22 49	23 04	23 20		23 49	00 19
Crossmyloof	d	22 09	22 23		22 52	23 07	23 23		23 52	00 22
Glasgow Central 15	a	22 21	22 29	22 38	22 59	23 15	23 29	23 36	23 59	00 28

Sundays

15 December to 10 May

		SR C	SR	SR	SR	SR	SR	SR	SR	SR	SR	SR		SR	SR	SR		SR	SR B 🍴	SR	SR	SR	SR	SR
Kilmarnock 3	d				08 55			09 55			10 55		and at the same minutes past each hour until		13 55				14 57			15 55		
Kilmaurs	d				08 59			09 59			10 59				13 59				15 01			15 59		
Stewarton	d				09 04			10 04			11 04				14 04				15 06			16 04		
Dunlop	d				09 09			10 09			11 09				14 09				15 11			16 09		
Barrhead	d				09 20			10 20			11 20				14 20				15 22			16 20		
Nitshill	d				09 23			10 23			11 23				14 23				15 25			16 23		
Priesthill & Darnley	d				09 25			10 25			11 25				14 25				15 27			16 25		
Kennishead	d				09 27			10 27			11 27				14 27				15 29			16 27		
East Kilbride	d		08 26	08 55		09 26	09 55		10 26	10 55		11 26		13 55		14 26		14 55		15 26	15 55		16 26	16 55
Hairmyres	d	00 02	08 30	08 59		09 30	09 59		10 30	10 59		11 30		13 59		14 30		14 59		15 30	15 59		16 30	16 59
Thorntonhall	d	00 04		09 02			10 02			11 02				14 02				15 02			16 02			17 02
Busby	d	00 07	08 35	09 05		09 35	10 05		10 35	11 05		11 35		14 05		14 35		15 05		15 35	16 05		16 35	17 05
Clarkston	d	00 10	08 38	09 08		09 38	10 08		10 38	11 08		11 38		14 08		14 38		15 08		15 38	16 08		16 38	17 08
Giffnock	d	00 14	08 42	09 12		09 42	10 12		10 42	11 12		11 42		14 12		14 42		15 12		15 42	16 12		16 42	17 12
Thornliebank	d	00 16	08 44	09 14		09 44	10 14		10 44	11 14		11 44		14 14		14 44		15 14		15 44	16 14		16 44	17 14
Pollokshaws West	d	00 19	08 47	09 17	09 31	09 48	10 17	10 31	10 47	11 17	11 31	11 47		14 17	14 31	14 47		15 17	15 33	15 47	16 17	16 31	16 47	17 17
Crossmyloof	d	00 22	08 50	09 20		09 51	10 20		10 50	11 20		11 50		14 20		14 50		15 20		15 50	16 20		16 50	17 20
Glasgow Central 15	a	00 28	08 56	09 26	09 40	09 57	10 26	10 40	10 57	11 26	11 40	11 56		14 26	14 40	14 56		15 26	15 43	15 56	16 26	16 40	16 56	17 26

		SR	SR		SR	SR	SR	SR	SR	SR	SR	SR	SR		SR	SR B 🍴	SR	SR	SR	SR	SR	SR
Kilmarnock 3	d	16 55				17 55			18 55			19 55				20 57						
Kilmaurs	d	16 59				17 59			18 59			19 59				21 01						
Stewarton	d	17 04				18 04			19 04			20 04				21 06						
Dunlop	d	17 09				18 09			19 09			20 09				21 11						
Barrhead	d	17 19				18 19			19 19			20 20				21 21						
Nitshill	d	17 23				18 23			19 23			20 23										
Priesthill & Darnley	d	17 25				18 25			19 25			20 25										
Kennishead	d	17 27				18 27			19 27			20 27										
East Kilbride	d		17 26		17 55		18 26	18 55		19 26	19 55		20 26		20 55		21 26	21 55	22 26	22 55	23 26	23 57
Hairmyres	d		17 30		17 59		18 30	18 59		19 30	19 59		20 30		20 59		21 30	21 59	22 30	22 59	23 30	00 02
Thorntonhall	d				18 02			19 02			20 02				21 02			22 02		23 02		00 05
Busby	d		17 35		18 05		18 35	19 05		19 35	20 05		20 35		21 05		21 35	22 05	22 35	23 05	23 35	00 08
Clarkston	d		17 38		18 08		18 38	19 08		19 38	20 08		20 38		21 08		21 38	22 08	22 38	23 08	23 38	00 11
Giffnock	d		17 42		18 12		18 42	19 12		19 42	20 12		20 42		21 12		21 42	22 12	22 42	23 12	23 42	00 14
Thornliebank	d		17 44		18 14		18 44	19 14		19 44	20 14		20 44		21 14		21 44	22 14	22 44	23 14	23 44	00 17
Pollokshaws West	d	17 31	17 47		18 17	18 31	18 47	19 17	19 31	19 47	20 17	20 31	20 47		21 17		21 47	22 17	22 47	23 17	23 47	00 20
Crossmyloof	d		17 50		18 20		18 50	19 20		19 50	20 20		20 50		21 20		21 50	22 20	22 50	23 20	23 50	00 23
Glasgow Central 15	a	17 40	17 56		18 26	18 40	18 56	19 26	19 40	19 56	20 26	20 40	20 56		21 26	21 35	21 56	22 26	22 56	23 28	23 56	00 30

A From Stranraer
B From Carlisle
C not 15 December. From East Kilbride

Table T222-R

16 December to 15 May

Glasgow Central - East Kilbride, Barrhead and Kilmarnock

Miles	Miles			SR	SR	SR	SR	SR A 🍴	SR	SR		SR	SR	SR	SR ◇ B	SR	SR	SR A 🍴	SR	SR		SR C	SR	SR	SR
0	0	**Glasgow Central** 15	d	06 12	06 26	06 47	06 54	07 09	07 13	07 24		07 37	07 42	07 52	08 08	08 15	08 22	08 38	08 48	08 57		09 13	09 18	09 27	09 43
2¼	2¼	Crossmyloof	d	06 18	06 32	06 53	07 00		07 19	07 30			07 50	08 00		08 22	08 29		08 56	09 04			09 25	09 34	
3¼	3¼	Pollokshaws West	d	06 21	06 35	06 56	07 03		07 22	07 33			07 52	08 02		08 24	08 32		08 59	09 06			09 27	09 37	
—	4¼	Thornliebank	d	06 24		06 59			07 25				07 55			08 27			09 02				09 30		
—	5¼	Giffnock	d	06 27		07 02			07 28				07 59			08 31			09 05				09 34		
—	6½	Clarkston	d	06 31		07 06			07 32				08 03			08 35			09 09				09 38		
—	7¼	Busby	d	06 34		07 09			07 36				08 10			08 38			09 12				09 41		
—	8½	Thorntonhall	d	06 37												08 41			09 15						
—	10	Hairmyres	d	06 41		07 15			07 42				08 16			08 45			09 19				09 47		
—	11½	**East Kilbride**	a	06 45		07 18			07 49				08 19			08 48			09 23				09 50		
4½	—	Kennishead	d		06 38		07 06			07 36				08 05			08 35			09 09				09 40	
5	—	Priesthill & Darnley	d		06 40		07 08			07 38				08 08			08 37			09 12				09 42	
5¾	—	Nitshill	d		06 43		07 11			07 41				08 11			08 40			09 15				09 45	
7½	—	**Barrhead**	d		06 48		07a15	07 22		07a45		07 51		08a15	08 22		08a45	08 51		09a19				09a50	09 55
16½	—	Dunlop	d		07 00			07 34				08 03			08 34			09 03				09 35			10 07
18¾	—	Stewarton	d		07 04			07 38				08 07			08 38			09 07				09 39			10 11
22	—	Kilmaurs	d		07 08			07 43				08 11			08 43			09 12				09 44			10 15
24¼	—	**Kilmarnock** 3	a		07 14			07 49				08 17			08 49			09 18				09 50			10 21

		SR	SR	SR A 🍴	SR	SR		SR	SR	SR	SR	SR	SR	SR	SR	SR		SR A 🍴	SR	SR	SR	SR	SR	SR A 🍴	SR
Glasgow Central 15	d	09 47	09 57	10 13	10 17	10 27		10 43	10 47	10 57	11 13	11 17	11 27	11 43	11 47	11 57		12 13	12 17	12 27	12 43	12 47	12 57	13 13	13 17
Crossmyloof	d	09 54	10 03		10 24	10 33			10 54	11 03		11 24	11 33		11 54	12 03			12 24	12 33		12 54	13 03		13 24
Pollokshaws West	d	09 56	10 06		10 26	10 36			10 56	11 06		11 26	11 36		11 56	12 06			12 26	12 36		12 56	13 06		13 26
Thornliebank	d	09 59			10 29				10 59			11 29			11 59				12 29			12 59			13 29
Giffnock	d	10 03			10 33				11 03			11 33			12 03				12 33			13 03			13 33
Clarkston	d	10 07			10 37				11 07			11 37			12 07				12 37			13 07			13 37
Busby	d	10 10			10 40				11 10			11 40			12 10				12 40			13 10			13 40
Thorntonhall	d	10 13							11 13						12 13							13 13			
Hairmyres	d	10 17			10 46				11 17			11 46			12 17				12 46			13 17			13 46
East Kilbride	a	10 20			10 49				11 20			11 49			12 20				12 49			13 20			13 49
Kennishead	d		10 09			10 39				11 09			11 39			12 09				12 39			13 09		
Priesthill & Darnley	d		10 11			10 41				11 11			11 41			12 11				12 41			13 11		
Nitshill	d		10 14			10 44				11 14			11 44			12 14				12 44			13 14		
Barrhead	d		10a19			10a49		10 55		11a19			11a49	11 55		12a19				12a49	12 55		13a19		
Dunlop	d			10 36				11 07			11 36			12 07				12 35			13 07			13 35	
Stewarton	d			10 40				11 11			11 40			12 11				12 39			13 11			13 39	
Kilmaurs	d			10 45				11 15			11 45			12 15				12 44			13 15			13 44	
Kilmarnock 3	a			10 51				11 21			11 51			12 21				12 50			13 21			13 50	

		SR		SR	SR	SR	SR ◇ B	SR	SR	SR	SR	SR		SR	SR	SR	SR	SR	SR	SR D 🍴	SR	SR		SR	SR
Glasgow Central 15	d	13 27		13 43	13 47	13 58	14 13	14 17	14 27	14 43	14 47	14 57		15 13	15 17	15 27	15 43	15 47	15 57	16 13	16 17	16 27		16 43	16 47
Crossmyloof	d	13 33			13 54	14 04		14 24	14 33		14 54	15 03			15 24	15 33		15 54	16 03		16 24	16 33			16 54
Pollokshaws West	d	13 36			13 56	14 07		14 26	14 36		14 56	15 06			15 26	15 36		15 56	16 06		16 26	16 36			16 56
Thornliebank	d				13 59			14 29			14 59				15 29			15 59			16 29				16 59
Giffnock	d				14 03			14 33			15 03				15 33			16 03			16 33				17 03
Clarkston	d				14 07			14 37			15 07				15 37			16 07			16 37				17 07
Busby	d				14 10			14 40			15 10				15 40			16 10			16 40				17 10
Thorntonhall	d				14 13						15 13							16 13			16 43				17 13
Hairmyres	d				14 17			14 46			15 17				15 46			16 17			16 47				17 17
East Kilbride	a				14 20			14 49			15 20				15 49			16 20			16 50				17 20
Kennishead	d	13 39				14 10			14 39			15 09				15 39			16 09			16 39			
Priesthill & Darnley	d	13 41				14 12			14 41			15 11				15 41			16 11			16 41			
Nitshill	d	13 44				14 15			14 44			15 14				15 44			16 14			16 44			
Barrhead	d	13a49		13 55		14a20			14a49	14 55		15a19				15a49	15 56		16a19	16 25		16a49		16 55	
Dunlop	d			14 07			14 36			15 07				15 37			16 08			16 37				17 07	
Stewarton	d			14 11			14 40			15 11				15 41			16 12			16 41				17 11	
Kilmaurs	d			14 15			14 44			15 15				15 45			16 16			16 46				17 15	
Kilmarnock 3	a			14 21			14 50			15 21				15 51			16 22			16 52				17 21	

		SR	SR	SR E	SR	SR	SR	SR A 🍴		SR	SR	SR	SR ◇ B	SR	SR	SR	SR	SR		SR A 🍴	SR	SR	SR	SR F	SR
Glasgow Central 15	d	16 57	17 01	17 13	17 20	17 27	17 33	17 42		17 48	17 58	18 04	18 13	18 19	18 27	18 43	18 47	18 57		19 13	19 17	19 33	19 47	20 13	20 17
Crossmyloof	d	17 03	17 07			17 33	17 39			17 56	18 04	18 11		18 26	18 35		18 54	19 03			19 24	19 39	19 54		20 24
Pollokshaws West	d	17 06	17 10			17 36	17 42			17 58	18 07	18 13		18 28	18 38		18 56	19 06			19 26	19 42	19 56		20 26
Thornliebank	d		17 13				17 45			18 01		18 16		18 31			18 59				19 29		19 59		20 29
Giffnock	d		17 16				17 48			18 05		18 20		18 35			19 03				19 33		20 03		20 33
Clarkston	d		17 20		17 33		17 52			18 09		18 24		18 39			19 07				19 37		20 07		20 37
Busby	d		17 23				17 55			18 12		18 27		18 43			19 10				19 40		20 10		20 40
Thorntonhall	d						17 58					18 30					19 13						20 13		
Hairmyres	d		17 29		17 44		18 02			18 18		18 34		18 49			19 17				19 46		20 17		20 46
East Kilbride	a		17 33		17 47		18 06			18 22		18 37		18 52			19 20				19 49		20 20		20 49
Kennishead	d	17 09				17 39					18 10				18 41			19 09				19 45			
Priesthill & Darnley	d	17 11				17 41					18 12				18 43			19 11				19 47			
Nitshill	d	17 14				17 44					18 15				18 46			19 14				19 50			
Barrhead	d	17a19		17 25		17a49		17 55			18a20		18 26		18a51	18 56		19a19		19 25		19 54		20 25	
Dunlop	d			17 37				18 07					18 38			19 08				19 37		20 06		20 37	
Stewarton	d			17 41				18 11					18 42			19 12				19 41		20 10		20 41	
Kilmaurs	d			17 46				18 16					18 46			19 16				19 46		20 14		20 46	
Kilmarnock 3	a			17 52				18 22					18 52			19 22				19 52		20 20		20 52	

A To Carlisle
B To Stranraer
C To New Cumnock
D To Newcastle
E To Girvan
F To Dumfries

Table T222-R

Glasgow Central - East Kilbride, Barrhead and Kilmarnock

Mondays to Fridays
16 December to 15 May

		SR	SR	SR A	SR	SR	SR	SR ◇ B	SR	SR	SR	SR C	SR
Glasgow Central 15	d	20 33	20 47	21 13	21 17	21 33	21 47	22 13	22 17	22 33	22 47	23 13	23 17
Crossmyloof	d	20 39	20 54		21 24	21 39	21 54		22 24	22 39	22 54	23 19	23 24
Pollokshaws West	d	20 42	20 56		21 26	21 42	21 56		22 26	22 42	22 56	23 22	23 26
Thornliebank	d		20 59		21 29		21 59		22 29		22 59		23 29
Giffnock	d		21 03		21 33		22 03		22 33		23 03		23 33
Clarkston	d		21 07		21 37		22 07		22 37		23 07		23 37
Busby	d		21 10		21 40		22 10		22 40		23 10		23 40
Thorntonhall	d		21 13				22 13				23 13		23 43
Hairmyres	d		21 17		21 46		22 17		22 46		23 17		23 47
East Kilbride	a		21 20		21 49		22 20		22 49		23 20		23 50
Kennishead	d	20 45				21 45				22 45		23 25	
Priesthill & Darnley	d	20 47				21 47				22 47		23 27	
Nitshill	d	20 50				21 50				22 50		23 30	
Barrhead	d	20 54		21 29		21 54		22 25		22 54		23 35	
Dunlop	d	21 07		21 41		22 06		22 37		23 06		23 47	
Stewarton	d	21 13		21 45		22 10		22 41		23 10		23 51	
Kilmaurs	d	21 17		21 50		22 14		22 46		23 14		23 55	
Kilmarnock 3	a	21 23		21 56		22 20		22 52		23 20		00 01	

Saturdays
21 December to 16 May

		SR	SR	SR	SR	SR	SR	SR A	SR	SR	SR	SR	SR ◇ B	SR	SR	SR A	SR	SR	SR D	SR	SR	SR	SR
Glasgow Central 15	d	00 12	00 18	06 12	06 29	06 47	06 54	07 07	07 20	07 37	07 47	07 53	08 08	08 17	08 23	08 37	08 47	08 57	09 13	09 17	09 27	09 43	09 47
Crossmyloof	d	00 18	00 24	06 18	06 35	06 53	07 00		07 26		07 54	08 00		08 24	08 29		08 54	09 03		09 25	09 34		09 54
Pollokshaws West	d	00 21	00 27	06 21	06 38	06 56	07 03		07 29		07 56	08 02		08 26	08 32		08 56	09 06		09 27	09 37		09 56
Thornliebank	d		00 30	06 24		06 59			07 32		07 59			08 29			08 59			09 30			09 59
Giffnock	d		00 33	06 27		07 02			07 35		08 03			08 33			09 03			09 34			10 03
Clarkston	d		00 37	06 31		07 06			07 39		08 07			08 37			09 07			09 38			10 07
Busby	d		00 40	06 34		07 09			07 42		08 10			08 40			09 10			09 41			10 10
Thorntonhall	d		00 43	06 37							08 13						09 13						10 13
Hairmyres	d		00 47	06 41		07 15			07 48		08 17			08 46			09 17			09 47			10 17
East Kilbride	a		00 51	06 45		07 18			07 52		08 20			08 49			09 20			09 50			10 20
Kennishead	d	00 24			06 41		07 06					08 05			08 35			09 09			09 40		
Priesthill & Darnley	d	00 26			06 43		07 08					08 08			08 37			09 11			09 42		
Nitshill	d	00 29			06 46		07 11					08 11			08 40			09 14			09 45		
Barrhead	d	00 33			06 51		07a15	07 22		07 51		08a15	08 22		08a45	08 51		09a19			09a50	09 55	
Dunlop	d	00 45			07 03			07 34		08 03			08 34			09 03			09 35			10 07	
Stewarton	d	00 49			07 07			07 38		08 07			08 38			09 07			09 39			10 11	
Kilmaurs	d	00 53			07 11			07 43		08 11			08 42			09 12			09 44			10 15	
Kilmarnock 3	a	00 59			07 17			07 49		08 17			08 48			09 18			09 50			10 21	

		SR	SR A	SR	SR	SR	SR	SR	SR	SR	SR	SR	SR	SR	SR A	SR	SR	SR	SR	SR	SR A	SR	SR
Glasgow Central 15	d	09 57	10 13	10 17	10 27	10 43	10 47	10 57	11 13	11 17	11 27	11 43	11 47	11 57	12 13	12 17	12 27	12 43	12 47	12 57	13 13	13 17	13 27
Crossmyloof	d	10 03		10 24	10 33		10 54	11 03		11 24	11 33		11 54	12 03		12 24	12 33		12 54	13 03		13 24	13 33
Pollokshaws West	d	10 06		10 26	10 36		10 56	11 06		11 26	11 36		11 56	12 06		12 26	12 36		12 56	13 06		13 26	13 36
Thornliebank	d			10 29			10 59			11 29			11 59			12 29			12 59			13 29	
Giffnock	d			10 33			11 03			11 33			12 03			12 33			13 03			13 33	
Clarkston	d			10 37			11 07			11 37			12 07			12 37			13 07			13 37	
Busby	d			10 40			11 10			11 40			12 10			12 40			13 10			13 40	
Thorntonhall	d						11 13						12 13						13 13				
Hairmyres	d			10 46			11 17			11 46			12 17			12 46			13 17			13 46	
East Kilbride	a			10 49			11 20			11 49			12 20			12 49			13 20			13 49	
Kennishead	d	10 09			10 39			11 09			11 39			12 09			12 39			13 09			13 39
Priesthill & Darnley	d	10 11			10 41			11 11			11 41			12 11			12 41			13 11			13 41
Nitshill	d	10 14			10 44			11 14			11 44			12 14			12 44			13 14			13 44
Barrhead	d	10a19			10a49	10 55		11a19			11a49	11 55		12a19			12a49	12 55		13a19			13a49
Dunlop	d		10 36			11 07			11 36			12 07			12 35			13 07			13 35		
Stewarton	d		10 40			11 11			11 40			12 11			12 39			13 11			13 39		
Kilmaurs	d		10 45			11 15			11 45			12 15			12 44			13 15			13 44		
Kilmarnock 3	a		10 51			11 21			11 51			12 21			12 50			13 21			13 50		

		SR	SR	SR	SR ◇ B	SR	SR	SR	SR	SR	SR	SR	SR	SR	SR	SR	SR E	SR	SR	SR	SR	SR
Glasgow Central 15	d	13 43	13 47	13 58	14 13	14 17	14 27	14 43	14 47	14 57	15 13	15 17	15 27	15 43	15 47	15 57	16 13	16 17	16 27	16 44	16 48	16 57
Crossmyloof	d		13 54	14 04		14 24	14 33		14 54	15 03		15 24	15 33		15 54	16 03		16 24	16 33		16 55	17 03
Pollokshaws West	d		13 56	14 07		14 26	14 36		14 56	15 06		15 26	15 36		15 56	16 06		16 26	16 36		16 57	17 06
Thornliebank	d		13 59			14 29			14 59			15 29			15 59			16 29			17 00	
Giffnock	d		14 03			14 33			15 03			15 33			16 03			16 33			17 04	
Clarkston	d		14 07			14 37			15 07			15 37			16 07			16 37			17 08	
Busby	d		14 10			14 40			15 10			15 40			16 10			16 40			17 11	
Thorntonhall	d		14 13						15 13						16 13			16 43			17 14	
Hairmyres	d		14 17			14 46			15 17			15 46			16 17			16 47			17 18	
East Kilbride	a		14 20			14 49			15 20			15 49			16 20			16 50			17 21	
Kennishead	d			14 10			14 39			15 09			15 39			16 09			16 39			17 09
Priesthill & Darnley	d			14 12			14 41			15 11			15 41			16 11			16 41			17 11
Nitshill	d			14 15			14 44			15 14			15 44			16 14			16 44			17 14
Barrhead	d	13 55		14a20			14a49	14 55		15a19			15a49	15 56		16a19	16 25		16a49	16 56		17a19
Dunlop	d	14 07			14 36			15 07			15 37			16 08			16 37			17 08		
Stewarton	d	14 11			14 40			15 11			15 41			16 12			16 41			17 12		
Kilmaurs	d	14 15			14 44			15 15			15 45			16 16			16 46			17 16		
Kilmarnock 3	a	14 21			14 50			15 21			15 51			16 22			16 52			17 22		

A To Carlisle
B To Stranraer
C To Dumfries
D To New Cumnock
E To Newcastle

Table T222-R

Glasgow Central - East Kilbride, Barrhead and Kilmarnock

Saturdays
21 December to 16 May

		SR A	SR	SR	SR B	SR	SR	SR C	SR	SR	SR	SR	SR	SR B	SR	SR	SR	SR D	SR	SR	SR	SR
Glasgow Central 15	d	17 13	17 17	17 27	17 43	17 47	17 57	18 13	18 17	18 27	18 43	18 47	18 57	19 13	19 17	19 33	19 47	20 13	20 17	20 33	20 47	21 13
Crossmyloof	d		17 24	17 33		17 54	18 03		18 24	18 35		18 54	19 03		19 24	19 39	19 54		20 24	20 39	20 54	
Pollokshaws West	d		17 26	17 36		17 56	18 06		18 26	18 38		18 56	19 06		19 26	19 42	19 56		20 26	20 42	20 56	
Thornliebank	d		17 29			17 59			18 29			18 59			19 29		19 59		20 29		20 59	
Giffnock	d		17 33			18 03			18 33			19 03			19 33		20 03		20 33		21 03	
Clarkston	d		17 37			18 07			18 37			19 07			19 37		20 07		20 37		21 07	
Busby	d		17 40			18 10			18 40			19 10			19 40		20 10		20 40		21 10	
Thorntonhall	d		17 43			18 13						19 13					20 13				21 13	
Hairmyres	d		17 47			18 17			18 46			19 17			19 46		20 17		20 46		21 17	
East Kilbride	a		17 50			18 20			18 49			19 20			19 49		20 20		20 49		21 20	
Kennishead	d			17 39			18 09			18 41			19 09			19 45				20 45		
Priesthill & Darnley	d			17 41			18 11			18 43			19 11			19 47				20 47		
Nitshill	d			17 44			18 14			18 46			19 14			19 50				20 50		
Barrhead	d	17 25		17a49	17 55		18a19	18 26		18a51	18 56		19a19	19 25		19 54		20 25		20 54		21 29
Dunlop	d	17 37			18 07			18 38			19 08			19 37		20 06		20 37		21 07		21 41
Stewarton	d	17 41			18 11			18 42			19 12			19 41		20 10		20 41		21 13		21 45
Kilmaurs	d	17 46			18 16			18 46			19 16			19 46		20 14		20 46		21 17		21 49
Kilmarnock 3	a	17 52			18 22			18 52			19 22			19 52		20 20		20 52		21 23		21 55

		SR	SR	SR	SR B	SR	SR	SR	SR	SR
Glasgow Central 15	d	21 18	21 34	21 47	22 13	22 17	22 33	22 47	23 13	23 17
Crossmyloof	d	21 24	21 40	21 54		22 24	22 39	22 54	23 19	23 24
Pollokshaws West	d	21 27	21 43	21 56		22 26	22 42	22 56	23 22	23 26
Thornliebank	d	21 30		21 59		22 29		22 59		23 29
Giffnock	d	21 33		22 03		22 33		23 03		23 33
Clarkston	d	21 37		22 07		22 37		23 07		23 37
Busby	d	21 40		22 10		22 40		23 10		23 40
Thorntonhall	d			22 13				23 13		23 43
Hairmyres	d	21 46		22 17		22 46		23 17		23 47
East Kilbride	a	21 49		22 20		22 49		23 20		23 50
Kennishead	d		21 46				22 45		23 25	
Priesthill & Darnley	d		21 48				22 47		23 27	
Nitshill	d		21 51				22 50		23 30	
Barrhead	d		21 58		22 25		22 54		23 35	
Dunlop	d		22 10		22 37		23 06		23 47	
Stewarton	d		22 14		22 41		23 10		23 51	
Kilmaurs	d		22 18		22 46		23 14		23 55	
Kilmarnock 3	a		22 24		22 52		23 20		00 01	

Sundays
15 December to 10 May

		SR	SR	SR		SR	SR	SR	SR B	SR	SR	SR		SR	SR	SR	SR	SR	SR	SR	SR	SR
Glasgow Central 15	d	08 03	08 18	08 48	and at the same minutes past each hour until	14 03	14 18	14 48	15 03	15 18	15 48	16 03	and at the same minutes past each hour until	18 18	18 48	19 03	19 18	19 48	20 18	20 48	21 18	21 48
Crossmyloof	d		08 24	08 54			14 24	14 54		15 24	15 54			18 24	18 54		19 24	19 54	20 24	20 54	21 24	21 54
Pollokshaws West	d	08 11	08 27	08 57		14 11	14 27	14 57	15 11	15 27	15 57	16 11		18 27	18 57	19 11	19 27	19 57	20 27	20 57	21 27	21 57
Thornliebank	d		08 30	09 00			14 30	15 00		15 30	16 00			18 30	19 00		19 30	20 00	20 30	21 00	21 30	22 00
Giffnock	d		08 33	09 03			14 33	15 03		15 33	16 03			18 33	19 03		19 33	20 03	20 33	21 03	21 33	22 03
Clarkston	d		08 37	09 07			14 37	15 07		15 37	16 07			18 37	19 07		19 37	20 07	20 37	21 07	21 37	22 07
Busby	d		08 40	09 10			14 40	15 10		15 40	16 10			18 40	19 10		19 40	20 10	20 40	21 10	21 40	22 10
Thorntonhall	d			09 13				15 13			16 13				19 13			20 13		21 13		22 13
Hairmyres	d		08 46	09 17			14 46	15 17		15 46	16 17			18 46	19 17		19 46	20 17	20 46	21 17	21 46	22 17
East Kilbride	a		08 50	09 21			14 50	15 21		15 50	16 21			18 50	19 21		19 50	20 21	20 50	21 21	21 50	22 21
Kennishead	d	08 14				14 14			15 14			16 14				19 14						
Priesthill & Darnley	d	08 16				14 16			15 16			16 16				19 16						
Nitshill	d	08 19				14 19			15 19			16 19				19 19						
Barrhead	d	08 23				14 23			15 24			16 23				19 23						
Dunlop	d	08 35				14 35			15 36			16 35				19 35						
Stewarton	d	08 39				14 39			15 40			16 39				19 39						
Kilmaurs	d	08 43				14 43			15 44			16 43				19 43						
Kilmarnock 3	a	08 49				14 49			15 50			16 49				19 49						

		SR B	SR	SR	SR
Glasgow Central 15	d	22 12	22 18	22 48	23 18
Crossmyloof	d		22 24	22 54	23 24
Pollokshaws West	d		22 27	22 57	23 27
Thornliebank	d		22 30	23 00	23 30
Giffnock	d		22 33	23 03	23 33
Clarkston	d		22 37	23 07	23 37
Busby	d		22 40	23 10	23 40
Thorntonhall	d			23 13	23 43
Hairmyres	d		22 46	23 17	23 47
East Kilbride	a		22 50	23 21	23 51
Kennishead	d				
Priesthill & Darnley	d				
Nitshill	d				
Barrhead	d	22 24			
Dunlop	d	22 36			
Stewarton	d	22 40			
Kilmaurs	d	22 44			
Kilmarnock 3	a	22 48			

A To Girvan
B To Carlisle
C To Stranraer
D To Dumfries

Table T223-F

Mondays to Fridays
16 December to 15 May

Newton, Neilston, Cathcart Circle and Glasgow Central

Miles	Miles	Miles		SR A	SR	SR	SR	SR A	SR	SR	SR A	SR		SR A	SR	SR	SR	SR A	SR	SR	SR A	SR A		SR
0	0	—	**Newton** 226 d		06 24		06 49			07 15					07 41		07 50							08 20
1½	1½	—	Kirkhill d		06 27		06 52			07 18					07 44		07 53							08 23
2¾	2¾	—	Burnside d		06 30		06 55			07 21					07 47		07 56							08 26
3¾	3¾	—	Croftfoot d		06 32		06 57			07 23					07 49		07 58							08 28
4¼	4¼	—	Kings Park d		06 34		06 59			07 25					07 51		08 02							08 30
—	—	0	**Neilston** d			06 29			06 58			07 24				07 41			07 55	08 07				
—	—	3¾	Patterton d			06 35			07 04			07 30				07 47			08 01	08 13				
—	—	4¾	Whitecraigs d			06 37			07 06			07 33				07 49			08 04	08 15				
—	—	5½	Williamwood d			06 39			07 08			07 35				07 51			08 07	08 17				
—	—	7	Muirend d			06 42			07 12			07 38				07 54			08 10	08 20				
4¾	—	7¾	Cathcart d	06 30		06 45		07 02	07 15		07 34	07 41		07 45		07 58		08 11	08 15		08 27	08 25		
—	5½	8½	Mount Florida d	06 32		06 47	07 03		07 17		07 36	07 43			07 55	08 00		08 14	08 17		08 29			08 34
—	6	9	Crosshill d	06 34		06 49	07 05		07 19		07 38	07 45			07 57	08 02		08 16	08 19		08 31			08 36
—	6½	9½	Queens Park d	06 36		06 51	07 07		07 21		07 40	07 47			07 59	08 05		08 18	08 22		08 33			08 39
—	6¾	9¾	Pollokshields East d	06 37		06 53	07 08		07 22		07 43	07 50			08 01	08 07		08 20	08 23		08 34			08 43
5¾	—	—	Langside d		06 38			07 05		07 29				07 47			08 06					08 28		
6¼	—	—	Pollokshaws East d		06 40			07 07		07 31				07 49			08 08					08 30		
6¾	—	—	Shawlands d		06 42			07 09		07 33				07 51			08 10					08 32		
7½	—	—	Maxwell Park d		06 44			07 11		07 35				07 53			08 12					08 34		
8	—	—	Pollokshields West d		06 48			07 13		07 37				07 55			08 14					08 36		
10	8¾	11¾	**Glasgow Central** 15 226 a	06 42	06 56	06 58	07 14	07 19	07 27	07 44	07 49	07 55		08 01	08 06	08 12	08 20	08 25	08 28	08 33	08 39	08 43		08 48

	SR A	SR	SR A	SR	SR	SR A	SR	SR		SR A	SR	SR	SR	SR A	SR	SR A	SR	SR		SR	SR A	SR	SR A	SR
Newton 226 d				08 31			09 02				09 19		09 49				10 19			10 49				11 19
Kirkhill d				08 36			09 09				09 22		09 52				10 22			10 52				11 22
Burnside d				08 39			09 12				09 25		09 55				10 25			10 55				11 25
Croftfoot d				08 42			09 14				09 27		09 57				10 27			10 57				11 27
Kings Park d				08 44			09 16				09 29		09 59				10 29			10 59				11 29
Neilston d		08 24			08 43			09 05				09 28			09 58			10 28				10 58		
Patterton d		08 30			08 49			09 11				09 34			10 04			10 34				11 04		
Whitecraigs d		08 33			08 51			09 13				09 36			10 06			10 36				11 06		
Williamwood d		08 35			08 53			09 15				09 38			10 08			10 38				11 08		
Muirend d		08 38			08 56			09 18				09 41			10 11			10 41				11 11		
Cathcart d	08 33	08 42	08 50		09 00	09 04		09 21		09 32		09 44		10 04	10 14	10 31		10 44			11 04	11 14	11 31	
Mount Florida d		08 44	08 52		09 02		09 20	09 23		09 34		09 46	10 03		10 16	10 33		10 46		11 03		11 16	11 33	
Crosshill d		08 46	08 54		09 04		09 22	09 25		09 36		09 48	10 05		10 18	10 35		10 48		11 05		11 18	11 35	
Queens Park d		08 49	08 56		09 06		09 24	09 27		09 38		09 50	10 07		10 20	10 37		10 50		11 07		11 20	11 37	
Pollokshields East d		08 51	08 58		09 07		09 25	09 29		09 39		09 52	10 08		10 22	10 39		10 52		11 08		11 22	11 39	
Langside d	08 36			08 49		09 07					09 34			10 06			10 34				11 06			11 34
Pollokshaws East d	08 38			08 51		09 09					09 36			10 08			10 36				11 08			11 36
Shawlands d	08 40			08 54		09 11					09 38			10 10			10 38				11 10			11 38
Maxwell Park d	08 42			08 56		09 13					09 40			10 12			10 40				11 12			11 40
Pollokshields West d	08 44			09 00		09 15					09 43			10 14			10 42				11 14			11 42
Glasgow Central 15 226 a	08 52	08 56	09 03	09 06	09 12	09 22	09 30	09 35		09 44	09 49	09 57	10 13	10 21	10 27	10 44	10 51	10 57		11 13	11 21	11 27	11 44	11 49

	SR	SR	SR A	SR		SR A	SR	SR	SR	SR A	SR	SR A	SR	SR		SR	SR A	SR	SR A	SR	SR	SR	SR A	SR
Newton 226 d		11 49					12 19		12 49				13 19			13 49				14 19		14 49		
Kirkhill d		11 52					12 22		12 52				13 22			13 52				14 22		14 52		
Burnside d		11 55					12 25		12 55				13 25			13 55				14 25		14 55		
Croftfoot d		11 57					12 27		12 57				13 27			13 57				14 27		14 57		
Kings Park d		11 59					12 29		12 59				13 29			13 59				14 30		14 59		
Neilston d	11 28			11 58				12 28			12 58			13 28				13 58			14 28			14 58
Patterton d	11 34			12 04				12 34			13 04			13 34				14 04			14 34			15 04
Whitecraigs d	11 36			12 06				12 36			13 06			13 36				14 06			14 36			15 06
Williamwood d	11 38			12 08				12 38			13 08			13 38				14 08			14 38			15 08
Muirend d	11 41			12 11				12 41			13 11			13 41				14 11			14 41			15 11
Cathcart d	11 44		12 04	12 14		12 31		12 44		13 04	13 14	13 31		13 44			14 04	14 14	14 31		14 44		15 04	15 14
Mount Florida d	11 46	12 03		12 16		12 33		12 46	13 03		13 16	13 33		13 46		14 03		14 16	14 33		14 46	15 03		15 16
Crosshill d	11 48	12 05		12 18		12 35		12 48	13 05		13 18	13 35		13 48		14 05		14 18	14 35		14 48	15 05		15 18
Queens Park d	11 50	12 07		12 20		12 37		12 50	13 07		13 20	13 37		13 50		14 07		14 20	14 37		14 50	15 07		15 20
Pollokshields East d	11 52	12 08		12 22		12 39		12 52	13 08		13 22	13 39		13 52		14 08		14 22	14 39		14 52	15 08		15 22
Langside d			12 06				12 34			13 06			13 34				14 06			14 35			15 06	
Pollokshaws East d			12 08				12 36			13 08			13 36				14 08			14 37			15 08	
Shawlands d			12 10				12 38			13 10			13 38				14 10			14 39			15 10	
Maxwell Park d			12 12				12 40			13 12			13 40				14 12			14 41			15 12	
Pollokshields West d			12 14				12 42			13 14			13 42				14 14			14 43			15 14	
Glasgow Central 15 226 a	11 57	12 13	12 21	12 27		12 44	12 50	12 57	13 13	13 21	13 27	13 44	13 49	13 57		14 13	14 21	14 27	14 44	14 51	14 57	15 13	15 24	15 27

		SR A	SR	SR	SR	SR A	SR	SR A	SR	SR		SR	SR A	SR	SR A	SR	SR	SR A	SR	SR		SR A	SR	SR
Newton 226 d			15 19		15 49				16 19			16 49					17 19			17 49				
Kirkhill d			15 22		15 52				16 22			16 52					17 22			17 52				
Burnside d			15 25		15 55				16 25			16 55					17 25			17 55				
Croftfoot d			15 27		15 57				16 27			16 57					17 27			17 57				
Kings Park d			15 29		15 59				16 29			16 59					17 31			17 59				
Neilston d				15 28			15 58			16 28				16 55		17 14			17 41				17 56	18 06
Patterton d				15 34			16 04			16 34				17 01		17 20			17 47				18 02	18 12
Whitecraigs d				15 36			16 06			16 36				17 03		17 22			17 50				18 04	18 14
Williamwood d				15 38			16 08			16 38				17 05		17 24			17 52				18 06	18 16
Muirend d				15 41			16 11			16 41				17 08		17 27			17 55				18 09	18 19
Cathcart d		15 31		15 44		16 07	16 14	16 31		16 44			17 04	17 12	17 23	17 30		17 41	17 58			18 04	18 12	18 22
Mount Florida d		15 33		15 46	16 03		16 16	16 33		16 46		17 03		17 14	17 25	17 32		17 43	18 00	18 03			18 14	18 24
Crosshill d		15 35		15 48	16 05		16 18	16 35		16 48		17 05		17 16	17 27	17 34		17 45	18 02	18 05			18 16	18 26
Queens Park d		15 37		15 50	16 07		16 20	16 37		16 50		17 07		17 18	17 29	17 36		17 47	18 04	18 07			18 18	18 28
Pollokshields East d		15 39		15 52	16 08		16 22	16 39		16 52		17 12		17 19	17 33	17 38		17 50	18 05	18 09			18 20	18 30
Langside d			15 34			16 10			16 34				17 06				17 35					18 06		
Pollokshaws East d			15 36			16 12			16 36				17 08				17 37					18 08		
Shawlands d			15 38			16 14			16 38				17 10				17 39					18 10		
Maxwell Park d			15 40			16 16			16 40				17 12				17 41					18 12		
Pollokshields West d			15 43			16 18			16 43				17 14				17 43					18 14		
Glasgow Central 15 226 a		15 44	15 51	15 57	16 13	16 24	16 27	16 44	16 53	16 57		17 17	17 22	17 24	17 39	17 43	17 49	17 56	18 10	18 14		18 20	18 25	18 35

A From Glasgow Central

Table T223-F

Mondays to Fridays
16 December to 15 May

Newton, Neilston, Cathcart Circle and Glasgow Central

	SR A	SR	SR	SR	SR A	SR		SR A	SR	SR	SR	SR A	SR	SR A	SR	SR		SR	SR A	SR	SR A	SR	SR	SR
Newton 226 d		18 19		18 49					19 19		19 49				20 19			20 49				21 19		21 49
Kirkhill d		18 22		18 52					19 22		19 52				20 22			20 52				21 23		21 52
Burnside d		18 25		18 55					19 25		19 55				20 25			20 55				21 26		21 55
Croftfoot d		18 27		18 58					19 27		19 57				20 27			20 57				21 28		21 57
Kings Park d		18 29		19 00					19 29		19 59				20 29			20 59				21 30		21 59
Neilston d			18 28			18 58				19 28			19 58			20 28				20 58			21 28	
Patterton d			18 34			19 04				19 34			20 04			20 34				21 04			21 34	
Whitecraigs d			18 36			19 06				19 36			20 06			20 36				21 06			21 36	
Williamwood d			18 38			19 08				19 38			20 08			20 38				21 08			21 38	
Muirend d			18 41			19 11				19 41			20 11			20 41				21 11			21 41	
Cathcart d	18 31		18 44		19 05	19 14		19 31		19 44		20 04	20 14	20 31		20 44			21 04	21 14	21 31		21 44	
Mount Florida d	18 33		18 46	19 03		19 16		19 33		19 46	20 03		20 16	20 33		20 46		21 03		21 16	21 33		21 46	22 03
Crosshill d	18 35		18 48	19 05		19 18		19 35		19 48	20 05		20 18	20 35		20 48		21 05		21 18	21 35		21 48	22 05
Queens Park d	18 37		18 50	19 07		19 20		19 37		19 50	20 07		20 20	20 37		20 50		21 07		21 20	21 37		21 50	22 07
Pollokshields East d	18 39		18 52	19 09		19 22		19 39		19 52	20 10		20 22	20 39		20 52		21 10		21 22	21 39		21 52	22 08
Langside d		18 34			19 07				19 34			20 07			20 34				21 06			21 35		
Pollokshaws East d		18 36			19 09				19 36			20 09			20 36				21 08			21 37		
Shawlands d		18 38			19 11				19 38			20 11			20 38				21 10			21 39		
Maxwell Park d		18 40			19 13				19 40			20 13			20 40				21 12			21 41		
Pollokshields West d		18 43			19 15				19 43			20 15			20 43				21 14			21 44		
Glasgow Central 15 226 a	18 44	18 51	18 57	19 14	19 21	19 27		19 44	19 51	19 57	20 15	20 22	20 27	20 45	20 51	20 57		21 15	21 21	21 27	21 44	21 51	21 57	22 13

	SR A	SR		SR A	SR	SR	SR	SR A	SR	SR A	SR	SR
Newton 226 d					22 19		22 49				23 19	
Kirkhill d					22 22		22 52				23 22	
Burnside d					22 25		22 55				23 25	
Croftfoot d					22 27		22 57				23 27	
Kings Park d					22 29		22 59				23 29	
Neilston d		21 58				22 28			22 58			23 28
Patterton d		22 04				22 34			23 04			23 34
Whitecraigs d		22 06				22 36			23 06			23 36
Williamwood d		22 08				22 38			23 08			23 38
Muirend d		22 11				22 41			23 11			23 41
Cathcart d	22 04	22 14		22 31		22 44		23 04	23 14	23 31		23 44
Mount Florida d		22 16		22 33		22 46	23 03		23 16	23 33		23 46
Crosshill d		22 18		22 35		22 48	23 05		23 18	23 35		23 48
Queens Park d		22 20		22 37		22 50	23 07		23 20	23 37		23 50
Pollokshields East d		22 22		22 39		22 52	23 09		23 22	23 39		23 52
Langside d	22 06				22 34			23 06			23 34	
Pollokshaws East d	22 08				22 36			23 08			23 36	
Shawlands d	22 10				22 38			23 10			23 38	
Maxwell Park d	22 12				22 40			23 12			23 40	
Pollokshields West d	22 14				22 43			23 14			23 43	
Glasgow Central 15 226 a	22 20	22 27		22 44	22 49	22 57	23 15	23 20	23 27	23 44	23 50	23 57

Saturdays
21 December to 16 May

	SR A	SR A	SR	SR	SR	SR	SR	SR	SR		SR	SR	SR	SR	SR A	SR	SR A	SR	SR		SR	SR A	SR	SR A
Newton 226 d			06 24		06 49		07 20		07 49			08 20		08 49				09 19			09 49			
Kirkhill d			06 27		06 52		07 23		07 52			08 23		08 52				09 22			09 52			
Burnside d			06 30		06 55		07 26		07 55			08 26		08 55				09 25			09 55			
Croftfoot d			06 32		06 57		07 28		07 57			08 28		08 57				09 27			09 57			
Kings Park d			06 34		06 59		07 30		07 59			08 30		08 59				09 29			09 59			
Neilston d				06 29		07 01		07 28			07 58		08 28			08 58			09 28				09 58	
Patterton d				06 35		07 07		07 34			08 04		08 34			09 04			09 34				10 04	
Whitecraigs d				06 37		07 09		07 36			08 06		08 36			09 06			09 36				10 06	
Williamwood d				06 39		07 11		07 38			08 08		08 38			09 08			09 38				10 08	
Muirend d				06 42		07 14		07 41			08 11		08 41			09 11			09 41				10 11	
Cathcart d	00 37	06 31		06 45		07 17		07 44			08 14		08 44		09 04	09 14	09 32		09 44			10 04	10 14	10 31
Mount Florida d	00 39	06 33		06 47	07 03	07 19		07 46	08 03		08 16		08 46	09 03		09 16	09 34		09 46		10 03		10 16	10 33
Crosshill d	00 41	06 35		06 49	07 05	07 21		07 48	08 05		08 18		08 48	09 05		09 18	09 36		09 48		10 05		10 18	10 35
Queens Park d	00 43	06 37		06 51	07 07	07 23		07 50	08 07		08 20		08 50	09 07		09 20	09 38		09 50		10 07		10 20	10 37
Pollokshields East d	00 44	06 38		06 53	07 08	07 25		07 52	08 08		08 22		08 52	09 08		09 22	09 39		09 52		10 08		10 22	10 39
Langside d			06 38				07 35					08 34			09 06			09 34				10 06		
Pollokshaws East d			06 40				07 37					08 36			09 08			09 36				10 08		
Shawlands d			06 42				07 39					08 38			09 10			09 38				10 10		
Maxwell Park d			06 44				07 41					08 40			09 12			09 40				10 12		
Pollokshields West d			06 48				07 43					08 43			09 14			09 43				10 14		
Glasgow Central 15 226 a	00 49	06 43	06 54	06 58	07 13	07 30	07 49	07 57	08 13		08 27	08 49	08 57	09 13	09 21	09 27	09 44	09 49	09 57		10 13	10 21	10 27	10 44

A From Glasgow Central

Table T223-F

Newton, Neilston, Cathcart Circle and Glasgow Central

Saturdays

21 December to 16 May

Station	SR	SR	SR	SR A	SR	SR A	SR	SR	SR	SR A	SR	SR A	SR	SR	SR	SR A	SR	SR A	SR	SR	SR
Newton 226 d	10 19		10 49				11 19		11 49				12 19		12 49				13 19		13 49
Kirkhill d	10 22		10 52				11 22		11 52				12 22		12 52				13 22		13 52
Burnside d	10 25		10 55				11 25		11 55				12 25		12 55				13 25		13 55
Croftfoot d	10 27		10 57				11 27		11 57				12 27		12 57				13 27		13 57
Kings Park d	10 29		10 59				11 29		11 59				12 29		12 59				13 29		13 59
Neilston d		10 28			10 58			11 28			11 58			12 28			12 58			13 28	
Patterton d		10 34			11 04			11 34			12 04			12 34			13 04			13 34	
Whitecraigs d		10 36			11 06			11 36			12 06			12 36			13 06			13 36	
Williamwood d		10 38			11 08			11 38			12 08			12 38			13 08			13 38	
Muirend d		10 41			11 11			11 41			12 11			12 41			13 11			13 41	
Cathcart d		10 44		11 04	11 14	11 31		11 44		12 04	12 14	12 31		12 44		13 04	13 14	13 31		13 44	
Mount Florida d		10 46	11 03		11 16	11 33		11 46	12 03		12 16	12 33		12 46	13 03		13 16	13 33		13 46	14 03
Crosshill d		10 48	11 05		11 18	11 35		11 48	12 05		12 18	12 35		12 48	13 05		13 18	13 35		13 48	14 05
Queens Park d		10 50	11 07		11 20	11 37		11 50	12 07		12 20	12 37		12 50	13 07		13 20	13 37		13 50	14 07
Pollokshields East d		10 52	11 08		11 22	11 39		11 52	12 08		12 22	12 39		12 52	13 08		13 22	13 39		13 52	14 08
Langside d	10 34			11 06			11 34			12 06			12 34			13 06			13 34		
Pollokshaws East d	10 36			11 08			11 36			12 08			12 36			13 08			13 36		
Shawlands d	10 38			11 10			11 38			12 10			12 38			13 10			13 38		
Maxwell Park d	10 40			11 12			11 40			12 12			12 40			13 12			13 40		
Pollokshields West d	10 42			11 14			11 42			12 14			12 42			13 14			13 42		
Glasgow Central 15 226 a	10 51	10 57	11 13	11 21	11 27	11 44	11 49	11 57	12 13	12 21	12 27	12 44	12 50	12 57	13 13	13 21	13 27	13 44	13 49	13 57	14 13

Station	SR A	SR	SR A	SR	SR	SR	SR A	SR	SR A	SR	SR	SR	SR A	SR	SR A	SR	SR	SR	SR A	SR	SR A	SR
Newton 226 d				14 19		14 49				15 19		15 49				16 19		16 49				17 19
Kirkhill d				14 22		14 52				15 22		15 52				16 22		16 52				17 22
Burnside d				14 25		14 55				15 25		15 55				16 25		16 55				17 25
Croftfoot d				14 27		14 57				15 27		15 57				16 27		16 57				17 27
Kings Park d				14 30		14 59				15 29		15 59				16 29		16 59				17 31
Neilston d		13 58			14 28			14 58			15 28			15 58			16 29			16 58		
Patterton d		14 04			14 34			15 04			15 34			16 04			16 35			17 04		
Whitecraigs d		14 06			14 36			15 06			15 36			16 06			16 37			17 06		
Williamwood d		14 08			14 38			15 08			15 38			16 08			16 39			17 08		
Muirend d		14 11			14 41			15 11			15 41			16 11			16 42			17 11		
Cathcart d	14 04	14 14	14 31		14 44		15 04	15 14	15 31		15 44		16 03	16 14	16 31		16 45		17 04	17 14	17 31	
Mount Florida d		14 16	14 33		14 46	15 03		15 16	15 33		15 46	16 03		16 16	16 33		16 47	17 03		17 16	17 33	
Crosshill d		14 18	14 35		14 48	15 05		15 18	15 35		15 48	16 05		16 18	16 35		16 49	17 05		17 18	17 35	
Queens Park d		14 20	14 37		14 50	15 07		15 20	15 37		15 50	16 07		16 20	16 37		16 51	17 07		17 20	17 37	
Pollokshields East d		14 22	14 39		14 52	15 08		15 22	15 39		15 52	16 08		16 22	16 39		16 53	17 08		17 22	17 39	
Langside d	14 06			14 35			15 06			15 34			16 06			16 34			17 06			17 35
Pollokshaws East d	14 08			14 37			15 08			15 36			16 08			16 36			17 08			17 37
Shawlands d	14 10			14 39			15 10			15 38			16 10			16 38			17 10			17 39
Maxwell Park d	14 12			14 41			15 12			15 40			16 12			16 40			17 12			17 41
Pollokshields West d	14 14			14 43			15 14			15 43			16 14			16 43			17 15			17 43
Glasgow Central 15 226 a	14 21	14 27	14 44	14 49	14 57	15 14	15 20	15 27	15 44	15 49	15 57	16 13	16 21	16 27	16 45	16 50	16 58	17 14	17 22	17 27	17 44	17 49

Station	SR	SR	SR A	SR	SR A	SR	SR	SR	SR A	SR	SR A	SR	SR	SR	SR A	SR	SR A	SR	SR	SR	SR A
Newton 226 d		17 49				18 19		18 49				19 19		19 49				20 19		20 49	
Kirkhill d		17 52				18 22		18 52				19 22		19 52				20 22		20 52	
Burnside d		17 55				18 25		18 55				19 25		19 55				20 25		20 55	
Croftfoot d		17 57				18 27		18 58				19 27		19 57				20 27		20 57	
Kings Park d		17 59				18 29		19 00				19 29		19 59				20 29		20 59	
Neilston d	17 28			17 58			18 28			18 58			19 28			19 58			20 28		
Patterton d	17 34			18 04			18 34			19 04			19 34			20 04			20 34		
Whitecraigs d	17 36			18 06			18 36			19 06			19 36			20 06			20 36		
Williamwood d	17 38			18 08			18 38			19 08			19 38			20 08			20 38		
Muirend d	17 41			18 11			18 41			19 11			19 41			20 11			20 41		
Cathcart d	17 44		18 04	18 14	18 31		18 44		19 05	19 14	19 31		19 44		20 04	20 14	20 31		20 44		21 04
Mount Florida d	17 46	18 03		18 16	18 33		18 46	19 03		19 16	19 33		19 46	20 03		20 16	20 33		20 46	21 03	
Crosshill d	17 48	18 05		18 18	18 35		18 48	19 05		19 18	19 35		19 48	20 05		20 18	20 35		20 48	21 05	
Queens Park d	17 50	18 07		18 20	18 37		18 50	19 07		19 20	19 37		19 50	20 07		20 20	20 37		20 50	21 07	
Pollokshields East d	17 52	18 08		18 22	18 39		18 52	19 09		19 22	19 39		19 52	20 10		20 22	20 39		20 52	21 09	
Langside d			18 06			18 34			19 07			19 34			20 06			20 34			21 06
Pollokshaws East d			18 08			18 36			19 09			19 36			20 08			20 36			21 08
Shawlands d			18 10			18 38			19 11			19 38			20 10			20 38			21 10
Maxwell Park d			18 12			18 40			19 13			19 40			20 12			20 40			21 12
Pollokshields West d			18 14			18 43			19 15			19 43			20 14			20 43			21 14
Glasgow Central 15 226 a	17 57	18 13	18 21	18 27	18 44	18 51	18 57	19 15	19 22	19 27	19 44	19 51	19 57	20 15	20 20	20 27	20 44	20 49	20 57	21 15	21 20

Station	SR	SR A	SR	SR	SR	SR A	SR	SR A	SR	SR	SR	SR A	SR	SR A	SR	SR
Newton 226 d			21 19		21 49				22 19		22 49				23 19	
Kirkhill d			21 23		21 52				22 22		22 52				23 22	
Burnside d			21 26		21 55				22 25		22 55				23 25	
Croftfoot d			21 28		21 57				22 27		22 57				23 27	
Kings Park d			21 30		21 59				22 29		22 59				23 29	
Neilston d	20 58			21 28			21 58			22 28			22 58			23 28
Patterton d	21 04			21 34			22 04			22 34			23 04			23 34
Whitecraigs d	21 06			21 36			22 06			22 36			23 06			23 36
Williamwood d	21 08			21 38			22 08			22 38			23 08			23 38
Muirend d	21 11			21 41			22 11			22 41			23 11			23 41
Cathcart d	21 14	21 31		21 44		22 04	22 14	22 31		22 44		23 04	23 14	23 31		23 44
Mount Florida d	21 16	21 33		21 46	22 03		22 16	22 33		22 46	23 03		23 16	23 33		23 46
Crosshill d	21 18	21 35		21 48	22 05		22 18	22 35		22 48	23 05		23 18	23 35		23 48
Queens Park d	21 20	21 37		21 50	22 07		22 20	22 37		22 50	23 07		23 20	23 37		23 50
Pollokshields East d	21 22	21 39		21 52	22 08		22 22	22 39		22 52	23 08		23 22	23 39		23 52
Langside d			21 35			22 06			22 34			23 06			23 34	
Pollokshaws East d			21 37			22 08			22 36			23 08			23 36	
Shawlands d			21 39			22 10			22 38			23 10			23 38	
Maxwell Park d			21 41			22 12			22 40			23 12			23 40	
Pollokshields West d			21 44			22 14			22 43			23 14			23 43	
Glasgow Central 15 226 a	21 27	21 44	21 51	21 57	22 13	22 25	22 27	22 44	22 49	22 57	23 13	23 20	23 27	23 44	23 50	23 57

A From Glasgow Central

Table T223-F

Newton, Neilston, Cathcart Circle and Glasgow Central

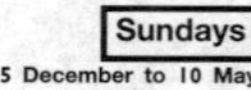

Sundays

15 December to 10 May

Station	SR	SR	SR	SR		SR	SR	SR	SR	SR	SR	SR	SR	SR	SR	SR	SR	SR	SR	SR	SR
Newton 226 d		09 09		09 39			13 09		13 39		14 09		14 39		15 09		15 39		16 09		16 39
Kirkhill d		09 12		09 42			13 12		13 42		14 12		14 42		15 12		15 42		16 12		16 42
Burnside d		09 15		09 45			13 15		13 45		14 15		14 45		15 15		15 45		16 15		16 45
Croftfoot d		09 17		09 47			13 17		13 47		14 17		14 47		15 17		15 47		16 17		16 47
Kings Park d		09 19		09 49			13 19		13 49		14 19		14 49		15 19		15 49		16 19		16 49
Neilston d	08 48		09 19			12 48		13 19		13 48		14 19		14 48		15 19		15 48		16 19	
Patterton d	08 54		09 25		and at the same minutes past each hour until	12 54		13 25		13 54		14 25		14 54		15 25		15 54		16 25	
Whitecraigs d	08 56		09 27			12 56		13 27		13 56		14 27		14 56		15 27		15 56		16 27	
Williamwood d	08 58		09 29			12 58		13 29		13 58		14 29		14 58		15 29		15 58		16 29	
Muirend d	09 01		09 32			13 01		13 32		14 01		14 32		15 01		15 32		16 01		16 32	
Cathcart d	09 05		09 36			13 05		13 36		14 07		14 35		15 05		15 36		16 05		16 35	
Mount Florida d	09 07		09 38	09 53		13 07		13 38	13 53	14 10		14 37	14 53	15 07		15 38	15 53	16 07		16 37	16 53
Crosshill d	09 09		09 40	09 55		13 09		13 40	13 55	14 12		14 39	14 55	15 09		15 40	15 55	16 09		16 39	16 55
Queens Park d	09 11		09 42	09 57		13 11		13 42	13 57	14 14		14 41	14 57	15 11		15 42	15 57	16 11		16 41	16 57
Pollokshields East d	09 12		09 43	09 58		13 12		13 43	13 58	14 16		14 43	14 58	15 12		15 43	15 58	16 12		16 43	16 58
Langside d		09 23					13 23				14 23				15 23				16 23		
Pollokshaws East d		09 25					13 25				14 25				15 25				16 25		
Shawlands d		09 27					13 27				14 27				15 27				16 27		
Maxwell Park d		09 29					13 29				14 29				15 29				16 29		
Pollokshields West d		09 32					13 32				14 32				15 32				16 32		
Glasgow Central 15 226 a	09 17	09 38	09 48	10 03		13 17	13 38	13 48	14 03	14 21	14 38	14 48	15 03	15 17	15 38	15 48	16 03	16 17	16 38	16 49	17 03

Station	SR	SR	SR	SR	SR	SR	SR	SR	SR	SR	SR	SR	SR	SR	SR	SR	SR	SR	SR	SR	SR	SR
Newton 226 d		17 09		17 39		18 09		18 39		19 09		19 39		20 09		20 39		21 09		21 39		22 09
Kirkhill d		17 12		17 42		18 12		18 42		19 12		19 42		20 12		20 42		21 12		21 42		22 12
Burnside d		17 15		17 45		18 15		18 45		19 15		19 45		20 15		20 45		21 15		21 45		22 15
Croftfoot d		17 17		17 47		18 17		18 47		19 17		19 47		20 17		20 47		21 17		21 47		22 17
Kings Park d		17 19		17 49		18 19		18 49		19 19		19 49		20 19		20 49		21 19		21 49		22 19
Neilston d	16 44		17 19		17 48		18 19		18 48		19 19		19 48		20 19		20 48		21 19		21 48	
Patterton d	16 50		17 25		17 54		18 25		18 54		19 25		19 54		20 25		20 54		21 25		21 54	
Whitecraigs d	16 52		17 27		17 56		18 27		18 56		19 27		19 56		20 27		20 56		21 27		21 56	
Williamwood d	16 54		17 29		17 58		18 29		18 58		19 29		19 58		20 29		20 58		21 29		21 58	
Muirend d	16 57		17 32		18 01		18 32		19 01		19 32		20 01		20 32		21 01		21 32		22 01	
Cathcart d	17 00		17 36		18 04		18 36		19 05		19 36		20 05		20 36		21 04		21 36		22 05	
Mount Florida d	17 02		17 38	17 53	18 06		18 38	18 53	19 07		19 38	19 53	20 07		20 38	20 53	21 08		21 38	21 53	22 09	
Crosshill d	17 04		17 40	17 55	18 08		18 40	18 55	19 09		19 40	19 55	20 09		20 40	20 55	21 10		21 40	21 55	22 11	
Queens Park d	17 06		17 42	17 57	18 10		18 42	18 57	19 11		19 42	19 57	20 11		20 42	20 57	21 12		21 42	21 57	22 13	
Pollokshields East d	17 08		17 43	17 58	18 12		18 43	18 58	19 12		19 43	19 58	20 12		20 43	20 58	21 14		21 43	21 58	22 14	
Langside d		17 23				18 23				19 23				20 23				21 23				22 23
Pollokshaws East d		17 25				18 25				19 25				20 25				21 25				22 25
Shawlands d		17 27				18 27				19 27				20 27				21 27				22 27
Maxwell Park d		17 29				18 29				19 29				20 29				21 29				22 29
Pollokshields West d		17 32				18 32				19 32				20 32				21 31				22 31
Glasgow Central 15 226 a	17 13	17 38	17 48	18 03	18 17	18 38	18 48	19 04	19 17	19 38	19 48	20 03	20 17	20 38	20 48	21 03	21 19	21 37	21 48	22 03	22 19	22 37

Station	SR	SR	SR	SR	SR
Newton 226 d		22 39		23 09	
Kirkhill d		22 42		23 12	
Burnside d		22 45		23 15	
Croftfoot d		22 47		23 17	
Kings Park d		22 49		23 19	
Neilston d	22 19		22 48		23 19
Patterton d	22 25		22 54		23 25
Whitecraigs d	22 27		22 56		23 27
Williamwood d	22 29		22 58		23 29
Muirend d	22 32		23 01		23 32
Cathcart d	22 36		23 06		23 36
Mount Florida d	22 39	22 53	23 10		23 38
Crosshill d	22 41	22 55	23 12		23 40
Queens Park d	22 43	22 57	23 14		23 42
Pollokshields East d	22 45	22 58	23 15		23 43
Langside d				23 23	
Pollokshaws East d				23 25	
Shawlands d				23 27	
Maxwell Park d				23 29	
Pollokshields West d				23 31	
Glasgow Central 15 226 a	22 50	23 03	23 20	23 37	23 48

Table T223-R

Mondays to Fridays
16 December to 15 May

Glasgow Central, Cathcart Circle, Neilston and Newton

Miles	Miles	Miles			SR A	SR	SR	SR	SR	SR A	SR	SR	SR	SR A	SR	SR	SR A	SR	SR	SR A	SR	SR	SR A
0	0	0	**Glasgow Central** 15 226	d	06 14	06 17	06 20	06 34	06 36	06 50	06 58	07 03	07 05	07 17	07 21	07 26	07 32	07 45	07 50	07 54	07 57	08 02	08 11
2¼	—	—	Pollokshields West	d	06 20				06 42			07 09		07 23				07 51		08 00			08 17
2¾	—	—	Maxwell Park	d	06 22				06 44			07 11		07 25				07 53		08 02			08 19
3½	—	—	Shawlands	d	06 24				06 46			07 13		07 27				07 55		08 04			08 21
3¾	—	—	Pollokshaws East	d	06 25				06 48			07 14		07 29				07 57		08 05			08 22
4¼	—	—	Langside	d	06 27				06 50			07 16		07 31				07 59		08 07			08 24
—	1¾	1¾	Pollokshields East	d		06 22	06 25	06 39		06 55	07 03		07 10		07 26	07 31	07 37				08 02	08 07	
—	2¼	2¼	Queens Park	d		06 23	06 27	06 40		06 56	07 04		07 11		07 27	07 33	07 38				08 03	08 08	
—	2½	2½	Crosshill	d		06 25	06 29	06 42		06 58	07 06		07 13		07 29	07 35	07 40				08 05	08 10	
—	3¼	3¼	Mount Florida	d		06 27	06 31	06 44		07 00	07 08		07 15		07 31	07 37	07 43				08 07	08 12	
5¼	—	4	Cathcart	d	06a30	06 29		06 46		07a02	07 10		07 20	07a34		07 39	07a45			08a11		08 14	08a27
—	—	4¾	Muirend	d		06 32		06 49			07 13		07 23			07 41			08 00			08 17	
—	—	6	Williamwood	d		06 35		06 52			07 16		07 26			07 44			08 03			08 20	
—	—	6¾	Whitecraigs	d		06 37		06 54			07 18		07 28			07 47			08 05			08 22	
—	—	7¾	Patterton	d		06 40		06 57			07 21		07 31			07 49			08 08			08 25	
—	—	11¾	**Neilston**	a		06 46		07 03			07 27		07 38			07 56			08 14			08 31	
5¾	4½	—	Kings Park	d			06 34		06 54			07 20			07 34			08 05			08 10		
6	4¾	—	Croftfoot	d			06 36		06 57			07 22			07 36			08 07			08 12		
7	5¼	—	Burnside	d			06 38		07 00			07 25			07 39			08 09			08 15		
8½	7¼	—	Kirkhill	a			06 41		07 03			07 28			07 42			08 12			08 18		
10	8¾	—	**Newton** 226	a			06 44		07 06			07 31			07 45			08 15			08 21		

		SR A	SR A	SR	SR	SR A	SR	SR	SR A	SR	SR A	SR	SR	SR	SR A	SR	SR A	SR	SR	SR	SR A	SR	
Glasgow Central 15 226	d	08 13	08 18	08 20	08 26	08 33	08 42	08 46	08 51	09 05	09 16	09 20	09 36	09 45	09 51	10 06	10 15	10 20	10 35	10 45	10 51	11 05	
Pollokshields West	d					08 40		08 52			09 22			09 51			10 21			10 51			
Maxwell Park	d					08 42		08 54			09 24			09 53			10 23			10 53			
Shawlands	d					08 44		08 56			09 26			09 55			10 25			10 55			
Pollokshaws East	d					08 45		08 57			09 27			09 56			10 26			10 56			
Langside	d					08 47		09 00			09 29			09 58			10 28			10 58			
Pollokshields East	d	08 18	08 23	08 26	08 31		08 47		08 57	09 10		09 25	09 41		09 56	10 11		10 25	10 40		10 56	11 10	and at the same minutes past each hour until
Queens Park	d	08 19	08 24	08 28	08 32		08 48		08 58	09 11		09 26	09 42		09 57	10 12		10 26	10 41		10 57	11 11	
Crosshill	d	08 21	08 26	08 30	08 34		08 50		09 00	09 13		09 28	09 44		09 59	10 14		10 28	10 43		10 59	11 13	
Mount Florida	d	08 23	08 28	08 32	08 36		08 52		09 02	09 15		09 30	09 46		10 01	10 16		10 30	10 45		11 01	11 15	
Cathcart	d	08a25	08a30		08 38	08a50	08 54		09a04	09 17	09a32		09 48		10a04	10 18	10a31		10 47		11a04	11 17	
Muirend	d				08 41		08 57			09 20			09 51			10 21			10 50			11 20	
Williamwood	d				08 44		09 00			09 23			09 54			10 24			10 53			11 23	
Whitecraigs	d				08 46		09 02			09 25			09 56			10 26			10 55			11 25	
Patterton	d				08 49		09 05			09 28			09 59			10 29			10 58			11 28	
Neilston	a				08 55		09 11			09 34			10 05			10 35			11 04			11 34	
Kings Park	d			08 35				09 04				09 34		10 04				10 34		11 04			
Croftfoot	d			08 37				09 06				09 36		10 06				10 36		11 06			
Burnside	d			08 39				09 08				09 38		10 08				10 38		11 08			
Kirkhill	a			08 42				09 11				09 41		10 11				10 41		11 11			
Newton 226	a			08 45				09 14				09 44		10 14				10 44		11 14			

		SR A	SR	SR	SR	SR A	SR	SR A	SR	SR	SR	SR A	SR	SR A	SR	SR	SR	SR A	SR	SR A	SR	SR	SR
Glasgow Central 15 226	d	13 15	13 20	13 35	13 45	13 51	14 05	14 15	14 20	14 35	14 45	14 51	15 06	15 15	15 20	15 35	15 45	15 51	16 07	16 15	16 20	16 35	16 45
Pollokshields West	d	13 21			13 51			14 21			14 51			15 21			15 51			16 21			16 51
Maxwell Park	d	13 23			13 53			14 23			14 53			15 23			15 53			16 23			16 53
Shawlands	d	13 25			13 55			14 25			14 55			15 25			15 55			16 25			16 55
Pollokshaws East	d	13 26			13 56			14 26			14 56			15 26			15 56			16 26			16 56
Langside	d	13 28			13 58			14 28			14 58			15 28			15 58			16 28			16 58
Pollokshields East	d		13 25	13 40		13 56	14 10		14 25	14 40		14 56	15 11		15 25	15 40		15 56	16 12		16 25	16 40	
Queens Park	d		13 26	13 41		13 57	14 11		14 26	14 41		14 57	15 12		15 26	15 41		15 57	16 13		16 27	16 41	
Crosshill	d		13 28	13 43		13 59	14 13		14 28	14 43		14 59	15 14		15 28	15 43		16 03	16 15		16 29	16 43	
Mount Florida	d		13 30	13 45		14 01	14 15		14 30	14 45		15 01	15 16		15 30	15 45		16 05	16 17		16 31	16 45	
Cathcart	d	13a31		13 47		14a04	14 17	14a31		14 47		15a04	15 18	15a31		15 47		16a07	16 19	16a31		16 47	
Muirend	d			13 50			14 20			14 50			15 21			15 50			16 22			16 50	
Williamwood	d			13 53			14 23			14 53			15 24			15 53			16 25			16 53	
Whitecraigs	d			13 55			14 25			14 55			15 26			15 55			16 27			16 55	
Patterton	d			13 58			14 28			14 58			15 29			15 58			16 30			16 58	
Neilston	a			14 04			14 34			15 04			15 35			16 04			16 36			17 04	
Kings Park	d		13 34		14 04				14 34		15 04				15 34		16 04				16 34		17 04
Croftfoot	d		13 36		14 06				14 36		15 06				15 36		16 06				16 36		17 06
Burnside	d		13 38		14 08				14 38		15 08				15 38		16 08				16 38		17 08
Kirkhill	a		13 41		14 11				14 41		15 11				15 41		16 11				16 41		17 11
Newton 226	a		13 44		14 14				14 44		15 14				15 44		16 14				16 44		17 14

		SR A	SR	SR A	SR	SR	SR A	SR	SR	SR	SR	SR A	SR	SR A	SR	SR	SR	SR A	SR	SR A	SR	SR
Glasgow Central 15 226	d	16 51	17 03	17 06	17 11	17 18	17 23	17 25	17 31	17 37	17 45	17 50	18 06	18 15	18 21	18 35	18 45	18 52	19 05	19 15	19 20	19 35
Pollokshields West	d			17 13			17 30				17 51			18 21			18 51			19 21		
Maxwell Park	d			17 15			17 32				17 53			18 23			18 53			19 23		
Shawlands	d			17 17			17 34				17 55			18 25			18 55			19 25		
Pollokshaws East	d			17 19			17 35				17 56			18 26			18 56			19 26		
Langside	d			17 21			17 37				17 58			18 28			18 59			19 28		
Pollokshields East	d	16 56	17 08		17 16			17 30	17 36	17 42		17 56	18 12		18 26	18 40		18 57	19 10		19 25	19 40
Queens Park	d	16 57	17 09		17 18			17 31	17 37	17 43		17 58	18 13		18 27	18 41		18 58	19 11		19 26	19 41
Crosshill	d	16 59	17 11		17 20			17 33	17 39	17 45		18 00	18 15		18 29	18 43		19 00	19 13		19 28	19 43
Mount Florida	d	17 01	17 13		17 22			17 35	17 41	17 47		18 02	18 17		18 31	18 45		19 02	19 15		19 30	19 45
Cathcart	d	17a04	17 15	17a23			17a40	17 37		17 49		18a04	18 19	18a31		18 47		19a05	19 17	19a31		19 47
Muirend	d		17 18			17 29		17 40		17 52			18 22			18 50			19 20			19 50
Williamwood	d		17 21			17 32		17 44		17 55			18 25			18 53			19 23			19 53
Whitecraigs	d		17 23			17 34		17 46		17 57			18 27			18 55			19 25			19 55
Patterton	d		17 26			17 37		17 49		18 00			18 30			18 58			19 28			19 58
Neilston	a		17 32			17 44		17 55		18 06			18 36			19 04			19 34			20 04
Kings Park	d				17 25				17 44		18 04				18 34		19 04				19 34	
Croftfoot	d				17 28				17 46		18 06				18 36		19 06				19 36	
Burnside	d				17 31				17 49		18 08				18 39		19 08				19 38	
Kirkhill	a				17 34				17 52		18 11				18 42		19 11				19 41	
Newton 226	a				17 40				17 57		18 14				18 45		19 14				19 44	

A To Glasgow Central

Table T223-R

Mondays to Fridays
16 December to 15 May

Glasgow Central, Cathcart Circle, Neilston and Newton

		SR	SR A	SR	SR A	SR	SR	SR	SR A	SR	SR A	SR	SR	SR	SR A	SR	SR A	SR	SR	SR	SR A	SR	SR A
Glasgow Central 15 226	d	19 45	19 52	20 05	20 15	20 20	20 35	20 45	20 50	21 05	21 15	21 20	21 35	21 45	21 50	22 05	22 15	22 20	22 35	22 45	22 50	23 05	23 15
Pollokshields West	d	19 51			20 21			20 51			21 21			21 51			22 21			22 51			23 21
Maxwell Park	d	19 53			20 23			20 53			21 23			21 53			22 23			22 53			23 23
Shawlands	d	19 55			20 25			20 55			21 25			21 55			22 25			22 55			23 25
Pollokshaws East	d	19 56			20 26			20 56			21 26			21 56			22 26			22 56			23 26
Langside	d	19 58			20 28			20 58			21 28			21 58			22 28			22 58			23 28
Pollokshields East	d		19 57	20 10		20 25	20 40		20 55	21 10		21 25	21 40		21 55	22 10		22 25	22 40		22 55	23 10	
Queens Park	d		19 58	20 11		20 26	20 41		20 56	21 11		21 26	21 41		21 56	22 11		22 26	22 41		22 56	23 11	
Crosshill	d		20 00	20 13		20 28	20 43		20 58	21 13		21 28	21 43		21 58	22 13		22 28	22 43		22 58	23 13	
Mount Florida	d		20 02	20 15		20 30	20 45		21 00	21 15		21 30	21 45		22 00	22 15		22 30	22 45		23 00	23 15	
Cathcart	d		20a04	20 17	20a31		20 47		21a04	21 17	21a31		21 47		22a04	22 17	22a31		22 47		23a04	23 17	23a31
Muirend	d			20 20			20 50			21 20			21 50			22 20			22 50			23 20	
Williamwood	d			20 23			20 53			21 23			21 53			22 23			22 53			23 23	
Whitecraigs	d			20 25			20 55			21 25			21 55			22 25			22 55			23 25	
Patterton	d			20 28			20 58			21 28			21 58			22 28			22 58			23 28	
Neilston	a			20 34			21 04			21 34			22 04			22 34			23 04			23 34	
Kings Park	d	20 04				20 34		21 04				21 34		22 04				22 34		23 04			
Croftfoot	d	20 06				20 36		21 06				21 36		22 06				22 36		23 06			
Burnside	d	20 08				20 38		21 08				21 38		22 08				22 38		23 08			
Kirkhill	a	20 11				20 41		21 11				21 41		22 11				22 41		23 11			
Newton 226	a	20 14				20 44		21 14				21 44		22 14				22 44		23 14			

		SR	SR FO
Glasgow Central 15 226	d	23 20	23 50
Pollokshields West	d		
Maxwell Park	d		
Shawlands	d		
Pollokshaws East	d		
Langside	d		
Pollokshields East	d	23 25	23 55
Queens Park	d	23 26	23 56
Crosshill	d	23 28	23 58
Mount Florida	d	23 30	23 59
Cathcart	d		
Muirend	d		
Williamwood	d		
Whitecraigs	d		
Patterton	d		
Neilston	a		
Kings Park	d	23 34	00 04
Croftfoot	d	23 36	00 06
Burnside	d	23 38	00 08
Kirkhill	a	23 41	00 11
Newton 226	a	23 44	00 14

Saturdays
21 December to 16 May

		SR B	SR	SR A	SR A	SR	SR	SR	SR	SR	SR	SR	SR	SR	SR	SR	SR	SR A	SR	SR A	SR	SR	SR
Glasgow Central 15 226	d		00 05	00 20	06 15	06 17	06 20	06 34	06 45	07 05	07 18	07 35	07 45	08 05	08 20	08 35	08 45	08 51	09 05	09 15	09 20	09 35	09 45
Pollokshields West	d			00 27	06 21				06 51				07 51				08 51			09 22			09 51
Maxwell Park	d			00 29	06 23				06 53				07 53				08 53			09 24			09 53
Shawlands	d			00 31	06 25				06 55				07 55				08 55			09 26			09 55
Pollokshaws East	d			00 32	06 26				06 56				07 56				08 56			09 27			09 56
Langside	d			00 34	06 28				06 59				07 58				08 58			09 29			09 58
Pollokshields East	d		00 10			06 22	06 25	06 39		07 10	07 23	07 40		08 10	08 25	08 40		08 56	09 10		09 25	09 40	
Queens Park	d		00 11			06 23	06 27	06 40		07 11	07 24	07 41		08 11	08 26	08 41		08 58	09 11		09 26	09 41	
Crosshill	d		00 13			06 25	06 29	06 42		07 13	07 26	07 43		08 13	08 28	08 43		09 00	09 13		09 28	09 43	
Mount Florida	d		00 15			06 27	06 31	06 44		07 15	07 28	07 45		08 15	08 30	08 45		09 02	09 15		09 30	09 45	
Cathcart	d		00 17	00a37	06a31	06 29		06 46		07 17		07 47		08 17		08 47		09a04	09 17	09a32		09 47	
Muirend	d		00 20			06 32		06 49		07 20		07 50		08 20		08 50			09 20			09 50	
Williamwood	d		00 23			06 35		06 52		07 23		07 53		08 23		08 53			09 23			09 53	
Whitecraigs	d		00 25			06 37		06 54		07 25		07 55		08 25		08 55			09 25			09 55	
Patterton	d		00 28			06 40		06 57		07 28		07 58		08 28		08 58			09 28			09 58	
Neilston	a		00 34			06 46		07 03		07 34		08 04		08 34		09 04			09 34			10 04	
Kings Park	d	00 04					06 34		07 05		07 31		08 05		08 33		09 04				09 34		10 04
Croftfoot	d	00 06					06 36		07 07		07 33		08 07		08 35		09 06				09 36		10 06
Burnside	d	00 08					06 38		07 09		07 36		08 09		08 38		09 08				09 38		10 08
Kirkhill	a	00 11					06 41		07 12		07 39		08 12		08 41		09 11				09 41		10 11
Newton 226	a	00 14					06 44		07 15		07 42		08 15		08 44		09 14				09 44		10 14

A To Glasgow Central **B** From Glasgow Central

Table T223-R

Glasgow Central, Cathcart Circle, Neilston and Newton

Saturdays

21 December to 16 May

		SR	SR	SR	SR	SR	SR	SR	SR		SR	SR	SR	SR	SR	SR		SR	SR	SR	SR	SR	SR	SR
		A		A				A			A				A			A				A		A
Glasgow Central 15 226	d	09 51	10 06	10 15	10 20	10 35	10 45	10 51	11 05		13 15	13 20	13 35	13 45	13 51	14 05		14 15	14 20	14 35	14 45	14 51	15 05	15 15
Pollokshields West	d			10 21			10 51				13 21			13 51				14 21			14 51			15 21
Maxwell Park	d			10 23			10 53				13 23			13 53				14 23			14 53			15 23
Shawlands	d			10 25			10 55				13 25			13 55				14 25			14 55			15 25
Pollokshaws East	d			10 26			10 56				13 26			13 56				14 26			14 56			15 26
Langside	d			10 28			10 58				13 28			13 58				14 28			14 58			15 28
Pollokshields East	d	09 56	10 11		10 25	10 40		10 56	11 10	and at		13 25	13 40		13 56	14 10			14 25	14 40		14 56	15 11	
Queens Park	d	09 57	10 12		10 26	10 41		10 57	11 11	the same		13 26	13 41		13 57	14 11			14 26	14 41		14 57	15 12	
Crosshill	d	09 59	10 14		10 28	10 43		10 59	11 13	minutes		13 28	13 43		13 59	14 13			14 28	14 43		14 59	15 14	
Mount Florida	d	10 01	10 16		10 30	10 45		11 01	11 15	past		13 30	13 45		14 01	14 15			14 30	14 45		15 01	15 16	
Cathcart	d	10a04	10 18	10a31		10 47		11a04	11 17	each	13a31		13 47		14a04	14 17		14a31		14 47		15a04	15 18	15a31
Muirend	d		10 21			10 50			11 20	hour until			13 50			14 20				14 50			15 21	
Williamwood	d		10 24			10 53			11 23				13 53			14 23				14 53			15 24	
Whitecraigs	d		10 26			10 55			11 25				13 55			14 25				14 55			15 26	
Patterton	d		10 29			10 58			11 28				13 58			14 28				14 58			15 29	
Neilston	a		10 35			11 04			11 34				14 04			14 34				15 04			15 35	
Kings Park	d				10 34		11 04					13 34		14 04					14 34		15 04			
Croftfoot	d				10 36		11 06					13 36		14 06					14 36		15 06			
Burnside	d				10 38		11 08					13 38		14 08					14 38		15 08			
Kirkhill	a				10 41		11 11					13 41		14 11					14 41		15 11			
Newton 226	a				10 44		11 14					13 44		14 14					14 44		15 14			

		SR	SR		SR	SR	SR	SR	SR	SR	SR	SR	SR		SR	SR	SR	SR	SR	SR	SR	SR	SR		SR
						A		A				A			A				A		A				
Glasgow Central 15 226	d	15 20	15 35		15 45	15 51	16 08	16 15	16 20	16 35	16 46	16 50	17 07		17 15	17 20	17 35	17 45	17 51	18 07	18 15	18 20	18 35		18 45
Pollokshields West	d				15 51			16 21			16 52				17 21			17 51			18 21				18 51
Maxwell Park	d				15 53			16 23			16 54				17 23			17 53			18 23				18 53
Shawlands	d				15 55			16 25			16 56				17 25			17 55			18 25				18 55
Pollokshaws East	d				15 56			16 26			16 57				17 26			17 56			18 26				18 56
Langside	d				15 58			16 28			16 59				17 28			17 58			18 28				18 59
Pollokshields East	d	15 25	15 40			15 56	16 13		16 25	16 40		16 55	17 12			17 25	17 40		17 56	18 12		18 26	18 40		
Queens Park	d	15 26	15 41			15 57	16 14		16 27	16 41		16 56	17 13			17 26	17 41		17 58	18 13		18 27	18 41		
Crosshill	d	15 28	15 43			15 59	16 16		16 29	16 43		16 58	17 15			17 28	17 43		18 00	18 15		18 29	18 43		
Mount Florida	d	15 30	15 45			16 01	16 18		16 31	16 45		17 00	17 17			17 30	17 45		18 02	18 17		18 31	18 45		
Cathcart	d		15 47			16a03	16 20	16a31		16 47		17a04	17 19		17a31		17 47		18a04	18 19	18a31		18 47		
Muirend	d		15 50				16 23			16 50			17 22				17 50			18 22			18 50		
Williamwood	d		15 53				16 26			16 53			17 25				17 53			18 25			18 53		
Whitecraigs	d		15 55				16 28			16 55			17 27				17 55			18 27			18 55		
Patterton	d		15 58				16 31			16 58			17 30				17 58			18 30			18 58		
Neilston	a		16 04				16 37			17 04			17 36				18 04			18 36			19 04		
Kings Park	d	15 34			16 04				16 34		17 04					17 34		18 04				18 34			19 04
Croftfoot	d	15 36			16 06				16 36		17 06					17 36		18 06				18 36			19 06
Burnside	d	15 38			16 08				16 38		17 08					17 38		18 08				18 39			19 08
Kirkhill	a	15 41			16 11				16 41		17 11					17 41		18 11				18 42			19 11
Newton 226	a	15 44			16 14				16 44		17 14					17 44		18 14				18 45			19 14

		SR	SR	SR	SR	SR	SR	SR	SR		SR	SR	SR	SR	SR	SR	SR	SR	SR		SR	SR	SR	SR	SR
		A		A				A			A				A		A					A		A	
Glasgow Central 15 226	d	18 52	19 05	19 15	19 20	19 35	19 45	19 50	20 05		20 15	20 20	20 35	20 45	20 50	21 05	21 15	21 20	21 36		21 45	21 51	22 05	22 15	22 20
Pollokshields West	d			19 21			19 51				20 21			20 51			21 21				21 51			22 21	
Maxwell Park	d			19 23			19 53				20 23			20 53			21 23				21 53			22 23	
Shawlands	d			19 25			19 55				20 25			20 55			21 25				21 55			22 25	
Pollokshaws East	d			19 26			19 56				20 26			20 56			21 26				21 56			22 26	
Langside	d			19 28			19 58				20 28			20 58			21 28				21 58			22 28	
Pollokshields East	d	18 57	19 10		19 25	19 40		19 55	20 10			20 25	20 40		20 55	21 10		21 25	21 41			21 56	22 10		22 25
Queens Park	d	18 58	19 11		19 26	19 41		19 56	20 11			20 26	20 41		20 56	21 11		21 26	21 42			21 57	22 11		22 26
Crosshill	d	19 00	19 13		19 28	19 43		19 58	20 13			20 28	20 43		20 58	21 13		21 28	21 44			21 59	22 13		22 28
Mount Florida	d	19 02	19 15		19 30	19 45		20 00	20 15			20 30	20 45		21 00	21 15		21 30	21 46			22 02	22 15		22 30
Cathcart	d	19a05	19 17	19a31		19 47		20a04	20 17		20a31		20 47		21a04	21 17	21a31		21 48			22a04	22 17	22a31	
Muirend	d		19 20			19 50			20 20				20 50			21 20			21 51				22 20		
Williamwood	d		19 23			19 53			20 23				20 53			21 23			21 54				22 23		
Whitecraigs	d		19 25			19 55			20 25				20 55			21 25			21 56				22 25		
Patterton	d		19 28			19 58			20 28				20 58			21 28			21 59				22 28		
Neilston	a		19 34			20 04			20 34				21 04			21 34			22 05				22 34		
Kings Park	d				19 34		20 04					20 34		21 04				21 34			22 04				22 34
Croftfoot	d				19 36		20 06					20 36		21 06				21 36			22 06				22 36
Burnside	d				19 38		20 08					20 38		21 08				21 38			22 08				22 38
Kirkhill	a				19 41		20 11					20 41		21 11				21 41			22 11				22 41
Newton 226	a				19 44		20 14					20 44		21 14				21 44			22 14				22 44

		SR	SR	SR	SR		SR	SR
				A			A	
Glasgow Central 15 226	d	22 35	22 45	22 50	23 05		23 15	23 20
Pollokshields West	d		22 51				23 21	
Maxwell Park	d		22 53				23 23	
Shawlands	d		22 55				23 25	
Pollokshaws East	d		22 56				23 26	
Langside	d		22 58				23 28	
Pollokshields East	d	22 40		22 55	23 10			23 25
Queens Park	d	22 41		22 56	23 11			23 26
Crosshill	d	22 43		22 58	23 13			23 28
Mount Florida	d	22 45		23 00	23 15			23 30
Cathcart	d	22 47		23a04	23 17		23a31	
Muirend	d	22 50			23 20			
Williamwood	d	22 53			23 23			
Whitecraigs	d	22 55			23 25			
Patterton	d	22 58			23 28			
Neilston	a	23 04			23 34			
Kings Park	d		23 04					23 34
Croftfoot	d		23 06					23 36
Burnside	d		23 08					23 38
Kirkhill	a		23 11					23 41
Newton 226	a		23 14					23 44

A To Glasgow Central

Table T223-R

Glasgow Central, Cathcart Circle, Neilston and Newton

Sundays

15 December to 10 May

		SR	SR	SR	SR	SR	SR	SR	SR	SR		SR	SR	SR	SR	SR	SR	SR	SR	SR		SR
Glasgow Central 15 226	d	08 23	08 36	08 55	09 08	09 23	09 36	09 53	10 08	10 23		10 36	10 53	11 08	11 23	11 36	11 53	12 08	12 23	12 36		12 55
Pollokshields West	d		08 42				09 42					10 42				11 42				12 42		
Maxwell Park	d		08 44				09 44					10 44				11 44				12 44		
Shawlands	d		08 46				09 46					10 46				11 46				12 46		
Pollokshaws East	d		08 47				09 47					10 47				11 47				12 47		
Langside	d		08 49				09 49					10 49				11 49				12 49		
Pollokshields East	d	08 28		09 00	09 13	09 28		09 58	10 13	10 28			10 58	11 13	11 28		11 58	12 13	12 28			13 00
Queens Park	d	08 29		09 01	09 14	09 29		09 59	10 14	10 29			10 59	11 14	11 29		11 59	12 14	12 29			13 01
Crosshill	d	08 31		09 03	09 16	09 31		10 01	10 16	10 31			11 01	11 16	11 31		12 01	12 16	12 31			13 03
Mount Florida	d	08 33		09 05	09 18	09 33		10 03	10 18	10 33			11 03	11 18	11 33		12 03	12 18	12 33			13 05
Cathcart	d	08 35		09 07		09 35		10 05		10 35			11 05		11 35		12 05		12 35			13 07
Muirend	d	08 38		09 10		09 38		10 08		10 38			11 08		11 38		12 08		12 38			13 10
Williamwood	d	08 41		09 13		09 41		10 11		10 41			11 11		11 41		12 11		12 41			13 13
Whitecraigs	d	08 43		09 15		09 43		10 13		10 43			11 13		11 43		12 13		12 43			13 15
Patterton	d	08 46		09 18		09 46		10 16		10 46			11 16		11 46		12 16		12 46			13 18
Neilston	a	08 52		09 24		09 52		10 22		10 52			11 22		11 52		12 22		12 52			13 24
Kings Park	d		08 54		09 21		09 54		10 21			10 54		11 21		11 54		12 21		12 54		
Croftfoot	d		08 56		09 23		09 56		10 23			10 56		11 23		11 56		12 23		12 56		
Burnside	d		08 58		09 26		09 58		10 26			10 58		11 26		11 58		12 26		12 58		
Kirkhill	a		09 01		09 29		10 01		10 29			11 01		11 29		12 01		12 29		13 01		
Newton 226	a		09 04		09 32		10 04		10 32			11 04		11 32		12 04		12 32		13 04		

		SR	SR	SR	SR		SR	SR	SR	SR		SR
Glasgow Central 15 226	d	13 08	13 23	13 36	13 53		22 08	22 23	22 36	22 53		23 08
Pollokshields West	d			13 42					22 42			
Maxwell Park	d			13 44					22 44			
Shawlands	d			13 46					22 46			
Pollokshaws East	d			13 47					22 47			
Langside	d			13 49					22 49			
Pollokshields East	d	13 13	13 28		13 58	and at	22 13	22 28		22 58		23 13
Queens Park	d	13 14	13 29		13 59	the same	22 14	22 29		22 59		23 14
Crosshill	d	13 16	13 31		14 01	minutes	22 16	22 31		23 01		23 16
Mount Florida	d	13 18	13 33		14 03	past	22 18	22 33		23 03		23 18
Cathcart	d		13 35		14 05	each		22 35		23 05		
Muirend	d		13 38		14 08	hour until		22 38		23 08		
Williamwood	d		13 41		14 11			22 41		23 11		
Whitecraigs	d		13 43		14 13			22 43		23 13		
Patterton	d		13 46		14 16			22 46		23 16		
Neilston	a		13 52		14 22			22 52		23 22		
Kings Park	d	13 21		13 54			22 21		22 54			23 21
Croftfoot	d	13 23		13 56			22 23		22 56			23 23
Burnside	d	13 26		13 58			22 26		22 58			23 26
Kirkhill	a	13 29		14 01			22 29		23 01			23 29
Newton 226	a	13 32		14 04			22 32		23 04			23 32

Table T224-F

Mondays to Fridays
16 December to 15 May

Edinburgh - Shotts, Carstairs, Motherwell and Glasgow Central

Miles	Miles	Station		SR MX	SR MX	SR	SR	XC	SR	TP	SR	XC	SR	SR	SR	SR	XC	TP	SR	SR	SR	SR	SR
				A	A			◇1		◇1 B		◇1 C					◇1 D	◇1 E					
0	0	Edinburgh [10] 230,238,242	d				05 53	06 25	06 40		06 55	07 27	07 41	07 58	08 21	08 57	09 12		09 25	09 56	10 21	10 25	10 55
1¼	1¼	Haymarket 230,238,242	d				05 57		06 45		07 00	07 32	07 46	08 03	08 27	09 01	09 16		09 30	10 00	10 26	10 30	11 01
3	3	Slateford	d				06 01				07 04				08 30				09 35			10 35	
3¾	3¾	Kingsknowe	d				06 04				07 07				08 33				09 38			10 39	
4¾	4¾	Wester Hailes	d				06 07				07 10				08 35				09 41			10 41	
7½	7½	Curriehill	d				06 11				07 14				08 38				09 45			10 45	
11	11	Kirknewton	d				06 17				07 20				08 43				09 51			10 51	
14	—	Livingston South	d				06 21		07 02		07 24			08 16	08 47	09 15			09 55	10 16		10 55	11 14
16¾	—	West Calder	d				06 25		07 06		07 27			08 20	08 50	09 19			09 58	10 20		10 59	11 18
18½	—	Addiewell	d				06 28				07 31				08 53				10 02			11 02	
21	—	Breich	d				06 32				07 34				08 57				10 05			11 06	
23¼	—	Fauldhouse	d				06 35				07 38				09 01				10 09			11 10	
26½	—	**Shotts**	d				06 47		07 17		07 53			08 38	09 17	09 37			10 20	10 38		11 17	11 35
28¼	—	Hartwood	d				06 49				07 56				09 20				10 23			11 20	
31½	—	Cleland	d				06 54				08 00				09 24				10 27			11 24	
33¼	—	Carfin	d	00 02			06 57				08 03				09 27				10 30			11 27	
34¼	—	Holytown	d	00 04			06 59				08 06				09 30				10 33			11 30	
—	28½	Carstairs	d			05 48				07 44			08 10								11 02		
—	—	Carluke 225	d		00 09	05 57							08 18								11 10		
—	—	Wishaw 225	d		00 15	06 06							08 28								11 16		
—	44½	**Motherwell** 225	a		00 22	06 13		07 04		07 59		08 14	08 34				09 54				11 23		
—	—		d			06 16		07 05		08 01		08 15	08 34				09 55	10 15			11 34		
36	—	Bellshill 225	d	00 08		06 22	07 06		07 30		08 10			08 50	09 35	09 50			10 38	10 49		11 36	11 47
38¾	—	Uddingston 225	d	00 12		06 28	07 13				08 15		08 39		09 40				10 42			11 42	
42	—	Cambuslang 225	d	00 18		06 33	07 18																
47¼	57¼	**Glasgow Central** [15] 225	a	00 30		06 42	07 29	07 21	07 52	08 20	08 28	08 31	08 56	09 10	09 55	10 10	10 15	10 32	10 56	11 10	11 55	11 57	12 09

Station		XC	TP	SR	SR	SR	SR	SR	XC	TP	SR	SR	SR	SR	SR	XC	SR	SR	SR	SR	SR	XC	TP
		◇1 F	◇1 E		G				◇1 H	◇1 E		G				◇1 I						◇1 J	◇1 E
Edinburgh [10] 230,238,242	d	11 11		11 25	11 51	11 58	12 27	12 55	13 11		13 26	13 53	13 56	14 25	14 56	15 12	15 26	15 49	15 57	16 25	16 57	17 12	
Haymarket 230,238,242	d	11 15		11 31	11 56	12 03	12 32	13 01	13 16		13 31	13 57	14 01	14 31	15 01	15 17	15 31	15 53	16 01	16 30	17 01	17 17	
Slateford	d			11 34			12 36				13 35			14 36			15 35			16 35			
Kingsknowe	d			11 37			12 39				13 39			14 39			15 39			16 38			
Wester Hailes	d			11 40			12 41				13 41			14 42			15 41			16 41			
Curriehill	d			11 44			12 45				13 45			14 46			15 45			16 45			
Kirknewton	d			11 50			12 51				13 51			14 52			15 51			16 51			
Livingston South	d			11 54		12 15	12 55	13 21			13 55		14 15	14 56	15 15		15 55		16 13	16 57	17 16		
West Calder	d			11 57		12 19	12 59	13 25			13 59		14 18	14 59	15 19		15 59		16 16	17 01	17 20		
Addiewell	d			12 01			13 02				14 02			15 03			16 02			17 04			
Breich	d			12 04			13 06				14 06			15 06			16 06			17 08			
Fauldhouse	d			12 08			13 10				14 10			15 10			16 10			17 12			
Shotts	d			12 19		12 36	13 18	13 38			14 18		14 35	15 17	15 37		16 19		16 33	17 18	17 35		
Hartwood	d			12 22			13 21				14 21			15 20			16 22			17 21			
Cleland	d			12 26			13 25				14 25			15 24			16 26			17 25			
Carfin	d			12 30			13 29				14 29			15 28			16 30			17 28			
Holytown	d			12 33			13 32				14 32			15 30			16 33			17 31			
Carstairs	d				12 49							14 33						16 16					
Carluke 225	d				12 58							14 42						16 24					
Wishaw 225	d				13 04							14 55											
Motherwell 225	a	11 54			13 09				13 54			15 02				15 54		16 31				17 55	
	d	11 55	12 22		13 10				13 55	14 20		15 06				15 55		16 32				17 56	18 21
Bellshill 225	d			12 38		12 49	13 37	13 50			14 37		14 48	15 36	15 50		16 38		16 47	17 35	17 48		
Uddingston 225	d			12 42			13 41				14 41			15 42			16 42			17 39			
Cambuslang 225	d																			17 45			
Glasgow Central [15] 225	a	12 11	12 39	12 56	13 24	13 09	13 56	14 10	14 12	14 38	14 56	15 25	15 09	15 56	16 09	16 12	16 55	16 51	17 07	17 55	18 09	18 11	18 39

A From Edinburgh
B From Manchester Piccadilly
C From Dunbar
D From Leeds
E From Manchester Airport
F From Birmingham New Street
G To Ayr
H From Bath Spa
I From Plymouth
J From Penzance

Table T224-F

Mondays to Fridays
16 December to 15 May

Edinburgh - Shotts, Carstairs, Motherwell and Glasgow Central

Station		SR	SR	SR	SR	SR	SR	SR	XC	TP	SR	GR	XC	TP	SR	SR FX	SR FO	SR
			A				A		◇1 B	◇1 C		D	◇1 E	◇1 C				
Edinburgh [10] 230,238,242	d	17 26	17 42	17 50	17 56		18 26	18 56	19 11		19 26	20 19	21 14		21 25	22 56	22 56	23 13
Haymarket 230,238,242	d	17 30	17 47	17 54	18 01		18 31	19 00	19 16		19 30	20 24	21 19		21 30	23 00	23 00	23 17
Slateford	d	17 34			18 04		18 36				19 34				21 34	23 04	23 04	23 22
Kingsknowe	d	17 37			18 07		18 39				19 37				21 37	23 07	23 07	23 25
Wester Hailes	d	17 40		18 00	18 10		18 42				19 40				21 40	23 10	23 10	23 27
Curriehill	d	17 44		18 04			18 45				19 44				21 44	23 13	23 13	23 31
Kirknewton	d	17 50		18 09			18 52				19 50				21 50	23 21	23 21	23 37
Livingston South	d	17 54		18 16	18 21			19 14			19 54				21 57	23 29	23 29	
West Calder	d	17 58		18 20	18 25			19 18			19 57				22 01	23 34	23 34	
Addiewell	d	18 01			18 28						20 01				22 04	23 37	23 37	
Breich	d	18 05			18 31						20 04				22 08	23 42	23 42	
Fauldhouse	d	18 09			18 35						20 08				22 12	23 46	23 46	
Shotts	d	18 19		18 31	18 49			19 35			20 19				22 22	23 51	23 51	
Hartwood	d	18 22			18 51						20 22				22 25	23 54	23 54	
Cleland	d	18 26			18 55						20 26				22 29	23 58	23 59	
Carfin	d	18 30			18 58						20 30				22 32	00 02	00 02	
Holytown	d	18 32			19 01						20 33				22 35	00 04	00 04	
Carstairs	d		18 13			18 38	19 13											23 59
Carluke 225	d		18 21			18 46	19 22											00 09
Wishaw 225	d		18 27			18 58	19 27											00 15
Motherwell 225	a		18 32			19 07	19 33		19 54			21 02	21 59					00 22
	d		18 33				19 34		19 55	20 22		21 04	22 01	22 22				
Bellshill 225	d	18 37		18 43	19 04			19 49			20 38				22 39	00 08	00 08	
Uddingston 225	d	18 41			19 10						20 42				22 43	00 12	00 11	
Cambuslang 225	d			18 52	19 16											00 18	00 17	
Glasgow Central [15] 225	a	18 56	18 53	19 07	19 28		19 54	20 10	20 15	20 39	20 56	21 26	22 21	22 40	22 55	00 30	00 29	

Saturdays
21 December to 16 May

Station		SR	SR	SR	SR	XC	SR	TP	SR	XC	SR	SR	SR	SR	XC	TP	SR	SR	SR	SR	SR	XC	TP
		F	F			◇1		◇1 G		◇1	A				◇1 H	◇1 C						◇1 I	◇1 C
Edinburgh [10] 230,238,242	d				05 53	06 22	06 40		06 55	07 26	07 53	07 56	08 28	08 58	09 12		09 27	09 57	10 24	10 27	10 57	11 11	
Haymarket 230,238,242	d				05 57		06 45		07 00	07 31	07 58	08 02	08 33	09 02	09 16		09 31	10 01	10 28	10 32	11 01	11 16	
Slateford	d				06 01				07 04				08 36				09 35			10 37			
Kingsknowe	d				06 04				07 07				08 40				09 38			10 39			
Wester Hailes	d				06 07				07 10				08 42				09 41			10 42			
Curriehill	d				06 11				07 14				08 46				09 45			10 45			
Kirknewton	d				06 17				07 20				08 52				09 51			10 51			
Livingston South	d				06 21		07 03		07 24			08 16	08 56	09 15			09 55	10 16		10 55	11 14		
West Calder	d				06 24		07 07		07 27			08 20	09 00	09 19			09 58	10 20		10 59	11 18		
Addiewell	d				06 28				07 31				09 03				10 02			11 02			
Breich	d				06 31				07 34				09 07				10 05			11 06			
Fauldhouse	d				06 35				07 38				09 11				10 09			11 10			
Shotts	d				06 47		07 19		07 53			08 38	09 18	09 37			10 18	10 38		11 17	11 35		
Hartwood	d				06 49				07 56				09 21				10 21			11 20			
Cleland	d				06 54				08 00				09 25				10 25			11 24			
Carfin	d	00 02			06 57				08 03				09 29				10 28			11 27			
Holytown	d	00 04			06 59				08 06				09 32				10 31			11 30			
Carstairs	d			05 48				07 45			08 31								11 07				
Carluke 225	d		00 09	05 57							08 39								11 19				
Wishaw 225	d		00 15	06 07							08 55								11 26				
Motherwell 225	a		00 22	06 16		07 05		07 59		08 13	09 00				09 54				11 32			11 54	
	d			06 18		07 06		08 01		08 14	09 01				09 57	10 21			11 34			11 55	12 22
Bellshill 225	d	00 08		06 24	07 08		07 31		08 10			08 50	09 37	09 50			10 36	10 49		11 36	11 47		
Uddingston 225	d	00 11		06 28	07 15				08 14				09 41				10 41			11 42			
Cambuslang 225	d	00 17		06 33	07 20																		
Glasgow Central [15] 225	a	00 29		06 42	07 30	07 22	07 53	08 20	08 28	08 30	09 24	09 10	09 56	10 10	10 14	10 38	10 56	11 10	11 54	11 57	12 09	12 12	12 39

A To Ayr
B From Penzance
C From Manchester Airport
D From London Kings Cross
E From Plymouth
F From Edinburgh
G From Manchester Piccadilly
H From Newcastle
I From Birmingham New Street

Table T224-F

Edinburgh - Shotts, Carstairs, Motherwell and Glasgow Central

Saturdays
21 December to 16 May

	SR		SR A	SR	SR	SR	XC ◇1 B	TP ◇1 C	SR	SR A	SR		SR	SR	XC ◇1 D	SR	SR A	SR	SR	SR	XC ◇1 E		TP ◇1 C	SR
Edinburgh 10 230,238,242 d	11 27		11 51	11 55	12 27	12 55	13 11		13 27	13 55	13 58		14 26	14 56	15 12	15 26	15 50	15 57	16 27	16 56	17 10			17 27
Haymarket 230,238,242 d	11 31		11 57	12 01	12 31	13 01	13 15		13 31	14 00	14 04		14 31	15 01	15 16	15 30	15 54	16 01	16 32	17 01	17 16			17 31
Slateford d	11 34				12 35				13 35				14 36			15 35			16 35					17 34
Kingsknowe d	11 37				12 39				13 39				14 39			15 39			16 38					17 37
Wester Hailes d	11 40				12 41				13 41				14 42			15 41			16 41					17 40
Curriehill d	11 44				12 45				13 45				14 46			15 45			16 45					17 44
Kirknewton d	11 50				12 51				13 51				14 52			15 51			16 51					17 50
Livingston South d	11 54			12 15	12 55	13 21			13 55		14 17		14 56	15 14		15 55		16 13	16 57	17 16				17 54
West Calder d	11 57			12 19	12 59	13 25			13 59		14 20		14 59	15 18		15 59		16 16	17 01	17 20				17 58
Addiewell d	12 01				13 02				14 02				15 03			16 02			17 04					18 01
Breich d	12 04				13 06				14 06				15 06			16 06			17 08					18 05
Fauldhouse d	12 08				13 10				14 10				15 10			16 10			17 12					18 09
Shotts d	12 16			12 36	13 17	13 38			14 17		14 35		15 17	15 37		16 19		16 33	17 16	17 35				18 19
Hartwood d	12 19				13 20				14 20				15 20			16 22			17 19					18 22
Cleland d	12 23				13 24				14 24				15 24			16 26			17 23					18 26
Carfin d	12 26				13 27				14 27				15 28			16 30			17 27					18 30
Holytown d	12 29				13 30				14 30				15 30			16 33			17 29					18 32
Carstairs d			12 48							14 33							16 32							
Carluke 225 d			12 56							14 41							16 41							
Wishaw 225 d			13 03							14 53							16 58							
Motherwell 225 a			13 08				13 54			15 03					15 54		17 05				17 54			
d			13 09				13 55	14 21		15 06					15 55		17 06				17 55		18 22	
Bellshill 225 d	12 34			12 49	13 35	13 50			14 35		14 48		15 35	15 50		16 38		16 50	17 34	17 48				18 37
Uddingston 225 d	12 39				13 40				14 40				15 40			16 42			17 38					18 41
Cambuslang 225 d																			17 43					
Glasgow Central 15 225 a	12 54		13 24	13 10	13 55	14 10	14 12	14 38	14 55	15 25	15 09		15 55	16 10	16 12	16 55	17 24	17 10	17 55	18 09	18 11		18 39	18 56

	SR A	SR	SR	SR A	SR	XC ◇1 E	TP ◇1 C		SR	XC ◇1 D	SR	SR	SR
Edinburgh 10 230,238,242 d	17 42	17 52	17 56	18 27	18 56	19 10			19 25	21 12	21 26	22 56	23 12
Haymarket 230,238,242 d	17 46	17 56	18 00	18 32	19 01	19 15			19 31	21 17	21 30	23 00	23 17
Slateford d			18 04	18 35					19 34		21 35	23 04	23 22
Kingsknowe d			18 07	18 38					19 37		21 38	23 07	23 25
Wester Hailes d		18 01	18 10	18 41					19 40		21 41	23 10	23 27
Curriehill d		18 04		18 44					19 44		21 45	23 13	23 31
Kirknewton d		18 10		18 51					19 50		21 51	23 21	23 37
Livingston South d		18 16	18 21		19 13				19 54		21 55	23 29	
West Calder d		18 20	18 25		19 17				19 57		21 58	23 34	
Addiewell d			18 28						20 01		22 02	23 37	
Breich d			18 31						20 04		22 05	23 42	
Fauldhouse d			18 35						20 08		22 09	23 46	
Shotts d		18 36	18 49		19 35				20 19		22 17	23 51	
Hartwood d			18 51						20 22		22 20	23 54	
Cleland d			18 55						20 26		22 24	23 59	
Carfin d			18 58						20 30		22 27	00 02	
Holytown d			19 01						20 33		22 30	00 04	
Carstairs d	18 12			19 13									23 57
Carluke 225 d	18 20			19 22									00 09
Wishaw 225 d	18 27			19 27									00 16
Motherwell 225 a	18 32			19 33		19 53				21 56			00 22
d	18 33			19 34		19 54	20 22			21 58			
Bellshill 225 d		18 48	19 04		19 49				20 39		22 35	00 08	
Uddingston 225 d			19 10						20 43		22 38	00 12	
Cambuslang 225 d		19 00	19 16									00 18	
Glasgow Central 15 225 a	18 53	19 11	19 27	19 54	20 10	20 15	20 40		20 56	22 20	22 55	00 30	

A To Ayr
B From Bristol Temple Meads
C From Manchester Airport
D From Plymouth
E From Penzance

Table T224-F

Edinburgh - Shotts, Carstairs, Motherwell and Glasgow Central

Sundays
15 December to 10 May

	SR A	SR A	SR	SR	SR		SR	XC ◇1	SR	SR	TP ◇1 B	SR	TP ◇1 C	XC ◇1 D	SR		SR	XC ◇1 E	TP ◇1 F	SR	SR	SR	XC ◇1 G	SR
Edinburgh 10 230,238,242 d								10 23		10 26				12 17			12 26	13 13				14 26	15 10	
Haymarket 230,238,242 d										10 30				12 21			12 30	13 18				14 30	15 14	
Slateford d										10 34							12 34					14 35		
Kingsknowe d										10 38							12 38					14 39		
Wester Hailes d										10 40							12 40					14 41		
Curriehill d										10 44							12 44					14 45		
Kirknewton d										10 50							12 50					14 51		
Livingston South d										10 55							12 54					14 55		
West Calder d										10 59							12 58					14 59		
Addiewell d										11 02							13 01					15 02		
Breich d										11 06							13 05					15 06		
Fauldhouse d										11 10							13 09					15 10		
Shotts d										11 18							13 16					15 18		
Hartwood d										11 21							13 19					15 20		
Cleland d										11 25							13 23					15 25		
Carfin d	00 02									11 28							13 26					15 28		
Holytown d	00 04									11 31							13 29					15 30		
Carstairs d																								
Carluke 225 d		00 09																						
Wishaw 225 d		00 16																						
Motherwell 225 a		00 22						11 03						12 59				13 55					15 55	
d			08 35	09 05	09 54		10 20	11 04	11 20		12 23	12 24	12 34	13 00	13 20			13 56	14 22	14 25	15 20		15 56	16 22
Bellshill 225 d	00 08		08 41	09 11	10 00		10 26		11 26	11 37		12 30			13 26		13 36			14 32	15 27	15 35		16 28
Uddingston 225 d	00 12		08 45	09 15	10 04		10 30		11 31	11 44		12 34			13 31		13 41			14 36	15 31	15 39		16 32
Cambuslang 225 d	00 18		08 50	09 20	10 09		10 35		11 36			12 39			13 36					14 40	15 35			16 37
Glasgow Central 15 225 a	00 30		09 01	09 31	10 20		10 45	11 28	11 47	12 03	12 46	12 48	12 55	13 19	13 46		13 59	14 14	14 42	14 50	15 46	16 00	16 12	16 46

	TP ◇1 F		TP ◇1 H	SR	SR	XC ◇1 I	SR	TP ◇1 F	SR	SR	XC ◇1 J		TP ◇1 F	SR	TP ◇1 H	SR	SR	XC ◇1 J	GR 1 K	SR	TP ◇1 F		SR
Edinburgh 10 230,238,242 d					16 26	17 11				18 26	19 18						20 26	21 12	21 22				
Haymarket 230,238,242 d					16 30	17 15				18 30	19 23						20 30	21 17	21 26				
Slateford d					16 34					18 34							20 34						
Kingsknowe d					16 38					18 38							20 38						
Wester Hailes d					16 40					18 40							20 40						
Curriehill d					16 44					18 44							20 44						
Kirknewton d					16 51					18 50							20 50						
Livingston South d					16 54					18 54							20 54						
West Calder d					16 58					18 58							20 58						
Addiewell d					17 01					19 01							21 01						
Breich d					17 05					19 05							21 05						
Fauldhouse d					17 09					19 09							21 09						
Shotts d					17 17					19 16							21 17						
Hartwood d					17 20					19 19							21 20						
Cleland d					17 24					19 23							21 24						
Carfin d					17 27					19 27							21 27						
Holytown d					17 30					19 29							21 30						
Carstairs d																							
Carluke 225 d																							
Wishaw 225 d																							
Motherwell 225 a						17 52					20 01							21 55	22 04				
d	16 24		17 10	17 20		17 53	18 22	18 24	19 22		20 02		20 23	20 24	21 16	21 20		21 56	22 05	22 20	22 29		23 20
Bellshill 225 d				17 27	17 38		18 28		19 28	19 37				20 30		21 26	21 37			22 27			23 26
Uddingston 225 d				17 31	17 44		18 32		19 32	19 44				20 34		21 30	21 41			22 31			23 30
Cambuslang 225 d				17 35			18 37		19 37					20 39		21 35				22 35			23 35
Glasgow Central 15 225 a	16 43		17 28	17 44	17 59	18 13	18 46	18 41	19 46	19 59	20 20		20 40	20 48	21 32	21 44	21 59	22 12	22 26	22 44	22 47		23 44

A not 15 December. From Edinburgh
B until 5 January, from 23 February until 29 March. From Manchester Airport
C from 12 January until 16 February, from 5 April. From Manchester Airport
D From Leeds
E From Sheffield
F From Manchester Airport
G From Birmingham New Street
H From Liverpool Lime Street
I From Bristol Temple Meads
J From Plymouth
K From London Kings Cross

Table T224-R

16 December to 15 May

Glasgow Central, Motherwell, Carstairs and Shotts - Edinburgh

Miles	Miles			SR MX	SR	XC	SR	SR	GR	SR	SR	SR	XC	SR	SR	XC	SR	SR	SR	SR	SR	XC	SR
				A		◇1 B			1 C				◇1 B			◇1 D			E			◇1 D	
0	0	**Glasgow Central** 15	225 d			06 01		06 16	06 48	07 00	07 05	07 13	07 48	08 03	08 17	09 00	09 04	09 17	09 33	10 03	10 16	11 00	11 03
5¼	—	Cambuslang	225 d					06 25				07 25											
8½	—	Uddingston	225 d					06 30				07 30			08 29			09 29			10 28		
11¼	—	Bellshill	225 d					06 34		07 16		07 34		08 20	08 33		09 18	09 33		10 18	10 33		11 18
—	12¼	**Motherwell**	225 a			06 15			07 03		07 20		08 03			09 14			09 56			11 14	
—	—		d		05 59	06 16	07 00		07 05		07 21		08 08			09 15			09 57			11 15	
—	—	Wishaw	225 d				07 07				07 34								10 03				
—	—	Carluke	225 d				07 17				07 40								10 09				
—	28½	Carstairs	d				07a25				07 49								10 18				
13¼	—	Holytown	d		06 06			06 38				07 40			08 38			09 38			10 38		
14	—	Carfin	d		06 09			06 40				07 42			08 40			09 40			10 40		
15¾	—	Cleland	d		06 13			06 43				07 45			08 43			09 43			10 43		
19	—	Hartwood	d		06 19			06 48				07 50			08 48			09 48			10 48		
20½	—	**Shotts**	d		06 23			07 00		07 30		08 02		08 35	09 00		09 34	09 58		10 35	10 54		11 33
24	—	Fauldhouse	d		06 29			07 05				08 07			09 05			10 03			10 59		
26¼	—	Breich	d		06 33			07 08				08 10			09 09			10 07			11 03		
28¾	—	Addiewell	d		06 37			07 12				08 14			09 13			10 10			11 08		
30½	—	West Calder	d	00 01	06 40			07 15		07 40		08 17		08 46	09 17		09 45	10 14		10 46	11 11		11 44
33¼	—	Livingston South	d	00 04	06 45			07 19		07 45		08 22		08 50	09 22		09 49	10 18		10 50	11 16		11 48
36¼	46¼	Kirknewton	d	00 08	06 53			07 23		07 48	08 06	08 26			09 27			10 22			11 23		
40¼	49¼	Curriehill	d	00 13	06 59			07 27		07 54	08 11	08 31			09 31			10 27			11 28		
42½	52½	Wester Hailes	d	00 17	07 02			07 30			08 15	08 35			09 34			10 30			11 32		
43½	53½	Kingsknowe	d	00 19	07 05			07 32			08 17	08 37			09 36			10 32			11 34		
44¼	54¼	Slateford	d	00 23	07 08			07 35			08 22	08 40			09 40			10 36			11 37		
46	56	Haymarket 230,238,242	d	00 31	07 12	06 57		07 39	07 48	08 06	08 32	08 46	08 51	09 05	09 47	09 54	10 03	10 42	10 53	11 04	11 43	11 57	12 04
47¼	57¼	**Edinburgh** 10 230,238,242	a	00 39	07 16	07 01		07 44	07 52	08 11	08 38	08 52	08 55	09 10	09 51	10 00	10 09	10 47	11 01	11 09	11 48	12 02	12 09

		SR	SR	SR	SR	XC	SR	SR	SR	SR	SR	XC	SR	SR	SR	SR	SR	XC	SR	SR	SR	SR	SR
			E			◇1 B				E		◇1 F			E			◇1 G			H		
Glasgow Central 15	225 d	11 16	11 46	12 03	12 16	13 00	13 03	13 17	14 03	14 06	14 16	15 00	15 03	15 16	15 47	16 03	16 16	17 00	17 02	17 16		18 03	18 17
Cambuslang	225 d																						
Uddingston	225 d	11 28			12 29			13 28			14 28			15 28			16 29			17u30	17 59		18 28
Bellshill	225 d	11 33		12 18	12 33		13 18	13 33	14 18		14 33		15 19	15 33		16 21	16 34		17 17	17 33	18 05	18 18	18 33
Motherwell	225 a		12 04			13 16				14 26		15 15			16 02			17 15			18 11		
	d		12 04			13 16				14 27		15 16			16 02			17 16			18 12		
Wishaw	225 d		12 10							14 32					16 07						18 19		
Carluke	225 d		12 16							14 38					16 13						18 25		
Carstairs	d		12 25							14 52					16 37						18a33		
Holytown	d	11 39			12 39			13 39			14 37			15 39			16 38			17 40			18 37
Carfin	d	11 41			12 40			13 41			14 39			15 41			16 40			17 41			18 39
Cleland	d	11 44			12 44			13 44			14 43			15 45			16 44			17 45			18 42
Hartwood	d	11 49			12 48			13 49			14 47			15 49			16 48			17 49			18 47
Shotts	d	11 52		12 36	12 58		13 33	13 57	14 36		15 01		15 35	16 03		16 38	17 01		17 33	17 59		18 37	18 59
Fauldhouse	d	11 59			13 02			14 01			15 05			16 08			17 05			18 04			19 03
Breich	d	12 03			13 06			14 05			15 09			16 12			17 09			18 08			19 07
Addiewell	d	12 08			13 10			14 09			15 13			16 15			17 13			18 11			19 11
West Calder	d	12 12		12 47	13 13		13 44	14 12	14 46		15 16		15 46	16 19		16 50	17 17		17 43	18 15		18 48	19 14
Livingston South	d	12 16		12 51	13 17		13 49	14 16	14 51		15 20		15 51	16 23		16 54	17 21		17 48	18 19		18 52	19 23
Kirknewton	d	12 20			13 22			14 20			15 24			16 27			17 25			18 23			19 27
Curriehill	d	12 25			13 27			14 25			15 29			16 32			17 30			18 28			19 32
Wester Hailes	d	12 29			13 30			14 29			15 33			16 35			17 33			18 31			19 34
Kingsknowe	d	12 31			13 32			14 31			15 35			16 37			17 35			18 33			19 36
Slateford	d	12 35			13 35			14 34			15 38			16 41			17 38			18 37			19 40
Haymarket 230,238,242	d	12 43	13 00	13 04	13 43	13 55	14 01	14 41	15 04	15 19	15 47	15 57	16 05	16 47	17 02	17 13	17 44	17 58	18 02	18 43		19 05	19 44
Edinburgh 10 230,238,242	a	12 48	13 07	13 10	13 48	13 59	14 06	14 46	15 10	15 26	15 52	16 02	16 12	16 52	17 06	17 18	17 48	18 03	18 06	18 49		19 09	19 49

		XC	SR	SR	SR	XC	SR	SR
		◇1 I			E	◇1		
Glasgow Central 15	225 d	19 00	19 03	19 16	19 46	21 05	21 16	23 03
Cambuslang	225 d							23 12
Uddingston	225 d			19 28			21 29	23 17
Bellshill	225 d		19 19	19 33			21 34	23 21
Motherwell	225 a	19 15			20 02	21 22		
	d	19 16			20 03	21 23		
Wishaw	225 d				20 09			
Carluke	225 d				20 15			
Carstairs	d				20 24			
Holytown	d			19 40			21 40	23 25
Carfin	d			19 42			21 43	23 27
Cleland	d			19 45			21 47	23 31
Hartwood	d			19 50			21 52	23 35
Shotts	d		19 37	20 00			21 56	23 45
Fauldhouse	d			20 05			22 02	23 50
Breich	d			20 09			22 06	23 54
Addiewell	d			20 12			22 10	23 57
West Calder	d		19 48	20 16			22 13	00 01
Livingston South	d		19 52	20 20			22 18	00 04
Kirknewton	d			20 24			22 23	00 08
Curriehill	d			20 29			22 29	00 13
Wester Hailes	d			20 32			22 33	00 17
Kingsknowe	d			20 34			22 35	00 19
Slateford	d			20 37			22 39	00 23
Haymarket 230,238,242	d	19 55	20 07	20 43	20 53		22 44	00 31
Edinburgh 10 230,238,242	a	19 59	20 12	20 47	20 59	22 22	22 50	00 39

A From Glasgow Central
B To Plymouth
C To London Kings Cross
D To Penzance
E From Ayr
F To Bristol Temple Meads
G To Birmingham New Street
H From Anderston
I To York

Table T224-R

21 December to 16 May

Glasgow Central, Motherwell, Carstairs and Shotts - Edinburgh

		SR	SR	SR	XC	SR	GR	SR	SR	SR	XC	SR	SR	XC	SR	SR	SR	SR	SR	XC	SR	SR	SR
		A			◇1 B		1 C				◇1 B			◇1 D						◇1 D			E
Glasgow Central 15	225 d		00 07		06 01	06 16	06 48	07 00	07 03	07 16	07 48	08 03	08 17	09 00	09 03	09 17	09 30	10 03	10 16	11 00	11 03	11 16	11 46
Cambuslang	225 d		00 15			06 25				07 24													
Uddingston	225 d		00 20			06 30				07 29			08 29			09 29			10 28			11 28	
Bellshill	225 d		00 25			06 34		07 16		07 34		08 20	08 33		09 18	09 33		10 18	10 33		11 18	11 33	
Motherwell	225 a				06 15		07 03		07 28		08 03			09 14			09 56			11 14			12 04
	d			05 59	06 16		07 04		07 29		08 08			09 15			09 57			11 15			12 04
Wishaw	225 d								07 34								10 03						12 10
Carluke	225 d								07 40								10 09						12 16
Carstairs	d								07 50								10 18						12 25
Holytown	d		00 29	06 06		06 38				07 40			08 38			09 38			10 38			11 39	
Carfin	d		00 31	06 09		06 40				07 42			08 40			09 40			10 40			11 41	
Cleland	d		00 34	06 13		06 43				07 45			08 43			09 43			10 43			11 44	
Hartwood	d		00 40	06 19		06 48				07 50			08 48			09 48			10 48			11 49	
Shotts	d		00 46	06 23		07 00		07 30		08 02		08 35	09 00		09 34	09 58		10 35	10 54		11 33	11 52	
Fauldhouse	d		00 51	06 29		07 05				08 07			09 05			10 03			10 59			11 59	
Breich	d			06 33		07 09				08 10			09 09			10 07			11 03			12 03	
Addiewell	d		00 57	06 37		07 12				08 14			09 12			10 10			11 08			12 08	
West Calder	d	00 01	01 00	06 40		07 15		07 40		08 17		08 46	09 16		09 45	10 14		10 46	11 11		11 44	12 12	
Livingston South	d	00 04	01 04	06 45		07 20		07 45		08 22		08 50	09 20		09 49	10 18		10 50	11 16		11 48	12 16	
Kirknewton	d	00 08		06 53		07 24		07 48	08 07	08 26			09 26			10 22			11 23			12 20	
Curriehill	d	00 13		06 59		07 29		07 54	08 12	08 31			09 30			10 27			11 28			12 25	
Wester Hailes	d	00 17		07 02		07 32			08 16	08 35			09 33			10 30			11 32			12 29	
Kingsknowe	d	00 19		07 05		07 34			08 18	08 37			09 35			10 32			11 34			12 31	
Slateford	d	00 23		07 08		07 38			08 21	08 40			09 38			10 36			11 37			12 35	
Haymarket 230,238,242	d	00 31	01 20	07 12	06 57	07 43	07 48	08 01	08 27	08 46	08 52	09 05	09 42	09 58	10 05	10 41	10 45	11 04	11 43	11 54	12 02	12 42	13 00
Edinburgh 10 230,238,242	a	00 39	01 26	07 16	07 01	07 48	07 52	08 06	08 34	08 52	08 56	09 10	09 48	10 03	10 11	10 47	10 50	11 11	11 48	12 01	12 06	12 48	13 06

		SR	SR	XC	SR	SR	SR	SR	SR	XC	SR	SR	SR	SR	SR	XC	SR	SR	SR	SR	XC	SR	SR
				◇1 B				E		◇1 F			E			◇1 G					◇1		
Glasgow Central 15	225 d	12 03	12 16	13 00	13 03	13 17	14 03	14 06	14 16	15 00	15 03	15 16	15 47	16 03	16 16	17 00	17 02	17 16	18 10	18 16	19 00	19 07	19 16
Cambuslang	225 d																						
Uddingston	225 d		12 29			13 28			14 28			15 28			16 29			17u30		18 28			19 28
Bellshill	225 d	12 18	12 33		13 18	13 33	14 18		14 33		15 19	15 33		16 21	16 34		17 18	17 33	18 24	18 33		19 22	19 33
Motherwell	225 a			13 16				14 24		15 15			16 03			17 14					19 14		
	d			13 16				14 25		15 16			16 07			17 15					19 15		
Wishaw	225 d							14 31					16 20										
Carluke	225 d							14 38					16 28										
Carstairs	d							14 50					16 37										
Holytown	d		12 39			13 39			14 37			15 39			16 38			17 40		18 37			19 40
Carfin	d		12 40			13 41			14 39			15 41			16 40			17 41		18 39			19 42
Cleland	d		12 44			13 44			14 43			15 45			16 44			17 45		18 42			19 45
Hartwood	d		12 48			13 49			14 47			15 49			16 48			17 49		18 47			19 50
Shotts	d	12 36	12 58		13 33	13 57	14 36		15 01		15 35	16 03		16 38	17 01		17 33	17 59	18 37	18 59		19 37	20 00
Fauldhouse	d		13 02			14 01			15 06			16 08			17 05			18 04		19 03			20 05
Breich	d		13 06			14 05			15 11			16 12			17 09			18 08		19 07			20 09
Addiewell	d		13 10			14 09			15 16			16 15			17 13			18 11		19 11			20 12
West Calder	d	12 47	13 13		13 44	14 12	14 46		15 19		15 46	16 19		16 50	17 16		17 43	18 15	18 48	19 15		19 48	20 16
Livingston South	d	12 51	13 17		13 49	14 16	14 51		15 24		15 51	16 23		16 54	17 20		17 48	18 19	18 52	19 20		19 52	20 20
Kirknewton	d		13 22			14 20			15 28			16 27			17 26			18 23		19 27			20 24
Curriehill	d		13 27			14 26			15 33			16 32			17 31			18 28		19 31			20 29
Wester Hailes	d		13 30			14 29			15 36			16 35			17 34			18 31		19 34			20 32
Kingsknowe	d		13 32			14 32			15 38			16 37			17 36			18 33		19 36			20 34
Slateford	d		13 35			14 36			15 41			16 40			17 39			18 37		19 40			20 38
Haymarket 230,238,242	d	13 03	13 42	13 58	14 03	14 47	15 03	15 17	15 46	15 57	16 04	16 44	17 01	17 13	17 47	17 58	18 05	18 43	19 12	19 47	19 53	20 07	20 45
Edinburgh 10 230,238,242	a	13 10	13 48	14 03	14 07	14 51	15 08	15 22	15 51	16 03	16 10	16 48	17 06	17 17	17 51	18 03	18 11	18 48	19 18	19 54	20 00	20 12	20 52

		SR	SR	SR
		E		
Glasgow Central 15	225 d	19 46	21 16	23 03
Cambuslang	225 d			23 12
Uddingston	225 d		21 29	23 17
Bellshill	225 d		21 34	23 21
Motherwell	225 a	20 03		
	d	20 04		
Wishaw	225 d	20 10		
Carluke	225 d	20 16		
Carstairs	d	20 25		
Holytown	d		21 40	23 25
Carfin	d		21 43	23 27
Cleland	d		21 47	23 30
Hartwood	d		21 52	23 35
Shotts	d		21 56	23 45
Fauldhouse	d		22 02	23 50
Breich	d		22 06	23 54
Addiewell	d		22 10	23 57
West Calder	d		22 13	00 02
Livingston South	d		22 19	00 05
Kirknewton	d		22 28	00 09
Curriehill	d		22 34	00 14
Wester Hailes	d		22 37	00 17
Kingsknowe	d		22 40	00 19
Slateford	d		22 42	00 23
Haymarket 230,238,242	d	20 54	22 47	00 31
Edinburgh 10 230,238,242	a	20 59	22 51	00 36

A From Glasgow Central
B To Plymouth
C To London Kings Cross
D To Penzance
E From Ayr
F To Bristol Temple Meads
G To Birmingham New Street

Table T224-R

Sundays

15 December to 10 May

Glasgow Central, Motherwell, Carstairs and Shotts - Edinburgh

			SR	SR	XC	XC	SR	XC	SR	XC	SR	XC	SR	XC	SR	XC
					◇1	◇1		◇1		◇1		◇1		◇1		◇1
			A		B	C ✠		C		D		E		F		
Glasgow Central 15	225	d		10 16	10 55	12 02	12 16	13 48	14 18	14 55	16 16	16 55	18 16	19 00	20 16	20 58
Cambuslang	225	d														
Uddingston	225	d		10 29			12 29		14 30		16 29		18 29		20 28	
Bellshill	225	d		10 34			12 34		14 34		16 33		18 33		20 33	
Motherwell	225	a			11 13	12 17		14 02		15 13		17 12		19 14		21 17
		d			11 14	12 18		14 03		15 13		17 13		19 15		21 18
Wishaw	225	d														
Carluke	225	d														
Carstairs		d														
Holytown		d		10 39			12 39		14 39		16 40		18 39		20 38	
Carfin		d		10 41			12 41		14 41		16 42		18 41		20 40	
Cleland		d		10 44			12 45		14 45		16 45		18 44		20 43	
Hartwood		d		10 49			12 49		14 49		16 50		18 49		20 48	
Shotts		d		10 59			12 58		14 58		16 58		18 58		20 57	
Fauldhouse		d		11 04			13 03		15 03		17 03		19 02		21 01	
Breich		d		11 08			13 07		15 07		17 07		19 06		21 05	
Addiewell		d		11 11			13 10		15 11		17 10		19 11		21 10	
West Calder		d	00 02	11 15			13 14		15 15		17 14		19 14		21 13	
Livingston South		d	00 05	11 19			13 18		15 21		17 19		19 19		21 18	
Kirknewton		d	00 09	11 25			13 27		15 27		17 25		19 28		21 27	
Curriehill		d	00 14	11 30			13 32		15 31		17 30		19 32		21 31	
Wester Hailes		d	00 17	11 33			13 35		15 34		17 33		19 35		21 34	
Kingsknowe		d	00 19	11 35			13 37		15 36		17 35		19 37		21 36	
Slateford		d	00 23	11 39			13 41		15 40		17 39		19 41		21 40	
Haymarket	230,238,242 ⛴	d	00 31	11 43	11 53	12 56	13 46	14 42	15 44	15 52	17 45	17 51	19 45	19 59	21 45	22 04
Edinburgh 10	230,238,242	a	00 36	11 47	11 57	13 01	13 50	14 47	15 49	15 57	17 49	17 56	19 49	20 04	21 49	22 08

A not 15 December. From Glasgow Central
B To Penzance
C To Plymouth
D To Bristol Temple Meads
E To Birmingham New Street
F To Newcastle

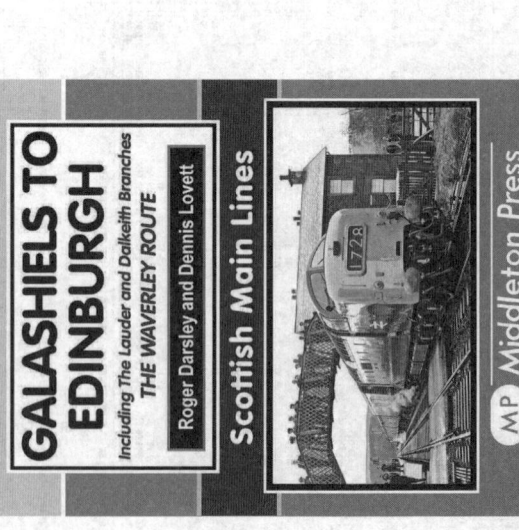

AVAILABLE FROM MP Middleton Press

GALASHIELS TO EDINBURGH

Including The Lauder and Dalkeith Branches
THE WAVERLEY ROUTE

Roger Darsley and Dennis Lovett

Scottish Main Lines

MP Middleton Press
EVOLVING THE ULTIMATE RAIL ENCYCLOPEDIA

Table T225-F

Mondays to Fridays

16 December to 15 May

Edinburgh, Lanark, Coatbridge, Motherwell, Whifflet, Larkhall and Hamilton - Glasgow

Miles	Miles	Miles	Miles	Miles			SR MX	SR MX	SR MX	SR	SR	SR	SR	SR	SR	SR	SR	SR	SR	SR	SR	SR	SR	SR
							A	B	B	C	D	D	E	D		F	D	E	C	D		G		D
—	—	—	0	—	**Edinburgh**	d																	05 53	
—	—	—	1¼	—	Haymarket ⛴	d																	05 57	
0	—	—	—	—	**Lanark**	d															06 21			
—	—	—	—	—	Carstairs	d									05 48									
8½	—	—	—	—	Carluke	d	00 01		00 09						05 57						06 31			
13	—	—	—	—	Wishaw	d	00 07		00 15						06 06						06 37			
—	—	—	34¼	—	Holytown	d		00 04															06 59	
15	—	—	—	—	Shieldmuir	d	00 10								06 10						06 41			
—	—	0	—	—	**Cumbernauld** 226	d														06 12				
—	—	1	—	—	Greenfaulds 226	d														06 14				
—	—	6½	—	—	Coatbridge Central	d														06 22				
—	—	7½	—	—	Whifflet	d														06 25				
16¼	0	11½	—	—	**Motherwell**	a	00 14		00 22						06 13					06 37	06 44			
						d				05 42	05 46	05 55		06 15	06 16		06 24		06 40	06 44	06 45			
—	4	—	—	—	Whifflet	d				05a49		06 02					06 31		06a48					06 59
—	5¼	—	—	—	Kirkwood	d						06 05					06 34							07 02
—	6	—	—	—	Bargeddie	d						06 08					06 37							07 05
—	7¾	—	—	—	Baillieston	d						06 12					06 41							07 08
—	8½	—	—	—	Mount Vernon	d						06 14					06 43							07 10
—	10	—	—	—	Carmyle	d						06 16					06 45							07 13
19	—	—	37	—	Bellshill	d		00 08							06 22						06 51		07 06	
21½	—	—	39¾	—	Uddingston	d		00 12							06 28	←					06 55	←	07 13	
—	—	12¼	—	—	Airbles	d					05 48			06 17		06 17				06 47		06 47		
—	—	—	—	0	**Larkhall**	d							06 00	→				06 33		→				
—	—	—	—	0¾	Merryton	d							06 02					06 35						
—	—	—	—	2¼	Chatelherault	d							06 05					06 38						
—	—	14½	—	3¾	**Hamilton Central**	d					05 54		06 09			06 23		06 42				06 52		
—	—	15½	—	4¾	Hamilton West	d					05 56		06 12			06 25		06 45				06 55		
—	—	17¼	—	6½	Blantyre	d					06 00		06 15			06 29		06 48				06 58		
—	—	21¼	—	9¼	Newton	d					06 04		06 19			06 33		06 53				07 02		
25	—	23¼	43	10¾	Cambuslang	d		00 18			06 07		06 23		06 33	06 36		06 56			07 00	07 06	07 18	
—	12½	25	—	12¾	Rutherglen	d					06 11	06 20	06 27			06 40	06 51	07 02				07 10		07 18
—	13¼	26	—	—	Dalmarnock	d					06 14	06 23	06 30			06 43	06 53					07 13		07 21
—	13¾	26¼	—	—	Bridgeton	d					06 16	06 25	06 32			06 45	06 55					07 15		07 23
—	15	27½	—	15¼	Argyle Street	d					06 19	06 28	06 35			06 48	06 59	07 07				07 18		07 27
29¾	—	—	47¼	—	**Glasgow Central H. Level** 15	a		00 30							06 42						07 11		07 29	
—	15½	28	—	15½	**Glasgow Central L. Level** 15	a					06 20	06 30	06 37			06 50	07 00	07 09				07 19		07 28
—	16	28½	—	16	Anderston	a					06 22	06 32	06 39			06 52	07 05	07 11				07 21		07 34
—	16½	29	—	16½	Exhibition Centre	a					06 24	06 34	06 41			06 54	07 07	07 13				07 24		07 36
—	17¾	30	—	17¾	**Partick** 226 ⛴	a					06 27	06 37	06 45			06 58	07 10	07 16				07 28		07 40
—	18½	30¼	—	18½	Hyndland 3 226	a					06 29	06 39	06 47			07 00	07 12	07 18				07 30		07 42

		SR	SR	SR	SR	SR	SR	SR	SR	SR	SR	SR	SR	SR	SR	TP	SR	SR	SR	SR	SR	SR
																◇1						
		E	D		F		D	D	H	I	E	G		G	H	J ✠		D	E	D		F
Edinburgh	d					06 40											06 55					
Haymarket ⛴	d					06 45											07 00					
Lanark	d			06 53									07 23								07 52	
Carstairs	d								07 13						07 35	07 44						
Carluke	d			07 03					07 22				07 33		07 48						08 02	
Wishaw	d			07 09					07 28				07 39		07 55						08 08	
Holytown	d														08 00		08 06					
Shieldmuir	d			07 13					07 32				07 42								08 13	
Cumbernauld 226	d							07 12														
Greenfaulds 226	d							07 14														
Coatbridge Central	d							07 22														
Whifflet	d							07 24				←										
Motherwell	a			07 16				07 32	07 35			07 32	07 45			07 59					08 18	
	d		07 15	07 16			07 21	07 44	07 35	07 43		07 44	07 46			08 01				08 16	08 18	
Whifflet	d						07 29	→		07a50								08 02				
Kirkwood	d						07 32											08 05				
Bargeddie	d						07 35											08 08				
Baillieston	d						07 39											08 12				
Mount Vernon	d						07 41											08 14				
Carmyle	d						07 43											08 17				
Bellshill	d			07 23		07 30			07 42				07 52		08 04		08 10				08 25	
Uddingston	d			07 27	←				07 47				07 56	←	08 08		08 15				08 29	←
Airbles	d		07 17		07 17							07 47		07 47						08 18		08 18
Larkhall	d	07 03	→								07 33	→							08 03	→		
Merryton	d	07 05									07 35								08 05			
Chatelherault	d	07 08									07 38								08 08			
Hamilton Central	d	07 12			07 23						07 43			07 53					08 12			08 24
Hamilton West	d	07 15			07 25						07 45			07 55					08 15			08 27
Blantyre	d	07 19			07 29						07 49			07 59					08 19			08 30
Newton	d	07 23			07 33						07 53			08 03					08 23			08 34
Cambuslang	d	07 27		07 31	07 36						07 57		08 01	08 07					08 27		08 34	08 38
Rutherglen	d	07 31			07 40		07 47		07 54		08 01			08 11	08 17			08 23	08 31			08 42
Dalmarnock	d				07 43		07 50				08 03			08 13				08 25	08 33			08 44
Bridgeton	d				07 45		07 52				08 05			08 15				08 27	08 35			08 46
Argyle Street	d	07 37			07 48		07 56		08 01		08 09			08 18	08 23			08 31	08 38			08 50
Glasgow Central H. Level 15	a			07 44		07 52							08 10			08 20	08 28				08 45	
Glasgow Central L. Level 15	a	07 39			07 50		07 57		08 03		08 11			08 20	08 25			08 32	08 40			08 51
Anderston	a	07 41			07 55		08 01		08 08		08 14			08 22	08 27			08 34	08 42			08 54
Exhibition Centre	a	07 43			07 57		08 04		08 11		08 17			08 24	08 29			08 36	08 44			08 56
Partick 226 ⛴	a	07 46			08 01		08 08		08 14		08 21			08 27	08 33			08 40	08 47			08 59
Hyndland 3 226	a	07 49			08 03		08 10		08 17		08 24			08 29	08 35			08 42	08 49			09 01

A From Lanark
B From Edinburgh
C To Cumbernauld
D To Dalmuir
E To Milngavie
F From Motherwell to Dalmuir
G From Cumbernauld to Dalmuir
H To Garscadden
I From Milngavie to Cumbernauld
J From Manchester Piccadilly

Table T225-F

Mondays to Fridays

16 December to 15 May

Edinburgh, Lanark, Coatbridge, Motherwell, Whifflet, Larkhall and Hamilton - Glasgow

	SR	SR	SR	SR	SR	SR		SR	SR	SR	SR	SR	SR	SR	SR	SR		SR	SR	SR	SR	SR	SR	SR
	A		B		C	A			D	A	C	A		E				A	C	B	A		D	A
Edinburgh d		07 41		07 58											08 21	08 57								
Haymarket d		07 46		08 03											08 27	09 01								
Lanark d								08 23					08 54									09 23		
Carstairs d		08 10																						
Carluke d		08 18						08 33					09 04									09 33		
Wishaw d		08 28						08 39					09 10									09 39		
Holytown d															09 30									
Shieldmuir d								08 42					09 14									09 42		
Cumbernauld 226 d						08 13															09 15			
Greenfaulds 226 d						08 15															09 17			
Coatbridge Central d						08 22															09 31			
Whifflet d						08 25			←												09 34			
Motherwell a		08 34				08 34		08 46	08 34				09 17								09 41	09 45		
d	08 22	08 34	08 43			08 47		08 47	08 47			09 15	09 17					09 23		09 43	09 45	09 47		
Whifflet d	08 30		08a50			→				08 58								09 30		09a50				09 58
Kirkwood d	08 33									09 01								09 33						10 01
Bargeddie d	08 36									09 04								09 36						10 04
Baillieston d	08 39									09 07								09 40						10 07
Mount Vernon d	08 41									09 09								09 42						10 09
Carmyle d	08 44									09 12								09 44						10 12
Bellshill d				08 50				08 54					09 24		09 35	09 50						09 54		
Uddingston d		08 39						08 58					09 28	←	09 40							09 58	←	
Airbles d									08 50			09 17		09 17							09 48		09 48	
Larkhall d					08 33						09 03	→							09 33		→			
Merryton d					08 35						09 05								09 35					
Chatelherault d					08 38						09 08								09 38					
Hamilton Central d					08 42				08 55		09 12			09 23					09 42				09 53	
Hamilton West d					08 45				08 58		09 15			09 25					09 45				09 56	
Blantyre d					08 48				09 01		09 18			09 29					09 48				09 59	
Newton d					08 52				09 05		09 22			09 33					09 52				10 06	
Cambuslang d					08 56			09 03	09 09		09 26		09 32	09 36					09 56			10 03	10 10	
Rutherglen d	08 48				09 01				09 13	09 17	09 31			09 40				09 49	10 00				10 14	10 17
Dalmarnock d	08 50				09 03				09 16	09 19	09 34			09 43				09 52	10 03				10 16	10 19
Bridgeton d	08 52				09 05				09 18	09 21	09 36			09 45				09 54	10 05				10 18	10 21
Argyle Street d	08 56				09 08				09 21	09 25	09 39			09 48				09 57	10 08				10 22	10 27
Glasgow Central H. Level 15 a		08 56		09 10				09 12					09 41		09 55	10 10						10 12		
Glasgow Central L. Level 15 a	08 57				09 10				09 23	09 26	09 40			09 50				09 59	10 09				10 23	10 28
Anderston a	09 00				09 12				09 25	09 29	09 42			09 52				10 04	10 11				10 27	10 33
Exhibition Centre a	09 02				09 14				09 27	09 31	09 44			09 54				10 06	10 13				10 29	10 36
Partick 226 a	09 06				09 17				09 31	09 35	09 48			09 58				10 10	10 16				10 33	10 40
Hyndland 3 226 a	09 08				09 19				09 33	09 37	09 50			10 00				10 12	10 18				10 35	10 42

	SR	TP		SR	SR	SR	SR	SR	SR	SR	SR	SR		SR	SR	SR	SR	SR	SR	SR	SR	SR		SR
	C	◇1 F		A		E			A	C	B	A			D	A	C	A		E	A			B
Edinburgh d							09 25	09 56														10 21		
Haymarket d							09 30	10 00														10 26		
Lanark d					09 53									10 23					10 53					
Carstairs d																						11 02		
Carluke d					10 03									10 33					11 03			11 10		
Wishaw d					10 10									10 40					11 11			11 16		
Holytown d							10 33																	
Shieldmuir d					10 15									10 45					11 14					
Cumbernauld 226 d												10 19												
Greenfaulds 226 d												10 21												
Coatbridge Central d												10 30												
Whifflet d												10 33												
Motherwell a					10 19							10 40		10 48					11 17			11 23		
d		10 15		10 18	10 19				10 23		10 45	10 46		10 48				11 15	11 17		11 23	11 34		11 45
Whifflet d									10 30		10a52					11 00					11 31			11a52
Kirkwood d									10 33							11 03					11 34			
Bargeddie d									10 36							11 06					11 37			
Baillieston d									10 40							11 09					11 40			
Mount Vernon d									10 42							11 11					11 42			
Carmyle d									10 44							11 14					11 45			
Bellshill d					10 26		10 38	10 49						10 55					11 24					
Uddingston d					10 30	←	10 42							10 59	←				11 28	←				
Airbles d				10 20		10 20						10 48			10 48			11 17		11 17				
Larkhall d	10 03			→						10 33		→					11 03	→						
Merryton d	10 05									10 35							11 05							
Chatelherault d	10 08									10 38							11 08							
Hamilton Central d	10 12					10 26				10 42					10 54		11 12			11 23				
Hamilton West d	10 15					10 28				10 45					10 56		11 15			11 25				
Blantyre d	10 18					10 32				10 48					11 00		11 18			11 29				
Newton d	10 22					10 36				10 52					11 05		11 23			11 33				
Cambuslang d	10 26				10 34	10 40				10 56				11 03	11 09		11 26		11 32	11 37				
Rutherglen d	10 31					10 44			10 49	11 00					11 14	11 19	11 30			11 41	11 49			
Dalmarnock d	10 33					10 47			10 51	11 03					11 17	11 21				11 44	11 52			
Bridgeton d	10 35					10 49			10 53	11 05					11 19	11 23				11 46	11 54			
Argyle Street d	10 38					10 52			10 57	11 08					11 23	11 26	11 36			11 49	11 57			
Glasgow Central H. Level 15 a		10 32			10 45		10 56	11 10						11 12					11 41			11 55		
Glasgow Central L. Level 15 a	10 40					10 54			10 58	11 09					11 24	11 28	11 38			11 50	11 59			
Anderston a	10 41					10 56			11 04	11 11					11 26	11 30	11 41			11 52	12 04			
Exhibition Centre a	10 43					10 58			11 06	11 13					11 28	11 32	11 43			11 54	12 06			
Partick 226 a	10 47					11 02			11 10	11 16					11 32	11 35	11 46			11 58	12 10			
Hyndland 3 226 a	10 49					11 04			11 12	11 18					11 34	11 37	11 48			12 00	12 12			

A To Dalmuir
B From Milngavie to Cumbernauld
C To Milngavie
D From Cumbernauld to Dalmuir
E From Motherwell to Dalmuir
F From Manchester Airport

Table T225-F

Mondays to Fridays

16 December to 15 May

Edinburgh, Lanark, Coatbridge, Motherwell, Whifflet, Larkhall and Hamilton - Glasgow

	SR	SR	SR	SR	SR	SR	SR	SR		SR	SR	TP	SR	SR	SR	SR	SR	SR		SR	SR	SR	SR	SR
			A	B		C	B	A			B	◇1 D		B	A	E	B	F		G		H	C	B
Edinburgh d	10 25	10 55											11 25							11 51	11 58			
Haymarket d	10 30	11 01											11 31							11 56	12 03			
Lanark d					11 23					11 53								12 23						
Carstairs d																				12 49				
Carluke d					11 33					12 03								12 33		12 58				
Wishaw d					11 40					12 10								12 40		13 04				
Holytown d	11 30												12 33											
Shieldmuir d					11 45					12 14								12 45						
Cumbernauld 226 d				11 19													12 19							
Greenfaulds 226 d				11 21													12 21							
Coatbridge Central d				11 30													12 30							
Whifflet d				11 33													12 33							
Motherwell a				11 40	11 48					12 17							12 40	12 48		13 09				
d				11 46	11 48					12 17	12 18	12 22		12 24		12 45	12 46	12 48		13 10				
Whifflet d							11 58							12 32		12a52								12 58
Kirkwood d							12 01							12 35										13 01
Bargeddie d							12 04							12 38										13 04
Baillieston d							12 07							12 41										13 07
Mount Vernon d							12 09							12 43										13 09
Carmyle d							12 12							12 46								←		13 12
Bellshill d	11 36	11 47			11 55					12 25			12 38					12 55			12 49	12 55		
Uddingston d	11 42				12 02	←				12 29			12 42					→				12 59	←	
Airbles d				11 48		11 48					12 20						12 48						12 48	
Larkhall d			11 33	→				12 03							12 33		→							
Merryton d			11 35					12 05							12 35									
Chatelherault d			11 38					12 08							12 38									
Hamilton Central d			11 42			11 54		12 13			12 26				12 42								12 54	
Hamilton West d			11 45			11 56		12 15			12 28				12 45								12 56	
Blantyre d			11 48			12 00		12 19			12 32				12 48								13 00	
Newton d			11 52			12 06		12 23			12 36				12 53								13 05	
Cambuslang d			11 56		12 06	12 09		12 26		12 34	12 39				12 56							13 03	13 09	
Rutherglen d			12 00			12 14	12 19	12 30			12 43			12 50	13 00								13 14	13 19
Dalmarnock d			12 03			12 16	12 21	12 33			12 46			12 52									13 16	13 21
Bridgeton d			12 05			12 18	12 23	12 35			12 48			12 54									13 18	13 23
Argyle Street d			12 08			12 22	12 27	12 38			12 51			12 58	13 06								13 22	13 27
Glasgow Central H. Level 15 a	11 57	12 09			12 15					12 45		12 39	12 56							13 24	13 09	13 12		
Glasgow Central L. Level 15 a			12 09			12 23	12 28	12 39			12 53			12 59	13 08								13 23	13 28
Anderston a			12 11			12 26	12 34	12 41			12 56			13 04	13 11								13 26	13 34
Exhibition Centre a			12 13			12 28	12 36	12 43			12 58			13 06	13 13								13 28	13 36
Partick 226 a			12 17			12 32	12 40	12 47			13 02			13 10	13 16								13 32	13 40
Hyndland 3 226 a			12 19			12 34	12 42	12 49			13 04			13 12	13 18								13 34	13 42

	SR	SR	SR	SR		SR	SR	SR	SR	SR	SR	SR	SR	SR		SR	SR	TP	SR	SR	SR	SR	SR	SR
	A					B	B	A	E	B		C	B	A			B	◇1 D		B	A	E	B	F
Edinburgh d			12 27	12 55															13 26					
Haymarket d			12 32	13 01															13 31					
Lanark d		12 53									13 23					13 53								14 23
Carstairs d																								
Carluke d		13 03									13 33					14 03								14 33
Wishaw d		13 09									13 40					14 09								14 40
Holytown d			13 32																14 32					
Shieldmuir d		13 12									13 45					14 12								14 45
Cumbernauld 226 d										13 17													14 19	
Greenfaulds 226 d										13 19													14 21	
Coatbridge Central d										13 30													14 30	
Whifflet d										13 33													14 33	
Motherwell a		13 15								13 40	13 48					14 15							14 40	14 48
d		13 16				13 18	13 19		13 45	13 45	13 48					14 16	14 18	14 20		14 22		14 45	14 46	14 48
Whifflet d							13 28		13a52				13 58							14 29		14a52		
Kirkwood d							13 31						14 01							14 32				
Bargeddie d							13 34						14 04							14 35				
Baillieston d							13 38						14 07							14 39				
Mount Vernon d							13 40						14 09							14 41				
Carmyle d							13 42						14 12							14 43				
Bellshill d		13 22	13 37	13 50							13 55					14 24			14 37					14 55
Uddingston d		13 26	13 41								14 02	←				14 29			14 41					→
Airbles d						13 20				13 47		13 47					14 20						14 48	
Larkhall d	13 03							13 33		→				14 03							14 33		→	
Merryton d	13 05							13 35						14 05							14 35			
Chatelherault d	13 08							13 38						14 08							14 38			
Hamilton Central d	13 13					13 26		13 42				13 53		14 12			14 26				14 42			
Hamilton West d	13 15					13 28		13 45				13 55		14 15			14 28				14 45			
Blantyre d	13 19					13 32		13 48				13 59		14 18			14 32				14 48			
Newton d	13 23					13 36		13 52				14 05		14 22			14 36				14 52			
Cambuslang d	13 26	13 31				13 39		13 56			14 06	14 10		14 26		14 33	14 39				14 56			
Rutherglen d	13 30					13 44	13 48	14 00				14 14	14 19	14 30			14 43			14 47	15 00			
Dalmarnock d	13 33					13 46	13 50	14 03				14 16	14 21	14 32			14 46			14 50	15 03			
Bridgeton d	13 35					13 48	13 52	14 05				14 18	14 23	14 34			14 48			14 52	15 05			
Argyle Street d	13 38					13 52	13 56	14 08				14 22	14 27	14 37			14 51			14 55	15 08			
Glasgow Central H. Level 15 a		13 40	13 56	14 10							14 15					14 45		14 38	14 56					
Glasgow Central L. Level 15 a	13 39					13 53	13 57	14 09				14 23	14 28	14 39			14 53			14 57	15 09			
Anderston a	13 41					13 55	14 03	14 11				14 26	14 34	14 41			14 55			15 04	15 11			
Exhibition Centre a	13 43					13 57	14 05	14 13				14 28	14 36	14 43			14 57			15 06	15 13			
Partick 226 a	13 47					14 01	14 09	14 17				14 31	14 40	14 46			15 01			15 10	15 17			
Hyndland 3 226 a	13 49					14 04	14 11	14 19				14 33	14 42	14 48			15 03			15 12	15 19			

A To Milngavie
B To Dalmuir
C From Cumbernauld to Dalmuir
D From Manchester Airport
E From Milngavie to Cumbernauld
F To Glasgow Central
G To Ayr
H From Lanark

Table T225-F

Edinburgh, Lanark, Coatbridge, Motherwell, Whifflet, Larkhall and Hamilton - Glasgow

Station			VT	SR	SR	SR	SR	SR	SR	SR		SR	SR	SR	SR	SR	SR	SR	SR		SR	SR	SR
			◇1 A ⊠	B		C	D	E	F	E	G		H			E	F	I	E		D		E	F	E
Edinburgh	d			13 53	13 56									14 25	14 56										
Haymarket	d			13 57	14 01									14 31	15 01										
Lanark	d										14 53									15 23					
Carstairs	d			14 33																					
Carluke	d			14 42							15 03									15 33					
Wishaw	d			14 55							15 09									15 40					
Holytown	d													15 30											
Shieldmuir	d										15 12									15 45					
Cumbernauld 226	d																		15 19						
Greenfaulds 226	d																		15 21						
Coatbridge Central	d																		15 30						
Whifflet	d																		15 33						
Motherwell	a			15 02							15 15								15 40	15 48					
	d		14 59	15 06						15 15	15 16					15 19		15 45	15 46	15 48					16 15
Whifflet	d							14 58								15 26		15a52					15 58		
Kirkwood	d							15 01								15 29							16 01		
Bargeddie	d							15 04								15 32							16 04		
Baillieston	d							15 07								15 36							16 07		
Mount Vernon	d							15 09								15 38							16 09		
Carmyle	d					←		15 12								15 40							16 12		
Bellshill	d				14 48	14 55					15 22			15 36	15 50					15 55					
Uddingston	d					14 59	←				15 26		←	15 42						16 02	←				
Airbles	d						14 48			15 17			15 17						15 48		15 48				16 17
Larkhall	d								15 03	→							15 33		→					16 03	→
Merryton	d								15 05								15 35							16 05	
Chatelherault	d								15 08								15 38							16 08	
Hamilton Central	d						14 54		15 13				15 23				15 42				15 54			16 12	
Hamilton West	d						14 56		15 15				15 25				15 45				15 56			16 15	
Blantyre	d						15 00		15 19				15 29				15 48				16 00			16 18	
Newton	d						15 05		15 23				15 33				15 53				16 05			16 22	
Cambuslang	d					15 03	15 09		15 26		15 31		15 36				15 56			16 06	16 09			16 26	
Rutherglen	d						15 14	15 18	15 30				15 40			15 47	16 01				16 13		16 18	16 30	
Dalmarnock	d						15 16	15 20	15 33				15 43			15 50					16 16		16 20	16 33	
Bridgeton	d						15 18	15 22	15 35				15 45			15 52					16 18		16 22	16 35	
Argyle Street	d						15 22	15 26	15 38				15 49			15 56	16 07				16 21		16 26	16 38	
Glasgow Central H. Level 15	a		15 15	15 25	15 09	15 12					15 40			15 56	16 09					16 15					
Glasgow Central L. Level 15	a						15 23	15 27	15 39				15 50			15 57	16 08				16 23		16 27	16 39	
Anderston	a						15 26	15 33	15 41				15 55			16 03	16 10				16 25		16 33	16 41	
Exhibition Centre	a						15 28	15 35	15 43				15 57			16 06	16 13				16 27		16 36	16 43	
Partick 226 ⛴	a						15 32	15 39	15 47				16 01			16 10	16 16				16 30		16 40	16 46	
Hyndland 3 226	a						15 34	15 42	15 49				16 03			16 12	16 18				16 32		16 42	16 48	

Station		SR	SR	SR	SR	SR	SR		SR	SR	SR	SR	SR	SR	SR	SR	SR		SR	SR	SR	SR	SR	SR	SR
			H		E		I			F	E		D	E	F	E			H			E	F	I	E
Edinburgh	d			15 26		15 49			15 57											16 25	16 57				
Haymarket	d			15 31		15 53			16 01											16 30	17 01				
Lanark	d	15 53										16 23					16 53								
Carstairs	d					16 16																			
Carluke	d	16 03				16 24						16 31					17 03								
Wishaw	d	16 09										16 40					17 09								
Holytown	d			16 33																17 31					
Shieldmuir	d	16 12										16 45					17 12								
Cumbernauld 226	d										16 19														17 19
Greenfaulds 226	d										16 21														17 21
Coatbridge Central	d										16 30														17 30
Whifflet	d										16 32														17 33
Motherwell	a	16 15				16 31					16 40	16 48					17 16								17 40
	d	16 16			16 19	16 32	16 45				16 46	16 48				17 15	17 17					17 20		17 46	17 46
Whifflet	d				16 28		16a52							16 58								17 29		17a53	
Kirkwood	d				16 31									17 01								17 32			
Bargeddie	d				16 34									17 04								17 35			
Baillieston	d				16 38									17 07								17 39			
Mount Vernon	d				16 40									17 09								17 41			
Carmyle	d				16 42									17 12								17 43			
Bellshill	d	16 23		16 38					16 47			16 55					17 24			17 35	17 48				
Uddingston	d	16 29	←	16 42								16 58	←				17 28		←	17 39					
Airbles	d		16 17								16 48		16 48			17 17			17 17						17 49
Larkhall	d									16 33	→				17 03	→							17 33		→
Merryton	d									16 35					17 05								17 35		
Chatelherault	d									16 38					17 08								17 38		
Hamilton Central	d		16 23							16 42			16 54		17 12				17 23				17 42		
Hamilton West	d		16 25							16 45			16 56		17 15				17 25				17 45		
Blantyre	d		16 29							16 48			17 00		17 18				17 29				17 48		
Newton	d		16 34							16 52			17 06		17 22				17 33				17 52		
Cambuslang	d	16 33	16 38							16 56		17 02	17 10		17 26		17 32		17 36	17 45			17 56		
Rutherglen	d		16 42		16 47					17 00			17 14	17 17	17 30				17 41			17 47	18 00		
Dalmarnock	d		16 44		16 49					17 02				17 19	17 33				17 43			17 50	18 03		
Bridgeton	d		16 46		16 51					17 04				17 21	17 35				17 45			17 52	18 05		
Argyle Street	d		16 50		16 55					17 08			17 19	17 25	17 38				17 49			17 56	18 08		
Glasgow Central H. Level 15	a	16 42		16 55		16 51			17 07			17 12					17 41			17 55	18 09				
Glasgow Central L. Level 15	a		16 51		16 56					17 09			17 21	17 26	17 39				17 50			17 57	18 09		
Anderston	a		16 53		17 03					17 11			17 23	17 29	17 41				17 52			18 03	18 11		
Exhibition Centre	a		16 55		17 06					17 13			17 25	17 31	17 43				17 54			18 05	18 13		
Partick 226 ⛴	a		16 59		17 10					17 17			17 28	17 38	17 47				17 58			18 10	18 16		
Hyndland 3 226	a		17 01		17 12					17 19			17 31	17 42	17 49				18 00			18 12	18 18		

A From London Euston
B To Ayr
C From Lanark
D From Cumbernauld to Dalmuir
E To Dalmuir
F To Milngavie
G From Glasgow Central
H From Motherwell to Dalmuir
I From Milngavie to Cumbernauld

Table T225-F

Edinburgh, Lanark, Coatbridge, Motherwell, Whifflet, Larkhall and Hamilton - Glasgow

Station		SR	SR		SR	SR	SR	SR	TP	SR	SR	SR	SR		SR	SR	SR	SR	SR	SR	SR	SR	SR		SR
			A		B	C		B	◇1 D ⚭		B	E	F			C	B		A			B	C		B
Edinburgh	d									17 26		17 42			17 50					17 56					
Haymarket	d									17 30		17 47			17 54					18 01					
Lanark	d	17 23					17 53											18 25							
Carstairs	d											18 13									18 38				
Carluke	d	17 33					18 03					18 21						18 35			18 46				
Wishaw	d	17 40					18 10					18 27						18 41			18 58				
Holytown	d									18 32										19 01					
Shieldmuir	d	17 45					18 13											18 45			19 03				
Cumbernauld 226	d																18 18								
Greenfaulds 226	d																18 20								
Coatbridge Central	d																18 29								
Whifflet	d																18 32		←						
Motherwell	a	17 48					18 16					18 32					18 40	18 48	18 40		19 07				
	d	17 49					18 17	18 17	18 21		18 23	18 33	18 45				18 48	18 48	18 48						19 15
Whifflet	d				17 58						18 31		18a52				→					18 58			
Kirkwood	d				18 01						18 34											19 01			
Bargeddie	d				18 04						18 37											19 04			
Baillieston	d				18 07						18 40											19 07			
Mount Vernon	d				18 09						18 42											19 09			
Carmyle	d				18 12						18 45											19 12			
Bellshill	d	17 56					18 25			18 37					18 43			18 55		19 04					
Uddingston	d	18 03	←				18 29			18 41								18 59		19 10					
Airbles	d		17 49					18 19											18 50						19 17
Larkhall	d					18 03										18 33							19 03		→
Merryton	d					18 05										18 35							19 05		
Chatelherault	d					18 08										18 38							19 08		
Hamilton Central	d		17 54			18 13		18 26								18 42			18 56				19 12		
Hamilton West	d		17 57			18 15		18 29								18 45			18 58				19 15		
Blantyre	d		18 00			18 19		18 32								18 48			19 02				19 18		
Newton	d		18 07			18 23		18 36								18 52			19 06				19 22		
Cambuslang	d	18 07	18 10			18 27	18 33	18 40							18 52	18 56		19 03	19 10	19 16			19 26		
Rutherglen	d		18 14		18 18	18 31		18 44			18 49					19 00			19 14			19 18	19 30		
Dalmarnock	d		18 17		18 21			18 46			18 52					19 03			19 17			19 21	19 32		
Bridgeton	d		18 19		18 23			18 48			18 54					19 05			19 19			19 23	19 34		
Argyle Street	d		18 22		18 27	18 37		18 51			18 57					19 08			19 22			19 26	19 38		
Glasgow Central H. Level 15	a	18 16					18 42		18 39	18 56		18 53			19 07			19 13		19 28					
Glasgow Central L. Level 15	a		18 24		18 28	18 38		18 53			18 59					19 09			19 24			19 27	19 39		
Anderston	a		18 27		18 34	18 40		18 55			19 01					19 11			19 26			19 29	19 41		
Exhibition Centre	a		18 29		18 36	18 42		18 57			19 03					19 13			19 28			19 31	19 43		
Partick 226 ⛴	a		18 33		18 40	18 47		19 00			19 07					19 17			19 32			19 35	19 47		
Hyndland 3 226	a		18 35		18 42	18 49		19 02			19 09					19 19			19 34			19 37	19 50		

Station		SR	SR	SR	SR	SR	SR	SR	SR		SR	SR	SR	SR	SR	SR	SR	TP	SR		SR	SR	SR	SR	SR
			G	B	E	F		C	B			A	B	C	B		G	◇1 D ⚭			B	C	F	B	
Edinburgh	d				18 26		18 56												19 26						
Haymarket	d				18 31		19 00												19 30						
Lanark	d	18 53									19 23					19 53									20 23
Carstairs	d				19 13																				
Carluke	d	19 03			19 22						19 33					20 03									20 33
Wishaw	d	19 09			19 27						19 40					20 11									20 39
Holytown	d																		20 33						
Shieldmuir	d	19 12									19 45					20 14									20 45
Cumbernauld 226	d								19 19															20 19	
Greenfaulds 226	d								19 21															20 21	
Coatbridge Central	d								19 30															20 30	
Whifflet	d								19 33			←												20 33	
Motherwell	a	19 15			19 33				19 40		19 48	19 40				20 17								20 40	20 48
	d	19 16		19 20	19 34	19 45			19 48		19 48	19 48			20 16	20 18		20 22			20 26		20 45	20 46	20 48
Whifflet	d			19 28		19a52			→				19 59								20 33		20a52		
Kirkwood	d			19 31									20 02								20 36				
Bargeddie	d			19 34									20 05								20 39				
Baillieston	d			19 38									20 08								20 43				
Mount Vernon	d			19 40									20 10								20 45				
Carmyle	d			19 42									20 13								20 47				
Bellshill	d	19 22					19 49				19 55					20 24			20 38						20 55
Uddingston	d	19 26	←								19 59					20 29	←		20 42						20 59
Airbles	d		19 17									19 50			20 18		20 18							20 48	
Larkhall	d							19 33						20 03	→							20 33		→	
Merryton	d							19 35						20 05								20 35			
Chatelherault	d							19 38						20 08								20 38			
Hamilton Central	d		19 23					19 42				19 56		20 12			20 25					20 44			
Hamilton West	d		19 25					19 45				19 58		20 15			20 28					20 46			
Blantyre	d		19 29					19 49				20 02		20 19			20 31					20 50			
Newton	d		19 33					19 53				20 06		20 24			20 36					20 54			
Cambuslang	d	19 31	19 36					19 56			20 03	20 10		20 27		20 34	20 40					20 57			21 03
Rutherglen	d		19 40	19 47				20 00				20 14	20 17	20 31			20 44				20 52	21 01			
Dalmarnock	d		19 43	19 49				20 03				20 16	20 20	20 34			20 47				20 55	21 04			
Bridgeton	d		19 45	19 51				20 05				20 18	20 22	20 36			20 49				20 57	21 06			
Argyle Street	d		19 48	19 55				20 08				20 22	20 25	20 39			20 52				21 00	21 09			
Glasgow Central H. Level 15	a	19 40			19 54		20 10				20 12					20 44		20 39	20 56						21 12
Glasgow Central L. Level 15	a		19 50	19 56				20 09				20 23	20 27	20 41			20 54				21 02	21 10			
Anderston	a		19 52	19 59				20 11				20 25	20 30	20 43			20 56				21 04	21 12			
Exhibition Centre	a		19 54	20 01				20 13				20 27	20 32	20 45			20 58				21 06	21 14			
Partick 226 ⛴	a		19 58	20 05				20 17				20 31	20 35	20 48			21 01				21 09	21 18			
Hyndland 3 226	a		20 00	20 07				20 19				20 33	20 37	20 50			21 03				21 11	21 20			

A From Cumbernauld to Dalmuir
B To Dalmuir
C To Milngavie
D From Manchester Airport
E To Ayr
F From Milngavie to Cumbernauld
G From Motherwell to Dalmuir

Table T225-F

16 December to 15 May

Edinburgh, Lanark, Coatbridge, Motherwell, Whifflet, Larkhall and Hamilton - Glasgow

		SR A	SR B	SR C	SR	SR B	SR B	VT ◇1 D ⊠	SR C	SR E	VT ◇1 D ⊠	SR B	SR	SR A	SR B	SR C	SR	SR B	SR B	TP ◇1 F	SR	SR C	SR E
Edinburgh	d																				21 25		
Haymarket	d																				21 30		
Lanark	d				20 52								21 23				21 53						
Carstairs	d																						
Carluke	d				21 02								21 33				22 03						
Wishaw	d				21 08								21 41				22 09						
Holytown	d																				22 35		
Shieldmuir	d				21 11								21 47				22 12						
Cumbernauld 226	d											21 21											
Greenfaulds 226	d											21 23											
Coatbridge Central	d											21 30											
Whifflet	d											21 33											
Motherwell	a				21 14							21 40	21 50				22 15						
	d				21 15	21 17	21 22	21 28		21 43	21 46	21 46	21 50				22 16	22 16	22 19	22 22			22 45
Whifflet	d		20 59				21 30			21a50					21 59				22 27				22a52
Kirkwood	d		21 02				21 33								22 02				22 30				
Bargeddie	d		21 05				21 36								22 05				22 33				
Baillieston	d		21 08				21 39								22 08				22 36				
Mount Vernon	d		21 10				21 41								22 10				22 38				
Carmyle	d		21 13				21 44								22 13				22 41				
Bellshill	d				21 21								21 57				22 23				22 39		
Uddingston	d	←			21 25								22 01	←			22 29				22 43		
Airbles	d	20 48				21 19						21 48		21 48				22 18					
Larkhall	d			21 03					21 33			→				22 03						22 33	
Merryton	d			21 05					21 35							22 05						22 35	
Chatelherault	d			21 08					21 38							22 08						22 38	
Hamilton Central	d	20 54		21 12		21 25			21 42					21 54		22 12		22 24				22 42	
Hamilton West	d	20 57		21 15		21 27			21 45					21 56		22 15		22 26				22 45	
Blantyre	d	21 00		21 18		21 31			21 48					22 00		22 18		22 30				22 48	
Newton	d	21 05		21 22		21 35			21 52					22 04		22 22		22 34				22 53	
Cambuslang	d	21 09		21 26	21 30	21 38			21 56				22 05	22 08		22 26	22 34	22 37				22 56	
Rutherglen	d	21 13	21 17	21 30		21 42	21 48		22 00					22 12	22 18	22 30		22 41	22 45			23 01	
Dalmarnock	d	21 15	21 20	21 32		21 45	21 51		22 02					22 15	22 20	22 33		22 44	22 47				
Bridgeton	d	21 17	21 22	21 34		21 47	21 53		22 04					22 17	22 22	22 35		22 46	22 49				
Argyle Street	d	21 21	21 25	21 37		21 50	21 56		22 07					22 20	22 26	22 38		22 49	22 53			23 07	
Glasgow Central H. Level 15	a				21 41			21 44			22 11		22 14				22 43			22 40	22 55		
Glasgow Central L. Level 15	a	21 22	21 27	21 39		21 51	21 58		22 09					22 22	22 27	22 39		22 51	22 54			23 08	
Anderston	a	21 24	21 29	21 41		21 53	22 00		22 11					22 24	22 29	22 41		22 53	22 58			23 10	
Exhibition Centre	a	21 26	21 31	21 43		21 55	22 02		22 13					22 26	22 31	22 43		22 55	23 00			23 12	
Partick 226	a	21 30	21 35	21 47		21 59	22 05		22 16					22 29	22 35	22 46		22 58	23 04			23 16	
Hyndland 3 226	a	21 32	21 37	21 49		22 01	22 07		22 18					22 31	22 37	22 48		23 00	23 06			23 18	

		SR G	SR	SR H	VT ◇1 D ⊠	SR B	SR C	SR	SR FO B	SR	SR FO C	SR FO	SR FX	SR	SR
Edinburgh	d											22 56	22 56		23 13
Haymarket	d											23 00	23 00		23 17
Lanark	d		22 23					22 51		23 21				23 51	
Carstairs	d														23 59
Carluke	d		22 33					23 01		23 31				00 01	00 09
Wishaw	d		22 40					23 07		23 37				00 07	00 15
Holytown	d											00 04	00 04		
Shieldmuir	d		22 44					23 10		23 40				00 10	
Cumbernauld 226	d	22 21													
Greenfaulds 226	d	22 23													
Coatbridge Central	d	22 31													
Whifflet	d	22 33													
Motherwell	a	22 41	22 47					23 13		23 43				00 14	00 22
	d	22 46	22 48		22 53			23 14	23 22						
Whifflet	d					22 58			23 29						
Kirkwood	d					23 01			23 32						
Bargeddie	d					23 04			23 35						
Baillieston	d					23 07			23 39						
Mount Vernon	d					23 09			23 41						
Carmyle	d					23 12			23 43						
Bellshill	d		22 55					23 20				00 08	00 08		
Uddingston	d		22 59	←				23 24				00 11	00 12		
Airbles	d	22 48		22 48											
Larkhall	d	→					23 03				23 33				
Merryton	d						23 05				23 35				
Chatelherault	d						23 08				23 38				
Hamilton Central	d			22 54			23 12				23 42				
Hamilton West	d			22 57			23 15				23 45				
Blantyre	d			23 00			23 18				23 48				
Newton	d			23 08			23 22				23 55				
Cambuslang	d		23 03	23 11			23 26	23 29			00 01	00 17	00 18		
Rutherglen	d			23 15		23 18	23 30		23 47		00 05				
Dalmarnock	d			23 18		23 21	23 33		23 50		00 06				
Bridgeton	d			23 20		23 23	23 35		23 52		00 08				
Argyle Street	d			23 23		23 26	23 38		23 55		00 11				
Glasgow Central H. Level 15	a		23 12		23 09			23 38				00 29	00 30		
Glasgow Central L. Level 15	a			23 24		23 28	23 39		23 57		00 13				
Anderston	a			23 26		23 30	23 41		23 59		00 15				
Exhibition Centre	a			23 28		23 32	23 43		00 02		00 17				
Partick 226	a			23 32		23 35	23 47		00 05		00 20				
Hyndland 3 226	a			23 34		23 37	23 49		00 07		00 22				

A From Cumbernauld to Dalmuir
B To Dalmuir
C To Milngavie
D From London Euston
E From Milngavie to Cumbernauld
F From Manchester Airport
G To Garscadden
H From Cumbernauld to Garscadden

Table T225-F

21 December to 16 May

Edinburgh, Lanark, Coatbridge, Motherwell, Whifflet, Larkhall and Hamilton - Glasgow

		SR A	SR B	SR C	SR C	SR D	SR E	SR E	SR F	SR E	SR	SR G	SR E	SR F	SR D	SR E	SR	SR H	SR	SR E	SR F	SR E	SR
Edinburgh	d																		05 53				
Haymarket	d																		05 57				
Lanark	d																06 22						06 53
Carstairs	d										05 48												
Carluke	d		00 01		00 09						05 57						06 32						07 03
Wishaw	d		00 07		00 15						06 07						06 38						07 09
Holytown	d			00 04															06 59				
Shieldmuir	d		00 10								06 12						06 41						07 13
Cumbernauld 226	d															06 13							
Greenfaulds 226	d															06 15							
Coatbridge Central	d															06 22							
Whifflet	d															06 25							
Motherwell	a		00 14		00 22						06 16					06 37	06 44						07 16
	d					05 42	05 46	05 55		06 15	06 18		06 24		06 40	06 44	06 45					07 15	07 16
Whifflet	d					05a49		06 02					06 31		06a48					06 59			
Kirkwood	d							06 05					06 34							07 02			
Bargeddie	d							06 08					06 37							07 05			
Baillieston	d							06 12					06 41							07 08			
Mount Vernon	d							06 14					06 43							07 10			
Carmyle	d							06 16					06 45							07 13			
Bellshill	d			00 08							06 24						06 51		07 08				07 23
Uddingston	d			00 11							06 28	←					06 55	←	07 15				07 27
Airbles	d						05 48			06 17		06 17				06 47		06 47				07 17	
Larkhall	d								06 00	→				06 33		→					07 03	→	
Merryton	d								06 02					06 35							07 05		
Chatelherault	d								06 05					06 38							07 08		
Hamilton Central	d						05 54		06 09			06 23		06 42				06 52			07 12		
Hamilton West	d						05 56		06 12			06 25		06 45				06 55			07 15		
Blantyre	d						06 00		06 15			06 29		06 48				06 58			07 19		
Newton	d						06 04		06 19			06 33		06 53				07 02			07 23		
Cambuslang	d	00 01		00 17			06 07		06 23		06 33	06 36		06 56			07 00	07 06	07 20		07 27		07 31
Rutherglen	d	00 05					06 11	06 20	06 27			06 40	06 51	07 02				07 10		07 18	07 31		
Dalmarnock	d	00 06					06 14	06 23	06 30			06 43	06 53					07 13		07 21			
Bridgeton	d	00 08					06 16	06 25	06 32			06 45	06 55					07 15		07 23			
Argyle Street	d	00 11					06 19	06 28	06 35			06 48	06 59	07 07				07 18		07 27	07 37		
Glasgow Central H. Level 15	a			00 29							06 42						07 13		07 30				07 41
Glasgow Central L. Level 15	a	00 13					06 20	06 30	06 37			06 50	07 00	07 09				07 19		07 28	07 39		
Anderston	a	00 15					06 22	06 32	06 39			06 52	07 05	07 11				07 21		07 34	07 41		
Exhibition Centre	a	00 17					06 24	06 34	06 41			06 54	07 07	07 13				07 24		07 36	07 43		
Partick 226	a	00 20					06 27	06 37	06 45			06 58	07 10	07 16				07 28		07 40	07 46		
Hyndland 3 226	a	00 22					06 29	06 39	06 47			07 00	07 12	07 18				07 30		07 42	07 49		

		SR G	SR	SR E	SR F	SR I	SR E	SR	SR H	TP ◇1 J	SR	SR E	SR F	SR E	SR	SR G	SR E	SR F	SR I	SR E	SR K	SR L	SR
Edinburgh	d		06 40								06 55											07 53	07 56
Haymarket	d		06 45								07 00											07 58	08 02
Lanark	d							07 23							07 52						08 23		
Carstairs	d									07 45												08 31	
Carluke	d							07 33							08 02						08 33	08 39	
Wishaw	d							07 39							08 08						08 39	08 55	
Holytown	d										08 06												
Shieldmuir	d							07 42							08 14						08 42		
Cumbernauld 226	d						07 12													08 13			
Greenfaulds 226	d						07 14													08 15			
Coatbridge Central	d						07 22													08 22			
Whifflet	d						07 24													08 25			
Motherwell	a						07 32	07 45		07 59					08 18					08 34	08 46	09 00	
	d			07 21		07 43	07 44	07 46		08 01				08 16	08 18		08 22		08 43	08 47	08 47	09 01	
Whifflet	d			07 29		07a50						08 02					08 30		08a50	→			
Kirkwood	d			07 32								08 05					08 33						
Bargeddie	d			07 35								08 08					08 36						
Baillieston	d			07 39								08 12					08 39						
Mount Vernon	d			07 41								08 14					08 41						
Carmyle	d			07 43								08 17					08 44						
Bellshill	d		07 31					07 52			08 10				08 25						08 56		08 50
Uddingston	d	←						07 56	←		08 14				08 29	←					→		
Airbles	d	07 17					07 47		07 47					08 18		08 18							
Larkhall	d				07 33		→						08 03	→				08 33					
Merryton	d				07 35								08 05					08 35					
Chatelherault	d				07 38								08 08					08 38					
Hamilton Central	d	07 23			07 43				07 53				08 12			08 24		08 42					
Hamilton West	d	07 25			07 45				07 55				08 15			08 27		08 45					
Blantyre	d	07 29			07 49				07 59				08 19			08 30		08 48					
Newton	d	07 33			07 53				08 03				08 23			08 34		08 52					
Cambuslang	d	07 36			07 57			08 01	08 07				08 27		08 33	08 38		08 56					
Rutherglen	d	07 40		07 47	08 01				08 11			08 23	08 31			08 42	08 48	09 01					
Dalmarnock	d	07 43		07 50	08 03				08 13			08 25	08 33			08 44	08 50	09 03					
Bridgeton	d	07 45		07 52	08 05				08 15			08 27	08 35			08 46	08 52	09 05					
Argyle Street	d	07 48		07 56	08 09				08 18			08 31	08 38			08 50	08 56	09 08					
Glasgow Central H. Level 15	a		07 53					08 10		08 20	08 28				08 42							09 24	09 10
Glasgow Central L. Level 15	a	07 50		07 57	08 11				08 20			08 32	08 40			08 51	08 57	09 10					
Anderston	a	07 55		08 01	08 14				08 22			08 34	08 42			08 54	09 00	09 12					
Exhibition Centre	a	07 57		08 04	08 17				08 24			08 36	08 44			08 56	09 02	09 14					
Partick 226	a	08 01		08 08	08 21				08 27			08 40	08 47			08 59	09 06	09 17					
Hyndland 3 226	a	08 03		08 10	08 24				08 29			08 42	08 49			09 01	09 08	09 19					

A From Larkhall to Milngavie
B From Lanark
C From Edinburgh
D To Cumbernauld
E To Dalmuir
F To Milngavie
G From Motherwell to Dalmuir
H From Cumbernauld to Dalmuir
I From Milngavie to Cumbernauld
J From Manchester Piccadilly
K To Glasgow Central
L To Ayr

Table T225-F

Saturdays

21 December to 16 May

Edinburgh, Lanark, Coatbridge, Motherwell, Whifflet, Larkhall and Hamilton - Glasgow

	SR		SR	SR	SR	SR	SR	SR	SR	SR	SR		SR	SR	SR	SR	SR	SR	SR	SR	SR		TP	SR
	A		B	C	D	C		E			C		D	F	C		B	C	D		C		◇1 G	
Edinburgh d									08 28	08 58														09 27
Haymarket d									08 33	09 02														09 31
Lanark d							08 54									09 23				09 52				
Carstairs d																								
Carluke d							09 04									09 33				10 02				
Wishaw d							09 10									09 40				10 09				
Holytown d									09 32															10 31
Shieldmuir d							09 13									09 44				10 13				
Cumbernauld 226 d															09 19									
Greenfaulds 226 d															09 21									
Coatbridge Central d															09 31									
Whifflet d			←												09 34									
Motherwell a			08 34				09 16								09 41	09 47				10 16				
d			08 47			09 15	09 16				09 23			09 43	09 45	09 47				10 16	10 18		10 21	
Whifflet d				08 58							09 30			09a50				09 58						
Kirkwood d				09 01							09 33							10 01						
Bargeddie d				09 04							09 36							10 04						
Baillieston d				09 07							09 40							10 07						
Mount Vernon d				09 09							09 42							10 09						
Carmyle d	←			09 12							09 44							10 12						
Bellshill d	08 56						09 23		09 37	09 50						09 54				10 23				10 36
Uddingston d	09 00						09 27	←	09 41							09 58	←			10 28				10 41
Airbles d			08 50			09 17		09 17							09 48		09 48				10 20			
Larkhall d					09 03	→							09 33		→				10 03					
Merryton d					09 05								09 35						10 05					
Chatelherault d					09 08								09 38						10 08					
Hamilton Central d			08 55		09 12			09 23					09 42				09 53		10 12		10 26			
Hamilton West d			08 58		09 15			09 25					09 45				09 56		10 15		10 28			
Blantyre d			09 01		09 18			09 29					09 48				09 59		10 18		10 32			
Newton d			09 05		09 22			09 33					09 52				10 06		10 22		10 36			
Cambuslang d	09 06		09 09		09 26		09 31	09 36					09 56			10 03	10 10		10 26	10 32	10 40			
Rutherglen d			09 13	09 17	09 31			09 40			09 49		10 00				10 14	10 17	10 31		10 44			
Dalmarnock d			09 16	09 19	09 34			09 43			09 52		10 03				10 16	10 19	10 33		10 47			
Bridgeton d			09 18	09 21	09 36			09 45			09 54		10 05				10 18	10 21	10 35		10 49			
Argyle Street d			09 21	09 25	09 39			09 48			09 57		10 08				10 22	10 27	10 38		10 52			
Glasgow Central H. Level 15 a	09 16						09 42		09 56	10 10						10 12				10 41			10 38	10 56
Glasgow Central L. Level 15 a			09 23	09 26	09 40			09 50			09 59		10 09				10 23	10 28	10 40		10 54			
Anderston a			09 25	09 29	09 42			09 52			10 04		10 11				10 27	10 33	10 41		10 56			
Exhibition Centre a			09 27	09 31	09 44			09 54			10 06		10 13				10 29	10 36	10 43		10 58			
Partick 226 a			09 31	09 35	09 48			09 58			10 10		10 16				10 33	10 40	10 47		11 02			
Hyndland 3 226 a			09 33	09 37	09 50			10 00			10 12		10 18				10 35	10 42	10 49		11 04			

	SR	SR	SR	SR	SR	SR	SR		SR	SR	SR	SR	SR	SR	SR	SR	SR		SR	SR	SR	SR	SR	SR
		C	D	F	C		B		C	D	C		E	C		F				D	C		B	C
Edinburgh d	09 57														10 24		10 27		10 57					
Haymarket d	10 01														10 28		10 32		11 01					
Lanark d						10 23						10 53										11 23		
Carstairs d															11 07									
Carluke d						10 33						11 03			11 19							11 33		
Wishaw d						10 40						11 09			11 26							11 40		
Holytown d																	11 30							
Shieldmuir d						10 45						11 13										11 45		
Cumbernauld 226 d					10 19																11 19			
Greenfaulds 226 d					10 21																11 21			
Coatbridge Central d					10 30																11 30			
Whifflet d					10 33																11 33			
Motherwell a					10 40	10 48						11 16			11 32						11 40	11 48		
d		10 23		10 45	10 46	10 48					11 15	11 17		11 23	11 34	11 45					11 46	11 48		
Whifflet d		10 30		10a52					11 00					11 31		11a52								11 58
Kirkwood d		10 33							11 03					11 34										12 01
Bargeddie d		10 36							11 06					11 37										12 04
Baillieston d		10 40							11 09					11 40										12 07
Mount Vernon d		10 42							11 11					11 42										12 09
Carmyle d		10 44							11 14					11 45										12 12
Bellshill d	10 49					10 55						11 25					11 36		11 47			11 55		
Uddingston d						10 59	←					11 29	←				11 42					12 02	←	
Airbles d					10 48		10 48				11 17		11 17								11 48		11 48	
Larkhall d			10 33		→					11 03	→									11 33	→			
Merryton d			10 35							11 05										11 35				
Chatelherault d			10 38							11 08										11 38				
Hamilton Central d			10 42				10 54			11 12			11 23							11 42			11 54	
Hamilton West d			10 45				10 56			11 15			11 25							11 45			11 56	
Blantyre d			10 48				11 00			11 18			11 29							11 48			12 00	
Newton d			10 52				11 05			11 23			11 33							11 52			12 06	
Cambuslang d			10 56			11 03	11 09			11 26		11 33	11 37							11 56		12 06	12 10	
Rutherglen d		10 49	11 00				11 14		11 19	11 30			11 41	11 49						12 00			12 14	12 19
Dalmarnock d		10 51	11 03				11 17		11 21				11 44	11 52						12 03			12 16	12 21
Bridgeton d		10 53	11 05				11 19		11 23				11 46	11 54						12 05			12 18	12 23
Argyle Street d		10 57	11 08				11 23		11 26	11 36			11 49	11 57						12 08			12 22	12 27
Glasgow Central H. Level 15 a	11 10					11 12						11 42			11 54		11 57		12 09			12 15		
Glasgow Central L. Level 15 a		10 58	11 09				11 24		11 28	11 38			11 50	11 59						12 09			12 23	12 28
Anderston a		11 04	11 11				11 26		11 30	11 41			11 52	12 04						12 11			12 26	12 34
Exhibition Centre a		11 06	11 13				11 28		11 32	11 43			11 54	12 06						12 13			12 28	12 36
Partick 226 a		11 10	11 16				11 32		11 35	11 46			11 58	12 10						12 17			12 32	12 40
Hyndland 3 226 a		11 12	11 18				11 34		11 37	11 48			12 00	12 12						12 19			12 34	12 42

A From Lanark
B From Cumbernauld to Dalmuir
C To Dalmuir
D To Milngavie
E From Motherwell to Dalmuir
F From Milngavie to Cumbernauld
G From Manchester Airport

Table T225-F

Saturdays

21 December to 16 May

Edinburgh, Lanark, Coatbridge, Motherwell, Whifflet, Larkhall and Hamilton - Glasgow

	SR	SR	SR		TP	SR	SR	SR	SR	SR	SR	SR	SR		SR	SR	SR	SR	SR	SR	SR	SR	SR	
	A		B		◇1 C		B	A	D	B	E	F			G	H	B	A				B	B	
Edinburgh d						11 27						11 51	11 55							12 27	12 55			
Haymarket d						11 31						11 57	12 01							12 31	13 01			
Lanark d		11 53									12 23								12 53					
Carstairs d												12 48												
Carluke d		12 03									12 33	12 56							13 03					
Wishaw d		12 10									12 40	13 03							13 09					
Holytown d						12 29														13 30				
Shieldmuir d		12 14									12 44								13 12					
Cumbernauld 226 d										12 19														
Greenfaulds 226 d										12 21														
Coatbridge Central d										12 30														
Whifflet d										12 33														
Motherwell a		12 17								12 40	12 47	13 08							13 15					
d		12 17	12 18		12 22		12 24		12 45	12 46	12 48	13 09							13 16			13 18	13 19	
Whifflet d							12 32		12a52								12 58						13 28	
Kirkwood d							12 35										13 01						13 31	
Bargeddie d							12 38										13 04						13 34	
Baillieston d							12 41										13 07						13 38	
Mount Vernon d							12 43										13 09						13 40	
Carmyle d							12 46								←		13 12						13 42	
Bellshill d		12 25				12 34					12 55		12 49		12 55				13 22	13 35	13 50			
Uddingston d		12 29				12 39					→				12 59	←			13 26	13 40				
Airbles d			12 20							12 48						12 48						13 20		
Larkhall d	12 03							12 33		→								13 03						
Merryton d	12 05							12 35										13 05						
Chatelherault d	12 08							12 38										13 08						
Hamilton Central d	12 13		12 26					12 42								12 54		13 13				13 26		
Hamilton West d	12 15		12 28					12 45								12 56		13 15				13 28		
Blantyre d	12 19		12 32					12 48								13 00		13 19				13 32		
Newton d	12 23		12 36					12 53								13 05		13 23				13 36		
Cambuslang d	12 26	12 34	12 39					12 56							13 03	13 09		13 26	13 31			13 39		
Rutherglen d	12 30		12 43				12 50	13 00								13 14	13 19	13 30				13 44	13 48	
Dalmarnock d	12 33		12 46				12 52									13 16	13 21	13 33				13 46	13 50	
Bridgeton d	12 35		12 48				12 54									13 18	13 23	13 35				13 48	13 52	
Argyle Street d	12 38		12 51				12 58	13 06								13 22	13 27	13 38				13 52	13 56	
Glasgow Central H. Level 15 a		12 45			12 39	12 54						13 24	13 10		13 12				13 40	13 55	14 10			
Glasgow Central L. Level 15 a	12 39		12 53				12 59	13 08								13 23	13 28	13 39				13 53	13 57	
Anderston a	12 41		12 56				13 04	13 11								13 26	13 34	13 41				13 55	14 03	
Exhibition Centre a	12 43		12 58				13 06	13 13								13 28	13 36	13 43				13 57	14 05	
Partick 226 a	12 47		13 02				13 10	13 16								13 32	13 40	13 47				14 01	14 09	
Hyndland 3 226 a	12 49		13 04				13 12	13 18								13 34	13 42	13 49				14 04	14 11	

	SR	SR	SR	SR	SR	SR	SR	SR	SR		SR	TP	SR	SR	SR	SR	SR	VT	SR		SR	SR	SR	SR
	A	D	B		H	B	A		B		B	◇1 C		A	D	B	E	◇1 I	F			G	H	B
Edinburgh d													13 27						13 55		13 58			
Haymarket d													13 31						14 00		14 04			
Lanark d				13 23				13 53									14 23							
Carstairs d																			14 33					
Carluke d				13 33				14 03									14 33		14 41					
Wishaw d				13 40				14 09									14 40		14 53					
Holytown d													14 30											
Shieldmuir d				13 45				14 12									14 44							
Cumbernauld 226 d			13 17													14 19								
Greenfaulds 226 d			13 19													14 21								
Coatbridge Central d			13 30													14 30								
Whifflet d			13 33													14 33								
Motherwell a			13 40	13 48				14 15								14 40	14 47		15 03					
d		13 45	13 45	13 48				14 16	14 18		14 19	14 21			14 45	14 46	14 48	14 59	15 06					
Whifflet d		13a52				13 58					14 29				14a52									14 58
Kirkwood d						14 01					14 32													15 01
Bargeddie d						14 04					14 35													15 04
Baillieston d						14 07					14 39													15 07
Mount Vernon d						14 09					14 41													15 09
Carmyle d						14 12					14 43											←		15 12
Bellshill d				13 55				14 24					14 35				14 55				14 48	14 55		
Uddingston d				14 02	←			14 29					14 40				→					14 59	←	
Airbles d			13 47		13 47				14 20							14 48							14 48	
Larkhall d	13 33		→				14 03							14 33		→								
Merryton d	13 35						14 05							14 35										
Chatelherault d	13 38						14 08							14 38										
Hamilton Central d	13 42				13 53		14 12		14 26					14 42									14 54	
Hamilton West d	13 45				13 55		14 15		14 28					14 45									14 56	
Blantyre d	13 48				13 59		14 18		14 32					14 48									15 00	
Newton d	13 52				14 05		14 22		14 36					14 52									15 05	
Cambuslang d	13 56			14 06	14 10		14 26	14 33	14 39					14 56								15 03	15 09	
Rutherglen d	14 00				14 14	14 19	14 30		14 43		14 47			15 00									15 14	15 18
Dalmarnock d	14 03				14 16	14 21	14 32		14 46		14 50			15 03									15 16	15 20
Bridgeton d	14 05				14 18	14 23	14 34		14 48		14 52			15 05									15 18	15 22
Argyle Street d	14 08				14 22	14 27	14 37		14 51		14 55			15 08									15 22	15 26
Glasgow Central H. Level 15 a				14 15				14 42				14 38	14 55					15 15	15 25		15 09	15 12		
Glasgow Central L. Level 15 a	14 09				14 23	14 28	14 39		14 53		14 57			15 09									15 23	15 27
Anderston a	14 11				14 26	14 34	14 41		14 55		15 04			15 11									15 26	15 33
Exhibition Centre a	14 13				14 28	14 36	14 43		14 57		15 06			15 13									15 28	15 35
Partick 226 a	14 17				14 31	14 40	14 46		15 01		15 10			15 17									15 32	15 39
Hyndland 3 226 a	14 19				14 33	14 42	14 48		15 03		15 12			15 19									15 34	15 42

A To Milngavie
B To Dalmuir
C From Manchester Airport
D From Milngavie to Cumbernauld
E To Glasgow Central
F To Ayr
G From Lanark
H From Cumbernauld to Dalmuir
I From London Euston

Table T225-F

Saturdays

21 December to 16 May

Edinburgh, Lanark, Coatbridge, Motherwell, Whifflet, Larkhall and Hamilton - Glasgow

		SR	SR	SR	SR	SR		SR	SR	SR	SR	SR	SR	SR	SR	SR		SR	SR	SR	SR	SR	SR	SR	SR
		A	B		C				B	A	D	B		E	B	A		B		C		B	A	D	B
Edinburgh	d					14 26		14 56													15 26				
Haymarket	d					14 31		15 01													15 30				
Lanark	d			14 53									15 23						15 53						
Carstairs	d																								
Carluke	d			15 03									15 33						16 03						
Wishaw	d			15 09									15 40						16 09						
Holytown	d					15 30															16 33				
Shieldmuir	d			15 12									15 45						16 12						
Cumbernauld 226	d											15 19													16 19
Greenfaulds 226	d											15 21													16 21
Coatbridge Central	d											15 30													16 30
Whifflet	d											15 33													16 32
Motherwell	a			15 15								15 40	15 48						16 15						16 40
	d		15 15	15 16					15 19		15 45	15 46	15 48					16 15	16 16			16 19		16 45	16 46
Whifflet	d								15 26		15a52				15 58							16 28		16a52	
Kirkwood	d								15 29						16 01							16 31			
Bargeddie	d								15 32						16 04							16 34			
Baillieston	d								15 36						16 07							16 38			
Mount Vernon	d								15 38						16 09							16 40			
Carmyle	d								15 40						16 12							16 42			
Bellshill	d			15 22		15 35		15 50					15 55						16 23		16 38				
Uddingston	d			15 26	←	15 40							16 02	←					16 29	←	16 42				
Airbles	d		15 17		15 17							15 48		15 48				16 17		16 17					16 48
Larkhall	d	15 03	→							15 33		→				16 03		→					16 33		→
Merryton	d	15 05								15 35						16 05							16 35		
Chatelherault	d	15 08								15 38						16 08							16 38		
Hamilton Central	d	15 13			15 23					15 42				15 54		16 12				16 23			16 42		
Hamilton West	d	15 15			15 25					15 45				15 56		16 15				16 25			16 45		
Blantyre	d	15 19			15 29					15 48				16 00		16 18				16 29			16 48		
Newton	d	15 23			15 33					15 53				16 05		16 22				16 33			16 52		
Cambuslang	d	15 26		15 31	15 36					15 56			16 06	16 09		16 26			16 33	16 36			16 56		
Rutherglen	d	15 30			15 40				15 47	16 01				16 13	16 18	16 30				16 42		16 47	17 00		
Dalmarnock	d	15 33			15 43				15 50					16 16	16 20	16 33				16 44		16 49	17 03		
Bridgeton	d	15 35			15 45				15 52					16 18	16 22	16 35				16 46		16 51	17 05		
Argyle Street	d	15 38			15 49				15 56	16 07				16 21	16 26	16 38				16 50		16 55	17 08		
Glasgow Central H. Level 15	a			15 40		15 55		16 10					16 15						16 43		16 55				
Glasgow Central L. Level 15	a	15 39			15 50				15 57	16 08				16 23	16 27	16 39				16 51		16 56	17 09		
Anderston	a	15 41			15 55				16 03	16 10				16 25	16 33	16 41				16 53		17 03	17 11		
Exhibition Centre	a	15 43			15 57				16 06	16 12				16 27	16 36	16 43				16 55		17 06	17 13		
Partick 226	a	15 47			16 01				16 10	16 16				16 30	16 40	16 46				16 59		17 10	17 17		
Hyndland 3 226	a	15 49			16 03				16 12	16 18				16 32	16 42	16 48				17 01		17 12	17 19		

		SR		SR	SR	SR	SR	SR	SR	SR	SR	SR		SR	SR	SR	SR	SR	SR	SR	SR	SR		SR	SR
		F		G		H	E	B	A	B		C				B	A	D	B		E	B		A	
Edinburgh	d			15 50	15 57									16 27	16 56										
Haymarket	d			15 54	16 01									16 32	17 01										
Lanark	d	16 23									16 53									17 23					17 53
Carstairs	d			16 32																					
Carluke	d	16 31		16 41							17 03									17 33					18 03
Wishaw	d	16 40		16 58							17 09									17 40					18 10
Holytown	d													17 29											
Shieldmuir	d	16 45									17 12									17 45					18 13
Cumbernauld 226	d																		17 19						
Greenfaulds 226	d																		17 21						
Coatbridge Central	d																		17 30						
Whifflet	d																		17 33						
Motherwell	a	16 48		17 05							17 15								17 40	17 48					18 16
	d	16 48		17 06						17 15	17 16					17 23		17 46	17 46	17 49					18 17
Whifflet	d							16 58								17 30		17a53				17 58			
Kirkwood	d							17 01								17 33						18 01			
Bargeddie	d							17 04								17 36						18 04			
Baillieston	d							17 07								17 40						18 07			
Mount Vernon	d							17 09								17 42						18 09			
Carmyle	d					←		17 12								17 44						18 12			
Bellshill	d	16 55			16 50	16 55					17 23			17 34	17 48					17 56					18 25
Uddingston	d	→				16 58	←				17 27	←		17 38						18 02	←				18 29
Airbles	d						16 48			17 17		17 17							17 49		17 49				
Larkhall	d								17 03	→							17 33		→					18 03	
Merryton	d								17 05								17 35							18 05	
Chatelherault	d								17 08								17 38							18 08	
Hamilton Central	d						16 54		17 12			17 23					17 42				17 54			18 13	
Hamilton West	d						16 56		17 15			17 25					17 45				17 57			18 15	
Blantyre	d						17 00		17 18			17 29					17 48				18 00			18 19	
Newton	d						17 06		17 22			17 33					17 52				18 07			18 23	
Cambuslang	d					17 02	17 10		17 26		17 31	17 36		17 43			17 56			18 06	18 10			18 27	18 33
Rutherglen	d						17 14	17 17	17 30			17 41				17 48	18 00				18 14	18 18		18 31	
Dalmarnock	d							17 19	17 33			17 43				17 51	18 03				18 17	18 21			
Bridgeton	d							17 21	17 35			17 45				17 53	18 05				18 19	18 23			
Argyle Street	d						17 19	17 25	17 38			17 49				17 57	18 08				18 22	18 27		18 37	
Glasgow Central H. Level 15	a			17 24	17 10	17 12					17 40			17 55	18 09					18 15					18 42
Glasgow Central L. Level 15	a						17 21	17 26	17 39			17 50				17 58	18 09				18 24	18 28		18 38	
Anderston	a						17 23	17 29	17 41			17 52				18 03	18 11				18 27	18 34		18 40	
Exhibition Centre	a						17 25	17 31	17 43			17 54				18 05	18 13				18 29	18 36		18 42	
Partick 226	a						17 28	17 38	17 47			17 58				18 10	18 16				18 33	18 40		18 47	
Hyndland 3 226	a						17 31	17 42	17 49			18 00				18 12	18 18				18 35	18 42		18 49	

A To Milngavie
B To Dalmuir
C From Motherwell to Dalmuir
D From Milngavie to Cumbernauld
E From Cumbernauld to Dalmuir
F To Glasgow Central
G To Ayr
H From Lanark

Table T225-F

Saturdays

21 December to 16 May

Edinburgh, Lanark, Coatbridge, Motherwell, Whifflet, Larkhall and Hamilton - Glasgow

		SR	TP	SR	SR	SR	SR	SR		SR	SR	SR	SR	SR	SR	SR	SR	SR		SR	SR	SR	SR	SR	SR
		A	◇1 B		A	C	D	E			A		F		A	E	A			G	A	C	D		E
Edinburgh	d			17 27		17 42				17 52				17 56								18 27		18 56	
Haymarket	d			17 31		17 46				17 56				18 00								18 32		19 01	
Lanark	d											18 23						18 53							
Carstairs	d					18 12																19 13			
Carluke	d					18 20						18 33						19 03				19 22			
Wishaw	d					18 27						18 40						19 09				19 27			
Holytown	d			18 32										19 01											
Shieldmuir	d											18 45						19 12							
Cumbernauld 226	d										18 18														
Greenfaulds 226	d										18 20														
Coatbridge Central	d										18 29														
Whifflet	d										18 32		←												
Motherwell	a					18 32					18 40	18 48	18 40					19 15				19 33			
	d	18 17	18 22		18 24	18 33	18 45				18 48	18 48	18 48				19 15	19 16			19 20	19 34	19 45		
Whifflet	d				18 31		18a52				→				18 58						19 28		19a52		
Kirkwood	d				18 34										19 01						19 31				
Bargeddie	d				18 37										19 04						19 34				
Baillieston	d				18 41										19 07						19 38				
Mount Vernon	d				18 43										19 09						19 40				
Carmyle	d				18 45										19 12						19 42				
Bellshill	d			18 37						18 48		18 55		19 04				19 22						19 49	
Uddingston	d			18 41								18 59		19 10				19 27		←					
Airbles	d	18 19											18 50				19 17			19 17					
Larkhall	d							18 33								19 03	→								19 33
Merryton	d							18 35								19 05									19 35
Chatelherault	d							18 38								19 08									19 38
Hamilton Central	d	18 26						18 42					18 56			19 12				19 23					19 42
Hamilton West	d	18 29						18 45					18 58			19 15				19 25					19 45
Blantyre	d	18 32						18 48					19 02			19 18				19 29					19 49
Newton	d	18 36						18 52					19 06			19 22				19 33					19 53
Cambuslang	d	18 40						18 56		19 00		19 03	19 10	19 16		19 26		19 31		19 36					19 56
Rutherglen	d	18 44			18 49			19 00					19 14		19 18	19 30				19 40	19 47				20 00
Dalmarnock	d	18 46			18 52			19 03					19 17		19 21	19 32				19 43	19 49				20 03
Bridgeton	d	18 48			18 54			19 05					19 19		19 23	19 34				19 45	19 51				20 05
Argyle Street	d	18 51			18 57			19 08					19 22		19 26	19 38				19 48	19 55				20 08
Glasgow Central H. Level 15	a		18 39	18 56		18 53				19 11		19 13		19 27				19 41				19 54		20 10	
Glasgow Central L. Level 15	a	18 53			18 59			19 09					19 24		19 27	19 39				19 50	19 56				20 09
Anderston	a	18 55			19 01			19 11					19 26		19 29	19 41				19 52	19 59				20 11
Exhibition Centre	a	18 57			19 03			19 13					19 28		19 31	19 43				19 54	20 01				20 13
Partick 226	a	19 00			19 07			19 17					19 32		19 35	19 47				19 58	20 05				20 17
Hyndland 3 226	a	19 02			19 09			19 19					19 34		19 37	19 50				20 00	20 07				20 19

		SR	SR	SR		SR	SR	SR	SR	SR	TP	SR	SR	SR		SR	SR	SR	SR	SR	SR	SR	SR	SR	
		A		F		A	E	A		G	◇1 B		A	E		A		F	D	A	E		A	A	
Edinburgh	d											19 25													
Haymarket	d											19 31													
Lanark	d		19 23						19 54								20 20					20 52			
Carstairs	d																								
Carluke	d		19 33						20 04								20 30					21 02			
Wishaw	d		19 39						20 10								20 36					21 08			
Holytown	d											20 33													
Shieldmuir	d		19 45						20 14								20 39					21 11			
Cumbernauld 226	d	19 19														20 19									
Greenfaulds 226	d	19 21														20 21									
Coatbridge Central	d	19 30														20 30									
Whifflet	d	19 33		←												20 33		←							
Motherwell	a	19 40	19 48	19 40					20 17							20 40	20 42	20 40				21 14			
	d	19 48	19 48	19 48				20 16	20 18		20 22		20 26			20 46	20 43	20 46	20 48			21 15	21 17	21 22	
Whifflet	d	→				19 59							20 33			→			20a55	21 00				21 30	
Kirkwood	d					20 02							20 36							21 03				21 33	
Bargeddie	d					20 05							20 39							21 06				21 36	
Baillieston	d					20 08							20 43							21 09				21 39	
Mount Vernon	d					20 10							20 45							21 11				21 41	
Carmyle	d					20 13							20 47							21 14				21 44	
Bellshill	d		19 55						20 25			20 39					20 49					21 21			
Uddingston	d		19 59						20 29	←		20 43					20 53					21 25			
Airbles	d			19 50				20 18		20 18								20 48					21 19		
Larkhall	d						20 03	→						20 33							21 03				
Merryton	d						20 05							20 35							21 05				
Chatelherault	d						20 08							20 38							21 08				
Hamilton Central	d			19 56			20 12			20 25				20 44				20 54			21 12		21 25		
Hamilton West	d			19 58			20 15			20 28				20 46				20 57			21 15		21 27		
Blantyre	d			20 02			20 19			20 31				20 50				21 00			21 18		21 31		
Newton	d			20 06			20 24			20 36				20 54				21 05			21 22		21 35		
Cambuslang	d		20 03	20 10			20 27		20 34	20 40				20 57			21 01	21 09			21 26	21 30	21 38		
Rutherglen	d			20 14		20 17	20 31			20 44			20 52	21 01				21 13		21 18	21 30		21 42	21 48	
Dalmarnock	d			20 16		20 20	20 34			20 47			20 55	21 04				21 15		21 21	21 32		21 45	21 51	
Bridgeton	d			20 18		20 22	20 36			20 49			20 57	21 06				21 17		21 23	21 34		21 47	21 53	
Argyle Street	d			20 22		20 25	20 39			20 52			21 00	21 09				21 21		21 26	21 37		21 50	21 56	
Glasgow Central H. Level 15	a		20 12						20 43		20 40	20 56					21 10					21 39			
Glasgow Central L. Level 15	a			20 23		20 27	20 41			20 54			21 02	21 10				21 22		21 27	21 39		21 51	21 58	
Anderston	a			20 25		20 30	20 43			20 56			21 04	21 12				21 24		21 29	21 41		21 53	22 00	
Exhibition Centre	a			20 27		20 32	20 45			20 58			21 06	21 14				21 26		21 31	21 43		21 55	22 02	
Partick 226	a			20 31		20 35	20 48			21 01			21 09	21 18				21 30		21 35	21 47		21 59	22 05	
Hyndland 3 226	a			20 33		20 37	20 50			21 03			21 11	21 20				21 32		21 37	21 49		22 01	22 07	

A To Dalmuir
B From Manchester Airport
C To Ayr
D From Milngavie to Cumbernauld
E To Milngavie
F From Cumbernauld to Dalmuir
G From Motherwell to Dalmuir

Table T225-F

Saturdays

21 December to 16 May

Edinburgh, Lanark, Coatbridge, Motherwell, Whifflet, Larkhall and Hamilton - Glasgow

		SR	SR	SR	SR	SR	SR	SR	SR	SR	SR	SR	SR	SR	SR	SR	SR	VT	SR	SR	SR	SR	SR
		A	B	C		D	C	A			C	C	A	B	E		F	◇1 G ⊡	C	A			
Edinburgh	d									21 26												22 56	
Haymarket ⇌	d									21 30												23 00	
Lanark	d				21 23				21 53							22 23					22 51		23 23
Carstairs	d																						
Carluke	d				21 33				22 03							22 33					23 01		23 33
Wishaw	d				21 41				22 09							22 40					23 07		23 39
Holytown	d									22 30												00 04	
Shieldmuir	d				21 47				22 12							22 44					23 10		23 42
Cumbernauld 226	d			21 21											22 21								
Greenfaulds 226	d			21 23											22 23								
Coatbridge Central	d			21 30											22 31								
Whifflet	d			21 33											22 33								
Motherwell	a			21 40	21 50				22 15						22 41	22 47					23 13		23 45
	d		21 46	21 46	21 50				22 16		22 16	22 19		22 45	22 46	22 48		22 53			23 14		
Whifflet	d		21a53				21 59					22 27		22a52					22 58				
Kirkwood	d						22 02					22 30							23 01				
Bargeddie	d						22 05					22 33							23 04				
Baillieston	d						22 08					22 36							23 07				
Mount Vernon	d						22 10					22 38							23 09				
Carmyle	d						22 13					22 41							23 12				
Bellshill	d				21 57				22 23	22 35						22 55					23 20	00 08	
Uddingston	d				22 01	←			22 29	22 38						23 00	←				23 24	00 12	
Airbles	d			21 48		21 48					22 18				22 48		22 48						
Larkhall	d	21 33		→				22 03					22 33		→					23 03			
Merryton	d	21 35						22 05					22 35							23 05			
Chatelherault	d	21 38						22 08					22 38							23 08			
Hamilton Central	d	21 42				21 54		22 12			22 24		22 42				22 54			23 12			
Hamilton West	d	21 45				21 56		22 15			22 26		22 45				22 57			23 15			
Blantyre	d	21 48				22 00		22 18			22 30		22 48				23 00			23 18			
Newton	d	21 52				22 04		22 22			22 34		22 53				23 08			23 22			
Cambuslang	d	21 56			22 05	22 08		22 26	22 33		22 37		22 56			23 04	23 11			23 26	23 30	00 18	
Rutherglen	d	22 00				22 12	22 18	22 30			22 41	22 45	23 01				23 15		23 18	23 30			
Dalmarnock	d	22 02				22 15	22 20	22 33			22 44	22 47					23 18		23 21	23 33			
Bridgeton	d	22 04				22 17	22 22	22 35			22 46	22 49					23 20		23 23	23 35			
Argyle Street	d	22 07				22 20	22 26	22 38			22 49	22 53	23 07				23 23		23 26	23 38			
Glasgow Central H. Level 15	a				22 14				22 44	22 55						23 13		23 09			23 39	00 30	
Glasgow Central L. Level 15	a	22 09				22 22	22 27	22 39			22 51	22 54	23 08				23 24		23 28	23 39			
Anderston	a	22 11				22 24	22 29	22 41			22 53	22 58	23 10				23 26		23 30	23 41			
Exhibition Centre	a	22 13				22 26	22 31	22 43			22 55	23 00	23 12				23 28		23 32	23 43			
Partick 226 ⇌	a	22 16				22 29	22 35	22 46			22 58	23 04	23 16				23 32		23 35	23 47			
Hyndland 3 226	a	22 18				22 31	22 37	22 48			23 00	23 06	23 18				23 34		23 37	23 49			

		SR	SR
Edinburgh	d		23 12
Haymarket ⇌	d		23 17
Lanark	d	23 51	
Carstairs	d		23 57
Carluke	d	00 01	00 09
Wishaw	d	00 07	00 16
Holytown	d		
Shieldmuir	d	00 10	
Cumbernauld 226	d		
Greenfaulds 226	d		
Coatbridge Central	d		
Whifflet	d		
Motherwell	a	00 14	00 22
	d		
Whifflet	d		
Kirkwood	d		
Bargeddie	d		
Baillieston	d		
Mount Vernon	d		
Carmyle	d		
Bellshill	d		
Uddingston	d		
Airbles	d		
Larkhall	d		
Merryton	d		
Chatelherault	d		
Hamilton Central	d		
Hamilton West	d		
Blantyre	d		
Newton	d		
Cambuslang	d		
Rutherglen	d		
Dalmarnock	d		
Bridgeton	d		
Argyle Street	d		
Glasgow Central H. Level 15	a		
Glasgow Central L. Level 15	a		
Anderston	a		
Exhibition Centre	a		
Partick 226 ⇌	a		
Hyndland 3 226	a		

A To Milngavie
B From Milngavie to Cumbernauld
C To Dalmuir
D From Cumbernauld to Dalmuir
E To Garscadden
F From Cumbernauld to Garscadden
G From London Euston

Table T225-F

Sundays

15 December to 10 May

Edinburgh, Lanark, Coatbridge, Motherwell, Whifflet, Larkhall and Hamilton - Glasgow

		SR	SR	SR	SR	SR	SR	SR	SR	SR	SR	SR	SR	SR	SR	SR	SR	SR	SR	SR	SR	SR	SR
		A	B	B	C		D	C		E	C	D	C		F	G		C	D		C	H	
Edinburgh	d																						
Haymarket ⇌	d																						
Lanark	d																			10 19			
Carstairs	d																						
Carluke	d	00 01		00 09																10 29			
Wishaw	d	00 07		00 16																10 35			
Holytown	d		00 04																				
Shieldmuir	d	00 10																		10 40			
Cumbernauld 226	d																						
Greenfaulds 226	d																						
Coatbridge Central	d																						
Whifflet	d																						
Motherwell	a	00 14		00 22																10 43			
	d				08 24	08 35	08 41	08 53	09 05		09 21	09 41	09 53	09 54			10 20	10 21	10 41	10 44	10 53		11 20
Whifflet	d						08 48					09 49							10 48				
Kirkwood	d						08 51					09 52							10 51				
Bargeddie	d						08 54					09 55							10 54				
Baillieston	d						08 58					09 58							10 58				
Mount Vernon	d						09 00					10 00							11 00				
Carmyle	d						09 02					10 03							11 02				
Bellshill	d		00 08			08 41			09 11					10 00			10 26			10 51			11 26
Uddingston	d		00 12			08 45			09 15					10 04	←		10 30			10 55			11 31
Airbles	d				08 26			08 55			09 23		09 55		09 55			10 23			10 55		
Larkhall	d									09 08			→			10 08						11 08	
Merryton	d									09 10						10 10						11 10	
Chatelherault	d									09 13						10 13						11 13	
Hamilton Central	d				08 32			09 02		09 17	09 32				10 02	10 17		10 32			11 02	11 17	
Hamilton West	d				08 35			09 05		09 20	09 35				10 05	10 20		10 35			11 05	11 20	
Blantyre	d				08 38			09 08		09 23	09 38				10 08	10 23		10 38			11 08	11 23	
Newton	d				08 42			09 12		09 27	09 42				10 12	10 27		10 42			11 13	11 27	
Cambuslang	d		00 18		08 46	08 50		09 16	09 20	09 31	09 46			10 09	10 16	10 31	10 35	10 46		10 59	11 18	11 31	11 36
Rutherglen	d				08 50		09 06	09 20		09 35	09 50	10 07			10 20	10 35		10 50	11 06		11 22	11 35	
Dalmarnock	d										09 52	10 09			10 22	10 37		10 52	11 09		11 24	11 37	
Bridgeton	d				08 54		09 10	09 24		09 39	09 54	10 11			10 24	10 39		10 54	11 11		11 26	11 39	
Argyle Street	d										09 58	10 14			10 28	10 43		10 58	11 14		11 30	11 43	
Glasgow Central H. Level 15	a		00 30			09 01			09 31					10 20			10 45			11 10			11 47
Glasgow Central L. Level 15	a				08 57		09 13	09 27		09 42	09 59	10 16			10 29	10 44		10 59	11 15		11 31	11 44	
Anderston	a										10 05	10 18			10 35	10 46		11 06	11 17		11 35	11 46	
Exhibition Centre	a				09 07		09 17	09 37		09 47	10 07	10 20			10 37	10 48		11 08	11 19		11 37	11 48	
Partick 226 ⇌	a				09 11		09 22	09 41		09 52	10 11	10 23			10 41	10 52		11 11	11 23		11 41	11 52	
Hyndland 3 226	a				09 14		09 24	09 44		09 54	10 14	10 25			10 44	10 54		11 14	11 25		11 44	11 54	

		SR	SR	SR	SR	SR	SR	TP	SR	SR	SR	TP	SR	SR	SR	SR	SR	SR	SR	SR	SR	SR	SR
			C	D		C	I	◇1 J ⚮	C		F	◇1 K ⚮	D		C	L			C	D		C	M
Edinburgh	d	10 26																12 26					
Haymarket ⇌	d	10 30																12 30					
Lanark	d				11 21									12 21							13 19		
Carstairs	d																						
Carluke	d				11 31									12 31							13 31		
Wishaw	d				11 37									12 37							13 37		
Holytown	d	11 31																13 29					
Shieldmuir	d				11 42									12 40							13 41		
Cumbernauld 226	d																						
Greenfaulds 226	d																						
Coatbridge Central	d																						
Whifflet	d																						
Motherwell	a				11 45									12 44							13 44		
	d		11 21	11 42	11 46	11 53		12 23	12 23	12 24		12 34	12 41	12 44	12 53		13 20		13 23	13 41	13 44	13 53	
Whifflet	d			11 49									12 49							13 49			
Kirkwood	d			11 52									12 52							13 52			
Bargeddie	d			11 55									12 55							13 55			
Baillieston	d			11 59									12 58							13 58			
Mount Vernon	d			12 01									13 00							14 00			
Carmyle	d			12 03									13 03							14 03			
Bellshill	d	11 37			11 52					12 30				12 51			13 26	13 36			13 51		
Uddingston	d	11 44			11 56					12 34	←			12 55			13 31	13 41			13 55		
Airbles	d		11 23			11 55			12 25		12 25				12 55				13 25			13 55	
Larkhall	d						12 08		→							13 08							14 08
Merryton	d						12 10									13 10							14 10
Chatelherault	d						12 13									13 13							14 13
Hamilton Central	d		11 30			12 02	12 17				12 32				13 02	13 17			13 32			14 02	14 17
Hamilton West	d		11 33			12 05	12 20				12 35				13 05	13 20			13 35			14 05	14 20
Blantyre	d		11 36			12 08	12 23				12 38				13 08	13 23			13 38			14 08	14 23
Newton	d		11 40			12 12	12 27				12 42				13 15	13 27			13 42			14 13	14 27
Cambuslang	d		11 44		12 01	12 16	12 31			12 39	12 47			12 59	13 18	13 31	13 36		13 46		14 00	14 16	14 32
Rutherglen	d		11 50	12 07		12 20	12 35				12 51		13 07		13 24	13 35			13 50	14 09		14 23	14 36
Dalmarnock	d		11 53	12 10		12 22	12 37				12 53		13 09		13 26	13 37			13 52	14 11		14 26	14 39
Bridgeton	d		11 55	12 12		12 24	12 39				12 55		13 11		13 28	13 39			13 54	14 13		14 28	14 41
Argyle Street	d		11 58	12 15		12 28	12 43				12 59		13 14		13 32	13 43			13 58	14 16		14 31	14 44
Glasgow Central H. Level 15	a	12 03			12 12			12 46		12 48		12 55		13 12			13 46	13 59			14 10		
Glasgow Central L. Level 15	a		12 00	12 16		12 29	12 44				13 00		13 16		13 33	13 44			13 59	14 18		14 33	14 45
Anderston	a		12 05	12 18		12 35	12 46				13 05		13 18		13 35	13 46			14 06	14 19		14 36	14 47
Exhibition Centre	a		12 07	12 20		12 37	12 48				13 07		13 20		13 37	13 48			14 08	14 21		14 38	14 49
Partick 226 ⇌	a		12 11	12 23		12 41	12 52				13 11		13 23		13 41	13 52			14 11	14 25		14 41	14 53
Hyndland 3 226	a		12 14	12 25		12 44	12 54				13 14		13 25		13 44	13 54			14 14	14 27		14 44	14 55

A not 15 December. From Lanark
B not 15 December. From Edinburgh
C To Milngavie
D To Balloch
E To Balloch. Forms tight booked connection out of 2C26.
F From Motherwell to Milngavie
G To Balloch. Forms tight booked connection out of 2C54.
H To Balloch. Forms tight booked connection out of 2C56.
I To Balloch. Forms tight booked connection out of 2C58.
J until 5 January, from 23 Feb[illegible]
K from 12 January until 16 February, from 5 April. From Manchester Airport
L To Balloch. Forms tight booked connection out of 2C48.
M To Balloch. Forms tight booked connection out of 2C50.

Edinburgh, Lanark, Coatbridge, Motherwell, Whifflet, Larkhall and Hamilton - Glasgow

		TP	SR	SR	SR	SR	SR	SR	SR	SR	SR	SR	SR	SR	SR	SR	SR	SR	SR	TP	SR	SR
		A	B		C	D		B	E			B	D		B	F	B		C	A		D
Edinburgh	d										14 26											
Haymarket	d										14 30											
Lanark	d						14 18							15 19							16 13	
Carstairs	d																					
Carluke	d						14 28							15 29							16 23	
Wishaw	d						14 35							15 37							16 29	
Holytown	d										15 30											
Shieldmuir	d						14 38							15 40							16 34	
Cumbernauld 226	d																					
Greenfaulds 226	d																					
Coatbridge Central	d																					
Whifflet	d																					
Motherwell	a						14 42							15 43							16 37	
	d	14 22	14 23	14 25		14 41	14 44	14 53		15 20		15 21	15 41	15 44	15 53		16 21	16 22		16 24	16 37	16 41
Whifflet	d					14 49							15 49									16 48
Kirkwood	d					14 52							15 52									16 51
Bargeddie	d					14 55							15 55									16 54
Baillieston	d					14 58							15 58									16 58
Mount Vernon	d					15 00							16 00									17 00
Carmyle	d					15 03							16 03									17 02
Bellshill	d			14 32			14 51			15 27	15 35			15 51				16 28			16 45	
Uddingston	d			14 36	←		14 55			15 31	15 39			15 55				16 32	←		16 52	
Airbles	d		14 25		14 25			14 55				15 23			15 55		16 23		16 23			
Larkhall	d		→						15 08							16 08	→					
Merryton	d								15 10							16 10						
Chatelherault	d								15 13							16 13						
Hamilton Central	d				14 32			15 02	15 17			15 32			16 02	16 17			16 32			
Hamilton West	d				14 35			15 05	15 20			15 35			16 05	16 20			16 35			
Blantyre	d				14 38			15 08	15 23			15 38			16 08	16 23			16 38			
Newton	d				14 42			15 12	15 27			15 42			16 15	16 27			16 42			
Cambuslang	d			14 40	14 46		14 59	15 16	15 31	15 35		15 46		15 59	16 19	16 31		16 37	16 46		16 56	
Rutherglen	d				14 50	15 07		15 20	15 35			15 50	16 08		16 24	16 35			16 50			17 06
Dalmarnock	d				14 52	15 09		15 22	15 37			15 53	16 11		16 27	16 38			16 52			17 09
Bridgeton	d				14 54	15 11		15 24	15 39			15 55	16 13		16 29	16 40			16 54			17 11
Argyle Street	d				14 58	15 14		15 28	15 43			15 58	16 16		16 32	16 43			16 58			17 14
Glasgow Central H. Level 15	a	14 42		14 50			15 10			15 46	16 00			16 10				16 46		16 43	17 05	
Glasgow Central L. Level 15	a				14 59	15 16		15 29	15 44			16 00	16 17		16 34	16 44			16 59			17 15
Anderston	a				15 05	15 18		15 35	15 46			16 05	16 19		16 36	16 47			17 06			17 17
Exhibition Centre	a				15 07	15 20		15 37	15 48			16 07	16 21		16 38	16 49			17 08			17 19
Partick 226	a				15 11	15 23		15 41	15 52			16 11	16 24		16 41	16 53			17 12			17 23
Hyndland 3 226	a				15 14	15 25		15 44	15 54			16 14	16 26		16 44	16 55			17 14			17 25

		SR	SR	TP	SR	SR	SR	SR	SR	SR	SR	SR	SR	SR	TP	SR	SR	SR	SR	SR	SR	SR	SR
		B	G	H			B	D		B	I	B		C	A		D	B	J	K		L	
Edinburgh	d					16 26																	18 26
Haymarket	d					16 30																	18 30
Lanark	d								17 20							18 13							
Carstairs	d																						
Carluke	d								17 30							18 23							
Wishaw	d								17 36							18 29							
Holytown	d					17 30																	19 29
Shieldmuir	d								17 39							18 32							
Cumbernauld 226	d																						
Greenfaulds 226	d																						
Coatbridge Central	d																						
Whifflet	d																						
Motherwell	a								17 42							18 36							
	d	16 53		17 10	17 20		17 21	17 41	17 44	17 53		18 21	18 22		18 24	18 37	18 40	18 53		19 21	19 22		
Whifflet	d							17 48									18 49						
Kirkwood	d							17 51									18 52						
Bargeddie	d							17 54									18 55						
Baillieston	d							17 58									18 58						
Mount Vernon	d							18 00									19 00						
Carmyle	d							18 02									19 03						
Bellshill	d				17 27	17 38			17 50				18 28			18 48					19 28		19 37
Uddingston	d				17 31	17 44			17 54				18 32	←		18 52					19 32	←	19 44
Airbles	d	16 55					17 23			17 55		18 23		18 23				18 55		19 23		19 23	
Larkhall	d		17 08								18 08	→							19 08	→			
Merryton	d		17 10								18 10								19 10				
Chatelherault	d		17 13								18 13								19 13				
Hamilton Central	d	17 02	17 17				17 32			18 02	18 17			18 32				19 02	19 17			19 32	
Hamilton West	d	17 05	17 20				17 35			18 05	18 20			18 35				19 05	19 20			19 35	
Blantyre	d	17 08	17 23				17 38			18 08	18 23			18 38				19 08	19 23			19 38	
Newton	d	17 12	17 27				17 42			18 16	18 29			18 42				19 12	19 27			19 42	
Cambuslang	d	17 16	17 31		17 35		17 46		17 59	18 19	18 34		18 37	18 46		18 56		19 16	19 31		19 37	19 46	
Rutherglen	d	17 20	17 35				17 50	18 06		18 24	18 38			18 50			19 07	19 22	19 35			19 50	
Dalmarnock	d	17 22	17 37				17 52	18 09															
Bridgeton	d	17 24	17 39				17 54	18 11		18 27	18 42			18 54			19 10	19 26	19 39			19 54	
Argyle Street	d	17 28	17 43				17 58	18 14															
Glasgow Central H. Level 15	a			17 28	17 44	17 59			18 08				18 46		18 41	19 06					19 46		19 59
Glasgow Central L. Level 15	a	17 29	17 44				17 59	18 15		18 32	18 45			18 57			19 14	19 30	19 42			19 57	
Anderston	a	17 35	17 46				18 05	18 17															
Exhibition Centre	a	17 37	17 48				18 07	18 19		18 38	18 49			19 07			19 18	19 37	19 47			20 07	
Partick 226	a	17 41	17 52				18 11	18 23		18 41	18 53			19 11			19 22	19 41	19 52			20 11	
Hyndland 3 226	a	17 44	17 54				18 14	18 25		18 44	18 55			19 14			19 24	19 44	19 54			20 14	

A From Manchester Airport
B To Milngavie
C From Motherwell to Milngavie
D To Balloch
E To Balloch. Forms tight booked connection out of 2C52.
F To Balloch. Forms tight booked connection out of 2C54.
G To Balloch. Forms tight booked connection out of 2C56.
H From Liverpool Lime Street
I To Balloch. Forms tight booked connection out of 2C58.
J To Balloch. Forms tight booked connection out of 2C48.
K To Motherwell
L From Motherwell to Hyndland continues to Motherwell

Edinburgh, Lanark, Coatbridge, Motherwell, Whifflet, Larkhall and Hamilton - Glasgow

		SR	SR	SR	SR	SR	TP	SR	SR	SR	SR	SR	SR	TP	SR	SR	SR	SR	SR	SR	SR	SR
		A		B	C	B	D		E	A		B	F	G			B	A		B	H	
Edinburgh	d															20 26						
Haymarket	d															20 30						
Lanark	d		19 19								20 19								21 19			
Carstairs	d																					
Carluke	d		19 29								20 29								21 29			
Wishaw	d		19 35								20 35								21 35			
Holytown	d															21 30						
Shieldmuir	d		19 40								20 38								21 38			
Cumbernauld 226	d																					
Greenfaulds 226	d																					
Coatbridge Central	d																					
Whifflet	d																					
Motherwell	a		19 43								20 42								21 42			
	d	19 41	19 44	19 53		20 21	20 23	20 24		20 41	20 44	20 53		21 16	21 20		21 21	21 41	21 44	21 53		22 20
Whifflet	d	19 48								20 48								21 49				
Kirkwood	d	19 51								20 51								21 52				
Bargeddie	d	19 54								20 54								21 55				
Baillieston	d	19 58								20 58								21 58				
Mount Vernon	d	20 00								21 00								22 00				
Carmyle	d	20 02								21 02								22 03				
Bellshill	d		19 50					20 30			20 50				21 26	21 37			21 51			22 27
Uddingston	d		19 54					20 34	←		20 55				21 30	21 41			21 55			22 31
Airbles	d			19 55		20 23			20 23			20 55					21 23			21 55		
Larkhall	d				20 08	→							21 08								22 08	
Merryton	d				20 10								21 10								22 10	
Chatelherault	d				20 13								21 13								22 13	
Hamilton Central	d			20 02	20 17				20 32			21 02	21 17				21 32			22 02	22 18	
Hamilton West	d			20 05	20 20				20 35			21 05	21 20				21 35			22 05	22 20	
Blantyre	d			20 08	20 23				20 38			21 08	21 23				21 38			22 08	22 24	
Newton	d			20 12	20 29				20 42			21 12	21 27				21 42			22 12	22 28	
Cambuslang	d		19 59	20 16	20 33			20 39	20 46		20 59	21 16	21 31		21 35		21 46		21 59	22 16	22 31	22 35
Rutherglen	d	20 06		20 20	20 37				20 50	21 06		21 20	21 35				21 50	22 07		22 20	22 36	
Dalmarnock	d																					
Bridgeton	d	20 10		20 24	20 41				20 54	21 10		21 24	21 39				21 54	22 10		22 24	22 40	
Argyle Street	d																					
Glasgow Central H. Level 15	a		20 09				20 40	20 48			21 08			21 32	21 44	21 59			22 08			22 44
Glasgow Central L. Level 15	a	20 14		20 28	20 45				20 57	21 14		21 27	21 42				21 57	22 14		22 27	22 43	
Anderston	a																					
Exhibition Centre	a	20 18		20 37	20 48				21 07	21 18		21 37	21 47				22 07	22 18		22 37	22 47	
Partick 226	a	20 22		20 41	20 53				21 12	21 22		21 41	21 52				22 11	22 22		22 41	22 52	
Hyndland 3 226	a	20 24		20 44	20 55				21 14	21 24		21 44	21 54				22 14	22 24		22 44	22 54	

		SR	TP	SR	SR	VT	SR	VT	SR	SR	SR
		B	D	A		I	J	I	K		
Edinburgh	d										
Haymarket	d										
Lanark	d				22 19						23 36
Carstairs	d										
Carluke	d				22 29						23 46
Wishaw	d				22 35						23 52
Holytown	d										
Shieldmuir	d				22 38						23 55
Cumbernauld 226	d										
Greenfaulds 226	d										
Coatbridge Central	d										
Whifflet	d										
Motherwell	a				22 42						23 59
	d	22 21	22 29	22 42	22 45	22 51	22 53	23 05		23 20	
Whifflet	d			22 49							
Kirkwood	d			22 52							
Bargeddie	d			22 55							
Baillieston	d			22 59							
Mount Vernon	d			23 01							
Carmyle	d			23 03							
Bellshill	d				22 51					23 26	
Uddingston	d				22 58					23 30	
Airbles	d	22 23					22 55				
Larkhall	d								23 08		
Merryton	d								23 10		
Chatelherault	d								23 13		
Hamilton Central	d	22 32					23 02		23 17		
Hamilton West	d	22 35					23 05		23 20		
Blantyre	d	22 38					23 08		23 23		
Newton	d	22 42					23 12		23 27		
Cambuslang	d	22 46			23 02		23 16		23 31	23 35	
Rutherglen	d	22 50		23 07			23 20		23 35		
Dalmarnock	d										
Bridgeton	d	22 54		23 11			23 24		23 39		
Argyle Street	d										
Glasgow Central H. Level 15	a		22 47		23 11	23 07		23 21		23 44	
Glasgow Central L. Level 15	a	22 57		23 14			23 27		23 42		
Anderston	a										
Exhibition Centre	a	23 07		23 18			23 37		23 50		
Partick 226	a	23 11		23 22			23 41		23 53		
Hyndland 3 226	a	23 14		23 24			23 44		23 56		

A To Balloch
B To Milngavie
C To Balloch. Forms tight booked connection out of 2C50.
D From Manchester Airport
E From Motherwell to Milngavie
F To Balloch. Forms tight booked connection out of 2C52.
G From Liverpool Lime Street
H To Balloch. Forms tight booked connection out of 2C54.
I From London Euston
J To Garscadden
K To Garscadden. Forms tight booked connection out of 2C56.

Table T225-R

Mondays to Fridays

16 December to 15 May

Glasgow - Hamilton, Larkhall, Whifflet, Motherwell, Coatbridge, Lanark and Edinburgh

Miles	Miles	Miles	Miles	Miles		SR MX A	SR MX A	SR	SR	SR B	SR	SR	SR C	SR	SR B	SR D	SR	SR	SR	SR C	SR	SR C	SR
0	0	—	0	—	Hyndland 3 226 d								06 07							06 17	06 22	06 32	
0¾	0¾	—	0¾	—	Partick 226 d								06 10							06 19	06 24	06 34	
2	2	—	2	—	Exhibition Centre d								06 13							06 22	06 28	06 38	
2½	2½	—	2¼	—	Anderston d								06 15							06 24	06 30	06 40	
3	3	—	3	—	Glasgow Central L. Level 15 a								06 16							06 26	06 31	06 42	
—	—	—	—	—	d								06 18							06 27	06 34	06 43	
—	—	0	—	0	Glasgow Central H. Level 15 d							06 16											06 52
3½	3½	—	3½	—	Argyle Street d								06 20							06 29	06 36	06 46	
—	4¾	—	4¾	—	Bridgeton d								06 23							06 32	06 39	06 50	
—	5¼	—	5¼	—	Dalmarnock d								06 25							06 34	06 41	06 52	
5	6	—	6	—	Rutherglen d								06 28							06 36	06 44	06 55	
7	8	—	—	4¾	Cambuslang d							06 25	06 31								06 47	06 59	07 02
8½	9½	—	—	—	Newton d								06 34								06 50	07 02	
11	12	—	—	—	Blantyre d								06 38								06 54	07 06	
12¾	13¾	—	—	—	Hamilton West d								06 41								06 57	07 09	
13¾	14¾	—	—	—	Hamilton Central d								06 44								07 00	07 13	
15½	—	—	—	—	Chatelherault d								06 49									07 18	
17	—	—	—	—	Merryton d								06 52									07 21	
17¾	—	—	—	—	Larkhall a								06 55									07 24	
—	17	—	—	—	Airbles d																07 06		
—	—	—	—	8¾	Uddingston d		00 03					06 30											07 06
—	—	—	—	11	Bellshill d		00 08					06 34											07 11
—	—	—	8½	—	Carmyle d															06 40			
—	—	—	10	—	Mount Vernon d															06 43			
—	—	—	10¾	—	Baillieston d															06 45			
—	—	—	12¾	—	Bargeddie d															06 48			
—	—	—	13¾	—	Kirkwood d															06 52			
—	—	—	14½	—	Whifflet d											06 25				06 56			
—	17¾	12½	18½	13¾	Motherwell a		00 15									06 37				07 09	07 08		07 17
—	—	—	—	—	d			05 42	05 48	05 55	05 59			06 22	06 24		06 40	06 50	07 00				07 18
—	21¼	—	—	—	Whifflet d			05 49		06a02					06a31		06 48						
—	22¾	—	—	—	Coatbridge Central d			05 52									06 52						
—	28¼	—	—	—	Greenfaulds 226 d			06 02									07 02						
—	29½	—	—	—	Cumbernauld 226 a			06 04									07 04						
—	—	—	—	15¾	Shieldmuir d				05 51					06 25				06 53	07 03				07 21
—	—	—	—	—	Holytown d						06 06	06 38											
—	—	15¾	—	17	Wishaw d				05 55					06 29				06 57	07 07				07 25
—	—	20¾	—	21¾	Carluke d	00 02			06 02					06 35				07 03	07 17				07 36
—	—	28½	—	—	Carstairs a														07 25				
—	—	—	—	30	Lanark a	00 14			06 13					06 46				07 15					07 47
—	—	56	—	—	Haymarket a						07 11	07 39											
—	—	57¾	—	—	Edinburgh a						07 16	07 44											

	SR B	SR	SR D	SR C	SR E	SR	SR	SR C	SR C	SR E	SR	SR B	SR C	SR	SR D	SR C	SR E	SR	SR C	SR C	SR E
Hyndland 3 226 d				06 48	06 52			07 04	07 17	07 23			07 35			07 48	07 57		08 05	08 17	08 23
Partick 226 d				06 50	06 54			07 06	07 19	07 25			07 37			07 50	07 59		08 07	08 20	08 25
Exhibition Centre d				06 53	06 58			07 10	07 22	07 29			07 41			07 53	08 03		08 11	08 23	08 29
Anderston d				06 55	07 00			07 12	07 24	07 31			07 43			07 55	08 05		08 13	08 25	08 31
Glasgow Central L. Level 15 a				06 57	07 02			07 14	07 26	07 33			07 44			07 57	08 06		08 15	08 26	08 33
d				06 58	07 06			07 16	07 26	07 36			07 46			07 58	08 07		08 16	08 27	08 36
Glasgow Central H. Level 15 d		07 05				07 13	07 20				07 51			08 17				08 20			
Argyle Street d				07 00	07 09			07 19	07 28	07 39			07 49			08 00	08 09		08 19	08 29	08 39
Bridgeton d				07 03	07 12			07 23	07 31	07 42			07 53			08 03	08 12		08 23	08 32	08 42
Dalmarnock d				07 05	07 14			07 25	07 33	07 44			07 55			08 05	08 14		08 25	08 34	08 44
Rutherglen d				07 07	07 17			07 28	07 35	07 47			07 58			08 07	08 16		08 28	08 37	08 47
Cambuslang d					07 21	07 25	07 28	07 31		07 51	07 59		08 03				08 20	08 29	08 32		08 51
Newton d					07 24			07 35		07 54			08 06				08 25		08 35		08 54
Blantyre d					07 28			07 39		07 58			08 10				08 29		08 39		08 58
Hamilton West d					07 31			07 42		08 01			08 13				08 32		08 42		09 01
Hamilton Central d					07 34			07 45		08 04			08 16				08 34		08 45		09 04
Chatelherault d								07 49					08 20						08 49		
Merryton d								07 52					08 23						08 52		
Larkhall a								07 55					08 26						08 55		
Airbles d					07 39					08 09							08 40				09 09
Uddingston d						07 30	07 33				08 04			08 29				08 34			
Bellshill d						07 34	07 39				08 09			08 33				08 39			
Carmyle d				07 11					07 40							08 12				08 41	
Mount Vernon d				07 14					07 42							08 14				08 44	
Baillieston d				07 16					07 45							08 17				08 46	
Bargeddie d				07 19					07 48							08 20				08 49	
Kirkwood d				07 23					07 52							08 24				08 53	
Whifflet d			07 24	07a29					07 56						08 25	08a29				08 57	
Motherwell a		07 20	07 32		07 42		07 46		08 07	08 12	08 17				08 34		08 42	08 45		09 04	09 12
d	07 21	07 21			07 43		07 47				08 17	08 22					08 43	08 47			
Whifflet d	07a29				07 50							08a30					08 50				
Coatbridge Central d					07 52												08 53				
Greenfaulds 226 d					08 02												09 00				
Cumbernauld 226 a					08 04												09 02				
Shieldmuir d							07 51				08 24							08 51			
Holytown d						07 40								08 38							
Wishaw d		07 34					07 58				08 28							08 56			
Carluke d		07 40					08 04				08 35							09 02			
Carstairs a		07 49																			
Lanark a							08 15				08 48							09 13			
Haymarket a		08 31				08 45								09 46							
Edinburgh a		08 38				08 52								09 51							

A From Glasgow Central
B To Dalmuir
C From Dalmuir
D From Cumbernauld to Dalmuir
E From Milngavie

Table T225-R

Mondays to Fridays

16 December to 15 May

Glasgow - Hamilton, Larkhall, Whifflet, Motherwell, Coatbridge, Lanark and Edinburgh

	SR A	SR A	SR	SR B	SR	SR C	SR D	SR	SR A	SR E	SR A	SR D	SR	SR B	SR A	SR A	SR C	SR D	SR	SR	SR A	SR A
Hyndland 3 226 d	08 33	08 49					08 57		09 06		09 17	09 27			09 35	09 47		09 53			10 06	10 17
Partick 226 d	08 35	08 51					08 59		09 08		09 20	09 29			09 38	09 49		09 55			10 08	10 19
Exhibition Centre d	08 39	08 54					09 02		09 11		09 23	09 33			09 41	09 52		09 59			10 12	10 22
Anderston d	08 41	08 56					09 05		09 13		09 25	09 35			09 44	09 54		10 01			10 14	10 24
Glasgow Central L. Level 15 a	08 43	08 58					09 06		09 15		09 26	09 36			09 45	09 56		10 03			10 16	10 26
d	08 44	08 58					09 08		09 16		09 27	09 38			09 49	09 57		10 06			10 18	10 27
Glasgow Central H. Level 15 d			08 51		09 17			09 21		09 33			09 50						10 16	10 20		
Argyle Street d	08 46	09 00					09 10		09 19		09 28	09 40			09 51	09 59		10 09			10 20	10 29
Bridgeton d	08 49	09 03					09 13		09 23		09 31	09 43			09 54	10 02		10 12			10 23	10 32
Dalmarnock d	08 51	09 05					09 15		09 25		09 33	09 45			09 56	10 04		10 14			10 25	10 34
Rutherglen d	08 53	09 07					09 17		09 28		09 35	09 47			09 58	10 06		10 17			10 28	10 37
Cambuslang d	08 57		09 00				09 21	09 29	09 33			09 51	09 58		10 01			10 21		10 28	10 32	
Newton d	09 02						09 24		09 36			09 54			10 08			10 24			10 36	
Blantyre d	09 07						09 28		09 40			09 58			10 12			10 28			10 40	
Hamilton West d	09 11						09 31		09 43			10 01			10 15			10 31			10 43	
Hamilton Central d	09 14						09 34		09 45			10 04			10 18			10 34			10 46	
Chatelherault d	09 19								09 50						10 21						10 50	
Merryton d	09 22								09 53						10 24						10 53	
Larkhall a	09 25								09 56						10 27						10 56	
Airbles d							09 39					10 09						10 40				
Uddingston d			09 05		09 29			09 34					10 03						10 28	10 33		
Bellshill d			09 10		09 33			09 41					10 08						10 33	10 38		
Carmyle d		09 11									09 40					10 12						10 41
Mount Vernon d		09 14									09 42					10 14						10 44
Baillieston d		09 16									09 45					10 17						10 46
Bargeddie d		09 19									09 48					10 20						10 49
Kirkwood d		09 23									09 52					10 24						10 53
Whifflet d		09a27				09 34					09 55					10a27	10 33					10 57
Motherwell a			09 18			09 41	09 42	09 47		09 56	10 07	10 12	10 17				10 40	10 42		10 45		11 04
d			09 19	09 23			09 43	09 48		09 57			10 17	10 23				10 45		10 48		
Whifflet d				09a30			09 50							10a30				10 52				
Coatbridge Central d							09 53											10 54				
Greenfaulds 226 d							10 00											11 02				
Cumbernauld 226 a							10 02											11 04				
Shieldmuir d			09 22					09 51					10 21							10 51		
Holytown d					09 38														10 38			
Wishaw d			09 26					09 55		10 03			10 26							10 55		
Carluke d			09 34					10 03		10 09			10 32							11 03		
Carstairs a										10 18												
Lanark a			09 45					10 15					10 43							11 14		
Haymarket a					10 41					10 53									11 42			
Edinburgh a					10 47					11 01									11 48			

	SR D	SR A	SR A	SR	SR B	SR	SR C	SR D	SR	SR A	SR E	SR A	SR D	SR	SR B	SR A	SR A	SR C	SR D	SR	SR
Hyndland 3 226 d	10 23	10 34	10 47					10 52		11 05		11 18	11 24			11 35	11 47		11 53		
Partick 226 d	10 25	10 37	10 49					10 55		11 08		11 20	11 26			11 37	11 49		11 55		
Exhibition Centre d	10 29	10 40	10 52					10 58		11 11		11 23	11 30			11 40	11 52		11 59		
Anderston d	10 31	10 42	10 54					11 01		11 13		11 25	11 32			11 43	11 54		12 01		
Glasgow Central L. Level 15 a	10 33	10 43	10 56					11 02		11 14		11 27	11 34			11 44	11 56		12 03		
d	10 36	10 44	10 57					11 06		11 17		11 28	11 36			11 46	11 56		12 06		
Glasgow Central H. Level 15 d				10 50		11 16			11 20		11 46			11 50						12 16	12 20
Argyle Street d	10 39	10 46	10 59					11 09		11 20		11 30	11 39			11 49	11 58		12 09		
Bridgeton d	10 42	10 49	11 02					11 12		11 23		11 33	11 42			11 53	12 01		12 12		
Dalmarnock d	10 44	10 51	11 04					11 14		11 26		11 35	11 44			11 55	12 03		12 14		
Rutherglen d	10 47	10 53	11 06					11 17		11 28		11 37	11 47			11 58	12 06		12 17		
Cambuslang d	10 51	10 57		11 00				11 21	11 28	11 32			11 51	11 58		12 01			12 21		12 28
Newton d	10 54	11 01						11 24		11 35			11 54			12 08			12 24		
Blantyre d	10 58	11 05						11 28		11 39			11 58			12 12			12 28		
Hamilton West d	11 01	11 08						11 31		11 42			12 01			12 15			12 31		
Hamilton Central d	11 04	11 15						11 33		11 45			12 04			12 18			12 34		
Chatelherault d		11 19								11 49						12 22					
Merryton d		11 22								11 52						12 25					
Larkhall a		11 25								11 55						12 28					
Airbles d	11 09							11 39					12 09						12 39		
Uddingston d				11 05		11 28			11 33					12 03						12 29	12 33
Bellshill d				11 10		11 33			11 38					12 08						12 33	12 38
Carmyle d			11 10									11 42					12 10				
Mount Vernon d			11 13									11 44					12 13				
Baillieston d			11 15									11 47					12 15				
Bargeddie d			11 18									11 50					12 18				
Kirkwood d			11 22									11 54					12 22				
Whifflet d			11a26				11 33					11 58					12a26	12 33			
Motherwell a	11 12			11 19			11 40	11 41	11 44		12 04	12 09	12 12	12 17				12 40	12 42		12 44
d				11 19	11 23			11 45	11 47		12 04			12 17	12 24				12 45		12 47
Whifflet d					11a31			11 52							12a32				12 52		
Coatbridge Central d								11 54											12 55		
Greenfaulds 226 d								12 02											13 02		
Cumbernauld 226 a								12 04											13 04		
Shieldmuir d				11 23					11 51					12 21							12 51
Holytown d						11 39														12 39	
Wishaw d				11 26					11 54		12 10			12 26							12 56
Carluke d				11 34					12 02		12 16			12 34							13 02
Carstairs a											12 25										
Lanark a				11 45					12 13					12 45							13 13
Haymarket a						12 43					13 00									13 43	
Edinburgh a						12 48					13 07									13 48	

A From Dalmuir
B To Dalmuir
C From Cumbernauld to Dalmuir
D From Milngavie
E From Ayr

Table T225-R

Mondays to Fridays

16 December to 15 May

Glasgow - Hamilton, Larkhall, Whifflet, Motherwell, Coatbridge, Lanark and Edinburgh

		SR A	SR A	SR B	SR C	SR	SR A	SR A	SR D	SR B	SR	SR	SR A	SR A	SR B	SR E	SR C	SR A	SR A	SR F	SR	SR D	SR B
Hyndland 226	d	12 04	12 17	12 27			12 35	12 49		12 57			13 05	13 17	13 27			13 35	13 47				13 57
Partick 226	d	12 07	12 20	12 29			12 37	12 52		12 59			13 07	13 19	13 29			13 37	13 49				13 59
Exhibition Centre	d	12 10	12 23	12 32			12 41	12 55		13 02			13 10	13 22	13 32			13 40	13 52				14 02
Anderston	d	12 13	12 25	12 35			12 43	12 57		13 05			13 13	13 24	13 35			13 43	13 54				14 05
Glasgow Central L. Level	a	12 14	12 26	12 36			12 45	12 58		13 06			13 14	13 26	13 36			13 44	13 56				14 06
	d	12 17	12 27	12 38			12 46	12 59		13 08			13 16	13 27	13 38			13 46	13 57				14 08
Glasgow Central H. Level	d					12 50					13 17	13 20				13 50				14 06	14 16		
Argyle Street	d	12 20	12 29	12 40			12 49	13 00		13 10			13 19	13 29	13 40			13 49	13 59				14 10
Bridgeton	d	12 23	12 32	12 43			12 53	13 03		13 13			13 23	13 32	13 43			13 53	14 02				14 13
Dalmarnock	d	12 26	12 34	12 45			12 55	13 05		13 15			13 25	13 34	13 45			13 55	14 04				14 15
Rutherglen	d	12 28	12 37	12 49			12 58	13 07		13 17			13 28	13 36	13 47			13 58	14 07				14 17
Cambuslang	d	12 32		12 52		12 58	13 01			13 21		13 28	13 32		13 51	13 58		14 01					14 21
Newton	d	12 35		12 55			13 08			13 24			13 35		13 54			14 08					14 24
Blantyre	d	12 39		12 59			13 12			13 28			13 39		13 58			14 12					14 28
Hamilton West	d	12 42		13 02			13 15			13 31			13 42		14 01			14 15					14 31
Hamilton Central	d	12 45		13 05			13 18			13 34			13 45		14 04			14 18					14 34
Chatelherault	d	12 50					13 22						13 49					14 22					
Merryton	d	12 53					13 25						13 52					14 25					
Larkhall	a	12 56					13 28						13 55					14 28					
Airbles	d			13 10						13 39					14 09								14 39
Uddingston	d					13 03					13 28	13 33				14 03					14 28		
Bellshill	d					13 08					13 33	13 39				14 08					14 33		
Carmyle	d		12 41					13 11						13 41					14 11				
Mount Vernon	d		12 44					13 14						13 43					14 14				
Baillieston	d		12 46					13 16						13 46					14 16				
Bargeddie	d		12 49					13 19						13 49					14 19				
Kirkwood	d		12 53					13 23						13 53					14 23				
Whifflet	d		12 57					13a27	13 33					13 56					14a27			14 33	
Motherwell	a		13 04	13 13		13 19			13 40	13 42		13 45		14 04	14 12	14 18				14 26		14 40	14 42
	d				13 19	13 19				13 45		13 48				14 18	14 22			14 27			14 45
Whifflet	d				13a28					13 52							14a29						14 52
Coatbridge Central	d									13 54													14 54
Greenfaulds 226	d									14 02													15 02
Cumbernauld 226	a									14 04													15 04
Shieldmuir	d					13 23						13 51				14 22							
Holytown	d										13 39										14 37		
Wishaw	d					13 26						13 55				14 25				14 32			
Carluke	d					13 34						14 02				14 32				14 38			
Carstairs	a																			14 47			
Lanark	a					13 45						14 14				14 44							
Haymarket	a										14 41									15 18	15 46		
Edinburgh	a										14 46									15 26	15 52		

		SR	SR A	SR A	SR B	SR C	SR A	SR A	SR	SR	SR D	SR B	SR	SR A	SR F	SR A	SR B	SR A	SR A	SR	SR C	SR	SR D
Hyndland 226	d		14 05	14 18	14 24		14 35	14 47				14 53		15 05		15 18	15 26	15 35	15 47				
Partick 226	d		14 07	14 21	14 26		14 37	14 49				14 55		15 07		15 20	15 29	15 38	15 49				
Exhibition Centre	d		14 10	14 24	14 29		14 40	14 52				14 59		15 11		15 23	15 32	15 41	15 52				
Anderston	d		14 13	14 26	14 32		14 42	14 54				15 01		15 13		15 25	15 34	15 43	15 54				
Glasgow Central L. Level	a		14 14	14 27	14 33		14 44	14 56				15 03		15 15		15 27	15 36	15 44	15 56				
	d		14 16	14 28	14 38		14 44	14 57				15 06		15 17		15 27	15 38	15 45	15 57				
Glasgow Central H. Level	d	14 20							14 50	15 16			15 20		15 47					15 50		16 16	
Argyle Street	d		14 19	14 30	14 40		14 46	14 59				15 09		15 20		15 29	15 40	15 47	15 59				
Bridgeton	d		14 23	14 33	14 43		14 49	15 02				15 12		15 23		15 32	15 43	15 50	16 02				
Dalmarnock	d		14 25	14 35	14 45		14 51	15 04				15 14		15 26		15 34	15 45	15 52	16 04				
Rutherglen	d		14 28	14 37	14 47		14 53	15 07				15 17		15 28		15 37	15 47	15 54	16 06				
Cambuslang	d	14 28	14 32		14 51		14 56		15 00			15 21	15 28	15 32			15 51	15 58		16 02			
Newton	d		14 35		14 54		15 00					15 24		15 35			15 54	16 01					
Blantyre	d		14 39		14 58		15 04					15 28		15 39			15 58	16 05					
Hamilton West	d		14 42		15 01		15 07					15 31		15 42			16 01	16 08					
Hamilton Central	d		14 45		15 04		15 13					15 34		15 45			16 04	16 13					
Chatelherault	d		14 49				15 18							15 49				16 18					
Merryton	d		14 52				15 21							15 52				16 21					
Larkhall	a		14 55				15 24							15 55				16 24					
Airbles	d				15 09							15 39					16 09						
Uddingston	d	14 33							15 05	15 28			15 33							16 06		16 29	
Bellshill	d	14 38							15 10	15 33			15 39							16 11		16 34	
Carmyle	d			14 41				15 11								15 41			16 11				
Mount Vernon	d			14 44				15 14								15 44			16 14				
Baillieston	d			14 46				15 16								15 46			16 16				
Bargeddie	d			14 49				15 19								15 49			16 19				
Kirkwood	d			14 53				15 23								15 53			16 23				
Whifflet	d			14 57				15a27			15 33					15 57			16a27				16 32
Motherwell	a	14 44		15 05	15 12				15 19		15 40	15 42	15 45		16 02	16 05	16 12			16 17			16 40
	d	14 45				15 19			15 19			15 45	15 48		16 02					16 18	16 19		
Whifflet	d					15a26						15 52									16a28		
Coatbridge Central	d											15 55											
Greenfaulds 226	d											16 03											
Cumbernauld 226	a											16 05											
Shieldmuir	d	14 49							15 23				15 51							16 21			
Holytown	d									15 39												16 38	
Wishaw	d	14 52							15 26				15 55		16 07					16 25			
Carluke	d	15 02							15 34				16 02		16 13					16 32			
Carstairs	a														16 37								
Lanark	a	15 13							15 45				16 13							16 43			
Haymarket	a									16 46					17 01							17 43	
Edinburgh	a									16 52					17 06							17 48	

A From Dalmuir
B From Milngavie
C To Dalmuir
D From Cumbernauld to Dalmuir
E To Glasgow Central
F From Ayr

Table T225-R

Mondays to Fridays

16 December to 15 May

Glasgow - Hamilton, Larkhall, Whifflet, Motherwell, Coatbridge, Lanark and Edinburgh

		SR A	SR	SR B	SR B	SR A	SR C	SR	SR B	SR B	SR D	SR	SR A	SR	SR	SR B	SR B	SR A	SR	SR	SR C	SR B
Hyndland 226	d	15 56		16 05	16 17	16 23			16 34	16 47			16 59			17 06	17 17	17 27				17 35
Partick 226	d	15 59		16 07	16 19	16 25			16 37	16 49			17 02			17 08	17 20	17 29				17 38
Exhibition Centre	d	16 02		16 11	16 22	16 29			16 40	16 52			17 05			17 12	17 23	17 32				17 42
Anderston	d	16 04		16 13	16 24	16 31			16 43	16 54		17 00	17 07			17 14	17 25	17 35	17 42			17 45
Glasgow Central L. Level	a	16 05		16 15	16 26	16 33			16 44	16 56		17 01	17 09			17 16	17 26	17 36	17 43			17 46
	d	16 07		16 16	16 27	16 36			16 46	16 56		17 02	17 09			17 17	17 27	17 37	17 44			17 48
Glasgow Central H. Level	d		16 20					16 50						17 16	17 20					17 50		
Argyle Street	d	16 10		16 19	16 29	16 39			16 49	16 58		17 04	17 11			17 19	17 29	17 39	17 46			17 51
Bridgeton	d	16 13		16 23	16 32	16 42			16 53	17 01			17 14			17 23	17 32	17 42				17 54
Dalmarnock	d	16 15		16 25	16 34	16 44			16 55	17 03			17 16			17 25	17 34	17 44				17 56
Rutherglen	d	16 17		16 28	16 37	16 47			16 58	17 05		17 10	17 18			17 28	17 37	17 47	17 51			17 59
Cambuslang	d	16 21	16 28	16 32		16 51		16 58	17 01				17 22		17 28	17 32		17 51		17 58		18 03
Newton	d	16 24		16 35		16 54			17 05				17 25			17 35		17 54				18 09
Blantyre	d	16 28		16 39		16 58			17 09				17 29			17 39		17 58				18 13
Hamilton West	d	16 31		16 42		17 01			17 12				17 32			17 42		18 01				18 16
Hamilton Central	d	16 34		16 45		17 04			17 15				17 34			17 45		18 04				18 18
Chatelherault	d			16 49					17 19							17 49						18 23
Merryton	d			16 52					17 22							17 52						18 26
Larkhall	a			16 55					17 25							17 55						18 29
Airbles	d	16 39				17 09							17 40					18 09				
Uddingston	d		16 33					17 03						17u30	17 33				17 59	18 04		
Bellshill	d		16 38					17 08				17 21		17 33	17 38				18 05	18 10		
Carmyle	d				16 41					17 10							17 41					
Mount Vernon	d				16 44					17 12							17 44					
Baillieston	d				16 46					17 15							17 46					
Bargeddie	d				16 49					17 18							17 49					
Kirkwood	d				16 53					17 22							17 53					
Whifflet	d				16 57					17a25	17 33						17 58					
Motherwell	a	16 42	16 45		17 04	17 12		17 19			17 40		17 42		17 48		18 05	18 12	18 11	18 17		
	d	16 45	16 45				17 20	17 20					17 46		17 49				18 12	18 17	18 23	
Whifflet	d	16 52					17a29						17 53								18a31	
Coatbridge Central	d	16 55											17 56									
Greenfaulds 226	d	17 07											18 06									
Cumbernauld 226	a	17 09											18 08									
Shieldmuir	d		16 49					17 23							17 52				18 15	18 21		
Holytown	d											17 26		17 40								
Wishaw	d		17 00					17 27				17 33			18 01				18 19	18 24		
Carluke	d		17 06					17 35				17 39			18 07				18 25	18 30		
Carstairs	a											17 48							18 33			
Lanark	a		17 17					17 46							18 19					18 41		
Haymarket	a													18 42								
Edinburgh	a													18 49								

		SR B	SR D	SR A	SR	SR	SR B	SR B	SR A	SR	SR C	SR B	SR B	SR D	SR A	SR B	SR	SR	SR E	SR B	SR A	SR	SR C
Hyndland 226	d	17 46		17 53			18 05	18 17	18 23			18 34	18 47		18 52	19 04				19 19	19 27		
Partick 226	d	17 49		17 56			18 07	18 19	18 25			18 37	18 49		18 54	19 07				19 21	19 29		
Exhibition Centre	d	17 52		17 59			18 10	18 22	18 29			18 40	18 52		18 58	19 10				19 24	19 32		
Anderston	d	17 54		18 02			18 13	18 24	18 31			18 43	18 54		19 00	19 13				19 26	19 34		
Glasgow Central L. Level	a	17 55		18 03			18 14	18 26	18 33			18 44	18 56		19 02	19 14				19 28	19 36		
	d	17 56		18 06			18 16	18 27	18 36			18 45	18 57		19 06	19 16				19 28	19 37		
Glasgow Central H. Level	d				18 17	18 21				18 50							19 16	19 21	19 46			19 50	
Argyle Street	d	17 58		18 09			18 19	18 29	18 39			18 48	18 59		19 09	19 19				19 30	19 39		
Bridgeton	d	18 01		18 12			18 23	18 32	18 42			18 53	19 02		19 12	19 22				19 33	19 42		
Dalmarnock	d	18 03		18 14			18 25	18 34	18 44			18 55	19 04		19 14	19 24				19 35	19 44		
Rutherglen	d	18 05		18 17			18 29	18 38	18 48			18 58	19 07		19 17	19 26				19 37	19 47		
Cambuslang	d			18 21		18 29	18 33		18 51	18 58		19 01			19 21	19 29		19 33			19 51	19 58	
Newton	d			18 24			18 36		18 54			19 05			19 24	19 33					19 54		
Blantyre	d			18 28			18 40		18 58			19 09			19 28	19 37					19 58		
Hamilton West	d			18 31			18 43		19 01			19 12			19 31	19 40					20 01		
Hamilton Central	d			18 34			18 46		19 04			19 15			19 34	19 43					20 04		
Chatelherault	d						18 50					19 19				19 48							
Merryton	d						18 53					19 22				19 51							
Larkhall	a						18 56					19 25				19 54							
Airbles	d			18 39					19 09						19 39						20 09		
Uddingston	d				18 28	18 34				19 03							19 28	19 37				20 03	
Bellshill	d				18 33	18 41				19 08							19 33	19 42				20 08	
Carmyle	d	18 10						18 42					19 11							19 41			
Mount Vernon	d	18 12						18 45					19 14							19 44			
Baillieston	d	18 15						18 47					19 16							19 46			
Bargeddie	d	18 18						18 50					19 19							19 49			
Kirkwood	d	18 22						18 54					19 23							19 53			
Whifflet	d	18a25	18 32					18 58					19a27	19 33						19 57			
Motherwell	a		18 40	18 42		18 47		19 05	19 12	19 18				19 40	19 42			19 48	20 02	20 08	20 12	20 14	
	d			18 45		18 48				19 19	19 20				19 45			19 49	20 03			20 18	20 26
Whifflet	d			18 52							19a28				19 52								20a33
Coatbridge Central	d			18 54											19 54								
Greenfaulds 226	d			19 02											20 02								
Cumbernauld 226	a			19 04											20 04								
Shieldmuir	d					18 51				19 22								19 53				20 22	
Holytown	d				18 37												19 40						
Wishaw	d					18 55				19 26								19 56	20 09			20 27	
Carluke	d					19 02				19 34								20 02	20 15			20 33	
Carstairs	a																		20 24				
Lanark	a					19 13				19 45								20 13				20 44	
Haymarket	a				19 43												20 42		20 53				
Edinburgh	a				19 49												20 47		20 59				

A From Milngavie
B From Dalmuir
C To Dalmuir
D From Cumbernauld to Dalmuir
E From Ayr

Table T225-R

Mondays to Fridays
16 December to 15 May

Glasgow - Hamilton, Larkhall, Whifflet, Motherwell, Coatbridge, Lanark and Edinburgh

		SR A	SR A	SR B	SR C	SR	SR A	SR A	SR C	SR	SR D	SR A	SR A	SR B	SR C	SR A	SR	SR	SR A	SR C	SR D	SR A
Hyndland 3 226	d	19 35	19 47		19 57		20 06	20 17	20 23			20 35	20 47		20 58	21 06			21 17	21 24		21 36
Partick 226 ⛴	d	19 38	19 50		19 59		20 08	20 20	20 25			20 37	20 50		21 00	21 09			21 20	21 26		21 38
Exhibition Centre	d	19 41	19 53		20 03		20 11	20 23	20 29			20 41	20 53		21 04	21 12			21 23	21 30		21 41
Anderston	d	19 44	19 55		20 05		20 13	20 25	20 31			20 43	20 55		21 06	21 14			21 25	21 32		21 43
Glasgow Central L. Level 15	a	19 45	19 56		20 06		20 15	20 26	20 33			20 45	20 56		21 07	21 15			21 26	21 34		21 45
	d	19 47	19 58		20 07		20 17	20 28	20 36			20 46	20 57		21 08	21 16			21 27	21 36		21 45
Glasgow Central H. Level 15	d					20 21					20 50						21 16	21 22				
Argyle Street	d	19 50	19 59		20 09		20 20	20 30	20 39			20 48	20 59		21 10	21 18			21 29	21 39		21 46
Bridgeton	d	19 54	20 02		20 12		20 23	20 33	20 42			20 51	21 02		21 13	21 21			21 32	21 42		21 49
Dalmarnock	d	19 56	20 04		20 14		20 26	20 35	20 44			20 53	21 04		21 15	21 23			21 34	21 44		21 51
Rutherglen	d	19 59	20 07		20 17		20 29	20 37	20 46			20 58	21 07		21 17	21 25			21 37	21 47		21 53
Cambuslang	d	20 02			20 21	20 29	20 32		20 49	20 58		21 01			21 21	21 28		21 33		21 50		21 57
Newton	d	20 08			20 26		20 35		20 53			21 08			21 24	21 32				21 54		22 00
Blantyre	d	20 12			20 30		20 39		20 57			21 12			21 28	21 36				21 58		22 05
Hamilton West	d	20 15			20 33		20 42		21 00			21 15			21 31	21 39				22 01		22 08
Hamilton Central	d	20 17			20 36		20 45		21 04			21 17			21 34	21 43				22 04		22 13
Chatelherault	d	20 22					20 49					21 22				21 48						22 18
Merryton	d	20 25					20 52					21 25				21 51						22 21
Larkhall	a	20 28					20 55					21 28				21 54						22 24
Airbles	d				20 41				21 09						21 39					22 09		
Uddingston	d					20 34				21 04							21 29	21 37				
Bellshill	d					20 39				21 09							21 34	21 42				
Carmyle	d		20 11					20 41					21 11						21 41			
Mount Vernon	d		20 14					20 44					21 14						21 44			
Baillieston	d		20 16					20 46					21 16						21 46			
Bargeddie	d		20 19					20 49					21 19						21 49			
Kirkwood	d		20 23					20 53					21 23						21 53			
Whifflet	d		20a27	20 33				20 58					21a27	21 33					21 57			
Motherwell	a			20 40	20 44	20 46		21 08	21 12	21 17				21 40	21 42			21 49	22 04	22 12		
	d				20 45	20 47				21 18	21 22				21 43			21 49			22 19	
Whifflet	d				20 52						21a30				21 51						22a27	
Coatbridge Central	d				20 55										21 55							
Greenfaulds 226	d				21 06										22 06							
Cumbernauld 226	a				21 08										22 08							
Shieldmuir	d					20 50				21 22								21 53				
Holytown	d																21 40					
Wishaw	d					20 54				21 25								21 56				
Carluke	d					21 02				21 33								22 02				
Carstairs	a																					
Lanark	a					21 13				21 44								22 13				
Haymarket ⛴	a																22 43					
Edinburgh	a																22 50					

		SR A	SR	SR E	SR C	SR	SR A	SR A	SR C	SR	SR FO D	SR A	SR A	SR	SR C	SR	SR A	SR A	SR C	SR FX	SR FO	SR FO A	SR FO A
Hyndland 3 226	d	21 47			21 58		22 06	22 18	22 28			22 34	22 47		22 58		23 05	23 17	23 28			23 35	23 48
Partick 226 ⛴	d	21 50			22 00		22 08	22 20	22 30			22 37	22 50		23 00		23 08	23 20	23 30			23 38	23 50
Exhibition Centre	d	21 53			22 04		22 11	22 23	22 34			22 40	22 53		23 04		23 12	23 23	23 34			23 41	23 54
Anderston	d	21 55			22 06		22 13	22 25	22 36			22 42	22 55		23 06		23 14	23 25	23 36			23 43	23 56
Glasgow Central L. Level 15	a	21 56			22 07		22 15	22 27	22 37			22 44	22 57		23 07		23 15	23 27	23 38			23 45	23 58
	d	21 57			22 08		22 17	22 27	22 38			22 46	22 57		23 08		23 17	23 27	23 38			23 46	23 59
Glasgow Central H. Level 15	d		21 50			22 20				22 50				23 03		23 20				23 50	23 50		
Argyle Street	d	21 59			22 10		22 20	22 29	22 40			22 49	22 59		23 10		23 20	23 29	23 40			23 49	00 03
Bridgeton	d	22 02			22 13		22 23	22 32	22 43			22 53	23 02		23 13		23 23	23 32	23 43			23 53	00 06
Dalmarnock	d	22 04			22 15		22 25	22 34	22 45			22 55	23 04		23 15		23 25	23 34	23 45			23 55	00 08
Rutherglen	d	22 07			22 17		22 29	22 37	22 47			22 58	23 07		23 17		23 28	23 37	23 48			23 58	00 12
Cambuslang	d		22 03		22 21	22 28	22 32		22 51	22 58		23 02		23 12	23 21	23 28	23 32		23 51	23 58	23 58	00 01	
Newton	d				22 24		22 35		22 54			23 07			23 24		23 35					00 05	
Blantyre	d				22 28		22 39		22 58			23 11			23 28		23 39					00 09	
Hamilton West	d				22 31		22 42		23 01			23 15			23 31		23 42					00 12	
Hamilton Central	d				22 34		22 45		23 04			23 17			23 33		23 46					00 15	
Chatelherault	d						22 50					23 22					23 50					00 19	
Merryton	d						22 53					23 25					23 53					00 22	
Larkhall	a						22 56					23 28					23 56					00 25	
Airbles	d				22 39				23 09						23 39								
Uddingston	d		22 07			22 33				23 03				23 17		23 33				00 03	00 03		
Bellshill	d		22 12			22 38				23 08				23 21		23 38				00 08	00 08		
Carmyle	d	22 11						22 41					23 11					23 41					00 17
Mount Vernon	d	22 14						22 44					23 14					23 44					00 20
Baillieston	d	22 16						22 46					23 16					23 46					00 23
Bargeddie	d	22 19						22 49					23 19					23 49					00 26
Kirkwood	d	22 23						22 53					23 23					23 53					00 32
Whifflet	d	22a27		22 33				22 57					23 27					23 57					00 36
Motherwell	a		22 18	22 41	22 42	22 46		23 04	23 12	23 17			23 34		23 41	23 44		00 05	00 01	00 15	00 16		00 44
	d		22 19		22 45	22 47				23 18	23 22		23 39			23 46					00 19		
Whifflet	d				22 52						23a29												
Coatbridge Central	d				22 55																		
Greenfaulds 226	d				23 08																		
Cumbernauld 226	a				23 10																		
Shieldmuir	d		22 23			22 50				23 22			23 42			23 49					00 22		
Holytown	d													23 25									
Wishaw	d		22 26			22 54				23 25			23 47			23 56					00 26		
Carluke	d		22 32			23 00				23 31			23 55			00 02					00 32		
Carstairs	a												00 05										
Lanark	a		22 43			23 11				23 42						00 14					00 42		
Haymarket ⛴	a													00 30									
Edinburgh	a													00 39									

A From Dalmuir
B From Cumbernauld to Dalmuir
C From Milngavie
D To Dalmuir
E From Cumbernauld to Garscadden

Table T225-R

Mondays to Fridays
16 December to 15 May

Glasgow - Hamilton, Larkhall, Whifflet, Motherwell, Coatbridge, Lanark and Edinburgh

		SR FO A
Hyndland 3 226	d	23 53
Partick 226 ⛴	d	23 55
Exhibition Centre	d	23 59
Anderston	d	00 02
Glasgow Central L. Level 15	a	00 03
	d	00 06
Glasgow Central H. Level 15	d	
Argyle Street	d	00 09
Bridgeton	d	00 12
Dalmarnock	d	00 14
Rutherglen	d	00 17
Cambuslang	d	00 21
Newton	d	00 24
Blantyre	d	00 28
Hamilton West	d	00 31
Hamilton Central	d	00 33
Chatelherault	d	
Merryton	d	
Larkhall	a	
Airbles	d	00 39
Uddingston	d	
Bellshill	d	
Carmyle	d	
Mount Vernon	d	
Baillieston	d	
Bargeddie	d	
Kirkwood	d	
Whifflet	d	
Motherwell	a	00 41
	d	
Whifflet	d	
Coatbridge Central	d	
Greenfaulds 226	d	
Cumbernauld 226	a	
Shieldmuir	d	
Holytown	d	
Wishaw	d	
Carluke	d	
Carstairs	a	
Lanark	a	
Haymarket ⛴	a	
Edinburgh	a	

Saturdays
21 December to 16 May

		SR B	SR C	SR C	SR B	SR	SR A	SR	SR	SR D	SR	SR	SR B	SR	SR D	SR E	SR	SR	SR B	SR	SR B	SR	SR D
Hyndland 3 226	d												06 07						06 17	06 22	06 32		
Partick 226 ⛴	d												06 10						06 19	06 24	06 34		
Exhibition Centre	d												06 13						06 22	06 28	06 38		
Anderston	d						00 02						06 15						06 24	06 30	06 40		
Glasgow Central L. Level 15	a						00 03						06 16						06 26	06 31	06 42		
	d						00 06						06 18						06 27	06 34	06 43		
Glasgow Central H. Level 15	d					00 07						06 16										06 50	
Argyle Street	d				00 03		00 09						06 20						06 29	06 36	06 46		
Bridgeton	d				00 06		00 12						06 23						06 32	06 39	06 50		
Dalmarnock	d				00 08		00 14						06 25						06 34	06 41	06 52		
Rutherglen	d				00 12		00 17						06 28						06 36	06 44	06 55		
Cambuslang	d	00 01				00 15	00 21					06 25	06 31							06 47	06 59	07 02	
Newton	d	00 05					00 24						06 34							06 50	07 02		
Blantyre	d	00 09					00 28						06 38							06 54	07 06		
Hamilton West	d	00 12					00 31						06 41							06 57	07 09		
Hamilton Central	d	00 15					00 33						06 44							07 00	07 13		
Chatelherault	d	00 19											06 49								07 18		
Merryton	d	00 22											06 52								07 21		
Larkhall	a	00 25											06 55								07 24		
Airbles	d						00 39													07 06			
Uddingston	d			00 03		00 20						06 30										07 07	
Bellshill	d			00 08		00 25						06 34										07 12	
Carmyle	d				00 17														06 40				
Mount Vernon	d				00 20														06 43				
Baillieston	d				00 23														06 45				
Bargeddie	d				00 26														06 48				
Kirkwood	d				00 32														06 52				
Whifflet	d				00 36											06 25			06 56				
Motherwell	a			00 16	00 44		00 41									06 37			07 09	07 09		07 18	
	d			00 19				05 42	05 48	05 55	05 59			06 22	06 24		06 40	06 50				07 18	07 21
Whifflet	d							05 49		06a02					06a31		06 48						07a29
Coatbridge Central	d							05 52									06 52						
Greenfaulds 226	d							06 02									07 02						
Cumbernauld 226	a							06 04									07 04						
Shieldmuir	d			00 22					05 51					06 25				06 53				07 22	
Holytown	d					00 29					06 06	06 38											
Wishaw	d			00 26					05 55					06 29				06 57				07 26	
Carluke	d		00 02	00 32					06 02					06 35				07 03				07 36	
Carstairs	a																						
Lanark	a		00 14	00 42					06 13					06 46				07 14				07 47	
Haymarket ⛴	a					01 20					07 11	07 42											
Edinburgh	a					01 26					07 16	07 48											

A From Milngavie
B From Dalmuir
C From Glasgow Central
D To Dalmuir
E From Cumbernauld to Dalmuir

Table T225-R

Saturdays

21 December to 16 May

Glasgow - Hamilton, Larkhall, Whifflet, Motherwell, Coatbridge, Lanark and Edinburgh

		SR	SR A	SR B	SR C	SR		SR	SR B	SR B	SR C	SR	SR D	SR B	SR	SR A		SR B	SR C	SR	SR B	SR B	SR C	SR B	SR B
Hyndland 226	d			06 48	06 52				07 04	07 17	07 23			07 35				07 48	07 57		08 05	08 17	08 23	08 33	08 49
Partick 226	d			06 50	06 54				07 06	07 19	07 25			07 37				07 50	07 59		08 07	08 20	08 25	08 35	08 51
Exhibition Centre	d			06 53	06 58				07 10	07 22	07 29			07 41				07 53	08 03		08 11	08 23	08 29	08 39	08 54
Anderston	d			06 55	07 00				07 12	07 24	07 31			07 43				07 55	08 05		08 13	08 25	08 31	08 41	08 56
Glasgow Central L. Level	a			06 57	07 02				07 14	07 26	07 33			07 44				07 57	08 06		08 15	08 26	08 33	08 43	08 58
	d			06 58	07 06				07 16	07 26	07 36			07 46				07 58	08 07		08 16	08 27	08 36	08 44	08 58
Glasgow Central H. Level	d	07 03				07 16		07 20				07 51			08 17					08 20					
Argyle Street	d			07 00	07 09				07 19	07 28	07 39			07 49				08 00	08 09		08 19	08 29	08 39	08 46	09 00
Bridgeton	d			07 03	07 12				07 23	07 31	07 42			07 53				08 03	08 12		08 23	08 32	08 42	08 49	09 03
Dalmarnock	d			07 05	07 14				07 25	07 33	07 44			07 55				08 05	08 14		08 25	08 34	08 44	08 51	09 05
Rutherglen	d			07 07	07 17				07 28	07 35	07 47			07 58				08 07	08 16		08 29	08 37	08 47	08 53	09 07
Cambuslang	d				07 21	07 24		07 28	07 32		07 51	07 59		08 03					08 20	08 29	08 32		08 51	08 57	
Newton	d				07 24				07 35		07 54			08 06					08 25		08 35		08 54	09 02	
Blantyre	d				07 28				07 39		07 58			08 10					08 29		08 39		08 58	09 07	
Hamilton West	d				07 31				07 42		08 01			08 13					08 32		08 42		09 01	09 11	
Hamilton Central	d				07 34				07 45		08 04			08 16					08 34		08 45		09 04	09 14	
Chatelherault	d								07 49					08 20							08 49			09 19	
Merryton	d								07 52					08 23							08 52			09 22	
Larkhall	a								07 55					08 26							08 55			09 25	
Airbles	d				07 39						08 09								08 40				09 09		
Uddingston	d					07 29		07 33				08 04			08 29					08 34					
Bellshill	d					07 34		07 39				08 09			08 33					08 39					
Carmyle	d			07 11						07 40								08 12				08 41			09 11
Mount Vernon	d			07 14						07 42								08 14				08 44			09 14
Baillieston	d			07 16						07 45								08 17				08 46			09 16
Bargeddie	d			07 19						07 48								08 20				08 49			09 19
Kirkwood	d			07 23						07 52								08 24				08 53			09 23
Whifflet	d		07 24	07a29						07 56						08 25		08a29				08 57			09a27
Motherwell	a	07 28	07 32		07 42			07 46		08 07	08 12	08 17				08 34			08 42	08 45		09 04	09 12		
	d	07 29			07 43			07 47				08 17	08 22						08 43	08 47					
Whifflet	d				07 50								08a30						08 50						
Coatbridge Central	d				07 52														08 53						
Greenfaulds 226	d				08 02														09 00						
Cumbernauld 226	a				08 04														09 02						
Shieldmuir	d							07 51				08 21								08 51					
Holytown	d					07 40									08 38										
Wishaw	d	07 34						07 57				08 24								08 54					
Carluke	d	07 40						08 03				08 30								09 02					
Carstairs	a	07 49																							
Lanark	a							08 14				08 43								09 13					
Haymarket	a	08 27				08 45									09 42										
Edinburgh	a	08 34				08 52									09 48										

		SR		SR D	SR	SR A	SR C	SR	SR B	SR	SR B	SR C		SR	SR D	SR B	SR B	SR A	SR C	SR	SR	SR B		SR B	SR C
Hyndland 226	d						08 57		09 06		09 17	09 27				09 35	09 47		09 53			10 06		10 17	10 23
Partick 226	d						08 59		09 08		09 20	09 29				09 38	09 49		09 55			10 08		10 19	10 25
Exhibition Centre	d						09 02		09 11		09 23	09 33				09 41	09 52		09 59			10 12		10 22	10 29
Anderston	d						09 05		09 13		09 25	09 35				09 44	09 54		10 01			10 14		10 24	10 31
Glasgow Central L. Level	a						09 06		09 15		09 26	09 36				09 45	09 56		10 03			10 16		10 26	10 33
	d						09 08		09 16		09 27	09 38				09 49	09 57		10 06			10 18		10 27	10 36
Glasgow Central H. Level	d	08 50			09 17			09 21		09 30				09 50						10 16	10 20				
Argyle Street	d						09 10		09 19		09 28	09 40				09 51	09 59		10 09			10 20		10 29	10 39
Bridgeton	d						09 13		09 23		09 31	09 43				09 54	10 02		10 12			10 23		10 32	10 42
Dalmarnock	d						09 15		09 25		09 33	09 45				09 56	10 04		10 14			10 25		10 34	10 44
Rutherglen	d						09 17		09 28		09 35	09 47				09 58	10 06		10 17			10 28		10 37	10 47
Cambuslang	d	09 00					09 21	09 29	09 33			09 51		09 58		10 01			10 21		10 28	10 32			10 51
Newton	d						09 24		09 36			09 54				10 08			10 24			10 36			10 54
Blantyre	d						09 28		09 40			09 58				10 12			10 28			10 40			10 58
Hamilton West	d						09 31		09 43			10 01				10 15			10 31			10 43			11 01
Hamilton Central	d						09 34		09 45			10 04				10 18			10 34			10 46			11 04
Chatelherault	d								09 50							10 21						10 50			
Merryton	d								09 53							10 24						10 53			
Larkhall	a								09 56							10 27						10 56			
Airbles	d						09 39					10 09							10 40						11 09
Uddingston	d	09 05			09 29			09 34						10 03						10 28	10 33				
Bellshill	d	09 10			09 33			09 41						10 08						10 33	10 38				
Carmyle	d										09 40						10 12							10 41	
Mount Vernon	d										09 42						10 14							10 44	
Baillieston	d										09 45						10 17							10 46	
Bargeddie	d										09 48						10 20							10 49	
Kirkwood	d										09 52						10 24							10 53	
Whifflet	d					09 34					09 55						10a27	10 33						10 57	
Motherwell	a	09 18				09 41	09 42	09 47		09 56	10 07	10 12		10 17				10 40	10 42		10 45			11 04	11 12
	d	09 18		09 23			09 43	09 48		09 57				10 17	10 23				10 45		10 48				
Whifflet	d			09a30			09 50								10a30				10 52						
Coatbridge Central	d						09 53												10 54						
Greenfaulds 226	d						10 00												11 02						
Cumbernauld 226	a						10 02												11 04						
Shieldmuir	d	09 22						09 51						10 21							10 51				
Holytown	d				09 38															10 38					
Wishaw	d	09 25						09 55		10 03				10 26							10 55				
Carluke	d	09 33						10 03		10 09				10 32							11 03				
Carstairs	a									10 18															
Lanark	a	09 44						10 15						10 43							11 14				
Haymarket	a				10 41					10 44										11 42					
Edinburgh	a				10 47					10 50										11 48					

A From Cumbernauld to Dalmuir
B From Dalmuir
C From Milngavie
D To Dalmuir

NRT DECEMBER 19 EDITION

Table T225-R

Saturdays

21 December to 16 May

Glasgow - Hamilton, Larkhall, Whifflet, Motherwell, Coatbridge, Lanark and Edinburgh

		SR A	SR A	SR	SR B	SR	SR C	SR D		SR	SR A	SR E	SR A	SR D	SR	SR B	SR A	SR A		SR C	SR D	SR	SR	SR A	SR A
Hyndland 226	d	10 34	10 47					10 52			11 05		11 18	11 24			11 35	11 47			11 53			12 04	12 17
Partick 226	d	10 37	10 49					10 55			11 08		11 20	11 26			11 37	11 49			11 55			12 07	12 20
Exhibition Centre	d	10 40	10 52					10 58			11 11		11 23	11 30			11 40	11 52			11 59			12 10	12 23
Anderston	d	10 42	10 54					11 01			11 13		11 25	11 32			11 43	11 54			12 01			12 13	12 25
Glasgow Central L. Level	a	10 43	10 56					11 02			11 14		11 27	11 34			11 44	11 56			12 03			12 14	12 26
	d	10 44	10 57					11 06			11 17		11 28	11 36			11 46	11 56			12 06			12 17	12 27
Glasgow Central H. Level	d			10 50		11 16				11 20		11 46			11 50							12 16	12 20		
Argyle Street	d	10 46	10 59					11 09			11 20		11 30	11 39			11 49	11 58			12 09			12 20	12 29
Bridgeton	d	10 49	11 02					11 12			11 23		11 33	11 42			11 53	12 01			12 12			12 23	12 32
Dalmarnock	d	10 51	11 04					11 14			11 26		11 35	11 44			11 55	12 03			12 14			12 26	12 34
Rutherglen	d	10 53	11 06					11 17			11 28		11 37	11 47			11 58	12 06			12 17			12 28	12 37
Cambuslang	d	10 57		11 00				11 21		11 28	11 32			11 51	11 58		12 01				12 21		12 28	12 32	
Newton	d	11 01						11 24			11 35			11 54			12 08				12 24			12 35	
Blantyre	d	11 05						11 28			11 39			11 58			12 12				12 28			12 39	
Hamilton West	d	11 08						11 31			11 42			12 01			12 15				12 31			12 42	
Hamilton Central	d	11 15						11 33			11 45			12 04			12 18				12 34			12 45	
Chatelherault	d	11 19									11 49						12 22							12 50	
Merryton	d	11 22									11 52						12 25							12 53	
Larkhall	a	11 25									11 55						12 28							12 56	
Airbles	d							11 39						12 09							12 39				
Uddingston	d			11 05		11 28				11 33					12 03							12 29	12 33		
Bellshill	d			11 10		11 33				11 38					12 08							12 33	12 38		
Carmyle	d		11 10										11 42					12 10							12 41
Mount Vernon	d		11 13										11 44					12 13							12 44
Baillieston	d		11 15										11 47					12 15							12 46
Bargeddie	d		11 18										11 50					12 18							12 49
Kirkwood	d		11 22										11 54					12 22							12 53
Whifflet	d		11a26				11 33						11 58					12a26		12 33					12 57
Motherwell	a			11 19			11 40	11 41		11 44		12 04	12 09	12 12	12 17					12 40	12 42		12 44		13 04
	d			11 19	11 23			11 45		11 47		12 04			12 17	12 24					12 45		12 47		
Whifflet	d				11a31			11 52								12a32					12 52				
Coatbridge Central	d							11 54													12 55				
Greenfaulds 226	d							12 02													13 02				
Cumbernauld 226	a							12 04													13 04				
Shieldmuir	d			11 23						11 51					12 21								12 51		
Holytown	d					11 39																12 39			
Wishaw	d			11 26						11 54		12 10			12 24								12 56		
Carluke	d			11 34						12 02		12 16			12 32								13 02		
Carstairs	a											12 25													
Lanark	a			11 45						12 13					12 43								13 13		
Haymarket	a					12 42						12 59										13 42			
Edinburgh	a					12 48						13 06										13 48			

		SR D	SR B	SR		SR A	SR A	SR C	SR D	SR	SR	SR A	SR A	SR D		SR	SR B	SR A	SR A	SR E	SR	SR C	SR D	SR	
Hyndland 226	d	12 27				12 35	12 49		12 57			13 05	13 17	13 27				13 35	13 47				13 57		
Partick 226	d	12 29				12 37	12 52		12 59			13 07	13 19	13 29				13 37	13 49				13 59		
Exhibition Centre	d	12 32				12 41	12 55		13 02			13 10	13 22	13 32				13 40	13 52				14 02		
Anderston	d	12 35				12 43	12 57		13 05			13 13	13 24	13 35				13 43	13 54				14 05		
Glasgow Central L. Level	a	12 36				12 45	12 58		13 06			13 14	13 26	13 36				13 44	13 56				14 06		
	d	12 38				12 46	12 59		13 08			13 16	13 27	13 38				13 46	13 57				14 08		
Glasgow Central H. Level	d			12 50						13 17	13 20					13 50				14 06	14 16			14 20	
Argyle Street	d	12 40				12 49	13 00		13 10			13 19	13 29	13 40				13 49	13 59				14 10		
Bridgeton	d	12 43				12 53	13 03		13 13			13 23	13 32	13 43				13 53	14 02				14 13		
Dalmarnock	d	12 45				12 55	13 05		13 15			13 25	13 34	13 45				13 55	14 04				14 15		
Rutherglen	d	12 49				12 58	13 07		13 17			13 28	13 36	13 47				13 58	14 07				14 17		
Cambuslang	d	12 52		12 58		13 01			13 21		13 28	13 32		13 51		13 58		14 01					14 21	14 28	
Newton	d	12 55				13 08			13 24			13 35		13 54				14 08					14 24		
Blantyre	d	12 59				13 12			13 28			13 39		13 58				14 12					14 28		
Hamilton West	d	13 02				13 15			13 31			13 42		14 01				14 15					14 31		
Hamilton Central	d	13 05				13 18			13 34			13 45		14 04				14 18					14 34		
Chatelherault	d					13 22						13 49						14 22							
Merryton	d					13 25						13 52						14 25							
Larkhall	a					13 28						13 55						14 28							
Airbles	d	13 10							13 39					14 09									14 39		
Uddingston	d			13 03						13 28	13 33					14 03					14 28			14 33	
Bellshill	d			13 08						13 33	13 39					14 08					14 33			14 38	
Carmyle	d						13 11						13 41						14 11						
Mount Vernon	d						13 14						13 43						14 14						
Baillieston	d						13 16						13 46						14 16						
Bargeddie	d						13 19						13 49						14 19						
Kirkwood	d						13 23						13 53						14 23						
Whifflet	d						13a27	13 33					13 56						14a27			14 33			
Motherwell	a	13 13		13 19				13 40	13 42		13 45		14 04	14 12		14 18				14 24		14 40	14 42	14 44	
	d		13 19	13 19					13 45		13 48					14 18	14 19			14 25			14 45	14 45	
Whifflet	d		13a28						13 52								14a29						14 52		
Coatbridge Central	d								13 54														14 54		
Greenfaulds 226	d								14 02														15 02		
Cumbernauld 226	a								14 04														15 04		
Shieldmuir	d			13 23							13 51					14 22								14 49	
Holytown	d									13 39											14 37				
Wishaw	d			13 26							13 55					14 25				14 31				14 52	
Carluke	d			13 34							14 02					14 32				14 38				15 02	
Carstairs	a																			14 47					
Lanark	a			13 45							14 14					14 43								15 13	
Haymarket	a									14 46										15 16	15 46				
Edinburgh	a									14 51										15 22	15 51				

A From Dalmuir
B To Dalmuir
C From Cumbernauld to Dalmuir
D From Milngavie
E From Ayr

Table T225-R

Saturdays

21 December to 16 May

Glasgow - Hamilton, Larkhall, Whifflet, Motherwell, Coatbridge, Lanark and Edinburgh

		SR A	SR A	SR B	SR C	SR A	SR A	SR	SR	SR D		SR B	SR	SR A	SR E	SR A	SR B	SR A	SR A	SR		SR C	SR	SR D	SR B
Hyndland ■ 226	d	14 05	14 18	14 24		14 35	14 47					14 53		15 05		15 18	15 26	15 35	15 47						15 56
Partick 226	d	14 07	14 21	14 26		14 37	14 49					14 55		15 07		15 20	15 29	15 38	15 49						15 59
Exhibition Centre	d	14 10	14 24	14 29		14 40	14 52					14 59		15 11		15 23	15 32	15 41	15 52						16 02
Anderston	d	14 13	14 26	14 32		14 42	14 54					15 01		15 13		15 25	15 34	15 43	15 54						16 04
Glasgow Central L. Level ■	a	14 14	14 27	14 33		14 44	14 56					15 03		15 15		15 27	15 36	15 44	15 56						16 05
	d	14 16	14 28	14 38		14 44	14 57					15 06		15 16		15 27	15 38	15 45	15 57						16 07
Glasgow Central H. Level ■	d							14 50	15 16				15 20		15 47					15 50			16 16		
Argyle Street	d	14 19	14 30	14 40		14 46	14 59					15 09		15 19		15 29	15 40	15 47	15 59						16 10
Bridgeton	d	14 23	14 33	14 43		14 49	15 02					15 12		15 23		15 32	15 43	15 50	16 02						16 13
Dalmarnock	d	14 25	14 35	14 45		14 51	15 04					15 14		15 25		15 34	15 45	15 52	16 04						16 15
Rutherglen	d	14 28	14 37	14 47		14 53	15 07					15 17		15 28		15 37	15 47	15 54	16 06						16 17
Cambuslang	d	14 32		14 51		14 56		15 00				15 21	15 28	15 32			15 51	15 58		16 02					16 21
Newton	d	14 35		14 54		15 00						15 24		15 35			15 54	16 01							16 24
Blantyre	d	14 39		14 58		15 04						15 28		15 39			15 58	16 05							16 28
Hamilton West	d	14 42		15 01		15 07						15 31		15 42			16 01	16 08							16 31
Hamilton Central	d	14 45		15 04		15 13						15 34		15 45			16 04	16 13							16 34
Chatelherault	d	14 49				15 18								15 49				16 18							
Merryton	d	14 52				15 21								15 52				16 21							
Larkhall	a	14 55				15 24								15 55				16 24							
Airbles	d			15 09								15 39					16 09								16 39
Uddingston	d							15 05	15 28				15 33							16 06			16 29		
Bellshill	d							15 10	15 33				15 39							16 11			16 34		
Carmyle	d		14 41				15 11									15 41			16 11						
Mount Vernon	d		14 44				15 14									15 44			16 14						
Baillieston	d		14 46				15 16									15 46			16 16						
Bargeddie	d		14 49				15 19									15 49			16 19						
Kirkwood	d		14 53				15 23									15 53			16 23						
Whifflet	d		14 57				15a27			15 33						15 57			16a27					16 32	
Motherwell	a		15 05	15 12				15 19		15 40		15 42	15 45		16 03	16 05	16 12			16 17				16 40	16 42
	d				15 19			15 19				15 45	15 48		16 07					16 18		16 19			16 45
Whifflet	d				15a26							15 52										16a28			16 52
Coatbridge Central	d											15 55													16 55
Greenfaulds 226	d											16 03													17 07
Cumbernauld 226	a											16 05													17 09
Shieldmuir	d							15 23					15 51							16 21					
Holytown	d								15 39														16 38		
Wishaw	d							15 26					15 55		16 20					16 25					
Carluke	d							15 34					16 02		16 28					16 32					
Carstairs	a														16 37										
Lanark	a							15 45					16 13							16 43					
Haymarket	a								16 43						17 01								17 46		
Edinburgh	a								16 48						17 06								17 51		

		SR	SR A	SR A	SR B	SR		SR C	SR A	SR A	SR D	SR B	SR	SR	SR A	SR A		SR B	SR	SR C	SR A	SR A	SR D	SR B	SR
Hyndland ■ 226	d		16 05	16 17	16 23				16 34	16 47		16 59			17 06	17 17		17 27			17 35	17 46		17 53	
Partick 226	d		16 07	16 19	16 25				16 37	16 49		17 02			17 08	17 20		17 29			17 38	17 49		17 56	
Exhibition Centre	d		16 11	16 22	16 29				16 40	16 52		17 05			17 12	17 23		17 32			17 44	17 52		17 59	
Anderston	d		16 13	16 24	16 31				16 43	16 54		17 07			17 14	17 25		17 35			17 46	17 54		18 02	
Glasgow Central L. Level ■	a		16 15	16 26	16 33				16 44	16 56		17 09			17 16	17 26		17 36			17 48	17 55		18 03	
	d		16 16	16 27	16 36				16 46	16 56		17 09			17 17	17 27		17 37			17 51	17 56		18 06	
Glasgow Central H. Level ■	d	16 20				16 50							17 16	17 20					17 50						18 16
Argyle Street	d		16 19	16 29	16 39				16 49	16 58		17 11			17 19	17 29		17 39			17 53	17 58		18 09	
Bridgeton	d		16 23	16 32	16 42				16 53	17 01		17 14			17 23	17 32		17 42			17 56	18 01		18 12	
Dalmarnock	d		16 25	16 34	16 44				16 55	17 03		17 16			17 25	17 34		17 44			17 58	18 03		18 14	
Rutherglen	d		16 28	16 37	16 47				16 58	17 05		17 18			17 28	17 37		17 47			18 01	18 05		18 17	
Cambuslang	d	16 28	16 32		16 51	16 58			17 01			17 22		17 28	17 32			17 51	17 58		18 05			18 21	
Newton	d		16 35		16 54				17 05			17 25			17 35			17 54			18 08			18 24	
Blantyre	d		16 39		16 58				17 09			17 29			17 39			17 58			18 12			18 28	
Hamilton West	d		16 42		17 01				17 12			17 32			17 42			18 01			18 15			18 31	
Hamilton Central	d		16 45		17 04				17 15			17 34			17 45			18 04			18 17			18 34	
Chatelherault	d		16 49						17 19						17 49						18 22				
Merryton	d		16 52						17 22						17 52						18 25				
Larkhall	a		16 55						17 25						17 55						18 28				
Airbles	d				17 09							17 40						18 09						18 39	
Uddingston	d	16 33				17 03							17u30	17 33					18 04						18 28
Bellshill	d	16 38				17 08							17 33	17 38					18 10						18 33
Carmyle	d			16 41						17 10						17 41						18 10			
Mount Vernon	d			16 44						17 12						17 44						18 12			
Baillieston	d			16 46						17 15						17 46						18 15			
Bargeddie	d			16 49						17 18						17 49						18 18			
Kirkwood	d			16 53						17 22						17 53						18 22			
Whifflet	d			16 57						17a25	17 33					17 58						18a25	18 32		
Motherwell	a	16 45		17 04	17 12	17 18					17 40	17 42		17 48		18 05		18 12	18 17				18 40	18 42	
	d	16 45				17 19		17 23				17 46		17 49					18 17	18 24				18 45	
Whifflet	d							17a30				17 53								18a31				18 52	
Coatbridge Central	d											17 56												18 54	
Greenfaulds 226	d											18 06												19 02	
Cumbernauld 226	a											18 08												19 04	
Shieldmuir	d	16 49				17 22								17 52					18 21						
Holytown	d												17 40												18 37
Wishaw	d	17 00				17 26								17 56					18 24						
Carluke	d	17 06				17 34								18 04					18 30						
Carstairs	a																								
Lanark	a	17 17				17 45								18 15					18 41						
Haymarket	a												18 43												19 46
Edinburgh	a												18 48												19 54

A From Dalmuir
B From Milngavie
C To Dalmuir
D From Cumbernauld to Dalmuir
E From Ayr

Table T225-R

Saturdays

21 December to 16 May

Glasgow - Hamilton, Larkhall, Whifflet, Motherwell, Coatbridge, Lanark and Edinburgh

		SR		SR A	SR A	SR B	SR	SR C	SR A	SR A	SR D	SR B		SR A	SR	SR	SR E	SR A	SR B	SR	SR C	SR A		SR A	SR D
Hyndland ■ 226	d			18 05	18 17	18 23			18 34	18 47		18 52		19 04				19 19	19 27			19 35		19 47	
Partick 226	d			18 07	18 19	18 25			18 37	18 49		18 54		19 07				19 21	19 29			19 38		19 50	
Exhibition Centre	d			18 10	18 22	18 29			18 40	18 52		18 58		19 10				19 24	19 32			19 41		19 53	
Anderston	d			18 13	18 24	18 31			18 43	18 54		19 00		19 13				19 26	19 34			19 44		19 55	
Glasgow Central L. Level ■	a			18 14	18 26	18 33			18 44	18 56		19 02		19 14				19 28	19 36			19 45		19 56	
	d			18 16	18 27	18 36			18 45	18 57		19 06		19 16				19 28	19 37			19 47		19 58	
Glasgow Central H. Level ■	d	18 20					18 50								19 16	19 21	19 46			19 50					
Argyle Street	d			18 19	18 29	18 39			18 48	18 59		19 09		19 19				19 30	19 39			19 50		19 59	
Bridgeton	d			18 23	18 32	18 42			18 53	19 02		19 12		19 22				19 33	19 42			19 54		20 02	
Dalmarnock	d			18 25	18 34	18 44			18 55	19 04		19 14		19 24				19 35	19 44			19 56		20 04	
Rutherglen	d			18 29	18 38	18 48			18 58	19 07		19 17		19 26				19 37	19 47			19 59		20 07	
Cambuslang	d	18 28		18 33		18 51	18 58		19 01			19 21		19 29		19 33			19 51	19 58		20 02			
Newton	d			18 36		18 54			19 05			19 24		19 33					19 54			20 08			
Blantyre	d			18 40		18 58			19 09			19 28		19 37					19 58			20 12			
Hamilton West	d			18 43		19 01			19 12			19 31		19 40					20 01			20 15			
Hamilton Central	d			18 46		19 04			19 15			19 34		19 43					20 04			20 17			
Chatelherault	d			18 50					19 19					19 48								20 22			
Merryton	d			18 53					19 22					19 51								20 25			
Larkhall	a			18 56					19 25					19 54								20 28			
Airbles	d					19 09						19 39							20 09						
Uddingston	d	18 33					19 03								19 28	19 37				20 03					
Bellshill	d	18 38					19 08								19 33	19 42				20 08					
Carmyle	d				18 42					19 11								19 41						20 11	
Mount Vernon	d				18 45					19 14								19 44						20 14	
Baillieston	d				18 47					19 16								19 46						20 16	
Bargeddie	d				18 50					19 19								19 49						20 19	
Kirkwood	d				18 54					19 23								19 53						20 23	
Whifflet	d				18 58					19a27	19 33							19 57						20a27	20 33
Motherwell	a	18 47			19 05	19 12	19 19				19 40	19 42				19 48	20 03	20 08	20 12	20 14					20 40
	d	18 48					19 19	19 20				19 45				19 49	20 04			20 18	20 26				
Whifflet	d							19a28				19 52									20a33				
Coatbridge Central	d											19 54													
Greenfaulds 226	d											20 02													
Cumbernauld 226	a											20 04													
Shieldmuir	d	18 51					19 23									19 53				20 22					
Holytown	d														19 40										
Wishaw	d	18 55					19 26									19 56	20 10			20 27					
Carluke	d	19 02					19 32									20 02	20 16			20 34					
Carstairs	a																20 25								
Lanark	a	19 13					19 43									20 13				20 45					
Haymarket	a														20 43		20 54								
Edinburgh	a														20 52		20 59								

		SR B	SR	SR A	SR A	SR B	SR	SR C		SR A	SR A	SR D	SR B	SR A	SR	SR	SR A	SR B		SR C	SR A	SR A	SR	SR F	SR B
Hyndland ■ 226	d	19 57		20 06	20 17	20 23				20 35	20 47		20 58	21 06			21 17	21 24			21 36	21 47			21 58
Partick 226	d	19 59		20 08	20 20	20 25				20 37	20 50		21 00	21 09			21 20	21 26			21 38	21 50			22 00
Exhibition Centre	d	20 03		20 11	20 23	20 29				20 41	20 53		21 04	21 12			21 23	21 30			21 41	21 53			22 04
Anderston	d	20 05		20 13	20 25	20 31				20 43	20 55		21 06	21 14			21 25	21 32			21 43	21 55			22 06
Glasgow Central L. Level ■	a	20 06		20 15	20 26	20 33				20 45	20 56		21 07	21 15			21 26	21 34			21 45	21 56			22 07
	d	20 07		20 17	20 28	20 35				20 46	20 57		21 08	21 16			21 27	21 36			21 45	21 57			22 08
Glasgow Central H. Level ■	d		20 21				20 51								21 16	21 20							21 50		
Argyle Street	d	20 09		20 20	20 30	20 37				20 48	20 59		21 10	21 18			21 29	21 39			21 46	21 59			22 10
Bridgeton	d	20 12		20 23	20 33	20 40				20 51	21 02		21 13	21 21			21 32	21 42			21 49	22 02			22 13
Dalmarnock	d	20 14		20 26	20 35	20 42				20 53	21 04		21 15	21 23			21 34	21 44			21 51	22 04			22 15
Rutherglen	d	20 17		20 29	20 37	20 45				20 59	21 07		21 17	21 25			21 37	21 47			21 53	22 07			22 17
Cambuslang	d	20 21	20 29	20 32		20 48	20 59			21 02			21 21	21 28		21 33		21 51			21 57		22 03		22 21
Newton	d	20 26		20 35		20 52				21 08			21 24	21 32				21 54			22 00				22 24
Blantyre	d	20 30		20 39		20 57				21 12			21 28	21 36				21 58			22 05				22 28
Hamilton West	d	20 33		20 42		21 00				21 15			21 31	21 39				22 01			22 08				22 31
Hamilton Central	d	20 36		20 45		21 04				21 17			21 34	21 43				22 04			22 13				22 34
Chatelherault	d			20 49						21 22				21 48							22 18				
Merryton	d			20 52						21 25				21 51							22 21				
Larkhall	a			20 55						21 28				21 54							22 24				
Airbles	d	20 41				21 09							21 39					22 09							22 39
Uddingston	d		20 34				21 04								21 29	21 37							22 07		
Bellshill	d		20 39				21 09								21 34	21 42							22 12		
Carmyle	d				20 41						21 11						21 41					22 11			
Mount Vernon	d				20 44						21 14						21 44					22 14			
Baillieston	d				20 46						21 16						21 46					22 16			
Bargeddie	d				20 49						21 19						21 49					22 19			
Kirkwood	d				20 53						21 23						21 53					22 23			
Whifflet	d				20 58						21a27	21 33					21 57					22a27		22 33	
Motherwell	a	20 44	20 46		21 08	21 12	21 19					21 40	21 42			21 49	22 04	22 12					22 18	22 41	22 42
	d	20 48	20 47				21 20	21 22					21 46			21 49				22 19			22 19		22 45
Whifflet	d	20 55						21a30					21 53							22a27					22 52
Coatbridge Central	d	20 57											21 56												22 55
Greenfaulds 226	d	21 06											22 07												23 08
Cumbernauld 226	a	21 08											22 09												23 10
Shieldmuir	d		20 50				21 24									21 53							22 23		
Holytown	d														21 40										
Wishaw	d		20 54				21 27									21 56							22 26		
Carluke	d		21 02				21 33									22 02							22 32		
Carstairs	a																								
Lanark	a		21 13				21 45									22 13							22 43		
Haymarket	a														22 46										
Edinburgh	a														22 51										

A From Dalmuir
B From Milngavie
C To Dalmuir
D From Cumbernauld to Dalmuir
E From Ayr
F From Cumbernauld to Garscadden

Table T225-R

Saturdays
21 December to 16 May

Glasgow - Hamilton, Larkhall, Whifflet, Motherwell, Coatbridge, Lanark and Edinburgh

		SR	SR A	SR A		SR B	SR	SR A	SR A	SR	SR B	SR	SR A	SR A		SR B	SR
Hyndland 3 226	d		22 06	22 18		22 28		22 34	22 47		22 58		23 05	23 17		23 28	
Partick 226	d		22 08	22 20		22 30		22 37	22 50		23 00		23 08	23 20		23 30	
Exhibition Centre	d		22 11	22 23		22 34		22 40	22 53		23 04		23 12	23 23		23 34	
Anderston	d		22 13	22 25		22 36		22 42	22 55		23 06		23 14	23 25		23 36	
Glasgow Central L. Level 15	a		22 15	22 27		22 37		22 44	22 57		23 07		23 15	23 27		23 38	
	d		22 17	22 27		22 38		22 46	22 57		23 08		23 17	23 27		23 38	
Glasgow Central H. Level 15	d	22 20					22 50			23 03		23 20					23 50
Argyle Street	d		22 20	22 29		22 40		22 49	22 59		23 10		23 20	23 29		23 40	
Bridgeton	d		22 23	22 32		22 43		22 53	23 02		23 13		23 23	23 32		23 43	
Dalmarnock	d		22 25	22 34		22 45		22 55	23 04		23 15		23 25	23 34		23 45	
Rutherglen	d		22 29	22 37		22 47		22 58	23 07		23 17		23 28	23 37		23 48	
Cambuslang	d	22 28	22 32			22 51	22 58	23 02		23 12	23 21	23 28	23 32			23 51	23 58
Newton	d		22 35			22 54		23 07			23 24		23 35				
Blantyre	d		22 39			22 58		23 11			23 28		23 39				
Hamilton West	d		22 42			23 01		23 15			23 31		23 42				
Hamilton Central	d		22 45			23 04		23 17			23 33		23 46				
Chatelherault	d		22 50					23 22					23 50				
Merryton	d		22 53					23 25					23 53				
Larkhall	a		22 56					23 28					23 56				
Airbles	d					23 09					23 39						
Uddingston	d	22 33					23 03			23 17		23 33					00 03
Bellshill	d	22 38					23 08			23 21		23 38					00 08
Carmyle	d			22 41					23 11					23 41			
Mount Vernon	d			22 44					23 14					23 44			
Baillieston	d			22 46					23 16					23 46			
Bargeddie	d			22 49					23 19					23 49			
Kirkwood	d			22 53					23 23					23 53			
Whifflet	d			22 57					23 27					23 57			
Motherwell	a	22 46		23 04		23 12	23 17		23 34		23 41	23 44		00 05		00 01	00 14
	d	22 47					23 18										
Whifflet	d																
Coatbridge Central	d																
Greenfaulds 226	d																
Cumbernauld 226	a																
Shieldmuir	d	22 50					23 22										
Holytown	d									23 25							
Wishaw	d	22 54					23 25										
Carluke	d	23 00					23 31										
Carstairs	a																
Lanark	a	23 11					23 42										
Haymarket	a									00 31							
Edinburgh	a									00 36							

Sundays
15 December to 10 May

		SR C	SR A	SR D	SR	SR E	SR	SR D	SR	SR E		SR B	SR	SR E	SR B	SR D	SR	SR	SR E	SR B		SR	SR E	SR B	SR D
Hyndland 3 226	d		08 15			08 45	08 55			09 15		09 25		09 45	09 55				10 15	10 25			10 45	10 55	
Partick 226	d		08 18			08 48	08 57			09 18		09 27		09 48	09 57				10 18	10 27			10 48	10 57	
Exhibition Centre	d		08 21			08 51	09 00			09 21		09 30		09 51	10 00				10 21	10 30			10 51	11 00	
Anderston	d													09 53	10 02				10 23	10 32			10 53	11 02	
Glasgow Central L. Level 15	a		08 23			08 53	09 03			09 23		09 33		09 54	10 04				10 24	10 34			10 54	11 04	
	d		08 25			08 56	09 06			09 25		09 37		09 56	10 05				10 25	10 37			10 56	11 06	
Glasgow Central H. Level 15	d				08 33				09 20				09 50				10 16	10 20				10 50			
Argyle Street	d													09 58	10 07				10 26	10 39			10 57	11 08	
Bridgeton	d		08 29			09 00	09 11			09 29		09 42		10 01	10 10				10 29	10 42			11 00	11 11	
Dalmarnock	d													10 03	10 12				10 31	10 44			11 02	11 13	
Rutherglen	d		08 34			09 05	09 15			09 34		09 47		10 05	10 14				10 33	10 46			11 05	11 15	
Cambuslang	d		08 37		08 42		09 19		09 29	09 37		09 50	09 59		10 18			10 29	10 37	10 50		10 59		11 19	
Newton	d		08 41				09 22			09 41		09 54			10 22				10 40	10 53				11 22	
Blantyre	d		08 45				09 26			09 45		09 58			10 26				10 44	10 57				11 26	
Hamilton West	d		08 48				09 29			09 48		10 01			10 29				10 47	11 00				11 29	
Hamilton Central	d		08 51				09 31			09 50		10 03			10 31				10 50	11 03				11 32	
Chatelherault	d		08 55							09 55									10 54						
Merryton	d		08 58							09 58									10 57						
Larkhall	a		09 01							10 01									11 00						
Airbles	d						09 37					10 09			10 37					11 08				11 37	
Uddingston	d	00 03			08 46				09 33				10 03				10 29	10 33				11 03			
Bellshill	d	00 08			08 52				09 39				10 09				10 34	10 38				11 09			
Carmyle	d					09 10								10 09									11 09		
Mount Vernon	d					09 13								10 12									11 12		
Baillieston	d					09 16								10 14									11 14		
Bargeddie	d					09 19								10 17									11 17		
Kirkwood	d					09 23								10 21									11 21		
Whifflet	d					09 27								10 25									11 25		
Motherwell	a	00 14			08 59	09 35	09 39		09 45			10 11	10 15	10 34	10 39			10 45		11 11		11 15	11 35	11 40	
	d			08 41				09 41	09 47							10 41		10 48							11 42
Whifflet	d			08a48				09a49								10a48									11a49
Coatbridge Central	d																								
Greenfaulds 226	d																								
Cumbernauld 226	a																								
Shieldmuir	d								09 51									10 51							
Holytown	d																10 39								
Wishaw	d								09 54									10 55							
Carluke	d								10 02									11 05							
Carstairs	a																								
Lanark	a								10 13									11 16							
Haymarket	a																11 42								
Edinburgh	a																11 47								

A From Dalmuir
B From Milngavie
C not 15 December. From Glasgow Central
D To Balloch
E From Balloch

Table T225-R

Sundays
15 December to 10 May

Glasgow - Hamilton, Larkhall, Whifflet, Motherwell, Coatbridge, Lanark and Edinburgh

		SR	SR A	SR B	SR	SR A		SR B	SR C	SR	SR	SR A	SR B	SR	SR A	SR B		SR C	SR	SR A	SR B	SR	SR A	SR B	SR C
Hyndland 3 226	d		11 15	11 25		11 45		11 55				12 15	12 25		12 45	12 55				13 15	13 25		13 45	13 55	
Partick 226	d		11 18	11 27		11 48		11 57				12 18	12 27		12 48	12 57				13 18	13 27		13 48	13 57	
Exhibition Centre	d		11 21	11 30		11 51		12 00				12 21	12 30		12 51	13 00				13 21	13 30		13 51	14 00	
Anderston	d		11 23	11 32		11 53		12 02				12 23	12 32		12 53	13 02				13 23	13 32		13 53	14 02	
Glasgow Central L. Level 15	a		11 24	11 34		11 54		12 04				12 24	12 34		12 54	13 04				13 24	13 34		13 54	14 04	
	d		11 25	11 37		11 56		12 06				12 25	12 35		12 56	13 06				13 25	13 37		13 56	14 06	
Glasgow Central H. Level 15	d	11 20			11 50					12 16	12 20			12 50					13 20			13 51			
Argyle Street	d		11 26	11 39		11 57		12 08				12 26	12 37		12 57	13 08				13 26	13 39		13 57	14 08	
Bridgeton	d		11 29	11 42		12 00		12 11				12 29	12 40		13 00	13 11				13 29	13 42		14 00	14 11	
Dalmarnock	d		11 31	11 44		12 02		12 13				12 31	12 42		13 02	13 13				13 31	13 44		14 02	14 13	
Rutherglen	d		11 33	11 46		12 05		12 15				12 34	12 46		13 05	13 15				13 33	13 46		14 05	14 15	
Cambuslang	d	11 29	11 37	11 50	11 59			12 18			12 29	12 38	12 50	12 59		13 18			13 29	13 37	13 50	14 00		14 18	
Newton	d		11 40	11 53				12 21				12 41	12 53			13 21				13 40	13 54			14 21	
Blantyre	d		11 44	11 57				12 25				12 45	12 57			13 25				13 44	13 58			14 25	
Hamilton West	d		11 47	12 00				12 28				12 48	13 00			13 28				13 47	14 01			14 28	
Hamilton Central	d		11 50	12 03				12 32				12 51	13 03			13 32				13 50	14 03			14 32	
Chatelherault	d		11 54									12 55								13 54					
Merryton	d		11 57									12 58								13 57					
Larkhall	a		12 00									13 01								14 00					
Airbles	d			12 08				12 38					13 08			13 37					14 09			14 37	
Uddingston	d	11 33			12 03					12 29	12 33			13 03					13 33			14 04			
Bellshill	d	11 39			12 09					12 34	12 38			13 09					13 38			14 09			
Carmyle	d					12 09									13 09								14 09		
Mount Vernon	d					12 12									13 12								14 12		
Baillieston	d					12 14									13 14								14 14		
Bargeddie	d					12 17									13 17								14 17		
Kirkwood	d					12 21									13 21								14 21		
Whifflet	d					12 25									13 25								14 25		
Motherwell	a	11 45		12 11	12 20	12 33		12 40			12 45		13 11	13 15	13 34	13 40			13 45		14 11	14 15	14 33	14 40	
	d	11 48							12 41		12 47							13 41	13 48						14 41
Whifflet	d								12a49									13a49							14a49
Coatbridge Central	d																								
Greenfaulds 226	d																								
Cumbernauld 226	a																								
Shieldmuir	d	11 51									12 51								13 51						
Holytown	d									12 39															
Wishaw	d	11 55									12 55								13 55						
Carluke	d	12 02									13 02								14 02						
Carstairs	a																								
Lanark	a	12 13									13 13								14 13						
Haymarket	a									13 45															
Edinburgh	a									13 50															

		SR		SR	SR A	SR B	SR	SR A	SR B	SR C	SR	SR A		SR B	SR	SR A	SR B	SR C	SR	SR	SR A	SR B		SR	SR A
Hyndland 3 226	d				14 15	14 25		14 45	14 55			15 15		15 25		15 45	15 55				16 15	16 25			16 45
Partick 226	d				14 18	14 27		14 48	14 57			15 18		15 27		15 48	15 57				16 18	16 27			16 48
Exhibition Centre	d				14 21	14 30		14 51	15 00			15 21		15 30		15 51	16 00				16 21	16 30			16 51
Anderston	d				14 23	14 32		14 53	15 02			15 23		15 32		15 53	16 02				16 23	16 32			16 53
Glasgow Central L. Level 15	a				14 24	14 34		14 54	15 04			15 24		15 34		15 54	16 04				16 24	16 34			16 54
	d				14 25	14 37		14 56	15 06			15 25		15 37		15 57	16 06				16 25	16 37			16 56
Glasgow Central H. Level 15	d	14 18		14 20			14 50				15 17				15 50				16 16	16 20				16 50	
Argyle Street	d				14 26	14 39		14 57	15 08			15 26		15 39		15 59	16 08				16 26	16 39			16 57
Bridgeton	d				14 29	14 42		15 00	15 11			15 29		15 42		16 02	16 11				16 29	16 42			17 00
Dalmarnock	d				14 31	14 44		15 02	15 13			15 31		15 44		16 04	16 13				16 31	16 44			17 02
Rutherglen	d				14 33	14 46		15 05	15 15			15 33		15 46		16 06	16 15				16 33	16 46			17 05
Cambuslang	d			14 29	14 37	14 50	14 59		15 18		15 26	15 37		15 50	15 59		16 18			16 29	16 37	16 50		16 58	
Newton	d				14 43	14 55			15 21			15 40		15 53			16 21				16 40	16 54			
Blantyre	d				14 47	14 59			15 25			15 44		15 57			16 25				16 44	16 58			
Hamilton West	d				14 50	15 02			15 28			15 47		16 00			16 28				16 47	17 01			
Hamilton Central	d				14 52	15 04			15 31			15 50		16 03			16 31				16 50	17 04			
Chatelherault	d				14 57							15 54									16 54				
Merryton	d				15 00							15 57									16 57				
Larkhall	a				15 03							16 00									17 00				
Airbles	d					15 10			15 36					16 08			16 36					17 09			
Uddingston	d	14 30		14 34			15 03				15 30				16 03				16 29	16 33				17 03	
Bellshill	d	14 34		14 39			15 09				15 35				16 09				16 33	16 38				17 08	
Carmyle	d							15 09								16 10									17 09
Mount Vernon	d							15 12								16 13									17 12
Baillieston	d							15 14								16 15									17 14
Bargeddie	d							15 17								16 18									17 17
Kirkwood	d							15 21								16 22									17 21
Whifflet	d							15 25								16 26									17 25
Motherwell	a			14 46		15 12	15 16	15 35	15 39		15 41			16 11	16 15	16 33	16 39			16 45		17 12		17 15	17 33
	d			14 47						15 41	15 42							16 41		16 48					
Whifflet	d									15a49								16a48							
Coatbridge Central	d																								
Greenfaulds 226	d																								
Cumbernauld 226	a																								
Shieldmuir	d			14 51							15 45									16 51					
Holytown	d	14 39																	16 40						
Wishaw	d			14 54							15 49									16 55					
Carluke	d			15 01							15 55									17 04					
Carstairs	a																								
Lanark	a			15 12							16 05									17 15					
Haymarket	a	15 44																	17 44						
Edinburgh	a	15 49																	17 49						

A From Balloch
B From Milngavie
C To Balloch

Table T225-R

Sundays

15 December to 10 May

Glasgow - Hamilton, Larkhall, Whifflet, Motherwell, Coatbridge, Lanark and Edinburgh

		SR	SR A	SR B	SR C	SR A	SR	SR C	SR A	SR B	SR	SR	SR C	SR A	SR	SR C	SR A	SR B	SR	SR C	SR A	SR	SR C
Hyndland 3	226 d		16 55		17 15	17 25		17 45	17 55				18 15	18 25		18 45	18 55			19 17	19 25		19 45
Partick	226 d		16 57		17 18	17 27		17 48	17 57				18 18	18 27		18 48	18 57			19 19	19 27		19 48
Exhibition Centre	d		17 00		17 21	17 30		17 51	18 00				18 21	18 30		18 51	19 00			19 22	19 30		19 51
Anderston	d		17 02		17 23	17 32		17 53	18 02														
Glasgow Central L. Level 15	a		17 04		17 24	17 34		17 54	18 04				18 23	18 34		18 54	19 03			19 25	19 33		19 54
	d		17 06		17 25	17 37		17 56	18 06				18 25	18 37		18 57	19 06			19 26	19 37		19 56
Glasgow Central H. Level 15	d	17 07					17 50				18 16	18 20			18 50				19 20			19 50	
Argyle Street	d		17 08		17 26	17 39		17 57	18 08														
Bridgeton	d		17 11		17 29	17 42		18 00	18 11				18 29	18 42		19 01	19 11			19 30	19 42		20 00
Dalmarnock	d		17 13		17 31	17 44		18 02	18 13														
Rutherglen	d		17 15		17 33	17 46		18 05	18 15				18 34	18 46		19 05	19 15			19 34	19 47		20 05
Cambuslang	d	17 15	17 18		17 37	17 51	17 58		18 18			18 29	18 37	18 49	19 00		19 19		19 29	19 37	19 50	19 59	
Newton	d		17 21		17 40	17 54			18 21				18 41	18 52			19 22			19 41	19 55		
Blantyre	d		17 25		17 44	17 58			18 25				18 45	18 56			19 26			19 45	19 59		
Hamilton West	d		17 28		17 47	18 01			18 28				18 48	18 59			19 29			19 48	20 02		
Hamilton Central	d		17 31		17 50	18 04			18 31				18 50	19 03			19 31			19 50	20 05		
Chatelherault	d				17 54								18 55							19 55			
Merryton	d				17 57								18 58							19 58			
Larkhall	a				18 00								19 01							20 01			
Airbles	d		17 36			18 10			18 36					19 08			19 37				20 10		
Uddingston	d	17 20					18 03				18 29	18 34			19 05				19 33			20 03	
Bellshill	d	17 27					18 08				18 33	18 39			19 10				19 38			20 08	
Carmyle	d							18 09								19 09							20 09
Mount Vernon	d							18 12								19 12							20 12
Baillieston	d							18 14								19 15							20 15
Bargeddie	d							18 17								19 18							20 18
Kirkwood	d							18 21								19 22							20 22
Whifflet	d							18 25								19 26							20 26
Motherwell	a	17 36	17 39			18 12	18 14	18 33	18 39			18 45		19 11	19 17	19 33	19 39		19 44		20 13	20 14	20 33
	d	17 37		17 41						18 40		18 46						19 41	19 46				
Whifflet	d			17a48						18a49								19a48					
Coatbridge Central	d																						
Greenfaulds	226 d																						
Cumbernauld	226 a																						
Shieldmuir	d	17 41										18 49							19 49				
Holytown	d										18 39												
Wishaw	d	17 44										18 53							19 53				
Carluke	d	17 50										19 00							19 59				
Carstairs	a																						
Lanark	a	18 01										19 11							20 10				
Haymarket	a										19 44												
Edinburgh	a										19 49												

		SR A	SR B	SR	SR	SR C	SR A	SR	SR C	SR D	SR B	SR	SR C	SR A	SR	SR C	SR A	SR B	SR	SR C	SR A	SR
Hyndland 3	226 d	19 55				20 15	20 25		20 45	20 55			21 15	21 25		21 45	21 55			22 15	22 25	
Partick	226 d	19 57				20 18	20 27		20 48	20 57			21 18	21 27		21 48	21 57			22 18	22 27	
Exhibition Centre	d	20 00				20 21	20 30		20 51	21 00			21 21	21 30		21 51	22 00			22 21	22 30	
Anderston	d																					
Glasgow Central L. Level 15	a	20 03				20 23	20 33		20 53	21 03			21 23	21 33		21 53	22 03			22 23	22 33	
	d	20 06				20 25	20 37		20 56	21 06			21 25	21 37		21 56	22 06			22 25	22 37	
Glasgow Central H. Level 15	d			20 16	20 20			20 50				21 20			21 50				22 20			22 50
Argyle Street	d																					
Bridgeton	d	20 11				20 29	20 42		21 00	21 11			21 29	21 42		22 00	22 11			22 29	22 42	
Dalmarnock	d																					
Rutherglen	d	20 15				20 34	20 46		21 05	21 15			21 34	21 46		22 05	22 15			22 34	22 47	
Cambuslang	d	20 19			20 29	20 37	20 49	20 58		21 19		21 29	21 37	21 49	21 58		22 19		22 28	22 37	22 50	22 58
Newton	d	20 22				20 41	20 52			21 22			21 41	21 53			22 22			22 41	22 54	
Blantyre	d	20 26				20 45	20 56			21 26			21 45	21 57			22 26			22 45	22 58	
Hamilton West	d	20 29				20 48	20 59			21 29			21 48	22 00			22 29			22 48	23 01	
Hamilton Central	d	20 31				20 50	21 03			21 31			21 50	22 03			22 31			22 50	23 03	
Chatelherault	d					20 55							21 55							22 55		
Merryton	d					20 58							21 58							22 58		
Larkhall	a					21 01							22 01							23 01		
Airbles	d	20 37					21 08			21 37				22 08			22 37				23 09	
Uddingston	d			20 28	20 33			21 03				21 34			22 03				22 33			23 03
Bellshill	d			20 33	20 38			21 08				21 39			22 08				22 38			23 08
Carmyle	d								21 09							22 09						
Mount Vernon	d								21 12							22 12						
Baillieston	d								21 15							22 15						
Bargeddie	d								21 18							22 18						
Kirkwood	d								21 22							22 22						
Whifflet	d								21 26							22 26						
Motherwell	a	20 39			20 44		21 11	21 14	21 33	21 39		21 45		22 11	22 14	22 33	22 39		22 44		23 11	23 15
	d		20 41		20 46						21 41	21 46						22 42	22 44			
Whifflet	d		20a48								21a49							22a49				
Coatbridge Central	d																					
Greenfaulds	226 d																					
Cumbernauld	226 a																					
Shieldmuir	d				20 49							21 50							22 48			
Holytown	d			20 38																		
Wishaw	d				20 53							21 53							22 51			
Carluke	d				20 59							21 59							22 57			
Carstairs	a																					
Lanark	a				21 11							22 10							23 08			
Haymarket	a			21 44																		
Edinburgh	a			21 49																		

A From Milngavie
B To Balloch
C From Balloch
D From Motherwell

Table T225-R

Sundays

15 December to 10 May

Glasgow - Hamilton, Larkhall, Whifflet, Motherwell, Coatbridge, Lanark and Edinburgh

		SR A	SR B	SR	SR B
Hyndland 3	226 d	22 45	22 55		23 25
Partick	226 d	22 48	22 57		23 27
Exhibition Centre	d	22 51	23 00		23 30
Anderston	d				
Glasgow Central L. Level 15	a	22 53	23 03		23 33
	d	22 56	23 06		23 37
Glasgow Central H. Level 15	d			23 22	
Argyle Street	d				
Bridgeton	d	23 00	23 11		23 42
Dalmarnock	d				
Rutherglen	d	23 05	23 14		23 47
Cambuslang	d		23 18	23 30	23 50
Newton	d		23 21		
Blantyre	d		23 25		
Hamilton West	d		23 28		
Hamilton Central	d		23 30		
Chatelherault	d				
Merryton	d				
Larkhall	a				
Airbles	d		23 36		
Uddingston	d			23 35	
Bellshill	d			23 40	
Carmyle	d	23 09			
Mount Vernon	d	23 12			
Baillieston	d	23 15			
Bargeddie	d	23 18			
Kirkwood	d	23 22			
Whifflet	d	23 26			
Motherwell	a	23 33	23 38	23 46	00 01
	d				
Whifflet	d				
Coatbridge Central	d				
Greenfaulds	226 d				
Cumbernauld	226 a				
Shieldmuir	d				
Holytown	d				
Wishaw	d				
Carluke	d				
Carstairs	a				
Lanark	a				
Haymarket	a				
Edinburgh	a				

A From Balloch
B From Milngavie

Table T226-F

Mondays to Fridays

16 December to 15 May

Edinburgh, Bathgate, Airdrie, Cumbernauld and Springburn - Glasgow - Milngavie, Dalmuir, Balloch and Helensburgh

Miles	Miles	Miles	Miles			SR	SR	SR	SR	SR	SR	SR	SR	SR	SR	SR	CS	SR	SR	SR	SR	SR	SR
						MX	MO	MO	MO	MX	MX	MX	MX	MX	MX								
						A	B	C	A	A	A	D	A	A	D	E	F ✕					G	
—	—	—	0	**Edinburgh** 228,230	d												04 50						
—	—	—	1¼	Haymarket 228,230	d						00 01												
—	—	—	4¾	Edinburgh Park 230	d						00 06												
—	—	—	12¾	Uphall	d						00 14												
—	—	—	14¾	Livingston North	d					00 01	00 17												
—	—	—	18¾	**Bathgate**	a					00 05	00 24												
—	—	—	—		d																		
—	—	—	21	Armadale	d																		
—	—	—	23¼	Blackridge	d																		
—	—	—	28¾	Caldercruix	d																		
—	—	—	31¼	Drumgelloch	d																		
—	—	0	33¼	**Airdrie**	d														05 32				
—	—	1	34¼	Coatdyke	d														05 34				
—	—	2	35¼	Coatbridge Sunnyside	d														05 36				
—	—	2¾	35¾	Blairhill	d														05 42				
—	—	5¼	38½	Easterhouse	d														05 46				
—	—	6¼	39½	Garrowhill	d														05 48				
—	—	7¼	40¾	Shettleston	d														05 51				
—	—	8	41½	Carntyne	d														05 53				
—	0	—	—	**Cumbernauld**	d																		
—	1	—	—	Greenfaulds	d																		
—	12¾	—	—	**Springburn**	d																		
—	13¼	—	—	Barnhill	d																		
—	14¼	—	—	Alexandra Parade	d																		
—	14¾	—	—	Duke Street	d										00 03								
—	15¼	10	43¼	Bellgrove	d									00 01	00 05				05 56				
—	15¾	10½	43¾	High Street	d									00 02	00 07				05 59				
—	16¼	11	44¼	**Glasgow Queen St LL**	a									00 04	00 09				06 01				
—	—	—	—		d									00 05	00 10		05u48		06 01				
—	17	11¾	45	Charing Cross	d									00 07	00 12				06 04				
0	—	—	—	Argyle Street 225	d																	06 19	
0½	—	—	—	**Glasgow Central LL** 225	a																	06 20	
—	—	—	—		d																	06 20	
1	—	—	—	Anderston 225	d																	06 22	
1½	—	—	—	Exhibition Centre 225	d																	06 24	
2¾	18¾	13½	47	**Partick** 225	d				00 01				00 01	00 11	00 16				06 08			06 27	
3½	19½	15¼	47½	Hyndland	d				00 03				00 03	00 13	00 19				06 10			06 30	
—	20	—	—	Jordanhill	d				00 05						00 24							06 32	
—	21	—	—	Scotstounhill	d			00 01	00 08						00 26							06 35	
—	21½	—	—	Garscadden	d			00a02	00 10					00a17	00a28							06 38	
—	22½	—	—	Yoker	d				00 12													06 40	
—	23¼	—	—	Clydebank	d				00 14													06 42	
4½	—	15¼	48½	Anniesland	d								00 06										
5	—	16¾	49¾	Westerton	d								00 09										
6¼	—	—	—	Bearsden	d																		
6¾	—	—	—	Hillfoot	d																		
7½	—	—	—	**Milngavie**	a																		
—	—	18	51	Drumchapel	d								00 12										
—	—	18¾	51¾	Drumry	d								00 14										
—	—	19¾	52¾	Singer	d								00 16										
—	24½	20½	53½	**Dalmuir** 227	a				00 18				00 19				06 04		06 19			06 46	
—	—	—	—		d								00 20			05 39	06 04	06 11	06 20	06 29	06 38		06 51
—	—	21¾	54¾	Kilpatrick	d							00 03								06 31			
—	—	23½	56½	Bowling	d							00 06								06 35			
—	—	26	59¼	Dumbarton East	d							00 11	00 28					06 18	06 28	06 39	06 46		06 58
—	—	26½	60	Dumbarton Central 227	d							00 13	00 31			05 48	06 15	06 21	06 30	06a42	06 49		07 00
—	—	26¾	60¼	Dalreoch	d		00 01					00 15	00 32					06 22	06 31		06 50		07 02
—	—	28½	—	Renton	d							00 18						06 25			06 53		
—	—	29½	—	Alexandria	d							00 20						06 28			06 56		
—	—	31¾	—	**Balloch**	a							00 24						06 32			07 00		
—	—	—	63½	Cardross	d	00 01	00 06						00 37						06 36				07 07
—	—	—	67¼	Craigendoran	d	00 07	00 11						00 42						06 41				07 12
—	—	—	68¼	**Helensburgh Central**	a	00 11	00 15						00 46						06 45				07 16
—	—	—	—	Helensburgh Upper 227	a											06 00	06 30						

A From Edinburgh
B From Airdrie
C From Larkhall. Forms tight booked connection out of 2C56.
D From Springburn
E From Glasgow Queen Street to Oban
F To Fort William
G From Motherwell

Table T226-F

Mondays to Fridays

16 December to 15 May

Edinburgh, Bathgate, Airdrie, Cumbernauld and Springburn - Glasgow - Milngavie, Dalmuir, Balloch and Helensburgh

		SR	SR	SR	SR	SR	SR	SR	SR	SR	SR	SR	SR	SR	SR	SR	SR	SR	SR	SR	SR	SR	SR
			A		B		A			A		B					C		B			A	
Edinburgh 228,230	d														06 07	06 22					06 37		06 51
Haymarket 228,230	d														06 11	06 26					06 41		06 55
Edinburgh Park 230	d														06 16	06 31					06 46		07 01
Uphall	d														06 24	06 39					06 54		07 09
Livingston North	d														06 27	06 43					06 58		07 13
Bathgate	a														06 32	06 48					07 02		07 17
	d							06 05	06 19						06 35	06 49					07 05		07 18
Armadale	d							06 10							06 39						07 09		
Blackridge	d							06 13							06 42						07 12		
Caldercruix	d							06 20							06 49						07 19		
Drumgelloch	d							06 23	06 32						06 52	07 02					07 22		07 31
Airdrie	d	05 57				06 16		06 28	06 35				06 46		06 57	07 05				07 16	07 27		07 34
Coatdyke	d					06 18			06 37				06 48			07 07				07 18	07 29		07 36
Coatbridge Sunnyside	d	06 01				06 21		06 31	06 40				06 51		07 01	07 10				07 21	07 31		07 39
Blairhill	d					06 23			06 42				06 53			07 12				07 23	07 34		07 41
Easterhouse	d					06 27			06 46				06 57			07 16				07 27			07 45
Garrowhill	d					06 30			06 49				07 00			07 19				07 30			07 48
Shettleston	d	06 12				06 32		06 43					07 02		07 12					07 32	07 40		
Carntyne	d	06 14				06 34		06 45					07 04		07 14					07 34	07 42		
Cumbernauld	d													06 12									
Greenfaulds	d													06 14									
Springburn	d			06 23							06 54							07 24					
Barnhill	d			06 24							06 55							07 25					
Alexandra Parade	d			06 27							06 58							07 28					
Duke Street	d			06 29							07 00							07 30					
Bellgrove	d	06 18		06 31		06 38		06 48			07 02		07 08		07 18			07 32		07 38	07 45		
High Street	d	06 20		06 33		06 40		06 50	06 56		07 04		07 10		07 20	07 26		07 34		07 40	07 48		07 55
Glasgow Queen St LL	a	06 22		06 35		06 42		06 52	06 58		07 06		07 12		07 22	07 28		07 36		07 42	07 50		07 57
	d	06 25		06 36		06 42		06 55	07 00		07 07		07 12		07 25	07 30		07 37		07 43	07 51		07 59
Charing Cross	d	06 27		06 38		06 44		06 58	07 03		07 09		07 15		07 28	07 32		07 39		07 46	07 54		08 01
Argyle Street 225	d		06 28		06 35		06 48			06 59		07 07		07 18			07 27		07 37			07 48	
Glasgow Central LL 225	a		06 30		06 37		06 50			07 00		07 09		07 19			07 28		07 39			07 50	
	d		06 30		06 38		06 51			07 03		07 09		07 20			07 33		07 39			07 53	
Anderston 225	d		06 32		06 39		06 52			07 05		07 11		07 22			07 34		07 41			07 55	
Exhibition Centre 225	d		06 34		06 42		06 54			07 07		07 13		07 24			07 36		07 43			07 57	
Partick 225	d	06 31	06 37	06 42	06 45	06 48	06 58	07 02	07 07	07 10	07 13	07 16	07 19	07 28	07 32	07 36	07 40	07 43	07 47	07 50	07 58	08 01	08 05
Hyndland	d	06 34	06 40	06 45	06 48	06 51	07 00	07 04	07 09	07 13	07 16	07 19	07 22	07 30	07 34	07 39	07 42	07 46	07 49	07 53	08 00	08 04	08 08
Jordanhill	d			06 47			07 02				07 18			07 32				07 48				08 06	
Scotstounhill	d			06 49			07 05				07 20			07 35				07 50				08 08	
Garscadden	d			06 51			07 07				07 22			07 37				07 52				08 10	
Yoker	d			06 54			07 09				07 25			07 39				07 55				08 13	
Clydebank	d			06 56			07 11				07 27			07 41				07 57				08 15	
Anniesland	d	06 37	06 43		06 51	06 54		07 07		07 16		07 22	07 25		07 37		07 45		07 52	07 56	08 05		
Westerton	d	06 40	06 46		06 54	06 57		07 10		07 19		07 25	07 28		07 40		07 48		07 55	07 59	08 08		
Bearsden	d	06 42			06 56			07 13				07 28			07 43				07 58		08 11		
Hillfoot	d	06 44			06 58			07 15				07 30			07 45				08 00		08 13		
Milngavie	a	06 48			07 02			07 18				07 33			07 48				08 03		08 16		
Drumchapel	d		06 48			07 00				07 21			07 30				07 51			08 02			
Drumry	d		06 50			07 02				07 23			07 32				07 53			08 04			
Singer	d		06 53			07 04				07 26			07 35				07 55			08 06			
Dalmuir 227	a		06 55	06 59		07 07	07 15		07 19	07 28	07 30		07 38	07 45		07 49	07 58	08 00		08 09		08 19	08 18
	d			07 00		07 08			07 20		07 31		07 39			07 50		08 01		08 10			08 19
Kilpatrick	d			07 03							07 34							08 04					
Bowling	d			07 06							07 37							08 07					
Dumbarton East	d			07 10		07 16			07 28		07 41		07 46			07 58		08 11		08 17			08 28
Dumbarton Central 227	d			07a13		07 19			07 30		07a44		07 49			08 00		08a14		08 20			08 30
Dalreoch	d					07 20			07 31				07 50			08 02				08 21			08 31
Renton	d					07 23							07 53							08 24			
Alexandria	d					07 26							07 56							08 27			
Balloch	a					07 30							08 00							08 31			
Cardross	d								07 36							08 07							08 36
Craigendoran	d								07 42							08 13							08 42
Helensburgh Central	a								07 45							08 16							08 45
Helensburgh Upper 227	a																						

A From Motherwell
B From Larkhall
C From Whifflet

Table T226-F

Mondays to Fridays

16 December to 15 May

Edinburgh, Bathgate, Airdrie, Cumbernauld and Springburn - Glasgow - Milngavie, Dalmuir, Balloch and Helensburgh

	SR	SR	SR	SR	SR	SR	SR	SR	SR	SR	SR	SR	SR	SR	SR	SR	SR	SR	SR	SR	SR	SR
	A		B		C	◇ D			B		E		C		A		A			C		
Edinburgh 228,230 d								07 06		07 23						07 38		07 55				08 05
Haymarket 228,230 d								07 10		07 28						07 42		07 59				08 10
Edinburgh Park 230 d								07 16		07 32						07 49		08 06				08 14
Uphall d								07 24		07 40						07 57		08 14				08 22
Livingston North d								07 28		07 44						08 00		08 18				08 26
Bathgate a								07 32		07 48						08 05		08 22				08 30
d								07 35		07 49						08 06		08 23				08 34
Armadale d								07 39								08 10						08 38
Blackridge d								07 42								08 13						08 42
Caldercruix d								07 49								08 20						08 48
Drumgelloch d								07 52		08 02						08 23		08 36				08 52
Airdrie d				07 45				07 56		08 05				08 16		08 27		08 39			08 46	08 56
Coatdyke d				07 47				07 58		08 07				08 18		08 29		08 41			08 48	
Coatbridge Sunnyside d				07 50				08 01		08 10				08 21		08 32		08 44			08 51	08 59
Blairhill d				07 52				08 03		08 12				08 23		08 34		08 46			08 53	
Easterhouse d				07 56						08 16				08 27				08 50			08 57	
Garrowhill d				07 59						08 19				08 30				08 53			09 00	
Shettleston d				08 01				08 09						08 32		08 40					09 02	09 11
Carntyne d				08 03				08 11						08 34		08 42					09 04	09 13
Cumbernauld d							07 12															
Greenfaulds d							07 14															
Springburn d		07 53										08 24							08 54			
Barnhill d		07 54										08 25							08 55			
Alexandra Parade d		07 57										08 28							08 58			
Duke Street d		07 59										08 30							09 00			
Bellgrove d		08 01		08 07				08 15				08 32		08 38		08 47			09 02		09 08	09 16
High Street d		08 03		08 09				08 17		08 26		08 34		08 40		08 50		09 00	09 04		09 10	09 19
Glasgow Queen St LL a		08 05		08 11				08 19		08 28		08 36		08 42		08 52		09 02	09 06		09 12	09 21
d		08 05		08 12				08 23		08 30		08 37		08 43		08 55		09 02	09 07		09 14	09 21
Charing Cross d		08 08		08 14				08 26		08 32		08 39		08 46		08 58		09 05	09 09		09 17	09 24
Argyle Street 225 d	07 56		08 01		08 09		08 18		08 23		08 31		08 38		08 50		08 56			09 08		
Glasgow Central LL 225 a	07 57		08 03		08 11		08 20		08 25		08 32		08 40		08 51		08 57			09 10		
d	08 00		08 07		08 13		08 20		08 25		08 33		08 40		08 52		08 59			09 10		
Anderston 225 d	08 02		08 09		08 15		08 22		08 27		08 34		08 42		08 54		09 00			09 12		
Exhibition Centre 225 d	08 04		08 11		08 17		08 24		08 30		08 37		08 44		08 56		09 02			09 14		
Partick 225 d	08 08	08 12	08 15	08 18	08 22		08 27	08 30	08 33	08 36	08 40	08 43	08 47	08 50	08 59	09 02	09 06	09 09	09 13	09 17	09 22	09 28
Hyndland d	08 11	08 14	08 18	08 21	08 25		08 30	08 33	08 36	08 39	08 43	08 46	08 50	08 53	09 02	09 05	09 08	09 11	09 15	09 20	09 24	09 30
Jordanhill d		08 16					08 32					08 48			09 04				09 17			
Scotstounhill d		08 19					08 34					08 50			09 07				09 20			
Garscadden d		08 21	08a25				08 37		08a40			08 53			09 09				09 22			
Yoker d		08 24					08 39					08 55			09 11				09 25			
Clydebank d		08 26					08 41					08 57			09 13				09 27			
Anniesland d	08 14			08 24	08 28			08 36			08 46		08 53	08 56		09 08	09 11			09 23	09 27	09 35
Westerton d	08 17			08 27	08 31			08 39			08 49		08 56	08 59		09 11	09 14			09 26	09 30	09 40
Bearsden d					08 33			08 41					08 58			09 13				09 28		09 42
Hillfoot d					08 35			08 43					09 00			09 15				09 30		09 44
Milngavie a					08 39			08 47					09 04			09 19				09 34		09 48
Drumchapel d	08 19			08 29							08 51			09 02			09 17				09 33	
Drumry d	08 21			08 31							08 53			09 04			09 19				09 35	
Singer d	08 24			08 34							08 56			09 06			09 21				09 37	
Dalmuir 227 a	08 27	08 29		08 37			08 45			08 49	08 58	09 00		09 09	09 17		09 24	09 20	09 30		09 40	
d		08 30		08 38		08 42				08 50		09 01		09 09				09 21	09 30		09 41	
Kilpatrick d		08 33										09 04							09 33			
Bowling d		08 36										09 07							09 36			
Dumbarton East d		08 40		08 46						08 58		09 11		09 17				09 29	09 40		09 48	
Dumbarton Central 227 d		08a43		08 48		08 52				09 00		09a14		09 19				09 31	09a43		09 51	
Dalreoch d				08 49						09 01				09 20				09 33			09 52	
Renton d				08 52										09 23							09 55	
Alexandria d				08 55										09 26							09 58	
Balloch a				08 59										09 30							10 02	
Cardross d										09 06								09 38				
Craigendoran d										09 11								09 44				
Helensburgh Central a										09 14								09 47				
Helensburgh Upper 227 a						09 05																

A From Motherwell
B From Carstairs
C From Larkhall
D From Glasgow Queen Street to Oban
E From Whifflet

Table T226-F

Mondays to Fridays

16 December to 15 May

Edinburgh, Bathgate, Airdrie, Cumbernauld and Springburn - Glasgow - Milngavie, Dalmuir, Balloch and Helensburgh

	SR	SR	SR	SR	SR	SR	SR	SR	SR	SR	SR	SR	SR	SR	SR	SR	SR	SR	SR	SR	SR
		A			B		C			C		B					◇ D	A		B	
Edinburgh 228,230 d			08 27					08 39	08 49					09 10		09 22					
Haymarket 228,230 d			08 33					08 45	08 55					09 15		09 27					
Edinburgh Park 230 d			08 38					08 50	09 01					09 20		09 31					
Uphall d			08 46					08 58	09 09					09 28		09 39					
Livingston North d			08 49					09 01	09 13					09 32		09 43					
Bathgate a			08 54					09 06	09 17					09 36		09 47					
d			08 54					09 08	09 18					09 37		09 49					
Armadale d								09 12						09 41							
Blackridge d								09 16						09 44							
Caldercruix d								09 22						09 51							
Drumgelloch d			09 07					09 26	09 31					09 54		10 01					
Airdrie d			09 10			09 16		09 29	09 34				09 46	09 58		10 05					10 16
Coatdyke d			09 12			09 18			09 36				09 48			10 07					10 18
Coatbridge Sunnyside d			09 15			09 21		09 33	09 39				09 51	10 01		10 10					10 21
Blairhill d			09 17			09 23			09 41				09 53			10 12					10 23
Easterhouse d			09 21			09 27			09 45				09 57			10 16					10 27
Garrowhill d			09 24			09 30			09 48				10 00			10 19					10 30
Shettleston d						09 32		09 44					10 02	10 13							10 32
Carntyne d						09 34		09 46					10 04	10 15							10 34
Cumbernauld d	08 13														09 15						
Greenfaulds d	08 15														09 17						
Springburn d				09 24							09 54								10 24		
Barnhill d				09 25							09 55								10 25		
Alexandra Parade d				09 28							09 58								10 28		
Duke Street d				09 30							10 00								10 30		
Bellgrove d				09 32		09 38		09 50			10 02		10 08	10 20					10 32		10 38
High Street d			09 31	09 34		09 40		09 52	09 55		10 04		10 10	10 22		10 26			10 34		10 40
Glasgow Queen St LL a			09 33	09 36		09 42		09 54	09 57		10 06		10 12	10 24		10 28			10 36		10 42
d			09 33	09 37		09 43		09 55	10 00		10 06		10 13	10 24		10 29			10 37		10 45
Charing Cross d			09 35	09 39		09 45		09 57	10 03		10 09		10 15	10 26		10 32			10 40		10 47
Argyle Street 225 d	09 21	09 25			09 39		09 48			09 57		10 08			10 22			10 27		10 38	
Glasgow Central LL 225 a	09 23	09 26			09 40		09 50			09 59		10 09			10 23			10 28		10 40	
d	09 24	09 28			09 41		09 51			10 03		10 09			10 26			10 32		10 40	
Anderston 225 d	09 25	09 29			09 42		09 52			10 04		10 11			10 27			10 34		10 41	
Exhibition Centre 225 d	09 27	09 32			09 44		09 55			10 06		10 13			10 29			10 36		10 43	
Partick 225 d	09 31	09 35	09 39	09 43	09 48	09 51	09 58	10 01	10 07	10 10	10 13	10 16	10 19	10 30	10 33	10 37		10 40	10 44	10 47	10 51
Hyndland d	09 33	09 38	09 42	09 46	09 50	09 55	10 01	10 04	10 09	10 12	10 15	10 19	10 22	10 33	10 36	10 40		10 43	10 46	10 49	10 54
Jordanhill d	09 35			09 48			10 03				10 17				10 38				10 48		
Scotstounhill d	09 38			09 50			10 05				10 20				10 40				10 51		
Garscadden d	09 40			09 52			10 08				10 22				10 43				10 53		
Yoker d	09 42			09 55			10 10				10 25				10 45				10 56		
Clydebank d	09 44			09 57			10 12				10 27				10 49				10 58		
Anniesland d		09 41			09 53	09 58		10 07		10 15		10 22	10 25	10 36				10 48		10 52	10 57
Westerton d		09 44			09 56	10 01		10 10		10 18		10 25	10 28	10 39				10 51		10 55	11 00
Bearsden d					09 59			10 12				10 27		10 41						10 58	
Hillfoot d					10 01			10 14				10 29		10 43						11 00	
Milngavie a					10 04			10 18				10 33		10 47						11 03	
Drumchapel d		09 46				10 03				10 21			10 30					10 53			11 03
Drumry d		09 48				10 05				10 23			10 32					10 55			11 05
Singer d		09 51				10 08				10 25			10 35					10 58			11 07
Dalmuir 227 a	09 48	09 53	09 51	10 00		10 10	10 16		10 19	10 28	10 30		10 37		10 53	10 49		11 00	11 01		11 10
d			09 52	10 01		10 11			10 20		10 30		10 38			10 50	10 55		11 02		11 11
Kilpatrick d				10 04							10 33								11 04		
Bowling d				10 07							10 36								11 07		
Dumbarton East d			10 00	10 11		10 19			10 28		10 40		10 46			10 58			11 12		11 18
Dumbarton Central 227 d			10 02	10a14		10 21			10 30		10a43		10 49			11 00	11 05		11a15		11 21
Dalreoch d			10 04			10 22			10 31				10 50			11 01					11 22
Renton d						10 25							10 53								11 25
Alexandria d						10 28							10 56								11 28
Balloch a						10 32							11 00								11 32
Cardross d			10 09						10 36							11 06					
Craigendoran d			10 15						10 41							11 12					
Helensburgh Central a			10 18						10 44							11 15					
Helensburgh Upper 227 a																	11 24				

A From Whifflet
B From Larkhall
C From Motherwell
D From Glasgow Queen Street to Oban

Table T226-F

Mondays to Fridays
16 December to 15 May

Edinburgh, Bathgate, Airdrie, Cumbernauld and Springburn - Glasgow - Milngavie, Dalmuir, Balloch and Helensburgh

	SR	SR A	SR	SR A	SR	SR B	SR	SR	SR	SR C	SR	SR	SR B	SR	SR A	SR	SR	SR A	SR	SR B	SR	SR
Edinburgh 228,230 d	09 38		09 52					10 08			10 22					10 37	10 52					11 07
Haymarket 228,230 ⇌ d	09 42		09 57					10 12			10 28					10 41	10 57					11 11
Edinburgh Park 230 d	09 47		10 02					10 17			10 34					10 46	11 03					11 16
Uphall d	09 55		10 10					10 25			10 42					10 54	11 11					11 25
Livingston North d	09 58		10 13					10 28			10 45					10 58	11 14					11 29
Bathgate a	10 03		10 18					10 33			10 50					11 02	11 19					11 33
d	10 04		10 19					10 35			10 50					11 07	11 20					11 34
Armadale d	10 08							10 39								11 11						11 38
Blackridge d	10 11							10 42								11 14						11 42
Caldercruix d	10 18							10 49								11 21						11 48
Drumgelloch d	10 21		10 31					10 52			11 03					11 24	11 33					11 52
Airdrie d	10 26		10 36				10 46	10 56			11 06			11 16		11 28	11 36				11 46	11 56
Coatdyke d			10 38				10 48				11 08			11 18			11 38				11 48	
Coatbridge Sunnyside d	10 30		10 40				10 51	11 00			11 11			11 21		11 31	11 41				11 51	12 00
Blairhill d			10 43				10 53				11 13			11 23			11 43				11 53	
Easterhouse d			10 47				10 57				11 17			11 27			11 47				11 57	
Garrowhill d			10 49				11 00				11 20			11 30			11 50				12 00	
Shettleston d	10 41						11 02	11 11						11 32		11 43					12 02	12 11
Carntyne d	10 43						11 04	11 13						11 34		11 45					12 04	12 13
Cumbernauld d									10 19													
Greenfaulds d									10 21													
Springburn d					10 54							11 24							11 54			
Barnhill d					10 55							11 25							11 55			
Alexandra Parade d					10 58							11 28							11 58			
Duke Street d					11 00							11 30							12 00			
Bellgrove d	10 47				11 02		11 08	11 17				11 32		11 38		11 48			12 02		12 08	12 17
High Street d	10 49		10 57		11 04		11 10	11 19			11 27	11 34		11 40		11 51	11 57		12 04		12 10	12 19
Glasgow Queen St LL 10 ⇌ a	10 51		10 59		11 06		11 12	11 21			11 29	11 36		11 42		11 53	11 59		12 06		12 12	12 21
d	10 52		11 00		11 07		11 13	11 22			11 31	11 37		11 42		11 55	12 00		12 07		12 13	12 22
Charing Cross d	10 55		11 02		11 09		11 15	11 25			11 34	11 39		11 45		11 57	12 02		12 10		12 16	12 25
Argyle Street 225 d		10 52		10 57		11 08			11 23	11 26			11 36		11 49			11 57		12 08		
Glasgow Central LL 15 225 a		10 54		10 58		11 09			11 24	11 28			11 38		11 50			11 59		12 09		
d		10 55		11 03		11 09			11 25	11 28			11 39		11 51			12 02		12 10		
Anderston 225 d		10 56		11 04		11 11			11 26	11 30			11 41		11 52			12 04		12 11		
Exhibition Centre 225 d		10 58		11 06		11 13			11 28	11 32			11 43		11 55			12 06		12 13		
Partick 225 ⇌ d	10 59	11 02	11 06	11 10	11 13	11 16	11 19	11 29	11 32	11 35	11 38	11 43	11 46	11 49	11 58	12 01	12 06	12 10	12 14	12 17	12 20	12 29
Hyndland 3 d	11 01	11 04	11 09	11 12	11 16	11 19	11 22	11 31	11 34	11 38	11 41	11 46	11 49	11 52	12 01	12 04	12 09	12 12	12 16	12 19	12 23	12 31
Jordanhill d		11 06			11 18				11 36			11 48			12 03				12 18			
Scotstounhill d		11 09			11 20				11 39			11 50			12 05				12 21			
Garscadden d		11 11			11 23				11 41			11 52			12 08				12 23			
Yoker d		11 13			11 25				11 43			11 55			12 10				12 25			
Clydebank d		11 15			11 27				11 45			11 57			12 12				12 27			
Anniesland d	11 06			11 15		11 22	11 25	11 36		11 44			11 52	11 55		12 07		12 15		12 22	12 26	12 37
Westerton d	11 10			11 18		11 25	11 28	11 40		11 47			11 55	11 58		12 10		12 18		12 25	12 29	12 41
Bearsden d	11 13					11 28		11 42					11 57			12 12				12 28		12 44
Hillfoot d	11 15					11 30		11 44					11 59			12 14				12 30		12 46
Milngavie a	11 18					11 33		11 48					12 04			12 18				12 33		12 49
Drumchapel d				11 21			11 31			11 50				12 00				12 21			12 31	
Drumry d				11 23			11 33			11 52				12 02				12 23			12 33	
Singer d				11 25			11 35			11 54				12 05				12 25			12 36	
Dalmuir 227 a		11 19	11 20	11 28	11 30		11 38		11 49	11 57	11 52	12 00		12 07	12 16		12 18	12 28	12 31		12 38	
d			11 21		11 31		11 38				11 53	12 01		12 08			12 19		12 31		12 39	
Kilpatrick d					11 34							12 04							12 34			
Bowling d					11 37							12 07							12 37			
Dumbarton East d			11 29		11 41		11 46				12 01	12 11		12 16			12 28		12 41		12 46	
Dumbarton Central 227 d			11 31		11a44		11 49				12 03	12a14		12 19			12 30		12a44		12 48	
Dalreoch d			11 32				11 50				12 04			12 20			12 32				12 50	
Renton d							11 53							12 23							12 53	
Alexandria d							11 56							12 26							12 55	
Balloch a							12 00							12 30							13 00	
Cardross d			11 37								12 09						12 37					
Craigendoran d			11 43								12 15						12 43					
Helensburgh Central a			11 46								12 18						12 46					
Helensburgh Upper 227 a																						

A From Motherwell
B From Larkhall
C From Whifflet

NRT DECEMBER 19 EDITION

Table T226-F

Mondays to Fridays
16 December to 15 May

Edinburgh, Bathgate, Airdrie, Cumbernauld and Springburn - Glasgow - Milngavie, Dalmuir, Balloch and Helensburgh

	SR ◇ A	SR	SR	SR B	SR	SR C	SR	SR	SR D	SR	SR D	SR	SR C	SR	SR	SR	SR	SR B	SR	SR C	SR
Edinburgh 228,230 d			11 23					11 37		11 54					12 06		12 24				
Haymarket 228,230 ⇌ d			11 27					11 42		11 59					12 12		12 28				
Edinburgh Park 230 d			11 33					11 47		12 04					12 18		12 33				
Uphall d			11 41					11 55		12 12					12 26		12 41				
Livingston North d			11 44					11 58		12 15					12 29		12 44				
Bathgate a			11 49					12 03		12 20					12 34		12 49				
d			11 51					12 05		12 21					12 36		12 49				
Armadale d								12 09							12 40						
Blackridge d								12 12							12 44						
Caldercruix d								12 19							12 50						
Drumgelloch d			12 03					12 22		12 34					12 54		13 02				
Airdrie d			12 07				12 16	12 27		12 37				12 46	12 57		13 06				13 16
Coatdyke d			12 09				12 18			12 39				12 48			13 08				13 18
Coatbridge Sunnyside d			12 12				12 21	12 30		12 42				12 51	13 01		13 10				13 21
Blairhill d			12 14				12 23			12 44				12 53			13 13				13 23
Easterhouse d			12 18				12 27			12 48				12 57			13 17				13 27
Garrowhill d			12 21				12 30			12 51				13 00			13 19				13 30
Shettleston d							12 32	12 42						13 02	13 12						13 32
Carntyne d							12 34	12 44						13 04	13 14						13 34
Cumbernauld d		11 19														12 19					
Greenfaulds d		11 21														12 21					
Springburn d					12 23							12 54							13 24		
Barnhill d					12 24							12 55							13 25		
Alexandra Parade d					12 27							12 58							13 28		
Duke Street d					12 29							13 00							13 30		
Bellgrove d					12 31		12 38	12 47				13 02		13 08	13 18				13 32		13 38
High Street d			12 28		12 34		12 40	12 50		12 58		13 04		13 10	13 20		13 27		13 34		13 40
Glasgow Queen St LL 10 ⇌ a			12 30		12 36		12 42	12 52		13 00		13 06		13 12	13 22		13 29		13 36		13 42
d			12 30		12 36		12 44	12 52		13 00		13 07		13 14	13 23		13 30		13 37		13 44
Charing Cross d			12 33		12 39		12 46	12 55		13 03		13 09		13 16	13 25		13 32		13 39		13 47
Argyle Street 225 d		12 22		12 27		12 38			12 51		12 58		13 06			13 22		13 27		13 38	
Glasgow Central LL 15 225 a		12 23		12 28		12 39			12 53		12 59		13 08			13 23		13 28		13 39	
d		12 24		12 33		12 40			12 55		13 03		13 09			13 25		13 33		13 40	
Anderston 225 d		12 26		12 34		12 41			12 56		13 04		13 11			13 26		13 34		13 41	
Exhibition Centre 225 d		12 28		12 36		12 43			12 58		13 06		13 13			13 28		13 36		13 43	
Partick 225 ⇌ d		12 32	12 37	12 40	12 43	12 47	12 50	12 59	13 02	13 07	13 10	13 13	13 16	13 20	13 29	13 32	13 36	13 40	13 43	13 47	13 51
Hyndland 3 d		12 34	12 39	12 42	12 45	12 49	12 53	13 01	13 04	13 09	13 12	13 16	13 19	13 23	13 32	13 35	13 39	13 42	13 45	13 49	13 53
Jordanhill d		12 36			12 47				13 06			13 18				13 37			13 47		
Scotstounhill d		12 39			12 50				13 09			13 21				13 39			13 50		
Garscadden d		12 41			12 52				13 11			13 23				13 41			13 52		
Yoker d		12 43			12 55				13 13			13 25				13 44			13 55		
Clydebank d		12 45			12 57				13 15			13 27				13 46			13 57		
Anniesland d				12 45		12 52	12 56	13 07			13 15		13 22	13 26	13 36			13 45		13 52	13 56
Westerton d				12 48		12 55	12 59	13 10			13 18		13 25	13 29	13 39			13 48		13 55	13 59
Bearsden d						12 58		13 12					13 27		13 42					13 58	
Hillfoot d						13 00		13 14					13 29		13 44					14 00	
Milngavie a						13 03		13 18					13 33		13 47					14 03	
Drumchapel d				12 51			13 02				13 21			13 32				13 51			14 02
Drumry d				12 53			13 04				13 23			13 34				13 53			14 04
Singer d				12 55			13 06				13 25			13 36				13 55			14 06
Dalmuir 227 a		12 49	12 50	12 58	13 00		13 09		13 19	13 19	13 28	13 31		13 39		13 50	13 48	13 58	14 00		14 09
d	12 43		12 51		13 01		13 10			13 20		13 31		13 39			13 49		14 00		14 10
Kilpatrick d					13 04							13 34							14 03		
Bowling d					13 07							13 37							14 06		
Dumbarton East d			12 58		13 11		13 17			13 28		13 42		13 47			14 00		14 10		14 17
Dumbarton Central 227 d	12 53		13 00		13a14		13 19			13 30		13a45		13 49			14 02		14a13		14 20
Dalreoch d			13 02				13 21			13 31				13 50			14 04				14 21
Renton d							13 24							13 53							14 24
Alexandria d							13 26							13 56							14 27
Balloch a							13 31							14 00							14 31
Cardross d			13 07							13 36							14 09				
Craigendoran d			13 13							13 42							14 14				
Helensburgh Central a			13 16							13 45							14 17				
Helensburgh Upper 227 a	13 05																				

A From Glasgow Queen Street to Oban
B From Whifflet
C From Larkhall
D From Motherwell

Table T226-F

Mondays to Fridays
16 December to 15 May

Edinburgh, Bathgate, Airdrie, Cumbernauld and Springburn - Glasgow - Milngavie, Dalmuir, Balloch and Helensburgh

Station			SR	SR	SR	SR	SR	SR	SR	SR	SR	SR	SR	SR	SR	SR	SR	SR	SR	SR	SR	SR	SR	SR
				A		A		B					C		B			A		A		B		
Edinburgh	228,230	d	12 37		12 54					13 05		13 23					13 38		13 51					14 09
Haymarket	228,230 ⛴	d	12 43		12 58					13 10		13 27					13 43		13 57					14 14
Edinburgh Park	230	d	12 48		13 04					13 16		13 32					13 47		14 03					14 19
Uphall		d	12 56		13 12					13 24		13 40					13 55		14 11					14 27
Livingston North		d	12 59		13 15					13 27		13 43					13 59		14 14					14 30
Bathgate		a	13 04		13 20					13 32		13 48					14 03		14 19					14 35
		d	13 05		13 20					13 35		13 49					14 05		14 20					14 36
Armadale		d	13 09							13 39							14 09							14 40
Blackridge		d	13 12							13 42							14 12							14 43
Caldercruix		d	13 19							13 49							14 19							14 50
Drumgelloch		d	13 22		13 33					13 52		14 01					14 22		14 32					14 53
Airdrie		d	13 27		13 36				13 46	13 56		14 06				14 16	14 26		14 36				14 46	14 57
Coatdyke		d			13 38				13 48			14 08				14 18			14 38				14 48	
Coatbridge Sunnyside		d	13 30		13 41				13 51	13 59		14 10				14 21	14 29		14 41				14 51	15 00
Blairhill		d			13 43				13 53			14 13				14 23			14 43				14 53	
Easterhouse		d			13 47				13 57			14 17				14 27			14 47				14 57	
Garrowhill		d			13 50				14 00			14 19				14 30			14 50				15 00	
Shettleston		d	13 42						14 02	14 11						14 32	14 41						15 02	15 12
Carntyne		d	13 44						14 04	14 13						14 34	14 43						15 04	15 14
Cumbernauld		d									13 17													
Greenfaulds		d									13 19													
Springburn		d					13 54							14 24							14 54			
Barnhill		d					13 55							14 25							14 55			
Alexandra Parade		d					13 58							14 28							14 58			
Duke Street		d					14 00							14 30							15 00			
Bellgrove		d	13 47				14 02		14 08	14 16				14 32		14 38	14 46				15 02		15 08	15 17
High Street		d	13 50		13 57		14 04		14 10	14 19		14 27		14 34		14 40	14 49		14 57		15 04		15 10	15 20
Glasgow Queen St LL 10	⛴	a	13 52		13 59		14 06		14 12	14 21		14 29		14 36		14 42	14 51		14 59		15 06		15 12	15 22
		d	13 52		14 00		14 06		14 14	14 21		14 30		14 37		14 43	14 52		15 00		15 07		15 13	15 22
Charing Cross		d	13 55		14 02		14 09		14 16	14 24		14 32		14 39		14 46	14 54		15 02		15 09		15 16	15 25
Argyle Street	225	d		13 52		13 56		14 08			14 22		14 27		14 37			14 51		14 55		15 08		
Glasgow Central LL 15	225	a		13 53		13 57		14 09			14 23		14 28		14 39			14 53		14 57		15 09		
		d		13 54		14 02		14 10			14 24		14 33		14 39			14 54		15 03		15 10		
Anderston	225	d		13 55		14 03		14 11			14 26		14 34		14 41			14 55		15 04		15 11		
Exhibition Centre	225	d		13 58		14 05		14 13			14 28		14 36		14 43			14 57		15 06		15 13		
Partick	225 ⛴	d	13 59	14 02	14 06	14 09	14 13	14 17	14 20	14 28	14 31	14 36	14 40	14 43	14 46	14 50	14 58	15 01	15 06	15 10	15 13	15 17	15 20	15 29
Hyndland 3		d	14 01	14 04	14 09	14 12	14 15	14 19	14 23	14 30	14 34	14 39	14 42	14 45	14 49	14 52	15 01	15 04	15 09	15 13	15 16	15 19	15 23	15 31
Jordanhill		d		14 06			14 17				14 36			14 47				15 06			15 18			
Scotstounhill		d		14 09			14 20				14 38			14 50				15 08			15 20			
Garscadden		d		14 11			14 22				14 40			14 52				15 10			15 23			
Yoker		d		14 13			14 25				14 43			14 55				15 13			15 25			
Clydebank		d		14 15			14 27				14 45			14 57				15 15			15 27			
Anniesland		d	14 06			14 15		14 22	14 26	14 36			14 45		14 52	14 55	15 06			15 16		15 22	15 26	15 36
Westerton		d	14 09			14 18		14 25	14 30	14 39			14 48		14 55	14 58	15 09			15 19		15 26	15 29	15 39
Bearsden		d	14 11					14 28		14 41					14 58		15 11					15 28		15 41
Hillfoot		d	14 13					14 30		14 43					15 00		15 14					15 30		15 43
Milngavie		a	14 17					14 33		14 47					15 03		15 18					15 34		15 47
Drumchapel		d				14 20			14 32				14 51			15 01				15 21			15 31	
Drumry		d				14 22			14 34				14 53			15 03				15 23			15 33	
Singer		d				14 25			14 37				14 55			15 05				15 26			15 36	
Dalmuir	227	a		14 19	14 18	14 28	14 30		14 39		14 49	14 50	14 58	15 00		15 08		15 19	15 19	15 28	15 30		15 38	
		d			14 19		14 30		14 40			14 51		15 00		15 08			15 20		15 31		15 39	
Kilpatrick		d					14 33							15 03							15 34			
Bowling		d					14 36							15 06							15 37			
Dumbarton East		d			14 28		14 40		14 47			14 58		15 10		15 17			15 28		15 41		15 47	
Dumbarton Central	227	d			14 30		14a43		14 50			15 00		15a13		15 19			15 30		15a44		15 50	
Dalreoch		d			14 31				14 51			15 02				15 21			15 31				15 51	
Renton		d							14 54							15 24							15 54	
Alexandria		d							14 57							15 26							15 57	
Balloch		a							15 01							15 31							16 01	
Cardross		d			14 36							15 07							15 36					
Craigendoran		d			14 42							15 13							15 42					
Helensburgh Central		a			14 45							15 16							15 45					
Helensburgh Upper	227	a																						

A From Motherwell **B** From Larkhall **C** From Whifflet

Table T226-F

Mondays to Fridays
16 December to 15 May

Edinburgh, Bathgate, Airdrie, Cumbernauld and Springburn - Glasgow - Milngavie, Dalmuir, Balloch and Helensburgh

Station			SR	SR	SR	SR	SR	SR	SR	SR	SR	SR	SR	SR	SR	SR	SR	SR	SR	SR	SR	SR	SR	SR
					A		B			C		C		B					◇ D 🍴	A		B		C
Edinburgh	228,230	d		14 21					14 36		14 53						15 07	15 23						
Haymarket	228,230 ⛴	d		14 27					14 41		14 57						15 12	15 27						
Edinburgh Park	230	d		14 34					14 45		15 03						15 17	15 32						
Uphall		d		14 42					14 53		15 11						15 26	15 40						
Livingston North		d		14 45					14 57		15 14						15 30	15 44						
Bathgate		a		14 50					15 01		15 19						15 34	15 48						
		d		14 50					15 04		15 20						15 35	15 49						
Armadale		d							15 08								15 39							
Blackridge		d							15 11								15 42							
Caldercruix		d							15 18								15 49							
Drumgelloch		d		15 03					15 21		15 32						15 52	16 01						
Airdrie		d		15 06				15 16	15 26		15 36				15 46		15 57	16 07					16 16	
Coatdyke		d		15 08				15 18			15 38				15 48			16 09					16 18	
Coatbridge Sunnyside		d		15 11				15 21	15 29		15 41				15 51		16 00	16 12					16 21	
Blairhill		d		15 13				15 23			15 43				15 53			16 14					16 23	
Easterhouse		d		15 17				15 27			15 47				15 57			16 18					16 27	
Garrowhill		d		15 20				15 30			15 50				16 00			16 21					16 30	
Shettleston		d						15 32	15 41						16 02		16 12						16 32	
Carntyne		d						15 34	15 43						16 04		16 14						16 34	
Cumbernauld		d	14 19													15 19								
Greenfaulds		d	14 21													15 21								
Springburn		d				15 24							15 54								16 24			
Barnhill		d				15 25							15 55								16 25			
Alexandra Parade		d				15 28							15 58								16 28			
Duke Street		d				15 30							16 00								16 30			
Bellgrove		d				15 32		15 38	15 46				16 02		16 08		16 17				16 32		16 38	
High Street		d		15 27		15 34		15 40	15 49		15 57		16 04		16 10		16 20	16 28			16 34		16 40	
Glasgow Queen St LL 10	⛴	a		15 29		15 36		15 42	15 51		15 59		16 06		16 12		16 22	16 30			16 36		16 42	
		d		15 30		15 37		15 43	15 51		16 00		16 07		16 12		16 26	16 31			16 37		16 44	
Charing Cross		d		15 33		15 39		15 46	15 54		16 03		16 09		16 15		16 29	16 33			16 39		16 47	
Argyle Street	225	d	15 22		15 26		15 38			15 49		15 56		16 07		16 21				16 26		16 38		16 50
Glasgow Central LL 15	225	a	15 23		15 27		15 39			15 50		15 57		16 08		16 23				16 27		16 39		16 51
		d	15 25		15 32		15 40			15 54		16 02		16 09		16 23				16 32		16 39		16 52
Anderston	225	d	15 26		15 33		15 41			15 55		16 04		16 11		16 25				16 34		16 41		16 53
Exhibition Centre	225	d	15 28		15 36		15 43			15 57		16 06		16 13		16 27				16 36		16 43		16 55
Partick	225 ⛴	d	15 32	15 37	15 40	15 43	15 47	15 50	15 58	16 01	16 07	16 10	16 13	16 16	16 19	16 30	16 34	16 37		16 40	16 43	16 46	16 51	16 59
Hyndland 3		d	15 34	15 39	15 42	15 46	15 49	15 53	16 00	16 04	16 10	16 13	16 16	16 19	16 22	16 33	16 36	16 40		16 43	16 46	16 49	16 56	17 01
Jordanhill		d	15 36			15 48				16 06			16 18			16 35					16 48			17 03
Scotstounhill		d	15 39			15 50				16 08			16 20			16 37					16 50			17 06
Garscadden		d	15 41			15 53				16 10			16 22			16 39					16 52			17 08
Yoker		d	15 44			15 55				16 13			16 25			16 42					16 55			17 10
Clydebank		d	15 46			15 57				16 15			16 27			16 44					16 57			17 12
Anniesland		d			15 47		15 52	15 56	16 06			16 16		16 22	16 25		16 39			16 46		16 52	16 59	
Westerton		d			15 50		15 55	15 59	16 10			16 19		16 25	16 28		16 42			16 49		16 56	17 02	
Bearsden		d					15 58		16 12					16 27			16 45					16 58		
Hillfoot		d					16 00		16 14					16 29			16 47					17 00		
Milngavie		a					16 03		16 18					16 33			16 51					17 04		
Drumchapel		d			15 53			16 01				16 21			16 30					16 51			17 04	
Drumry		d			15 55			16 03				16 23			16 32					16 53			17 06	
Singer		d			15 57			16 06				16 26			16 35					16 56			17 09	
Dalmuir	227	a	15 50	15 49	16 00	16 00		16 08		16 19	16 19	16 28	16 30		16 37	16 49		16 51		17 00	17 00		17 11	17 16
		d		15 50		16 01		16 09			16 20		16 30		16 38			16 52	16 56		17 01		17 12	
Kilpatrick		d				16 04							16 33								17 03			
Bowling		d				16 07							16 36								17 06			
Dumbarton East		d		15 58		16 11		16 17			16 28		16 40		16 46			16 59			17 11		17 19	
Dumbarton Central	227	d		16 00		16a14		16 19			16 30		16a43		16 49			17 01	17 07		17a14		17 21	
Dalreoch		d		16 01				16 21			16 31				16 50			17 03					17 23	
Renton		d						16 24							16 53								17 26	
Alexandria		d						16 27							16 56								17 28	
Balloch		a						16 31							17 00								17 32	
Cardross		d		16 06							16 36							17 08						
Craigendoran		d		16 11							16 42							17 13						
Helensburgh Central		a		16 15							16 45							17 16						
Helensburgh Upper	227	a																	17 20					

A From Whifflet
B From Larkhall
C From Motherwell
D From Glasgow Queen Street to Oban

Table T226-F

Mondays to Fridays

16 December to 15 May

Edinburgh, Bathgate, Airdrie, Cumbernauld and Springburn - Glasgow - Milngavie, Dalmuir, Balloch and Helensburgh

		SR	SR	SR A	SR	SR B	SR	SR	SR	SR	SR C	SR	SR B	SR	SR A	SR	SR	SR A	SR	SR B	SR	SR
Edinburgh 228,230	d	15 38	15 52						16 07	16 22						16 41	16 54					17 08
Haymarket 228,230 ⇌	d	15 42	15 57						16 12	16 27						16 46	16 58					17 13
Edinburgh Park 230	d	15 47	16 02						16 17	16 33						16 51	17 04					17 19
Uphall	d	15 55	16 10						16 25	16 41						16 59	17 12					17 27
Livingston North	d	15 58	16 14						16 29	16 45						17 03	17 16					17 31
Bathgate	a	16 03	16 18						16 34	16 49						17 07	17 20					17 35
	d	16 04	16 19						16 35	16 50						17 08	17 21					17 36
Armadale	d	16 08							16 39							17 12						17 40
Blackridge	d	16 12							16 42							17 16						17 43
Caldercruix	d	16 18							16 49							17 22						17 50
Drumgelloch	d	16 22	16 32						16 52	17 02						17 26	17 33					17 53
Airdrie	d	16 26	16 36				16 46		16 58	17 06				17 16		17 29	17 37				17 46	17 57
Coatdyke	d		16 38				16 48			17 08				17 18			17 39				17 48	
Coatbridge Sunnyside	d	16 29	16 40				16 51		17 01	17 10				17 21		17 33	17 41				17 51	18 00
Blairhill	d		16 43				16 53			17 13				17 23			17 44				17 53	
Easterhouse	d		16 47				16 57			17 17				17 27			17 48				17 57	
Garrowhill	d		16 49				17 00			17 19				17 30			17 50				18 00	
Shettleston	d	16 41					17 02		17 13					17 32		17 44					18 02	18 12
Carntyne	d	16 43					17 04		17 15					17 34		17 46					18 04	18 14
Cumbernauld	d							16 19														
Greenfaulds	d							16 21														
Springburn	d				16 54							17 24							17 52			
Barnhill	d				16 55							17 25							17 53			
Alexandra Parade	d				16 58							17 28							17 56			
Duke Street	d				17 00							17 30							17 58			
Bellgrove	d	16 46			17 02		17 08		17 18			17 32		17 38		17 50			18 00		18 08	18 17
High Street	d	16 49	16 57		17 04		17 10		17 21	17 27		17 34		17 40		17 52	17 58		18 02		18 10	18 20
Glasgow Queen St LL 10 ⇌	a	16 51	16 59		17 06		17 12		17 23	17 29		17 36		17 42		17 54	18 00		18 04		18 12	18 22
	d	16 55	17 00		17 07		17 14		17 24	17 29		17 37		17 43		17 55	18 00		18 06		18 12	18 22
Charing Cross	d	16 57	17 02		17 09		17 16		17 28	17 32		17 39		17 46		17 58	18 03		18 09		18 15	18 25
Argyle Street 225	d			16 55		17 08		17 19			17 25		17 38		17 49			17 56		18 08		
Glasgow Central LL 15 225	a			16 56		17 09		17 21			17 26		17 39		17 50			17 57		18 09		
	d			17 02		17 10		17 21			17 27		17 40		17 51			18 02		18 09		
Anderston 225	d			17 04		17 11		17 23			17 29		17 41		17 52			18 03		18 11		
Exhibition Centre 225	d			17 06		17 13		17 25			17 35		17 43		17 55			18 06		18 13		
Partick 225 ⇌	d	17 02	17 07	17 10	17 13	17 17	17 20	17 29	17 32	17 36	17 40	17 43	17 47	17 50	17 58	18 02	18 07	18 10	18 13	18 16	18 19	18 29
Hyndland 3	d	17 04	17 09	17 12	17 16	17 19	17 23	17 31	17 34	17 38	17 42	17 46	17 49	17 52	18 01	18 04	18 09	18 12	18 15	18 19	18 22	18 31
Jordanhill	d				17 18			17 33				17 48			18 03				18 17			
Scotstounhill	d				17 20			17 36				17 50			18 05				18 20			
Garscadden	d				17 22			17 38				17 53			18 08				18 22			
Yoker	d				17 25			17 40				17 55			18 10				18 24			
Clydebank	d				17 27			17 42				17 57			18 12				18 26			
Anniesland	d	17 07		17 15		17 22	17 26		17 38		17 45		17 52	17 55		18 07		18 15		18 22	18 25	18 36
Westerton	d	17 10		17 18		17 25	17 29		17 41		17 48		17 55	17 58		18 10		18 18		18 25	18 28	18 39
Bearsden	d	17 13				17 28			17 44				17 58			18 13				18 27		18 41
Hillfoot	d	17 15				17 30			17 46				18 00			18 15				18 29		18 43
Milngavie	a	17 18				17 33			17 49				18 03			18 18				18 33		18 47
Drumchapel	d			17 21			17 31				17 51			18 01				18 21			18 31	
Drumry	d			17 23			17 33				17 53			18 03				18 23			18 33	
Singer	d			17 25			17 36				17 55			18 05				18 25			18 35	
Dalmuir 227	a		17 19	17 28	17 32		17 38	17 46		17 50	17 58	18 00		18 08	18 16		18 19	18 28	18 30		18 38	
	d		17 20		17 33		17 39			17 51		18 01		18 09			18 20		18 30		18 38	
Kilpatrick	d				17 35							18 04							18 33			
Bowling	d				17 38							18 07							18 36			
Dumbarton East	d		17 28		17 43		17 48			17 58		18 11		18 16			18 28		18 40		18 46	
Dumbarton Central 227	d		17 30		17a46		17 50			18 00		18a14		18 19			18 30		18a43		18 48	
Dalreoch	d		17 32				17 52			18 02				18 20			18 31				18 49	
Renton	d						17 55							18 23							18 52	
Alexandria	d						17 57							18 26							18 55	
Balloch	a						18 02							18 30							18 59	
Cardross	d		17 37							18 07							18 36					
Craigendoran	d		17 42							18 12							18 42					
Helensburgh Central	a		17 45							18 15							18 45					
Helensburgh Upper 227	a																					

A From Motherwell
B From Larkhall
C From Whifflet

NRT DECEMBER 19 EDITION

Table T226-F

Mondays to Fridays

16 December to 15 May

Edinburgh, Bathgate, Airdrie, Cumbernauld and Springburn - Glasgow - Milngavie, Dalmuir, Balloch and Helensburgh

		SR ◇ A ✠	SR	SR	SR B	SR	SR C	SR	SR D	SR	SR D	SR	SR	SR C	SR	SR	SR	SR B	SR	SR	SR C	SR	SR D
Edinburgh 228,230	d			17 22						17 38		17 53				18 04			18 23				
Haymarket 228,230 ⇌	d			17 27						17 43		17 57				18 08			18 27				
Edinburgh Park 230	d			17 32						17 48		18 04				18 13			18 32				
Uphall	d			17 40						17 56		18 12				18 21			18 40				
Livingston North	d			17 44						18 00		18 15				18 25			18 44				
Bathgate	a			17 49						18 04		18 20				18 30			18 48				
	d			17 49						18 05		18 20				18 35			18 50				
Armadale	d									18 09						18 39							
Blackridge	d									18 13						18 42							
Caldercruix	d									18 19						18 49							
Drumgelloch	d			18 02						18 23		18 33				18 52			19 02				
Airdrie	d			18 06				18 16		18 28		18 36			18 46	18 58			19 06			19 17	
Coatdyke	d			18 08				18 18				18 38			18 48				19 08			19 19	
Coatbridge Sunnyside	d			18 10				18 21		18 31		18 41			18 51	19 01			19 11			19 22	
Blairhill	d			18 13				18 23				18 43			18 53				19 13			19 24	
Easterhouse	d			18 17				18 27				18 47			18 57				19 17			19 28	
Garrowhill	d			18 19				18 30				18 50			19 00				19 20			19 31	
Shettleston	d							18 32		18 43					19 02	19 13						19 33	
Carntyne	d							18 34		18 45					19 04	19 15						19 35	
Cumbernauld	d		17 19														18 18						
Greenfaulds	d		17 21														18 20						
Springburn	d					18 23							18 53							19 24			
Barnhill	d					18 24							18 54							19 25			
Alexandra Parade	d					18 27							18 57							19 28			
Duke Street	d					18 29							18 59							19 30			
Bellgrove	d					18 31		18 38		18 48			19 01		19 08	19 18				19 32		19 39	
High Street	d			18 26		18 34		18 40		18 51		18 57	19 03		19 10	19 20			19 28	19 34		19 41	
Glasgow Queen St LL 10 ⇌	a			18 28		18 36		18 42		18 53		18 59	19 05		19 12	19 22			19 30	19 36		19 43	
	d			18 29		18 36		18 44		18 57		19 02	19 07		19 14	19 23			19 33	19 38		19 44	
Charing Cross	d			18 32		18 39		18 47		18 59		19 06	19 10		19 17	19 25			19 36	19 40		19 47	
Argyle Street 225	d		18 22		18 27		18 37		18 51		18 57			19 08			19 22	19 26			19 38		19 48
Glasgow Central LL 15 225	a		18 24		18 28		18 38		18 53		18 59			19 09			19 24	19 27			19 39		19 50
	d		18 26		18 33		18 39		18 53		18 59			19 10			19 24	19 28			19 40		19 51
Anderston 225	d		18 27		18 34		18 40		18 55		19 01			19 11			19 26	19 29			19 41		19 52
Exhibition Centre 225	d		18 29		18 36		18 43		18 57		19 03			19 13			19 28	19 32			19 44		19 55
Partick 225 ⇌	d		18 33	18 36	18 40	18 43	18 47	18 51	19 00	19 03	19 07	19 10	19 14	19 17	19 21	19 29	19 32	19 35	19 41	19 44	19 48	19 51	19 58
Hyndland 3	d		18 36	18 39	18 42	18 45	18 49	18 54	19 03	19 06	19 09	19 13	19 16	19 19	19 23	19 31	19 34	19 38	19 43	19 47	19 50	19 54	20 01
Jordanhill	d		18 38			18 47			19 05				19 18				19 36			19 49			20 03
Scotstounhill	d		18 40			18 50			19 07				19 21				19 39			19 51			20 05
Garscadden	d		18 42			18 52			19 09				19 23				19 41			19 53			20 08
Yoker	d		18 45			18 55			19 12				19 26				19 43			19 56			20 10
Clydebank	d		18 47			18 57			19 14				19 28				19 45			19 58			20 12
Anniesland	d				18 45		18 52	18 57		19 09	19 12			19 23	19 26	19 34		19 41			19 53	19 57	
Westerton	d				18 48		18 55	19 00		19 12	19 15			19 26	19 29	19 40		19 44			19 56	20 00	
Bearsden	d						18 58			19 14				19 28		19 42					19 59		
Hillfoot	d						19 00			19 16				19 30		19 44					20 01		
Milngavie	a						19 03			19 20				19 34		19 48					20 04		
Drumchapel	d				18 51			19 02			19 18				19 32			19 46				20 02	
Drumry	d				18 53			19 04			19 20				19 34			19 48				20 04	
Singer	d				18 55			19 07			19 22				19 36			19 51				20 07	
Dalmuir 227	a		18 53	18 48	18 58	19 00		19 09	19 18		19 25	19 21	19 31		19 39		19 49	19 53	19 52	20 01		20 09	20 16
	d	18 42		18 49		19 01		19 10				19 22	19 31		19 40				19 53	20 01		20 10	
Kilpatrick	d					19 03							19 34							20 04			
Bowling	d					19 06							19 37							20 07			
Dumbarton East	d			18 56		19 11		19 18				19 30	19 41		19 47				20 01	20 11		20 18	
Dumbarton Central 227	d	18 52		18 58		19a14		19 21				19 32	19a44		19 50				20 03	20a14		20 21	
Dalreoch	d			19 00				19 22				19 33			19 51				20 04			20 22	
Renton	d							19 25							19 54							20 25	
Alexandria	d							19 28							19 57							20 28	
Balloch	a							19 32							20 01							20 32	
Cardross	d			19 05								19 38							20 09				
Craigendoran	d			19 10								19 44							20 15				
Helensburgh Central	a			19 13								19 47							20 18				
Helensburgh Upper 227	a	19 04																					

A From Glasgow Queen Street to Oban
B From Whifflet
C From Larkhall
D From Motherwell

Table T226-F

Mondays to Fridays

16 December to 15 May

Edinburgh, Bathgate, Airdrie, Cumbernauld and Springburn - Glasgow - Milngavie, Dalmuir, Balloch and Helensburgh

	SR	SR A	SR	SR	SR	SR B	SR	SR	SR C	SR B	SR	SR	SR	SR A	SR A	SR B	SR	SR	SR	SR	SR C
Edinburgh 228,230 d	18 37		18 53	19 06								19 22	19 40					19 52	20 06		
Haymarket 228,230 d	18 41		18 58	19 11								19 27	19 44					19 57	20 10		
Edinburgh Park 230 d	18 47		19 03	19 16								19 31	19 49					20 03	20 15		
Uphall d	18 55		19 11	19 24								19 39	19 57					20 11	20 23		
Livingston North d	18 59		19 15	19 28								19 43	20 00					20 15	20 26		
Bathgate a	19 03		19 19	19 32								19 47	20 05					20 19	20 31		
d	19 05		19 20									19 49						20 20			
Armadale d	19 09		19 24									19 53						20 24			
Blackridge d	19 12		19 27									19 57						20 27			
Caldercruix d	19 19		19 34									20 03						20 34			
Drumgelloch d	19 22		19 37									20 07						20 37			
Airdrie d	19 28		19 41				19 46					20 17						20 47			
Coatdyke d							19 48					20 19						20 49			
Coatbridge Sunnyside d	19 31		19 44				19 51					20 21						20 51			
Blairhill d							19 53					20 24						20 54			
Easterhouse d							19 57					20 28						20 58			
Garrowhill d							20 00					20 30						21 00			
Shettleston d	19 43						20 02					20 33						21 03			
Carntyne d	19 45						20 04					20 35						21 05			
Cumbernauld d								19 19												20 19	
Greenfaulds d								19 21												20 21	
Springburn d					19 53						20 24						20 54				
Barnhill d					19 54						20 25						20 55				
Alexandra Parade d					19 57						20 28						20 58				
Duke Street d					19 59						20 30						21 00				
Bellgrove d	19 48				20 01		20 08				20 32	20 39					21 02	21 08			
High Street d	19 51		20 00		20 04		20 10				20 35	20 41					21 04	21 11			
Glasgow Queen St LL 10 a	19 53		20 02		20 06		20 12				20 37	20 43					21 06	21 13			
d	19 54		20 03		20 06		20 12				20 40	20 48					21 09	21 18			
Charing Cross d	19 58		20 05		20 08		20 15				20 45	20 50					21 15	21 21			
Argyle Street 225 d		19 55				20 08		20 22	20 25	20 39				20 52	21 00	21 09				21 21	21 25
Glasgow Central LL 15 225 a		19 56				20 09		20 23	20 27	20 41				20 54	21 02	21 10				21 22	21 27
d		19 57				20 10		20 24	20 28	20 41				20 54	21 02	21 11				21 23	21 28
Anderston 225 d		19 59				20 11		20 25	20 30	20 43				20 56	21 04	21 12				21 24	21 29
Exhibition Centre 225 d		20 01				20 13		20 27	20 32	20 45				20 58	21 06	21 14				21 26	21 32
Partick 225 d	20 02	20 05	20 09		20 12	20 17	20 20	20 31	20 35	20 48	20 51	20 55		21 01	21 09	21 18	21 21	21 25		21 30	21 35
Hyndland 3 d	20 04	20 07	20 12		20 15	20 19	20 22	20 33	20 38	20 51	20 54	20 57		21 04	21 12	21 20	21 23	21 28		21 32	21 38
Jordanhill d					20 17			20 35			20 56			21 06			21 25			21 34	
Scotstounhill d					20 19			20 38			20 58			21 08			21 28			21 37	
Garscadden d					20 22			20 40			21 00			21 10			21 30			21 39	
Yoker d					20 24			20 42			21 03			21 13			21 33			21 41	
Clydebank d					20 26			20 44			21 05			21 15			21 35			21 43	
Anniesland d	20 07	20 10				20 22	20 25		20 41	20 54		21 00			21 15	21 23		21 31			21 41
Westerton d	20 10	20 13				20 25	20 28		20 44	20 57		21 03			21 18	21 26		21 34			21 44
Bearsden d	20 13					20 28				20 59						21 29					
Hillfoot d	20 15					20 30				21 01						21 31					
Milngavie a	20 18					20 33				21 05						21 34					
Drumchapel d		20 16					20 31		20 46			21 06			21 20			21 36			21 46
Drumry d		20 18					20 33		20 48			21 08			21 22			21 38			21 48
Singer d		20 20					20 35		20 51			21 10			21 25			21 41			21 51
Dalmuir 227 a		20 23	20 21		20 29		20 38	20 48	20 53		21 08	21 13		21 19	21 27		21 38	21 43		21 47	21 53
d			20 22		20 30		20 39				21 09	21 14					21 39	21 44			
Kilpatrick d					20 33						21 12						21 41				
Bowling d					20 36						21 15						21 44				
Dumbarton East d			20 30		20 40		20 47				21 19	21 24					21 49	21 54			
Dumbarton Central 227 d			20 33		20a43		20 51				21 22	21 27					21 51	21 56			
Dalreoch d			20 34				20 54				21 23	21 29					21 53	21 58			
Renton d							20 57				21 26						21 56				
Alexandria d							21 00				21 29						21 58				
Balloch a							21 04				21 33						22 03				
Cardross d			20 39									21 34						22 03			
Craigendoran d			20 45									21 40						22 09			
Helensburgh Central a			20 49									21 43						22 13			
Helensburgh Upper 227 a																					

A From Motherwell B From Larkhall C From Whifflet

Table T226-F

Mondays to Fridays

16 December to 15 May

Edinburgh, Bathgate, Airdrie, Cumbernauld and Springburn - Glasgow - Milngavie, Dalmuir, Balloch and Helensburgh

	SR A	SR	SR	SR B	SR B	SR A	SR	SR	SR	SR C	SR A	SR	SR	SR B	SR B	SR A	SR	SR	SR	SR C	SR	SR A
Edinburgh 228,230 d			20 22					20 54					21 20					21 52				
Haymarket 228,230 d			20 29					20 58					21 26					21 56				
Edinburgh Park 230 d			20 34					21 03					21 31					22 01				
Uphall d			20 42					21 11					21 39					22 09				
Livingston North d			20 46					21 14					21 42					22 12				
Bathgate a			20 50					21 19					21 47					22 17				
d			20 52					21 19					21 49					22 19				
Armadale d			20 56					21 23					21 53					22 23				
Blackridge d			20 59					21 27					21 57					22 27				
Caldercruix d			21 06					21 33					22 03					22 33				
Drumgelloch d			21 09					21 37					22 07					22 37				
Airdrie d			21 17					21 47					22 17					22 47				
Coatdyke d			21 19					21 49					22 19					22 49				
Coatbridge Sunnyside d			21 21					21 51					22 21					22 51				
Blairhill d			21 24					21 54					22 24					22 54				
Easterhouse d			21 28					21 58					22 28					22 58				
Garrowhill d			21 30					22 00					22 30					23 00				
Shettleston d			21 33					22 03					22 33					23 03				
Carntyne d			21 35					22 05					22 35					23 05				
Cumbernauld d									21 21										22 21			
Greenfaulds d									21 23										22 23			
Springburn d		21 23					21 54					22 27					22 54				23 24	
Barnhill d		21 24					21 55					22 28					22 55				23 25	
Alexandra Parade d		21 27					21 58					22 31					22 58				23 28	
Duke Street d		21 29					22 00					22 33					23 00				23 30	
Bellgrove d		21 31	21 38				22 02	22 08				22 35	22 39				23 02	23 08			23 32	
High Street d		21 33	21 41				22 04	22 11				22 37	22 42				23 04	23 11			23 34	
Glasgow Queen St LL 10 a		21 35	21 43				22 06	22 13				22 39	22 44				23 06	23 13			23 36	
d		21 39	21 47				22 09	22 17				22 41	22 47				23 09	23 17			23 37	
Charing Cross d		21 45	21 49				22 15	22 20				22 46	22 50				23 15	23 20			23 39	
Argyle Street 225 d	21 37			21 50	21 56	22 07			22 20	22 26	22 38			22 49	22 53	23 07			23 23	23 26		23 38
Glasgow Central LL 15 225 a	21 39			21 51	21 58	22 09			22 22	22 27	22 39			22 51	22 54	23 08			23 24	23 28		23 39
d	21 39			21 52	21 58	22 09			22 22	22 28	22 39			22 51	22 57	23 09			23 25	23 28		23 40
Anderston 225 d	21 41			21 53	22 00	22 11			22 24	22 29	22 41			22 53	22 58	23 10			23 26	23 30		23 41
Exhibition Centre 225 d	21 43			21 55	22 02	22 13			22 26	22 32	22 43			22 55	23 01	23 12			23 28	23 32		23 43
Partick 225 d	21 47	21 50	21 53	21 59	22 05	22 16	22 19	22 24	22 29	22 35	22 46	22 50	22 54	22 58	23 04	23 16	23 19	23 24	23 32	23 35	23 43	23 47
Hyndland 3 d	21 49	21 52	21 56	22 01	22 08	22 19	22 22	22 26	22 32	22 38	22 49	22 52	22 56	23 01	23 07	23 18	23 22	23 26	23 34	23 38	23 46	23 49
Jordanhill d		21 54		22 03			22 24		22 34			22 54		23 03			23 24		23 36		23 48	
Scotstounhill d		21 57		22 05			22 26		22 36			22 57		23 05			23 26		23 39		23 50	
Garscadden d		21 59		22 07			22 29		22 38			22 59		23 08			23 29		23a41		23 53	
Yoker d		22 01		22 10			22 32		22 41			23 02		23 10			23 31				23 55	
Clydebank d		22 03		22 12			22 34		22 43			23 04		23 12			23 34				23 57	
Anniesland d	21 52		21 59		22 11	22 22		22 29		22 41	22 52		22 59		23 10	23 21		23 29		23 41		23 52
Westerton d	21 55		22 02		22 14	22 25		22 32		22 44	22 55		23 02		23 13	23 24		23 32		23 44		23 55
Bearsden d	21 58					22 27					22 57					23 27						23 58
Hillfoot d	22 00					22 29					22 59					23 29						23 59
Milngavie a	22 03					22 33					23 03					23 33						00 03
Drumchapel d			22 04		22 16			22 35		22 46			23 05		23 15			23 35		23 46		
Drumry d			22 06		22 18			22 37		22 48			23 07		23 17			23 37		23 48		
Singer d			22 09		22 21			22 39		22 51			23 09		23 20			23 39		23 51		
Dalmuir 227 a		22 07	22 11	22 16	22 23		22 37	22 42	22 47	22 53		23 07	23 12	23 16	23 22		23 37	23 42		23 53	23 58	
d		22 08	22 13				22 37	22 43				23 08	23 13				23 37	23 43			23 59	
Kilpatrick d		22 10					22 40					23 10					23 39				00 03	
Bowling d		22 13					22 43					23 13					23 42				00 06	
Dumbarton East d		22 18	22 23				22 47	22 52				23 18	23 22				23 47	23 52			00 11	
Dumbarton Central 227 d		22 20	22 25				22 49	22 54				23 20	23 24				23 49	23 54			00 13	
Dalreoch d		22 22	22 27				22 52	22 56				23 22	23 26				23 52	23 56			00 15	
Renton d		22 25					22 55					23 25					23 55				00 18	
Alexandria d		22 28					22 57					23 27					23 57				00 20	
Balloch a		22 32					23 02					23 32					00 02				00 24	
Cardross d			22 32					23 01					23 31					00 01				
Craigendoran d			22 38					23 08					23 38					00 07				
Helensburgh Central a			22 42					23 12					23 42					00 11				
Helensburgh Upper 227 a																						

A From Larkhall B From Motherwell C From Whifflet

Table T226-F

Mondays to Fridays

16 December to 15 May

Edinburgh, Bathgate, Airdrie, Cumbernauld and Springburn - Glasgow - Milngavie, Dalmuir, Balloch and Helensburgh

		SR	SR FO A	SR	SR	SR	SR	SR
Edinburgh 228,230	d	22 24		22 52	23 09	23 37		23 56
Haymarket 228,230	d	22 28		22 56	23 13	23 42		00 01
Edinburgh Park 230	d	22 33		23 01	23 18	23 48		00 06
Uphall	d	22 41		23 09	23 26	23 56		00 14
Livingston North	d	22 44		23 12	23 29	00 01		00 17
Bathgate	a	22 49		23 17	23 34	00 05		00 24
	d	22 50		23 17	23 35			
Armadale	d	22 54		23 21	23 39			
Blackridge	d	22 57		23 25	23 42			
Caldercruix	d	23 04		23 31	23 49			
Drumgelloch	d	23 07		23 35	23 52			
Airdrie	d	23 17		23 39	23a55			
Coatdyke	d	23 20		23 41				
Coatbridge Sunnyside	d	23 24		23 43				
Blairhill	d	23 27		23 46				
Easterhouse	d	23 32		23 50				
Garrowhill	d	23 36		23 52				
Shettleston	d	23 39		23 55				
Carntyne	d	23 42		23 57				
Cumbernauld	d							
Greenfaulds	d							
Springburn	d						23 54	
Barnhill	d						23 55	
Alexandra Parade	d						23 58	
Duke Street	d						00 03	
Bellgrove	d	23 47		00 01			00 05	
High Street	d	23 50		00 02			00 07	
Glasgow Queen St LL 10	a	23 52		00 04			00 09	
	d	23 54		00 05			00 10	
Charing Cross	d	23 57		00 07			00 12	
Argyle Street 225	d		23 55					
Glasgow Central LL 15 225	a		23 57					
	d		23 57					
Anderston 225	d		23 59					
Exhibition Centre 225	d		00 02					
Partick 225	d	00 01	00 05	00 11			00 16	
Hyndland 3	d	00 03	00 07	00 13			00 19	
Jordanhill	d						00 24	
Scotstounhill	d						00 26	
Garscadden	d			00a17			00a28	
Yoker	d							
Clydebank	d							
Anniesland	d	00 06	00 11					
Westerton	d	00 09	00 14					
Bearsden	d							
Hillfoot	d							
Milngavie	a							
Drumchapel	d	00 12	00 16					
Drumry	d	00 14	00 18					
Singer	d	00 16	00 21					
Dalmuir 227	a	00 19	00 23					
	d	00 20						
Kilpatrick	d							
Bowling	d							
Dumbarton East	d	00 28						
Dumbarton Central 227	d	00 31						
Dalreoch	d	00 32						
Renton	d							
Alexandria	d							
Balloch	a							
Cardross	d	00 37						
Craigendoran	d	00 42						
Helensburgh Central	a	00 46						
Helensburgh Upper 227	a							

A From Motherwell

NRT DECEMBER 19 EDITION

Table T226-F

Saturdays

21 December to 16 May

Edinburgh, Bathgate, Airdrie, Cumbernauld and Springburn - Glasgow - Milngavie, Dalmuir, Balloch and Helensburgh

		SR A	SR A	SR A	SR B	SR A	SR C	SR A	SR B	SR D	SR E	CS F ✕	SR	SR	SR	SR	SR C	SR	SR	SR C	SR	SR D	SR
Edinburgh 228,230	d											04 50											
Haymarket 228,230	d			00 01																			
Edinburgh Park 230	d			00 06																			
Uphall	d			00 14																			
Livingston North	d		00 01	00 17																			
Bathgate	a		00 05	00 24																			
	d																						
Armadale	d																						
Blackridge	d																						
Caldercruix	d																						
Drumgelloch	d																						
Airdrie	d													05 32					05 57				06 16
Coatdyke	d													05 34									06 18
Coatbridge Sunnyside	d													05 36					06 01				06 21
Blairhill	d													05 42									06 23
Easterhouse	d													05 46									06 27
Garrowhill	d													05 48									06 30
Shettleston	d													05 51					06 12				06 32
Carntyne	d													05 53					06 14				06 34
Cumbernauld	d																						
Greenfaulds	d																						
Springburn	d																				06 23		
Barnhill	d																				06 24		
Alexandra Parade	d																				06 27		
Duke Street	d								00 03												06 29		
Bellgrove	d							00 01	00 05					05 56					06 18		06 31		06 38
High Street	d							00 02	00 07					05 59					06 20		06 33		06 40
Glasgow Queen St LL 10	a							00 04	00 09					06 01					06 22		06 35		06 42
	d							00 05	00 10			05u48		06 01					06 25		06 36		06 42
Charing Cross	d							00 07	00 12					06 04					06 27		06 38		06 44
Argyle Street 225	d									00 11							06 19			06 28		06 35	
Glasgow Central LL 15 225	a									00 13							06 20			06 30		06 37	
	d									00 13							06 20			06 30		06 38	
Anderston 225	d									00 15							06 22			06 32		06 39	
Exhibition Centre 225	d						00 02			00 17							06 24			06 34		06 42	
Partick 225	d					00 01	00 05	00 11	00 16	00 20				06 08			06 27		06 31	06 37	06 42	06 45	06 48
Hyndland 3	d					00 03	00 07	00 13	00 19	00 23				06 10			06 30		06 34	06 40	06 45	06 48	06 51
Jordanhill	d								00 24								06 32				06 47		
Scotstounhill	d								00 26								06 35				06 49		
Garscadden	d							00a17	00a28								06 38				06 51		
Yoker	d																06 40				06 54		
Clydebank	d																06 42				06 56		
Anniesland	d					00 06	00 11			00 26									06 37	06 43		06 51	06 54
Westerton	d					00 09	00 14			00 29									06 40	06 46		06 54	06 57
Bearsden	d									00 31									06 42			06 56	
Hillfoot	d									00 33									06 44			06 58	
Milngavie	a									00 37									06 48			07 02	
Drumchapel	d					00 12	00 16													06 48			07 00
Drumry	d					00 14	00 18													06 50			07 02
Singer	d					00 16	00 21													06 53			07 04
Dalmuir 227	a					00 19	00 23					06 04		06 19			06 46			06 55	06 59		07 07
	d					00 20					05 39	06 04	06 11	06 20	06 29	06 38		06 51			07 00		07 08
Kilpatrick	d				00 03										06 31						07 03		
Bowling	d				00 06										06 35						07 06		
Dumbarton East	d				00 11	00 28							06 18	06 28	06 39	06 46		06 58			07 10		07 16
Dumbarton Central 227	d				00 13	00 31					05 48	06 15	06 21	06 30	06a42	06 49		07 00			07a13		07 19
Dalreoch	d				00 15	00 32							06 22	06 31		06 50		07 02					07 20
Renton	d				00 18								06 25			06 53							07 23
Alexandria	d				00 20								06 28			06 56							07 26
Balloch	a				00 24								06 32			07 00							07 30
Cardross	d	00 01				00 37								06 36				07 07					
Craigendoran	d	00 07				00 42								06 41				07 12					
Helensburgh Central	a	00 11				00 46								06 45				07 16					
Helensburgh Upper 227	a										06 00	06 30											

A From Edinburgh
B From Springburn
C From Motherwell
D From Larkhall
E From Glasgow Queen Street to Oban
F To Fort William

Table T226-F

Saturdays
21 December to 16 May

Edinburgh, Bathgate, Airdrie, Cumbernauld and Springburn - Glasgow - Milngavie, Dalmuir, Balloch and Helensburgh

Station		SR A	SR	SR	SR A	SR	SR B	SR	SR	SR	SR	SR C	SR	SR B	SR	SR	SR A	SR	SR A	SR	SR	SR B	SR ◇ D
Edinburgh 228,230	d									06 07	06 22					06 36		06 49					
Haymarket 228,230 ⛴	d									06 11	06 27					06 41		06 55					
Edinburgh Park 230	d									06 16	06 32					06 46		07 01					
Uphall	d									06 24	06 40					06 54		07 09					
Livingston North	d									06 27	06 44					06 58		07 13					
Bathgate	a									06 32	06 49					07 02		07 17					
	d		06 05	06 19						06 35	06 49					07 05		07 18					
Armadale	d		06 10							06 39						07 09							
Blackridge	d		06 13							06 42						07 12							
Caldercruix	d		06 20							06 49						07 19							
Drumgelloch	d		06 23	06 32						06 52	07 02					07 22		07 31					
Airdrie	d		06 28	06 35				06 46		06 57	07 05				07 16	07 27		07 34			07 45		
Coatdyke	d			06 37				06 48			07 07				07 18	07 29		07 36			07 47		
Coatbridge Sunnyside	d		06 31	06 40				06 51		07 01	07 10				07 21	07 31		07 39			07 50		
Blairhill	d			06 42				06 53			07 12				07 23	07 34		07 41			07 52		
Easterhouse	d			06 46				06 57			07 16				07 27			07 45			07 56		
Garrowhill	d			06 49				07 00			07 19				07 30			07 48			07 59		
Shettleston	d		06 43					07 02		07 12					07 32	07 40					08 01		
Carntyne	d		06 45					07 04		07 14					07 34	07 42					08 03		
Cumbernauld	d								06 13														
Greenfaulds	d								06 15														
Springburn	d					06 54							07 24							07 53			
Barnhill	d					06 55							07 25							07 54			
Alexandra Parade	d					06 58							07 28							07 57			
Duke Street	d					07 00							07 30							07 59			
Bellgrove	d		06 48			07 02		07 08		07 18			07 32		07 38	07 45				08 01	08 07		
High Street	d		06 50	06 56		07 04		07 10		07 20	07 26		07 34		07 40	07 48		07 55		08 03	08 09		
Glasgow Queen St LL 10 ⛴	a		06 52	06 58		07 06		07 12		07 22	07 28		07 36		07 42	07 50		07 57		08 05	08 11		
	d		06 55	07 00		07 07		07 12		07 25	07 30		07 37		07 43	07 51		07 59		08 05	08 12		
Charing Cross	d		06 58	07 03		07 09		07 15		07 28	07 32		07 39		07 46	07 54		08 01		08 08	08 14		
Argyle Street 225	d	06 48			06 59		07 07		07 18			07 27		07 37			07 48		07 56			08 09	
Glasgow Central LL 15 225	a	06 50			07 00		07 09		07 19			07 28		07 39			07 50		07 57			08 11	
	d	06 51			07 03		07 09		07 20			07 33		07 39			07 53		08 00			08 13	
Anderston 225	d	06 52			07 05		07 11		07 22			07 34		07 41			07 55		08 02			08 15	
Exhibition Centre 225	d	06 54			07 07		07 13		07 24			07 36		07 43			07 57		08 04			08 17	
Partick 225 ⛴	d	06 58	07 02	07 07	07 10	07 13	07 16	07 19	07 28	07 32	07 36	07 40	07 43	07 47	07 50	07 58	08 01	08 05	08 08	08 12	08 18	08 22	
Hyndland 3	d	07 00	07 04	07 09	07 13	07 16	07 19	07 22	07 30	07 34	07 39	07 42	07 46	07 49	07 53	08 00	08 04	08 08	08 11	08 14	08 21	08 25	
Jordanhill	d	07 02				07 18			07 32				07 48				08 06			08 16			
Scotstounhill	d	07 05				07 20			07 35				07 50				08 08			08 19			
Garscadden	d	07 07				07 22			07 37				07 52				08 10			08 21			
Yoker	d	07 09				07 25			07 39				07 55				08 13			08 24			
Clydebank	d	07 11				07 27			07 41				07 57				08 15			08 26			
Anniesland	d		07 07		07 16		07 22	07 25		07 37		07 45		07 52	07 56	08 05			08 14		08 24	08 28	
Westerton	d		07 10		07 19		07 25	07 28		07 40		07 48		07 55	07 59	08 08			08 17		08 27	08 31	
Bearsden	d		07 13				07 28			07 43				07 58		08 11						08 33	
Hillfoot	d		07 15				07 30			07 45				08 00		08 13						08 35	
Milngavie	a		07 18				07 33			07 48				08 03		08 16						08 39	
Drumchapel	d				07 21			07 30				07 51			08 02				08 19		08 29		
Drumry	d				07 23			07 32				07 53			08 04				08 21		08 31		
Singer	d				07 26			07 35				07 55			08 06				08 24		08 34		
Dalmuir 227	a	07 15		07 19	07 28	07 30		07 38	07 45		07 49	07 58	08 00		08 09		08 19	08 18	08 27	08 29	08 37		
	d			07 20		07 31		07 39			07 50		08 01		08 10			08 19		08 30	08 38		08 42
Kilpatrick	d					07 34							08 04							08 33			
Bowling	d					07 37							08 07							08 36			
Dumbarton East	d			07 28		07 41		07 46			07 58		08 11		08 17			08 28		08 40	08 46		
Dumbarton Central 227	d			07 30		07a44		07 49			08 00		08a14		08 20			08 30		08a43	08 48		08 52
Dalreoch	d			07 31				07 50			08 02				08 21			08 31			08 49		
Renton	d							07 53							08 24						08 52		
Alexandria	d							07 56							08 27						08 55		
Balloch	a							08 00							08 31						08 59		
Cardross	d			07 36							08 07							08 36					
Craigendoran	d			07 42							08 13							08 42					
Helensburgh Central	a			07 45							08 16							08 45					
Helensburgh Upper 227	a																						09 05

A From Motherwell
B From Larkhall
C From Whifflet
D From Glasgow Queen Street to Oban

Table T226-F

Saturdays
21 December to 16 May

Edinburgh, Bathgate, Airdrie, Cumbernauld and Springburn - Glasgow - Milngavie, Dalmuir, Balloch and Helensburgh

Station		SR	SR	SR	SR A	SR	SR B	SR	SR C	SR	SR C	SR	SR	SR B	SR	SR	SR	SR A	SR	SR	SR B	SR
Edinburgh 228,230	d		07 07	07 20						07 37		07 49				08 08			08 25			
Haymarket 228,230 ⛴	d		07 11	07 24						07 42		07 53				08 12			08 29			
Edinburgh Park 230	d		07 16	07 30						07 47		07 58				08 17			08 34			
Uphall	d		07 24	07 40						07 55		08 06				08 25			08 42			
Livingston North	d		07 27	07 43						07 59		08 10				08 29			08 45			
Bathgate	a		07 32	07 48						08 03		08 15				08 33			08 50			
	d		07 35	07 49						08 06		08 20				08 34			08 51			
Armadale	d		07 39							08 10						08 38						
Blackridge	d		07 42							08 13						08 42						
Caldercruix	d		07 49							08 20						08 48						
Drumgelloch	d		07 52	08 02						08 23		08 33				08 52			09 04			
Airdrie	d		07 56	08 05				08 16		08 27		08 39			08 46	08 56			09 08			09 16
Coatdyke	d		07 58	08 07				08 18		08 29		08 41			08 48				09 10			09 18
Coatbridge Sunnyside	d		08 01	08 10				08 21		08 32		08 44			08 51	08 59			09 12			09 21
Blairhill	d		08 03	08 12				08 23		08 34		08 46			08 53				09 15			09 23
Easterhouse	d			08 16				08 27				08 50			08 57				09 19			09 27
Garrowhill	d			08 19				08 30				08 53			09 00				09 21			09 30
Shettleston	d		08 09					08 32		08 40					09 02	09 11						09 32
Carntyne	d		08 11					08 34		08 42					09 04	09 13						09 34
Cumbernauld	d	07 12															08 13					
Greenfaulds	d	07 14															08 15					
Springburn	d					08 24							08 54							09 24		
Barnhill	d					08 25							08 55							09 25		
Alexandra Parade	d					08 28							08 58							09 28		
Duke Street	d					08 30							09 00							09 30		
Bellgrove	d		08 15			08 32		08 38		08 47			09 02		09 08	09 16				09 32		09 38
High Street	d		08 17	08 26		08 34		08 40		08 50		09 00	09 04		09 10	09 19			09 29	09 34		09 40
Glasgow Queen St LL 10 ⛴	a		08 19	08 28		08 36		08 42		08 52		09 02	09 06		09 12	09 21			09 31	09 36		09 42
	d		08 23	08 30		08 37		08 43		08 55		09 02	09 07		09 14	09 21			09 32	09 37		09 43
Charing Cross	d		08 26	08 32		08 39		08 46		08 58		09 05	09 09		09 17	09 24			09 34	09 39		09 45
Argyle Street 225	d	08 18			08 31		08 38		08 50		08 56			09 08			09 21	09 25			09 39	
Glasgow Central LL 15 225	a	08 20			08 32		08 40		08 51		08 57			09 10			09 23	09 26			09 40	
	d	08 20			08 33		08 40		08 52		08 59			09 10			09 24	09 28			09 41	
Anderston 225	d	08 22			08 34		08 42		08 54		09 00			09 12			09 25	09 29			09 42	
Exhibition Centre 225	d	08 24			08 37		08 44		08 56		09 02			09 14			09 27	09 32			09 44	
Partick 225 ⛴	d	08 27	08 30	08 36	08 40	08 43	08 47	08 50	08 59	09 02	09 06	09 09	09 13	09 17	09 22	09 28	09 31	09 35	09 39	09 43	09 48	09 51
Hyndland 3	d	08 30	08 33	08 39	08 43	08 46	08 50	08 53	09 02	09 05	09 08	09 11	09 15	09 20	09 24	09 30	09 33	09 38	09 41	09 46	09 50	09 55
Jordanhill	d	08 32				08 48			09 04				09 17				09 35			09 48		
Scotstounhill	d	08 34				08 50			09 07				09 20				09 38			09 50		
Garscadden	d	08 37				08 53			09 09				09 22				09 40			09 52		
Yoker	d	08 39				08 55			09 11				09 25				09 42			09 55		
Clydebank	d	08 41				08 57			09 13				09 27				09 44			09 57		
Anniesland	d		08 36		08 46		08 53	08 56		09 08	09 11			09 23	09 27	09 35		09 41			09 53	09 58
Westerton	d		08 39		08 49		08 56	08 59		09 11	09 14			09 26	09 30	09 40		09 44			09 56	10 01
Bearsden	d		08 41				08 58			09 13				09 28		09 42					09 59	
Hillfoot	d		08 43				09 00			09 15				09 30		09 44					10 01	
Milngavie	a		08 47				09 04			09 19				09 34		09 48					10 04	
Drumchapel	d				08 51			09 02			09 17				09 33			09 46				10 03
Drumry	d				08 53			09 04			09 19				09 35			09 48				10 05
Singer	d				08 56			09 06			09 21				09 37			09 51				10 08
Dalmuir 227	a	08 45		08 49	08 58	09 00		09 09	09 17		09 24	09 20	09 30		09 40		09 48	09 53	09 51	10 00		10 10
	d			08 50		09 01		09 09				09 21	09 30		09 41				09 52	10 01		10 11
Kilpatrick	d					09 04							09 33							10 04		
Bowling	d					09 07							09 36							10 07		
Dumbarton East	d			08 58		09 11		09 17				09 29	09 40		09 48				10 00	10 11		10 19
Dumbarton Central 227	d			09 00		09a14		09 19				09 31	09a43		09 51				10 02	10a14		10 21
Dalreoch	d			09 01				09 20				09 33			09 52				10 04			10 22
Renton	d							09 23							09 55							10 25
Alexandria	d							09 26							09 58							10 28
Balloch	a							09 30							10 02							10 32
Cardross	d			09 06								09 38							10 09			
Craigendoran	d			09 11								09 44							10 15			
Helensburgh Central	a			09 14								09 47							10 18			
Helensburgh Upper 227	a																					

A From Whifflet
B From Larkhall
C From Motherwell

Table T226-F

Saturdays
21 December to 16 May

Edinburgh, Bathgate, Airdrie, Cumbernauld and Springburn - Glasgow - Milngavie, Dalmuir, Balloch and Helensburgh

	SR	SR	SR	SR	SR	SR	SR	SR	SR	SR	SR	SR	SR	SR	SR	SR	SR	SR	SR	SR	SR	SR
	A			A		B					◇ C	D		B			A		A		B	
Edinburgh 228,230 d		08 41	08 49					09 10		09 23						09 37		09 53				
Haymarket 228,230 d		08 46	08 54					09 15		09 27						09 42		09 57				
Edinburgh Park 230 d		08 50	08 58					09 20		09 32						09 47		10 02				
Uphall d		08 58	09 07					09 28		09 40						09 55		10 10				
Livingston North d		09 02	09 10					09 32		09 43						09 58		10 13				
Bathgate a		09 06	09 15					09 36		09 48						10 03		10 18				
d		09 08	09 18					09 37		09 49						10 04		10 19				
Armadale d		09 12						09 41								10 08						
Blackridge d		09 16						09 44								10 11						
Caldercruix d		09 22						09 51								10 18						
Drumgelloch d		09 26	09 31					09 54		10 01						10 21		10 31				
Airdrie d		09 29	09 34				09 46	09 58		10 05					10 16	10 26		10 36				10 46
Coatdyke d			09 36				09 48			10 07					10 18			10 38				10 48
Coatbridge Sunnyside d		09 33	09 39				09 51	10 01		10 10					10 21	10 30		10 40				10 51
Blairhill d			09 41				09 53			10 12					10 23			10 43				10 53
Easterhouse d			09 45				09 57			10 16					10 27			10 47				10 57
Garrowhill d			09 48				10 00			10 19					10 30			10 49				11 00
Shettleston d		09 44					10 02	10 13							10 32	10 41						11 02
Carntyne d		09 46					10 04	10 15							10 34	10 43						11 04
Cumbernauld d									09 19													
Greenfaulds d									09 21													
Springburn d					09 54								10 24							10 54		
Barnhill d					09 55								10 25							10 55		
Alexandra Parade d					09 58								10 28							10 58		
Duke Street d					10 00								10 30							11 00		
Bellgrove d		09 50			10 02		10 08	10 20					10 32		10 38	10 47				11 02		11 08
High Street d		09 52	09 55		10 04		10 10	10 22		10 26			10 34		10 40	10 49		10 57		11 04		11 10
Glasgow Queen St LL 10 a		09 54	09 57		10 06		10 12	10 24		10 28			10 36		10 42	10 51		10 59		11 06		11 12
d		09 55	10 00		10 06		10 13	10 24		10 29			10 37		10 45	10 52		11 00		11 07		11 13
Charing Cross d		09 57	10 03		10 09		10 15	10 26		10 32			10 40		10 47	10 55		11 02		11 09		11 15
Argyle Street 225 d	09 48			09 57		10 08			10 22			10 27		10 38			10 52		10 57		11 08	
Glasgow Central LL 15 225 a	09 50			09 59		10 09			10 23			10 28		10 40			10 54		10 58		11 09	
d	09 51			10 03		10 09			10 26			10 32		10 40			10 55		11 03		11 09	
Anderston 225 d	09 52			10 04		10 11			10 27			10 34		10 41			10 56		11 04		11 11	
Exhibition Centre 225 d	09 55			10 06		10 13			10 29			10 36		10 43			10 58		11 06		11 13	
Partick 225 d	09 58	10 01	10 07	10 10	10 13	10 16	10 19	10 30	10 33	10 37		10 40	10 44	10 47	10 51	10 59	11 02	11 06	11 10	11 13	11 16	11 19
Hyndland 3 d	10 01	10 04	10 09	10 12	10 15	10 19	10 22	10 33	10 36	10 40		10 43	10 46	10 49	10 54	11 01	11 04	11 09	11 12	11 16	11 19	11 22
Jordanhill d	10 03				10 17				10 38				10 48				11 06			11 18		
Scotstounhill d	10 05				10 20				10 40				10 51				11 09			11 20		
Garscadden d	10 08				10 22				10 43				10 53				11 11			11 23		
Yoker d	10 10				10 25				10 45				10 56				11 13			11 25		
Clydebank d	10 12				10 27				10 49				10 58				11 15			11 27		
Anniesland d		10 07		10 15		10 22	10 25	10 36				10 48		10 52	10 57	11 06			11 15		11 22	11 25
Westerton d		10 10		10 18		10 25	10 28	10 39				10 51		10 55	11 00	11 10			11 18		11 25	11 28
Bearsden d		10 12				10 27		10 41						10 58		11 13					11 28	
Hillfoot d		10 14				10 29		10 43						11 00		11 15					11 30	
Milngavie a		10 18				10 33		10 47						11 03		11 18					11 33	
Drumchapel d				10 21			10 30					10 53			11 03				11 21			11 31
Drumry d				10 23			10 32					10 55			11 05				11 23			11 33
Singer d				10 25			10 35					10 58			11 07				11 25			11 35
Dalmuir 227 a	10 16		10 19	10 28	10 30		10 37		10 53	10 49		11 00	11 01		11 10		11 19	11 20	11 28	11 30		11 38
d			10 20		10 30		10 38			10 50	10 55		11 02		11 11			11 21		11 31		11 38
Kilpatrick d					10 33								11 04							11 34		
Bowling d					10 36								11 07							11 37		
Dumbarton East d			10 28		10 40		10 46			10 58			11 12		11 18			11 29		11 41		11 46
Dumbarton Central 227 d			10 30		10a43		10 49			11 00	11 05		11a15		11 21			11 31		11a44		11 49
Dalreoch d			10 31				10 50			11 01					11 22			11 32				11 50
Renton d							10 53								11 25							11 53
Alexandria d							10 56								11 28							11 56
Balloch a							11 00								11 32							12 00
Cardross d			10 36							11 06								11 37				
Craigendoran d			10 41							11 12								11 43				
Helensburgh Central a			10 44							11 15								11 46				
Helensburgh Upper 227 a											11 24											

A From Motherwell
B From Larkhall
C From Glasgow Queen Street to Oban
D From Whifflet

Table T226-F

Saturdays
21 December to 16 May

Edinburgh, Bathgate, Airdrie, Cumbernauld and Springburn - Glasgow - Milngavie, Dalmuir, Balloch and Helensburgh

	SR	SR	SR	SR	SR	SR	SR	SR	SR	SR	SR	SR	SR	SR	SR	SR	SR	SR	SR	SR	SR
			A			B		C			C		B			◇ D			A		B
Edinburgh 228,230 d	10 08			10 23					10 41	10 54					11 08			11 19			
Haymarket 228,230 d	10 12			10 27					10 46	10 58					11 12			11 23			
Edinburgh Park 230 d	10 17			10 33					10 50	11 04					11 17			11 28			
Uphall d	10 25			10 41					10 58	11 12					11 26			11 36			
Livingston North d	10 28			10 44					11 02	11 15					11 29			11 39			
Bathgate a	10 33			10 49					11 06	11 20					11 34			11 44			
d	10 35			10 50					11 07	11 20					11 34			11 51			
Armadale d	10 39								11 11						11 38						
Blackridge d	10 42								11 14						11 42						
Caldercruix d	10 49								11 21						11 48						
Drumgelloch d	10 52			11 03					11 24	11 33					11 52			12 03			
Airdrie d	10 56			11 06			11 16		11 28	11 36				11 46	11 56			12 07			
Coatdyke d				11 08			11 18			11 38				11 48				12 09			
Coatbridge Sunnyside d	11 00			11 11			11 21		11 31	11 41				11 51	12 00			12 12			
Blairhill d				11 13			11 23			11 43				11 53				12 14			
Easterhouse d				11 17			11 27			11 47				11 57				12 18			
Garrowhill d				11 20			11 30			11 50				12 00				12 21			
Shettleston d	11 11						11 32		11 43					12 02	12 11						
Carntyne d	11 13						11 34		11 45					12 04	12 13						
Cumbernauld d		10 19															11 19				
Greenfaulds d		10 21															11 21				
Springburn d					11 24							11 54								12 23	
Barnhill d					11 25							11 55								12 24	
Alexandra Parade d					11 28							11 58								12 27	
Duke Street d					11 30							12 00								12 29	
Bellgrove d	11 17				11 32		11 38		11 48			12 02		12 08	12 17					12 31	
High Street d	11 19			11 27	11 34		11 40		11 51	11 57		12 04		12 10	12 19			12 28		12 34	
Glasgow Queen St LL 10 a	11 21			11 29	11 36		11 42		11 53	11 59		12 06		12 12	12 21			12 30		12 36	
d	11 22			11 31	11 37		11 42		11 55	12 00		12 07		12 13	12 22			12 30		12 36	
Charing Cross d	11 25			11 34	11 39		11 45		11 57	12 02		12 10		12 16	12 25			12 33		12 39	
Argyle Street 225 d		11 23	11 26			11 36		11 49			11 57		12 08				12 22		12 27		12 38
Glasgow Central LL 15 225 a		11 24	11 28			11 38		11 50			11 59		12 09				12 23		12 28		12 39
d		11 25	11 28			11 39		11 51			12 02		12 10				12 24		12 33		12 40
Anderston 225 d		11 26	11 30			11 41		11 52			12 04		12 11				12 26		12 34		12 41
Exhibition Centre 225 d		11 28	11 32			11 43		11 55			12 06		12 13				12 28		12 36		12 43
Partick 225 d	11 29	11 32	11 35	11 38	11 43	11 46	11 49	11 58	12 01	12 06	12 10	12 14	12 17	12 20	12 29		12 32	12 37	12 40	12 43	12 47
Hyndland 3 d	11 31	11 34	11 38	11 41	11 46	11 49	11 52	12 01	12 04	12 09	12 12	12 16	12 19	12 23	12 31		12 34	12 39	12 42	12 45	12 49
Jordanhill d		11 36			11 48			12 03				12 18					12 36			12 47	
Scotstounhill d		11 39			11 50			12 05				12 21					12 39			12 50	
Garscadden d		11 41			11 52			12 08				12 23					12 41			12 52	
Yoker d		11 43			11 55			12 10				12 25					12 43			12 55	
Clydebank d		11 45			11 57			12 12				12 27					12 45			12 57	
Anniesland d	11 36		11 44			11 52	11 55		12 07		12 15		12 22	12 26	12 37				12 45		12 52
Westerton d	11 40		11 47			11 55	11 58		12 10		12 18		12 25	12 29	12 41				12 48		12 55
Bearsden d	11 42					11 57			12 12				12 28		12 44						12 58
Hillfoot d	11 44					11 59			12 14				12 30		12 46						13 00
Milngavie a	11 48					12 04			12 18				12 33		12 49						13 03
Drumchapel d			11 50				12 00				12 21			12 31					12 51		
Drumry d			11 52				12 02				12 23			12 33					12 53		
Singer d			11 54				12 05				12 25			12 36					12 55		
Dalmuir 227 a		11 49	11 57	11 52	12 00		12 07	12 16		12 18	12 28	12 31		12 38			12 49	12 50	12 58	13 00	
d				11 53	12 01		12 08			12 19		12 31		12 39		12 43		12 51		13 01	
Kilpatrick d					12 04							12 34								13 04	
Bowling d					12 07							12 37								13 07	
Dumbarton East d				12 01	12 11		12 16			12 28		12 41		12 46				12 58		13 11	
Dumbarton Central 227 d				12 03	12a14		12 19			12 30		12a44		12 48		12 53		13 00		13a14	
Dalreoch d				12 04			12 20			12 32				12 50				13 02			
Renton d							12 23							12 53							
Alexandria d							12 26							12 55							
Balloch a							12 30							13 00							
Cardross d				12 09						12 37								13 07			
Craigendoran d				12 15						12 43								13 13			
Helensburgh Central a				12 18						12 46								13 16			
Helensburgh Upper 227 a																13 05					

A From Whifflet
B From Larkhall
C From Motherwell
D From Glasgow Queen Street to Oban

Table T226-F

Saturdays
21 December to 16 May

Edinburgh, Bathgate, Airdrie, Cumbernauld and Springburn - Glasgow - Milngavie, Dalmuir, Balloch and Helensburgh

		SR	SR	SR A	SR	SR A	SR	SR B	SR	SR	SR	SR	SR C	SR	SR B	SR	SR	SR A	SR	SR A	SR	SR B	SR
Edinburgh 228,230	d		11 37		11 55					12 07		12 22					12 37		12 53				
Haymarket 228,230 ⛴	d		11 42		11 59					12 12		12 27					12 42		12 57				
Edinburgh Park 230	d		11 47		12 05					12 17		12 33					12 46		13 03				
Uphall	d		11 55		12 13					12 25		12 41					12 54		13 11				
Livingston North	d		11 58		12 16					12 29		12 44					12 58		13 14				
Bathgate	a		12 03		12 21					12 33		12 49					13 02		13 19				
	d		12 05		12 21					12 36		12 49					13 05		13 20				
Armadale	d		12 09							12 40							13 09						
Blackridge	d		12 12							12 44							13 12						
Caldercruix	d		12 19							12 50							13 19						
Drumgelloch	d		12 22		12 34					12 54		13 02					13 22		13 33				
Airdrie	d	12 16	12 27		12 37				12 46	12 57		13 06				13 16	13 27		13 36				13 46
Coatdyke	d	12 18			12 39				12 48			13 08				13 18			13 38				13 48
Coatbridge Sunnyside	d	12 21	12 30		12 42				12 51	13 01		13 10				13 21	13 30		13 41				13 51
Blairhill	d	12 23			12 44				12 53			13 13				13 23			13 43				13 53
Easterhouse	d	12 27			12 48				12 57			13 17				13 27			13 47				13 57
Garrowhill	d	12 30			12 51				13 00			13 19				13 30			13 50				14 00
Shettleston	d	12 32	12 42						13 02	13 12						13 32	13 42						14 02
Carntyne	d	12 34	12 44						13 04	13 14						13 34	13 44						14 04
Cumbernauld	d										12 19												
Greenfaulds	d										12 21												
Springburn	d						12 54							13 24							13 54		
Barnhill	d						12 55							13 25							13 55		
Alexandra Parade	d						12 58							13 28							13 58		
Duke Street	d						13 00							13 30							14 00		
Bellgrove	d	12 38	12 47				13 02		13 08	13 18				13 32		13 38	13 47				14 02		14 08
High Street	d	12 40	12 50		12 58		13 04		13 10	13 20		13 27		13 34		13 40	13 50		13 57		14 04		14 10
Glasgow Queen St LL 10 ⛴	a	12 42	12 52		13 00		13 06		13 12	13 22		13 29		13 36		13 42	13 52		13 59		14 06		14 12
	d	12 44	12 52		13 00		13 07		13 14	13 23		13 30		13 37		13 44	13 52		14 00		14 06		14 14
Charing Cross	d	12 46	12 55		13 03		13 09		13 16	13 25		13 32		13 39		13 47	13 55		14 02		14 09		14 16
Argyle Street 225	d			12 51		12 58		13 06			13 22		13 27		13 38			13 52		13 56		14 08	
Glasgow Central LL 15 225	a			12 53		12 59		13 08			13 23		13 28		13 39			13 53		13 57		14 09	
	d			12 55		13 03		13 09			13 25		13 33		13 40			13 54		14 02		14 10	
Anderston 225	d			12 56		13 04		13 11			13 26		13 34		13 41			13 55		14 03		14 11	
Exhibition Centre 225	d			12 58		13 06		13 13			13 28		13 36		13 43			13 58		14 05		14 13	
Partick 225 ⛴	d	12 50	12 59	13 02	13 07	13 10	13 13	13 16	13 20	13 29	13 32	13 36	13 40	13 43	13 47	13 51	13 59	14 02	14 06	14 09	14 13	14 17	14 20
Hyndland 8	d	12 53	13 01	13 04	13 09	13 12	13 16	13 19	13 23	13 32	13 35	13 39	13 42	13 45	13 49	13 53	14 01	14 04	14 09	14 12	14 15	14 19	14 23
Jordanhill	d			13 06			13 18				13 37			13 47				14 06			14 17		
Scotstounhill	d			13 09			13 21				13 39			13 50				14 09			14 20		
Garscadden	d			13 11			13 23				13 41			13 52				14 11			14 22		
Yoker	d			13 13			13 25				13 44			13 55				14 13			14 25		
Clydebank	d			13 15			13 27				13 46			13 57				14 15			14 27		
Anniesland	d	12 56	13 07			13 15		13 22	13 26	13 36			13 45		13 52	13 56	14 06			14 15		14 22	14 26
Westerton	d	12 59	13 10			13 18		13 25	13 29	13 39			13 48		13 55	13 59	14 09			14 18		14 25	14 30
Bearsden	d		13 12					13 27		13 42					13 58		14 11					14 28	
Hillfoot	d		13 14					13 29		13 44					14 00		14 13					14 30	
Milngavie	a		13 18					13 33		13 47					14 03		14 17					14 33	
Drumchapel	d	13 02				13 21			13 32				13 51			14 02				14 20			14 32
Drumry	d	13 04				13 23			13 34				13 53			14 04				14 22			14 34
Singer	d	13 06				13 25			13 36				13 55			14 06				14 25			14 37
Dalmuir 227	a	13 09		13 19	13 19	13 28	13 31		13 39		13 50	13 48	13 58	14 00		14 09		14 19	14 18	14 28	14 30		14 39
	d	13 10			13 20		13 31		13 39			13 49		14 00		14 10			14 19		14 30		14 40
Kilpatrick	d						13 34							14 03							14 33		
Bowling	d						13 37							14 06							14 36		
Dumbarton East	d	13 17			13 28		13 42		13 47			14 00		14 10		14 17			14 28		14 40		14 47
Dumbarton Central 227	d	13 19			13 30		13a45		13 49			14 02		14a13		14 20			14 30		14a43		14 50
Dalreoch	d	13 21			13 31				13 50			14 04				14 21			14 31				14 51
Renton	d	13 24							13 53							14 24							14 54
Alexandria	d	13 26							13 56							14 27							14 57
Balloch	a	13 31							14 00							14 31							15 01
Cardross	d				13 36							14 09							14 36				
Craigendoran	d				13 42							14 14							14 42				
Helensburgh Central	a				13 45							14 17							14 45				
Helensburgh Upper 227	a																						

A From Motherwell B From Larkhall C From Whifflet

Table T226-F

Saturdays
21 December to 16 May

Edinburgh, Bathgate, Airdrie, Cumbernauld and Springburn - Glasgow - Milngavie, Dalmuir, Balloch and Helensburgh

		SR	SR	SR	SR A	SR	SR B	SR	SR	SR C	SR	SR C	SR	SR B	SR	SR	SR	SR	SR A	SR	SR B	SR	SR
Edinburgh 228,230	d	13 07		13 23					13 37		13 52					14 09		14 23					14 37
Haymarket 228,230 ⛴	d	13 11		13 27					13 42		13 57					14 14		14 27					14 42
Edinburgh Park 230	d	13 16		13 32					13 47		14 02					14 19		14 32					14 46
Uphall	d	13 24		13 40					13 55		14 10					14 27		14 40					14 55
Livingston North	d	13 28		13 43					13 59		14 14					14 30		14 44					14 59
Bathgate	a	13 32		13 48					14 03		14 18					14 35		14 48					15 03
	d	13 35		13 49					14 05		14 20					14 36		14 50					15 04
Armadale	d	13 39							14 09							14 40							15 08
Blackridge	d	13 42							14 12							14 43							15 11
Caldercruix	d	13 49							14 19							14 50							15 18
Drumgelloch	d	13 52		14 01					14 22		14 32					14 53		15 03					15 21
Airdrie	d	13 56		14 06				14 16	14 26		14 36				14 46	14 57		15 06				15 16	15 26
Coatdyke	d			14 08				14 18			14 38				14 48			15 08				15 18	
Coatbridge Sunnyside	d	13 59		14 10				14 21	14 29		14 41				14 51	15 00		15 11				15 21	15 29
Blairhill	d			14 13				14 23			14 43				14 53			15 13				15 23	
Easterhouse	d			14 17				14 27			14 47				14 57			15 17				15 27	
Garrowhill	d			14 19				14 30			14 50				15 00			15 20				15 30	
Shettleston	d	14 11						14 32	14 41						15 02	15 12						15 32	15 41
Carntyne	d	14 13						14 34	14 43						15 04	15 14						15 34	15 43
Cumbernauld	d		13 17														14 19						
Greenfaulds	d		13 19														14 21						
Springburn	d					14 24							14 54							15 24			
Barnhill	d					14 25							14 55							15 25			
Alexandra Parade	d					14 28							14 58							15 28			
Duke Street	d					14 30							15 00							15 30			
Bellgrove	d	14 16				14 32		14 38	14 46				15 02		15 08	15 17				15 32		15 38	15 46
High Street	d	14 19		14 27		14 34		14 40	14 49		14 57		15 04		15 10	15 20		15 27		15 34		15 40	15 49
Glasgow Queen St LL 10 ⛴	a	14 21		14 29		14 36		14 42	14 51		14 59		15 06		15 12	15 22		15 29		15 36		15 42	15 51
	d	14 21		14 30		14 37		14 43	14 52		15 00		15 07		15 13	15 22		15 30		15 37		15 43	15 51
Charing Cross	d	14 24		14 32		14 39		14 46	14 54		15 02		15 09		15 16	15 25		15 33		15 39		15 46	15 54
Argyle Street 225	d		14 22		14 27		14 37			14 51		14 55		15 08			15 22		15 26		15 38		
Glasgow Central LL 15 225	a		14 23		14 28		14 39			14 53		14 57		15 09			15 23		15 27		15 39		
	d		14 24		14 33		14 39			14 54		15 03		15 10			15 25		15 32		15 40		
Anderston 225	d		14 26		14 34		14 41			14 55		15 04		15 11			15 26		15 33		15 41		
Exhibition Centre 225	d		14 28		14 36		14 43			14 57		15 06		15 13			15 28		15 36		15 43		
Partick 225 ⛴	d	14 28	14 31	14 36	14 40	14 43	14 46	14 50	14 58	15 01	15 06	15 10	15 13	15 17	15 20	15 29	15 32	15 37	15 40	15 43	15 47	15 50	15 58
Hyndland 8	d	14 30	14 34	14 39	14 42	14 45	14 49	14 52	15 01	15 04	15 09	15 13	15 16	15 19	15 23	15 31	15 34	15 39	15 42	15 46	15 49	15 53	16 00
Jordanhill	d		14 36			14 47				15 06			15 18				15 36			15 48			
Scotstounhill	d		14 38			14 50				15 08			15 20				15 39			15 50			
Garscadden	d		14 40			14 52				15 10			15 23				15 41			15 53			
Yoker	d		14 43			14 55				15 13			15 25				15 44			15 55			
Clydebank	d		14 45			14 57				15 15			15 27				15 46			15 57			
Anniesland	d	14 36			14 45		14 52	14 55	15 06			15 16		15 22	15 26	15 36			15 47		15 52	15 56	16 06
Westerton	d	14 39			14 48		14 55	14 58	15 09			15 19		15 26	15 29	15 39			15 50		15 55	15 59	16 10
Bearsden	d	14 41					14 58		15 11					15 28		15 41					15 58		16 12
Hillfoot	d	14 43					15 00		15 14					15 30		15 43					16 00		16 14
Milngavie	a	14 47					15 03		15 18					15 34		15 47					16 03		16 18
Drumchapel	d				14 51			15 01				15 21			15 31				15 53			16 01	
Drumry	d				14 53			15 03				15 23			15 33				15 55			16 03	
Singer	d				14 55			15 05				15 26			15 36				15 57			16 06	
Dalmuir 227	a		14 49	14 50	14 58	15 00		15 08		15 19	15 19	15 28	15 30		15 38		15 50	15 49	16 00	16 00		16 08	
	d			14 51		15 00		15 08			15 20		15 31		15 39			15 50		16 01		16 09	
Kilpatrick	d					15 03							15 34							16 04			
Bowling	d					15 06							15 37							16 07			
Dumbarton East	d			14 58		15 10		15 17			15 28		15 41		15 47			15 58		16 11		16 17	
Dumbarton Central 227	d			15 00		15a13		15 19			15 30		15a44		15 50			16 00		16a14		16 19	
Dalreoch	d			15 02				15 21			15 31				15 51			16 01				16 21	
Renton	d							15 24							15 54							16 24	
Alexandria	d							15 26							15 57							16 27	
Balloch	a							15 31							16 01							16 31	
Cardross	d			15 07							15 36							16 06					
Craigendoran	d			15 13							15 42							16 11					
Helensburgh Central	a			15 16							15 45							16 15					
Helensburgh Upper 227	a																						

A From Whifflet B From Larkhall C From Motherwell

Table T226-F

Saturdays
21 December to 16 May

Edinburgh, Bathgate, Airdrie, Cumbernauld and Springburn - Glasgow - Milngavie, Dalmuir, Balloch and Helensburgh

		SR	SR	SR	SR	SR	SR	SR	SR	SR	SR	SR	SR	SR	SR	SR	SR	SR	SR	SR	SR	SR
		A		A		B					◇ C 🛏	D		B		A			A		B	
Edinburgh 228,230	d		14 52						15 08	15 22							15 37	15 53				
Haymarket 228,230 ⛴	d		14 57						15 12	15 27							15 41	15 57				
Edinburgh Park 230	d		15 02						15 17	15 32							15 47	16 02				
Uphall	d		15 10						15 25	15 40							15 55	16 10				
Livingston North	d		15 14						15 29	15 43							15 58	16 14				
Bathgate	a		15 18						15 33	15 48							16 03	16 18				
	d		15 20						15 35	15 49							16 04	16 19				
Armadale	d								15 39								16 08					
Blackridge	d								15 42								16 12					
Caldercruix	d								15 49								16 18					
Drumgelloch	d		15 32						15 52	16 01							16 22	16 32				
Airdrie	d		15 36				15 46		15 57	16 07					16 16		16 26	16 36				16 46
Coatdyke	d		15 38				15 48			16 09					16 18			16 38				16 48
Coatbridge Sunnyside	d		15 41				15 51		16 00	16 12					16 21		16 29	16 40				16 51
Blairhill	d		15 43				15 53			16 14					16 23			16 43				16 53
Easterhouse	d		15 47				15 57			16 18					16 27			16 47				16 57
Garrowhill	d		15 50				16 00			16 21					16 30			16 49				17 00
Shettleston	d						16 02		16 12						16 32		16 41					17 02
Carntyne	d						16 04		16 14						16 34		16 43					17 04
Cumbernauld	d							15 19														
Greenfaulds	d							15 21														
Springburn	d				15 54								16 24							16 54		
Barnhill	d				15 55								16 25							16 55		
Alexandra Parade	d				15 58								16 28							16 58		
Duke Street	d				16 00								16 30							17 00		
Bellgrove	d				16 02		16 08		16 17				16 32		16 38		16 46			17 02		17 08
High Street	d		15 57		16 04		16 10		16 20	16 28			16 34		16 40		16 49	16 57		17 04		17 10
Glasgow Queen St LL 10 ⛴	a		15 59		16 06		16 12		16 22	16 30			16 36		16 42		16 51	16 59		17 06		17 12
	d		16 00		16 07		16 12		16 26	16 31			16 37		16 44		16 55	17 00		17 07		17 14
Charing Cross	d		16 03		16 09		16 15		16 29	16 33			16 39		16 47		16 57	17 02		17 09		17 16
Argyle Street 225	d	15 49		15 56		16 07		16 21				16 26		16 38		16 50			16 55		17 08	
Glasgow Central LL 15 225	a	15 50		15 57		16 08		16 23				16 27		16 39		16 51			16 56		17 09	
	d	15 54		16 02		16 09		16 23				16 32		16 39		16 52			17 02		17 10	
Anderston 225	d	15 55		16 04		16 10		16 25				16 34		16 41		16 53			17 04		17 11	
Exhibition Centre 225	d	15 57		16 06		16 13		16 27				16 36		16 43		16 55			17 06		17 13	
Partick 225 ⛴	d	16 01	16 07	16 10	16 13	16 16	16 19	16 30	16 34	16 37		16 40	16 43	16 46	16 51	16 59	17 02	17 07	17 10	17 13	17 17	17 20
Hyndland 3	d	16 04	16 10	16 13	16 16	16 19	16 22	16 33	16 36	16 40		16 43	16 46	16 49	16 56	17 01	17 04	17 09	17 12	17 16	17 19	17 23
Jordanhill	d	16 06			16 18			16 35					16 48			17 03				17 18		
Scotstounhill	d	16 08			16 20			16 37					16 50			17 06				17 20		
Garscadden	d	16 10			16 22			16 39					16 52			17 08				17 22		
Yoker	d	16 13			16 25			16 42					16 55			17 10				17 25		
Clydebank	d	16 15			16 27			16 44					16 57			17 12				17 27		
Anniesland	d			16 16		16 22	16 25		16 39			16 46		16 52	16 59		17 07		17 15		17 22	17 26
Westerton	d			16 19		16 25	16 28		16 42			16 49		16 56	17 02		17 10		17 18		17 25	17 29
Bearsden	d					16 27			16 45					16 58			17 13				17 28	
Hillfoot	d					16 29			16 47					17 00			17 15				17 30	
Milngavie	a					16 33			16 51					17 04			17 18				17 33	
Drumchapel	d			16 21			16 30					16 51			17 04				17 21			17 31
Drumry	d			16 23			16 32					16 53			17 06				17 23			17 33
Singer	d			16 26			16 35					16 56			17 09				17 25			17 36
Dalmuir 227	a	16 19	16 19	16 28	16 30		16 37	16 49		16 51		17 00	17 00		17 11	17 16		17 19	17 28	17 32		17 38
	d		16 20		16 30		16 38			16 52	16 56		17 01		17 12			17 20		17 33		17 39
Kilpatrick	d				16 33								17 03							17 35		
Bowling	d				16 36								17 06							17 38		
Dumbarton East	d		16 28		16 40		16 46			16 59			17 11		17 19			17 28		17 43		17 48
Dumbarton Central 227	d		16 30		16a43		16 49			17 01	17 07		17a14		17 21			17 30		17a46		17 50
Dalreoch	d		16 31				16 50			17 03					17 23			17 32				17 52
Renton	d						16 53								17 26							17 55
Alexandria	d						16 56								17 28							17 57
Balloch	a						17 00								17 32							18 02
Cardross	d		16 36							17 08								17 37				
Craigendoran	d		16 42							17 13								17 42				
Helensburgh Central	a		16 45							17 16								17 45				
Helensburgh Upper 227	a										17 20											

A From Motherwell
B From Larkhall
C From Glasgow Queen Street to Oban
D From Whifflet

NRT DECEMBER 19 EDITION

Table T226-F

Saturdays
21 December to 16 May

Edinburgh, Bathgate, Airdrie, Cumbernauld and Springburn - Glasgow - Milngavie, Dalmuir, Balloch and Helensburgh

		SR	SR	SR	SR	SR	SR	SR	SR	SR	SR	SR	SR	SR	SR	SR	SR	SR	SR	SR	SR	SR	SR
					A		B		C			C		B			◇ D 🛏			A		B	
Edinburgh 228,230	d		16 07	16 24						16 42	16 52					17 07			17 23				
Haymarket 228,230 ⛴	d		16 11	16 28						16 47	16 57					17 12			17 27				
Edinburgh Park 230	d		16 16	16 33						16 52	17 03					17 17			17 32				
Uphall	d		16 25	16 41						17 00	17 11					17 26			17 40				
Livingston North	d		16 29	16 45						17 03	17 15					17 29			17 44				
Bathgate	a		16 33	16 49						17 08	17 20					17 34			17 48				
	d		16 35	16 50						17 08	17 21					17 36			17 49				
Armadale	d		16 39							17 12						17 40							
Blackridge	d		16 42							17 16						17 43							
Caldercruix	d		16 49							17 22						17 50							
Drumgelloch	d		16 52	17 02						17 26	17 33					17 53			18 02				
Airdrie	d		16 58	17 06				17 16		17 29	17 37				17 46	17 57			18 06				18 16
Coatdyke	d			17 08				17 18			17 39				17 48				18 08				18 18
Coatbridge Sunnyside	d		17 01	17 10				17 21		17 33	17 41				17 51	18 00			18 10				18 21
Blairhill	d			17 13				17 23			17 44				17 53				18 13				18 23
Easterhouse	d			17 17				17 27			17 48				17 57				18 17				18 27
Garrowhill	d			17 19				17 30			17 50				18 00				18 19				18 30
Shettleston	d		17 13					17 32		17 44					18 02	18 12							18 32
Carntyne	d		17 15					17 34		17 46					18 04	18 14							18 34
Cumbernauld	d	16 19																17 19					
Greenfaulds	d	16 21																17 21					
Springburn	d					17 24							17 52								18 23		
Barnhill	d					17 25							17 53								18 24		
Alexandra Parade	d					17 28							17 56								18 27		
Duke Street	d					17 30							17 58								18 29		
Bellgrove	d		17 18			17 32		17 38		17 50			18 00		18 08	18 17					18 31		18 38
High Street	d		17 21	17 27		17 34		17 40		17 52	17 58		18 02		18 10	18 20			18 26		18 34		18 40
Glasgow Queen St LL 10 ⛴	a		17 23	17 29		17 36		17 42		17 54	18 00		18 04		18 12	18 22			18 28		18 36		18 42
	d		17 24	17 29		17 37		17 43		17 55	18 00		18 06		18 12	18 22			18 29		18 36		18 44
Charing Cross	d		17 28	17 32		17 39		17 46		17 58	18 03		18 09		18 15	18 25			18 32		18 39		18 47
Argyle Street 225	d	17 19			17 25		17 38		17 49			17 57		18 08				18 22		18 27		18 37	
Glasgow Central LL 15 225	a	17 21			17 26		17 39		17 50			17 58		18 09				18 24		18 28		18 38	
	d	17 21			17 27		17 40		17 51			18 02		18 09				18 26		18 33		18 39	
Anderston 225	d	17 23			17 29		17 41		17 52			18 03		18 11				18 27		18 34		18 40	
Exhibition Centre 225	d	17 25			17 35		17 43		17 55			18 06		18 13				18 29		18 36		18 43	
Partick 225 ⛴	d	17 29	17 32	17 36	17 40	17 43	17 47	17 50	17 58	18 02	18 07	18 10	18 13	18 16	18 19	18 29		18 33	18 36	18 40	18 43	18 47	18 51
Hyndland 3	d	17 31	17 34	17 38	17 42	17 46	17 49	17 52	18 01	18 04	18 09	18 12	18 15	18 19	18 22	18 31		18 36	18 39	18 42	18 45	18 49	18 54
Jordanhill	d	17 33				17 48			18 03				18 17					18 38			18 47		
Scotstounhill	d	17 36				17 50			18 05				18 20					18 40			18 50		
Garscadden	d	17 38				17 53			18 08				18 22					18 42			18 52		
Yoker	d	17 40				17 55			18 10				18 24					18 45			18 55		
Clydebank	d	17 42				17 57			18 12				18 26					18 47			18 57		
Anniesland	d		17 38		17 45		17 52	17 55		18 07		18 15		18 22	18 25	18 36				18 45		18 52	18 57
Westerton	d		17 41		17 48		17 55	17 58		18 10		18 18		18 25	18 28	18 39				18 48		18 55	19 00
Bearsden	d		17 44				17 58			18 13				18 27		18 41						18 58	
Hillfoot	d		17 46				18 00			18 15				18 29		18 43						19 00	
Milngavie	a		17 49				18 03			18 18				18 33		18 47						19 03	
Drumchapel	d				17 51			18 01				18 21			18 31					18 51			19 02
Drumry	d				17 53			18 03				18 23			18 33					18 53			19 04
Singer	d				17 55			18 05				18 25			18 35					18 55			19 07
Dalmuir 227	a	17 46		17 50	17 58	18 00		18 08	18 16		18 19	18 28	18 30		18 38			18 53	18 48	18 58	19 00		19 09
	d			17 51		18 01		18 09			18 20		18 30		18 38		18 42		18 49		19 01		19 10
Kilpatrick	d					18 04							18 33								19 03		
Bowling	d					18 07							18 36								19 06		
Dumbarton East	d			17 58		18 11		18 16			18 28		18 40		18 46				18 56		19 11		19 18
Dumbarton Central 227	d			18 00		18a14		18 19			18 30		18a43		18 48		18 52		18 58		19a14		19 21
Dalreoch	d			18 02				18 20			18 31				18 49				19 00				19 22
Renton	d							18 23							18 52								19 25
Alexandria	d							18 26							18 55								19 28
Balloch	a							18 30							18 59								19 32
Cardross	d			18 07							18 36								19 05				
Craigendoran	d			18 12							18 42								19 10				
Helensburgh Central	a			18 15							18 45								19 13				
Helensburgh Upper 227	a																19 04						

A From Whifflet
B From Larkhall
C From Motherwell
D not 2 May. From Glasgow Queen Street to Oban

Table T226-F

Saturdays

21 December to 16 May

Edinburgh, Bathgate, Airdrie, Cumbernauld and Springburn - Glasgow - Milngavie, Dalmuir, Balloch and Helensburgh

	SR A	SR	SR A	SR	SR	SR B	SR	SR	SR	SR C	SR	SR	SR B	SR	SR A	SR	SR A	SR	SR	SR	SR B
Edinburgh 228,230 d		17 38		17 50				18 08			18 24					18 39		18 52	19 07		
Haymarket 228,230 d		17 42		17 55				18 12			18 28					18 43		18 57	19 11		
Edinburgh Park 230 d		17 47		18 03				18 17			18 33					18 48		19 02	19 17		
Uphall d		17 55		18 11				18 25			18 41					18 56		19 10	19 25		
Livingston North d		17 59		18 14				18 28			18 44					18 59		19 14	19 29		
Bathgate a		18 04		18 19				18 33			18 49					19 04		19 18	19 33		
d		18 05		18 20				18 35			18 50					19 05		19 20			
Armadale d		18 09						18 39								19 09		19 24			
Blackridge d		18 13						18 42								19 12		19 27			
Caldercruix d		18 19						18 49								19 19		19 34			
Drumgelloch d		18 23		18 33				18 52			19 02					19 22		19 37			
Airdrie d		18 28		18 36			18 46	18 58			19 06			19 17		19 28		19 41			
Coatdyke d				18 38			18 48				19 08			19 19							
Coatbridge Sunnyside d		18 31		18 41			18 51	19 01			19 11			19 22		19 31		19 44			
Blairhill d				18 43			18 53				19 13			19 24							
Easterhouse d				18 47			18 57				19 17			19 28							
Garrowhill d				18 50			19 00				19 20			19 31							
Shettleston d		18 43					19 02	19 13						19 33		19 43					
Carntyne d		18 45					19 04	19 15						19 35		19 45					
Cumbernauld d									18 18												
Greenfaulds d									18 20												
Springburn d					18 53							19 24								19 53	
Barnhill d					18 54							19 25								19 54	
Alexandra Parade d					18 57							19 28								19 57	
Duke Street d					18 59							19 30								19 59	
Bellgrove d		18 48			19 01		19 08	19 18				19 32		19 39		19 48				20 01	
High Street d		18 51		18 57	19 03		19 10	19 20			19 28	19 34		19 41		19 51		20 00		20 04	
Glasgow Queen St LL [10] a		18 53		18 59	19 05		19 12	19 22			19 30	19 36		19 43		19 53		20 02		20 06	
d		18 57		19 02	19 07		19 14	19 23			19 33	19 38		19 44		19 54		20 03		20 06	
Charing Cross d		18 59		19 06	19 10		19 17	19 25			19 36	19 40		19 47		19 58		20 05		20 08	
Argyle Street 225 d	18 51		18 57			19 08			19 22	19 26			19 38		19 48		19 55				20 08
Glasgow Central LL [15] 225 a	18 53		18 59			19 09			19 24	19 27			19 39		19 50		19 56				20 09
d	18 53		18 59			19 10			19 24	19 28			19 40		19 51		19 57				20 10
Anderston 225 d	18 55		19 01			19 11			19 26	19 29			19 41		19 52		19 59				20 11
Exhibition Centre 225 d	18 57		19 03			19 13			19 28	19 32			19 44		19 55		20 01				20 13
Partick 225 d	19 00	19 03	19 07	19 10	19 14	19 17	19 21	19 29	19 32	19 35	19 41	19 44	19 48	19 51	19 58	20 02	20 05	20 09		20 12	20 17
Hyndland [3] d	19 03	19 06	19 10	19 13	19 16	19 19	19 23	19 31	19 34	19 38	19 43	19 47	19 50	19 54	20 01	20 04	20 07	20 12		20 15	20 19
Jordanhill d	19 05				19 18				19 36			19 49			20 03					20 17	
Scotstounhill d	19 07				19 21				19 39			19 51			20 05					20 19	
Garscadden d	19 09				19 23				19 41			19 53			20 08					20 22	
Yoker d	19 12				19 26				19 43			19 56			20 10					20 24	
Clydebank d	19 14				19 28				19 45			19 58			20 12					20 26	
Anniesland d		19 09	19 13			19 23	19 26	19 34		19 41			19 53	19 57		20 07	20 10				20 22
Westerton d		19 12	19 16			19 26	19 29	19 40		19 44			19 56	20 00		20 10	20 13				20 25
Bearsden d		19 14				19 28		19 42					19 59			20 13					20 28
Hillfoot d		19 16				19 30		19 44					20 01			20 15					20 30
Milngavie a		19 20				19 34		19 48					20 04			20 18					20 33
Drumchapel d			19 18				19 32			19 46				20 02			20 16				
Drumry d			19 20				19 34			19 48				20 04			20 18				
Singer d			19 23				19 36			19 51				20 07			20 20				
Dalmuir 227 a	19 18		19 25	19 21	19 31		19 39		19 49	19 53	19 52	20 01		20 09	20 16		20 23	20 21		20 29	
d				19 22	19 31		19 40				19 53	20 01		20 10				20 22		20 30	
Kilpatrick d					19 34							20 04								20 33	
Bowling d					19 37							20 07								20 36	
Dumbarton East d				19 30	19 41		19 47				20 01	20 11		20 18				20 30		20 40	
Dumbarton Central 227 d				19 32	19a44		19 50				20 03	20a14		20 21				20 33		20a43	
Dalreoch d				19 33			19 51				20 04			20 22				20 34			
Renton d							19 54							20 25							
Alexandria d							19 57							20 28							
Balloch a							20 01							20 32							
Cardross d				19 38							20 09							20 39			
Craigendoran d				19 44							20 15							20 45			
Helensburgh Central a				19 47							20 18							20 49			
Helensburgh Upper 227 a																					

A From Motherwell B From Larkhall C From Whifflet

Table T226-F

Saturdays

21 December to 16 May

Edinburgh, Bathgate, Airdrie, Cumbernauld and Springburn - Glasgow - Milngavie, Dalmuir, Balloch and Helensburgh

	SR	SR	SR A	SR B	SR	SR	SR	SR C	SR C	SR B	SR	SR	SR	SR	SR A	SR B	SR	SR	SR C	SR C	SR B	SR
Edinburgh 228,230 d						19 22	19 38					19 52	20 08					20 21				
Haymarket 228,230 d						19 27	19 42					19 57	20 12					20 25				
Edinburgh Park 230 d						19 32	19 47					20 03	20 17					20 30				
Uphall d						19 40	19 55					20 11	20 25					20 38				
Livingston North d						19 43	19 58					20 15	20 28					20 42				
Bathgate a						19 48	20 03					20 19	20 33					20 46				
d						19 49						20 20						20 52				
Armadale d						19 53						20 24						20 56				
Blackridge d						19 57						20 27						20 59				
Caldercruix d						20 03						20 34						21 06				
Drumgelloch d						20 07						20 37						21 09				
Airdrie d	19 46					20 17						20 47						21 17				
Coatdyke d	19 48					20 19						20 49						21 19				
Coatbridge Sunnyside d	19 51					20 21						20 51						21 21				
Blairhill d	19 53					20 24						20 54						21 24				
Easterhouse d	19 57					20 28						20 58						21 28				
Garrowhill d	20 00					20 30						21 00						21 30				
Shettleston d	20 02					20 33						21 03						21 33				
Carntyne d	20 04					20 35						21 05						21 35				
Cumbernauld d		19 19												20 19								
Greenfaulds d		19 21												20 21								
Springburn d					20 24						20 54						21 23					21 54
Barnhill d					20 25						20 55						21 24					21 55
Alexandra Parade d					20 28						20 58						21 27					21 58
Duke Street d					20 30						21 00						21 29					22 00
Bellgrove d	20 08				20 32	20 39					21 02	21 08					21 31	21 38				22 02
High Street d	20 10				20 35	20 41					21 04	21 11					21 33	21 41				22 04
Glasgow Queen St LL [10] a	20 12				20 37	20 43					21 06	21 13					21 35	21 43				22 06
d	20 12				20 40	20 48					21 09	21 18					21 39	21 47				22 09
Charing Cross d	20 15				20 45	20 50					21 15	21 21					21 45	21 49				22 15
Argyle Street 225 d		20 22	20 25	20 39				20 52	21 00	21 09				21 21	21 26	21 37			21 50	21 56	22 07	
Glasgow Central LL [15] 225 a		20 23	20 27	20 41				20 54	21 02	21 10				21 22	21 27	21 39			21 51	21 58	22 09	
d		20 24	20 28	20 41				20 54	21 02	21 11				21 23	21 28	21 39			21 52	21 58	22 09	
Anderston 225 d		20 25	20 30	20 43				20 56	21 04	21 12				21 24	21 29	21 41			21 53	22 00	22 11	
Exhibition Centre 225 d		20 27	20 32	20 45				20 58	21 06	21 14				21 26	21 32	21 43			21 55	22 02	22 13	
Partick 225 d	20 20	20 31	20 35	20 48	20 51	20 55		21 01	21 09	21 18	21 21	21 25		21 30	21 35	21 47	21 50	21 53	21 59	22 05	22 16	22 19
Hyndland [3] d	20 22	20 33	20 38	20 51	20 54	20 57		21 04	21 12	21 20	21 23	21 28		21 32	21 38	21 49	21 52	21 56	22 01	22 08	22 19	22 22
Jordanhill d		20 35			20 56			21 06			21 25			21 34			21 54		22 03			22 24
Scotstounhill d		20 38			20 58			21 08			21 28			21 37			21 57		22 05			22 26
Garscadden d		20 40			21 00			21 10			21 30			21 39			21 59		22 07			22 29
Yoker d		20 42			21 03			21 13			21 33			21 41			22 01		22 10			22 32
Clydebank d		20 44			21 05			21 15			21 35			21 43			22 03		22 12			22 34
Anniesland d	20 25		20 41	20 54		21 00			21 15	21 23		21 31			21 41	21 52		21 59		22 11	22 22	
Westerton d	20 28		20 44	20 57		21 03			21 18	21 26		21 34			21 44	21 55		22 02		22 14	22 25	
Bearsden d				20 59						21 29						21 58					22 27	
Hillfoot d				21 01						21 31						22 00					22 29	
Milngavie a				21 05						21 34						22 03					22 33	
Drumchapel d	20 31		20 46			21 06			21 20			21 36			21 46			22 04		22 16		
Drumry d	20 33		20 48			21 08			21 22			21 38			21 48			22 06		22 18		
Singer d	20 35		20 51			21 10			21 25			21 41			21 51			22 09		22 21		
Dalmuir 227 a	20 38	20 48	20 53		21 08	21 13		21 19	21 27		21 38	21 43		21 47	21 53		22 07	22 11	22 16	22 23		22 37
d	20 39				21 09	21 14					21 39	21 44					22 08	22 13				22 37
Kilpatrick d					21 12						21 41						22 10					22 40
Bowling d					21 15						21 44						22 13					22 43
Dumbarton East d	20 47				21 19	21 24					21 49	21 54					22 18	22 23				22 47
Dumbarton Central 227 d	20 51				21 22	21 27					21 51	21 56					22 20	22 25				22 49
Dalreoch d	20 54				21 23	21 29					21 53	21 58					22 22	22 27				22 52
Renton d	20 57				21 26						21 56						22 25					22 55
Alexandria d	21 00				21 29						21 58						22 28					22 57
Balloch a	21 04				21 33						22 03						22 32					23 02
Cardross d						21 34						22 03						22 32				
Craigendoran d						21 40						22 09						22 38				
Helensburgh Central a						21 43						22 13						22 42				
Helensburgh Upper 227 a																						

A From Whifflet B From Larkhall C From Motherwell

Table T226-F

Saturdays

21 December to 16 May

Edinburgh, Bathgate, Airdrie, Cumbernauld and Springburn - Glasgow - Milngavie, Dalmuir, Balloch and Helensburgh

		SR	SR	SR A	SR B	SR	SR	SR C	SR C	SR B	SR	SR	SR	SR A	SR	SR B	SR	SR	SR	SR	SR	SR
Edinburgh 228,230	d	20 54					21 21					21 52					22 22	22 52	23 09	23 39	23 54	
Haymarket 228,230 ⇌	d	20 58					21 26					21 56					22 26	22 56	23 13	23 43	23 58	
Edinburgh Park 230	d	21 03					21 31					22 01					22 31	23 01	23 18	23 48	00 03	
Uphall	d	21 11					21 39					22 09					22 39	23 09	23 26	23 56	00 11	
Livingston North	d	21 14					21 42					22 12					22 42	23 12	23 29	00 01	00 14	
Bathgate	a	21 19					21 47					22 17					22 47	23 17	23 34	00 05	00 19	
	d	21 19					21 49					22 19					22 50	23 17	23 35			
Armadale	d	21 23					21 53					22 23					22 54	23 21	23 39			
Blackridge	d	21 27					21 57					22 27					22 57	23 25	23 42			
Caldercruix	d	21 33					22 03					22 33					23 04	23 31	23 49			
Drumgelloch	d	21 37					22 07					22 37					23 07	23 35	23 52			
Airdrie	d	21 47					22 17					22 47					23 17	23 39	23a55			
Coatdyke	d	21 49					22 19					22 49					23 20	23 41				
Coatbridge Sunnyside	d	21 51					22 21					22 51					23 24	23 43				
Blairhill	d	21 54					22 24					22 54					23 27	23 46				
Easterhouse	d	21 58					22 28					22 58					23 32	23 50				
Garrowhill	d	22 00					22 30					23 00					23 36	23 52				
Shettleston	d	22 03					22 33					23 03					23 39	23 55				
Carntyne	d	22 05					22 35					23 05					23 42	23 57				
Cumbernauld	d		21 21										22 21									
Greenfaulds	d		21 23										22 23									
Springburn	d					22 27					22 54				23 24							23 54
Barnhill	d					22 28					22 55				23 25							23 55
Alexandra Parade	d					22 31					22 58				23 28							23 58
Duke Street	d					22 33					23 00				23 30							00 03
Bellgrove	d	22 08				22 35	22 39				23 02	23 08			23 32		23 47	00 01				00 05
High Street	d	22 11				22 37	22 42				23 04	23 11			23 34		23 50	00 02				00 07
Glasgow Queen St LL 10 ⇌	a	22 13				22 39	22 44				23 06	23 13			23 36		23 52	00 04				00 09
	d	22 17				22 41	22 47				23 09	23 17			23 37		23 54	00 05				00 10
Charing Cross	d	22 20				22 46	22 50				23 15	23 20			23 39		23 57	00 07				00 12
Argyle Street 225	d		22 20	22 26	22 38			22 49	22 53	23 07			23 23	23 26		23 38						
Glasgow Central LL 15 225	a		22 22	22 27	22 39			22 51	22 54	23 08			23 24	23 28		23 39						
	d		22 22	22 28	22 39			22 51	22 57	23 09			23 25	23 28		23 40						
Anderston 225	d		22 24	22 29	22 41			22 53	22 58	23 10			23 26	23 30		23 41						
Exhibition Centre 225	d		22 26	22 32	22 43			22 55	23 01	23 12			23 28	23 32		23 43						
Partick 225 ⇌	d	22 24	22 29	22 35	22 46	22 50	22 54	22 58	23 04	23 16	23 19	23 24	23 32	23 35	23 43	23 47	00 02	00 11				00 16
Hyndland 3	d	22 26	22 32	22 38	22 49	22 52	22 56	23 01	23 07	23 18	23 22	23 26	23 34	23 38	23 46	23 49	00 03	00 13				00 19
Jordanhill	d		22 34			22 54		23 03			23 24		23 36		23 48							00 24
Scotstounhill	d		22 36			22 57		23 05			23 26		23 39		23 50							00 26
Garscadden	d		22 38			22 59		23 08			23 29		23a41		23 53			00a17				00a28
Yoker	d		22 41			23 02		23 10			23 31				23 55							
Clydebank	d		22 43			23 04		23 12			23 34				23 57							
Anniesland	d	22 29		22 41	22 52		22 59		23 10	23 21		23 29		23 41		23 52	00 06					
Westerton	d	22 32		22 44	22 55		23 02		23 13	23 24		23 32		23 44		23 55	00 09					
Bearsden	d				22 57					23 27						23 58						
Hillfoot	d				22 59					23 29						23 59						
Milngavie	a				23 03					23 33						00 03						
Drumchapel	d	22 35		22 46			23 05		23 15			23 35		23 46			00 12					
Drumry	d	22 37		22 48			23 07		23 17			23 37		23 48			00 14					
Singer	d	22 39		22 51			23 09		23 20			23 39		23 51			00 16					
Dalmuir 227	a	22 42	22 47	22 53		23 07	23 12	23 16	23 22		23 37	23 42		23 53	23 58		00 19					
	d	22 43				23 08	23 13				23 37	23 43			23 59		00 20					
Kilpatrick	d					23 10					23 39				00 03							
Bowling	d					23 13					23 42				00 06							
Dumbarton East	d	22 52				23 18	23 22				23 47	23 52			00 11		00 28					
Dumbarton Central 227	d	22 54				23 20	23 24				23 49	23 54			00 13		00 31					
Dalreoch	d	22 56				23 22	23 26				23 52	23 56			00 15		00 32					
Renton	d					23 25					23 55				00 18							
Alexandria	d					23 27					23 57				00 20							
Balloch	a					23 32					00 02				00 24							
Cardross	d	23 01					23 31					00 01					00 37					
Craigendoran	d	23 08					23 38					00 07					00 42					
Helensburgh Central	a	23 12					23 42					00 11					00 46					
Helensburgh Upper 227	a																					

A From Whifflet
B From Larkhall
C From Motherwell

Table T226-F

Sundays

15 December to 10 May

Edinburgh, Bathgate, Airdrie, Cumbernauld and Springburn - Glasgow - Milngavie, Dalmuir, Balloch and Helensburgh

		SR A	SR A	SR B	SR A	SR A	SR A	SR B	SR	SR	SR	SR	SR C	SR C	SR	SR C	SR D	SR ◇ E 🍴	SR	SR C	SR C	SR	SR C
Edinburgh 228,230	d																		08 38			09 05	
Haymarket 228,230 ⇌	d																		08 42			09 09	
Edinburgh Park 230	d						00 03												08 48			09 16	
Uphall	d						00 11												09 01			09 29	
Livingston North	d		00 01				00 14												09 04			09 32	
Bathgate	a		00 05				00 19												09 09			09 37	
	d											08 06							09 09			09 37	
Armadale	d											08 10							09 13			09 41	
Blackridge	d											08 14							09 17			09 45	
Caldercruix	d											08 20							09 23			09 51	
Drumgelloch	d											08 24							09 27			09 55	
Airdrie	d									07 57		08 27			08 57				09 30			09 58	
Coatdyke	d									07 59		08 29			08 59				09 32			10 00	
Coatbridge Sunnyside	d									08 02		08 32			09 02				09 35			10 03	
Blairhill	d									08 05		08 35			09 05				09 37			10 06	
Easterhouse	d									08 09		08 39			09 09				09 41			10 10	
Garrowhill	d									08 11		08 41			09 11				09 44			10 12	
Shettleston	d									08 14		08 44			09 14				09 46			10 15	
Carntyne	d									08 16		08 46			09 16				09 48			10 17	
Cumbernauld	d																						
Greenfaulds	d																						
Springburn	d																						
Barnhill	d																						
Alexandra Parade	d																						
Duke Street	d							00 03															
Bellgrove	d					00 01		00 05		08 19		08 49			09 19				09 52			10 20	
High Street	d					00 02		00 07		08 21		08 51			09 21				09 54			10 22	
Glasgow Queen St LL 10 ⇌	a					00 04		00 09		08 23		08 53			09 23				09 56			10 24	
	d					00 05		00 10		08 24		08 54			09 24				09 56			10 25	
Charing Cross	d					00 07		00 12		08 27		08 57			09 27				09 58			10 27	
Argyle Street 225	d																			09 58	10 14		10 28
Glasgow Central LL 15 225	a																			09 59	10 16		10 29
	d												09 04	09 15		09 34	09 45			10 04	10 16		10 34
Anderston 225	d																			10 05	10 18		10 35
Exhibition Centre 225	d												09 08	09 18		09 38	09 48			10 07	10 20		10 37
Partick 225 ⇌	d				00 02	00 11		00 16		08 31		09 01	09 12	09 22	09 31	09 42	09 52		10 02	10 12	10 23	10 31	10 42
Hyndland 3	d				00 03	00 13		00 19		08 34		09 04	09 16	09 24	09 34	09 45	09 54		10 05	10 15	10 25	10 34	10 45
Jordanhill	d							00 24						09 26			09 56				10 27		
Scotstounhill	d							00 26						09 29			09 59				10 30		
Garscadden	d					00a17		00a28						09 31			10 01				10 32		
Yoker	d								08 34		09 04			09 34			10 04				10 34		
Clydebank	d								08 36		09 06			09 36			10 06				10 36		
Anniesland	d				00 06					08 37		09 07	09 19		09 37	09 48			10 08	10 18		10 37	10 48
Westerton	d				00 09					08 40		09 10	09 22		09 40	09 51			10 11	10 21		10 40	10 51
Bearsden	d												09 25			09 55				10 25			10 55
Hillfoot	d												09 27			09 57				10 27			10 57
Milngavie	a												09 30			10 00				10 30			11 00
Drumchapel	d				00 12					08 42		09 12			09 42				10 13			10 42	
Drumry	d				00 14					08 44		09 14			09 44				10 15			10 44	
Singer	d				00 16					08 47		09 17			09 47				10 18			10 47	
Dalmuir 227	a				00 19				08 39	08 49	09 09	09 19		09 39	09 49		10 09		10 20		10 39	10 49	
	d				00 20				08 40	08 50	09 10	09 20		09 40	09 50		10 10	10 16	10 21		10 40	10 50	
Kilpatrick	d			00 03					08 42		09 12			09 42			10 12				10 43		
Bowling	d			00 06					08 45		09 15			09 45			10 15				10 46		
Dumbarton East	d			00 11	00 28				08 50	08 58	09 20	09 28		09 50	09 58		10 20		10 28		10 50	10 58	
Dumbarton Central 227	d			00 13	00 31				08 52	09 00	09 22	09 30		09 52	10 00		10 22	10 26	10 30		10 52	11 00	
Dalreoch	d			00 15	00 32				08 53	09 01	09 23	09 31		09 53	10 01		10 23		10 32		10 54	11 01	
Renton	d			00 18					08 56		09 26			09 56			10 26				10 57		
Alexandria	d			00 20					08 59		09 29			09 59			10 29				10 59		
Balloch	a			00 24					09 03		09 33			10 03			10 33				11 03		
Cardross	d	00 01			00 37					09 06		09 36			10 06				10 37			11 06	
Craigendoran	d	00 07			00 42					09 11		09 41			10 11				10 42			11 11	
Helensburgh Central	a	00 11			00 46					09 15		09 45			10 15				10 46			11 15	
Helensburgh Upper 227	a																	10 38					

A not 15 December. From Edinburgh
B not 15 December. From Springburn
C From Motherwell
D From Larkhall. Forms tight booked connection out of 2C26.
E From Glasgow Queen Street to Oban

Table T226-F

Sundays

15 December to 10 May

Edinburgh, Bathgate, Airdrie, Cumbernauld and Springburn - Glasgow - Milngavie, Dalmuir, Balloch and Helensburgh

		SR A	SR	SR B	SR B	SR	SR B	SR C	SR	SR B	SR ◇ D ⌶	SR B	SR	SR B	SR E	SR	SR B	SR B	SR	SR B	SR F	SR	SR B
Edinburgh 228,230	d		09 38			10 06			10 40				11 10			11 40			12 09			12 41	
Haymarket 228,230 ⇌	d		09 42			10 10			10 44				11 14			11 44			12 13			12 45	
Edinburgh Park 230	d		09 48			10 15			10 49				11 19			11 49			12 19			12 50	
Uphall	d		10 01			10 28			10 57				11 27			11 57			12 27			12 58	
Livingston North	d		10 04			10 31			11 00				11 30			12 00			12 30			13 01	
Bathgate	a		10 09			10 36			11 05				11 35			12 05			12 35			13 06	
	d		10 09			10 36			11 06				11 36			12 06			12 37			13 06	
Armadale	d		10 13			10 40			11 10				11 40			12 10			12 41			13 10	
Blackridge	d		10 17			10 44			11 14				11 44			12 14			12 44			13 14	
Caldercruix	d		10 23			10 50			11 20				11 50			12 20			12 51			13 20	
Drumgelloch	d		10 27			10 54			11 24				11 54			12 24			12 54			13 24	
Airdrie	d		10 30			10 57			11 27				11 57			12 27			12 58			13 27	
Coatdyke	d		10 32			10 59			11 29				11 59			12 29			13 00			13 29	
Coatbridge Sunnyside	d		10 35			11 02			11 32				12 02			12 32			13 03			13 32	
Blairhill	d		10 37			11 05			11 35				12 05			12 35			13 05			13 35	
Easterhouse	d		10 41			11 09			11 39				12 09			12 39			13 09			13 39	
Garrowhill	d		10 44			11 11			11 41				12 11			12 41			13 12			13 41	
Shettleston	d		10 46			11 14			11 44				12 14			12 44			13 14			13 44	
Carntyne	d		10 48			11 16			11 46				12 16			12 46			13 16			13 46	
Cumbernauld	d																						
Greenfaulds	d																						
Springburn	d																						
Barnhill	d																						
Alexandra Parade	d																						
Duke Street	d																						
Bellgrove	d		10 52			11 19			11 49				12 19			12 49			13 20			13 49	
High Street	d		10 54			11 21			11 51				12 21			12 51			13 22			13 51	
Glasgow Queen St LL 10 ⇌	a		10 56			11 23			11 53				12 23			12 53			13 24			13 53	
	d		10 56			11 24			11 54				12 24			12 54			13 24			13 54	
Charing Cross	d		10 58			11 27			11 57				12 27			12 57			13 27			13 57	
Argyle Street 225	d	10 43		10 58	11 14		11 30	11 43		11 58		12 15		12 28	12 43		12 59	13 14		13 32	13 43		13 58
Glasgow Central LL 15 225	a	10 44		10 59	11 15		11 31	11 44		12 00		12 16		12 29	12 44		13 00	13 16		13 33	13 44		13 59
	d	10 45		11 04	11 16		11 34	11 45		12 04		12 16		12 34	12 45		13 04	13 16		13 34	13 45		14 04
Anderston 225	d	10 46		11 06	11 17		11 35	11 46		12 05		12 18		12 35	12 46		13 05	13 18		13 35	13 46		14 06
Exhibition Centre 225	d	10 48		11 08	11 19		11 37	11 48		12 07		12 20		12 37	12 48		13 07	13 20		13 37	13 48		14 08
Partick 225 ⇌	d	10 52	11 02	11 12	11 23	11 32	11 42	11 52	12 01	12 12		12 23	12 31	12 42	12 52	13 01	13 12	13 23	13 31	13 42	13 52	14 01	14 12
Hyndland 3	d	10 54	11 05	11 15	11 25	11 34	11 45	11 54	12 04	12 15		12 25	12 34	12 45	12 54	13 04	13 15	13 25	13 34	13 45	13 54	14 04	14 15
Jordanhill	d	10 56			11 27			11 56				12 27			12 56			13 27			13 56		
Scotstounhill	d	10 59			11 29			11 59				12 30			12 59			13 30			13 59		
Garscadden	d	11 01			11 31			12 01				12 32			13 01			13 32			14 01		
Yoker	d	11 04			11 34			12 04				12 34			13 04			13 34			14 04		
Clydebank	d	11 06			11 36			12 06				12 36			13 06			13 36			14 06		
Anniesland	d		11 08	11 18		11 37	11 48		12 07	12 18			12 37	12 48		13 07	13 18		13 37	13 48		14 07	14 18
Westerton	d		11 11	11 21		11 40	11 51		12 10	12 21			12 40	12 51		13 10	13 21		13 40	13 51		14 10	14 21
Bearsden	d			11 25			11 55			12 25				12 55			13 25			13 55			14 25
Hillfoot	d			11 27			11 57			12 27				12 57			13 27			13 57			14 27
Milngavie	a			11 30			12 00			12 30				13 00			13 30			14 00			14 30
Drumchapel	d		11 13			11 42			12 12				12 42			13 12			13 42			14 12	
Drumry	d		11 15			11 44			12 14				12 44			13 14			13 44			14 14	
Singer	d		11 18			11 47			12 17				12 47			13 17			13 47			14 17	
Dalmuir 227	a	11 09	11 20		11 39	11 49		12 09	12 19			12 39	12 49		13 09	13 19		13 39	13 49		14 09	14 19	
	d	11 10	11 21		11 40	11 50		12 10	12 20		12 34	12 40	12 50		13 10	13 20		13 40	13 50		14 10	14 20	
Kilpatrick	d	11 12			11 42			12 12				12 43			13 12			13 43			14 12		
Bowling	d	11 15			11 45			12 15				12 46			13 15			13 46			14 15		
Dumbarton East	d	11 20	11 29		11 50	11 58		12 20	12 28			12 50	12 58		13 20	13 28		13 50	13 58		14 20	14 28	
Dumbarton Central 227	d	11 22	11 31		11 52	12 00		12 22	12 30		12 47	12 52	13 00		13 22	13 30		13 52	14 00		14 22	14 30	
Dalreoch	d	11 23	11 32		11 53	12 01		12 23	12 31			12 54	13 01		13 23	13 31		13 54	14 01		14 23	14 31	
Renton	d	11 26			11 56			12 26				12 57			13 26			13 57			14 26		
Alexandria	d	11 29			11 59			12 29				12 59			13 29			13 59			14 29		
Balloch	a	11 33			12 03			12 33				13 03			13 33			14 03			14 33		
Cardross	d		11 37			12 06			12 36				13 06			13 36			14 06			14 36	
Craigendoran	d		11 42			12 11			12 41				13 11			13 41			14 11			14 41	
Helensburgh Central	a		11 46			12 15			12 45				13 15			13 45			14 15			14 45	
Helensburgh Upper 227	a										12 59												

A From Larkhall. Forms tight booked connection out of 2C54.
B From Motherwell
C From Larkhall. Forms tight booked connection out of 2C56.
D From Glasgow Queen Street to Oban
E From Larkhall. Forms tight booked connection out of 2C58.
F From Larkhall. Forms tight booked connection out of 2C48.

Table T226-F

Sundays

15 December to 10 May

Edinburgh, Bathgate, Airdrie, Cumbernauld and Springburn - Glasgow - Milngavie, Dalmuir, Balloch and Helensburgh

		SR A	SR	SR A	SR B	SR	SR A	SR A	SR	SR A	SR C	SR	SR A	SR A	SR	SR A	SR D	SR	SR A	SR A	SR	SR A
Edinburgh 228,230	d		13 09			13 40			14 09			14 41			15 10			15 40			16 09	
Haymarket 228,230 ⇌	d		13 14			13 46			14 13			14 45			15 15			15 44			16 14	
Edinburgh Park 230	d		13 19			13 50			14 20			14 50			15 21			15 49			16 19	
Uphall	d		13 28			13 58			14 28			14 58			15 29			15 57			16 27	
Livingston North	d		13 31			14 02			14 32			15 01			15 32			16 00			16 31	
Bathgate	a		13 36			14 06			14 36			15 06			15 37			16 05			16 35	
	d		13 36			14 06			14 37			15 06			15 37			16 06			16 38	
Armadale	d		13 40			14 10			14 41			15 10			15 41			16 10			16 42	
Blackridge	d		13 44			14 14			14 45			15 14			15 44			16 14			16 45	
Caldercruix	d		13 50			14 20			14 51			15 20			15 51			16 20			16 52	
Drumgelloch	d		13 54			14 24			14 55			15 24			15 54			16 24			16 55	
Airdrie	d		13 57			14 27			14 58			15 27			15 58			16 27			16 59	
Coatdyke	d		13 59			14 29			15 00			15 29			16 00			16 29			17 01	
Coatbridge Sunnyside	d		14 02			14 32			15 03			15 32			16 03			16 32			17 03	
Blairhill	d		14 05			14 35			15 05			15 35			16 05			16 35			17 06	
Easterhouse	d		14 09			14 39			15 09			15 39			16 09			16 39			17 10	
Garrowhill	d		14 11			14 41			15 12			15 41			16 12			16 41			17 12	
Shettleston	d		14 14			14 44			15 14			15 44			16 14			16 44			17 15	
Carntyne	d		14 16			14 46			15 16			15 46			16 16			16 46			17 17	
Cumbernauld	d																					
Greenfaulds	d																					
Springburn	d																					
Barnhill	d																					
Alexandra Parade	d																					
Duke Street	d																					
Bellgrove	d		14 19			14 49			15 20			15 49			16 20			16 49			17 20	
High Street	d		14 21			14 51			15 22			15 51			16 22			16 51			17 22	
Glasgow Queen St LL 10 ⇌	a		14 23			14 53			15 24			15 53			16 24			16 53			17 24	
	d		14 24			14 54			15 24			15 54			16 24			16 54			17 25	
Charing Cross	d		14 27			14 57			15 27			15 57			16 27			16 57			17 27	
Argyle Street 225	d	14 16		14 31	14 44		14 58	15 14		15 28	15 43		15 58	16 16		16 32	16 43		16 58	17 14		17 28
Glasgow Central LL 15 225	a	14 18		14 33	14 45		14 59	15 16		15 29	15 44		16 00	16 17		16 34	16 44		16 59	17 15		17 29
	d	14 18		14 34	14 46		15 04	15 16		15 34	15 45		16 04	16 17		16 34	16 46		17 04	17 16		17 34
Anderston 225	d	14 19		14 36	14 47		15 05	15 18		15 35	15 46		16 05	16 19		16 36	16 47		17 06	17 17		17 35
Exhibition Centre 225	d	14 21		14 38	14 49		15 07	15 20		15 37	15 48		16 07	16 21		16 38	16 49		17 08	17 19		17 37
Partick 225 ⇌	d	14 25	14 31	14 42	14 53	15 01	15 12	15 23	15 31	15 42	15 52	16 01	16 12	16 24	16 31	16 42	16 53	17 01	17 12	17 23	17 31	17 42
Hyndland 3	d	14 27	14 34	14 45	14 55	15 04	15 15	15 25	15 34	15 45	15 54	16 04	16 15	16 26	16 34	16 45	16 55	17 04	17 15	17 25	17 34	17 45
Jordanhill	d	14 29			14 57			15 27			15 56			16 28			16 57			17 27		
Scotstounhill	d	14 31			15 00			15 30			15 59			16 31			17 00			17 29		
Garscadden	d	14 33			15 02			15 32			16 01			16 33			17 02			17 31		
Yoker	d	14 36			15 05			15 35			16 04			16 35			17 05			17 34		
Clydebank	d	14 38			15 07			15 37			16 06			16 37			17 07			17 36		
Anniesland	d		14 37	14 48		15 07	15 18		15 37	15 48		16 07	16 18		16 37	16 48		17 07	17 18		17 37	17 48
Westerton	d		14 40	14 51		15 10	15 21		15 40	15 51		16 10	16 21		16 40	16 51		17 10	17 21		17 40	17 51
Bearsden	d			14 55			15 25			15 55			16 25			16 55			17 25			17 55
Hillfoot	d			14 57			15 27			15 57			16 27			16 57			17 27			17 57
Milngavie	a			15 00			15 30			16 00			16 30			17 00			17 30			18 00
Drumchapel	d		14 42			15 12			15 42			16 12			16 42			17 12			17 42	
Drumry	d		14 44			15 14			15 44			16 14			16 44			17 14			17 44	
Singer	d		14 47			15 17			15 47			16 17			16 47			17 17			17 47	
Dalmuir 227	a	14 41	14 49		15 10	15 19		15 40	15 49		16 09	16 19		16 40	16 49		17 10	17 19		17 39	17 49	
	d	14 41	14 50		15 11	15 20		15 41	15 50		16 10	16 20		16 40	16 50		17 11	17 20		17 40	17 50	
Kilpatrick	d	14 43			15 13			15 43			16 12			16 43			17 13			17 42		
Bowling	d	14 46			15 16			15 46			16 15			16 46			17 16			17 45		
Dumbarton East	d	14 51	14 58		15 21	15 28		15 51	15 58		16 20	16 28		16 50	16 58		17 21	17 28		17 50	17 58	
Dumbarton Central 227	d	14 53	15 00		15 23	15 30		15 53	16 00		16 22	16 30		16 52	17 00		17 23	17 30		17 52	18 00	
Dalreoch	d	14 54	15 01		15 24	15 31		15 54	16 01		16 23	16 31		16 54	17 01		17 24	17 31		17 53	18 01	
Renton	d	14 57			15 27			15 57			16 26			16 57			17 27			17 56		
Alexandria	d	15 00			15 30			16 00			16 29			16 59			17 30			17 59		
Balloch	a	15 03			15 34			16 03			16 33			17 03			17 34			18 03		
Cardross	d		15 06			15 36			16 06			16 36			17 06			17 36			18 06	
Craigendoran	d		15 11			15 41			16 11			16 41			17 11			17 41			18 11	
Helensburgh Central	a		15 15			15 45			16 15			16 45			17 15			17 45			18 15	
Helensburgh Upper 227	a																					

A From Motherwell
B From Larkhall. Forms tight booked connection out of 2C50.
C From Larkhall. Forms tight booked connection out of 2C52.
D From Larkhall. Forms tight booked connection out of 2C54.

Table T226-F

Sundays
15 December to 10 May

Edinburgh, Bathgate, Airdrie, Cumbernauld and Springburn - Glasgow - Milngavie, Dalmuir, Balloch and Helensburgh

	SR	SR	SR	SR	SR	SR	SR	SR	SR	SR	SR	SR	SR	SR	SR	SR	SR	SR	SR	SR	SR	SR
	A		B	◇ C	B		B	D		B	B		B	E			F	B		B	G	
Edinburgh 228,230 d		16 40				17 10			17 40			18 09			18 40	19 10						19 40
Haymarket 228,230 d		16 44				17 14			17 44			18 13			18 44	19 14						19 44
Edinburgh Park 230 d		16 49				17 20			17 49			18 20			18 49	19 19						19 49
Uphall d		16 58				17 28			17 57			18 28			18 57	19 27						19 57
Livingston North d		17 01				17 31			18 00			18 31			19 00	19 30						20 00
Bathgate a		17 06				17 36			18 05			18 36			19 05	19 35						20 05
d		17 06				17 36			18 06			18 36			19 06							20 06
Armadale d		17 10				17 40			18 10			18 40			19 10							20 10
Blackridge d		17 14				17 44			18 14			18 44			19 14							20 14
Caldercruix d		17 20				17 50			18 20			18 50			19 20							20 20
Drumgelloch d		17 24				17 54			18 24			18 54			19 24							20 24
Airdrie d		17 27				17 57			18 27			18 57			19 27				19 57			20 27
Coatdyke d		17 29				17 59			18 29			18 59			19 29				19 59			20 29
Coatbridge Sunnyside d		17 32				18 02			18 32			19 02			19 32				20 02			20 32
Blairhill d		17 35				18 05			18 35			19 05			19 35				20 05			20 35
Easterhouse d		17 39				18 09			18 39			19 09			19 39				20 09			20 39
Garrowhill d		17 41				18 11			18 41			19 11			19 41				20 11			20 41
Shettleston d		17 44				18 14			18 44			19 14			19 44				20 14			20 44
Carntyne d		17 46				18 16			18 46			19 16			19 46				20 16			20 46
Cumbernauld d																						
Greenfaulds d																						
Springburn d																						
Barnhill d																						
Alexandra Parade d																						
Duke Street d																						
Bellgrove d		17 49				18 19			18 49			19 19			19 49				20 19			20 49
High Street d		17 51				18 21			18 51			19 21			19 51				20 21			20 51
Glasgow Queen St LL 10 a		17 53				18 23			18 53			19 23			19 53				20 23			20 53
d		17 54				18 24			18 54			19 24			19 54				20 24			20 54
Charing Cross d		17 57				18 27			18 57			19 27			19 57				20 27			20 57
Argyle Street 225 d	17 43		17 58		18 14																	
Glasgow Central LL 15 225 a	17 44		17 59		18 15																	
d	17 45		18 04		18 16		18 34	18 46		19 04	19 15		19 34	19 45			20 04	20 15		20 34	20 46	
Anderston 225 d	17 46		18 05		18 17																	
Exhibition Centre 225 d	17 48		18 07		18 19		18 38	18 49		19 08	19 18		19 38	19 48			20 08	20 18		20 38	20 49	
Partick 225 d	17 52	18 01	18 12		18 23	18 31	18 42	18 53	19 01	19 12	19 22	19 31	19 42	19 52	20 01		20 12	20 22	20 31	20 42	20 53	21 01
Hyndland 3 d	17 54	18 04	18 15		18 25	18 34	18 45	18 55	19 04	19 17	19 24	19 34	19 45	19 54	20 04		20 15	20 24	20 34	20 45	20 55	21 04
Jordanhill d	17 56				18 27			18 57			19 26			19 56				20 26			20 57	
Scotstounhill d	17 59				18 29			19 00			19 29			19 59				20 29			20 59	
Garscadden d	18 01				18 31			19 02			19 31			20 01				20 31			21 01	
Yoker d	18 04				18 34			19 05			19 34			20 04				20 34			21 04	
Clydebank d	18 06				18 36			19 07			19 36			20 06				20 36			21 06	
Anniesland d		18 07	18 18			18 37	18 48		19 07	19 20		19 37	19 48		20 07		20 18		20 37	20 48		21 11
Westerton d		18 10	18 21			18 40	18 51		19 10	19 23		19 40	19 51		20 10		20 21		20 40	20 51		21 14
Bearsden d			18 25				18 55			19 25			19 55				20 25			20 55		
Hillfoot d			18 27				18 57			19 27			19 57				20 27			20 57		
Milngavie a			18 30				19 00			19 31			20 00				20 30			21 00		
Drumchapel d		18 12				18 42			19 12			19 42			20 12				20 42			21 16
Drumry d		18 14				18 44			19 14			19 44			20 14				20 44			21 18
Singer d		18 17				18 47			19 17			19 47			20 17				20 47			21 21
Dalmuir 227 a	18 09	18 19			18 39	18 49		19 10	19 19		19 39	19 49		20 09	20 19			20 39	20 49		21 09	21 23
d	18 10	18 20		18 36	18 40	18 50		19 11	19 20		19 40	19 50		20 10	20 20			20 40	20 50		21 10	21 23
Kilpatrick d	18 12				18 42			19 13			19 42			20 12				20 42			21 12	
Bowling d	18 15				18 45			19 16			19 45			20 15				20 45			21 15	
Dumbarton East d	18 20	18 28			18 50	18 58		19 21	19 28		19 50	19 58		20 20	20 28			20 50	20 58		21 20	21 31
Dumbarton Central 227 d	18 22	18 30		18 47	18 52	19 00		19 23	19 30		19 52	20 00		20 22	20 30			20 52	21 00		21 22	21 33
Dalreoch d	18 23	18 31			18 53	19 01		19 24	19 31		19 53	20 01		20 23	20 31			20 53	21 01		21 23	21 34
Renton d	18 26				18 56			19 27			19 56			20 26				20 56			21 26	
Alexandria d	18 29				18 59			19 30			19 59			20 29				20 59			21 29	
Balloch a	18 33				19 03			19 34			20 03			20 33				21 03			21 33	
Cardross d		18 36				19 06			19 36			20 06			20 36				21 06			21 39
Craigendoran d		18 41				19 11			19 41			20 11			20 41				21 11			21 44
Helensburgh Central a		18 45				19 15			19 45			20 15			20 45				21 15			21 48
Helensburgh Upper 227 a				18 59																		

A From Larkhall. Forms tight booked connection out of 2C56.
B From Motherwell
C From Glasgow Queen Street to Oban
D From Larkhall. Forms tight booked connection out of 2C58.
E From Larkhall. Forms tight booked connection out of 2C48.
F From Motherwell to Milngavie continues to Motherwell
G From Larkhall. Forms tight booked connection out of 2C50.

Table T226-F

Sundays
15 December to 10 May

Edinburgh, Bathgate, Airdrie, Cumbernauld and Springburn - Glasgow - Milngavie, Dalmuir, Balloch and Helensburgh

	SR	SR	SR	SR	SR	SR	SR	SR	SR	SR	SR	SR	SR	SR	SR	SR	SR	SR	SR	SR
		A	A		A	B		A	A		A	C		A	A		A	D		
Edinburgh 228,230 d	20 10						20 40						21 40						22 40	23 18
Haymarket 228,230 d	20 16						20 44						21 44						22 44	23 22
Edinburgh Park 230 d	20 20						20 49						21 49						22 49	23 27
Uphall d	20 28						20 57						21 57						22 57	23 35
Livingston North d	20 32						21 01						22 00						23 00	23 38
Bathgate a	20 36						21 05						22 05						23 05	23 43
d							21 06						22 06						23 06	
Armadale d							21 10						22 10						23 10	
Blackridge d							21 14						22 14						23 14	
Caldercruix d							21 20						22 20						23 20	
Drumgelloch d							21 24						22 24						23 24	
Airdrie d				20 57			21 27			21 57			22 27			22 57			23 27	
Coatdyke d				20 59			21 29			21 59			22 29			22 59			23 29	
Coatbridge Sunnyside d				21 02			21 32			22 02			22 32			23 02			23 32	
Blairhill d				21 05			21 35			22 05			22 35			23 05			23 35	
Easterhouse d				21 09			21 39			22 09			22 39			23 09			23 39	
Garrowhill d				21 11			21 41			22 11			22 41			23 11			23 41	
Shettleston d				21 14			21 44			22 14			22 44			23 14			23 44	
Carntyne d				21 16			21 46			22 16			22 46			23 16			23 46	
Cumbernauld d																				
Greenfaulds d																				
Springburn d																				
Barnhill d																				
Alexandra Parade d																				
Duke Street d																				
Bellgrove d				21 19			21 49			22 19			22 49			23 19			23 49	
High Street d				21 21			21 51			22 21			22 51			23 21			23 51	
Glasgow Queen St LL 10 a				21 23			21 53			22 23			22 53			23 23			23 53	
d				21 24			21 54			22 24			22 54			23 24			23 54	
Charing Cross d				21 27			21 57			22 27			22 57			23 27			23 57	
Argyle Street 225 d																				
Glasgow Central LL 15 225 a																				
d		21 04	21 15		21 34	21 45		22 04	22 15		22 34	22 45		23 04	23 15		23 34	23 47		
Anderston 225 d																				
Exhibition Centre 225 d		21 08	21 18		21 38	21 48		22 08	22 18		22 38	22 48		23 08	23 18		23 38	23 50		
Partick 225 d		21 12	21 22	21 31	21 42	21 52	22 01	22 12	22 22	22 31	22 42	22 52	23 01	23 12	23 22	23 31	23 42	23 54	00 01	
Hyndland 3 d		21 15	21 24	21 34	21 45	21 54	22 04	22 15	22 24	22 34	22 45	22 54	23 04	23 15	23 24	23 34	23 45	23 56	00 03	
Jordanhill d			21 26			21 56			22 26			22 56			23 26		23 47	23 58	00 05	
Scotstounhill d			21 29			21 59			22 29			22 59			23 29		23 49	00 01	00 08	
Garscadden d			21 31			22 01			22 31			23 01			23 31		23a51	00a02	00 10	
Yoker d			21 34			22 04			22 34			23 04			23 34				00 12	
Clydebank d			21 36			22 06			22 36			23 06			23 36				00 14	
Anniesland d		21 18		21 37	21 48		22 07	22 18		22 37	22 48		23 07	23 18		23 37				
Westerton d		21 21		21 40	21 51		22 10	22 21		22 40	22 51		23 10	23 21		23 40				
Bearsden d		21 25			21 55			22 25			22 55			23 25						
Hillfoot d		21 27			21 57			22 27			22 57			23 27						
Milngavie a		21 30			22 00			22 30			23 01			23 30						
Drumchapel d				21 42			22 12			22 42			23 12			23 42				
Drumry d				21 44			22 14			22 44			23 14			23 44				
Singer d				21 47			22 17			22 47			23 17			23 47				
Dalmuir 227 a			21 39	21 49		22 09	22 19		22 39	22 49		23 09	23 19		23 39	23 49			00 18	
d			21 40	21 50		22 10	22 20		22 40	22 50		23 10	23 20		23 40	23 50				
Kilpatrick d			21 42			22 12			22 42			23 12			23 42					
Bowling d			21 45			22 15			22 45			23 15			23 45					
Dumbarton East d			21 50	21 58		22 20	22 28		22 50	22 58		23 20	23 28		23 50	23 58				
Dumbarton Central 227 d			21 52	22 00		22 22	22 30		22 52	23 00		23 22	23 30		23 52	23 59				
Dalreoch d			21 53	22 01		22 23	22 31		22 53	23 01		23 23	23 31		23 53	00 01				
Renton d			21 56			22 26			22 56			23 26			23 56					
Alexandria d			21 59			22 29			22 59			23 29			23 59					
Balloch a			22 03			22 33			23 03			23 33			00 03					
Cardross d				22 06			22 36			23 06			23 36			00 06				
Craigendoran d				22 11			22 41			23 11			23 41			00 11				
Helensburgh Central a				22 15			22 45			23 15			23 46			00 15				
Helensburgh Upper 227 a																				

A From Motherwell
B From Larkhall. Forms tight booked connection out of 2C52.
C From Larkhall. Forms tight booked connection out of 2C54.
D From Larkhall. Forms tight booked connection out of 2C56.

Table T226-R

Mondays to Fridays
16 December to 15 May

Helensburgh, Balloch, Dalmuir and Milngavie - Glasgow - Springburn, Cumbernauld, Airdrie, Bathgate and Edinburgh

Miles	Miles	Miles	Miles	Station		SR MX A	SR MX A	SR MX A	SR	SR	SR	SR	SR	SR	SR B	SR	SR C	SR C	SR	SR	SR B	SR	SR
—	—	—	—	**Helensburgh Upper** 227	d																		
0	—	—	—	**Helensburgh Central**	d															05 56			
1¼	—	—	—	Craigendoran	d															05 59			
4¼	—	—	—	Cardross	d															06 04			
—	0	—	—	**Balloch**	d																		06 07
—	1	—	—	Alexandria	d																		06 09
—	2¼	—	—	Renton	d																		06 12
8	3¾	—	—	Dalreoch	d															06 09			06 15
8¼	4	—	—	Dumbarton Central 227	d															06 11			06 17
9	4¾	—	—	Dumbarton East	d															06 13			06 19
11¾	7½	—	—	Bowling	d																		
13½	9¼	—	—	Kilpatrick	d																		
14¾	10½	0	0	**Dalmuir** 227	a															06 20			06 27
—	—	—	—		d									05 47	05 51	05 58	06 00		06 12	06 21	06 16		06 28
15½	11¼	—	0¾	Singer	d			00 01							05 53	06 00					06 18		06 30
16½	12¼	—	1¾	Drumry	d			00 03							05 56	06 02					06 21		06 33
17¼	13	—	2½	Drumchapel	d			00 06							05 58	06 05					06 23		06 35
—	—	—	—	**Milngavie**	d																		
—	—	—	—	Hillfoot	d																		
—	—	—	—	Bearsden	d																		
18½	14¼	—	3¾	Westerton	d			00 08							06 01	06 08					06 26		06 38
19¾	15½	—	5	Anniesland	d			00 11							06 04	06 11					06 29		06 41
—	—	1¼	—	Clydebank	d									05 49			06 02		06 14				
—	—	2¼	—	Yoker	d									05 51			06 04		06 16				
—	—	3¼	—	Garscadden	d							05 45	05 49	05 54			06 07		06 19				
—	—	3¾	—	Scotstounhill	d							05 47	05 51	05 57			06 09		06 21				
—	—	4¾	—	Jordanhill	d							05 49	05 53	05 59			06 14		06 23				
20¾	16½	5¼	6	Hyndland [3]	d			00 14			05 37	05 52	05 56	06 01	06 07	06 14	06 17	06 22	06 25	06 28	06 32	06 35	06 44
21¼	17	6	6½	**Partick** 225 ⛴	d			00 17			05 39	05 54	05 58	06 04	06 10	06 16	06 19	06 24	06 28	06 31	06 34	06 38	06 46
—	—	—	8¼	Exhibition Centre 225	a										06 13		06 22	06 27			06 37		
—	—	—	8¾	Anderston 225	a										06 15		06 24	06 30			06 40		
—	—	—	8¾	**Glasgow Central LL** [15] 225	a										06 16		06 26	06 31			06 42		
—	—	—	9¼	Argyle Street 225	a										06 19		06 28	06 35			06 45		
23¼	19	7¾	—	Charing Cross	d			00 21			05 43	05 59	06 02	06 08		06 21			06 32	06 35		06 42	06 51
24	19¾	8½	—	**Glasgow Queen St LL** [10] ⛴	a			00 23			05 45	06 01	06 04	06 10		06 23			06 34	06 37		06 44	06 53
—	—	—	—		d			00 23			05 45	06 01	06 05	06 16		06 23			06 34	06 38		06 45	06 54
24½	20¼	9	—	High Street	d			00 25			05 47	06 03	06 07	06 18		06 26			06 36	06 40		06 47	06 56
25	20¾	9½	—	Bellgrove	d			00 27			05 49		06 09	06 20		06 28			06 38			06 49	06 58
—	21¼	10	—	Duke Street	d								06 11						06 41				
—	21½	10¼	—	Alexandra Parade	d								06 12						06 42				
—	22¾	11¼	—	Barnhill	d								06 15						06 45				
—	23	11¾	—	Springburn	a								06 17						06 47				
—	—	23½	—	Greenfaulds	d																		
—	—	24½	—	Cumbernauld	a																		
26¾	—	—	—	Carntyne	d		00 02	00 31			05 53			06 24		06 31						06 52	07 02
27½	—	—	—	Shettleston	d		00 03	00 33			05 55			06 27		06 34						06 55	07 04
28¾	—	—	—	Garrowhill	d		00 06	00 36				06 11				06 36				06 47			07 07
29¾	—	—	—	Easterhouse	d		00 08	00 38				06 13				06 39				06 50			07 09
32½	—	—	—	Blairhill	d		00 12	00 42				06 17				06 43				06 54			07 13
33	—	—	—	Coatbridge Sunnyside	d		00 15	00 45			06 04	06 20		06 35		06 45				06 56		07 03	07 16
34	—	—	—	Coatdyke	d		00 17	00 47				06 22				06 48				06 59			07 18
35	—	—	—	**Airdrie**	d		00 20	00a51			06 09	06 29		06 42		06a52				07 02		07 08	07a22
36½	—	—	—	Drumgelloch	d		00 23				06 12	06 32		06 45						07 05		07 11	
39½	—	—	—	Caldercruix	d		00 27				06 16			06 49								07 15	
45	—	—	—	Blackridge	d	00 03	00 33				06 22			06 55								07 21	
47¼	—	—	—	Armadale	d	00 07	00 37				06 25			06 59								07 24	
49¾	—	—	—	**Bathgate**	a	00 11	00 41				06 29	06 44		07 03						07 17		07 28	
—	—	—	—		d				05 46	06 16	06 30	06 45		07 06						07 17		07 31	
52¾	—	—	—	Livingston North	d				05 50	06 20	06 34	06 50		07 11						07 22		07 35	
55¾	—	—	—	Uphall	d				05 53	06 23	06 37	06 53		07 15						07 25		07 38	
64½	—	—	—	Edinburgh Park 230	d				06 02	06 32	06 47	07 02		07 26						07 33		07 48	
67	—	—	—	Haymarket 228,230 ⛴	a				06 07	06 39	06 51	07 06		07 32						07 42		07 52	
68¼	—	—	—	**Edinburgh** 228,230	a				06 12	06 46	06 56	07 13		07 38						07 48		07 58	

A From Helensburgh Central
B To Larkhall
C To Motherwell

Table T226-R

Mondays to Fridays
16 December to 15 May

Helensburgh, Balloch, Dalmuir and Milngavie - Glasgow - Springburn, Cumbernauld, Airdrie, Bathgate and Edinburgh

Station		SR A	SR	SR	SR	SR B	SR	SR	SR C	SR C	SR	SR	SR B	SR	SR	SR A	SR	SR	SR	SR B	SR	SR	SR C
Helensburgh Upper 227	d																						
Helensburgh Central	d				06 26							06 56							07 26				
Craigendoran	d				06 29							06 59							07 29				
Cardross	d				06 34							07 04							07 34				
Balloch	d							06 37							07 07							07 37	
Alexandria	d							06 39							07 09							07 39	
Renton	d							06 42							07 12							07 42	
Dalreoch	d				06 39			06 45				07 09			07 15				07 39			07 45	
Dumbarton Central 227	d			06 26	06 41			06 47			06 56	07 11			07 17		07 26		07 41			07 46	
Dumbarton East	d			06 28	06 43			06 49			06 58	07 13			07 19		07 28		07 43			07 48	
Bowling	d			06 33							07 03						07 33						
Kilpatrick	d			06 36							07 07						07 36						
Dalmuir 227	a			06 39	06 50			06 56			07 10	07 20			07 26		07 39		07 50			07 56	
	d	06 33		06 41	06 51	06 48		06 58	07 02		07 11	07 21	07 19		07 28	07 33	07 40		07 51	07 49		07 57	08 02
Singer	d					06 50		07 00					07 21		07 30					07 51		07 59	
Drumry	d					06 52		07 03					07 23		07 33					07 53		08 01	
Drumchapel	d					06 55		07 05					07 26		07 35					07 56		08 04	
Milngavie	d		06 38				06 54			07 09				07 24				07 41			07 54		
Hillfoot	d		06 41				06 57			07 12				07 27				07 44			07 57		
Bearsden	d		06 43				06 59			07 14				07 29				07 46			07 59		
Westerton	d		06 46			06 57	07 02	07 08		07 17			07 28	07 32	07 38			07 49		07 59	08 02	08 06	
Anniesland	d		06 49			07 00	07 05	07 11		07 20			07 31	07 35	07 41			07 53		08 02	08 05	08 10	
Clydebank	d	06 35		06 43					07 04		07 13					07 35	07 42						08 04
Yoker	d	06 37		06 45					07 06		07 15					07 37	07 44						08 06
Garscadden	d	06 40		06 48					07 09		07 19					07 40	07 47						08 10
Scotstounhill	d	06 42		06 50					07 11		07 21					07 42	07 49						08 12
Jordanhill	d	06 45		06 53					07 15		07 24					07 45	07 52						08 15
Hyndland [3]	d	06 48	06 52	06 55	06 58	07 04	07 08	07 14	07 17	07 23	07 26	07 29	07 35	07 38	07 44	07 48	07 54	07 57	08 00	08 05	08 08	08 13	08 17
Partick 225 ⛴	d	06 50	06 54	06 57	07 00	07 06	07 10	07 16	07 19	07 25	07 28	07 31	07 37	07 40	07 46	07 50	07 56	07 59	08 02	08 07	08 11	08 16	08 20
Exhibition Centre 225	a	06 53	06 57			07 09			07 22	07 28			07 40			07 53		08 02		08 10			08 23
Anderston 225	a	06 55	07 00			07 12			07 24	07 31			07 43			07 55		08 05		08 13			08 25
Glasgow Central LL [15] 225	a	06 57	07 02			07 14			07 26	07 33			07 44			07 57		08 06		08 15			08 26
Argyle Street 225	a	06 59	07 07			07 18			07 28	07 37			07 48			07 59		08 09		08 18			08 29
Charing Cross	d			07 01	07 05		07 14	07 21			07 32	07 36		07 45	07 51		08 01		08 07		08 15	08 20	
Glasgow Queen St LL [10] ⛴	a			07 03	07 07		07 16	07 23			07 34	07 38		07 47	07 53		08 03		08 09		08 17	08 22	
	d			07 04	07 07		07 17	07 24			07 35	07 38		07 47	07 53		08 03		08 09		08 18	08 23	
High Street	d			07 06	07 09		07 19	07 26			07 37	07 40		07 49	07 56		08 05		08 11		08 20	08 26	
Bellgrove	d			07 08			07 21	07 28			07 39			07 51	07 58		08 07				08 22	08 28	
Duke Street	d			07 10							07 41						08 09						
Alexandra Parade	d			07 11							07 42						08 11						
Barnhill	d			07 14							07 45						08 14						
Springburn	a			07 16							07 47						08 16						
Greenfaulds	d		08 02															09 00					
Cumbernauld	a		08 04															09 02					
Carntyne	d						07 24	07 32						07 55	08 01						08 25	08 31	
Shettleston	d						07 27	07 34						07 57	08 04						08 28	08 34	
Garrowhill	d				07 17			07 37				07 48			08 06				08 19			08 36	
Easterhouse	d				07 19			07 39				07 50			08 09				08 21			08 39	
Blairhill	d				07 23			07 43				07 54			08 13				08 25			08 43	
Coatbridge Sunnyside	d				07 26		07 35	07 46				07 57		08 06	08 15				08 28		08 36	08 45	
Coatdyke	d				07 28			07 48				07 59			08 18				08 30			08 48	
Airdrie	d				07 31		07 40	07a52				08 02		08 11	08a22				08 34		08 41	08a51	
Drumgelloch	d				07 34		07 43					08 05		08 14					08 37		08 44		
Caldercruix	d						07 47							08 18							08 48		
Blackridge	d						07 53							08 24							08 54		
Armadale	d						07 56							08 28							08 57		
Bathgate	a				07 47		08 00					08 18		08 32					08 50		09 01		
	d				07 47		08 01					08 18		08 36					08 53		09 01		
Livingston North	d				07 52		08 06					08 23		08 41					08 57		09 06		
Uphall	d				07 55		08 09					08 26		08 44					09 00		09 09		
Edinburgh Park 230	d				08 03		08 19					08 34		08 55					09 11		09 19		
Haymarket 228,230 ⛴	a				08 09		08 25					08 38		09 01					09 15		09 24		
Edinburgh 228,230	a				08 14		08 32					08 45		09 07					09 21		09 29		

A To Whifflet
B To Larkhall
C To Motherwell

Table T226-R

Mondays to Fridays

16 December to 15 May

Helensburgh, Balloch, Dalmuir and Milngavie - Glasgow - Springburn, Cumbernauld, Airdrie, Bathgate and Edinburgh

		SR A	SR	SR ◇ B	SR	SR C	SR	SR	SR	SR D	SR	SR	SR	SR C	SR	SR	SR A	SR	SR A	SR	SR C	SR	SR
Helensburgh Upper 227	d			07 42																			
Helensburgh Central	d				07 56			08 05					08 26							08 54			
Craigendoran	d				07 59			08 08					08 29							08 57			
Cardross	d			07 50	08 04			08 14					08 34							09 04			
Balloch	d								08 07							08 37							09 07
Alexandria	d								08 09							08 39							09 09
Renton	d								08 12							08 42							09 12
Dalreoch	d				08 09			08 20	08 15				08 39			08 45				09 09			09 15
Dumbarton Central 227	d		07 51	07 59	08 11			08 22	08 17		08 26		08 41			08 47		08 56		09 11			09 17
Dumbarton East	d		07 53		08 13			08 24	08 19		08 28		08 43			08 49		08 58		09 13			09 19
Bowling	d		07 58								08 32							09 03					
Kilpatrick	d		08 01								08 35							09 06					
Dalmuir 227	a		08 05		08 20				08 26		08 38		08 50			08 56		09 09		09 21			09 26
	d		08 11		08 23	08 16			08 27	08 35	08 39		08 51	08 50		08 58	09 03	09 10		09 22	09 20		09 28
Singer	d			08a11		08 18			08 29					08 52		09 00					09 22		09 30
Drumry	d					08 20			08 32					08 54		09 02					09 24		09 33
Drumchapel	d					08 23			08 34					08 57		09 05					09 27		09 35
Milngavie	d	08 09					08 21					08 40			08 55				09 11			09 25	
Hillfoot	d	08 12					08 24					08 43			08 58				09 14			09 28	
Bearsden	d	08 14					08 26					08 45			09 00				09 16			09 30	
Westerton	d	08 17				08 25	08 29		08 37			08 48		08 59	09 03	09 07			09 19		09 29	09 33	09 38
Anniesland	d	08 20				08 29	08 32		08 43			08 53		09 03	09 06	09 10			09 23		09 32	09 36	09 41
Clydebank	d		08 13							08 37	08 42						09 05	09 12					
Yoker	d		08 15							08 39	08 44						09 07	09 14					
Garscadden	d		08 18							08 42	08 46						09 10	09 17					
Scotstounhill	d		08 20							08 44	08 48						09 12	09 19					
Jordanhill	d		08 23							08 46	08 52						09 15	09 22					
Hyndland 3	d	08 23	08 26		08 30	08 33	08 36		08 46	08 49	08 54	08 57	09 00	09 06	09 09	09 14	09 17	09 24	09 27	09 30	09 35	09 39	09 44
Partick 225 ⛴	d	08 25	08 28		08 32	08 35	08 38	08 44	08 48	08 51	08 56	08 59	09 03	09 08	09 11	09 16	09 20	09 26	09 29	09 32	09 38	09 41	09 46
Exhibition Centre 225	a	08 28				08 38				08 54		09 02		09 11			09 23		09 32		09 41		
Anderston 225	a	08 31				08 41				08 56		09 04		09 13			09 25		09 35		09 43		
Glasgow Central LL 15 225	a	08 33				08 43				08 58		09 06		09 15			09 26		09 36		09 45		
Argyle Street 225	a	08 37				08 46				09 00		09 09		09 18			09 28		09 39		09 50		
Charing Cross	d		08 33		08 37		08 43	08 49	08 53		09 01		09 07		09 15	09 21		09 31		09 37		09 45	09 51
Glasgow Queen St LL 10 ⛴	a		08 35		08 39		08 45	08 51	08 55		09 03		09 09		09 17	09 23		09 33		09 39		09 47	09 53
	d		08 35		08 39		08 46	08 52	08 55		09 03		09 11		09 18	09 24		09 33		09 40		09 48	09 54
High Street	d		08 38		08 42		08 48	08 54	08 57		09 06		09 13		09 20	09 26		09 36		09 43		09 50	09 56
Bellgrove	d		08 40				08 50		08 59		09 08				09 22	09 28		09 38				09 52	09 58
Duke Street	d		08 42								09 10							09 40					
Alexandra Parade	d		08 43								09 11							09 41					
Barnhill	d		08 46								09 14							09 44					
Springburn	a		08 48					09 03			09 16							09 46					
Greenfaulds	d											10 00											
Cumbernauld	a											10 02											
Carntyne	d						08 54		09 03						09 25	09 32						09 55	10 02
Shettleston	d						08 56		09 05						09 28	09 34						09 58	10 04
Garrowhill	d				08 49				09 08				09 21			09 37				09 50			10 07
Easterhouse	d				08 52				09 10				09 23			09 39				09 53			10 09
Blairhill	d				08 56				09 14				09 27			09 43				09 57			10 13
Coatbridge Sunnyside	d				08 58		09 05		09 17				09 30		09 36	09 46				09 59		10 06	10 16
Coatdyke	d				09 01				09 19				09 32			09 48				10 02			10 18
Airdrie	d				09 05		09 10		09a25				09 36		09 41	09a52				10 05		10 11	10a22
Drumgelloch	d				09 08		09 13						09 39		09 44					10 08		10 14	
Caldercruix	d						09 17								09 48							10 18	
Blackridge	d						09 23								09 54							10 24	
Armadale	d						09 26								09 58							10 27	
Bathgate	a				09 20		09 30						09 51		10 02					10 20		10 31	
	d				09 22		09 31						09 52		10 02					10 22		10 32	
Livingston North	d				09 27		09 35						09 57		10 07					10 26		10 36	
Uphall	d				09 30		09 39						10 00		10 10					10 29		10 39	
Edinburgh Park 230	d				09 38		09 47						10 08		10 18					10 39		10 47	
Haymarket 228,230 ⛴	a				09 43		09 53						10 16		10 25					10 45		10 53	
Edinburgh 228,230	a				09 48		09 58						10 24		10 31					10 51		10 58	

A To Motherwell
B From Oban to Glasgow Queen Street
C To Larkhall
D To Whifflet

Table T226-R

Mondays to Fridays

16 December to 15 May

Helensburgh, Balloch, Dalmuir and Milngavie - Glasgow - Springburn, Cumbernauld, Airdrie, Bathgate and Edinburgh

		SR A	SR	SR	SR	SR B	SR	SR	SR C	SR C	SR	SR	SR B	SR	SR	SR A	SR	SR	SR	SR B	SR	SR
Helensburgh Upper 227	d																					
Helensburgh Central	d				09 26							09 56							10 26			
Craigendoran	d				09 29							09 59							10 29			
Cardross	d				09 34							10 04							10 34			
Balloch	d							09 37							10 07							10 37
Alexandria	d							09 39							10 09							10 39
Renton	d							09 42							10 12							10 42
Dalreoch	d				09 39			09 45				10 09			10 15				10 39			10 45
Dumbarton Central 227	d			09 22	09 41			09 46			09 57	10 11			10 16			10 26	10 41			10 47
Dumbarton East	d			09 24	09 43			09 48			09 59	10 13			10 18			10 28	10 43			10 49
Bowling	d			09 29							10 03							10 33				
Kilpatrick	d			09 33							10 06							10 36				
Dalmuir 227	a			09 36	09 51			09 56			10 10	10 20			10 26			10 39	10 50			10 58
	d	09 33		09 41	09 52	09 50		09 58	10 03		10 11	10 21	10 18		10 27	10 33		10 40	10 55	10 49		10 59
Singer	d					09 52		10 00					10 20		10 29					10 51		11 01
Drumry	d					09 54		10 02					10 23		10 32					10 53		11 03
Drumchapel	d					09 57		10 05					10 26		10 34					10 56		11 06
Milngavie	d		09 39				09 55			10 09				10 24			10 38				10 55	
Hillfoot	d		09 42				09 58			10 12				10 27			10 41				10 58	
Bearsden	d		09 44				10 00			10 14				10 29			10 43				11 00	
Westerton	d		09 47			10 00	10 03	10 07		10 17			10 28	10 32	10 37		10 46			10 59	11 03	11 08
Anniesland	d		09 50			10 03	10 06	10 11		10 20			10 31	10 35	10 41		10 49			11 02	11 06	11 11
Clydebank	d	09 35		09 43					10 05		10 13					10 35		10 42				
Yoker	d	09 37		09 45					10 07		10 15					10 37		10 44				
Garscadden	d	09 40		09 48					10 10		10 19					10 40		10 48				
Scotstounhill	d	09 42		09 50					10 12		10 21					10 42		10 50				
Jordanhill	d	09 45		09 53					10 15		10 24					10 45		10 53				
Hyndland 3	d	09 47	09 53	09 56	10 00	10 06	10 09	10 14	10 17	10 23	10 26	10 29	10 34	10 38	10 44	10 47	10 52	10 55	11 02	11 05	11 09	11 14
Partick 225 ⛴	d	09 49	09 55	09 58	10 02	10 08	10 12	10 16	10 19	10 25	10 28	10 31	10 37	10 40	10 46	10 49	10 55	10 58	11 04	11 08	11 11	11 17
Exhibition Centre 225	a	09 52	09 58			10 11			10 22	10 28			10 40			10 52	10 58			11 11		
Anderston 225	a	09 54	10 01			10 14			10 24	10 31			10 42			10 54	11 00			11 13		
Glasgow Central LL 15 225	a	09 56	10 03			10 16			10 26	10 33			10 43			10 56	11 02			11 14		
Argyle Street 225	a	09 58	10 07			10 20			10 28	10 37			10 46			10 59	11 07			11 18		
Charing Cross	d			10 03	10 07		10 16	10 21			10 32	10 35		10 44	10 51			11 02	11 09		11 15	11 21
Glasgow Queen St LL 10 ⛴	a			10 05	10 09		10 18	10 23			10 34	10 37		10 46	10 53			11 04	11 11		11 17	11 23
	d			10 05	10 09		10 18	10 24			10 35	10 38		10 47	10 54			11 05	11 12		11 18	11 24
High Street	d			10 08	10 11		10 20	10 26			10 37	10 40		10 49	10 56			11 07	11 14		11 20	11 26
Bellgrove	d			10 10			10 22	10 28			10 39			10 51	10 58			11 09			11 22	11 28
Duke Street	d			10 12							10 41							11 11				
Alexandra Parade	d			10 13							10 42							11 12				
Barnhill	d			10 16							10 45							11 15				
Springburn	a			10 18							10 47							11 17				
Greenfaulds	d		11 02														12 02					
Cumbernauld	a		11 04														12 04					
Carntyne	d						10 26	10 32						10 54	11 04						11 25	11 32
Shettleston	d						10 28	10 34						10 57	11 06						11 28	11 34
Garrowhill	d				10 19			10 37				10 47			11 09				11 22			11 37
Easterhouse	d				10 21			10 39				10 50			11 11				11 24			11 39
Blairhill	d				10 25			10 43				10 54			11 15				11 28			11 43
Coatbridge Sunnyside	d				10 28		10 37	10 46				10 56		11 05	11 18				11 31		11 36	11 46
Coatdyke	d				10 30			10 48				10 59			11 20				11 33			11 48
Airdrie	d				10 33		10 41	10a52				11 04		11 10	11a24				11 36		11 41	11a52
Drumgelloch	d				10 36		10 44					11 07		11 13					11 39		11 44	
Caldercruix	d						10 48							11 17							11 48	
Blackridge	d						10 54							11 23							11 54	
Armadale	d						10 58							11 26							11 57	
Bathgate	a				10 49		11 02					11 19		11 30					11 52		12 01	
	d				10 52		11 02					11 22		11 31					11 52		12 02	
Livingston North	d				10 56		11 07					11 26		11 35					11 57		12 06	
Uphall	d				10 59		11 10					11 29		11 38					12 00		12 09	
Edinburgh Park 230	d				11 07		11 18					11 38		11 47					12 08		12 18	
Haymarket 228,230 ⛴	a				11 12		11 22					11 46		11 51					12 12		12 24	
Edinburgh 228,230	a				11 18		11 28					11 51		11 57					12 19		12 30	

A To Whifflet
B To Larkhall
C To Motherwell

Table T226-R

Mondays to Fridays

16 December to 15 May

Helensburgh, Balloch, Dalmuir and Milngavie - Glasgow - Springburn, Cumbernauld, Airdrie, Bathgate and Edinburgh

		SR A	SR A	SR	SR ◇ B	SR	SR C	SR	SR	SR D	SR	SR	SR ◇ E	SR	SR C	SR	SR	SR A	SR	SR A	SR	SR C	SR
Helensburgh Upper 227	d				10 44								11 16										
Helensburgh Central	d					10 56								11 26							11 50		
Craigendoran	d					10 59								11 29							11 53		
Cardross	d					11 04								11 34							11 59		
Balloch	d								11 07								11 37						
Alexandria	d								11 09								11 39						
Renton	d								11 12								11 42						
Dalreoch	d					11 09			11 15					11 39			11 45				12 04		
Dumbarton Central 227	d			10 54	11 01	11 11			11 17			11 22	11 29	11 41			11 47		11 56		12 06		
Dumbarton East	d			10 56		11 13			11 19			11 24		11 43			11 49		11 58		12 08		
Bowling	d			11 00								11 28							12 03				
Kilpatrick	d			11 04								11 31							12 06				
Dalmuir 227	a			11 07	11 12	11 22			11 26			11 34	11 38	11 52			11 57		12 09		12 19		
	d	11 04		11 11		11 23	11 19		11 28	11 31		11 41		11 53	11 49		11 58	12 03	12 10		12 20	12 19	
Singer	d						11 21		11 30						11 51		12 00					12 21	
Drumry	d						11 23		11 33						11 53		12 03					12 23	
Drumchapel	d						11 26		11 35						11 56		12 05					12 26	
Milngavie	d		11 09					11 24			11 39					11 54				12 11			12 25
Hillfoot	d		11 12					11 27			11 42					11 57				12 14			12 28
Bearsden	d		11 14					11 29			11 44					11 59				12 16			12 30
Westerton	d		11 17				11 29	11 32	11 38		11 47				11 58	12 02	12 08			12 19		12 29	12 33
Anniesland	d		11 20				11 32	11 35	11 41		11 50				12 01	12 05	12 11			12 24		12 32	12 37
Clydebank	d	11 06		11 13						11 35		11 43						12 05	12 12				
Yoker	d	11 08		11 15						11 37		11 45						12 07	12 14				
Garscadden	d	11 11		11 19						11 40		11 49						12 10	12 17				
Scotstounhill	d	11 13		11 21						11 42		11 51						12 12	12 19				
Jordanhill	d	11 16		11 25						11 45		11 54						12 15	12 21				
Hyndland 3	d	11 18	11 24	11 27		11 30	11 35	11 38	11 44	11 47	11 53	11 56		12 00	12 04	12 08	12 14	12 17	12 23	12 27	12 30	12 35	12 40
Partick 225 ⛴	d	11 20	11 26	11 29		11 33	11 37	11 41	11 46	11 49	11 55	11 58		12 03	12 07	12 10	12 17	12 20	12 26	12 29	12 32	12 37	12 42
Exhibition Centre 225	a	11 23	11 29				11 40			11 52	11 58				12 10			12 23		12 32		12 40	
Anderston 225	a	11 25	11 32				11 42			11 54	12 01				12 12			12 25		12 34		12 43	
Glasgow Central LL 15 225	a	11 27	11 34				11 44			11 56	12 03				12 14			12 26		12 36		12 45	
Argyle Street 225	a	11 29	11 38				11 48			11 58	12 07				12 18			12 29		12 39		12 48	
Charing Cross	d			11 33		11 37		11 45	11 51			12 02		12 07		12 15	12 21		12 30		12 37		12 46
Glasgow Queen St LL 10 ⛴	a			11 35		11 39		11 47	11 53			12 04		12 09		12 17	12 23		12 32		12 39		12 48
	d			11 36		11 40		11 47	11 54			12 05		12 10		12 17	12 24		12 33		12 39		12 49
High Street	d			11 38		11 42		11 49	11 56			12 07		12 12		12 19	12 26		12 36		12 42		12 51
Bellgrove	d			11 40				11 51	11 58			12 09				12 21	12 28		12 38				12 53
Duke Street	d			11 42								12 11							12 40				
Alexandra Parade	d			11 43								12 12							12 41				
Barnhill	d			11 46								12 15							12 44				
Springburn	a			11 48								12 17							12 46				
Greenfaulds	d										13 02												
Cumbernauld	a										13 04												
Carntyne	d							11 55	12 02							12 25	12 32						12 56
Shettleston	d							11 57	12 04							12 27	12 34						12 59
Garrowhill	d					11 49			12 07					12 19			12 37				12 49		
Easterhouse	d					11 52			12 09					12 22			12 39				12 52		
Blairhill	d					11 56			12 13					12 26			12 43				12 56		
Coatbridge Sunnyside	d					11 58		12 06	12 16					12 28		12 36	12 46				12 58		13 07
Coatdyke	d					12 01			12 18					12 31			12 48				13 01		
Airdrie	d					12 05		12 10	12a22					12 34		12 40	12a52				13 04		13 12
Drumgelloch	d					12 08		12 13						12 37		12 43					13 07		13 15
Caldercruix	d							12 17								12 47							13 19
Blackridge	d							12 23								12 53							13 25
Armadale	d							12 27								12 57							13 28
Bathgate	a					12 21		12 31						12 50		13 01					13 20		13 32
	d					12 23		12 31						12 51		13 01					13 22		13 36
Livingston North	d					12 28		12 36						12 56		13 06					13 27		13 40
Uphall	d					12 31		12 39						12 59		13 09					13 30		13 43
Edinburgh Park 230	d					12 39		12 48						13 09		13 18					13 38		13 53
Haymarket 228,230 ⛴	a					12 46		12 53						13 16		13 27					13 46		13 57
Edinburgh 228,230	a					12 51		13 00						13 21		13 33					13 51		14 02

A To Motherwell
B From Mallaig to Glasgow Queen Street
C To Larkhall
D To Whifflet
E From Oban to Glasgow Queen Street

Table T226-R

Mondays to Fridays

16 December to 15 May

Helensburgh, Balloch, Dalmuir and Milngavie - Glasgow - Springburn, Cumbernauld, Airdrie, Bathgate and Edinburgh

		SR	SR A	SR	SR	SR	SR B	SR	SR	SR C	SR	SR C	SR	SR B	SR	SR	SR A	SR	SR	SR	SR B	SR
Helensburgh Upper 227	d																					
Helensburgh Central	d					12 26							12 55							13 26		
Craigendoran	d					12 29							12 58							13 29		
Cardross	d					12 34							13 03							13 34		
Balloch	d	12 07							12 37							13 07						
Alexandria	d	12 09							12 39							13 09						
Renton	d	12 12							12 42							13 12						
Dalreoch	d	12 15				12 39			12 45				13 08			13 15				13 39		
Dumbarton Central 227	d	12 17		12 26		12 41			12 47		12 56		13 10			13 17		13 26		13 41		
Dumbarton East	d	12 19		12 28		12 43			12 49		12 58		13 12			13 19		13 28		13 43		
Bowling	d			12 33							13 03							13 33				
Kilpatrick	d			12 36							13 06							13 36				
Dalmuir 227	a	12 28		12 39		12 52			12 57		13 09		13 22			13 26		13 39		13 53		
	d	12 29	12 33	12 40		12 53	12 49		12 58	13 03	13 10		13 23	13 19		13 27	13 33	13 40		13 54	13 49	
Singer	d	12 31					12 51		13 00					13 21		13 29					13 51	
Drumry	d	12 33					12 53		13 03					13 23		13 32					13 53	
Drumchapel	d	12 36					12 56		13 05					13 26		13 34					13 56	
Milngavie	d				12 41			12 54				13 11			13 25				13 40			13 54
Hillfoot	d				12 44			12 57				13 14			13 28				13 43			13 57
Bearsden	d				12 46			12 59				13 16			13 30				13 45			13 59
Westerton	d	12 39			12 49		12 59	13 03	13 08			13 19		13 29	13 33	13 37			13 48		13 59	14 02
Anniesland	d	12 42			12 54		13 02	13 06	13 11			13 24		13 32	13 36	13 40			13 53		14 02	14 05
Clydebank	d		12 35	12 42						13 05	13 12						13 35	13 42				
Yoker	d		12 37	12 44						13 07	13 14						13 37	13 44				
Garscadden	d		12 40	12 47						13 10	13 17						13 40	13 47				
Scotstounhill	d		12 42	12 49						13 12	13 19						13 42	13 49				
Jordanhill	d		12 47	12 52						13 15	13 22						13 45	13 52				
Hyndland 3	d	12 45	12 49	12 54	12 57	13 01	13 05	13 09	13 14	13 17	13 24	13 27	13 30	13 35	13 39	13 43	13 47	13 54	13 57	14 01	14 05	14 08
Partick 225 ⛴	d	12 48	12 52	12 56	12 59	13 03	13 07	13 11	13 16	13 19	13 26	13 29	13 33	13 37	13 41	13 45	13 49	13 56	13 59	14 03	14 07	14 11
Exhibition Centre 225	a		12 55		13 02		13 10			13 22		13 32		13 40			13 52		14 02		14 10	
Anderston 225	a		12 57		13 04		13 12			13 24		13 34		13 42			13 54		14 04		14 12	
Glasgow Central LL 15 225	a		12 58		13 06		13 14			13 26		13 36		13 44			13 56		14 06		14 14	
Argyle Street 225	a		13 00		13 09		13 18			13 28		13 39		13 48			13 58		14 09		14 18	
Charing Cross	d	12 52		13 01		13 07		13 15	13 21		13 31		13 37		13 46	13 50		14 01		14 08		14 15
Glasgow Queen St LL 10 ⛴	a	12 54		13 03		13 09		13 17	13 23		13 33		13 39		13 48	13 52		14 03		14 10		14 17
	d	12 55		13 03		13 12		13 18	13 24		13 33		13 40		13 48	13 54		14 03		14 10		14 18
High Street	d	12 57		13 06		13 14		13 20	13 26		13 36		13 42		13 50	13 56		14 06		14 13		14 20
Bellgrove	d	12 59		13 08				13 22	13 28		13 38				13 52	13 58		14 08				14 22
Duke Street	d			13 10							13 40							14 10				
Alexandra Parade	d			13 11							13 41							14 11				
Barnhill	d			13 14							13 44							14 14				
Springburn	a			13 16							13 46							14 16				
Greenfaulds	d				14 02														15 02			
Cumbernauld	a				14 04														15 04			
Carntyne	d	13 03						13 25	13 32						13 56	14 02						14 25
Shettleston	d	13 05						13 28	13 34						13 58	14 04						14 28
Garrowhill	d	13 08				13 22			13 37				13 49			14 07				14 20		
Easterhouse	d	13 10				13 24			13 39				13 52			14 09				14 23		
Blairhill	d	13 14				13 28			13 43				13 56			14 13				14 27		
Coatbridge Sunnyside	d	13 17				13 31		13 36	13 46				13 58		14 07	14 16				14 29		14 36
Coatdyke	d	13 19				13 33			13 48				14 01			14 18				14 32		
Airdrie	d	13a23				13 36		13 41	13a52				14 05		14 11	14a22				14 35		14 41
Drumgelloch	d					13 39		13 44					14 08		14 14					14 38		14 44
Caldercruix	d							13 48							14 18							14 48
Blackridge	d							13 54							14 24							14 54
Armadale	d							13 57							14 28							14 57
Bathgate	a					13 52		14 01					14 21		14 32					14 50		15 01
	d					13 52		14 01					14 21		14 32					14 52		15 02
Livingston North	d					13 57		14 06					14 26		14 37					14 57		15 06
Uphall	d					14 00		14 09					14 29		14 40					15 00		15 09
Edinburgh Park 230	d					14 09		14 17					14 39		14 48					15 10		15 17
Haymarket 228,230 ⛴	a					14 15		14 24					14 44		14 54					15 15		15 22
Edinburgh 228,230	a					14 24		14 31					14 49		14 59					15 21		15 29

A To Whifflet
B To Larkhall
C To Motherwell

Table T226-R

Mondays to Fridays
16 December to 15 May

Helensburgh, Balloch, Dalmuir and Milngavie - Glasgow - Springburn, Cumbernauld, Airdrie, Bathgate and Edinburgh

Station		SR	SR A	SR A	SR	SR	SR B	SR	SR	SR C	SR	SR	SR	SR B	SR	SR	SR A	SR	SR ◇ D 🍴	SR A	SR	SR B	SR
Helensburgh Upper 227	d																		14 43				
Helensburgh Central	d					13 56							14 26								14 56		
Craigendoran	d					13 59							14 29								14 59		
Cardross	d					14 04							14 34								15 04		
Balloch	d	13 37							14 07							14 37							
Alexandria	d	13 39							14 09							14 39							
Renton	d	13 42							14 12							14 42							
Dalreoch	d	13 45				14 09			14 15				14 39			14 45					15 09		
Dumbarton Central 227	d	13 46			13 58	14 11			14 17			14 26	14 41			14 47		14 55	15 02		15 11		
Dumbarton East	d	13 48			14 00	14 13			14 19			14 28	14 43			14 49		14 57			15 13		
Bowling	d				14 05							14 33						15 01					
Kilpatrick	d				14 08							14 36						15 04					
Dalmuir 227	a	13 57			14 11	14 22			14 26			14 39	14 52			14 56		15 07	15 12		15 22		
	d	13 57	14 03		14 11	14 23	14 19		14 27	14 32		14 41	14 53	14 49		14 57	15 03	15 09			15 23	15 19	
Singer	d	13 59					14 21		14 29					14 51		14 59						15 21	
Drumry	d	14 02					14 23		14 32					14 53		15 02						15 23	
Drumchapel	d	14 04					14 26		14 34					14 56		15 04						15 26	
Milngavie	d			14 09				14 24			14 39				14 54					15 11			15 25
Hillfoot	d			14 12				14 27			14 42				14 57					15 14			15 28
Bearsden	d			14 14				14 29			14 44				14 59					15 16			15 30
Westerton	d	14 07		14 17			14 29	14 32	14 37		14 47			14 59	15 02	15 07				15 19		15 29	15 33
Anniesland	d	14 10		14 20			14 32	14 35	14 40		14 50			15 02	15 05	15 11				15 23		15 32	15 36
Clydebank	d		14 05		14 14					14 34		14 43					15 05	15 12					
Yoker	d		14 07		14 16					14 36		14 45					15 07	15 14					
Garscadden	d		14 10		14 18					14 40		14 49					15 10	15 16					
Scotstounhill	d		14 12		14 20					14 42		14 51					15 12	15 18					
Jordanhill	d		14 16		14 25					14 44		14 54					15 15	15 21					
Hyndland ■	d	14 13	14 18	14 24	14 27	14 31	14 35	14 38	14 43	14 47	14 53	14 56	15 01	15 05	15 08	15 15	15 18	15 23		15 26	15 30	15 35	15 39
Partick 225 ⛴	d	14 16	14 21	14 26	14 29	14 33	14 37	14 40	14 45	14 49	14 55	14 59	15 03	15 07	15 11	15 17	15 20	15 26		15 29	15 33	15 38	15 41
Exhibition Centre 225	a		14 24	14 29			14 40			14 52	14 58			15 10			15 23			15 32		15 41	
Anderston 225	a		14 26	14 31			14 42			14 54	15 01			15 13			15 25			15 34		15 43	
Glasgow Central LL 15 225	a		14 27	14 33			14 44			14 56	15 03			15 15			15 27			15 36		15 44	
Argyle Street 225	a		14 29	14 39			14 46			14 58	15 07			15 18			15 29			15 39		15 46	
Charing Cross	d	14 21			14 33	14 38		14 45	14 50			15 03	15 08		15 15	15 22		15 30			15 37		15 46
Glasgow Queen St LL 10 ⛴	a	14 23			14 35	14 40		14 47	14 52			15 05	15 10		15 17	15 24		15 32			15 39		15 48
	d	14 24			14 36	14 40		14 47	14 54			15 05	15 10		15 17	15 25		15 33			15 40		15 48
High Street	d	14 26			14 38	14 42		14 50	14 56			15 08	15 12		15 19	15 27		15 36			15 42		15 50
Bellgrove	d	14 28			14 40			14 52	14 58			15 10			15 21	15 29		15 38					15 52
Duke Street	d				14 42							15 12						15 40					
Alexandra Parade	d				14 44							15 13						15 41					
Barnhill	d				14 47							15 16						15 44					
Springburn	a				14 49							15 18						15 46					
Greenfaulds	d										16 03												
Cumbernauld	a										16 05												
Carntyne	d	14 32						14 55	15 04						15 25	15 33							15 56
Shettleston	d	14 34						14 58	15 06						15 27	15 37							15 58
Garrowhill	d	14 37				14 50			15 09				15 20			15 40					15 49		
Easterhouse	d	14 39				14 52			15 11				15 22			15 42					15 52		
Blairhill	d	14 43				14 56			15 15				15 26			15 46					15 56		
Coatbridge Sunnyside	d	14 46				14 59		15 06	15 18				15 29		15 36	15 49					15 58		16 07
Coatdyke	d	14 48				15 01			15 20				15 31			15 51					16 01		
Airdrie	d	14a52				15 04		15 11	15a24				15 35		15 40	15a55					16 04		16 11
Drumgelloch	d					15 07		15 14					15 38		15 43						16 07		16 14
Caldercruix	d							15 18							15 47								16 18
Blackridge	d							15 24							15 53								16 24
Armadale	d							15 27							15 57								16 28
Bathgate	a					15 20		15 31					15 50		16 01						16 20		16 32
	d					15 21		15 32					15 52		16 01						16 21		16 32
Livingston North	d					15 26		15 36					15 56		16 06						16 25		16 37
Uphall	d					15 29		15 39					15 59		16 09						16 28		16 40
Edinburgh Park 230	d					15 38		15 47					16 09		16 17						16 38		16 48
Haymarket 228,230 ⛴	a					15 43		15 53					16 16		16 23						16 43		16 53
Edinburgh 228,230	a					15 48		15 59					16 24		16 28						16 48		17 00

A To Motherwell
B To Larkhall
C To Whifflet
D From Mallaig to Glasgow Queen Street

NRT DECEMBER 19 EDITION

Table T226-R

Mondays to Fridays
16 December to 15 May

Helensburgh, Balloch, Dalmuir and Milngavie - Glasgow - Springburn, Cumbernauld, Airdrie, Bathgate and Edinburgh

Station		SR	SR A	SR	SR	SR	SR B	SR	SR	SR C	SR C	SR	SR	SR B	SR	SR	SR A	SR	SR	SR	SR B	SR	SR
Helensburgh Upper 227	d																						
Helensburgh Central	d					15 26							15 55						16 21				
Craigendoran	d					15 29							15 58						16 24				
Cardross	d					15 34							16 03						16 30				
Balloch	d	15 07							15 37							16 06							16 37
Alexandria	d	15 09							15 39							16 08							16 39
Renton	d	15 12							15 42							16 11							16 42
Dalreoch	d	15 15				15 39			15 45				16 08			16 14			16 35				16 45
Dumbarton Central 227	d	15 17		15 26		15 41			15 47			15 56	16 10			16 15		16 26	16 36				16 47
Dumbarton East	d	15 19		15 28		15 43			15 49			15 58	16 12			16 17		16 28	16 38				16 49
Bowling	d			15 33								16 03						16 32					
Kilpatrick	d			15 36								16 06						16 35					
Dalmuir 227	a	15 26		15 39		15 53			15 57			16 09	16 22			16 26		16 38	16 46				16 56
	d	15 27	15 33	15 40		15 54	15 49		15 58	16 03		16 11	16 23	16 19		16 28	16 33	16 39	16 49		16 49		16 57
Singer	d	15 29					15 51		16 00					16 21		16 30					16 51		16 59
Drumry	d	15 32					15 53		16 02					16 23		16 32					16 53		17 02
Drumchapel	d	15 34					15 56		16 05					16 26		16 35					16 56		17 04
Milngavie	d				15 40			15 54			16 09				16 25					16 41		16 56	
Hillfoot	d				15 43			15 57			16 12				16 28					16 44		16 59	
Bearsden	d				15 45			15 59			16 14				16 30					16 46		17 01	
Westerton	d	15 37			15 48		15 59	16 02	16 07		16 17			16 28	16 33	16 37				16 49	16 59	17 04	17 07
Anniesland	d	15 40			15 53		16 02	16 05	16 10		16 20			16 31	16 36	16 41				16 54	17 02	17 07	17 10
Clydebank	d		15 35	15 42						16 05		16 13					16 35	16 41					
Yoker	d		15 37	15 44						16 07		16 15					16 37	16 43					
Garscadden	d		15 40	15 47						16 10		16 19					16 40	16 47					
Scotstounhill	d		15 42	15 49						16 12		16 21					16 42	16 49					
Jordanhill	d		15 45	15 51						16 15		16 24					16 45	16 51					
Hyndland ■	d	15 43	15 47	15 53	15 56	16 01	16 05	16 08	16 13	16 17	16 23	16 26	16 30	16 34	16 39	16 44	16 47	16 53	16 56	16 59	17 06	17 10	17 14
Partick 225 ⛴	d	15 45	15 49	15 56	15 59	16 03	16 07	16 11	16 16	16 19	16 25	16 28	16 33	16 37	16 42	16 46	16 49	16 56	16 59	17 02	17 08	17 12	17 16
Exhibition Centre 225	a		15 52		16 02		16 10			16 22	16 28			16 40			16 52			17 05	17 11		
Anderston 225	a		15 54		16 04		16 13			16 24	16 31			16 42			16 54			17 07	17 14		
Glasgow Central LL 15 225	a		15 56		16 05		16 15			16 26	16 33			16 44			16 56			17 09	17 16		
Argyle Street 225	a		15 58		16 08		16 18			16 28	16 37			16 48			16 58			17 11	17 19		
Charing Cross	d	15 50		16 00		16 08		16 15	16 21			16 33	16 37		16 46	16 51		17 00	17 04			17 17	17 21
Glasgow Queen St LL 10 ⛴	a	15 52		16 02		16 10		16 17	16 23			16 35	16 39		16 48	16 53		17 02	17 06			17 19	17 23
	d	15 54		16 03		16 11		16 18	16 24			16 35	16 40		16 49	16 54		17 03	17 07			17 19	17 24
High Street	d	15 56		16 05		16 13		16 20	16 26			16 37	16 42		16 51	16 56		17 05	17 09			17 22	17 26
Bellgrove	d	15 58		16 07				16 22	16 28			16 39			16 53	16 58		17 07				17 24	17 28
Duke Street	d			16 09								16 41						17 09					
Alexandra Parade	d			16 11								16 43						17 11					
Barnhill	d			16 14								16 46						17 14					
Springburn	a			16 16								16 48						17 16					
Greenfaulds	d				17 07															18 06			
Cumbernauld	a				17 09															18 08			
Carntyne	d	16 02						16 25	16 32						16 57	17 02						17 27	17 32
Shettleston	d	16 04						16 28	16 34						16 59	17 04						17 30	17 34
Garrowhill	d	16 07				16 21			16 37				16 49			17 07			17 16				17 37
Easterhouse	d	16 09				16 23			16 39				16 52			17 09			17 19				17 39
Blairhill	d	16 13				16 27		16 34	16 43				16 56		17 06	17 13			17 23			17 36	17 43
Coatbridge Sunnyside	d	16 16				16 30		16 37	16 46				16 58		17 08	17 16			17 25			17 39	17 46
Coatdyke	d	16 18				16 32		16 39	16 48				17 01		17 11	17 18			17 28			17 41	17 48
Airdrie	d	16a22				16 36		16 42	16a52				17 05		17 15	17a22			17 31			17 45	17a52
Drumgelloch	d					16 39		16 45					17 08		17 18				17 34			17 48	
Caldercruix	d							16 49							17 22							17 52	
Blackridge	d							16 55							17 28							17 58	
Armadale	d							16 59							17 32							18 01	
Bathgate	a					16 51		17 03					17 20		17 36				17 46			18 05	
	d					16 52		17 03					17 23		17 37				17 47			18 06	
Livingston North	d					16 57		17 08					17 28		17 42				17 51			18 10	
Uphall	d					17 00		17 11					17 31		17 45				17 54			18 13	
Edinburgh Park 230	d					17 10		17 19					17 40		17 54				18 02			18 22	
Haymarket 228,230 ⛴	a					17 16		17 23					17 47		18 05				18 08			18 26	
Edinburgh 228,230	a					17 21		17 29					17 52		18 10				18 17			18 33	

A To Whifflet
B To Larkhall
C To Motherwell

Table T226-R

Mondays to Fridays

16 December to 15 May

Helensburgh, Balloch, Dalmuir and Milngavie - Glasgow - Springburn, Cumbernauld, Airdrie, Bathgate and Edinburgh

	SR A	SR	SR A	SR	SR B	SR ◇ C	SR	SR D	SR	SR	SR	SR	SR B	SR	SR	SR A	SR A	SR	SR	SR B	SR
Helensburgh Upper 227 d						17 00															
Helensburgh Central d				16 54								17 26							17 56		
Craigendoran d				16 57								17 29							17 59		
Cardross d				17 02								17 34							18 04		
Balloch d									17 09						17 37						
Alexandria d									17 11						17 39						
Renton d									17 14						17 42						
Dalreoch d				17 07					17 17			17 39			17 45				18 09		
Dumbarton Central 227 d		16 56		17 09		17 14			17 19		17 26	17 41			17 47			17 56	18 11		
Dumbarton East d		16 58		17 11					17 21		17 28	17 43			17 49			17 58	18 13		
Bowling d		17 03									17 33							18 03			
Kilpatrick d		17 06									17 36							18 06			
Dalmuir 227 a		17 09		17 19		17 24			17 29		17 39	17 50			17 56			18 09	18 20		
d	17 03	17 10		17 20	17 19			17 33	17 30		17 41	17 51	17 49		17 57	18 03		18 11	18 21	18 18	
Singer d					17 21				17 32				17 51		17 59					18 20	
Drumry d					17 23				17 34				17 53		18 02					18 23	
Drumchapel d					17 26				17 37				17 56		18 04					18 26	
Milngavie d			17 11				17 24			17 39				17 54			18 09				18 24
Hillfoot d			17 14				17 27			17 42				17 57			18 12				18 27
Bearsden d			17 16				17 29			17 44				17 59			18 14				18 29
Westerton d			17 19		17 29		17 32		17 40	17 47			17 59	18 02	18 07		18 17			18 28	18 32
Anniesland d			17 23		17 32		17 35		17 46	17 50			18 02	18 05	18 10		18 20			18 31	18 35
Clydebank d	17 05	17 12						17 35			17 43					18 05		18 13			
Yoker d	17 07	17 14						17 37			17 45					18 07		18 15			
Garscadden d	17 10	17 17						17 40			17 49					18 10		18 19			
Scotstounhill d	17 12	17 19						17 42			17 51					18 12		18 21			
Jordanhill d	17 15	17 21						17 44			17 54					18 15		18 25			
Hyndland 3 d	17 17	17 24	17 27	17 30	17 35		17 38	17 46	17 49	17 53	17 56	18 00	18 05	18 08	18 13	18 17	18 23	18 27	18 30	18 34	18 38
Partick 225 ⛴ d	17 20	17 26	17 29	17 32	17 38		17 41	17 49	17 52	17 56	17 59	18 02	18 07	18 11	18 15	18 19	18 25	18 29	18 32	18 37	18 40
Exhibition Centre 225 a	17 23		17 32		17 41			17 52		17 59			18 10			18 22	18 28			18 40	
Anderston 225 a	17 25		17 34		17 44			17 54		18 01			18 12			18 24	18 31			18 42	
Glasgow Central LL 15 225 a	17 26		17 36		17 46			17 55		18 03			18 14			18 26	18 33			18 44	
Argyle Street 225 a	17 29		17 39		17 50			17 57		18 07			18 18			18 28	18 37			18 47	
Charing Cross d		17 31		17 37			17 45		17 56		18 03	18 07		18 15	18 20			18 33	18 37		18 44
Glasgow Queen St LL 10 ⛴ a		17 33		17 39			17 47		17 58		18 05	18 09		18 17	18 22			18 35	18 39		18 46
d		17 33		17 39			17 48		17 59		18 06	18 10		18 17	18 23			18 36	18 39		18 47
High Street d		17 35		17 42			17 50		18 01		18 08	18 13		18 19	18 26			18 38	18 41		18 49
Bellgrove d		17 37					17 52		18 03		18 10			18 21	18 28			18 40			18 51
Duke Street d		17 39									18 12							18 42			
Alexandra Parade d		17 41									18 13							18 43			
Barnhill d		17 44									18 16							18 46			
Springburn a		17 46									18 18							18 48			
Greenfaulds d										19 02											
Cumbernauld a										19 04											
Carntyne d							17 55		18 07					18 25	18 32						18 54
Shettleston d							17 58		18 09					18 27	18 34						18 57
Garrowhill d				17 49					18 12			18 20			18 37				18 49		
Easterhouse d				17 52					18 14			18 23			18 39				18 51		
Blairhill d				17 56					18 18			18 27			18 43				18 55		
Coatbridge Sunnyside d				17 58			18 06		18 21			18 29		18 36	18 46				18 58		19 05
Coatdyke d				18 01					18 23			18 32			18 48				19 00		
Airdrie d				18 04			18 11		18a27			18 35		18 40	18a52				19 04		19 10
Drumgelloch d				18 07			18 14					18 38		18 43					19 07		19 13
Caldercruix d							18 18							18 47							19 17
Blackridge d							18 24							18 53							19 23
Armadale d							18 27							18 57							19 26
Bathgate a				18 20			18 31					18 51		19 01					19 20		19 30
d				18 22			18 32					18 52		19 02					19 22		19 31
Livingston North d				18 26			18 36					18 56		19 06					19 27		19 35
Uphall d				18 29			18 39					18 59		19 09					19 30		19 38
Edinburgh Park 230 d				18 39			18 47					19 10		19 17					19 39		19 48
Haymarket 228,230 ⛴ a				18 47			18 54					19 15		19 22					19 47		19 54
Edinburgh 228,230 a				18 52			18 59					19 22		19 28					19 52		19 59

A To Motherwell
B To Larkhall
C From Oban to Glasgow Queen Street
D To Whifflet

Table T226-R

Mondays to Fridays

16 December to 15 May

Helensburgh, Balloch, Dalmuir and Milngavie - Glasgow - Springburn, Cumbernauld, Airdrie, Bathgate and Edinburgh

	SR	SR A	SR	SR	SR	SR B	SR	SR C	SR	SR C	SR	SR B	SR	SR A	SR	SR	SR B	SR	SR	SR C	SR C	SR
Helensburgh Upper 227 d																						
Helensburgh Central d					18 22						18 54								19 32			
Craigendoran d					18 25						18 57								19 35			
Cardross d					18 30						19 02								19 40			
Balloch d	18 07						18 38						19 07									19 43
Alexandria d	18 09						18 40						19 09									19 45
Renton d	18 12						18 43						19 12									19 48
Dalreoch d	18 15				18 35		18 46				19 07		19 15						19 45			19 51
Dumbarton Central 227 d	18 17			18 26	18 37		18 48		18 54		19 11		19 17		19 26				19 47			19 57
Dumbarton East d	18 19			18 28	18 39		18 50		18 56		19 13		19 19		19 28				19 49			19 59
Bowling d				18 33					19 01						19 33							20 04
Kilpatrick d				18 36					19 04						19 36							20 07
Dalmuir 227 a	18 26			18 39	18 49		18 57		19 07		19 21		19 26		19 39				19 57			20 10
d	18 27	18 33		18 40	18 50	18 48	18 58	19 03	19 10		19 22	19 19	19 28	19 34	19 40		19 50		19 59	20 02		20 11
Singer d	18 29					18 50	19 00					19 21	19 30				19 52		20 01			
Drumry d	18 32					18 53	19 03					19 23	19 33				19 54		20 03			
Drumchapel d	18 34					18 55	19 05					19 27	19 35				19 57		20 06			
Milngavie d			18 38							19 09						19 41					20 09	
Hillfoot d			18 41							19 12						19 44					20 12	
Bearsden d			18 43							19 15						19 46					20 14	
Westerton d	18 37		18 46			18 58	19 08			19 18		19 29	19 38			19 49	20 00		20 08		20 17	
Anniesland d	18 40		18 49			19 01	19 11			19 23		19 32	19 41			19 54	20 03		20 11		20 20	
Clydebank d		18 35		18 43				19 05	19 12					19 36	19 42					20 04		20 13
Yoker d		18 37		18 45				19 07	19 14					19 38	19 44					20 06		20 16
Garscadden d		18 40		18 47				19 10	19 17					19 41	19 47					20 10		20 19
Scotstounhill d		18 42		18 49				19 12	19 19					19 43	19 49					20 12		20 21
Jordanhill d		18 45		18 52				19 16	19 21					19 45	19 52					20 15		20 24
Hyndland 3 d	18 43	18 47	18 52	18 55	18 58	19 04	19 14	19 19	19 24	19 27	19 30	19 35	19 44	19 47	19 54	19 57	20 06		20 14	20 17	20 23	20 26
Partick 225 ⛴ d	18 45	18 49	18 54	18 57	19 01	19 07	19 16	19 21	19 26	19 29	19 32	19 38	19 46	19 50	19 56	19 59	20 08		20 17	20 20	20 25	20 29
Exhibition Centre 225 a		18 52	18 57			19 10		19 24		19 32		19 41		19 53		20 02	20 11			20 23	20 28	
Anderston 225 a		18 54	19 00			19 12		19 26		19 34		19 43		19 55		20 05	20 13			20 25	20 31	
Glasgow Central LL 15 225 a		18 56	19 02			19 14		19 28		19 36		19 45		19 56		20 06	20 15			20 26	20 33	
Argyle Street 225 a		18 58	19 07			19 18		19 30		19 39		19 49		19 59		20 09	20 18			20 29	20 37	
Charing Cross d	18 50			19 01	19 05		19 20		19 31		19 36		19 51		20 01				20 21			20 33
Glasgow Queen St LL 10 ⛴ a	18 52			19 03	19 07		19 22		19 33		19 38		19 53		20 03				20 23			20 35
d	18 52			19 04	19 07		19 23		19 33		19 39		19 54		20 03				20 23			20 35
High Street d	18 55			19 06	19 09		19 25		19 36		19 41		19 56		20 06				20 25			20 37
Bellgrove d	18 57			19 08			19 27		19 38				19 58		20 08				20 27			20 39
Duke Street d				19 10					19 40						20 10							20 41
Alexandra Parade d				19 11					19 41						20 11							20 43
Barnhill d				19 15					19 44						20 14							20 46
Springburn a				19 17					19 46						20 16							20 48
Greenfaulds d			20 02													21 06						
Cumbernauld a			20 04													21 08						
Carntyne d	19 01						19 30						20 02						20 31			
Shettleston d	19 03						19 33						20 04						20 33			
Garrowhill d	19 06						19 35						20 07						20 36			
Easterhouse d	19 08						19 38						20 09						20 38			
Blairhill d	19 12						19 42						20 13						20 42			
Coatbridge Sunnyside d	19 15				19 22		19 44				19 53		20 16						20 45			
Coatdyke d	19 17						19 47						20 18						20 47			
Airdrie d	19a21				19 26		19a49				19 58		20a22						20 50			
Drumgelloch d					19 29						20 01								20 53			
Caldercruix d					19 33						20 05								20 57			
Blackridge d					19 39						20 11								21 03			
Armadale d					19 43						20 14								21 07			
Bathgate a					19 47						20 18								21 11			
d					19 47						20 19							20 48	21 13			
Livingston North d					19 52						20 23							20 52	21 18			
Uphall d					19 55						20 26							20 55	21 21			
Edinburgh Park 230 d					20 04						20 34							21 03	21 33			
Haymarket 228,230 ⛴ a					20 10						20 39							21 08	21 38			
Edinburgh 228,230 a					20 15						20 44							21 13	21 44			

A To Whifflet
B To Larkhall
C To Motherwell

Table T226-R

Mondays to Fridays

16 December to 15 May

Helensburgh, Balloch, Dalmuir and Milngavie - Glasgow - Springburn, Cumbernauld, Airdrie, Bathgate and Edinburgh

		SR	SR	SR	SR	SR	SR	SR	SR	SR	SR	SR	SR	SR	SR	SR	SR	SR	SR	SR	SR	SR
		A		B			A		◇ C	D	D		A		B			A		D		D
Helensburgh Upper 227	d								20 37													
Helensburgh Central	d		20 02					20 32						21 02					21 32			
Craigendoran	d		20 05					20 35						21 05					21 35			
Cardross	d		20 10					20 40						21 10					21 40			
Balloch	d				20 14							20 46				21 14					21 44	
Alexandria	d				20 16							20 48				21 16					21 46	
Renton	d				20 19							20 51				21 19					21 49	
Dalreoch	d		20 15		20 22			20 45				20 55		21 15		21 24			21 45		21 52	
Dumbarton Central 227	d		20 17		20 26			20 47	20 52			20 56		21 17		21 26			21 47		21 56	
Dumbarton East	d		20 19		20 28			20 49				20 58		21 19		21 28			21 49		21 58	
Bowling	d				20 33							21 03				21 33					22 03	
Kilpatrick	d				20 36							21 06				21 36					22 06	
Dalmuir 227	a		20 26		20 39			20 57	21 03			21 09		21 28		21 39			21 58		22 09	
	d	20 19	20 28	20 33	20 40		20 50	20 58		21 03		21 11	21 20	21 29	21 33	21 40		21 50	21 59	22 03	22 10	
Singer	d	20 21	20 30				20 52	21 00					21 22	21 31				21 52	22 01			
Drumry	d	20 23	20 32				20 54	21 03					21 24	21 33				21 54	22 04			
Drumchapel	d	20 26	20 35				20 57	21 05					21 27	21 36				21 57	22 06			
Milngavie	d					20 44					21 10						21 44					22 14
Hillfoot	d					20 47					21 13						21 47					22 17
Bearsden	d					20 49					21 15						21 49					22 19
Westerton	d	20 29	20 37			20 52	21 00	21 08			21 18		21 30	21 38			21 52	21 59	22 09			22 22
Anniesland	d	20 32	20 40			20 55	21 03	21 11			21 21		21 33	21 41			21 55	22 03	22 12			22 25
Clydebank	d			20 35	20 43					21 05		21 13			21 35	21 42				22 05	22 12	
Yoker	d			20 37	20 45					21 07		21 15			21 37	21 44				22 07	22 14	
Garscadden	d			20 40	20 47					21 10		21 19			21 40	21 47				22 10	22 17	
Scotstounhill	d			20 42	20 49					21 12		21 21			21 42	21 49				22 12	22 19	
Jordanhill	d			20 45	20 53					21 15		21 25			21 45	21 52				22 15	22 22	
Hyndland 3	d	20 35	20 43	20 47	20 55	20 58	21 06	21 14		21 17	21 24	21 27	21 36	21 44	21 47	21 54	21 58	22 06	22 15	22 18	22 24	22 28
Partick 225	d	20 37	20 46	20 50	20 57	21 00	21 09	21 16		21 20	21 26	21 29	21 38	21 47	21 50	21 56	22 00	22 08	22 17	22 20	22 26	22 30
Exhibition Centre 225	a	20 40		20 53		21 03	21 12			21 23	21 29		21 41		21 53		22 03	22 11		22 23		22 33
Anderston 225	a	20 43		20 55		21 06	21 14			21 25	21 32		21 43		21 55		22 06	22 13		22 25		22 36
Glasgow Central LL 15 225	a	20 45		20 56		21 07	21 15			21 26	21 34		21 45		21 56		22 07	22 15		22 27		22 37
Argyle Street 225	a	20 48		20 59		21 09	21 17			21 29	21 37		21 46		21 59		22 09	22 18		22 29		22 39
Charing Cross	d		20 50		21 02			21 21				21 33		21 51		22 01			22 21		22 31	
Glasgow Queen St LL 10	a		20 52		21 04			21 23				21 35		21 53		22 03			22 23		22 33	
	d		20 53		21 04			21 23				21 36		21 53		22 03			22 25		22 33	
High Street	d		20 55		21 07			21 25				21 38		21 55		22 06			22 27		22 36	
Bellgrove	d		20 57		21 09			21 27				21 40		21 57		22 08			22 29		22 38	
Duke Street	d				21 11							21 42				22 10					22 40	
Alexandra Parade	d				21 12							21 43				22 11					22 41	
Barnhill	d				21 15							21 46				22 14					22 44	
Springburn	a				21 17							21 48				22 16					22 46	
Greenfaulds	d					22 06											23 08					
Cumbernauld	a					22 08											23 10					
Carntyne	d		21 01					21 31						22 01					22 32			
Shettleston	d		21 03					21 33						22 03					22 35			
Garrowhill	d		21 06					21 36						22 06					22 37			
Easterhouse	d		21 08					21 38						22 08					22 40			
Blairhill	d		21 12					21 42						22 12					22 44			
Coatbridge Sunnyside	d		21 15					21 45						22 15					22 46			
Coatdyke	d		21 17					21 47						22 17					22 49			
Airdrie	d		21 21					21 50						22 21					22 52			
Drumgelloch	d		21 24					21 53						22 24					22 55			
Caldercruix	d		21 28					21 57						22 28					22 59			
Blackridge	d		21 34					22 03						22 34					23 05			
Armadale	d		21 38					22 07						22 38					23 08			
Bathgate	a		21 42					22 11						22 42					23 12			
	d		21 44					22 11						22 42					23 13			
Livingston North	d		21 49					22 16						22 47					23 17			
Uphall	d		21 52					22 19						22 50					23 20			
Edinburgh Park 230	d		22 04					22 31						23 00					23 28			
Haymarket 228,230	a		22 08					22 36						23 05					23 38			
Edinburgh 228,230	a		22 14					22 41						23 12					23 43			

A To Larkhall
B To Whifflet
C From Mallaig to Glasgow Queen Street
D To Motherwell

NRT DECEMBER 19 EDITION

Table T226-R

Mondays to Fridays

16 December to 15 May

Helensburgh, Balloch, Dalmuir and Milngavie - Glasgow - Springburn, Cumbernauld, Airdrie, Bathgate and Edinburgh

		SR	SR	SR	SR	SR	SR	SR	SR	SR	SR	SR	SR FO	SR	SR FO	SR	CS	SR FO	SR	SR
		A		B		C	A		C		◇ D	C	A		C		E	C		
Helensburgh Upper 227	d										22 49						23 26			
Helensburgh Central	d		22 02					22 31						23 02					23 32	
Craigendoran	d		22 05					22 34						23 05					23 35	
Cardross	d		22 10					22 40						23 10					23 40	
Balloch	d				22 14					22 44						23 14				23 44
Alexandria	d				22 16					22 46						23 16				23 46
Renton	d				22 19					22 49						23 19				23 49
Dalreoch	d		22 15		22 22			22 45		22 52				23 15		23 22			23 45	23 52
Dumbarton Central 227	d		22 17		22 26			22 47		22 54	23 02			23 17		23 24	23 41		23 47	23 55
Dumbarton East	d		22 19		22 28			22 49		22 56				23 19		23 26			23 49	23 57
Bowling	d				22 33					23 00						23 31				
Kilpatrick	d				22 36					23 03						23 34				
Dalmuir 227	a		22 26		22 39			22 56		23 06	23 11			23 26		23 37	23 52		23 56	00 08
	d	22 18	22 29	22 33	22 40		22 49	22 59	23 03	23 11			23 19	23 29	23 33		23 53		23 59	
Singer	d	22 20	22 31				22 51	23 01					23 21	23 31					00 01	
Drumry	d	22 23	22 33				22 53	23 03					23 23	23 33					00 03	
Drumchapel	d	22 26	22 36				22 56	23 06					23 26	23 36					00 06	
Milngavie	d					22 44						23 14						23 39		
Hillfoot	d					22 47						23 17						23 42		
Bearsden	d					22 49						23 19						23 44		
Westerton	d	22 28	22 38			22 52	22 59	23 08				23 22	23 28	23 38				23 47	00 08	
Anniesland	d	22 31	22 41			22 55	23 02	23 11				23 25	23 32	23 41				23 50	00 11	
Clydebank	d			22 35	22 42				23 05	23 13					23 35					
Yoker	d			22 37	22 44				23 07	23 15					23 37					
Garscadden	d			22 40	22 47				23 10	23 18					23 40					
Scotstounhill	d			22 42	22 49				23 12	23 20					23 42					
Jordanhill	d			22 45	22 52				23 15	23 22					23 45					
Hyndland 3	d	22 34	22 44	22 47	22 54	22 58	23 05	23 14	23 17	23 24		23 28	23 35	23 44	23 48			23 53	00 14	
Partick 225	d	22 37	22 47	22 50	22 56	23 00	23 08	23 17	23 20	23 27		23 30	23 38	23 47	23 50			23 55	00 17	
Exhibition Centre 225	a	22 40		22 53		23 03	23 11		23 23			23 33	23 41		23 53			23 58		
Anderston 225	a	22 42		22 55		23 06	23 14		23 25			23 36	23 43		23 56			00 01		
Glasgow Central LL 15 225	a	22 44		22 57		23 07	23 15		23 27			23 38	23 45		23 58			00 03		
Argyle Street 225	a	22 48		22 59		23 09	23 19		23 29			23 40	23 48		00 02			00 07		
Charing Cross	d		22 51		23 01			23 21		23 31				23 51					00 21	
Glasgow Queen St LL 10	a		22 53		23 03			23 23		23 33				23 53			00s15		00 23	
	d		22 53		23 03			23 23		23 33				23 53					00 23	
High Street	d		22 55		23 06			23 25		23 36				23 55					00 25	
Bellgrove	d		22 57		23 08			23 27		23 38				23 57					00 27	
Duke Street	d				23 10					23 40										
Alexandra Parade	d				23 11					23 41										
Barnhill	d				23 14					23 44										
Springburn	a				23 16					23 46										
Greenfaulds	d																			
Cumbernauld	a																			
Carntyne	d		23 01					23 31						00 02					00 31	
Shettleston	d		23 03					23 33						00 03					00 33	
Garrowhill	d		23 06					23 36						00 06					00 36	
Easterhouse	d		23 08					23 38						00 08					00 38	
Blairhill	d		23 12					23 42						00 12					00 42	
Coatbridge Sunnyside	d		23 15					23 45						00 15					00 45	
Coatdyke	d		23 17					23 47						00 17					00 47	
Airdrie	d		23 20					23 50						00 20					00a51	
Drumgelloch	d		23 23					23 53						00 23						
Caldercruix	d		23 27					23 57						00 27						
Blackridge	d		23 33					00 03						00 33						
Armadale	d		23 37					00 07						00 37						
Bathgate	a		23 41					00 11						00 41						
	d																			
Livingston North	d																			
Uphall	d																			
Edinburgh Park 230	d																			
Haymarket 228,230	a																			
Edinburgh 228,230	a																			

A To Larkhall
B To Carstairs
C To Motherwell
D From Oban to Glasgow Queen Street
E From Fort William to London Euston

21 December to 16 May

Helensburgh, Balloch, Dalmuir and Milngavie - Glasgow - Springburn, Cumbernauld, Airdrie, Bathgate and Edinburgh

	SR A	SR A	SR A	SR	SR	SR	SR	SR	SR	SR B	SR	SR C	SR C	SR	SR	SR B	SR	SR	SR D	SR	SR	SR
Helensburgh Upper 227 d																						
Helensburgh Central d															05 56							06 26
Craigendoran d															05 59							06 29
Cardross d															06 04							06 34
Balloch d																		06 07				
Alexandria d																		06 09				
Renton d																		06 12				
Dalreoch d															06 09			06 15				06 39
Dumbarton Central 227 d															06 11			06 17			06 26	06 41
Dumbarton East d															06 13			06 19			06 28	06 43
Bowling d																					06 33	
Kilpatrick d																					06 36	
Dalmuir 227 a															06 20			06 27			06 39	06 50
d									05 47	05 51	05 58	06 00		06 12	06 21	06 16		06 28	06 33		06 41	06 51
Singer d			00 01							05 53	06 00					06 18		06 30				
Drumry d			00 03							05 56	06 02					06 21		06 33				
Drumchapel d			00 06							05 58	06 05					06 23		06 35				
Milngavie d																				06 38		
Hillfoot d																				06 41		
Bearsden d																				06 43		
Westerton d			00 08							06 01	06 08					06 26		06 38		06 46		
Anniesland d			00 11							06 04	06 11					06 29		06 41		06 49		
Clydebank d									05 49			06 02		06 14					06 35		06 43	
Yoker d									05 51			06 04		06 16					06 37		06 45	
Garscadden d							05 45	05 49	05 54			06 07		06 19					06 40		06 48	
Scotstounhill d							05 47	05 51	05 57			06 09		06 21					06 42		06 50	
Jordanhill d							05 49	05 53	05 59			06 14		06 23					06 45		06 53	
Hyndland ■ d			00 14			05 37	05 52	05 56	06 01	06 07	06 14	06 17	06 22	06 25	06 28	06 32	06 35	06 44	06 48	06 52	06 55	06 58
Partick 225 ⇌ d			00 17			05 39	05 54	05 58	06 04	06 10	06 16	06 19	06 24	06 28	06 31	06 34	06 38	06 46	06 50	06 54	06 57	07 00
Exhibition Centre 225 a										06 13		06 22	06 27			06 37			06 53	06 57		
Anderston 225 a										06 15		06 24	06 30			06 40			06 55	07 00		
Glasgow Central LL ■ 225 a										06 16		06 26	06 31			06 42			06 57	07 02		
Argyle Street 225 a										06 19		06 28	06 35			06 45			06 59	07 07		
Charing Cross d			00 21			05 43	05 59	06 02	06 08		06 21			06 32	06 35		06 42	06 51			07 01	07 05
Glasgow Queen St LL ■ ⇌ a			00 23			05 45	06 01	06 04	06 10		06 23			06 34	06 37		06 44	06 53			07 03	07 07
d			00 23			05 45	06 01	06 05	06 16		06 23			06 34	06 38		06 45	06 54			07 04	07 07
High Street d			00 25			05 47	06 03	06 07	06 18		06 26			06 36	06 40		06 47	06 56			07 06	07 09
Bellgrove d			00 27			05 49		06 09	06 20		06 28			06 38			06 49	06 58			07 08	
Duke Street d								06 11						06 41							07 10	
Alexandra Parade d								06 12						06 42							07 11	
Barnhill d								06 15						06 45							07 14	
Springburn a								06 17						06 47							07 16	
Greenfaulds d																				08 02		
Cumbernauld a																				08 04		
Carntyne d		00 02	00 31			05 53			06 24		06 31						06 52	07 02				
Shettleston d		00 03	00 33			05 55			06 27		06 34						06 55	07 04				
Garrowhill d		00 06	00 36				06 11				06 36				06 47			07 07				07 17
Easterhouse d		00 08	00 38				06 13				06 39				06 50			07 09				07 19
Blairhill d		00 12	00 42				06 17				06 43				06 54			07 13				07 23
Coatbridge Sunnyside d		00 15	00 45			06 04	06 20		06 35		06 45				06 56		07 03	07 16				07 26
Coatdyke d		00 17	00 47				06 22				06 48				06 59			07 18				07 28
Airdrie d		00 20	00a51			06 09	06 29		06 42		06a52				07 02		07 08	07a22				07 31
Drumgelloch d		00 23				06 12	06 32		06 45						07 05		07 11					07 34
Caldercruix d		00 27				06 16			06 49								07 15					
Blackridge d	00 03	00 33				06 22			06 55								07 21					
Armadale d	00 07	00 37				06 25			06 59								07 24					
Bathgate a	00 11	00 41				06 29	06 44		07 03						07 17		07 28					07 47
d				05 46	06 16	06 30	06 45		07 03						07 17		07 31					07 47
Livingston North d				05 50	06 20	06 34	06 49		07 08						07 22		07 35					07 52
Uphall d				05 53	06 23	06 37	06 52		07 11						07 25		07 38					07 55
Edinburgh Park 230 d				06 03	06 31	06 46	07 03		07 21						07 33		07 48					08 03
Haymarket 228,230 ⇌ a				06 07	06 36	06 50	07 07		07 31						07 38		07 53					08 09
Edinburgh 228,230 a				06 12	06 43	06 55	07 12		07 36						07 43		07 59					08 15

A From Helensburgh Central
B To Larkhall
C To Motherwell
D To Whifflet

Table T226-R

Saturdays

21 December to 16 May

Helensburgh, Balloch, Dalmuir and Milngavie - Glasgow - Springburn, Cumbernauld, Airdrie, Bathgate and Edinburgh

	SR A	SR	SR	SR B	SR B	SR	SR	SR A	SR	SR	SR C	SR	SR	SR	SR A	SR	SR	SR B	SR B	SR	SR ◇ D 🚌	SR
Helensburgh Upper 227 d																					07 42	
Helensburgh Central d							06 56							07 26								07 56
Craigendoran d							06 59							07 29								07 59
Cardross d							07 04							07 34							07 50	08 04
Balloch d			06 37							07 07							07 37					
Alexandria d			06 39							07 09							07 39					
Renton d			06 42							07 12							07 42					
Dalreoch d			06 45				07 09			07 15				07 39			07 45					08 09
Dumbarton Central 227 d			06 47			06 56	07 11			07 17		07 26		07 41			07 46			07 51	07 59	08 11
Dumbarton East d			06 49			06 58	07 13			07 19		07 28		07 43			07 48			07 53		08 13
Bowling d						07 03						07 33								07 58		
Kilpatrick d						07 07						07 36								08 01		
Dalmuir 227 a			06 56			07 10	07 20			07 26		07 39		07 50			07 56			08 05		08 22
d	06 48		06 58	07 02		07 11	07 21	07 19		07 28	07 33	07 40		07 51	07 49		07 57	08 02		08 11		08 23
Singer d	06 50		07 00					07 21		07 30					07 51		07 59				08a11	
Drumry d	06 52		07 03					07 23		07 33					07 53		08 01					
Drumchapel d	06 55		07 05					07 26		07 35					07 56		08 04					
Milngavie d		06 54			07 09				07 24				07 41			07 54			08 09			
Hillfoot d		06 57			07 12				07 27				07 44			07 57			08 12			
Bearsden d		06 59			07 14				07 29				07 46			07 59			08 14			
Westerton d	06 57	07 02	07 08		07 17			07 28	07 32	07 38			07 49		07 59	08 02	08 06		08 17			
Anniesland d	07 00	07 05	07 11		07 20			07 31	07 35	07 41			07 53		08 02	08 05	08 10		08 20			
Clydebank d				07 04		07 13					07 35	07 42						08 04		08 13		
Yoker d				07 06		07 15					07 37	07 44						08 06		08 15		
Garscadden d				07 09		07 19					07 40	07 47						08 10		08 18		
Scotstounhill d				07 11		07 21					07 42	07 49						08 12		08 20		
Jordanhill d				07 15		07 24					07 45	07 52						08 15		08 23		
Hyndland ■ d	07 04	07 08	07 14	07 17	07 23	07 26	07 29	07 35	07 38	07 44	07 48	07 54	07 57	08 00	08 05	08 08	08 13	08 17	08 23	08 26		08 30
Partick 225 ⇌ d	07 06	07 10	07 16	07 19	07 25	07 28	07 31	07 37	07 40	07 46	07 50	07 56	07 59	08 02	08 07	08 11	08 16	08 20	08 25	08 28		08 32
Exhibition Centre 225 a	07 09			07 22	07 28			07 40			07 53		08 02		08 10			08 23	08 28			
Anderston 225 a	07 12			07 24	07 31			07 43			07 55		08 05		08 13			08 25	08 31			
Glasgow Central LL ■ 225 a	07 14			07 26	07 33			07 44			07 57		08 06		08 15			08 26	08 33			
Argyle Street 225 a	07 18			07 28	07 37			07 48			07 59		08 09		08 18			08 29	08 37			
Charing Cross d		07 14	07 21			07 32	07 36		07 45	07 51		08 01		08 07		08 15	08 20			08 33		08 37
Glasgow Queen St LL ■ ⇌ a		07 16	07 23			07 34	07 38		07 47	07 53		08 03		08 09		08 17	08 22			08 35		08 39
d		07 17	07 24			07 35	07 38		07 47	07 53		08 03		08 09		08 18	08 23			08 35		08 39
High Street d		07 19	07 26			07 37	07 40		07 49	07 56		08 05		08 11		08 20	08 26			08 38		08 42
Bellgrove d		07 21	07 28			07 39			07 51	07 58		08 07				08 22	08 28			08 40		
Duke Street d						07 41						08 09								08 42		
Alexandra Parade d						07 42						08 11								08 43		
Barnhill d						07 45						08 14								08 46		
Springburn a						07 47						08 16								08 48		
Greenfaulds d													09 00									
Cumbernauld a													09 02									
Carntyne d		07 24	07 32						07 55	08 01						08 25	08 31					
Shettleston d		07 27	07 34						07 57	08 04						08 28	08 34					
Garrowhill d			07 37				07 48			08 06				08 19			08 36					08 49
Easterhouse d			07 39				07 50			08 09				08 21			08 39					08 52
Blairhill d			07 43				07 54			08 13				08 25			08 43					08 56
Coatbridge Sunnyside d		07 35	07 46				07 57		08 06	08 15				08 28		08 36	08 45					08 58
Coatdyke d			07 48				07 59			08 18				08 30			08 48					09 01
Airdrie d		07 40	07a52				08 03		08 11	08a22				08 34		08 41	08a51					09 05
Drumgelloch d		07 43					08 06		08 14					08 37		08 44						09 08
Caldercruix d		07 47							08 18							08 48						
Blackridge d		07 53							08 24							08 54						
Armadale d		07 56							08 28							08 57						
Bathgate a		08 00					08 19		08 32					08 50		09 01						09 20
d		08 01					08 23		08 36					08 53		09 01						09 22
Livingston North d		08 05					08 28		08 41					08 57		09 06						09 27
Uphall d		08 08					08 32		08 44					09 00		09 09						09 30
Edinburgh Park 230 d		08 18					08 42		08 55					09 11		09 19						09 38
Haymarket 228,230 ⇌ a		08 23					08 48		09 01					09 15		09 24						09 45
Edinburgh 228,230 a		08 31					08 55		09 06					09 22		09 30						09 51

A To Larkhall
B To Motherwell
C To Whifflet
D From Oban to Glasgow Queen Street

Table T226-R

Saturdays

21 December to 16 May

Helensburgh, Balloch, Dalmuir and Milngavie - Glasgow - Springburn, Cumbernauld, Airdrie, Bathgate and Edinburgh

		SR A	SR	SR	SR B	SR	SR	SR	SR A	SR	SR	SR C	SR	SR C	SR	SR A	SR	SR	SR B	SR	SR	SR
Helensburgh Upper 227	d																					
Helensburgh Central	d							08 26							08 54							09 26
Craigendoran	d							08 29							08 57							09 29
Cardross	d							08 34							09 04							09 34
Balloch	d			08 07							08 37							09 07				
Alexandria	d			08 09							08 39							09 09				
Renton	d			08 12							08 42							09 12				
Dalreoch	d			08 15				08 39			08 45				09 09			09 15				09 39
Dumbarton Central 227	d			08 17		08 26		08 41			08 47		08 56		09 11			09 17			09 22	09 41
Dumbarton East	d			08 19		08 28		08 43			08 49		08 58		09 13			09 19			09 24	09 43
Bowling	d					08 32							09 03								09 29	
Kilpatrick	d					08 35							09 06								09 33	
Dalmuir 227	a			08 26		08 38		08 50			08 56		09 09		09 21			09 26			09 36	09 51
	d	08 16		08 27	08 35	08 39		08 51	08 50		08 58	09 03	09 10		09 22	09 20		09 28	09 33		09 41	09 52
Singer	d	08 18		08 29					08 52		09 00					09 22		09 30				
Drumry	d	08 20		08 32					08 54		09 02					09 24		09 33				
Drumchapel	d	08 23		08 34					08 57		09 05					09 27		09 35				
Milngavie	d		08 21				08 40			08 55				09 11			09 25			09 39		
Hillfoot	d		08 24				08 43			08 58				09 14			09 28			09 42		
Bearsden	d		08 26				08 45			09 00				09 16			09 30			09 44		
Westerton	d	08 25	08 29	08 37			08 48		08 59	09 03	09 07			09 19		09 29	09 33	09 38		09 47		
Anniesland	d	08 29	08 32	08 43			08 53		09 03	09 06	09 10			09 23		09 32	09 36	09 41		09 50		
Clydebank	d				08 37	08 42						09 05	09 12						09 35		09 43	
Yoker	d				08 39	08 44						09 07	09 14						09 37		09 45	
Garscadden	d				08 42	08 46						09 10	09 17						09 40		09 48	
Scotstounhill	d				08 44	08 48						09 12	09 19						09 42		09 50	
Jordanhill	d				08 46	08 52						09 15	09 22						09 45		09 53	
Hyndland [3]	d	08 33	08 36	08 46	08 49	08 54	08 57	09 00	09 06	09 09	09 14	09 17	09 24	09 27	09 30	09 35	09 39	09 44	09 47	09 53	09 56	10 00
Partick 225 ⛴	d	08 35	08 38	08 48	08 51	08 56	08 59	09 03	09 08	09 11	09 16	09 20	09 26	09 29	09 32	09 38	09 41	09 46	09 49	09 55	09 58	10 02
Exhibition Centre 225	a	08 38			08 54		09 02		09 11			09 23		09 32		09 41			09 52	09 58		
Anderston 225	a	08 41			08 56		09 04		09 13			09 25		09 35		09 43			09 54	10 01		
Glasgow Central LL [15] 225	a	08 43			08 58		09 06		09 15			09 26		09 36		09 45			09 56	10 03		
Argyle Street 225	a	08 46			09 00		09 09		09 18			09 28		09 39		09 50			09 58	10 07		
Charing Cross	d		08 43	08 53		09 01		09 07		09 15	09 21		09 31		09 37		09 45	09 51			10 03	10 07
Glasgow Queen St LL [10] ⛴	a		08 45	08 55		09 03		09 09		09 17	09 23		09 33		09 39		09 47	09 53			10 05	10 09
	d		08 46	08 55		09 03		09 11		09 18	09 24		09 33		09 40		09 48	09 54			10 05	10 09
High Street	d		08 48	08 57		09 06		09 13		09 20	09 26		09 36		09 43		09 50	09 56			10 08	10 11
Bellgrove	d		08 50	08 59		09 08				09 22	09 28		09 38				09 52	09 58			10 10	
Duke Street	d					09 10							09 40								10 12	
Alexandra Parade	d					09 11							09 41								10 13	
Barnhill	d					09 14							09 44								10 16	
Springburn	a					09 16							09 46								10 18	
Greenfaulds	d						10 00													11 02		
Cumbernauld	a						10 02													11 04		
Carntyne	d		08 54	09 03						09 25	09 32						09 55	10 02				
Shettleston	d		08 56	09 05						09 28	09 34						09 58	10 04				
Garrowhill	d			09 08				09 21			09 37				09 50			10 07				10 19
Easterhouse	d			09 10				09 23			09 39				09 53			10 09				10 21
Blairhill	d			09 14				09 27			09 43				09 57			10 13				10 25
Coatbridge Sunnyside	d		09 05	09 17				09 30		09 36	09 46				09 59		10 06	10 16				10 28
Coatdyke	d			09 19				09 32			09 48				10 02			10 18				10 30
Airdrie	d		09 10	09a25				09 36		09 41	09a52				10 05		10 11	10a22				10 33
Drumgelloch	d		09 13					09 39		09 44					10 08		10 14					10 36
Caldercruix	d		09 17							09 48							10 18					
Blackridge	d		09 23							09 54							10 24					
Armadale	d		09 26							09 58							10 27					
Bathgate	a		09 30					09 51		10 02					10 20		10 31					10 49
	d		09 31					09 52		10 02					10 22		10 32					10 49
Livingston North	d		09 35					09 56		10 07					10 26		10 36					10 54
Uphall	d		09 38					09 59		10 10					10 29		10 39					10 57
Edinburgh Park 230	d		09 47					10 08		10 18					10 39		10 48					11 05
Haymarket 228,230 ⛴	a		09 53					10 14		10 24					10 48		10 54					11 09
Edinburgh 228,230	a		09 59					10 19		10 30					10 53		11 00					11 14

A To Larkhall **B** To Whifflet **C** To Motherwell

Table T226-R

Saturdays

21 December to 16 May

Helensburgh, Balloch, Dalmuir and Milngavie - Glasgow - Springburn, Cumbernauld, Airdrie, Bathgate and Edinburgh

		SR A	SR	SR	SR B	SR B	SR	SR	SR A	SR	SR	SR C	SR	SR	SR	SR A	SR	SR	SR B	SR B	SR	SR ◇ D	SR
Helensburgh Upper 227	d																					10 44	
Helensburgh Central	d							09 56							10 26								10 56
Craigendoran	d							09 59							10 29								10 59
Cardross	d							10 04							10 34								11 04
Balloch	d			09 37							10 07							10 37					
Alexandria	d			09 39							10 09							10 39					
Renton	d			09 42							10 12							10 42					
Dalreoch	d			09 45				10 09			10 15				10 39			10 45					11 09
Dumbarton Central 227	d			09 46			09 57	10 11			10 16			10 26	10 41			10 47			10 54	11 01	11 11
Dumbarton East	d			09 48			09 59	10 13			10 18			10 28	10 43			10 49			10 56		11 13
Bowling	d						10 03							10 33							11 00		
Kilpatrick	d						10 06							10 36							11 04		
Dalmuir 227	a			09 56			10 10	10 20			10 26			10 39	10 50			10 58			11 07	11 12	11 22
	d	09 50		09 58	10 03		10 11	10 21	10 18		10 27	10 33		10 40	10 55	10 49		10 59	11 04		11 11		11 23
Singer	d	09 52		10 00					10 20		10 29					10 51		11 01					
Drumry	d	09 54		10 02					10 23		10 32					10 53		11 03					
Drumchapel	d	09 57		10 05					10 26		10 34					10 56		11 06					
Milngavie	d		09 55			10 09				10 24			10 38				10 55			11 09			
Hillfoot	d		09 58			10 12				10 27			10 41				10 58			11 12			
Bearsden	d		10 00			10 14				10 29			10 43				11 00			11 14			
Westerton	d	10 00	10 03	10 07		10 17			10 28	10 32	10 37		10 46			10 59	11 03	11 08		11 17			
Anniesland	d	10 03	10 06	10 11		10 20			10 31	10 35	10 41		10 49			11 02	11 06	11 11		11 20			
Clydebank	d				10 05		10 13					10 35		10 42					11 06		11 13		
Yoker	d				10 07		10 15					10 37		10 44					11 08		11 15		
Garscadden	d				10 10		10 19					10 40		10 48					11 11		11 19		
Scotstounhill	d				10 12		10 21					10 42		10 50					11 13		11 21		
Jordanhill	d				10 15		10 24					10 45		10 53					11 16		11 25		
Hyndland [3]	d	10 06	10 09	10 14	10 17	10 23	10 26	10 29	10 34	10 38	10 44	10 47	10 52	10 55	11 02	11 05	11 09	11 14	11 18	11 24	11 27		11 30
Partick 225 ⛴	d	10 08	10 12	10 16	10 19	10 25	10 28	10 31	10 37	10 40	10 46	10 49	10 55	10 58	11 04	11 08	11 11	11 17	11 20	11 26	11 29		11 33
Exhibition Centre 225	a	10 11			10 22	10 28			10 40			10 52	10 58			11 11			11 23	11 29			
Anderston 225	a	10 14			10 24	10 31			10 42			10 54	11 00			11 13			11 25	11 32			
Glasgow Central LL [15] 225	a	10 16			10 26	10 33			10 43			10 56	11 02			11 14			11 27	11 34			
Argyle Street 225	a	10 20			10 28	10 37			10 46			10 59	11 07			11 18			11 29	11 38			
Charing Cross	d		10 16	10 21			10 32	10 35		10 44	10 51			11 02	11 09		11 15	11 21			11 33		11 37
Glasgow Queen St LL [10] ⛴	a		10 18	10 23			10 34	10 37		10 46	10 53			11 04	11 11		11 17	11 23			11 35		11 39
	d		10 18	10 24			10 35	10 38		10 47	10 54			11 05	11 12		11 18	11 24			11 36		11 40
High Street	d		10 20	10 26			10 37	10 40		10 49	10 56			11 07	11 14		11 20	11 26			11 38		11 42
Bellgrove	d		10 22	10 28			10 39			10 51	10 58			11 09			11 22	11 28			11 40		
Duke Street	d						10 41							11 11							11 42		
Alexandra Parade	d						10 42							11 12							11 43		
Barnhill	d						10 45							11 15							11 46		
Springburn	a						10 47							11 17							11 48		
Greenfaulds	d												12 02										
Cumbernauld	a												12 04										
Carntyne	d		10 26	10 32						10 54	11 04						11 25	11 32					
Shettleston	d		10 28	10 34						10 57	11 06						11 28	11 34					
Garrowhill	d			10 37				10 47			11 09				11 22			11 37					11 49
Easterhouse	d			10 39				10 50			11 11				11 24			11 39					11 52
Blairhill	d			10 43				10 54			11 15				11 28			11 43					11 56
Coatbridge Sunnyside	d		10 37	10 46				10 56		11 05	11 18				11 31		11 36	11 46					11 58
Coatdyke	d			10 48				10 59			11 20				11 33			11 48					12 01
Airdrie	d		10 41	10a52				11 04		11 10	11a24				11 36		11 41	11a52					12 05
Drumgelloch	d		10 44					11 07		11 13					11 39		11 44						12 08
Caldercruix	d		10 48							11 17							11 48						
Blackridge	d		10 54							11 23							11 54						
Armadale	d		10 58							11 26							11 57						
Bathgate	a		11 02					11 19		11 30					11 52		12 01						12 21
	d		11 02					11 22		11 31					11 52		12 02						12 23
Livingston North	d		11 07					11 26		11 35					11 57		12 06						12 28
Uphall	d		11 10					11 29		11 38					12 00		12 09						12 31
Edinburgh Park 230	d		11 19					11 37		11 48					12 09		12 19						12 39
Haymarket 228,230 ⛴	a		11 24					11 43		11 55					12 16		12 24						12 45
Edinburgh 228,230	a		11 30					11 48		12 00					12 22		12 29						12 51

A To Larkhall
B To Motherwell
C To Whifflet
D From Mallaig to Glasgow Queen Street

Table T226-R

Saturdays

21 December to 16 May

Helensburgh, Balloch, Dalmuir and Milngavie - Glasgow - Springburn, Cumbernauld, Airdrie, Bathgate and Edinburgh

	SR	SR	SR	SR	SR	SR	SR	SR	SR	SR	SR	SR	SR	SR	SR	SR	SR	SR	SR	SR	SR
	A			B			◇ C		A			D		D		A			B		
Helensburgh Upper 227 d							11 16														
Helensburgh Central d								11 26							11 50						
Craigendoran d								11 29							11 53						
Cardross d								11 34							11 59						
Balloch d			11 07								11 37							12 07			
Alexandria d			11 09								11 39							12 09			
Renton d			11 12								11 42							12 12			
Dalreoch d			11 15					11 39			11 45				12 04			12 15			
Dumbarton Central 227 d			11 17			11 22	11 29	11 41			11 47		11 56		12 06			12 17		12 26	
Dumbarton East d			11 19			11 24		11 43			11 49		11 58		12 08			12 19		12 28	
Bowling d						11 28							12 03							12 33	
Kilpatrick d						11 31							12 06							12 36	
Dalmuir 227 a			11 26			11 34	11 38	11 52			11 57		12 09		12 19			12 28		12 39	
d	11 19		11 28	11 31		11 41		11 53	11 49		11 58	12 03	12 10		12 20	12 19		12 29	12 33	12 40	
Singer d	11 21		11 30						11 51		12 00					12 21		12 31			
Drumry d	11 23		11 33						11 53		12 03					12 23		12 33			
Drumchapel d	11 26		11 35						11 56		12 05					12 26		12 36			
Milngavie d		11 24			11 39					11 54				12 11			12 25				12 41
Hillfoot d		11 27			11 42					11 57				12 14			12 28				12 44
Bearsden d		11 29			11 44					11 59				12 16			12 30				12 46
Westerton d	11 29	11 32	11 38		11 47				11 58	12 02	12 08			12 19		12 29	12 33	12 39			12 49
Anniesland d	11 32	11 35	11 41		11 50				12 01	12 05	12 11			12 24		12 32	12 37	12 42			12 54
Clydebank d				11 35		11 43						12 05	12 12						12 35	12 42	
Yoker d				11 37		11 45						12 07	12 14						12 37	12 44	
Garscadden d				11 40		11 49						12 10	12 17						12 40	12 47	
Scotstounhill d				11 42		11 51						12 12	12 19						12 42	12 49	
Jordanhill d				11 45		11 54						12 15	12 21						12 47	12 52	
Hyndland d	11 35	11 38	11 44	11 47	11 53	11 56		12 00	12 04	12 08	12 14	12 17	12 23	12 27	12 30	12 35	12 40	12 45	12 49	12 54	12 57
Partick 225 d	11 37	11 41	11 46	11 49	11 55	11 58		12 03	12 07	12 10	12 17	12 20	12 26	12 29	12 32	12 37	12 42	12 48	12 52	12 56	12 59
Exhibition Centre 225 a	11 40			11 52	11 58				12 10			12 23		12 32		12 40			12 55		13 02
Anderston 225 a	11 42			11 54	12 01				12 12			12 25		12 34		12 43			12 57		13 04
Glasgow Central LL 225 a	11 44			11 56	12 03				12 14			12 26		12 36		12 45			12 58		13 06
Argyle Street 225 a	11 48			11 58	12 07				12 18			12 29		12 39		12 48			13 00		13 09
Charing Cross d		11 45	11 51			12 02		12 07		12 15	12 21		12 30		12 37		12 46	12 52		13 01	
Glasgow Queen St LL a		11 47	11 53			12 04		12 09		12 17	12 23		12 32		12 39		12 48	12 54		13 03	
d		11 47	11 54			12 05		12 10		12 17	12 24		12 33		12 39		12 49	12 55		13 03	
High Street d		11 49	11 56			12 07		12 12		12 19	12 26		12 36		12 42		12 51	12 57		13 06	
Bellgrove d		11 51	11 58			12 09				12 21	12 28		12 38				12 53	12 59		13 08	
Duke Street d						12 11							12 40							13 10	
Alexandra Parade d						12 12							12 41							13 11	
Barnhill d						12 15							12 44							13 14	
Springburn a						12 17							12 46							13 16	
Greenfaulds d					13 02																14 02
Cumbernauld a					13 04																14 04
Carntyne d		11 55	12 02							12 25	12 32						12 56	13 03			
Shettleston d		11 57	12 04							12 27	12 34						12 59	13 05			
Garrowhill d			12 07					12 19			12 37				12 49			13 08			
Easterhouse d			12 09					12 22			12 39				12 52			13 10			
Blairhill d			12 13					12 26			12 43				12 56			13 14			
Coatbridge Sunnyside d		12 06	12 16					12 28		12 36	12 46				12 58		13 07	13 17			
Coatdyke d			12 18					12 31			12 48				13 01			13 19			
Airdrie d		12 10	12a22					12 34		12 40	12a52				13 04		13 12	13a23			
Drumgelloch d		12 13						12 37		12 43					13 07		13 15				
Caldercruix d		12 17								12 47							13 19				
Blackridge d		12 23								12 53							13 25				
Armadale d		12 27								12 57							13 28				
Bathgate a		12 31						12 50		13 01					13 20		13 32				
d		12 31						12 52		13 01					13 22		13 33				
Livingston North d		12 36						12 57		13 06					13 27		13 37				
Uphall d		12 39						13 00		13 09					13 30		13 40				
Edinburgh Park 230 d		12 47						13 09		13 17					13 39		13 48				
Haymarket 228,230 a		12 52						13 14		13 23					13 45		13 53				
Edinburgh 228,230 a		12 57						13 21		13 29					13 51		13 58				

A To Larkhall
B To Whifflet
C From Oban to Glasgow Queen Street
D To Motherwell

Table T226-R

Saturdays

21 December to 16 May

Helensburgh, Balloch, Dalmuir and Milngavie - Glasgow - Springburn, Cumbernauld, Airdrie, Bathgate and Edinburgh

	SR	SR	SR	SR	SR	SR	SR	SR	SR	SR	SR	SR	SR	SR	SR	SR	SR	SR	SR	SR	SR	SR
		A			B		B		A			C				A			B	B		
Helensburgh Upper 227 d																						
Helensburgh Central d	12 26							12 55							13 26							13 56
Craigendoran d	12 29							12 58							13 29							13 59
Cardross d	12 34							13 03							13 34							14 04
Balloch d				12 37							13 07							13 37				
Alexandria d				12 39							13 09							13 39				
Renton d				12 42							13 12							13 42				
Dalreoch d	12 39			12 45				13 08			13 15				13 39			13 45				14 09
Dumbarton Central 227 d	12 41			12 47		12 56		13 10			13 17		13 26		13 41			13 46			13 58	14 11
Dumbarton East d	12 43			12 49		12 58		13 12			13 19		13 28		13 43			13 48			14 00	14 13
Bowling d						13 03							13 33								14 05	
Kilpatrick d						13 06							13 36								14 08	
Dalmuir 227 a	12 52			12 57		13 09		13 22			13 26		13 39		13 53			13 57			14 11	14 22
d	12 53	12 49		12 58	13 03	13 10		13 23	13 19		13 27	13 33	13 40		13 54	13 49		13 57	14 03		14 11	14 23
Singer d		12 51		13 00					13 21		13 29					13 51		13 59				
Drumry d		12 53		13 03					13 23		13 32					13 53		14 02				
Drumchapel d		12 56		13 05					13 26		13 34					13 56		14 04				
Milngavie d			12 54				13 11			13 25				13 40			13 54			14 09		
Hillfoot d			12 57				13 14			13 28				13 43			13 57			14 12		
Bearsden d			12 59				13 16			13 30				13 45			13 59			14 14		
Westerton d		12 59	13 03	13 08			13 19		13 29	13 33	13 37			13 48		13 59	14 02	14 07		14 17		
Anniesland d		13 02	13 06	13 11			13 24		13 32	13 36	13 40			13 53		14 02	14 05	14 10		14 20		
Clydebank d					13 05	13 12						13 35	13 42						14 05		14 14	
Yoker d					13 07	13 14						13 37	13 44						14 07		14 16	
Garscadden d					13 10	13 17						13 40	13 47						14 10		14 18	
Scotstounhill d					13 12	13 19						13 42	13 49						14 12		14 20	
Jordanhill d					13 15	13 22						13 45	13 52						14 16		14 25	
Hyndland d	13 01	13 05	13 09	13 14	13 17	13 24	13 27	13 30	13 35	13 39	13 43	13 47	13 54	13 57	14 01	14 05	14 08	14 13	14 18	14 24	14 27	14 31
Partick 225 d	13 03	13 07	13 11	13 16	13 19	13 26	13 29	13 33	13 37	13 41	13 45	13 49	13 56	13 59	14 03	14 07	14 11	14 16	14 21	14 26	14 29	14 33
Exhibition Centre 225 a		13 10			13 22		13 32		13 40			13 52		14 02		14 10			14 24	14 29		
Anderston 225 a		13 12			13 24		13 34		13 42			13 54		14 04		14 12			14 26	14 31		
Glasgow Central LL 225 a		13 14			13 26		13 36		13 44			13 56		14 06		14 14			14 27	14 33		
Argyle Street 225 a		13 18			13 28		13 39		13 48			13 58		14 09		14 18			14 29	14 39		
Charing Cross d	13 07		13 15	13 21		13 31		13 37		13 46	13 50		14 01		14 08		14 15	14 21			14 33	14 38
Glasgow Queen St LL a	13 09		13 17	13 23		13 33		13 39		13 48	13 52		14 03		14 10		14 17	14 23			14 35	14 40
d	13 12		13 18	13 24		13 33		13 40		13 48	13 54		14 03		14 10		14 18	14 24			14 36	14 40
High Street d	13 14		13 20	13 26		13 36		13 42		13 50	13 56		14 06		14 13		14 20	14 26			14 38	14 42
Bellgrove d			13 22	13 28		13 38				13 52	13 58		14 08				14 22	14 28			14 40	
Duke Street d						13 40							14 10								14 42	
Alexandra Parade d						13 41							14 11								14 44	
Barnhill d						13 44							14 14								14 47	
Springburn a						13 46							14 16								14 49	
Greenfaulds d														15 02								
Cumbernauld a														15 04								
Carntyne d			13 25	13 32						13 56	14 02						14 25	14 32				
Shettleston d			13 28	13 34						13 58	14 04						14 28	14 34				
Garrowhill d	13 22			13 37				13 49			14 07				14 20			14 37				14 50
Easterhouse d	13 24			13 39				13 52			14 09				14 23			14 39				14 52
Blairhill d	13 28			13 43				13 56			14 13				14 27			14 43				14 56
Coatbridge Sunnyside d	13 31		13 36	13 46				13 58		14 07	14 16				14 29		14 36	14 46				14 59
Coatdyke d	13 33			13 48				14 01			14 18				14 32			14 48				15 01
Airdrie d	13 36		13 41	13a52				14 05		14 11	14a22				14 35		14 41	14a52				15 04
Drumgelloch d	13 39		13 44					14 08		14 14					14 38		14 44					15 07
Caldercruix d			13 48							14 18							14 48					
Blackridge d			13 54							14 24							14 54					
Armadale d			13 57							14 28							14 57					
Bathgate a	13 52		14 01					14 21		14 32					14 50		15 01					15 20
d	13 52		14 01					14 21		14 32					14 52		15 02					15 21
Livingston North d	13 57		14 06					14 26		14 37					14 57		15 06					15 26
Uphall d	14 00		14 09					14 29		14 40					15 00		15 09					15 29
Edinburgh Park 230 d	14 08		14 18					14 39		14 48					15 08		15 17					15 38
Haymarket 228,230 a	14 15		14 23					14 43		14 54					15 13		15 23					15 42
Edinburgh 228,230 a	14 21		14 29					14 48		15 01					15 18		15 29					15 48

A To Larkhall
B To Motherwell
C To Whifflet

Table T226-R

Saturdays

21 December to 16 May

Helensburgh, Balloch, Dalmuir and Milngavie - Glasgow - Springburn, Cumbernauld, Airdrie, Bathgate and Edinburgh

		SR A	SR	SR	SR B	SR	SR	SR	SR A	SR	SR	SR C	SR	SR ◇ D	SR C	SR	SR A	SR	SR	SR B	SR	SR	SR
Helensburgh Upper	227 d													14 43									
Helensburgh Central	d							14 26								14 56							15 26
Craigendoran	d							14 29								14 59							15 29
Cardross	d							14 34								15 04							15 34
Balloch	d			14 07							14 37								15 07				
Alexandria	d			14 09							14 39								15 09				
Renton	d			14 12							14 42								15 12				
Dalreoch	d			14 15				14 39			14 45					15 09			15 15				15 39
Dumbarton Central	227 d			14 17			14 26	14 41			14 47		14 55	15 02		15 11			15 17		15 26		15 41
Dumbarton East	d			14 19			14 28	14 43			14 49		14 57			15 13			15 19		15 28		15 43
Bowling	d						14 33						15 01								15 33		
Kilpatrick	d						14 36						15 04								15 36		
Dalmuir	227 a			14 26			14 39	14 52			14 56		15 07	15 12		15 22			15 26		15 39		15 53
	d	14 19		14 27	14 32		14 41	14 53	14 49		14 57	15 03	15 09			15 23	15 19		15 27	15 33	15 40		15 54
Singer	d	14 21		14 29					14 51		14 59						15 21		15 29				
Drumry	d	14 23		14 32					14 53		15 02						15 23		15 32				
Drumchapel	d	14 26		14 34					14 56		15 04						15 26		15 34				
Milngavie	d		14 24			14 39				14 54					15 11			15 25				15 40	
Hillfoot	d		14 27			14 42				14 57					15 14			15 28				15 43	
Bearsden	d		14 29			14 44				14 59					15 16			15 30				15 45	
Westerton	d	14 29	14 32	14 37		14 47			14 59	15 02	15 07				15 19		15 29	15 33	15 37			15 48	
Anniesland	d	14 32	14 35	14 40		14 50			15 02	15 05	15 11				15 23		15 32	15 36	15 40			15 53	
Clydebank	d				14 34		14 43					15 05	15 12							15 35	15 42		
Yoker	d				14 36		14 45					15 07	15 14							15 37	15 44		
Garscadden	d				14 40		14 49					15 10	15 16							15 40	15 47		
Scotstounhill	d				14 42		14 51					15 12	15 18							15 42	15 49		
Jordanhill	d				14 44		14 54					15 15	15 21							15 45	15 51		
Hyndland 3	d	14 35	14 38	14 43	14 47	14 53	14 56	15 01	15 05	15 08	15 15	15 18	15 23		15 26	15 30	15 35	15 39	15 43	15 47	15 53	15 56	16 01
Partick	225 d	14 37	14 40	14 45	14 49	14 55	14 59	15 03	15 07	15 11	15 17	15 20	15 26		15 29	15 33	15 38	15 41	15 45	15 49	15 56	15 59	16 03
Exhibition Centre	225 a	14 40			14 52	14 58			15 10			15 23			15 32		15 41			15 52		16 02	
Anderston	225 a	14 42			14 54	15 01			15 13			15 25			15 34		15 43			15 54		16 04	
Glasgow Central LL 15	225 a	14 44			14 56	15 03			15 15			15 27			15 36		15 44			15 56		16 05	
Argyle Street	225 a	14 46			14 58	15 07			15 18			15 29			15 39		15 46			15 58		16 08	
Charing Cross	d		14 45	14 50			15 03	15 08		15 15	15 22		15 30			15 37		15 46	15 50		16 00		16 08
Glasgow Queen St LL 10	a		14 47	14 52			15 05	15 10		15 17	15 24		15 32			15 39		15 48	15 52		16 02		16 10
	d		14 47	14 54			15 05	15 10		15 17	15 25		15 33			15 40		15 48	15 54		16 03		16 11
High Street	d		14 50	14 56			15 08	15 12		15 19	15 27		15 36			15 42		15 50	15 56		16 05		16 13
Bellgrove	d		14 52	14 58			15 10			15 21	15 29		15 38					15 52	15 58		16 07		
Duke Street	d						15 12						15 40								16 09		
Alexandra Parade	d						15 13						15 41								16 11		
Barnhill	d						15 16						15 44								16 14		
Springburn	a						15 18						15 46								16 16		
Greenfaulds	d					16 03																17 07	
Cumbernauld	a					16 05																17 09	
Carntyne	d		14 55	15 04						15 25	15 33							15 56	16 02				
Shettleston	d		14 58	15 06						15 27	15 37							15 58	16 04				
Garrowhill	d			15 09				15 20			15 40					15 49			16 07				16 21
Easterhouse	d			15 11				15 22			15 42					15 52			16 09				16 23
Blairhill	d			15 15				15 26			15 46					15 56			16 13				16 27
Coatbridge Sunnyside	d		15 06	15 18				15 29		15 36	15 49					15 58		16 07	16 16				16 30
Coatdyke	d			15 20				15 31			15 51					16 01			16 18				16 32
Airdrie	d		15 11	15a24				15 35		15 40	15a55					16 04		16 11	16a22				16 36
Drumgelloch	d		15 14					15 38		15 43						16 07		16 14					16 39
Caldercruix	d		15 18							15 47								16 18					
Blackridge	d		15 24							15 53								16 24					
Armadale	d		15 27							15 57								16 28					
Bathgate	a		15 31					15 50		16 01						16 20		16 32					16 51
	d		15 32					15 52		16 01						16 21		16 32					16 52
Livingston North	d		15 36					15 56		16 06						16 25		16 37					16 57
Uphall	d		15 39					15 59		16 09						16 28		16 40					17 00
Edinburgh Park	230 d		15 47					16 08		16 17						16 39		16 48					17 10
Haymarket	228,230 a		15 53					16 13		16 24						16 45		16 53					17 16
Edinburgh	228,230 a		15 59					16 18		16 30						16 50		16 59					17 21

A To Larkhall
B To Whifflet
C To Motherwell
D From Mallaig to Glasgow Queen Street

Table T226-R

Saturdays

21 December to 16 May

Helensburgh, Balloch, Dalmuir and Milngavie - Glasgow - Springburn, Cumbernauld, Airdrie, Bathgate and Edinburgh

		SR A	SR	SR	SR B	SR B	SR	SR	SR A	SR	SR	SR C	SR	SR	SR	SR A	SR	SR	SR B	SR	SR B	SR
Helensburgh Upper	227 d																					
Helensburgh Central	d							15 55						16 21								16 54
Craigendoran	d							15 58						16 24								16 57
Cardross	d							16 03						16 30								17 02
Balloch	d			15 37							16 06							16 37				
Alexandria	d			15 39							16 08							16 39				
Renton	d			15 42							16 11							16 42				
Dalreoch	d			15 45				16 08			16 14			16 35				16 45				17 07
Dumbarton Central	227 d			15 47			15 56	16 10			16 15		16 26	16 36				16 47		16 56		17 09
Dumbarton East	d			15 49			15 58	16 12			16 17		16 28	16 38				16 49		16 58		17 11
Bowling	d						16 03						16 32							17 03		
Kilpatrick	d						16 06						16 35							17 06		
Dalmuir	227 a			15 57			16 09	16 22			16 26		16 38	16 46				16 56		17 09		17 19
	d	15 49		15 58	16 03		16 11	16 23	16 19		16 28	16 33	16 39	16 49		16 49		16 57	17 03	17 10		17 20
Singer	d	15 51		16 00					16 21		16 30					16 51		16 59				
Drumry	d	15 53		16 02					16 23		16 32					16 53		17 02				
Drumchapel	d	15 56		16 05					16 26		16 35					16 56		17 04				
Milngavie	d		15 54			16 09				16 25					16 41		16 56				17 11	
Hillfoot	d		15 57			16 12				16 28					16 44		16 59				17 14	
Bearsden	d		15 59			16 14				16 30					16 46		17 01				17 16	
Westerton	d	15 59	16 02	16 07		16 17			16 28	16 33	16 37				16 49	16 59	17 04	17 07			17 19	
Anniesland	d	16 02	16 05	16 10		16 20			16 31	16 36	16 41				16 54	17 02	17 07	17 10			17 23	
Clydebank	d				16 05		16 13					16 35	16 41						17 05	17 12		
Yoker	d				16 07		16 15					16 37	16 43						17 07	17 14		
Garscadden	d				16 10		16 19					16 40	16 47						17 10	17 17		
Scotstounhill	d				16 12		16 21					16 42	16 49						17 12	17 19		
Jordanhill	d				16 15		16 24					16 45	16 51						17 15	17 21		
Hyndland 3	d	16 05	16 08	16 13	16 17	16 23	16 26	16 30	16 34	16 39	16 44	16 47	16 53	16 56	16 59	17 06	17 10	17 14	17 17	17 24	17 27	17 30
Partick	225 d	16 07	16 11	16 16	16 19	16 25	16 28	16 33	16 37	16 42	16 46	16 49	16 56	16 59	17 02	17 08	17 12	17 16	17 20	17 26	17 29	17 32
Exhibition Centre	225 a	16 10			16 22	16 28			16 40			16 52			17 05	17 11			17 23		17 32	
Anderston	225 a	16 13			16 24	16 31			16 42			16 54			17 07	17 14			17 25		17 34	
Glasgow Central LL 15	225 a	16 15			16 26	16 33			16 44			16 56			17 09	17 16			17 26		17 36	
Argyle Street	225 a	16 18			16 28	16 37			16 48			16 58			17 11	17 19			17 29		17 39	
Charing Cross	d		16 15	16 21			16 33	16 37		16 46	16 51		17 00	17 04			17 17	17 21		17 31		17 37
Glasgow Queen St LL 10	a		16 17	16 23			16 35	16 39		16 48	16 53		17 02	17 06			17 19	17 23		17 33		17 39
	d		16 18	16 24			16 35	16 40		16 49	16 54		17 03	17 07			17 19	17 24		17 33		17 39
High Street	d		16 20	16 26			16 37	16 42		16 51	16 56		17 05	17 09			17 22	17 26		17 35		17 42
Bellgrove	d		16 22	16 28			16 39			16 53	16 58		17 07				17 24	17 28		17 37		
Duke Street	d						16 41						17 09							17 39		
Alexandra Parade	d						16 43						17 11							17 41		
Barnhill	d						16 46						17 14							17 44		
Springburn	a						16 48						17 16							17 46		
Greenfaulds	d														18 06							
Cumbernauld	a														18 08							
Carntyne	d		16 25	16 32						16 57	17 02						17 27	17 32				
Shettleston	d		16 28	16 34						16 59	17 04						17 30	17 34				
Garrowhill	d			16 37				16 49			17 07			17 16				17 37				17 49
Easterhouse	d			16 39				16 52			17 09			17 19				17 39				17 52
Blairhill	d		16 34	16 43				16 56		17 06	17 13			17 23			17 36	17 43				17 56
Coatbridge Sunnyside	d		16 37	16 46				16 58		17 08	17 16			17 25			17 39	17 46				17 58
Coatdyke	d		16 39	16 48				17 01		17 11	17 18			17 28			17 41	17 48				18 01
Airdrie	d		16 42	16a52				17 05		17 15	17a22			17 31			17 44	17a52				18 04
Drumgelloch	d		16 45					17 08		17 18				17 34			17 47					18 07
Caldercruix	d		16 49							17 22							17 51					
Blackridge	d		16 55							17 28							17 57					
Armadale	d		16 59							17 32							18 01					
Bathgate	a		17 03					17 20		17 36				17 46			18 05					18 20
	d		17 03					17 23		17 36				17 47			18 05					18 22
Livingston North	d		17 08					17 28		17 41				17 51			18 10					18 26
Uphall	d		17 11					17 31		17 45				17 54			18 13					18 29
Edinburgh Park	230 d		17 19					17 40		17 54				18 02			18 22					18 39
Haymarket	228,230 a		17 23					17 50		18 01				18 08			18 27					18 46
Edinburgh	228,230 a		17 29					17 55		18 06				18 13			18 33					18 51

A To Larkhall
B To Motherwell
C To Whifflet

Table T226-R

Saturdays

21 December to 16 May

Helensburgh, Balloch, Dalmuir and Milngavie - Glasgow - Springburn, Cumbernauld, Airdrie, Bathgate and Edinburgh

	SR A	SR	SR B	SR	SR	SR	SR	SR A	SR	SR	SR C	SR C	SR	SR	SR A	SR	SR	SR B	SR	SR	SR	SR A
Helensburgh Upper 227 d																						
Helensburgh Central d							17 26							17 56							18 22	
Craigendoran d							17 29							17 59							18 25	
Cardross d							17 34							18 04							18 30	
Balloch d				17 09						17 37							18 07					
Alexandria d				17 11						17 39							18 09					
Renton d				17 14						17 42							18 12					
Dalreoch d				17 17			17 39			17 45				18 09			18 15				18 35	
Dumbarton Central 227 d				17 19		17 26	17 41			17 47			17 56	18 11			18 17			18 26	18 37	
Dumbarton East d				17 21		17 28	17 43			17 49			17 58	18 13			18 19			18 28	18 39	
Bowling d						17 33							18 03							18 33		
Kilpatrick d						17 36							18 06							18 36		
Dalmuir 227 a				17 29		17 39	17 50			17 56			18 09	18 20			18 26			18 39	18 49	
d	17 19		17 33	17 30		17 41	17 51	17 49		17 57	18 03		18 11	18 21	18 18		18 27	18 33		18 40	18 50	18 48
Singer d	17 21			17 32				17 51		17 59					18 20		18 29					18 50
Drumry d	17 23			17 34				17 53		18 02					18 23		18 32					18 53
Drumchapel d	17 26			17 37				17 56		18 04					18 26		18 34					18 55
Milngavie d		17 24			17 39				17 54			18 09				18 24			18 38			
Hillfoot d		17 27			17 42				17 57			18 12				18 27			18 41			
Bearsden d		17 29			17 44				17 59			18 14				18 29			18 43			
Westerton d	17 29	17 32		17 40	17 47			17 59	18 02	18 07		18 17			18 28	18 32	18 37		18 46			18 58
Anniesland d	17 32	17 35		17 46	17 50			18 02	18 05	18 10		18 20			18 31	18 35	18 40		18 49			19 01
Clydebank d			17 35			17 43					18 05		18 13					18 35		18 43		
Yoker d			17 37			17 45					18 07		18 15					18 37		18 45		
Garscadden d			17 40			17 49					18 10		18 19					18 40		18 47		
Scotstounhill d			17 42			17 51					18 12		18 21					18 42		18 49		
Jordanhill d			17 44			17 54					18 15		18 25					18 45		18 52		
Hyndland 3 d	17 35	17 38	17 46	17 49	17 53	17 56	18 00	18 05	18 08	18 13	18 17	18 23	18 27	18 30	18 34	18 38	18 43	18 47	18 52	18 55	18 58	19 04
Partick 225 ⛴ d	17 38	17 41	17 49	17 52	17 56	17 59	18 02	18 07	18 11	18 15	18 19	18 25	18 29	18 32	18 37	18 40	18 45	18 49	18 54	18 57	19 01	19 07
Exhibition Centre 225 a	17 41		17 52		17 59			18 10			18 22	18 28			18 40			18 52	18 57			19 10
Anderston 225 a	17 46		17 54		18 01			18 12			18 24	18 31			18 42			18 54	19 00			19 12
Glasgow Central LL 15 225 a	17 48		17 55		18 03			18 14			18 26	18 33			18 44			18 56	19 02			19 14
Argyle Street 225 a	17 52		17 57		18 07			18 18			18 28	18 37			18 47			18 58	19 07			19 18
Charing Cross d		17 45		17 56		18 03	18 07		18 15	18 20			18 33	18 37		18 44	18 50			19 01	19 05	
Glasgow Queen St LL 10 ⛴ a		17 47		17 58		18 05	18 09		18 17	18 22			18 35	18 39		18 46	18 52			19 03	19 07	
d		17 48		17 59		18 06	18 10		18 17	18 23			18 36	18 40		18 47	18 52			19 04	19 07	
High Street d		17 50		18 01		18 08	18 13		18 19	18 26			18 38	18 42		18 49	18 55			19 06	19 09	
Bellgrove d		17 52		18 03		18 10			18 21	18 28			18 40			18 51	18 57			19 08		
Duke Street d						18 12							18 42							19 10		
Alexandra Parade d						18 13							18 43							19 11		
Barnhill d						18 16							18 46							19 15		
Springburn a						18 18							18 48							19 17		
Greenfaulds d					19 02														20 02			
Cumbernauld a					19 04														20 04			
Carntyne d		17 55		18 07					18 25	18 32						18 54	19 01					
Shettleston d		17 58		18 09					18 27	18 34						18 57	19 03					
Garrowhill d				18 12			18 20			18 37				18 49			19 06					
Easterhouse d				18 14			18 23			18 39				18 52			19 08					
Blairhill d				18 18			18 27			18 43				18 56			19 12					
Coatbridge Sunnyside d		18 06		18 21			18 29		18 36	18 46				18 58		19 05	19 15				19 22	
Coatdyke d				18 23			18 32			18 48				19 01			19 17					
Airdrie d		18 11		18a27			18 35		18 40	18a52				19 04		19 10	19a21				19 26	
Drumgelloch d		18 14					18 38		18 43					19 07		19 13					19 29	
Caldercruix d		18 18							18 47							19 17					19 33	
Blackridge d		18 24							18 53							19 23					19 39	
Armadale d		18 27							18 57							19 26					19 43	
Bathgate a		18 31					18 51		19 01					19 20		19 30					19 47	
d		18 32					18 52		19 02					19 21		19 31					19 47	
Livingston North d		18 36					18 56		19 06					19 26		19 35					19 52	
Uphall d		18 39					18 59		19 09					19 29		19 38					19 55	
Edinburgh Park 230 d		18 47					19 09		19 17					19 38		19 48					20 03	
Haymarket 228,230 ⛴ a		18 53					19 15		19 22					19 43		19 54					20 09	
Edinburgh 228,230 a		18 59					19 22		19 28					19 48		19 59					20 15	

A To Larkhall B To Whifflet C To Motherwell

Table T226-R

Saturdays

21 December to 16 May

Helensburgh, Balloch, Dalmuir and Milngavie - Glasgow - Springburn, Cumbernauld, Airdrie, Bathgate and Edinburgh

	SR ◇ A 🍴	SR	SR B	SR	SR B	SR	SR C	SR	SR D	SR	SR	SR C	SR	SR	SR B	SR B	SR	SR C	SR	SR D	SR
Helensburgh Upper 227 d	18 31																				
Helensburgh Central d						18 54								19 32					20 02		
Craigendoran d						18 57								19 35					20 05		
Cardross d						19 02								19 40					20 10		
Balloch d		18 38						19 07									19 43				20 14
Alexandria d		18 40						19 09									19 45				20 16
Renton d		18 43						19 12									19 48				20 19
Dalreoch d		18 46				19 07		19 15						19 45			19 51		20 15		20 22
Dumbarton Central 227 d	18 44	18 48		18 54		19 11		19 17		19 26				19 47			19 57		20 17		20 26
Dumbarton East d		18 50		18 56		19 13		19 19		19 28				19 49			19 59		20 19		20 28
Bowling d				19 01						19 33							20 04				20 33
Kilpatrick d				19 04						19 36							20 07				20 36
Dalmuir 227 a	18 53	18 57		19 07		19 21		19 26		19 39				19 57			20 10		20 26		20 39
d		18 58	19 03	19 10		19 22	19 19	19 28	19 34	19 40		19 50		19 59	20 02		20 11	20 19	20 28	20 33	20 40
Singer d		19 00					19 21	19 30				19 52		20 01				20 21	20 30		
Drumry d		19 03					19 23	19 33				19 54		20 03				20 23	20 32		
Drumchapel d		19 05					19 27	19 35				19 57		20 06				20 26	20 35		
Milngavie d					19 09						19 41					20 09					
Hillfoot d					19 12						19 44					20 12					
Bearsden d					19 15						19 46					20 14					
Westerton d		19 08			19 18		19 29	19 38			19 49	20 00		20 08		20 17		20 29	20 37		
Anniesland d		19 11			19 23		19 32	19 41			19 54	20 03		20 11		20 20		20 32	20 40		
Clydebank d			19 05	19 12					19 36	19 42					20 04		20 13			20 35	20 43
Yoker d			19 07	19 14					19 38	19 44					20 06		20 16			20 37	20 45
Garscadden d			19 10	19 17					19 41	19 47					20 10		20 19			20 40	20 47
Scotstounhill d			19 12	19 19					19 43	19 49					20 12		20 21			20 42	20 49
Jordanhill d			19 16	19 21					19 45	19 52					20 15		20 24			20 45	20 53
Hyndland 3 d		19 14	19 19	19 24	19 27	19 30	19 35	19 44	19 47	19 54	19 57	20 06		20 14	20 17	20 23	20 26	20 35	20 43	20 47	20 55
Partick 225 ⛴ d		19 16	19 21	19 26	19 29	19 32	19 38	19 46	19 50	19 56	19 59	20 08		20 17	20 20	20 25	20 29	20 37	20 46	20 50	20 57
Exhibition Centre 225 a			19 24		19 32		19 41		19 53		20 02	20 11			20 23	20 28		20 40		20 53	
Anderston 225 a			19 26		19 34		19 43		19 55		20 05	20 13			20 25	20 31		20 43		20 55	
Glasgow Central LL 15 225 a			19 28		19 36		19 45		19 56		20 06	20 15			20 26	20 33		20 45		20 56	
Argyle Street 225 a			19 30		19 39		19 49		19 59		20 09	20 18			20 29	20 36		20 48		20 59	
Charing Cross d		19 20		19 31		19 36		19 51		20 01				20 21			20 33		20 50		21 02
Glasgow Queen St LL 10 ⛴ a		19 22		19 33		19 38		19 53		20 03				20 23			20 35		20 52		21 04
d		19 23		19 33		19 39		19 54		20 03				20 23			20 35		20 53		21 04
High Street d		19 25		19 36		19 41		19 56		20 06				20 25			20 37		20 55		21 07
Bellgrove d		19 27		19 38				19 58		20 08				20 27			20 39		20 57		21 09
Duke Street d				19 40						20 10							20 41				21 11
Alexandra Parade d				19 41						20 11							20 43				21 12
Barnhill d				19 44						20 14							20 46				21 15
Springburn a				19 46						20 16							20 48				21 17
Greenfaulds d											21 06										
Cumbernauld a											21 08										
Carntyne d		19 30						20 02						20 31					21 01		
Shettleston d		19 33						20 04						20 33					21 03		
Garrowhill d		19 35						20 07						20 36					21 06		
Easterhouse d		19 38						20 09						20 38					21 08		
Blairhill d		19 42						20 13						20 42					21 12		
Coatbridge Sunnyside d		19 44				19 53		20 16						20 45					21 15		
Coatdyke d		19 47						20 18						20 47					21 17		
Airdrie d		19a49				19 58		20a22						20 50					21 21		
Drumgelloch d						20 01								20 53					21 24		
Caldercruix d						20 05								20 57					21 28		
Blackridge d						20 11								21 03					21 34		
Armadale d						20 14								21 07					21 38		
Bathgate a						20 18								21 11					21 42		
d						20 19							20 48	21 13					21 44		
Livingston North d						20 23							20 52	21 18					21 49		
Uphall d						20 26							20 55	21 21					21 52		
Edinburgh Park 230 d						20 34							21 03	21 32					22 01		
Haymarket 228,230 ⛴ a						20 40							21 08	21 38					22 08		
Edinburgh 228,230 a						20 45							21 13	21 44					22 13		

A From Oban to Glasgow Queen Street
B To Motherwell
C To Larkhall
D To Whifflet

Table T226-R

Saturdays
21 December to 16 May

Helensburgh, Balloch, Dalmuir and Milngavie - Glasgow - Springburn, Cumbernauld, Airdrie, Bathgate and Edinburgh

		SR	SR	SR	SR	SR	SR	SR	SR	SR	SR	SR	SR	SR	SR	SR	SR	SR	SR	SR	SR	SR	SR
			A		◇ B	C	C		A		D			A		C		C	A		C		C
Helensburgh Upper 227	d				20 37																		
Helensburgh Central	d			20 32						21 02					21 32					22 02			
Craigendoran	d			20 35						21 05					21 35					22 05			
Cardross	d			20 40						21 10					21 40					22 10			
Balloch	d							20 46				21 14					21 44					22 14	
Alexandria	d							20 48				21 16					21 46					22 16	
Renton	d							20 51				21 19					21 49					22 19	
Dalreoch	d			20 45				20 55		21 15		21 24			21 45		21 52			22 15		22 22	
Dumbarton Central 227	d			20 47	20 52			20 56		21 17		21 26			21 47		21 56			22 17		22 26	
Dumbarton East	d			20 49				20 58		21 19		21 28			21 49		21 58			22 19		22 28	
Bowling	d							21 03				21 33					22 03					22 33	
Kilpatrick	d							21 06				21 36					22 06					22 36	
Dalmuir 227	a			20 57	21 03			21 09		21 28		21 39			21 58		22 09			22 26		22 39	
	d		20 50	20 58		21 03		21 11	21 20	21 29	21 33	21 40		21 50	21 59	22 03	22 10		22 18	22 29	22 33	22 40	
Singer	d		20 52	21 00					21 22	21 31				21 52	22 01				22 20	22 31			
Drumry	d		20 54	21 03					21 24	21 33				21 54	22 04				22 23	22 33			
Drumchapel	d		20 57	21 05					21 27	21 36				21 57	22 06				22 26	22 36			
Milngavie	d	20 44					21 10						21 44					22 14					22 44
Hillfoot	d	20 47					21 13						21 47					22 17					22 47
Bearsden	d	20 49					21 15						21 49					22 19					22 49
Westerton	d	20 52	21 00	21 08			21 18		21 30	21 38			21 52	21 59	22 09			22 22	22 28	22 38			22 52
Anniesland	d	20 55	21 03	21 11			21 21		21 33	21 41			21 55	22 03	22 12			22 25	22 31	22 41			22 55
Clydebank	d					21 05		21 13			21 35	21 42				22 05	22 12				22 35	22 42	
Yoker	d					21 07		21 15			21 37	21 44				22 07	22 14				22 37	22 44	
Garscadden	d					21 10		21 19			21 40	21 47				22 10	22 17				22 40	22 47	
Scotstounhill	d					21 12		21 21			21 42	21 49				22 12	22 19				22 42	22 49	
Jordanhill	d					21 15		21 25			21 45	21 52				22 15	22 22				22 45	22 52	
Hyndland 3	d	20 58	21 06	21 14		21 17	21 24	21 27	21 36	21 44	21 47	21 54	21 58	22 06	22 15	22 18	22 24	22 28	22 34	22 44	22 47	22 54	22 58
Partick 225 ⛴	d	21 00	21 09	21 16		21 20	21 26	21 29	21 38	21 47	21 50	21 56	22 00	22 08	22 17	22 20	22 26	22 30	22 37	22 47	22 50	22 56	23 00
Exhibition Centre 225	a	21 03	21 12			21 23	21 29		21 41		21 53		22 03	22 11		22 23		22 33	22 40		22 53		23 03
Anderston 225	a	21 06	21 14			21 25	21 32		21 43		21 55		22 06	22 13		22 25		22 36	22 42		22 55		23 06
Glasgow Central LL 15 225	a	21 07	21 15			21 26	21 34		21 45		21 56		22 07	22 15		22 27		22 37	22 44		22 57		23 07
Argyle Street 225	a	21 09	21 17			21 29	21 37		21 46		21 59		22 09	22 18		22 29		22 39	22 48		22 59		23 09
Charing Cross	d			21 21				21 33		21 51		22 01			22 21		22 31			22 51		23 01	
Glasgow Queen St LL 10 ⛴	a			21 23				21 35		21 53		22 03			22 23		22 33			22 53		23 03	
	d			21 23				21 36		21 53		22 03			22 25		22 33			22 53		23 03	
High Street	d			21 25				21 38		21 55		22 06			22 27		22 36			22 55		23 06	
Bellgrove	d			21 27				21 40		21 57		22 08			22 29		22 38			22 57		23 08	
Duke Street	d							21 42				22 10					22 40					23 10	
Alexandra Parade	d							21 43				22 11					22 41					23 11	
Barnhill	d							21 46				22 14					22 44					23 14	
Springburn	a							21 48				22 16					22 46					23 16	
Greenfaulds	d	22 07											23 08										
Cumbernauld	a	22 09											23 10										
Carntyne	d			21 31						22 01					22 32					23 01			
Shettleston	d			21 33						22 03					22 35					23 03			
Garrowhill	d			21 36						22 06					22 37					23 06			
Easterhouse	d			21 38						22 08					22 40					23 08			
Blairhill	d			21 42						22 12					22 44					23 12			
Coatbridge Sunnyside	d			21 45						22 15					22 46					23 15			
Coatdyke	d			21 47						22 17					22 49					23 17			
Airdrie	d			21 50						22 21					22 52					23 20			
Drumgelloch	d			21 53						22 24					22 55					23 23			
Caldercruix	d			21 57						22 28					22 59					23 27			
Blackridge	d			22 03						22 34					23 05					23 33			
Armadale	d			22 07						22 38					23 08					23 37			
Bathgate	a			22 11						22 42					23 12					23 41			
	d			22 11						22 42					23 13								
Livingston North	d			22 16						22 47					23 17								
Uphall	d			22 19						22 50					23 20								
Edinburgh Park 230	d			22 30						23 00					23 31								
Haymarket 228,230 ⛴	a			22 36						23 04					23 36								
Edinburgh 228,230	a			22 41						23 09					23 42								

A To Larkhall
B From Mallaig to Glasgow Queen Street
C To Motherwell
D To Whifflet

Table T226-R

Saturdays
21 December to 16 May

Helensburgh, Balloch, Dalmuir and Milngavie - Glasgow - Springburn, Cumbernauld, Airdrie, Bathgate and Edinburgh

		SR	SR	SR	SR	SR	SR	SR	SR	SR	SR
		A		B		◇ C	B				
Helensburgh Upper 227	d					22 50					
Helensburgh Central	d		22 31					23 02		23 32	
Craigendoran	d		22 34					23 05		23 35	
Cardross	d		22 40					23 10		23 40	
Balloch	d				22 44				23 14		23 44
Alexandria	d				22 46				23 16		23 46
Renton	d				22 49				23 19		23 49
Dalreoch	d		22 45		22 52			23 15	23 22	23 45	23 52
Dumbarton Central 227	d		22 47		22 54	23 03		23 17	23 24	23 47	23 55
Dumbarton East	d		22 49		22 56			23 19	23 26	23 49	23 57
Bowling	d				23 00				23 31		
Kilpatrick	d				23 03				23 34		
Dalmuir 227	a		22 56		23 06	23 12		23 26	23 37	23 56	00 08
	d	22 49	22 59	23 03	23 11			23 29		23 59	
Singer	d	22 51	23 01					23 31		00 01	
Drumry	d	22 53	23 03					23 33		00 03	
Drumchapel	d	22 56	23 06					23 36		00 06	
Milngavie	d						23 14				
Hillfoot	d						23 17				
Bearsden	d						23 19				
Westerton	d	22 59	23 08				23 22	23 38		00 08	
Anniesland	d	23 02	23 11				23 25	23 41		00 11	
Clydebank	d			23 05	23 13						
Yoker	d			23 07	23 15						
Garscadden	d			23 10	23 18						
Scotstounhill	d			23 12	23 20						
Jordanhill	d			23 15	23 22						
Hyndland 3	d	23 05	23 14	23 17	23 24		23 28	23 44		00 14	
Partick 225 ⛴	d	23 08	23 17	23 20	23 27		23 30	23 47		00 17	
Exhibition Centre 225	a	23 11		23 23			23 33				
Anderston 225	a	23 14		23 25			23 36				
Glasgow Central LL 15 225	a	23 15		23 27			23 38				
Argyle Street 225	a	23 19		23 29			23 40				
Charing Cross	d		23 21		23 31			23 51		00 21	
Glasgow Queen St LL 10 ⛴	a		23 23		23 33			23 53		00 23	
	d		23 23		23 33			23 53		00 23	
High Street	d		23 25		23 36			23 55		00 25	
Bellgrove	d		23 27		23 38			23 57		00 27	
Duke Street	d				23 40						
Alexandra Parade	d				23 41						
Barnhill	d				23 44						
Springburn	a				23 46						
Greenfaulds	d										
Cumbernauld	a										
Carntyne	d		23 31					00 02		00 31	
Shettleston	d		23 33					00 03		00 33	
Garrowhill	d		23 36					00 06		00 36	
Easterhouse	d		23 38					00 08		00 38	
Blairhill	d		23 42					00 12		00 42	
Coatbridge Sunnyside	d		23 45					00 15		00 45	
Coatdyke	d		23 47					00 17		00 47	
Airdrie	d		23 50					00 20		00a51	
Drumgelloch	d		23 53					00 23			
Caldercruix	d		23 57					00 27			
Blackridge	d		00 03					00 33			
Armadale	d		00 07					00 37			
Bathgate	a		00 11					00 41			
	d										
Livingston North	d										
Uphall	d										
Edinburgh Park 230	d										
Haymarket 228,230 ⛴	a										
Edinburgh 228,230	a										

A To Larkhall
B To Motherwell
C From Oban to Glasgow Queen Street

Table T226-R

Sundays

15 December to 10 May

Helensburgh, Balloch, Dalmuir and Milngavie - Glasgow - Springburn, Cumbernauld, Airdrie, Bathgate and Edinburgh

	SR A	SR A	SR A	SR	SR	SR	SR B	SR	SR C	SR C	SR	SR	SR B	SR C	SR	SR C	SR C	SR	SR	SR B	SR C	SR
Helensburgh Upper 227 d																						
Helensburgh Central d								07 55				08 25			08 55				09 25			09 55
Craigendoran d								07 58				08 28			08 58				09 28			09 58
Cardross d								08 03				08 33			09 03				09 33			10 03
Balloch d									08 09				08 39			09 09				09 39		
Alexandria d									08 11				08 41			09 11				09 41		
Renton d									08 14				08 44			09 14				09 44		
Dalreoch d								08 08	08 17			08 38	08 47		09 08	09 17			09 38	09 47		10 08
Dumbarton Central 227 d								08 10	08 18			08 40	08 48		09 10	09 18			09 40	09 48		10 10
Dumbarton East d								08 12	08 20			08 42	08 50		09 12	09 20			09 42	09 50		10 12
Bowling d									08 25				08 55			09 25				09 55		
Kilpatrick d									08 28				08 58			09 28				09 58		
Dalmuir 227 a								08 19	08 31			08 49	09 01		09 19	09 31			09 49	10 01		10 19
d						07 46	08 01	08 20	08 32			08 50	09 02		09 20	09 32			09 50	10 02		10 20
Singer d			00 01			07 48		08 22				08 52			09 22				09 52			10 22
Drumry d			00 03			07 50		08 25				08 55			09 25				09 55			10 25
Drumchapel d			00 06			07 53		08 27				08 57			09 27				09 57			10 27
Milngavie d														09 11			09 41				10 11	
Hillfoot d														09 14			09 44				10 14	
Bearsden d														09 16			09 46				10 16	
Westerton d			00 08			07 55		08 30				09 00		09 19	09 30		09 49		10 00		10 19	10 30
Anniesland d			00 11			07 59		08 33				09 03		09 22	09 33		09 52		10 03		10 22	10 33
Clydebank d							08 04		08 34				09 04			09 34				10 04		
Yoker d							08 06		08 36				09 06			09 36				10 06		
Garscadden d							08 09		08 39				09 09			09 39				10 09		
Scotstounhill d							08 11		08 41				09 11			09 41				10 11		
Jordanhill d							08 13		08 43				09 13			09 43				10 13		
Hyndland 3 d			00 14			08 02	08 15	08 36	08 45	08 55		09 06	09 15	09 25	09 36	09 45	09 55		10 06	10 15	10 25	10 36
Partick 225 ⛴ d			00 17		08 01	08 05	08 18	08 38	08 48	08 57	09 01	09 08	09 18	09 27	09 38	09 48	09 57	10 01	10 08	10 18	10 27	10 38
Exhibition Centre 225 a							08 21		08 51	09 00			09 21	09 30		09 51	10 00			10 21	10 30	
Anderston 225 a																09 53	10 02			10 23	10 32	
Glasgow Central LL 15 225 a							08 23		08 53	09 03			09 23	09 33		09 54	10 04			10 24	10 34	
Argyle Street 225 a																09 57	10 07			10 26	10 39	
Charing Cross d			00 21		08 05	08 09		08 43			09 05	09 13			09 43			10 05	10 13			10 43
Glasgow Queen St LL 10 ⛴ a			00 23		08 07	08 11		08 45			09 07	09 15			09 45			10 07	10 15			10 45
d			00 23		08 07	08 11		08 45			09 07	09 15			09 45			10 07	10 15			10 45
High Street d			00 25		08 09	08 13		08 47			09 09	09 17			09 47			10 09	10 17			10 47
Bellgrove d			00 27		08 11	08 15		08 49			09 11	09 19			09 49			10 11	10 19			10 49
Duke Street d											09 13							10 13				
Alexandra Parade d											09 15							10 15				
Barnhill d											09 18							10 18				
Springburn a					08 20						09 20							10 20				
Greenfaulds d																						
Cumbernauld a																						
Carntyne d		00 02	00 31			08 19		08 53				09 23			09 53				10 23			10 53
Shettleston d		00 03	00 33			08 21		08 55				09 25			09 55				10 25			10 55
Garrowhill d		00 06	00 36			08 24		08 58				09 28			09 58				10 28			10 58
Easterhouse d		00 08	00 38			08 26		09 00				09 30			10 00				10 30			11 00
Blairhill d		00 12	00 42			08 30		09 04				09 34			10 04				10 34			11 04
Coatbridge Sunnyside d		00 15	00 45			08 33		09 07				09 37			10 07				10 37			11 07
Coatdyke d		00 17	00 47			08 35		09 09				09 39			10 09				10 39			11 09
Airdrie d		00 20	00a51			08 38		09 12				09 42			10 12				10 42			11 12
Drumgelloch d		00 23				08 41		09 15				09 45			10 15				10 45			11 15
Caldercruix d		00 27				08 45		09 19				09 49			10 19				10 49			11 19
Blackridge d	00 03	00 33				08 51		09 25				09 55			10 25				10 55			11 25
Armadale d	00 07	00 37				08 55		09 29				09 59			10 29				10 59			11 29
Bathgate a	00 11	00 41				08 59		09 33				10 03			10 33				11 03			11 33
d				07 55		08 59		09 34				10 04			10 34				11 04			11 34
Livingston North d				07 59		09 04		09 39				10 09			10 38				11 08			11 38
Uphall d				08 02		09 07		09 42				10 12			10 41				11 11			11 41
Edinburgh Park 230 d				08 10		09 16		09 53				10 23			10 52				11 19			11 49
Haymarket 228,230 ⛴ a				08 21		09 27		10 03				10 33			10 56				11 24			11 59
Edinburgh 228,230 a				08 26		09 32		10 08				10 38			11 01				11 29			12 04

A not 15 December. From Helensburgh Central **B** To Larkhall **C** To Motherwell

Table T226-R

Sundays

15 December to 10 May

Helensburgh, Balloch, Dalmuir and Milngavie - Glasgow - Springburn, Cumbernauld, Airdrie, Bathgate and Edinburgh

	SR A	SR A	SR	SR	SR B	SR A	SR	SR A	SR A	SR	SR	SR B	SR A	SR	SR A	SR A	SR	SR	SR B	SR A	SR	SR A
Helensburgh Upper 227 d																						
Helensburgh Central d				10 25			10 55				11 25			11 55				12 25			12 55	
Craigendoran d				10 28			10 58				11 28			11 58				12 28			12 58	
Cardross d				10 33			11 03				11 33			12 03				12 33			13 04	
Balloch d	10 09				10 39			11 09				11 39			12 09				12 39			13 09
Alexandria d	10 11				10 41			11 11				11 41			12 11				12 41			13 11
Renton d	10 14				10 44			11 14				11 44			12 14				12 44			13 14
Dalreoch d	10 17			10 38	10 47		11 08	11 17			11 38	11 47		12 08	12 17			12 38	12 47		13 09	13 17
Dumbarton Central 227 d	10 18			10 40	10 48		11 10	11 18			11 40	11 48		12 10	12 18			12 40	12 48		13 10	13 18
Dumbarton East d	10 20			10 42	10 50		11 12	11 20			11 42	11 50		12 12	12 20			12 42	12 50		13 12	13 20
Bowling d	10 25				10 55			11 25				11 55			12 25				12 55			13 25
Kilpatrick d	10 28				10 58			11 28				11 58			12 28				12 58			13 28
Dalmuir 227 a	10 31			10 49	11 01		11 19	11 31			11 49	12 01		12 19	12 31			12 49	13 01		13 20	13 31
d	10 32			10 50	11 02		11 20	11 32			11 50	12 02		12 20	12 32			12 50	13 02		13 21	13 32
Singer d				10 52			11 22				11 52			12 22				12 52			13 23	
Drumry d				10 55			11 25				11 55			12 25				12 55			13 25	
Drumchapel d				10 57			11 27				11 57			12 27				12 57			13 28	
Milngavie d		10 41				11 11			11 41				12 11			12 41				13 11		
Hillfoot d		10 44				11 14			11 44				12 14			12 44				13 14		
Bearsden d		10 46				11 16			11 46				12 16			12 46				13 16		
Westerton d		10 49		11 00		11 19	11 30		11 49		12 00		12 19	12 30		12 49		13 00		13 19	13 30	
Anniesland d		10 52		11 03		11 22	11 33		11 52		12 03		12 22	12 33		12 52		13 03		13 22	13 33	
Clydebank d	10 34				11 04			11 34				12 04			12 34				13 04			13 34
Yoker d	10 36				11 06			11 36				12 06			12 36				13 06			13 36
Garscadden d	10 39				11 09			11 39				12 09			12 39				13 09			13 39
Scotstounhill d	10 41				11 11			11 41				12 11			12 41				13 11			13 41
Jordanhill d	10 43				11 13			11 43				12 13			12 43				13 13			13 43
Hyndland 3 d	10 45	10 55		11 06	11 15	11 25	11 36	11 45	11 55		12 06	12 15	12 25	12 36	12 45	12 55		13 06	13 15	13 25	13 36	13 45
Partick 225 ⛴ d	10 48	10 57	11 01	11 08	11 18	11 27	11 38	11 48	11 57	12 01	12 08	12 18	12 27	12 38	12 48	12 57	13 01	13 08	13 18	13 27	13 38	13 48
Exhibition Centre 225 a	10 51	11 00			11 21	11 30		11 51	12 00			12 21	12 30		12 51	13 00			13 21	13 30		13 51
Anderston 225 a	10 53	11 02			11 23	11 32		11 53	12 02			12 23	12 32		12 53	13 02			13 23	13 32		13 53
Glasgow Central LL 15 225 a	10 54	11 04			11 24	11 34		11 54	12 04			12 24	12 34		12 54	13 04			13 24	13 34		13 54
Argyle Street 225 a	10 57	11 07			11 26	11 39		11 57	12 07			12 26	12 37		12 57	13 07			13 26	13 39		13 57
Charing Cross d			11 05	11 13			11 43			12 05	12 13			12 43			13 05	13 13			13 43	
Glasgow Queen St LL 10 ⛴ a			11 07	11 15			11 45			12 07	12 15			12 45			13 07	13 15			13 45	
d			11 07	11 15			11 45			12 07	12 15			12 45			13 07	13 15			13 45	
High Street d			11 09	11 17			11 47			12 09	12 17			12 47			13 09	13 17			13 47	
Bellgrove d			11 11	11 19			11 49			12 11	12 19			12 49			13 11	13 19			13 49	
Duke Street d			11 13							12 13							13 13					
Alexandra Parade d			11 15							12 15							13 15					
Barnhill d			11 18							12 18							13 18					
Springburn a			11 20							12 20							13 20					
Greenfaulds d																						
Cumbernauld a																						
Carntyne d				11 23			11 53				12 23			12 53				13 23			13 53	
Shettleston d				11 25			11 55				12 25			12 55				13 25			13 55	
Garrowhill d				11 28			11 58				12 28			12 58				13 28			13 58	
Easterhouse d				11 30			12 00				12 30			13 00				13 30			14 00	
Blairhill d				11 34			12 04				12 34			13 04				13 34			14 04	
Coatbridge Sunnyside d				11 37			12 07				12 37			13 07				13 37			14 07	
Coatdyke d				11 39			12 09				12 39			13 09				13 39			14 09	
Airdrie d				11 42			12 12				12 42			13 12				13 42			14 12	
Drumgelloch d				11 45			12 15				12 45			13 15				13 45			14 15	
Caldercruix d				11 49			12 19				12 49			13 19				13 49			14 19	
Blackridge d				11 55			12 25				12 55			13 25				13 55			14 25	
Armadale d				11 59			12 29				12 59			13 29				13 59			14 29	
Bathgate a				12 03			12 33				13 03			13 33				14 03			14 33	
d				12 04			12 34				13 04			13 34				14 04			14 34	
Livingston North d				12 08			12 38				13 08			13 38				14 08			14 38	
Uphall d				12 11			12 41				13 11			13 41				14 11			14 41	
Edinburgh Park 230 d				12 19			12 49				13 22			13 49				14 19			14 49	
Haymarket 228,230 ⛴ a				12 24			12 55				13 26			13 54				14 24			14 55	
Edinburgh 228,230 a				12 29			13 00				13 33			13 59				14 29			15 03	

A To Motherwell **B** To Larkhall

Table T226-R

Sundays

15 December to 10 May

Helensburgh, Balloch, Dalmuir and Milngavie - Glasgow - Springburn, Cumbernauld, Airdrie, Bathgate and Edinburgh

Station		SR	SR	SR	SR	SR	SR	SR	SR	SR	SR	SR	SR	SR	SR	SR	SR	SR	SR	SR	SR	SR
		A			B	A		A	A			B	◇ C	A		A	A			B	A	
Helensburgh Upper 227	d												14 40									
Helensburgh Central	d			13 25			13 55				14 25				14 55				15 25			15 55
Craigendoran	d			13 28			13 58				14 28				14 58				15 28			15 58
Cardross	d			13 33			14 03				14 33				15 03				15 33			16 03
Balloch	d				13 39			14 09				14 39				15 09				15 39		
Alexandria	d				13 41			14 11				14 41				15 11				15 41		
Renton	d				13 44			14 14				14 44				15 14				15 44		
Dalreoch	d			13 38	13 47		14 08	14 17			14 38	14 47			15 08	15 17			15 38	15 47		16 08
Dumbarton Central 227	d			13 40	13 48		14 10	14 18			14 40	14 48	14 56		15 10	15 18			15 40	15 48		16 10
Dumbarton East	d			13 42	13 50		14 12	14 20			14 42	14 50			15 12	15 20			15 42	15 50		16 12
Bowling	d				13 55			14 25				14 55				15 25				15 55		
Kilpatrick	d				13 58			14 28				14 58				15 28				15 58		
Dalmuir 227	a			13 49	14 01		14 19	14 31			14 49	15 01	15 05		15 19	15 31			15 49	16 01		16 19
	d			13 50	14 02		14 20	14 32			14 50	15 02			15 20	15 32			15 50	16 02		16 20
Singer	d			13 52			14 22				14 52				15 22				15 52			16 22
Drumry	d			13 55			14 25				14 55				15 25				15 55			16 25
Drumchapel	d			13 57			14 27				14 57				15 27				15 57			16 27
Milngavie	d	13 41				14 11			14 41					15 11			15 41				16 11	
Hillfoot	d	13 44				14 14			14 44					15 14			15 44				16 14	
Bearsden	d	13 46				14 16			14 46					15 16			15 46				16 16	
Westerton	d	13 49		14 00		14 19	14 30		14 49		15 00			15 19	15 30		15 49		16 00		16 19	16 30
Anniesland	d	13 52		14 03		14 22	14 33		14 52		15 03			15 22	15 33		15 52		16 03		16 22	16 33
Clydebank	d				14 04			14 34				15 04				15 34				16 04		
Yoker	d				14 06			14 36				15 06				15 36				16 06		
Garscadden	d				14 09			14 39				15 09				15 39				16 09		
Scotstounhill	d				14 11			14 41				15 11				15 41				16 11		
Jordanhill	d				14 13			14 43				15 13				15 43				16 13		
Hyndland 3	d	13 55		14 06	14 15	14 25	14 36	14 45	14 55		15 06	15 15		15 25	15 36	15 45	15 55		16 06	16 15	16 25	16 36
Partick 225 ⛴	d	13 57	14 01	14 08	14 18	14 27	14 38	14 48	14 57	15 01	15 08	15 18		15 27	15 38	15 48	15 57	16 01	16 08	16 18	16 27	16 38
Exhibition Centre 225	a	14 00			14 21	14 30		14 51	15 00			15 21		15 30		15 51	16 00			16 21	16 30	
Anderston 225	a	14 02			14 23	14 32		14 53	15 02			15 23		15 32		15 53	16 02			16 23	16 32	
Glasgow Central LL 15 225	a	14 04			14 24	14 34		14 54	15 04			15 24		15 34		15 54	16 04			16 24	16 34	
Argyle Street 225	a	14 07			14 26	14 39		14 57	15 07			15 26		15 39		15 58	16 07			16 26	16 39	
Charing Cross	d		14 05	14 13			14 43			15 05	15 13				15 43			16 05	16 13			16 43
Glasgow Queen St LL 10 ⛴	a		14 07	14 15			14 45			15 07	15 15				15 45			16 07	16 15			16 45
	d		14 07	14 15			14 45			15 07	15 15				15 45			16 07	16 15			16 45
High Street	d		14 09	14 17			14 47			15 09	15 17				15 47			16 09	16 17			16 47
Bellgrove	d		14 11	14 19			14 49			15 11	15 19				15 49			16 11	16 19			16 49
Duke Street	d		14 13							15 13								16 13				
Alexandra Parade	d		14 15							15 15								16 15				
Barnhill	d		14 18							15 18								16 18				
Springburn	a		14 20							15 20								16 20				
Greenfaulds	d																					
Cumbernauld	a																					
Carntyne	d			14 23			14 53				15 23				15 53				16 23			16 53
Shettleston	d			14 25			14 55				15 25				15 55				16 25			16 55
Garrowhill	d			14 28			14 58				15 28				15 58				16 28			16 58
Easterhouse	d			14 30			15 00				15 30				16 00				16 30			17 00
Blairhill	d			14 34			15 04				15 34				16 04				16 34			17 04
Coatbridge Sunnyside	d			14 37			15 07				15 37				16 07				16 37			17 07
Coatdyke	d			14 39			15 09				15 39				16 09				16 39			17 09
Airdrie	d			14 42			15 12				15 42				16 12				16 42			17 12
Drumgelloch	d			14 45			15 15				15 45				16 15				16 45			17 15
Caldercruix	d			14 49			15 19				15 49				16 19				16 49			17 19
Blackridge	d			14 55			15 25				15 55				16 25				16 55			17 25
Armadale	d			14 59			15 29				15 59				16 29				16 59			17 29
Bathgate	a			15 03			15 33				16 03				16 33				17 03			17 33
	d			15 04			15 33				16 04				16 34				17 04			17 34
Livingston North	d			15 08			15 38				16 08				16 38				17 08			17 38
Uphall	d			15 11			15 41				16 11				16 41				17 11			17 41
Edinburgh Park 230	d			15 19			15 49				16 19				16 51				17 19			17 54
Haymarket 228,230 ⛴	a			15 24			15 55				16 24				16 56				17 24			17 58
Edinburgh 228,230	a			15 29			16 00				16 29				17 01				17 29			18 03

A To Motherwell B To Larkhall C From Mallaig to Glasgow Queen Street

NRT DECEMBER 19 EDITION

Table T226-R

Sundays

15 December to 10 May

Helensburgh, Balloch, Dalmuir and Milngavie - Glasgow - Springburn, Cumbernauld, Airdrie, Bathgate and Edinburgh

Station		SR	SR	SR	SR	SR	SR	SR	SR	SR	SR	SR	SR	SR	SR	SR	SR	SR	SR	SR	SR	SR	SR
		A	A			B	A		A	A			B	A		A	A			◇ C	B	A	
Helensburgh Upper 227	d																			18 31			
Helensburgh Central	d				16 25			16 55				17 25			17 55				18 25				18 55
Craigendoran	d				16 28			16 58				17 28			17 58				18 28				18 58
Cardross	d				16 33			17 03				17 33			18 03				18 33				19 04
Balloch	d	16 09				16 39			17 09				17 39			18 09					18 39		
Alexandria	d	16 11				16 41			17 11				17 41			18 11					18 41		
Renton	d	16 14				16 44			17 14				17 44			18 14					18 44		
Dalreoch	d	16 17			16 38	16 47		17 08	17 17			17 38	17 47		18 08	18 17			18 38		18 50		19 09
Dumbarton Central 227	d	16 18			16 40	16 48		17 10	17 18			17 40	17 48		18 10	18 18			18 40	18 47	18 51		19 10
Dumbarton East	d	16 20			16 42	16 50		17 12	17 20			17 42	17 50		18 12	18 20			18 42		18 53		19 12
Bowling	d	16 25				16 55			17 25				17 55			18 25					18 58		
Kilpatrick	d	16 28				16 58			17 28				17 58			18 28					19 01		
Dalmuir 227	a	16 31			16 49	17 01		17 19	17 31			17 49	18 01		18 19	18 31			18 49	18 58	19 04		19 20
	d	16 32			16 50	17 02		17 20	17 32			17 50	18 02		18 20	18 32			18 50		19 04		19 21
Singer	d				16 52			17 22				17 52			18 22				18 52				19 23
Drumry	d				16 55			17 25				17 55			18 25				18 55				19 25
Drumchapel	d				16 57			17 27				17 57			18 27				18 57				19 28
Milngavie	d		16 41				17 11			17 41				18 11			18 41					19 11	
Hillfoot	d		16 44				17 14			17 44				18 14			18 44					19 14	
Bearsden	d		16 46				17 16			17 46				18 16			18 46					19 16	
Westerton	d		16 49		17 00		17 19	17 30		17 49		18 00		18 19	18 30		18 49		19 00			19 19	19 30
Anniesland	d		16 52		17 03		17 22	17 33		17 52		18 03		18 22	18 33		18 52		19 03			19 22	19 33
Clydebank	d	16 34				17 04			17 34				18 04			18 34					19 06		
Yoker	d	16 36				17 06			17 36				18 06			18 36					19 08		
Garscadden	d	16 39				17 09			17 39				18 09			18 39					19 11		
Scotstounhill	d	16 41				17 11			17 41				18 11			18 41					19 13		
Jordanhill	d	16 43				17 13			17 43				18 13			18 43					19 15		
Hyndland 3	d	16 45	16 55		17 06	17 15	17 25	17 36	17 45	17 55		18 06	18 15	18 25	18 36	18 45	18 55		19 06		19 17	19 25	19 36
Partick 225 ⛴	d	16 48	16 57	17 01	17 08	17 18	17 27	17 38	17 48	17 57	18 01	18 08	18 18	18 27	18 38	18 48	18 57	19 01	19 08		19 19	19 27	19 38
Exhibition Centre 225	a	16 51	17 00			17 21	17 30		17 51	18 00			18 21	18 30		18 51	19 00				19 22	19 30	
Anderston 225	a	16 53	17 02			17 23	17 32		17 53	18 02													
Glasgow Central LL 15 225	a	16 54	17 04			17 24	17 34		17 54	18 04			18 23	18 34		18 54	19 03				19 25	19 33	
Argyle Street 225	a	16 57	17 07			17 26	17 39		17 57	18 07													
Charing Cross	d			17 05	17 13			17 43			18 05	18 13			18 43			19 05	19 13				19 43
Glasgow Queen St LL 10 ⛴	a			17 07	17 15			17 45			18 07	18 15			18 45			19 07	19 15				19 45
	d			17 07	17 15			17 45			18 07	18 15			18 45			19 07	19 15				19 45
High Street	d			17 09	17 17			17 47			18 09	18 17			18 47			19 09	19 17				19 47
Bellgrove	d			17 11	17 19			17 49			18 11	18 19			18 49			19 11	19 19				19 49
Duke Street	d			17 13							18 13							19 13					
Alexandra Parade	d			17 15							18 15							19 15					
Barnhill	d			17 18							18 18							19 18					
Springburn	a			17 20							18 20							19 20					
Greenfaulds	d																						
Cumbernauld	a																						
Carntyne	d				17 23			17 53				18 23			18 53				19 23				19 53
Shettleston	d				17 25			17 55				18 25			18 55				19 25				19 55
Garrowhill	d				17 28			17 58				18 28			18 58				19 28				19 58
Easterhouse	d				17 30			18 00				18 30			19 00				19 30				20 00
Blairhill	d				17 34			18 04				18 34			19 04				19 34				20 04
Coatbridge Sunnyside	d				17 37			18 07				18 37			19 07				19 37				20 07
Coatdyke	d				17 39			18 09				18 39			19 09				19 39				20 09
Airdrie	d				17 42			18 12				18 42			19 12				19a43				20 12
Drumgelloch	d				17 45			18 15				18 45			19 15								20 15
Caldercruix	d				17 49			18 19				18 49			19 19								20 19
Blackridge	d				17 55			18 25				18 55			19 25								20 25
Armadale	d				17 59			18 29				18 59			19 29								20 29
Bathgate	a				18 03			18 33				19 03			19 33								20 33
	d				18 04			18 34				19 04			19 33								20 34
Livingston North	d				18 08			18 38				19 08			19 37								20 38
Uphall	d				18 11			18 41				19 11			19 40								20 41
Edinburgh Park 230	d				18 19			18 52				19 19			19 48								20 52
Haymarket 228,230 ⛴	a				18 24			18 56				19 24			19 54								20 56
Edinburgh 228,230	a				18 29			19 01				19 29			19 59								21 01

A To Motherwell B To Larkhall C From Oban to Glasgow Queen Street

Table T226-R

Sundays
15 December to 10 May

Helensburgh, Balloch, Dalmuir and Milngavie - Glasgow - Springburn, Cumbernauld, Airdrie, Bathgate and Edinburgh

	SR	SR	SR	SR	SR	SR	SR	SR	SR	SR	SR	SR	SR	SR	SR	SR	SR	SR	SR	SR	SR
	A	A			B	A		A	C			B	◇ D	A		A	A			B	A
Helensburgh Upper 227 d													20 40								
Helensburgh Central d				19 25			19 55				20 25				20 55				21 25		
Craigendoran d				19 28			19 58				20 28				20 58				21 28		
Cardross d				19 33			20 03				20 33				21 03				21 33		
Balloch d	19 09				19 39			20 09				20 38				21 09				21 39	
Alexandria d	19 11				19 41			20 11				20 40				21 11				21 41	
Renton d	19 14				19 44			20 14				20 43				21 14				21 44	
Dalreoch d	19 17			19 38	19 47		20 08	20 17			20 38	20 46			21 08	21 17			21 38	21 47	
Dumbarton Central 227 d	19 18			19 40	19 48		20 10	20 18			20 40	20 47	20 53		21 10	21 18			21 40	21 48	
Dumbarton East d	19 20			19 42	19 50		20 12	20 20			20 42	20 49			21 12	21 20			21 42	21 50	
Bowling d	19 25				19 55			20 25				20 54				21 25				21 55	
Kilpatrick d	19 28				19 58			20 28				20 57				21 28				21 58	
Dalmuir 227 a	19 31			19 49	20 01		20 19	20 31			20 49	21 00	21 04		21 19	21 31			21 49	22 01	
d	19 32			19 50	20 02		20 20	20 32			20 50	21 02			21 20	21 32			21 50	22 02	
Singer d				19 52			20 22				20 52				21 22				21 52		
Drumry d				19 55			20 25				20 55				21 25				21 55		
Drumchapel d				19 57			20 27				20 57				21 27				21 57		
Milngavie d		19 41				20 11			20 41					21 11			21 41				22 11
Hillfoot d		19 44				20 14			20 44					21 14			21 44				22 14
Bearsden d		19 46				20 16			20 46					21 16			21 46				22 16
Westerton d		19 49		20 00		20 19	20 30		20 49		21 00			21 19	21 30		21 49		22 00		22 19
Anniesland d		19 52		20 03		20 22	20 33		20 52		21 03			21 22	21 33		21 52		22 03		22 22
Clydebank d	19 34				20 04			20 34				21 04				21 34				22 04	
Yoker d	19 36				20 06			20 36				21 06				21 36				22 06	
Garscadden d	19 39				20 09			20 39				21 09				21 39				22 09	
Scotstounhill d	19 41				20 11			20 41				21 11				21 41				22 11	
Jordanhill d	19 43				20 13			20 43				21 13				21 43				22 13	
Hyndland 3 d	19 45	19 55		20 06	20 15	20 25	20 36	20 45	20 55		21 06	21 15		21 25	21 36	21 45	21 55		22 06	22 15	22 25
Partick 225 ⛴ d	19 48	19 57	20 01	20 08	20 18	20 27	20 38	20 48	20 57	21 01	21 08	21 18		21 27	21 38	21 48	21 57	22 01	22 08	22 18	22 27
Exhibition Centre 225 a	19 51	20 00			20 21	20 30		20 51	21 00			21 21		21 30		21 51	22 00			22 21	22 30
Anderston 225 a																					
Glasgow Central LL 15 225 a	19 54	20 03			20 23	20 33		20 53	21 03			21 23		21 33		21 53	22 03			22 23	22 33
Argyle Street 225 a																					
Charing Cross d			20 05	20 13			20 43			21 05	21 13				21 43			22 05	22 13		
Glasgow Queen St LL 10 ⛴ a			20 07	20 15			20 45			21 07	21 15				21 45			22 07	22 15		
d			20 07	20 15			20 45			21 07	21 15				21 45			22 07	22 15		
High Street d			20 09	20 17			20 47			21 09	21 17				21 47			22 09	22 17		
Bellgrove d			20 11	20 19			20 49			21 11	21 19				21 49			22 11	22 19		
Duke Street d																					
Alexandra Parade d																					
Barnhill d																					
Springburn a			20 20							21 20								22 20			
Greenfaulds d																					
Cumbernauld a																					
Carntyne d				20 23			20 53				21 23				21 53				22 23		
Shettleston d				20 25			20 55				21 25				21 55				22 25		
Garrowhill d				20 28			20 58				21 28				21 58				22 28		
Easterhouse d				20 30			21 00				21 30				22 00				22 30		
Blairhill d				20 34			21 04				21 34				22 04				22 34		
Coatbridge Sunnyside d				20 37			21 07				21 37				22 07				22 37		
Coatdyke d				20 39			21 09				21 39				22 09				22 39		
Airdrie d				20a43			21 12				21a43				22 12				22a43		
Drumgelloch d							21 15								22 15						
Caldercruix d							21 19								22 19						
Blackridge d							21 25								22 25						
Armadale d							21 29								22 29						
Bathgate a							21 33								22 33						
d							21 34								22 34						
Livingston North d							21 38								22 38						
Uphall d							21 41								22 41						
Edinburgh Park 230 d							21 52								22 49						
Haymarket 228,230 ⛴ a							21 56								22 55						
Edinburgh 228,230 a							22 01								23 01						

A To Motherwell
B To Larkhall
C From Motherwell to Glasgow Central LL continues to Motherwell
D From Mallaig to Glasgow Queen Street

Table T226-R

Sundays
15 December to 10 May

Helensburgh, Balloch, Dalmuir and Milngavie - Glasgow - Springburn, Cumbernauld, Airdrie, Bathgate and Edinburgh

	SR	SR	SR	SR	SR	SR	CS	SR	SR	SR
		A	A				🛏 B ⛴ ✕			A
Helensburgh Upper 227 d							22 39			
Helensburgh Central d	21 55				22 25			22 55		
Craigendoran d	21 58				22 28			22 58		
Cardross d	22 03				22 33			23 03		
Balloch d		22 09				22 39			23 09	
Alexandria d		22 11				22 41			23 11	
Renton d		22 14				22 44			23 14	
Dalreoch d	22 08	22 17			22 38	22 47		23 08	23 17	
Dumbarton Central 227 d	22 10	22 18			22 40	22 48	22 54	23 10	23 18	
Dumbarton East d	22 12	22 20			22 42	22 50		23 12	23 20	
Bowling d		22 25				22 55			23 25	
Kilpatrick d		22 28				22 58			23 28	
Dalmuir 227 a	22 19	22 31			22 49	23 01	23 06	23 19	23 31	
d	22 20	22 32			22 50	23 01	23 06		23 31	
Singer d	22 22				22 52					
Drumry d	22 25				22 55					
Drumchapel d	22 27				22 57					
Milngavie d			22 41							23 11
Hillfoot d			22 44							23 14
Bearsden d			22 46							23 16
Westerton d	22 30		22 49		23 00					23 19
Anniesland d	22 33		22 52		23 03					23 22
Clydebank d		22 34				23 03			23 33	
Yoker d		22 36				23a05			23a35	
Garscadden d		22 39								
Scotstounhill d		22 41								
Jordanhill d		22 43								
Hyndland 3 d	22 36	22 45	22 55		23 06					23 25
Partick 225 ⛴ d	22 38	22 48	22 57	23 01	23 08					23 27
Exhibition Centre 225 a		22 51	23 00							23 30
Anderston 225 a										
Glasgow Central LL 15 225 a		22 53	23 03							23 33
Argyle Street 225 a										
Charing Cross d	22 43			23 05	23 13					
Glasgow Queen St LL 10 ⛴ a	22 45			23 07	23 15		23s29			
d	22 45			23 07	23 15					
High Street d	22 47			23 09	23 17					
Bellgrove d	22 49			23 11	23 19					
Duke Street d										
Alexandra Parade d										
Barnhill d										
Springburn a				23 20						
Greenfaulds d										
Cumbernauld a										
Carntyne d	22 53				23 23					
Shettleston d	22 55				23 25					
Garrowhill d	22 58				23 28					
Easterhouse d	23 00				23 30					
Blairhill d	23 04				23 34					
Coatbridge Sunnyside d	23 07				23 37					
Coatdyke d	23 09				23 39					
Airdrie d	23 12				23a43					
Drumgelloch d	23 15									
Caldercruix d	23 19									
Blackridge d	23 25									
Armadale d	23 29									
Bathgate a	23 33									
d										
Livingston North d										
Uphall d										
Edinburgh Park 230 d										
Haymarket 228,230 ⛴ a										
Edinburgh 228,230 a										

A To Motherwell
B From Fort William to London Euston

Table T227-F

Glasgow Queen Street - Oban, Fort William and Mallaig

Mondays to Fridays
16 December to 27 March

Miles	Miles			SR	SR	CS	WR	SR		SR	SR	WR		SR	SR	SR	SR	SR FX	SR FO
					◇	🛏 🍴		◇ 🛒		◇ 🛒	◇ 🛒			◇ A 🛒		◇ 🛒	◇ 🛒	◇ A 🛒	◇ A 🛒
—	—	Edinburgh 228	d			04 50													
0	0	**GlasgowQueenSt** 10 226 ⛴	d	05 20		05u48		08 23		10 33	12 24					16 36	18 23		
10	10	Dalmuir 226	d	05 39		06 04		08 42		10 55	12 43					16 56	18 42		
16½	16½	Dumbarton Central 226	d	05 48		06 15		08 52		11 05	12 53					17 07	18 52		
25½	25½	Helensburgh Upper	a	06 00		06 30		09 05		11 24	13 05					17 20	19 04		
—	—		d	06 03		06 32		09 07		11 27	13 08					17 22	19 07		
32¼	32¼	Garelochhead	d	06 14		06 45		09 18		11 40	13 19					17 33	19 18		
43	43	Arrochar & Tarbet	d	06 34		07 09		09 38		12 00	13 39					17 57	19 37		
51	51	Ardlui	d	06 52		07x24		09 51		12 14	13 56					18 10	19 51		
59¾	59¾	**Crianlarich**	a	07 08		07 45		10 07		12 30	14 12					18 26	20 07		
—	—		d	07 18		07 46		10 15	10 21	12 33	14 18			14 24		18 29	20 14	20 20	20 20
64¾	—	Tyndrum Lower	d	07 27				10 24		12 41	14 26					18 37	20 22		
76¾	—	Dalmally	d	07 51				10 42		12 59	14 44				17 05	18 55	20 40		
79½	—	Loch Awe	d	07 56				10 47		13 04	14 49				17 10	19 04	20 45		
83½	—	Falls of Cruachan §	d																
88½	—	Taynuilt	d	08 11				11 03		13 20	15 05				17 24	19 19	21 00		
95¼	—	Connel Ferry	d	08 22				11 14		13 30	15 15				17 34	19 29	21 11		
101½	—	**Oban**	a	08 35				11 27		13 43	15 28				17 47	19 42	21 24		
—	64½	Upper Tyndrum	d			08 00			10 32					14 35				20 31	20 31
—	72¼	Bridge of Orchy	d			08 17			10 48					14 49				20 45	20 45
—	87¾	Rannoch	d			08 44			11 09					15 12				21 08	21 08
—	95	Corrour	d			08 59			11 21					15 24				21 20	21 20
—	105	Tulloch	d			09 20			11 38					15 40				21 36	21 36
—	110¾	Roy Bridge	d			09x31			11 48					15 50				21 46	21 46
—	114	Spean Bridge	d			09 38			11 55					15 56				21 53	21 56
—	122¾	**Fort William**	a			09 57			12 08					16 09				22 06	22 09
—	—		d		08 30		10 15		12 12			14 40		16 19				22 11	22 16
—	125	Banavie	d		08 36				12 19					16 25				22 18	22 23
—	126	Corpach	d		08 42				12 23					16 30				22 24	22 28
—	129	Loch Eil Outward Bound	d		08 49				12 30					16 36				22 31	22 34
—	132¾	Locheilside	d		08x53				12x34					16x40				22x35	22x38
—	139¾	Glenfinnan	d		09 05				12 46					16 55				22 47	22 50
—	148½	Lochailort	d		09x19				13x01					17x09				23x02	23x05
—	153¾	Beasdale	d		09x28				13x10					17x18				23x11	23x14
—	156¾	Arisaig	d		09 38				13 19					17 27				23 20	23 23
—	161¼	Morar	d		09 46				13 27					17 36				23 28	23 31
—	164¾	**Mallaig**	a		09 53		12 26		13 34			16 42		17 43				23 35	23 38

Mondays to Fridays
30 March to 15 May

		SR	SR	CS	WR	SR		SR	WR	SR			SR	SR	SR	SR FX	SR FO
			◇	🛏 🍴		◇ 🛒		◇ 🛒		◇ 🛒				◇ 🛒	◇ 🛒	◇ A 🛒	◇ A 🛒
Edinburgh 228	d			04 50													
GlasgowQueenSt 10 226 ⛴	d	05 20		05u48		08 23		10 33		12 24				16 36	18 23		18 23
Dalmuir 226	d	05 39		06 04		08 42		10 55		12 43				16 56	18 42		18 42
Dumbarton Central 226	d	05 48		06 15		08 52		11 05		12 53				17 07	18 52		18 52
Helensburgh Upper	a	06 00		06 30		09 05		11 24		13 05				17 20	19 04		19 04
	d	06 03		06 32		09 07		11 27		13 08				17 22	19 07		19 07
Garelochhead	d	06 14		06 45		09 18		11 40		13 19				17 33	19 18		19 18
Arrochar & Tarbet	d	06 34		07 09		09 38		12 00		13 39				17 57	19 37		19 37
Ardlui	d	06 52		07x24		09 51		12 14		13 56				18 10	19 51		19 51
Crianlarich	a	07 08		07 45		10 07		12 30		14 12				18 26	20 07		20 07
	d	07 18		07 46		10 15	10 21	12 33		14 18	14 24			18 29	20 14	20 20	20 20
Tyndrum Lower	d	07 27				10 24		12 41		14 26				18 37	20 22		
Dalmally	d	07 51				10 42		12 59		14 44			17 05	18 55	20 40		
Loch Awe	d	07 56				10 47		13 04		14 49			17 10	19 04	20 45		
Falls of Cruachan §	d					10 52		13 09		14 54				19 09	20 50		
Taynuilt	d	08 11				11 03		13 20		15 05			17 24	19 19	21 00		
Connel Ferry	d	08 22				11 14		13 30		15 15			17 34	19 29	21 11		
Oban	a	08 35				11 27		13 43		15 28			17 47	19 42	21 24		
Upper Tyndrum	d			08 00			10 32				14 35					20 31	20 31
Bridge of Orchy	d			08 17			10 48				14 49					20 45	20 45
Rannoch	d			08 44			11 09				15 12					21 08	21 08
Corrour	d			08 59			11 21				15 24					21 20	21 20
Tulloch	d			09 20			11 38				15 40					21 36	21 36
Roy Bridge	d			09x31			11 48				15 50					21 46	21 46
Spean Bridge	d			09 38			11 55				15 56					21 53	21 56
Fort William	a			09 57			12 08				16 09					22 06	22 09
	d		08 30		10 15		12 12		14 40		16 19					22 11	22 16
Banavie	d		08 36				12 19				16 25					22 18	22 23
Corpach	d		08 42				12 23				16 30					22 24	22 28
Loch Eil Outward Bound	d		08 49				12 30				16 36					22 31	22 34
Locheilside	d		08x53				12x34				16x40					22x35	22x38
Glenfinnan	d		09 05				12 46				16 55					22 47	22 50
Lochailort	d		09x19				13x01				17x09					23x02	23x05
Beasdale	d		09x28				13x10				17x18					23x11	23x14
Arisaig	d		09 38				13 19				17 27					23 20	23 23
Morar	d		09 46				13 27				17 36					23 28	23 31
Mallaig	a		09 53		12 26		13 34		16 42		17 43					23 35	23 38

§ Summer station only
A 🛒 to Fort William

Table T227-F

Glasgow Queen Street - Oban, Fort William and Mallaig

Saturdays
21 December to 21 March

		SR	SR	CS	WR	SR		SR	SR	WR		SR	SR	SR	SR
			◇	🛏 🍴		◇ 🛒		◇ 🛒	◇ 🛒			◇ A 🛒	◇ 🛒	◇ 🛒	◇ A 🛒
Edinburgh 228	d			04 50											
GlasgowQueenSt 10 226 ⛴	d	05 20		05u48		08 25		10 33	12 24				16 36	18 22	
Dalmuir 226	d	05 39		06 04		08 42		10 55	12 43				16 56	18 42	
Dumbarton Central 226	d	05 48		06 15		08 52		11 05	12 53				17 07	18 52	
Helensburgh Upper	a	06 00		06 30		09 05		11 24	13 05				17 20	19 04	
	d	06 03		06 32		09 07		11 27	13 08				17 22	19 07	
Garelochhead	d	06 14		06 45		09 18		11 40	13 19				17 33	19 18	
Arrochar & Tarbet	d	06 34		07 09		09 38		12 00	13 39				17 57	19 37	
Ardlui	d	06 52		07x24		09 51		12 14	13 56				18 10	19 53	
Crianlarich	a	07 08		07 45		10 07		12 30	14 12				18 26	20 09	
	d	07 18		07 46		10 15	10 21	12 33	14 18			14 24	18 29	20 15	20 20
Tyndrum Lower	d	07 27				10 24		12 41	14 26				18 37	20 23	
Dalmally	d	07 51				10 42		12 59	14 44				18 55	20 41	
Loch Awe	d	07 56				10 47		13 04	14 49				19 04	20 46	
Falls of Cruachan §	d														
Taynuilt	d	08 11				11 03		13 20	15 05				19 19	21 01	
Connel Ferry	d	08 22				11 14		13 30	15 15				19 29	21 12	
Oban	a	08 35				11 27		13 43	15 28				19 42	21 25	
Upper Tyndrum	d			08 00			10 32					14 35			20 31
Bridge of Orchy	d			08 17			10 48					14 49			20 45
Rannoch	d			08 44			11 09					15 12			21 08
Corrour	d			08 59			11 21					15 24			21 20
Tulloch	d			09 20			11 38					15 40			21 36
Roy Bridge	d			09x31			11 48					15 50			21 46
Spean Bridge	d			09 38			11 55					15 56			21 53
Fort William	a			09 57			12 08					16 09			22 06
	d		08 30		10 15		12 12			14 40		16 19			22 11
Banavie	d		08 36				12 19					16 25			22 18
Corpach	d		08 42				12 23					16 30			22 24
Loch Eil Outward Bound	d		08 49				12 30					16 36			22 31
Locheilside	d		08x53				12x34					16x40			22x35
Glenfinnan	d		09 05				12 46					16 55			22 47
Lochailort	d		09x19				13x01					17x09			23x02
Beasdale	d		09x28				13x10					17x18			23x11
Arisaig	d		09 38				13 19					17 27			23 20
Morar	d		09 46				13 27					17 36			23 28
Mallaig	a		09 53		12 26		13 34			16 42		17 43			23 35

Saturdays
28 March to 16 May

		SR	SR	CS	WR	SR		SR	WR	SR			SR	SR		SR
			◇	🛏 🍴		◇ 🛒		◇ 🛒		◇ 🛒			◇ 🛒	◇ B 🛒		◇ A 🛒
Edinburgh 228	d			04 50												
GlasgowQueenSt 10 226 ⛴	d	05 20		05u48		08 25		10 33		12 24			16 36	18 23		
Dalmuir 226	d	05 39		06 04		08 42		10 55		12 43			16 56	18 42		
Dumbarton Central 226	d	05 48		06 15		08 52		11 05		12 53			17 07	18 52		
Helensburgh Upper	a	06 00		06 30		09 05		11 24		13 05			17 20	19 04		
	d	06 03		06 32		09 07		11 27		13 08			17 22	19 07		
Garelochhead	d	06 14		06 45		09 18		11 40		13 19			17 33	19 18		
Arrochar & Tarbet	d	06 34		07 09		09 38		12 00		13 39			17 57	19 37		
Ardlui	d	06 52		07x24		09 51		12 14		13 56			18 10	19 53		
Crianlarich	a	07 08		07 45		10 07		12 30		14 12			18 26	20 09		
	d	07 18		07 46		10 15	10 21	12 33		14 18	14 24		18 29	20 15	20 20	20 20
Tyndrum Lower	d	07 27				10 24		12 41		14 26			18 37	20 23		
Dalmally	d	07 51				10 42		12 59		14 44			18 55	20 41		
Loch Awe	d	07 56				10 47		13 04		14 49			19 04	20 46		
Falls of Cruachan §	d					10 52		13 09		14 54			19 09	20 51		
Taynuilt	d	08 11				11 03		13 20		15 05			19 19	21 01		
Connel Ferry	d	08 22				11 14		13 30		15 15			19 29	21 12		
Oban	a	08 35				11 27		13 43		15 28			19 42	21 25		
Upper Tyndrum	d			08 00			10 32				14 35				20 31	20 31
Bridge of Orchy	d			08 17			10 48				14 49				20 45	20 45
Rannoch	d			08 44			11 09				15 12				21 08	21 08
Corrour	d			08 59			11 21				15 24				21 20	21 20
Tulloch	d			09 20			11 38				15 40				21 36	21 36
Roy Bridge	d			09x31			11 48				15 50				21 46	21 46
Spean Bridge	d			09 38			11 55				15 56				21 53	21 53
Fort William	a			09 57			12 08				16 09				22 06	22 06
	d		08 30		10 15		12 12		14 40		16 19				22 11	22 11
Banavie	d		08 36				12 19				16 25				22 18	22 18
Corpach	d		08 42				12 23				16 30				22 24	22 24
Loch Eil Outward Bound	d		08 49				12 30				16 36				22 31	22 31
Locheilside	d		08x53				12x34				16x40				22x35	22x35
Glenfinnan	d		09 05				12 46				16 55				22 47	22 47
Lochailort	d		09x19				13x01				17x09				23x02	23x02
Beasdale	d		09x28				13x10				17x18				23x11	23x11
Arisaig	d		09 38				13 19				17 27				23 20	23 20
Morar	d		09 46				13 27				17 36				23 28	23 28
Mallaig	a		09 53		12 26		13 34		16 42		17 43				23 35	23 35

§ Summer station only
A 🛒 to Fort William
B not 2 May

Table T227-F

Glasgow Queen Street - Oban, Fort William and Mallaig

Sundays
15 December to 22 March

		SR	WR	SR	SR		SR	SR	SR
		◇ 🍴		◇	◇ 🍴		◇ 🍴	◇ 🍴	
Edinburgh 228	d								22 40
GlasgowQueenSt 10 226	d	09 56			12 20		18 21		23 54
Dalmuir 226	d	10 16			12 34		18 36		00a18
Dumbarton Central 226	d	10 26			12 47		18 47		
Helensburgh Upper	a	10 38			12 59		18 59		
	d	10 41			13 06		19 05		
Garelochhead	d	10 52			13 18		19 16		
Arrochar & Tarbet	d	11 12			13 38		19 36		
Ardlui	d	11 28			13 56		19 51		
Crianlarich	a	11 45			14 12		20 07		
	d	11 47			14 18	14 24	20 14	20 20	
Tyndrum Lower	d	11 56			14 26		20 22		
Dalmally	d	12 15			14 44		20 40		
Loch Awe	d	12 20			14 49		20 45		
Falls of Cruachan §	d				14 54				
Taynuilt	d	12 38			15 04		21 00		
Connel Ferry	d	12 50			15 14		21 11		
Oban	a	13 04			15 27		21 24		
Upper Tyndrum	d					14 35		20 31	
Bridge of Orchy	d					14 49		20 47	
Rannoch	d					15 12		21 08	
Corrour	d					15 24		21 20	
Tulloch	d					15 40		21 36	
Roy Bridge	d					15 50		21 46	
Spean Bridge	d					15 56		21 53	
Fort William	a					16 09		22 06	
	d		10 15	12 12		16 19		22 14	
Banavie	d			12 19		16 25		22 20	
Corpach	d			12 23		16 30		22 25	
Loch Eil Outward Bound	d			12 30		16 36		22 31	
Locheilside	d			12x34		16x40		22x35	
Glenfinnan	d			12 46		16 55		22 47	
Lochailort	d			13x01		17x09		23x02	
Beasdale	d			13x10		17x18		23x11	
Arisaig	d			13 19		17 27		23 20	
Morar	d			13 27		17 36		23 28	
Mallaig	a		12 26	13 34		17 43		23 35	

Sundays
29 March to 10 May

		SR	WR	SR	WR	SR		SR		SR
		◇ 🍴		◇		◇ 🍴		◇ 🍴		
Edinburgh 228	d									22 40
GlasgowQueenSt 10 226	d	09 56				12 20		18 21		23 54
Dalmuir 226	d	10 16				12 34		18 36		00a18
Dumbarton Central 226	d	10 26				12 47		18 47		
Helensburgh Upper	a	10 38				12 59		18 59		
	d	10 41				13 06		19 05		
Garelochhead	d	10 52				13 18		19 16		
Arrochar & Tarbet	d	11 12				13 38		19 36		
Ardlui	d	11 28				13 56		19 51		
Crianlarich	a	11 45				14 12		20 07		
	d	11 47				14 18	14 24	20 14	20 20	
Tyndrum Lower	d	11 56				14 26		20 22		
Dalmally	d	12 15				14 44		20 40		
Loch Awe	d	12 20				14 49		20 45		
Falls of Cruachan §	d	12 25				14 54		20 50		
Taynuilt	d	12 38				15 04		21 00		
Connel Ferry	d	12 50				15 14		21 11		
Oban	a	13 04				15 27		21 24		
Upper Tyndrum	d						14 35		20 31	
Bridge of Orchy	d						14 49		20 47	
Rannoch	d						15 12		21 08	
Corrour	d						15 24		21 20	
Tulloch	d						15 40		21 36	
Roy Bridge	d						15 50		21 46	
Spean Bridge	d						15 56		21 53	
Fort William	a						16 09		22 06	
	d		10 15	12 12	14 40		16 19		22 14	
Banavie	d			12 19			16 25		22 20	
Corpach	d			12 23			16 30		22 25	
Loch Eil Outward Bound	d			12 30			16 36		22 31	
Locheilside	d			12x34			16x40		22x35	
Glenfinnan	d			12 46			16 55		22 47	
Lochailort	d			13x01			17x09		23x02	
Beasdale	d			13x10			17x18		23x11	
Arisaig	d			13 19			17 27		23 20	
Morar	d			13 27			17 36		23 28	
Mallaig	a		12 26	13 34	16 42		17 43		23 35	

§ Summer station only

Table T227-R

Mallaig, Fort William and Oban - Glasgow Queen Street

Mondays to Fridays
16 December to 27 March

Miles	Miles			SR	SR	SR	SR	SR	WR	SR	SR	SR	SR		SR	SR	CS	WR
				◇ 🍴	◇ A 🍴	◇ 🍴	◇ 🍴	◇		◇ 🍴		◇ A 🍴	◇ 🍴		◇	◇ 🍴	B 🛏 ✕	
—	0	**Mallaig**	d		06 03		10 08		14 10			16 05			18 15			18 40
—	3	Morar	d		06 09		10 15					16 12			18 22			
—	7½	Arisaig	d		06 19		10 25					16 21			18 31			
—	11	Beasdale	d		06x24		10x30					16x27			18x37			
—	15¾	Lochailort	d		06x33		10x39					16x36			18x46			
—	25	Glenfinnan	d		06 51		10 59					16 54			19 04			
—	31½	Locheilside	d		07x00		11x08					17x02			19x12			
—	35¼	Loch Eil Outward Bound	d		07 07		11 15					17 10			19 20			
—	38¾	Corpach	d		07 13		11 21					17 16			19 26			
—	39¾	Banavie	d		07 17		11 25					17 20			19 30			
—	41½	**Fort William**	a		07 25		11 32		16 03			17 28			19 37			20 31
—	—		d		07 44		11 40					17 37					19 50	
—	50¼	Spean Bridge	d		07 57		11 56					17 51					20 09	
—	53½	Roy Bridge	d		08 04		12 02					17 57					20x17	
—	59¼	Tulloch	d		08 15		12 14					18 08					20 30	
—	69¼	Corrour	d		08 32		12 30					18 25					20 53	
—	76½	Rannoch	d		08 47		12 42					18 38					21 08	
—	92	Bridge of Orchy	d		09 07		13 03					18 58					21 37	
—	99¾	Upper Tyndrum	d		09 23		13 19					19 14					21 55	
0	—	**Oban**	d	05 21		08 57		12 11		14 41	16 11		18 11			20 37		
6¼	—	Connel Ferry	d	05 32		09 08		12 23		14 52	16 22		18 22			20 48		
13	—	Taynuilt	d	05 44		09 20		12 35		15 06	16 34		18 33			21 01		
18½	—	Falls of Cruachan §	d															
22	—	Loch Awe	d	05 57		09 35		12 50		15 21	16 49		18 48			21 15		
24¾	—	Dalmally	d	06 03		09 40		13 00		15 26	16a54		18 56			21 20		
36¾	—	Tyndrum Lower	d	06 22		09 59		13 20		15 45			19 15			21 39		
42	104½	**Crianlarich**	a	06 31	09 31	10 08	13 27	13 32		15 54		19 22	19 27			21 48	22 06	
—	—		d	06 33	09 33	10 14	13 37			15 56		19 32				21 48	22 08	
50¾	113¼	Ardlui	d	06 51	09 52	10 29	13 55			16 11		19 52				22 04	22x28	
58¾	121¼	Arrochar & Tarbet	d	07 10	10 06	10 43	14 09			16 27		20 06				22 18	22 46	
69½	132	Garelochhead	d	07 30	10 32	11 04	14 31			16 49		20 26				22 38	23 12	
76¼	138¾	Helensburgh Upper	a	07 40	10 42	11 15	14 41			16 59		20 37				22 49	23 25	
—	—		d	07 42	10 44	11 16	14 43			17 00		20 37				22 49	23 26	
85¼	147¾	Dumbarton Central 226	a	07 56	10 59	11 29	14 59			17 13		20 51				23 02	23 40	
92½	154¼	Dalmuir 226	a		11 12	11 38	15 12			17 24		21 03				23 11	23 52	
101½	164¼	**GlasgowQueenSt** 10 226	a	08 39	11 36	12 03	15 36			17 49		21 24				23 33	00s15	
—	—	Edinburgh 228	a															

Mondays to Fridays
30 March to 15 May

		SR	SR	SR	SR	SR	WR	SR	SR	SR	SR		SR	SR	CS	WR
		◇ 🍴	◇ A 🍴	◇ 🍴	◇ 🍴	◇ B 🍴		◇ 🍴		◇ A 🍴	◇ 🍴		◇	◇ 🍴	B 🛏 ✕	
Mallaig	d		06 03		10 08		14 10			16 05			18 15			18 40
Morar	d		06 09		10 15					16 12			18 22			
Arisaig	d		06 19		10 25					16 21			18 31			
Beasdale	d		06x24		10x30					16x27			18x37			
Lochailort	d		06x33		10x39					16x36			18x46			
Glenfinnan	d		06 51		10 59					16 54			19 04			
Locheilside	d		07x00		11x08					17x02			19x12			
Loch Eil Outward Bound	d		07 07		11 15					17 10			19 20			
Corpach	d		07 13		11 21					17 16			19 26			
Banavie	d		07 17		11 25					17 20			19 30			
Fort William	a		07 25		11 32		16 03			17 28			19 37			20 31
	d		07 44		11 40					17 37					19 50	
Spean Bridge	d		07 57		11 56					17 51					20 09	
Roy Bridge	d		08 04		12 02					17 57					20x17	
Tulloch	d		08 15		12 14					18 08					20 30	
Corrour	d		08 32		12 30					18 25					20 53	
Rannoch	d		08 47		12 42					18 38					21 08	
Bridge of Orchy	d		09 07		13 03					18 58					21 37	
Upper Tyndrum	d		09 23		13 19					19 14					21 55	
Oban	d	05 21		08 57		12 11		14 41	16 11		18 11			20 37		
Connel Ferry	d	05 32		09 08		12 23		14 52	16 22		18 22			20 48		
Taynuilt	d	05 44		09 20		12 35		15 06	16 34		18 33			21 01		
Falls of Cruachan §	d			09 28		12 43		15 14			18 42					
Loch Awe	d	05 57		09 35		12 50		15 21	16 49		18 48			21 15		
Dalmally	d	06 03		09 40		13 00		15 26	16a54		18 56			21 20		
Tyndrum Lower	d	06 22		09 59		13 20		15 45			19 15			21 39		
Crianlarich	a	06 31	09 31	10 08	13 27	13 32		15 54		19 22	19 27			21 48	22 06	
	d	06 33	09 33	10 14	13 37			15 56		19 32				21 48	22 08	
Ardlui	d	06 51	09 52	10 29	13 55			16 11		19 52				22 04	22x28	
Arrochar & Tarbet	d	07 10	10 06	10 43	14 09			16 27		20 06				22 18	22 46	
Garelochhead	d	07 30	10 32	11 04	14 31			16 49		20 26				22 38	23 12	
Helensburgh Upper	a	07 40	10 42	11 15	14 41			16 59		20 37				22 49	23 25	
	d	07 42	10 44	11 16	14 43			17 00		20 37				22 49	23 26	
Dumbarton Central 226	a	07 56	10 59	11 29	14 59			17 13		20 51				23 02	23 40	
Dalmuir 226	a		11 12	11 38	15 12			17 24		21 03				23 11	23 52	
GlasgowQueenSt 10 226	a	08 39	11 36	12 03	15 36			17 49		21 24				23 33	00s15	
Edinburgh 228	a															

§ Summer station only

A 🍴 from Fort William

B 🍴 from Crianlarich

Table T227-R

Saturdays
21 December to 21 March

Mallaig, Fort William and Oban - Glasgow Queen Street

		SR	SR	SR	SR	SR	WR	SR	SR	SR	SR	WR	SR
		◇	◇	◇	◇	◇		◇	◇	◇	◇		◇
			A						A				
		⌶	⌶	⌶	⌶			⌶	⌶	⌶			⌶
Mallaig	d		06 03		10 08		14 10		16 05		18 15	18 40	
Morar	d		06 09		10 15				16 12		18 22		
Arisaig	d		06 19		10 25				16 21		18 31		
Beasdale	d		06x24		10x30				16x27		18x37		
Lochailort	d		06x33		10x39				16x36		18x46		
Glenfinnan	d		06 51		10 59				16 54		19 04		
Locheilside	d		07x00		11x08				17x02		19x12		
Loch Eil Outward Bound	d		07 07		11 15				17 10		19 20		
Corpach	d		07 13		11 21				17 16		19 26		
Banavie	d		07 17		11 25				17 20		19 30		
Fort William	a		07 25		11 32		16 03		17 28		19 37	20 31	
	d		07 44		11 40				17 37				
Spean Bridge	d		07 57		11 56				17 51				
Roy Bridge	d		08 04		12 02				17 57				
Tulloch	d		08 15		12 14				18 08				
Corrour	d		08 32		12 30				18 25				
Rannoch	d		08 47		12 42				18 36				
Bridge of Orchy	d		09 07		13 03				19 01				
Upper Tyndrum	d		09 23		13 19				19 17				
Oban	d	05 21		08 57		12 11		16 11		18 11			20 38
Connel Ferry	d	05 32		09 08		12 23		16 22		18 22			20 49
Taynuilt	d	05 44		09 20		12 35		16 34		18 33			21 02
Falls of Cruachan §	d												
Loch Awe	d	05 57		09 35		12 50		16 49		18 48			21 16
Dalmally	d	06 03		09 40		13 00		16 54		18 56			21 21
Tyndrum Lower	d	06 22		09 59		13 20		17 13		19 15			21 40
Crianlarich	a	06 31	09 31	10 08	13 27	13 32		17 22	19 25	19 30			21 49
	d	06 33	09 33	10 14	13 37			17 24	19 36				21 49
Ardlui	d	06 51	09 52	10 29	13 55			17 42	19 52				22 05
Arrochar & Tarbet	d	07 10	10 06	10 43	14 09			17 56	20 06				22 19
Garelochhead	d	07 30	10 32	11 04	14 31			18 19	20 26				22 39
Helensburgh Upper	a	07 40	10 42	11 15	14 41			18 29	20 36				22 50
	d	07 42	10 44	11 16	14 43			18 31	20 37				22 50
Dumbarton Central 226	a	07 56	10 59	11 29	14 59			18 44	20 51				23 03
Dalmuir 226	a		11 12	11 38	15 12			18 53	21 03				23 12
GlasgowQueenSt 10 226 ⛴	a	08 41	11 37	12 06	15 36			19 18	21 25				23 33
Edinburgh 228	a												

Saturdays
28 March to 16 May

		SR	SR	SR	SR	SR	WR	SR	SR	SR	SR	WR	SR
		◇	◇	◇	◇	◇		◇	◇	◇	◇		◇
			A			B			A				
		⌶	⌶	⌶	⌶	⌶		⌶	⌶	⌶			⌶
Mallaig	d		06 03		10 08		14 10		16 05		18 15	18 40	
Morar	d		06 09		10 15				16 12		18 22		
Arisaig	d		06 19		10 25				16 21		18 31		
Beasdale	d		06x24		10x30				16x27		18x37		
Lochailort	d		06x33		10x39				16x36		18x46		
Glenfinnan	d		06 51		10 59				16 54		19 04		
Locheilside	d		07x00		11x08				17x02		19x12		
Loch Eil Outward Bound	d		07 07		11 15				17 10		19 20		
Corpach	d		07 13		11 21				17 16		19 26		
Banavie	d		07 17		11 25				17 20		19 30		
Fort William	a		07 25		11 32		16 03		17 28		19 37	20 31	
	d		07 44		11 40				17 37				
Spean Bridge	d		07 57		11 56				17 51				
Roy Bridge	d		08 04		12 02				17 57				
Tulloch	d		08 15		12 14				18 08				
Corrour	d		08 32		12 30				18 25				
Rannoch	d		08 47		12 42				18 36				
Bridge of Orchy	d		09 07		13 03				19 01				
Upper Tyndrum	d		09 23		13 19				19 17				
Oban	d	05 21		08 57		12 11		16 11		18 11			20 38
Connel Ferry	d	05 32		09 08		12 23		16 22		18 22			20 49
Taynuilt	d	05 44		09 20		12 35		16 34		18 33			21 02
Falls of Cruachan §	d			09 28		12 43		16 42		18 42			
Loch Awe	d	05 57		09 35		12 50		16 49		18 48			21 16
Dalmally	d	06 03		09 40		13 00		16 54		18 56			21 21
Tyndrum Lower	d	06 22		09 59		13 20		17 13		19 15			21 40
Crianlarich	a	06 31	09 31	10 08	13 27	13 32		17 22	19 25	19 30			21 49
	d	06 33	09 33	10 14	13 37			17 24	19 36				21 49
Ardlui	d	06 51	09 52	10 29	13 55			17 42	19 52				22 05
Arrochar & Tarbet	d	07 10	10 06	10 43	14 09			17 56	20 06				22 19
Garelochhead	d	07 30	10 32	11 04	14 31			18 19	20 26				22 39
Helensburgh Upper	a	07 40	10 42	11 15	14 41			18 29	20 36				22 50
	d	07 42	10 44	11 16	14 43			18 31	20 37				22 50
Dumbarton Central 226	a	07 56	10 59	11 29	14 59			18 44	20 51				23 03
Dalmuir 226	a		11 12	11 38	15 12			18 53	21 03				23 12
GlasgowQueenSt 10 226 ⛴	a	08 41	11 37	12 06	15 36			19 18	21 25				23 33
Edinburgh 228	a												

§ Summer station only
A ⌶ from Fort William
B ⌶ from Crianlarich

Table T227-R

Sundays
15 December to 22 March

Mallaig, Fort William and Oban - Glasgow Queen Street

		SR	SR	WR	SR	SR	SR	CS	SR	WR
								B		
		◇	◇		◇	◇	◇		◇	
			A							
		⌶	⌶		⌶	⌶	⌶	✕		
Mallaig	d		10 08	14 10		16 05			18 15	18 40
Morar	d		10 15			16 12			18 22	
Arisaig	d		10 25			16 21			18 31	
Beasdale	d		10x30			16x27			18x37	
Lochailort	d		10x39			16x36			18x46	
Glenfinnan	d		10 59			16 54			19 04	
Locheilside	d		11x08			17x02			19x12	
Loch Eil Outward Bound	d		11 15			17 10			19 20	
Corpach	d		11 21			17 16			19 26	
Banavie	d		11 25			17 20			19 30	
Fort William	a		11 32	16 03		17 28			19 37	20 31
	d		11 40			17 37		19 00		
Spean Bridge	d		11 56			17 51		19 19		
Roy Bridge	d		12 02			17 57		19x25		
Tulloch	d		12 14			18 08		19 39		
Corrour	d		12 30			18 25		19 59		
Rannoch	d		12 42			18 38		20 14		
Bridge of Orchy	d		13 03			18 58		20 47		
Upper Tyndrum	d		13 19			19 14		21 05		
Oban	d	12 11			16 11		18 11			
Connel Ferry	d	12 27			16 26		18 22			
Taynuilt	d	12 38			16 38		18 33			
Falls of Cruachan §	d									
Loch Awe	d	12 53			16 53		18 48			
Dalmally	d	12 59			16 58		18 56			
Tyndrum Lower	d	13 17			17 17		19 15			
Crianlarich	a	13 26	13 32		17 26	19 22	19 27	21 16		
	d	13 37			17 27	19 32		21 18		
Ardlui	d	13 55			17 43	19 52		21x38		
Arrochar & Tarbet	d	14 09			17 57	20 06		21 57		
Garelochhead	d	14 29			18 19	20 26		22 23		
Helensburgh Upper	a	14 40			18 29	20 37		22 36		
	d	14 40			18 31	20 40		22 39		
Dumbarton Central 226	a	14 53			18 47	20 53		22 54		
Dalmuir 226	a	15 05			18 58	21 04		23 06		
GlasgowQueenSt 10 226 ⛴	a	15 25			19 18	21 19		23s29		
Edinburgh 228	a									

Sundays
29 March to 10 May

		SR	SR	WR	SR	SR	SR	CS	SR	WR
								B		
		◇	◇		◇	◇	◇		◇	
			A							
		⌶	⌶		⌶	⌶	⌶	✕		
Mallaig	d		10 08	14 10		16 05			18 15	18 40
Morar	d		10 15			16 12			18 22	
Arisaig	d		10 25			16 21			18 31	
Beasdale	d		10x30			16x27			18x37	
Lochailort	d		10x39			16x36			18x46	
Glenfinnan	d		10 59			16 54			19 04	
Locheilside	d		11x08			17x02			19x12	
Loch Eil Outward Bound	d		11 15			17 10			19 20	
Corpach	d		11 21			17 16			19 26	
Banavie	d		11 25			17 20			19 30	
Fort William	a		11 32	16 03		17 28			19 37	20 31
	d		11 40			17 37		19 00		
Spean Bridge	d		11 56			17 51		19 19		
Roy Bridge	d		12 02			17 57		19x25		
Tulloch	d		12 14			18 08		19 39		
Corrour	d		12 30			18 25		19 59		
Rannoch	d		12 42			18 38		20 14		
Bridge of Orchy	d		13 03			18 58		20 47		
Upper Tyndrum	d		13 19			19 14		21 05		
Oban	d	12 11			16 11		18 11			
Connel Ferry	d	12 27			16 26		18 22			
Taynuilt	d	12 38			16 38		18 33			
Falls of Cruachan §	d	12 46			16 46		18 42			
Loch Awe	d	12 53			16 53		18 48			
Dalmally	d	12 59			16 58		18 56			
Tyndrum Lower	d	13 17			17 17		19 15			
Crianlarich	a	13 26	13 32		17 26	19 22	19 27	21 16		
	d	13 37			17 27	19 32		21 18		
Ardlui	d	13 55			17 43	19 52		21x38		
Arrochar & Tarbet	d	14 09			17 57	20 06		21 57		
Garelochhead	d	14 29			18 19	20 26		22 23		
Helensburgh Upper	a	14 40			18 29	20 37		22 36		
	d	14 40			18 31	20 40		22 39		
Dumbarton Central 226	a	14 53			18 47	20 53		22 54		
Dalmuir 226	a	15 05			18 58	21 04		23 06		
GlasgowQueenSt 10 226 ⛴	a	15 25			19 18	21 19		23s29		
Edinburgh 228	a									

§ Summer station only
A ⌶ from Crianlarich

Table T228-F

Edinburgh - Falkirk High - Glasgow Queen Street

Mondays to Fridays

16 December to 15 May

Miles	Station																									
				SR MX 1	SR	SR	SR 1	SR	SR 1	SR	SR 1	SR 1 ☕	SR	SR 1 ☕	SR 1 ☕	SR	SR 1 ☕	SR 1 ☕	SR	SR 1 ☕	SR 1 ☕	SR	SR 1 ☕	SR 1 ☕
0	**Edinburgh**	225,230,242	d		05 03	05 33	06 00	06 04	06 30	06 33	06 45	07 00	07 03	07 15	07 30	07 35	07 45	08 00	08 05	08 15	08 30	08 35	08 45	09 00
1¼	Haymarket	225,230,242	d		05 07	05 37	06 04	06 08	06 34	06 37	06 49	07 04	07 07	07 19	07 35	07 39	07 49	08 06	08 12	08 20	08 37	08 41	08 50	09 05
17½	Linlithgow	230	d	00 02	05 22	05 52	06 17	06 23	06 46	06 54	07 02		07 23	07 32	07 48	07 56	08 04		08 28	08 33		08 58	09 05	
22¼	Polmont	230	d	00 07	05 26	05 57	06 21	06 27	06 51	06 59		07 19	07 27		07 53	08 00		08 27	08 33	08 38		09 03	09 09	
25½	**Falkirk High**		d	00 12	05b34	06b08	06 26	06b35	06 55	07b05	07 09	07 24	07b33	07 39	07 57	08b06	08 12	08 32	08b40	08 43	08 57	09b10	09 14	09 22
35¾	Croy	230	a	00 21			06 34		07 04		07 19			07 48	08 06			08 40			09 06			09 31
41	Lenzie	230	a	00 26													08 24							
44	Bishopbriggs	230	a																					
47¼	**Glasgow Queen Street**	230	a	00 36	06 16	06 51	06 48	07 14	07 18	07 48	07 37	07 44	08 15	08 03	08 23	08 45	08 36	08 53	09 23	09 06	09 18	09 52	09 34	09 43

Station																								
			SR	SR 1 ☕	SR 1 ☕	SR	SR 1 ☕	SR 1 ☕	SR	SR 1 ☕	SR 1 ☕	SR	SR 1 ☕	SR 1 ☕	SR	SR 1 ☕	SR 1 ☕	SR	SR 1 ☕	SR 1 ☕	SR	SR 1 ☕	SR 1 ☕	SR
Edinburgh	225,230,242	d	09 04	09 15	09 30	09 35	09 45	10 00	10 03	10 15	10 30	10 33	10 45	11 00	11 04	11 15	11 30	11 34	11 45	12 00	12 04	12 15	12 30	12 34
Haymarket	225,230,242	d	09 09	09 20	09 34	09 39	09 49	10 04	10 08	10 19	10 34	10 37	10 49	11 04	11 08	11 19	11 34	11 38	11 49	12 06	12 09	12 20	12 35	12 39
Linlithgow	230	d	09 25	09 35		09 54	10 02		10 24	10 34		10 54	11 02		11 24	11 32		11 53	12 02		12 25	12 33		12 55
Polmont	230	d	09 29	09 39		09 59	10 06		10 29	10 38		10 58	11 06		11 29	11 36		11 58	12 06		12 30	12 38		12 59
Falkirk High		d	09b36	09 44	09 55	10b10	10 11	10 22	10b40	10 43	10 52	11b10	11 11	11 22	11b37	11 41	11 52	12b10	12 11	12 23	12b40	12 42	12 53	13b08
Croy	230	a			10 03			10 30			11 01			11 30			12 00			12 32			13 02	
Lenzie	230	a																						
Bishopbriggs	230	a																						
Glasgow Queen Street	230	a	10 20	10 06	10 15	10 50	10 30	10 43	11 21	11 03	11 13	11 54	11 30	11 42	12 24	12 00	12 14	12 51	12 33	12 44	13 21	13 00	13 14	13 52

Station																							
			SR 1 ☕	SR 1 ☕	SR	SR 1 ☕	SR 1 ☕	SR	SR 1 ☕	SR 1 ☕	SR	SR 1 ☕	SR 1 ☕	SR	SR 1 ☕	SR 1 ☕	SR	SR 1 ☕	SR 1 ☕	SR	SR 1 ☕	SR 1 ☕	SR
Edinburgh	225,230,242	d	12 45	13 00	13 04	13 15	13 30	13 35	13 45	14 00	14 03	14 15	14 30	14 39	14 45	15 00	15 04	15 15	15 30	15 35	15 45	16 00	16 03
Haymarket	225,230,242	d	12 50	13 05	13 08	13 20	13 34	13 39	13 49	14 04	14 10	14 21	14 36	14 44	14 49	15 05	15 08	15 20	15 34	15 39	15 49	16 04	16 08
Linlithgow	230	d	13 06		13 24	13 33		13 54	14 02		14 28	14 33		15 00	15 04		15 24	15 33		15 54	16 02		16 23
Polmont	230	d	13 11		13 28	13 37		13 58	14 06		14 32	14 38		15 04	15 09		15 28	15 38		15 58	16 06		16 28
Falkirk High		d	13 15	13 25	13b38	13 42	13 52	14b10	14 11	14 22	14b40	14 42	14 53	15b10	15 13	15 22	15b40	15 43	15 52	16b10	16 11	16 22	16b37
Croy	230	a		13 34			14 00			14 31			15 02			15 31			16 00			16 30	
Lenzie	230	a																					
Bishopbriggs	230	a																					
Glasgow Queen Street	230	a	13 33	13 45	14 21	14 01	14 12	14 51	14 30	14 43	15 21	15 02	15 14	15 51	15 31	15 43	16 22	16 05	16 13	16 51	16 35	16 45	17 20

Station																							
			SR 1 ☕	SR 1 ☕	SR	SR 1 ☕	SR 1 ☕	SR	SR 1 ☕	SR 1 ☕	SR	SR 1 ☕	SR 1 ☕	SR	SR 1 ☕	SR 1 ☕	SR	SR 1 ☕	SR 1	SR	SR 1	SR 1	SR	SR 1 ☕
Edinburgh	225,230,242	d	16 15	16 30	16 37	16 45	17 00	17 05	17 15	17 30	17 34	17 45	18 00	18 07	18 15	18 30	18 34	18 45	19 00	19 03	19 15	19 30	19 35	19 45
Haymarket	225,230,242	d	16 21	16 34	16 43	16 50	17 05	17 09	17 20	17 34	17 38	17 50	18 04	18 12	18 20	18 34	18 38	18 49	19 04	19 08	19 20	19 34	19 39	19 49
Linlithgow	230	d	16 34		16 58	17 05		17 26	17 34		17 53	18 03		18 29	18 33		18 54	19 02		19 24	19 33	19 49	19 54	20 03
Polmont	230	d	16 38		17 03	17 10		17 31	17 39		17 58	18 08		18 34	18 38		18 58	19 07		19 28	19 37		19 59	20 08
Falkirk High		d	16 43	16 52		17 14	17 23		17 43	17 52		18 13	18 23		18 42	18 52		19 11	19 22		19 42	19 57		20 12
Croy	230	a		17 00			17 32			18 01			18 31			19 01			19 31			20 05		20 20
Lenzie	230	a								18 06														
Bishopbriggs	230	a																						
Glasgow Queen Street	230	a	17 03	17 12	17 52	17 33	17 44	18 18	18 06	18 15	18 51	18 33	18 44	19 21	19 05	19 13	19 53	19 31	19 43	20 23	20 00	20 17	20 53	20 32

Station										
			SR 1	SR 1	SR 1	SR 1	SR 1	SR 1	SR 1	SR 1
Edinburgh	225,230,242	d	20 15	20 45	21 15	21 45	22 15	22 45	23 15	23 45
Haymarket	225,230,242	d	20 20	20 49	21 21	21 49	22 20	22 49	23 21	23 49
Linlithgow	230	d	20 33	21 02	21 35	22 02	22 33	23 06	23 34	00 02
Polmont	230	d	20 37	21 06	21 40	22 06	22 38	23 10	23 39	00 07
Falkirk High		d	20 42	21 11	21 44	22 11	22 42	23 15	23 43	00 12
Croy	230	a	20 50	21 19	21 53	22 19	22 51	23 23	23 53	00 21
Lenzie	230	a							23 58	00 26
Bishopbriggs	230	a							00 03	
Glasgow Queen Street	230	a	21 02	21 31	22 06	22 31	23 02	23 36	00 09	00 36

Saturdays

21 December to 16 May

Station																								
			SR 1	SR	SR	SR 1	SR	SR 1	SR	SR 1 ☕	SR	SR 1 ☕	SR 1 ☕	SR	SR 1 ☕	SR 1 ☕	SR	SR 1 ☕	SR 1 ☕	SR	SR 1 ☕	SR 1 ☕	SR	SR 1 ☕
Edinburgh	225,230,242	d		05 03	05 33	06 00	06 04	06 30	06 33	07 00	07 03	07 15	07 30	07 33	07 45	08 00	08 05	08 15	08 30	08 35	08 45	09 00	09 07	09 15
Haymarket	225,230,242	d		05 07	05 37	06 04	06 08	06 34	06 37	07 04	07 07	07 19	07 35	07 38	07 49	08 05	08 09	08 19	08 36	08 40	08 50	09 06	09 12	09 20
Linlithgow	230	d	00 02	05 22	05 52	06 17	06 23	06 47	06 53		07 23	07 32	07 48	07 55	08 02		08 24	08 32		08 55	09 05		09 27	09 35
Polmont	230	d	00 07	05 26	05 57	06 21	06 27	06 51	06 58	07 19	07 27		07 53	07 59		08 23	08 29	08 37		09 00	09 10		09 31	09 39
Falkirk High		d	00 12	05b34	06b08	06 26	06b35	06 55	07b05	07 24	07b33	07 39	07 57	08b05	08 10	08 27	08b40	08 42	08 54	09b10	09 14	09 23	09b37	09 44
Croy	230	a	00 21			06 34		07 04				07 48	08 05			08 36			09 04			09 32		
Lenzie	230	a	00 26												08 22									
Bishopbriggs	230	a													08 27									
Glasgow Queen Street	230	a	00 36	06 15	06 49	06 46	07 14	07 18	07 48	07 42	08 20	08 03	08 17	08 48	08 37	08 51	09 21	09 03	09 18	09 56	09 35	09 44	10 20	10 05

b Falkirk Grahamston

Table T228-F

Saturdays

21 December to 16 May

Edinburgh - Falkirk High - Glasgow Queen Street

Station																							
			SR 1 ☕	SR	SR 1 ☕	SR 1 ☕	SR	SR 1 ☕	SR 1 ☕	SR	SR 1 ☕	SR 1 ☕	SR	SR 1 ☕	SR 1 ☕	SR	SR 1 ☕	SR 1 ☕	SR	SR 1 ☕	SR 1 ☕	SR	SR 1 ☕
Edinburgh	225,230,242	d	09 30	09 33	09 45	10 00	10 04	10 15	10 30	10 34	10 45	11 00	11 05	11 15	11 30	11 33	11 45	12 00	12 03	12 15	12 30	12 34	12 45
Haymarket	225,230,242	d	09 34	09 38	09 49	10 05	10 08	10 21	10 35	10 38	10 49	11 05	11 09	11 20	11 34	11 38	11 49	12 04	12 08	12 20	12 34	12 38	12 49
Linlithgow	230	d		09 53	10 02		10 24	10 34		10 55	11 04		11 25	11 32		11 54	12 02		12 25	12 33		12 53	13 03
Polmont	230	d		09 58	10 06		10 29	10 38		10 59	11 09		11 30	11 37		11 59	12 06		12 30	12 38		12 58	13 07
Falkirk High		d	09 54	10b10	10 11	10 23	10b40	10 43	10 53	11b10	11 13	11 23	11b37	11 41	11 53	12b10	12 11	12 24	12b40	12 42	12 52	13b10	13 12
Croy	230	a	10 02			10 31			11 01			11 31			12 02			12 32			13 00		
Lenzie	230	a																					
Bishopbriggs	230	a																					
Glasgow Queen Street	230	a	10 14	10 50	10 31	10 43	11 21	11 01	11 13	11 54	11 32	11 44	12 22	12 00	12 14	12 51	12 34	12 44	13 22	13 03	13 12	13 52	13 33

Station																								
			SR 1 ☕	SR	SR 1 ☕	SR 1 ☕	SR	SR 1 ☕	SR 1 ☕	SR	SR 1 ☕	SR 1 ☕	SR	SR 1 ☕	SR 1 ☕	SR	SR 1 ☕	SR 1 ☕	SR	SR 1 ☕	SR 1 ☕	SR	SR 1 ☕	SR 1 ☕
Edinburgh	225,230,242	d	13 00	13 03	13 15	13 30	13 34	13 45	14 00	14 04	14 15	14 30	14 33	14 45	15 00	15 05	15 15	15 30	15 34	15 45	16 00	16 04	16 15	16 30
Haymarket	225,230,242	d	13 04	13 08	13 19	13 34	13 38	13 49	14 07	14 11	14 19	14 34	14 38	14 49	15 04	15 09	15 20	15 34	15 38	15 49	16 04	16 08	16 19	16 35
Linlithgow	230	d		13 24	13 33		13 55	14 02		14 26	14 33		14 57	15 02		15 24	15 32		15 54	16 02		16 23	16 32	
Polmont	230	d		13 28	13 37		13 59	14 06		14 30	14 37		15 02	15 07		15 28	15 37		15 58	16 06		16 28	16 37	
Falkirk High		d	13 22	13b38	13 42	13 52	14b10	14 11	14 25	14b40	14 42	14 52	15b10	15 11	15 22	15b40	15 41	15 51	16b11	16 11	16 22	16b37	16 41	16 52
Croy	230	a	13 30			14 00			14 33			15 00			15 30			16 00			16 30			17 01
Lenzie	230	a																						
Bishopbriggs	230	a																						
Glasgow Queen Street	230	a	13 42	14 23	14 06	14 12	14 50	14 33	14 45	15 21	15 01	15 12	15 54	15 31	15 42	16 22	16 01	16 13	16 51	16 31	16 42	17 20	17 01	17 13

Station																							
			SR	SR 1 ☕	SR 1 ☕	SR	SR 1 ☕	SR 1 ☕	SR	SR 1 ☕	SR 1 ☕	SR	SR 1 ☕	SR 1 ☕	SR	SR 1 ☕	SR 1 ☕	SR	SR 1	SR 1	SR	SR 1 ☕	SR 1
Edinburgh	225,230,242	d	16 37	16 45	17 00	17 03	17 15	17 30	17 33	17 45	18 00	18 05	18 15	18 30	18 34	18 45	19 00	19 03	19 15	19 30	19 33	19 45	20 15
Haymarket	225,230,242	d	16 43	16 50	17 05	17 08	17 20	17 34	17 38	17 49	18 04	18 09	18 20	18 35	18 39	18 50	19 04	19 08	19 20	19 34	19 37	19 49	20 21
Linlithgow	230	d	16 59	17 06		17 25	17 33		17 53	18 02		18 24	18 32		18 54	19 02		19 24	19 33	19 49	19 55	20 01	20 34
Polmont	230	d	17 03	17 11		17 29	17 37		17 57	18 07		18 28	18 37		18 58	19 07		19 29	19 38		19 59	20 06	20 39
Falkirk High		d	17b10	17 15	17 23	17b37	17 42	17 52	18b10	18 12	18 22	18b40	18 41	18 53	19b10	19 11	19 21	19b40	19 42	19 56	20b07	20 10	20 43
Croy	230	a			17 31			18 00			18 30			19 01			19 30			20 05		20 19	20 52
Lenzie	230	a						18 06															
Bishopbriggs	230	a																					
Glasgow Queen Street	230	a	17 52	17 33	17 43	18 17	18 03	18 14	18 50	18 32	18 42	19 21	19 01	19 14	19 50	19 30	19 42	20 24	20 03	20 21	20 54	20 34	21 06

Station									
			SR 1	SR 1	SR 1	SR 1	SR 1	SR 1	SR 1
Edinburgh	225,230,242	d	20 45	21 15	21 45	22 15	22 45	23 15	23 45
Haymarket	225,230,242	d	20 50	21 20	21 49	22 19	22 49	23 20	23 49
Linlithgow	230	d	21 03	21 33	22 02	22 32	23 06	23 33	00 02
Polmont	230	d	21 07	21 38	22 06	22 36	23 10	23 37	00 07
Falkirk High		d	21 12	21 42	22 11	22 41	23 15	23 42	00 12
Croy	230	a	21 20	21 51	22 19	22 49	23 23	23 50	00 21
Lenzie	230	a						23 55	00 26
Bishopbriggs	230	a						23 59	
Glasgow Queen Street	230	a	21 32	22 02	22 31	23 01	23 36	00 08	00 36

Sundays

15 December to 10 May

Station																							
			SR 1 A	SR 1	SR 1 ☕	SR 1	SR 1	SR 1 ☕	SR 1 ☕	SR 1 ☕	SR 1 ☕	SR 1 ☕	SR 1 ☕	SR 1 ☕	SR 1 ☕	SR 1 ☕	SR 1	SR 1 ☕	SR 1 ☕	SR 1 ☕	SR 1 ☕	SR 1 ☕	SR 1	SR 1 ☕
Edinburgh	225,230,242	d		08 00	08 30	09 00	09 30	10 00	10 30	11 00	11 30	12 00	12 30	13 00	13 30	14 00	14 30	15 00	15 30	16 00	16 30	17 00	17 30	18 00
Haymarket	225,230,242	d		08 04	08 34	09 04	09 34	10 04	10 34	11 04	11 34	12 06	12 34	13 04	13 34	14 04	14 34	15 04	15 34	16 04	16 34	17 05	17 34	18 04
Linlithgow	230	d	00 02	08 24	08 54	09 23	09 52	10 22	10 47	11 17	11 47	12 19	12 47	13 17	13 47	14 17	14 47	15 17	15 47	16 17	16 47	17 17	17 47	18 17
Polmont	230	d	00 07	08 29		09 28		10 27		11 22		12 23		13 21		14 21		15 21		16 21		17 22		18 21
Falkirk High		d	00 12	08 33	09 01	09 32	09 59	10 31	10 54	11 26	11 54	12 28	12 54	13 26	13 54	14 26	14 54	15 26	15 54	16 26	16 54	17 26	17 54	18 26
Croy	230	a	00 21	08 41	09 09	09 41	10 08	10 40	11 02	11 35	12 03	12 36	13 05	13 34	14 02	14 34	15 02	15 34	16 04	16 35	17 04	17 35	18 03	18 35
Lenzie	230	a	00 26																					
Bishopbriggs	230	a																						
Glasgow Queen Street	230	a	00 36	08 54	09 22	09 53	10 20	10 52	11 14	11 48	12 18	12 48	13 18	13 48	14 14	14 46	15 14	15 48	16 20	16 48	17 19	17 48	18 19	18 46

Station													
			SR 1 ☕	SR 1 ☕	SR 1	SR 1	SR 1	SR 1	SR 1	SR 1	SR 1	SR 1	SR 1
Edinburgh	225,230,242	d	18 30	19 00	19 30	20 00	20 30	21 00	21 30	22 00	22 30	23 00	23 30
Haymarket	225,230,242	d	18 34	19 04	19 34	20 04	20 34	21 04	21 34	22 04	22 34	23 04	23 34
Linlithgow	230	d	18 47	19 17	19 47	20 17	20 47	21 17	21 47	22 17	22 47	23 16	23 46
Polmont	230	d		19 21		20 22		21 21		22 21		23 21	23 51
Falkirk High		d	18 54	19 26	19 54	20 26	20 54	21 26	21 54	22 26	22 54	23 25	23 55
Croy	230	a	19 02	19 35	20 03	20 35	21 02	21 35	22 02	22 35	23 02	23 34	00 04
Lenzie	230	a											
Bishopbriggs	230	a											
Glasgow Queen Street	230	a	19 14	19 50	20 15	20 47	21 14	21 47	22 14	22 46	23 14	23 47	00 16

A not 15 December

b Falkirk Grahamston

Table T228-R

Mondays to Fridays

16 December to 15 May

Glasgow Queen Street - Falkirk High - Edinburgh

Miles		SR	SR	SR	SR	SR	SR	SR	SR	SR	SR	SR	SR	SR	SR	SR	SR	SR	SR	SR	SR	SR
		MX 1			1		1	1		1 trolley	1 trolley		1 trolley	1		1 trolley	1 trolley		1 trolley	1 trolley		1 trolley
0	**Glasgow Queen Street** 10 230 d		05 26	05 56	06 00	06 25	06 30	06 45	06 56	07 00	07 15	07 26	07 30	07 45	07 55	08 00	08 15	08 26	08 30	08 45	08 56	09 00
3¼	Bishopbriggs 230 d																					
6¾	Lenzie 3 230 d						06 38			07 08												
11½	Croy 3 230 d							06 55					07 42			08 11			08 42			09 11
21¾	**Falkirk High** 3 d	00 04	06b07	06b36	06 18	07b08	06 51	07 04	07b36	07 20	07 33	08b08	07 51	08 04	08b40	08 22	08 32	09b07	08 51	09 04	09b37	09 20
25	Polmont 3 230 a	00 08	06 12	06 41	06 22	07 13	06 55		07 41	07 24	07 37	08 13		08 08	08 45	08 26		09 12		09 08	09 42	
29¾	Linlithgow 230 a	00 14	06 17	06 46	06 27	07 18	07 00	07 11	07 46	07 29	07 42	08 18	07 58	08 14	08 51		08 39	09 17		09 13	09 47	
46	Haymarket 225,230,242 a	00s27	06 33	07 01	06s42	07 35	07s18	07s24	08 02	07s46	07s58	08 35	08s12	08s28	09 08	08s42	08s54	09 36	09s12	09s28	10 05	09s39
47¼	**Edinburgh** 10 225,230,242 a	00 34	06 38	07 07	06 49	07 41	07 23	07 29	08 08	07 55	08 03	08 42	08 18	08 35	09 13	08 48	09 03	09 41	09 18	09 33	10 10	09 44

	SR	SR	SR	SR	SR	SR	SR	SR	SR	SR	SR	SR	SR	SR	SR	SR	SR	SR	SR	SR	SR
	1 trolley		1 trolley	1 trolley		1 trolley	1 trolley		1 trolley	1 trolley		1 trolley	1 trolley		1 trolley	1 trolley		1 trolley	1 trolley		1 trolley
Glasgow Queen Street 10 230 d	09 15	09 24	09 30	09 45	09 56	10 00	10 15	10 25	10 30	10 45	10 55	11 00	11 15	11 26	11 30	11 45	11 54	12 00	12 15	12 27	12 30
Bishopbriggs 230 d																					
Lenzie 3 230 d																					
Croy 3 230 d			09 40			10 10			10 40			11 10			11 41			12 11			12 42
Falkirk High 3 d	09 34	10b07	09 49	10 03	10b36	10 19	10 33	11b07	10 49	11 03	11b36	11 19	11 33	12b07	11 49	12 04	12b37	12 20	12 33	13b07	12 50
Polmont 3 230 a	09 38	10 12		10 07	10 41		10 37	11 12		11 07	11 41		11 37	12 13		12 08	12 42		12 37	13 12	
Linlithgow 230 a	09 43	10 17		10 12	10 46		10 42	11 17		11 12	11 46		11 42	12 18		12 14	12 47		12 42	13 17	
Haymarket 225,230,242 a	09s57	10 34	10s07	10s29	11 05	10s38	10s56	11 33	11s07	11s26	12 05	11s37	12s00	12 33	12s07	12s27	13 06	12s38	12s56	13 35	13s08
Edinburgh 10 225,230,242 a	10 03	10 41	10 13	10 36	11 10	10 44	11 04	11 40	11 12	11 31	12 12	11 43	12 05	12 40	12 15	12 34	13 11	12 43	13 04	13 41	13 14

	SR	SR	SR	SR	SR	SR	SR	SR	SR	SR	SR	SR	SR	SR	SR	SR	SR	SR	SR	SR	SR	SR
	1 trolley		1 trolley	1 trolley		1 trolley	1 trolley		1 trolley	1 trolley		1 trolley	1 trolley		1 trolley	1 trolley		1 trolley	1 trolley		1 trolley	1 trolley
Glasgow Queen Street 10 230 d	12 45	12 56	13 00	13 15	13 26	13 30	13 45	13 55	14 00	14 15	14 26	14 30	14 45	14 56	15 00	15 15	15 24	15 30	15 45	15 56	16 00	16 15
Bishopbriggs 230 d																						
Lenzie 3 230 d																						
Croy 3 230 d			13 11			13 42			14 10			14 41			15 11			15 41			16 10	
Falkirk High 3 d	13 03	13b37	13 20	13 33	14b07	13 51	14 03	14b37	14 19	14 33	15b07	14 50	15 03		15 20	15 33		15 50	16 04		16 19	16 33
Polmont 3 230 a	13 07	13 42		13 37	14 12		14 07	14 42		14 37	15 12		15 07	15 42		15 37	16 12		16 08	16 42		16 37
Linlithgow 230 a	13 12	13 47		13 42	14 17		14 12	14 47		14 42	15 17		15 12	15 47		15 42	16 17		16 13	16 47		16 42
Haymarket 225,230,242 a	13s30	14 08	13s38	14s04	14 34	14s12	14s30	15 05	14s37	14s57	15 35	15s10	15s27	16 04	15s38	16s01	16 33	16s08	16s27	17 05	16s37	16s57
Edinburgh 10 225,230,242 a	13 36	14 13	13 44	14 09	14 39	14 21	14 35	15 10	14 42	15 03	15 41	15 16	15 33	16 09	15 44	16 06	16 38	16 15	16 33	17 11	16 42	17 03

	SR	SR	SR	SR	SR	SR	SR	SR	SR	SR	SR	SR	SR	SR	SR	SR	SR	SR	SR	SR	SR	SR
		1 trolley	1 trolley		1 trolley	1 trolley		1 trolley		1 trolley		1 trolley	1 trolley		1 trolley	1 trolley		1 trolley	1		1	1 trolley
Glasgow Queen Street 10 230 d	16 25	16 30	16 45	16 55	17 00	17 15	17 25	17 30	17 33	17 45	17 57	18 00	18 15	18 26	18 30	18 45	18 56	19 00	19 15	19 25	19 30	19 45
Bishopbriggs 230 d									17 39													
Lenzie 3 230 d									17 44													
Croy 3 230 d		16 41			17 11			17 41				18 11			18 42			19 10				19 56
Falkirk High 3 d		16 50	17 06		17 19	17 33		17 49	18b00	18 04		18 20	18 33		18 51	19 03		19 19	19 33	20b09	19 49	20 04
Polmont 3 230 a	17 14		17 10	17 42	17 23		18 14	17 53	18 05	18 09	18 42		18 37	19 12		19 07	19 42		19 37	20 14	19 53	20 08
Linlithgow 230 a	17 19		17 15	17 47		17 40	18 20	17 59	18 11	18 15	18 47		18 42	19 17		19 12	19 47		19 42	20 19	19 59	20 14
Haymarket 225,230,242 a	17 35	17s09	17s28	18 08	17s40	17s54	18 35	18s12		18s31	19 07	18s38	18s57	19 37	19s09	19s29	20 03	19s40	20s00	20 35	20s15	20s29
Edinburgh 10 225,230,242 a	17 40	17 14	17 33	18 13	17 45	17 59	18 40	18 18		18 37	19 12	18 43	19 02	19 42	19 15	19 34	20 09	19 46	20 05	20 41	20 20	20 36

	SR	SR	SR	SR	SR	SR	SR	SR
	1	1	1	1	1	1	1	1
Glasgow Queen Street 10 230 d	20 15	20 45	21 15	21 45	22 15	22 45	23 15	23 45
Bishopbriggs 230 d								
Lenzie 3 230 d								
Croy 3 230 d	20 26	20 57	21 26	21 57	22 26	22 56	23 25	23 56
Falkirk High 3 d	20 35	21 05	21 35	22 06	22 35	23 04	23 34	00 04
Polmont 3 230 a	20 39	21 09	21 39	22 10	22 39	23 08	23 38	00 08
Linlithgow 230 a	20 44	21 15	21 44	22 15	22 44	23 14	23 43	00 14
Haymarket 225,230,242 a	20s57	21s28	21s57	22s29	23s01	23s29	23s57	00s27
Edinburgh 10 225,230,242 a	21 03	21 33	22 02	22 34	23 09	23 34	00 04	00 34

Saturdays

21 December to 16 May

	SR	SR	SR	SR	SR	SR	SR	SR	SR	SR	SR	SR	SR	SR	SR	SR	SR	SR	SR	SR	SR	SR
	1			1		1		1 trolley	1 trolley		1 trolley	1		1 trolley	1 trolley		1 trolley	1 trolley		1 trolley	1 trolley	
Glasgow Queen Street 10 230 d		05 26	05 56	06 00	06 25	06 30	06 56	07 00	07 15	07 26	07 30	07 45	07 55	08 00	08 15	08 28	08 30	08 45	08 55	09 00	09 15	09 26
Bishopbriggs 230 d																						
Lenzie 3 230 d						06 38		07 08														
Croy 3 230 d						06 43					07 42			08 11			08 42			09 10		
Falkirk High 3 d	00 04	06b07	06b36	06 18	07b07	06 52	07b36	07 20	07 33	08b08	07 51	08 03	08b39	08 20	08 32	09b07	08 51	09 03	09b37	09 19	09 33	10b07
Polmont 3 230 a	00 08	06 12	06 41	06 22	07 12	06 56	07 41	07 24	07 37	08 13		08 07	08 44	08 25		09 12		09 07	09 42		09 37	10 12
Linlithgow 230 a	00 14	06 17	06 46	06 27	07 17	07 01	07 46	07 30	07 42	08 18	07 58	08 12	08 52		08 39	09 17		09 13	09 47		09 42	10 17
Haymarket 225,230,242 a	00s27	06 33	07 01	06s40	07 35	07s18	08 05	07s46	07s57	08 37	08s12	08s31	09 08	08s41	08s55	09 34	09s12	09s28	10 04	09s37	10s01	10 33
Edinburgh 10 225,230,242 a	00 34	06 39	07 06	06 46	07 40	07 24	08 11	07 55	08 03	08 44	08 18	08 38	09 13	08 48	09 02	09 39	09 18	09 33	10 10	09 42	10 07	10 38

b Falkirk Grahamston

Table T228-R

Saturdays

21 December to 16 May

Glasgow Queen Street - Falkirk High - Edinburgh

	SR	SR	SR	SR	SR	SR	SR	SR	SR	SR	SR	SR	SR	SR	SR	SR	SR	SR	SR	SR	SR
	1 trolley	1		1 trolley	1 trolley		1 trolley	1 trolley		1 trolley	1 trolley		1 trolley	1 trolley		1 trolley	1 trolley		1 trolley	1 trolley	
Glasgow Queen Street 10 230 d	09 30	09 45	09 56	10 00	10 15	10 25	10 30	10 45	10 55	11 00	11 15	11 26	11 30	11 45	11 54	12 00	12 15	12 27	12 30	12 45	12 55
Bishopbriggs 230 d																					
Lenzie 3 230 d																					
Croy 3 230 d	09 41			10 11			10 41			11 10			11 42			12 11			12 42		
Falkirk High 3 d	09 49	10 03	10b36	10 19	10 33	11b08	10 50	11 03	11b36	11 19	11 33	12b07	11 50	12 03	12b37	12 20	12 32	13b07	12 51	13 03	13b37
Polmont 3 230 a		10 07	10 41		10 37	11 13		11 07	11 41		11 37	12 12		12 07	12 42		12 36	13 12		13 07	13 42
Linlithgow 230 a		10 12	10 46		10 42	11 18		11 12	11 46		11 42	12 17		12 13	12 47		12 42	13 17		13 12	13 47
Haymarket 225,230,242 a	10s08	10s27	11 06	10s37	10s58	11 35	11s17	11s28	12 05	11s38	11s57	12 33	12s09	12s28	13 07	12s38	12s56	13 33	13s09	13s29	14 05
Edinburgh 10 225,230,242 a	10 15	10 34	11 11	10 42	11 04	11 41	11 22	11 33	12 10	11 44	12 02	12 38	12 14	12 33	13 12	12 43	13 01	13 40	13 14	13 34	14 11

	SR	SR	SR	SR	SR	SR	SR	SR	SR	SR	SR	SR	SR	SR	SR	SR	SR	SR	SR	SR	SR	SR
	1 trolley	1 trolley		1 trolley	1 trolley		1 trolley	1 trolley		1 trolley	1 trolley		1 trolley	1 trolley		1 trolley	1 trolley		1 trolley	1 trolley		1 trolley
Glasgow Queen Street 10 230 d	13 00	13 15	13 25	13 30	13 45	13 57	14 00	14 15	14 25	14 30	14 45	14 55	15 00	15 15	15 25	15 30	15 45	15 55	16 00	16 15	16 27	16 30
Bishopbriggs 230 d																						
Lenzie 3 230 d																						
Croy 3 230 d	13 10			13 40			14 11			14 41			15 10			15 40			16 10			16 41
Falkirk High 3 d	13 19	13 33	14b07	13 49	14 03	14b37	14 20	14 33	15b07	14 50	15 03	15b37	15 19	15 33	16b07	15 49	16 03	16b37	16 19	16 33	17b05	16 50
Polmont 3 230 a		13 37	14 12		14 07	14 42		14 37	15 12		15 07	15 42		15 37	16 12		16 07	16 42		16 37	17 14	
Linlithgow 230 a		13 42	14 17		14 12	14 47		14 42	15 17		15 12	15 47		15 42	16 17		16 12	16 47		16 42	17 19	
Haymarket 225,230,242 a	13s37	13s58	14 34	14s07	14s31	15 06	14s38	14s57	15 34	15s09	15s27	16 05	15s37	16s00	16 32	16s09	16s28	17 06	16s37	16s57	17 35	17s08
Edinburgh 10 225,230,242 a	13 43	14 03	14 40	14 12	14 36	15 11	14 43	15 04	15 39	15 14	15 33	16 12	15 42	16 07	16 40	16 14	16 33	17 14	16 43	17 02	17 40	17 14

	SR	SR	SR	SR	SR	SR	SR	SR	SR	SR	SR	SR	SR	SR	SR	SR	SR	SR	SR	SR	SR
	1		1 trolley	1 trolley		1 trolley	1 trolley		1 trolley	1 trolley		1 trolley	1 trolley		1 trolley	1		1	1 trolley	1	1
Glasgow Queen Street 10 230 d	16 45	16 55	17 00	17 15	17 24	17 30	17 45	17 57	18 00	18 15	18 26	18 30	18 45	18 55	19 00	19 15	19 26	19 30	19 45	20 15	20 45
Bishopbriggs 230 d																					
Lenzie 3 230 d																					
Croy 3 230 d			17 10			17 41			18 12			18 41			19 10				19 56	20 26	20 57
Falkirk High 3 d	17 06	17b38	17 19	17 33	18b10	17 49	18 04	18b37	18 21	18 33	19b07	18 50	19 03	19b37	19 19	19 33	20b09	19 48	20 04	20 35	21 06
Polmont 3 230 a	17 10	17 43	17 23		18 15	17 53	18 09	18 42		18 37	19 12		19 07	19 42		19 37	20 14	19 53	20 08	20 39	21 10
Linlithgow 230 a	17 15	17 48		17 40	18 20	17 59	18 15	18 47		18 42	19 17		19 12	19 47		19 42	20 19	19 58	20 14	20 44	21 15
Haymarket 225,230,242 a	17s28	18 08	17s39	17s53	18 35	18s12	18s31	19 03	18s39	18s56	19 36	19s08	19s26	20 02	19s39	19s58	20 34	20s12	20s27	20s58	21s28
Edinburgh 10 225,230,242 a	17 33	18 14	17 44	17 59	18 40	18 17	18 37	19 08	18 44	19 02	19 41	19 13	19 31	20 07	19 44	20 03	20 39	20 19	20 32	21 06	21 33

	SR	SR	SR	SR	SR	SR
	1	1	1	1	1	1
Glasgow Queen Street 10 230 d	21 15	21 45	22 15	22 45	23 15	23 45
Bishopbriggs 230 d						
Lenzie 3 230 d						
Croy 3 230 d	21 26	21 57	22 26	22 56	23 26	23 56
Falkirk High 3 d	21 35	22 06	22 35	23 04	23 35	00 04
Polmont 3 230 a	21 39	22 10	22 39	23 08	23 39	00 08
Linlithgow 230 a	21 44	22 15	22 44	23 14	23 44	00 14
Haymarket 225,230,242 a	22s00	22s29	22s58	23s31	23s59	00s27
Edinburgh 10 225,230,242 a	22 06	22 34	23 03	23 36	00 04	00 34

Sundays

15 December to 10 May

	SR	SR	SR	SR	SR	SR	SR	SR	SR	SR	SR	SR	SR	SR	SR	SR	SR	SR	SR	SR	SR	SR
	1 A	1	1 trolley	1 trolley	1 trolley	1 trolley	1 trolley	1 trolley	1 trolley	1 trolley	1 trolley	1 trolley	1	1 trolley	1	1	1	1 trolley	1 trolley	1 trolley	1 trolley	1 trolley
Glasgow Queen Street 10 230 d		07 56	08 30	09 00	09 30	10 00	10 30	11 00	11 30	12 00	12 30	13 00	13 30	14 00	14 30	15 00	15 30	16 00	16 30	17 00	17 30	18 00
Bishopbriggs 230 d																						
Lenzie 3 230 d																						
Croy 3 230 d		08 07	08 40	09 11	09 41	10 12	10 41	11 11	11 41	12 11	12 41	13 11	13 41	14 11	14 41	15 11	15 41	16 11	16 41	17 11	17 41	18 11
Falkirk High 3 d	00 04	08 16	08 49	09 19	09 49	10 20	10 49	11 20	11 50	12 20	12 50	13 20	13 50	14 20	14 50	15 20	15 49	16 20	16 50	17 20	17 50	18 20
Polmont 3 230 a	00 08	08 20	08 53		09 53		10 53		11 54		12 58		13 54		14 54		15 53		16 54		17 54	
Linlithgow 230 a	00 14	08 26	08 58	09 26	09 59	10 27	10 59	11 29	11 59	12 27	13 04	13 27	13 59	14 27	14 59	15 27	16 01	16 27	16 59	17 27	17 59	18 27
Haymarket 225,230,242 a	00s27	08 50	09s18	09s45	10s17	10s43	11s12	11s45	12s12	12s41	13s20	13s40	14s12	14s45	15s12	15s40	16s17	16s43	17s12	17s40	18s17	18s40
Edinburgh 10 225,230,242 a	00 34	08 55	09 24	09 50	10 22	10 49	11 17	11 50	12 17	12 47	13 25	13 46	14 17	14 50	15 17	15 45	16 23	16 48	17 17	17 46	18 22	18 45

	SR	SR	SR	SR	SR	SR	SR	SR	SR	SR	SR
	1 trolley	1 trolley	1	1	1	1	1	1	1	1	1
Glasgow Queen Street 10 230 d	18 30	19 00	19 30	20 00	20 30	21 00	21 30	22 00	22 30	23 00	23 30
Bishopbriggs 230 d											
Lenzie 3 230 d											
Croy 3 230 d	18 41	19 11	19 41	20 11	20 41	21 11	21 41	22 11	22 41	23 11	23 41
Falkirk High 3 d	18 50	19 19	19 50	20 20	20 50	21 20	21 50	22 20	22 50	23 20	23 50
Polmont 3 230 a	18 54		19 54		20 54		21 54		22 54		23 54
Linlithgow 230 a	18 59	19 26	19 59	20 27	20 59	21 27	21 59	22 27	22 59	23 27	23 59
Haymarket 225,230,242 a	19s12	19s40	20s12	20s41	21s12	21s40	22s18	22s40	23s12	23s40	00s12
Edinburgh 10 225,230,242 a	19 17	19 45	20 18	20 46	21 17	21 45	22 23	22 45	23 17	23 45	00 17

A not 15 December

b Falkirk Grahamston

Table T229-F

Mondays to Fridays
16 December to 15 May

Edinburgh and Glasgow Queen Street - Perth, Inverness, Dundee, Aberdeen, Dyce and Inverurie

Miles	Miles	Miles	Miles	Miles			SR MO	SR MX	SR MX	SR MX	SR	SR	CS	SR	SR	SR	XC	SR	SR	SR	SR	SR	SR	SR
							◇1 A 🛒	◇1 A	◇ A	◇ B	◇1		■ C 🛏 ✕	◇		1	◇1 🛒	◇1			◇1 🛒			◇
—	0	—	0	0	**Edinburgh** ■10 242	d						05 19						05 30				05 49	06 19	06 29
—	1¼	—	1¼	1¼	Haymarket 242	d						05 23						05 35				05 53	06 23	06 33
—	5½	—	5½	—	Edinburgh Gateway	d																		06 39
—	13¼	—	13¼	—	Inverkeithing 242	d												05 49						06 49
—	26	—	26	—	Kirkcaldy 242	d												06 04						07 05
—	33¼	—	33¼	—	Markinch	d				00 05								06 13						07 15
—	39¼	—	39¼	—	Ladybank	d				00 12								06 20						07 22
—	42¼	—	—	—	Springfield	d																		
—	44½	—	—	—	Cupar	d				00 18								06 27						
—	51	—	—	—	Leuchars ■5	a				00 25								06 33						
—	—	—	—	—	St Andrews Bus Station	a																		
—	—	—	—	—	St Andrews Bus Station	d																		
—	—	—	—	—	Leuchars ■3	d				00 25								06 34						
0	—	0	—	—	**Glasgow Queen St.** ■10 230	d															05 53			
21	—	21	—	28¼	Larbert 230	d						05 51									06 14	06 21	06 51	
29	—	29	—	36½	Stirling 230	d						06 00									06 23	06 30	07a01	
32½	—	32½	—	40	Bridge of Allan 230	d						06 04										06 34		
34½	—	34½	—	42	Dunblane 230	d						06a08									06 31	06a37		
46¾	—	46¾	—	54¼	Gleneagles	d															06 44			
62½	—	62½	57	70¾	**Perth**	a															07 00			07 47
—	—	—	—	—		d			00 15		05 03					05 55			06 42		07 02			07 48
79¾	—	—	—	88	Invergowrie	d																		08 05
83¾	59¾	—	—	—	**Dundee**	a			00 36	00 41						06 24		06 48	07 04		07 23			08 13
—	—	—	—	—		d								05 39		06 25	06 42	06 49	07 05		07 24			
87¼	63¼	—	—	—	Broughty Ferry	d								05 46		06 32			07 12					
89	65	—	—	—	Balmossie	d																		
89¾	65¾	—	—	—	Monifieth	d								05 50					07 16					
92¾	68¾	—	—	—	Barry Links	d																		
93½	69½	—	—	—	Golf Street	d																		
94	70	—	—	—	Carnoustie	d								05 56		06 40		07 03	07 22		07 36			
100¼	76¼	—	—	—	Arbroath	a								06 02		06 46	06 57	07 10	07 30		07 42			
—	—	—	—	—		d								06 03		06 47	07 00	07 12			07 43			
114	90	—	—	—	Montrose	a								06 21		07 02	07 13	07 25			07 56			
—	—	—	—	—		d								06 26	06 39	07 03	07 15	07 27		07 42	07 57			
124	100	—	—	—	Laurencekirk	d								06 38	06 51			07 38		07 54				
138¼	114¼	—	—	—	Stonehaven	d	00 04	00 08						06 52	07 05	07 26	07 38	07 51		08 08	08 18			
146½	122½	—	—	—	Portlethen	d		00 17						07 01	07 14	07 35		08 00		08 17				
154½	130½	—	—	—	**Aberdeen**	a	00 21	00 29						07 13	07 28	07 47	07 56	08 12		08 29	08 35			
—	—	—	—	—		d								07 21	07 30	07 49				08 40				
160¾	136¾	—	—	—	Dyce 240	a								07 29	07 38	07 57				08 49				
171½	147½	—	—	—	**Inverurie** 240	a								07 42	07 52	08 11								
—	—	78	72½	86¾	Dunkeld & Birnam	d					05 21													
—	—	91	85½	99¾	Pitlochry	d					05 34													
—	—	97¾	92¼	106	Blair Atholl	d					05 44													
—	—	121	116¾	130¾	Dalwhinnie	d					06 10													
—	—	131¾	126¾	140½	Newtonmore	d					06 20													
—	—	134	129½	143¼	Kingussie	d					06 49		07 20											
—	—	145¾	141¼	155	Aviemore	d					07 03		07 45											
—	—	152¾	148¼	162	Carrbridge	d					07 23		07 58											
—	—	180	175	188¾	**Inverness**	a					07 53		08 42	09 35										

A From Glasgow Queen Street
B From Edinburgh
C From London Euston

Table T229-F

Mondays to Fridays
16 December to 15 May

Edinburgh and Glasgow Queen Street - Perth, Inverness, Dundee, Aberdeen, Dyce and Inverurie

		SR	SR	SR	SR	SR	SR	SR	SR	SR	SR	SR	SR	SR	SR	SR	SR	SR	SR	SR	SR	SR
			◇	◇1 🛒			◇1 🛒	◇1 🛒		◇		◇	◇		◇1 🛒	◇1 🛒		◇1 🛒		◇		◇1 🛒
Edinburgh ■10 242	d	06 48	07 00		07 20		07 29			07 34	07 46	07 59		08 18	08 31			08 34	08 49	08 58	09 19	09 28
Haymarket 242	d	06 52	07 04		07 24		07 35			07 38	07 52	08 07		08 23	08 36			08 40	08 53	09 03	09 23	09 33
Edinburgh Gateway	d		07 10							07 44		08 12						08 47		09 09		
Inverkeithing 242	d		07 20							07 55		08 23								09 22		
Kirkcaldy 242	d		07 36				08 05			08 11		08 39						09 10		09 38		
Markinch	d		07 45							08 20		08 49						09 19		09 47		
Ladybank	d		07 53							08 27		08 57								09 54		
Springfield	d											09 01										
Cupar	d		07 59									09 05								10 00		
Leuchars ■5	a		08 06				08 26					09 12			09 29					10 07		10 21
St Andrews Bus Station	a																					
St Andrews Bus Station	d																					
Leuchars ■3	d		08 06				08 27					09 13			09 30					10 07		10 22
Glasgow Queen St. ■10 230	d			07 07				07 41					08 10			08 40						
Larbert 230	d	07 21			07 52						08 25			08 56					09 24		09 54	
Stirling 230	d	07 29		07 35	08 01			08u09			08 33		08 37	09 04		09 10			09 33		10 02	
Bridge of Allan 230	d	07 33			08 05						08 37		08 41	09 08					09 37		10 06	
Dunblane 230	d	07a37		07 42	08a08			08 18			08a40		08 46	09a11					09a40		10a10	
Gleneagles	d												08 57									
Perth	a			08 10				08 44		08 53			09 13			09 45		09 50				
	d			08 11				08 45					09 14			09 46		09 51				
Invergowrie	d												09 31									
Dundee	a		08 22				08 42	09 07				09 27	09 39		09 46	10 07				10 23		10 36
	d		08 24				08 43	09 08				09 29			09 47	10 08				10 24		10 38
Broughty Ferry	d		08 31									09 36			09 53					10 31		
Balmossie	d																					
Monifieth	d		08 35									09 40										
Barry Links	d																					
Golf Street	d																					
Carnoustie	d		08 41									09 46								10 38		
Arbroath	a		08 49				08 59	09 23				09 54			10 05	10 24				10 46		10 56
	d						09 00	09 24							10 06	10 25						10 57
Montrose	a						09 13	09 37							10 20	10 41						11 10
	d					08 59	09 14	09 38	09 53						10 20	10 42	10 51					11 11
Laurencekirk	d					09 11			10 05								11 03					
Stonehaven	d					09 25	09 35		10 19						10 43	11 03	11 17					11 32
Portlethen	d					09 34			10 28								11 26					
Aberdeen	a					09 48	09 56	10 14	10 39						11 01	11 21	11 38					11 50
	d					09 50			10 40								11 41					
Dyce 240	a					09 58			10 49								11 49					
Inverurie 240	a					10 12			11 02								12 03					
Dunkeld & Birnam	d			08 32																		
Pitlochry	d			08 46														10 20				
Blair Atholl	d			08 56														10 30				
Dalwhinnie	d			09 21														10 56				
Newtonmore	d			09 32																		
Kingussie	d			09 37														11 09				
Aviemore	d			09 49														11 25				
Carrbridge	d			10 00																		
Inverness	a			10 28														11 59				

Table T229-F

Mondays to Fridays
16 December to 15 May

Edinburgh and Glasgow Queen Street - Perth, Inverness, Dundee, Aberdeen, Dyce and Inverurie

	SR	SR	SR	SR	SR	SR	SR	SR	GR	SR	SR	SR	SR	SR	SR	SR	SR	SR	SR	SR	SR	SR
	◇	◇1 ⚒		◇		◇	◇1 ⚒		1 A	◇1 ⚒		◇1 ⚒		◇		◇1 ⚒	◇1 ⚒		◇		◇	◇1 ⚒
Edinburgh 10 242 d				09 36	09 48	09 59		10 18	10 28			10 36	10 48	11 02	11 20	11 32			11 37	11 48	12 00	
Haymarket 242 d				09 40	09 53	10 07		10 23	10 33			10u41	10 53	11 06	11 24	11 37			11 41	11 52	12 05	
Edinburgh Gateway d				09 46		10 12						10 47		11 12					11 48		12 12	
Inverkeithing 242 d				09 58		10 23			10 48			10u58		11 22					11 58		12 22	
Kirkcaldy 242 d				10 14		10 39			11 05			11u14		11 38					12 14		12 38	
Markinch d				10 24		10 47						11 23		11 47					12 24		12 47	
Ladybank d				10 31		10 55						11 30		11 54					12 32		12 54	
Springfield d																						
Cupar d						11 01								12 00							13 00	
Leuchars 5 a						11 07			11 28					12 07		12 22					13 07	
St Andrews Bus Station a																						
St Andrews Bus Station d																						
Leuchars 5 d						11 08			11 30					12 07		12 23					13 07	
Glasgow Queen St. 10 230 d	09 07	09 40					10 10			10 40							11 38					12 08
Larbert 230 d					10 22			10 54					11 22		11 53					12 22		
Stirling 230 d	09 39	10 09			10 30		10 36	11 02		11 07			11 30		12 01		12 13			12 30		12 35
Bridge of Allan 230 d					10 34		10 41	11 06					11 34		12 05					12 34		12 41
Dunblane 230 d	09 47				10a38		10 45	11a09					11a38		12a09					12a37		12 45
Gleneagles d	09 58						10 57															
Perth a	10 14	10 39		10 55			11 14			11 38		11 55					12 43		12 56			13 13
d	10 17	10 40					11 16			11 39		11 56					12 44					13 14
Invergowrie d	10 35																					
Dundee a	10 41	11 02				11 24			11 44	12 01				12 23		12 37	13 05				13 21	
d		11 07				11 25			11 45	12 02				12 24		12 38	13 06				13 24	
Broughty Ferry d						11 31								12 31							13 31	
Balmossie d																						
Monifieth d						11 36								12 36								
Barry Links d																						
Golf Street d																						
Carnoustie d						11 41								12 42							13 38	
Arbroath a		11 23				11 50			12 01	12 17				12 50		12 59	13 22				13 46	
d		11 24							12 03	12 18						13 00	13 23					
Montrose a		11 48							12 17	12 31							13 36					
d		11 49	12 04						12 19	12 32	12 43						13 37	13 45				
Laurencekirk d			12 16								12 55							13 56				
Stonehaven d		12 15	12 30						12 43		13 09					13 32		14 10				
Portlethen d			12 39								13 18							14 19				
Aberdeen a		12 35	12 51						13 02	13 12	13 30					13 49	14 13	14 31				
d			12 53								13 32							14 32				
Dyce 240 a			13 01								13 41							14 40				
Inverurie 240 a			13 15								13 54							14 54				
Dunkeld & Birnam d							11 39															13 31
Pitlochry d							11 52					12 24										13 45
Blair Atholl d												12 34										13 55
Dalwhinnie d												13 00										
Newtonmore d												13 10										
Kingussie d							12 36					13 16										14 30
Aviemore d							12 48					13 33										14 42
Carrbridge d												13 42										
Inverness a							13 25					14 11										15 22

A From Leeds

NRT DECEMBER 19 EDITION

Table T229-F

Mondays to Fridays
16 December to 15 May

Edinburgh and Glasgow Queen Street - Perth, Inverness, Dundee, Aberdeen, Dyce and Inverurie

	SR	SR	SR	SR	SR	SR	SR	SR	SR	SR	SR	SR	SR	SR	SR	GR	SR	SR	SR	SR	SR
		◇1 ⚒	◇1 ⚒		◇		◇		◇1 ⚒	◇1 ⚒		◇1 ⚒		◇		1 A	◇1 ⚒		◇		◇
Edinburgh 10 242 d	12 21	12 30			12 37	12 49	13 00	13 20	13 30			13 33	13 50	14 03	14 20	14 29			14 37	14 50	15 00
Haymarket 242 d	12 25	12 35			12 41	12 53	13 05	13 24	13 36			13u40	13 54	14 07	14 24	14 34			14 41	14 54	15 05
Edinburgh Gateway d					12 47		13 11					13 46		14 13					14 47		15 11
Inverkeithing 242 d					12 57		13 21							14 25		14 51			14 58		15 21
Kirkcaldy 242 d					13 13		13 37					14u11		14 41		15 08			15 14		15 37
Markinch d					13 23		13 46					14 20		14 50					15 23		15 46
Ladybank d					13 30		13 53							14 57					15 31		15 53
Springfield d																					
Cupar d							13 59							15 03							15 59
Leuchars 5 a		13 23					14 06		14 26					15 10		15 31					16 06
St Andrews Bus Station a																					
St Andrews Bus Station d																					
Leuchars 5 d		13 24					14 06		14 26					15 10		15 32					16 06
Glasgow Queen St. 10 230 d			12 39							13 40							14 39				
Larbert 230 d	12 53					13 29		13 53					14 22		14 54					15 24	
Stirling 230 d	13 01		13 07			13 37		14 01		14 07			14 31		15 02		15 08			15 32	
Bridge of Allan 230 d	13 05					13 41		14 05					14 35		15 06					15 36	
Dunblane 230 d	13a09					13a45		14a08					14a38		15a10					15a40	
Gleneagles d			13 24																		
Perth a			13 40		13 54					14 41		14 48					15 39		15 56		
d			13 42							14 42		14 50					15 40				
Invergowrie d																					
Dundee a		13 37	14 03				14 22		14 40	15 03				15 24		15 46	16 01				16 22
d		13 39	14 05				14 23		14 41	15 05				15 26		15 49	16 02				16 23
Broughty Ferry d							14 30							15 33							16 30
Balmossie d																					
Monifieth d							14 34														16 34
Barry Links d																					
Golf Street d																					
Carnoustie d							14 40							15 40							16 40
Arbroath a		13 56	14 20				14 48		14 57	15 21				15 49		16 05	16 18				16 48
d		13 57	14 21						14 58	15 22						16 06	16 19				
Montrose a		14 10	14 34							15 41						16 21	16 33				
d		14 11	14 35	14 49						15 42	15 50					16 22	16 33	16 49			
Laurencekirk d				15 01							16 02							17 01			
Stonehaven d		14 32	14 56	15 15					15 32		16 16					16 46		17 15			
Portlethen d				15 24							16 25							17 24			
Aberdeen a		14 50	15 14	15 36					15 50	16 21	16 37					17 04	17 11	17 35			
d				15 45													17 24	17 37			
Dyce 240 a				15 53													17 32	17 45			
Inverurie 240 a				16 07													17 45	17 59			
Dunkeld & Birnam d												15 06									
Pitlochry d												15 20									
Blair Atholl d												15 30									
Dalwhinnie d												15 55									
Newtonmore d																					
Kingussie d												16 09									
Aviemore d												16 21									
Carrbridge d																					
Inverness a												16 54					19 37				

A From London Kings Cross

Table T229-F

Mondays to Fridays

16 December to 15 May

Edinburgh and Glasgow Queen Street - Perth, Inverness, Dundee, Aberdeen, Dyce and Inverurie

	SR	SR	SR	SR	SR	SR	SR	SR		SR	SR	SR	SR	SR	GR	SR	SR	SR		SR	SR	SR	SR	SR
	◇1 🛒		◇1 🛒	◇1 🛒		◇		◇			◇1 🛒			◇1 🛒	■ 1 A 🍽					◇	B		◇1 🛒	
Edinburgh 10 242 d		15 20	15 28			15 35	15 48	16 03		16 20	16 28				16 34	16 35	16 49	17 01			17 19	17 19	17 36	
Haymarket 242 d		15 24	15 33			15 40	15 53	16 07		16 24	16u33				16 39	16 39	16 53	17 06			17 23	17 23	17 42	
Edinburgh Gateway d						15 48		16 13								16 45		17 13						
Inverkeithing 242 d						15 58		16 23								16 57		17 23						
Kirkcaldy 242 d						16 14		16 39								17 13		17 39						
Markinch d						16 23		16 48								17 23		17 48						
Ladybank d						16 30		16 55								17 30		17 56						
Springfield d																		18 00						
Cupar d								17 01			17 18							18 04					18 32	
Leuchars 5 a			16 20					17 08			17 24							18 11					18 38	
St Andrews Bus Station 🚌 a																								
St Andrews Bus Station 🚌 d																								
Leuchars 3 d			16 21					17 08			17 25							18 12					18 39	
Glasgow Queen St. 10 230 d	15 08			15 39									16 10	16 42						17 09				
Larbert 230 d		15 53					16 22			16 54							17 25			17 34	17 54	17 54		
Stirling 230 d	15 37	16 01					16 30			17 02			16 37		17 17		17 33			17 45	18a02	18 13		
Bridge of Allan 230 d	15 43	16 05					16 34			17 06			16 41				17 38			17 50		18 19		
Dunblane 230 d	15 47	16a09					16a38			17a10			16 46				17a41			17 55		18a23		
Gleneagles d													16 58		17 35					18 08				
Perth a	16 16			16 37		16 54							17 14	17 41	17 53	17 58				18 24				
d	16 17			16 38									17 19	17 46	18 00					18 25				
Invergowrie d													17 37							18 43				
Dundee a			16 35	17 00				17 24			17 38		17 44	18 08				18 28		18 49			18 56	
d			16 39	17 01				17 25			17 40		17 49	18 09				18 29					18 57	
Broughty Ferry d								17 32					17 56					18 36						
Balmossie d													17 59					18 39						
Monifieth d								17 36					18 02					18 42						
Barry Links d													18 06					18 46						
Golf Street d													18 08					18 49						
Carnoustie d				17 13				17 42					18 11	18 23				18 51						
Arbroath a			16 58	17 19				17 50			18 05		18 19	18 30				18 59					19 13	
d			16 59	17 20							18 06			18 31									19 14	
Montrose a			17 12	17 33							18 21			18 44									19 27	
d			17 13	17 34	18 08						18 23	18 35		18 45									19 28	19 35
Laurencekirk d					18 20							18 47												19 47
Stonehaven d			17 34	17 55	18 34						18 44	19 01											19 49	20 01
Portlethen d					18 43							19 10												20 10
Aberdeen a			17 52	18 13	18 55						19 01	19 22		19 28									20 06	20 22
d					18 56							19 24												
Dyce 240 ✈ a					19 05							19 32												
Inverurie 240 a					19 18							19 46												
Dunkeld & Birnam d	16 36																							
Pitlochry d	16 50														18 31									
Blair Atholl d	17 00																							
Dalwhinnie d																								
Newtonmore d	17 33																							
Kingussie d	17 38														19 16									
Aviemore d	17 50														19 29									
Carrbridge d	17 59																							
Inverness a	18 27														20 06									

A From London Kings Cross

B To Alloa

Table T229-F

Mondays to Fridays

16 December to 15 May

Edinburgh and Glasgow Queen Street - Perth, Inverness, Dundee, Aberdeen, Dyce and Inverurie

	SR	SR	SR	SR		SR	XC	SR	GR	SR	SR	SR	SR	SR		SR	SR	GR	SR	SR	SR	SR	XC	SR
	◇1 🛒	◇1 🛒		◇		◇1 🛒	◇1 A		■ 1 B 🍽	◇1 🛒		◇		◇		◇		■ 1 B 🍽	◇1 🛒	◇1 🛒	◇1 🛒	◇	◇1 C	
Edinburgh 10 242 d		17 42	17 49	18 04			18 11	18 20	18 33			18 43	18 49	19 02			19 19	19 25	19 34		19 41	19 58	20 14	
Haymarket 242 d		17u47	17 54	18 08			18 17	18 24	18 38			18 47	18 53	19 06			19 23	19 30	19 39		19 46	20 04	20 19	
Edinburgh Gateway d		17 53		18 14								18 53		19 12							19 52	20 12		
Inverkeithing 242 d				18 24			18 31		18 55			19 03		19 22							20 03	20 26	20 33	
Kirkcaldy 242 d		18 21		18 40			18 46		19 13			19 19		19 38							20 18	20 48		
Markinch d		18 30		18 49			18 56					19 29		19 47							20 27	20 56	21 05	
Ladybank d		18 37		18 57			19 04					19 38		19 54							20 34	21 04	21 13	
Springfield d																								
Cupar d				19 03			19 13							20 01					20 22			21 10	21 21	
Leuchars 5 a				19 10			19 19		19 39					20 07					20 28			21 16	21 28	
St Andrews Bus Station 🚌 a																								
St Andrews Bus Station 🚌 d																								
Leuchars 3 d				19 10			19 20		19 40					20 08					20 29			21 17	21 29	
Glasgow Queen St. 10 230 d	17 40					18 06				18 41						19 07				19 38				
Larbert 230 d			18 24			18 29		18 55					19 22				19 53							
Stirling 230 d	18 09		18 34			18 40		19 03		19 08			19 31			19 37	20 01	20a16		20 10				
Bridge of Allan 230 d			18 38			18 44		19 07					19 35			19 41	20 05							
Dunblane 230 d	18 16		18a42			18 49		19a10		19 15			19a38			19 45	20a08							
Gleneagles d	18 33					19 01				19 28						19 57								
Perth a	18 49	19 02				19 18				19 44		20 02				20 13				20 40	20 58			
d	18 50	19 03				19 21				19 45						20 14				20 41	20 59			
Invergowrie d																20 31								
Dundee a	19 12			19 24			19 33		19 54	20 07				20 23		20 38			20 43	21 04		21 33	21 43	
d	19 15						19 36		19 57	20 08									20 44	21 06				
Broughty Ferry d																								
Balmossie d																								
Monifieth d																								
Barry Links d																								
Golf Street d																								
Carnoustie d	19 26																							
Arbroath a	19 33						19 51		20 13	20 24									20 59	21 22				
d	19 34						19 52		20 15	20 25									21 00	21 23				
Montrose a	19 47						20 05		20 30	20 38									21 13	21 36				
d	19 49						20 06		20 31	20 39	20 50								21 14	21 37				22 00
Laurencekirk d											21 02									21 48				22 12
Stonehaven d	20 10						20 27		20 55		21 16									22 01				22 26
Portlethen d											21 25													22 35
Aberdeen a	20 27						20 44		21 15	21 19	21 37								21 50	22 19				22 47
d											21 39													22 50
Dyce 240 ✈ a											21 47													22 58
Inverurie 240 a											22 01													23 12
Dunkeld & Birnam d		19 19				19 37															21 15			
Pitlochry d		19 33				19 50															21 35			
Blair Atholl d						19 59															21 45			
Dalwhinnie d						20 24															22 16			
Newtonmore d						20 34															22 27			
Kingussie d		20 16				20 39															22 32			
Aviemore d		20 28				20 51															22 44			
Carrbridge d																					22 53			
Inverness a		21 01				21 27															23 21			

A From Plymouth

B From London Kings Cross

C From Penzance

Table T229-F

Mondays to Fridays
16 December to 15 May

Edinburgh and Glasgow Queen Street - Perth, Inverness, Dundee, Aberdeen, Dyce and Inverurie

		GR	SR	SR	SR	SR	SR	SR	SR	SR		SR	SR	SR
		1 A	◇1		◇	◇	◇1	◇1	◇	◇		◇	◇	B
Edinburgh 10 242	d	20 32			20 40	21 08	21 43		22 11	22 37			23 06	23 13
Haymarket 242	d	20 37			20 44	21 12	21 47		22 15	22 41			23 12	23a17
Edinburgh Gateway	d				20 50	21 19			22 22	22 48			23 20	
Inverkeithing 242	d	20 53			21 00	21 33			22 36	23 02			23 34	
Kirkcaldy 242	d	21 11			21 17	21 54	22 15		22 58	23 24			23 56	
Markinch	d				21 26	22 03			23 09	23 33			00 05	
Ladybank	d				21 33	22 10			23 18	23 40			00 12	
Springfield	d								23 23					
Cupar	d					22 16			23 26				00 18	
Leuchars 5	a	21 37				22 23	22 39		23 33				00 25	
St Andrews Bus Station	a													
St Andrews Bus Station	d													
Leuchars 3	d	21 39				22 23	22 39		23 33				00 25	
Glasgow Queen St. 10 230	d		20 40					21 40				23 09		
Larbert 230	d											23 29		
Stirling 230	d		21 06					22 09				23 38		
Bridge of Allan 230	d											23 42		
Dunblane 230	d		21 16									23 46		
Gleneagles	d		21 29									23 58		
Perth	a		21 45		21 57			22 39		00 04		00 14		
	d		21 46					22 40				00 15		
Invergowrie	d		22 04											
Dundee	a	21 53	22 11			22 39	22 53	23 01	23 48			00 36	00 41	
	d	21 54	22 12				22 54	23 02						
Broughty Ferry	d							23 10						
Balmossie	d													
Monifieth	d							23 14						
Barry Links	d													
Golf Street	d													
Carnoustie	d		22 23					23 20						
Arbroath	a	22 10	22 30				23 11	23 29						
	d	22 12	22 31				23 11	23 30						
Montrose	a	22 26	22 44				23 25	23 43						
	d	22 28	22 45	23 02			23 26	23 44						
Laurencekirk	d			23 14				23 55						
Stonehaven	d	22 52		23 28			23 48	00 08						
Portlethen	d			23 37				00 17						
Aberdeen	a	23 11	23 20	23 49			00 06	00 29						
	d													
Dyce 240	a													
Inverurie 240	a													
Dunkeld & Birnam	d													
Pitlochry	d													
Blair Atholl	d													
Dalwhinnie	d													
Newtonmore	d													
Kingussie	d													
Aviemore	d													
Carrbridge	d													
Inverness	a													

A From London Kings Cross
B To Motherwell

NRT DECEMBER 19 EDITION

Table T229-F

Saturdays
21 December to 16 May

Edinburgh and Glasgow Queen Street - Perth, Inverness, Dundee, Aberdeen, Dyce and Inverurie

		SR	SR	SR	SR	SR	CS	SR	SR	SR		XC	SR	SR	SR	SR	SR	SR	SR	SR		SR	SR	SR	SR
		◇1 A	◇ A	◇ B	◇1		C ✕	◇		1		◇1	◇1			◇1			◇			◇	◇1		
Edinburgh 10 242	d					05 18							05 30				05 49	06 18	06 28	06 48		07 00		07 22	
Haymarket 242	d					05 23							05 35				05 53	06 23	06 32	06 52		07 04		07 27	
Edinburgh Gateway	d																		06 39			07 10			
Inverkeithing 242	d												05 49						06 49			07 20			
Kirkcaldy 242	d												06 04						07 06			07 36			
Markinch	d			00 05									06 13						07 15			07 45			
Ladybank	d			00 12									06 20						07 22			07 53			
Springfield	d																								
Cupar	d			00 18									06 27									07 59			
Leuchars 5	a			00 25									06 33									08 06			
St Andrews Bus Station	a																								
St Andrews Bus Station	d																								
Leuchars 3	d			00 25									06 34									08 06			
Glasgow Queen St. 10 230	d															05 53							07 07		
Larbert 230	d					05 51										06 14	06 21	06 52		07 21				07 56	
Stirling 230	d					06 00										06 23	06 30	07 01		07 29			07 35	08 04	
Bridge of Allan 230	d					06 04											06 34	07 05		07 33				08 08	
Dunblane 230	d					06a08										06 31	06a37	07a09		07a37			07 42	08a11	
Gleneagles	d															06 43									
Perth	a															07 00			07 47				08 10		
	d		00 15		05 03					06 00				06 42		07 02			07 48				08 11		
Invergowrie	d																		08 05						
Dundee	a		00 36	00 41						06 24			06 48	07 04		07 23			08 13			08 22			
	d									06 25		06 42	06 49	07 05		07 24						08 24			
Broughty Ferry	d									06 32				07 12								08 31			
Balmossie	d																								
Monifieth	d													07 16								08 35			
Barry Links	d																								
Golf Street	d																								
Carnoustie	d									06 40			07 03	07 22		07 36						08 41			
Arbroath	a									06 46		06 57	07 10	07 30		07 42						08 49			
	d									06 47		07 00	07 12			07 43									
Montrose	a									07 02		07 13	07 25			07 56									
	d							06 26	06 39	07 03		07 15	07 27		07 42	07 57									08 59
Laurencekirk	d							06 38	06 51				07 38		07 54										09 11
Stonehaven	d	00 08						06 52	07 05	07 26		07 38	07 51		08 08	08 18									09 25
Portlethen	d	00 17						07 01	07 14	07 35			08 00		08 17										09 34
Aberdeen	a	00 29						07 13	07 28	07 47		07 56	08 12		08 29	08 35									09 48
	d							07 21	07 30	07 49					08 40										09 50
Dyce 240	a							07 29	07 38	07 57					08 49										09 58
Inverurie 240	a							07 42	07 52	08 11															10 12
Dunkeld & Birnam	d				05 21																		08 32		
Pitlochry	d				05 34																		08 46		
Blair Atholl	d				05 44																		08 56		
Dalwhinnie	d				06 10																		09 21		
Newtonmore	d				06 20																		09 32		
Kingussie	d				06 49		07 20																09 37		
Aviemore	d				07 03		07 45																09 49		
Carrbridge	d				07 23		07 58																10 00		
Inverness	a				07 53		08 42	09 35															10 28		

A From Glasgow Queen Street
B From Edinburgh
C From London Euston

Table T229-F

Saturdays
21 December to 16 May

Edinburgh and Glasgow Queen Street - Perth, Inverness, Dundee, Aberdeen, Dyce and Inverurie

Station			SR	SR	SR	SR	SR	SR	SR	SR	SR	SR	SR	SR	SR	SR	SR	SR	SR	SR	SR	SR	SR	SR
			◇1 ⊼	◇1 ⊼		◇		◇	◇		◇1 ⊼	◇1 ⊼		◇1 ⊼		◇		◇1 ⊼	◇	◇1 ⊼		◇		◇
Edinburgh 10	242	d	07 29			07 33	07 54	08 00		08 18	08 28			08 33	08 51	09 01	09 19	09 29				09 38	09 49	10 02
Haymarket	242	d	07 34			07 37	07 58	08 07		08 22	08 33			08 38	08 55	09 06	09 23	09 34				09 42	09 53	10 07
Edinburgh Gateway		d				07 44		08 12						08 46		09 12						09 48		10 12
Inverkeithing	242	d				07 55		08 23								09 22						09 58		10 23
Kirkcaldy	242	d	08 05			08 11		08 39						09 10		09 38						10 14		10 39
Markinch		d				08 20		08 49						09 19		09 47						10 24		10 47
Ladybank		d				08 27		08 57								09 54						10 31		10 55
Springfield		d						09 01																
Cupar		d						09 05								10 00								11 01
Leuchars 5		a	08 26					09 12			09 27					10 07		10 22						11 07
St Andrews Bus Station		a																						
St Andrews Bus Station		d																						
Leuchars 3		d	08 27					09 13			09 27					10 07		10 23						11 08
Glasgow Queen St. 10	230	d		07 41					08 10			08 41							09 07	09 40				
Larbert	230	d					08 28			08 57					09 26		09 54						10 22	
Stirling	230	d		08u09			08 36		08 41	09 05		09 10			09 34		10 02		09 39	10 08			10 30	
Bridge of Allan	230	d					08 40		08 45	09 09					09 38		10 06						10 34	
Dunblane	230	d		08 18			08a43		08 49	09a12					09a41		10a10		09 47				10a38	
Gleneagles		d							09 00										09 58					
Perth		a		08 44		08 53			09 16			09 45		09 50					10 14	10 39		10 55		
		d		08 45					09 17			09 46		09 51					10 17	10 40				
Invergowrie		d							09 35										10 35					
Dundee		a	08 42	09 07				09 27	09 42		09 46	10 07				10 21		10 37	10 41	11 02				11 24
		d	08 43	09 08				09 29			09 47	10 08				10 24		10 38		11 07				11 25
Broughty Ferry		d						09 36			09 53					10 31								11 31
Balmossie		d																						
Monifieth		d						09 40																11 36
Barry Links		d																						
Golf Street		d																						
Carnoustie		d						09 46								10 38								11 41
Arbroath		a	08 59	09 23				09 54			10 05	10 24				10 46		10 56		11 23				11 50
		d	09 00	09 24							10 06	10 25						10 57		11 24				
Montrose		a	09 13	09 37							10 20	10 41						11 10		11 48				
		d	09 14	09 38	09 53						10 20	10 42	10 51					11 11		11 49	12 04			
Laurencekirk		d			10 05								11 03								12 16			
Stonehaven		d	09 35		10 19						10 43	11 03	11 17					11 32		12 10	12 30			
Portlethen		d			10 28								11 26								12 39			
Aberdeen		a	09 56	10 14	10 39						11 01	11 21	11 38					11 50		12 29	12 51			
		d			10 40								11 41								12 53			
Dyce	240 ✈	a			10 49								11 49								13 01			
Inverurie	240	a			11 02								12 03								13 15			
Dunkeld & Birnam		d																						
Pitlochry		d												10 20										
Blair Atholl		d												10 30										
Dalwhinnie		d												10 56										
Newtonmore		d																						
Kingussie		d												11 09										
Aviemore		d												11 25										
Carrbridge		d																						
Inverness		a												11 59										

Table T229-F

Saturdays
21 December to 16 May

Edinburgh and Glasgow Queen Street - Perth, Inverness, Dundee, Aberdeen, Dyce and Inverurie

Station			SR	SR	GR	SR	SR	SR	SR	SR	SR	SR	SR	SR	SR	SR	SR	SR	SR	SR	SR	SR	SR
			◇1 ⊼		■ 1 A ⊏	◇1 ⊼		◇1 ⊼		◇		◇1 ⊼	◇1 ⊼		◇		◇	◇1 ⊼		◇1 ⊼	◇1 ⊼		◇
Edinburgh 10	242	d		10 20	10 28			10 37	10 49	11 02	11 23	11 30			11 35	11 48	12 02		12 19	12 30			12 37
Haymarket	242	d		10 24	10 33			10u42	10 53	11 06	11 27	11 35			11 39	11 54	12 06		12 23	12 35			12 41
Edinburgh Gateway		d						10 47		11 12					11 45		12 12						12 47
Inverkeithing	242	d			10 48			10u58		11 22					11 58		12 22						12 57
Kirkcaldy	242	d			11 05			11u14		11 38					12 14		12 38						13 13
Markinch		d						11 23		11 47					12 24		12 47						13 23
Ladybank		d						11 30		11 54					12 32		12 54						13 30
Springfield		d																					
Cupar		d								12 00							13 00						
Leuchars 5		a			11 28					12 07		12 20					13 07			13 23			
St Andrews Bus Station		a																					
St Andrews Bus Station		d																					
Leuchars 3		d			11 30					12 07		12 21					13 07			13 24			
Glasgow Queen St. 10	230	d	10 08			10 39							11 38					12 07			12 40		
Larbert	230	d		10 53					11 25		11 59					12 22			12 53				
Stirling	230	d	10 36	11 01		11 07			11 33		12 07		12 13			12 30		12 35	13 01		13 07		
Bridge of Allan	230	d	10 41	11 05					11 37		12 11					12 34		12 41	13 05				
Dunblane	230	d	10 45	11a09					11a40		12a14					12a37		12 45	13a09				
Gleneagles		d	10 57																		13 24		
Perth		a	11 14			11 38		11 55					12 43	12 56				13 13			13 40		13 54
		d	11 16			11 39		11 56					12 44					13 14			13 42		
Invergowrie		d																					
Dundee		a			11 44	12 01				12 23		12 35	13 05				13 21			13 37	14 03		
		d			11 45	12 02				12 24		12 38	13 06				13 24			13 39	14 05		
Broughty Ferry		d								12 31							13 31						
Balmossie		d																					
Monifieth		d								12 36													
Barry Links		d																					
Golf Street		d																					
Carnoustie		d								12 42							13 38						
Arbroath		a			12 01	12 17				12 50		12 59	13 22				13 46			13 56	14 20		
		d			12 03	12 18						13 00	13 23							13 57	14 21		
Montrose		a			12 17	12 31							13 36							14 10	14 34		
		d			12 19	12 32	12 43						13 37	13 45						14 11	14 35	14 49	
Laurencekirk		d					12 55							13 56								15 01	
Stonehaven		d			12 43		13 09					13 32		14 10						14 32	14 56	15 15	
Portlethen		d					13 18							14 19								15 24	
Aberdeen		a			13 02	13 12	13 30					13 49	14 13	14 31						14 50	15 14	15 36	
		d					13 32							14 32								15 45	
Dyce	240 ✈	a					13 41							14 40								15 53	
Inverurie	240	a					13 54							14 54								16 07	
Dunkeld & Birnam		d	11 39															13 31					
Pitlochry		d	11 52					12 24										13 45					
Blair Atholl		d						12 34										13 55					
Dalwhinnie		d						13 00															
Newtonmore		d						13 10															
Kingussie		d	12 36					13 16										14 30					
Aviemore		d	12 48					13 33										14 42					
Carrbridge		d						13 42															
Inverness		a	13 25					14 11										15 22					

A From Leeds

Table T229-F

Saturdays
21 December to 16 May

Edinburgh and Glasgow Queen Street - Perth, Inverness, Dundee, Aberdeen, Dyce and Inverurie

Station		SR	SR ◇	SR	SR ◇1 🛒	SR ◇1 🛒	SR	SR ◇1 🛒	SR	SR ◇	SR	GR ■ 1 A 🍴	SR ◇1 🛒	SR	SR ◇	SR	SR ◇	SR ◇1 🛒	SR	SR ◇1 🛒	SR ◇1 🛒	SR	SR ◇
Edinburgh 10 242	d	12 49	13 03	13 20	13 28			13 31	13 49	14 04	14 18	14 29			14 37	14 48	15 00		15 19	15 28			15 36
Haymarket 242	d	12 53	13 07	13 24	13 33			13u38	13 53	14 08	14 22	14 34			14 41	14 52	15 04		15 23	15 35			15 40
Edinburgh Gateway	d		13 13					13 45		14 15					14 47		15 11						15 46
Inverkeithing 242	d		13 23							14 25		14 51			14 58		15 21						15 57
Kirkcaldy 242	d		13 39					14u08		14 41		15 08			15 14		15 37						16 13
Markinch	d		13 48					14 17		14 50					15 23		15 46						16 22
Ladybank	d		13 55							14 57					15 31		15 53						16 29
Springfield	d																						
Cupar	d		14 01							15 03							15 59						
Leuchars 5	a		14 08		14 26					15 10		15 31					16 06			16 20			
St Andrews Bus Station	a																						
St Andrews Bus Station	d																						
Leuchars 3	d		14 08		14 26					15 10		15 32					16 06			16 21			
Glasgow Queen St. 10 230	d					13 39							14 39					15 08			15 38		
Larbert 230	d	13 23		13 53					14 23		14 53					15 22			15 52				
Stirling 230	d	13 31		14 01		14 08			14 31		15 01		15 08			15 31		15 37	16 01				
Bridge of Allan 230	d	13 35		14 05					14 35		15 05					15 35		15 42	16 05				
Dunblane 230	d	13a39		14a08					14a38		15a09					15a38		15 47	16a08				
Gleneagles	d																						
Perth	a					14 41		14 48					15 39		15 56			16 16			16 37		16 54
	d					14 42		14 50					15 40					16 17			16 38		
Invergowrie	d																						
Dundee	a		14 22		14 40	15 03				15 25		15 46	16 01				16 22			16 35	17 00		
	d		14 23		14 41	15 05				15 26		15 48	16 02				16 23			16 39	17 01		
Broughty Ferry	d		14 30							15 33							16 30						
Balmossie	d																						
Monifieth	d		14 34														16 34						
Barry Links	d																						
Golf Street	d																						
Carnoustie	d		14 40							15 40							16 40				17 13		
Arbroath	a		14 48		14 57	15 21				15 49		16 04	16 18				16 48			16 58	17 19		
	d				14 58	15 22						16 05	16 19							16 59	17 20		
Montrose	a					15 41						16 21	16 33							17 12	17 33		
	d					15 42	15 50					16 22	16 33	16 49						17 13	17 34	18 08	
Laurencekirk	d						16 02							17 01								18 20	
Stonehaven	d				15 32		16 16					16 46		17 15						17 34	17 55	18 34	
Portlethen	d						16 25							17 24								18 43	
Aberdeen	a				15 50	16 21	16 37					17 06	17 11	17 35						17 52	18 13	18 55	
	d												17 24									18 56	
Dyce 240	a												17 32									19 05	
Inverurie 240	a												17 45									19 18	
Dunkeld & Birnam	d							15 06										16 36					
Pitlochry	d							15 20										16 50					
Blair Atholl	d							15 30										17 00					
Dalwhinnie	d							15 55															
Newtonmore	d																	17 33					
Kingussie	d							16 09										17 38					
Aviemore	d							16 21										17 50					
Carrbridge	d																	17 59					
Inverness	a							16 54					19 37					18 27					

A From London Kings Cross

Table T229-F

Saturdays
21 December to 16 May

Edinburgh and Glasgow Queen Street - Perth, Inverness, Dundee, Aberdeen, Dyce and Inverurie

Station		SR	SR ◇	SR	SR ◇1 🛒	SR	SR	SR ◇1 🛒	GR ■ 1 A 🍴	SR	SR	SR	SR ◇	SR B	SR ◇1 🛒	SR	SR ◇1 🛒	SR ◇1 🛒	SR	SR ◇1 🛒	XC ◇1 C	SR
Edinburgh 10 242	d	15 48	16 01	16 21	16 28				16 34	16 36	16 49	17 01		17 20	17 37			17 41	17 48		18 12	18 21
Haymarket 242	d	15 52	16 05	16 25	16u33				16 39	16 40	16 54	17 06		17 24	17 42			17u47	17 53		18 16	18 25
Edinburgh Gateway	d		16 11							16 47		17 13						17 53				
Inverkeithing 242	d		16 22							16 57		17 23									18 29	
Kirkcaldy 242	d		16 38							17 13		17 39						18 21			18 45	
Markinch	d		16 46							17 23		17 48						18 30			18 54	
Ladybank	d		16 54							17 30		17 56						18 37			19 01	
Springfield	d											18 00										
Cupar	d		17 00		17 18							18 04			18 32						19 08	
Leuchars 5	a		17 06		17 24							18 11			18 38						19 14	
St Andrews Bus Station	a																					
St Andrews Bus Station	d																					
Leuchars 3	d		17 07		17 25							18 12			18 39						19 15	
Glasgow Queen St. 10 230	d						16 10	16 42					17 09				17 40			18 09		
Larbert 230	d	16 22		16 53							17 26		17 34	17 53					18 23	18 29		18 55
Stirling 230	d	16 30		17 01			16 37	17 13	17 17		17 34		17 45	18a00			18 13		18 31	18 40		19 03
Bridge of Allan 230	d	16 34		17 05			16 41				17 39		17 50						18 35	18 44		19 07
Dunblane 230	d	16a38		17a09			16 46				17a42		17 55				18 20		18a39	18 49		19a10
Gleneagles	d						16 58		17 35				18 08				18 33			19 01		
Perth	a						17 14	17 42	17 53	17 58			18 24				18 49	19 02		19 18		
	d						17 19	17 46	18 00				18 25				18 50	19 03		19 21		
Invergowrie	d						17 37						18 43									
Dundee	a		17 23		17 38		17 44	18 08				18 28	18 49		18 56		19 12				19 28	
	d		17 25		17 40		17 49	18 09				18 29			18 57		19 15				19 33	
Broughty Ferry	d		17 32				17 56					18 36										
Balmossie	d						17 59					18 39										
Monifieth	d		17 36				18 02					18 42										
Barry Links	d						18 06					18 46										
Golf Street	d						18 08					18 49										
Carnoustie	d		17 42				18 11	18 23				18 51					19 26					
Arbroath	a		17 50		18 05		18 19	18 30				18 59			19 13		19 33				19 48	
	d				18 06			18 31							19 14		19 34				19 49	
Montrose	a				18 21			18 44							19 27		19 47				20 02	
	d				18 23	18 35		18 45							19 28	19 35	19 49				20 03	
Laurencekirk	d					18 47										19 47						
Stonehaven	d				18 44	19 01									19 49	20 01	20 10				20 24	
Portlethen	d					19 10										20 10						
Aberdeen	a				19 01	19 22		19 28							20 06	20 22	20 27				20 42	
	d					19 24																
Dyce 240	a					19 32																
Inverurie 240	a					19 46																
Dunkeld & Birnam	d																	19 19		19 37		
Pitlochry	d								18 31									19 33		19 50		
Blair Atholl	d																			19 59		
Dalwhinnie	d																			20 24		
Newtonmore	d																			20 34		
Kingussie	d								19 16									20 16		20 39		
Aviemore	d								19 29									20 28		20 53		
Carrbridge	d																					
Inverness	a								20 06									21 01		21 29		

A From London Kings Cross
B To Alloa
C From Plymouth

Table T229-F

Saturdays
21 December to 16 May

Edinburgh and Glasgow Queen Street - Perth, Inverness, Dundee, Aberdeen, Dyce and Inverurie

	GR	SR	SR	SR	SR	SR	SR	SR	SR	SR	SR	SR	XC	SR	SR	SR	SR	SR	SR	SR	SR	SR	SR	SR
	■1 A 🍽	◇1 🛒		◇		◇	◇		◇1 🛒	◇1 🛒	◇1 🛒	◇	◇1 B		◇1		◇	◇	◇1	◇1	◇	◇	◇	C
Edinburgh 10 242 d	18 35			18 42	18 49	19 00		19 19	19 34		19 39	20 01	20 12				20 38	21 05	21 43		22 12	22 37	23 09	23 12
Haymarket 242 d	18 40			18 46	18 53	19 04		19 24	19 39		19 44	20 05	20 17				20 44	21 09	21 47		22 16	22 41	23 13	23a16
Edinburgh Gateway d				18 52		19 10					19 50	20 12					20 50	21 16			22 23	22 48	23 21	
Inverkeithing 242 d	18 58			19 02		19 22					20 01	20 26	20 35				21 00	21 30			22 37	23 02	23 34	
Kirkcaldy 242 d	19 16			19 19		19 38					20 16	20 48	20 55				21 17	21 51	22 15		22 59	23 24	23 56	
Markinch d				19 29		19 47					20 25	20 56	21 05				21 26	22 00			23 08	23 33	00 05	
Ladybank d				19 38		19 54					20 32	21 04	21 13				21 33	22 08			23 18	23 40	00 12	
Springfield d																					23 23			
Cupar d						20 01			20 22			21 10	21 20					22 14			23 26		00 18	
Leuchars 5 a	19 41					20 07			20 28			21 16	21 26					22 21	22 39		23 33		00 25	
St Andrews Bus Station a																								
St Andrews Bus Station d																								
Leuchars 3 d	19 43					20 08			20 29			21 17	21 28					22 22	22 39		23 33		00 25	
Glasgow Queen St. 10 230 d		18 39					19 07			19 38					20 39					21 41				
Larbert 230 d					19 23			19 53																
Stirling 230 d		19 08			19 31		19 37	20 01		20 10					21 06					22 09				
Bridge of Allan 230 d					19 35		19 41	20 05																
Dunblane 230 d		19 15			19a38		19 45	20a09							21 16									
Gleneagles d		19 28					19 57								21 29									
Perth a		19 44		20 02			20 13			20 40	20 57				21 45		21 57			22 39		00 05		
d		19 45					20 14			20 41	20 59				21 46					22 40				
Invergowrie d							20 31								22 04									
Dundee a	19 57	20 07				20 23	20 38		20 43	21 04		21 33	21 43		22 11			22 38	22 53	23 01	23 47		00 41	
d	19 58	20 08							20 44	21 06					22 12				22 54	23 02				
Broughty Ferry d																				23 10				
Balmossie d																								
Monifieth d																				23 14				
Barry Links d																								
Golf Street d																								
Carnoustie d															22 23					23 20				
Arbroath a	20 14	20 24							20 59	21 22					22 30				23 11	23 29				
d	20 16	20 25							21 00	21 23					22 31				23 11	23 30				
Montrose a	20 30	20 38							21 13	21 36					22 44				23 25	23 43				
d	20 32	20 39	20 50						21 14	21 37				22 00	22 45	23 02			23 26	23 44				
Laurencekirk d			21 02							21 48				22 12		23 14				23 55				
Stonehaven d	20 56		21 16							22 01				22 26		23 28			23 48	00 08				
Portlethen d			21 25											22 35		23 37				00 17				
Aberdeen a	21 16	21 21	21 37						21 50	22 19				22 47	23 20	23 49			00 06	00 29				
d			21 39											22 50										
Dyce 240 a			21 47											22 58										
Inverurie 240 a			22 01											23 12										
Dunkeld & Birnam d											21 15													
Pitlochry d											21 35													
Blair Atholl d											21 45													
Dalwhinnie d											22 10													
Newtonmore d											22 21													
Kingussie d											22 26													
Aviemore d											22 38													
Carrbridge d											22 47													
Inverness a											23 15													

A From London Kings Cross
B From Plymouth
C To Motherwell

Table T229-F

Sundays
15 December to 10 May

Edinburgh and Glasgow Queen Street - Perth, Inverness, Dundee, Aberdeen, Dyce and Inverurie

	SR	SR	XC	GR	SR	SR	SR	SR	SR	SR	SR	SR	SR	SR	SR	SR	SR	GR	SR	SR	SR	SR
	◇ A	◇1 B	◇1	■1 🍽	◇1	◇1 🛒	◇1 🛒	◇1 🛒	◇1 🛒	◇1 🛒	◇	◇1 🛒	◇1 🛒	◇1 🛒	◇	◇1 🛒	◇1 🛒	■1 C 🍽	◇1 D 🛒	◇1 🛒		◇1 🛒
Edinburgh 10 242 d			08 04	09 10	09 17		09 29		10 50		11 32		12 41		13 34		13 57	14 33			15 34	
Haymarket 242 d			08 09	09 15	09 21		09 34		10 54		11 36		12 46		13 38		14 01	14 39			15 38	
Edinburgh Gateway d					09 28		09 41				11 42				13 44		14 07				15 44	
Inverkeithing 242 d			08 25	09 33	09 45		09 54		11 07		11 52		13 00		13 56		14 18	14 54			15 54	
Kirkcaldy 242 d			08 41	09 50	10 07		10 10		11 23		12 08		13 15		14 12		14 34	15 11			16 10	
Markinch d	00 05				10 15		10 19				12 17				14 21						16 23	
Ladybank d	00 12				10 23		10 26				12 25				14 29						16 31	
Springfield d																						
Cupar d	00 18		08 58		10 29						12 31				14 35						16 37	
Leuchars 5 a	00 25		09 04	10 13	10 35				11 46		12 38		13 37		14 42			15 34			16 44	
St Andrews Bus Station a																						
St Andrews Bus Station d																						
Leuchars 3 d	00 25		09 05	10 14	10 36				11 47		12 39		13 38		14 43			15 36			16 45	
Glasgow Queen St. 10 230 d						09 37		10 45		11 11		11 45		12 43		13 45			14 38	14 50		15 45
Larbert 230 d						10 02				11 32									14 59			
Stirling 230 d						10 11		11 11		11 41		12 11		13 10		14 12			15 08	15 17		16 12
Bridge of Allan 230 d																						
Dunblane 230 d						10 18		11 18		11 48		12 18		13 17		14 19			15 15	15 26		16 18
Gleneagles d						10 31				12 00		12 29				14 32			15 27			16 30
Perth a						10 47	10 52	11 43		12 18		12 45		13 41		14 49	15 10		15 44	15 54		16 46
d						10 48	10 53	11 44		12 19		12 46		13 43		14 50	15 14		15 46	15 56		16 47
Invergowrie d																						
Dundee a	00 41		09 18	10 28	10 51	11 10		12 06			12 53	13 08	13 51	14 04	14 57	15 11		15 50		16 17	16 59	17 09
d			09 20	10 30	10 52	11 11						13 10	13 53	14 08		15 12		15 51		16 19		17 10
Broughty Ferry d						11 19																
Balmossie d																						
Monifieth d																						
Barry Links d																						
Golf Street d																						
Carnoustie d						11 26										15 24						
Arbroath a			09 35	10 46	11 08	11 33		12 26	12 26			13 26	14 08	14 23		15 30		16 07		16 34		17 26
d			09 36	10 47	11 09	11 34		12 27	12 27			13 26	14 09	14 24		15 31		16 09		16 35		17 26
Montrose a			09 49	11 02	11 23	11 47		12 41	12 41			13 40	14 22	14 37		15 44		16 23		16 48		17 40
d			09 50	11 03	11 23	11 48		12 41	12 41			13 41	14 23	14 38		15 45		16 25		16 49		17 41
Laurencekirk d						11 59							14 34									17 53
Stonehaven d		00 08	10 11	11 27	11 45	12 12		13 04	13 04			14 03	14 47	14 59		16 06		16 49		17 10		18 06
Portlethen d		00 17			11 54	12 20										16 15						
Aberdeen a		00 29	10 28	11 47	12 06	12 34		13 22	13 22			14 21	15 05	15 17		16 27		17 08		17 27		18 24
d																						
Dyce 240 a																						
Inverurie 240 a																						
Dunkeld & Birnam d							11 10			12 38							15 31					
Pitlochry d							11 24			12 52							15 44		16 14			
Blair Atholl d							11 34										15 53					
Dalwhinnie d							11 59										16 22					
Newtonmore d							12 10										16 33					
Kingussie d							12 15			13 36							16 38		16 56			
Aviemore d							12 28			13 49							16 50		17 09			
Carrbridge d							12 37			14 01							16 59					
Inverness a							13 16			14 30							17 29		17 45			

A not 15 December. From Edinburgh
B not 15 December. From Glasgow Queen Street
C From London Kings Cross. The Northern Lights
D To Elgin

Table T229-F

Sundays

15 December to 10 May

Edinburgh and Glasgow Queen Street - Perth, Inverness, Dundee, Aberdeen, Dyce and Inverurie

Station		SR	SR	SR	GR	SR	SR	SR	SR	SR	XC	GR	SR	SR	SR	SR	SR	SR
		◇1 🛒	◇1	◇1 🛒	1 A 🍴	◇1		◇1 B 🛒	◇	◇1 C 🛒	◇1 D	1 E 🍴	◇	◇1 F 🛒	◇1	◇1 🛒	◇	
Edinburgh 10	242 d	15 50	16 05		16 32	17 05	17 34		17 50		18 13	18 36	19 15		21 00		22 26	23 34
Haymarket	242 d	15 55	16 10		16 37	17 10	17 38		17 54		18 18	18 41	19 19		21 05		22 30	23 38
Edinburgh Gateway	d	16 02					17 44		18 00				19 26				22 37	23 45
Inverkeithing	242 d	16 12	16 25			17 24	17 54		18 10		18 31	18 56	19 40		21 19		22 51	23a58
Kirkcaldy	242 d	16 28	16 40			17 40	18 10		18 26		18 47	19 13	20 02		21 34		23 13	
Markinch	d	16 37	16 49				18 19		18 36		18 56		20 11		21 43		23 22	
Ladybank	d	16 44					18 27				19 03		20 18		21 50		23 29	
Springfield	d																	
Cupar	d		17 01				18 33				19 10		20 25		21 57		23 36	
Leuchars 5	a		17 07			18 01	18 40				19 16	19 36	20 32		22 03		23 43	
St Andrews Bus Station	a																	
St Andrews Bus Station	d																	
Leuchars 5	d		17 08			18 02	18 41				19 17	19 37	20 32		22 04		23 43	
Glasgow Queen St. 10	230 d			16 45				17 45		18 11				19 44		21 44		
Larbert	230 d									18 31								
Stirling	230 d			17 12	17 19			18 13		18 41				20 11		22 11		
Bridge of Allan	230 d																	
Dunblane	230 d									18 47				20 18		22 18		
Gleneagles	d				17 36					18 59				20 30		22 30		
Perth	a	17 08		17 40	17 53			18 45	19 05	19 16				20 47		22 47		
	d	17 11		17 42	18 00			18 46		19 17				20 48		22 48		
Invergowrie	d																	
Dundee	a		17 22	18 03		18 16	18 57	19 09			19 30	19 51	20 48	21 10	22 18	23 09	23 59	
	d		17 23	18 05		18 17		19 10			19 35	19 53		21 12	22 19	23 10		
Broughty Ferry	d		17 31												22 27			
Balmossie	d																	
Monifieth	d																	
Barry Links	d																	
Golf Street	d																	
Carnoustie	d		17 38					19 22								23 22		
Arbroath	a		17 45	18 20		18 34		19 28			19 50	20 09		21 27	22 38	23 28		
	d		17 46	18 21		18 35		19 29			19 51	20 10		21 28	22 39	23 29		
Montrose	a		17 59	18 34		18 48		19 44			20 04	20 25		21 41	22 52	23 42		
	d		18 00	18 35		18 49		19 44			20 05	20 26		21 42	22 53	23 43		
Laurencekirk	d							19 56						21 53				
Stonehaven	d		18 21	18 56		19 10		20 10			20 26	20 50		22 06	23 14	00 04		
Portlethen	d					19 18									23 23			
Aberdeen	a		18 38	19 14		19 30		20 28			20 43	21 10		22 24	23 35	00 21		
	d																	
Dyce	240 a																	
Inverurie	240 a																	
Dunkeld & Birnam	d	17 27								19 33								
Pitlochry	d	17 41			18 31					19 46								
Blair Atholl	d									19 56								
Dalwhinnie	d									20 20								
Newtonmore	d									20 31								
Kingussie	d	18 24			19 16					20 36								
Aviemore	d	18 37			19 32					20 48								
Carrbridge	d									20 57								
Inverness	a	19 10			20 09					21 25								

A From London Kings Cross. The Highland Chieftain
B 🛒 to Dundee
C To Elgin
D From Plymouth
E From London Kings Cross
F 🛒 from Dundee

Table T229-R

Mondays to Fridays

16 December to 15 May

Inverurie, Dyce, Aberdeen, Dundee, Inverness and Perth - Glasgow Queen Street and Edinburgh

Miles	Miles	Miles	Miles	Miles	Station		SR	GR	SR	SR	SR	SR	XC	SR	SR	SR	SR	SR	SR	SR	SR	SR	SR	SR
								1 A 🍴	◇	◇	◇	◇	◇1 B				◇1	◇1		◇		◇	◇1 🛒	◇
—	—	0	0	0	**Inverness**	d																05 36		
—	—	28	28	28	Carrbridge	d																		
—	—	34¾	34¾	34¾	Aviemore	d																06 13		
—	—	46½	46½	46½	Kingussie	d																06 28		
—	—	49¼	49¼	49¼	Newtonmore	d																		
—	—	59½	59½	59½	Dalwhinnie	d																06 41		
—	—	82¾	82¾	82¾	Blair Atholl	d																07 12		
—	—	89½	89½	89½	Pitlochry	d																07 26		
—	—	102½	102½	102½	Dunkeld & Birnam	d																07 39		
0	0	—	—	—	**Inverurie**	240 d																		
10¾	10¾	—	—	—	Dyce	240 d																		
17	17	—	—	—	**Aberdeen**	240 a																		
—	—	—	—	—		d	05 05										05 39	05 48	06 19				06 38	
27	27	—	—	—	Portlethen	d	05 16												06 30					
33	33	—	—	—	Stonehaven	d	05 24											06 04	06 38				06 54	
47½	47½	—	—	—	Laurencekirk	d	05 38												06 52					
57½	57½	—	—	—	Montrose	a	05 50										06 11	06 23	07 04				07 13	
—	—	—	—	—		d											06 12	06 24					07 14	
71¼	71¼	—	—	—	Arbroath	a											06 25	06 38					07 28	
—	—	—	—	—		d								06 06			06 27	06 39			07 12		07 29	07 43
77½	77½	—	—	—	Carnoustie	d								06 13				06 46			07 18			07 50
78	78	—	—	—	Golf Street	d								06 15										07 51
79	79	—	—	—	Barry Links	d								06 18										07 54
82	82	—	—	—	Monifieth	d								06 22							07 24			07 58
82¾	82¾	—	—	—	Balmossie	d								06 25										08 01
84½	84½	—	—	—	Broughty Ferry	d								06 28							07 28			08 04
88¼	88¼	—	—	—	**Dundee**	a								06 36			06 46	06 58			07 36		07 45	08 12
—	—	—	—	—		d					05 43	06 02	06 33				06 49	06 59		07 09	07 37		07 49	08 15
92¼	—	—	—	100¾	Invergowrie	d					05 48													08 20
109½	—	118	118	118	**Perth**	a					06 07						07 14					07 56	08 09	08 40
—	—	—	—	—		d			05 12	05 17	06 09				06 55	07 01	07 15					07 58	08 10	08 41
125	—	133¾	—	133¾	Gleneagles	d				05 32	06 28					07 16	07 30						08 25	08 56
136½	—	146	—	146	Dunblane	230 d				05 46	06 42					07 30	07 44							09 09
139	—	148	—	148	Bridge of Allan	230 d				05 50	06 45					07 33	07 48							09 12
142½	—	151½	—	151½	Stirling	230 d		05 26		05 54	06 50					07 38	07 55						08 43	09 16
150½	—	159½	—	159½	Larbert	230 d				06 03						07 46	08 04							
172	—	180½	—	—	**Glasgow Queen St.** 10	230 a				06 37	07 29					08 19	08 32						09 11	09 49
—	96½	—	—	—	Leuchars 5	a						06 14	06 45					07 10		07 21	07 50			
—	—	—	—	—	St Andrews Bus Station	a																		
—	—	—	—	—	St Andrews Bus Station	d																		
—	—	—	—	—	Leuchars 5	d						06 15	06 46					07 11		07 22	07 50			
—	102¾	—	—	—	Cupar	d						06 22	06 55					07 19		07 29	07 58			
—	105	—	—	—	Springfield	d														07 34				
—	108½	—	135¾	—	Ladybank	d			05 38			06 30	07 03		07 31					07 38		08 20		
—	114¼	—	141	—	Markinch	d			05 46			06 38	07 11		07 38					07 46	08 11	08 28		
—	121½	—	149	—	Kirkcaldy	242 d			05 56			06 48	07 22		07 48			07 37		07 57	08 22	08 38		
—	134½	—	161¾	—	Inverkeithing	242 d			06 19			07 11	07 40		08 04					08 19	08 38	08 54		
—	142	—	169½	—	Edinburgh Gateway	d			06 33			07 23			08 15					08 31	08 50	09 05		
—	146¼	—	173¾	186½	Haymarket	242 a		06 11	06 42			07 30	07 58		08 22			08 18		08 40	09 00	09 11		
—	147½	—	175	187¾	**Edinburgh** 10	242 a		06 17	06 49			07 35	08 04		08 29			08 24		08 48	09 08	09 16		

A not 16 December. To London Kings Cross
B To Plymouth

Table T229-R

Mondays to Fridays

16 December to 15 May

Inverurie, Dyce, Aberdeen, Dundee, Inverness and Perth - Glasgow Queen Street and Edinburgh

		SR	SR	SR	SR	SR	GR	XC	SR	GR	SR	SR	SR	SR	SR	SR	SR	SR	SR	GR	SR	SR
		◇1 A 🛒	◇	◇1 🛒		◇1 B	1 C 🍴	1 D 🛒	◇	1 E 🍴		◇	◇1 🛒	◇1 🛒	◇1 🛒	◇		◇	◇1	1 C 🍴	◇	◇1 🛒
Inverness	d	04 56		06 48						07 55				08 45								09 44
Carrbridge	d													09 13								
Aviemore	d			07 24						08 32				09 22								10 28
Kingussie	d			07 36						08 45				09 36								10 40
Newtonmore	d													09 41								
Dalwhinnie	d																					10 53
Blair Atholl	d																					11 16
Pitlochry	d			08 17						09 28				10 20								11 26
Dunkeld & Birnam	d			08 32										10 34								11 39
Inverurie 240	d	06 37			06 53						07 58											
Dyce 240 ✈	d	06 53			07 05						08 10						09 07					
Aberdeen 240	a	07 03			07 15						08 20						09 16					
	d	07 07			07 18	07 38	07 52	08 20			08 30		08 51		09 04		09 18		09 44	09 52		
Portlethen	d				07 29						08 41						09 29					
Stonehaven	d	07 27			07 37	07 54	08 10	08 37			08 49				09 20		09 37			10 10		
Laurencekirk	d				07 51						09 03						09 51					
Montrose	a	07 46			08 03	08 13	08 31	08 57			09 15		09 23		09 39		10 03		10 16	10 31		
	d	07 47				08 14	08 33	08 59					09 24		09 40				10 20	10 33		
Arbroath	a	08 00				08 28	08 48	09 13					09 37		09 54				10 34	10 48		
	d	08 01				08 29	08 49	09 14	09 23				09 39		09 55	10 06			10 35	10 49	11 03	
Carnoustie	d					08 36			09 30							10 12					11 09	
Golf Street	d																					
Barry Links	d																					
Monifieth	d															10 18					11 15	
Balmossie	d																					
Broughty Ferry	d								09 37							10 22					11 19	
Dundee	a	08 19				08 48	09 06	09 31	09 44				09 55		10 14	10 30			10 51	11 06	11 27	
	d	08 22	08 29			08 50	09 08	09 33	09 45				09 57		10 20	10 31			10 55	11 08	11 28	
Invergowrie	d																					
Perth	a			08 49		09 10				09 56			10 17	10 51					11 15			11 56
	d			08 52		09 14				09 58		10 05	10 18	10 53				11 02	11 17			11 58
Gleneagles	d									10 15				11 08								
Dunblane 230	d													11 21								
Bridge of Allan 230	d													11 26								
Stirling 230	d					09 43				10 34			10 48	11 32					11 48			
Larbert 230	d																					
Glasgow Queen St. 10 230	a					10 10							11 18	12 07					12 20			
Leuchars 5	a		08 41				09 20	09 45	09 58						10 31	10 43				11 21	11 40	
St Andrews Bus Station	a																					
St Andrews Bus Station	d																					
Leuchars 5	d		08 42				09 22	09 46	09 58						10 32	10 44				11 24	11 41	
Cupar	d		08 49					09 53	10 05							10 51					11 48	
Springfield	d																					
Ladybank	d		08 56					10 01	10 13			10 26				10 59		11 23			11 55	
Markinch	d		09 03					10 08	10 20			10 34				11 06		11 31			12 02	
Kirkcaldy 242	d		09 14	09 28			09 47	10 18	10 30			10 45				11 16		11 42		11 49	12 13	12 32
Inverkeithing 242	d		09 36				10 03	10 34	10 46			11 03				11 32		11 58		12 05	12 29	12 47
Edinburgh Gateway ✈	d		09 46	09 53					10 57			11 17				11 43		12 09			12 41	12 58
Haymarket 242	a	09 24	09 56	10 00			10 19	10 48	11 08	11 15		11 28			11 31	11 52		12 15		12 20	12 49	13 09
Edinburgh 10 242	a	09 31	10 01	10 07			10 25	10 54	11 13	11 21		11 33			11 37	11 57		12 21		12 26	12 54	13 15

A 🛒 from Aberdeen
B Forms booked connection out of 1B08.
C To London Kings Cross
D To Penzance
E To London Kings Cross. The Highland Chieftain

Table T229-R

Mondays to Fridays

16 December to 15 May

Inverurie, Dyce, Aberdeen, Dundee, Inverness and Perth - Glasgow Queen Street and Edinburgh

		SR	SR	SR	SR	SR	SR	SR	SR	SR	SR	SR	SR	SR	SR	SR	SR	SR	SR	SR	SR	SR	SR
			◇1 🛒	◇1	◇		◇	◇1 🛒	◇1 🛒	◇1	◇		◇	◇1 🛒	◇1 🛒	◇	◇1 🛒		◇1 🛒	◇1 🛒	◇		◇
Inverness	d							10 46									12 50						
Carrbridge	d																13 24						
Aviemore	d							11 24									13 33						
Kingussie	d							11 37									13 45						
Newtonmore	d																13 50						
Dalwhinnie	d																						
Blair Atholl	d																14 21						
Pitlochry	d							12 24									14 31						
Dunkeld & Birnam	d							12 37									14 45						
Inverurie 240	d	10 00										12 00						13 01				13 57	
Dyce 240 ✈	d	10 12										12 12						13 13				14 09	
Aberdeen 240	a	10 22										12 22						13 23				14 19	
	d	10 24	10 46	11 02		11 25			11 45	12 07		12 27		12 47	13 12			13 25	13 50	13 56		14 22	
Portlethen	d	10 35				11 36						12 37						13 36				14 33	
Stonehaven	d	10 43		11 18		11 44				12 24		12 46						13 44		14 12		14 41	
Laurencekirk	d	10 57				11 58						12 59						13 58				14 55	
Montrose	a	11 09	11 18	11 37		12 10			12 20	12 45		13 11		13 20	13 44			14 10	14 22	14 31		15 07	
	d		11 19	11 38					12 21	12 45				13 22	13 45				14 23	14 35			
Arbroath	a		11 32	11 52					12 34	12 59				13 35	13 58				14 36	14 49			
	d		11 33	11 53			12 08		12 35	12 59	13 09			13 37	13 59	14 09			14 37	14 50			15 05
Carnoustie	d						12 14				13 15					14 15							15 11
Golf Street	d																						
Barry Links	d																						
Monifieth	d						12 20				13 21					14 21							15 17
Balmossie	d																						
Broughty Ferry	d						12 24				13 25					14 25							15 21
Dundee	a		11 50	12 09			12 32		12 51	13 16	13 33			13 53	14 16	14 33			14 54	15 06			15 29
	d		11 57	12 11	12 16		12 36		12 54	13 18	13 34			13 57	14 21	14 36			14 57	15 08	15 13		15 30
Invergowrie	d				12 21																15 18		
Perth	a		12 17		12 39			12 54	13 15					14 17			15 02		15 17		15 36		
	d		12 18		12 40			13 02	13 16				14 00	14 18			15 07		15 19		15 37		
Gleneagles	d				12 55																15 52		
Dunblane 230	d				13 08																16 07		
Bridge of Allan 230	d				13 12																16 11		
Stirling 230	d		12 47		13 16				13 45					14 48					15 48		16 15		
Larbert 230	d																						
Glasgow Queen St. 10 230	a		13 18		13 55				14 18					15 18					16 18		16 48		
Leuchars 5	a			12 22			12 48			13 31	13 46				14 32	14 49				15 19			15 42
St Andrews Bus Station	a																						
St Andrews Bus Station	d																						
Leuchars 5	d			12 23			12 49			13 31	13 47				14 33	14 49				15 20			15 43
Cupar	d						12 56				13 54					14 56							15 50
Springfield	d																						
Ladybank	d			12 34			13 03				14 01		14 21			15 04							15 57
Markinch	d			12 42			13 10	13 30			14 08		14 31			15 11	15 42						16 04
Kirkcaldy 242	d						13 21	13 41			14 19		14 42			15 21	15 52						16 15
Inverkeithing 242	d						13 37				14 35		15 00			15 37	16 07						16 31
Edinburgh Gateway ✈	d						13 47	14 14			14 45		15 12			15 48	16 16						16 42
Haymarket 242	a			13 18			13 57	14 20		14 24	14 55		15 24		15 28	15 54	16 26			16 22			16 53
Edinburgh 10 242	a			13 23			14 05	14 27		14 30	15 00		15 29		15 33	15 59	16 34			16 31			16 58

Table T229-R

Mondays to Fridays
16 December to 15 May

Inverurie, Dyce, Aberdeen, Dundee, Inverness and Perth - Glasgow Queen Street and Edinburgh

	SR	SR	SR	GR	SR	SR	SR	SR	SR	SR	SR	SR	SR	SR	SR	SR	SR	SR	SR	SR	SR
	◇	◇1	◇1	1		◇	◇1	◇	◇	◇1		◇	◇1	◇1	1	◇1	◇		◇	◇1	
		🛒	🛒	A 🍴		B	🛒		C				🛒	🛒						🛒	
Inverness d			14 50										15 56								
Carrbridge d													16 28								
Aviemore d			15 26										16 37								
Kingussie d			15 38										16 49								
Newtonmore d													16 54								
Dalwhinnie d			15 52																		
Blair Atholl d													17 25								
Pitlochry d			16 21										17 35								
Dunkeld & Birnam d			16 37										17 49								
Inverurie 240 d					14 54						15 48							17 00			
Dyce 240 ✈ d					15 06						16 00							17 13			
Aberdeen 240 a					15 16						16 10							17 22			
d		14 45		14 52	15 18		15 38			16 00	16 12			16 32	16 39	17 15		17 25		17 39	
Portlethen d					15 29						16 23				16 50			17 35			
Stonehaven d				15 10	15 37					16 18	16 31				16a58			17 44		17 55	
Laurencekirk d					15 51						16 45							17 57		18 08	
Montrose a		15 17		15 31	16 03		16 10			16 37	16 57			17 06		17 50		18 09		18 17	
d		15 18		15 33			16 11			16 43				17 12		17 51				18 22	
Arbroath a		15 31		15 48			16 25			16 58				17 26		18 04				18 36	
d		15 32		15 49			16 26	15 59		17 00		17 09		17 27		18 05	18 18			18 37	18 47
Carnoustie d								16 06		17 07		17 16					18 25				18 54
Golf Street d																					
Barry Links d																					
Monifieth d								16 12				17 21					18 30				19 00
Balmossie d																					
Broughty Ferry d								16 16				17 26					18 35				19 04
Dundee a		15 49		16 06			16 43	16 24		17 19		17 33		17 43		18 22	18 42			18 53	19 12
d		15 51		16 08			16 45	16 50		17 24		17 34		17 49		18 24	18 43			18 57	
Invergowrie d							16 50														
Perth a		16 11	16 54				17 11						18 06	18 10						19 17	
d	16 06	16 13	16 56			17 03	17 12						18 07	18 12					19 11	19 20	
Gleneagles d			17 11				17 27														
Dunblane 230 d			17 25				17 40							18 37							
Bridge of Allan 230 d			17 28																		
Stirling 230 d		16s44	17 33				17 46							18 43						19 49	
Larbert 230 d																					
Glasgow Queen St. 10 230 ⛴ a		17 17	18 09				18 23							19 09						20 26	
Leuchars 5 a				16 20				17 02		17 35		17 47				18 37	18 56				
St Andrews Bus Station 🚌 a																					
St Andrews Bus Station 🚌 d																					
Leuchars 5 d				16 22				17 03		17 36		17 47				18 37	18 59				
Cupar d								17 10				17 54					19 06				
Springfield d									←			17 59									
Ladybank d	16 37					17 24		17 18	17 24			18 03	18 29				19 14		19 32		
Markinch d	16 44					→		17 25	17 32			18 11	18 37				19 21		19 40		
Kirkcaldy 242 d	16 55			16 48				17 36	17 48			18 21	18 49				19 31		19 51		
Inverkeithing 242 d	17 11			17 05				17 58	18 04			18 37	19 04				19 47		20 07		
Edinburgh Gateway ⛴✈ d	17 22							18 12	18 16			18 48	19 18				19 58		20 18		
Haymarket 242 ⛴ a	17 32			17 20				18 19	18 23	18 28		18 55	19 25			19 33	20 05		20 26		
Edinburgh 10 242 a	17 37			17 26				18 24	18 28	18 33		19 01	19 31			19 38	20 10		20 31		

A To London Kings Cross
B To Edinburgh
C From Perth

NRT DECEMBER 19 EDITION

Table T229-R

Mondays to Fridays
16 December to 15 May

Inverurie, Dyce, Aberdeen, Dundee, Inverness and Perth - Glasgow Queen Street and Edinburgh

	SR	SR	SR	GR	SR	SR	SR	SR	SR	SR	SR	SR	SR	SR	SR	SR	SR	SR	SR	SR	XC	SR FX	SR FO
		◇	◇1	1	◇	◇1		◇1	◇	◇1	◇1	◇		◇1		◇1	◇1	◇1			◇1	1	1
		🛒	🛒	A 🍴		🛒				🛒	🛒												
Inverness d		15 27	17 27							18 53							20 17						
Carrbridge d			17 59							19 20							21 01						
Aviemore d			18 08							19 33							21 10						
Kingussie d			18 19							19 45							21 22						
Newtonmore d										19 50							21 26						
Dalwhinnie d										20 01							21 38						
Blair Atholl d										20 24							22 00						
Pitlochry d			19 02							20 34							22 13						
Dunkeld & Birnam d			19 19							20 48							22 26						
Inverurie 240 d		17 19											19 25							20 51			
Dyce 240 ✈ d		17 38											19 37							21 03			
Aberdeen 240 a		17 47											19 47							21 13			
d	17 48	18 00		18 18		18 40		19 16			19 45		19 49	20 11	20 28	20 44		21 07		21 15	21 35	22 26	23 23
Portlethen d	17 59	18 11											20 03		20 38					21 26		22 37	23 34
Stonehaven d	18 07	18a19		18 36				19 32					20 11	20 27	20 47	21 00				21 34	21 52	22 46	23 43
Laurencekirk d	18 21												20 25		21 00					21 48		22 59	23 56
Montrose a	18 33			18 57		19 13		19 51			20 17		20 37	20 47	21 12	21 21		21 40		22 00	22 12	23 09	00 06
d				18 59		19 14		19 52			20 18			20 48		21 22		21 41			22 13	23 10	00 07
Arbroath a				19 14		19 27		20 06			20 36			21 01		21 36		21 54			22 27	23 24	00 21
d				19 15		19 28	19 38	20 07			20 37	20 49		21 02		21 37		21 55	22 07		22 28	23 24	00 21
Carnoustie d							19 44	20 16				20 56							22 14			23 31	00 28
Golf Street d																							
Barry Links d																							
Monifieth d							19 50												22 19				
Balmossie d																							
Broughty Ferry d							19 54					21 03							22 24			23 38	00 35
Dundee a				19 32		19 45	20 02	20 28			20 59	21 11		21 19		21 53		22 12	22 32		22 44	23 46	00 45
d				19 34		19 46		20 30	20 43		21 01			21 21		21 56		22 13			22 49	23 49	00 46
Invergowrie d																						23 54	00 51
Perth a			19 36			20 09				21 05	21 21					22 16	22 43					00 12	01 10
d			19 37		20 02	20 10				21 06	21 22					22 17	22 44						
Gleneagles d			19 52			20 25										22 32							
Dunblane 230 d			20 06														23 09						
Bridge of Allan 230 d			20 11														23 13						
Stirling 230 d			20 17			20 46					21 51					22 50	23 19						
Larbert 230 d																							
Glasgow Queen St. 10 230 ⛴ a			20 45			21 15					22 21					23 21	23 57						
Leuchars 5 a				19 46				20 41	20 55					21 32				22 24			23 01		
St Andrews Bus Station 🚌 a																							
St Andrews Bus Station 🚌 d																							
Leuchars 5 d				19 48				20 42	20 56					21 33				22 25			23 02		
Cupar d									21 03					21 40				22 33			23 09		
Springfield d																							
Ladybank d					20 24				21 10					21 47				22 40			23 17		
Markinch d					20 32				21 17	21 36				21 55				22 47			23 24		
Kirkcaldy 242 d				20 13	20 42				21 28	21 45				22 04				22 57			23 36		
Inverkeithing 242 d				20 29	20 58				21 50												23 51		
Edinburgh Gateway ⛴✈ d					21 09				22 04	22 09													
Haymarket 242 ⛴ a				20 44	21 16			21 28	22 13	22 18				22 42				23 24			00 05		
Edinburgh 10 242 a				20 50	21 21			21 34	22 18	22 23				22 47				23 29			00 10		

A To Leeds

Table T229-R

Saturdays
21 December to 16 May

Inverurie, Dyce, Aberdeen, Dundee, Inverness and Perth - Glasgow Queen Street and Edinburgh

		SR 1 A	SR	SR ◇	SR	SR ◇	SR ◇	XC ◇1 B	SR	SR	SR ◇1	SR ◇1	SR	SR ◇	SR	SR ◇	SR ◇1 (trolley)	SR ◇	SR ◇1 C (trolley)	SR ◇	SR ◇1 (trolley)	SR	SR ◇1 D
Inverness	d															05 36			04 56		06 48		
Carrbridge	d																						
Aviemore	d															06 13					07 24		
Kingussie	d															06 28					07 36		
Newtonmore	d																						
Dalwhinnie	d															06 41							
Blair Atholl	d															07 12							
Pitlochry	d															07 26					08 17		
Dunkeld & Birnam	d															07 39					08 32		
Inverurie 240	d																		06 37			06 53	
Dyce 240 ✈	d																		06 53			07 05	
Aberdeen 240	a																		07 03			07 15	
	d		05 05								05 39	05 48	06 19				06 38		07 07			07 18	07 38
Portlethen	d		05 16										06 30									07 29	
Stonehaven	d		05 24									06 04	06 38				06 54		07 27			07 37	07 54
Laurencekirk	d		05 38										06 52									07 51	
Montrose	a		05 50								06 11	06 23	07 04				07 13		07 46			08 03	08 13
	d	00 07									06 12	06 24					07 14		07 47				08 14
Arbroath	a	00 21									06 25	06 38					07 28		08 00				08 28
	d	00 21							06 06		06 27	06 39			07 12		07 29	07 43	08 01				08 29
Carnoustie	d	00 28							06 13			06 46			07 18			07 50					08 36
Golf Street	d								06 15									07 51					
Barry Links	d								06 18									07 54					
Monifieth	d								06 22						07 24			07 58					
Balmossie	d								06 25									08 01					
Broughty Ferry	d	00 35							06 28						07 28			08 04					
Dundee	a	00 45							06 36		06 46	06 58			07 36		07 45	08 12	08 19				08 48
	d	00 46				05 53	06 02	06 33			06 49	06 59		07 09	07 37		07 49	08 13	08 22	08 29			08 50
Invergowrie	d	00 51				05 58												08 18					
Perth	a	01 10				06 16					07 14					07 56	08 09	08 36			08 49		09 10
	d			05 17	05 35	06 19				06 55	07 15					07 58	08 10	08 37			08 51		09 14
Gleneagles	d			05 32		06 34					07 30						08 25	08 52					
Dunblane 230	d			05 46		06 47					07 44							09 06					
Bridge of Allan 230	d			05 50		06 51					07 48							09 09					
Stirling 230	d			05 54		06 56					07 55						08 43	09 13					09 43
Larbert 230	d			06 03		07 04					08 04												
Glasgow Queen St. 10 230 ⛴	a			06 36		07 30					08 31						09 11	09 49					10 11
Leuchars 5	a						06 14	06 45				07 10		07 21	07 50					08 41			
St Andrews Bus Station 🚌	a																						
St Andrews Bus Station 🚌	d																						
Leuchars 5	d						06 15	06 46				07 11		07 22	07 50					08 42			
Cupar	d						06 22	06 55				07 19		07 29	07 58					08 49			
Springfield	d													07 34									
Ladybank	d				05 57		06 30	07 03		07 31				07 38		08 20				08 56			
Markinch	d				06 05		06 38	07 11		07 38				07 46	08 11	08 28				09 03			
Kirkcaldy 242	d				06 15		06 48	07 22		07 48		07 37		07 57	08 22	08 38				09 14	09 27		
Inverkeithing 242	d				06 38		07 11	07 39		08 04				08 19	08 38	08 54				09 36			
Edinburgh Gateway ⛴✈	d				06 51		07 23			08 15				08 31	08 49	09 05				09 46	09 52		
Haymarket 242 ⛴	a				07 00		07 30	07 58		08 22		08 18		08 41	08 57	09 12			09 23	09 53	09 58		
Edinburgh 10 242	a				07 05		07 36	08 03		08 27		08 24		08 47	09 02	09 17			09 29	09 58	10 05		

A From Aberdeen
B To Plymouth
C (trolley) from Aberdeen
D Forms booked connection out of 1B08.

Table T229-R

Saturdays
21 December to 16 May

Inverurie, Dyce, Aberdeen, Dundee, Inverness and Perth - Glasgow Queen Street and Edinburgh

		GR 1 A (sleeper)	XC ◇1 B (trolley)	SR ◇	GR 1 C (sleeper)	SR	SR ◇	SR ◇1 (trolley)	SR ◇1 (trolley)	SR ◇1 (trolley)	SR ◇	SR	SR ◇	SR ◇1	GR 1 A (sleeper)	SR ◇	SR ◇1 (trolley)	SR	SR ◇1 (trolley)	SR ◇1	SR ◇	SR	SR ◇
Inverness	d				07 55				08 45								09 44						
Carrbridge	d								09 13														
Aviemore	d				08 32				09 22								10 28						
Kingussie	d				08 45				09 36								10 40						
Newtonmore	d								09 41														
Dalwhinnie	d																10 53						
Blair Atholl	d																11 16						
Pitlochry	d				09 28				10 20								11 26						
Dunkeld & Birnam	d								10 34								11 39						
Inverurie 240	d					07 58												10 00					
Dyce 240 ✈	d					08 10						09 07						10 12					
Aberdeen 240	a					08 20						09 16						10 22					
	d	07 52	08 20			08 30		08 51		09 04		09 18		09 44	09 52			10 24	10 46	11 02		11 25	
Portlethen	d					08 41						09 29						10 35				11 36	
Stonehaven	d	08 10	08 37			08 49				09 20		09 37			10 10			10 43		11 18		11 44	
Laurencekirk	d					09 03						09 51						10 57				11 58	
Montrose	a	08 31	08 57			09 15		09 23		09 39		10 03		10 16	10 31			11 09	11 18	11 37		12 10	
	d	08 33	08 59					09 24		09 40				10 20	10 33				11 19	11 38			
Arbroath	a	08 48	09 13					09 37		09 54				10 34	10 48				11 32	11 52			
	d	08 49	09 14	09 23				09 39		09 55	10 06			10 35	10 49	11 03			11 33	11 53			12 08
Carnoustie	d			09 30							10 12					11 09							12 14
Golf Street	d																						
Barry Links	d																						
Monifieth	d										10 18					11 15							12 20
Balmossie	d																						
Broughty Ferry	d			09 37							10 22					11 19							12 24
Dundee	a	09 06	09 31	09 44				09 55		10 14	10 30			10 51	11 06	11 27			11 50	12 09			12 32
	d	09 08	09 33	09 45				09 57		10 20	10 31			10 55	11 08	11 28			11 57	12 11	12 16		12 36
Invergowrie	d																				12 21		
Perth	a				09 56			10 17	10 51					11 15			11 56		12 17		12 39		
	d				09 58		10 05	10 18	10 53				11 02	11 17			11 58		12 18		12 40		
Gleneagles	d				10 15				11 08												12 55		
Dunblane 230	d								11 21												13 08		
Bridge of Allan 230	d								11 26												13 12		
Stirling 230	d				10 33			10 48	11 32					11 47					12 47		13 16		
Larbert 230	d																						
Glasgow Queen St. 10 230 ⛴	a							11 18	12 10					12 19					13 18		13 49		
Leuchars 5	a	09 20	09 45	09 58						10 31	10 44				11 21	11 40				12 22			12 48
St Andrews Bus Station 🚌	a																						
St Andrews Bus Station 🚌	d																						
Leuchars 5	d	09 22	09 46	09 58						10 32	10 44				11 24	11 41				12 23			12 49
Cupar	d		09 53	10 05							10 51					11 48							12 56
Springfield	d																						
Ladybank	d		10 01	10 13			10 26				10 59		11 23			11 55				12 34			13 03
Markinch	d		10 08	10 20			10 34				11 06		11 31			12 02				12 42			13 10
Kirkcaldy 242	d	09 47	10 18	10 30			10 45				11 16		11 42		11 49	12 13	12 32						13 21
Inverkeithing 242	d	10 03	10 34	10 46			11 03				11 32		11 58		12 05	12 29	12 47						13 37
Edinburgh Gateway ⛴✈	d			10 57			11 17				11 43		12 09			12 39	12 57						13 47
Haymarket 242 ⛴	a	10 19	10 48	11 03	11 13		11 24			11 28	11 50		12 16		12 20	12 45	13 03			13 24			13 54
Edinburgh 10 242	a	10 26	10 54	11 08	11 19		11 29			11 33	11 55		12 21		12 26	12 50	13 09			13 29			13 59

A To London Kings Cross
B To Penzance
C To London Kings Cross. The Highland Chieftain

Table T229-R

Saturdays

21 December to 16 May

Inverurie, Dyce, Aberdeen, Dundee, Inverness and Perth - Glasgow Queen Street and Edinburgh

	SR	SR	SR	SR	SR	SR	SR	SR	SR	SR	SR	SR	SR	SR	SR	SR	SR	SR	SR	GR	SR
	◇1	◇1	◇1	◇		◇	◇1	◇1	◇	◇1		◇1	◇1	◇		◇	◇	◇1	◇1	▪ 1	
																				A	
	🛒	🛒					🛒	🛒		🛒		🛒	🛒					🛒	🛒	⊡	
Inverness d	10 46									12 50									14 50		
Carrbridge d										13 24											
Aviemore d	11 24									13 33									15 26		
Kingussie d	11 37									13 45									15 38		
Newtonmore d										13 50											
Dalwhinnie d																			15 52		
Blair Atholl d										14 21											
Pitlochry d	12 24									14 31									16 21		
Dunkeld & Birnam d	12 37									14 45									16 37		
Inverurie 240 d					12 00						13 01				13 57						14 54
Dyce 240 ✈ d					12 12						13 13				14 09						15 06
Aberdeen 240 a					12 22						13 23				14 19						15 16
d		11 45	12 07		12 27		12 47	13 12			13 25	13 50	13 56		14 22			14 45		14 52	15 18
Portlethen d					12 37						13 36				14 33						15 29
Stonehaven d			12 24		12 46						13 44		14 12		14 41					15 10	15 37
Laurencekirk d					12 59						13 58				14 55						15 51
Montrose a		12 20	12 45		13 11		13 20	13 44			14 10	14 22	14 31		15 07			15 17		15 31	16 03
d		12 21	12 45				13 22	13 45				14 23	14 35					15 18		15 33	
Arbroath a		12 34	12 59				13 35	13 58				14 36	14 49					15 31		15 48	
d		12 35	12 59	13 09			13 37	13 59	14 09			14 37	14 50			15 05		15 32		15 49	
Carnoustie d				13 15					14 15							15 11					
Golf Street d																					
Barry Links d																					
Monifieth d				13 21					14 21							15 17					
Balmossie d																					
Broughty Ferry d				13 25					14 25							15 21					
Dundee a		12 51	13 16	13 33			13 53	14 16	14 33			14 54	15 06			15 29		15 49		16 06	
d		12 54	13 18	13 34			13 57	14 21	14 35			14 57	15 08	15 13		15 30		15 51		16 08	
Invergowrie d														15 18							
Perth a	12 54	13 15					14 17			15 02		15 17		15 36				16 11	16 54		
d	13 02	13 16				14 00	14 18			15 07		15 19		15 37			16 06	16 13	16 55		
Gleneagles d														15 52					17 10		
Dunblane 230 d														16 07					17 23		
Bridge of Allan 230 d														16 11					17 27		
Stirling 230 d		13 45					14 48					15 48		16 15				16s44	17 32		
Larbert 230 d																					
Glasgow Queen St. 10 230 ⛴ a		14 19					15 18					16 18		16 48				17 17	18 08		
Leuchars 5 a			13 31	13 46				14 32	14 47				15 19			15 43				16 20	
St Andrews Bus Station 🚌 a																					
St Andrews Bus Station 🚌 d																					
Leuchars 5 d			13 31	13 47				14 33	14 48				15 20			15 44				16 23	
Cupar d				13 54					14 55							15 51					
Springfield d																					
Ladybank d				14 01		14 21			15 02							15 58	16 38				
Markinch d	13 31			14 08		14 31			15 09	15 42						16 05	16 46				
Kirkcaldy 242 d	13 42			14 19		14 42			15 20	15 52						16 16	16 56			16 48	
Inverkeithing 242 d				14 35		15 00			15 36	16 07						16 32	17 12			17 05	
Edinburgh Gateway ⛴✈ d	14 10			14 45		15 12			15 46	16 16						16 42	17 23				
Haymarket 242 ⛴ a	14 21		14 27	14 52		15 18		15 26	15 52	16 26			16 20			16 52	17 29			17 20	
Edinburgh 10 242 a	14 29		14 32	14 57		15 24		15 31	15 57	16 34			16 27			16 57	17 34			17 26	

A To London Kings Cross

Table T229-R

Saturdays

21 December to 16 May

Inverurie, Dyce, Aberdeen, Dundee, Inverness and Perth - Glasgow Queen Street and Edinburgh

	SR	SR	SR	SR	SR	SR	SR	SR	SR	SR	SR	SR	SR	SR	SR	SR	SR	SR	SR	SR	SR	SR
	◇	◇1	◇	◇	◇1		◇	◇1	◇1	◇1	◇		◇	◇1		◇1		◇1	◇	◇1		◇1
	A			B																		
		🛒						🛒	🛒					🛒		🛒		🛒		🛒		
Inverness d								15 56								17 27						
Carrbridge d								16 28								17 59						
Aviemore d								16 37								18 08						
Kingussie d								16 49								18 19						
Newtonmore d								16 54														
Dalwhinnie d																						
Blair Atholl d								17 25														
Pitlochry d								17 35								19 02						
Dunkeld & Birnam d								17 49								19 19						
Inverurie 240 d						15 48						17 00										
Dyce 240 ✈ d						16 00						17 13										
Aberdeen 240 a						16 10						17 22										
d		15 38			16 00	16 12			16 32	17 15		17 25		17 39			17 48	18 18		18 40		19 16
Portlethen d						16 23						17 35					17 59					
Stonehaven d					16 18	16 31						17 44		17 55			18 07	18 36				19 32
Laurencekirk d						16 45						17 57		18 08			18 21					
Montrose a		16 10			16 37	16 57			17 06	17 50		18 09		18 17			18 33	18 57		19 13		19 51
d		16 11			16 43				17 12	17 51				18 22				18 59		19 14		19 52
Arbroath a		16 25			16 58				17 26	18 04				18 36				19 12		19 27		20 06
d		16 26	15 59		17 00		17 09		17 27	18 05	18 18			18 37	18 47			19 14		19 28	19 38	20 07
Carnoustie d			16 06		17 07		17 16				18 25				18 54						19 44	20 16
Golf Street d																						
Barry Links d																						
Monifieth d			16 12				17 21				18 30				19 00						19 50	
Balmossie d																						
Broughty Ferry d			16 16				17 26				18 35				19 04						19 54	
Dundee a		16 43	16 24		17 19		17 33		17 43	18 22	18 42			18 53	19 12			19 31		19 45	20 02	20 28
d		16 45	16 50		17 24		17 34		17 49	18 24	18 43			18 57				19 33		19 46		20 30
Invergowrie d		16 50																				
Perth a		17 11						18 06	18 10					19 17		19 36				20 09		
d	17 03	17 12						18 07	18 12				19 11	19 20		19 37			20 02	20 10		
Gleneagles d		17 27														19 52				20 25		
Dunblane 230 d		17 40							18 37							20 06						
Bridge of Allan 230 d																20 11						
Stirling 230 d		17 46							18 43					19 49		20 17				20 46		
Larbert 230 d																						
Glasgow Queen St. 10 230 ⛴ a		18 20							19 11					20 27		20 45				21 16		
Leuchars 5 a			17 02		17 35		17 47			18 37	18 58							19 45				20 41
St Andrews Bus Station 🚌 a																						
St Andrews Bus Station 🚌 d																						
Leuchars 5 d			17 03		17 36		17 47			18 37	18 59							19 46				20 42
Cupar d			17 10				17 54				19 06											
Springfield d				←			17 59															
Ladybank d	17 24		17 18	17 24			18 03	18 29			19 14		19 32						20 24			
Markinch d	↪		17 25	17 32			18 11	18 37			19 21		19 40						20 32			
Kirkcaldy 242 d			17 36	17 48			18 21	18 46			19 31		19 51					20 12	20 43			
Inverkeithing 242 d			17 58	18 05			18 37	19 03			19 47		20 07					20 28	20 59			
Edinburgh Gateway ⛴✈ d			18 12	18 18			18 48	19 13			19 58		20 18						21 10			
Haymarket 242 ⛴ a			18 20	18 24	18 28		18 54	19 19		19 31	20 04		20 26					20 44	21 16			21 29
Edinburgh 10 242 a			18 28	18 31	18 34		18 59	19 25		19 36	20 11		20 31					20 49	21 20			21 36

A To Edinburgh

B From Perth

Table T229-R

Saturdays
21 December to 16 May

Inverurie, Dyce, Aberdeen, Dundee, Inverness and Perth - Glasgow Queen Street and Edinburgh

Station		SR ◇	SR ◇1 🍴	SR ◇1 🍴	SR ◇	SR	SR ◇1	SR	SR ◇1	SR ◇1	SR	SR	XC ◇1	SR 1
Inverness	d		18 53											
Carrbridge	d		19 20											
Aviemore	d		19 33											
Kingussie	d		19 45											
Newtonmore	d		19 50											
Dalwhinnie	d		20 01											
Blair Atholl	d		20 24											
Pitlochry	d		20 34											
Dunkeld & Birnam	d		20 48											
Inverurie 240	d					19 25						20 51		
Dyce 240 ✈	d					19 37						21 03		
Aberdeen 240	a					19 47						21 13		
	d			19 45		19 49	20 11	20 28	20 44	21 07		21 15	21 35	22 26
Portlethen	d					20 03		20 38				21 26		22 37
Stonehaven	d					20 11	20 27	20 47	21 00			21 34	21 52	22 46
Laurencekirk	d					20 25		21 00				21 48		22 59
Montrose	a			20 17		20 37	20 47	21 12	21 21	21 40		22 00	22 12	23 09
	d			20 18			20 48		21 22	21 41			22 13	23 10
Arbroath	a			20 36			21 01		21 36	21 54			22 27	23 24
	d			20 37	20 49		21 02		21 37	21 55	22 07		22 28	23 24
Carnoustie	d				20 56						22 14			23 31
Golf Street	d													
Barry Links	d													
Monifieth	d										22 19			
Balmossie	d													
Broughty Ferry	d				21 03						22 24			23 38
Dundee	a			20 59	21 11		21 19		21 53	22 12	22 32		22 44	23 46
	d	20 43		21 01			21 21		21 56	22 13			22 49	
Invergowrie	d													
Perth	a		21 06	21 21					22 16					
	d		21 07	21 22					22 17					
Gleneagles	d								22 32					
Dunblane 230	d													
Bridge of Allan 230	d													
Stirling 230	d			21 51					22 52					
Larbert 230	d													
Glasgow Queen St. 10 230 ⛴	a			22 21					23 22					
Leuchars 5	a	20 55					21 32			22 24			23 01	
St Andrews Bus Station 🚌	a													
St Andrews Bus Station 🚌	d													
Leuchars 5	d	20 56					21 33			22 25			23 02	
Cupar	d	21 03					21 40			22 33			23 09	
Springfield	d													
Ladybank	d	21 10					21 47			22 40			23 17	
Markinch	d	21 17	21 36				21 55			22 47			23 24	
Kirkcaldy 242	d	21 28	21 45				22 04			22 57			23 34	
Inverkeithing 242	d	21 50											23 49	
Edinburgh Gateway ⛴✈	d	22 04	22 08											
Haymarket 242 ⛴	a	22 13	22 17				22 36			23 24			00 03	
Edinburgh 10 242	a	22 18	22 22				22 43			23 29			00 08	

Table T229-R

Sundays
15 December to 10 May

Inverurie, Dyce, Aberdeen, Dundee, Inverness and Perth - Glasgow Queen Street and Edinburgh

Station		SR ◇	SR	SR ◇	SR ◇1	SR ◇	SR	SR	SR ◇1 🍴	GR 1 A 🍽	SR	SR ◇	GR 1 B 🍽	SR ◇1 🍴	SR	XC ◇1 C	SR ◇1 🍴	SR ◇1 D 🍴	GR 1 E 🍽	SR	SR ◇	SR ◇1 🍴	SR ◇1
Inverness	d												09 40				10 53						
Carrbridge	d												10 11										
Aviemore	d												10 22				11 28						
Kingussie	d												10 35				11 39						
Newtonmore	d												10 40										
Dalwhinnie	d																11 52						
Blair Atholl	d												11 14										
Pitlochry	d												11 27				12 23						
Dunkeld & Birnam	d												11 41				12 38						
Inverurie 240	d																	11 03					
Dyce 240 ✈	d																	11 15					
Aberdeen 240	a																	11 25					
	d								09 24	09 47				10 33		11 10		11 29	11 47			12 30	12 44
Portlethen	d																						12 55
Stonehaven	d								09 41	10 05				10 49		11 27		11 45	12 05			12 47	13 05
Laurencekirk	d								09 54														13 18
Montrose	a								10 03	10 26				11 08		11 47		12 04	12 26			13 08	13 27
	d								10 04	10 28				11 09		11 49		12 05	12 28			13 08	13 28
Arbroath	a								10 17	10 43				11 23		12 03		12 19	12 43			13 22	13 41
	d								10 18	10 44				11 24		12 04		12 20	12 44			13 23	13 42
Carnoustie	d								10 25														13 49
Golf Street	d																						
Barry Links	d																						
Monifieth	d																						
Balmossie	d																						
Broughty Ferry	d								10 33														13 57
Dundee	a								10 41	11 01				11 40		12 21		12 36	13 01			13 40	14 05
	d	07 24			08 45		09 24		10 42	11 04		11 20		11 42		12 22		12 38	13 03		13 20	13 43	14 06
Invergowrie	d																						
Perth	a				09 05				11 02				11 59	12 02			12 56	12 58				14 04	
	d			08 50	09 06	09 16		10 10	11 04				12 01	12 06			12 58	13 03				14 06	
Gleneagles	d				09 21	09 31		10 25	11 19				12 17					13 18					
Dunblane 230	d				09 34	09 43		10 39	11 32				12 29	12 39				13 31				14 33	
Bridge of Allan 230	d					09 47		10 43															
Stirling 230	d		09 10		09 40	09 51		10 47	11 39		11 49		12 37	12 45	12 49			13 37		13 49		14 40	
Larbert 230	d		09 17		09 49	10 00		10 56			11 57				12 57					13 57			
Glasgow Queen St. 10 230 ⛴	a				10 14				12 06					13 13				14 05				15 09	
Leuchars 5	a	07 36					09 36			11 16		11 32				12 34			13 15		13 32		14 17
St Andrews Bus Station 🚌	a																						
St Andrews Bus Station 🚌	d																						
Leuchars 5	d	07 37					09 37			11 18		11 33				12 35			13 18		13 33		14 18
Cupar	d	07 44					09 44					11 40				12 43					13 40		
Springfield	d																						
Ladybank	d	07 52		09 11			09 52					11 48				12 50					13 48		
Markinch	d	07 59		09 19			09 59					11 55				12 58	13 26				13 55		
Kirkcaldy 242	d	08 10		09 30			10 10			11 43		12 06				13 08	13 36		13 44		14 06		14 41
Inverkeithing 242	d	08 32		09 52			10 32			11 59		12 22				13 24	13 51		14 05		14 22		14 56
Edinburgh Gateway ⛴✈	d	08 49		10 09			10 46					12 33					14 00				14 33		
Haymarket 242 ⛴	a	08 58	09 55	10 18		10 40	10 55	11 35		12 16	12 28	12 40	13 11		13 30	13 37	14 09		14 20	14 28	14 40		15 16
Edinburgh 10 242	a	09 03	10 00	10 23		10 46	11 01	11 40		12 22	12 33	12 47	13 19		13 36	13 43	14 15		14 26	14 33	14 45		15 24

A To London Kings Cross. The Northern Lights
B To London Kings Cross. The Highland Chieftain
C To Plymouth
D 🍴 from Aberdeen
E To London Kings Cross

Table T229-R

Sundays

15 December to 10 May

Inverurie, Dyce, Aberdeen, Dundee, Inverness and Perth - Glasgow Queen Street and Edinburgh

		SR	SR	SR	GR	SR	SR	SR	SR	SR	SR	SR	SR	SR	SR	SR	SR	SR	SR	SR	SR	SR	SR	XC	SR
			◇1 ⊼	◇1 ⊼	1 A (seat)		◇	◇1 ⊼	◇1 ⊼	◇1 ⊼		◇1 ⊼	◇1 ⊼	◇	◇1 ⊼	◇1 ⊼	◇1 ⊼	◇1	◇	◇1 B ⊼	◇1 ⊼	◇1 C ⊼	◇1 ⊼	◇1	
Inverness	d		12 41					13 32					15 22			16 26					18 52				
Carrbridge	d		13 12													16 59					19 25				
Aviemore	d		13 21					14 08					15 57			17 08					19 34				
Kingussie	d		13 37					14 20					16 08			17 20					19 46				
Newtonmore	d		13 42																		19 51				
Dalwhinnie	d																				20 02				
Blair Atholl	d		14 13													17 53					20 25				
Pitlochry	d		14 23					15 01					16 50			18 03					20 35				
Dunkeld & Birnam	d		14 38										17 04			18 20					20 49				
Inverurie 240	d																								
Dyce 240	d																								
Aberdeen 240	a																								
	d			13 34	13 47				14 33	15 08		15 31			16 31		17 04	17 45		19 04		19 38	20 05	21 30	22 28
Portlethen	d									15 19													20 16		22 38
Stonehaven	d			13 50	14 05				14 50	15 28		15 48			16 47		17 20	18 01		19 21		19 54	20 25	21 47	22 47
Laurencekirk	d											16 02						18 14					20 38		23 01
Montrose	a			14 09	14 26				15 11	15 49		16 12			17 06		17 39	18 23		19 42		20 13	20 47	22 07	23 11
	d			14 10	14 28				15 11	15 49		16 12			17 07		17 43	18 24		19 45		20 14	20 48	22 08	23 11
Arbroath	a			14 24	14 43				15 25	16 03		16 26			17 21		17 57	18 38		19 59		20 28	21 01	22 22	23 25
	d			14 25	14 44				15 26	16 03		16 26			17 22		17 58	18 39		19 59		20 29	21 02	22 23	23 26
Carnoustie	d									16 10										20 06					23 33
Golf Street	d																								
Barry Links	d																								
Monifieth	d																								
Balmossie	d																								
Broughty Ferry	d																			20 14					23 40
Dundee	a			14 41	15 01				15 43	16 23		16 43			17 38		18 14	18 55		20 21		20 45	21 19	22 39	23 48
	d			14 43	15 03		15 15		15 45	16 24		16 44		17 21	17 40		18 17	18 58	19 16	20 22		20 50	21 20	22 41	23 49
Invergowrie	d																								
Perth	a		14 55	15 03				15 29	16 07			17 04	17 21		18 00	18 37		19 18			21 06	21 10			00 13
	d		14 56	15 04				15 30	16 09			17 05	17 23		18 01	18 39		19 20			21 08	21 15			
Gleneagles	d			15 20								17 20						19 35				21 30			
Dunblane 230	d		15 22	15 34					16 36			17 33			18 26	19 05						21 44			
Bridge of Allan 230	d																								
Stirling 230	d	14 49	15 28	15 40		15 49			16 43		16 49	17 40			18 32	19 11		19 52				21 50			
Larbert 230	d	14 57	15 36			15 57					16 57					19 20						21 59			
Glasgow Queen St. 10 230	a		15 58	16 16					17 12			18 09			19 09	19 42		20 21				22 23			
Leuchars 5	a				15 15		15 27			16 36				17 33			18 28		19 28	20 35			21 31	22 53	
St Andrews Bus Station	a																								
St Andrews Bus Station	d																								
Leuchars 5	d				15 17		15 28			16 37				17 34			18 29		19 29	20 35			21 32	22 54	
Cupar	d						15 35							17 41					19 36				21 40	23 01	
Springfield	d																								
Ladybank	d						15 43	15 52					17 44	17 49					19 44		21 30		21 47	23 09	
Markinch	d						15 50	15 59					17 52	17 57					19 51		21 40		21 54	23 16	
Kirkcaldy 242	d				15 43		16 01	16 09		17 03			18 01	18 07			18 52		20 02	21 02	21 49		22 04	23 26	
Inverkeithing 242	d				16 00		16 17	16 24		17 19			18 16	18 23			19 07		20 24	21 18	22 04		22 19	23 42	
Edinburgh Gateway	d						16 28	16 33					18 26	18 34					20 38		22 14				
Haymarket 242	a	15 29			16 18	16 28	16 35	16 42		17 34	17 35		18 35	18 41			19 21		20 47	21 33	22 22		22 33	23 55	
Edinburgh 10 242	a	15 36			16 24	16 33	16 40	16 48		17 40	17 40		18 42	18 46			19 26		20 52	21 38	22 28		22 38	00 01	

A To London Kings Cross   **B** ⊼ to Dundee   **C** ⊼ from Dundee

Table T230-F

16 December to 15 May

Edinburgh, Glasgow Queen Street and Falkirk Grahamston - Stirling, Alloa and Dunblane

Miles	Miles	Miles			SR MX	SR MO	SR MX	SR MX	SR MX	SR	SR	SR	SR	SR	SR	SR	SR	SR	SR	SR	SR	SR	SR
					◇ A	◇ A	B	C	1 D	E		E	◇1 F ⊼			1 E	E		1 G	1 G	1 E	E	
0	—	—	**Edinburgh** 10	d						05 03	05 19	05 33		05 49		06 00	06 04	06 19			06 30	06 33	
1¼	—	—	Haymarket	d						05 07	05 23	05 37		05 53		06 04	06 08	06 23			06 34	06 37	
3¾	—	—	Edinburgh Park	d						05 11	05 27	05 42		05 57			06 12	06 27				06 42	
17½	—	—	Linlithgow	d					00 02	05 22		05 52				06 17	06 23				06 46	06 54	
22¼	—	—	Polmont 3	d					00 07	05 26		05 57				06 21	06 27				06 51	06 59	
—	0	0	**Glasgow Queen Street** 10	d									05 53		06 19				06 30	06 45			06 48
—	3¼	3¼	Bishopbriggs	d											06 24								06 55
—	6¼	6¼	Lenzie 3	d				00 02							06 28				06a37				06 59
—	11½	11½	Croy 3	d				00 07	00a21						06 33	06a34				06a55	07a04		07 04
25½	—	—	**Falkirk Grahamston** 3	d			00 02			05 34	05 45	06 08		06 15			06 35	06 45				07 05	
27	—	—	Camelon 4	d			00 05			05a37	05 48	06a11		06 18			06a38	06 48				07a08	
28¼	21	21	Larbert	d		00 11	00 12	00 18			05 51		06 14	06 21	06 46			06 51					07 16
36½	29	29	**Stirling**	a		00 19	00 20	00 25			05 59		06 22	06 29	06 55			07 01					07 23
—	—	—		d	00 06	00 20	00 21				06 00		06 23	06 30									07 24
—	—	35¾	**Alloa**	a																			07 40
40	32½	—	Bridge of Allan	d	00 11	00 24	00 25				06 04			06 34									
42	34½	—	**Dunblane**	a	00 15	00 28	00 28				06 08		06 30	06 37									

		SR	SR	SR	SR	SR	SR	SR	SR	SR	SR	SR	SR	SR	SR	SR	SR	SR	SR	SR	SR	SR	SR
		1 E		1 G ⊼	E	◇1 H ⊼		1 G ⊼	1 E ⊼		◇1 F ⊼		1 E ⊼	E	1 E ⊼		1 G ⊼	◇ I		1 E ⊼	E		1 G ⊼
Edinburgh 10	d	06 45	06 48		07 03				07 15	07 20			07 30	07 35	07 45	07 46				08 00	08 05	08 18	
Haymarket	d	06 49	06 52		07 07				07 19	07 24			07 35	07 39	07 49	07 52				08 06	08 12	08 23	
Edinburgh Park	d		06 57		07 12					07 28				07 45		07 58					08 18	08 28	
Linlithgow	d	07 02			07 23				07 32				07 48	07 56	08 04						08 28		
Polmont 3	d				07 27								07 53	08 00						08 27	08 33		
Glasgow Queen Street 10	d			07 00		07 07	07 20	07 30			07 41	07 49					08 00	08 10	08 20				08 30
Bishopbriggs	d						07 26					07 55							08 27				
Lenzie 3	d			07a07			07 31					07 59			08a24				08 31				
Croy 3	d	07a19					07 36	07a42	07a48			08 04	08a06				08a10		08 37	08a40			08a42
Falkirk Grahamston 3	d		07 15		07 33					07 46				08 06		08 19					08 40	08 48	
Camelon 4	d		07 18		07a36					07 49				08a09		08 22					08a43	08 51	
Larbert	d		07 21				07 48			07 52		08 15				08 25			08 48			08 56	
Stirling	a		07 29			07 33	07 55			08 00		08 28				08 32		08 37	08 55			09 03	
	d		07 29			07 35	07 56			08 01	08u09	08 29				08 33		08 37				09 04	
Alloa	a											08 38											
Bridge of Allan	d		07 33				08 00			08 05						08 37		08 41				09 08	
Dunblane	a		07 37			07 41	08 03			08 08	08 17					08 40		08 45				09 11	

		SR	SR	SR	SR	SR	SR	SR	SR	SR	SR	SR	SR	SR	SR	SR	SR	SR	SR	SR	SR	SR	SR
		E	◇1 F ⊼			1 G ⊼	E	◇ I			1 G ⊼	E	◇1 F ⊼			1 G ⊼	E	◇1 H ⊼			1 G ⊼	E	◇1 F ⊼
Edinburgh 10	d	08 35			08 49		09 04			09 19		09 35			09 48		10 03			10 18		10 33	
Haymarket	d	08 41			08 53		09 09			09 23		09 39			09 53		10 08			10 23		10 37	
Edinburgh Park	d	08 46			08 58		09 13			09 28		09 43			09 58		10 13			10 29		10 42	
Linlithgow	d	08 58					09 25					09 54					10 24					10 54	
Polmont 3	d	09 03					09 29					09 59					10 29					10 58	
Glasgow Queen Street 10	d		08 40	08 50		09 00		09 07	09 20		09 30		09 40	09 52		10 00		10 10	10 21		10 30		10 40
Bishopbriggs	d			08 56					09 26					09 57					10 26				
Lenzie 3	d			09 00					09 30					10 01					10 30				
Croy 3	d			09 05		09a11			09 36		09a40			10 07		10a10			10 36		10a40		
Falkirk Grahamston 3	d	09 10			09 18		09 36			09 48		10 10			10 15		10 40			10 47		11 10	
Camelon 4	d	09a13			09 21		09a39			09 51		10a13			10 18		10a43			10 50		11a13	
Larbert	d			09 16	09 24				09 47	09 54				10 17	10 22				10 47	10 54			
Stirling	a		09 09	09 25	09 32			09 38	09 55	10 02			10 07	10 25	10 29			10 36	10 55	11 01			11 06
	d			09 26	09 33			09 39		10 02				10 26	10 30			10 36		11 02			
Alloa	a			09 35										10 35									
Bridge of Allan	d				09 37					10 06					10 34			10 41		11 06			
Dunblane	a				09 40			09 46		10 10					10 38			10 45		11 09			

		SR	SR	SR	SR	SR	SR	SR	SR	SR	SR	SR	SR	SR	SR	SR	SR	SR	SR	SR	SR	SR
				1 G ⊼	E			1 G ⊼	E	◇1 F ⊼			1 G ⊼	E	◇1 H ⊼			1 G ⊼	E	◇1 F ⊼		
Edinburgh 10	d		10 48		11 04		11 20		11 34			11 48		12 04			12 21		12 34			12 49
Haymarket	d		10 53		11 08		11 24		11 38			11 52		12 09			12 25		12 39			12 53
Edinburgh Park	d		10 57		11 12		11 28		11 43			11 57		12 14			12 29		12 44			12 59
Linlithgow	d				11 24				11 53					12 25					12 55			
Polmont 3	d				11 29				11 58					12 30					12 59			
Glasgow Queen Street 10	d	10 51		11 00		11 21		11 30		11 38	11 51		12 00		12 08	12 21		12 30		12 39	12 48	
Bishopbriggs	d	10 57				11 26					11 57					12 26					12 55	
Lenzie 3	d	11 01				11 30					12 01					12 30					13 00	
Croy 3	d	11 06		11a10		11 36		11a41			12 06		12a11			12 36		12a42			13 05	
Falkirk Grahamston 3	d		11 15		11 37		11 47		12 10			12 16		12 40			12 47		13 08			13 19
Camelon 4	d		11 18		11a40		11 50		12a13			12 19		12a43			12 50		13a11			13 22
Larbert	d	11 17	11 22			11 47	11 53				12 17	12 22				12 47	12 53				13 16	13 29
Stirling	a	11 24	11 29			11 54	12 01			12 11	12 24	12 29			12 34	12 55	13 01			13 06	13 24	13 37
	d	11 25	11 30			11 55	12 01				12 25	12 30			12 35		13 01				13 25	13 37
Alloa	a	11 34									12 34										13 35	
Bridge of Allan	d		11 34			11 59	12 05					12 34			12 41		13 05					13 41
Dunblane	a		11 38			12 02	12 09					12 37			12 44		13 09					13 45

A From Glasgow Queen Street to Perth
B From Edinburgh
C From Glasgow Queen Street
D From Edinburgh to Glasgow Queen Street
E To Glasgow Queen Street
F To Aberdeen
G To Edinburgh
H To Inverness
I To Dundee

Table T230-F

Edinburgh, Glasgow Queen Street and Falkirk Grahamston - Stirling, Alloa and Dunblane

Mondays to Fridays
16 December to 15 May

		SR	SR		SR	SR	SR	SR	SR	SR	SR	SR	SR		SR	SR	SR	SR	SR	SR	SR	SR	SR		SR
		[1] A 🛒	B				[1] A 🛒	B	◇[1] C 🛒			[1] A 🛒	B				[1] A 🛒	B	◇[1] D 🛒			[1] A 🛒	B		◇[1] D 🛒
Edinburgh [10]	d		13 04			13 20		13 35			13 50		14 03			14 20		14 39			14 50		15 04		
Haymarket	d		13 08			13 24		13 39			13 54		14 10			14 24		14 44			14 54		15 08		
Edinburgh Park	d		13 13			13 28		13 43			13 58		14 15			14 30		14 49			14 58		15 13		
Linlithgow	d		13 24					13 54					14 28					15 00					15 24		
Polmont [3]	d		13 28					13 58					14 32					15 04					15 28		
Glasgow Queen Street [10]	d	13 00			13 18		13 30		13 40	13 52		14 00			14 18		14 30		14 39	14 48		15 00			15 08
Bishopbriggs	d				13 25					13 57					14 26					14 56					
Lenzie [3]	d				13 29					14 01					14 30					15 00					
Croy [3]	d	13a11			13 35		13a42			14 06		14a10			14 36		14a41			15 06		15a11			
Falkirk Grahamston [3]	d		13 38			13 46		14 10			14 16		14 40			14 48		15 10			15 18		15 40		
Camelon [4]	d		13a41			13 49		14a13			14 19		14a43			14 51		15a13			15 21		15a43		
Larbert	d				13 46	13 53				14 17	14 22				14 47	14 54				15 16	15 24				
Stirling	a				13 53	14 00			14 06	14 24	14 30				14 54	15 02			15 07	15 24	15 32				15 36
	d				13 55	14 01				14 25	14 31				14 55	15 02				15 24	15 32				15 37
Alloa	a									14 34										15 34					
Bridge of Allan	d				13 59	14 05					14 35				14 59	15 06					15 36				15 43
Dunblane	a				14 02	14 08					14 38				15 02	15 10					15 40				15 46

		SR	SR	SR	SR	SR	SR	SR	SR		SR	SR	SR	SR	SR	GR	SR	SR	SR		SR	SR	SR	SR	SR
				[1] A 🛒	B			[1] A 🛒	B		E			[1] A 🛒		[1] F	B				[1] A 🛒		B	◇ G	
Edinburgh [10]	d		15 20		15 35		15 48		16 03				16 20			16 34	16 37		16 49				17 05		
Haymarket	d		15 24		15 39		15 53		16 08				16 24			16 39	16 43		16 53				17 09		
Edinburgh Park	d		15 28		15 43		15 59		16 12				16 29				16 47		16 58				17 14		
Linlithgow	d				15 54				16 23								16 58						17 26		
Polmont [3]	d				15 58				16 28								17 03						17 31		
Glasgow Queen Street [10]	d	15 21		15 30		15 48		16 00			16 10	16 19		16 30	16 33			16 48			17 00	17 03		17 09	17 20
Bishopbriggs	d	15 26				15 54						16 25			16 38			16 55				17 08			17 26
Lenzie [3]	d	15 30				15 58						16 29			16 42			17 00				17 13			17 30
Croy [3]	d	15 36		15a41		16 04		16a10				16 35		16a41				17 05			17a10				17 36
Falkirk Grahamston [3]	d		15 47		16 10		16 16		16 37				16 48			17 02			17 19						
Camelon [4]	d		15 50		16a13		16 19		16a40				16 51				17a13		17 22				17a40		
Larbert	d	15 47	15 53			16 15	16 22					16 46	16 54		16 58			17 16	17 25			17 29		17 34	17 47
Stirling	a	15 56	16 01			16 22	16 30				16 36	16 55	17 02		17 06	17 16		17 23	17 33			17 37		17 42	17 54
	d		16 01			16 23	16 30				16 37		17 02					17 24	17 33					17 45	17 55
Alloa	a					16 32												17 33							
Bridge of Allan	d		16 05				16 34				16 41		17 06						17 38					17 50	17 59
Dunblane	a		16 09				16 38				16 45		17 10						17 41					17 54	18 02

		SR	SR	SR	SR			SR	SR	SR	SR	SR	SR	SR	SR	SR		SR	SR	SR	SR	SR	SR	SR	SR
		[1] A 🛒	H	◇[1] C 🛒				B			[1] A 🛒	◇[1] D 🛒	B			[1] A 🛒		B	◇[1] C 🛒			[1] A 🛒	B	◇ G	
Edinburgh [10]	d				17 19			17 34		17 49			18 07		18 20			18 34			18 49		19 03		
Haymarket	d				17 23			17 38		17 54			18 12		18 24			18 38			18 53		19 08		
Edinburgh Park	d				17 28			17 43		18 00			18 18		18 28			18 42			18 57		19 12		
Linlithgow	d							17 53					18 29					18 54					19 24		
Polmont [3]	d							17 58					18 34					18 58					19 28		
Glasgow Queen Street [10]	d	17 30	17 33	17 40					17 53		18 00	18 06		18 20		18 30			18 41	18 51		19 00		19 07	19 21
Bishopbriggs	d		17 39						17 58					18 25						18 56					19 26
Lenzie [3]	d		17 44						18 02					18 29						19 00					19 30
Croy [3]	d	17a40							18 07		18a11			18 35		18a42				19 05		19a10			19 36
Falkirk Grahamston [3]	d		18a00		17 48					18 18					18 47						19 16				
Camelon [4]	d				17 51			18a13		18 21			18a43		18 50			19a13			19 19		19a43		
Larbert	d				17 54				18 18	18 24		18 29		18 47	18 55					19 16	19 22				19 47
Stirling	a			18 08	18 02				18 29	18 33		18 38		18 54	19 02				19 07	19 23	19 30			19 36	19 55
	d			18 09	18 10	18 13			18 33	18 34		18 40			19 03				19 08	19 24	19 31			19 37	
Alloa	a				18 20				18 42											19 33					
Bridge of Allan	d					18 19				18 38		18 44			19 07						19 35			19 41	
Dunblane	a			18 15		18 23				18 42		18 48			19 10				19 14		19 38			19 45	

		SR		SR	GR	SR	SR	SR	SR	SR	SR	SR		SR	SR	SR	SR	SR	SR	SR	SR	SR		SR	SR
				◇[1] C 🛒	[1] I	[1] A 🛒		[1] B	B	[1] B 🛒				[1] A		[1] B	◇[1] C		[1] A		[1] B			[1] A	
Edinburgh [10]	d	19 19			19 25			19 30	19 35	19 45	19 49	20 01				20 15		20 33			20 45	21 03			
Haymarket	d	19 23			19 30			19 34	19 39	19 49	19 54	20 07				20 20		20 37			20 49	21 07			
Edinburgh Park	d	19 28							19 43		20 00	20 11						20 41				21 11			
Linlithgow	d							19 49	19 54	20 03	20 16	20 22				20 33		20 52			21 02	21 23			
Polmont [3]	d								19 59	20 08	20 21	20 26				20 37		20 56			21 06	21 27			
Glasgow Queen Street [10]	d			19 38		19 45	19 50							20 15	20 19		20 40		20 45	20 50				21 15	21 21
Bishopbriggs	d						19 55								20 25					20 56					21 26
Lenzie [3]	d						19 59								20 29					21 00					21 30
Croy [3]	d					19a55	20 04	20a05		20a20				20a26	20 35	20a50			20a56	21 05	21a19			21a26	21 36
Falkirk Grahamston [3]	d	19 46			19 56						20 26	20 32						21 02				21 33			
Camelon [4]	d	19 49							20a11		20 29	20 35						21 05				21 36			
Larbert	d	19 53					20 15				20 33	20 38			20 45			21 08		21 16		21 39			21 47
Stirling	a	20 00		20 09	20 16		20 24				20 40	20 45			20 53		21 05	21 15		21 26		21 46			21 57
	d	20 01					20 25					20 46			20 53		21 06	21 16		21 27		21 47			
Alloa	a						20 34													21 36					
Bridge of Allan	d	20 05										20 50			20 57			21 20				21 51			
Dunblane	a	20 08										20 53			21 01		21 15	21 23				21 54			

A To Edinburgh
B To Glasgow Queen Street
C To Aberdeen
D To Inverness
E To Arbroath
F From London Kings Cross to Inverness
G To Dundee
H To Markinch
I From London Kings Cross

Table T230-F

Edinburgh, Glasgow Queen Street and Falkirk Grahamston - Stirling, Alloa and Dunblane

Mondays to Fridays
16 December to 15 May

		SR	SR	SR		SR	SR	SR	SR	SR	SR	SR	SR	SR		SR	SR	SR	SR	SR	SR	SR	SR	SR	
		[1] A	◇[1] B			[1] C		[1] A		[1] C		[1] A		[1] C			[1] A	◇ D		[1] C		[1] A	◇ E		
Edinburgh [10]	d	21 15		21 33				21 45	22 01			22 15	22 33				22 45		23 03			23 15		23 33	
Haymarket	d	21 22		21 37				21 49	22 07			22 20	22 37				22 49		23 07			23 21		23 37	
Edinburgh Park	d			21 41					22 11				22 43						23 12					23 41	
Linlithgow	d	21 35		21 52				22 02	22 22			22 33	22 54				23 06		23 23			23 34		23 52	
Polmont [3]	d	21 40		21 56				22 06	22 26			22 38	22 58				23 10		23 27			23 39		23 56	
Glasgow Queen Street [10]	d		21 40			21 45	21 51			22 15	22 20			22 45		22 51		23 09		23 15	23 20		23 38		
Bishopbriggs	d						21 57				22 26					22 56					23 25				
Lenzie [3]	d						22 01				22 30					23 00					23 29				
Croy [3]	d	21a53				21a57	22 06	22a19		22a26	22 36	22a51		22a55		23 05	23a23			23a25	23 35	23a53			
Falkirk Grahamston [3]	d			22 02					22 32				23 04						23 33					00 02	
Camelon [4]	d			22 05					22 35				23 07						23 36					00 05	
Larbert	d			22 08			22 17		22 38		22 47		23 10			23 16		23 29	23 39		23 47			00 12	
Stirling	a		22 07	22 15			22 26		22 46		22 56		23 18			23 23		23 37	23 47		23 55		00 05	00 20	
	d			22 16			22 27		22 47				23 19			23 25		23 38	23 47		23 57		00 06	00 21	
Alloa	a						22 36									23 35					00 06				
Bridge of Allan	d			22 20					22 51				23 23					23 42	23 51				00 11	00 25	
Dunblane	a			22 23					22 54				23 26					23 46	23 55				00 15	00 28	

		SR	SR	SR
		[1] C		[1] A
Edinburgh [10]	d			23 45
Haymarket	d			23 49
Edinburgh Park	d			
Linlithgow	d			00 02
Polmont [3]	d			00 07
Glasgow Queen Street [10]	d	23 45	23 51	
Bishopbriggs	d		23 57	
Lenzie [3]	d		00 02	
Croy [3]	d	23a55	00 07	00a21
Falkirk Grahamston [3]	d			
Camelon [4]	d			
Larbert	d		00 18	
Stirling	a		00 25	
	d			
Alloa	a			
Bridge of Allan	d			
Dunblane	a			

Saturdays
21 December to 16 May

		SR	SR	SR	SR	SR	SR	SR	SR	SR		SR	SR	SR	SR	SR	SR	SR	SR	SR		SR	SR	SR	SR
		◇ F	G	H	[1] I	A		A	◇[1] B 🛒				[1] A	A		[1] C	[1] A	A				[1] C 🛒	A	◇[1] J 🛒	
Edinburgh [10]	d					05 03	05 18	05 33		05 49			06 00	06 04	06 18		06 30	06 33		06 48			07 03		
Haymarket	d					05 07	05 23	05 37		05 53			06 04	06 08	06 23		06 34	06 37		06 52			07 07		
Edinburgh Park	d					05 11	05 27	05 42		05 57				06 12	06 27			06 42		06 57			07 12		
Linlithgow	d				00 02	05 22		05 52					06 17	06 23			06 47	06 53					07 23		
Polmont [3]	d				00 07	05 26		05 57					06 21	06 27			06 51	06 58					07 27		
Glasgow Queen Street [10]	d								05 53			06 19				06 30			06 50			07 00		07 07	07 20
Bishopbriggs	d											06 24							06 55						07 27
Lenzie [3]	d			00 02								06 28				06 38			06 59			07a07			07 32
Croy [3]	d			00 07	00a21							06 33	06a34			06a43	07a04		07 04						07 37
Falkirk Grahamston [3]	d		00 02			05 34	05 45	06 08		06 15				06 35	06 46			07 05		07 15			07 33		
Camelon [4]	d		00 05			05a37	05 48	06a11		06 18				06a38	06 49			07a08		07 18			07a36		
Larbert	d		00 12	00 18			05 51		06 14	06 21		06 46			06 52				07 16	07 21					07 48
Stirling	a		00 20	00 25			05 59		06 22	06 29		06 55			07 00				07 23	07 29				07 33	07 55
	d	00 06	00 21				06 00		06 23	06 30					07 01				07 24	07 29				07 35	07 56
Alloa	a																		07 34						
Bridge of Allan	d	00 11	00 25				06 04			06 34					07 05					07 33					08 00
Dunblane	a	00 15	00 28				06 08		06 30	06 37					07 09					07 37				07 41	08 03

		SR	SR	SR	SR	SR		SR	SR	SR	SR	SR	SR	SR	SR	SR		SR	SR	SR	SR	SR	SR	SR	SR
		[1] C 🛒	[1] A 🛒		[1] A 🛒	A		◇[1] B 🛒		[1] A 🛒		[1] C 🛒	[1] A 🛒	A	◇ D				[1] C 🛒	A	◇[1] B 🛒			[1] C 🛒	A
Edinburgh [10]	d		07 15	07 22	07 30	07 33				07 45	07 54		08 00	08 05				08 18		08 35			08 51		09 07
Haymarket	d		07 19	07 27	07 35	07 38				07 49	07 58		08 05	08 09				08 22		08 40			08 55		09 12
Edinburgh Park	d			07 33		07 43					08 04			08 13				08 28		08 45			09 02		09 16
Linlithgow	d		07 32		07 48	07 55				08 02				08 24						08 55					09 27
Polmont [3]	d				07 53	07 59							08 23	08 29						09 00					09 31
Glasgow Queen Street [10]	d	07 30						07 41	07 50			08 00			08 10	08 21			08 30		08 41	08 50		09 00	
Bishopbriggs	d								07 55							08 28						08 57			
Lenzie [3]	d								07 59	08a22						08 32						09 01			
Croy [3]	d	07a42	07a48		08a05				08 05			08a10	08a36			08 38			08a42			09 06		09a10	
Falkirk Grahamston [3]	d					08 05					08 22			08 40				08 47		09 10			09 20		09 37
Camelon [4]	d			07 53		08a08					08 25			08a43				08 50		09a13			09 23		09a40
Larbert	d			07 56					08 15		08 28					08 49		08 57				09 17	09 26		
Stirling	a			08 03					08 28		08 35				08 40	08 56		09 04			09 09	09 25	09 34		
	d			08 04				08u09	08 29		08 36				08 41			09 05				09 26	09 34		
Alloa	a								08 38													09 35			
Bridge of Allan	d			08 08							08 40				08 45			09 09					09 38		
Dunblane	a			08 11				08 17			08 43				08 49			09 12					09 41		

A To Glasgow Queen Street
B To Aberdeen
C To Edinburgh
E To Perth
F From Glasgow Queen Street to Perth
G From Edinburgh
I From Edinburgh to Glasgow Queen Street
J To Inverness

Edinburgh, Glasgow Queen Street and Falkirk Grahamston - Stirling, Alloa and Dunblane

		SR	SR	SR	SR	SR	SR	SR	SR	SR	SR	SR	SR	SR	SR	SR	SR	SR	SR	SR	SR	SR	SR
		◇			1		◇1			1		◇1			1		◇1			1			
		A			B	C	D			B	C	E			B	C	D			B	C		
					🍴		🍴			🍴		🍴			🍴		🍴			🍴			
Edinburgh 10	d			09 19		09 33			09 49		10 04			10 20		10 34			10 49		11 05		11 23
Haymarket	d			09 23		09 38			09 53		10 08			10 24		10 38			10 53		11 09		11 27
Edinburgh Park	d			09 28		09 43			09 57		10 13			10 29		10 44			10 58		11 13		11 34
Linlithgow	d					09 53					10 24					10 55					11 25		
Polmont 3	d					09 58					10 29					10 59					11 30		
Glasgow Queen Street 10	d	09 07	09 22		09 30		09 40	09 50		10 00		10 08	10 21		10 30		10 39	10 51		11 00		11 22	
Bishopbriggs	d		09 27					09 57					10 26					10 57				11 27	
Lenzie 3	d		09 31					10 01					10 30					11 01				11 31	
Croy 3	d		09 37		09a41			10 07		10a11			10 36		10a41			11 06		11a10		11 37	
Falkirk Grahamston 3	d			09 48		10 10			10 15		10 40			10 47		11 10			11 18		11 37		11 51
Camelon 4	d			09 51		10a13			10 18		10a43			10 50		11a13			11 21		11a40		11 54
Larbert	d		09 48	09 54				10 17	10 22				10 47	10 53				11 17	11 25			11 48	11 59
Stirling	a	09 38	09 55	10 02			10 07	10 25	10 29			10 36	10 55	11 01			11 06	11 24	11 32			11 55	12 06
	d	09 39		10 02				10 26	10 30			10 36		11 01				11 25	11 33			11 56	12 07
Alloa	a							10 35										11 34					
Bridge of Allan	d			10 06					10 34			10 41		11 05					11 37			12 00	12 11
Dunblane	a	09 46		10 10					10 38			10 45		11 09					11 40			12 03	12 14

		SR	SR	SR	SR	SR	SR	SR	SR	SR	SR	SR	SR	SR	SR	SR	SR	SR	SR	SR	SR	SR
		1		◇1			1		◇1			1		◇1			1				1	
		B	C	D			B	C	E			B	C	D			B	C			B	C
		🍴		🍴			🍴		🍴			🍴		🍴			🍴				🍴	
Edinburgh 10	d		11 33			11 48		12 03			12 19		12 34			12 49		13 03		13 20		13 34
Haymarket	d		11 38			11 54		12 08			12 23		12 38			12 53		13 08		13 24		13 38
Edinburgh Park	d		11 43			11 58		12 12			12 28		12 42			12 58		13 12		13 28		13 43
Linlithgow	d		11 54					12 25					12 53					13 24				13 55
Polmont 3	d		11 59					12 30					12 58					13 28				13 59
Glasgow Queen Street 10	d	11 30		11 38	11 51		12 00		12 07	12 21		12 30		12 40	12 48		13 00		13 19		13 30	
Bishopbriggs	d				11 56					12 26					12 55				13 25			
Lenzie 3	d				12 00					12 30					13 00				13 29			
Croy 3	d	11a42			12 06		12a11			12 36		12a42			13 05		13a10		13 35		13a40	
Falkirk Grahamston 3	d		12 10			12 16		12 40			12 47		13 10			13 16		13 38		13 46		14 10
Camelon 4	d		12a13			12 19		12a43			12 50		13a13			13 19		13a41		13 49		14a13
Larbert	d				12 17	12 22				12 47	12 53				13 16	13 23			13 46	13 53		
Stirling	a			12 11	12 24	12 29			12 34	12 55	13 01			13 06	13 24	13 30			13 53	14 00		
	d				12 25	12 30			12 35		13 01				13 25	13 31			13 55	14 01		
Alloa	a				12 34										13 35							
Bridge of Allan	d					12 34			12 41		13 05					13 35			13 59	14 05		
Dunblane	a					12 37			12 44		13 09					13 39			14 02	14 08		

		SR	SR	SR	SR	SR	SR	SR	SR	SR	SR	SR	SR	SR	SR	SR	SR	SR	SR	SR	SR	SR	SR
		◇1			1				1		◇1			1		◇1			1				1
		D			B	C			B	C	E			B	C	E			B	C			B
		🍴			🍴				🍴		🍴			🍴		🍴			🍴				🍴
Edinburgh 10	d			13 49		14 04		14 18		14 33			14 48		15 05			15 19		15 34		15 48	
Haymarket	d			13 53		14 11		14 22		14 38			14 52		15 09			15 23		15 38		15 52	
Edinburgh Park	d			13 57		14 15		14 28		14 43			14 57		15 13			15 28		15 43		15 58	
Linlithgow	d					14 26				14 57					15 24					15 54			
Polmont 3	d					14 30				15 02					15 28					15 58			
Glasgow Queen Street 10	d	13 39	13 53		14 00		14 20		14 30		14 39	14 51		15 00		15 08	15 21		15 30		15 50		16 00
Bishopbriggs	d		13 58				14 26					14 56					15 26				15 55		
Lenzie 3	d		14 02				14 30					15 00					15 30				15 59		
Croy 3	d		14 07		14a11		14 36		14a41			15 06		15a10			15 36		15a40		16 04		16a10
Falkirk Grahamston 3	d			14 15		14 40		14 46		15 10			15 16		15 40			15 46		16 11		16 16	
Camelon 4	d			14 18		14a43		14 49		15a13			15 19		15a43			15 49		16a14		16 19	
Larbert	d		14 18	14 23			14 47	14 53				15 16	15 22				15 47	15 52			16 15	16 22	
Stirling	a	14 07	14 25	14 30			14 54	15 00			15 07	15 24	15 30			15 36	15 56	16 00			16 22	16 30	
	d		14 26	14 31			14 55	15 01				15 24	15 31			15 37		16 01			16 23	16 30	
Alloa	a		14 35									15 34									16 32		
Bridge of Allan	d			14 35			14 59	15 05					15 35			15 42		16 05				16 34	
Dunblane	a			14 38			15 02	15 09					15 38			15 46		16 08				16 38	

		SR	SR	SR	SR	SR	SR	GR	SR	SR	SR	SR	SR	SR	SR	SR	SR	SR	SR	SR	SR	SR	SR
						1	◇1	1				1		◇			1		◇1			1	
		C	F			B	D	G	C			B	C	A			B	C	D			B	C
						🍴	🍴	🛏				🍴					🍴		🍴			🍴	
Edinburgh 10	d	16 04			16 21			16 34	16 37		16 49		17 03			17 20		17 33			17 48		18 05
Haymarket	d	16 08			16 25			16 39	16 43		16 54		17 08			17 24		17 38			17 53		18 09
Edinburgh Park	d	16 12			16 29				16 48		16 59		17 13			17 28		17 42			17 58		18 13
Linlithgow	d	16 23							16 59				17 25					17 53					18 24
Polmont 3	d	16 28							17 03				17 29					17 57					18 28
Glasgow Queen Street 10	d		16 10	16 19		16 30	16 42			16 51		17 00		17 09	17 21		17 30		17 40	17 53		18 00	
Bishopbriggs	d			16 25						16 56					17 26					17 58			
Lenzie 3	d			16 29						17 00					17 30					18 02			
Croy 3	d			16 35		16a41				17 05		17a10			17 36		17a40			18 07		18a12	
Falkirk Grahamston 3	d	16 37			16 47			17 02	17 10		17 20		17 37			17 46		18 10			18 16		18 40
Camelon 4	d	16a40			16 50				17a13		17 23		17a40			17 49		18a13			18 19		18a43
Larbert	d			16 46	16 53					17 16	17 26			17 34	17 47	17 53				18 18	18 23		
Stirling	a		16 36	16 55	17 01		17 12	17 16		17 23	17 34			17 42	17 54	18 00			18 12	18 25	18 30		
	d		16 37		17 01					17 24	17 34			17 45	17 55	18 06			18 13	18 28	18 31		
Alloa	a									17 33						18 15				18 37			
Bridge of Allan	d		16 41		17 05						17 39			17 50	17 59						18 35		
Dunblane	a		16 45		17 09						17 42			17 54	18 02				18 19		18 39		

A To Dundee
B To Edinburgh
C To Glasgow Queen Street
D To Aberdeen
E To Inverness
F To Arbroath
G From London Kings Cross to Inverness

Edinburgh, Glasgow Queen Street and Falkirk Grahamston - Stirling, Alloa and Dunblane

		SR	SR	SR	SR	SR	SR	SR	SR	SR	SR	SR	SR	SR	SR	SR	SR	SR	SR	SR	SR	SR	SR
		◇1			1		◇1			1		◇			◇1	1	1			1			1
		A			B	C	D			B	C	E			D	B	C	C		C			B
		🍴			🍴		🍴			🍴					🍴	🍴				🍴			
Edinburgh 10	d			18 21		18 34			18 49		19 03			19 19			19 30	19 33		19 45	19 48	20 03	
Haymarket	d			18 25		18 39			18 53		19 08			19 24			19 34	19 37		19 49	19 54	20 07	
Edinburgh Park	d			18 29		18 43			18 58		19 14			19 28				19 42			19 58	20 11	
Linlithgow	d					18 54					19 24						19 49	19 55		20 01	20 09	20 22	
Polmont 3	d					18 58					19 29							19 59		20 06	20 14	20 26	
Glasgow Queen Street 10	d	18 09	18 20		18 30		18 39	18 51		19 00		19 07	19 21		19 38	19 45			19 51				20 15
Bishopbriggs	d		18 26					18 56					19 26						19 56				
Lenzie 3	d		18 30					19 00					19 30						20 00				
Croy 3	d		18 36		18a41			19 05		19a10			19 36			19a55	20a05		20 05	20a19			20a26
Falkirk Grahamston 3	d			18 47		19 10			19 16		19 40			19 47				20 07			20 19	20 32	
Camelon 4	d			18 50		19a13			19 19		19a43			19 50				20a10			20 22	20 35	
Larbert	d	18 29	18 47	18 55				19 16	19 23				19 47	19 53					20 16		20 29	20 38	
Stirling	a	18 38	18 54	19 02			19 07	19 23	19 30			19 36	19 54	20 01	20 09				20 23		20 37	20 45	
	d	18 40		19 03			19 08	19 24	19 31			19 37		20 01					20 24			20 46	
Alloa	a							19 33											20 33				
Bridge of Allan	d	18 44		19 07					19 35			19 41		20 05								20 50	
Dunblane	a	18 48		19 10			19 14		19 38			19 45		20 09								20 53	

		SR	SR	SR	SR	SR	SR	SR	SR	SR	SR	SR	SR	SR	SR	SR	SR	SR	SR	SR	SR	SR
			1	◇1		1		1		1		1	◇1		1		1		1		1	
			C	D		B		C		B		C	D		B		C		B		C	
Edinburgh 10	d		20 15		20 33			20 45	21 03			21 15		21 33			21 45	22 03			22 15	22 33
Haymarket	d		20 21		20 37			20 50	21 07			21 20		21 37			21 49	22 07			22 19	22 37
Edinburgh Park	d				20 41				21 11					21 41				22 11				22 43
Linlithgow	d		20 34		20 52			21 03	21 22			21 33		21 52			22 02	22 22			22 32	22 54
Polmont 3	d		20 39		20 56			21 07	21 26			21 38		21 56			22 06	22 26			22 36	22 58
Glasgow Queen Street 10	d	20 18		20 39		20 45	20 51			21 15	21 20		21 41		21 45	21 51			22 15	22 22		
Bishopbriggs	d	20 25					20 56				21 25					21 57				22 27		
Lenzie 3	d	20 29					21 00				21 29					22 01				22 31		
Croy 3	d	20 35	20a52			20a57	21 05	21a20		21a26	21 35	21a51			21a57	22 06	22a19		22a26	22 37	22a49	
Falkirk Grahamston 3	d				21 02				21 32					22 02				22 32				23 04
Camelon 4	d				21 05				21 35					22 05				22 35				23 07
Larbert	d	20 45			21 08		21 16		21 38		21 46			22 08		22 17		22 38		22 48		23 10
Stirling	a	20 53		21 05	21 15		21 26		21 45		21 57		22 07	22 15		22 26		22 46		22 58		23 18
	d	20 53		21 06	21 16		21 27		21 46					22 16		22 27		22 47				23 19
Alloa	a						21 36									22 36						
Bridge of Allan	d	20 57			21 20				21 50					22 20				22 51				23 23
Dunblane	a	21 01		21 15	21 23				21 53					22 23				22 54				23 26

		SR	SR	SR	SR	SR	SR	SR	SR	SR	SR	SR	SR	SR
		1		1	◇		1		1	◇		1		1
		B		C	F		B		C	F		B		C
Edinburgh 10	d			22 45		23 03			23 15		23 33			23 45
Haymarket	d			22 49		23 07			23 20		23 37			23 49
Edinburgh Park	d					23 12					23 41			
Linlithgow	d			23 06		23 23			23 33		23 52			00 02
Polmont 3	d			23 10		23 27			23 37		23 56			00 07
Glasgow Queen Street 10	d	22 45	22 51		23 09		23 15	23 19		23 37		23 45	23 50	
Bishopbriggs	d		22 56					23 25					23 57	
Lenzie 3	d		23 00					23 29					00 02	
Croy 3	d	22a55	23 05	23a23			23a25	23 35	23a50			23a55	00 07	00a21
Falkirk Grahamston 3	d					23 33					00 02			
Camelon 4	d					23 36					00 05			
Larbert	d		23 17		23 29	23 39		23 46			00 12		00 17	
Stirling	a		23 27		23 37	23 47		23 55		00 05	00 20		00 25	
	d		23 27		23 38	23 47		23 57		00 06	00 21			
Alloa	a		23 37					00 06						
Bridge of Allan	d				23 42	23 51				00 11	00 25			
Dunblane	a				23 46	23 55				00 15	00 28			

Sundays

15 December to 10 May

		SR	SR	SR	SR	SR	SR	SR	SR	SR	SR	SR	SR	SR	SR	SR	SR	SR	SR	SR	SR	SR	SR
		◇			1	1	1	1	1	1	1	1	1	◇1		1		1	1	1	◇1		1
		G	H	I	J	B	B	C	C	B	B	C	C	D		B		C	B	C	D		B
							🍴		🍴	🍴	🍴			🍴		🍴		🍴	🍴	🍴	🍴		🍴
Edinburgh 10	d							08 00	08 30			09 00	09 30		09 35			10 00		10 30		10 35	
Haymarket	d							08 04	08 34			09 04	09 34		09 39			10 04		10 34		10 39	
Edinburgh Park	d														09 43							10 43	
Linlithgow	d				00 02			08 24	08 54			09 23	09 52		09 59			10 22		10 47		10 54	
Polmont 3	d				00 07			08 29				09 28			10 03			10 27				10 58	
Glasgow Queen Street 10	d					07 56	08 30			09 00	09 30			09 37		10 00	10 15		10 30		10 45		11 00
Bishopbriggs	d																10 20						
Lenzie 3	d			00 02										09 46			10 24						
Croy 3	d			00 07	00a21	08a06	08a40	08a41	09a09	09a10	09a40	09a41	10a08			10a11	10 30	10a40	10a40	11a02			11a10
Falkirk Grahamston 3	d		00 02												10 09							11 04	
Camelon 4	d		00 05												10 12							11 07	
Larbert	d		00 12	00 17										10 02	10 15		10 40					11 10	
Stirling	a		00 20	00 25										10 10	10 23		10 53				11 11	11 18	
	d	00 06	00 21											10 11	10 23		10 54				11 11	11 18	
Alloa	a																11 03						
Bridge of Allan	d	00 11	00 25												10 27							11 22	
Dunblane	a	00 15	00 28											10 17	10 31						11 17	11 26	

A To Inverness
B To Edinburgh
C To Glasgow Queen Street
D To Aberdeen
E To Dundee
F To Perth
G not 15 December. From Glasgow Queen Street to Perth
H not 15 December. From Edinburgh
I not 15 December. From Glasgow Queen Street
J not 15 December. From Edinburgh to Glasgow Queen Street

Table T230-F

Sundays
15 December to 10 May

Edinburgh, Glasgow Queen Street and Falkirk Grahamston - Stirling, Alloa and Dunblane

		SR ◇1 A		SR	SR 1 B	SR	SR 1 C	SR 1 B	SR ◇1 D	SR	SR 1 C	SR		SR 1 B	SR	SR 1 C	SR 1 B	SR ◇1 D	SR	SR 1 C	SR	SR 1 B		SR	SR 1 C
Edinburgh	d				11 00	11 07		11 30		11 34				12 00	12 06		12 30		12 36			13 00		13 05	
Haymarket	d				11 04	11 11		11 34		11 38				12 06	12 11		12 34		12 40			13 04		13 09	
Edinburgh Park	d					11 15				11 44					12 15				12 44					13 13	
Linlithgow	d				11 17	11 26		11 47		11 56				12 19	12 26		12 47		12 56			13 17		13 24	
Polmont	d				11 22	11 30				12 00				12 23	12 30				13 01			13 21		13 28	
Glasgow Queen Street	d	11 11		11 15			11 30		11 45		12 00	12 15				12 30		12 43		13 00	13 15				13 30
Bishopbriggs	d			11 20								12 20									13 20				
Lenzie	d			11 24								12 24									13 24				
Croy	d			11 30	11a35		11a40	12a03			12a10	12 30		12a36		12a40	13a05			13a10	13 30	13a34			13a40
Falkirk Grahamston	d					11 36				12 06					12 36				13 06					13 34	
Camelon	d					11 39				12 09					12 39				13 09					13 37	
Larbert	d	11 32		11 40		11 44				12 12		12 40			12 44				13 13		13 40			13 44	
Stirling	a	11 40		11 48		11 54			12 11	12 20		12 51			12 55			13 09	13 20		13 48			13 54	
	d	11 41		11 49					12 11	12 20		12 52						13 10	13 21		13 49				
Alloa	a			11 58								13 01									13 58				
Bridge of Allan	d									12 24									13 25						
Dunblane	a	11 47							12 17	12 28								13 16	13 28						

		SR 1 B	SR ◇1 D	SR	SR 1 C	SR	SR 1 B	SR		SR 1 C	SR 1 B	SR ◇1 E	SR ◇1 D	SR	SR 1 C	SR	SR 1 B	SR		SR 1 C	SR 1 B	SR ◇1 D	SR	SR 1 C	SR
Edinburgh	d	13 30		13 37			14 00	14 06			14 30			14 36			15 00	15 06			15 30		15 36		
Haymarket	d	13 34		13 41			14 04	14 10			14 34			14 41			15 04	15 10			15 34		15 40		
Edinburgh Park	d			13 45				14 14						14 45				15 14					15 44		
Linlithgow	d	13 47		13 56			14 17	14 26			14 47			14 56			15 17	15 26			15 47		15 55		
Polmont	d			14 00			14 21	14 30						15 00			15 21	15 30					16 00		
Glasgow Queen Street	d		13 45		14 00	14 15				14 30		14 38	14 50		15 00	15 15				15 30		15 45		16 00	16 15
Bishopbriggs	d					14 20										15 20									16 20
Lenzie	d					14 24										15 24									16 24
Croy	d	14a02			14a10	14 30	14a34			14a40	15a02				15a10	15 30	15a34			15a40	16a04			16a10	16 30
Falkirk Grahamston	d			14 06				14 36						15 06				15 36					16 05		
Camelon	d			14 09				14 39						15 09				15 42					16 08		
Larbert	d			14 12		14 40		14 44				14 59		15 14		15 40		15 47					16 12		16 40
Stirling	a		14 11	14 20		14 48		14 54				15 07	15 16	15 22		15 48		15 54				16 11	16 19		16 48
	d		14 12	14 20		14 49						15 08	15 17	15 22		15 49						16 12	16 20		16 49
Alloa	a					14 58										15 58									16 58
Bridge of Allan	d			14 24										15 26									16 24		
Dunblane	a		14 18	14 28								15 14	15 23	15 30								16 18	16 27		

		SR 1 B	SR	SR 1 C		SR 1 B	SR ◇1 D	GR 1 F	SR	SR 1 C	SR	SR 1 B	SR	SR 1 C		SR 1 B	SR ◇1 D	SR	SR 1 C	SR ◇1 E	SR	SR 1 B	SR G	SR 1 C
Edinburgh	d	16 00	16 06			16 30		16 32	16 36			17 00	17 04			17 30		17 35				18 00	18 06	
Haymarket	d	16 04	16 10			16 34		16 37	16 41			17 05	17 09			17 34		17 39				18 04	18 11	
Edinburgh Park	d		16 14						16 46				17 14					17 43					18 16	
Linlithgow	d	16 17	16 26			16 47			16 58			17 17	17 26			17 47		17 54				18 17	18 28	
Polmont	d	16 21	16 30						17 03			17 22	17 32					17 58				18 21	18 33	
Glasgow Queen Street	d			16 30			16 45			17 00	17 15			17 30			17 45		18 00	18 11	18 16			18 30
Bishopbriggs	d										17 20										18 21			
Lenzie	d										17 24										18 25			
Croy	d	16a35		16a40		17a04				17a10	17 30	17a35		17a40		18a03			18a10		18 31	18a35		18a40
Falkirk Grahamston	d		16 36					17 02	17 10				17 38					18 04					18 40	
Camelon	d		16 39						17 13				17 41					18 07					18 43	
Larbert	d		16 44						17 17		17 40		17 44					18 10		18 31	18 41		18 50	
Stirling	a		16 54				17 11	17 16	17 25		17 48		17 52				18 12	18 18		18 40	18 49		18 59	
	d								17 26		17 49							18 18		18 41	18 50		19 03	
Alloa	a										17 58										18 59			
Bridge of Allan	d								17 30									18 22					19 08	
Dunblane	a								17 33									18 26		18 47			19 12	

		SR 1 B	SR	SR 1 C	SR	SR 1 B	SR 1 C	SR 1 B	SR ◇1 D	SR		SR 1 C	SR	SR 1 B	SR 1 C	SR 1 B	SR	SR 1 C	SR	SR 1 B		SR 1 C	SR 1 B	SR ◇1 D	SR
Edinburgh	d	18 30	18 35			19 00		19 30		19 36				20 00		20 30	20 35			21 00			21 30		21 35
Haymarket	d	18 34	18 39			19 04		19 34		19 40				20 04		20 34	20 39			21 04			21 34		21 39
Edinburgh Park	d		18 43							19 44							20 43								21 43
Linlithgow	d	18 47	18 54			19 17		19 47		19 55				20 17		20 47	20 54			21 17			21 47		21 54
Polmont	d		18 58			19 21				19 59				20 22			20 58			21 21					21 58
Glasgow Queen Street	d			19 00	19 15		19 30		19 44			20 00	20 15		20 30			21 00	21 15			21 30		21 44	
Bishopbriggs	d				19 20								20 20						21 20						
Lenzie	d				19 24								20 24						21 25						
Croy	d	19a02		19a10	19 30	19a35	19a40	20a03				20a10	20 30	20a35	20a40	21a02		21a10	21 30	21a35		21a40	22a02		
Falkirk Grahamston	d		19 04							20 05							21 04								22 04
Camelon	d		19 07							20 08							21 07								22 07
Larbert	d		19 10		19 40					20 11			20 40				21 10		21 41						22 10
Stirling	a		19 18		19 48				20 10	20 19			20 48				21 18		21 48					22 10	22 18
	d		19 18		19 49				20 11	20 19			20 49				21 18		21 49					22 11	22 18
Alloa	a				19 58								20 58						21 59						
Bridge of Allan	d		19 22							20 23							21 22								22 22
Dunblane	a		19 26						20 17	20 27							21 26							22 17	22 26

A To Inverness
B To Glasgow Queen Street
C To Edinburgh
D To Aberdeen
E To Elgin
F From London Kings Cross to Inverness. The Highland Chieftain
G To Perth

Table T230-F

Sundays
15 December to 10 May

Edinburgh, Glasgow Queen Street and Falkirk Grahamston - Stirling, Alloa and Dunblane

		SR 1 A	SR	SR 1 B		SR 1 A	SR 1 B	SR ◇ C	SR 1 A	SR 1 B	SR 1 A	SR ◇ C	SR 1 B
Edinburgh	d			22 00			22 30	22 35		23 00			23 30
Haymarket	d			22 04			22 34	22 41		23 04			23 34
Edinburgh Park	d							22 45					
Linlithgow	d			22 17			22 47	22 58		23 16			23 46
Polmont	d			22 21				23 03		23 21			23 51
Glasgow Queen Street	d	22 00	22 15			22 30			23 00		23 30	23 44	
Bishopbriggs	d		22 20									23 50	
Lenzie	d		22 24									23 54	
Croy	d	22a10	22 30	22a35		22a40	23a02		23a10	23a34	23a40	23 59	00a04
Falkirk Grahamston	d							23 10					
Camelon	d							23 14					
Larbert	d		22 40					23 19				00 11	
Stirling	a		22 48					23 28				00 19	
	d		22 49					23 28				00 20	
Alloa	a		22 58										
Bridge of Allan	d							23 33				00 24	
Dunblane	a							23 37				00 28	

A To Edinburgh
B To Glasgow Queen Street
C To Perth

MP Middleton Press New Title for Jan 2020

Table T230-R

Dunblane, Alloa and Stirling - Falkirk Grahamston, Glasgow Queen Street and Edinburgh

Mondays to Fridays

16 December to 15 May

Miles	Miles	Miles		SR MX	SR MO	SR MX	SR MX	GR	SR	SR	SR	SR	SR	SR	SR	SR	SR	SR	SR	SR	SR	SR
				1 A	1 A	1 B	1 A	1 C			◇ D	B	1 B		B	1 A	1 B			1 B	1 A	◇ E
0	0	—	**Dunblane** d						05 14		05 46			06 03					06 32			06 42
2	2	—	Bridge of Allan d						05 17		05 50			06 06					06 35			06 45
—	—	0	**Alloa** d															06 17				
5½	5½	6¾	**Stirling** a						05 21		05 54			06 10				06 26	06 39			06 49
—	—	—	d					05 26	05 42	05 49	05 54			06 11				06 26	06 41			06 50
13½	13½	14¾	Larbert d						05 50	05 57	06 03			06 19				06 34	06 49			
—	15	—	Camelon 4 d						05 53			06 04		06 22	06 32				06 52			
—	16½	—	**Falkirk Grahamston** 3 d					05 42	05 56			06 07		06 25	06 36				06 55			
24	—	25¼	Croy 3 d		00 04		00 21			06 10	06 15					06 34		06 44		06 55	07 04	
29¼	—	30½	Lenzie 3 d				00 27			06 15	06 21						06 38	06 49				
32¼	—	33½	Bishopbriggs d	00 03						06 19	06 26							06 53				
34½	—	35¾	**Glasgow Queen Street** 10 a	00 09	00 16		00 36			06 27	06 37					06 48		07 00			07 18	07 29
—	19½	—	Polmont 3 d			00 09			06 01			06 12	06 22		06 41		06 55					
—	24¼	—	Linlithgow d			00 14			06 07			06 18	06 27		06 47		07 01			07 11		
—	38	—	Edinburgh Park d						06 17			06 28		06 42	06 57				07 16			
—	40½	—	Haymarket d			00s27		06 13	06 22			06 34	06s42	06 48	07 02		07s18		07 21	07s24		
—	41¾	—	**Edinburgh** 10 225,242 a			00 34		06 17	06 26			06 38	06 49	06 53	07 07		07 23		07 26	07 29		

	SR	SR	SR	SR	SR	SR	SR	SR	SR	SR	SR	SR	SR	SR	SR	SR	SR	SR	SR	SR	SR	SR
	B	1 B ☕		1 A				1 B ☕	B	1 B ☕	1 A ☕	D		1 A ☕		◇1 F	1 B	B	1 B ☕	1 A ☕		
Dunblane d						07 02						07 30				07 44						07 58
Bridge of Allan d						07 05						07 33				07 48						08 01
Alloa d							07 13						07 31								07 53	
Stirling a						07 09	07 22					07 37	07 40			07 53					08 02	08 05
d			06 56		07 04	07 11	07 24					07 38	07 43		07 50	07 55					08 03	08 08
Larbert d			07 04		07 12	07 19	07 32					07 46	07 50		07 58	08 04					08 11	08 16
Camelon 4 d	07 05					07 22			07 33				07 54					08 05				08 20
Falkirk Grahamston 3 d	07 08					07 25			07 36				07 57					08 08				08 26
Croy 3 d			07 15	07 19	07 24		07 41			07 42	07 48	07 58		08 06	08 10				08 11		08 24	
Lenzie 3 d		07 08	07 20		07 29		07 47					08 05			08 16					08 24	08 30	
Bishopbriggs d			07 24		07 33		07 51					08 10			08 20						08 34	
Glasgow Queen Street 10 a			07 32	07 37	07 40		07 58				08 03	08 19		08 23	08 29	08 32				08 36	08 42	
Polmont 3 d	07 13	07 24						07 37	07 41								08 09	08 13	08 26			
Linlithgow d	07 18	07 29						07 43	07 47	07 58							08 14	08 19				
Edinburgh Park d	07 29					07 43			07 57				08 14					08 29				08 43
Haymarket d	07 36	07s46				07 51		07s58	08 02	08s12			08 21				08s28	08 35	08s42			08 51
Edinburgh 10 225,242 a	07 41	07 55				07 58		08 03	08 08	08 18			08 31				08 35	08 42	08 48			08 58

	SR	SR	SR	SR	SR	SR	SR	SR	SR	SR	SR	SR	SR	SR	SR	SR	SR	SR	SR	SR	SR
	1 B ☕	B	1 A ☕	1 B ☕			◇1 F ☕	1 A ☕	1 B ☕	B	1 B ☕			1 A ☕	◇ G	1 B ☕	B	1 B ☕			◇1 H
Dunblane d					08 16	08 30							09 00		09 09					09 29	
Bridge of Allan d					08 19	08 33							09 03		09 12					09 32	
Alloa d												08 44									
Stirling a					08 24	08 37						08 53	09 07		09 16					09 36	
d					08 25	08 38	08 43					08 54	09 11		09 16				09 23	09 36	09 43
Larbert d					08 32	08 46						09 02	09 19						09 31	09 44	
Camelon 4 d		08 37				08 54				09 04			09 22				09 34			09 47	
Falkirk Grahamston 3 d		08 40				08 57				09 07			09 25				09 37			09 55	
Croy 3 d			08 41	08 42	08 44			09 06			09 11	09 12		09 31				09 40	09 42		
Lenzie 3 d					08 49							09 17							09 47		
Bishopbriggs d					08 53							09 21							09 51		
Glasgow Queen Street 10 a			08 53		08 59		09 11	09 18				09 30		09 43	09 49				09 58		10 10
Polmont 3 d		08 45							09 08	09 12						09 38	09 42				
Linlithgow d	08 40	08 51							09 13	09 18						09 43	09 48				
Edinburgh Park d		09 03				09 15				09 28			09 42				09 58			10 12	
Haymarket d	08s54	09 09		09s12		09 21			09s28	09 36	09s39		09 50			09s57	10 05	10s07		10 20	
Edinburgh 10 225,242 a	09 03	09 13		09 18		09 26			09 33	09 41	09 44		09 55			10 03	10 10	10 13		10 28	

A From Edinburgh
B From Glasgow Queen Street
C not 16 December. To London Kings Cross
D From Perth
E From Dundee
F From Aberdeen
G From Arbroath
H From Aberdeen. Forms booked connection out of 1B08.

Table T230-R

16 December to 15 May

Dunblane, Alloa and Stirling - Falkirk Grahamston, Glasgow Queen Street and Edinburgh

	SR	SR	SR	SR	SR	SR	SR	SR	SR	SR	SR	GR	SR	SR	SR	SR	SR	SR	SR	SR	SR	SR
	1 A ☕	1 B ☕	B	1 B ☕			1 A ☕	1 B ☕	B	1 B ☕		1 C		1 A ☕	◇1 D ☕	1 B ☕	B	1 B ☕			1 A ☕	
Dunblane d						10 02							10 32							11 02		
Bridge of Allan d						10 05							10 35							11 05		
Alloa d					09 44														10 44			
Stirling a					09 53	10 09							10 39						10 53	11 09		
d					09 54	10 11					10 24	10 34	10 41		10 48				10 54	11 11		11 24
Larbert d					10 02	10 19					10 32		10 49						11 02	11 19		11 32
Camelon 4 d			10 04			10 22			10 33				10 52				11 04			11 22		
Falkirk Grahamston 3 d			10 07			10 25			10 36			10 49	10 55				11 07			11 25		
Croy 3 d	10 04			10 10	10 12		10 31			10 40	10 41			11 02				11 10	11 12		11 31	11 41
Lenzie 3 d					10 17						10 47								11 17			11 46
Bishopbriggs d					10 21						10 51								11 21			11 50
Glasgow Queen Street 10 a	10 15				10 27		10 43				10 58			11 13	11 18				11 27		11 42	11 57
Polmont 3 d		10 07	10 12					10 37	10 41							11 07	11 12					
Linlithgow d		10 12	10 18					10 42	10 47							11 12	11 17					
Edinburgh Park d			10 28			10 42			10 57				11 14				11 27			11 42		
Haymarket d		10s29	10 35	10s38		10 50		10s56	11 05	11s07		11 17	11 21			11s26	11 34	11s37		11 49		
Edinburgh 10 225,242 a		10 36	10 41	10 44		10 58		11 04	11 10	11 12		11 21	11 26			11 31	11 40	11 43		11 53		

	SR	SR	SR	SR	SR	SR	SR	SR	SR	SR	SR	SR	SR	SR	SR	SR	SR	SR	SR	SR	SR
	◇1 E ☕	1 B ☕	B	1 B ☕		1 A ☕	◇1 D	1 B ☕	B	1 B ☕			1 A ☕		1 B ☕	B	1 B ☕		1 A ☕	◇1 D ☕	1 B ☕
Dunblane d	11 21				11 35							12 02		12 16				12 32			
Bridge of Allan d	11 26				11 38							12 05		12 19				12 35			
Alloa d											11 44										
Stirling a	11 31				11 42						11 53	12 09		12 23				12 39			
d	11 32				11 42		11 48				11 54	12 11		12 25				12 41		12 47	
Larbert d					11 50						12 02	12 19		12 33				12 49			
Camelon 4 d			11 33		11 53				12 04			12 22				12 34		12 52			
Falkirk Grahamston 3 d			11 36		11 56				12 07			12 25				12 37		12 55			
Croy 3 d				11 41		12 01				12 11	12 12		12 32	12 42			12 42		13 02		
Lenzie 3 d											12 17			12 47							
Bishopbriggs d											12 21			12 51							
Glasgow Queen Street 10 a	12 07					12 14	12 20				12 30		12 44	12 57					13 14	13 18	
Polmont 3 d		11 37	11 41					12 09	12 13						12 37	12 42					13 07
Linlithgow d		11 42	11 46					12 14	12 19						12 42	12 48					13 12
Edinburgh Park d			11 56		12 13				12 29			12 43				12 58		13 13			
Haymarket d		12s00	12 06	12s07	12 21			12s27	12 34	12s38		12 49			12s56	13 06	13s08	13 22			13s30
Edinburgh 10 225,242 a		12 05	12 12	12 15	12 27			12 34	12 40	12 43		12 53			13 04	13 11	13 14	13 27			13 36

	SR	SR	SR	SR	SR	SR	SR	SR	SR	SR	SR	SR	SR	SR	SR	SR	SR	SR	SR	SR	SR	SR
	B	1 B ☕			1 A ☕	◇ F		1 B ☕	B	1 B ☕		1 A ☕	◇1 D ☕	1 B ☕	B	1 B ☕			1 A ☕	1 B ☕	B	1 B ☕
Dunblane d				13 00		13 08					13 32							14 02				
Bridge of Allan d				13 03		13 12					13 35							14 05				
Alloa d			12 44														13 44					
Stirling a			12 53	13 07		13 16					13 39						13 53	14 09				
d			12 54	13 11		13 16	13 24				13 41		13 45				13 54	14 11				
Larbert d			13 02	13 19			13 32				13 49						14 02	14 19				
Camelon 4 d	13 04			13 22					13 34		13 52				14 04			14 22			14 34	
Falkirk Grahamston 3 d	13 07			13 25					13 37		13 55				14 07			14 25			14 37	
Croy 3 d		13 11	13 12		13 34		13 42			13 42		14 01				14 10	14 12		14 31			14 4
Lenzie 3 d			13 17				13 47										14 17					
Bishopbriggs d			13 21				13 51										14 21					
Glasgow Queen Street 10 a			13 29		13 45	13 55	13 58					14 12	14 18				14 27		14 43			
Polmont 3 d	13 12							13 37	13 42					14 07	14 12					14 37	14 42	
Linlithgow d	13 17							13 42	13 47					14 12	14 17					14 42	14 48	
Edinburgh Park d	13 27			13 42					14 01		14 13				14 27			14 44			14 58	
Haymarket d	13 35	13s38		13 50				14s04	14 08	14s12	14 21			14s30	14 34	14s37		14 52		14s57	15 06	15s1
Edinburgh 10 225,242 a	13 41	13 44		13 55				14 09	14 13	14 21	14 28			14 35	14 39	14 42		14 56		15 03	15 10	15 1

	SR	SR	SR	SR	SR	SR	SR	SR	SR	SR	SR	SR	SR	SR	SR	SR	SR	SR	SR	SR	SR
			1 A ☕	◇1 D ☕	1 B ☕	B	1 B ☕			1 A ☕	1 B ☕	B	1 B ☕			1 A ☕	◇1 D ☕	1 B ☕	B	1 B ☕	
Dunblane d	14 16	14 32							15 02					15 16	15 32						
Bridge of Allan d	14 19	14 35							15 05					15 19	15 35						
Alloa d								14 44													15 44
Stirling a	14 23	14 39						14 53	15 09					15 23	15 39						15 53
d	14 25	14 41		14 48				14 54	15 11					15 24	15 41		15 48				15 54
Larbert d	14 32	14 49						15 02	15 19					15 32	15 49						16 02
Camelon 4 d		14 52				15 04			15 22			15 34			15 52				16 04		
Falkirk Grahamston 3 d		14 55				15 07			15 25						15 55						
Croy 3 d	14 44		15 02				15 11	15 13		15 31			15 41	15 42		16 01				16 10	16 12
Lenzie 3 d	14 49							15 18						15 47							16 17
Bishopbriggs d	14 53							15 22						15 51							16 21
Glasgow Queen Street 10 a	14 59		15 14	15 18				15 28		15 43				15 57		16 13	16 18				16 31
Polmont 3 d					15 07	15 12					15 37	15 42						16 08	16 12		
Linlithgow d					15 12	15 17					15 42	15 47						16 13	16 18		
Edinburgh Park d		15 14				15 27			15 42			15 57			16 12				16 28		
Haymarket d		15 22			15s27	15 35	15s38		15 50		16s01	16 05	16s08		16 20			16s27	16 34	16s37	
Edinburgh 10 225,242 a		15 26			15 33	15 41	15 44		15 56		16 06	16 09	16 15		16 24			16 33	16 38	16 42	

A From Edinburgh
B From Glasgow Queen Street
C From Inverness to London Kings Cross. The Highland Chieftain
D From Aberdeen
E From Inverness
F From Dundee

Table T230-R

Mondays to Fridays

16 December to 15 May

Dunblane, Alloa and Stirling - Falkirk Grahamston, Glasgow Queen Street and Edinburgh

	SR	SR 1 A ✠	SR ◇ B	SR 1 C ✠	SR C	SR 1 C ✠	SR	SR	SR 1 A ✠	SR 1 C ✠	SR C	SR 1 C ✠	SR	SR	SR 1 A ✠	SR 1 C ✠	SR C	SR 1 C ✠	SR	SR ◇ 1 D ✠	SR	SR 1 A ✠
Dunblane d	16 00		16 07					16 32						16 58						17 25	17 33	
Bridge of Allan d	16 03		16 11					16 35						17 01						17 28	17 36	
Alloa d													16 44									
Stirling a	16 07		16 15					16 39					16 53	17 05						17 32	17 40	
d	16 11		16 15				16 24	16 40					16 54	17 07					17 24	17 33	17 41	
Larbert d	16 19						16 32	16 49					17 02	17 19					17 32		17 48	
Camelon 4 d	16 22				16 34			16 52			17 02			17 22			17 34				17 52	
Falkirk Grahamston 3 d	16 25							16 55						17 25							17 55	
Croy 3 d		16 31				16 41	16 42		17 01			17 11	17 12		17 32			17 41	17 42			18 01
Lenzie 3 d							16 47						17 18						17 48			18 06
Bishopbriggs d							16 51						17 22						17 52			
Glasgow Queen Street 10 ⇌ a		16 45	16 48				16 58		17 12				17 28		17 44				18 03	18 09		18 15
Polmont 3 d				16 37	16 42					17 10	17 14	17 24					17 42	17 54				
Linlithgow d				16 42	16 47					17 15	17 19					17 41	17 47	17 59				
Edinburgh Park ⇌ d	16 42				16 57			17 13			17 29			17 44			17 57				18 13	
Haymarket ⇌ d	16 50			16s57	17 06	17s09		17 20		17s28	17 36	17s40		17 52		17s54	18 09	18s12			18 20	
Edinburgh 10 225,242 a	16 55			17 03	17 11	17 14		17 25		17 33	17 40	17 45		17 57		17 59	18 13	18 18			18 26	

	SR ◇ 1 E ✠	SR 1 C ✠	SR C	SR 1 C ✠	SR	SR	SR 1 A ✠	SR	SR 1 C ✠	SR C	SR 1 C ✠	SR	SR ◇ 1 E ✠	SR 1 A ✠	SR 1 C ✠	SR C	SR 1 C ✠	SR	SR	SR 1 A	SR
Dunblane d	17 40					18 02		18 12					18 37						19 00		
Bridge of Allan d						18 05		18 15											19 03		
Alloa d					17 45							18 25						18 47			
Stirling a	17 45				17 54	18 09		18 19				18 34	18 42					18 56	19 07		
d	17 46				17 55	18 12		18 20				18 38	18 43					18 56	19 09		19 24
Larbert d					18 03	18 20		18 28				18 46						19 04	19 19		19 31
Camelon 4 d			18 06			18 23				18 34		18 54				19 04			19 22		
Falkirk Grahamston 3 d						18 26						18 57							19 25		
Croy 3 d				18 11	18 14		18 32	18 42			18 42			19 02			19 10	19 13		19 31	19 41
Lenzie 3 d					18 19			18 47										19 18			19 46
Bishopbriggs d					18 23			18 51										19 22			19 50
Glasgow Queen Street 10 ⇌ a	18 23				18 29		18 44	18 59					19 09	19 13				19 28		19 43	19 56
Polmont 3 d		18 10	18 14						18 37	18 42					19 07	19 12					
Linlithgow d		18 15	18 20						18 42	18 47					19 13	19 18					
Edinburgh Park ⇌ d			18 30			18 43				18 57		19 14				19 28			19 42		
Haymarket ⇌ d		18s31	18 35	18s38		18 52			18s57	19 07	19s09	19 19			19s29	19 38	19s40		19 51		
Edinburgh 10 225,242 a		18 37	18 40	18 43		18 57			19 02	19 12	19 15	19 25			19 34	19 42	19 46		19 55		

	SR 1 C	SR C	SR 1 C	SR	SR 1 C ✠	SR 1 A	SR ◇ 1 E ✠	SR	SR C	SR	SR 1 A ✠	SR ◇ 1 D ✠	SR 1 C	SR	SR	SR 1 A	SR ◇ 1 E ✠	SR 1 C	SR	SR	SR 1 A	SR 1 C
Dunblane d				19 34						19 59		20 06			20 33					21 04		
Bridge of Allan d				19 37						20 02		20 11			20 36					21 07		
Alloa d								19 44											20 44			
Stirling a				19 41				19 53		20 06		20 16			20 40				20 53	21 11		
d				19 41			19 49	19 55		20 11		20 17		20 24	20 41		20 46		20 54	21 11		
Larbert d				19 49				20 03		20 19				20 32	20 48				21 02	21 19		
Camelon 4 d		19 33		19 52					20 06	20 22					20 52					21 22		
Falkirk Grahamston 3 d				19 55					20 09	20 25					20 55					21 25		
Croy 3 d					19 56	20 05		20 12			20 21		20 26	20 41		20 50		20 57	21 11		21 19	21 26
Lenzie 3 d								20 17						20 47					21 17			
Bishopbriggs d								20 21						20 51					21 21			
Glasgow Queen Street 10 ⇌ a						20 17	20 26	20 29			20 32	20 45		20 57		21 02	21 15		21 27		21 31	
Polmont 3 d	19 37	19 42	19 54		20 09				20 14	20 30			20 39		21 00			21 10		21 30		21 39
Linlithgow d	19 42	19 47	19 59		20 14				20 20	20 36			20 44		21 05			21 15		21 36		21 44
Edinburgh Park ⇌ d		19 57		20 14					20 30	20 46					21 15					21 46		
Haymarket ⇌ d	20s00	20 04	20s15	20 22	20s29				20 35	20 53			20s57		21 23			21s28		21 51		21s57
Edinburgh 10 225,242 a	20 05	20 09	20 20	20 28	20 36				20 41	20 59			21 03		21 27			21 33		21 55		22 02

	SR	SR	SR 1 A	SR ◇ 1 E ✠	SR 1 C	SR 1 A	SR	SR	SR 1 C	SR	SR	SR 1 A	SR ◇ 1 E	SR 1 C	SR	SR 1 A	SR ◇ 1 D	SR 1 C	SR	SR	SR
Dunblane d	21 14	21 33						22 04			22 33						23 09		23 21		
Bridge of Allan d	21 17	21 36						22 07			22 36						23 13		23 24		
Alloa d							21 44								22 44						23 48
Stirling a	21 22	21 40					21 53	22 11			22 40				22 53		23 17		23 28		23 57
d	21 24	21 41		21 51			21 59	22 11		22 25	22 41		22 50		22 56		23 19		23 28	23 33	
Larbert d	21 32	21 49					22 07	22 19		22 32	22 49				23 04				23 36	23 40	
Camelon 4 d		21 52						22 22			22 52								23 39		
Falkirk Grahamston 3 d		21 55						22 25			22 55								23 42		
Croy 3 d	21 42		21 53		21 57	22 19	22 23		22 26	22 42		22 51		22 56	23 13	23 23		23 25		23 50	
Lenzie 3 d	21 47						22 28			22 47					23 18					23 55	
Bishopbriggs d	21 51						22 32			22 51					23 22					23 59	
Glasgow Queen Street 10 ⇌ a	21 57		22 06	22 21		22 31	22 39			22 57		23 02	23 21		23 29	23 36	23 57			00 06	
Polmont 3 d		22 00			22 10			22 30	22 39		23 00			23 09				23 38	23 47		
Linlithgow d		22 06			22 16			22 40	22 44		23 06			23 14				23 44	23 53		
Edinburgh Park ⇌ d		22 16						22 50			23 16								00 03		
Haymarket ⇌ d		22 22			22s29			22 58	23s01		23 21			23s29				23s57	00 08		
Edinburgh 10 225,242 a		22 26			22 34			23 05	23 09		23 25			23 34				00 04	00 12		

A From Edinburgh
B From Dundee
C From Glasgow Queen Street
D From Inverness
E From Aberdeen

Table T230-R

Mondays to Fridays

16 December to 15 May

Dunblane, Alloa and Stirling - Falkirk Grahamston, Glasgow Queen Street and Edinburgh

	SR 1 A	SR 1 B
Dunblane d		
Bridge of Allan d		
Alloa d		
Stirling a		
d		
Larbert d		
Camelon 4 d		
Falkirk Grahamston 3 d		
Croy 3 d	23 53	23 56
Lenzie 3 d	23 58	
Bishopbriggs d	00 03	
Glasgow Queen Street 10 ⇌ a	00 09	
Polmont 3 d		00 09
Linlithgow d		00 14
Edinburgh Park ⇌ d		
Haymarket ⇌ d		00s27
Edinburgh 10 225,242 a		00 34

Saturdays

21 December to 16 May

	SR 1 A	SR 1 B	SR 1 A	SR	SR	SR ◇ C	SR B	SR 1 B	SR	SR B	SR 1 A	SR 1 B	SR	SR	SR B	SR 1 A	SR 1 B ✠	SR	SR ◇ D	SR	SR	SR 1 B ✠
Dunblane d				05 32		05 46			06 03					06 32					06 47	07 02		
Bridge of Allan d				05 35		05 50			06 06					06 35					06 51	07 05		
Alloa d													06 17								07 10	
Stirling a				05 39		05 54			06 10				06 26	06 39					06 55	07 09	07 19	
d				05 42	05 49	05 54			06 11				06 26	06 41				06 49	06 56	07 11	07 24	
Larbert d				05 50	05 57	06 03			06 19				06 34	06 49				06 57	07 04	07 19	07 32	
Camelon 4 d				05 53			06 04		06 22	06 33				06 52	07 04					07 22		
Falkirk Grahamston 3 d				05 56			06 07		06 25	06 36				06 55	07 07					07 25		
Croy 3 d			00 21		06 10	06 15					06 34	06 43	06 44			07 04		07 08			07 41	
Lenzie 3 d			00 27		06 15	06 21							06 49				07 08	07 13			07 47	
Bishopbriggs d	00 03				06 19	06 26							06 53					07 17			07 51	
Glasgow Queen Street 10 ⇌ a	00 09		00 36		06 28	06 36					06 46		07 00			07 18		07 23	07 30		07 58	
Polmont 3 d		00 09		06 01			06 12	06 22		06 41		06 56			07 12		07 25					07 37
Linlithgow d		00 14		06 07			06 18	06 27		06 47		07 02			07 18		07 30					07 42
Edinburgh Park ⇌ d				06 17			06 28		06 42	06 57				07 16	07 29					07 44		
Haymarket ⇌ d		00s27		06 24			06 33	06s40	06 47	07 02		07s18		07 22	07 35		07s46			07 51		07s57
Edinburgh 10 225,242 a		00 34		06 29			06 39	06 46	06 52	07 06		07 24		07 27	07 40		07 55			07 58		08 03

	SR B	SR 1 B ✠	SR	SR 1 A ✠	SR 1 A ✠	SR	SR ◇ 1 E	SR 1 A ✠	SR 1 B	SR B	SR 1 B ✠	SR	SR	SR 1 A ✠	SR	SR 1 B ✠	SR B	SR 1 B ✠	SR	SR ◇ 1 E ✠	SR 1 A ✠	SR 1 B ✠
Dunblane d			07 32				07 44						07 58		08 16				08 30			
Bridge of Allan d			07 35				07 48						08 01		08 19				08 33			
Alloa d												07 53										
Stirling a			07 39				07 53					08 02	08 05		08 24				08 37			
d			07 43			07 50	07 55					08 03	08 08		08 25				08 38	08 43		
Larbert d			07 50			07 58	08 04					08 11	08 16		08 32				08 46			
Camelon 4 d	07 33		07 54							08 05			08 20				08 36		08 54			
Falkirk Grahamston 3 d	07 36		07 57							08 08			08 26				08 39		08 57			
Croy 3 d		07 42		07 48	08 06	08 09					08 11	08 24		08 36	08 42			08 42			09 04	
Lenzie 3 d						08 14	08 19	08 23				08 29			08 48							
Bishopbriggs d						08 18		08 27				08 34			08 52							
Glasgow Queen Street 10 ⇌ a				08 03	08 17	08 25	08 31	08 37				08 44		08 51	09 00					09 11	09 18	
Polmont 3 d	07 41								08 07	08 13	08 25						08 45					09 08
Linlithgow d	07 47	07 58							08 13	08 19						08 40	08 52					09 13
Edinburgh Park ⇌ d	07 57		08 14							08 29			08 46				09 02		09 15			
Haymarket ⇌ d	08 05	08s12	08 20						08s31	08 37	08s41		08 54			08s55	09 09	09s12	09 21			09s28
Edinburgh 10 225,242 a	08 11	08 18	08 25						08 38	08 44	08 48		08 59			09 02	09 13	09 18	09 26			09 33

	SR B	SR 1 B ✠	SR	SR	SR 1 A ✠	SR ◇ F	SR 1 B ✠	SR B	SR 1 B ✠	SR	SR	SR ◇ 1 G	SR 1 A ✠	SR 1 B	SR B	SR 1 B ✠	SR	SR	SR 1 A ✠	SR	SR 1 B ✠
Dunblane d				09 01		09 06					09 29							10 02			
Bridge of Allan d				09 04		09 09					09 32							10 05			
Alloa d			08 44														09 44				
Stirling a			08 53	09 08		09 13					09 36						09 53	10 09			
d			08 54	09 11		09 13				09 23	09 36	09 43					09 54	10 11		10 24	
Larbert d			09 02	09 19						09 31	09 44						10 02	10 19		10 32	
Camelon 4 d	09 04			09 22				09 34			09 47				10 04			10 22			
Falkirk Grahamston 3 d	09 07			09 25				09 37			09 55				10 07			10 25			
Croy 3 d		09 10	09 12		09 32				09 41	09 42			10 03			10 11	10 12		10 31	10 41	
Lenzie 3 d			09 17							09 47							10 17			10 47	
Bishopbriggs d			09 21							09 51							10 21			10 51	
Glasgow Queen Street 10 ⇌ a			09 29		09 44	09 49				09 59		10 11	10 14				10 28		10 43	10 57	
Polmont 3 d	09 12						09 37	09 42						10 07	10 12						10 37
Linlithgow d	09 17						09 42	09 47						10 12	10 18						10 42
Edinburgh Park ⇌ d	09 27			09 42				09 57			10 12				10 28			10 43			
Haymarket ⇌ d	09 35	09s37		09 50			10s01	10 05	10s08		10 20			10s27	10 34	10s37		10 53			10s58
Edinburgh 10 225,242 a	09 39	09 42		09 56			10 07	10 10	10 15		10 27			10 34	10 38	10 42		10 58			11 04

A From Edinburgh
B From Glasgow Queen Street
D From Dundee
E From Aberdeen
G From Aberdeen. Forms booked connection out

Table T230-R

Saturdays

21 December to 16 May

Dunblane, Alloa and Stirling - Falkirk Grahamston, Glasgow Queen Street and Edinburgh

		SR	GR	SR	SR	SR	SR	SR	SR	SR	SR	SR	SR	SR	SR	SR	SR	SR	SR	SR	SR	SR
		A	1 B	1 A		1 C	◇1 D	1 A	A	1 A			1 C		◇1 E	1 A	A	1 A		1 C	◇1 D	1 A
Dunblane	d				10 32							11 02			11 21				11 34			
Bridge of Allan	d				10 35							11 05			11 26				11 37			
Alloa	d										10 44											
Stirling	a				10 39						10 53	11 09			11 31				11 41			
	d		10 33		10 41		10 48				10 54	11 11		11 24	11 32				11 42		11 47	
Larbert	d				10 49						11 02	11 19		11 32					11 50			
Camelon 4	d	10 33			10 52				11 05			11 22					11 33		11 53			
Falkirk Grahamston 3	d	10 36	10 48		10 55				11 08			11 25					11 36		11 56			
Croy 3	d			10 41		11 02				11 10	11 13		11 32	11 41				11 42		12 02		
Lenzie 3	d										11 18			11 46								
Bishopbriggs	d										11 22			11 50								
Glasgow Queen Street 10	a					11 13	11 18				11 29		11 44	11 57	12 10					12 14	12 19	
Polmont 3	d	10 41						11 07	11 13							11 37	11 41					12 08
Linlithgow	d	10 47						11 12	11 19							11 42	11 46					12 13
Edinburgh Park	d	10 57			11 15				11 29			11 42					11 57		12 14			
Haymarket	d	11 07	11 14	11s17	11 21			11s28	11 35	11s38		11 47				11s57	12 06	12s09	12 20			12s28
Edinburgh 10 225,242	a	11 11	11 19	11 22	11 26			11 33	11 41	11 44		11 54				12 02	12 10	12 14	12 25			12 33

		SR	SR	SR	SR	SR	SR	SR	SR	SR	SR	SR	SR	SR	SR	SR	SR	SR	SR	SR	SR	SR	SR
		A	1 A			1 C		1 A	A	1 A		1 C	◇1 D	1 A	A	1 A			1 C	◇ F	1 A	A	1 A
Dunblane	d				12 02		12 16				12 32							13 00		13 08			
Bridge of Allan	d				12 05		12 19				12 35							13 03		13 12			
Alloa	d			11 44													12 44						
Stirling	a			11 53	12 09		12 23				12 39						12 53	13 07		13 16			
	d			11 54	12 11		12 25				12 41		12 47				12 54	13 11		13 16			
Larbert	d			12 02	12 19		12 33				12 49						13 02	13 19					
Camelon 4	d	12 04			12 22				12 34		12 52				13 04			13 22				13 34	
Falkirk Grahamston 3	d	12 07			12 25				12 37		12 55				13 07			13 25				13 37	
Croy 3	d		12 11	12 12		12 33	12 42			12 42		13 01				13 10	13 12		13 31				13 40
Lenzie 3	d			12 17			12 47										13 17						
Bishopbriggs	d			12 21			12 51										13 21						
Glasgow Queen Street 10	a			12 30		12 44	12 58					13 12	13 18				13 28		13 42	13 49			
Polmont 3	d	12 12						12 37	12 42					13 07	13 12						13 37	13 42	
Linlithgow	d	12 18						12 42	12 48					13 12	13 17						13 42	13 47	
Edinburgh Park	d	12 28			12 43				12 58		13 13				13 27			13 42				13 57	
Haymarket	d	12 34	12s38		12 49			12s56	13 08	13s09	13 20			13s29	13 33	13s37		13 49			13s58	14 05	14s07
Edinburgh 10 225,242	a	12 38	12 43		12 54			13 01	13 12	13 14	13 26			13 34	13 40	13 43		13 55			14 03	14 11	14 12

		SR	SR	SR	SR	SR	SR	SR	SR	SR	SR	SR	SR	SR	SR	SR	SR	SR	SR	SR	SR	SR	SR
				1 C	◇1 D	1 A	A	1 A			1 C	1 A	A	1 A			1 C	◇1 D	1 A	A	1 A		
Dunblane	d		13 32							14 02					14 17	14 32							15 02
Bridge of Allan	d		13 35							14 05					14 20	14 35							15 05
Alloa	d								13 44													14 44	
Stirling	a		13 39						13 53	14 09					14 24	14 39						14 53	15 09
	d	13 24	13 41		13 45				13 54	14 11					14 26	14 41		14 48				14 54	15 11
Larbert	d	13 32	13 49						14 02	14 19					14 33	14 49						15 02	15 19
Camelon 4	d		13 52				14 04			14 22			14 34			14 52				15 04			15 22
Falkirk Grahamston 3	d		13 55				14 07			14 25			14 37			14 55				15 07			15 25
Croy 3	d	13 42		14 01				14 11	14 12		14 33			14 41	14 43		15 01				15 10	15 13	
Lenzie 3	d	13 47							14 17						14 48							15 18	
Bishopbriggs	d	13 51							14 21						14 52							15 22	
Glasgow Queen Street 10	a	13 57		14 12	14 19				14 29		14 45				14 58		15 12	15 18				15 28	
Polmont 3	d					14 07	14 12					14 37	14 42						15 07	15 12			
Linlithgow	d					14 12	14 17					14 42	14 48						15 12	15 17			
Edinburgh Park	d		14 13				14 27			14 44			14 58			15 13				15 27			15 42
Haymarket	d		14 19			14s31	14 35	14s38		14 51		14s57	15 06	15s09		15 20			15s27	15 35	15s37		15 50
Edinburgh 10 225,242	a		14 24			14 36	14 40	14 43		14 58		15 04	15 11	15 14		15 25			15 33	15 39	15 42		15 56

		SR	SR	SR	SR	SR	SR	SR	SR	SR	SR	SR	SR	SR	SR	SR	SR	SR	SR	SR	SR	SR
		1 C	1 A	A	1 A			1 C	◇1 D	1 A	A	1 A			1 C	◇ F	1 A	A	1 A			1 C
Dunblane	d					15 16	15 32							16 00		16 07					16 32	
Bridge of Allan	d					15 19	15 35							16 03		16 11					16 35	
Alloa	d												15 44									
Stirling	a					15 23	15 39						15 53	16 07		16 15					16 39	
	d					15 24	15 41		15 48				15 54	16 11		16 15				16 24	16 40	
Larbert	d					15 32	15 49						16 02	16 19						16 32	16 49	
Camelon 4	d			15 34			15 52				16 04			16 22				16 34			16 52	
Falkirk Grahamston 3	d			15 37			15 55				16 07			16 25				16 37			16 55	
Croy 3	d	15 31			15 40	15 42		16 00				16 10	16 12		16 31				16 41	16 42		17 01
Lenzie 3	d					15 47							16 17							16 47		
Bishopbriggs	d					15 51							16 21							16 51		
Glasgow Queen Street 10	a	15 42				15 58		16 13	16 18				16 28		16 42	16 48				16 58		17 13
Polmont 3	d		15 37	15 42						16 07	16 12						16 37	16 42				
Linlithgow	d		15 42	15 47						16 12	16 17						16 42	16 47				
Edinburgh Park	d			15 57			16 12				16 27			16 43				16 57			17 14	
Haymarket	d		16s00	16 06	16s09		16 21			16s28	16 32	16s37		16 50			16s57	17 08	17s08		17 20	
Edinburgh 10 225,242	a		16 07	16 12	16 14		16 27			16 33	16 40	16 43		16 54			17 02	17 14	17 14		17 26	

A From Glasgow Queen Street
B From Inverness to London Kings Cross. The Highland Chieftain
C From Edinburgh
D From Aberdeen
E From Inverness
F From Dundee

Table T230-R

Saturdays

21 December to 16 May

Dunblane, Alloa and Stirling - Falkirk Grahamston, Glasgow Queen Street and Edinburgh

		SR	SR	SR	SR	SR	SR	SR	SR	SR	SR	SR	SR	SR	SR	SR	SR	SR	SR	SR	SR	SR
		1 A	A	1 A			1 B	1 A	A	1 A		◇1 C		1 B	◇1 D	1 A	A	1 A			1 B	1 A
Dunblane	d					16 58						17 23	17 32		17 40					18 02		
Bridge of Allan	d					17 01						17 27	17 35							18 05		
Alloa	d				16 44														17 45			
Stirling	a				16 53	17 05						17 31	17 39		17 45				17 54	18 09		
	d				16 54	17 07					17 24	17 32	17 40		17 46				17 55	18 12		
Larbert	d				17 02	17 19					17 32		17 48						18 03	18 20		
Camelon 4	d		17 02			17 22			17 35				17 52				18 05			18 23		
Falkirk Grahamston 3	d		17 05			17 25			17 38				17 55				18 10			18 26		
Croy 3	d			17 10	17 12		17 32			17 41	17 43			18 01				18 12	18 14		18 31	
Lenzie 3	d				17 17						17 48			18 06					18 19			
Bishopbriggs	d				17 21						17 52								18 23			
Glasgow Queen Street 10	a				17 27		17 43				18 00	18 08		18 14	18 20				18 29		18 42	
Polmont 3	d	17 10	17 14	17 23					17 43	17 54						18 10	18 15					18 37
Linlithgow	d	17 15	17 20					17 40	17 48	17 59						18 15	18 20					18 42
Edinburgh Park	d		17 30			17 44			17 58				18 13				18 30			18 43		
Haymarket	d	17s28	17 36	17s39		17 51		17s53	18 08	18s12			18 21			18s31	18 35	18s39		18 51		18s56
Edinburgh 10 225,242	a	17 33	17 40	17 44		17 56		17 59	18 14	18 17			18 27			18 37	18 40	18 44		18 56		19 02

		SR	SR	SR	SR	SR	SR	SR	SR	SR	SR	SR	SR	SR	SR	SR	SR	SR	SR	SR	SR	SR	SR
		A	1 A			◇1 D	1 B	1 A	A	1 A			1 B		1 A	A	1 A		1 A	1 B	◇1 D		A
Dunblane	d			18 12		18 37						19 00						19 34					
Bridge of Allan	d			18 15								19 03						19 37					
Alloa	d				18 20						18 45											19 44	
Stirling	a			18 19		18 42					18 54	19 07						19 41				19 53	
	d			18 20		18 43					18 55	19 09		19 24				19 41			19 49	19 54	
Larbert	d			18 28	18 46						19 02	19 19		19 31				19 49				20 02	
Camelon 4	d	18 34			18 54				19 04			19 22				19 33		19 52					20 06
Falkirk Grahamston 3	d	18 37			18 57				19 07			19 25				19 37		19 55					20 09
Croy 3	d		18 41	18 42			19 02			19 10	19 12		19 30	19 41					19 56	20 05		20 13	
Lenzie 3	d			18 47							19 17			19 46								20 18	
Bishopbriggs	d			18 51							19 21			19 50								20 22	
Glasgow Queen Street 10	a			18 58		19 11	19 14				19 27		19 42	19 57						20 21	20 27	20 30	
Polmont 3	d	18 42						19 07	19 12						19 37	19 42	19 53		20 09				20 14
Linlithgow	d	18 47						19 12	19 17						19 42	19 47	19 58		20 14				20 20
Edinburgh Park	d	18 57			19 14				19 28			19 42				19 57		20 12					20 30
Haymarket	d	19 03	19s08		19 19			19s26	19 36	19s39		19 50			19s58	20 02	20s12	20 21	20s27				20 35
Edinburgh 10 225,242	a	19 08	19 13		19 25			19 31	19 41	19 44		19 57			20 03	20 07	20 19	20 27	20 32				20 39

		SR	SR	SR	SR	SR	SR	SR	SR	SR	SR	SR	SR	SR	SR	SR	SR	SR	SR	SR	SR	SR	SR
			1 B	◇1 C	1 A			1 B	◇1 D	1 A			1 B	1 A			1 B	◇1 D	1 A	1 B			1 A
Dunblane	d	19 59		20 06			20 33					21 04			21 14	21 33						22 03	
Bridge of Allan	d	20 02		20 11			20 36					21 07			21 17	21 36						22 06	
Alloa	d										20 44										21 44		
Stirling	a	20 06		20 16			20 40				20 53	21 11			21 22	21 40					21 53	22 10	
	d	20 11		20 17		20 24	20 41		20 46		20 54	21 11			21 24	21 41		21 51			21 59	22 11	
Larbert	d	20 19				20 32	20 48				21 02	21 19			21 32	21 49					22 07	22 19	
Camelon 4	d	20 22					20 52					21 22				21 53						22 22	
Falkirk Grahamston 3	d	20 25					20 55					21 25				21 56						22 25	
Croy 3	d		20 19		20 26	20 41		20 52		20 57	21 11		21 20	21 26	21 42		21 51		21 57	22 19	22 23		22 26
Lenzie 3	d					20 47					21 17				21 47						22 28		
Bishopbriggs	d					20 51					21 21				21 51						22 32		
Glasgow Queen Street 10	a		20 34	20 45		20 57		21 06	21 16		21 28		21 32		21 57		22 02	22 21		22 31	22 39		
Polmont 3	d	20 30			20 39		21 00			21 10		21 30		21 39		22 01			22 10			22 30	22 39
Linlithgow	d	20 36			20 45		21 05			21 15		21 36		21 44		22 07			22 16			22 36	22 44
Edinburgh Park	d	20 46					21 15					21 46				22 17						22 46	
Haymarket	d	20 51			20s58		21 23			21s28		21 51		22s00		22 22			22s29			22 51	22s58
Edinburgh 10 225,242	a	20 55			21 06		21 27			21 33		21 55		22 06		22 26			22 34			22 55	23 03

		SR	SR	SR	SR	SR	SR	SR	SR	SR	SR	SR	SR	SR
				1 B	◇1 D	1 A		1 B	1 A				1 B	1 A
Dunblane	d		22 33							23 14				
Bridge of Allan	d		22 36							23 17				
Alloa	d						22 44					23 48		
Stirling	a		22 40				22 53			23 21		23 57		
	d	22 25	22 41		22 52		22 56			23 21	23 26			
Larbert	d	22 32	22 49				23 04			23 29	23 34			
Camelon 4	d		22 52							23 33				
Falkirk Grahamston 3	d		22 55							23 38				
Croy 3	d	22 42		22 49		22 56	23 13	23 23	23 26		23 43		23 50	23 56
Lenzie 3	d	22 47					23 18				23 48		23 55	
Bishopbriggs	d	22 51					23 22				23 52		23 59	
Glasgow Queen Street 10	a	22 57		23 01	23 22		23 28	23 36			23 58		00 08	
Polmont 3	d		23 00			23 09			23 39	23 44				00 09
Linlithgow	d		23 06			23 14			23 45	23 49				00 14
Edinburgh Park	d		23 16							23 59				
Haymarket	d		23 21			23s31			23s59	00 04				00s27
Edinburgh 10 225,242	a		23 25			23 36			00 04	00 11				00 34

A From Glasgow Queen Street
B From Edinburgh
C From Inverness
D From Aberdeen

Table T230-R

Sundays

15 December to 10 May

Dunblane, Alloa and Stirling - Falkirk Grahamston, Glasgow Queen Street and Edinburgh

		SR	SR	SR	SR	SR	SR	SR	SR	SR	SR	SR	SR	SR	SR	SR	SR	SR	SR	SR	SR	SR	SR
		1	1	1	1	1	1	1		1	1		◇1	◇	1	1	1	1			1	1	
		A	B	C	C ⊼	D	D ⊼	C ⊼		D	C ⊼		E	F	D	C ⊼	D ⊼	C ⊼		F	D ⊼	C ⊼	
Dunblane	d												09 34	09 43						10 39			11 01
Bridge of Allan	d													09 47						10 43			11 04
Alloa	d											09 16							10 16				
Stirling	a											09 25	09 40	09 51					10 25	10 47			11 08
	d								09 10			09 26	09 40	09 51					10 26	10 47			11 09
Larbert	d								09 17			09 34	09 49	10 00					10 34	10 56			11 17
Camelon 4	d								09 21					10 05						11 01			11 21
Falkirk Grahamston 3	d								09 24					10 08						11 04			11 24
Croy 3	d		00 21	08 07	08 40	08 42	09 10	09 11		09 41	09 41	09 45			10 08	10 12	10 40	10 41	10 43		11 03	11 11	
Lenzie 3	d		00 27									09 50	10 02						10 49				
Bishopbriggs	d											09 54							10 53				
Glasgow Queen Street 10	a		00 36			08 54	09 22			09 53		10 00	10 14		10 20		10 52		10 59		11 14		
Polmont 3	d	00 09		08 21	08 53				09 30		09 54			10 14				10 54		11 09			11 29
Linlithgow	d	00 14		08 26	08 59			09 27	09 35		09 59			10 21		10 28		10 59		11 16		11 30	11 35
Edinburgh Park	d								09 45					10 34						11 30			11 45
Haymarket	d	00s27		08 51	09s18			09s45	09 55		10s17			10 40		10s43		11s12		11 36		11s45	11 56
Edinburgh 10 225,242	a	00 34		08 55	09 24			09 50	10 00		10 22			10 46		10 49		11 17		11 40		11 50	12 01

		SR	SR	SR	SR	SR	SR	SR	SR	SR	SR	GR	SR	SR	SR	SR	SR	SR	SR	SR	SR	SR
		1	1		◇1		1	1		1		1	◇1	1		1	1		1	1		◇1
		D ⊼	C ⊼		G ⊼		D ⊼	C ⊼		D ⊼		H	G ⊼	C ⊼		D ⊼	C ⊼		D ⊼	C		I ⊼
Dunblane	d				11 32				12 01			12 29	12 39					13 01				13 31
Bridge of Allan	d								12 04									13 04				
Alloa	d			11 16							12 16										13 16	
Stirling	a			11 25	11 38				12 08		12 25	12 35	12 44					13 08			13 25	13 36
	d			11 26	11 39	11 49			12 09		12 26	12 37	12 45		12 49			13 09			13 26	13 37
Larbert	d			11 34		11 57			12 17		12 34				12 57			13 17			13 34	
Camelon 4	d					12 00			12 21						13 00			13 21				
Falkirk Grahamston 3	d					12 03			12 24			12 51			13 03			13 24				
Croy 3	d	11 35	11 41	11 43			12 04	12 11		12 37	12 43			12 41		13 05	13 11		13 35	13 41	13 43	
Lenzie 3	d			11 49							12 49										13 49	
Bishopbriggs	d			11 53							12 53										13 53	
Glasgow Queen Street 10	a	11 48		11 59	12 06		12 18			12 48	12 59		13 13			13 18			13 48		13 59	14 05
Polmont 3	d		11 54			12 08			12 29					12 59	13 08			13 29		13 54		
Linlithgow	d		11 59			12 14		12 27	12 34					13 04	13 14		13 27	13 34		13 59		
Edinburgh Park	d					12 24			12 44						13 25			13 44				
Haymarket	d		12s12			12 29		12s41	12 49			13 13		13s20	13 30		13s40	13 49		14s12		
Edinburgh 10 225,242	a		12 17			12 33		12 47	12 54			13 19		13 25	13 36		13 46	13 54		14 17		

		SR	SR	SR	SR	SR	SR	SR	SR	SR	SR	SR	SR	SR	SR	SR	SR	SR	SR	SR	SR	SR	SR
			1	1		1	1		◇1		1	1		1	◇1	1		◇1		1	1		1
			D ⊼	C ⊼		D ⊼	C		G ⊼		D	C		D ⊼	J ⊼	C		G ⊼		D ⊼	C ⊼		D ⊼
Dunblane	d				14 01				14 33				15 01		15 22			15 34				16 01	
Bridge of Allan	d				14 04								15 04									16 04	
Alloa	d							14 16									15 18						
Stirling	a				14 08			14 25	14 39				15 08		15 27		15 27	15 39				16 08	
	d	13 49			14 10			14 26	14 40	14 49			15 10		15 28		15 32	15 40	15 49			16 09	
Larbert	d	13 57			14 19			14 34		14 57			15 19		15 36		15 41		15 57			16 17	
Camelon 4	d	14 00			14 24					15 00			15 24						16 00			16 21	
Falkirk Grahamston 3	d	14 03			14 27					15 03			15 27						16 03			16 24	
Croy 3	d		14 03	14 11		14 35	14 41	14 43			15 03	15 11		15 35		15 41	15 54			16 04	16 11		16 35
Lenzie 3	d							14 49									16 01						
Bishopbriggs	d							14 53									16 06						
Glasgow Queen Street 10	a		14 14			14 46		14 59	15 09		15 14			15 48	15 58		16 12	16 16		16 20			16 48
Polmont 3	d	14 08			14 33		14 54			15 08			15 33			15 54			16 08			16 29	
Linlithgow	d	14 14		14 27	14 40		14 59			15 14		15 27	15 40			16 01			16 14		16 28	16 34	
Edinburgh Park	d	14 24			14 54					15 24			15 55						16 24			16 45	
Haymarket	d	14 29		14s45	15 00		15s12			15 30		15s40	16 01			16s17			16 29		16s43	16 50	
Edinburgh 10 225,242	a	14 33		14 50	15 06		15 17			15 36		15 45	16 06			16 23			16 33		16 48	16 54	

		SR	SR	SR	SR	SR	SR	SR	SR	SR	SR	SR	SR	SR	SR	SR	SR	SR	SR	SR	SR	SR
		1		◇1		1	1		1	1		◇1	1	1		1	1		◇1	1	◇1	1
		C ⊼		G ⊼		D ⊼	C ⊼		D ⊼	C ⊼		G ⊼	D	C ⊼		D ⊼	C ⊼		G ⊼	D ⊼	J ⊼	C ⊼
Dunblane	d			16 36				17 01				17 33			18 01				18 26		19 05	
Bridge of Allan	d							17 04							18 04							
Alloa	d		16 16								17 16							18 16				
Stirling	a		16 25	16 42				17 08			17 25	17 39			18 08			18 25	18 31		19 10	
	d		16 26	16 43	16 49			17 10			17 26	17 40			18 09			18 27	18 32		19 11	
Larbert	d		16 34		16 57			17 19			17 34				18 17			18 36			19 20	
Camelon 4	d				17 00			17 22							18 21							
Falkirk Grahamston 3	d				17 03			17 25							18 24							
Croy 3	d	16 41	16 43			17 04	17 11		17 35	17 41	17 43		18 03	18 11		18 35	18 41	18 48		19 03		19 11
Lenzie 3	d		16 49								17 49							18 55				
Bishopbriggs	d		16 53								17 53							18 59				
Glasgow Queen Street 10	a		16 59	17 12		17 19			17 48		17 59	18 09	18 19			18 46		19 06	19 09	19 14	19 42	
Polmont 3	d	16 54			17 08			17 31		17 54					18 29		18 54					
Linlithgow	d	16 59			17 14		17 27	17 38		17 59				18 27	18 34		18 59					19 27
Edinburgh Park	d				17 24			17 50							18 44							
Haymarket	d	17s12			17 35		17s40	17 55		18s17				18s40	18 49		19s12					19s40
Edinburgh 10 225,242	a	17 17			17 40		17 46	18 00		18 22				18 45	18 54		19 17					19 45

A not 15 December. From Glasgow Queen Street
B not 15 December. From Edinburgh
C From Glasgow Queen Street
D From Edinburgh
E From Dundee
F From Perth
G From Aberdeen
H From Inverness to London Kings Cross. The Highland Chieftain
I From Inverurie
J From Inverness

Table T230-R

Sundays

15 December to 10 May

Dunblane, Alloa and Stirling - Falkirk Grahamston, Glasgow Queen Street and Edinburgh

		SR	SR	SR	SR	SR	SR	SR	SR	SR	SR	SR	SR	SR	SR	SR	SR	SR	SR	SR	SR	SR	SR
			1	1		1	◇1	1		1	1		1	1		1	1		1	◇1	1		1
			A ⊼	B		A	C	B		A	B		A	B		A	B		A	C ⊼	B		A
Dunblane	d	19 11							20 01						21 01					21 44		22 01	
Bridge of Allan	d	19 14							20 04						21 04							22 04	
Alloa	d				19 16							20 16						21 16					
Stirling	a	19 18			19 25				20 08			20 25			21 08			21 25		21 49		22 08	
	d	19 18			19 26		19 52		20 09			20 26			21 09			21 26		21 50		22 09	
Larbert	d	19 26			19 34				20 17			20 34			21 17			21 34		21 59		22 17	
Camelon 4	d	19 30							20 21						21 21							22 21	
Falkirk Grahamston 3	d	19 33							20 24						21 24							22 24	
Croy 3	d		19 35	19 41	19 43	20 03		20 11		20 36	20 41	20 43	21 03	21 11		21 35	21 41	21 43	22 03		22 11		22 35
Lenzie 3	d				19 49							20 49						21 49		22 13			
Bishopbriggs	d				19 53							20 53						21 53					
Glasgow Queen Street 10	a		19 50		19 59	20 15	20 21			20 47		20 59	21 14			21 47		21 59	22 14	22 23			22 46
Polmont 3	d	19 38		19 54					20 29		20 54				21 29		21 54					22 29	
Linlithgow	d	19 43		19 59				20 28	20 34		20 59			21 27	21 34		21 59				22 27	22 34	
Edinburgh Park	d	19 54							20 45						21 45							22 44	
Haymarket	d	20 03		20s12				20s41	20 50		21s12			21s40	21 51		22s18				22s40	22 51	
Edinburgh 10 225,242	a	20 07		20 18				20 46	20 54		21 17			21 45	21 56		22 23				22 45	22 58	

		SR	SR	SR	SR	SR
		1	1	1	1	1
		B	A	B	A	B
Dunblane	d					
Bridge of Allan	d					
Alloa	d					
Stirling	a					
	d					
Larbert	d					
Camelon 4	d					
Falkirk Grahamston 3	d					
Croy 3	d	22 41	23 03	23 11	23 35	23 41
Lenzie 3	d					
Bishopbriggs	d					
Glasgow Queen Street 10	a		23 14		23 47	
Polmont 3	d	22 54				23 54
Linlithgow	d	22 59		23 27		23 59
Edinburgh Park	d					
Haymarket	d	23s12		23s40		00s12
Edinburgh 10 225,242	a	23 17		23 45		00 17

A From Edinburgh
B From Glasgow Queen Street
C From Aberdeen

Table T231-F

Mondays to Fridays
16 December to 15 May

Motherwell, Glasgow Queen Street - Falkirk Grahamston

		SR	SR	SR	SR	SR	SR	SR	SR	SR		SR	SR	SR	SR	SR	SR	SR	SR	SR		SR	SR	SR	SR
Motherwell	d		05 42			06 40			07 43				08 43			09 43			10 45				11 45		
Whifflet	d		05 49			06 48			07 50				08 50			09 50			10 52				11 52		
Coatbridge Central	d		05 52			06 52			07 52				08 53			09 53			10 54				11 54		
Glasgow Queen Street	d	05 26		05 56	06 25		06 56	07 26		07 55		08 26		08 56	09 24		09 56	10 25		10 55		11 26		11 54	12 27
Springburn	d	05 31		06 01	06 31		07 01	07 33		08 02		08 32		09 02	09 33		10 02	10 32		11 00		11 32		12 03	12 33
Stepps	d	05 40		06 09	06 40		07 10	07 42		08 10		08 41		09 10	09 41		10 10	10 40		11 10		11 41		12 12	12 41
Gartcosh	d	05 44		06 12	06 44		07 14	07 45		08 14		08 44		09 14	09 45		10 14	10 44		11 14		11 45		12 15	12 45
Greenfaulds	d	05 50	06 02	06 18	06 50	07 02	07 20	07 51	08 02	08 20		08 50	09 00	09 20	09 51	10 00	10 20	10 50	11 02	11 20		11 51	12 02	12 21	12 51
Cumbernauld	d	05 53	06a04	06 21	06 53	07a04	07 23	07 54	08a04	08 23		08 53	09a02	09 23	09 54	10a02	10 23	10 53	11a04	11 23		11 54	12a04	12 24	12 53
Camelon	d	06 04		06 32	07 05		07 33	08 05		08 37		09 04		09 34	10 04		10 33	11 04		11 33		12 04		12 34	13 04
Falkirk Grahamston	a	06 06		06 34	07 07		07 36	08 07		08 40		09 06		09 36	10 07		10 36	11 06		11 36		12 07		12 37	13 06

		SR	SR	SR	SR	SR		SR	SR	SR	SR	SR	SR	SR	SR	SR		SR	SR	SR	SR	SR	SR	SR	SR
Motherwell	d	12 45			13 45				14 45			15 45			16 45				17 46			18 45			19 45
Whifflet	d	12 52			13 52				14 52			15 52			16 52				17 53			18 52			19 52
Coatbridge Central	d	12 55			13 54				14 54			15 55			16 55				17 56			18 54			19 54
Glasgow Queen Street	d		12 56	13 26		13 55		14 26		14 56	15 24		15 56	16 25		16 55		17 25		17 57	18 26		18 56	19 25	
Springburn	d		13 02	13 33		14 02		14 32		15 03	15 32		16 02	16 31		17 02		17 32		18 02	18 33		19 01	19 32	
Stepps	d		13 11	13 42		14 11		14 41		15 11	15 41		16 10	16 39		17 10		17 40		18 11	18 42		19 10	19 41	
Gartcosh	d		13 14	13 45		14 14		14 44		15 14	15 44		16 14	16 43		17 14		17 44		18 14	18 45		19 13	19 44	
Greenfaulds	d	13 02	13 20	13 51	14 02	14 20		14 50	15 02	15 20	15 50	16 03	16 20	16 49	17 07	17 20		17 50	18 06	18 21	18 51	19 02	19 19	19 50	20 02
Cumbernauld	d	13a04	13 23	13 54	14a04	14 23		14 53	15a04	15 23	15 53	16a05	16 23	16 52	17a09	17 23		17 53	18a08	18 23	18 54	19a04	19 22	19 53	20a04
Camelon	d		13 34	14 04		14 34		15 04		15 34	16 04		16 34	17 02		17 34		18 06		18 34	19 04		19 33	20 06	
Falkirk Grahamston	a		13 36	14 07		14 36		15 06		15 36	16 07		16 36	17 05		17 37		18 08		18 36	19 07		19 35	20 09	

		SR		SR	SR	SR	SR	SR	SR	SR	SR	SR		SR
Motherwell	d				20 45			21 43			22 45			
Whifflet	d				20 52			21 51			22 52			
Coatbridge Central	d				20 55			21 55			22 55			
Glasgow Queen Street	d	19 56		20 28		21 05	21 36		22 07	22 36		23 06		23 57
Springburn	d	20 02		20 34		21 12	21 43		22 14	22 44		23 13		00 04
Stepps	d	20 10		20 42		21 20	21 51		22 23	22 53		23 21		00 12
Gartcosh	d	20 14		20 46		21 24	21 55		22 27	22 57		23 25		00 16
Greenfaulds	d	20 20		20 52	21 06	21 33	22 01	22 06	22 33	23 03	23 08	23 31		00 22
Cumbernauld	d	20 23		20a54	21a08	21 36	22a03	22a08	22 36	23a05	23a10	23 34		00a24
Camelon	d	20 33				21 57			22 57			23 49		
Falkirk Grahamston	a	20 36				21 59			23 00			23 52		

Saturdays
21 December to 16 May

		SR	SR	SR	SR	SR	SR	SR	SR	SR		SR	SR	SR	SR	SR	SR	SR	SR	SR		SR	SR	SR	SR
Motherwell	d		05 42			06 40			07 43				08 43			09 43			10 45				11 45		
Whifflet	d		05 49			06 48			07 50				08 50			09 50			10 52				11 52		
Coatbridge Central	d		05 52			06 52			07 52				08 53			09 53			10 54				11 54		
Glasgow Queen Street	d	05 26		05 56	06 25		06 56	07 26		07 55		08 28		08 55	09 26		09 56	10 25		10 55		11 26		11 54	12 27
Springburn	d	05 31		06 01	06 31		07 01	07 33		08 02		08 33		09 02	09 32		10 02	10 32		11 02		11 33		12 03	12 33
Stepps	d	05 40		06 10	06 40		07 10	07 42		08 10		08 41		09 11	09 41		10 10	10 41		11 10		11 41		12 12	12 41
Gartcosh	d	05 44		06 14	06 44		07 14	07 45		08 14		08 45		09 14	09 45		10 14	10 44		11 14		11 45		12 15	12 45
Greenfaulds	d	05 50	06 02	06 20	06 50	07 02	07 20	07 51	08 02	08 20		08 51	09 00	09 20	09 51	10 00	10 20	10 50	11 02	11 20		11 51	12 02	12 21	12 51
Cumbernauld	d	05 53	06a04	06 23	06 53	07a04	07 23	07 54	08a04	08 23		08 53	09a02	09 23	09 54	10a02	10 23	10 53	11a04	11 23		11 54	12a04	12 24	12 53
Camelon	d	06 04		06 33	07 04		07 33	08 05		08 36		09 04		09 34	10 04		10 33	11 05		11 33		12 04		12 34	13 04
Falkirk Grahamston	a	06 06		06 36	07 07		07 36	08 07		08 39		09 06		09 36	10 07		10 36	11 08		11 36		12 07		12 37	13 06

		SR	SR	SR	SR	SR		SR	SR	SR	SR	SR	SR	SR	SR	SR		SR	SR	SR	SR	SR	SR	SR	SR
Motherwell	d	12 45			13 45				14 45			15 45			16 45				17 46			18 45			19 45
Whifflet	d	12 52			13 52				14 52			15 52			16 52				17 53			18 52			19 52
Coatbridge Central	d	12 55			13 54				14 54			15 55			16 55				17 56			18 54			19 54
Glasgow Queen Street	d		12 55	13 25		13 57		14 25		14 55	15 25		15 55	16 27		16 55		17 24		17 57	18 26		18 55	19 26	
Springburn	d		13 02	13 32		14 02		14 32		15 02	15 32		16 02	16 32		17 02		17 32		18 03	18 34		19 01	19 32	
Stepps	d		13 11	13 40		14 11		14 40		15 10	15 40		16 10	16 40		17 10		17 40		18 11	18 41		19 10	19 40	
Gartcosh	d		13 14	13 44		14 14		14 44		15 14	15 44		16 14	16 43		17 14		17 44		18 15	18 45		19 13	19 44	
Greenfaulds	d	13 02	13 20	13 50	14 02	14 20		14 50	15 02	15 20	15 50	16 03	16 20	16 49	17 07	17 20		17 50	18 06	18 21	18 51	19 02	19 19	19 50	20 02
Cumbernauld	d	13a04	13 23	13 53	14a04	14 23		14 53	15a04	15 23	15 53	16a05	16 23	16 52	17a09	17 23		17 53	18a08	18 23	18 53	19a04	19 22	19 53	20a04
Camelon	d		13 34	14 04		14 34		15 04		15 34	16 04		16 34	17 02		17 35		18 06		18 34	19 04		19 33	20 06	
Falkirk Grahamston	a		13 36	14 07		14 36		15 06		15 36	16 06		16 36	17 05		17 37		18 08		18 36	19 06		19 35	20 09	

		SR		SR	SR	SR	SR	SR	SR	SR	SR	SR		SR
Motherwell	d				20 48			21 46			22 45			
Whifflet	d				20 55			21 53			22 52			
Coatbridge Central	d				20 57			21 56			22 55			
Glasgow Queen Street	d	19 57		20 28		21 07	21 37		22 11	22 36		23 06		23 55
Springburn	d	20 02		20 33		21 12	21 43		22 15	22 44		23 13		00 02
Stepps	d	20 10		20 41		21 20	21 51		22 23	22 53		23 21		00 10
Gartcosh	d	20 14		20 45		21 24	21 55		22 27	22 57		23 25		00 14
Greenfaulds	d	20 20		20 51	21 06	21 33	22 01	22 07	22 33	23 03	23 08	23 31		00 20
Cumbernauld	d	20 23		20a54	21a08	21 36	22a03	22a09	22 36	23a05	23a10	23 34		00a22
Camelon	d	20 33				21 48			22 57			23 49		
Falkirk Grahamston	a	20 36				21 51			23 00			23 52		

Table T231-F

Sundays
15 December to 10 May

Motherwell, Glasgow Queen Street - Falkirk Grahamston

		SR		SR	SR	SR	SR	SR
Motherwell	d							
Whifflet	d							
Coatbridge Central	d							
Glasgow Queen Street	d	08 26	and hourly until	19 26	20 22	21 26	22 26	23 04
Springburn	d	08 31		19 31	20 27	21 31	22 31	23 09
Stepps	d	08 40		19 40	20 36	21 40	22 40	23 17
Gartcosh	d	08 44		19 44	20 40	21 44	22 44	23 21
Greenfaulds	d	08 50		19 50	20 46	21 50	22 50	23 27
Cumbernauld	d	08a52		19a52	20a48	21a52	22a52	23a30
Camelon	d							
Falkirk Grahamston	a							

SUNDAY RETURN TIMES

Table T231-R

Sundays
15 December to 10 May

Falkirk Grahamston - Glasgow Queen Street, Motherwell

		SR	SR		SR		SR	SR		SR
Falkirk Grahamston	d									
Camelon	d									
Cumbernauld	d	09 12	10 12	and hourly until	13 12		14 12	15 12	and hourly until	23 12
Greenfaulds	d	09 15	10 15		13 15		14 15	15 15		23 15
Gartcosh	d	09 22	10 22		13 22		14 22	15 22		23 22
Stepps	d	09 25	10 25		13 25		14 25	15 25		23 25
Springburn	d	09 34	10 34		13 34		14 34	15 34		23 34
Glasgow Queen Street	a	09 40	10 39		13 39		14 41	15 39		23 39
Coatbridge Central	d									
Whifflet	d									
Motherwell	a									

Table T231-R

Mondays to Fridays
16 December to 15 May

Falkirk Grahamston - Glasgow Queen Street, Motherwell

		SR	SR	SR	SR	SR	SR	SR	SR	SR	SR	SR	SR	SR	SR	SR	SR	SR	SR	SR	SR	SR	SR
Falkirk Grahamston	d	05 34	.	06 08	06 35	.	07 05	07 33	.	08 06	08 11	08 40	.	09 10	09 36	.	10 10	10 40	.	11 10	11 37	.	12 10
Camelon	d	05 37	.	06 11	06 38	.	07 08	07 36	.	08 09	08 14	08 43	.	09 13	09 39	.	10 13	10 43	.	11 13	11 40	.	12 13
Cumbernauld	d	05 48	06 12	06 22	06 48	07 12	07 19	07 48	08 13	08 19	08 28	08 54	09 15	09 25	09 54	10 19	10 24	10 54	11 19	11 24	11 54	12 19	12 24
Greenfaulds	d	05 50	06 14	06 24	06 50	07 14	07 21	07 51	08 15	08 22	.	08 56	09 17	09 28	09 56	10 21	10 26	10 56	11 21	11 26	11 56	12 21	12 26
Gartcosh	d	05 57	.	06 31	06 57	.	07 28	07 58	.	08 28	.	09 03	.	09 34	10 03	.	10 33	11 03	.	11 33	12 03	.	12 33
Stepps	d	06 01	.	06 35	07 01	.	07 32	08 01	.	08 32	.	09 06	.	09 38	10 07	.	10 37	11 07	.	11 37	12 07	.	12 37
Springburn	d	06 10	.	06 44	07 09	.	07 41	08 10	.	08 40	08 47	09 15	.	09 47	10 15	.	10 45	11 16	.	11 46	12 16	.	12 46
Glasgow Queen Street	a	06 16	.	06 51	07 14	.	07 48	08 15	.	08 45	08 56	09 23	.	09 52	10 20	.	10 50	11 21	.	11 54	12 24	.	12 51
Coatbridge Central	d	.	06 22	.	.	07 22	.	.	08 22	.	.	.	09 31	.	.	10 30	.	.	11 30	.	.	12 30	.
Whifflet	d	.	06 25	.	.	07 24	.	.	08 25	.	.	.	09 34	.	.	10 33	.	.	11 33	.	.	12 33	.
Motherwell	a	.	06 37	.	.	07 32	.	.	08 34	.	.	.	09 41	.	.	10 40	.	.	11 40	.	.	12 40	.

		SR	SR	SR	SR	SR	SR	SR	SR	SR	SR	SR	SR	SR	SR	SR	SR	SR	SR	SR	SR	SR
Falkirk Grahamston	d	12 40	.	13 08	13 38	.	14 10	14 40	.	15 10	15 40	.	16 10	16 37	.	.	.	.	.	.	.	.
Camelon	d	12 43	.	13 11	13 41	.	14 13	14 43	.	15 13	15 43	.	16 13	16 40	.	17 13	17 40	.	18 13	18 43	.	19 13
Cumbernauld	d	12 55	13 17	13 22	13 54	14 19	14 24	14 54	15 19	15 24	15 54	16 19	16 24	16 51	17 19	17 24	17 52	18 18	18 24	18 54	19 19	19 24
Greenfaulds	d	12 57	13 19	13 24	13 56	14 21	14 26	14 56	15 21	15 26	15 57	16 21	16 26	16 53	17 21	17 27	17 54	18 20	18 26	18 56	19 21	19 26
Gartcosh	d	13 04	.	13 31	14 03	.	14 33	15 03	.	15 33	16 04	.	16 33	17 00	.	17 34	18 01	.	18 33	19 03	.	19 33
Stepps	d	13 08	.	13 35	14 07	.	14 37	15 07	.	15 37	16 08	.	16 37	17 04	.	17 37	18 05	.	18 37	19 07	.	19 37
Springburn	d	13 16	.	13 43	14 16	.	14 46	15 16	.	15 46	16 16	.	16 46	17 13	.	17 46	18 13	.	18 46	19 16	.	19 46
Glasgow Queen Street	a	13 21	.	13 52	14 21	.	14 51	15 21	.	15 51	16 22	.	16 51	17 20	.	17 52	18 18	.	18 51	19 21	.	19 53
Coatbridge Central	d	.	13 30	.	.	14 30	.	.	15 30	.	.	16 30	.	.	17 30	.	.	18 29	.	.	19 30	.
Whifflet	d	.	13 33	.	.	14 33	.	.	15 33	.	.	16 32	.	.	17 33	.	.	18 32	.	.	19 33	.
Motherwell	a	.	13 40	.	.	14 40	.	.	15 40	.	.	16 40	.	.	17 40	.	.	18 40	.	.	19 40	.

		SR	SR	SR	SR	SR	SR	SR	SR	SR	SR	SR
Falkirk Grahamston	d	.	.	.	.	.	21 26	.	.	22 37	.	23 39
Camelon	d	19 43	.	20 11	.	.	21 29	.	.	22 40	.	23 42
Cumbernauld	d	19 54	20 19	20 24	21 13	21 21	21 43	22 15	22 21	22 52	23 15	23 54
Greenfaulds	d	19 56	20 21	20 27	21 16	21 23	21 46	22 18	22 23	22 54	23 17	23 57
Gartcosh	d	20 03	.	20 34	21 23	.	21 52	22 25	.	23 01	23 24	00 04
Stepps	d	20 07	.	20 37	21 26	.	21 56	22 28	.	23 05	23 27	00 07
Springburn	d	20 16	.	20 46	21 35	.	22 05	22 37	.	23 13	23 36	00 15
Glasgow Queen Street	a	20 23	.	20 53	21 43	.	22 10	22 42	.	23 18	23 42	00 20
Coatbridge Central	d	.	20 30	.	.	21 30	.	.	22 31	.	.	.
Whifflet	d	.	20 33	.	.	21 33	.	.	22 33	.	.	.
Motherwell	a	.	20 40	.	.	21 40	.	.	22 41	.	.	.

Saturdays
21 December to 16 May

		SR	SR	SR	SR	SR	SR	SR	SR	SR	SR	SR	SR	SR	SR	SR	SR	SR	SR	SR	SR	SR	SR
Falkirk Grahamston	d	05 34	.	06 08	06 35	.	07 05	07 33	.	08 05	08 40	.	09 10	09 37	.	10 10	10 40	.	11 10	11 37	.	12 10	12 40
Camelon	d	05 37	.	06 11	06 38	.	07 08	07 36	.	08 08	08 43	.	09 13	09 40	.	10 13	10 43	.	11 13	11 40	.	12 13	12 43
Cumbernauld	d	05 48	06 13	06 22	06 48	07 12	07 19	07 48	08 13	08 20	08 54	09 19	09 24	09 54	10 19	10 24	10 54	11 19	11 25	11 54	12 19	12 24	12 55
Greenfaulds	d	05 50	06 15	06 24	06 50	07 14	07 21	07 51	08 15	08 22	08 56	09 21	09 26	09 56	10 21	10 26	10 56	11 21	11 28	11 56	12 21	12 26	12 57
Gartcosh	d	05 57	.	06 31	06 57	.	07 28	07 58	.	08 29	09 03	.	09 33	10 03	.	10 33	11 03	.	11 35	12 03	.	12 33	13 04
Stepps	d	06 01	.	06 35	07 01	.	07 32	08 02	.	08 32	09 07	.	09 36	10 07	.	10 36	11 07	.	11 38	12 07	.	12 37	13 08
Springburn	d	06 10	.	06 44	07 09	.	07 41	08 15	.	08 41	09 16	.	09 50	10 15	.	10 45	11 16	.	11 47	12 16	.	12 46	13 16
Glasgow Queen Street	a	06 15	.	06 49	07 14	.	07 48	08 20	.	08 48	09 21	.	09 56	10 20	.	10 50	11 21	.	11 54	12 22	.	12 51	13 22
Coatbridge Central	d	.	06 22	.	.	07 22	.	.	08 22	.	.	09 31	.	.	10 30	.	.	11 30	.	.	12 30	.	.
Whifflet	d	.	06 25	.	.	07 24	.	.	08 25	.	.	09 34	.	.	10 33	.	.	11 33	.	.	12 33	.	.
Motherwell	a	.	06 37	.	.	07 32	.	.	08 34	.	.	09 41	.	.	10 40	.	.	11 40	.	.	12 40	.	.

		SR	SR	SR	SR	SR	SR	SR	SR	SR	SR	SR	SR	SR	SR	SR	SR	SR	SR	SR	SR	SR	SR
Falkirk Grahamston	d	.	13 10	13 38	.	14 10	14 40	.	15 10	15 40	.	16 11	16 37	.	17 10	17 37	.	18 10	18 40	.	19 10	19 40	.
Camelon	d	.	13 13	13 41	.	14 13	14 43	.	15 13	15 43	.	16 14	16 40	.	17 13	17 40	.	18 13	18 43	.	19 13	19 43	.
Cumbernauld	d	13 17	13 24	13 54	14 19	14 24	14 54	15 19	15 24	15 54	16 19	16 24	16 51	17 19	17 24	17 51	18 18	18 24	18 54	19 19	19 24	19 54	20 19
Greenfaulds	d	13 19	13 26	13 56	14 21	14 26	14 56	15 21	15 26	15 57	16 21	16 27	16 53	17 21	17 27	17 53	18 20	18 26	18 56	19 21	19 26	19 56	20 21
Gartcosh	d	.	13 33	14 03	.	14 33	15 03	.	15 33	16 04	.	16 34	17 00	.	17 34	18 00	.	18 33	19 03	.	19 33	20 03	.
Stepps	d	.	13 37	14 07	.	14 37	15 07	.	15 37	16 07	.	16 37	17 04	.	17 37	18 03	.	18 37	19 07	.	19 37	20 07	.
Springburn	d	.	13 46	14 16	.	14 45	15 16	.	15 46	16 16	.	16 46	17 13	.	17 46	18 12	.	18 45	19 16	.	19 45	20 16	.
Glasgow Queen Street	a	.	13 52	14 23	.	14 50	15 21	.	15 54	16 22	.	16 51	17 20	.	17 52	18 17	.	18 50	19 21	.	19 50	20 24	.
Coatbridge Central	d	13 30	.	.	14 30	.	.	15 30	.	.	16 30	.	.	17 30	.	.	18 29	.	.	19 30	.	.	20 30
Whifflet	d	13 33	.	.	14 33	.	.	15 33	.	.	16 32	.	.	17 33	.	.	18 32	.	.	19 33	.	.	20 33
Motherwell	a	13 40	.	.	14 40	.	.	15 40	.	.	16 40	.	.	17 40	.	.	18 40	.	.	19 40	.	.	20 40

		SR	SR	SR	SR	SR	SR	SR	SR	SR
Falkirk Grahamston	d	20 07	.	.	21 26	.	.	22 37	.	23 39
Camelon	d	20 10	.	.	21 29	.	.	22 40	.	23 42
Cumbernauld	d	20 24	21 13	21 21	21 43	22 15	22 21	22 52	23 15	23 52
Greenfaulds	d	20 26	21 16	21 23	21 46	22 18	22 23	22 54	23 17	23 55
Gartcosh	d	20 33	21 23	.	21 52	22 25	.	23 01	23 24	00 02
Stepps	d	20 37	21 26	.	21 56	22 28	.	23 05	23 27	00 06
Springburn	d	20 46	21 35	.	22 05	22 37	.	23 13	23 36	00 14
Glasgow Queen Street	a	20 54	21 40	.	22 10	22 42	.	23 18	23 41	00 19
Coatbridge Central	d	.	.	21 30	.	.	22 31	.	.	.
Whifflet	d	.	.	21 33	.	.	22 33	.	.	.
Motherwell	a	.	.	21 40	.	.	22 41	.	.	.

See previous page for Sunday times.

Table T232-F

Mondays to Fridays
16 December to 15 May

Glasgow Queen Street - Maryhill and Anniesland

Miles			SR	SR	SR	SR	SR	SR	SR	SR	SR	SR	SR	SR	SR	SR	SR	SR	SR	SR	SR	SR	SR
0	**Glasgow Queen Street** 10	d	06 33	07 03	07 34	08 03	08 33	09 03	09 33	10 03	10 36	11 03	11 33	12 04	12 35	13 03	13 34	14 03	14 34	15 03	15 33	16 03	16 39
2¼	Ashfield	d	06 39	07 08	07 39	08 08	08 40	09 08	09 38	10 08	10 42	11 08	11 38	12 09	12 40	13 08	13 39	14 08	14 39	15 08	15 39	16 08	16 45
3	Possilpark & Parkhouse	d	06 42	07 11	07 42	08 11	08 43	09 11	09 41	10 11	10 45	11 11	11 41	12 12	12 43	13 11	13 42	14 11	14 42	15 11	15 41	16 11	16 48
3¼	Gilshochill	d	06 44	07 13	07 44	08 13	08 45	09 13	09 43	10 13	10 47	11 13	11 43	12 14	12 45	13 13	13 44	14 13	14 44	15 13	15 43	16 13	16 50
4¼	Summerston	d	06 46	07 15	07 46	08 15	08 47	09 15	09 45	10 15	10 49	11 15	11 45	12 16	12 47	13 15	13 46	14 15	14 46	15 15	15 46	16 15	16 52
4¾	**Maryhill**	d	06 48	07 17	07 48	08 17	08 49	09 17	09 47	10 17	10 51	11 17	11 47	12 18	12 49	13 16	13 48	14 17	14 48	15 16	15 47	16 17	16 54
5½	Kelvindale	d	06 50	07 19	07 50	08 19	08 51	09 19	09 49	10 19	10 53	11 19	11 49	12 20	12 51	13 18	13 50	14 19	14 50	15 18	15 50	16 19	16 56
6¼	**Anniesland** 226	a	06 53	07 22	07 53	08 22	08 54	09 22	09 52	10 22	10 56	11 22	11 52	12 23	12 54	13 21	13 53	14 22	14 53	15 21	15 53	16 22	16 59

		SR	SR	SR	SR	SR	SR	SR	SR	SR	SR		SR	SR
Glasgow Queen Street 10	d	17 06	17 36	18 03	18 37	19 03	19 33	20 02	20 35	21 02	21 33	and every 30 minutes until	23 03	23 34
Ashfield	d	17 11	17 41	18 09	18 42	19 08	19 38	20 08	20 40	21 08	21 38		23 08	23 39
Possilpark & Parkhouse	d	17 14	17 44	18 12	18 45	19 11	19 41	20 11	20 43	21 11	21 41		23 11	23 42
Gilshochill	d	17 16	17 46	18 14	18 47	19 13	19 43	20 13	20 45	21 13	21 43		23 13	23 44
Summerston	d	17 18	17 48	18 16	18 49	19 15	19 45	20 15	20 47	21 15	21 45		23 15	23 46
Maryhill	d	17 20	17 50	18 18	18 51	19 16	19 47	20 17	20 48	21 17	21 47		23 17	23 48
Kelvindale	d	17 22	17 52	18 20	18 53	19 18	19 49	20 19	20 50	21 19	21 49		23 19	23 50
Anniesland 226	a	17 25	17 55	18 23	18 56	19 21	19 52	20 22	20 53	21 22	21 52		23 22	23 53

Saturdays
21 December to 16 May

		SR	SR	SR	SR	SR	SR	SR	SR	SR	SR	SR	SR	SR	SR	SR	SR	SR	SR	SR	SR	SR	SR
Glasgow Queen Street 10	d	00 03	06 33	07 03	07 34	08 03	08 35	09 03	09 33	10 03	10 36	11 03	11 33	12 03	12 35	13 03	13 33	14 03	14 34	15 03	15 33	16 03	16 39
Ashfield	d	00 08	06 39	07 08	07 39	08 08	08 40	09 08	09 38	10 08	10 42	11 08	11 38	12 09	12 40	13 08	13 39	14 08	14 39	15 08	15 39	16 08	16 45
Possilpark & Parkhouse	d	00 11	06 42	07 11	07 42	08 11	08 43	09 11	09 41	10 11	10 45	11 11	11 41	12 12	12 43	13 11	13 42	14 11	14 42	15 11	15 41	16 11	16 48
Gilshochill	d	00 13	06 44	07 13	07 44	08 13	08 45	09 13	09 43	10 13	10 47	11 13	11 43	12 14	12 45	13 13	13 44	14 13	14 44	15 13	15 43	16 13	16 50
Summerston	d	00 15	06 46	07 15	07 46	08 15	08 47	09 15	09 45	10 15	10 49	11 15	11 45	12 16	12 47	13 15	13 46	14 15	14 46	15 15	15 46	16 15	16 52
Maryhill	d	00 17	06 48	07 17	07 48	08 17	08 49	09 17	09 47	10 17	10 51	11 17	11 47	12 18	12 49	13 16	13 48	14 17	14 48	15 16	15 47	16 17	16 54
Kelvindale	d	00 19	06 50	07 19	07 50	08 19	08 51	09 19	09 49	10 19	10 53	11 19	11 49	12 20	12 51	13 18	13 50	14 19	14 50	15 18	15 50	16 19	16 56
Anniesland 226	a	00 22	06 53	07 22	07 53	08 22	08 54	09 22	09 52	10 22	10 56	11 22	11 52	12 23	12 54	13 21	13 53	14 22	14 53	15 21	15 53	16 22	16 59

		SR	SR	SR	SR	SR	SR	SR	SR	SR		SR	SR
Glasgow Queen Street 10	d	17 06	17 36	18 04	18 35	19 03	19 33	20 03	20 35	21 03	and every 30 minutes until	23 03	23 34
Ashfield	d	17 11	17 41	18 09	18 42	19 08	19 38	20 08	20 40	21 08		23 08	23 39
Possilpark & Parkhouse	d	17 14	17 44	18 12	18 45	19 11	19 41	20 11	20 43	21 11		23 11	23 42
Gilshochill	d	17 16	17 46	18 14	18 47	19 13	19 43	20 13	20 45	21 13		23 13	23 44
Summerston	d	17 18	17 48	18 16	18 49	19 15	19 45	20 15	20 47	21 15		23 15	23 46
Maryhill	d	17 20	17 50	18 18	18 51	19 16	19 47	20 17	20 48	21 17		23 17	23 48
Kelvindale	d	17 22	17 52	18 20	18 53	19 18	19 49	20 19	20 50	21 19		23 19	23 50
Anniesland 226	a	17 25	17 55	18 23	18 56	19 21	19 52	20 22	20 53	21 22		23 22	23 53

Sundays
15 December to 10 May

		SR		SR
Glasgow Queen Street 10	d	09 33	and hourly until	18 33
Ashfield	d	09 38		18 38
Possilpark & Parkhouse	d	09 41		18 41
Gilshochill	d	09 43		18 43
Summerston	d	09 45		18 45
Maryhill	d	09 47		18 47
Kelvindale	d	09 49		18 49
Anniesland 226	a	09 52		18 52

Table T232-R

Mondays to Fridays
16 December to 15 May

Anniesland and Maryhill - Glasgow Queen Street

Miles			SR	SR	SR	SR	SR	SR		SR	SR	SR	SR	SR	SR	SR	SR	SR		SR	SR	SR	SR	SR	SR
							◇ ⊥																		
0	**Anniesland** 226	d	06 32	07 05	07 32	08 02		08 31		09 04	09 34	10 05	10 35	11 05	11 29	12 05	12 35	13 02		13 26	14 05	14 35	15 05	15 26	16 02
0¾	Kelvindale	d	06 34	07 07	07 34	08 04		08 33		09 06	09 36	10 07	10 37	11 07	11 31	12 07	12 37	13 04		13 28	14 07	14 37	15 07	15 28	16 04
1½	**Maryhill**	d	06 36	07 09	07 36	08 06	08 24	08 35		09 08	09 38	10 09	10 39	11 09	11 33	12 09	12 39	13 06		13 30	14 09	14 39	15 09	15 30	16 06
2	Summerston	d	06 38	07 11	07 38	08 08		08 37		09 10	09 40	10 11	10 41	11 11	11 35	12 11	12 41	13 08		13 32	14 11	14 41	15 11	15 32	16 08
3	Gilshochill	d	06 40	07 13	07 40	08 10		08 39		09 12	09 42	10 13	10 43	11 13	11 37	12 13	12 43	13 10		13 34	14 13	14 43	15 13	15 34	16 10
3¼	Possilpark & Parkhouse	d	06 42	07 15	07 42	08 12	08 28	08 41		09 14	09 44	10 15	10 45	11 15	11 39	12 15	12 45	13 12		13 36	14 15	14 45	15 15	15 36	16 12
4	Ashfield	d	06 45	07 18	07 45	08 15		08 44		09 17	09 47	10 18	10 48	11 18	11 42	12 18	12 48	13 15		13 39	14 18	14 48	15 18	15 39	16 19
6¼	**Glasgow Queen Street** 10	a	06 57	07 24	07 55	08 26	08 39	08 50		09 27	09 55	10 24	10 54	11 24	11 51	12 27	12 54	13 25		13 49	14 24	14 54	15 24	15 48	16 28

		SR	SR	SR		SR	SR	SR	SR	SR	SR	SR	SR	SR		SR	SR	SR
Anniesland 226	d	16 30	17 05	17 36		18 02	18 35	19 05	19 26	19 57	20 28	20 58	21 28	22 03		22 35	23 02	23 32
Kelvindale	d	16 32	17 07	17 38		18 04	18 37	19 07	19 28	19 59	20 30	21 00	21 30	22 05		22 37	23 04	23 34
Maryhill	d	16 34	17 09	17 40		18 06	18 39	19 09	19 30	20 01	20 33	21 02	21 32	22 07		22 39	23 06	23 36
Summerston	d	16 36	17 11	17 42		18 08	18 41	19 11	19 32	20 03	20 34	21 04	21 34	22 09		22 41	23 08	23 38
Gilshochill	d	16 38	17 13	17 44		18 10	18 43	19 13	19 34	20 05	20 37	21 06	21 36	22 11		22 43	23 10	23 40
Possilpark & Parkhouse	d	16 40	17 15	17 46		18 12	18 45	19 15	19 36	20 07	20 39	21 08	21 38	22 13		22 45	23 12	23 42
Ashfield	d	16 43	17 18	17 49		18 15	18 48	19 18	19 39	20 10	20 42	21 11	21 41	22 16		22 48	23 15	23 46
Glasgow Queen Street 10	a	16 54	17 24	17 56		18 26	18 54	19 24	19 48	20 20	20 50	21 19	21 50	22 25		22 54	23 26	23 58

Saturdays
21 December to 16 May

		SR	SR	SR	SR	SR	SR	SR	SR	SR		SR	SR	SR	SR	SR	SR	SR	SR	SR		SR	SR	SR	SR
						◇ ⊥																			
Anniesland 226	d	06 32	07 05	07 35	08 07		08 36	09 05	09 27	10 05		10 35	11 05	11 29	12 05	12 35	13 02	13 26	14 05	14 35		15 05	15 26	16 02	16 30
Kelvindale	d	06 34	07 07	07 37	08 09		08 38	09 07	09 29	10 07		10 37	11 07	11 31	12 07	12 37	13 04	13 28	14 07	14 37		15 07	15 28	16 04	16 32
Maryhill	d	06 36	07 09	07 39	08 11	08 24	08 40	09 09	09 31	10 09		10 39	11 09	11 33	12 09	12 39	13 06	13 30	14 09	14 39		15 09	15 30	16 06	16 34
Summerston	d	06 38	07 11	07 41	08 13		08 42	09 11	09 33	10 11		10 41	11 11	11 35	12 11	12 41	13 08	13 32	14 11	14 41		15 11	15 32	16 08	16 36
Gilshochill	d	06 40	07 13	07 43	08 15		08 44	09 13	09 35	10 13		10 43	11 13	11 37	12 13	12 43	13 10	13 34	14 13	14 43		15 13	15 34	16 10	16 38
Possilpark & Parkhouse	d	06 42	07 15	07 45	08 17	08 28	08 46	09 15	09 37	10 15		10 45	11 15	11 39	12 15	12 45	13 12	13 36	14 15	14 45		15 15	15 36	16 12	16 40
Ashfield	d	06 45	07 18	07 48	08 20		08 49	09 18	09 40	10 18		10 48	11 18	11 42	12 18	12 48	13 15	13 39	14 18	14 48		15 18	15 39	16 15	16 43
Glasgow Queen Street 10	a	06 53	07 26	07 54	08 28	08 41	08 57	09 25	09 49	10 24		10 54	11 25	11 50	12 25	12 55	13 25	13 46	14 26	14 54		15 24	15 45	16 25	16 54

		SR	SR	SR	SR	SR		SR	SR	SR	SR	SR	SR	SR	SR	SR
Anniesland 226	d	17 05	17 36	18 02	18 35	19 05		19 26	19 57	20 28	20 58	21 28	22 03	22 35	23 02	23 32
Kelvindale	d	17 07	17 38	18 04	18 37	19 07		19 28	19 59	20 30	21 00	21 30	22 05	22 37	23 04	23 34
Maryhill	d	17 09	17 40	18 06	18 39	19 09		19 30	20 01	20 33	21 02	21 32	22 07	22 39	23 06	23 36
Summerston	d	17 11	17 42	18 08	18 41	19 11		19 32	20 03	20 34	21 04	21 34	22 09	22 41	23 08	23 38
Gilshochill	d	17 13	17 44	18 10	18 43	19 13		19 34	20 05	20 37	21 06	21 36	22 11	22 43	23 10	23 40
Possilpark & Parkhouse	d	17 15	17 46	18 12	18 45	19 15		19 36	20 07	20 39	21 08	21 38	22 13	22 45	23 12	23 42
Ashfield	d	17 18	17 49	18 15	18 48	19 18		19 39	20 10	20 42	21 11	21 41	22 16	22 48	23 15	23 45
Glasgow Queen Street 10	a	17 24	17 56	18 24	18 54	19 24		19 45	20 18	20 50	21 19	21 50	22 25	22 54	23 25	23 54

Sundays
15 December to 10 May

		SR	SR		SR	SR	SR	SR	SR	SR
Anniesland 226	d	10 05	11 06	and hourly until	14 06	15 00	16 06	17 06	18 06	19 10
Kelvindale	d	10 07	11 08		14 08	15 02	16 08	17 08	18 08	19 12
Maryhill	d	10 09	11 10		14 10	15 04	16 10	17 10	18 10	19 14
Summerston	d	10 11	11 12		14 12	15 06	16 12	17 12	18 12	19 16
Gilshochill	d	10 13	11 14		14 14	15 08	16 14	17 14	18 14	19 18
Possilpark & Parkhouse	d	10 15	11 16		14 16	15 10	16 16	17 16	18 16	19 20
Ashfield	d	10 18	11 19		14 19	15 13	16 19	17 19	18 19	19 23
Glasgow Queen Street 10	a	10 24	11 25		14 25	15 19	16 25	17 25	18 25	19 29

Table T238-F

Mondays to Fridays
16 December to 15 May

Dunbar and North Berwick - Edinburgh and Haymarket

Miles	Miles			SR	SR	XC	SR	GR	SR	SR	SR	GR		SR	GR	SR	SR	SR	XC	SR	SR	SR		XC	SR
						◇1 A ⊥		■ 1 ⊏				■ 1 ⊏			■ 1 ⊏				◇1 ⊥					◇1 ⊥	
0	—	**North Berwick**	d	06 08	06 47		07 18			07 55	08 46			09 29		10 29		11 28		12 28		13 28			14 28
—	0	**Dunbar**	d			07 00		07 42				08 56			09 57		11 02		11 40		13 01			13 42	
4½	10¼	Drem	d	06 15	06 54		07 25			08 03	08 53			09 37		10 37		11 36		12 36		13 36			14 37
9	14¾	Longniddry	d	06 20	07 00		07 31			08 09	08 58			09 42		10 42		11 41		12 41		13 41			14 42
12½	18¼	Prestonpans	d	06 25	07 05		07 36		08 03	08 14	09 03			09 47		10 47		11 45		12 46		13 45			14 47
14¾	20½	Wallyford	d	06 28	07 08		07 39		08 06	08 18	09 06			09 50		10 50		11 48		12 49		13 48			14 50
17	22¾	Musselburgh	d	06 32	07 12		07 43		08 11	08 22	09 10			09 55		10 54	11 21	11 52		12 53	13 19	13 52			14 54
22¼	28	**Edinburgh** 10 225,230,242	a	06 39	07 19	07 22	07 50	08 07	08 18	08 29	09 16	09 21		10 01	10 20	11 00	11 27	11 59	12 04	12 59	13 30	13 59		14 07	15 00
—	—		d			07 27	07 52								10 28										
23½	29¼	**Haymarket** 225,230,242	a			07 31	07 56								10 31										

		SR	SR	XC	SR	SR	SR	XC		SR	SR	SR	SR	XC	SR	SR	GR	XC		SR
				◇1 ⊥				◇1 B ⊥						◇1 B ⊥			■ 1 ⊏	◇1		
North Berwick	d		15 28		16 27		17 29			17 56	18 29	19 02	19 29		20 27	21 27				22 28
Dunbar	d	15 06		15 42		17 06		17 45						19 46			21 43	21 51		
Drem	d		15 36		16 36		17 38				18 39	19 10	19 36		20 36	21 36				22 36
Longniddry	d		15 41		16 41		17 43				18 44	19 15	19 42		20 41	21 41				22 41
Prestonpans	d		15 46		16 46		17 49				18 49	19 20	19 47		20 46	21 45				22 46
Wallyford	d		15 49		16 49		17 52				18 52	19 24	19 51		20 49	21 48				22 49
Musselburgh	d	15 23	15 53		16 53	17 23	17 56			18 13	18 56	19 31	19 55		20 53	21 52				22 53
Edinburgh 10 225,230,242	a	15 32	15 59	16 06	16 59	17 33	18 02	18 07		18 19	19 02	19 41	20 02	20 10	20 59	21 59	22 08	22 14		23 00
	d							18 11						20 14						
Haymarket 225,230,242	a							18 15						20 17						

Saturdays
21 December to 16 May

		SR	SR	GR	SR	GR	SR	SR	GR	SR		SR	SR	SR	XC	SR	SR	SR	SR	SR		XC	SR	SR	SR
				■ 1 ⊏		■ 1 ⊏			■ 1 ⊏						◇1 ⊥							◇1 ⊥			
North Berwick	d	06 08	07 17		08 17		09 17	09 48		10 16		10 51		11 17		11 50	12 17	12 50		13 18			13 51	14 17	14 51
Dunbar	d			07 41		08 54			09 56				11 11		11 39				13 05			13 40			
Drem	d	06 15	07 24		08 25		09 25	09 55		10 23		10 58		11 24		11 57	12 25	12 57		13 26			13 58	14 24	14 58
Longniddry	d	06 21	07 30		08 30		09 30	10 00		10 28		11 04		11 29		12 03	12 30	13 03		13 31			14 04	14 29	15 03
Prestonpans	d	06 26	07 35		08 34		09 35	10 05		10 33		11 09		11 34		12 07	12 35	13 08		13 36			14 09	14 34	15 08
Wallyford	d	06 30	07 39		08 37		09 38	10 08		10 36		11 12		11 37		12 10	12 38	13 11		13 40			14 12	14 37	15 11
Musselburgh	d	06 34	07 43		08 41		09 43	10 12		10 40		11 16	11 29	11 41		12 14	12 42	13 15	13 22	13 44			14 16	14 41	15 15
Edinburgh 10 225,230,242	a	06 41	07 49	08 07	08 48	09 19	09 49	10 18	10 23	10 48		11 22	11 39	11 47	12 05	12 21	12 49	13 21	13 35	13 52		14 05	14 22	14 49	15 22
	d								10 28																
Haymarket 225,230,242	a								10 31																

		SR	SR	XC	SR	SR		SR	SR	SR	XC	SR	SR	SR	SR	XC		SR	SR	XC	GR	SR
				◇1 ⊥							◇1 B ⊥					◇1 B ⊥				◇1	■ 1 ⊏	
North Berwick	d		15 17		15 50	16 17		16 50		17 18		17 51	18 20	18 51	19 18			20 17	21 17			22 22
Dunbar	d	15 04		15 42					17 08		17 45					19 46				21 46	22 12	
Drem	d		15 25		15 59	16 24		16 58		17 26		18 01	18 28	18 59	19 25			20 26	21 24			22 29
Longniddry	d		15 30		16 04	16 29		17 03		17 31		18 06	18 33	19 04	19 30			20 32	21 29			22 35
Prestonpans	d		15 35		16 09	16 34		17 08		17 35		18 11	18 37	19 09	19 35			20 36	21 34			22 40
Wallyford	d		15 38		16 12	16 37		17 11		17 38		18 14	18 40	19 12	19 38			20 40	21 37			22 43
Musselburgh	d	15 25	15 43		16 16	16 44		17 15	17 30	17 42		18 18	18 44	19 16	19 42			20 44	21 41			22 47
Edinburgh 10 225,230,242	a	15 38	15 49	16 06	16 22	16 50		17 24	17 42	17 51	18 06	18 24	18 51	19 23	19 49	20 08		20 50	21 48	22 08	22 38	22 53
	d										18 12					20 12						
Haymarket 225,230,242	a										18 15					20 16						

Sundays
15 December to 10 May

		GR	SR	SR	GR	SR	SR	XC	GR	SR		SR	XC	SR	SR	XC	SR	SR	XC	SR		GR	SR	XC	SR	GR
		■ 1 ⊏			■ 1 ⊏			◇1 ⊥	■ 1 ⊏				◇1 ⊥			◇1 B ⊥			◇1 ⊥			■ 1 ⊏		◇1 ⊥		■ 1 ⊏
North Berwick	d		10 24	11 20		12 20	13 20			14 20		15 20		16 20	17 20		18 20	19 20		20 20			21 20		22 20	
Dunbar	d	10 04			11 33			13 36	13 50				15 37			17 38			19 35			20 49		21 45		23 13
Drem	d		10 31	11 27		12 27	13 27			14 27		15 27		16 27	17 27		18 27	19 27		20 27			21 27		22 27	
Longniddry	d		10 37	11 33		12 33	13 33			14 33		15 33		16 33	17 33		18 33	19 33		20 33			21 33		22 33	
Prestonpans	d		10 42	11 38		12 38	13 38			14 38		15 38		16 38	17 38		18 38	19 38		20 38			21 38		22 38	
Wallyford	d		10 45	11 41		12 41	13 41			14 41		15 41		16 41	17 41		18 41	19 41		20 41			21 41		22 41	
Musselburgh	d		10 49	11 45		12 45	13 45			14 45		15 45		16 45	17 45		18 45	19 45		20 45			21 45		22 45	
Edinburgh 10 225,230,242	a	10 28	10 59	11 52	11 58	12 52	13 52	13 58	14 18	14 52		15 51	15 59	16 51	17 52	17 59	18 52	19 53	19 59	20 52		21 12	21 52	22 06	22 52	23 38
	d															18 13						21 22				
Haymarket 225,230,242	a															18 16						21 25				

A ⊥ from Edinburgh

B ⊥ to Edinburgh

Table T238-R

Mondays to Fridays

16 December to 15 May

Haymarket and Edinburgh - North Berwick and Dunbar

Miles	Miles			TP MX	TP MO	GR	XC	SR	SR	SR		XC	SR	SR	SR	XC	SR	SR	SR	XC		SR	SR	SR	XC
				◇1 [trolley]	◇1 [trolley]	■ 1 [restaurant]	◇1 A [trolley]	B				◇1 A [trolley]				■ ◇1 C [trolley]				◇1 [trolley]					◇1 [trolley]
0	0	Haymarket 225,230,242 ⇌	d				06 57					08 51				10 50									
1¼	1¼	Edinburgh 10 225,230,242	a				07 01					08 55				10 54									
—	—		d	05 14	05 17	05 48	07 10	07 14	08 15	08 42		09 07	09 43	10 13	10 42	11 06	11 42	12 11	12 43	13 08		13 41	14 15	14 41	15 08
6½	6½	Musselburgh	d					07 21	08 21	08 48			09 49	10 19	10 48		11 49	12 18	12 49			13 48	14 21	14 48	
8¾	8¾	Wallyford	d					07 25		08 52			09 53		10 52		11 53		12 53			13 52		14 52	
11	11	Prestonpans	d					07 28		08 56			09 56		10 55		11 56		12 56			13 55		14 55	
14½	14½	Longniddry	d					07 33		09 01			10 01		11 00		12 01		13 01			14 00		15 00	
19	19	Drem	d					07 39		09 07			10 07		11 06		12 08		13 07			14 05		15 05	
—	29¼	Dunbar	a	05 44	05 44	06 09	07 31					09 27		10 38		11 26		12 38		13 29			14 40		15 28
23½	—	North Berwick	a					07 47	08 39	09 16			10 16		11 14		12 16		13 16			14 13		15 14	

		SR	SR	SR	XC	SR		GR	SR	XC	SR	GR	SR	SR	XC	SR		GR	SR	GR FO	SR FX	TP	SR FO	SR
					◇1 [trolley]			■ 1 [restaurant]		◇1 [trolley]		■ 1 [restaurant]			◇1 [trolley]			■ 1 [restaurant]		■ 1 [restaurant]		◇1 [trolley]		
Haymarket 225,230,242 ⇌	d							17 22	17 44	17 58					19 55			20 46						
Edinburgh 10 225,230,242	a							17 26	17 51	18 03					19 59			20 50						
	d	15 41	16 36	16 42	17 07	17 16		17 30	17 53	18 08	18 17	18 30	18 45	19 45	20 03	20 39		21 00	21 43	22 00	22 07	22 14	23 01	23 12
Musselburgh	d	15 47	16 43	16 49		17 22			17 59		18 23		18 53	19 52		20 48			21 50		22 15		23 10	23 18
Wallyford	d	15 51		16 53		17 26			18 03		18 27		18 57	19 57		20 52			21 54					23 22
Prestonpans	d	15 54		16 56		17 30			18 06		18 30		19 00	20 00		20 55			21 57					23 25
Longniddry	d	15 59		17 01		17 35			18 11		18 35		19 06	20 05		21 00			22 02					23 30
Drem	d	16 05		17 07		17 40			18 16		18 40		19 13	20 11		21 06			22 08					23 36
Dunbar	a		17 01		17 27			17 51		18 28		18 53			20 23			21 21		22 21	22 44	22 50	23 34	
North Berwick	a	16 14		17 15		17 49			18 24		18 48		19 21	20 19		21 14			22 16					23 55

Saturdays

21 December to 16 May

		TP	GR	XC	SR	SR	XC	SR	SR	SR		SR	SR	XC	SR	SR	SR	SR	SR	XC		SR	SR	SR	SR
		◇1 [trolley]	■ 1 [restaurant]	◇1 A [trolley]			◇1 A [trolley]							◇1 [trolley]						◇1 [trolley]					
Haymarket 225,230,242 ⇌	d			06 57			08 52							10 50											
Edinburgh 10 225,230,242	a			07 01			08 56							10 54											
	d	05 14	05 48	07 07	07 40	08 40	09 08	09 11	09 39	10 10		10 13	10 40	11 08	11 11	11 40	12 09	12 12	12 40	13 09		13 12	13 40	14 10	14 13
Musselburgh	d				07 46	08 46		09 17	09 45	10 16		10 20	10 47		11 18	11 46	12 15	12 19	12 47			13 18	13 46	14 16	14 20
Wallyford	d				07 50	08 50		09 21	09 49			10 24	10 51		11 22	11 50		12 23	12 51			13 22	13 50		14 24
Prestonpans	d				07 53	08 53		09 24	09 52			10 27	10 54		11 25	11 53		12 26	12 54			13 25	13 53		14 27
Longniddry	d				07 58	08 58		09 29	09 57			10 32	10 59		11 30	11 58		12 31	12 59			13 30	13 58		14 32
Drem	d				08 04	09 04		09 35	10 03			10 38	11 04		11 35	12 04		12 36	13 04			13 35	14 04		14 38
Dunbar	a	05 44	06 09	07 28			09 28			10 36				11 28			12 37			13 29				14 36	
North Berwick	a				08 12	09 12		09 43	10 11			10 46	11 12		11 43	12 13		12 45	13 12			13 45	14 12		14 46

		SR	XC	SR	SR	SR		SR	SR	XC	SR	GR	SR	XC	SR	SR		GR	SR	GR	SR	SR	SR	SR
			◇1 [trolley]							◇1 [trolley]		■ 1 [restaurant]		◇1 [trolley]				■ 1 [restaurant]		■ 1 [restaurant]				
Haymarket 225,230,242 ⇌	d											17 21		17 58										
Edinburgh 10 225,230,242	a											17 26		18 03										
	d	14 40	15 08	15 11	15 40	16 10		16 16	16 40	17 08	17 11	17 30	17 41	18 07	18 14	18 41		19 00	19 40	20 00	20 35	21 38	22 09	23 11
Musselburgh	d	14 46		15 17	15 46	16 16		16 23	16 46		17 17		17 48		18 20	18 47			19 47		20 44	21 44	22 15	23 17
Wallyford	d	14 50		15 21	15 50	16 20			16 50		17 21		17 52		18 24	18 51			19 51		20 48	21 48		23 21
Prestonpans	d	14 53		15 24	15 53	16 23			16 53		17 24		17 55		18 27	18 54			19 54		20 51	21 52		23 24
Longniddry	d	14 58		15 29	15 58	16 28			16 58		17 29		18 00		18 33	18 59			19 59		20 56	21 57		23 29
Drem	d	15 04		15 35	16 04	16 33			17 04		17 35		18 08		18 38	19 05			20 04		21 02	22 03		23 35
Dunbar	a		15 28					16 46		17 30		17 51		18 28				19 20		20 21			22 34	
North Berwick	a	15 12		15 43	16 12	16 42			17 12		17 43		18 16		18 46	19 13			20 12		21 11	22 12		23 54

Sundays

15 December to 10 May

		SR	SR	XC	SR	SR	XC	SR	SR	XC		SR	SR	XC	GR	SR	XC	SR	GR	SR		GR	XC	SR	GR	SR
				◇1 [trolley]			◇1 [trolley]			◇1 A [trolley]				◇1 [trolley]	■ 1 [restaurant]		◇1 A [trolley]		■ 1 [restaurant]			■ 1 [restaurant]	◇1		■ 1 [restaurant]	
Haymarket 225,230,242 ⇌	d						12 56			14 42							17 51						19 59			
Edinburgh 10 225,230,242	a						13 01			14 47							17 56						20 04			
	d	09 33	10 33	11 05	11 36	12 33	13 08	13 36	14 33	15 08		15 36	16 37	17 08	17 30	17 33	18 06	18 33	19 00	19 33		20 00	20 18	20 33	21 00	21 33
Musselburgh	d	09 39	10 39		11 42	12 39		13 42	14 39			15 42	16 43			17 39		18 39		19 39				20 39		21 39
Wallyford	d	09 43	10 43		11 46	12 43		13 46	14 43			15 46	16 47			17 43		18 43		19 43				20 43		21 43
Prestonpans	d	09 46	10 46		11 49	12 46		13 49	14 46			15 49	16 50			17 46		18 46		19 46				20 46		21 46
Longniddry	d	09 51	10 51		11 54	12 51		13 54	14 51			15 54	16 55			17 51		18 51		19 51				20 51		21 51
Drem	d	09 58	10 58		12 01	12 58		14 01	14 58			16 01	17 01			17 58		18 58		19 58				20 58		21 58
Dunbar	a			11 25			13 28			15 28				17 28	17 51		18 27		19 21			20 21	20 39		21 20	
North Berwick	a	10 06	11 06		12 09	13 06		14 09	15 06			16 09	17 09			18 06		19 06		20 06				21 06		22 06

A [trolley] from Edinburgh
B until 3 April, MX from 7 April
C ◇ from Edinburgh ■ to Edinburgh

Table T239-F

Mondays to Fridays

16 December to 27 March

Inverness - Kyle of Lochalsh, Thurso and Wick

Miles	Miles			SR	SR	SR	SR		SR	SR	SR	SR		SR	SR	SR	SR		SR FO
				◇	◇	◇ [trolley]	◇			◇	◇ [trolley]				◇	◇ [trolley]			
0	0	Inverness	d	07 00	08 55	10 41	10 56		11 42	13 35	14 00	14 50		17 12	17 54	18 33	21 06		23 33
10	10	Beauly	d	07 15	09 10		11 13		11 59	13 50	14 15	15 05		17 27	18 09		21 21		23 48
13	13	Muir of Ord	d	07 23	09 16	11 01	11 19		12 09	13 56	14 23	15 11		17 33	18 15	18 52	21 27		23 54
16	16	Conon Bridge	d	07 31	09 23		11 26		12 16	14 03	14 31	15 18		17 41	18 23	18 59	21 34		00 01
18¾	18¾	Dingwall	d	07 39	09 29	11 12	11 32		12a21	14 11	14 37	15 24		17 47	18 29	19 06	21 40		00 07
—	30½	Garve	d		09 52		11 55			14 33					18 53				
—	36	Lochluichart	d		09x59		12x02			14x41					19x01				
—	40¼	Achanalt	d		10x06		12x09			14x47					19x07				
—	46½	Achnasheen	d		10 18		12 21			15 04					19 20				
—	59¼	Achnashellach	d		10x36		12x39			15x21					19x37				
—	64½	Strathcarron	d		10 48		12 53			15 33					19 49				
—	67	Attadale	d		10x51		12x56			15x36					19x52				
—	72	Stromeferry	d		11 05		13 10			15 50					20 06				
—	75¾	Duncraig	d		11x12		13x17			15x57					20x13				
—	77	Plockton	d		11 17		13 22			16 02					20 18				
—	78½	Duirinish	d		11x20		13x25			16x05					20x21				
—	82¼	Kyle of Lochalsh	a		11 30		13 35			16 15					20 31				
28½	—	Alness	d	07 51		11 24					14 49	15 36		17 59		19 18	21 52		00 19
31½	—	Invergordon	d	07 58		11 30					14 54	15a41		18 04		19 26	21 57		00 24
40¾	—	Fearn	d	08 11		11 42					15 07			18 17		19 39	22 10		00 37
44¼	—	Tain	d	08 17		11 49					15 13			18 24		19 47	22a16		00a43
57¾	—	Ardgay	d	08 33		12 05					15 29			18a39		20 03			
61	—	Culrain	d	08x37		12x09					15x33					20x07			
61½	—	Invershin	d	08x38		12x10					15x34					20x08			
67	—	Lairg	d	08 53		12 21					15 45					20 20			
77	—	Rogart	d	09x06		12x34					15x58					20x33			
84½	—	Golspie	d	09 18		12 46					16 10					20 45			
87	—	Dunrobin Castle	d																
90½	—	Brora	d	09 29		12 57					16 21					20 55			
101½	—	Helmsdale	d	09 47		13 12					16 36					21 10			
111	—	Kildonan	d	09x59		13x24					16x48					21x22			
118¼	—	Kinbrace	d	10x09		13x34					16x58					21x32			
125¾	—	Forsinard	d	10 21		13 46					17 12					21 44			
134	—	Altnabreac	d	10x29		13x54					17x20					21x52			
143	—	Scotscalder	d	10x38		14x03					17x29					22x01			
147¼	—	Georgemas Junction	a	10 45		14 10					17 36					22 08			
—	—		d	10 49		14 14					17 40					22 12			
154	—	Thurso	a	10 59		14 24					17 50					22 22			
—	—		d	11 02		14 27					17 53					22 25			
160¾	—	Georgemas Junction	d	11 14		14 39					18 05					22 37			
175	—	Wick	a	11 31		14 56					18 22					22 54			

Mondays to Fridays

30 March to 15 May

		SR	SR	SR	SR		SR	SR	SR	SR		SR	SR	SR	SR		SR FO
		◇	◇	◇ [trolley]	◇			◇	◇ [trolley]				◇	◇ [trolley]			
Inverness	d	07 00	08 55	10 41	10 56		11 42	13 35	14 00	14 50		17 12	17 54	18 33	21 06		23 33
Beauly	d	07 15	09 10		11 13		11 59	13 50	14 15	15 05		17 27	18 09		21 21		23 48
Muir of Ord	d	07 23	09 16	11 01	11 19		12 09	13 56	14 23	15 11		17 33	18 15	18 52	21 27		23 54
Conon Bridge	d	07 31	09 23		11 26		12 16	14 03	14 31	15 18		17 41	18 23	18 59	21 34		00 01
Dingwall	d	07 39	09 29	11 12	11 32		12a21	14 11	14 37	15 24		17 47	18 29	19 06	21 40		00 07
Garve	d		09 52		11 55			14 33					18 53				
Lochluichart	d		09x59		12x02			14x41					19x01				
Achanalt	d		10x06		12x09			14x47					19x07				
Achnasheen	d		10 18		12 21			15 04					19 20				
Achnashellach	d		10x36		12x39			15x21					19x37				
Strathcarron	d		10 48		12 53			15 33					19 49				
Attadale	d		10x51		12x56			15x36					19x52				
Stromeferry	d		11 05		13 10			15 50					20 06				
Duncraig	d		11x12		13x17			15x57					20x13				
Plockton	d		11 17		13 22			16 02					20 18				
Duirinish	d		11x20		13x25			16x05					20x21				
Kyle of Lochalsh	a		11 30		13 35			16 15					20 31				
Alness	d	07 51		11 24					14 49	15 36		17 59		19 18	21 52		00 19
Invergordon	d	07 58		11 30					14 54	15a41		18 04		19 26	21 57		00 24
Fearn	d	08 11		11 42					15 07			18 17		19 39	22 10		00 37
Tain	d	08 17		11 49					15 13			18 24		19 47	22a16		00a43
Ardgay	d	08 33		12 05					15 29			18a39		20 03			
Culrain	d	08x37		12x09					15x33					20x07			
Invershin	d	08x38		12x10					15x34					20x08			
Lairg	d	08 53		12 21					15 45					20 20			
Rogart	d	09x06		12x34					15x58					20x33			
Golspie	d	09 18		12 46					16 10					20 45			
Dunrobin Castle	d	09x20		12x48					16x12								
Brora	d	09 29		12 57					16 21					20 55			
Helmsdale	d	09 47		13 12					16 36					21 10			
Kildonan	d	09x59		13x24					16x48					21x22			
Kinbrace	d	10x09		13x34					16x58					21x32			
Forsinard	d	10 21		13 46					17 12					21 44			
Altnabreac	d	10x29		13x54					17x20					21x52			
Scotscalder	d	10x38		14x03					17x29					22x01			
Georgemas Junction	a	10 45		14 10					17 36					22 08			
	d	10 49		14 14					17 40					22 12			
Thurso	a	10 59		14 24					17 50					22 22			
	d	11 02		14 27					17 53					22 25			
Georgemas Junction	d	11 14		14 39					18 05					22 37			
Wick	a	11 31		14 56					18 22					22 54			

NRT DECEMBER 19 EDITION

Table T239-F

Inverness - Kyle of Lochalsh, Thurso and Wick

Saturdays
21 December to 21 March

		SR	SR ◇ A ⊥	SR ◇	SR ◇ ⊥	SR ◇	SR	SR ◇	SR ◇ ⊥	SR	SR	SR ◇	SR ◇ ⊥	SR	SR
Inverness	d		07 00	08 55	10 41	10 56	11 42	13 35	14 00	14 50	17 12	17 54	18 33	21 06	23 33
Beauly	d		07 15	09 10		11 13	11 59	13 50	14 15	15 05	17 27	18 09		21 21	23 48
Muir of Ord	d		07 23	09 16	11 01	11 19	12 09	13 56	14 23	15 11	17 33	18 15	18 52	21 27	23 54
Conon Bridge	d	00 01	07 31	09 23		11 26	12 16	14 03	14 31	15 18	17 41	18 23	18 59	21 34	00 01
Dingwall	d	00 07	07 39	09 29	11 12	11 32	12a21	14 11	14 37	15 24	17 47	18 29	19 06	21 40	00 07
Garve	d			09 52		11 55		14 33				18 53			
Lochluichart	d			09x59		12x02		14x41				19x01			
Achanalt	d			10x06		12x09		14x47				19x07			
Achnasheen	d			10 18		12 21		15 04				19 20			
Achnashellach	d			10x36		12x39		15x21				19x37			
Strathcarron	d			10 48		12 53		15 33				19 49			
Attadale	d			10x51		12x56		15x36				19x52			
Stromeferry	d			11 05		13 10		15 50				20 06			
Duncraig	d			11x12		13x17		15x57				20x13			
Plockton	d			11 17		13 22		16 02				20 18			
Duirinish	d			11x20		13x25		16x05				20x21			
Kyle of Lochalsh	a			11 30		13 35		16 15				20 31			
Alness	d	00 19	07 51		11 24				14 49	15 36	17 59		19 18	21 52	00 19
Invergordon	d	00 24	07 58		11 30				14 54	15a41	18 04		19 26	21 57	00 24
Fearn	d	00 37	08 11		11 42				15 07		18 17		19 39	22 10	00 37
Tain	d	00a43	08 17		11 49				15 13		18 24		19 47	22a16	00a43
Ardgay	d		08 33		12 05				15 29		18a39		20 03		
Culrain	d		08x37		12x09				15x33				20x07		
Invershin	d		08x38		12x10				15x34				20x08		
Lairg	d		08 53		12 21				15 45				20 20		
Rogart	d		09x06		12x34				15x58				20x33		
Golspie	d		09 18		12 46				16 10				20 45		
Dunrobin Castle	d														
Brora	d		09 29		12 57				16 21				20 55		
Helmsdale	d		09 47		13 12				16 36				21 10		
Kildonan	d		09x59		13x24				16x48				21x22		
Kinbrace	d		10x09		13x34				16x58				21x32		
Forsinard	d		10 21		13 46				17 12				21 44		
Altnabreac	d		10x29		13x54				17x20				21x52		
Scotscalder	d		10x38		14x03				17x29				22x01		
Georgemas Junction	a		10 45		14 10				17 36				22 08		
	d		10 49		14 14				17 40				22 12		
Thurso	a		10 59		14 24				17 50				22 22		
	d		11 02		14 27				17 53				22 25		
Georgemas Junction	d		11 14		14 39				18 05				22 37		
Wick	a		11 31		14 56				18 22				22 54		

Saturdays
28 March to 16 May

		SR	SR ◇ A ⊥	SR ◇	SR ◇ ⊥	SR ◇	SR	SR ◇	SR ◇ ⊥	SR	SR	SR ◇	SR ◇ ⊥	SR	SR
Inverness	d		07 00	08 55	10 41	10 56	11 42	13 35	14 00	14 50	17 12	17 54	18 33	21 06	23 33
Beauly	d		07 15	09 10		11 13	11 59	13 50	14 15	15 05	17 27	18 09		21 21	23 48
Muir of Ord	d		07 23	09 16	11 01	11 19	12 09	13 56	14 23	15 11	17 33	18 15	18 52	21 27	23 54
Conon Bridge	d	00 01	07 31	09 23		11 26	12 16	14 03	14 31	15 18	17 41	18 23	18 59	21 34	00 01
Dingwall	d	00 07	07 39	09 29	11 12	11 32	12a21	14 11	14 37	15 24	17 47	18 29	19 06	21 40	00 07
Garve	d			09 52		11 55		14 33				18 53			
Lochluichart	d			09x59		12x02		14x41				19x01			
Achanalt	d			10x06		12x09		14x47				19x07			
Achnasheen	d			10 18		12 21		15 04				19 20			
Achnashellach	d			10x36		12x39		15x21				19x37			
Strathcarron	d			10 48		12 53		15 33				19 49			
Attadale	d			10x51		12x56		15x36				19x52			
Stromeferry	d			11 05		13 10		15 50				20 06			
Duncraig	d			11x12		13x17		15x57				20x13			
Plockton	d			11 17		13 22		16 02				20 18			
Duirinish	d			11x20		13x25		16x05				20x21			
Kyle of Lochalsh	a			11 30		13 35		16 15				20 31			
Alness	d	00 19	07 51		11 24				14 49	15 36	17 59		19 18	21 52	00 19
Invergordon	d	00 24	07 58		11 30				14 54	15a41	18 04		19 26	21 57	00 24
Fearn	d	00 37	08 11		11 42				15 07		18 17		19 39	22 10	00 37
Tain	d	00a43	08 17		11 49				15 13		18 24		19 47	22a16	00a43
Ardgay	d		08 33		12 05				15 29		18a39		20 03		
Culrain	d		08x37		12x09				15x33				20x07		
Invershin	d		08x38		12x10				15x34				20x08		
Lairg	d		08 53		12 21				15 45				20 20		
Rogart	d		09x06		12x34				15x58				20x33		
Golspie	d		09 18		12 46				16 10				20 45		
Dunrobin Castle	d		09x20		12x48				16x12						
Brora	d		09 29		12 57				16 21				20 55		
Helmsdale	d		09 47		13 12				16 36				21 10		
Kildonan	d		09x59		13x24				16x48				21x22		
Kinbrace	d		10x09		13x34				16x58				21x32		
Forsinard	d		10 21		13 46				17 12				21 44		
Altnabreac	d		10x29		13x54				17x20				21x52		
Scotscalder	d		10x38		14x03				17x29				22x01		
Georgemas Junction	a		10 45		14 10				17 36				22 08		
	d		10 49		14 14				17 40				22 12		
Thurso	a		10 59		14 24				17 50				22 22		
	d		11 02		14 27				17 53				22 25		
Georgemas Junction	d		11 14		14 39				18 05				22 37		
Wick	a		11 31		14 56				18 22				22 54		

A ⊥ from Lairg

Table T239-F

Inverness - Kyle of Lochalsh, Thurso and Wick

Sundays
29 March to 10 May

		SR	SR	SR ◇	SR	SR	SR ◇ ⊥	SR
Inverness	d		09 40	10 59	12 53	15 33	17 54	21 08
Beauly	d		09 55	11 15	13 08	15 48	18 09	21 23
Muir of Ord	d		10 01	11 21	13 14	15 56	18 15	21 29
Conon Bridge	d	00 01	10 08	11 28	13 21	16 03	18 22	21 36
Dingwall	d	00 07	10 14	11 34	13 27	16 09	18 31	21 42
Garve	d			11 58				
Lochluichart	d			12x06				
Achanalt	d			12x12				
Achnasheen	d			12 25				
Achnashellach	d			12x43				
Strathcarron	d			12 55				
Attadale	d			12x58				
Stromeferry	d			13 12				
Duncraig	d			13x19				
Plockton	d			13 24				
Duirinish	d			13x27				
Kyle of Lochalsh	a			13 37				
Alness	d	00 19	10 26		13 39	16 21	18 43	21 54
Invergordon	d	00 24	10 32		13 45	16a26	18 48	22 00
Fearn	d	00 37	10 44		13 57		19 01	22 12
Tain	d	00a43	10a50		14a03		19 07	22a18
Ardgay	d						19 23	
Culrain	d						19x27	
Invershin	d						19x28	
Lairg	d						19 42	
Rogart	d						19x55	
Golspie	d						20 07	
Dunrobin Castle	d							
Brora	d						20 18	
Helmsdale	d						20 33	
Kildonan	d						20x45	
Kinbrace	d						20x55	
Forsinard	d						21 07	
Altnabreac	d						21x15	
Scotscalder	d						21x24	
Georgemas Junction	a						21 31	
	d						21 35	
Thurso	a						21 45	
	d						21 48	
Georgemas Junction	d						22 00	
Wick	a						22 17	

Sundays
15 December to 22 March

		SR	SR	SR ◇	SR	SR	SR ◇ ⊥	SR
Inverness	d		09 40	10 59	12 53	15 33	17 54	21 08
Beauly	d		09 55	11 15	13 08	15 48	18 09	21 23
Muir of Ord	d		10 01	11 21	13 14	15 56	18 15	21 29
Conon Bridge	d	00 01	10 08	11 28	13 21	16 03	18 22	21 36
Dingwall	d	00 07	10 14	11 34	13 27	16 09	18 31	21 42
Garve	d			11 58				
Lochluichart	d			12x06				
Achanalt	d			12x12				
Achnasheen	d			12 25				
Achnashellach	d			12x43				
Strathcarron	d			12 55				
Attadale	d			12x58				
Stromeferry	d			13 12				
Duncraig	d			13x19				
Plockton	d			13 24				
Duirinish	d			13x27				
Kyle of Lochalsh	a			13 37				
Alness	d	00 19	10 26		13 39	16 21	18 43	21 54
Invergordon	d	00 24	10 32		13 45	16a26	18 48	22 00
Fearn	d	00 37	10 44		13 57		19 01	22 12
Tain	d	00a43	10a50		14a03		19 07	22a18
Ardgay	d						19 23	
Culrain	d						19x27	
Invershin	d						19x28	
Lairg	d						19 42	
Rogart	d						19x55	
Golspie	d						20 07	
Dunrobin Castle	d							
Brora	d						20 18	
Helmsdale	d						20 33	
Kildonan	d						20x45	
Kinbrace	d						20x55	
Forsinard	d						21 07	
Altnabreac	d						21x15	
Scotscalder	d						21x24	
Georgemas Junction	a						21 31	
	d						21 35	
Thurso	a						21 45	
	d						21 48	
Georgemas Junction	d						22 00	
Wick	a						22 17	

Table T239-R

Mondays to Fridays
30 March to 15 May

Wick, Thurso and Kyle of Lochalsh - Inverness

Miles	Miles			SR	SR	SR	SR	SR	SR	SR	SR	SR	SR	SR	SR	SR	SR
						◇	◇	◇ 🍴		◇	◇		◇ 🍴	◇	◇ 🍴		
0	—	**Wick**	d				06 18	08 02					12 34		16 00		
14¼	—	Georgemas Junction	d				06 36	08 20					12 52		16 18		
21	—	**Thurso**	a				06 46	08 30					13 02		16 28		
—	—		d				06 50	08 34					13 06		16 32		
27¾	—	Georgemas Junction	a				07 00	08 44					13 16		16 42		
—	—		d				07 03	08 47					13 19		16 45		
32	—	Scotscalder	d					08x52					13x24		16x50		
41	—	Altnabreac	d					09x02					13x34		17x00		
49¼	—	Forsinard	d				07 27	09 13					13 47		17 11		
56¾	—	Kinbrace	d					09x22					13x56		17x20		
64	—	Kildonan	d				07x45	09x32					14x06		17x30		
73½	—	Helmsdale	d				08 00	09 46					14 21		17 44		
84½	—	Brora	d				08 16	10 02					14 36		18 00		
88	—	Dunrobin Castle	d					10x07					14x42		18x05		
90½	—	Golspie	d				08 25	10 12					14 47		18 10		
98	—	Rogart	d				08x34	10x21					14x55		18x19		
108	—	Lairg	d		06 26		08 52	10 38					15 12		18 36		
113½	—	Invershin	d		06x34			10x46					15x20		18x44		
114	—	Culrain	d		06x35			10x47					15x21		18x45		
117¼	—	Ardgay	d	06 14	06 43		09 07	10 54					15 30		18 52	19 28	
130¼	—	Tain	d	06 30	06 59		09 23	11 10					15 46		19 08	19 46	22 21
134¼	—	Fearn	d	06 36	07 05		09 29	11 16					15 53			19 52	22 27
143½	—	Invergordon	d	06 49	07 19		09 42	11 31				15 51	16 06		19 25	20 05	22 40
146½	—	Alness	d	06 55	07 25		09 48	11 36				15 56	16 11			20 11	22 45
—	0	**Kyle of Lochalsh**	d			06 11				12 08	13 46			17 13			
—	3¾	Duirinish	d			06x20				12x16	13x54			17x21			
—	5¼	Plockton	d			06 27				12 21	13 59			17 26			
—	6½	Duncraig	d			06x29				12x23	14x01			17x28			
—	10¼	Stromeferry	d			06 39				12 33	14 11			17 38			
—	15¼	Attadale	d			06x50				12x44	14x22			17x49			
—	17¾	Strathcarron	d			06 58				12 52	14 34			17 57			
—	23	Achnashellach	d			07x06				13x00	14x42			18x05			
—	35¾	Achnasheen	d			07 26				13 20	15 03			18 25			
—	42	Achanalt	d			07x35				13x29	15x12			18x34			
—	46¼	Lochluichart	d			07x42				13x36	15x18			18x41			
—	51¾	Garve	d			07 53				13 47	15 29			18 52			
156¼	63¾	Dingwall	d	07 08	07 38	08 16	10 01	11 53	12 45	14 10	15 52	16 11	16 26	19 19	19 41	20 24	22 58
159¼	66¼	Conon Bridge	d	07 14	07 44	08 22	10 06	11 58	12 50	14 15	15 57	16 16	16 31	19 24		20 29	23 03
162	69¼	Muir of Ord	d	07 22	07 51	08 30	10 14	12 06	12 58	14 22	16 04	16 24	16 39	19 31	19 52	20 37	23 11
164¾	72¼	Beauly	d	07 28	07 57	08 35	10 20	12 11	13 04	14 27	16 09	16 29	16 45	19 36		20 42	23 16
175	82¼	**Inverness**	a	07 43	08 12	08 50	10 35	12 26	13 21	14 42	16 27	16 46	17 02	19 54	20 10	20 57	23 31

Mondays to Fridays
16 December to 27 March

		SR	SR	SR	SR	SR	SR	SR	SR	SR	SR	SR	SR	SR	SR
				◇	◇	◇ 🍴		◇	◇		◇ 🍴	◇	◇ 🍴		
Wick	d				06 18	08 02					12 34		16 00		
Georgemas Junction	d				06 36	08 20					12 52		16 18		
Thurso	a				06 46	08 30					13 02		16 28		
	d				06 50	08 34					13 06		16 32		
Georgemas Junction	a				07 00	08 44					13 16		16 42		
	d				07 03	08 47					13 19		16 45		
Scotscalder	d					08x52					13x24		16x50		
Altnabreac	d					09x02					13x34		17x00		
Forsinard	d				07 27	09 13					13 47		17 11		
Kinbrace	d					09x22					13x56		17x20		
Kildonan	d				07x45	09x32					14x06		17x30		
Helmsdale	d				08 00	09 46					14 21		17 44		
Brora	d				08 16	10 02					14 36		18 00		
Dunrobin Castle	d														
Golspie	d				08 25	10 12					14 47		18 10		
Rogart	d				08x34	10x21					14x55		18x19		
Lairg	d		06 26		08 52	10 38					15 12		18 36		
Invershin	d		06x34			10x46					15x20		18x44		
Culrain	d		06x35			10x47					15x21		18x45		
Ardgay	d	06 14	06 43		09 07	10 54					15 30		18 52	19 28	
Tain	d	06 30	06 59		09 23	11 10					15 46		19 08	19 46	22 21
Fearn	d	06 36	07 05		09 29	11 16					15 53			19 52	22 27
Invergordon	d	06 49	07 19		09 42	11 31				15 51	16 06		19 25	20 05	22 40
Alness	d	06 55	07 25		09 48	11 36				15 56	16 11			20 11	22 45
Kyle of Lochalsh	d			06 11				12 08	13 46			17 13			
Duirinish	d			06x20				12x16	13x54			17x21			
Plockton	d			06 27				12 21	13 59			17 26			
Duncraig	d			06x29				12x23	14x01			17x28			
Stromeferry	d			06 39				12 33	14 11			17 38			
Attadale	d			06x50				12x44	14x22			17x49			
Strathcarron	d			06 58				12 52	14 34			17 57			
Achnashellach	d			07x06				13x00	14x42			18x05			
Achnasheen	d			07 26				13 20	15 03			18 25			
Achanalt	d			07x35				13x29	15x12			18x34			
Lochluichart	d			07x42				13x36	15x18			18x41			
Garve	d			07 53				13 47	15 29			18 52			
Dingwall	d	07 08	07 38	08 16	10 01	11 53	12 45	14 10	15 52	16 11	16 26	19 19	19 41	20 24	22 58
Conon Bridge	d	07 14	07 44	08 22	10 06	11 58	12 50	14 15	15 57	16 16	16 31	19 24		20 29	23 03
Muir of Ord	d	07 22	07 51	08 30	10 14	12 06	12 58	14 22	16 04	16 24	16 39	19 31	19 52	20 37	23 11
Beauly	d	07 28	07 57	08 35	10 20	12 11	13 04	14 27	16 09	16 29	16 45	19 36		20 42	23 16
Inverness	a	07 43	08 12	08 50	10 35	12 26	13 21	14 42	16 27	16 46	17 02	19 54	20 10	20 57	23 31

Table T239-R

Saturdays
21 December to 21 March

Wick, Thurso and Kyle of Lochalsh - Inverness

		SR	SR	SR	SR	SR	SR	SR	SR	SR	SR	SR	SR	SR	SR	SR
					◇	◇ 🍴	◇ 🍴		◇	◇		◇ 🍴	◇	◇ 🍴		
Wick	d					06 18	08 02					12 34		16 00		
Georgemas Junction	d					06 36	08 20					12 52		16 18		
Thurso	a					06 46	08 30					13 02		16 28		
	d					06 50	08 34					13 06		16 32		
Georgemas Junction	a					07 00	08 44					13 16		16 42		
	d					07 03	08 47					13 19		16 45		
Scotscalder	d						08x52					13x24		16x50		
Altnabreac	d						09x02					13x34		17x00		
Forsinard	d					07 27	09 13					13 47		17 11		
Kinbrace	d						09x22					13x56		17x20		
Kildonan	d					07x45	09x32					14x06		17x30		
Helmsdale	d					08 00	09 46					14 21		17 44		
Brora	d					08 16	10 02					14 36		18 00		
Dunrobin Castle	d															
Golspie	d					08 25	10 12					14 47		18 10		
Rogart	d					08x34	10x21					14x55		18x19		
Lairg	d			06 26		08 52	10 38					15 12		18 36		
Invershin	d			06x34			10x46					15x20		18x44		
Culrain	d			06x35			10x47					15x21		18x45		
Ardgay	d		06 14	06 43		09 07	10 54					15 30		18 52	19 28	
Tain	d	00 46	06 30	06 59		09 23	11 10					15 46		19 08	19 46	22 21
Fearn	d		06 36	07 05		09 29	11 16					15 53			19 52	22 27
Invergordon	d	01 03	06 49	07 19		09 42	11 31				15 51	16 06		19 25	20 05	22 40
Alness	d		06 55	07 25		09 48	11 36				15 56	16 11			20 11	22 45
Kyle of Lochalsh	d				06 11				12 08	13 46			17 13			
Duirinish	d				06x20				12x16	13x54			17x21			
Plockton	d				06 27				12 21	13 59			17 26			
Duncraig	d				06x29				12x23	14x01			17x28			
Stromeferry	d				06 39				12 33	14 11			17 38			
Attadale	d				06x50				12x44	14x22			17x49			
Strathcarron	d				06 58				12 52	14 34			17 57			
Achnashellach	d				07x06				13x00	14x42			18x05			
Achnasheen	d				07 26				13 20	15 03			18 25			
Achanalt	d				07x35				13x29	15x12			18x34			
Lochluichart	d				07x42				13x36	15x18			18x41			
Garve	d				07 53				13 47	15 29			18 52			
Dingwall	d	01 19	07 08	07 38	08 16	10 01	11 53	12 45	14 10	15 52	16 11	16 26	19 19	19 41	20 24	22 58
Conon Bridge	d		07 14	07 44	08 22	10 06	11 58	12 50	14 15	15 57	16 16	16 31	19 24		20 29	23 03
Muir of Ord	d	01a31	07 22	07 51	08 30	10 14	12 06	12 58	14 22	16 04	16 24	16 39	19 31	19 52	20 37	23 11
Beauly	d		07 28	07 57	08 35	10 20	12 11	13 04	14 27	16 09	16 29	16 45	19 36		20 42	23 16
Inverness	a		07 43	08 12	08 50	10 35	12 26	13 21	14 42	16 27	16 46	17 02	19 54	20 10	20 57	23 31

Saturdays
28 March to 16 May

		SR	SR	SR	SR	SR	SR	SR	SR	SR	SR	SR	SR	SR	SR	SR
					◇	◇ 🍴	◇ 🍴		◇	◇		◇ 🍴	◇	◇ 🍴		
Wick	d					06 18	08 02					12 34		16 00		
Georgemas Junction	d					06 36	08 20					12 52		16 18		
Thurso	a					06 46	08 30					13 02		16 28		
	d					06 50	08 34					13 06		16 32		
Georgemas Junction	a					07 00	08 44					13 16		16 42		
	d					07 03	08 47					13 19		16 45		
Scotscalder	d						08x52					13x24		16x50		
Altnabreac	d						09x02					13x34		17x00		
Forsinard	d					07 27	09 13					13 47		17 11		
Kinbrace	d						09x22					13x56		17x20		
Kildonan	d					07x45	09x32					14x06		17x30		
Helmsdale	d					08 00	09 46					14 21		17 44		
Brora	d					08 16	10 02					14 36		18 00		
Dunrobin Castle	d						10x07					14x42		18x05		
Golspie	d					08 25	10 12					14 47		18 10		
Rogart	d					08x34	10x21					14x55		18x19		
Lairg	d			06 26		08 52	10 38					15 12		18 36		
Invershin	d			06x34			10x46					15x20		18x44		
Culrain	d			06x35			10x47					15x21		18x45		
Ardgay	d		06 14	06 43		09 07	10 54					15 30		18 52	19 28	
Tain	d	00 46	06 30	06 59		09 23	11 10					15 46		19 08	19 46	22 21
Fearn	d		06 36	07 05		09 29	11 16					15 53			19 52	22 27
Invergordon	d	01 03	06 49	07 19		09 42	11 31				15 51	16 06		19 25	20 05	22 40
Alness	d		06 55	07 25		09 48	11 36				15 56	16 11			20 11	22 45
Kyle of Lochalsh	d				06 11				12 08	13 46			17 13			
Duirinish	d				06x20				12x16	13x54			17x21			
Plockton	d				06 27				12 21	13 59			17 26			
Duncraig	d				06x29				12x23	14x01			17x28			
Stromeferry	d				06 39				12 33	14 11			17 38			
Attadale	d				06x50				12x44	14x22			17x49			
Strathcarron	d				06 58				12 52	14 34			17 57			
Achnashellach	d				07x06				13x00	14x42			18x05			
Achnasheen	d				07 26				13 20	15 03			18 25			
Achanalt	d				07x35				13x29	15x12			18x34			
Lochluichart	d				07x42				13x36	15x18			18x41			
Garve	d				07 53				13 47	15 29			18 52			
Dingwall	d	01 19	07 08	07 38	08 16	10 01	11 53	12 45	14 10	15 52	16 11	16 26	19 19	19 41	20 24	22 58
Conon Bridge	d		07 14	07 44	08 22	10 06	11 58	12 50	14 15	15 57	16 16	16 31	19 24		20 29	23 03
Muir of Ord	d	01a31	07 22	07 51	08 30	10 14	12 06	12 58	14 22	16 04	16 24	16 39	19 31	19 52	20 37	23 11
Beauly	d		07 28	07 57	08 35	10 20	12 11	13 04	14 27	16 09	16 29	16 45	19 36		20 42	23 16
Inverness	a		07 43	08 12	08 50	10 35	12 26	13 21	14 42	16 27	16 46	17 02	19 54	20 10	20 57	23 31

Table T239-R

Sundays
29 March to 10 May

Wick, Thurso and Kyle of Lochalsh - Inverness

		SR	SR	SR	SR ◇ 🍴	SR	SR ◇	SR
Wick	d				11 58			
Georgemas Junction	d				12 16			
Thurso	a				12 26			
	d				12 30			
Georgemas Junction	a				12 40			
	d				12 43			
Scotscalder	d				12x48			
Altnabreac	d				12x58			
Forsinard	d				13 09			
Kinbrace	d				13x18			
Kildonan	d				13x28			
Helmsdale	d				13 42			
Brora	d				13 58			
Dunrobin Castle	d				14x03			
Golspie	d				14 08			
Rogart	d				14x17			
Lairg	d				14 33			
Invershin	d				14x41			
Culrain	d				14x42			
Ardgay	d				14 49			
Tain	d	00 46	10 55	14 08	15 05			22 23
Fearn	d		11 01	14 14	15 11			22 29
Invergordon	d	01 03	11 14	14 27	15 24	16 31		22 42
Alness	d		11 19	14 32	15 30	16 36		22 47
Kyle of Lochalsh	d						15 12	
Duirinish	d						15x20	
Plockton	d						15 25	
Duncraig	d						15x27	
Stromeferry	d						15 37	
Attadale	d						15x48	
Strathcarron	d						15 56	
Achnashellach	d						16x04	
Achnasheen	d						16 24	
Achanalt	d						16x33	
Lochluichart	d						16x40	
Garve	d						16 51	
Dingwall	d	01 19	11 35	14 45	15 43	16 49	17 14	23 00
Conon Bridge	d		11 40	14 50	15 48	16 54	17 19	23 05
Muir of Ord	d	01a31	11 48	14 57	15 55	17 02	17 26	23 13
Beauly	d		11 53	15 02	16 01	17 07	17 32	23 18
Inverness	a		12 08	15 17	16 16	17 22	17 47	23 33

Sundays
15 December to 22 March

		SR	SR	SR	SR ◇ 🍴	SR	SR ◇	SR
Wick	d				11 58			
Georgemas Junction	d				12 16			
Thurso	a				12 26			
	d				12 30			
Georgemas Junction	a				12 40			
	d				12 43			
Scotscalder	d				12x48			
Altnabreac	d				12x58			
Forsinard	d				13 09			
Kinbrace	d				13x18			
Kildonan	d				13x28			
Helmsdale	d				13 42			
Brora	d				13 58			
Dunrobin Castle	d							
Golspie	d				14 08			
Rogart	d				14x17			
Lairg	d				14 33			
Invershin	d				14x41			
Culrain	d				14x42			
Ardgay	d				14 49			
Tain	d	00 46	10 55	14 08	15 05			22 23
Fearn	d		11 01	14 14	15 11			22 29
Invergordon	d	01 03	11 14	14 27	15 24	16 31		22 42
Alness	d		11 19	14 32	15 30	16 36		22 47
Kyle of Lochalsh	d						15 12	
Duirinish	d						15x20	
Plockton	d						15 25	
Duncraig	d						15x27	
Stromeferry	d						15 37	
Attadale	d						15x48	
Strathcarron	d						15 56	
Achnashellach	d						16x04	
Achnasheen	d						16 24	
Achanalt	d						16x33	
Lochluichart	d						16x40	
Garve	d						16 51	
Dingwall	d	01 19	11 35	14 45	15 43	16 49	17 14	23 00
Conon Bridge	d		11 40	14 50	15 48	16 54	17 19	23 05
Muir of Ord	d	01a31	11 48	14 57	15 55	17 02	17 26	23 13
Beauly	d		11 53	15 02	16 01	17 07	17 32	23 18
Inverness	a		12 08	15 17	16 16	17 22	17 47	23 33

Table T240-F

Mondays to Fridays
16 December to 15 May

Aberdeen and Elgin - Inverness

Miles			SR ◇	SR ◇	SR ◇[1]	SR ◇ A	SR B	SR [1] C	SR ◇[1]	SR B	SR	SR B	SR	SR ◇ 🍴	SR B	SR	SR B	SR	SR ◇ 🍴	SR	SR B	SR	SR B
0	**Aberdeen**	d			06 22	07 21	07 30	07 49	08 22	08 40	08 58	09 50		10 12	10 40	11 06	11 41		11 56	12 30	12 53	13 08	13 32
6¼	Dyce ✈	d			06 30	07 30	07 39	07 58	08 31	08a49	09 07	09 59		10 21	10 49	11 15	11 50		12 05	12 39	13 02	13 17	13 41
17	**Inverurie**	a			06 41	07 42	07 52	08 11	08 43		09 20	10 12		10 33	11 02	11 28	12 03		12 17	12 52	13 15	13 30	13 54
—		d			06 43	07 43			08 43					10 34					12 17				
27½	Insch	d			06 55	07 55			08 56					10 47					12 30				
40¾	Huntly	d			07 14	08 12			09 12					11 03					12 46				
53¼	Keith	d			07 29	08 26			09 27					11 18					13 01				
71¼	**Elgin**	d	07 06	07 29	07 56	08 52			09 50				10 55	11 41				12 38	13 26				
83½	Forres	d	07 19	07 42	08 09	09 05			10 03				11 08	11 54				12 51	13 39				
93¾	Nairn	d	07 31	07 53	08 19	09 17			10 16				11 20	12 05				13 02	13 50				
108¼	**Inverness**	a	07 48	08 10	08 36	09 35			10 33				11 37	12 23				13 19	14 07				

		SR	SR ◇[1] 🍴	SR	SR B	SR	SR ◇ 🍴	SR B	SR	SR	SR	SR	SR ◇[1] D 🍴	SR B	SR	SR ◇ 🍴	SR B	SR B	SR	SR ◇ 🍴	SR	SR B	SR ◇[1]
Aberdeen	d		13 43	14 05	14 32	15 04	15 27	15 45	16 00	16 26	16 55		17 24	17 37	17 57	18 20	18 56	19 24	19 57	20 19	20 57	21 39	22 00
Dyce ✈	d		13 51	14 14	14 41	15 13	15 36	15 54	16 09	16 35	17 04		17 33	17 46	18 06	18 29	19 05	19 33	20 07	20 28	21 06	21 48	22 08
Inverurie	a		14 02	14 27	14 54	15 26	15 48	16 07	16 22	16 48	17 17		17 45	17 59	18 19	18 41	19 18	19 46	20 20	20 40	21 19	22 01	22 19
	d		14 03				15 48						17 46			18 42				20 40			22 20
Insch	d		14 16				16 01						17 59			18 55				20 53			22 33
Huntly	d		14 32				16 17						18 15			19 11				21 10			22 50
Keith	d		14 47				16 41						18 30			19 26				21 24			23 05
Elgin	d	14 42	15 19				17 02					18 06	18 54			19 47				21 47			23 24
Forres	d	14 56	15 32				17 15					18 19	19 07			20 00				22 00			23 37
Nairn	d	15 07	15 43				17 30					18 30	19 18			20 11				22 11			23 48
Inverness	a	15 26	16 00				17 48					18 48	19 37			20 28				22 28			00 05

		SR B
Aberdeen	d	22 50
Dyce ✈	d	22 59
Inverurie	a	23 12
	d	
Insch	d	
Huntly	d	
Keith	d	
Elgin	d	
Forres	d	
Nairn	d	
Inverness	a	

Saturdays
21 December to 16 May

		SR ◇	SR ◇	SR ◇[1]	SR ◇ B	SR B	SR [1] C	SR ◇	SR B	SR	SR B	SR	SR ◇ 🍴	SR B	SR	SR B	SR	SR ◇ 🍴	SR	SR B	SR	SR B	SR
Aberdeen	d			06 22	07 21	07 30	07 49	08 22	08 40	08 58	09 50		10 12	10 40	11 06	11 41		11 56	12 30	12 53	13 08	13 32	
Dyce ✈	d			06 30	07 30	07 39	07 58	08 31	08a49	09 07	09 59		10 21	10 49	11 15	11 50		12 05	12 39	13 02	13 17	13 41	
Inverurie	a			06 41	07 42	07 52	08 11	08 43		09 20	10 12		10 33	11 02	11 28	12 03		12 17	12 52	13 15	13 30	13 54	
	d			06 43	07 43			08 43					10 34					12 17					
Insch	d			06 55	07 55			08 56					10 47					12 30					
Huntly	d			07 14	08 12			09 12					11 03					12 46					
Keith	d			07 29	08 26			09 27					11 18					13 01					
Elgin	d	07 06	07 29	07 56	08 52			09 50				10 55	11 41				12 38	13 26					14 42
Forres	d	07 19	07 42	08 09	09 05			10 03				11 08	11 54				12 51	13 39					14 56
Nairn	d	07 31	07 53	08 19	09 17			10 16				11 20	12 05				13 02	13 50					15 07
Inverness	a	07 48	08 10	08 36	09 35			10 33				11 37	12 23				13 19	14 07					15 26

		SR ◇[1] 🍴	SR B	SR	SR ◇ 🍴	SR B	SR	SR	SR	SR	SR ◇[1] D 🍴	SR	SR ◇ 🍴	SR B	SR B	SR	SR ◇ 🍴	SR	SR B	SR ◇[1]	SR B
Aberdeen	d	13 43	14 32	15 04	15 27	15 45	16 00	16 26	16 55		17 24	17 57	18 20	18 56	19 24	19 57	20 19	20 57	21 39	22 00	22 50
Dyce ✈	d	13 51	14 41	15 13	15 36	15 54	16 09	16 35	17 04		17 33	18 06	18 29	19 05	19 33	20 07	20 28	21 06	21 48	22 08	22 59
Inverurie	a	14 02	14 54	15 26	15 48	16 07	16 22	16 48	17 17		17 45	18 19	18 41	19 18	19 46	20 20	20 40	21 19	22 01	22 19	23 12
	d	14 03			15 48						17 46		18 42				20 40			22 20	
Insch	d	14 16			16 01						17 59		18 55				20 53			22 33	
Huntly	d	14 32			16 17						18 15		19 11				21 10			22 50	
Keith	d	14 47			16 41						18 30		19 26				21 24			23 05	
Elgin	d	15 19			17 02					18 06	18 54		19 47				21 47			23 24	
Forres	d	15 32			17 15					18 19	19 07		20 00				22 00			23 37	
Nairn	d	15 43			17 30					18 30	19 18		20 11				22 11			23 48	
Inverness	a	16 00			17 48					18 48	19 37		20 28				22 28			00 05	

A From Dundee
B From Montrose
C From Perth
D From Glasgow Queen Street

Table T240-F

Sundays
15 December to 10 May

Aberdeen and Elgin - Inverness

		SR ◇1 🛒	SR 1	SR 1	SR ◇1 🛒	SR 1	SR ◇1 🛒	SR 1	SR 1	SR ◇1 🛒	SR 1	SR ◇ 🛒
Aberdeen	d	10 02	10 34	12 25	13 00	14 28	15 23	15 50	16 49	18 02	20 37	21 28
Dyce ✈	d	10 10	10 43	12 34	13 09	14 37	15 31	15 58	16 58	18 10	20 46	21 37
Inverurie	a	10 22	10 56	12 47	13 21	14 50	15 42	16 12	17 11	18 21	20 59	21 49
	d	10 23			13 21		15 43			18 22		21 49
Insch	d	10 36			13 34		15 56			18 35		22 02
Huntly	d	10 52			13 51		16 12			18 51		22 21
Keith	d	11 07			14 05		16 34			19 06		22 35
Elgin	d	11 27			14 25		16 59			19 30		22 55
Forres	d	11 40			14 38		17 12			19 43		23 08
Nairn	d	11 50			14 49		17 23			19 53		23 19
Inverness	a	12 08			15 07		17 40			20 10		23 37

SUNDAY RETURN TIMES

NRT DECEMBER 19 EDITION

Table T240-R

Sundays
15 December to 10 May

Inverness and Elgin - Aberdeen

		SR ◇1 A	SR ◇1 🛒	SR 1	SR ◇1 🛒	SR 1	SR 1	SR ◇1 🛒	SR 1	SR ◇1 🛒	SR ◇1 B 🛒	SR 1	SR ◇1 🛒	SR ◇1 B
Inverness	d		10 00		12 35			15 30		17 07	18 00		21 07	21 42
Nairn	d		10 16		12 51			15 45		17 23	18 16		21 22	21 59
Forres	d		10 27		13 02			15 55		17 34	18 27		21 32	22 10
Elgin	d		10 40		13 14			16 08		17 47	18a39		21 45	22a23
Keith	d		11 00		13 34			16 28		18 08			22 06	
Huntly	d		11 20		13 50			16 44		18 22			22 21	
Insch	d		11 36		14 06			17 00		18 38			22 37	
Inverurie	a		11 47		14 17			17 12		18 50			22 48	
	d	11 03	11 48	12 55	14 18	14 58	16 19	17 12	17 30	18 50		21 04	22 49	
Dyce ✈	d	11 15	12 00	13 07	14 31	15 10	16 31	17 24	17 42	19 03		21 16	23 01	
Aberdeen	a	11 25	12 10	13 17	14 40	15 20	16 41	17 34	17 52	19 12		21 26	23 10	

A To Glasgow Queen Street B From Glasgow Queen Street

Table T240-R

Mondays to Fridays
16 December to 15 May

Inverness and Elgin - Aberdeen

Miles			SR ◇1 A	SR B	SR	SR ◇1 🛒	SR B	SR	SR	SR B	SR ◇	SR B	SR	SR ◇ 🛒	SR	SR	SR B	SR	SR ◇1 🛒	SR	SR B	SR	SR B
0	**Inverness**	d	04 56			06 01					07 14			09 01	09 59				11 02	11 48			
15	Nairn	d	05 12			06 17					07 30			09 18	10 15				11 19	12 05			
24¾	Forres	d	05 23			06 28					07 41			09 29	10 26				11 29	12 16			
37	**Elgin**	d	05 35			06 40					07 57			09 53	10a40				11 42	12a30			
55	Keith	d	05 55			07 00					08 18			10 13					12 01				
67½	Huntly	d	06 09			07 14		07 48			08 39			10 28					12 16				
80¾	Insch	d	06 24			07 30		08 04			08 56			10 48					12 32				
91¼	**Inverurie**	a	06 36			07 41		08 15			09 08			10 59					12 43				
—		d	06 37	06 53	07 20	07 42	07 58	08 16	08 46		09 08	10 00	10 35	11 00		11 33	12 00	12 21	12 44		13 01	13 32	13 57
102	Dyce ✈	d	06 53	07 05	07 32	07 55	08 10	08 28	08 58	09 07	09 21	10 12	10 47	11 12		11 45	12 12	12 33	12 57		13 13	13 44	14 09
108¼	**Aberdeen**	a	07 03	07 15	07 42	08 04	08 20	08 38	09 08	09 16	09 30	10 22	10 57	11 22		11 55	12 22	12 43	13 06		13 23	13 54	14 19

		SR ◇ 🛒	SR	SR	SR B	SR	SR B	SR ◇ 🛒	SR	SR	SR B	SR ◇ C 🛒	SR	SR	SR	SR	SR ◇1 🛒	SR B	SR ◇1	SR	SR	SR ◇
Inverness	d	12 44	13 33					14 29				15 27	16 49				17 14		18 14	19 02		20 32
Nairn	d	13 02	13 50					14 45				15 44	17 05				17 32		18 30	19 19		20 48
Forres	d	13 13	14 01					14 56				15 55	17 16				17 42		18 41	19 30		20 59
Elgin	d	13 27	14a14					15 09				16 17	17a29				18 01		18 55	19a43		21a13
Keith	d	13 47						15 29				16 37					18 21		19 16			
Huntly	d	14 02						15 43				16 52					18 43		19 39			
Insch	d	14 18						16 01				17 07					18 59		19 55			
Inverurie	a	14 29						16 13				17 19					19 10		20 06			
	d	14 30		14 40	14 54	15 21	15 48	16 14	16 27	16 46	17 00	17 19		17 48	18 20	18 45	19 11	19 25	20 07		20 23	
Dyce ✈	d	14 42		14 52	15 06	15 33	16 00	16 27	16 39	16 58	17 13	17 38		18 00	18 32	18 57	19 24	19 37	20 19		20 35	
Aberdeen	a	14 52		15 02	15 16	15 43	16 10	16 36	16 49	17 08	17 22	17 47		18 10	18 42	19 07	19 34	19 47	20 29		20 45	

		SR B	SR	SR	SR ◇
Inverness	d				21 33
Nairn	d				21 49
Forres	d				22 00
Elgin	d				22 13
Keith	d				22 33
Huntly	d				22 50
Insch	d				23 06
Inverurie	a				23 17
	d	20 51	21 27	22 18	23 17
Dyce ✈	d	21 03	21 39	22 30	23 30
Aberdeen	a	21 13	21 49	22 40	23 39

Saturdays
21 December to 16 May

		SR ◇1 A	SR B	SR	SR ◇1 🛒	SR B	SR	SR B	SR ◇	SR B	SR	SR ◇ 🛒	SR	SR	SR B	SR	SR ◇1 🛒	SR	SR B	SR	SR B	SR ◇ 🛒	SR
Inverness	d	04 56			06 01				07 14			09 01	09 59				11 02	11 48				12 44	13 33
Nairn	d	05 12			06 17				07 30			09 18	10 15				11 19	12 05				13 02	13 50
Forres	d	05 23			06 28				07 41			09 29	10 26				11 29	12 16				13 13	14 01
Elgin	d	05 35			06 40				07 57			09 53	10a40				11 42	12a30				13 27	14a14
Keith	d	05 55			07 00				08 18			10 13					12 01					13 47	
Huntly	d	06 09			07 14				08 39			10 28					12 16					14 02	
Insch	d	06 24			07 30				08 56			10 48					12 32					14 18	
Inverurie	a	06 36			07 41				09 08			10 59					12 43					14 29	
	d	06 37	06 53	07 20	07 42	07 58	08 28		09 08	10 00	10 35	11 00		11 33	12 00	12 21	12 44		13 01	13 32	13 57	14 30	
Dyce ✈	d	06 53	07 05	07 32	07 55	08 10	08 40	09 07	09 21	10 12	10 47	11 12		11 45	12 12	12 33	12 57		13 13	13 44	14 09	14 42	
Aberdeen	a	07 03	07 15	07 42	08 04	08 20	08 50	09 16	09 30	10 22	10 57	11 22		11 55	12 22	12 43	13 06		13 23	13 54	14 19	14 52	

		SR B	SR	SR B	SR ◇ 🛒	SR	SR	SR B	SR ◇ 🛒	SR	SR	SR	SR ◇1 🛒	SR B	SR ◇	SR	SR	SR ◇	SR B	SR	SR	SR ◇
Inverness	d				14 29				15 27	16 49			17 14		18 14	19 02		20 32				21 33
Nairn	d				14 45				15 44	17 05			17 32		18 30	19 19		20 48				21 49
Forres	d				14 56				15 55	17 16			17 42		18 41	19 30		20 59				22 00
Elgin	d				15 09				16 17	17a29			18 01		18 55	19a43		21a13				22 13
Keith	d				15 29				16 37				18 21		19 16							22 33
Huntly	d				15 43				16 52				18 43		19 39							22 50
Insch	d				16 01				17 07				18 59		19 55							23 06
Inverurie	a				16 13				17 19				19 10		20 06							23 17
	d	14 54	15 21	15 48	16 14	16 27	16 46	17 00	17 19		17 48	18 45	19 11	19 25	20 07		20 23		20 51	21 27	22 18	23 17
Dyce ✈	d	15 06	15 33	16 00	16 27	16 39	16 58	17 13	17 38		18 00	18 57	19 24	19 37	20 19		20 35		21 03	21 39	22 30	23 30
Aberdeen	a	15 16	15 43	16 10	16 36	16 49	17 08	17 22	17 47		18 10	19 07	19 34	19 47	20 29		20 45		21 13	21 49	22 40	23 39

A To Edinburgh B To Montrose C To Stonehaven

← See Sunday times, left.

Table T242-F

Mondays to Fridays
16 December to 15 May

Edinburgh - Dunfermline, Kirkcaldy and Glenrothes with Thornton

Miles	Miles	Station		SR MX ◇ A	SR ◇1 B	SR	SR	SR ◇ C	SR	SR ◇ D	SR	SR	SR ◇1 B	SR ◇ E	SR F	SR ◇ D	SR F	SR	SR F	SR ◇1 G	SR	SR	SR ◇ D
0	0	**Edinburgh** 10	d		05 30	06 08	06 16	06 29	06 33	07 00	07 09	07 16	07 29	07 34	07 37	07 59	08 08	08 15	08 23	08 34	08 38	08 45	08 58
1¼	1¼	Haymarket	d		05 35	06 12	06 20	06 33	06 38	07 04	07 14	07 20	07 35	07 38	07 42	08 07	08 15	08 19	08 28	08 40	08 44	08 51	09 03
4½	4½	South Gyle	d			06 17	06 25		06 46		07 19				07 48			08 24	08a33		08 49	08 57	
—	—	Edinburgh Gateway	d			06 19		06 39		07 10		07 26		07 44		08 12	08 20			08 47		08 59	09 09
9½	9½	Dalmeny	d			06 25	06 31		06 53		07 25	07 32			07 54			08 31			08 55	09 05	
11¼	11¼	North Queensferry	d			06 29	06 35		06 56		07 29	07 35			07 58			08 34			08 59	09 09	
13¾	13¾	Inverkeithing	d		05 49	06 33	06 39	06 49	07 01	07 20	07 33	07 39		07 55	08 02	08 23	08 31	08 38			09 03	09 13	09 22
—	14¾	Rosyth	d				06 42					07 43						08 42				09 16	
—	17	**Dunfermline Town**	d				06 47					07 48						08 47				09 21	
—	18¾	Dunfermline Queen Margaret	d				06 51					07 51						08 50				09 25	
—	22¾	Cowdenbeath	d	00 02			06 57					07 58						08 57				09 31	
—	25	Lochgelly	d	00 08			07 03					08 03						09 02				09 37	
—	27¾	Cardenden	d	00 12			07 07					08 07						09 06				09 41	
14¾	—	Dalgety Bay	d			06 36			07 04		07 36				08 05		08 34				09 06		
17½	—	Aberdour	d			06 41			07 09		07 41				08 10		08 39				09 11		
20¼	—	Burntisland	d			06 45			07 13		07 45				08 14		08 43				09 15		
22¾	—	Kinghorn	d			06 50			07 17		07 50				08 19		08 48				09 20		
25¾	—	Kirkcaldy	d		06a03	06a57		07a05	07 22	07a36	07 55		08a04	08a10	08 29	08a38	08 53			09a09	09 25		09a38
30¾	30¾	Glenrothes With Thornton 2	a	00 18			07 16		07 33		08 03	08 17			08 43		09 03	09 16			09 36	09 50	

Station		SR F	SR	SR	SR ◇ E	SR	SR	SR ◇ D	SR	SR	GR ■ 1 H	SR ◇1 G	SR	SR	SR ◇ D	SR	SR	SR ◇ E	SR	SR	SR ◇ D	SR	SR
Edinburgh 10	d	09 02	09 07	09 18	09 36	09 41	09 51	09 59	10 07	10 19	10 28	10 36	10 41	10 48	11 02	11 07	11 15	11 37	11 42	11 49	12 00	12 09	12 18
Haymarket	d	09 07	09 11	09 22	09 40	09 45	09 55	10 07	10 11	10 23	10 33	10u41	10 45	10 54	11 06	11 11	11 22	11 41	11 46	11 53	12 05	12 15	12 22
South Gyle	d	09a11		09 28		09 51				10 28			10 50				11 27		11 51				12 27
Edinburgh Gateway	d		09 18		09 46		10 01	10 12	10 17			10a47		10 59	11 12	11 17		11 48		12 00	12 12	12 21	
Dalmeny	d		09 24	09 34		09 57	10 07		10 23	10 35			10 56	11 05		11 23	11 34		11 58	12 06		12 27	12 33
North Queensferry	d		09 27	09 38		10 01	10 10		10 26	10 38			11 00	11 09		11 26	11 37		12 01	12 10		12 30	12 37
Inverkeithing	d		09 31	09 42	09 58	10 05	10 14	10 23	10 30	10 42	10 48		11 04	11 13	11 22	11 30	11 41	11 58	12 05	12 14	12 22	12 34	12 41
Rosyth	d			09 45			10 18			10 46				11 16			11 45			12 17			12 44
Dunfermline Town	d			09 50			10 23			10 51				11 21			11 50			12 22			12 49
Dunfermline Queen Margaret	d			09 54			10 27			10 54				11 25			11 53			12 26			12 53
Cowdenbeath	d			10a03			10 33			11a03				11 31			12a00			12 32			13a00
Lochgelly	d						10 39							11 37						12 38			
Cardenden	d						10 42							11 41						12 42			
Dalgety Bay	d		09 34			10 08			10 33				11 07			11 33			12 08			12 37	
Aberdour	d		09 39			10 13			10 38				11 12			11 38			12 13			12 42	
Burntisland	d		09 43			10 17			10 42				11 16			11 42			12 17			12 46	
Kinghorn	d		09 48			10 22			10 47				11 21			11 47			12 22			12 51	
Kirkcaldy	d		09 53		10a14	10 27		10a38	10 52		11a04		11 26		11a38	11 52		12a14	12 27		12a38	12 56	
Glenrothes With Thornton 2	a		10 04			10 38	10 50		11 03				11 37	11 49		12 03			12 39	12 51		13 06	

Station		SR ◇ E	SR	SR	SR ◇ D	SR	SR	SR ◇1 G	SR	SR	SR ◇ D	SR	SR	GR ■ 1 I	SR ◇ E	SR	SR	SR ◇ D	SR	SR	SR ◇ E	SR
Edinburgh 10	d	12 37	12 42	12 49	13 00	13 08	13 23	13 33	13 41	13 48	14 03	14 07	14 23	14 29	14 37	14 40	14 49	15 00	15 07	15 17	15 35	15 38
Haymarket	d	12 41	12 46	12 53	13 05	13 14	13 27	13u40	13 45	13 54	14 07	14 12	14 28	14 34	14 41	14 46	14 53	15 05	15 11	15 22	15 40	15 45
South Gyle	d		12 51				13 32		13 50				14 32			14 51				15 27		15 50
Edinburgh Gateway	d	12 47		12 59	13 11	13 19		13a45		13 59	14 13	14 17			14 47		14 59	15 11	15 17		15 48	
Dalmeny	d		12 57	13 05		13 25	13 38		13 57	14 05		14 25	14 39			14 57	15 05		15 23	15 34		15 57
North Queensferry	d		13 01	13 08		13 29	13 41		14 00	14 09		14 28	14 42			15 01	15 08		15 26	15 37		16 00
Inverkeithing	d	12 57	13 05	13 12	13 21	13 33	13 45		14 04	14 13	14 25	14 32	14 46	14 51	14 58	15 05	15 12	15 21	15 30	15 41	15 58	16 04
Rosyth	d			13 16			13 50			14 17			14 50				15 16			15 45		
Dunfermline Town	d			13 21			13 55			14 22			14 55				15 21			15 50		
Dunfermline Queen Margaret	d			13 24			13 59			14 25			14 58				15 24			15 53		
Cowdenbeath	d			13 31			14a07			14 32			15a06				15 31			16a02		
Lochgelly	d			13 36						14 37							15 36					
Cardenden	d			13 40						14 41							15 40					
Dalgety Bay	d		13 08			13 36			14 07			14 35				15 08			15 33			16 07
Aberdour	d		13 13			13 41			14 12			14 40				15 13			15 38			16 12
Burntisland	d		13 17			13 45			14 16			14 44				15 17			15 42			16 16
Kinghorn	d		13 22			13 50			14 21			14 49				15 22			15 47			16 21
Kirkcaldy	d	13a13	13 27		13a37	13 55			14 26		14a41	14 54		15a06	15a13	15 27		15a37	15 52		16a14	16 26
Glenrothes With Thornton 2	a		13 37	13 50		14 06			14 37	14 51		15 05				15 38	15 50		16 04			16 37

A From Edinburgh to Perth
B To Aberdeen
C To Dundee
D To Arbroath
E To Perth
F From Tweedbank
G To Inverness
H From Leeds to Aberdeen
I From London Kings Cross to Aberdeen

NRT DECEMBER 19 EDITION

Table T242-F

Mondays to Fridays
16 December to 15 May

Edinburgh - Dunfermline, Kirkcaldy and Glenrothes with Thornton

Station		SR	SR ◇ A	SR	SR	SR B	SR	SR	SR A	SR	SR	SR	SR ◇1 C	SR	SR	SR ◇ D	XC ◇1 E	SR F	SR	SR	GR ■ 1 G	SR ◇ B	SR
Edinburgh 10	d	15 45	16 03	16 08	16 19	16 35	16 38	16 48	17 01	17 11	17 16	17 19	17 42	17 45	17 56	18 04	18 11		18 14	18 25	18 33	18 43	18 50
Haymarket	d	15 49	16 07	16 12	16 23	16 39	16 44	16 52	17 06	17 15	17 21	17 24	17u47	17 51	18 01	18 08	18 17		18 20	18 29	18 38	18 47	18 54
South Gyle	d				16 28		16 49			17 21		17 30		17 57					18 25				18 59
Edinburgh Gateway	d	15 56	16 13	16 18		16 45	16 51	16 59	17 13		17 27		17 53		18 06	18 14				18 35		18 53	
Dalmeny	d	16 02		16 23	16 35		16 57	17 04			17 33	17 37		18 04	18 12			18 28	18 32	18 41			19 06
North Queensferry	d	16 06		16 27	16 38		17 01	17 08			17 37	17 41		18 08	18 16				18 36	18 44			19 09
Inverkeithing	d	16 10	16 23	16 31	16 42	16 57	17 05	17 12	17 23	17 32	17 41	17 46		18 13	18 20	18 24	18 31	18 36	18 41	18 50	18 55	19 03	19 13
Rosyth	d	16 13			16 46			17 16		17 37		17 51			18 23					18 53			19 17
Dunfermline Town	d	16 18			16 51			17 21		17 43		17 56			18 28					18 58			19 22
Dunfermline Queen Margaret	d	16 22			16 54			17 24		17 48		18 02			18 32					19 02			19 25
Cowdenbeath	d	16 28			17a01			17a31		17 56		18 09			18 38					19 08			19 32
Lochgelly	d	16 34								18 02		18 16			18 44					19 14			19 37
Cardenden	d	16 38								18 07		18a23			18 48					19 18			19 41
Dalgety Bay	d			16 34			17 08				17 45			18 16				18 39	18 44				
Aberdour	d			16 39			17 13				17 50			18 21				18 44	18 49				
Burntisland	d			16 43			17 17				17 54			18 25				18 48	18 53				
Kinghorn	d			16 48			17 22				17 59			18 30				18 53	18 58				
Kirkcaldy	d		16a39	16 53		17a13	17 27		17a39		18a05		18a20	18 35		18a40	18a45	18a57	19 03		19a11	19a19	
Glenrothes With Thornton 2	a	16 47		17 04			17 38			18 18				18 45	18 57				19 15	19 27			19 51

Station		SR ◇ D	SR	SR	SR ◇1 C	SR	SR ◇ D	XC ◇1 H	GR ■ 1 G	SR ◇ B	SR	SR ◇ D	SR ◇1 I	SR B	SR ◇ D	SR ◇ B	SR ◇ D	SR ◇ B
Edinburgh 10	d	19 02	19 13	19 20	19 41	19 53	19 58	20 14	20 32	20 40	20 51	21 08	21 43	21 49	22 11	22 37	23 06	23 19
Haymarket	d	19 06	19 17	19 24	19 46	19 57	20 04	20 19	20 37	20 44	20 55	21 12	21 47	21 54	22 15	22 41	23 12	23 23
South Gyle	d		19 22			20 02	20 10				21 00	21 17			22 20	22 46	23 17	23 28
Edinburgh Gateway	d	19 12		19 30	19 52		20 12			20 50	21 02	21 19		22 00	22 22	22 48	23 20	23 30
Dalmeny	d		19 28	19 36		20 08	20 18				21 08	21 25		22 06	22 28	22 54	23 27	23 36
North Queensferry	d		19 32	19 39		20 12	20 22				21 12	21 29		22 09	22 32	22 58	23 30	23 40
Inverkeithing	d	19 22	19 36	19 43	20 03	20 16	20 26	20a32	20 53	21 00	21 16	21 33		22 13	22 36	23 02	23 34	23 44
Rosyth	d			19 47		20 19					21 19			22 17				23 47
Dunfermline Town	d			19 52		20 24					21 24			22 22				23 52
Dunfermline Queen Margaret	d			19 55		20 28					21 28			22 25				23 56
Cowdenbeath	d			20 02		20 34					21 34			22 32				00 02
Lochgelly	d			20 07		20 40					21 40			22 37				00 08
Cardenden	d			20 11		20 44					21 44			22 41				00 12
Dalgety Bay	d		19 39				20 29					21 36			22 39	23 05	23 37	
Aberdour	d		19 44				20 34					21 41			22 44	23 10	23 42	
Burntisland	d		19 48				20 38					21 45			22 48	23 14	23 45	
Kinghorn	d		19 53				20 43					21 49			22 53	23 19	23 51	
Kirkcaldy	d	19a38	19a58		20a17		20a47		21a09	21a16		21a54	22a15		22a57	23a23	23a56	
Glenrothes With Thornton 2	a			20 21		20 53					21 53			22 48				00 18

Saturdays
21 December to 16 May

Station		SR ◇ J	SR ◇1 I	SR	SR ◇ D	SR	SR ◇ A	SR	SR	SR ◇1 I	SR ◇ B	SR	SR ◇ A	SR	SR	SR ◇1 C	SR	SR	SR ◇ A	SR	SR	SR ◇ B	SR
Edinburgh 10	d		05 30	06 14	06 28	06 36	07 00	07 10	07 16	07 29	07 33	07 37	08 00	08 10	08 13	08 33	08 37	08 40	09 01	09 07	09 18	09 38	09 41
Haymarket	d		05 35	06 18	06 32	06 40	07 04	07 14	07 20	07 34	07 37	07 41	08 07	08 14	08 18	08 38	08 43	08 48	09 06	09 11	09 22	09 42	09 46
South Gyle	d			06 23		06 45		07 20				07 48			08 24		08 49	08 52			09 27		09 51
Edinburgh Gateway	d			06 25	06 39	06 47	07 10		07 26		07 44		08 12	08 20		08 46		08 55	09 12	09 17		09 48	
Dalmeny	d			06 31		06 53		07 26	07 32			07 54			08 31		08 55	09 01		09 25	09 33		09 57
North Queensferry	d			06 35		06 57		07 30	07 35			07 58			08 34		08 59	09 04		09 29	09 37		10 01
Inverkeithing	d		05 49	06 39	06 49	07 01	07 20	07 34	07 39		07 55	08 02	08 23	08 31	08 38		09 03	09 08	09 22	09 33	09 41	09 58	10 05
Rosyth	d			06 42					07 43						08 42			09 12			09 44		
Dunfermline Town	d			06 47					07 48						08 47			09 17			09 49		
Dunfermline Queen Margaret	d			06 51					07 51						08 50			09 20			09 53		
Cowdenbeath	d	00 02		06 57					07 58						08 57			09 27			10a00		
Lochgelly	d	00 08		07 03					08 03						09 02			09 32					
Cardenden	d	00 12		07 07					08 07						09 06			09 36					
Dalgety Bay	d					07 04		07 37				08 05		08 34			09 06			09 36			10 08
Aberdour	d					07 08		07 42				08 10		08 39			09 11			09 41			10 13
Burntisland	d					07 12		07 46				08 14		08 43			09 15			09 45			10 17
Kinghorn	d					07 17		07 51				08 19		08 48			09 20			09 50			10 22
Kirkcaldy	d		06a03		07a05	07 22	07a36	07 56		08a04	08a10	08 29	08a38	08 53		09a09	09 25		09a38	09 55		10a14	10 27
Glenrothes With Thornton 2	a	00 18		07 16		07 33		08 06	08 17			08 43		09 03	09 16		09 36	09 46		10 06			10 38

A To Arbroath
B To Perth
C To Inverness
D To Dundee
E From Plymouth to Aberdeen
F From Glasgow Queen Street to Markinch
G From London Kings Cross to Aberdeen
H From Penzance to Dundee
I To Aberdeen
J From Edinburgh to Perth

Table T242-F

Saturdays
21 December to 16 May

Edinburgh - Dunfermline, Kirkcaldy and Glenrothes with Thornton

		SR	SR ◇ A	SR	SR	GR ■1 B	SR ◇1 C	SR	SR	SR ◇ A	SR	SR	SR ◇ D	SR	SR	SR ◇ A	SR	SR	SR ◇ D	SR	SR	SR ◇ A
Edinburgh 10	d	09 51	10 02	10 07	10 20	10 28	10 37	10 44	10 48	11 02	11 07	11 18	11 35	11 42	11 51	12 02	12 08	12 18	12 37	12 41	12 49	13 03
Haymarket	d	09 55	10 07	10 13	10 24	10 33	10u42	10 48	10 53	11 06	11 11	11 22	11 39	11 46	11 55	12 06	12 12	12 22	12 41	12 45	12 53	13 07
South Gyle	d				10 29			10 53				11 27		11 51				12 27		12 51		
Edinburgh Gateway	d	10 01	10 12	10 18			10a47		10 59	11 12	11 17		11 45		12 00	12 12	12 18		12 47		12 59	13 13
Dalmeny	d	10 06		10 24	10 36			10 59	11 05		11 23	11 34		11 58	12 06		12 24	12 33		12 57	13 05	
North Queensferry	d	10 10		10 28	10 39			11 03	11 09		11 26	11 37		12 01	12 10		12 27	12 37		13 01	13 08	
Inverkeithing	d	10 14	10 23	10 32	10 43	10 48		11 07	11 13	11 22	11 30	11 41	11 58	12 05	12 14	12 22	12 31	12 41	12 57	13 05	13 12	13 23
Rosyth	d	10 18			10 47				11 16			11 45			12 17			12 44			13 16	
Dunfermline Town	d	10 22			10 52				11 21			11 50			12 22			12 49			13 21	
Dunfermline Queen Margaret	d	10 26			10 55				11 25			11 53			12 26			12 53			13 24	
Cowdenbeath	d	10 32			11a02				11 31			12a00			12 32			13a00			13 31	
Lochgelly	d	10 38							11 37						12 38						13 36	
Cardenden	d	10 42							11 41						12 42						13 40	
Dalgety Bay	d			10 35				11 10			11 33			12 08			12 34			13 08		
Aberdour	d			10 40				11 15			11 38			12 13			12 39			13 13		
Burntisland	d			10 44				11 19			11 42			12 17			12 43			13 17		
Kinghorn	d			10 49				11 24			11 47			12 22			12 48			13 22		
Kirkcaldy	d		10a38	10 54		11a04		11 29		11a38	11 52		12a14	12 27		12a38	12 53		13a13	13 27		13a39
Glenrothes With Thornton 2	a	10 50		11 05				11 39	11 49		12 03			12 39	12 51		13 04			13 37	13 50	

		SR	SR	SR ◇1 C	SR	SR	SR ◇ A	SR	SR	GR ■1 E	SR ◇ D	SR	SR	SR ◇ A	SR	SR	SR ◇ D	SR	SR	SR ◇ A	SR	SR	SR D
Edinburgh 10	d	13 11	13 18	13 31	13 42	13 49	14 04	14 08	14 23	14 29	14 37	14 41	14 49	15 00	15 07	15 18	15 36	15 40	15 44	16 01	16 06	16 18	16 36
Haymarket	d	13 15	13 22	13u38	13 46	13 54	14 08	14 14	14 27	14 34	14 41	14 45	14 53	15 04	15 11	15 22	15 40	15 45	15 49	16 05	16 10	16 23	16 40
South Gyle	d		13 27		13 51				14 32			14 50				15 27		15 50				16 28	
Edinburgh Gateway	d	13 21		13a44		14 00	14 15	14 19			14 47		14 59	15 11	15 17		15 46		15 56	16 11	16 16		16 47
Dalmeny	d	13 27	13 33		13 57	14 09		14 25	14 39			14 57	15 05		15 23	15 34		15 57	16 02		16 21	16 35	
North Queensferry	d	13 30	13 37		14 00	14 12		14 28	14 42			15 01	15 08		15 26	15 37		16 00	16 06		16 25	16 38	
Inverkeithing	d	13 34	13 41		14 04	14 17	14 25	14 32	14 46	14 51	14 58	15 05	15 12	15 21	15 30	15 41	15 57	16 04	16 10	16 22	16 29	16 42	16 57
Rosyth	d		13 44			14 20			14 50				15 16			15 45			16 13			16 46	
Dunfermline Town	d		13 49			14 25			14 55				15 21			15 50			16 18			16 51	
Dunfermline Queen Margaret	d		13 53			14 29			14 58				15 24			15 53			16 22			16 54	
Cowdenbeath	d		14a00			14 35			15a06				15 31			16a02			16 28			17a01	
Lochgelly	d					14 40							15 36						16 34				
Cardenden	d					14 44							15 40						16 38				
Dalgety Bay	d	13 37			14 07			14 35				15 08			15 33			16 07			16 32		
Aberdour	d	13 42			14 12			14 40				15 13			15 38			16 12			16 37		
Burntisland	d	13 46			14 16			14 44				15 17			15 42			16 16			16 41		
Kinghorn	d	13 51			14 21			14 49				15 22			15 47			16 21			16 46		
Kirkcaldy	d	13 56			14 26		14a41	14 54		15a06	15a13	15 27		15a37	15 52		16a12	16 26		16a37	16 51		17a13
Glenrothes With Thornton 2	a	14 07			14 37	14 51		15 05				15 38	15 50		16 04			16 37	16 47		17 02		

		SR	SR	SR A	SR	SR	SR	SR ◇1 C	SR	XC ◇1 F	SR	SR	GR ■1 E	SR ◇ D	SR	SR ◇ G	SR	SR	SR ◇1 C	SR	SR ◇ G	XC ◇1 H
Edinburgh 10	d	16 42	16 49	17 01	17 05	17 13	17 23	17 41	17 47	18 12	18 15	18 28	18 35	18 42	18 49	19 00	19 13	19 20	19 39	19 50	20 01	20 12
Haymarket	d	16 46	16 53	17 06	17 11	17 17	17 27	17u47	17 51	18 16	18 20	18 32	18 40	18 46	18 53	19 04	19 17	19 24	19 44	19 54	20 05	20 17
South Gyle	d	16 51			17 17		17 32		17 58		18 24				18 59		19 22			19 59	20 10	
Edinburgh Gateway	d	16 53	16 59	17 13		17 24		17 53				18 37		18 52		19 10		19 30	19 50		20 12	
Dalmeny	d	16 59	17 04			17 30	17 38		18 05		18 31	18 43			19 06		19 28	19 36		20 05	20 18	
North Queensferry	d	17 03	17 08			17 34	17 42		18 09		18 34	18 47			19 09		19 32	19 39		20 09	20 22	
Inverkeithing	d	17 07	17 12	17 23	17 28	17 38	17 46		18 13	18 29	18 38	18 51	18 58	19 02	19 13	19 22	19 36	19 43	20 01	20 13	20 26	20 35
Rosyth	d		17 16		17 32		17 49					18 54			19 17			19 47		20 16		
Dunfermline Town	d		17 21		17 37		17 54					18 59			19 22			19 52		20 21		
Dunfermline Queen Margaret	d		17 24		17 41		17 58					19 03			19 25			19 55		20 25		
Cowdenbeath	d		17a31		17 48		18 04					19 09			19 32			20 02		20 31		
Lochgelly	d				17 54		18 10					19 15			19 37			20 07		20 37		
Cardenden	d				17 58		18 14					19 19			19 41			20 11		20 41		
Dalgety Bay	d	17 10				17 42			18 16		18 41						19 39				20 29	
Aberdour	d	17 15				17 47			18 21		18 46						19 44				20 34	
Burntisland	d	17 19				17 51			18 25		18 50						19 48				20 38	
Kinghorn	d	17 24				17 56			18 30		18 55						19 53				20 43	
Kirkcaldy	d	17 29		17a39		18a02		18a20	18 35	18a43	19 00		19a13	19a19		19a38	19a58		20a15		20a47	20a51
Glenrothes With Thornton 2	a	17 40			18 07		18 23		18 45		19 11	19 28			19 51			20 21		20 50		

A To Arbroath
B From Leeds to Aberdeen
C To Inverness
D To Perth
E From London Kings Cross to Aberdeen
F From Plymouth to Aberdeen
G To Dundee
H From Plymouth to Dundee

Table T242-F

Saturdays
21 December to 16 May

Edinburgh - Dunfermline, Kirkcaldy and Glenrothes with Thornton

		SR ◇ A	SR	SR ◇ B	SR ◇1 C	SR A	SR ◇ B	SR ◇ A	SR ◇ B	SR ◇ A
Edinburgh 10	d	20 38	20 51	21 05	21 43	21 51	22 12	22 37	23 09	23 19
Haymarket	d	20 44	20 55	21 09	21 47	21 55	22 16	22 41	23 13	23 23
South Gyle	d		21 00	21 14			22 21	22 46	23 18	23 28
Edinburgh Gateway	d	20 50	21 02	21 16		22 03	22 23	22 48	23 21	23 30
Dalmeny	d		21 08	21 22		22 09	22 29	22 54	23 27	23 36
North Queensferry	d		21 12	21 26		22 12	22 33	22 58	23 30	23 40
Inverkeithing	d	21 00	21 16	21 30		22 16	22 37	23 02	23 34	23 44
Rosyth	d		21 19			22 20				23 47
Dunfermline Town	d		21 24			22 25				23 52
Dunfermline Queen Margaret	d		21 28			22 28				23 56
Cowdenbeath	d		21 34			22 35				00 02
Lochgelly	d		21 40			22 40				00 08
Cardenden	d		21 44			22 44				00 12
Dalgety Bay	d			21 33			22 40	23 05	23 37	
Aberdour	d			21 38			22 45	23 10	23 42	
Burntisland	d			21 42			22 49	23 14	23 46	
Kinghorn	d			21 46			22 54	23 19	23 51	
Kirkcaldy	d	21a16		21a51	22a15		22a58	23a23	23a56	
Glenrothes With Thornton 2	a		21 53			22 51				00 18

Sundays
15 December to 10 May

		SR ◇ D	XC ◇1 C	GR ■1 C	SR ◇1 C	SR ◇1 E	SR	SR	SR ◇1 C	SR	SR	SR ◇ B	SR	SR	SR ◇1 C	SR	SR	SR ◇ B	SR ◇1 E	SR	SR	GR ■1 F	SR
Edinburgh 10	d		08 04	09 10	09 17	09 29	09 55	10 15	10 50	10 55	11 15	11 32	11 55	12 15	12 41	12 55	13 15	13 34	13 57	14 00	14 15	14 33	14 55
Haymarket	d		08 09	09 15	09 21	09 34	09 59	10 19	10 54	10 59	11 19	11 36	11 59	12 21	12 46	12 59	13 19	13 38	14 01	14 04	14 19	14 39	14 59
South Gyle	d				09 26		10 04	10 24		11 04	11 24		12 04	12 26		13 04	13 24			14 09	14 24		15 04
Edinburgh Gateway	d				09 28	09 41	10 06	10 26		11 06	11 26	11 42	12 06	12 28		13 06	13 26	13 44	14 07	14 11	14 26		15 06
Dalmeny	d				09 34		10 12	10 32		11 12	11 32		12 12	12 34		13 12	13 32			14 17	14 32		15 12
North Queensferry	d				09 41		10 19	10 36		11 16	11 36		12 16	12 38		13 16	13 36			14 21	14 36		15 16
Inverkeithing	d		08 25	09 33	09 45	09 54	10 23	10 40	11 07	11 20	11 40	11 52	12 20	12 42	13 00	13 20	13 40	13 56	14 18	14 25	14 40	14 54	15 20
Rosyth	d						10 26			11 23			12 23			13 23				14 28			15 23
Dunfermline Town	d						10 31			11 28			12 28			13 28				14 33			15 28
Dunfermline Queen Margaret	d						10 35			11 32			12 32			13 32				14 37			15 32
Cowdenbeath	d	00 02					10 41			11 38			12 38			13 38				14 43			15 38
Lochgelly	d	00 08					10 47			11 44			12 44			13 44				14 49			15 44
Cardenden	d	00 12					10 51			11 48			12 48			13 48				14 53			15 48
Dalgety Bay	d				09 48			10 43			11 43			12 45			13 43				14 43		
Aberdour	d				09 53			10 48			11 48			12 50			13 48				14 48		
Burntisland	d				09 57			10 52			11 52			12 54			13 52				14 52		
Kinghorn	d				10 02			10 57			11 57			12 59			13 57				14 57		
Kirkcaldy	d		08a39	09a48	10a06	10a09		11 02	11a23		12 02	12a08		13 04	13a14		14 02	14a12	14a34		15 02	15a10	
Glenrothes With Thornton 2	a	00 18					11 00	11 13		11 57	12 13		12 57	13 16		13 57	14 13			15 02	15 15		15 57

		SR	SR B	SR ◇1 E	SR	SR ◇1 C	SR	SR	SR ◇1 C	SR	SR B	SR ◇ A	SR	XC ◇1 G	SR	GR ■1 H	SR ◇ A	SR ◇ B	SR	SR	SR ◇1 C	SR	SR	SR ◇ B	SR
Edinburgh 10	d	15 17	15 34	15 50	15 55	16 05	16 15	16 55	17 05	17 16	17 34	17 50	17 55	18 13	18 17	18 36	18 55	19 15	19 55	20 15	21 00	21 15	21 55	22 26	23 34
Haymarket	d	15 21	15 38	15 55	15 59	16 10	16 19	16 59	17 10	17 20	17 38	17 54	17 59	18 18	18 22	18 41	18 59	19 19	20 00	20 19	21 05	21 19	21 59	22 30	23 38
South Gyle	d	15 26			16 04		16 24	17 04		17 25			18 04		18 26		19 04	19 24	20 04	20 24		21 24	22 04	22 35	23 43
Edinburgh Gateway	d	15 28	15 44	16 02	16 06		16 26	17 06		17 27	17 44	18 00	18 06		18 29		19 06	19 26	20 07	20 26		21 26	22 06	22 37	23 45
Dalmeny	d	15 34			16 12		16 32	17 12		17 33			18 12		18 35		19 12	19 32	20 13	20 32		21 32	22 12	22 43	23 51
North Queensferry	d	15 38			16 16		16 36	17 16		17 37			18 16		18 38		19 16	19 36	20 16	20 36		21 36	22 16	22 47	23 55
Inverkeithing	d	15 42	15 54	16 12	16 20	16 25	16 40	17 20	17 24	17 41	17 54	18 10	18 20	18 31	18 42	18 56	19 20	19 40	20 20	20 40	21 19	21 40	22 20	22 51	23a58
Rosyth	d				16 23			17 23					18 23				19 23		20 24				22 23		
Dunfermline Town	d				16 28			17 28					18 28				19 28		20 29				22 28		
Dunfermline Queen Margaret	d				16 32			17 32					18 32				19 32		20 32				22 32		
Cowdenbeath	d				16 38			17 38					18 38				19 38		20 39				22 38		
Lochgelly	d				16 44			17 44					18 44				19 44		20 44				22 44		
Cardenden	d				16 48			17 48					18 48				19 48		20 48				22 48		
Dalgety Bay	d	15 45					16 43			17 44					18 45			19 43		20 43		21 43		22 54	
Aberdour	d	15 50					16 48			17 49					18 50			19 48		20 48		21 48		22 59	
Burntisland	d	15 54					16 52			17 53					18 54			19 52		20 52		21 52		23 03	
Kinghorn	d	15 59					16 57			17 58					18 59			19 57		20 57		21 57		23 08	
Kirkcaldy	d	16 04	16a10	16a27		16a39	17 02		17a39	18 03	18a10	18a26		18a45	19 04	19a11		20a01		21 02	21a33	22a04		23a12	
Glenrothes With Thornton 2	a	16 18			16 57		17 13	17 57		18 14			18 57		19 15		19 57		20 58	21 13			22 57		

A To Perth
B To Dundee
C To Aberdeen
D not 15 December. From Edinburgh to Perth
E To Inverness
F From London Kings Cross to Aberdeen. The Northern Lights
G From Plymouth to Aberdeen
H From London Kings Cross to Aberdeen

Table T242-R

Mondays to Fridays
16 December to 15 May

Glenrothes with Thornton, Kirkcaldy and Dunfermline - Edinburgh

Miles	Miles			XC MX	SR MX	GR	SR	SR	SR	SR	SR	SR	SR	SR	XC	SR	SR	SR	SR	SR	SR	SR	SR
				◇1 A	◇ B	1 C	◇ B	D		D	◇ E		B	F	◇1 G		◇1 A	B		◇ E		H	
0	0	Glenrothes With Thornton 2	d					06 02		06 26			06 53			07 19					07 47		08 09
5	—	**Kirkcaldy**	d				05 56		06 30		06 48			07 12	07 22	07 27	07 37	07 48		07 57		08 22	
8	—	Kinghorn	d				06 01		06 35		06 53			07 17		07 32				08 01			
10½	—	Burntisland	d				06 06		06 39		06 58			07 21		07 37				08 06			
13¼	—	Aberdour	d				06 10		06 44		07 02			07 25		07 41				08 11			
16	—	Dalgety Bay	d				06 15		06 49		07 07			07 30		07 46				08 16			
—	3½	Cardenden	d					06 09		06 33			07 01						07 35		07 54		08 16
—	5¾	Lochgelly	d					06 13		06 37			07 05						07 40		08 00		08 20
—	8	Cowdenbeath	d					06 19		06 43			07 11						07 47		08 06		08 26
—	12	Dunfermline Queen Margaret	d					06 25		06 49		07 06	07 16						07 53		08 12		08 32
—	13¾	**Dunfermline Town**	d					06 29		06 53		07 09	07 20						07 57		08 17		08 35
—	16	Rosyth	d					06 32		06 57		07 13	07 23						08 02		08 21		08 39
17½	17½	Inverkeithing	d		00 02		06 19	06 37	06 52	07 01	07 11	07 17	07 27	07 33	07 40	07 50		08 04	08 07	08 19	08 26	08 38	08 43
19½	19½	North Queensferry	d		00 04		06 23	06 41	06 56	07 05		07 21	07 31			07 54					08 32		08 47
21¼	21¼	Dalmeny	d		00 08		06 27	06 45	07 00	07 09	07 17		07 35	07a39		07 58			08 15	08 25			08 51
—	—	Edinburgh Gateway	d		00 14		06 33	06 51		07 15	07 23		07 41			08 04		08 15		08 31		08 50	
26¾	26¾	South Gyle	d		00 16		06 35	06 54	07 07			07 30	07 44			08 06			08 22		08 41		08 59
29½	29½	Haymarket	d	00 06	00 23	06 13	06 43	07 00	07 13	07 23	07 30	07 36	07 54		08 00	08 15	08 19	08 22	08 30	08 40	08 54	09 00	09 07
30¼	30¼	**Edinburgh 10**	a	00 10	00 27	06 17	06 49	07 05	07 19	07 27	07 35	07 44	08 01		08 04	08 21	08 24	08 29	08 35	08 48	09 01	09 08	09 13

		SR	SR	SR	SR	SR	SR	SR	GR	SR	SR	SR	XC	SR	SR	SR	SR	SR	SR	SR	SR	SR	SR
		◇ I			◇ E	◇1 I		J	1 K	L			1 M		◇ H		◇ B			◇ H			◇ B
Glenrothes With Thornton 2	d		08 35	08 44			09 11	09 24			09 37	09 52				10 27		10 40	10 52			11 21	
Kirkcaldy	d	08 38	08 43		09 14	09 28		09 34	09 47	←		10 00	10 18		10 30	10 35	10 45		11 01	11 16		11 29	11 42
Kinghorn	d		08 48		09 18			09 38		09 38		10 05				10 40			11 05			11 34	
Burntisland	d		08 52		09 23			→		09 43		10 10				10 45			11 10			11 39	
Aberdour	d		08 56		09 27					09 48		10 14				10 49			11 14			11 43	
Dalgety Bay	d		09 01		09 32					09 53		10 19				10 54			11 19			11 48	
Cardenden	d			08 51			09 18				09 44							10 47					
Lochgelly	d			08 55			09 22				09 48							10 51					
Cowdenbeath	d			09 01			09 28				09 54			10 22				10 57			11 21		
Dunfermline Queen Margaret	d			09 07			09 34				10 00			10 27				11 03			11 26		
Dunfermline Town	d			09 10			09 37				10 03			10 31				11 06			11 30		
Rosyth	d			09 14			09 41				10 07			10 34				11 10			11 33		
Inverkeithing	d	08 54	09 14	09 18	09 36		09 48		10 03	10 07	10 11	10 22	10 34	10 38	10 46	10 58	11 03	11 14	11 22	11 32	11 38	11 52	11 58
North Queensferry	d		09 18	09 22						10 11	10 15			10 42		11 02		11 18	11 26		11 42		
Dalmeny	d		09 22	09 26						10 15	10 19			10 46		11 06		11 22	11 30		11 46		
Edinburgh Gateway	d	09 05	09 28	09 32	09 46	09 53				10 21	10 25				10 57	11 12	11 17	11 28		11 43		12 03	12 09
South Gyle	d			09 34			10 01					10 33		10 52					11 36		11 52		
Haymarket	d	09 12	09 35	09 42	09 57	10 00	10 09		10 20	10 28	10 33	10 40	10 50	10 59	11 09	11 25	11 28	11 36	11 43	11 53	11 59	12 11	12 16
Edinburgh 10	a	09 16	09 39	09 47	10 01	10 07	10 13		10 25	10 34	10 37	10 47	10 54	11 04	11 13	11 29	11 33	11 40	11 47	11 57	12 03	12 15	12 21

		GR	SR	SR	SR	SR	SR	SR	SR	SR	SR	SR	SR	SR	SR	SR	SR	SR	SR	SR	SR	SR
		1 K			◇ H		◇1 I				◇ H			◇1 I			◇ H			◇ B		
Glenrothes With Thornton 2	d		11 38	11 51				12 29	12 43	12 53			13 25		13 41	13 54			14 23		14 41	14 53
Kirkcaldy	d	11 49		11 59	12 13		12 32	12 38		13 02	13 21		13 33	13 41		14 03	14 19		14 32	14 42		15 02
Kinghorn	d			12 04				12 42		13 07			13 38			14 07			14 36			15 06
Burntisland	d			12 09				12 47		13 12			13 43			14 12			14 41			15 11
Aberdour	d			12 13				12 51		13 16			13 47			14 17			14 46			15 16
Dalgety Bay	d			12 18				12 56		13 21			13 52			14 22			14 51			15 21
Cardenden	d		11 45						12 50						13 48						14 48	
Lochgelly	d		11 49						12 54						13 52						14 52	
Cowdenbeath	d		11 55			12 23			13 00			13 24			13 58			14 24			14 58	
Dunfermline Queen Margaret	d		12 01			12 28			13 06			13 29			14 04			14 29			15 04	
Dunfermline Town	d		12 04			12 32			13 09			13 33			14 07			14 33			15 07	
Rosyth	d		12 08			12 35			13 13			13 36			14 11			14 36			15 11	
Inverkeithing	d	12 05	12 12	12 21	12 29	12 39	12 47	13 11	13 17	13 25	13 37	13 41	13 56		14 15	14 25	14 35	14 40	14 54	15 00	15 15	15 24
North Queensferry	d		12 16	12 25		12 43		13 15	13 21	13 29		13 45	14 00		14 19	14 29		14 44	14 58		15 19	15 28
Dalmeny	d		12 20	12 29		12 47		13 19	13 25	13 33		13 49	14 04		14 23	14 33		14 50	15 02		15 23	15 32
Edinburgh Gateway	d		12 26		12 41		12 58	13 25	13 31		13 47		14 10	14 14	14 29		14 45		15 08	15 12	15 29	
South Gyle	d			12 35		12 53				13 39		13 55				14 39		14 56				15 38
Haymarket	d	12 22	12 36	12 42	12 50	13 00	13 10	13 34	13 38	13 48	13 59	14 04	14 17	14 21	14 36	14 47	14 56	15 02	15 17	15 25	15 38	15 48
Edinburgh 10	a	12 26	12 40	12 46	12 54	13 04	13 15	13 39	13 42	13 54	14 05	14 10	14 24	14 27	14 43	14 52	15 00	15 07	15 23	15 29	15 44	15 54

A From Aberdeen
B From Perth
C not 16 December. From Stirling to London Kings Cross
D From Markinch
E From Dundee
F To Glasgow Queen Street
G From Dundee to Plymouth
H From Arbroath
I From Inverness
J To Edinburgh
K From Aberdeen to London Kings Cross
L From Glenrothes With Thornton
M From Aberdeen to Penzance

Table T242-R

Mondays to Fridays
16 December to 15 May

Glenrothes with Thornton, Kirkcaldy and Dunfermline - Edinburgh

		SR	SR	SR	SR	SR	SR	SR	SR	SR	GR	SR	SR	SR	SR	SR	SR	SR	SR	SR	SR	SR
		◇ A		B	◇1 C		B	◇ A		B	1 D	◇ E		B		◇ A	◇ E		◇ A		◇1 C	
Glenrothes With Thornton 2	d			15 20		15 43	15 52			16 19			16 41	16 52	17 06			17 49		18 22		18 47
Kirkcaldy	d	15 21		15 29	15 52		16 00	16 15		16 28	16 48	16 55		17 00		17 36	17 48		18 21	18 32	18 49	
Kinghorn	d			15 34			16 05			16 32				17 05		17 40				18 38		
Burntisland	d			15 39			16 10			16 37				17 10		17 45				18 44		
Aberdour	d			15 43			16 14			16 42				17 14		17 50				18 50		
Dalgety Bay	d			15 48			16 19			16 47				17 19		17 55				18 56		
Cardenden	d					15 50							16 48		17 13			17 56				18 58
Lochgelly	d					15 54							16 52		17 17			18 00				19 02
Cowdenbeath	d		15 28			16 00			16 26				16 58		17 23			18 06				19 08
Dunfermline Queen Margaret	d		15 33			16 06			16 31				17 04		17 29			18 12				19 14
Dunfermline Town	d		15 37			16 09			16 35				17 07		17 32			18 15				19 17
Rosyth	d		15 40			16 13			16 38				17 11		17 36			18 19				19 21
Inverkeithing	d	15 37	15 45	15 52	16 07	16 17	16 23	16 31	16 42	16 50	17 05	17 11	17 16	17 23	17 40	17 58	18 04	18 23	18 37	19 00	19 04	19 26
North Queensferry	d		15 49	15 56		16 21	16 27		16 46				17 20	17 27	17 44	18 02		18 27				19 30
Dalmeny	d		15 53	16 00		16 25	16 31		16 50				17 24	17 31	17 48	18 06		18 31		19 08		19 34
Edinburgh Gateway	d	15 48		16 06	16 16	16 31		16 42				17 22		17 37	17 54	18 12	18 15		18 48		19 18	19 40
South Gyle	d		15 59				16 37		16 56	17 02			17 30	17 39	17 56			18 37		19 15		
Haymarket	d	15 54	16 09	16a12	16 27	16 40	16a43	16 54	17 03	17a10	17 22	17 33	17 38	17a47	18 04	18 19	18 24	18 45	18 56	19 23	19 26	19 50
Edinburgh 10	a	15 59	16 14		16 34	16 44		16 58	17 08		17 26	17 37	17 43		18 10	18 24	18 28	18 52	19 01	19 31	19 31	19 56

		SR	SR	SR	SR	SR	GR	SR	SR	SR	SR	SR	SR	SR	SR	SR	SR	SR	XC	SR
			◇ A			◇ E	1 F			◇ E		◇ G	◇1 C	◇1 H			◇1 H		◇1 H	◇ E
Glenrothes With Thornton 2	d	19 03		19 18	19 30			20 05			21 07					22 05				23 26
Kirkcaldy	d	19 12	19 31		19 38	19 51	20 13		20 27	20 42		21 28	21 45	22 04	22 10		22 57	23 09	23 36	
Kinghorn	d	19 16			19 43				20 32			21 32			22 15			23 14		
Burntisland	d	19 21			19 48				20 36			21 37			22 19			23 18		
Aberdour	d	19 26			19 52				20 41			21 41			22 24			23 23		
Dalgety Bay	d	19 31			19 57				20 46			21 46			22 29			23 28		
Cardenden	d			19 25				20 12			21 14					22 12				23 34
Lochgelly	d			19 29				20 16			21 18					22 16				23 38
Cowdenbeath	d			19 35				20 22			21 24					22 22				23 44
Dunfermline Queen Margaret	d			19 40				20 28			21 30					22 28				23 49
Dunfermline Town	d			19 44				20 31			21 33					22 31				23 53
Rosyth	d			19 47				20 35			21 37					22 35				23 56
Inverkeithing	d	19 34	19 47	19 51	20 01	20 07	20 29	20 39	20 50	20 58	21 41	21 50			22 33	22 40		23 31	23 51	00 02
North Queensferry	d	19 38		19 55	20 05			20 43	20 54		21 45	21 54			22 37	22 44		23 35		00 04
Dalmeny	d	19 42		19 59	20 09			20 47	20 58		21 49	21 58			22 41	22 48		23 39		00 08
Edinburgh Gateway	d		19 58	20 05		20 18		20 53		21 09	21 55	22 04	22 09			22 54		23 45		00 14
South Gyle	d	19 48			20 15				21 04		21 57				22 47	22 56		23 47		00 16
Haymarket	d	19 58	20 06	20 12	20 23	20 26	20 46	21 00	21 13	21 16	22 06	22 14	22 19	22 43	22 56	23 03	23 25	23 56	00 06	00 23
Edinburgh 10	a	20 02	20 10	20 19	20 31	20 31	20 50	21 04	21 17	21 21	22 10	22 18	22 23	22 47	23 01	23 09	23 29	00 01	00 10	00 27

Saturdays
21 December to 16 May

		XC	SR	SR	SR	SR	XC	SR	SR	SR	SR	SR	SR	SR	SR	SR	SR	SR	SR	SR	SR	GR	SR
		◇1 H	◇ E	E	I	◇ G	◇1 J		◇1 H	E		◇ G	A		◇ C			◇ G	◇1 C		K	1 D	L
Glenrothes With Thornton 2	d				06 24			07 19			07 37			08 08		08 35	08 46			09 11	09 24		
Kirkcaldy	d			06 15		06 48	07 22	07 27	07 37	07 48		07 57	08 22		08 38	08 43		09 14	09 27		09 33	09 47	←
Kinghorn	d			06 20		06 53		07 32				08 01				08 48		09 18			09 37		09 37
Burntisland	d			06 25		06 58		07 37				08 06				08 52		09 23			→		09 42
Aberdour	d			06 29		07 02		07 41				08 11				08 56		09 27					09 47
Dalgety Bay	d			06 34		07 07		07 46				08 16				09 01		09 32					09 52
Cardenden	d				06 32						07 45			08 15			08 53			09 18			
Lochgelly	d				06 36						07 49			08 19			08 57			09 22			
Cowdenbeath	d				06 42						07 55			08 25			09 03			09 28			
Dunfermline Queen Margaret	d				06 47						08 00			08 31			09 09			09 34			
Dunfermline Town	d				06 51						08 04			08 34			09 12			09 37			
Rosyth	d				06 54						08 07			08 38			09 16			09 41			
Inverkeithing	d		00 02	06 38	06 59	07 11	07 39	07 50		08 04	08 11	08 19	08 38	08 43	08 54	09 15	09 20	09 36		09 47		10 03	10 07
North Queensferry	d		00 04	06 42	07 03			07 54			08 15			08 47		09 19	09 24						10 11
Dalmeny	d		00 08	06 45	07 07	07 17		07 58			08 19	08 25		08 51		09 23	09 28						10 15
Edinburgh Gateway	d		00 14	06 51	07 13	07 23		08 04		08 15		08 31	08 49		09 05	09 29	09 34	09 46	09 52				10 21
South Gyle	d		00 16	06 53				08 06			08 25			08 59			09 36			09 59			
Haymarket	d	00 06	00 23	07 01	07 20	07 31	07 59	08 14	08 19	08 23	08 32	08 42	08 58	09 06	09 12	09 38	09 43	09 54	09 59	10 08		10 21	10 29
Edinburgh 10	a	00 10	00 27	07 05	07 24	07 36	08 03	08 21	08 24	08 27	08 36	08 47	09 02	09 10	09 17	09 43	09 47	09 58	10 05	10 13		10 26	10 34

A From Arbroath
B To Tweedbank
C From Inverness
D From Aberdeen to London Kings Cross
E From Perth
F From Aberdeen to Leeds
G From Dundee
H From Aberdeen
I From Markinch
J From Dundee to Plymouth
K To Edinburgh
L From Glenrothes With Thornton

Table T242-R

Glenrothes with Thornton, Kirkcaldy and Dunfermline - Edinburgh

Saturdays

21 December to 16 May

		SR	SR	XC	SR	SR	SR	SR	SR	SR	SR	SR	SR	SR	GR	SR	SR	SR	SR	SR	SR	SR
				◇1 A ⊼		◇ B		◇ C			◇ B			◇ C	1 D ⊏			◇ B		◇1 E ⊼		
Glenrothes With Thornton 2	d	09 38	09 53				10 27		10 40	10 53			11 21			11 41	11 51				12 29	12 42
Kirkcaldy	d		10 01	10 18		10 30	10 35	10 45		11 02	11 16		11 29	11 42	11 49		11 59	12 13		12 32	12 38	
Kinghorn	d		10 06				10 40			11 07			11 34				12 04				12 42	
Burntisland	d		10 11				10 45			11 12			11 39				12 09				12 47	
Aberdour	d		10 15				10 49			11 16			11 43				12 13				12 51	
Dalgety Bay	d		10 20				10 54			11 21			11 48				12 18				12 56	
Cardenden	d	09 45							10 47							11 48						12 49
Lochgelly	d	09 49							10 51							11 52						12 53
Cowdenbeath	d	09 55			10 22				10 57			11 21				11 58			12 23			12 59
Dunfermline Queen Margaret	d	10 01			10 27				11 03			11 26				12 04			12 28			13 05
Dunfermline Town	d	10 04			10 31				11 06			11 30				12 07			12 32			13 08
Rosyth	d	10 08			10 34				11 10			11 33				12 11			12 35			13 12
Inverkeithing	d	10 12	10 24	10 34	10 38	10 46	10 58	11 03	11 14	11 25	11 32	11 38	11 52	11 58	12 05	12 15	12 21	12 29	12 39	12 47	13 11	13 16
North Queensferry	d	10 16			10 42		11 02		11 18	11 29		11 42				12 19	12 25		12 43		13 15	13 20
Dalmeny	d	10 20			10 46		11 06		11 22	11 33		11 46				12 23	12 29		12 47		13 19	13 24
Edinburgh Gateway	d	10 26				10 57	11 12	11 17	11 28		11 43		12 03	12 09		12 29		12 39		12 57	13 25	13 30
South Gyle	d		10 35		10 52					11 39		11 52					12 35		12 53			
Haymarket	d	10 33	10 43	10 50	10 59	11 03	11 21	11 25	11 37	11 47	11 51	11 59	12 09	12 17	12 22	12 36	12 42	12 46	13 00	13 04	13 32	13 37
Edinburgh 10	a	10 37	10 47	10 54	11 03	11 08	11 25	11 29	11 41	11 52	11 55	12 03	12 15	12 21	12 26	12 40	12 47	12 50	13 04	13 09	13 36	13 41

		SR	SR	SR	SR	SR	SR	SR	SR	SR	SR	SR	SR	SR	SR	SR	SR	SR	SR	SR	SR	SR	SR
			◇ B			◇1 E ⊼			◇ B			◇ C			◇ B			◇1 E ⊼			◇ B		
Glenrothes With Thornton 2	d	12 53			13 21		13 41	13 54			14 23		14 41	14 53			15 20		15 43	15 53			16 19
Kirkcaldy	d	13 02	13 21		13 29	13 42		14 03	14 19		14 32	14 42		15 02	15 20		15 29	15 52		16 01	16 16		16 28
Kinghorn	d	13 07			13 34			14 07			14 36			15 06			15 34			16 06			16 32
Burntisland	d	13 12			13 39			14 12			14 41			15 11			15 39			16 11			16 37
Aberdour	d	13 16			13 43			14 17			14 46			15 16			15 43			16 15			16 42
Dalgety Bay	d	13 21			13 48			14 21			14 51			15 21			15 48			16 20			16 47
Cardenden	d						13 48						14 48						15 50				
Lochgelly	d						13 52						14 52						15 54				
Cowdenbeath	d			13 28			13 58			14 28			14 58			15 23			16 00			16 26	
Dunfermline Queen Margaret	d			13 33			14 04			14 33			15 04			15 28			16 06			16 31	
Dunfermline Town	d			13 37			14 07			14 37			15 07			15 32			16 09			16 35	
Rosyth	d			13 40			14 11			14 40			15 11			15 35			16 13			16 38	
Inverkeithing	d	13 25	13 37	13 44	13 52		14 15	14 25	14 35	14 44	14 54	15 00	15 15	15 24	15 36	15 40	15 52	16 07	16 17	16 24	16 32	16 42	16 50
North Queensferry	d	13 29		13 48	13 56		14 19	14 29		14 48	14 58		15 19	15 28		15 44	15 56		16 21	16 28		16 46	
Dalmeny	d	13 33		13 52	14 00		14 23	14 33		14 52	15 02		15 23	15 32		15 48	16 00		16 25	16 32		16 50	
Edinburgh Gateway	d		13 47		14 06	14 10	14 29		14 45		15 08	15 12	15 29		15 46		16 06	16 16	16 31		16 42		
South Gyle	d	13 39		13 58				14 39		14 58				15 38		15 54				16 39		16 56	17 02
Haymarket	d	13 46	13 54	14 09	14 13	14 22	14 36	14 45	14 53	15 07	15 15	15 19	15 38	15 48	15 53	16 02	16 13	16 27	16 38	16 49	16 52	17 03	17 12
Edinburgh 10	a	13 51	13 59	14 14	14 18	14 29	14 40	14 50	14 57	15 11	15 19	15 24	15 43	15 54	15 57	16 09	16 17	16 34	16 42	16 55	16 57	17 11	17 19

		GR	SR	SR	SR	SR	SR	SR	SR	SR	SR	SR	SR	SR	SR	SR	SR	SR	SR	SR	SR	SR
		1 D ⊏	◇ C				◇ B	◇ C		◇ B	F	◇1 E ⊼	G		◇ B			◇ C	◇1 H ⊼			◇ C
Glenrothes With Thornton 2	d			16 41	16 53	17 08			17 44		18 24			18 51		19 17	19 30			20 05		
Kirkcaldy	d	16 48	16 56		17 01		17 36	17 48		18 21	18 34	18 46	⟵		19 31		19 38	19 51	20 12		20 27	20 43
Kinghorn	d				17 06		17 40				18 39		18 39				19 43				20 31	
Burntisland	d				17 11		17 45				⟶		18 44				19 48				20 35	
Aberdour	d				17 15		17 50						18 48				19 52				20 40	
Dalgety Bay	d				17 20		17 55						18 53				19 57				20 45	
Cardenden	d			16 48		17 15			17 51					18 58		19 24				20 12		
Lochgelly	d			16 52		17 19			17 55					19 02		19 28				20 16		
Cowdenbeath	d			16 58		17 25			18 01					19 08		19 34				20 22		
Dunfermline Queen Margaret	d			17 04		17 31			18 07					19 14		19 40				20 28		
Dunfermline Town	d			17 07		17 34			18 10					19 17		19 43				20 31		
Rosyth	d			17 11		17 38			18 14					19 21		19 47				20 35		
Inverkeithing	d	17 05	17 12	17 16	17 24	17 42	17 58	18 05	18 18	18 37		19 03	19 07	19 26	19 47	19 51	20 01	20 07	20 28	20 39	20 50	20 59
North Queensferry	d			17 20	17 28	17 46	18 02		18 22				19 11	19 30		19 55	20 05			20 43	20 54	
Dalmeny	d			17 24	17 32	17 50	18 06		18 26				19 15	19 34		19 59	20 09			20 47	20 57	
Edinburgh Gateway	d		17 23	17 30	17 38	17 56	18 12	18 18		18 48		19 13		19 40	19 58	20 05		20 18		20 53		21 10
South Gyle	d				17 40	17 58			18 32				19 21				20 15				21 03	
Haymarket	d	17 21	17 30	17 39	17 48	18 04	18 21	18 25	18 41	18 55		19 21	19 28	19 51	20 05	20 14	20 23	20 27	20 45	21 00	21 10	21 16
Edinburgh 10	a	17 26	17 34	17 43	17 53	18 09	18 28	18 31	18 45	18 59		19 25	19 32	19 56	20 11	20 18	20 28	20 31	20 49	21 04	21 14	21 20

A From Aberdeen to Penzance
B From Arbroath
C From Perth
D From Aberdeen to London Kings Cross
E From Inverness
F To Edinburgh
G From Glenrothes With Thornton
H From Aberdeen

Table T242-R

Glenrothes with Thornton, Kirkcaldy and Dunfermline - Edinburgh

Saturdays

21 December to 16 May

		SR	SR	SR	SR	SR	SR	SR	SR	XC	SR
			◇ A	◇1 B ⊼	◇1 C			◇1 C		◇1 C	◇ D
Glenrothes With Thornton 2	d	21 07				22 05					23 25
Kirkcaldy	d		21 28	21 45	22 04	22 10		22 57	23 09	23 34	
Kinghorn	d		21 32			22 15			23 14		
Burntisland	d		21 37			22 19			23 18		
Aberdour	d		21 41			22 24			23 23		
Dalgety Bay	d		21 46			22 29			23 28		
Cardenden	d	21 14					22 12				23 33
Lochgelly	d	21 18					22 16				23 37
Cowdenbeath	d	21 24					22 22				23 43
Dunfermline Queen Margaret	d	21 30					22 28				23 48
Dunfermline Town	d	21 33					22 31				23 52
Rosyth	d	21 37					22 35				23 55
Inverkeithing	d	21 41	21 50			22 33	22 39		23 31	23 49	23 59
North Queensferry	d	21 45	21 54			22 37	22 43		23 35		00 04
Dalmeny	d	21 49	21 58			22 41	22 47		23 39		00 08
Edinburgh Gateway	d	21 55	22 04	22 08			22 53		23 45		00 14
South Gyle	d	21 57				22 47	22 55		23 47		00 16
Haymarket	d	22 06	22 14	22 18	22 37	22 59	23 03	23 25	23 56	00 04	00 24
Edinburgh 10	a	22 10	22 18	22 22	22 43	23 03	23 07	23 29	00 01	00 08	00 28

Sundays

15 December to 10 May

		XC	SR	SR	SR	SR	SR	SR	SR	GR	SR	SR	SR	XC	SR	SR	SR	GR	SR	SR	SR	SR	SR
		◇1 E	◇ F	◇ A	◇ D	A	◇ D			1 G ⊏	◇ A			◇1 H		◇1 B ⊼		1 I ⊏	◇ A			◇1 C	
Glenrothes With Thornton 2	d						10 15	11 02	11 15			12 03	12 15		13 04		13 18			14 03	14 15		15 04
Kirkcaldy	d			08 10	09 30	10 10		11 11		11 43	12 06	12 11		13 08	13 13	13 36		13 44	14 06	14 11		14 41	15 13
Kinghorn	d			08 15	09 34	10 15		11 15				12 16			13 17					14 16			15 17
Burntisland	d			08 19	09 39	10 19		11 20				12 21			13 22					14 21			15 22
Aberdour	d			08 24	09 44	10 24		11 25				12 25			13 27					14 25			15 27
Dalgety Bay	d			08 29	09 49	10 29		11 30				12 30			13 32					14 30			15 32
Cardenden	d						10 22		11 22				12 22				13 25				14 22		
Lochgelly	d						10 27		11 26				12 26				13 29				14 26		
Cowdenbeath	d						10 32		11 32				12 32				13 35				14 32		
Dunfermline Queen Margaret	d						10 38		11 38				12 38				13 41				14 38		
Dunfermline Town	d						10 41		11 41				12 41				13 44				14 41		
Rosyth	d						10 45		11 45				12 45				13 48				14 45		
Inverkeithing	d			08 32	09 52	10 32	10 49	11 33	11 49	11 59	12 22	12 34	12 49	13 24	13 35	13 51	13 54	14 05	14 22	14 34	14 49	14 56	15 35
North Queensferry	d		00 04	08 36	09 56	10 36	10 53	11 37	11 53			12 38	12 53		13 39		13 58			14 38	14 53		15 39
Dalmeny	d		00 08	08 43	10 03	10 40	10 57	11 41	11 57			12 42	12 57		13 43		14 02			14 42	14 57		15 43
Edinburgh Gateway	d		00 14	08 49	10 09	10 46	11 03	11 47	12 03		12 33	12 48	13 03		13 49	14 00	14 08		14 33	14 48	15 03		15 49
South Gyle	d		00 16	08 51	10 11	10 48	11 05	11 49	12 05			12 50	13 05		13 51		14 10			14 50	15 05		15 51
Haymarket	d	00 04	00 24	08 59	10 19	10 56	11 14	11 58	12 13	12 18	12 41	12 59	13 13	13 39	14 00	14 11	14 17	14 21	14 41	14 58	15 13	15 17	16 00
Edinburgh 10	a	00 08	00 28	09 03	10 23	11 01	11 18	12 02	12 18	12 22	12 47	13 04	13 18	13 43	14 06	14 15	14 21	14 26	14 45	15 02	15 18	15 24	16 04

		SR	GR	SR	SR	SR	SR	SR	SR	SR	SR	SR	SR	SR	SR	SR	SR	SR	SR	SR	SR	SR	SR	SR	SR	XC
			1 I ⊏	◇ A	◇1 B ⊼			◇1 C ⊼			◇1 B ⊼	◇ A			◇1 C ⊼			◇ A	◇1 C			◇1 B ⊼	◇1 C ⊼			◇1 C
Glenrothes With Thornton 2	d	15 17				16 09	16 20		17 02	17 15			18 04	18 16		18 59	19 17			20 59	21 15				22 59	
Kirkcaldy	d		15 43	16 01	16 09	16 17		17 03	17 11		18 01	18 07	18 12		18 52	19 07		20 02	21 02	21 07		21 49	22 04	22 13	23 07	23 26
Kinghorn	d					16 22			17 15				18 17			19 12		20 07		21 12				22 17	23 12	
Burntisland	d					16 27			17 20				18 22			19 17		20 11		21 17				22 22	23 17	
Aberdour	d					16 31			17 25				18 26			19 21		20 16		21 21				22 27	23 21	
Dalgety Bay	d					16 36			17 30				18 31			19 26		20 21		21 26				22 32	23 26	
Cardenden	d	15 24					16 27			17 22				18 23			19 24				21 22					
Lochgelly	d	15 28					16 31			17 26				18 27			19 28				21 26					
Cowdenbeath	d	15 34					16 37			17 32				18 33			19 34				21 32					
Dunfermline Queen Margaret	d	15 40					16 43			17 38				18 39			19 40				21 38					
Dunfermline Town	d	15 43					16 46			17 41				18 42			19 43				21 41					
Rosyth	d	15 47					16 50			17 45				18 46			19 47				21 45					
Inverkeithing	d	15 51	16 00	16 17	16 24	16 40	16 54	17 19	17 33	17 49	18 16	18 23	18 35	18 50	19 07	19 30	19 51	20 24	21 18	21 30	21 49	22 04	22 19	22 35	23 30	23 42
North Queensferry	d	15 55				16 44	16 58		17 37	17 53			18 39	18 54		19 34	19 55	20 28		21 34	21 53			22 39	23 34	
Dalmeny	d	15 59				16 48	17 02		17 41	17 57			18 43	18 58		19 38	19 59	20 32		21 38	21 57			22 43	23 38	
Edinburgh Gateway	d	16 05		16 28	16 33	16 54	17 08		17 47	18 03	18 26	18 34	18 49	19 04		19 44	20 05	20 38		21 44	22 03	22 14		22 49	23 44	
South Gyle	d	16 07				16 56	17 10		17 49	18 05			18 51	19 06		19 46	20 07	20 40		21 46	22 05			22 51	23 46	
Haymarket	d	16 15	16 20	16 36	16 43	17 02	17 18	17 34	17 58	18 13	18 36	18 42	18 59	19 15	19 22	19 54	20 17	20 48	21 34	21 54	22 17	22 24	22 34	23 00	23 52	23 57
Edinburgh 10	a	16 21	16 24	16 40	16 48	17 07	17 23	17 40	18 02	18 20	18 42	18 46	19 03	19 19	19 26	20 01	20 21	20 52	21 38	21 59	22 21	22 28	22 38	23 04	23 57	00 01

A From Dundee
B From Inverness
C From Aberdeen
D From Perth
E not 15 December. From Aberdeen
F not 15 December. From Perth
G From Aberdeen to London Kings Cross. The Northern Lights
H From Aberdeen to Plymouth
I From Aberdeen to London Kings Cross

Table T243-F

Mondays to Fridays

16 December to 15 May

Edinburgh - Newcraighall - Tweedbank

Miles			SR MO A	SR MX A	SR	SR	SR	SR	SR	SR	SR	SR	SR	SR	SR	SR	SR	SR	SR	SR	SR	SR	SR
0	**Edinburgh** 226,230	d			05 44	06 21	06 49	07 22	07 51	08 23	08 51	09 24	09 55	10 24	10 54	11 25	11 53	12 23	12 53	13 25	13 55	14 25	14 54
4	Brunstane	d		00 01	05 51	06 29	06 57	07 30	08 00	08 31	09 03	09 31	10 02	10 31	11 01	11 32	12 03	12 31	13 03	13 32	14 02	14 32	15 02
4¾	**Newcraighall**	d		00 05	05 55	06 33	07 01	07 34	08 04	08 35	09 07	09 35	10 06	10 35	11 05	11 36	12 07	12 35	13 07	13 36	14 06	14 36	15 06
5¾	Shawfair	d		00 08	06 02	06 36	07 04	07 37	08 07	08 38	09 10	09 38	10 09	10 38	11 08	11 39	12 10	12 38	13 10	13 39	14 09	14 39	15 09
8¼	Eskbank	d		00 13	06 08	06 41	07 11	07 42	08 12	08 43	09 14	09 43	10 14	10 43	11 13	11 44	12 14	12 43	13 14	13 44	14 14	14 44	15 13
9¾	Newtongrange	d		00 16	06 12	06 44	07 14	07 45	08 15	08 46	09 17	09 46	10 17	10 46	11 16	11 47	12 17	12 46	13 17	13 47	14 17	14 47	15 16
12	Gorebridge	d		00 21	06 20	06 49	07 19	07 50	08 20	08 51	09 22	09 51	10 22	10 51	11 21	11 52	12 22	12 51	13 22	13 52	14 22	14 52	15 21
26¼	Stow	d		00 40		07 06	07 36	08 07	08 37	09 08		10 08		11 08		12 09		13 08		14 09		15 09	
36½	Galashiels	d	00 04	00 49	06 44	07 15	07 45	08 16	08 46	09 17	09 46	10 17	10 46	11 17	11 45	12 18	12 46	13 17	13 46	14 18	14 46	15 18	15 45
38½	**Tweedbank**	a	00 09	00 54	06 48	07 19	07 49	08 20	08 50	09 21	09 51	10 21	10 50	11 21	11 49	12 22	12 51	13 21	13 51	14 22	14 50	15 22	15 50

		SR	SR	SR B	SR B	SR B	SR B	SR	SR	SR	SR	SR	SR FO	SR FX	SR	SR FO	SR FX
Edinburgh 226,230	d	15 24	15 50					18 24	18 54	19 24	19 53	20 53	21 53	21 53	22 54	23 54	23 54
Brunstane	d	15 31	16 01	16 32	17 02	17 31	18 03	18 31	19 02	19 31	20 03	21 04	22 00	22 00	23 04	00 01	00 01
Newcraighall	d	15 35	16 05	16 36	17 06	17 35	18 07	18 35	19 06	19 35	20 07	21 08	22 04	22 04	23 08	00 05	00 05
Shawfair	d	15 38	16 08	16 39	17 09	17 38	18 10	18 38	19 09	19 38	20 10	21 11	22 07	22 07	23 11	00 08	00 08
Eskbank	d	15 43	16 13	16 44	17 13	17 43	18 15	18 43	19 14	19 43	20 15	21 16	22 12	22 12	23 16	00 13	00 13
Newtongrange	d	15 46	16 16	16 47	17 16	17 46	18 18	18 46	19 17	19 46	20 18	21 19	22 15	22 15	23 19	00 16	00 16
Gorebridge	d	15 51	16 21	16 52	17 21	17 51	18 23	18 51	19 22	19 51	20 23	21 24	22 20	22 20	23 24	00 21	00 21
Stow	d	16 08		17 09	17 39	18 08	18 40	19 08	19 39	20 08	20 40	21 41	22 37	22 37	23 41	00 38	00 40
Galashiels	d	16 17	16 46	17 18	17 48	18 17	18 49	19 17	19 48	20 17	20 49	21 50	22 46	22 46	23 50	00 47	00 49
Tweedbank	a	16 22	16 50	17 22	17 52	18 21	18 54	19 21	19 52	20 21	20 53	21 54	22 50	22 51	23 55	00 52	00 54

Saturdays

21 December to 16 May

		SR A	SR	SR	SR	SR	SR	SR	SR	SR	SR	SR	SR	SR	SR	SR	SR	SR	SR	SR	SR	SR	SR
Edinburgh 226,230	d		05 55	06 20	06 51	07 22	07 53	08 24	08 52	09 22	09 53	10 25	10 55	11 23	11 54	12 25	12 55	13 24	13 56	14 26	14 53	15 26	15 54
Brunstane	d	00 01	06 02	06 28	06 58	07 31	08 04	08 32	09 00	09 30	10 02	10 32	11 04	11 32	12 02	12 32	13 03	13 32	14 03	14 32	15 03	15 33	16 03
Newcraighall	d	00 05	06 06	06 32	07 02	07 34	08 07	08 36	09 04	09 34	10 06	10 36	11 08	11 36	12 06	12 36	13 07	13 36	14 07	14 36	15 07	15 37	16 06
Shawfair	d	00 08	06 09	06 36	07 07	07 37	08 10	08 39	09 10	09 38	10 09	10 39	11 11	11 39	12 09	12 39	13 11	13 39	14 10	14 39	15 10	15 40	16 10
Eskbank	d	00 13	06 14	06 41	07 12	07 42	08 15	08 44	09 14	09 43	10 14	10 44	11 16	11 44	12 14	12 44	13 16	13 44	14 15	14 44	15 15	15 45	16 14
Newtongrange	d	00 16	06 17	06 44	07 15	07 45	08 18	08 47	09 17	09 46	10 17	10 47	11 19	11 47	12 17	12 47	13 19	13 47	14 18	14 47	15 18	15 48	16 17
Gorebridge	d	00 21	06 22	06 49	07 20	07 50	08 23	08 52	09 22	09 51	10 22	10 52	11 24	11 52	12 22	12 52	13 24	13 52	14 23	14 52	15 23	15 53	16 22
Stow	d	00 38		07 06	07 37	08 07	08 40	09 09		10 08		11 09		12 09		13 09		14 09		15 09		16 10	
Galashiels	d	00 47	06 46	07 15	07 46	08 16	08 49	09 18	09 46	10 17	10 47	11 18	11 47	12 18	12 47	13 18	13 48	14 18	14 48	15 19	15 47	16 19	16 47
Tweedbank	a	00 52	06 50	07 19	07 50	08 20	08 53	09 22	09 50	10 21	10 51	11 22	11 52	12 22	12 51	13 22	13 52	14 22	14 52	15 23	15 51	16 23	16 51

		SR	SR	SR	SR	SR	SR	SR	SR	SR	SR	SR	SR
Edinburgh 226,230	d	16 24	16 54	17 22	17 54	18 25	18 54	19 25	19 53	20 53	21 56	22 55	23 54
Brunstane	d	16 32	17 04	17 30	18 02	18 33	19 04	19 34	20 02	21 03	22 03	23 02	00 01
Newcraighall	d	16 36	17 08	17 34	18 06	18 37	19 08	19 38	20 06	21 07	22 07	23 06	00 05
Shawfair	d	16 39	17 11	17 38	18 10	18 40	19 11	19 41	20 09	21 10	22 10	23 09	00 09
Eskbank	d	16 44	17 15	17 43	18 14	18 45	19 16	19 45	20 14	21 15	22 15	23 14	00 14
Newtongrange	d	16 47	17 18	17 46	18 17	18 48	19 19	19 48	20 17	21 18	22 18	23 17	00 17
Gorebridge	d	16 52	17 23	17 51	18 22	18 53	19 24	19 53	20 22	21 23	22 23	23 22	00 22
Stow	d	17 09	17 41	18 08	18 40	19 10	19 41	20 11	20 39	21 40	22 40	23 39	00 39
Galashiels	d	17 18	17 49	18 17	18 49	19 19	19 50	20 20	20 48	21 49	22 48	23 48	00 48
Tweedbank	a	17 22	17 54	18 21	18 53	19 23	19 54	20 25	20 52	21 53	22 53	23 52	00 53

Sundays

15 December to 10 May

		SR C	SR	SR	SR	SR	SR	SR	SR	SR	SR	SR	SR	SR	SR	SR	SR
Edinburgh 226,230	d		09 11	10 11	11 13	12 11	13 11	14 11	15 11	16 11	17 12	18 11	19 12	20 11	21 12	22 12	23 11
Brunstane	d	00 01	09 18	10 18	11 20	12 18	13 18	14 20	15 18	16 20	17 19	18 19	19 19	20 19	21 19	22 20	23 18
Newcraighall	d	00 05	09 22	10 22	11 24	12 22	13 22	14 24	15 22	16 24	17 23	18 23	19 23	20 23	21 23	22 24	23 22
Shawfair	d	00 09	09 25	10 25	11 27	12 25	13 25	14 27	15 25	16 27	17 26	18 27	19 26	20 26	21 26	22 27	23 25
Eskbank	d	00 14	09 30	10 30	11 32	12 30	13 30	14 32	15 30	16 32	17 31	18 32	19 31	20 31	21 32	22 32	23 30
Newtongrange	d	00 17	09 33	10 33	11 35	12 33	13 33	14 35	15 33	16 35	17 34	18 35	19 34	20 34	21 34	22 35	23 33
Gorebridge	d	00 22	09 38	10 38	11 40	12 38	13 38	14 40	15 38	16 40	17 39	18 40	19 39	20 39	21 39	22 40	23 38
Stow	d	00 39	09 55	10 55	11 57	12 55	13 55	14 57	15 55	16 57	17 56	18 57	19 56	20 56	21 56	22 57	23 55
Galashiels	d	00 48	10 04	11 04	12 06	13 04	14 04	15 06	16 04	17 06	18 05	19 06	20 05	21 05	22 05	23 06	00 04
Tweedbank	a	00 53	10 08	11 08	12 10	13 08	14 08	15 10	16 08	17 10	18 09	19 10	20 09	21 09	22 09	23 10	00 09

A From Edinburgh
B From Glenrothes With Thornton
C not 15 December. From Edinburgh

NRT DECEMBER 19 EDITION

Table T243-R

Mondays to Fridays

16 December to 15 May

Tweedbank - Newcraighall - Edinburgh

Miles			SR MX A	SR	SR	SR B	SR B	SR C	SR C	SR	SR	SR	SR	SR	SR	SR	SR	SR	SR	SR	SR	SR	SR
0	**Tweedbank**	d		05 20	05 58	06 28	06 58	07 26	07 59	08 28	08 59	09 29	10 00	10 29	10 58	11 28	12 01	12 29	12 59	13 28	13 59	14 30	15 01
2	Galashiels	d		05 24	06 02	06 32	07 02	07 30	08 03	08 32	09 03	09 33	10 04	10 33	11 02	11 32	12 05	12 33	13 03	13 32	14 03	14 34	15 05
11¾	Stow	d		05 33	06 11	06 41	07 11	07 39	08 12	08 41		09 42		10 42		11 41		12 42		13 41		14 43	
26½	Gorebridge	d		05 50	06 28	06 58	07 28	07 56	08 29	08 58	09 28	09 59	10 29	10 59	11 27	11 58	12 30	12 59	13 28	13 58	14 28	15 00	15 30
28¾	Newtongrange	d	00 01	05 53	06 31	07 01	07 31	08 00	08 33	09 01	09 31	10 02	10 32	11 02	11 30	12 01	12 33	13 02	13 31	14 01	14 31	15 03	15 33
30¼	Eskbank	d	00 04	05 56	06 34	07 04	07 34	08 03	08 36	09 04	09 34	10 05	10 35	11 05	11 33	12 04	12 36	13 05	13 34	14 04	14 34	15 06	15 36
32¾	Shawfair	d	00 10	06 00	06 40	07 08	07 38	08 07	08 40	09 08	09 38	10 09	10 39	11 09	11 38	12 08	12 40	13 09	13 38	14 09	14 38	15 12	15 42
33¾	**Newcraighall**	d	00 14	06 04	06 44	07 13	07 42	08 11	08 44	09 12	09 42	10 13	10 43	11 13	11 42	12 12	12 44	13 13	13 42	14 13	14 42	15 16	15 46
34½	Brunstane	d	00 17	06 08	06 47	07 18	07 47	08 14	08 48	09 16	09 46	10 17	10 47	11 17	11 45	12 16	12 48	13 17	13 46	14 17	14 46	15 20	15 50
38½	**Edinburgh** 226,230	a	00 24	06 15	06 55	07 27	07 57	08 21	08 57	09 23	09 54	10 24	10 54	11 24	11 52	12 28	12 55	13 25	13 54	14 24	14 56	15 29	15 56

		SR	SR	SR	SR	SR	SR	SR	SR	SR	SR	SR	SR	SR FO	SR FX
Tweedbank	d	15 29	15 57	16 30	17 00	17 30	17 59	18 28	18 59	19 31	20 29	21 29	22 29	23 28	23 28
Galashiels	d	15 33	16 01	16 34	17 04	17 34	18 03	18 32	19 03	19 35	20 33	21 33	22 33	23 32	23 32
Stow	d	15 42	16 10	16 43	17 13	17 43		18 41		19 44	20 42	21 42	22 42	23 41	23 41
Gorebridge	d	15 59	16 27	17 00	17 30	18 00	18 28	18 58	19 28	20 01	20 59	21 59	22 59	23 58	23 58
Newtongrange	d	16 02	16 31	17 03	17 33	18 03	18 32	19 01	19 31	20 04	21 02	22 02	23 02	00 01	00 01
Eskbank	d	16 05	16 34	17 06	17 36	18 06	18 35	19 04	19 34	20 07	21 05	22 05	23 05	00 04	00 04
Shawfair	d	16 09	16 38	17 12	17 40	18 10	18 39	19 08	19 38	20 11	21 09	22 15	23 10	00 08	00 10
Newcraighall	d	16 13	16 42	17 16	17 44	18 14	18 43	19 13	19 43	20 15	21 14	22 19	23 14	00 12	00 14
Brunstane	d	16 17	16 45	17 20	17 48	18 22	18 46	19 16	19 48	20 19	21 17	22 23	23 17	00 16	00 17
Edinburgh 226,230	a	16 26	16 52	17 29	17 55	18 35	18 53	19 23	19 55	20 26	21 24	22 32	23 26	00 23	00 24

Saturdays

21 December to 16 May

		SR A	SR	SR	SR	SR	SR	SR	SR	SR	SR	SR	SR	SR	SR	SR	SR	SR	SR	SR	SR	SR	SR
Tweedbank	d		05 28	05 58	06 29	06 59	07 30	07 59	08 32	08 59	09 31	10 01	10 31	11 02	11 31	12 01	12 31	13 01	13 32	14 02	14 32	15 03	15 31
Galashiels	d		05 32	06 02	06 33	07 03	07 34	08 03	08 36	09 03	09 35	10 05	10 35	11 06	11 35	12 05	12 35	13 05	13 36	14 06	14 36	15 07	15 35
Stow	d		05 41	06 11	06 42	07 12	07 43	08 12	08 45		09 44		10 44		11 44		12 44		13 45		14 45		15 44
Gorebridge	d		05 58	06 28	06 59	07 29	08 00	08 29	09 01	09 28	10 00	10 30	11 01	11 31	12 01	12 30	13 01	13 30	14 02	14 31	15 02	15 32	16 01
Newtongrange	d	00 01	06 01	06 31	07 02	07 32	08 03	08 32	09 05	09 31	10 04	10 33	11 04	11 34	12 04	12 33	13 04	13 33	14 05	14 34	15 05	15 35	16 04
Eskbank	d	00 04	06 04	06 34	07 05	07 35	08 06	08 35	09 08	09 34	10 07	10 36	11 07	11 37	12 07	12 36	13 07	13 36	14 08	14 37	15 08	15 38	16 07
Shawfair	d	00 08	06 11	06 40	07 10	07 39	08 13	08 39	09 14	09 38	10 11	10 40	11 11	11 41	12 11	12 40	13 13	13 43	14 12	14 41	15 13	15 42	16 11
Newcraighall	d	00 12	06 15	06 44	07 14	07 43	08 17	08 43	09 18	09 42	10 15	10 44	11 15	11 45	12 15	12 44	13 17	13 47	14 16	14 45	15 17	15 46	16 15
Brunstane	d	00 16	06 18	06 47	07 18	07 47	08 20	08 47	09 21	09 46	10 19	10 48	11 22	11 49	12 21	12 50	13 20	13 51	14 22	14 49	15 22	15 50	16 22
Edinburgh 226,230	a	00 23	06 25	06 55	07 27	07 58	08 29	08 56	09 28	09 58	10 28	10 55	11 29	11 59	12 28	13 00	13 29	13 58	14 29	14 59	15 28	15 59	16 29

		SR	SR	SR	SR	SR	SR	SR	SR	SR	SR	SR	SR
Tweedbank	d	16 02	16 31	17 01	17 31	18 01	18 33	19 03	19 31	20 32	21 31	22 31	23 31
Galashiels	d	16 06	16 35	17 05	17 35	18 05	18 37	19 07	19 35	20 36	21 35	22 35	23 35
Stow	d		16 44		17 44		18 46		19 44	20 45	21 44	22 44	23 44
Gorebridge	d	16 31	17 00	17 30	18 01	18 30	19 03	19 32	20 01	21 02	22 01	23 01	00 02
Newtongrange	d	16 34	17 04	17 33	18 04	18 33	19 06	19 35	20 04	21 05	22 04	23 04	00 04
Eskbank	d	16 37	17 07	17 36	18 07	18 36	19 09	19 38	20 07	21 08	22 07	23 07	00 07
Shawfair	d	16 41	17 14	17 43	18 11	18 40	19 19	19 42	20 14	21 14	22 11	23 11	00 11
Newcraighall	d	16 45	17 18	17 47	18 15	18 44	19 23	19 46	20 18	21 18	22 15	23 15	00 15
Brunstane	d	16 49	17 22	17 50	18 22	18 50	19 26	19 50	20 21	21 22	22 19	23 19	00 19
Edinburgh 226,230	a	16 59	17 30	17 58	18 33	18 59	19 34	19 59	20 28	21 30	22 26	23 26	00 26

Sundays

15 December to 10 May

		SR D	SR	SR	SR	SR	SR	SR	SR	SR	SR	SR	SR	SR	SR	SR	SR
Tweedbank	d		08 45	09 45	10 45	11 45	12 45	13 45	14 45	15 45	16 45	17 45	18 45	19 45	20 45	21 45	22 46
Galashiels	d		08 49	09 49	10 49	11 49	12 49	13 49	14 49	15 49	16 49	17 49	18 49	19 49	20 49	21 49	22 50
Stow	d		08 58	09 58	10 58	11 58	12 58	13 58	14 58	15 58	16 58	17 58	18 58	19 58	20 58	21 58	22 59
Gorebridge	d	00 02	09 15	10 15	11 15	12 15	13 15	14 15	15 15	16 15	17 15	18 15	19 15	20 15	21 15	22 15	23 16
Newtongrange	d	00 04	09 18	10 18	11 18	12 18	13 18	14 18	15 18	16 18	17 18	18 18	19 18	20 18	21 18	22 18	23 19
Eskbank	d	00 07	09 21	10 21	11 21	12 21	13 21	14 21	15 21	16 21	17 21	18 21	19 21	20 21	21 21	22 21	23 22
Shawfair	d	00 11	09 25	10 25	11 26	12 25	13 25	14 26	15 25	16 26	17 25	18 29	19 25	20 25	21 25	22 26	23 26
Newcraighall	d	00 15	09 29	10 29	11 30	12 29	13 29	14 30	15 29	16 30	17 29	18 33	19 29	20 29	21 29	22 30	23 30
Brunstane	d	00 19	09 33	10 33	11 33	12 33	13 33	14 34	15 33	16 34	17 33	18 36	19 33	20 33	21 33	22 34	23 34
Edinburgh 226,230	a	00 26	09 40	10 40	11 42	12 40	13 40	14 41	15 42	16 43	17 40	18 43	19 40	20 40	21 40	22 41	23 42

A From Tweedbank
B To Glenrothes With Thornton
C To South Gyle
D not 15 December. From Tweedbank

CS — Sleeper trains LONDON - SCOTLAND

All trains in this table convey 🛏 1, 2 cl., (2) (reservation compulsory) ✕ and 🍷. Only available for overnight journeys.

	⑦	⑦	⑦	Ⓐ	Ⓐ	Ⓐ	⑦ ◐	⑦ ◐	Ⓐ ◐	Ⓐ ◐
London Euston **151/2/3** d.	2059**g**	2059**g**	2059**g**	2115	2115	2115	2330**h**	2330**h**	2350	2350
Watford Junction d.	2120**f**	2120**f**	2120**f**	2133	2133	2133	2350**f**	2350**f**	0010	0010
Crewe **151 152 153 154** d.	2340**f**	2340**f**	2340**f**	2350	2350	2350	|	|	|	|
Preston **154** d.	0033**f**	0033**f**	0033**f**	0056	0056	0056	|	|	|	|
Carlisle **154** a.	|	|	|	|	|	|	0445**f**	0445**f**	0513	0513
Motherwell a.	|	|	|	|	|	|	|	0700	|	0700
Glasgow Central **154** ⊠ a.	|	|	|	|	|	|	|	0722	|	0722
Edinburgh Waverley **154** ⊠ a.	|	|	|	|	|	|	0723**k**	...	0723	...
Dundee **222** a.	0605	|	|	0605	|	|	...	...	...	...
Aberdeen **222** a.	0740	|	|	0740	|	|	...	...	...	...
Perth **223** a.	...	0541	|	...	0541	|	...	...	...	...
Inverness **223** a.	...	0842	|	...	0842	|	...	...	...	...
Fort William **218** a.	...	...	0957	...	...	0957	...	...	...	...

	⑦	⑦	Ⓐ	Ⓐ	Ⓐ	Ⓐ	Ⓐ	⑦	⑦	⑦
Fort William **218** d.	...	...	...	...	1950	...	...	1900	...	...
Inverness **223** d.	...	...	...	...	|	2045	...	|	2026	...
Perth **223** d.	...	...	...	...	|	2327	...	|	2307	...
Aberdeen **222** d.	...	...	...	...	|	|	2143	|	|	2143
Dundee **222** d.	...	...	...	...	|	|	2309	|	|	2309
Edinburgh Waverley **154** d.	2315	...	2340	...	|	|	|	|	|	|
Glasgow Central **154** d.	|	2315**r**	|	2340	|	|	|	|	|	|
Motherwell d.	|	2331**f**	|	2359	|	|	|	|	|	|
Carlisle **154** d.	0141**f**	0141**f**	0144	0144	|	|	|	|	|	|
Preston **154** a.	0304**f**	0304**f**	|	|	0432	0432	0432	0429**f**	0429**f**	0429**f**
Crewe **151 152 153 154** a.	|	|	|	|	0537	0537	0537	0537**f**	0537**f**	0537**f**
Watford Junction a.	0638**f**	0638**f**	0643	0643	|	|	|	|	|	|
London Euston **151/2/3** ◧ a.	0707	0707	0707	0707	0749	0749	0749	0749**t**	0749**t**	0749**t**

f – Until Mar. 29.
g – From Apr. 5 departs 2027.
h – From Apr. 5 departs 2134.
k – From Apr. 5 arrives 0515.
r – From Apr. 5 departs 2145.
t – From Apr. 5 arrives 0905.
◐ – Sleeping-car passengers may occupy their cabins from 2200.
◧ – Sleeping-car passengers from Edinburgh and Glasgow may occupy their cabins until 0730; from Inverness, Aberdeen and Fort William until 0800.
⊠ – Sleeping-car passengers may occupy their cabins until 0800 following arrival at these stations.

Products for sale from European Rail Timetable Limited

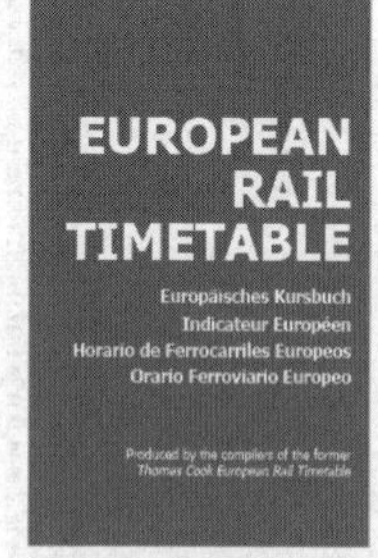

2nd Edition of the
Rail Map Europe.
£11.99 + p&p

Subscribe to the ERT from
£100

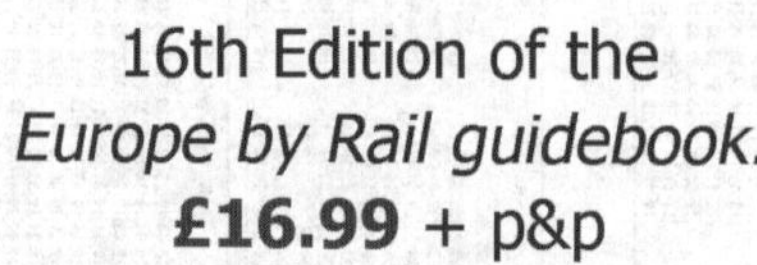

16th Edition of the
Europe by Rail guidebook.
£16.99 + p&p

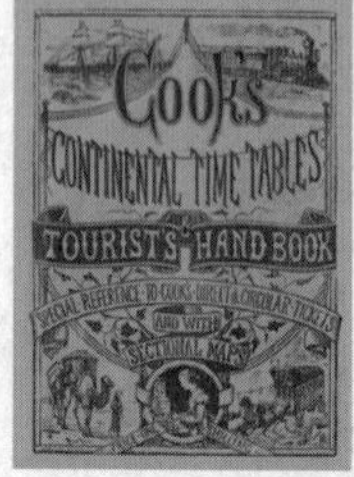

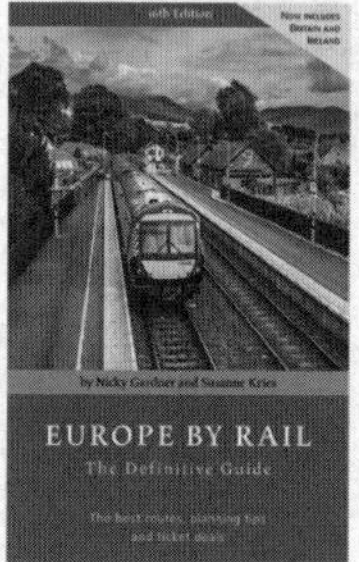

Reprint of the 1873 edition of
Cook's Continental Time Tables & Tourist's Hand Book.
£13.99 + p&p

Order on-line at **www.europeanrailtimetable.eu**
Telephone **01832 270198**

Published in Winter 2019/20

ISBN: 978 1 910356 36 4

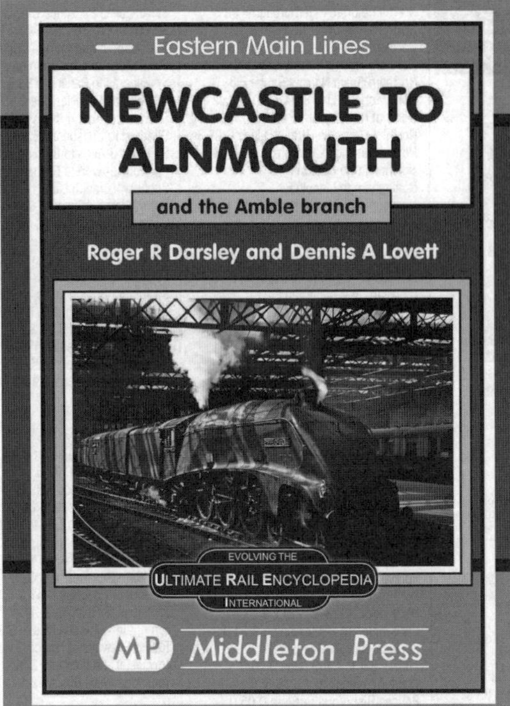

This journey on one of the country's premier routes, leaves Newcastle Central and travels through the city's northern suburbs, then the collieries of the county's south east coalfield to end at Alnmouth in the history and beauty of Northumberland.

ISBN: 978 1 910356 42 5

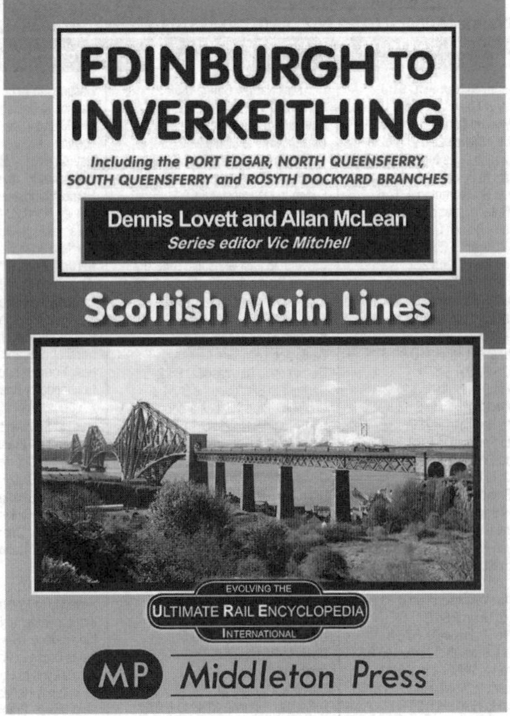

The crossing of the Forth Estuary provided a challenge up to the opening of the Forth Bridge in 1890. The original route via Kirkliston required passengers to change to the ferry before rejoining trains to complete their journeys. Both routes and the connecting lines are covered in this album.

Leisurely armchair journeys back in time.
Each station is visited in geographical order.
Photographs give a visual history of each location.
Over 400 albums bound in attractive glossy hardback covers - £18.95 (post-free)

Please request our brochure or visit *www.middletonpress.co.uk.*

Our website includes the INDEX TO STATIONS, containing all Middleton Press albums. Simply search for a station and find the relevant albums.

MP Middleton Press

Easebourne Lane, Midhurst, West Sussex, GU29 9AZ

Tel: 01730 813169 • sales@middletonpress.co.uk • www.middletonpress.co.uk

EVOLVING THE
ULTIMATE RAIL ENCYCLOPEDIA
INTERNATIONAL

Easebourne Midhurst GU29 9AZ. Tel:01730 813169

A-978 0 906520 B- 978 1 873793 C- 978 1 901706 D-978 1 904474
E - 978 1 906008 F - 978 1 908174 G - 978 1 910356

Our RAILWAY titles are listed below. Please check availability by looking at our website **www.middletonpress.co.uk,** telephoning us or by requesting a Brochure which includes our LATEST RAILWAY TITLES also our TRAMWAY, TROLLEYBUS, MILITARY and COASTAL series.

email:info@middletonpress.co.uk

A
Abergavenny to Merthyr C 91 8
Abertillery & Ebbw Vale Lines D 84 5
Aberystwyth to Carmarthen E 90 1
Allhallows - Branch Line to A 62 8
Alton - Branch Lines to A 11 6
Ambergate to Buxton G 28 9
Andover to Southampton A 82 6
Ascot - Branch Lines around A 64 2
Ashburton - Branch Line to B 95 4
Ashford - Steam to Eurostar B 67 1
Ashford to Dover A 48 2
Austrian Narrow Gauge D 04 3
Avonmouth - BL around D 42 5
Aylesbury to Rugby D 91 3

B
Baker Street to Uxbridge D 90 6
Bala to Llandudno E 87 1
Banbury to Birmingham D 27 2
Banbury to Cheltenham E 63 5
Bangor to Holyhead F 01 7
Bangor to Portmadoc E 72 7
Barking to Southend C 80 2
Barmouth to Pwllheli E 53 6
Barry - Branch Lines around D 50 0
Bartlow - Branch Lines to F 27 7
Basingstoke to Salisbury A 89 4
Bath Green Park to Bristol C 36 9
Bath to Evercreech Junction A 60 4
Beamish 40 years on rails E94 9
Bedford to Wellingborough D 31 9
Berwick to Drem F 64 2
Berwick to St. Boswells F 75 8
B'ham to Tamworth & Nuneaton F 63 5
Birkenhead to West Kirby F 61 1
Birmingham to Wolverhampton E253
Blackburn to Hellifield F 95 6
Bletchley to Cambridge D 94 4
Bletchley to Rugby E 07 9
Bodmin - Branch Lines around B 83 1
Boston to Lincoln F 80 2
Bournemouth to Evercreech Jn A 46 8
Bournemouth to Weymouth A 57 4
Bradshaw's History F18 5
Bradshaw's Rail Times 1850 F 13 0
Branch Lines series - see town names
Brecon to Neath D 43 2
Brecon to Newport D 16 6
Brecon to Newtown E 06 2
Brighton to Eastbourne A 16 1
Brighton to Worthing A 03 1
Bristol to Taunton D 03 6
Bromley South to Rochester B 23 7
Bromsgrove to Birmingham D 87 6
Bromsgrove to Gloucester D 73 9
Broxbourne to Cambridge F16 1
Brunel - A railtour D 74 6
Bude - Branch Line to B 29 9
Burnham to Evercreech Jn B 68 0
Buxton to Stockport G 32 6

C
Cambridge to Ely D 55 5
Canterbury - BLs around B 58 9
Cardiff to Dowlais (Cae Harris) E 47 5
Cardiff to Pontypridd E 95 6
Cardiff to Swansea E 42 0
Carlisle to Hawick E 85 7
Carmarthen to Fishguard E 66 6
Caterham & Tattenham Corner B251
Central & Southern Spain NG E 91 8
Chard and Yeovil - BLs a C 30 7
Charing Cross to Dartford A 75 8
Charing Cross to Orpington A 96 3
Cheddar - Branch Line to B 90 9
Cheltenham to Andover C 43 7
Cheltenham to Redditch D 81 4
Chesterfield to Lincoln G 21 0
Chester to Birkenhead F 21 5
Chester to Manchester F 51 2
Chester to Rhyl E 93 2
Chester to Warrington F 40 6
Chichester to Portsmouth A 14 7
Clacton and Walton - BLs to F 04 8
Clapham Jn to Beckenham Jn B 36 7
Cleobury Mortimer - BLs a E 18 5
Clevedon & Portishead - BLs to D180
Consett to South Shields E 57 4
Cornwall Narrow Gauge D 56 2
Corris and Vale of Rheidol E 65 9
Coventry to Leicester G 00 5
Craven Arms to Llandeilo E 35 2
Craven Arms to Wellington E 33 8
Crawley to Littlehampton A 34 5
Crewe to Manchester F 57 4
Crewe to Wigan G 12 8
Cromer - Branch Lines around C 26 0
Cromford and High Peak G 35 7
Croydon to East Grinstead B 48 0
Crystal Palace & Catford Loop B 87 1
Cyprus Narrow Gauge E 13 0

D
Darjeeling Revisited F 09 3
Darlington Leamside Newcastle E 28 4
Darlington to Newcastle D 98 2
Dartford to Sittingbourne B 34 3
Denbigh - Branch Lines around F 32 1
Derby to Chesterfield G 11 1
Derby to Stoke-on-Trent F 93 2
Derwent Valley - BL to the D 06 7
Devon Narrow Gauge E 09 3
Didcot to Banbury D 02 9
Didcot to Swindon C 84 0
Didcot to Winchester C 13 0
Diss to Norwich G 22 7
Dorset & Somerset NG D 76 0
Douglas - Laxey - Ramsey E 75 8
Douglas to Peel C 88 8
Douglas to Port Erin C 55 0
Douglas to Ramsey D 39 5
Dover to Ramsgate A 78 9
Drem to Edinburgh G 06 7
Dublin Northwards in 1950s E 31 4
Dunstable - Branch Lines to E 27 7

E
Ealing to Slough C 42 0
Eastbourne to Hastings A 27 7
East Cornwall Mineral Railways D 22 7
East Croydon to Three Bridges A 53 6
Eastern Spain Narrow Gauge E 56 7
East Grinstead - BLs to A 07 9
East Kent Light Railway A 61 1
East London - Branch Lines of C 44 4
East London Line B 80 0
East of Norwich - Branch Lines E 69 7
Effingham Junction - BLs a A 74 1
Ely to Norwich C 90 1
Enfield Town & Palace Gates D 32 6
Epsom to Horsham A 30 7
Eritrean Narrow Gauge E 38 3
Euston to Harrow & Wealdstone C 89 5
Exeter to Barnstaple B 15 2
Exeter to Newton Abbot C 49 9
Exeter to Tavistock B 69 5
Exmouth - Branch Lines to B 00 8

F
Fairford - Branch Line to A 52 9
Falmouth, Helston & St. Ives C 74 1
Fareham to Salisbury A 67 3
Faversham to Dover B 05 3
Felixstowe & Aldeburgh - BL to D 20 3
Fenchurch Street to Barking C 20 8
Festiniog - 50 yrs of enterprise C 83 3
Festiniog 1946-55 E 01 7
Festiniog in the Fifties B 68 8
Festiniog in the Sixties B 91 6
Ffestiniog in Colour 1955-82 F 25 3
Finsbury Park to Alexandra Pal C 02 8
French Metre Gauge Survivors F 88 8
Frome to Bristol B 77 0

G
Gainsborough to Sheffield G 17 3
Galashiels to Edinburgh F 52 9
Gloucester to Bristol D 35 7
Gloucester to Cardiff D 66 1
Gosport - Branch Lines around A 36 9
Greece Narrow Gauge D 72 2
Guildford to Redhill A 63 5

H
Hampshire Narrow Gauge D 36 4
Harrow to Watford D 14 2
Harwich & Hadleigh - BLs to F 02 4
Harz Revisited F 62 8
Hastings to Ashford A 37 6
Hawick to Galashiels F 36 9
Hawkhurst - Branch Line to A 66 6
Hayling - Branch Line to A 12 3
Hay-on-Wye - BL around D 92 0
Haywards Heath to Seaford A 28 4
Hemel Hempstead - BLs to D 88 3
Henley, Windsor & Marlow - BLa C77 2
Hereford to Newport D 54 8
Hertford & Hatfield - BLs a E 58 1
Hertford Loop E 71 0
Hexham to Carlisle D 75 3
Hexham to Hawick F 08 6
Hitchin to Peterborough D 07 4
Holborn Viaduct to Lewisham A 81 9
Horsham - Branch Lines to A 02 4
Hull, Hornsea and Withernsea G 27 2
Huntingdon - Branch Line to A 93 2

I
Ilford to Shenfield C 97 0
Ilfracombe - Branch Line to B 21 3
Ilkeston to Chesterfield G 26 5
Ipswich to Diss F 81 9
Ipswich to Saxmundham C 41 3
Isle of Man Railway Journey F 94 9
Isle of Wight Lines - 50 yrs C 12 3
Italy Narrow Gauge F 17 8

K
Kent Narrow Gauge C 45 1
Kettering to Nottingham F 82-6
Kidderminster to Shrewsbury E 10 9
Kingsbridge - Branch Line to C 98 7
Kings Cross to Potters Bar E 62 8
King's Lynn to Hunstanton F 58 1
Kingston & Hounslow Loops A 83 3
Kingswear - Branch Line to C 17 8

L
Lambourn - Branch Line to C 70 3
Launceston & Princetown - BLs C 19 2
Leek - Branch Line From G 01 2
Leicester to Burton F 85 7
Leicester to Nottingham G 15 9
Lewisham to Dartford A 92 5
Lincoln to Cleethorpes F 56 7
Lincoln to Doncaster G 03 6
Lines around Stamford F 98 7
Lines around Wimbledon B 75 6
Lines North of Stoke G 29 6
Liverpool Street to Chingford D 01 2
Liverpool Street to Ilford C 34 5
Llandeilo to Swansea E 46 8
London Bridge to Addiscombe B 20 6
London Bridge to East Croydon A 58 1
Longmoor - Branch Lines to A 41 3
Looe - Branch Line to C 22 2
Loughborough to Ilkeston G 24 1
Loughborough to Nottingham F 68 0
Lowestoft - BLs around E 40 6
Ludlow to Hereford E 14 7
Lydney - Branch Lines around E 26 0
Lyme Regis - Branch Line to A 45 1
Lynton - Branch Line to B 04 6

M
Machynlleth to Barmouth E 54 3
Maesteg and Tondu Lines F 06 2
Majorca & Corsica Narrow Gauge F 41 3
Mansfield to Doncaster G 23 4
March - Branch Lines around B 09 1
Market Drayton - BLs around F 67 3
Market Harborough to Newark F 86 4
Marylebone to Rickmansworth D 49 4
Melton Constable to Yarmouth Bch E031
Midhurst - Branch Lines of E 78 9
Midhurst - Branch Lines to F 00 0
Minehead - Branch Line to A 80 2
Mitcham Junction Lines B 01 5
Monmouth - Branch Lines to E 20 8
Monmouthshire Eastern Valleys D 71 5
Moretonhampstead - BL to C 27 7
Moreton-in-Marsh to Worcester D 26 5
Morpeth to Bellingham F 87 1
Mountain Ash to Neath D 80 7

N
Newark to Doncaster F 78 9
Newbury to Westbury C 66 6
Newcastle to Alnmouth G 36 4
Newcastle to Hexham D 69 2
Newport (IOW) - Branch Lines to A 26 0
Newquay - Branch Lines to C 71 0
Newton Abbot to Plymouth C 60 4
Newtown to Aberystwyth E 41 3
Northampton to Peterborough F 92 5
North East German NG D 44 9
Northern Alpine Narrow Gauge F 37 6
Northern France Narrow Gauge C 75 8
Northern Spain Narrow Gauge E 83 3
North London Line B 94 7
North of Birmingham F 55 0
North of Grimsby - Branch Lines G 09 8
North Woolwich - BLs around C 65 9
Nottingham to Boston F 70 3
Nottingham to Lincoln F 43 7
Nuneaton to Loughborough G 08 1

O
Ongar - Branch Line to E 05 5
Orpington to Tonbridge B 03 9
Oswestry - Branch Lines around E 60 4
Oswestry to Whitchurch E 81 9
Oxford to Bletchley D 57 9
Oxford to Moreton-in-Marsh D 15 9

P
Paddington to Ealing C 37 6
Paddington to Princes Risborough C819
Padstow - Branch Line to B 54 1
Peebles Loop G 19 7
Pembroke and Cardigan - BLs to F 29 1
Peterborough to Kings Lynn E 32 1
Peterborough to Lincoln F 89 5
Peterborough to Newark F 72 7
Plymouth - BLs around B 98 5
Plymouth to St. Austell C 63 5
Pontypool to Mountain Ash D 65 4
Pontypridd to Merthyr F 14 7
Pontypridd to Port Talbot E 86 4
Porthmadog 1954-94 - BLa B 31 2
Portmadoc 1923-46 - BLa B 13 8
Portsmouth to Southampton A 31 4
Portugal Narrow Gauge E 67 3
Potters Bar to Cambridge D 70 8
Preston to Blackpool G 16 6
Princes Risborough - BL to D 05 0
Princes Risborough to Banbury C 85 7

R
Railways to Victory C 16 1
Reading to Basingstoke B 27 5
Reading to Didcot C 79 6
Reading to Guildford A 47 5
Redhill to Ashford A 73 4
Return to Blaenau 1970-82 C 64 2
Rhyl to Bangor F 15 4
Rhymney & New Tredegar Lines E 48 2
Rickmansworth to Aylesbury D 61 6
Romania & Bulgaria NG E 23 9
Romneyrail C 32 1
Ross-on-Wye - BLs around E 30 7
Ruabon to Barmouth E 84 0
Rugby to Birmingham E 37 6
Rugby to Loughborough F 12 3
Rugby to Stafford F 07 9
Rugeley to Stoke-on-Trent F 90 1
Ryde to Ventnor A 19 2

RAIL TIMES FOR GREAT BRITAIN please request details

S
Salisbury to Westbury B 39 8
Salisbury to Yeovil B 06 0
Sardinia and Sicily Narrow Gauge F 50 5
Saxmundham to Yarmouth C 69 7
Saxony & Baltic Germany Revisited F 71 0
Saxony Narrow Gauge D 47 0
Scunthorpe to Doncaster G 34 0
Seaton & Sidmouth - BLs to A 95 6
Selsey - Branch Line to A 04 8
Sheerness - Branch Line to B 16 2
Sheffield towards Manchester G 18 0
Shenfield to Ipswich E 96 3
Shrewsbury - Branch Line to A 86 4
Shrewsbury to Chester E 70 3
Shrewsbury to Crewe F 48 2
Shrewsbury to Ludlow E 21 5
Shrewsbury to Newtown E 29 1
Sirhowy Valley Line E 12 3
Sittingbourne to Ramsgate A 90 1
Skegness & Mablethorpe - BL to F 84 0
Slough to Newbury C 56 7
South African Two-foot gauge E 51 2
Southampton to Bournemouth A 42 0
Southend & Southminster BLs E 76 5
Southern Alpine Narrow Gauge F 22 2
Southern France Narrow Gauge C 47 5
South London Line B 46 6
South Lynn to Norwich City F 03 1
Southwold - Branch Line to A 15 4
Spalding - Branch Lines around E 52
Spalding to Grimsby F 65 9 6
Stafford to Chester F 34 5
Stafford to Wellington F 59 8
St Albans to Bedford D 08 1
St. Austell to Penzance C 67 3
St. Boswell to Berwick F 44 4
Steaming Through Isle of Wight A 56
Stourbridge to Wolverhampton E 16 1
St. Pancras to Barking D 68 5
St. Pancras to Folkestone E 88 8
St. Pancras to St. Albans C 78 9
Stratford to Cheshunt F 53 6
Stratford-u-Avon to Birmingham D 77
Stratford-u-Avon to Cheltenham C 25
Sudbury - Branch Lines to F 19 2
Surrey Narrow Gauge C 87 1
Sussex Narrow Gauge C 68 0
Swaffham - Branch Lines around F 97
Swanage to 1999 - BL to A 33 8
Swanley to Ashford B 45 9
Swansea - Branch Lines around F 38 3
Swansea to Carmarthen E 59 8
Swindon to Bristol C 96 3
Swindon to Gloucester D 46 3
Swindon to Newport D 30 2
Swiss Narrow Gauge C 94 9

T
Talyllyn 60 E 98 7
Tamworth to Derby F 76 5
Taunton to Barnstaple B 60 2
Taunton to Exeter C 82 6
Taunton to Minehead F 39 0
Tavistock to Plymouth B 88 6
Tenterden - Branch Line to A 21 5
Three Bridges to Brighton A 35 2
Tilbury Loop C 86 4
Tiverton - BLs around C 62 8
Tivetshall to Beccles D 41 8
Tonbridge to Hastings A 44 4
Torrington - Branch Lines to B 37 4
Tourist Railways of France G 04 3
Towcester - BLs around E 39 0
Tunbridge Wells BLs A 32 1

U
Upwell - Branch Line to B 64 0
Uttoxeter to Buxton G 33 3
Uttoxeter to Macclesfield G 05 0

V
Victoria to Bromley South A 98 7
Victoria to East Croydon A 40 6
Vivarais Revisited E 08 6

W
Walsall Routes F 45 1
Wantage - Branch Line to D 25 8
Wareham to Swanage 50 yrs D 09 8
Waterloo to Windsor A 54 3
Waterloo to Woking A 38 3
Watford to Leighton Buzzard D 45 6
Wellingborough to Leicester F 73 4
Welshpool to Llanfair E 49 9
Wenford Bridge to Fowey C 09 3
Westbury to Bath B 55 8
Westbury to Taunton C 76 5
West Cornwall Mineral Rlys D 48 7
West Croydon to Epsom B 08 4
West German Narrow Gauge D 93 7
West London - BLs of C 50 5
West London Line B 84 8
West Wiltshire - BLs of D 12 8
Weymouth - BLs A 65 9
Willesden Jn to Richmond B 71 8
Wimbledon to Beckenham C 58 1
Wimbledon to Epsom B 62 6
Wimborne - BLs around A 97 0
Wirksworth - Branch Lines to G 10 4
Wisbech - BLs around C 01 7
Witham & Kelvedon - BLs a E 82 6
Woking to Alton A 59 8
Woking to Portsmouth A 25 3
Woking to Southampton A 55 0
Wolverhampton to Shrewsbury E 44 4
Wolverhampton to Stafford F 79 6
Worcester to Birmingham D 97 5
Worcester to Hereford D 38 8
Worthing to Chichester A 06 2
Wrexham to New Brighton F 47 5
Wroxham - BLs around F 31 4

Y
Yeovil - 50 yrs change C 38 3
Yeovil to Dorchester A 76 5
Yeovil to Exeter A 91 8
York to Scarborough F 23 9